BOOK PRICES:
USED AND RARE,
1996

BOOK PRICES: USED AND RARE, 1996

Edited by
Edward N. Zempel
and
Linda A. Verkler

THE SPOON RIVER PRESS

Published by:
The Spoon River Press
2319-C West Rohmann Avenue
Peoria, Illinois 61604
(309) 672-2665
Fax: (309) 672-7853

ISBN 0-930358-14-7

Manufactured in the United States of America

This book is printed on acid-free paper meeting the standards of the American National Standard for Permanence of Paper for Library Materials.

Introduction

Book Prices: Used and Rare, 1996 is the fourth volume in a series of book price guides. Published annually, *Book Prices: Used and Rare* is a reference for the secondhand and antiquarian book dealer, general and rare book librarian, and the private collector seeking to place a value on a book. The nearly 32,000 titles in the present volume have been selected from the 1995 catalogs of over 190 book dealers and auction houses in the United States and the United Kingdom. The dealers who provided catalogs—and kindly gave their permission to reproduce their entries—represent a broad spectrum of the American and British book trade, not only geographically, but in the subject matter range and the price range of the books offered.

With a large variety of possible subject categories, we have attempted to balance the entries in this guide. Our general goal has been to provide pricing information on books in those subject categories and that price range most likely to be found in the day-to-day trade of the average generalist bookseller. This volume, then, contains entries on books in a wide variety of subject areas. Among them are modern first editions, travel and voyages, Americana and the West, natural history, science, medicine, art, architecture, children's literature, and books on books. Only books published in English have been listed. Though this guide includes several entries for books priced over $5,000 and some entries for books priced under $20, 90 percent of the titles listed in this guide are priced between $20 and $300.

All prices are given in both U.S. dollars and pounds sterling.

Entry Alphabetizing

Entries have been alphabetized word-for-word by the author's surname. Every effort has been made to present the correct spelling of surnames. However, variant spellings were sometimes found, especially in names beginning with de and De, le and Le, Mac and Mc, etc. (Such inconsistencies extend also to the entry of such names in reference works and library catalog files.)

Names preceded by de or de la should correctly be alphabetized under the family surname. For example, Simone de Beauvoir should be alphabetized under B—i.e., Beauvoir, Simone de. However, in the interests of clarity, ease of reference, and in anticipation of where many readers would first look, we have alphabetized such names under D. The same practice was used for surnames beginning with di, le, la, von, etc. Please take this into consideration when searching for an entry for a particular author. If not in one place, the name may be in another.

In the case of U.S. government publications such as House and Senate documents, the user is advised to check for the title of the work, as well as for the work's author. Some works have been entered with the government agency as the author. For example, publications of the Bureau of American Ethnology (BAE) have generally been alphabetized under BAE.

An entry for which the author is unknown has been alphabetized in the general list by its title. Pseudonymous entries give, if known, the author's real name in parentheses after the pseudonym. Generally, in the interest of more efficient alphabetizing, military ranks and other titles have been deleted from the author's name.

Some edited works (letters, diaries, and journals, especially) were listed in catalogs under the name of the author; others were listed under the name of the editor. In searching such titles in this guide, check first under the name of the author, and then under the name of the editor. Though there are exceptions, translated works have generally been entered under the name of the author, not the translator.

Entry Information

Each entry in *Book Prices: Used and Rare* includes the following information (when offered in the catalog): author's name (in CAPITAL letters), title of book, publisher and/or place and date of publication, condition, the price at which the book was cataloged or sold at auction, and the name (perhaps shortened) of the dealer or auction house that cataloged or auctioned the book. The key to these dealer and auction house abbreviations is found in the listing of contributing book dealers and auction houses, which begins on page 8.

If the condition of the book is not noted, it may be assumed that the book is in good or better collectible condition. Specific faults are usually listed in parentheses following the general condition of the book or its dust jacket. In the case of modern first editions, careful attention was given to noting those defects, both of the dust jacket and the book itself, affecting the book's value. The following are general definitions applying to a book's condition.

As New: In "as published" condition. The dust jacket (dj), if issued with the book, must be flawless.

Very Fine (VF): Nearly as new.

Fine: Without defect, but not "as new."

Near Fine (NF): Approaching Fine condition.

Very Good (VG): Minimal wear with no defects.

Good: In average condition.

Poor: Text complete, but book worn and binding defective.

Ex-library copies and book club editions are noted.

First editions are so noted. All titles are hardcover, unless the entry mentions otherwise. Every book is presumed to be in its original binding unless the entry mentions otherwise.

A dust jacket (dj) is mentioned when present. The dust jacket is assumed to be in the same general condition as the book unless the entry mentions otherwise. Slipcases also are noted.

In the case of certain older books, where collation is a factor in determining the book's edition, the collation (if given in the dealer's catalog) has been provided. Generally, if mentioned in the dealer's catalog description, folding maps, folding plates, and folding illustrations have been noted in the entry, regardless of the value of the book. In the case of entries for limited editions, the number of copies in the edition has been noted, if included in the catalog entry.

When a "point" (a typographical or binding feature bearing on the edition of the book and thus on its value) was mentioned in the book dealer's catalog entry, we have included that "point" in our entry. For some Americana entries we have also included the Howes reference number included in the dealer's catalog entry (for example, Howes E 231). These numbers are keyed to entries in the second edition of *U.S.iana* by Wright Howes. Similarly, some entries carry numbers referencing the *Bibliography of American Literature* (BAL), e.g., BAL 14356.

For some titles we have provided multiple entries, suggesting a price agreement or a price range, usually across a range of conditions or editions. As mentioned, most of the entries provide information on books in the $20-$300 price range. Generally, then—though there are exceptions—this guide does not contain entries for unique copies, association copies, or books published in very small limited editions. While most of the books listed are hardcovers, prices on some vintage paperback first editions also have been included.

The prices listed are retail prices at which the books were cataloged or sold at auction in 1995.

Auction Prices

Those books sold at auction are identified by an asterisk following the name of the auction house. In the case of books sold by the following auction houses, the prices listed in this guide include the buyer's premium: Christie's South Kensington; Robert C. Eldred Co., Inc.; Metropolitan Book Auction; Sotheby's; Swann Galleries, Inc.; and Waverly Auctions, Inc. In the case of books sold by the other auction houses, the price listed is the "hammer price," which is the price called out by the auctioneer when sale is made to the successful bidder. These hammer prices do not include the buyer's premium charged by the auction house. The buyer's premium charged is as follows: Baltimore Book Company, Inc., 10%; Freeman\Fine Arts of Philadelphia, Inc., 10%; Kane Antiquarian Auction, 5%; New Hampshire Book Auctions, 10%; Oinenon Book Auctions, 10%; Pacific Book Auction Galleries, 15%; The Scribe's Perch, 10%; Samuel Yudkin and Associates, 10%; and Zubal Auction Company, 10%.

Identifying First Editions

First Editions: A Guide to Identification is the standard reference for identifying first editions. To receive information on this book, now in its third edition, send your name and address to the publisher: The Spoon River Press, 2319-C West Rohmann Avenue, Peoria, IL 61604. The Spoon River Press also publishes and distributes a wide range of books about books. Write, call (309-672-2665), or fax (309-672-7853) for our free catalog.

Abbreviations

To allow the inclusion of as much useful information as possible, certain standard abbreviations were used. A list of those abbreviations is on page 14.

A Caution

The prices listed in this guide are not the prices that book dealers will pay for the books listed. The prices listed are the prices at which dealers offered books for sale in 1995 or the prices at which auction houses sold books at auction in 1995. See Auction Prices (above).

Like any other retail business, the selling of rare, scarce, and used books depends on a markup for its profitability. The price a dealer is willing to pay for a book depends on its condition and scarcity, as well as the demand for the book.

In the case of cataloged books, the catalog prices listed in this guide are the prices at which the books were advertised for retail sale. The books may not have sold at these prices.

Standing Orders

Book Prices: Used and Rare is published annually in March. Annual volumes may be placed on standing order *at preferential discounts well below the post-publication price.*

Annual volumes on standing order will be shipped in March each year. To place *Book Prices: Used and Rare* on standing order, contact the publisher for an order form: The Spoon River Press, 2319-C West Rohmann Avenue, Peoria, IL 61604. Send no payment. An invoice will be enclosed with the book when it is shipped.

We are intent on making *Book Prices: Used and Rare* the most comprehensive, affordable, and useful book price guide obtainable. If you have suggestions on how future annual editions might be improved regarding focus or coverage, please let us know.

Contributing Book Dealers and Auction Houses

We are grateful to the book dealers and auction houses listed below. They generously provided copies of their 1995 catalogs (and, in the case of auction houses, prices realized lists) for our use in compiling this price guide. The name in parentheses below the name of the dealer or auction house is the name by which the catalog entries of that dealer or auction house are identified in this guide. Names followed by an asterisk are the names of auction houses.

Richard H. Adelson
(ADELSON)
North Pomfret, VT 05053
(802) 457-2608

Charles Agvent
(AGVENT)
291 Linden Road
Mertztown, PA 19539
(610) 682-4750

Antic Hay Rare Books
(ANTIC HAY)
P.O. Box 2185
Asbury Park, NJ 07712
(908) 774-4590

Appelfeld Gallery
(APPELFELD)
1372 York Avenue
New York, NY 10021
(212) 988-7835

Archaeologia
(ARCHAEOLOGIA)
707 Carlston Avenue
Oakland, CA 94610
(510) 832-1405

Archer's Used and Rare Books
(ARCHER)
104 S. Lincoln Street
Kent, OH 44240
(216) 673-0945

Argonaut Book Shop
(ARGONAUT)
786-792 Sutter Street
San Francisco, CA 94109
(415) 474-9067

Argosy Book Store, Inc.
(ARGOSY)
116 East 59th Street
New York, NY 10022
(212) 753-4455

David Aronovitz
(ARONOVITZ)
781 E. Snell Road
Rochester, MI 48306
(810) 651-8799

Ars Artis
(ARS ARTIS)
31 Abberbury Road
Oxford OX4 4ET
United Kingdom

Ash Rare Books
(ASH)
25 Royal Exchange
Threadneedle Street
London EC3V 3LP
United Kingdom

The Associates
(ASSOCIATES)
P.O. Box 4747
Falls Church, VA 22044-0747
(703) 578-3810

Authors of the West
(AUTHORS OF WEST)
191 Dogwood Drive
Dundee, OR 97115
(503) 538-8132

Gene W. Baade
(BAADE)
824 Lynnwood Avenue NE
Renton, WA 98056
(206) 271-6481

Gary A. Backman
(BACKMAN)
1005 Woodland Drive
Santa Paula, CA 93060
(805) 525-2647

Baltimore Book Company, Inc.
(BALTIMORE*)
2114 N. Charles Street
Baltimore, MD 21218
(410) 659-0550

Beasley Books
(BEASLEY)
1533 W. Oakdale
Chicago, IL 60657
(312) 472-4528

Benchmark Books
(BENCHMARK)
3269 S. Main Street
Suite 250 (2nd floor)
Salt Lake City, UT 84115
(801) 486-3111

Steven C. Bernard
(BERNARD)
15011 Plainfield Lane
Darnestown, MD 20874
(301) 948-8423

Between the Covers
(BETWEEN THE COVERS)
132 Kings Highway East
Haddonfield, NJ 08033
(609) 354-7665

David Bickersteth
(BICKERSTETH)
4 South End
Bassingbourn, Royston
Hertsfordshire SG8 5NG
United Kingdom

Matthew Biscotti & Company
(BISCOTTI)
481 Route 45 South
Austinburg, OH 44010
(216) 275-1310

Black Sun Books
(BLACK SUN)
157 East 57th Street
New York, NY 10022
(212) 688-6622

Frederick C. Blake
(BLAKE)
11 Oakway Drive
Stony Brook, NY 11790-1231

Blue Mountain Books
(BLUE MOUNTAIN)
P.O. Box 363
Catskill, NY 12414
(518) 943-4771

Bohling Book Company
(BOHLING)
P.O. Box 204
Decatur, MI 49045
(616) 423-8786

Nelson Bond
(BOND)
4724 Easthill Drive
Roanoke, VA 24018
(540) 774-2674

The Book Block
(BOOK BLOCK)
8 Loughlin Avenue
Cos Cob, CT 06807
(203) 629-2990

The Book Broker
(BOOK BROKER)
P.O. Box 1283
Charlottesville, VA 22902
(804) 296-2194

The Book Market
(BOOK MARKET)
Box 74
Altadena, CA 91003-0074
(818) 797-9527

Bookcell Books
(BOOKCELL)
Box 506
Haverford, PA 19041
(610) 649-4933

Bookmark, Children's Books
(BOOKMARK)
Fortnight, Wick Down
Broad Hinton, Swindon
Wiltshire SN4 9NR
United Kingdom

Books & Birds
(BOOKS & BIRDS)
519 E. Middle Turnpike
Manchester, CT 06040
(203) 649-3449

Meyer Boswell Books, Inc.
(BOSWELL)
2141 Mission Street
San Francisco, CA 94110
(415) 255-6400

Judith Bowman—Books
(BOWMAN)
Pound Ridge Road
Bedford, NY 10506
(914) 234-7543

Bromer Booksellers
(BROMER)
607 Boylston Street
Boston, MA 02116
(617) 247-2818

Brooks Books
(BROOKS)
P.O. Box 21473
Concord, CA 94521
(510) 672-4566

Michael Brown
(BROWN)
4421 Osage Avenue
Philadelphia, PA 19104
(215) 387-2290

Brian Buckley
(BUCKLEY)
The Chrysalis Press
11 Convent Close
Kenilworth
Warwickshire CV8 2FQ
United Kingdom

James Burmester
(BURMESTER)
Manor House Farm
North Stoke, Bath BA1 9AT
United Kingdom

Richard Cady
(CADY)
1927 North Hudson Avenue
Chicago, IL 60614
(312) 944-0856

Andrew Cahan
(CAHAN)
3000 Blueberry Lane
Chapel Hill, NC 27516
(919) 968-0538

The Captain's Bookshelf, Inc.
(CAPTAIN'S BOOKSHELF)
31 Page Avenue
Asheville, NC 28801
(704) 253-6631

Cattermole 20th Century
Children's Books
(CATTERMOLE)
9880 Fairmount Road
Newbury, OH 44065
(216) 338-3253

Nicholas Certo
(CERTO)
P.O. Box 322
Circleville, NY 10919
(914) 361-1190

Children's Book Adoption Agency
(BOOK ADOPTION)
P.O. Box 643
Kensington, MD 20895-0643
(301) 565-2834

Christie's South Kensington
(CHRISTIE'S*)
85 Old Brompton Road
London SW7 3LD
United Kingdom

Stan Clark Military Books
(CLARK)
915 Fairview Avenue
Gettysburg, PA 17325
(717) 337-1728

Clearwater Books
(CLEARWATER)
19 Matlock Road
Ferndown
Dorset BH22 8QT
United Kingdom

G. W. Connolly
(CONNOLLY)
2810 Kansas Avenue
Joplin, MO 64804-2931
(417) 624-5602

Claude Cox
(COX)
College Gateway Bookshop
3 & 5 Silent Street
Ipswich IP1 1TF
United Kingdom

Thomas Cullen
(CULLEN)
Box 134
Cattaraugus, NY 14719
(716) 257-5121

James Cummins, Bookseller
(CUMMINS)
699 Madison Avenue
New York, NY 10021
(212) 688-6441

D & D Galleries
(D & D)
Box 8413
Somerville, NJ 08876
(908) 874-3162

Dawson's Book Shop
(DAWSON)
535 N. Larchmont Blvd.
Los Angeles, CA 90004
(213) 469-2186

Joseph A. Dermont
(DERMONT)
P.O. Box 654
Onset, MA 02558
(508) 295-4760

The Doctor's Library
(DOCTOR'S LIBRARY)
P.O. Box 423
Jersey City, NJ 07303-0423
(800) 225-0912

Dower House
(DOWER)
Box 76
Athol, MA 01331
(508) 249-2335

Dramatis Personae
(DRAMATIS)
P.O. Box 1070
Sheffield, MA 01257
(413) 229-7735

Dumont Maps & Books of the West
(DUMONT)
P.O. Box 10250
Santa Fe, NM 87504
(505) 988-1076

I. D. Edrich
(EDRICH)
17 Selsdon Road
London E11 2QF
United Kingdom

Francis Edwards
(EDWARDS)
The Old Cinema
Castle Street, Hay-on-Wye
Via Hereford HR3 5DF
United Kingdom

Francis Edwards of London
(EDWARDS)
13 Great Newport Street
Charing Cross Road
London WC2H 7JA
United Kingdom

Robert C. Eldred Co., Inc.
(ELDRED*)
P.O. Box 796
East Dennis, MA 02641
(508) 385-3116

Else Fine Books
(ELSE FINE)
P.O. Box 43
Dearborn, MI 48121
(313) 582-1080

Europa Books
(EUROPA)
15 Luttrell Avenue
London SW15 6PD
United Kingdom

Joseph J. Felcone, Inc.
(FELCONE)
P.O. Box 366
Princeton, NJ 08542
(609) 924-0539

Five Quail Books
(FIVE QUAIL)
8540 N. Central Avenue, #27
Phoenix, AZ 85020-3577
(602) 861-0548

Freeman\ Fine Arts
of Philadelphia, Inc.
(FREEMAN*)
1808-10 Chestnut Street
Philadelphia, PA 19103
(215) 563-9275

Fuller and Saunders, Books
(FULLER & SAUNDERS)
1531 33rd Street NW
Washington, DC 20007
(800) 655-4693

W. Bruce Fye
(FYE)
1607 N. Wood Avenue
Marshfield, WI 54449
(715) 384-8128

John Gach Books
(GACH)
5620 Waterloo Road
Columbia, MD 21045
(410) 465-9023

R. A. Gekoski
(GEKOSKI)
Pied Bull Yard
15a Bloomsbury Square
London WC1A 2LP
United Kingdom

Michael Gibbs
(GIBBS)
P.O. Box 33271
Los Gatos, CA 95031
(408) 395-1937

Michael Ginsberg Books, Inc.
(GINSBERG)
Box 402
Sharon, MA 02067
(617) 784-8181

Edwin V. Glaser Rare Books
(GLASER)
P.O. Box 1765
Sausalito, CA 94966
(415) 332-1194

Glenn Books
(GLENN)
4503 Genessee, 2nd floor
Kansas City, MO 64111
(816) 561-9989

James Tait Goodrich
(GOODRICH)
214 Everett Place
Englewood, NJ 07631
(201) 567-0199

William A. Graf
(GRAF)
717 Clark Street
Iowa City, IA 52240-5640
(319) 337-7748

Gravesend Books
(GRAVESEND)
Box 235
Pocono Pines, PA 18350
(717) 646-3317

David A. H. Grayling
(GRAYLING)
Lyvennet
Crosby Ravensworth,
Penrith, Cumbria CA10 3JP
United Kingdom

John R. Gretton
(GRETTON)
5 Quebec Road
Dereham
Norfolk NR19 2DP
United Kingdom

Peter J. Hadley
(HADLEY)
132 Corve Street
Ludlow
Shropshire SY8 2PG
United Kingdom

Emmett Harrington
(HARRINGTON)
P.O. Box 27326
San Francisco, CA 94127
(415) 587-4604

Hartfield Fine and Rare Books
(HARTFIELD)
117 Dixboro Road
Ann Arbor, MI 48105
(313) 662-6035

Richard Hatchwell
(HATCHWELL)
The Old Rectory
Little Somerford
Chippenham
Wiltshire SN15 5JW
United Kingdom

Robert G. Hayman
(HAYMAN)
Box 188
Carey, OH 43316
(419) 396-6933

Heinoldt Books
(HEINOLDT)
1325 W. Central Avenue
South Egg Harbor, NJ 08215
(609) 965-2284

Joshua Heller Rare Books, Inc.
(HELLER)
P.O. Box 39114
Washington, DC 20016-9114
(202) 966-9411

John Henly
(HENLY)
Brooklands, Walderton
Chichester
West Sussex PO18 9EE
United Kingdom

Heritage Book Shop, Inc.
(HERITAGE)
8540 Melrose Avenue
Los Angeles, CA 90069
(310) 659-3674

The Hermitage Bookshop
(HERMITAGE)
290 Fillmore Street
Denver, CO 80206-5020
(303) 388-6811

High Latitude
(HIGH LATITUDE)
P.O. Box 11254
Bainbridge Island, WA 98110
(206) 842-0202

Hobbyhorse Books
(HOBBYHORSE)
P.O. Box 591
Ho-Ho-Kus, NJ 07423
(201) 327-4717

R. F. G. Hollett & Son
(HOLLETT)
6 Finkle Street, Sedbergh
Cumbria LA10 5BZ
United Kingdom

David J. Holmes
(HOLMES)
230 S. Broad Street, 3rd floor
Philadelphia, PA 19102
(215) 735-1083

Houle Rare Books & Autographs
(HOULE)
7260 Beverly Blvd.
Los Angeles, CA 90036-2537
(213) 937-5858

J. & J. House Booksellers
(HOUSE)
731 Unionville Road
Kennett Square, PA 19348
(610) 444-0490

Murray Hudson
(HUDSON)
P.O. Box 163
Halls, TN 38040
(800) 748-9946

James Jaffe Rare Books
(JAFFE)
P.O. Box 496
Haverford, PA 19041
(610) 649-4221

Janus Books
(JANUS)
P.O. Box 40787
Tucson, AZ 85717
(520) 881-8192

Kane Antiquarian Auction
(KANE*)
1525 Shenkel Road
Pottstown, PA 19465
(610) 323-5289

Kenneth Karmiole
(KARMIOLE)
P.O. Box 464
Santa Monica, CA 90404
(310) 451-4342

John K. King Books
(KING)
901 W. Lafayette Blvd.
Detroit, MI 48226
(313) 961-0622

Lame Duck Books
(LAME DUCK)
90 Moraine Street
Jamaica Plain, MA 02130
(617) 522-6657

Edward J. Lefkowicz, Inc.
(LEFKOWICZ)
P.O. Box 630
Fairhaven, MA 02719
(508) 997-6839

George Lenz
(LENZ)
336 New York Avenue
Huntington, NY 11743
(516) 427-3744

Barry R. Levin
(LEVIN)
720 Santa Monica Blvd
Santa Monica, CA 90401
(310) 458-6111

Lien's Book Shop
(LIEN)
57 South 9th Street
Minneapolis, MN 55402
(612) 332-7081

Robert F. Lucas
(LUCAS)
P.O. Box 63
Blandford, MA 01008
(413) 848-2061

M & S Rare Books
(M & S)
Box 2594, East Side Station
Providence, RI 02906
(401) 421-1050

MacDonnell Rare Books
(MACDONNELL)
9307 Glenlake Drive
Austin, TX 78730
(512) 345-4139

Robert A. Madle
(MADLE)
4406 Bestor Drive
Rockville, MD 20853
(301) 460-4712

Maggs Bros. Ltd.
(MAGGS)
50 Berkeley Square
London W1X 6EL
United Kingdom

Marlborough Rare Books, Ltd.
(MARLBOROUGH)
144-146 New Bond Street
London W1Y 9FD
United Kingdom

C. J. Martin
(MARTIN)
45 New Mill Lane
Mansfield
Woodhouse NG19 9BU
United Kingdom

David A. McClintock
(MCCLINTOCK)
1454 Sheridan Avenue NE
Warren, OH 44483
(216) 372-4425

McGowan Book Company
(MCGOWAN)
39 Kimberly Drive
Durham, NC 27707
(919) 403-1503

Metropolitan Book Auction
(METROPOLITAN*)
110 West 19th Street
New York, NY 10011
(212) 463-0200

Middle Earth Books
(MIDDLE EARTH)
P.O. Box 81906
Rochester Hills, MI 48308-1906
(810) 656-4989

Frank Mikesh
(MIKESH)
1356 Walden Road
Walnut Creek, CA 94596
(510) 934-9243

Hartley Moorhouse Books
(MOORHOUSE)
10 Ashchurch Terrace
London W12 9SL
United Kingdom

Mordida Books
(MORDIDA)
P.O. Box 79322
Houston, TX 77279
(713) 467-4280

Nicholas C. Morrell, Ltd.
(MORRELL)
77 Falkland Road
Kentish Town
London NW5 2XB
United Kingdom

V. J. Moss
(MOSS)
83 Chaigley Road
Longridge
Preston PR3 3TQ
United Kingdom

Murder by the Book
(MURDER BY THE BOOK)
1281 North Main Street
Providence, RI 02904
(401) 331-9140

My Bookhouse
(MY BOOKHOUSE)
27 S. Sandusky Street
Tiffin, OH 44883
(419) 447-9842

New Hampshire Book Auctions
(NEW HAMPSHIRE*)
P.O. Box 460
Weare, NH 03281
(603) 529-7432

Oak Knoll Books
(OAK KNOLL)
414 Delaware Street
New Castle, DE 19720
(302) 328-7232

October Farm
(OCTOBER FARM)
2609 Branch Road
Raleigh, NC 27610
(919) 772-0482

Oinonen Book Auctions
(OINONEN*)
P.O. Box 470
Sunderland, MA 01375
(413) 665-3253

The Old London Bookshop
(OLD LONDON)
P.O. Box 922
Bellingham, WA 98227-0922
(360) 647-8946

Oregon Territorial Books
(OREGON)
P.O. Box 22
Sublimity, OR 97385
(503) 769-7356

Other Worlds Bookstore
(OTHER WORLDS)
1281 N. Main Street
Providence, RI 02904-1827
(401) 331-9140

Pacific Book Auction Galleries
(PACIFIC*)
139 Townsend Street, Suite 305
San Francisco, CA 94107
(415) 896-2665

Parmer Books
(PARMER)
7644 Forrestal Road
San Diego, CA 92120-2203
(619) 287-0693

Ian Patterson
(PATTERSON)
21 Bateman Street
Cambridge CB2 1NB
United Kingdom

Dick Perier—Books
(PERIER)
P.O. Box 1
Vancouver, WA 98666
(360) 696-2033

The Petersfield Bookshop
(PETERSFIELD)
16A Chapel Street
Petersfield
Hampshire GU32 3DS
United Kingdom

R & A Petrilla, Booksellers
(PETRILLA)
Box 306
Roosevelt, NJ 08555-0306
(609) 426-4999

Pettler & Lieberman Booksellers
(PETTLER & LIEBERMAN)
8033 Sunset Blvd #977
Los Angeles, CA 90046
(310) 474-2479

Phillip J. Pirages
(PIRAGES)
P.O. Box 504
McMinnville, OR 97128
(800) 962-6666

R. Plapinger
(PLAPINGER)
P.O. Box 1062
Ashland, OR 97520
(503) 488-1220

The Poetry Bookshop
(POETRY BOOKSHOP)
West House, Broad Street
Hay-on-Wye
Via Hereford HR3 5DB
United Kingdom

Polyanthos Park Avenue Books
(POLYANTHOS)
P.O. Box 343
Huntington, NY 11743
(516) 271-5558

Wallace D. Pratt, Bookseller
(PRATT)
1801 Gough Street, #304
San Francisco, CA 94109
(415) 673-0178

Larry W. Price Books
(PRICE)
353 NW Maywood Drive
Portland, OR 97210-3333
(503) 221-1410

Quest Rare Books
(QUEST)
774 Santa Ynez
Stanford, CA 94305
(415) 324-3119

William Reese Co.
(REESE)
409 Temple Street
New Haven, CT 06511
(203) 789-8081

Revere Books
(REVERE)
P.O. Box 420
Revere, PA 18953
(610) 847-2709

Alice Robbins, Bookseller
(ROBBINS)
3002 Round Hill Road
Greensboro, NC 27408
(910) 282-1964

Rostenberg & Stern, Rare Books
(ROSTENBERG & STERN)
40 East 88th Street
New York, NY 10128
(212) 831-6628

Sadlon's
(SADLON)
1207 Fox River Drive
De Pere, WI 54115
(414) 336-6665

Savona Books
(SAVONA)
9 Wilton Road
Hornsea
North Humberside HU18 1QU
United Kingdom

Andrew Sclanders
(SCLANDERS)
11 Albany Road
Stroud Green
London N4 4RR
United Kingdom

The Scribe's Perch
(SCRIBE'S PERCH*)
P.O. Box 3295
Newport, RI 02840
(401) 849-8426

Second Life Books, Inc.
(SECOND LIFE)
P.O. Box 242
Lanesborough, MA 01237
(413) 447-8010

Florian J. Shasky
(SHASKY)
970 Terra Bella Avenue, Suite 1
Mountain View, CA 94043
(415) 967-5330

Ed Smith Books
(SMITH)
P.O. Box 66
Oak View, CA 93022
(805) 649-2844

A. Sokol Books
(SOKOL)
Berghersh Place
Witnesham, Ipswich
Suffolk IP6 9EZ
United Kingdom

Sotheby's
(SOTHEBY'S*)
34-35 New Bond Street
London W1A 2AA
United Kingdom

Henry Sotheran Ltd.
(SOTHERAN)
2 Sackville Street
Piccadilly
London W1X 2DP
United Kingdom

Andrew Stewart
(STEWART)
11 High Street
Helpringham
Lincolnshire NG34 9RA
United Kingdom

Sumner & Stillman
(SUMNER & STILLMAN)
P.O. Box 973
Yarmouth, ME 04096
(207) 846-6070

Swann Galleries, Inc.
(SWANN*)
104 E. 25th Street
New York, NY 10010
(212) 254-4710

Michael Taylor Rare Books
(MICHAEL TAYLOR)
The Gables, 8 Mendham Lane
Harleston
Norfolk IP20 9DE
United Kingdom

Peter Taylor & Son
(PETER TAYLOR)
1, Ganders Ash
Leavesden, Watford
Hertfordshire WD2 7HE
United Kingdom

Robert Temple
(TEMPLE)
65 Mildmay Road
London N1 4PU
United Kingdom

Terramedia Books
(TERRAMEDIA)
12 Leighton Road
Wellesley, MA 02181
(617) 237-6485

Tiger Books
(TIGER)
Yew Tree Cottage
Westbere, Canterbury
Kent CT2 0HH
United Kingdom

Truepenny Books Inc.
(TRUEPENNY)
2509 N. Campbell Avenue
Tucson, AZ 85719
(520) 881-4822

H. E. Turlington Books
(TURLINGTON)
P.O. Box 190
Carrboro, NC 27510-0190
(919) 968-3656

D. Turpen Books
 of Mexico & the West
(TURPEN)
P.O. Box 8736
Albuquerque, NM 87198
(505) 268-5323

Turtle Island Booksellers
(TURTLE ISLAND)
2067 Center Street
Berkeley, CA 94704
(510) 540-5422

The Typographeum Bookshop
(TYPOGRAPHEUM)
246 Bennington Road
Francestown, NH 03043

Len Unger Rare Books
(UNGER)
Hancock Park Terrace
631 N. Wilcox Avenue, 3B
Los Angeles, CA 90004
(213) 962-7929

T. S. Vandoros Rare Books
(VANDOROS)
5827 Highland Terrace
Middleton, WI 53562
(608) 836-8254

Virgo Books
(VIRGO)
Little Court
South Wraxall, Bradford-on-Avon
Wiltshire BA15 2SE
United Kingdom

Wantagh Rare Book Co.
(WANTAGH)
Box 605
Neversink, NY 12765-0605

Rob Warren of Skyline Books
(WARREN)
13 West 18th Street
New York, NY 10011
(212) 759-5463

Andrew D. Washton
(WASHTON)
411 East 83rd Street
New York, NY 10028
(212) 481-0479

Waverly Auctions, Inc.
(WAVERLY*)
4931 Cordell Avenue
Bethesda, MD 20814
(301) 951-8883

Jeff Weber Rare Books
(WEBER)
P.O. Box 3368
Glendale, CA 91221-0368
(818) 848-9704

Wheldon & Wesley
(WHELDON & WESLEY)
Lytton Lodge
Codicote, Hitchin
Hertfordshire SG4 8TE
United Kingdom

David White
(WHITE)
17 High Street
Bassingbourn, Royston
Hertfordshire SG8 5NE
United Kingdom

F. E. Whitehart, Rare Books
(WHITEHART)
40 Priestfield Road
Forest Hill
London SE23 2RS
United Kingdom

Edna Whiteson, ABA
(WHITESON)
66 Belmont Avenue
Cockfosters
Hertfordshire EN4 9LA
United Kingdom

Avril Whittle, Bookseller
(WHITTLE)
Swarthgill House
Garsdale, Nr. Sedbergh
Cumbria LA10 5PD
United Kingdom

Nigel Williams
(WILLIAMS)
22 Cecil Court
London WC2N 4HE
United Kingdom

Words Etcetera
(WORDS ETC)
6 West Street
Blandford
Dorset DT11 7AJ
United Kingdom

Worldwide Antiquarian
(WORLDWIDE)
P.O. Box 410391
Cambridge, MA 02141-0004
(617) 876-6220

Samuel Yudkin & Associates
(YUDKIN*)
A232, The Woodner, Box A117
3636 16th Street NW
Washington, DC 20010
(202) 232-6249

Zubal Auction Company
(ZUBAL*)
2969 W. 25th Street
Cleveland, OH 44113
(216) 241-7640

ABBREVIATIONS

To present the maximum amount of information, we have used the following abbreviations in editing the entries in this guide. Most of these abbreviations are standard.

4to	a book with a height of approximately 12"	extrem(s)	extremities	OUP	Oxford University Press
8vo	a book with a height of approximately 9"	facs	facsimile	pb	paperback
12mo	a book with a height of approximately 7-8"	fep	free end paper, front end paper, front free end paper, flyleaf	perf	perforated
add'l	additional	fig(s)	figure(s)	Phila	Philadelphia
aeg	all edges gilt	fldg	folding, fold-out, folded	pict	pictorial
adv	advance	fr	front	prelims	preliminary pages
als	autograph letter, signed	frontis	frontispiece	plt(s)	plate(s)
assoc	association	FSG	Farrar, Straus, and Giroux	pg/pp	page(s)
BAE	Bureau of American Ethnology	G&D	Grosset & Dunlap	port(s)	portrait(s)
BAL	Bibliography of American Literature	GC	Garden City	promo	promotional
Balt	Baltimore	GPO	Government Printing Office	pseud	pseudonym
bd(s)	board(s)	grn	green	ptd	printed
bkpl(s)	bookplate(s)	hb	hardback, hardcover	ptg	printing
brn	brown	hist	historical	ptr	printer
b/w	black and white	HMSO	Her (His) Majesty's Stationery Office	pub's	publisher's
C&W	Chatto & Windus	illus	illustration(s), illustrated, illustrator	rev	revised, reviser
ca	circa	imp	impression	rev copy	review copy
cat(s)	catalog(s)	incl	included, including	rep	rear end paper, rear free end paper
CCC	Collins Crime Club	inscrip	non-authorial inscription	rt	right
cent	century	L.A.	Los Angeles	rmdr mk	remainder mark
cl	cloth	LEC	Limited Editions Club	rpt	reprint
comp	compiler/complimentary	lib	library	rptd	reprinted
contemp	contemporary	litho	lithograph, lithographic	S&S	Simon & Schuster
CUP	Cambridge University Press	lg	large	SF	San Francisco
cvr(s)	cover(s)	ll	leaves	sig(s)	non-authorial signature(s); signature(s) (gathering of book pages)
cvrd	covered	ltd	limited	sl	slight, slightly, minor, marginally
dbl	double	lt	light, lightly, moderately	sm	small
DCC	Doubleday Crime Club	mk(s)	mark(s), marking(s)	soc	society
dec	decorative, decorated	mkd	marked	SPCK	Society for the Promotion of Christian Knowledge
diag(s)	diagram(s)	MMA	Metropolitan Museum of Art	subs	subscription
dj	dust jacket, dust wrapper	mod	modern	supp	supplement
dk	dark	MOMA	Museum of Modern Art	teg	top edge gilt
dknd	darkened	ms	manuscript	tls	typed letter, signed
dkng	darkening	mtd	mounted	tp	title page
dup	duplicate	n.d.	no date	trans	translated, translator, translation
dwgs	drawings	n.p.	no place, no publisher	univ	university
ed(s)	editor(s), edited by, edition(s)	NAL	New American Library	unptd	unprinted
emb	embossed	NF	near fine	VF	very fine
engr(s)	engraving(s), engraved	#	number	VG	very good
enlgd	enlarged	NY	New York	vol(s)	volume(s)
ep(s)	endpaper(s)	NYGS	New York Graphic Society	w/	with
esp	especially	o/w	otherwise	w/o	without
et al	and others	OJ	Orange Judd		
ex-lib	ex-library	orig	original		
ex-libris	bookplate present				

A

A'BECKETT, GILBERT ABBOTT. The Comic History of England. (London): Punch Office, 1847-1848. 1st ed, 1st issue. 2 vols. Uncut. Orig purple cl, gilt. (Foxed; last text pg vol 1, contents pg vol 2 partly loose; spines faded.) *Maggs.* $187/£120

A'BECKETT, GILBERT ABBOTT. The Comic History of Rome. (London): Bradbury, Evans, n.d. (ca 1852). 1st ed. xii,308pp; 10 hand-colored wood engrs. 19th cent calf, marbled bds, grn spine label. (Sl rubbed.) *Karmiole.* $175/£112

A1. (Pseud of Florence Anthony.) Cruelty. Boston, 1973. 1st Amer ed, 1st bk. Fine in NF dj. *Polyanthos.* $45/£29

A1. (Pseud of Florence Anthony.) Cruelty. Boston: Houghton Mifflin, 1973. 1st ed, 1st bk. Fine in dj. *Lame Duck.* $150/£96

ABBE, DOROTHY. The Dwiggins Marionettes. NY: Abrams, n.d. 1st ed. 22 tipped-in color plts. VF in ptd acetate dj. *Captain's Bookshelf.* $50/£32

ABBEY, CHARLES A. Before the Mast in the Clippers. (By Harpur Allen Gosnell.) NY: Derrydale, 1937. 1st ed. One of 950. 1/2 cl. Fine. *Lefkowicz.* $165/£106

ABBEY, EDWARD. The Fool's Progress. NY: Holt, (1988). 1st ed. Fine in dj. *Hermitage.* $30/£19

ABBEY, EDWARD. The Monkey Wrench Gang. Phila/NY: J.B. Lippincott, (1975). 1st ed. Black bds, red cl spine. VG in dj. *Dawson.* $150/£96

ABBEY, J. R. Life in England in Aquatint and Lithography, 1770-1860. Curwen Press, 1953. 1st ed. Ltd to 400 numbered. Color frontis, 32 collotype plts. Brn cl (sl bumped, upper hinge sl cracked), red morocco spine label. Abbey's bkpl. *Maggs.* $499/£320

ABBEY, J. R. Travel in Aquatint and Lithography 1770-1860.... Folkestone/London: Dawsons of Pall Mall, 1972. Rpt. 4to. 2 vols. Color frontis, 36 plts. Brn cl. Djs (1 w/sm tear). *Maggs.* $187/£120

ABBOT, ROBERT. A Hand of Fellowship.... London: Nathaniel Butter, 1623. Vellum. (Inscrips, tp sl chipped; dknd.) *Metropolitan*.* $100/£64

Abbot. (By Walter Scott.) Edinburgh: Longman et al, 1820. 1st ed. 3 vols. Brn 1/2 calf, marbled bds, gilt panels. Fine (bkpls, browned or foxed). *Antic Hay.* $250/£160

Abbotsford and Newstead Abbey. (By Washington Irving.) John Murray, 1835. 1st ed. 19th cent 1/2 russia, gilt back (upper joint partly cracked). *Hatchwell.* $78/£50

ABBOTT, ASA APPLETON. Pioneer Family of the West. Cleveland, (1926). Ptd presentation card. Cl-backed bds (dknd, spine dull, flaked). *Bohling.* $20/£13

ABBOTT, BERENICE. Changing New York. NY: Dutton, 1939. 1st ed. 97 photo plts. (Owner stamps, ep gutters dknd), else NF in VG dj. *Cahan.* $475/£304

ABBOTT, BERENICE. Hound and Horn. NY: H&H, 1932. 4 full-pg repros. Good in wrappers. *Smith.* $35/£22

ABBOTT, BERNICE. Lisette Model. NY: Millerton, 1979. Dj (chipped). *Edwards.* $55/£35

ABBOTT, CARLISLE. Recollections of a California Pioneer. NY: Neale Pub Co, 1917. 1st ed. Frontis port. Orange cl, gilt. (Ink inscrip), o/w Fine. *Pacific*.* $138/£88

ABBOTT, CHARLES. A Treatise of the Law Relative to Merchant Ships and Seamen.... London: E. & R. Brooke et al, 1802. 1st ed. New 1/4 calf (browned). Usable only (ex-lib). *Boswell.* $275/£176

ABBOTT, EDWIN ABBOTT. Flatland, a Romance of Many Dimensions. Oxford: Basil Blackwell, 1950. 5th ed, rev. Pict bds encased in plastic (sl rubbed, soiled). *Bohling.* $10/£6

ABBOTT, HENRY G. Abbott's American Watchmaker and Jeweler. Chicago: Hazlitt & Walker, 1910. 1st ed. 204pp. 2 fldg illus. (Paper uniformly browned.) Maroon cl (spine ends frayed). *Weber.* $60/£38

ABBOTT, HENRY G. Antique Watches and How to Establish Their Age. Chicago: George K. Hazlitt, (1897). 1st ed. Blue cl. Fine. *Weber.* $90/£58

ABBOTT, JOHN. Exposition of the Principles of Abbott's Hydraulic Engine. Boston, 1835. 7 wood-engr plts. (Lower corner waterstained.) Orig 1/2 cl (worn, shabby). *Maggs.* $70/£45

ABBOTT, LYMAN. Henry Ward Beecher. Hartford: Amer Pub Co, 1887. 1st ed. Tp bears 2nd (inkstamped) imprint of 'Winter & Co., Springfield, Mass.' Brn cl, gilt. Fine. *Sumner & Stillman.* $70/£45

ABBOTT, MAUDE E. (ed). Appreciations and Reminiscences of Sir William Osler, Bart; with Bibliographies. (Binding title.) Montreal: Privately issued, (January 1927). 2nd imp, enlgd, corrected. Ltd to 1500 numbered. Frontis port, (6),xl,634 (sic 644)pp. VG (spine sl dull, lt shelfwear). *Glaser.* $185/£119

ABBOTT, WILLIS J. Battlefields of '61. NY, (1889). 1st ed. 356pp. Pict cl. VG+. *Pratt.* $40/£26

ABC in Living Models.... Bookano, n.d. (ca 1935). 8vo. All stand-up shaped pictures in Nice condition. Cl spine, pict bds. VG (fr hinge repaired). *Bookmark.* $78/£50

ABC Jingles. Syracuse: Hanford, 1920. 12mo. (13)pp. Nice in color-ptd self-wrappers (1-inch spine tear, lt foxing). *Bromer.* $45/£29

ABC of Nature. NY: McLoughlin Bros, 1884. 4to. Dbl-pg word list. Illus linen w/4 letter color illus blocks. (Linen pp dknd; linen edges sl worn), o/w VG. *Dower.* $125/£80

ABC of the Apple Pie. NY: McLoughlin Bros, 1899. Little Linen Series. 12mo. 8pp. Red linen. Good+. *Dower.* $65/£42

ABDILL, GEORGE B. Civil War Railroads. Seattle: Superior, (1961). 1st ed. VG+ in dj. *Bohling.* $30/£19

ABE, KOBO. Friends. Donald Keene (trans). NY: Grove, 1969. 1st ed. NF (sl yellowed) in wraps. *Else Fine.* $35/£22

ABE, KOBO. Secret Rendezvous. NY: Knopf, 1979. 1st ed. Fine in Fine dj. *Else Fine.* $30/£19

ABEL, ANNIE H. The American Indian as Slaveholder and Secessionist.... Cleveland: A.H. Clark, 1915-25. 3 vols. Red cl. (Ex-lib #s to spines, perf stamps tps), o/w VG set. Howes A9. *Reese.* $600/£385

ABEL, JOHN JACOB. Investigator, Teacher, Prophet, 1857-1938. Balt: Williams & Wilkins, 1957. 1st ed. Frontis, 2-sided plt, table. VG. *Glaser.* $75/£48

ABELL, MRS. L. G. The Skillful Housewife's Book. NY: Moore, 1858. 35th thousand. 216pp+ads. VG. *Second Life.* $85/£54

ABERCROMBIE, JOHN. Inquiries Concerning the Intellectual Powers, and the Investigation of Truth. NY: Harper, 1833. 2nd Edinburgh ed. (ii),349,(13)pp. Ptd bds (sl worn). VG. *Gach.* $50/£32

ABERNETHY, ALONZO (comp). Dedication of Monuments Erected by the State of Iowa...November 12 to 26, 1906. (Des Moines: State of IA), 1908. 30 plts, 4 maps. Maroon cl (rebound). Fine. *Graf.* $40/£26

ABERNETHY, JOHN. Surgical and Physiological Essays. 1793-7. 1st ed. 3 parts in 1 vol w/separate tps. viii,208pp; 3 plts. 1/4 morocco (rebound). (Lib stamp tps), o/w VG. *Whitehart.* $593/£380

ABERNETHY, JOHN. Surgical Observations on Diseases Resembling Syphilis; and on Diseases of the Urethra. 1810. 234pp (sl foxed, lib stamp tp). New 1/2 red morocco. *Whitehart.* $172/£110

ABERNETHY, JOHN. Surgical Observations on Diseases Resembling Syphilis; and on Diseases of the Urethra. 1814. 3rd ed. 234pp (lib stamps, sigs). New 1/2 calf. *Whitehart.* $125/£80

ABERNETHY, JOHN. Surgical Observations on the Constitutional Origin and Treatment of Local Diseases and Aneurisms. Vol I. London: Longman et al, 1820. 5th ed. xii,341pp. Uncut. Orig bds (rubbed, worn), paper spine label. VG. *Glaser.* $100/£64

ABERNETHY, JOHN. Surgical Observations on the Constitutional Origin and Treatment of Local Diseases. 1829. 11th ed. xii,346pp (sl foxed). New paper spine, binding, eps. (Bd edges damaged.) *Whitehart.* $94/£60

ABERNETHY, JOHN. Surgical Observations on the Constitutional Origin and Treatment of Local Diseases; and on Aneurysms.... Phila, 1811. 1st Amer ed. 325pp. Full leather. Good (extrems scuffed, worn). *Doctor's Library.* $250/£160

ABERNETHY, JOHN. Surgical Observations. (Part the First.) 1804. 1st ed. 264pp. New 1/2 blue morocco (rebound). (Lib stamps prelims) o/w VG. *Whitehart.* $218/£140

ABERNETHY, JOHN. Surgical Observations. Part the Second. 1806. 1st ed. viii,246pp (lib stamps prelims). *Whitehart.* $218/£140

ABERT, JAMES W. Through the Country of the Comanche Indians in the Fall of the Year 1845. John Galvin (ed). (SF): John Howell, 1970. One of 5000. Deckle edge. Beige cl, gilt. Fine in plain dj (lt soiled). *Bohling.* $60/£38

ABERT, JAMES W. Through the Country of the Comanche Indians in the Fall of the Year 1845. John Galvin (ed). SF: John Howell, 1970. Color frontis, 2 fldg maps. VF. *Oregon.* $75/£48

ABERT, JAMES W. Through the Country of the Comanche Indians, in the Fall of the Year 1845. John Galvin (ed). (SF): John Howell, 1970. One of 5000. 26 plts, 2 fldg maps. Tan cl, gilt. Fine in Fine dj. Howes A10. *Harrington.* $85/£54

ABERT, JAMES W. Western America in 1846-1847. The Original Travel Diary.... John Galvin (ed). (SF): John Howell, 1966. 2nd ed. Ltd to 3000 ptd by Lawton & Alfred Kennedy. Frontis, 13 color plts, 2 plans, 2 fldg maps. Tan cl, gilt. VF. *Argonaut.* $100/£64

ABERT, JAMES W. Western America in 1846-1847.... John Galvin (ed). SF: John Howell Books, 1966. 15 color dwgs, 2 fldg maps. Fine in acetate dj. *Graf.* $75/£48

ABISH, WALTER. Alphabetical Africa. NY, 1974. 1st ed. NF in NF dj (spine creased). *Warren.* $30/£19

ABRAHAM, GEORGE D. The Complete Mountaineer. London: Methuen, 1907. 1st ed. 75 plts. (Rebacked in matching levant morocco gilt.) *Hollett.* $133/£85

ABRAHAM, GEORGE D. Swiss Mountain Climbs. London: Mills & Boon, 1911. 1st ed. 24 plts. Box-bound cl, gilt. (Upper joint strained, reps sl stained.) *Hollett.* $101/£65

ABRAHAM, J. J. The Surgeon's Log. NY: Dutton, 1912. Dec cvr. Good. *Scribe's Perch*.* $20/£13

ABRAHAM, J. J. The Surgeon's Lot. London, 1911. 2nd ed. (Feps lt browned; rebound, spine sl rubbed.) *Edwards.* $39/£25

ABRAHAMS, PETER. The Fury of Rachel Monette. NY: Macmillan, 1980. 1st ed. VF in dj. *Mordida.* $50/£32

ABRAHAMS, PETER. The Path of Thunder. NY: Harper, (1948). 1st US ed. VG+ in VG+ dj. *Pettler & Lieberman.* $50/£32

ABRAHAMS, PETER. Tell Freedom. London: Faber, (1954). 1st British ed. NF in NF dj (price-clipped). *Pettler & Lieberman.* $40/£26

ABRAHAMS, PETER. A Wreath for Udomo. London, 1956. 1st Eng ed. Very Nice in dj. *Clearwater.* $47/£30

ABRAHAMSEN, DAVID. The Murdering Mind. NY: Harper & Row, (1973). 1st ed. Inscribed. VG. *Gach.* $25/£16

ABRAMOVITZ, I. (ed). The Great Prisoners, Anthology. NY, 1946. 1st ed. VG in dj (frayed). *Typographeum.* $50/£32

ABRAMS, ALBERT. Transactions of the Antiseptic Club. NY, 1895. 1st ed. 205pp. VG (backstrip soiled, spotted). *Fye.* $100/£64

ABSE, DANNIE. Some Corner of an English Field. London, 1956. 1st Eng ed. Nice in dj (sl torn). *Clearwater.* $39/£25

Account of the Roman Antiquities Preserved in the Museum of Chesters.... (By E. A. Wallis Budge.) London: Gilbert & Rivington, 1907. Map. *Archaeologia.* $65/£42

Account of the Wreck of H.M. Sloop 'Osprey'.... (By Henry Moon.) Landport: Annett & Robinson, 1858. 1st ed. (xii),127pp; ptd errata slip. Orig cl, ptd paper label. *Lefkowicz.* $475/£304

ACHAD, FRATER. The Egyptian Revival. Chicago, 1923. 1st ed. #104/1001. Signed. Foldout. (Cvr lt worn), o/w NF. *Middle Earth.* $245/£157

ACHEBE, CHINUA. Hopes and Impediments. NY, 1989. 1st ed. Fine in Fine dj. *Smith.* $20/£13

ACHEBE, CHINUA. A Man of the People. NY: John Day, 1966. 1st Amer ed. VG in VG- dj (worn, 1-inch tear). *Revere.* $20/£13

ACHEBE, CHINUA. No Longer at Ease. NY: Obolensky, 1961. 1st US ed. Inscribed. (Sl shelfworn), else NF in VG+ dj (spine faded, 1/2-inch tear spine head). *Lame Duck.* $200/£128

ACIER, MARCEL (ed). From Spanish Trenches. Mod Age, 1937. 1st ed. Wraps (dull). Contents Good. *Whiteson.* $23/£15

ACKER, KATHY. The Adult Life of Toulouse Lautrec. NY: TVRT Press, 1978. 1st ed. NF in illus wraps. *Lame Duck.* $65/£42

ACKER, KATHY. The Childlike Life of the Black Tarantula. NY: Turt, 1978. 1st trade ed. NF wrappers (rear panel rubbed). *Warren.* $30/£19

ACKER, KATHY. Hello, I'm Erica Jong. NY: Contact II Publications, 1982. 1st ed. Fine in stapled black wraps. *Lame Duck.* $85/£54

ACKERKNECHT, ERWIN H. A Short History of Medicine. NY: Ronald, (1955). 1st ed. VG. *Glaser.* $40/£26

ACKERLEY, J. R. Hindoo Holiday. London, 1932. 1st ed. (Cvr edges sl cockled, something removed from ep.) Dj. *Typographeum.* $75/£48

ACKERLEY, J. R. Hindoo Holiday. London, 1932. 1st Eng ed. Good in dj (sl nicked, rubbed). *Clearwater.* $101/£65

ACKERLEY, J. R. Hindoo Holiday: An Indian Journal. NY: Viking, 1932. 1st Amer ed. Fine in dj (sm chips, price-clipped). *Captain's Bookshelf.* $125/£80

ACKERLEY, J. R. My Dog Tulip. London: Secker & Warburg, 1956. 1st ed. VG (lacks dj). *Captain's Bookshelf.* $40/£26

ACKERLEY, J. R. My Father and Myself. NY: Coward, (1969). 1st Amer ed. NF in NF dj. *Captain's Bookshelf.* $35/£22

ACKERLEY, J. R. The Prisoners of War. London, 1925. 1st Eng ed, 1st bk. Very Nice (name; spine label sl rubbed). *Clearwater.* $86/£55

ACKERMAN, JAMES S. The Architecture of Michelangelo. NY: Viking, (1961). 1st ed. Blue cl. Good in dj (chipped). *Karmiole*. $60/£38

ACKERMAN, PHYLLIS. Ritual Bronzes of Ancient China. NY: Dryden, 1945. 1st ed. 66 plts. (Cl sl rubbed, spine sl frayed, ex-lib, sticker fr cvr), o/w VG. *Worldwide*. $25/£16

ACKERMAN, PHYLLIS. Ritual Bronzes of Ancient China. NY: Dryden, 1945. 1st ed. Frontis, 66 plts. Black cl, gilt. Good. *Karmiole*. $50/£32

Ackermann's New Drawing Book of Light and Shadow. London: R. Ackermann, 1812 (plts dated 1809). Tp,ii,6 ff. explanations, 24 aquatint plts (dampstaining, discoloration). 1/2 straight-grain morocco (worn), orig yellow ptd label. *Marlborough*. $390/£250

ACKERMANN, J. S. The Architecture of Michelangelo. London: Zwemmer, 1961. 2 vols. 83 plts. (Cl sl worn.) *Ars Artis*. $195/£125

ACKLAND, VALENTINE. For Sylvia: An Honest Account. NY: Norton, (1986). 1st Amer ed. Rev flyer laid in. Fine in dj. *Reese*. $15/£10

ACKLAND, VALENTINE. The Nature of the Moment. London: C&W, 1973. 1st ed. Relevant clippings laid in. Fine in dj. *Reese*. $25/£16

ACKLEY, W. WORTH. Tales of the Sea and Other Poems. Prairie City, IL: Decker, (1949). 1st ed. Signed. Fine in dj (spine tanned). *Dermont*. $45/£29

ACKROYD, PETER. Chatterton. NY: Grove, (1987). 1st ed. Signed. Fine in dj. *Antic Hay*. $50/£32

ACKROYD, PETER. Dickens. Stevenson, 1990. 1st UK ed. Signed. Mint in Mint dj. *Martin*. $23/£15

ACKROYD, PETER. Dressing Up. London, 1979. 1st Eng ed. Fine in dj. *Clearwater*. $78/£50

ACKROYD, PETER. Dressing Up. NY, 1979. 1st Amer ed. Fine in dj. *Clearwater*. $62/£40

ACKROYD, PETER. English Music. NY: Knopf, 1992. 1st ed. Signed. Fine in dj. *Antic Hay*. $45/£29

ACKROYD, PETER. Ezra Pound and His World. London, 1980. 1st Eng ed. Fine in dj (sl sunned). *Clearwater*. $31/£20

ACKROYD, PETER. Hawksmoor. NY: Harper & Row, (1985). 1st ed. Signed. Fine in dj. *Antic Hay*. $75/£48

ACKROYD, PETER. The Last Testament of Oscar Wilde. NY: Harper & Row, (1983). 1st ed. Fine in dj (faint stain, sm tear). *Antic Hay*. $25/£16

ACKROYD, PETER. T. S. Eliot. Hamish Hamilton, 1984. 1st ed. (Spine head bruised), o/w Fine in dj. *Poetry Bookshop*. $23/£15

ACOSTA, OSCAR ZEN. The Revolt of the Cockroach People. SF: Straight Arrow, (1973). 1st ed. VG+ in VG dj. *Pettler & Lieberman*. $30/£19

ACTON, ELIZA. Modern Cookery. London: Longman, Greene et al, 1868. xxxi,643,32pp; 8 steel-engr plts. Mod 1/2 levant morocco, gilt. VG (lt spotted). *Hollett*. $281/£180

ACTON, HAROLD. Cornelian: A Fable. London: C&W, (1928). 1st ed. One of 550 numbered, signed. NF in dj (spine sl dknd). *Captain's Bookshelf*. $150/£96

ACTON, HAROLD. The Last Medici. Faber, 1932. 1st Eng ed. Bright (cvrs sl mkd). *Clearwater*. $31/£20

ACTON, HAROLD. Modern Chinese Poetry. Harold Acton & Ch'en Shih-Hsiang (trans). Duckworth, 1936. 1st Eng ed. Nice (cvrs sl mkd). *Clearwater*. $86/£55

ACTON, HAROLD. Nancy Mitford, A Memoir. NY, 1975. 1st ed. VG in dj. *Typographeum*. $25/£16

ACTON, HAROLD. Prince Isidore. London, 1950. 1st Eng ed. Very Nice in dj (sl chipped, chafed). *Clearwater*. $55/£35

ACTON, HAROLD. Tuscan Villas. London: Thames & Hudson, (1973). 1st ed. 126 photogravure plts, 34 color plts. Fine in dj. *Captain's Bookshelf*. $125/£80

Acts of the Legislature of the State of Michigan, Passed at the First and Extra Sessions, of 1835 and 1836. Detroit: J.S. Bagg, 1836. 396pp. Contemp 1/4 calf, leather label, marbled bds. (Text lt browned; sl worn), else VG. *Brown*. $100/£64

ACWORTH, BERNARD. The Cuckoo and Other Bird Mysteries. London, 1944. 1st ed. Grn cl. VG. *Price*. $29/£19

ADAM, G. MERCER. From Savagery to Civilization. Toronto: Rose, 1885. 390pp; 12 ports. Pict cl (rubbed). *Adelson*. $60/£38

ADAM, HANS-CHRISTIAN and RAINER FABIAN. Masters of Early Travel Photography. NY: Vendome, 1983. 1st ed. NF in NF dj. *Smith*. $125/£80

ADAMS, A. John James Audubon, a Biography. London, 1967. Eng ed. Dj (sl frayed). *Maggs*. $19/£12

ADAMS, ALEXANDER B. Geronimo: A Biography. NY: Putnam, (1971). 1st ed. VG in dj. *Lien*. $30/£19

ADAMS, ANDY. Cattle Brands. A Collection of Western Camp-Fire Stories. Boston/NY: Houghton Mifflin, (1934). NF in dj (sl worn). *Sadlon*. $20/£13

ADAMS, ANDY. The Corporal Segundo. Austin: Encino, 1968. One of 750 numbered, signed by Wilson M. Hudson (ed). Cl, pict bds. NF. *Reese*. $45/£29

ADAMS, ANDY. The Log of a Cowboy. Boston: Houghton Mifflin, 1903. 1st ed. 6 plts. Dec cvr. Good. *Scribe's Perch**. $42/£27

ADAMS, ANDY. The Outlet. Boston: Houghton Mifflin, 1905. 1st ed. Pict olive cl stamped in gold/red/white/black. Fine (ink name fep, lt soil 2pp; sl rubbed). *Argonaut*. $60/£38

ADAMS, ANDY. The Outlet. London: Constable, 1905. 1st British ed. Pict mustard cl stamped in gold/red/white/black. (Corners sl jammed, spine sl faded), else Very Nice. *Argonaut*. $40/£26

ADAMS, ANDY. A Texas Matchmaker. Boston/NY: Houghton Mifflin, 1904. 1st ed. Pict olive cl stamped in gold/red/white/black. NF (eps renewed, sm tear 1 leaf; rubbed). *Argonaut*. $40/£26

ADAMS, ANDY. Why the Chisholm Trail Forks and Other Tales of the Cattle Country. Wilson M. Hudson (ed). Austin: Univ of TX, 1956. 1st ed. Mustard cl stamped in black. Fine in pict dj (spine faded). *Argonaut*. $45/£29

ADAMS, ANSEL and EDWARD JOESTING. An Introduction to Hawaii. SF: 5 Associates, (1964). 1st ed. Fine in Fine dj. *Book Market*. $60/£38

ADAMS, ANSEL and NANCY NEWHALL. Death Valley. SF: 5 Associates, 1959. 2nd ed. 24 b/w, 10 color plts. NF in pict wrappers (extrems sl worn). *Harrington*. $75/£48

ADAMS, ANSEL and NANCY NEWHALL. The Tetons and the Yellowstone. Redwood City: 5 Associates, 1970. 1st ed. Fine in NF dj. *Smith*. $125/£80

ADAMS, ANSEL. Born Free and Equal. NY: US Camera, 1944. 1st ed. VG (name stamp) in ptd wrappers (corner creased). *Cahan*. $400/£256

ADAMS, ANSEL. The Camera. Boston: NYGS, 1980. 1st ed thus. Fine in Fine dj. *Smith*. $35/£22

ADAMS, ANSEL. The Eloquent Light. SF: Sierra Club, 1963. 1st ed. VG+ in VG+ dj. *Smith*. $125/£80

ADAMS, ANSEL. Examples. Boston: NYGS, 1983. 1st ed. Fine in Fine dj. *Smith*. $90/£58

ADAMS, ANSEL. Images 1923-1974. Boston: NYGS, 1981. Signed. Fine in dj (browned). *Argosy*. $100/£64

ADAMS, ANSEL. Making a Photograph. London/NY: Studio, 1935. 32 tipped-in b/w plts. Cl-backed pict bds. (Eps, text lt spotted; edges sl rubbed.) Dj (lt soiled, chipped; loss at corners, spine). *Edwards*. $70/£45

ADAMS, ANSEL. My Camera in the National Parks. Boston, 1950. 1st ed. Signed. Stiff spiral wraps (well worn). *King*. $300/£192

ADAMS, ANSEL. My Camera in the National Parks. Yosemite Nat'l Park: Virginia Adams, 1950. 1st ed. Signed. 30 b/w photo plts. Spiral bound bds (sl soiled, rubbed). NF. *Harrington*. $275/£176

ADAMS, ANSEL. My Camera in Yosemite Valley. Yosemite National Park/Boston: Houghton Mifflin, 1949. Folio. NF in orig spiral-backed photographic wrappers. *Sadlon*. $275/£176

ADAMS, ANSEL. Photographs of the Southwest. Boston, (1976). 1st ed. VG in dj (sl yellowed, price-clipped). *King*. $95/£61

ADAMS, ANSEL. Photographs of the Southwest. Boston: NYGS, 1976. 1st ed. Signed. Fine in Fine dj. *Smith*. $150/£96

ADAMS, ANSEL. The Portfolios of Ansel Adams. Boston: NYGS, 1977. 2nd ptg. 92 full-pg plts. (Half-title lt foxed), else Fine in dj. *Cahan*. $20/£13

ADAMS, ANSEL. The Portfolios of Ansel Adams. Boston: NYGS, 1977. 1st ed. VG + in VG dj (sl damp-stained). *Smith*. $80/£51

ADAMS, ANSEL. The Print. NY: Morgan & Morgan, 1968. 1st ed thus. VG + in VG dj. *Smith*. $35/£22

ADAMS, ANSEL. Yosemite and the Range of Light. Boston: NYGS, 1979. 3rd ptg. One of special ed prepared for Time/Life subs w/Adams's sig on bkpl. VG in VG dj. *Smith*. $200/£128

ADAMS, ANSEL. Yosemite Valley. Redwood City: 5 Associates, 1967. VG + in wrappers. *Smith*. $30/£19

ADAMS, ARTHUR FREDERICK. Terra Cotta of the Italian Renaissance. Terra Cotta Assoc, 1928. *Edwards*. $39/£25

ADAMS, BILL et al. The Antique Bowie Knife Book. Conyers, GA: Museum Pub Co, (1990). 1st ed. Ltd to 1100. As New in dj. *Lien*. $300/£192

ADAMS, CHARLES FRANCIS. Lee at Appomattox and Other Papers. Boston, 1902. 1st ed. (Cvr sl worn), o/w Fine. *Pratt*. $35/£22

ADAMS, DANIEL. The Scholar's Arithmetic. Leominster: The Author, 1805. 3rd ed. 216pp. Orig leather spine, marbled paper-cvrd bds. (Text browned; bds rubbed), else Good. *Brown*. $15/£10

ADAMS, DOUGLAS. The Hitch-Hikers Guide to the Galaxy. Pan Books, 1979. True 1st ed. Fine in wrappers. *Words Etc*. $39/£25

ADAMS, DOUGLAS. So Long, and Thanks for All the Fish. Pan, 1984. 1st UK ed. Fine in dj, hologram on fr panel. *Williams*. $19/£12

ADAMS, ELEANOR B. (ed). Bishop Tamaron's Visitation of New Mexico 1760. Albuquerque, 1954. 1st ed. Pb. Fine. *Turpen*. $28/£18

ADAMS, ELIZ and D. REDSTONE. Bow Porcelain. Faber, 1981. 1st ed. Mint in dj. *Whittle*. $31/£20

ADAMS, FREDERICK UPHAM. John Henry Smith. A Humorous Romance of Outdoor Life. NY: Doubleday, Page, 1905. 1st ed. Pict label. NF (fore-edge, extrems lt rubbed). *Captain's Bookshelf*. $125/£80

ADAMS, H. and H. The Smaller British Birds. London, 1874. 32 color plts (1 margin frayed). Gilt edges. Grn cl (sl worn, loose). *Maggs*. $94/£60

ADAMS, H. G. and H. B. The Smaller British Birds. London, 1894. iv,252pp (lt spotted; upper hinge cracked, lower hinge sl tender); 32 color plts. Teg. Gilt-illus cl (sl rubbed, sl bumped). *Edwards*. $70/£45

ADAMS, HANNAH. A View of Religions. Boston: John West Folsom, (1791). 2nd ed. 410pp, errata leaf. Full calf (rebound). *Second Life*. $125/£80

ADAMS, HENRY. History of the United States.... NY: Scribner, 1889-90. 1st ed. 4 vols. VG- (spines faded, tips worn). Howes A53. *Agvent*. $150/£96

ADAMS, HENRY. Mont Saint Michel and Chartres. NY: LEC, 1957. One of 1500 numbered, signed by Samuel Chamberlain (photos). 59 photo plts. Gilt leather label. VG in marbled bd slipcase. *Argosy*. $125/£80

ADAMS, HERBERT. The Golf House Murder. Phila: Lippincott, 1933. 1st ed. NF (w/o dj). *Mordida*. $55/£35

ADAMS, J. HOWE. History of David Hayes Agnews Life. Phila, 1892. 1st ed. 1/2 leather. VG. *Argosy*. $75/£48

ADAMS, JAMES T. Album of American History. NY, 1944-1951. 1st ed. 5 vols. Some vols in djs. *Ginsberg*. $100/£64

ADAMS, JAMES T. The Lost Hunter. NY: Debry, 1856. 1st ed. 462,(4)pp. *Ginsberg*. $100/£64

ADAMS, JOHN M. Viruses and Colds: The Modern Plague. NY, 1967. 1st ed. VG in Good dj. *Doctor's Library*. $30/£19

ADAMS, JOHN QUINCY. The Jubilee of the Constitution. NY: Berford, 1848. 136pp. 1/4 morocco. (Sl foxed, recently rebound), o/w VG. *Worldwide*. $145/£93

ADAMS, JOHN QUINCY. Writings, 1779-1823. Worthington C. Ford (ed). NY, 1913-1917. 1st ed. 7 vols. (Spine sl faded few vols.) *Ginsberg*. $275/£176

ADAMS, JOHN. The Works of John Adams...with a Life of the Author...by His Grandson Charles Francis Adams. Boston, 1856. 1st ed. 10 vols. Black cl (spine wear few vols). *Ginsberg*. $650/£417

ADAMS, LEONIE. High Falcon and Other Poems. NY, 1931. 1st ed. VG. *Bond*. $60/£38

ADAMS, MARY STILL. Autobiography of.... L.A.: Buckingham, 1893. 288pp. (Worn.) *Dawson*. $30/£19

ADAMS, MRS. Letters of...the Wife of John Adams.... Boston: Little, Brown, 1841. 3rd ed. 2 vols. Frontis port (offsetting), 208; 282pp. Fine. *Second Life*. $85/£54

ADAMS, PHILIP R. Auguste Rodin. Hyperion, 1945. 40 plts. Good. *Goodrich*. $35/£22

ADAMS, R. CHARLES. Intravenous Anaesthesia. NY: Hoeber, (1944). 1st ed. (Sl worn.) Dj (frayed). *Oinonen**. $50/£32

ADAMS, RAMON F. Come an' Get It. Norman: Univ of OK, (1952). 1st ed. 2-tone cl, gilt lettering. Fine (bkpl) in pict dj (sl chipped). *Argonaut*. $45/£29

ADAMS, RAMON F. Come an' Get It. The Story of the Old Cowboy Cook. Norman: Univ of OK, (1952). 1st ed. Inscribed. Fine in NF dj. *Sadlon*. $65/£42

ADAMS, RAMON F. The Cowboy and His Humor. Austin: Encino, 1968. 1st ed. #222/850. Signed. Pict bds. VF. *Argonaut*. $90/£58

ADAMS, RAMON F. Cowboy Lingo. Boston: Houghton Mifflin, 1936. 1st ed, 1st bk. Fine in dj (sl chipped, lt rubbed). *Argonaut*. $150/£96

ADAMS, RAMON F. The Cowman and His Code of Ethics. Austin: Encino, 1969. 1st ed. #186/850. Signed. Uncut. Pict bds. VF. *Argonaut*. $90/£58

ADAMS, RAMON F. The Cowman and His Philosophy. Austin: Encino, 1967. 1st ed. #94/750. Signed by Adams and William Wittliff of Encino Press. 1/2 cl, pict bds. VF. *Argonaut*. $90/£58

ADAMS, RAMON F. The Cowman Says It Salty. Tucson: Univ of AZ, (1971). 1st ed. Gilt-lettered grn cl. VF in pict dj. *Argonaut*. $75/£48

ADAMS, RAMON F. A Fitting Death for Billy the Kid. Norman: Univ of OK, (1960). 1st ed. VG in dj. *Perier*. $50/£32

ADAMS, RAMON F. A Fitting Death for Billy the Kid. Norman: Univ of OK, (1960). 1st ed. VF in pict dj. *Argonaut.* $75/£48

ADAMS, RAMON F. (ed). From the Pecos to the Powder, a Cowboy's Autobiography. Norman: Univ of OK, (1965). 1st ed. Frontis. Gilt-lettered olive/gray cl, pict stamped in black. VF in pict dj (sl rubbed). *Argonaut.* $50/£32

ADAMS, RAMON F. From the Pecos to the Powder. Norman: Univ of OK, (1965). 1st ed. Good. *Lien.* $40/£26

ADAMS, RAMON F. The Old-Time Cowhand. NY: Macmillan, 1961. 1st trade ed. Signed. Tan cl stamped in gold/red. VF in pict dj (spine faded). *Argonaut.* $75/£48

ADAMS, RAMON F. The Old-Time Cowhand. NY: Macmillan, 1961. One of 350 numbered, signed by Adams and Nick Eggenhofer (illus). Pict cl stamped in brn, gilt-lettered spine. VF in pub's slipcase, paper label. *Argonaut.* $225/£144

ADAMS, RAMON F. Six-Guns and Saddle Leather. Norman: Univ of OK, (1954). 1st ed. VG in dj. *Lien.* $75/£48

ADAMS, RAMON F. Western Words. Norman: Univ of OK, (1968). New ed, rev, enlgd. Gilt-lettered blue cl. VF in pict dj (spine faded). *Argonaut.* $75/£48

ADAMS, RAMON F. and HOMER BRITZMAN. Charles M. Russell, the Cowboy Artist. Pasadena: Trail's End, 1957. Good in dj (sl worn). *Dumont.* $50/£32

ADAMS, RAMON F. and HOMER BRITZMAN. Charles M. Russell, the Cowboy Artist: A Biography, with Charles M. Russell, the Cowboy Artist: A Bibliography by Karl Yost. Pasadena: Trail's End Pub Co, (1948). 'Collector's Edition' ltd to 600 sets. 2 vols. 12 color plts. 1/2 black leather, gilt lettering, black cl-cvrd bds. Fine in pub's slipcase (worn). *Argonaut.* $250/£160

ADAMS, RAMON F. and HOMER BRITZMAN. Charles M. Russell, the Cowboy Artist: A Biography. Pasadena: Trail's End, (1948). 1st ed. 11 color plts. Burgundy cl (sl stained). Dj (tears internally repaired w/tape). *Karmiole.* $85/£54

ADAMS, RAMON F. and HOMER BRITZMAN. Charles M. Russell, the Cowboy Artist: A Biography. Pasadena: Trail's End, (1954). 2nd ed. 12 color plts. Maroon cl, gilt-lettered spine. Fine. *Argonaut.* $100/£64

ADAMS, RAMON F. and HOMER E. BRITZMAN. Charles M. Russell, the Cowboy Artist: A Biography. Pasadena, (1948). 1st ed. VG. *Truepenny.* $75/£48

ADAMS, RICHARD C. A Delaware Indian Legend and the Story of Their Troubles. Washington: Privately published, 1899. 1st ed. 72,3pp. Maroon cl (rubbed, spotted, spine sl faded, extrem wear beginning), gilt. Internally Fine. Overall VG. *Harrington.* $125/£80

ADAMS, RICHARD. The Iron Wolf and Other Stories. Allen Lane, 1980. 1st UK ed. Fine in dj. *Williams.* $19/£12

ADAMS, RICHARD. The Legend of Te Tuna. London: Sidgwick & Jackson, (1986). 1st trade ed. Ul de Rico (illus). Fine in dj. *Between The Covers.* $50/£32

ADAMS, RICHARD. The Plague Dogs. Allen Lane, 1977. 1st UK ed. Fine in dj. *Williams.* $23/£15

ADAMS, RICHARD. Shardik. NY: S&S, (1974). 1st ed. NF in dj. *Antic Hay.* $15/£10

ADAMS, RICHARD. Traveller. NY, 1988. 1st ed. Fine in Fine dj. *Pratt.* $17/£11

ADAMS, RICHARD. The Tyger Voyage. London: Cape, (1976). 1st Eng ed. Signed by Adams and Nicola Bayley (illus). 8vo. 31pp. Glazed illus bds. Fine. *Dower.* $75/£48

ADAMS, RICHARD. Watership Down. NY: Macmillan, (1972). 1st Amer ed. NF in dj (sl worn, soiled). *Waverly*.* $49/£31

ADAMS, ROBERT. The Architecture and Art of Early Hispanic Colorado. (Boulder): CO Assoc Univ Press, 1974. 1st ed. Map. Fine in dj (price-clipped). *Cahan.* $85/£54

ADAMS, ROBERT. Denver. Denver: CO Assoc Univ Press, 1977. 1st ed. Signed. Fine in New pict dj. *Cahan.* $75/£48

ADAMS, ROBERT. From the Missouri West. Millerton, NY: Aperture, 1980. 1st ed. Signed. Fine in illus dj. *Cahan.* $65/£42

ADAMS, ROBERT. Our Lives and Our Children. Millerton, NY: Aperture, 1983. 1st ed. NF in pict stiff wrappers. *Cahan.* $30/£19

ADAMS, ROBERT. Summer Nights. NY: Aperture, 1985. 1st ed. Fine in VG dj. *Cahan.* $35/£22

ADAMS, ROBERT. A Treatise on Rheumatic Gout.... London, 1857. 1st ed. 362pp. Orig tooled cl bds. Good (extrems worn). *Doctor's Library.* $200/£128

ADAMS, ROBERT. White Churches of the Plains. Boulder: CO Assoc Univ Press, 1970. 1st ed, 1st bk. Frontis. Fine in dj (price-clipped). *Cahan.* $85/£54

ADAMS, SAMUEL HOPKINS. The Flying Death. NY: McClure, 1908. 1st ed. (Bumped, lt soil, spine dk.) Lacks dj. *Metropolitan*.* $57/£37

ADAMS, SAMUEL HOPKINS. The Great American Fraud. NY, 1906. 1st ed. VG. *Fye.* $75/£48

ADAMS, W. I. LINCOLN. Photographing in Old England. NY: Baker & Taylor, 1910. 1st ed. Frontis. Aeg. Gilt-titled illus cl. (Eps foxed), else VG. *Cahan.* $50/£32

ADAMS, W. L. History of Medicine and Surgery from the Earliest Times. Portland: Geo. H. Himes, 1888. 178pp. (Wraps soiled; spine chipped.) *Perier.* $95/£61

ADAMS, WILLIAM HOWARD. Atget's Gardens. GC: Doubleday, 1979. 1st ed. 76 full-pg b/w plts. (Owner stamp), else NF in pict stiff wrappers. *Cahan.* $20/£13

ADCOCK, MARION ST. JOHN. The Littlest One. Harrap, 1914. 1st ed. Margaret Tarrant (illus). 4to. 41pp; 4 mtd color plts. Pict cl. (Edges rubbed), else VG. *Bookmark.* $39/£25

ADDAMS, CHARLES. Black Maria. NY: S&S, 1960. Stated 1st ptg. Good in Poor dj. *Scribe's Perch*.* $22/£14

ADDAMS, CHARLES. Chas Addams' Mother Goose. NY: Windmill, 1967. 1st ed. 9 x 12 1/4. 56pp. Fine in dj. *Cattermole.* $75/£48

ADDAMS, JANE. The Long Road of Woman's Memory. NY: Macmillan, 1916. 1st ed. Inscribed. (Sl shelfworn, address stamp), else Fine in blue cl-cvrd bds. *Lame Duck.* $450/£288

ADDINGTON, ANTHONY. An Essay on the Sea-Scurvy. Reading: C. Micklewright, 1753. 1st ed. vii, 47pp (foxed, few ll reinforced in gutter), erratum slip pasted to verso A4. Good. *Glaser.* $250/£160

ADDISON, A. C. and W. H. MATTHEWS. A Deathless Story or the 'Birkenhead' and Its Heroes. London, 1906. Frontis, map. Grn cl (shaken; prize certificate fep), gilt. *Maggs.* $47/£30

ADDISON, FRANK (ed). The Wellcome Excavations in the Sudan. London: OUP, 1949-51. 3 vols. 203 plts. Good in dj (tattered). *Archaeologia.* $375/£240

ADDISON, JOSEPH et al. The Spectator. Robert Halsband (ed). London: LEC, 1970. One of 1500 numbered, signed by Lynton Lamb (illus). 16 hand-colored plts. Dec cl, leather spine label. Mint in bd slipcase. *Argosy.* $125/£80

ADDISON, JOSEPH. Notes Upon the Twelve Books of Paradise Lost. London: Jacob Tonson, 1719. 1st sep ed. (Some pp tanned), o/w internally VG in contemp calf (bds, fly detached; notes on pastedowns, flies). *Poetry Bookshop.* $39/£25

ADDISON, JOSEPH. Remarks on Several Parts of Italy. London: Jacob Tonson, 1705. 1st ed. (10),534,(10)pp. Tree calf (rebacked, edgewear), morocco spine label. *Dawson.* $150/£96

ADDISON, JOSEPH. The Works of the Late Right Honorable.... Birmingham: John Baskerville at Shakespear's Head, 1761. 4 vols. 4to. Full red morocco, gilt. (Bkpls; bumped, rubbed), o/w Handsome. *Metropolitan*.* $517/£331

ADDISON, THOMAS. A Collection of the Published Writings. London, 1868. 1st ed. 242pp. VG. *Fye.* $250/£160

ADDISON, THOMAS. A Collection of the Published Writings. London: New Sydenham Soc, 1869. xxxi,239pp; 7 plts. (Ex-lib; rebacked.) *White.* $86/£55

ADDISON, WILLIAM. English Fairs and Markets. London: Batsford, 1953. 1st Eng ed. VG in dj (sl rubbed, price-clipped). *Hadley.* $47/£30

ADDISON, WILLIAM. Worthy Dr. Fuller. London: Dent, 1951. VG + in dj. *Bookcell.* $18/£12

Address of the People of Great Britain to the Inhabitants of America. (By John Dalrymple.) London: T. Cadell, 1775. 1st ed, 1st ptg. Complete w/half-title. Sl trimmed. 19th-cent 3/4 red morocco, marbled bds (rubbed, fr cvr detached). Howes D36. *Freeman*.* $120/£77

Addresses Delivered at the Annual Dinner of the Lincoln Club of Los Angeles 1921-1940. L.A.: Privately ptd, 1940. Ltd to 200 numbered. Teg. Leather-backed cl. (Sl wear.) *King.* $45/£29

ADDY, SIDNEY OLDALL. Church and Manor. London, 1913. 1st ed. Frontis port. (Feps lt browned.) *Edwards.* $47/£30

ADE, GEORGE. True Bells. NY: Harper, 1904. 1st ed. Inscribed. (Spine lettering rubbed), else Fine in dec cl. *Captain's Bookshelf.* $75/£48

ADELER, MAX. Elbow-Room. Phila, (1876). 1st Amer ed. NF (spine sl rubbed). *Polyanthos.* $45/£29

ADELER, MAX. Out of the Hurly-Burly. Phila, NY, Boston, Chicago/SF: 'To-Day' Pub/F. Dewing, 1874. 1st ed. Red-brn cl. Fine. *Sumner & Stillman.* $95/£61

ADLEMAN, R. and G. WALTON. The Champagne Campaign. NY, 1973. VG in VG dj. *Clark.* $30/£19

ADLER, ELMER. Breaking into Print. NY: S&S, 1937. 1st ed. Fine in dj. *Dermont.* $35/£22

ADLER, KATHLEEN and TAMAR GARB. Berthe Morisot. Phaidon, 1987. 1st ed. Color frontis port, 48 color plts. Dj. *Edwards.* $31/£20

ADNEY, EDWIN T. and HOWARD I. CHAPPELLE. The Bark Canoes and Skin Boats of North America. Washington: Smithsonian Inst, 1964. VG. *Perier.* $45/£29

ADOLPH, E. F. et al. Physiology of Man in the Desert. NY: Interscience, 1947. (Rear cvr lt spotted.) Dj (edgewear). *Dawson.* $40/£26

ADOLPHUS, J. H. The Royal Exile. London, 1821. 2 vols. 15 plts (2 color). Contemp calf (worn). *Argosy.* $200/£128

ADRIAN, E. D. The Physical Background of Perception...1946. Oxford: Clarendon, 1947. VG. *Argosy.* $60/£38

Adventures in Americana, 1492-1897...from the Library of Herschel V. Jones. NY, 1928. 2 vols. (Bkpls, part of fep excised 1 vol; sl rubbed.) *Swann*.* $57/£37

Adventures of a Colonist; or, Godfrey Arabin the Settler. (By Thomas M'Combie.) London: John & Daniel A. Darling, (1845). 1st ed. 274pp. Orig grn cl. (Corners bumped, sl shelfwear), else VG. *Brown.* $250/£160

Adventures of Little Red Riding Hood. London: J.L. Marks, n.d. 8vo. 8 leaves, incl cvrs (sl dknd, 3 leaves torn, repaired w/document tape, ink notes); 8 hand-colored wood engrs. Orig yellow wraps (rebacked in cl, chipped, soiled, stained). Fair. *Blue Mountain.* $75/£48

Adventures of Mickey Mouse Book I. Phila: David McKay, (1931). 1st ed. 7.5x5.5. Unpaged. Color pict bds. (Sl wear spine ends), else Nice in dj (spine, edges chipped). *King.* $1,250/£801

Adventures of Mickey Mouse. Book 1. Phila: David McKay, (1931). 8vo. Pict illus bds (sl rubbed; sl hand-soil inside). *Metropolitan*.* $661/£424

Adventures of Mickey Mouse. Book 1. David McKay, 1931. 5.5x7.5. Pict bds. Good + (rep removed; rubbed, chipped). *My Bookhouse.* $110/£71

Adventures of Mickey Mouse. Book 2. Phila: David McKay, 1932. 8vo. Pict illus bds (chipped, scratches; name, pp sl soiled). *Metropolitan*.* $172/£110

Adventures of Peregrine Pickle. (By Tobias Smollett.) London: Strahan, Rivington et al, 1784. 7th ed. 4 vols. Engr frontis each vol, (xii)268; 298; 282; 304pp. Full contemp calf, gilt. Attractive set. *Hartfield.* $395/£253

Adventures of Robert Drury, During Fifteen Years Captivity on the Island of Madagascar.... Hull: Stodart & Craggs, 1807. Rpt. Copper engr frontis, xii,460pp; 1 plt. Later calf, marbled bds. *Karmiole.* $175/£112

Adventures of Roderick Random.... (By Tobias Smollett.) London: A. Millar (et al), 1763. 6th ed. 2 vols. Frontis each vol. Contemp calf. (Heavy offsetting to early/late margins; spine sl chipped), else Good set. *Reese.* $40/£26

Adventures of Ulysses. (By Charles Lamb.) London: M.J. Godwin, 1819. 2nd ed. 12mo. 148pp. Uncut. Pub's paper-backed bds (spine worn). VG (tp sl foxed). *Second Life.* $300/£192

AEGINATA, PAUL OF. The Seven Books of Paulus Aeginata. London: Sydenham Soc, 1844-46-47. 3 vols. Orig bds. VG set (newly rebacked). *Goodrich.* $375/£240

AESCULAPIUS. The Magnetism of Sin. London: Greening, 1901. 1st ed. (Sm dealer plt on pastedown; rubbed, sl soiled, spine sl dknd.) *Metropolitan*.* $34/£22

AESOP. Aesop's Fables. Mt. Vernon, NY: Peter Pauper, 1965. Prob 1st ed. Eric Carle (illus). 4 1/2 x 7 1/2. 62pp. Fine in dj. *Cattermole.* $20/£13

AESOP. Aesop's Fables. Boston: Gambit, 1975. 1st ed. David Levine (illus). 7 1/4 x 10. 103pp. Fine in dj. *Cattermole.* $25/£16

AESOP. Aesop's Fables. NY: Rizzoli, 1991. 1st ed. John Hejduk (illus). 10 x 10 1/4. 30pp. Fine in dj. *Cattermole.* $25/£16

AESOP. Aesop's Fables: A New Version, Chiefly from Original Sources. (By Thomas James.) London: Murray, 1848. 1st ed thus. John Tenniel (illus). 8vo. xxv,232,12pp. Morocco, gilt. (Tps lt foxed), else Fine. *Bromer.* $400/£256

AESOP. The Fables of Aesop and Others. J. & R. Tonson, 1737. 4th ed. 12mo. Engr frontis, 196 text illus by Elisha Kirkall. 18th cent sheep (joints cracked, worn, lacks label). *Hatchwell.* $187/£120

AESOP. The Fables of Aesop. London: Hodder & Stoughton, 1909. Ltd to 750 numbered, signed by Edmund Detmold. Lg 4to. (100)ff, 25 color plts. Gilt-stamped linen. Fine. *Bromer.* $2,000/£1,282

AESOP. The Fables of Aesop. Roger L'Estrange (trans). Golden Cockerel, 1926. Ltd to 350. Celia M. Fiennes (engrs). 4to. 94pp. Unopened. VF. *Bromer.* $300/£192

AESOP. Fables of Aesop. (By Roger L'Estrange.) London: Golden Cockerel, 1926. One of 350 numbered. 1/4 cl. *Swann*.* $138/£88

AESOP. Fables of Aesop. (By Roger L'Estrange.) Paris: Harrison of Paris, 1931. One of 595. Alexander Calder (illus). Sm 4to. Dj, slipcase. *Swann*.* $690/£442

AESOP. Fables of Aesop. According to Roger L'Estrange. (Paris): Harrison of Paris, (1931). Ltd to 595 numbered. 8vo. Alexander Calder (illus). Dec paper dj. *Black Sun.* $550/£353

AESOP. Fables. V. S. Vernon Jones (trans). London, 1912. One of 1450 numbered, signed by Arthur Rackham (illus). 4to. 13 tipped-in color plts, guards. Later black niger, gilt. Announcement for 1912 exhibition of Rackham's orig artwork for this bk mtd on frontis verso. *Swann*.* $920/£590

AESOP. Fables. V.S. Vernon Jones (trans). London, 1912. One of 1450 numbered, signed by Arthur Rackham (illus). 13 tipped-in color plts, guards. Cl-backed bds (recased, hinges reinforced; bkpl). Cl slipcase. *Swann*.* $977/£626

AESOP. Fables. Roger L'Estrange (trans). London, 1936. One of 325 numbered, signed by Stephen Gooden (illus). Lg 8vo. Engr tp, 11 plts. Vellum. (Binder's blanks lt foxed.) Pub's bd slipcase. *Swann*.* $373/£239

AESOP. The Fables.... William Caxton (trans). Newtown: Gregynog, 1931 (i.e., 1932). One of 250 numbered. Folio. 37 wood-engr illus by Agnes Miller Parker. Orig tan sheep (spine sl scuffed). *Swann*.* $2,760/£1,769

AESOP. Fabularum Aesopicarum Delectus. Oxford: Johan Croke, 1698. 8vo. Frontis, engr tp, (16),128,(7)pp. Full calf (hinges broken). Contents VG. *New Hampshire*.* $120/£77

AESOP. Twelve Fables of Aesop. NY: MOMA, (1954). One of 975 signed by Antonio Frasconi (illus) and Joseph Blumenthal (ptr). Dec cl. Slipcase. *Swann*.* $258/£165

AFFORD, MAX. Death's Mannikins. NY: Appleton-Century, 1937. 1st Amer ed. VG (name; rubbed) in dj (worn, ends chipped, rear panel dampstained). *Metropolitan*.* $34/£22

AFLALO, F. G. The Sportsman's Book for India. London: Marshall, 1904. 1st ed. 5 maps (2 fldg). Grn pict cl. VG. *Terramedia.* $200/£128

AFLALO, F. G. and R. B. MARSTON. British Salt-Water Fishes. London: Hutchinson, 1904. 1st ed. 17 color plts. VG. *Hollett.* $70/£45

AGASSIZ, ALEXANDER. Three Cruises on the...Survey Steamer 'Blake'...from 1877 to 1880. Boston: Riverside, 1888. 2 vols. (Bds sl worn.) Internally Fine. *Goodrich.* $125/£80

AGASSIZ, ELIZABETH C. (ed.) Louis Agassiz, His Life and Correspondence. Boston, 1886. 4th ed. 2 vols. 794pp; 12 plts. Teg. Blue cl, gilt. (Sl edgewear), else VG. *Price.* $59/£38

AGASSIZ, ELIZABETH C. and ALEXANDER. Seaside Studies in Natural History: Marine Animals of Massachusetts Bay. Boston: Ticknor & Fields, 1865. 1st ed. 155pp. Blind-stamped cl (spine ends chipped). *Argosy.* $150/£96

AGASSIZ, ELIZABETH C. and ALEXANDER. Seaside Studies in Natural History: Marine Animals of Massachusetts Bay. Radiates. Boston: Houghton Mifflin, 1865. 1st ed. 157pp. Blind-stamped dec cl. NF. *Mikesh.* $45/£29

AGASSIZ, L. Geological Sketches. Boston/NY, 1893-94. 2 vols. *Wheldon & Wesley.* $94/£60

AGASSIZ, L. Methods of Study in Natural History. Boston: Ticknor & Field, 1863. 1st ed. 319pp + 21pp ads. Blind-stamped dec cl. VG. *Mikesh.* $47/£30

Age of Bruegel: Netherlandish Drawings in the Sixteenth Century. Washington: Nat'l Gallery of Art, 1986. Good in wraps. *Washton.* $35/£22

Age of Chivalry. Art in Plantagenet England 1200-1400. London: Royal Academy, 1987. Good in wrappers (sl worn). *Washton.* $145/£93

AGEE, JAMES and WALKER EVANS. Let Us Now Praise Famous Men. Boston: Houghton Mifflin, 1941. 1st ed. 8vo. 31 photos. VG in dj (price-clipped; spine ends sl wear; rear panel sl dusty). *Cahan.* $550/£353

AGEE, JAMES. A Death in the Family. Franklin Library, 1979. Fine. *Smith.* $20/£13

AGEE, JAMES. Letters of James Agee to Father Flye. NY: Braziller, 1962. 1st ed. Fine in NF dj. *Hermitage.* $40/£26

AGEE, JAMES. The Morning Watch. London, 1952. 1st Eng ed. Very Nice in dj (sl torn, nicked, dust-mkd). *Clearwater.* $78/£50

AGEE, JAMES. Permit Me Voyage. New Haven: Yale Univ, 1934. 1st ed, 1st bk. Fine in dj (sl rubbed, lt dampstain to lower spine). *Jaffe.* $650/£417

AGUET, ISABELLE. A Pictorial History of the Slave Trade. Bonnie Christen (trans). (Geneva): Minerva, (1971). 1st ed. NF (lt soiled) in NF dj (lamination irregularities). *Between The Covers.* $75/£48

AGUILAR, GRACE. The Mother's Recompense. Groombridge, 1875. 25th ed. Pub's cat. Aeg. Orig beveled bds. Good (spotted, new eps, ink inscrip recto frontis; spine bumped). *Tiger.* $19/£12

AHLEFELDT-BILLE, G. Tandalla. London, 1951. 1st Eng ed. Map, 32 plts. (1 cancellation, 2 lib stamps on tp, not affecting text; cl sl worn.) *Maggs.* $195/£125

AHMED, ROLLO. I Rise: The Life Story of a Negro. London: John Long, (1937). 1st ed. (Sm name, prelims foxed), else Fine in VG dj (sm spine hole, sm tears). *Between The Covers.* $150/£96

AIDOO, AMA ATA. Our Sister Killjoy or Reflections from a Black Eyed Squint. NY: NOK Publishers Intl, 1979. 1st ed. NF in VG dj (long tears tape-repaired to verso). *Lame Duck.* $45/£29

AIKEN, CONRAD. Bring! Bring! and Other Stories. NY: Boni & Liveright, 1925. 1st ed. Fine in NF dj (spine sl faded; sm nicks). *Between The Covers.* $125/£80

AIKEN, CONRAD. Collected Poems. NY: OUP, 1953. 1st ed. Dec maroon cl. NF (rubbed) in dj (price-clipped). *Blue Mountain.* $45/£29

AIKEN, CONRAD. The Collected Short Stories of Conrad Aiken. Cleveland/NY: World, (1960). 1st ed. Fine in NF dj (short tears, lt worn). *Between The Covers.* $75/£48

AIKEN, CONRAD. King Coffin. NY: Scribner, 1935. 1st ed. Gilt cl. Fine in Good dj (chips, creases). *Reese.* $50/£32

AIKEN, CONRAD. Senlin. London, 1925. 2nd binding, in blue bds (spine sl chafed; inscrip). *Clearwater.* $70/£45

AIKEN, CONRAD. The Short Stories of.... NY: Duell, Sloane & Pearce, (1950). 1st ed. VG in dj (sunned, closed snag). *Reese.* $18/£12

AIKEN, CONRAD. The Soldier. CT: Poets of the Year, New Directions, (1944). 1st Amer ed. Wraps. Fine in dj (spine lt chipped, sunned). *Polyanthos.* $20/£13

AIKEN, CONRAD. Thee. A Poem. NY, 1967. 1st Amer ed. Fine in dj (spine lt sunned, sm tear rear panel). *Polyanthos.* $25/£16

AIKEN, JOAN. The Silence of Herondale. NY: Doubleday, 1964. 1st ed. Fine in Fine dj. *Old London.* $20/£13

AIKEN, JOAN. The Wolves of Willoughby Chase. London, 1962. 1st Eng ed. Fine (inscrip) in dj (price-clipped). *Clearwater.* $47/£30

AIKENS, CHARLOTTE A. Studies in Ethics for Nurses. Phila, 1928. 2nd ed. Grn cl bds. VG. *Doctor's Library.* $50/£32

AIKIN, J. Letters from a Father to His Son, on Various Topics.... Phila: Ptd by Samuel Harrison Smith, 1794. 328pp (sl foxed). Contemp calf (rubbed, bumped, spine chipped, sm piece out spine bottom, lower joints split), red leather spine label. Internally NF. *Blue Mountain.* $35/£22

AIKIN, LUCY. The Life of Joseph Addison. London: Longman et al, 1843. 1st ed. 2 vols. xii,250; viii,256pp, engr port. Mod 1/2 levant morocco, gilt, dbl contrasting spine labels. *Hollett.* $187/£120

AIKIN, LUCY. Memoirs of the Court of King James the First. London: Longman et al, 1822. 2nd ed. 2 vols. 444; 413pp. Uncut. Orig paper-backed bds, paper label. VG (wear). *Second Life.* $125/£80

AINGER, ALFRED. Lectures and Essays. London: Macmillan, 1905. 1st ed. 2 vols. Blue cl (old paper lib labels spine feet). *Burmester.* $39/£25

AINSLIE, KATHLEEN. At Great-Aunt Martha's. London: Castell Bros, n.d. (1905). 1st ed. Oblong 8vo. Unpaginated. Grey color illus bds (rubbed, sl soiled), cl spine. Contents Clean. *Dower.* $75/£48

AINSLIE, KATHLEEN. What I Did. London: Castell Bros, n.d. 1st ed. 16mo. Illus paper sewn w/cording. VG + . *Dower.* $135/£87

AINSWORTH, ED. Beckoning Desert. Englewood Cliffs, NJ, 1962. Inscribed. NF in dj (chipped). *Five Quail.* $35/£22

AINSWORTH, ED. The Cowboy in Art. NY: World, (1968). #222/1000 of deluxe ed. Aeg. Full brn leather, gilt. Fine in Fine slipcase. *Harrington.* $180/£115

AINSWORTH, ED. Golden Checkerboard. Palm Desert: Desert-Southwest, (1965). 1st ed. Dj. *Dawson.* $100/£64

AINSWORTH, WILLIAM HARRISON. Cardinal Pole: or, The Days of Philip and Mary. London: Chapman & Hall, 1863. 1st ed. 3 vols. Grn cl (short slits in cl at joints all vols) blocked in blind, gilt. Good (lib label inside each vol). *Bickersteth.* $172/£110

AINSWORTH, WILLIAM HARRISON. Cardinal Pole; or, The Days of Philip and Mary. London, 1863. 1st ed. 3 vols. (Shaken; lib label upper cvrs.) *Words Etc.* $62/£40

AINSWORTH, WILLIAM HARRISON. Historical Romances. Phila: George Barrie, n.d. (ca 1900). 20 vols. Teg. Gilt-dec blue cl. *Kane*.* $80/£51

AINSWORTH, WILLIAM HARRISON. Jack Sheppard: A Romance. G. Routledge, 1854. 27 steel engr plts by George Cruikshank. 19th cent full lt brn calf gilt, gilt panelled back, teg (joints neatly repaired), orig red cl cvrs bound in at end. *Hatchwell.* $117/£75

AINSWORTH, WILLIAM HARRISON. The Tower of London. H.G. Bohn, 1844. 5th ed. 40 steel engr plts after George Cruikshank. (Sl foxing.) 20th cent 1/2 red morocco gilt, gilt panelled back, teg; orig red cl cvrs bound in at end. *Hatchwell.* $117/£75

AINSWORTH, WILLIAM HARRISON. Windsor Castle: An Historical Romance. London: Colburn, 1843. New ed. George Cruikshank and Tony Johannot (illus). 1/4 leather marbled bds (worn, spine cracked). *Yudkin*.* $55/£35

AIRS, MALCOLM. The Making of the English Country House 1500-1640. Architectural Press, 1975. VG in dj, cased. *Peter Taylor.* $30/£19

AIRY, GEORGE BIDDELL. Mathematical Tracts on the Lunar and Planetary Theories.... Cambridge: J. & J.J. Deighton, 1831. 2nd ed. v,410pp; 5 fldg plts at rear (prelims, plts lt spotted; hinges sl tender). 1/2 calf, marbled bds (rubbed). *Edwards.* $117/£75

AIRY, OSMOND. Charles II. Paris: Goupil, 1901. Ltd numbered ed. Hand-colored frontis, guards. Full blue calf. VG. *Argosy.* $200/£128

AITKEN, JOHN. Principles of Midwifery, or Puerperal Medicine. London: John Murray, n.d. (1786). 3rd ed. Frontis port, 210pp + 8pp list, ads (eps loose; ex-lib), 31 fldg copper plts. 1/2 calf (cvrs detached, spine split, worn). *Argosy.* $300/£192

AITKEN, R. B. Great Game Animals of the World. NY: Macmillan, 1968. 1st ed. Dec eps. Good. *Mikesh.* $30/£19

AITKEN, RUSSELL BARNETT. Great Game Animals of the World. NY: Macmillan, n.d. (1968). VG + in VG dj. *Backman.* $75/£48

AITON, WILLIAM. Hortus Kewensis; or, A Catalogue of the Plants Cultivated in the Royal Botanic Garden at Kew.... London: Longman et al, 1810-13. 2nd ed. 5 vols. Orig bds (spines worn, lt rubbed). *Christie's*.* $456/£292

AKELEY, M. L. J. Carl Akeley's Africa. NY: Dodd, 1929. 1st ed. 4 maps. Blind-stamped pict cl. NF in Fair dj. *Mikesh.* $25/£16

AKSYONOV, VASSILY. The Burn. NY: Random House, 1984. 1st US ed. Signed. NF in NF dj (lt worn, edge tear). *Lame Duck.* $125/£80

AKSYONOV, VASSILY. It's Time, My Love, It's Time. Nashville: Aurora, 1970. 1st US ed. NF in VG dj (edgetears, fr lt rubbed). *Lame Duck.* $45/£29

Aladdin or the Wonderful Lamp. NY: McLoughlin Bros, n.d. (1880s). 1st Amer ed. 10x7. 24 chromolitho transformation pp at center fold. Color pict bds (lose, extrems chipped, spine perished). *King.* $95/£61

ALBACH, JAMES R. Annals of the West: Embracing a Concise Account of Principal Events Which Have Occurred in the Western States and Territories.... Pittsburg: W.S. Haven Book and Job Printer, 1856. 3rd ed, 1st ptg. (Lt foxing.) Later cl, gilt. Howes P231. *Sadlon.* $60/£38

ALBAUGH, WILLIAM A. III and RICHARD D. STEUART. The Original Confederate Colt. NY: Greenberg, 1953. 1st ed. Pub's dec cl. (Few sm spots rear cvr), else VG. *Cahan.* $75/£48

ALBAUGH, WILLIAM A. III. More Confederate Faces. (Washington: ABS Printers, 1972.) 1st ed. Ltd to 400. Pristine in NF dj. *Mcgowan.* $200/£128

ALBEE, EDWARD. A Delicate Balance. London, 1968. 1st Eng ed. Fine in dj (clipped). *Clearwater.* $39/£25

ALBEE, EDWARD. Tiny Alice. Cape, 1965. 1st UK ed. VG + in dj. *Williams.* $23/£15

ALBEE, EDWARD. Tiny Alice. NY: Atheneum, 1965. 1st ed. Signed. Fine in Fine dj. *Lenz.* $150/£96

ALBEE, EDWARD. Who's Afraid of Virginia Woolf? London: Cape, 1964. 1st UK ed. Fine in VG dj. *Williams.* $62/£40

ALBEE, EDWARD. The Zoo Story and Other Plays. London: Cape, (1962). 1st ed. NF in dj. *Hermitage.* $100/£64

ALBEE, FRED HOUDLETT. Bone-Graft Surgery. Phila: W.B. Saunders, 1917. (Cl sl rubbed, spine faded.) Internally Clean. *Goodrich.* $125/£80

ALBERT, ALLEN D. (ed). History of the Forty-Fifth Regiment: Pennsylvania Veteran Volunteer Infantry, 1861-1865. Williamsport, PA: Grit, 1912. 1st ed. VG (extrems lt rubbed). *Cahan.* $150/£96

ALBERT, DANIEL and HAROLD SCHEIE. A History of Ophthalmology at the University of Pennsylvania. Springfield, 1965. 1st ed. VG in dj. *Fye.* $75/£48

ALBERT, HERMAN W. Odyssey of a Desert Prospector. Norman: Univ of OK, (1967). 1st ed. Fine in dj, plastic jacket. *Bohling.* $20/£13

ALBERT, HERMAN W. Odyssey of a Desert Prospector. Norman: Univ of OK, (1967). 1st ed. Dj. *Dawson.* $30/£19

ALBERT, NEIL. The January Corpse. NY: Walker, 1991. 1st ed. Signed. VF in dj. *Mordida.* $85/£54

ALBERTI, LEON BATTISTA. On Painting. John R. Spencer (trans). New Haven, 1956. Good in dj. *Washton.* $25/£16

Alberto Giacometti. Peter Selz (intro). GC: MOMA, (1965). 2-tone cl. VG in dj (yellowed, sl torn). *King.* $35/£22

ALBERTS, ROBERT C. The Most Extraordinary Adventures of Major Robert Stobo. Boston: Houghton, Mifflin, 1965. 1st ed. VG (pencilling margins, rep) in dj. *Lien.* $35/£22

ALBERTSON, CHRIS. Bessie. London: Barrie & Jenkins, 1972. 1st UK ed. Fine in dj (lt used). *Beasley.* $35/£22

ALBION, ROBERT GREENHALGH. The Rise of New York Port (1815-1860). NY: Scribner, 1939. 1st ed. *Lefkowicz.* $50/£32

ALBRAND, MARTHA. Nightmare in Copenhagen. London, (1954). 1st ed. VG in dj. *Argosy.* $35/£22

Albrecht Durer, Master Printmaker. Boston: Museum of Fine Arts, 1971. (Ink underlining.) *Washton.* $75/£48

ALBRIZZI, ISABELLA. The Works of Antonio Canova.... London, 1824. Folio. Vols 1 and 2 (of 3). Engr frontis ports, 99 line-engr plts, all mtd India-proofs. Contemp navy morroco (joints rubbed), gilt. *Swann*.* $230/£147

ALBUCASIS. On Surgery and Instruments.... M. S. Spink and G. L. Lewis (trans). London, 1973. 1st ed. VG in dj. *Fye.* $125/£80

ALCIPHRON. Epistles...the Domestic Manners, the Courtesans and Parasites of Greece.... Wm. Beloe (trans). London, 1791. 1st Eng ed. 1/2 straight-grain maroon morocco (sl worn), gilt. *Kane*.* $95/£61

Alcoholics Anonymous. NY, 1965. 2nd ed. Blue cl (worn), bronze-tooled spine lettering. Good (lacks fep, 1/2-title pp). *Doctor's Library.* $30/£19

Alcoholics Anonymous. NY, 1969. 2nd ed, 10th ptg. Blue cl, bronze-tooled spine lettering. NF. *Doctor's Library.* $50/£32

Alcoholics Anonymous. NY, 1973. 2nd ed, 15th ptg. Blue cl (sl worn), bronze-tooled spine lettering. VG. *Doctor's Library.* $50/£32

Alcoholics Anonymous. NY, 1973. 2nd ed, 14th ptg. Blue cl, bronze-tooled spine lettering. Fine in NF dj. *Doctor's Library.* $100/£64

ALCOTT, A. BRONSON. Concord Days. Boston: Roberts, 1872. 1st ed. Gilt-stamped grn cl. (Ink inscrip, sl discoloration lower corner text block; spine extrems rubbed), else Good. BAL 114. *Reese.* $30/£19

ALCOTT, A. BRONSON. Ralph Waldo Emerson, Philosopher and Seer.... Boston: Cupples & Hurd, (1888). Denoted 2nd ed. Paper label (rubbed). Good (ink inscrip rep, foxing). BAL 133. *Reese.* $30/£19

ALCOTT, A. BRONSON. Sonnets and Canzonets. Boston: Roberts, 1882. 1st ed. Teg. Gilt/black-dec brn cl. VG. BAL 124. *Reese.* $65/£42

ALCOTT, A. BRONSON. Table-Talk. Boston: Roberts, 1877. 1st ed. Grn cl, gilt. (Name, sm snag fep), o/w VG. BAL 117. *Reese.* $45/£29

ALCOTT, A. BRONSON. Tablets. Boston: Roberts, 1868. 1st ed, in primary binding. Teg. Gilt brn cl. (1/2-title neatly excised), o/w Fine. BAL 112. *Reese.* $60/£38

ALCOTT, LOUISA M. Jack and Jill. Boston: Roberts Bros, 1880. 1st ed. Blue pict cl, gilt. VF. BAL 195. *Macdonnell.* $200/£128

ALCOTT, LOUISA M. Jo's Boys, and How They Turned Out. Boston: Roberts Bros, 1886. 1st ed, 1st state (bulks 1 1/16 inches). Brn cl, gilt. (Fr hinge paper starting to crack), else Fine. BAL 211. *Macdonnell.* $100/£64

ALCOTT, LOUISA M. Little Men. Boston: Roberts, 1871. 1st ed, 1st issue, w/signature mk 'l.' Grn cl (sl rubbing). Very Nice (sig). BAL 167. *Second Life.* $350/£224

ALCOTT, LOUISA M. Little Women. Boston: Roberts Bros, 1868, 1869. 1st ed. 2 vols. 8vo. 341pp + (6)pp ads; 359pp + (8)pp ads. May Alcott (illus). Part First is 1st ptg w/price of $1.25 ptd on 3rd pg of terminal ads. Part Second is in 1st state w/no notice for Little Women, Part First at pg iv. Gilt-stamped cl. (Partial bkpl removal vol 1; Part Second extrems lt rubbed, spine sl cocked), else Fine in leather-backed cl dropback box. BAL 158-159. *Bromer.* $7,500/£4,808

ALCOTT, LOUISA M. Little Women. Boston: Little, Brown, 1923. 8 color plts by Jessie Willcox Smith. Color plt laid down fr cvr. VG. *New Hampshire*.* $80/£51

Alden's Oxford Guide. Oxford: Alden, (1887). 13th ed. iv,113,(i)pp + 24pp ads. Red cl. *Bickersteth.* $39/£25

ALDEN, JOHN B. Alden's Home Atlas of the World. NY: John B. Alden, 1887. 96pp (sl foxed). Red cl (faded). *Hudson.* $275/£176

ALDEN, JOHN RICHARD. General Gage in America. Baton Rouge: LA State Univ, 1948. 1st ed. VG. *Lien.* $30/£19

ALDIN, CECIL. An Artist's Model. London: H.F.&G. Witherby, (1930). 1st Eng ed. 4to. 80pp; 20 color plts. Beige cl. VG in dj (piece missing from plt). *Dower.* $250/£160

ALDIN, CECIL. Mac. London: Humphrey Milford, n.d. ca 1915. 25 full-pg color plts. Cl-backed dec pict bds (sm crack fr cvr). *Argosy.* $150/£96

ALDIN, CECIL. Mrs. Tickler's Caravan. NY: Scribner, 1931. 1st Amer ed. 4to. 91pp. Illus eps. Blue cl, color picture label. VG. *Dower.* $95/£61

ALDIN, CECIL. Scarlet to M.F.H. NY: Scribner, (1933). 1st Amer ed. (Spine sl faded, worn), o/w Fine in dj (lacks upper 3 inches spine panel). *Hermitage.* $125/£80

ALDINGTON, RICHARD (trans). French Comedies of the XVIIIth Century.... London/NY: Routledge/Dutton, (1923). 1st ed, 1st binding. Cl, leather spine label. (Ink inscrip pastedown; spine dkng), o/w VG. *Reese.* $30/£19

ALDINGTON, RICHARD. A. E. Housman and W. B. Yeats. Two Lectures. Hurst/Berksshre: Peacocks, 1955. One of 350 ptd. Blue buckram. Very Nice. No dj, as issued. *Clearwater.* $55/£35

ALDINGTON, RICHARD. All Men Are Enemies. London: C&W, 1933. 1st ed, trade issue. Gilt cl. (Pencil inscrip), else NF in VG dj (spine tanned). *Reese.* $50/£32

ALDINGTON, RICHARD. All Men Are Enemies. London: C&W, 1933. One of 100 signed. Cl-backed patterned bds (spine, extrems sl faded). Fine. *Pirages.* $95/£61

ALDINGTON, RICHARD. Balls and Another Book for Suppression. Draguignan: Melissa Press, 1962. 1st ptg under Count Potocki's imprint. Fine in ptd wrappers. *Reese.* $25/£16

ALDINGTON, RICHARD. The Colonel's Daughter. London: C&W, 1931. 1st ed. Ltd to 210 numbered, specially ptd, bound, signed. Teg. Grn cl (spine sunned, scattered fox mks). VG. *Reese.* $100/£64

ALDINGTON, RICHARD. The Crystal World. (1937.) 1st ed. (Upper cvr sl faded.) *Bickersteth*. $31/£20

ALDINGTON, RICHARD. D. H. Lawrence: An Appreciation. Middlesex: Penguin Bks, (1950). 1st ed. NF in ptd wraps. *Antic Hay*. $25/£16

ALDINGTON, RICHARD. Death of a Hero. London: C&W, 1929. 1st Eng ed. Black cl, gilt. Dj. *Maggs*. $78/£50

ALDINGTON, RICHARD. Death of a Hero. London: C&W, 1929. 1st British ed. Gilt black cl. NF in Good dj (extrems tanned, sl soiled, chips, sm internal reinforcements). *Reese*. $125/£80

ALDINGTON, RICHARD. A Dream in the Luxembourg. London, 1930. #230/308 signed. *Typographeum*. $50/£32

ALDINGTON, RICHARD. The Eaten Heart. London: C&W, 1933. 1st British ed. Inscribed. Gilt cl. (Lt foxing to eps, edges), else Nice in dj (spine tanned, sm tear). *Reese*. $175/£112

ALDINGTON, RICHARD. Exile and Other Poems. London: Allen & Unwin, (1923). 1st ed. Ltd to 750. Gilt cl. Fine in VG dj (spine rubbed, chips). *Reese*. $85/£54

ALDINGTON, RICHARD. Images of War. Boston, 1921. Amer issue, sheets of Allen & Unwin 1st ed w/cancel tp. (Name; spine sl rubbed.) *Clearwater*. $78/£50

ALDINGTON, RICHARD. Images, (1910-1915). (London): Poetry Bookshop, n.d. (1915). 1st ed, 1st bk. Sewn ptd pict wraps (sl dust-soiled). *Kane**. $120/£77

ALDINGTON, RICHARD. Images. London: Egoist, (1919). 1st ed. Linen, bds, paper labels. (Spine label worn), o/w Very Nice. *Reese*. $75/£48

ALDINGTON, RICHARD. Jane Austen. Pasadena: Ampersand, 1948. Very Nice (fep sl mkd from label removal) in tissue wrapper. *Clearwater*. $78/£50

ALDINGTON, RICHARD. Last Straws. Paris: Hours, 1930. Ltd to 200 (of 700) numbered, signed. Grn 'suede' cl. VG (cvrs discolored, worn). *Antic Hay*. $125/£80

ALDINGTON, RICHARD. Lawrence of Arabia: A Biographical Enquiry. London: Collins, 1955. 1st ed. NF (ink name) in dj (worn, chipped). *Antic Hay*. $27/£17

ALDINGTON, RICHARD. Love and the Luxembourg. NY: Covici Friede, 1930. 1st ed. One of 475 numbered, signed by author & Frederic Warde (designer). Fine (bare rubbed spine). *Beasley*. $75/£48

ALDINGTON, RICHARD. Pinorman. London, (1954). VG in dj (sl frayed). *King*. $25/£16

ALDINGTON, RICHARD. Portrait of a Genius, But.... London, 1950. 1st ed. VG in dj (sl soiled, torn). *Typographeum*. $40/£26

ALDINGTON, RICHARD. Stepping Heavenward. Florence: G. Orioli, 1931. Ltd to 808 numbered, signed. NF in dj (lg tear fr panel). *Antic Hay*. $60/£38

ALDINGTON, RICHARD. War and Love. Boston: Four Seas, 1919. 1st Amer ed. Patterned bds (sl rubbed). Fine. *Polyanthos*. $50/£32

ALDINGTON, WILLIAM (trans). The Golden Asse of Lucius Apuleius. London: John Lane, Bodley Head, 1923. One of 3000 numbered. 8 b/w, 8 color plts. Teg. Brn cl (bumped), gilt. Internally NF. *Blue Mountain*. $40/£26

ALDISS, BRIAN. The Canopy of Time. Faber, 1959. 1st ed. (Burn mk rear cvr edge), else VG+ in Nice dj (2 sm chips). *Certo*. $40/£26

ALDISS, BRIAN. Dracula Unbound. London: Grafton, 1991. 1st ed. Signed presentation. Fine in dj. *Virgo*. $70/£45

ALDISS, BRIAN. Earthworks. London: Faber & Faber, (1965). 1st ed. Signed, inscribed. Dj. *Swann**. $69/£44

ALDISS, BRIAN. Frankenstein Unbound. NY: Random, (1973). 1st Amer ed. (Sl fading bd edges; sm erasure fr fly), else Fine in NF dj (lt stain). *Between The Covers*. $45/£29

ALDISS, BRIAN. Galaxies Like Grains of Sand. (NY): NAL, (1960). 1st ed. Pb orig. NF. *Antic Hay*. $25/£16

ALDISS, BRIAN. Greybeard. NY: Harcourt, (1964). 1st ed. Fine in dj (sm stain spine, lt soil). *Metropolitan**. $80/£51

ALDISS, BRIAN. Intangibles Inc. and Other Stories. London, 1969. 1st Eng ed. Nice (sl spotted) in dj (sl mkd, water-stained). *Clearwater*. $39/£25

ALDISS, BRIAN. Report on Probability A. London: Faber, 1968. 1st ed. VG in dj. *Hollett*. $31/£20

ALDISS, BRIAN. A Rude Awakening. NY: Random House, (1978). 1st Amer ed. NF in dj. *Antic Hay*. $20/£13

ALDISS, BRIAN. Space Time and Nathaniel. London: Faber & Faber, 1957. 1st ed. (Dust spotting to top edge), else Fine in NF dj (head of spine sl worn). *Certo*. $200/£128

ALDRED, CYRIL. Jewels of the Pharoahs: Egyptian Jewellery of the Dynastic Period. NY: Praeger, (1971). Good. *Archaeologia*. $85/£54

ALDRED, CYRIL. Middle Kingdom Art in Ancient Egypt: 2300-1590 B.C. London: Alec Tiranti, 1956. Good in dj. *Archaeologia*. $35/£22

ALDRICH, BESS STREETER. A White Bird Flying. D. Appleton, 1931. 1st ed. Fine in VG dj (sl chipped). *Authors Of West*. $40/£26

ALDRICH, LORENZO D. A Journal of the Overland Route to California and the Gold Mines. L.A.: Dawson's Book Shop, 1950. Fldg map in pocket. Ptd bds (bkpl; sm dknd spot fr cvr), cl spine, paper spine label. *Dawson*. $100/£64

ALDRICH, THOMAS BAILEY. The Ballad of Babie Bell and Other Poems. NY, 1859. 1st issue. Fine (bkpl; spine top rubbed). *Polyanthos*. $75/£48

ALDRICH, THOMAS BAILEY. A Book of Songs and Sonnets. (Boston): Riverside Press, 1906. One of 430 numbered. Signed, inscribed loose paper slip dated Sept. 27, 1886 laid in. Prospectus tipped in at rear. Grn handmade paper bds, emb cameo port fr bd. VG (ends sl worn, spine soiled). *Waverly**. $22/£14

ALDRICH, THOMAS BAILEY. Marjorie Daw and Other People. Boston: James R. Osgood, 1873. 1st ed. (Name fep), o/w NF in cl-cvrd bds, gilt. *Mordida*. $200/£128

ALDRICH, THOMAS BAILEY. Ponkapog Papers. Boston: Houghton Mifflin, 1903. 1st ed. Teg. Black cl, gilt. Very Nice. BAL 393. *Cady*. $25/£16

ALDRICH, THOMAS BAILEY. The Story of a Bad Boy. Boston: Fields, Osgood, 1870. 1st ed, 1st issue (w/'scattered' on p14, 'abroad' on p197, 'The Uncle Sam Series' on 1st pg of ads). 23pp ads dated 1870. Grn cl, gilt spine. VG (spine sl dull, sl shelfworn). *Sumner & Stillman*. $195/£125

ALDRICH, THOMAS BAILEY. Two Bites at a Cherry and Other Tales. Boston: Houghton, Mifflin, 1894. 1st ed. Dec maroon cl. VG (ink name). BAL 368. *Antic Hay*. $45/£29

ALDRICH, THOMAS BAILEY. The Writings of Thomas Bailey Aldrich. Boston, 1897. 1st ed. 8 vols. *Ginsberg*. $75/£48

ALDRICH, THOMAS BAILEY. Wyndham Towers. Boston/NY: Houghton, Mifflin, 1890. 1st ed. Grn cl, gilt, vellum spine. Orig brn ribbon marker. Fine in NF dj (sl edgeworn). *Sumner & Stillman*. $195/£125

ALDRIDGE, JAMES. Gold and Sand: Stories. London, (1960). 1st ed. Fine in dj. *Argosy*. $40/£26

ALDRIDGE, JAMES. The Hunter. London, (1950). 1st ed. VG in dj. *Argosy*. $40/£26

ALDRIDGE, WILLIAM. Narrative of the Life of John Marrant of New York, in North America, with Account of the Conversion of the King of the Cherokees and His Daughter. London: Farncombe, (ca 1900). (Bkpl.) Orig ptd wrappers. Slipcase. Howes A111. *Ginsberg*. $125/£80

ALECHINSKY, PIERRE. By the Artist. NY: Abrams, (1977). Dj. *Swann**. $115/£74

ALEICHEM, SHOLOM. The Great Fair. Tamara Kahana (trans). NY: Noonday, 1955. 1st Amer ed. Dwg by Marc Chagall. NF in dj (lt rubbed, soiled). *Antic Hay*. $30/£19

ALESHKOVSKY, YUZ. Kangaroo. NY: FSG, 1986. 1st ed. Fine in dj. *Lame Duck*. $20/£13

ALEXANDER, A. S. The Veterinary Adviser. NY: OJ, 1943. 6 photo plts. Grn cl, gilt. VG. *Price*. $19/£12

ALEXANDER, DAVID. A Sound of Horses. Indianapolis: Bobbs-Merrill, 1966. 1st ed. VG in Good+ dj. *October Farm*. $38/£24

ALEXANDER, E. P. The American Civil War. London: Siegle, Hill, 1908. Good (shelfworn). Howes A114. *Cullen*. $100/£64

ALEXANDER, EDWARD PORTER. Military Memoirs of a Confederate. NY: Scribner, 1907. 1st ed. VG. Howes A114. *Mcgowan*. $275/£176

ALEXANDER, FRANCES and SIDNEY (eds). The Berenson Collection. Milano: Arti Grafiche Ricordi, (1964). 1st ed. 102 plts. Maroon buckram. Good in illus dj (few tears). *Karmiole*. $185/£119

ALEXANDER, HENRY. The Cairngorms. Scottish Mountaineering Club, 1950. Fine in dj. *Petersfield*. $31/£20

ALEXANDER, J. A. The Life of George Chaffey, A Story of Irrigation Beginnings in California and Australia. Melbourne: Macmillan, 1928. 1st ed. Frontis port, 7 maps (1 fldg). Lt blue cl. (Spotting fr cvr), else Fine in dj (chipped). *Argonaut*. $75/£48

ALEXANDER, JOHN H. Mosby's Men. NY: Neale, 1907. 1st ed. Port. Dec cl (ex-lib w/spine numbers, emb lib stamp tp; bkpls). Howes A120. *Ginsberg*. $150/£96

ALEXANDER, LLOYD. The Foundling. NY: Holt Rinehart, 1973. 1st ed. Margot Zemach (illus). 6 1/4 x 9 1/2. 88pp. VG in dj. *Cattermole*. $25/£16

ALEXANDER, LLOYD. The Four Donkeys. NY: Holt, Rinehart & Winston, (1972). 1st ed. Sm 4to. Frontis, 40pp; 8 full-pg, 2 dbl-pg illus by Lester Abrams. Dec pink bds (sl rubbed, chip), gilt. VG in pict dj (soiled). *Blue Mountain*. $20/£13

ALEXANDER, MRS. Through Fire to Fortune. Bernhard Tauchnitz, 1900. Copyright ed. Sprinkled edges. Contemp 1/2 leather, marbled bds. Good. *Tiger*. $31/£20

ALEXANDER, WILLIAM. The History of Women. London: Strahan & Cadell, 1779. 1st ed. 4to. 2 vols in 1. 368pp + index; 344pp + index. New cl (rebound). Nice (trimmed rather close). *Second Life*. $600/£385

ALFORD, THOMAS WILDCAT. Civilization. Norman: Univ of OK, 1936. 1st ed. Paper spine label. Fine in VG dj (spine ends, corners chipped). *Harrington*. $80/£51

ALGER, HORATIO, JR. Bertha's Christmas Vision: An Autumn Sheaf. Boston: Brown, Bazin, 1856. 1st ed, 1st bk. Sm 8vo. Frontis, extra pict tp. Red cl stamped in blind, gilt. (1st few ll dampstained; sl worn, sm tear spine). *Oinonen**. $300/£192

ALGER, HORATIO, JR. From Canal Boy to President. NY: Anderson, 1881. 1st ed, later issue, w/o errata slip at p267, etc. 8vo. Pict blue cl stamped in black, gilt. (Foxed, soiled, sl worn.) *Oinonen**. $40/£26

ALGER, HORATIO, JR. From Farm Boy to Senator. NY: Ogilvie, (1882). 1st ed. 8vo. (Sl foxed, sm piece torn last ad leaf w/loss.) Pict brn cl (shelfworn). *Oinonen**. $50/£32

ALGER, HORATIO, JR. Mark Mason's Victory. NY: A.L. Burt, n.d. (1899). 1st ed, 1st issue w/pub's street address '97-99-101 Reade Street' on 1st pg of ads. 14pp undated ads. Pict blue-gray cl. NF (sticker fr pastedown; sl shelfworn). *Sumner & Stillman*. $375/£240

ALGER, HORATIO, JR. Tattered Tom; or, the Story of a Street Arab. Boston: Loring, (1871). 1st ed. 8vo. (Contemp private lib stamp tp; worn, shaken, spotted, sl stained, soiled.) *Oinonen**. $50/£32

ALGER, HORATIO, JR. The Young Miner, or Tom Nelson in California. Boston: Loring, (1879). 1st ed. Woodcut frontis, 1/2-title illus, 288pp. Plum cl, gilt. (Bumped, spine sl faded, worn), o/w VG. *Pacific**. $150/£96

ALGER, HORATIO, JR. The Young Outlaw. Boston: Loring, (1875). 1st ed, 1st issue. Frontis, engr tp. Grn cl (extrems sl worn). *Appelfeld*. $100/£64

ALGREN, NELSON. Chicago: City on the Make. GC: Doubleday, 1951. 1st ed. (Bkpl fep), else NF in dj (sl rubbed). *Hermitage*. $50/£32

ALGREN, NELSON. Chicago: City on the Make. GC: Doubleday, 1951. 1st ed. Signed. Fine (worn) in dj (price-clipped). *Captain's Bookshelf*. $150/£96

ALGREN, NELSON. Somebody in Boots. NY: Vanguard, 1935. One of 770; 1st bk. Good (ex-lib, date stamps; worn). *Beasley*. $65/£42

ALGREN, NELSON. Somebody in Boots. NY: Vanguard, 1935. 1st ed, 1st bk. Fine in pict dj (3 archival internal mends, 2 sm chips, spine sl dknd). *Captain's Bookshelf*. $1,250/£801

ALGREN, NELSON. A Walk on the Wild Side. NY: Farrar, Straus & Cudahy, (1956). 1st ed. (Bkpl), o/w VG in dj (rear panel soiled). *Bernard*. $40/£26

ALGREN, NELSON. Who Lost an American? NY: Macmillan, (1963). 1st Amer ed. Gray cl-backed pink bds. VG (top edges sl soiled, spine sl stained, rubbed; corners 2 blanks spotted) in dj (soiled, sl chipped). *Blue Mountain*. $15/£10

Ali Baba. London: Dean & Son, n.d. Dean Diploma Series #105. 4to. 10pp, 4pp heavy bds. Cl hinges each pg. Heavy color illus bds. (Lt edgewear, corners sl rubbed), o/w VG. *Dower*. $150/£96

ALI, MUHAMMAD with RICHARD DURHAM. The Greatest: My Own Story. NY, (1975). Signed. Cl-backed bds. Dj. *Argosy*. $150/£96

Alice, Where Art Thou? Guinness, n.d. Illus wrappers. (Top corners creased), o/w VG. *Words Etc*. $39/£25

ALIKI. A Medieval Feast. NY: Crowell, 1983. Stated 1st ed. Signed, inscribed w/sketch by author. VG in VG dj. *Scribe's Perch**. $20/£13

ALINDER, JAMES. Ansel Adams: 50 Years of Portraits. (Carmel, CA): Friends of Photography, 1978. 1st ed. 26 full-pg b/w plts. NF in pict stiff wrappers. *Cahan*. $25/£16

ALIREZA, MARIANNE. At the Drop of a Veil. Boston: Houghton Mifflin, 1971. 1st ed. VG in dj. *Worldwide*. $22/£14

ALLAN, JOYCE. Australian Shells. Melbourne, 1950. 1st ed. Color frontis, 11 color plts, 32 b/w plts. Dj (sl chipped). *Edwards*. $55/£35

ALLAN, MEA. The Hookers of Kew: 1785-1911. London: Michael Joseph, 1967. 1st ed. Color frontis port, fldg table. Fine in dj. *Quest*. $110/£71

ALLAN, MEA. The Tradescants. London, 1964. Color frontis. Good. *Brooks*. $66/£42

ALLAN, MEA. William Robinson. 1838-1935. London: Faber & Faber, 1982. 1st ed. As New. *Quest*. $40/£26

ALLAN, P. B. M. The Book-Hunter at Home. London, 1922. One of 500. VG in 2-tone brn cl. *Moss*. $34/£22

ALLAN, P. B. M. The Book-Hunter at Home. NY: Putnam, 1922. 2nd Amer ed. One of 500. 1/4 cl, bds. Nice (sm bkpl; corners sl nicked). *Reese*. $45/£29

ALLAN, WILLIAM. The Army of Northern Virginia in 1862. Boston, 1892. 1st ed. 537pp. VG (ex-lib; spine label, cvr worn). *Pratt*. $275/£176

ALLAND, ALEXANDER, SR. Jessie Tarbox Beals: First Woman News Photographer. NY: Camera/Graphic Press, 1978. 1st ed. 95 full-pg b/w plts. Pict eps. Silhouette on cl. Fine (owner stamp) in illus dj. *Cahan*. $60/£38

ALLANSON, GEORGE G. A Segment of Minnesota History.... Wheaton, MN: Wheaton Gazette, n.d. (ca 1940s). Paper cvrs. VG. *Lien*. $25/£16

ALLBEURY, TED. Palomino Blonde. London: Peter Davies, 1975. 1st ed. (Name, lt spotting pg edges), o/w Fine in dj. *Mordida*. $65/£42

ALLBUTT, T. CLIFFORD. Arteriosclerosis. London, 1925. (Ex-libris, stamp tp; lt worn), o/w VG. *Doctor's Library*. $35/£22

ALLBUTT, T. CLIFFORD. The Historical Relations of Medicine and Surgery to the End of the Sixteenth Century.... London: Macmillan, 1905. 1st ed. Fine (bkpl). *Glaser*. $100/£64

ALLBUTT, T. CLIFFORD. On Visceral Neuroses. Phila: University Press, 1884. 1st Amer ed. viii,(104)pp (lib stamp tp, bkpl). Emb mauve cl. *Gach*. $85/£54

ALLDERIDGE, PATRICIA. The Late Richard Dadd 1817-1886. Tate Gallery, 1974. Frontis port, map. Dj. *Edwards*. $31/£20

ALLDRIDGE, T. J. The Sherbro and Its Hinterland. London: Macmillan, 1901. 1st ed. Frontis, 2 fldg maps (1 in rear pocket). Unopened. Blue gilt pict cl (trace of lib stamp on spine), else VG. *Terramedia*. $250/£160

ALLEGRETTO, MICHAEL. Blood Stone. NY: Scribner, 1988. 1st ed. VF in dj. *Mordida*. $30/£19

ALLEGRO, JOHN. The Sacred Mushroom and the Cross. Hodder & Stoughton, 1970. 1st ed. 2 color plts. Good. *Sclanders*. $19/£12

Allen Press Bibliography. (Greenbrae), 1985. One of 750. (Bkpl, stamp of Library of Congress.) *Swann**. $103/£66

ALLEN, ARTHUR C. The Skin: A Clinicopathologic Treatise. St. Louis, 1954. VG. *Argosy*. $45/£29

ALLEN, BETSY. The Green Island Mystery. G&D, 1949. 5x7.5. 205pp. Lists to #11. VG + (shelfworn) in dj (worn, 1-inch closed tear). *My Bookhouse*. $25/£16

ALLEN, BETSY. The Peril in Pink. G&D, 1955. 5x7.5. 182pp. Lists to #11. VG + (sl worn) in dj (sl edgeworn). *My Bookhouse*. $50/£32

ALLEN, BETSY. Puzzle in Purple. G&D, 1948. 5x7.5. 213pp. Lists to #9. VG + (sl shelfworn) in dj (sl edgeworn, price-clipped). *My Bookhouse*. $20/£13

ALLEN, BETSY. The Secret of Black Cat Gulch. G&D, 1948. 5x7.5. 206pp. Caramel brn cl (sl shelfworn). Lists to #6. VG + in dj (sl edgeworn). *My Bookhouse*. $20/£13

ALLEN, C. L. Cabbage, Cauliflower and Allied Vegetables from Seed to Harvest. NY: OJ, 1901. 1st ed. Grn cl, gilt. VG. *Price*. $24/£15

ALLEN, CARROLL W. Local and Regional Anesthesia. Phila, 1914. 1st ed. (Ex-lib.) Buckram. *Argosy*. $45/£29

ALLEN, CHARLES DEXTER. American Bookplates. London: George Bell, 1895. 1st trade ed. Grn cl, gilt. (Hinge paper cracked), else Fine. *Macdonnell*. $125/£80

ALLEN, CHARLES DEXTER. Classified List of Early American Bookplates. (DeVinne Press, 1894.) One of 350. 88pp. VG in ptd wraps (lacks rear wrapper; bkpls). *Bohling*. $30/£19

ALLEN, CHARLES DEXTER. Ex Libris. Essays of a Collector. Boston/NY: Lamson, Wolffe, 1896. #439/750. Frontis. Teg. Gilt cl (Spine sl dknd), else VG. *Reese*. $60/£38

ALLEN, CLIFFORD (ed). Michigan Log Marks. East Lansing: WPA, 1942. (Few pp creased.) Wraps (sl worn). *King*. $25/£16

ALLEN, EDGAR V. et al. Peripheral Vascular Diseases. Phila, 1947. 1st ed. Red cl bds (extrems sl worn). VG. *Doctor's Library*. $45/£29

ALLEN, EDWARD W. North Pacific. NY, 1936. VG. *High Latitude*. $20/£13

ALLEN, EDWARD W. The Vanishing Frenchman: The Mysterious Disappearance of La Perouse. Rutland: Charles E. Tuttle, (1959). 1st ed. 16 plts. Blue cl, silver spine title. Fine in pict dj (price-clipped). *Pacific**. $23/£15

ALLEN, EVERETT S. Arctic Odyssey. NY, 1962. 1st ed. Inscribed. VG in dj. *High Latitude*. $25/£16

ALLEN, EVERETT S. Children of the Light. Boston, c. 1973. 1st ed. VG in dj (frayed). *High Latitude*. $22/£14

ALLEN, F. H. (ed). Bibliography of Henry David Thoreau. Boston: HM Co, 1908. One of 530. Frontis port. Uncut. VG (ex-lib). *Mikesh*. $85/£54

ALLEN, F. J. The Great Church Towers of England. CUP, 1932. 52 full-pg plts. Good. *Scribe's Perch**. $26/£17

ALLEN, FLETCHER. A Wayfarer in North Africa: Tunisia and Algeria. Boston/NY: Houghton Mifflin, 1931. 1st ed. 16 plts. Partly unopened. (Sl rubbed), o/w VG. *Worldwide*. $10/£6

ALLEN, FRED C. Hand Book of the New York State Reformatory at Elmira. Summary Press, 1927. 87 plts, long fldg port. (Fr hinge cracked, inscrip.) Red cl (bumped). *Bohling*. $25/£16

ALLEN, G. The Evolutionist at Large, Vignettes from Nature, and Force and Energy. NY: Humboldt, n.d. (ca 1880). 3 vols in 1. 50; 55; 55pp + ads. Blind-stamped dec cl. VG + . *Mikesh*. $35/£22

ALLEN, G. M. The Mammals of China and Mongolia. Pt. 1 (all published). NY, 1938. 1st ed. *Maggs*. $179/£115

ALLEN, GRANT. Dumaresq's Daughter. C&W, 1893. New ed. Pub's cat dated July 1893. Pict bds (hinges, corners rubbed). Good. *Tiger*. $50/£32

ALLEN, GRANT. Miss Cayley's Adventures. London: Grant Richards, 1899. 1st ed. (Bkpl; sm spine tear), o/w NF in pict blue cl-cvrd bds, gilt. *Mordida*. $135/£87

ALLEN, GRANT. The Reluctant Hangman and Other Stories of Crime. Boulder: Aspen, 1973. 1st ed thus, pb orig. Fine in wrappers, as issued. *Janus*. $25/£16

ALLEN, GRANT. What's Bred in the Bone. London: Titbits Offices, 1891. 1st ed. 1/2 title not called for, imprint leaf at end, iv,414,(ii)pp. Dec eps; top edges uncut. Blue buckram, gilt. (Spine dknd), o/w Nice. *Temple*. $86/£55

ALLEN, H. WARNER. Number Three Saint James's Street. London, 1950. (Bkpl.) Dj (sl chipped, lt soiled). *Edwards*. $23/£15

ALLEN, HERVEY. Anthony Adverse. NY: Farrar & Rinehart, 1933. 1st ed. NF in dj. *Lame Duck*. $350/£224

ALLEN, HERVEY. Bedford Village. NY: Farrar & Rinehart, (1944). 1st ed. (Lt soiled, bumped.) Dj (frayed). *Hermitage*. $40/£26

ALLEN, HERVEY. Toward the Morning. NY: Rinehart, (1948). 1st ed. NF in dj (lt worn, frayed). *Hermitage*. $40/£26

ALLEN, IVAN. Atlanta from the Ashes. Atlanta, GA: Ruralist Press, 1928. Signed, ltd presentation copy. Cl, beveled bds (spine gilt rubbed). *Sadlon*. $15/£10

ALLEN, J. FISK. A Practical Treatise on the Culture and Treatment of the Grape Vine. Boston: Dutton & Wentworth, 1848. 2nd ed. Frontis, 247pp. (Spine ends worn.) M&s. $200/£128

ALLEN, JAMES LANE. The Choir Invisible. London/NY: Macmillan, 1897. 1st ed.
(viii),361pp + (i)blank + (ii)verso blank, integral ad leaf at end. Laid-paper eps; teg, others uncut. Lt blue buckram, gilt. Nice (cvrs sl faded). Temple. $28/£18

ALLEN, JAMES LANE. Flute and Violin and Other Kentucky Tales and Romances. NY: Harper, 1891. 1st ed, 1st bk. (Spine ends sl rubbed.) BAL 451. Sadlon. $100/£64

ALLEN, JAY. Forty Carets. NY: Random House, (1969). 1st ed. Fine in dj (edges sl dkng). Between The Covers. $75/£48

ALLEN, JOHN HOUGHTON. Southwest. Phila, 1952. 1st ed. Pict cl. Fine in dj (sl edgewear). Baade. $35/£22

ALLEN, JOHN LOGAN. Passage Through the Garden. Urbana: Univ of IL, (1975). 1st ed. VG in dj. Lien. $45/£29

ALLEN, LADY and SUSAN JELLICOE. The New Small Garden. London: Architectural Press, 1956. Fine in dj (worn). Quest. $25/£16

ALLEN, LAWRENCE J. et al. The Trans Alaska Pipeline. Seattle: Scribe, 1975-77. 3 vols. Leatherette-backed bds. VG in djs. High Latitude. $95/£61

ALLEN, LEWIS F. History of the Short-Horn Cattle. Buffalo: The Author, 1883. 2nd ed. 280pp (sigs). Brn cl, gilt. (Edges sl frayed, rear inner hinge cracked). Karmiole. $150/£96

ALLEN, LEWIS M. Printing with the Handpress. NY: Van Nostrand Reinhold, (1969). 2nd ptg. Folio. Black pict brn cl. NF in dj. House. $100/£64

ALLEN, LIEUT. and HENRY R. SCHOOLCRAFT. Expedition to Northwest Indians...in 1832. (Washington, 1834.) 1st ed. 68pp; fldg map (sm tape repair, 1-inch tear). Old marbled wraps (worn). Kane*. $180/£115

ALLEN, M. Falconry in Arabia. London: Orbin, 1980. 1st ed. Map. Fine in NF dj. Mikesh. $45/£29

ALLEN, MISS A. J. Ten Years in Oregon. Ithaca, 1848. 1st ed, 2nd issue, w/o frontis found in 1st issue, but w/appendix on pp401-30 entitled 'Col. Fremont's Adventures in Crossing California Mountain' and consisting of excerpts from Fremont's Narrative...of 1845. 430pp (lt foxing). Good (edgeworn, spine ends sl frayed, corners bumped). Howes A131. Reese. $225/£144

ALLEN, R. B. (trans). The Saga of Gisli. NY: Harcourt Brace, (1936). Stated 1st ed. Rockwell Kent (illus). Dec cvr. Good in dj (chipped). Scribe's Perch*. $32/£21

ALLEN, RICHARD. Covered Bridges of the Middle West. NY: Bonanza, 1970. 1st ed thus. Fine in dj. Archer. $17/£11

ALLEN, STEPHEN and W. H. PILSBURY. History of Methodism in Maine, 1793-1886. Augusta: Press of Charles E. Nash, 1887. xvi,650,282pp. (Dull, rubbed.) Zubal*. $17/£11

ALLEN, TED. Willie the Squowse. Cape, 1977. 1st ed. Quentin Blake (illus). 8vo. 57pp. Fine in pict dj. Bookmark. $27/£17

ALLEN, W. E. D. Russian Embassies to the Georgian Kings (1589-1605). Cambridge: Hakluyt Soc, 1970. 2 vols. Color frontis, 16 plts, 8 maps. Blue cl, gilt. VG. Parmer. $65/£42

ALLEN, W. W. and R. B. AVERY. California Gold Book. SF/Chicago: Donohue & Henneberry, 1893. 1st ed. iv,3-439pp. Lt blue cl (spine ends, corners worn, lt soiled), gilt. VG. Argonaut. $125/£80

ALLEN, WALTER C. Hendersonia. Highland Park: the Author, 1973. 1st ed. NF (sl spine wear). Beasley. $125/£80

ALLEN, WILLIAM A. Adventures with Indians and Game or Twenty Years in the Rocky Mountains. Chicago, 1903. Port. 3/4 calf, marbled bds. Internally VG (hinges worn, weak). Howes A165. Reese. $200/£128

ALLEN, WILLIAM. An American Biographical and Historical Dictionary.... Cambridge: William Hilliard, 1809. 1st ed. Frontis port, viii,632pp; fldg engr chart. (Lt wormed, foxed.) Early calf covering orig calf. Karmiole. $150/£96

ALLEN, WILLIAM. The History of Norridgewock. Norridgewock, 1849. 1st ed. Add'l vignette title, 5 (of 6) litho plts. Orig cl (sl worn, bumped, sl frayed). Howes A164. Freeman*. $15/£10

ALLEN, WINTHROP S. G. Civil War Letters of Winthrop S.G. Allen. Harry Pratt (ed). (Springfield, IL, 1932.) Port. Fine in ptd wraps. Wantagh. $25/£16

ALLEN, WOODY. Side Effects. NY: Random House, (1980). 1st ed. Cl-backed bds. Fine in dj (sl worn). Holmes. $45/£29

ALLEN, WOODY. Side Effects. NY: Random House, (1980). 1st ed. Signed. Fine in Fine dj. Metropolitan*. $143/£92

ALLEN, Z. Defense of the Rhode Island System of Treatment of the Indians.... Providence, 1876. 34pp. Dec cvr. Good (hinge cracks). Scribe's Perch*. $18/£12

ALLENDE, ISABEL. Of Love and Shadows. Margaret Sayers Peden (trans). NY: Knopf, 1987. 1st ed in English. Promo postcard loosely inserted. Nice in dj. Ash. $31/£20

ALLEY, FELIX E. Random Thoughts and Musings of a Mountaineer. Salisbury, NC, (1941). 1st ed. (Rear bd dampstained), else VG in dj (worn). Bohling. $20/£13

ALLEY, G. Observations on the Hydragyria. 1810. xx,104pp; 3 color plts. (Cvr sl dust-stained.) Whitehart. $312/£200

ALLEYNE, MARGARET. (Pseud of K. J. Burrell.) The Story of Mr. Prettimouse. London, (1946.) 1st ed. Mary B. Robinson (illus). Lg 16mo. 44pp, 23 color illus (8 full-pg). White paper bds, upper cvr ptd in color (prize label inside fr cvr dated 1946). Dj (sl worn). Cox. $23/£15

ALLIBONE, S. AUSTIN. Critical Dictionary of English Literature and British and American Authors.... Phila: Lippincott, 1871. 2nd issue. 3 vols. (Extrems sl worn), o/w VG. New Hampshire*. $170/£109

ALLINGHAM, E. A Romance of the Rostrum. London: Witherby, 1924. Orig sales brochure tipped in; notice attached fr pastedown. Good (lt foxed). Blake. $75/£48

ALLINGHAM, MARGERY. The Beckoning Lady. London: C&W, 1955. 1st ed. (Name, lt spotting pg edges), o/w VG in dj (chipped, long closed tear base of spine). Mordida. $45/£29

ALLINGHAM, MARGERY. The China Governess. GC: Doubleday, 1952. 1st ed. NF in NF dj. Else Fine. $40/£26

ALLINGHAM, MARGERY. Hide My Eyes. London: C&W, 1958. 1st ed. (Name, eps dknd, edges lt spotted), o/w VG in dj (price-clipped, chip, closed tears). Mordida. $35/£22

ALLINGHAM, MARGERY. The Tiger in the Smoke. C&W, 1952. 1st ed. VG in dj (sl worn, chipped). Ash. $62/£40

ALLINSON, T. R. Medical Essays. London: Fowler, 1901-1902. 5 vols in 1. Frontis port. (Sm tear tp vol 1.) 1/2 leather (spine top chipped). White. $101/£65

ALLISON, WILLIAM. Memories of Men and Horses. NY: Brentano's, (1924). 1st Amer ed. Good+ (old stain rear cvr). Agvent. $35/£22

ALLIX, CHARLES. Carriage Clocks, Their History and Development. (Suffolk, 1974.) 1st ed. 16 color plts. Navy blue cl. Dj (worn). *Weber.* $65/£42

ALLMAN, NORWOOD F. Shanghai Lawyer. NY: Whittlesey House, 1943. Sound in dj (worn, chipped). *Boswell.* $45/£29

ALLRED, B. W. The Life of a Horse and Buggy Stage Line Operator. Falls Church, VA: Potomac Corral of the Westerners, 1972. Ltd to 200 signed. VF. *Gibbs.* $25/£16

ALLSOPP, BRUCE (ed). Historic Architecture of Newcastle upon Tyne. Oriel, 1970. Rev 2nd ed. VG in dj (creased). *Hadley.* $28/£18

ALLSOPP, BRUCE. Decoration and Furniture. London, 1952-53. 1st ed. 2 vols. VG in djs. *Argosy.* $150/£96

Almanac for Thirty-Niners. (By the Works Progress Administration.) Stanford: James Ladd Delkin, (1938). 1st ed. Frontis. VF. *Argonaut.* $45/£29

Almanack for the Year of Christ 1850. (London, 1849.) (58x33mm), 13ff, fldg plt mtd as 2 leaves. Aeg. Orig brn morocco, gilt w/beige, grn, red onlays. In matching contemp slipcase. Excellent. *Marlborough.* $351/£225

Along Highways in Old Virginia. Richmond, 1920s. Dbl map. Pict wraps. (Spine worn, creased, stamps on cvr.) *Bohling.* $15/£10

Along the San Antonio River. San Antonio: City of San Antonio, 1941. 1st ed. VG in wraps. *Gibbs.* $35/£22

Alphabet of Children's Names. Nelson, n.d. 4to. (14)pp. (1903 inscrip; sl mkd, worn, spine fold grazed), else VG in pict wraps. *Bookmark.* $75/£48

ALSCHULER, ROSE and L. HATTWICK. Painting and Personality. Chicago: Univ of Chicago, 1951. 3rd ptg. 2 vols. (Spine ends 1 vol discolored), else Fine in djs (spines stained). *Beasley.* $45/£29

ALTER, J. CECIL. Early Utah Journalism: A Half Century of Forensic Warfare.... Salt Lake City: UT Hist Soc, 1938. Fabricoid (spine sl faded). *Dawson.* $50/£32

ALTER, J. CECIL. Jim Bridger. Norman: Univ of OK, (1962). 1st ptg of new ed. (Inscrip), else VF in dj (spine faded). *Argonaut.* $60/£38

ALTER, J. CECIL. Through the Heart of the Scenic West. Salt Lake City: Shepard Bk Co, 1927. Ltd to 1000. Signed. VG. *Lien.* $45/£29

ALTHAM, H. S. and E. W. SWANTON. A History of Cricket. 1962. 1st ed. 2 vols. Djs (sl chipped). *Edwards.* $47/£30

ALVARADO, JUAN BAUTISTA. Vignettes of Early California. John H. R. Polt (trans). SF: Book Club of CA, 1982. Ltd to 650 ptd. Frontis port, ms facs pg. Cl-backed dec bds, paper spine label. Prospectus laid in. Fine in dj. *Pacific*.* $35/£22

ALVAREZ, JULIA. How the Garcia Girls Lost Their Accents. (Chapel Hill, NC): Algonquin, 1991. 1st ed. New in New dj. *Bernard.* $45/£29

ALVAREZ, WALTER C. Nervousness, Indigestion, and Pain. NY, 1943. 1st ed. VG. *Doctor's Library.* $50/£32

ALVORD, CLARENCE W. The Mississippi Valley in British Politics. Cleveland: A.H. Clark, 1917. 2 vols. 4 color maps. Teg, unopened. (Vol 1 prelim roughly opened), else Fine set. Howes A195. *Bohling.* $300/£192

ALVORD, CLARENCE W. and LEE BIDGOOD. The First Explorations of the Trans-Allegheny Region by the Virginians 1650-1674. Cleveland: Clark, 1912. 1st ed. 2 maps, 4 facs. (Spine sl discolored.) Howes A194. *Ginsberg.* $175/£112

ALVORD, CLARENCE W. and CLARENCE EDWARD CARTER (eds). Collections of the Illinois Historical Library British Series Volumes 1-3. Springfield: IL State Hist Library, 1915-1921. 3 vols. (Ex-lib, blindstamps, rubberstamps, call #s on spines, spine lettering faded, shelfworn), else Good. *Brown.* $75/£48

AMARAL, A. Mustang: Life and Legends of Nevada's Wild Horses. Reno: Univ of NV, 1977. 1st ed. Fine in Fine dj. *Mikesh.* $30/£19

AMBERG, GEORGE. Art in Modern Ballet. (NY, 1946.) *Swann*.* $46/£29

AMBLER, CHARLES HENRY. History of Transportation in the Ohio Valley.... Glendale, CA: A.H. Clark, 1932. Fldg map. Teg. Blue cl, gilt. VG + (lt bumped). *Bohling.* $110/£71

AMBLER, ERIC. The Ability to Kill. NY: Mysterious, (1987). Ltd to 250 numbered, signed. Fine in slipcase. *Antic Hay.* $65/£42

AMBLER, ERIC. The Ability to Kill. Bodley Head, 1963. 2nd issue, w/Bodkin Adams passage excised. Fine (sm label) in VG dj. *Williams.* $14/£9

AMBLER, ERIC. Dirty Story. NY, 1967. 1st ed. Signed. Fine in Fine dj. *Smith.* $25/£16

AMBLER, ERIC. Doctor Frigo. Weidenfeld, 1974. 1st UK ed. Fine in dj. *Williams.* $19/£12

AMBLER, ERIC. Journey into Fear. NY: Knopf, 1940. 1st ed. (Stamp, plt removed fr pastedown, stamp rep; sl shelfwear.) Dj (price-clipped, corners through, edgeworn, chipped). *Metropolitan*.* $92/£59

AMBLER, ERIC. A Kind of Anger. Bodley Head, 1964. 1st UK ed. NF in VG dj (sm nicks, price-clipped). *Williams.* $14/£9

AMBLER, ERIC. The Levanter. Weidenfeld, 1972. 1st UK ed. Fine in VG + dj. *Williams.* $19/£12

AMBLER, ERIC. The Night-Comers. Heinemann, 1956. 1st UK ed. VG in VG + dj. *Williams.* $28/£18

AMBLER, ERIC. Passage of Arms. Heinemann, 1959. 1st UK ed. VG (sm stamps) in dj. *Williams.* $23/£15

AMBLER, ERIC. Passage of Arms. NY: Knopf, 1960. 1st Amer ed. NF in bright dj (spine sl chipped). *Hermitage.* $35/£22

AMBLER, ERIC. State of Siege. NY: Knopf, 1956. 1st Amer ed. Rev slip laid in. Fine in dj (faded). *Hermitage.* $45/£29

AMBROSE, STEPHEN E. Crazy Horse and Custer. NY: Doubleday, (1975). 1st ed. VG in dj. *Lien.* $55/£35

American Angler's Guide. (By John J. Brown.) NY: H. Long & John J. Brown, 1850. 4th ed. 332pp + ads. Gilt-pict cl. (Lt foxed; cvr faded), o/w VG. *New Hampshire*.* $75/£48

American Anti-Slavery Almanac, for 1838.... Boston: Hitchcock, 1838. 46-pg pamphlet, sewn gathers. (Browning, lt dampstains, cvr rather faded.) *Metropolitan*.* $51/£33

American Armies and Battlefields in Europe: A History.... Washington: GPO, 1938. 3 lg fldg maps rear pocket. *Dawson.* $50/£32

AMERICAN ART ASSOCIATION. The Stephen H. Wakeman Collection of Books. NY: American Art Assoc, 1924. 1st ed. Grn cl, paper label. Fine. *Macdonnell.* $100/£64

American Country Houses of Today, Chiefly for Moderate Incomes. NY: Architectural Book Pub Co, 1917. (Lt wear, soil.) *Freeman*.* $35/£22

American Fish and How to Catch Them. (By M. C. Weidmeyer.) NY: Harper, 1885. 1st ed. 95pp. Grn cl. VG + . *Bowman.* $80/£51

American Lady's Preceptor. Balt: Coale et al, 1815. 2nd ed. 300pp (lacks fep). Calf-backed bds (rubbed, worn). VG. *Second Life.* $135/£87

American Memoranda, by a Mercantile Man.... (By James Lumsden.) Glasgow, 1844. (4),60pp. (Bkpl, hinges broken, spine worn), else Good. Howes L568. *Reese.* $125/£80

American Spectator, or Matrimonial Preceptor. Boston: David West, 1797. Frontis (offsetting on title; sl damp-staining). Contemp tree calf (rubbed, fr cvr detached), gilt-paneled spine, leather label. *Freeman*. $90/£58

American Stage of To-Day. NY: P.F. Collier, 1910. 1st ed. Mod cl. VG. *Dramatis Personae.* $120/£77

AMERY, L. S. (ed). The Times' History of the War in South Africa, 1899-1900. London: Sampson Low, Marston, 1900. 7 vols. Red cl. VG. *Zubal*. $190/£122

AMES, FISHER. Works. Boston: T.B. Wait, 1809. 1st ed. Engr frontis port, xxxi,(vi),519pp (lt browned, sl foxed). Old polished tree calf (lt worn, sl scuffed), orig red leather spine label. Cvrs VG. *Baltimore*. $90/£58

AMES, WINSLOW. Drawings of the Masters. Italian Drawings from the 15th to the 19th Century. Boston, 1963. 94 color plts. Good in wrappers. *Washton.* $15/£10

AMHERST, ALICIA. A History of Gardening in England. London: Quaritch, 1896. 2nd ed. (Fr hinge tender), else Beautiful in gilt-pict grn cl. *Captain's Bookshelf.* $125/£80

AMIET, PIERRE. Art of the Ancient Near East. NY: Abrams, 1980. 158 plts, 115 plans and elevations, 41 dwgs, 6 reconstructions, map. (Bkpl.) Dj. *Archaeologia.* $250/£160

AMIRANASHVILI, SHALVA. Georgian Metalwork from Antiquity to the 18th Century. London, 1971. 109 color plts. Good in dj. *Washton.* $40/£26

AMIS, KINGSLEY with ROBERT CONQUEST. The Egyptologists. NY: Random House, (1966). 1st Amer ed. NF in dj (sm tears). *Antic Hay.* $35/£22

AMIS, KINGSLEY. The Alteration. Cape, 1976. 1st UK ed. NF in dj (price-clipped). *Williams.* $25/£16

AMIS, KINGSLEY. The Anti-Death League. NY: Harcourt, Brace & World, (1966). 1st ed. NF in dj (sl worn, few sm tears). *Antic Hay.* $45/£29

AMIS, KINGSLEY. The Crime of the Century. NY: Mysterious Press, 1989. Ltd to 100 signed. Fine in slipcase. *Words Etc.* $78/£50

AMIS, KINGSLEY. Dear Illusion. Covent Garden Press, 1972. Ltd to 600. Fine in wraps. *Martin.* $44/£28

AMIS, KINGSLEY. Ending Up. Cape, 1974. 1st UK ed. Fine in NF dj. *Williams.* $31/£20

AMIS, KINGSLEY. The Fantasy Poets—Number Twenty-Two. Swinford, Eynsham: Fantasy Press, 1954. VG in wrappers (lower lt spotted; staples rusted). *Gekoski.* $273/£175

AMIS, KINGSLEY. Girl, 20. London: Cape, 1971. 1st UK ed. VG (sm stain bottom edge) in dj. *Williams.* $19/£12

AMIS, KINGSLEY. The Green Man. NY: Harcourt, Brace & World, (1970). 1st Amer ed. Fine in NF dj. *Hermitage.* $40/£26

AMIS, KINGSLEY. The Green Man. London: Cape, 1969. 1st UK ed. VG + in dj (sl bumped). *Williams.* $31/£20

AMIS, KINGSLEY. Jake's Thing. London: Hutchinson, (1978). 1st ed. Fine in dj. *Antic Hay.* $35/£22

AMIS, KINGSLEY. The James Bond Dossier. London: Cape, (1965). 1st ed. Fine in dj. *Reese.* $40/£26

AMIS, KINGSLEY. Lucky Jim's Politics. Conservative Political Centre, 1968. 1st UK ed. VG in wraps. *Williams.* $34/£22

AMIS, KINGSLEY. Lucky Jim. London, 1953. 1st Eng ed. Good (spine sl faded). *Clearwater.* $125/£80

AMIS, KINGSLEY. Memoirs. Hutchinson, 1991. 1st UK ed. Fine in dj. *Williams.* $19/£12

AMIS, KINGSLEY. New Maps of Hell. Gollancz, 1961. 1st ed. Good in dj (sl mkd). *Whiteson.* $23/£15

AMIS, KINGSLEY. The Old Devils. London Ltd Eds, 1986. One of 250 specially bound, signed. NF in tissue. *Clearwater.* $62/£40

AMIS, KINGSLEY. One Fat Englishman. London: Gollancz, 1963. 1st Eng ed. NF in dj (browned). *Antic Hay.* $40/£26

AMIS, KINGSLEY. The Riverside Villas Murder. London: Jonathan Cape, (1973). 1st Eng ed. Paper-cvrd bds. Fine in dj. *Antic Hay.* $35/£22

AMIS, KINGSLEY. Russian Hide and Seek. London: Hutchinson, 1980. 1st UK ed. NF in dj. *Williams.* $23/£15

AMIS, KINGSLEY. Socialism and the Intellectuals. Fabian Tract 304, 1957. 1st ed. VG in wrappers (spine rubbed). *Buckley.* $55/£35

AMIS, KINGSLEY. Stanley and the Women. Hutchinson, 1984. 1st UK ed. Fine in dj. *Williams.* $23/£15

AMIS, KINGSLEY. You Can't Do Both. London Ltd Eds, 1994. One of 150 specially bound, signed. Fine in tissue. *Clearwater.* $55/£35

AMIS, MARTIN. Dead Babies. NY: Knopf, 1975. 1st US ed. NF in dj (nick). *Lame Duck.* $150/£96

AMIS, MARTIN. Invasion of the Space Invaders. London: Hutchinson, 1982. 1st ed. NF in illus glossy wraps. *Lame Duck.* $250/£160

AMIS, MARTIN. London Fields. London, 1989. 1st Eng ed. Signed. Fine in dj. *Clearwater.* $55/£35

AMIS, MARTIN. Other People. London, 1981. 1st Eng ed. NF in dj. *Clearwater.* $78/£50

AMIS, MARTIN. The Rachel Papers. NY, 1974. 1st Amer ed. NF in NF dj. *Warren.* $150/£96

AMIS, MARTIN. The Rachel Papers. NY: Knopf, 1974. 1st US ed, 1st bk. NF in dj (sm tear, sl crease). *Bernard.* $100/£64

AMIS, MARTIN. Success. NY: Harmony, (1978). 1st US ed. Fine in Fine dj. *Fuller & Saunders.* $25/£16

AMIS, MARTIN. Time's Arrow. London: Cape/London Ltd Eds, 1991. One of 200 numbered, signed. Marble paper-cvrd bds. Fine in glassine dj. *Moorhouse.* $55/£35

AMMONS, A. R. Changing Things. Palaemon, (1981). One of 100 numbered. Signed. Fine in silver-foil wrappers. *Dermont.* $60/£38

AMMONS, A. R. Northfield Poems. Ithaca: Cornell Univ, (1966). 1st ed. Fine in VG + dj (sl rubbing). *Between The Covers.* $85/£54

AMORY, CLEVELAND. The Cat Who Came for Christmas. Boston: Little, Brown, (1987). 1st ed. Signed. Fine in dj (sm nicks). *Captain's Bookshelf.* $60/£38

AMORY, COPLEY, JR. Persian Days. Boston/NY: Houghton Mifflin, 1929. 1st ed. 32 plts. (Sl foxed; rubbed, spine frayed), o/w Good. *Worldwide.* $14/£9

AMORY, R. and R. L. EMERSON. Wharton and Stille's Medical Jurisprudence. Vol II: Poisons. Rochester, NY, 1905. 5th ed. Vol II only, but complete in itself. xxxi,858pp. Contemp calf (rebacked). 2 spine labels, 1 orig. *Whitehart.* $148/£95

AMORY, THOMAS C. Transfer of Erin: or The Acquisition of Ireland by England. Phila: Lippincott, 1877. 1st ed. 654,(1)pp. Irish grn cl (rear inner hinge starting, corners worn), gilt spine. NF. *Argonaut.* $175/£112

AMOS, SHELDON. Political and Legal Remedies for War. NY: Harper, 1880. Orig (?) bds. Sound (rubbed, worn). *Boswell.* $250/£160

AMPHLETT, F. H. Everybody's Book on Angling. Brindley & Howe, c. 1903. *Petersfield.* $34/£22

AMUNDSEN, ROALD and LINCOLN ELLSWORTH. First Crossing of the Polar Sea. NY: George H. Doran, 1927. Fldg map. (Shelfwear), else VG. *Parmer.* $125/£80

AMUNDSEN, ROALD. My Polar Flight. London: Hutchinson, n.d. (1925). Map. VG. *High Latitude.* $65/£42

AMUNDSEN, ROALD. The South Pole. A. G. Chater (trans). London/NY: John Murray/Lee Keedick, 1913. 1st Amer ed. Sm 4to. 2 vols. Frontis port. Teg. Blue cl, gilt. Fine. *Appelfeld.* $600/£385

AMUNDSEN, ROALD. The South Pole. An Account of the Norwegian Antarctic Expedition in the 'Fram,' 1910-1912. London: John Murray, 1912. 1st ed in English. 2 vols. xxxv,392; xi,449pp, 3 fldg maps. Teg. Red dec cl. VG. *High Latitude.* $750/£481

ANAGNOS, MICHAEL. The Education of the Blind in the United States of America: Its Principles, Development and Results. Boston: Geo. H. Ellis, 1904. 23pp + 3-pg ptd checklist dated November, 1895, tipped in. 1st ed thus. Contemp 3/4 calf over pebbled cl (sm chip spine top, corners rubbed, joints tender). NF. *Glaser.* $60/£38

ANAN'YEV, M. G. (ed). New Soviet Surgical Apparatus and Instruments and Their Application. John B. Elliott (trans). NY: Pergamon, 1961. 1st ed in English. VG. *Glaser.* $50/£32

Ananga-Ranga. A. F. F. and B. F. R. (trans). (Pseuds of F. F. Arbuthnot and R. F. Burton.) Cosmopoli: Kama Shastra Soc of London and Benares, 1885. xvi,144pp. Orig imitation vellum (rubbed), gilt. *Adelson.* $285/£183

Anastasius, or Memoirs of a Greek. (By Thomas Hope.) John Murray, 1820. 3rd ed. 3 vols. Fldg map (folds reinforced). Orig bds. Good (lt spotting; rebacked, orig backstrips relaid, spine labels rubbed, chipped). *Tiger.* $70/£45

ANATOLI, A. Babi Yar. David Floyd (trans). NY: FSG, (1970). 1st Amer ed. Fine in dj (sl rubbed). *Antic Hay.* $25/£16

Anatomy of Melancholy, What It Is, with All the Kinds, Causes, Symptoms, Prognostics and Several Cures of It.... (By Robert Burton.) Longman et al, 1827. 13th ed. 2 vols. xxiv,461,(1); (iv),612pp. Marbled edges, eps. Contemp polished calf (both hinges vol 1 cracked through; bds held by 4 cords), gilt, dbl morocco labels. *Cox.* $86/£55

Anatomy of Melancholy. (By Robert Burton.) Oxford: Henry Cripps, 1632. 4th ed. Engr tp. (1st leaf strengthened on recto, sl browned, soiled.) 19th-cent bds (rubbed), polished calf back, tips, gilt spine, morocco label. *Oinonen*.* $450/£288

Anatomy of Melancholy. (By Robert Burton.) London: Ptd & are to be sould by H. Cripps & Lodo Lloyd, 1652. 6th ed, 2nd issue w/1652 title-leaf and 1651 Cripps and Crook colophon on final leaf. (6),78,(6),723,(11)pp (inscrips, lt foxing, discolorations, marginal nicks, blemishes). Old calf. VG. *Reese.* $550/£353

Anatomy of Melancholy. (By Robert Burton.) London, 1852. 5th ed. 670pp. Woodcut inserted fr pastedown. 1/4 leather, marbled bds (worn). Good (inner hinges cracked). *Doctor's Library.* $50/£32

ANBUREY, THOMAS. Travels Through the Interior Parts of America. Boston: Houghton Mifflin, 1923. Ltd to 575. 2 vols. Map. Good (rebound; ex-lib). Howes A226. *Lien.* $95/£61

ANDERS, CURT. Fighting Confederates. NY, 1968. 1st ed. VG+ in VG+ dj. *Pratt.* $35/£22

ANDERSEN, HANS CHRISTIAN and GRANDFATHER DREWSEN. Christine's Picture Book. NY: Holt, 1985. 1st ed. 10 x 12 1/4. 266pp. VG in dj. *Cattermole.* $30/£19

ANDERSEN, HANS CHRISTIAN. The Complete Andersen. Jean Hersholt (trans). NY: LEC, 1949. One of 1500 signed by Fritz Kredel (illus). 6 vols. Cl-backed pict bds. VG. *Argosy.* $400/£256

ANDERSEN, HANS CHRISTIAN. The Emperor's New Clothes. Boston: Houghton Mifflin, 1949. 4th ed. Virginia Lee Burton (illus). 7 1/2 x 9. 44pp. VG in dj. *Cattermole.* $25/£16

ANDERSEN, HANS CHRISTIAN. Fairy Tales. London, (1932). One of 525 numbered, signed by Arthur Rackham (illus). 4to. 12 color plts, guards. Pict eps. Orig vellum, gilt. *Swann*.* $1,495/£958

ANDERSEN, HANS CHRISTIAN. Fairy Tales. NY: Brentano's, (n.d.). 1st ed thus. Harry Clarke (illus). 16 tipped-in color plts, tissue guards, 24 full-pg b/w illus. VG (rear hinge sl damaged). *Certo.* $195/£125

ANDERSEN, HANS CHRISTIAN. The Little Mermaid. Natick, MA, 1984. 1st US ed. Chihiro Iwasaki (illus). 8 1/2 x 11 1/2. 32pp. Glossy bds. Fine in dj. *Cattermole.* $25/£16

ANDERSEN, HANS CHRISTIAN. The Nightingale. NY: Harper & Row, 1965. 1st ed. Signed by Nancy Ekholm Burkert (illus). 9x11. 32pp, high-quality paper; 1/2 title ptd in black. Fine in dj. *Cattermole.* $45/£29

ANDERSEN, HANS CHRISTIAN. The Sand-Hills of Jutland. Boston: Ticknor & Fields, 1860. 1st Amer ed. (iv),267pp. Brn cl (bumped, spine ends chipped, fr joint starting), gilt (faded). Good. *Blue Mountain.* $45/£29

ANDERSEN, HANS CHRISTIAN. The Steadfast Tin Soldier. NY: Macmillan Happy Hour, 1934. George M. Richards (illus). 5 3/4 sq. Pict bds. Good. *Cattermole.* $20/£13

ANDERSEN, HANS CHRISTIAN. Stories. London, (1911). One of 750 numbered, signed by Edmund Dulac (illus). 4to. 28 tipped-in color plts, guards. Vellum gilt, silk ties. (Bkpl.) *Swann*.* $1,610/£1,032

ANDERSEN, HANS CHRISTIAN. The Tumble-Bug and Other Tales. NY: HBJ, 1940. 1st ed. Hertha List (illus). 7 1/4 x 9 1/4. 166pp. Fine. *Cattermole.* $40/£26

ANDERSEN, HANS CHRISTIAN. The Ugly Duckling. NY: Macmillan, 1955. 1st US ed. Johannes Larsen (illus). 10 1/4 x 8 1/2. 54pp. Pict bds. Fine in dj. *Cattermole.* $25/£16

ANDERSEN, HANS CHRISTIAN. What the Moon Saw and Other Tales. H.W. Dulken (trans). Routledge, 1871. Rpt. Pict beveled bds. A. W. Bayes (illus), Brothers Dalziel (engr). Good (sl spotted, new fep; spine bumped, chipped, corners rubbed). *Tiger.* $44/£28

ANDERSEN, HANS. Andersen's Fairy Tales. NY: Cupples & Leon, (1923). John R. Neill (illus). 4to. 180pp; 3 color illus incl label. Blue cl, gilt. (Spine ends sl bumped, rubbed), o/w VG. *Dower.* $85/£54

ANDERSEN, HANS. Danish Fairy Legends and Tales with a Memoir by Author. Caroline Peachey (trans). London: Addey, 1852. 2nd (enlgd) ed. 12mo. 532pp (fep, rep professionally replaced). Red cl. *Dower.* $125/£80

ANDERSEN, HANS. Fairy Tales. London: Hodder & Stoughton, (1924). One of 500 on lg paper and signed by Kay Nielsen (illus). Lg 4to. 12 mtd color plts. Gilt-stamped vellum (buckled, spotted, spine heel rubbed). *Appelfeld.* $1,850/£1,186

ANDERSEN, HANS. Fairy Tales. Mrs. H. B. Paoll (trans). London/NY, 1890. viii,670pp. (Feps lt browned, hinges cracked, sl shaken; joints sl rubbed, spine sl bumped.) *Edwards.* $31/£20

ANDERSEN, HANS. Hans Andersen's Fairy Tales. London: Boots the Chemist, n.d. W. Heath Robinson (illus). 4to. 320pp (fore-edge, several pp foxed); 16 color plts tipped in, 79 b/w illus. Red cl, gilt. VG in VG dj (spine top tape-repaired, rear cvr sl dknd). *Dower.* $500/£321

ANDERSEN, HANS. Stories from Hans Andersen. London: Hodder & Stoughton, (1911). 1st trade ed. Sm folio. 28 tipped-in color plts by Edmund Dulac. Gilt-dec brn cl. (Spine sl bumped), o/w VG++. *Dower.* $400/£256

ANDERSON, A. W. The Coming of the Flowers. NY: Farrar, Straus and Young, n.d. Fine. *Quest.* $35/£22

ANDERSON, AENEAS. A Narrative of the British Embassy to China, in the Years 1792, 1793, and 1794. Dublin: P. Byrne, 1796. 2nd ed. xxiv,304pp. Marbled eps, all edges marbled. 1/2 morocco, marbled bds, gilt. (Sl foxed; sl rubbed), o/w VG. *Worldwide.* $275/£176

ANDERSON, ANNE. The Anne Anderson Fairy-Tale Book. NY: Thos. Nelson, n.d. c. 1928. 1st ed thus. Lg 4to. 190pp; 12 full-pg color illus. Grey cl, color pict label. (Sm ink spot tp), else VG+. *Dower.* $175/£112

ANDERSON, BARRY C. Lifeline to the Yukon. Seattle, c. 1983. 1st ed. Fine in dj. *High Latitude.* $25/£16

ANDERSON, BERN. Surveyor of the Sea: The Life and Voyages of Captain George Vancouver. Toronto: Univ of Toronto, (1960). 1st ed. Map. (Spine sunned.) *Lefkowicz.* $65/£42

ANDERSON, C. W. Bobcat. NY: Macmillan, 1949. 1st ed. VG in Good- dj. *October Farm.* $45/£29

ANDERSON, C. W. Deep Through the Heart. NY: Macmillan, 1940. 1st ed. VG in Good dj. *October Farm.* $45/£29

ANDERSON, C. W. Heads Up—Heels Down. NY: Macmillan, 1944. VG in Good dj. *October Farm.* $25/£16

ANDERSON, C. W. The Outlaw. NY: Macmillan, 1967. 1st ed. 7 x 9 1/4. 99pp. Fine in dj. *Cattermole.* $30/£19

ANDERSON, C. W. Salute. NY: Macmillan, 1940. 1st ed. VG in Good- dj. *October Farm.* $45/£29

ANDERSON, CHARLES ROBERTS (ed). Journal of a Cruise to the Pacific Ocean, 1842-1844, in the Frigate United States.... Durham: Duke Univ, 1937. 1st ed. Frontis. Blue cl. (Spine faded), else Fine. *Argonaut.* $50/£32

ANDERSON, CHARLES ROBERTS (ed). Journal of a Cruise to the Pacific Ocean, 1842-1844.... Durham: Duke Univ, 1937. 1st ed. 7 plts. Blue cl, gilt spine. (Spine sl faded), else NF. *Pacific*.* $23/£15

ANDERSON, CHESTER. The Butterfly Kid. Boston: Gregg, 1977. 1st hb ed. Inscribed, signed. (Sl rubbed.) *Swann*.* $69/£44

ANDERSON, E. B. Seven Gardens or Sixty Years of Gardening. Michael Joseph, 1973. VG in dj. *Hadley.* $19/£12

ANDERSON, EVA GREENSLIT. Dog-Team Doctor: The Story of Dr. Romig. Caldwell: Caxton, 1940. (Fore-edge stained.) Dk grn cl, gilt. *Parmer.* $45/£29

ANDERSON, FRANK MALOY. The Mystery of 'A Public Man.' Minneapolis, (1948). Dj. *Wantagh.* $30/£19

ANDERSON, FRANK. The Complete Book of 169 Redoute Roses. NY: Abbeville, (1979). 169 color plts. Fine in dj. *Quest.* $45/£29

ANDERSON, GALUSHA. The Story of a Border City During the Civil War. Boston: Little, Brown, 1908. 1st ed. Frontis, 8 plts. Color pict cl. VG. *Petrilla.* $45/£29

ANDERSON, HENRY. The Medical and Surgical Aspects of Aviation. London, 1919. 1st ed. (Ex-lib; recased). *Fye.* $300/£192

ANDERSON, ISABEL. The Great Sea-Horse. Boston: Little, Brown, 1909. One of 300. 24 tipped-in color plts. Full gilt-dec vellum. VG in dj (sl worn, soiled). *New Hampshire*.* $280/£179

ANDERSON, ISABEL. A Yacht in Mediterranean Seas. Boston: Marshall Jones, 1930. 1st ed. Color frontis, 86 plts. (1st few leaves sl damp), o/w VG in dj (torn, soiled). *Worldwide.* $45/£29

ANDERSON, J. The Book of British Topography. London, 1881. 1st ed. xvi,472pp. Brn cl. Good (bkpl). *Moss.* $86/£55

ANDERSON, J. (ed). The New Practical Gardener and Modern Horticulturist. London, (c 1870). iv,988pp; 27 chromolitho plts (5 dbl-pg), 12 plain plts (4 dbl-pg). (Color plt sl foxed.) 1/2 calf, gilt. *Henly.* $281/£180

ANDERSON, JAMES DOUGLAS. Making the American Thoroughbred...1800-1845. Nashville: Granger Williams, 1946. 2nd ptg. 1/4 leather. VG. *October Farm.* $65/£42

ANDERSON, JOHN Q. (ed). Tales of Frontier Texas. Dallas: SMU, 1966. 1st ed. Fine in dj. *Gibbs.* $25/£16

ANDERSON, JOSEPH. Recollections of a Peninsular Veteran. London, 1913. Frontis port (loose). Red cl (unevenly faded, sm stain fr cvr), gilt. *Maggs.* $156/£100

ANDERSON, M. D. The Imagery of British Churches. John Murray, 1955. VG in dj (creased, chipped). *Hadley.* $25/£16

ANDERSON, MARY AUDENTIA SMITH. Ancestry and Posterity of Joseph Smith and Emma Hale. Independence, 1929. 1st ed. Frontis, fldg chart. (Fr hinge cracked, lt edgeworn, spine discolored), o/w VG. *Benchmark.* $500/£321

ANDERSON, MAXWELL. Storm Operation. Washington, 1944. 1st ed. Fine in dj. *Argosy.* $40/£26

ANDERSON, MILES et al. Prosthetic Principles—Above Knee Amputations. Raymond E. Sollars (ed). Springfield, (1960). VG in dj. *Argosy.* $60/£38

ANDERSON, MILES H. Functional Bracing of the Upper Extremities. Raymond E. Sollars (ed). Springfield, (1958). 1st ed. VG in dj. *Argosy.* $60/£38

ANDERSON, NANCY MAE. Swede Homestead. Caldwell: Caxton, 1942. 1st ed. (Ink name), else VG in dj (torn). *Perier.* $40/£26

ANDERSON, PAUL L. Pictorial Photography. Phila: Lippincott, 1917. 1st ed. Good. *Smith.* $60/£38

ANDERSON, POUL. Is There Life on Other Worlds? Crowell, 1963. 1st ed. Fine in dj. *Madle.* $35/£22

ANDERSON, POUL. Perish by the Sword. NY: Macmillan, 1959. 1st ed. Signed. Fine in VG dj (sl wear). *Old London.* $135/£87

ANDERSON, POUL. Satan's World. NY: Doubleday, (1969). 1st ed. Dj (lt rubbed). *Swann*.* $69/£44

ANDERSON, POUL. Three Hearts and Three Lions. NY: Doubleday, 1961. 1st ed. Dj (sl soiled). *Swann*.* $69/£44

ANDERSON, POUL. Time and the Stars. NY: Doubleday, 1964. 1st ed. Inscribed, signed. Dj. *Swann*.* $69/£44

ANDERSON, R. C. The Rigging of Ships in the Days of the Spritsail Topmast, 1600-1720. Salem, MA: Marine Research Soc, 1927. 1st ed. 24 plts. Blue buckram (spine faded, soiled). *Karmiole.* $75/£48

ANDERSON, R. P. A Personal Journal of the Siege of Lucknow. T. Carnegy Anderson (ed). London, 1858. 2nd imp. xii,110pp + ads. Yellow cl (stained, faded). *Maggs.* $250/£160

ANDERSON, RICHARD. Lightning Conductors. London: F.N. Spon, 1880. 1st ed. Wood-engr frontis, xv,256pp. (Upper joint tender, strip cut top tp, ink spots fore-edge; sl worn, spine head frayed.) *Hollett.* $133/£85

ANDERSON, ROBERT. An Artillery Officer in the Mexican War, 1846-7: Letters of Robert Anderson, Captain 3rd Artillery, U.S.A.... NY: Putnam, 1911. 1st ed. (Bkpl removed; lt discoloration over lib #s spine.) *Ginsberg.* $100/£64

ANDERSON, RUFUS. The Hawaiian Islands.... Boston: Gould & Lincoln, 1864. 2nd ed. 450,(6)pp (ink #s fep); fldg map. VG (spine sl worn, sunned). *Agvent.* $175/£112

ANDERSON, RUFUS. A Heathen Nation Evangelized. Boston: Congregational Pub, 1870. 1st ed. Engr frontis port, xxiv,408pp (lt aged, foxed, lacks rear blank); engr full-pg map. Red-brn cl, gilt. Cvrs Good (stained, discolored). *Baltimore*.* $70/£45

ANDERSON, RUFUS. Memoir of Catherine Brown. Phila, (1831). Later ed. Frontis, 138pp. Calf-backed marbled bds. Howes A235. *Wantagh.* $100/£64

ANDERSON, SHERWOOD. Dark Laughter. NY: Boni & Liveright, 1925. One of 350 numbered, signed. White parchment-backed black bds (spine spotted), gilt. Fine in VG black slipcase (rubbed, broken at top) w/color pict paper label. *Blue Mountain.* $125/£80

ANDERSON, SHERWOOD. Letters of Sherwood Anderson. Howard Mumford Jones (ed). Boston: Little, Brown, (1953). 1st ed. VG in dj. *Turtle Island.* $45/£29

ANDERSON, SHERWOOD. Many Marriages. NY: Huebsch, 1923. 1st ed. Top edge stained orange. Fine in VG white dj (lt nicked, dust soiled, 2 sm spots spine). *Reese.* $125/£80

ANDERSON, SHERWOOD. Nearer the Grass Roots, and...An Account of a Journey: Elizabethton. SF: Westgate, 1929. #203/500. Signed. Grn patterned-paper cvrd bds, black cl spine strip. NF. *Harrington.* $80/£51

ANDERSON, SHERWOOD. Nearer the Grass Roots. SF: Westgate Press, 1929. One of 500 numbered, signed. Superb (sl bump bottom pp) in orig glassine dj. *Between The Covers.* $275/£176

ANDERSON, SHERWOOD. Sherwood Anderson's Notebook. NY: Boni & Liveright, 1926. 1st ed. One of 225 numbered, signed. Grn cl-backed marbled bds, label. VF. *Macdonnell.* $150/£96

ANDERSON, WILLIAM MARSHALL. The Rocky Mountain Journals of...The West in 1834. Dale L. Morgan and Eleanor Towles Harris (eds). San Marino: Huntington Library, 1967. 1st ed. Ltd to 1500. Frontis port. Fine in pict dj. *Argonaut.* $150/£96

ANDERSSON, ARON. English Influence in Norwegian and Swedish Figure Sculpture in Wood 1220-1270. Stockholm, 1949. Map. Lib morocco-backed cl bds (rebound; spine sl discolored, spine #s; ex-lib, ink stamp). *Edwards.* $117/£75

ANDERSSON, C. J. Lake Ngami. NY: Dix, Edwards, 1857 (c. 1856). 55 engrs. Blind-stamped dec cl. VG (ex-lib). *Mikesh.* $125/£80

ANDERSSON, CHARLES JOHN. The Okavango River. NY: Harper, 1861. Engr tp, xx,21-414pp; 16 plts, 2 ads, fldg map. Blue pict cl (spine faded, ends worn), gilt. *Adelson.* $185/£119

ANDERTON, JOHANA GAST. Twentieth Century Dolls from Bisque to Vinyl. North Kansas City, 1974. Rev ed. Dj (sl chipped, spine head loss). *Edwards.* $59/£38

ANDES, L. E. Drying Oils, Boiled Oil, and Solid and Liquid Driers. London: Scott, Greenwood, 1901. VG. *Savona.* $23/£15

ANDRADE, CYRIL. Old English Pottery. London, 1924. Ltd to 500. *Petersfield.* $70/£45

ANDRE, JOHN. Andre's Journal. Henry Cabot Lodge (ed). Boston: Bibliophile Soc, 1903. One of 467 (of 487) unnumbered sets. 2 vols. Frontis ports, each signed in pencil. Teg, untrimmed. Full vellum, gilt. Cvrs VG (lt dusty, smudged). Howes A239. *Baltimore*.* $260/£167

ANDREAE, BERNARD. The Art of Rome. Robert Erich Wolf (trans). NY: Abrams, 1977. 900 plts/plans. VG in dj, pub's slipcase. *Turtle Island.* $150/£96

ANDREE, S. A. The Andree Diaries. London, 1931. Fldg map. Good (lt foxed, spine faded, spotted). *High Latitude.* $30/£19

ANDREE, S. A. Andree's Story. NY, 1930. 2 1897 extracts from Century Magazine tipped in back. (Unevenly faded), else Good. *High Latitude.* $25/£16

ANDREW, JOHN. An Address to the Graduating Class of the Medical School in the University at Cambridge. Boston, 1864. 1st ed. 28pp. VG in wrappers. *Fye.* $60/£38

ANDREW, LAUREL B. The Early Temples of the Mormons.... Albany: State Univ of NY, 1978. 1st ed. Fine in dj. *Perier.* $17/£11

ANDREWS, C. L. Sitka, The Chief Factory of the Russian American Company. Caldwell: Caxton, 1945. 3rd ed. VG. *Perier.* $22/£14

ANDREWS, C. L. Wrangell and the Gold of Cassiar. Seattle: Luke Tinker, 1937. VG in wraps. *Perier.* $35/£22

ANDREWS, C. M. The Colonial Period of American History. Yale, 1934, 1936, 1937, 1938. 1st ed. 4 vols. Good (shelfworn). Howes A252. *Scribe's Perch*.* $110/£71

ANDREWS, CLARENCE L. The Eskimo and His Reindeer in Alaska. Caldwell, ID: Caxton, 1939. Frontis map. Fine in dj (sl chipped). *High Latitude.* $60/£38

ANDREWS, EDMUND and THOMAS LACEY. The Mortality of Surgical Operations in the Upper Lake States, Compared with That of Other Regions. Chicago, 1877. 123pp. (Ex-lib.) Ptd wrappers (lacks end wrapper). *Argosy.* $40/£26

ANDREWS, EDWARD D. The Community Industries of the Shakers. Albany: Univ of the State of NY, 1933. 1st ed. NF in wraps (corner crease; lt soil). *Beasley.* $40/£26

ANDREWS, EDWARD D. The Gift to Be Simple: Songs, Dances and Rituals of the American Shakers. NY: J.J. Augustin, 1940. 1st ed. Frontis. Paper labels. (Foreedge stained), else VG in illus dj. *Cahan.* $45/£29

ANDREWS, EDWARD D. The People Called Shakers. NY: Oxford, 1953. 1st ed. NF in dj (tears, creases). *Agvent.* $45/£29

ANDREWS, EDWARD D. and FAITH. Religion in Wood. IN Univ, 1969. 2nd ptg. 79pp of plts. Dj (lt soiled, chipped). *Edwards.* $47/£30

ANDREWS, KENNETH. Nook Farm, Mark Twain's Hartford Circle. Cambridge: Harvard Univ, 1950. 1st ed. Fine in dj (chipped). *Macdonnell.* $35/£22

ANDREWS, L. Grammar of the Hawaiian Language. Honolulu: Mission Press, 1854. (1)leaf; 156pp (foxed, browned). Contemp sheep-backed bds (shelfworn). *Oinonen*.* $160/£103

ANDREWS, R. C. On the Trail of Ancient Man. NY: Putnam, (Apr 1930). Dec eps. NF. *Mikesh.* $27/£17

ANDREWS, R. McCANTS. John Merrick: A Biographical Sketch. (Durham, NC: Seeman Printery, 1920.) 1st ed. VG- (spine sl sunned, spine extrems worn). *Between The Covers.* $185/£119

ANDREWS, RALPH W. Picture Gallery Pioneers 1850-1875.... Seattle: Superior, (1964). 1st ed. Fine in VG dj. *Perier.* $35/£22

ANDREWS, ROY CHAPMAN. Across Mongolian Plains. NY, 1921. Dj (chipped). *Edwards.* $39/£25

ANDREWS, STEPHEN PEARL. Discoveries in Chinese or the Symbolism of the Primitive Characters of the Chinese System of Writing. NY: Charles B. Norton, 1854. 1st ed. NF. *Captain's Bookshelf*. $150/£96

ANDREWS, TAILER (comp). Animal Stories for Children. NY: J.H. Sears, (1927). Marguerite Kirmse (illus). 4to. color frontis, viii,241pp + 3pp pub's cat. Black cl (lt bumped), gilt (sl rubbed), mtd cvr illus. VG. Internally Fine. *Blue Mountain*. $75/£48

ANDREWS, WILLIAM. At the Sign of the Barber's Pole. Cottingham: J.R. Tutin, 1904. Relevant cuttings laid on eps. VG. *Hollett*. $70/£45

ANDREWS, WILLIAM. Bygone England. London, 1892. 1st ed. 258pp + (ii)pub's ads (prelims lt browned, bkpl). Dec eps; teg. Gilt device upper bd. (Spine sl dknd.) *Edwards*. $31/£20

ANDREWS, WILLIAM. The Doctor in History, Literature, Folk-Lore, Etc. London, 1896. 1st ed. 287pp. VG. *Fye*. $175/£112

ANDREWS, WILLIAM. England in the Days of Old. London: William Andrews, 1897. 1st ed. (iv),279,(x)pp. Teg. Cl, beveled bds (extrems sl rubbed), gilt. *Hollett*. $55/£35

ANDREWS, WILLIAM. The Heavenly Jerusalem: A Mediaeval Song.... NY: Scribner, 1908. 1st ed. Beautiful in dec french-fold wrappers (outer wrapper chipped), slipcase (worn). *Captain's Bookshelf*. $125/£80

ANDREYEV, LEONID. Abyss. John Cournos (trans). Waltham St. Lawrence, 1929. One of 500. 4 Nice wood engrs. Teg. Black buckram-backed plum paper bds (sl mkd), spine gilt. Nice. *Cady*. $50/£32

ANDRIST, RALPH K. The Long Death. NY: Macmillan, 1967. *Dumont*. $30/£19

Anecdotes of Mr. Hogarth. London: Thomas Cook and G. & J. Robinson, 1803. Thomas Cook (engrs). Contemp 1/2 calf (sl rubbed), gilt. *Hollett*. $78/£50

ANGAS, GEORGE F. Polynesia. London: SPCK, 1866. xii,436,4ads pp; fldg map, 6 plts. Blue pict cl (rubbed). *Adelson*. $250/£160

Angel in the House. (By Coventry Patmore.) Boston: Ticknor & Fields, 1856. 1st Amer ed. Blindstamped brn cl. Fine. *Sumner & Stillman*. $85/£54

ANGELL, G. T. Autobiographical Sketches and Personal Recollections. Boston: Amer Human Educ Soc, n.d. (ca 1883). 3 vols in 1. Photo port. Blind-stamped dec cl. NF. *Mikesh*. $25/£16

ANGELL, JOSEPH K. Treatise on the Law of Watercourses. Boston: Little & Brown, 1840. 3rd ed. Old 1/2 calf (edges worn), gilt. *Hollett*. $55/£35

ANGELOU, MAYA. All God's Children Need Traveling Shoes. NY: Random House, (1986). 1st trade ed. Cl-backed bds. VG in illus dj. *Petrilla*. $20/£13

ANGELOU, MAYA. All God's Children Need Traveling Shoes. Franklin Center, PA: Franklin Library, 1986. Signed 1st ed. Fine in dec full leather. *Lame Duck*. $100/£64

ANGELOU, MAYA. I Know Why the Caged Bird Sings. NY: Random House, (1969). 1st ed, 1st bk. Fine in Fine dj. *Bernard*. $150/£96

ANGELOU, MAYA. I Know Why the Caged Bird Sings. NY: Random House, (1969). 1st ed. 1st state w/top edge stained in red. Fine in dj (spine ends sl worn). *Cahan*. $150/£96

ANGELOU, MAYA. Wouldn't Take Nothing for My Journey Now. NY: Random House, (1993). 1st ed. #113/500 numbered, signed. Maroon cl. Fine in maroon slipcase. *Lucas*. $100/£64

ANGIER, BELLE SUMNER. The Garden Book of California. SF: Paul Elder, (1906). 20 full-pg photos. Pict linen. *Dawson*. $35/£22

ANGLE, PAUL M. The Chicago Historical Society 1856-1956. NY/Chicago/SF: Rand McNally, (1956). 1st ed, w/prospectus laid in. NF in pub's pict slipcase. *Sadlon*. $20/£13

ANGLE, PAUL M. (ed). The Lincoln Reader. New Brunswick: Rutgers Univ, 1947. 1st ed. NF in VG dj (chipped). *Mcgowan*. $25/£16

ANGLE, PAUL M. (ed). Pioneers: Narratives of Noah Harris Letts and Thomas Allen Banning 1825-1865. Chicago: Lakeside, Christmas, 1972. Dk blue cl (sl water spotted). *Sadlon*. $10/£6

ANGLE, PAUL M. and EARL SCHENCK MIERS (eds). Poetry and Prose by A. Lincoln. Kingsport, TN: Kingsport, (1956). One of 1500 ptd. White, tan cl binding. Fine. *Graf*. $27/£17

Angler's Diary and Fisherman...1868. London: Horace Cox, 1868. Grn wraps. *Metropolitan**. $57/£37

Anglo-Irish Essays. (By William K. Magee.) Dublin/London: Talbot/Unwin, 1917. 1st ed. Paper label. (Cl, labels sl dustmkd), else Good. *Reese*. $20/£13

Animal ABC. Buffalo: Hayes Lithographic, (ca 1880). 4to. 8pp color lithos. Good in color pict wrappers (sl rubbed). *Houle*. $150/£96

Animate Creation. NY: Selmar Hess, (1885). 5 vols (of 6). 22 VG chromolithos. Dec cl (shabby, spotted). *New Hampshire**. $120/£77

ANIOL, CLAUDE B. San Antonio, City of Missions. NY: Hastings House, 1942. 1st ed. Fine in dj (sm tear). *Gibbs*. $15/£10

ANNABEL, RUSSELL. Hunting and Fishing in Alaska. NY, 1948. 1st ed. (Sl worn.) Dj (chipped, frayed). *Oinonen**. $225/£144

ANNABEL, RUSSELL. Tales of a Big Game Guide. NY: Derrydale, (1938). One of 950 numbered. 3/4 burlap (sl worn), leather spine label. *Oinonen**. $160/£103

ANNABEL, RUSSELL. Tales of a Big Game Guide. NY: Derrydale, (1938). One of 950 numbered. Cl, buckram back, tips, leather spine label, gilt. (Sl worn.) *Oinonen**. $250/£160

ANNAHEIM, HANS et al. Across the Alps. Berne, (1959). 1st ed. 91 plts. VG in dj (sl soiled, sm tear). *King*. $35/£22

Annals of Lloyd's Register. London: Lloyd's Register, 1884. x,166pp, photo port, fldg table. (New fep; label pastedown.) Aeg. Cl, beveled bds. VG. *Hollett*. $47/£30

Annals of the Propagation of the Faith. Paris/London, 1840-1866. Vols 1-28 from July 1839-1866. Fldg map vol 1. 3/4 polished leather, gilt, marbled bds, edges. (Vol 1 lacks pp97-138; 1861 bound after 1862.) Very Attractive set. Howes A279. *Bohling*. $850/£545

ANNESLEY, MAUDE. Shadow-Shapes. London, 1911. 1st ed. Good. *Madle*. $25/£16

ANNESLEY, MICHAEL. Spy-Counter Spy. London: Stanley Paul, (1946). 1st ed. Fine in dj (lt soil, sm scrapes, nicks). *Mordida*. $45/£29

ANNGELL, T. Ravens, Crows, Magpies and Jays. Seattle: Univ of WA, 1978. 1st ed. Blind-stamped dec cl. Fine in Fine dj. *Mikesh*. $37/£24

ANNO, MITSUMASA. Anno's Aesop. London: Reinhardt, 1990. 1st ed. 9 x 10 3/4. 64pp. Glossy bds. Fine. *Cattermole*. $50/£32

ANNO, MITSUMASA. Anno's Alphabet. NY: Crowell, 1975. 1st ed. 9 1/4 x 10. 64pp. Pict bds. VG in dj. *Cattermole*. $30/£19

ANNO, MITSUMASA. Anno's Medieval World. NY: Philomel, 1980. 1st US ed. VG in dj (price-clipped). *Scribe's Perch**. $20/£13

ANNO, MITSUMASA. Anno's USA. NY: Philomel, 1983. Signed, ltd ed in slipcase. 9 1/4 x 10. 32pp. VG. *Cattermole*. $150/£96

ANNO, MITSUMASA. Magical Midnight Circus. NY/Tokyo: Weatherhill, 1972. Stated 1st ed. VG in dj (price-clipped). *Scribe's Perch**. $20/£13

ANNO, MITSUMASA. Topsy-Turvies. NY/Tokyo: Walker/Weatherhill, 1970. Stated 1st ed, 1st bk. VG in dj (price-clipped). *Scribe's Perch**. $30/£19

ANNO, MITSUMASA. Upside-Downers. NY/Tokyo: Weatherhill, 1971. Stated 1st ed. Good +. *Scribe's Perch**. $20/£13

Annual 1927 (No. V). London: Palestine Exploration Fund, 1929. Frontis, 22 plts. Orig ptd bds (corners sl bumped). *Archaeologia*. $150/£96

Annual of Advertising and Editorial Art and Design. Number 33. NY, 1954. VG (cvr lt scuffed). *Truepenny*. $45/£29

Annual of Advertising and Editorial Art and Design. Number 35. (NY, 1956). Pict bds (lt soiled, worn). VG. *Truepenny*. $45/£29

Annual Report of American History Association 1918. Washington, 1920. 1st ed. VG. *Turpen*. $150/£96

Annual Report of the Adjutant General of the State of Michigan, for the Years 1865-6. Vol. I. Lansing, 1866. 253, errata slip, 371pp. Lib buckram (rebound). *Bohling*. $25/£16

Annual Report of the Board of Regents of the Smithsonian Institution...1884. Washington: GPO, 1885. 1st ed. viii,458pp. VG (rubbed, scuffed, spine faded, frayed). *Worldwide*. $25/£16

Annual Report of the Board of Regents of the Smithsonian Institution...for the Year Ending June 30 1891. Washington, 1892. xvii,869pp (ink stamps feps). Black cl (wear, chip upper bd). *Edwards*. $31/£20

Annual Report of the Board of Regents of the Smithsonian Institution...for the Year Ending June 30 1901. Washington, 1903. (Ink stamps feps; cl sl worn.) *Edwards*. $31/£20

Annual Report of the Board of Regents of the Smithsonian Institution...for the Year Ending June 30 1924. Washington, 1925. (Ink stamps feps.) Gilt cl. *Edwards*. $25/£16

Annual Report of the Board of Regents of the Smithsonian Institution...for the Year Ending June 30, 1888. Washington, 1890. xxii,876pp. Orig cl (expertly rebacked), orig backstrip laid down. (Edgeworn), else VG. *Reese*. $125/£80

Annual Report of the Board of Regents of the Smithsonian Institution...for the Year Ending June 30, 1895. Washington, 1897. xx,1080pp. Orig cl (expertly rebacked, edgeworn, spine gilt dull), orig backstrip laid down. VG. *Reese*. $200/£128

Annual Report of the Board of Regents of the Smithsonian Institution...Part II. Washington, 1886. xi,(1),939pp; 2 fldg maps. VG. Howes C416. *Reese*. $500/£321

Annual Report of the Chief of Engineers to the Secretary of War for the Year 1877. Part II. Washington: GPO, 1877. 27 maps (11 fldg); 10 fldg charts. (Fr cvr, spine detached from text block; rear cvr hanging by cord.) Contents VG. *Waverly**. $165/£106

Annual Report of the Chief of Engineers to the Secretary of War for the Year 1879. Part III. Washington: GPO, 1879. 9 fldg maps, 5 fldg charts. (Pencil mk tp; sl worn, spine frayed), else VG. *Waverly**. $176/£113

Annual Report of the Commissioner of the General Land Office for the Fiscal Year Ending June 30, 1881(-1891). 11 vols. 244-949pp each, index in each; 1884 & 1885 w/lg fldg color map. Full govt leather (scuffed; 1 vol w/detached bds, rest w/hinges splitting). *Bohling*. $200/£128

Annual Report of the Secretary of the Interior. Washington, 1856. Good. *Zubal**. $80/£51

Annual Reports Made to the Governor of the State of Ohio...1861. Part II. Columbus: R. Nevins, 1862. 1st ed. 1/2 leather. VG. *Archer*. $32/£21

ANOLE, HUNTER. Let's Ride to Hounds. NY: Derrydale, 1929. Ltd to 850 unnumbered. VG. *October Farm*. $45/£29

ANOUILH, JEAN. Poor Bitos. Lucienne Hill (trans). London: Methuen, (1964). 1st Eng ed. Paper-cvrd bds. Fine in dj (sl rubbed). *Antic Hay*. $25/£16

ANOUILH, JEAN. The Rehearsal. P. H. Johnson & Kitty Black (trans). NY: Coward-McCann, (1962). 1st Amer ed. Fine in dj (sl worn, price-clipped). *Antic Hay*. $25/£16

ANOUILH, JEAN. Restless Heart. L. Hill (trans). London, 1957. 1st ed. Dj (sl frayed, torn). *Typographeum*. $12/£8

ANSON, GEORGE. A Voyage Round the World in the Years MDCCXL, I, II, III, IV. London: The Author, 1748. 1st ed. 4to. (xxxiv),417pp, 42 fldg plts and maps. Tan 1/4 morocco (rebound), grn spine label. VG. *Terramedia*. $900/£577

ANSON, GEORGE. A Voyage Round the World in the Years MDCCXL, I, II, III, IV. London, 1767. 12th ed. 42 engr plts, maps. Prosaic mod binding. *Yudkin**. $450/£288

ANSON, GEORGE. A Voyage Round the World, in the Years MDCCXL,I,III,IV. (Compiled by Richard Walter.) London: John & Paul Knapton, 1748. 3rd ed. 3 fldg maps. Contemp polished calf, gilt. *Parmer*. $650/£417

ANSON, P. F. Fashions in Church Furnishings 1840-1940. London, 1965. 2nd ed. 18 plts. Sound. *Ars Artis*. $39/£25

ANSON, WALTER VERNON. The Life of Admiral Lord Anson. London: John Murray, 1912. 1st ed. *Lefkowicz*. $60/£38

ANSORGE, W. J. Under the African Sun. London: William Heinemann, 1899. 1st ed. xiv + 355pp; 2 color plts. All edges uncut. (Grn pict cl sl rubbed, sm red scuff), o/w Good. *Sotheran*. $390/£250

ANSORGE, W. J. Under the African Sun. NY: Longmans, Green, 1899. 1st Amer ed. 2 color plts. (Foxing throughout; spine skewed, 2 sm ink spots), o/w VG. *Hermitage*. $225/£144

ANSTED, D. The Great Stone Book of Nature. Phila: George W. Childs, 1863. 335pp. (Lt dampstains leaves, plts), else VG. *Blake*. $75/£48

ANSTEY, F. The Brass Bottle. Appleton, 1900. 1st US ed. Red pict cl, gilt. VG. *Certo*. $50/£32

ANSTEY, F. The Man from Blankley's and Other Sketches. London: Longmans, Green, 1893. 1st ed. Frontis, (viii),151,(i)pp, pub's ads verso last leaf. 1/4 Japanese vellum, gilt, ribbed lt blue paper-cvrd bds. Nice (cvrs sl worn). *Temple*. $45/£29

Anthony Van Dyck. Washington: Nat'l Gallery of Art, 1990. Good in wraps. *Washton*. $75/£48

ANTHONY, EARL. Picking Up the Gun: A Report on the Black Panthers. NY: Dial, 1970. 1st ed. Fine in dj (sl rubbed). *Between The Covers*. $65/£42

ANTHONY, EDGAR WATERMAN. A History of Mosaics. Boston, (1935). (Fr cvr spotted, spine dull.) *Swann**. $46/£29

ANTHONY, KATHERINE. Louisa May Alcott. Cresset, 1939. Good (ink inscrip, lt spotted; spine bumped) in dj (grubby, closed tears). *Tiger*. $23/£15

ANTONINUS, MARCUS AURELIUS. The Thoughts... George Long (trans). London, 1909. One of 500 numbered. 12 tipped-in color plts by William Russell Flint. Limp vellum, silk ties. Dj (lacks sm piece spine top); bd slipcase (cracked). *Swann**. $149/£96

APLIN, O. V. The Birds of Oxfordshire. OUP, 1889. Color frontis, vii,217pp; fldg map. (Sl bumped, spine sl rubbed.) *Edwards.* $62/£40

APOLLINAIRE, GUILLAUME. The Poet Assassinated. Ron Padgett (trans). NY/Chicago/SF: Holt, Rinehart & Winston, (1968). 1st ed. Jim Dine (illus). 4to. 128pp. Pict eps. Pict white cl (soiled). NF. *Blue Mountain.* $45/£29

Appeal to the Justice and Interests of the People of Great Britain.... (By Arthur Lee.) London: J. Almon, 1775. 2nd ed. (Tp soiled.) Mod 1/2 calf, marbled bds. Howes L183. *Freeman*.* $220/£141

APPEL, BENJAMIN. The Raw Edge. NY, 1958. 1st Amer ed. NF in NF dj. *Polyanthos.* $25/£16

Apple Pie ABC. NY: McLoughlin Bros, 1888. 10x7.5. (14)pp. Linen bk (very worn, soiled, fr cvr badly chipped). *King.* $25/£16

APPLE, MAX. The Oranging of America and Other Stories. NY: Grossman, 1976. 1st ed, 1st bk. (Inscrip), o/w NF in dj (price-clipped). *Bernard.* $30/£19

APPLEGATE, JESSE A. A Day with the Cow Column in 1843. Joseph Schafer (ed). Chicago: Caxton Club, 1934. One of 300 ptd. Top edge stained red. Gray cl blocked in red. Fine. *Cady.* $85/£54

APPLEGATE, JESSE A. Westward Journeys. Martin Ridge (ed). Chicago: (Lakeside Classic), 1989. Dbl color map. Teg. Brn cl, gilt. Fine. *Bohling.* $20/£13

Appleton's Dictionary of Machines, Mechanics, Engine-Work, and Engineering. NY: Appleton, 1856. 2 vols. Leather-backed cl (sl rubbed), gilt spines. Contents VG. *New Hampshire*.* $60/£38

Appleton's General Guide to the United States and Canada.... NY, 1892. xvi,602pp; fldg map rear pocket (split). Orig roan, limp bds (worn, scuffed, chipped). Internally VG. *Reese.* $125/£80

Appleton's Hand-Book of American Travel. Western Tour. NY: D. Appleton, 1873. Lg fldg hand-colored frontis map, (12, ads),x,321,(13, ads)pp; 3 sm fldg hand-colored maps, 2 fldg b/w maps, 2 full-pg b/w maps. Red cl stamped in gilt. Overall Fine (lt rubbed). *Argonaut.* $175/£112

APPLETON, G. W. The Ingenious Captain Cobbs. London: Long, (1906). 1st ed. (Spine discolored, head frayed.) *Metropolitan*.* $51/£33

APPLETON, JOHN. Beginners' Book of Chemistry. Chautauqua, 1888. 254pp. 12 color lithos. VG. *Bookcell.* $50/£32

APPLETON, LE ROY H. Indian Art of the Americas. NY: Scribner, (1950). 1st ed. 79 full-pg color plts. VG in dj (sl worn). *Lien.* $75/£48

APPLETON, VICTOR. The Movie Boys Under Fire. GC Pub, (1926). 5x7. 218pp + ads. Lists 17 titles on rear. Beautiful (sm chips) in pict wraps. *My Bookhouse.* $25/£16

APPLETON, VICTOR. Tom Swift Among the Diamond Makers. Grossett, 1911. VG. *Madle.* $20/£13

APPLETON, VICTOR. Tom Swift and His Big Dirigible. G&D, 1930. 1st ed. 5x7.5. 214pp + ads. Tan pict cl. Lists to #32. VG+ (1933 Christmas seal on fep; sl shelfworn) in dj (edgeworn, spine faded). *My Bookhouse.* $65/£42

APPLETON, VICTOR. Tom Swift and His Big Tunnel. G&D, 1916. 5x7.5. 218pp + ad. Tan pict cl. Lists to #33. (Bumped), else VG+ in dj (worn, stained). *My Bookhouse.* $30/£19

APPLETON, VICTOR. Tom Swift and His Chest of Secrets. G&D, 1925. 5x7.5. 216pp + ads. Tan pict cl (sl shelfworn). Lists to #29. VG+ in dj (chips, sl edgeworn). *My Bookhouse.* $50/£32

APPLETON, VICTOR. Tom Swift and His Electric Locomotive. G&D, 1922. 5x7.5. 212pp + ads. Tan pict cl. Lists to #33. VG (worn) in dj (worn). *My Bookhouse.* $45/£29

APPLETON, VICTOR. Tom Swift and His Motorboat. G&D, 1910. 5x7.5. 212pp + ads. Tan pict cl (soil, shelfworn). Lists to #22. VG in 2-color dj (edges ragged). *My Bookhouse.* $35/£22

APPLETON, VICTOR. Tom Swift and His Ocean Airport. G&D, 1934. 5x7.5. 214pp + ads. Orange cl. VG (bumped, shelfworn, spotted; lacks dj). *My Bookhouse.* $40/£26

APPLETON, VICTOR. Tom Swift and His Planet Stone. G&D, 1935. 5x7.5. 203pp + ad. Orange cl. (Name, address stamp; bumped, worn, stained), else VG. *My Bookhouse.* $65/£42

APPLETON, VICTOR. Tom Swift and His Submarine Boat. G&D, 1910. Lists to #28. VG+ (sl shelfworn) in dj (sl edgeworn, chip). *My Bookhouse.* $50/£32

APPLETON, VICTOR. Tom Swift and His Television Detector. Racine, WI: Whitman, 1933. Pict buckram-cvrd bds. VG+ (pp toned) in VG+ dj. *Book Adoption.* $50/£32

APPLETON, VICTOR. Tom Swift Circling the Globe. Grossett, 1927. 1st ed. NF. *Madle.* $25/£16

APPLETON, VICTOR. Tom Swift in the Land of Wonders. G&D, 1917. 5x7.5. 218pp + ad. Orange cl (sl shelfworn). Lists to #36. VG+ in dj (edgeworn, spine faded). *My Bookhouse.* $45/£29

April Baby's Book of Tunes.... (By Mary Annette Beauchamp Russell.) London: Macmillan, 1900. 1st ed. Obl 8vo. 77pp (p73 torn in margin, several pp soiled); 6 full-pg plts by Kate Greenaway. Pict cl. *Argosy.* $150/£96

APTHEKER, HERBERT (ed). A Documentary History of the Negro People in the United States. NY: Citadel, (1951). 1st ed. Dk red cl, gilt. VG. *Petrilla.* $40/£26

APULEIUS, LUCIUS. De Cupidinis et Psyches Amoribus. (London: Vale, 1901.) One of 310. Charles Ricketts (illus). 1/4 cl (backstrip lacks sm portions). *Swann*.* $149/£96

Arabian Nights Entertainments. London/(Edinburgh): T. Longman/(Bell & Bradfute et al), 1792. 8 vols. (Lt spotted.) Contemp tree calf (bumped, lt rubbed, spine head vol 1 chipped), gilt, contrasting morocco lettering pieces. *Christie's*.* $666/£427

Arabian Nights. London: Hodder & Stoughton, (1924). 1st ed thus. Lg 4to. 12 full-pg color plts by E.J. Detmold tipped in, lettered tissue guards. Gilt-dec cream cl. (Lt tan spotting, spine ends sl bumped), o/w VG. *Dower.* $750/£481

ARAGON, LOUIS. The Century Was Young. NY: Duell, Sloan & Pearce, 1941. 1st US ed. VG in VG dj (worn). *Lame Duck.* $45/£29

ARAGON, LOUIS. Residential Quarter. NY: Harcourt, Brace, (1938). 1st Amer ed. Fine in pict dj (sl worn). *Hermitage.* $75/£48

ARBER, AGNES. Herbals, Their Origin and Evolution. CUP, 1912. 1st ed. Frontis. (Ink name, eps tanned, spine dknd), o/w Good. *Reese.* $100/£64

ARBER, AGNES. Herbals.... Cambridge, 1938. New ed. *Swann*.* $80/£51

ARBERRY, A. J. Discourses of Rumi. London: Murray, 1961. 1st ed. VG in dj. *Worldwide.* $45/£29

ARBERRY, A. J. More Tales from the Masnavi. London: Allen & Unwin, 1963. 1st ed. VG in dj. *Worldwide.* $35/£22

ARBUS, DIANE. Diane Arbus. Doon Arbus (ed). Millerton: Aperture, 1972. 1st ed, 1st issue w/photo of 2 girls in raincoats. Pict paper over bds. (Eps, cl lt soiled, owner stamp), else VG. *Cahan.* $125/£80

ARBUS, DIANE. Magazine Work. Millerton: Aperture, 1984. 1st ed. NF in NF dj. *Smith*. $75/£48

ARBUTHNOT, J. An Essay Concerning the Nature of Ailments and the Choice of Them. 1756. 4th ed. xxxii,365pp (lib stamps). Full calf (joints weak). *Whitehart*. $281/£180

ARBUTHNOT, J. An Essay Concerning the Nature of Ailments, and the Choice of Them. 1731. xxxii,232pp (foxed, new eps). Full calf (rebacked). *Whitehart*. $390/£250

ARBUTHNOT, THOMAS S. African Hunt. NY: Norton, 1954. 1st ed. Inscribed. VG in dj. *Terramedia*. $100/£64

ARCHBOLD, JOHN FREDERICK. A Collection of the Forms and Entries...in the Courts of King's Bench.... NY: Edward B. Gould, 1828. Contemp sheep (joints cracked). *Boswell*. $85/£54

Archer's Manual: The Art of Shooting with the Long Bow.... Phila: R.H. Hobson, 1830. 1st ed. Inserted frontis, 1 add'l plt. Orig cl-backed grn paper-cvrd bds (rubbed, lt worn, old spine repair, rear cvr detached; pp browned, last 2 ll trimmed at bottom margin, sig). Grn fldg cl box. *Kane**. $300/£192

ARCHER, JEFFREY. Not a Penny More, Not a Penny Less. Cape, 1976. 1st UK ed. (Production flaw final text pg, blank), o/w NF in dj. *Williams*. $117/£75

ARCHER, JEFFREY. Shall We Tell the President? Cape, 1977. 1st UK ed. Fine in dj. *Williams*. $78/£50

ARCHER, M. Natural History Drawings in the India Office Library. London, 1962. Dj (sl soiled). *Maggs*. $34/£22

ARCHER, WILLIAM. About the Theatre. London: T. Fisher Unwin, 1886. 1st ed. Frontis port, plts. (Lt foxing.) *Dramatis Personae*. $60/£38

ARCHER, WILLIAM. The Pirate's Progress. NY, 1918. (Pp browned; cvrs soiled), else Good in wraps. *King*. $22/£14

ARCHIBALD, JOE. Full Count. Macrae Smith, 1956. 1st ed. VG in VG dj. *Plapinger*. $45/£29

Architectural Drawings from the Collection of the Royal Institute of British Architects. London: Royal Inst of British Architects, 1961. Good in wraps. *Washton*. $15/£10

ARCIERI, JOHN. The Circulation of the Blood in Andrea Cesalpino of Arezzo. NY, 1945. 1st ed. VG. *Fye*. $75/£48

Arctic Bibliography. Washington: Arctic Inst of North America, 1953-66. 1st ed. Vols 1-13. *Ginsberg*. $1,150/£737

Arctic Regions: A Narrative of Discovery and Adventure. London: T. Nelson, 1853. Frontis, 237pp. Brn emb cl, gilt. (Inscrip, bkpl, clipping tipped to tp verso; lt worn, spine sl faded.) *Parmer*. $75/£48

ARD, WILLIAM. The Perfect Frame. Hammond, 1953. 1st Eng ed, 1st bk. NF in NF dj. *Certo*. $25/£16

ARDIZZONE, EDWARD. Diary of a War Artist. London, 1974. 1st Eng ed. Fine in dj (sl torn, rubbed). *Clearwater*. $47/£30

ARDIZZONE, EDWARD. Lucy Brown and Mr. Grimes. Bodley Head, 1970. Rev, redrawn; 1st ed thus. 4to. 48pp; 24 color, 26 b/w illus. Pict bds. Fine in pict dj (mk on back, sm closed tear fr top edge). *Bookmark*. $37/£24

ARDIZZONE, EDWARD. Lucy Brown and Mr. Grimes. London: OUP, n.d. 1st ed. Signed, inscribed presentation. Folio. Cl-backed bds (shelfworn). Dj (chipped, torn, soiled). *Oinonen**. $650/£417

ARDIZZONE, EDWARD. Tim and Ginger. Henry T. Walck, 1965. 8x10. VG+ (sl shelfworn) in dj (sl edgeworn). *My Bookhouse*. $30/£19

AREY, LESLIE. Northwestern University Medical School 1859-1959. Chicago, 1959. 1st ed. VG. *Fye*. $50/£32

ARGENTI, PHILIP P. The Costumes of Chios.... London: B.T. Batsford, (1953). Ltd to 500. Color frontis, 110 plts (88 color). Blue cl, gilt. Fine in dj. *Karmiole*. $500/£321

ARIAS, P. E. A History of 1,000 Years of Greek Vase Painting. NY: Abrams, n.d. (ca 1961). 54 tipped-in color plts. Good in Poor dj. *Scribe's Perch**. $160/£103

ARIAS, P. E. A History of 1000 Years of Greek Vase Painting. NY: Abrams, (1962). Signed presentation. 329 plts (52 color, hand-mtd). Good. *Archaeologia*. $375/£240

ARIEL. (Pseud of Buckner H. Payne.) The Negro: What Is His Ethnological Status? Cincinnati: The Proprietor, 1872. Enlgd ed. 172,(4)pp. Grn cl. Good. *Karmiole*. $150/£96

ARIES, PHILIPPE. Images of Man and Death. Janet Lloyd (trans). Harvard Univ, 1985. 1st ed. 9 color plts. Dj. *Edwards*. $39/£25

Arikara Indians of South Dakota. Vermillion, SD: University Museum, 1941. Pb. Good. *Lien*. $30/£19

ARIS, ERNEST. The Story of Tinkaboo Mouse. Humphrey Milford, n.d. (1919). 1st ed. 12mo. Color frontis, (36)pp (eps foxed); 18 full-pg silhouettes. Horizontal pict bds. (Edges rubbed), else VG. *Bookmark*. $47/£30

ARIS, ERNEST. Wee Bits o' Things. Gale & Polden, (1913). 1st ed. 'Playtime Picture Book.' 16mo. 49pp; 10 color plts. Pict bds, cl spine. NF. *Bookmark*. $70/£45

ARIS, ERNEST. Wee Jenny Mouse. Gale & Polden, (1913). 1st ed. 'Playtime Picture Book.' 16mo. 49pp; 10 color plts. Pict bds (sl rubbed), cl spine. VG+. *Bookmark*. $55/£35

ARISTOPHANES. The Frogs. NY: LEC, 1937. Ltd to 1500 ptd, signed by John Austen (engr). Orig prospectus laid in. VG. *Truepenny*. $60/£38

ARISTOPHANES. Lysistrata.... NY: LEC, 1934. One of 1500 numbered, signed by Pablo Picasso (illus). Sm folio. Orig bds. 1/4 morocco slipcase. *Swann**. $2,760/£1,769

ARISTOTLE. On the Parts of Animals. W. Ogle (trans). London, 1882. 1st ed in English. 263pp. VG. *Fye*. $200/£128

ARKELL, A. J. Early Khartoum: An Account of the Excavation.... London: OUP, 1949. Inscribed presentation. 113 plts. (Lower corners of bds sl discolored.) *Archaeologia*. $475/£304

ARKELL, A. J. A History of the Sudan from the Earliest Times to 1821. London: Univ of London, 1961. 2nd ed. 24 plts, 11 maps. (Sig.) Dj. *Archaeologia*. $45/£29

ARKELL, W. The Geology of Oxford. Oxford, 1947. (Few ll sl cockled.) Dj. *Maggs*. $31/£20

ARLEN, MICHAEL. The Green Hat, a Romance. NY: George H. Doran, 1925. One of 175 signed. Black paper-cvrd bds (paper split, chipped at joints), gilt, w/ptd grn paper spine label. (Plt removed rear pastedown), else NF internally. *Blue Mountain*. $65/£42

ARLEN, MICHAEL. The Green Hat. London: Collins, (1924). 1st ed. NF in dj (lt chipped, sm tears). *Captain's Bookshelf*. $150/£96

ARLEN, MICHAEL. The Romantic Lady. London: Collins, (1921). 1st ed. (Sm inscrip, offset to eps), o/w Nice in Good dj (sl nicks, corners split). *Reese*. $75/£48

ARMES, ETHEL. Stratford Hall: The Great House of the Lees. Garrett & Massie, 1936. 1st ed. VG in Good dj. *Book Broker*. $110/£71

ARMES, GEORGE A. Ups and Downs of an Army Officer. Washington, 1900. 1st ed. Pict cl (corners sl discolored, spine faded). Howes A316. *Ginsberg*. $225/£144

ARMITAGE, MERLE. Accent on America. NY: E. Weyhe, 1944. Ltd to 325 signed. Dk blue cl (spine faded). NF. *Blue Mountain.* $35/£22

ARMITAGE, MERLE. Dance Memoranda. Edwin Corle (ed). NY: Duell Sloan & Pearce, (1946). 1st ed. Inscribed presentation. 210 photo plts. Cl spine. Good in dj. *Karmiole.* $60/£38

ARMITAGE, MERLE. Stella Dysart of Ambrosia Lake. NY: Duell, Sloan & Pearce, (1959). 1st ltd ed. Fine in dj (lt soiled). *Hermitage.* $45/£29

ARMITT, M. L. The Church of Grasmere. Kendal: Titus Wilson, 1912. 1st ed. (Sig fep.) Blue cl (rubbed). *Hollett.* $39/£25

ARMITT, M. L. Rydal. Kendal: Titus Wilson, 1916. 1st ed. Color frontis, fldg pedigree, add'l map tipped in. Uncut. Mod 1/2 levant morocco, gilt. VG. *Hollett.* $148/£95

ARMOUR, MARGARET (trans). The Nibelungenlied. NY: LEC, 1960. One of 1500 numbered, signed by Edy Legrand (illus). Sm folio. (Lt worn.) Glassine wrapper (sl frayed), slipcase. *Oinonen*.* $30/£19

ARMS, CEPHAS. The Long Road to California. Mt. Pleasant, MI: John Cumming, (1985). One of 487. Fine. *Bohling.* $30/£19

ARMS, D. N. Churches of France. NY: Macmillan, Oct 1929. 1st ed. 51 full-pg guarded repros. (Sunned), o/w Good+. *Scribe's Perch*.* $24/£15

ARMSTRONG, A. LESLIE. Rhodesian Archaeological Expedition (1929). London: Royal Anthropological Inst, n.d. (1931). Rpt. 2 color plts (1 fldg), 8 plts at end. Grn ptd wrappers. *Morrell.* $23/£15

ARMSTRONG, EDWARD A. Bird Display. CUP, 1942. 22 plts. (Bkpl; cl sl soiled, sl wrinkled upper bd, spine faded.) *Edwards.* $23/£15

ARMSTRONG, HARRY G. Principles and Practice of Aviation Medicine. Balt, 1940. 2nd ed. VG. *Doctor's Library.* $50/£32

ARMSTRONG, J. et al. Catalogue of the Western Scottish Fossils.... Glasgow, 1876. Fldg map, 4 litho plts. (Sl worn.) *Maggs.* $31/£20

ARMSTRONG, JOHN and CHARLES W. UPHAM. Lives of Anthony Wayne and Sir Henry Vane. NY: Harper, 1839. x,403pp; extra engr tp. Orig cl (spotted). *Bohling.* $15/£10

ARMSTRONG, M. F. and H. W. LUDLOW. Hampton and Its Students. NY: Putnam, 1874. Fldg engr frontis, 256pp. Dec cvr (head frayed). Good. *Scribe's Perch*.* $26/£17

ARMSTRONG, MARGARET. The Man with No Face. NY: Random House, (1940). 1st ed. VG in Good dj (creased, sun, soil, short tears). *Metropolitan*.* $23/£15

ARMSTRONG, MOSES K. The Early Empire Builders of the West. St. Paul: E.W. Porter, 1901. 1st ed thus. (Few pp margins smoked; rebound), else Good. *Brown.* $35/£22

ARMSTRONG, N. A. D. After Big Game in the Upper Yukon. London, (1937). 1st ed. (Sl worn, sl foxed.) *Oinonen*.* $100/£64

ARMSTRONG, N. A. D. After Big Game in the Upper Yukon. London, 1937. (2nd imp.) 3 maps. VG+. *Mikesh.* $137/£88

ARMSTRONG, NELSON. Nuggets of Experience: Narrative of the Sixties and Other Days.... (L.A.), 1906. 1st ed. *Ginsberg.* $100/£64

ARMSTRONG, ROBERT BRUCE. Musical Instruments. Part I. The Irish and the Highland Harps. Edinburgh, ca 1904. Inscribed. 24 full-pg b/w engrs. (Sl foxing; rubbed, bumped, shaken.) *Metropolitan*.* $115/£74

ARMSTRONG, WALTER. Gainsborough and His Place in English Art. London, 1899. 1899 rpt. Ltd to 250. 214pp; 62 photogravures, 10 lithos. Teg. Fine 3/4 red leather, raised bands, gilt. (Sl foxed, sl bumped, rubbed), else Attractive. *King.* $495/£317

ARMSTRONG, WALTER. Sir Henry Raeburn. London: (Ballantyne), 1901. Ltd ed. 61 lg photogravure plts, guards, 8 sm copper plts. Teg; uncut. (Binding waterstained, damaged.) *Argosy.* $100/£64

ARMSTRONG, WALTER. Sir Joshua Reynolds, First President of the Royal Academy. London, 1900. 1st ed. Ltd to 1100. 6 lithos, 78 photogravures. Teg. (Bkpl removed, eps spotted; sl bumped), else VG in dj (defective). *King.* $250/£160

ARMSTRONG, WALTER. Turner. London/NY: T. Agnew/Scribner, 1902. One of 1000 numbered, initialed by pub. Gilt maroon cl, beveled bds. (Inner hinges split), else Contents VG. *Waverly*.* $55/£35

ARNASON, H. H. The Sculptures of Houdon. NY: OUP, 1975. 143 plts. Fine in dj. *Europa.* $101/£65

Arnheim Lift, Diary of a Glider Pilot. London: Pilot Press, 1945. 1st ed. Frontis map. (Pencil inscrip), o/w Nice in dj (lt worn). *Reese.* $30/£19

ARNHEIM, RUDOLF. Art and Visual Perception. Berkeley/L.A., 1954. Good in dj. *Washton.* $50/£32

ARNOLD, AUGUSTUS. Nefario. London: Allison & Busby, (1974). 1st ed. Fine in dj (sl wear). *Between The Covers.* $75/£48

ARNOLD, EDMUND. On Medical Provision for Railroads.... NY, 1862. 47pp. VG in wrappers. *Fye.* $75/£48

ARNOLD, EDWIN. Indian Idylls, from the Sanskrit of the Mahabarata. London: Trubner, n.d. (c. 1883). 2nd ed. xiii,282pp, ads. Orange cl. VG. *Terramedia.* $30/£19

ARNOLD, EDWIN. Japonica. NY: Scribner, 1892. 2nd US ptg. Illus brn cl over bds. NF. *Old London.* $75/£48

ARNOLD, EDWIN. The Light of Asia. Avon, CT: LEC, 1976. One of 2000 numbered, signed by Ayers Houghtelling (illus). 8 color plts. Patterned cl. Mint in bd slipcase. *Argosy.* $150/£96

ARNOLD, EDWIN. Poems. Narrative and Lyrical. Oxford: Francis Macpherson, 1853. 1st ed. Dk purple cl (faded, bumped). Good. *Maggs.* $55/£35

ARNOLD, EVE. In America. NY: Random House, 1983. 1st ed. NF in NF dj. *Smith.* $30/£19

ARNOLD, F. H. Flora of Sussex. London, 1907. 2nd ed. Color plt, dbl-pg map. Fine. *Henly.* $39/£25

ARNOLD, FOSTER W. Shrubs for the Milder Counties. London: Country Life, 1948. 1st ed. 41 plts. Dj (repaired). *Quest.* $65/£42

ARNOLD, H. J. P. William Henry Fox Talbot, Pioneer of Photography and Man of Science. 1977. (Spine ends sl defective, cvr edge sl dented), o/w VG in dj. *Whitehart.* $39/£25

ARNOLD, ISAAC. The Life of Abraham Lincoln. Chicago, 1885. One of 375 numbered. Frontis port. *Swann*.* $161/£103

ARNOLD, MATTHEW. Discourses in America. Macmillan, 1889. VG (spine bumped, lt spotted). *Tiger.* $56/£36

ARNOLD, MATTHEW. God and the Bible. NY: Macmillan, 1875. 1st Amer issue (British sheets, NY title). (Cl lt soiled, spine sl rolled, sm nicks crown), else VG. *Reese.* $55/£35

ARNOLD, MATTHEW. Letters of Matthew Arnold 1848-1888. G. W. Russell (ed). London: Macmillan, 1895. 1st ed, 2nd imp. 2 vols. VG (eps sl tanned, few pencil notes). *Reese.* $35/£22

ARNOLD, MATTHEW. Matthew Arnold's Notebooks. London: Smith, Elder, 1902. 1st ed. Frontis port. White straight-grain ribbed cl (spine worn, bumped, nicked). *Maggs.* $47/£30

ARNOLD, OREN. Sun in Your Eyes. Albuquerque: Univ of NM, (1947). 1st ed. Illus eps. VG in dj (sl worn). *Lien.* $25/£16

ARNOLD, RALPH. A Yeoman of Kent. London: Constable, 1949. 1st ed. Color frontis, 19 plts, pedigree. Dj (sl chipped). *Hollett.* $47/£30

ARNOLD, ROBERT. Scientific Fact and Metaphysical Reality. London, 1904. 1st ed. VG + . *Middle Earth.* $45/£29

ARNOLD, THOMAS W. and ADOLF GROHMANN. The Islamic Book. (London): Pegasus, 1929. One of 375 numbered. Folio. 104 plts. (Spine faded.) *Swann*.* $488/£313

ARNOLD, THOMAS W. and J. V. S. WILKINSON. The Library of A. Chester Beatty: A Catalogue of the Indian Miniatures. Oxford: John Johnson, 1936. 3 vols. 103 plts, 19 mtd color. (Cl affected by damp.) *Christie's*.* $736/£472

ARNOLD, W. H. First Editions of Bryant, Emerson, Hawthorne, Holmes, Longfellow, Lowell, Thoreau, Whittier. Jamaica, NY: Marion, 1901. 1st ed. One of 1200 ptd. Brn ptd wrappers (expertly rebacked in cl). VG. *Macdonnell.* $65/£42

ARNOLD, W. H. First Report of a Book-Collector. NY: Dodd, Mead, 1898. 1st trade ed. One of 220. Uncut, unopened. 3/4 red cl, bds, labels, gilt. Nice (gilt rubbed from spine label). *Macdonnell.* $300/£192

ARNOLD, W. H. Ventures in Book Collecting. NY, 1923. Good. *Moss.* $25/£16

ARNOLD, W. H. Ventures in Book Collecting. NY/London, 1923. Frontis port, color plt. (Eps lt spotted, few margins browned; edges lt browned.) *Edwards.* $55/£35

ARNOLD, W. H. Ventures in Book-Collecting. NY: Scribner, 1923. 1st ed. Cl-backed bds, gilt. (Fep neatly excised), else Fine. *Macdonnell.* $50/£32

ARNOT, HUGO. A Collection and Abridgement of Celebrated Criminal Trials in Scotland, from A.D. 1536, to 1784. Glasgow: A. Napier, 1812. 2nd (and last) ed. 3/4 sheep over marbled bds (joints rubbed). Attractive. *Boswell.* $275/£176

ARNOTT, NEIL. On the Smokeless Fire-Place. London: Longmans, 1855. 1st ed. xii,232pp + 24pp pub's ads. (Margins lt browned, lt spotted, lacks leaf after tp.) Uncut. Emb cl (spine faded, sl worn, sl loss to ends). *Edwards.* $148/£95

ARNOW, HARRIET. Hunter's Horn. NY: Macmillan, (1949). 1st ed. Fine in dj (lt worn). *Hermitage.* $60/£38

ARNOW, HARRIETTE SIMPSON. Flowering of the Cumberland. NY: Macmillan, (1963). 1st ed. VG in dj. *Lien.* $35/£22

ARNOW, HARRIETTE SIMPSON. Seedtime on the Cumberland. NY: Macmillan, 1960. 1st ed. VG in dj. *Lien.* $40/£26

ARNOW, HARRIETTE SIMPSON. The Weedkiller's Daughter. NY: Knopf, 1970. 1st ed. VF in dj (sl rubbed). *Else Fine.* $40/£26

ARONIN, BEN. The New Mother Goose Rhymes. NY: Consolidated Book, (1943). 1st ed. Fridolf Johnson (illus). 4to. 128pp. Pict eps. Color pict bds (rubbed). VG in matching dj (chipped, 2 holes fr panel). *Blue Mountain.* $20/£13

ARONSON, J. K. An Account of the Foxglove and Its Medical Uses, 1785-1985. London, 1985. 1st ed. VG. *Fye.* $125/£80

Around the Horn in '49. (By George C. Webster.) Wethersfield: Rev. L.J. Hall, 1898. 2nd ed. 252pp. Maroon cl. (Sl rubbing joints, spine), o/w Fine. *Hermitage.* $250/£160

ARP, JEAN. Sculpture: His Last 10 Years. NY: Abrams, n.d. English ed. Dj. *Metropolitan*.* $172/£110

ARRABAL, FERNANDO. The Burial of the Sardine. London: Calder & Boyars, 1966. 1st British ed. (Fr bd sl warped), else NF in dj (price-clipped, soiled). *Lame Duck.* $35/£22

ARRABAL, FERNANDO. Guernica and Other Plays. NY: Grove, 1969. 1st US ed, wraps issue. Rev copy, slip laid in. NF in illus wraps. *Lame Duck.* $25/£16

ARRHENIUS, SVANTE. Immunochemistry. NY: Macmillan, 1907. 1st ed in English. Red cl. VG (ex-lib). *White.* $133/£85

ARRINGTON, ALFRED W. The Rangers and Regulators of the Tanaha. NY, (1856). Frontis, 397pp + 10pp ads; 5 plts. Blind/gilt-stamped cl. NF. Howes A340. *Reese.* $500/£321

ARRINGTON, LEONARD J. and DAVIS BITTON. The Mormon Experience: A History of the Latter-Day Saints. London, 1979. 1st British ed. (Stamps), o/w NF in dj (corner cut). *Benchmark.* $30/£19

ARROWSMITH, JAMES. The Paper-Hanger's Companion. Phila: Henry Carey Baird, 1887. Later ptg of 1852 ed. 108pp, 32 ads. Gilt/blind emb cl. (Sm nick top edge), else VG. *Cahan.* $85/£54

Art in Italy 1600-1700. Detroit: Inst of Arts, 1965. Good. *Washton.* $45/£29

Art of Bookbinding. (By Henry Parry.) London: Baldwin, Cradock & Joy, 1818. Frontis, title vignette. 1/2 calf, spine gilt in compartments, grn morocco spine label, marbled bds (sl worn, edges rubbed; bk labels). Not in orig ptd bds on which, unlike the tp, appeared the author's name and which carries the date 1817 on some copies & 1818 on others. *Maggs.* $1,326/£850

Art of Manual Defence; or System of Boxing.... London: Ptd for G. Kearsley, 1799. 3rd ed. 2 p.l., (7)-9,(1)pp,(1)leaf,(xiii)-xxxv,(1),133,(9)pp (lt foxed); 10 engr plts (clean but for lt foxing to frontis). 19th-cent cl (extrems sl worn, sl soiled). Internally Excellent. *Pirages.* $375/£240

Art of Preserving the Feet. (By H. Colburn.) 1819. 3rd ed. xvi,239pp (foxed, browned; ink stain in margin). Later bds, paper label. *Whitehart.* $390/£250

ARTAUD, ANTONIN. The Theatre and Its Double. NY: Grove, 1958. 1st US ed. NF in dj (verso lt foxed). *Lame Duck.* $35/£22

ARTHUR, ELIZABETH. Bad Guys. NY: Knopf, 1986. 1st ed. (Corners sl bumped), else Fine in NF dj (sl soiled, lt pencil mk, stamp). *Between The Covers.* $65/£42

ARTHUR, GEORGE. Life of Lord Kitchener. London: Macmillan, 1920. 1st ed. 3 vols. 11 plts and maps. Sound set (cl sl mkd). *Cox.* $23/£15

ARTHUR, ROBERT. Treatment and Prevention of Decay of the Teeth. Phila: Lippincott, 1871. 1st ed. xii,(13)-256pp (perforated lib stamp tp, bkpl). Lib buckram. VG (ex-lib). *Glaser.* $225/£144

ARTHUR, STANLEY CLISBY. Jean Laffite, Gentleman Rover. New Orleans: Harmonson, 1952. Inscribed. Dj. *Dawson.* $40/£26

Arts and Artisans in Philadelphia. Phila: Butler, 1872. Mtd photo plt. (Edgewear.) *Freeman*.* $60/£38

ARUNDALE, GEORGE S. The Lotus Fire. Madras, India: Theosophical Pub House, 1939. 1st ed. Red cl (bumped, rubbed, sl stained), gilt. Good (top edge half-title, frontis dampstained red). *Blue Mountain.* $45/£29

As Great a Man as Nelson...The Life of the Most Noble the Marquis Cornwallis...in the American and Indian War. (By Charles Cornwallis.) London, n.d. Frontis port. Mod cl. *Swann**. $316/£203

ASBJORNSEN, PETER CHRISTEN and JORGEN MOE. East of the Sun and West of the Moon. London, (1914). 25 tipped-in color plts by Kay Nielsen, guards. (Contemp sig.) Pict eps. Gilt-pict navy cl (spine corners sl frayed, sl shaken). *Swann**. $1,035/£663

ASBURY, HERBERT. The Barbary Coast. NY: GC, 1933. 1st ed. 7 plts. (Sl rubbed, soiled), o/w VG. *Worldwide*. $15/£10

ASBURY, HERBERT. The Devil of Pei Ling. Macy-Macius, 1927. 1st ed. Yellow cl spine sunned, else VG. *Certo*. $25/£16

ASBURY, HERBERT. Gem of the Prairie. NY: Knopf, 1950. 1st ed. (Sl shelfwear), else Good. *Brown*. $12/£8

ASCHAFFENBURG, GUSTAV. Crime and Its Repression. Adalbert Albrecht (trans). Boston: Little, Brown, 1913. 1st ed in English. Red cl. VG. *Gach*. $50/£32

ASDELL, S. A. Patterns of Mammalian Reproduction. London: Constable, (1965). 2nd ed. Fine in VG + dj. *Mikesh*. $30/£19

ASH, EDWARD C. The Practical Dog Book. NY: Derrydale, 1931. 1st Amer ed. One of 500. Color frontis, 43 plts. Black cl. (Sm stains cvrs, sl shaken), o/w VG. *Cummins*. $150/£96

ASHBERY, JOHN. Self-Portrait in a Convex Mirror. NY, (1975). 1st ed. VG in dj. *Argosy*. $45/£29

ASHBERY, JOHN. Self-Portrait in a Convex Mirror. NY: Viking, (1975). 1st ed. Signed. Fine in Fine dj. *Lenz*. $75/£48

ASHBERY, JOHN. Some Trees. New Haven: Yale Univ, 1956. 1st ed. Signed. Fine in dj (spine sl dknd). *Lenz*. $300/£192

ASHBERY, JOHN. Sunrise in Suburbia. NY: Phoenix Bk Shop, 1968. One of 100 numbered, signed. Fine in wrappers. *Lenz*. $150/£96

ASHBERY, JOHN. Three Madrigals. (NY: Poet's Press, 1968.) 1st ed. One of 150 numbered (of 162), signed. NF in dec violet wrappers (lt sun strike fore-edge). *Reese*. $100/£64

ASHBROOK, H. The Murder of Steven Kester. NY: Coward-McCann, 1931. 1st ed. Nice (sl shelfworn) in dj (short tears, ends worn). *Metropolitan**. $51/£33

ASHBURN, P. M. History of the Medical Department of the U.S. Army. Boston, 1929. 1st ed. (Sl waterstained.) *Argosy*. $85/£54

ASHBY, R. C. Out Went the Taper. NY: Macmillan, 1934. 1st Amer ed. (Bumped, sunned, soil.) Dj (edges, corners worn). *Metropolitan**. $28/£18

ASHBY, THOMAS. The Roman Campagna in Classical Times. London: Ernest Benn, (1970). (Sig.) Dj. *Archaeologia*. $65/£42

ASHBY, THOMAS. Turner's Visions of Rome. London/NY, 1925. 12 tipped-in color, 16 b/w plts. (Lt spotting.) Cl-backed dec bds (edges sl faded, corners worn), paper title label upper bd, spine. *Edwards*. $39/£25

ASHBY, WILLIAM. Tales Without Hate. Newark: Newark Preservation and Landmarks Committee, 1980. 1st ed. VG in white perfectbound wrappers (sl soiled). *Between The Covers*. $45/£29

ASHDOWN, CHARLES H. British Castles. London: A&C Black, 1911. 32 color plts. Pict cl (sl rubbed). *Edwards*. $47/£30

ASHE, R. P. Chronicles of Uganda. NY: Randolph, 1895. 1st Amer ed. Frontis, xiv,480pp. Blue gilt pict cl (sl worn), else VG. *Terramedia*. $125/£80

ASHE, THOMAS. Travels in America, Performed in the Year 1806. London, 1809. Mod cl (spotted). Howes A352. *Swann**. $115/£74

ASHE, THOMAS. Travels in America. London: Richard Phillips, 1809. 316,(iv)pp (foxed). Paper wrappers. *Edwards*. $117/£75

ASHER, DON. The Piano Sport. NY: Atheneum, 1966. 1st ed, 1st bk. Fine in dj (lt soiled, rubbed). *Hermitage*. $35/£22

ASHLEY, CLIFFORD W. Whaleships of New Bedford. Boston/NY, 1929. 1st ed. One of 1035. Signed. 60 plts. (Spine sl faded.) *Lefkowicz*. $275/£176

ASHLEY, CLIFFORD W. Whaleships of New Bedford.... Boston, 1929. 1st ed. Ltd to 1035. 60 plts. Good (sl dknd, worn). *King*. $165/£106

ASHLEY, CLIFFORD W. The Yankee Whaler. NY, (1942). (3rd ed.) Frontis; 15 color plts, 111 b/w plts. Fine in dj (lt rubbed). *Lefkowicz*. $100/£64

ASHLEY, CLIFFORD W. The Yankee Whaler. Boston/NY: Houghton Mifflin, 1926. 1st ed. One of 1625. London issue binding. Grn cl back. (Lacks half-title/limitation leaf, else VF in pub's box (worn). Howes A356. *Lefkowicz*. $350/£224

ASHLEY, CLIFFORD W. The Yankee Whaler. Boston: Houghton Mifflin, 1926. 1st ed. 16 color plts. Beautiful in pict dj (sm chips). Howes A356. *Captain's Bookshelf*. $375/£240

ASHLEY, WILLIAM H. The West of William H. Ashley...1822-1838. Dale L. Morgan (ed). Denver: Old West Pub, 1964. 1st trade ed. Fldg map. Pict cl. VF. *Argonaut*. $225/£144

ASHLEY-COOPER, JOHN. The Great Salmon Rivers of Scotland. London: Gollancz, 1980. 1st ed. 9 colored plts, 12 maps. Mint in dj. *Hollett*. $70/£45

ASHTON, DORE. Richard Lindner. NY, (1969). 1st ed. Frontis, 186 plts (51 mtd). VG in dj. *Argosy*. $185/£119

ASHTON, DORE. Rosa Bonheur, a Life and a Legend. NY: Viking, (1981). 1st ed. Nice (name, ex-libris) in dj. *Second Life*. $40/£26

ASHTON, JAMES M. Ice-Bound. NY/London: Putnam, 1928. 1st ed. Fldg sketch map. VG (lt shelfworn, bumped). *Parmer*. $50/£32

ASHTON, JOHN. Chap-Books of the Eighteenth Century. London, 1882. Extra illus mtd fr fly. Brn cl (sl worn, soiled; fr hinge stressed), gilt. *Freeman**. $70/£45

ASHTON, JOHN. Old Times. London: John C. Nimmo, 1885. 1st ed. xii,354,29pp. Teg, uncut. (Roughly rebacked.) *Hollett*. $47/£30

ASHTON, LEIGH. Samplers. London: Medici Soc, 1926. 1st ed. 6 color, 72 monochrome plts. VG in dj (cvrd w/adhesive film). *Hollett*. $70/£45

ASIMOV, ISAAC. The Asimov Chronicles. Arlington Heights: Dark Harvest, 1989. 1st ed. One of 500 numbered, signed. Fine in Fine dj, slipcase. *Other Worlds*. $75/£48

ASIMOV, ISAAC. Casebook of the Black Widowers. GC: DCC, 1980. 1st ed. Fine in dj (price-clipped). *Mordida*. $45/£29

ASIMOV, ISAAC. The Dream, Benjamin's Dream, and Benjamin's Bicentennial Blast. NY: Privately ptd, 1976. 1st ed. Tissue dj (worn). *Swann**. $92/£59

ASIMOV, ISAAC. Earth Is Room Enough. NY: Doubleday, 1957. 1st ed. Signed. Dj (lt worn). *Swann**. $161/£103

ASIMOV, ISAAC. Fantastic Voyage II. NY: Doubleday, 1967. 1st ed. One of 450 numbered, signed. Leather. Matching slipcase. *Swann**. $69/£44

ASIMOV, ISAAC. Fantastic Voyage. Boston: Houghton Mifflin, 1966. 1st ed. VF in dj (neatly reinforced w/tape, sm tears, wrinkles rear panel). *Pirages.* $95/£61

ASIMOV, ISAAC. Foundation and Earth. GC: Doubleday, 1986. 1st ed. One of 300 numbered, signed, w/ribbon marker, aeg, bound in leather. Fine in matching slipcase, no dj as issued. *Other Worlds.* $200/£128

ASIMOV, ISAAC. Foundation. NY: Gnome, 1951. 1st ed. Excellent in VG dj (yellowed, wrinkled, chipped, reinforced). *Pirages.* $125/£80

ASIMOV, ISAAC. The Gods Themselves. Doubleday, 1972. 1st ed. NF in dj. *Madle.* $50/£32

ASIMOV, ISAAC. The Gods Themselves. NY: Doubleday, 1972. Signed. (Erasure fep; lt worn.) Dj (lt worn, rear soiled). *Swann*.* $172/£110

ASIMOV, ISAAC. I, Robot. NY: Gnome, (1950). 1st ed, binding A. (Sl cocked.) Excellent dj. *Kane*.* $625/£401

ASIMOV, ISAAC. In the Beginning. NY, 1981. 1st ed. NF in NF dj. *Smith.* $20/£13

ASIMOV, ISAAC. The Naked Sun. GC: Doubleday, 1957. 1st ed. (Soiled, rubbed.) Dj (soiled, rubbed). *Metropolitan*.* $172/£110

ASIMOV, ISAAC. The Naked Sun. London, 1958. 1st Eng ed. VG in dj (spine sl dust-soiled). *Words Etc.* $78/£50

ASIMOV, ISAAC. Nemesis. NY: Doubleday, (1989). 1st ed. Fine in dj. *Antic Hay.* $20/£13

ASIMOV, ISAAC. Nemesis. NY: Doubleday, (1989). 1st ed. One of 500 numbered, signed. Fine in slipcase, no dj as issued. *Other Worlds.* $125/£80

ASIMOV, ISAAC. Nightfall and Other Stories. GC: Doubleday, 1969. 1st ed. NF (bkpl) in dj (browned, sl worn, 2-inch tear outer fold rear flap). *Metropolitan*.* $46/£29

ASIMOV, ISAAC. Pebble in the Sky. GC, 1950. 1st ed, 1st bk. Excellent dj. *Kane*.* $325/£208

ASIMOV, ISAAC. Pebble in the Sky. GC: Doubleday, 1950. 1st ed. (Lt stains, soil.) Dj (worn, stained, spine losses). *Metropolitan*.* $57/£37

ASIMOV, ISAAC. Pebble in the Sky. NY: Doubleday, 1950. 1st ed, 1st bk. Signed. (Tape stains eps; lt worn.) Dj (worn, rubbed, lacks rear flap). *Swann*.* $172/£110

ASIMOV, ISAAC. Prelude to Foundation. NY: Doubleday, 1988. One of 500 numbered, signed. Imitation leather. Slipcase, mailing carton. *Swann*.* $69/£44

ASIMOV, ISAAC. The Robots of Dawn. GC: Doubleday, 1983. 1st ed. Inscribed. VF in dj. *Mordida.* $65/£42

ASIMOV, ISAAC. The Robots of Dawn. Huntington Woods: Phantasia, 1983. 1st ed. One of 750 signed. Dj, slipcase. *Swann*.* $80/£51

ASIMOV, ISAAC. The Union Club Mysteries. GC: Doubleday, 1983. 1st ed. Inscribed. VF in dj. *Mordida.* $65/£42

ASIMOV, ISAAC. A Whiff of Death. Walker, (1968). 1st hb ed. (Pg edges sl browned), else Fine in Fine dj. *Certo.* $100/£64

ASINOF, ELIOT. Eight Men Out: The Black Sox and the 1919 World Series. NY: Holt, Rinehart & Winston, (1963). True 1st ed. VG + in Good dj (edgeworn, price-clipped, tape-repaired). *Fuller & Saunders.* $65/£42

ASINOF, ELIOT. Man on Spikes. McGraw Hill, 1955. 1st ed. VG in Good dj. *Plapinger.* $70/£45

ASKIN, JOHN. The John Askin Papers, 1747-1820. Milo M. Quaife (ed). Detroit, 1928-1931. 1st ed. 2 vols. Orig 1/2 morocco. (Sm emb lib stamps, bkpl removed.) Howes A359. *Ginsberg.* $250/£160

ASKINS, CHARLES. Game Bird Shooting. NY, 1931. VG. *Truepenny.* $45/£29

ASLANAPA, OKTAY. Turkish Art and Architecture. NY: Praeger, (1971). 1st ed. 67 plans, 3 maps. Fine in dj (price-clipped). *Captain's Bookshelf.* $175/£112

ASLIN, ELIZABETH. E. W. Godwin: Furniture and Interior Decoration. John Murray, 1986. VG in dj. *Hadley.* $28/£18

ASLIN, ELIZABETH. Nineteenth Century English Furniture. Faber & Faber, 1962. 4 color, 135 b/w plts. Dj. *Edwards.* $62/£40

ASPLUND, KARL. Anders Zorn: His Life and Work. London: The Studio, 1921. 1/4 imitation vellum (backstrip lt spotted), gilt. *Swann*.* $103/£66

ASQUITH, CYNTHIA (ed). The Black Cap. London: Hutchinson, (1929). 1st ed. Dk blue cl (spine very faded, edges foxed). Internally VG. *Certo.* $40/£26

ASQUITH, CYNTHIA (ed). Not Long for This World. Telegraph, 1936. 1st ed. VG in dj (sl frayed). *Madle.* $65/£42

ASQUITH, CYNTHIA. Portrait of Barrie. NY, 1955. 1st ed. VG in dj. *Typographeum.* $20/£13

ASQUITH, CYNTHIA. This Mortal Coil. Sauk City: Arkham House, 1947. 1st ed. Fine (sl bumped) in VG dj (lt browned, lt wear). *Metropolitan*.* $34/£22

ASQUITH, HERBERT. Pillicock Hill. Heinemann, 1926. 1st ed. A. H. Watson (illus). 8vo. 88pp. Maroon cl, gilt. VG. *Bookmark.* $27/£17

Assassination of Abraham Lincoln...and the Attempted Assassination of William H. Seward...and Frederick W. Seward. Washington, 1867. Engr frontis port. 1/2 morocco (fr cvr loose, backstrip defective). *Swann*.* $69/£44

ASTLE, THOMAS. The Origin and Progress of Writing.... London: C&W, 1876. Rpt of 2nd ed. Engr frontis, xxiv,240pp; 32 plts (9 dbl-pg, 7 hand-colored, 1 ptd in sepia). Teg, rest uncut. Good (lib stamps) in orig 1/2 grn roan, crimson cl sides (rubbed, fr cvr splash-mkd). *Cox.* $86/£55

ASTOR, JOHN JACOB. A Journey into Other Worlds. NY: Appleton, 1894. 1st ed. Blue cl dec in silver/gold (sl rubbed, sl frayed). VG (fr hinge sl cracked; owner stamp each prelim, 1st text leaf). *Waverly*.* $38/£24

Atalanta's Garland: Being the Book of the Edinburgh University Women's Union, 1926. Edinburgh: T&A Constable, (1926). 1st ed. One of 2000 ptd. 12 plts. 1st state binding: cl-backed patterned bds, paper label. Fine in ptd dj (top edge sl chipped). *Cahan.* $150/£96

ATCHLEY, S. C. Wild Flowers of Attica. W. B. Turrill (ed). London, 1938. 22 color plts. Good. *Henly.* $59/£38

ATGET, EUGENE. A Vision of Paris. NY: Macmillan, 1963. 1st ed. Inscribed in year of pub. VG + in VG dj. *Smith.* $400/£256

ATGET, EUGENE. A Vision of Paris. Arthur D. Trottenberg (ed). NY: Macmillan, (1980). Reissue of 1963 ed. Fine in NF dj. *Cahan.* $50/£32

ATHEARN, ROBERT G. High Country Empire, The High Plains and Rockies. NY: McGraw-Hill, (1960). 1st ed. Grn cl. (Spine head sl jammed), else Fine in dj (lt rubbed). *Argonaut.* $30/£19

ATHEARN, ROBERT G. High Country Empire. NY: McGraw-Hill, (1960). 1st ed. VG in dj. *Lien.* $30/£19

ATHEARN, ROBERT G. Union Pacific Country. Chicago: Rand McNally, (1971). 1st ed. VG + in dj (lt chipped). *Bohling.* $45/£29

ATHEARN, ROBERT G. William Tecumseh Sherman and the Settlement of the West. Norman: Univ of OK, (1956). 1st ed. (Bkpl), o/w Fine in NF dj (extrems sl worn). *Harrington*. $50/£32

ATHEARN, ROBERT G. William Tecumseh Sherman and the Settlement of the West. Norman: Univ of OK, 1956. 1st ed. Good in dj (tape-repaired). *Archer*. $25/£16

ATHERTON, FAXON DEAN. The California Diary of Faxon Dean Atherton. Doyce B. Nunis (ed). SF: CA Hist Soc, 1964. #118/325 signed by Nunis. Frontis port, fldg map, 5 fldg facs. Blue cl, gilt. Fine in slip-case, ptd spine label. *Pacific**. $161/£103

ATHERTON, GERTRUDE. California, an Intimate History. NY, 1914. 1st ed. Frontis. Teg. VG+. *Turpen*. $35/£22

ATHERTON, GERTRUDE. The Gorgeous Isle. NY, 1908. 1st ed. 4 full-pg color plts, pict eps by C. Coles Phillips. Pict cl (sl worn; ink name). *King*. $22/£14

ATHERTON, GERTRUDE. The Splendid Idle Forties. NY: Macmillan, 1902. 1st ed. Frontis, 7 plts. Red cl, dec stamped. VF (sm spot rear cvr, corner sl jammed, lt rubbed). *Argonaut*. $90/£58

ATHERTON, JOHN. The Fly and the Fish. NY: Macmillan, 1951. Stated 1st ptg. 2 color plts. Good- in Good-dj. *Scribe's Perch**. $50/£32

ATHERTON, LEWIS. The Cattle Kings. Bloomington: IN Univ, (1961). 1st ed. Frontis. White cl (sm stains). Fine in pict dj (sl chipped). *Argonaut*. $40/£26

ATIL, ESIN. Kalila Wa Dimna. Washington: Smithsonian, 1981. 1st ed. 10x10. 60pp. VG in dj. *Cattermole*. $25/£16

ATKEY, BERTRAM. The Midnight Mystery. NY: D. Appleton-Century, 1928. 1st ed. Pub's file copy w/rubber stamp fep. VG in VG dj. *Mcclintock*. $50/£32

ATKINSON, EDWARD. Treatise Upon the Science of Nutrition. Boston, 1896. 4th ed. 254pp. Grn cl. Good (extrems worn). *Doctor's Library*. $45/£29

ATKINSON, J. BEAVINGTON. An Art Tour to Northern Capitals of Europe. 1873. xii,455pp. (Pencil notes; spine head sl bumped.) *Edwards*. $70/£45

ATKINSON, J. C. British Birds' Eggs and Nests, Popularly Described. Routledge, n.d. (1880s). viii,182pp + ad leaf; 12 chromolitho plts, lg fldg chart (torn along fold) in end pocket. Good in pict blocked cl. *Cox*. $31/£20

ATKINSON, T. D. Local Style in English Architecture. Batsford, 1947. VG in dj. *Hadley*. $23/£15

ATKINSON, T. W. Oriental and Western Siberia. NY: Harper, 1858. 1st US ed. 533pp + ad leaf (lt foxing, aging); lg fldg b/w engr map. Blind brn cl (lower cvr edges sl stained, worn), gilt. Text VG. *Baltimore**. $70/£45

ATKINSON, T. W. Travels in the Region of the Upper and Lower Amoor. NY: Harper, 1860. 1st Amer ed. Frontis, xii,448pp, ads, fldg map. Brn gilt pict cl. VG. *Terramedia*. $125/£80

ATKINSON, WILLIAM B. (ed). The Physicians and Surgeons of the United States. Phila, 1878. 1st ed. 788pp. Orig 1/2 sheep (scuffed, rear hinge splitting). *King*. $250/£160

Atlas of Essex County, Massachusetts. Boston: Geo. H. Walker, 1884. 178pp. Leather-backed cl. (Several leaves creased; cl worn), o/w Contents VG. *New Hampshire**. $475/£304

Atlas of New Bedford City, Massachusetts. Boston: Geo. H. Walker, 1881. 79pp; 16 maps, 12 plts. Leather-backed cl (extrems worn). *New Hampshire**. $140/£90

Atlas of the World at War. Indianapolis/NY, 1918. VG (once folded) in pict wraps. *Hudson*. $135/£87

ATLEE, WASHINGTON L. General and Differential Diagnosis of Ovarian Tumors.... Phila, 1873. 1st ed. 482pp. (Spine top frayed.) *Argosy*. $300/£192

ATTERIDGE, A. HILLIARD. Towards Khartoum. London, 1897. Frontis, xxiv,357pp, map. Grn cl (worn), gilt. *Maggs*. $125/£80

Attractions of an Excursion upon the Great Lakes. (Buffalo): Lake Superior Transit, 1880. 60pp; 4 color litho plts, sm fldg map. Color litho wraps (sl worn, sm spots, crease). Text Good (map, 1 plt loose). *Baltimore**. $20/£13

ATWATER, CALEB. An Essay on Education. Cincinnati: Kendall & Henry, 1841. 1st ed. vii,123pp. Contemp cl (staining). (Name stamp tp), else VG. *Cahan*. $275/£176

ATWATER, CALEB. The Indians of the Northwest.... Columbus, OH: N.p., (1831). 1st ed. viii,296pp. Orig calf spine, grn bds (rubbed, joints cracked, spine chipped). Howes A379. *Karmiole*. $175/£112

ATWATER, CALEB. Remarks Made on a Tour to Prairie du Chien; Thence to Washington City in 1829. Columbus, OH, 1831. 1st ed. 296pp. New cl, leather label. Howes A377. *Ginsberg*. $300/£192

ATWATER, CALEB. Remarks Made on a Tour to Prairie du Chien; Thence to Washington City, in 1829. Columbus, (OH), 1831. 1st ed. 296pp (ep loose, fr inner hinge weak). Contemp calf-backed marbled bds. Howes A379. *M & S*. $425/£272

ATWOOD, MARGARET. Bluebeard's Egg. (Toronto): McClelland & Stewart, (1983). 1st ed. Fine in dj. *Hermitage*. $35/£22

ATWOOD, MARGARET. Cat's Eye. Bloomsbury, 1989. 1st ed. NF in dj. *Words Etc*. $25/£16

ATWOOD, MARGARET. Dancing Girls and Other Stories. (Toronto): McClelland & Stewart, (1977). 1st ed. Fine in dj. *Hermitage*. $75/£48

ATWOOD, MARGARET. Good Bones. Canada, 1992. Ltd to 150 signed. Fine in wrappers. *Words Etc*. $39/£25

ATWOOD, MARGARET. Lady Oracle. Toronto: McClelland & Stewart, (1976). 1st ed. Signed. Fine in dj (sl wear). *Lenz*. $150/£96

ATWOOD, MARGARET. The Robber Bride. Franklin Center, PA: Franklin Library, 1993. True 1st US ed. Signed. Fine in dec full leather. *Lame Duck*. $65/£42

ATWOOD, MARGARET. You Are Happy. NY: Harper, (1974). 1st Amer ed. (Sl rubbing), else Fine in dj. *Between The Covers*. $65/£42

AUBERT, ALVIN. Against the Blues. Detroit: Broadside, (1972). 1st ed. (Extrems sl dknd), else NF in stapled wrappers. *Between The Covers*. $35/£22

AUBIER, DOMINIQUE. Fiesta in Pamplona. London/Paris: Photography Magazine/Robert Delpire, 1956. 1st ed. NF. *Cahan*. $75/£48

AUBREY, JOHN. Miscellanies upon Various Subjects. John Russell Smith, 1857. 4th ed. Frontis port, xvi,227 + 40pp pub's cat. (Cl chipped head of backstrip.) *Cox*. $23/£15

AUBURY, LEWIS E. (ed). The Structural and Industrial Materials of California. SF: CA State Mining Bureau, 1906. 1st ed. Fldg frontis map, frontis. Brn cl. (Spine faded), else Fine. *Argonaut*. $60/£38

AUDEN, W. H. About the House. London: Faber & Faber, (1966). 1st British ed. NF in dj. *Reese*. $30/£19

AUDEN, W. H. The Age of Anxiety. NY: Random House, (1947). 1st ed. One of 3500. Fine in VG dj (sm tear mended on verso). *Reese*. $85/£54

AUDEN, W. H. Another Time. NY: Random House, (1940). 1st ed. One of 1500 ptd. (Ep gutters sl tanned), o/w Fine in NF dj (lt smudged). *Reese*. $150/£96

AUDEN, W. H. A Certain World. NY: Viking, (1970). 1st US ed. NF in dj. *Antic Hay.* $45/£29

AUDEN, W. H. City Without Walls and Other Poems. London: Faber & Faber, (1969). 1st ed. Fine in dj. *Reese.* $45/£29

AUDEN, W. H. The Collected Poetry of W.H. Auden. NY: Random House, (1945). 1st ed. Fine in dj (spine sl sunned). *Reese.* $150/£96

AUDEN, W. H. The Dance of Death. Faber & Faber, (1933). 1st ed. Grn bds (sl rubbed, sl discoloration top cvr). Good (scattered foxing) in dj (rubbed, sl chipped). *Ash.* $117/£75

AUDEN, W. H. The Dance of Death. London: Faber, (1933). 1st ed. One of 1200. Grn bds. VF in dj. *Jaffe.* $350/£224

AUDEN, W. H. The Dyer's Hand. NY, 1962. 1st ed. NF in NF dj. *Smith.* $25/£16

AUDEN, W. H. Good-Bye to the Mezzogiorno. Milan, 1958. 1st ed. Fine in ptd self wraps w/wraparound band. *Polyanthos.* $25/£16

AUDEN, W. H. Look, Stranger! London, 1936. 1st Eng ed. Bright (cvrs lt dknd). *Clearwater.* $39/£25

AUDEN, W. H. Look, Stranger! London: Faber & Faber, 1936. Inscribed. VG (owner stamp; unevenly faded, sm stain spine) in dj (sl chipped, spine faded). *Gekoski.* $624/£400

AUDEN, W. H. Making, Knowing, and Judging...An Inaugural Lecture.... Oxford: Clarendon Press, 1956. 1st ed. (Sl use at overlap edges), else NF in ptd wrappers. *Reese.* $50/£32

AUDEN, W. H. Nones. NY: Random House, (1951). 1st ed. Signed. Fine in dj (spine head chipped). *Jaffe.* $225/£144

AUDEN, W. H. Nones. NY, 1951. 1st Amer ed. Fine in dj (spine lt sunned, sm chips, sm edge tear, sl soiled). *Polyanthos.* $25/£16

AUDEN, W. H. On This Island. NY: Random House, (1937). 1st Amer ed. Fine in dj (sl dknd). *Reese.* $100/£64

AUDEN, W. H. Poems. NY: Random House, (1934). 1st ed. One of 1575 ptd. Fine in VG dj (sm edge tears). *Reese.* $275/£176

AUDEN, W. H. et al. The Rise and Fall of the City of Mahagonny. Boston, 1976. 1st Amer ed. Frontis port. Fine in dj. *Polyanthos.* $30/£19

AUDEN, W. H. Selected Poems. London: Faber & Faber, (1938). 1st ed. Gilt cl. (Lower edge rubbed), else NF in dj (lt spots, sm nicks). *Reese.* $150/£96

AUDEN, W. H. The Shield of Achilles. London: Faber & Faber, (1955). 1st British ed. Fine in VG dj (nicks, tears). *Reese.* $35/£22

AUDEN, W. H. Spain. Faber, 1937. 1st UK ed. Fine in wraps. *Williams.* $156/£100

AUDEN, W. H. Spain. London: Faber & Faber, 1937. (Sm patch soil upper wrapper.) *Gekoski.* $195/£125

AUDEN, W. H. Two Songs. NY: Phoenix Book Shop, 1968. 1st ed. One of 100 (of 126) numbered, signed. Fine in wrappers. *Jaffe.* $250/£160

AUDEN, W. H. and CHRISTOPHER ISHERWOOD. The Ascent of F6. Faber & Faber, (1936). 1st ed. 2000 ptd. Nice in dj (sl nicked, torn). *Ash.* $94/£60

AUDEN, W. H. and LOUIS MacNEICE. Letters from Iceland. London, 1937. 1st ed. (Spine sl rubbed, sunned), else VG. (Lacks dj.) *Buckley.* $31/£20

AUDLJO, JOHN. Journal of a Visit to Constantinople, and Some of the Greek Islands, in the Spring and Summer of 1833. London: Longmans et al, 1835. 1st ed. Engr tp, xii,259pp; 2 (of 7) plts. Recent 1/2 morocco. VG (bkpls). *Worldwide.* $165/£106

AUDSLEY, GEORGE A. and JAMES L. BOWES. Keramic Art of Japan. 1881. xii,(ii),304pp; 32 plts (ink stamps). (Margins browned, few sl chipped, sl thumbed; new eps; ex-lib; rebound, sl soiled, spine sl faded, spine #s.) *Edwards.* $101/£65

AUDSLEY, W. and G. Cottage, Lodge and Villa Architecture. W. Mackenzie, n.d. (c. 1860). 58pp (intro); fldg table at rear. Orig 1/2 leather (worn, mkd), raised bands to spine, gilt. VG. *Whittle.* $234/£150

AUDSLEY, W. and G. Polychromatic Decoration. London, 1882. 32pp; 36 color plts. (Ex-lib, perf stamps to plt margins; extrems frayed.) *King.* $195/£125

AUDUBON, J. J. The 1826 Journal...an Account of His Journey to England and Scotland.... NY, 1987. Dj. *Maggs.* $31/£20

AUDUBON, J. J. Audubon's America. Donald Culross Peattie (ed). Boston: Houghton Mifflin, 1940. Color frontis port, 16 color plts (15 dbl). VG + in dj (dknd, lt chipped). *Bohling.* $30/£19

AUDUBON, J. J. Birds of America. NY, 1856. 4to. 7 vols. 500 hand-colored lithos. (Some pp torn, browned, dampstained; some plts sl browning, minor wrinkling.) 3/4 leather, marbled bds (hinges cracked, bds bumped). *Metropolitan*.* $17,000/£10,897

AUDUBON, J. J. The Birds of America. London, 1937. 500 color plts. (Rubbed.) *Maggs.* $81/£52

AUDUBON, J. J. The Birds of America. NY, 1937. #140/2500. Port, tp repro, 500 color plts. Orig bds, buckram back. Fine in slipcase. *Wheldon & Wesley.* $78/£50

AUDUBON, J. J. Birds of America. NY, 1942. 435 color plts. (Eps, fore-edge foxed; sl worn, spine dull), o/w Contents VG. *New Hampshire*.* $30/£19

AUDUBON, J. J. Birds of America. NY, 1946. Frontis port, 435 color plts. Dj (sl chipped). *Edwards.* $55/£35

AUDUBON, J. J. Journal of John James Audubon Made During His Trip to New Orleans in 1820-1 (and) Journal of...1840-1843. Howard Corning (ed). Boston: Club of Odd Volumes, 1929. Ltd to 225 sets. 2 vols. Uncut. Muslin-backed gold-stamped blue bds, ptd paper spine labels. Boxed. Howes A386, A387. *Ginsberg.* $400/£256

AUDUBON, J. J. Journal of...Made While Obtaining Subscriptions to His 'Birds of America,' 1840-1843.... Howard Corning (ed). Cambridge, MA, 1939. New ed. Paper spine label. Howes A387. *Ginsberg.* $125/£80

AUDUBON, J. J. Letters of John James Audubon, 1826-1840. Boston, 1930. 1st ed. One of 225 sets ptd. 2 vols. Lt blue bds, muslin spines. Howes A388. *Ginsberg.* $450/£288

AUDUBON, J. J. The Original Water-Color Paintings by J.J. Audubon for the Birds of America. M.B. Davidson (ed). NY: Amer Heritage, (1966). Gilt-dec cl. NF in VG dj. *Mikesh.* $60/£38

AUDUBON, J. J. The Original Water-Color Paintings...for the Birds of America. NY: American Heritage, 1966. 1st ed. 2 vols. 431 plts. Fine in slipcase (sl worn). *Waverly*.* $66/£42

AUDUBON, J. J. The Quadrupeds of North America. NY: V.G. Audubon, 1851, 1851, 1854. 4to. 3 vols. Complete w/155 hand-colored plts (plt 3 trimmed). Marbled eps. All orig wraps bound in at rear, incl rare wrapper from issue #31. Grn full leather (spines sunned), gilt. *Metropolitan*.* $8,000/£5,128

AUDUBON, J. J. Selected Birds and Quadrupeds of North America. Montreal: Optimum, 1978. 1st ed. 2 vols. Silk eps, aeg. Full gilt-dec leather. VF in Fine slipcase. *Mikesh.* $125/£80

AUDUBON, J. J. A Synopsis of the Birds of North America. Edinburgh, 1839. Orig cl (rebacked). Cl slipcase. *Swann*.* $103/£66

AUDUBON, J. J. The Viviparous Quadrupeds of North America. NY, 1854. Vol 3 only. (Spine missing.) *Metropolitan*.* $2,185/£1,401

AUDUBON, J. J. and J. BACHMAN. The Quadrupeds of North America. NY: V.G. Audubon, 1854. 1st 8vo ed. Vol 3 (only). Lg 8vo. 55 NF hand-colored litho plts (sl toned, minor marginal foxing). Aeg. Recent 1/2 calf, marbled bds, ribbed gilt spine. Very Bright. *Waverly*.* $1,650/£1,058

AUDUBON, J. J. and J. BACHMAN. The Viviparous Quadrupeds of North America, Volume 2. NY: V.G. Audubon, 1851. 1st ed. 334pp + subs list. Spine label. (Spine ends worn), else VG +. *Mikesh.* $200/£128

AUDUBON, J. J. and J. BACHMAN. The Viviparous Quadrupeds of North America. Vol 1-2 (of 3) of the text (only). NY: Audubon, 1846-51. 1st ed. Vol 1-2 (of 3) of the text (only). (Sig, bkpl.) Contemp purple cl (stained, worn, ptd labels almost flaked away). *Maggs.* $179/£115

AUDUBON, J. W. Audubon's Western Journal: 1849-1850. Cleveland: A.H. Clark, 1906. 1st ed. Frontis port, fldg map. Uncut. Grn cl, gilt spine. (Bump), o/w NF. *Pacific*.* $138/£88

AUDUBON, J. W. The Drawings of John Woodhouse Audubon, Illustrating His Adventures Through Mexico and California 1849-1850. SF: Book Club of CA, 1957. Ltd to 400 ptd. 34 collotype plts. Prospectus laid in. Cl-backed dec bds, gilt-stamped morocco spine label. Fine. *Pacific*.* $207/£133

AUEL, JEAN M. The Clan of the Cave Bear. NY, (1980). 1st ed, 1st bk. Cl-backed bds. VG in dj (sm tear). *King.* $75/£48

AUER, HARRY A. Camp Fires in the Yukon. Cincinnati: Stewart & Kidd, 1917. 1st ed, 2nd ptg. 17 plts, 2 maps. Grn cl, gilt. NF (sl worn). *Parmer.* $150/£96

AUER, MICHEL. The Illustrated History of the Camera from 1839 to the Present. D. B. Tubbs (trans). Boston: NYGS, (1975). 1st US ed. Red bds. NF in dj. *Waverly*.* $66/£42

AUGHEY, JOHN H. The Fighting Preacher. Chicago, 1899. 1st ed. 361pp. VG + in VG + plain plastic dj. *Pratt.* $185/£119

AUGHEY, JOHN H. The Iron Furnace. Phila: William S. & Alfred Martien, 1863. 1st ed. 296pp; port, 2 plts. (Piece torn from fep.) Diced grn cl (ends sl scuffed), gilt spine title. *Petrilla.* $50/£32

AUGHEY, JOHN H. Tupelo. Lincoln, NE: State Journal, 1888. 1st ed. 606pp. (Shelfworn, rubbed), else Good. *Brown.* $35/£22

AUGUSTINE, SAINT. The Confessions. Phila: Lippincott, 1900. #95/150 for the US. Frontis engr. Teg, uncut. Full vellum (sl worn), gilt, yapped edges, ribbon ties, marbled eps. VG (sl waterstains 2 blank prelims). *Hartfield.* $185/£119

AUGUSTINE, SAINT. The Confessions. Temple Scott (ed). Edward Bouberie Pusey (trans). London: C&W, (1921, 1909). Color frontis, facs tp, 10 full-pg color illus. Marbled eps, aeg. Full tan calf, gilt-stamped brn morocco label, raised bands. VG. *Houle.* $250/£160

AULDE, JOHN. The Pocket Pharmacy. NY, 1901. 2nd ed. VG (sl worn). *Doctor's Library.* $60/£38

AULT, PHIL. Wires West. NY: Dodd, Mead, 1974. VG in dj. *Dumont.* $25/£16

Aunt Kate's Conjuring and Parlor Magic. Dundee: John Leng, n.d. (c. 1900). VG in color pict wraps. *Dramatis Personae.* $45/£29

Aunt Mary's Tales, for the Entertainment and Improvement of Little Boys. (By Mary Robson Hughes.) NY: For D. Bliss, 1817. 1st and only Amer ed. 12mo. Wood-engr frontis, iv,174pp (owner stamps). Contemp pink bds (shelfworn, soiled), red roan back. *Oinonen*.* $120/£77

Aunt Sally; or, The Cross the Way of Freedom. Cincinnati: American Reform Tract & Book Soc, 1859. 216,(7)cat pp (browned, spotted). Good (discolored). *Zubal*.* $65/£42

AURAND, A. MONROE, JR. Historical Account of the Mollie Maguires and James 'McKenna' McParlan. Harrisburg: Aurand Press, 1940. 1st ed. Pb. NF (stamp fr wrap). *Beasley.* $75/£48

AUSCHER, E. S. A History and Description of French Porcelain. London, 1905. Ltd to 1250 numbered. 24 color plts. Teg. (Tp detached; bkpl; rubbed, cvr dent, scratch.) *King.* $100/£64

AUSCHER, E. S. A History and Description of French Porcelain. William Burton (trans). London: Cassell, 1905. 1st ed. 24 color plts. (Lt accession stamp verso tp, few marginal blindstamps.) 2-tone cl gilt (sl dknd, scratched, recased). *Hollett.* $133/£85

AUSTEN, JANE. Emma. London: Macmillan, 1896. 1st Thomson ed, 'Peacock Series' issue. Fine. *Reese.* $60/£38

AUSTEN, JANE. Lady Susan. Oxford: Clarendon, 1925. 1st separate ed. Uncut. Bds, cl spine, ptd paper label. *Bickersteth.* $39/£25

AUSTEN, JANE. Lady Susan. Oxford: Clarendon, 1925. One of 250. Paper label. VG. *Argosy.* $150/£96

AUSTEN, JANE. Love and Friendship and Other Early Works.... NY: Stokes, (1922). 1st Amer ed. One of 250. Fine in both ptd paper and flowered cl djs. *Argosy.* $250/£160

AUSTEN, JANE. Northanger Abbey. NY: LEC, 1971. #1029/1500 signed by Clarke Hutton (illus). Fine in slipcase. *Hermitage.* $100/£64

AUSTEN, JANE. The Novels and Letters of Jane Austen. R. Brimley Johnson (ed). NY/Phila: Frank S. Holby, 1906. One of 1250 numbered. 12 vols. Teg. Good (spots, labels dknd, discolored). *Reese.* $400/£256

AUSTEN, JANE. Pride and Prejudice. London: George Allen, 1894. 1st ed. Hugh Thompson (illus). Aeg. Pict cl, gilt. Fine. *Holmes.* $125/£80

AUSTEN, JANE. Sense and Sensibility. Richard Bentley, 1833. Frontis. Orig cl. (Spine bumped, chipped, sunned; spine labels chipped.) VG. *Tiger.* $234/£150

AUSTEN, JANE. Sense and Sensibility. London: George Allen, 1899. 1st thus. Chris Hammond (illus). Teg. Forest grn cl, gilt. *Glenn.* $100/£64

AUSTEN, JOHN. The ABC of Pen and Ink Rendering. 1937. 1st ed. Dj (sl chipped). *Edwards.* $62/£40

AUSTEN-LEIGH, J. E. A Memoir of Jane Austen. London: Richard Bentley, 1871. 2nd ed. Blank before half-title, engr facs, (2),(x),364pp; engr facs. 1926 newspaper clipping laid in. Eps coated brn; uncut. Dk grn ribbed cl, blind, gilt. Nice (eps foxed, offsetting; sl foxed). *Temple.* $218/£140

AUSTEN-LEIGH, R. The Story of a Printing House. Spottiswoode, 1912. Uncut. Fine in 1/4 cl. *Moss.* $25/£16

AUSTER, PAUL. Auggie Wren's Christmas Story. Delos, 1990. Ltd to 300. Fine in marbled paper-cvrd wrappers. *Words Etc.* $39/£25

AUSTER, PAUL. Disappearances. Woodstock, NY: Overlook, (1988). 1st ed. Fine (name) in dj (sl used). *Dermont.* $25/£16

AUSTER, PAUL. In the Country of Last Things. NY: Viking, (1987). 1st ed. Fine in dj. *Hermitage.* $45/£29

AUSTER, PAUL. Leviathan. NY: Viking, 1992. 1st ed. Inscribed. Fine in Fine dj. *Beasley.* $45/£29

AUSTER, PAUL. Moon Palace. London: Faber, 1989. 1st UK ed. Fine in dj. *Williams.* $28/£18

AUSTIN, F. BRITTEN. A Saga of the Sword. NY, 1929. 1st ed. NF in NF dj. *Mcclintock.* $25/£16

AUSTIN, G. W. Henry Wadsworth Longfellow, His Life, His Works, His Friendships. Boston: Lee & Shepard, 1883. 1st ed. Brn pict cl, gilt. VF. *Macdonnell*. $20/£13

AUSTIN, GABRIEL. The Library of Jean Grolier: A Preliminary Catalogue. NY: Grolier Club, 1971. 1st ed. One of 1000. *Swann**. $57/£37

AUSTIN, HUGH. Death Has Seven Faces. NY: Scribner, 1949. 1st ed. (Label removed.) o/w VG in dj. *Mordida*. $35/£22

AUSTIN, JOHN. The Province of Jurisprudence Determined. London: John Murray, 1832. 1/2 calf (rebacked, rubbed), marbled edges. Fresh. *Boswell*. $2,500/£1,603

AUSTIN, MARGOT. Gabriel Churchkitten. NY: Dutton, 1942. 1st ed. 8 3/4 x 10. 32pp. Cl spine. Good. *Cattermole*. $20/£13

AUSTIN, MARY. The Arrow Maker: A Drama in 3 Acts. NY: Duffield, 1911. 1st ed. Paper label. (Stamps; lt worn.) *Dawson*. $75/£48

AUSTIN, MARY. Isidro. Houghton Mifflin, 1905. 1st ed. Color frontis, 3 color plts. Dec eps. Gilt pict cl. VG. *Oregon*. $60/£38

AUSTIN, MARY. The Land of Journey's Ending. NY: Century, (1924). 1st ed. (5 prelims nicked.) Pict cl (tip fr cvr bumped). Dj (lt worn). *Dawson*. $150/£96

AUSTIN, MARY. The Land of Little Rain. Boston: Houghton Mifflin, (1903). 1st ed. VG (foxed, pencil note pg xi; sl edgeworn, sl stain fr bd). *Fuller & Saunders*. $100/£64

AUSTIN, MARY. The Land of Little Rain. Boston: Houghton Mifflin, 1950. 1st Ansel Adams illus ed. Fine in dj (spine head sl rubbed). *Sadlon*. $145/£93

AUSTIN, MARY. The Land of Little Rain. Boston: Houghton Mifflin, 1950. 1st ed thus. 48 b/w plts from photos by Ansel Adams. Yellow cl. Fine in NF dj. *Harrington*. $150/£96

AUSTIN, MARY. The Lands of the Sun. Boston: Houghton Mifflin, 1927. 1st ed. (Spine extrems lt worn, couple sm spots.) *Dawson*. $75/£48

AUSTIN, MARY. Lost Borders. NY: Harper, 1909. 1st ed. 7 full-pg illus. Pict cl. *Dawson*. $100/£64

AUSTIN, MARY. A Woman of Genius. GC: Doubleday, Page, 1912. 1st ed. VG. *Reese*. $35/£22

AUSTIN, THOMAS R. (comp). The Well-Spent Life. Louisville, 1878. Ltd ed. 48pp; engr port. Ptd wraps (sl soiled, edgeworn). *Bohling*. $45/£29

AUTENRIETH, WILHELM. Laboratory Manual for the Detection of Poisons and Powerful Drugs. William H. Warren (trans). Phila, (1915). Color plt. (Ex-lib; lower hinge broken.) *Argosy*. $50/£32

AUTENRIETH, WILHELM. Laboratory Manual for the Detection of Poisons and Powerful Drugs. Phila, 1921. 5th ed. Brn cl. VG (extrems sl worn). *Doctor's Library*. $75/£48

Author's Love: Being the Unpublished Letters of Prosper Merimee's 'Inconnue.' (By Elizabeth Balch.) London/NY: Macmillan, 1889. 1st ed. 2 vols. (xxiv),205,(i),(ii)pp,2pp integral ads; (iv),223,(i)pp. Lower edges rough trimmed, others uncut. Brownish black buckram, gilt. (Sl foxed; spines sl worn), o/w Very Nice. *Temple*. $86/£55

Autobiography of an English Soldier in the United States Army. (By George Ballentine.) NY: Stringer & Townsend, 1853. 1st US ed. Engr frontis, extra tp, xii,(9)-288pp (sl foxed, aged, 1 sig lt sprung, early bkpl, later ink handstamp eps). Lt yellow eps. Dk grn blind cl, gilt. Cvrs VG (sl worn, few sm holes upper joint). Howes B77. *Baltimore**. $35/£22

AUTON, C. (Pseud of Augustus Hoppin.) Recollections of Auton House. Boston, 1881. 1st ed. 8.5x6.5. 99pp. Cl-backed bds (extrems frayed). *King*. $35/£22

AVALLONE, MICHAEL. The Case of the Violent Virgin. London: W.H. Allen, 1960. 1st ed. Fine (name) in dj (lt soiled, spine lt browned). *Metropolitan**. $34/£22

AVARY, MYRTA LOCKETT (ed). A Virginia Girl in the Civil War, 1861-1865. NY: D. Appleton, 1903. 1st ed. Teg. (Sm spot top margin 2 leaves), else NF. *Cahan*. $100/£64

AVARY, MYRTA LOCKETT. Dixie After the War. NY: Doubleday, Page, 1906. 1st ed. 32 plts. Teg. (Sl rubbed, soiled.) Internally VG. *Worldwide*. $30/£19

AVEBURY, LORD. The Scenery of England. London, 1902. Frontis, fldg map. (Feps sl browned, bkpl.) Gilt-emb cl. *Edwards*. $39/£25

AVEDON, RICHARD. Avedon Photographs 1947-1977. NY: FSG, 1978. 1st ed. Signed. VG+ in VG+ dj. *Smith*. $225/£144

AVEDON, RICHARD. In the American West: 1979-1984. NY: Abrams, 1985. 1st ed. 109 full-pg b/w photos. Mtd photo fr/rear cvrs. NF (sl worn) in acetate dj (lt scuffed). *Cahan*. $150/£96

AVEDON, RICHARD. Nothing Personal. NY: Atheneum, 1964. 1st ed. Ptd paper over bds. VG (sl soiled, spine ends sl worn; owner stamp) in pub's slipcase (lt soiled, 1 end separating). *Cahan*. $250/£160

AVEDON, RICHARD. Observations. NY: S&S, (1959). 1st ed. VF in ptd bds, w/glassine dj, matching slipcase (lt soiled). *Bromer*. $300/£192

AVEDON, RICHARD. Observations. NY: S&S, 1959. 1st ed. Ptd glazed bds. VG (name) in slipcase (sl worn). *Cahan*. $250/£160

AVEDON, RICHARD. Portraits. NY: FSG, 1976. 1st ed. 84 b/w plts. (Stamp lower edge, owner stamp), else VG. *Cahan*. $35/£22

AVEDON, RICHARD. Portraits. NY: FSG, 1976. 1st ed. Signed, dated in year of pub. 84 b/w plts. Fine in dj. *Cahan*. $200/£128

AVERELL, WILLIAM WOODS. Ten Years in the Saddle, The Memoirs of William Wood Averall, 1851-1868. Edward K. Eckert & Nicholas J. Amato (eds). San Rafael, (1978). 1st ed. Fine in Fine dj. *Pratt*. $30/£19

AVERILL, ESTHER and LILA STANLEY. Powder. Paris: Domino Press, 1933. #71 of ltd ed. Signed by Feodor Rojankovsky (illus). 7 1/2 x 10 1/4. 32pp. VG (ex-lib, mks) in wraps. *Cattermole*. $75/£48

AVERILL, ESTHER. The Cat Club. NY: Harper, 1944. 1st ed. 5 1/4 x 7 1/2. 32pp. Fine. *Cattermole*. $60/£38

AVERILL, ESTHER. Jenny's First Party. NY: Harper, 1948. 1st ed. 5 x 7 1/2. 32pp. VG. *Cattermole*. $35/£22

AVERILL, ESTHER. When Jenny Lost Her Scarf. NY: Harper, 1951. 1st ed. 5 x 7 1/2. 32pp. VG in dj. *Cattermole*. $100/£64

AVERILL, GERALD. Ridge Runner. Phila: Lippincott, 1948. 1st ed. Ptd paper over bds. VG. *Bowman*. $22/£14

AVERILL, NAOMI. Choochee. NY: G&D, 1937. 1st ed, 1st bk. 9 3/4 x 9 1/2. 40pp. Pict bds. VG in dj. *Cattermole*. $100/£64

AVERY, GILLIAN. A Likely Lad. NY: Holt, 1971. 1st US ed. Faith Jacques (illus). 5 1/2 x 8 1/2. 223pp. Fine in dj. *Cattermole*. $30/£19

AVERY, P. O. History of the Fourth Illinois Cavalry Regiment. Humbolt, NE: Enterprise, 1903. 1st ed. Errata pasted inside fr cvr. *Ginsberg*. $375/£240

AVERY, RUFUS and STEPHEN HEMPSTEAD. Narrative of Jonathan Rathbun with Accurate Accounts.... (New London, 1840?) 1st ed. (4),80pp. Howes A423. *Ginsberg*. $175/£112

AWDRY, W. 04. Tank Engine Thomas Again. Leicester: Edmund Ward, 1949. 1st ed. C. Reginald Dalby (illus). Sm obl 24mo. Pict paper-cvrd bds. VG in Good+ dj (chipped). *Book Adoption*. $40/£26

AWDRY, W. 06. Henry the Green Engine. Leicester: Edmund Ward, 1951. 1st ed. C. R. Dalby (illus). 4 1/4 x 5 1/2. Pict cl. NF in VG dj (chipped). *Book Adoption*. $45/£29

AWDRY, W. 08. Gordon the Big Engine. Leicester: Edmund Ward, 1953. 1st ed. C. Reginald Dalby (illus). Sm obl 24mo. Pict paper-cvrd bds. VG+ in Good+ dj (chipped, cellotape remnants). *Book Adoption*. $40/£26

AWDRY, W. 23. Enterprising Engines. London: Kaye & Ward, 1968. 1st ed. G. and P. Edwards (illus). 4 1/4 x 5 1/2. Pict paper-cvrd bds. VG in Good+ dj (chipped, sm tears). *Book Adoption*. $40/£26

AYCKBOURN, ALAN. Joking Apart and Two Other Plays. Chatto, 1979. 1st UK ed. NF in dj. *Williams*. $39/£25

AYCKBOURN, ALAN. The Norman Conquests. London, 1975. VG (inscrip, sl bumped) in NF dj. *Buckley*. $31/£20

AYCKBOURN, ALAN. Sisterly Feelings and Taking Steps. Chatto, 1981. 1st UK ed. Fine in dj. *Williams*. $39/£25

AYER, MARGARET. Made in Thailand. NY: Knopf, 1964. 1st ed. Frontis. (Ex-lib; cl sl rubbed), o/w VG. *Worldwide*. $22/£14

AYER, SARAH CONNELL. Diary, 1805-1835. Portland, ME, 1910. 1st ed. Paper over bds, linen spine. Good (sl pencil to text; hinge cracks) in Good slipcase. *Scribe's Perch**. $32/£21

AYMAR, B. (ed). Treasury of Snake Lore: From the Garden of Eden to Snakes of Today, Etc. NY: Greenberg, 1956. 1st ed. Fine in VG+ dj. *Mikesh*. $27/£17

AYME, MARCEL. The Magic Pictures. NY: Harper, 1954. 1st ed. Maurice Sendak (illus). 5 1/2 x 8 1/2. 117pp. VG. *Cattermole*. $75/£48

AYRE, JOSEPH. Practical Observations on the Nature and Treatment of Marasmus.... Northampton, MA: Simeon Butler, 1822. 1st Amer ed. 219,(1)pp. Complete w/errata slip pasted to final leaf. Orig speckled calf, red leather spine label. (Notes rear ep, rear pastedown, sig, lt browning; extrems sl worn.) NF. *Glaser*. $250/£160

AYRES, PAUL. (Pseud of Edward Aarons.) Dead Heat. Drexel Hill: Bell, 1950. 1st ed. NF in dj (sm spine chips). *Janus*. $45/£29

AYRTON, MICHAEL (ed). Hogarth's Drawings. London: Avalon, 1948. 1st ed. VG in dj (price-clipped, few repairs to verso). *Hollett*. $70/£45

AYRTON, MICHAEL. The Midas Consequence. London: Secker & Warburg, 1974. 1st ed. VG in dj. *Hollett*. $47/£30

AYRTON, MICHAEL. The Testament of Daedalus. Methuen, 1962. 1st UK ed. Fine in VG dj (sl browned, closed tear). *Williams*. $23/£15

AYRTON, MICHAEL. Tittivulus. London: Max Reinhardt, (1953). 1st ed. Fine in dj (sl worn). *Antic Hay*. $20/£13

AZARIAN, MARY. The Tale of John Barleycorn. Boston: Godine, 1982. 1st ed. 9 1/2 x 10 3/4. 40pp. Fine in dj. *Cattermole*. $25/£16

B

B., B. (Pseud of D.J. Watkins-Pitchford.) The Shooting Man's Bedside Book. NY: Scribner, 1948. 1st ed. VG+ (inscrip) in VG dj. *Backman*. $30/£19

B., M. (Max Brand.) The Thunderer. NY: Derrydale, 1933. One of 950. (Worn, spine sl dknd.) *Oinonen**. $50/£32

BABB, T. A. In the Bosom of the Comanches. Amarillo, TX, (1912). 1st ed. Signed, dated. (Marginal dampstain affecting upper corner of text pp, eps browned.) Red cl, gilt, black on spine. (Very worn, water spotting, hinges expertly repaired), o/w Internally Clean, NF. Howes B3. *Harrington*. $250/£160

BABBITT, E. L. The Allegheny Pilot. Freeport, PA, 1855. 64pp; 16 maps, 4pp ads at fr, 12pp directory at rear. Ptd wraps (worn, spotted, backstrip chipped away.) Howes B5. *Bohling*. $650/£417

BABCOCK, BERNIE. Hallerloogy, the Story of a Little Arkansas Negro Boy Who Took a Ride with Santa Claus. Perry, AR, 1943. 1st ed. Signed. 48pp. NF in orig stiff dec wrappers. *Mcgowan*. $45/£29

BABCOCK, HAVILAH. The Education of Pretty Boy. NY: Holt, 1960. 1st ed. VF in dj. *Bowman*. $200/£128

BABCOCK, PHILIP H. Falling Leaves; Tales from a Gun Room. NY: Derrydale, (1937). One of 950 numbered. Gilt-stamped cl (sl shelfworn). *Oinonen**. $110/£71

BABCOX, PETER and DEBORAH (eds). The Conspiracy. NY: Dell, 1969. Pb orig. (Sm chip fr cvr, sl rubbed), o/w NF-. *Sclanders*. $12/£8

BACH, RICHARD. Stranger to the Ground. NY, 1963. 1st ed, 1st bk. NF in NF dj (rear panel sl rubbed, edgewear). *Warren*. $75/£48

BACHE, FRANKLIN. The Pharmacopoeia of the United States of America. Phila, 1864. 1st ed, 2nd ptg. 399pp. VG. *Fye*. $300/£192

BACHELLER, IRVING. A Man for the Ages. Indianapolis: Bobbs-Merrill, (1919). Signed. Brn bds, lt brn cl spine, gilt stamping. VG (edgewear, fr hinge weak). *Bohling*. $40/£26

BACHMAN, RICHARD. (Pseud of Stephen King.) Roadwork. London: New English Library, 1983. 1st UK ed. Pb orig. VG (bkseller stamp flyleaf, sl creased). *Williams*. $28/£18

BACHMANN, INGEBORG. The Thirtieth Year. NY: Knopf, 1964. 1st US ed. NF in VG+ dj (price-clipped, sl surface loss spine). *Lame Duck*. $25/£16

BACHMEYER, ARTHUR (ed). Hospital Trends and Developments 1940-1946. NY, 1948. 1st ed. VG. *Fye*. $75/£48

BACK, GEORGE. Narrative of an Expedition in H.M.S. Terror...in the Years 1836-7. London: John Murray, 1838. vii,456pp; 12 plts, fldg map (expertly backed). Uncut. Orig cl (hinges repaired). VG. *High Latitude*. $650/£417

BACK, GEORGE. Narrative of the Arctic Land Expedition to the Mouth of the Great Fish River...1833, 1834, and 1835.... Phila: E.L. Carey & A. Hart, 1836. 1st Amer ed. (4 ads),456pp; fldg map. Uncut. Orig bds, ptd paper spine label. VG (lt foxing). *Lefkowicz*. $175/£112

BACK, GEORGE. Narrative of the Arctic Land Expedition...in the Years 1833, 1834, and 1835. London, 1836. Map, 15 plts. (Lt foxed, browned, label.) 1/2 morocco, gilt. *Swann**. $230/£147

BACK, HOWARD. The Waters of Yellowstone. NY: Dodd Mead, 1938. 1st ed. NF. *Bowman*. $180/£115

BACKUS, ISAAC. Diary of Isaac Backus. William G. McLoughlin (ed). Providence: Brown Univ, (1979). 3 vols. Fine. *Bohling*. $45/£29

Backwoods of Canada. (By Catherine Parr Traill.) London: Charles Knight, 1836. 1st ed, 2nd issue, w/Appendix B starting p326 and text finishing p351. viii,351pp, half-title, wood-engr port, map. Contemp 1/2 calf (lt rubbed). *Burmester*. $195/£125

BACON, ALICE MABEL. Japanese Girls and Women. Boston/NY: Houghton Mifflin (Riverside), 1902. Rev enlgd ed, 16th imp. (Cl sl rubbed), o/w VG. *Worldwide*. $18/£12

BACON, FRANCIS. The Essays or Counsels Civill and Morall. NY: LEC, 1944. #904/1100 signed by Bruce Rogers (designer). Cl-backed dec bds. Fine in tissue dj, drop lid box (sl worn). *Hermitage*. $175/£112

BACON, FRANCIS. Of the Advancement and Proficience of Learning or the Partitions of Sciences. Oxford: Lichfield, 1640. 1st ed in English, expanded; 2nd issue, w/colophon dated 1640, but w/other points as in 1st issue. Port, engr title (both w/fraying, tears, versos strengthened, title leaf w/piece clipped away w/loss; some leaves w/margins restored, sl soil, stains). Old calf (rubbed, recased). *Oinonen**. $450/£288

BACON, FRANCIS. Of the Advancement and Proficience of Learning. London: Thomas Williams, 1674. 2nd ed. (30),38,(14),322,(20)pp (fep corner torn), port. W/the orig blanks. Contemp calf (rubbed, sm chip spine). VG. Engr bkpl of John Wentworth. *Reese*. $375/£240

BACON, FRANCIS. Of the Proficience and Advancement of Learning. B. Montagu (ed). London: William Pickering, 1851. xvi,341pp. Teg, rest uncut. (Eps spotted), o/w Good in contemp crimson roan, raised bands, grn morocco label. *Cox*. $39/£25

BACON, FRANCIS. Works. Phila: M. Murphy, 1876. 3 vols. cxvii,454pp (fr hinge cracked, rear hinge starting; feps, tp partly detached); viii,589pp (fr hinge cracked); xv,584pp (hinges cracked). Dk blue cl (rubbed, bumped; spine tear vol 1, fr joint partly split; rear joint vol 2 partly split; vol 3 cl dampstained, sl bubbled), mtd spine label (chipped). Good reading copy. *Blue Mountain*. $35/£22

BACON, FRED P. (ed). History of the Second Pilgrimage to Richmond, by the Knights Templar of Massachusetts and Rhode Island, May, 1881. Boston, 1882. 148pp. Good. *Hayman*. $15/£10

BACON, JOHN. The Town Officer's Guide, Containing a Compilation of the General Laws of Massachusetts.... Haverhill: E.W. Reinhart, 1825. Contemp mottled sheep (spine chipped). Pretty. *Boswell*. $150/£96

BACON, ROGER. The Opus Majus of Roger Bacon. Robert Belle Burke (trans). Phila: Univ of PA, 1928. 1st ed thus. 2 vols. Frontis each vol, 6 plts. NF set. *Glaser*. $385/£247

BACOU, ROSELINE. Drawings in the Louvre. London, 1968. 100 plts. Good in dj. *Washton*. $35/£22

BADAWY, ALEXANDER. Architecture in Ancient Egypt and the Near East. Cambridge: MIT, (1978). 5 maps. Good. *Archaeologia*. $125/£80

BADAWY, ALEXANDER. A History of Egyptian Architecture...1580-1085 B.C. Berkeley/L.A.: Univ of CA, 1968. 16 plts. Good. *Archaeologia*. $225/£144

BADDELEY, JOHN F. The Rugged Flanks of the Caucasus. London, 1940. 1st ed. 2 vols. Port, 7 fldg maps, 39 plts. Fine. *Maggs*. $702/£450

BADEN-POWELL, R. Boy Scouts Beyond the Seas. London: C. Arthur Pearson, 1913. 7 (of 8) plts. Red cl (rubbed, sl soiled, fr hinge cracked). VG. *Waverly**. $71/£46

BADEN-POWELL, R. Sport in War. London: Heinemann, 1900. 1st ed. (Spine ends sl rubbed.) *Hollett*. $101/£65

BADER, BARBARA. Aesop and Company. Boston: Houghton Mifflin, 1991. 1st ed. Arthur Gelsert (illus). 8 1/4 x 10 1/4. 48pp. Fine in dj. *Cattermole*. $20/£13

BADER, BARBARA. American Picturebooks from Noah's Ark to the Beast Within. NY: Macmillan, (1976). 1st ed. Fine in dj. *Oak Knoll*. $95/£61

BADGER, G. PERCY. A Guide to Malta and Gozo. Malta, 1881. Fldg frontis map (taped to rear), 320pp (1st 3 leaves lack sm portion inner upper corner, fep, maps taped to hinge, lt margin browning). Red cl (lt soiled, spine sl chipped), gilt. *Edwards*. $117/£75

BADLAM, ALEXANDER. The Wonders of Alaska. SF: Bancroft, 1890. 1st ed. vii,(2),152pp (fore-edge spotted). Dec grey cl (shelfwear). VG. *Parmer*. $90/£58

BAE. 6th Annual Report. Washington: GPO, 1888. 2 fldg maps in pocket. (Sl mkd, lib stamp), else Good. *High Latitude*. $90/£58

BAE. 9th Annual Report. Washington, 1892. Grn cl. VG-. *Perier*. $97/£62

BAE. 12th Annual Report. Washington, 1894. 742pp; 42 plts, fldg map in pocket. Olive cl (hinges weak, cvrs worn). *Parmer*. $120/£77

BAE. 14th Annual Report. Washington, 1896. 1st ed. Fine. *Turpen*. $175/£112

BAE. 18th Annual Report 1896-97. Part 2. Washington: GPO, 1899. 67 dbl-pg maps. (1st 25 leaves fore-edges chewed; spine dull, ends rubbed, hinges tender.) *Sadlon*. $125/£80

BAE. 19th Annual Report 1897-98. Parts I and II. Washington: GPO, 1900. (Extrems rubbed, sl abrasions cvrs.) *Sadlon*. $125/£80

BAE. 20th Annual Report 1898-99. By W. H. Holmes. Washington: GPO, 1903. (Extrems rubbed, 1-inch spine tear.) *Sadlon*. $75/£48

BAE. 21st Annual Report. Washington, 1903. 69 plts. (Edgeworn), else Good. *Perier*. $300/£192

BAE. 22nd Annual Report 1900-1901. Parts I and II. Washington: GPO, 1904. (Extrems rubbed, few sl spots, abrasions.) *Sadlon*. $125/£80

BAE. 22nd Annual Report...Part 2. Washington, 1904. 1st ed. Grn cl. VG. *Archer*. $50/£32

BAE. 30th Annual Report. Washington, 1915. 7 plts (1 color). Good. *Scribe's Perch**. $26/£17

BAE. 33rd Annual Report. Washington, 1919. 95 plts. Grn cl. VG. *Perier*. $80/£51

BAE. 44th Annual Report. Washington, 1928. 98 plts. (Spine faded), else VG. *Parmer*. $145/£93

BAE. 48th Annual Report. Washington, 1933. Ptd grn wrappers (lt edgewear). *Dawson*. $50/£32

BAEDEKER, KARL. Belgium and Holland Including the Grand-Duchy of Luxembourg. Leipsic: Karl Baedeker, 1897. 12th ed. lxii,418pp, 14 maps, 21 plans (1 w/frayed edges). Good (extrems sl worn). *Cox*. $28/£18

BAEDEKER, KARL. Belgium and Holland Including the Grand-Duchy of Luxembourg. Leipzig, 1905. 14th ed. 15 maps, 30 plans. VG (underlining). *Bohling*. $20/£13

BAEDEKER, KARL. The Eastern Alps. Leipzig, 1911. 12th ed. 73 maps, 16 plans, 11 panoramas. All edges marbled. (Hinges cracked; spine rubbed, loss to head.) *Edwards*. $31/£20

BAEDEKER, KARL. Egypt and the Sudan. Leipzig, 1929. 8th rev ed. Flexible cl (spine sunned, torn, ex-lib). *King*. $60/£38

BAEDEKER, KARL. Egypt. Leipsig: Karl Baedeker, 1902. 5th remodelled ed. 23 maps, 66 plans. Red cl (sl rubbed), gilt. VG. *Hollett*. $187/£120

BAEDEKER, KARL. Great Britain. Leipzig, 1906. 6th ed. 22 maps, 58 plans, fldg panorama. All edges marbled. (Foxing; spine sl faded, rubbed, sl worn.) *Edwards*. $47/£30

BAEDEKER, KARL. Great Britain. Leipzig: Karl Baedeker, 1910. 7th ed. Frontis map, xvi,624pp; 28 maps, 65 plans, panorama. Red cl, gilt. (Sm fold repair frontis), o/w Excellent. *Hollett*. $47/£30

BAEDEKER, KARL. Greece. Leipzig, 1909. 4th rev ed. 16 maps, 30 plans, 2 diags. (Lacks fldg panorama; 1st gathering detached.) All edges marbled. *Edwards.* $47/£30

BAEDEKER, KARL. Italy from the Alps to Naples. Leipsic, 1904. 24 (of 26) maps, incl fldg frontis map (folds split). *Bohling.* $12/£8

BAEDEKER, KARL. Italy. Handbook for Travellers. Third Part.... London, 1896. 12th rev ed. xlviii,416pp, 25 maps (frontis map edges chipped), 17 plans. (Label remnants upper bd.) *Edwards.* $23/£15

BAEDEKER, KARL. The Mediterranean Sea Port and Sea Routes.... Leipzig: Baedeker, 1911. 1st ed. 38 maps, 49 plans. (Frontis map sl torn; rubbed, spine torn), o/w VG. *Worldwide.* $75/£48

BAEDEKER, KARL. Palestine and Syria. Leipzig, 1912. 5th ed. 21 maps, 56 plans, fldg panorama. All edges marbled. Dj (sl chipped, split, portion detached). *Edwards.* $195/£125

BAEDEKER, KARL. Paris and Environs with Routes from London to Paris. Leipzig, 1904. 15th rev ed. 13 maps. VG (marginalia, 1 plan in index split). *Bohling.* $20/£13

BAEDEKER, KARL. Paris and Environs.... Leipzig, 1907. 16th rev ed. 14 maps, 38 plans. All edges marbled. (Spine sl rubbed, chipped.) *Edwards.* $31/£20

BAEDEKER, KARL. The Rhine from Rotterdam to Constance. Leipzig, 1900. 14th rev ed. 45 maps, 25 plans. All edges marbled. (Spine faded, sl chipped.) *Edwards.* $23/£15

BAEDEKER, KARL. The Rhine, Including the Black Forest and the Vosges. Leipzig, 1911. 17th rev ed. 69 maps, 59 plans. All edges marbled. (Feps lt browned; spine sl rubbed, faded.) *Edwards.* $23/£15

BAEDEKER, KARL. The Rhine. Leipzig, 1926. 18th rev ed. 102 maps and plans (1 fore-edge chipped). All edges marbled. (Spine faded, sm split.) *Edwards.* $31/£20

BAEDEKER, KARL. Southern Germany. Leipzig, 1914. 12th rev ed. 37 maps, 50 plans. All edges marbled. (Sl rubbed.) *Edwards.* $31/£20

BAEDEKER, KARL. Spain and Portugal. Handbook for Travellers. Leipsic: Baedeker, 1901. 2nd ed. 7 maps, 45 (of 47) plans. (Sl rubbed), o/w Good. *Worldwide.* $30/£19

BAEDEKER, KARL. Switzerland. Coblenz/Leipsic: Karl Baedeker, 1873. 6th ed. xlii,427pp. 22 maps, 10 plans, 7 panoramas. Red cl (neatly recased; fep replaced). *Hollett.* $101/£65

BAEDEKER, KARL. Switzerland. Leipzig, 1907. 22nd ed. 69 maps, 18 plans, 11 panoramas. All edges marbled. (Browning; spine sl faded.) *Edwards.* $25/£16

BAEDEKER, KARL. Travellers Manual of Conversation. Leipzig, n.d. c.(1881). Stereotype ed. ix,331pp. All edges marbled. (Lt browned, upper hinge cracked; spine chipped, fading.) *Edwards.* $55/£35

BAEDEKER, KARL. Tyrol and the Dolomites. Leipzig, 1927. 13th rev ed. 65 maps, 19 plans, 11 panoramas. All edges marbled. (Sl shaken, spine faded, sl mkd.) *Edwards.* $23/£15

BAEDEKER, KARL. The United States with an Excursion into Mexico Handbook for Travellers. Leipsic, 1899. 2nd Amer ed. c,579pp; 19 maps, 24 plans. VG. *Reese.* $275/£176

BAEGERT, JOHANN JAKOB. Observations in Lower California. Berkeley: UC, 1952. Map. Fine in dj (lt wear). Howes B29. *Bohling.* $45/£29

BAER, KURT. Architecture of the California Missions. Berkeley/L.A.: Univ of CA, 1958. 1st ed. Brn cl, gilt. Fine in pict dj. *Pacific*.* $35/£22

BAER, WARREN. The Duke of Sacramento, a Comedy in Four Acts.... SF: Grabhorn Press, 1934. One of 550. Cl-backed dec bds, paper spine label. Fine. *Harrington.* $55/£35

BAERLEIN, ANTHONY. Daze, the Magician. London: Barker, 1936. 1st ed. VG (soil) in dj (lg chips, losses, worn). *Metropolitan*.* $51/£33

BAGBY, GEORGE. Dead Drunk. GC: DCC, 1953. 1st ed. (Pp sl dknd), o/w Fine in dj (sl wear spine top). *Mordida.* $35/£22

BAGBY, GEORGE. The Three-Time Losers. GC: DCC, 1958. 1st ed. Fine in dj (sl wear spine ends). *Mordida.* $35/£22

BAGENAL, N. B. Fruit Growing. Modern Cultural Methods. London, 1945. 2nd imp. 8 color, 32 plain plts. Good in dj. *Henly.* $28/£18

BAGGULEY, W. H. (ed). Andrew Marvell: Tercentenary Tributes. London, 1922. One of 1000 ptd. Buckram (sl mkd, scratched). *Clearwater.* $70/£45

BAGLEY, CLARENCE B. Indian Myths of the Northwest. Seattle: Lowman & Hanford, 1930. 1st ed. Signed. (Spine label chipped), else VG. *Perier.* $75/£48

BAGLEY, HELEN. Sand in My Shoe. Twenty-Nine Palms: Calico Press, (1978). 1st ed. Frontis. Tan cl. Fine in dj. *Argonaut.* $45/£29

BAGNOLD, ENID. National Velvet. NY: Morrow, 1935. 1st ed. Fine (owner stamp) in dj (short tear, abrasion fr flap, sl worn). *Metropolitan*.* $86/£55

BAGOT, RICHARD. My Italian Year. Leipzig: Bernhard Tauschnitz, 1912. Copyright ed. Photo laid on fep, press cutting of letter from Bagot loosely inserted. Contemp 1/2 calf (few sm scratches), gilt, raised bands, dbl spine labels. *Hollett.* $47/£30

BAHR, A. W. Old Chinese Porcelain and Works of Art in China. London, 1911. 121 plts, incl 12 color. (Corners worn.) *Argosy.* $175/£112

BAIER, LESLEY K. Walker Evans at Fortune, 1945-1965. Wellesley, MA: Wellesley College Museum, 1977. 1st ed. (Owner stamp), else VG in pict stiff wrappers. *Cahan.* $15/£10

BAIGELL, MATTHEW. Albert Bierstadt. NY: Watson-Guptill, (1981). 1st ed. 32 plts, erratum. VG in dj. *Lien.* $30/£19

BAIGELL, MATTHEW. Thomas Hart Benton. NY, (1974). One of 350 numbered, signed by Benton. Leather, gilt. *Swann*.* $258/£165

BAIL, HAMILTON VAUGHN. Views of Harvard. A Pictorial Record to 1860. Cambridge: Harvard Univ, 1949. 1st ed. Fine in dj (sl edgewear). *Sadlon.* $40/£26

Bailey's Franklin Almanac, for the Year of Our Lord 1830.... Phila: Lydia R. Bailey, (1829). (35)pp; 13 woodcuts. (Name; edge frayed; 1st few ll dknd; foxing), else Good in stitched wrappers. *Cahan.* $35/£22

BAILEY, A. M. and R. J. NEIDRACH. Birds of Colorado. Denver: Museum of Natural Hist, 1965. 1st ed. 2 vols. 124 full-pg color repros. NF. *Mikesh.* $150/£96

BAILEY, CAROLYN SHERWIN. Tops and Whistles: True Stories of Early American Toys and Children. NY: Viking, 1937. 1st ed. 20 full-pg illus. VG (sm stain) in dj (sm stain; worn). *Cahan.* $45/£29

BAILEY, COLIN J. Catalogue of the Collection of Drawings. Volume V. German Nineteenth-Century Drawings. Oxford: Ashmolean Museum, 1987. Good in dj. *Washton.* $65/£42

BAILEY, DAVID and PETER EVANS. Goodbye Baby and Amen. NY: Coward-McCann, 1969. 1st Amer ed, on Eng sheets. (Cl sl faded, rubbed), else VG. *Cahan.* $85/£54

BAILEY, FLORA L. Some Sex Beliefs and Practices in the Navaho Community. Cambridge: Peabody Museum, 1950. VF in heavy brn wraps. *Five Quail.* $35/£22

BAILEY, FLORENCE M. Birds of New Mexico. NM Dept Game & Fish, 1928. 1st ed. 76 full-color plts. Grn cl, gilt. VG. *Price.* $195/£125

BAILEY, FREDERICK RANDOLPH and ADAM MARION MIILER. Text-Book of Embryology. NY, 1911. 2nd ed. Grn cl bds (sl worn). VG. *Doctor's Library.* $45/£29

BAILEY, H. and W. J. BISHOP. Notable Names in Medicine and Surgery. Springfield, 1959. 3rd ed. VG. *Fye.* $90/£58

BAILEY, H. C. The Apprehensive Dog. GC: DCC, 1942. 1st Amer ed. VG in dj (spine faded, wear along folds, short closed tears, chipped). *Mordida.* $45/£29

BAILEY, H. C. Meet Mr. Fortune. GC: DCC, 1942. 1st Amer ed. Fine in VG dj (price-clipped, spine ends chipping, closed crease-tears, stain back panel). *Mordida.* $45/£29

BAILEY, H. C. Mr. Fortune Speaking. NY: E.P. Dutton, 1931. 1st Amer ed. Fine in VG dj (spine ends chipped, frayed, 1-inch piece missing back panel, chip, wear to folds). *Mordida.* $45/£29

BAILEY, H. C. Nobody's Vineyard. GC: DCC, 1942. 1st Amer ed. VG in dj (spine ends, corners chipped, closed tears). *Mordida.* $40/£26

BAILEY, H. C. Nobody's Vineyard. GC: Doubleday, 1942. 1st ed. NF (bkpl) in dj (tape-mended). *Beasley.* $30/£19

BAILEY, H. C. The Queen of Spades. GC: DCC, 1944. 1st Amer ed. VG in dj (spine ends, corners sl worn, crease-tear back panel). *Mordida.* $40/£26

BAILEY, H. C. The Wrong Man. London: Macdonald, (1946). 1st Eng ed. Fine in VG dj (chip, sl wear spine top, short closed tears). *Mordida.* $65/£42

BAILEY, HAROLD H. The Birds of Florida. Balt: The Author, 1925. Ltd ed. Inscribed. 76 full-pg color plts, fldg map. Brn buckram. Good. *Karmiole.* $185/£119

BAILEY, L. H. The Standard Cyclopedia of Horticulture. NY: Macmillan, 1939. 3 vol ed. 24 color, 96 halftone plts. Fine set. *Quest.* $165/£106

BAILEY, L. H. The Standard Cyclopedia of Horticulture. NY, 1943. Corrected ed. 3 vols. 24 color, 96 halftone plts. Grn cl. VG+ (eps tanned, text edges sl spotted) in djs (chipped). *Brooks.* $175/£112

BAILEY, L. H. with G. H. M. LAWRENCE. The Garden of Bellflowers in North America. NY, 1953. Color frontis, 50 b/w plts. VG in dj. *Brooks.* $45/£29

BAILEY, LYNN R. If You Take My Sheep. Pasadena, CA: Westernlore, 1980. 1st ed. VG in dj (sl worn). *Lien.* $30/£19

BAILEY, N. An Universal Etymological English Dictionary.... R. Ware, 1753. 15th ed. (952)pp (margin trimmed from tp foot). Contemp panelled calf (newly rebacked), orig morocco label. *Cox.* $101/£65

BAILEY, PHILIP A. Golden Mirages. NY: Macmillan, 1940. 1st ed. Frontis, 24 full-pg illus, 8 maps. Dj (wear top edge, top tips bumped). *Dawson.* $30/£19

BAILEY, PHILIP JAMES. The Mystic and Other Poems. Boston: Ticknor & Fields, 1856. 1st Amer ed. 12pp ads dated Nov 1855. Blind-stamped brn cl. Fine. *Sumner & Stillman.* $50/£32

BAILEY, V. H. Skyscrapers of New York. NY: W.E. Rudge, 1928. 1st ed. Frontis, 23 sketches. Paper-cvrd bds, cl spine. Dj (sm nicks, tears). *Marlborough.* $273/£175

BAILEY, WILLIAM WHITMAN. My Boyhood at West Point. Providence, RI, 1891. 1st ed. Ltd to 250. PNRISSHS Series 4, #12. 38pp. NF in ptd wrappers. *Mcgowan.* $45/£29

BAILLIE, G. H. Britten's Old Clocks and Watches and Their Makers. NY, (1956). Fldg frontis. VG in dj. *Argosy.* $125/£80

BAILLIE, G. H. Britten's Old Clocks and Watches. NY: Bonanza, 1956. 7th ed. 183 plts. 1/4 blue cl, bds. Fine in dj. *Weber.* $20/£13

BAILLIE, G. H. Clocks and Watches: An Historical Bibliography. Volume 1. London: NAG, (1951). 1st ed. VG in dj (very worn). *Weber.* $75/£48

BAILLIE, G. H. Watches, Their History, Decoration and Mechanism. London: Methuen, (1929). 1st ed. Color frontis. Red cl. (Back hinge starting.) *Weber.* $200/£128

BAILLIE, G. H. Watchmakers and Clockmakers of the World. London: Methuen, (1929). 1st ed. Teg. Red cl. (Lt spotting), else Fine. Inscribed by Hyde & Sons, Jewellers, Southgate. *Weber.* $200/£128

BAILLIE, G. H. Watchmakers and Clockmakers of the World. London: NAG, (1951). 3rd ed. Brn cl. (Spine ends sl frayed), else VG. *Weber.* $25/£16

BAILLIE, G. H. Watchmakers and Clockmakers of the World. London: N.A.G. Press, 1976. 2 vols. 14pp maps. VG in djs. *Hollett.* $101/£65

BAILLIE, JOANNA. Miscellaneous Plays. London/Edinburgh: Longman et al/A. Constable, 1804. 1st ed. (New eps.) Contemp tree calf (edgewear, rebacked), leather labels. Contents VG. *Dramatis Personae.* $80/£51

BAILLIE, JOHN. A Memoir of Captain W. T. Bate. NY: Carter, 1859. 1st ed. Frontis, 278pp. (Cl sl worn, soiled; fore-edge sl stained, ex-lib, #), o/w VG. *Worldwide.* $45/£29

BAILLIE, MARIANNE. Lisbon in the Years 1821, 1822 and 1823. John Murray, 1824. 2 vols. (Sl spotted; sig fep.) Contemp 1/2 leather, marbled bds (lacks 1 spine label; hinges, corners rubbed). Good. *Tiger.* $125/£80

BAILLIE, MATTHEW. The Morbid Anatomy of Some of the Most Important Parts of the Human Body. Albany, 1795. 1st Amer ed. (2)leaves, viii,248pp, (6)leaves (foxed, sl stains). Contemp calf (rubbed). *Oinonen*.* $170/£109

BAILLIE, MATTHEW. The Morbid Anatomy of Some of the Most Important Parts of the Human Body. Albany: Barber & Southwick, 1795. 1st Amer ed. Contemp Amer sheep (joints, spine cracked; browned, contemp name, lib bkpl). *Maggs.* $164/£105

BAILLIE, MATTHEW. The Morbid Anatomy of Some of the Most Important Parts of the Human Body. 1797. 2nd ed. xxxvi,460pp (foxed). Contemp leather (rebacked). *Whitehart.* $281/£180

BAILLIE, MRS. W. W. Days and Nights of Shikar. London, 1921. Color frontis. Nice (lt foxed). *Grayling.* $101/£65

BAILLIE-GROHMAN, W. A. Fifteen Years' Sport and Life in the Hunting Grounds of Western America and British Columbia. London: Horace Cox, 1900. 1st ed. 3 fldg maps in rear pocket. Grn cl. (Soiled, shaken), else VG. *Cummins.* $350/£224

BAILLIE-GROHMAN, W. A. Fifteen Years' Sport and Life in the Hunting Grounds of Western America and British Columbia. London: Horace Cox, 1900. 1st ed. Frontis photo port, 2pp ('press opinions'); xii,407pp; 15 photo plts. Pale grn cl (sl mkd, fore-edge lt spotted), gilt. Superbly Bright. *Sotheran.* $465/£298

BAIN, F. W. (trans). The Ashes of God. NY/London: Putnam/Knickerbocker, 1911. 1st Amer ed. 8vo. Frontis, xxiii,152pp, 6pp pub's cat (2 rear pp roughly opened). Dk blue cl (bumped, soiled, edges dknd, spine faded), gilt. Good. *Blue Mountain.* $25/£16

BAIN, IAIN. The Watercolours and Drawings of Thomas Bewick and His Workshop Apprentices. (Hants/Detroit): Winchester/Omnigraphics, 1989. 1 vol different color cl. *Europa.* $86/£55

BAINBRIDGE, BERYL. The Bottle Factory Outing. NY: Braziller, (1975). 1st Amer ed. NF in dj (nick, sl worn). *Antic Hay.* $25/£16

BAINBRIDGE, BERYL. A Weekend with Claud. London: New Authors Ltd, 1967. 1st UK ed, 1st bk. VG + in VG dj (sl creased, sm closed tear). *Williams.* $86/£55

BAINBRIDGE, BERYL. Winter Garden. London: Duckworth, 1980. 1st ed. Very Nice in dj. *Virgo.* $31/£20

BAINBRIDGE, H. C. Peter Carl Faberge, Goldsmith and Jeweller to the Russian Imperial Court. London, (1949). Folio. Dj. *Swann*.* $69/£44

BAINBRIDGE, H. C. Peter Carl Faberge, Goldsmith and Jeweller to the Russian Imperial Court. London: Spring Books, (1966). Rpt. Color frontis, 128 plts. Mustard cl. VG (stamp) in dj. *Weber.* $45/£29

BAINBRIDGE, H. C. Peter Carl Faberge, Goldsmith and Jeweller to the Russian Imperial Court.... London: Batsford, (1949). 1st trade ed. One of 750. Tipped-in errata slip. 126 photo plts. Crimson cl (sl rubbed; sl aged; portions of chipped dj laid in at fr). *Baltimore*.* $40/£26

BAINBRIDGE, H. C. Peter Carl Faberge, Goldsmith and Jeweller to the Russian Imperial Court.... London: Batsford, (1949). Orig ed, pub at 7 pounds, 7 shillings. 127 plts (18 color). Red cl. Good in dj. *Karmiole.* $100/£64

BAINBRIDGE, H. C. Twice Seven. NY, 1934. 1st Amer ed. VG (spine sunned, extrems sl rubbed). *Polyanthos.* $25/£16

BAINES, EDWARD. History of the Cotton Manufacture in Great Britain. London: Fisher & Jackson, (1835). Good (new eps; rebacked; ex-lib). *Bookcell.* $85/£54

BAIRD, JAMES. Ishmael. Balt: Johns Hopkins, 1956. 1st ed. Fine in dj. *Lefkowicz.* $30/£19

BAIRD, JOSEPH A., JR. 1849-1869: California's Pictorial Letter Sheets. SF: Magee, 1967. 1st ed. One of 475 ptd. *Ginsberg.* $300/£192

BAIRD, W. DAVID. Peter Pitchlynn: Chief of the Choctaws. Norman: Univ of OK, (1972). 1st ed. Frontis port. VF in dj. *Argonaut.* $45/£29

BAIRD, W. DAVID. The Quapaw Indians. Norman: Univ of OK, (1980). 1st ed. VG in dj. *Lien.* $30/£19

BAKELESS, JOHN. Background to Glory: The Life of George Rogers Clark. Phila: Lippincott, 1957. 1st ed. Frontis. VG (margins pencilled) in dj (sl worn). *Lien.* $40/£26

BAKER, BLANCH M. Theatre and Allied Arts: A Guide to Books.... NY: Wilson, 1952. 1st ed. *Ginsberg.* $75/£48

BAKER, CHARLES H., JR. Blood of the Lamb. NY/Toronto: Rinehart, 1946. 1st ed. Rev slip laid in. (2pp offset), else VG in dj (lt edgeworn). *Cahan.* $65/£42

BAKER, CHARLES H., JR. The Gentleman's Companion. NY: Derrydale, 1930. Ltd to 1250. 2 vols. VG. *Truepenny.* $175/£112

BAKER, CHARLES H., JR. The Gentleman's Companion.... NY, 1939. One of 1250. 2 vols. Frontis each vol. Box (worn). *Kane*.* $60/£38

BAKER, CLYDE. Modern Gunsmithing. Plantersville: Small Arms, 1933. 2nd ed. VG in VG dj (soiled). *Bowman.* $30/£19

BAKER, DENYS VAL (ed). London Aphrodite. (1955). 1st ed. Fine in dj (sl rubbed). *Polyanthos.* $25/£16

BAKER, DENYS VAL. The Face in the Mirror. Sauk City: Arkham House, 1971. 1st ed. VF in dj (spine lt sunned). *Bromer.* $50/£32

BAKER, E. C. S. The Game-Birds of India, Burma and Ceylon. Volume II. London, 1921. 19 color plts, 2 maps, 6 plain plts. Orig 1/2 morocco (sl faded; marginal foxing). *Wheldon & Wesley.* $78/£50

BAKER, E. C. S. The Game-Birds of India, Burma and Ceylon. Volume III. London: Bombay Natural Hist Soc, 1921. 1st ed. 19 color plts, 2 color maps, 6 b/w plts. Teg. 1/2 leather, cl. (Few pen notes, rear cvr stained), else VG. *Mikesh.* $125/£80

BAKER, ERNEST. The Highlands with Rope and Rucksack. London: Witherby, 1923. 1st ed. 20 plts. (Edges, 1/2-title lt spotted; cl faded.) Dj (sl chipped). *Hollett.* $78/£50

BAKER, GEORGE. The Soul of a Skunk. London: Eric Partridge, 1930. One of 25 (of 1000) numbered, signed. Red cl. VG. *Argosy.* $65/£42

BAKER, HENRY. The Microscope Made Easy. London, 1754. 4th ed. xvi,324pp (lacks rep); 14 plts (8 fldg), fldg table. Full leather (corners rubbed), newer spine. Good (fr hinge weak). *Scribe's Perch*.* $200/£128

BAKER, HERBERT. Cecil Rhodes. OUP, 1934. 1st ed. Dj (chipped, sl soiled). *Edwards.* $23/£15

BAKER, HOUSTON, JR. A Many-Colored Coat of Dreams: The Poetry of Countee Cullen. Detroit: Broadside, 1974. 1st ed. Pb. Fine. *Beasley.* $45/£29

BAKER, HOUSTON, JR. No Matter Where You Travel, You Still Be Black. Detroit: Lotus, 1979. 1st ed. Pb. Fine. *Beasley.* $40/£26

BAKER, HOUSTON, JR. Singers of Daybreak. Washington: Howard Univ, 1974. 1st ed. Fine in NF dj. *Beasley.* $45/£29

BAKER, J. G. Handbook of the Amaryllideae. London, 1888. (Sl browned, new eps, ex-lib w/notes, insertions; cl repaired.) *Maggs.* $81/£52

BAKER, JEANNIE. Where the Forest Meets the Sea. NY: Greenwillow, 1987. 1st US ed. 8 3/4 x 11 1/4. 32pp. Glossy bds. As New in dj. *Cattermole.* $25/£16

BAKER, JOHN EARL. Explaining China. London: Philpot, 1927. 1st ed. 16 plts, 5 dbl-pg maps. (Sl rubbed, ex-lib, #, stamps reverse plts), o/w VG. *Worldwide.* $28/£18

BAKER, NICHOLSON. The Mezzanine. NY: W&N, (1988). 1st ed, 1st bk. Signed. NF in NF dj. *Robbins.* $125/£80

BAKER, NICHOLSON. The Mezzanine. NY: Weidenfeld & Nicholson, (1988). 1st ed. Fine in Fine dj. *Fuller & Saunders.* $80/£51

BAKER, NICHOLSON. Room Temperature. NY: Grove Weidenfeld, 1990. 1st ed. Signed. Fine in Fine dj. *Beasley.* $100/£64

BAKER, NICHOLSON. U and I. Granta Books, 1991. 1st UK ed. Fine in dj. *Williams.* $19/£12

BAKER, R. S. Woodrow Wilson Life and Letters. Doubleday, Page, 1927. Stated 1st ed. 2 vols. (Stains, bumps), o/w Good + . *Scribe's Perch*.* $24/£15

BAKER, RICHARD M. Death Stops the Bells. NY: Scribner, 1938. 1st ed. Fine in dj (panels sl creasing, corners sl worn). *Mordida.* $45/£29

BAKER, RUSSELL. So This Is Depravity. NY: Congdon & Lattes, (1980). 1st ed. One of 500 numbered, signed. Fine in slipcase. *Hermitage.* $75/£48

BAKER, SAMUEL W. The Albert N'Yanza, Great Basin of the Nile, and Explorations of the Nile Sources. London: Macmillan, 1866. 2 vols. Vol 1: 8 plts incl frontis (2 loose w/edges frayed), 2 chromolitho maps (1 fldg w/tears); Vol 2: 7 plts incl chromolitho frontis. Lacks 2 maps called for on p358 (not issued?). 1/2 calf, cl bds (edges, spine worn, repaired chip). *Waverly*.* $143/£92

BAKER, SAMUEL W. The Albert N'Yanza, Great Basin of the Nile, and Explorations of the Nile Sources. London: Macmillan, 1867. 1st ed. 2 vols. Frontis port, xxx,371; tinted litho frontis, x,(ii),372pp, 1/2-title in vol 2; 2 maps (1 fldg), 12 engr plts. (Fldg map torn, repaired; sl foxing each vol.) Grn cl (sl rubbed, stained), gilt. Generally VG. *Morrell.* $195/£125

BAKER, SAMUEL W. The Albert Nyanza, Great Basin of the Nile, and Explorations of the Nile Sources. London/Phila: Macmillan/Lippincott, 1866. Frontis port, xxvi,516pp; lg fldg map; erratum tipped in. Dk grn cl, gilt. Good+ (interior hinge, spine repaired; dated inscrip; corner wear). *Backman.* $75/£48

BAKER, SAMUEL W. The Albert Nynanza, Great Basin of the Nile. London: Macmillan, 1866. 1-vol ed. xxvi,516pp; map. Brn 1/2 morocco. VG. *Terramedia.* $125/£80

BAKER, SAMUEL W. Eight Years in Ceylon. London: Longmans, Green, 1902. xvi,376pp; 6 full-pg wood-engr illus. (Bkpls, prelims sl browned), o/w VG. *Sotheran.* $133/£85

BAKER, SAMUEL W. Eight Years' Wanderings in Ceylon. London, 1855. xii,423pp (marginal browning); 5 chromolitho plts (lacks 1; lacks pp.xi-xiv, all supplied in photocopy). Blind-emb cl (faded, rebacked, much of orig spine laid down). *Edwards.* $39/£25

BAKER, SAMUEL W. Eight Years' Wanderings. NY: Lovell, n.d. (ca 1890). 323pp. (Cl sl rubbed, sl soiled), o/w VG. *Worldwide.* $16/£10

BAKER, SAMUEL W. Explorations of the Nile Tributaries of Abyssinia. Hartford: O.D. Case, 1868. 1st Amer ed. 2 maps (1 fldg). Nice (plt loose; edges rubbed, spine ends frayed). *Hermitage.* $200/£128

BAKER, SAMUEL W. Explorations of the Nile Tributaries of Abyssinia. Hartford, 1869. Contents VG (lt worn, spine sl faded). *New Hampshire**. $45/£29

BAKER, SAMUEL W. Ismailia: A Narrative of the Expedition to Central Africa. NY: Harper, 1875. 1st Amer ed. 542pp; 2 colored maps (1 fldg). Brn gilt pict cl. Nice. *Terramedia.* $200/£128

BAKER, SAMUEL W. The Nile Tributaries of Abyssinia. London, 1867. 1st ed. Frontis port, xxii,(i),596pp (lt browning, hinges taped); 23 plts (w/o plt of Coor as issued? but w/extra plt pg 485), 2 maps (1 fldg). Gilt-illus cl (spine worn, recased, splits repaired). *Edwards.* $195/£125

BAKER, SAMUEL W. The Nile Tributaries of Abyssinia. London: Macmillan, 1871. 3rd ed. xx,568pp; 25 plts. Unopened. Blue gilt pict cl (sl worn), else VG. *Terramedia.* $200/£128

BAKER, SAMUEL W. The Nile Tributaries of Abyssinia. London: Macmillan, 1894. 413pp; 2 maps, 23 plts. (Lt rubbed.) *Adelson.* $60/£38

BAKER, SAMUEL W. The Nile Tributaries of Abyssinia. London, 1908. 2 maps (1 fldg). Blind-ruled cl, gilt. *Edwards.* $31/£20

BAKER, SAMUEL W. The Nile Tributaries of Abyssinia.... London: Macmillan, 1874. New ed. xx,414pp + 56pp ads; 2 maps (1 fldg), 24 wood engrs. Later 1/2 dk brn morocco (rebound), brn cl, gilt spine. *Karmiole.* $100/£64

BAKER, SAMUEL W. The Rifle and Hound in Ceylon. NY: Lovell, n.d. (ca 1920). (Sl foxed; tattered, soiled, spine torn), o/w Good in wraps. *Worldwide.* $20/£13

BAKER, SAMUEL W. Wild Beasts and Their Ways. London, 1890. 1st ed. 2 vols. Nice (plts lt foxed, feps vol 2 mkd, sl creased). *Grayling.* $195/£125

BAKER, WILLARD F. Bob Dexter and the Storm Mountain Mystery. Cupples & Leon, 1925. 5x7.5. 250pp + ads. Gray pict cl. Lists to this title. VG (bumped) in dj (worn, spotted). *My Bookhouse.* $20/£13

BAKER, WILLIAM AVERY. Colonial Vessels. Barre: Barre Pub, 1962. 1st ed. 3 sheets of plans laid in. *Lefkowicz.* $45/£29

BAKER, WILLIAM AVERY. The Mayflower and Other Colonial Vessels. (Annapolis): Naval Inst, (1983). 1st Amer ed. Dj. *Lefkowicz.* $40/£26

BAKER, WILLIAM B. The Life and Labours of the Rev. Daniel Baker.... Phila: Presbyterian Board of Publication, 1858. 3rd ed. Port, 560pp. (Text sl spotted, lacks eps; worn, soiled, spine loss), else Good. *Brown.* $25/£16

BALANCHINE, GEORGE. Choreography. NY: Eakins Press, (1983). 1st ed. Ltd to 2000 ptd. Port. Beige linen, blue paper spine label. Good. *Karmiole.* $150/£96

BALCH, THOMAS WILLING. The Alabama Arbitration. Phila, 1900. 1st ed. VG. *Wantagh.* $35/£22

BALDRY, A. L. Contemporary Figure Painters. The Studio, n.d. 24 color plts tipped in. (Upper hinge sl cracked, feps lt foxed.) Blind emb cl. *Edwards.* $39/£25

BALDRY, A. L. Modern Mural Decoration. London: Georges Newnes, 1902. 1st ed. Pict eps; aeg. Blue cl, gilt. (Rubbed), else Fine. *Glenn.* $150/£96

BALDRY, GEORGE. The Rabbit Skin Cap. London: Collins, 1939. 1st ed. Color frontis, 12 full-pg illus by Edward Seago. Coarse-weave cl. VG in dj. *Hollett.* $70/£45

BALDWIN, ALICE BLACKWOOD. An Army Wife on the Frontier...1867-1877. Salt Lake City, (1975). 1st ed. Ltd to 1200. Fine in Fine dj. *Pratt.* $45/£29

BALDWIN, C. L. Quinquivara. NY: Gemor, 1944. 1st ed. Ltd to 300. Inscribed presentation. Pict white bds. Fine in tissue dj. *Blue Mountain.* $95/£61

BALDWIN, CHARLES N. Universal Biographical Dictionary.... Richmond, VA: White, 1826. Frontis, 44pp. Orig full calf, dec spine. *Ginsberg.* $100/£64

BALDWIN, ELMER. History of La Salle County, Illinois. Chicago: Rand, McNally, 1877. Frontis photo, 552pp; 3 full-pg maps. Gilt-dec cl (discolored). *Cullen.* $125/£80

BALDWIN, J. H. Large and Small Game of Bengal and the North-Western Provinces of India. London: Kegan Paul, 1883. 2nd ed. xxiv,380pp. Grn gilt pict cl. (Name on tp, slight wear, recased), else VG. *Terramedia.* $200/£128

BALDWIN, JAMES and MARGARET MEAD. A Rap on Race. Phila: Lippincott, (1971). 1st ed. Fine in dj (few sm tears). *Captain's Bookshelf.* $35/£22

BALDWIN, JAMES. Another Country. NY, 1962. 1st Amer ed. Fine (spine lt rubbed) in dj (spine lt sunned, lt rubbed, sm tear spine, price-clipped). *Polyanthos.* $75/£48

BALDWIN, JAMES. The Devil Finds Work. London, 1976. 1st Eng ed. Fine in dj. *Clearwater.* $31/£20

BALDWIN, JAMES. Giovanni's Room. NY: Dial, 1956. 1st ed. VG (name) in dj (very worn, lg chip fr flap). *Metropolitan**. $57/£37

BALDWIN, JAMES. If Beale Street Could Talk. NY: Dial, 1974. One of 250 numbered, signed. Fine in Fine slipcase. *Lenz.* $300/£192

BALDWIN, JAMES. Just Above My Head. NY: Dial, (1979). One of 500 numbered, signed. Fine in Fine slipcase. *Lenz.* $200/£128

BALDWIN, JAMES. Little Man Little Man. (London): Michael Joseph, (1976). 1st ed. Signed by Baldwin. Fine in Fine dj. *Lenz.* $125/£80

BALDWIN, JAMES. Little Man Little Man. NY: Dial Press, (1976). 1st ed. Rev copy; pub photo, prospectus laid in. Yoran Cazac (illus). Pict bds. VF in dj (sl chip). *Bromer.* $110/£71

BALDWIN, JAMES. Notes of a Native Son. Boston: Beacon, 1955. 1st ed. NF in VG dj (spine faded, short tear). *Lame Duck.* $125/£80

BALDWIN, LELAND D. The Keelboat Age on Western Waters. Univ of Pittsburgh, 1941. 1st ed. VG in dj. *Lien.* $75/£48

BALDWIN, LELAND D. Whiskey Rebels: The Story of a Frontier Uprising. Univ of Pittsburgh, 1939. 1st ed. VG in dj. *Lien.* $50/£32

BALDWIN, MUNSON. With Brass and Gas: An Illustrated...Chronicle of Ballooning in Mid-19th Century America. Beacon, 1967. VG. *Bookcell.* $20/£13

BALDWIN, S. P. and S. C. KENDEIGH. Physiology of the Temperature of Birds. Cleveland: Museum of Natural History, 1932. 1st ed. 23 tables. VG +. *Mikesh.* $47/£30

BALDWIN, T. W. Shakspeare's 'Love's Labor's Won': New Evidence from the Account Books of an Elizabethan Bookseller. Carbondale: Southern IL Univ, 1957. 1st ed of 2500. Black cl spine, gilt title, vellum patterned paper over bd. Fine in dj (price-clipped, several tears). *Heller.* $45/£29

BALDWIN, THOMAS. Introduction to Irish Farming. London: Macmillan, 1874. 1st ed. 169pp (ex-lib, name stamps, final text leaf torn, sl loss). Flexible cl. *Second Life.* $45/£29

BALE, FLORENCE GRATIOT. Galena's Yesterdays. Waukegan, IL: Skokie Press, (1931-1939). 2 vols. Orig pict ptd wrappers (soft vertical crease 1st vol). *Sadlon.* $15/£10

BALFOUR, ARTHUR JAMES. Essays Speculative and Political. London: Hodder & Stoughton, 1920. 1st ed. VG (bkpl; sm faded spine label, few nicks). *Burmester.* $31/£20

BALFOUR-KINNEAR, G. P. R. Flying Salmon. London, 1947. 1st ed. *Petersfield.* $50/£32

BALFOUR-KINNEAR, G. P. R. Spinning Salmon. Longmans, (1938). (Fore-edge sl foxed; binding sl faded.) *Petersfield.* $62/£40

BALL, CHARLES. The History of the Indian Mutiny. London: London Ptg & Pub Co, (1858-1859). 1st ed in bk form bound up from orig parts. 2 vols. Engr frontispieces, extra tps, (iv),(1)-32,2,(viii),33-(648); (4),viii,(664)pp. Contemp 1/2 calf (sl rubbed, worn). Good (sl thumbed, foxed; marginal nicks, tears, 2 plts torn, affecting image). *Ash.* $304/£195

BALL, ELIZA CRAUFURD. The Christian Armour. NY: (Scribner), 1866. 4to. 31 leaves. Aeg, inner dentelles, marbled eps. Full brn morocco, beveled bds, heavily emb in blind, gilt-dec, sunken oval panels in which title appears above/below shield, sword; spine w/5 raised bands, gilt dec, no title. Fine. *Book Block.* $1,250/£801

BALL, J. DYER. The Chinese at Home. London: Religious Tract Soc, 1911. 1st ed. 7 color plts, color tp, 21 monochrome plts. Pict cl (spine faded), gilt. *Hollett.* $133/£85

BALL, J. DYER. Things Chinese. NY: Scribner, 1906. 4th ed. (Margin pencil mks; sl rubbed, soiled, sl silverfished), o/w VG. *Worldwide.* $35/£22

BALL, JAMES M. Modern Ophthalmology. Phila, 1904. 1st ed. VG. *Doctor's Library.* $75/£48

BALL, JAMES M. The Sack-'em-Up Men. Edinburgh, 1928. 1st ed. 60 Fine plts. VG. *Argosy.* $75/£48

BALL, JOHN. Ball's Alpine Guide to the Western Alps. London: Longmans, Green, 1898. New ed. xlix,612pp; 10 fldg color maps, errata list loosely inserted. Beige cl. VG (inner joint sl weak, repaired). *Sotheran.* $101/£65

BALL, JOHN. Edwards: Flight Test Center of the U.S.A.F. NY: Duell, Sloan & Pearce, (1962). 1st US ed. Bkpl of Dr. Julian Wolff laid in. VG in VG dj (lt wear). *Gravesend.* $40/£26

BALL, JOHN. The Eyes of Buddha. Boston: Little, Brown, 1976. 1st ed. Good + (sl cocked) in Good + dj (tear lower edge). *Old London.* $20/£13

BALL, JOHN. The Kiwi Target. NY: Carroll & Graf, 1989. 1st ed. Fine in Fine dj. *Old London.* $15/£10

BALL, JOHN. The Western Alps. London: Longmans, Green, 1898. New ed. Lg fldg map frontis (sl torn), 612pp; 9 fldg maps. (Spine sl snagged.) *Hollett.* $117/£75

BALL, RICHARD. Hounds Will Meet. London/NY: Country Life/Scribner, 1931. 16 full-pg b/w plts by Lionel Edwards. VG in Good- dj. *October Farm.* $45/£29

BALL, TIMOTHY H. Northwestern Indiana from 1800 to 1900. La Porte, IN, 1900. 1st ed. 4 fldg maps, port. (Sm rubber stamp.) Howes B71. *Ginsberg.* $175/£112

BALL, W. VALENTINE. Reminiscences and Letters of Sir Robert Ball. Boston, 1915. 1st Amer ed. 9 photo plts. Teg. Blue cl, gilt. (Ex-lib, perforations tp), else VG. *Price.* $34/£22

Ballads and Lyrics of Love. C&W, 1908. 1st ed. Tall 8vo. xvii,180pp; 10 color plts by Byam Shaw. Teg. VG (cl sl faded). *Bookmark.* $39/£25

BALLANTYNE, R. M. Fighting the Whales. London: James Nisbet, 1886. 12mo. Frontis, (iii),124pp + 2pp ads (soiled, stained); 2 plts. Blue cl (cocked, bumped, rubbed, soiled, starting). Good. *Blue Mountain.* $25/£16

BALLANTYNE, R. M. In the Track of the Troops: A Tale of Modern War. James Nisbet, 1881. New ed. Pub's cat. Pict beveled bds (spine bumped, chipped, sl sunned; sm mk upper cvr). Good (sig, inner hinges cracked). *Tiger.* $53/£34

BALLANTYNE, R. M. The Prairie Chief. James Nisbet, (1886). 4th thousand. Contemp 1/2 leather, marbled bds, raised bands (spine sl sunned). VG (sl thumb mks). *Tiger.* $41/£26

BALLANTYNE, R. M. The Prairie Chief. James Nisbet, n.d. 7th ed. Pub's cat (several pp missing). Pict cl (spine bumped, chipped). Good. *Tiger.* $39/£25

BALLANTYNE, R. M. The World of Ice or, The Whaling Cruise of 'The Dolphin.' T. Nelson, 1877. Rpt. Pict cl (spine bumped, chipped; hinges, corners rubbed). Good (prize label fr pastedown, fore-edge spotted). *Tiger.* $41/£26

BALLARD, ADOLPHUS. The Domesday Inquest. London, 1906. 1st ed. Gilt-edged cl. (Feps lt browned, lib bkpl; spine sl faded.) *Edwards.* $39/£25

BALLARD, GEORGE. Memoirs of British Ladies. London: T. Evans, 1775. 3rd ed. 320pp + index. Contemp calf. VG. *Second Life.* $350/£224

BALLARD, J. G. Crash. NY: FSG, (1973). 1st Amer ed. (Sl fading top edges), o/w NF in dj. *Hermitage.* $85/£54

BALLARD, J. G. The Crystal World. NY: FSG, 1966. 1st ed. Fine (sl faded) in dj (foxing, wear). *Metropolitan*.* $23/£15

BALLARD, J. G. The Day of Creation. London: Gollancz, 1987. 1st Eng ed. Signed. Fine in dj. *Hadley.* $39/£25

BALLARD, J. G. The Day of Creation. London: Gollancz, 1987. One of 100 numbered, signed. Fine in cl slipcase, not issued in dj. *Certo.* $125/£80

BALLARD, J. G. Empire of the Sun. Gollancz, 1984. 1st UK ed. Signed. Mint in Mint 1st state dj w/2 quotes back panel. *Martin.* $31/£20

BALLARD, J. G. Empire of the Sun. London, 1984. True 1st ed. Fine in NF dj. *Warren.* $75/£48

BALLARD, J. G. High-Rise. London: Cape, (1975). 1st ed. Dj. *Swann*.* $80/£51

BALLARD, J. G. The Inner Landscape. London: Allison & Busby, 1969. 1st Eng ed. VG in dj (rubbed, few creases). *Hadley.* $31/£20

BALLARD, J. G. Love and Napalm: Export U.S.A. NY, 1972. 1st Amer ed. Fine in Fine dj. *Warren.* $50/£32

BALLARD, J. G. The Unlimited Dream Company. NY: Holt, Rinehart & Winston, (1979). 1st Amer ed. Black cl-backed grn bds, gilt. Fine in NF dj (sl bumped, spine head chipped). *Blue Mountain.* $20/£13

BALLARD, J. G. The Unlimited Dream Company. London: Cape, 1979. 1st ed. Fine in dj. *Virgo.* $31/£20

BALLARD, JULIA P. Among the Moths and Butterflies. NY: Putnam, 1893. 367,237pp. Dec cvr, spine. Good + . *Scribe's Perch*.* $16/£10

BALLARD, W. T. Hot Dam. Greenwich, CT: Gold Medal #964, 1960. 1st ed, pb orig. (Lt crease; nick spine foot), else NF. *Murder By The Book.* $15/£10

BALLIETT, WHITNEY. Dinosaurs in the Morning. Phila: Lippincott, 1962. 1st ed. Fine in Fine dj (sl sunned spine). *Beasley.* $125/£80

BALLIETT, WHITNEY. The Sound of Surprise. NY: Dutton, 1959. 1st ed, 1st bk. Fine in Fine dj. *Beasley.* $125/£80

BALLOU, DANIEL ROSS. The Military Services of Maj. Gen. Ambrose Everett Burnside in the Civil War. Providence, RI, 1914. 1st eds. Ltd to 250. PNRISSHS Series 7, #8, 9. 2 vols. NF in ptd wrappers. *Mcgowan.* $65/£42

BALLOU, ELLEN B. The Building of the House. Boston: Houghton, Mifflin, 1970. 1st ed, 2nd ptg. Grn cl, gilt. VF. *Macdonnell.* $25/£16

BALLOU, M. M. The New Eldorado. Boston: Houghton Mifflin, 1890. 2nd ed. xi,352pp. Dec cl. VG. *High Latitude.* $40/£26

BALLOU, M. M. Under the Southern Cross, or Travels in Australia, Tasmania, New Zealand, Samoa, and Other Pacific Islands. Boston, 1888. 1st ed. 405pp. Good. *Hayman.* $20/£13

BALNIEL, LORD and KENNETH CLARK (eds). A Commemorative Catalogue of the Exhibition of Italian Art Held...January-March 1930. London, Royal Academy, 1931. 2 vols. 1 plt, 252 collotype plts. Internally VG (cl lt worn, sl soiled). *Washton.* $150/£96

BALSTON, THOMAS. English Wood-Engraving 1900-1950. Art & Technics, 1951. Fine dj. *Petersfield.* $31/£20

BALSTON, THOMAS. The Life of Jonathan Martin.... London: Macmillan, 1945. 1st ed. 16 plts. VG in dj (lt spotted). *Hollett.* $39/£25

BALSTON, THOMAS. The Wood-Engravings of Robert Gibbings. London: Art & Technics, 1949. 1st ed, 2nd ptg. Grn cl. (Spine faded), else Very Nice. *Turtle Island.* $45/£29

Baltimore City Directory 1920. Balt: R.L. Polk, 1920. Fldg map at fr. Maroon/grn cl w/ads. (Tp creased, torn; cvrs stained, worn.) Map Good; text Sound. *Baltimore*.* $200/£128

Baltimore City Directory for the Year Commencing April 1st, 1912. Balt: R.L. Polk, 1912. Black/yellow cl w/ptd ads. (Sl worn, sl dusty.) *Baltimore*.* $180/£115

BALTZ, LEWIS. Park City. Albuquerque/NY: Art Space/Castelli Graphics, 1980. 1st ed. 102 b/w photo plts. Fine in pict dj. *Cahan.* $175/£112

BALZAC, HONORE DE. See DE BALZAC, HONORE

BAMBARA, TONI CADE. The Salt Eaters. NY: Random House, (1980). 1st ed. Cl-backed bds. VG in dj (lt chipped). *Petrilla.* $30/£19

Bancroft's Official Guide Map, City and County of San Francisco. SF: A.L. Bancroft, 1873. Fldg into orig cl cvrs. *Dawson.* $150/£96

BANCROFT, FREDERIC W. and HENRY C. MARBLE. Surgical Treatment of the Motor-Skeletal System. Phila, 1951. 2nd ed. 2 vols. Good (underlining; worn). *Doctor's Library.* $75/£48

BANCROFT, GRIFFING. The Flight of the Least Petrel. NY: Putnam, 1932. Inscribed by Margaret Bancroft. Fldg map (sm marginal tear). Black cl (sl shelfwear). VG + in dj (clipped, worn). *Parmer.* $65/£42

BANCROFT, HUBERT HOWE. California Inter Pocula. SF: History Co, 1888. 1st ed. French cl (newly bound), leather labels. Fine. *Argonaut.* $75/£48

BANCROFT, HUBERT HOWE. California Pastoral. SF, 1888. 1st ed. vi,808pp. All edges marbled. Orig full calf. VG + . Howes B91. *Turpen.* $100/£64

BANCROFT, HUBERT HOWE. History of Alaska 1730-1885. SF: History Co, 1890. 775pp. Fine (rebound). *Perier.* $150/£96

BANCROFT, HUBERT HOWE. History of British Columbia 1792-1887. SF, 1887. 1st ed. 3 vols. xxxi,792pp. All edges marbled. Orig full calf. (2-inch crack rear joint), o/w VG. Howes B91. *Turpen.* $95/£61

BANCROFT, HUBERT HOWE. History of Mexico 1516-1887. SF, 1883-88. 1st ed. 6 vols. All edges marbled. Orig full calf. (1-inch chip from spine top vol 1), o/w VG + . Howes B91. *Turpen.* $210/£135

BANCROFT, HUBERT HOWE. History of Nevada, Colorado and Wyoming 1540-1888. SF, 1890. 1st ed. xvii,828pp. All edges marbled. Orig full calf. (2-inch crack rear joint, corner worn), o/w VG. *Turpen.* $95/£61

BANCROFT, HUBERT HOWE. History of Oregon 1834-1888. SF, 1886-88. 1st ed. 2 vols. xvii,789; xv,808pp. All edges marbled. Orig full calf. (Joints cracked), o/w VG + . *Turpen.* $150/£96

BANCROFT, HUBERT HOWE. History of the Life of Leland Stanford: A Character Study. Oakland: Biobooks, 1952. Ltd to 750. 2-tone red cl. Fine. *Argonaut.* $60/£38

BANCROFT, HUBERT HOWE. History of the North Mexican States and Texas, 1531-1889. SF: A.L. Bancroft/The History Co, 1884/1889. 2 vols. x1viii,751; xvi,814pp, fldg map. Newly bound in French cl, red/black leather labels. Fine. Howes B91. *Argonaut.* $300/£192

BANCROFT, HUBERT HOWE. History of the Northwest Coast. SF: History Co, 1886. 2 vols. 735;768pp. Red cl. VG. *Perier.* $135/£87

BANCROFT, HUBERT HOWE. History of Utah 1540-1886. SF, 1889. 1st ed. xx,808pp. All edges marbled. Orig full calf. VG + . *Turpen.* $100/£64

BANCROFT, HUBERT HOWE. Literary Industries. SF: The History Co, 1890. 1st ed. Frontis port, vii,808pp. Newly bound in French cl, red/black leather labels. Fine. *Argonaut.* $90/£58

BANCROFT, HUBERT HOWE. Literary Industries: A Memoir. NY: Harper, 1891. Inscribed. Frontis (loose), 446pp + ads. (Sl worn.) *Dawson.* $50/£32

BANCROFT, HUBERT HOWE. Popular Tribunals. SF: The History Co, 1887. 1st ed. 2 vols. xiii,749; viii,772pp; fldg map, facs. Newly bound in French cl, red/black leather labels (dampstaining some leaf edges vol 1), else Fine. *Argonaut.* $175/£112

BANCROFT, HUBERT HOWE. Register of Pioneer Inhabitants of California, 1542 to 1848. L.A.: Dawson's Book Shop, 1964. Blue cl (sl rubbed, sm dent fr cvr). NF. *Argonaut.* $45/£29

BANCROFT, HUBERT HOWE. The Works of Hubert Howe Bancroft: The Native Races. SF: A.L. Bancroft, 1882. 1st ed. 5 vols. xlix,(1),797; x,805; x,796; viii,807; xii,796pp; 3 different prospectuses in Fine condition. Brn cl, emb cvr design, gilt spine title. (Sl shelfworn), o/w Fine set. *Pacific*.* $207/£133

BANCROFT, P. The World's Finest Minerals and Crystals. NY: Viking, c 1973. VG in dj. *Blake.* $125/£80

BANDEL, EUGENE. Frontier Life in the Army, 1854-1861. Ralph P. Bieber (ed). Olga Bandel and Richard Jente (trans). Glendale: Clark, 1932. 1st ed. One of 1060. Teg. Red cl. Fine. *Argonaut.* $150/£96

BANDELIER, ADOLPH F. The Southwestern Journals of Adolph F. Bandelier. Charles H. Lange et al (eds). Albuquerque: Univ of NM, 1966, 1970, 1975, 1984. 1st eds. Each vol signed by all eds. VF set in djs. *Argonaut.* $350/£224

BANDELIER, ADOLPH F. The Southwestern Journals of Adolph F. Bandelier. Charles H. Lange et al (eds). Albuquerque: Univ of NM, 1966-1975. 1st ed. 3 vols. Different cl each vol, in djs (sl cocked). *Dawson.* $150/£96

BANDELIER, ADOLPH F. The Unpublished Letters of Adolph F. Bandelier. NY: Charles P. Everitt, 1942. One of 295. Fldg letter repro. Fine in dj (reinforced, sl dusty). *Gibbs.* $425/£272

BANDINI, JOSE. A Description of California in 1828. Doris Marion Wright (trans). Berkeley, CA: Friends of the Bancroft Library, 1951. 1st ed. Ltd to 400 ptd. 2 ports. Fine. *Argonaut.* $60/£38

Banditti of the Plains.... (By A.S. Mercer.) SF: Grabhorn Press, 1935. Arvilla Parker (illus). Ad leaflet laid in. (Tape mk inside cvrs), else VG. *Heinoldt.* $135/£87

BANFIELD, E. J. My Tropic Island. London, 1913. 3rd imp. Dec cl. (Browning; extrems rubbed.) *Edwards.* $31/£20

BANGS, JOHN KENDRICK. Mr. Munchausen. Boston: Noyes, Platt, 1901. 1st ed. This issue has Small, Maynard copyright overprinted w/Noyes, Platt handstamp on copyright pg. 8vo. 15 color plts by Peter Newell. Color pict cl (sl worn). *Oinonen*.* $30/£19

BANGS, JOHN KENDRICK. Tiddledywink Tales. Griffith Farran, c., ads dated 1891. 1st Eng ed. Charles Howard Johnson (illus). 8vo. 236+32pp. Dec grey cl (spine sl dknd, sl wear). VG. *Bookmark.* $31/£20

BANGS, JOHN KENDRICK. The Water Ghost and Others. NY, 1894. 1st ed. Pict cl. Fine. *Argosy.* $65/£42

BANHAM, REYNER. The Architecture of the Well-Tempered Environment. Univ of Chicago, 1984. 2nd rev ed. VG. *Hadley.* $25/£16

BANKART, GEORGE P. The Art of the Plasterer. Batsford, 1908. Teg. (Upper hinge sl tender, feps lt browned, ink stamp; corners, joints sl rubbed, spine head sl bumped, sm split.) *Edwards.* $195/£125

BANKOFF, GEORGE. The Story of Plastic Surgery. London, 1952. 1st ed. VG. *Fye.* $125/£80

BANKS, IAIN. Consider Phlebas. Macmillan, (1987). 1st ed. Inscribed, signed, dated. VG in dj. *Ash.* $62/£40

BANKS, IAIN. The Player of Games. London: Macmillan, (1988). 1st ed. One of 201 numbered, signed. Matching slipcase. *Swann*.* $80/£51

BANKS, IAIN. Walking on Glass. Macmillan, 1985. 1st UK ed. Fine in dj. *Williams.* $55/£35

BANKS, IAIN. The Wasp Factory. London: Macmillan, 1984. 1st ed, 1st bk. Fine in dj. *Lame Duck.* $150/£96

BANKS, LOUIS ALBERT. Censor Echoes, or Words That Burned.... Portland, OR, 1882. Frontis port, 162pp; 8 engr illus. VG (extrems sl worn). *Reese.* $85/£54

BANKS, LYNNE REID. The L-Shaped Room. London: Chatto, 1960. 1st UK ed. VG (ink name, date; sl bumped) in dj. *Williams.* $28/£18

BANKS, MARY ROSS. Bright Days in the Old Plantation Time. Boston/NY, 1882. 1st ed. 266,(2)pp. Pict gilt-stamped cl. VG. *Wantagh.* $75/£48

BANKS, MIKE. High Arctic. London, 1957. Color frontis. VG in dj. *High Latitude.* $25/£16

BANKS, OLIVER. The Caravaggio Obsession. Boston: Little, Brown, (1984). 1st ed. Fine in Fine dj. *Unger.* $40/£26

BANKS, RUSSELL. Searching for Survivors. NY: Fiction Collective, 1975. 1st ed. Fine in dj. *Hermitage.* $35/£22

BANKS, SAM W. and HAROLD LAUFMAN. Surgical Exposures of the Extremities. Phila, 1953. 1st ed. NF. *Doctor's Library.* $50/£32

BANKSON, RUSSELL. The Klondike Nugget. Caldwell: Caxton, 1935. 1st ed. VG in Poor dj (torn). *Perier.* $75/£48

BANNERMAN, D. A. The Birds of the British Isles. London, 1953-63. 12 vols. 387 color plts by G. E. Lodge. Good in djs. *Henly.* $515/£330

BANNERMAN, D. A. The Birds of West and Equatorial Africa. Oliver & Boyd, 1953. 1st ed. 2 vols. 54 plts (30 color). Red cl (sl mkd), gilt. VG set (hinge sl strained). *Hollett.* $148/£95

BANNERMAN, D. A. The Birds of West and Equatorial Africa. Edinburgh, 1953. 2 vols. 54 plts (30 color). (Sl browned; sl scruffy.) *Maggs.* $70/£45

BANNERMAN, D. A. The Canary Islands, Their History, Natural History and Scenery. London, 1922. Unopened. (Sl worn.) Dj (tattered). *New Hampshire*.* $60/£38

BANNERMAN, D. A. and W. MARY. Birds of Cyprus. Edinburgh/London, 1958. 1st ed. 16 color, 15 b/w plts, fldg map. (Ink stamp fep.) VG in dj (sl chipped). *Edwards.* $273/£175

BANNERMAN, HELEN. Little Black Sambo. (Cleveland: Harter, 1931.) 4to. 8 full-pg color illus by Fern Bisel Peat. Color pict wraps (sl worn, few crimps). *Waverly*.* $121/£78

BANNERMAN, HELEN. Sambo and the Twins. NY: Stokes, 1936. 1st Amer ed. Sm 8vo. 90pp. Fine (bkpl) in color Bannerman dj (lt chipped, soiled). *Bromer.* $185/£119

BANNERMAN, HELEN. The Story of Little Black Sambo. NY: Frederick A. Stokes, (ca 1920). 12mo. Ochre cl, color pict bds (rubbed, bumped). VG. *Houle.* $225/£144

BANNING, WILLIAM and GEORGE HUGH. Six Horses. NY: Century, (1930). 1st ed. Orig dec black cl. Fine in dj (chipped). *Argonaut.* $100/£64

BANNISTER, DON. Long Day at Shiloh. London: R&KP, (1981). Correct 1st ed. Fine in dj (price-clipped). *Captain's Bookshelf.* $60/£38

BANNON, ANN. Beebo Brinker. Greenwich: Gold Medal, 1962. 1st ed. Pb. NF (name). *Beasley.* $30/£19

BANNON, ANTHONY. The Photo-Pictorialists of Buffalo. Buffalo: Media Study, 1981. 1st ed. Ltd to 2500. 49 plts. VG (name) in pict stiff wrappers (lt rubbed). *Cahan.* $45/£29

BANNON, JOHN FRANCIS. Bolton and the Spanish Borderlands. Norman, 1968. 2nd ptg. Pb. 4 maps. VF in NF dj. *Turpen.* $55/£35

BANNON, JOHN FRANCIS. The Mission Frontier in Sonora 1620-87. NY, 1955. 1st ed. VF. *Turpen.* $45/£29

BANTA, R. E. The Ohio. NY, (1949). 1st ed. One of signed, ltd ed. VG (bkpl) in dj. *Hayman.* $25/£16

BANTA, R. E. The Ohio. NY: Rinehart, 1949. 1st ed. VG+. *Archer.* $15/£10

BANTA, WILLIAM and J. W. CALDWELL, JR. Twenty-Seven Years on the Texas Frontier. Council Hill, OK, (1933). Frontis port. Fine in ptd wraps. Howes B109. *Bohling.* $60/£38

BANTING, W. Letter on Corpulence.... London, 1864. 3rd ed. iv,5-50pp (soiled). Wrappers (spine worn). *Maggs.* $47/£30

BANTOCK, NICK. Sabine's Notebook: In Which the Extraordinary Correspondence of Griffin and Sabine Continues. SF: Chronicle Books, (1992). 1st ed. Fine in dj. *Between The Covers.* $85/£54

BANVILLE, JOHN. The Book of Evidence. London, 1989. 1st Eng ed. Fine in dj. *Clearwater*. $31/£20

BANVILLE, JOHN. Doctor Copernicus. London: Secker & Warburg, 1976. 1st UK ed. Signed. NF in dj (spine sl sunned; removed label). *Moorhouse*. $62/£40

BANVILLE, JOHN. Mefisto. London: Secker & Warburg, 1986. 1st ed. Fine in Fine dj. *Revere*. $30/£19

BANVILLE, JOHN. Nightspawn. NY: Norton, 1971. 1st US ed. Fine (last pg soiled) in VG dj. *Beasley*. $45/£29

BARAKA, IMANU AMIRI. Hard Facts. People's War, (1975). 1st ed. Fine in red stapled wrappers. *Dermont*. $25/£16

Barbarities of the Enemy, Exposed in a Report of the Committee of the House.... Worcester: Dunnell Remark, 1814. 192pp. Full calf (sl worn). (Foxed), o/w contents VG. Howes B112. *New Hampshire**. $170/£109

BARBEAU, MARIUS and EDWARD SAPIR. Folk Songs of French Canada. New Haven: Yale, 1925. 1st ed. Good (sl rubbed). *Reese*. $50/£32

BARBEAU, MARIUS. Indian Days in the Canadian Rockies. Toronto: Macmillan, 1923. 1st ed. Color frontis. Cl-backed bds, paper labels. VG in dj (chipped, few closed tears). *Cahan*. $125/£80

BARBEAU, MARIUS. Pathfinders in the North Pacific. Caldwell: Caxton/Ryerson, 1958. 1st US ed. Dec eps. Tan cl. (Head, edges foxed, soiled), else VG in VG dj. *Parmer*. $65/£42

BARBEAU, MARIUS. Totem Poles. Nat'l Museum of Canada, (1950). 2 vols. VG in wraps. *Perier*. $150/£96

BARBER, H. The Aeroplane Speaks. NY, 1918. 7th ed. 40pp of plts. *Whitehart*. $39/£25

BARBER, JOEL. Wild Fowl Decoys. GC: Garden City, 1937. VG + in VG dj (edge tears, chipped; 2-inch tear at back). *Backman*. $100/£64

BARBER, JOHN and HENRY HOWE. Historical Collections of the State of New-York. NY, 1841. Map. Pub's sheep (worn). *Swann**. $126/£81

BARBER, JOHN. Connecticut Historical Collections.... New Haven: Durrie & Peck & Barber, (1838). 1st ed. 560pp (lt foxed throughout), 6 full-pg engrs, dbl-fold hand-colored map. Marbled eps. Orig full calf (hinges rubbed), spine fully gilt. Attractive. Howes B120. *Cullen*. $125/£80

BARBER, OLIVE. Meet Me in Juneau. Portland: Binfords & Mort, 1960. 1st ed. Signed. Dec yellow cl. (Heel, ep spot), else VG in dj (worn). *Parmer*. $25/£16

BARBER, R. H. A Supplementary Bibliography of Hawking, Etc. Westminster: Fielding, 1943. One of 1000. Pict wraps. Fine in Fine custom slipcase. *Mikesh*. $55/£35

BARBEY, DANIEL. Macarthur's Amphibious Navy. Annapolis: US Naval Inst, 1969. 1st ed. Fine in dj (torn). *Archer*. $25/£16

BARBIERE, JOE. Scraps from the Prison Table at Camp Chase and Johnson's Island. Doylestown, 1868. Litho map. Pub's cl (fr joint, spine ends frayed, cvrs spotted; lt dampstained, browned). *Swann**. $126/£81

BARBOSA, DUARTE. A Description of the Coasts of East Africa and Malabar in...16th Century. London: Hakluyt Soc, 1866. xi,236pp. Mod cl. (Ex-lib.) *Adelson*. $50/£32

BARBOUR, RALPH H. Finkler's Field. Appleton, 1911. 1st ed. Emb pict cvr. VG. *Plapinger*. $60/£38

BARBOUR, RALPH H. The Junior Trophy. Appleton, 1913. 1st ed. 5x7.5. 310pp. Red cl, pict paste-on. (Bumped), else VG + in dj (chipped) w/baseball illus. *My Bookhouse*. $35/£22

BARBOUR, RALPH H. Lovell Leads Off. Appleton, 1928. VG. *Plapinger*. $50/£32

BARBOUR, RALPH H. Merrit Leads the Nine. Appleton, 1936. 1st ed. VG + . *Plapinger*. $65/£42

BARBOUR, RALPH H. New Boy at Hilltop. Appleton, 1910. 1st ed. Pict cvr. Good + . *Plapinger*. $45/£29

BARBOUR, RALPH H. Right Tackle Todd. Dodd Mead, (1924). 1st ed. 5x7.5. 291pp. Brn cl (worn). VG (lacks dj). *My Bookhouse*. $12/£8

BARBOUR, RALPH H. The Score is Tied. Appleton, 1937. Later ptg. VG. *Plapinger*. $60/£38

BARBOUR, RALPH H. Southworth Scores. Appleton, 1934. 1st ed. Sm pict cvr. Good + (sl cocked). *Plapinger*. $65/£42

BARBOUR, RALPH H. Tod Hale on the Nine. Dodd Mead, 1929. 1st ed. Pict cvr. VG. *Plapinger*. $65/£42

BARBOUR, RALPH H. Weatherby's Inning. Appleton, 1903. Later ptg. Good. *Plapinger*. $20/£13

BARBOUR, RALPH H. Winning His Game. Appleton, 1917. Later ptg. VG. *Plapinger*. $50/£32

BARBOUR, T. A Contribution to the Zoogeography of the West Indies.... Cambridge: Harvard, Mar. 1914. 1st ed. 1 plt. Uncut. Fine in wraps. *Mikesh*. $60/£38

BARBOUR, T. Reptiles and Amphibians. Boston: Houghton Mifflin, (1934). Rev ed. NF. *Mikesh*. $25/£16

BARBOUR, T. Sphaerodactylus. Cambridge: Harvard, Dec 1921. 1st ed. 26 plts. Uncut. Fine in wraps. *Mikesh*. $65/£42

BARBUT, JACQUES. The Genera Insectorum of Linnaeus Exemplified by Various Specimens of English Insects Drawn from Nature. London: (J. Dixwell for J. Sewell), 1781. 1st ed. 4to. Text in English and French. 2-pg subs list w/paragraph of Errata & Desiderata below; extensive Index and Directions to Binder follows text. 20 brilliantly hand-colored plts of insects, incl lg fldg plt; directly before Index are 2 lg plain fldg plts; all of which are by James Newton from dwgs by Author. Full contemp acid calf, enclosed thin ribbon border both cvrs; smooth rounded spine, gilt dec, morocco lettering piece. Attractive (extrems lt worn). *Book Block*. $1,500/£962

BARCLAY, J. An Inquiry into the Opinions, Ancient and Modern, Concerning Life and Organization. Edinburgh, 1822. xvi,542pp (sl foxed). Orig full calf (spine sl rubbed). *Whitehart*. $187/£120

BARCLAY, J. The Muscular Motions of the Human Body. Edinburgh, 1808. xxii,591pp (lt foxed). New 1/2 morocco. *Whitehart*. $374/£240

BARCLAY, ROBERT. An Apology for the True Christian Divinity.... Newport: James Franklin, 1729. 1st Amer ed. 6th ed in English. 8vo. (12),524,(32)pp (washed, few sidenotes cropped). Old sheep (rebacked), orig backstrip, mod morocco spine labels added. *Swann**. $575/£369

BARCLAY-ALLARDICE, ROBERT. Agricultural Tour in the United States and Upper Canada, with Miscellaneous Notices. Edinburgh, 1842. xxiii,(1),181pp + 1 ad leaf, half-title. (Bkpl, sig, 2 leaves repaired upper corner; spine sunned, extrems worn), else VG. Howes B132. *Reese*. $400/£256

BARCROFT, H. and H. J. C. SWAN. Sympathetic Control of Human Blood Vessels. London: Edward Arnold, 1953. 1st ed. Fine. *Glaser*. $35/£22

BARDSLEY, SAMUEL ARGENT. Medical Reports of Cases and Experiments.... London, 1807. 1st ed. 8vo. 336pp (waterstains, esp to prelims). Contemp mottled calf (worn, hinges cracked). *Argosy*. $600/£385

BARDSWELL, F. A. The Herb-Garden. London: A&C Black, 1911. 16 tipped-in color plts, guards. Dec cvr, spine. Good (text lt foxed). *Scribe's Perch**. $60/£38

BARETTI, JOSEPH. A Journey from London to Genoa.... Centaur, 1970. Facs of orig 1770 ed, from 2nd. 2 vols in 1. VG in dj. *Cox*. $44/£28

BARING, MAURICE. Punch and Judy and Other Essays. London: Heinemann, (1924). 1st ed. VG. *Dramatis Personae*. $30/£19

BARING-GOULD, S. (ed). A Book of Nursery Songs and Rhymes. London: Methuen, 1895. xvi,160pp. Teg, uncut. Orig black buckram (spine sl frayed), gilt. *Hollett*. $117/£75

BARING-GOULD, S. Curiosities of Olden Times. Edinburgh: John Grant, 1896. Rev, enlgd ed. (8)301 + ad leaf. (Lacks fep; cl lt soiled), o/w Good. *Cox*. $23/£15

BARING-GOULD, S. Curious Myths of the Middle Ages. Boston: Roberts Bros, 1867. 1st Amer ed, 1st series. Frontis. Gilt grn cl (spine crown lt worn). Good (fox mks tissue guard, sm spots ep). *Reese*. $35/£22

BARING-GOULD, S. Curious Myths of the Middle Ages. Rivingtons, 1868. 1st ed. Woodcut frontis, (8)374 + 32pp pub's cat. Sound (gathering sl sprung; sl faded, rubbed). *Cox*. $39/£25

BARING-GOULD, S. Family Names and Their Story. London, 1910. 1st ed. (Feps lt browned, bkpl.) *Edwards*. $39/£25

BARING-GOULD, S. Historic Oddities and Strange Events. London, 1891. Second Series. 372pp. (Sl fading to bds, spine sl dknd, sl soil.) *Edwards*. $56/£36

BARING-GOULD, S. The Land of Teck and Its Neighbourhood. John Lane/Bodley Head, 1911. Fldg map. Good (sl spotting; spine bumped, sunned, cvrs sl mkd). *Tiger*. $25/£16

BARING-GOULD, WILLIAM S. Nero Wolfe of West Thirty-Fifth Street.... NY: Viking, (1969). 1st US ed. NF in VG dj (ink name, lt wear). *Gravesend*. $75/£48

BARKAS, GEOFFREY. The Camouflage Story. London: Cassell, 1952. 1st ed. Fine in VG- dj (chipped). *Archer*. $25/£16

BARKER, CECILY. Flower Fairies of the Autumn. London: Blackie, n.d. c. 1939. Inscribed 8/7/39. 16mo. Blue illus eps (ep gutters, several pp sl stained). Brn checked bds, color label. VG in VG dj. *Dower*. $50/£32

BARKER, CECILY. Flower Fairies of the Wayside. London/Glasgow: Blackie & Son, n.d. 12mo. Blue illus eps. Brn checked bds, illus paste label. VG in VG dj. *Dower*. $75/£48

BARKER, CLIVE. Books of Blood. Volumes 1-6. London: Weidenfeld & Nicolson, (1985-86). 1st hb ed vols 3-6, 1st separate hb ed vols 1-2. Djs. *Swann**. $149/£96

BARKER, CLIVE. Books of Blood. Volumes 4-6. L.A.: Scream, 1987-91. Each vol one of 333 signed by Barker and Harry O. Morris (illus). Dec imitation leather. Slipcases. *Swann**. $161/£103

BARKER, CLIVE. The Damnation Game. London: Weidenfeld & Nicolson, (1985). 1st ed. Dj. *Swann**. $69/£44

BARKER, CLIVE. The Damnation Game. London: Weidenfeld & Nicolson, (1985). 1st ed. One of 250 numbered, signed. Pub's cl slipcase. *Swann**. $115/£74

BARKER, CLIVE. The Great and Secret Show. NY: Harper, (1989). 1st ed. Fine in NF dj. *Antic Hay*. $25/£16

BARKER, CLIVE. The Great and Secret Show. London: Collins, 1989. 1st ed. One of 500 numbered, signed. Imitation leather. Fldg case. *Swann**. $80/£51

BARKER, CLIVE. In the Flesh. NY, 1986. 1st Amer ed. Signed. Fine in Fine dj. *Warren*. $75/£48

BARKER, CLIVE. Weaveworld. NY: Poseidon, (1987). Ltd to 500 numbered, signed. Fine in slipcase. *Antic Hay*. $150/£96

BARKER, ERNEST. Social and Political Thought in Byzantium from Justinian to the Last Palaeologues. Oxford: Clarendon, 1957. (Name tp, plt removed inside back cvr), o/w Fine. *Europa*. $44/£28

BARKER, EUGENE C. The Life of Stephen F. Austin, Founder of Texas 1793-1836. Austin, 1949. 2nd ed. 7 plts, 2 maps (1 dbl, 1 fldg). Fine in dj (lt worn, spine lacks sm piece). Howes B137. *Bohling*. $30/£19

BARKER, EUGENE C. The Life of Stephen F. Austin, Founder of Texas, 1793-1836. Nashville: Cokesbury, 1925. 1st ed. 2 maps. Good (ex-lib). Howes B137. *Lien*. $55/£35

BARKER, EUGENE C. The Life of Stephen F. Austin, Founder of Texas. Nashville: Cokesbury, 1925. #234/250. Signed. VG. *Gibbs*. $250/£160

BARKER, FORDYCE. On Sea-Sickness. NY: Appleton, 1870. 36pp. Aeg. Limp bds (stained). *Goodrich*. $45/£29

BARKER, GEORGE. The Dead Seagull. London: John Lehmann, 1950. 1st ed. NF in illus dj, w/promo wraparound band. *Cahan*. $50/£32

BARKER, GEORGE. The True Confession of George Barker. NY, 1964. 1st Amer ed. Fine in dj (3 sm edge tears, price-clipped). *Polyanthos*. $25/£16

BARKER, JAMES P. The Log of a Limejuicer. NY: Huntington, 1933. 2nd ptg. Fldg color map. Beige cl. VG in dj (lt worn). *Parmer*. $65/£42

BARKER, LEWELLYS F. Time and the Physician: The Autobiography of Lewellys F. Barker. NY, 1942. 1st ed. Inscribed. VG in dj (tattered). *Doctor's Library*. $50/£32

BARKER, NICHOLAS. The Oxford University Press and the Spread of Learning 1478-1978. Clarendon, 1978. 336 plts (4 color). Dj (sl soiled, chipped). *Edwards*. $117/£75

BARKER, NICHOLAS. Stanley Morison. (London): Macmillan, (1972). 1st ed. 16 plts. Fine in dj (short tears). *Heller*. $50/£32

BARLETT, LANDELL. The Vanguard of Venus. NY: Experimenter Pub Co, 1928. 1st ed. Fine in wrappers. *Hermitage*. $100/£64

BARLETT, ROBERT A. and RALPH T. HALE. The Last Voyage of the Karluk Flagship of Vilhjalmur Stefansson's Canadian Arctic Expedition of 1913-1916. Boston: Small, Maynard, c. 1916. 1st ed. Map. VG. *High Latitude*. $70/£45

BARLEY, M. W. The English Farmhouse and Cottage. London: RKP, 1961. 24 plts. Sound. *Ars Artis*. $39/£25

BARLOW, JANE. Mavreen's Fairing and Other Stories. London: J.M. Dent, 1895. 1st ed. Wood-engr frontis, half-title, tp, 5 plts, all ptd in sepia; (viii),191,(i)pp. Pale grn coated eps; teg, edges uncut. Mottled pale and lt grn Fine buckram, gilt. (Sl foxed), o/w Very Nice. *Temple*. $31/£20

BARLOW, JOEL. The Vision of Columbus. Hartford, 1787. 1st ed. 6pp sub's names at end. Envelope of contemp reviews, ads tipped in at rear. (Lt foxed.) Full later dk blue crushed morocco, gilt. BAL 865. *Kane**. $200/£128

BARLOW, N. (ed). Darwin's Ornithological Notes. London: British Museum, 1963. 1st ed. NF in wraps. *Mikesh*. $37/£24

BARMAN, CHRISTIAN. The Bridge. London/NY: John Lane/Dodd, Mead, (1926). 1st ed. 24 color plts by Frank Brangwyn. Partially unopened; untrimmed. Natural linen. Fine in VG dj (lt chipped). *House*. $180/£115

BARNARD, EVAN G. and E. E. DALE (eds). A Rider of the Cherokee Strip. Boston, 1936. 1st ed. Fine in dj (edgewear, price-clipped). Howes B147. *Baade*. $75/£48

BARNARD, FREDERICK. A Series of Character Sketches from Dickens. London, 1884-1887. 1st ed. 3 vols in 1. 18 full-pg photogravure plts. Teg. (Foxed; cvrs worn, sl spotted.) *King*. $195/£125

BARNARD, HENRY. School Architecture. NY, 1850. 4th ed. 425pp, index (bkpl, ink note). Old sheep (rubbed, spine sl chipped). *King.* $95/£61

BARNARD, ROBERT. Bodies. London: Collins, 1986. 1st ed. Fine in Fine dj. *Janus.* $45/£29

BARNARD, ROBERT. Death of an Old Goat. NY: Walker, (1977). 1st ed. Fine in Fine dj. *Metropolitan*.* $40/£26

BARNEBY, WILLIAM HENRY. The New Far West and the Old Far East. London: Stanford, 1889. 1st ed. Presentation copy. (10),312,(8)pp, 3 fldg color maps, 8 plts. Pict cl. Very Nice. *Ginsberg.* $300/£192

BARNES, ALBERT. The Church and Slavery. Phila: Parry & McMillan, 1857. 1st ed. 196,(16)pp. (Extrems sl worn), else VG. *Mcgowan.* $150/£96

BARNES, CLARE, JR. John F. Kennedy Scrimshaw Collector. Boston/Toronto: Little, Brown, (1969). 1st ed. VG in dj (worn). *Waverly*.* $44/£28

BARNES, DJUNA. Creatures in an Alphabet. NY: Dial Press, (1982). 1st ed. Cl-cvrd bds. (Bump), else Fine in dj. *Bromer.* $50/£32

BARNES, DJUNA. Ryder. NY, 1928. 1st ed. Blue cl. VG in dj (price-clipped, fr corner lacks piece). *Argosy.* $250/£160

BARNES, GEORGE C. Denver, the Man. Wilmington, 1949. 1st ed. Fine. *Turpen.* $55/£35

BARNES, JAMES M. A Guide to Good Golf. NY: Dodd, Mead, 1925. 7th ed. Grn cl, pict cvr label. Fine in VG dj. *Pacific*.* $29/£19

BARNES, JOSEPH K. The Medical and Surgical History of the War of the Rebellion, Medical Parts: One, Two, and Three. Washington, 1870-1888. 1st ed. 3 vols. Grn cl. Vols 1 & 2 Good (extrems worn), Vol 3 (binding shaken, spine torn). *Doctor's Library.* $750/£481

BARNES, JULIAN. Before She Met Me. London: Cape, 1982. 1st UK ed. Fine in dj. *Moorhouse.* $62/£40

BARNES, JULIAN. Flaubert's Parrot. NY: Knopf, 1985. 1st Amer ed. Fine in dj (sm tear, price-clipped). *Antic Hay.* $40/£26

BARNES, JULIAN. A History of the World in 10 1/2 Chapters. London: Cape, 1989. 1st UK ed. Fine in dj. *Moorhouse.* $31/£20

BARNES, JULIAN. Talking It Over. Cape, 1991. 1st UK ed. Fine in dj. *Williams.* $19/£12

BARNES, LINDA. Blood Will Have Blood. NY: Avon, 1982. 1st ed. Pb orig. (Spine, top corner fr cvr creased), o/w VG in wrappers. *Mordida.* $35/£22

BARNES, LINDA. Cities of the Dead. NY: St. Martin's, 1986. 1st ed. Fine in dj (short closed tear). *Mordida.* $45/£29

BARNES, LINDA. Coyote. NY: Delacorte, 1990. 1st ed. Fine in dj (creases top fr panel). *Mordida.* $35/£22

BARNES, R. G. The Complete Poems of R. G. Barnes. (SF: Press of Robert Grabhorn & Andrew Hoyem, c. 1972.) 1st ed. One of 150 ptd. Frontis illus in red. Orange bds, label, tied in Japanese manner. NF. *Heller.* $40/£26

BARNES, R. MONEY. The British Army of 1914. London, 1968. 8 color plts. Red cl. Dj. *Maggs.* $47/£30

BARNES, R. MONEY. A History of the Regiments and Uniforms of the British Army. Seeley Service, 1954. 3rd ed. 24 color plts. VG (sl marginalia). *Cox.* $39/£25

BARNES, R. MONEY. The Uniforms and History of the Scottish Regiments Britain-Canada-Australia-New Zealand-South Africa. Seeley Service, (1956). 1st ed. 12 color plts. VG (lt margin notes). *Cox.* $39/£25

BARNES, ROBERT. Obstetric Operations Including the Treatment of Hemorrhage. NY: Appleton, 1870. xv-483pp. (Lib bkpl; cl rubbed, worn.) *Goodrich.* $85/£54

BARNES, WILLIAM. Poems, Partly of Rural Life. J.R. Smith, 1846. 1st ed. vii,(i),144pp (presentation inscrip); index in this copy left at end. Orig cl (fr cvr lt mkd), paper label (chipped). *Cox.* $140/£90

BARNES, WILLIAM. Rural Poems. Boston: Roberts Bros, 1869. 1st ed. 6 Fine woodcuts. Beveled edges, gilt design fr cvr (worn). Contents Fine. *New Hampshire*.* $100/£64

BARNESBY, NORMAN. Medical Chaos and Crime. NY, 1910. 1st ed. VG (inner hinges starting). *Doctor's Library.* $50/£32

BARNEY, MARY. A Biographical Memoir of the Late Commodore Joshua Barney. Boston, 1832. 1st ed. 328pp. (Lacks port, ex-lib; spine perished, cvrs detached.) *King.* $65/£42

BARNEY, MARY. A Biographical Memoir of the Late Commodore Joshua Barney. Boston: Gray, 1832. 1st ed. (16),238pp; port. Orig cl-backed bds, paper spine label. Howes B160. *Ginsberg.* $150/£96

BARNITZ, ALBERT and JENNIE. Life in Custer's Cavalry. Robert M. Utley (ed). New Haven: Yale Univ, 1977. 1st ed. VG in dj. *Lien.* $60/£38

BARNSTONE, HOWARD. The Galveston That Was. NY/Houston: Macmillan/Museum of Fine Arts, 1966. 1st ed. (Owner stamp), else NF in illus dj (spine rubbed). *Cahan.* $100/£64

BARNSTONE, HOWARD. The Galveston That Was. NY/Houston: Macmillan/Museum of Fine Arts, 1966. 1st ed. Inscribed. (Name), else Fine in NF dj. *Cahan.* $135/£87

BARNUM, H. L. The Spy Unmasked. NY, 1828. 1st ed. Map (repaired), 5 plts, extra-illus w/add'l 39 plts; complete w/ads. (Sl tears, dampstaining.) Late 19th-cent 3/4 morocco (spine gone, cvrs detached). Howes B161. *Freeman*.* $20/£13

BARNUM, P. T. The Life of P. T. Barnum. NY: Redfield, 1855. 1st ed. W/pict circus bkpl of 'Waterman Brown, Woburn, Mass.' affixed to fr pastedown. 8vo. 404pp + 4pp ads. Orig cl. (Shelfworn, soiled, sl stained, foxed.) *Oinonen*.* $60/£38

BARNUM, P. T. Struggles and Triumphs. Buffalo: Warren, Johnson, 1872. Frontis port, 870pp. Nice. *Bohling.* $25/£16

BARNUM, P. T. Struggles and Triumphs. George S. Bryan (ed). NY/London: Knopf, 1927. 2 vols. VG in slipcase (sl soiled, worn), paper labels. *Waverly*.* $44/£28

Baroque III 1620-1700. London: Matthiesen Fine Arts, 1986. 34 color plts. Good in wrappers (sl nicked). *Washton.* $40/£26

BARR, E. OSMUN. Flying Men and Medicine: The Effects of Flying Upon the Human Body. NY, 1943. 1st ed. (Ex-lib.) *Fye.* $60/£38

BARR, LOUISE FARROW. Presses of Northern California and Their Books, 1900-1933. Berkeley: Book Arts Club, Univ of CA, 1934. Ltd to 400 numbered. Grn cl (spine faded), leather spine label (rubbed). *Karmiole.* $150/£96

BARR, NEVADA. Bittersweet. NY: St. Martin's, 1984. 1st ed. Fine in dj (crease inner fr flap). *Mordida.* $250/£160

BARR, NEVADA. Track of the Cat. NY: Putnam, 1993. 1st ed. VF in VF dj. *Unger.* $100/£64

BARRAS. Memoirs of Barras. George Duruy (ed). Charles E. Roche (trans). London, 1895-6. 4 vols. ci,457; xxi,659; xlii,644; xxxix,681pp. Partly unopened. Brn cl. *Maggs.* $218/£140

BARRELL, J. and G. LOUGHLIN. The Lithology of Connecticut. Hartford: SGNHS, 1910. Pb. Good. *Blake.* $45/£29

BARRETT, FRANCIS. The Magus. NY: University Books, 1967. Fine in VG dj. *Middle Earth.* $99/£63

BARRETT, FRANKLIN A. Caughley and Coalport Porcelain. Leigh-on-Sea, (1951). 1st ed. Ltd to 500 numbered. (Sl worn.) *King.* $100/£64

BARRETT, FRANKLIN A. and ARTHUR L. THORPE. Derby Porcelain 1750-1848. London: Collectors' Book Club, 1973. 8 color plts. VG in dj (price-clipped). *Hollett.* $70/£45

BARRETT, J. O. History of 'Old Abe,' the Live War Eagle of the Eighth Regiment Wisconsin Volunteers. Chicago, 1865. 1st ed. 71pp; 2 color plts, map. Later 1/2 cl, bds. (Corners bumped, extrems sl frayed), else VG. *Reese.* $450/£288

BARRETT, J. O. Old Abe: The Live War-Eagle of Wisconsin.... Madison, WI, 1876. 2nd ed. Map, port. Pict wrappers. 1/4 morocco slipcase. *Swann*.* $69/£44

BARRETT, JOSEPH H. Life of Abraham Lincoln. Cincinnati: Moore et al, 1865. 1st ed. (1st, last leaves sl foxing.) Orig calf (unskillfully rebacked in leather, part of orig backstrip laid on; rubbed). *Sadlon.* $20/£13

BARRETT, LINDSAY. Song for Mumu. Washington: Howard Univ, 1974. 1st Amer ed. Fine in VG dj (creased, rubbed). *Between The Covers.* $50/£32

BARRETT, TIMOTHY. Nagashizuki. North Hills: Bird & Bull, 1979. One of 300 numbered. Prospectus laid in. 1/4 morocco. *Swann*.* $316/£203

BARRETT, WILLIAM E. The Left Hand of God. GC: Doubleday, 1951. 1st ed. Fine in Fine dj (2 nicks rear panel). *Unger.* $65/£42

BARRETT, WILLIAM E. The Lilies of the Field. London: Heinemann, (1963). 1st Eng ed. Inscribed. Fine in dj. *Between The Covers.* $150/£96

BARRIE, J. M. The Admirable Crichton. London, (1914). One of 500 numbered, signed by Hugh Thomson (illus). 20 tipped-in color plts, guards. Gilt-blocked vellum, silk ties. Cl slipcase. *Swann*.* $488/£313

BARRIE, J. M. Better Dead. London: Swan et al, 1888. 1st ed, 1st bk. Pict wrappers (spine expertly restored). 1/2 morocco slipcase. *Appelfeld.* $400/£256

BARRIE, J. M. Courage. NY: Scribner, 1922. 1st Amer ed. Inscribed. Pale grn bds. Fine in 1/2 morocco slipcase. *Appelfeld.* $100/£64

BARRIE, J. M. An Edinburgh Eleven. London: Office of 'British Weekly,' 1889. 1st ed. 4pp undated ads. Lt brn cl. NF (2 bkpls; lt soil). *Sumner & Stillman.* $75/£48

BARRIE, J. M. The Greenwood Hat. London, 1937. 1st ed. (Loose; lacks dj.) *Typographeum.* $15/£10

BARRIE, J. M. Half Hour. NY: Scribner, 1914. 1st ed. Grn cl. Fine. *Antic Hay.* $25/£16

BARRIE, J. M. Jess. Boston: Dana Estes, (1898). 1st ed, 2nd issue, w/ads for Laura E. Richards' bks bound in rear. Grn cl. VG (lacks rear ep; spine sl dknd). *Antic Hay.* $25/£16

BARRIE, J. M. Margaret Ogilvy. London: Hodder & Stoughton, 1896. 1st Eng ed. 4pp undated ads. Dk blue cl, beveled. VG (spine faded). *Sumner & Stillman.* $40/£26

BARRIE, J. M. Peter and Wendy. NY: Scribner, 1911. 1st ed. 8vo. Frontis, illus tp, 11 plts. Gilt-pict cl (lt rubbed; name). *Swann*.* $258/£165

BARRIE, J. M. Peter Pan in Kensington Gardens. London, 1906. Signed by Arthur Rackham (illus). 4to. 50 tipped-in color plts, guards. (Prelims foxed, bkpl.) Cl slipcase. *Swann*.* $517/£331

BARRIE, J. M. Peter Pan in Kensington Gardens. London, 1906. One of 500 numbered, signed by Arthur Rackham (illus). 4to. 50 tipped-in color plts, guards. Orig vellum, gilt, silk ties (detached). Morocco-edged marbled bd slipcase. *Swann*.* $3,680/£2,359

BARRIE, J. M. Peter Pan in Kensington Gardens. London: Hodder & Stoughton, 1906. 1st trade ed. 4to. 50 color plts by Arthur Rackham. Gilt-pict red cl (lt rubbed). *Swann*.* $747/£479

BARRIE, J. M. Peter Pan in Kensington Gardens. NY, 1913. 8vo. 126pp, 16 color plts by Arthur Rackham. Grn cl (sl soiled), gilt, Rackham color plt inset fr cvr. VG. *Truepenny.* $45/£29

BARRIE, J. M. Peter Pan or The Boy Who Would Not Grow Up. London: Hodder & Stoughton, 1928. 1st pub ed. Sm 8vo. Blue cl, paper labels. Fine in dj (spine ends sl sunned, rubbed). *Dramatis Personae.* $125/£80

BARRIE, J. M. Quality Street. London, (1913). One of 1000 numbered, signed by Hugh Thomson (illus). 22 tipped-in color plts, guards. Gilt-blocked vellum, silk ties. Cl slipcase. *Swann*.* $258/£165

BARRIE, J. M. Quality Street. London: Hodder & Stoughton, n.d. (1913). 4to. 198pp; 22 VG tipped-in color plts by Hugh Thompson. Dec cvr, spine. (Sl bumped), o/w Good+. *Scribe's Perch*.* $55/£35

BARRIE, J. M. Quality Street. London: Hodder & Stoughton, n.d. (1913). One of 1000 numbered, signed by Hugh Thomson (illus). 4to. Full vellum (sl shelfworn, soiled), gilt. *Oinonen*.* $160/£103

BARRIE, J. M. Sentimental Tommy. NY: Scribner, 1896. 1st Amer ed. Brn cl dec in gold/grn. Fine. *Sumner & Stillman.* $50/£32

BARRIE, J. M. A Tillyloss Scandal. NY: Lovell, Coryell, (1893). 1st ed, 1st issue, w/pub's address listed as '43, 47 and 47 East Tenth Street.' Teg. Blue cl. VG (ink name). *Antic Hay.* $150/£96

BARRIE, J. M. Tommy and Grizel. London: Cassell, 1900. 1st ed. 8pp ads dated '9.00.' Black cl. Fine. *Sumner & Stillman.* $50/£32

BARRIE, J. M. When a Man's Single. London: Hodder & Stoughton, 1888. 1st Eng ed. Teg. Blue buckram, gilt. VG in grn-blue morocco leather and cl slipcase, gilt. *Antic Hay.* $175/£112

BARRIE, J. M. The Works. Kirriemuir Edition. London: Hodder & Stoughton, 1913. 1st ed. #344/1000 signed by pubs. 10 vols. 8vo. VG (inner joints vol 1 sl strained) in orig 1/4 blue cl, gray bds, gilt. *Maggs.* $601/£385

BARRINGTON, EMILIE ISABEL. The Life, Letters and Work of Frederick Leighton. London: George Allen, 1906. 1st ed. 2 vols. 158 guarded plts mtd on gray card. Teg, uncut. Dec cl gilt (spines sl faded, mottled). *Hollett.* $218/£140

BARROW, JOHN. A Chronological History of Voyages into the Arctic Regions. London: John Murray, 1819. (6),379,48pp (inscrip, bkpl); fldg map (sm tape repair verso), 3 woodcuts. Orig bds (rebacked). *Parmer.* $550/£353

BARROWS, R. M. (ed). The Kit Book for Soldiers, Sailors and Marines. Chicago: Consolidated Book Pub, 1942. 1st issue. VG+ in illus paper-cvrd bds. *Lame Duck.* $250/£160

BARROWS, R. M. (ed). The Kit Book for Soldiers, Sailors and Marines. Chicago: Consolidated Book Publishers, 1943. 1st ed, 2nd issue. Pict paper-cvrd bds. (Margins browned), o/w NF. *Bernard.* $100/£64

BARROWS, WILLIAM. The General. Boston: Lee & Shepard, 1869. 1st ed. iv,268pp; 4 plts. (Foxed, few pencil/pen mks; edges worn, spine ends frayed), o/w Good. *Worldwide.* $45/£29

BARRUS, CLARA. Nursing the Insane. NY: Macmillan, 1908. 1st ed. Grn cl (ex-lib). *Gach.* $50/£32

BARRY, E. A Treatise on the Three Different Digestions, and Discharges of the Human Body.... 1763. 2nd ed. xvi,384pp. Full leather (binding sl loose). *Whitehart.* $281/£180

BARRY, LOUISE. The Beginning of the West...1540-1854. Topeka: KS State Hist Soc, (1972). 1st ed. VG in dj. *Lien.* $35/£22

BARRY, T. A. and B. A. PATTEN. Men and Memories of San Francisco in the Spring of '50. SF: A.L. Bancroft, 1873. 296pp. Blind/gold-stamped grn cl (lt spotting, wear). *Dawson.* $150/£96

BARRY, WILLIAM E. Chronicles of Kennebunk. N.p., 1923. 1st ed. Rockwell Kent (illus). Paper label. NF in orig glassine wrapper (chipped, repaired). *Sadlon.* $150/£96

BARRYMORE, LIONEL. Mr. Cantonwise: A Moral Tale. Boston: Little Brown, (1953). (Name; inked out name, #; sl rubbed), else NF in VG dj (lt wear, 2 sm spine stains). *Between The Covers.* $65/£42

BARSNESS, L. The Bison in Art. Flagstaff: Northland, 1977. 1st ed. VG in color pict wraps. *Mikesh.* $30/£19

BARSTOW, STAN. A Kind of Loving. London: Michael Joseph, 1960. 1st UK ed. VG + in dj. *Williams.* $47/£30

BART, THOMAS HANMER. The Garden Book of Sir Thomas Hanmer Bart. London: Gerald Howe, 1933. 1st ed thus. One of 900 ptd. Teg. Very Nice in dj (lt used). *Reese.* $85/£54

BARTH, HENRY. Travels and Discoveries in North and Central Africa. NY: Harper, 1857-1859. 1st US ed. 3 vols. 657; 709,ad leaf; 800pp (lt aging, few ll w/residue or offsetting from dried flowers; ink stamp eps); fldg engr map w/orig hand-coloring. Dk brn blind cl (spine ends chipped, snagged, edges worn), gilt. *Baltimore*.* $140/£90

BARTH, JEAN BAPTISTE and HENRY-LOUIS ROGER. A Manual of Auscultation and Percussion. Francis G. Smith (trans). Phila, 1845. 1st ed. Orig cl. VG. *Argosy.* $125/£80

BARTH, JOHN. Chimera. Deutsch, 1974. 1st UK ed. NF in VG + dj. *Williams.* $56/£36

BARTH, JOHN. The Floating Opera. NY: Appleton, (1956). 1st ed. (Lt shelfwear.) Dj (spine sunned, lt stains, wear). *Metropolitan*.* $115/£74

BARTH, JOHN. Giles Goat-Boy. London, 1967. 1st Eng ed. Very Nice in dj. *Clearwater.* $39/£25

BARTH, JOHN. Letters. NY, (1979). 1st ed. Ltd to 500 numbered, signed. Cl-backed bds. VG in slipcase. *King.* $75/£48

BARTH, JOHN. Letters. NY: Putnam, (1979). 1st trade ed. Silver variant dj. Black cl-backed lt gray bds (rubbed, lt spotted; top edge fr bd soiled), gilt. Internally Fine in VG dj (rubbed, bumped). *Blue Mountain.* $20/£13

BARTH, JOHN. Lost in the Funhouse. GC: Doubleday, 1968. One of 250 numbered, signed. Fine in Fine slipcase. *Lenz.* $175/£112

BARTH, JOHN. The Sot-Weed Factor. London, 1961. 1st Eng ed. Very Nice in dj (clipped). *Clearwater.* $39/£25

BARTH, JOHN. Todd Andrews to the Author. Northridge, CA: Lord John, 1979. One of 300 numbered, signed. Fine. *Lenz.* $100/£64

BARTHEL, T. S. The Eighth Land: The Polynesian Discovery and Settlement of Easter Island. A. Martin (trans). Honolulu: Univ of HI, 1978. 1st ed. Fine in Fine dj. *Mikesh.* $30/£19

BARTHELEMY, D. and J. T. MILIK (eds). Discoveries in the Judean Desert (of Jordan). Oxford: Clarendon, (1956). Vol 1 (only). 37 plts. Good in dj. *Archaeologia.* $150/£96

BARTHELME, DONALD. Come Back, Dr. Caligari. London: Eyre & Spottiswoode, (1966). 1st British ed. Fine (edges sl soiled) in dj (price-clipped, dknd, short tear rear flap). *Metropolitan*.* $57/£37

BARTHELME, DONALD. The Dead Father. NY, 1975. 1st Amer ed. Fine in dj (sl creased). *Polyanthos.* $25/£16

BARTHELME, DONALD. Great Days. NY, 1979. 1st Amer ed. Fine in dj. *Polyanthos.* $20/£13

BARTHELME, DONALD. Sixty Stories. NY: Putnam, (1981). One of 500 numbered, signed. Fine in Fine slipcase. *Lenz.* $150/£96

BARTHELME, DONALD. The Slightly Irregular Fire Engine. NY: FSG, 1971. 1st ed in 1st state dj w/o NBA sticker. Fine in Fine dj. *Bernard.* $75/£48

BARTHOLOMEW, CHARLES. Mechanical Toys. London, 1979. 1st ed. Dbl-pg color tp. Dj. *Edwards.* $31/£20

BARTHOLOMEW, ED. Houston Story. Houston: Frontier, 1951. 2nd ptg. Signed. VG (paper dknd) in pict wrapper. *Bohling.* $30/£19

BARTHOLOMEW, J. Handy Reference Atlas of the World. London: Walker, 1896. 5th ed. Map. 80 loose sheets w/tp. *Yudkin*.* $65/£42

BARTHOLOMEW, J. The Pocket Atlas of the World. London: John Walker, 1886. 2nd ed. 54 double-pg color maps, 60pp index. Limp maroon morocco (broken, needs rebacking). *Hudson.* $120/£77

BARTLETT, ALICE HUNT. Caesar. The Undefeated. London: Cecil Palmer, 1929. 1st ed. Frontis, 24 full-pg illus. Uncut, partly unopened. Pict cvrs. Fine (sl offsetting eps). *Polyanthos.* $60/£38

BARTLETT, HENRIETTA and ALFRED POLLARD. A Census of Shakespeare's Plays in Quarto 1594-1709. New Haven/London: Yale Univ/Humphrey Milford, 1916. One of 500. Untrimmed, unopened. 1/2 cl. NF in slipcase (broken). *Waverly*.* $66/£42

BARTLETT, JOHN RUSSELL. Dictionary of Americanisms. NY, 1848. 1st ed. xxvii,412pp (lib mks, name clipped tp). Pub's cl (sl worn). *Oinonen*.* $140/£90

BARTLETT, JOHN RUSSELL. Personal Narrative of Explorations and Incidents in Texas, New Mexico, California, Sonora and Chihuahua. NY: Appleton, 1854. 1st ed. 2 vols. Fldg frontis (sl foxing), fldg map (repaired tear), 16 litho-tint views (offsetting). Blind panelled ribbed cl (extrems sl rubbed), gilt. Howes B201. *Sadlon.* $700/£449

BARTLETT, JOHN RUSSELL. Personal Narrative of Explorations and Incidents...During the Years 1850, '51, '52 and '53. NY: D. Appleton, 1854. 1st ed. 2 vols in 1. 8 7/8x5 5/8. 16 full-pg lithos, fldg map. Blind, gold-stamped cl. *Dawson.* $750/£481

BARTLETT, ROBERT A. The Log of Bob Bartlett. NY, 1928. 1st ed. (Spine sl spotted), else VG. *High Latitude.* $25/£16

BARTLETT, ROBERT A. Sails Over Ice. NY: Scribner, 1934. Fine in dj (sl chipped). *High Latitude.* $50/£32

BARTLETT, W. H. The Nile Boat; or Glimpses of the Land of Egypt. London, 1850. 2nd ed. Engr tp, 34 plts, 17 cuts. (Ex-lib, bkpl, stamps, paper spine label; gathering pulled.) Gilt-pict cl (worn, backstrip torn). *New Hampshire*.* $60/£38

BARTLETT, W. H. Walks About the City and Environs of Jerusalem. London: Hall, Virtue, (1880). Engr frontis, tp engr, 4 maps, 24 plts. Aeg. Contemp crushed morocco, gilt. Fine. *Andrew Stewart.* $234/£150

BARTLETT, W. H. Walks About the City and Environs of Jerusalem. London: George Virtue, n.d. (ca 1844). 1st ed. Tinted frontis, (12),224pp; fldg map. Teg. 1/2 brn morocco, marbled bds. Good. *Karmiole.* $200/£128

BARTLETT, W. H. Walks About the City of Jerusalem and Its Environs. London: Hall, Virtue, (n.d.) c1845. 2nd ed. Engr tp, frontis, xp255pp + (16)pp pub's cat. Contemp dk red full morocco (upper joint sl rubbed), spine gilt in 6 compartments. VG (lacks fep, ink inscrip). *Sotheran.* $309/£198

BARTLETT, W. P. Happenings. L.A.: Times-Mirror, 1927. 2nd ed. Fine in VG dj. *Book Market.* $45/£29

BARTOL, B. H. A Treatise on the Marine Boilers of the United States. Phila: Ptd by R.W. Barnard, 1851. 143pp (sl offsetting, few mks). Emb cl (worn, faded). *Parmer.* $300/£192

BARTON, CLARA. The Red Cross: A History of This Remarkable International Movement in the Interest of Humanity. Washington, 1898. 1st ed. 684pp. VG. *Fye.* $75/£48

BARTON, D. PLUNKET et al. The Story of Our Inns of Court. London: G.T. Foulis, 1924? (Worn, faded.) *Boswell.* $65/£42

BARTON, FREDERICK. The El Cholo Feeling. Atlanta: Peachtree Pub, (1985). 1st ed, 1st bk. NF in VG + dj. *Pettler & Lieberman.* $25/£16

BARTON, GEORGE. Adventures of the World's Greatest Detectives. Phila: John C. Winston, 1909. 1st ed. (Spine sl dknd), o/w VG in pict cvrs (w/o dj). *Mordida.* $45/£29

BARTON, LUCY. Historic Costume for the Stage. Boston, 1935. 1st ed. Signed, dated 1939. Color frontis. VG in grn dec cl. *Smith.* $20/£13

BARTON, MICHAEL. Goodmen: The Character of Civil War Soldiers. Univ Park, PA, (1981). 1st ed. Fine in Fine dj. *Pratt.* $30/£19

BARTON, ROSE. Familiar London. A&C Black, 1904. 1st ed. 61 color plts (1 detached; feps lt browned). Dec cl (rubbed, spine faded). *Edwards.* $117/£75

BARTON, STUART. Monumental Follies. (Worthing): Lyle Publications, 1972. (Inscrip), else VG in dj. *Hadley.* $28/£18

BARTON, WILLIAM P. C. A Flora of North America. Phila: M. Carey, 1821 (-1822). 1st ed. Vols I and II (of 3). 70 hand-colored engr plts (some dampstaining sl affecting plts; leaves lt browned). Contemp 1/2 roan, marbled bds (worn). *Christie's*.* $421/£270

BARTON, WILLIAM P. C. Vegetable Materia Medica of the United States. Phila: M. Carey, 1817-1818. 1st ed. 2 vols. 4to. 273,(i),xvi; (9)-243pp (sl foxed, aged, sl smudges) incl sub's list end vol 2; 50 full-pg (1 fldg) hand-colored engr plts (lt aged, foxed, finger mks). Plain eps, bulked edges spattered. Orig scarlet sheep, marbled bds (sl worn, scuffed, joints cracked), raised bands, gilt. *Baltimore*.* $2,300/£1,474

BARTRAM, WILLIAM. Travels Through North and South Carolina, Georgia, East and West Florida. Phila, 1791. Fldg map (defective), 5 (of 8) plts (several defective). Contemp sheep (worn; browned throughout). *Swann*.* $431/£276

BARTTELOT, W. G. Major Barttelot's Diary on the Congo. London: Richard Bentley, 1890. 3rd ed. xi,413pp, 2 fldg maps. (Spine dknd, lt soiled.) *Hollett.* $187/£120

BARUCH, DOROTHY WALTER. I Like Automobiles. NY: John Day, 1931. 1st ed, 1st bk. Gyo Fujikawa (illus). 6 1/2 x 8 1/2. 52pp. VG. *Cattermole.* $75/£48

BARWICK, G. F. The Reading Room of the British Museum. London: Ernest Benn, 1929. 1st ed. VG (inscrip, sl dusty). *Reese.* $30/£19

BASEDOW, HERBERT. Knights of the Boomerang. Sydney: Endeavour Press, 1935. 1st ed. Frontis, 8 plts (ptd recto/verso). Pale blue cl. Fine (lt foxing). *Morrell.* $94/£60

BASKIN, LEONARD. Ars Anatomica. NY: Medicina Rara, 1972. #226/2500 signed. Fine in slipcase (sl edgeworn). *Metropolitan*.* $115/£74

BASKIN, R. N. Reminiscences of Early Utah. Salt Lake, 1914. 1st ed. Inscribed. Good+ (sl bowed, fr hinge cracked, corners bumped, cvr waterstained). *Benchmark.* $75/£48

BASON, F. T. A Bibliography of the Writings of William Somerset Maugham. London, 1931. Signed. Partly unopened. Red cl (spine faded, sl stained). *Maggs.* $16/£10

BASS, RICK. Oil Notes. Boston, 1989. 1st ed. Fine in Fine dj. *Smith.* $15/£10

BASS, RICK. Oil Notes. London: Collins, 1989. 1st British ed. Fine in Fine dj. *Revere.* $30/£19

BASS, RICK. Wild to the Heart. Harrisburg: Stackpole, (1987). 1st ed. Fine in Fine dj. *Robbins.* $75/£48

BASSANI, GIORGIO. The Garden of the Finzi-Continis. London: Faber & Faber, 1965. 1st British ed. NF in dj. *Lame Duck.* $50/£32

BASSETT, JOHN SPENCER. The Life of Andrew Jackson. NY, 1911. 1st ed. 2 vols. 2 maps. *Wantagh.* $50/£32

BASSETT, JOHN. The Medical Reports of John Y. Bassett, M.D.: The Alabama Student. Springfield, 1941. 1st ed. VG. *Fye.* $60/£38

BASSETT, SAM. Royal Marine. London, (1962). 1st ed. VG + in VG + dj. *Pratt.* $30/£19

BATAILLE, GEORGES. Blue of Noon. Harry Matthews (trans). London: Marion Boyars, 1979. 1st ed in English. VG + in dj (price-clipped). *Lame Duck.* $50/£32

BATCHELDER, JAMES. Multum in Parvo. SF: Pacific, 1892. 1st ed. Presentation binding, inscribed. Aeg. Full blind-stamped morocco (extrems sl scuffed), gilt. Howes B232. *Sadlon.* $150/£96

BATCHELLER, GEORGE CLINTON. Golden Hours from Mother Goose. Phila: Sunshine Printery, n.d. 4to. (Few plts creased; sl shaken.) Pict bds (shelfworn). *Oinonen*.* $60/£38

BATCHELOR, JOHN CALVIN. American Falls. NY: Norton, (1985). 1st ed. (Corner bumped), else Fine in dj. *Between The Covers.* $65/£42

BATEMAN, G. C. Fresh-Water Aquaria. London: Upcott Gill, n.d. (1892). 2nd ed. 353pp + 19pp pub's cat. Dec cl. (Sl dust-staining), o/w Good. *Savona.* $28/£18

BATEMAN, THOMAS. Delineations of Cutaneous Diseases. London: Henry Bohn, 1840. New ed. viiipp; 72 color plts. 1/2 morocco, marbled bds (spine relaid). Nice. *White.* $374/£240

BATES, ALBERT C. (comp). The Two Putnams. Hartford: CT Hist Soc, 1931. Deckle edge, unopened. Cl-backed bds. Fine. *Bohling.* $40/£26

BATES, CHARLOTTE FISKE (ed). The Longfellow Birthday Book. Boston: Houghton, Mifflin, 1881. 1st ed. Brn dec cl, gilt. NF. BAL 12593. *Macdonnell.* $35/£22

BATES, EDWARD. The Diary of Edward Bates 1859-1866. Howard K. Beale (ed). Washington, 1933. (Spine labelling faded), o/w VG + . *Pratt.* $40/£26

BATES, GEORGE LATIMER. Handbook of the Birds of West Africa. 1930. 1st ed. (Sl wrinkling, marginal staining; cl worn w/sl extrem loss, rebacked, orig spine laid down.) *Edwards.* $39/£25

BATES, H. E. An Aspidistra in Babylon. Michael Joseph, (1960). 1st ed. Nice (edges lt spotted) in dj (sl browned). *Ash.* $31/£20

BATES, H. E. The Bride Comes to Evensford. London, 1943. 1st ed. VG in dj (lt rubbed). *Words Etc.* $39/£25

BATES, H. E. The Country of White Clover. Michael Joseph, (1952). 1st ed, secondary issue w/plain top edge, later (25/-) version of Broom Lynne dj, ptd in black on pale blue. VG in dj (spine sl sunned). *Ash.* $31/£20

BATES, H. E. Cut and Come Again. London, 1935. 1st ed. Dj (sl rubbed). *Words Etc.* $148/£95

BATES, H. E. The Day of Glory. London, 1945. 1st Eng ed. Very Nice in dj. *Clearwater.* $55/£35

BATES, H. E. Down the River. NY: Holt, 1937. 81 wood engrs by Agnes Miller Parker. Good in Fair dj (torn). *Scribe's Perch**. $35/£22

BATES, H. E. The Duet. Grayson Books, 1935. One of 285 signed. Very Nice (sl foxed). *Clearwater.* $172/£110

BATES, H. E. The Face of England. London: Batsford, (1952). 1st ed. Gilt cl. Fine in NF dj. *Reese.* $45/£29

BATES, H. E. The Fallow Land. London, 1932. 1st ed. VG in dj (spine sl dknd). *Words Etc.* $140/£90

BATES, H. E. The Feast of July. Michael Joseph, (1954). 1st ed, 1st issue, in grn dj. Nice in dj (sl rubbed). *Ash.* $39/£25

BATES, H. E. Flowers and Faces. (Waltham Saint Lawrence): Golden Cockerel, (1935.) One of 325 numbered, signed. Grn morocco, gilt, by Sangorski & Sutcliffe. *Swann**. $546/£350

BATES, H. E. The Four Beauties. Michael Joseph, (1968). 1st ed. Nice in dj (sl mkd). *Ash.* $39/£25

BATES, H. E. The Golden Oriole. Michael Joseph, (1962). 1st ed. (Edges sl browned, spotted), o/w Nice in dj (lt worn). *Ash.* $31/£20

BATES, H. E. The Grapes of Paradise. Boston, 1960. 1st Amer ed. Nice in dj (sl frayed, chafed). *Clearwater.* $31/£20

BATES, H. E. The Hessian Prisoner. London, 1930. One of 550 signed. Buckram. Very Nice. *Clearwater.* $140/£90

BATES, H. E. Mrs. Esmond's Life. London: Privately ptd, 1931. One of 50 w/ms leaf bound in. VG (bkpl, bottom edge 1st 4 pp sl dampstained). *Certo.* $100/£64

BATES, H. E. Mrs. Esmond's Life. London: Privately ptd, 1931. One of 300 signed. Yellow buckram. Very Nice. *Clearwater.* $109/£70

BATES, H. E. My Uncle Silas. London, 1939. 1st Eng ed. Edward Ardizzone (illus). (Inscrip, eps, fore-edges foxed; cvrs sl mkd.) *Clearwater.* $78/£50

BATES, H. E. Now Sleeps the Crimson Petal. Joseph, 1961. 1st ed. Fine in Fine dj. *Whiteson.* $25/£16

BATES, H. E. The Poacher. NY: Macmillan, 1935. 1st US ed. (Sunned), o/w Fine in Fine dj. *Beasley.* $50/£32

BATES, H. E. The Scarlet Sword. Boston, 1951. 1st Amer ed. (Sl bumped.) Dj (chafed, nicked). *Clearwater.* $47/£30

BATES, H. E. Seven Tales and Alexander. Scholartis Press, 1929. One of 1000. VG (bds lt mkd) in VG dj (sl edgewear, sl browned, lt chipped). *Williams.* $78/£50

BATES, H. E. The Story Without an End, and the Country Doctor. London: White Owl, 1932. 1st ed. #40/125 signed. Woodcut frontis. Teg. Beige cl, beveled bds, gilt spine. Fine. *Vandoros.* $175/£112

BATES, H. E. Sugar for the Horses, New Uncle Silas Stories. London: Michael Joseph, (1957). 1st Eng ed. Ed Ardizzone (illus). 8vo. 120pp. Blue cl. VG. *Dower.* $65/£42

BATES, H. E. The Two Sisters. London, 1926. 1st Eng ed. Bright. *Clearwater.* $86/£55

BATES, H. E. When the Green Woods Laugh. Michael Joseph, (1960). 1st ed. Nice (sl signs of age) in dj. *Ash.* $39/£25

BATES, H. E. The White Admiral. Dennis Dobson, (1968). 1st ed. Excellent in dj. *Ash.* $117/£75

BATES, H. E. The Yellow Meads of Asphodel. Michael Joseph, (1976). 1st ed. Nice in dj. *Ash.* $47/£30

BATES, HENRY WALTER. The Naturalist on the River Amazons. London, 1873. 3rd ed. x,394pp. Marbled eps, edges. Full prize calf (sl rubbed; bkpl), gilt, morocco label. *Edwards.* $55/£35

BATES, J. C. (ed). History of the Bench and Bar of California. SF: Bench & Bar, 1912. Straight grained crimson morocco (rubbed), gilt. Attractive. *Boswell.* $225/£144

BATES, JOSEPH D., JR. The Art of the Atlantic Salmon Fly. Boston: Godine, 1987. 1st trade ed. Color frontis, 25 color plts. As New in dj; still in blister-pack wrap. *Bowman.* $50/£32

BATES, KATHARINE LEE. Little Robin Stay-Behind. NY: Woman's Press, 1923. 12mo. 229pp. Dec paper over bds, linen spine. Good+ in dj (chipped). *Scribe's Perch**. $15/£10

BATES, MOLLY BRYANT. Incidents on Land and Water; or, Four Years on the Pacific Coast. Boston: French, 1857. 1st ed. Frontis, 336pp. Dec cl (crown chipped). *Ginsberg.* $125/£80

BATES, RALPH. The Olive Field. NY: Dutton, (1936). 1st Amer ed. Pict cl (Stamp fep), o/w VG in dj (lt edgewear, nicks, creased tears). *Reese.* $50/£32

BATES, SAMUEL P. The Battle of Chancellorsville. Meadville, PA, 1882. 1st ed. 261pp (ink name); 2 ports, 3 maps. (Heavily worn, ends frayed, spotted, stained.) *King.* $65/£42

BATESON, F. W. (comp). The Cambridge Bibliography of English Literature. CUP, 1940. 1st ed. 4 vols. Gilt cl. VG in djs (sl nicked, frayed). *Reese.* $175/£112

BATESON, GREGORY. Steps to an Ecology of Mind: Collected Essays.... SF: Chandler, (1972). 1st ed. Blue-grey cl. VG in dj. *Gach.* $125/£80

BATSFORD, HARRY and CHARLES FRY. The Face of Scotland. London: Batsford, (1933). 1st UK ed. VG (pp aged). *Gravesend.* $25/£16

BATSFORD, HARRY and CHARLES FRY. The Massacre of Glencoe. London, 1933. 1st ed. Cream cl. (Spine dknd), o/w VG. *Words Etc.* $31/£20

BATTERSBY, MARTIN. Trompe l'Oeil. London, 1974. 1st UK ed. Dj (sl chipped, faded). *Edwards.* $75/£48

Battle of the Aleutians. (By Dashiell Hammett.) (Adak, AK: 29th Engineers, 1944.) 1st ed. VG in wraps (sl soiled, rubbed; upper corner sl creased). *Waverly**. $110/£71

BAUDELAIRE, CHARLES PIERRE. The Mirror of Baudelaire. Charles Henri Ford (ed). Norfolk: New Directions, (1942). Drawing by Henri Matisse. (1/2-title, colophon pg sl stained by acid migration from cardboard cvrs.) VG in wrappers. *Graf.* $15/£10

BAUDELAIRE, CHARLES. Flowers of Evil. NY: LEC, 1971. #1029/1500 signed by Pierre-Yves Tremois (illus). Fine in slipcase. *Hermitage.* $125/£80

BAUDELAIRE, CHARLES. Intimate Journals. Christopher Isherwood (trans). London: Methuen, 1949. One of 750 ptd. Blue buckram (corner tip bumped, spine sl faded). Very Nice in dj (torn, ragged). *Clearwater.* $78/£50

BAUDELAIRE, CHARLES. The Painter of Modern Life, and Other Essays. J. Mayne (ed). London: Phaidon, 1964. Color frontis, 53 plts hors-texte. (Ex-lib, sm stamp margin tp.) Nice in dj. *Europa.* $28/£18

BAUDESSON, HENRY. Indo-China and Its Primitive People. E. Appleby Holt (trans). London: Hutchinson, n.d. (1912). 1st Eng ed. (Sl text foxing.) 16 plts, incl frontis. Blue cl (few mks), gilt. *Morrell.* $62/£40

BAUDOUIN, FRANS. Rubens. NY, 1977. Good in dj. *Washton.* $75/£48

BAUER, JACK. Surfboats and Horse Marines, US Naval Operations in the Mexican War 1846-48. Annapolis, (1969). 1st ed. Fine in VG dj. *Turpen.* $75/£48

BAUER, MAX. Precious Stones.... London, 1904. 20 plts. Orig 3/4 red morocco (extrems rubbed). *Freeman**. $100/£64

BAUER, PAUL. The Siege of Nanga. London, 1956. 1st Eng ed. VG in dj. *King.* $35/£22

BAUGHMAN, ROBERT W. Kansas in Maps. Topeka: KS State Hist Soc, 1961. 1st trade ed. 90 maps. Tan linen, gilt. Fine in NF dj. *Harrington*. $80/£51

BAUM, DWIGHT JAMES. The Work of Dwight James Baum, Architect. NY: William Helburn, 1927. 191 plts. (Sl internal soil.) Blue cl (worn, soiled, sl warped), gilt. *Freeman**. $140/£90

BAUM, JAMES. Savage Abyssinia. NY, 1927. 1st US ed. (Cl spine dknd, chipped.) *Edwards*. $47/£30

BAUM, JAMES. Unknown Ethiopia. NY, (1937). Frontis, dbl-pg map. Red cl. VG. *Terramedia*. $30/£19

BAUM, L. FRANK. Dorothy and the Wizard in Oz. Chicago, (1908). 1st ed, 1st state, secondary binding w/o 'THE' at spine foot. 16 color plts by John R. Neill. Orig blue cl (sl spotted; ink name), pict onlay. *Kane**. $400/£256

BAUM, L. FRANK. Dorothy and the Wizard in Oz. Chicago: Reilly & Britton, (1908). 1st ed, 1st issue, w/picture of Dorothy on ownership pg and dwg of Ozma, w/words 'The End' as final illus (p257). 8vo. 16 full-pg color plts by John R. Neill. Lt blue cl (soiled, worn, lower hinge repaired, spine chipped), paper pict cvr pastedown, gilt, 'THE REILLY & BRITTON CO.' on spine. *Glenn*. $500/£321

BAUM, L. FRANK. Dorothy and the Wizard of Oz. Chicago, (1908). 1st ed, 1st issue, w/pub's ad on half-title listing 3 works; w/last gathering in 10 leaves. 8vo. 16 color plts by John R. Neill. Orig cl, full-size color pict fr cvr label. Excellent in secondary binding w/shortened pub's imprint on spine. Dj (corners chipped, clean tear fr panel, sm pieces missing spine ends w/partial loss of imprint). Dj design identical to that of 1st issue binding, w/longer imprint. *Swann**. $2,530/£1,622

BAUM, L. FRANK. Dorothy and the Wizard of Oz. Chicago: Reilly & Britton, (1908). 1st ed. 16 full-color plts (lacks plt facing p146). Secondary binding w/o 'Co.' (worn). Contents, plts VG. *New Hampshire**. $75/£48

BAUM, L. FRANK. The Emerald City of Oz. Chicago: Reilly & Britton, (1910). 1st ed, 1st issue, w/ads listing 'The Road To Oz' through 'John Dough and the Cherub,' all 16 color plts illus by John R. Neill embellished w/grn metallic ink, inserted pict eps in black/orange. 8vo. 296pp. 1st binding 1-1/4 inches thick of lt blue cl, color pict paper label fr cvr embellished w/grn metallic ink, spine lettered in black w/rabbit in silver/black. (Lt dampstain edge of few ll and plts w/edges sl rippled.) *House*. $900/£577

BAUM, L. FRANK. The Emerald City of Oz. Chicago: Reilly & Britton, (1910). 1st ed, 1st issue. 4to. 296pp; 16 full-pg color plts by John R. Neill, each w/metallic-grn ink. Pict eps ptd in orange/black. Blue cl, ptd paper label. Fine. *Bromer*. $950/£609

BAUM, L. FRANK. Glinda of Oz. Chicago, (1920). 1st ed of Baum's last Oz bk. 8vo. 12 color plts by John R. Neill. Fldg color map of Oz laid in, w/Oz flag on verso, that was distributed w/all Oz bks sold in 1920 as promo for the series. (Map reproduces w/sl changes the feps for 1914 orig ed of Tik-Tok of Oz.) Orig cl w/full-size color pict fr cvr label. (Contemp ink inscrip.) Dj (spine ends sl worn). *Swann**. $2,070/£1,327

BAUM, L. FRANK. A Kidnapped Santa Claus. NY/Indianapolis: Bobbs-Merrill, (1969). 1st ed. Richard Rosenblum (illus). 8vo. 45pp (1-inch tear tp). Grn cl. VG + in dj (edge, spine sl torn). *Dower*. $35/£22

BAUM, L. FRANK. The Land of Oz. Chicago: Reilly & Britton, ca 1917. 4to. 287pp; 12 color plts. Pict tan cl (sl worn, soiled). Contents VG. *New Hampshire**. $90/£58

BAUM, L. FRANK. The Life and Adventures of Santa Claus. Indianapolis, (1902). 1st ed, 2nd state, w/Bobbs-Merrill imprint, etc. Sq 8vo. (Few plts sl wrinkled, edgetorn; sl soiled, few pp creased.) Pict cl (sl shelfworn). *Oinonen**. $90/£58

BAUM, L. FRANK. Little Dorothy and Toto of Oz, Also the Cowardly Lion and the Hungry Tiger of Oz. Chicago, 1939. Reissue. 1st ptg coded 'CS 3-39' on tp verso. John R. Neill (illus). Internally VG (edges rubbed). *Mcclintock*. $25/£16

BAUM, L. FRANK. The Lost Princess of Oz. Chicago, (1917). 1st ed, 1st issue, w/pub's ad on ownership pg verso listing this as last of 10 Oz titles. 8vo. 12 color plts by John R. Neill. Orig cl, full-size color pict fr cvr label. (Contemp pencil sig.) Dj (top/bottom edges sl worn, sm surface imperfection affecting 1 letter fr panel, sl cellotape repair verso rear panel). *Swann**. $2,990/£1,917

BAUM, L. FRANK. The Magic of Oz. Chicago, (1919). 1st ed, 1st issue, w/pub's ad on ownership pg verso listing this as last of 11 Oz titles. 8vo. 12 color plts by John R. Neill. Orig cl, full-size color pict fr cvr label. (Contemp pencil sig.) Dj (top/bottom edges sl worn). *Swann**. $2,300/£1,474

BAUM, L. FRANK. The Master Key. Indianapolis: Bowen Merrill, (1901). 1st ed, 1st issue. 12 full-pg color plts by F. Y. Corey. Pict paste-on label fr cvr. NF. *Captain's Bookshelf*. $300/£192

BAUM, L. FRANK. The Master Key. Indianapolis: Bowen-Merrill, (1901). 1st ed, 3rd state, made up of 16pp gatherings, w/pub's name on c. 1 25/32 inches long. Frontis by F. Y. Cory. Olive grn cl, gilt, lurid pict onlay. (Ink name dated 1904, sm smudge half-title, spine sl rubbed), o/w Fine. *Reese*. $150/£96

BAUM, L. FRANK. The New Wizard of Oz. Indianapolis: Bobbs-Merrill, (after 1920). Lg 8vo. 8 color plts by W. W. Denslow. (Sl marginal damping to plts; smudging; inscrip.) Table of Contents calls for pp209-210 to contain Instructions for Waddles, but no evidence those pp bound in. Grn cl (lt soiled, rubbed), plt mtd to fr cvr. VG in remnants of dj. *Waverly**. $38/£24

BAUM, L. FRANK. Ozma of Oz. Chicago, (1907, i.e., 1911). 1st ed, 2nd issue, w/O in Ozma missing p11, line 6; illus p(221) in b/w; pub's ad at end dec w/designs for Baum's The Sea Fairies (1911), which is advertised on dj. This is last issue to incl color pict eps. John R. Neill (illus). 8vo. (Edges lt spotted.) Dj (corners chipped, spine ends lack portions). *Swann**. $690/£442

BAUM, L. FRANK. Ozma of Oz. Toronto: Copp, Clark, (1941). Red cl. (Sl crack rear hinge; 2-inch tears bottoms of pp83, 93, 103), o/w Good. *Scribe's Perch**. $65/£42

BAUM, L. FRANK. The Patchwork Girl of Oz. Chicago: Reilly & Britton, (1913). 1st ed, 1st state, 1st binding. 4to. 340,(8)pp. John R. Neill (illus). 'Chap. Three' positioned incorrectly on p35. Lt grn cl, the 1st binding color, stamped in grn/red/yellow w/illus. Fine. *Bromer*. $850/£545

BAUM, L. FRANK. Phoebe Daring. Chicago: Reilly & Britton, (1912). 1st ed. Joseph Pierre Nuyttens (illus). Dec fr panel. Nice (spine skewed, dknd). *Hermitage*. $200/£128

BAUM, L. FRANK. The Purple Dragon and Other Fantasies. Fictioneer, 1976. 1st ed. Tim Kirk (illus). Fine in Fine dj. *Certo*. $30/£19

BAUM, L. FRANK. Rinkitink in Oz. Chicago, (1916). 1st ed, 1st issue, w/o pub's ad. 8vo. 12 color plts by John R. Neill. Orig cl, full-size color pict fr cvr label. (Contemp ink sig.) Dj (top/bottom edges sl worn). *Swann**. $3,680/£2,359

BAUM, L. FRANK. Rinkitink in Oz. Reilly & Lee, (1935). Color frontis. Grn cl. Good + . *Scribe's Perch**. $65/£42

BAUM, L. FRANK. The Road to Oz. Chicago, (1909). 1st ed, 1st ptg in earliest binding: lt grn cl, pub's name in upper/lower case. Pict cl (lt soil rear cvr). *Kane**. $450/£288

BAUM, L. FRANK. The Royal Book of Oz.... Chicago, (1921). 1st ed, 1st issue, w/plts coated on picture side only; 1st state of plt facing p255, w/'Scarecorw's' in caption. Although Baum, who had died in 1919, is listed as author on cvr and tp, bk was written entirely by Ruth Plumly Thompson. 8vo. 12 color plts by John R. Neill. Orig cl w/full-size color pict fr cvr label. (Contemp ink inscrip, sig.) Dj (top/bottom edges sl worn, 2 sl repairs on verso). *Swann**. $2,185/£1,401

BAUM, L. FRANK. The Scarecrow of Oz. Chicago, (1915). 1st ed, 1st issue, w/pub's ad on half-title verso listing this as the last of 6 Oz titles. 8vo. 12 color plts by John R. Neill. Orig cl, full-size color pict fr cvr label. Dj (top/bottom edges sl worn, spine smudge). *Swann**. $3,680/£2,359

BAUM, L. FRANK. The Surprising Adventures of the Magical Monarch of Mo, and His People. Chicago: M.A. Donohoe, n.d. (ca 1913). 2nd ed, 1st state w/all 12 orig color plts. Frank Verbeck (illus). Sq 8vo. (8),238pp. Blue cl (sl soiled), mtd color illus. *Karmiole*. $100/£64

BAUM, L. FRANK. Tik-Tok of Oz. Reilly & Lee, (1935). Red cl (rear bd mottled). Good (rear pastedown silverfished 4 inches at bottom). *Scribe's Perch**. $50/£32

BAUM, L. FRANK. The Wizard of Oz Waddle Book. NY: Blue Ribbon Books, (1934). 1st Blue Ribbon ed, 2nd state. Lt olive cl, no imprint at base of spine. (Lacks Waddles; ink name fep, spine sl skewed), o/w VF. *Hermitage*. $175/£112

BAUM, L. FRANK. The Wonderful Wizard of Oz. Chicago: Hill, 1900. 1st ed, 2nd issue. (Bds very worn, stained, frayed, loss to head, heel, lacks endsheets; nearly disbound.) *Metropolitan**. $184/£118

BAUM, L. FRANK. The Wonderful Wizard of Oz. West Hatfield: Pennyroyal Press, 1985. One of 350 numbered, signed by Barry Moser (illus). Lg 4to. Gilt-stamped white bds (lt worn). Cl slipcase as issued. *Oinonen**. $400/£256

BAUMANN, JOHN. Old Man Crow's Boy. NY: Wm. Morrow, 1948. 1st ed. Fine in NF dj. *Sadlon*. $40/£26

BAUMEISTER, R. The Cleaning and Sewerage of Cities. NY, 1891. 281pp. Good (extrems worn). *Doctor's Library*. $50/£32

BAUMGARTNER, LEONA and JOHN F. FULTON. A Bibliography of the Poem Syphilis Sive Morbus Gallicus by Girolamo Fracastoro of Verona. New Haven: Yale Univ, 1935. 1st ed. Unopened. Fine. *Glaser*. $60/£38

BAUR, JOHN E. Christmas on the American Frontier, 1800-1900. Caldwell: Caxton, 1961. 1st ed. Color frontis. Red cl. Fine in pict dj. *Argonaut*. $50/£32

BAUSCH, RICHARD. Real Presence. NY: Dial, (1980). 1st ed. Signed, inscribed (1994). (Lt rmdr spray bottom edge), else Fine in dj. *Waverly**. $27/£17

BAX, ARNOLD. Farewell, My Youth. London, 1943. 1st Eng ed. Very Nice (bumped) in dj (sl chipped, nicked). *Clearwater*. $39/£25

BAXTER, J. H. Statistics, Medical and Anthropological of the Provost-Marshal-General's Bureau...During the Late War of the Rebellion.... Washington: GPO, 1875. 2 vols. lxxxvii,568; xxviii,767pp. Orig cl (worn; newly recased saving spines). *Goodrich*. $295/£189

BAXTER, JAMES PHINNEY (ed). Sir Ferdinando Gorges and His Province of Maine. Boston: Prince Soc, 1890. One of 250 sets. 3 vols. Ptd wrappers (detached vol 3), o/w Very Nice set. Howes B250. *Bohling*. $300/£192

BAXTER, JAMES PHINNEY. Pioneers of New France in New England. Albany: Munsell, 1894. 1st ed. (2),450pp. Ptd yellow bds (worn). Howes B249. *Ginsberg*. $150/£96

BAY, J. CHRISTIAN. The Fortune of Books.... Chicago: Walter M. Hill, (1941). 1st ed. Teg. Fine. *Graf*. $100/£64

BAYARD, RALPH. Lone-Star Vanguard. St. Louis: Vincentian, 1945. Good (ex-lib, pocket removed). *Lien*. $20/£13

BAYER, HERBERT. Herbert Bayer: Photographic Works. Leland Rice (intro). (L.A.): Arco Center for Visual Art, 1977. 1st ed. Ltd to 2500. (Owner stamp, 1 corner sl crimped), else VG in illus stiff wrappers. *Cahan*. $65/£42

BAYER, OLIVER WELD. An Eye for an Eye. GC: DCC, 1945. 1st ed. Fine in dj. *Mordida*. $45/£29

BAYLEY, NICOLA. Nicola Bayley's Book of Nursery Rhymes. Cape, 1975. 1st ed, 1st bk. 4to. (32)pp (top margins lt dampmkd, sm spots). Pict bds. (Spine ends knocked), else VG. *Bookmark*. $47/£30

BAYLEY, NICOLA. Nursery Rhymes. London: Cape, (1975). 1st Eng ed. Signed. 8vo. Unpaginated. Glazed illus bds. Fine. *Dower*. $65/£42

BAYLEY, NICOLA. One Old Oxford Ox. Cape, 1977. 1st ed. 4to. 12 color plts. Glossy pict bds. Fine. *Bookmark*. $27/£17

BAYLIS, T. HENRY. The Temple Church and Chapel of St. Ann.... London: George Philip, 1895. Cl-backed bds (worn). *Boswell*. $85/£54

BAYLISS, MARGUERITE F. Bolinvar. NY: Derrydale, 1937. One of 950 numbered sets. Vol 1 signed. 2 vols. (Sl worn, spines sunned.) *Oinonen**. $50/£32

BAYLISS, MARGUERITE F. Bolinvar. NY: Derrydale, 1937. 1st ed. #310/950. 2 vols. Red cl (Spines sl faded), else Fine in bd slipcase (sl worn). *Cummins*. $75/£48

BAYLISS, W. M. Principles of General Physiology. London: Longmans Green, 1915. 1st ed. (Ex-lib.) Red cl (rebacked, spine laid down). *White*. $86/£55

BAYLOR, ARMISTED KEITH. Abdul. An Allegory. (NY): Privately ptd by (Derrydale), 1930. One of 500. Marbled eps. Black cl (Sm stain running through top of gutter), o/w VG. *Cummins*. $400/£256

BAYLOR, GEORGE. Bull Run to Bull Run. Richmond: B.F. Johnson, 1900. 1st ed. (Bkpl, sm rubber lib stamp tp), else near Mint. *Mcgowan*. $275/£176

BAYNE, P. The Life and Letters of Hugh Miller. London, 1871. 2 vols. 2 tinted vignette tps, 4 plts (2 ports, chromolitho view, letter facs). Contemp 1/2 red calf (worn, fr joint vol 1 cracking, vol 2 repaired), gilt spines. *Maggs*. $53/£34

BAYNES, H. G. Mythology of the Soul: A Research into the Unconscious from Schizophrenic Dreams and Drawings. London: Routledge/Kegan Paul, (1955). 50 plts. Blue cl. VG in dj. *Gach*. $100/£64

BAYNES, PAULINE. Victoria and the Golden Bird. London/Glasgow: Blackie, n.d. (1947). Probable 1st ed, 1st bk. 7 1/4 x 9 3/4. 32pp. Cl spine. VG. *Cattermole*. $100/£64

BAZIN, G. A Galley of Flowers. London, 1960. Dj (sl worn). *Maggs*. $19/£12

BAZIN, GERMAIN. The Baroque. Principles, Styles, Modes, Themes. Greenwich, 1968. 418 plts (24 color). Good in dj. *Washton*. $50/£32

BAZIN, HERVE. Viper in the Fist. NY: Prentice-Hall, 1951. 1st US ed. VG (offsetting eps; bds foxed) in VG dj (spine faded, verso foxed). *Lame Duck*. $45/£29

BEACH, REX. Oh Shoot! NY: Harper, 1921. 1st ed. VG. *Bowman*. $20/£13

BEACH, REX. Oh, Shoot!—Confessions of an Agitated Sportsman. NY/London: Harper, (1921), July 1922. Frontis. VG (lt stain cvr) in VG dj (lt stain). *Backman.* $60/£38

BEACH, S. A. et al. The Apples of New York. Albany, 1905. 2 vols. Dec cl. Good (hinges weak, fr hinge vol 2 cracked). *Scribe's Perch**. $85/£54

BEACH, S. A. et al. The Apples of New York. Albany: J.B. Lyons, 1905. 2 vols. Gilt-dec cl (sl edgeworn, bumped). *Metropolitan**. $115/£74

BEACH, SYLVIA. Shakespeare and Company. NY: Harcourt, Brace, (1959). 1st Amer ed. NF in VG dj. *Metropolitan**. $57/£37

BEACH, W. The American Practice Condensed, or the Family Physician. Cincinnati: Moore, Wilstach, 1862. 20th ed. Engr frontis, xlviii-873pp + pub's ads. Orig full sheep (recently rebacked; browning). *Goodrich.* $125/£80

BEACH, WILLIAM N. In the Shadow of Mount McKinley. NY: Derrydale, 1931. One of 750 numbered. Fldg map. Gilt-stamped blue cl (lt worn). *Oinonen**. $325/£208

BEACH, WILLIAM N. In the Shadow of Mount McKinley. NY: Derrydale, 1931. One of 750 numbered. Fldg map. (Lt worn.) Dj (sl soiled, frayed, sm cellotape repair spine). *Oinonen**. $400/£256

BEADLE, ERASTUS F. To Nebraska in '57, a Diary of Erastus F. Beadle. NY Public Library, 1923. Frontis facs, 2 plts. Ptd wraps (lt soiled, spine ends chipped). *Bohling.* $40/£26

BEADLE, J. H. Life in Utah; or, The Mysteries and Crimes of Mormonism.... Phila: National Pub Co, (1870). 1st ed, 1st issue. Fldg map. Contemp blind-stamped calf (rebacked, corners rubbed; lt foxed). *Sadlon.* $50/£32

BEADLE, J. H. Life in Utah; or, The Mysteries and Crimes of Mormonism.... Phila, 1870. 1st ed. Frontis, 540pp + ads, fldg map. (Fr hinge neatly cracked; lt edgewear), o/w VG. *Benchmark.* $90/£58

BEADLE, J. H. Polygamy, or the Mysteries and Crimes of Mormonism.... (N.p., c. 1904.) This copy incl chapter 29, 'New Testimony Proving That Mormons Violate the Laws and Defy the Government.' Pict cl, gilt, marbled edges (dust soiled, tips sl worn). *Shasky.* $50/£32

BEADLE, J. H. Polygamy; or, The Mysteries and Crimes of Mormonism.... N.p., n.d. (1904). (Spine sl lightened.) *Sadlon.* $30/£19

BEADLE, J. H. The Undeveloped West. Phila, (1873). 1st ed. 15,823 pp. (Rebound.) *Heinoldt.* $35/£22

BEADLE, J. H. Western Wilds and the Men Who Redeem Them. Cincinnati, 1878. Dbl-pg map frontis, 624pp. Marbled eps, edges. Red-brn beveled bds, gilt. VG (cvr, spine edges lt scuffed). Howes B269. *Five Quail.* $125/£80

BEAGLE, PETER. A Fine and Private Place. Viking, 1960. 1st ed, 1st bk. Fine in dj (corners sl worn, sm closed tear rear panel). *Certo.* $60/£38

BEAL, MERRILL D. The Story of Man in Yellowstone. Caldwell: Caxton, 1949. 1st ed. VG in VG dj. *Perier.* $30/£19

BEALE, JAMES (comp). The Battle Flags of the Army of the Potomac at Gettysburg, Penna. July, 1st, 2d, and 3d, 1863. Phila: James Beale, 1885. 1st ed. #66/125 numbered, signed. 35 leaves; 32 Superb color plts. Later cl. (2 sm owner stamps, sm lib stamp), else NF. *Mcgowan.* $2,250/£1,442

BEALE, JOSEPH HENRY. A Treatise on Criminal Pleading and Practice. Boston: Little, Brown, 1899. Contemp sheep (rubbed). Sound. *Boswell.* $75/£48

BEALE, LIONEL S. How to Work with the Microscope. London: Harrison, 1865. 3rd ed. Frontis, 272pp; 56 plts. VG. *Savona.* $70/£45

BEALE, MORRIS. The Washington Senators: An 87-Year History of the World's Oldest Baseball Club.... DC: Columbia, 1947. 1st ed. VG + (lt foxed) in VG + dj (spine sunned). *Fuller & Saunders.* $95/£61

BEALS, CARLTON. Black River. Phila: Lippincott, 1934. (Name erased fep), else Fine in metallic silver-color bds, NF dj (lt soiled, crown sl rubbed). *Between The Covers.* $85/£54

BEAMISH, NORTH LUDLOW. Discovery of America by the Northmen, in the Tenth Century.... London: Boone, 1841. 1st ed. 239,(10)pp; 2 fldg maps, fldg table, fldg plt. Contemp 1/2 calf. Howes B277. *Ginsberg.* $150/£96

BEAN, JACOB. 17th Century Italian Drawings in the Metropolitan Museum of Art. NY, 1979. (Sl soiled, sl shaken.) *Washton.* $25/£16

BEAN, W. J. Trees and Shrubs Hardy in the British Isles. London: John Murray, 1929. 5th ed. 2 vols. Gilt-dec spine (rubbed, sl shaken). *Quest.* $85/£54

BEAN, W. J. Trees and Shrubs. London, 1950. 7th ed. 3 vols. Djs (sl chipped). *Edwards.* $117/£75

BEANE, J. F. From Forecastle to Cabin: The Story of a Cruise...in Pursuit of Whales. NY: Editor Pub Co, 1905. Port, fldg map. (Orig buff sailcl soiled), else VG. *High Latitude.* $160/£103

BEARD, GEORGE M. A Practical Treatise on Nervous Exhaustion.... NY: William Wood, 1880. 1st ed. (ii),xx,198,(2)pp. Good (shelfworn, fr bd stained). *Gach.* $200/£128

BEARD, GEORGE M. and A. D. ROCKWELL. A Practical Treatise on the Medical and Surgical Uses of Electricity. NY: William Wood, 1875. 2nd rev, enlgd ed. (iv),(xxx),794,(4)pp. Panelled grn cl (lt spotted; joints, edges rubbed), gilt spine. Good + . *Gach.* $250/£160

BEARD, GEORGE M. and A. D. ROCKWELL. A Practical Treatise on the Medical and Surgical Uses of Electricity. NY, 1881. 3rd ed. 758pp. Good (extrems worn). *Doctor's Library.* $150/£96

BEARD, JAMES. Delights and Prejudices. NY: Atheneum, 1964. 1st ed. Fine in dj (edgetorn). *Perier.* $50/£32

BEARDSLEY, AUBREY. Last Letters of Aubrey Beardsley. London, 1904. 1st Eng ed. Good (sl mkd, handled, rubbed). *Clearwater.* $86/£55

BEARDSLEY, AUBREY. The Later Works. London: John Lane, Bodley Head, 1920. 174 plts. Mod 1/2 levant morocco gilt. Very Nice. *Hollett.* $187/£120

BEARDSLEY, AUBREY. The Letters of Aubrey Beardsley. Maas et al (eds). London: Cassell, 1971. 1st ed. (Fr corners sl bruised), o/w Very Nice in dj (sl soiled, nicked, price-clipped). *Virgo.* $70/£45

BEARDSLEY, AUBREY. A Second Book of Fifty Drawings. NY: John Lane, 1899. 1st ed, Amer issue. Port. Crimson cl, gilt. (Eps, plt borders foxed; spine faded), o/w Good. *Reese.* $125/£80

BEARDSLEY, AUBREY. Under the Hill and Other Essays in Prose and Verse. London/NY: John Lane, Bodley Head, 1904. 1st ed, ordinary issue. Port. Blue cl, gilt. (Sl foxed, spine rubbed), o/w VG. *Reese.* $300/£192

BEARDSLEY, AUBREY. Under the Hill. London: John Lane, Bodley Head, 1921. 3rd ed. Frontis. Grn cl. VG (bkpl) in dj (chipped, lacks pieces). *Turtle Island.* $145/£93

BEARSS, EDWIN C. and A. M. GIBSON. Fort Smith. Norman: Univ of OK, (1969). 1st ed. VG in dj (sl worn). *Lien.* $30/£19

BEATIE, RUSSEL H. Saddles. London, 1981. Dj. *Edwards.* $39/£25

BEATNIFFE, R. The Norfolk Tour. Norwich, 1808. 6th ed. 392pp; fldg map. Good + (recased). *Scribe's Perch**. $20/£13

BEATON, CECIL and GAIL BUCKLAND. The Magic Image. Boston/Toronto: Little, Brown, 1975. 1st Amer ed. Fine in dj (lt worn). *Cahan.* $85/£54

BEATON, CECIL. Air of Glory. London: HMSO, 1941. 1st Eng ed. Very Nice in dj (chipped, mkd, spotted, torn, repaired). *Clearwater.* $70/£45

BEATON, CECIL. Ashcombe: The Story of a Fifteen-Year Lease. Batsford, 1949. 1st ed. (Inscrip), else VG in dj (chipped, rubbed, closed tears). *Hadley.* $39/£25

BEATON, CECIL. Ballet. London, 1951. 1st Eng ed. Very Nice in dj (chipped, price-clipped). *Clearwater.* $39/£25

BEATON, CECIL. Ballet. NY: Doubleday, 1951. 1st ed. Grey/black cl. Fine in dj. *Appelfeld.* $85/£54

BEATON, CECIL. Beaton Portraits. London: Nat'l Portrait Gallery, HMSO, 1968. 1st ed. Frontis self-port. (Owner stamp, lt worn), else VG in plain stiff wrappers, illus dj. *Cahan.* $25/£16

BEATON, CECIL. Beaton. NY: Viking, 1980. 1st ed. VG+ in VG+ dj. *Smith.* $50/£32

BEATON, CECIL. Cecil Beaton's Fair Lady. NY, (1964). 1st ed. Inscribed. Pict cl. Dj (torn). *Argosy.* $60/£38

BEATON, CECIL. Cecil Beaton's New York. Phila: Lippincott, (1938). 1st ed. Color frontis. Brn morocco, marbled bds, gilt, black spine labels. Good. *Karmiole.* $85/£54

BEATON, CECIL. Cecil Beaton's Scrapbook. Batsford, 1937. 1st Eng ed. 1/2 cl, wallpaper sides. Good (spine, edges chafed). *Clearwater.* $101/£65

BEATON, CECIL. History Under Fire. London: Batsford, (1941). 1st ed. VG in dj (lt chipped). *Reese.* $45/£29

BEATON, CECIL. India. (Bombay): Thacker, 1945. 1st ed. VG in gray cl. *Hadley.* $62/£40

BEATON, CECIL. Portrait of New York. London: Batsford, 1948. Frontis. (Owner stamp, ink name, sm stain on fr), else VG w/dj fragments. *Cahan.* $45/£29

BEATON, GEORGE. (Pseud of Gerald Brenan.) Jack Robinson. London, 1933. 1st Eng ed. (Ex-lib; label removed fr cvr, cvrs mkd, handled.) *Clearwater.* $39/£25

BEATON, GEORGE. (Pseud of Gerald Brenan.) Jack Robinson: A Picaresque Novel. London: C&W, 1933. 1st bk. Inscribed presentation. VG (cl sl worn) in dj (chipped, torn, spine dknd). *Gekoski.* $585/£375

BEATON, KENDALL. Enterprise in Oil. NY, 1957. Dj (sl chipped). *Edwards.* $39/£25

BEATTIE, GEORGE WILLIAM and HELEN PRUITT BEATTIE. Heritage of the Valley: San Bernardino's First Century. Pasadena: San Pasqual, 1939. 1st ed. Fldg map. Gold-stamped. Dj (tear). *Dawson.* $150/£96

BEATTIE, WILLIAM. Switzerland. London: George Virtue, 1836. 1st ed. 2 vols. Extra engr tps, 106 steel-engr plts, fldg engr map vol 2. Aeg. Crimson sheep, plain brn cl, gilt. (Text, plts sl foxed, lt aged, map edge ragged; spines worn, scuffed, chipped, 1 vol w/spine top torn.) Texts Good. *Baltimore*.* $350/£224

BEATTY, JOHN. Memoirs of a Volunteer, 1861-1863. Harvey S. Ford (ed). NY, (1946). 1st ed. Map. *Wantagh.* $30/£19

BEATY, RICHARD E. The Blue Ridge Boys. Front Royal: The Author, (c. 1938). Paper cvrs (soiled). *Book Broker.* $45/£29

BEAUCHAMP, WILLIAM M. Aboriginal Place Names of New York. Albany: NY State Ed Dept, 1907. Good in wraps (spine dknd, chipped). *Brown.* $20/£13

BEAUCLERK, HELEN. For the Love of the Foolish Angel. London: Collins, 1929. 1st ed. Frontis by Edmund Dulac. (Feps browned.) Patterned cl, gilt. Dj (sl creased). *Hollett.* $55/£35

BEAUFORT, DUKE OF and MOWBRAY MORRIS. Hunting. Badminton Library, 1894. 7th ed. Dec brn cl (backstrip sl dull). *Petersfield.* $39/£25

BEAUMAN, KATHARINE BENTLEY. Wings on Her Shoulders. London, (?1945). Very Nice (cvrs sl spotted) in dj (mkd, chipped). *Clearwater.* $86/£55

BEAUMONT, CHARLES. Charles Beaumont: Selected Stories. Arlington Heights: Dark Harvest, 1988. 1st ed. One of 500 numbered, signed by Bloch, Bradbury, Ellison, Etchison and 11 other contributors. Fine in dj in slipcase. *Other Worlds.* $175/£112

BEAUMONT, CHARLES. The Hunger and Other Stories. NY: Putnam, (1957). 1st ed. Fine (sl shelfworn) in VG dj (extrems lt worn). *Metropolitan*.* $69/£44

BEAUMONT, CHARLES. Selected Stories. Arlington Heights, IL: Dark Harvest, 1988. 1st trade ed. Dj. *Swann*.* $46/£29

BEAUMONT, CHARLES. Selected Stories. Roger Anker (ed). Arlington Heights, IL: Dark Harvest, 1988. One of 500 numbered, signed by Anker, Christopher Beaumont (preface) and 14 other contributors. Dj, pub's bd slipcase. *Swann*.* $115/£74

BEAUMONT, CYRIL W. The History of Harlequin. London: C.W. Beaumont, 1926. One of 325. 5 hand-colored plts. Ptd bds, vellum spine. *Appelfeld.* $250/£160

BEAUMONT, CYRIL W. The Monte Carlo Russian Ballet. London, 1934. 1st ed. Fine. *Polyanthos.* $30/£19

BEAUMONT, CYRIL W. Serge Diaghilev. London: C.W. Beaumont, 1933. 1st ed. 7 plts. (Cvr sl soiled, chipped; fep excised). *Shasky.* $25/£16

BEAUMONT, CYRIL W. A Short History of Ballet. 1933. 1st ed. VG. *Words Etc.* $19/£12

BEAUMONT, CYRIL W. The Vic-Wells Ballet. London, 1935. 1st ed. Fine. *Polyanthos.* $30/£19

BEAUMONT, FRANCIS and JOHN FLETCHER. The Maides Tragedy. NY: Cheshire House, 1932. Ltd to 1200 numbered. Teg. Leather backed marbled bds. VG (bkpl) in poor slipcase. *King.* $65/£42

BEAUMONT, ROBERTS. Carpets and Rugs. Benn, 1924. 1st ed. 14 color plts, 1 fldg. Blue cl, gilt spine. VG. *Words Etc.* $55/£35

BEAUMONT, WILLIAM. Experiments and Observations on the Gastric Juice, and the Physiology of Digestion. Plattsburgh: F.P. Allen, 1833. 1st ed. One of 1000 ptd. 8vo. 280pp (foxed). Mod 1/2 brn levant. *Argosy.* $2,000/£1,282

BEAUMONT, WILLIAM. Experiments and Observations on the Gastric Juice, and the Physiology of Digestion. Plattsburgh: F.P. Allen, 1833. 1st ed. 8vo. 280pp (early owner sig on tp; lt foxing to prelims). Orig bds (rebacked in cl, w/paper spine label replicating orig). VG in 1/2 morocco fldg clamshell box. *Glaser.* $2,400/£1,538

BEAUMONT, WILLIAM. Experiments and Observations on the Gastric Juice, and the Physiology of Digestion. Boston: (Harvard Univ), 1929. Facs of 1833 1st ed. Frontis port. Cl-backed bds, paper spine label. VF in ptd dj (sl soiled, mkd, sl frayed). *Pirages.* $150/£96

BEAVER, C. MASTEN. Fort Yukon Trader——Three Years in an Alaskan Wilderness. NY: Exposition Press, (1955). 1st ed. VG in VG dj. *Perier.* $35/£22

BEAVER, HERBERT. Reports and Letters of...1836-1838. Thomas E. Jessett (ed). (Portland, OR): Champoeg, 1959. 1st ed. One of 750 ptd. Uncut. Grn cl lettered in gold/white. Fine. *Argonaut.* $60/£38

BEAVER, PATRICK. A History of Tunnels. Citadel, 1973. 1st Amer ed. VG+. *Bookcell.* $30/£19

BEAZLEY, J. D. The Development of Attic Black-Figure. Berkeley/L.A., 1951. 49 plts. Good. *Washton.* $75/£48

BECHER, H. C. R. A Trip to Mexico. Toronto: Willing & Williamson, 1800. 1st ed. vii,183pp; 13 albumen photos. Orig gilt-dec cl. (1st, last leaf strengthened; recased, lt worn, new eps), else VG. *Cahan.* $300/£192

BECHSTEIN, JOHANN MATTHAUS. Cage and Chamber-Birds. Henry Gardiner Adams (ed). London: H.G. Bohn, 1853. xvi,500pp; 31 hand-colored engr plts, incl frontis. (Sl browned, few sl creases, tears.) Contemp pebble-grain grn morocco (neatly rejointed, corners worn, sl rubbed, backstrip dknd, scuffed), gilt. Internally Excellent. *Pirages.* $450/£288

BECHSTEIN, LUDWIG and RANDALL JARRELL. The Rabbit Catcher. NY: Macmillan, 1961. 1st ed. Ugo Fontana (illus). 9 3/4 x 13. 36pp. Glossy bds. VG. *Cattermole.* $15/£10

BECHTEL, EDWIN DE T. Jacques Callot. NY, 1955. 100 plts, 3 gatefolds. Good in dj. *Washton.* $45/£29

BECK, JAMES M. The Evidence in the Case. NY: Putnam, 1914. Grn cl (spine faded), gilt. Good. *Boswell.* $50/£32

BECK, T. R. and J. B. Elements of Medical Jurisprudence. 1836. 5th ed. xviii,1010pp (ink sig crossed out, lt foxed, lt pencil mks). 1/2 morocco, marbled bds (sl worn). *Whitehart.* $125/£80

BECKE, LOUIS and WALTER JEFFERY. The Naval Pioneers of Australia. London: Murray, 1899. 1st ed. x,313pp. (Eps browned; worn, faded; ex-lib, spine sticker), o/w Good. *Worldwide.* $35/£22

BECKE, LOUIS. Rodman the Boatsteerer and Other Stories. London: T. Fisher Unwin, 1898. 1st ed. Ad leaf before tp; (viii),331,(i),(xii)pp + 12pp integral ads. Teg, others uncut. Ribbed dk grn cl, gilt. (Cvrs sl dull), o/w Nice. *Temple.* $28/£18

BECKER, G. Geology of the Comstock Lode and the Washoe District. Washington: USGS, 1882. xv,422pp. (Map atlas not present.) Good. *Blake.* $200/£128

BECKER, J. E. Sexual Life of Japan. N.p.: Privately ptd, n.d. (1905). 3rd ed. Later red 1/2 morocco. VG. *Terramedia.* $300/£192

BECKER, STEPHEN. When the War Is Over. NY: Random House, (1969). 1st ed. Navy blue cl. Fine in NF dj (sl bumped). *Blue Mountain.* $20/£13

BECKETT, R. B. Hogarth. London, 1949. 202 plts. Good. *Washton.* $75/£48

BECKETT, SAMUEL. All That Fall. NY, (1957). Specially bound, ltd to 100 numbered. Cl-backed bds. (Sl extrem discolor), else VG. *King.* $200/£128

BECKETT, SAMUEL. Come and Go. London: Calder & Boyars, (1967). 1st Eng ed. One of 100 numbered, signed. Fine in cardbd slipcase. *Between The Covers.* $600/£385

BECKETT, SAMUEL. Film. Faber, 1972. 1st ed. VG in wrappers. *Words Etc.* $31/£20

BECKETT, SAMUEL. From an Abandoned Work. London, 1958. 1st ed. VG in glassine wrapper. *Words Etc.* $31/£20

BECKETT, SAMUEL. How It Is. London: John Calder, 1964. 1st ed in English. Fine in Excellent dj (sl wrinkled, sl soiled). *Pirages.* $100/£64

BECKETT, SAMUEL. Ill Seen, Ill Said. NY: Grove, 1981. 1st English trans. Fine in NF dj (long scratch rear panel). *Lame Duck.* $35/£22

BECKETT, SAMUEL. Mercier and Camier. NY: Grove, 1974. 1st English trans. (Upper edges sl faded), else Fine in dj. *Lame Duck.* $50/£32

BECKETT, SAMUEL. Molloy, Malone Dies, The Unnamable. (Paris): Olympia, 1959. 1st complete ed. (Spine creased), else Fine in ptd wraps. *Hadley.* $31/£20

BECKETT, SAMUEL. Molloy. Paris: Olympia, 1955. VG in dec self-wrappers. *Williams.* $187/£120

BECKETT, SAMUEL. Murphy. NY, 1957. 1st Amer ed. Fine in NF dj (spine sunned). *Warren.* $100/£64

BECKETT, SAMUEL. Poems in English. NY: Grove, 1963. 1st ptg this ed. VF in ptd paper cvrs. *Pirages.* $30/£19

BECKETT, SAMUEL. Proust. London: C&W, 1931. 1st ed. Dec bds. Dj (browned, dampstained; spine head loss, cracks). *Metropolitan*.* $86/£55

BECKETT, SAMUEL. Six Residua. Calder, 1972. Pb orig. VG + . *Williams.* $23/£15

BECKETT, SAMUEL. Stories and Texts for Nothing. NY: Grove, (1967). 1st Amer ed. Fine in dj (lt rubbed). *Hermitage.* $75/£48

BECKETT, SAMUEL. Three Occasional Pieces. Faber, 1982. 1st UK ed. Fine in wraps, as issued. *Williams.* $9/£6

BECKETT, SAMUEL. The Unnamable. NY: Grove, 1958. Ltd to 100 numbered. Cl-backed bds. NF. *Words Etc.* $148/£95

BECKETT, SAMUEL. Waiting for Godot. Faber, 1956. 1st UK ed. NF in VG dj. *Williams.* $148/£95

BECKETT, SAMUEL. Watt. Paris: Olympia, (1958). 2nd ed. Dec bds. VG in dj (spine fraying). *Reese.* $65/£42

BECKETT, SAMUEL. Worstward Ho. NY: Grove, 1983. 1st ed. Fine in dj. *Lame Duck.* $50/£32

BECKFORD, PETER. Thoughts upon Hunting.... J. Debrett, 1802. 4th ed. Frontis (lt browned), 1/2 title, 2 plts. 19th cent grn calf gilt, gilt panelled back w/red morocco label, marbled edges (cvrs sl mkd). *Hatchwell.* $195/£125

BECKFORD, RUTH. Katherine Dunham: A Biography. NY: Marcel Dekker, (1979). 1st ed. Fine in dj. *Between The Covers.* $50/£32

BECKFORD, WILLIAM. The History of the Caliph Vathek; and European Travels. Ward Lock, 1891. xxvi,549pp; port. Sound (cl lt rubbed, soiled). *Cox.* $19/£12

BECKFORD, WILLIAM. The Journal of William Beckford in Portugal and Spain 1787-88. Boyd Alexander (ed). London, 1954. 1st ed. VG in dj. *Gretton.* $31/£20

BECKFORD, WILLIAM. Vathek. Herbert B. Grimsditch (trans). London: Nonesuch, 1929. Ltd to 1550. Uncut. Orig 1/4 vellum (corners sl rubbed), gilt. *Hollett.* $101/£65

BECKMAN, H. and N. HINCHEY. The Large Springs of Missouri. Rolla, 1944. Wrappers (sl worn). *Maggs.* $19/£12

BECKMANN, JOHN. A History of Inventions, Discoveries, and Origins. London: Bohn, 1846. 4th ed. 2 vols. 2 frontis ports. (Inscrip both vols.) *Rostenberg & Stern.* $85/£54

BECKMANN, JOHN. A History of Inventions, Discoveries, and Origins. London: Bohn, 1846. 2 vols. 1000 + pp. Nice. *Bookcell.* $100/£64

BECKWITH, JOHN. The Art of Constantinople. An Introduction to Byzantine Art 330-1453. London: Phaidon, 1961. 1st ed. Fine in dj. *Europa.* $25/£16

BECKWITH, MARTHA WARREN. Black Roadways: A Study of Jamaican Folk Life. Chapel Hill: Univ of NC, 1929. 1st ed. Frontis, color fldg map. VG in dj (chipped). *Cahan.* $45/£29

BECOTTE, MICHAEL. Space Capsule. Carlisle, MA: Pentacle, 1975. 1st ed. 51 full-pg sepia photos. Fine in illus stiff wrappers. *Cahan.* $25/£16

BEDARD, MICHAEL. Emily. NY: Doubleday, 1992. 1st ed. Barbara Cooney (illus). 10 3/4 x 9 1/4. 32pp. Cl spine. Fine in dj. *Cattermole.* $32/£21

BEDDARD, F. E. A Book of Whales. London/NY: Murray/Putnam, 1900. 1st ed. 40 plts. Blind-stamped dec cl. VG + . *Mikesh.* $125/£80

BEDE, CUTHBERT. (Pseud of Edward Bradley.) Little Mr. Bouncer and His Friend Verdant Green. Boston: Little, Brown, 1893. Amer ed. #32/250. Frontis port, xv,292pp. Ptd spine label (chipped, dknd). Nice interior. (Edgewear.) *Bohling.* $20/£13

BEDE, THE VENERABLE. The History of the Church of England. Stratford-upon-Avon: Shakespeare Head, 1930. One of 475 sets. 2 vols. Uncut, unopened. Linen-backed bds. Cl slipcase. *Swann*.* $402/£258

BEDELL, L. FRANK. The Shetland Pony. Ames: IA State Univ, 1959. 1st ed. VG. *October Farm.* $40/£26

BEDFORD, GUNNING S. Lecture on Obstetrics and the Diseases of Women and Children. NY, 1848. 26pp. (Ex-lib.) Orig ptd wrappers. *Argosy.* $50/£32

BEDFORD, GUNNING S. The Principles and Practice of Obstetrics. NY: Wm. Wood, 1862. 2nd ed. xxxvii,731pp. Orig cl (rebacked), orig spine. *Goodrich.* $115/£74

BEDFORD, SYBILLE. A Compass Error. Collins, (1968). 1st ed. Nice in dj (sl rubbed). *Ash.* $31/£20

BEDINI, SYLVIO A. The Life of Benjamin Banneker. NY: Scribner, (1972). 1st ed. Fine (bd edges sl soiled) in NF dj (sl spine tanned). *Between The Covers.* $75/£48

BEE, CLAIR. Triple-Threat Trouble. G&D, 1960. 1st ed. 5x7.5. 182pp. Last title listed. VG+ (sl shelfworn) in dj (edgetears). *My Bookhouse.* $50/£32

BEEBE, LUCIUS and CHARLES CLEGG. U.S. West. The Saga of Wells Fargo. NY: E.P. Dutton, 1949. 1st ed. Dec cl. Fine in pict dj (lt worn; spine lacks sm piece). *Argonaut.* $75/£48

BEEBE, LUCIUS. Fallen Stars. Boston: Cornhill, (1921). 1st ed. Gray-grn bds, ptd paper label. VG. *Houle.* $150/£96

BEEBE, LUCIUS. Mansions on Rails. Berkeley: Howell-North, 1959. #579/1950. Signed. Tipped-in color frontis, fldg pocket plt. Fine in slipcase. *Bohling.* $110/£71

BEEBE, WILLIAM. Galapagos: World's End. NY: Putnam, 1924. 2nd ptg. 8 plts. Dec eps. Good. *Scribe's Perch*.* $50/£32

BEEBE, WILLIAM. A Monograph of the Pheasants. London, 1918-22. One of 600 numbered sets. 4 vols. Folio. 90 color plts, 88 photogravure plts, 20 maps. (Vol 1 spine ends worn, vol 2 spine faded.) *Swann*.* $2,070/£1,327

BEEBE, WILLIAM. Pheasant Jungles. NY/London: Putnam (Knickerbocker), 1927. 1st ed. 46 photo plts. (Cl sl rubbed, soiled), o/w VG. *Worldwide.* $24/£15

BEEBE, WILLIAM. Pheasants: Their Lives and Homes. GC/NY, 1926. 1st ed. 2 vols. VG. *Truepenny.* $250/£160

BEEBE, WILLIAM. Pheasants: Their Lives and Homes. NY: Doubleday, Doran, 1931. 2 vols. Grn cl (speckled, spines sunned, bumped). *Metropolitan*.* $60/£38

BEECHER, CATHERINE E. Letters to the People on Health and Happiness. NY: Harper, 1855. 1st ed. (194),(30)pp. Emb Victorian cl. (Gutter, lower margin 1 leaf torn), else VG. *Gach.* $85/£54

BEECHER, EDWARD. Narrative of Riots at Alton.... Alton, (IL): George Holton, 1838. 1st ed. 159pp. Orig cl (faded), ptd paper spine label. Howes B307. *M & S.* $300/£192

BEECHER, HENRY W. Pleasant Talk About Flowers and Farming. Edinburgh/London: Strahan/Sampson Low, 1859. 2nd ed. x,270pp. Dec cl (hinges cracked), gilt. *Quest.* $40/£26

BEECHER, LYMAN. A Plea for the West. Cincinnati: Truman & Smith, 1835. 2nd ed. 190pp. Later cl. *M & S.* $75/£48

BEECHER, LYMAN. Six Sermons on the Nature, Occasions, Signs, Evils; and Remedy of Intemperance. NY, 1827. 1st ed. 104pp (foxed). Orig tooled cl bds. Good (worn, cvrs faded). *Doctor's Library.* $50/£32

BEECHEY, FREDERICK WILLIAM. Crew of the Blossom's Barge Erecting a Post for Captn Franklin Near Refuge Inlet. London: Henry Colburn & Richard Bentley, 1830. (Verso, margins of sheet lt soiled), else VG. Howes B309. *Parmer.* $45/£29

BEEDE, A. M. Sitting Bull—Custer. Bismarck, ND, (1913). 1st ed. Limp suede. (Badly stained.) *King.* $35/£22

BEEDHAM, R. JOHN. Wood Engraving. London: Faber & Faber, 1938. 5th ed. VG in dj. *Michael Taylor.* $20/£13

BEEDING, FRANCIS. Death Walks in Eastrepps. NY: Mystery League, 1931. 1st Amer ed. NF in dj (edge tear, sl rubbed, rear panel missing). *Polyanthos.* $25/£16

BEEDING, FRANCIS. He Could Not Have Slipped. NY: Harper, 1939. 1st ed. Fine in dj (few sm tears). *Antic Hay.* $25/£16

BEEDOME, THOMAS. Select Poems Divine and Humane. Bloomsbury: Nonesuch, 1928. Ltd to 1250. Full limp parchment w/pigskin thongs. VF in cream paper-cvrd slipcase (lt worn). *Truepenny.* $125/£80

BEEK, MARTIN A. Atlas of Mesopotamia. H. H. Rowley (ed). D. R. Welsh (trans). London: Nelson, 1962. 22 color maps. Burgundy buckram. (Bkpl.) *Turtle Island.* $75/£48

BEER, THOMAS. Hanna. NY: Knopf, 1929. One of 250 numbered, signed. Patterned bds. VG- (spine sl dknd, sm chip fr bd). *Antic Hay.* $50/£32

BEER, THOMAS. Stephen Crane, a Study in American Letters. NY: Knopf, 1923. 1st ed. Fine in Fine dj. *Macdonnell.* $100/£64

BEERBOHM, MAX. And Even Now. London, 1920. 1st Eng ed. (Sl faded, sl bumped.) Dj. *Clearwater.* $70/£45

BEERBOHM, MAX. Around Theatres. London: Heinemann, 1924. 1st ed, issued as vols 8 & 9 of the collected ed of the 'Works,' each vol being ltd to 780 copies. 2 vols. Uncut. Buckram, paper spine labels. VG. *Dramatis Personae.* $150/£96

BEERBOHM, MAX. Around Theatres. London: Heinemann, 1924. One of 780 sets, 750 for sale. 2 vols. (Offsetting, eps browned, prelims sl foxed; edges spotted), o/w VG in djs (soiled, browned, chipped; lg pieces missing spine ends). *Virgo.* $624/£400

BEERBOHM, MAX. Caricatures by Max from the Collection in the Ashmolean Museum. OUP, (1958). 1st ed. VG in dec wraps. *Ash.* $39/£25

BEERBOHM, MAX. Catalogue of the Caricatures of Max Beerbohm. Cambridge, MA: Harvard Univ, 1972. 1st ed. Mint in dj. *Argosy.* $85/£54

BEERBOHM, MAX. The Dreadful Dragon of Hay Hill. London, 1928. 1st ed. Color frontis. 1/2 cl. VG in dj. *Argosy.* $100/£64

BEERBOHM, MAX. Fifty Caricatures. London: Heinemann, 1913. 1st ed. (Prelims sl foxed.) Pict cl. Very Nice. *Holmes.* $95/£61

BEERBOHM, MAX. The Happy Hypocrite. London: John Lane, (1915). 1st ed thus. George Sheringham (illus). Full pict linen (spine sl dknd). *Appelfeld.* $125/£80

BEERBOHM, MAX. The Happy Hypocrite. London: John Lane, Bodley Head, (1918). 1st illus ed, trade issue. Frontis. Pict cl. (Lt foxing; spine sl tanned, few bubbles, smudges rear bd), else VG. *Reese.* $75/£48

BEERBOHM, MAX. The Happy Hypocrite. New Fairfield: Bruce Rogers/October House, 1955. One of 600. Lilac/purple dec paper bds, gilt. (Bk label pasted to ep), o/w Fine in glassine dj (chipped). *Heller.* $75/£48

BEERBOHM, MAX. Lytton Strachey. CUP, 1943. 1st ed. (Edges lt spotted), o/w VG in wraps. *Ash.* $31/£20

BEERBOHM, MAX. Mainly on the Air. NY: Knopf, 1958. 1st Amer ed. Fine in dj. *Antic Hay.* $20/£13

BEERBOHM, MAX. Max Beerbohm's Letters to Reggie Turner. Rupert Hart-Davis (ed). Phila: Lippincott, 1965. 1st ed. NF in VG dj (price-clipped, internal mends to tears). *Antic Hay.* $20/£13

BEERBOHM, MAX. Max's Nineties. Drawings 1892-1899. London, 1958. 1st Eng ed. Buckram-backed bds. Very Nice in dj. *Clearwater.* $62/£40

BEERBOHM, MAX. Observations. London: Heinemann, 1925. 1st ed. Color frontis, 51 plts. Yellow cl. (Crown sl torn, corners bumped; dusty), else VG. *Hermitage.* $65/£42

BEERBOHM, MAX. Observations. London: Heinemann, 1925. 1st ed. Yellow cl. Fine in dj (nicked). *Appelfeld.* $150/£96

BEERBOHM, MAX. Rossetti and His Circle. Heinemann, (1922). 1st ed. #178/380 signed. Color frontis, 22 color plts, guards. Aeg. White buckram (sl soiled), gilt. *Bickersteth.* $172/£110

BEERBOHM, MAX. A Survey. London, 1921. 1st ed. 51 mtd illus. Red cl. VG. *Argosy.* $125/£80

BEERBOHM, MAX. Things New and Old. London: Heinemann, 1923. 1st ed. One of 380 numbered w/extra plt, signed. Color frontis, 16 mtd color plts. Extraneous Beerbohm plt taped to fr pastedown. White cl. *Swann*.* $258/£165

BEERBOHM, MAX. A Variety of Things. NY: Knopf, 1928. 1st Amer ed. One of 2000 numbered. Black cl (fr cvr lt spotting), gilt. Internally NF in dj (chipped, torn, spine faded). *Blue Mountain.* $25/£16

BEERBOHM, MAX. The Works of Max Beerbohm. John Lane, Bodley Head, 1896. 1st British ed. Red cl (spine sl worn, sl dknd), paper label, both spare labels intact. Good. *Ash.* $304/£195

BEERBOHM, MAX. The Works of Max Beerbohm. London: Heinemann, 1922-1928. One of 780 sets signed. 10 vols. 8vo. 1/2 calf, gilt. *Swann*.* $1,265/£811

BEERBOHM, MAX. The Works.... NY, 1896. 1st ed. One of 1000 (400 pulped). (Foxed; spine top lt rubbed, sm tear.) *Kane*.* $80/£51

BEERBOHM, MAX. Zuleika Dobson. London, 1911. 1st issue, in smooth cl. (Name, foxed; mkd, hinges cracking.) *Clearwater.* $55/£35

BEERBOHM, MAX. Zuleika Dobson. London: Heinemann, 1911. 1st ed. (Scattered foxing, rubbing, sm stain; nameplt fr pastedown.) Emb smooth brn cl. VG. *Antic Hay.* $150/£96

BEERBOHM, MAX. Zuleika Dobson. London: Heinemann, 1911. 1st ed. Smooth brn cl (lt bumped). *Swann*.* $230/£147

BEERBOHM, MAX. Zuleika Dobson. NY: John Lane, 1912. 1st Amer ed. Pict cl (lt rubbed). *Argosy.* $50/£32

BEERS, F. W. Atlas of Worcester County, Massachusetts. NY, 1870. Cl, leather back, tips. (Worn, spine crudely taped, soil, sl stains.) Internally Sound. *Oinonen*.* $130/£83

BEERS, FRANK. The Green Signal or Life on the Rail. Kansas City, MO: Franklin Hudson, (c. 1904). Port, 6 plts. VG (paper dknd) in pict wraps (spine top chipped). *Bohling.* $30/£19

BEERS, HENRY A. A Wordlet About Whitman in Four Americans. YUP, 1919. 1st Amer ed. Ptd bds. NF. *Polyanthos.* $25/£16

BEESLEY, LAWRENCE. The Loss of the SS. Titanic: Its Story and Its Lessons. Boston: Houghton Mifflin, 1912. 1st US ed. VG (cvrs lt worn). *Gravesend.* $150/£96

BEETON, ISABELLA. Beeton's Every-Day Cookery and Housekeeping Book. Ward, Lock & Tyler, n.d. (1872). 1st ed. viii,lxiv,404,(4)pp (leaf refastened w/frayed edges); 4 dbl-pg plts, direction card pasted to 1/2 title. 2-tone cl (rebacked), gilt-lettered backstrip. *Cox.* $47/£30

BEETON, ISABELLA. The Book of Household Management. London: Ward Lock, c. 1917. New ed. 32 color plts. Orig 1/4 leather (rubbed), gilt. VG. *Hollett.* $117/£75

BEGBIE, J. WARBURTON. Selections from the Works of the Late J. Warburton Begbie. Dyce Duckworth (ed). New Sydenham Soc, 1882. xxiv,422pp; port. *Bickersteth.* $37/£24

BEGLEY, JOHN. Western Missionary Priest. (Wichita, KS, 1894.) 1st ed. 205pp. Howes G316. *Ginsberg.* $300/£192

BEGLEY, LOUIS. Wartime Lies. NY: Knopf, 1991. 1st ed, 1st bk. As New in dj. *Captain's Bookshelf.* $150/£96

BEGLEY, W. E. Visnu's Flaming Wheel: The Iconography of the Sudarsana-Cakra. NY: NY Univ, 1973. 1st ed. 80 photo plts. Maroon cl. Good. *Karmiole.* $50/£32

BEHAN, BRENDAN. Borstal Boy. London, 1958. 1st ed. VG in dj. *Typographeum.* $45/£29

BEHAN, BRENDAN. Brendan Behan's Island. NY, 1962. 1st Amer ed. Fine in dj (spine sl sunned, sm edge tear). *Polyanthos.* $30/£19

BEHAN, BRENDAN. Brendan Behan's New York. (NY): Bernard Geis, (1964). 1st ed. Paul Hogarth (illus). Fine in dj (sm tear). *Antic Hay.* $45/£29

BEHAN, BRENDAN. Hold Your Hour and Have Another. London: Hutchinson, (1963). 1st ed. Fine in NF dj. *Antic Hay.* $45/£29

BEHAN, BRENDAN. The Hostage. NY: Grove, 1958. 1st US ed. NF in dj. *Lame Duck.* $45/£29

BEHAN, JOHN M. Dogs of War. NY: Scribner, (1946). Dj (sl tattered). *Dawson.* $30/£19

BEHRENS, CHARLES (ed). Atomic Medicine. NY, 1949. VG. *Fye.* $150/£96

BEHRENS, CHARLES (ed). Atomic Medicine. Balt, 1959. 3rd ed. VG. *Fye.* $50/£32

BEHRMAN, S. N. Wine of Choice. NY: Random House, (1938). Rev copy w/slip laid in. Fine in dj (extrems sl tanned). *Between The Covers.* $75/£48

BEINHART, LARRY. No One Rides for Free. NY: William Morrow, 1986. 1st ed. VF in dj. *Mordida.* $45/£29

BEISNER, MONIKA. Fantastic Toys. London: Abelard-Schuman, 1973. 1st ed, 1st issue, 1st bk. Rev copy w/detailed slip incl. Lg sq 4to. (24)pp (crease fep). Red bds. Fine in pict dj. *Bookmark.* $47/£30

BEK, WILLIAM. The German Settlement Society of Philadelphia and Its Colony Hermann, Missouri. Phila: Americana Germanica, 1907. 1st ed. Grn cl. Fine. *Archer.* $25/£16

BEKASSY, FERENC. Adriatica and Other Poems. Hogarth, 1925. 1st ed. Marbled paper-cvrd bds. (Spine ends sl nicked), o/w VG. *Words Etc.* $117/£75

BELDAM, G. W. and J. H. TAYLOR. Golf Faults Illustrated. London: George Newnes, (c. 1900). New, enlgd ed. Gilt-lettered brn cl, pict cvr label. (Spine ends lt rubbed), else VG. *Pacific*.* $173/£111

BELDEN, JACK. China Shakes the World. London: Gollancz, 1950. 1st ed. Nice. *Patterson.* $31/£20

BELDEN, JOSIAH. Josiah Belden 1841 California Overland Pioneer. Doyce B. Nunis, Jr. (ed). Georgetown, CA: Talisman, 1962. One of 750. Fine in dj. *Bohling.* $30/£19

BELDEN, L. BURR. Death Valley Heroine and Source Accounts of the 1849 Travelers. San Bernardino: Inland Printing, (1954). Ltd to 250. VG. *Perier.* $45/£29

BELDEN, L. BURR. Goodbye, Death Valley! Palm Desert: Desert Magazine, (1956). 1st ed. VG in wraps. *Book Market.* $20/£13

BELDEN, L. BURR. Mines of Death Valley. Glendale: La Siesta, 1966. Ltd to 300. Signed. Fine in Fine unptd, textured dj. *Book Market.* $40/£26

BELDEN, L. W. An Account of Jane C. Rider, the Springfield Somnambulist.... Springfield, IL: G. & C. Merriam, 1834. 1st ed. 134,(6)pp + 4pp ads. (Lt foxed.) Pub's tan cl (lt rubbed, spine base gouge, lacks paper spine label). *Gach.* $285/£183

BELKNAP, D. P. The Probate Law and Practice of Califonia.... SF: A.L. Bancroft, 1873. 3rd ed. Contemp sheep (worn, chafed). *Boswell.* $150/£96

BELKNAP, GEORGE E. Deep-Sea Soundings in the North Pacific Ocean.... Washington: GPO, 1874. 1st ed. 52pp (fep torn); 19 plts (3 fldg), 10 lg fldg color plans, charts, maps. Grn cl, gilt. *Karmiole.* $150/£96

BELKNAP, GEORGE NICHOLAS. Oregon Imprints 1845-1870. Eugene, (1968). Pict eps. Pict cl. Fine in dj. *Bohling.* $30/£19

BELKNAP, WALDRON PHOENIX. American Colonial Painting. Cambridge, 1959. 1st ed. (Spine sunned), else VG in slipcase. *King.* $65/£42

BELL, A. Climatology and Mineral Waters of the United States. NY: W. Wood, 1885. Brn cl (sl worn). *Maggs.* $37/£24

BELL, A. MORTON. Locomotives. London: Virtue, 1946. 5th ed. 2 vols. Fldg color frontis. VG. *Glaser.* $150/£96

BELL, B. A System of Surgery. Edinburgh, 1801. 7th ed. 7 vols. 478pp, 48 plts; 472pp; 445pp, 11 plts; 588pp, 29 plts; 581pp, 28 plts; 536pp, 20 plts; 460pp, 26 plts. (Sl foxed.) Full calf (worn). *Whitehart.* $390/£250

BELL, C. Engravings of the Arteries. 1811. 3rd ed. viii,54pp (lt foxed); 14 plts. New 1/2 cl. *Whitehart.* $390/£250

BELL, CHARLES. Essays on the Anatomy of Expression in Painting. London, 1806. 1st ed. 4to. 186pp (new eps). 1/2 leather, marbled bds. Fine. *Fye.* $1,500/£962

BELL, CHARLES. An Exposition of the Natural System of the Nerves of the Human Body. Phila, 1825. 1st Amer ed. 165pp, 3 engr plts (2 fldg; 1 torn). Contemp sheep (worn, fr cvr loose; ex-lib). *Argosy.* $300/£192

BELL, CHARLES. The Hand: Its Mechanism and Vital Endowments as Evincing Design. London, 1833. 2nd ed. 314pp. 1/2 leather. VG. *Fye.* $400/£256

BELL, CHARLES. The Hand: Its Mechanism and Vital Endowments as Evincing Design. London: William Pickering, 1837. 4th ed. Contemp calf. (Lib bkpl fr pastedown; sm split spine top, spine lt chipped), o/w VG. *White.* $101/£65

BELL, CHARLES. Letters Concerning the Diseases of the Urethra. Boston: W. Wells & T.B. Wait, 1811. 1st Amer ed. (viii),(13)-155,(6),(2 ads)pp (inscrips); 6 plts (foxed, offsetted). Orig 1/2 morocco (scuffed). VG. *Glaser.* $225/£144

BELL, CURRER. (Pseud of Charlotte Bronte.) The Professor, a Tale. London: Smith, Elder, 1857. 1st ed. 2 vols. 2pp ads vol 1, 8pp ads vol 2 (undated). New eps. Contemp polished calf (recently rebacked), raised bands, gilt, red/grn morocco labels. Excellent (sl smudged, creased; bds sl chafed). *Pirages.* $650/£417

BELL, CURRER. (Pseud of Charlotte Bronte.) The Professor. London: Smith, Elder, 1857. 1st ed, 1st binding, w/ads from June 1857. 2 vols. 8vo. 294,2; 258,8,16pp. Blindstamped purple cl, gilt spine. (Spines, lower corners faded.) *Bromer.* $3,500/£2,244

BELL, CURRER. (Pseud of Charlotte Bronte.) Shirley. London: Smith, Elder, 1860. New ed. iv,534,(4)pp, (ink name tp). Contemp 1/2 calf (sl worn), gilt. *Hollett.* $47/£30

BELL, CURRER. (Pseud of Charlotte Bronte.) Villette. London: Smith, Elder, 1853. 1st ed. 3 vols. 12pp ads vol 1 dated Jan 1853. Blind-stamped olive-brn cl. VG set (vol 3 rebacked retaining orig spine, eps; vols 1-2 ends chipped). *Sumner & Stillman.* $1,650/£1,058

BELL, DOUGLAS. Wellington's Officers. London, 1938. 6 plts. Red cl (unevenly faded). *Maggs.* $70/£45

BELL, EDWARD PRICE. Is the Ku Klux Klan Constructive or Destructive? Girard, KS: Haldeman-Julius, (1924). 1st ed. 2 ports. (Paper tanning.) Ptd stiff wraps. *Petrilla.* $40/£26

BELL, GEORGE JOSEPH. Principles of the Law of Scotland. Edinburgh: Oliver & Boyd, 1833. 3rd ed. Contemp 1/4 calf (rubbed). Sound. *Boswell.* $225/£144

BELL, GERTRUDE. The Earlier Letters of Gertrude Bell. Elsa Richmond (ed). NY: Liveright, (1937). Frontis, 7 plts. Good in dj (tattered). *Archaeologia.* $65/£42

BELL, GERTRUDE. The Letters of Gertrude Bell. Florence Bell (ed). NY: Liveright, (1927). 2 vols. Frontis, 30 plts, fldg map. (Sigs; spine sl faded.) *Archaeologia.* $125/£80

BELL, HORACE. On the Old West Coast, Being Further Reminiscences of a Ranger. Lanier Bartlett (ed). NY: William Morrow, 1930. 1st ed. Paper labels. (Sl shelfwear), else Good. *Brown.* $30/£19

BELL, HORACE. Reminiscences of a Ranger, Or Early Times in Southern California. L.A.: Yarnell, Caystile & Mathes, 1881. 1st ed. 457pp. Black/gold-stamped grn pict cl (inner hinges sl weak, lt wear to tips, spine ends). *Dawson.* $350/£224

BELL, J. Discourses on the Nature and Cure of Wounds. Edinburgh, 1800. 2 vols bound in 1. x,250; 235pp; 2 plts. Contemp bds (rebacked). *Whitehart.* $281/£180

BELL, J. H. B. A Progress in Mountaineering. London: Oliver & Boyd, 1950. 1st ed. 10 maps. Dj (sl worn, chipped, piece missing top lower panel). Nice. *Hollett.* $117/£75

BELL, JAMES B. The Homoeopathic Therapeutics of Diarrhoea, Dysentery, Cholera, Cholera Morbus, Cholera Infantum.... Phila: Boericke & Tafel, 1881. 2nd ed. 275pp. Good. *Goodrich.* $85/£54

BELL, JOHN. On Regimen and Longevity.... Phila, 1942. 1st ed. Full calf. VG. *Argosy.* $75/£48

BELL, JOHN. The Pilgrim and the Pioneer. Lincoln: Internat'l Pub Assoc, (1906). Errata. Good (spine lettering faded). *Lien.* $40/£26

BELL, JOHN. The Principles of Surgery. NY, 1810. 1st Amer ed. 562pp (foxing, browning); 7 engr plts. Contemp full calf (spine worn, lacks orig labels). *Goodrich.* $195/£125

BELL, JOHN. The Principles of Surgery.... NY, 1812. 2nd ed. 562pp. Old calf (worn, 1 corner fr cvr off, very stained; recent ink inscrips). *King.* $95/£61

BELL, JOHN. Report of the Importance and Economy of Sanitary Measures to Cities. NY, 1859. 243pp. (Fep taped; lacks 1-inch spine piece.) *Fye.* $200/£128

BELL, JOSEPHINE. Crime in Our Time. London: Nicholas Vane, 1962. 1st ed. NF in VG + dj (lt soiled, 2 sm chips). *Janus*. $35/£22

BELL, JOSEPHINE. Death at the Medical Board. Longmans, 1944. 1st UK ed. Fine in VG dj (lt edgewear, sl spine loss). *Williams*. $31/£20

BELL, JOSEPHINE. A Well-Known Face. London: Hodder, 1960. 1st UK ed. VG in dj (sl browned). *Williams*. $23/£15

BELL, M. C. Little Yellow Wang-Lo. Grant Richards, 1903. 1st ed. 32mo. 95pp; 24 color plts. (Eps sl foxed, sm mk fr hinge), else contents Bright. Striped grn cl (fingermkd, spine sl discolored, rubbed). Sound. *Bookmark*. $133/£85

BELL, MADISON SMARTT. Doctor Sleep. San Diego, 1991. 1st Amer ed. Signed. Mint in dj. *Polyanthos*. $35/£22

BELL, MALCOLM, JR. Major Butler's Legacy. Athens, GA, (1987). 1st ed. 2-tone cl. VG in dj. *King*. $30/£19

BELL, MALCOLM. Edward Burne-Jones: A Record and Review. London, 1892. Ltd to 390 numbered. 130pp (loosening). Teg. Cream buckram (soiled, dknd), gilt. *King*. $185/£119

BELL, SAMUEL D. Justice and Sheriff, Practical Forms.... Concord: G. Parker Lyon, 1843. 1st ed. Contemp sheep (very worn). Sound (lacks eps). *Boswell*. $150/£96

BELL, SOLOMON. Tales of Travels West of the Mississippi. Boston: Gray & Bowen, 1830. 1st ed. Frontis, 162pp, dbl-pg map. VG (rebound). Howes S739. *Oregon*. $795/£510

BELL, THOMAS. The Anatomy, Physiology, and Diseases of the Teeth. London, 1835. 2nd ed. 11 engr full pg plts. (Foxed.) Mod bds. *Argosy*. $300/£192

BELL, THOMAS. A History of British Quadrupeds Including the Cetacae. London, 1874. 2nd ed. xviii,474,2pp; 160 wood engrs. (Spine faded.) *Henly*. $47/£30

BELL, THOMAS. A History of British Quadrupeds. London: John van Voorst, 1837. 1st ed. xviii,526pp. (Joints tender), o/w Fine. *Hollett*. $117/£75

BELL, VICTOR C. Popular Essays on the Care of the Teeth and Mouth. NY, 1911. 9th ed. NF. *Doctor's Library*. $50/£32

BELL, W. D. M. Karamojo Safari. NY: Harcourt Brace, 1949. 1st ed. VG + in VG dj (chipped). *Bowman*. $125/£80

BELL, W. D. M. The Wanderings of an Elephant Hunter. London, 1923. 1/4 linen (2-inch tear rear joint). Good. *Scribe's Perch**. $135/£87

BELL, W. D. M. The Wanderings of an Elephant Hunter. London, 1958. VG in dj (frayed). *Grayling*. $55/£35

BELL, W. H. The Quiddities of an Alaskan Trip. Portland, OR: C.A. Steel, 1873. Unpaginated (67pp). (New ep, sl marginal tear 2 ll, no loss; new cl strip over spine), else VG. *High Latitude*. $290/£186

BELL, W. H. The Quiddities of an Alaskan Trip. Portland: C.A. Steel, 1873. 1st ed. 66pp. T.p. in facs. Good (refurbished). *Perier*. $175/£112

BELL, WILLIAM (ed). Poetry from Oxford in Wartime. London: Fortune Press, (1945). Bl cloth. Fine in dj (sl soiled rear panel). *Dermont*. $200/£128

BELL, WILLIAM A. New Tracks in North America. Albuquerque, 1965. Facs rpt of 2-vol ed (1869, London). 20 lithos, 3 plts, 22 woodcuts. Black cl. VF in VG + dj w/acrylic protector. Howes B330. *Five Quail*. $85/£54

BELL, WILLIAM A. New Tracks in North America. Albuquerque: Horn & Wallace, 1965. Fldg map. VG in dj. *Dumont*. $65/£42

BELL, WILLIAM E. Carpentry Made Easy. Phila, 1891. 2nd ed. 152pp; 44 full-pg plts. Contents Clean (hinge cracks, 3-inch tear fr joint). *Scribe's Perch**. $20/£13

BELL, WILLIAM GARDNER. The Snake: A Noble and Various River. The Westerners, 1969. #70/250, signed. Map. Ptd bds. (Bds sl faded, soiled), else VG. *Bohling*. $22/£14

BELLAH, JAMES WARNER. Soldier's Battle. Gettysburg. NY, (1962). 1st ed. Fine in dj (sm tear, sl worn). *Pratt*. $75/£48

BELLAMY, D. The Great Seasons. London: Hodder & Stoughton, 1981. 1st ed. Gilt-dec bds. Fine in Fine dj. *Mikesh*. $25/£16

BELLAMY, EDWARD. Looking Backward 2000-1887. Boston, 1888. 1st ed, 1st issue. Pub's grn cl (soiled; lib bkpl). *Swann**. $80/£51

BELLAMY, H. S. and P. ALLEN. The Calendar of Tihuanaco. London: Faber & Faber, (1956). 1st ed. (Ink-stamp tp.) Dj. *Archaeologia*. $65/£42

BELLE, FRANCIS P. Life and Adventures of the Celebrated Bandit Joaquin Murrieta. Chicago: Reagan, 1925. 1st ed thus. Ltd to 925. VF in dj. *Perier*. $97/£62

BELLER, E. A. Caricatures of the 'Winter King' of Bohemia. Oxford, 1928. 25 full-pg plts. (Sl bumped.) *Washton*. $85/£54

BELLET, SAMUEL. Clinical Disorders of the Heart Beat. Phila, 1953. 1st ed. Grn cl bds (waterstain lower corner, sl worn). VG. *Doctor's Library*. $50/£32

BELLING, JOHN. The Use of the Microscope: A Handbook.... NY, 1930. 1st ed. VG (bkpl; extrems sl worn). *Doctor's Library*. $65/£42

BELLOC, HILAIRE. Avril. London, 1945. 1st ed. Fine dj. *Petersfield*. $16/£10

BELLOC, HILAIRE. The Bad Child's Book of Beasts. London: Duckworth, (1896). 1st ed. 4to. Gray pict paper bds (spine dknd, corners worn). VG (inscrip). *Maggs*. $187/£120

BELLOC, HILAIRE. The Battle Ground. Cassell, 1936. 1st ed. VG in dj. *Whiteson*. $23/£15

BELLOC, HILAIRE. The Book of the Bayeux Tapestry. London: Chatto, 1914. 1st Eng ed. Bright (sticker remains fep; cvrs sl mkd). *Clearwater*. $62/£40

BELLOC, HILAIRE. The Emerald of Catherine the Great. London, 1926. 1st Eng ed. 21 dwgs by G.K. Chesterton. (Cvrs sl spotted.) Dj (frayed). *Clearwater*. $70/£45

BELLOC, HILAIRE. A General Sketch of the European War. London, (1915). 1st ed. (Sl worn, cvrs dknd.) *King*. $35/£22

BELLOC, HILAIRE. The Highway and Its Vehicles. London: The Studio Limited, 1926. 1st ed. #426/1250. 131 full-pg plts. Grn beveled cl bds, gilt. Very Nice. *Vandoros*. $250/£160

BELLOC, HILAIRE. Lambkin's Remains. Proprietor's of JCR, 1900. Good (bkpl; spine bumped, lt sunned). *Tiger*. $39/£25

BELLOC, HILAIRE. On Nothing and Kindred Subjects. Methuen, 1908. 1st ed. (Lt spotted.) Teg. Dec spine title, gilt. (Sm ink? stain upper bd.) Dj remains loosely inserted. *Edwards*. $39/£25

BELLOC, HILAIRE. One Thing and Another. London: Hollis & Carter, 1955. 1st ed. VG in dj (frayed). *Cox*. $16/£10

BELLOC, HILAIRE. The Path to Rome. Allen, 1902. 1st Eng ed. Bright (inscrip, fr hinge sl tender). *Clearwater*. $62/£40

BELLOC, HILAIRE. The Stane Street. Constable, 1913. 1st ed. (Sl dull, sl rubbed), else Good. *Whiteson*. $22/£14

BELLOSTE, AUGUSTIN. The Hospital Surgeon. Vol II. London: John Clarke, 1729. 1st ed in English. (8),344,(8)pp (scribbling feps, lt browned, bkpl). Contemp calf (worn, rear hinge cracked), raised spine bands, gilt spine compartments. Good. *Glaser.* $450/£288

BELLOW, SAUL. The Adventures of Augie March. NY, 1953. 1st ed, 2nd issue, w/unstained top. VG in 1st issue dj (lt worn) w/o reviews for this bk. *Argosy.* $75/£48

BELLOW, SAUL. Dangling Man. NY: Vanguard, (1944). 1st ed. (Cl sl soiled, spine sl leaning), else VG in dj (spine sunned, chipped, rubbed, tape to verso). *Pacific*.* $489/£313

BELLOW, SAUL. The Dean's December. NY: Harper & Row, (1982). One of 500 numbered, signed. Fine in Fine slipcase. *Lenz.* $125/£80

BELLOW, SAUL. The Dean's December. London, 1982. 1st ed. (Sl shaken), o/w VG in dj. *Words Etc.* $23/£15

BELLOW, SAUL. Henderson the Rain King. (London): Weidenfeld & Nicolson, (1959). 1st Eng ed. (Spine cocked), o/w Fine in dj (sl rubbed, dusty). *Jaffe.* $150/£96

BELLOW, SAUL. Herzog. NY, 1964. 1st Amer ed. Fine (spine sl rubbed, faint spots fr cvr) in dj (sl rubbed, price-clipped). *Polyanthos.* $25/£16

BELLOW, SAUL. Herzog. London: Weidenfeld & Nicholson, 1965. 1st ed. Fine in dj (sl worn). *Else Fine.* $50/£32

BELLOW, SAUL. Humboldt's Gift. NY: Viking, 1975. 1st ed. Fine in Fine dj. *Else Fine.* $60/£38

BELLOW, SAUL. Mosby's Memoirs and Other Stories. NY: Viking, (1968). 1st ed. Fine in dj (spine dknd). *Hermitage.* $45/£29

BELLOW, SAUL. Recent American Fiction. Washington: Reference Dept, Library of Congress, 1963. 1st ed. Fine in ptd wrappers. *Cahan.* $25/£16

BELLOW, SAUL. The Victim. NY: Vanguard, (1947). 1st ed. VG in dj (chipped, stains, browned). *Pacific*.* $109/£70

BELLOW, SAUL. The Victim. NY: Vanguard, (1947). 1st ed. Fine (sm owner #) in dj (sm tear rear panel). *Dermont.* $300/£192

BELLOWS, ALBERT J. The Philosophy of Eating. NY, 1867. 1st ed. (Spine dknd, ends frayed.) *King.* $35/£22

BELLOWS, GEORGE. George W. Bellows, His Lithographs. NY: Knopf, 1927. (Browning.) Pub's box (broken). *Metropolitan*.* $34/£22

BELLOWS, GEORGE. The Paintings. NY, 1929. (Ex-lib; extrems worn.) *Swann*.* $92/£59

BELLOWS, J. G. (ed). Contemporary Ophthalmology Honoring Sir Stewart Duke-Elder. Balt, 1972. *Whitehart.* $39/£25

BELT, ELMER. Leonardo the Anatomist. Univ of KS, 1955. 1st ed. Belt's greeting card encl, complete w/plt of genito-urinary system which has been excised in some copies. Fine in dj. *Glaser.* $65/£42

BELY, ANDREI. St. Petersburg. London: Weidenfeld & Nicolson, 1960. 1st Eng ed. (Edges foxed), else VG + in VG dj. *Lame Duck.* $25/£16

BELZONI, G. Narrative of the Operations and Recent Discoveries...in Egypt and Nubia.... London: John Murray, 1822. 3rd ed. 2 vols. Frontis port, 859pp; 2 plts, 1 map. 1/2 calf antique, 5 raised bands. *Archaeologia.* $650/£417

BEMELMANS, LUDWIG. The Castle No. 9. NY: Viking, 1937. 1st ed. VG in dj (browned, chipped, loss to head/heel). *Metropolitan*.* $86/£55

BEMELMANS, LUDWIG. The Castle No. 9. NY: Viking, Nov 1937. 1st ed. 8vo. Unpaginated. (Dog-eared pg, sl cvr stains), o/w Good- in dj (tattered, soiled). *Scribe's Perch*.* $40/£26

BEMELMANS, LUDWIG. The Donkey Inside. NY: Viking, 1941. 1st ed. 6 x 8 3/4. 224pp; 4 dbl-pg color plts. Dec eps. Fine in dj. *Cattermole.* $75/£48

BEMELMANS, LUDWIG. The Happy Place. Boston: LB, 1952. 1st ed. 5 1/2 x 8 1/2. 58pp. VG in dj. *Cattermole.* $75/£48

BEMELMANS, LUDWIG. Madeline in London. NY: Viking, (1961). 1st ed. Signed. Fine in VG dj. *Metropolitan*.* $460/£295

BEMELMANS, LUDWIG. Madeline's Christmas. NY: Viking, (1985). Uncorrected color proofs. VG in wraps. *Metropolitan*.* $115/£74

BEMELMANS, LUDWIG. Madeline's Rescue. NY: Viking, 1953. 1st ed. Tall 4to. (Sl worn.) Dj (sl frayed). *Oinonen*.* $200/£128

BEMELMANS, LUDWIG. Madeline. NY: S&S, 1939. 1st ed. 9 x 12 1/4. 48pp. Pict bds. VG. *Cattermole.* $45/£29

BEMELMANS, LUDWIG. Marina. NY: Harper Row, 1962. 1st ed. Pub's name overwritten w/mask dingbats on c. pg, new name added. 11 3/4 x 10 1/4. 32pp. Pict bds. VG. *Cattermole.* $40/£26

BEMELMANS, LUDWIG. My Life in Art. NY: Harper, 1958. 1st ed. 10 x 12 3/4. 80pp. VG in dj. *Cattermole.* $75/£48

BEMELMANS, LUDWIG. Parsley. NY: Harper, 1955. 1st ed. 12 3/4 x 10 1/4. 47pp. VG in dj. *Cattermole.* $150/£96

BEMELMANS, LUDWIG. Small Beer. NY: Viking, 1939. 1st trade ed. VG in dj. *Turtle Island.* $45/£29

BEMELMANS, LUDWIG. Sunshine. NY: S&S, 1950. 1st ed. 9 1/4 x 12 1/4. 40pp. Pict bds. VG in dj. *Cattermole.* $125/£80

BEMELMANS, LUDWIG. Welcome Home! NY: Harper, 1960. 1st ed. 12 1/2 x 10 1/4. 22pp. Cl spine, pict bds. Good. *Cattermole.* $100/£64

BEMISS, ELIJAH. Dyer's Companion in Two Parts.... NY: E. Duyckinck, 1815. 2nd ed. Orig full calf (worn, rubbed, spine very worn; pp lt browned, 1pg w/1.5-inch tear). *Kane*.* $160/£103

BENCHLEY, NATHANIEL. Lassiter's Folly. NY, 1971. 1st Amer ed. NF in dj (spine sl rubbed). *Polyanthos.* $25/£16

BENCHLEY, NATHANIEL. One to Grow On. NY, (1958). 1st ed. Signed, inscribed presentation. *Argosy.* $35/£22

BENCHLEY, NATHANIEL. Side Street. NY: HB&Co, (1950). 1st ed, 1st bk. Fine in Fine dj (sm tears, sm nick). *Between The Covers.* $100/£64

BENCHLEY, PETER. Jaws. Deutsch, 1974. 1st UK ed. (Sm mk fep), o/w Fine in VG + dj (lt creased). *Williams.* $23/£15

BENCHLEY, ROBERT. Chips Off the Old Benchley. NY: Harper, (1949). 1st ed. NF in NF dj. *Bernard.* $50/£32

BENDANN, E. Death Customs. NY, 1930. 1st Amer ed. (Bkpl crudely removed; spine top bumped, worn.) *King.* $35/£22

BENDER, LAURETTA. Psychopathology of Children with Organic Brain Disorders. Springfield, IL, (1956). Buckram. VG in dj. *Argosy.* $50/£32

BENDIRE, CHARLES. Life Histories of North American Birds. Washington: GPO, 1892-1895. 1st ed. 2 vols. viii,446; x,518pp; 19 color litho plts. Later buckram: vol 1 grn, black gilt spine label; vol 2 burgundy, red leather spine label. Good. *Karmiole.* $200/£128

BENEDICT, F. G. and R. C. LEE. Hibernation and Marmot Physiology. Washington: Carnegie, 1938. 1st ed. 2 plts. (Sl margin pen notes), else VG + in wraps. *Mikesh*. $37/£24

BENEDICT, FRANCIS G. The Physiology of Large Reptiles. Washington, DC: Carnegie Inst, 1932. Brn cl (ex-lib, spine # removed). VG. *Price*. $95/£61

BENEDICT, PINCKNEY. Town Smokes. Princeton: Ontario Rev Press, (1987). 1st ed. 1st bk. Fine in wrappers as issued. *Between The Covers*. $85/£54

BENESCH, OTTO. Collected Writings. Volume III. German and Austrian Art of the 15th and 16th Centuries. London, 1972. Good in dj. *Washton*. $60/£38

BENESCH, OTTO. Rembrandt as a Draughtsman. London, 1960. Good in dj. *Washton*. $60/£38

BENESCH, OTTO. Rembrandt. Phaidon, 1947. 292 plts. (Spine lt faded.) *Edwards*. $39/£25

BENESCH, OTTO. Venetian Drawings of the Eighteenth Century in America. NY, 1947. 57 plts. Good in dj (sl soiled). *Washton*. $40/£26

BENET, STEPHEN VINCENT. John Brown's Body. NY: Book-of-the-Month Club, 1980. 1st ptg. 2-tone maroon/red cl, orange paper title label; brn ribbon marker; top edge red. VF in ptd tan dj, maroon cl slipcase. *Heller*. $125/£80

BENET, WILLIAM ROSE. Merchants from Cathay. NY: Century, 1913. 1st ed, 1st bk. Grn cl. VG. *Antic Hay*. $60/£38

BENEZET, ANTHONY and JOHN WESLEY. Views of American Slavery, Taken a Century Ago. Phila: Assoc of Friends, 1858. 2 vols in 1. 138pp (feps removed). Blind-stamped cl (spine ends lt chipped), gilt. *Petrilla*. $40/£26

BENFORD, GREGORY. Timescape. NY: S&S, (1980). 1st ed. Dj. *Swann**. $69/£44

BENFORD, ROBERT. Doctors in the Sky. Springfield, 1955. 1st ed. VG in dj. *Fye*. $50/£32

BENGSTON, JIM. Afterwords. N.p.: Jim Bengston, (1978). 1st ed, 1st bk. VG in pict stiff wrappers. *Cahan*. $40/£26

BENHAM, W. G. Playing Cards: The History and Secrets of the Pack. London: Spring Books, n.d. Good in Good dj (chipped). *Scribe's Perch**. $24/£15

BENHAM, WILLIAM. Old St. Paul's Cathedral. Seeley, 1902. Pub's cl (faded, spine worn), gilt. *Peter Taylor*. $31/£20

BENJAMIN, ASHER. The Architect, or Practical House Carpenter.... Boston: Sanborn, Carter, Bazin, (1857). 119pp; 64 engr plts. Buckram. (Blindstamp tp), else Good. *Cahan*. $285/£183

BENJAMIN, ASHER. Practical House Carpenter. Boston, 1830. 1st ed. 119pp, 64 copperplt engrs. (Foxing.) Contemp 1/2 morocco (lacks spine label). *Ginsberg*. $400/£256

BENJAMIN, HARRY. The Transsexual Phenomenon. NY: Julian, 1966. 1st ed. Dj (spine sl chipped). *Edwards*. $25/£16

BENJAMIN, S. G. W. The Atlantic Islands as Resorts of Health and Pleasure. NY: Harper, 1878. 1st ed. 274pp + (3) ads. Gilt/black pict brn cl (lt worn). Clean. *House*. $80/£51

BENKARD, ERNST. Undying Faces: A Collection of Death Masks. Margaret M. Green (trans). London: Hogarth, 1929. 1st ed. (Ex-lib w/stamps, eps sl browned; cvrs sl rubbed, soiled), o/w VG (lacks dj). *Virgo*. $70/£45

Bennett's Handbook for Travellers in Norway.... 1913. 30th ed. Fldg map (taped to verso), 4 plans. (Spine sl faded.) *Edwards*. $31/£20

BENNETT, ALAN. Forty Years On. London: Faber, (1969). 1st ed, clbound issue. Fine in NF dj (sm nicks). *Reese*. $35/£22

BENNETT, ARNOLD. The Bright Island. London: Golden Cockerel, 1924. One of 200 signed. Teg. Full limp vellum (sl soiled). *Appelfeld*. $125/£80

BENNETT, ARNOLD. The Card. London: Methuen, 1911. 1st UK ed. VG. *Williams*. $55/£35

BENNETT, ARNOLD. Clayhanger. NY: E.P. Dutton, 1910. 1st Amer ed. Good. *Cox*. $31/£20

BENNETT, ARNOLD. Don Juan de Marana. London: T. Werner Laurie, 1923. Signed, ltd ed. Gray bds, vellum spine, paper label. Fine. *Appelfeld*. $85/£54

BENNETT, ARNOLD. Elsie and the Child. London: Cassell, 1924. 1st UK ed. VG in dj (2 sm chips, few closed tears, wear). *Williams*. $148/£95

BENNETT, ARNOLD. The Great Adventure. London: Methuen, 1913. 1st ed. (Sigs.) *Hollett*. $23/£15

BENNETT, ARNOLD. Lillian. London: Cassell, (1922). 1st ed. (Bds sl rubbed), else NF in NF dj (sm nicks extrems; spine foxed). *Between The Covers*. $150/£96

BENNETT, ARNOLD. A Man from the North. London: John Lane, Bodley Head, 1898. 1st UK ed, 1st bk. Inserted ads dated 1897. VG (bds unevenly faded, spine lt stained). *Williams*. $148/£95

BENNETT, ARNOLD. The Matador of the Five Towns and Other Stories. London, 1912. 1st Eng ed. Very Nice. *Clearwater*. $47/£30

BENNETT, ARNOLD. Mr. Prohack. Methuen, 1922. 1st ed. Good. *Whiteson*. $34/£22

BENNETT, ARNOLD. The Old Wives' Tale. Oxford: LEC, 1941. #904/1500 numbered, signed by John Austen (illus). 2 vols. Cl-backed paper-cvrd bds. Fine in djs, pub's slipcase (lt worn). *Hermitage*. $100/£64

BENNETT, ARNOLD. Our Women. London: Cassell, 1920. 1st ed. (Spine sl nicked.) *Hollett*. $55/£35

BENNETT, ARNOLD. The Price of Love. NY: Harper, 1914. 1st Amer ed. (Ink name fep), else NF. *Hermitage*. $25/£16

BENNETT, ARNOLD. Tales of the Five Towns. London: C&W, 1905. 1st ed. Blue dec cl. 1/2 morocco slipcase. *Appelfeld*. $50/£32

BENNETT, ARNOLD. Teresa of Watling Street. London: C&W, 1904. 1st ed. Maroon dec cl. 1/2 morocco slipcase. *Appelfeld*. $45/£29

BENNETT, ARNOLD. These Twain. Metheun, 1916. 1st ed. (Sig.) Gilt spine. Nice. *Buckley*. $47/£30

BENNETT, ARNOLD. Venus Rising from the Sea. London: Cassell, 1931. One of 350 signed by E. McKnight Kauffer (illus). 4to. 12 full-pg plts. Gray ptd cl bds. Fine in orig slipcase. *Bromer*. $750/£481

BENNETT, C. M. Tim Kane's Treasure. NY: E.P. Dutton, (1931). Stated 1st ed. Good. *Hayman*. $15/£10

BENNETT, CHARLES H. and ROBERT B. BROUGH. Shadow and Substance. London, 1860. 8vo. 30 plts. (Sl shaken, sl foxed.) Pub's cl (sl worn) stamped in blind, gilt. *Oinonen**. $110/£71

BENNETT, E. ARNOLD. Polite Farces for the Drawing-Room. London: Lamley, 1900. 1st ed. Teg, others uncut. Red buckram, gilt. VG (inscrip; spine sl faded). *Maggs*. $172/£110

BENNETT, FRANK M. The Steam Navy of the United States. Pittsburgh: W.T. Nicholson, 1896. 1st ed. xi,953pp (ink name). Blue cl (soil, spine ends sl rubbed). VG. *Argonaut*. $150/£96

BENNETT, H. S. English Books and Readers 1475-1557. Cambridge: CUP, 1969. 2nd ed. Red cl (ex-lib w/stamp on title, shelf mk). Dj (stuck down). *Maggs*. $28/£18

BENNETT, HAL. Insanity Runs in Our Family. GC: Doubleday, 1977. 1st ed. (Corners sl bumped), else NF in VG dj (lt worn, sm chips, tears). *Between The Covers*. $50/£32

71

BENNETT, HAL. Seventh Heaven. GC: Doubleday, 1976. 1st ed. Fine in NF dj (sl soiled). *Between The Covers*. $65/£42

BENNETT, IRA E. History of the Panama Canal, Its Construction and Builders. Washington, D.C.: Historic Pub Co, 1915. 1st ed. Color frontis. Dk grn cl, gilt-lettered spine. VF. *Argonaut*. $175/£112

BENNETT, JAMES. Overland Journey to California. NY, 1932. Ltd to 200. Wrappers. Howes B357. *Ginsberg*. $50/£32

BENNETT, JOHN C. The History of the Saints. Boston: Leland & Whiting, 1842. 1st ed. Port, 344pp. (Sl wear, spine sl frayed, card pocket rear pastedown), else Good. Howes B358. *Brown*. $275/£176

BENNETT, JOHN. Letters to a Young Lady.... Newburyport: John Mycall, (1792). 1st ed. 2 vols in 1. 156; 168pp + 12pp ads. Orig calf (corner chipped), red spine label. *Karmiole*. $100/£64

BENNETT, JOHN. Letters to a Young Lady.... NY: Duyckinck, 1716 (i.e. 1796). 1st NY ed. 2 vols in 1. 115; 116pp + ads (eps stained). Contemp calf (lacks leather label). VG. *Second Life*. $150/£96

BENNETT, JOHN. Letters to a Young Lady.... Worcester: Isiah Thomas, 1798. 4th Amer ed. 2 vols in 1. 300pp (foxing). Contemp calf (scuffing, hinges loose). Good. *Second Life*. $150/£96

BENNETT, L. G. and WM. H. HAIGH. History of the Thirty-Sixth Regiment Illinois Volunteers, During the War of the Rebellion. Aurora, IL: Knickerbocker & Hodder, 1876. 808pp. Fair (water staining). *Lien*. $125/£80

BENNETT, LERONE, JR. Before the Mayflower. Chicago: Johnson, 1962. 1st ed. Fine in dj (lt used, few sm tears). *Captain's Bookshelf*. $75/£48

BENNETT, LERONE, JR. The Negro Mood and Other Essays. Chicago: Johnson, 1964. 1st ed. Fine in dj (sl rubbed). *Between The Covers*. $55/£35

BENNETT, LERONE, JR. Pioneers in Protest. Chicago: Johnson, (1968). 1st ed. (Eps sl offset from flaps), else Fine in VG + dj (crown sl worn). *Between The Covers*. $55/£35

BENNETT, NORMAN R. (ed). Stanley's Despatches to the New York Herald 1871-1872, 1874-1877. Boston Univ, 1970. 1st ed. Dj (sl chipped). *Edwards*. $39/£25

BENNETT, PAUL A. (ed). Books and Printing. Cleveland: World, (1951). Rev ed. Fine in dj (few chips, tape repair). *Dermont*. $40/£26

BENNETT, PAUL A. (ed). Books and Printing: A Treasury for Typophiles. Cleveland: World, (1951). 1st ed. Gray cl. Fine in VG + dj (spine sl chipped). *House*. $35/£22

BENNETT, RAINEY. The Secret Hiding Place. World, 1960. 1st ed. Oblong 8vo. Unpaginated. NF. *Dower*. $35/£22

BENNETT, WHITMAN. A Practical Guide to American Nineteenth Century Color Plate Books with Supplement No. 1. NY: Bennett Book Studios, 1949. 1st ed. Errata mtd to fr pastedown. 4-pg supp in self-wraps. Sound (sl rubbed, faded; supp creased). *Waverly**. $60/£38

BENSELL, ROYAL A. All Quiet on the Yamhill. Gunter Barth (ed). Eugene: Univ of OR Books, 1959. 1st ed. Fldg map, 2 plts. Fine in dj (sl rubbed). *Argonaut*. $45/£29

BENSON, A. C. From a College Window. London, 1906. 1st ed. *Typographeum*. $18/£12

BENSON, A. C. The Thread of Gold. NY: Dutton, 1907. 1st ed. Teg. Red cl, gilt. VG. *Antic Hay*. $35/£22

BENSON, A. C. and LAWRENCE WEAVER (eds). Everybody's Book of the Queen's Doll's House. London: Daily Telegraph/Methuen, 1924. 1st ed. Color frontis, port, 10 color plts. (Lt spotting; sl faded, lower bd sl water-stained.) Dj (repaired). *Edwards*. $39/£25

BENSON, ADOLPH B. (ed). Peter Kalm's Travels in North America. NY, 1937. Signed, inscribed. 2 vols. Fldg map vol 2. Good + in Good slipcase. Howes K5. *Scribe's Perch**. $75/£48

BENSON, ALLAN L. A Way to Prevent War. Girard: Appeal to Reason, 1915. 1st ed. Blue cl, gilt. Fine. *Beasley*. $65/£42

BENSON, E. F. Charlotte Bronte. London: Longmans, 1932. 1st ed. Port. Gilt cl. (Bkpl), o/w Fine in VG dj (chip, nicks). *Reese*. $50/£32

BENSON, E. F. The Climber. London, 1908. 1st ed. Brn cl, gilt. (Name; spine sl discolored, corners rubbed), o/w VG. *Words Etc*. $94/£60

BENSON, E. F. The Freaks of Mayfair. T.N. Foulis, 1916. 1st ed. Teg, uncut. Brick red buckram, gilt. (Spine dknd), o/w VG. *Words Etc*. $101/£65

BENSON, E. F. The Life of Alcibiades. 1928. 1st ed. (Prelims lt foxed), o/w VG. *Words Etc*. $86/£55

BENSON, E. F. Mr. Teddy. T. Fisher Unwin, (1917). 1st ed. Nice (prelims, edges foxed). *Ash*. $62/£40

BENSON, E. F. Sheaves. London, 1908. 1st ed. Brn cl, gilt. (Spine sl discolored, corners rubbed), o/w VG. *Words Etc*. $94/£60

BENSON, E. F. Trouble for Lucia. London: Hodder & Stoughton, 1939. 1st ed. VG in dj (spine browned, sm inner edge mend). *Reese*. $30/£19

BENSON, FRANK W. Etchings and Drypoints. Vol. 4. Boston: Houghton, Mifflin, 1929. Ltd to 600 numbered, w/orig pencil signed drypoint etching by artist inserted as frontis. 1/4 cl (sl soiled, edgeworn, spine ends frayed), label (browned). Contents VG (sl foxed, sl dampstain upper pg edges). *Waverly**. $385/£247

BENSON, FRANK W. Etchings and Drypoints. Vol. 5. Boston: Houghton, Mifflin, 1959. Ltd to 400 numbered so illus and w/artist's signature to drypoint etching inserted as frontis (this copy w/o artist's signature). (Old tape stains, residue eps.) 1/4 cl. VG. *Waverly**. $275/£176

BENSON, J. L. Bamboula at Kourion: The Necropolis and the Finds Excavated by J. F. Daniel. Phila: Univ of PA, (1972). Frontis, 74 plts. Good in dj (torn). *Archaeologia*. $50/£32

BENSON, JAMES W. Time and Time-Tellers. London: Robert Hardwicke, 1875. 1st ed. Frontis, vii,189pp. Gilt-stamped grn cl. *Weber*. $55/£35

BENSON, L. The Cacti of the U.S. and Canada. Stanford Univ, 1982. 1st ed. Fine in Fine dj. *Mikesh*. $95/£61

BENSON, STELLA. Twenty. NY: Macmillan, 1918. 1st ed. Fine in VG + dj (chip fr panel). *Between The Covers*. $125/£80

BENT, CHARLES. History of Whiteside County, Illinois From Its First Settlement to the Present Time.... Morrison, IL, 1877. 1st ed. Frontis, color map. Buckram. *Wantagh*. $100/£64

BENT, CHARLES. History of Whiteside County, Illinois. Morrison, IL: n.p. (ptd by L.P. Allen in Clinton, IA), 1877. 1st ed. Hand-colored frontis map, (2),536pp. Contemp calf (lt worn), leather spine label. *Karmiole*. $125/£80

BENT, J. THEODORE. The Ruined Cities of Mashonaland. London: Longmans, Green, 1893. xvii,427,24ads pp; fldg map. Pict cl (lt rubbed). *Adelson*. $225/£144

BENT, J. THEODORE. The Ruined Cities of Mashonaland. London: Longman's, 1902. New impression (rpt of 3rd ed). Frontis. Contemp gilt red full morocco. Fine. *Terramedia*. $150/£96

BENT, J. THEODORE. The Sacred City of the Ethiopians. London: Longman's, 1893. 1st ed. Frontis, xv,309pp,24pp ads; fldg colored map. Maroon gilt pict cl. VG. *Terramedia*. $250/£160

BENTHAM, JEREMY. The Works of Jeremy Bentham. John Bowring (ed). Edinburgh: William Tait, 1843. 11 vols. Contemp morocco (worn, joints cracked), extra gilt. Clean. *Boswell*. $1,500/£962

BENTLEY, E. C. Clerihews Complete. London: Werner Laurie, 1951. 1st ed. VG in pict dj (sl frayed). *Cox*. $28/£18

BENTLEY, E. C. More Biography. London: Methuen, (1929). 1st UK ed. Good (ink name, date fep; foreedge foxed) in VG dj (lt wear). *Gravesend*. $50/£32

BENTLEY, E. C. Trent Intervenes. London: Nelson, 1938. 1st UK ed. Fine in dj (rear panel rubbed, sl residual tape mks). *Williams*. $546/£350

BENTLEY, E. C. The Woman in Black. NY: Century, 1913. 1st Amer ed. (Bkpl, inner hinges weak; spine ends frayed.) *Metropolitan**. $57/£37

BENTLEY, E. C. and H. WARNER ALLEN. Trent's Own Case. London: Constable, 1936. 1st ed. Fine in dj. *Mordida*. $750/£481

BENTLEY, E. C. and H. WARNER ALLEN. Trent's Own Case. NY: Knopf, 1936. 1st Amer ed. (Sl browned.) Dj (edgeworn, corners through, spine crease, sm tape on inside). *Metropolitan**. $40/£26

BENTLEY, HARRY C. and RUTH S. LEONARD. Bibliography of Works on Accounting by American Authors. Boston, 1934-35. 2 vols. (Cl sl worn, spine gilt faded vol 2.) *Oinonen**. $50/£32

BENTLEY, JOHN A. The Submerged Tenth. London: Constable, 1933. 1st ed. VG. *Patterson*. $47/£30

BENTLEY, WILLIAM. The Diary of William Bentley, D.D. Salem: Essex Inst, 1905-14. 1st ed. 4 vols. Good (ex-lib, labels removed spines, emb tps, pp5-12 vol 3 torn in margin; bumped). *Scribe's Perch**. $110/£71

BENTON, FRANK. Cowboy Life on the Sidetrack.... Denver: Western Stories Syndicate, (1903). 1st ed. NF (name; 2 sm spots fr cvr, sl rubbed). *Argonaut*. $75/£48

BENTON, J. A. The California Pilgrim. Sacramento: Solomon Alter, 1853. 1st ed. 261pp (tp lt stained, feps partly stuck at gutter to pastedowns); 6 woodcut plts. Later cl (sl edgeworn, frayed). *Waverly**. $55/£35

BENTON, JOEL. A Unique Story of a Marvellous Career. Edgewood, 1891. 621pp (dknd). Dec cl (rubbed). VG. *Bohling*. $30/£19

BENTON, THOMAS HART. An Artist in America. NY, (1937). 1st ed. Signed. Dj. *Swann**. $138/£88

BENTON, THOMAS HART. Thirty Years' View. NY: Appleton, 1854. 2 vols. Frontis port, ix,739; frontis view, 788pp. (Spines faded), else Very Nice. *Bohling*. $120/£77

Beowulf. NY: Random House, 1932. #528/950. 8 full-pg lithos by Rockwell Kent. Deckled edges. Fabric bds, stamped design. (Bumped, frayed.) *Metropolitan**. $50/£32

Beowulf. NY: Random House, 1932. #328/950 signed with Rockwell Kent's (illus) thumbprint. Dec cvr. Good (crack at p1). *Scribe's Perch**. $140/£90

BERENSON, BERNARD. Homeless Paintings of the Renaissance. Bloomington, 1970. Good. *Washton*. $100/£64

BERENSON, BERNARD. The Italian Painters of the Renaissance. Phaidon, 1952. 416 plts (16 color tipped in). (Bkpl.) Dj (chipped). *Edwards*. $39/£25

BERENSON, BERNARD. Italian Pictures of the Renaissance. A List of the Principal Artists and Their Works with an Index of Places. London, 1957. 2 vols. Good in djs (sl worn). *Washton*. $350/£224

BERENSON, BERNARD. The Passionate Sightseer. NY, 1960. (Sm stain rear cvr.) *Washton*. $20/£13

BERENSON, BERNARD. Piero Della Francesca, or the Ineloquent in Art. NY, 1954. 48 plts. Good in dj. *Washton*. $35/£22

BERENSON, BERNARD. Studies in Medieval Painting. New Haven: Yale Univ, 1930. 1st ed. 168 plts. Blue cl (sl frayed), gilt. *Karmiole*. $125/£80

BERGER, JOHN A. Fernand Lungren. Santa Barbara: Schauer, 1936. 1st ed. Frontis, 18 plts (3 color). Blue cl, paper spine label. Fine in dj. *Karmiole*. $100/£64

BERGER, KLAUS. Gericault. Drawings and Watercolours. NY, 1946. 52 plts. Good in dj. *Washton*. $60/£38

BERGER, ROBERT W. Antoine le Pautre. NY, 1969. Good. *Washton*. $75/£48

BERGER, THOMAS. Crazy in Berlin. NY: Scribner, (1958). 1st ed. Fine in VG dj (lacks sm piece, chipped, spine sl sunned, rubbed). *Pacific**. $127/£81

BERGER, THOMAS. Granted Wishes. Northridge: Lord John, 1984. One of 250 numbered, signed. Fine. *Antic Hay*. $100/£64

BERGER, THOMAS. The Houseguest. Weidenfeld, 1989. 1st UK ed. Fine in dj. *Williams*. $16/£10

BERGER, THOMAS. Little Big Man. NY, 1964. 1st ed. NF (tip sl bumped) in VG + dj (sl rubbed). *Warren*. $175/£112

BERGER, THOMAS. Little Big Man. London: Eyre & Spottiswoode, 1965. 1st UK ed. VG in dj (few 1-inch closed tears). *Williams*. $55/£35

BERGER, THOMAS. Nowhere. Methuen, 1986. 1st UK ed. Fine in dj. *Williams*. $19/£12

BERGER, THOMAS. Reinhart in Love. NY, (1962). 1st ed. VG in dj. *Argosy*. $50/£32

BERGHOLD, ALEXANDER. The Indians Revenge; or, Days of Horror. SF: P.J. Thomas, 1891. 1st ed in English. Frontis, 240pp, 6 plts. (Mottling fr cvr), o/w VG. Howes B373. *Oregon*. $100/£64

BERGIN, THOMAS G. Dante Alighieri: The Divine Comedy. NY: Grossman, 1969. 3 vols. Leonard Baskin (illus). Pub's box. *Metropolitan**. $143/£92

BERGLER, EDMUND. The Superego. NY: Grune & Stratton, 1952. 1st ed. Fine in NF dj (internal reinforcements). *Beasley*. $40/£26

BERGMAN, PETER M. The Chronological History of the Negro in America. NY: Harper, (1969). 1st ed. NF in NF dj. *Captain's Bookshelf*. $45/£29

BERGMAN, RAY. Fresh Water Bass. Phila: Penn, 1942. 1st trade ed. Bright blue cl. Fine. *Bowman*. $60/£38

BERINGER, JOHANN. The Lying Stones of Dr. Johann Bartholomew Adam Beringer.... Berkeley, 1963. 1st ed in English. VG in dj. *Fye*. $25/£16

BERJEAU, J. The Homoeopathic Treatment of Syphilis, Gonorrhoea Spermatorrhoea, and Urinary Diseases. Phila: Boericke & Tafel, n.d. ca 1870. 256pp. (Cl worn), else Good. *Goodrich*. $85/£54

BERKEBILE, DON. Carriage Terminology. Washington: Smithsonian, 1979. 3rd ptg. (Corners bumped), o/w Fine. No dj as issued. *October Farm*. $65/£42

BERKELEY, ANTHONY. Mr. Pidgeon's Island. GC: Crime Club, 1934. 1st Amer ed. Nice in dj (extrems lt worn). *Metropolitan**. $345/£221

BERKELEY, EDMUND CALLIS. Giant Brains: Or, Machines That Think. NY: John Wiley, (1949). 1st ed. VG. *Glaser*. $135/£87

BERKELEY, EDMUND CALLIS. Symbolic Logic and Intelligent Machines. NY: Reinhold, (1959). 1st ed. NF (sigs). *Glaser.* $75/£48

BERKELEY, GEORGE. The Works. 1705-1752. Clarendon, 1901. 4 vols. Frontis port. (Eps lt spotted, bkpl; spines sl discolored.) *Edwards.* $117/£75

BERKELEY, GRANTLEY F. Reminiscences of a Huntsman. London/NY, 1897. New ed. Color frontis, (xxii),344pp (lt spotting). Teg, rest uncut. 1/2 japon, marbled bds (edges lt soiled, rubbed), leather spine title label (sl rubbed). *Edwards.* $39/£25

BERKELEY, WILLIAM N. Laboratory Work with Mosquitoes. NY, 1902. 1st ed. Grn cl. VG. *Doctor's Library.* $40/£26

Berkeley: The First Seventy-Five Years. Berkeley: Gillick Press, 1941. 1st ed. Fine (spine sl dknd). *Argonaut.* $50/£32

BERKEY, C. Geology of the New York City. Albany: NYSM, 1911. VG. *Blake.* $125/£80

BERKMAN, ALEXANDER and EMMA GOLDMAN. Anarchism on Trial with Portraits. NY: Mother Earth, 1917. 1st ed. NF in wraps (offsetting; store stamp). *Beasley.* $125/£80

BERKMAN, ALEXANDER. Prison Memoirs of an Anarchist. NY: Mother Earth, 1912. 1st ed. Frontis. 3/4 calf. *M & S.* $200/£128

BERKOFF, STEVEN. A Prisoner in Rio. Hutchinson, 1989. 1st UK ed. Fine in dj. *Williams.* $23/£15

BERKY, ANDREW S. Practitioner in Physick: A Biography of Abraham Wagner, 1717-1763. Pennsburg, PA: Schwenkfelder Library, 1954. 1st ed. Fldg facs. Cl-backed patterned bds, paper label. VG. *Cahan.* $35/£22

BERNACCHI, L. C. Saga of the 'Discovery.' London/Glasgow: Blackie, 1938. 1st ed. 3 maps (1 fldg). Blue cl. (Edges foxed), else VG. *Parmer.* $125/£80

BERNAL, IGNACIO. The Olmec World. Berkeley/L.A.: Univ of CA, 1969. Frontis. Good. *Archaeologia.* $45/£29

BERNANOS, GEORGES. Joy. Louise Varese (trans). NY: Pantheon, 1946. 1st ed. VG + (offsetting eps, lt dampstain upper pg edges) in VG dj (lt worn, sl chipped). *Lame Duck.* $35/£22

BERNANOS, GEORGES. Mouchette. J. C. Whitehouse (trans). NY: Holt et al, (1966). 1st ed. NF in dj (sl worn, browned). *Antic Hay.* $20/£13

BERNANOS, GEORGES. The Star of Satan. NY: Macmillan, 1940. 1st US ed. VG in VG- dj (spine faded). *Lame Duck.* $40/£26

Bernard Shaw and Fascism. (London): Favil, n.d. (1927). Fine in ptd wraps, stapled. *Dramatis Personae.* $60/£38

BERNARD, BRUCE (ed). Vincent. By Himself. London, 1985. 1st UK ed. 319 plts. News clippings loosely inserted. Dj. *Edwards.* $39/£25

BERNARD, CLAUDE. An Introduction to the Study of Experimental Medicine. NY, 1927. 1st ed in English. Fine (ex-lib). *Fye.* $100/£64

BERNARDETE, M. J. and ROLFE HUMPHRIES (eds). ...And Spain Sings. NY: Vanguard, 1937. 1st ed. Nice (sl dusty) in Good dj (2 sm chips). *Reese.* $45/£29

BERNE, HELMUT and GOTTFRIED GRUBER. Greek Temples, Theatres, and Shrines. NY: Abrams, n.d. (ca 1962). (Sl internal soil; sl shaken, worn, soiled.) Dj (chipped). *Freeman*.* $70/£45

BERNERS, LORD. The Camel. London, 1936. 1st Eng ed. Very Nice in dj. *Clearwater.* $70/£45

BERNERS, LORD. Count Omega. London, 1941. 1st Eng ed. Frontis. Nice in dj (sl mkd). *Clearwater.* $55/£35

BERNERS, LORD. A Distant Prospect. London, 1945. 1st Eng ed. Frontis. Very Nice (sl foxed) in dj (clipped). *Clearwater.* $39/£25

BERNERS, LORD. Far from the Madding War. London, 1941. 1st Eng ed. Very Nice (bkpl) in dj (sl torn, nicked). *Clearwater.* $55/£35

BERNFELD, SIEGFRIED. The Psychology of the Infant. Rosetta Hurwitz (trans). NY: Brentano's, 1929. 1st ed. (Spine ends sl frayed), o/w NF. *Beasley.* $85/£54

BERNHARD, THOMAS. Correction. NY: Knopf, 1979. 1st US ed. (2 rmdr stamps lower edge), else NF in VG + dj (worn). *Lame Duck.* $35/£22

BERNHARD, THOMAS. The Lime Works. Sophie Wilkins (trans). NY: Knopf, 1973. 1st Amer ed. Fine in dj. *Hermitage.* $35/£22

BERNHEIM, BERTRAM. The Story of Johns Hopkins: Four Great Doctors and the Medical School They Created. NY, 1948. 1st ed. VG. *Fye.* $45/£29

BERNHEIMER, CHARLES L. Rainbow Bridge. NY, 1924. 1st ed. Frontis, 3 maps. Teg. Internally VG + (spotting rear cvr, spine dull, ends lt scuffed). *Five Quail.* $55/£35

BERNSTEIN, ALINE. The Journey Down. NY: Knopf, 1938. 1st ed. Good (lt dust soiling) in dj (edgewear, flaws lower spine panel). *Reese.* $25/£16

BERNSTEIN, JERROLD G. Handbook of Drug Therapy in Psychiatry. Boston: John Wright/PSG, 1983. 1st ed. Inscribed. Ptd brn cl. (Lt mkd, ex-lib.) *Gach.* $25/£16

BERRA, YOGI and TIL FERDENZI. Behind the Plate. Argonaut, 1962. 1st ed. VG + in Good + dj. *Plapinger.* $45/£29

BERRI, D. G. Monograms, Historical and Practical. London, 1869. 47pp + 20 full-pg plts. Aeg. Gilt-stamped pub's cl (lt worn, joints tender). Clean. *Truepenny.* $125/£80

BERRIAULT, G. The Descent. Atheneum, 1960. 1st ed, 1st bk. VG + in VG dj (rubbed). *Aronovitz.* $22/£14

BERRIGAN, TED. Red Wagon. Chicago: The Yellow Press, 1976. 1st Amer ed. Signed, inscribed. Fine in dj. *Polyanthos.* $30/£19

BERRILL, N. J. Sex and the Nature of Things. NY: Dodd, Mead, 1954. 1st ed. VG (name tp, ex-libris). *Second Life.* $20/£13

BERRISFORD, JUDITH. The Wild Garden. Faber, 1966. 1st ed. VG in dj. *Hadley.* $23/£15

BERROW, NORMAN. Words Have Wings. London: Ward Lock, 1946. 1st ed. (Edges spotting), o/w Fine in dj (price-clipped, wear along edges, spine base). *Mordida.* $100/£64

BERRY, A. J. Henry Cavendish. London: Hutchinson, (1960). 1st ed. Fine in dj. *Glaser.* $35/£22

BERRY, DON. A Majority of Scoundrels—An Informal History of the Rocky Mountain Fur Company. NY: Harper, (1961). 1st ed. Maps rear pocket. Fine in Fine dj. *Perier.* $85/£54

BERRY, DON. Moontrap. Viking, (1962). 1st ed. Fine in Fine dj. *Authors Of West.* $50/£32

BERRY, JAMES and STEPHEN G. LEE. A Cromwellian Major General. OUP, 1938. Color frontis, fldg color map. (Feps lt browned; spine rubbed.) *Edwards.* $55/£35

BERRY, WENDELL. The Country of Marriage. NY: HBJ, (1973). 1st ed. Fine in Fine dj (extrems sl dknd). *Between The Covers.* $85/£54

BERRY, WENDELL. An Eastward Look. Berkeley: Sand Dollar, 1974. One of 376. Fine in yellow stapled wraps. *Lame Duck.* $50/£32

BERRY, WENDELL. Findings. (Iowa City, IA): Prairie Press, 1969. 1st ed. Cl-backed dec bds. Fine in dj. *Jaffe.* $100/£64

BERRY, WENDELL. The Hidden Wound. Boston: Houghton Mifflin, 1970. 1st ed. (Spine cocked), o/w Fine in dj (price-clipped). *Jaffe.* $45/£29

BERRY, WENDELL. Horses. (Monterey, KY: Larkspur Press, 1975.) 1st ed. One of 949 ptd. Fine in wrappers. *Jaffe.* $25/£16

BERRY, WENDELL. November Twenty Six Nineteen Hundred Sixty Three. (NY: Braziller, 1964.) Ltd ed. Signed by Berry & Ben Shahn (illus). NF in slipcase (sl mkd). *Waverly*.* $93/£60

BERRY, WENDELL. Sayings and Doings. (Lexington, KY): Gnomon Press, (1975). 1st ed. (Spine sl dknd), o/w Fine. *Jaffe.* $25/£16

BERRY, WENDELL. The Unforeseen Wilderness. Lexington: Univ Press of KY, 1971. 1st ed. VG (name) in dj. *Cahan.* $100/£64

BERRYMAN, JOHN. Berryman's Sonnets. NY: Farrar, (1967). 1st ed. (Top edge lt sunned), else NF in dj. *Reese.* $40/£26

BERRYMAN, JOHN. His Toy, His Dream, His Rest. NY: FSG, (1968). 1st ed. Fine in dj (sticker stain rear panel). *Jaffe.* $75/£48

BERRYMAN, JOHN. Short Poems. NY, (1967). 1st ed. VG in dj. *Argosy.* $40/£26

BERRYMAN, JOHN. Stephen Crane. (NY, 1950.) 1st ed. VG in dj (spine frayed, rubbed). *King.* $95/£61

BERTHOUD, ROGER. Graham Sutherland. London: Faber, 1982. 1st ed. 10 color, 90 monochrome plts. Dj. *Hollett.* $55/£35

BERTHRONG, DONALD J. The Cheyenne and Arapaho Ordeal. Norman, (1976). 1st ed. VG+ in VG+ dj. *Pratt.* $30/£19

BERTHRONG, DONALD J. The Southern Cheyennes. Norman: Univ of OK, (1963). 1st ed. VG in dj. *Lien.* $50/£32

BERTI, LUCIANO. Masaccio. University Park/London, 1967. 80 plts. Good. *Washton.* $95/£61

BERTO, GIUSEPPE. The Sky Is Red. NY: New Directions, 1948. 1st ed in English. VG (pg edges, bds foxed) in VG- dj (tears). *Lame Duck.* $35/£22

BERTON, KATHLEEN. Moscow: An Architectural History. Vista, 1977. 1st ed in English. VG in dj. *Hadley.* $39/£25

BERTON, PIERRE. The Impossible Railway. NY: Knopf, 1972. 1st US ed. 27 maps. Fine in VG dj (inscrip). *Graf.* $25/£16

BERTRAM, JAMES G. The Harvest of the Sea. London: John Murray, 1865. 1st ed. Wood-engr frontis, xvi,519pp; 32-pg pub's cat at end. Grn cl, gilt. Excellent. *Burmester.* $140/£90

BERVE, HELMUT and GOTTFRIED GRUBEN. Greek Temples, Theaters and Shrines. NY: Abrams, (1962). 212 plts (36 color, tipped-in). Good in dj. *Archaeologia.* $350/£224

BERZELIUS, J. The Use of the Blowpipe in Chemistry and Mineralogy. J.D. Whitney (trans). Boston: William D. Ticknor, 1845. 1st Amer ptg. xv,237pp + 2pp ads; 4 plts. Recent 1/2 blue morocco, marbled paper over bds. Good (lt waterstain). *Blake.* $250/£160

BESANT, WALTER and JAMES RICE. My Little Girl. C&W, 1887. New ed. Pub's cat dated March 1888. Pict bds (spine bumped, corners rubbed). Good. *Tiger.* $23/£15

BESKOW, ELSA. Aunt Green, Aunt Brown, and Aunt Lavender. NY: Harper, 1928. 1st ed. 13 x 9 3/4. 32pp. Price sticker fep w/1st pub'd price. Cl spine. Good (rubbed, lt soil on cvr). *Cattermole.* $200/£128

BESKOW, ELSA. Pelle's New Suit. NY: Harper, n.d. (1929). Possible 1st. 12 1/2 x 9; Cl spine, pict bds. Good (rubbed). *Cattermole.* $35/£22

BESKOW, ELSA. The Tale of the Little, Little Old Woman. Edinborough: Floris, 1988. 1st ed thus. 9 1/2 x 10 1/4. 32pp. Cl spine, glossy bds. Fine. *Cattermole.* $35/£22

BESSON, MAURICE. The Scourge of the Indies. Everard Thornton (trans). NY: Random House, 1929. 1st ed. One of 1040. 4 hand-colored plts. (Bkpl; sl rubbed, faded, spine ends sl frayed), o/w VG. *Worldwide.* $75/£48

BEST, CHARLES H. Selected Papers of.... Univ of Toronto, (1963). 1st ed thus. Frontis, 13 plts (7 color). Fine in dj. *Glaser.* $95/£61

BEST, ELSDON. The Maori As He Was. Wellington: Dominion Museum, 1952. 3rd imp. Grn cl. VG in dj (worn). *Parmer.* $45/£29

BEST, J. J. Excursions in Albania. London: Wm. H. Allen, 1842. 1st ed. xii,359pp,(1) errata/directions; fldg engr map, engr plt. Contemp polished calf (joints well repaired), spine elaborately gilt, new red label gilt. VG (bkpl). *Morrell.* $187/£120

BEST, J. W. Indian Shikar Notes. Allahabad: Pioneer Press, 1922. 2nd ed. Lg fldg map. Grn cl. VG. *Terramedia.* $100/£64

BEST, THOMAS. A Concise Treatise on the Art of Angling: Confirmed by Actual Experience...to Which Will Be Added The Compleat Fly-Fisher.... (Market Drayton), 1992. One of 175 numbered, signed by Mary Parry (binder). Grn/yellow dec paper, toning cl spine, paper title labels; brn eps. Fine. *Heller.* $145/£93

BESTE, RICHARD. The Wabash; or, Adventure of an English Gentleman's Family in the Interior of America.... London, 1855. 1st ed. 2 vols. (12),329; (8),352pp; 2 plts, color litho frontis views. (Vol 1 lacks ep, sl stained; vol 2 lacks tp corner, sigs starting, sl stained, spine mended.) Howes B401. *Ginsberg.* $150/£96

BESTER, ALFRED. The Light Fantastic. Berkley, 1976. 1st ed. Fine in dj (sl frayed). *Madle.* $15/£10

BESTER, ALFRED. The Stars My Destination. (NY, 1979.) Ltd to 3000 numbered, signed by Bester, Byron Preiss (panel configs), & Howard Chaykin (illus). Silver bds. (Sl worn, 2 bumped corners; lacks slipcase.) *King.* $75/£48

BESTOR, GEORGE CLINTON. Prelude to Murder. NY: Dial, (1936). 1st ed. Bright in dj (rubbed, short tears, creases, few lg chips). *Metropolitan*.* $23/£15

BETJEMAN, JOHN et al. The Englishman's Country.... W. J. Turner (ed). London: Collins, 1945. 1st ptg of omnibus issue. Gilt cl. Nice (pencil inscrip) in dj (lt worn). *Reese.* $45/£29

BETJEMAN, JOHN and JOHN PIPER. Shropshire. Faber, 1951. 1st Eng ed. NF (name, ink ticks) in dj (sl torn). *Clearwater.* $86/£55

BETJEMAN, JOHN and GEOFFREY TAYLOR (eds). English, Scottish and Welsh Landscape 1700-c.1860. London: Muller, (1944). 1st ed. Pict cl. Fine in NF dj. *Reese.* $75/£48

BETJEMAN, JOHN and DAVID VAISEY. Victorian and Edwardian Oxford from Old Photographs. Batsford, (1971). 1st ed. Fine. *Bickersteth.* $39/£25

BETJEMAN, JOHN. Archie and the Strict Baptists. (Chatham: W. & J. Mackay, 1977.) 1st ed. Phillida Gili (illus). Yellow cl-cvrd bds. (Sl bump), else Fine in dj. *Bromer.* $50/£32

BETJEMAN, JOHN. The Book Collectors Fair at the National Book League. London, 1966. 1st Eng ed. Single leaf. *Clearwater.* $31/£20

BETJEMAN, JOHN. Continual Dew. A Little Book of Bourgeois Verse. London, 1937. 1st Eng ed. Very Nice (inscrip) in dj (sl rubbed, nicked). *Clearwater.* $187/£120

BETJEMAN, JOHN. Cornwall Illustrated, in a Series of Views.... Architectural Press, 1935. 2nd ed. Ringbound pict card cvrs (lt creased). *Cox.* $47/£30

BETJEMAN, JOHN. Cornwall. Faber, (1939?). Rev 2nd ed. White cl (sl bruised). Dj (torn, frayed). *Clearwater.* $70/£45

BETJEMAN, JOHN. Cornwall. A Shell Guide. London: Faber, 1966. 2nd imp. Very Nice in dj. *Clearwater.* $31/£20

BETJEMAN, JOHN. English Cities and Small Towns. London, 1943. 1st ed. Illus bds. VG in dj (rubbed). *Words Etc.* $12/£8

BETJEMAN, JOHN. First and Last Loves. London, 1952. 1st Eng ed. Very Nice (inscrip) in dj (frayed, mkd). *Clearwater.* $55/£35

BETJEMAN, JOHN. Ghastly Good Taste. London: Chapman & Hall, 1933. 1st ed, 2nd issue (leaf 119-120 is a cancel). Fldg plt, errata slip, extra label. (Unevenly dknd/faded, lt rubbed.) Contents VG (lt foxing). *Waverly*.* $60/£38

BETJEMAN, JOHN. High and Low. London: John Murray, (1966). 1st ed, trade issue. Gilt cl. (Top edge dusty), else Nice in dj (price-clipped). *Reese.* $30/£19

BETJEMAN, JOHN. London's Historic Railway Stations. London: John Murray, 1972. 1st Eng ed. VG in dj (sl creased). *Hadley.* $47/£30

BETJEMAN, JOHN. A Nip in the Air. London, 1974. 1st Eng ed. Fine in dj. *Clearwater.* $23/£15

BETJEMAN, JOHN. Old Lights for New Chancels. London, 1940. 1st Eng ed. Fine (fr hinge repaired, new eps). *Clearwater.* $39/£25

BETJEMAN, JOHN. An Oxford University Chest. London, 1938. Teg. Cl-backed marbled bds (ex-lib, ink stamps, fep affixed to pastedown; faint spine #), gilt. *Edwards.* $31/£20

BETJEMAN, JOHN. A Pictorial History of English Architecture. Murray, 1972. NF in dj. *Hadley.* $25/£16

BETJEMAN, JOHN. Poems in the Porch. London, 1954. 1st Eng ed. Card wrappers. *Clearwater.* $39/£25

BETJEMAN, JOHN. Summoned by Bells. 1960. 1st ed. VG in dj (spine head torn w/loss). *Words Etc.* $12/£8

BETJEMAN, JOHN. Vintage London. London: Collins, 1942. 1st ed. 11 tipped-in color plts. (Sl foxing), else NF in VG+ dj (lt worn). *Between The Covers.* $75/£48

BETT, W. R. The Infirmities of Genius. London, 1952. 1st ed. VG. *Fye.* $65/£42

BETTEN, H. L. Upland Game Shooting. Phila: Penn, 1940. 1st ed, 1st ptg. Color frontis, 8 color plts. VG (lt spot cvr, water stain) in Good+ dj (edge tears). *Backman.* $75/£48

BETTMANN, OTTO L. A Pictorial History of Medicine. Springfield, 1956. 1st ed. VG in Good dj. *Doctor's Library.* $60/£38

BETTS, CHARLES WYLLYS. Visitors' Hand Book of Old Point Comfort, Virginia and Vicinity. Ptd by Students of Hampton Inst, 1893. 6th ed. 114,(1)pp; map. Tied in ptd wraps (worn, spine ends torn). *Bohling.* $35/£22

BETTS, DORIS. The Gentle Insurrection and Other Stories. NY: Putnam, (1954). 1st ed, 1st bk. VG+ in dj (spine ends sl worn, rear panel lt soiled). *Bernard.* $125/£80

BEURDELEY, MICHEL. Chinese Trade Porcelain. Diana Imber (trans). Rutland/Tokyo: Charles E. Tuttle, (1962). 1st US ed. 24 tipped-in color plts. Maroon cl (sm stain upper joint), gilt. Pict dj (sl worn, chipped). *Baltimore*.* $60/£38

BEURDELEY, MICHEL. Chinese Trade Porcelain. Rutland/Tokyo: Tuttle, (1963). 2nd ed. 24 tipped-in color plts. Good+ in Good+ dj, Good+ slipcase. *Scribe's Perch*.* $30/£19

BEVAN, BERNARD. History of Spanish Architecture. London, 1938. (Lt foxed.) *Washton.* $85/£54

BEVAN, BERNARD. History of Spanish Architecture. London: Batsford, 1938. Frontis, 94 plts, 2 fldg maps. (Sm lib stamp tp, verso; cvr every other plt just touching surface; gilt lib spine #), else Good. *Ars Artis.* $70/£45

BEVAN, E. The Honey Bee. London, 1870. 3rd rev, enlgd ed. Frontis, xxiv,(i),394pp; 12 color, 9 plain plts. (Cl sl used, sm tear rear joint.) *Wheldon & Wesley.* $156/£100

BEVAN, EDWYN. Jerusalem Under the High-Priests. London: Arnold, 1912. 2nd imp. (Sl foxed; sl rubbed, spine sl frayed), o/w VG. *Worldwide.* $65/£42

BEVERIDGE, ALBERT J. Abraham Lincoln 1809-1858. Boston/NY: Houghton Mifflin, 1928. 1st ed. 2 vols. VG set (lower corners sl damped). *Mcgowan.* $150/£96

BEVERIDGE, ALBERT J. Abraham Lincoln, 1809-1858. Boston, 1928. Standard Library ed. 4 vols. VG+. *Pratt.* $95/£61

BEVERIDGE, ALBERT J. The Life of John Marshall. Boston: Houghton Mifflin, 1916. 4 vols. 3/4 brn morocco (sl rubbed). Pretty. *Boswell.* $450/£288

BEVERIDGE, THOMAS J. English Renaissance Woodwork 1660-1730. NY/London, 1921. 80 plts. Cl-backed bds (sl worn, spine faded, chipped). *Edwards.* $156/£100

BEWICK, THOMAS. Bewick to Dovaston, Letters 1824-1828. Gordon Williams (ed). London: Nattali & Maurice, (1968). 1st ed. Frontis. Parchment spine, gilt. Dj. *Bickersteth.* $39/£25

BEWICK, THOMAS. Birds. Newcastle: David Esslemont, 1984. One of 250 hand-ptd by Esslemont, this one of 147 bound in 1/4 cl, patterned paper over bds, matching dj. 24 engrs. Fine. *Michael Taylor.* $226/£145

BEWICK, THOMAS. A General History of Quadrupeds. London, 1791. 2nd ed. x,483pp (2 tears repaired pp 284-5). Calf (rebacked, preserving label). *Henly.* $140/£90

BEWICK, THOMAS. A History of British Birds. Newcastle, 1805. 2 vols. Later 19th-cent red morocco (spines dknd), gilt. *Swann*.* $287/£184

BEWICK, THOMAS. A History of British Birds. Newcastle: for T. Bewick: sold by him, and Longman & Rees, London, 1805. 3rd ed vol 1, 2nd ed vol 2. Lg Paper copy. 2 vols. Contemp diced russia gilt, gilt dec backs, aeg. Fine. *Hatchwell.* $780/£500

BEWICK, THOMAS. Memoir of Thomas Bewick Written by Himself 1822-28. London, 1924. Fine. *Wheldon & Wesley.* $117/£75

BEWICK, THOMAS. A Memoir.... Montague Weekley (ed). Cresset, 1961. Frontis. Dj (sl foxed). *Maggs.* $25/£16

BEWICK, THOMAS. Thomas Bewick's Fables of Aesop. (London), 1980. 1/2 calf. Cl fldg case. *Swann*.* $230/£147

BEYER, W. F. and O. F. KEYDEL (eds). Deeds of Valor...How American Heroes Won the Medal of Honor. Detroit, 1906. 2 vols. 32 color plts. VG. *New Hampshire*.* $70/£45

BEYLE, MARIE-HENRI. The Red and the Black. NY: LEC, 1947. #904/1500 numbered, signed by Rafaello Busoni (illus). Leather-backed cl. Fine in pub's slipcase (sl used). *Hermitage.* $75/£48

Bhagavad Gita: The Song Celestial. Edwin Arnold (trans). Bombay: LEC, 1965. One of 1500 numbered, signed by Y. G. Srimati (illus). 15 mtd color plts. Patterned silk. Mint in fldg linen slipcase w/ties. *Argosy.* $150/£96

BHUSHAN, JAMILA BRIJ. Indian Jewellery, Ornaments, and Decorative Designs. Bombay, (1935). 1st ed. Cl-backed bds (shaken). Swann*. $230/£147

BIANCHINO, GLORIA et al. Italian Fashion. NY, (1987). 2 vols. Djs, bd slipcase. Swann*. $57/£37

BIANCO, MARGERY. Poor Cecco. NY, (1925). 1st Amer ed, 2nd issue. 7 color plts by Arthur Rackham. (Bkpl, sl soil.) Blue cl (worn, lt soiled), gilt. Freeman*. $90/£58

BIANCO, MARGERY. Winterbound. Viking, 1936. 1st ed. Kate Seredy (illus). 5.5x8.5. 234pp. VG+ in dj (sl edgeworn). My Bookhouse. $45/£29

BIANCO, PAMELA. The Valentine Party. Phila/NY: Lippincott, 1954. 1st Amer ed. 8vo. 28pp. Illus eps. Yellow cl. Dj (missing sm piece lower corner, spine ends). Dower. $45/£29

BIART, L. Adventures of a Young Naturalist. NY, 1871. 491pp; 64 engr plts. Pict cl, gilt. Fine. Henly. $33/£21

BIBBY, GEOFFREY. Looking for Dilmun. NY: Knopf, 1969. 1st ed. NF in dj. Worldwide. $22/£14

BIBER, SAMUEL. The Romance of Fur. Sydney: W.C. Penfold, 1935. VG. Perier. $30/£19

BIBESCO, MARTHE. The Veiled Wanderer. Roland Gant (trans). London: Falcon, 1949. 1st Eng ed. Fine (name) in dj (sl torn, dust-mkd, price-clipped). Clearwater. $39/£25

Bibliography of State Participation in the Civil War, 1861-1866. Washington: GPO, 1913. Rev, enlgd ed. 1/2 leather (worn, spine partly lacking, tape-repaired). Contents VG. Waverly*. $22/£14

Bibliography of Swinburne. (By Richard H. Shepherd.) London: George Redway, 1887. 4th rev expanded ed. One of 250 ptd. Unopened. Full gilt vellum (sl spotted). Good. Reese. $85/£54

BICK, EDGAR M. Source Book of Orthopedics. Balt, 1948. 2nd ed. Blue cl. NF. Doctor's Library. $250/£160

BICKEL, KARL A. The Mangrove Coast. NY: Coward-McCann, 1942. 1st ed. 32 photo plts. Pict label on fr, spine label. VG (bkpl) in photo-illus dj (spine faded, edges chipped). Cahan. $200/£128

BICKEL, LENNARD. Shackleton's Forgotten Argonauts. (Melbourne): Macmillan of Australia, 1982. As New in dj. High Latitude. $30/£19

Bickerstaff's Boston Almanack...1780. Boston: Draper et al, n.d. (Very worn, bottom portions of fr wrapper, 1st 2 leaves missing, affecting text.) New Hampshire*. $90/£58

BICKHAM, WILLIAM D. From Ohio to the Rocky Mountains. Dayton, 1879. 178pp. Dk grn cl (lt worn, spine ends chipped), blind-emb fr cvr, gilt spine. Bohling. $65/£42

BICKHAM, WILLIAM D. Rosencrans' Campaign with the Fourteenth Army Corps, of the Army of the Cumberland.... Cincinnati: Moore, 1863. 1st ed. Frontis map, 476pp (lacks fep). Howes B422. Ginsberg. $250/£160

BICKNELL, T. W. Story of Dr. John Clarke. Providence, 1915. Stated 1st ed. Grn lib buckram. Good (ex-lib). Scribe's Perch*. $20/£13

BIDDLE, ANTHONY F. DREXEL. The Second Froggy Fairy Book. London, 1900. 8th thousand. Anne Pennock & Gustave Verbeek (illus). 8x5.5. 127pp. Teg. Nice color dec pict cl. (Sl loose, worn.) King. $50/£32

BIDDLE, FRANCIS. Mr. Justice Holmes. NY: Scribner, 1942. Grn cl (worn). Boswell. $45/£29

BIDDLE, TYRREL E. The Corinthian Yachtsman or Hints on Yachting. Norie & Wilson, 1886. Frontis. (Binding faded.) Petersfield. $22/£14

BIDDLECOMBE, GEORGE. The Art of Rigging. Salem: Marine Research Soc, 1925. Best ed. 17 plts, tables. NF in dj (sl spotted). Lefkowicz. $95/£61

BIDDLECOMBE, GEORGE. The Art of Rigging.... Salem: Marine Research Soc, 1925. 1st ed. 17 plts. Dk grn cl, gilt-lettered spine. Fine (bkpl). Argonaut. $125/£80

BIDDULPH, JOHN. The Pirates of Malabar.... London, 1907. 1st ed. Frontis, map. (Feps lt browned; spine tail sl chipped.) Edwards. $39/£25

BIDDULPH, JOHN. Stringer Lawrence. London, 1901. 5 plts (1 color), fldg map. Blue pict cl (sl worn). Maggs. $86/£55

BIDMAN, DAVID. The Complete Graphic Works of William Blake. NY, 1978. 1st ed. Fine in dj. Argosy. $200/£128

BIDWELL, GEORGE. Forging His Chains. NY/Hartford: Bidwell, 1889. 560pp. Good (rubbed). Zubal*. $35/£22

BIDWELL, JOHN. Echoes of the Past About California. [With] In Camp and Cabin. By John Steele. Milo Milton Quaife (ed). Chicago: Lakeside, Christmas, 1928. Dk red cl (spine ends, corners rubbed, sm spots cvrs, rear inner hinge cracked). Sadlon. $10/£6

BIDWELL, JOHN. Echoes of the Past. Chico, CA: Chico Advertiser, (n.d., but 1914). 1st separate ed. Grn ptd wrappers. (Spine worn.) NF. Howes B432. Harrington. $85/£54

BIEBER, MARGARETE. Ancient Copies: Contributions to the History of Greek and Roman Art. NY Univ, 1977. 1st ed. VF in dj. Hermitage. $45/£29

BIEBER, MARGARETE. The History of the Greek and Roman Theater. Princeton: Princeton Univ, 1961. 2nd ed. VG in dj. Turtle Island. $75/£48

BIEBER, RALPH P. Marching with the Army of the West 1846-48, SW Hist #IV. Glendale, 1936. 1st ed. VF. No dj as issued. Turpen. $150/£96

BIEBER, RALPH P. (ed). The Southwest Historical Series. Glendale: A.H. Clark, 1931-43. 12 vols incl index vol. Teg. Uniform red cl. Overall VG (some vols w/spines sunned, heads fraying). All internally Fine. Howes S791, G70, H72. Reese. $2,500/£1,603

BIEDL, ARTUR. The Internal Secretory Organs: Their Physiology and Pathology. NY: William Wood, 1913. 1st Amer ed. Panelled thatched grn buckram (lib stamp tp, spine #s), gilt spine. Gach. $75/£48

BIERCE, AMBROSE and GUSTAVE ADOLPH DANZIGER. The Monk and the Hangman's Daughter. Chicago, 1892. 1st ed. 166pp. (Ex-lib; worn, soiled.) King. $45/£29

BIERCE, AMBROSE. The Devil's Dictionary. NY, 1972. One of 1500 numbered, signed by Fritz Kredel (illus). 1/2 leather (lt worn). Slipcase. Oinonen*. $60/£38

BIERCE, AMBROSE. My Favorite Murder. N.p., n.d. (ca 1916). Unauthorized ed. VG in ptd wrappers. Argosy. $25/£16

BIERCE, AMBROSE. The Shadow on the Dial and Other Essays. SF: A.M. Robertson, 1909. 1st ed. 249pp. (Sl offsetting eps), else Fine in dj (sl faded). Hermitage. $275/£176

BIERCE, AMBROSE. The Shadow on the Dial and Other Essays. S.O. Howes (ed). SF: A.M. Robertson, 1909. 1st ed. Dec brn cl (spine ends, extrems sl frayed). VG. BAL 1127. Antic Hay. $125/£80

BIERCE, AMBROSE. Tales of Soldiers and Civilians. NY: Lovell, Coryell, (1891). 300pp. Unrecorded variant binding: grn cl stamped in gold on spine, black on cvr. Good (lt foxing; shelfwear). Cullen. $55/£35

BIERCE, AMBROSE. Tales of Soldiers and Civilians. SF, 1891. 1st ed. Pub's gilt-lettered cl (rubbed, bumped; lib bkpl). Swann*. $103/£66

BIERCE, AMBROSE. Tales of Soldiers and Civilians. NY: LEC, 1943. #904/1500 numbered, signed by Paul Landacre (illus). Pict cl, leather. (Extrems sl rubbed), else Very Nice. Hermitage. $75/£48

BIERCE, AMBROSE. Twenty-One Letters. Samuel Loveman (ed). Cleveland, 1922. Ltd to 950 numbered. (Sl rubbed, spotted.) *King.* $85/£54

BIETENHOLZ, PETER G. (ed). Contemporaries of Erasmus. Toronto: Univ of Toronto, c. 1985-87. 3 vols. Pict cl (sl worn). Contents VG. *New Hampshire*.* $70/£45

BIGELOW, FRANCIS HILL. Historic Silver of the Colonies and Its Makers. NY: Macmillan, 1917. 1st ed. VG. *New Hampshire*.* $50/£32

BIGELOW, FRANCIS HILL. Historic Silver of the Colonies and Its Makers. NY: Macmillan, 1917. 1st ed. Pict cl (spine ends lt rubbed). *Sadlon.* $65/£42

BIGELOW, HENRY J. A Lecture Introductory to the Course of Surgery.... Boston, 1850. 1st ed. 24pp. VG in wrappers. *Fye.* $100/£64

BIGELOW, HENRY J. Orthopedic Surgery and Other Medical Papers. Boston, 1900. 1st ed. VG. *Fye.* $100/£64

BIGELOW, HORATIO. Gunnerman's Gold. Huntington, 1943. Ltd to 1000. VG. *Truepenny.* $95/£61

BIGELOW, HORATIO. Gunnerman's Gold. Huntington: Standard, 1943. 1st ed. #261/1000. Photo eps. VG + in VG white dj (edge tears; foxed). *Backman.* $145/£93

BIGELOW, HORATIO. Gunnerman. NY: Derrydale, (1939). 1st ed. #442/950. NF. *Mcgowan.* $75/£48

BIGELOW, J. Memoir of the Life and Public Service of John Charles Fremont. NY, 1856. 1st ed. 480pp. Pub's cl (spine sunned). Good. *Scribe's Perch*.* $20/£13

BIGELOW, JACOB. Brief Expositions of Rational Medicine.... Boston, 1858. 1st ed. 69pp. VG. *Fye.* $125/£80

BIGELOW, JACOB. Discourse on Self-Limited Diseases.... Boston: Nathan Hale, 1835. 46pp. (Lower blank margin dampstained; lib stamp fr wrap, shelving #), o/w Clean in orig ptd wrappers, protective bds. *Goodrich.* $395/£253

BIGELOW, JACOB. Nature in Disease. Boston, 1854. 1st ed. 391pp. VG. *Fye.* $225/£144

BIGELOW, JACOB. A Treatise on the Materia Medica.... Boston, 1822. 424pp. (New eps, stamp, foxing). Recent 1/4 leather, marbled bds. *Fye.* $300/£192

BIGELOW, JOHN, JR. The Campaign of Chancellorsville, a Strategic and Tactical Study. New Haven: Yale Univ, (1910). 1st ed. #534/1000 ptd. 39 color maps, 5 plans. (Ex-libris; pp101-102 in facs.) Later cl. *Mcgowan.* $150/£96

BIGELOW, JOHN, JR. The Campaign of Chancellorsville. New Haven: Yale Univ, (1910). 1st ed. Ltd to 1000. Errata, 39 color maps, 3 sketches, 5 plans. (Upper rt-hand corner sl damped), else VG. *Mcgowan.* $850/£545

BIGELOW, JOHN, JR. On the Bloody Trail of Geronimo. L.A.: Westernlore, 1958. 1st bk ed. One of 750. Illus by Frederic Remington et al. Maroon blind-stamped cl, gilt. (Bkpl), o/w Fine in NF dj. *Harrington.* $50/£32

BIGELOW, JOHN. Jamaica in 1850. NY/London: Putnam, 1851. 1st ed. iv,214pp. (Sl foxed; rubbed, spine faded, chipped, frayed; ex-lib, # spine), o/w Good. *Worldwide.* $65/£42

BIGELOW, JOHN. The Mystery of Sleep. NY, 1924. VG (sl worn). *Doctor's Library.* $50/£32

BIGELOW, MELVILLE M. Elements of the Law of Torts for the Use of Students. Boston: Little, Brown, 1896. Contemp sheep (rubbed). Sound. *Boswell.* $75/£48

BIGGERS, EARL DERR. The Black Camel. Indianapolis, (1929). 1st Amer ed. NF (spine sl sunned, extrems sl rubbed). *Polyanthos.* $30/£19

BIGGERS, EARL DERR. Charlie Chan Carries On. Bobbs Merrill, (1930). 1st ed. VG in VG dj (shallow spine head chipping). *Certo.* $135/£87

BIGGERS, EARL DERR. Earl Derr Biggers Tells Ten Stories. Indianapolis, (1933). 1st ed. NF. *Mcclintock.* $27/£17

BIGGERS, EARL DERR. Seven Keys to Baldpate. Indianapolis, (1913). 1st ed. VG. *Mcclintock.* $45/£29

BIGGLE, LLOYD. The Still Small Voice of Trumpets. Doubleday, 1968. 1st ed. NF in dj. *Madle.* $15/£10

BIGGS, DONALD C. Conquer and Colonize. San Rafael, (1977). 1st ed. Fine in Fine dj. *Pratt.* $20/£13

BIGGS, DONALD C. The Pony Express: Creation of the Legend. SF: Privately ptd, 1956. One of 500. Stiff wrappers. *Dawson.* $30/£19

BIGGS, JOHN R. Woodcuts, Wood Engravings, Linocuts and Prints by Related Methods.... London: Blandford, 1958. 1st ed. VG in dj. *Michael Taylor.* $47/£30

BIGGS, WILLIAM. Narrative of the Captivity of William Biggs Among the Kickapoo Indians in Illinois in 1788. (N.p.): Heartman's Hist Series, 1922. One of 81 ptd. Orig bds, paper label fr cvr. Howes B443. *Ginsberg.* $175/£112

BIGLAND, EILEEN. The Lake of the Royal Crocodiles. NY, 1939. 1st ed. 8 color plts, 2 maps. Grn cl, gilt. VG. *Price.* $29/£19

Biglow Papers. (By James Russell Lowell.) Boston: Ticknor & Fields, 1867. 1st Amer ed, 1st ptg (w/'are getting' on pxvi line 5; w/TF device at spine foot). Grn cl. NF (sl foxed). *Sumner & Stillman.* $95/£61

BILBO, JACK. Out of My Mind. London: Modern Art Gallery, 1946. 1st ed. VG in dj. *Hollett.* $47/£30

BILL, ALFRED HOYT. The Beleagured City Richmond, 1861-1865. NY: Knopf, 1946. 1st ed. VG. *Mcgowan.* $25/£16

BILL, M. (ed). Le Corbusier and P. Jeanneret. The Complete Architectural Works. Vol III: 1934-1938. Thames & Hudson, 1964. Sound. *Ars Artis.* $70/£45

BILLEB, EMIL W. Mining Camp Days. Berkeley: Howell-North, 1968. 1st ed. Fine in dj. *Argonaut.* $45/£29

BILLINGS, JOHN D. Hardtack and Coffee. Richard Harwell (ed). Chicago: Lakeside Classic, 1960. Fine. *Wantagh.* $25/£16

BILLINGS, JOHN S. Description of the Johns Hopkins Hospital. Balt, 1890. 1st ed. 4to. 116pp + 56 plts. Recent 1/4 leather, marbled bds. VG. *Fye.* $1,400/£897

BILLINGS, JOHN S. Report of the Mortality and Vital Statistics of the United States...(June 1, 1880). Part II (only, of a 2-part set). Washington: GPO, 1886. 803pp. (Lt browning; cl worn, rubbed; spine lettering faded.) *Goodrich.* $125/£80

BILLINGTON, RAY ALLEN. Westward Expansion. NY, 1949. 1st ed. NF in dj (edgewear, sm hole in back). *Baade.* $125/£80

BILLROTH, THEODOR. Historical Studies on the Nature and Treatment of Gunshot Wounds from the Fifteenth Century to the Present Time. New Haven: Nathan Smith Medical Club, 1933. 1st bk ed in English. Fine. *Glaser.* $150/£96

BILLROTH, THEODOR. Lectures on Surgical Pathology and Therapeutics. London: New Sydenham Soc, 1877/78. 2 vols. x,438; xi,543pp. Orig brn cl (rebacked, retaining backstrips). *White.* $55/£35

BILLROTH, THEODOR. The Medical Sciences in the German Universities. NY, 1924. 1st ed in English. VG. *Fye.* $100/£64

BINDLOSS, HAROLD. In the Niger Country. Edinburgh: Wm. Blackwood, 1898. x,338pp; 2 maps (1 color fldg). VG. *Adelson.* $50/£32

BINGHAM, HIRAM. Inca Land, Explorations in the Highlands of Peru. Boston: Houghton Mifflin, 1922. 1st ed. Blue cl (lt rubbed). VG. *Hermitage.* $75/£48

BINGHAM, JOHN A. Trial of the Conspirators for the Assassination of President Lincoln.... Washington, 1865. 122pp. Ptd wrapper (sl worn). Contents VG. *New Hampshire**. $130/£83

BINGHAM, JOHN. God's Defector. London: Macmillan, 1976. 1st ed. Fine in dj. *Mordida.* $35/£22

BINGHAM, JOHN. Vulture in the Sun. London: Gollancz, 1971. 1st ed. Fine in dj (price-clipped). *Mordida.* $40/£26

BINGLEY, THOMAS. Tales About Travellers: Their Perils, Adventures, and Discoveries. NY: Wiley & Putnam, 1844. 1st Amer ed. Sq 12mo. Full-pg frontis, guard; vi + 190pp (lt foxing; sig sprung); 7 full-pg engrs. Yellow eps. Tooled cl on bds, gilt vignette upper cvr (spine chipped, corners rubbed). VG. *Hobbyhorse.* $90/£58

BINGLEY, W. Useful Knowledge. Vol. I. Minerals. London: Baldwin, Cradock & Joy, 1821. 3rd ed. viii,279pp. Contemp full tooled calf, gilt. VG (fr joint tender). *Blake.* $250/£160

BINNEY, GEORGE. With Seaplane and Sledge in the Arctic. NY: Geo. H. Doran, 1926. Fldg map. VG (cl sl soiled). *High Latitude.* $70/£45

BINNS, ARCHIE. Peter Skene Ogden: Fur Trader. Portland: Binfords & Mort, (1967). 1st ed. 2 dbl-pg maps. Fine in pict dj (lt worn). *Argonaut.* $45/£29

BINNS, R. W. A Century of Potting in the City of Worcester...1751 to 1851. London/Worcester, 1865. 1st ed. xx,228pp. Teg. Emb cl, gilt device. (Margins lt browned, upper hinge cracked; edges sl soiled, rubbed, spine sl discolored, head bumped.) *Edwards.* $156/£100

BINYON, LAURENCE. The Drawings and Engravings of William Blake. London: The Studio, 1922. 1st ed. 1/2 vellum (sl soiled, esp spine, crown sl torn, rear bd lt damped bottom edge, fr hinge tender). Contents Clean (sl foxing, eps browned). *Waverly**. $44/£28

BINYON, LAURENCE. The Drawings and Engravings of William Blake. Geoffrey Holme (ed). London: The Studio, 1922. 104 plts (incl 16 color tipped in). Teg, rest uncut. Japon-backed bds, gilt. (Feps browned, hinges cracked, tp sl spotted; edges sl worn, soiled.) *Edwards.* $70/£45

BINYON, LAURENCE. The Drawings and Engravings of William Blake. Geoffrey Holme (ed). London: The Studio, 1922. One of 200. 104 plts (16 color), 2 ports. Full vellum, gilt. VF in fldg box (lacks ties). *Kane**. $200/£128

BINYON, LAURENCE. Dutch Etchers of the Seventeenth Century. London: Seeley, 1905. 4 plts. Cl-backed bds, paper spine label (worn). *Hollett.* $62/£40

BINYON, LAURENCE. The Engraved Designs of William Blake. London: Ernest Benn, 1926. 2 vols. 20 color plts, 62 collotypes + 82 extra illus in the portfolio. VG in dj (sl rubbed, dknd), cl portfolio w/ties. *Hollett.* $304/£195

BINYON, LAURENCE. The Followers of William Blake. London, 1925. 79 plts (6 tipped-in color). Brn cl (frayed, scuffed), gilt. Contents VG. *Yudkin**. $50/£32

BINYON, LAURENCE. Second Book of London Visions. London: Elkin Mathews, 1899. 1st ed. Dec blue-gray wrappers (sl edgeworn). NF. *Sumner & Stillman.* $135/£87

BINYON, LAURENCE. The Wonder Night. (London: Faber & Faber, n.d.) 1st ed. VG in sewn ptd wraps. *Antic Hay.* $25/£16

BINYON, T. J. Murder Will Out: The Detective in Fiction. NY: OUP, 1989. 1st US ed. Fine in Fine dj. *Janus.* $25/£16

Biographies of Physicians and Surgeons, Illustrated. Chicago, 1904. Full leather (fr bd nearly detached). Contents Fine. *Fye.* $300/£192

BION. The Construction and Principle Uses of Mathematical Instruments. London: Holland Press, 1972. Facs. One of 500. Dj (soiled, faded). *Weber.* $100/£64

BIRCH, G. H. London Churches of XVII and XVIIIth Century.... London: Batsford, 1896. xviii,2ff,24pp; 64 plts (loose). 1/2 leather (sl worn). *Ars Artis.* $133/£85

BIRCH, JONATHAN. Fifty-One Original Fables with Morals and Ethical Index. London: Hamilton, Adams, 1833. 1st ed. 8vo. Full-pg frontis, 251pp; 85 orig wood engrs by Robert Cruikshank. Aeg. Tan calf, gilt. (Spine edges sl worn), else VF. *Bromer.* $475/£304

BIRCH, SAMUEL. History of Ancient Pottery. London: John Murray, 1858. 1st ed. 2 vols. 12 color plts. 3/4 leather (scuffed), marbled bds (rubbed). VG (foxed, name). *Old London.* $200/£128

BIRCH, SAMUEL. History of Ancient Pottery. 1873. New rev ed. xv,644pp (foxed); 13 plts. (Spine sl chipped.) *Edwards.* $75/£48

BIRD, BRANDON. Downbeat for a Dirge. NY: Dodd Mead, 1952. 1st ed. Fine in dj (lt soiled, 2 sm tears). *Mordida.* $50/£32

BIRD, GOLDING. Urinary Deposits: Their Diagnosis, Pathology, and Therapeutical Indications. Blanchard & Lea, 1859. 382pp. (Sl foxed), o/w Excellent. *Bookcell.* $75/£48

BIRD, ISABELLA. Six Months Among the...Sandwich Islands. NY: Putnam, 1881. 318pp; fldg map, 3 plts. Pict cl (rubbed). *Adelson.* $50/£32

BIRD, ISABELLA. Six Months...in the Sandwich Islands. London, 1876. 2nd ed. 318pp + 2pp ads; fldg map. Good- (ex-lib). *Scribe's Perch**. $36/£23

BIRD, ISABELLA. Unbeaten Tracks in Japan. NY, n.d. c.(1880). 2 vols in 1 as issued. xxiii,407; xiii,392pp (lt margin browning); fldg map. Dec eps. Gilt-dec cl (rubbed, spine chipped). *Edwards.* $70/£45

BIRD, ROBERT MONTGOMERY. The City Looking Glass. Arthur Hobson Quinn (ed). NY: Colophon, 1933. 1st ed. One of 465. Paper label. (Lt offsetting eps), else Fine in dj. BAL 1177. *Reese.* $45/£29

BIRDWOOD, LORD. Khaki and Gown. London, 1941. 4 color maps. Blue cl (sl worn). *Maggs.* $47/£30

BIRKBECK, MORRIS. Letters from Illinois. London: Taylor & Hessey, 1818. 1st Eng ed. 1/4 marbled calf over marbled bds, leather spine label. Fine. Howes B467. *Sadlon.* $175/£112

BIRKBECK, MORRIS. Notes on a Journey in America, from the Coast of Virginia to the Territory of Illinois. London, 1818. 3rd ed. Fldg frontis map, 163pp + ads. Contemp 3/4 calf, marbled bds, leather label. (Offsetting tp; fr bd scuffed), else Very Nice. Howes B468. *Reese.* $225/£144

BIRKBECK, MORRIS. Notes on a Journey in America.... London, 1818. 2nd ed. 16pp ads. Engr fldg map, hand-colored in outline, laid in (from another copy?) w/trimmed margins. Lib buckram. Howes B468. *Swann**. $138/£88

BIRKBY, CAREL. Limpopo Journey. 1939. 1st ed. Dj (chipped). *Edwards.* $39/£25

BIRKENHEAD, EARL OF. Fourteen English Judges. London: Cassell, 1926. 3/4 crimson morocco (sl rubbed), gilt. Pretty. *Boswell.* $350/£224

BIRKET-SMITH, KAJ. The Eskimos. London: Methuen, (1936). VG (edges sl discolored) in Good dj. *High Latitude.* $55/£35

BIRKETT, H. F. The Book of Overton. London: J&E Bumpus, 1928. 1st ed. Paper spine label (lt mkd; bkpl). *Hollett.* $39/£25

BIRKHEAD, EDITH. The Tale of Terror: A Study of the Gothic Romance. London: Constable, 1921. 1st ed. (Eps browned, scattered foxing), else VG. *Certo.* $45/£29

BIRLEY, ERIC. Research on Hadrian's Wall. Kendal: Titus Wilson, 1961. 1st ed. 18 plts. (Eps sl browned.) Dj. *Hollett.* $86/£55

BIRMINGHAM, GEORGE. (Pseud of James O. Hannay.) Gossamer. London: Methuen, (1915). 1st ed. VG in pict dj (sl chipped). *Reese.* $45/£29

BIRMINGHAM, GEORGE. (Pseud of James O. Hannay.) Inisheeny. London: Methuen, (1920). 1st ed. Sample fr dj panel tipped in. Nice (top edge dusty, sl cocked) in dj (lt chipped). *Reese.* $45/£29

BIRNBAUM, A. Green Eyes. NY: Golden, 1953. 2nd ed. 10 1/2 x 12. 32pp. Glossy bds. VG. *Cattermole.* $50/£32

BIRNBAUM, MARTIN. Oscar Wilde: Fragments and Memories. NY, 1914. One of 250 numbered. Cl-backed bds. NF. *Clearwater.* $70/£45

BIRNEY, CATHERINE. Sarah and Angelina Grimke. Boston: Lee & Shephard, 1885. 1st ed. 319pp. Brn cl (sl worn, paper adhered rear cvr). Good (ex-lib, stamp tp). *Second Life.* $35/£22

BIRNEY, HOFFMAN. Forgotten Canon. Phila: Penn Co, 1934. (Name; fr hinge tender), else NF in VG dj (chips). *Five Quail.* $35/£22

BIRNEY, HOFFMAN. Roads to Roam. Phila, 1930. 1st ed. Frontis. (Cvr lt soiled, faded, else VG +. *Five Quail.* $35/£22

BIRNMBAUM, MARTIN. Oscar Wilde: Fragments and Memories. NY: James F. Drake, 1914. 1st ed. One of 250. Frontis. Cl-backed paper over bds, paper label fr cvr. Fine in orig glassine wrapper. *Cahan.* $100/£64

BIRRELL, AUGUSTINE. The Collected Essays and Addresses 1880-1920. Dent, 1922. 1st ed. 2 vols. (Backstrips sl faded.) *Cox.* $39/£25

BIRRELL, AUGUSTINE. Frederick Locker-Lampson, a Character Sketch.... London, 1920. Uncut. Cl spine. (Cvr wear, foxing.) *King.* $30/£19

BIRRELL, AUGUSTINE. A Rogue's Memoirs. London: Arthur L. Humphreys, 1912. 1st ed. 5 mtd head/tail pieces. (Prelims sl spotted, fep edges browned.) Teg. Full dec gilt suede (spine, upper bd lt faded.) *Edwards.* $55/£35

Birthday Book. Random House, (1931). One of 1850 numbered, signed by Rockwell Kent (illus). Good + (edge sl dampstained). *Certo.* $40/£26

BISCHOF, WERNER. Japan. NY: S&S, 1954. 1st Amer ed. NF in dj (worn). *Cahan.* $50/£32

BISCHOFF, WILLIAM NORBERT. Jesuits in Old Oregon, 1840-1940. Caldwell, ID: Caxton Ptrs, 1945. VG. *Bohling.* $22/£14

BISHOP, A. W. Loyalty on the Frontier. St. Louis, 1863. 1st ed. Inscribed. 228pp. (Worn; spine edge frayed; 1-inch corner piece off rear cvr; inner stains, foxing; last 30pp corners worn away.) Howes B474. *Wantagh.* $85/£54

BISHOP, CLAIRE. The Five Chinese Brothers. NY: Coward McCann, 1938. 1st ed. Kurt Wiese (illus). 9 3/4 x 6 3/4. 52pp. Pict bds, cl spine. VG. *Cattermole.* $500/£321

BISHOP, ELIZABETH (ed). The Diary of Helena Morley. NY: Farrar, Straus & Cudahy, (1957). 1st ed. NF in dj (sl worn, price-clipped). *Antic Hay.* $25/£16

BISHOP, GEORGE. New-England Judged, by the Spirit of the Lord.... London: T. Sowle, 1703-02. 2nd ed. Three parts in 1 vol. (6),231,(3),235-498,(2),3-212,(11),(3)pp. Later 18th-cent calf. (Worn, lacks 1/2 of spine; spotting to text, few pp corners missing, no loss), o/w Good. Howes B481. *Brown.* $400/£256

BISHOP, HARRIET E. Floral Home. NY: Sheldon, Blakeman, 1857. 1st ed. 342pp; 10 plts. VG (lt foxed, browned). *Second Life.* $225/£144

BISHOP, I. B. Among the Tibetans. NY, (1894). 159pp. Dec cvr. Good-. *Scribe's Perch*.* $50/£32

BISHOP, J. A Visit to the Farm. London: Dean & Munday/A.K. Newman, n.d. (ca 1835). Sq 12mo. 30pp + 1pg list on lower wrapper; 8 VF hand-colored full-pg wood engrs incl frontis. Dec buff stiff paper wrappers (edges lt soiled), else Fine. *Hobbyhorse.* $325/£208

BISHOP, J. LEANDER. A History of American Manufactures from 1608 to 1860. Phila: Edward Young, 1861-1864. 1st ed. 2 vols. 11,xii,(13)-642,(1); Frontis, 826pp. Pebbled cl (dull, spine extrems rubbed). VG set. Howes B476. *Glaser.* $150/£96

BISHOP, JIM. The Day Lincoln Was Shot. NY, 1955. 1st ed. VG +. *Pratt.* $22/£14

BISHOP, JOHN PEALE. The Collected Essays. Edmund Wilson (ed). NY, (1948). 1st ed. VG in dj. *Argosy.* $50/£32

BISHOP, MICHAEL. Catalogue: Winter-Spring, 1974. N.p. (Venice, CA): Michael Bishop, 1974. (Name stamp, pencil address), else Fine in pict stiff wrappers. *Cahan.* $60/£38

BISHOP, MICHAEL. One Winter in Eden. (Sauk City): Arkham House, (1983). 1st ed. VF in VF dj. *Mcclintock.* $40/£26

BISHOP, MORRIS. Champlain; the Life of Fortitude. London: McDonald, 1949. Fldg map. Interior clean. Dj (chipped, stained). *Dumont.* $20/£13

BISHOP, MRS. J. F. The Yangtze Valley and Beyond. London: John Murray, 1899. 1st ed. xv,557pp; fldg map. Teg, uncut. Dec cl (sl dknd), gilt. *Hollett.* $343/£220

BISHOP, NATHANIEL. Four Months in a Sneak-Box. Boston, 1879. Pub's gilt-pict cl. *Swann*.* $373/£239

BISHOP, NATHANIEL. Voyage of the Paper Canoe. Boston: Lee & Shepard, 1878. 1st ed. xv,351pp; 10 maps, 6 full-pg illus. (Frontis frayed, new eps, ex-lib), o/w Good. *Worldwide.* $45/£29

BISHOP, RICHARD E. Bishop's Birds. Phila, 1936. One of 1050. 73 plts. Pict cl (spine sl dknd). *Kane*.* $150/£96

BISHOP, RICHARD E. Bishop's Wildfowl. MN: Brown & Bigelow, 1948. 1st ltd ed. Mission leather. NF. *Books & Birds.* $200/£128

BISHOP, RICHARD E. Wildfowl. (St. Paul, 1948.) One of ltd 1st ed. Inscribed. 12 color plts, port. Full dec leather. Orig box (worn). *Kane*.* $275/£176

BISHOP, SETH SCOTT. Diseases of the Ear, Nose and Throat and Their Accessory Cavities. Phila, 1898. 2nd ed. 554pp. Red cl bds (worn). Good. *Doctor's Library.* $125/£80

BISHOP, W. J. and S. GOLDIE. A Bio-Bibliography of Florence Nightingale. London: Dawsons, 1962. Blue cl, gilt-lettered spine. Protective wrappers. *Maggs.* $140/£90

BISHOP, WILLIAM HENRY. Old Mexico and Her Lost Provinces. NY, 1883. 1st ed. 509pp. Blind-stamped red cl, gilt. (Cvr sl soiled), o/w Fine. No dj as issued. *Turpen.* $88/£56

BISHOP, WILLIAM WARNER. The Backs of Books and Other Essays in Librarianship. Balt: Williams & Wilkins, 1926. 1st ed. Unopened. Paper spine label. VF in dj (chipped, sl yellowed). *Oak Knoll.* $35/£22

BISSOONDATH, NEIL. Digging up the Mountains. NY, 1986. 1st ed, 1st bk. Fine in dj. *Buckley.* $16/£10

BITHELL, RICHARD. A Counting-House Dictionary. London: Routledge, 1883. 2nd ed. Leather-backed bds. (Ex-lib.) Sound. *Boswell.* $150/£96

BITTING, SAMUEL TILDEN. Rural Land Ownership Among the Negroes of Virginia.... Charlottesville, VA, 1915. 1st ed. NF in orig stiff ptd wrappers. *Mcgowan.* $75/£48

BIXBY-SMITH, SARAH. Adobe Days. Cedar Rapids: Torch, 1925. 1st ed. Brn-stamped dec bds, white linen spine, paper spine label. *Dawson.* $50/£32

BJERREGAARD, C. H. A. Sufi Interpretations of the Quatrains of Omar Khayyam and Fitzgerald. NY: J.F. Taylor, 1902. Color frontis. Gray paper-cvrd bds (spine faded, spotted). Contents VG. *New Hampshire**. $30/£19

Black Yeomanry: Life on St. Helena Island. NY: Holt, (1930). 1st ed. Fine in dj (lt used, sm internal mend). *Captain's Bookshelf.* $125/£80

Black's Guide to Cornwall. London, 1923. 24th ed. 4 color plts, 7 maps and plans (1 fldg). (Sl margin browning.) Illus laid down to upper bd (spine faded). *Edwards.* $23/£15

Black's Picturesque Guide to the English Lakes. Edinburgh: A&C Black, 1849. 3rd ed. xxiv,252pp; 2 steel-engr plts (edges dampstained), 4 maps. Blind-stamped red cl (rebacked in matching morocco, gilt). *Hollett.* $133/£85

Black's Picturesque Guide to the English Lakes. Edinburgh, 1872. 17th ed. xxx,293pp + 88pp ads; 2 fldg maps (1 torn, no loss). (Spine sl chipped.) *Edwards.* $39/£25

Black's Picturesque Guide to the English Lakes. Edinburgh: A&C Black, 1879. 19th ed. xxv,293,112pp. Blind-stamped grn cl, gilt. Fine. *Hollett.* $78/£50

Black's Picturesque Tourist and Road and Railway Guide Book Through England and Wales. Edinburgh: A&C Black, 1851. 2nd ed. xx,538pp + 24pp ads; 7 plts, 25 maps (lacks 1). Ms folio fldg sheet laid in. Good (inner hinges cracked, backstrip browned). *Cox.* $55/£35

Black's Picturesque Tourist and Road and Railway Guide Book Through England and Wales. Edinburgh: A&C Black, 1856. 4th ed. 544pp + 56pp ads; lg fldg map on oil cl at rear. (Lacks spine.) Maps Good; book Poor. *Scribe's Perch**. $28/£18

BLACK, ARCHIBALD. American Airport Designs. NY: Lehigh Portland Cement, (1930). Blue wrappers (chipped, lt worn, soiled). *Freeman**. $60/£38

BLACK, HENRY CAMPBELL, A Dictionary of Law, Containing Definitions.... St. Paul: West, 1891. 1st ed. Orig sheep (rubbed, fr joint cracked). Sound. *Boswell.* $450/£288

BLACK, J. ANDERSON and MADGE GARLAND. A History of Fashion. London, 1975. Dj, pict slipcase. *Edwards.* $47/£30

BLACK, MARY. Summerfield Farm. NY: Viking, 1951. 1st ed. VG in Good dj. *October Farm.* $25/£16

BLACK, ROBERT L. Little Miami Railroad. Cincinnati, n.d. (1936?). Fldg map. Deckled edge. VG + in dj (soiled, chipped). *Bohling.* $55/£35

BLACK, SAMUEL. A Journal of a Voyage from Rocky Mountain Portage in Peace River...in Summer 1824. E.E. Rich (ed). London: Hudson's Bay Record Soc, 1955. 3 plts, fldg map. Blue cl. (Sl faded, corners bumped), else NF. *Parmer.* $150/£96

BLACK, WILLIAM. Adventures in Thule: Three Stories for Boys. Macmillan, 1883. Pub's cat. VG (spine bumped; hinges, corners sl rubbed). *Tiger.* $34/£22

BLACK, WILLIAM. The Beautiful Wretch. The Four Macnicols. The Pupil of Aurelius. Macmillan, 1881. 3 vols. Pub's cat dated April 1881 vol I. Good (spines bumped, chipped, dull; rubbed, sl mkd; sl spotted). *Tiger.* $55/£35

BLACK, WILLIAM. Judith Shakespeare. Macmillan, 1884. 3 vols. Pub's cat dated May 1884 vol I. Good (sl spotting; spines bumped, chipped, sunned, hinges rubbed, sm vents). *Tiger.* $47/£30

BLACK, WILLIAM. A Practical Treatise on Brewing. London, 1854. 5th ed. xi,249pp + 24pp pub's list (lt marginal browning, hinges cracked). Blind-emb cl (spine chipped, joints splitting, fading). *Edwards.* $55/£35

BLACKADDER, H. HOME. Observations on Phagedaena Gangraenosa. In Two Parts. Edinburgh: Balfour & Clarke, 1818. xvi,180pp. Uncut. Orig bds (spine, joints worn). Internally Clean. *Goodrich.* $195/£125

BLACKBEARD, BILL. Sherlock Holmes in America. NY: Abrams, (1981). 1st US ed. VG (cvr lt bumped) in VG dj. *Gravesend.* $70/£45

BLACKBURN, HENRY. Randolph Caldecott. London, 1886. Mtd photo frontis port (lt spotted), xvi,216pp. Teg. (Spine sl faded, chipped.) *Edwards.* $47/£30

BLACKBURN, HENRY. Randolph Caldecott. London, 1886. 1st ed. 8vo. Mtd photo frontis port. (Sl foxed.) Aeg. Pict cl (shelfworn). *Oinonen**. $60/£38

BLACKBURN, HENRY. Randolph Caldecott. London: Sampson Low et al, 1887. 4th ed. 210pp. Grn cl, gilt. Good + (fr hinge cracking; shelfworn). *My Bookhouse.* $55/£35

BLACKBURN, I. W. Intracranial Tumors Among the Insane.... Washington: GPO, 1903. 1st ed. 71 plts, author's ptd complimentary slip. Pebbled ruled grn cl (lib spine #s, stamps), gilt. Jelliffe's name stamp, bkpl. *Gach.* $125/£80

BLACKBURN, JOHN. Bury Him Darkly. NY: Putnam, (1970). 1st ed. NF in dj (sl soiled). *Antic Hay.* $45/£29

BLACKBURN, PAUL. In, On, or About the Premises. NY: Grossman, 1968. 1st Amer ed. NF in illus wrappers. *Turtle Island.* $20/£13

BLACKBURN, PAUL. The Nets. NY: Trobar, 1961. 1st ed. Fine (spine dknd) in wraps. *Beasley.* $60/£38

BLACKFORD, L. MINOR. Mine Eyes Have Seen the Glory.... Harvard Univ, 1954. 1st ed. VG (eps sl foxed, top edges sl soiled) in VG dj. *Book Broker.* $25/£16

BLACKFORD, MRS. The Scottish Orphans. Phila: J.B. Perry, 1843. 1st ed. 24mo. 123pp; 2 full-pg woodcuts. Illus grn bds. Good + . *Dower.* $35/£22

BLACKFORD, SUSAN LEIGH (comp). Letters from Lee's Army or Memoirs of Life In and Out of the Army in Virginia During the War Between the States. NY: Scribner, 1947. 1st trade ed. NF in VG dj. *Mcgowan.* $65/£42

BLACKFORD, W. W. War Years with Jeb Stuart. NY, 1945. 1st ed. VG + in dj (sl chipping). *Pratt.* $60/£38

BLACKMORE, R. A Treatise of Consumptions and Other Distempers Belonging to the Breasts and Lungs. 1724. xxxx,224pp (sl foxed; worming lower margin). New full calf. *Whitehart.* $281/£180

BLACKMORE, R. D. Lorna Doone. London, 1910. Dulverton ed. One of 250 numbered. Full morocco (lt rubbed). *Argosy.* $125/£80

BLACKMORE, R. D. Lorna Doone: A Romance of Exmoor. Sampson Low, Son, & Marston, 1869. 1st ed. 3 vols. 8vo. 8 leaves of ads end of vol 3. (Sl soil throughout.) Orig blue cl (rebacked retaining orig spines, rather rubbed, stained), binder's ticket of W. Bone on rear pastedown vol 1. *Sotheby's**. $897/£575

BLACKMUR, R. P. Dirty Hands or the True-Born Censor. Cambridge: Minority Press, 1930. 1st ed. Fine in wrappers. *Jaffe.* $175/£112

BLACKMUR, R. P. The Double Agent. NY: Arrow Editions, (1935). 1st ed. Fine in dj (lt rubbed, spine dknd). *Jaffe.* $100/£64

BLACKMUR, R. P. The Expense of Greatness. NY: Arrow Editions, (1940). 1st ed. Fine in VG dj (spine sunned). *Hermitage.* $75/£48

BLACKMUR, R. P. From Jordan's Delight. NY: Arrow Editions, (1937). 1st ed. Fine in dj (price-clipped, price stamp inner fr flap). *Jaffe.* $100/£64

BLACKMUR, R. P. Language as Gesture, Essays in Poetry. NY: Harcourt, Brace, (1952). 1st ed. Fine in dj. *Jaffe.* $35/£22

BLACKMUR, R. P. T.S. Eliot. (N.p.): Hound & Horn, 1928. 1st ed, 1st bk. Good in wrappers (chipped, worn, 2 internal tape mends). *Jaffe.* $225/£144

BLACKSTONE, WILLIAM. An Analysis of the Laws of England. Oxford: Clarendon, 1762. 5th ed. Contemp calf (sl rubbed). *Boswell.* $850/£545

BLACKSTONE, WILLIAM. Commentaries on the Laws of England. London: T. Cadell, 1791. 11th ed. 4 vols. Contemp calf (joints cracking, worn, rubbed). Usable set. *Boswell.* $650/£417

BLACKSTONE, WILLIAM. Commentaries on the Laws of England. NY: W.E. Dean, 1836. 2 vols. Contemp sheep (rubbed, foxed). Well Preserved set. *Boswell.* $650/£417

BLACKSTONE, WILLIAM. Commentaries on the Laws of England...to which is Added an Analysis by Baron Field....A New Edition...by Christian, Archbold and Chitty. NY: Collins & Hannay...W.E. Dean, Printer, 1830. New ed. 2 vols. Contemp sheep (rubbed, foxed). Well Preserved. *Boswell.* $650/£417

BLACKWELDER, BERNICE. Great Westerner. The Story of Kit Carson. Caldwell: Caxton, 1962. 1st ed. Frontis port. Tan cl lettered in red. Fine in pict dj (spine dknd). *Argonaut.* $60/£38

BLACKWELL, ALICE STONE. Songs of Russia. (Chicago): The Author, 1906. Red cl. VG. *Second Life.* $75/£48

BLACKWOOD, ALGERNON with WILFRED WILSON. The Wolves of God and Other Fey Stories. Dutton, 1921. 1st ed. Variant binding blue cl; cvr, spine red stamped. NF. *Certo.* $125/£80

BLACKWOOD, ALGERNON. Day and Night Stories. Dutton, (1917). 1st US ed. (Eps sl browned), else NF. *Certo.* $50/£32

BLACKWOOD, ALGERNON. The Doll and One Other. Sauk City, 1946. 1st ed. Fine in Fine dj. *Mcclintock.* $45/£29

BLACKWOOD, ALGERNON. Dudley and Gilderoy. London: Benn, 1929. 1st ed. 5 3/4 x 8 3/4. 281pp. Good (worn, lt soil). *Cattermole.* $50/£32

BLACKWOOD, ALGERNON. The Education of Uncle Paul. London: Macmillan, 1909. 1st ed. Pub's cat rear. Red cl, gilt, teg. (Spine lt sunned), else Fresh. *Certo.* $175/£112

BLACKWOOD, ALGERNON. The Extra Day. London: Macmillan, 1915. 1st ed. Blue cl, gilt. (Sl whitened at points), else NF. *Certo.* $100/£64

BLACKWOOD, ALGERNON. The Extra Day. NY: Macmillan, 1915. 1st ed. Grn cl, gilt. (Edges sl foxed), else NF in pict dj (1/2-inch chips at spine ends, 1x2-inch chip upper right corner). *Certo.* $150/£96

BLACKWOOD, ALGERNON. Incredible Adventures. Macmillan, 1914. 1st US ed. Grn bds; cvr, spine gilt. (Sm spot fore edge), else Fresh. *Certo.* $95/£61

BLACKWOOD, ALGERNON. Jimbo: A Fantasy. London: Macmillan, 1909. 1st ed. Red cl, blind-stamped, gilt. (Bkpl, label fr pastedown; spine sunned, 2 spine tips bumped), else VG. *Certo.* $200/£128

BLACKWOOD, ALGERNON. Jimbo: A Fantasy. NY: Macmillan, 1909. 1st US ed. Beige paper-cvrd bds, ruled and stamped in black. (Spine sl sunned), else NF. *Certo.* $85/£54

BLACKWOOD, ALGERNON. A Prisoner in Fairyland. London: Macmillan, 1913. 1st ed. 2pp pub's ads bound in rear offering Blackwood titles through 'Pan's Garden'. Grn cl, cvr stamped black, spine gilt. (Fr hinge strained; eps foxed), else VG. *Certo.* $90/£58

BLACKWOOD, ALGERNON. Shocks. NY, (1936). 1st ed. VG (cvr soil). *Mcclintock.* $35/£22

BLACKWOOD, ALICIA. Scutari, the Bosphorus and the Crimea. Ventnor, Isle of Wight, 1857. Vol 1 only (of 2). Litho title, 10 litho plts (2 fldg), each stamped on blank verso. Wraps (soiled, worn, dampstaining affecting plts). *Waverly*.* $49/£31

BLADES, WILLIAM. Books in Chains and Other Bibliographical Essays. London: Elliot Stock, 1892. 1st ed. xl,232pp. Grn cl, beveled edges. Fine. *Oak Knoll.* $45/£29

BLADES, WILLIAM. The Enemies of Books. London: Trubner, 1880. 1st ed. Frontis port, 8p.l., 110pp,(1)leaf; 6 plts. Marbled eps. Grn 1/2 morocco, marbled paper sides, raised bands, gilt. Orig paper wrappers bound in. (Leather faded, sl rubbed), o/w Excellent. *Pirages.* $100/£64

BLADES, WILLIAM. Fishing Flies and Fly Tying. Harrisburg: Stackpole & Heck, 1951. 1st ed. Color frontis, 5 add'l color plts. Grn buckram, gilt. Fine in VG dj. *Biscotti.* $55/£35

BLAGDEN, CYPRIAN. The Stationers' Company: A History, 1403-1959. Cambridge: Harvard Univ, 1960. Dj. *Rostenberg & Stern.* $25/£16

BLAIKIE, WILLIAM G. The Personal Life of David Livingstone. NY: Harper, 1881. xix,504pp; port, fldg map. (Ends frayed.) *Adelson.* $45/£29

BLAINE, JAMES G. Twenty Years of Congress: From Lincoln to Garfield. Norwich: Henry Bill, 1884-1886. 1st ed. 2 vols. Steel-engr frontis port, fldg map rear vol 1. Floral eps, marbled edges. Brn cl, beveled bds, gilt. Cvrs VG (sl rubbed, shelfworn; ex-lib w/mks to eps). *Baltimore*.* $20/£13

BLAINE, JOHN. The Veiled Raiders. G&D, 1965. 5x7.5. 178pp. Pict bds (sl shelfworn, bumped). Lists to this title. VG+. *My Bookhouse.* $50/£32

BLAIR, MARIA. Matthew Fontaine Maury. Richmond, VA: Whittet & Shepperson, 1918. 1st ed. 13pp. NF in ptd wrappers. *Mcgowan.* $37/£24

BLAIR, MILLARD F. Practical Tree Surgery. Boston, 1937. VG-. *Brooks.* $65/£42

BLAIR, ROBERT. The Grave. London: T. Bensley, 1808. 1st ed. Folio. Frontis, extra engr tp (both foxed), 11 plts (sm brn stains few plts) by William Blake, port by T. Phillips. Later full polished calf, raised bands, red leather spine labels, gilt. Cl case. *Kane*.* $800/£513

BLAIR, WALTER A. A Raft Pilot's Log: A History of the Great Rafting Industry on the Upper Mississippi, 1840-1915. Cleveland: Clark, 1930. 1st ed. One of 1254. Signed. Frontis port, fldg map. Gilt-lettered cl (sl spots fr cvr, lt rubbing spine ends). Fine. *Argonaut.* $250/£160

BLAIR, WILLIAM. An Opium-Eater in America and The Fratricide's Death. Aurora, NY: Wells College, (1941). #22/150 for sale, plus 32 for presentation. Victor Hammer (illus). Blue-gray bds, ptd spine label. VG. *Heller.* $125/£80

BLAIS, MARIE-CLAIRE. A Season in the Life of Emmanuel. Derek Coltman (trans). NY: FSG, (1966). 1st ed. NF in dj. *Antic Hay.* $25/£16

BLAISDELL, LOWELL L. The Desert Revolution: Baja California, 1911. Madison: Univ of WI, 1962. Frontis. Dj. *Dawson.* $50/£32

Blake's Illuminated Books. Princeton: Princeton Univ, (1992). 1st ed thus. Vols 1 and 2 (of 5). Fine in djs. *Waverly*.* $71/£46

BLAKE, CHRISTOPHER. The Fair Ladies of Chartres Street. New Orleans: Beale, 1965. 1st ed, 1st bk. Signed. NF in dj (lt rubbed). *Cahan.* $25/£16

BLAKE, CLAGETTE. Charles Elliot R.N. 1801-1875, a Servant of Britain Overseas. London: Cleaver-Hume, (1960). Errata slip. VG + in dj (edgeworn). *Bohling.* $20/£13

BLAKE, E. VALE. (ed). Arctic Experiences. NY: Harper, 1874. 1st ed. 486pp + (6)pp ads, incl frontis (sm lib stamp title, sl browned; new eps). Grn cl (corners sl rubbed, sm shelf label spine, spine well repaired), gilt. Good. *Morrell.* $273/£175

BLAKE, EVARTS I. (ed). San Francisco, a Brief Biographical Sketch of Some of the Most Prominent Men.... SF: Press Pacific, 1902. 1st ed. Gilt-lettered black cl. (Sl fading, sl wear), else Fine. *Argonaut.* $60/£38

BLAKE, G. S. The Stratigraphy of Palestine and Its Building Stones. Jerusalem, (1935). Map. New cl. Orig wrapper bound in. Fine. *Henly.* $39/£25

BLAKE, J. L. Conversations on Natural Philosophy. Gould, Kendall, 1847. Frontis, 246pp (lacks fep; internal joints weak), 17 plts. Leather (worn). Good. *Bookcell.* $75/£48

BLAKE, MARION ELIZABETH. Ancient Roman Construction in Italy from the Prehistoric Period to Augustus. Washington, DC: Carnegie Inst, 1947. Signed, dated. 57 plts. (Few sm holes inner joint 1st 2 blank ll, bkpl; sl shelfwear at edges.) *Archaeologia.* $175/£112

BLAKE, NICHOLAS. (Pseud of Cecil Day-Lewis.) The Private Wound. London: Collins, 1968. 1st UK ed. NF in VG dj. *Williams.* $34/£22

BLAKE, NICHOLAS. (Pseud of Cecil Day-Lewis.) A Tangled Web. London: Collins, 1956. 1st UK ed. VG + in dj (spine top sl pushed). *Williams.* $59/£38

BLAKE, NICHOLAS. (Pseud of Cecil Day-Lewis.) The Worm of Death. London: Collins, 1961. 1st UK ed. NF in VG dj (sl edgeworn, sm chip). *Williams.* $44/£28

BLAKE, PETER. Marcel Breuer: Architect and Designer. NY: MOMA, 1949. 1st ed. VG. *Hollett.* $101/£65

BLAKE, PETER. The Master Builders. Victor Gollancz, 1960. 1st ed. Dj. *Edwards.* $39/£25

BLAKE, QUENTIN. Mr. Magnolia. Cape, 1980. 1st ed. 4to. (32)pp. Glossy pict bds. Fine. *Bookmark.* $47/£30

BLAKE, QUENTIN. Mrs. Armitage on Wheels. Cape, 1987. 1st ed. 4to. (32)pp. Glossy pict bds. Fine. *Bookmark.* $34/£22

BLAKE, QUENTIN. Snuff. Cape, 1973. 1st ed. 4to. (32)pp. Pict bds. (Tips rubbed), else VG + . *Bookmark.* $39/£25

BLAKE, W. O. (ed). The History of Slavery and the Slave Trade.... Columbus, OH, 1861. 866pp (foxing). Full leather, dec spine. Good. *Scribe's Perch*. $55/£35

BLAKE, WILLIAM. All Religions Are One. Paris: Trianon, (1970). One of 662. 10 plts in facs. Excellent in orig box. *Kane*. $110/£71

BLAKE, WILLIAM. America. London: Trianon, 1963. One of 480 numbered. (Pencil marginalia.) Morocco-backed bds (lt worn). Slipcase. *Oinonen*. $160/£103

BLAKE, WILLIAM. Blake's Illustrations of Dante. London: Trianon, 1978. One of 376 (of 440) numbered. Obl folio. 12 plts. Orig 1/4 brn morocco. Cl slipcase. *Swann*. $345/£221

BLAKE, WILLIAM. The Book of Ahania. London: Trianon, 1973. One of 750 numbered. Morocco-backed bds (lt worn). Slipcase. *Oinonen*. $120/£77

BLAKE, WILLIAM. The Book of Los. Paris: Trianon, (1976). One of 538. 5 plts in facs. Excellent in orig box. *Kane*. $110/£71

BLAKE, WILLIAM. The Book of Thel. London: Fredk. Hollyer, 1924. One of 125 numbered. Color facs leaves tipped to larger sheets. Good (gutters, eps browned; spine sl worn). *Reese.* $125/£80

BLAKE, WILLIAM. The Book of Thel. (London/NY: Gollancz/Payson & Clarke, 1928.) 1st ed of color facs of BM copy. One of 1700 numbered. Gilt-dec cl. (Spine sl dull, bkpl), else Nice. *Reese.* $100/£64

BLAKE, WILLIAM. The Book of Thel. London: Trianon, 1965. One of 380 numbered. (Lt pencil marginalia.) 1/2 morocco (sl worn). Slipcase (sl scuffed). *Oinonen*. $180/£115

BLAKE, WILLIAM. The Complete Writings of William Blake. Geoffrey Keynes (ed). London/NY: Nonesuch/Random House, 1957. One of 4735 ptd. Cl, marbled bds. Fine. *Reese.* $45/£29

BLAKE, WILLIAM. Europe, a Prophecy. Trianon, 1969. One of 480 numbered. Morocco-backed bds (lt worn). Slipcase. *Oinonen*. $140/£90

BLAKE, WILLIAM. The Great Gates of Paradise. London: Trianon, 1968. One of 650 numbered. 3 vols. (Lt worn.) Cl slipcase. *Oinonen*. $130/£83

BLAKE, WILLIAM. Illustrations of the Book of Job. NY: Pierpont Morgan Library, 1935. 6 separate paperbound bks. Fine in clbound clamshell case (soiled, sunned, bumped, rubbed). *Metropolitan*. $373/£239

BLAKE, WILLIAM. Illustrations to the Divine Comedy of Dante. NY: Da Capo, 1968. One of 1100, this copy unnumbered and mkd 'not for sale.' Blue-gray coarse cl-cvrd portfolio, black lettering. Plts Fine. *Baltimore*. $130/£83

BLAKE, WILLIAM. Jerusalem. Trianon, 1974. One of 500 numbered. Morocco-backed bds (lt worn). Slipcase. *Oinonen*. $230/£147

BLAKE, WILLIAM. Letters from William Blake to Thomas Butts, 1800-1803. Oxford: Clarendon, 1926. 1st ed. One of 350. 10 inserted facs letters. 1/4 cl, marbled bds (lt soiled, rubbed, sm stain spine). VG (sl foxed). *Waverly*. $60/£38

BLAKE, WILLIAM. The Marriage of Heaven and Hell. Trianon, (1960). One of 526. 27 plts in facs. Excellent in orig box. *Kane*. $225/£144

BLAKE, WILLIAM. The Marriage of Heaven and Hell. (Maastricht): Halcyon, 1928. One of 325. (Edges lt worn.) Paper label. Good. *Reese.* $50/£32

BLAKE, WILLIAM. The Marriage of Heaven and Hell. London: Trianon, 1960. One of 480 numbered. (Pencil marginalia.) 1/2 morocco (lt worn). Slipcase (sl scuffed). *Oinonen*. $250/£160

BLAKE, WILLIAM. Milton: A Poem. Paris: Trianon, (1967). One of 426. 50 plts in facs. Excellent in orig box. *Kane*. $250/£160

BLAKE, WILLIAM. The Note-Book of William Blake: Called the Rossetti Manuscript. Geoffrey Keynes (ed). London: Nonesuch, 1935. One of 650 numbered. Teg; untrimmed. Blue buckram, gilt leather spine label. Fine. *Argosy.* $150/£96

BLAKE, WILLIAM. The Notebook of William Blake. David V. Erdman (ed). Oxford: Clarendon, 1973. 1st ed. Photo, typographic facs. Fine in dj (lt rubbed). *Hermitage.* $75/£48

BLAKE, WILLIAM. Pencil Drawings by William Blake. Geoffrey Keynes (ed). London: Nonesuch, 1927. #1260/1550 ptd at Chiswick Press. Linen-backed bds. (Bkpl fr paste-down, bds sl bowed), o/w VG. *Hermitage.* $200/£128

BLAKE, WILLIAM. Pencilled Drawings. Geoffrey Keynes (ed). London: Nonesuch, 1956. One of 1440 numbered. (Sl worn.) Dj (chipped, frayed). *Oinonen*. $60/£38

BLAKE, WILLIAM. The Poems of William Blake. Aileen Ward (ed). Cambridge: LEC, 1973. One of 1500 numbered. 12 tipped-in color plts. Prospectus laid in. 1/4 morocco, cl bds. Fine in slipcase. *Waverly**. $66/£42

BLAKE, WILLIAM. The Poetical Works of William Blake. Edwin John Ellis (ed). London: C&W, 1906. 1st ed thus. 2 vols. Port, engr frontis. Teg. Red buckram (spines sunned, sl rubbed, sizing flecked), paper labels. Internally Very Nice (bkpl). *Reese*. $85/£54

BLAKE, WILLIAM. The Prophetic Writings of William Blake. D. Sloss and J. Wallis (eds). Oxford: Clarendon, 1926. 1st ed. 2 vols. 12 facs plts. Djs (partly toned). *Waverly**. $66/£42

BLAKE, WILLIAM. The Prophetic Writings of.... D. J. Sloss and J. P. R. Wallis (eds). Oxford: Clarendon, 1926. 1st ed. 2 vols. 10 facs illus, incl fldg frontis (detached but present; 3 sm tears vol 1 w/o loss of text). Uncut, unopened. Djs. *Argosy*. $150/£96

BLAKE, WILLIAM. Selections from the Writings of William Blake. London: Kegan Paul, 1893. 1st ed thus. Teg. Full vellum. (2 sm spots), else Fine. *Captain's Bookshelf*. $75/£48

BLAKE, WILLIAM. The Song of Los. Paris: Trianon, (1975). One of 458. 8 plts in facs. Excellent in orig box. *Kane**. $110/£71

BLAKE, WILLIAM. Songs of Experience. (London: Ernest Benn, 1927.) 1st ed of color facs of BM copy. Gilt-dec cl. NF. *Reese*. $125/£80

BLAKE, WILLIAM. Songs of Innocence. Paris: Trianon, (1954). One of 1600. Facs of Lessing J. Rosenwald copy of 1789 ed. Inscribed by Rosenwald. 30 plts in facs. Excellent (rubbed) in orig box. *Kane**. $160/£103

BLAKE, WILLIAM. Songs of Innocence. (NY: Minton, Balch, 1926.) Amer issue of color facs of BM copy. Gilt-dec cl. (Sm bkpl, nick), o/w NF. *Reese*. $125/£80

BLAKE, WILLIAM. There Is No Natural Religion. Trianon, 1971. One of 540 numbered. 2 vols. 1/2 morocco (lt worn). Marbled slipcase. *Oinonen**. $110/£71

BLAKE, WILLIAM. Visions of the Daughters of Albion. Trianon, (1959). One of 446, this copy unnumbered. 11 facs plts. Excellent in orig box. *Kane**. $225/£144

BLAKE, WILLIAM. William Blake's Engravings. Geoffrey Keynes (ed). London: Faber & Faber, (1950). 1st ed. VG in dj (chipped). *Hermitage*. $100/£64

BLAKE, WILLIAM. William Blake's Illuminated Books. NY: Grolier Club, 1953. One of 400. 8 plts, guards. Blue buckram, gilt spine. (Bottom edge rear cvr sl dented), o/w Fine. *Argosy*. $150/£96

BLAKE, WILLIAM. The Writings of.... Geoffrey Keynes (ed). London, 1925. One of 1500. 3 vols. 1/4 vellum, marbled bds (spines sl soiled). *Kane**. $160/£103

BLAKEMORE, KENNETH. Snuff Boxes. London, 1976. 1st UK ed. Dj. *Edwards*. $31/£20

BLAKEY, LEONARD S. The Sale of Liquor in the South. NY: Columbia Univ, 1912. 1st ed. Gilt-titled cl. (Tips rubbed), else NF. *Cahan*. $60/£38

BLAKEY, ROBERT. Old Faces in New Masks. London, 1859. 1st ed. Add'l tp, frontis by George Cruikshank. Later straight-grain morocco (joints cracked, orig backstrip bound in; several ll loose). *Swann**. $92/£59

BLANC, LOUIS. Letters on England. London: Sampson, Low, 1866. 1st ed. 2 vols. 1/4 bound leather (powdery, flaking), marbled paper-cvrd bds. Good. *Beasley*. $150/£96

BLANCHARD, ELIZABETH and MANLY WADE WELLMAN. The Life and Times of Sir Archie 1805-1833. Chapel Hill: Univ of NC, 1958. 1st ed. VG in Good dj. *October Farm*. $45/£29

BLANCHARD, FESSENDEN S. Block Island to Nantucket. Princeton, NJ, (1961). 1st ed. Red cl. VG. *Bohling*. $28/£18

BLANCHARD, LEOLA HOWARD. Conquest of Southwest Kansas. Wichita: Wichita Eagle, (1931). 1st ed. Pict cl. NF. *Glenn*. $75/£48

BLANCHARD, RUFUS. The Discovery and Conquests of the North West.... Chicago, 1880. (Lt worn, soiled.) *Freeman**. $60/£38

BLANCHARD, RUFUS. The Discovery and Conquests of the Northwest Including the Early History of Chicago, Detroit, Vincennes, St. Louis.... Chicago: Cushing, Thomas, 1880. 486pp + 30pp Washington's Journal of a Tour to the Ohio in 1753; 7 maps, 11 views. VG (extrems lt rubbed). Howes B508. *House*. $160/£103

BLANCK, JACOB. Bibliography of American Literature. New Haven: Yale Univ, various dates. 9 vols complete. (Name; rubbed.) *Oak Knoll*. $950/£609

BLANCK, JACOB. Peter Parley to Penrod: A Bibliographical Description of the Best-Loved American Juvenile Books. NY: Bowker, 1938. 1st ed. One of 500. *Ginsberg*. $125/£80

BLANCO, ANTONIO DE FIERRO. (Pseud of Walter Nordhoff.) Journey of the Flame, One Year in the Life of Juan Obrigon. Boston, 1933. 1st ed. Good +. *Turpen*. $25/£16

BLANCO, RICHARD L. Wellington's Surgeon General: Sir James McGrigor. Duke Univ, 1974. 8 plts. Dj. *Maggs*. $47/£30

BLAND, DAVID. A Bibliography of Book Illustration. London: Nat'l Book League, 1955. Dec paper wrappers, ptd label. (Sm spot fr cvr, spine faded), else VG. *Heller*. $25/£16

BLAND, JANE COOPER. Currier and Ives: A Manual for Collectors. GC: Doubleday, Doran, (1931). Untrimmed. Tan buckram, gilt. (Spine dknd, lettering lt, cvrs sl spotted.) Text Good (lt aged). *Baltimore**. $15/£10

BLANDFORD, GEORGE FIELDING. Insanity and Its Treatment.... NY: William Wood, 1886. 3rd Amer ed. (x),379,(1)pp; 9 plts, each w/descrip leaf. Dec russet cl (rear bd spotted). Good. *Gach*. $50/£32

BLANEY, HENRY. Journal of Voyages to China and Return...1851-1853. Boston: Privately ptd, 1913. Frontis (inscrip). Unopened. Lt blue paper over bds. (Spine dknd), else Fine. *Parmer*. $75/£48

BLANK, CLAIR. Beverly Gray's Surprise. McLoughlin, 1955. 5x7.5. 182pp. Glossy pict bds (edgeworn, pulled at spine). Good + (pp yellowed). *My Bookhouse*. $20/£13

BLANKENSHIP, RUSSELL. And There Were Men. NY, 1942. 1st ed. Dec cl. Fine (pencil inscrip) in dj. *Baade*. $30/£19

BLANSHARD, FRANCES. Portraits of Wordsworth. London: Allen & Unwin, 1959. 1st ed. 48pp of collotype plts. VG in dj (defective). *Hollett*. $55/£35

BLANTON, WYNDHAM. Medicine in Virginia in the Nineteenth Century. Richmond, 1933. 1st ed. VG. *Fye*. $200/£128

BLASCO IBANEZ, VICENTE. The Borgias. NY: Dutton, 1930. 1st US ed. (Stain lower corner pp), else VG + in VG dj. *Lame Duck*. $45/£29

BLASINGAME, IKE. Dakota Cowboy—My Life in the Old Days. NY: Putnam, (1958). VG in dj. *Perier*. $60/£38

BLATCH, HARRIOT STANTON. Mobilizing Woman-Power. NY: The Woman's Press, 1918. 1st ed. Very Nice. *Second Life*. $85/£54

BLATCHFORD, THOMAS W. Hydrophobia: Its Origin and Development.... Phila, 1856. 1st separate ed. 104pp, stitched. (Dampstains; ex-lib.) *Argosy*. $45/£29

BLATTY, WILLIAM PETER. The Exorcist. NY: Harper, (1971). 1st ed. Inscribed. Fine in dj (tear). *Between The Covers.* $175/£112

BLAVATSKY, HELENA PETROVNA. From the Caves and Jungles of Hindostan. London: Theosophical Soc, 1892. 1st ed. 318pp + ads. Pub's cl. VG (name stamp). *Second Life.* $125/£80

BLAYLOCK, JAMES. The Paper Grail. Easton Press, (1991). Signed. Maroon leather, gilt. VG. *Yudkin*.* $30/£19

BLEACKLEY. A Tour in Southern Asia (Indo-China, Malaya, Java, Sumatra, and Ceylon, 1925-1926). London: John Lane, Bodley Head, 1928. 1st ed. 17 plts. (Sl foxing; sl rubbed, soiled, spine sl faded), o/w VG. *Worldwide.* $45/£29

BLECH, GUSTAVUS M. and CHARLES LYNCH. Medical Tactics and Logistics. Springfield, 1934. 1st ed. VG in dj (worn). *Doctor's Library.* $45/£29

BLEECK, OLIVER. (Pseud of Ross Thomas.) The Brass Go-Between. NY: Morrow, 1969. 1st ed. Fine (sl shelfworn) in dj (soiled). *Metropolitan*.* $132/£85

BLEECK, OLIVER. (Pseud of Ross Thomas.) The Highbinders. NY: Morrow, 1973. 1st ed. Fine in Fine dj. *Beasley.* $75/£48

BLEECK, OLIVER. (Pseud of Ross Thomas.) The Highbinders. NY: William Morrow, 1974. 1st ed. Fine in dj. *Mordida.* $85/£54

BLEECK, OLIVER. (Pseud of Ross Thomas.) The Highbinders. NY: William Morrow, 1974. 1st ed. Fine in dj. *Mordida.* $85/£54

BLEECK, OLIVER. (Pseud of Ross Thomas.) Protocol for a Kidnapping. NY: Morrow, 1971. 1st ed. Fine in dj (sl wrinkle). *Else Fine.* $250/£160

BLEGBOROUGH, R. Facts and Observations Respecting the Air-Pump Vapour-Bath.... 1803. Frontis, 152pp (sl foxed). Orig bds (corners worn). *Whitehart.* $140/£90

BLEGVAD, LENORE. Hark! Hark! The Dogs Do Bark. NY: Atheneum, 1976. 1st ed. Erik Blegvad (illus). 6 3/4 x 8 1/4. 36pp. Fine in dj. *Cattermole.* $30/£19

BLEGVAD, LENORE. Mittens for Kittens. NY: Atheneum, 1974. 1st ed. Erik Blegvad (illus). 6 3/4 x 8 1/4. 36pp. Fine in dj. *Cattermole.* $30/£19

BLEGVAD, LENORE. Mr. Jensen and Cat. NY, 1965. 1st ed. Erik Blegvad (illus). 6 1/4 x 7 1/4. 32pp. Fine in dj. *Cattermole.* $30/£19

BLEGVAD, LENORE. This Little Pig-a-Wig. NY: Atheneum, 1978. 1st ed. Erik Blegvad (illus). 6 3/4 x 8 1/4. 32pp. Fine in dj. *Cattermole.* $32/£21

BLEVINS, WINFRED. Charbonneau: Man of Two Dreams. Nash, (1975). 1st ed. Signed. Fine in Fine dj. *Authors Of West.* $40/£26

BLIGH, WILLIAM. Bligh's Voyage in the Resource from Coupang to Batavia, Together with the Log of His Subsequent Passage to England.... (London): Golden Cockerel, 1937. One of 350. Peter Barker-Mill (illus). (Sl foxing; cvrs sl soiled.) *Lefkowicz.* $900/£577

BLIGH, WILLIAM. The Voyage of the Bounty's Launch as Related in William Bligh's Despatch to the Admiralty and the Journal of John Fryer. (London): Golden Cockerel, 1934. 1st ed. One of 300. Folio. Robert Gibbings (illus). (Lt foxing, mainly eps, prelims.) 2-tone cl. *Lefkowicz.* $800/£513

BLIGH, WILLIAM. A Voyage to the South Seas. Adelaide, South Australia: LEC, 1975. One of 2000 numbered, signed by Geoffrey C. Ingleton (illus) and designer. 4 full-pg color plts. Pict cl, leather spine label. Mint in bd slipcase. *Argosy.* $175/£112

BLIGH, WILLIAM. A Voyage to the South Seas. Adelaide: LEC, 1975. One of 2000 numbered, signed by Alan Villiers (intro) and Geoffrey C. Ingleton (illus). Full pict cl, leather label. Fine in slipcase. *Hermitage.* $150/£96

BLINN, CAROL J. On Becoming Three and Thirty: Being a Brief History and Description of Warwick Press.... (N.p.): Warwick, 1976. #105/150 signed by Blinn & printer. Linocut tp. Fine in grn paste paper wrappers, ptd label. *Heller.* $50/£32

BLISH, HELEN H. A Pictographic History of the Oglala Sioux. Lincoln: Univ of NE, (1967). 1st ed. VG in slipcase. *Lien.* $100/£64

BLISH, JAMES. The Seedling Stars. NY: Gnome, 1957. 1st Amer ed. Fine (pp browned) in dj (2 sm tears). *Polyanthos.* $25/£16

BLISS, GEORGE. Historical Memoir of the Western Railroad. Springfield, MA, 1863. 190pp + 1pg errata. Ptd wraps (sl soiled, spine chipped, corners stained). *Bohling.* $85/£54

BLISS, GEORGE. Reminiscences of Service in the First Rhode Island Cavalry. Providence, 1878. Orig ptd wraps. Fine. *Wantagh.* $45/£29

BLISS, THEODORE. Theodore Bliss, Publisher and Bookseller. Ptd for private circulation, 1911. VG (label removed tp; lt soiled). *Bohling.* $27/£17

BLITZ, SIGNOR. Fifty Years in the Magic Circle. Hartford: Belknap & Bliss, 1871. 1st ed. Steel-engr frontis port, 432pp + 4pp ads at rear (few sigs sl loose, hinges lt cracked, edges sl browned). Brn coated eps. Red-brn pict cl (ends lt nicked). *Baltimore*.* $80/£51

BLIVEN, BRUCE. The Wonderful Writing Machine. NY: Random House, (1954). 1st ed. Dj (wrinkled, spotted). *Oak Knoll.* $35/£22

BLIXEN, KAREN. Winter's Tales. Putnam, (1942). 1st ed. Nice in dj (sl sunned). *Ash.* $62/£40

BLOCH, ROBERT. The Dead Beat. NY: S&S, 1960. 1st ed. (Interior browning.) Dj (creased, soil, foxing). *Metropolitan*.* $23/£15

BLOCH, ROBERT. Dragons and Nightmares. Balt: Mirage, 1968. 1st ed. Fine (inscribed bkpl) in NF dj (spine ends lt worn). *Metropolitan*.* $63/£40

BLOCH, ROBERT. Night World. S&S, 1972. 1st ed. NF in NF dj. *Certo.* $45/£29

BLOCH, ROBERT. Night World. S&S, 1972. 1st ed. NF in NF dj. *Certo.* $45/£29

BLOCH, ROBERT. The Opener of the Way. Spearman, 1974. 1st British ed. NF in dj. *Madle.* $35/£22

BLOCH, ROBERT. Out of the Mouths of Graves. Mysterious, 1979. Trade issue. Fine in Fine dj. *Certo.* $35/£22

BLOCH, ROBERT. Out of the Mouths of Graves. NY: Mysterious, 1979. 1st ed. One of 250 numbered, signed. Fine in Fine dj, slipcase (sl wear). *Janus.* $100/£64

BLOCH, ROBERT. Screams. San Rafael: Underwood Miller, 1989. 1st collected ed. Part of ltd issue signed, this one of few mkd 'presentation copy.' Dj, slipcase. *Swann*.* $69/£44

BLOCH, ROBERT. The Selected Stories. L.A.: Underwood Miller, 1987. 1st trade ed. *Swann*.* $57/£37

BLOCH, ROBERT. The Selected Stories. L.A.: Underwood Miller, 1987. 1st ed. One of 500 numbered, signed. 3 vols. Imitation leather. Cl slipcase. *Swann*.* $172/£110

BLOCK, A. Sir J. M. Barrie, His First Editions: Points and Values. London: W.G. Foyle, 1933. 1st ed. Blue cl, gilt. *Maggs.* $16/£10

BLOCK, EUGENE B. Great Stagecoach Robbers of the West. Doubleday, (1962). VG in dj. *Perier.* $30/£19

BLOCK, LAWRENCE and HAROLD KING. Code of Arms. NY: Richard Marek, 1981. 1st ed. Fine in dj. *Mordida*. $40/£26

BLOCK, LAWRENCE. The Burglar Who Studied Spinoza. NY: Random House, 1980. 1st ed. Inscribed. VF in dj. *Mordida*. $65/£42

BLOCK, LAWRENCE. Burglars Can't Be Choosers. NY: Random House, 1977. 1st ed. One of 1000 numbered, signed. (Lower corners bumped), o/w Fine in dj (crease inner fr flap). *Mordida*. $65/£42

BLOCK, LAWRENCE. Death Pulls a Doublecross. Gold Medal s1162, (1961). 1st ed. Pb original. VG + (spine crease). *Certo*. $25/£16

BLOCK, LAWRENCE. Eight Million Ways to Die. NY: Arbor House, 1982. 1st ed. VG (spine rubbed) in dj (edgeworn). *Metropolitan**. $63/£40

BLOCK, LAWRENCE. Five Little Rich Girls. London: Allison & Busby, 1984. 1st hb ed. VF in dj. *Mordida*. $75/£48

BLOCK, LAWRENCE. In the Midst of Death. London: Robert Hale, 1979. 1st hb ed. Fine in dj (sl wear spine ends). *Mordida*. $100/£64

BLOCK, LAWRENCE. Out on the Cutting Edge: A Matt Scudder Mystery. NY: William Morrow, 1989. 1st ed. Inscribed. Fine in Fine dj. *Janus*. $30/£19

BLOCK, LAWRENCE. Random Walk. NY: Tor, 1988. 1st ed. VF in dj. *Mordida*. $40/£26

BLOCK, LAWRENCE. Sometimes They Bite. NY: Arbor House, 1983. 1st ed. Signed. VF in dj. *Mordida*. $65/£42

BLOCK, LAWRENCE. When the Sacred Ginmill Closes. NY: Arbor House, 1986. 1st ed. VF in dj. *Mordida*. $40/£26

BLODGET, LORIN. Climatology of the United States and of the Temperate Latitudes of the North American Continent. Phila: Lippincott, 1857. 1st ed. 536pp; 12 fldg maps (sm acid stain, crack 1 extrem), chart. Largely unopened. Emb cl. (Sigs; maps, 1 gathering sl foxed; sl faded), o/w VF. *Pirages*. $475/£304

BLODGETT, HENRY WILLIAMS. Autobiography of Henry W. Blodgett. Waukegan, IL, 1906. 1st ed. Howes B540. *Ginsberg*. $300/£192

BLOMBERG, ROLF. Chavante, an Expedition to the Tribes of the Mato Grosso. Reginald Spink (trans). NY: Taplinger, (1961). 1st Amer ed. Fine in NF dj. *Mcgowan*. $35/£22

BLOMEFIELD, M. The Bulleymung Pit. Faber, 1946. 1st ed. (Top edge sl discolored), else Good in dj (dull, sl torn). *Whiteson*. $22/£14

BLOMFIELD, REGINALD. A History of Renaissance Architecture in England 1500-1800. 1897. 2 vols. xix,186; x,(187-431)pp. (Ex-lib, sm ink stamps plts, tp; bkpl, few margins thumbed.) Lib morocco-backed cl bds (rebound; spines sl rubbed, faded, spine #s). *Edwards*. $94/£60

BLOOD, BENJAMIN. Optimism—The Lesson of Ages. Boston: Bela Marsh, 1860. 1st ed. VG. *Beasley*. $175/£112

BLOOD, BINDON. Four Score Years and Ten. London, 1933. Frontis, 7 plts. Black cl (spotted), gilt. *Maggs*. $78/£50

BLOOM, HAROLD. The Anxiety of Influence. NY: OUP, 1973. 1st ed. Gilt blue cl. NF in VG dj (sl chipped, price-clipped). *Blue Mountain*. $15/£10

BLOOM, J. HARVEY. Folk Lore, Old Customs and Superstitions in Shakespeare Land. London, 1929. (Ink stamp tp, last leaf, ex-lib, bkpl; lt soiled, spine #s.) *Edwards*. $44/£28

BLOOM, LANSING BARTLETT. Early Vaccination in New Mexico. Santa Fe: Hist Soc of NM, n.d. (ca 1924-25). 12pp. (Sl dknd, soiled.) Ptd wraps. *Bohling*. $12/£8

BLOOMFIELD, B. C. Philip Larkin; a Bibliography 1933-1976. Faber & Faber, (1979). 1st ed. Fine in dj. *Ash*. $31/£20

BLOOMFIELD, B. C. W. H. Auden: A Bibliography; The Early Years Through 1955. Charlottesville: Bibliographical Soc of Univ of VA, 1964. 1st ed. VG. *Cahan*. $25/£16

BLOOMFIELD, MAX. Bloomfield's Illustrated Historical Guide.... St. Augustine, FL, 1885. 2 fldg maps. VG. *Wantagh*. $100/£64

BLOOMFIELD, PAUL. Imaginary Worlds: Or, The Evolution of Utopia. London: Hamish Hamilton, (1932). 1st ed. (Cl unevenly sunned, rear hinge cracked), else VG + . *Other Worlds*. $50/£32

Blossoms of Morality. London: E. Newbery, 1796. 2nd ed. 1st John Bewick ed. 12mo. x,221pp; 47 woodcut vignettes by Bewick. 19th cent 3/4 red morocco, marbled bds. (Extrems lt rubbed), else Fine. *Bromer*. $550/£353

BLOUNT, ROY, JR. About Three Bricks Shy of a Load. Boston/Toronto: Little, Brown, (1974). 1st ed, 1st bk. Fine in Fine dj. *Bernard*. $45/£29

BLOUNT, WALTER PUTNAM and JOHN H. MOE. The Milwaukee Brace. Balt: Williams & Wilkins, (1973). 1st ed. Fine. *Glaser*. $50/£32

BLOUNT, WALTER PUTNAM. Fractures in Children. Balt: Williams & Wilkins, (1968). 1st ed, 9th ptg. VG. *Glaser*. $35/£22

Blue Book of Map Making. Whitney-Graham, n.d. 20 maps tipped in. (Extrems, lower cvr lt rubbed.) Paper label. *Sadlon*. $50/£32

BLUMENTHAL, JOSEPH. Art of the Printed Book 1455-1955. Bodley Head, 1974. 126 plts. (Bkpl.) VG in 2-tone cl. *Cox*. $44/£28

BLUMENTHAL, JOSEPH. Art of the Printed Book, 1455-1955. NY/Boston, (1973). 1st ptg. 125 full-pg plts. VG in dj. *Truepenny*. $75/£48

BLUMENTHAL, JOSEPH. The Printed Book in America. Boston: David R. Godine, (1977). 1st ed. Later 1/4 calf, marbled paper-cvrd bds. Fine in slipcase. *Oak Knoll*. $95/£61

BLUMENTHAL, JOSEPH. The Printed Book in America. London, 1977. 1st ed. Dj. *Typographeum*. $35/£22

BLUMENTHAL, JOSEPH. Typographic Years. Grolier Club, (1982). One of 300. This designated 'printer's copy'. Fine in slipcase. *Dermont*. $35/£22

BLUMLEIN, MICHAEL. The Brains of Rats. L.A.: Scream, 1990. 1st ed. One of 250 numbered, signed by Blumlein and Michael McDowell (intro). Leatherette. Dj, slipcase. *Swann**. $57/£37

BLUNDEN, EDMUND. English Poems. London: Cobden-Sanderson, 1925. 1st ed. Uncut. Fine (prelims, margins foxing) in dj (spine sunned, rubbed; side sl torn, sm edge chips). *Polyanthos*. $30/£19

BLUNDEN, EDMUND. Halfway House: A Miscellany of New Poems. London: Cobden Sanderson, 1932. 1st ed. Fine in VG dj (sl soiled). *Virgo*. $28/£18

BLUNDEN, EDMUND. The Poems of Edmund Blunden. London: Cobden-Sanderson, 1930. #1/200 (of 210) numbered, signed. (Eps sl browned), o/w Nice. *Gekoski*. $351/£225

BLUNDEN, EDMUND. The Shepherd and Other Poems of Peace and War. NY: Knopf, 1922. 1st ed, Amer issue. Cl, dec bds, paper spine label. Good. *Reese*. $30/£19

BLUNDEN, EDMUND. Undertones of War. GC, 1929. 1st ed. Good (worn). *King*. $35/£22

BLUNDEN, EDMUND. Winter Nights. London: Faber & Gwyer, 1928. 1st ed, deluxe issue. One of 500 numbered, signed. (Spine sl dkng), else NF. *Reese*. $75/£48

BLUNT, ANTHONY and HEREWARD L. COOKE. The Roman Drawings of the XVII and XVIII Centuries in the Collection of Her Majesty the Queen at Windsor Castle. London: Phaidon, 1960. 66 plts. VF in dj (sm tear). *Europa*. $53/£34

BLUNT, ANTHONY. Art and Architecture in France 1500-1700. Harmondsworth, 1954. 1st ed. 192 plts hors-texte. VF (bkpl). *Europa*. $44/£28

BLUNT, ANTHONY. Art and Architecture in France 1500-1700. Harmondsworth, 1957. 2nd ed. 192 plts. (Spine sl faded, rubbed.) *Washton*. $50/£32

BLUNT, ANTHONY. Artistic Theory in Italy 1450-1600. Oxford, 1956. 2nd imp. 12 plts hors-texte. Fine. *Europa*. $28/£18

BLUNT, ANTHONY. Nicolas Poussin. NY, 1967. 2 vols. 265 plts vol 2. Good in djs, slipcase. *Washton*. $150/£96

BLUNT, ANTHONY. Philibert de l'Orme. London: Zwemmer, 1958. 67 plts. Fine. *Europa*. $101/£65

BLUNT, EDMUND M. The American Coast Pilot. NY: Edmund & George W. Blunt, 1827. 11th ed. xvi,676,(4 appendix, 16 ad)pp; 20 charts. (Lt water-stains, esp margins of 1st ll, some charts misfolded, some foxing.) Orig calf. *Lefkowicz*. $250/£160

BLUNT, WILFRED. Of Flowers and Village. London: Hamish Hamilton, 1963. 1st ed. Fine in dj. *Quest*. $35/£22

BLUNT, WILFRID. The Art of Botanical Illustration. New Naturalist, 1950. 1st ed. Grn buckram. (Corner faded), o/w VG in dj (sl soiled). *Words Etc*. $70/£45

BLUNT, WILFRID. The Art of Botanical Illustration. NY, 1951. Dj. *Swann**. $57/£37

BLUNT, WILFRID. The Art of Botanical Illustration. NY, 1951. 47 color, 32 b/w plts. VG in dj (sunned, sm tears). *Brooks*. $87/£56

BLUNT, WILFRID. The Compleat Naturalist, a Life of Linnaeus. London, 1971. 2nd imp. Dj. *Maggs*. $25/£16

BLUNT, WILFRID. Flower Books and Their Illustrators. National Book League, 1950. VG in dec cvrs. *Moss*. $17/£11

BLUNT, WILFRID. My Diaries, 1888-1914. NY, 1921. 1st Amer ed. One of 1500 ptd. 2 vols. (Name, eps replaced 1 vol; sl rubbed, bumped, spine labels chafed.) *Clearwater*. $70/£45

BLUNT, WILFRID. Sebastiano. London: James Barrie, 1956. 1st ed. Dj (sl worn, chipped). *Hollett*. $55/£35

BLUTIG, EDUARD. The Stupid Joke. (NY): Fantod Press, 1990. Ltd to 500. Signed by Edward Gorey (illus) under pseud of Regera Dowdy. Fine in ptd wrappers. *Bromer*. $35/£22

BLY, ROBERT. The Man in the Black Coat Turns. NY: Dial, 1981. 1st ed. Signed. Fine in Fine dj. *Revere*. $40/£26

BLY, ROBERT. The Moon on a Fencepost. (Greensboro): Unicorn, 1988. 1st ed. Fine in wraps. *Turlington*. $25/£16

BLYTH, HENRY. Caro, the Fatal Passion. NY: Coward et al, (1973). 1st US ed. VG (name tp, ex-libris) in dj (sl worn). *Second Life*. $20/£13

BLYTHE, RONALD. A Treasonable Growth. London, 1960. 1st Eng ed. Very Nice (2 corners bumped) in dj. *Clearwater*. $39/£25

BLYTON, ENID. Here Comes Noddy Again. Sampson Low, Marston, n.d. (1951). 1st ed. Beek (illus). 8vo. 61pp (marginal fingering, mks). Pict bds. (Edges rubbed), else VG in remains of pict dj (soiled). #4, ptd price 3s/6d. *Bookmark*. $39/£25

BLYTON, ENID. Jolly Story Book. London, 1944. 1st ed. VG (inscrip) in dj (very torn). *Words Etc*. $9/£6

BLYTON, ENID. Mr. Tumpy and His Caravan. McNaughton, 1951. 7.5x10. Pict bds (sl shelfworn). VG in dj (chipped, edges ragged). *My Bookhouse*. $25/£16

BLYTON, ENID. Noddy's New Big Book. Sampson Low, Marston, n.d. 1st ed. 4to. (74)pp. Pict bds, cl spine. VG ('Picture to Color' neatly done) in pict dj (chipped). *Bookmark*. $23/£15

BOADEN, JAMES. Memoirs of Mrs. Siddons. Phila, 1827. 1st Amer ed. 22,382pp (browned). Uncut. Cl-backed bds (stained), ptd paper label. VG. *M & S*. $100/£64

BOAL, SAM. The Hemingway I Know. NY, 1957. 1st Amer ed. NF in pict wrappers. *Polyanthos*. $20/£13

BOARDMAN, JOHN et al. Greek Art and Architecture. NY: Abrams, (1967). 372 plts (52 color, tipped-in), map. Good in dj (sl chipped). *Archaeologia*. $175/£112

BOARDMAN, JOHN. Archaic Greek Gems. Evanston, IL: Northwestern Univ, 1968. 1st ed. Red cl, gilt. Good in dj. *Karmiole*. $50/£32

BOARDMAN, JOHN. Athenian Black Figure Vases. NY: OUP, 1974. (Bkpl.) *Archaeologia*. $25/£16

BOARDMAN, JOHN. Athenian Red Figure Vases: The Archaic Period. London: Thames & Hudson, (1975). Good in stiff wrappers. *Archaeologia*. $25/£16

BOARDMAN, JOHN. Greek Gems and Finger Rings. NY: Abrams, (1972). 1st ed. Blue cl. Good in dj. *Karmiole*. $200/£128

BOARDMAN, JOHN. Greek Gems and Finger Rings: Early Bronze Age to Late Classical. London: Thames & Hudson, (1970). 51 color plts. Good in dj (sl shelfworn). *Archaeologia*. $250/£160

BOAS, FRANK. Handbook of American Indian Languages. BAE Bulletin 40. Washington: GPO, 1911/1922. 2 vols. VG. *Lien*. $100/£64

BOAS, FRANZ. Anthropology and Modern Life. NY: Norton, (1928). 1st ed. (Bkpl), else Fine in Good+ dj (spine lacks bottom 1 inch; few sm chips). *Between The Covers*. $100/£64

BOAS, FRANZ. Handbook of American Indian Languages. Part 1. BAE Bulletin 40. Washington: GPO, 1911. Uncut. VG in wraps (edges cracked). *Yudkin**. $60/£38

BOAS, FRANZ. Kathlamet Texts. BAE Bulletin 26. Washington: GPO, 1901. Frontis. VG. *Lien*. $25/£16

BOAS, FRANZ. Tsimshian Texts. BAE Bulletin 27. Washington: GPO, 1902. (Extrems rubbed, sm lightened spots lower cvr.) *Sadlon*. $20/£13

BOAS, FRANZ. Tsimshian Texts. BAE Bulletin 27. Washington: GPO, 1902. VG. *Lien*. $30/£19

BOAS, FREDERICK S. (ed). Songs and Lyrics from the English Playbooks. London: Cresset, 1945. 1st ed. 8 tinted plts. (Few spots.) Dj (lt rubbed). *Hollett*. $47/£30

BOATRIGHT, MODY C. Folklore of the Oil Industry. Dallas: SMU, 1963. 1st ed. Pict cl. (Name blacked out fep), else Fine in Good dj. *Connolly*. $35/£22

BOBART, H. H. Basketwork Through the Ages. OUP, 1936. VG (eps foxed, browned). *Peter Taylor*. $30/£19

Bobby Bear. Racine, WI: Whitman, 1935. Sq 8vo. 3 Fine pop-ups. (Foxing.) Flexible cardbd pict cvrs (bumped, crease, tears, bk coming loose from cvrs). *Metropolitan**. $69/£44

BOCCACCIO, GIOVANNI. The Decameron of Giovanni Boccacci...Now First Completely Done into English Prose and Verse. London: Villon Soc, 1886. 1st ed of Payne's version. #297 of unspecified #. 3 vols. Teg. Full parchment (sl mottled, rubbed) over bds stamped in gilt. VG. *Reese*. $150/£96

BOCCACCIO, GIOVANNI. The Decameron of Giovanni Boccaccio. Richard Aldington (trans). GC: Garden City, (1949). One of 1500 signed by Rockwell Kent (illus). 2 vols. 18 full-pg illus. Teg. Dk red cl, gilt spine. Fine in slipcase (extrems worn) w/dec tps both sides. *Heller.* $400/£256

BODANSKY, MEYER. Introduction to Physiological Chemistry. NY, 1938. 4th ed. VG. *Doctor's Library.* $50/£32

BODDIE, JOHN BENNETT. Seventeenth Century Isle of Wight County Virginia. Chicago: Chicago Law Ptg, 1938. 1st ed. (Ex-lib, bkpl, blind stamp, call # on spine), else Good. *Brown.* $40/£26

BODE, WILHELM. Florentine Sculptors of the Renaissance. London: Methuen, (1908). 1st ed. 96 b/w plts. Grn cl, spine gilt. (Lt foxing prelims; sm ding rear bd), o/w Fine. *Hermitage.* $100/£64

BODE, WINSTON. Portrait of Pancho. Austin: Pemberton, 1965. #44/150 signed. Full brn leather, gilt. Fine in slipcase. *Bohling.* $300/£192

BODECKER, N. M. It's Raining Said John Twaining. NY: Atheneum, 1973. 1st ed. 8 3/4 x 7 1/2. 32pp. VG. *Cattermole.* $15/£10

BODECKER, N. M. Miss Jaster's Garden. NY: Golden, 1972. 2nd ed. 9 1/2 x 12 3/4. 28pp. Glossy bds. Fine; no dj as issued. *Cattermole.* $50/£32

BODECKER, N. M. The Mushroom Center Disaster. NY: Atheneum, 1974. 1st ed. Erik Blegvad (illus). 5 3/4 x 7. 48pp. Fine in dj. *Cattermole.* $25/£16

BODENHEIM, MAXWELL. Bringing Jazz. NY: Horace Liveright, 1930. 1st ed. NF in dj (spine extrems chipped, sm sticker fr flap; lt soiled). *Captain's Bookshelf.* $75/£48

BODFISH, HARTSON H. Chasing the Bowhead. Cambridge: Harvard Univ, 1936. 9 plts. Teg. VG (sl worn). *High Latitude.* $100/£64

BODILLY, R. B. The Voyage of Captain Thomas James for the Discovery of the Northwest Passage, 1631. London/Toronto: J.M. Dent, 1928. Fldg map. (Lacks fep), else VG. *High Latitude.* $35/£22

BODKIN, M. White Magic. London: Chapman & Hal, 1897. 1st ed. (Rubbed.) *Metropolitan*.* $115/£74

BOEHME, JACOB. Six Theosophic Points and Other Writings. J.R. Earle (trans). London: Constable, 1919. 1st ed. VG+. *Middle Earth.* $95/£61

BOESSENECKER, JOHN. Badge and Buckshot. Norman: Univ of OK, (1988). 1st ed. 2 maps. VF in pict dj. *Argonaut.* $50/£32

BOETHIUS, AXEL. The Golden House of Nero. Ann Arbor: Univ of MI, (1960). (3 blind emb stamps 1st 3 ll.) Dj. *Archaeologia.* $125/£80

BOGAN, LOUISE. Achievement in American Poetry 1900-1950. Chicago: Henry Regnery, 1951. 1st ed. Fine in dj. *Jaffe.* $35/£22

BOGAN, LOUISE. The Blue Estuaries. NY: FSG, (1968). 1st ed. Mint in dj. *Jaffe.* $125/£80

BOGAN, LOUISE. Body of This Death. NY: Robert M. McBride, 1923. 1st ed, 1st bk. Cl-backed bds. Fine in dj (sl worn, faded). *Jaffe.* $350/£224

BOGAN, LOUISE. Dark Summer. NY: Scribner, 1929. 1st ed. Cl-backed bds, ptd labels. (Sig), o/w Fine in dj (rubbed, spine faded). *Jaffe.* $225/£144

BOGAN, LOUISE. Selected Criticism: Poetry and Prose. NY: Noonday, 1955. 1st ed. Fine in dj (price-clipped, lt dust-soiled, torn). *Jaffe.* $45/£29

BOGAN, LOUISE. The Sleeping Fury. NY: Scribner, 1937. 1st ed. (Eps lt offset), o/w Fine in dj (sl chipped). *Jaffe.* $150/£96

BOGAN, LOUISE. What the Woman Lived. Ruth Limmer (ed). NY: Harcourt Brace Jovanovich, (1973). 1st ed. Fine in dj (sl edgeworn, sm tear). *Jaffe.* $35/£22

BOGAN, PHEBE M. Yaqui Indian Dances of Tucson, Arizona. Tucson: The Archeological Soc, 1925. 1st ed. Brn fabrikoid (sl edgewear). NF. *Harrington.* $45/£29

BOGARDE, DIRK. Voices in the Garden. London: Chatto, 1981. 1st UK ed. NF in dj. *Williams.* $14/£9

BOGER, ALNOD J. The Story of General Bacon. London, 1903. Frontis port, plt. (Prelims, final leaves foxed.) Blue cl (sl worn), gilt. *Maggs.* $125/£80

BOGG, EDMUND. A Thousand Miles of Wandering in the Border Country. Newcastle/York: Mawson, Swan & Morgan/John Sampson, 1898. xv,364pp. Pict cl (very faded). *Hollett.* $55/£35

BOGG, EDMUND. Two Thousand Miles of Wandering in the Border Country, Lakeland and Ribblesdale. Leeds/York: The Author/John Sampson, 1898. xxii,364,264pp (blind stamps feps). 1/2 morocco (joints cracked), gilt, raised bands. Very Attractive. *Hollett.* $250/£160

BOGGS, MAE H. B. My Playhouse Was a Concord Coach. Oakland: The Author, (1942). 8 fldg maps inserted. Blue cl, gilt spine title, blind-stamped cvr dec. Fine. Howes B570. *Pacific*.* $230/£147

BOGGS, MAE H. B. My Playhouse Was a Concord Coach. (Oakland: Howell-North, 1942.) 1st ed. 8 fldg maps, plts. Blue cl. Howes B570. *Ginsberg.* $500/£321

BOGGS, SAMUEL S. Eighteen Months a Prisoner Under the Rebel Flag. Lovington, IL: The Author, 1887. 1st ed. 96pp. VG in wrappers (fr cvr chipped, attached by cellophane tape; lacks rear cvr, last pg sl chipped). *Connolly.* $65/£42

BOGOSIAN, ERIC. Sex, Drugs, Rock and Roll. NY: HarperCollins, 1991. 1st ed. Signed. Fine in Fine dj. *Beasley.* $45/£29

BOGUE, BENJAMIN N. Stammering; Its Cause and Cure. Indianapolis, 1926. VG. *Argosy.* $35/£22

BOGUET, HENRY. An Examen of Witches Drawn from Various Trials. Montague Summers (ed). E. Allen Ashwin (trans). London: John Rodker, 1929. Ltd to 1275 (this unnumbered). Uncut. Good in orig stained vellum-backed blue cl (backstrip faded). *Cox.* $70/£45

BOID, CAPTAIN. A Description of Azores. London, 1834. Fldg map, 4 plts. (Lt foxing.) Orig bds (worn, soiled, spine gone). *Freeman*.* $60/£38

BOID, EDWARD. A Concise History and Analysis of the Principal Styles of Architecture. Ptd by G.B. Whittaker, 1835. 2nd ed. xx,212,11pp (ink stamp fep, prelims sl spotted); 13 plts. Orig full calf (sl discolored; ex-lib). *Edwards.* $70/£45

BOK, HANNES. Beauty and the Beasts. Gerry de la Ree (ed). Saddle River, NJ: Gerry de la Ree, 1958. 1st ed. One of 1300 numbered. This copy inscribed, signed by de la Ree. Fine in Fine dj. *Mcclintock.* $110/£71

BOKUM, HERMANN. The Testimony of a Refugee from East Tennessee. Phila: Ptd for Gratuitous Distribution, 1863. 24pp. (Text, wrappers sl dampstained), else Good. *Brown.* $25/£16

BOLAM, GEORGE. Wild Life in Wales. London, 1913. *Wheldon & Wesley.* $62/£40

BOLAM, GEORGE. Wild Life in Wales. London, 1913. 1st ed. Teg. (Spine lt sunned, sl rubbed.) *Edwards.* $78/£50

BOLAND, JOHN. Fatal Error. London: Boardman, 1962. 1st ed. VG in dj (price-clipped, 2 sm closed tears). *Mordida.* $30/£19

BOLDUAN, CHARLES FREDERICK. Immune Sera. NY: John Wiley, 1908. 3rd ed. (Sig, note fep; ex-lib mks on cvr.) *White.* $39/£25

BOLIN, C. Narrative of the Life and Adventures of Major C. Bolin, Alias David Butler. Palo Alto: Lewis Osborne, 1966. Full-size repro of pg from Nevada Democrat describing Bolin's execution laid in. VG + (cl sl faded) in plain dj (worn, dknd). Bohling. $25/£16

BOLL, HEINRICH. Absent Without Leave. NY: McGraw-Hill, 1965. 1st US ed. VG + in dj (price-clipped). Lame Duck. $45/£29

BOLL, HEINRICH. Acquainted with the Night. Richard Graves (trans). NY: Holt, (1954). 1st ed. Fine in NF dj. Antic Hay. $35/£22

BOLL, HEINRICH. The Bread of Those Early Years. NY: McGraw-Hill, 1976. 1st US ed. (Lt shelfworn), else NF in VG + dj (1-inch tear). Lame Duck. $25/£16

BOLL, HEINRICH. The Lost Honour of Katharina Blum. L. Vennewitz (trans). London, 1975. 1st ed. Dj. Typographeum. $22/£14

BOLL, HEINRICH. A Soldier's Legacy. Leila Vennewitz (trans). London: Secker & Warburg, (1985). 1st Eng ed. Fine in dj. Antic Hay. $20/£13

BOLLIGER, MAX. The Golden Apple. NY: Atheneum, 1970. 1st ed. Celestino Platti (illus). 8 1/2 x 12. 32pp. Pict bds, cl spine. Fine in dj. Cattermole. $20/£13

BOLLIGER, MAX. Noah and the Rainbow. NY: Crowell, 1972. 1st ed. Helga Alchinger (illus). 9x12. 26pp. VG in dj. Cattermole. $15/£10

BOLLINGER, EDWARD T. and FREDERICK BAUER. The Moffat Road. Denver: Sage Books, (1962). One of 2000. Signed by both. Color plt. Fine in dj. Bohling. $100/£64

BOLLINGER, JAMES W. Lincoln: Statesman and Logician. Davenport, IA: Privately ptd, 1944. Ltd to 500. Inscribed presentation. Fine in dj. Graf. $75/£48

BOLSCHE, W. Haeckel, His Life and Work.... Joseph McCabe (trans). London, 1906. (Fep cut away; sl worn.) Maggs. $28/£18

BOLTON and COE. American Samplers. N.p. (Boston): MA Soc of Colonial Dames, 1921. 126 photo plts. Dec pastedown cvr. (Spine faded, sl foxing, rear hinge crack), o/w Good. Scribe's Perch*. $120/£77

BOLTON, ARTHUR T. The Architecture of Robert and James Adam (1758-1794). London: Country Life, 1922. 1st ed. 2 vols. Frontis each vol (vol 2 in color). Teg. Lt grn cl (lt soiled, sm labels removed from spines). Karmiole. $350/£224

BOLTON, ARTHUR T. The Architecture of Robert and James Adam (1758-1794). London: Country Life, 1922. 2 vols. Color frontis vol 2. Teg. Christie's*. $456/£292

BOLTON, CHARLES KNOWLES. On the Wooing of Martha Pitkin.... Boston: Copeland & Day, 1894. Ltd to 350 ptd. Signed, dated Dec 24, 1894. (28)pp. 1/4 leather, marbled bds (worn, esp bottom edges), ptd label fr cvr. Internally VG. New Hampshire*. $10/£6

BOLTON, HENRY. The Follies of Science at the Court of Rudolph II 1576-1612. Milwaukee, 1904. 1st ed. VG. Fye. $75/£48

BOLTON, HERBERT E. Anza's California Expeditions. Berkeley: Univ of CA, 1930. 1st ed. 5 vols. Uncut. Blue cl, gilt spines. Fine. Pacific*. $489/£313

BOLTON, HERBERT E. Athanase de Mezieres and the Louisiana-Texas Frontier 1768-80. NY, 1914. 1st ed. 3 vols. VG +. No dj as issued. Howes B584. Turpen. $495/£317

BOLTON, HERBERT E. The Colonization of North America 1492-1783. NY, 1925. Dk blue cl, gilt. (1/2-inch nick rear cvr), o/w VG. Turpen. $48/£31

BOLTON, HERBERT E. Fray Juan Crespi: Missionary Explorer on the Pacific Coast, 1769-1774. Berkeley, CA, 1927. 1st ed. 11 maps, plts. Howes B586. Ginsberg. $150/£96

BOLTON, HERBERT E. History of the Americas, a Syllabus with Maps. Berkeley, 1928. 1st ed. 92 maps. NF. Turpen. $45/£29

BOLTON, HERBERT E. In the South San Joaquin Ahead of Garces...and A Short Reading List on the History of Kern County by John D. Henderson. Bakersfield: Kern County Hist Soc, 1935. Rev ed. Ptd wrappers. Shasky. $30/£19

BOLTON, HERBERT E. Outpost of Empire. NY: Knopf, 1931. 1st ed. 11 maps. Gilt-lettered spine. Fine (sig on fep). Argonaut. $100/£64

BOLTON, HERBERT E. Pageant in the Wilderness, Story of the Escalante Expedition to the Interior Basin 1776.... Salt Lake City, 1950. 1st ed. Frontis, 2 fldg maps pocket. Fine in VG dj. Turpen. $100/£64

BOLTON, HERBERT E. Rim of Christendom, Biography of Eusebio Francisco Kino. NY, 1936. 1st ed. Signed, inscribed. 8 fldg maps. VG + in dj (chipped). Howes B587. Turpen. $150/£96

BOLTON, HERBERT E. Rim of Christendom. NY: Macmillan, 1936. 1st ed. Good (ex-lib, rubberstamps; spine #). Howes B587. Brown. $40/£26

BOLTON, HERBERT E. Texas in the Middle Eighteenth Century. Berkeley: Univ of CA, 1915. 1st ed. 12 maps, 1 facs. Good (ex-lib, bkpls, stamp). Howes B589. Agvent. $135/£87

BOLTON, HERBERT E. Texas in the Middle Eighteenth Century: Studies in Spanish Colonial History and Administration. Berkeley: Univ of CA, 1915. 1st ed. Lg fldg map at rear. Uncut. Ptd gray wrappers (sl chipped, sm corner piece lacking), else VF. Custom made clamshell box, leather labels. Howes B589. Argonaut. $350/£224

BOLTON, J. S. The Brain in Health and Disease. 1914. Whitehart. $62/£40

Bomba, the Merry Old King and Other Stories. NY, (1902). 10x7.5. Unpaged. Glazed pict bds (worn, sl stained). King. $50/£32

BONAR, H. The Desert of Sinai. NY: Carter, 1857. Frontis, 408pp. Pub's cl, dec spine. Good. Scribe's Perch*. $65/£42

BOND, BEVERLY W., JR. (ed). The Courses of the Ohio River. Cincinnati, 1942. 2 fldg maps. (Sl bumped), else VG. King. $35/£22

BOND, DOUGLAS D. The Love and Fear of Flying. NY: IUP, 1952. 1st ed. (Sm price oblit fep), else Fine in dj (lt used, sm tears, chip). Beasley. $45/£29

BOND, EARL D. and KENNETH E. APPEL. The Treatment of Behavior Disorders Following Encephalitis. NY: Commonwealth Fund Div of Publications, 1931. 1st ed. Blue cl. Jelliffe's name stamp, bkpl. VG in dj (chipped). Gach. $50/£32

BOND, FRANCIS. Gothic Architecture in England. London: Batsford, 1906. (4 leaves of table of contents and intro are bound out of order before tp; sl shaken), o/w VG. New Hampshire*. $90/£58

BOND, FRANCIS. Screens and Galleries in English Churches. London: Frowde, 1908. (Cl sl worn.) Ars Artis. $28/£18

BOND, FRANCIS. Woodcarvings in English Churches. I. Misericords. London: OUP, 1910. 1st ed. Blue cl (spine sl dull; feps lt spotted, lib label fep). Hollett. $70/£45

BOND, JAMES. Birds of the West Indies. Boston: Houghton Mifflin, 1961. 1st ed. Dec cl. NF in Good+ dj. Mikesh. $27/£17

BOND, JAMES. Birds of the West Indies. Boston: Houghton Mifflin, 1971. 3rd ed. NF in Good dj. Books & Birds. $20/£13

BOND, JAMES. Field Guide to the Birds of the West Indies. NY, 1947. Color frontis. Dj (chipped). Edwards. $39/£25

BOND, JULIAN. Black Candidates: Southern Campaign Experiences. Atlanta: Voter Education Project/Southern Regional Council, (1969). 1st ed. (Corners of last few pp sl soiled, lt creased), else NF in stapled wrappers. *Between The Covers*. $100/£64

BOND, MICHAEL. Paddington at Large. NY: HM, 1963. 1st ed. Peggy Fortnum (illus). 5 1/2 x 8 1/4. 128pp. VG in dj. *Cattermole*. $30/£19

BOND, NELSON. Exiles of Time. Prime Press, 1949. One of 112 specially bound, numbered, signed. Partly unopened. Fine in paper-cvrd slipcase, not issued in dj. *Certo*. $200/£128

BOND, NELSON. Nightmares and Daydreams. Sauk City: Arkham House, 1968. 1st ed. Fine in dj (sm tear spine). *Bromer*. $50/£32

BONE, MUIRHEAD. The Western Front. London: Country Life, 1917. 2 vols. 200 plts. (Vol 1 cocked, prelims foxed.) Cl-backed bds (worn, soiled, bumped). *Waverly**. $60/£38

BONE, P. J. The Guitar and Mandolin, Biographies of Celebrated Players and Composers. London: Schott & Co, 1954. 2nd ed, enlgd. Red cl, gilt. VG (lt wear). *Cullen*. $150/£96

BONE, STEPHEN. The Landscapes of Britain. London: A&C Black, 1949. 2nd ed. 24 color plts. (Eps lt spotted.) Dj (sl soiled, chipped w/some loss). *Edwards*. $31/£20

BONE, STEPHEN. The West Coast of Scotland. London: Faber, 1952. 1st ed. VG in dj. *Hollett*. $47/£30

BONELLI, WILLIAM G. Billion Dollar Blackjack. Beverly Hills: Civic Research, (1954). 1st ed. NF in pict dj (sl chipped). *Argonaut*. $90/£58

BONER, CHARLES. Chamois Hunting in the Mountains of Bavaria and the Tyrol. Chapman & Hall, 1860. 2nd ed. xiii,446pp; 7 color litho plts (lt spotting). Contemp blue calf (rebacked, repaired). Good. *Bickersteth*. $250/£160

BONHOTE, J. L. Birds of Britain. A&C Black, 1907. 1st ed. 100 color plts. Teg. Good in dec cl, gilt. *Cox*. $62/£40

BONHOTE, J. L. (ed). Practical Bird-Keeping.... London: West, Newman, 1913. 1st ed. Color frontis. VG. *Agvent*. $45/£29

BONNARD, GEORGES A. (ed). Gibbon's Journey from Geneva to Rome...20 April to 2 October, 1764. London: Thomas Nelson, (1961). Frontis, 11 plts. Good in dj. *Archaeologia*. $45/£29

BONNER, CAMPBELL. Studies in Magical Amulets, Chiefly Graeco-Egyptian. Ann Arbor: Univ of MI, 1950. 25 plts. (Sig fep.) *Archaeologia*. $450/£288

BONNER, T. D. The Life and Adventures of James P. Beckwourth.... NY: Harper & Bros, 1856. 1st ed. Frontis port, 537pp + ad leaf at end. Blind-stamped red cl (spine sl chipped, tips sl worn). *Dawson*. $275/£176

BONNER, THOMAS N. The Kansas Doctor.... Lawrence, KS, 1959. Fine in dj. *Argosy*. $30/£19

BONNEY, JOSEPH L. Murder Without Clues. NY: Carrick & Evans, 1940. 1st ed. Inscribed. VG in dj (soiled). *Mordida*. $45/£29

BONNEY, T. G. et al. The Mediterranean. NY: Pott, 1902. 1st ed. 17 plts. Teg. (Sl rubbed, soiled, spine sl frayed), o/w VG. *Worldwide*. $30/£19

BONNYCASTLE, J. An Introduction to Astronomy. London, 1796. 1st ed. 431pp; 20 plts (some frayed from improper fldg). Old calf (detached, lacks spine label). *King*. $350/£224

BONNYCASTLE, J. An Introduction to Mensuration and Practical Geometry.... Phila, 1848. xii,288pp (writing fr blank). Contemp sheep (sl worn, rubbed), leather label. *Whitehart*. $62/£40

BONNYCASTLE, R. H. Spanish America. Phila: Abraham Small, 1819. 1st Amer ed. Fldg map, fldg hand-colored chart. Calf, gilt. Presentable (browning throughout, map creased incorrectly, few tears starting). *Hermitage*. $400/£256

BONSAL, STEPHEN. Edward Fitzgerald Beale: A Pioneer in the Path of Empire 1822-1903. NY: Putnam, 1912. 1st ed. (Ink inscrip, overall lt wear), o/w Fine. Howes B608. *Hermitage*. $200/£128

BONSELS, WALDEMAR. An Indian Journey. NY: Boni, 1928. 1st ed. Frontis, engr tp, 7 plts. (Bkpl; sl rubbed), o/w VG. *Worldwide*. $18/£12

BONSER, WILFRID. A Bibliography of Folklore. London, 1961. *Edwards*. $39/£25

BONTEMPS, ARNA and JACK CONROY. Slappy Hooper, the Wonderful Sign Painter. Boston: HMCo, 1946. 1st ed. Ursula Koering (illus). Oblong 4to. Fine in NF dj (sl foxed, tears neatly repaired internally). *Between The Covers*. $650/£417

BONTEMPS, ARNA and JACK CONROY. They Seek a City. GC: Doubleday, Doran, 1945. 1st ed. Grn cl (mottling). Good in Very Nice pict dj. *Captain's Bookshelf*. $125/£80

BONTEMPS, ARNA. Frederick Douglass: Slave-Fighter-Freeman. NY: Knopf, 1959. 1st ed. Advance Review Copy w/slip laid in. Harper Johnson (illus). Fine in dj (black marker to spine). *Between The Covers*. $65/£42

BONTEMPS, ARNA. Mr. Kelso's Lion. Phila/NY: Lippincott, (1970). 1st ed. Len Ebert (illus). NF in VG+ dj (price-clipped, sm tears). *Between The Covers*. $100/£64

BONVALOT, GABRIEL. Across Tibet. NY: Cassell, 1892. 1st ed in English. xiii,417pp; fldg map fr pocket. Uncut. Pict cl (spine tail, corners sl rubbed), bright gilt. Good. *Sotheran*. $437/£280

BONVALOT, GABRIEL. Through the Heart of Asia, Over Pamir to India. London: Chapman & Hall, 1889. 1st Eng ed. 2 vols. xv,281; x,255pp + 4 uncut ad leaves; fldg map. Uncut. Pict cl, gilt. (Sm dent spines), o/w Beautiful. *Sotheran*. $546/£350

BONVALOT, GABRIEL. Through the Heart of Asia. C. B. Pitman (trans). London: Chapman & Hall, 1889. 1st ed. 2 vols. Lg 8vo. xxii,281; x,255pp + 8 ads; fldg map. Blue gilt pict cl. Fine set. *Terramedia*. $750/£481

BONWICK, JAMES. The Lost Tasmanian Race. London: Sampson Low et al, 1884. 1st ed. (viii),216pp. Pict cl (sl soiled, spine tail sl bumped). Good. *Sotheran*. $234/£150

Book of Common Prayer. Cambridge, 1762. 3rd ed. (John Baskerville, ptr.) 19th-cent diced calf (sig, old ink hymn fep, soil, dampstaining, foxing; worn, edges rubbed). *Freeman**. $50/£32

Book of Common Prayer. (London: Essex House Press, 1903.) One of 400. Pigskin-backed oak bds, wrought-iron clasps (1 lacks leather strap). *Swann**. $747/£479

Book of Common Prayer. Boston: Merrymount, 1930. One of 500. Maroon pigskin. Fine. *Swann**. $1,265/£811

Book of Costume.... (By Mary Margaret Egerton.) London, 1847. New ed. Gilt-pict cl (edges dknd). *Swann**. $57/£37

Book of Job.... NY: LEC, 1946. One of 1950. Signed by Arthur Szyk (illus). Tipped-in color illus. (Tape stains fep.) Box (rubbed). *Kane**. $90/£58

Book of Kells: Reproductions from the Manuscript in Trinity College Dublin. NY, 1974. 1st Amer ed. Slipcase (frayed). *Freeman**. $50/£32

Book of Mormon.... Liverpool, 1898. 623pp (lacks 1/2 rep). Orig full pebbled leather (edges, spine worn, lacks portion spine crown, spine crack). Good. *Benchmark*. $75/£48

Book of Photographs from the Collection of Sam Wagstaff. NY: Gray Press, 1978. 1st ed. (Pict stiff wrappers sl worn), o/w NF. *Cahan.* $30/£19

Book of Pictures in Roland Park, Baltimore, Maryland. (Balt, 1912.) (Sl internal wear; corners bumped, lt worn.) *Freeman*.* $50/£32

Book of the Dead. London, 1894. 2nd ed. Folio. 37 dbl-pg color plts. 1/2 morocco (extrems rubbed). *Swann*.* $287/£184

Bookbinding in America, 1680-1910: From the Collection of Frederick E. Maser. Bryn Mawr College Library, 1983. VF. *Truepenny.* $45/£29

Booklover's Almanac. NY, 1893/4. #123/400. Full blue morocco, gilt. *Petersfield.* $90/£58

BOOKWALTER, JOHN W. Siberia and Central Asia. Springfield, OH, 1899. 1st ed. xxxi,548pp. Pict cl. (Corners sl bumped), o/w NF. *Sotheran.* $468/£300

Boon, The Mind of the Race, The Wild Asses of the Devil, and The Last Trump. (By H. G. Wells.) London: T. Fisher Unwin, (1915). 1st ed. Dk grn cl, gilt. Fine (bkpl, orig purchase invoice loosely laid in, rep sl cracked). *Sumner & Stillman.* $250/£160

BOONE AND CROCKETT CLUB. North American Big Game Records. Pittsburgh: B&C, 1971. Color frontis. VF in VG+ dj. *Bowman.* $90/£58

BOONE AND CROCKETT CLUB. Records of North American Big Game. NY: Holt, 1964. 1st ptg. Color frontis. Fine+ in VG dj. *Bowman.* $125/£80

BOOTH, ANDREW D. and KATHLEEN H. V. Automatic Digital Calculators. London: Butterworths, 1953. 1st ed. Frontis, 3 plts. VG. *Glaser.* $175/£112

BOOTH, J. B. (ed). Seventy Years of Song. Hutchinson, (1943). 1st ed. VG in pict wraps (sl rubbed). *Ash.* $31/£20

BOOTH, SALLY SMITH. Hung, Strung, and Potted---A History of Eating Habits in Colonial America. NY: Clarkson N. Potter, 1971. 1st ed. VG in dj. *Perier.* $25/£16

BOOTH, STEPHEN. The Book Called Hollinshed's Chronicles. SF: (Tuscany), 1968. One of 500, w/orig leaf from 1587 ed tipped in. *Swann*.* $126/£81

BOOTH, WILLIAM. In Darkest England and the Way Out. London: Intl Headquarters of the Salvation Army, (1890). 1st ed. Fldg chromolitho frontis. Contents VG (worn, lt soiled). *Waverly*.* $38/£24

BOOTHBY, GUY. Farewell Nikola. London: Ward-Lock, 1901. 1st ed. Sound (pict insert fr panel, white spine enamel flaking). *Else Fine.* $85/£54

BOOTHE, CLARE. Kiss the Boys Good-Bye. NY: Random House, (1939). 1st ed. Fine in dj (sl soiling). *Between The Covers.* $85/£54

BOOTS, TIFFNEY. Five Men. London: Royal, 1905. 1st ed. (Brittle fep), else Fine in red cl. *Between The Covers.* $150/£96

BORCHERT, WOLFGANG. The Man Outside. London: Hutchinson, 1952. 1st ed in English. VG+ (upper pg edges soiled) in VG dj (loss spine foot). *Lame Duck.* $50/£32

BORCHERT, WOLFGANG. The Sad Geraniums. NY: Ecco, 1973. 1st US ed. Fine in NF dj (price-clipped). *Lame Duck.* $25/£16

BORCOMAN, JAMES. Charles Negre, 1820-1880. Ottawa: Nat'l Gallery of Canada, 1976. 1st ed. 203 plts. (Owner stamp), else NF in stiff wrappers, mtd circular photo. *Cahan.* $85/£54

BORCOMAN, JAMES. Eugene Atget, 1857-1927. Ottawa: Nat'l Gallery of Canada, 1984. 1st ed. Full-pg frontis, 24 plts. Fine in dj (lt rubbed). *Cahan.* $30/£19

BORDEAUX, WILLIAM J. Sitting Bull, TaTanka-Iyotaka. N.p., n.d. (c. 1957). 1st ed. Frontis port. Pict orange wrappers, ptd in black w/frontis port repeated on fr cvr. Fine. *Argonaut.* $75/£48

BORDEN, SPENCER. Arab Horses and the Crabbet Stud. Ft. Collins: Caballus, 1973. Ltd to 1500. VG. *October Farm.* $45/£29

Border and Bastille. (By George Alfred Lawrence.) NY: W.I. Pooley, (1863). 1st ed. xii,291pp. Pub's dec cl. (Spine ends sl chipped), else VG. *Cahan.* $125/£80

Border and Bastille. (By George Alfred Lawrence.) NY: W.I. Pooley, (1863). xii,291pp (lacks rep, bkpl). Textured cl. VG. *Reese.* $150/£96

BORGES, JORGE LUIS. In Praise of Darkness. Norman Thomas di Giovanni (trans). NY: Dutton, 1974. 1st ed in English. Fine in dj. *Captain's Bookshelf.* $60/£38

BORGES, JORGE LUIS. A Personal Anthology. Anthony Kerrigan (trans). NY: Grove, (1967). 1st US ed. Fine in VG- dj (smudges, sm creased edge tear). *Reese.* $75/£48

BORGIA, ANTHONY. Life in the World Unseen and More About Life in the World Unseen. NY: Citadel, 1957. 1st Amer ed. 2 vols. Fine in VG+ djs, VG+ box. *Middle Earth.* $45/£29

BORROW, GEORGE. The Bible in Spain. Ulick R. Burke (ed). London, 1896. 2 vols. Red cl, gilt. (Spine sl rubbed.) *Gretton.* $25/£16

BORROW, GEORGE. Lavengro. London: LEC, 1936. Ltd to 1500 signed by Barnett Freedman (illus). 2 vols. 16 full-pg color lithos. Full mulberry linen. Fine set in slipcase (lt worn). *Truepenny.* $95/£61

BORROW, GEORGE. Lavengro: The Scholar---the Gypsy---the Priest. London: John Murray, 1851. 1st ed. One of 3000 ptd. 3 vols. Engr frontis port vol 1 (foxed), 32pp pub's cats end of vols 1 & 2, dated respectively Feb and Jan 1851. Pale yellow coated eps (sl cracked); top edges uncut, others rough-trimmed. Ribbed blind-ruled dk grn cl (worn vol 1), paper spine labels (1 rubbed, all chipped). Text Nice. *Temple.* $86/£55

BORROW, GEORGE. The Romany Rye. London: Cresset, 1948. VG in dj (price-clipped). *Hollett.* $19/£12

BORROW, GEORGE. Wild Wales: Its People, Language, and Scenery. London: John Murray, 1862. 1st ed. One of 1000 ptd. 3 vols. Paper labels (chipped). Internally VG (bkpls; joints cracking, mended; worn). *Reese.* $175/£112

BORROW, GEORGE. The Zincali. London: Murray, 1841. 1st ed, w/half-titles. One of 750 ptd. 2 vols. Contemp 3/4 calf (rubbed). *Oinonen*.* $160/£103

BORROW, GEORGE. The Zincali. Murray, 1845. 1st ed thus. Signed by pub. 2 vols in 1. 1/2 black calf, blind-dec backstrip. *Petersfield.* $172/£110

BORSI, FRANCO. Bernini. NY, 1984. Good. *Washton.* $150/£96

BORTHWICK, J. D. Three Years in California. Oakland: Biobooks, 1948. 1st Amer ed. Ltd 1000. 8 color plts, lg color fldg map. (Sl bump to fr bd), o/w Fine. Howes B622. *Cahan.* $50/£32

BOSE, JAGADIS CHUNDER. The Nervous Mechanism of Plants. London: Longmans, Green, 1926. Good (ex-lib w/stamp tp, # to faded spine). *Savona.* $28/£18

BOSQUI, EDWARD. Memoirs of Edward Bosqui. Oakland: Holmes, 1952. One of 350 ptd. Frontis. Patterned dk cl, paper spine label, extra label bound in. *Dawson.* $100/£64

BOSSOM, ALFRED C. An Architectural Pilgrimage in Old Mexico. NY, 1924. Frontis, 110 plts at rear. (Margins lt browned; cl sl soiled, spine rubbed.) *Edwards.* $86/£55

BOSTOCK, JOHN ASHTON. Letters from India and the Crimea. London, 1896. Frontis port, xviii,270pp. Grn cl (sl worn). Maggs. $187/£120

BOSTON, CHARLES K. (Pseud of Frank Gruber.) The Silver Jackass. NY: Reynal & Hitchcock, 1941. 1st ed. Fine in pict silver dj (lt rubbed). Else Fine. $135/£87

BOSTON, LUCY. An Enemy at Green Knowe. London: Faber, 1964. 1st ed. Peter Boston (illus). 5 1/2 x 8. 150pp. Good in dj. Cattermole. $40/£26

BOSTON, LUCY. The Guardians of the House. London: Bodley Head, 1974. 1st ed. Peter Boston (illus). 5 1/2 x 8 3/4. 53pp. Fine in dj. Cattermole. $50/£32

BOSTON, LUCY. The Guardians of the House. NY: Atheneum, 1975. 1st US ed. Peter Boston (ilus). 5 3/4 x 8 1/2. 52pp. Fine in dj. Cattermole. $30/£19

BOSTON, LUCY. Memory in a House. NY: Bodley Head, 1973. 1st ed. 5 1/2 x 8 3/4. 142pp. VG in dj. Cattermole. $100/£64

BOSTON, LUCY. Nothing Said. London: Bodley Head, 1971. 1st ed. Peter Boston (illus). 5 1/4 x 8. 58pp. VG (inscrip) in dj. Cattermole. $50/£32

BOSTON, LUCY. The Stones of Green Knowe. London: Bodley Head, 1976. 1st ed. Peter Boston (illus). 5 1/4 x 8. 119pp. VG (inscrip) in dj. Cattermole. $75/£48

BOSWELL, JAMES. Boswell in Holland 1763-64.... Frederick A. Pottle (ed). Heinemann, 1952. 1st ed. Frontis. Good. Cox. $12/£8

BOSWELL, JAMES. Boswell on the Grand Tour: Germany and Switzerland 1764. Frederick A. Pottle (ed). London, 1953. Ltd ed. 1/2 parchment. VG in box. Argosy. $75/£48

BOSWELL, JAMES. Boswell's Column. London: William Kimber, (1951). 1st British ed. (Spine sl dknd, lt soiled), else VG. Reese. $30/£19

BOSWELL, JAMES. Boswell's Life of Johnson. London: Navarre Soc, 1924. Rpt of 1791 ed, w/Additions and Corrections of 1793. 3 vols. 20 photogravure etchings, 50 half-tone plts, facs autograph letter. Teg. Pict cl, gilt. VG set. Hartfield. $265/£170

BOSWELL, JAMES. Boswell's Life of Johnson. George Birbeck Hill (ed). Oxford/NY: Clarendon/Macmillan, 1887. 1st ed. 6 vols. 14 ports, maps, facs. Uncut. Grn cl, gilt titles. VG (bkpl; wear). Hartfield. $395/£253

BOSWELL, JAMES. Boswell's Life of Samuel Johnson Together with Boswell's Journal of a Tour to the Hebrides and Johnson's Diary of a Journey into North Wales. Oxford: Clarendon, 1934-50. 1st ptg. 7 vols. VG set (extrems sl worn). Reese. $350/£224

BOSWELL, JAMES. The Correspondence of James Boswell with David Garrick, Edmund Burke, and Edmond Malone (ed). London: Heinemann, (1986). 1st ed. (Sm sticker mk ep), else Fine in dj. Reese. $65/£42

BOSWELL, JAMES. The Journal of a Tour to Corsica.... S.C. Roberts (ed). Cambridge, 1923. 1st separate ed. Uncut. VG in cl-backed bds, paper label, spare at end. Cox. $23/£15

BOSWELL, JAMES. The Journal of a Tour to the Hebrides with Samuel Johnson. Avon, CT: LEC, 1974. One of 2000 numbered. 10 color plts. Teg. 1/2 crushed levant, gilt spine, raised bands. Mint in bd slipcase. Argosy. $125/£80

BOSWELL, JAMES. The Journal of a Tour to the Hebrides, with Samuel Johnson, LL.D. London: T. Cadell & W. Davies, Strand, 1813. 6th ed. Engr frontis port, 460pp. Full speckled calf, black leather label w/gilt. (Corners lt bumped), else Very Nice. Turtle Island. $350/£224

BOSWELL, JAMES. Letters of James Boswell to the Rev. W. J. Temple. London: Sidgwick & Jackson, 1908. 1st ed thus. Port. VG (sm nick joint). Reese. $35/£22

BOSWELL, JAMES. Letters of James Boswell. C. B. Tinker (ed). Oxford, 1924. 1st ed. 2 vols. (Owner stamp; bumped, rubbed, dknd.) King. $65/£42

BOSWELL, JAMES. The Life of Samuel Johnson, LL.D. Boston/Salem: W. Andrews & L. Blake/Cushing & Appleton, 1807. 1st Amer ed. 3 vols. Frontis port vol 1, 500; 512; 543pp (lt foxing). Uncut. Contemp marbled bds (spines worn, 1 vol broken, cvrs becoming detached), orig ptd paper labels. VG. M & S. $325/£208

BOSWELL, JAMES. The Life of Samuel Johnson, LL.D.... Alexander Chalmers (ed). London: T. Cadell (et al), 1822. 9th ed. 4 vols. Frontis port vol 1. Very Nice (paper on spines of vols 1, 4 imperfect; chip vol 2 spine). Reese. $350/£224

BOSWELL, JAMES. The Life of Samuel Johnson. Henry Baldwin for Charles Dilly, 1791. 1st ed, 1st state vol 1 w/misprint 'gve' for 'give' on S4r, all 7 cancels listed by Pottle. 2 vols. 4to. Engr frontis port after Reynolds, round robin and plt showing facs of Johnson's hand vol 2, w/o initial blank vol 2. (Foxing to margins of sigs Uu-Zz vol 1.) Old panelled tree and mottled calf (rebacked in morocco gilt, repairs to corners, new eps w/initials and # of restorer). Sotheby's*. $4,126/£2,645

BOSWELL, JAMES. The Life of Samuel Johnson. London: Henry Baldwin for Charles Dilly, 1791. 1st ed. Port (lt foxed), 2 plts. Complete w/blanks, 7 cancels; leaf S4r (vol1, p135) in 2nd state having word 'give' correctly. (Lt spotting, bkpl.) Contemp full gilt-paneled calf (fr cvr vol 1 soiled, affected by mildew, joints, extrems scuffed), morocco labels. Freeman*. $1,400/£897

BOSWELL, JAMES. The Life of Samuel Johnson. London: John Murray, 1839. New ed. 10 vols. Sm 8vo. Marbled eps, ribbon markers. Teg. Fine grained blue 1/4 morocco, marbled bds, spines gilt. NF (sl rubbed, bkpls; tears to few frontispieces, 1/2 titles). Antic Hay. $500/£321

BOSWELL, JAMES. The Life of Samuel Johnson.... London: John Murray, 1839. 5 vols. 3/4 navy blue polished calf, gilt spines, red leather labels. Fine. Appelfeld. $375/£240

BOSWELL, JAMES. Private Papers from Malahide Castle, in the Collection of Lt. Col. Ralph H. Isham. NY, 1928-34. 1st ed. One of 570. Vols 1-18 (of 21; lacks 3 supplementary vols). (Spines faded.) Slipcases (sm piece missing top panel vols 1, 4). Swann*. $747/£479

BOSWELL, ROBERT. Dancing in the Movies. Iowa City: Univ of IA, (1986). 1st ed, 1st bk. As New in dj. Captain's Bookshelf. $150/£96

BOSWORTH, CLARENCE. Breeding. NY: Derrydale, 1939. Ltd to 1250. VG. October Farm. $60/£38

Botanical Keepsake; An Arrangement of British Plants. London, 1846. x,233,iipp; 28 hand-colored plts. (Cl sl faded; neatly rebacked, preserving spine.) Henly. $153/£98

Botanist's Calendar and Pocket Flora. London: B&J White, 1797. 2 vols. Engr tp, vi,264; 266-396+94pp index. Orig bds restored, reinforced paper spine. Quest. $195/£125

BOTCHER, A. Cranes, Their Construction, Mechanical Equipment and Working. A. Tolhausen (trans). 1908. 63 plts, 41 tables. VG in later cl. Whitehart. $101/£65

BOTKIN, B. A. (ed). Lay My Burden Down. Chicago: Univ of Chicago, (1945). 1st ed. Fine in VG- dj (price-clipped, 2 chips, external tape repairs). Between The Covers. $65/£42

BOTTOMLEY, WILLIAM LAWRENCE. Spanish Details. NY: William Helburn, 1924. 1st ed. Color frontis. Red cl, gilt. (Sl flecking to cvrs), o/w Fine. House. $220/£141

BOTTRALL, RONALD. The Palisades of Fear. London: Editions Poetry, 1949. 1st Eng ed. Fine in Superb dj (neatly repaired tear). *Clearwater.* $55/£35

BOUBAT, EDOUARD. Woman. NY: Braziller, 1972. 1st ed. Signed. 64 full-pg plts. VG+ in VG dj. *Smith.* $175/£112

BOUCHARD, CHARLES. Lectures on Auto-Intoxication in Disease, or Self-Poisoning of the Individual. Phila, 1907. 2nd ed. Good (lacks fep; worn). *Doctor's Library.* $50/£32

BOUCHER, ANTHONY. The Case of the Baker Street Irregulars. NY, 1940. 1st ed. NF in VG dj (rubbed, chipped). *Mcclintock.* $95/£61

BOUCHER, JOHN NEWTON. William Kelly: A True History of the So-Called Bessemer Process. Greensburg, PA: The Author, 1924. 1st ed. Port. (Ex-lib, bkpl, cardpocket; spine #, cl lt soiled), else Good. *Brown.* $15/£10

BOUCHER, JONATHAN. Reminiscences of an American Loyalist 1738-1739. Boston/NY: Houghton Mifflin, 1925. 1st ed. Ltd to 575. NF. Howes B640. *Mcgowan.* $95/£61

BOUCHER, JONATHAN. A View of the Causes and Consequences of the American Revolution. London, 1797. 1st ed. Complete w/half-title. Uncut. (ink inscrip, sl dampstaining back matter, new eps.) Orig bds (rebacked, worn). *Freeman*.* $140/£90

BOUCHETTE, JOSEPH. A Topographical Description of the Province of Lower Canada.... London: W. Faden, 1815. 1st ed. Frontis port, 7 maps, 2 charts (calls for 17 plts). White paper-cvrd bds (rebound), patterned paper spine. *Metropolitan*.* $143/£92

BOUDRYE, LOUIS NAPOLEON. Historic Records of the Fifth New York Cavalry, First Ira Harris Guard. Albany, NY: S.R. Gray, 1865. 1st ed. 358pp. VG (2 plts sl jutting out; extrems worn). *Mcgowan.* $225/£144

BOUGHTON, ALICE. Photographing the Famous. NY: Avondale, (1928). 1st Amer ed. 28 full-pg photos. Contents NF (cvrs rubbed, sl soiled). *Polyanthos.* $95/£61

BOULE, M. and H. V. VALLOIS. Fossil Men. NY: Dryden, 1957. 1st ed. Pict cl. VG. *Mikesh.* $30/£19

BOULENGER, G. A. The Tailless Batrachians of Europe. London: Ray Soc, 1897-1898. 1st ed. 2 vols. 376pp + ads; 24 plts, 124 engrs, 6 fldg maps. Full contemp reptile leather. (Lacks 1/2-titles, p.i-iv vol 2), else VG+. *Mikesh.* $200/£128

BOULGER, G. S. Familiar Trees. First (and Second) Series. London: (Cassell, 1885-88.) 1st ed. 2 vols. 80 chromolithos. Aeg. Pub's gray cl, gilt dec. Brilliant. *Book Block.* $325/£208

BOULTON, DAVID (ed). Voices from the Crowd Against the H Bomb. Peter Owen, 1964. 1st ed. VG in dj. *Words Etc.* $23/£15

BOULTON, R. Traveling with the Birds, a Book on Bird Migration. Chicago/NY, 1933. 1st ed. (Cl rubbed.) *Maggs.* $37/£24

BOULTON, WILLIAM B. Sir Joshua Reynolds P.R.A. London, 1905. 1st ed. (Lt spotted.) Marbled eps; teg. 1/2 calf, cl bds, gilt spine, leather label. *Edwards.* $31/£20

BOUQUET, A. C. European Brasses. Batsford, 1967. 1st ed. 32 plts. (Ex-lib, ink stamp verso tp, label removed fep; bds lt soiled, sl bumped, #s.) *Edwards.* $55/£35

BOURJAILY, VANCE. Country Matters: Collected Reports from the Fields of Iowa and Other Places. NY: Dial, 1973. 1st ed. Fine in dj (sl rubbing). *Between The Covers.* $50/£32

BOURJAILY, VANCE. The End of My Life. NY: Scribner, 1947. 1st bk. Good+ in dj (chipped, lt soiled). *Scribe's Perch*.* $25/£16

BOURJAILY, VANCE. The Girl in the Abstract Bed. NY: Tiber, (1954). 1st ed. One of 1500 numbered. Cardbd portfolio (sl soiled). *Black Sun.* $100/£64

BOURJAILY, VANCE. The Man Who Knew Kennedy. (NY, 1967.) 1st ed. VG in dj. *Argosy.* $30/£19

BOURKE, JOHN G. An Apache Campaign in the Sierra Madre. NY: Scribner, (1958). Rpt. Fine in dj (lt worn). *Argonaut.* $35/£22

BOURKE, JOHN G. On the Border with Crook. NY, (1891). 1st ed. 491pp. Pict cvr. VG (2 pp torn out, replaced w/typed pp; lacks 6 plts, of 7). *Pratt.* $125/£80

BOURKE, JOHN. Baroque Churches of Central Europe. Faber & Faber, 1958. 1st ed. Color frontis. (Eps sl browned.) Dj (sl ragged, spine lt faded). *Edwards.* $31/£20

BOURKE, THOMAS. A Concise History of the Moors in Spain. London: F.C. & J. Rivington/J. Hatchard, 1811. 1st ed. xlii,278pp; complete w/half-title. Old calf-backed blue bds (rubbed, rebacked in coarse blue cl, old calf backstrip laid down). *Karmiole.* $150/£96

BOURKE-WHITE, MARGARET. Eyes on Russia. NY: S&S, 1931. 1st ed. 40 plts (1 w/sl soiled margins). VG (sl worn, soiled; lacks dj). *Waverly*.* $132/£85

BOURKE-WHITE, MARGARET. Portrait of Myself. NY: S&S, 1963. VG in spiral-bound ptd wrappers (spiral split, wrappers lt soiled). *Cahan.* $20/£13

BOURKE-WHITE, MARGARET. Shooting the Russian War. NY: S&S, 1942. 1st ed, 3rd ptg. (Sl bumped), else VG in dj (worn, fragmented). *Cahan.* $25/£16

BOURKE-WHITE, MARGARET. Shooting the Russian War. NY: S&S, 1942. 1st ed. Fine in dj (lt frayed). *Reese.* $75/£48

BOURLIERE, F. Mammals of the World: Their Life and Habits. NY: Knopf, 1955. 1st ed. Dec eps. Pict cl. NF in VG dj. *Mikesh.* $25/£16

BOURNE, E. E. The History of Wells and Kennebunk. Portland, 1875. 797pp; 5 ports & plts. Good. *Scribe's Perch*.* $38/£24

BOURNE, GEORGE. Change in the Village. London, 1912. 1st ed. (Feps lt browned; spine sl discolored, rubbed.) *Edwards.* $39/£25

BOURNE, GEORGE. Memoirs of a Surrey Labourer. London, 1907. 1st ed. (1st, last ll lt foxed; spine sl chipped, discolored.) *Edwards.* $39/£25

BOURNE, GEORGE. William Smith. London, 1920. 1st ed. (Edges lt foxed; spine sl faded, frayed.) *Edwards.* $39/£25

BOURNE, GILBERT C. A Text-Book of Oarsmanship. London: OUP, 1925. 1st ed. Blue cl, gilt device fr cvr. (Spine faded), else NF. *Cummins.* $250/£160

BOURNE, JOHN A. Treatise on the Steam Engine in Its Various Applications.... 1862. 6th ed. x,(1),495pp; 36 plts (of 37). Orig 3/4 calf. (Very worn, spine stripped; piece cut out of fep), o/w VG. *Whitehart.* $140/£90

BOURNE, RANDOLPH. Youth and Life. Boston: Houghton Mifflin, 1913. 1st ed, 1st bk. Teg. Grn cl, gilt. NF (spine sl dknd). *Reese.* $150/£96

BOUSQUET, JACQUES. Mannerism. The Painting and Style of the Late Renaissance. NY, 1964. Good. *Washton.* $125/£80

BOUTCHER, WILLIAM. A Treatise on Forest-Trees. Edinburgh, 1775. 1/2 straight-grained grn morocco (sl rubbed). Sound (lacks engr frontis; notes eps). *Petersfield.* $218/£140

BOUTELL, CHARLES. English Heraldry. London/NY, 1871. 2nd ed. xix,347pp (prelims, tp sl spotted, bkpl). Marbled eps, edges. 1/2 calf, marbled bds, dec gilt spine, raised bands. *Edwards.* $47/£30

BOUTELL, CHARLES. Monumental Brasses and Slabs. London, 1847. xv,235pp + (vi)ads (lt spotting). Gilt device upper bd. (Edges, spine faded; upper hinge sl tender; upper joint sl split; sl bumped.) *Edwards.* $78/£50

BOUTON, NATHANIEL. The History of Concord, N.H. Concord, 1856. 1st ed. 786pp, VG map. (Orig cvr taped at joints, spine ends), o/w VG. *New Hampshire**. $45/£29

BOUTWELL, GEORGE S. Reminiscences of Sixty Years in Public Affairs. NY, 1902. 1st ed. 2 vols. Leather spine labels. *Ginsberg.* $75/£48

BOUVIER, JACQUELINE and LEE BOUVIER. One Special Summer. NY: Delacorte, 1974. 1st ed. One of 500 numbered, signed by both. Folio. Fine in pub's slipcase (lt sunned). *Unger.* $850/£545

BOVA, BEN (ed). The Science Fiction Hall of Fame. Volume 2, Parts A and B. NY: Doubleday, (1973). 1st eds. 2 vols. Djs. *Swann**. $46/£29

BOVILL, E. W. The Golden Trade of the Moors. OUP, 1958. 1st ed. 8 maps (1 fldg). Dj (sl rubbed). *Edwards.* $55/£35

BOVINI, GIUSEPPE. Ravenna Mosaics.... Greenwich, CT: NYGS, (1956). Dj (lt worn); slipcase (browned). *Kane**. $35/£22

BOWDEN, B. V. (ed). Faster Than Thought...Digital Computing Machines. London: Isaac Pitman, (1957). 1st ed, 3rd ptg. Frontis, 18 plts, 2 fldg charts. Fine in dj. *Glaser.* $125/£80

BOWDEN, CHARLES. Red Line. NY: Norton, (1989). 1st ed. Signed. Fine in dj. *Between The Covers.* $50/£32

BOWDITCH, C. P. (ed). Mexican and Central American Antiquities, Calendar Systems, and History. GPO, 1904. 49 full-pg plts. Good- (hinge cracks). *Scribe's Perch**. $42/£27

BOWDITCH, N. I. A History of the Massachusetts General Hospital.... Boston: Ptd by the Trustees from Bowditch Fund, 1872. 2nd ed. Presentation bkpl from Trustees. Frontis, 734pp. Grn cl (sl worn). VG + . *Lucas.* $150/£96

BOWDITCH, N. I. Memoir of Nathaniel Bowditch. Boston: Little, Brown, 1840. 2nd ed. 172pp; 2 ports. Internally VG (cvrs faded). *Parmer.* $250/£160

BOWDITCH, NATHANIEL. The New American Practical Navigator. Newburyport: Edmund M. Blunt, 1802. 1st ed. Lg fldg frontis map in facs, 592pp + 10pp ads (browned, worn, foxed, sl stains, tp lacks corner, some ll dog-eared, new blanks); 7 b/w copper plts, charts (foxed). Recent full calf, raised bands, gilt, black spine label. Cvrs Fine. Recent clamshell leather/bd box. Howes B657. *Baltimore**. $350/£224

BOWDITCH, NATHANIEL. The New American Practical Navigator.... NY: E. & G.W. Blunt, 1846. (xvi),318,(2 blank),451,(1 blank, 2 ads)pp; 13 charts, plts. Orig calf, red leather label. (Dampstaining inner margin; ink stain bottom inner corner; ad labels.) *Lefkowicz.* $250/£160

BOWDITCH, NATHANIEL. Report of the Board of Trustees of the Massachusetts General Hospital...January 26, 1848. Boston: John Wilson, 1848. Engr frontis, 72pp. Mod 1/4 blue morocco, paper bds. (Lt foxing), o/w VG. *Goodrich.* $595/£381

BOWEN, ELIZABETH. Bowen's Court. NY: Knopf, 1942. 1st Amer ed. VF in dj. *Hermitage.* $45/£29

BOWEN, ELIZABETH. Encounters: Early Stories. London: Sidgwick & Jackson, 1949. 1st ed thus. NF in dj (rubbed). *Antic Hay.* $20/£13

BOWEN, ELIZABETH. Eva Trout. London: Cape, 1969. 1st Eng ed. VG in dj. *Hollett.* $31/£20

BOWEN, ELIZABETH. The Hotel. NY: Lincoln Mac Veagh/Dial, 1928. 1st ed. Fine in dj (minor nicks edges). *Associates.* $40/£26

BOWEN, ELIZABETH. A Time in Rome. London, 1960. 1st Eng ed. Nice (spine foot sl damaged, sl bumped) in dj. *Clearwater.* $31/£20

BOWEN, ELIZABETH. A World of Love. London: Jonathan Cape, (1955). 1st Eng ed. Fine in dj (sl soiled, sl sunned). *Antic Hay.* $35/£22

BOWEN, FRANK C. The Golden Age of Sail. London: Halton & Truscott Smith, 1925. 1st ed. One of 1500 numbered. Frontis, 91 full-pg illus, 12 tipped-in color plts. Gilt-lettered dec blue cl. (Fep fore-edge neatly re-inforced), else Fine. *Argonaut.* $175/£112

BOWEN, FRANK C. Sailing Ships of the London River. London: Sampson et al, n.d. (ca 1925). (Sl soil; wear, edges sl frayed.) *Freeman**. $15/£10

BOWEN, N. L. The Evolution of the Igneous Rocks. Princeton, 1928. 1st ed. Fine. *Henly.* $50/£32

BOWEN, PETER. Kelly Blue. NY: Crown, 1991. 1st ed. (Rmdr mk pg edge tops), o/w Fine in dj. *Mordida.* $40/£26

BOWEN, PETER. Yellowstone Kelly. Ottawa, IL: Jameson, 1987. 1st ed. VF in dj. *Mordida.* $45/£29

BOWEN, ROBERT SIDNEY. Make Mine Murder. NY: Checkerbooks, (1949). Good (leaves aging) in pict wrappers (lt wear, bkst stamp inside). *Gravesend.* $25/£16

BOWEN, ROBERT SIDNEY. Red Randall's One-Man War. G&D, 1946. 5x7.5. 215pp (acidic). VG + (shelfworn) in dj (chipped). *My Bookhouse.* $30/£19

BOWER, B. M. Dark Horse. Little, Brown, 1931. 1st ed. Fine in dj (spine ends badly clipped). *Authors Of West.* $30/£19

BOWER, B. M. The Heritage of the Sioux. Boston: Little, Brown, (1916). 1st ed. Fine (bkpl) in NF dj (edge-torn). *Unger.* $250/£160

BOWER, DONALD E. Fred Rosenstock, a Legend in Books and Art. Flagstaff, 1976. 1st ed. Frontis port. Fine in Fine dj. *Turpen.* $48/£31

BOWER, WARD T. Alaska Fishery and Fur-Seal Industries: 1943. Washington: GPO, 1944. Stencilled errata laid in. (Sl faded), else Fine in gray ptd wraps. *Parmer.* $27/£17

BOWES, JAMES. Japanese Marks and Seals. London: Henry Sotheran, 1882. Color frontis, ix,379pp; dbl-pg map. (Bkpl.) Lib buckram gilt. *Hollett.* $281/£180

BOWIE, THEODORE and DIETER THIMME (eds). The Carrey Drawings of the Parthenon Sculptures. Bloomington: IN Univ, (1971). Good. *Archaeologia.* $200/£128

BOWLES, JANE. The Collected Works of Jane Bowles. NY: FSG, (1966). 1st ed. Fine in dj. *Captain's Bookshelf.* $75/£48

BOWLES, JANE. In the Summer House. NY, 1954. 1st Amer ed. Fine (spine top sl rubbed) in dj (spine lt sunned). *Polyanthos.* $95/£61

BOWLES, JANE. Plain Pleasures. London: Peter Owen, (1966). 1st ed. Fine in dj (lt rubbed, clipped, pub's price increase label on flap). *Reese.* $40/£26

BOWLES, PAUL. Collected Stories 1939-1976. Santa Barbara, CA: Black Sparrow, 1979. One of 300 numbered, signed. Fine in Fine clear acetate dj. *Lenz.* $150/£96

BOWLES, PAUL. Let It Come Down. London: Lehmann, 1952. 1st Eng ed. Nice (fore-edges very foxed, title-hinge tender) in Attractive dj (foxed). *Clearwater.* $86/£55

BOWLES, PAUL. Let It Come Down. NY, 1952. 1st ed. VG in VG dj (internally strengthened). *Warren.* $50/£32

BOWLES, PAUL. A Little Stone. London: John Lehmann, (1950). 1st ed, 1st issue in lt grn cl. Fine in dj (lt worn, price-clipped). *Hermitage.* $200/£128

BOWLES, PAUL. Midnight Mass. Santa Barbara: Black Sparrow, 1981. 1st ed. One of 350 signed. Ptd paper bds, cl spine. Fine. *Turtle Island.* $125/£80

BOWLES, PAUL. The Sheltering Sky. London: John Lehmann, 1949. 1st UK ed. (Fore-edge sl spotted; cl sl sunned at extrems), o/w VG in dj (price-clipped; lt worn; chipped). *Moorhouse*. $94/£60

BOWLES, PAUL. The Spider's House. Random House, 1955. 1st ed. VG+ in VG dj (spine ends chipped). *Certo*. $45/£29

BOWLES, PAUL. Things Gone and Things Still Here. Santa Barbara: Black Sparrow, 1977. 1st ed. Ltd to 250 signed. Cl-backed dec bds. As New in acetate dj. *Jaffe*. $100/£64

BOWLES, PAUL. Up Above the World. NY: S&S, (1966). 1st ed. Fine in dj (sm tear spine head). *Captain's Bookshelf*. $100/£64

BOWLES, PAUL. Without Stopping. NY, 1972. 1st ed. NF in NF dj (2 nearly invisible tape repairs inside). *Warren*. $40/£26

BOWLES, PAUL. Yallah. NY: McDowell, Obolensky, (1957). 1st ed in English; ptd in Switzerland. (Crease fep), o/w NF in VG dj (sm chips, wrinkles, laminate peeled away). *Reese*. $200/£128

BOWLES, PAUL. Yallah. NY, 1957. 1st ed. NF in VG dj. *Warren*. $150/£96

BOWLES, SAMUEL. Across the Continent.... Springfield, MA, 1865. 1st ed, 1st issue. 452pp; fldg map. *Ginsberg*. $125/£80

BOWLES, SAMUEL. Across the Continent: A Summer's Journey...with Speaker Colfax. Springfield: Samuel Bowles, 1866. 2nd ed, incl add'l chapter. (2),xx,452,6pp; lg fldg hand-colored map. Mod 1/2 brn calf, bds (rebound). Fine. *Harrington*. $110/£71

BOWLES, SAMUEL. Our New West. Hartford: Hartford, 1869. 1st ed. Frontis port, map, 12 plts. Gray cl (rebound), gilt-lettered red leather spine label. Fine. *Argonaut*. $75/£48

BOWLKER, CHARLES. The Art of Angling; or Complete Fly-Fisher.... Birmingham: Swinney & Hawkins, (1785). 3rd ed. Engr frontis. (Prelims starting; foxing.) 19th-cent 3/4 brn calf. VG. *Cummins*. $250/£160

BOWMAN, J. N. and ROBERT F. HEIZER. Anza and the Northwest Frontier of New Spain. Highland Park: Southwest Museum, 1967. 1st ed. Frontis port, 2 maps. Gilt-lettered grn cl. Fine. *Argonaut*. $45/£29

BOWNAS, SAMUEL and JOHN RICHARDSON. The Journals of the Lives and Travels of.... Phila: William Dunlap, 1759. 1st Amer ed. Complete w/3 tps (1st chipped, not affecting text, ink sigs; dampstaining). Contemp sheep (rubbed). Howes B668. *Freeman**. $130/£83

BOWNAS, SAMUEL. An Account of the Life, Travels, and Christian Experiences...of Samuel Bownas. London: Ptd by Luke Hinde, 1756. 1st ed. viii,3-198,(2)pp (incl ad leaf at back). Contemp calf (rubbed, extrems worn, nicked). Internally VF (inscrip, 1 leaf stained, lt creasing). Howes B668. *Pirages*. $175/£112

BOWRA, C. M. Edith Sitwell. Monaco: Lyrebird, 1947. 1st ed. Port. (Spine toe split), else VG in ptd wrappers. *Reese*. $20/£13

BOX, EDGAR. (Pseud of Gore Vidal.) Death Before Bedtime. NY: Dutton, 1953. 1st ed. Fine in VG dj (spine ends nicked, worn; corners worn, sm closed tears). *Mordida*. $100/£64

BOX, EDGAR. (Pseud of Gore Vidal.) Death Likes It Hot. NY: Dutton, (1954). 1st ed. VG+ in VG+ dj (spine head chipped). *Unger*. $225/£144

Boyd's Philadelphia Blue Book. 1906. (Phila, 1906.) Blue cl (edgeworn, lt soiled, sl shaken), gilt. *Freeman**. $50/£32

BOYD, A. W. A Country Parish. London: Collins, 1951. 1st ed. VG in dj (sl dknd). *Cox*. $70/£45

BOYD, ARTHUR. Etchings and Lithographs. Lund Humphries, 1971. 1st ed. 6 lithos. Fine in dj (sl soiled). *Whittle*. $23/£15

BOYD, JOYCE. My Farm in Lion Country. London, 1933. Good (lt foxing, ex-lib; cvrs rubbed). *Grayling*. $55/£35

BOYD, LAWRENCE VISSCHER. Successful Homes by.... Phila, (1926). Signed, inscribed. (Lt worn, soiled.) *Freeman**. $140/£90

BOYD, THOMAS. Mad Anthony Wayne. NY: Scribner, 1929. #311/530 slipcased, signed. Frontis port. Yellow bds, blue cl backstrip. Fine in VG+ slipcase (worn). *Harrington*. $75/£48

BOYD, THOMAS. Through the Wheat. NY, 1927. 1st Amer ed, 1st bk. Fine (spine sl sunned). *Polyanthos*. $50/£32

BOYD, WILLIAM. School Ties. Penguin, 1985. Simultaneous pb 1st ed. Fine. *Williams*. $19/£12

BOYD, WILLIAM. A Textbook of Pathology. Phila, 1941. 3rd ed. VF (Sm water stain pp, underlining) in dj. *Doctor's Library*. $35/£22

BOYD, WILLIAM. A Textbook of Pathology: An Introduction to Medicine. Phila, 1947. 5th ed. 30 color plts. Red cl bds (extrems sl worn; fr inner hinge cracked). VG. *Doctor's Library*. $60/£38

BOYENSEN, HJALMAR HJORTH. A Commentary on the Works of Henrik Ibsen. NY: Macmillan, 1894. 1st Amer ed. Inscribed. VG. *Dramatis Personae*. $40/£26

BOYER, ALEXIS. The Lectures of Boyer upon Diseases of the Bones.... A. Richearand (comp). M. Farrell (trans). Phila, 1805. 1st Amer ed. 2 vols in 1. 368pp (upper section fep torn away, sig), 7 engr plts (1 dbl); separate 1/2-title vol 2. Contemp calf. *Argosy*. $275/£176

BOYKIN, EDWARD. Beefsteak Raid. NY, (1960). 1st ed. VG+ in dj (worn). *Pratt*. $45/£29

BOYKIN, R. M. Captain Alexander Hamilton Boykin. NY: Privately ptd, 1942. Good+. *Scribe's Perch**. $50/£32

BOYLE, FREDERICK. The Culture of Greenhouse Orchids Old System and New. London, 1902. 1st ed. 3 color plts. Teg. Red cl, gilt. VG (ex-lib, spine # removed). *Price*. $95/£61

BOYLE, JOHN. Remarks on the Life and Writings of Dr., Jonathan Swift. London, 1752. 3rd ed. Engr frontis port, 214,4pp+2pp ads (tanned, sl foxed; pp211-end detached but present; index leaf torn). Contemp full leather. Poor. *Scribe's Perch**. $40/£26

BOYLE, KAY. Avalanche. NY: S&S, 1944. 1st ed. NF in VG dj (nicked, spine sl tanned). *Reese*. $35/£22

BOYLE, KAY. Death of a Man. NY: Harcourt, 1936. 1st ed. Fine (sl sunned) in NF dj (sl dknd; chips). *Beasley*. $65/£42

BOYLE, KAY. The Seagull on the Step. NY: Knopf, 1955. 1st ed. (Ep gutters sl foxed), else VG in dj (edgeworn). *Reese*. $30/£19

BOYLE, T. CORAGHESSAN. Budding Prospects. NY: Viking, (1984). Fine in dj. *Between The Covers*. $100/£64

BOYLE, T. CORAGHESSAN. Budding Prospects. NY: Viking, 1984. 1st ed. Fine (sl rubbed) in NF dj (edge tears). *Beasley*. $50/£32

BOYLE, T. CORAGHESSAN. Descent of Man. London, 1980. 1st ed, 1st bk. Fine in dj. *Polyanthos*. $75/£48

BOYLE, T. CORAGHESSAN. East Is East. NY: Viking, (1990). 1st ed. Fine in dj. *Turtle Island*. $30/£19

BOYLE, T. CORAGHESSAN. If the River Was Whiskey. NY, 1989. 1st ed. Signed. Fine in NF dj. *Warren*. $75/£48

BOYLE, T. CORAGHESSAN. The Road to Wellville. NY: Viking, (1993). 1st ed. Signed. VF in VF dj. *Unger.* $50/£32

BOYLE, T. CORAGHESSAN. Water Music. Boston: Little, Brown, 1981. 1st ed. Fine in dj. *Lame Duck.* $125/£80

BOYLE, T. CORAGHESSAN. World's End. Macmillan, 1987. 1st UK ed. NF in dj. *Williams.* $31/£20

BOYNTON, CHARLES B. The History of the Navy During the Rebellion. NY: D. Appleton, 1867-68. 1st ed. 2 vols. 576; 579,(1)pp,(8, ads) (name on tps). 9 steel-engr ports, steel-engr plt, 14 wood-engr plts, 10 full-pg tinted lithos. Gilt-lettered dec grn cl (name; corners lt worn). Fine. *Argonaut.* $300/£192

BOYNTON, M. F. (ed). Louis Agassiz Fuertes: His Life Briefly Told and His Correspondence Edited. NY: OUP, 1956. 1st ed. 16 plts. VG + in Fair dj. *Mikesh.* $40/£26

BOZ (ed). (Pseud of Charles Dickens.) Memoirs of Joseph Grimaldi. Routledge, 1853. New ed. George Cruikshank (illus). Pub's cat. Orig cl. (Rebacked, orig backstrip relaid, corners rubbed.) Good. *Tiger.* $41/£26

BOZ (ed). (Pseud of Charles Dickens.) Memoirs of Joseph Grimaldi. Charles Whitehead (rev). Richard Bentley, 1846. 2nd ed (1st ptg of Whitehead's revisions). Frontis port (lt browned), xviii,211pp; 10 plts (lt spotting) by George Cruikshank. Good in later 19th cent 1/2 crimson calf, backstrip gilt, morocco label, marbled edges. *Cox.* $187/£120

BOZ (ed). (Pseud of Charles Dickens.) The Pic Nic Papers. Henry Colburn, 1841. George Cruikshank, Phiz (H.K. Browne) & E. J. Hamerton (illus). 3 vols. Pub's cat vol II dated May 1841, pub's ads vol III. Orig cl. Good (plts spotted, new eps; rebacked, orig backstrips relaid, corners rubbed). *Tiger.* $468/£300

BOZ. (Pseud of Charles Dickens.) Oliver Twist. Richard Bentley, 1838. 1st issue of this scarce title, complete w/fire-side plt in vol 3. 3 vols. Fine set (foxed, few pp sl creased) in Attractive mod 1/4 leather, marbled bds, red leather labels, gilt. *Williams.* $1,396/£895

BOZMAN, JOHN LEEDS. A Sketch of the History of Maryland During the Three First Years After Its Settlement. Balt, 1811. 1st ed. Port (offsetting on title). Contemp full tree calf (extrems rubbed), red leather label. Howes B680. *Freeman*.* $40/£26

BRABY, DOROTHEA. The Way of Wood Engraving. London: The Studio, 1953. 1st ed. How to Do It series #46. VG in dj (lt rubbed, stained). *Michael Taylor.* $31/£20

BRACKEN, THOMAS. Musings in Maoriland. Dunedin, New Zealand: Keirle, 1890. viii,359pp; 20 plts. Gilt-pict cl. VG. *Adelson.* $65/£42

BRACKENRIDGE, H. M. History of the Western Insurrection in Western Pennsylvania.... Pittsburgh: W.S. Haven, 1859. 336pp. Grn cl (soiled, rubbed). Nice interior. Howes B685. *Bohling.* $150/£96

BRACKENRIDGE, H. M. History of the Western Insurrection in Western Pennsylvania...1794. Pittsburgh, 1859. 1st ed. (Lacks fep; spine mostly gone, cvrs detached.) Howes B685. *Freeman*.* $30/£19

BRACKENRIDGE, H. M. Recollections of Persons and Places in the West. Phila, (1834). 1st ed. 244pp. Orig cl, new leather back. Howes B687. *M & S.* $225/£144

BRACKENRIDGE, HUGH HENRY and PHILIP FRENEAU. Father Bombo's Pilgrimage to Mecca. (Princeton): Princeton Univ Library, (1975). 1st complete ptg. Comp slip laid in. Cl, paper-cvrd bds. Fine in unptd glassine dj, as issued. *Between The Covers.* $45/£29

BRACKETT, ALBERT G. History of the United States Cavalry.... NY, 1865. 1st ed. 337,(2)pp (lacks fep). Howes B692. *Ginsberg.* $250/£160

BRACKETT, LEIGH. Stranger at Home. S&S, 1946. 1st ed. (Lt bumped), else Fine in dj (sm chip rear). *Aronovitz.* $45/£29

BRACKETT, OLIVER (ed). An Encyclopaedia of English Furniture. London, 1927. 310 plts. VG. *Argosy.* $75/£48

BRACKETT, OLIVER. English Furniture Illustrated. London: Spring Books, n.d. (c. 1950). 2nd ed. 240 plts. VG. *Waverly*.* $22/£14

BRACKETT, OLIVER. English Furniture Illustrated. H. Clifford Smith (ed). London: Ernest Benn, 1950. 240 plts. Fine in dj. *Hollett.* $117/£75

BRADBURY, FREDERICK. History of Old Sheffield Plate. London: Macmillan, 1912. 1st ed. Frontis. (Lib stamps feps, tp verso; prelims sl fingered; spine ends frayed, lower hinge splitting.) *Hollett.* $148/£95

BRADBURY, MALCOLM. Eating People Is Wrong. London, 1959. 1st ed, 1st bk. Nice in dj (sl browned, chipped). *Buckley.* $62/£40

BRADBURY, RAY. Beyond 1984. NY: Targ, 1979. One of 350 signed. Fine in acetate. *Clearwater.* $78/£50

BRADBURY, RAY. Dark Carnival. Sauk City: Arkham House, 1947. 1st ed, 1st bk. NF in dj (2-inch chip spine heel, edgewear). *Captain's Bookshelf.* $300/£192

BRADBURY, RAY. Fahrenheit 451. NY: Ballantine, (1953). 1st ed. Very Nice in pict stiff wrappers (corners sl worn). *Reese.* $65/£42

BRADBURY, RAY. Fahrenheit 451. LEC, 1982. One of 2000 signed by Bradbury and Joseph Mugnaini (illus). 4 color plts (3 dbl-pg fldg). LEC newsletter, warning about binding fragility laid in. Aluminum foil over bds. VF in matching lined pub's slipcase. *Pirages.* $225/£144

BRADBURY, RAY. The Golden Apples of the Sun. Hart-Davis, 1953. 1st UK ed. VG (sm faded patches, 2 sm stamps fep) in dj (sl edgewear, chips, price-clipped). *Williams.* $47/£30

BRADBURY, RAY. The Golden Apples of the Sun. GC: Doubleday, 1953. 1st ed. VG + in dj (lt soiled). *Bernard.* $175/£112

BRADBURY, RAY. The Halloween Tree. Knopf, 1972. 1st ed. Fine in dj. *Madle.* $75/£48

BRADBURY, RAY. I Sing the Body Electric. Knopf, 1969. 1st ed. Blue cl (edges sl faded). VG + in dj (sm creased tear). *Certo.* $48/£31

BRADBURY, RAY. I Sing the Body Electric. NY, 1969. 1st ed. Fine in Fine dj. *Warren.* $75/£48

BRADBURY, RAY. The Machineries of Joy. S&S, 1964. 1st ed. (1-inch tear fep), else NF in NF dj. *Certo.* $45/£29

BRADBURY, RAY. The Machineries of Joy. London: Hart-Davis, 1964. 1st Eng ed. VG in dj. *Hadley.* $70/£45

BRADBURY, RAY. A Medicine for Melancholy. NY, 1959. 1st ed. Dj (sm tape repairs). *Swann*.* $172/£110

BRADBURY, RAY. The October Country. NY, (1955). 1st ed. Inscribed. Dj (worn). *Swann*.* $373/£239

BRADBURY, RAY. The Silver Locusts. London, (1951). 1st British ed. Dj (archival tape reinforcement to edges). *Swann*.* $172/£110

BRADBURY, RAY. Switch on the Night. NY: Pantheon, 1955. 1st ed. Madeleine Geklere (illus). 7 x 8 1/2. 48pp. Pict bds (edgeworn, sl shaken). Good. *Cattermole.* $25/£16

BRADBURY, RAY. The Toynbee Convector. NY: Knopf, 1988. 1st ed. One of 350 numbered, signed. Pict slipcase. *Swann*.* $230/£147

BRADBURY, RAY. The Wonderful Ice Cream Suit and Other Plays. NY: Bantam, 1972. 1st ed. Pb orig. Unread. NF. *Warren.* $40/£26

BRADFIELD, SCOTT. The History of Luminous Motion. London, 1989. 1st ed. Fine in Fine dj. *Smith.* $25/£16

BRADFORD, ALDEN. History of Massachusetts...1620 to 1820. Boston, 1835. 1st ed. 480pp; fldg map. Cl-backed bds, ptd paper label. Very Nice. Howes B697. *M&s.* $125/£80

BRADFORD, CHARLES. The Angler's Guide. Richmond Hill: Nassau, 1908. Red cl. VG + . *Bowman.* $75/£48

BRADFORD, EDWARD and ROBERT LOVETT. A Treatise on Orthopedic Surgery. NY, 1890. 1st ed. 783pp. VG (hinges starting, extrems sl worn, spine chipped, cracked). *Doctor's Library.* $200/£128

BRADFORD, EDWARD E. Life of Admiral of the Fleet Sir Arthur Knyvet Wilson. London, 1923. Frontis port, 5 plts, 2 plans. Dj. *Maggs.* $47/£30

BRADFORD, EDWARD H. and ROBERT W. LOVETT. Treatise on Orthopedic Surgery. NY: William Wood, 1905. 3rd ed. Good (sl shelfworn). *Glaser.* $85/£54

BRADFORD, ERNLE. The Great Siege. London, 1961. 1st ed. Dj (sl rubbed). *Edwards.* $31/£20

BRADFORD, JOHN. Ancient Landscapes. London, 1957. 1st ed. 75 plts. Dj (chipped). *Edwards.* $31/£20

BRADFORD, PERRY. Born with the Blues. NY: Oak, 1965. 1st ed. Pb. NF. *Beasley.* $45/£29

BRADFORD, ROARK. John Henry. NY: Harper, (1931). 1st ed. NF in dj (sl chipped). *Pettler & Lieberman.* $25/£16

BRADFORD, WILLIAM J. A. Notes on the Northwest, or Valley of the Upper Missisippi (sic). NY/London: Wiley & Putnam, 1846. vii,302pp. Nice (foxing, spine ends chipped). Howes B704. *Bohling.* $175/£112

BRADFORD, WILLIAM J. A. Notes on the Northwest, or Valley of the Upper Missisippi (sic).... NY: Wiley & Putnam, 1846. 1st ed. 302pp (lt foxed). Brn cl (sl rubbed overall). VG + . Howes B704. *Harrington.* $200/£128

BRADLEY, A. G. Highways and Byways in South Wales. London, 1903. (1st few leaves sl foxed.) *Petersfield.* $23/£15

BRADLEY, A. G. Highways and Byways in the Lake District. London: Macmillan, 1908. VG. *Hollett.* $31/£20

BRADLEY, CUTHBERT. The Foxhound of the Twentieth Century. London, 1914. 16 color, 16 b/w plts, 10 maps. Buckram-backed cl. (Margins lt browned, bkpl, hinges tender; corners rubbed w/sl cl loss, sl bumped, sl soiled, rubbed.) *Edwards.* $94/£60

BRADLEY, DAVID. South Street. NY, 1975. 1st ed. VG in VG dj (fr panel lacks sm piece, sm tears). *Warren.* $75/£48

BRADLEY, EDITH. The Story of the English Abbeys Told in Counties. Volume 1: The Northern Counties. London: Robert Hale, 1938. 1st ed. Map. VG in dj (edges lt chipped, worn). *Hollett.* $47/£30

BRADLEY, ELIZA. An Authentic Narrative of the Shipwreck and Sufferings of Mrs. Eliza Bradley. NY: Ptd by J.H. Turney, 1832. Fldg frontis (sm tear, sl dknd, fold worn), 108pp (lt foxed); 2-pg plt. Orig ptd blue bds (bumped, soiled, rebacked spine heavily worn). VG. *Blue Mountain.* $125/£80

BRADLEY, J. D. et al. British Tortricoid Moths. London: Ray Soc, 1973-79. 2 vols. 90 plts (45 color). Fine set in dj. *Hollett.* $218/£140

BRADLEY, J. W. A Manual of Illumination on Paper and Vellum. London: Winsor & Newton, 1860. 76pp, 16-pg ad at end, 12 litho illus. Orig wrappers (soiled, lower cvr detached). *Maggs.* $62/£40

BRADLEY, JAMES H. The March of the Montana Column. Norman: Univ of OK, (1961). 1st ed thus. Map. Grey cl. (Bkpl), o/w NF in NF dj. *Harrington.* $85/£54

BRADLEY, JAMES H. The March of the Montana Column.... Edgar I. Stewart (ed). Norman: Univ of OK, (1961). VG in dj. *Lien.* $75/£48

BRADLEY, MARION ZIMMER. The Mists of Avalon. NY, 1982. 1st ed. VG in dj. *Argosy.* $65/£42

BRADLEY, MARION ZIMMER. The Mists of Avalon. NY: Knopf, 1982. 1st ed. Fine in dj. *Captain's Bookshelf.* $100/£64

BRADLEY, MARY H. Caravans and Cannibals. NY/London: Appleton, 1923. 1st ed. Frontis, map. Grn cl. VG. *Terramedia.* $75/£48

BRADLEY, MARY H. On the Gorilla Trail. NY/London: Appleton, 1922. 1st ed. 47 plts. (Sl rubbed), o/w VG. *Worldwide.* $20/£13

BRADLEY, OMAR N. A Soldier's Story. NY, (1951). Signed, inscribed presentation. (Inner fr hinge cracked, cvrs sl soiled), else Good in dj (creased, sl torn). *King.* $100/£64

BRADLEY, VAN ALLEN. The Book Collector's Handbook of Values. 1978-1979. NY: Putnam, (1978). 3rd ed. Fine in dj (worn). *Oak Knoll.* $50/£32

BRADNER, ENOS. Northwest Angling. NY: A.S. Barnes, 1950. 1st ed. Blue-grn cl (top edge faded), gilt. Internally Fine in NF dj. *Biscotti.* $35/£22

BRADSHAW, HAROLD. The Indians of Connecticut. Privately ptd, 1935. 1st ed. VG in wraps. *Oregon.* $25/£16

BRADSTREET, ANNE. The Works of Anne Bradstreet in Prose and Verse. John Harvard Ellis (ed). Charlestown: Abram E. Cutter, 1867. 1st ed thus. One of 350 numbered, initialled by Cutter. 4to. Frontis, lxxvi,434pp, port. Mod 3/4 morocco, marbled bds, gilt. NF. *Reese.* $650/£417

BRADSTREET, ANNE. The Works of Anne Bradstreet. Jeannine Hensley (ed). Cambridge: Belknap/Harvard, 1967. 1st ed thus. Frontis. Fine (inscrip) in VG dj. *Reese.* $35/£22

BRADSTREET, DUDLEY. The Life and Uncommon Adventures. G. S. Dudley (ed). John Hamilton, (1929). Rpt. Facs letter tipped in. (Label, stamps verso tp), o/w Good. *Cox.* $12/£8

BRADY, CYRUS TOWNSEND. Recollections of a Missionary in the Great West. NY: Scribner, 1900. 1st ed. Frontis port. Teg. Blue cl, gilt. Fine. *Harrington.* $55/£35

BRADY, CYRUS TOWNSEND. Secret Service. NY, 1912. 1st ed. Pict cl. (Lt worn), o/w Fine. *Pratt.* $25/£16

BRAGG, BENJAMIN. Surprising Voyage of Captain Bragg, in a Journey to Discover the North Pole.... London: Walker, n.d. (ca 184?). 211pp; plt, fldg map. (Bkpl removed, sm emb lib stamp.) Orig pict cl (hinges chipped). *Ginsberg.* $500/£321

BRAGG, L. The Development of X-Ray Analysis. 1975. (Lib #s to spine), o/w VG in dj (sl torn). *Whitehart.* $39/£25

BRAGG, MELVYN. For Want of a Nail. Secker & Warburg, (1965). 1st ed, 1st bk. Signed, dated (1990). Nice (sl dusty) in dj (sl browned). *Ash.* $70/£45

BRAGG, MELVYN. The Maid of Buttermere. Hodder, 1987. 1st UK ed. Fine in dj. *Williams.* $14/£9

BRAGG, WILLIAM. From the National Gallery Laboratory. London, 1940. 50 plts. Buckram. Fine. *Europa.* $19/£12

BRAHAM, ALLAN. The Architecture of the French Enlightenment. Thames & Hudson, 1980. Dj. *Edwards.* $55/£35

BRAIDER, DONALD. Solitary Star. NY, (1974). 1st ed. Fine in dj (lt worn). *Pratt.* $20/£13

BRAIDWOOD, LINDA. Digging Beyond the Tigris. NY: Henry Schuman, (1953). Dj (tattered). *Archaeologia*. $35/£22

BRAINARD, DAVID L. The Outpost of the Lost. Bessie Rowland James (ed). Indianapolis: Bobbs-Merrill, c. 1929. VG in dj (worn). *High Latitude*. $45/£29

BRAINE, JOHN. The Jealous God. London: Eyre & Spottiswoode, 1964. 1st Eng ed. Paper-cvrd bds. NF in dj (sm tear). *Antic Hay*. $30/£19

BRAINE, JOHN. Life at the Top. London: Eyre & Spottiswoode, 1962. 1st Eng ed. Paper-cvrd bds. NF (eps sl browned) in dj (sl worn). *Antic Hay*. $35/£22

BRAINERD, C. N. My Diary. NY: Egbert, Bourne, 1868. 45pp. Ptd wraps (lt soiled, spine chipped). *Bohling*. $110/£71

BRAITHWAITE, R. The British Moss-Flora. London, 1887-1905. 3 vols. 128 plts. (Foxing, esp ends.) *Henly*. $218/£140

BRAITHWAITE, WILLIAM S. (ed). Anthology of Magazine Verse for 1918 and Year Book of American Poetry. Boston: Small, Maynard, (1918). 1st ed. Teg. Paper labels. (Few bumps extrems), else VG. *Reese*. $35/£22

BRAITHWAITE, WILLIAM S. (ed). The Book of Elizabethan Verse. London: C&W, 1908. 1st (British) ed. Frontis. Gilt full vellum, leather label, pict crest each cvr. (Binder's feps excised; cvrs sl bowed), o/w VG. *Reese*. $65/£42

BRAIVE, MICHEL F. The Era of the Photograph. London: Thames & Hudson, 1966. 1st Eng ed. Fine in pict dj, plain slipcase. *Cahan*. $200/£128

BRAKE, HEZEKIAH. On Two Continents, a Long Life's Experience. Topeka: Crane, 1896. 240pp; 2 ports. Gilt cl (spine ends frayed, some etching; bkpl). VG. Howes B178. *Bohling*. $60/£38

BRAM, JOSEPH. An Analysis of Inca Militarism. NY: J.J. Augustin, 1941. 1st ed. VG. *Cahan*. $40/£26

BRAMAH, ERNEST. The Eyes of Max Carrados. London: Richards, 1923. 1st ed. (Edges rubbed.) Lacks dj. *Metropolitan**. $103/£66

BRAMAH, ERNEST. The Kai Lung Omnibus. London: Philip Allan, 1936. 1st complete ed. (Few spots foreedge.) *Hollett*. $47/£30

BRAMAH, ERNEST. Kai Lung Unrolls His Mat. GC, 1928. 1st ed. (Pict bd cvr rubbed.) Interior Good. *Mcclintock*. $20/£13

BRAMAH, ERNEST. Kai Lung's Golden Hours. NY, (1923). 1st ed. Good. *Mcclintock*. $20/£13

BRAMAH, ERNEST. Kai Lung's Golden Hours. London, 1924. 1st ed. One of 250. Signed. Cl-backed bds, grn leather spine label, gilt. *Kane**. $95/£61

BRAMAH, ERNEST. Kai Lung's Golden Hours. London: Grant Richards, 1929. 1st ed. #46/250 signed. Fine in dj (lt rubbed). *Hermitage*. $275/£176

BRAMAH, ERNEST. The Specimen Case. NY: Doran, 1925. 1st ed. (Edges rubbed.) *Metropolitan**. $23/£15

BRAMAH, ERNEST. The Wallet of Kai Lung. London: Grant Richards, 1900. 1st UK ed, 1st issue in lt grn cl measuring 1.5 inches thick. NF in pict bds (spine sl worn). *Williams*. $390/£250

BRANCH, E. DOUGLAS. The Cowboy and His Interpreters. NY: D. Appleton, 1926. 1st ed. Pict rust cl stamped in black. (Feps sl dknd from newspaper clipping), else Fine in pict dj (soiled, lt worn). Howes B721. *Argonaut*. $150/£96

BRANCH, E. DOUGLAS. The Hunting of the Buffalo. NY: D. Appleton, 1929. 1st ed. Blue-grn cl, ptd paper labels. (Ink stain spine, label sl dknd, spotted), else Fine. *Argonaut*. $90/£58

BRANCH, EDGAR M. (ed). Clemens of the Call: Mark Twain in San Francisco. Univ of CA, 1969. 1st ed. Fine in Fine dj. *Authors Of West*. $50/£32

BRAND, CHRISTIANNA. The Three-Cornered Halo. London: Michael Joseph, 1957. 1st ed. (Lt spotting feps), o/w Fine in dj (sl wear spine top). *Mordida*. $65/£42

BRAND, JOHN. Observations on Popular Antiquities. Henry Ellis (rev by). London: F.C. & J. Rivington, 1813. 1st ed. 2 vols. Lg paper copy. 4to. Teg. 3/4 grn morocco, grn cl sides, gilt spines. (Lt foxing, bkpls), else Fine. *Cummins*. $600/£385

BRAND, MAX. (Pseud of Frederick Faust.) The Guns of Dorking Hollow. NY: Dodd Mead, 1965. 1st hb ed. Fine in dj (price-clipped). *Mordida*. $45/£29

BRAND, MAX. (Pseud of Frederick Faust.) Hired Guns. NY: Dodd, Mead, 1948. 1st ed. VG in dj (nicked). *Houle*. $85/£54

BRAND, MAX. (Pseud of Frederick Faust.) Smiling Charlie. NY: Dodd, Mead, 1927. 1st ed. Illus eps. Fine in Fine dj. *Unger*. $300/£192

BRAND, MAX. (Pseud of Frederick Faust.) Torture Trail. NY: Dodd Mead, 1965. 1st hb ed. Fine in dj. *Mordida*. $45/£29

BRANDEIS, LOUIS D. Letters of Louis D. Brandeis. Vol. III. M. Urofsky and D. Levy (eds). Albany: SUNY, 1973. 1st ed. (Bumped), o/w Fine in VG dj. *Archer*. $25/£16

BRANDEIS, LOUIS D. Other People's Money and How the Bankers Use It. NY: Frederick A. Stokes, (1914). 1st ed, 1st bk. Brn cl (bumped, sl spotted), gilt (dknd). Internally NF. *Blue Mountain*. $125/£80

BRANDEIS, LOUIS D. Other People's Money and How the Bankers Use It. NY: Frederick A. Stokes, 1934. (Pencilling), else VG in dj (defective). *Boswell*. $85/£54

BRANDER, A. Wild Animals of Central India. London: Arnold, 1923. 1st ed. Maroon cl. (Blindstamp tp), else Fine. *Terramedia*. $150/£96

BRANDES, RAY. Frontier Military Posts of Arizona. Globe, AZ: Dale Stuart King, 1960. (Spine ends sl worn, lt dust soiling), else Good in wrappers. *Brown*. $20/£13

BRANDON, RAPHAEL and J. ARTHUR. An Analysis of Gothick Architecture. London, 1847. 2 vols. vii,118pp, 53 + 105 plts. 1/2 leather (rubbed). *Ars Artis*. $117/£75

BRANDON, RAPHAEL and J. ARTHUR. An Analysis of Gothick Architecture. London, 1849. 'New Edition.' 2 vols. (Bkpls, few plts loose; spines frayed, vol 2 spine torn, soiled.) *King*. $150/£96

BRANDON, WILLIAM. The Men and the Mountain. NY: William Morrow, 1955. 1st ed. (Spine head sl bumped), else Fine in dj (lt rubbed, soiled). *Argonaut*. $30/£19

BRANDT, BILL (ed). The Land: Twentieth Century Landscape Photographs. London: Gordon Fraser, 1975. 1st ed. 48 full-pg b/w photo plts. (Corner crimpled, lt rubbed), else VG in pict stiff wrappers. *Cahan*. $25/£16

BRANDT, BILL. Bill Brandt: Nudes 1945-1980. Boston: NYGS, 1980. 1st ed. 100 b/w full-pg plts. NF (staple removal fep, stickers fep, rear pastedown) in NF dj. *Smith*. $125/£80

BRANDT, BILL. Camera in London. London: Focal Press, 1948. 1st ed. Dj (worn, soiled). *Hollett*. $70/£45

BRANDT, BILL. Literary Britain. London: Cassell, 1951. 1st ed. 100 full-pg b/w photos. VG (inscrip). *Cahan*. $100/£64

BRANDT, BILL. London in the Thirties. NY: Pantheon, 1983. 1st ed. Fine in Fine dj. *Smith*. $65/£42

BRANDT, BILL. Perspective of Nudes. NY: Amphoto, 1961. 1st ed. 92 full-pg b/w images. VG+ in VG dj (chipped, rubbed, piece missing top edge). Smith. $300/£192

BRANDT, BILL. Perspective of Nudes. NY: AMPHOTO, 1961. 1st ed. 90 gravure photo plts. Patterned bds. Fine in dj. Cahan. $375/£240

BRANDT, HERBERT. Alaska Bird Trails. Cleveland, OH: Bird Research, 1943. Inscribed, signed. Fine in dj. Cullen. $175/£112

BRANGWYN, FRANK and HAYTER PRESTON. Windmills. London/NY, 1923. Stated 1st ed. 16 full-pg color plts. Dec cvr. Good. Scribe's Perch*. $40/£26

BRANGWYN, FRANK. Catalogue of the Etched Work. London, 1912. (Fr hinge cracked.) 1/4 vellum, leather spine label (worn). Swann*. $103/£66

BRANN, W. C. Brann the Iconoclast. Waco, TX: Herz, 1898. 2 vols. 464; 463pp. Good. Scribe's Perch*. $25/£16

BRANNER, R. Manuscript Painting in Paris During the Reign of Saint Louis. Berkeley: Univ of CA, 1977. Blue cl. Mint in dj. Maggs. $86/£55

BRANNON, C. and A. Brannon's Shilling Pocket Guide to the Isle of Wight. London, n.d. (1883). New ed. Frontis map, 2 full-pg engr plts. VG in stiff pict grn wrappers. Words Etc. $94/£60

BRANNON, PETER A. The Organization of the Confederate Postoffice Department at Montgomery and a Story of the Thomas Welsh Provisional Stamped Envelope.... Montgomery, 1960. 1st ed. Fine in Fine dj. Pratt. $85/£54

BRANNT, W. India Rubber, Gutta-Percha, and Balata. Phila, 1900. 1st ed. (Cl faded, worn.) Maggs. $37/£24

BRANSON, H. C. The Pricking Thumb. NY: S&S, 1942. 1st ed. Fine in dj (price-clipped, spine ends sl worn). Mordida. $85/£54

BRAQUE, GEORGES. Georges Braque: His Graphic Work. NY: Abrams, (1961). 1st Amer ed. Fine in dj (lt soiled). Hermitage. $75/£48

BRAQUE, GEORGES. His Complete Graphic Work. NY: Abrams, n.d. (Eps lt stained.) Dj. Metropolitan*. $23/£15

BRASCH, FREDERICK E. (ed). Sir Isaac Newton, 1727-1927. Balt: Williams & Wilkins, 1928. 1st ed. Frontis port. Teg. Fine in dj. Glaser. $100/£64

BRASHER, REX. Birds and Trees of North America. Chickadee Valley, CT: Rex Brasher Assoc, 1929. Ltd to 500. Oblong folio. 68 hand-colored plts. Leather, dec bds. Fine. Metropolitan*. $2,185/£1,401

BRASHER, REX. Birds and Trees of North America. Chickadee Valley, CT: Rex Brasher Assoc, 1931. Ltd to 500. Oblong folio. 76 hand-colored plts. Leather, dec bds. Fine. Metropolitan*. $1,840/£1,179

BRASHER, REX. Birds and Trees of North America. NY: Rowman & Littlefield, 1961. 1st ed. 4 vols. 875 full-color plts. VG in wooden holding case. New Hampshire*. $200/£128

BRASHLER, WILLIAM. Bingo Long Traveling All Stars. Harper & Row, 1973. 1st ed. Fine in VG dj. Plapinger. $50/£32

BRASSAI. Brassai: The Secret Paris. NY: Pantheon, 1976. VG (rubbed, closed tears) in VG dj. Smith. $85/£54

BRASSAI. Camera in Paris. London/NY: Focal Press, 1949. 1st ed. White cl (ends sl worn). NF in VG dj (chip). Cahan. $325/£208

BRASSAI. Fiesta in Seville. NY, 1956. 1st ed. VG in VG dj (price-clipped; sl shelfwear). Warren. $85/£54

BRASSINGTON, W. SALT (ed). A History of the Art of Bookbinding.... London: Elliot Stock, 1894. 1st ed. xvi,277pp (ex-lib, stamps); 10 color plts. Contemp leather-backed cl (sl worn). Cox. $133/£85

BRATBY, JOHN. Breakdown. Cleveland/NY: World, (1960). 1st Amer ed. Black cl-backed pict red/black bds, gilt. NF in pict dj (sl rubbed, chipped). Blue Mountain. $35/£22

BRATT, JOHN. Trails of Yesterday. Lincoln: University Publishing, 1921. 1st ed. Signed presentation by Mrs. John Bratt. VG. Howes B725. Perier. $275/£176

BRAUN, HUGH. English Abbeys. Faber, 1971. VG in dj. Hadley. $23/£15

BRAUN, KATHY. Kangaroo and Kangaroo. NY: Doubleday, 1965. 1st ed. J. McMullen (illus). Oblong 8vo. 36pp. Illus eps. Illus bds. NF. Dower. $25/£16

BRAUN, LILIAN JACKSON. The Cat Who Lived High. NY: Putnam, 1990. 1st ed. VF in dj. Mordida. $30/£19

BRAUNFELS, WOLFGANG. Monastries of Western Europe. Thames & Hudson, 1972. 1st ed. Dj. Edwards. $44/£28

BRAUNSTEIN, H. TERRY. Windows. (Rochester): Visual Studies Workshop/William Blake Press, 1982. 1st ed. Fine in dj. Cahan. $50/£32

BRAUTIGAN, RICHARD. Five Poems. Berkeley: Serendipity Bks, 1971. 1st ed. Broadside. Fine. Sclanders. $39/£25

BRAUTIGAN, RICHARD. Revenge of the Lawn. London: Jonathan Cape, 1972. 1st UK ed. VG in dj (sl rubbed). Cox. $16/£10

BRAUTIGAN, RICHARD. The San Francisco Weather Report. SF: Graham Mackintosh, 1968. 1st ed. Broadside. Fine. Sclanders. $94/£60

BRAWNER, A. H., JR. Our South American Trip. N.p., 1940. 1st ed. Cl-backed textured paper over bds. (Sl foxing eps), else NF. Cahan. $25/£16

BRAY, MRS. Life of Thomas Stothard, R.A. London, 1851. 18 tipped-in vignettes. Aeg. Red full morocco, ribbed spines. VG in orig slipcase. Yudkin*. $200/£128

BRAYER, HERBERT O. The Cattle Barons' Rebellion Against Law and Order. Evanston, IL: Branding Iron, 1955. Ltd ed rpt. Fine. Gibbs. $25/£16

BRAYTON, MATTHEW. Indian Captive: A Narrative of the Adventures and Sufferings of Matthew Brayton.... Fostoria, OH: Gray Ptg, 1896. 2nd ed. Later cl-backed stiff wrappers, orig upper wrapper laid on. Good (top corner tp expertly repaired). Howes B736. Sadlon. $200/£128

BRAZIER, MARY A. B. A History of the Electrical Activity of the Brain. NY, (1961). VG in dj. Argosy. $60/£38

BREA, L. BERNABO. Sicily Before the Greeks. London: Thames & Hudson, (1957). 7 maps. Good in dj. Archaeologia. $35/£22

Bread-Winners. By a Lady of Boston. (By Susan D. Nickerson.) Boston: Nichols & Hall, 1871. 1st ed. 295pp. M & S. $100/£64

BREAKENRIDGE, WILLIAM M. Helldorado, Bringing the Law to the Mesquite. Boston, 1928. 1st ed. VG+. Pratt. $85/£54

BREAKENRIDGE, WILLIAM M. Helldorado. Boston/NY: Houghton Mifflin, 1928. 1st ed. Frontis port. Fine (name) in pict dj (soiled, lt worn, 1-inch piece lacking fore-edge). Argonaut. $150/£96

BREARLEY, HARRY C. Time Telling Through the Ages. NY: Doubleday, Page, 1919. Frontis, 24 plts. (Fr inner hinge cracked, bkpl.) Teg. Appreciation by Dr. Frank Crane laid in. 1/4 linen, blue bds (spine ends frayed), paper spine label (rubbed). Weber. $20/£13

BREASTED, JAMES HENRY. A History of the Ancient Egyptians. NY: Scribner, 1913. 4 maps, 3 plans. (Sig.) Archaeologia. $25/£16

BREAZEALE, J. F. The Pima and His Basket. Tucson: AZ Hist & Archaeological Soc, 1923. Black-stamped tan cl. Dawson. $35/£22

BRECHER, RUTH and EDWARD M. (eds). An Analysis of Human Sexual Response. Boston: Little, Brown, (1959). 1st ed. Inscribed. VG in dj. *Gach.* $40/£26

BRECHT, BERTOLT. Selected Poems. NY: Reynal & Hitchcock, 1947. 1st ed. VG + in VG dj. *Lame Duck.* $65/£42

BRECHT, BERTOLT. Seven Plays. Eric Bentley (ed). NY: Grove, (1961). 1st ed thus. Fine in dj. *Hermitage.* $35/£22

BRECHT, BERTOLT. Tales from the Calendar. Yvonne Kapp & Michael Hamburger (trans). London: Methuen, (1961). 1st Eng ed. NF in dj. *Hermitage.* $35/£22

BRECK, JOSEPH. The Flower Garden. NY: A.O. Moore, 1861. New ed. xii,395 + 12pp ads (prelims lt foxed, last few ll stained). Blind-stamped cl, gilt. *Quest.* $45/£29

BRECKINRIDGE, SOPHONISBA. The Illinois Poor Law and Its Administration. Chicago: Univ of Chicago, 1939. *Boswell.* $45/£29

BREDIUS, ABRAHAM. Rembrandt. The Complete Edition of the Paintings. London, 1969. 3rd ed. (Ex-lib.) *Washton.* $75/£48

BREE, CHARLES ROBERT. A History of the Birds of Europe, Not Observed in the British Isles. George Bell, 1875/76. 2nd ed. 5 vols. 4to. xii,150; iv,171; iv,176; iv,180; (4),175pp + pub's cat inserted end each vol; 253 hand-colored plts. Partly unopened. (Backstrip ends frayed.) Internally Fine set. *Cox.* $702/£450

BREED, R. S. et al. Bergey's Manual of Determinative Bacteriology. London: Bailliere, Tindall & Cox, 1948. 6th ed. VG. *Savona.* $39/£25

BREEDEN, JAMES O. Joseph Jones, M.D., Scientist of the Old South. Lexington, (1975). 1st ed. Fine in dj (sm back piece torn away, lt wear). *Pratt.* $25/£16

BREEN, PATRICK. Diary of Patrick Breen, One of the Donner Party. Frederick J. Teggart (ed). Berkeley: Univ of CA, 1910. 1st ed. Frontis photo plt. VG in ptd wrappers. *Shasky.* $35/£22

BREEN, PATRICK. Diary of Patrick Breen, One of the Donner Party. Frederick J. Teggart (ed). Berkeley, CA: Univ of CA, July 1910. 1st ed. Frontis. Fine in orig ptd wrappers. *Sadlon.* $45/£29

BREESKIN, ADELYN D. The Graphic Work of Mary Cassatt. NY, 1948. Cl-backed dec bds. Dj (lt stain spine). *Swann*.* $402/£258

BREEZE, DAVID J. and BRIAN DOBSON. Hadrian's Wall. London: Allen Lane, 1976. 1st ed. 29 plts, 14 tables. VG in dj. *Hollett.* $39/£25

BREHM, ALFRED E. From the North Pole to the Equator. London: Blackie, 1896. 592pp; 22 plts. Red pict cl. VG. *Adelson.* $85/£54

BREIHAN, CARL W. and CHARLES H. ROSAMOND. The Bandit Belle. Seattle, (1970). 1st ed. Pict cl. Fine. *Perier.* $30/£19

BREITBACH, JOSEPH. Report on Bruno. Michael Bullock (trans). NY: Knopf, 1964. 1st Amer ed. Fine in dj. *Antic Hay.* $35/£22

BREITIGAM, GERALD. Morvich. NY: Rotary, 1922. 1st ed. Good (vertical crease fr cvr). *October Farm.* $65/£42

BREMER, FREDERIKA. The Homes of the New World. Mary Howitt (trans). NY: Harper, 1853. 1st US ed. 2 vols. 651; 654pp (soiled). VG (fr hinge cl sl wormed). Howes B745. *Second Life.* $325/£208

BREMER, FREDERIKA. Homes of the New World: Impressions of America. Mary Howitt (trans). NY: Harper, 1853. 1st Amer ed. 2 vols. 651; 652pp. Fair. Howes B745. *Lien.* $300/£192

BREMNER, M. D. K. The Story of Dentistry. NY, 1946. 2nd ed. VG. *Fye.* $75/£48

BRENAN, GERALD. Personal Record 1920-1972. London: Cape, 1974. 1st ed. Very Nice (bkpl) in dj (nicked, chipped, sl creased top edge). *Virgo.* $47/£30

BRENAN, GERALD. South from Granada. London: Hamish Hamilton, 1957. 1st ed. (Sl offsetting, name fep), o/w Very Nice in dj (sl soiled, nicked, chipped, price-clipped). *Virgo.* $62/£40

BRENNAN, JOSEPH PAYNE. The Borders Just Beyond. Grant, (1986). One of 750 signed. Fine in Fine dj. *Certo.* $40/£26

BRENNAN, JOSEPH PAYNE. The Casebook of Lucius Leffing. Macabre House, 1973. 1st ed. Fine in dj (sm creased tear). *Certo.* $50/£32

BRENNAN, JOSEPH PAYNE. Chronicles of Lucius Leffing. Donald M. Grant, 1977. 1st ed. Fine in Fine dj. *Certo.* $40/£26

BRENNAN, JOSEPH PAYNE. As Evening Advances. Crystal Visions, 1978. One of 400 numbered, signed. Fine in wraps. *Certo.* $35/£22

BRENNAN, JOSEPH PAYNE. Nightmare Need. Sauk City: Arkham House, 1964. 1st ed. One of 500 ptd. Fine in Fine dj (pin hole). *Mcclintock.* $195/£125

BRENNAN, JOSEPH PAYNE. Nightmare Need. Sauk City: Arkham House, 1964. 1st ed. One of 500. NF in NF dj (spine, fr panel edges rubbed). *Other Worlds.* $225/£144

BRENNAN, JOSEPH PAYNE. Nine Horrors and a Dream. Sauk City, WI, 1958. 1st ed. Signed. One of 1200 ptd. Fine in Fine dj. *Mcclintock.* $200/£128

BRENNAN, JOSEPH PAYNE. Nine Horrors: And a Dream. Sauk City: Arkham House, 1958. 1st ed. NF in dj. *Other Worlds.* $150/£96

BRENNAN, JOSEPH PAYNE. Stories of Darkness and Dread. Sauk City, WI, 1973. 1st ed. Fine in NF dj (edges sl shelfworn). *Mcclintock.* $20/£13

BRENNAN, LOUIS A. Tree of Arrows. NY: Macmillan, (1964). 1st ed. (Spine head sl rubbed), o/w Fine in dj. *Sadlon.* $15/£10

BRENNAND, W. Hindu Astronomy. London: Straker, 1896. 1st ed. xv,329pp. (Inner hinges cracked; worn, spine top frayed, lacks spine bottom, spine tears, ex-lib, spine #), o/w Good. *Worldwide.* $35/£22

BRENNECKE, J. The Hunters and the Hunted. NY, 1957. VG in VG dj. *Clark.* $45/£29

BRENT-DYER, ELINOR. Althea Joins the Chalet School. Chambers, (1969). 1st ed. 8vo. Frontis by D. Brooke, 175pp. Fine in pict dj. *Bookmark.* $140/£90

BRENT-DYER, ELINOR. The Chalet School Triplets. Chambers, n.d. (1963). 1st ed. 8vo. Frontis by D. Brooke, 218pp. (Sm streak top spine-edge), else VF in pict dj (few repaired tears). *Bookmark.* $94/£60

BRERETON, AUSTIN. The Life of Henry Irving. London, 1908. 1st ed. Presentation copy. 2 vols. 1 photogravure plt, 22 collotype plts. (Ex-lib, bkpl.) Fore, lower edge uncut. (Cl lt soiled.) *Edwards.* $101/£65

BRERETON, F. S. Tom Stapleton the Boy Scout. Blackie, 1911. 1st ed. 8vo. Color frontis, 287pp; 6 mono plts by Gordon Browne. Pict cl, gilt. (Sl rubbed), else VG. *Bookmark.* $70/£45

BRESLAUER, BERNARD H. and ROLAND FOLTER. Bibliography: Its History and Development. NY: Grolier Club, 1984. 1st ed. One of 600. *Swann*.* $57/£37

BRETON, NICHOLAS. A Mad World My Masters and Other Prose Works. Ursula Kentish-Wright (ed). London: Cressett, 1929. Ltd to 500 sets. 2 vols. Teg. Grn 'gilt cloud' patterned cl, red leather labels. NF. *Cady.* $75/£48

BRETT, SIMON. Dead Giveaway. London: Gollancz, 1985. 1st ed. Fine in dj. *Mordida.* $45/£29

BRETT, SIMON. A Series of Murders. London: Victor Gollancz, 1989. 1st ed. VF in dj. *Mordida.* $50/£32

BRETT, SIMON. What Bloody Man Is That? London: Victor Gollancz, 1987. 1st ed. Signed. VF in dj. *Mordida*. $65/£42

BRETTELL, RICHARD R. Paper and Light. Boston/London: David R. Godine/Kudos & Godine, 1984. NF in illus dj. *Cahan*. $50/£32

BRETZ, J. HARLEN. The Grand Coulee. NY: Amer Geog Soc, 1932. 1st ed. Color fldg map, 8 stereo views in pocket. Grey/black cl. VG. *Price*. $48/£31

BREWER, GIL. Backwoods Teaser. Greenwich: Fawcett, 1960. 1st ed. Unread. VF in wrappers. *Mordida*. $35/£22

BREWER, JAMES NORRIS. A Descriptive and Historical Account of Various Palaces and Public Buildings (English and Foreign) with Biographical Notices.... London: Giling, 1821. 4 ff prelims,153 ff n.n., 25 engr plts (lt foxed). Contemp diced calf, spine gilt. Good. *Marlborough*. $390/£250

BREWER, JOSIAH. A Residence at Constantinople, in the Year 1827. New Haven: Durrie & Peck, 1830. 2nd ed. Fldg engr frontis, 384pp (foxed); fldg hand-colored map. Contemp calf, gilt black leather spine label. *Karmiole*. $200/£128

BREWER, LUTHER A. Leigh Hunt and Charles Dickens: The Skimpole Caricature. Cedar Rapids, IA: Torch Press, Christmas 1930. 1st ed. Ltd to 300. Paper over bds, cl spine; gold spine lettering. Mint. *Graf*. $50/£32

BREWER, LUTHER. Wanderings in London. Cedar Rapids: Torch, 1925. One of 300 ptd. Parchment-backed bds (backstrip foxed). VG. *Agvent*. $35/£22

BREWER, ROY. Eric Gill: The Man Who Loved Letters. London: Frederick Muller, 1973. 1st ed. Gray cl. Fine in dj. *Heller*. $50/£32

BREWER, WILLIAM H. Such a Landscape! (Yosemite): Yosemite Assoc, Sequoia Nat. Hist Assoc, 1987. 1st ed. #165/500 signed by William Alsup (intro). Frontis, 39 plts. 1/2 cl, bds. VF. *Argonaut*. $125/£80

BREWER, WILLIAM H. Up and Down California in 1860-1864. New Haven: Yale Univ, 1930. 1st ed. 32 plts, fldg map. Unopened. Fine. Howes B754. *Sadlon*. $175/£112

BREWER, WILLIAM H. Up and Down California in 1860-1864. Francis P. Farquhar (ed). New Haven: Yale Univ, 1930. 1st ed. Inscribed presentation signed by Francis P. Farquhar (ed). Frontis, fldg map. Gilt-lettered dk blue cl (few lt smudges fr cvr). Fine. *Argonaut*. $225/£144

BREWER, WILLIS. Alabama: Her History, Resources, War Record, and Public Men. Montgomery: Barrett & Brown, 1872. 712pp (lt spotted). VG (spine lightened). Howes B755. *Zubal**. $100/£64

BREWER-BONERIGHT, SARAH and HARRIET BONERIGHT-CLOSZ. Reminiscences of Newcastle, Iowa 1848. Des Moines, 1921. 1st ed. Pict cl (faded). *Ginsberg*. $100/£64

BREWERTON, GEORGE D. Incidents of Travel in New Mexico. Ashland: Lewis Osborne, 1969. One of 1400, this unnumbered. (Soiled.) In plain dj (chipped, soiled). *Bohling*. $15/£10

BREWINGTON, M. V. and DOROTHY. The Marine Paintings and Drawings in the Peabody Museum. Salem, MA, 1968. 1st ed. Dj. *Eldred's**. $176/£113

BREWSTER, DAVID. The Life of Sir Isaac Newton. John Murray, 1831. 1st ed. xv,366pp; engr port. New eps. Mod bds, ptd paper spine label. *Bickersteth*. $117/£75

BREWSTER, DAVID. A Treatise on Magnetism. Edinburgh: A&C Black, 1837. 1st ed. Fldg frontis map. Contemp cl. VG. *Argosy*. $500/£321

BREWSTER, JAMES H. The Conveyance of Estates in Fee by Deed. Indianapolis: Bobbs-Merrill, 1904. Contemp sheep (worn, rubbed). Sound. *Boswell*. $75/£48

BREY, WILLIAM. John Carbutt on the Frontiers of Photography. Cherry Hill, NJ: Willowdale, 1984. 1st ed. Fine in illus stiff wrappers. *Cahan*. $25/£16

BRICE, MARSHALL M. The Stonewall Brigade Band. McClure, (c. 1967). 1st ed. Inscribed presentation copy. (Ink title bottom edge), o/w VG. *Book Broker*. $45/£29

BRICKEL, A. C. J. Surgical Treatment of Hand and Forearm Infections. St. Louis, 1939. 1st ed. Grn cl. NF. *Doctor's Library*. $75/£48

BRICKHILL, PAUL. The Great Escape. London: Faber, 1951. 1st UK ed. NF in dj. *Williams*. $55/£35

Brickwork in Italy. Chicago: Amer Brick Face Assoc, 1925. Color frontis, 329 plts, map. Fine. *Quest*. $85/£54

BRIDGE, HORATIO. Journal of an African Cruiser. Nathaniel Hawthorne (ed). NY: Wiley & Putnam, 1845. 1st ed, 2nd issue. One of 1500 (of 2000 ptd). Orig grn cl, gilt. Bound w/Headley's Letter from Italy, as issued. VG (sl dampstain lower margin, spine rubbed). BAL 7597. *Macdonnell*. $300/£192

BRIDGE, HORATIO. Journal of an African Cruiser. Nathaniel Hawthorne (ed). NY: Putnam, 1853. vi,179pp. Orig cl (crudely rebacked). *Adelson*. $35/£22

BRIDGE, HORATIO. Personal Recollections of Nathaniel Hawthorne. NY: Harper, 1893. 1st ed. Lt blue cl, gilt. Fine. BAL IV:34:col.1. *Macdonnell*. $85/£54

BRIDGE, NORMAN. The Marching Years. NY: Duffield, 1920. 1st ed. Dec cl. *Ginsberg*. $75/£48

BRIDGES, ROBERT. Eros and Psyche. (Newtown): Gregynog, 1935. One of 300. 4to. 24 wood-engr illus. Prospectus laid in. Orig gilt-blocked pigskin (rear cvr lt spotted). White cl slipcase (lt soiled). *Swann**. $805/£516

BRIDGES, ROBERT. The Necessity of Poetry. Oxford: Clarendon, 1918. (Edges lt spotted, worn), else Fine in blue paper wrappers. *Heller*. $50/£32

BRIDGES, ROBERT. The Testament of Beauty. NY: OUP, 1930. 1st Amer ed. As New. *Bond*. $17/£11

BRIDGETT, R. C. Sea-Trout Fishing. London, 1929. 1st ed. 19 plts (3 color). (Edges lt spotted.) Dj (spotted, sl chipped, faded). *Edwards*. $39/£25

BRIDGMAN, LEONARD (ed). Jane's All the World's Aircraft 1943-44. London, 1944. Blue cl (spotted). *Maggs*. $273/£175

Brief Notices of a Small Number of the Shakespeare Rarities That Are Preserved.... London, 1885. 2nd ed. 24pp. (Ex-lib, ink stamp tp, last leaf; inner hinges cracked, sl shaken; lt soiled.) *Edwards*. $23/£15

BRIERLEY, HARRY. Transvestism: A Handbook with Case Studies.... Oxford: Pergamon, (1979). 1st ed. Ptd tan laminated bds. (Sheets sl damp-crinkled), else VG. *Gach*. $35/£22

BRIEUX. Damaged Goods. Phila: John C. Winston, (1913). 1st ed. NF in dj (sl chipped). *Antic Hay*. $35/£22

BRIFFAULT, ROBERT. The Mothers. NY: Macmillan, 1927. 1st ed. 3 vols. VG set. *Second Life*. $175/£112

BRIGGS, CARL and CLYDE F. TRUDELL. Quarterdeck and Saddlehorn. Glendale: Clark, 1983. 1st ed. One of 1027. VF. *Argonaut*. $75/£48

BRIGGS, ERNEST E. Angling and Art in Scotland. Longmans, 1908. 32 color plts. Pict cl. *Petersfield*. $62/£40

BRIGGS, HAROLD E. Frontiers of the Northwest. NY: D. Appleton-Century, 1940. 1st ed. Frontis, 31 plts, 7 maps. Gilt-lettered brn cl. (Bkpl), else Fine. *Argonaut*. $100/£64

BRIGGS, K. M. Abbey Lubber, Banshees and Boggarts. NY: Pantheon, 1979. 1st US ed. Yvonne Gilbert (illus). 6 1/2 x 9 1/2. 159pp. VG in dj. *Cattermole*. $15/£10

BRIGGS, K. M. The Personnel of Fairyland. Cambridge, MA: Robert Bentley, 1954. 1st US ed. 5 1/2 x 8. 228pp. Good (ex-lib, mks) in dj. *Cattermole*. $15/£10

BRIGGS, L. CABOT. Bullterriers. The Biography of a Breed. NY: Derrydale, c. 1940. One of 500. Presentation copy. (Sl soiled), o/w VG. *New Hampshire**. $310/£199

BRIGGS, L. VERNON. The Manner of Man That Kills: Spencer—Czolgosz—Richeson. Boston: Richard G. Badger, (1921). 1st ed. Inscribed. 16 half-tones. Ruled straight-grained grn cl. VG. *Gach*. $100/£64

BRIGGS, M. S. Baroque Architecture. London, 1913. (Cl sl worn.) *Ars Artis*. $55/£35

BRIGGS, M. S. Baroque Architecture. NY, 1967. Rpt of 1913 ed. Good in dj. *Washton*. $50/£32

BRIGGS, M. S. The English Farmhouse. London: Batsford, 1953. 1st ed. Sound in dj (sl frayed). *Ars Artis*. $23/£15

BRIGGS, RAYMOND. Father Christmas. London: Hamish Hamilton, 1973. 1st ed. Lg 8vo. 32pp. Pict bds. VG. *Hollett*. $55/£35

BRIGGS, RAYMOND. Father Christmas. NY: Coward McCann, 1973. 1st ed. 9x10. 32pp. VG in dj. *Cattermole*. $25/£16

BRIGGS, WALTER. Without Noise of Arms. Flagstaff, 1976. 1st ed. 10 full-pg oils, 15 maps and charts. White cl. VG. *Five Quail*. $65/£42

BRIGHAM, AMARIAH. Remarks on the Influence of Mental Cultivation and Mental Excitement upon Health. Phila: Lea & Blanchard, 1845. 3rd ed. (ii),xxviii,(37)-204,(2)pp. Pub's cl (worn, fr bd detached). *Gach*. $85/£54

BRIGHAM, CLARENCE S. Paul Revere's Engravings. Worcester, MA: Amer Antiquarian Soc, 1954. 77 plts. VG in dj (dknd, frayed). *Bohling*. $120/£77

BRIGHT, RICHARD. Clinical Memoirs on Abdominal Tumours and Intumescence. G. H. Barlow (ed). London: New Sydenham Soc, 1860. xviii,326pp; 79 woodcuts. Orig brn cl (rebacked, spine relaid), gilt. Clean (bkpls). *White*. $70/£45

BRIGHTON, J. G. Admiral of the Fleet, Sir Provo W. P. Wallis. London, 1892. ix,299pp (1 marginal tear, no loss); 14 plts. Black cl (recased), gilt. *Maggs*. $156/£100

BRIGHTWELL, D. BARRON. Concordance to the Entire Works of Alfred Tennyson. London, 1869. Port, 477pp. Mod buckram. (Ex-lib.) *Argosy*. $75/£48

BRILL, CHARLES J. Conquest of the Southern Plains. Oklahoma City: Golden Saga, 1938. Fldg plt. VG. *Dumont*. $95/£61

BRILL, EDITH. The Golden Bird. NY: Atheneum, 1976. 6th ed. Jan Plenkowski (illus). 6 1/4 x 8 1/4. 118pp. Fine in dj. *Cattermole*. $50/£32

BRILLAT-SAVARIN, JEAN ANTHELME. The Physiology of Taste, or Meditations on Transcendental Gastronomy. London: Peter Davies, 1925. One of 750. Untrimmed. Vellum-backed marbled paper bds (sl worn, sl soiled, sl yellowed, chafed), gilt spine. Internally Fine. *Pirages*. $225/£144

BRILLIANT, RICHARD. Pompeii: A.D. 79. NY: Clarkson N. Potter, (1979). Good in dj. *Archaeologia*. $65/£42

BRIM, CHARLES. Medicine in the Bible, the Pentateuch, Torah. NY, 1936. 1st ed. VG. *Fye*. $130/£83

BRIN, DAVIS. Earth. NY: Bantam, (1990). One of 342 signed. Morocco. Tissue dj, pub's mailing carton. *Swann**. $80/£51

BRINE, MARY D. Grandma's Attic Treasures. NY: Dutton, 1893. 8vo. 94pp, 8 color lithos. Aeg. VF in color-illus bds, orig dj (lt chipped, browned). *Bromer*. $275/£176

BRININSTOOL, E. A. A Trooper with Custer, and Other Historic Incidents of the Battle of the Little Big Horn. Volume I (all published). Columbus: Hunter-Trader-Trapper, 1925. 1st ed. Tipped-in errata slip, photo frontis. Yellow cl stamped in blue. Cvrs VG (sl dusty, spine lettering faded). *Baltimore**. $100/£64

BRININSTOOL, E. A. Troopers with Custer. Harrisburg, PA, (1952). (Lacks fep; cvrs sl dknd.) *King*. $30/£19

BRINK, ANDRE (trans). File on a Diplomat. London: Longmans, 1967. 1st Eng ed. VG in dj. *Hollett*. $31/£20

BRINK, ANDRE. A Dry White Season. London: W.H. Allen, 1979. 1st ed. VG (label) in VG dj (price-clipped; tear spine base). *Between The Covers*. $85/£54

BRINK, ANDRE. Rumours of Rain. NY: Morrow, 1978. 1st ed. Fine in dj (sl worn). *Antic Hay*. $35/£22

BRINK, CAROL RYRIE. Lad with a Whistle. Macmillan, 1941. 1st ed. Robert Ball (illus). 6x8. 235pp. VG + (sl shelfworn) in dj (sl edgeworn). *My Bookhouse*. $25/£16

BRINKERHOFF, DERICKSEN M. A Collection of Sculpture in Classical and Early Christian Antioch. NY, 1970. Good. *Washton*. $50/£32

BRINTON, CHRISTIAN. Modern Art at the Sesqui-Centennial Exhibition. NY, 1926. Color wrappers. *Swann**. $345/£221

BRINTON, DANIEL G. Essays of an Americanist. Phila: David McKay, (1890). 1st ed. xii,17-489pp. (Lt rubbed), else VG. *Cahan*. $125/£80

BRION, MARCEL. The Medici. NY, 1969. Good. *Washton*. $25/£16

BRISBIN, JAMES S. (ed). Belden, the White Chief. Cincinnati/NY: C.F. Vent, 1870. 1st ed, 1st issue binding of orig royal blue pebbled cl (sl edgeworn), w/gilt cvr vignettes; subsequent issues were in brn or plum cl, w/blind vignettes. 513pp (sl aged, lt foxed). Howes B781. *Baltimore**. $100/£64

BRISCOE, EDWARD G. Diary of a Short-Timer in Vietnam. NY: Vantage, 1970. 1st ed. NF in dj (edge tears, sm chip). *Associates*. $125/£80

BRISSOT DE WARVILLE, J. P. New Travels in the United States, Performed in 1788. Boston, 1797. 276,(3)pp, fldg table. Contemp calf, morocco spine label. (Hinges loosening.) Howes B784. *Ginsberg*. $300/£192

BRISTED, JOHN. America and Her Resources. London, 1818. 1st British ed. xvi,504pp (lt foxed). Mod 1/2 morocco, marbled bds, gilt spine. VG. Howes B785. *Reese*. $225/£144

BRISTOL, SHERLOCK. The Pioneer Preacher: An Autobiography. NY/Chicago, (1887). 330pp + illus, ads; port. Internally VG. (Cl sl soiled, hinges broken, bkpl removed.) *Reese*. $350/£224

BRISTOWE, J. S. A Treatise on the Theory and Practice of Medicine. London, 1876. xxxiii,1166pp (sl foxed). (New eps, few pencil notes; cl worn, dust-stained), o/w VG. *Whitehart*. $55/£35

British Cowhide Leathers. London: British Leather Fdn, n.d. (ca 1960). 16pp, 34 circular leather samples. Calf-backed bds, leather label upper cvr. *Marlborough*. $101/£65

British Historical Portraits. A Selection from the National Portrait Gallery with Biographical Notes. 1957. Good. *Washton*. $35/£22

British Librarian: Exhibiting a Compendious Review or Abstract of Our Most Scarce, Useful, and Valuable Books. (By W. Oldys.) London, 1738. 402pp (sl browning; tp, last leaf repaired). Mod 1/2 calf, raised bands, red morocco label. *Moss.* $250/£160

BRITTAIN, H. A. Architectural Principles in Arthrodesis. Edinburgh, 1942. 1st ed. VG. *Doctor's Library.* $75/£48

BRITTAIN, VERA. Not Without Honour. London, 1924. 1st Eng ed. Good (foxing; cvrs sl mkd). *Clearwater.* $47/£30

BRITTAIN, VERA. The Rebel Passion. NY: Fellowship, (1964). 1st US ed. Fine (no dj). *Second Life.* $40/£26

BRITTEN, EMMA H. Art Magic, Or Mundane, Sub-Mundane, and Super-Mundane Spiritism. Chicago: Progressive Thinker, 1898. x,366pp (Lt chips spine, cvr), o/w VG. *Middle Earth.* $95/£61

BRITTEN, EMMA H. The Faiths, Facts, and Frauds of Religious History. London: John Heywood, 1889. iv,128pp (fr hinge cracked, soiling, few pp corners creased). Purple cl (bumped, rubbed, stained, extrems faded, spine chipped), gilt. Good. *Blue Mountain.* $50/£32

BRITTEN, EMMA H. Ghost Land, or Researches into the Mysteries of Occultism.... Chicago: Progressive Thinker, 1897. 1st ed. 357pp + 20pp cat at rear (pp browned, hinges cracked); port, tipped-in errata at fr. Cranberry cl stamped in silver. *Baltimore*.* $30/£19

BRITTEN, EMMA H. Ghost Land; or Researches into the Mysteries of Occultism.... Boston: For the ed, 1876. (2),484,(4)pp (tp sl soiled). 1/2 leather, marbled bds, gilt spine. VG. *New Hampshire*.* $35/£22

BRITTEN, F. J. Britten's Watch and Clock Maker's Handbook. London, 1978. 16th ed. (Ex-lib, bkpl, ink stamp.) Dj (spine faded). *Edwards.* $39/£25

BRITTEN, F. J. Old Clocks and Watches and Their Makers. London: E.&F. Spon, (1932). 6th ed. Red cl, ptd in black (spine faded; back upper corner sharply bumped). *Weber.* $100/£64

BRITTEN, F. J. Old Clocks and Watches and Their Makers. London: Batsford, 1904. 2nd ed. Maroon Cl (worn, inner hinge cracked; bkpl). *Weber.* $75/£48

BRITTEN, F. J. Old English Clocks (The Wetherfield Collection). London: Lawrence & Jellicoe, 1907. Ltd to 320 numbered. Tall 4to. Color frontis. Teg. Maroon buckram, gilt. (Spine ends sl frayed, back freckled), else VG. *Weber.* $600/£385

BRITTEN, F. J. On the Springing and Adjusting of Watches. London/NY: E. & F.N. Spon/Spon & Chamberlain, 1898. 152pp (tp, final index ll browned; offsetting). Gray-grn black-stamped cl. (Sig, rubbed), else VG. *Weber.* $40/£26

BRITTEN, F. J. Watch and Clock Makers' Handbook, Dictionary and Guide.... Brooklyn, NY: Chemical Pub, 1938. 14th ed. Red cl (sm stains, corner showing; bkpl removed). *Weber.* $25/£16

BRITTON, LEWIS W. Town Portraits. Chicago: Black Cat, 1934. One of 200. Unopened. Patterned bds, cl spine. VG (sl soiled, rubbed). *Bohling.* $20/£13

BRITTON, NATHANIEL LORD and ADDISON BROWN. Illustrated Flora of Northern U.S. and Canada. 1896, 1898, 1939. 1st ed. 3 vols. xii,612; iv,643; xiv,588pp. Contents Fine (4 hinges cracked). *Quest.* $95/£61

BRIX, MAURICE. List of Philadelphia Silversmiths and Allied Artificers from 1682 to 1850. Phila: Privately ptd, 1920. 1st ed. One of 300, this unnumbered and out-of-series. Frontis. Untrimmed. Ptd lt grn wraps over plain thin bds, hand-lettered spine. (Lt pencil mks; sl dusty, worn, chipped, upper cvr separated.) *Baltimore*.* $80/£51

BRIZZOLARA, JOHN. Wirecutter. GC: Doubleday, 1987. 1st ed, 1st bk. Inscribed. Fine in dj (sl edgewear). *Janus.* $25/£16

BROADHEAD, G. C. Reports on the Geological Survey of the State of Missouri, 1855-1871. Jefferson City, 1873. 324,vipp; 3 color plts, 9 dbl color maps. Good + (spine faded, sl loose). *Bohling.* $50/£32

BROCH, HERMANN. The Death of Virgil. NY: Pantheon, 1945. 1st ed. VG + in VG dj (spine tanned, chips, tears). *Lame Duck.* $300/£192

BROCH, HERMANN. The Death of Virgil. London: Routledge, 1946. 1st British ed. (Bump), else NF in VG dj (spine tanned). *Lame Duck.* $250/£160

BROCH, HERMANN. The Guiltless. Boston: Little Brown, (1950). 1st ed in English. NF in NF dj. *Fuller & Saunders.* $25/£16

BROCK, A. A History of Fireworks. London: George G. Harrap, 1949. VG (lt foxed) in dj. *Blake.* $125/£80

BROCK, ALICE MAY. Alice's Restaurant Cookbook. NY: Random House, (1969). 1st ed. NF in dj (lt rubbed), w/Arlo Guthrie's often missing record tipped in at rear, as issued. *Captain's Bookshelf.* $60/£38

BROCKETT, JOSHUA ARTHUR. Zipporah: The Maid of Midian. (Chicago: Ustafrican B.P. & D., 1926). 1st ed. VG (bds sl splayed, fr bd lt spotting). Lacks dj, presumably as issued. *Between The Covers.* $285/£183

BROCKETT, JOSHUA. Zipporah the Maid of Midian. Chicago: n.p., 1926. 1st ed. Photo frontis. VG + in cl-cvrd bds (lt shelfworn, lt mildew fr bd). *Lame Duck.* $285/£183

BROCKETT, L. P. Handbook of the United States and Guide to Emigration.... NY: Gaylord Watson, 1887. 211pp + ads. VG. *Second Life.* $75/£48

BROCKMAN, E. P. Congenital Club-Foot (Talipes Equinovarus). NY: William Wood, 1930. 1st Amer ed. NF (2 sm binding stains). *Glaser.* $45/£29

BRODHEAD, L. W. The Delaware Water Gap. Phila: Sherman, 1870. 2nd ed. Color frontis, 276pp. Grn cl (mottled). VG. *Cullen.* $45/£29

BRODIE, B. C. Pathological and Surgical Observations on the Diseases of the Joints. 1834. 3rd ed. viii,344pp (prelims foxed). 1/2 cl, marbled bds. *Whitehart.* $140/£90

BRODIE, BENJAMIN C. Lectures Illustrative of Certain Local Nervous Affections. London: Longman et al, 1837. 1st ed. iv,88pp + pub's cat dated Feb 1837 inserted at fr. Uncut. Drab bds (spine chipped). Jelliffe's name stamp, bkpl. Fine (lib stamp tp). *Gach.* $375/£240

BRODIE, FAWN M. No Man Knows My History: The Life of Joseph Smith. NY: Knopf, 1945. 1st ed. Good in dj (worn; chipped). *Lien.* $30/£19

BRODKEY, HAROLD. The Runaway Soul. NY: FSG, (1991). 1st ed. Inscribed, w/pub's slips. Fine in dj (sl worn). *Metropolitan*.* $115/£74

BRODRICK, M. and A. A. MORTON. A Concise Dictionary of Egyptian Archaeology. London: Methuen, (1922). (Sig.) *Archaeologia.* $45/£29

BRODSKY, JOSEPH. A Part of Speech. NY, 1980. 1st Amer ed. Fine in dj. *Polyanthos.* $25/£16

BRODSKY, JOSEPH. Selected Poems. George L. Kline (trans). (Middlesex): Penguin, (1973). 1st ed, pb orig. Fine in wrappers. *Jaffe.* $45/£29

BRODSKY, JOSEPH. Selected Poems. NY: Harper & Row, (1973). 1st ed. Fine in dj. *Antic Hay.* $45/£29

BRODSKY, JOSEPH. To Urania. NY: Farrar Straus, (1988). One of 150 numbered, signed. Fine in Fine slipcase. *Lenz.* $125/£80

BRODSKY, JOSEPH. To Urania. NY: FSG, (1988). 1st ed. Fine in dj. *Jaffe.* $25/£16

BRODZKY, HORACE. Henri Gaudier-Brzeska. London: Faber & Faber, 1933. Frontis. Red cl 9spine faded), gilt. VG (eps spotted). *Heller*. $80/£51

BROMFIELD, LOUIS. Awake and Rehearse. NY: Frederick A. Stokes, (1929). 1st ed. Good. *Hayman*. $20/£13

BROMLEY, JOHN. The Clockmaker's Library. London: Sotheby, 1977. 1st ed. VG in dj. *Weber*. $22/£14

BROMMELLE, NORMAN and PERRY SMITH (eds). Conservation and Restoration of Pictorial Art. London, 1976. 2nd ed. Pict bds (sm nick). *Washton*. $85/£54

BRONK, WILLIAM. Life Supports: New and Selected Poems. SF: North Point, 1981. 1st ed. Signed. Fine in Fine dj. *Lenz*. $75/£48

BRONK, WILLIAM. Silence and Metaphor. NY: Elizabeth Press, 1975. Ltd to 400 ptd. VG in ptd wrappers. *Cox*. $28/£18

BRONOWSKI, J. For Wilhelmina, Queen of the Netherlands. (Cambridge: W. Heffer & Sons, 1929). 1st ed, 1st bk. Inscribed. Fine in saddlestitched wrappers (lt stain fr wrap). *Between The Covers*. $250/£160

BRONSON, S. A. John Sherman, What He Has Said and Done.... Cincinnati, 1888. 1st ed. 277pp. (Sl cvr wear), o/w Fine. *Pratt*. $35/£22

BRONSON, WILFRID S. Children of the Sea. NY: Harcourt, 1940. 1st ed. 8vo. Color frontis. Pict eps. VG in pict dj (nicks). *Houle*. $150/£96

BRONTE, CHARLOTTE, EMILY, AND ANNE. The Novels of.... London: J.M. Dent, 1922. 6 vols. Edmund Dulac (illus). Marbled eps. Teg. 3/4 tan calf, leather spine labels. Very Nice. *Holmes*. $1,000/£641

BRONTE, CHARLOTTE. Jane Eyre. Temple Scott (ed). Edinburgh: John Grant, 1924. Thornton ed. 2 vols. Frontis port, 10 b/w plts. Top edge stained gray, uncut. Gilt-stamped grn cl. VG in djs. *Houle*. $150/£96

BRONTE, CHARLOTTE. The Spell. An Extravaganza. G.E. MacLean (ed). London: Oxford/Humphrey Milford, 1931. 1st ed. Unopened. Dec parchment, bds. Fine in dj (lt tanned, nicked). *Reese*. $50/£32

BRONTE, EMILY. Poems. London: Selwyn & Blunt, 1923. One of 500 numbered. Port. Cl, dec bds, paper label. VG. *Reese*. $50/£32

BRONTE, EMILY. Wuthering Heights. NY: Random House, 1931. Ltd to 450 numbered, signed by Claire Leighton (illus). 12 wood engrs. Uncut, unopened. Black cl, gilt. Good in orig pub's box. *Karmiole*. $400/£256

BRONTMAN, L. On Top of the World. London, 1938. Fldg map. VG. *High Latitude*. $20/£13

BROOK, HARRY ELLINGTON. The Land of Sunshine Southern California. L.A.: World's Fair Assn, 1893. 112pp; fldg map. (Spine expertly repaired), else Good. *Dumont*. $55/£35

BROOKE, HENRY. A Guide to the Stars. London, 1820. 12 plts. (Lt foxing, soiling.) Orig bds (worn, soiled, spine gone, fr cvr detaching), paper label. *Freeman**. $20/£13

BROOKE, JOCELYN. The Crisis in Bulgaria, or Ibsen to the Rescue! London, 1956. 1st Eng ed. Very Nice in dj (rear panel lacks piece). *Clearwater*. $55/£35

BROOKE, JOCELYN. The Dog at Clambercrown. London, 1955. 1st Eng ed. (Sl bumped, spine sl faded.) Dj (repaired). *Clearwater*. $55/£35

BROOKE, JOCELYN. The Elements of Death. Aldington: Hand & Flower, 1952. 1st Eng ed. Fine in card wrappers. *Clearwater*. $39/£25

BROOKE, JOCELYN. The Flower in Season. London, 1952. 1st Eng ed. Very Nice (stain fr cvr through dj) in dj. *Clearwater*. $39/£25

BROOKE, JOCELYN. The Image of a Drawn Sword. London, 1950. 1st Eng ed. (Sl leak from top dyed edge.) Dj (sl torn, chipped). *Clearwater*. $55/£35

BROOKE, JOCELYN. A Mine of Serpents. London, 1949. 1st Eng ed. Very Nice (1st few leaves sl creased) in dj (sl torn, mkd). *Clearwater*. $55/£35

BROOKE, JOCELYN. Ronald Firbank. London, 1951. 1st Eng ed. Very Nice in dj (dusty). *Clearwater*. $31/£20

BROOKE, JOCELYN. The Wild Orchids of Britain. London: Bodley Head, (1950). 1st ed. Brn cl. Fine in dj. *Appelfeld*. $200/£128

BROOKE, RUPERT. 1914. Five Sonnets. London, 1915. 1st ed. VG in wrappers (sl soiled). *Words Etc*. $78/£50

BROOKE, RUPERT. The Collected Poems of Rupert Brooke. NY: Editions for the Armed Services, (1945). Nice in illus ptd wrappers. *Turtle Island*. $15/£10

BROOKE, RUPERT. John Webster and the Elizabethan Drama. London, 1916. 1st ed. (Spine paper label browned), o/w VG. *Buckley*. $117/£75

BROOKE, RUPERT. John Webster and the Elizabethan Drama. NY: John Lane, 1916. 1st Amer ed. (Spine sunned), else VG. *Hermitage*. $40/£26

BROOKE, RUPERT. Letters from America. NY: Scribner, 1916. 1st ed. VG. *Waverly**. $22/£14

BROOKE, RUPERT. The Prose of Rupert Brooke. Christopher Hassall (ed). London: Sidgwick & Jackson, (1956). VG in dj. *Turtle Island*. $30/£19

BROOKE, SYLVIA. Queen of the Head Hunters. NY: Morrow, 1972. 1st US ed. 16 plts. VG in dj. *Worldwide*. $18/£12

BROOKE-RAWLE, W. Gregg's Cavalry Fight at Gettysburg. Phila, 1884. 29pp. Ptd wraps. (Tape repair fr cvr, map; rear cvr detached but present), o/w Good. *Scribe's Perch**. $120/£77

BROOKES, R. The Art of Angling.... London: W. Lowndes, 1793. New ed. Frontis. Uncut. Orig stiff wraps (worn, fr wrap detached, spine ends lt eroded). *Kane**. $80/£51

BROOKES, R. Brookes's General Gazetteer Improved; or, A New and Compendious Geographical Dictionary. Phila/Richmond, 1812. 11 maps. Orig sheep (spine foot frayed; lt dampstained). *Swann**. $149/£96

BROOKES, R. The General Practice of Physic.... London: J. Newbery, 1763. 4th ed. 2 vols. (Stamps tps, leaf torn w/loss, replaced in ms.) Contemp polished calf (worn). *Goodrich*. $175/£112

BROOKES, R. An Introduction to Physic and Surgery.... London, 1754. viii,536pp. Contemp leather (rebacked w/new label). (Top margin tp, some pp discolored), o/w VG. *Whitehart*. $289/£185

BROOKNER, ANITA. The Genius of the Future. London: Phaidon, 1971. 1st ed. Fine in dj (price-clipped, spine lt faded). *Lame Duck*. $100/£64

BROOKNER, ANITA. Hotel Du Lac. Cape, 1984. 1st UK ed. Fine in dj. *Williams*. $86/£55

BROOKNER, ANITA. Look at Me. Cape, 1983. 1st UK ed. NF in dj. *Williams*. $62/£40

BROOKS, ALFRED HULSE. Blazing Alaska's Trails. Univ of AK, 1953. 1st ed. VG in VG dj. *Perier*. $40/£26

BROOKS, C. M. et al. Humors, Hormones, and Neurosecretions.... NY, 1962. 1st ed. VG in dj. *Fye*. $60/£38

BROOKS, GWENDOLYN. The Bean Eaters. NY, (1960). 1st ed. (Ex-lib w/mks.) Good dj (sm ink #). *King*. $35/£22

BROOKS, GWENDOLYN. Maud Martha. NY, (1953). 1st ed. Cl-backed bds. (Ink name, date; ends sl soiled), else Good in dj (stained, torn, chipped). *King*. $65/£42

BROOKS, GWENDOLYN. Riot. Detroit: Broadside, 1969. 1st ed. (Rear wrap sl rubbed, tanned), else Fine in stapled wrappers. *Between The Covers*. $50/£32

BROOKS, GWENDOLYN. A Street in Bronzeville. NY, 1945. 1st ed, 1st bk. (Extrems sl worn), else Nice in dj (sl chipped, price-clipped). *King*. $395/£253

BROOKS, GWENDOLYN. Very Young Poets. (Chicago): Brooks, (1983). 1st ed. Signed. Fine (corner sl bumped) in stapled wrappers. *Between The Covers*. $75/£48

BROOKS, J. TYRWHITT. (Pseud of Henry Vizetelly.) Four Months Among the Gold-Finders in California. NY: D. Appleton, 1849. 1st Amer ed. 94,(2)pp; map. Orig ptd wrappers bound in brn calf over marbled bds, black/brn spine labels. (Sl rubbed.) Howes V134. *Karmiole*. $375/£240

BROOKS, JEREMY. Henry's War. London: Macmillan, 1962. 1st ed. Fine in dj. *Hermitage*. $40/£26

BROOKS, JUANITA. John Doyle Lee: Zealot—Pioneer Builder—Scapegoat. Glendale: Clark, 1962. 2nd ptg in red cl, issued simultaneously w/1st ptg. One of 2323. Frontis port, 16 plts. Red cl. VF in dj (sl chipped, soiled). *Argonaut*. $90/£58

BROOKS, JUANITA. John Doyle Lee: Zealot.... Glendale, 1961. True 1st ed, 1st ptg. Frontis, port. NF. *Benchmark*. $360/£231

BROOKS, JUANITA. The Mountain Meadows Massacre. Stanford Univ, 1950. 1st ed. Inscribed. Map frontis. Dec cl. Fine in dj (chipped). *Connolly*. $95/£61

BROOKS, JUANITA. Quicksand and Cactus. Salt Lake, 1982. 1st ed, 2nd ptg. Frontis, port. VG in dj. *Benchmark*. $30/£19

BROOKS, NOAH. The Fairport Nine. Scribner, 1880. 1st ed. Pict cvr. VG (sm chip upper spine). *Plapinger*. $550/£353

BROOKS, NOAH. Our Baseball Club. Dutton, 1884. 1st ed. Pict cvr. Good+ (spine worn; 1st, last pp dampstained). *Plapinger*. $550/£353

BROOKS, NOAH. Washington in Lincoln's Time. Herbert Mitgang (ed). NY: Rinehart, (1958). Dj. *Dawson*. $30/£19

BROOKS, PHILLIPS. Letters of Travel. NY: Dutton, 1893. 1st ed. v,386pp. Teg. (Spine, corners frayed, spine sl dampstained), o/w VG. *Worldwide*. $14/£9

BROOKS, U. R. Butler and His Cavalry.... Columbia, SC, 1909. Good- (pp wrinkled). *Scribe's Perch**. $75/£48

BROOKS, VAN WYCK. The Flowering of New England. (NY): Dutton, 1936. 1st ed, 1st ptg. Fine in VG dj. *Macdonnell*. $25/£16

BROOKS, VAN WYCK. New England: Indian Summer 1865-1915. (NY): Dutton, 1940. 1st ed. Ltd to 997 numbered, signed. (Spine spotted, lt worn.) Contents VG. *New Hampshire**. $30/£19

BROOKS, VAN WYCK. The World of Washington Irving. (NY): Dutton, 1944. 1st ed, 1st ptg. Fine in VG dj. *Macdonnell*. $25/£16

BROOKS, WALTER R. Freddy and the Baseball Team from Mars. NY: Knopf, 1955. 1st ed. Kurt Wiese (illus). Lg 12mo. Illus eps. Pict cl. VG+; contents NF. *Book Adoption*. $75/£48

BROOKS, WALTER R. Freddy Rides Again. NY: Knopf, 1951. 1st ed. Kurt Wiese (illus). 5 1/2 x 8. 240pp. VG. *Cattermole*. $50/£32

BROOKS, WALTER R. The Story of Freginald. NY: Knopf, 1936. 1st ed. Kurt Wiese (illus). Lg 12mo. Lib cl (ex-lib, cvr worn). Good+. *Book Adoption*. $75/£48

BROOKS, WILLIAM E. Lee of Virginia. Indianapolis, (1932). 1st ed. VG. *Pratt*. $40/£26

BROOKS, WILLIAM. The Foundations of Zoology. NY, 1899. 1st ed. 339pp. (Ex-lib.) *Fye*. $75/£48

BROOMELL, I. N. and P. FISCHELIS. Anatomy and Histology of the Mouth and Teeth. London: Kimpton, 1917. 5th ed. VG. *Savona*. $39/£25

BROONZY, WILLIAM and YANNICK BRUYNOGHE. Big Bill Blues. London: Cassell, 1955. US issue. Fine in Grove Press dj (sl used). *Beasley*. $65/£42

BROPHY, BRIGID. The Snow Ball/The Finishing Touch. Cleveland: World, (1963). 1st ed. Fine in dj (sl worn, price-clipped). *Antic Hay*. $35/£22

BROPHY, JOHN. Britain's Home Guard. London, 1945. 1st Eng ed. 19 color plts. Very Nice in dj (torn, frayed). *Clearwater*. $39/£25

BROSS, WILLIAM. Biographical Sketch of the Late Gen. B.J. Sweet. Chicago: Jansen, McClurg, 1878. 1st ed. 28pp + 4pp ads; full-pg map. Orig wraps. (Sl rubbed), o/w VG. *Worldwide*. $65/£42

BROSSARD, CHANDLER. The Bold Saboteurs. NY: Farrar, Straus & Young, 1953. 1st ed. Signed. (Extrems sl shelfworn), else NF in VG+ dj (spine faded, lt worn). *Lame Duck*. $150/£96

BROSSARD, CHANDLER. The Double View. NY, 1960. 1st ed. VG in dj. *Argosy*. $25/£16

BROSSARD, CHANDLER. The Girls in Rome. NY: Signet, 1961. 1st ed. Pb orig. Fine (few sm dents). *Beasley*. $35/£22

BROTHWELL, D. R. (ed). The Skeletal Biology of Earlier Human Populations. Oxford: Pergamon, 1968. 1st ed. Fine. *Mikesh*. $25/£16

BROUGH, ROBERT. The Life of Sir John Falstaff. London: Longman, Brown, 1858. 1st ed. 20 etchings by George Cruikshank. Teg. Full tan polished calf (expertly rebacked, orig spine laid down, corners worn, orig cl cvr bound in at end). *Appelfeld*. $300/£192

BROUGHAM, H. L. Lives of Men of Letters and Science Who Flourished in the Time of George III. 1845. Frontis port, xv,517pp. (Stamp fep, inner hinge sl cracked; spine ends sl defective, corners sl worn), o/w VG. *Whitehart*. $62/£40

BROUGHTON, H. H. Electric Cranes, Their Design, Construction and Application.... n.d. (1911). 3/4 morocco. (Spine rubbed), o/w VG. *Whitehart*. $62/£40

BROUGHTON, RHODA. Nancy. Bentley, 1873. 1st Eng ed. 3 vols. (Feps stained 1 vol, lacks 1/2 titles; bindings cocked, sections loosening from stitching.) *Clearwater*. $70/£45

BROUN, HEYWOOD. The Fifty-First Dragon. Englewood Cliffs, NJ: Prentice-Hall, 1968. 1st ed thus. Ed Emberly (illus). 5 1/4 x 7 1/4. 48pp. VG in dj. *Cattermole*. $15/£10

BROUN, HEYWOOD. Seeing Things at Night. NY, 1921. 1st Amer ed, 1st bk. Fine (name, piece of dj pasted inside fr cvr; spine, corners sl rubbed). *Polyanthos*. $50/£32

BROUSSAIS, F. J. V. A Treatise on Physiology Applied to Pathology. Phila, 1828. 2nd ed. 600pp (yellowed). Orig leather bds (detached). Fair (binding shaken). *Doctor's Library*. $35/£22

BROUWER, B. Anatomical, Phylogenetical and Clinical Studies on the Central Nervous System. Balt, 1927. (Sm tear 1 pg; ink sig, sm label fep; spine sl damaged.) *Whitehart*. $62/£40

BROUWS, JEFFREY. Twenty-Six Abandoned Gasoline Stations. Santa Barbara: Handjob Press, 1992. One of 1000 numbered. Fine in stiff wrappers, Fine tissue dj. *Smith*. $40/£26

BROWDER, EARL and BILL LAWRENCE. Next Steps to Win the War in Spain. NY: Workers Library, 1938. 1st ed. Nice in wrappers. *Patterson*. $31/£20

BROWER, CHARLES D. Fifty Years Below Zero. NY: Dodd, Mead, 1942. 1st ed. VG in dj. *High Latitude*. $35/£22

BROWER, DAVID (ed). Not Man Apart. SF: Sierra Club, (1965). 1st ed. VG in dj (sl wrinkled). *King*. $65/£42

BROWN, A. SAMLER. Madeira, Canary Islands and Azores. Simpkin, Marshall, 1932. 14th ed. 22 fldg maps. Pict cl (sl soiled, mkd). Sound. *Cox*. $23/£15

BROWN, ALAN K. Sawpits in the Spanish Red Woods, 1787-1849. San Mateo County Hist Assoc, 1966. 1st ed. One of 750 ptd. Frontis map, 2 plts. Gilt-lettered grn cl. Fine. *Argonaut*. $40/£26

BROWN, ALEXANDER. The Cabells and Their Kin.... Garrett & Massie, 1939. 2nd ed. (Several index pp archivally repaired.) *Book Broker*. $100/£64

BROWN, ALFRED. Old Masterpieces in Surgery. Omaha: Privately ptd, 1928. 1st ed. 57 plts. VG. *Fye*. $200/£128

BROWN, ALICE. The Wind Between the Worlds. Macmillan, 1920. 1st ed. VG +. *Certo*. $30/£19

BROWN, B. Astronomical Atlases, Maps and Charts. 1968. VG. *Whitehart*. $70/£45

BROWN, B. Talking Pictures. 1932. 2nd ed. (Pencil sig; cl dull.) *Whitehart*. $39/£25

BROWN, CHARLES BROCKDEN. The Novels of Charles Brockden Brown. Phila: David McKay, 1887. Ltd to 500 numbered sets. 6 vols. Frontis port. Vellum-like spines, grn bds (sl soiled). BAL 1516. *Karmiole*. $150/£96

BROWN, D. ALEXANDER. The Galvanized Yankees. Urbana: Univ of IL, 1963. 1st ed. VG in dj. *Lien*. $45/£29

BROWN, D. MACKENZIE (ed). China Trade Days in California.... Berkeley: Univ of CA, 1947. 1st ed. 2 ports. Fine. *Argonaut*. $45/£29

BROWN, DAVID L. Three Years in the Rocky Mountains. (NY: Eberstadt, 1950.) One of 100. *Ginsberg*. $75/£48

BROWN, DEE and MARTIN F. SCHMITT. Trail Driving Days. NY, 1952. 1st ed. Folio. Good. *Heinoldt*. $50/£32

BROWN, DEE. Hear That Lonesome Whistle Blow. NY: HR&W, (1977). 1st ed. Fine in Fine dj. *Agvent*. $25/£16

BROWN, DEE. Kildeer Mountain. NY, (1983). 1st ed. Fine in Fine dj. *Pratt*. $22/£14

BROWN, EVERETT SOMERVILLE. The Constitutional History of the Louisiana Purchase, 1803-1812. Berkeley: Univ of CA, 1920. 1st ed. Uncut. Gilt-lettered blue cl. VF. *Argonaut*. $125/£80

BROWN, F. MARTIN and BERNARD HEINEMAN. Jamaica and Its Butterflies. London: E.W. Classey Ltd, 1972. 1st ed. Color frontis, 10 color plts, 2 maps. Beige cl, gilt. Fine in dj. *Karmiole*. $75/£48

BROWN, FREDRIC. And the Gods Laughed: A Collection of Science Fiction and Fantasy. West Bloomfield: Phantasia, 1987. 1st ed. One of 475 numbered. Unnumbered presentation copy signed by Brown and Mack Reynolds. Fine in Fine dj, slipcase. *Janus*. $150/£96

BROWN, FREDRIC. Angels and Spaceships. Dutton, 1954. 1st ed. (Top edge sl dusty.) NF in dj (spine browned, lettering illegible). *Certo*. $60/£38

BROWN, FREDRIC. The Case of the Dancing Sandwiches. Volcano, HI: Dennis McMillan, 1985. 1st ed. Ltd to 400 numbered, signed by Lawrence Block (intro). VF in VF dj. *Murder By The Book*. $100/£64

BROWN, FREDRIC. Death Has Many Doors. Dutton, 1951. 1st ed. (Dust along fore-edge.) VG + in dj (short closed tears, sl rubbed). *Certo*. $100/£64

BROWN, FREDRIC. The Deep End. NY, 1952. 1st ed. Nice in dj (sl worn). *King*. $125/£80

BROWN, FREDRIC. The Deep End. NY: Dutton, 1952. 1st ed. Fine in dj (short closed tears, sl corner wear). *Mordida*. $200/£128

BROWN, FREDRIC. Here Comes a Candle. NY: Dutton, 1950. 1st ed. (Faint tape mks external cvrs), o/w VG in dj (corners, folds worn). *Mordida*. $65/£42

BROWN, FREDRIC. Homicide Sanitarium. San Antonio: Dennis McMillan, 1984. 1st ed. One of 300 numbered, signed by Bill Pronzini (intro). VF in dj. *Mordida*. $125/£80

BROWN, FREDRIC. The Office. Dutton, 1958. 1st ed. (Edges worn, spine lt dknd), else VG + in dj (spine rubbed, few closed tears, wear). *Murder By The Book*. $95/£61

BROWN, FREDRIC. Paradox Lost and Twelve Other Great Science Fiction Stories. Random House, (1973). 1st ed. (Top pg edges dusty), else Fine in Fine dj. *Certo*. $45/£29

BROWN, FREDRIC. Rogue in Space. NY: Dutton, 1957. 1st ed. VG + (spine sl slant) in dj (edgewear, lt chipping). *Other Worlds*. $95/£61

BROWN, FREDRIC. The Screaming Mimi. NY: Dutton, 1949. 1st ed. (Newspaper rev removed from fep), o/w VG in dj (spine dknd, chipped). *Mordida*. $85/£54

BROWN, FREDRIC. The Shaggy Dog and Other Murders. NY: Dutton, 1963. 1st ed. VG (lib seal fly) in dj (soiled, extrems worn). *Metropolitan**. $207/£133

BROWN, FREDRIC. Space on My Hands. Chicago: Shasta, (1951). 1st ed. Signed. Bright (stamp fep, tp) in dj (lt toned, few nicks, crimps). *Waverly**. $176/£113

BROWN, FREDRIC. What Mad Universe. NY: Dutton, 1949. 1st ed. Blue bds. (Bkpl; sl shelfworn), else Fine in dj (toning rear panel, spine head sl frayed, short tears). *Waverly**. $132/£85

BROWN, G. BALDWIN. The Art of the Cave Dweller. 1928. Color frontis, 95 b/w plts, 4 maps (lt spotted). (Feps browned.) *Edwards*. $55/£35

BROWN, GEORGE D. From Coast to Coast. Simsbury, CT: The Author, 1923. Signed. 7 plts. VG + in ptd wraps w/mtd illus. *Bohling*. $60/£38

BROWN, GEORGE S. Brown's Abridged Journal, Containing a Brief Account of the Life, Trials and Travels of Geo. S. Brown, Six Years a Missionary in Liberia, West Africa. Troy, NY: Prescott, 1849. 1st ed. 392pp. Dec cl (joint top starting). *Ginsberg*. $300/£192

BROWN, GEORGE. Melanesians and Polynesians. London, 1910. (Lacks frontis, 5 plts supplied in photocopy; bds sl dampstained, spine sl faded.) *Edwards*. $47/£30

BROWN, GOULD. The Grammar of English Grammars. NY, 1860. 5th ed. Port. Orig sheep, leather labels (scuffed). *Freeman**. $25/£16

BROWN, HENRY COLLINS. The Story of Old New York. NY: Dutton, 1934. 1st ed. Facs 1839 NYC map laid in. VG (spine sunned). *Archer*. $17/£11

BROWN, HENRY. A Narrative of the Anti-Masonick Excitement in the Western Part of the State of New York....1826, '7, '8 and a Part of 1829. Batavia, NY: Ptd by Adams & M'Cleary, 1829. 1st ed. (8),244pp (foxing). Contemp bds, spine neatly cvrd w/mod tan paper. *Karmiole*. $150/£96

BROWN, IRVING. Nights and Days on the Gypsy Trail. NY/London: Harper, 1922. 16 photo plts. (Spine faded), o/w Good. *Scribe's Perch**. $22/£14

BROWN, J. The Forester, a Practical Treatise on the Planting...of Forest Trees. London, 1851. 2nd ed. xiv,526pp. Good. *Henly*. $50/£32

BROWN, J. H. Spectropia. London: Griffith & Farran, 1864. 3rd ed. 11pp + 15 hand-color plts. Cl-backed ptd bds (lt soiled, edgewear). (Lacks final plt), o/w VG. *Hollett*. $273/£175

BROWN, J. WOOD. The Builders of Florence. London: Methuen, 1907. 1st ed. Teg, uncut. Good in blue cl (backstrip sl faded, sl worn), gilt. *Cox.* $62/£40

BROWN, J. WOOD. An Enquiry into the Life and Legend of Michael Scot. Edinburgh: David Douglas, 1897. 1st ed. Frontis, xvi,281,(1),20(ads)pp; plt. Teg. VG (ex-lib). *Glaser.* $100/£64

BROWN, JAMES BERRY. Journal of a Journey Across the Plains in 1859. George R. Stewart (ed). SF: Book Club of CA, 1970. One of 450. Pict bds. Fine. *Harrington.* $75/£48

BROWN, JESSE and A. M. WILLARD. The Black Hills Trails. John T. Milek (ed). Rapid City, SD: Rapid City Journal Co, 1924. 1st ed. Frontis. Grn cl, gilt-lettered spine (lt rubbed). Fine. Howes B850. *Argonaut.* $225/£144

BROWN, JOHN and JAMES C. MALIN. John Brown and the Legend of Fifty-Six. Phila: Amer Philosophical Soc, 1942. 1st ed. 2 maps (1 fldg). NF. *Worldwide.* $45/£29

BROWN, JOHN HULL. Early American Beverages. Rutland, VT, (1966). 1st ed. VG in dj. *King.* $45/£29

BROWN, JOHN. I Was a Tramp. London: Selwyn & Blount, 1934. 2nd imp. Nice. *Patterson.* $47/£30

BROWN, JONATHAN and J. H. ELLIOTT. A Palace for a King. New Haven/London, 1980. Good. *Washton.* $35/£22

BROWN, JONATHAN. Murillo and His Drawings. Princeton, 1976. Good in dj. *Washton.* $90/£58

BROWN, KENNETH. The Medchester Club. NY: Derrydale, 1938. Ltd to 950. VG+. *October Farm.* $50/£32

BROWN, LARRY. Dirty Work. (Chapel Hill, NC): Algonquin, 1989. 1st ed. Signed. Fine in Fine dj. *Bernard.* $60/£38

BROWN, LARRY. Facing the Music. Chapel Hill: Algonquin, 1988. 1st ed, 1st bk. Fine in dj. *Between The Covers.* $85/£54

BROWN, LOUIS A. The Salisbury Prison, a Case Study of Confederate Military Prisons 1861-1865. Wendell, NC, 1980. Fine. *Bohling.* $30/£19

BROWN, M. L. Firearms in Colonial America. Washington: Smithsonian, 1980. Fine in dj. *Bohling.* $35/£22

BROWN, MALCOLM and ORIN CASSMORE. Migratory Cotton Pickers in Arizona. Washington: WPA/GPO, 1939. 1st ed. VG in wraps (wear). *Beasley.* $25/£16

BROWN, MARCIA. The Blue Jackal. NY: Scribner, 1977. 1st ed. 8 1/4 x 10 1/4. 32pp. Fine in dj. *Cattermole.* $30/£19

BROWN, MARGARET W. The Dresses of the First Ladies of the White House. Washington: Smithsonian, 1952. 1st ed. Supplements from 1954, 1958, 1963 bound in at rear. Grn cl, rose bds (lt soiled), ptd paper label. *Karmiole.* $50/£32

BROWN, MARGARET WISE. The Country Noisy Book. NY: Wm R. Scott, 1940. 1st ed. Leonard Weisgard (illus). 7 1/4 x 9. 32pp. Pict bds. VG in dj (sl edge tears, chips). *Cattermole.* $100/£64

BROWN, MARGARET WISE. The Dark Wood of the Golden Birds. NY: Harper, 1950. 1st ed. Leonard Weisgard (illus). 5 3/4 x 8 1/2. 60pp. Cl spine, pict bds. VG (inscrip) in dj (lt soil, sl rubbed). *Cattermole.* $50/£32

BROWN, MARGARET WISE. David's Little Indian. NY: Young Scott, 1956. 1st ed. Remy Charlip (illus). 5 1/4 x 6 1/4. 32pp. VG in dj (sl rubbed, few chips). *Cattermole.* $125/£80

BROWN, MARGARET WISE. The Fish with the Deep Sea Smile. NY: Dutton, 1938. 1st ed. Roberta Rauch (illus). 6 1/4 x 9. 128pp. Pict cl. VG. *Cattermole.* $60/£38

BROWN, MARGARET WISE. Fox Eyes. NY: Pantheon, 1951. 1st ed. Jean Charlot (illus). 5 3/4 x 8 1/2. 32pp. VG in dj. *Cattermole.* $150/£96

BROWN, MARGARET WISE. The Seashore Noisy Book. NY: Harper, 1941. Probable 1st ed. Leonard Weisgard (illus). 7 x 8 1/2. 32pp. VG. *Cattermole.* $60/£38

BROWN, MARGARET WISE. Shhhhhh...Bang. NY: Harper, 1943. 1st ed. Robert De Veyrac (illus). 8 1/4 x 10 1/4. 40pp. Cl spine, pict bds. Good (inscrip, lt soil). *Cattermole.* $50/£32

BROWN, MARGARET WISE. The Steamroller. NY: Walker & Co, 1974. 1st ed. Evaline Ness (illus). 9 x 7 1/4. 32pp. VG in dj. *Cattermole.* $35/£22

BROWN, MARGARET WISE. They All Saw It. NY: Harper, 1944. 1st ed. 9 x 11 1/2. 32pp. Cl spine, pict bds. VG. *Cattermole.* $100/£64

BROWN, MARK H. The Plainsmen of the Yellowstone. NY: Putnam, 1961. 9 maps. Good in dj. *Dumont.* $45/£29

BROWN, MARK H. and W. R. FELTON. Before Barbed Wire: L.A. Huffman, Photographer on Horseback. NY: Holt, (1956). 1st ed. 124 photos. VG in dj (sl worn). *Lien.* $40/£26

BROWN, MERLE BLINN. Eight Rattles and a Button. San Antonio: Naylor, (1967). Pict fabricoid. Dj. *Dawson.* $25/£16

BROWN, MRS. HUGH. Lady in Boomtown. Palo Alto, CA: Amer West, 1968. 1st ed. 32 photo plts. Pink cl. VG in dj (chipped). *Price.* $29/£19

BROWN, PAUL. Aintree, Grand Nationals—Past and Present. NY: Derrydale, 1930. Ltd to 850. (Sl wear, cvr spotting.) *King.* $185/£119

BROWN, PAUL. Three Rings. NY: Scribner, 1938. 1st ed. 8 1/2 x 10 1/2. 76pp. VG in dj. *Cattermole.* $100/£64

BROWN, RITA MAE. A Plain Brown Rapper. CA: Diana Press, 1976. 1st ed. Fine in wrappers. *Warren.* $95/£61

BROWN, ROBERT E. The Book of the Landed Estate. London, 1869. 1st ed. xiii,505pp + 16pp pub's list. Gilt-dec roan-backed cl. (Lt browning; edges faded, spine rubbed, sm split.) *Edwards.* $62/£40

BROWN, ROBERT L. Colorado Ghost Towns, Past and Present. Caldwell, ID: Caxton, 1972. 1st ed. VG in dj (piece cut from spine bottom). *Heinoldt.* $25/£16

BROWN, ROSELLEN. Street Games. GC: Doubleday, 1974. 1st ed. Fine (name, address) in NF dj (rear tear). *Beasley.* $45/£29

BROWN, RUSSELL A. Sherlock Holmes and the Mysterious Friend of Oscar Wilde. NY: St. Martin's, (1988). 1st US ed. VG in VG dj (sl wear). *Gravesend.* $35/£22

BROWN, SAMUEL R. The Western Gazetteer. Auburn, NY, 1817. 1st ed, 3rd issue. 360pp (name stamp, foxed, lacks fep, pp311-312 badly torn, hinges loose). Old tree calf (scuffed). *King.* $250/£160

BROWN, SANGER II. The Sex Worship and Symbolism of Primitive Races. Boston: Richard G. Badger, (1916). 1st ed. Ptd grn cl. Jelliffe's bkpl. VG (lib stamp tp, spine #s). *Gach.* $30/£19

BROWN, STERLING A. et al (eds). The Negro Caravan. NY: Citadel, (1941). Cream cl (smudged). *Petrilla.* $40/£26

BROWN, STERLING. The Last Ride of Wild Bill. Detroit: Broadside, 1975. 1st ed. Pb. NF. *Beasley.* $40/£26

BROWN, STEVE. Doberman Champions of America 1960 thru 1964. Lakeport, 1966. 1st ed. VG. *October Farm.* $45/£29

BROWN, SUSAN ANNA (comp). Home Topics. NY: Century, (1881). 1st ed. 564pp. Brn cl (sl worn, hinges loose). Good (ex-lib). *Second Life.* $85/£54

BROWN, THADDEUS C. S. et al. Behind the Guns. C. C. Walton (ed). Carbondale, (1965). 1st ed. #660/1000. Fine in slipcase. *Pratt.* $50/£32

BROWN, THEODORE M. Margaret Bourke-White, Photojournalist. Ithaca: Andrew Dickson White Museum of Art, Cornell Univ, 1972. 1st ed. Cl-backed illus paper over bds. (Owner stamp), else NF in ptd acetate wrapper (chipped). *Cahan.* $65/£42

BROWN, THOMAS. An Account of the People Called Shakers. Troy, NY: Parker & Bliss, 1812. 372pp (sl dknd, stained). Full leather (scuffed, fr hinge split, fr cvr nearly detached). *Bohling.* $90/£58

BROWN, THOMAS. Taxidermist's Manual. NY: OJ, n.d. Amer rev ed, from 20th Eng ed. 111pp + 7pp ads. Rust cl (rubbed, lt frayed), gilt. *Bohling.* $30/£19

BROWN, THORVALD T. The Enigma of Drug Addiction. Springfield, IL: Charles C. Thomas, 1963. 2nd ptg. VG + in dj. *Sclanders.* $23/£15

BROWN, W. NORMAN. The Swastika: A Study of the Nazi Claims of Its Aryan Origin. NY: Emerson Bks, (1933). Orig ptd wrappers (spine sl dknd). *Sadlon.* $20/£13

BROWN, WALTER L. Manual of Assaying Gold, Silver, Copper and Lead Ores. Chicago, 1883. 1st ed. 318pp. Brn cl, gilt. (Edgewear), else Good. *Price.* $35/£22

BROWN, WILLIAM COMPTON. The Indian Side of the Story. Spokane: C.W. Hill, (1961). 1st ed. Signed. VG. *Perier.* $97/£62

BROWN, WILLIAM F. How to Train Hunting Dogs. NY, (1942). VG (ink name ep). *Truepenny.* $15/£10

BROWN, WILLIAM F. Retriever Gun Dogs. NY: A.S. Barnes, 1945. Ltd to 5000. Grn cl, orange lettering. NF in pict dj (chipped). *Biscotti.* $15/£10

BROWN, WILLIAM HARVEY. On the South African Frontier. London: Sampson, Low, 1899. 1st ed. Frontis, xxii,430pp; 2 fldg colored maps. Red gilt cl (spine sl sunned), else VG. *Terramedia.* $300/£192

BROWN, WILLIAM SYMINGTON. The Capability of Women to Practice the Healing Art. Boston: Ripley, 1859. 1st ed. 15pp. VG in ptd wraps, mtd in cardbd binder. *Second Life.* $85/£54

BROWN, WILLIAM W. Narrative of...a Fugitive Slave. Boston: Anti-Slavery Office, 1847. 1st ed. Port, 110pp. (Sl waterstained throughout; cl quite rubbed, worn.) Howes B874. *M & S.* $425/£272

BROWN, WILLIAM W. The Negro in the American Rebellion. Boston: Lee & Shepard, 1867. 1st ed. xvi,380pp. (Sl worn), else VG. *Brown.* $100/£64

BROWN-SEQUARD, CHARLES E. Lectures on the Diagnosis and Treatment of the Principal Forms of Paralysis of the Lower Extremities. Phila: Collins, 1861. 188pp. (Cl sl worn, faded, spine bottom chipped), else Good. *Goodrich.* $795/£510

BROWNE, ANTHONY. Through the Magic Mirror. NY: Greenwillow, 1977. 1st US ed. 10 1/4 x 8 1/4. 32pp. Fine in dj. *Cattermole.* $50/£32

BROWNE, BELMORE. The Conquest of Mt. McKinley. Boston, 1956. VG in dj (torn, creased). *King.* $45/£29

BROWNE, D. G. and E. V. TULLETT. Bernard Spilsbury. London: Harrap, 1951. VG. *Savona.* $19/£12

BROWNE, DOUGLAS G. and E. V. TULLETT. The Scalpel of Scotland Yard: The Life of Sir Bernard Spilsbury. NY, 1952. 1st ed. Grn cl. VG in Good dj. *Doctor's Library.* $45/£29

BROWNE, FRANCIS I. (ed). Bugle-Echoes. NY, 1886. 1st ed. 336pp. Gilt edges. Pict cl. (Cvr wear), o/w Fine. *Pratt.* $30/£19

BROWNE, HOWARD. The Taste of Ashes. NY: S&S, 1957. 1st ed. Fine (lt browned) in VG dj (edgeworn). *Metropolitan*.* $161/£103

BROWNE, J. and J. TAYLOR. Reports on the Mineral Resources of the United States. Washington, 1868. 674,72pp. Good (foxed). *Blake.* $85/£54

BROWNE, J. H. BALFOUR. The Medical Jurisprudence of Insanity. SF: Sumner Whitney, 1880. 2nd US ed. (714)pp. Contemp legal sheepskin (joints cracked, spine shelfworn), red/black leather spine labels. Good (fep edges sl frayed). *Gach.* $175/£112

BROWNE, J. ROSS. Adventures in Apache Country. NY, 1869. 1st ed. 535pp + ads. (Ink name tp nearly faded away; lt wear spine extrems.) VG. Howes B875. *Truepenny.* $300/£192

BROWNE, J. ROSS. Adventures in Apache Country. NY: Harper, 1869. 535,5ads pp. Blue cl (rubbed, frayed). Howes B875. *Adelson.* $325/£208

BROWNE, J. ROSS. Crusoe's Island. NY: Harper, 1867. Inscribed. vii,9-436pp. Brn cl (lt rubbed). Howes B876. *Adelson.* $375/£240

BROWNE, J. ROSS. A Dangerous Journey. Palo Alto: Arthur Lites, 1950. One of 1000. VG in dj. *Dumont.* $55/£35

BROWNE, J. ROSS. Explorations in Lower California 1868. Tucson, 1952. Fine. *Turpen.* $18/£12

BROWNE, J. ROSS. J. Ross Browne, His Letters, Journals and Writings. Lina Fergusson Browne (ed). Albuquerque, 1969. 1st ed. Fine in Fine dj. *Turpen.* $28/£18

BROWNE, J. ROSS. Muleback to the Convention: Letters of J. Ross Browne. SF: Book Club of CA, 1950. 1st ed. Ltd to 400. Port; bound-in facs. Illus paper over bds. Fine. *Cahan.* $60/£38

BROWNE, J. ROSS. A Peep at Washoe or, Sketch of Adventure in Virginia City.... Palo Alto: Lewis Osborne, 1968. Ltd to 1400 numbered. Frontis port. Grn cl, silver decs. Fine. *Argonaut.* $45/£29

BROWNE, J. ROSS. Resources of the Pacific Slope.... NY, 1869. 1st ed. 678pp + supp by Alexander S. Taylor (fep, fr pastedown sl dampstained). Lt blue cl. VG. *Turpen.* $295/£189

BROWNE, J. ROSS. Washoe Revisited. Oakland: Biobooks, 1957. Rpt of 1869 ed. Ltd to 500. NF. Howes B875. *Cahan.* $35/£22

BROWNE, JAMES. A History of the Highlands. London: A. Fullarton, 1845. 4 vols. 40 engr plts (some damp-stained), fldg map hand colored in outline. Blind-stamped cl (sl faded, rubbed; joint cracked, roughly repaired; damping), gilt. *Hollett.* $101/£65

BROWNE, JEFFERSON BEALE. Key West, the Old and the New. St. Augustine: Record, 1912. 1st ed. (Cl sl damped), else VG. *Mcgowan.* $150/£96

BROWNE, JUNIUS HENRI. Four Years in Secessia. Chicago/London, 1865. (vi),450pp; 8 plts. VG (lt foxed). *Wantagh.* $35/£22

BROWNE, JUNIUS HENRI. The Great Metropolis. Hartford: Amer Pub Co, 1869. 700,4pp. (Sl shaken, worn, spine tear.) Internally VG. *Worldwide.* $25/£16

BROWNE, M. Practical Taxidermy. London, (1884). 2nd ed. viii,354pp; plan, 4 plts. *Wheldon & Wesley.* $62/£40

BROWNE, NINA E. A Bibliography of Nathaniel Hawthorne. Boston/NY: Houghton, Mifflin, 1905. 1st ed. One of 550 numbered. Uncut. Cl, paper label. (Fading), else Fine. *Macdonnell.* $85/£54

BROWNE, THOMAS. Christian Morals. London: J. Payne, 1756. 2nd ed. (4),lxi,(10),8-136pp, incl 1/2-title (sl pencil mks, 1 leaf torn). Contemp calf (worn, fr joint partly split). *Waverly*.* $104/£67

BROWNE, THOMAS. Christian Morals. Cambridge: CUP, 1904. Rpt. Ltd to 250. Unopened. Parchment-backed gray bds, ptd title label. Nice. *Cady.* $30/£19

BROWNE, THOMAS. Letter to a Friend, 1690. London: Frederick Etchells & Hugh Macdonald, 1924. One of 425 numbered. Bds, paper label. VG. *Reese*. $45/£29

BROWNE, THOMAS. Posthumous Works. London: E. Curll & R. Gosling, 1712. 1st ed. Frontis port, 22 other engr plts, incl 4 fldg plts (1 torn, few shaved). Contents Sound (lt browned, foxed; binding defective, lacks fr bd; rear bd, later spine worn). *Waverly**. $60/£38

BROWNE, THOMAS. Religio Medici and Other Essays. London: Chapman & Hall, (1911). Laid deckled-edge paper. Uncut, teg. Bound by Sangorski & Sutcliffe in polished burgundy calf, gilt. Good. *Goodrich*. $125/£80

BROWNE, THOMAS. Religio Medici, Hydriotaphia, and the Letter to a Friend. London, 1869. 196pp. VG. *Fye*. $75/£48

BROWNE, THOMAS. Religio Medici. London: J. Torbuck, 1736. New ed. Engr frontis, 150 leaves. Contemp 1/4 vellum, marbled bds (worn, spine chipped). *Goodrich*. $250/£160

BROWNE, THOMAS. Religio Medici. Geoffrey Keynes (ed). Eugene: Univ of OR/LEC, 1939. Ltd to 1500 ptd, signed by John Henry Nash (ptr). 1/4 natural linen, marbled bds. VG +. *Truepenny*. $85/£54

BROWNE, THOMAS. The Works of Sir Thomas Browne. Charles Sayle (ed). Edinburgh, 1927. 3 vols. Cl-backed bds, leather labels. VG. *Fye*. $125/£80

BROWNE, THOMAS. The Works of the Learned Sr. Thomas Brown.... London: T. Bassett, 1686. 1st collected ed. Sm folio. (xxii),316, (317-28 table), (14), 102, (8), 52, (6), 103pp (104 blank,105-107 index,108 blank); engr port. (Lt foxing, margin notes, leaf Ccc1 and Ggg1 w/tears; bkpl.) Contemp full calf (skillfully rebacked), raised bands. Tight. *Goodrich*. $595/£381

BROWNE, THOMAS. The Works. London: Basset Ric. Chiswell, etc, 1686. 1st collected ed. Tp in red/black (dusty), full-pg mtd engr frontis port. Full polished chestnut calf (rebound in period style), orig leather label laid down. Contents Fine. *Hartfield*. $895/£574

BROWNE, THOMAS. The Works. Charles Sayle (ed). Edinburgh: John Grant, 1927. 3 vols. 5 plts. Uncut. Good set in orig buckram-backed bds, morocco labels. *Cox*. $59/£38

BROWNE, THOMAS. The Works.... Geoffrey Keynes (ed). Faber & Faber, 1964. 4 vols. 12 plts, facs. VG in djs (sl rubbed). *Cox*. $70/£45

BROWNE, TURNER and ELAINE PARTNOW. Macmillan Biographical Encyclopedia of Photographic Artists and Innovators. NY: Macmillan, 1982. 1st ed. Cl-backed paper over bds. NF in dj (edge-chipped). *Cahan*. $85/£54

BROWNELL, HENRY HOWARD. The Pioneer Heroes of the New World. Cincinnati, 1856. Pub's emb morocco (extrems worn). *Swann**. $69/£44

BROWNING, ELIZABETH BARRETT. Aurora Leigh. NY: C.S. Francis, 1857. 1st Amer ed, 1st ptg. Brn cl (sl rubbed), gilt. Fine. *Macdonnell*. $85/£54

BROWNING, ELIZABETH BARRETT. The Greek Christian Poets and the English Poets. London: Chapman & Hall, 1863. 1st ed. Purple cl, gilt. VG. *Macdonnell*. $85/£54

BROWNING, ELIZABETH BARRETT. The Letters of Elizabeth Barrett Browning. F. G. Kenyon (ed). London, 1897. 1st ed. 2 vols. Frontis + facs. VG. *Gretton*. $47/£30

BROWNING, ELIZABETH BARRETT. Poems Before Congress. London: Chapman & Hall, 1860. 1st ed. Half-title, ad leaf at end. Red cl (sl worn). Good. *Maggs*. $117/£75

BROWNING, ELIZABETH BARRETT. The Seraphim, and Other Poems. London: Saunders & Otley, 1838. 1st ed. Top, fore-edge uncut. Blind-dec purple cl (unevenly faded), gilt. VG. *Maggs*. $390/£250

BROWNING, ELIZABETH BARRETT. Sonnets from the Portugese. London, 1897. One of 300. Blue paper bds. (Foxing; spine, paper label dknd; sl worn.) Contents VG (feps offset) in custom wood slipcase, hand-wrought sterling silver centerpiece mtd to cvr. *Waverly**. $198/£127

BROWNING, J. M. and M. S. A History of Browning Guns from 1831. Ogden, (UT): PP, 1942. 1st ed. Emb black cl. VF. *Bowman*. $40/£26

BROWNING, ORVILLE HICKMAN. Diary of...1850-1881. Theodore Calvin Pease (ed). Springfield: IL State Hist Library, 1925-33. 2 vols. Buckram, gilt. VG +. *Bohling*. $45/£29

BROWNING, ROBERT and ELIZABETH BARRETT. Letters of Robert and Elizabeth Barrett Browning 1845-1846. London, 1899. 1st ed. 2 vols. VG. *Gretton*. $47/£30

BROWNING, ROBERT. Aristophanes' Apology. Boston: James R. Osgood, 1875. 1st ed. VG (ink name). *Antic Hay*. $50/£32

BROWNING, ROBERT. Asolando: Fancies and Facts. London: Smith, Elder, 1890. 1st ed. (Spine faded, eps lt foxed), o/w VG. *Hermitage*. $150/£96

BROWNING, ROBERT. The Complete Works. NY, (1898). 12 vols. 8vo. Frontispieces. Contemp 1/2 brn calf, gilt, spines in 6 compartments, crimson morocco lettering pieces in 2. *Swann**. $747/£479

BROWNING, ROBERT. Dramatic Idyls. Smith, Elder, 1879. 1st ed. (vi),143,(3)pp (inscrip). Grey eps, beveled edges, uncut. Silk finish citron cl (sl water splashes lower cvr), gilt. Nice. *Cox*. $39/£25

BROWNING, ROBERT. Dramatic Idyls. London: Smith, Elder, 1879. 1st ed. Dec cl. Early binding w/o 'First Series' on spine. Good (2 bkpls). *Antic Hay*. $50/£32

BROWNING, ROBERT. Dramatis Personae. Boston: Ticknor & Fields, 1864. 1st Amer ed. Brn cl stamped in gilt/blind. (Sm nick fep fore-edge), o/w Nice. *Reese*. $50/£32

BROWNING, ROBERT. Ferishtah's Fancies. Smith, Elder, 1884. 1st ed. (viii),143,(9)pp (inscrip). Grey eps, beveled edges, top edge uncut. Dk grn cl (lower cvr lt mkd), gilt. VG. *Cox*. $39/£25

BROWNING, ROBERT. A History of Golf, the Royal and Ancient Game. London: J.M. Dent, (1955). 1st ed. (Inscrip), else VG in VG- dj (chipped, tear). *Pacific**. $184/£118

BROWNING, ROBERT. The Inn Album. London: Smith, Elder, 1875. 1st ed. Olive-grn cl. VG (bkpl). *Antic Hay*. $50/£32

BROWNING, ROBERT. Jocoseria. Smith, Elder, 1883. 1st ed. (viii),143,(5)pp. Grey eps, beveled edges, top edge uncut. Rose cl (lt rubbed, backstrip faded). *Cox*. $31/£20

BROWNING, ROBERT. The Pied Piper of Hamelin. London: Routledge, (1888). 1st ed w/Kate Greenaway illus. Pict bds (corners sl worn), linen spine. Very Nice. *Appelfeld*. $250/£160

BROWNING, ROBERT. The Pied Piper of Hamelin. London, (1934). One of 410 numbered, signed by Arthur Rackham (illus). 8vo. 4 color plts. Pict eps. Orig limp vellum, gilt. (Bkpl.) Pub's bd slipcase (spine ends sl worn). *Swann**. $747/£479

BROWNING, ROBERT. The Pied Piper of Hamelin. London: Harrap, 1939. 1st ed thus. Arthur Rackham (illus). Color frontis. VG in orig dec wrappers (sl torn, spine defective). *Hollett*. $55/£35

BROWNING, ROBERT. The Ring and the Book. L.A.: LEC, 1949. One of 1500 signed by Carl Schultheiss (illus). 2 vols. 16 copper engrs. Leather-backed bds. Fine in cl slipcase. *Argosy.* $125/£80

BROWNING, ROBERT. La Saisiaz: The Two Poets of Croisic. London: Smith, Elder, 1878. 1st Eng ed. (Sm label, sm hole fep; sm ink name tp.) Dec blue-grn cl. VG. *Antic Hay.* $50/£32

BROWNLEE, RICHARD S. Gray Ghosts of the Confederacy. Baton Rouge, (1958). 1st ed. Signed. (Cvr wear), o/w VG + in VG + dj. *Pratt.* $60/£38

BROWNLOW, W. G. Sketches of the Rise, Progress and Decline of Secession. Phila, 1862. 1st ed. 458pp + ads. Good. *Scribe's Perch*.* $20/£13

BROWSE, LILLIAN. Degas Dancers. London: Faber & Faber, (1949). 12 mtd color plts. Teg. Buckram, gilt leather spine label. VG. *Argosy.* $125/£80

BRUCE, C. G. The Assault on Mount Everest 1922. London, 1923. 1st ed. (Sl foxed, rubbed, sl spotted.) *King.* $150/£96

BRUCE, DAVID. Sun Pictures. Greenwich: NYGS, 1974. 1st Amer ed. (Owner stamp), else VG in illus stiff wrappers. *Cahan.* $45/£29

BRUCE, J. COLLINGWOOD. The Hand-Book to the Roman Wall. London/Newcastle-upon-Tyne: Longmans, Green/Andrew Reid, 1885. 3rd ed. Frontis and port, viii,272pp; 9 etched plts, 8 full-pg illus, lg extending color map. Grn cl (sl scratched, rubbed), gilt. *Hollett.* $257/£165

BRUCE, J. COLLINGWOOD. The Hand-Book to the Roman Wall. Ian A. Richmond (ed). Newcastle-upon-Tyne, 1947. 10th ed. Lg extending map. Dj (creased, chipped). *Hollett.* $16/£10

BRUCE, J. COLLINGWOOD. The Hand-Book to the Roman Wall. Robert Blair (ed). London/Newcastle-upon-Tyne: Longman, Green/Andrew Reid, 1895. 4th ed. Frontis port (sl spotted), 279pp; lg fldg map. (Cl sl worn.) *Hollett.* $39/£25

BRUCE, JAMES. Classic and Historic Portraits. London: Hurst & Blackett, 1853. 1st ed. 2 vols. Nice (cl sl bubbled, few smudges, spines sunned). *Reese.* $60/£38

BRUCE, JAMES. Interesting Narrative of the Travels of James Bruce, Esq. into Abyssinia.... Boston: Samuel Etheridge, 1798. 2nd Amer ed. vii,388pp. Mod 1/2 leather (extrems sl worn), cl bds. (Foxed, fr inner hinge cracked), o/w Contents VG. *New Hampshire*.* $95/£61

BRUCE, LENNY. How to Talk Dirty and Influence People. (Chicago): Playboy, (1965). 1st ed. NF in VG dj (rubbed, few tears; price-clipped). *Antic Hay.* $50/£32

BRUCE, LEO. Death on Allhallowe'en. London: W.H. Allen, 1970. 1st ed. Fine in dj (sl wear spine ends). *Mordida.* $65/£42

BRUCE, LEO. Murder in Miniature. Chicago: Academy Chicago, 1992. 1st Amer ed. VF in dj. *Mordida.* $35/£22

BRUCE, PHILIP ALEXANDER. Economic History of Virginia in the Seventeenth Century. NY: Macmillan, 1896. 1st ed. 2 vols. Fldg map frontis, 634; 647pp. (Vol 1 separated from casing), o/w Good. Howes B888. *Scribe's Perch*.* $35/£22

BRUCE, PHILIP ALEXANDER. Economic History of Virginia in the Seventeenth Century. NY: Macmillan, 1896. 1st ed. 2 vols. xix,634, fldg map; vi,647pp,(4)ads. Teg. (Sm bleach spots both vols, spines sl mottled), else NF. Howes B888. *Cahan.* $65/£42

BRUCE, PHILIP ALEXANDER. Social Life of Virginia in the Seventeenth Century. Lynchburg, VA, 1927. 2nd ed. Uncut, unopened. (Sm tears top margins 5 leaves), else Fine. *Wantagh.* $25/£16

BRUCE, ROBERT. The Fighting Norths and Pawnee Scouts. Lincoln, NE, 1932. 1st ed. Map. VG + in pict wraps. *Pratt.* $37/£24

BRUCE, WILLIAM N. (ed). Sir A. Henry Layard: Autobiography and Letters.... London: John Murray, 1903. 1st ed. 2 vols. Frontispieces, 9 plts, 2 fldg maps. (Bkpls; corner bumped, sl shelfwear.) *Archaeologia.* $250/£160

BRUCE-MITFORD, R. L. S. (ed). Recent Archaeological Excavations in Britain. London, 1956. 1st ed. VG-. *Gretton.* $16/£10

BRUETTE, WILLIAM. American Duck, Goose, and Brant Shooting. NY: G. Howard Watt, 1929. 1st ed. Color frontis. Dec eps. Gilt dec. VG + (spine sl faded). *Backman.* $95/£61

BRUFF, J. GOLDSBOROUGH. Gold Rush: The Journals, Drawings and Other Papers of J. Goldsborough Bruff...(1849-1851). Georgia Willis Read and Ruth Gaines (eds). NY: Columbia Univ, 1944. 1st ed. 2 vols. Color frontis. 1/2 cl, bds. NF. Howes R91. *Harrington.* $250/£160

BRUFF, J. GOLDSBOROUGH. Gold Rush: The Journals, Drawings, and Other Papers of J. Goldsborough Bruff.... Georgia Willis Read and Ruth Gaines (eds). NY: Columbia Univ, 1949. Rpt. Color frontis. Overall Fine (sl remains from removed bkpl). *Argonaut.* $100/£64

BRUFF, J. GOLDSBOROUGH. Gold Rush: The Journals, Drawings, and Other Papers...April 2, 1849 - July 20, 1851. Georgia Willis Read and Ruth Gaines (eds). NY: Columbia Univ, 1944. 1st ed. 2 vols. Gray bds, black cl spine, gilt. Fine (lacks slipcase). *Pacific*.* $195/£125

BRUMMER GALLERY. Brancusi Exhibition. NY, 1926. Wrappers. *Swann*.* $258/£165

BRUNNER, JOHN. No Future in It. Doubleday, 1962. 1st US ed. VG in dj. *Madle.* $35/£22

BRUNNER, JOHN. The Wrong End of Time. Doubleday, 1971. 1st ed. Fine in dj (sl soiled). *Madle.* $30/£19

BRUNO, GUIDO. Adventures in American Bookshops, Antique Stores and Auction Rooms. Detroit: Douglas Book Shop, 1922. #429/1000. Brn cl, ptd paper label on backstrip. VG. *Heller.* $50/£32

BRUNS, HENRY P. Angling Books of the Americas. Atlanta: Angler's Press, 1975. 26 b/w plts. Grn buckram, gilt. VF. *Biscotti.* $135/£87

BRUNSON, ALFRED. Going West, the Pioneer Work of Alfred Brunson. Cedar Rapids, IA: For friends of Torch Press, Christmas 1951. One of 400. Frontis port. 1/2 cl, ptd title label. VG. *Bohling.* $40/£26

BRUNTON, LAUDER. Modern Developments of Harvey's Work. London, 1894. 35pp. VG. *Fye.* $75/£48

BRUNTON, LAUDER. Therapeutics of the Circulation. London: John Murray, 1908. 1st ed. Errata slip. Blue cl, crest fr cvr. (Ink marginalia), o/w VG. *White.* $78/£50

BRUSSEL, I. R. Anglo-American First Editions 1826-1900.... London, 1935-1936. Ltd to 500. 2 vols. 2 frontispieces, 22 plts. Partly unopened. Vellum-look backed marbled bds, gilt. *Maggs.* $218/£140

BRUSSEL, JACK. Ecce Homo/George Grosz. NY: Mahoney & Reese, 1965. Ltd ed. Pub's slipcase (sl soiled). *Metropolitan*.* $74/£47

BRUSSEL, JAMES A. Casebook of a Crime Psychiatrist. NY: Bernard Geis, (1968). 1st ed. Inscribed. Gold cl-backed orange bds. VG. *Gach.* $28/£18

BRY, DORIS. Alfred Stieglitz: Photographer. Boston: Museum of Fine Arts, 1965. 1st ed. 62 plts. (Owner stamp), else Fine in stiff wrappers. *Cahan.* $35/£22

Bryan's Dictionary of Painters and Engravers. G. Bell, 1915/19. 4th ed, rpt. 5 vols. Good set in 2-tone cl (backstrips faded, lt rubbed). *Cox*. $117/£75

BRYAN, ASHLEY. Ashley Bryan. (NY: Atheneum, 1985). 1st ed. Fine. *Between The Covers*. $35/£22

BRYAN, ASHLEY. Walk Together Children. NY: Atheneum, 1974. 1st ed. 10 1/4 x 8 1/4. 53pp. VG (ex-lib, mks) in dj. *Cattermole*. $25/£16

BRYAN, DANIEL. The Mountain Muse. Harrisonburg: The Author, 1813. 1st ed. 252pp (soiled, lacks feps). Contemp calf (neatly rebacked), red morocco spine label, gilt. *Karmiole*. $200/£128

BRYAN, J. III. The Sword over the Mantle. McGraw Hill, (c. 1960). 1st ed. VG in Good dj. *Book Broker*. $25/£16

BRYAN, JOHN ALBURY. Missouri's Contribution to American Architecture. (St. Louis), 1928. Grn cl (sl soiled, warped), gilt. *Freeman**. $60/£38

BRYAN, JOHN E. Bulbs. Portland, 1989. 2 vols. Fine in djs. *Brooks*. $99/£63

BRYAN, MARGARET. A Compendious System of Astronomy. London: The Author, 1797. 1st ed. Engr frontis (spotted), 17 engr plts. Sprinkled edges. Contemp calf (rubbed), gilt spine, spine label (almost torn away). *Christie's**. $228/£146

BRYAN, MICHAEL. A Biographical and Critical Dictionary of Painters and Engravers. London, 1816. 2 vols. Frontis port (sl offset). xlix, 709; 822pp (ink stamp tps, 1st pg text; lt spotting), 5 plts. Full calf (extrems sl rubbed, worn; hinges cracked, bds sl scuffed; dec gilt spines (sl rubbed), leather title labels. *Edwards*. $156/£100

BRYAN, MICHAEL. Dictionary of Painters and Engravers, Biographical and Critical. London: Bell, 1886-9. New ed. 2 vols. vii,754; vii,771pp incl supp, 5 plts. Teg. Dk grn 1/2 morocco (extrems rubbed). Good set. *Europa*. $55/£35

BRYAN, MICHAEL. (Pseud of Brian Moore.) Intent to Kill. London: Eyre, 1956. 1st UK ed. VG in dj (sl rubbed, edgeworn). *Williams*. $94/£60

BRYAN, WILLIAM S. and ROBERT ROSE. A History of the Pioneer Families of Missouri. Columbia, MO: Lucas Bros, (1935). Facs of 1876 ed. Frontis. VG. Howes B901. *Lien*. $125/£80

BRYAN, WILLIAM S. and ROBERT ROSE. A History of the Pioneer Families of Missouri.... St. Louis: Bryan, Brand, 1876. iv,528pp (fep corner removed); 2 plts w/composite ports. Blue cl (frayed, spotted, soiled), gilt. Good+. Howes B901. *Bohling*. $225/£144

BRYANT, BILLY. Children of Ol' Man River. NY: Lee Furman, (1936). Apparent 1st ed. Fldg facs. Red cl. VG+ (name clipped fep) in dj (chipped). *Bohling*. $30/£19

BRYANT, BILLY. Children of Ol' Man River. Martin Ridge (ed). Chicago: Lakeside Classic, 1988. Teg. Brn cl, gilt. Fine. *Bohling*. $20/£13

BRYANT, EDWIN. What I Saw in California. NY: D. Appleton, 1848. 1st ed. 455pp. Orig emb gray-grn cl, gilt spine. (Lt foxed, eps sl discolored; spine faded), o/w VG. *Pacific**. $489/£313

BRYANT, EDWIN. What I Saw in California...in the Years 1846, 1847. Santa Ana, CA: Fine Arts, 1936. Color frontis; map. Orig calf-backed bds (fr cvr worn), leather spine label. *Ginsberg*. $175/£112

BRYANT, THOMAS. A Manual for the Practice of Surgery. Phila, 1881. 3rd Amer ed. 1005pp. Full leather (worn, fr cvr detached but present). Fair. *Doctor's Library*. $50/£32

BRYANT, WILLIAM CULLEN (ed). Picturesque America, or the Land We Live In.... NY: D. Appleton, (1872-74). 2 vols. 50 steel engrs. (Foxing.) Full gilt-dec leather (sl rubbed, faded). Handsome set. *Metropolitan**. $345/£221

BRYANT, WILLIAM CULLEN (ed). Picturesque America. NY: D. Appleton, (1872-74). 2 vols. 49 steel-engr plts incl frontis, tps. Aeg. Full blind-, gilt-stamped morocco (extrems worn). Contents VG. *Waverly**. $330/£212

BRYANT, WILLIAM CULLEN (ed). Picturesque America.... NY, (1872-74). 2 vols. 47 engr plts, incl add'l titles. Pub's 1/2 leather (scuffed; lib stamps tp versos, bkpls), gilt. *Swann**. $258/£165

BRYANT, WILLIAM CULLEN. Poems. Cambridge, 1821. 1st ed. 12mo. Extraneous signed frontis port. Ptd paper-cvrd bds (sl soiled, spine chipped; foxing, offset to blanks, pastedowns). 1/2 morocco slipcase. *Swann**. $805/£516

BRYCE, JAMES. Impressions of South Africa. NY: Century, 1898. 2nd ed. xxvi,499pp; 3 fldg color maps. Teg. (Sl rubbed, soiled; ex-lib, spine #), o/w VG. *Worldwide*. $15/£10

BRYCE, JAMES. Studies in History and Jurisprudence. NY: OUP, 1901. New 1/4 morocco (notes on tp), else Very Nice. *Boswell*. $275/£176

BRYCE, WILLIAM MOIR. Holyrood. London, 1914. 1st ed. #99/200. 49 mtd plts. Marbled eps; teg. Gilt-edged 1/2 morocco, cl bds (sl rubbed, sl soiled). *Edwards*. $39/£25

BRYDEN, H. A. Horn and Hound. London, 1927. 1st ed. (Lt browned; spine faded.) *Edwards*. $31/£20

BRYDGES, CHARLES JOHN. Letters of Charles John Brydges, 1879-1882. Hartwell Bowsfield (ed). Winnipeg: Hudson's Bay Record Soc, 1977. Ltd ed issued to subs. VG in dj. *Lien*. $40/£26

BRYDONE, P. A Tour Through Sicily and Malta, in a Series of Letters to William Beckford.... NY: Evert Duyckinck, 1813. 1st Amer ed. viii,276pp (foxed). 19th-cent 1/2 calf, marbled bds, tan morocco spine label (rubbed). *Karmiole*. $150/£96

BRYHER, WINIFRED. The Fourteenth of October. London: Collins, 1954. 1st ed. VG in dj. *Hollett*. $47/£30

BRYHER. Roman Wall. London, 1955. 1st ed. VG in dj (sl creased, rubbed). *Words Etc*. $16/£10

BUCHAN, JOHN (ed). Essays and Apothegms of Francis Lord Bacon. London: Walter Scott, 1894. 1st ed, early state. Ad block inserted. VG in grn bds, gilt. *Williams*. $195/£125

BUCHAN, JOHN. The Adventures of Sir Edward Leithen. London: Hodder & Stoughton, (1935). 1st collected ed. Linen cl, black/blue lettering. (Bkpl, sm # tp verso, lib stamp pg edges), else Clean. *Turtle Island*. $65/£42

BUCHAN, JOHN. The African Colony. Edinburgh: Wm. Blackwood, 1903. 1st ed. 2 fldg maps. (Lt rubbed.) *Adelson*. $275/£176

BUCHAN, JOHN. Augustus. London: Hodder & Stoughton, (1937). 1st UK ed. Grn cl. VG (sl foxed). *Gravesend*. $35/£22

BUCHAN, JOHN. The Battle of the Somme. NY: George H. Doran, (1917). 1st US ed. Pict cl. Good (pencil inscrip, fore-edge lt stained; fr hinge split). *Gravesend*. $35/£22

BUCHAN, JOHN. The Battle of the Somme: First Phase. London: Thomas Nelson, (1916). 1st UK ed. Blue bds (worn, soiled, backstrip frayed). Good. *Gravesend*. $50/£32

BUCHAN, JOHN. The Blanket of the Dark. Hodder & Stoughton, 1931. 1st ed. (Edges sl spotted), o/w VG in dj (lt worn, nicked). *Ash*. $117/£75

BUCHAN, JOHN. The Blanket of the Dark. Hodder, 1931. 1st UK ed. VG (ink inscrip) in Good dj (sl grubby, tears strengthened, sm stamp rear panel). *Williams*. $70/£45

BUCHAN, JOHN. A Book of Escapes and Hurried Journeys. London, 1922. 1st ed. (Sl rubbed), o/w VG. *Words Etc.* $55/£35

BUCHAN, JOHN. Castle Gay. Boston: Houghton Mifflin, 1930. 1st US ed. VG (pencil name, label removed fep; worn, soiled). *Gravesend.* $25/£16

BUCHAN, JOHN. Castle Gay. London: Hodder & Stoughton, 1930. 1st ed. Fine in pict dj (sm spine chips, 2-inch closed tear). *Else Fine.* $135/£87

BUCHAN, JOHN. The Causal and the Casual in History: The Rede Lecture 1929. CUP, 1929. 1st UK ed. Lt brn bds (spine lt worn). VG (ink name, address). *Gravesend.* $60/£38

BUCHAN, JOHN. The Courts of the Morning. London: Hodder & Stoughton, (1929). 1st ed. VG (dated inscrip, pencil mks on bk list; fep map, reps discolored). *Gravesend.* $25/£16

BUCHAN, JOHN. The Dancing Floor. London: Hodder & Stoughton, (1926). 1st ed. Lt blue cl. Good (ink name; hinges split). *Gravesend.* $20/£13

BUCHAN, JOHN. A Five-Fold Salute to Adventure. London: Hodder & Stoughton, (1939). 1st UK ed. Variant w/red cvr title. Good (fr hinge split, spine dknd). *Gravesend.* $35/£22

BUCHAN, JOHN. The Four Adventures of Richard Hannay. London: Hodder & Stoughton, 1930. 1st ed. (Owner stamp, spine sl dknd), o/w Fine in dj (spine top sl frayed). *Mordida.* $250/£160

BUCHAN, JOHN. The Free Fishers. Boston: Houghton Mifflin, 1934. 1st US ed. Good (pencil name; worn, soiled, stain). *Gravesend.* $20/£13

BUCHAN, JOHN. The Free Fishers. London: Hodder, 1934. 1st UK ed. VG (cvrs sl mkd) in dj (top edge lacks pieces). *Williams.* $59/£38

BUCHAN, JOHN. Greenmantle. London: Hodder & Stoughton, 1916. 1st UK ed. Dk grn cl (soiled, fr hinge split). Good (lacks fep, ink name, date). *Gravesend.* $30/£19

BUCHAN, JOHN. Grey Weather. London: John Lane, 1899. 1st Eng ed. (Lacks fep, bottom edge 1 leaf chipped; hinges cracking, cvrs faded, extrems stringbruised.) *Clearwater.* $78/£50

BUCHAN, JOHN. A History of the Great War. Boston, 1922. Autograph ed. Ltd to 500 numbered, signed. 8 vols. Cl-backed bds, paper labels. (Extrems worn), else Good set. *King.* $350/£224

BUCHAN, JOHN. Homilies and Recreations. London: Thomas Nelson, (1926). 1st UK ed. #3/200 signed. VG (ink name, place, date, pencil name; lt bumped). *Gravesend.* $150/£96

BUCHAN, JOHN. The House of the Four Winds. London: Hodder & Stoughton, (1935). 1st UK ed. Grn cl (sl worn), gilt. VG (fore-edge foxed). *Gravesend.* $30/£19

BUCHAN, JOHN. The House of the Four Winds. London: Hodder, 1935. 1st UK ed. Fine in Good dj (rubbed, sl edge loss). *Williams.* $117/£75

BUCHAN, JOHN. Huntingtower. London: Hodder & Stoughton, (1922). 1st ed. Lt blue cl. VG (ink name, address; fr cvr lt faded). *Gravesend.* $35/£22

BUCHAN, JOHN. The Island of Sheep. London: Hodder & Stoughton, (1936). 1st UK ed. Grn cl, gilt. VG in VG dj (worn, torn, aged, spine faded). *Gravesend.* $125/£80

BUCHAN, JOHN. Lake of Gold. Boston: Houghton Mifflin, 1941. 1st US ed. VG in VG dj (4 sm holes fr panel). *Gravesend.* $45/£29

BUCHAN, JOHN. The Last Secrets. London, 1923. 1st ed. (Cl sl worn), o/w VG. *Words Etc.* $55/£35

BUCHAN, JOHN. Lord Minto. London, 1924. 1st ed. Frontis. Pub's cl, gilt. (Spine, lower panel sl faded), o/w VG. *Words Etc.* $34/£22

BUCHAN, JOHN. The Marquis of Montrose. London, 1913. 1st ed. Pub's buckram, gilt. (Guards foxed, extrems sl dknd), o/w VG. *Words Etc.* $34/£22

BUCHAN, JOHN. The Marquis of Montrose. London, 1913. 1st Eng ed. Buckram (sl handled, mkd). Good (ink family tree rep, inscrip, bkpl). *Clearwater.* $55/£35

BUCHAN, JOHN. The Massacre of Glencoe. 1933. 1st ed. Cream cl. (Spine dknd), o/w VG. *Words Etc.* $50/£32

BUCHAN, JOHN. Memory Hold-the-Door. London: Hodder & Stoughton, 1940. 1st UK ed. Blue-grn cl (bumped). VG (inscrip, date) in dj (worn, lt torn, soiled, inside corner cut). *Gravesend.* $35/£22

BUCHAN, JOHN. Mountain Meadow. Boston: Houghton Mifflin, 1941. 1st US ed. Good (ink names, dates, fr hinge split; worn). *Gravesend.* $15/£10

BUCHAN, JOHN. Mr. Standfast. NY: George H. Doran, (1919). 1st US ed. Yellow-grn cl. VG. *Gravesend.* $40/£26

BUCHAN, JOHN. Mr. Standfast. London: Hodder & Stoughton, 1919. 1st ed. (Feps browned.) Blue cl. *Hollett.* $47/£30

BUCHAN, JOHN. Musa Piscatrix. London/Chicago: John Lane/A.C. McClurg, 1896. 1st ed. 16pp ads dated 1896. 6 sepia plts. Blue cl, gilt. (Spine sl faded), else Fine. *Sumner & Stillman.* $325/£208

BUCHAN, JOHN. The Novel and the Fairy Tale. London: English Assoc, 1931. 1st Eng ed. VG in ptd wraps. *Hadley.* $23/£15

BUCHAN, JOHN. Oliver Cromwell. London: Hodder & Stoughton, (1934). 1st UK ed. Grn cl, gilt. VG. *Gravesend.* $45/£29

BUCHAN, JOHN. Oliver Cromwell. Boston: Houghton Mifflin, 1934. 1st US ed. VG (backstrip label faded, loose). *Gravesend.* $30/£19

BUCHAN, JOHN. The Power-House. Edinburgh/London, 1916. 1st Eng ed. (Name, paper brittle, browned; sl faded, hinges weak.) *Clearwater.* $62/£40

BUCHAN, JOHN. The Runagates Club. London, 1928. 1st ed. Pub's cl. (Lt foxing, inner hinge weak), o/w VG. *Words Etc.* $23/£15

BUCHAN, JOHN. Scholar Gipsies. London: John Lane, Bodley Head, 1896. Frontis, 16-pg cat. Cl-backed linen over bds, spine gilt, pict upper cvr. VG (bkpl, ink sig fep, sl rubs, smudges). *Reese.* $150/£96

BUCHAN, JOHN. Sick Heart River. London: Hodder & Stoughton, (1941). 1st UK ed. Dk grn cl. VG (ink name, place, date, fore-edge foxed) in VG dj (worn, torn). *Gravesend.* $40/£26

BUCHAN, JOHN. Sick Heart River. 1941. 1st ed. Pub's grn cl. (Prelims lt foxed), o/w VG in pict dj (creased, sl chipped). *Words Etc.* $56/£36

BUCHAN, JOHN. Sir Walter Scott. London: Cassell, (1932). 1st UK ed. Grn cl, gilt. VG (bkpl, label). *Gravesend.* $25/£16

BUCHAN, JOHN. The Thirty-Nine Steps. London: Blackwood, 1915. 1st UK ed. VG (sm stain spine bottom). *Williams.* $390/£250

BUCHAN, JOHN. Witch Wood. Boston: Houghton Mifflin, 1927. 1st US ed. Black cl (sl worn). VG. *Gravesend.* $25/£16

BUCHAN, JOHN. Witch Wood. London: Hodder & Stoughton, 1927. 1st UK ed. Lt blue cl (soiled, spine discolored). Good (eps foxed). *Gravesend.* $25/£16

BUCHAN, WILLIAM. Domestic Medicine. London: W. Strahan, T. Cadell, 1781. 7th ed. xx,523pp (1/2-title soiled, creased, tp spotted, sm tear text leaf; last ll index soiled, creased). Mod 1/2 morocco, gilt. *Hollett.* $117/£75

BUCHAN, WILLIAM. Domestic Medicine. 1790. 11th ed. xxxvi,748pp (foxing). Contemp calf (joints weak). *Whitehart.* $109/£70

BUCHAN, WILLIAM. Domestic Medicine. 1813. 21st ed. xl,762pp (foxed). 1/2 leather, marbled bds; Leather spine label incorrectly reads 18th ed. *Whitehart.* $94/£60

BUCHAN, WILLIAM. Domestic Medicine. Boston, 1825. 652pp + ads (foxing). Full leather Poor. Book Good- (lacks fr bd). *Scribe's Perch*.* $22/£14

BUCHANAN, ANGUS. Wild Life in Canada. London: John Murray, 1920. 2nd ptg. Dec cl. VG. *High Latitude.* $45/£29

BUCHANAN, EDNA. Nobody Lives Forever. NY: Random House, 1990. 1st ed. VF in dj. *Mordida.* $35/£22

BUCHANAN, R. The Culture of the Grape, and Wine-Making. Cincinnati: Moore et al, 1855. 5th ed. 142pp (sl foxed). VG. *Agvent.* $150/£96

Buck Rogers in the 25th Century. NY: Random House, 1980. 1st ptg. Chuck McVicker (illus). Pop-up bk. 8vo. Glazed pict paper-cvrd bds. VG +. *Book Adoption.* $25/£16

BUCK, ALBERT H. The Growth of Medicine from the Earliest Times to About 1800. New Haven: Yale Univ, 1917. Good. *Goodrich.* $65/£42

BUCK, DANIEL. Indian Outbreaks. Minneapolis: Ross & Haines, 1965. VG in dj. Howes B914. *Lien.* $25/£16

BUCK, FRANKLIN A. A Yankee Trader in the Gold Rush. Katherine A. White (comp). Boston/NY: Houghton Mifflin, 1930. 1st ed. Frontis. Grn cl. VG in pict dj (badly chipped). *Pacific*.* $63/£40

BUCK, H. S. A Study in Smollett. New Haven: Yale Univ, 1925. 1st ed. Paper label. *Macdonnell.* $35/£22

BUCK, PEARL. Kinfolk. NY: John Day, (1949). 1st ed. NF in NF dj. *Captain's Bookshelf.* $45/£29

BUCK, SOLON J. The Granger Movement: A Study...1870-1880. Cambridge, 1913. 1st ed. (Sm emb lib stamp, bkpl removed.) Howes B916. *Ginsberg.* $75/£48

BUCK, SOLON J. Travel and Description 1765-1865. Springfield, IL: IL State Hist Library, 1914. (Soil, wear, top edge rear cvr chewed.) *Waverly*.* $44/£28

BUCK, SOLON J. and ELIZABETH HAWTHORN BUCK. The Planting of Civilization in Western Pennsylvania. Pittsburgh: Univ of Pittsburgh, 1939. Gray cl. NF in Good dj. *Zubal*.* $22/£14

BUCKBEE, EDNA BRYAN. The Saga of Old Tuolomne. NY: Press of the Pioneers, 1935. 1st ed. 'Autographed edition,' but not signed. (Clipping tipped in fr pastedown.) Red cl. Fine in dj (chipped, price-clipped). *Harrington.* $90/£58

BUCKINGHAM, JAMES S. America, Historical, Statistic, and Descriptive. NY, 1841. 2 vols. Engr frontis port, xii,(13)-514,(1); add'l frontis, xiii,(blank),(9)-516pp; fldg map. Mod 3/4 morocco, marbled bds, gilt spine. NF. Howes B921. *Reese.* $250/£160

BUCKINGHAM, JAMES S. Canada, Nova Scotia, New Brunswick, and the Other British Provinces in North America. London, (1843). Pub's cl (spine ends frayed; plts very foxed). *Swann*.* $57/£37

BUCKINGHAM, NASH. Blood Lines. NY: Derrydale, (1938). Ltd to 1250. VG +. *Truepenny.* $250/£160

BUCKINGHAM, NASH. De Shootinest Gent'man. NY, 1941. 1st ed. Signed, inscribed. VG. *Truepenny.* $150/£96

BUCKINGHAM, NASH. Game Bag, Tales of Shooting and Fishing. NY, (1945). Ltd to 1250 numbered, signed. 2-tone cl. (Edges spotted), else Nice. *King.* $150/£96

BUCKINGHAM, NASH. Game Bag: Tales of Shooting and Fishing. NY, (1945). Ltd to 1250 signed. VG. *Truepenny.* $200/£128

BUCKINGHAM, NASH. Mark Right! Tales of Shooting and Fishing. NY: Derrydale, (1936). 1st ed. #940/1250. Color medallion fr cvr. Fine. *Cummins.* $350/£224

BUCKINGHAM, NASH. Ole Miss'. NY: Derrydale, (1937). One of 1250 numbered. Frontis. Pict cvr vignette. (Sl worn.) *Oinonen*.* $180/£115

BUCKINGHAM, NASH. Ole Miss'. NY: Derrydale, 1937. #1249/1250. Pict pastedown cvr. Good +. *Scribe's Perch*.* $100/£64

BUCKINGHAM, NASH. Tattered Coat. NY, (1944). Ltd to 995 signed. Pict cl. VG. *Truepenny.* $150/£96

BUCKLAND, FRANK T. Curiosities of Natural History. London, 1883-85. Popular ed. 4 vols. 11 plts. (Rebacked preserving spines; sl soiled.) *Henly.* $41/£26

BUCKLAND, FRANK T. Fish Hatching. London: Tinsley Bros, 1863. xv,268pp + 4pp ads. Grn cl, gilt. VG (bkpl, lt dampstain fr cvr). *Bohling.* $30/£19

BUCKLAND, FRANK T. Natural History of British Fishes. London, 1883. 1st ed. (Stamped address tp; cl scruffy.) *Maggs.* $28/£18

BUCKLAND, GAIL. Reality Recorded. Greenwich, CT: NYGS, 1974. 1st Amer ed. (Owner stamp, tips lt rubbed), else Fine in illus dj. *Cahan.* $35/£22

BUCKLAND, WILLIAM. Geology and Mineralogy. London, 1836. 1st ed. 2 vols. 599; 128pp; lg hand-colored fldg map, 68 engr plts. Marbled eps. Brn 1/2 leather, gilt, marbled bds, ribbed spine. VG (ex-lib). *Price.* $350/£224

BUCKLE, HENRY THOMAS. Essays.... NY: Appleton, 1863. 1st US ed. 209pp. VG (lib bkpl). *Second Life.* $125/£80

BUCKLE, RICHARD (ed). Costumes and Curtains from the Diaghilev and de Basil Ballets. NY: Viking, (1972). Ltd to 750 numbered. Pink bds. Good in dj. *Karmiole.* $125/£80

BUCKLEY, ARTHUR. Card Control. Springfield, IL: The Author, (1946). 1st ed, 1st ptg. Blue cl. Fine. *Glenn.* $85/£54

BUCKLEY, ARTHUR. Principles and Deceptions. Springfield, IL: Williamson Press, (1948). 1st ed, 1st ptg. Blue cl. Fine. *Glenn.* $75/£48

BUCKLEY, THOMAS C. (ed). Rendezvous: Selected Papers...1981. St. Paul, MN: North Amer Fur Trade Conference, (1984). 1st ed. Pb. VG. *Lien.* $25/£16

BUCKLEY, WILLIAM F., JR. Mongoose R.I.P. NY: Random House, 1987. 1st ed. Inscribed. VF in dj. *Mordida.* $45/£29

BUCKLEY, WILLIAM F., JR. See You Later Alligator. GC: Doubleday, 1985. 1st ed. Fine in dj (price-clipped). *Mordida.* $25/£16

BUCKNILL, JOHN A. The Birds of Surrey. London: R.H. Porter, 1900. 1st ed. Photo frontis, 5 plts, lg fldg map. Teg. Pale brn cl (spine sl dknd), gilt. Internally Perfect. *Sotheran.* $231/£148

BUCKSTEIN, JACOB. Peptic Ulcer.... NY, 1930. 1/2 cl. VG. *Argosy.* $50/£32

BUCKTON, A. M. Eager Heart, a Christmas Mystery Play. Elkin Mathews & Marrot, 1931. 1st Knowles illus ed. Horace J. Knowles (illus). 4to. 68pp; 10 full-pg illus. B/w pict initials, eps. Silver-dec cl. VG in dj (defective). *Bookmark.* $55/£35

BUCOVICH, MARIO. Manhattan Magic. NY: The Author, 1937. 1st ed. 85 gravure plts. VG in illus spiral-bound wrappers (worn). *Cahan.* $60/£38

BUDDEN, C. W. English Gothic Churches. London: Batsford, (1933). 40 plts. Sound. *Ars Artis.* $23/£15

BUDGE, E. A. WALLIS. Amulets and Talismans. NY: University Books, 1961. VG+ in VG- dj. *Middle Earth*. $50/£32

BUDGE, E. A. WALLIS. Babylonian Life and History. London, 1925. 2nd ed. 11 plts. (Feps lt browned; sl rubbed, spine faded, chipped.) *Edwards*. $39/£25

BUDGE, E. A. WALLIS. Book of the Dead. London, 1890. 20pp; facs, 37 dbl-pg color plts. (Ex-lib, ink stamps, table of plts torn, repaired, margins thumbed; lib cl, #s.) *Edwards*. $195/£125

BUDGE, E. A. WALLIS. The Book of the Dead. London: British Museum, 1895. clv,377pp. Teg, uncut. Black 1/2 calf, gilt (scraped). VG. *Hollett*. $234/£150

BUDGE, E. A. WALLIS. The Book of the Dead. Chicago/London: Open Court/Kegan Paul, Trench, Trubner, 1901. 1st Amer illus ed. 3 vols. Teg. Grn ribbed cl, gilt. Clean. *House*. $100/£64

BUDGE, E. A. WALLIS. The Book of the Dead. NY: University Books, 1960. 15 frontis plts. Fine in VG dj. *Middle Earth*. $35/£22

BUDGE, E. A. WALLIS. The Book of the Kings of Egypt.... London: Kegan Paul et al, 1908. 2 vols. Good. *Archaeologia*. $250/£160

BUDGE, E. A. WALLIS. Cook's Handbook for Egypt and the Egyptian Sudan. London, 1921. (Cvrs rubbed; map torn.) *King*. $75/£48

BUDGE, E. A. WALLIS. Egyptian Magic. NY: University Books, 1958. 22 plts. Fine in VG dj. *Middle Earth*. $25/£16

BUDGE, E. A. WALLIS. Egyptian Sculptures in the British Museum. London: British Museum, 1914. 54 plts. Red cl over bds. NF. *Old London*. $350/£224

BUDGE, E. A. WALLIS. The Gods of the Egyptians. Chicago: Open Court, 1904. 1st ed. 2 vols. 98 chromolitho plts, incl vol 2 frontis. Blind-stamped red cl (spines sl faded, vol 1 lt soiled, lib # spine; text sl foxed, removed cardpocket mks rep). *Karmiole*. $300/£192

BUDGE, E. A. WALLIS. A Hieroglyphic Vocabulary to the Theban Recension of the Book of the Dead. London: Kegan Paul et al, 1911. (Fep sl torn.) *Archaeologia*. $75/£48

BUDGE, E. A. WALLIS. A History of Egypt from the End of the Neolithic Period to the Death of Cleopatra VII, B.C. 30. NY: Henry Frowde, 1902. 8 vols complete. (Ink stamp tp each vol.) Uniform cl. *Archaeologia*. $250/£160

BUDGE, E. A. WALLIS. A History of Ethiopia. London, 1928. 1st ed. 2 vols. Frontis ports, 47 plts, fldg map. (Ex-lib, bkpl, marginal ink stamps affecting most plts; vol 2 chipped, spines faded w/labels removed, edges sl discolored.) *Edwards*. $234/£150

BUDGE, E. A. WALLIS. The Mummy: A Handbook of Egyptian Funerary Archaeology. Cambridge: CUP, 1925. 38 plts. (Inscrip, bkpl.) Dj (tattered). *Archaeologia*. $150/£96

BUDGE, E. A. WALLIS. The Nile. London: Thos. Cook, 1892. 2nd ed. Frontis map, xvi,374pp. Gilt-pict limp cl. Good. *Archaeologia*. $65/£42

BUDGE, E. A. WALLIS. The Nile. London/Cairo, 1893. 3rd ed. 425pp. Limp cl, rounded corners, dec cvr. Good (fr hinge tender). *Scribe's Perch**. $28/£18

BUDGE, E. A. WALLIS. The Nile. London: Thos. Cook, 1902. 8th ed. Frontis map. (Sig.) Gilt-pict limp cl. *Archaeologia*. $75/£48

BUDGE, E. A. WALLIS. The Nile. London: Thomas Cook, 1910. 11th ed. 2 frontis maps, fldg map. Limp cl (sl worn; sl shaken), gilt. *Hollett*. $55/£35

BUDGE, E. A. WALLIS. Osiris and the Egyptian Resurrection. London: Philip Lee Warner, 1911. 1st ed. 2 vols. 2 long fldg color frontispieces, 2 lg fldg plts. Teg. Red cl (spines faded; lib rubberstamps bottom edges). *Karmiole*. $300/£192

BUDGE, E. A. WALLIS. Tutankhamen: Amenism, Atenism, and Egyptian Monotheism. London: Martin Hopkinson, 1923. 1st ed. Frontis; 11 plts. Brn cl. (Sm dk spot fr cvr), o/w VG. *House*. $65/£42

BUDGEN, FRANK. James Joyce and the Making of Ulysses. London: Grayson & Grayson, (1934). 1st ed. Frontis. Spine label. (Sm tan spot spine), o/w NF in Good dj (narrow loss spine crown, sm nicks, tears). *Reese*. $65/£42

BUDRYS, ALGIS. Rogue Moon. Greenwich, CT: Fawcett, (1960). 1st ed. Pb orig. VG- (dknd, several pp foxed). *Antic Hay*. $15/£10

BUECHNER, FREDERICK. A Long Day's Dying. NY: Knopf, 1950. 1st ed. VF in dj. *Hermitage*. $85/£54

BUEL, JESSE. The Farmer's Companion. Boston: Marsh et al, 1840. 2nd ed. 303pp + ads. Mod bds, paper label. Nice. *Second Life*. $95/£61

BUELL, M. H. Li'l Lulu: Her Train Ride to Grandma's. Springfield, MA: McLoughlin, 1946. 8vo. Unpaginated. Pict paper over bds. Good- in Good- dj. *Scribe's Perch**. $60/£38

BUFFET, BERNARD. Lithographs, 1952-1966. NY: Tudor, (1968). 1st ed in English. 66 full-pg repros, 10 orig color lithos. Color pict wraps. VF in Fine dj, orig clear plastic outer protective wrapper, orig bd slipcase (edges sl worn). *Baltimore**. $350/£224

BUFFET-CHAILIE, LAURENCE. Flower Decoration in European Homes. NY: Morrow, n.d. (1969). 41 color plts tipped in. Fine in dj (repaired). *Quest*. $50/£32

BUHLER, CURT F. Early Books and Manuscripts. (NY): Grolier Club & Pierpont Morgan Library, 1973. *Freeman**. $45/£29

BUIST, ROBERT. American Flower Garden Directory. NY: OJ, 1854. New ed. xvi,342pp + ads. Nice (extrems worn). *Quest*. $65/£42

BUKOWSKI, CHARLES. All the Assholes in the World and Mine. Bensenville, IL: Open Skull, 1966. 1st ed. One of 400. NF in wraps. *Sclanders*. $156/£100

BUKOWSKI, CHARLES. Crucifix in a Deathhand: New Poems, 1963-65. NY, 1965. 1st ed. Ltd to 3100 signed. Wrap-around band laid in. Wraps (extrems worn). *King*. $200/£128

BUKOWSKI, CHARLES. Factotum. Black Sparrow, 1975. Trade issue of 675. Fine in unptd mylar cvr as issued. *Certo*. $80/£51

BUKOWSKI, CHARLES. Hot Water Music. Black Sparrow, 1983. One of 400 numbered, signed. Fine in glassine dj. *Sclanders*. $109/£70

BUKOWSKI, CHARLES. If You Let Them Kill You, They Will. Santa Rosa: Black Sparrow, 1989. Ltd to 226 numbered, handbound, signed. Cl-backed illus bds (sl soiled). *King*. $75/£48

BUKOWSKI, CHARLES. In the Shadow of the Rose. Santa Rosa: Black Sparrow, 1991. Ltd to 750 numbered, signed. This copy add'lly inscribed. Black cl-backed dec cream bds, paper spine label. Fine in plain grn dj. *Blue Mountain*. $450/£288

BUKOWSKI, CHARLES. Luck. Santa Rosa: Black Sparrow, (1987). Ltd to 226 numbered, signed w/caricature. Largely unopened. Black cl-backed dec bds. Fine. *Blue Mountain*. $60/£38

BUKOWSKI, CHARLES. Relentless as the Tarantula. Detroit, MI: Planet Detroit Chapbooks, (1966). Signed, w/dwg. Pict stapled tan wraps. Fine. *Blue Mountain*. $150/£96

BUKOWSKI, CHARLES. War All the Time. Poems 1981-1984. Black Sparrow, 1984. One of 400 numbered, signed. Fine in glassine dj (sl rubbed). *Sclanders.* $94/£60

BULEY, R. CARLYLE. The Old Northwest Pioneer Period, 1815-1840. Indianapolis: IN Hist Soc, 1950. 1st ed. 2 vols. VG in slipcase. *Lien.* $60/£38

BULGAKOV, MIKHAIL. The Master and Margarita. NY: Harper & Row, 1967. 1st ed in English. NF in dj. *Lame Duck.* $85/£54

BULKLEY, L. DUNCAN. On the Use of the Solid Rubber Bandage in the Treatment of Eczema and Ulcers of the Leg. NY, 1878. 21pp, sewed. VG. *Argosy.* $35/£22

BULL, H. J. The Cruise of the 'Antarctic' to the South Polar Regions. London: Edward Arnold, 1896. 1st ed. Frontis, (12),243pp; 11 plts. (Margin of 1st 2 gatherings stained.) Cl-backed bds (rebound), morocco label; pict cl (badly faded, stained) preserved at end. *Cox.* $70/£45

BULLARD, F. LAURISTAN. Abraham Lincoln and the Widow Bixby. New Brunswick: Rutgers Univ, 1946. 1st ed. *Wantagh.* $20/£13

BULLARD, F. LAURISTON. Lincoln in Marble and Brass. New Brunswick, NJ, (1952). 1st ed. Fine in dj (lt wear, chipping). *Pratt.* $27/£17

BULLARD, JOHN M. The Greens as I Knew Them. New Bedford, 1964. 1st ed. Inscribed. Fine in dj. *Lefkowicz.* $65/£42

BULLEN, FRANK. The Cruise of the Cachalot. London: Smith, Elder, 1898. 1st ed. Frontis, map. Gilt-pict blue cl. Fine. *Swann*.* $103/£66

BULLEN, FRANK. The Cruise of the Cachalot. London, 1900. 2nd ed. Map, 8 plts. *Wheldon & Wesley.* $55/£35

BULLEN, FRANK. The Log of a Sea-Waif. NY: Appleton, 1899. 1st Amer ed. 8 plts. Dec cl. VG (lacks fep). *Agvent.* $35/£22

BULLEN, FRANK. The Log of a Sea-Waif. NY: D. Appleton, 1899. 370pp. Dec lt grn cl, gilt. VG. *Parmer.* $45/£29

BULLEN, GEORGE (ed). Caxton Celebration 1877. London: N. Truebner, (1877). 472pp (pencil mks, ink dates in margins, offset tp). Generally VG (cvr wear). *Heller.* $100/£64

BULLEN, HENRY LEWIS. Civilization Rests on Printing. Chicago: Black Cat, 1938. One of 250. (5) French-fold pp, colophon. NF in string-tied ptd wrappers. *Cahan.* $15/£10

BULLETT, GERALD. The Snare of the Fowler. NY, 1936. 1st Amer ed. Fine (name) in dj (spine sunned, few nicks). *Polyanthos.* $30/£19

BULLINS, ED. The Duplex: A Black Fable in Four Movements. NY: Morrow, 1971. 1st ed. Fine in NF dj (fr panel lamination sl wrinkled, flaps sl discolored). *Between The Covers.* $85/£54

BULLINS, ED. Four Dynamite Plays. NY: Morrow, 1972. 1st ed. Fine (pg edges sl dknd) in dj (sm tear fr panel). *Between The Covers.* $75/£48

BULLINS, ED. The Hungered One. NY: William Morrow, 1971. 1st ed. Fine in dj (1-inch tear). *Lame Duck.* $45/£29

BULLINS, ED. The Reluctant Rapist. NY: Harper, (1973). 1st ed. (Paperclip indentation, some rust to 1st few pp), else Fine in NF dj (spine lt worn). *Between The Covers.* $65/£42

BULLINS, ED. The Theme Is Blackness. NY: Morrow, 1973. 1st ed. Fine in dj (sm tear fr flap). *Between The Covers.* $75/£48

BULLOCK, BARBARA. Wynn Bullock. SF: Scrimshaw, 1971. 1st ed. 63 plts. Gray cl, inset photo fr cvr. (Owner stamp), else Fine. *Cahan.* $250/£160

BULLOCK, CHARLES J. (ed). The China Sea Directory. Volume III. London: Admiralty, 1874. (xii),632pp; fldg index chart. Limp cl. *Lefkowicz.* $150/£96

BULLOCK, HELEN. The Williamsburg Art of Cookery. Williamsburg: Colonial Williamsburg, 1947. 4th ed. Frontis. Full leather. VG. *Bohling.* $15/£10

BULLOCK, WILLIAM. Preserving Objects of Natural History. London: The Proprietor, 1818. 2nd ed. (4),36pp, incl 1/2-title; 2 engr plts; 4 leaves inserted blanks (1 partly filled). Contemp marbled bds (dknd, worn), gilt calf spine, maroon label. Contents VG (fep split in hinge). *Waverly*.* $66/£42

BULPIN, T. V. The Ivory Trail. Cape Town, 1954. 1st ed. NF in dj. *Grayling.* $47/£30

BUMPUS, T. F. A Guide to Gothic Architecture. n.d. (c. 1914). 143 full-pg plts. Tan/black pict cl. Good (text lt foxed). *Whittle.* $23/£15

BUNBURY, HENRY. Narratives of Some Passages in the Great War with France. London, 1854. xxiv,471pp; 4 maps. Red cl (sl worn, headcaps repaired). *Maggs.* $273/£175

BUNIN, IVAN. Memories and Portraits. GC: Doubleday, 1951. 1st ed. NF in dj (sl worn, sm tear). *Antic Hay.* $35/£22

BUNKER, GEORGE R. (ed). Alexey Brodovitch and His Influence. Phila: Phila College of Art, 1972. 1st ed. (Name stamp), else Fine in stiff black wrappers. *Cahan.* $100/£64

BUNN, MATTHEW. Journal of the Adventures of.... Chicago, 1962. One of 2000. Ptd wrappers. Howes B952. *Ginsberg.* $25/£16

BUNNELL, PETER C. Harry Callahan. 38th Venice Biennial, 1978, United States Pavilion. (NY): Internat'l Exhibitions Committee of Amer Federation of Arts, 1978. 1st ed. Signed by Callahan. Frontis port, 32 b/w, 1 color plt. (Owner stamp), else NF in pict stiff wrappers. *Cahan.* $85/£54

BUNNELL, STERLING. Surgery of the Hand. London, 1944. 1st ed, 4th imp. Good (extrems worn). *Doctor's Library.* $200/£128

BUNNELL, STERLING. Surgery of the Hand. Phila, 1956. 3rd ed. NF (bkpl, stamps fep). *Doctor's Library.* $100/£64

BUNNER, H. C. More 'Short Sixes.' NY: Keppler & Schwarzmann, 1894. 1st ed. Brn linen bds (dusty, faded, spine dknd), stamped in brn, gilt. VG (inscrip fep). BAL 1927. *Hermitage.* $40/£26

BUNTING, BASIL. Collected Poems. Fulcrum, 1968. One of 1000. NF in dj (chipped, rubbed). *Poetry Bookshop.* $31/£20

BUNTING, BASIL. Loquitur. Fulcrum, (1965). One of 774 (ex 1000) in the ordinary ed. Plain lt gray cardboard bds (Polythene dj sl cockled), o/w Fine. *Poetry Bookshop.* $78/£50

BUNTING, BASIL. Version of Horace. Holborn: Guidonis Londinensis, 1972. One of 300 numbered. Folded sheet. Fine in ptd envelope. *Dermont.* $25/£16

BUNYAN, JOHN. Grace Abounding to the Chief of Sinners. Lancaster: John Bear, 1843. 188pp. Aeg. Orig blind/gilt-emb cl. (Sl shelfworn), else VG. *Brown.* $25/£16

BUNYAN, JOHN. The Pilgrim's Progress. NY: Century, 1898. 1st ed. Folio. xx,184pp. Dec litho paper on bds, gilt, grn cl spine. Near Mint. *Hobbyhorse.* $200/£128

BUNYAN, JOHN. The Pilgrim's Progress. (London), 1899. One of 750 numbered. Woodcut frontis by Reginald Savage. Vellum. *Swann*.* $172/£110

BUNYAN, JOHN. The Pilgrim's Progress. The Strand: Essex House, 1899. Ltd to 750. Woodcut frontis, 426pp. Orig full vellum (sl soil). *Cullen.* $200/£128

BUNYAN, JOHN. The Pilgrim's Progress. London: Henry Frowde, 1904. George Cruikshank (illus). Patterned eps; teg. Red 1/4 morocco, red cl, gilt, 5 raised bands. VG (bkpl). *Antic Hay*. $50/£32

BUNYAN, JOHN. The Pilgrim's Progress. Nonesuch, 1928. Marbled cl bds. (Eps browned; spine sl dknd, sl frayed), o/w VG. *Michael Taylor*. $62/£40

BUNYAN, JOHN. The Pilgrim's Progress. NY: LEC, 1941. #904/1500 numbered. William Blake (illus). Fine in pub's slipcase. *Hermitage*. $150/£96

BUNYAN, JOHN. The Pilgrim's Progress. Boston: Isaiah Thomas, Jun. 1817. Genuine Edition, with Notes. Complete in 2 parts, continuous pagination. Sm 8vo. Full-pg woodcut frontis, vii,302pp; 9 full-pg cuts. (Damp stains throughout, some margins repaired w/loss; browning.) Full leather on bds (sl scuffed, corners rubbed), gilt on black spine label. Good. *Hobbyhorse*. $200/£128

BUNYAN, JOHN. The Pilgrim's Progress. G. B. Harrison (ed). NY: LEC, 1941. 29 watercolor illus by William Blake. Leather label. VG. *Argosy*. $200/£128

BUNYARD, EDWARD A. Old Garden Roses. London: Country Life, 1936. Color frontis. (Lt foxing.) Aeg. Fine full red morocco (sl rubbed), spine gilt in 6 compartments. Slipcase. *Oinonen**. $130/£83

BURBANK, LUTHER. Luther Burbank, His Methods and Discoveries and Their Practical Application.... NY/London: Luther Burbank, 1914. 1st ed. 12 vols. Incl engr dedication leaf bound into vol 1, signed by Secretary of the Luther Burbank Soc. 105 mtd prints. Teg. Red cl, gilt-lettered spines (lt faded; fore-edge sl foxed), port mtd fr cvr each vol as issued. Fine. *Argonaut*. $375/£240

BURBANK, LUTHER. Luther Burbank: His Methods and Discoveries and Their Practical Application. NY/London, 1914/1915. 12 vols, each w/tipped-in color frontis. Untrimmed. VG. *Zubal**. $190/£122

BURBRIDGE, F. W. The Gardens of the Sun. London, 1880. xviii,(i),364pp + 24pp pub's ads. (Lt browned; bkpl; dec cl corners rubbed, sl worn, rebacked w/much of orig spine laid down.) *Edwards*. $117/£75

BURCH, JOHN P. Charles W. Quantrill: A True History of His Guerrilla Warfare...During the Civil War of 1861 to 1865. Vega, TX, 1923. 1st ed. (Bkpl.) *Wantagh*. $45/£29

BURCHARD, H. Report of the Director of the Mint Upon the Production of the Precious Metals in the United States...1884. Washington, 1885. 644pp. Recent red cl. *Blake*. $150/£96

BURCHARD, PETER. One Gallant Rush. NY: St. Martin's, (1965). 1st ed. 3 maps. Blue cl. VG in pict dj. *Petrilla*. $35/£22

BURCHETT, WILFRED. My Visit to the Liberated Zones of South Vietnam. Hanoi: Foreign Languages Pub, 1966. 3rd ed. Wraps. Fine in Fine dj. *Beasley*. $45/£29

BURCHETT, WILFRED. North of the 17th Parallel. Hanoi: The Author, 1955. 1st ed. (Spine chipped, frayed; edges worn), o/w VG in orig wrappers. *Patterson*. $39/£25

BURCKHARDT, JOHN LEWIS. Travels in Nubia. London: John Murray, 1822. 2nd ed. 4to. Etched frontis port, 3 engr maps (2 fldg). Marbled edges. Contemp tan polished calf (scuffed, stained), gilt, raised bands. *Appelfeld*. $1,250/£801

BURCKHARDT, TITUS. Sacred Art in East and West. Lord Northbourne (trans). 1967. 1st ed. 16 plts. Dj (lt soiled). *Edwards*. $23/£15

BURDICK, ARTHUR J. The Prospectors Manual. L.A.: George Rice, 1905. 1st ed. Pict cl (soiled, worn). Good. *Perier*. $25/£16

BURDICK, USHER L. Life and Exploits of John Goodall. Watford City, ND: McKenzie County Farmer, 1931. 1st ed. VG in wrappers. *Lien*. $30/£19

BURDIN, J. A Course of Medical Studies. 1803. 3 vols. xxxiv,428; xii,447; xii,436pp (eps lt foxed). Orig marbled bds (corner vol 3 knocked). *Whitehart*. $250/£160

BURDON, WILLIAM. Life and Character of Bonaparte, from His Birth to the 15th of August, 1804. Newcastle upon Tyne: K. Anderson, May 30, 1805. 2nd ed. Frontis port, 296pp + 8pp ads (foxing). Later 3/4 red leather (hinges rubbed, spine lt chipped), gilt. *Bohling*. $70/£45

BUREAU OF AMERICAN ETHNOLOGY. See BAE

BURGER, J. F. African Jungle Memories. London, 1958. 1st ed. Excellent in dj (spine lacks top inch, frayed). *Grayling*. $70/£45

BURGES, ARNOLD. The American Kennel and Sporting Field. NY, 1876. 1st ed. 201pp. (Ink inscrip; cvrs poor; fr cvr, 1/2 of spine detached.) *King*. $50/£32

BURGES, BARTHOLOMEW. A Series of Indostan Letters. NY, (1790). Engr tp, frontis. (Lacks last leaf.) Contemp calf (rubbed, cvrs detached, rebacked). *Freeman**. $20/£13

BURGES, TRISTRAM. Battle of Lake Erie with Notices of Commodore Elliot's Conduct in That Engagement. Providence: Brown/Cady, 1839. 132pp. (Lib handstamp tp; sl wear, spine end lt worn), else Good. *Brown*. $60/£38

BURGESS, ANTHONY. 1985. Hutchinson, 1978. 1st UK ed. NF in dj. *Williams*. $19/£12

BURGESS, ANTHONY. 99 Novels. The Best in English Since 1939. NY, 1984. 1st Amer ed. NF (sm edge rub) in dj. *Polyanthos*. $30/£19

BURGESS, ANTHONY. The Age of the Grand Tour. Elek, 1967. 1st ed. VG in dj (torn, internally repaired). *Words Etc*. $94/£60

BURGESS, ANTHONY. A Clockwork Orange. NY: Norton, (1963). 1st US ed. Fine in NF dj (lt soiled, bumped). *Unger*. $225/£144

BURGESS, ANTHONY. A Clockwork Orange. Heinemann, 1962. 1st issue black bds. NF in dj (spine sl faded, worn; sm closed tear bottom fr panel). *Williams*. $975/£625

BURGESS, ANTHONY. A Clockwork Orange. London: Heinemann, 1962. 1st issue in black cl. (Sm blue star stamped on fep), o/w Excellent in dj (sl chipped). *Gekoski*. $1,170/£750

BURGESS, ANTHONY. Coaching Days of England. London, 1966. 24 color plts. Dec eps. Dj (torn, repaired). *Edwards*. $148/£95

BURGESS, ANTHONY. Coaching Days of England. London: Elek/Internat'l Book Soc, 1966. 1st ed. 24 color plts. VG in Good+ dj. *Scribe's Perch**. $70/£45

BURGESS, ANTHONY. Devil of a State. London: Heinemann, (1961). 1st ed. Fine in dj (sl worn). *Antic Hay*. $50/£32

BURGESS, ANTHONY. The Devil's Mode. London: Hutchinson, 1989. 1st UK ed. Fine in dj. *Williams*. $19/£12

BURGESS, ANTHONY. Earthly Powers. NY, 1980. 1st Amer ed. Fine in dj. *Polyanthos*. $25/£16

BURGESS, ANTHONY. The End of the World News. Hutchinson, 1982. 1st UK ed. Fine in dj. *Williams*. $23/£15

BURGESS, ANTHONY. Enderby's Dark Lady. Hutchinson, 1984. 1st UK ed. NF in dj (price-clipped). *Williams*. $19/£12

BURGESS, ANTHONY. Enderby's Dark Lady. London, 1984. 1st ed. Fine in Fine dj. *Smith*. $15/£10

BURGESS, ANTHONY. The Kingdom of the Wicked. Franklin Library, 1985. 1st US ed. Signed. Fine in dec binding. *Williams*. $44/£28

BURGESS, ANTHONY. The Pianoplayers. Hutchinson, 1986. 1st UK ed. VG+ in dj (spine lt bumped, price-clipped). *Williams*. $12/£8

BURGESS, ANTHONY. The Pianoplayers. NY, 1986. 1st Amer ed. NF in NF dj. *Polyanthos*. $25/£16

BURGESS, ANTHONY. The Right to an Answer. Heinemann, 1960. 1st UK ed. VG in dj (fr flap lt scuffed). *Williams*. $101/£65

BURGESS, ANTHONY. Tremor of Intent. Heinemann, 1966. 1st UK ed. Fine in NF dj. *Williams*. $75/£48

BURGESS, ANTHONY. Tremor of Intent. NY, 1966. 1st Amer ed. Fine in dj (rear panel sl sunned, sl rubbed). *Polyanthos*. $25/£16

BURGESS, ANTHONY. Urgent Copy. London: Jonathan Cape, (1968). 1st ed. NF (corner sl bumped) in Fine dj. *Antic Hay*. $45/£29

BURGESS, ANTHONY. The Worm and the Ring. Heinemann, 1961. VG (lt foxed) in dj (rear lt foxed, corners sl worn, price-clipped). *Williams*. $546/£350

BURGESS, F. F. R. Sporting Fire-Arms for Bush and Jungle. London, 1884. 1st ed. (Sl worn.) *Oinonen**. $120/£77

BURGESS, FRED. Antique Jewellery and Trinkets. London: George Routledge, 1919. 1st ed, 1st ptg. Pict cl. VG (pp browned). *Blake*. $125/£80

BURGESS, FRED. Chats on Household Curios. London: T. Fisher Unwin, 1914. 1st ed. (Spotted, mkd, name erased fep.) *Hollett*. $47/£30

BURGESS, FRED. Silver, Pewter, and Sheffield Plate. London: George Routledge, 1921. Gilt pict dk grn cl. VG+. *House*. $35/£22

BURGESS, GELETT. Bayside Bohemia. SF: Book Club of CA, 1954. One of 375. 4 facs (2 fldg). Dec cl. Fine. *Harrington*. $65/£42

BURGESS, GELETT. Bayside Bohemia. SF: Book Club of CA, 1954. 1st ed. Ltd to 375 ptd. 4 facs (2 fldg). Rendition of 'The Purple Cow' laid in. Fine. *Argonaut*. $75/£48

BURGESS, GELETT. Goops and How to Be Them. London: Methuen, 1900. 1st Eng ed. Sq 8vo. Brn pict cl. Nice. *Appelfeld*. $150/£96

BURGESS, JOHN. Bugle in the Wilderness. NY: Vanguard, (1958). 1st ed. (Stain fr pastedown), else Fine in Fine dj (sm tear). *Between The Covers*. $45/£29

BURGESS, OPIE RUNDLE. Bisbee Not So Long Ago. San Antonio: Naylor, 1967. VG (name) in dj. *Dumont*. $45/£29

BURGESS, THORNTON. The Adventures of Danny Meadow Mouse. Boston: Little Brown, (1944). 1st ed thus. Bedtime Story-Book. 8vo. 94pp; 8 full-pg color illus by Harrison Cady. Illus eps. Yellow illus bds (edgewear, corners sl bumped), red cl label. Good+. *Dower*. $45/£29

BURGESS, THORNTON. The Adventures of Jimmy Skunk. Boston: Little Brown, 1947. 1st ed thus. 8vo. 94pp; 10 full-pg color illus by Harrison Cady. Illus eps. Yellow illus bds, red cl spine. VG in Fair dj. *Dower*. $50/£32

BURGESS, THORNTON. The Burgess Flower Book for Children. Boston: Little Brown, May 1923. 8vo. 350pp. Pict pastedown cvr. Good. *Scribe's Perch**. $27/£17

BURGESS, THORNTON. Longlegs the Heron. Boston: Little Brown, 1927. 1st ed. 8vo. 207pp (faint damp mk tp); 8 full-pg color plts by Harrison Cady. Grn cl, color pict label. VG. *Dower*. $95/£61

BURGIN, RICHARD. Conversations with Jorge Luis Borges. NY: Holt, Rinehart & Winston, (1969). 1st ed. Fine in NF dj (sm section lamination peeled). *Antic Hay*. $35/£22

BURGOYNE, J. A State of the Expedition from Canada as Land Before the House of Commons.... London: J. Almon, 1780. 1st ed. 4to. 5 fldg maps in back, 1 large linen-backed fldg map in fr (sl tears along folds; very sl foxing). 1/2 leather (leather spine lacks lg pieces). *Metropolitan**. $1,092/£700

BURHANS, ROBERT D. The First Special Service Force. Washington, (1947). 1st ed. (Removal mks eps; few pp repaired; rubbed.) *King*. $200/£128

BURKE, EDMUND. On Conciliation With the Colonies. LEC, 1975. #872/2000. Signed by Lynd Ward (illus). Dec cvrs. Fine in Fine box (sm chip). *Polyanthos*. $100/£64

BURKE, EDMUND. On Conciliation with the Colonies. (NY): LEC, 1975. #417/2000 signed by Lynd Ward (illus). Fine in slipcase. *Hermitage*. $125/£80

BURKE, EDMUND. A Philosophical Inquiry into the Origin of Our Ideas of the Sublime and Beautiful. London: Thos. Tegg, 1810. Engr frontis, 172pp. Uncut. Ptd pub's bds (considerably worn, faded). Contents Excellent. *Hartfield*. $125/£80

BURKE, EDMUND. Three Memorials on French Affairs. London: F. & C. Rivington, 1797. Contemp tree calf (rubbed, upper bd detached, lower joint cracked, spine chipped), morocco spine label. *Edwards*. $133/£85

BURKE, JAMES D. Jan Both: Paintings, Drawings, and Prints. NY, 1976. Good. *Washton*. $75/£48

BURKE, JAMES LEE. Heaven's Prisoners. NY, 1988. 1st ed. Signed. Fine in Fine dj. *Smith*. $50/£32

BURKE, JAMES LEE. Lay Down My Sword and Shield. NY: Crowell, 1971. 1st ed. Signed. (Pg edges foxed), o/w Fine in dj (price-clipped, short closed tears). *Mordida*. $750/£481

BURKE, JAMES LEE. The Lost Get-Back Boogie. Baton Rouge: LA State Univ, 1986. 1st ed. Signed. Fine in dj (price-clipped). *Mordida*. $250/£160

BURKE, JAMES LEE. The Neon Rain. Holt, 1987. 1st ed. Fine in Fine dj. *Certo*. $85/£54

BURKE, JAMES LEE. A Stained White Radiance. NY: Hyperion, 1992. 1st ed. VF in dj. *Mordida*. $45/£29

BURKE, JAMES LEE. Two for Texas. NY: Pocket Books, 1972. Pb orig. VG- in wraps. *Warren*. $45/£29

BURKE, JAMES W. Missions of Old Texas. NY, 1971. 1st ed. Fine in Fine dj. *Turpen*. $25/£16

BURKE, JOHN. A Hard Day's Night. Pan Books, 1964. 1st ed. VG in orig pict paper cvrs. *Cox*. $23/£15

BURKE, JOSEPH and COLIN CALDWELL. Hogarth: The Complete Engravings. NY: Abrams, (n.d., ca 1968). VG in dj. *Argosy*. $150/£96

BURKE, MARIE LOUISE. Little Music. Aquarius, 1948. Ltd to 300. Dec bds, natural canvas spine. VF. *Truepenny*. $30/£19

BURKE, PHYLLIS. Atomic Candy. NY: Atlantic Monthly, 1989. 1st ed. Fine in Fine dj. *Revere*. $25/£16

BURKE, THOMAS. East of Mansion House. Doran, 1926. 1st ed. NF in dj (chipped). *Madle*. $50/£32

BURKE, THOMAS. East of Mansion House. London: Cassell, 1928. 1st ed. Fine in pict dj (soiled, sm chips). *Else Fine*. $85/£54

BURKE, THOMAS. The English Townsman. Batsford, 1946. 1st ed. Color frontis. (Eps, edges spotted.) Dj (lt spotted, sl chipped). *Edwards*. $23/£15

BURKHARDT, FRANK A. Pioneer Days of George H. A. Burkhardt. (L.A., 1935.) VG in ptd wraps. *Bohling*. $16/£10

BURLACE, J. B. (ed). Rowland Ward's Sportsman's Handbook to Collecting and Preserving Trophies and Specimens. London: R. Ward, (1923). 11th ed. 7 plts. VG. *Mikesh.* $65/£42

BURLE, AUBREY. The Stone Circles of the British Isles. Yale Univ, 1976. 1st ed. 36 plts. Dj (sl rubbed). *Edwards.* $31/£20

BURLEIGH, BENNET. The Natal Campaign. London, 1900. Frontis port. Contemp calf, gilt. Good. *Maggs.* $156/£100

BURLEIGH, THOMAS D. Birds of Idaho. Caldwell: Caxton, 1972. Fine in VG dj. *Perier.* $50/£32

BURLETON, SOLOMON STEVENS. An Officer of the Line. Hartford: Church Missions Pub Co, 1911. 1st ed. *Ginsberg.* $75/£48

BURLINGAME, EUGENE W. The Grateful Elephant. New Haven: Yale Univ, 1923. 1st ed thus. Lg 8vo. Color frontis, 172pp; 22 full-pg b/w illus by Dorothy Lathrop. Beige illus cl. VG in VG dj. *Dower.* $150/£96

BURN, RICHARD. The Justice of the Peace, and Parish Officer. (London): A. Millar, 1755. 1st ed. 2 vols. Mod 1/4 calf, orig labels preserved. Good set. *Boswell.* $1,250/£801

BURNABY, FRED. A Ride to Khiva. NY: Harper, 1877. 403pp; 1 (of 3) color fldg map (tears) in rear pocket. Good (foxing, sl shaken; edges rubbed, spine frayed, corners worn). *Worldwide.* $45/£29

BURNABY, FRED. A Ride to Khiva. NY: Harper, 1877. 1st ed. 401pp; 3 fldg color maps. (Cl sl rubbed), o/w VG. *Worldwide.* $65/£42

BURNAND, FRANCIS. Records and Reminiscences. Methuen, 1904. 3rd ed. 2 vols. 32 plts. (Lacks loosely inserted facs letters.) Teg, others uncut. Sound (cl sl dusty). *Cox.* $23/£15

BURNE-JONES, EDWARD. Letters to Kate. Macmillan, 1925. 1st ed. 24 plts. VG in Holland-backed bds, paper label. *Cox.* $39/£25

BURNET, GILBERT. Bishop Burnet's History of His Own Time.... London: Ptd for the Company of Booksellers, 1725-1734. 6 vols. Old full polished calf (lt worn). *Kane*.* $110/£71

BURNET, JACOB. Notes on the Early Settlement of the North-Western Territory. Cincinnati: Derby, Bradley, 1847. Frontis port, 501pp, errata slip, 16 pp ads (ink names, foxing). Orig cl (worn, extrems chipped). Howes B997. *Bohling.* $110/£71

BURNET, JOHN et al. Engravings from the Pictures of the National Gallery. London: John Pye for Assoc Engrs, 1840. 29 engr plts (several spotted). Contemp maroon 1/2 morocco (worn). *Christie's*.* $562/£360

BURNET, JOHN. A Treatise on Painting in Four Parts. London: Carpenter, 1837, 1836, 1838, 1843. 2nd, 5th, 5th, 5th eds, respectively. 73pp, 7 plts; 31pp, 9 plts; 45pp, 8 plts; 64pp + 2pp ads, 8 plts. Later plain bds. (Some plts sl browned), o/w Fine. *Europa.* $125/£80

BURNET, MACFARLANE. The Integrity of the Body. Cambridge, MA: Harvard Univ, 1962. 1st ed. Good in dj. *White.* $23/£15

BURNETT, FRANCES HODGSON. Little Lord Fauntleroy. NY, 1886. 1st ed. Gilt-pict cl (sl askew). *Swann*.* $103/£66

BURNETT, FRANCES HODGSON. Sarah Crewe, or What Happened at Miss Minchin's. Scribner, (1888). 1st ed. 7x8.5. 83pp. Brn cl, gilt. (Fr hinge cracking; shelfworn), else VG. *My Bookhouse.* $40/£26

BURNETT, FRANCES HODGSON. The White People. Harper, (1917). 1st ed. Pict cl. NF. *Certo.* $30/£19

BURNETT, PETER H. Recollections and Opinions of an Old Pioneer. NY: D. Appleton, 1880. 1st ed. xiv,448pp + 6pp ads. Black/gold-stamped dk yellow cl (spotting to rear cvr, lacks rfep, sl marginal staining). *Dawson.* $300/£192

BURNETT, W. R. Adobe Walls. NY: Knopf, (1953). 1st ed. VG + in VG + dj. *Pettler & Lieberman.* $40/£26

BURNETT, W. R. The Asphalt Jungle. Knopf, 1949. 1st ed. (Name stamp tp, bottom pg edges.) VG in VG dj. *Certo.* $45/£29

BURNETT, W. R. The Asphalt Jungle. NY: Knopf, 1949. 1st ed. Fine in dj (lt worn). *Else Fine.* $175/£112

BURNETT, W. R. High Sierra. NY: Knopf, 1940. 1st ed. VG in VG dj (edges frayed). *Unger.* $250/£160

BURNETT, W. R. Iron Man. Dial, 1930. 1st ed. VG + in dj (short tears, very sm spine chips). *Certo.* $50/£32

BURNETT, W. R. Underdog. NY: Knopf, 1957. 1st ed. Fine in dj. *Mordida.* $45/£29

BURNETT, W. R. Vanity Row. NY: Knopf, 1952. 1st ed. Fine in VG dj (long closed tears, internal tape mends, sl rubbed). *Mordida.* $35/£22

BURNEY, FRANCES. The Diary and Letters.... Bickers, 1911. 2 vols. 2 plts. (Backstrips sl worn), o/w Good set in orig buckram. *Cox.* $39/£25

BURNEY, FRANCES. The Early Diary...1768-1778. Annie Raine Ellis (ed). G. Bell, 1913. 2 vols. Brn cl. Sound set. *Cox.* $19/£12

BURNEY, JAMES. History of the Buccaneers of America. Unit Library, 1902. 2nd separate ed. Red limp morocco, gilt. *Cox.* $19/£12

BURNHAM, GEORGE P. The Game Fowl; for the Pit, or the Spit. Melrose, MA, 1877. 1st ed. Chromolitho frontis (tissue torn), 26 wood-engrs; newscuttings inserted together w/signed agreement for a main at Wedruth, 2 1/2pp. Brn cl. *Hatchwell.* $234/£150

BURNINGHAM, JOHN. Around the World in Eighty Days. London: Cape, 1972. 1st ed. 8 1/2 x 10 3/4. 97pp. VG in dj. *Cattermole.* $30/£19

BURNINGHAM, JOHN. Come Away from the Water, Shirley. London: Cape, 1977. 1st ed. 10 3/4 x 8 3/4. 32pp. Glossy bds. Fine. *Cattermole.* $60/£38

BURNINGHAM, JOHN. Mr. Gumpy's Motor Car. NY: Crowell, 1976. 1st US ed. 10 1/2 sq. 32pp. Fine in dj. *Cattermole.* $24/£15

BURNINGHAM, JOHN. Mr. Gumpy's Outing. NY: Holt, 1970. 1st US ed. 10 1/2 sq. 32pp. Fine in dj. *Cattermole.* $32/£21

BURNINGHAM, JOHN. Seasons. Indianapolis: Bobbs Merrill, 1971. 1st US ed. 9 3/4 x 12. 32pp. Fine in dj. *Cattermole.* $50/£32

BURNS, ALLAN. Observations on the Surgical Anatomy of the Head and Neck. Edinburgh, 1811. 1st ed. 8vo. 8 + 415pp (lower margin tp cut away removing date); 10 plts. Old calf (spine worn, upper hinge repaired; ex-lib), else Good. *Argosy.* $600/£385

BURNS, EUGENE. Advanced Fly Fishing. Harrisburg: Stackpole, 1953. 1st ed. Color frontis. VF. *Bowman.* $75/£48

BURNS, HELEN. Salton Sea Story. Thermal: The Author, (1952). Pict wrappers (edgewear, nick). *Dawson.* $25/£16

BURNS, JOHN HORNE. The Gallery. NY: Harper, (1947). 1st ed, 1st bk. Fine in dj (lt worn). *Hermitage.* $100/£64

BURNS, JOHN. The Principles of Midwifery; Including the Diseases of Women and Children. Phila, 1823. 223pp. Vol 2 only. Full leather (worn). Good. *Doctor's Library.* $50/£32

BURNS, KATHLEEN S. and HENRY T. WYSE. Embroidery and Stencilling. Edinburgh, Sept 1910. 17 diags, 20 photo plts. Dec grn cl. Good+ (worn). *Whittle.* $55/£35

BURNS, REX. Angle of Attack. NY: Harper & Row, 1979. 1st ed. Fine in NF dj. *Janus.* $25/£16

BURNS, REX. Speak for the Dead. NY: Harper & Row, 1978. 1st ed. Fine in dj. *Mordida.* $45/£29

BURNS, ROBERT. The Glenriddell Manuscripts. Phila: John Gribbel, 1914. Full pigskin (spine chipped). *Argosy.* $75/£48

BURNS, ROBERT. Letters of Robert Burns. Boston: Wills & Lilly, 1820. 1st Amer ed. 2 vols in 1. 248; 197pp. Contemp calf, spine gilt. (Lt text foxing, ink name; binding lt rubbed), else VG. *Reese.* $65/£42

BURNS, ROBERT. The Poetry. W. E. Henley and T. F. Henderson (eds). Edinburgh: T.C. & E.C. Jack, 1896. 4 vols. Teg, untrimmed. Dec cream cl (spines sl dknd), gilt. Very Nice set. *Hollett.* $117/£75

BURNS, TEX. (Pseud of Louis L'Amour.) Hopalong Cassidy and the Rustlers of West Fork. London: Hodder & Stoughton, (1951). 1st Eng ed. Fine in NF dj (lt stain top corners flaps). *Between The Covers.* $285/£183

BURNS, TEX. (Pseud of Louis L'Amour.) Hopalong Cassidy, Trouble-Shooter. London: Hodder & Stoughton, (1953). 1st Eng ed. (Foxing), else VG in VG+ dj (price-clipped; short tears; crown lt wear). *Between The Covers.* $250/£160

BURNSIDE, WESLEY M. Maynard Dixon, Artist of the West. Provo: Brigham Young Univ, (1974). 1st trade ed. 32 color plts. Tan cl, brn leatherette backstrip. Fine in NF dj (sl soiled). *Harrington.* $100/£64

BURR, AARON. The Private Journal of Aaron Burr, During His Residence of Four Years in Europe. NY: Harper, 1838. 1st ed. 2 vols. Grn cl, gilt. (Sl foxing throughout.) *Hermitage.* $175/£112

BURR, ANNA R. Weir Mitchell. NY: Duffield, 1929. Clean in dj, orig box (joints splitting). *Goodrich.* $50/£32

BURR, FREDERIC M. Life and Works of Alexander Anderson, M.D., the First American Wood Engraver. NY: Burr Bros, 1893. 1st ed. Ltd to 725 numbered, signed. 210pp; 3 ports, 30 plts. Mod cl, leather spine label. Fine. *Oak Knoll.* $200/£128

BURRA, EDWARD. Well, Dearie! William Chappell (ed). London, 1985. 1st ed. Fine in dj. *Words Etc.* $55/£35

BURRAGE, HENRY S. Gettysburg and Lincoln. NY, 1906. 1st ed. Pict cl (Cvr sl worn), o/w Fine. *Pratt.* $45/£29

BURRAGE, HENRY S. History of the Baptists in Maine. Portland, ME: Marks, 1904. 1st ed. *Ginsberg.* $100/£64

BURRAGE, WALTER L. (ed). A Guide Book of Boston for Physicians Prepared for the Fifty-Seventh Annual Session of the American Medical Association...1906. Boston: Merrymount, 1906. 4 maps. (Sm break fore-edge), o/w Fine in pict ptd wrappers. *Sadlon.* $45/£29

BURRARD, G. Big Game Hunting in the Himalayas and Tibet. NY: Frederick A. Stokes, (1925?). 1st (?) Amer ed. Sheets of the Eng 1st ed, w/Stokes' tp. 8 maps, 23 half-tone plts. Blue cl (spine faded). VG. *Cummins.* $175/£112

BURRARD, G. The Modern Shotgun. NY, 1931-31-32. 3 vols. (Owner stamps; sl worn.) *Oinonen*.* $200/£128

BURRELL, HARRY. The Platypus. Sydney, 1927. 1st ed. Color frontis, 34 photo plts. Maroon cl. VG. *Price.* $95/£61

BURRIS-MEYER, HAROLD and EDWARD C. COLE. Theatres and Auditoriums. NY: Reinhold, 1949. 1st ed. (Extrems rubbed, skewed), else VG. *Cahan.* $45/£29

BURROUGHES, DOROTHY. The Little Pigs Who Sailed Away. London: Hutchinson's Books, n.d. c. 1950. 1st Eng ed. Oblong 8vo. 47pp. Tan cl (fade stain rear, sm stain fr, spine ends worn). Good+. *Dower.* $45/£29

BURROUGHS, EDGAR RICE. Apache Devil. Tarzana: Edgar Rice Burroughs, (1933). 1st ed. Fine (tp lt foxed; dj fr panel laid in). Heins AD 1. *Turtle Island.* $50/£32

BURROUGHS, EDGAR RICE. At the Earth's Core. Chicago: A.C. McClurg, 1922. 1st ed. 9 b/w plts. (Piece torn bottom corner pp239-240, no loss; rear inner hinge cracked; fr cvr lt spotted), o/w VG. *Bernard.* $125/£80

BURROUGHS, EDGAR RICE. At the Earth's Core. Chicago: A.C. McClurg, 1922. 1st ed. VG (top, fore-edge spotted; most of dj fr panel laid down on ep). Heins AEC 1. *Turtle Island.* $350/£224

BURROUGHS, EDGAR RICE. At the Earth's Core. Chicago: McClurg, 1922. 1st ed, w/ptr's imprint at base of c. pg. 8vo. 9 plts. NF in dj (sl dust-soiled, edges lt rubbed, two 3-inch tears, no loss, 2 sm closed tears). *Kane*.* $1,600/£1,026

BURROUGHS, EDGAR RICE. Back to the Stone Age. Tarzana: Edgar Rice Burroughs, (1937). 1st ed. Fine (fore-edge lt spotted) in Fine dj. Heins BSA 1. *Turtle Island.* $475/£304

BURROUGHS, EDGAR RICE. The Bandit of Hell's Bend. NY: G&D, (1926). Rpt ed. Fine (fore-edge, pp top sl foxed). Heins BHB 2. *Turtle Island.* $35/£22

BURROUGHS, EDGAR RICE. The Beasts of Tarzan. NY: A.L. Burt, (1917). Rpt ed. NF (bkpl, fore-edge spotted; sl cocked; image from dj laid down on eps). Heins BTa 3. *Turtle Island.* $65/£42

BURROUGHS, EDGAR RICE. The Beasts of Tarzan. Chicago: McClurg, 1916. 1st Amer ed. NF (spine sl sunned, fr hinge starting). *Polyanthos.* $150/£96

BURROUGHS, EDGAR RICE. The Beasts of Tarzan. Chicago: McClurg, 1916. 1st ed, 1st issue w/'W.F. Hall Printing Company, Chicago' at bottom of copyright pg. Grn cl. VG. *New Hampshire*.* $160/£103

BURROUGHS, EDGAR RICE. Beyond Thirty and Man Eater. NY: Science-Fiction & Fantasy, 1957. 1st ed. One of 3000. Fine in NF dj (sl foxing fr panel, internally). Heins BTh 1. *Turtle Island.* $45/£29

BURROUGHS, EDGAR RICE. Carson of Venus. Tarzana: Edgar Rice Burroughs, (1939). 1st ed. Fine in NF dj. Heins CV 1. *Turtle Island.* $425/£272

BURROUGHS, EDGAR RICE. The Cave Girl. Chicago: A.C. McClurg, 1925. 1st ed. VG (rep foxed, pg edges spotted; entire dj fr panel laid in). Heins CaG 1. *Turtle Island.* $65/£42

BURROUGHS, EDGAR RICE. The Chessmen of Mars. Chicago: A.C. McClurg, 1922. 1st ed. NF (top, fore-edge spotted; most of dj fr panel laid down on rep). Heins CM 1. *Turtle Island.* $85/£54

BURROUGHS, EDGAR RICE. The Chessmen of Mars. Chicago: A.C. McClurg, 1922. 1st ed. (Fr cvr dj illus pasted to back pastedown ep; fep sl browned, rep offsetting; spine sl faded, edges foxed), o/w Fine. *Levin.* $165/£106

BURROUGHS, EDGAR RICE. The Deputy Sheriff of Comanche County. Tarzana: Burroughs, (1940). 1st ed, 1st issue (laminated) dj. Exceptional. *Swann*.* $488/£313

BURROUGHS, EDGAR RICE. The Deputy Sheriff of Comanche County. Tarzana: Edgar Rice Burroughs, (1941). 1st ed. Fine (fore-edge sl foxed) in dj. Heins DS 1. *Turtle Island.* $500/£321

BURROUGHS, EDGAR RICE. The Edgar Rice Burroughs Library of Illustrations. West Plains, MO, (1976). One of 2000 numbered. 3 vols. Pict labels inlaid on cvrs. Fine. *Argosy.* $350/£224

BURROUGHS, EDGAR RICE. The Efficiency Expert. House of Greystoke, 1966. 1st ed. Frontis. VG in wraps. *Certo.* $25/£16

BURROUGHS, EDGAR RICE. Escape on Venus. Tarzana: Edgar Rice Burroughs, (1946). 1st ed. Fine (fore-edge sl spotted) in NF dj (short closed tear, sm red mks back panel). Heins EV 1. *Turtle Island.* $200/£128

BURROUGHS, EDGAR RICE. Escape on Venus. Tarzana: Burroughs, 1946. 1st ed. Fine (sl worn, few spots on fr, sm closed tears, creases spine head). *Metropolitan*.* $92/£59

BURROUGHS, EDGAR RICE. The Eternal Lover. Chicago: A.C. McClurg, 1925. 1st ed. NF (spine lt mottled). Heins EL 1. *Turtle Island.* $125/£80

BURROUGHS, EDGAR RICE. A Fighting Man of Mars. NY: Metropolitan Books, (1931). 1st ed. Fine (Christmas presentation). Heins FMM 1. *Turtle Island.* $110/£71

BURROUGHS, EDGAR RICE. The Girl from Hollywood. NY, (1923). 1st ed, 2nd binding. Mesh red cl stamped in yellow-grn ink. VG (ink name blank ep). *Truepenny.* $125/£80

BURROUGHS, EDGAR RICE. The Girl from Hollywood. NY: Macaulay, (1923). 1st ed, 2nd state binding: pict red (but not pebbled) cl, grn lettering. NF (top, fore-edge spotted). Heins GH 2. *Turtle Island.* $75/£48

BURROUGHS, EDGAR RICE. The Girl from Hollywood. NY: Macauley, (1923). 1st ed, 1st issue. Frontis. (Sm hole spine corner; bottom corner tips sl frayed), o/w VG. *Bernard.* $75/£48

BURROUGHS, EDGAR RICE. The Gods of Mars. NY: G&D, (1919). Rpt ed. NF (most of dj fr panel laid down ep). Heins GM 3. *Turtle Island.* $65/£42

BURROUGHS, EDGAR RICE. I Am a Barbarian. Tarzana, CA: ERB, (1967). 1st ed. Fine in NF dj (sm tear). *Bernard.* $65/£42

BURROUGHS, EDGAR RICE. Jungle Girl. Tarzana: Edgar Rice Burroughs, (1932). 1st ed, no statement. Fine (spine crown sl rubbed, dkng). Heins JG 1. *Turtle Island.* $85/£54

BURROUGHS, EDGAR RICE. Jungle Tales of Tarzan. Chicago, 1919. 1st ed. (Lt soil.) *Swann*.* $69/£44

BURROUGHS, EDGAR RICE. Jungle Tales of Tarzan. London: Methuen, 1919. 1st UK ed. VG (ink name; spine sl dull). *Williams.* $75/£48

BURROUGHS, EDGAR RICE. The Lad and the Lion. Tarzana: Edgar Rice Burroughs, (1938). 1st ed. NF (glue offset eps) in Fine dj. Heins LL 1. *Turtle Island.* $500/£321

BURROUGHS, EDGAR RICE. Land of Terror. Tarzana: Edgar Rice Burroughs, (1944). 1st ed. (Eps lt foxed; cl lt mottled), else Fine in dj (2 short closed tears). Heins LT 1. *Turtle Island.* $325/£208

BURROUGHS, EDGAR RICE. The Land That Time Forgot. Chicago: A.C. McClurg, 1924. 1st ed. NF (top, fore-edges lt spotted; 2 spots woven into cl). Heins LTF 1. *Turtle Island.* $100/£64

BURROUGHS, EDGAR RICE. Llana of Gathol. Tarzana: Burroughs, (1948). 1st ed. Fine in dj (sm spine chip). *Levin.* $125/£80

BURROUGHS, EDGAR RICE. Llana of Gathol. Tarzana: Edgar Rice Burroughs, (1948). 1st ed. Fine in dj (spine spotted, sm closed tear rear panel). Heins LG 1. *Turtle Island.* $125/£80

BURROUGHS, EDGAR RICE. Llana of Gathol. Tarzana, 1948. 1st Amer ed. Fine (spine sl creased, lt sunned; sl rubbed). *Polyanthos.* $35/£22

BURROUGHS, EDGAR RICE. Lost on Venus. Tarzana: Edgar Rice Burroughs, (1935). 1st ed. Fine (fore-edge sl spotted) in Fine dj (short closed tear, spine sl mottled). Heins LV 1. *Turtle Island.* $400/£256

BURROUGHS, EDGAR RICE. The Mad King. Chicago: A.C. McClurg, 1926. 1st ed, w/all points uncorrected. Fine (tp, top of pp lt foxed; spine sl faded). Heins MK 1. *Turtle Island.* $200/£128

BURROUGHS, EDGAR RICE. The Master Mind of Mars. Chicago: A.C. McClurg, 1928. 1st ed. Fine (most of dj fr panel laid in). Heins MMM 1. *Turtle Island.* $75/£48

BURROUGHS, EDGAR RICE. The Master Mind of Mars. Methuen, 1939. 1st Eng ed. VG in VG pict dj (sl soiled, worn). *Aronovitz.* $325/£208

BURROUGHS, EDGAR RICE. The Monster Men. Chicago: A.C. McClurg, 1929. 1st ed. Fine (2 sm spots fore-edge; most of dj fr panel laid in, offsetting fep). Heins MMe 1. *Turtle Island.* $175/£112

BURROUGHS, EDGAR RICE. The Moon Maid. Chicago: A.C. McClurg, 1926. 1st ed. NF (name, top, fore-edge spotted; extrems sl worn). Heins MMa 1. *Turtle Island.* $65/£42

BURROUGHS, EDGAR RICE. The Mucker. NY: G&D, (1922). Rpt ed. VG (spine lt sunned, fr panel mottled). Heins M 3. *Turtle Island.* $45/£29

BURROUGHS, EDGAR RICE. The Mucker. NY: Canaveral, 1963. 1st thus. NF in NF- dj (price-clipped). *Other Worlds.* $35/£22

BURROUGHS, EDGAR RICE. The Outlaw of Torn. Chicago: A.C. McClurg, 1927. 1st ed. NF (top, fore-edge foxed). Heins OT 1. *Turtle Island.* $65/£42

BURROUGHS, EDGAR RICE. Pellucidar. Chicago: A.C. McClurg, 1923. 1st ed. NF (fore-edge, pg top spotted; most of dj fr panel laid down on fep, offsetting). Heins P 1. *Turtle Island.* $50/£32

BURROUGHS, EDGAR RICE. Pirates of Venus. Tarzana: Edgar Rice Burroughs, (1934). 1st ed. (Spine spotted), else NF (fr, spine panels of dj laid in). Heins PV 1. *Turtle Island.* $375/£240

BURROUGHS, EDGAR RICE. A Princess of Mars. NY: G&D, (1918). Rpt ed. Frontis, 1 plt. Gray-grn cl. VG (portion of dj fr panel laid down on ep). Heins PM 2/3. *Turtle Island.* $45/£29

BURROUGHS, EDGAR RICE. The Return of Tarzan. NY: A.L. Burt, (1916). Rpt ed. VG (bkpl; top, fore-edge of pp foxed; most of dj fr panel laid down on fep). Heins RT 7. *Turtle Island.* $65/£42

BURROUGHS, EDGAR RICE. The Return of Tarzan. A.L. Burt, (n.d.) Early rpt. VG in dj (sm spine tears, heavy dust). *Certo.* $45/£29

BURROUGHS, EDGAR RICE. The Return of Tarzan. Chicago: A.C. McClurg, 1915. 1st ed. Grn cl (extrems rubbed), gilt. VG. *House.* $350/£224

BURROUGHS, EDGAR RICE. Savage Pellucidar. NY: Canaveral, 1963. 1st ed. (Name on fr pastedown), o/w NF in dj. *Bernard.* $75/£48

BURROUGHS, EDGAR RICE. The Son of Tarzan. Chicago, 1917. 1st ed, 2nd ptg or state w/dedication to his son incl. VG+. *Mcclintock.* $145/£93

BURROUGHS, EDGAR RICE. The Son of Tarzan. NY: A.L. Burt, 1918. Rpt ed. NF (bkpl; top, fore-edges spotted; most of dj fr panel laid down). Heins ST 6. *Turtle Island.* $55/£35

BURROUGHS, EDGAR RICE. Swords of Mars. Tarzana: Edgar Rice Burroughs, (1936). 1st ed. Fine (fore-edge sl spotted) in dj. Heins SWM 1. *Turtle Island.* $750/£481

BURROUGHS, EDGAR RICE. Synthetic Men of Mars. Tarzana, CA: ERB, (1940). 1st ed in 1st state (laminated) dj. 5 b/w plts. Fine in NF dj (rear panel sl soiled). *Bernard.* $500/£321

BURROUGHS, EDGAR RICE. Synthetic Men of Mars. Tarzana: Burroughs, (1940). 1st ed. (Owner stamp fep), else NF in dj (wear, fraying). *Other Worlds.* $300/£192

BURROUGHS, EDGAR RICE. Synthetic Men of Mars. Tarzana: Edgar Rice Burroughs, (1940). 1st ed. NF (sm spots) in VF dj. Heins SMM 1. *Turtle Island.* $500/£321

BURROUGHS, EDGAR RICE. Tanar of Pellucidar. NY, (1930). 1st ed. Dj (chips). *Swann*.* $149/£96

BURROUGHS, EDGAR RICE. Tanar of Pellucidar. NY: Metropolitan Books, (1930). 1st ed. Fine (pg tops sl discolored). Heins TP 1. *Turtle Island.* $75/£48

BURROUGHS, EDGAR RICE. Tarzan and 'The Foreign Legion.' Tarzana: Burroughs, (1947). 1st ed. Frontis, 4 b/w plts. Royal blue cl (lt shelfworn). Good in pict dj (lt worn, sl chipped). *Baltimore*.* $100/£64

BURROUGHS, EDGAR RICE. Tarzan and 'The Foreign Legion.' Tarzana: Edgar Rice Burroughs, (1947). 1st ed. Fine in dj (spine spotted, inside foxed, 2 short closed tears). Heins FL 1. *Turtle Island.* $75/£48

BURROUGHS, EDGAR RICE. Tarzan and the Ant Men. Chicago: A.C. McClurg, (1924). 1st ed. NF (fore-edge spotted; most of entire dj laid down on rep, pastedown). Heins AM 1. *Turtle Island.* $450/£288

BURROUGHS, EDGAR RICE. Tarzan and the City of Gold. Tarzana: Edgar Rice Burroughs, (1933). 1st ed. NF (most of dj fr panel laid in). Heins CiG 1. *Turtle Island.* $175/£112

BURROUGHS, EDGAR RICE. Tarzan and the City of Gold. London: John Lane, 1936. 1st UK ed. NF (bds unevenly faded) in VG dj. *Williams.* $390/£250

BURROUGHS, EDGAR RICE. Tarzan and the Forbidden City. Tarzana: Edgar Rice Burroughs, (1938). 1st ed. Fine (top edge bds sl spotted) in Fine dj. Heins FC 1. *Turtle Island.* $500/£321

BURROUGHS, EDGAR RICE. Tarzan and the Golden Lion. Chicago: A.C. McClurg, (1923). 1st ed. Gold/mustard cl. NF (top, fore-edges lt spotted; most of dj fr panel laid down on fep). Heins GL 1. *Turtle Island.* $350/£224

BURROUGHS, EDGAR RICE. Tarzan and the Golden Lion. Chicago: McClurg, 1923. 1st ed, 1st issue. J. Allen St. John (illus). VG in dj (soiled, archival repair 1/3 lower spine). *Captain's Bookshelf.* $750/£481

BURROUGHS, EDGAR RICE. Tarzan and the Golden Lion. London: Methuen, 1924. 1st UK ed. Fine. *Williams.* $75/£48

BURROUGHS, EDGAR RICE. Tarzan and the Golden Lion. London: Methuen, 1924. 1st UK ed. NF in dj (considerable repair to rear; browned). *Williams.* $460/£295

BURROUGHS, EDGAR RICE. Tarzan and the Jewels of Opar. NY, (1918). 1st rpt ed. Unique Cunneo-Henneberry Co., Chicago imprint on tp verso. Unrecorded binding variant: lt blue cl (lt soiled, nicked). VG (fr hinge cracked) in dj. *Mcclintock.* $195/£125

BURROUGHS, EDGAR RICE. Tarzan and the Jewels of Opar. NY: A.L. Burt, (1919). Rpt ed. Nice (bkpl, fr cvr spotted, most of dj fr panel laid in). Heins JO 3. *Turtle Island.* $75/£48

BURROUGHS, EDGAR RICE. Tarzan and the Jewels of Opar. Methuen, 1919. 1st Eng ed. Good. *Aronovitz.* $55/£35

BURROUGHS, EDGAR RICE. Tarzan and the Jewels of Opar. London: Methuen, 1919. 1st UK ed. VG (ink name; spine faded, corner bumped). *Williams.* $62/£40

BURROUGHS, EDGAR RICE. Tarzan and the Leopard Men. Tarzana: Edgar Rice Burroughs, (1935). 1st ed. Fine (fr panel spotted) in Fine dj. Heins LeM 1. *Turtle Island.* $600/£385

BURROUGHS, EDGAR RICE. Tarzan and the Lion Man. Tarzana: Edgar Rice Burroughs, (1934). 1st ed. Fine (fore-edge spotted; most of dj fr panel laid down fep). Heins LiM 1. *Turtle Island.* $125/£80

BURROUGHS, EDGAR RICE. Tarzan and the Lost Empire. NY: Metropolitan Books, (1929). 1st ed. NF (tp foxed, pg edges spotted, lt stain inside rear gutter half-title; spine lt sunned). Heins LE 1. *Turtle Island.* $75/£48

BURROUGHS, EDGAR RICE. Tarzan and the Lost Empire. NY: Metropolitan Books, (1929). 1st ed. Stunning in dj (spine heel sl rubbed). *Captain's Bookshelf.* $1,000/£641

BURROUGHS, EDGAR RICE. Tarzan and the Lost Empire. NY: Metropolitan, (1929). 1st ed. Frontis. (Lt worn, bumped.) *Swann*.* $69/£44

BURROUGHS, EDGAR RICE. Tarzan and the Lost Empire. London: Cassell, 1931. 1st UK ed. VG (sl foxed; bds sl spotted) in pict dj (sl edgeworn). *Williams.* $585/£375

BURROUGHS, EDGAR RICE. Tarzan at the Earth's Core. NY: Metropolitan Books, (1930). 1st ed. NF (top, fore-edge lt spotted; most of wraparound pict dj laid in, offsetting). Heins TEC 1. *Turtle Island.* $125/£80

BURROUGHS, EDGAR RICE. Tarzan at the Earth's Core. NY: Metropolitan, (1930). 1st ed, later issue, w/Metropolitan tp and 'Grosset & Dunlap' at spine foot. In G&D dj (chipped). *Kane*.* $120/£77

BURROUGHS, EDGAR RICE. Tarzan at the Earth's Core. NY: Metropolitan, (1930). 1st ed. (Offset fep, pastedown), else Fine in dj (internally repaired, lt chipped). *Captain's Bookshelf.* $500/£321

BURROUGHS, EDGAR RICE. Tarzan Lord of the Jungle. Chicago: A.C. McClurg, 1928. 1st ed. Fine (top, fore-edge lt spotted; dj fr panel laid in). Heins LJ 1. *Turtle Island.* $375/£240

BURROUGHS, EDGAR RICE. Tarzan of the Apes. NY: A.L. Burt, (1915). Rpt ed. NF (bkpl, pg edges spotted; most of fr/rear panels of wraparound dj laid down on eps). Heins TA 5. *Turtle Island.* $65/£42

BURROUGHS, EDGAR RICE. Tarzan the Invincible. Tarzana: Edgar Rice Burroughs, (1931). 1st ed. (Presentation, sm stain tp; sm spots spine), else Fine. Heins TI 1. *Turtle Island.* $50/£32

BURROUGHS, EDGAR RICE. Tarzan the Magnificent. Tarzana: Edgar Rice Burroughs, (1939). 1st ed. NF in dj (sm closed tear). Heins TaM 1. *Turtle Island.* $475/£304

BURROUGHS, EDGAR RICE. Tarzan the Terrible. Chicago: A.C. McClurg, 1921. 1st ed. Red cl (spine sl creased, ends sl worn, sm blip in cl). NF (bkpl). Heins TTe 1. *Turtle Island.* $55/£35

BURROUGHS, EDGAR RICE. Tarzan the Untamed. Chicago: A.C. McClurg, 1920. 1st ed. NF (bkpl). Heins TU 1. *Turtle Island.* $125/£80

BURROUGHS, EDGAR RICE. Tarzan the Untamed. Chicago: A.C. McClurg, 1920. 1st ed. (Pg edges, eps lt soiled, inscrip.) NF in dj (sl soiled, sm holes, sm chips, tears at edges). *Waverly*.* $715/£458

BURROUGHS, EDGAR RICE. Tarzan Triumphant. Tarzana: Edgar Rice Burroughs, (1932). 1st ed though not stated. NF (lg lt stains fep, tp). Heins TTr 1. *Turtle Island.* $75/£48

BURROUGHS, EDGAR RICE. Tarzan's Quest. Tarzana: Edgar Rice Burroughs, (1936). 1st ed. Fine in Fine dj (internal foxing, lamination separating). Heins TQ 1. *Turtle Island.* $350/£224

BURROUGHS, EDGAR RICE. Tarzan, Lord of the Jungle. Chicago: McClurg, 1928. (Lib label fep, 1/2 title partly detached, 1 plt loose; cl lt worn.) Swann*. $126/£81

BURROUGHS, EDGAR RICE. Thuvia. NY: G&D, (1921). Rpt ed. VG (spine ends sl rubbed; most of dj fr panel laid down on fep). Heins TMM 3. Turtle Island. $55/£35

BURROUGHS, EDGAR RICE. The War Chief. Chicago: A.C. McClurg, 1927. 1st ed. NF (top, fore-edge lt spotted; dj fr panel laid in). Heins WC 1. Turtle Island. $400/£256

BURROUGHS, EDGAR RICE. The War Chief. Chicago: A.C. McClurg, 1927. 1st ed. Orange cl. Nice in pict dj (water stain on spine, extrems soiled, chipped). Glenn. $800/£513

BURROUGHS, EDGAR RICE. The Warlord of Mars. NY: G&D, (1920). Rpt ed. VG (sm chip bd fore-edge, spine ends sl rubbed; most of dj fr panel laid on fep). Heins WM 3. Turtle Island. $45/£29

BURROUGHS, JOHN ROLFE. Where the Old West Stayed Young. NY, 1962. 1st ed. Pict cl, bds. (Bkpl; lower corner sl bumped), o/w VG in dj (chipped, worn). Baade. $55/£35

BURROUGHS, JOHN ROLFE. Where the Old West Stayed Young. NY: William Morrow, 1962. 1st ed. Fine in dj (sl rubbed). Argonaut. $75/£48

BURROUGHS, JOHN. The Breath of Life. Boston: Houghton Mifflin, 1915. 1st ed. Frontis. Fine in dj (sl chipped). Second Life. $85/£54

BURROUGHS, JOHN. Camping and Tramping with Roosevelt. Boston: Houghton Mifflin, 1907. Ltd to 250. Unopened, fore-edge untrimmed. VG. Books & Birds. $75/£48

BURROUGHS, JOHN. In the Catskills. Boston, 1910. 1st ed. 24 photo plts. Teg. Grn dec cl, gilt. VG. Price. $34/£22

BURROUGHS, JOHN. In the Catskills. Boston: Houghton Mifflin, 1910. 1st ed. Teg. Pict cl, gilt. VG+. Bowman. $45/£29

BURROUGHS, PAUL. Southern Antiques. Garrett & Massie, (c. 1931). VG- (cvr sl spotted, edges browned). Book Broker. $75/£48

BURROUGHS, STEPHEN. Memoirs of Stephen Burroughs. Albany, 1811. 2 vols in 1. Contemp sheep. (Browned.) Howes B1022. Swann*. $92/£59

BURROUGHS, STEPHEN. Memoirs of Stephen Burroughs. Albany: B.D. Packard, 1811. 1st ed thus. 2 vols in 1. 248; 148pp. Contemp calf. (Sl rubbed, scuffed; text sl browned), else Good. Howes B1022. Brown. $75/£48

BURROUGHS, STEPHEN. Memoirs of the Notorious Stephen Burroughs of New Hampshire. NY: Dial, 1924. 1st ed. (Ink underlining; last leaves, back cvr affected by damp; sl rubbed.) Worldwide. $32/£21

BURROUGHS, WILLIAM S. The Adding Machine. Seaver Books, (1986). 1st US ed. Fine in Fine dj. Certo. $27/£17

BURROUGHS, WILLIAM S. Doctor Benway. Santa Barbara: Bradford Morrow, 1979. 1st ed. One of 150 signed, numbered. Fine in dj. Turtle Island. $150/£96

BURROUGHS, WILLIAM S. Electronic Revolution. Cambridge: Blackmoor Head, 1971. Trade issue of 450. VG+ in wraps (sl dust soiled). Certo. $65/£42

BURROUGHS, WILLIAM S. Interzone. James Grauerholz (ed). NY: Viking, (1989). 1st ed. Fine (rmdr stripe) in dj. Turtle Island. $35/£22

BURROUGHS, WILLIAM S. The Naked Lunch. Paris: Olympia, (1965). 3rd ptg of Traveller's Companion ed. (Corner bumped), else Very Nice in ptd wrappers. Reese. $20/£13

BURROUGHS, WILLIAM S. The Naked Lunch. 1964. 1st Eng ed. VG in dj. Words Etc. $78/£50

BURROUGHS, WILLIAM S. The Place of Dead Roads. NY: Holt Rinehart, (1984). One of 300 numbered, signed. Fine in Fine slipcase. Lenz. $150/£96

BURROUGHS, WILLIAM S. and ALLEN GINSBERG. The Yage Letters. (SF): City Lights, (1975). 2nd ed. Signed by both. Fine in wrappers. Lenz. $100/£64

BURROW, E. I. Elements of Conchology. London, 1844. New (4th) ed. xix,245pp; 28 plts (25 hand-colored). (Fep removed; cl sl worn.) Wheldon & Wesley. $265/£170

BURROW, E. J. Burrow's Guide to the Lake District. Cheltenham: Ed J Burrow, (c.1920). 9th ed. VG in stiff pict wrappers. Hollett. $19/£12

BURROW, E. J. Eton College Portfolio. Cheltenham, ca 1887. 12 mtd orig etchings, each signed in pencil. (Tp, 1st plt foxed), o/w Contents VG. (Cl worn, soiled, fr inner hinge cracked.) New Hampshire*. $70/£45

BURROWS, HAROLD. Biological Actions of Sex Hormones. Cambridge, 1945. 1st ed. VG. Argosy. $75/£48

BURROWS, JACK. John Ringo: The Gunfighter Who Never Was. Tucson: Univ of AZ, (1987). 1st ed. Map. VG in dj. Lien. $25/£16

BURROWS, LARRY. Larry Burrows: Compassionate Photographer. NY: Time-Life, 1972. 1st ed. (Inscrip; spine sl faded), else Fine in pub's slipcase (sl rubbed), mtd color photo plt. Cahan. $165/£106

BURRUS, ERNEST J. Kino and the Cartography of Northwestern New Spain. (Tucson): AZ Pioneers' Hist Soc, 1965. Ltd to 750. Folio. 23 plts (17 maps). Rose cl, gilt. Good. Karmiole. $250/£160

BURRUS, ERNEST J. Kino and the Cartography of Northwestern New Spain. Tucson: AZ Pioneers' Hist Soc, 1965. 1st ed. One of 750 ptd by Lawton & Alfred Kennedy. Red cl, gilt. VF. Argonaut. $200/£128

BURT, OLIVE WOOLLEY (ed). American Murder Ballads and Their Stories. NY: OUP, 1958. Tan bds (stained, bumped). VG in dj (stained, chipped). Blue Mountain. $20/£13

BURT, WILLIAM and BELLA HUBBARD. Reports...on the Geography, Topography and Geology of the U.S. Surveys of the Mineral Region of the South Shore of Lake Superior, for 1845. Detroit, 1845. 12mo. Lg fldg map. Pub's cl. (Sm holes, short tears), o/w Fine. Howes B1027. Swann*. $690/£442

BURTON, ANTHONY. Josiah Wedgwood. Stein & Day, 1976. 1st ed. VG (sl shelfworn) in dj (edge-worn). My Bookhouse. $25/£16

BURTON, E. F. Reminiscences of Sport in India. London: Allen, 1885. 1st ed. xi,419pp + 44 ads. Brn gilt pict cl. VG. Terramedia. $400/£256

BURTON, E. MILBY. South Carolina Silversmiths 1690-1860. Charleston: Charleston Museum, (1968). 1st ed. Inscribed. Fine in dj (lt rubbed, 2-inch tear fr panel). Captain's Bookshelf. $100/£64

BURTON, GIDEON. Reminiscences of.... Cincinnati: G.P. Houston, 1895. Frontis port, 152pp. Gilt title, top. Nice (new eps). Bohling. $40/£26

BURTON, JOHN HILL. A History of the Reign of Queen Anne. Edinburgh/London, 1880. Inscribed. 3 vols. Dec gilt cl. Bkpl of George Healey. Argosy. $100/£64

BURTON, RICHARD F. Camoens: His Life and His Lusiads. London: Quaritch, 1881. 1st issue. 2 vols. viii,366; 367-738pp. Grn cl (rubbed, ex-lib). Adelson. $50/£32

BURTON, RICHARD F. (trans). The Carmina of Caius Valerius Catullus.... London: The Translators, 1894. Ltd to 1000. Frontis, (xxiv),313pp. Frontis. Orig bds, vellum spine. (Bkpl; eps lt foxed; corners worn, spine dknd), else Nice. Argonaut. $275/£176

BURTON, RICHARD F. Etruscan Bologna: A Study. London: Smith, Elder, 1876. Fldg frontis, xii,errata,275pp. Blue cl (rubbed, ends worn). Adelson. $225/£144

BURTON, RICHARD F. First Footsteps in East Africa. London: Longman et al, 1856. 1st ed, 2nd issue (1st issue bound in dull violet cl). Lg 8vo. 4 color plts, 2 maps. Pub's brick red cl (expertly rebacked, bd edges faded). Very Bright (bkpl, binder's ticket pastedowns). Book Block. $1,250/£801

BURTON, RICHARD F. The Gold-Mines of Midian and the Ruined Midianite Cities. London: Kegan Paul, 1878. 1st ed. xvi,395pp,(iii) appendix,(i) blank + (i) ad (lacks 1/2-title, ads to rear; some corners sl creasing), fldg map. Mod 1/2 calf (rebound), marbled bds, garish spine gilt. Edwards. $468/£300

BURTON, RICHARD F. The Highlands of the Brazil. London: Tinsley Bros, 1869. 1st ed, 1st issue. 2 vols. 8vo. Frontis, xii,443pp, fldg map; frontis, viii,478,(2)pp ads; 1/2-titles, add'l tps w/vignettes. (Foxing throughout, lib plts removed from pastedowns.) Grn cl (spines sl rubbed, lt damp spotting upper cvrs), gilt vignettes fr cvrs. Sound. Morrell. $1,014/£650

BURTON, RICHARD F. The Jew, the Gypsy, and El Islam. W. H. Wilkins (ed). Chicago/NY: Stone, 1898. 1st ed. Frontis, xix,351pp. Teg. (Bkpl removed inner fr cvr; sl rubbed), o/w VG. Worldwide. $250/£160

BURTON, RICHARD F. The Kasidah of Haji-Abdu Elyezdi. Phila: David McKay, (1931). 1st ed w/Willy Pogany illus. Full navy blue morocco, gilt-stamped strapwork on cvrs, maroon leather spine labels; dec eps, edges gilt. Fine in custom-made slipcase. Appelfeld. $250/£160

BURTON, RICHARD F. The Lake Regions of Central Africa. London: Longman, 1860. 1st ed. 2 vols. 8vo. xvii,412; vii,468pp; 12 chromoxylographic plts, fldg map. Contemp or later blue 1/2 morocco. (Lt dampstain, marginal browning most plts), else VG. Terramedia. $1,000/£641

BURTON, RICHARD F. The Lake Regions of Central Africa. London: Longman, Green et al, 1860. 1st ed. 2 vols. 8vo. Engr fldg map, 11 color wood engrs. 1/2-titles present. Aeg; marbled eps, edges. Full later polished calf, gilt spines, grn morocco labels. Clean. Cummins. $1,500/£962

BURTON, RICHARD F. The Land of Midian (Revisited). London, 1879. 1st ed. 2 vols. xxviii,338; vii,319pp + 32pp pub's list (fore-edge creasing), 10 plain plts (sl staining), 5 color lithos (lacks color litho plt), fldg map. Mod shiny 1/2 calf (rebound), marbled bds, garish spine gilt, labels. Edwards. $624/£400

BURTON, RICHARD F. Os Lusiadas. London: Quaritch, 1880. 1st issue. 2 vols. xx,250; ii,251-471pp. Grn cl (rubbed, ex-lib). Adelson. $60/£38

BURTON, RICHARD F. Personal Narrative of a Pilgrimage to El-Medinah and Meccah. NY: Putnam, 1856. 1st US ed (so stated). Litho frontis, extra tp, 492pp (lacks fep, sig sprung, sl aged, foxed); fldg engr map. Brn coated eps. Blind brn cl (sl worn, spotted, spine frayed, sm tear), gilt. Cvrs Sound. Baltimore*. $40/£26

BURTON, RICHARD F. Vikram and the Vampire or Tales of Hindu Devilry. London: Longmans, Green, 1870. xxiv,319pp; 16 plts. Mod cl. VG. Adelson. $145/£93

BURTON, RICHARD F. Wanderings in Three Continents. W. H. Wilkins (ed). London: Hutchinson, 1901. 1st ed. Port, 4 plts. Red buckram (lt rubbed, spine faded). Adelson. $200/£128

BURTON, RICHARD F. and CHARLES F. TYRWHITT DRAKE. Unexplored Syria. London, 1872. 1st ed. 2 vols. 360; 400pp (joints tender, starting). Gold mustard-colored cl. (Spine tops frayed, soiled, dknd), o/w Clean. Truepenny. $850/£545

BURTON, RICHARD. A Christmas Story. NY: William Morrow, 1964. 1st ed, 1st bk. Lydia Fruhauf (illus). VF in dj. Bromer. $95/£61

BURTON, RICHARD. Literary Inklings. Boston: Copeland & Day, 1898. 1st ed. Inscribed presentation copy. Paper spine label. (Sig; lt rubbing, label sl dknd), else VG. Reese. $35/£22

BURTON, ROBERT. The Anatomy of Melancholy. London, 1804. 10th ed. 2 vols in 1. 1065pp (fep removed, rep tattered; bkpl). 1/4 leather, marbled bds (worn). Good. Doctor's Library. $100/£64

BURTON, ROBERT. The Anatomy of Melancholy. London: B. Blake, 1838. 16th ed. Frontis, viii,744pp. Marbled edges. Calf-backed marbled bds, gilt spine. Good (hinges, joints repaired, reinforced). Gach. $85/£54

BURTON, ROBERT. The Anatomy of Melancholy. London, 1849. Fine engr frontis, 748pp. VG. Fye. $100/£64

BURTON, ROBERT. The Anatomy of Melancholy. Boston: William Veazie, 1861. New ed. Ltd to 75. 3 vols. Facs frontis, 500; 467; 514pp. 3/4 morocco, marbled bds (lt rubbed). VG. Glaser. $300/£192

BURTON, ROBERT. The Anatomy of Melancholy. Floyd Dell and Paul Jordan-Smith (eds). NY: George H. Doran, 1927. One of 500. 2 vols. Frontis facs vol 2. Teg, rest untrimmed. 1/2 vellum, tan paper bds, gilt. (Sl soiled), o/w Fine. Pirages. $125/£80

BURTON, WILLIAM. A History and Description of English Earthenware and Stoneware.... London: Cassell, 1904. 1st ed. #669/1450. 24 color, 93 half-tone plts. Good in red cl. Cox. $70/£45

BURY, ADRIAN. Francis Towne. 1962. Color frontis, 44 plts (6 color). Dj (spine head sl chipped). Edwards. $62/£40

BURY, ADRIAN. Joseph Crawhall: The Man and the Artist. London: Charles Skilton, (1958). Ltd to 975 numbered. Teg. Yellow buckram, mtd color plt. Good. Karmiole. $200/£128

BURY, ADRIAN. Shadow of Eros. London, 1952. One of 247 numbered. 25j plts. Uncut. Brn 3/4 levant. Fine. Argosy. $150/£96

BURY, WILLIAM COUTTS KEPPEL and G. LACY HILLIER. Cycling. London: Longmans, Green, 1887. 1st ed. (xiv),458,(iv)pp. Pict cl. (Rep cracking, edges sl spotted, sl strained), o/w Nice. Ash. $133/£85

BUSBEY, L. WHITE. Uncle Joe Cannon: The Story of a Pioneer American. NY: Henry Holt, (1927). 1st ed. NF. Sadlon. $15/£10

BUSEY, JOHN W. and DAVID G. MARTIN. Regimental Strengths and Losses at Gettysburg. Balt, 1982. 1st ed. Ltd to 1000. Fine. Pratt. $30/£19

BUSH, EGBERT. In the Grip of the Expert. NY: Broadway, 1904. 1st ed. Lacks dj. Metropolitan*. $23/£15

BUSH, GEORGE. A Grammar of the Hebrew Language. NY, 1835. Pub's cl (spine faded, ends frayed w/loss), gilt. Swann*. $115/£74

BUSH-BROWN, L. Men with Green Pens: Lives of the Great Writers on Plants in Early Times. Phila: Dorrance, 1964. 1st ed. 12 photo plts. Fine in NF dj. Mikesh. $30/£19

BUSH-BROWN, L. and J. Portraits of Philadelphia Gardens. Phila: Dorrance, 1929. Inscribed by both. 83 plans. Paper title cvr, spine (sl worn). (Edgewear), else VG. Quest. $125/£80

BUSHNELL, DAVID. The Choctaw of Bayou Lacomb, St. Tammany Parish, Louisiana. BAE Bulletin 48. Washington: GPO, 1909. 22 plts. VG. *Lien.* $15/£10

BUSHNELL, DAVID. Native Villages and Village Sites East of the Mississippi. BAE Bulletin 69. 1919. 1st ed. Signed presentation. Color frontis map. VG. *Oregon.* $25/£16

BUSHNELL, DAVID. Villages of the Algonquian, Siouan and Caddoan Tribes West of the Mississippi. BAE Bulletin 77. Washington: GPO, 1922. Inscribed. (Spine ends, corners sl rubbed, sm lightened spots.) *Sadlon.* $45/£29

BUSHNELL, G. H. S. and ADRIAN DIGBY. Ancient American Pottery. London: Faber & Faber, (1955). 84 plts (4 color), 2 maps, table. Good in dj. *Archaeologia.* $65/£42

BUSK, DOUGLAS. The Delectable Mountains. London, (1947). Fldg map. VG in dj (edgeworn). *King.* $25/£16

BUTEN, DAVID. 18th-Century Wedgwood. NY: Methuen, 1980. 1st ed. 20 color plts. Cl-backed bds. VG in dj. *Hollett.* $55/£35

BUTLER, A. J. The Ancient Coptic Churches of Egypt. Oxford, 1884. 2 vols. 2 frontispieces, xx,377; xii,409pp. Sound. *Ars Artis.* $133/£85

BUTLER, ALBAN. The Lives of the Primitive Fathers, Martyrs, and Other Principal Saints. Edinburgh: J.P. Cochlane, 1798. 3rd ed. 12 vols in 6. 8vo. Full speckled calf. Good + (sealing wax tp each vol; hinges starting). *Old London.* $600/£385

BUTLER, ARTHUR G. Birds of Great Britain and Ireland. Hull: Brumby & Clark, n.d. (ca 1908). 1st ed. 2 vols. 115 color litho plts. Gray over blue cl (extrems sl rubbed), gilt. *Karmiole.* $375/£240

BUTLER, CHARLES. The American Lady. Phila: Hogan & Thompson, 1849. xii,(13)-288pp. Aeg. VG. *Second Life.* $65/£42

BUTLER, ELIZABETH BEARDSLEY. Women and the Trades. NY: Charities Publication Committee, 1909. 1st ed. Frontis, 77 tables. Gilt-titled cl. (Rubbed, sl soiled), else VG. *Cahan.* $200/£128

BUTLER, FRANCES ANNE. Journal. Phila: Carey et al, 1835. 1st US ed. 252 + ads; 218pp + ads. Untrimmed. Muslin (spine faded), paper label (sl chipped). Very Nice (bkpl, sl foxed, hinge sl tender). Howes B1051. *Second Life.* $325/£208

BUTLER, FRANCES ANNE. Poems. London: Washbourne et al, 1844. 1st UK ed. 144pp + 16pp ads. (Cl sl faded, hinges tender, spine extrems chipped.) *Second Life.* $175/£112

BUTLER, FRANK HEDGES. Wine and the Wine Lands of the World. London: Unwin, (1926). 1st ed. Frontis port, 55 full-pg photos. Marbled eps; teg. 3/4 gilt-stamped red morocco over cl, gilt. Fine. *Houle.* $225/£144

BUTLER, GERALD. Kiss the Blood Off My Hands. NY: F&R, (1946). 1st ed. (Lt wear; few pp sl bent), else NF in NF dj (rubbing; lt wear spine; sm tear). *Between The Covers.* $175/£112

BUTLER, GUY. The Dove Returns. London, 1956. 1st ed. Errata slip. NF in dj (spine sl sunned, extrems sl rubbed). *Polyanthos.* $25/£16

BUTLER, JOHN C. Historical Record of Macon and Central Georgia.... Macon, GA, 1879. 1st ed. 351pp + (28)pp ads; inserted slip. Dec cl. Howes B1056. *Ginsberg.* $300/£192

BUTLER, JOSEPHINE E. Native Races and the War. London/Newcastle, Gay & Bird/Mawson et al, 1900. 1st ed. Blue cl (spine, edges worn; corners bumped). VG. *Patterson.* $47/£30

BUTLER, LIONEL and CHRIS GIVEN-WILSON. Medieval Monasteries of Great Britain. Joseph, 1979. NF in dj. *Hadley.* $39/£25

BUTLER, MARGARET MANOR. The Lakewood Story. NY, 1949. Presentation copy. VG + . *Bohling.* $15/£10

BUTLER, ROBERT OLEN. The Alleys of Eden. Horizon, (1981). 1st ed, 1st book. Fine in Fine dj. *Certo.* $45/£29

BUTLER, S. Luck, or Cunning, as the Main Means of Organic Modification. London: Fifeld, (1920). 2nd ed. Blind-stamped dec cl. VG + in VG dj. *Mikesh.* $75/£48

BUTLER, SAMUEL. The Authoress of the Odyssey. London: A.C. Fifield, (1897). 1st ed. Frontis, 275pp. Red cl, blind/gilt. VG. *Hartfield.* $195/£125

BUTLER, SAMUEL. Butleriana. A. T. Bartholomew (ed). Bloomsbury, 1932. Ltd to 800. 8 tipped-in collotype repros. Teg. Tan niger morocco-backed Cockerel marbled bds, gilt. Very Nice. *Cady.* $45/£29

BUTLER, SAMUEL. Erewhon Revisited. London: Grant Richards, 1901. 1st ed. 1pg undated ads. Red cl. NF (cl sl dknd). *Sumner & Stillman.* $225/£144

BUTLER, SAMUEL. Erewhon. Newtown: Gregynog, 1932. One of 300 numbered. Brn morocco, gilt. 1/4 morocco fldg case. *Swann*.* $747/£479

BUTLER, SAMUEL. Hudibras. Glasgow, 1763. New ed. Contemp full calf. Sound. *Gretton.* $47/£30

BUTLER, SAMUEL. Hudibras. London, 1772. 3rd ed. 2 vols. Frontis port, 36,424,Index; 446pp,Index; 16 plts (1 fldg). Marbled eps, edges. Full leather, gilt. (Hinges, joints tender, rear hinge vol 2 tape-repaired, spine chips.) *Scribe's Perch*.* $110/£71

BUTLER, SAMUEL. Hudibras. Troy, NY: Ptd by Wright, Goodenow & Stockwell, 1806. 1st Amer ed. x,286,(14)pp. Orig calf (sl rubbed), red leather spine label. *Karmiole.* $100/£64

BUTLER, SAMUEL. Hudibras. London, 1819. 1st ed w/these illus. 2 vols. 12 aquatint plts by Clark. (Foxing, soiling.) 19th-cent 3/4 calf (rubbed). *Oinonen*.* $100/£64

BUTLER, SAMUEL. Hudibras.... London: Charles & Henry Baldwyn, 1819. 3 vols. 11 engr plts, 28 mtd woodcut vignettes; extra-illus w/60 hand-colored engr ports. Later 19th-cent red straight-grain morocco (spines dknd, ends worn; foxed, several text ll trimmed, inlaid to size). *Swann*.* $172/£110

BUTLER, SAMUEL. The Way of All Flesh. NY: LEC, 1936. #904/1500 numbered, signed by Ward Johnson (illus). 2 vols. Full leather. Fine in pub's slipcase. *Hermitage.* $100/£64

BUTLER, W. F. The Wild North Land. London: Sampson Low et al, 1874. 3rd ed. Frontis, xii,358pp + 48pp pub's cat dated Oct 1873; lg fldg map, 15 plts. Pict grn cl (rubbed, faded). Sound (inner hinges cracked). *Cox.* $59/£38

BUTLER, WILLIAM. The Land of the Veda. NY: Nelson & Phillips, (1871). 9th ed. Aeg. Brn full-morocco, gilt spine. VG (sl rubbed). *Antic Hay.* $225/£144

BUTLIN, M. The Paintings and Drawings of William Blake. New Haven: Yale Univ, 1981. 1st ed. 2 vols. NF (inner hinges cracked) in djs. *Waverly*.* $121/£78

BUTOR, MICHEL. A Change of Heart. NY: S&S, 1957. 1st US ed. (Corners bruised), else VG + in VG dj (chipped, edgetorn). *Lame Duck.* $35/£22

BUTOR, MICHEL. Letters from the Antipodes. Athens: OH Univ, (1981). 1st Amer ed. Fine in dj. *Hermitage.* $25/£16

BUTT-THOMPSON, F. W. West African Secret Societies. London: H.F. & G. Witherby, 1929. 1st ed. Map. Blue cl (lt rubbed). *Karmiole.* $75/£48

BUTTERFIELD, C. W. An Historical Account of the Campaign Against Sandusky Under Colonel William Crawford in 1872. Cincinnati, 1873. 1st ed. VG (rebound; ex-lib w/few mks). Howes B1062. *Mcclintock.* $125/£80

BUTTERFIELD, H. The Origins of Modern Science, 1300-1800. NY: Macmillan, 1957. Rev 2nd ed. NF in dj. *Glaser.* $35/£22

Butterworth's Universal Penman or the Beauties of Writing Delineated.... Laurie & Whittle, Nov. 12, 1799. Presumably the 2nd ed. Obl folio. Engr tp (sl torn, soiled), 2 dedication leaves, 28 plts. (Lacks plt 14, outer 1/2 plt 8, lg corners plts 9, 10; last leaf torn, mtd; short tears throughout, incl middle every pg). Imperfect in old marbled wrappers (roughly rebacked). *Hatchwell.* $156/£100

BUTTERWORTH, HEZEKIAH. Zigzag Journeys in the Levant.... Boston: Estes & Lauriat, 1886. Frontis, 304pp. Orig ptd bds (shelfwear, spine sl chipped). *Archaeologia.* $65/£42

BUTTINGER, JOSEPH. The Smaller Dragon: A Political History of Vietnam. NY: Praeger, (1958). 1st ed. VG+ in VG+ dj. *Fuller & Saunders.* $25/£16

BUTTLES, JANET R. The Queens of Egypt. London: Constable, 1908. 20 plts (2 color). (Sig, pencil notes, fep chipped; spine chipped, extrems worn.) *Archaeologia.* $85/£54

BUTTS, MARY. Ashe of Rings. London: Wishart, 1933. 1st British ed. Good (sm bkseller label, foxing) in dj (lt soiled, chips, tears). *Reese.* $85/£54

BUXTON, CHARLES (ed). Memoirs of Sir Thomas Fowell Buxton. London, 1849. 3rd ed. xi,508pp (ex-lib, bkpls, ink stamps). Marbled eps. Later 1/2 morocco, marbled bds (rubbed, loss to spine head, corners). *Edwards.* $25/£16

BUXTON, DAVID. Travels in Ethiopia. London: Ernest Ben, 1957. 2nd ed. Frontis, 72 photo plts. VG in dj. *Worldwide.* $25/£16

BUXTON, EDWARD NORTH. Short Stalks, or Hunting Camps. London: Edward Stanford, 1893. 2nd ed. xiii,405pp. Tan pict cl. VG. *Terramedia.* $150/£96

BUXTON, GENE. The Bees Wedding. Adelphi Quality, n.d. ca 1940. 1st ed. Tall 8vo. 64pp; 8 color plts by Kenneth Hunter. Illus bds. VG in pict dj (frayed). *Bookmark.* $23/£15

BUXTON, THOMAS FOWELL. The African Slave Trade.... London, 1839. 2nd ed. Orig cl (rebacked; leaf of contemp notes mtd fr pastedown); orig backstrip. *Swann*.* $149/£96

BUZZATI, DINO. The Bears' Famous Invasion of Sicily. Frances Cobb (trans). (NY): Pantheon, (1947). 1st Amer ed. 4to. 16 color plts. VG in dj (chip, nicks, sm tears). *Houle.* $85/£54

By-Laws of the Orphan House of Charleston, South Carolina. Charleston: Steam-Power Presses, 1861. 1st ed. 40pp. Yellow ptd wraps. (Few leaves stained), o/w VG. *Second Life.* $150/£96

BYAM, W. W. A Sketch of the State of Chiapas, Mexico. (L.A., 1897.) Color frontis, 3 maps. Grn/beige cl, gilt title. (2pp pencilled letter rep, lib stamp inside back cvr, fep removed; sl rubbed, soiled.) *Bohling.* $85/£54

BYARS, WILLIAM VINCENT (ed). An American Commoner. St. Louis: H.L. Conard, 1900. (Hinges badly cracked.) *Boswell.* $25/£16

BYATT, A. S. The Game. London: C&W, 1967. 1st ed. NF in VG- dj (sl soiled, sm chips, spine sl tanned). *Between The Covers.* $175/£112

BYATT, A. S. Possession. London, 1990. 1st Eng ed. NF in dj. *Clearwater.* $39/£25

BYATT, A. S. Still Life. London, 1985. 1st Eng ed. Fine in dj. *Clearwater.* $55/£35

BYATT, A. S. The Virgin in the Garden. London: C&W, 1978. 1st UK ed. Fine in dj (price-clipped). *Moorhouse.* $47/£30

BYATT, A. S. Wordsworth and Coleridge in Their Time. London, 1970. 1st ed. NF in dj. *Words Etc.* $55/£35

BYERS, ALMA. The Inverness Murder. NY: Dial, (1935). 1st ed. (Spine sl worn.) Dj (short tears, wear). *Metropolitan*.* $28/£18

BYINGTON, MARGARET F. Homestead: The Households of a Mill Town. Paul Underwood Kellogg (ed). NY: (Russell Sage) Charities Pub Committee, 1910. 1st ed. Fldg illus; map. Gilt-titled cl. (Rubbed; fr inner hinge starting; red underlining), else Good. *Cahan.* $125/£80

BYNE, ARTHUR and MILDRED STAPLEY. Rejeria of the Spanish Renaissance. NY: Hispanic Soc Publications, 1914. Presentation copy. Color frontis, 26 plts. Fine (ex-lib). *Quest.* $115/£74

BYNE, ARTHUR and MILDRED STAPLEY. Spanish Architecture of the Sixteenth Century. NY/London: Putnam, 1917. 80 plts. Sound. *Ars Artis.* $70/£45

BYNNER, WITTER (ed). The Sonnets of Frederick Goddard Tuckerman. NY: Knopf, 1931. 1st ed. (Eps sl dust spotted), o/w Nice in dj (spine tanned). *Reese.* $30/£19

BYNNER, WITTER. Journey with Genius. (London): Peter Nevill, (1953). 1st Eng ed. NF (eps lt browned) in dj (sl worn, sl stained). *Antic Hay.* $30/£19

BYRD, CECIL K. A Bibliography of Illinois Imprints 1814-1858. Chicago: Univ of Chicago, (1966). 1st ed. Fine in dj. *Sadlon.* $40/£26

BYRD, RICHARD E. Alone. NY, 1938. 1st ed. Signed. VG. *High Latitude.* $30/£19

BYRD, RICHARD E. Alone. NY: Putnam, 1938. One of 225 numbered, signed. Teg, others uncut. Orig full blue morocco. Fine. *High Latitude.* $450/£288

BYRD, RICHARD E. Discovery. The Story of the Second Byrd Antarctic Expedition. NY: Putnam, 1935. 1st ed. Signed. Blue cl (sl rubbed). Illus dj (chipped, creased). *Karmiole.* $75/£48

BYRD, RICHARD E. Little America. Aerial Exploration in the Antarctic. NY: Putnam, 1930. One of 1000 numbered of Author's Autograph Ed, signed. Gravure frontis port, 2 fldg maps. Uncut. Parchment paperbacked bds. (Spine sl soiled), else VG. *High Latitude.* $180/£115

BYRD, RICHARD E. Skyward. NY, 1928. 1st ed. Photogravure frontis. VG. *High Latitude.* $30/£19

BYRD, WILLIAM. The Writings of Colonel William Byrd of Westover in Virginia Esqr. John Spencer Bassett (ed). NY: Doubleday, Page, 1901. 1st ed. 3 plts. Buck. (Lacks frontis, some leaves frayed; edges heavily rubbed, ex-lib), o/w Good. *Worldwide.* $20/£13

BYRD, WILLIAM. The Writings of.... John Spencer Bassett (ed). NY, 1901. One of 500. 4 plts. 1/4 art vellum, bds. Cl dj (worn). Howes B1077. *Ginsberg.* $175/£112

BYRON, LORD. Beppo, a Venetian Story. London: John Murray, 1818. 5th ed. (iv),51pp, half-title, 12-pg pub's cat at end. Uncut. Orig drab wrappers (spine ends sl worn). Fine. *Burmester.* $117/£75

BYRON, LORD. The Bride of Abydos, a Turkish Tale. London: John Murray, 1813. 1st ed. Teg. Full brn morocco (rubbed), gilt, raised bands. Attractive. *Appelfeld.* $200/£128

BYRON, LORD. The Bride of Abydos. London: John Murray, 1813. 1st ed, 1st issue, w/errata uncorrected. (iv),72pp, errata slip. Later drab bds. Early owner added extra ms text to this copy: extra 6 lines added to p45 in 2nd ed, extra 2 lines following line 653, long add'l note p71. *Burmester.* $78/£50

BYRON, LORD. Byron's Letters and Journals. R.E. Prothero (ed). London: John Murray, 1922. 6 vols. Lt blue cl, gilt. VG. *Gretton.* $75/£48

BYRON, LORD. Childe Harold's Pilgrimage. London: John Murray, 1845. 'Gift Book' ed. Frontis, xvi,227pp (lt browned, soiled). Good (ep renewed) in ribbed blue cl. *Cox.* $55/£35

BYRON, LORD. Finden's Landscape and Portrait to the Life of Lord Byron. London: John Murray, 1833. 3 vols. Dec silk-cvrd bds (soiled, frayed; inner hinges split). *Metropolitan**. $175/£112

BYRON, LORD. Hebrew Melodies. London: J. Murray, 1815. 1st ed, 1st issue w/ad for Jacqueline on verso of E4 and w/titles and 1/2-titles for both vols of Byron Works bound in at rear. (Mod sigs; old sig 1/2 title at rear; lt foxing few pp.) Aeg. Full tan calf, ribbed gilt spine (sl scuffed) in 6 panels, 2 gilt leather labels. Bright overall. *Waverly**. $319/£204

BYRON, LORD. Hebrew Melodies. London: John Murray, 1815. 1st ed, later issue, w/half-title, 1 ad leaf. Later polished tan calf, red morocco spine label, by Riviere. *Swann**. $126/£81

BYRON, LORD. Lara, a Tale / Jacqueline, a Tale. London: John Murray, 1814. 1st ed, w/half-title. Later polished grn calf, red morocco spine label, gilt, by Zaehnsdorf. *Swann**. $92/£59

BYRON, LORD. Letters and Journals of Lord Byron. London: John Murray, 1830. 1st ed. 2 vols. Engr frontis (offset onto tp), viii,670; (ii),832pp, errata leaf (lacks half-titles). Contemp calf (rebacked), Signet Library arms on cvrs. *Burmester*. $234/£150

BYRON, LORD. Letters and Journals of Lord Byron. London: Murray, 1830. 2 vols. (viii),670pp + 2pp ads dated Jan 1830; frontis port, 823pp + errata, 16pp pub's cat dated Jan 1831. (Foxed.) Orig bds (recased, edgeworn); backstrip, ptd labels (chipped) laid down (new eps). Untrimmed, vol 2 mostly unopened. *Bohling*. $50/£32

BYRON, LORD. Mazeppa. John Murray, 1819. 1st ed. (iv),69,(1)pp (lacks final ad leaf). New calf-backed marbled paper bds, morocco label. *Cox*. $86/£55

BYRON, LORD. Poems. John Murray, 1816. 2nd ed. 39,(1)pp (lacks 1/2-title). New linen-backed marbled paper bds, morocco label. *Cox*. $70/£45

BYRON, LORD. Poems. London: J. Murray, 1816. 1st ed, 2nd issue w/terminal leaf containing the poem 'To Samuel Rogers' (recto) and 'Notes' (verso). (Sl foxed, tp lt soiled; inscrips, bkpls w/adhesive stains.) Aeg. Full tan calf (corners worn, joints starting, cvrs sl bowed), ribbed gilt spine in 6 panels, 2 gilt leather labels. Aeg. Bright overall. *Waverly**. $121/£78

BYRON, LORD. Poems. London: John Murray, 1816. 1st ed, 2nd 'issue' on unwatermkd paper, w/add'l poem 'To Samuel Rogers, Esq.,' and title on 1/2-title between double rules. 4pp May 1816 cat in rear. Mod 1/2 pseudo-tree calf, patterned bds. Attractive. *Reese*. $275/£176

BYRON, LORD. The Poetical Works. John Murray, 1853. New ed. 6 vols. Port. Marbled ends, edges. Full citron calf, dbl-rule borders to sides, gilt, raised bands, dbl grn/red labels. Nice set. *Cox*. $234/£150

BYRON, LORD. Sardanapalus, a Tragedy. The Two Foscari, a Tragedy. Cain, a Mystery. John Murray, 1821. 1st ed. viii,439,(1)pp. Contemp calf (rebacked, corners repaired), gilt borders, morocco label. *Cox*. $117/£75

BYRON, LORD. The Siege of Corinth [and] Parisina. London: John Murray, 1816. 1st ed. 4pp ads dated Feb 1816. Orig unptd drab wrappers (w/'Siege of Corinth' handwritten on fr cvr). VG (spine ends chipped, sl edgeworn) in cl case. *Sumner & Stillman*. $425/£272

BYRON, LORD. The Siege of Corinth. A Poem. Parisina. A Poem. London: John Murray, 1816. 1st ed. W/half-title, but lacks final ads. Later polished tan calf, red morocco spine label, by Riviere. *Swann**. $103/£66

BYRON, LORD. Voyage of H.M.S. Blonde to the Sandwich Islands. London: Murray, 1826. 1st ed. 4to. xi,260pp; 15 plts and maps (2 fldg, linen-backed). Mod 1/4 red morocco. (Foxing, mostly marginal; few marginal repairs), else VG. *Terramedia*. $1,500/£962

BYRON, LORD. Werner, a Tragedy. John Murray, 1823. 1st ed, 1st issue. (viii),188pp; 10 pg cat bound in; 8 pp list. Uncut in orig wrappers. (Worn, chipped; water spots rear cvr, last few ll.) *Cullen*. $325/£208

BYRON, LORD. The Works of the Right Honorable Lord Byron. London: John Murray, 1815-1819. 1st collected Eng ed. 7 vols. xviii,(ii),218; (xii),202,(ii); (vi),228; viii,203,(ii); (ii),vi,(iv),184; (viii),187,(i),4 ads; (iv),273,(iii)pp. Marbled edges. Contemp 3/4 grn calf, marbled bds (rubbed, bumped, spine ends chipped, 1-inch piece gone vol 4 tail), gilt. VG set; internally NF (sl foxed, 1 sig loose). *Blue Mountain*. $350/£224

BYRON, LORD. The Works. London, 1815-16. 4 vols. 1/4 brn morocco, marbled bds (sl rubbed; lib stamp tps, few other ll). *Kane**. $85/£54

BYRON, LORD. The Works. Phila: R.W. Pomeroy, 1825. 1st this ed. 8 vols. Uncut. Pub's bds (paper spines, labels renewed). Good (pp dknd; early bkseller ticket). *Hartfield*. $450/£288

BYRON, LORD. The Works. London: John Murray, 1898-1901. 13 vols. Frontispieces. Teg. Blue cl (lt worn, spine ends lt frayed), gilt. *Freeman**. $70/£45

BYRON, ROBERT. Imperial Pilgrimage. 1937. 1st ed. Wrappers. VG in dj (sl torn). *Words Etc*. $55/£35

BYRON, ROBERT. Imperial Pilgrimage. London Transport, 1937. 1st Eng ed. Good in card wrappers, dj (stained). *Clearwater*. $31/£20

BYRON, ROBERT. The Road to Oxiana. London, 1937. Map. *Petersfield*. $28/£18

C

C. DE LA B., MADAME. Life in Mexico During a Residence of 2 Years. London, 1843. 1st ed. 436pp. 3/4 kid, marbled bds, red kid label (sm chip), gilt, raised bands. Fine. *Turpen*. $395/£253

C.3.3. (Pseud of Oscar Wilde.) The Ballad of Reading Goal. Leonard Smithers, 1898. 2nd ed. (Sl mkd, spine bumped, sunned, rubbed.) Good. *Tiger*. $25/£16

CABELL, JAMES BRANCH. Ballades from the Hidden Way. NY: Crosby Gaige, 1928. #247/831 signed. Dec cvrs gilt. Fine (name, sm tear fep; sl rubbed). *Polyanthos*. $30/£19

CABELL, JAMES BRANCH. Chivalry. NY: Harper, 1909. 1st ed. (Bkpl remains), o/w Fine. *Hermitage*. $125/£80

CABELL, JAMES BRANCH. The Cords of Vanity. NY: McBride, 1920. 1st rev ed. (Name fr pastedown; spine gilt sl tarnished), else NF in VG- dj (spine hole, extrems lt chipped, sl soiling). *Between The Covers*. $125/£80

CABELL, JAMES BRANCH. Figures of Earth. NY, 1925. 1st Amer ed. Pict cvrs, gilt. Fine (spine top sl bumped) in dj (spine sl sunned, sl chipped, lt soiled). *Polyanthos*. $40/£26

CABELL, JAMES BRANCH. The Jewel Merchants. NY, 1921. 1st ed. #25/100 numbered, signed. As New in Perfect dj. *Bond*. $400/£256

CABELL, JAMES BRANCH. Jurgen. NY: Robert M. McBride, 1919. 1st ed, 1st issue. (Bkpl, top edge lt dusted), else NF in VG dj (shallow loss spine head, chips, short edgetears). *Lame Duck*. $2,500/£1,603

CABELL, JAMES BRANCH. Jurgen: A Comedy of Errors. Westport, (1976). One of 2000 signed by Virgil Burnett (illus). VG in slipcase (bumped). *Truepenny*. $50/£32

CABELL, JAMES BRANCH. Some of Us. NY, 1930. #424/1295 signed. Uncut. Fine (spine lt sunned, 2 corners sl rubbed). *Polyanthos*. $35/£22

CABELL, JAMES BRANCH. Something About Eve. McBride, 1927. Ltd to 850 signed. Orig 1/2 vellum, bds. VG. *Cullen*. $50/£32

CABELL, JAMES BRANCH. Something About Eve. NY: Robert M. McBride, 1927. 1st ed. NF in dj (spine sl sunned). *Turtle Island*. $50/£32

CABELL, JAMES BRANCH. Taboo. NY, 1921. #702/920. Fine (bkpl) in dj (spine sunned, pieces missing, torn). *Polyanthos*. $25/£16

CABELL, JAMES BRANCH. Domnei: A Comedy of Woman Worship. NY: McBride, 1920. 1st ed w/this title. (Sl wear spine ends), else Fine in Fine dj (lt crease; sl dknd along center). *Between The Covers*. $150/£96

CABELL, JAMES BRANCH. The King Was in His Counting House. NY: F&R, (1938). 1st ed. (Bkpl; spine cl, edges faded), thus VG- in VG dj (lt stains rear panel; extrems sl chipped). *Between The Covers*. $75/£48

CABELL, JAMES BRANCH. Preface to the Past. NY: McBride, (1936). 1st ed. (Sl tarnish gold spine lettering), else Fine in VG dj (price-clipped; extrem chips). *Between The Covers*. $85/£54

CABELL, SEARS WILSON. The Bulldog Longstreet at Gettysburg and Chickamauga. Atlanta: Ruralist, 1938. 1st ed. NF in ptd wrappers. *Mcgowan*. $37/£24

CABLE, GEORGE W. The Cavalier. NY, 1901. 1st Amer ed. Pict cvrs, gilt. NF (2 name stamps; cvrs sl soiled). *Polyanthos*. $30/£19

CABLE, GEORGE W. The Grandissimes. NY, 1899. 1st Amer ed. Teg, uncut. Pict cvrs. NF (spine lt sunned, lt rubbed). *Polyanthos*. $50/£32

CABOT, HUGH (ed). Modern Urology. Phila, 1918. 1st ed. 2 vols. VG. *Doctor's Library*. $100/£64

CABOT, WILLIAM B. In Northern Labrador. Boston: Richard C. Badger, c. 1912. Teg. VG (sl worn). *High Latitude*. $80/£51

CACCIARELLI, ROBERT. Forceps in Obstetrics. Newark, NJ, 1943. 1st ed. (Pencil mks; cl chipped head, tail.) *Argosy*. $60/£38

CACKLER, CHRISTIAN. Recollections of an Old Settler. Kent Courier, 1904. (Paper dknd, fragile, last leaf loose.) Recent black cl, gilt. Howes C13. *Bohling*. $30/£19

CADWALLADER, SYLVANUS. Three Years with General Grant. Benjamin J. Thomas (ed). NY, 1955. 1st ed. Fine in dj (lt wear). *Pratt*. $40/£26

CADY, JOHN H. Arizona's Yesterday. Patagonia, 1915. 6 plts. (Cvrs spotted), else Good. Howes C16. *Dumont*. $90/£58

CADY, JOHN H. Arizona's Yesterday: Being the Narrative of John H. Cady, Pioneer. (Patagonia, AZ, 1916.) Ptd pict wrappers (mended). Howes C16. *Ginsberg*. $100/£64

CAESAR, GENE. King of the Mountain Men. The Life of Jim Bridger. NY: E.P. Dutton, 1961. 1st ed. 4 dbl-pg maps. Gilt-lettered blue cl. Fine in dj (spine faded). *Argonaut*. $60/£38

CAESAR, JULIUS. Julius Caesar's Commentaries. A Modern Rendering by Somerset De Chair. London, 1951. Ltd to 320. 14 engrs. Red/orange buckram-backed blue buckram bds, gilt. Very Nice. *Cady*. $125/£80

CAFFYN, WILLIAM. Seventy-One Not Out, the Reminiscences of William Caffyn. Blackwood, 1899. 32pp ads at rear. (Few pp foxed; binding sl faded.) *Petersfield*. $47/£30

CAGE, JOHN and LOIS LONG. The Mud Book. NY: Abrams, 1988. 1st ed. 5 1/4 sq. 44pp. Fine in dj. *Cattermole*. $35/£22

CAGE, JOHN. Empty Words. Middletown, CT: Wesleyan Univ, (1979). 1st ed. (Sl rubbed), o/w Fine in dj (sl rubbed, price-clipped, ink price inside fr flap). *Jaffe*. $125/£80

CAHALANE, V. H. Biological Survey of Katmai National Monument. Washington: Smithsonian, Aug. 1959. 1st ed. 17 plts, fldg map. NF in wraps. *Mikesh*. $25/£16

CAHAN, ABRAHAM. Yekl: A Tale of the New York Ghetto. NY: D. Appleton, 1896. 1st ed. Good (foxed, eps spotted; rubbed, finger-soiled, spine ends worn). *Cahan*. $125/£80

CAHILL, HOLGER. George O. 'Pop' Hart. NY, 1928. One of 250 numbered, signed by Hart and Cahill. Signed frontis litho, 24 repros. (Backstrip imperfect.) *Swann**. $172/£110

CAHILL, JAMES. Chinese Painting. NY: Crown, 1972. 2nd ed. VG. *Worldwide*. $35/£22

CAIN, JAMES M. The Butterfly. NY, 1946. 1st ed. VG+ in VG dj. *Smith*. $20/£13

CAIN, JAMES M. The Butterfly. NY: Knopf, 1947. 1st ed. Fine in dj (sl rubbed). *Else Fine*. $70/£45

CAIN, JAMES M. Galatea. NY: Knopf, 1953. 1st ed. Fine in NF dj. *Hermitage*. $25/£16

CAIN, JAMES M. Galatea. NY: Knopf, 1953. 1st ed. Signed. VG+ in VG+ dj. *Bernard*. $300/£192

CAIN, JAMES M. The Postman Always Rings Twice. London: Jonathan Cape, 1934. 1st ed. (Name, sl cocked), else NF in NF dj (center crease). *Associates*. $500/£321

CAIN, JAMES M. Serenade. NY: Knopf, 1937. 1st ed. (Spine corners sl worn), o/w VG+ in color photocopy dj. *Bernard*. $75/£48

CAIN, JAMES M. Sinful Woman. NY: Avon, (1947). Pb orig. (Pp lt browned), else Fine in stapled wrappers, digest format. *Between The Covers*. $125/£80

CAIN, JAMES M. Three of Hearts. Robert Hale, (1949). 1st British ed. (Top edge sl dusty), o/w VG in dj (sl worn, chipped). *Ash*. $55/£35

CAIN, PAUL. Fast One. GC: Doubleday Doran, 1933. 1st ed. VG (soiling; extrems sl frayed). *Between The Covers*. $200/£128

CAINE, HALL. The Manxman. NY, 1895. 1st Amer ed, lg paper ed. Ltd to 250 numbered, signed. 2 vols. 529pp, port. Teg. Full gilt-stamped vellum (cvrs dknd). *King*. $75/£48

CAIRNS, HUNTINGTON. Law and the Social Sciences. NY: Harcourt, Brace/Kegan Paul et al, 1935. 1st ed. Inscribed. Blue-grn cl. VG. *Gach*. $65/£42

CALDECOTT, RANDOLPH. The Hey Diddle Diddle Picture Book.... Frederick Warne, n.d. (c.1907). 4 bks in 1. Obl format. (2),24,24,24,24pp (sm margin tears); 24 plts. Good in pict linen (sl rubbed, soiled). *Cox*. $39/£25

CALDECOTT, RANDOLPH. More 'Graphic' Pictures. London, 1887. 71pp (hinges cracked). Cl-backed pict bds (rubbed). *Argosy*. $125/£80

CALDECOTT, RANDOLPH. A Sketch-Book of R. Caldecott's. London/NY: Routledge, n.d. (1883). 1st ed. Oblong 8vo. 48pp. Grey cl-backed bds (sl worn, rubbed, cl sl bubbled rear cvr, hinge sl cracked). Internally Clean. *Dower*. $125/£80

CALDER, ISABEL M. Colonial Captivities, Marches and Journeys. NY, 1935. 1st ed. 2 plts. *Wantagh*. $75/£48

CALDER-MARSHALL, ARTHUR. A Crime Against Cania. Waltham Saint Lawrence, 1934. One of 250 signed. Teg. 1/4 black morocco, ptd cl over bds, gilt. VG (sl shelfworn). *Heller*. $200/£128

CALDERWOOD, W. L. The Life of the Salmon. London: Edward Arnold, 1907. 1st ed. 8 plts. (Edges, eps spotted.) Pict ribbed cl, gilt. Very Attractive. *Hollett.* $55/£35

CALDICOTT, J. The Values of Old English Silver and Sheffield Plate, from the XVth to the XIXth Centuries. J. Starkie Gardner (ed). London: Bemrose, 1906. 1st ed. 87 plts. Good in blue cl, gilt. *Cox.* $86/£55

CALDWELL, CHARLES. Autobiography.... Phila, 1855. 1st ed. Port, 454pp. VG. *Argosy.* $85/£54

CALDWELL, ELSIE NOBLE. Alaska Trail Dogs. NY, 1945. 1st ed. Map. Good (sl spotted). *High Latitude.* $25/£16

CALDWELL, ERSKINE. Certain Women. Heinemann, 1958. 1st UK ed. VG in dj. *Williams.* $19/£12

CALDWELL, ERSKINE. Claudelle. Heinemann, 1959. 1st UK ed. VG in dj. *Williams.* $19/£12

CALDWELL, ERSKINE. The Courting of Susie Brown. Falcon Press, (1952). 1st British ed. Nice (bkseller stamp fr fly, edges lt spotted, sl mk top cvr) in dj. *Ash.* $31/£20

CALDWELL, ERSKINE. A House in the Uplands. Falcon Press, (1947). 1st British ed. Nice (sl mks, sm flaws) in dj (lt rubbed). *Ash.* $31/£20

CALDWELL, ERSKINE. Tenant Farmer. NY: Phalanx, (1935). 1st ed. Fine in orig ptd grn wrappers. *Bromer.* $225/£144

CALDWELL, ERSKINE. We Are the Living. NY, 1933. 1st ed. VG in VG dj. *Smith.* $25/£16

Calendar of the Correspondence of Thomas Jefferson. Washington, 1894-95. 2 vols (of 3). 541; 593pp. Full calf (scuffed, lib mks). *Bohling.* $30/£19

CALHOUN, ARTHUR W. A Social History of the American Family from Colonial Times to the Present. Cleveland: Clark, 1917-9. 1st ed. 3 vols. (Vol 3 w/few barely visible #s to spine.) Howes C27. *Ginsberg.* $350/£224

CALHOUN, MARY. Depend on Katie John. NY: Harper, 1961. 1st ed. Paul Frame (illus). 5 1/2 x 8 1/4. 181pp. VG in dj. *Cattermole.* $20/£13

California Illustrated. (By J. M. Letts.) NY: William Holdredge, 1852. 1st ed. 224pp; 48 litho plts. (All plts foxed; fr cvr, tp, ep separated together; spine lacks covering.) Howes L300. *New Hampshire*.* $140/£90

California. NY: WPA, 1939. 1st ed, 1st ptg. Lg fldg map in cvr pocket. Grn cl (lt worn, soiled). Dj (worn, chipped). *Freeman*.* $30/£19

CALKINS, E. A. A Biographical Sketch of Gen. Philo White, of Whitestown, N.Y. Milwaukee: Symes, Swain, 1880. 16pp, stitched w/o wraps. Nice. *Bohling.* $15/£10

CALKINS, JOHN S. Olive Grower's Handbook. Pomona, 1896. 30pp. Ptd wrappers. *Dawson.* $40/£26

CALKINS, ROBERT G. Illuminated Books of the Middle Ages. Ithaca, 1986. (Few ink notes; spine sl bumped.) Wrappers. *Washton.* $25/£16

CALL, R. ELLSWORTH. Mammoth Cave, Kentucky. Two Hundred Miles Underground (cvr title). Louisville & Nashville RR Co, ca 1902. 4th ed. VG in pict wraps (paper label added). *Bohling.* $25/£16

CALLAGHAN, MORLEY. More Joy in Heaven. NY: Random House, 1937. 1st ed. Fine in NF dj (sm chip fr panel). *Beasley.* $100/£64

CALLAGHAN, MORLEY. No Man's Meat. Paris: Edward W. Titus, 1931. Ltd to 525 numbered, signed. Fine. *Antic Hay.* $275/£176

CALLAGHAN, MORLEY. They Shall Inherit the Earth. NY: Random House, 1935. 1st ed. Fine in VG dj (sl chipping; dknd spine). *Beasley.* $65/£42

CALLAHAN, HARRY. Color. 1941-1980. Providence: Matrix, 1980. 1st ed. Signed. Fine in slipcase (lt sunned) w/inset photo. *Smith.* $200/£128

CALLAHAN, HARRY. Harry Callahan. (Tucson): Center for Creative Photography, Univ of AZ, (1980). 1st ed. 8 color, 2 b/w plts. NF in ptd wrappers. *Cahan.* $20/£13

CALLAHAN, HARRY. Harry Callahan: Photographs. Santa Barbara: El Mochuelo Gallery, 1964. 1st ed. Ltd to 1500. Signed. Black cl, silver lettering. (Eps discolored), o/w NF in slipcase. *Cahan.* $750/£481

CALLAHAN, HARRY. The Multiple Image. Chicago: Press of Inst of Design, 1961. 1st ed. VG in pict stiff wrappers (lt soiled). *Cahan.* $125/£80

CALLAHAN, SEAN (ed). The Photographs of Margaret Bourke-White. Boston: NYGS, 1972. 1st ed. (Owner stamp), else Fine in dj (sl edgeworn). *Cahan.* $60/£38

CALLANDINE, GEORGE. The Diary of Colour-Serjeant George Callandine, 19th Foot, 1793-1837. M. L. Ferrar (ed). London, 1922. Grn cl (sl mkd). *Maggs.* $117/£75

CALLAWAY, NICHOLAS (ed). Georgia O'Keeffe: One Hundred Flowers. NY, 1987. Folio. 100 color repros. Dj, pub's shipping box. *Swann*.* $69/£44

CALLENDER, JAMES THOMSON. Sketches of the History of America. Phila, 1798. 1st ed. (Tp damaged, repaired and mtd, text affected; browning, spotting.) Mod cl (lt worn, soiled). *Freeman*.* $45/£29

CALLERY, BERNADETTE G. and ELIZABETH A. MOSIMANN (comps). The Tradition of Fine Bookbinding in the Twentieth Century. Pittsburgh, 1979. Cl-backed pict bds. *Edwards.* $39/£25

CALLOWAY, CAB. Of Minnie the Moocher and Me. NY: Crowell, 1976. 1st ed. Inscribed. Fine in Fine dj. *Beasley.* $100/£64

CALTHROP, DION CLAYTON. The Charm of Gardens. A&C Black, 1910. 32 color plts. (Sl mainly marginal spotting.) Teg. Dec cl, gilt illus upper bd (chipped, spine faded). *Edwards.* $39/£25

CALTHROP, DION CLAYTON. English Costume. I. Early English. A&C Black, 1906. 1st ed. 10 color plts. (Feps sl browned.) Teg. *Edwards.* $31/£20

CALVERLEY, C. S. Verses and Translations. Cambridge, 1862. 2nd ed. Good. *Typographeum.* $25/£16

CALVERT, A. F. Spain. London: Allen & Unwin, 1909. 46 color plts. Teg. (Cl sl worn.) *Ars Artis.* $78/£50

CALVERT, HARRY. The Journals and Correspondence of General Sir Harry Calvert....Harry Verney (ed). London, 1853. 544pp + ads; 2 fldg maps (1 w/marginal repair, no loss). Mod 1/2 morocco, gilt, marbled bds. *Maggs.* $156/£100

CALVERT, J. The Gold Rocks of Great Britain and Ireland.... London, 1853. xx,324,ii,xpp. (Lib stamp verso tp; neatly rebacked, preserving spine.) *Henly.* $212/£136

CALVERT, W. The Wife's Manual, or Prayers, Thoughts, and Songs.... London: (Longman et al), 1861. 3rd ed. Binder's ticket rear pastedown. (Prelims, last ll foxed.) Aeg, gauffered. Pub's textured cl (spine lt worn), beveled bds, blind-blocked border dec, gilt. Bound by Leighton and Son and Hodge. Nice. *Book Block.* $195/£125

CALVIN, ROSS. River of the Sun. Albuquerque, 1946. 1st ed. NF in VG tan dj. *Turpen.* $48/£31

CALVINO, ITALO. Cosmicomics. NY, 1968. 1st Amer ed. NF (name) in NF dj (edgewear). *Warren.* $50/£32

CALVINO, ITALO. If on a Winter's Night a Traveller. NY: Harcourt Brace Jovanovich, 1981. 1st US ed. NF in dj. *Lame Duck.* $50/£32

CALVINO, ITALO. Italian Fables. NY: Orion, 1959. 1st US ed. Michael Train (illus). 7 1/2 x 9. 242pp. VG in dj. *Cattermole.* $50/£32

CALVINO, ITALO. Italian Fables. NY: Orion, 1959. 1st US ed. NF in VG dj (tears tape-mended to verso). *Lame Duck.* $85/£54

CALVINO, ITALO. Mr. Palomar. San Diego: Harcourt Brace Jovanovich, 1985. 1st US ed. Fine in dj. *Lame Duck.* $35/£22

CALVINO, ITALO. The Nonexistent Knight and The Cloven Viscount. NY: Random House, (1962). 1st Amer ed. (Name), else Fine in VG dj (rubbed, lt worn). *Between The Covers.* $85/£54

CALVINO, ITALO. The Path to the Nest of Spiders. Boston: Beacon, 1957. 1st US ed. (Pg edges lt foxed, sticker residue fep), else VG+ in VG+ dj. *Lame Duck.* $95/£61

CALVINO, ITALO. T Zero. NY: Harcourt, Brace & World, 1967. 1st ed. (Date fep), else NF in dj. *Lame Duck.* $175/£112

CALVINO, ITALO. Under the Jaguar Sun. NY, 1988. 1st ed. Fine in Fine dj. *Smith.* $15/£10

CALVINO, ITALO. The Uses of Literature. San Diego: Harcourt Brace Jovanovich, 1986. 1st US ed. Fine in dj (price-clipped). *Lame Duck.* $35/£22

Cambrian Travellers Guide. (By George Nicholson.) Stourport, 1813. 2nd ed. Fldg frontis map (photocopy), xiii,1468pp (ink stamp). Mod cl (rebound). *Edwards.* $62/£40

CAMERON, G. R. Pathology of the Cell. Edinburgh, 1952. 64 plts. (Corner sl bumped), o/w VG in dj. *Whitehart.* $75/£48

CAMERON, H. K. A List of Monumental Brasses on the Continent of Europe. London, 1970. Good. *Washton.* $35/£22

CAMERON, JULIA MARGARET. Victorian Photographs of Famous Men and Fair Women. Boston, (1973). 48 full-pg plts. VG in dj. *Argosy.* $75/£48

CAMERON, NIGEL. The Face of China As Seen by Photographers and Travelers, 1860-1912. Millerton, NY: Aperture, 1978. 1st ed. Frontis. (Eps sl wrinkled), else Fine in illus dj. *Cahan.* $45/£29

CAMERON, VERNEY L. Across Africa. NY: Harper, 1877. 1st Amer ed. Frontis, xvi,508pp,8pp ads; fldg map in pocket. Grn gilt pict cl (label remnants spine), else VG. *Terramedia.* $200/£128

CAMERON, W. J. From Cape Town to the Belgian Congo. Chicago: Privately Pub, 1929. 1st ed. Frontis port. Teg. Gilt-dec bds. VG. *Mikesh.* $25/£16

CAMM, DOM BEDE. Pilgrim Paths in Latin Lands. London, 1923. 1st ed. Teg. Gilt-dec cl (lib bkpl; spine sl rubbed). *Edwards.* $47/£30

CAMP, CHARLES L. (ed). 1792-1881. James Clyman, Frontiersman. Portland, OR, (1960). 2nd ed. One of 1450 ptd by Lawton Kennedy. Port. Gilt cl. VF. Howes C81. *Reese.* $150/£96

CAMP, CHARLES L. Desert Rats. (Berkeley): Friends of the Bancroft Library, 1966. *Dawson.* $15/£10

CAMP, F. B. American Soldier Ballads. L.A.: Geo. Rice, 1917. 1st ed. Pict cl. *Dawson.* $30/£19

CAMP, RAYMOND R. Duck Boats: Blinds: Decoys. NY: Knopf, 1952. 1st ed. 2 color plts. 1/2 black cl, turquoise cl-cvrd bds. Fine in Fine pict dj. *Biscotti.* $125/£80

CAMP, RAYMOND R. The Hunter's Encyclopedia. Harrisburg, (1949). VG. *Truepenny.* $45/£29

CAMP, SAMUEL G. The Fine Art of Fishing. NY: Outing, 1915. 2-tone dec cl. VG+. *Bowman.* $15/£10

CAMP, WADSWORTH. The Gray Mask. GC: Doubleday, 1920. 1st ed. Good (spine ends lt bumped, sl shaken) in dj (creases, chips, soil, loss to head, heel). *Metropolitan*.* $28/£18

CAMPA, ARTHUR L. (ed). Brand Book of the Denver Westerners. Boulder, CO: Johnson, (1966). 1st ed. Ltd to 735. VG in dj. *Lien.* $50/£32

Campaigns of Napoleon Buonaparte, Embracing the Events of His Unexampled Military Career.... Boston: Charles Gaylord, 1835. Fldg frontis view, 422,xpp. (Paper dknd, foxed; reps removed; rebacked, backstrip title laid down.) *Bohling.* $30/£19

Campaigns of Walker's Texas Division. By a Private Soldier. (By Joseph Palmer Blessington.) NY: the Author, 1875. 1st ed. 314pp (Sl cvr speckling, sl wear to extrems), else VG. Howes B533. *Mcgowan.* $550/£353

CAMPBELL, BRUCE. The Mystery of the Plumed Serpent. G&D, 1962. 1st ed. 5x7.5. 176pp. Tan tweed cl (sl shelfworn). Lists to this title. VG in dj (sl edgeworn, sm tears). *My Bookhouse.* $100/£64

CAMPBELL, CHARLES et al (eds). Problems of Personality. London: Routledge/Kegan Paul, (1925). 1st ed. Early issue w/undated ads listing 1st 30 vols in series as ready. Blue-grn cl (sl rubbed, lt shelfworn). Good+ (inscrip). *Gach.* $65/£42

CAMPBELL, CHARLES. The Traveller's Complete Guide Through Belgium, Holland and Germany. London: Sherwood, Neely & Jones, 1815. 3 fldg maps. (2 closed tears to map; foxed, offset.) Contemp 1/2 calf, marbled bds (sl worn), gilt spine. *Waverly*.* $44/£28

CAMPBELL, DONALD. A Narrative of the Extraordinary Adventures, and Sufferings by Shipwreck and Imprisonment. London: Vernor & Hood, 1796. Frontis, xi,276pp. Contemp 1/2 morocco. (Lt foxing; edges rubbed, hinges tender), o/w Good. *Worldwide.* $190/£122

CAMPBELL, DUGALD. In the Heart of Bantuland. Phila: Lippincott, 1922. 1st Amer ed. Photo frontis; fldg map. Gray cl. Good. *Karmiole.* $75/£48

CAMPBELL, DUGALD. On the Trail of the Veiled Tuareg. Phila: Lippincott, n.d. (ca 1930). 1st ed. 16 plts, fldg map. Gilt-stamped blue cl. Good. *Karmiole.* $75/£48

CAMPBELL, GEORGE. A Handy Book on the Eastern Question. London, 1876. 1st ed. xvii,212pp+4pp pub's ads; fldg map (torn, sl foxed; extrems rubbed, spine sl chipped). *Edwards.* $55/£35

CAMPBELL, GORDON. My Mystery Ships. Hodder, (1928). Color frontis. (Sl foxed.) *Petersfield.* $19/£12

CAMPBELL, J. RAMSEY (ed). New Tales of the Cthulhu Mythos. (Sauk City, WI): Arkham House, 1980. 1st ed. One of 3647. New in New dj. *Bernard.* $100/£64

CAMPBELL, JANE C. The Money-Maker, and Other Tales. NY etc.: J.C. Derby et al, 1854. 1st ed. Buff eps. Ribbed blue cl (chipped), blind, gilt. VG (foxed, lt dusty). *Temple.* $14/£9

CAMPBELL, JOHN F. History and Bibliography of the New American Practical Navigator and the American Coast Pilot. Salem: Peabody Museum, 1964. 1st ed. One of 1000. VF. *Lefkowicz.* $125/£80

CAMPBELL, JOHN LORD. The Lives of the Chief Justices of England. NY: James Cockcroft, 1873-75. 6 vols. Grn cl, gilt. VG set (sl worn). *Boswell.* $350/£224

CAMPBELL, JOHN LORD. Shakespeare's Legal Acquirements Considered. NY: Appleton, 1859. 1st Amer ed. Crimson cl (faded), gilt. Sound. *Boswell.* $250/£160

CAMPBELL, JOHN W. The Black Star Passes. Reading: Fantasy, (1953). 1st ed, 1st binding. One of 500 w/signed, numbered leaf tipped in. Purple cl, gilt-lettered spine. VG dj. *Kane*.* $110/£71

CAMPBELL, JOHN W. From Unknown Worlds. London, (1952). 1st Eng, 1st hb ed. Fine in NF dj (edges, folds sl rubbed). *Mcclintock.* $40/£26

CAMPBELL, JOHN W. The Incredible Planet. Reading: Fantasy, 1949. 1st ed. Dj. *Swann*.* $69/£44

CAMPBELL, JOHN W. The Mightiest Machine. Providence: Hadley, (1935). 1st ed. Variant red Dj (chipped, worn, price-clipped). *Swann**. $69/£44

CAMPBELL, JOHN. A Personal Narrative of Thirteen Years Service...for the Suppression of Human Sacrifice. London: Hurst & Blackett, 1864. 1st ed. ix,320pp (tp sl browned) + (viii) pub's cat; fldg map at rear. Uncut. Pict maroon cl (spine sl faded, extrems sl bumped), gilt. *Sotheran*. $304/£195

CAMPBELL, JOHN. The Spanish Empire in America.... London, 1747. (Pp dknd.) Full leather (possibly recovered). *Metropolitan**. $287/£184

CAMPBELL, L. The Life of James Clerk Maxwell with Selections from His Correspondence and Occasional Writings. 1884. xv,421,32pp. (Spine sl defective, discolored, fr cvr sl mkd), o/w VG. *Whitehart*. $55/£35

CAMPBELL, LORNE. The Early Flemish Pictures in the Collection of Her Majesty the Queen. Cambridge, 1985. Good in dj, slipcase (sl worn). *Washton*. $145/£93

CAMPBELL, MARJORIE WILKINS. The North West Company. Toronto: Macmillan, 1957. 1st Canadian ed. 4 plts. Fine in dj (worn). *Argonaut*. $45/£29

CAMPBELL, MARY MASON. The New England Buttr'y Shelf Almanac. NY: World, (1970). 1st ed. Tasha Tudor (illus). 8vo. 302pp. VG in VG dj. *Dower*. $65/£42

CAMPBELL, PATRICK. Travels in the Interior Inhabited Parts of North America in the Years 1791 and 1792. H. H. Langton (ed). Toronto: Champlain Soc, 1937. One of 550 ptd. Howes C101. *Ginsberg*. $300/£192

CAMPBELL, RAMSEY. Cold Print. (Santa Cruz): Scream Press, (1985). 1st ed. One of 250 signed, numbered. Fine in dj, slipcase. *Other Worlds*. $150/£96

CAMPBELL, RAMSEY. Demons by Daylight. Sauk City, 1973. 1st ed. Fine in Fine dj. *Mcclintock*. $45/£29

CAMPBELL, RAMSEY. The Doll Who Ate His Mother. Bobbs Merrill, 1976. 1st ed. (Bkpl fr pastedown), else Fine in Fine dj. *Certo*. $95/£61

CAMPBELL, RAMSEY. The Face That Must Die. Santa Cruz: Scream, 1983. 1st ed. Signed by Campbell and Robert Bloch (intro). Fine in VG dj. *Metropolitan**. $69/£44

CAMPBELL, RAMSEY. The Height of the Scream. Sauk City: Arkham House, 1976. 1st Amer ed. VF in dj (spine sl discolored). *Bromer*. $75/£48

CAMPBELL, RAMSEY. Incarnate. Macmillan, 1983. 1st ed. NF in dj. *Madle*. $35/£22

CAMPBELL, RAMSEY. The Inhabitant of the Lake. Sauk City: Arkham House, 1964. 1st ed. Fine in dj (browned, sl worn). *Metropolitan**. $69/£44

CAMPBELL, RAMSEY. Scared Stiff. L.A.: Scream, (1987). 1st ed. One of 250 numbered, signed by Campbell and J. K. Potter (illus). Slipcase. *Swann**. $57/£37

CAMPBELL, REAU. Complete Guide and Descriptive Book of the Yellowstone Park. Chicago, 1914. Rev 2nd ed. Map. Fine in wraps. *Perier*. $50/£32

CAMPBELL, ROY. Adamastor. London, 1930. 1st Eng ed. Fine in 2 djs (1 of each issue). *Clearwater*. $47/£30

CAMPBELL, ROY. The Georgiad. London: Boriswood, 1931. 1st ed. Fine (spine heel sl rubbed) in dj (sm corner chips). *Polyanthos*. $35/£22

CAMPBELL, ROY. Portugal. London, 1957. 1st ed. *Typographeum*. $50/£32

CAMPBELL, ROY. Talking Bronco. London: Faber & Faber, 1946. 1st ed. VG in dj (sl frayed, repaired). *Cox*. $23/£15

CAMPBELL, RUTH. The Cat Whose Whiskers Slipped. Boston/Joliet/NY: P.F. Volland, (1925). 10th ed. 8vo. 50 leaves, incl pict eps. Pict blue cl (rubbed, bumped). VG. *Blue Mountain*. $15/£10

CAMPBELL, T. E. Colonial Caroline: A History of Caroline County, Virginia. Dietz, (c. 1954). VG- (cvr insect spotted) in Good dj (faded, few tears). *Book Broker*. $75/£48

CAMPBELL, T. J. The Upper Tennessee. Chattanooga, TN: The Author, 1932. 1st ed. Fine. *Wantagh*. $50/£32

CAMPBELL, THOMAS. Diary of a Visit to England in 1775. James L. Clifford (ed). Cambridge, 1947. 1st ed. 2 plts. VG in dj (soiled). *Cox*. $23/£15

CAMPBELL, THOMAS. Gertrude of Wyoming. London: Longman et al, 1809. 1st ed. Errata slip. 1/4 mottled calf over marbled bds (spine ends chipped, fr hinge cracked). *Sadlon*. $100/£64

CAMPBELL, THOMAS. Gertrude of Wyoming. London: The Author, 1809. 1st ed. Aeg. (4), 134pp, errata slip tipped in. Full gilt-stamped black morocco (spine rubbed). *M & S*. $200/£128

CAMPBELL, THOMAS. The Jesuits, 1534-1921. NY: Encyclopedia Press, 1921. 1st ed. 2 vols. VG. *Worldwide*. $35/£22

CAMPBELL, THOMAS. The Poetical Works. W. Alfred Hill (ed). London: George Bell, 1890. Collected ed. Aeg. Full red morocco, gilt. VG (spine sl dknd, joints sl chafed). *Sumner & Stillman*. $75/£48

CAMPBELL, TOM W. Two Fighters and Two Fines. Little Rock, 1941. 2nd ed. VG (hinges weak). *Bohling*. $12/£8

CAMPBELL, W. D. Beyond the Border. Westminster/NY: Constable/R.H. Russell, 1898. 1st ed. Aeg. Grn cl (spine sl faded, knocked), gilt. *Maggs*. $117/£75

CAMPBELL, W. G. The New World. London, 1871. 208pp. VG. *Reese*. $125/£80

CAMPBELL, WALTER. The Book Lover's Southwest. Norman: Univ of OK, (1955). 1st ed. VF in VF dj. *Book Market*. $65/£42

CAMPBELL, WALTER. The Booklover's Southwest, a Guide to Good Reading. Norman, 1955. 1st ed. VG in VG dj. *Turpen*. $45/£29

CAMPBELL, WALTER. The Old Forest Ranger. London: Routledge, 1869. xv,359pp; 6 plts. Red gilt-pict cl. VG. *Adelson*. $60/£38

CAMPBELL, WILL D. Brother to a Dragonfly. NY, 1977. 1st ed. VG (3 owner stamps) in VG dj. *Smith*. $15/£10

CAMPBELL, WILLIAM CAREY. A Colorado Colonel and Other Sketches. Topeka, KS, 1901. (Piece cut from fep; sl worn.) *Hayman*. $25/£16

CAMPBELL, WILLIAM W. Annals of Tryon County. NY, 1831. 1st ed. 191,(1),78pp (lt foxing), fldg facs, fldg map. Contemp full calf (sl scuffing, chipping), red calf label. Good. Howes C103. *Cullen*. $250/£160

CAMPDEN, R. N. Architecture of the Western Reserve 1800-1900. Case Western Reserve Univ, 1971. Sound. *Ars Artis*. $47/£30

CAMPER, CHARLES and J. W. KIRKLEY. Historical Record of the First Regiment Maryland Infantry. Washington: Gibson Bros, 1871. 1st ed. x,312pp. (Edgewear), else NF. Howes C104. *Mcgowan*. $350/£224

CAMPER, PETRUS. The Works. London: C. Dilly, 1794. 1st ed in English. 2 parts in 1 vol. Engr frontis port, 17 fldg engr plts (clean tear 1 plt; margins sl browned, some leaves lt soiled, spotted). Later bds (worn). *Christie's**. $315/£202

CAMPION, THOMAS. The Works of Dr. Thomas Campion. A. H. Bullen (ed). London: Privately ptd, 1889. Ltd to 400 numbered. xxvi,406pp. Aeg. Contemp blue morocco (spine sl faded; lib bkpl) by Riviere & Son. *Karmiole*. $150/£96

CAMSELL, CHARLES. Son of the North. Toronto: Ryerson Press, (1955). 2nd ptg. VG in VG dj. *Perier.* $32/£21

CAMSELL, CHARLES. Son of the North. Toronto: Ryerson, 1954. VG in dj (frayed). *High Latitude.* $30/£19

CAMUS, ALBERT. Exile and the Kingdom. Justin O'Brien (trans). London: Hamish Hamilton, (1958). 1st Eng ed. Paper-cvrd bds. NF in VG dj (sl worn, sm stain, chips). *Antic Hay.* $35/£22

CAMUS, ALBERT. Resistance, Rebellion, and Death. Justin O'Brien (trans). NY: Knopf, 1961. 1st Amer ed. Cl-backed bds. (Bkseller label rep), o/w Fine in dj. *Jaffe.* $50/£32

Can This Be Beeton? Guinness, n.d. (1956). Fine in illus wrappers. *Words Etc.* $31/£20

CANADA, J. W. Life at Eighty. (La Porte, TX, 1952.) 1st ed. Inscribed. W/o later 6-pg addendum. (Top edge rear bd snagged, cl dull.) *Bohling.* $30/£19

CANDEE, HELEN CHURCHILL. The Tapestry Book. NY: Tudor Pub Co, (1935). New ed. 1st thus. Dec cl. Fine (w/o dj). *Hermitage.* $50/£32

CANDLER, ALLEN D. (comp). The Confederate Records of the State of Georgia. Atlanta: Chas. P. Byrd, 1909-1911. 1st ed. Vols 1-4, 6. Vol 5 never pub. Vols 1-3 orig cl, vols 4, 6 later cl. (Inner hinges cracked vols 1, 2), else VG set. *Mcgowan.* $1,250/£801

CANDLER, E. On the Edge of the World. London: Cassell, 1919. 1st ed. (x),278pp; map, 35 photo plts. Pict cl, gilt. VG. *Sotheran.* $125/£80

CANETTI, ELIAS. Auto-Da Fe. Cape, 1946. 1st UK ed. VG (cvrs sl whitened) in dj (sl browned, sl loss spine top). *Williams.* $187/£120

CANETTI, ELIAS. Auto-Da-Fe. NY, (1946). 1st Amer ed. Fine (bkpl) in dj (2 sm spine tears, edges lt rubbed). *Polyanthos.* $35/£22

CANETTI, ELIAS. The Tower of Babel. NY: Knopf, 1947. 1st US ed. VG (bd edges, spine faded) in dj (sl dampstained fr panel). *Lame Duck.* $65/£42

CANFIELD, DOROTHY. The Day of Glory. NY: Holt, 1919. 1st ed. Fine in VG dj (lt chip rear panel; extrem chips). *Between The Covers.* $100/£64

CANKAR, IVAN. The Baliff Yerney and His Rights. Sidonie Yeras & H. C. Sewall Grant (trans). London: John Rodker, 1930. 1st ed thus. NF (sl soiled, sm red star rep) in dj (sl browned, interior spine repair). *Antic Hay.* $27/£17

CANNELL, J. C. The Secrets of Houdini. Hutchinson, 1931. 2nd imp. 16 half-tone plts. Good (sl rubbed, faded). *Cox.* $39/£25

Cannon Collection of Italian Paintings of the Renaissance. Princeton, 1936. Good. *Washton.* $60/£38

CANNON, FRANK J. and H. J. O'HIGGINS. Under the Prophet in Utah. Boston: Clark, 1911. Frontis port. Good (ex-lib). *Scribe's Perch*.* $22/£14

CANNON, GEORGE QUALE. Writings from the 'Western Standard,' Published in San Francisco, California. Liverpool, 1864. 1st ed. 512pp. Marbled eps, edges. Orig full dec leather (lt worn; crown, spine foot sl worn, chipped; hinges cracked, expertly repaired). Overall VG +. Pencil autograph of Amasa M. Lyman. *Benchmark.* $700/£449

CANNON, JANELL. Stellaluna. NY: HBJ, 1993. 1st ed. 10 1/4 sq. 48pp. Glossy bds. Fine in dj. *Cattermole.* $100/£64

CANNON, LE GRAND B. Personal Reminiscences of the Rebellion, 1861-1866. NY, 1895. 228pp; port. 1/2 cl. Good (fep mostly excised; spine stains). *Wantagh.* $75/£48

CANNON, MILES. Waiilatpu—Its Rise and Fall. Boise: Capital News, 1915. 1st ed. VG in wraps. *Perier.* $97/£62

CANNON, WALTER B. Bodily Changes in Pain, Hunger, Fear and Rage. NY: Appleton, 1929. 2nd ed. VG. *White.* $59/£38

CANTACUZINO, SHERBAN (ed). Architectural Conservation in Europe. Architectural Press, 1975. NF in dj. *Hadley.* $23/£15

CANTOR, G. Contributions to the Founding of the Theory of Transfinite Numbers. P. E. B. Jourdain (trans). Chicago/London, 1915. (Spine ends sl worn, cl dust stained.) *Whitehart.* $39/£25

CANTWELL, R. Alexander Wilson, Naturalist and Pioneer. Phila/NY, 1961. (Sl bumped.) Dj. *Maggs.* $28/£18

CANTWELL, ROBERT. Laugh and Lie Down. Farrar & Rinehart, (1931). 1st ed. VG +. *Authors Of West.* $40/£26

CAPA, CORNELL (ed). Robert Capa, 1913-1954. NY: Grossman, 1974. (Owner stamp), else VG in pict stiff wrappers (crease). *Cahan.* $25/£16

CAPA, CORNELL and RICHARD WHELAN (eds). Robert Capa Photographs. NY, (1985). 1st ed. VG in dj. *Argosy.* $85/£54

CAPA, ROBERT and IRWIN SHAW. Report on Israel. NY, 1950. 1st ed. VG + in VG dj (chipped). *Warren.* $45/£29

CAPA, ROBERT. Robert Capa. NY: Paragraphic, 1969. 1st ed. NF in wrappers. *Smith.* $35/£22

CAPA, ROBERT. Slightly Out of Focus. NY: Holt, (1947). 1st ed. (Sl soiled), else Fine in dj (lt worn; unfaded; 2 sm chips crown edge). *Between The Covers.* $100/£64

CAPA, ROBERT. Slightly Out of Focus. NY: Henry Holt, 1947. 1st ed. (Owner stamp), o/w VG, dj remnants laid in. *Cahan.* $30/£19

CAPEK, KAREL. I Had a Dog and a Cat. NY: Macmillan, 1941. 1st US ed. VG + in VG dj (price-clipped). *Lame Duck.* $65/£42

CAPEK, KAREL. Intimate Things. NY: Putnam, 1936. 1st ed. VG in VG- dj (soiled, chipped). *Lame Duck.* $65/£42

CAPEK, KAREL. Krakatit. Lawrence Hyde (trans). NY, 1925. 1st Amer ed. Fine (spine label rubbed). *Polyanthos.* $60/£38

CAPEK, KAREL. Meteor. NY: Putnam, 1935. 1st US ed. VG + (lt ofsetting feps) in VG dj (worn, sm tears). *Lame Duck.* $75/£48

CAPONIGRO, PAUL. Landscape. NY: McGraw-Hill, 1975. 1st ed. 74 b/w photo plts. (Owner stamp), else Fine in illus stiff wrappers. *Cahan.* $30/£19

CAPONIGRO, PAUL. Megaliths. Boston: NYGS, 1986. 1st ed. Blind-emb cl. Fine in pict dj. *Cahan.* $125/£80

CAPOTE, TRUMAN. Breakfast at Tiffany's. London: Hamish Hamilton, (1958). 1st British ed. (Edges tanned), else VG in dj. *Reese.* $35/£22

CAPOTE, TRUMAN. Breakfast at Tiffany's. NY: Random House, 1958. 1st ed. (Bump), else NF in dj (spine sl faded). *Lame Duck.* $275/£176

CAPOTE, TRUMAN. The Dogs Bark. NY, 1973. 1st ed. VG in VG dj (sl wrinkled). *Smith.* $20/£13

CAPOTE, TRUMAN. The Grass Harp. (NY): Random House, (1951). 1st ed, 1st binding. (Spine sl dknd), o/w Fine in dj (sl rubbed). *Jaffe.* $125/£80

CAPOTE, TRUMAN. The Grass Harp. (NY): Random House, (1951). 1st ed, 1st binding. Signed at later date, 1956 publicity photo laid in. VG + (sl dknd) in VG dj (chipped). *Reese.* $175/£112

CAPOTE, TRUMAN. In Cold Blood. NY: Random House, (1965). One of 500 numbered, signed. Fine in Fine slipcase. *Lenz.* $475/£304

CAPOTE, TRUMAN. In Cold Blood. NY, 1965. 1st Amer ed. Fine (spine heel sl rubbed) in dj (few sm tears; rubbed). *Polyanthos.* $35/£22

CAPOTE, TRUMAN. Miriam. Mankato, MN: Creative Education, (1982). 1st separate ed. Signed. Illus lib binding. Fine. *Bernard.* $175/£112

CAPOTE, TRUMAN. The Muses Are Heard. NY: Random House, (1956). 1st ed. (Fr cvr design lt faded.) Dj (sl soil, chip). *Glenn.* $95/£61

CAPOTE, TRUMAN. Music for Chameleons. NY: Random House, (1980). 1st ed, trade issue. Rev flyer, photo laid in. Fine in dj. *Reese.* $50/£32

CAPOTE, TRUMAN. Music for Chameleons. NY: Random House, (1980). One of 350 numbered, signed. Fine in Fine slipcase. *Lenz.* $300/£192

CAPOTE, TRUMAN. Music for Chameleons. NY: Random House, (1980). 1st ed. Ltd to 350 signed. VF in slipcase. *Jaffe.* $350/£224

CAPOTE, TRUMAN. One Christmas. NY: Random House, (1983). 1st ed, trade issue. Rev slip, flyer, photo laid in. VF in slipcase. *Reese.* $50/£32

CAPOTE, TRUMAN. One Christmas. NY: Random House, (1983). 1st ed. #55/300 signed. Fine (sm water spot limitation pg) in illus pub's box. *Metropolitan*.* $143/£92

CAPOTE, TRUMAN. Other Voices, Other Rooms. NY: Random House, (1948). 1st ed. NF in VG dj. *Metropolitan*.* $172/£110

CAPOTE, TRUMAN. Other Voices, Other Rooms. London, 1948. 1st Eng ed. Nice in dj (reinforced, ragged). *Clearwater.* $55/£35

CAPOTE, TRUMAN. The Thanksgiving Visitor. NY, 1967. 1st Amer ed. Fine in Fine box. *Polyanthos.* $60/£38

CAPOTE, TRUMAN. A Tree of Night and Other Stories. NY, 1949. 1st Amer ed. Fine (spine sl bumped) in dj (spine lt sunned, few chips, rubbed, sl creased; strengthened internally). *Polyanthos.* $45/£29

CAPOTE, TRUMAN. A Tree of Night. NY, (1949). 1st ed. VG in dj. *Argosy.* $150/£96

CAPOTE, TRUMAN. Trilogy. NY: Macmillan, 1969. 1st ed. NF in dj (price-clipped). *Lame Duck.* $50/£32

CAPP, B. Astrology and the Popular Press, English Almanacs 1500-1800. Faber, 1979. 1st ed. Fine in dj. *Moss.* $31/£20

CAPPE, CATHERINE. Memoirs of the Life of the Late.... Boston: Wells & Lilly, 1824. 1st US ed. 406pp. Contemp calf. VG. *Second Life.* $75/£48

CAPPER, BENJAMIN PITTS. A Topographical Dictionary of the United Kingdom. London, 1825. 46 engr maps (lt foxed). Calls for 47 maps, incl 2 maps of Wales; this copy bound w/1 fldg map of Wales. Uncut. (Casing loose.) *Freeman*.* $130/£83

CAPPS, BENJAMIN. The Trail to Ogallala. NY: Duell, Sloan & Pearce, (1964). 1st ed. Brn cl-backed brn-veined pale grn bds. Fine in VG dj (bumped, rear flap sl soiled). *Blue Mountain.* $35/£22

CAPPS, STEPHEN R. Geology of the Alaska Railroad Region. Washington: GPO, 1940. 1st ed. 10 plts, incl 3 lg fldg color maps in rear pocket. Stiff wraps. (Rubbed, sl dampstained, soiled, 1st 40pp wrinkled), o/w Good. *Worldwide.* $35/£22

CAPPS, STEPHEN R. Geology of the Alaska Railroad Region. Washington: GPO, 1940. USGS Bull 907. 7 plts, 3 Fine lg color maps in pocket. Fine in ptd wrap. *Parmer.* $60/£38

CAPPS, STEPHEN R. and J. B. MERTIE. Geology of the Upper Matanuska Valley, Alaska. Washington: GPO, 1927. USGS Bull 791. 16 plts, 2 maps in pocket. VG in ptd wraps. *Parmer.* $35/£22

CAPSTICK, PETER HATHAWAY. Last Horizons. Mississippi, 1989. 1st ed. #322/2500 signed. Silken eps; aeg. Dec gilt mod morocco. *Edwards.* $47/£30

CAPSTICK, PETER HATHAWAY. Maneaters. Mississippi, 1981. 1st ed. #322/5000 signed. Silken eps; aeg. Dec gilt mod morocco. *Edwards.* $55/£35

CARD, ORSON SCOTT. Hot Sleep. NY: Baronet, (1979). 1st ed. Wrappers. *Swann*.* $92/£59

CARD, ORSON SCOTT. The Memory of Earth. NY: Tor, (1992). 1st ed. One of 300 (of 325) numbered, signed. Imitation leather. Pub's imitation leather slipcase. *Swann*.* $69/£44

CARD, ORSON SCOTT. A Planet Called Treason. NY: St. Martins, (1979). 1st ed. NF- in NF dj (1/4-inch closed tear). *Other Worlds.* $85/£54

CARD, ORSON SCOTT. Songmaster. NY: Dial, (1980). 1st ed. NF in dj (nicked). *Other Worlds.* $100/£64

CARD, ORSON SCOTT. Xenocide. NY: Tor, 1991. 1st ed. One of 300 numbered, signed. Leather. Slipcase. *Swann*.* $103/£66

CARDUCCI, CARLO. Gold and Silver Treasures of Ancient Italy. Greenwich, CT: NYGS, (1963). 1st ed. 95 plts. Gray cl, gilt. Good in illus dj (sl chipped). *Karmiole.* $50/£32

CAREW, JAN. The Third Gift. Boston: Little, Brown, (1974). 1st ed. The Dillons (illus). Fine in NF dj (sm tear, sl rubbed). *Between The Covers.* $75/£48

CAREW, THOMAS. A Rapture. London: Golden Cockerel, 1927. One of 375 numbered. *Swann*.* $80/£51

CAREY, A. MERWYN. American Firearms Makers. Crowell, 1953. 1st ed. VG (spotting, mostly eps; shelfworn) in dj (edgeworn). *My Bookhouse.* $35/£22

CAREY, EDITH F. Channel Islands. A&C Black, 1904. 1st ed. Fldg map, 76 color plts, guards. Teg, others uncut. Dec cl (sl shaken, backstrip dull, sl rubbed). Sound. *Cox.* $70/£45

CAREY, H. C. The Slave Trade, Domestic and Foreign. Phila: Parry & McMillan, 1856. 2nd ed. (2),426pp. (Shelfworn, edgeworn, spine top discolored), else Good. *Brown.* $100/£64

CAREY, H. E. One River. Falcon Press, 1952. 1st ed. Dj (chipped). *Edwards.* $31/£20

CAREY, HENRY. The Thrilling Story of Famous Boot Hill. Dodge City: Herbert Etrick, 1937. 1st ed. Good in wraps. *Perier.* $15/£10

CAREY, PETER with RAY LAWRENCE. Bliss—The Film. Faber, 1986. Pb orig. Fine. *Williams.* $19/£12

CAREY, PETER. The Fat Man in History. London, 1980. 1st Eng ed, 1st bk. Very Nice (sl bumped) in dj. *Clearwater.* $55/£35

CAREY, PETER. Oscar and Lucinda. Faber & Faber, (1988). 1st ed. Nice in dj (sl mkd). *Ash.* $31/£20

CAREY, PETER. The Tax Inspector. Faber, 1991. 1st UK ed. Fine in dj. *Williams.* $19/£12

CAREY, PETER. The Tax Inspector. NY, 1992. 1st Amer ed. Signed. Fine in dj. *Polyanthos.* $30/£19

CAREY, PETER. The Tax Inspector. NY: Knopf, 1992. 1st Amer ed. Signed. VF in Fine dj. *Revere.* $35/£22

CAREY, S. P. William Carey. London, 1923. 2nd ed. (1 plt loose, sl frayed; cl scuffed.) *Maggs.* $17/£11

CAREY, WILLIAM. Travel and Adventure in Tibet. London: Hodder & Stoughton, 1902. 1st ed. Grn pict cl. (Contents shaken), else VG. *Terramedia.* $200/£128

CAREY, WILLIAM. Travel and Adventure in Tibet. London: Hodder & Stoughton, 1902. 1st ed. 285pp (lib stamp tp). Pict grn cl stamped in white, spine gilt. VG. *Sotheran.* $226/£145

CAREY, WILLIAM. Wrecked on the Fejees. Nantucket: Inquirer/Mirror, 1928. Internally Fine. Ptd wraps (corners chipped), stapled as issued. *Parmer.* $47/£30

CARILLO, CHARLES. Shepherd Avenue. Boston/NY: Atlantic Monthly, 1986. 1st ed. Brn cl-backed rust bds (sl bumped), gilt. NF in Fine dj. *Blue Mountain.* $20/£13

CARINS, M. L. Grand Lake (Colorado): The Pioneers. Denver: World, 1946. 1st ed. VG+. *Mikesh.* $45/£29

CARLE, ERIC. The Bad-Tempered Ladybug. London: Hamish Hamilton, 1977. 1st ed. 8 1/2 x 8 3/4. 16pp. Glossy bds. Fine. *Cattermole.* $25/£16

CARLE, ERIC. The Mixed-Up Chameleon. NY: Crowell, 1975. 1st ed. 8 1/2 x 11 1/2. 28pp. Cl spine, glossy bds. VG. *Cattermole.* $40/£26

CARLETON, J. H. The Battle of Buena Vista. NY: Harper, 1848. 2 fldg maps (lt foxed, short tears). Mod simulated 1/2 morocco, marbled bds. Binding NF (contents lt foxed). *Waverly*.* $71/£46

CARLETON, J. H. The Prairie Logbooks. Chicago: Caxton Club, 1943. Ltd to 300 ptd. Teg. Blue cl-backed brn bds, spine gilt. Very Nice. *Cady.* $50/£32

CARLEY, KENNETH. Minnesota in the Civil War. Minneapolis, (1961). 1st ed. Fine in Fine dj. *Pratt.* $32/£21

CARLING, JOHN. The Weird Picture. Little Brown, 1905. 1st ed. VG (bkpl, name) in pict cl. *Certo.* $25/£16

CARLISLE, ANTHONY. An Essay on the Disorders of Old Age, and on the Means for Prolonging Human Life. Phila: Edward Earle, 1819. 1st Amer ed. iv,(5)-74pp (new extra eps, lt marginal dampstains, lt pencil underlining). Untrimmed, unopened. Mod brushed calf, morocco label fr cvr. VG. *Glaser.* $175/£112

CARLISLE, D. T. The Belvidere Hounds. NY: Derrydale, 1935. One of 1250. Cl-backed pict bds (sl soiled, worn). Contents VG. *Waverly*.* $88/£56

CARLL, LEWIS BUFFETT. A Treatise on the Calculus of Variations. NY: John Wiley, 1881. 1st ed. xvii,568pp (lacks fep). VG. *Glaser.* $135/£87

CARLQUIST, SHERWIN. Hawaii: A Natural History. NY: Natural History Press, 1970. 1st ed. Fine in Fine dj. *Book Market.* $75/£48

CARLSON, NATALIE SAVAGE. Alphonse That Bearded One. NY: Harcourt, Brace, 1954. 1st ed. Nicolas Mordvinoff (illus). 6 1/2 x 8 1/4. 78pp. Fine (lt soil fep) in dj. *Cattermole.* $60/£38

CARLUCCIO, LUIGI. Alberto Giacometti: A Sketchbook of Interpretive Drawings. NY: Abrams, n.d. (Pp, dj sunned around edges.) *Metropolitan*.* $115/£74

CARLYLE, ALEXANDER. Autobiography. Edinburgh: Blackwood, 1861. 3rd ed. Frontis. Uncut. Good. *Stewart.* $31/£20

CARLYLE, J. D. Poems Suggested Chiefly by Scenes in Asia-Minor, Syria, and Greece.... London: Ptd by William Bulmer, 1805. 1st ed. 149pp; 2 engr views. Orig full leather (spine rough, outer hinges cracked, extrems worn). Contents VG. *New Hampshire*.* $60/£38

CARLYLE, J. D. Specimens of Arabian Poetry. Cambridge, 1796. Full red morocco. (Inscrip; neatly re-backed), o/w VG. *Petersfield.* $122/£78

CARLYLE, JANE WELSH. Letters and Memorials of.... James Anthony Froude (ed). London: Longmans, Green, 1883. 1st ed. 3 vols. 397; 399; 341pp + 24pp ads. (Sl nick spine top vol 1), o/w Fine. *Second Life.* $125/£80

CARLYLE, JANE WELSH. New Letters and Memorials of Jane Welsh Carlyle. NY: John Lane, 1903. 1st ed. 2 vols. Red cl. VG (ink name, wear). *Antic Hay.* $50/£32

CARLYLE, THOMAS. New Letters of Thomas Carlyle. NY: John Lane, 1904. 1st ed. 2 vols. Red cl. VG (wear, browning, ink name). *Antic Hay.* $50/£32

CARLYLE, THOMAS. Oliver Cromwell's Letters and Speeches: With Elucidations. London: Chapman & Hall, 1850. 3rd ed. 4 vols. Frontis port. Marbled eps, edges. Period tan calf, gilt, brn/dk blue morocco spine labels. (Bkpls, name stamps; rear cvr vol 1 nearly detached, spine chipped), else NF set. *Pacific*.* $86/£55

CARLYLE, THOMAS. Past and Present. London: Chapman & Hall, 1843. 1st ed (2000 ptd). Orig cl stamped in gilt/blind. (Inner hinges cracking, top edge spotted, spine frayed), else Good. *Reese.* $75/£48

CARLYLE, THOMAS. Sartor Resartus. London: Geo. Bell, 1898. 1st ed w/these illus. Edmund J. Sullivan (illus). Gilt-stamped cl, gilt top. Fine. *Appelfeld.* $85/£54

CARLYLE, THOMAS. Sartor Resartus. (Hammersmith, 1907.) One of 300. (Fore-edges sl spotted.) Limp vellum. Cl slipcase. *Swann*.* $316/£203

CARLYLE, THOMAS. Selected Works, Reminiscences and Letters. Julian Symons (ed). Rupert Hart-Davis, 1955. VG. *Cox.* $19/£12

CARMALT, C. et al. Studies in Cancer and Allied Subjects. Vol IV. NY, 1913. 100 plts. (Sl worn, bkpl fep), o/w VG. *Whitehart.* $55/£35

CARMAN, BLISS. Ode on the Coronation of King Edward. Boston: L.C. Page, 1902. 1st public ed. Inscribed, signed. Good (edgewear). BAL 2651. *Reese.* $45/£29

CARMER, CARL. The Hudson. NY: Rinehart, 1938. 1st ed. Good (spine sunned). *Archer.* $12/£8

CARNAC, CAROL. Copy for Crime. GC: DCC, 1951. 1st ed. Fine in dj (sl worn). *Else Fine.* $30/£19

CARNAC, CAROL. A Double for Detection. London: Macdonald, 1945. 1st ed. Fine in dj (sl wear spine ends, corners). *Mordida.* $75/£48

CARNE, JOHN. Syria, the Holy Land and Asia Minor. London: Peter Jackson, Late Fisher, mid 19th cent. 3 vols. 122 b/w engrs, 2 maps. (Foxing.) Gilt-dec red cl (rubbed, bumped, torn at tips). *Metropolitan*.* $287/£184

CARNE, JOHN. Syria, the Holy Land.... London: Fisher, (1836-1838). 1st ed. 3 vols. Engr title each vol, 117 engr plts, 2 engr maps (spotting). Gilt edges. Contemp morocco (extrems lt worn), gilt. *Christie's*.* $526/£337

CARNEGIE, ANDREW. An American Four-in-Hand in Britain. NY: Scribner, 1907. Later ed. 1911 signed presentation. Black coated eps. Red cl (lt worn, spine sl dknd; name erased, sm hole tp, ink stamps blanks), gilt. *Baltimore*.* $40/£26

CARNOCHAN, F. G. and H. C. ADAMSON. The Empire of the Snakes. NY: Stokes, 1935. 2nd ptg. 15 photo plts. Grn cl. VG in dj (torn). *Price.* $24/£15

CARNOT, S. Reflections on the Motive Power of Heat.... R. H. Thurston (trans). NY: Amer Soc of Mechanical Engineers, 1943. Frontis port. Ptd bds, cl spine. VG. *Glaser.* $60/£38

CAROLINO, PEDRO. The New Guide of the Conversation in Portuguese and English in Two Parts. Mark Twain (intro). Boston: James R. Osgood, 1883. 1st ed. (xiv)(182)pp. Unbound, uncut, unopened. Laid in cl folder; 1/2 blue morocco slipcase, ribbed gilt-lettered spine. Mint. BAL 3412. *D & D.* $400/£256

CAROLINO, PEDRO. The New Guide of the Conversation in Portuguese and English. Boston: James R. Osgood, 1883. 1st ed. Orig flexible brn cl lettered in black. Fine (sl rubbed). BAL 3412. *Macdonnell.* $250/£160

CARPENTER, EDMUND. They Became What They Beheld. NY: Outerbridge & Dienstfrey/Ballantine Book, 1970. 1st ed. (Owner stamp), else VG in silver-foil illus dj. *Cahan.* $35/£22

CARPENTER, EDWARD (ed). A House of Kings. London, 1966. 1st ed. 3 color plts. Dj (sl chipped, soiled). *Edwards.* $39/£25

CARPENTER, EDWARD. Pagan and Christian Creeds: Their Origin and Meaning. NY, (1920). 1st Amer ed. Fine (spine sl rubbed). *Polyanthos.* $30/£19

CARPENTER, EDWIN (ed). A Bibliography of the Writings of Noah Webster. Emily Ellsworth Ford Skeel (comp). NY Public Library, 1958. One of 500. 26 full-pg illus. *Dawson.* $60/£38

CARPENTER, G. A Naturalist in East Africa. Oxford, 1925. Map, 2 color plts. (Sl soiled, worn.) *Maggs.* $59/£38

CARPENTER, HUMPHREY. The Inklings. London, 1978. 1st ed. Dj. *Typographeum.* $20/£13

CARPENTER, R. R. M. Game Trails in Idaho and Alaska. Privately ptd, (1940). 1st ed. #67/400. Inscribed. Blue cl, gilt title on brn field upper cvr (cvrs soiled). Internally Fine. *Cummins.* $325/£208

CARPENTER, WILLIAM B. Introduction to the Study of the Foraminifera. London, 1862. xxii,319pp; 22 plts (waterstained). *Henly.* $75/£48

CARPENTER, WILLIAM B. The Microscope and Its Revelations. London: Churchill, 1881. 6th ed. Frontis, xxxii,882pp + 8pp ads; 25 plts. VG (spine sl worn). *Savona.* $94/£60

CARPENTER, WILLIAM B. The Microscope and Its Revelations. Phila: Presley Blakiston, 1881. 6th ed. 882pp; 26 plts. Blind-stamped cl. (Ex-lib, lib seal stamped to verso of plts, loose in binding.) *Argosy.* $125/£80

CARPENTER, WILLIAM B. The Microscope and Its Revelations. Wood, 1883. 2 vols. (Ex-lib, rubber stamp title leaves; corner tip, head of backstrip worn), o/w Good+. *Bookcell.* $60/£38

CARPENTER, WILLIAM B. The Microscope and Its Revelations. W.H. Dallinger (ed). London: J. & A. Churchill, 1891. 7th ed. Frontis. (Lt spotting.) Pub's cl (spine ends sl worn, extrems rubbed). *Christie's*.* $70/£45

CARPENTER, WILLIAM B. Principles of Human Physiology. London: Churchill, 1846. 3rd ed. xxiv,776pp + 32pp pub's cat; 3 plts, 175 engrs. Orig cl (rebacked), orig spine relaid. Good (bkpl, plts foxed). *Savona.* $70/£45

CARPENTER, WILLIAM B. Principles of Mental Physiology.... 1896. 7th ed. lxiii,737pp. (Eps lt foxed, fep discolored; hinges, sections cracked; spine, corners sl worn.) *Whitehart.* $62/£40

CARPENTIER, ALEJO. The Kingdom of This World. LEC, (1987). Ltd to 750. Signed by John Hersey (intro) and Roberto Juarez (illus). Orig prospectus laid in. Hand bound in 1/2 black Nigerian Oasis goatskin over burgundy Japanese cl bds. Mint in orig slipcase. *Truepenny.* $400/£256

CARR, CALEB. Casing the Promised Land. NY: Harper, 1980. 1st ed, 1st bk. Fine in dj (sm closed tear). *Else Fine.* $150/£96

CARR, CAMILLUS. A Cavalryman in Indian Country. Ashland: Lewis Osborne, 1974. 1st ed in bk form. One of 600. 1/2 cl, paper-cvrd bds, paper spine label. (Sl bumped), else NF. *Brown.* $35/£22

CARR, HERBERT R. C. and GEORGE A. LISTER. The Mountains of Snowdonia. London, 1925. 1st ed. Color frontis. (Feps lt browned; spine lt faded, chipped.) *Edwards.* $78/£50

CARR, J. COMYNS. Coasting Bohemia. London: Macmillan, 1914. 1st ed. (Sl rubbed), o/w VG. *Worldwide.* $15/£10

CARR, JAMES F. (comp). Mantle Fielding's Dictionary of American Painters, Sculptors and Engravers. NY, 1965. (Fore-edge splashed), else VG. *Waverly*.* $44/£28

CARR, JOHN DICKSON. Dark of the Moon. NY: Harper & Row, 1967. 1st ed. Fine in dj. *Mordida.* $45/£29

CARR, JOHN DICKSON. Death-Watch. NY: Harper, 1935. 1st ed. Fine (name, corner bump; lacks dj). *Janus.* $50/£32

CARR, JOHN DICKSON. The Hungry Goblin. NY: Harper & Row, (1972). 1st ed. Fine in dj (lt worn). *Hermitage.* $40/£26

CARR, JOHN DICKSON. The Life of Sir Arthur Conan Doyle. NY: Harper, (1949). 1st US ed. Good (cvrs worn, 2 tape remnants fep). *Gravesend.* $25/£16

CARR, JOHN DICKSON. The Life of Sir Arthur Conan Doyle. NY: Harper, (1949). 1st ed. VG in dj (chipped, edgeworn, sig). *Turtle Island.* $35/£22

CARR, JOHN DICKSON. The Life of Sir Arthur Conan Doyle. London: John Murray, 1949. 1st ed. (Initials fep, edges foxed), o/w VG in dj (price-clipped, internal tape mends). *Mordida.* $55/£35

CARR, JOHN DICKSON. Scandal at High Chimneys. London, 1959. 1st ed. NF in dj (few spine nicks). *Polyanthos.* $35/£22

CARR, JOHN DICKSON. The Third Bullet and Other Stories. NY: Harper, 1954. 1st ed. Fine (corner sl bumped) in NF dj. *Janus.* $85/£54

CARR, JOHN DICKSON. The Waxworks Murder. Melbourne/London: George Jaboor/Hamish Hamilton, (1944). 1st Australian ed. Stapled wrappers. (Paper browned, sm dampstain rear panel), else VG. *Turtle Island.* $55/£35

CARR, JOHN. Pioneer Days in California: Historical and Personal Sketches. Eureka: Times Pub Co, 1891. 1st ed. Frontis port, 452pp. Blue cl (spotted; corners, spine ends very worn; gilt rubbed away). Internally Fine, but Good-. Howes C167. *Harrington.* $150/£96

CARR, JOHN. Pioneer Days in California: Historical and Personal Sketches. Eureka: Times Pub Co, 1891. 1st ed. Frontis port, 452pp. Grn cl, gilt spine. (Tp partly detached; gilt dull), o/w NF. Howes C167. *Pacific*.* $195/£125

CARR, JOHN. A Vulcan Among the Argonauts. SF: George Fields, 1936. One of 500. Signed by Robin Lampson (ed). Pict tan cl. Fine. *Argonaut.* $75/£48

CARR, M. F. Life Among the Shakers. NY: Wemple, (188-). 1st ed. 36pp. Color litho cvrs. Fine. *Agvent.* $125/£80

CARR, ROBERT. Beyond Infinity. Reading, PA: Fantasy Press, 1951. 1st ed. 12mo. VG+ in VG dj. *Book Adoption.* $35/£22

CARR, ROBERT. Cowboy Lyrics. Chicago: Conkey, 1908. 1st ed. Teg. Grn cl, gilt. (Few pp torn), o/w VG. *Archer.* $25/£16

CARRINGTON, FRANCES C. My Army Life and the Fort Phil. Kearney Massacre.... Phila/London: Lippincott, 1910. 1st ed. 3 maps. Dk grn ribbed cl. (Text lt aged, ink handstamp.) Howes C172. *Baltimore*.* $35/£22

CARRINGTON, FRANCES C. My Army Life and the Fort Phil. Kearney Massacre.... Phila: Lippincott, 1911. Fldg map. Good (cvrs sl spotted). Howes C172. *Lien.* $65/£42

CARRINGTON, MARGARET I. Absaraka Home of the Crows. Milo M. Quaife (ed). Chicago: Lakeside, Christmas, 1950. Dk red cl (sl spotted). *Sadlon.* $20/£13

CARROLL, B. R. (ed). Historical Collections of South Carolina. NY: Harper, 1836. 1st ed. 2 vols. Lg fldg map. (Paper spine labels worn off, white lib #s spines.) Contents VG. Howes C178. *New Hampshire*.* $260/£167

CARROLL, DANIEL B. Henri Mercier and the American Civil War. Princeton, 1971. 1st ed. Fine in Fine dj. *Pratt.* $25/£16

CARROLL, H. BAILEY. The Texan Santa Fe Trail. Canyon, TX: Panhandle Plains Hist Soc, 1951. 1st ed. Box, ptd spine label. *Ginsberg.* $150/£96

CARROLL, H. BAILEY. The Texan Santa Fe Trail. Canyon, TX: Panhandle-Plains Hist Soc, 1951. 1st ed. Inscribed. Fine in slipcase (top edge taped). *Gibbs.* $125/£80

CARROLL, JAMES A. The First Ten Years. Memoirs of a Fort Yukon Trapper, 1911-1922. NY: Exposition Press, (1957). 1st ed. Signed. Author's photo laid in. VG in dj (edgetorn). *Perier.* $40/£26

CARROLL, JIM. The Book of Nods. (NY): Viking, (1986). 1st ed. Advance rev copy w/slip, photo of Carroll, publicity release laid in. New in New dj. *Bernard.* $75/£48

CARROLL, JOHN M. (ed). The Arrest and Killing of Sitting Bull. Glendale: Clark, 1986. 1st ed. One of 350 numbered, signed. Color frontis. Dec cl, red/blue guidon. *Ginsberg.* $125/£80

CARROLL, JOHN M. The Black Military Experience in the American West. NY: Liveright, (1971). 1st trade ed. 63 full-pg illus. Pict eps. VG in pict dj. *Petrilla.* $95/£61

CARROLL, JOHN M. (ed). The Papers of the Order of Indian Wars. Fort Collins, (1975). 1st ed. Fine in dj (lt worn, chipped, 2 sm tears repaired w/tape). *Pratt.* $55/£35

CARROLL, LEWIS. (Pseud of C. L. Dodgson.) Alice in Wonderland and Through the Looking-Glass and What Alice Found There. Chicago: Rand McNally, (1916). Lg 8vo. 242pp; 14 full-pg color plts by Milo Winter. Dk grn linen, gilt, pict label. Fine. *Bromer.* $100/£64

CARROLL, LEWIS. (Pseud of C. L. Dodgson.) Alice in Wonderland. Girard, KS: Haldeman-Julius, n.d. 1st Haldeman-Julius ed. 12mo. 115pp + (5)pp ads. (Edges browned), else Nice in blue-gray wrappers. *Turtle Island.* $15/£10

CARROLL, LEWIS. (Pseud of C. L. Dodgson.) Alice in Wonderland. London/Melbourne/Toronto: Ward, Lock, n.d. (1916). 2nd Tarrant ed. 8vo. 48 color plts by Margaret Tarrant. Forest grn cl, color pict cvr pastedown. (Lt foxed), else Fine. *Glenn.* $110/£71

CARROLL, LEWIS. (Pseud of C. L. Dodgson.) Alice Through the Looking Glass. Max Parrish, 1950. 1st ed thus. Lg 8vo. 151pp; 8 color plts by Hugh Gee. Pict bds, cl spine. VG in pict dj (defective). *Bookmark.* $47/£30

CARROLL, LEWIS. (Pseud of C. L. Dodgson.) Alice's Adventures in Wonderland and Through the Looking Glass. NY: Harper, c. (1949). Folio. 160pp; 24 full-pg color illus by Leonard Weisgard. Grn illus eps. VG in VG dj (edges sl chipped). *Dower.* $50/£32

CARROLL, LEWIS. (Pseud of C. L. Dodgson.) Alice's Adventures in Wonderland and Through the Looking Glass. Collins, n.d. (1930 inscrip). Lg 4to. 143pp (mks, sl spotted); 8 mtd color plts by Harry Rountree, tissue guard remnants. Gilt-pict grn cl (spine faded). Good+. *Bookmark.* $28/£18

CARROLL, LEWIS. (Pseud of C. L. Dodgson.) Alice's Adventures in Wonderland. Berkeley: Univ of CA, (1982). 1st ptg of trade ed. Folio. Orig wood engr initialed by Barry Moser. Red cl. Red cl portfolio; both in red cl slipcase. *Waverly*.* $104/£67

CARROLL, LEWIS. (Pseud of C. L. Dodgson.) Alice's Adventures in Wonderland. Boston: Lee & Shepard, 1869. 1st ed ptd in America. Aeg. Orig grn cl, gilt. Bright (recased, spine ends reinforced; long tear 1 leaf repaired). *Macdonnell.* $600/£385

CARROLL, LEWIS. (Pseud of C. L. Dodgson.) Alice's Adventures in Wonderland. Boston, 1872. Early ed. John Tenniel (illus). 7.5x5. 192pp. (Long ink inscrip, inner fr hinge cracked; worn, frayed, binding broken.) *King.* $35/£22

CARROLL, LEWIS. (Pseud of C. L. Dodgson.) Alice's Adventures in Wonderland. NY: LEC, 1932. #832/1500 ptd by William Edwin Rudge, designed by Frederic Warde. John Tenniel (illus). Full dec gilt brn morocco. Fine in slipcase (sl dknd). *Hermitage.* $300/£192

CARROLL, LEWIS. (Pseud of C. L. Dodgson.) Alice's Adventures in Wonderland. CA: Pennyroyal, 1982. 1st ed. Barry Moser (illus). Pub's cl-backed bds. Dj. *D & D.* $125/£80

CARROLL, LEWIS. (Pseud of C. L. Dodgson.) Alice's Adventures in Wonderland. John Lane/Bodley Head, n.d. Lg 8vo. 152pp (eps lt foxed, spots); 8 color plts by W. H. Walker. Illus brn cl. VG+. *Bookmark.* $55/£35

CARROLL, LEWIS. (Pseud of C. L. Dodgson.) Alice's Adventures in Wonderland...with a Poem by Austin Dobson. London, (1907). One of 1130 numbered. 4to. 13 tipped-in color plts by Arthur Rackham, guards. Pict eps. Orig white cl (spine lt soiled; feps browned), gilt. *Swann*.* $1,150/£737

CARROLL, LEWIS. (Pseud of Charles L. Dodgson.) Alice's Adventures Under Ground. London: Macmillan, 1886. 1st ed. 12mo. Orig red cl lettered in gilt. Fine. *Cummins.* $750/£481

CARROLL, LEWIS. (Pseud of C. L. Dodgson.) Alice's Adventures Underground. London: Macmillan, 1886. 1st ed, 1st binding. Aeg. Red cl, gilt. VG (fr hinge cracked). *Macdonnell.* $150/£96

CARROLL, LEWIS. (Pseud of C. L. Dodgson.) Feeding the Mind. London: C&W, 1906. 1st ed. Cl, ptd bds. VG. *Antic Hay.* $125/£80

CARROLL, LEWIS. (Pseud of C. L. Dodgson.) The Hunting of the Snark. Boston: James R. Osgood, 1876. 1st Amer ed. 12mo. 9 illus by Henry Holliday. Pict bds (spine, tips rubbed, sm paper loss extrems). *Swann*.* $632/£405

CARROLL, LEWIS. (Pseud of Charles L. Dodgson.) The Hunting of the Snark. London: Macmillan, 1876. 1st ed. Henry Holiday (illus). Aeg. Pub's black-stamped gray/tan cl (lt overall browning, spine head, foot sl rubbed). *D & D.* $650/£417

CARROLL, LEWIS. (Pseud of C. L. Dodgson.) The Letters of Lewis Carroll. Morton N. Cohen (ed). NY: OUP, 1979. 2 vols. Frontispieces. Blue cl, gilt. Fine in VG violet dec slipcase (bumped, corners chipped). *Blue Mountain.* $45/£29

CARROLL, LEWIS. (Pseud of C. L. Dodgson.) The Letters of Lewis Carroll. Morton N. Cohen (ed). NY: OUP, 1979. 1st Amer ed. 2 vols. Fine set in pub's slipcase (lt worn). *Hermitage.* $60/£38

CARROLL, LEWIS. (Pseud of C. L. Dodgson.) Phantasmagoria and Other Poems. London: Macmillan, 1869. 1st ed, 1st issue, w/integral title-leaf. Sm 8vo. viii,202pp (inner joints broken). Aeg. Gilt-pict blue cl (shelfworn, spine tips sl chipped). *Oinonen*.* $70/£45

CARROLL, LEWIS. (Pseud of C. L. Dodgson.) Sylvie and Bruno Concluded. London: Macmillan, 1893. 1st Eng ed, 1st issue, w/chapter 8 in table of contents given as pg 110 instead of pg 113. Aeg. Red cl, gilt. NF (foxing, scattered spotting to eps). *Antic Hay.* $125/£80

CARROLL, LEWIS. (Pseud of C. L. Dodgson.) Sylvie and Bruno. Macmillan, 1889. 1st ed. 8vo. xxiii,400pp,3pp ads; 46 illus by Harry Furniss. Aeg. Red cl (rubbed, spine chipped, worn), gilt-pict roundels. Internally VG. *Bookmark.* $34/£22

CARROLL, LEWIS. (Pseud of C. L. Dodgson.) Sylvie and Bruno. Macmillan, 1890. 1st Amer ed. 5x8. 395pp. Red cl, gilt. VG (lacks flyleaf; bumped, shelfworn). *My Bookhouse.* $50/£32

CARROLL, LEWIS. (Pseud of C. L. Dodgson.) A Tangled Tale. London, 1885. 1st ed. A.B. Frost (illus). Sm 8vo. Aeg. Gilt-pict red cl (sl worn, soiled). *Freeman*.* $30/£19

CARROLL, LEWIS. (Pseud of C. L. Dodgson.) Through the Looking Glass and What Alice Found There. Boston/NY: Lee & Shepard/Dillingham, 1872. 1st Amer ed w/imprint and error p21. John Tenniel (illus). 8vo. Blue cl (cocked, spine dknd, ends frayed). Good. *Waverly*.* $93/£60

CARROLL, LEWIS. (Pseud of C. L. Dodgson.) Through the Looking Glass and What Alice Found There. NY/London: Harper, 1902. Peter Newell (illus). 8vo. Frontis port, xvi,211pp; 40 full-pg plts. VF (inscrip) in crimson cl, gilt, protected by matching canvas dj (bottom wear, spine sunned). *Bromer.* $175/£112

CARROLL, LEWIS. (Pseud of C. L. Dodgson.) Through the Looking Glass and What Alice Found There. NY: Harper, 1902. 1st ed thus. Peter Newell (illus). 8vo. VG (sig; lt soiled, worn). *Waverly*.* $77/£49

CARROLL, LEWIS. (Pseud of C. L. Dodgson.) Through the Looking Glass and What Alice Found There. NY/London: Harper, 1912. 8vo. Photogravure frontis port, 40 full-pg illus by Peter Newell. Pict white bds. *Swann*.* $69/£44

CARROLL, LEWIS. (Pseud of Charles L. Dodgson.) Through the Looking Glass.... London, 1872. 1st ed, 1st state, w/'wade' on p21. 1/2 blue morocco (rebound; cvrs, feps detached, spine lacks pieces; lt offset ink stains 2pp). *Kane*.* $225/£144

CARROLL, REBECCA. I Know What the Red Clay Looks Like. NY: Crown Trade Paperbacks, 1994. Uncorrected proof. Fine in illus red wraps (sm nudge). *Lame Duck.* $45/£29

CARRUTH, HAYDEN. Loneliness, An Outburst of Hexasyllables. (West Burke, VT): Janus Press, 1976. Ltd to 150 signed by Carruth and Claire Van Vliet (illus). 8vo. (16)pp, frenchfold. 2 color relief prints. Ptd on Japanese paper. Blue cl. VF. *Bromer.* $175/£112

CARRUTH, HAYDEN. The Norfolk Poems of Hayden Carruth (1 June to 1 September 1961). Iowa City: Prairie, (1962). 1st ed. Fine in dj. *Graf.* $35/£22

CARSE, ROBERT. Department of the South. Columbia, 1961. 1st ed. Fine in dj (3 sm pieces torn away). *Pratt.* $60/£38

CARSON, EDWARD. The War on German Submarines.... London: T. Fisher Unwin, 1917. 1st separate ed. NF in ptd self wrappers (ink name). *Reese.* $20/£13

CARSON, JOHN. Doc Middleton, the Unwickedest Outlaw. (Santa Fe: Press of the Territorian, 1966.) 1st ed. One of 1000. Port. Fine in wraps. *Bohling.* $20/£13

CARSON, RACHEL L. Under the Sea-Wind. NY: S&S, 1941. 1st ed, 1st bk. (Sm lt stain prelim pg), else Fine in VG- dj (2 chips; dampstaining, scraping top edge). *Between The Covers.* $125/£80

CARSON, RACHEL. Silent Spring. Boston: Houghton, Mifflin, 1962. 1st ed. NF (top edge lt spotted) in dj (tape repairs; price-clipped, worn). *Antic Hay.* $75/£48

CARSTENSEN, A. RIIS. Two Summers in Greenland. London: Chapman & Hall, 1890. 1st ed. xxxipp, 28 full-pg illus, fldg map at rear. Pict blue cl, gilt. Attractive (corners sl bumped). *Sotheran.* $200/£128

CARTER, ANGELA. Nights at the Circus. C&W/Hogarth, (1984). 1st ed. Nice (sl bruised) in dj. *Ash.* $31/£20

CARTER, ANGELA. Sleeping Beauty and Other Fairy Tales. NY: Schocken, 1984. 1st US ed. Michael Foreman (illus). 8 x 11 1/4. 128pp. VG in dj. *Cattermole.* $32/£21

CARTER, DAGNY. Four Thousand Years of China's Art. NY: Ronald, 1948. 1st ed. Map. (Cl sl rubbed), o/w VG. *Worldwide.* $45/£29

CARTER, FORREST. The Vengeance Trail of Josey Wales. (NY): Delacorte, (1976). Fine in Fine dj (sm crease fr flap). *Between The Covers.* $275/£176

CARTER, FREDERICK. D.H. Lawrence and the Body Mystical. London: Denis Archer, 1932. 1st ed. #69/250. Frontis port. Paper over thin bds, dec cvr. Good-. *Scribe's Perch*.* $50/£32

CARTER, GEORGE GOLDSMITH. Forgotten Ports of England. London: Evans, 1952. Frontis map. (Cl sl spotted.) Dj (short tear to top of upper hinge). *Hollett.* $70/£45

CARTER, H. B. His Majesty's Spanish Flock. Sydney, 1964. Dj (sl worn). *Maggs.* $31/£20

CARTER, HARRY. Wolvercote Mill: A Study in Paper-Making at Oxford. Oxford: OUP, 1957. 1st ed. Color frontis. Blue cl. Fine in dj. *House.* $65/£42

CARTER, HARVEY LEWIS. Dear Old Kit. Norman: Univ of OK, (1968). 1st ed. 5 maps. VF in dj. *Argonaut.* $125/£80

CARTER, HODDING. Doomed Road of Empire, The Spanish Trail of Conquest. NY: McGraw-Hill, (1963). 1st ed. Red cl. Fine in dj (spine dknd). *Argonaut.* $35/£22

CARTER, HODDING. Flood Crest. NY: Rinehart, (1947). 1st ed. VG in dj (internal archival tissue reinforcements). *Turtle Island.* $30/£19

CARTER, HODDING. Flood Crest. NY: Rinehart, (1947). 1st ed. Very Nice in VG dj (lt shelfworn). *Reese.* $50/£32

CARTER, JOHN (ed). Clerihews, an Unofficial Supplement to 'Biography for Beginners.' (Cambridge): Rampant Lions, 1938. NF in black ptd wrappers. *Heller.* $75/£48

CARTER, JOHN and PERCY H. MUIR. Printing and the Mind of Man. London/NY: Cassell/Holt, Rinehart & Winston, (1967). 1st ed. Brick-red cl, gilt. VG dj (price-clipped). *Baltimore*.* $80/£51

CARTER, JOHN and PERCY H. MUIR. Printing and the Mind of Man. NY: Holt, Rinehart, & Winston, (1967). 1st Amer ed. NF in dj. *Waverly*.* $88/£56

CARTER, JOHN and PERCY H. MUIR. Printing and the Mind of Man. London/NY: Cassell/Holt, Rinehart, Winston, 1967. 1st ed. VF in dj (spine sl browned). *Pirages.* $100/£64

CARTER, JOHN and GRAHAM POLLARD. An Enquiry into the Nature of Certain Nineteenth Century Pamphlets. London/NY, 1934. 1st ed. Red cl (sl askew, spine faded). *Swann*.* $92/£59

CARTER, JOHN and GRAHAM POLLARD. An Enquiry into the Nature of Certain Nineteenth Century Pamphlets. London/NY, 1934. 1st ed. Inscribed, signed by Carter. VG in dj (spine lt faded, sl chipped). *Truepenny.* $350/£224

CARTER, JOHN and GRAHAM POLLARD. An Enquiry into the Nature of Certain Nineteenth Century Pamphlets. London/NY: Constable/Scribner, 1934. 1st ed. 4 plts. VF in dj (sl faded, smudged), vinyl chemise, hard-shell box w/sliding top panel. *Pirages.* $250/£160

CARTER, JOHN and GRAHAM POLLARD. The Firm of Charles Ottley, Landon and Co. Rupert Hart-Davis, 1948. 1st ed. 3 facs plts. Stiff paper wrappers (sl frayed). *Cox.* $31/£20

CARTER, JOHN. ABC for Book Collectors. Hart-Davis, 1952. 1st ed. VG in dj. *Moss.* $34/£22

CARTER, JOHN. Taste and Technique in Book Collecting. NY: R.R. Bowker, 1948. 1st Amer ed. VG in dj (sl frayed). *Reese*. $30/£19

CARTER, JOHN. Victorian Fiction, Exhibition of Original Editions, 1947. London, 1947. Illus ed. VG in dj. *Gretton*. $23/£15

CARTER, LIN. Dreams from R'lyeh. Sauk City: Arkam House, 1975. 1st ed. Fine in Fine dj. *Other Worlds*. $30/£19

CARTER, ROBERT GOLDTHWAITE. Four Brothers in Blue, or Sunshine and Shadows of the War of the Rebellion. Washington: Gibson Bros, 1913. True 1st ed ltd to 80; the 'imperfect' ed because pagination incorporated from journal appearances in the Maine Bugle. This issue more scarce, desirable of the 2 issues because the 'perfect' ed was ltd to 100 and had no plts. VG. *Mcgowan*. $2,250/£1,442

CARTER, SAMUEL, III. The Siege of Atlanta, 1864. NY, (1973). 1st ed. Fine in Fine dj. *Pratt*. $30/£19

CARTER, T. D. Hoofed Mammals of the World. NY: Scribner, (1971). 2nd ed. Blind-stamped silver dec cl. NF in VG dj. *Mikesh*. $45/£29

CARTER, THOMAS. Medals of the British Army. London: Groombridge, 1861. 3 vols in 1. viii,185; x,185; viii,192pp; 19 color plts. 3/4 scarlet levant morocco gilt, raised bands. VG. *Hollett*. $507/£325

CARTIER-BRESSON, HENRI. About Russia. NY: Viking, 1974. 1st ed in English. 141 b/w photo plts. (Sig, 1 sig loose), else Fine in dj. *Cahan*. $75/£48

CARTIER-BRESSON, HENRI. Cartier-Bresson's France. Francois Nourissier (text). NY, (1971). 1st Amer ed. VG in dj. *King*. $50/£32

CARTIER-BRESSON, HENRI. The Decisive Moment. NY, (1952). Pamphlet laid in. (Spine ends lt worn, sl rubbed.) Dj (defective). *Kane**. $225/£144

CARTIER-BRESSON, HENRI. The Decisive Moment. NY/Paris: S&S/Verve, (1952). 1st Amer ed. Pamphlet of descriptions laid in. Pict bds (sl worn, bowed). VG in Good dj (torn, soiled, frayed). *Waverly**. $143/£92

CARTIER-BRESSON, HENRI. The Europeans. S&S/Editions Verve, 1955. 1st ed. VG (sl worn). *Words Etc*. $429/£275

CARTIER-BRESSON, HENRI. The Europeans. NY: S&S, 1955. 1st US ed. 114 full-pg plts. Bk of captions laid in. Illus bds. Fine in glassine dj, ptd flaps. *Cahan*. $550/£353

CARTIER-BRESSON, HENRI. The Face of Asia. NY: Viking, 1972. (Owner stamp), else NF in dj. *Cahan*. $75/£48

CARTIER-BRESSON, HENRI. The Face of Asia. NY: Viking, 1972. 1st ed. NF in NF dj. *Smith*. $100/£64

CARTIER-BRESSON, HENRI. Man and Machines. NY: Viking, 1971. 1st ed. NF in Good dj (badly chipped). *Smith*. $60/£38

CARTIER-BRESSON, HENRI. The People of Moscow. NY, Sept 1955. 1st ed. Coarse-textured cl. VG in dj (chipped). *Scribe's Perch**. $50/£32

CARTIER-BRESSON, HENRI. The Photographs of Henri Cartier-Bresson. NY: MOMA, 1947. 1st ed. Fine in Fine dj. *Smith*. $95/£61

CARTLIDGE, BARBARA. Twentieth-Century Jewelry. NY, (1985). VG in dj. *Argosy*. $85/£54

CARTWRIGHT, JULIA. Italian Gardens of the Renaissance.... London: Smith, 1914. 1st ed. Pub's cl (sl faded, soiled). VG. *Second Life*. $35/£22

CARUSO, JOHN ANTHONY. The Appalachian Frontier. Indianapolis: Bobbs-Merrill, (1959). 1st ed. VG in dj. *Lien*. $40/£26

CARUSO, JOHN ANTHONY. The Great Lakes Frontier. Indianapolis: Bobb-Merrill, (1961). 1st ed. VG in dj. *Lien*. $40/£26

CARUSO, JOHN ANTHONY. The Great Lakes Frontier: An Epic of the Old Northwest. Indianapolis/NY: Bobbs-Merrill, (1961). 1st ed. Fine in NF dj. *Sadlon*. $20/£13

CARUSO, JOHN ANTHONY. The Mississippi Valley Frontier. Indianapolis: Bobbs-Merrill, (1966). 1st ed. VG (lt pencil) in dj. *Lien*. $40/£26

CARUSO, JOHN ANTHONY. The Southern Frontier. Indianapolis: Bobbs-Merrill, (1963). 1st ed. VG in dj. *Lien*. $40/£26

CARUTHERS, WILLIAM. Loafing Along Death Valley Trails. Shoshone: Death Valley, (1951). 2nd ed. Pict cl in Dj. *Dawson*. $20/£13

CARUTHERS, WILLIAM. Loafing Along Death Valley Trails. Palm Desert, CA, 1951. 8 photo plts. Red cl, gilt. VG in dj. *Price*. $48/£31

CARVALHO, SOLOMON NUNES. Incidents of Travel and Adventure in the Far West. Bertram Wallace Korn (ed). Phila: Jewish Pub Soc of America, 1954. Centenary ed. VG in Fine dj. *Bohling*. $35/£22

CARVER, CLIFFORD. Bookplates of Princeton and Princetonians. Princeton, 1912. #139/500 signed. (Lt wear, soil.) *Freeman**. $30/£19

CARVER, JONATHAN. Journals of Jonathan Carver and Related Documents, 1766-1770. John Parker (ed). MN Hist Soc, 1976. Fine in dj (sm tear). *Bohling*. $20/£13

CARVER, JONATHAN. Three Years' Travels Throughout the Interior Part of North America.... Walpole, NH: Isaiah Thomas, 1813. Rpt. 280pp. Orig calf, marbled bds. Good. Howes C215. *Karmiole*. $185/£119

CARVER, JONATHAN. Travels Through the Interior Parts of North America in the Years 1766, 1767, 1768. Dublin: S. Price et al, 1779. 1st Dublin ed. 2 copper engr plts, fldg map. 3/4 calf over marbled bds, leather spine label. (Sm lib stamp), o/w Nice. Howes C215. *Sadlon*. $1,000/£641

CARVER, JONATHAN. Travels Through the Interior Parts of North America, in the Years 1766, 1767, and 1768. London, 1778. 1st ed. 8vo. 2 maps, 4 plts. Contemp sheep. Nice. Howes C215. *Swann**. $1,840/£1,179

CARVER, JONATHAN. Travels Through the Interior Parts of North America...1766, 1767, 1768.... London, 1781. 3rd and best ed. (2),22,(20),543,(21)pp; 6 plts, 2 fldg maps (1 color). Mod 1/2 calf, marbled bds, spine gilt, leather label. (Heavily foxed, 1 leaf of index professionally reinforced at fore-edge not affecting text), else VG. Howes C215. *Reese*. $3,500/£2,244

CARVER, RAYMOND. Cathedral. NY, 1983. 1st ed. Fine in dj. *Argosy*. $65/£42

CARVER, RAYMOND. Fires: Essays. Poems. Stories. Santa Barbara: Capra, 1983. 1st hb trade ed. Signed. Fine in ptd bds w/o dj, as issued. *Captain's Bookshelf*. $250/£160

CARVER, RAYMOND. If It Please You. Northridge, CA: Lord John Press, 1984. 1st ed. Ltd to 200 signed. VF. *Bromer*. $175/£112

CARVER, RAYMOND. If It Please You. Northridge: Lord John, 1984. One of 26 signed, lettered copies. Fine in bds as issued. *Between The Covers*. $350/£224

CARVER, RAYMOND. Portraits. NY: Ecco Press, 1987. 1st ed. Fine in Fine dj. *Smith*. $45/£29

CARVER, RAYMOND. The Stories of Raymond Carver. (London): Picador, (1983). 1st ed. Fine in pict wrappers (sm tear fr panel). *Captain's Bookshelf*. $275/£176

CARVER, RAYMOND. Ultramarine. NY: Random House, (1986). 1st ed. Signed. Fine in dj. *Between The Covers*. $150/£96

CARVER, RAYMOND. What We Talk About When We Talk About Love. NY, 1981. 1st ed. NF in Fine dj. *Warren.* $95/£61

CARVER, RAYMOND. Where I'm Calling From. NY, (1988). 1st ed. Fine in dj. *Argosy.* $100/£64

CARVER, RAYMOND. Where I'm Calling From. NY: Atlantic Monthly, (1988). One of 250 signed. Fine in Fine slipcase. *Lenz.* $275/£176

CARVER, RAYMOND. Where Water Comes Together with Other Water. NY, (1985). 1st ed. VG in dj. *Argosy.* $50/£32

CARVER, RAYMOND. Will You Please Be Quiet, Please? NY: McGraw-Hill, (1976). 1st ed. Nf in dj (lt worn, soiled, label mk fr flap). *Waverly*.* $209/£134

CARVIC, HERON. Picture Miss Seeton. NY: Harper & Row, 1968. 1st Amer ed. VF in dj. *Mordida.* $35/£22

CARY, EDWARD. George William Curtis. Boston/NY: Houghton Mifflin, 1894. 1st ed. Maroon cl, gilt. Fine. *Macdonnell.* $30/£19

CARY, JOYCE. Aissa Saved. NY: Harper, (1962). 1st Amer ed, 1st bk. Fine in dj (sl soiling). *Between The Covers.* $45/£29

CARY, JOYCE. The Case for African Freedom. London: Secker, 1941. 1st Eng ed. Good (name, tp hinge tender) in card wrappers, dj. *Clearwater.* $39/£25

CARY, JOYCE. The Horse's Mouth. London: Michael Joseph, 1957. One of 1500. Bds, morocco label. Slipcase. *Swann*.* $172/£110

CARY, JOYCE. Power in Men. London: Liberal Book Club, 1939. True 1st ed. Issued w/o dj. (2 corners bumped), else VG. *Buckley.* $47/£30

CARY, VIRGINIA. Letters on Female Character. Richmond, VA: A(riel) Works, 1828. 1st ed. 199pp (inner margins sl stained, esp last 50 pp). Leather-backed bds. Good (foxed). *Second Life.* $235/£151

CARY, VIRGINIA. Letters on Female Character. Richmond, VA: Ariel Works, 1830. 2nd ed. 220pp (tps sl stained). Leather-backed bds. Good (sigs, foxed). *Second Life.* $150/£96

CASANOVA. Life and Memoirs.... Dunning Gribble (ed). Routledge, 1930. 2 vols. Djs (1 w/piece torn away, cl faded). *Cox.* $39/£25

CASANOVA. The Memoirs of Jacques Casanova de Seingalt. Arthur Machen (trans). Haarlem, Holland: LEC, 1972. One of 1500 numbered, signed by Rene Ben Sussan (illus). 16 color plts. Dec cl, gilt vellum spine label. Mint in bd slipcase. *Argosy.* $125/£80

CASANOVA. The Memoirs of. Arthur Machen (trans). Edinburgh: LEC, 1940. One of 1500 numbered. 8 vols. Cl-backed bds (sl worn). 2 slipcases (broken). *Oinonen*.* $70/£45

CASANOVA. The Memoirs of.... Arthur Machen (trans). Casanova Soc, 1922. #1/1000 sets. 12 vols. Frontispieces. Teg, rest uncut. Japon-backed bds. (Marginal pencil notes; edges lt faded, sl rubbed, spines sl soiled.) *Edwards.* $195/£125

CASATI, GAETANO. Ten Years in Equatoria and the Return with Emin Pasha. Mrs. J. Randolph Clay (trans). London, 1891. 2 vols. Frontis, 59 plts (10 colored). (Lacks fldg maps.) Pict cl. *Argosy.* $150/£96

CASATI, GAETANO. Ten Years in Equatoria. London/NY: Warne, 1891. 2nd ed. 2 vols. 2 frontispieces, xxi,376; xv,347pp; 4 fldg maps in rear pockets. Brn gilt pict cl. (Leaves of 1 vol lt dampstained bottom), else Fine. *Terramedia.* $300/£192

Case of Great Britain and America.... (By Gervaise Parker Bushe.) London: T. Becket, 1769 (i.e., 1768). 1st ed. (Lacks 1/2 title, ex-lib.) 19th-cent 1/4 morocco, marbled bds (spine, extrems rubbed). Howes B1039. *Freeman*.* $110/£71

CASEY, JOHN. Spartina. NY: Knopf, 1989. 1st ed. Fine (sig) in dj. *Captain's Bookshelf.* $50/£32

CASEY, ROBERT J. The Texas Border. Indianapolis, (1950). 1st ed. Pamphlet guide present. (Spine dull, sl worn.) *King.* $30/£19

CASH, W. J. The Mind of the South. NY: Knopf, 1941. 1st ed. NF (sm lib stamp) in dj (few sm chips, spine sl dknd). *Captain's Bookshelf.* $350/£224

CASKEY, L. D. and J. D. BEAZLEY. Attic Vase Paintings in the Museum of Fine Arts, Boston. Boston: Museum of Fine Arts, 1931-63. 3 vols in 6 parts. Text vols sm folio in orig ptd wrappers (sm chip upper corner vol 1), o/w Fine. Plt vols lg folio in orig cl-backed portfolios (sl shelfwear to corners), ties. Interior Fine. *Archaeologia.* $1,500/£962

CASPER, JOHANN LUDWIG. A Handbook of the Practice of Forensic Medicine Based upon Personal Experience. George William Balfour (trans). London: New Sydenham Soc, 1861. 1st ed in English. 4 vols. xvi,317; vii,331; x,417; xvi,364pp. Emb Victorian cl (joints, edges worn, spines 2 vols torn). Good set. *Gach.* $175/£112

CASSADY, NEAL. The First Third. (SF): City Lights, (1971). NF (sl rubbed) in perfectbound wrappers. *Between The Covers.* $65/£42

CASSADY, NEAL. The First Third. SF: City Lights, 1971. 1st ed ($3 cvr price). NF in wraps. *Sclanders.* $39/£25

CASSERLY, GORDON. Tiger Girl. London: Philip Allan, 1934. 1st ed. Orange cl. VG. *Certo.* $125/£80

CASSINO, SAMUEL. The Naturalist's Directory 1884. Boston, 1884. 1st ed. 191pp. Contents Fine (eps, cvr waterstained). *Fye.* $100/£64

CASSON, LIONEL. The Ancient Mariners: Seafarers and Sea Fighters of the Mediterranean in Ancient Times. NY: Macmillan, 1959. 16 plts, 4 maps. Good in dj (tattered). *Archaeologia.* $35/£22

CASSON, LIONEL. Travel in the Ancient World. Toronto: Hakkert, 1974. 4 maps. (Bkpl.) Dj (shelfwear). *Archaeologia.* $35/£22

CASSOU, JEAN. Jenkins. Abrams, 1963. VG + in dj (sl yellowed). *My Bookhouse.* $25/£16

CASTANEDA, CARLOS. The Eagle's Gift. London, 1981. 1st ed. Fine in dj. *Words Etc.* $23/£15

CASTANEDA, CARLOS. Journey to Ixtlan: The Lessons of Don Juan. NY: S&S, (1972). 1st ed. Brn cl, gilt. VG in pict dj. *Blue Mountain.* $30/£19

CASTANEDA, CARLOS. A Separate Reality. NY, 1971. 1st ed. (Name), o/w Fine in Fine dj. *Warren.* $40/£26

CASTANEDA, CARLOS. The Teachings of Don Juan: A Yaqui Way of Knowledge. Berkeley: Univ of CA, 1968. 1st ed, 1st bk. Fine in dj (used, inch-square chip fr panel). *Captain's Bookshelf.* $125/£80

CASTELLOTE, RAMON. The Handbook of Fencing. London/NY: Ward, Lock, (1882). 1st ed. vi,42pp + 8pp cat, ads on pastedowns, eps. Pict limp brn cl (rubbed, stained, sl bubbled). VG. *Blue Mountain.* $20/£13

CASTERET, NORBERT. Ten Years Under the Earth. NY, 1939. 3rd ptg. Grn cl. (Ex-lib, stamp tp), else VG. *Price.* $29/£19

CASTIGLIONI, ARTURO. A History of Medicine. NY, 1947. 2nd ed. VG. *Fye.* $150/£96

CASTIGLIONI, ARTURO. The Renaissance of Medicine in Italy. Balt, 1934. 1st ed. (Protective tissue guard glued to tp.) *Fye.* $60/£38

Castle of Otranto. (By Horace Walpole.) William Marshal (trans). London: J. Dodsley, 1791. 6th ed. xxiv,200pp. Contemp mottled calf (rebacked), much of orig backstrip laid down. (Tanning), else Nice. *Reese.* $85/£54

CASTLE, AGNES and EGERTON. Our Sentimental Garden. Phila: Lippincott, 1914. 1st Amer ed. 8 color plts. Pict tp, eps. Fine (hinges strengthened). *Quest.* $65/£42

CASTLE, WILLIAM B. and GEORGE R. MINOT. Pathological Physiology and Clinical Description of the Anemias. NY: OUP, (1936). 1st separate ed. Fine. *Glaser*. $125/£80

CASTLEMAN, ALFRED L. The Army of the Potomac. Milwaukee: Strickland, 1863. 1st ed. 288,(6)pp (lacks rep). Howes C230. *Ginsberg*. $300/£192

CASTLEMON, HARRY. Winged Arrow's Medicine. Chicago, (1901). Pict cvr. VG. *Pratt*. $27/£17

Catalan Art from the Ninth to the Fifteenth Centuries. (By Christian Zervos.) Heinemann, 1937. 223 b/w plts. Pub's wraparound loosely inserted. (Margins sl browned; cl sl soiled.) *Edwards*. $117/£75

Catalogue of an Exhibition of Drawings by Sir Max Beerbohm Entitled 'Max' in Retrospect. London: Ernest Brown & Phillips; Leicester Galleries, (May 1952). 1st ed. NF in ptd wrappers. *Holmes*. $50/£32

Catalogue of an Exhibition of Nineteenth Century Bookbindings. Chicago: Caxton Club, 1898. One of 127. Cl, ptd bds. NF in slipcase (worn). *Dermont*. $250/£160

Catalogue of Another Exhibition of Caricatures by Max Beerbohm. Ernest Brown & Phillips, 1921. 1st ed. (Sl vertical crease), o/w VG in stapled wraps. *Ash*. $39/£25

Catalogue of Paintings. Volume III. Cambridge: Fitzwilliam Museum, 1977. 64 plts. Good in dj (worn). *Washton*. $50/£32

Catalogue of the Books and Manuscripts of Robert Louis Stevenson in the Library of...Henry Elkins Widener. Phila, 1913. One of 150. Teg. Contemp 3/4 dk blue morocco (joints, extrems rubbed; bkpl), gilt, raised bands. *Freeman**. $90/£58

Catalogue of the Library and Literary Manuscripts of the Late Sir Max Beerbohm, Removed from Rapallo.... London: Sotheby, 12 and 13 December 1960. (Ink/pencil notes), o/w Good in ptd wrappers (sl soiled, sl worn). *Holmes*. $35/£22

Catalogue of the Library of the Late John Fletcher Hurst. NY: Anderson Auction, 1904. 3/4 morocco, marbled paper bds. Fine (presentation). *Metropolitan**. $150/£96

Catalogue of the Printed Books and Pamphlets in the Library of the Royal Microscopical Society. London: R.M.S., 1929. VG. *Savona*. $78/£50

Catalogue Raisonne of Books Printed and Published at the Doves Press. (Hammersmith), 1908. One of 300. Linen-backed bds. *Swann**. $138/£88

CATANZARO, RONALD J. (ed). Alcoholism: The Total Treatment Approach. Springfield, IL: Charles C. Thomas, (1968). Presentation copy. Ptd crimson cl. (Lib bkpl, rear pocket), else Fine. *Gach*. $30/£19

CATCOTT, E. J. and J. F. SMITHCORS (eds). Progress in Feline Practice, Including Caged Birds and Exotic Animals. Santa Barbara, 1966, 1971. 1st ed. 2 vols. Fine in VG + slipcase. *Mikesh*. $45/£29

CATE, WIRT ARMISTEAD. Lucius Q. C. Lamar Secession and Reunion. Chapel Hill: Univ of NC, (1935). 1st ed. #22/400 signed. VG in VG dj. *Mcgowan*. $250/£160

Cathedrals and Abbey Churches of England. London, n.d. (1920s or '30s). 16 full-pg color plts by Cecil Aldin. (Cvr very faded, lt scuffed.) Internally VG (bkpl). *Truepenny*. $30/£19

CATHELL, D. W. Book on the Physician Himself from Graduation to Old Age. Phila: F.A. Davis, 1931. 'Crowning ed.' Frontis port. Fine. *Glaser*. $45/£29

CATHELL, D. W. The Physician Himself and What He Should Add to His Scientific Acquirements. Balt, 1883. 3rd ed. 208pp. VG. *Fye*. $75/£48

CATHER, WILLA. Alexander's Bridge. Boston: Houghton, Mifflin, (1922). (2nd ed.) VG in dj (soiled, chipped, spine sl dknd, shelfworn), later chemise, slipcase. *Pacific**. $115/£74

CATHER, WILLA. Alexander's Bridge. London: Heinemann, 1912. 1st British ed. F. Graham Cootes (illus). (Lt offset dj flaps to eps) else VG in dj (sm tears; creases fr, rear panels, soil), later chemise, slipcase. *Pacific**. $1,380/£885

CATHER, WILLA. April Twilights. Boston: Richard G. Badger, 1903. 1st ed, 1st bk. Gray bds; paper spine, cvr labels. (Fr cvr label sl ciscolored), else NF in later chemise, 1/2 morocco slipcase. *Pacific**. $2,588/£1,659

CATHER, WILLA. Death Comes for the Archbishop. NY: Knopf, 1927. 1st ed. Fine in VG- dj (2 sm chips; sl dkng). *Between The Covers*. $550/£353

CATHER, WILLA. Death Comes for the Archbishop. NY: Knopf, 1927. 1st ed. VG in dj (creases, sm repair verso), later chemise, slipcase. *Pacific**. $633/£406

CATHER, WILLA. A Lost Lady. NY: LEC, 1983. One of 1500 signed by William Bailey (illus). Frontis etching, 4 full-pg b/w illus. Plum eps; aeg. Burgundy leather spine, tips; burgundy/plum floral patterned cl bds. Fine in plum paper bd slipcase. *Heller*. $135/£87

CATHER, WILLA. A Lost Lady. NY: Knopf, Sept 1923. 1st trade ed. Grn cl, title at top of spine, 'of' correct line 19, p174. Good. *Scribe's Perch**. $37/£24

CATHER, WILLA. Lucy Gayheart. NY: Knopf, 1935. 1st ed. #270/749 signed. Teg. Blue cl, gilt spine. Fine in NF dj (offset from slipcase, lacks sm piece fr panel), slipcase. *Pacific**. $288/£185

CATHER, WILLA. My Antonia. Boston: Houghton, Mifflin, (1926). New ed. Signed, inscribed, dated 1927. VG in later chemise, slipcase. *Pacific**. $920/£590

CATHER, WILLA. My Antonia. London: Heinemann, 1919. 1st Eng ed. NF in dj, later chemise, slipcase. *Pacific**. $1,265/£811

CATHER, WILLA. My Mortal Enemy. NY, 1926. 1st ed. One of 220 signed. Cl-backed dec bds (ex-lib). *Argosy*. $150/£96

CATHER, WILLA. My Mortal Enemy. NY: Knopf, 1926. 1st ed. Fine in dj (sl worn). *Hayman*. $125/£80

CATHER, WILLA. My Mortal Enemy. NY: Knopf, 1926. 1st trade ed. 1/2 cl, bds. (Spine sl dull), else NF in dj, later chemise, VG slipcase (tape-repaired). *Pacific**. $184/£118

CATHER, WILLA. Not Under Forty. London: Cassell, (1936). 1st British ed. VG in dj (spine sl rubbed w/loss, sl dknd), later chemise, slipcase. *Pacific**. $40/£26

CATHER, WILLA. Not Under Forty. NY: Knopf, 1936. 1st ed, trade issue. Good (cl dusty) in dj (spine tanned, sm edge tear). *Reese*. $30/£19

CATHER, WILLA. Not Under Forty. NY: Knopf, 1936. Ltd to 333 numbered, signed. Lt red cl. Good in dj (browned, lt soiled, 2 sm closed tears), pub's slipcase (browned, edges rubbed). *Karmiole*. $300/£192

CATHER, WILLA. Not Under Forty. NY: Knopf, 1936. 1st ed. #35/333 signed. Orange cl, gilt. Fine in NF oversize dj (offset from slipcase), slipcase. *Pacific**. $489/£313

CATHER, WILLA. The Novels and Stories of Willa Cather. Boston: Houghton, Mifflin, 1937-1941. Autograph ed. #68/970 signed on limitation pg, vol 1. 13 vols. Teg. Riverside Press binding: 3/4 dk brn French levant morocco, rose cl, gilt-lettered spines, raised bands. Fine. *Pacific**. $4,888/£3,133

CATHER, WILLA. O Pioneers! Boston: Houghton, Mifflin, 1913. 1st ed w/'June 1913' on c. pg. Frontis, guard. 1st binding: lt yellow-brn vertical ribbed cl. (Bkpl; spine ends lt rubbed), else VG in later chemise, slipcase. *Pacific**. $374/£240

CATHER, WILLA. Obscure Destinies. NY: Knopf, 1932. 1st ed, trade issue. Paper labels. Good (spine sunned) in yellow dj (price-clipped, tanned). *Reese.* $45/£29

CATHER, WILLA. Obscure Destinies. NY: Knopf, 1932. 1st ed. Price-clipped as issued. (Dj spines sunned), else VG in dj. *Pacific*.* $63/£40

CATHER, WILLA. The Old Beauty and Others. Knopf, 1948. 1st ed. (Inscrip), else Fine in VG dj. *Authors Of West.* $30/£19

CATHER, WILLA. One of Ours. NY: Knopf, 1922. 1st ed. #333/345 signed. Batik bds, coarse linen spine, paper spine label. (Spine head bumped), else NF. *Pacific*.* $403/£258

CATHER, WILLA. The Professor's House. NY: Knopf, 1925. 1st ed. Fine in dj, later chemise, slipcase. *Pacific*.* $489/£313

CATHER, WILLA. Sapphira and the Slave Girl. NY, 1940. 1st ed. Ltd to 520 numbered, signed. Teg. Cl-backed bds. (Sl rubbed; spine sl sunned; lacks dj, slipcase.) *King.* $295/£189

CATHER, WILLA. Sapphira and the Slave Girl. NY: Knopf, 1940. 1st ed. #418/520 on Rives Liampre paper, signed. Teg. Grn cl-backed bds, gilt. Fine in NF dj (offset from slipcase, spine sl browned), slipcase. *Pacific*.* $518/£332

CATHER, WILLA. Shadows on the Rock. NY: Knopf, 1931. 1st ed, trade issue. Paper spine label. Good (spine sunned) in dj (spine tanned). *Reese.* $35/£22

CATHER, WILLA. The Song of the Lark. Boston: Houghton, Mifflin, 1915. 1st ed, 2nd issue w/'moments' on p8, 3rd line from bottom; ad notice of 3 titles by Cather in panel rule is on verso of 2nd leaf, facing tp. 2nd issue binding: vertical rib blue cl, gilt. (Bkpl, name; spine foot sl shelfworn), else Fine in chemise, slipcase. *Pacific*.* $150/£96

CATHER, WILLA. The Song of the Lark. Boston: Houghton, Mifflin, 1915. 1st ed, 1st issue w/'moment' for 'moments' p8, 3rd line from bottom; ad notice of 3 titles by Cather in panel rule is on c. pg instead of on verso of 2nd leaf, facing tp. 1st issue binding: blue smooth (instead of vertical rib) cl. (Spine foot sl shelfworn), else Fine in chemise, slipcase. *Pacific*.* $431/£276

CATHERWOOD, JOHN. A New Method of Curing the Apoplexy. London: W. Taylor et al, 1715. viii,77pp (blank between pp58-59). Contemp 1/4 calf, marbled bds (recently rebacked). (Lt foxing), else VG. *Goodrich.* $595/£381

CATICH, EDWARD M. Eric Gill, His Social and Artistic Roots. Iowa City: Prairie Press, 1964. 1st ed. Cl-backed bds. Photo of Catich laid in. Fine in pict dj. *Shasky.* $50/£32

CATICH, EDWARD M. Letters Redrawn from the Trajan Inscription in Rome. Davenport, IA, 1961. Inscribed. Orange buckram, gilt. VG in matching slipcase. *Heller.* $250/£160

CATICH, EDWARD M. The Trajan Inscription in Rome. Davenport, IA: Catfish Press, (1961). 2nd ed. Tns of author to purchaser. 94 loose plts (plt 1 edge browned), o/w VG in Good+ fldg case (corner bumped). *Scribe's Perch*.* $55/£35

CATLIN, GEORGE. The Breath of Life.... NY: John Wiley, 1872. 76pp. (Spine rubbed, dknd), o/w VG. *New Hampshire*.* $85/£54

CATLIN, GEORGE. Catlin's North American Indian Portfolio. Chicago: Swallow, 1970. Ltd to 1000. 25 2-tone plts. VG. *Lien.* $200/£128

CATLIN, GEORGE. Illustrations of the Manners, Customs and Condition of the North American Indians: In a Series of Letters.... London: Henry G. Bohn, 1845. 5th ed. 2 vols. 264; 266pp (marginal foxing, pencil notes); 180 etched plts (offsetting), 3 maps (1 fldg). Full period gilt-ruled black morocco (corners, edges sl worn). VG+. Howes C241. *Harrington.* $600/£385

CATLIN, GEORGE. Illustrations of the Manners, Customs, and Condition of the North American Indians. London: Bohn, 1866. 10th ed. 2 vols. Lg 8vo. Red cl (very worn; foxing, soil inside). *Metropolitan*.* $575/£369

CATLIN, GEORGE. Illustrations of the Manners, Customs, and Condition of the North American Indians. Vol 1. London: Bohn, 1857. 9th ed. Map (not orig). Red cl. (Foxed, ex-lib, cvrs poor.) *Yudkin*.* $130/£83

CATLIN, GEORGE. Letters and Notes on the Manners, Customs, and Condition of the North American Indians. London, 1841. 2nd ed. 2 vols. viii,264; viii,266pp, frontis, 176 plts, 3 maps (1 fldg). Marbled eps. Contemp 1/2 morocco, purple cl (sm sunned strip vol 2), gilt-stamped leather spine labels. VG. Howes C241. *Oregon.* $850/£545

CATLIN, GEORGE. Letters and Notes on the Manners, Customs, and Condition of the North American Indians. London: David Bogue, 1844. 2 vols. 264; 266pp. Fldg map. Good (rebacked). Howes C241. *Lien.* $450/£288

CATLIN, GEORGE. North American Indians. Edinburgh, 1926. Vol 1 (of 2). Uncut. Gilt-pict cl (sl worn). *Oinonen*.* $180/£115

CATLIN, GEORGE. North American Indians: Being Letters and Notes...1832-1839. Phila: Leary, 1913. 2 vols. 180 plts, maps. Pict dec cl (ex-lib spine mks, bkpls removed). Howes C241. *Ginsberg.* $200/£128

CATTELLE, W. The Diamond. NY, 1911. 1st ed. 9 plts. Purple cl, gilt. VG. *Price.* $75/£48

CATTELLE, W. The Diamond. NY: John Lane, 1911. Good (faded). *Blake.* $100/£64

CATTERMOLE, R. The Book of Raphael's Cartoons. Henry G. Bohn, 1845. 1st ed. Engr frontis port, (4),185pp; 7 engr plts. Uncut. Good in orig red cl (lt dust-soiled), gilt. *Cox.* $55/£35

CATTON, BRUCE. Banners at Shenendoah. GC, 1955. 1st ed. VG+ in dj (lt wear). *Pratt.* $20/£13

CATTON, BRUCE. Grant Takes Command. Boston, (1969). 1st ed. Fine in dj (lt wear). *Pratt.* $25/£16

CATULLUS. Catulli Carmina. London: Curwen Press, 1929. Vellum. Slipcase. *Swann*.* $57/£37

CAUDILL, REBECCA. Up and Down the River. NY: Winston, 1951. 1st ed. Decie Merwin (illus). 6 x 8 1/4. 115pp. Fine in dj. *Cattermole.* $25/£16

CAUGHEY, JOHN WALTON. Hubert Howe Bancroft, Historian of the West. Berkeley: Univ of CA, 1946. 1st ed. Frontis port. VF. *Argonaut.* $50/£32

CAUGHEY, JOHN WALTON. Hubert Howe Bancroft. Berkeley: Univ of CA, 1946. 1st ed. VG in dj. *Lien.* $30/£19

CAULDWELL, FRANK. (Pseud of Francis King.) The Firewalkers. John Murray, (1956). 1st ed. Good in dj (sl rubbed, sunned). *Ash.* $39/£25

CAULFIELD, JAMES. The High Court of Justice. London, 1820. 1st ed extra illus. Aeg. Full panelled calf (fr cvr detached), gilt. *Kane*.* $65/£42

CAUMONT, MRS. Wilbourne Hall. T. Fisher Unwin, 1885. 2 vols. Pub's cats both vols dated 1884. Good (margin spotting, soiling; spines bumped, chipped; hinges, corners rubbed). *Tiger.* $47/£30

CAUTE, DAVID. The Demonstration. Heinemann, 1978. 1st UK ed. Fine in NF dj. *Williams.* $16/£10

CAUTLEY, H. M. Suffolk Churches and Their Treasures. London, 1975. 4th ed. 3 color plts, map. Sound in dj, slipcase. *Ars Artis*. $47/£30

CAUTLEY, MARJORIE S. Garden Design. NY, 1935. Color spectrum plt, 5 color overlays. (Cl rear cvr sl bubbled, discolored.) *Brooks*. $55/£35

CAVADA, F. F. Libby Life——Experiences of a Prisoner of War in Richmond, Va., 1863-4. Phila, 1865. 221pp. Good (ink name, foxed, middle sig pulled; shaken, spine worn). *Wantagh*. $40/£26

CAVAFY, C. P. Homage to Cavafy. Danbury, NH: Addison House, (1978). 1st ed. Ptd wrapper over stiff bds. (Wrappers mottled), else Fine. *Turtle Island*. $55/£35

CAVE, RODERICK. The Private Press. NY, (1971). Fine in dj. *Truepenny*. $50/£32

CAVENDISH, GEORGE. The Life and Death of Cardinal Wolsey. Boston, 1905. Ltd to 1030. Uncut. Dec cvrs, gilt. Fine (spine sl sunned, corners rubbed, sm spots rear cvr). *Polyanthos*. $60/£38

CAVENDISH, GEORGE. The Life of Cardinal Wolsey. London, 1827. 2nd ed. Facs, 8 plts. (Lt foxing.) Contemp full polished tan calf (scuffed, sl soiled, joints stressed), gilt, raised bands, red morocco label. *Freeman**. $40/£26

CAVENDISH, GEORGE. The Life of Thomas Wolsey, Cardinal Archbishop of York. Kelmscott Press, 1893. One of 250 ptd. (10),iv,287,(7)pp. Full vellum, grn ribbon ties. Fine (sm stamp). *Michael Taylor*. $897/£575

CAVENDISH, HENRY. The Electrical Researches of the Honourable Henry Cavendish, FRS. J. Clerk-Maxwell (ed). Cambridge, 1879. 1st ed, 1st issue w/only 1pg pub's ads. xxiv,454pp, 3 plts of facs, 1pg pub's ads. Plum cl. (Sm lib stamps mostly in blank margins), o/w Very Nice. *Whitehart*. $281/£180

CAVENDISH. Card Essays, Clay's Decisions, and Card-Table Talk. London: Thomas de la Rue, 1879. (Foxed, bumped, rubbed.) *Metropolitan**. $17/£11

Caverns of Luray. Balt, 1893. Fldg frontis map, 50pp; map. VG in ptd wraps (chipped). *Bohling*. $50/£32

CAWEIN, MADISON. Nature-Notes and Impressions. In Prose and Verse. NY, 1906. 1st Amer ed. Teg, uncut. Fine (spine sl sunned). *Polyanthos*. $35/£22

CAWEIN, MADISON. So Many Ways. Chicago: P.F. Volland, 1911. 1st ed. French-folded leaves. Pict bds (lt rubbed, hinge puncture), gilt. VG. BAL 3027. *Cahan*. $20/£13

CAWLEY, A. C. (ed). Sir Gawain and the Green Knight. NY: LEC, 1971. One of 1500 numbered, signed by Cyril Satorsky (illus). Full linen. Mint in bd slipcase. *Argosy*. $125/£80

CAWLEY, A. C. (ed). Sir Gawain and the Green Knight. NY: LEC, 1971. #1029/1500 signed by Cyril Satorsky (illus). Fine in slipcase. *Hermitage*. $175/£112

CAXTON, WILLIAM. The History of Reynard the Fox. (Hammersmith: Kelmscott, 1892.) One of 300. Vellum, silk ties. *Swann**. $1,955/£1,253

CECIL, EVELYN. Children's Gardens. London: Macmillan, 1902. Frontis. Pict blue cl. NF. *Quest*. $60/£38

CECIL, HENRY. The Asking Price. London: Michael Joseph, 1966. 1st ed. Inscribed. Fine in dj. *Mordida*. $50/£32

CECIL, HENRY. Friends at Court. London: Michael Joseph, 1958. Sound (worn). *Boswell*. $25/£16

CECIL, HENRY. Independent Witness. London: Michael Joseph, 1963. 1st ed. Fine in dj (short closed tears). *Mordida*. $45/£29

CECIL, HENRY. Ways and Means. London, 1952. 1st ed. VG in dj. *Typographeum*. $30/£19

CECIL, HENRY. A Woman Named Anne. London: Michael Joseph, 1967. 1st ed. Fine in dj (spine sl dknd). *Mordida*. $45/£29

CELA, CAMILO JOSE. The Hive. NY: FSG, 1953. 1st US ed. NF in VG + dj (sl worn). *Lame Duck*. $50/£32

Celebrated Collection of Americana Formed by the Late Thomas Winthrop Streeter. NY. 1st ed. 8 vols. Fine. No dj as issued. Orig glassine. *Turpen*. $750/£481

Celebrated Collection of Americana Formed by the Late Thomas Winthrop Streeter. NY: Parke-Bernet Galleries, 1966, plus later dates. 7 vols. Blue cl, gilt. (Few spines sl sunned), o/w Fine set in glassine djs. *Biscotti*. $750/£481

Celebrated Collection of Americana Formed by the Late Thomas Winthrop Streeter. NY, 1966-1969. 1st ed. 7 vols & index. Tall 8vo. *Ginsberg*. $750/£481

Celebrated Collection of Americana Formed by the Late Thomas Winthrop Streeter. NY: Parke-Bernet, 1966-70. 8vo. 8 vols. Bds, except Index in cl. *Swann**. $575/£369

Celebrated Collection of Americana Formed by the Late Thomas Winthrop Streeter. Vol 1. NY. 1st ed. NF. *Turpen*. $65/£42

Celebrated Collection of Americana Formed by the Late Thomas Winthrop Streeter. Vol 7. NY: Parke-Bernet, 1969. Gilt-titled blue paper over bds. As New. *Bowman*. $100/£64

Celebrated Collection of Americana Formed by the Late Thomas Winthrop Streeter. Vol 8, index. NY. 1st ed. NF. *Turpen*. $85/£54

Celebrated Collection of Americana Formed by the Late Thomas Winthrop Streeter. Vol 8, index. NY: Parke-Bernet Galleries, 1970. Fine. *Wantagh*. $75/£48

CELINE, LOUIS-FERDINAND. Castle to Castle. Ralph Mannheim (trans). NY: Delacorte, 1968. 1st US ed. NF in VG + dj. *Lame Duck*. $35/£22

CELINE, LOUIS-FERDINAND. Journey to the End of Night. John Marks (trans). London: Chatto, 1934. 1st Eng ed. Very Nice (eps sl foxed). *Clearwater*. $78/£50

CELINE, LOUIS-FERDINAND. Mea Culpa, the Life and Work of Semmelweis. Boston, 1937. 1st Amer ed. NF (spine lt sunned). *Polyanthos*. $45/£29

CELINE, LOUIS-FERDINAND. Rigadoon. NY: Delacorte, 1974. 1st ed in English. NF in dj. *Lame Duck*. $45/£29

CELLINI, BENVENUTO. The Life of Benvenuto Cellini. John Addington Symonds (ed). NY, 1906. 2 vols. Marbled eps; teg. 1/2 blue morocco, gilt spines. VG + (ink inscrip). *Truepenny*. $150/£96

CELLINI, BENVENUTO. Life Written by Himself.... J. Addington Symonds (ed). NY: Brentano's, 1906. 2 vols. 40 plts, tissue guards. Teg, others uncut. (Backstrips lt faded.) *Cox*. $23/£15

CELLINI, BENVENUTO. Life.... Thomas Nugent (trans). London: T. Davies, 1771. 1st ed in English. 2 vols. Frontis ports. Old full polished calf. (Sigs a, b vol 2 bound after tp; last 6 leaves of sig c bound properly vol 2.) *Kane**. $150/£96

CELLINI, BENVENUTO. The Life.... Robert H. Hobart Cust (ed). Navarre Soc, 1935. 2 vols. Blue cl (lt rubbed, soiled). Good. *Cox*. $19/£12

CENDRARS, BLAISE. Little Black Stories for Little White Children. NY: Payson & Clark, 1929. 1st ed. Pierre Pinsard (illus). 7 1/2 x 9 1/2. 138pp. Good. *Cattermole*. $90/£58

CENDRARS, BLAISE. Panama. NY, 1931. 1st ed. One of 300. Signed by Cendrars and John Dos Passos (trans). Unopened. Pict wraps (lower spine eroded, dknd; lt worn). *Kane**. $35/£22

CENDRARS, BLAISE. Panama. NY: Harper, 1931. 1st ed. John Dos Passos (illus). 7 3/4 x 9 3/4. 157pp. Good (lt soil, backstrip starting). *Cattermole*. $50/£32

CENDRARS, BLAISE. Panama. John Dos Passos (trans). NY: Harper, 1931. 1st ed. NF in wrappers (sig) in NF dj. *Warren.* $95/£61

CENDRARS, BLAISE. Sutter's Gold. NY, (1926). 1st Amer ed. (Ink name; fr hinge cracked; cvrs worn), else VG in dj (sl frayed; edge-torn). *King.* $50/£32

Centennial History of Akron 1825-1925. Summit Co Hist Soc, 1925. Map, 8pp plts. (Name ep; worn, spine dknd.) *Bohling.* $35/£22

Centeola; and Other Tales. (By Daniel P. Thompson.) NY: Carleton, 1864. 1st ed. 312pp. (Spine faded.) BAL 19976, binding A. *M & S.* $125/£80

CERF, BENNETT. At Random. NY, (1977). Fine in dj. *Truepenny.* $20/£13

CERVANTES. Don Quixote. NY: Modern Library, (1946). Frontis, 10 dbl-pg color plts by Salvador Dali. Color pict paper over bds, linen spine. Good+ in ptd clear plastic dj (chipped). *Scribe's Perch*.* $40/£26

CERVANTES. The History and Adventures of the Renowned Don Quixote. Dr. Smollett (trans). London: Cooke's Edition, ca 1798. 5 vols. Contemp tree calf (worn). *Swann*.* $138/£88

CERVANTES. The Ingenious Gentleman Don Quixote de la Mancha. PA: Franklin Library, 1976. Gustave Dore (illus). Satin eps, ribbon marker, aeg. Brn fine-grained full morocco leather. NF. *Antic Hay.* $75/£48

CERVANTES. The Life and Exploits of Don Quixote de la Mancha. Charles Jarvis (trans). Knight & Lacey, 1824. 1st ed. 'Incorrect' leaf of 'Directions for placing the plates' not present. 2 vols. Engr, ptd tps; 24 engr plts. Woodcuts not signed by artist, (Robert) Cruikshank, but some signed by engraver, Sears. 19th cent 1/2 calf, gilt backs (joints cracked; head/tail bands sl rubbed). *Hatchwell.* $62/£40

CESBRON, GILBERT. The Innocents of Paris. M. Waldman (trans). Boston: Houghton, Mifflin, 1946. 1st ed. NF in dj. *Antic Hay.* $25/£16

CESCINSKY, HERBERT and ERNEST R. GRIBBLE. Early English Furniture and Woodwork. London: Routledge, 1922. 2 vols. Color frontispieces. (Eps lt spotted; sl shaken.) 2-tone cl (sl soiled, corners sl bumped). *Edwards.* $234/£150

CESCINSKY, HERBERT and ERNEST R. GRIBBLE. Early English Furniture and Woodwork. London: Waverley, 1922. 1st ed. 2 vols. Folio. Color frontispieces w/ptd guards. Teg. 2-tone cl, calf spine label. (Rubbed, stained; label vol 1 chipped, name, stamp), else VG. *Cahan.* $175/£112

CESCINSKY, HERBERT and GEORGE LELAND HUNTER. English and American Furniture. NY: GC Pub Co, 1929. (Flyleaves spotted.) VG in dj (sl worn). *Hollett.* $101/£65

CESCINSKY, HERBERT and MALCOLM R. WEBSTER. English Domestic Clocks. NY: Bonanza, (1968). Rpt. 1/4 maroon cl, bds (rubbed). Dj. *Weber.* $45/£29

CESCINSKY, HERBERT. The Old English Master Clockmakers. London: Routledge, 1938. 1st ed. Black cl. Dj (worn). *Weber.* $100/£64

CESINSKY, HERBERT. The Old English Master Clockmakers and Their Clocks 1670-1820. Routledge, 1938. 1st ed. Good. *Cox.* $109/£70

CHABON, MICHAEL. The Mysteries of Pittsburg. NY: Morrow, (1988). 1st ed. Signed. Fine in Fine dj. *Unger.* $50/£32

CHABON, MICHAEL. The Mysteries of Pittsburgh. NY: Morrow, 1988. 1st ed, 1st bk. VF in VF dj (Macmillan of Canada sticker over price). *Revere.* $35/£22

CHACE, ELIZABETH BUFFUM and LUCY BUFFUM LOVELL. Two Quaker Sisters. From the Original Diaries of.... NY, (1937). 1st ed. VG. *Mcgowan.* $75/£48

CHACE, ELIZABETH BUFFUM and LUCY BUFFUM LOVELL. Two Quaker Sisters.... NY: Liveright, (1937). 1st ed. VG. *Second Life.* $25/£16

CHADWICK, ALBERT A. Little Churches of France. 1930. 25pp; 125 plts. Unbound in bds w/ties as issued. (Sl soiled.) *Edwards.* $140/£90

CHADWICK, J. Radioactivity and Radioactive Substances. 1921. Pict cl. (Spine ends sl defective, corners sl worn), o/w VG. *Whitehart.* $39/£25

CHADWICK, JOHN. The Decipherment of Linear B. CUP, 1958. 1st ed. Frontis port, plt, fldg chart. Dj (spine head sl chipped). *Edwards.* $23/£15

CHADWICK, LESTER. Baseball Joe at Yale. Cupples & Leon, 1913. Later ptg. Good+ in Good dj. *Plapinger.* $40/£26

CHADWICK, LESTER. Baseball Joe in the World Series. Cupples & Leon, 1917. Later ptg. VG in Good dj. *Plapinger.* $40/£26

CHADWICK, LESTER. Baseball Joe in the World Series. Cupples & Leon, 1917. 5x7.5. 242pp + ads. Gray pict cl (sl shelfworn). Lists to #14. VG+ in dj (edgeworn, esp spine). *My Bookhouse.* $45/£29

CHADWICK, LESTER. Baseball Joe of the Silver Stars. Cupples & Leon, 1912. Later ptg. Good+ in Good+ dj. *Plapinger.* $40/£26

CHADWICK, LESTER. Baseball Joe, Champion of the League. Cupples & Leon, 1925. Later ptg. VG in VG dj. *Plapinger.* $45/£29

CHADWICK, LESTER. Baseball Joe, Home Run King. Cupples & Leon, 1922. Later ptg. Good+ in Good dj. *Plapinger.* $40/£26

CHADWICK, LESTER. Baseball Joe, Saving the League. Cupples & Leon, 1923. Later ptg. VG in VG dj. *Plapinger.* $50/£32

CHADWICK, OWEN. Mackenzie's Grave. 1959. 1st ed. Frontis port, map. Dj (sl chipped). *Edwards.* $23/£15

CHAFFERS, WILLIAM and H. M. CUNDALL. The New Keramic Gallery. London: Reeves & Turner, 1926. 3rd ed. 2 vols. 8 color plts. Uncut. (Name stamp some prelims), o/w Fine in djs. *Hollett.* $117/£75

CHAFFERS, WILLIAM. The Keramic Gallery. London, 1907. 2nd ed. 5 full-pg color plts. Dec cvrs. (Hinge cracks), o/w Good. *Scribe's Perch*.* $40/£26

CHAFFERS, WILLIAM. Marks and Monograms on European and Oriental Pottery and Porcelain. Frederick Litchfield et al (eds). London, 1946. 14th rev ed. (Eps sl spotted; extrems rubbed.) *Edwards.* $39/£25

CHAFFERS, WILLIAM. Marks and Monograms on Pottery and Porcelain. London: Bickers, 1872. 3rd ed. viii,778,(vi)pp. Teg. Gilt cl, beveled bds (extrems sl worn). *Hollett.* $62/£40

CHAGALL, MARC. The Ceiling of the Paris Opera. NY: Frederick A. Praeger, 1966. 1st ed. Litho frontis, 6 color lithos, fldg study in rear pocket. VF in dj, glassine wrapper, slipcase. *Hermitage.* $400/£256

CHAGALL, MARC. Lithographs. Monte Carlo: Andre Sauret, (1963). Vol 2 only. 11 litho plts. Dj, bd slipcase. *Swann*.* $862/£553

CHAGALL, MARC. The Lithographs.... Monte Carlo/NY: Andre Sauret, (1960). Folio. Vol 1 only. 11 color lithos. Dj. *Swann*.* $1,610/£1,032

Chainbearer: or, The Little-Page Manuscripts. (By James Fenimore Cooper.) NY: Burgess, Stringer, 1845. 1st Amer ed. 2 vols in 1. Trimmed. Later lib leather-backed binding (shabby; foxed). BAL 3917. *New Hampshire*.* $50/£32

CHALFANT, W. A. Death Valley: The Facts. Stanford: Stanford Univ, 1930. 1st ed. Pict cl binding. VG. *Graf.* $25/£16

CHALFANT, W. A. Death Valley: The Facts. Stanford: Stanford Univ, 1930. 1st ed. Frontis. Pict cl. (Few margin pencil mks; extrems lt worn.) *Dawson.* $30/£19

CHALFANT, W. A. Outposts of Civilization. Boston: Christopher, (1928). Fine in Fine dj. *Book Market.* $100/£64

CHALFANT, W. A. Outposts of Civilization. Boston: Christopher, 1928. (Sig, extrems lt worn.) *Dawson.* $100/£64

CHALFANT, W. A. The Story of Inyo. (N.p.): The Author, 1922. 1st ed. Fldg map, errata slip. Blind-stamped cl. Fine. *Book Market.* $100/£64

CHALFANT, W. A. The Story of Inyo. N.p.: The Author, 1922. 1st ed. Fldg map. (Spine extrems, tips sl worn.) *Dawson.* $75/£48

CHALFANT, W. A. Tales of the Pioneers. Stanford: Stanford Univ, (1942). 1st ed. Pict cl. Dj (lt chipped). *Dawson.* $30/£19

CHALKLEY, LYMAN. Chronicles of the Scotch-Irish Settlement in Virginia. Balt, 1866. 3 vols. VG. *Wantagh.* $135/£87

CHALMERS, A. K. The Health of Glasgow 1818-1925, an Outline. Ptd by Authority of the Corporation, 1930. Good. *White.* $55/£35

CHALMERS, JOHN W. Fur Trade Governor. Edmonton: Inst of Applied Art, 1960. 1st ptg. Signed. Blue cl, black titles. (Stamp fep), o/w VG in dj. *Parmer.* $35/£22

CHALMERS, LIONEL. An Account of the Weather and Diseases of South-Carolina. (Charleston, 1947.) Port. VG in ptd wrappers. *Argosy.* $45/£29

CHALMERS, MARY. Come to the Doctor, Harry. NY: Harper & Row, 1981. 1st ed. 4x6. 32pp. Pict bds. Fine in dj. *Cattermole.* $30/£19

CHALMERS, P. R. A Fisherman's Angles. London/NY, (1931). VG. *Truepenny.* $45/£29

CHALMERS, P. R. Mine Eyes unto the Hills. London: A&C Black, 1931. 1st ed. 8 Fine colored plts. (Spine faded.) *Hollett.* $62/£40

CHALMERS, P. R. Sport and Travel in East Africa. London: Allan, 1934. 1st ed. 2 color fldg maps. (Lacks 3rd map), else Good+. *Mikesh.* $37/£24

CHALMERS, PATRICK. Forty Fine Ladies. London/NY: Eyre & Spottiswoode/Scribner, 1929. 1st ed. (Fr cvr chewed), else VG. *October Farm.* $65/£42

CHALMERS, PATRICK. The Horn. NY: Scribner, 1938. 1st ed. Color frontis, 22 full-pg b/w dwgs by Lionel Edwards. VG in Good+ dj. *October Farm.* $85/£54

CHAMBERLAIN, J. L. Yale University. Boston: R. Herndon, 1900. 1/2 morocco (scuffed, ends worn, lower joints splitting). *Waverly*.* $66/£42

CHAMBERLAIN, JACOB CHESTER. First Editions of the Works of Nathaniel Hawthorne. NY: Grolier Club, 1904. 1st ed. Uncut. Fine in ptd wrappers. *Macdonnell.* $85/£54

CHAMBERLAIN, PAUL M. It's About Time. NY, 1941. 1st ed. (Sl staining lower gutter last few pp), else Good in dj (badly chipped). *King.* $125/£80

CHAMBERLAIN, SAMUEL and NARCISSA. Southern Interiors of Charleston, South Carolina. NY: Hastings House, 1956. 1st ed. Color frontis. VG in dj (chipped). *Cahan.* $25/£16

CHAMBERLAIN, SAMUEL. My Confession. NY, 1956. 1st ed. Dbl-pg panorama. Fine in Fine dj. *Turpen.* $25/£16

CHAMBERLAIN, SAMUEL. Recollections of a Rogue. London: Museum Press Ltd, (1957). 1st ed. Frontis. Red cl. Fine in pict dj. *Argonaut.* $75/£48

CHAMBERLAIN, SAMUEL. Sketches of Northern Spanish Architecture in Pen, Pencil and Wash. NY: Architectural Book Pub, (1926). 51 Fine plts laid in pub's ptd folder w/tie. (Label to spine), o/w Fine. *New Hampshire*.* $135/£87

CHAMBERLIN, EVERETT. Chicago and Its Suburbs. Chicago, 1874. 8vo. Fldg map. This copy w/ads interleaved through vol. Pub's cl (very worn). *Swann*.* $1,092/£700

CHAMBERLIN, HARRY D. Training Hunters, Jumpers and Hacks. NY: Derrydale, 1937. 1st ed. #1235/1250. Grn cl (sl worn), gilt, black cl spine (faded). Internally Fine in brn morocco-backed cl fldg box. *Cummins.* $125/£80

CHAMBERLIN, T. Geology of Wisconsin. Vol. IV only. Milwaukee: Commissioners of Public Ptg, 1882. xxiv,779pp; 3 tinted plts, 27 plts w/explanatory ll. VG (emb stamp of J. Hall tp; 1st sig sl shaken; sl foxed). *Blake.* $100/£64

CHAMBERLIN, W. J. The Bark and Timber Beetles of North America, North of Mexico. Corvallis: OSC Coop., 1939. 1st ed. 5 plts. VG in stiff wraps. *Mikesh.* $37/£24

Chambers's Stepping-Stones to Literature...Book V. In Gardens Fair. London: W. & R. Chambers, n.d. 1st ed. Dec cl. Lib of Thomas Hardy, w/Max Gate booklabel. VG. *Holmes.* $75/£48

CHAMBERS, ANDREW JACKSON. Recollections. (N.p., 1947.) 1/2 calf, marbled bds, leather label. VG. Howes C270. *Reese.* $200/£128

CHAMBERS, B. M. Salt Junk. Naval Reminiscences, 1881-1906. London, 1927. Color frontis, 4 plts. Blue cl (spine faded). *Maggs.* $55/£35

CHAMBERS, CHARLES E. S. Golfing: A Handbook to the Royal and Ancient Game.... Edinburgh: W. & R. Chambers, 1887. 1st ed. Chromolitho frontis port. Pict grn cl. NF. *Pacific*.* $920/£590

CHAMBERS, DAVID. Joan Hassall, Engravings and Drawings. Private Libraries Assoc, 1985. One of 2500 (1250 for sale). Black cl. *Michael Taylor.* $37/£24

CHAMBERS, E. T. D. The Ouananiche and Its Canadian Environment. NY: Harper, 1896. 1st ed. xx,357pp+ad; 15 plts. Teg. Grn cl (spine dknd, rubbed), gilt-titled. NF internally. *Blue Mountain.* $65/£42

CHAMBERS, G. L. Wellington's Battlefields Illustrated. Bussaco. London, 1910. Frontis, fldg panorama, 7 fldg maps in rear pocket. Pict maroon cl. (Sl shaken.) *Maggs.* $156/£100

CHAMBERS, HENRY E. Mississippi Valley Beginnings. NY/London: Putnam, 1922. 13 plts and maps. Good (lt foxed; worn, dull). *Bohling.* $50/£32

CHAMBERS, JULIUS. The Mississippi River and Its Wonderful Valley. NY: Putnam, 1910. 1st ed. Teg. (Extrems sl rubbed), else Good. *Brown.* $30/£19

CHAMBERS, LENOIR. Stonewall Jackson. NY: William Morrow, 1959. 1st ed, 2nd ptg. 2 vols. VG set. *Mcgowan.* $65/£42

CHAMBERS, R. The Book of Days. London: W&R Chambers, n.d. 2 vols. Crimson cl (spines faded, worn, few mks, joint strained), gilt. Good set. *Hollett.* $86/£55

CHAMBERS, ROBERT and EDWARD L. Explorations into the Nature of the Living Cell. Cambridge, 1961. 1st ed. VG in Good dj. *Doctor's Library.* $40/£26

CHAMBERS, ROBERT W. The King in Yellow. Chicago: Neely, 1895. 1st ed, 1st issue. VG (spine, edges sl dknd). *Between The Covers.* $250/£160

CHAMBERS, ROBERT W. The King in Yellow. Harpers, 1902. 1st illus ed. (Eps replaced.) Dec yellow cl (spine dull). Good+. *Certo.* $30/£19

CHAMBERS, ROBERT W. The Mystery of Choice. NY: D. Appleton, 1897. 1st ed. VG in pict cl-cvrd bds, gilt. *Mordida.* $150/£96

CHAMBERS, ROBERT W. Quick Action. Appleton, (1914). 1st ed. Cvr port. VG + . *Certo.* $45/£29

CHAMBERS, ROBERT W. The Talkers. Doran, (1923). 1st ed. (Bkpl; cvrs sl mkd), else VG. *Certo.* $30/£19

CHAMBERS, WILLIAM. American Slavery and Colour. London, 1861. 2nd Eng ed, enlgd. (Sl wear spine ends), else VG. *Mcgowan.* $150/£96

CHAMBERS, WILLIAM. Things as They Are in America. London/Edinburgh, 1854. vi,364,(2)pp (bkpls, hinges cracked; spine ends frayed). Good. Howes C275. *Reese.* $300/£192

CHAMBERS, WILLIAM. A Treatise on Civil Architecture. London: J. Dixwell, 1768. 2nd ed. 2ff,iv,86pp; 49 (ex 50) engr plts (lacks plt p36). New 1/2 cl. *Ars Artis.* $234/£150

CHAMBERS, WILLIAM. A Treatise on the Decorative Part of Civil Architecture. W. H. Leeds (ed). London, 1862. Port, viii,336pp; 28 + 54 plts. (1 pg of memorial, 1 or 2 letters of text restored), else Good. *Ars Artis.* $234/£150

CHAMPION, F. W. The Jungle in Sunlight and Shadow. NY: Scribner, 1934. 1st ed. 95 full-pg photos. VG. *Mikesh.* $45/£29

CHAMPION, F. W. With a Camera in Tiger-Land. NY: Doubleday, 1928. 1st ed. 73 full-pg photos. VG. *Mikesh.* $35/£22

CHAMPLAIN, SAMUEL. Narrative of a Voyage to the West Indies and Mexico in 1599-1602. London: Hakluyt Soc, 1859. 10,xcix,48pp; 12 plts (4 color). Mod cl. (Ex-lib.) *Adelson.* $80/£51

CHANCELLOR, E. BERESFORD. Life in Regency and Early Victorian Times. Batsford, n.d. (c. 1926). Color frontis, 79 b/w plts. (Feps sl browned.) Dj (sl chipped). *Edwards.* $44/£28

CHANCELLOR, E. BERESFORD. The Lives of the Rakes. London: Philip Allan, 1924-1925. Ltd to 300 signed. 6 vols. Blue cl, dec orange bds, paper spine labels. Fine. *Karmiole.* $175/£112

CHANCELLOR, E. BERESFORD. Picturesque Architecture in Paris, Etc. London: Architectural Press, 1928. 26 color plts. Good (shaken, bumped, spine sl sunned). *Metropolitan*.* $10/£6

CHANDLER, ALLISON. Trolley Through the Countryside. Denver: Sage Books, (1963). Buckram. VG in dj (frayed, soiled). *Bohling.* $45/£29

CHANDLER, DAVID. The Campaigns of Napoleon. London, 1966. Dj. *Maggs.* $109/£70

CHANDLER, RAYMOND. The Big Sleep. NY: Knopf, 1939. 1st ed. (Bkshop stamp fep), o/w VG. *Mordida.* $150/£96

CHANDLER, RAYMOND. The Big Sleep. NY: Knopf, 1939. True 1st ed w/'First Edition' ptd copyright pg. (Spine sl creased, extrems sl rubbed.) *Hollett.* $281/£180

CHANDLER, RAYMOND. The Big Sleep. NY: Knopf, 1939. 1st bk. VG (browning; 2 owner sigs fr pastedown, ep; 2nd ep creased) in dj (sl rubbed, creased; shallow chipping head, base of spine and corners; 2-inch clean cut center upper panel). *Gekoski.* $4,446/£2,850

CHANDLER, RAYMOND. The High Window. NY: Knopf, 1942. 1st ed. VG in dj (internal tape mends, spine ends, corners chipped, folds worn, spine dknd). *Mordida.* $650/£417

CHANDLER, RAYMOND. The Lady in the Lake. London: Hamish Hamilton, 1944. 1st UK ed. VG in dj (sl edgeworn, nicked, sl loss spine extrems, tape mks to verso). *Williams.* $663/£425

CHANDLER, RAYMOND. The Little Sister. London: Hamilton, 1949. 1st UK ed. VG (ink name; cvrs faded) in dj (edgeworn, spine sl faded, sl loss spine extrems). *Williams.* $257/£165

CHANDLER, RAYMOND. The Long Good-Bye. London, 1953. 1st Eng ed. VG in dj (badly creased, torn, chipped, 1-inch loss spine foot, 1-cm loss spine head). *Words Etc.* $78/£50

CHANDLER, RAYMOND. The Long Good-Bye. London: Hamilton, 1953. 1st UK ed. VG + (sl foxed, tp lacks sm piece) in dj (rubbed, edgeworn, tape-repaired to rear). *Williams.* $140/£90

CHANDLER, RAYMOND. Playback. Hamish Hamilton, (1958). 1st ed. Nice in dj (sl worn, nicked). *Ash.* $117/£75

CHANDLER, RAYMOND. Playback. London: Hamish Hamilton, 1958. 1st ed. (Feps sl dkng), o/w Fine in dj. *Mordida.* $200/£128

CHANDLER, RAYMOND. The Simple Art of Murder. London: Hamish Hamilton, 1950. 1st Eng ed. Fine in dj (wear, nicks, chip, short closed tears). *Mordida.* $250/£160

CHANDLER, RAYMOND. The Smell of Fear. London: Hamish Hamilton, 1965. 1st ed. Fine in dj (price-clipped). *Mordida.* $250/£160

CHANDLER, RAYMOND. Spanish Blood. Cleveland/NY: World, (1946). 1st ptg. (Pp lt browned), else Fine in NF dj (spine foot sl worn). *Between The Covers.* $85/£54

CHANDLER, RAYMOND. Spanish Blood. Cleveland: World, 1946. Stated 1st ptg. Dec cvr, spine. Good + (pp sl browned) in Good + dj. *Scribe's Perch*.* $37/£24

CHANDLER, RICHARD. The Life of William Waynflete, Bishop of Winchester.... London: White & Cochrane, 1811. One of 50 lg paper copies on special paper; holograph note on prelim to this effect, signed by pub. Frontis, xvi,(2),428pp, engr dedication leaf; 4 plts. Orig panelled calf (rebacked; rubbed), old spine laid down; gilt. *Karmiole.* $150/£96

CHANDLER, ROBERT. Russian Folk Tales. NY: Random House, 1980. Ivan Billbin (illus). 9x11. 78pp. Cl spine. VG in dj. *Cattermole.* $40/£26

CHANDLESS, WILLIAM. A Visit to Salt Lake. London: Smith, Elder, 1857. 1st ed. xii,346pp + 24pp ads dated 20 June 1859; fldg map at fr. Emb orange cl. (Reps sl soiled, map creased; backstrip faded, cl sl soiled), o/w Excellent. Howes C286. *Pirages.* $750/£481

CHANDOS, JOHN. Boys Together: English Public Schools 1800-1864. New Haven/London: Yale Univ, (1984). 1st Amer ed. Rust cl (top edge soiled, lt stain fr cvr). VG (sm red stains fr pastedown, eps) in dj (sl chipped, soiled). *Blue Mountain.* $25/£16

CHANG, KWANG-CHIH. The Archaeology of Ancient China. New Haven/London: Yale Univ, 1963. 1st ed. VG (ex-lib) in dj. *Worldwide.* $25/£16

CHANNING, MARK. Nine Lives. Lippincott, (1937). 1st ed. Orange cl. (Spine sl dknd), else VG. *Certo.* $25/£16

CHANNING, WILLIAM E. The Duty of the Free States, Remarks Suggested by the Case of the Creole. Boston: William Crosby, 1842. 93pp. Dec emb cl, gilt. (Foxed; faded, spine frayed), o/w VG. *Cahan.* $100/£64

CHANSLER, WALTER S. The River Trapper. Columbus, OH, 1928. 1st ed. Dec grn cl. Good. *Price.* $18/£12

CHAPELLE, HOWARD I. American Sailing Craft. NY: Crown, 1939. Color frontis. Blue cl. VG in dj (ruined). *Parmer.* $55/£35

CHAPELLE, HOWARD I. The History of American Sailing Ships. NY: W.W. Norton, 1935. 2nd ptg. Frontis, 16 plts. Beige cl. (Sl foxed, soiled), else VG in dj (worn). *Parmer*. $45/£29

CHAPELLE, HOWARD I. The National Watercraft Collection. Washington: GPO, (1960). VG. *Perier*. $45/£29

CHAPIN, E. H. Duties of Young Men. Boston: George W. Briggs, 1849. Rev ed. 12mo. iv,203pp + 3pp list (ink name fep). Blind-stamped grn cl on bds (lt faded, sl chipped), gilt, gilt edges. Internally Fine. *Hobbyhorse*. $55/£35

CHAPIN, E. H. Moral Aspects of City Life. NY: Kiggins & Kellogg, 1854. 191pp. Black cl, gilt spine. VG (sl worn). *Lucas*. $75/£48

CHAPIN, LON F. Thirty Years in Pasadena: With an Historical Sketch.... N.p.: (Southwest Publishing), 1929. Vol I (all pub). Gold-stamped black cl (most of gold flaked off, wear to spine extrems). *Dawson*. $100/£64

CHAPMAN, A. P. F. et al. The Game of Cricket. Phila, n.d. 41 plts. (Spine sl sunned.) *Edwards*. $31/£20

CHAPMAN, ABEL. Bird-Life of the Borders, Records of Wild Sport and Natural History. London, 1889. 1st ed. (Cl sl worn.) *Maggs*. $86/£55

CHAPMAN, ABEL. Bird-Life of the Borders. London, 1889. 14 plts. (Sl worn, scuffed.) *Maggs*. $55/£35

CHAPMAN, ABEL. First Lessons in the Art of Wildfowling. London, 1896. 1st ed. 36 illus by author, 3 by C. Whymper. Ads at both ends; (sl foxed). Grn cl. *Hatchwell*. $172/£110

CHAPMAN, ABEL. First Lessons in the Art of Wildfowling. London: Horace Cox, 1896. 1st ed. Extending frontis, xi,270pp. Marbled edges. Full crimson calf prize binding, raised bands, gilt spines (tops sl abraded). *Hollett*. $250/£160

CHAPMAN, ABEL. Savage Sudan. 1921. Frontis map. (Recased, spine repaired, cl upper joint sl wrinkled, sm split head upper joint.) *Edwards*. $148/£95

CHAPMAN, ABEL. Savage Sudan.... London: Gurney & Jackson, 1921. 1st ed. Map. Grn gilt pict cl (sm spine puncture), else VG. *Terramedia*. $350/£224

CHAPMAN, ALLEN. The Radio Boys at Mountain Pass. G&D, 1922. 5x7.5. 218pp + ads. Lists to #5. VG + (sl shelfworn) in dj (chipped). *My Bookhouse*. $32/£21

CHAPMAN, ALLEN. Ralph in the Switch Tower. G&D, 1907. 5x7.5. 263pp + ads. Pict cl. Lists to #6. VG + (shelfworn) in dj (sl edgeworn, spine mar). *My Bookhouse*. $40/£26

CHAPMAN, C. The Ocean Waves; Travels by Land and Sea. London, 1875. 1st ed. Presentation copy. (2),295,(2)pp. *Ginsberg*. $300/£192

CHAPMAN, CHARLES E. Colonial Hispanic America: A History. NY, 1933. 1st ed. Frontis. (Underlining, marginalia), o/w VG. *Turpen*. $35/£22

CHAPMAN, CHARLES E. Colonial Hispanic America: A History. NY: Macmillan, 1933. 1st ed. Inscribed, signed. 7 maps. Maroon cl, gilt-lettered spine. Fine. *Argonaut*. $75/£48

CHAPMAN, CHARLES E. The Founding of Spanish California. The Northwestward Expansion of New Spain, 1687-1783. NY, 1916. 1st ed. Frontis, 6 maps. Rev slip laid in. (Perf tp), o/w Fine. *Turpen*. $60/£38

CHAPMAN, CHARLES E. A History of California: The Spanish Period. NY, 1921. 1st ed. Frontis, 3 maps (1 fldg). (Rear inner hinge tender), o/w VG. *Turpen*. $50/£32

CHAPMAN, CHARLES E. A History of California: The Spanish Period. NY: Macmillan, 1926. 3 maps and illus. Blue cl. (Sm tear 2 pg edges), o/w Fine. *Pacific**. $29/£19

CHAPMAN, F. SPENCER. The Jungle Is Neutral. London, 1949. Fldg map. Beige cl (sl soiled). *Maggs*. $62/£40

CHAPMAN, FRANK. Autobiography of a Bird-Lover. NY: Appleton, 1933. 1st ed. VG (inscrip crossed out). *Agvent*. $35/£22

CHAPMAN, ISAAC A. A Sketch of the History of Wyoming. Wilkesbarre, PA, 1830. 209pp + errata (paper dknd). Full leather (worn, hinges repaired). Howes C292. *Bohling*. $30/£19

CHAPMAN, JOHN. Sea-Sickness and How to Prevent It.... London, 1868. 2nd ed. VG in mod wrappers. *Argosy*. $45/£29

CHAPMAN, MARIA WESTON. Right and Wrong in Massachusetts. Boston, 1839. Pub's cl (spine foot chipped). *Swann**. $103/£66

CHAPMAN, NATHANIEL. Elements of Therapeutics and Materia Medica. Phila, 1823-24. 3rd ed. 2 vols. (Ex-lib.) Contemp calf (rubbed). *Argosy*. $400/£256

CHAPMAN, OLIVE MURRAY. Across Lapland. London, 1932. 1st ed. 8 color, 62 b/w plts, sketch map. Dj (chipped, sl loss). *Edwards*. $78/£50

CHAPMAN, PRISCILLA. Hindoo Female Education. London: Seeley & Burnside, 1839. 1st ed. (178)pp. Pub's cl. VG (ex-lib, spine #, 2 ink stamps). *Second Life*. $150/£96

CHAPMAN, TONY and HUGH FOOT (eds). Humour and Laughter: Theory, Research and Applications. London: John Wiley, (1976). 1st ed. Inscribed. Blue fabrikoid. VG in dj (chipped). *Gach*. $40/£26

CHAPMAN, WILLIAM. A Pathfinder in South Central Africa. London, 1910. Nice (lt foxing) in pict cl. *Grayling*. $47/£30

CHAPPELL, EDWARD. Narrative of a Voyage to Hudson's Bay.... London, 1817. 1st ed. 279pp (bkpl, ink name), fldg map. Calf (nicely rebacked, sl worn, lt foxing). *King*. $450/£288

CHAPPELL, WARREN. Anatomy of Lettering. NY/Toronto, (1935). 1st ed. VG in dj. *Truepenny*. $45/£29

CHAPPELLE, HOWARD I. Boatbuilding. NY: Norton, 1941. Stated 1st ed. Good in Poor dj. *Scribe's Perch**. $32/£21

CHAPTAL, M. F. A. Elements of Chemistry. Buckingham, 1806. 3rd Amer ed. 3 vols in 1. 612pp. Calf. (Sm tear fep repaired, 2 index leaves sl wrinkled, foxing), o/w Good. *Bookcell*. $135/£87

CHAPUIS, ALFRED and EDMOND DROS. Automata; A Historical and Technological Study. Alec Reid (trans). NY: Central Book, 1958. 1st ed in English. 18 color plts. Red cl, gilt. (Stamp; corner bumped, spine top sl frayed), o/w VG. *Weber*. $200/£128

CHAPUIS, ALFRED and EUGENE JAQUET. The History of the Self-Winding Watch, 1770-1931. NY: Central Book, 1956. 1st ed in English. Color plts, 16 tipped-in figs. Grn cl (stamp; spine faded.) *Weber*. $35/£22

CHAPUT, DONALD. Francois X. Aubry, Trader, Trailmaker and Voyageur in the Southwest, 1846-1854. Glendale, CA: A.H. Clark, 1975. 1st ed. Good. *Heinoldt*. $25/£16

CHAPUT, DONALD. Francois X. Aubry...1846-54. Glendale, 1975. 1st ed. One of 1274. Frontis, 5 maps. (Top edges stained blue, by Clark binding error. Blue cl unlike rest of series in red.) VF. No dj as issued. *Turpen*. $45/£29

CHAPUT, DONALD. Francois X. Aubry: Trader, Trailmaker, and Voyageur in the Southwest, 1846-1854. Glendale: Clark, 1975. 1st ed. One of 1274. 5 maps (1 fldg). VF. *Argonaut*. $40/£26

CHARAKA CLUB. The Proceedings of.... Volume 5. NY, 1919. Ltd ed. *Fye*. $150/£96

145

CHARCOT, JEAN-MARTIN. Clinical Lectures on Senile and Chronic Diseases. William S. Tuke (trans). London: New Sydenham Soc, 1881. xvi,307pp; 6 plts. (Sm lib stamp tp; spine ends bumped), o/w VG. *White*. $78/£50

CHARCOT, JEAN-MARTIN. Clinical Lectures on the Diseases of Old Age. Leigh H. Hunt (trans). NY: William Wood, 1881. 1st Amer ed. (iv),(xvi),280,(2)pp. Stamped brn cl, gilt spine. VG. *Gach*. $175/£112

CHARCOT, JEAN-MARTIN. Lectures on Bright's Diseases of the Kidneys.... Henry Millard (trans). NY, 1878. 1st ed in English. 2 chromo-litho plts. (Spine top worn.) *Argosy*. $175/£112

Charles A. Swedlund: Photographs. Cobden, IL: Anna Press, 1973. 1st ed. Ltd to 2000. 24 full-pg b/w photos. (Owner stamp, lt crease 1 corner), else VG in pict stiff wrappers. *Cahan*. $45/£29

Charles Meryon. Prints and Drawings. New Haven: Yale Univ Art Gallery, 1974. Good in wraps (sl soiled). *Washton*. $25/£16

CHARLIP, REMY and BURTON SUPREE. Harlequin and the Gift of Many Colors. NY: Parents, 1973. 1st ed. 7 1/2 x 10 1/4. 32pp. Fine in dj. *Cattermole*. $30/£19

CHARLIP, REMY. Arm in Arm. NY: Parents, 1969. 1st ed. 7 1/2 x 10 1/4. 40pp. Pict bds. Fine. *Cattermole*. $25/£16

Charter of Kansas City. Kansas City: Lawton, Havens & Burnap, 1889. 135pp + index (fr hinge cracked). Tan buckram (rebacked), early bds. *Parmer*. $30/£19

Chartered Surveyor, His Training and His Work. Westminster: Chartered Surveyor's Inst, (1932). 1st ed. Ephemera laid in. (Lt soil, corners bumped.) VG. *Reese*. $55/£35

CHARTERIS, EVAN. The Life and Letters of Sir Edmund Gosse. 1931. 1st ed. VG. *Words Etc*. $23/£15

CHARTERIS, LESLIE. The Saint Goes West. London: Hodder & Stoughton, 1942. 1st ed. (Sm stain rep; lt spotted, sl worn.) Dj (chipped, creased). *Metropolitan**. $28/£18

CHARTERIS, LESLIE. The Saint on the Spanish Main. GC: DCC, 1955. 1st ed. (Bottom edges cvrs shelfworn), o/w Fine in dj (internal tape reinforcing). *Mordida*. $65/£42

CHARTERS, SAMUEL B. and LEONARD KUNSTADT. Jazz. A History of the New York Scene. GC: Doubleday, 1962. 1st ed. Fine in dj (lt used). *Beasley*. $50/£32

CHARYN, JEROME. The 7th Babe. Arbor House, 1979. 1st ed. Signed. Fine in VG dj (lt soil). *Plapinger*. $125/£80

CHASE, A. W. Dr. Chase's Recipes. Ann Arbor, 1872. New ed. 400pp (lt foxed). Black gilt morocco (worn, spine chipped). Good. *Doctor's Library*. $75/£48

CHASE, J. SMEATON and CHARLES FRANCIS SAUNDERS. The California Padres and Their Missions. Boston: Houghton Mifflin, 1915. 1st ed. Uncut. Blue cl, gilt. Fine (sl rubbed). *Pacific**. $40/£26

CHASE, J. SMEATON. California Desert Trails. Boston: Houghton Mifflin, 1919. 1st ed. 31 full-pg illus. Pict cl (spine extrems, tips sl worn; spine faded), gilt. *Dawson*. $45/£29

CHASE, J. SMEATON. Our Araby: Palm Springs and the Garden of the Sun. NY: J.J. Little & Ives, 1923. Rev, enlgd ed. 9 full-pg illus, fldg map rear pocket. Pict cl. *Dawson*. $40/£26

CHASE, J. SMEATON. Yosemite Trails. Boston: Houghton Mifflin, 1911. Map, 16 plts. Blue pict cl. VG. *Adelson*. $65/£42

CHASE, JAMES HADLEY. The Flesh of the Orchid. Jarrolds, (1948). 1st ed. NF in dj (sl spine wear, price-clipped w/new price imptd). *Certo*. $75/£48

CHASTELLUX, FRANCOIS. Travels in North-America, in the Years 1780, 1781, and 1782. London, 1787. 1st ed in English. 2 vols. 2 maps, 3 plts. Mod 1/4 morocco. Howes C324. *Swann**. $488/£313

CHATTERTON, E. KEBLE. Old Ship Prints. London: John Lane, (1927). 1st ed. 15 color, 95 b/w plts. VG (spine sl frayed). *Agvent*. $65/£42

CHATTERTON, E. KEBLE. Old Ship Prints. London: Spring Books, 1965. 69 plts (9 color). VG in dj. *Hollett*. $47/£30

CHATTERTON, E. KEBLE. Ships and Ways of Other Days. Phila, 1913. Teg. Blue cl (lt worn), gilt, color cvr label. *Freeman**. $30/£19

CHATTERTON, FREDERICK (ed). Shop Fronts: A Selection of English, American and Continental Examples. Cleveland, OH: Carl Wendelin Kuehnym, 1927. 1st ed. Cl-backed paper over bds. (Stamp pastedown; rubbed, dknd), else VG. *Cahan*. $75/£48

CHATTERTON, THOMAS. The Works of...Containing His Life, by G. Gregory...and Miscellaneous Poems. Robert Southey and J. Cottle (eds). London: Ptd by Biggs & Cottle, 1803. 1st ed. 3 vols. Frontis each vol, fldg plt. Contemp 3/4 calf, marbled bds. (Bkpls, sigs, plts foxed; sl rubbed), o/w Nice. *Reese*. $200/£128

CHATTO, WILLIAM ANDREW. Facts and Speculations on the Origin and History of Playing Cards. London, 1848. (Shelfworn, shaken, spine edge torn.) *Oinonen**. $70/£45

CHATWIN, BRUCE and PAUL THEROUX. Patagonia Revisited. (Wiltshire): Russell, (1985). One of 250 numbered, signed by both. Dec cl bds. Fine in unptd glassine dj. *Between The Covers*. $300/£192

CHATWIN, BRUCE and PAUL THEROUX. Patagonia Revisited. Boston: Houghton, Mifflin, 1986. 1st Amer trade ed. Fine in dj. *Antic Hay*. $35/£22

CHATWIN, BRUCE. The Attractions of France. London: Colophon, 1993. Ltd to 175 numbered in Murillo card cvrs. New. *Buckley*. $47/£30

CHATWIN, BRUCE. In Patagonia. London: Cape, (1977). 1st ed, 1st bk. (Name, address), o/w Fine in dj. *Captain's Bookshelf*. $750/£481

CHATWIN, BRUCE. In Patagonia. London: Cape, 1977. 1st UK ed, 1st bk. (Spine top bumped), else Fine in dj. *Williams*. $624/£400

CHATWIN, BRUCE. Lady Lisa Lyon. Blond & Briggs, 1983. 1st ed. Pb issue. Fine. *Sclanders*. $47/£30

CHATWIN, BRUCE. On the Black Hill. NY: Viking, (1983). 1st ed. NF in dj. *Antic Hay*. $20/£13

CHATWIN, BRUCE. On the Black Hill. London, 1982. 1st Eng ed. Very Nice (spine, corner sl bumped) in dj. *Clearwater*. $47/£30

CHATWIN, BRUCE. The Songlines. (NY): Viking, (1987). 1st Amer ed. Fine in dj. *Antic Hay*. $45/£29

CHATWIN, BRUCE. The Songlines. London: London Ltd Eds, (1987). 1st ed. One of 150 specially bound, signed. Cl-backed marbled bds. Mint in glassine dj. *Jaffe*. $375/£240

CHATWIN, BRUCE. The Songlines. Franklin Center, PA: Franklin Library, 1987. 1st ed. Signed. Special statement prepared by Chatwin for this ed. Full dec gilt-stamped leather. Fine. *Lame Duck*. $250/£160

CHAUCER, DANIEL. (Pseud of Ford Madox Ford.) The New Humpty-Dumpty. London: John Lane, 1912. 1st ed. Dec cl. Good (foxed; sl worn). *Holmes*. $750/£481

CHAUCER, GEOFFREY. The Canterbury Tales. J.U. Nicolson (trans). NY: Covici Friede, (1934). Rockwell Kent (illus). (Dust in margins dozen pp), o/w VG in Good- dj. *Scribe's Perch**. $24/£15

CHAUCER, GEOFFREY. The Canterbury Tales. London, 1913. One of 500 numbered sets, signed by William Russell Flint (illus). 3 vols. 36 mtd color plts. Limp vellum (sl discolored), silk ties. Cl slipcase. Swann*. $747/£479

CHAUCER, GEOFFREY. The Canterbury Tales. London: Medici Soc, 1929. 24 color plts. (Lt faded.) Hollett. $62/£40

CHAUCER, GEOFFREY. The Complete Works. W. W. Skeat (ed). OUP, 1894-97. 7 vols. Fine. Andrew Stewart. $211/£135

CHAUCER, GEOFFREY. Flower and the Leaf. (London: Edward Arnold, 1902.) Ltd to 165. 8vo. 45pp. 1 full-pg, 1 dbl-pg hand-colored illus by Edith Harwood. Full vellum, blind-stamped w/rose logo, motto, 'Soul is Form.' VF. Bromer. $600/£385

CHAUCER, GEOFFREY. The Romaunt of the Rose. London: Florence Press, 1908. One of 500 numbered. 20 tipped-in color plts, guards. (Eps foxed.) Limp vellum, silk ties. Cl slipcase. Swann*. $402/£258

CHAUCER, GEOFFREY. Troilus and Cressida. George Philip Krapp (trans). London: LEC, 1939. #904/1500 numbered, signed by George W. Jones (printer). Cl-backed dec bds. Fine in slipcase. Hermitage. $100/£64

CHAUCER, GEOFFREY. The Woorkes Of. (London: John Kyngston for John Wight, 1561.) 5th ed, 2nd issue. Folio. 2 woodcut 1/2 titles, woodcut illus leaf B1, dec initials. (Lacks 10 ll, sig 'pi'(4ll: tp + 3prelims) and sig 3N (6ll); trimmed, sl loss few running heads; sm tear gutter leaf A2, text affected but complete; sm hole leaf 3D w/sl loss of text; sl dampstaining, marginal worming; back matter soiled, worn; o 19th-cent calf (rubbed, fr cvr detached). Freeman*. $1,000/£641

CHAUCER, GEOFFREY. The Works of.... Cleveland/NY: World, (1958). 1st ed thus. Simulated pigskin stamped in blind/gilt. Fine in dj (nick, lt dust-smudged). Reese. $175/£112

CHAUCER, GEOFFREY. The Works.... (London: Basilisk, 1974.) One of 515 numbered sets. 2 vols. Folio. Orig patterned linen. Bd slipcase. Swann*. $805/£516

CHAUNDY, LESLIE. A Bibliography of the First Editions of the Works of Maurice Baring. London: Dulau, 1925. 1st ed. Ltd to 250. (Bkpl.) Uncut. Cox. $39/£25

CHAVEZ, ANGELICO. Dominguez-Escalante Journal, Their Expedition...1776. Ted Warner (ed). Provo, 1976. 1st ed. Pb. Fine. Turpen. $55/£35

CHAVEZ, ANGELICO. My Penitente Land, Reflections on Spanish New Mexico. Albuquerque, (1974). 1st ed. (Underlining), o/w Fine in VG dj. Turpen. $45/£29

CHAVEZ, ANGELICO. Our Lady of the Conquest. Santa Fe, 1948. Ltd ed. Pb. Frontis port. NF. Turpen. $30/£19

CHAYEFSKY, PADDY. Television Plays. NY: S&S, 1955. 1st bk. Fine in Fine dj (sl rubbed). Between The Covers. $150/£96

CHAYEFSKY, PADDY. The Tenth Man. NY, (1960). 1st ed. VG in dj. Argosy. $40/£26

CHEADLE, W. B. Cheadle's Journal of a Trip Across Canada 1862-1863. Ottawa, 1931. Fldg map. Limp cl. VG. Reese. $100/£64

CHEESMAN, E. Six-Legged Snakes in New Guinea. London: Harrap, 1949. 1st ed. 11 dwgs. Fine in Fine dj. Mikesh. $35/£22

CHEESMAN, R. E. In Unknown Arabia. London: Macmillan, 1926. 1st ed. Lg fldg map colored in outline tipped to rear pastedown, 32 plts. Teg. Olive cl, gilt. (Sm tear map margin; sm lib stamp tp; sl rubbed, stained, upper hinge repaired.) VG. Morrell. $452/£290

CHEETHAM, JAMES. The Life of Thomas Paine. NY: Southwick & Pelsue, 1809. 1st ed. (Browned.) Calf, bds. Howes C336. Rostenberg & Stern. $125/£80

CHEEVER, GEORGE B. Wanderings of a Pilgrim in the Shadow of Mont Blanc and the Jungfrau Alp. Aberdeen/Ipswich: George Clark/J.M. Burton, 1848. 310pp + 2 ads, 1/2-title. (Few spots.) Blind-stamped cl (extrems sl rubbed), gilt. Hollett. $133/£85

CHEEVER, HENRY T. Life in the Sandwich Islands. NY: A.S. Barnes, 1851. 1st ed. Engr tp, 355pp (lt foxed); map, 5 plts. Red pict cl (lt rubbed). Adelson. $225/£144

CHEEVER, JOHN. The Day the Pig Fell into the Well. Northridge, CA: Lord John, 1978. One of 275 numbered, signed. Fine. Lenz. $125/£80

CHEEVER, JOHN. The Leaves, the Lion-Fish and the Bear. L.A.: Sylvester & Orphanos, 1980. One of 330 numbered, signed. Fine. Lenz. $125/£80

CHEEVER, JOHN. The Stories of.... NY: Knopf, 1978. 1st ed. Signed. (Sl worn) dj (sl worn). Metropolitan*. $57/£37

CHEEVER, JOHN. The Wapshot Scandal. NY: Harper, (1964). VG+ (spine sl mottled) in Fine dj (sl rubbed). Between The Covers. $200/£128

CHEEVER, SUSAN. Looking for Work. NY: S&S, (1979). 1st ed. (Sl wear extrems), o/w Fine in dj. Hermitage. $30/£19

CHEKHOV, ANTON. Don Juan. Basil Ashmore (trans). (London): Nevill, (1952). 1st ed. NF in dj. Antic Hay. $45/£29

CHEKHOV, ANTON. The Sea Gull. Stark Young (trans). NY: Scribner, 1939. 1st ed in English. NF (pastedowns sl dknd) in dj (lt edgeworn, sm tears). Antic Hay. $35/£22

Chelsea Song Book. London: Cresset, n.d. (ca 1930?). VG in 1/4 grn cl, illus bds. Michael Taylor. $44/£28

Chemistry of Penicillin. Princeton Univ, 1949. Black cl. VG (lib stamp fep). White. $148/£95

CHENERY, WILLIAM H. Fourteenth Regiment Rhode Island Artillery (Colored), in the War to Preserve the Union, 1861-1865. Providence, 1898. VG. New Hampshire*. $140/£90

CHERRY, P. P. The Western Reserve and Early Ohio. Akron: R.L. Fouse, 1921. 1st ed. VG+. Archer. $40/£26

CHERRY-GARRARD, APSLEY. The Worst Journey in the World. Antarctic 1910-1913. London: The Author, 1951. 1st ptg to contain author's Postscript dated 1948. 9 plts, 4 maps. VG in dj (sl chipped). High Latitude. $55/£35

CHERRY-GARRARD, APSLEY. The Worst Journey in the World: Antarctic 1910-1911. London: Constable, 1922. 1st ed, 1st issue, w/the 10 fldg panoramas. 8vo. 2 vols. 53 plts from art by Edward A. Wilson. VG set (sl foxed; sl worn, spine labels lt dknd, chipped). Parmer. $1,900/£1,218

CHERRY-GARRARD, APSLEY. The Worst Journey in the World: Antarctic 1910-1913. NY: Doran, (1922). 1st Amer ed ptd from the English sheets. 2 vols. Edward A. Wilson et al (illus). NF in orig cl-backed bds, paper spine labels (sl browned); orig djs (spines sunned); custom black cl slipcase. Captain's Bookshelf. $1,250/£801

CHERRYH, C. J. Cyteen. (NY): Warner, (1988). 1st ed. Dj. Swann*. $57/£37

CHERUBINI. Pinocchio in Africa. Boston, (1911). Once Upon a Time Series. Charles Copeland (illus). 7x4. 152pp. Pict cl (ends sl frayed, sl discolor; ink inscrip). King. $25/£16

CHESBRO, GEORGE C. Two Songs the Archangel Sings. NY: Atheneum, 1986. 1st ed. Fine in Fine dj. Janus. $30/£19

CHESBRO, GEORGE C. Two Songs the Archangel Sings. NY: Atheneum, 1986. 1st ed. Inscribed. VF in dj. Mordida. $45/£29

CHESELDEN, WILLIAM. The Anatomy of the Human Body. 1756. 7th ed. Frontis plt, vi,348pp (ink sigs half-title, sl foxed); 40 copper plts. New cl. *Whitehart.* $218/£140

CHESELDEN, WILLIAM. The Anatomy of the Human Body. London: J.F. & C. Rivington et al, 1778. 11th ed. 40 engr copperplts. Contemp calf. (Recently re-backed, not matching leather; eps renewed, upper margin tp repaired, foxing, browning, lacks engr frontis.) *Goodrich.* $135/£87

CHESELDEN, WILLIAM. The Anatomy of the Human Body. Boston, Jan 1806. Stated 2nd US ed. 352pp (tanned, bkpl, rubber stamp bottom edge, lib blind-stamps); 40 full-pg copper plts. Full contemp leather (rubbed; hinge, joint cracks). Good-. *Scribe's Perch*.* $50/£32

CHESNEY, ALAN. The Johns Hopkins Hospital and the Johns Hopkins University School of Medicine, A Chronicle. Balt, 1943, 1958, 1963. 1st eds. 3 vols. VG. *Fye.* $200/£128

CHESNEY, ALAN. The Johns Hopkins Hospital and the Johns Hopkins University School of Medicine. Volume 1. 1867-1893. Balt, 1943. 1st ed. VG. *Fye.* $75/£48

CHESSMAN, CARYL. Cell 2455 Death Row. NY: Pren-tice-Hall, (1954). 1st ed. VG in dj (nicks). *Houle.* $65/£42

CHESTER, ALDEN. Courts and Lawyers of New York, a History, 1609-1925. NY: Amer Hist Soc, 1925. 3 vols. 3/4 buckram (worn), gilt. Sound set. *Boswell.* $250/£160

CHESTER, SAMUEL BEACH. Anomalies of the English Law. Boston: Little, Brown, 1912. *Boswell.* $65/£42

CHESTERFIELD, EARL OF. Letters Written by the Late Philip Dormer Stanhope to His Son.... London, 1774. 4th ed. 2 vols. Frontis port. Contemp calf (hinges mended). *Argosy.* $300/£192

CHESTERFIELD, PHILIP DORMER. Lord Chesterfield's Advice to His Son, on Men and Manners.... London: For W. Richardson, 1793. 6th ed. (xii),(206)pp. Con-temp marbled bds. Good (pencil mks; worn). *Ash.* $78/£50

CHESTERMAN, W. D. Guide to Richmond and the Bat-tlefields. Richmond: Ptd by James E. Goode, 1881. 1st ed. 66+6pp ads, map. Good in wrappers (wear, lt soiling). *Brown.* $25/£16

CHESTERTON, G. K. The Autobiography of.... NY, 1936. 1st Amer ed. (Sl bumped, spine light), else Good. *King.* $25/£16

CHESTERTON, G. K. The Ball and the Cross. London: Wells Gardner, Darton, 1910. 1st UK ed. (Foxed), else Fine in VG dj (spine sl dull). *Williams.* $148/£95

CHESTERTON, G. K. The Ballad of the White Horse. NY, 1911. 1st ed. VG. *Typographeum.* $45/£29

CHESTERTON, G. K. The Club of Queer Trades. 1905. 1st ed. (Spine faded, extrems bumped), o/w VG. *Words Etc.* $78/£50

CHESTERTON, G. K. The Coloured Lands. London: Sheed & Ward, 1938. 1st ed. Cl-backed dec bds (sl soiled). *Cox.* $39/£25

CHESTERTON, G. K. The Coloured Lands. London: Sheed & Ward, 1938. 1st ed. Fine in dj (sm stain, abrasion where tape removed). *Antic Hay.* $85/£54

CHESTERTON, G. K. The Common Man. London: Sheed & Ward, 1950. 1st UK ed. NF in dj. *Williams.* $31/£20

CHESTERTON, G. K. Divorce Versus Democracy. Lon-don: York Books, 1916. 1st ed. Nice (edges sl creased, sl foxed) in sewn wrappers. *Patterson.* $31/£20

CHESTERTON, G. K. Five Types. London, 1910. 1st ed thus. Ptd paper-cvrd bds. NF in case (worn). *Buckley.* $39/£25

CHESTERTON, G. K. George Bernard Shaw. London: John Lane, 1910. 1st ed. Good (bkpl, inscrip, eps foxed; spine sl dull). *Reese.* $25/£16

CHESTERTON, G. K. Gloria in Profundis. Curwen Press, 1927. 1st UK ed. VG in ptd wrappers (spine fold sl split). *Williams.* $23/£15

CHESTERTON, G. K. Gloria in Profundis. NY: W.E. Rudge, 1927. 1st Amer ed. One of 27 ptd. Fine in ptd wrappers. *Reese.* $125/£80

CHESTERTON, G. K. Heretics. London: John Lane, 1905. 1st UK ed. Fine. *Williams.* $117/£75

CHESTERTON, G. K. The Incredulity of Father Brown. London, 1926. 1st Eng ed. *Clearwater.* $62/£40

CHESTERTON, G. K. The Incredulity of Father Brown. London: Cassell, 1926. 1st UK ed. (Top, fore-edge sl spotted; spine lt faded), o/w VG. *Moorhouse.* $47/£30

CHESTERTON, G. K. The Judgement of Doctor Johnson. Sheed & Ward, 1930. 1st ed. Buckram, gilt. (Edges sl faded), o/w VG. *Words Etc.* $19/£12

CHESTERTON, G. K. The Man Who Knew Too Much. London: Cassell, 1922. 1st UK ed. Grn cl (spine sl faded; top edge sl dusty; eps sl browned), o/w VG. *Moorhouse.* $23/£15

CHESTERTON, G. K. The Man Who Knew Too Much. NY: Harper, 1922. 1st Amer ed. Fine in VG dj (spine chipped, sm stain, fr panel lt rubbed). *Mordida.* $200/£128

CHESTERTON, G. K. Manalive. Thomas Nelson, 1912. 1st ed. Color frontis. (Margins, feps lt browned.) Blind-emb grn cl (sl bumped, nick), gilt spine. *Edwards.* $39/£25

CHESTERTON, G. K. The Napoleon of Notting Hill. London: John Lane, 1904. 1st Eng ed. Pict cl (sl mkd, bumped, spine head sl chafed). VG (bkpl, foxed). *Clearwater.* $117/£75

CHESTERTON, G. K. The Paradoxes of Mr. Pond. Dodd, Mead, 1937. 1st ed. VG+ in dj. *Authors Of West.* $60/£38

CHESTERTON, G. K. The Poet and the Lunatics. Lon-don: Cassell, 1929. 1st UK ed. (Top edge sl dusty; sl bumped), o/w NF. *Moorhouse.* $23/£15

CHESTERTON, G. K. The Resurrection of Rome. NY, 1930. 1st Amer ed. Fine (name stamp; spine, edges sunned). *Polyanthos.* $25/£16

CHESTERTON, G. K. The Return of Don Quixote. Lon-don: Chatto, 1927. 1st UK ed. NF in VG dj (sl edge-worn, spine sl faded, sm closed tear fr panel). *Williams.* $187/£120

CHESTERTON, G. K. The Scandal of Father Brown. Lon-don: Cassell, (1935). 1st ed. (Bkpl), else NF. *Certo.* $50/£32

CHESTERTON, G. K. The Secret of Father Brown. Lon-don, 1927. 1st ed. (Prelims browned, upper cvr mkd), o/w VG. *Words Etc.* $16/£10

CHESTERTON, G. K. St. Francis of Assisi. London, (1923). 1st ed. VG in dj (spine top chipped). *Buckley.* $31/£20

CHESTERTON, G. K. St. Thomas Aquinas. NY, 1933. 1st Amer ed. Good in dj (chipped, dknd). *King.* $40/£26

CHESTERTON, G. K. What I Saw in America. Hodder & Stoughton, 1922. 1st ed. (Margins, eps lt browned; sl faded, corners sl worn, few sm splash mks.) *Ed-wards.* $39/£25

CHESTNUTT, CHARLES W. Conjure Tales. Ray An-thony Shepard (ed). London: Collins, 1973. 1st UK ed. John Ross and Clare Romano (illus). 6x9. 99pp. Fine in dj. *Cattermole.* $30/£19

CHETLAIN, AUGUSTUS L. Recollections of Seventy Years. Galena: Gazette Pub Co, 1899. 1st ed. Frontis port (foxed), 304pp; errata slip. VG (bkpl). *Wantagh.* $125/£80

CHETWOOD, W. R. The Voyages and Adventures of Capt. Robert Boyle. London, 1771. vi,9-276pp. 1/2 calf, red label. (Hinges worn.) *Adelson.* $75/£48

CHEVALIER, MAURICE. My Paris. NY: Macmillan, 1972. 1st ed. (Ink note, price mkd out w/ink), else VG in illus dj (rubbed, lamination peeling). *Cahan.* $45/£29

CHEVES, W. R. Snow Ridges and Pillboxes. N.p., 1945. 1st ed. VG. *Clark.* $150/£96

CHEVREUL, M. E. The Principles of Harmony and Contrast of Colors. NY: Reinhold, 1967. *Metropolitan*.* $51/£33

CHEVREUL, M. E. The Principles of Harmony and Contrast of Colours, and Their Application to the Arts. Martel (trans). London: Longman, 1854. xxxi,431pp + 24pp ads; 4 plts hors-texte. Contemp blue emb cl. (Corners, joints sl worn), o/w Fine. *Europa.* $94/£60

CHEYNE, GEORGE. The English Malady. 1734. 3rd ed. xxxii,370pp (torn corner fep, pencil mks, prelims sl foxed). Old calf (joints weak). *Whitehart.* $374/£240

CHEYNE, GEORGE. An Essay of Health and Long Life. London, 1725. 5th ed. xx,(xxiv),232pp. New leather spine, paper-cvrd bds. (Bottom margin tp defective, neatly repaired; contemp ink inscrips), o/w VG. *Whitehart.* $234/£150

CHEYNE, GEORGE. An Essay of Health and Long Life. 1745. 9th ed. xlvii,232pp (eps sl foxed). Full calf (sl rubbed). *Whitehart.* $109/£70

CHEYNE, GEORGE. An Essay of Health and Long Life. London: G. Strahan, 1745. 10th ed. (42),(1),232pp (tp remargined, foxing, lt browning). Later full calf, raised bands. Clean. *Goodrich.* $95/£61

CHEYNE, GEORGE. The Natural Method of Cureing the Diseases of the Body, and of the Mind Depending on the Body. London: G. Strahan, 1742. 3rd ed. (xviii),316pp. Contemp full calf, raised spine bands (ends chipped, fr hinge splitting but firm). Clean. *White.* $133/£85

CHEYNEY, PETER. A Tough Spot for Cupid. London: Vallancey, 1945. Collected ed. Fine in dj (crease-tear fr panel, short closed tears). *Mordida.* $25/£16

CHIANG, YEE. The Silent Traveller. London: Country Life, 1942. (Fep removed; tp, fore-edge spotted.) Dj (sl rubbed, price-clipped). *Hollett.* $19/£12

CHIARENZA, CARL. Aaron Siskind: Pleasures and Terrors. Boston, 1982. 1st ed. Fine in dj. *Cahan.* $100/£64

Chicago Business Directory. Chicago, (1886). 14pp ads + cvr ads. Pict ptd cl. VG. *Sadlon.* $40/£26

Child's Book on Slavery. Cincinnati: American Reform Tract & Book Soc, 1857. 16mo. 143pp + 4pp ads. (Lacks rep; cl worn, spine lettering dull), else Good. *Brown.* $65/£42

Child's Pictorial Mentor, for the Year, Containing Amusing Instruction.... Worcester: S.A. Howland, 1845. 2nd ed. Sm 8vo. Full-pg VF litho frontis, 58pp (2 dated ink dedications fep, lacks rep, sl foxing); 12 full-pg lithos. Orig pict lt blue stiff paper wrappers (soiled, rubbed, chipped), black roan spine. *Hobbyhorse.* $200/£128

Child's Remembrancer; A Memoir of Bowyer Smith...1811.... (NY): Amer Tract Soc, 1825. 16mo. Full-pg wood engr frontis,24pp + 1pg ad lower wrapper. (2 ink sigs.) Fine in buff pict paper wrappers. *Hobbyhorse.* $100/£64

CHILD, ANDREW. Overland Route to California. L.A.: N.A. Kovach, 1946. Trade ed. Map. Grn cl, gilt spine. Fine in pict dj. *Pacific*.* $34/£22

CHILD, ANDREW. Overland Route to California. L.A.: N.A. Kovach, 1946. Ltd to 750. Map. VF in dj. *Perier.* $40/£26

CHILD, BENJAMIN H. From Fredericksburg to Gettysburg. Providence, RI, 1895. 1st ed. Ltd to 250. PNRISSHS Series 5, #4. 36pp. NF in ptd wrappers. *Mcgowan.* $45/£29

CHILD, HAROLD (ed). Aucassin and Nicolete. London: A&C Black, 1911. 1st ed thus. 4to. 132pp; 6 full-pg color illus by Anne Anderson. Dec cream cl bds (sl soiled). VG. *Dower.* $150/£96

CHILD, HEATHER. Calligraphy Today: Twentieth Century Tradition and Practice. A&C Black, 1988. Dec card. Fine. *Whittle.* $23/£15

CHILD, L. MARIA. The Frugal Housewife. London: Tegg, 1839. 19th ed. Engr frontis, 183pp. Aeg. Very Nice (sig) in pub's cl. BAL 3104. *Second Life.* $150/£96

CHILD, L. MARIA. Letters from New York. NY/Boston: Francis, 1843. 1st ed. One of 1500. 288pp (tp, prelims foxed). Pub's cl (sl soiled). Good. BAL 3144. *Second Life.* $75/£48

CHILD, LYDIA MARIE. The Little Girl's Own Book. NY: Samuel Colman, 1838. Sq 12mo. viii,288pp (sl foxing). 13 wood engrs signed by John H. Hall. Pict dec paper on bds (professionally rebacked), orig eps (sl discolored); gilt spine, edges. Fine. BAL 3108. *Hobbyhorse.* $300/£192

CHILD, THEODORE. Wimples and Crisping Pins, Being Studies in the Coiffure and Ornaments of Women. NY: Harper, 1895. 1st ed. 55 plts. Dec cl. VG. *Agvent.* $50/£32

Children's Instructive Poetry. NY: T.W. Strong, n.d. (1860s?). 10x7. 8 hand-colored lg woodcuts. Pict wraps (sl spotting, rubbed, soiled, spine torn). *King.* $75/£48

CHILDRESS, ALICE. Like One of the Family. Brooklyn: Independence, (1956). 1st ed, 1st bk. (Spine sl rubbed), else Fine in NF dj (lt soiled). *Between The Covers.* $150/£96

CHILDRESS, ALICE. A Short Walk. NY: Coward, McCann & Geoghegan, (1979). 1st ed. Fine in VG dj (crease fr panel). *Bernard.* $50/£32

CHILDRESS, MARK. Tender. NY, 1990. 1st Amer ed. Fine in NF dj. *Polyanthos.* $30/£19

Chin P'Ing Mei: The Adventurous History of Hsi Men and His Six Wives. NY: Putnam, 1940. 1st ed. 2 vols. (Cl sl rubbed, soiled), o/w VG. *Worldwide.* $35/£22

Chinese Pottery of the Han, T'ang and Sung Dynasties. NY, 1917. 16 tipped-in color plts. Dec paper over bds, linen spine. Good. *Scribe's Perch*.* $75/£48

CHING, R. New Zealand Birds. Auckland: Reed, Methuen, 1986. 1st ed. 40 color, 40 b/w dwgs. Fine in Fine dj. *Mikesh.* $125/£80

CHINIQUY, FATHER. The Priest, the Woman, and the Confessional. Chicago: Craig, 1888. 296pp. VG (paper browned, hinges tender). *Second Life.* $35/£22

CHIPMAN, DANIEL. Life of Hon. Nathaniel Chipman, LL.D., Formerly Member of the United States Senate, and Chief Justice of the State of Vermont. Boston: Little, 1846. 1st ed. (12),402pp. Orig cl. *Ginsberg.* $100/£64

CHIPMAN, N. P. The Tragedy of Andersonville. The Author, 1911. 1st ed. (Cvrs heavily worn, dknd.) *King.* $60/£38

CHIPMAN, N. P. The Tragedy of Andersonville. Sacramento, CA, 1911. 2nd ed. Later buckram, gilt. *Wantagh.* $65/£42

CHIPPENDALE, THOMAS. The Gentleman and Cabinet-Maker's Director. NY: Towse, 1938. Facs of 1762 3rd ed. 200 plts + 10pp supp + 100pp ads. Good. *Scribe's Perch*.* $60/£38

Chisholm's White Mountain Guide-Book. (By Moses Foster Sweetser.) Portland: Chisholm Bros, (c. 1880). (10),140,(8)pp; 8 plts/ads, fldg color map. Good (pg torn w/o loss) in pink ptd wraps (chipped). *Bohling.* $65/£42

CHISHOLM, DANIEL. The Civil War Notebook of Daniel Chisholm. NY, (1989). 1st ed. Fine in Fine dj. *Mcgowan.* $35/£22

CHISHOLM, HUGH et al (eds). Hellas: A Tribute to Classical Greece. NY: J.J. Augustin, (1944). 2nd rev ed. (Owner stamp), else VG in dj (worn). *Cahan.* $35/£22

CHITTENDEN, F. J. (ed). Dictionary of Gardening. London, 1951. 1st ed. 4 vols. Good in djs. *Henly.* $133/£85

CHITTENDEN, HIRAM M. The American Fur Trade of the Far West. Stanford: Academic Reprints, (1954). 3rd ed. 2 vols. Fldg map. Purple cl, gilt. (Spines faded), o/w NF. Howes C390. *Harrington.* $80/£51

CHITTENDEN, HIRAM M. The American Fur Trade of the Far West. NY, 1902. 1st ed. 3 vols. Frontis, fldg map. VG (bkpl each vol; hinge sl tender, rubbed). Howes C390. *Reese.* $750/£481

CHITTENDEN, HIRAM M. The American Fur Trade of the Far West. NY: Harper, 1902. 1st ed. 3 vols. Map, plan, 3 facs. (Joints, cvrs worn.) Howes C390. *Ginsberg.* $600/£385

CHITTENDEN, HIRAM M. The American Fur Trade of the Far West. Stanford: Academic Reprints, 1954. Rpt of 1902 ed. 2 vols. Lg fldg map. VF in pict djs. *Argonaut.* $95/£61

CHITTENDEN, HIRAM M. History of Early Steamboat Navigation on the Missouri River. NY: Francis P. Harper, 1903. 1st ed. Ltd to 950. 2 vols. 16 plts. (Lt foxing eps; stain gutter vol 2 affecting 1st few leaves; name eps), else VG. Howes C399. *Cahan.* $450/£288

CHITTENDEN, HIRAM M. History of Early Steamboat Navigation on the Missouri River. Minneapolis: Ross & Haines, 1962. Rpt of 1st ed. One of 1500. 2 vols in 1. Map. (Bkpl.) VF in pict dj. Howes C391. *Argonaut.* $90/£58

CHITTENDEN, HIRAM M. The Yellowstone National Park, Historical and Descriptive. St. Paul: J.E. Haynes, (1924). New, enlgd ed. Frontis, 15 plts, fldg map. Good (bkpl, spine dull). *Bohling.* $25/£16

CHITTENDEN, LUCIUS E. Invisible Siege. San Diego, CA, 1969. 1st ed. Ltd to 1500. Fine in orig box. *Wantagh.* $45/£29

CHITTENDEN, RUSSELL. History of the Sheffield Scientific School of Yale University, 1846-1922. New Haven, 1928. Signed, ltd ed. 2 vols. 1/2 leather. VG. *Fye.* $125/£80

CHITTENDEN, RUSSELL. The Nutrition of Man. Stokes, 1907. VG in vinyl dj. *Bookcell.* $55/£35

CHITTY, JOSEPH. A Practical Treatise on the Law of Nations.... Boston: Bradford & Read, 1812. Contemp sheep (rebacked, worn, foxed). Usable. *Boswell.* $350/£224

CHOATE, JOSEPH HODGES. Arguments and Addresses of Joseph Hodges Choate.... Frederick C. Hicks (ed). St. Paul: West Pub Co, 1926. Sound (worn, rubbed). *Boswell.* $45/£29

Chocolate-Plant (Theobroma Cacao) and Its Products. Dorchester, MA, 1891. 40pp (ink inscrip). Gilt-stamped pict brn bds (worn, most of backstrip gone). *King.* $50/£32

CHOLMONDELEY, MARY. Prisoners. London: Hutchinson, 1906. 1st ed. 2pp undated ads, 24pp ads dated Aug 1906. Reddish-brn cl. VG (foxed; cl discolored). *Sumner & Stillman.* $65/£42

CHOLMONDELEY-PENNELL, H. Complete Guide Fly Fishing. London, 1870. *Petersfield.* $62/£40

CHOLMONDELEY-PENNELL, H. Fishing Gossip or Stray Leaves from the Note-Books of Several Anglers. A&C Black, 1866. Frontis, plt; 2pp ads at rear. 1/2 dk maroon morocco (rebound). *Petersfield.* $81/£52

CHOLMONDELEY-PENNELL, H. Fishing: Salmon and Trout. London: Longman, 1901. VG + . *Bowman.* $50/£32

CHOLMONDELEY-PENNELL, H. The Modern Practical Angler. Routledge, 1884. 4th ed. *Petersfield.* $41/£26

CHOPPING, RICHARD. The Fly. NY, (1965). 1st ed, only bk. Cl-backed bds. VG in dj (sl worn, foxed; price-clipped). *King.* $50/£32

CHOPPING, RICHARD. The Fly. London: Secker, 1965. 1st UK ed. Fine in dj. *Williams.* $37/£24

CHORLTON, WILLIAM. The Cold Grapery, from Direct American Practice. NY: J.C. Riker, 1853. 1st ed. Frontis, 95pp. (Lt water stained throughout; fr cvr nearly detached.) *M&s.* $100/£64

CHOULANT, LUDWIG. History and Bibliography of Anatomic Illustration. M. Frank (trans). Chicago, 1920. 1st ed in English. VG. *Fye.* $350/£224

CHRIST-JANER, ALBERT. Boardman Robinson. Univ of Chicago, (1946). 1st ed. Fine in NF dj. *Agvent.* $125/£80

CHRISTENSEN, ERWIN. Primitive Art. Crowell, (1955). 1st ed. VG in Good + dj. *Oregon.* $75/£48

Christian Imagery in French Nineteenth Century Art 1789-1906. NY: Shepherd Gallery, 1980. Good in wraps. *Washton.* $30/£19

CHRISTIAN, EDGAR. Unflinching. A Diary of Tragic Adventure. London: John Murray, 1947. 3rd ptg. Map. VG. *High Latitude.* $35/£22

CHRISTIAN, PAUL. The History and Practice of Magic. James Kirkup & Julian Shaw (trans). London: Forge Press, 1952. 1st Eng ed. 2 vols. Teg. Grn cl, beveled sides. Fine. *House.* $200/£128

CHRISTIAN, W. E. Rhymes of the Rookies. Sunny Side of Soldier Service. NY: Dodd, Mead, 1917. 1st ed. Pict cl, gilt. (Spine title sl rubbed), o/w Fine. *Sadlon.* $20/£13

CHRISTIE, AGATHA. The Adventure of the Christmas Pudding. Collins, 1960. 1st UK ed. Fine (ink inscrip) in VG + dj. *Williams.* $25/£16

CHRISTIE, AGATHA. Akhnaton. Dodd, 1973. 1st ed. Fine in dj. *Murder By The Book.* $45/£29

CHRISTIE, AGATHA. And Then There Were None. NY, 1940. 1st ed (no statement of ptg on cp pg). Top stain red. Tan cl, red lettering. VG + . *Smith.* $25/£16

CHRISTIE, AGATHA. Appointment with Death. London: Collins, 1938. 1st UK ed. VG (flyleaf hinge sl cracked). *Williams.* $56/£36

CHRISTIE, AGATHA. At Bertram's Hotel. NY, (1965). 1st Amer ed. Cl-backed bds. VG in dj. *King.* $35/£22

CHRISTIE, AGATHA. The Big Four. NY, 1927. 2nd ed. Top stain orange. NF in dec cl. *Smith.* $25/£16

CHRISTIE, AGATHA. The Big Four. NY: Dodd Mead, 1927. 1st Amer ed. (Spine sl dknd), o/w VG. *Mordida.* $65/£42

CHRISTIE, AGATHA. Cat Among the Pigeons. London: Crime Club, (1959). 1st ed. NF in dj (rubbed, sl nicked, short tears). *Metropolitan*.* $28/£18

CHRISTIE, AGATHA. Cat Among the Pigeons. London: Crime Club, (1959). 1st ed. Fine (name, address; spine sl rubbed) in dj (edges lt rubbed, sm tears). *Polyanthos.* $35/£22

CHRISTIE, AGATHA. Crooked House. London: CCC, 1949. 1st ed. (Pg edges sl spotted), o/w VG in dj (price-clipped, tape mends; chips to spine, back panel; crease tears). *Mordida.* $45/£29

CHRISTIE, AGATHA. Death Comes as the End. Collins, 1945. 1st UK ed. VG + (lacks dj). *Williams.* $28/£18

CHRISTIE, AGATHA. Death Comes as the End. Collins, 1945. 1st UK ed. NF (spine sl faded) in VG + dj (spine sl faded, nicks). *Williams.* $156/£100

CHRISTIE, AGATHA. Evil Under the Sun. NY: Dodd, Mead, 1941. 1st Amer ed. VG in dj (chipped). *Houle.* $225/£144

CHRISTIE, AGATHA. The Golden Ball and Other Stories. NY: Dodd, Mead, 1971. 1st ed. Fine (2 corner bumps) in Fine dj. *Janus.* $50/£32

CHRISTIE, AGATHA. Hercule Poirot's Early Cases. NY: Dodd, Mead, 1974. 1st US ed. Fine in Fine dj. *Janus.* $25/£16

CHRISTIE, AGATHA. Hickory Dickory Dock. London: Crime Club, (1955). 1st ed. NF (name; spine top lt sunned) in dj (edges lt rubbed, rear panel lt soiled). *Polyanthos.* $35/£22

CHRISTIE, AGATHA. The Hollow. Collins, 1946. 1st UK ed. NF in VG dj (sm closed tears). *Williams.* $94/£60

CHRISTIE, AGATHA. The Hollow. London: Samuel French Ltd, 1952. 1st UK ed. Good only (ink name) in pict wrappers (creased, browned, stained). *Williams.* $56/£36

CHRISTIE, AGATHA. The Hound of Death and Other Stories. London: Odhams, (1933). 1st ed. Good + (spine sunned, cvrs sl mkd). *Certo.* $35/£22

CHRISTIE, AGATHA. The Hound of Death. Odhams, 1933. 1st ed. VG in dj (worn, torn, chipped). *Aronovitz.* $175/£112

CHRISTIE, AGATHA. The Hound of Death. London: Odhams, 1933. 1st UK ed. VG + in Nice dj (spine sl scuffed, closed tear rear panel). *Williams.* $250/£160

CHRISTIE, AGATHA. The Labours of Hercules. Collins, 1947. 1st UK ed. VG in dj (edgewear, rubbed, sm closed tears, chips). *Williams.* $86/£55

CHRISTIE, AGATHA. The Man in the Brown Suit. London: Bodley Head, 1924. 1st UK ed. VG (ink name; sl stained, spine sl creased). *Williams.* $507/£325

CHRISTIE, AGATHA. The Moving Finger. London: Collins, 1943. 1st UK ed. NF (fep sl creased) in dj (sl edgeworn, sm chip). *Williams.* $351/£225

CHRISTIE, AGATHA. Mrs. McGinty's Dead. NY: Dodd, Mead, 1952. 1st ed. VG (head, heel rubbed through) in dj (chipped, torn, soiled, stained). *Metropolitan*. $46/£29

CHRISTIE, AGATHA. The Murder at the Vicarage. NY: Dodd, Mead, 1930. 1st US ed. Grn cl. VG. *Gravesend.* $40/£26

CHRISTIE, AGATHA. A Murder Is Announced. London: Collins, 1950. 1st UK ed. NF in VG dj (sl rubbed, nicked, creased). *Williams.* $55/£35

CHRISTIE, AGATHA. The Murder of Roger Ackroyd. London: Collins, 1926. 1st UK ed. Good + (fr hinge damaged, repaired, spine top creased). *Williams.* $257/£165

CHRISTIE, AGATHA. The Murder of Roger Ackroyd. London: Collins, 1926. 1st UK ed. VG (spine extrems sl rubbed). *Williams.* $351/£225

CHRISTIE, AGATHA. The Murder on the Links. London: Bodley Head, 1923. 1st UK ed. VG- (sl rubbed, rear cvr sl stained). *Williams.* $1,482/£950

CHRISTIE, AGATHA. The Mystery of the Blue Train. London: Collins, (1928). 1st UK ed. VG (spine sl faded, sl rubbed). *Williams.* $304/£195

CHRISTIE, AGATHA. N or M? NY: Dodd Mead, 1941. 1st Amer ed. (Edges sl dknd), o/w Fine in dj (price-clipped, 2 sm tears spine ends; corners, folds sl worn) *Mordida.* $200/£128

CHRISTIE, AGATHA. N or M? NY: Dodd, 1941. 1st US ed. (Lt sticker dkng fep), o/w Fine in dj (lt used; lt skinned mk). *Beasley.* $175/£112

CHRISTIE, AGATHA. Ordeal by Innocence. London: Collins, 1958. 1st ed. (Lt foxed), o/w NF in dj (lt used). *Murder By The Book.* $60/£38

CHRISTIE, AGATHA. Pale Horse. London: Collins, 1961. 1st ed. Fine in dj (lt worn). *Murder By The Book.* $40/£26

CHRISTIE, AGATHA. Peril at End House. Dodd, 1932. 1st US ed. VG + . *Murder By The Book.* $25/£16

CHRISTIE, AGATHA. A Pocket Full of Rye. Collins, 1953. 1st UK ed. Fine in NF dj (price-clipped). *Williams.* $55/£35

CHRISTIE, AGATHA. Poems. London: Collins, 1973. Uncorrected advance proofs. NF in wrappers, as issued. *Janus.* $65/£42

CHRISTIE, AGATHA. Poirot Loses a Client. NY, 1937. 1st Amer ed. (Sl worn.) *King.* $25/£16

CHRISTIE, AGATHA. The Secret Adversary. London: Bodley Head, 1922. 1st UK ed. VG (lacks fep, spine top sl nicked). *Williams.* $1,365/£875

CHRISTIE, AGATHA. Sparkling Cyanide. Collins, 1945. 1st UK ed. Fine in VG dj (lt edgewear). *Williams.* $109/£70

CHRISTIE, AGATHA. Taken at the Flood. Collins, 1948. 1st UK ed. VG (lacks dj). *Williams.* $19/£12

CHRISTIE, AGATHA. Taken at the Flood. Collins, 1948. 1st UK ed. NF in VG dj (sl edgewear, creased, sm chip). *Williams.* $75/£48

CHRISTIE, AGATHA. Taken at the Flood. London: CCC, 1948. 1st ed. VG in dj (tape mends, lg piece missing back panel, corners chipped). *Mordida.* $45/£29

CHRISTIE, AGATHA. They Came to Baghdad. London: Collins, 1951. 1st UK ed. Fine in NF dj. *Williams.* $70/£45

CHRISTIE, AGATHA. Three Blind Mice. NY: Dodd, Mead, 1948. 1st ed. (Extrems worn through.) Dj (soiled, loss). *Metropolitan*. $51/£33

CHRISTIE, AGATHA. Towards Zero. Collins, 1944. 1st UK ed. VG (lacks fep) in dj (sl foxed, closed tears, spine chipped). *Williams.* $39/£25

CHRISTIE, AGATHA. Towards Zero. London: Collins, 1944. 1st UK ed. VG + in dj. *Williams.* $429/£275

CHRISTMAN, ENOS. One Man's Gold. Florence Morrow Christman (ed). NY: Whittlesey House, 1930. 1st ed. Good. *Lien.* $30/£19

CHRISTY, BYRON. Clown Joke Book. NY: F.A. Brady, (1859). 1st ed. Frontis, 64,(6)pp pub ads; 2 plts. Pict wraps (chipped, transparent tape repair spine, rear wrap gone). *Petrilla.* $50/£32

CHRISTY, CUTHBERT. Big Game and Pygmies. London: Macmillan, 1924. 1st ed. Color fldg map. Gilt-dec cl. VG + . *Mikesh.* $175/£112

CHRISTY, CUTHBERT. Big Game and Pygmies. London: Macmillan, 1924. 1st ed. Frontis, fldg color map. Blue gilt pict cl. (Few leaves opened carelessly), else Fine. *Terramedia.* $200/£128

CHRISTY, HOWARD CHANDLER. The American Girl. NY: Moffat, Yard, 1906. 1st ed. 15 (of 16) color plts. Grn cl (sl worn), color pict label (sl dusty, spotted), gilt. Text Good (hinges retightened, some plts reinserted w/edge tears, chipping, some guards torn/lacking). *Baltimore*. $40/£26

CHRISTY, HOWARD CHANDLER. Drawings. NY: Moffat Yard, 1905. Cl-backed pict bds (ends worn, extrems rubbed). *Argosy.* $175/£112

CHRISTY, THOMAS. Thomas Christy's Road Across the Plains. Denver: Old West, 1969. Frontis; 95 maps. As New. *Dumont.* $45/£29

CHRISTY, THOMAS. Thomas Christy's Road Across the Plains. Robert Becker (ed). Denver: Old West, 1969. Frontis port, 94 strip maps. Pict cl. VG + in dj (dknd, edgeworn). *Bohling.* $45/£29

Chronological Detail of Events in Which Oliver Cromwell Was Engaged from...1640 to...1658.... (By James Caulfield.) Westminster: Michael Stace, 1810. 1/2 morocco, marbled bds (rubbed), gilt. *Kane*.* $200/£128

CHUBB, I. M. Little Pickaninnies. Racine: Whitman, 1929. 20pp incl Fair pict wraps. 10 full-pg color illus. Contents Clean. *Scribe's Perch*.* $70/£45

CHUINARD, ELDON G. Only One Man Died. Glendale: A.H. Clark, 1979. 1st ed. Frontis, dbl-pg map. Red cl. Dj. *Dawson.* $100/£64

CHURCH, A. H. Josiah Wedgwood, Master Potter.... London, 1903. New ed. (Pencil notes on frontis recto; spine ends worn.) *Swann*.* $57/£37

CHURCH, A. H. et al. Some Minor Arts as Practised in England. London: Seeley, 1894. Grn buckram, gilt. VG (inscrip; shelfworn). *Heller.* $150/£96

CHURCH, ALBERT COOK. American Fishermen. James B. Connolly (text). NY: Norton, (1940). 1st ed. 261 plts. (Cvrs lt soil, shelfwear.) Internally Clean. *Lefkowicz.* $65/£42

CHURCH, ALBERT COOK. Whale Ships and Whaling. NY: W.W. Norton, (1938). 1st ed. VG in dj (torn, taped). *Perier.* $97/£62

CHURCH, ALFRED J. Roman Life in the Days of Cicero. London, 1884. 4th thousand. xi,(iv),291pp; 12 ink-photo plts. Marbled eps, edges. Contemp prize gilt calf (sl rubbed; bkpl), morocco spine label. *Edwards.* $31/£20

CHURCH, ARCHIBALD. Diseases of the Nervous System (Modern Clinical Medicine). NY, 1910. 1st ed. 5 color plts. Grn cl bds (sl worn). VG. *Doctor's Library.* $75/£48

CHURCH, GEORGE EARL and CLEMENTS R. MARKHAM (eds). Aborigines of South America. London, 1912. 1st ed. Frontis port, lg fldg map. Red cl (spine sl faded; lt foxed). *Maggs.* $148/£95

CHURCH, JERRY. Journal of Travels, Adventures, and Remarks, of Jerry Church.... A. Monroe Aurand, Jr. (ed). Harrisburg, PA: Aurand, 1933. Orig cl rpt of 1845 ed. Howes C404. *Ginsberg.* $100/£64

CHURCH, PEGGY POND. The House at Otowi Bridge: The Story of Edith Warner and Los Alamos. Univ of NM, (1959). 1st ed. Fine in VG dj. *Authors Of West.* $30/£19

CHURCH, RICHARD. The Golden Sovereign. London: Heinemann, 1957. 1st ed. (Sl shaken.) Dj (lt worn, chipped). *Hollett.* $19/£12

CHURCH, RICHARD. Twelve Noon. 1936. 1st ed. NF in dj (spine sl tanned). *Words Etc.* $19/£12

CHURCH, THOMAS. The History of Philip's War.... Exeter, 1834. Frontis. (Bk label, sm portion excised upper margin tp.) Contemp sheep. Cl slipcase. Howes C405. *Swann*.* $201/£129

CHURCH, W. S. Legal and Business Forms. SF: Bender-Moss, 1911. Orig buckram (worn). Sound. *Boswell.* $30/£19

CHURCH, WILLIAM CONANT. The Life of John Ericsson. NY: Scribner, 1906-7. 2 vols. VG. *Wantagh.* $45/£29

CHURCHILL, CLAIRE WARNER. South of the Sunset. NY: Rufus Rockwell Wilson, 1936. 1st ed. VG in dj (sl worn). *Lien.* $50/£32

CHURCHILL, FLEETWOOD. On the Diseases of Infants and Children. Phila, 1856. 2nd Amer ed. 735pp. Fair (binding shaken, spine tape-repaired). *Doctor's Library.* $75/£48

CHURCHILL, J. FRANCIS. Treatise on the Immediate Cause and the Specific Treatment of Pulmonary Phthisis and Tubercular Diseases. NY, (1859). 112pp, sewn. VG. *Argosy.* $85/£54

CHURCHILL, ROBERT. Churchill's Shotgun Book. NY: Knopf, 1955. 1st ed. 1/2 blue cl, ivory linen-cvrd bds. NF in ptd dj (chipped). *Biscotti.* $40/£26

CHURCHILL, SIDNEY J. A. and CYRIL G. E. BUNT. The Goldsmiths of Italy. London: Martin Hopkinson, 1926. 1st ed. Mtd color frontis, 20 plts. (Few prelims sl waterstained to corner.) Teg. Blue cl, gilt. *Karmiole.* $200/£128

CHURCHILL, WINSTON S. An Address by the Rt. Hon. Winston S. Churchill...December 26th, 1941. Stamford, CT: Overbrook Press, 1942. 1st ptg in this format. One of 1000. Paper label (sl tanned), o/w Fine. *Reese.* $175/£112

CHURCHILL, WINSTON S. An Address...Delivered Before a Joint Meeting of the Two Houses of Congress on Wednesday, May 19, 1943. (Wrapper title.) Washington: GPO, 1943. 1st ed, House issue. Fine in ptd wrappers. *Reese.* $250/£160

CHURCHILL, WINSTON S. The Collected Works. Frederick Woods (ed). Library of Imperial History, 1973-1976. Centenary ed. Ltd to 3000. 34 vols. The Collected Essays. Michael Wolff (ed). Library of Imperial History, 1976. Centenary ed. Ltd to 3000. Uniformly bound in orig vellum gilt. Aeg. Slipcases. *Sotheby's*.* $2,153/£1,380

CHURCHILL, WINSTON S. The Dawn of Liberation. Cassell, (1945). 1st ed. Nice (edges lt spotted, sl mks) in dj (sl nicked, chipped). *Ash.* $39/£25

CHURCHILL, WINSTON S. A History of the English-Speaking Peoples. London: Cassell, 1956-1958. 1st ed. 4 vols. Red cl, gilt spines. Excellent in Fine pict djs. *Vandoros.* $425/£272

CHURCHILL, WINSTON S. Ian Hamilton's March...Together with Extracts from the Diary of Lieutenant H. Frankland.... London: Longmans, Green, 1900. 1st ed (5000 ptd). Frontis, fldg map, terminal ads, inserted 32-pg cat. Deep red cl stamped in gilt. (Prelims foxed, spine crown sl soft), o/w Very Nice in slipcase. *Reese.* $850/£545

CHURCHILL, WINSTON S. Into Battle. Cassell, (1941). 1st ed, 1st issue, w/o inserted leaf. Good (edges sl spotted) in dj (sl creased, chipped). *Ash.* $39/£25

CHURCHILL, WINSTON S. Liberalism and the Social Problem. London: Hodder & Stoughton, 1909. 1st ed (5000 ptd). Plum cl (spine sl dknd, bumped), gilt. VG in slipcase. *Reese.* $900/£577

CHURCHILL, WINSTON S. London to Ladysmith via Pretoria. London: Longmans, Green, 1900. 1st ed. 3 fldg maps (1 color). Beige pict cl (sl soiled, rubbed). Good (foxing, 1 map torn). *Morrell.* $296/£190

CHURCHILL, WINSTON S. London to Ladysmith via Pretoria. London: Longmans, Green, 1900. 1st ed. 32-pg inserted terminal cat. (Edges sl foxed, lt smudges.) Pict tan cl stamped in black/red/gilt. VG (fr inner hinge sl cracking) in slipcase. *Reese.* $750/£481

CHURCHILL, WINSTON S. London to Ladysmith via Pretoria. NY: Longmans, Green, 1900. 1st Amer ed. Teg. Red cl, gilt. (Sm mend 1st map; fore-edges lt creased, sl soil), o/w Good in slipcase. *Reese.* $300/£192

CHURCHILL, WINSTON S. Lord Randolph Churchill. London: Macmillan, 1906. 1st ed. 2 vols. Ports. Largely unopened. Plum cl, gilt. (Sm bkseller label pastedowns, spines sl dknd), o/w Nice. *Reese.* $500/£321

CHURCHILL, WINSTON S. Marlborough, His Life and Times. Harrap, 1933, 1934, 1936, 1938. 1st UK ed. 4 vols. VG (bds vols 1, 2, 3 unevenly faded; lack djs). *Williams.* $351/£225

CHURCHILL, WINSTON S. Marlborough, His Life and Times. George G. Harrap, 1933-1938. 1st ed. 4 vols. Errata slips, fldg maps. Orig plum buckram. Fine in djs. *Sotheby's**. $1,524/£977

CHURCHILL, WINSTON S. Marlborough, His Life and Times. London: Harrap, 1933-1938. 1st trade ed. 4 vols. Gilt polished buckram. (Extrems 1st 3 vols sunned), o/w VG set. *Reese.* $300/£192

CHURCHILL, WINSTON S. My African Journey. London: Hodder & Stoughton, 1908. 1st ed, 1st binding. Frontis, 16-pg terminal cat. Pict red cl stamped in black/gray/gray-blue. VG (edges lt foxed, ink name dated year of pub rep, sm nick spine crown, cl lt smudged) in slipcase. *Reese.* $600/£385

CHURCHILL, WINSTON S. My African Journey. London: Hodder, 1908. 1st UK ed. VG (spine sl faded). *Williams.* $702/£450

CHURCHILL, WINSTON S. My Early Life, a Roving Commission. London: Butterworth, (1930). 1st ed, 2nd state, w/half-title a cancel, listing 12 titles. Bright purple cl. VG (edges lt foxed) in cl slipcase. *Reese.* $100/£64

CHURCHILL, WINSTON S. Onwards to Victory. War Speeches.... Charles Eade (ed). London: Cassell, (1944). 1st ed. Fine in VG dj. *Reese.* $75/£48

CHURCHILL, WINSTON S. A Roving Commission, My Early Life. NY: Scribner, 1930. 1st US ed. Port. Gilt cl. Dull in cl slipcase. *Reese.* $30/£19

CHURCHILL, WINSTON S. Savrola. London: Hodder & Stoughton, 1915. 2nd Cheap ed. Good. *Clearwater.* $31/£20

CHURCHILL, WINSTON S. Savrola. A Tale of the Revolution in Laurania. London: Longmans, Green, 1900. 1st British ptg (1500 copies). This copy has copyright notice on title verso. (Bkseller blindstamp ep.) Dk grn cl (spine sl dknd, lt rubs, lower joint sl cracking), gilt. Nice in cl slipcase. *Reese.* $750/£481

CHURCHILL, WINSTON S. Savrola. A Tale of the Revolution in Laurania. NY: Longmans, Green, 1900. 1st ed, preceding British ptg. Dk blue cl, gilt. (Ink inscrip, smk mk from once tipped-in bkpl), o/w NF in fldg cl case. *Reese.* $950/£609

CHURCHILL, WINSTON S. The Second World War. Cassell, (1948-1954). 1st British ed. 6 vols. 8vo. Recent 1/2 crimson morocco, banded, gilt. (Edges sl spotted), o/w VG set. *Ash.* $702/£450

CHURCHILL, WINSTON S. The Second World War. London, 1948-1954. 1st ed. 6 vols. VG in djs. *Words Etc.* $117/£75

CHURCHILL, WINSTON S. A Speech by the Prime Minister.... London, August 20, 1940. 1st Eng ed. Ptd wrappers (sl mkd). *Clearwater.* $78/£50

CHURCHILL, WINSTON S. A Speech by the Prime Minister...August 20, 1940. (London: Ministry of Information, 1940.) 1st ed. VG in pale blue wrappers (sl foxed, mkd). *Reese.* $500/£321

CHURCHILL, WINSTON S. The Story of the Malakand Field Force. London: Longmans, 1897. 1st UK ed, 1st bk, 1st issue w/ads dated 12/97 and lacking errata slip. (Rubbed patch upper bd from removed name), else VG. *Williams.* $3,892/£2,495

CHURCHILL, WINSTON S. The Story of the Malakand Field Force. Longmans Green, 1898. 1st ed. 8vo. Maps, 32-pg cat at end dated 12/97. Orig cl (spine sl soiled). VG. *Sotheby's**. $1,794/£1,150

CHURCHILL, WINSTON S. The Story of the Malakand Field Force. Longmans Green, 1898. 1st ed, 1st state w/o errata slip. 8vo. Unopened. Pub's cat at end. (Sl dampstain outer margin 1 plan, sl foxing toward final leaves.) Black eps. Apple grn cl lettered in gilt. Matching collector's box. VF. *Sotheby's**. $3,409/£2,185

CHURCHILL, WINSTON S. The Story of the Malakand Field Force. London: Longmans, Green, 1898. 1st ed, 1st bk; preferred state w/o errata slip tipped in prior to 1st map. 1st ptg consisted of 2000 copies, of which a number of copies were exported to US. Ptgs for Colonial ed and 'Silver Library' ed followed shortly. Frontis, 32pp, terminal cat, 2 fldg maps. Apple grn cl stamped in gilt. (Sm bkpl, pencil name dated in year of pub, foxing to eps, edges), o/w externally NF in fldg cl case. *Reese.* $5,000/£3,205

CHURCHILL, WINSTON S. Thoughts and Adventures. London: Butterworth, (1932). 1st ed. Port. (Ink inscrip, foxing early and late.) Gilt cl (quite rubbed). Sound in cl slipcase. *Reese.* $75/£48

CHURCHILL, WINSTON. Dr. Jonathan. NY: Macmillan, 1919. 1st ed. Fine in VG dj (sl chipped, spine lettering affected). *Antic Hay.* $50/£32

CHURCHMAN, JOHN. An Account of the Gospel Labors, and Christian Experiences, of...John Churchman. Phila, 1779. 1st ed. 256pp. Orig calf (scuffed, worn). Sound. *Reese.* $225/£144

CHURCHMAN, JOHN. An Account of the Gospel Labours, and Christian Experiences of...John Churchman. London, 1780. 1st British ed. viii,351pp. Contemp calf (expertly rebacked), orig leather spine label. Good. *Reese.* $150/£96

CHURCHWARD, ALBERT. The Signs and Symbols of Primordial Man. London, 1910. xxiii,449pp; 17 plts (14 color, 1 fldg; 1 b/w fldg), fldg map. (Feps lt foxed, hinges cracked; lt soiled, spine sl faded, chipped.) *Edwards.* $117/£75

CHUTE, CAROLYN. The Beans. London: C&W, 1985. 1st British ed. NF (sl sticker remains fep) in NF dj. *Revere.* $35/£22

CIANFRANI, THEODORE. A Short History of Obstetrics and Gynecology. Springfield, 1960. 1st ed. (Exlib, mkd.) *Fye.* $75/£48

CIARDI, JOHN. 39 Poems. New Brunswick: Rutgers, 1959. 1st ed. NF (eps foxing) in VG+ dj (sl rubbing; sm tears). *Between The Covers.* $50/£32

CIARDI, JOHN. An Alphabestiary. Phila: Lippincott, (1965). 1st ed. Milton Hebald (illus). Blind-stamped olive grn cl bds. VF in cranberry slipcase. *Bromer.* $50/£32

CIARDI, JOHN. Homeward to America. NY: Holt, (1940). 1st ed, 1st bk. (Name; sm smudge fr pastedown), else Fine in NF dj (price-clipped; sl rubbing). *Between The Covers.* $125/£80

CIARDI, JOHN. The Monster Den. NY: Lippincott, (1966). 1st ed. Edward Gorey (illus). Fine in dj (price-clipped). *Bromer.* $65/£42

CIBBER, COLLEY. An Apology for the Life of Colley Cibber, Comedian.... (Tyford): Golden Cockerel, 1925. #89/450. 2 vols. Deckled edges, partially unopened. Cl-backed bds. VG. *Dramatis Personae.* $150/£96

CICERO, M. TULLIUS. Correspondence. R. Y. Tyrrell and L. C. Purser (eds). Dublin Univ, 1904-33. Vol 1, 3rd ed; vols 2-6, 2nd ed. (Lacks Index vol.) *Stewart.* $195/£125

Cinderella, or, The Little Glass Slipper. NY/St. Louis: Nafis & Comish, n.d. 8vo. 16pp, incl cvrs (edges sl chipped, sl foxed); 8 hand-colored wood engrs. Orig pict yellow wraps (soiled, creased, spine splitting). Good. *Blue Mountain.* $125/£80

Cinderella. NY: McLoughlin Bros, n.d. (1880s). 1st Amer ed. 10x7. 24 chromolitho transformation pp at center fold. (Sl adhesion mks center pp, ink name, tear top margin, incl cvr.) Color pict bds (loose, extrems chipped, spine poor). *King.* $75/£48

CIORAN, E. M. A Short History of Decay. NY: Viking, 1975. 1st ed in English. NF in NF dj. *Lame Duck.* $45/£29

CIORAN, E. M. The Trouble with Being Born. NY: Viking, 1976. 1st US ed. NF in dj (sl loss extrems, edges). *Lame Duck*. $45/£29

CIPRIANI, LEONETTO. California and Overland Diaries of Count Leonetto Cipriani, 1853 through 1871. (Portland): Champoeg, 1962. 1st ed in English. One of 750. Gilt-dec red cl. (Spine sl dknd), o/w NF. *Harrington*. $50/£32

Circus ABC. NY: Saalfield, (1910). 8x5. (5)pp ptd in color on cl. Pict limp cl (rubbed). *King*. $40/£26

CIRLOT, J. E. A Dictionary of Symbols. Jack Sage (trans). NY: Philosophical Library, 1962. 1st ed. 32 plts. Black cl, gilt. Fine. *Hartfield*. $45/£29

CISCO, JAY GUY. Historic Sumner County Tennessee with Genealogies of the Bledsoe, Cage and Douglas Families. Nashville: Folk-Keelin, 1909. #320/500. VG. *Perier*. $45/£29

CISNEROS, JOSE. Riders Across the Centuries, Horsemen of the Spanish Borderlands. El Paso, 1984. 1st ed. Rev copy. Frontis. VF in VF dj. *Turpen*. $45/£29

CISNEROS, SANDRA. Woman Hollering Creek. (London): Bloomsbury, (1993). 1st UK ed. NF in pict wraps. *Robbins*. $25/£16

CIST, CHARLES. Sketches and Statistics of Cincinnati in 1851. Cincinnati, 1851. Frontis, 363pp. Good (inscrip, bkpl, sl foxed, frayed). Howes C412. *Ginsberg*. $125/£80

CIST, CHARLES. Sketches and Statistics of Cincinnati in 1851. Cincinnati: Wm. H. Moore, 1851. Frontis, viii,13-363pp (bkpl, date, stamp, stain fep); 31 plts. Clean exterior (spine ends, lower corners lt frayed). *Bohling*. $120/£77

Civil Record of Major General Winfield S. Hancock, During His Administration in Louisiana and Texas. N.p., 1871. 1st ed. 32pp. (2 sm WY Hist Geological Soc stamps), else VG in ptd wrappers. *Mcgowan*. $250/£160

Civil War Maps in the National Archives. Washington: GPO, 1964. 1st ed. NF in stiff ptd wrappers. *Mcgowan*. $35/£22

CLAFLIN, BERT. American Waterfowl. NY: Knopf, 1952. 1st ed. Color frontis. 1/2 red cl, rust-colored cl. Fine in NF pict dj. *Biscotti*. $100/£64

CLAMPITT, AMY. The Kingfisher. NY: Knopf, 1983. 1st ed. Fine in dj (price-clipped, price sticker inner fr flap). *Jaffe*. $50/£32

CLAMPITT, AMY. What the Light Was Like. NY: Knopf, 1985. 1st ed. Fine in dj. *Jaffe*. $65/£42

CLANCY, TOM. Clear and Present Danger. NY: Putnam, (1989). 1st ed. Signed. Fine in Fine dj. *Unger*. $125/£80

CLANCY, TOM. Clear and Present Danger. London, 1989. 1st ed. VG in dj (sl creased, short tear spine head). *Words Etc*. $23/£15

CLANCY, TOM. The Hunt for Red October. Annapolis: Naval Inst, (1984). 1st ed. Red cl (sl bumped). Dj (sl creased, soiled, extrems sl chipped). *Freeman**. $180/£115

CLANCY, TOM. The Hunt for Red October. Annapolis: Naval Inst, (1984). 1st ed. W/o price on dj, w/o any ed statement on c. pg. Red cl (sl shelfworn), silver spine lettering. VG dj (1 flap corner sl creased). *Baltimore**. $185/£119

CLANCY, TOM. The Hunt for Red October. Annapolis: Naval Institute, (1984). 1st ed, 1st bk. (Sm smudge fep; bds lt worn.) NF in Fine dj (sl wear). *Between The Covers*. $550/£353

CLANCY, TOM. The Hunt for Red October. Annapolis: Naval Inst, 1984. 1st ed. Fine (sl worn) in VG dj. *Metropolitan**. $373/£239

CLANCY, TOM. Red Storm Rising. NY: Putnam, (1986). 1st ed. NF (sm stain fore edge) in dj (sm interior stain). *Antic Hay*. $35/£22

CLANCY, TOM. Red Storm Rising. NY: Putnam, (1986). Fine in VG + dj (lt worn). *Between The Covers*. $85/£54

CLANCY, TOM. Submarine. NY: Putnam, 1993. #149/300 'specially bound,' signed. No dj, as issued. NF in NF slipcase. *Scribe's Perch**. $160/£103

CLANCY, TOM. Without Remorse. NY: Putnam, 1993. #235/600 'specially bound,' signed. No dj, as issued. NF in NF slipcase. *Scribe's Perch**. $100/£64

CLAPHAM, A. W. English Romanesque Architecture. Oxford, 1934. 47 plts hors texte. (Spine sunned.) *Washton*. $110/£71

CLAPHAM, RICHARD. The Book of the Fox. NY: Derrydale, 1931. 1st ed. One of 750. (Spine, bds faded.) *Cummins*. $65/£42

CLAPHAM, RICHARD. The Book of the Otter. London: Heath Cranton, 1922. 1st ed. 13 plts. Blue cl (sl rubbed), gilt. *Hollett*. $55/£35

CLAPHAM, RICHARD. Sport on Fell, Beck, and Tarn. London: Heath Cranton, 1924. 1st ed. (1/2-title spotted.) *Hollett*. $55/£35

CLAPP, HERBERT C. A Tabular Handbook of Auscultation and Percussion. NY, 1897. 12th ed. 101pp. Grn cl bds (sl worn). VG. *Doctor's Library*. $50/£32

CLAPP, THEODORE. Autobiographical Sketches and Recollections, During a Thirty-Five Years' Residence in New Orleans. Boston: Phillips, Sampson, 1857. 1st ed. Frontis port, viii,419pp + ads. (Foxed; worn, shaken; backstrip torn, chipped.) Howes C425. *Bohling*. $45/£29

CLAPPERTON, R. H. and W. HENDERSON. Modern Paper-Making. Waverley, 1929. 1st ed. Grained cl, gilt. (Lt worn, sl mkd), o/w VG. *Whittle*. $47/£30

CLARE, JOHN. The Hue and Cry: A Tale of the Times. Eric Robinson (ed). Market Drayton, 1990. One of 125 numbered, signed by Nicholas Parry (binder). Gold-colored toile. Fine. *Heller*. $175/£112

CLARE, JOHN. Poems Descriptive of Rural Life and Scenery. Taylor & Hessey, 1820. 1st ed, 1st bk. xxxii,222,(10)pp; 1/2 title, 5-line errata slip, 10pp ads (lacks blank before half-title). Later 19th cent 1/2 grn morocco (extrems rubbed), patterned cl sides, gilt backstrip. Nice. *Cox*. $390/£250

CLARE, JOHN. Sketches in the Life of John Clare Written by Himself. Cobden-Sanderson, 1931. 1st ed. (Cl faded; spotted), o/w VG. *Poetry Bookshop*. $94/£60

CLARE, JOHN. The Village Minstrel and Other Poems. Taylor & Hessey, 1821. 1st ed. 2 vols. xxviii,216; (viii),211,(5)pp; 1/2 titles each vol, engr port (spotted) vol 1, 4pp ads end vol 2. Later 19th cent 1/2 grn morocco (extrems rubbed), patterned cl sides, gilt backstrips. (Copies have been recorded w/2 ad ll inserted end vol 1.) VG. *Cox*. $343/£220

CLARE, JOHN. The Village Minstrel, and Other Poems. London: Taylor & Hessey, and E. Drury, 1821. 1st ed. 2 vols. Half-titles, engr port. (Spotted.) Contemp olive calf (neatly rebacked), gilt. *Burmester*. $468/£300

CLAREMONT, L. The Gem-Cutter's Craft. London: Bell, 1906. Frontis. Teg. VG (spine faded). *Savona*. $62/£40

Clarence Buckingham Collection of Japanese Prints. Chicago: Art Institute, 1965. One of 1000. Fine in slipcase (sl worn). *Waverly**. $104/£67

CLARENDON, EDWARD. The History of the Rebellion and Civil Wars in England…. Oxford, 1702-04. 1st ed. 3 vols. Frontis each vol. (Ink notes margin 1 leaf.) Mod full leather, gilt. *Kane**. $400/£256

CLARENDON, EDWARD. Life of Edward, Earl of Clarendon.... Oxford: Clarendon, 1760. 2 vols. Full calf (sl worn, fr hinges cracked). *New Hampshire**. $80/£51

CLARK and WACKERBARTH. The Red Couch. NY: Van Der Marck, 1985. 1st ed. NF in VG + dj. *Smith*. $65/£42

CLARK, A. H. A Complete Roster of Colonel David Waterbury Jr.'s Regiment of Connecticut Volunteers. NY, 1897. 1st ed. 20pp. Good in ptd wraps (sl tears spine). *Scribe's Perch**. $17/£11

CLARK, ALEXANDER. The Old Log Schoolhouse. Phila: Leary, Getz, 1861. 1st ed. (Extrems sl rubbed.) *Sadlon*. $20/£13

CLARK, ALLEN C. Greenleaf and Law in the Federal City. Washington: Press of W.F. Roberts, 1901. (Age-spotted, rubbed.) *Zubal**. $16/£10

CLARK, ARTHUR C. A Fall of Moondust. NY: HBW, (1961). 1st ed. Fine in Fine dj (3 tears rear panel). *Between The Covers*. $250/£160

CLARK, C. M. Picturesque Ohio. Cincinnati: Cranston & Curts, (1887). Columbian ed. 238pp. Brn cl. VG + . *Bohling*. $15/£10

CLARK, D. H. Superstars. How Stellar Explosions Shape the Destiny of Our Universe. NY, 1984. *Whitehart*. $23/£15

CLARK, EDNA MARIA. Ohio Art and Artists. Richmond: Garrett & Massie, (1932). Blue cl (sl worn, extrems frayed, cvr stain). *Bohling*. $120/£77

CLARK, ELEANOR. Rome and a Villa. NY, 1952. 1st ed. Fine in dj. *Argosy*. $40/£26

CLARK, EMMONS. History of the Seventh Regiment of New York, 1806-1889. Vol I only. NY: 7th Regiment, 1890. 498 pp; color plt. Fair (pp roughly opened). *Lien*. $50/£32

CLARK, FREDERICK THICKSTUN. In the Valley of Havilah. NY: Frank F. Lovell, (1890). 1st ed. 282pp. Mottled bds (spine paper flaked off; bkpl). *Dawson*. $75/£48

CLARK, GEORGE ROGERS. George Rogers Clark Papers 1781-1784. James Alton James (ed). Springfield: IL State Hist Library, (1926). Buckram (spine dull). Good. *Bohling*. $25/£16

CLARK, GEORGE T. Leland Stanford: War Governor of California, Railroad Builder, and Founder of Stanford University. Stanford Univ, 1931. 1st ed. Frontis port. Maroon cl (spine head sl rubbed), gilt. Fine. *Argonaut*. $60/£38

CLARK, H. Catalogue of Halticidae in the Collection of the British Museum. Part I: Physapodes and Oedipodes. 1860. xii,302pp; 5 plts. (Ex-lib, stamps on all prelims, some text pp, plts; labels feps.) *Whitehart*. $28/£18

CLARK, H. F. The English Landscape Garden. Pleiades, 1948. VG in VG dj (sl dusty). *Hadley*. $39/£25

CLARK, H. H. Lost in Pompeii. Lothrop, 1883. 1st ed. VG. *Madle*. $30/£19

CLARK, ISAAC NEWTON. Isaac Newton Clark: A Personal Sketch by Himself. Philip Wendell Cranwell (ed). Kansas City, 1917. 1st ed. *Ginsberg*. $75/£48

CLARK, J. A Treatise on Pulmonary Consumption. 1835. xxxiii,399pp. Old bds (rebacked). *Whitehart*. $109/£70

CLARK, J. W. and T. M. HUGHES. The Life and Letters of the Reverend Adam Sedgwick. CUP, 1890. 1st ed. 2 vols. xiii,539; vii,640pp. VG set (ex-lib). *Glaser*. $150/£96

CLARK, JAMES A. and MICHEL T. HALBOUTY. Spindletop. NY: Random House, (1952). 1st ed. VG in dj (sl worn). *Lien*. $40/£26

CLARK, JAMES L. Trails of the Hunted. Boston: Little, Brown, 1928. 1st ed. Frontis. VG (spine edgewear; fr inner hinge chipped) *Backman*. $45/£29

CLARK, JOHN. Hunza: Lost Kingdom of the Himalayas. NY: Funk & Wagnals, 1956. 1st ed. 16 plts. VG in dj (torn). *Worldwide*. $28/£18

CLARK, JOSEPH G. Lights and Shadows of Sailor Life.... Boston: Mussey, 1848. 324pp; 6 woodcut plts (browned). Orig cl (spine ends worn). Howes C442. *Lefkowicz*. $200/£128

CLARK, KENNETH. The Drawings by Sandro Botticelli for Dante's Divine Comedy. NY: Harper, (1976). 1st Amer ed. VF in dj. *Hermitage*. $85/£54

CLARK, KENNETH. Feminine Beauty. NY: Rizzoli, (1980). 1st ed. Very nice (name, ex-libris) in dj (mouse nibbling). *Second Life*. $45/£29

CLARK, KENNETH. Leonardo da Vinci. NY/Cambridge, 1939. 68 plts. (Sl worn.) *Washton*. $35/£22

CLARK, KENNETH. Leonardo da Vinci. Cambridge: CUP, 1952. 2nd ed. 68 plts. Good. *Washton*. $45/£29

CLARK, KENNETH. Piero della Francesca. London, 1951. Orig ed. 7 tipped-in color plts. (Ink underlining.) Dj (worn). *Washton*. $60/£38

CLARK, KENNETH. Rembrandt and the Italian Renaissance. London, 1966. 1st ed. Color frontis port, 181 plts. (Margins lt browned.) Dj (sl chipped). *Edwards*. $31/£20

CLARK, MARK. Calculated Risk. London, 1951. Frontis. Dj. *Maggs*. $39/£25

CLARK, MARY HIGGINS. Aspire to the Heavens. A Portrait of George Washington. NY: Meredith Press, 1968. 1st ed, 1st bk. Fine in dj (lt used; spine lt stained). *Beasley*. $200/£128

CLARK, R. B. Dynamics in Metazoan Evolution. London: OUP, (1967). Corrected ed. Fine in VG dj. *Mikesh*. $25/£16

CLARK, ROBERT (ed). Golf: A Royal and Ancient Game. London: Macmillan, 1893. 2nd ed. Teg. Pict gilt-stamped grn cl, gilt spine. (Inscrip, dampstain reps; extrems rubbed, fr cvr sl discolored), else VG. *Pacific**. $316/£203

CLARK, ROBERT STERLING and ARTHUR DE C. SOWERBY. Through Shen-Kan: The Account of the Clark Expedition in North China, 1908-9. London: T. Fisher Unwin, 1912. 1st ed. Frontis map, fldg map in rear pocket, 6 color plts, 58 photographic plts. (Lt soil, bubbling to cl), o/w VG. *Hermitage*. $450/£288

CLARK, ROLAND. Gunner's Dawn. NY: Derrydale, 1937. One of 950. Etched frontis signed by Clark; 14 b/w, 5 color plts. Orig box (worn). *Kane**. $350/£224

CLARK, ROLAND. Roland Clark's Etchings. NY: Derrydale, 1938. #789/800. Orig signed etching. Fine in box (worn). *Metropolitan**. $350/£224

CLARK, RONALD. The Day the Rope Broke. London, (1965). 1st ed. VG in dj (sl used). *King*. $35/£22

CLARK, RONALD. The Early Alpine Guides. NY, 1950. 1st Amer ed. VG in dj (sl frayed). *King*. $25/£16

CLARK, RONALD. An Eccentric in the Alps. London, (1959). 1st ed. (Spine stained), else Good in dj. *King*. $40/£26

CLARK, STERLING B. F. How Many Miles from St. Jo? SF: Privately ptd, 1929. 5 plts & facs. Maroon cl-backed marbled bds, spine gilt, onlaid color paper woodcut fr bd. Fine in plain dj. *Cady*. $50/£32

CLARK, STERLING B. F. How Many Miles from St. Jo?... Together with a Brief Autobiography of James Phelan.... SF: Privately Ptd, 1929. 1st ed. 5 plts. Cl-backed pict marbled bds, compliments slip tipped in, erratum tipped in back. VG in plain parchment wrapper as issued. *Shasky*. $55/£35

CLARK, SUSIE C. The Round-Trip from the Hub to the Golden Gate. Boston: Lee & Shepard, 1890. 1st ed. 193pp. VG in ptd wraps (2-inch closed tear). VG. *Second Life.* $75/£48

CLARK, THOMAS D. The Kentucky. NY: Farrar, (1942). 1st ed. Map. Pict eps. Grn cl. VG in dj (nicked, sm chip). *Houle.* $150/£96

CLARK, THOMAS D. The Southern Country Editor. Indianapolis, (1948). 1st ed. Dj. *Ginsberg.* $35/£22

CLARK, THOMAS D. The Southern Country Editor. NY/Indianapolis, 1948. 1st ed. *Wantagh.* $30/£19

CLARK, THOMAS D. Travels in the New South, a Bibliography. Norman: Univ of OK, (1962). 1st ptg. 2 vols. Red cl. Fine in djs (sl soiled). *Bohling.* $200/£128

CLARK, TOM. The Last Gas Station and Other Stories. Santa Barbara: Black Sparrow, 1980. 1st ed. Fine. *Metropolitan*.* $57/£37

CLARK, TOM. Who Is Sylvia? (Berkeley): Blue Wind Press, (1979). 1st ed. Fine in dj (sm tear). *Between The Covers.* $45/£29

CLARK, VICTOR S. History of Manufactures in the United States, 1860-1914. Washington: Carnegie Inst of Washington, 1928. 1st ed. Navy buckram (sl worn, rubbed; lt foxed, pencil notes.) *Baltimore*.* $40/£26

CLARK, W. C. and J. L. KINGSTON. The Skyscraper: A Study in the Economic Height of Modern Office Buildings. NY, (1930). Frontis. Pict bds (lt worn, lt soiled). *Freeman*.* $30/£19

CLARK, W. E. LE GROS. The Tissues of the Body. Oxford, 1945. 2nd ed. VG in dj (tattered). *Doctor's Library.* $85/£54

CLARK, WALTER VAN TILBURG. The Ox-Bow Incident. NY: Random House, (1940). 1st ed. Top edge blue-gray. Tan cl (spine, edges sun-dknd, sl worn, hinges dknd). Pict dj (worn, upper fold separated, chipped, spine lacks top 2 inches). *Baltimore*.* $40/£26

CLARK, WALTER VAN TILBURG. The Track of the Cat. NY: Random House, (1949). 1st ed. (Bottom spine edge sl bumped), o/w Fine in NF dj (sl rubbed). *Bernard.* $75/£48

CLARK, WALTER VAN TILBURG. The Watchful Gods. NY, 1950. 1st ed. VG in VG dj. *Smith.* $15/£10

CLARK, WALTER. The Papers of Walter Clark. Chapel Hill: Univ of NC, (1948-50). 1st ed. 2 vols. NF set. *Mcgowan.* $125/£80

CLARK, WILLIAM BELL. Ben Franklin's Privateers. Baton Rouge: LA State Univ, (1956). 1st ed. Dj. *Lefkowicz.* $35/£22

CLARK, WILLIAM L. Hand-Book of Criminal Law. St. Paul: West Pub Co, 1907. 2nd ed by Francis B. Tiffany. Contemp sheep (very rubbed). *Boswell.* $50/£32

CLARK, WILLIAM L. Reminiscences of a Reformer's Life. Milan, IL, 1913. 1st ed. Ptd wraps (sl worn, soiled). *Wantagh.* $45/£29

CLARKE, A. An Essay on Warm, Cold, and Vapour Bathing.... London: Henry Colburn, 1820. 5th ed. xii,232pp. Orig bds (backstrip worn, joints started). VG. *Glaser.* $100/£64

CLARKE, ALLEN. Windmill Land. London: J.M. Dent, 1916. 1st ed. 32 plts, map. (Prelims sl mkd; 1 leaf soiled, margin sl defective.) Later cl, panel; orig lettering laid on spine. *Hollett.* $70/£45

CLARKE, ARTHUR C. 2001: A Space Odyssey. NY: NAL, (1968). 1st ed. (Corners sl bumped), else Fine in Fine dj (lt foxing inside). *Between The Covers.* $350/£224

CLARKE, ARTHUR C. 2001: A Space Odyssey. NY: NAL, 1968. 1st ed. (Top edge lt foxed), else NF in dj (verso lt foxed). *Lame Duck.* $350/£224

CLARKE, ARTHUR C. 2010: Odyssey Two. Granada, 1982. 1st UK ed. Fine in dj (price-clipped). *Williams.* $19/£12

CLARKE, ARTHUR C. 2010: Odyssey Two. Huntington Woods: Phantasia, 1982. 1st ed. One of 650 signed, numbered. Fine in dj, slipcase. *Other Worlds.* $150/£96

CLARKE, ARTHUR C. Expedition to Earth. NY: Ballantine Books, (1953). 1st ed. Fine in VG dj (sl worn). *Metropolitan*.* $149/£96

CLARKE, ARTHUR C. A Fall of Moondust. NY: Harcourt, Brace, & World, (1961). 1st ed. (Sl soiled.) Dj (sl browned, lt edgeworn, short tears). *Metropolitan*.* $46/£29

CLARKE, ARTHUR C. Interplanetary Flight. NY: Harper, (1950). Apparent 1st Amer ed; 1st bk. NF in dj (toned, dusty, edgewear, sm waterspot). *Waverly*.* $33/£21

CLARKE, ARTHUR C. Islands in the Sky. London, 1952. 1st British ed. NF in dj (soiled, frayed). *Madle.* $75/£48

CLARKE, ARTHUR C. The Other Side of the Sky. London, 1961. 1st ed. VG in dj. *Words Etc.* $70/£45

CLARKE, ARTHUR C. Profiles of the Future. Harper, 1962. 1st ed. NF in dj (frayed). *Madle.* $25/£16

CLARKE, ARTHUR C. Reach for Tomorrow. NY: Ballantine, 1956. 1st ed. Pb orig. VG in wraps. *Warren.* $25/£16

CLARKE, ARTHUR C. The Songs of Distant Earth. NY, (1986). 1st ed. Fine in dj. *Argosy.* $30/£19

CLARKE, ARTHUR C. The Songs of Distant Earth. NY: Del Rey, 1986. 1st ed. One of 500 signed. Fine in slipcase (lt rubbed). *Metropolitan*.* $86/£55

CLARKE, ASA BEMENT. Travels in Mexico and California. Boston, 1852. 1st ed. Mod lib buckram, orig wrappers bound in. Full-pg inscrip by Clarke's daughter(?) on inserted leaf. Howes C451. *Swann*.* $316/£203

CLARKE, BASIL F. L. The Building of the Eighteenth-Century Church. London: SPCK, 1963. 15 plts. Sound in dj. *Ars Artis.* $33/£21

CLARKE, BASIL F. L. Church Builders of the Nineteenth Century. London, 1938. 1st ed. Cl (sl bruised). VG-. *Gretton.* $23/£15

CLARKE, BASIL F. L. Parish Churches of London. Batsford, 1966. (Bkpl), else VG in dj (creased, rubbed). *Hadley.* $55/£35

CLARKE, BASIL F. L. and JOHN BETJEMAN. English Churches. Vista, 1964. 1st ed. VG in dj (sl browned, spine faded). *Hadley.* $39/£25

CLARKE, CHARLES G. The Men of the Lewis and Clark Expedition. Glendale: A.H. Clark, 1970. 1st ed. Frontis. Red cl. *Dawson.* $100/£64

CLARKE, DWIGHT L. Stephen Watts Kearny, Soldier of the West. Norman, (1961). 1st ed. VG+ in dj (lt wear). *Pratt.* $75/£48

CLARKE, EDWARD H. The Relation of Drugs to Treatment. Boston, 1856. 1st ed. 28pp. VG in ptd wrappers. *Argosy.* $45/£29

CLARKE, EDWARD H. Sex in Education; or, A Fair Chance for Girls. Boston: Osgood, 1873. 2nd ed. 181pp. (Spine faded, sl foxed), o/w VG. *Second Life.* $150/£96

CLARKE, EDWARD H. Sex in Education; or, A Fair Chance for Girls. Boston: Osgood, 1874. Later ed. 181pp. (Spine faded, sl chipped), o/w Good. *Second Life.* $75/£48

CLARKE, ERNEST E. A Handbook of Plant Form. Batsford, 1904. 1st ed. 100 plts. Grn cl (stained, fingermks, prize label). Good. *Whittle.* $44/£28

CLARKE, FRANCES M. Thomas Simpson and His Times. NY, 1929. 1st ed. Presentation. Frontis. VG (lib card pocket removed). *Glaser*. $85/£54

CLARKE, H. et al. Miner's Manual United States, Alaska, the Klondike. Chicago: Callaghan, 1898. 1st ptg. 404pp; lg fldg map. Buckram, leather spine label. Good. *Blake*. $125/£80

CLARKE, L. LANE. Objects for the Microscope. London: Groombridge, 1877. 5th ed. viii,230pp (prelim repaired); 8 color plts. Pict grn/gilt cl. VG. *Savona*. $39/£25

CLARKE, L. LANE. Objects for the Microscope. London: Groombridge, 1887. 7th ed. 230pp; 8 color plts. Aeg. Dec red/gilt cl. VG. *Savona*. $44/£28

CLARKE, LEWIS and MILTON. Narratives of the Sufferings of Lewis and Milton Clarke...During a Captivity.... Boston: Bela Marsh, 1846. 2nd ed. 144pp; 2 ports. (Text lt spotted; cl rubbed, worn), else Good. Howes C457. *Brown*. $100/£64

CLARKE, MARY ANNE. The Rival Princes. NY: Longworth, 1810. 1st US ed. 2 vols in 1. Frontis, vi,180pp (sl dknd). Later bds (taped). VG. *Second Life*. $125/£80

CLARKE, MRS. STANLEY. From the Deck of Yacht. London: Remington, 1882. 1st ed. (iv),134pp. Nice (dec cl sl worn; edges, prelims sl spotted). *Ash*. $62/£40

CLARKE, S. A. Pioneer Days of Oregon History. Portland: J.K. Gill, 1905. 1st ed. 2 vols. Grn cl, gilt. Arthur H. Clark Co. cancel pasted over orig pub's imprint on tps. (2 corners sl bumped), o/w NF. *Harrington*. $225/£144

CLARKE, SOMERS and R. ENGELBACH. Ancient Egyptian Masonry: The Building Craft. London: OUP, 1930. 1st ed. Frontis, map. (Bkpl.) Gilt-pict cl (bds sl rubbed). *Archaeologia*. $450/£288

CLARKE, T. WOOD. The Bloody Mohawk. NY, 1940. 1st ed. Good. *Mcclintock*. $15/£10

CLARKSON, ROSETTA E. Green Enchantment. NY: Macmillan, 1940. 1st ed. Frontis. NF. *Quest*. $35/£22

CLARKSON, THOMAS. History...Rise, Progress...of Abolition of African Slave Trade.... NY: Taylor, 1836. 3 vols. 276; 298; 296pp; 3 plts. Orig cl (spines faded). *Adelson*. $75/£48

CLARKSON, THOMAS. Memoirs of the Private and Public Life of William Penn. London: Ptd by Richard Taylor, 1813. 2 vols. xii,520; 500pp (browned). Mod cl (rebound). *Edwards*. $70/£45

CLARKSON, THOMAS. A Portraiture of Quakerism. NY: Samuel Stansbury, 1806. 1st US ed. 3 vols. viii,363; ix,382; vii,372pp (browned, sl foxed, ink sigs). Early black sheep, marbled bds (worn, sl scuffed, chipped). *Baltimore**. $90/£58

Classical Dictionary of the Vulgar Tongue. (By Francis Grose.) London: Hooper & Wigstead, 1796. 3rd ed. xvi,B1-Hh2pp. Old speckled calf (sl rubbed, scraped), gilt, spine label. *Hollett*. $187/£120

CLATER, FRANCIS. Every Man His Own Cattle Doctor. Phila: Abm. Small, 1815. 1st Amer ed. 256,(8)pp. Orig calf-backed ptd bds (water staining). *M&s*. $300/£192

CLAVELL, JAMES. King Rat. Boston: Little, Brown, (1962). 1st ed. (Bumps, lt stains, discoloration.) Dj (edgeworn, loss spine ends, stamp inside fr flap). *Metropolitan**. $80/£51

CLAVELL, JAMES. Noble House. NY: Delacorte, (1981). One of 500 numbered, signed. Fine in Fine slipcase. *Lenz*. $125/£80

CLAVELL, JAMES. Shogun. NY: Atheneum, 1975. 1st ed. Fine in Fine dj (sm tear, sl wrinkle). *Between The Covers*. $150/£96

CLAVELL, JAMES. Whirlwind. NY: Wm. Morrow, (1986). 1st trade ed. Signed. Fine in Fine dj. *Bernard*. $50/£32

CLAVERS, MARY. (Pseud of Caroline Matilda Kirkland.) A New Home: Who'll Follow? NY/Boston: C.S. Francis/J.H. Francis, 1839. 1st ed, 1st bk. 317pp incl half-title, 2pp ads (lt foxed). VG (extrems lt frayed). BAL 11143. Howes K184. *Bohling*. $400/£256

CLAXTON, FLORENCE. The Adventures of a Woman in Search of Her Rights. London: Thomas Owen, (ca 1865). 1st ed. Cl-backed pict paper bds (lt soiled, bumped). VG. *Captain's Bookshelf*. $250/£160

CLAY, S. The Present-Day Rock Garden. London, 1954. 2nd ed. 56 plts. Good in dj (chipped). *Henly*. $55/£35

CLAYDEN, P. W. Samuel Sharpe; Egyptologist and Translator of the Bible. London: Kegan Paul, Trench, 1883. iv,320,48pp (sig). *Archaeologia*. $85/£54

CLAYTON, ELLEN CREATHORNE. Queens of Song. London: Smith, Elder, 1863. 1st ed. 2 vols. Burgundy moire (rebound), 3/4 burgundy levant, moire eps. VG. *Old London*. $125/£80

CLAYTON, P. B. and B. R. LEFTWICH. The Pageant of Tower Hill.... Longmans, Green, 1933. 1st ed. Color frontis. (Fep removed), o/w Good. *Cox*. $23/£15

CLAYTON, VICTORIA V. White and Black Under the Old Regime. Milwaukee/London, 1899. 1st ed. 195pp; port. *Wantagh*. $75/£48

CLEAVELAND, P. An Elementary Treatise on Mineralogy and Geology. Boston: Cummings & Hilliard, 1822. 2nd ed. 2 vols in 1. xii,818pp, errata. Mod grn cl, paper spine label. (Sl dampstained, sl cockled), else VG. *Blake*. $450/£288

CLEAVER, DENIS. On the Air. Collins, (1947). 1st ed. G.W. Backhouse (illus). 8vo. Color frontis, 96pp. Dec cl. VG + in pict dj (chipped). *Bookmark*. $23/£15

CLEAVER, ELDRIDGE. Soul on Ice. NY, 1968. 1st Amer ed, 1st bk. Fine (spine extrems sl rubbed) in dj (price-clipped, sl rubbed). *Polyanthos*. $30/£19

CLEAVER, ELIZABETH. The Enchanted Caribou. NY: Atheneum, 1985. 1st US ed. 10 3/4 x 8 1/2. 32pp. VG in dj. *Cattermole*. $35/£22

CLEAVER, ELIZABETH. The Miraculous Hind. NY: Holt, 1973. 1st ed. 12 1/2 x 9 1/2. 64pp. Fine in dj. *Cattermole*. $45/£29

CLEAVES, FREEMAN. Meade of Gettysburg. Norman, 1960. 1st ed. VG + in VG + dj. *Pratt*. $65/£42

CLECKLEY, HERVEY. The Mask of Sanity. St. Louis: Mosby, 1950. 2nd ed. (Spine ends lt worn), o/w NF. *Beasley*. $60/£38

CLECKLEY, HERVEY. The Mask of Sanity: An Attempt to Clarify Some Issues.... St. Louis: C.V. Mosby, 1941. 1st ed. Ptd ruled red cl. NF in dj (lt chipped). *Gach*. $100/£64

CLEGHORN, GEORGE. Observations on the Epidemical Diseases of Minorca...1744 to 1749. Phila: F. Nichols, 1809. 1st Amer ed. xviii,184pp. Orig tree calf (spine ends sl chipped). Bkpl, sig of William Webb. VG. *Glaser*. $525/£337

CLELAND, JOHN. Memoirs of a Coxcomb. Fortune Press, 1926. #528/575. (Rebound.) *Edwards*. $62/£40

CLELAND, JOHN. Memoirs of Fanny Hill. Paris: Isidore Liseux, 1911. Ltd to 350. 24 full-pg illus, some in 2 states. 1/4 black cl, dec paper-cvrd bds. *D & D*. $295/£189

CLELAND, ROBERT G. Pathfinders. L.A., 1929. 1st ed. 3 maps. VG. *Turpen*. $75/£48

CLELAND, ROBERT G. The Place Called Sespe: The History of a California Ranch. San Marino: Huntington Library, 1957. 3rd ed, 1st trade ed. Fldg frontis map. Brn cl, gilt-stamped morocco spine label. (Fep sl discolored), o/w Fine. *Pacific**. $23/£15

CLELAND, ROBERT G. This Reckless Breed of Men. NY: Knopf, 1950. 1st ed. Color frontis, 4 maps. Pict emb blue cl, gilt spine. VF in pict dj. *Argonaut.* $60/£38

CLELAND, ROBERT G. and FRANK B. PUTNAM. Isaias W. Hellman and the Farmers and Merchants Bank. San Marino: Huntington Library, 1965. 1st ed. Frontis port. Black cl. VF in dj (spine dknd). *Argonaut.* $35/£22

CLEMENS, WILL. Mark Twain, His Life and Work. SF: Clemens, 1892. 1st ed. Orig pict ptd wrappers. (Sl rubbed, lt soiled.) BAL II:251. *Macdonnell.* $125/£80

CLEMENT, F. W. Nitrous Oxide-Oxygen Anesthesia: McKesson-Clement Viewpoint and Technique. London, 1939. 1st ed. 70 engrs. Grn-tooled cl bds. VG. *Doctor's Library.* $40/£26

CLEMENT, HAL. Iceworld. NY: Gnome, (1953). 1st ed. VG in VG dj (soil, short tears). *Metropolitan*.* $34/£22

CLEMENT, HAL. Some Notes on Xi Bootis. (Chicago: Advent, 1960.) 1st ed. Signed as both Clement and Harry C. Stubbs. Pict wrappers. *Swann*.* $69/£44

CLEMENT, MAUD C. The History of the Pittsyvania County, Virginia. Lynchburg, VA: Bell, 1929. 1st ed. (Bkpl removed; sm paper spine label.) *Ginsberg.* $75/£48

CLEMENTS, ROBERT J. Michelangelo's Theory of Art. NY, 1961. 2nd ed. 20 plts. Good. *Washton.* $45/£29

CLEMMER, JEAN. Canned Candies. 1969. Dj (edges lt browned). *Edwards.* $28/£18

CLERGUE, LUCIEN. Naissances d'Aphrodite. NY: Brussel & Brussel, 1966. 1st ed. NF in dj (chipped, creased). *Cahan.* $75/£48

CLERGUE, LUCIEN. Nude Work Shop. NY: Viking/Studio, 1982. 1st ed. VG (cl spotted) in NF dj. *Smith.* $65/£42

CLERK, N. W. (Pseud of C.S. Lewis.) A Grief Observed. London: Faber, 1961. 1st UK ed. NF (ink name, eps browned) in VG dj (sl browned, spine rubbed). *Williams.* $117/£75

CLERKE, A. M. A Popular History of Astronomy During the Nineteenth Century. Edinburgh, 1885. xiv,468pp (bkpl, perf stamp tp; last text pp; spine discolored, lib label, ends sl worn, back hinge cracked). *Whitehart.* $62/£40

CLEUGH, JAMES. Secret Enemy. London: Thames & Hudson, 1954. 1st ed. Good in dj. *White.* $19/£12

CLEVELAND, H. W. S. Hints to Riflemen. NY, 1864. 1st ed. Pub's cl (shelfworn, spine head torn). *Oinonen*.* $60/£38

CLEVENGER, S. V. Spinal Concussion: Surgically Considered as a Cause of Spinal Injury.... Phila: Davis, 1889. iv,(1),359pp. Internally Clean (stamp tp; cl worn). *Goodrich.* $395/£253

CLIFFE, JOHN HENRY. Notes and Recollections of an Angler. London: Hamilton, Adams, 1860. 1st ed. xii,254,(ii)pp. Blind-stamped cl (sl dknd), gilt. *Hollett.* $187/£120

CLIFFE, JOHN HENRY. Notes and Recollections of an Angler. London: Hamilton, 1870. 2nd ed. 254pp + ads. Partly unopened. Gilt-pict brn cl. VG +. *Bowman.* $60/£38

CLIFFORD, ANNE. The Diary of the Lady of.... London, 1923. 1st ed. 4 ports, fldg table. *Edwards.* $23/£15

CLIFFORD, DEREK and TIMOTHY. John Crome. Greenwich: NYGS, (1968). 1st Amer ed. Fine in dj (lt rubbed). *Hermitage.* $75/£48

CLIFFORD, DEREK. A History of Garden Design. London: Faber & Faber, 1962. 1st ed. Fine in dj. *Quest.* $110/£71

CLIFFORD, DEREK. A History of Garden Design. NY, 1963. *Maggs.* $37/£24

CLIFFORD, HENRY. Henry Clifford V.C. His Letters and Sketches from the Crimea. NY, 1956. 1st ed. Fine in NF dj. *Mcgowan.* $45/£29

CLIFFORD, ISIDORE E. and R. E. Crown, Bar, and Bridge-Work. London: Simpkin, Marshall, 1885. 1st ed. Signed presentation copy. 26pp, 10 color plts. VG (top inch backstrip chipped, sl dusty). *Glaser.* $135/£87

CLIFFORD, JAMES L. Young Sam Johnson. NY: McGraw-Hill, 1955. 1st ed. Inscribed presentation. Map. Good (backstrip sl dknd). *Cox.* $23/£15

CLIFT, WILLIAM. Certain Places. Santa Fe: William Clift Editions, 1987. 1st ed. Letter from Ray DeMoulin to Robert Sobieszek laid in. Fine in Fine dj. *Smith.* $175/£112

CLIFTON, F. Hippocrates Upon Air, Water, and Situation.... 1734. Frontis plt, xxxxii,388pp (top of tp cut off). Marbled eps. New morocco. *Whitehart.* $281/£180

CLIFTON, F. The State of Physick Ancient and Modern. 1732. xl,192,134pp (sl foxed). Orig calf (rubbed). *Whitehart.* $281/£180

CLIFTON, MARK and FRANK RILEY. They'd Rather Be Right. NY: Gnome, 1957. 1st ed. Fine (interior browning; sl soil, short closed tears). *Metropolitan*.* $69/£44

CLIFTON, MARK and FRANK RILEY. They'd Rather Be Right. NY: Gnome, 1957. 1st ed. Fine in dj (nicked). *Other Worlds.* $100/£64

CLIFTON, VIOLET. The Book of Talbot. NY: Harcourt, Brace, 1933. Frontis port. VG (sl shelfwear). *Parmer.* $35/£22

CLINCH, GEORGE. English Costume from Prehistoric Times to the End of the Eighteenth Century. London, 1909. 1st ed. (Tp lt browned, lib bkpl; spine lt faded, sl split.) *Edwards.* $31/£20

CLINE, WALTER M. The Muzzle-Loading Rifle. WV: Standard Ptg & Pub Co, 1942. 1st ed. VG. *Hollett.* $133/£85

Clinical Lectures and Reports by the Medical and Surgical Staff of the London Hospital. London: John Churchill, 1864-1867. Vols 1 through 4. (Paper brittle, browning, foxing; vols 2 and 3 newly rebacked), else Good set. *Goodrich.* $750/£481

CLINTON, HENRY. Observations on Earl Cornwallis' Answer. Phila: Campbell, 1866. 1st Amer ed. One of 250 ptd. 35,116pp; fldg table. Ptd wrappers. Howes C499. *Ginsberg.* $75/£48

CLISE, MICHELE DURKSON. Ophelia's World. NY: Potter, 1984. 1st ed. 7 3/4 x 10 1/4. 128pp. VG (ex-lib, few mks) in dj. *Cattermole.* $20/£13

CLOAK, EVELYN CAMPBELL. Glass Paperweights. London, 1969. 1st UK ed. Dj (browned, sl chipped). *Edwards.* $39/£25

CLOKEY, RICHARD M. and WILLIAM H. ASHLEY. Enterprise and Politics in the Trans-Mississippi West. Norman: Univ of OK, (1980). 1st ed. 9 maps. VF in pict dj. *Argonaut.* $50/£32

CLOUD, C. CAREY and HAROLD B. LENTZ. Goldilocks and the Three Bears. Blue Ribbon, 1934. Pop-up. 8x9. Pict bds (chipped). VG (finger mks, soil, sm tear last pop-up not affecting pop-up ability). *My Bookhouse.* $200/£128

CLOUGH, ARTHUR HUGH. Poems with a Memoir. Cambridge: Macmillan, 1862. 1st collected ed. xxvii,(i),259,(1)pp, pub's 16-pg list dated 1.7.62. Brn eps. Grn honeycomb cl, gilt. VG. *Cox.* $70/£45

CLOUSTON, THOMAS SMITH. Clinical Lectures on Mental Diseases. Phila/NY: Lea Bros, 1904. 4th Amer ed, 1st ptg. 29 plts (28 w/descrip text leaf not included in pagination). Panelled pebbled crimson cl. Jelliffe's name stamp. VG (fep excised; stamp, rear pocket, spine #s). *Gach.* $65/£42

CLOUSTON, THOMAS SMITH. Neuroses of Development, Being the Morison Lectures for 1890. Edinburgh/London: Oliver & Boyd/Simpkin et al, 1891. 1st ed. viii,138pp; 9 plts. Panelled crimson cl, gilt spine (faded, lt worn). VG. *Gach.* $285/£183

CLOUSTON, THOMAS SMITH. Unsoundness of Mind. NY, 1911. 1st Amer ed. VG. *Argosy.* $60/£38

CLOUSTON, W. A. The Book of Noodles...or, Fools and Their Follies. London: Elliot Stock, 1888. 1st ed. xx,228pp. Leather-backed cl-cvrd bds. (Spine cvrd w/masking tape), o/w VG. *Gach.* $35/£22

CLOWES, G. S. LAIRD. Sailing Ships. London, 1930-32. 1st eds. 2 vols. 66 plts. Ptd wrappers (sl shelfworn). *Lefkowicz.* $85/£54

CLOWES, WILLIAM. Selected Writings of William Clowes, 1544-1604. F. N. L. Poynter (ed). London, 1948. VG. *Fye.* $75/£48

CLUM, WOODWORTH. Apache Agent. NY, (1936). 1st ed. VG + (ex-lib). *Pratt.* $85/£54

CLUNE, FRANK. Murders on Maunga-Tapu, a History of the Crimes Committed...in the Year 1866. Sydney: Angus & Robertson, 1959. *Boswell.* $45/£29

CLUTE, WILLARD N. Our Ferns in Their Haunts. NY, 1901. 8 color plts. Pristine. *Brooks.* $40/£26

CLUTTON, CECIL and GEORGE DANIELS. Watches. London: Batsford, (1965). 1st British ed. 2 color plts. Violet cl. VG (stamp). *Weber.* $17/£11

CLUTTON, CECIL and GEORGE DANIELS. Watches. NY: Viking, (1965). 1st Amer ed. 2 color plts. Violet cl. Fine in dj (short tear). *Weber.* $45/£29

CLUTTON, CECIL and GEORGE DANIELS. Watches; a Complete History of the Technical and Decorative Development of the Watch. NY: Sotheby, (1979). 3rd ed. 16 color plts. Black cl. Fine in dj (extrems sl worn). *Weber.* $100/£64

CLUTTON-BROCK, ARTHUR. The Miracle of Love and Other Poems. London: Julian Editions, 1926. Ltd to 450. Teg, others uncut. Black buckram-backed brn paper bds, gilt. Very Nice. *Cady.* $45/£29

CLYNES, MICHAEL. (Pseud of P. C. Doherty.) The Poisoned Chalice. London: Headline, 1992. 1st ed. VF in dj. *Mordida.* $45/£29

CLYNES, MICHAEL. (Pseud of P. C. Doherty.) The White Rose Murders. London: Headline, 1991. 1st ed. Fine in dj. *Mordida.* $45/£29

COAKLEY, CORNELIUS GODFREY. A Manual of Diseases of the Nose and Throat. Phila, 1899. 1st ed. 536pp. Good (inner hinges cracked; worn). *Doctor's Library.* $60/£38

Coastline. Britain's Threatened Heritage. Greenpeace, 1987. 1st ed. (Ink annotation to text), o/w VG in dj (corner nicked). *Words Etc.* $39/£25

COATES, HAROLD WILSON. Stories of Kentucky Feuds. Knoxville, TN: Holmes-Darst Coal Corp, (1942). 1st ed thus. VG. *Mcgowan.* $45/£29

COATES, HENRY. American Trotting and Pacing Horse. Phila: Winston, 1905. 2nd ed. (Plt loose; shelfworn.) *October Farm.* $38/£24

COATES, JOHN BOYD, JR. (ed). Internal Medicine in World War II: Volume II, Infectious Diseases. Washington, 1963. 1st ed. Gilt-tooled maroon leatherette cl bds. VG (sm water stain lower corner). *Doctor's Library.* $50/£32

COATES, JOHN BOYD, JR. (ed). Preventive Medicine in World War II: Volume V, Communicable Diseases Transmitted Through Contact or by Unknown Means. Washington, DC, 1960. 1st ed. Gilt-tooled maroon leatherette cl bds. VG. *Doctor's Library.* $50/£32

COATES, ROBERT M. The Hour After Westerly and Other Stories. Harcourt, Brace, (1957). 1st ed. NF (sl dust-mkd) in dj (sm tears). *Certo.* $35/£22

COATES, THOMAS F. G. Hector Macdonald, or the Private Who Became a General. London, 1900. Frontis port. Pict cl (worn, lib sticker upper cvr). *Maggs.* $47/£30

COATS, A. The Quest for Plants, a History of the Horticultural Explorers. London, 1969. Dj (sl torn). *Maggs.* $37/£24

COATS, A. The Treasury of Flowers. London, 1975. Dj. *Maggs.* $23/£15

COATS, PETER (ed). The House and Garden Book of Garden Decoration. London: Collins, 1970. 1st ed. Fine in dj. *Quest.* $85/£54

COATSWORTH, ELIZABETH. Alice-All-by-Herself. Harrap, 1938. 1st UK ed. Marguerite de Angeli (illus). 6x9. 205pp. (Spine, top edge faded; sl shelfworn), o/w VG + in dj (sl edgeworn). *My Bookhouse.* $60/£38

COATSWORTH, ELIZABETH. Night and the Cat. NY: Macmillan, 1950. 1st ed. Foujita (illus). 7 1/4 x 9 3/4. 55pp. VG in dj. *Cattermole.* $50/£32

COBB, HUMPHREY. Paths of Glory. NY: Viking, 1935. 1st ed, 1st bk. Deckle-edged. Pink/blue cl (sl soiled), gilt. Internally Fine in dj (rubbed, soiled). *Blue Mountain.* $40/£26

COBB, IRVIN S. Maine (Cobb's America Guyed Books). NY: Doran, (1924). 1st ed. Pict paper-cvrd bds. Fine in NF dj. *Hermitage.* $35/£22

COBB, IRVIN S. On an Island That Cost $24.00. NY: Doran, 1926. 1st ed. NF in emb cvrs in pict dj (sl worn). *Else Fine.* $35/£22

COBB, LYMAN. The Evil Tendencies of Corporal Punishment as a Means of Moral Discipline.... NY: Mark H. Newman, 1847. Emb cl (rubbed, lt foxed), gilt. Sound. *Boswell.* $175/£112

COBB, THOMAS. The Castaways of Meadow Bank. E. V. Lucas (ed). Methuen, (1901). 1st ed. #1 in 'The Little Blue Books' series. Sm 8vo. 191pp; 4 illus by A. E. Buckland. Bkpl of Sybil Corbett. Blue cl. (Spotting), else VG. *Bookmark.* $23/£15

COBB, W. MONTAGUE. The First Negro Medical Society...1884-1939. Washington, 1939. 1st ed. (Ex-lib.) *Fye.* $75/£48

COBBE, FRANCES POWER. Darwinism in Morals, and Other Essays. London, 1872. 1st ed. 399pp. VG. *Fye.* $100/£64

COBBETT, WILLIAM. The English Gardener. London: The Author, 1829. 1st ed. Unpaginated. 1/2 morocco, marbled bds, raised spine bands, leather spine label, gilt. (Fep frayed, prelims stained; last few ll foxed), else VG. *Quest.* $240/£154

COBBETT, WILLIAM. The English Gardener. London, 1833. iv,338pp (spotted); fldg plt (sl foxed). Orig bds (rebacked). *Henly.* $133/£85

COBBETT, WILLIAM. Letters to Edward Thornton Written in the Years 1797 to 1800. G. D. H. Cole (ed). Oxford, 1937. 1st ed. VG in dj (lt soiled). *Cox.* $23/£15

COBBETT, WILLIAM. Life and Adventures of Peter Porcupine. London, 1927. #469/1800. Color frontis. Uncut, unopened. Fine (spine top sl chipped, heel sl rubbed, few sm spots, edges sl rubbed). *Polyanthos.* $35/£22

COBBETT, WILLIAM. Life and Adventures of Peter Porcupine.... London: Nonesuch, 1927. 1st ed. #1439/1800. Hand-colored frontis. Cl-backed marbled bds (corners worn). Sound. *Cox.* $31/£20

COBBETT, WILLIAM. Life of Andrew Jackson, President of the United States of America. NY: Harper, 1834. Frontis port, 196pp + 20pp ads. Ptd spine label (dknd, chipped). Good (foxed; worn, frayed). *Bohling.* $20/£13

COBBETT, WILLIAM. Rural Rides in the Southern, Western and Eastern Countries of England.... London: Peter Davies, 1930. #30/1000. 3 vols. Cl-backed marbled bds (spines chipped, soiled). Edwards. $273/£175

COBBETT, WILLIAM. The Woodlands: or A Treatise on Preparing the Ground for Planting.... London, 1825. 1st ed. (344)pp, (2 ads). Contemp tree calf. Good. Henly. $172/£110

COBBOLD, RALPH P. Innermost Asia. London: Heinemann, 1900. 1st ed. Frontis, 4 maps (1 fldg). Contemp brn 1/2 morocco. (Sl rubbed, sm lib stamp), else VG. Terramedia. $400/£256

COBDEN-SANDERSON, T. J. The Ideal Book or Book Beautiful. Hammersmith, 1900. One of 300. (Bkpl.) Limp vellum. Swann*. $575/£369

COBDEN-SANDERSON, T. J. The Journals of Thomas James Cobden-Sanderson, 1879-1922. London: Richard Cobden-Sanderson, 1926. 1st ed. Ltd to 1050. 5 full-pg plts. (Bkpl; rubbed.) Oak Knoll. $275/£176

COBLENTZ, STANTON A. Villains and Vigilantes, the Story of James King of William and Pioneer Justice in California. NY: Thomas Yoseloff, 1957. Boswell. $45/£29

COBLENTZ, STANTON. When the Birds Fly South. Wings Press, 1945. 1st ed. Fine in dj (frayed). Madle. $50/£32

COBLENTZ, STANTON. When the Birds Fly South. Wings, 1945. 1st ed. VG in dj (edges browned, dust streaking). Certo. $30/£19

COBURN, ALVIN LANGDON. Alvin Langdon Coburn, Photographer. Helmut & Alison Gernsheim (ed). London: Faber & Faber, 1966. 1st ed. 64 full-pg gravure plts. (Owner stamp), else VG in dj. Cahan. $85/£54

COBURN, ALVIN LANGDON. Men of Mark. London/NY: Duckworth/Mitchell Kennerley, 1913. 1st ed. 33 tipped-in hand-pulled photogravures w/tissue guards. Linen w/gilt title. (Tips, lower binding edge bumped; spine soiled, dknd; lt foxing; bkpl), else VG. Cahan. $1,500/£962

COBURN, ALVIN LANGDON. More Men of Mark. NY: Knopf, 1922. 1st ed. 33 Fine collotypes w/guards. Linen-backed patterned bds (rubbed, scraped; dknd along spine; fr hinge sl loose). Cahan. $325/£208

COCHRAN-PATRICK, R. W. Records of the Coinage of Scotland. Edinburgh: Edmonston & Douglas, 1876. 1st ed. 2 vols. (2),xii,ccii,296; (6),360pp; 16 photogravure plts. 1/2 yellow morocco (spines lt rubbed; bkpls), marbled bds, gilt. Karmiole. $350/£224

COCHRANE, JOHN DUNDAS. Narrative of a Pedestrian Journey...1820, 1821, 1822, and 1823. London: John Murray, 1824. 1st ed. xvi,564pp (w/o maps). (Bkpl to pastedown; browning.) Contemp 1/2 calf, cl bds (joints sl rubbed), gilt-edged raised bands, leather spine label. Edwards. $117/£75

Cock Robin. NY: McLoughlin Bros, 1893. 9x6.5. (12)pp, 4 color illus. Color pict wraps (wear, loose). Nice. King. $40/£26

COCKBURN, HENRY THOMAS. Life of Lord Jeffrey with a Selection from His Correspondence. Edinburgh: A&C Black, 1852. 2nd ed. 2 vols. 1/4 crimson calf (rubbed), marbled edges. Attractive. Boswell. $250/£160

COCKE, CHARLES FRANCIS. Recollections of Wilton Egerton Mingea, 1855-1938. Privately ptd, 1965. VG-. Book Broker. $35/£22

COCKER, EDWARD. Cocker's English Dictionary.... London: T. Norris, 1715. 2nd ed. Unpaginated. Aeg. Orig mottled calf (nicely rebacked; many fore-edge margins reinforced). Karmiole. $150/£96

COCKERELL, DOUGLAS. Bookbinding as a School Subject. G.W. Russell & Son, Ltd., Hitchen, c. 1930. 4 vols (vol 1 is 2nd ptg). Wrappers (upper cvr vol 1 sl rust stained). Maggs. $55/£35

COCKERELL, DOUGLAS. Bookbinding, and the Care of Books. London, 1901. 1st ed. 1/4 holland on ptd paper bds (sl faded). Hatchwell. $39/£25

COCKERELL, DOUGLAS. Bookbinding, and the Care of Books. London: John Hogg, 1901. 1st ed. Frontis. Cl-backed bds (sl rubbed, lt sunned). Good. Reese. $30/£19

COCKERELL, SYDNEY C. Old Testament Miniatures. NY: Braziller, (1975). 1st ed. Folio. 238 color plts. Natural buckram. Fine in pict dj. House. $90/£58

COCKERELL, SYDNEY C. and J. TEBBUTT. Thirty Recent Bindings. Foss, K.D. Duval, (1980). Frontis, 25 color plts (3 fldg). Wrappers. Maggs. $34/£22

COCKS, ANNA SOMERS. An Introduction to Courtly Jewellery. London: V&A, 1980. Good. Washton. $15/£10

COCKS, DOROTHY. The Etiquette of Beauty. NY: Doran, (1927). 1st ed. Fine (ex-libris) in dj (sl chipped). Second Life. $45/£29

COCKTON, HENRY. Stanley Thorn. Phila: Lea & Blanchard, 1841. 1st Amer ed. Orig grn cl, gilt. Nice. Macdonnell. $200/£128

COCTEAU, JEAN. The Difficulty of Being. NY: Coward-McCann, 1967. 1st US ed. VG+ in dj. Lame Duck. $35/£22

COCTEAU, JEAN. The Infernal Machine. Carl Wildman (trans). London, 1936. 1st Eng ed. Very Nice in dj (sl torn, long slit fr panel). Clearwater. $55/£35

COCTEAU, JEAN. My Contemporaries. Phila: Chilton, 1968. 1st ed. (Marker star fep), else NF in NF dj. Lame Duck. $20/£13

COCTEAU, JEAN. Opium. NY: Grove, 1958. 1st ed. NF (lt soiling) in glassine dj. Beasley. $75/£48

COCTEAU, JEAN. Opium. The Diary of an Addict. Ernest Boyd (trans). Allen & Unwin, 1933. 1st UK ed. VG-. Sclanders. $19/£12

COCTEAU, JEAN. The Typewriter. Ronald Duncan (trans). Dennis Dobson, 1947. 1st UK ed. NF in Cocteau dj (sl rubbed). Sclanders. $39/£25

Code of Virginia. Richmond, 1849. 900pp (lacks fep, foxed). Full leather. Good+. Scribe's Perch*. $55/£35

Code of Virginia. Ritchie Dunnavant, 1860. 2nd ed. 1016pp (pp xi, xii lack lower 1/2; pp xiii, iv present but slit off; foxed). Contemp full leather (worn). Fair. Book Broker. $45/£29

CODMAN, JOHN. The Mormon Country. NY, 1874. 1st ed. Frontis map, 225pp + ads. (Few ll yellowed; tp; map waterstained; spine chipped), o/w VG. Benchmark. $95/£61

CODRESCU, ANDREI. License to Carry a Gun. Chicago: Big Table, 1970. 1st ed, 1st bk. Inscribed. Fine in NF dj. Lame Duck. $150/£96

CODY, LIZA. Bad Company. London: Collins, 1982. 1st UK ed. Good (new fep; spine crease) in VG- dj (spine bottom sl worn). Williams. $62/£40

CODY, LIZA. Head Case. Collins, 1985. 1st UK ed. Fine in NF dj. Williams. $39/£25

CODY, LIZA. Rift. Collins, 1988. 1st UK ed. NF in VG dj (sm closed tear). Williams. $25/£16

COE, GEORGE W. Frontier Fighter, the Autobiography.... Doyce B. Nunis, Jr. (ed). Chicago: Lakeside Classic, 1984. Teg. Dk brn cl, gilt. Fine. Bohling. $20/£13

COE, MICHAEL D. Lords of the Underworld: Masterpieces of Classic Maya Ceramics. Princeton: Art Museum, (1978). 20 fldg color plts. Good in dj. Archaeologia. $125/£80

COE, MICHAEL D. The Maya Scribe and His World. NY: Grolier Club, 1973. One of 1000. *Swann**. $115/£74

COE, TUCKER. (Pseud of Donald E. Westlake.) Murder Among Children. NY: Random House, 1967. 1st ed. Fine in dj (sl worn). *Else Fine*. $95/£61

COETZEE, J. M. Age of Iron. Secker, 1990. 1st UK ed. Fine in dj. *Williams*. $16/£10

COETZEE, J. M. Dusklands. Johannesburg, (South Africa): Ravan, 1974. 1st ed, 1st bk. NF (sl foxing) in dj (sm mends w/clear tape, sl foxing). *Antic Hay*. $300/£192

COETZEE, J. M. Life and Times of Michael K. Johannesburg: Ravan, (1983). 1st ed. NF (corners sl bumped) in dj. *Antic Hay*. $50/£32

COETZEE, J. M. Life and Times of Michael K. Secker, 1983. 1st UK ed. Fine in Fine dj. *Martin*. $28/£18

COFFIN, CHARLES CARLETON. Marching to Victory, The Second Period of the War of the Rebellion Including the Year 1863. NY, 1889. Contemp rpt. 491pp & ads. Pict cl. (Spine chipped, back cvr stained), o/w VG + . *Pratt*. $22/£14

COFFIN, CHARLES CARLETON. The Seat of Empire. Boston: Fields, Osgood, 1870. viii,232pp; 6 plts, lg fldg map. Gilt-pict cl. VG. *Adelson*. $60/£38

COFFIN, CHARLES CARLETON. Winning His Way. Boston, 1887. Rpt. 258pp. Pict cl. (Spine faded), o/w VG. *Pratt*. $20/£13

COFFIN, DAVID R. The Villa in the Life of Renaissance Rome. Princeton, 1979. Good. *Washton*. $100/£64

COFFIN, LEWIS A. et al. Small French Buildings. NY, 1921. Good. *Washton*. $60/£38

COFFIN, LEWIS A. et al. Small French Buildings. NY, 1926. 183 photo plts and dwgs. VG (sm stain fr cvr). *Truepenny*. $60/£38

COFFIN, LEWIS A. and ARTHUR C. HOLDEN. Brick Architecture of the Colonial Period in Maryland and Virginia. NY: Architectural Book Pub Co, 1919. 118 plts. Dk blue cl (worn, soiled), gilt. *Freeman**. $70/£45

COFFIN, MORSE H. The Battle of Sand Creek. Alan W. Farley (ed). Waco, TX: W.M. Morrison, 1965. 1st bk ed. One of 300. Brn cl. Fine. *Harrington*. $45/£29

COFFIN, WILLIAM F. 1812; the War, and Its Moral: A Canadian Chronicle. Montreal, 1864. *Swann**. $46/£29

COGAN, SARA G. (comp). Pioneer Jews of the California Mother Lode, 1849-1880. Berkeley: Western Jewish History Center, 1968. 1st ed. Frontis map. Gilt-lettered black cl. Fine. *Argonaut*. $50/£32

COGSWELL, MOSES PEARSON. The Gold Rush Diary of Moses Pearson Cogswell of New Hampshire. Elmer Munson Hunt (ed). (Concord): NH Hist Soc, (1949). 1st separate ptg. Paper-backed bds, pict cvr label. Fine. *Pacific**. $52/£33

COHELEACH, GUY. The Big Cats. NY: Abrams, (1982). Dj (sl soiled). *Freeman**. $45/£29

COHEN, ANTHEA. Angel Without Mercy. GC: Doubleday, 1984. 1st US ed. Advance review copy. Fine in dj (sl edgewear). *Janus*. $25/£16

COHEN, FELIX S. Handbook of Federal Indian Law. Washington: GPO, 1942. Fair (inner hinges repaired). *Lien*. $50/£32

COHEN, I. B. Introduction to Newton's Principia. Cambridge, 1971. 16 plts. VG in dj. *Whitehart*. $62/£40

COHEN, I. B. Some Early Tools of American Science. Cambridge, MA: Harvard Univ, 1950. 1st ed. Red cl. Fine. *Weber*. $45/£29

COHEN, LEONARD. Death of a Lady's Man. NY, 1978. 1st ed. NF in NF dj. *Warren*. $40/£26

COHEN, LEONARD. The Spice-Box of Earth. Toronto: McCelland & Stewart, 1961. 1st ed. Pb. VG + (sl rubbed; name). *Beasley*. $35/£22

COHEN, LEONARD. The Spice-Box of Earth. (Toronto: McClelland & Stewart, 1961.) 1st ed. Red patterned eps. Gilt-stamped black cl, patterned bds. VG in dj (sq cutout to reveal cvr port). *Houle*. $95/£61

COHEN, MORTON. Rider Haggard. London: Hutchinson, 1960. 1st ed. Dj (spine sl chipped). *Edwards*. $23/£15

COHEN, OCTAVUS. Romance in the First Degree. NY: Macmillan, 1944. 1st ed. NF in dj (edges rubbed). *Else Fine*. $40/£26

COHEN, OCTAVUS. The Townsend Murder Mystery. NY: Appleton-Century, 1933. 1st ed. (Bumped, shelfworn.) Dj (soiled, worn). *Metropolitan**. $40/£26

COHN, ISIDORE. Rudolph Matas. GC, 1960. 1st ed. VG. *Argosy*. $85/£54

COHN, NORMAN. The Pursuit of the Millennium. London: Secker & Warburg, 1957. 1st ed. 9 plts, map. VG in dj. *Cox*. $39/£25

COHN, WILLIAM. Chinese Painting. Phaidon, 1948. 1st ed. 224 plts. (Bkpl; spine faded.) *Edwards*. $44/£28

COHNHEIM, JULIUS. Lectures on General Pathology. Vol 1: The Pathology of the Circulation. London: New Sydenham Soc, 1889. xviii,528pp. (Lt spotted.) *White*. $23/£15

COHNHEIM, JULIUS. Lectures on General Pathology. Vol 2: The Pathology of Nutrition. London: New Sydenham Soc, 1889. 529-821pp. (lt spotted.) *White*. $23/£15

COILLARD, FRANCOIS. On the Threshold of Central Africa. Catherine W. McIntosh (ed). NY: Amer Tract Soc, 1903. 2nd ed. Frontis port, fldg map. Red gilt cl (sl worn). Internally VG. *Terramedia*. $100/£64

COKE, EDWARD. The Fourth Part of the Institutes of the Laws of England. London: John Streater et al, 1671. 5th ed. Frontis port. Mod speckled calf (browned), else Attractive. *Boswell*. $750/£481

COKE, EDWARD. The Third Part of the Institutes of the Laws of England. London: A. Crooke et al, 1671. 5th ed. Mod speckled calf. (Embrowning, w/o port.) Attractive. *Boswell*. $850/£545

COKE, EDWARD. The Third Part of the Institutes of the Laws of England...(and) The Fourth Part of the Institutes.... London: A. Crooke, 1671. 5th eds. (Corner 1st port torn away, not affecting image), else Very Fresh. Contemp calf (new label). *Boswell*. $1,500/£962

COKE, HENRY J. A Ride Over the Rocky Mountains to California.... London: Richard Bentley, 1852. 1st ed. x,388,(2)pp. Brn cl, gilt spine. (Tp partly separated; rebacked, orig spine laid down), o/w VG. Howes C548. *Pacific**. $316/£203

COKE, HENRY J. Tracks of a Rolling Stone. London, 1905. Port. VG (sl soiled, edgeworn, spine sunned). Howes C549. *Reese*. $300/£192

COKE, VAN DEREN (ed). One Hundred Years of Photographic History. Albuquerque: Univ of NM, 1975. 1st ed. 110 b/w plts. Fine in pict dj. *Cahan*. $35/£22

COKE, VAN DEREN. The Painter and the Photograph. Albuquerque: Univ of NM, 1972. Rev, enlgd ed. Fine in dj. *Cahan*. $125/£80

COLBERT, E. H. The Dinosaur Book: The Ruling Reptiles and Their Relatives. NY: Amer Museum of Natural History, 1945. 1st ed. Pict cl. VG. *Mikesh*. $25/£16

COLCQUORN, JOHN. The Moor and the Loch. Blackwood, 1884. 6th ed. 2 vols. Grn gilt-dec cl. (Inscrip), o/w VG. *Petersfield*. $97/£62

COLDEN, CADWALLADER. Colden Letter Books. 1760-1775. NY Hist Soc, 1876-77. 2 vols. 495; 531pp, index vol 2. (Lib stamps; vol 1 spine top chipped.) *Bohling.* $35/£22

COLDEN, CADWALLADER. The History of the Five Indian Nations of Canada. London, 1747. 8vo. Engr fldg map. Contemp calf. Howes C560. *Swann*.* $1,495/£958

COLDSTREAM, J. N. Knossos. The Sanctuary of Demeter. Oxford: British School of Archaeology at Athens, (1975). 100 plts. Good. *Archaeologia.* $85/£54

COLE COLLABORATORS. Radiologic Exploration of the Mucosa of the Gastro-Intestinal Tract. Saint Paul, 1934. 1/4 leather. NF. *Doctor's Library.* $150/£96

COLE, A. C. The Methods of Microscopical Research. London: Bailliere, Tindall & Cox, 1895. 2nd ed. 207pp + ads, 42pp pub's cat. VG. *Savona.* $44/£28

COLE, CORNELIUS. California Three Hundred and Fifty Years Ago. SF/NY, 1888/1887. 1st ed. 333pp. Old lib buckram. Good (tear near binding of tp, frontis; old tape, ex-lib). *Baade.* $30/£19

COLE, CYRENUS. Anna Marcella's Book of Verse. Cedar Rapids, IA: Torch Press, Aug 11, 1912. #6/125. Inscribed. Laid-in ptd presentation poem w/facs sig of Marcella. Pattern paper over bds; white cl spine; teg. Fine. *Graf.* $37/£24

COLE, EMMA. The Life and Sufferings of Miss Emma Cole. Boston: M. Aurelius, 1844. 1st ed. Frontis, 36pp. (Frontis, 1st few leaves stained, sl affecting text; text dampstained), else Good (lacks wrappers). *Brown.* $75/£48

COLE, ERNEST. House of Bondage. NY: Ridge Press, 1967. 1st ed. VG in cl over bds. *Smith.* $60/£38

COLE, F. J. A History of Comparative Anatomy from Aristotle to the Eighteenth Century. London, 1944. 1st ed. Fine (ex-lib). *Fye.* $95/£61

COLE, GAROLD L. Travels in America. Norman: Univ of OK, (1984). 1st ed. VG in dj. *Lien.* $38/£24

COLE, GEORGE E. Early Oregon. Jottings of Personal Recollections of a Pioneer of 1850. (Spokane): The Author, (1905). 1st ed. Fine in dj (torn). *Perier.* $85/£54

COLE, GEORGE E. Early Oregon. Jottings of Personal Recollections of a Pioneer of 1850. Spokane, 1905. VG in dj (chipped). *Reese.* $75/£48

COLE, H. M. The European Theater of Operations: The Lorraine Campaign. Washington: Hist Division Dept of the Army, 1950. 1st ed. 50 maps, lg map rear pocket. Fine. *Graf.* $25/£16

COLE, HARRY ELLSWORTH. Stagecoach and Tavern Tales of the Old Northwest. Cleveland: A. H. Clark, 1930. Dbl map frontis. Teg. Navy cl, gilt. VG +. *Bohling.* $60/£38

COLE, HARRY ELLSWORTH. Stagecoach and Tavern Tales of the Old Northwest. Cleveland: Clark, 1930. 1st ed. One of 1505. Teg. Blue cl. (Spine, fr cvr sl spotted, corners sl bumped), else Fine. *Argonaut.* $90/£58

COLE, R. H. Mental Diseases: A Text-Book of Psychiatry.... London: Univ of London, 1913. 1st ed. 7 monochrome photolithos. Ptd panelled blue-grey cl (crown chipped, sl shaken), gilt spine. Jelliffe's name stamp, bkpl. Good+ (lib stamps to tp, other ll; whited spine #s, rear pocket). *Gach.* $65/£42

COLE, RALPH D. Thirty-Seventh Division in the World War 1917-1918. Columbus, OH, 1926-29. 2 vols. Blue cl (extrems rubbed), gilt. VG +. *Bohling.* $40/£26

COLE, WILLIAM. A Journal of My Journey to Paris in the Year 1765. F.G. Stokes (ed). London, 1931. 1st ed. Fldg map. VG. *Gretton.* $39/£25

COLEMAN, A. D. The Grotesque in Photography. NY: Summit, 1977. 1st ed. (Name stamp), else Fine in illus stiff wrappers. *Cahan.* $50/£32

COLEMAN, EVELYN J. et al. The Collector's Encyclopedia of Dolls. London, 1970. 1st UK ed. 46 color plts. Dj (sl chipped, spine lt faded). *Edwards.* $70/£45

COLEMAN, J. WALTER. The Molly Maguire Riots. Richmond: Garrett & Massie, 1936. 1st ed. NF in dj (very worn, internally mended tears). *Beasley.* $50/£32

COLEMAN, LOUIS C. and LEO RIEMAN. Captain John Mullan; His Life. Montreal: Payette Radio Ltd, 1968. Fine. *Perier.* $75/£48

COLEMAN, MRS. GEORGE P. Virginia Silhouettes. Dietz, 1934. #84/235. Good+ (foxed; binding weak). *Book Broker.* $50/£32

COLEMAN, W. S. British Butterflies, Figures and Descriptions of Every Native Species, Etc. London, (1886). 18th ed. 179pp + ads, 15 litho plts. Gilt-dec cl. VG. *Mikesh.* $45/£29

COLERIDGE, CHRISTABEL ROSE. Jack O'Lanthorn. London: Walter Smith & Innes, 1889. 1st ed. 2 vols. Red cl (spines faded, rubbed, sm splits lower joints). *Burmester.* $140/£90

COLERIDGE, ERNEST HARTLEY. The Life of Thomas Coutts, Banker. London: John Lane, Bodley Head, 1920. 1st ed. 2 vols. 47 plts. Uncut. Cl-backed bds, gilt. VG. *Hollett.* $117/£75

COLERIDGE, HENRY NELSON. Six Months in the West Indies, in 1825. London: Murray, 1832. 3rd ed. (viii),311pp; fldg map. Lib cl. VG (ex-lib, lib # spine). *Worldwide.* $65/£42

COLERIDGE, SAMUEL TAYLOR. Biographia Literaria or Biographical Sketches of My Literary Life and Opinions. Henry N. and Sara Coleridge (eds). London: William Pickering, 1847. 2nd ed. 2 vols in 3. Orig cl, ptd spine labels. (Bkpls; labels worn, edges sunned), o/w VG set. *Reese.* $125/£80

COLERIDGE, SAMUEL TAYLOR. The Complete Works. NY, 1863-64. 7 vols. Port. (Sl shaken.) Contemp 1/2 tan calf, marbled bds, edges. (Rubbed.) *Freeman*.* $50/£32

COLERIDGE, SAMUEL TAYLOR. Confessions of an Inquiring Spirit. Henry Nelson Coleridge (ed). London: William Pickering, 1840. 1st ed. 95pp. 3/4 gilt-dec brn morocco, marbled bds (sl rubbed). VG. *Lucas.* $125/£80

COLERIDGE, SAMUEL TAYLOR. Letters, Conversations and Recollections of S. T. Coleridge. Thomas Allsop (ed). London: Groombridge/Waterlow, 1858. 2nd ed. (xii),251pp. Brn cl (spine top repaired). *Burmester.* $70/£45

COLERIDGE, SAMUEL TAYLOR. Poems. (Hammersmith): Kelmscott, (1896). One of 300. 8vo. Orig limp vellum, silk ties. *Swann*.* $920/£590

COLERIDGE, SAMUEL TAYLOR. The Poetical and Dramatic Works. J.J. Chidley, 1844. New ed. iv,464pp (faint trace of stamp across ptd tp); extra engr tp, frontis. Orig cl blocked in blind on sides, in gold on backstrip. *Cox.* $44/£28

COLERIDGE, SAMUEL TAYLOR. The Rime of the Ancient Mariner. London, 1876. 1st Dore ed. 14pp; 38 full-pg plts by Gustave Dore. Aeg. Fine full red leather, gilt. (Old waterstain top edge text block; sl scuffed), else Very Attractive. *King.* $495/£317

COLERIDGE, SAMUEL TAYLOR. The Rime of the Ancient Mariner. NY: Harper, 1876. 1st Amer ed. Tp vignette, 41 illus, 12pp of text. Gilt-pict cl (corners worn, spine ends frayed). *Argosy.* $150/£96

COLERIDGE, SAMUEL TAYLOR. The Rime of the Ancient Mariner. Bristol: Douglas Cleverdon, 1929. One of 400 numbered. 1/4 cl. *Swann*.* $488/£313

COLERIDGE, SAMUEL TAYLOR. Selected Poems. London: Nonesuch, 1935. One of 500 numbered. Orange vellum, gold signature ties. Slipcase. *Swann**. $230/£147

COLERIDGE, SAMUEL TAYLOR. Specimens of the Table Talk of the Late Samuel Taylor Coleridge. London, 1835. 1st ed. 2 vols. Frontispieces. W/index, half-titles, ads. 1/2 calf (sl rubbed). Fine. *Polyanthos*. $150/£96

COLERIDGE, SAMUEL TAYLOR. The Table Talk and Omnia. Oxford, 1917. Frontis. VG. *Cox*. $16/£10

COLERIDGE, SARA. Memoirs and Letters of Sara Coleridge. E. Coleridge (ed). NY: Harper, 1874. 1st US ed. xxxi,528,4pp; 2 engr ports. Cl over beveled bds (sl mkd), gilt. *Hollett*. $101/£65

COLERIDGE-TAYLOR, S. Twenty-Four Negro Melodies. Boston: Oliver Ditson, (1905). Pb ed. VG (pp sl browned; few sm tears extrems, canvas spine sl rubbed) in stiff card wrappers. *Between The Covers*. $375/£240

COLERIDGE-TAYLOR, S. Twenty-Four Negro Melodies. Boston: Oliver Ditson, 1905. 1st ed. Wraps. Fine in Fine dj (sm chips rear panel). *Beasley*. $225/£144

COLES, JOHN. Summer Travelling in Iceland. London, 1882. 1st ed. Frontis, (xiv),x,270pp; lg fldg map, 9 plts. Blue cl, gilt. *Maggs*. $273/£175

COLES, ROBERT. The Darkness and the Light. NY: Aperture, 1974. 1st ed. 65 b/w plts by Doris Ulmann. Fine in NF dj. *Cahan*. $100/£64

COLES, ROBERT. Dorothea Lange: Photographs of a Lifetime. Millerton, NY: Aperture, 1982. 1st ed. Fine in pict dj. *Cahan*. $85/£54

COLETTE. Belles Saisons: A Colette Scrapbook. NY: FSG, (1978). 1st ed. Fine in dj (lt wear, sm slice rear panel). *Antic Hay*. $25/£16

COLETTE. Duo. Indianapolis: Bobbs-Merrill, (1974). 1st Amer ed. NF (sm ink name) in dj. *Antic Hay*. $25/£16

COLETTE. The Other One. NY: Farrar Straus & Cudahy, 1960. 1st US ed. VG+ in dj (spine sl faded, rear lt foxed). *Lame Duck*. $25/£16

COLETTE. The Pure and the Impure. NY: FSG, (1967). 1st ed. NF in dj (lt worn, sm tears). *Antic Hay*. $25/£16

COLL, CARTER. A Mirror of Nature. L.A. County Museum of Art, 1982. Good in wraps. *Washton*. $25/£16

Collection of All Such Acts...as Have Passed Since the Session of 1801. Richmond: Ptd by S. Pleasants, 1808. Vol II only. vi,167,(1),322pp (foxed, ink sig). Contemp yapp style calf (stained, worn, edges frayed). *Waverly**. $49/£31

Collection of Poems.... (Robert Dodsley, ed.) London: R. & J. Dodsley, 1763. 6 vols. Contemp full calf (worn, rubbed, spines chipped, flaking). *Kane**. $45/£29

Collection of Sundry Publications, and Other Documents, in Relation to the Attack Made During the Late War Upon the Private Armed Brig General Armstrong.... NY: J. Gray, 1833. iv,55pp (55 misnumbered 45). Later 1/2 leather, marbled bds. Nice (lt foxing). Howes C582. *Bohling*. $100/£64

Collection of the Facts and Documents Relative to the Death of Major General Alexander Hamilton. (By William Coleman.) NY, 1804. 1st ed. (Sl internal spotting.) Contemp calf (rubbed, cvrs detached). *Freeman**. $50/£32

Collection of the Facts and Documents Relative to the Death of Major-General Alexander Hamilton. (By William Coleman.) NY, 1804. Contemp sheep (skillfully rebacked). Howes C572. *Swann**. $80/£51

Colleen Moore's Doll House. NY, 1935. Pict wraps (worn). *King*. $15/£10

COLLES, A. Selections from the Work of Abraham Colles. R. McDonnell (ed). New Sydenham Soc, 1881. Frontis port, xvi,431pp. Blind-stamped cl. (Cl worn; lib mks on spine, fep, tp), o/w VG. *Whitehart*. $55/£35

COLLET, STEPHEN. (Pseud of Thomas Byrley.) Relics of Literature. London, 1823. 400pp; extra-illus, w/19 engr plts. Marbled eps, edges. Full diced calf, gilt. VG. *Argosy*. $150/£96

Collier's New Photographic History of the World's War...1918. NY: P.F. Collier, (1918). Cvr photo illus laid down. (Edgewear, shaken.) *Dawson*. $35/£22

COLLIER, JEREMY. A Short View of the Immorality, and Profaneness of the English Stage. London: S. Keble, R. Sare, & M. Hindmarsh, 1698. 1st ed. 8 p.l., 288pp (bkpl, 3 leaves sl torn, lt foxed, rep stuck to pastedown). Contemp calf (label remnants spine, sm cracks to spine, sm splits top of joints, corners sl worn, cvrs sl dull). Internally Excellent. *Pirages*. $550/£353

COLLIER, JEREMY. A Short View of the Profaneness and Immorality of the English Stage. London: G. Strahan, Williamson, Osborne, 1730. 5th ed, corrected. 437pp + (3 bk ads). Recent vinyl, raised bands, gilt red leather label. Good (names, foxing). *Hartfield*. $185/£119

COLLIER, JOHN PAYNE. A Bibliographical and Critical Account of the Rarest Books in the English Language.... NY: David G. Francis & Scribner, 1866. 4 vols. 1/2 morocco (sl worn, hinge repaired; bk label). *Moss*. $94/£60

COLLIER, JOHN PAYNE. New Facts Regarding the Life of Shakespeare. London: Thomas Rodd, 1835. 1st ed. 55pp (lib ink stamp tp, last leaf; hinges repaired). Uncut. Mod cl (rebacked, bds lt soiled, rubbed). *Edwards*. $55/£35

COLLIER, JOHN PAYNE. Punch and Judy. NY: Rimington & Hooper, 1929. #334/376 ptd. 28 illus by George Cruikshank. Frontis. Cl-backed bds (soiling, wear), paper spine label (rubbed). *Dramatis Personae*. $60/£38

COLLIER, JOHN PAYNE. Punch and Judy. NY: LEC, 1937. #904/1500 numbered. 24 color sketches by George Cruikshank. Full leather. Fine in tissue dj, bd folder, pub's slipcase (sl worn). *Hermitage*. $125/£80

COLLIER, JOHN PAYNE. The Tragical Comedy or Comical Tragedy of Punch and Judy. NY: LEC, 1937. One of 1500 numbered. Full blindstamped leather (lt rubbed). Slipcase (scuffed). *Oinonen**. $70/£45

COLLIER, JOHN. The Devil and All. London: Nonesuch, 1934. One of 1000 numbered, signed. Grn cl, beveled bds, 3 gold foil panels inset fr bd. (Edges sl dknd, foil insets flaking), else NF in acetate dj (torn, incomplete) w/gold foil turn-ins (wrinkled, flaking). *Waverly**. $33/£21

COLLIER, JOHN. Fancies and Goodnights. Doubleday, 1951. 1st ed. Fine in dj (lt chipped). *Madle*. $100/£64

COLLIER, JOHN. Fancies and Goodnights. NY, 1951. Good (sl bumped, creased) in dj (torn, chipped). *Clearwater*. $78/£50

COLLIER, JOHN. His Monkey Wife or, Married to a Chimp. London: Peter Davies, 1930. 1st ed, 1st bk. (Top edge sl dusty), o/w Fine in VG+ dj (spine sunned, sl edge nicks). *Reese*. $350/£224

COLLIER, JOHN. His Monkey Wife. Appleton, 1931. 1st ed. VG. *Madle*. $20/£13

COLLIER, JOHN. Tom's A-Cold. London: Macmillan, 1933. 1st ed. Leather spine label (sl chipped). VG (inscrip). *Certo*. $45/£29

COLLIER, JOHN. Witch's Money. NY, 1940. Ltd to 350. Signed. Fine (spine sunned, cvrs sl bubbled). *Polyanthos*. $75/£48

COLLIER, RICHARD. The Plague of the Spanish Lady. NY: Atheneum, 1974. 1st ed. Good in dj. *White*. $23/£15

COLLIER, V. F. W. Dogs of China and Japan in Nature and Art. NY: Frederick A. Stokes, (1921). 1st Amer ed. 7 color plts (1 dbl-pg). Yellow cl over bds. Good. *Karmiole*. $200/£128

COLLIER, WILLIAM ROSS and EDWIN VICTOR WESTRATE. The Reign of Soapy Smith. London: Cassell, 1936. 1st ed. 14 plts. (Few spots.) *Hollett*. $39/£25

COLLIGNON, CHARLES. The Miscellaneous Works of Charles Collignon, M.D.... Cambridge: Hodson, 1786. (5),345pp, errata leaf; 1/2-title. Calf (joints weak). *Goodrich*. $125/£80

COLLIN, PAUL RIES. Calling Bridge. OUP, 1976. 1st ed. 8vo. 86pp; 12 Fine b/w illus by Harold Jones. VG + in pict dj (edge-creased). *Bookmark*. $23/£15

COLLING, JAMES K. Details of Gothic Architecture. London, 1852/56. 2 vols. 8pp,38 + 23 + 3 plts; 27pp,54 + 11 plts (vol I 2nd series plt 2 margin repaired, tidemark corner 1st ff vol II). (Cl sl worn, spotted, guttapercha binding loose.) *Ars Artis*. $133/£85

COLLING, JAMES K. Details of Gothic Architecture. Batsford, n.d. (1856). 1st ed in bk form. 2 vols. 8pp, 95 litho plts, guards; 27pp, 85 litho plts. VG in brn cl (sl rubbed, inner hinges reinforced), gilt. *Cox*. $133/£85

COLLING, SUSAN. Frogmorton. London: Collins, (1955). 1st Eng ed. E.H. Shepard (illus). 8vo. Blue bds. VG in VG dj. *Dower*. $55/£35

COLLINGWOOD, STUART DODGSON. The Life and Letters of Lewis Carroll (Rev. C.L. Dodgson). London: T. Fisher Unwin, 1898. 1st ed. Dec grn cl spine (faded to brn). VG. *Captain's Bookshelf*. $75/£48

COLLINGWOOD, W. G. The Lake Counties. London: Frederick Warne, 1932. 1st ed thus. 16 color plts, lg fldg map. VG. *Hollett*. $78/£50

COLLINGWOOD, W. G. The Life of John Ruskin. London: Methuen, 1900. 2nd ed. Nice. *Patterson*. $31/£20

COLLINGWOOD, W. G. The Limestone Alps of Savoy. London, 1884. xxiii,206pp. Largely unopened, uncut. (Upper fore-edge cvr dampstained.) Glassine dj (torn). *Henly*. $75/£48

COLLINGWOOD, W. G. and JON STEFANSSON. A Pilgrimage to the Saga-Steads of Iceland. Ulverston: W. Holmes, 1899. 1st ed. x,187pp, w/map. Blue cl (sl rubbed, mkd). Very Nice. *Hollett*. $429/£275

COLLINS, A. FREDERICK. Experimental Television. Boston: Lothrop et al, (1932). 1st ed. Frontis. Pict cl. NF. *Glaser*. $225/£144

COLLINS, A. H. Symbolism of Animals and Birds Represented in English Church Architecture. London: Pitman, 1913. (Emb lib stamps plt margins.) *Ars Artis*. $33/£21

COLLINS, DENNIS. Indian's Last Fight; or, The Dull Knife Raid. (Girard, KS, 1915.) 1st ed. Howes C590. *Ginsberg*. $300/£192

COLLINS, H. R. Threads of History: Americana Recorded on Cloth 1775 to the Present. Washington: Smithsonian, 1979. 16pp color plts. Dec cvr. Good + in dj (chipped). *Scribe's Perch**. $65/£42

COLLINS, JOHN A. The Monthly Offering. Boston: Anti-Slavery Office, 1841. (Foxing; shaken, rubbed, bumped.) *Metropolitan**. $69/£44

COLLINS, JOHN S. My Experiences in the West. Colton Storm (ed). Chicago: Lakeside, 1970. Frontis, fldg map. Teg. Fine in glassine dj. Reissue of Howes C594. *Cahan*. $20/£13

COLLINS, MAX ALLAN. The Baby Blue Rip-Off. NY: Walker, 1983. 1st ed. Fine in Fine dj. *Janus*. $50/£32

COLLINS, MAX ALLAN. Kill Your Darlings. NY: Walker, 1984. 1st ed. Fine in Fine dj. *Janus*. $45/£29

COLLINS, MAX ALLAN. Midnight Haul. Woodstock: Foul Play, 1986. 1st ed. VF in dj. *Mordida*. $30/£19

COLLINS, MAX ALLAN. Nice Weekend for Murder. NY: Walker, 1986. 1st ed. VF in dj. *Mordida*. $30/£19

COLLINS, MAX ALLAN. No Cure for Death. NY: Walker, 1983. 1st ed. Fine in Fine dj. *Janus*. $45/£29

COLLINS, VERE H. Talks with Thomas Hardy at Max Gate 1920-1922. Guernsey: Toucan Press, 1971. Ltd to 300. Fine in wrappers. *Words Etc*. $47/£30

COLLINS, WILKIE. Armadale. Smith, Elder, 1866. 2 vols. Sprinkled edges. Contemp 1/2 leather, marbled bds (re-spined, corners rubbed), raised bands. Good (bkpls). *Tiger*. $936/£600

COLLINS, WILKIE. The Moonstone. NY, 1868. 1st Amer ed. 223pp. VG (bkpl, margins soiled; brn cl lt worn, spine chipped). *Truepenny*. $95/£61

COLLINS, WILKIE. The Moonstone. NY: Harper, 1868. 1st Amer ed. (Heel clipped, edges worn through, lt browned, spotted.) *Metropolitan**. $230/£147

COLLINS, WILKIE. My Miscellanies. Sampson Low, 1863. Late issue in tan cl (1st issue bound in grn). 2 vols. Good (lt spotted, bkpls, lib #s; spines bumped, chipped). *Tiger*. $624/£400

COLLINS, WILKIE. My Miscellanies. London: Sampson, Low, 1863. 1st ed. 2 vols. 16pp ads dated Nov 1863 each vol. Primary binding of 'grass-grn diagonal-wide-bead-grain cl, greenish buff eps.' (Bkpl removed, feps sl cracked; sl shelfworn.) *Sumner & Stillman*. $975/£625

COLLINS, WILKIE. No Name. NY: Harper, 1863. 1st Amer ed. Lavender cl, gilt. VG (spine sl chafed). *Macdonnell*. $150/£96

COLLINS, WILKIE. The Woman in White. Sampson, Low, 1860. 1st ed. 3 vols. 8vo. (Pub's ads absent from end of vol 3; sl foxing.) Later 1/4 red morocco, gilt. *Sotheby's**. $1,076/£690

COLLINS, WILLIAM. The Poems of William Collins.... Edmund Blunden (ed). London: Etchells & MacDonald, 1929. One of 500 (of 550) numbered. Frontis. Paper label. (Forecorners bumped), else NF in dj (chipped). *Reese*. $45/£29

COLLINS, WILLIAM. The Poetical Works. H. Nicolas (ed). London: William Pickering, 1830. 1st ed thus. Engr frontis port, lxxii,(2),150pp. Aeg. VG in contemp 1/2 red morocco, cl sides (hinges rubbed). *Cox*. $28/£18

COLLINSON, CLIFFORD W. Life and Laughter 'Midst the Cannibals. London, n.d. c.(1926). 3rd ed. Presentation copy. Frontis port. (Lt marginal browning, rear few leaves roughly opened; sl spotted, recased w/sl loss spine tail.) *Edwards*. $39/£25

COLLINSON, FRANK. Life in the Saddle. Mary Whatley Clarke (ed). Norman: Univ of OK, 1963. 1st ed. Fine in dj. *Gibbs*. $25/£16

COLLIS, MAURICE. Cortes and Montezuma. NY, 1955. 1st Amer ed. (Sm damp circle spine foot, rear cvr), o/w Fine in NF dj. *Turpen*. $25/£16

COLLIS, MAURICE. The First Holy One. Faber, 1948. 1st ed. 16 plts, 4 maps. Dj (torn). *Edwards*. $23/£15

COLLIS, MAURICE. Siamese White. London: Faber & Faber, 1936. 1st ed. 4 maps (1 fldg). (Ex-lib, pencil notes; sl rubbed, soiled, lib # spine), o/w VG. *Worldwide*. $22/£14

COLLIS, MAURICE. Stanley Spencer: A Biography. London, 1962. 1st ed. VG in dj (sl torn, sl loss). *Words Etc*. $19/£12

COLLIS, SEPTIMA M. A Woman's Trip to Alaska. NY, c. 1890. Fldg frontis (finger smudge on back), map. Dec cl. VG (new eps). *High Latitude*. $30/£19

COLLIS, SEPTIMA M. A Woman's War Record. NY, 1889. 1st ed. 78pp (ink inscrip); 8 photos (lacks 1). Teg. (Cl worn, spotted.) King. $50/£32

COLLODI, CARLO. The Adventures of Pinocchio. NY: Macmillan, 1926. 4to. 404pp (few sl flaws, edge tears). Pict cl (shelfworn, sl soiled). Oinonen*. $80/£51

COLLODI, CARLO. The Adventures of Pinocchio. NY: Knopf, 1988. 1st US ed. Roberto Innocenti (illus). 8 3/4 x 11 3/4. 142pp. Fine in dj. Cattermole. $35/£22

COLOMB, R. N. Slave Catching in the Indian Ocean. London, 1873. 1st ed. 8vo. xi,503pp; fldg map, 8 plts. Mod 1/2 calf, gilt. Maggs. $1,287/£825

Colorado: A Guide to the Highest State. Workers of the Writers' Program (comp). NY: Hastings House, (1948). Good. Lien. $25/£16

COLQUHOUN, ARCHIBALD. The Key of the Pacific. Westminster: Archibald Constable, 1895. 1st ed. Association copy. xvii,(i),443pp (sig, lt foxed); lg fldg map at rear; errata slip tipped in. Untrimmed, partly unopened. Blue-grn, ribbed lt brn cl (sl worn), gilt. Cvrs Good. Baltimore*. $80/£51

COLQUHOUN, ARCHIBALD. The Mastery of the Pacific. NY: Macmillan, 1904. 44 plts. (Lt rubbed.) Adelson. $40/£26

COLQUHOUN, ARCHIBALD. Overland to China. NY/London: Harper, 1900. 1st ed. 4 color fldg maps. (Ex-lib; lib spine label removed, cl sl rubbed), o/w VG. Worldwide. $45/£29

COLQUHOUN, ARCHIBALD. Overland to China. NY/London: Harper, 1900. 1st Amer ed. 4 color fldg maps. Blue cl. VG. Terramedia. $100/£64

COLQUHOUN, J. Rocks and Rivers. London: J. Murray, 1849. 1st ed. 1/2 leather, marbled bds. VG. Mikesh. $137/£88

COLT, MARGARETTA BARTON. Defend the Valley. NY, (1940). 1st ed. Fine in Fine dj. Pratt. $32/£21

COLT, MIRIAM DAVIS. A Heroine of the Frontier: Miriam Davis Colt in Kansas, 1856. J. Christian Bay (ed). Cedar Rapids: Privately ptd, Christmas 1941. Port. Title label. Fine in plain dj (chipped, soiled). Bohling. $20/£13

COLT, MIRIAM DAVIS. Went to Kansas.... Watertown, 1862. 1st ed. 294pp (lacks fep). Howes C616. Ginsberg. $450/£288

COLTHARP, LURLINE. The Tongue of the Tirilones. Univ of AL, 1965. VG+ in dj. Zubal*. $65/£42

COLTON, CALVIN. The Life and Times of Henry Clay. NY: A.S. Barnes, 1846. 2 vols. 504; 504pp; 2 engrs. (Lt foxed; hinges repaired vol 1, extrems worn.) Cullen. $50/£32

COLTON, HAROLD. Black Sand. Albuquerque: Univ of NM, 1960. 1st ed. NF in dj. Archer. $35/£22

COLTON, MATTHEW. (Pseud of Walter Camp.) Frank Armstrong's Second Term. A.L. Burt, 1911. Rpt. VG in Good+ dj. Plapinger. $45/£29

COLTON, RAY C. The Civil War in the Western Territories. Norman: Univ of OK, (1959). 1st ed. 7 maps. Fine in dj (sl chipped). Argonaut. $35/£22

COLTON, WALTER. The California Diary. Oakland: Biobooks, 1948. One of 1000. Map, 6 plts, fldg facs, 6 ports on 1 sheet. Marbled eps. Red pebbled cl, gilt. (Gilt faded), else NF. Howes C625. Parmer. $65/£42

COLTON, WALTER. Deck and Port. NY, 1850. 1st ed, 2nd issue. Frontis port, map, 4 hand-colored plts. Pub's cl (lacks spine ends). Howes C624. Swann*. $69/£44

COLTON, WALTER. Deck and Port. NY: A.S. Barnes, 1850. 1st ed. Frontis port (backed; new eps), 408pp, 4 tinted litho plts, 20-pg pub's cat. Blind-stamped brn cl (wear to tips, spine ends, along rear joint). Dawson. $125/£80

COLTON, WALTER. Deck and Port. NY, 1852. 1st ed, later ptg. Engr frontis port, 408pp; 4 color litho views. Ptd eps and only Sarony listed, not Sarony & Major. (Foxed, spine dknd.) Howes C624. New Hampshire*. $90/£58

COLTON, WALTER. Deck and Port. NY: A.S. Barnes, 1852. Steel-engr frontis port, 408pp; map, 4 litho plts. Grn cl, gilt. (Lt foxed; spine faded, lt water spots on cvrs), o/w VG. Howes C624. Pacific*. $57/£37

COLTON, WALTER. Deck and Port. NY: A.S. Barnes, 1854. 408pp; map, 5 plts. Dec cl (rubbed, faded, end frayed). Howes C624. Adelson. $120/£77

COLTON, WALTER. Land and Lee in the Bosphorus and Aegean, Or Views of Athens and Constantinople. Henry T. Cheever (ed). NY: A.S. Barnes, 1851. 2nd ed. Frontis, 366pp (foxing), 1 plt, 11-pg pub's cat. Blind/gold-stamped brn cl (sl wear to tips, spine ends, 1-in crack along fr joint). Dawson. $100/£64

COLTON, WALTER. The Sea and the Sailor: Notes on France and Italy.... NY: A.S. Barnes, 1851. 1st ed. Frontis port, 437 pp, 1 engr plt, 8-pg pub's cat. Blind/gold-stamped blue cl (crack in cl along fr joint, but sound). Dawson. $100/£64

COLTON, WALTER. Ship and Shore in Madeira, Lisbon and the Mediterranean. NY: A.S. Barnes, 1852. 3rd? ed. Frontis, 313pp (foxing), engr plt, 14-pg pub's cat. Blind/gold-stamped brn cl (sl loose; tips, spine ends worn). Dawson. $75/£48

COLTON, WALTER. Three Years in California. (Stanford): Stanford Univ, (1949). 1st ed of facs rpt of 1850 1st ed. Frontis port, 6 full-pg ports, 1 map. Yellow cl. VF in dj (sl chipped). Argonaut. $45/£29

COLTON, WALTER. Three Years in California. NY, 1850. 1st ed. 456pp (eps sl foxed), map, 6 ports, 6 sep illus. 3/4 morocco (recased), marbled bds. Fine. Howes C625. Turpen. $85/£54

COLTON, WALTER. Three Years in California. NY, 1850. 1st ed. 456pp. (Foxed; rear fly defective; cvrs worn, spine chipped; fold-out torn, repaired w/thread.) King. $100/£64

COLTON, WALTER. Three Years in California. NY: A.S. Barnes, 1850. 1st ed. 456pp (foxing, spotted); 6 litho plts, 6 engr ports, fldg facs (2 short tears). Blind/gold-stamped red cl (rebacked, orig spine laid down, edgewear, spine sunned). Dawson. $250/£160

COLTON, WALTER. Three Years in California. NY: A.S. Barnes, 1850. 1st ed. Frontis port, 456pp; 5 engr port plts, 6 engr plts, 1 map, 1 fldg facs. Red cl, gilt. (Lt foxed, 2 sm tears facs, skillfully repaired w/archival tape), o/w Fine. Howes C625. Pacific*. $431/£276

COLUM, MARY and PADRAIC. Our Friend James Joyce. London: Gollancz, 1959. 1st ed. Fine (copyright obliteration) in NF dj. Antic Hay. $27/£17

COLUM, PADRAIC. The Adventures of Odysseus and the Tale of Troy. NY, (1918). 1st ed. Willy Pogany (illus). VG. Argosy. $45/£29

COLUM, PADRAIC. Castle Conquer. NY, 1923. 1st Amer ed. Fine. Polyanthos. $25/£16

COLUM, PADRAIC. Creatures. With Drawings by Boris Artzybasheff. NY: Macmillan, 1927. 1st ed. Signed, dated. Pict eps. Cl-backed patterned bds, gilt spine. Nice (waterstains) in pict dj (closed tears, few nicks). Vandoros. $150/£96

COLUM, PADRAIC. Dramatic Legends and Other Poems. NY: Macmillan, 1922. 1st Amer ed. Signed. Paper labels. VG. Reese. $30/£19

COLVER, ANNE. Mr. Lincoln's Wife. NY/Chicago et al: Rinehart & Winston, 1965. 1st ed. VG in dj. Worldwide. $14/£9

COLVIN, F. F. and E. R. GORDON. Diary of the 9th (Q.R.) Lancers During the South African Campaign, 1899 to 1902. S. Kensington: Cecil Roy, 1904. 1st ed. Fldg map in rear pocket. Aeg. 2-toned cl, gilt emblem. (Inner hinges starting), else NF. *Mcgowan.* $250/£160

COLVIN, H. M. A Biographical Dictionary of English Architects 1660-1840. John Murray, 1954. 1st ed. (Ex-lib, sm ink stamp, bkpl, piece of paper adhered p311; spine #s.) Dj (sl shaved). *Edwards.* $39/£25

COLVIN, IAN D. The Cape of Adventure, Being Strange and Notable Discoveries.... London: Jack, 1912. 25 plts. (Edges sl rubbed, spine sl faded), o/w VG. *Worldwide.* $18/£12

COLVIN, SIDNEY. Early Engraving and Engravers in England (1545-1695). London, 1905. (Ex-lib, ink stamp tp verso, bkpl, sl crease tp.) Teg, rest uncut. Morocco-backed cl bds (sl rubbed, spine lt faded, #s). *Edwards.* $312/£200

COLWELL, EILEEN. Round About and Long Ago. Boston: Houghton Mifflin, 1974. 1st US ed. Anthony Colbert (illus). 6 1/4 x 9. 125pp. VG in dj. *Cattermole.* $20/£13

COLWELL, ERNEST CADMAN and HAROLD R. WILLOUGHBY. The Four Gospels of Karahissar. Chicago, 1936. 2 vols. 13plts vol 1, 137 plts vol 2. (Spine tops lt sunned.) *Washton.* $250/£160

COLWELL, MAX. Whaling Around Australia. London: Angus & Robertson, (1970). VG in dj. *High Latitude.* $25/£16

COLWIN, LAURIE. Another Marvelous Thing. NY: Knopf, 1986. 1st ed. Cl-backed bds. As New in dj. *Jaffe.* $45/£29

COLWIN, LAURIE. Shine On, Bright and Dangerous Object. NY: Viking, 1975. 1st ed. Fine in dj (2 sm nicks). *Captain's Bookshelf.* $75/£48

COLYAR, A. S. Life and Times of Andrew Jackson, Soldier, Statesman, President. Nashville, 1904. 2 vols. 6 plts. Teg. Maroon cl. VG (bkpls, pencil notes; spines sl faded, dull). *Bohling.* $40/£26

COMAN, EDWIN T., JR. and HELEN M. GIBBS. Time, Tide and Timber: A Century of Pope and Talbot. Stanford Univ, (1949). 1st ed. Fldg chart. Fine in dj (sl rubbed). *Argonaut.* $50/£32

Combat Divisions of World War II (Army of the United States). Washington, DC: Army Times, (1946). 1st ed. VG (pp foxed; backstrip worn) in orig ptd wrappers. *Mcgowan.* $45/£29

COMBE, ANDREW. Treatise on the Physiological and Moral Management of Infancy. Phila: Carey & Hart, 1842. 3rd Amer ed. (xii),307,(7)pp. Orig cl, paper label (chipped; hinges cracked). *Gach.* $75/£48

COMBE, WILLIAM. The Tour of Doctor Syntax in Search of the Picturesque (together with) The Tour...in Search of Consolation (together with) The Tour...in Search of a Wife. London: Nattali & Bond, (1817). 9th ed. 3 vols. 80 Fine hand-colored plts by Thomas Rowlandson. 19th-cent 3/4 calf over marbled bds, all edges marbled, gilt, red/black spine labels. NF set. *Captain's Bookshelf.* $750/£481

COMBERMERE, VISCOUNT. Memoirs and Correspondence of Field-Marshal Viscount Combermere from His Family Papers. Mary, Viscountess Combermere & W. W. Knollys (eds). London, 1866. 2 vols. 2 frontis ports, xiii,403; x,434pp; plan. Black 1/2 morocco, grn bds, gilt. *Maggs.* $390/£250

COMBS, BARRY B. Westward to Promontory. Palo Alto: Amer West, (1969). VG + in dj (sl worn). *Bohling.* $30/£19

Come Not, Lucifer! A Romantic Anthology. London: Westhouse, (1945). 1st ed. NF in NF dj. *Other Worlds.* $45/£29

COMEAU, N. A. Life and Sport on the Lower St. Lawrence and Gulf.... London, (1912). 2nd issue. Dk blue cl (hinges stained, few lt blotches sides), gilt. *Maggs.* $50/£32

COMFORT, J. W. The Practice of Medicine on Thomsonian Principles.... Phila: A. Comfort, 1843. 1st ed. 15,514,(1)pp (pencil notes). Full contemp leather, label. *M&s.* $300/£192

Comic Adventures of Old Dame Trot, and Her Cat. London: Grant & Griffith, n.d. (ca 1845). 12mo. Full-pg wood engr frontis port, 17pp (few pp corners creased); 16 1/2-pg color engrs. (Ink dedication inside upper wrapper.) Buff stiff paper wrappers (soiled, creased, sl chipped). Internally VG. *Hobbyhorse.* $240/£154

Comic Latin Grammar. London: Charles Tilt, 1840. 1st ed. 8 plts by John Leech. 3/4 blue morocco, gilt-paneled spine, raised bands, gilt top. Nice. *Appelfeld.* $150/£96

COMMAGER, HENRY STEELE. The Blue and the Gray. Indianapolis/NY, (1950). 1st ed. 2 vols. VG. *Wantagh.* $45/£29

COMMAGER, HENRY STEELE. The Blue and the Gray. NY, (1950). 1st of the 1 vol ed. VG + in VG + dj. *Pratt.* $30/£19

Compendium of the Enumeration of the Inhabitants and Statistics of the United States.... Washington: Thomas Allen, 1841. 379pp (sl browned, lt foxed). Orig calf, plain bds, red leather spine label. (Dusty, spine torn, chipped, edges peeling). *Baltimore*.* $140/£90

Compilation of Narratives of Explorations in Alaska. Washington: GPO, 1900. (Edgewear), else VG. *Perier.* $425/£272

Compleat and Humorous Account of All the Remarkable Clubs and Societies in the Cities of London and Westminster.... London: J. Wren, 1756. 7th ed. xii,(2),327pp (lacks prelim blank). Contemp sheep (spine extrems chipped, hinges cracking). Internally Clean. *Reese.* $125/£80

Compleat History of Thomas Kouli Kan Sovereign of Persia. (By Jean Antoine Du Cerceau?) London: J. Brinkley, 1742. 2 parts in 1. Engr frontis port; 163,116pp; triple fold map. Contemp calf; spine gilt (upper joint cracked). Good. *Cullen.* $400/£256

Complete Work of Michelangelo. 1965. 2 vols. 1040 b/w, 32 color plts. (Pencil notes.) Djs (cellotaped to spine heads), slipcase. *Edwards.* $70/£45

COMPTON, JAMES R. Andersonville. Des Moines, 1887. 1st ed. 98pp. (Index pg partially torn, blank fep torn out), o/w VG. *Pratt.* $70/£45

COMPTON, PIERS. Marshal Ney. London, 1937. Frontis port, 3 plts. Red cl. *Maggs.* $62/£40

COMPTON-BURNETT, IVY. Darkness and Day. London, 1951. 1st Eng ed. Very Nice in dj (nicked, sl foxed). *Clearwater.* $39/£25

COMPTON-BURNETT, IVY. A Heritage and Its History. London: Gollancz, 1959. 1st ed. Good in dj (sl soiled, edges torn). *Holmes.* $25/£16

COMPTON-BURNETT, IVY. A Heritage and Its History. London: Gollancz, 1959. 1st ed. Comp copy w/pub's slip laid in. Fine in dj (spine sl dknd). *Captain's Bookshelf.* $50/£32

COMPTON-BURNETT, IVY. Men and Wives. London, 1931. 1st Eng ed. Very Nice. *Clearwater.* $70/£45

COMPTON-BURNETT, IVY. Two Worlds and Their Ways. London, 1949. 1st Eng ed. Very Nice in dj (sl rubbed). *Clearwater.* $39/£25

COMRIE, JOHN. History of Scottish Medicine. 1932. 2nd ed. 2 vols. VG. *Fye.* $175/£112

COMRIE, JOHN. History of Scottish Medicine. London: Wellcome Hist Medical Museum, 1932. 2nd ed. 2 vols. Excellent. *Pirages.* $125/£80

COMSTOCK, J. An Introduction to Mineralogy. NY: Pratt, Woodford, 1845. 3rd ed. 369pp. Full calf. (Foxed; rubbed), else Good. *Blake*. $100/£64

COMSTOCK, WILLIAM PHILLIPS. Garages and Motor Boat Houses. NY, (1911). 1/2 cl, bds (sl wear). *Freeman**. $70/£45

CONANT, A. J. Foot-prints of Vanished Races in the Mississippi Valley. St. Louis, 1879. 1st ed. 122pp. (Exlib; spine chipped; cvrs dknd.) *King*. $45/£29

CONANT, A. J. Foot-Prints of Vanished Races in the Mississippi Valley. St. Louis: Chancy R. Barns, 1879. 1st ed. Frontis, x,122pp (lt foxed). Good (spine worn). *Cahan*. $50/£32

CONANT, A. J. Foot-Prints of Vanished Races in the Mississippi Valley. St. Louis: Chancy R. Barns, 1879. 1st ed. viii,122pp. Red-brn cl, gilt. Good (sl browned; sl dusty, worn). *Baltimore**. $100/£64

CONARD, HOWARD LOUIS. Uncle Dick Wootten, the Pioneer Frontiersman.... Milo M. Quaife (ed). Chicago: Lakeside Classic, 1957. Map. Teg. Blue cl (spine dknd), gilt. VG + . *Bohling*. $20/£13

CONARD, HOWARD LOUIS. Uncle Dick Wootten. Milo M. Quaife (ed). Chicago: Lakeside, Christmas, 1957. Dk blue cl. NF. *Sadlon*. $30/£19

CONDER, CLAUDE REIGNER. Syrian Stone-Lore. London, 1886. 3 fldg maps. (Lt wear.) *Freeman**. $40/£26

CONDIE, FRANCIS. Practical Treatise on the Diseases of Children. Phila, 1844. 1st ed. 642pp. Good (lt internal foxing; rebound in cl). *Doctor's Library*. $135/£87

CONDIT, IRA J. The Fig. Waltham, MA, 1947. 1st ed. Frontis. *Edwards*. $47/£30

CONDON, RICHARD. The Manchurian Candidate. NY: McGraw-Hill, (1959). 1st ed. Fine (spine base sl rubbing) in VG + dj (sm nicks, spine sl fading). *Between The Covers*. $250/£160

CONDON, RICHARD. The Manchurian Candidate. NY: McGraw-Hill, 1959. 1st ed. (Name stamps eps, pg edges dknd), o/w VG in dj (spine chipped, frayed, sl faded). *Mordida*. $45/£29

CONDON, RICHARD. A Talent for Loving. NY: McGraw-Hill, 1961. 1st ed. Fine in dj (lt soiled, spine sl faded, chip). *Mordida*. $45/£29

CONDON, RICHARD. The Venerable Bead. Franklin Center, PA, 1992. 1st ed. Signed, ltd ed. Full red dec emb leather. *Argosy*. $50/£32

CONDON, T. Oregon Geology: A Revision of 'The Two Islands.' Portland: Gill, (1910). 2nd ed. 30 plts. News clipping on author laid in. (Spine ends rubbed), else VG. *Mikesh*. $45/£29

CONE, MARY. Two Years in California. Chicago: Griggs, 1876. 1st ed. 238pp. VG. *Second Life*. $125/£80

Confessions of an English Opium-Eater. (By Thomas de Quincey.) Phila, 1823. 1st Amer ed. Uncut. Orig bds (worn), paper spine label (worn, chipped). Custom slipcase, protective sleeve. *Freeman**. $120/£77

CONFUCIUS. The Analects of Confucius. NY: LEC, 1970. #1029/1500 signed by Tseng Yu-Ho (illus). Chinese silk. Fine in clamshell slipcase. *Hermitage*. $125/£80

CONFUCIUS. The Analects of Confucius. Lionel Giles (trans). NY: LEC, 1970. One of 1500 numbered, signed by Tseng Yu-Ho (illus). Shaded orange cl overlaid w/gilt pattern, paper spine label. Cream cl dropback box, Chinese calligraphy on fr; red button, string tie. (Corners of drop-back box loose), else Fine. *Heller*. $150/£96

CONFUCIUS. The Analects of Confucius. Lionel Giles (trans). NY: LEC, 1970. One of 1500 numbered, signed by Tseng Yu-Ho (illus). 12 dbl-pg color plts. Dec cl. Mint in cl clamshell box. *Argosy*. $175/£112

CONGER, SARAH PIKE. Letters from China with Particular Reference to the Empress Dowager and the Women of China. Chicago: McClurg, 1909. 1st ed. Map called for in tp not present. (All eds handled do not include map.) Bk complete. Teg. (Cl sl rubbed, spine frayed, faded, ex-lib, spine label), o/w VG. *Worldwide*. $30/£19

CONGREVE, WILLIAM. The Complete Works of.... Montague Summers (ed). Nonesuch, 1923. 4 vols. Uncut. Buckram-backed bds (bkpls; corners worn), paper spine label. *Argosy*. $350/£224

CONGREVE, WILLIAM. Plays. London: J. Tonson in the Strand, 1735. 2 vols. Contemp full sheep. VG (1 rebacked w/orig spine laid down, other w/cracked fr hinge). *Sumner & Stillman*. $170/£109

CONKLING, ROSCOE P. and MARGARET B. The Butterfield Overland Mail, 1857-1869. Volume III, Atlas. Glendale: Clark, 1947. 1st ed. One of 1260. 77 plts, 3 lg fldg maps. Gilt-lettered red cl. Fine. *Argonaut*. $250/£160

CONN, GEORGE. The Arabian Horse in America. Woodstock: Countryman, 1957. 1st ed. VG in Good dj. *October Farm*. $30/£19

CONNELL, EVAN S. The Connoisseur. NY: Knopf, 1974. 1st ed. Fine in NF dj. *Hermitage*. $30/£19

CONNELL, EVAN S. The Diary of a Rapist. NY: S&S, (1966). 1st ed. NF in dj (sm tears, sl wear). *Antic Hay*. $25/£16

CONNELL, EVAN S. The Diary of a Rapist. NY: S&S, 1966. 1st ed. VG in VG dj (spine top worn). *Revere*. $35/£22

CONNELL, EVAN S. A Long Desire. NY: Holt, Rinehart & Winston, (1979). 1st ed. Fine in Fine dj. *Fuller & Saunders*. $25/£16

CONNELL, EVAN S. Son of the Morning Star. SF: North Point, 1984. 1st ed. VF in VF dj. *Else Fine*. $135/£87

CONNELLEY, WILLIAM E. History of Kansas State and People. Chicago/NY: American Hist Soc, 1928. 1st ed. 5 vols. Marbled eps, edges. Navy blue cl. (Puncture upper joint vol 2), o/w Fine set. *Glenn*. $200/£128

CONNELLEY, WILLIAM E. Quantrill and the Border Wars. Cedar Rapids, IA, 1910. 1st ed. Howes C689. *Ginsberg*. $125/£80

CONNELLEY, WILLIAM E. Wild Bill and His Era: The Life and Adventures of James Butler Hickok. NY: Press of the Pioneers, 1933. 1st ed. Ltd to 200. Pict cl, gilt. NF. Howes C690. *Sadlon*. $100/£64

CONNELLY, MARC. The Green Pastures. NY: Farrar & Rinehart, 1930. One of 550 numbered, signed by Connelly & Robert Edmond Jones (illus). Color frontis, pict tp, 11 Fine b/w plts (clipping removed from rear pastedown, plt removed from fr pastedown). Teg. Grn paper-cvrd bds (sl rubbed at extrems), gilt. *Blue Mountain*. $175/£112

CONNELLY, MICHAEL. The Black Echo. Boston: Little Brown, 1992. 1st ed. VF in dj. *Mordida*. $50/£32

CONNER, SEYMOUR V. (ed). Texas Treasury Papers. Austin: TX State Library, 1955. 1st ed. 3 vols. Wraps. Fine. *Gibbs*. $175/£112

CONNETT, EUGENE V. (ed). American Big Game Fishing. NY: Derrydale, (1935). One of 850. 65 plts (5 color). Uncut. Blue cl (sl worn), gilt. *Oinonen**. $425/£272

CONNETT, EUGENE V. (ed). American Sporting Dogs. NY: D. Van Nostrand, 1948. Stated 1st ed. Frontis. Gilt lettering. VG (sm stain back edge). *Backman*. $55/£35

CONNETT, EUGENE V. Duck Decoys. NY: D. Van Nostrand, 1953. 1st ed. Color frontis. Rust-colored cl, gilt. Fine in pict dj (tattered). *Biscotti*. $65/£42

CONNETT, EUGENE V. My Friend the Trout. Princeton: Van Nostrand, 1961. 1st ed. VF in dj. *Bowman*. $120/£77

CONNETT, EUGENE V. Random Casts. NY, (1939). One of 1075. 13 plts. (Sm tear preface leaf neatly tape-repaired.) *Kane**. $110/£71

CONNETT, EUGENE V. (ed). Yachting in North America. NY, (1948). 1st ed. VG. *Argosy*. $85/£54

CONNICK, CHARLES J. Adventures in Light and Color. NY, (1937). 2nd ptg. 42 mtd color plts, 48 collotype. VG. *Argosy*. $175/£112

CONNICK, CHARLES J. Adventures in Light and Color. 1937. 1st ed. Frontis, 41 color plts tipped in, 48 b/w plts. (Eps spotted; sl rubbed.) *Edwards*. $117/£75

CONNINGTON, J. C. Death at Swathling Court. London: Ernest Benn, 1926. 1st ed. (Lt sunned, soiled.) *Metropolitan**. $28/£18

CONNINGTON, J. J. No Past Is Dead. Boston: Little Brown, 1942. 1st Amer ed. VG in dj (sm chips spine ends). *Mordida*. $50/£32

CONNOLLY, CYRIL (ed). Horizon Stories. NY: Vanguard, (1946). 1st ed. VG in dj. *Turtle Island*. $25/£16

CONNOLLY, CYRIL. The Condemned Playground. Routledge, 1945. 1st ed. (Cl sl stained), o/w VG in dj (stained, nicked). *Poetry Bookshop*. $31/£20

CONNOLLY, CYRIL. Enemies of Promise. London, (1938). 1st ed. (Rubbed.) *Argosy*. $50/£32

CONNOLLY, CYRIL. Enemies of Promise. London, 1938. 1st ed. VG in dj (worn). *Buckley*. $31/£20

CONNOLLY, CYRIL. Les Pavillons. NY, 1962. 1st Amer ed. Nice (cvrs sl mkd). *Clearwater*. $47/£30

CONNOLLY, CYRIL. The Missing Diplomats. London: Queen Anne Press, 1952. 1st ed. Plain wrappers w/ptd label in ptd yellow dj. (Dj edges browned), else Nice. *Turtle Island*. $55/£35

CONNOLLY, CYRIL. A Romantic Friendship, Letters to Noel Blakiston. London, 1975. 1st ed. VG in dj. *Typographeum*. $25/£16

CONNOR, RALPH. The Rock and the River. McClelland & Stewart, (1931). 1st Canadian ed. Inscribed, signed by 'Charles W. Gordon / Ralph Connor.' VG in dj (foxed). *Authors Of West*. $20/£13

CONNOR, SEYMOUR V. Adventure in Glory, Saga of Texas 1836-49. Austin, 1965. 1st ed. Fine in Fine dj. *Turpen*. $28/£18

CONNOR, SEYMOUR V. Explorers and Settlers, Historic Places Commemorating Early Exploration and Settlement of U.S. Washington, 1968. 1st ed. VG. *Turpen*. $20/£13

CONNOR, SEYMOUR V. and JIMMY M. SKAGGS. Broadcloth and Britches, the Santa Fe Trade. College Station: TX A&M Univ, (1977). 1st ed. 4 maps. Yellow cl. VF in pict dj. *Argonaut*. $50/£32

CONOLLY, JOHN. An Inquiry Concerning the Indications of Insanity.... London: John Taylor, 1830. 1st ed, 1st bk. vi,496pp. Mod beige cl, leather label. VG. *Gach*. $950/£609

CONOLLY, JOHN. The Treatment of the Insane Without Mechanical Restraints. London: Smith, Elder, 1856. 1st ed. xii,380pp + pub's cat dated Oct 1856. Emb brn cl (hinges strengthened, rebacked; orig spine laid down w/part of top and bottom chipped away), gilt spine. Good+ (lib stamps tp). *Gach*. $1,850/£1,186

CONRAD, BARNARBY. Encyclopaedia of Bullfighting. London, 1962. Illus 2-tone cl (bds sl warped). *Edwards*. $31/£20

CONRAD, JACK RANDOLPH. The Horn and the Sword. London: MacGibbon & Kee, 1959. 1st UK ed. 32 plts. Dj. *Edwards*. $39/£25

CONRAD, JESSIE. A Handbook of Cookery for a Small House. Heinemann, (1923). 1st ed. Patterned cl. VG (eps, edges sl spotted) in dj (sl browned). *Ash*. $78/£50

CONRAD, JESSIE. A Handbook of Cookery. London: Heinemann, (1923). 1st ed. Fine in dj (spine sl dknd, sl rubbed). *Between The Covers*. $225/£144

CONRAD, JESSIE. Joseph Conrad As I Knew Him. London, 1926. 1st Eng ed. Good (foxing, clippings pasted to feps). *Clearwater*. $31/£20

CONRAD, JOSEPH with FORD MADOX HUEFFER. The Nature of a Crime. London: Duckworth, (1924). 1st ed. NF in dj (sl wear, sm tears). *Antic Hay*. $125/£80

CONRAD, JOSEPH and FORD MADOX HUEFFER. The Nature of a Crime. London: Duckworth, (1924). 1st ed. Orange cl. Fine in dj (sl nicked). *Appelfeld*. $125/£80

CONRAD, JOSEPH and FORD MADOX HUEFFER. Romance. NY: McClure Phillips, 1904. 1st Amer ed. Fine (spine sl rubbed). *Between The Covers*. $250/£160

CONRAD, JOSEPH. The Arrow of Gold. London: T. Fisher Unwin, (1919). 1st British ed, state w/'A' in running head pg67 intact, 3 titles listed opposite title. VG. *Reese*. $50/£32

CONRAD, JOSEPH. The Arrow of Gold. Fisher Unwin, 1919. 1st UK ed. Fine in VG dj (sl edgewear, browned, 1.5 inch closed tear fr panel). *Williams*. $390/£250

CONRAD, JOSEPH. The Arrow of Gold. London, 1919. 1st ed. (Cl faded), else VG. *Buckley*. $19/£12

CONRAD, JOSEPH. The Arrow of Gold. London: T. Fisher Unwin, 1919. 1st Eng ed. VG. *Hollett*. $39/£25

CONRAD, JOSEPH. The Dover Patrol, a Tribute. Canterbury: For Private Circulation, 1922. 1st ed. One of 75 ptd. Uncut, unopened. NF in orig pale blue-grn ptd wrappers. NF. *Macdonnell*. $375/£240

CONRAD, JOSEPH. The Heart of Darkness. NY: LEC, 1969. #1029/1500 signed by Robert Shore (illus). Fine in slipcase. *Hermitage*. $85/£54

CONRAD, JOSEPH. Joseph Conrad's Letters to His Wife. London: Privately ptd, 1927. 1st ed. #60/220 signed by Jessie Conrad. Teg. NF (bkpl removed; cvrs rubbed). *Polyanthos*. $45/£29

CONRAD, JOSEPH. Joseph Conrad's Letters to R. B. Cunninghame Graham. C. T. Watts (ed). Cambridge, 1969. 1st ed. VF in dj. *Bromer*. $50/£32

CONRAD, JOSEPH. Last Essays. London: Dent, 1926. 1st ed. Grn cl, gilt. Fine in dj (chipped). *Macdonnell*. $50/£32

CONRAD, JOSEPH. Last Essays. London: J.M. Dent, 1926. 1st ed. Emb grn cl. NF in dj (dkng, sm chips, tears). *Antic Hay*. $125/£80

CONRAD, JOSEPH. Letters from Conrad: 1895 to 1924. Edward Garnett (ed). London: Nonesuch, 1928. One of 925 numbered. Buckram (sl spotted, mkd). Nice. *Clearwater*. $78/£50

CONRAD, JOSEPH. Letters of Joseph Conrad to Richard Curle. NY: Crosby Gaige, 1928. Frontis port. Marbled bds, linen spine, label, gilt top. *Appelfeld*. $125/£80

CONRAD, JOSEPH. Lord Jim. Blackwood, 1900. Blackwood's Colonial Library ed. Poor (pg corners waterstained; cvrs shabby) in card wrappers (partially defective spine repaired). *Clearwater*. $78/£50

CONRAD, JOSEPH. Lord Jim. London: William Blackwood, 1900. 1st ed. 8vo. Grn cl blocked in black. (Inner fr hinge starting, sig.) Fldg slipcase. *Swann**. $575/£369

CONRAD, JOSEPH. The Mirror of the Sea. NY: Harper, 1906. 1st Amer ed. (Ink name, browning eps due to offset from former dj.) Pict blue cl (sl soiled). NF. *Antic Hay*. $85/£54

CONRAD, JOSEPH. The Nigger of the Narcissus. London: Heinemann, 1898. 1st Eng ed. (Sig; nick fr cvr, bumped, spine lt rubbed.) *Swann**. $115/£74

CONRAD, JOSEPH. The Nigger of the Narcissus. LEC, 1965. One of 1500 signed by Millard Sheets (illus). Dk blue morocco-backed cl bds. Mint in tissue dj (yellowed, brittle, chipped), Mint pub's slipcase. *Pirages*. $75/£48

CONRAD, JOSEPH. Nostromo, a Tale of the Seaboard. LEC, 1961. One of 1500 signed by Lima de Freitas (illus). LEC newsletter laid in. Burlap-backed linen bds, cl label. (Tissue dj sl torn), o/w Mint in pub's silver slipcase (chafed). *Pirages*. $100/£64

CONRAD, JOSEPH. Nostromo. London: Harper, 1904. (Fore-edge sl foxed, rep lt creased), else Fine. *Gekoski*. $1,014/£650

CONRAD, JOSEPH. Notes on Life and Letters. London: Dent, 1921. 1st ed. Grn cl, gilt. VF in dj (chip). *Macdonnell*. $50/£32

CONRAD, JOSEPH. Notes on My Books. London: Heinemann, 1921. 1st ed, ltd issue. One of 250 numbered, signed. 1/4 vellum, ptd spine label (rubbed; bkpl). *Swann**. $201/£129

CONRAD, JOSEPH. One Day More. GC: Doubleday, Page, 1920. One of 377 numbered, signed. VG (cvrs worn). *Lenz*. $300/£192

CONRAD, JOSEPH. One Day More. NY, 1920. 1st ed. Ltd to 377 signed, numbered. Parchment spine, tips. (Spine sl worn), else NF. *Black Sun*. $400/£256

CONRAD, JOSEPH. An Outcast of the Islands. London: T. Fisher Unwin, 1896. 1st Eng ed. Good (name; fr hinge cracked, rear hinge tender; binding sl cocked, cvrs sl mkd, corners chafed). *Clearwater*. $312/£200

CONRAD, JOSEPH. The Rescue. GC: Doubleday, Page, 1920. 1st US ed. Navy cl (sl shelfworn), gilt. Pict dj (sl dusty, chipped, lacks bottom 3 inches of spine). *Baltimore**. $30/£19

CONRAD, JOSEPH. The Rescue. London, 1920. 1st Eng ed. Dj (sl dknd, ink date spine). *Swann**. $57/£37

CONRAD, JOSEPH. The Rescue. London: Dent, 1920. 1st ed. Fine in dj (2 short tears). *Between The Covers*. $500/£321

CONRAD, JOSEPH. The Rover. London: T. Fisher Unwin, (1923). 1st Eng ed. VG (eps browned) in dj (worn, sm tears, spine head chipped). *Antic Hay*. $75/£48

CONRAD, JOSEPH. The Rover. GC: Doubleday, Page, 1923. 1st ed. Full leather. (Sl sunned), else Fine. *Metropolitan**. $86/£55

CONRAD, JOSEPH. The Rover. London, 1923. 1st ed. (Pg edges foxed), o/w VG in dj (spine browned, extrems sl chipped). *Buckley*. $109/£70

CONRAD, JOSEPH. The Rover. NY: Doubleday, Page, 1923. 1st Amer ed. Blue cl, gilt. Fine in VG dj. *Macdonnell*. $75/£48

CONRAD, JOSEPH. The Rover. Toronto: Ryerson, 1923. 1st Canadian issue of British ed, comprised of British sheets, integral title-leaf, and binding w/Ryerson imprint at spine toe. Red cl, gilt. Good (crease rep, couple smudges). *Reese*. $100/£64

CONRAD, JOSEPH. A Set of Six. London: Methuen, (1908). 1st ed, later issue w/rear ads dated June. Blue cl blocked in red. *Swann**. $69/£44

CONRAD, JOSEPH. The Shadow Line. London: J.M. Dent, (1917). 1st ed. Dec grn cl. VG (browning). *Antic Hay*. $85/£54

CONRAD, JOSEPH. The Shadow-Line: A Confession. London: Dent, (1917). 1st ed. Lt grn cl (sl rubbed). VG. *Houle*. $125/£80

CONRAD, JOSEPH. The Sisters. NY: Crosby Gaige, 1928. 1st ed. One of 926 ptd. Uncut. Red marbled bds, black leather label, gilt. (Sl rubbed), else Fine. *Macdonnell*. $100/£64

CONRAD, JOSEPH. The Sisters. NY: Crosby Gaige, 1928. Ltd to 926. Marbled bds. VG. *Truepenny*. $125/£80

CONRAD, JOSEPH. Suspense. London: Dent, 1925. 1st ed. Fine in variant gray cl binding w/o eps, as issued. Pict dj (lt edgewear, spine head sl chipped). *Captain's Bookshelf*. $150/£96

CONRAD, JOSEPH. Suspense. London: Dent, 1925. 1st ed. (Fore-edge foxing; frontis puckering), else NF in NF dj (sm nick crown; tear rear panel). *Between The Covers*. $350/£224

CONRAD, JOSEPH. Suspense. London: J.M. Dent, 1925. 1st ed. Purple cl (sl scuffed). VG (ink name). *Antic Hay*. $75/£48

CONRAD, JOSEPH. Suspense. London: J.M. Dent, 1925. 1st ed. Maroon cl. Fine in dj (worn). *Appelfeld*. $200/£128

CONRAD, JOSEPH. Suspense. NY: Doubleday, Page, 1925. 1st Amer ed. Ltd to 377 numbered. Teg, uncut. Parchment bds, gilt. (Rubbed), else VF in inner tissue dj, outer blue ptd dj, box (cracked) w/label. *Macdonnell*. $275/£176

CONRAD, JOSEPH. Tales of Hearsay. London: T. Fisher Unwin, (1925). 1st ed. VG (bkpl, eps browned) in dj (soiled, chipped, sm stain). *Antic Hay*. $75/£48

CONRAD, JOSEPH. Tales of Hearsay. London: T. Fisher Unwin, (1925). (Offsetting eps, edges foxed), else VG in dj (lt soiled, creased, spine chipped). *Hermitage*. $125/£80

CONRAD, JOSEPH. Tales of Hearsay. London: T. Fisher Unwin, (1925). 1st ed. (Sl foxing fore-edge, else Fine in NF dj (nicks base fr panel). *Between The Covers*. $375/£240

CONRAD, JOSEPH. Tales of Hearsay. London: Unwin, (1925). 1st ed. Gilt-stamped dk grn cl. VG. *Houle*. $125/£80

CONRAD, JOSEPH. Tales of Unrest. London: T. Fisher Unwin, 1898. 1st Eng ed. Grn cl (sl bumped). *Swann**. $103/£66

CONRAD, JOSEPH. Tales of Unrest. NY, 1898. 1st ed. 348pp (ink name 1/2-title verso). Teg. Tan cl stamped in brn. VG. *Truepenny*. $200/£128

CONRAD, JOSEPH. Twixt Land and Sea. London: J.M. Dent, 1912. 1st ed. Grn cl. Fine. *Appelfeld*. $200/£128

CONRAD, JOSEPH. Typhoon and Other Stories. London: Heinemann, 1903. 1st Eng ed, 1st issue. Gilt-pict gray cl (lt rubbed; 3 bkpls, sig). *Swann**. $172/£110

CONRAD, JOSEPH. Typhoon and Other Stories. London: Heinemann, 1903. One of 500 ptd. Windmill device tp. Gray cl. Fine. *Appelfeld*. $250/£160

CONRAD, JOSEPH. Typhoon. NY/London: Putnam, 1902. 1st ed. 1st issue grn cl cvr, w/picture of ship foundering in high seas done in blue/orange. VF. *Bromer*. $650/£417

CONRAD, JOSEPH. Under Western Eyes. NY: Harper, 1911. 1st Amer ed. Gilt-stamped blue cl. Fine. *Swann**. $103/£66

CONRAD, JOSEPH. Victory. An Island Tale. London: Methuen, (1915). 1st ed. Red cl (spine lt sunned). *Swann**. $172/£110

CONRAD, JOSEPH. Victory: An Island Tale. GC: Doubleday, 1915. Gilt-stamped dk blue cl (sl rubbed). VG. *Houle*. $125/£80

CONRAD, JOSEPH. Within the Tides. London: J.M. Dent, 1915. 1st ed. *Swann**. $172/£110

CONRAD, JOSEPH. Youth and Two Other Stories. London: Blackwood, 1902. 1st ed. Grn cl (spine head rubbed, sl loss). *Swann**. $287/£184

CONRAD, JOSEPH. Youth: A Narrative. Edinburgh: Blackwood, 1902. 1st ed, earliest issue, w/ads dated 10/02. Grn cl. VG (lt rubbed, sl frayed). *Hermitage*. $275/£176

CONRAD, MRS. JOSEPH. Did Joseph Conrad Return as a Spirit? Webster Groves, MO: Int'l Mark Twain Soc, 1932. Excellent in orig wrappers. *Gekoski*. $117/£75

CONRAT, MASSIE and RICHARD. Executive Order 9066: The Internment of 110,000 Japanese Americans. N.p.: CA Hist Soc, 1972. 1st ed. (Owner stamp, corners sl creased, lt rubbed), else VG in illus stiff wrappers. *Cahan*. $30/£19

CONROY, FRANK. Stop-time. NY: Viking, (1967). 1st ed. Signed. Fine in dj (sl wrinkled). *Lenz*. $75/£48

CONROY, JACK and ANNA BONTEMPS. Slappy Hooper the Wonderful Sign Painter. Boston: Houghton Mifflin, 1946. 1st ed. Ursula Koering (illus). 4to. VG + (bd edges lt foxed) in dj (verso foxed, short edgetears). *Lame Duck*. $650/£417

CONROY, PAT. The Great Santini. Boston: HMCo, 1976. 1st ed. Fine in NF dj (spine sl foxed). *Between The Covers*. $150/£96

CONROY, PAT. The Great Santini. Boston: Houghton Mifflin, 1976. 1st ed. (Glue stain fep), o/w Fine in dj (lt worn). *Hermitage*. $100/£64

CONROY, PAT. The Great Santini. Boston: Houghton Mifflin, 1976. 1st ed. Fine in dj. *Lame Duck*. $150/£96

CONROY, PAT. The Prince of Tides. Boston: HMCo, 1986. Fine in Fine dj. *Between The Covers*. $75/£48

CONROY, PAT. The Prince of Tides. Boston: Houghton Mifflin, 1986. 1st ed. Fine in dj. *Lame Duck*. $50/£32

CONROY, PAT. The Water Is Wide. Boston: Houghton Mifflin, 1972. 1st ed. NF in dj (chips to spine top). *Lame Duck*. $450/£288

CONSTABLE, W. G. The Painter's Workshop. Oxford, 1954. 24 plts. Good in dj. *Washton*. $35/£22

CONSTANTINE, K. C. The Blank Page. NY: Saturday Review, 1974. 1st ed. VG (sl sunned) in dj (sl sunned). *Metropolitan**. $138/£88

CONSTANTINE, K. C. The Man Who Liked Slow Tomatoes. Boston: Godine, 1982. 1st ed. Fine in dj (spine sl dknd). *Mordida*. $75/£48

CONSTANTINE, MILDRED. Tina Modotti: A Fragile Life. London/NY: Paddington, 1975. 1st ed, US issue. Fine in illus dj. *Cahan*. $75/£48

Constitution of the State of New Mexico 1850. Santa Fe: Stagecoach, (1965). One of 350. Frontis map. Fine in dj. *Bohling*. $30/£19

Contributions to Medical and Biological Research Dedicated to Sir William Osler...in Honour of His Seventieth Birthday July 12th, 1919. (Charles Loomis Dana, ed.) NY: Paul B. Hoeber, 1919. Ltd to 1600 sets. 2 vols. (xxii),(650)pp, 29 plts; (xiv),651-1268,(2)pp, 25 plts. Ptd panelled blue buckram. VG set. *Gach*. $200/£128

Contributions to the Historical Society of Montana. Vol II. Helena, 1896. 1st ed. Frontis, 409pp; 2 plts. VG (binding sl soiled). *Oregon*. $120/£77

Conversations on Chemistry.... (By Jane Marcet.) N.p.: Sydney's Press, 1814. Frontis, xii,358,18,(8)pp; 11 plts. Old calf (rubbed). *Karmiole*. $150/£96

CONWAY, MARTIN. The Van Eycks and Their Followers. London: John Murray, 1921. 1st ed. 24 plts. (Spine gilt faded.) *Hollett*. $101/£65

CONWAY, W. MARTIN. The Alps from End to End. Westminster, 1895. 1st ed. xii + 403pp (lt browning, bkpl removed from pastedown), 100 full-pg illus by A.D. M'Cormick. Teg. Gilt-ruled 2-tone cl (fading, sm splits heads of joints). *Edwards*. $117/£75

CONWAY, W. MARTIN. The Bolivian Andes. NY: Harper, 1901. 1st ed. 55 photo plts, 3 full-pg illus. (Sig tp, sl marginal foxing, rubbed.) *Maggs*. $390/£250

CONWAY, W. MARTIN. With Ski and Sledge over Arctic Glaciers. NY: M.F. Mansfield, 1898. vi(4)240pp; 14 plts, fldg map. Good (spine ends chipped; ex-lib). *High Latitude*. $90/£58

Cook's Tourist's Handbook for Switzerland. London: Thomas Cook, 1879. 1st ed. Fldg frontis map, viii,241pp + 32pp ads. Good in brn bds (sl rubbed). *Cox*. $55/£35

COOK, A. J. The Bee-Keeper's Guide. Lansing, MI, 1891. 14th ed, 16th thousand. 461pp + ads. Brn cl. VG. *Second Life*. $50/£32

COOK, A. J. The Bee-Keeper's Guide. Chicago, 1910. 19th ed, 21st thousand. Frontis port. (Feps lt browned; sl bumped.) Gilt motif spine. *Edwards*. $55/£35

COOK, A. J. Manual of the Apiary. Chicago, 1879. 4th ed. Color frontis, guard (torn), 302pp + (vi) index + (xii) ads. (Ex-lib, ink stamp tp, bkpl pastedown, margins browned, some sl thumbed; fep sl torn w/o loss; edges sl rubbed.) *Edwards*. $47/£30

COOK, CYRIL. The Life and Work of Robert Hancock. Chapman & Hall, 1948. 1st ed. Frontis port, 7 plts. (Cl lt soiled.) *Edwards*. $195/£125

COOK, DAVID J. Hands Up. Norman: Univ of OK, (1958). 1st ptg of new ed. Illus bds. Fine in dj. *Bohling*. $22/£14

COOK, DAVID J. Hands Up. Denver, 1897. Enlgd 2nd ed. Frontis port + another port, ii,442pp. Maroon cl (spine sl dull, ends frayed), gilt. VG. Howes C728. *Bohling*. $150/£96

COOK, DAVID J. Hands Up; or, Thirty-Five Years of Detective Life in the Mountains and on the Plains. John W. Cook (comp). Denver: W.F. Robinson, 1897. 1st rev ed. 442pp. (Cl sl worn, spine sl frayed; inner hinges cracked), else Good. Howes C728. *Brown*. $100/£64

COOK, E. T. (ed). The Century Book of Gardening. London/NY: Country Life, (1903). Color frontis. (Sl worn, very soiled.) *Maggs*. $33/£21

COOK, EARNSHAW. Hollica Snooze. Rindge, NH, 1957. 1st ed. Blue cl, gilt. VG in dj (chipped). *Price*. $45/£29

COOK, FREDERICK A. Through the First Antarctic Night 1898-1899. NY: Doubleday & McClure, 1900. 4 color plts, map. Teg, others uncut. Dec cl. VG (new eps). *High Latitude*. $500/£321

COOK, G. H. The English Mediaeval Parish Church. Phoenix House, 1955. 2nd ed. 54 plans. VG. *Peter Taylor*. $23/£15

COOK, G. H. The Mediaeval Parish Church. London: Batsford, 1961. (3rd ed.) 179 plt illus, 25 plans. Sound in dj (torn). *Ars Artis*. $33/£21

COOK, GEORGE CRAM. The Spring. NY: Frank Shay, 1921. 1st ed. (Lt wear, soil), else NF- in wraps. *Beasley*. $100/£64

COOK, J. Bibliography of the Writings of Charles Dickens.... London: Frank Kerslake, 1879. Frontis. 1/2 cl (worn, upper cvr detached, orig wrappers bound in; bk label). *Maggs*. $47/£30

COOK, JAMES and JAMES KING. A Voyage to the Pacific Ocean Undertaken.... London: 1784. Atlas vol only. Pub w/o title. 62 engr plts, 1 color, 2 engr dbl-pg charts, fldg map. (1 plt torn affecting text, closed tear 1 plt margin, lt spotting; inscrip.) Later 1/2 morocco, cl (scuffed). *Christie's**. $4,914/£3,150

COOK, JAMES H. Fifty Years on the Old Frontier....
Yale, 1923. 1st ed. (Ex-lib, label removed spine,
bumped, nicked), o/w Good + . Scribe's Perch*.
$42/£27

COOK, JAMES H. Fifty Years on the Old Frontier....
New Haven: Yale Univ, 1923. 1st ed. (Sl soiled.)
Shasky. $50/£32

COOK, JAMES H. Fifty Years on the Old Frontier....
Norman, 1957. 1st ed thus. Fine in dj (worn,
chipped). Pratt. $37/£24

COOK, JAMES. The Three Famous Voyages Round the
World.... Ward, Lock, n.d. (1888/89). Mtd frontis,
xx,1152,(6)pp ads (few ll refastened w/bruised edges,
lt wear, signs of hand coloring few illus); 24 plts. Pict
cl (rebacked, new eps), orig backstrip. Cox. $70/£45

COOK, JOEL. France Historic and Romantic. Phila:
Winston, 1906. 2 vols. 50 photo plts, guards. Teg. 1/2
leather, dec spines, marbled bds. Good-. Scribe's
Perch*. $26/£17

COOK, JOHN R. The Border and the Buffalo. Milo M.
Quaife (ed). Chicago: Lakeside, Christmas, 1938. Dk
red cl (spotted). Sadlon. $15/£10

COOK, JOSEPH. Labor, with Preludes on Current
Events. Boston: Houghton, Osgood, 1880. 1st ed. NF.
Beasley. $50/£32

COOK, R. L. The Concord Saunterer. Middlebury, VT:
Middlebury College Press, 1940. 1st ed. One of 600
ptd. Ptd bds, dj. Fine (text pencilling) in Very Nice dj
(few chips). BAL 20156. Macdonnell. $100/£64

COOK, R. M. Greek Painted Pottery. London, 1972.
2nd ed. 56 plts. Dj (spine sl faded, sl chipped). Edwards. $31/£20

COOK, THEODORE A. Henley Races: With Details of
Regattas from 1903 to 1914 Inclusive. London: OUP,
1919. 1st ed. Blue cl, gilt medallion fr cvr. (Spine
faded), else NF. Cummins. $150/£96

COOK, THEODORE A. Rowing at Henley. London:
OUP, 1919. 1st ed. Diags, map in rear cvr pocket.
Blue cl, gilt emb medallion fr cvr. (Spine faded, lacks
1 pocket diag), else NF. Cummins. $125/£80

COOKE, ALISTAIR. Douglas Fairbanks, the Making of a
Screen Character. NY: MOMA, (1940). 1st ed. (Spine
sl sunned), else VG. King. $20/£13

COOKE, C. E. and A. E. VAN VOGT. Hypnotism Handbook. NY, 1956. 1st ed. Good in dj (tattered). Doctor's Library. $25/£16

COOKE, EDMUND VANCE. Baseballogy. Chicago:
Forbes, 1912. 1st ed. VG (chip to paper cvr of unptd
spine). Beasley. $75/£48

COOKE, EDWARD WILLIAM. View of the Old and
New London Bridges, with Scientific and Historical
Notices...and a Concise Essay on Bridges by George
Rennie. London: Brown & Syrett, 1833. Lg folio.
Tp,1f,vi + 24pp (sl foxing), 12 etched plts. 1/2 mo-
rocco (edges, corners rubbed). Marlborough.
$1,092/£700

COOKE, GEORGE. Loddiges Botanical Cabinet. London, 1827. Vol 8 only. 100 hand-colored copper
engrs. (Lacks spine.) Metropolitan*. $862/£553

COOKE, GRACE McGOWAN. Their First Formal Call.
NY: Harper, 1906. 1st ed. 8vo. 55pp, 14 full-pg illus
by Peter Newell. Fine in red cl, illus label, ptd glassine dj (lt chipped). Bromer. $250/£160

COOKE, JAMES. Mellificivm Chirurgiae; or, the Marrow of Chirurgery. London: T. Hodgkin/W. Marshall,
1688. 4th ed. Complete w/all plts. Engr frontis,
(8),616pp; 11 plts (several w/tears repaired). Recent
full calf (sl foxed, lt dampstaining). Very Clean. Goodrich. $1,195/£766

COOKE, JOHN ESTEN. Mohun or The Last Days of Lee
and His Paladins. Charlottesville, 1937. Fine in dj (sl
chipped). Pratt. $45/£29

COOKE, JOHN ESTEN. Mohun, or, The Last Days of
Lee and His Paladins.... Charlottesville, 1936. VG in
dj (worn). King. $50/£32

COOKE, JOHN ESTEN. Stonewall Jackson and the Old
Stonewall Brigade. Richard Barksdale Harwell (ed).
Charlottesville, (1954). 1st ed. VG (ex-lib) in dj (spine
faded). Pratt. $45/£29

COOKE, M. C. Handbook of British Fungi. London,
1871. 2 vols in 1. 7 plts (1 color). New cl. Good (ex-
lib; sm stain upper margin frontis, few sm stamps).
Wheldon & Wesley. $86/£55

COOKE, PHILIP ST. GEORGE et al. Exploring Southwestern Trails, 1846-1854. Ralph P. Bieber (ed). Glendale: Clark, 1938. 1st ed. One of 1067. Teg. Red cl.
Fine. Argonaut. $125/£80

COOKE, PHILIP ST. GEORGE. The Conquest of New
Mexico and California. Oakland: Biobooks, 1942
(sic), actually 1952. One of 600. Fldg map. Red cl.
(Gilt dull), o/w Fine. Howes C738. Harrington.
$50/£32

COOKE, PHILIP ST. GEORGE. The Conquest of New
Mexico and California. Albuquerque, 1964. Facs rpt
of 1878 ed. Fine in NF dj. Howes C138. Turpen.
$30/£19

COOKE, PHILIP ST. GEORGE. The Conquest of New
Mexico and California; An Historical and Personal
Narrative. NY, 1878. 1st ed. Inscribed. 307pp; fldg
map. (Joints, spine lt worn.) Howes C738. Ginsberg.
$600/£385

COOKE, PHILIP ST. GEORGE. Scenes and Adventures
in the Army; or, Romance of Military Life. Phila,
1859. 2nd ed. 432pp. Contemp 1/2 morocco.
(Owner gilt initials stamped on spine.) Howes C740.
Ginsberg. $450/£288

COOKE, THOMAS. The Universal Letter-Writer.... London: T. Deighton, 1814. Engr frontis, (216)pp. Orig
sheep (sl mks, flaws). Good. Ash. $94/£60

COOKRIDGE, E. H. The Baron of Arizona. NY: John
Day, 1967. Map. Good in dj (worn). Dumont.
$25/£16

COOKRIDGE, E. H. The Third Man. London, 1968. 1st
ed. VG in dj. Typographeum. $30/£19

COOLE, P. G. and E. NEUMAN. The Orpheus Clocks.
London: Hutchinson, 1972. 1st ed. P. Foulkes (trans).
7 color plts. Red cl. Fine in dj. Weber. $25/£16

COOLEY, JEROME EUGENE. Recollections of Early
Days in Duluth. Duluth: The Author, 1925. Frontis
port. (Ink note p72; edgeworn.) Bohling. $85/£54

COOLEY, THOMAS M. A Treatise on the Law of Torts.
Chicago: Callaghan, 1888. 2nd ed. Very Nice in full
mod mottled sheep. Boswell. $250/£160

COOLEY, WILLIAM DESBOROUGH. The Negroland
of the Arabs Examined and Explained. London, 1841.
1st ed. 8vo. xvi,143,(2)ads pp (faint lib stamp to margin of preface); lg fldg map. Orig blind-stamped cl (rebacked, old spine laid down). Maggs. $897/£575

COOLIDGE, DANE. Death Valley Prospectors. NY: E.P.
Dutton, 1937. 1st ed. 16 full-pg illus. (Spine extrems,
tips sl worn.) Dawson. $40/£26

COOLIDGE, DANE. Horse-Ketchum. NY: Dutton,
(1930). 1st ed. Fine in Fine dj. Book Market. $75/£48

COOLIDGE, DANE. Last of the Seris. NY: E.P. Dutton,
1939. 1st ed. Gray cl. VG (sl foxed) in dj (worn). Parmer. $50/£32

COOLIDGE, DANE. Silver Hat. NY: Dutton, 1934. 1st
ed. VG + in VG dj (torn). Book Market. $40/£26

COOLIDGE, DANE. Wally Laughs-Easy. Dutton, 1939.
1st ed. Fine in Nice dj (chipped). Authors Of West.
$30/£19

COOLIDGE, MARY ROBERTS. The Rain Makers. Bos-
ton/NY, 1929. 1st ed. 23 plts. Blue-grn cl. NF in Fine
slipcase. Five Quail. $60/£38

COOLIDGE, MARY ROBERTS. Why Women Are So. NY: Holt, 1912. 2nd ptg. Fine in NF dj. *Second Life.* $45/£29

COOLIDGE, RICHARD. Statistical Report on the Sickness and Mortality in the Army of the United States.... Washington, 1856. 1st ed. 703pp. Leather label. (Skillfully rebacked.) *Fye.* $275/£176

COOLIDGE, RICHARD. Statistical Report on the Sickness and Mortality in the Army of the United States.... Washington, 1860. 1st ed. 515pp; hand-colored fldg map. VG. *Fye.* $275/£176

COOMBS, DAVID. Churchill, His Paintings. London: Hamish Hamilton, (1967). 1st ed. NF (sig) in dj (sm chip spine). *Reese.* $125/£80

COOMBS, DAVID. Churchill: His Paintings. NY: World, 1967. Dj (edge sl frayed). *Metropolitan*.* $201/£129

COOMBS, DAVID. Sport and the Countryside in English Paintings, Watercolours and Prints. Oxford: Phaidon, 1978. 1st ed. VG in VG dj. *October Farm.* $65/£42

COOMBS, JOHN HARTLEY (ed). Dr. Livingstone's 17 Years' Explorations and Adventures in the Wilds of Africa. Phila/Chicago: Lloyd/Bronson & Fobes, 1857. 1st ed. 334pp; fldg color map. (Ep corners missing, corner last leaf missing w/sl loss; no cvrs), o/w VG. *Worldwide.* $30/£19

COON, CARLETON S. The Races of Europe. NY, 1939. 1st ed. 16 maps, 46 plts. (Discoloring.) *Edwards.* $31/£20

COON, CARLETON S. The Seven Caves. NY: Knopf, 1957. 1st ed. 31 plts. (Sl rubbed.) *Worldwide.* $18/£12

COONEY, BARBARA. Miss Rumphius. NY: Viking, 1982. 1st ed. 10 1/2 x 8 1/4. 30pp. Cl spine. Fine in dj. *Cattermole.* $75/£48

COOPER, ASTLEY. The Lectures of Sir Astley Cooper.... 1824/5/7. 3 vols. viii,352pp; vi,458pp, 4 plts; 538pp, 2 plts. Orig 1/2 blue calf, gilt spines. Fine. *Whitehart.* $1,014/£650

COOPER, ASTLEY. Lectures on the Principles and Practice of Surgery. 1835. 8th ed. viii,612pp (foxed). 1/2 vellum (rubbed). *Whitehart.* $75/£48

COOPER, ASTLEY. Observations on the Structure and Diseases of the Testis. B. B. Cooper (ed). 1841. 2nd ed. xiii,328pp (lib stamps throughout); 14 color plts. (Fr bd loose but repaired w/sellotape). *Whitehart.* $437/£280

COOPER, ASTLEY. A Treatise on Dislocations and Fractures of the Joints. B. B. Cooper (ed). 1842. New ed. xxxi,576pp (prelims sl foxed). Orig cl (rebacked). *Whitehart.* $218/£140

COOPER, ASTLEY. A Treatise on Dislocations and on Fractures of the Joints. 1826. 5th ed. xxiv,518pp; 34 plts (sl foxed). Old 1/2 calf (worn, joints weak). *Whitehart.* $437/£280

COOPER, C. S. The Outdoor Monuments of London. London, 1928. 1st ed. Dj (ragged). *Edwards.* $50/£32

COOPER, DOUGLAS. The Courtauld Collection. London Univ (Athlone Press), 1954. Frontis port, 90 plts. (Fep sl damaged), o/w Fine in dj (torn, repaired). *Europa.* $55/£35

COOPER, DOUGLAS. Picasso Theatre. NY, (1968). Pict cl. Ptd acetate dj. *Kane*.* $75/£48

COOPER, DOUGLAS. Picasso Theatre. NY: Abrams, (1968). (Sl worn.) Plasticine wrapper. *Oinonen*.* $60/£38

COOPER, ERWIN. Aqueduct Empire: a Guide to Water in California.... Glendale: Clark, 1968. 1st ed. One of 2589. VF in pict dj. *Argonaut.* $60/£38

COOPER, FREDERIC TABER. Rider's California. NY: Macmillan, 1925. 28 maps and plans (1 fldg). Good (edgeworn). *Dumont.* $45/£29

COOPER, IRVING S. St. Barnabus Symposium on Surgical Therapy of Extrapyramidal Disorders. NY, 1956. (Cl lt worn), else VG. *Goodrich.* $65/£42

COOPER, J. M. W. Game Fowls, Their Origin and History. West Chester, PA: Privately ptd, 1869. 1st ed. 304pp; 2 Nice color plts. Brn cl, gilt. (Lt flecks cvr, plts sl foxed), else Good. *Price.* $195/£125

COOPER, J. M. W. Game Fowls, Their Origin and History.... West Chester: The Author, 1869. Standard Ed. 2 color frontispieces, 304pp. (Spine sunned, worn; lt soiled), o/w Good. *Brown.* $100/£64

COOPER, JAMES FENIMORE. The Deerslayer. London: Richard Bentley, 1841. 2nd ed. 3 vols. Half-titles. Contemp dk blue 1/2 calf (old ms shelf mks lower labels), gilt. Fine. BAL 3895. *Burmester.* $156/£100

COOPER, JAMES FENIMORE. The Deerslayer. NY: Scribner, 1925. 1st ed thus. 9 full-pg color illus by N. C. Wyeth. Pict eps. VF in pict dj (sl used). *Captain's Bookshelf.* $500/£321

COOPER, JAMES FENIMORE. The Deerslayer: or The First War-Path. Phila: Lee & Blanchard, 1841. 1st ed. 2 vols. 12mo. Purple cl (faded), ptd spine labels (rubbed). BAL 3895. *Swann*.* $1,265/£811

COOPER, JAMES FENIMORE. The Deerslayer: or, The First Warpath. Phila: Lea & Blanchard, 1841. 1st ed. 2 vols. (Vol 1 top margin edges sl dampstained; sm wormhole upper cvr, lower margin edge prelims vol 1; sl worming vol 2 upper margin edge prelims; foxing.) Orig cl, paper spine labels. (Cvrs rubbed, dampstained.) 3/4 brn morocco clamshell box w/linen bds, trays, raised bands, leather spine labels. BAL 3895. *Sadlon.* $800/£513

COOPER, JAMES FENIMORE. History of the Navy of the United States of America. NY, 1856. 15 plts. Contemp 1/2 calf, marbled bds, edges. (Scuffed.) *Freeman*.* $60/£38

COOPER, JAMES FENIMORE. The Last of the Mohicans, a Narrative of 1757.... Phila: Carey & Lea, 1826. 2 vols. 8vo. 1/2 leather, marble paper bds. (Sl loss to bds; sl bumped; foxing, browning.) *Metropolitan*.* $1,840/£1,179

COOPER, JAMES FENIMORE. The Pathfinder. (NY): LEC, 1965. #417/1500 signed by Richard Powers (illus). Fine in slipcase. *Hermitage.* $85/£54

COOPER, JAMES FENIMORE. The Pilot. NY: LEC, 1968. #1029/1500 signed by Robert M. Quackenbush (illus). Fine in slipcase. *Hermitage.* $85/£54

COOPER, JAMES FENIMORE. The Pilot: A Tale of the Sea.... NY: Charles Wiley, 1823. 2 vols. 1/2 leather, marbled paper bds. (Foxing, browning, paper abrasions; sl frayed.) *Metropolitan*.* $172/£110

COOPER, JAMES FENIMORE. The Pioneers. Richard Bentley, 1849. Frontis, xi,460pp. *Bickersteth.* $34/£22

COOPER, JAMES FENIMORE. The Prairie. Menasha, WI: LEC, 1940. One of 1500 signed by John Steuart Curry (illus). Pict cl backed in deerskin. VG in box. *Argosy.* $175/£112

COOPER, JAMES FENIMORE. The Works of James Fenimore Cooper. NY: W.A. Townsend, 1861. 30 vols. Engr frontispieces, titles. 1/2 dk grn morocco over marbled bds. 1/4-inch gilt raised bands. Fine set. *Hermitage.* $1,750/£1,122

COOPER, JOHN R. The Southpaw's Secret. Cupples & Leon, 1947. 5.5x7.5. 212pp (acidic). VG+ (sl shelfworn) in dj (edgeworn, folds lt dampstained). *My Bookhouse.* $25/£16

COOPER, JOHN SPENCER. Rough Notes of Seven Campaigns in Portugal, Spain, France, and America.... Carlisle, 1914. 2nd ed. Maroon cl (sm split lower joint). *Maggs.* $187/£120

COOPER, PAGE and ROGER TREAT. Man O'War. NY: Messner, 1950. 1st ed. VG. *October Farm.* $45/£29

COOPER, SAMUEL. The First Lines of the Practice of Surgery. Boston, 1828. 3rd Amer ed. 458pp (water stained); 9 plts. Full leather (sl worn). Good. *Doctor's Library.* $100/£64

COOPER, SAMUEL. A Treatise on the Diseases of the Joints. Hanover, NH: Justin Hinds, 1811. 2nd Amer ed. 165pp. Old 2-toned paper cvrd bds (paper gone back cvr). *M&s.* $200/£128

COOPER, SUSAN ROGERS. Houston in the Rearview Mirror. NY: St. Martin's, 1990. 1st ed. Signed. VF in dj. *Mordida.* $85/£54

COOPER, SUSAN ROGERS. Other People's Houses. NY: St. Martin's, 1990. 1st ed. Signed. VF in dj. *Mordida.* $65/£42

COOPER, SUSAN. Over Sea, Under Stone. NY: HBJ, 1965. 2nd ed. Margery Gill (illus). 5 1/2 x 8 1/4. 252pp. VG in dj. *Cattermole.* $30/£19

COOPER, SUSAN. The Selkie Girl. NY: Macmillan, 1986. 1st ed. Warwick Hutton (illus). 8 1/2 x 10 1/4. 32pp. Fine in dj. *Cattermole.* $25/£16

COOPER, SUSAN. The Silver Cow. NY: Atheneum, 1983. 1st ed. Warwick Hutton (illus). 8 1/2 x 10 1/4. 32pp. Fine in dj. *Cattermole.* $25/£16

COOPER, SUSAN. Silver on the Tree. NY: Atheneum, 1977. 1st ed. 5 3/4 x 9 1/2. VG in dj. *Cattermole.* $40/£26

COOPER, SUSAN. Tam Lin. NY: Macmillan, 1991. 1st ed. Warwick Hutton (illus). 8 1/2 x 10. 32pp. Cl spine. Fine in dj. *Cattermole.* $20/£13

COOPER, W. HEATON. The Lakes. London: Frederick Warne, 1966. 1st ed. Signed. 17 color plts. Pict cl. VG in dj. *Hollett.* $101/£65

COOPER, W. HEATON. The Tarns of Lakeland. Grasmere: Heaton Cooper Studio, 1970. 2nd ed. Signed. 16 color plts. VG in dj. *Hollett.* $101/£65

COOPER, WILLIAM M. A History of the Rod.... London: John Camden Hotten, 1869. 1st ed. x,544,(32,ads)pp. (Fr joint strengthened w/tape, rear hinge tender, 2 ad ll sl torn w/sl loss; sl rubbed.) *Hollett.* $101/£65

COOPER, WILLIAM. Scenes from Married Life. London: Macmillan, 1961. 1st ed. VG in dj. *Hollett.* $55/£35

COOPER-KING, C. The British Army and Auxiliary Forces. London: Cassell, 1893. Subs ed. 2 vols. viii,119; viii,112pp. Aeg. Orig bkseller's invoice loosely inserted. Pub's 1/2 morocco (sl rubbed), gilt. *Hollett.* $218/£140

COOVER, ROBERT. Pricksongs and Descants. Cape, 1971. 1st UK ed. Fine in VG + dj. *Williams.* $31/£20

COOVER, ROBERT. The Public Burning. NY, 1977. 1st Amer ed. Signed. NF in NF dj. *Polyanthos.* $30/£19

COOVER, ROBERT. A Theological Position. NY: Dutton, 1972. 1st ed. VG + (stamp 1/2 title, top edge lt foxed) in dj (price-clipped, chip). *Lame Duck.* $175/£112

COOVER, ROBERT. The Universal Baseball Association, Inc. NY: Random House, 1968. 1st ed. NF in dj (nick). *Lame Duck.* $200/£128

COOVER, ROBERT. The Universal Baseball Association, Inc. J. Henry Waugh, Prop. NY: Random House, (1968). 1st ed. Fine in dj. *Captain's Bookshelf.* $150/£96

COOVER, ROBERT. The Universal Baseball Association. London: Rupert Hart-Davis, 1970. 1st ed. Signed. Fine in Fine dj. *Lenz.* $150/£96

COPE, CHRISTOPHER. Phoenix Frustrated. Constable, 1986. 26 maps. Fine. *Peter Taylor.* $19/£12

COPE, THOMAS P. Philadelphia Merchant: The Diary of Thomas P. Cope 1800-1851. E. C. Harrison (ed). South Bend, IN, 1978. 1st ed. VG in dj (chipped). *Scribe's Perch*.* $50/£32

COPELAND, ESTELLA M. Overland by Auto in 1913. Indianapolis: InHS, 1981. Frontis. VG + in ptd wraps. *Bohling.* $12/£8

COPELAND, FAYETTE. Kendall of the Picayune.... Norman, 1943. 1st ed. 2 maps. (Ex-lib), o/w VG. *Turpen.* $25/£16

COPELAND, R. MORRIS. Country Life. Boston: Henry P.B. Jewett, 1859. 1st ed. Dbl-pg color litho frontis, x,813pp; 7 plts. (Spine dulled), else Fine. *Quest.* $245/£157

COPLAND, AARON. Nonet for Strings. London: Boosey & Hawkes, (1962). Signed presentation. VG in ptd lt brn wraps (lt rubbed). *Baltimore*.* $60/£38

COPLEY, H. The Game Fishes of Africa. London, 1952. 24 plts. *Wheldon & Wesley.* $39/£25

COPPARD, A. E. The Bells of Heaven. London: White Owl, (1933). (Bkpl), else VG. *Certo.* $30/£19

COPPARD, A. E. Clorinda Walks in Heaven. London: Golden Cockerel, 1922. 1st ed, 1st issue. One of 1200 ptd. Uncut. Fine in cl-backed yellow bds, paper label; ptd dj (sl faded, frayed). *Cox.* $101/£65

COPPARD, A. E. Collected Poems. NY: Knopf, 1928. 1st Amer ed. VG in dj (sl used, nicked). *Reese.* $30/£19

COPPARD, A. E. Count Stefan. Waltham Saint Lawrence, 1928. One of 600. Robert Gibbings (engrs). 1/4 yellow buckram, marbled paper over bds, gilt. VG (spine faded). *Heller.* $150/£96

COPPARD, A. E. Emergency Exit. NY: Random House, (1934). Ltd to 350 signed. Dec buckram cl. Fine. *Antic Hay.* $100/£64

COPPARD, A. E. Fearful Pleasures. Sauk City: Arkham House, (1946). 1st ed. Dj (sm stain, sl rubbed). *Swann*.* $57/£37

COPPARD, A. E. The Field of Mustard. (London): Jonathan Cape, (1926). 1st trade ed. VG in dj (worn, soiled, spine browned). *Antic Hay.* $40/£26

COPPARD, A. E. Ninepenny Flute. London, 1937. 1st Eng ed. Very Bright (cvrs sl mottled) in dj. *Clearwater.* $70/£45

COPPARD, A. E. Pink Furniture. London, 1930. 1st Eng ed. Fine in dj (sl nicked). *Clearwater.* $39/£25

COPPARD, A. E. Polly Oliver. London, 1935. 1st Eng ed. Very Nice in dj (sl mkd, frayed). *Clearwater.* $62/£40

COPPENS, CHARLES. Moral Principles and Medical Practice, the Basis of Medical Jurisprudence. Cincinnati, 1897. 1st ed. 222pp. VG. *Fye.* $100/£64

COPPENS, MARTIEN. Gothic Choir-Stalls in the Netherlands. Amsterdam: Elsevier, (1954). 1st ed. 2 vols. 139 plts. Gray cl. Good in djs. *Karmiole.* $85/£54

COPPER, BASIL. And Afterward, the Dark: Seven Tales. (Sauk City): Arkham House, 1977. 1st ed. Fine in dj. *Other Worlds.* $20/£13

COPPER, BASIL. The Black Death. Fedogan & Bremer, 1991. Ltd to 100 signed by Copper and Stefanie Kate Hawks (illus). As New in dj, boxed. *Certo.* $75/£48

COPPER, BASIL. The Curse of the Fleers. St. Martin's, 1976. 1st ed. Review sheet laid in. Fine in Fine dj. *Certo.* $50/£32

COPPER, BASIL. From Evil's Pillow. Sauk City: Arkham House, 1973. 1st ed. VF in dj (lt sunned). *Bromer.* $65/£42

COPPER, BASIL. The House of the Wolf. (Sauk City): Arkham House, (1983). 1st ed. NF in dj. *Other Worlds.* $30/£19

COPPER, BASIL. Voices of Doom. St. Martins/Robert Hale, 1980. 1st ed, US issue. Rev copy, slip laid in. Fine in dj (inner flaps dust spotted). *Certo.* $50/£32

COPPER, BASIL. When Footsteps Echo. NY: St. Martin's, (1975). 1st Amer ed. Dj. *Swann*.* $69/£44

COPPINGER, JOSEPH. The American Practical Brewer and Tanner. NY: Van Winkle & Wiley, 1815. 1st ed. vii,(3),(11)-246,(2)pp. Later marbled bds, cl spine. Good (ex-lib, ink #s tp, foxed, browned). *Glaser.* $450/£288

COPPINGER, JOSEPH. The American Practical Brewer and Tanner.... NY: Van Winkle & Wiley, 1815. 1st ed. 246,(2)pp; errata slip. Entirely untrimmed. Orig paper-cvrd bds (skillfully rebacked in period style). (Foxed throughout, occasional dampstaining), else Very Nice. *Felcone.* $500/£321

COPPINGER, R. W. Cruise of the 'Alert.' London: W. Swan Sonnenschein, 1883. 1st ed. Engr frontis, xiii,(iii),256pp (foxing), 1/2-title, 15 plts. Dec grn cl (stained, rubbed, sm hole spine, upper hinge cracking). *Morrell.* $218/£140

COPPOLA, ELEANOR. Notes. NY: S&S, (1979). 1st ed. (Sm bkstore sticker), else Fine in NF dj (extrems lt rubbed, price-clipped). *Between The Covers.* $50/£32

COPWAY, GEORGE. The Traditional History and Characteristic Sketches of the Ojibway Nation. London: Gilpin, 1850. 1st ed. (12), 298pp. Orig cl bds (faded). Howes C772. *Ginsberg.* $450/£288

CORBETT, JAMES. The Somerville Case. London: Herbert Jenkins, (1949). 1st ed. VG in dj (spine ends, corners chipped, closed crease-tears). *Mordida.* $35/£22

CORBETT, JIM. Death Is My Shadow. London: Herbert Jenkins, (1947). 1st ed. VG in dj (price-clipped, spine ends frayed, corners chipped, few sm closed tears). *Mordida.* $40/£26

CORBETT, JIM. Man-Eaters of Kumaon. (NY): OUP, 1946. 1st US ed. Dj (sl chipped). *Edwards.* $31/£20

CORBETT, JIM. Man-Eaters of Kumaon. NY: OUP, 1946. 1st ed. VG in dj. *Worldwide.* $25/£16

CORBETT, JIM. The Man-Eating Leopard of Rudraprayag. London: Oxford, (1954). 1st illus ed. R. Sheppard (illus). VG. *Mikesh.* $30/£19

CORBETT, JIM. The Man-Eating Leopard of Rudraprayag. London, 1948. 1st ed. (Spine faded, lower corners bumped.) *Grayling.* $23/£15

CORBETT, JIM. Tree Tops. London: Oxford, 1955. 1st ed. NF in VG dj. *Mikesh.* $37/£24

CORBETT, JULIAN S. England in the Seven Years' War. London, 1907. 1st ed. 2 vols. 6 maps and plans. Contemp red 1/2 calf (sl mkd), gilt spines. *Maggs.* $187/£120

CORBIN, BERNARD and WILLIAM KERKA. Steam Locomotives of the Burlington Route. Red Oak, IA: Thos. D. Murphy, 1960. 1st ed. Color frontis. Black cl. Fine in NF dj. *Harrington.* $100/£64

CORBIN, BERNARD and WILLIAM KERKA. Steam Locomotives of the Burlington Route. (Red Oak, IA, 1960.) Color frontis. Black buckram, gilt. Fine in dj. *Bohling.* $100/£64

CORBIN, HENRY. Creative Imagination in the Sufism of Ibn 'Arabi. Ralph Manheim (trans). Princeton, NJ: Princeton Univ, 1969. 1st ed. 5 plts (1 color). (Sl rubbed), o/w VG. *Worldwide.* $70/£45

CORDRY, MRS. T. A. The Story of the Marking of the Santa Fe Trail. Topeka: Crane, 1915. Fldg map. VG. *Dumont.* $65/£42

CORELLI, MARIE. Cameos. London: Hutchinson, (1896). 1st ed. Grn cl, gilt, vcr inset. VG. *Certo.* $45/£29

CORK, RICHARD. David Bomberg. Tate Gallery, 1988. 1st ed. Fine in wrappers. *Words Etc.* $34/£22

CORKE, HELEN. Lawrence and Apocalypse. London, 1933. 1st ed. VG in dj (sunned, sl chipped). *Buckley.* $31/£20

CORKRAN, DAVID H. The Cherokee Frontier...1740-62. Norman: Univ of OK, (1962). 1st ed. VG in dj (sl worn). *Lien.* $35/£22

CORLE, EDWIN. Burro Alley. NY: Duell, Sloan & Pearce, (1938). One of 1500 numbered, signed. Fine in VG+ dj (lt soiled, sl edgewear). *Bernard.* $85/£54

CORLE, EDWIN. Death Valley and the Creek Called Furnace. L.A.: Ward Ritchie, (1962). 25 Ansel Adams plts. (Sl foxing.) Dj. *Dawson.* $60/£38

CORLE, EDWIN. The Gila—River of the Southwest. NY: Rinehart, 1951. 1st ed. Yellow cl. Fine. *Five Quail.* $30/£19

CORLE, EDWIN. Listen, Bright Angel. NY, 1946. 1st ed. Map. NF in VG+ dj (sl chips). *Five Quail.* $40/£26

CORN, ALFRED. All Roads at Once. NY: Viking, 1976. 1st ed, 1st bk. Signed. Fine in dj. *Lame Duck.* $100/£64

CORNARO, LEWIS. Sure and Certain Methods of Attaining a Long and Healthful Life. London: D. Midwinter & A. Ward, 1737. 5th ed. 197pp (sig fep). Contemp leather (old reback retaining orig spine, label). Nice. *White.* $133/£85

CORNARO, LOUIS. How to Live Long: The Discourses and Letters of Louis Cornaro. Passaic, NJ, 1916. 1st ed. Grn cl. NF. *Doctor's Library.* $40/£26

CORNELL, KATHARINE. I Wanted to Be an Actress, the Autobiography of.... NY, (1939). 1st ed. Ltd to 550 numbered, signed. (Cvrs sunned.) *King.* $60/£38

CORNELL, SARAH SOPHIA. Cornell's Physical Geography. NY: D. Appleton, 1883. 104pp. Tan pict bds (rubbed). *Hudson.* $125/£80

CORNER, WILLIAM. San Antonio De Bexar—A Guide and History. San Antonio, 1890. 166pp, 27pp ads. 16 plts. VG. Howes C 778. *Perier.* $150/£96

CORNET, JOSEPH. A Survey of Zairian Art. Raleigh, NC: NC Museum of Art, 1978. 1st ed. Black/gold cl. Good in dj. *Karmiole.* $100/£64

CORNFORD, FRANCES. Different Days. London, 1928. One of 500 ptd. Nice (sl mkd, handled). *Clearwater.* $70/£45

CORNFORTH, JOHN. Country Houses in Britain—Can They Survive? Country Life, 1974. NF in wrappers. *Hadley.* $23/£15

CORNS, A. R. and A. SPARKE. A Bibliography of Unfinished Books in the English Language. London: Bernard Quaritch, 1915. Ltd to 300. Blue cl (sl chipped, rubbed, sm tear upper joint). *Maggs.* $70/£45

CORNWALL, BRUCE. Life Sketch of Pierre B. Cornwall. SF: A.M. Robertson, 1906. 1st ed. Signed presentation. Orig 3/4 black leather, marbled bds (rebacked to match; corners, edges lt worn; ex-lib, bkpl, stamps on inner cvr, 3 cat descriptions pasted to prelims). Overall Fine. Howes C780. *Argonaut.* $325/£208

CORNWALL, L. PETER and JACK W. FARRELL. Ride the Sandy River. (Edmonds, WA): Pacific Fast Mail, (1973). 1st ed. Pict eps. Fine in dj. *Bohling.* $50/£32

CORNWALLIS, EARL. An Answer to That Part of the Narrative of Lieutenant-General Sir Henry Clinton.... London: J. Debrett, 1783. 1st ed. Errata, fldg table. (Lacks 4pp ads.) Contemp marbled bds. *Freeman*.* $160/£103

CORNWELL, BERNARD. Sharpe's Eagle. NY: Viking, 1981. 1st US ed. Fine in Fine dj. *Unger.* $100/£64

CORNWELL, BERNARD. Sharpe's Gold. London: Collins, 1981. 1st ed. Fine in Fine dj. *Unger.* $100/£64

CORNWELL, PATRICIA D. All That Remains. NY: Scribner, 1992. 1st Amer ed. VF in dj. *Mordida.* $45/£29

CORNWELL, PATRICIA D. Body of Evidence. NY: Scribner, 1991. 1st ed. VF in dj. *Mordida*. $100/£64

CORPE, HILDA. Prisoner Beyond the Chindwin. London, 1955. 8 plts. Mint cl in dj. *Maggs*. $23/£15

CORREDOR-MATHEOS, J. Miro's Posters. (Secaucus): Chartwell, (1980). 119 plts. Fine in dj. *Waverly**. $44/£28

CORRELL, CHARLES J. and FREEMAN F. GOSDEN. Here They Are...Amos 'N' Andy. NY: Ray Long & Richard R. Smith, 1931. 1st ed. Fine in NF dj (sl edgewear, spine sl hand-soiled). *Associates*. $200/£128

CORRELL, D. S. Native Orchids of North America. Waltham: Chronica Botanica, 1950. Frontis, 146 full-pg plts. Fine. *Quest*. $60/£38

CORRELL, D. S. and H. B. Aquatic and Wetland Plants of Southwestern United States. Washington, DC, 1972. Orig EPA ed. (Sm stamps fep, tp), else VG +. *Brooks*. $115/£74

Correspondence, Papers and Documents, of Dates from 1856 to 1882...of the Province of Ontario. Toronto, 1882. 504 w/index pp. Fldg map. 3/4 leather (extrems scuffed). *King*. $95/£61

CORRIGAN, DOUGLAS. That's My Story. NY: Dutton, 1938. 1st ed. Signed presentation. Blue cl, red stamping. Internally VG (spine, edges lt sunned). *Baltimore**. $35/£22

CORRIN, SARA and STEPHEN. The Pied Piper of Hamelin. London: Faber & Faber, (1988). 1st ed thus. Errol Le Cain (illus). 4to. Unpaginated. Glazed illus bds. Fine. *Dower*. $45/£29

CORRINGTON, JULIAN D. Working with the Microscope. NY, 1941. 1st ed. Grn cl bds (sl worn). VG. *Doctor's Library*. $40/£26

CORROYER, EDOUARD. Gothic Architecture. Walter Armstrong (ed). 1893. (Lt spotted, bkpl; spine sl soiled.) *Edwards*. $31/£20

CORSO, GREGORY. Long Live Man. NY: New Directions, (1962). 1st Amer ed. Signed. Dec wraps (lt edge rubbed). NF (name). *Polyanthos*. $25/£16

CORSON, RICHARD. Fashions in Hair. London: Peter Owen, 1966. 2nd imp. VG (sl loose, edgeworn). *Metropolitan**. $80/£51

CORTAZAR, JULIO. 62: A Model Kit. NY, 1972. 1st Amer ed. Fine (edge sl rubbed) in dj (sm edge nicks). *Polyanthos*. $25/£16

CORTAZAR, JULIO. A Manual For Manuel. NY: Pantheon, (1978). 1st Amer ed. Fine in dj (price-clipped; tear). *Between The Covers*. $75/£48

CORTAZAR, JULIO. The Winners. NY, 1965. 1st Amer ed, 1st bk. NF in NF dj. *Polyanthos*. $50/£32

CORTHELL, E. L. A Histories of the Jetties at the Mouth of the Mississippi River. John Wiley, 1880. 1st ed. 383pp. VG- (map borders torn, sm spine holes, corners rubbed). *Book Broker*. $75/£48

CORTI, COUNT. A History of Smoking. London, (1931). (Lt wear, soil.) *Freeman**. $30/£19

CORVO, BARON. (Pseud of Frederick Rolfe.) The Armed Hands and Other Stories and Pieces. Cecil Woolf (ed). Cecil & Amelia Woolf, 1974. #38/200. Fine in glassine wrapper, slipcase. *Cox*. $47/£30

CORVO, BARON. (Pseud of Frederick Rolfe.) The Cardinal Prefect of Propaganda. Cecil Woolf (ed). London: Nicholas Vane, 1957. 1st ed. One of 60 unnumbered. Inscribed by Woolf. Teg. Linen-backed Cockerell bds. (Sl rubbed), else NF. *Reese*. $225/£144

CORVO, BARON. (Pseud of Frederick Rolfe.) Chronicles of the House of Borgia. NY: Dutton, 1901. 1st Amer ed. (Circular stain 2 plts), else VG. *Captain's Bookshelf*. $75/£48

CORVO, BARON. (Pseud of Frederick Rolfe.) The Desire and Pursuit of the Whole. London/Toronto/Melbourne/Sydney: Cassell, (1934). 1st ed, in rmdr binding. Grn cl titled in grn within dk grn rectangle on spine. Fine in lt blue-grn dj ptd/dec in black. *Blue Mountain*. $75/£48

CORVO, BARON. (Pseud of Frederick Rolfe.) Don Renato. Cecil Woolf (ed). London, 1963. 1st Eng ed. Fine in dj. *Clearwater*. $62/£40

CORVO, BARON. (Pseud of Frederick Rolfe.) Hadrian the Seventh. Chatto, 1904. Scarce 1st issue (Woolf A6a). One of 700. VG- (lt foxed, 2 sm bksellers' stamps; bds lt bumped). *Williams*. $546/£350

CORVO, BARON. (Pseud of Frederick Rolfe.) Hadrian the Seventh. NY: Knopf, 1925. 1st US ed. VG + (rear bd bumped, note rear pastedown) in VG dj (chips). *Lame Duck*. $175/£112

CORVO, BARON. (Pseud of Frederick Rolfe.) A History of the Borgias. NY: Modern Library, 1931. Good. *Cox*. $12/£8

CORVO, BARON. (Pseud of Frederick Rolfe.) Letters to Pirie-Gordon and Leonard Moore. London: Nicholas Vane, 1959/60. 1st Eng ed. 2 vols. Vol 1: #128/350; Vol 2: #101/290. (Bkpls; vol 1 spine sl mkd), else Very Nice set. *Hadley*. $218/£140

CORVO, BARON. (Pseud of Frederick Rolfe.) Nicholas Crabbe or the One and the Many: A Romance. (NY): New Directions, (1958). 1st ed. Fine in Fine dj (sl dkng). *Between The Covers*. $85/£54

CORVO, BARON. (Pseud of Frederick Rolfe.) Nicholas Crabbe. London, 1958. 1st Eng ed. Fine in dj. *Clearwater*. $55/£35

CORVO, BARON. (Pseud of Frederick Rolfe.) Nicholas Crabbe. London, 1958. 1st ed. Dj (sl frayed). *Typographeum*. $65/£42

CORVO, BARON. See also ROLFE, FREDERICK

COSENTINO, F. J. Edward Marshall Boehm 1913-1969. N.p.: E.M. Boehm Inc, 1970. 1st ed. 40 full-pg color plts. NF in VG + slipcase. *Mikesh*. $35/£22

COSGRAVE, GEORGE. Early California Justice. The History of the United States District Court...of California 1849-1944. SF: Grabhorn, 1948. One of 400. Red linen cl. (Tp sl mkd; cl worn, spine faded, chipped), o/w Nice. *Boswell*. $175/£112

COSTANSO, MIGUEL. Diary of...Portola Expedition of 1769-70. Berkeley, 1911. 1st ed. Pb. Frontis. Fine. Howes C795. *Turpen*. $55/£35

COSULICH, BERNICE. Tucson. Tucson, 1953. Map. Fine in Fine dj. *Turpen*. $25/£16

COTCHETT, LUCRETIA EDDY. The Evolution of Furniture. Batsford, 1938. 1st ed. Fore, lower edge uncut. (Lt spotted.) *Edwards*. $39/£25

COTT, H. B. Adaptive Coloration in Animals. 1940. Color frontis, 48 plts. (Lib stamp verso tp, lib label remains fep.) Lib binding. *Whitehart*. $39/£25

COTT, JONATHAN. He Dreams What Is Going on Inside His Head. SF: Straight Arrow, 1973. 1st ptg. NF in wrappers (lt creasing). *Sclanders*. $16/£10

COTTAM, C. Food Habits of North American Diving Ducks. Washington: USDA, Apr 1939. 1st ed. 4 color plts. VG + in wraps. *Mikesh*. $25/£16

COTTERELL, H. H. Old Pewter, Its Makers and Marks. London: Batsford, 1929. 1st ed. 76 plts, 7 fldg plts. Fine in dj (reinforced). *Hollett*. $234/£150

COTTLE, JOSEPH. Early Recollections. London: Longman/Hamilton, Adams, 1837. 1st ed. 2 vols. xxviii,325; (viii),346,(2)pp, half-titles, 6 engr ports. Later roan-backed cl bds (spine tops sl worn, old paper lib labels spine feet). *Burmester*. $234/£150

COTTON, CHARLES. The Wonders of the Peake. London: Charles Brome, 1699. 4th ed. (4),86pp (lacks fep). Blank A1 present. Old calf (hinges rubbed), red morocco spine label. *Karmiole.* $175/£112

COTTON, HENRY A. The Defective, Delinquent and Insane.... Princeton, 1921. 1st ed. Grn cl (sl worn; fep removed). VG. *Doctor's Library.* $50/£32

COTTON, WILLIAM (ed). Sir Joshua Reynolds' Notes and Observations on Pictures.... 1859. xii,107pp + (i) (tp margin lt spotted). Uncut. Emb cl (spine sl bumped). *Edwards.* $86/£55

COTTRELL, LEONARD. The Bull of Minos. London: Evans, 1953. 1st ed. 33 plts. NF in dj. *Worldwide.* $12/£8

COTTRELL, LEONARD. The Lost Pharaohs. London: Evans, (1950). 1st ed. Frontis. Dj (torn). *Archaeologia.* $35/£22

COTTRELL, LEONARD. Realms of Gold. Greenwich, CT: NYGS, 1963. 1st ed. 32 plts, 2 maps. VG in dj (torn). *Worldwide.* $20/£13

COUCH, JONATHAN. A History of the Fishes of the British Islands. London: George Bell, 1877. 4 vols. Lg 8vo. 252 hand-colored plts. Gilt pict, titled blue blind dec cl (extrems lt worn). Attractive. *House.* $950/£609

COUCH, WILLIAM, JR. (ed). New Black Playwrights: An Anthology. Baton Rouge: LA State Univ, (1969). VG in dj (repaired). *Petrilla.* $35/£22

COUES, ELLIOTT (ed). History of the Expedition Under the Command of Lewis and Clark. NY: Francis P. Harper, 1893. Ltd to 200. Frontis ports, 1364pp, index vol 4. Good. Howes L317. *Lien.* $1,000/£641

COUES, ELLIOTT and JOEL ASAPH ALLEN. Monographs of North American Rodentia. Washington, 1877. x,1091pp, 5 plts. (Ex-lib, ink stamp, labels; hinge cracked, reps sl soiled; chipped, joint split, fraying.) *Edwards.* $78/£50

COUES, ELLIOTT. Birds of the North-West. Boston, 1877. xi,791pp (1st, last ll w/sm tears fore-edge). Mod cl (rebound), spine label. *Edwards.* $39/£25

COUES, ELLIOTT. Birds of the Northwest: A Hand-Book of the Ornithology.... Washington: USDI, 1874. 1st ed. 791pp. VG. *Mikesh.* $95/£61

COUES, ELLIOTT. The Expeditions of Zebulon Montgomery Pike. Minneapolis: Ross & Haines, 1965. 3 vols in 2. 6 fldg maps in rear pocket. Fine in slipcase (worn). *Dumont.* $120/£77

COUES, ELLIOTT. The Fur-Bearing Animals of North America. Washington, 1877. 20 plts. (Worn, sl stained, fr joint split.) *Maggs.* $37/£24

COUES, ELLIOTT. The Manuscript Journals of Alexander Henry...and of David Thompson. Minneapolis: Ross & Haines, 1965. One of 1500. 2 vols. Frontis vol 1; fldg maps rear pocket vol 2. Fine set in box (edge splitting). *Dumont.* $55/£35

COUES, ELLIOTT. Third Installment of American Ornithological Bibliography. Washington: USDI/GS, 1879. 1st ed. 521-1072pp + appendix. (Pg 1 chipped, lacks fr cvr), else VG in wraps. *Mikesh.* $45/£29

COULIN, C. Drawings by Architects, from 9th Century to the Present Day. NY: Reinhold, 1962. 65 plts. Sound in dj. *Ars Artis.* $55/£35

COULSON, W. On the Diseases of the Hip-Joint. 1837. viii,112pp. Color eps. VG. *Whitehart.* $437/£280

COULTER, E. MERTON. The Confederate States of America. Baton Rouge, 1950. 1st ed. VG + in dj (worn, chipped). *Pratt.* $37/£24

COULTER, E. MERTON. Travels in the Confederate States, a Bibliography. Norman: Univ of OK, 1948. 1st ed. Fine in dj (chipped, soiled). *Oak Knoll.* $75/£48

COULTER, JOHN. Adventures on the Western Coast of South America.... London: Longman, Brown, 1847. 1st ed. 2 vols. (v),viii-xxiv,288; xii,278pp, 1/2-titles (foxing throughout). Contemp 1/2 roan, marbled bds (sl rubbed, few wormholes affecting spine feet, sm hole upper spine vol 2). Sound. Howes C802. *Morrell.* $218/£140

COULTON, G. G. Social Life in Britain from the Conquest to the Reformation. CUP, 1919. Rev ed. 40 plts. Uncut. Buckram, gilt. VG in dj (frayed, neatly strengthened). *Peter Taylor.* $45/£29

Country Life Picture Book of the Lake District. London: Country Life, 1953. 1st ed. 58 full-pg plts. VG in dj. *Hollett.* $31/£20

Country Scenes, in Easy Lessons for Children. London: Darton & Harvey, 1834. 12mo. 16pp + 2pp + 1pg list lower wrapper; 8 VF 1/2-pg hand-colored wood engrs. Orig brn stiff paper wrappers (sunned). Internally Fine. *Hobbyhorse.* $300/£192

COURTHION, PIERRE. Georges Rouault. NY: Abrams, (1961). 1st ed. Fine in dj (lt soiled). *Hermitage.* $125/£80

COURTHOPE, W. J. A History of English Poetry. London, 1926. 6 vols. Fldg table. (Lt pencilling.) Dj. *Argosy.* $150/£96

COURTNEY, W. P. and D. N. SMITH. A Bibliography of Samuel Johnson. Oxford: Clarendon, 1925. Ltd to 350. Black cl, paper spine label (sl worn), spare label inserted at end. *Maggs.* $133/£85

COUSE, ERWINA L. and MARGUERITE MAPLE. Button Classics. Chicago: Lightner, (1942). 2nd ed. (Extrems rubbed), else NF. *Bromer.* $275/£176

COUSINS, GEORGE (comp). From Island to Island in the South Seas. London: London Missionary Soc, 1894. 2nd ed. 124,2pp; fldg map. Blue pict cl. Fine. *Burmester.* $39/£25

COUSINS, SHEILA. (Pseud of Graham Greene and Ronald Matthews.) To Beg I Am Ashamed: An Autobiography of a London Prostitute. Paris: N.p., (1938). NF (paper sl dknd, lt spine creases, lt worn) in wrappers. *Between The Covers.* $300/£192

COUSTILLAS, PIERRE. Gissing and Turgenev. London: Enitharmon, 1981. One of 250. Signed presentation. 12pp. Fine in wrappers. *Virgo.* $31/£20

COUTS, CAVE JOHNSON. From San Diego to the Colorado in 1849. William McPherson (ed). L.A.: Arthur M. Ellis, 1932. 3 full-pg illus. Cl spine, paper spine label (bottom bd tips sl worn; bkpl). *Dawson.* $125/£80

COVARRUBIAS, MIGUEL. The Eagle, the Jaguar, and the Serpent: Indian Art of the Americas. NY: Knopf, 1954. 1st ed. 12 color plts, 48 plts following text. Dec tan cl, black cl spine. Fine in VG + dj. *Harrington.* $100/£64

COVARRUBIAS, MIGUEL. Indian Art of Mexico and Central America. NY, 1957. 1st ed. 12 color plts. 2-tone dec cl. VG. *Argosy.* $125/£80

COVARRUBIAS, MIGUEL. Indian Art of Mexico and Central America. NY, 1957. 1st ed. Inscribed. Cl slipcase, sleeve. *Swann*.* $258/£165

COVARRUBIAS, MIGUEL. Island of Bali. NY, 1937. 1st ed. 2-tone cl. VG in dj (sl frayed). *King.* $45/£29

COVARRUBIAS, MIGUEL. The Prince of Wales and Other Famous Americans. NY, 1925. 1/4 cl. *Swann*.* $201/£129

COVENTRY, CHARLES B. Epidemic Cholera.... Buffalo, 1849. 1st ed. 119pp. Orig cl. Fine. *Argosy.* $40/£26

COVENTRY, FRANCIS. The History of Pompey the Little.... Golden Cockerel, 1926. #332/400. Frontis by David Jones. Uncut, partly unopened. Good in buckram-backed bds (backstrip dknd, sl mkd). *Cox.* $133/£85

COVILLE, FREDERICK VERNON. Botany of the Death Valley Expedition. Washington: Dept of Agriculture, 1893. Frontis, (iv),viii,364pp, 21 full-pg litho plts, lg fldg map (sm margin tear). Marbled bds (rubbing, fr joint starting), leather spine, tips. *Dawson.* $300/£192

COWAN, HARRISON J. Time and Its Measurement. Cleveland/NY: World, (1958). 1st ed. Dj (worn). *Weber.* $25/£16

COWAN, J. Diseases of the Heart. 1914. New binder's cl. (Few pp sl discolored.) *Whitehart.* $125/£80

COWAN, ROBERT E. A Bibliography of the Spanish Press of California, 1833-1845. SF: Robert Ernest Cowan, 1919. Ptd white wrappers (sl overall soiling). *Dawson.* $100/£64

COWAN, ROBERT G. A Bibliography of the History of California and the Pacific West, 1510-1906. Columbus, OH, 1952. Good. *Heinoldt.* $125/£80

COWARD, NOEL. Australia Visited 1940. London, 1941. 1st ed. Frontis port. NF in ptd wraps (lt soiled). *Polyanthos.* $25/£16

COWARD, NOEL. Conversation Piece. London, 1934. 1st ed. VG in Good+ dj. *Smith.* $15/£10

COWARD, NOEL. Nude with Violin. NY, 1958. 1st Amer ed. Fine in dj (sm edge tear). *Polyanthos.* $30/£19

COWARD, NOEL. Point Valaine. NY, 1935. 1st Amer ed. Fine (cvrs sunned unevenly) in dj (sm edge tears, chips). *Polyanthos.* $35/£22

COWARD, NOEL. Post-Mortem. NY, 1931. 1st Amer ed. NF (spine lt rubbed) in dj (spine missing pieces, sm edge chips). *Polyanthos.* $30/£19

COWARD, NOEL. Present Laughter. NY, 1947. 1st Amer ed. Fine (spine sl bumped) in dj (sm edge piece missing, sm edge chips). *Polyanthos.* $30/£19

COWARD, NOEL. Quadrille. NY, 1955. 1st Amer ed. Fine (spine sl rubbed) in dj (edges lt rubbed). *Polyanthos.* $35/£22

COWARD, NOEL. Sirocco. London, 1927. 1st ed. VG in wrappers. *Smith.* $15/£10

COWARD, NOEL. This Happy Breed. NY, 1947. 1st Amer ed. Fine (spine heel sl bumped) in dj (spine sunned, 3 sm chips). *Polyanthos.* $45/£29

COWARD, NOEL. A Withered Nosegay. 1922. 1st ed. Yellow cl. (Sl dusty), o/w VG. *Words Etc.* $101/£65

COWARD, NOEL. A Withered Nosegay. London: Christophers, 1922. 1st Eng ed. Bright (bkpl; cvrs sl spotted, faded). *Clearwater.* $70/£45

COWARD, T. The Birds of the British Isles. London: Wayside & Woodland, 1920-26. 2nd impression vol 1. 3 vols. Purple cl (vol 1 soiled, sm white paint spots; vol 2 fr joint splitting, inscrips), gilt. *Maggs.* $44/£28

COWDRY, E. V. (ed). Arteriosclerosis: A Survey of the Problem. NY, 1933. 1st ed. VG. *Fye.* $150/£96

COWDRY, E. V. (ed). Problems of Aging: Biological and Medical Aspects. Balt, 1939. 1st ed. VG. *Fye.* $75/£48

COWLEY, ABRAHAM. The Works of Mr. Abraham Cowley.... London: Henry Herringman, 1693. 8th ed. Port. Orig panelled morocco (worn, rebacked in 19th-cent calf), gilt. *Cullen.* $250/£160

COWLEY, CHARLES. Illustrated History of Lowell. Boston/Lowell: Lee & Shepard/Sargeant & Merrill, 1868. Rev ed. 235pp; 34 ports, fldg map. Good (cl sl worn, nicked, cl sl tender). *Second Life.* $75/£48

COWLEY, MALCOLM. Blue Juniata: Poems. NY, 1929. 1st ed. As New. *Bond.* $150/£96

COWLEY, MALCOLM. Exile's Return: A Literary Odyssey of the 1920s. NY: LEC, 1981. One of 2000 signed by Berenice Abbott (photos) and Cowley. Cl-backed dec bds. Fine in orig glassine dj, pub's slipcase. *Cahan.* $175/£112

COWPER, H. S. The Art of Attack. Ulverston, 1906. VG. *New Hampshire*.* $30/£19

COWPER, WILLIAM. The Correspondence of.... Thomas Wright (ed). NY/London: Dodd, Mead/Hodder & Stoughton, 1904. 1st ed. 4 vols complete. 3 maps (2 fldg at end of vol 4). Teg, uncut. Dk red cl (sl rubbed), ptd paper spine labels. VG. *Houle.* $225/£144

COWPER, WILLIAM. The Diverting History of John Gilpin.... (Christmas, 1952.) One of 1600 ptd. Ronald Searle (illus). 45 collotype repros. Fine in pict wrappers. *Cox.* $55/£35

COWPER, WILLIAM. Poems in Two Volumes. J. Johnson, 1794/95. 6th ed. 2 vols. xii,368; (viii),389,(3)pp ad and blank. Contemp tree calf, red morocco labels. VG. *Cox.* $117/£75

COWPER, WILLIAM. Private Correspondence of William Cowper, Esq. London: Henry Colburn, 1824. 1st ed. 2 vols. Frontis ports. 1/2 title to vol 1 only, as issued. Uncut. Mod cl, hand-titled spine. (Foxed, tps offset), o/w VG. *Poetry Bookshop.* $195/£125

COWPER, WILLIAM. Private Correspondence.... John Johnson (ed). London: Henry Colburn et al, 1824. 2nd ed. 2 vols. Untrimmed. Later cl, gilt labels. (Frontispieces sl discolored, foxed, offsetting tps), o/w VG. *Reese.* $60/£38

Cowper, Illustrated by a Series of Views. London: Vernor & Hood, 1803. 1st ed. 13 etched plts (lt foxed). Aeg. Early full tan morocco (scuffed, soiled, edgeworn), gilt. Contents VG (sl marginal worming toward rear). *Waverly*.* $99/£63

COX, CHARLES E. John Tobias, Sportsman. NY: Derrydale, (1937). One of 950 numbered. Gilt-stamped cl (sl worn). *Oinonen*.* $60/£38

COX, CHARLES E. John Tobias, Sportsman. NY: Derrydale, (1937). Ltd to 950. VG. *Truepenny.* $95/£61

COX, E. A History of Gardening in Scotland. London, 1935. Dj (sl defective). *Maggs.* $41/£26

COX, E. Plant Hunting in China. London, 1961. Rpt. Wrappers. *Maggs.* $19/£12

COX, EDWARD GODFREY. A Reference Guide to the Literature of Travel. NY: Greenwood, (1969). 3 vols. (Sl worn.) *Oinonen*.* $135/£87

COX, G. V. Recollections of Oxford. Macmillan, 1870. 2nd ed. (viii),460pp. Cl gilt. *Bickersteth.* $59/£38

COX, GEOFFREY. Defence of Madrid. London: Gollancz, 1937. Good (ink name, inscrip) in limp orange cl wrappers (sl tanned, corners creased). *Reese.* $45/£29

COX, HARVEY. Chinese Ivory Sculpture. NY: Bonanza, 1946. 1st ed. 48 plts. VG in dj. *Worldwide.* $40/£26

COX, J. CHARLES. Churchwarden's Accounts from the Fourteenth Century to the Close of the Seventeenth Century. Methuen, 1913. 1st ed. 14 plts. Good in red cl, gilt. *Cox.* $39/£25

COX, J. CHARLES. English Church Fittings, Furniture and Accessories. London: Batsford, n.d. (1923). 1st ed. (Spine faded.) Internally Good. *Ars Artis.* $33/£21

COX, J. CHARLES. Pulpits, Lecterns, and Organs in English Churches. London: OUP, 1915. 1st ed. Blue cl (spine sl dull, mkd; joints cracking, bkpl, sl shaken). *Hollett.* $70/£45

COX, JAMES. My Native Land. St. Louis: Blair, 1895. 1st ed. 400pp. Good. *Lien.* $35/£22

COX, PALMER. Brownie Year Book. NY: McLoughlin Bros, (1895). 12x10. (23)pp (sl defects); 12 full-pg color plts. Color pict glazed bds (loose, worn); label stating that this book is compliments of the Managers of 'Palmer Cox's Brownies.' *King.* $150/£96

COX, PALMER. Queer People with Paws and Claws. Phila: Hubbard, 1888. Pict bds (well rubbed, extrems through; lt interior browning, soil). *Metropolitan**. $80/£51

COX, PALMER. Queer People with Paws, Claws, Wings, Stings, and Others without Either, Etc. Phila: Hubbard, 1894. Sm 4to. Pict bds (corners worn). *Appelfeld*. $125/£80

COX, PALMER. Queerie Queer with Hands, Wings, and Claws. Buffalo, n.d. (early 1900s?). 10x7.5. Unpaged. (Ink inscrip, some pp torn, lacks fep, rep defective, inner hinges cracked.) Color pict bds (worn, spine chipped). *King*. $60/£38

COX, ROSS. Adventures on the Columbia River.... NY: J&J Harper, 1832. 1st Amer ed. 335pp (some tape mended, 4 in facs). Blue buckram (rebound). Good. Howes C822. *Lien*. $75/£48

COX, SANFORD C. Recollections of the Early Settlement of the Wabash Valley. Lafayette: Courier Steam, 1860. 1st ed. 160pp. Howes C823. *Ginsberg*. $250/£160

COX, WARREN E. Chinese Ivory Sculpture. NY: Crown, (1946). 1st ed. #749/1250 numbered, signed. 48 photo plts. Gilt-lettered cl. VF in dj (sl chipped). *Argonaut*. $150/£96

COXE, JOHN REDMAN. The Writings of Hippocrates and Galen.... Phila: Lindsay & Blakiston, 1846. xvi,682pp. Orig full sheep. (Foxing; rubbed, lacks spine label), else Good. *Goodrich*. $175/£112

COY, OWEN C. California County Boundaries. Berkeley: CA Hist Survey Commission, 1923. (Lib stamps, fr hinge starting), else Good. *Dumont*. $75/£48

COYKENDALL, RALF. Duck Decoys and How to Rig Them. NY: Henry Holt, 1955. Stated 1st ed. Decoy eps. VG in VG dj (edge tears, lt soiled). *Backman*. $55/£35

COYNER, DAVID H. The Lost Trappers. David J. Weber (ed). Albuquerque: Univ of NM, (1970). 1st ed w/added notations and intro. Red cl. Fine in dj. *Argonaut*. $45/£29

COYNER, DAVID H. The Lost Trappers; A Collection of Interesting Scenes and Events in the Rocky Mountains.... Cincinnati: James, 1847. 1st ed. 255,(7 ads)pp. New marble bds w/calf spine, raised bands, black leather label. Howes C836. *Ginsberg*. $750/£481

COZZENS, FREDERIC S. The Sparrowgrass Papers. NY, 1856. 1st state. Frontispieces. Fine (spine sl rubbed). BAL 3998. *Polyanthos*. $50/£32

COZZENS, FREDERIC S. Yachts and Yachting. NY: Cassell, (1888). New, rev ed. (8),11-200pp. Dec cl (sl rubbed). VG. *Lefkowicz*. $175/£112

COZZENS, ISSACHAR. A Geological History of Manhattan or New York Island, Together with a Map of the Island.... NY: W.E. Dean, 1843. 1st ed. 114pp (foxed), incl subs list, color fldg map, 8 color plts and tables. Orig cl (rebacked). *M & S*. $300/£192

COZZENS, JAMES GOULD. Cock Pit. NY: Morrow, 1928. 1st ed. Black cl stamped in orange. VG. *Argosy*. $150/£96

CRABB, JAMES. The Gipsies' Advocate. London: Nisbet et al, 1832. 3rd ed. 190pp. Orig brn cl, spine label. Good. *Karmiole*. $85/£54

CRABBE, GEORGE II. The Life of George Crabbe. Cresset, 1947. 1st ed. VG in dj (worn). *Poetry Bookshop*. $9/£6

CRABBE, GEORGE. The Library. London: De la More, 1931. 1st ed thus. Edward Ardizzone (illus). Pict bds. VG. *Hollett*. $133/£85

CRABBE, GEORGE. Poems. London: J. Hatchard, 1807. 1st ed. xxvi,256pp, 1/2-title. Contemp 1/2 calf, (mod amateur reback), paper label. (Gatherings spotted), o/w Good. *Cox*. $44/£28

CRABBE, GEORGE. Poems. J. Hatchard, 1812. 6th ed. 2 vols. xlv,(3),127; (2),223pp; bound w/o 1/2-titles. (Lt spotted). Good in contemp rose 1/2 roan (lt rubbed), gilt-lettered, marbled sides. *Cox*. $47/£30

CRABBE, GEORGE. Tales of the Hall. Boston: Wells & Lilly, 1819. 1st Amer ed. 2 vols. Bkpls of Mary Morison and of 'R.S.M.' (Sl foxed; spines sl torn, worn, spine labels dknd, worn), o/w Good. *Holmes*. $275/£176

CRABBE, GEORGE. Tales of the Hall. London: John Murray, 1819. 1st ed. 2 vols. 1/2 tan calf (expertly recased, preserving contemp bds; bkpl), maroon labels. *Maggs*. $78/£50

CRABBE, GEORGE. Works. London: John Murray, 1823. Lg paper ed. 5 vols. 31 engr plts. Uncut. Later labeled patterned cl. VG. *Argosy*. $175/£112

CRACE, JIM. Continent. London, 1986. 1st ed, 1st bk. Fine in Fine dj. *Smith*. $20/£13

CRACKANTHORPE, HUBERT. Last Studies. London: Heinemann, 1897. 1st ed. (Cvrs sl soiled, worn), o/w Good. *Holmes*. $150/£96

CRACKANTHORPE, HUBERT. Sentimental Studies and a Set of Village Tales. London: Heinemann, 1895. 1st ed. (Spine sl mkd, soiled), else Good. *Holmes*. $175/£112

CRACKANTHORPE, HUBERT. Vignettes. London: Bodley Head, 1896. 1st ed. Uncut. Vellum (spine sunned). Fine (lt rubbed, cvrs lt soiled). *Polyanthos*. $35/£22

CRADDOCK, CHARLES EGBERT. (Pseud of Mary N. Murfree.) In the Clouds. Ward, Lock & Bowden, 1894. New ed. Pict bds (spine bumped, chipped; hinges, corners rubbed; cvrs sl mkd). Good (spotted, margins soiled). *Tiger*. $19/£12

CRADDOCK, CHARLES EGBERT. (Pseud of Mary N. Murfree.) In the Tennessee Mountains. Boston: Houghton Mifflin, 1884. 1st ed. 322pp + 12pp ads. (Scuff), else VG. *Brown*. $20/£13

CRAFT, WILLIAM and ELLEN. Running a Thousand Miles for Freedom. London: William Tweedie, 1861. 2nd ed. Frontis, 109pp + 3pp ads. Ptd wraps. (Rubbed, chipped, spine loss), else Good. *Brown*. $100/£64

CRAIB, ALEXANDER. America and the Americans. London, 1892. Inscribed. 325pp. Dec cl. *Reese*. $150/£96

CRAIG, A. R. Modern Palmistry. NY, 1867. 1st ed. 320pp. Gilt dec cvr (lt wear). VG + . *Middle Earth*. $95/£61

CRAIG, ALEC. Suppressed Books. Cleveland, 1963. 1st Amer ed. Fine (bkpl) in NF dj. *Polyanthos*. $25/£16

CRAIG, EDWARD GORDON. Paris Diary, 1932-1933. North Hills: Bird & Bull, 1982. One of 350 numbered. Prospectus laid in. 1/4 morocco. *Swann**. $92/£59

CRAIG, EDWARD GORDON. Woodcuts and Some Words. NY: E.P. Dutton, (1924). 1st Amer ed. E.P. Dutton imprint pasted over London imprint on tp. (Bkpl, lt foxing prelims; overall dkng), else VG. *Hermitage*. $100/£64

CRAIG, EDWARD GORDON. Woodcuts and Some Words. London/Toronto: Dent, 1924. 1st ed, w/o limitation, plts unmtd. Ptd bds. (Spine sl faded), o/w Very Nice. *Europa*. $75/£48

CRAIG, HUGH (ed). Johnson's Household Book of Nature.... NY: Henry J. Johnson, c. 1880. 2 vols. 74 chromo plts. 1/2 leather, cl bds. (Fr inner hinge vol 1 cracked; sl worn), o/w Contents VG. *New Hampshire**. $120/£77

CRAIG, MAURICE. Dublin 1660-1860: A Social and Architectural History. (NY): Coward-McCann, n.d. (c 1962). 1st Amer ed. Fldg map. VG in dj. *Hadley.* $94/£60

CRAIG, NEVILLE B. History of Pittsburgh. Pittsburgh, 1917. New ed. 3 maps (2 fldg, 1 dbl). Teg. VG +. Howes C844. *Bohling.* $35/£22

CRAIGHEAD, J. G. The Story of Marcus Whitman. Phila: Presbyterian Board, 1900. 2nd ptg. (Spine worn), else VG. *Perier.* $35/£22

CRAIGHEAD, J. J. et al. A Definitive System for Analysis of Grizzly Bear Habitat and Other Wilderness Resources.... Missoula: Univ of MT, 1982. 1st ed. VG in color pict wraps. *Mikesh.* $20/£13

CRAIGHEAD, JAMES. The Lost Empire. Oswego, IL: Bond, (1926). 1st ed. Inscribed by Mr. and Mrs. Craighead. Prospectus laid in. (Spine sl lightened.) *Sadlon.* $15/£10

CRAIK, GEORGE L. English Causes Celebres; or Reports of Remarkable Trials. London: Charles Knight, 1844. 3/4 morocco, spine gilt. Pretty (browned). *Boswell.* $175/£112

CRAIK, GEORGE L. The English of Shakespeare. London, 1875. 5th ed. xvi,350pp + (i) ads. (Ink stamp tp, last leaf, ex-lib, bkpl; text cracked; spine faded.) *Edwards.* $55/£35

CRAIK, HENRY. The Life of Jonathan Swift. Macmillan, 1894. 2nd ed. 2 vols. Frontis, xxvi,382; frontis, x,377pp; ad leaf each vol. Uncut. (Backstrips sl faded.) Good set. *Cox.* $39/£25

CRAIK, JOHN L. The New Zealanders.... London: Nattali, 1847. iv,424pp; map. Mod cl, leather label. VG. *Adelson.* $175/£112

CRAIS, ROBERT. Stalking the Angel. NY: Bantam, 1989. 1st ed. VF in dj. *Mordida.* $45/£29

CRAKES, SYLVESTER, JR. Five Years a Captive Among the Black-Feet Indians. Columbus, 1858. 244pp (lt soil, foxing; neat repairs fore-edge several leaves; lacks frontis); 5 plts. Later 3/4 calf (extrems rubbed), spine gilt, orig cl mtd at rear. Good. Howes C850. *Reese.* $1,500/£962

CRAM, GEORGE F. Cram's Unrivaled Family Atlas of the World. Chicago: Henry S. Stebbins, 1884. 197pp; plt. Dk brn cl. Fine (sm tear fr hinge). *Hudson.* $395/£253

CRAM, RALPH ADAMS. Farm Houses, Manor Houses, Minor Chateaux and Small Churches from the Eleventh to Sixteenth Centuries in...France. NY: Architectural Bk Pub Co, (1917). 1st ed. 5pp + 94 full-pg plts. VG. *Truepenny.* $65/£42

CRAM, RALPH ADAMS. Impressions of Japanese Architecture and the Allied Arts. NY: Baker & Taylor, (1905). 1st ed. Frontis, 57 sepia photos. Teg, uncut. Gilt/blind-stamped maroon cl (sl rubbed, bumped). VG. *Houle.* $150/£96

CRAMP, ARTHUR. Nostrums and Quackery...Volume 2. Chicago, 1921. 1st ed. VG. *Fye.* $75/£48

CRAMPTON, C. GREGORY. Land of Living Rock. NY, 1972. 1st ed. 16 color plts, 17 color maps. Black cl. Fine in NF dj w/acrylic protector. *Five Quail.* $40/£26

CRAMPTON, C. GREGORY. Standing Up Country. NY, 1965. 1st ed. 2 maps. Grn/white cl. Fine in VG + full-color dj. *Five Quail.* $75/£48

CRAMPTON, FRANK A. Deep Enough. Denver: Sage Books, (1956). (Cl sl spotting.) Dj (lt edgewear). *Dawson.* $40/£26

CRANE, FRANCES. The Ultraviolet Widow. NY: Random House, 1956. 1st ed. Fine in dj (sl wear spine ends, corners). *Mordida.* $45/£29

CRANE, HART. The Bridge. NY: LEC, 1981. Mint in pub's box. *Argosy.* $150/£96

CRANE, HART. The Letters of...1916-1932. Brom Weber (ed). NY: Hermitage House, 1952. 1st ed. Black cl, gilt. NF in VG dj (rubbed, chipped; flap folds torn). *Blue Mountain.* $50/£32

CRANE, JAMES. The Past, Present and Future of the Pacific. SF, 1856. 8vo. 79pp (lt foxed). Later grn cl. Overall VG. Howes C861. *Reese.* $750/£481

CRANE, NATHALIE. Pocahontas. NY: Dutton, (1930). #137/155 signed. Teg. Paper over bds, dec cvr. Good in clear plastic dj, Fair slipcase. *Scribe's Perch*.* $18/£12

CRANE, STEPHEN and ROBERT BARR. The O'Ruddy. NY: Frederick A. Stokes, (1903). 1st ed. Frontis. Beige cl pict dec in grn/black. NF (inscrip; sl askew). *Sumner & Stillman.* $125/£80

CRANE, STEPHEN. Active Service. London: Heinemann, 1899. 1st Eng ed. (iv),316pp, 32pg inserted pub's cat. Uncut. Buff glazed art canvas. Nice. *Temple.* $78/£50

CRANE, STEPHEN. Great Battles of the World. Phila, 1901. 1st Amer ed. Teg. Dec cvrs, gilt. Fine (extrems lt rubbed). BAL 4094. *Polyanthos.* $95/£61

CRANE, STEPHEN. The Little Regiment. NY, 1896. 1st ed, 1st ptg. (Lt worn.) BAL 4076. *Kane*.* $110/£71

CRANE, STEPHEN. The Little Regiment. NY: Appleton, 1896. 1st state; ads begin w/'Gilbert Parker's Best Books.' vi,196pp + 6pp ads; pub's device tp; meets all points. Dec cvr. Good. *Scribe's Perch*.* $65/£42

CRANE, STEPHEN. The Little Regiment. NY: D. Appleton, 1896. 1st ed. Top edge stained, rest uncut. Oatmeal cl. VF. *Maggs.* $109/£70

CRANE, STEPHEN. The Little Regiment. London: Heinemann, 1897. 1st Eng ed. Ad leaf, 1/2-title, 16pp ads. Japon vellum eps; uncut, lower edges rough-trimmed. Dk grn buckram. (Margins lt browned, lt foxed; label removed fr cvr, spine sl faded), o/w Nice. *Temple.* $47/£30

CRANE, STEPHEN. Maggie, a Girl of the Streets. NY, 1896. 1st pub ed, 1st state, 1st bk; tp ptd in upper/lower case letters. NF (bkpl). BAL 4075. *Kane*.* $200/£128

CRANE, STEPHEN. Maggie, a Girl of the Streets. LEC, 1974. #394/2000 signed by Sigmund Abeles (illus). Fine in slipcase. *Hermitage.* $100/£64

CRANE, STEPHEN. The Monster and Other Stories. NY: Harper, 1899. 1st ed. Red-orange cl (spine lt aged), gilt. BAL 4085. *Macdonnell.* $200/£128

CRANE, STEPHEN. The Open Boat and Other Stories. London: Heinemann, 1898. 1st Eng ed. Grn cl (sl soiled, sm tear spine head). VG. BAL 4080. *Captain's Bookshelf.* $175/£112

CRANE, STEPHEN. The Red Badge of Courage. NY: Random House, (1931). One of 980 numbered. Cl-backed bds (spine crown sl rubbed), spine label (top chipped). Good. Internally NF. *Reese.* $50/£32

CRANE, STEPHEN. The Red Badge of Courage. NY: D. Appleton, 1896. 2nd ed. (ii),233pp (early cat entries mtd rear pastedown). Tan cl (rubbed, stained, spine dknd). Good. *Blue Mountain.* $50/£32

CRANE, STEPHEN. The Red Badge of Courage. NY: D. Appleton, 1896. 1st ed, 2nd ptg. 233,(4)pp. Good + (sl cocked, sl speckled). *Mcgowan.* $150/£96

CRANE, STEPHEN. The Red Badge of Courage. SF: Grabhorn, 1931. One of 980. Valenti Angelo (illus). 1/4 cl. *Swann*.* $138/£88

CRANE, STEPHEN. The Red Badge of Courage. MA: Pennyroyal Editions, 1984. 1st ed. Barry Moser (illus). Pub's tan cl, orig matching slipcase. *D & D.* $125/£80

CRANE, STEPHEN. The Third Violet. Heinemann, 1897. 1st British ed. Fawn-colored linen (sl wear, spine sl dknd, cvrs sl discolored). Good (sl foxing). *Ash.* $62/£40

CRANE, STEPHEN. The Third Violet. NY, 1897. 1st ed. 203pp. (Ink name; cvrs dknd, rubbed.) *King.* $75/£48

CRANE, STEPHEN. The Third Violet. NY: D. Appleton, 1897. 1st ed. Orig cream buckram, gilt. Fine. BAL 4078. *Macdonnell.* $200/£128

CRANE, VERNER W. The Southern Frontier 1670-1732. Durham, 1928. 1st ed. Fldg map. (Ex-lib), o/w VG. Howes C865. *Turpen.* $45/£29

CRANE, WALTER. The Bases of Design. London: George Bell, 1898. 1st ed. xix,365,(x)pp. Teg, uncut. (Upper joint cracked, label fep, tp spotted; worn, spine faded.) *Hollett.* $101/£65

CRANE, WALTER. A Floral Fantasy in an Old English Garden. London/NY: Harper, 1899. Folio. 46 full-pg color plts. Illus eps. Cream cl (age stains). VG+. *Dower.* $325/£208

CRANE, WALTER. Legends for Lionel. Cassell, 1887. 1st ed, 1st issue dated 9.87 (i.e., Sept 1887) at base of 1st pg of ads. 4to. 40pp, 8pp ads; 39 color plts. Fore-edges in uncut folds, unopened as issued. Lion-patterned eps. Pict pink bds, cl spine. (Sl rubbed), else Fine. *Bookmark.* $343/£220

CRANE, WALTER. Queen Summer. London, 1891. 1st ed. (Spine shot, corners heavily rubbed), o/w VG. *Words Etc.* $56/£36

CRANE, WALTER. Queen Summer. London: Cassell, 1891. Cl-backed pict bds (soiled). *Argosy.* $125/£80

CRAPSEY, ADELAIDE. Verse. NY, 1922. 1st Amer ed. Patterned bds (sl rubbed). NF (tears lower margins 2 prelims; spine, label sunned). *Polyanthos.* $25/£16

CRAUFURD, ALEXANDER H. General Craufurd and His Light Division. London, (1891). Frontis port, xiv,298pp. Grn cl (spotted). *Maggs.* $234/£150

CRAVEN, AVERY. The Coming of the Civil War. NY: Scribner, 1942. 1st ed. (Spine sl soiled.) *Shasky.* $30/£19

CRAVEN, THOMAS. Treasury of American Prints. NY, (1929). 1st ed. Folio. Fine in slipcase (worn). *Heinoldt.* $75/£48

CRAVEN, TUNIS AUGUSTUS MACDONOUGH. A Naval Campaign in the Californias, 1846-1849. John Haskell Kemble (ed). SF: Book Club of CA, (1973). Ltd to 400 ptd. Frontis, 3 color plts. Orig announcement laid in. Dec cl. VF. *Argonaut.* $75/£48

CRAWFORD, F. MARION. Corleone. A Tale of Sicily. London: Macmillan, 1897. 1st ed. 2 vols. Blue cl stamped in gilt/yellow. (Lt rubbed, few mks), o/w VG set. BAL 4201. *Reese.* $225/£144

CRAWFORD, F. MARION. Love in Idleness: A Bar Harbour Tale. London: Macmillan, 1894. 1st pub ed. (iv),(158),(ii)pp, integral ad leaf. Uncut. Limp mottled blue linen wrappers, copper dec. (Eps lt foxed; copper sl dull), o/w Fine. *Temple.* $28/£18

CRAWFORD, F. MARION. Man Overboard. Macmillan, 1903. 1st ed. Dec cl. (Sm spot cvr corner), else VG. *Certo.* $50/£32

CRAWFORD, F. MARION. To Leeward. Houghton Mifflin, 1884. VG. *Madle.* $25/£16

CRAWFORD, J. MARSHALL. Mosby and His Men. NY, 1867. 1st ed. 375pp. (Ink inscrip; cvrs worn, spine frayed.) *King.* $150/£96

CRAWFORD, JOE (ed). The Black Photographers Annual. Volume 3. Brooklyn: Black Photographers Annual, 1976. 1st ed. VG in pict stiff wrappers. *Cahan.* $50/£32

CRAWFORD, JOHN. Chinese Calligraphy and Painting in the Collection of John M. Crawford. NY, 1962. One of 850. Inscribed, signed. Folio. Slipcase. *Swann*.* $172/£110

CRAWFORD, JOHN. Chinese Calligraphy and Painting in the Collection of John M. Crawford. NY: Pierpont Morgan Library, 1962. 1st ed. Fine. *Terramedia.* $50/£32

CRAWFORD, LEWIS F. The Medora-Deadwood Stage Line. Bismarck: Capitol Book Co, 1925. 1st ed. (Sig), else VG in ptd wrappers. *Brown.* $35/£22

CRAWFORD, LEWIS F. The Medora-Deadwood Stage Line. Bismarck, March 1925. 1st ed. Good in ptd wrappers (dust-soiled). *Lucas.* $40/£26

CRAWFORD, LEWIS F. Rekindling Camp Fires. Bismarck: Capital Book Co, 1926. 1st ed. Map. Good. Howes C872. *Lien.* $80/£51

CRAWFORD, MARY CAROLINE. Old Boston Days and Ways. Boston: Little Brown, 1909. 1st ed. 48 plts. (Sl rubbed, shaken), o/w Good. *Worldwide.* $20/£13

CRAWFORD, MARY CAROLINE. The Romance of Old New England Churches. Boston: Page, 1907. 2nd imp. 16 plts. (Ink underlining; sl rubbed, soiled), o/w VG. *Worldwide.* $15/£10

CRAWFORD, MARY CAROLINE. Romantic Days in Old Boston. Boston: Little Brown, 1910. 63 plts. Teg. (Ink underlining; sl rubbed, spine tear), o/w VG. *Worldwide.* $15/£10

CRAWFORD, MEDOREM. Journal of Medorem Crawford. Eugene: Star Job Office, 1897. 1st separate ptg. 26pp. VG in self-wraps, stapled as issued. Howes C874. *Brown.* $75/£48

CRAWFORD, MEDOREM. Journal of Medorem Crawford: An Account of His Trip Across the Plains...1842.... Eugene, OR, 1897. 1st separate ed. 26pp. Stapled. Howes C874. *Ginsberg.* $100/£64

CRAWFORD, THOMAS EDGAR. The West of the Texas Kid, 1881-1910. Jeff C. Dykes (ed). Norman: Univ of OK, (1962). 1st ed. Fine in dj, plastic jacket. *Bohling.* $22/£14

CRAWFORD, WILLIAM. The Keepers of Light. Dobbs Ferry, NY: Morgan & Morgan, 1979. NF in illus stiff wrappers. *Cahan.* $30/£19

CRAYON, GEOFFREY. (Pseud of Washington Irving.) Bracebridge Hall; or The Humorists. John Murray, 1822. 1st Eng ed. 2 vols. 19th cent 1/2 red morocco, gilt panelled backs, marbled edges. *Hatchwell.* $195/£125

CRAYON, GEOFFREY. (Pseud of Washington Irving.) Sketch Book of Geoffrey Crayon. NY, 1819-20. 7 parts in 2 vols. W/all BAL 1st ptg points. Lacks terminal blanks parts 1, 2; contains 'Legend of Sleepy Hollow'. Later full brn calf (rubbed, other faults; joints cracked, leather labels gone; minor internal foxing). BAL 10106. *Freeman*.* $500/£321

CREASEY, JOHN. Death of a Racehorse. London: Hodder & Stoughton, 1959. 1st ed. Fine in dj (spine top sl creased). *Mordida.* $35/£22

CREASEY, JOHN. The Inferno. NY: Walker, (1965). 1st Amer ed. Rev copy w/inserted slip. Fine in dj (soiled). *Antic Hay.* $27/£17

CREASEY, JOHN. The Toff and the Spider. London: Hodder & Stoughton, 1965. 1st ed. Fine in dj (sl soiling). *Janus.* $45/£29

CREASY, E. S. History of the Ottoman Turks. London: Richard Bentley, 1858. 2 vols. Fldg frontis maps. Teg. 3/4 vellum, grn cl, morocco spine labels. (Bkpls), else NF. *Pacific*.* $126/£81

CREDLE, ELLIS. Down Down the Mountain. NY: Nelson/JLG, 1934. 1st ed. Signed. 9 1/4 x 11 1/4. 48pp. VG in dj. *Cattermole.* $150/£96

CREED, R. S. et al. Reflex Activity of the Spinal Cord. Oxford, 1923. 1st ed. (Spine rubbed, worn.) *Argosy.* $150/£96

CREELEY, ROBERT. The Finger. L.A.: Black Sparrow, 1968. Ltd to 250 numbered, signed. 4 full-pg illus. NF in ptd brn wraps (corners sl creased). *Blue Mountain.* $35/£22

CREELEY, ROBERT. Hello. NY: New Directions, (1978). 1st ed. Signed bkpl tipped in. Fine in dj (yellowed). *Metropolitan*.* $57/£37

CREELEY, ROBERT. Listen. L.A.: Black Sparrow, 1972. Ltd to 250 numbered, signed. Orange cl-backed tan bds, spine label. Fine in acetate dj. *Blue Mountain.* $35/£22

CREELEY, ROBERT. Thirty Things. L.A.: Black Sparrow, 1974. One of 250 numbered, signed. Black cl-backed tan bds, ptd spine label. Fine in acetate dj. *Blue Mountain.* $50/£32

CREELEY, ROBERT. The Whip. Worcester: Migrant Bks, 1957. 1st ed. NF in wrappers (mild staining). *Sclanders.* $156/£100

CREGAR, R. P. The Description and Laws of the Game of Boston.... Phila, 1883. 1st ed. 39pp. *Ginsberg.* $100/£64

CREIGHTON, C. A History of Epidemics in Britain. Cambridge, 1891-94. 1st ed. 2 vols. (Sig; cl sl worn, scuffed.) *Maggs.* $125/£80

CREIGHTON, C. Illustrations of Unconscious Memory in Disease.... London, 1886. VG. *Argosy.* $60/£38

CREIGHTON, C. Illustrations of Unconscious Memory in Disease.... NY: J.H. Vail, 1886. 1st Amer ed. xvi,212pp (lib stamps tp, other ll). Emb panelled grn cl, gilt spine. *Gach.* $50/£32

CRELLIN, JOHN K. Medical Care in Pioneer Illinois. Springfield, IL, 1982. 1st ed. (Marginal damp-staining), o/w VG in VG dj. *Doctor's Library.* $30/£19

CRELLY, WILLIAM R. The Painting of Simon Vouet. New Haven/London, 1962. Sm 4to. Good in dj. *Washton.* $600/£385

Creole Tourist's Guide and Sketch Book to the City of New Orleans.... Creole Pub Co, n.d. 'Latest ed.' Fldg color map (protrudes, sl edgeworn). Pict wraps (sl worn, short tear; 1921 inscrip). *Bohling.* $24/£15

CRESPELLE, JEAN-PAUL. The Fauves. CT: NYGS, n.d. VG in VG dj. *Metropolitan*.* $69/£44

CRESSON, JOSHUA. Meditations Written During the Prevalence of the Yellow Fever in the City of Philadelphia in the Year 1793. London: W. Phillips, 1803. 1st ed. x,26pp (sig). Orig marbled wrappers. *Maggs.* $133/£85

CRESSWELL, BEATRICE. The Royal Progress of King Pepito. SPCK, n.d. (1889). 1st ed. Sm 4to. 48pp (eps foxed); 12 color plts by Kate Greenaway. Pict buff bds (surface-paper stripped from spine, bds mkd, rubbed), ads on back. Sound. *Bookmark.* $109/£70

CRESSWELL, NICHOLAS. Journal 1774-1777. NY: Dial, 1924. 1st ed. Frontis port, 12,287pp. Good (hinge cracks, bumped). *Scribe's Perch*.* $25/£16

CREWS, HARRY. Car. NY: William Morrow, 1972. 1st US ed. Fine in NF dj. *Lame Duck.* $200/£128

CREWS, HARRY. The Enthusiast. (Winston-Salem, NC): Palaemon, (1981). One of 200 signed. New. *Bernard.* $175/£112

CREWS, HARRY. Karate Is a Thing of the Spirit. NY: Wm. Morrow, 1971. 1st ed. One of 5942. Fine in Fine dj. *Bernard.* $175/£112

CREWS, HARRY. Karate Is a Thing of the Spirit. NY: Wm. Morrow, 1971. 1st ed. One of 5,942. Signed. Fine in Fine dj. *Bernard.* $225/£144

CREWS, HARRY. Karate Is a Thing of the Spirit. London, 1972. 1st Eng ed. Bright (cvrs sl rubbed) in dj (torn, chafed). *Clearwater.* $55/£35

CREWS, HARRY. Naked in Garden Hills. NY: Wm. Morrow, 1969. 1st ed. One of 5500. (Name, address, phone, date on fep; edgewear), o/w VG in 1st issue dj (lt yellowed, spotted). *Bernard.* $175/£112

CREYKE, W. R. Book of Modern Receipts...for Producing All Kinds of Enamel, Underglaze, and Majolica Colours. Hanley: Hitchings, 1884. 1st ed. Tp,96pp. Blue cl, gilt. *Marlborough.* $304/£195

CRICHTON, MICHAEL. The Andromeda Strain. London: Cape, (1969). 1st Eng ed. VG (lt wear) in VG- dj (short tears corners). *Between The Covers.* $100/£64

CRICHTON, MICHAEL. The Andromeda Strain. NY: Knopf, 1969. 1st ed. Fine in Fine dj (flap creases). *Between The Covers.* $250/£160

CRICHTON, MICHAEL. Congo. London: Allen Lane, 1981. 1st UK ed. NF in dj. *Williams.* $39/£25

CRICHTON, MICHAEL. Electronic Life: How to Think About Computers. NY: Knopf, 1983. 1st ed. Fine in dj (sm tear). *Captain's Bookshelf.* $75/£48

CRICHTON, MICHAEL. The Great Train Robbery. London, 1975. 1st ed. VG in dj. *Typographeum.* $15/£10

CRICHTON, MICHAEL. The Great Train Robbery. NY: Knopf, 1975. 1st ed. (Sl fading bds), else Fine in Fine dj (price-clipped). *Between The Covers.* $100/£64

CRICHTON, MICHAEL. Jasper Johns. NY: Abrams, (1977). Inscribed. 128 lg plts, 6 fldg plts. VG in dj. *Argosy.* $500/£321

CRICHTON, MICHAEL. Jurassic Park. Century, 1991. #737/750. Proof copy. Fine in illus wraps. *Williams.* $117/£75

CRICHTON, MICHAEL. The Terminal Man. NY: Knopf, (1972). 1st ed. Inscribed. Fine in NF dj (flap creased). *Unger.* $150/£96

CRICHTON, MICHAEL. The Terminal Man. NY: Knopf, 1972. 1st ed. Fine in dj. *Mordida.* $65/£42

CRICHTON, MICHAEL. Travels. NY: Knopf, 1988. 1st ed. NF in dj. *Worldwide.* $18/£12

CRICHTON, ROBERT. The Secret of Santa Vittoria. London, 1967. 1st ed. Dj. *Typographeum.* $18/£12

Cries of New York. NY: Harbor, 1931. 1st ed. Cl, dec bds. Fine in glassine dj. *Dermont.* $25/£16

CRILE, GEORGE. Diseases Peculiar to Civilized Man.... Amy Rowland (ed). NY, 1934. 1st ed. Fldg table. VG. *Argosy.* $50/£32

CRILE, GEORGE. The Origin and Nature of the Emotions. Phila: W.B. Saunders, 1915. 1st ed. Ptd grn cl (sl stained). Jelliffe's name stamp. Good (lib stamp tp, spine #s). *Gach.* $75/£48

Criminal Recorder. Phila: Carey, 1812. 280pp. Contemp calf. VG. *Second Life.* $225/£144

CRIPPS, WILFRED JOSEPH. Old English Plate.... London: John Murray, 1878. 1st ed. xvi,432pp + 32pp pub's cat. Sound (extrems rubbed). *Cox.* $31/£20

CRIPPS-DAY, FRANCIS H. et al. The Manor Farm...to Which Are Added Reprint-Facsimiles of the Boke of Husbandry...by Walter of Henley...and The Book of Thrift...by James Bellot. London: Quaritch, 1931. 1st ed thus. Teg. Vellum, bds. VG. *Reese.* $75/£48

CRISP, F. Medieval Gardens. Catherine Childs Paterson (ed). London: John Lane, 1924. One of 1000. 2 vols. 140,xivpp; 229; 332 plts. Teg. Dec cl (sm stain fr cvr 1 vol, sl worn). Internally Excellent. *Ars Artis.* $390/£250

CRISP, QUENTIN. All This and Bevin Too. London: Nicholson & Watson, 1943. 1st Eng ed. Mervyn Peake (illus). VG in pict wrappers (spine worn, sl spotted, dusty). *Clearwater.* $195/£125

CRISP, QUENTIN. Colour in Display. London: Blandford, 1938. 1st Eng ed, 1st bk. Complete w/linen colour-chart. Good (tp torn). *Clearwater.* $47/£30

CRISP, QUENTIN. How to Become a Virgin. NY, 1981. 1st ed. Fine in Fine dj. *Warren.* $35/£22

CRISP, QUENTIN. Manners from Heaven. London, 1984. 1st ed. Dj. *Typographeum.* $20/£13

CRISPIN, E. Holy Disorders. London: Gollancz, 1945. 1st UK ed. VG in dj (spine sl browned, sl edgeworn). *Williams.* $187/£120

CRISPIN, E. The Moving Toyshop. Phila: Lippincott, 1946. 1st Amer ed. (Pg edges lt spotted), o/w VG in dj (sl wear, closed tears). *Mordida.* $45/£29

CROCKET, S. R. The Black Douglas. Doubleday McClure, 1899. 1st US ed. VG +. *Certo.* $30/£19

CROCKETT, DAVID. Adventures of Davy Crockett Told Mostly by Himself. NY, 1955. Rpt of 1934 ed. (Sl worn), o/w VG. *Turpen.* $30/£19

CROCKETT, DAVY. The Crockett Almanacks: Nashville Series, 1835-1838. Franklin J. Meine (ed). Caxton Club, 1955. Ltd ed of 600. Fine. *Authors Of West.* $60/£38

CROCKETT, W. S. The Scott Country. London: A&C Black, 1911. 4th ed. Map. Port inset upper bd (sl rubbed). *Hollett.* $12/£8

CROFT, ANDREW. Polar Exploration. London: A&C Black, 1939. 8 plts, 8 maps. Blue cl. (Edges lt foxed, sl worn, soiled.) *Parmer.* $35/£22

CROFT, HELEN DOWNER. The Downs, the Rockies—and Desert Gold. Caldwell: Caxton, 1961. 1st ed. VG in dj (sl worn). *Brown.* $15/£10

CROFT-COOK, RUPERT. Feasting with Panthers. NY: Holt, Rinehart Winston, (1967). 1st ed. VG in dj. *Turtle Island.* $35/£22

CROFT-COOKE, RUPERT. The Verdict of You All. London, 1955. 1st Eng ed. (Rear cvr mkd.) Dj (sl frayed, mkd). *Clearwater.* $31/£20

CROFT-MURRAY, EDWARD and PAUL HULTON. Catalogue of British Drawings. Volume One: XVI and XVII Centuries. Supplemented by a List of Foreign Artists' Drawings...by Christopher White. London, 1960. 304 plts (8 color). Good. *Washton.* $225/£144

CROFTON, ALGERNON. Poker: Its Laws and Principles with a Full Exposition of Mathematical Odds. R. F. Foster (ed). NY: Wycil & Co, 1915. Brn cl (rubbed, sl soiled, sm sticker fr cvr), gilt. *Cummins.* $75/£48

CROFTS, FREEMAN WILLS. 12-30 from Croydon. London: Hodder & Stoughton, 1934. 1st ed. (Sunned, bds dampstained.) Dj (browned, losses at extrems). *Metropolitan*.* $402/£258

CROFTS, FREEMAN WILLS. Antidote to Venom. London: Hodder & Stoughton, 1938. 1st ed. Fine in dj (nicks, short closed tears). *Mordida.* $800/£513

CROFTS, FREEMAN WILLS. Anything to Declare? Hodder, 1957. 1st UK ed. VG in dj (sl dusty). *Williams.* $47/£30

CROFTS, FREEMAN WILLS. Enemy Unseen. NY: Dodd, Mead, 1945. 1st ed. (Soil, stains.) Dj (edgewear, chips). *Metropolitan*.* $92/£59

CROFTS, FREEMAN WILLS. Fear Comes to Chalfont. NY: Dodd, Mead, 1942. 1st Amer ed. NF in VG dj (rubbed, short tear, crease). *Metropolitan*.* $184/£118

CROFTS, FREEMAN WILLS. Found Floating. London: Hodder & Stoughton, 1937. 1st ed. (Sunned, frayed.) Dj (chipped). *Metropolitan*.* $460/£295

CROFTS, FREEMAN WILLS. Golden Ashes. NY: Dodd, Mead, 1940. 1st Amer ed. VG in dj (worn, torn). *Metropolitan*.* $69/£44

CROFTS, FREEMAN WILLS. Inspector French's Greatest Case. Collins, n.d. (Rubbed, worn, shaken.) Dj (extrem losses, worn). *Metropolitan*.* $92/£59

CROFTS, FREEMAN WILLS. Many a Slip. Hodder, 1955. 1st UK ed. Good (bds worn, mkd; spine hinge sl damaged) in dj (sm chip bottom fr panel). *Williams.* $28/£18

CROFTS, FREEMAN WILLS. Murderers Make Mistakes. London: Hodder & Stoughton, 1947. (Bds lt stained.) Dj (surface worn, soiled, short tears). *Metropolitan*.* $69/£44

CROFTS, FREEMAN WILLS. The Mystery of the Sleeping Car Express. London: Hodder & Stoughton, 1956. NF in VG dj (sl browned, price-clipped). *Metropolitan*.* $80/£51

CROFTS, FREEMAN WILLS. The Strange Case of Dr. Earle. NY: Dodd, Mead, 1933. 1st ed. VG in dj (extrems worn, soiled). *Metropolitan*.* $230/£147

CROFTS, FREEMAN WILLS. Sudden Death. NY: Harper, 1932. 1st ed. Sharp in dj (1-inch tear fr top, chipped, worn), wraparound ad intact. *Metropolitan*.* $373/£239

CROFTS, FREEMAN WILLS. Tragedy in the Hollow. NY: Dodd, Mead, 1939. 1st ed. VG in dj (worn, 2 sm losses, rear panel yellowed). *Metropolitan*.* $103/£66

Crofutt's Trans-Continental Tourist's Guide. NY: Geo. A. Crofutt, 1871. 3rd vol, 2nd annual rev. 215,(7),8pp; lg color fldg map. (Faded, extrems sl worn.) Contents VG (map folds splitting). *New Hampshire*.* $140/£90

CROFUTT, GEORGE A. Croffutt's New Overland Tourist and Pacific Coast Guide. Omaha: Overland, 1880. 281pp. (Back cvr creased), else Good. *Perier.* $60/£38

CROGHAN, GEORGE. Army Life on the Western Frontier. Francis Paul Prucha (ed). Norman: Univ of OK, (1958). 1st ed. Map. (Sm ink sig). Fine in pict dj (lt rubbed). *Argonaut.* $50/£32

CROGHAN, JOHN. Rambles in the Mammoth Cave, During the Year 1844. Louisville, KY, 1845. 1st ed. 101pp, errata, lg fldg map, 6 lithos. Contemp 1/2 morocco. Howes C905. *Ginsberg.* $400/£256

CROKER, JOHN WILSON. The Correspondence and Diaries.... Louis J. Jennings (ed). John Murray, 1884. 1st ed. 3 vols. Frontis, xii,434; viii,423; viii,397 + 32pp pub's cat dated May 1884. VG set. *Cox.* $70/£45

CROLL, P. C. Ancient and Historic Landmarks in the Lebanon Valley. Phila: Lutheran Publication Soc, 1895. Als attached to fr pastedown. 334pp. (Fr hinge cracked), else VG. *Zubal*.* $20/£13

CROM, THEODORE R. Horological Shop Tools 1700 to 1900. Melrose, FL: (The Author), 1980. 1st ed. Inscribed. 21 color plts. Brn cl. Fine. *Weber.* $100/£64

CROMBIE, MICHAEL. The House of Horror. London: Arthur Gray, n.d. 1st British ed. Dj (spine faded, interior reinforcement). *Metropolitan*.* $51/£33

Cromwelliana. A Chronological Detail of Events in which Oliver Cromwell Was Engaged.... (By James Caulfield.) Westminster: Machell Stace, 1810. 1st ed. (6),196,(2)pp; 5 copper engrs. Uncut. 19th cent calf, marbled bds (lt rubbed). *Karmiole.* $250/£160

CRON, GRETCHEN. The Roaring Veldt. NY: Putnam, 1930. 1st ed. (Dj flap tipped in fep.) Red cl, gilt lettering. VG (lt wear spine edges; adhesive mks on back; 1-inch strip clipped from fep). *Backman.* $65/£42

CRONIN, A. J. Adventures in Two Worlds. Gollancz, 1952. 1st UK ed. VG (sl foxed) in dj (sl discolored, sl spine top loss). *Williams.* $19/£12

CRONIN, A. J. Beyond This Place. Gollancz, 1953. 1st UK ed. VG (fep crease) in dj. *Williams.* $23/£15

CRONIN, A. J. The Citadel. London: Gollancz, 1937. VG (fep sl foxed; bds sl mottled) in VG dj (spine sl faded, lt spots). *Between The Covers.* $85/£54

CRONIN, A. J. Shannon's Way. Gollancz, 1948. 1st UK ed. VG in dj (sl faded). *Williams.* $23/£15

CRONIN, FRANCIS D. Under the Southern Cross. Washington, (1951). 1st ed. (Rubbed, spotted.) *King.* $65/£42

CRONIN, VINCENT. The Last Migration. NY: Dutton, 1957. 1st ed. VG in dj (tattered). *Worldwide.* $18/£12

CRONISE, TITUS. Natural Wealth of California. SF: Bancroft, 1868. 1st ed. 696pp + plts. Fine. *Book Market.* $200/£128

CRONLEY, JAY. Screwballs. Doubleday, 1980. 1st ed. Fine in VG + dj. *Plapinger.* $50/£32

CROOK, GEORGE. General Crook: His Autobiography. Martin F. Schmitt (ed). Norman: Univ of OK, 1946. 1st ed. VG in dj (sl worn, taped). *Lien.* $65/£42

CROOKE, GEORGE. The Twenty-First Regiment of Iowa Volunteer Infantry. Milwaukee, 1891. 1st ed. 232pp. (Few sl stains.) *Wantagh.* $150/£96

CROOKSHANK, EDGAR (ed). History and Pathology of Vaccination. Volume 2. Selected Essays. London, 1889. 1st ed. 610pp. VG. *Fye.* $175/£112

CROOME, A. C. M. Fifty Years of Sport. Oxford/Cambridge, 1913. 2 vols. Marbled eps, teg. Full blind-ruled morocco (sl rubbed), gilt-edged dec device upper bds. *Edwards.* $218/£140

CROSBY, CARESSE. The Passionate Years. London, 1955. 1st Eng ed. Very Nice in dj (repaired). *Clearwater.* $55/£35

CROSBY, PERCY. A Cartoonist's Philosophy. McLean, VA, (1931). 1st ed. Signed. 252pp (name, address stamp tp; flies discolored from newspaper rev); 10 full-pg plts. (Cvrs soiled, worn.) *King.* $95/£61

CROSFIELD, THOMAS. The Diary of Thomas Crosfield, M.A., M.B.D.... OUP, 1935. 1st ed. Frontis port, 3 facs. (Extrems sl worn.) *Hollett.* $70/£45

CROSS, AMANDA. Death in a Tenured Position. NY: Dutton, 1981. 1st ed. VF in dj. *Mordida.* $30/£19

CROSS, AMANDA. In the Last Analysis. NY: Macmillan, 1964. 1st ed. (Bottom edges eps, cvrs sl tape residue), o/w VG in dj (faded). *Mordida.* $65/£42

CROSS, AMANDA. Poetic Justice. NY, 1970. 1st Amer ed. Fine in dj. *Polyanthos.* $25/£16

CROSS, ARTHUR LYON. Eighteenth Century Documents Relating to the Royal Forests.... NY: Macmillan, 1928. *Boswell.* $75/£48

CROSS, IRA B. (ed). Frank Roney, Irish Rebel and California Labor Leader, an Autobiography. Berkeley: Univ of CA, 1931. 1st ed. Gilt-lettered grn cl. Fine. *Argonaut.* $125/£80

CROSS, JAMES WALTER. George Eliot's Life as Related in Her Letters and Journals. Edinburgh/London: William Blackwood, 1885. 1st ed. 3 vols. Mauve cl, gilt. (Sm chip vol 3), else Nice. *Macdonnell.* $275/£176

CROSS, M. I. and MARTIN J. COLE. Modern Microscopy. London: Bailliere, Tindall & Cox, 1895. 2nd ed. 182pp. VG. *Savona.* $31/£20

CROSS, R. W. JEREMY. The True Masonic Chart, or Hieroglyphic Monitor. New Haven: T.G. Woodward, 1824. Full contemp calf (very rubbed, bumped). *Metropolitan*.* $57/£37

CROSS, RALPH HERBERT. The Early Inns of California, 1844-1869. SF: (Cross & Brandt), 1954. 1st ed. One of 500 ptd. Frontis, fldg map. Uncut. VF. *Argonaut.* $75/£48

CROSSLEY, ANTHONY. The Floating Line for Salmon and Sea-Trout. Methuen, 1939. 1st ed. (Eps sl discolored.) *Petersfield.* $39/£25

CROSSLEY, FRED H. English Church Monuments 1150-1550. Batsford, 1933. New ed. Buckram (spine dull). VG-. *Gretton.* $23/£15

CROSSLEY, FRED H. English Church Monuments A.D. 1150-1550. Batsford, n.d. c.(1921). (Cl lt soiled, paint mk rear bd, edges sl rubbed.) *Edwards.* $47/£30

CROSSLEY, FRED H. Timber Building in England from Early Times to the End of the Seventeenth Century. London: Batsford, 1951. 1st ed. VG in pict dj (rear dknd). *Cox.* $55/£35

CROSSLEY-HOLLAND, KEVIN (trans). Beowulf. London: Folio Soc, 1973. 2nd ptg. Frontis, 125pp (sm mk fr pastedown); 7 plts by Virgil Burnett. Brn cl (spine sl rubbed). NF in Good tan paper-cvrd slipcase (chipped). *Blue Mountain.* $15/£10

CROTHERS, SAMUEL M. The Children of Dickens. NY, 1925. 1st Amer ed. NF (bkpl, sl foxed; spine sl sunned, extrems sl rubbed). *Polyanthos.* $60/£38

CROTHERS, SAMUEL M. Meditations on Votes for Women. Boston, 1914. 1st ed. Good (ex-lib). *Second Life.* $25/£16

CROUCH, JOSEPH. Puritanism and Art. 1910. (Prelims, tp lt spotted, feps browned.) *Edwards.* $55/£35

CROUSE, DAVID ELDRIDGE. The Ohio Gateway. NY: Scribner, 1938. Orange cl. VG in dj (chipped, deep tear). *Bohling.* $15/£10

CROUSE, NELLIS M. The Search for the Northwest Passage. NY: Columbia Univ, 1934. 1st ed. Fldg map. Fine. *Perier.* $60/£38

CROWE, EYRE. With Thackeray in America. London, 1893. Frontis, xii,179,(1)pp. (Inner hinges cracked), else VG. *Reese.* $150/£96

CROWE, EYRE. With Thackeray in America. NY, 1893. xvi,179,8pp. *Wantagh.* $35/£22

CROWE, J. A. and G. B. CAVALCASELLE. A History of Painting in Italy Umbria Florence and Siena from the Second to the Sixteenth Century. Vol I. Early Christian Art. Langton Douglas & Tancred Borenius (eds). NY, 1903. Blue cl (shelfwear). *Washton.* $40/£26

CROWE, J. A. and G. B. CAVALCASELLE. A History of Painting in Italy Umbria Florence and Siena from the Second to the Sixteenth Century. Vol VI. Sienese and Florentine Masters of the Sixteenth Century. Langton Douglas & Tancred Borenius (eds). London, 1914. Blue cl (shelfwear). *Washton.* $40/£26

CROWE, J. H. V. General Smuts' Campaign in East Africa. London, 1918. Frontis port, 4 fldg maps. Red cl (spine faded). *Maggs.* $234/£150

CROWE, JOHN. The Book of Trout Lore. NY: A.S. Barnes, 1947. 1st ed. Blue cl. Fine in pict dj (chipped). *Biscotti.* $25/£16

CROWE, SYLVIA. Garden Design. Country Life, 1965. 3rd imp. VG in dj. *Hadley.* $39/£25

CROWE, SYLVIA. Tomorrow's Landscape. London: Architectural Press, 1956. Fine. *Quest.* $25/£16

CROWELL, PERS. Beau Dare. NY: Whittlesey House, 1946. 1st ed. VG (sl shelfworn). *October Farm.* $25/£16

CROWLEY, ALEISTER. The Blue Equinox. Detroit: Universal Pub, 1919. 1st ed. Color frontis. Dec cvr (spine lt chipped). VG- (10pp mkd). *Middle Earth.* $295/£189

CROWLEY, ALEISTER. The Collected Works of Aleister Crowley. Soc for the Propagation of Religious Truth, 1905-07. 1st ed. 3 vols. Black camel hair. VG in paper wrappers. *Middle Earth.* $800/£513

CROWLEY, ALEISTER. Jephthah and Other Mysteries Lyrical and Dramatic. London: Kegan Paul, 1899. 1st Eng ed. Internally Sound. (Bds atrocious.) *Clearwater.* $78/£50

CROWLEY, ALEISTER. Little Essays Toward Truth. London: Private Issue, 1938. 1st ed. Foldout. Dec cvr. (Name), o/w Fine. *Middle Earth.* $295/£189

CROWLEY, ALEISTER. Moonchild. Mandrake, 1929. 1st ed. (Cvrs sl mkd, spine head rubbed), o/w VG. *Words Etc.* $70/£45

CROWLEY, ALEISTER. Moonchild. London: Mandrake, 1929. 1st ed. (Brn spot ep), else VG in VG dj (lacking 1/2-inch spine head; sm chip spine base & upper left corner fr panel). *Certo*. $300/£192

CROWLEY, ALEISTER. The Stratagem and Other Stories. London: Mandrake, (1929). 1st ed. Black cl-backed gold 'snakeskin' textured bds, ptd paper label. Very Nice. *Cady*. $50/£32

CROWLEY, ALEISTER. The Stratagem and Other Stories. London: Mandrake, (1929). 1st ed. VG (bds sl bowed; fep browned) in dj (browned; spine ends sl chipped). *Certo*. $225/£144

CROWLEY, JOHN. Beasts. GC: Doubleday, 1976. 1st ed. (Lower corners bumped), else Fine in dj. *Other Worlds*. $30/£19

CROWLEY, JOHN. The Deep. GC: Doubleday, (1975). 1st ed, 1st bk. Fine in VG dj (internal repair; lt crease fr panel). *Between The Covers*. $175/£112

CROWLEY, MART. The Boys in the Band. NY: FSG, (1968). 1st ed. VG in Nice dj (nick). *Ash*. $148/£95

CROWQUILL, ALFRED (ed). Phantasmagoria of Fun. London, 1843. 2 vols. Mod 1/2 brn levant, orig cl backstrips bound in. (Lib stamps tp versos, bkpls.) *Swann**. $103/£66

CROWTHER, ROBERT. Pop-Up Machines. London: Walker, 1988. 1st ed. 9 x 10 3/4. 6pp; 28 working pop-ups. Glossy bds. Fine. *Cattermole*. $50/£32

CROXALL, SAMUEL. The Fables of Aesop. London: J.F. & C. Rivington, 1786. 13th ed. Frontis, (xxxii),329,(iii)pp (lacks last 2 ll index). Mod full calf, gilt. *Hollett*. $101/£65

CRUIKSHANK, GEORGE. Cruikshankiana, an Assemblage of the Most Celebrated Works of George Cruikshank. London: Thomas McLean, n.d. 50 (of 68) folio plts. Wraps (soiled). *Metropolitan**. $69/£44

CRUIKSHANK, GEORGE. George Cruikshank's Omnibus. Laman Blanchard (ed). London: Bell & Daldy, 1869. 'New Ed.' Very Nice (bkpl). *Reese*. $35/£22

CRUIKSHANK, GEORGE. My Sketch Book. London: Charles Tilt, (1833-1836). Orig 9 parts. 1st ed, w/later state of 2nd plt in Pt 5; wrappers of pts 2, 7 varying from those described by Cohn. 37 hand-colored plts. Contents VG. Orig illus wraps (several parts skillfully rebacked; few cvrs soiled, stained; tears, creases). Later full morocco pull-off case. *Waverly**. $253/£162

CRUIKSHANK, GEORGE. My Sketchbook. (London): George Cruikshank, 1834-6. 1st ed in bk form. Engr tp, 36 hand-colored plts. Aeg. Full polished calf, gilt. (Upper joint cracking, spine chip), o/w VG. *Reese*. $250/£160

Cruise of the Eight Hundred to and Through Palestine. NY: Christian Herald, 1905. 1st ed. 212 photo plts, 4 color plts. (Sl rubbed), o/w VG. *Worldwide*. $35/£22

CRUMLEY, JAMES. Dancing Bear. NY: Random House, 1983. 1st ed. Fine in dj (crease back panel). *Mordida*. $65/£42

CRUMLEY, JAMES. The Mexican Tree Duck. Bristol, England: Scorpion Press, 1993. One of 75 numbered, signed. *Murder By The Book*. $125/£80

CRUMLEY, JAMES. One to Count Cadence. NY: Random House, (1969). 1st ed, 1st bk. NF in dj (short tear). *Captain's Bookshelf*. $250/£160

CRUMLEY, JAMES. One to Count Cadence. Random House, 1969. 1st ed. (Sm name label, date fr pastedown), else Fine in Fine dj. *Certo*. $200/£128

CRUMLEY, JAMES. The Pigeon Shoot. Neville, 1987. One of 350 numbered, signed. Fine in mylar dj. *Certo*. $125/£80

CRUMLEY, JAMES. The Pigeon Shoot. Santa Barbara: Neville, 1987. 1st ed. One of 350 numbered, signed. VF; no dj as issued. *Mordida*. $125/£80

CRUMLEY, JAMES. Whores. Missoula, MT: Dennis McMillan, 1988. 1st ed. Ltd to 475 signed, numbered. Fine in dj. *Murder By The Book*. $100/£64

CRUMLEY, JAMES. The Wrong Case. Random House, 1975. 1st ed. Fine in Fine dj (edges sl dknd). *Certo*. $375/£240

CRUMP, SPENCER. Black Riot in Los Angeles, the Story of the Watts Tragedy. L.A.: Trans-Anglo, (1966). 1st ed. Frontis. White cl. Fine in pict dj. *Argonaut*. $75/£48

CRUMP, SPENCER. Redwoods, Iron Horses and the Pacific. L.A.: Trans-Anglo, (1963). 1st ed. Fine in dj (lt chipped). *Argonaut*. $40/£26

CRUMPTON, H. J. and W. B. The Adventures of Two Alabama Boys.... Montgomery: Paragon, 1912. 1st ed. (Shelfworn, edgeworn), else Good. Howes C937. *Brown*. $125/£80

CRUNDEN, JOHN. Convenient and Ornamental Architecture Consisting of the Original Designs. London, 1791. 70 plts complete. Leather, bds. (Staining; lg losses on bds, bumped, hinges split.) *Metropolitan**. $400/£256

CUADRA, PABLO. The Jaguar and the Moon. Thomas Merton (trans). Greensboro: Unicorn, 1971. 1st ed. One of 500 in bds. Fine. *Turlington*. $100/£64

CULBERTSON, ANNE VIRGINIA. Banjo Talks. Indianapolis: Bobbs Merrill, (1905). 1st ed. (White spine lettering rubbed), else Fine in pict cl. *Captain's Bookshelf*. $125/£80

CULBERTSON, THADDEUS A. et al. Journal of an Expedition to the Mauvaises Terres and the Upper Missouri in 1850. BAE Bulletin 147. Washington, 1952. Ptd wrappers. Howes C941. *Ginsberg*. $50/£32

CULLEN, COUNTEE. The Ballad of the Brown Girl. NY: Harper, 1927. Trade ed. Fine in box (worn, piece missing bottom edge). *Beasley*. $125/£80

CULLEN, COUNTEE. The Lost Zoo. NY: Harper, 1940. 1st ed. Charles Sebree (illus). 6 1/4 x 9 1/4. 72pp. VG. *Cattermole*. $150/£96

CULLEN, COUNTEE. One Way to Heaven. NY: Harpers, 1932. 1st ed. (Sm inscrip, spine label sl rubbed), else NF in VG dj (price-clipped, faded spine, extrems sm chips). *Between The Covers*. $700/£449

CULLEN, THOMAS F. The Spirit of Serra. North Providence, ca 1935. 1st ed. Frontis. VG. *Turpen*. $35/£22

CULLEN, WILLIAM. First Lines of the Practice of Physic. NY: L. Nichols, 1801. 2 vols in 1. 326; 294,(x)pp. Contemp full calf, black leather spine label. Good (browned, sl foxed; sl worn, scuffed). *Baltimore**. $110/£71

CULLISON, IRENE MARGARET. Mother Goose Finger Plays. Phila: George W. Jacobs, 1915. 4to. Tipped-in color frontis, 32pp. Cl-backed pict bds. Fine. *Hollett*. $101/£65

CULPEPER, NICHOLAS. The British Herbal and Family Physician to Which Is Added a Dispensatory.... Halifax: Garlick, 1837. In two parts. 410; 317pp; 59 plts (52 hand-colored). Orig tree calf (later rebacked w/gilt calf, orig eps). Very Clean. *Goodrich*. $595/£381

CULPEPER, NICHOLAS. The Complete Herbal.... London: Thomas Kelly, 1845. (4),(1)-398,(4)pp, 20 color plts, port (foxed, offset to guard; lt tanning margins of text and plts). Old calf, bds (worn). Good. *Reese*. $175/£112

CULPEPER, NICHOLAS. The Complete Herbal...English Physician Enlarged. London, 1835. New ed. Contemp 1/2 calf, marbled bds. Good (sl used). *Gretton*. $117/£75

CULPEPPER, NICHOLAS. Culpepper's English Family Phisician.... London: W. Locke, 1792. 2 vols in 1. 73 b/w plts bound in at rear (dampstains to tops of plts; hasty color to tps, frontis; crude binding, few repairs). *Metropolitan**. $69/£44

CULVER, FRANCIS BARNUM. Blooded Horses of Colonial Days. Balt: The Author, 1922. Spiral binding, stiff black wraps, ptd title label. Nice. *Bohling.* $18/£12

CUMBERLAND, MARTEN. The Crime School. London: Eldon Press, (1949). 1st ed. (Pg edges lt spotted), o/w Fine in dj. *Mordida.* $45/£29

CUMHAIL, P. W. Investing in Clocks and Watches. NY: Clarkson N. Potter, (1967). 1st Amer ed. Brownish-gray cl, VG in dj. *Weber.* $15/£10

CUMING, FORTESCUE. Sketches of a Tour to the Western Country, Through the States of Ohio and Kentucky. Pittsburgh, 1810. 1st ed. 12mo. Contemp tree sheep (skillfully rebacked, partially retipped; bound w/o feps). Cl fldg case. Howes C947. *Swann*.* $1,380/£885

CUMING, FORTESCUE. Sketches of a Tour to the Western Country. Reuben Gold Thwaites (ed). Cleveland: A.H. Clark, 1904. 1st ed thus. Teg. (Spine rubbed, faded), else VG. Howes C947. *Cahan.* $85/£54

CUMMING, GORDON. At Home in Fiji. London: William Blackwood, 1881. 2nd ed. 2 vols. ix,293; viii,323pp; 7 full-pg photo plts, fldg map rear vol 1. Contemp 1/2 calf, marbled bds. Good (extrems sl rubbed, lt spotting). *Sotheran.* $273/£175

CUMMING, R. GORDON. Five Years of a Hunter's Life in the Far Interior of South Africa. NY: Harper, 1850. 1st Amer ed. 2 vols. Pub's cl (sl worn; foxed). *Oinonen*.* $70/£45

CUMMING, ROBERT. Picture Fictions. N.p.: Robert Cumming, 1973. 2nd ptg, 1st bk. NF in pict stiff wrappers. *Cahan.* $30/£19

CUMMING, WILLIAM P. The Southeast in Early Maps. Princeton, NJ, 1958. VG in dj (stained, worn). *King.* $350/£224

CUMMINGS, E. E. CIOPW. NY: Covici Friede, 1931. One of 391 numbered, signed. 4to. Burlap cvrd bds. Nice (well-repaired fr joint). *Beasley.* $750/£481

CUMMINGS, E. E. Eimi. NY: Covici Friede, 1933. One of 1381 numbered, signed. Fine. *Lenz.* $275/£176

CUMMINGS, E. E. Eimi. (NY: Covici, Friede, 1933.) One 1381 numbered, signed. Yellow cl. Fine in dj (sl edgewear, few internally repaired tears). Bkpls, initials on dj of Paul Horgan. *Antic Hay.* $475/£304

CUMMINGS, E. E. Fairy Tales. NY: Harcourt, Brace & World, (1965). 1st ed. John Eaton (illus). (Spine lt sunned), else VF in pict dj (sl tear). *Bromer.* $85/£54

CUMMINGS, E. E. Is 5. NY: Boni & Liveright, 1936. 1st ed. VG (lacks dj). *Warren.* $85/£54

CUMMINGS, E. E. Santa Claus, A Morality. NY: Holt, (1946). 1st ed, trade issue (1500 thus). Fine in VG dj (edgewear, sm chips spine extrems). *Reese.* $40/£26

CUMMINGS, E. E. Santa Claus. Paris: Editions de l'Herne, 1974. 9 pencil-signed etchings by Alexander Calder. Fine in dec clamshell box (sl sunned). *Metropolitan*.* $3,105/£1,990

CUMMINGS, JACOB A. An Introduction to Ancient and Modern Geography.... Boston: Cummings & Hilliard, 1823. 9th ed. 340,8pp; 1 plt. Marbled bds, calf spine. (Ex-lib.) *Hudson.* $90/£58

CUMMINS, SARAH J. Autobiography and Reminiscences of.... (Freewater, OR: The Author, 1914.) Port. VG + in gray ptd wraps. Howes C951. *Bohling.* $65/£42

CUMSTON, CHARLES. An Introduction to the History of Medicine to the Time of the Pharaohs. NY, 1926. 1st ed. VG. *Fye.* $75/£48

CUNARD, NANCY. Grand Man. London, 1954. 1st Eng ed. Good (edges spotted, faded, bumped) in dj (nicked). *Clearwater.* $39/£25

CUNARD, NANCY. Releve into Maquis. Derby: Grasshopper Press, 1944. 1st ed. Ltd to 250. Single folded leaf. (Sl creased), o/w Nice. *Ash.* $31/£20

CUNDALL, H. M. Birket Foster R.W.S. London: A&C Black, 1906. Frontis port, 73 color plts, guards, 78 monochrome plts, all hors-texte. Teg, rest uncut. Later crimson 1/2 calf, gilt spine, raised cords. Brilliant. *Europa.* $226/£145

CUNDALL, H. M. Birket Foster. A&C Black, 1906. 1st ed. Frontis port (edges chipped), 73 color plts. Teg. Dec cl (upper joint split; sl soiled, spine chipped, sl loss). *Edwards.* $94/£60

CUNDALL, H. M. (ed). William Callow, an Autobiography. A&C Black, 1908. 1st ed. Frontis port, 22 color plts. Teg. Dec cl (Bkpl, feps lt spotted; sl chipped.) *Edwards.* $44/£28

CUNDALL, H. M. (ed). William Callow. R.W.S., F.R.G.S. London: A&C Black, 1908. 1st ed. 22 color plts, 9 monochrome plts. Dec cl, gilt. VG. *Hollett.* $117/£75

CUNDALL, JOSEPH. A Brief History of Wood Engraving from Its Invention. London: Sampson, Low, Marston, 1895. 1st ed. Frontis, x,132pp. Teg. Pict cl, gilt, beveled edges. (Fep corner clipped), else VG. *Connolly.* $35/£22

CUNDALL, JOSEPH. A Brief History of Wood-Engraving from Its Invention. London, 1895. 1st ed. 132pp. VG in dec cl. *Moss.* $41/£26

CUNEO, JOHN R. Robert Rogers of the Rangers. NY: OUP, 1959. 1st ed. VG (lt pencilling) in dj. *Lien.* $35/£22

CUNNINGHAM, ALEXANDER. History of Great Britain.... London: A. Strahan & T. Cadell, 1787. Apparent 1st ed. 2 vols. All edges speckled red/blue, marbled eps. Contemp speckled calf (ends starting, sl corner wear), smooth spines (chipped, scuffed) gilt-tooled in 6 compartments, black leather labels. Contents VG. *Waverly*.* $220/£141

CUNNINGHAM, ALLAN. The Life of Sir David Wilkie.... London: John Murray, 1843. 3 vols. 1/2 leather (very worn, 1 cvr detached). Contents VG. *Yudkin*.* $30/£19

CUNNINGHAM, C. Victorian and Edwardian Town Halls. London: RKP, 1981. Sound in dj. *Ars Artis.* $55/£35

CUNNINGHAM, CAROLINE. The Talking Stone. NY: Knopf, 1939. 1st ed. Richard Floethe (illus). 6 1/4 x 9 1/2. 118pp. VG. *Cattermole.* $20/£13

CUNNINGHAM, CHARLES HENRY. The Audiencia in the Spanish Colonies. Berkeley: Univ of CA, 1919. 1st ed. Blue cl, gilt-lettered spine. Fine (sig). *Argonaut.* $150/£96

CUNNINGHAM, E. V. The Case of the Russian Diplomat. NY: Holt, Rinehart & Winston, 1978. 1st ed. Fine in NF dj. *Janus.* $20/£13

CUNNINGHAM, E. V. Sally. NY: William Morrow, 1967. 1st ed. Fine in Fine dj. *Janus.* $25/£16

CUNNINGHAM, EDITH PERKINS. Owls Nest, a Tribute to Sarah Elliott Perkins. Privately ptd, 1907. 3/4 morocco, 5 raised bands, gilt. VG (bkpl; edgewear). Howes C593. *Bohling.* $60/£38

CUNNINGHAM, FRANK. General Stand Watie's Confederate Indians. San Antonio: Naylor, (1959). 1st ed. NF in VG dj (chipped). *Mcgowan.* $125/£80

CUNNINGHAM, IMOGEN. Imogen Cunningham: Photographs. Margery Mann (intro). Seattle/London: Univ of WA, 1971. 1st ed, 2nd ptg. 94 full-pg b/w photos. (Owner stamp), else Fine in dj. *Cahan.* $75/£48

CUNNINGHAM, PETER. The Story of Nell Gwyn: and the Sayings of Charles the Second. Bradbury & Evans, 1852. 1st ed. xi,(i),212pp, 8-pg pub's list. Cl simulating leather, gilt. *Cox.* $47/£30

CUNNINGHAM, PHILLIS and ALAN MANSFIELD. English Costume for Sports and Outdoor Recreation. Adam & Charles, 1969. 1st ed. Color frontis, 64 plts. Dj (sl chipped). *Edwards.* $47/£30

CUNNINGHAME GRAHAM, R. B. See GRAHAM, R. B. CUNNINGHAME

CUNYNGHAME, HENRY. On the Theory and Practice of Art-Enameling upon Metals. Westminster: Archibald Constable, 1899. 1st ed. 135pp. (Spine dknd, lt soil), else VG. *Hermitage*. $50/£32

Cups and Their Customs. (By Henry Porter and George E. Roberts.) London: John van Voorst, 1863. 1st ed. Hand-colored extra tp, (2),vi,52pp. Glazed pict bds, gilt. (Neatly rebacked, eps rejointed, gilt faded), o/w Nice. *Ash*. $70/£45

Curiosities of Human Nature. (By Samuel Griswold Goodrich.) Boston: Bradbury, Soden, 1843. 1st ed. 2 vols. Sm 8vo. Wood engr frontis, vi,320pp + 2pp list lower wrappers. Dec paper wrappers (ink sig fr cvrs; dusted; vol 1 spine tender). Fine set in mod handmade box. *Hobbyhorse*. $425/£272

CURL STEVENS, JAMES. The Victorian Celebration of Death. David & Charles, 1972. 1st ed. VG in dj. *Hadley*. $31/£20

CURLE, ALEXANDER. The Treasure of Trapprain. Glasgow: Maclehose, Jackson, 1923. 1st ed. 41 full-pg plts. (Eps dknd from dj flaps), o/w VG. *New Hampshire**. $75/£48

CURLE, RICHARD. The Last Twelve Years of Joseph Conrad. London: Sampson Low, Marston, 1928. 1st British ed. Port. (Sm ink note), o/w Nice in dj (tanned, edgetorn). *Reese*. $30/£19

CURLING, JONATHAN. Janus Weathercock. The Life of Thomas Griffiths Wainewright. 1794-1847. London: Thomas Nelson, 1938. 1st ed. Top edge stained purple. Pink cl, gilt. (Inscrip; unevenly faded.) *Maggs*. $39/£25

CURNOCK, GEORGE C. (ed). Hospitals Under Fire but the Lamp Still Burns. London: Allen & Unwin, (1941). Advance rev copy of 1st ed, so imprinted. VG in ptd wrappers (extrems tanned). *Reese*. $35/£22

CURRAN, DALE. Dupree Blues. NY: Knopf, 1948. 1st ed. Fine (fr hinge starting) in dj (lt used, chipped). *Beasley*. $30/£19

CURRENT, KAREN. Photography and the Old West. NY: Abrams, 1986. Fine in dj. *Cahan*. $40/£26

CURREY, LLOYD W. and DENNIS G. KRUSKA. Bibliography of Yosemite, the Central and the Southern High Sierra, and the Big Trees, 1839-1900. L.A./Palo Alto: Dawson's Book Shop/William P. Wreden, 1992. One of 300 ptd. Cl spine. *Dawson*. $250/£160

CURRIE, BARTON and AUGUSTIN McHUGH. Officer 666. NY: H. K. Fly, (1912). 1st ed. Frontis, 3 plts. Dec cvr. Good. *Hayman*. $35/£22

CURRIE, BARTON. Fishers of Books. Boston: Little, Brown, 1931. 1st trade ed. Label. Fine in VG pict dj. *Macdonnell*. $65/£42

CURRIER, ERNEST M. Marks of Early American Silversmiths. Kathryn C. Buhler (ed). Portland, ME, 1938. Teg, partly uncut. (Corners worn.) *Argosy*. $125/£80

CURRIER, THOMAS FRANKLIN and ELEANOR M. TILTON. A Bibliography of Oliver Wendell Holmes. NY Univ, 1953. 1st ed. Frontis port. Fine. *Glaser*. $125/£80

CURRIER, THOMAS FRANKLIN and ELEANOR M. TILTON. A Bibliography of Oliver Wendell Holmes. NY, 1953. 1st ed. VG. *Fye*. $100/£64

CURRY, GEORGE. George Curry, 1861-1947: An Autobiography. H.B. Hening (ed). (Albuquerque): Univ of NM, (1958). 1st ed. Port. VF in dj. *Argonaut*. $45/£29

CURRY, JABEZ LAMAR MONROE. Civil History of the Government of the Confederate States with Some Personal Reminiscences. Richmond, VA: B.F. Johnson, 1901. 1st ed. VG (extrems sl worn). *Mcgowan*. $45/£29

CURTIES, HENRY. The Queen's Gate Mystery. Boston: Dana Estes, 1908. 1st Amer ed. Fine in pict cvrs (lacks dj). *Mordida*. $65/£42

CURTIN, JEREMIAH. Creation Myths of Primitive Americans. Boston: Little, Brown, 1898. 1st ed. 532pp. (Extrems worn), o/w VG. *New Hampshire**. $80/£51

CURTIN, L. S. M. Healing Herbs of the Upper Rio Grande. Santa Fe: Laboratory of Anthropology, 1947. 1st ed. Good in dj (worn, chipped). *Dumont*. $100/£64

Curtis's Botanical Magazine. Vol 136 of Series. London, 1910. 60 hand-colored plts. 3/4 leather (call tag remnants spine; lib bkpl). VG. *Metropolitan**. $600/£385

CURTIS, CHARLES H. Orchids. London: Putnam, 1950. 1st ed. 30 color plts, 40 b/w photo plts. Grn cl, gilt. VG. *Price*. $65/£42

CURTIS, CHARLES P. and RICHARD C. Hunting in Africa East and West. Boston, 1925. 1st ed. (Sl browned; spine sl discolored.) *Edwards*. $70/£45

CURTIS, EDWARD. Indian Days of the Long Ago. Yonkers-on-Hudson: World, 1915. 2nd ptg. Signed. Fine. *Oregon*. $325/£208

CURTIS, GEORGE TICKNOR. Life of Daniel Webster. NY: D. Appleton, 1870. 3rd ed. 2 vols. Contemp 3/4 morocco (sl worn). Attractive. *Boswell*. $250/£160

CURTIS, GEORGE WILLIAM. Nile Notes of a Howadji. (By George William Curtis.) NY: Harper, 1851. 1st ed. 2 tps, 320pp (foxing). Marbled eps. 3/4 blue morocco (orig cl cvrs bound in at rear, spine sl chipped), 5 raised bands. *Archaeologia*. $85/£54

CURTIS, JOHN. Harvey's Views on the Use of the Circulation of Blood. NY, 1915. Frontis (loose). (Ex-lib.) *Goodrich*. $45/£29

CURTIS, MATTOON M. The Book of Snuff and Snuff Boxes. NY, (1935). (Corners bumped, sl wear.) *King*. $35/£22

CURTIS, MATTOON M. The Story of Snuff and Snuff Boxes. NY, 1935. 1st ed. 59 plts. Top edges red. VG. *New Hampshire**. $70/£45

CURTIS, NATALIE (ed). The Indians' Book. NY: Harper, 1907. 1st ed. Dec tan cl (sl rubbed, worn), paper spine label (corner chipped). NF. *Harrington*. $235/£151

CURTIS, NATALIE (comp). Songs and Tales from the Dark Continent.... NY: G. Schirmer, (1920). 1st ed. 8 plts. Dec ivory cl. VG. *Petrilla*. $100/£64

CURTIS, NEWTON MARTIN. From Bull Run to Chancellorsville. NY, 1906. 1st ed. Signed. Gilt edge. Pict cl. (Cvr lt spotting), o/w VG + . *Pratt*. $85/£54

CURTIS, PAUL A. American Game Shooting. NY: Dutton, 1927. 1st ed. VG. *Bowman*. $20/£13

CURTIS, PAUL A. Sportsmen All. NY, (1938). One of 950. 12 plts. (Lg bkpl.) *Kane**. $100/£64

CURTIS, PAUL A. Sportsmen All. NY: Derrydale, (1938). One of 950 numbered. Gilt-dec cl (sl worn). *Oinonen**. $80/£51

CURTIS, PAUL A. Sportsmen All. NY: Derrydale, (1938). Ltd to 950. Fine. *Truepenny*. $95/£61

CURTIS, PAUL A. Sportsmen All. NY: Derrydale, 1938. 1st ed. #704/950. Black cl, gilt. (Gilt sl dull), else Fine. *Cummins*. $100/£64

CURTISS, DANIEL S. Western Portraiture and Emigrant's Guide. NY, 1852. 1st ed. 351,18pp; fldg map. Howes C967. *Ginsberg*. $375/£240

CURTISS, DANIEL S. Western Portraiture, and Emigrant's Guide: A Description of Wisconsin, Illinois, and Iowa. NY: J.H. Colton, 1852. 1st ed. 351,18(ads)pp; fldg map tipped on fep (few tears at folds). Good (bkpl; spine extrems worn). Howes C967. *Wantagh*. $225/£144

CURTISS, DANIEL S. Western Portraiture, and Emigrants' Guide: A Description of Wisconsin, Illinois, and Iowa. NY: J.H. Colton, 1852. 1st ed. 351pp + 18pp ads, lg fldg map. (Cl faded; inner fr hinge cracked.) Howes C967. *M & S.* $250/£160

CURWEN, H. A History of Booksellers Old and New. C&W, (1873). 1st ed. 483pp. Gilt-dec cl. Good. *Moss.* $62/£40

CURWOOD, JAMES OLIVER. The Country Beyond. Cosmopolitan, 1922. 1st ed. VG+ in VG+ dj. *Authors Of West.* $50/£32

CURZON, ROBERT. Visits to Monasteries in the Levant. John Murray, 1881. 6th ed. xx,(2),373pp + 32pp pub's cat (stamp 1/2-title); 18 wood engrs. Maroon cl (sl rubbed), gilt. *Cox.* $39/£25

CUSHING, FRANK HAMILTON. My Adventures in Zuni. Santa Fe: Peripatetic, (1941). One of 400. VG+ in dj (price-clipped, dknd, sl chipped). *Bohling.* $375/£240

CUSHING, FRANK. The Nation of the Willows. Flagstaff: Northland, (1965). 1st ed. Fine in Fine dj. *Oregon.* $45/£29

CUSHING, HARVEY and LEO M. DAVIDOFF. Studies in Acromegaly. (Chicago, 1927.) Uncut. (Ex-lib.) Wrappers. *Argosy.* $50/£32

CUSHING, HARVEY. A Bibliography of the Writings of Harvey Cushing.... Springfield, 1939. Ltd to 500. Good (ex-lib, usual mks). *Goodrich.* $95/£61

CUSHING, HARVEY. A Bio-Bibliography of Andreas Vesalius. NY: Schuman, 1943. Ltd to 800. 1/4 grn morocco, linen bds, armorial crest. (Lt rubbing), else NF. *Goodrich.* $495/£317

CUSHING, HARVEY. From a Surgeon's Journal. Phila: Little Brown, 1936. Fine in dj (tattered, worn). *Goodrich.* $115/£74

CUSHING, HARVEY. Harvey Cushing's Seventieth Birthday Party.... Springfield: Thomas, 1939. Ltd to 350. (Ex-lib.) *Goodrich.* $75/£48

CUSHING, HARVEY. The Life of Sir William Osler. Oxford, 1925. 1st ed, 3rd imp. 2 vols. (Ex-lib; cl rubbed, mkd, 1-inch chip spine vol 1.) *Goodrich.* $55/£35

CUSHING, HARVEY. The Life of Sir William Osler. Oxford, 1925. 1st ed. 2 vols. (Cl rubbed.) *Maggs.* $70/£45

CUSHING, HARVEY. The Life of Sir William Osler. Oxford, 1925. 1st ed, 2nd imp. 2 vols. VG (lt rubbed). *Goodrich.* $125/£80

CUSHING, HARVEY. Papers Relating to the Pituitary Body, Hypothalamus and Parasympathetic Nervous System. Springfield, 1932. 1st ed. Good (cvr worn, faded). *Doctor's Library.* $400/£256

CUSHING, HARVEY. Papers Relating to the Pituitary Body, Hypothalamus and Parasympathetic Nervous System. Springfield: Charles C. Thomas, 1932. 1st collected ed. Grn cl. Fine. *Glaser.* $450/£288

CUSHING, HARVEY. The Pituitary Body and Its Disorders. Phila: Lippincott, (1912). 1st ed, 1st issue. 1st bk. 8vo. Color frontis, x,341pp; lg fldg plt. Red cl. NF (stamp, sig; edges sl shelfworn). *Glaser.* $650/£417

CUSHING, HARVEY. Studies in Intracranial Physiology and Surgery.... OUP, 1926. VG. *Goodrich.* $495/£317

CUSHMAN, CLARA M. Tientsin Scribbles. Leominster, MA: Boutwell, Owens, 1925. 1st ed. (Lacks fep; cl sl rubbed), o/w VG. *Worldwide.* $18/£12

CUSHNY, A. R. The Action and Uses in Medicine of Digitalis and Its Allies. 1925. Frontis port. (Pencil mks, sig, some sections cracked, spine worn.) *Whitehart.* $28/£18

CUSHNY, A. R. Biological Relations of Optically Isomeric Substances. Balt, 1926. 1st ed. VG in orig wrappers (worn). *Argosy.* $45/£29

CUSS, T. P. CAMERER. The Camerer Cuss Book of Antique Watches. Suffolk: Antique Collectors' Club, (1976). Rev, enlgd ed. 8 color plts. VG in dj (sm tear). *Weber.* $30/£19

CUSSLER, CLIVE. Deep Six. NY: S&S, (1984). 1st ed. Fine in dj. *Antic Hay.* $25/£16

CUSSLER, CLIVE. Treasure. NY: S&S, 1988. 1st ed. Fine in dj. *Mordida.* $45/£29

CUSSLER, CLIVE. Vixen 03. NY: Viking, 1978. 1st ed. Fine in dj. *Mordida.* $65/£42

CUST, LIONEL. The Cenci, A Study in Murder. London: Mandrake, 1929. Cl-backed dec bds (chipped). Usable. *Boswell.* $50/£32

CUSTER, ELIZABETH B. Boots and Saddles, or Life in Dakota with General Custer. NY: Harper, 1885. 1st ed. Bibliographers report 1st issue lacked both port and sm map; this copy apparently from 2nd issue or unrecorded variant issue, as it lacks map w/no evidence of removal. Frontis port, 312pp (lt aged, ink handstamp eps). Brn coated eps. Brn pict cl. Cvrs VG (sl rubbed, sl frayed). Howes C980. *Baltimore*.* $50/£32

CUSTER, ELIZABETH B. Boots and Saddles. NY: Harper, 1885. 312pp. Dec cvr. Good (hinge cracks). Howes C980. *Scribe's Perch*.* $28/£18

CUSTER, ELIZABETH B. Boots and Saddles. NY: Harper, 1885. 1st ed, 2nd issue (w/frontis and map). Pict bds. VG. Howes C980. *Archer.* $75/£48

CUSTER, ELIZABETH B. Following the Guidon. NY: Harper, 1899. 1st ed. Grn cl stamped in gilt/blue/red/white/black. Very Nice (ink inscrip; lt wear, abrasion). *Hermitage.* $100/£64

CUTCLIFFE, H. C. The Art of Trout Fishing on Rapid Streams. London: Sampson Low, Marston, n.d. (c. 1900). VG. *Hollett.* $70/£45

CUTLER, B. D. Sir James M. Barrie, a Bibliography.... NY: Greenberg, 1931. Ltd to 1000 numbered. Color frontis. Unopened. Canvas-backed bds (spine sl faded), paper spine label. *Maggs.* $62/£40

CUTLER, CARL. Greyhounds of the Sea. NY: Putnam, 1930. 1st ed. Blue cl (faded). *Eldred's*.* $33/£21

CUTLER, CARL. The Story of the American Clipper Ship, Greyhounds of the Sea. NY: Halcyon House, 1930. 1st ed. 8 color, 3 duotone, 31 b/w plts; 13 plts dwgs. VG. *Worldwide.* $28/£18

CUTLER, CHARLES D. Northern Painting from Pucelle to Bruegel. NY, 1968. Good in dj. *Washton.* $40/£26

CUTLER, WILLIAM P. and JULIA P. Life, Journals, and Correspondence of Rev. Manasseh Cutler, LL.D. Cincinnati: Clarke, 1888. 1st ed. 2 vols. (12),524; (4),495,(10),(2)pp. *Ginsberg.* $250/£160

CUTOLO, SALVATORE R. Bellevue Is My Home. NY, 1956. 1st ed. VG in dj (worn). *Doctor's Library.* $40/£26

CUTTER, CHARLES. Cutter's Guide to the Hot Springs of Arkansas. St. Louis, 1890. 61,(3)pp; fldg map. Orig ptd wraps. *Wantagh.* $65/£42

CUTTER, CHARLES. Guide to the Hot Springs of Arkansas. St. Louis, 1882. 2 fldg maps. Ptd wrappers (chipped, worn), recent cl case. *Maggs.* $31/£20

CUTTER, DONALD C. Malaspina in California. (SF): John Howell-Books, 1960. 1st ed. Ltd to 1000 ptd. Frontis map, 18 plts (2 color), 2 fldg tables. Gilt-lettered, dec tan cl. VF. *Argonaut.* $90/£58

CUTTER, DONALD C. Malaspina in California. SF, 1960. Ltd to 1000 ptd by Lawton Kennedy. Frontis map, fldg table. Partially unopened. Gilt cl. VF. *Reese.* $125/£80

CUTTING, S. The Fire Ox and Other Years. NY, 1940. 1st ed. 3 maps, 3 color plts. (Cl sl mkd.) *Wheldon & Wesley.* $78/£50

CUTTS, EDWARD L. Scenes and Characters of the Middle Ages. London: Simpkin et al, 1926. 6th ed. *Boswell.* $45/£29

CUVIER, GEORGES L. C. The Animal Kingdom. London: Geo. B. Whittaker, 1827-1835. 16 vols. 11 hand-colored, 787 uncolored etched plts. (Sl foxing.) Contemp 1/2 calf (sl rubbed, sl variations). Nice set. *Metropolitan**. $718/£460

Cyclopedia of Automobile Engineering. Chicago: Amer Technical Soc, 1912. 4 vols. Recent red cl. VG. *Waverly**. $99/£63

D

D' ORLEANS, HENRY. From Tonkin to India. Hamley Bent (trans). NY: Dodd, Mead, 1898. 1st Amer ed. Frontis, xii,467pp; fldg map. Orange-brn cl w/silver lettering & pict on cvrs. (Slight wear), else VG. *Terramedia.* $150/£96

D'ANCEMONT, R. The Historical and Unrevealed Memoirs of the Political and Private Life of Napoleon Buonaparte. N.p. (London), 1820. 3rd ed. 172pp (bkpl); 2 facs. Teg. 3/4 red leather (spine top chipped), gilt. *King.* $125/£80

D'ANNUNZIO, GABRIELE. The Child of Pleasure. Arthur Symons (trans). London: Heinemann, 1898. 1st ed in English. VG (eps sl foxed, bkstore label fep, offsetting fr pastedown) in cl-cvrd bds. *Lame Duck.* $65/£42

D'ANNUNZIO, GABRIELE. Episcopo and Company. Myrta Leonora Jones (trans). Chicago: Herbert S. Stone, 1896. 1st ed in English. xiii,(i),122,(iii)pp. Teg, deckle-edged. Gilt grn cl. NF. *Blue Mountain.* $95/£61

D'ANTIGNAC, MUNROE. Georgia's Navy, 1861. Griffin, GA: Goen Printing, 1945. 1st ed. NF in ptd wrappers. *Mcgowan.* $37/£24

D'ANVILLE, MONSIEUR. Compendium of Ancient Geography. NY: M'Dermut and D.D. Auden, 1814. 1st US ed. 2 vols. Red cl over bds. NF. *Old London.* $100/£64

D'ARBLAY, MADAME. The Diary and Letters of Madame D'Arblay. Muriel Masefield (ed). Routledge, 1931. Good (sig; spine bumped, sl sunned; lacks dj). *Tiger.* $25/£16

D'ARBLAY, MADAME. The Diary and Letters of.... Charlotte Barrett (ed). London: Sonnenschein, 1893. Rpt. 4 vols. 586; 601; 592; 486pp. Blue cl (sl rubbed). VG set. *Second Life.* $150/£96

D'ARCH SMITH, TIMOTHY. Love in Earnest. London, 1970. 1st ed. NF (spine side sl creased) in dj (price-clipped, sl rubbed). *Polyanthos.* $25/£16

D'ARCH SMITH, TIMOTHY. Love in Earnest. London, 1970. 1st Eng ed. Good (name) in dj (worn). *Clearwater.* $31/£20

D'AULAIRE, INGRI and EDGAR PARIN. Children of the Northlights. NY: Viking, 1935. 1st ed. 9 x 12. Cl spine, pict bds. VG in dj (chipped, 2 x 3 price clip). *Cattermole.* $125/£80

D'AULAIRE, INGRI and EDGAR PARIN. Columbus. NY: Doubleday, 1955. 1st ed. 9 x 12 1/2. 57pp. Cl spine, pict bds. VG. *Cattermole.* $40/£26

D'AULAIRE, INGRI and EDGAR PARIN. The Conquest of the Atlantic. NY: Viking, 1933. 1st ed. 4to. 55pp, errata slip. Beige cl. VG. *Dower.* $75/£48

D'AULAIRE, INGRI and EDGAR PARIN. East of the Sun and West of the Moon. NY: Viking, (1969). 1st ed thus. 4to. 224pp; 6 full-pg etchings, 16 full-pg wash dwgs. Illus bds. NF. *Dower.* $45/£29

D'AULAIRE, INGRI and EDGAR PARIN. George Washington. NY: Doubleday, 1936. 1st ed. 8 3/4 x 12 1/2. 56pp. Cl spine. Good. *Cattermole.* $60/£38

D'AULAIRE, INGRI and EDGAR PARIN. Ola and Blakken. NY: Doubleday, 1933. 1st ed. 9 x 12 1/4. 40pp. Cl spine. Good (rebound). *Cattermole.* $90/£58

D'AULAIRE, INGRI and EDGAR PARIN. Wings for Per. NY: Doubleday, 1944. 1st ed. 9 1/4 x 12 1/4. 40pp. Cl spine, pict bds. VG in dj. *Cattermole.* $100/£64

D'AUREVILLY, BARBEY. The Anatomy of Dandyism. D.B. Wyndham Lewis (trans). London, 1928. #298/500. Teg, rest uncut. (Sl rubbed, upper joint sl split, spine sl bumped.) *Edwards.* $70/£45

D'AUREVILLY, BARBEY. Bewitched. Harper, 1928. 1st ed. VG in most of dj. *Madle.* $35/£22

D'AUREVILLY, BARBEY. What Never Dies. Sebastian Melmouth (trans). Privately ptd, 1928. #16/25 w/extra plts. Frontis in 2 states; 9 handcolored plts. 3/4 morocco, gilt-dec spine, raised bands. Fine (edges sl rubbed). *Polyanthos.* $250/£160

D'AVIELLA, GOBLET. The Migration of Symbols. Westminster, 1894. (xxvii),277pp + (ii); 6 plts. Uncut. (Rebacked, much of orig discolored spine laid down; hinges repaired.) *Edwards.* $70/£45

D'HARNONCOURT, RENE. The Hole in the Wall. NY: Knopf, 1931. 1st ed. 10 3/4 x 8 1/4. Fine in dj (sm chip bottom front). *Cattermole.* $1,500/£962

D'OLLONE, VICOMTE DE. In Forbidden China. Bernard Miall (trans). London, 1912. 2nd imp. Frontis port, dbl-pg map. (Lt browning; spine sl rubbed, faded.) *Edwards.* $39/£25

D'OOGE, MARTIN L. The Acropolis of Athens. NY/London: Macmillan, 1908. 7 plans (1 color, fldg). Burgundy cl (lt faded). *Turtle Island.* $55/£35

D'ORLEANS, LOUIS PHILIPPE ALBERT. History of the Civil War in America. John Page Nicholson (ed vols 3 and 4). Phila: Potter & Coates, (1875-88). 1st ed in English. 4 vols. (Extrems sl worn), else VG set. *Mcgowan.* $425/£272

D., H. (Hilda Doolittle.) Helen in Egypt. New Directions, (1961). 1st ed. Fine in dj. *Argosy.* $45/£29

D., H. (Hilda Doolittle.) Hippolytus Temporizes. Boston, 1927. 1st Amer ed. Ltd to 500 (of 550). Uncut. Fine (name). *Polyanthos.* $60/£38

da COSTA, J. M. Harvey and His Discovery. Phila, 1879. 1st ed. Inscribed. (Inscrip tp, bkpl.) (Cl worn, hole in spine patched.) *Maggs.* $44/£28

DA COSTA, JOHN CHALMERS. Selections from the Papers and Speeches. Phila, 1931. 1st ed. Blue cl. NF. *Doctor's Library.* $50/£32

DA VINCI, LEONARDO. Leonardo da Vinci's Note-Books. NY, 1935. VG in dj. *Fye.* $50/£32

DA VINCI, LEONARDO. The Literary Works of Leonardo Da Vinci. Jean Paul Richter (ed). London: OUP, 1939. 2nd ed. 2 vols. 122 plts. Orig buckram, gilt. VG. *Hollett.* $234/£150

DABBS, EDITH M. Face of an Island. NY: Grossman, 1971. 1st ed, 2nd issue (w/imprint changed from The R.L. Bryan Co. to Grossman). (Owner stamp), else VG in dj (edgeworn, lt soiled). *Cahan.* $125/£80

DABNEY, ROBERT LEWIS. Life and Campaigns of Lieut.-Gen. Thomas J. Jackson, (Stonewall Jackson). NY: Blelock, 1866. 1st ed. Frontis, x,(2),742,(1)pp. Photo eps. Later cl, orig spine label. Internally NF. Howes D2. *Mcgowan.* $150/£96

DADD, GEORGE H. The Modern Horse Doctor, Treating on Disease and Lameness in Horses. NY, 1900. New ed. Brn tooled cl. VG. *Doctor's Library.* $45/£29

DAGLEY, RICHARD. Death's Doings. London: J. Andrews & W. Cole, 1826. 1st ed. 24 etched plts incl extra tp. Blue-grn eps. Later dk grn calf, grn cl, raised bands, gilt. (Sl aged, foxed; lt scuffed, lacks spine label.) Baltimore*. $100/£64

DAGLISH, E. F. Animals in Black and White. NY: Morrow, 1938. 1st ed. Pict cl. Good + . Mikesh. $30/£19

DAHL, G. L. Portals, Doorways and Windows of France. NY: Archit. Pubs, 1925. 209 plts. Sound. Ars Artis. $55/£35

DAHL, G. L. Portals, Doorways and Windows of France. NY: Architectural Book, 1925. Frontis, 209 plts. (Cl sl faded, spine tail split.) Dj (spine faded, torn). Edwards. $75/£48

DAHL, ROALD. Boy: Tales of Childhood. NY: FSG, (1984). Ltd to 200 numbered. Signed. Fine in slipcase. Antic Hay. $150/£96

DAHL, ROALD. Boy: Tales of Childhood. NY: FSG, (1984). 1st ed. Ltd to 200 signed. 8vo. As New in slipcase. Jaffe. $225/£144

DAHL, ROALD. Charlie and the Chocolate Factory. NY: Knopf, 1964. 1st ed. Joseph Schindelman (illus). 6 1/4 x 9 1/2. 162pp. VG in dj (chips, lt soil). Cattermole. $75/£48

DAHL, ROALD. Danny the Champion of the World. NY, (1975). 1st Amer ed. Fine in NF dj (price-clipped). Polyanthos. $35/£22

DAHL, ROALD. Danny the Champion of the World. NY: Knopf, 1975. 1st ed. Jill Bennett (illus). 6 1/4 x 9 1/2. 198pp. 1/2 cl. VG in dj. Cattermole. $25/£16

DAHL, ROALD. Dirty Beasts. NY: FSG, 1983. 1st ed. Rosemary Fawcett (illus). 8 3/4 x 11 1/4. 32pp. VG in dj. Cattermole. $35/£22

DAHL, ROALD. The Magic Finger. Allen & Unwin, 1966. 1st ed. William Pene du Bois (illus). Lg 8vo. 41pp (fingermks, almost-erased inscrip, figures). Pict bds (sl dusty). VG. Bookmark. $62/£40

DAHL, ROALD. The Magic Finger. NY: Harper Row, 1966. 1st ed. Pene Du Bois (illus). 7 3/4 x 9. 41pp. Cl spine. Fine in dj. Cattermole. $50/£32

DAHL, ROALD. Matilda. Jonathan Cape, 1988. 1st ed. Quentin Blake (illus). Lg 8vo. 240pp. VG + in pict dj. Bookmark. $34/£22

DAHL, ROALD. More Tales of the Unexpected. Michael Joseph, 1980. 1st UK ed. NF in dj. Williams. $25/£16

DAHL, ROALD. Roald Dahl's Guide to Railway Safety. British Railways Board, 1991. 1st UK ed. Fine in illus wraps. Williams. $14/£9

DAHL, ROALD. Someone Like You. Secker & Warburg, 1954. 1st Eng ed. VG in dj (spine ends chipped). Certo. $20/£13

DAHL, ROALD. Switch Bitch. NY: Knopf, 1974. 1st ed. NF (bd edges fading) in NF dj (spine faded). Between The Covers. $45/£29

DAHL, ROALD. The Witches. NY: FSG, (1983). 1st ed. Ltd to 300 signed by Dahl and Quentin Blake (illus). 8vo. Mint in slipcase. Jaffe. $250/£160

DAHL, ROALD. The Wonderful Story of Henry Sugar and Six More. NY: Knopf, 1977. 1st US ed. 5 1/2 x 8 1/2. 225pp. 1/2 cl. VG in dj. Cattermole. $25/£16

DAHLBERG, EDWARD. Bottom Dogs. London, (1929). 1st trade ed. (Sl wear). King. $125/£80

DAHLBERG, EDWARD. Bottom Dogs. NY: S&S, 1930. 1st US ed. Fine in NF dj (sl sunned spine). Beasley. $150/£96

DAHLBERG, EDWARD. The Confessions of Edward Dahlberg. NY: Braziller, (1971). One of 200 numbered, signed. Fine in Fine slipcase. Lenz. $150/£96

DAHLBERG, EDWARD. The Sorrows of Priapus. (Norfolk): New Directions, (1957). 1st ed. Fine in dj (chipped, lt faded). Hermitage. $35/£22

DAIKEN, LESLIE. Children's Toys Throughout the Ages. NY: Praeger, 1958. Stated 1st US ed. Good (lt foxing) in Good dj. Scribe's Perch*. $20/£13

DAINTON, COURTNEY. Clock Jacks and Bee Boles. London: Phoenix House, 1957. 1st ed. VG in dj. Hollett. $39/£25

DAIX, PIERRE and GEORGES BOUDAILLE. Picasso. The Blue and Rose Periods. Greenwich, CT: NYGS, (1966). 61 tipped-in color plts. Dj (price-clipped); box. Kane*. $120/£77

DAKE, H. C. and JACK DE MENT. Ultra-Violet Light and Its Applications. Brooklyn, NY, 1942. 1st ed. VG in dj (worn). Doctor's Library. $40/£26

Dakota Wowapi Wakan Kin. NY: Amer Bible Soc, 1891. Orig sheep (scuffed, rear joint split, sewing cracked, open after eps). Overall VG. Waverly*. $121/£78

DALBY, MILTON A. The Sea Saga of Dynamite Johnny O'Brien.... Seattle: Lowman & Hanford, 1933. VG (lt wear). High Latitude. $40/£26

DALE, EDWARD EVERETT and GASTON LITTON. Cherokee Cavaliers. Norman: Univ of OK, 1939. 1st ed. VG in dj (sl worn). Lien. $75/£48

DALE, EDWARD EVERETT. Cow Country in Transition. (Torch Press), 1937. Inscribed presentation. Ptd wraps (edges faded, lt vertical crease); laid in protective folder. Bohling. $12/£8

DALE, EDWARD EVERETT. Frontier Ways. Austin: Univ of TX, (1959). 1st ed. VF in pict dj. Argonaut. $45/£29

DALE, EDWARD EVERETT. The Indians of the Southwest. Norman, 1949. 1st ed. (Sl bumped, sl worn.) King. $25/£16

DALE, EDWARD EVERETT. The Range Cattle Industry. Norman: Univ of OK, 1930. 1st ed. Grn cl (spine, edges faded). (Sl foxing), o/w NF. Howes D20. Harrington. $225/£144

DALE, EDWARD EVERETT. The Range Cattle Industry. Norman: Univ of OK, 1930. 1st ed. Frontis, title map. Grn cl (spine faded). NF (name; tp foxed) in dj (lt worn, chipped, inside spine reinforced). Howes D20. Argonaut. $300/£192

DALE, T. F. The History of the Belvoir Hunt. Westminster, 1899. 429pp (edges, ends foxed), fldg map. Teg. (Rubbed, dknd, hinges loose, bumped.) King. $35/£22

DALGLIESH, ALICE. The Davenports and Cherry Pie. Scribner, 1949. 1st ed. Flavia Gag (illus). 6x8.5. 196pp. VG + (eps sl browned; sl shelfworn) in dj (sl edgeworn). My Bookhouse. $40/£26

DALI, SALVADOR and PHILIPPE HALSMAN. Dali's Mustache. S&S, (1954). 1st ed. Pict bds (corners sl worn). VG + . Certo. $45/£29

DALI, SALVADOR. Catalogue Raisonne of Etchings and Mixed-Media Prints, 1924-1980. Ralf Michler and Lutz W. Lopsinger (eds). (Munich): Prestel, (1994). 1st ed in English. Cranberry cl. Fine in Fine color pict dj. Baltimore*. $90/£58

DALI, SALVADOR. Conquest of the Irrational. NY: Julien Levy, (1935). 1st ed. Color frontis, 35 photo repros. NF in photo stiff wrappers (margins sl browned). Turtle Island. $200/£128

DALI, SALVADOR. Dali, a Study of His Art-in-Jewels. Greenwich: NYGS, c 1970. 3rd ed. 36 full color tipped-in plts; 3pp, 1plt supplement laid-in. Fine in slipcase. Blake. $65/£42

DALI, SALVADOR. Dali. Fifty Secrets of Magic Craftmanship. Haakon M. Chevalier (trans). NY: Dial, 1948. 1st Amer ed. Black cl (bumped, rubbed, soiled), gilt. VG in pict dj (chipped, torn at edges). *Blue Mountain.* $125/£80

DALI, SALVADOR. Fifty Secrets of Magic Craftsmanship. Haakon M. Chevalier (trans). NY: Dial, 1948. 1st Amer ed. Gilt-stamped black cl. (Lt tape residue fep.) Illus dj (sl chipped). *Karmiole.* $150/£96

DALI, SALVADOR. Hidden Faces. NY: Dial, 1944. 1st ed. Frontis. NF in dj (chipped, sl rubbed). *Hermitage.* $75/£48

DALI, SALVADOR. The Secret Life of Salvador Dali. Haakon Chevalier (trans). London: Vision Press, 1949. Ltd to 1000. Dbl-pg color title, 1 color plt, 16 monochrome plts. Mod 1/2 black levant morocco gilt, buckram bds. Excellent (lt fingering). *Hollett.* $218/£140

DALL, WILLIAM H. Alaska and Its Resources. Boston: Lee & Shepard, 1870. xii,627(1)pp; 13 plts, fldg map. Dec cl. VG (new eps). *High Latitude.* $275/£176

DALL, WILLIAM H. et al. Alaska: History, Geography, Resources, Volume II. NY: Doubleday, 1901. 1st ed. Color frontis. Teg. Gilt-emb cl. VG (ex-lib). *Mikesh.* $95/£61

DALLIMORE, W. Holly, Yew and Box with Notes on Other Evergreens. London, 1908. 1st ed. 41 plts. Pict cl, gilt. (Ex-lib, stamps on tp, plts; new eps.) *Henly.* $50/£32

DALLIMORE, W. and A. BRUCE JACKSON. A Handbook of Coniferae. London, 1923. 1st ed. 32 plts. (Feps lt browned; sl rubbed.) *Edwards.* $86/£55

DALRYMPLE, JOHN. Memoirs of Great Britain and Ireland. London, 1771-88. 2nd ed. 2 vols. Contemp speckled calf, raised bands, gilt, 2 leather title labels. (Vol 2 lacks 1; joints cracked, vol 2 spine cracking, sl chipped; bkpl.) *Edwards.* $133/£85

DALTON, CHARLES. With the Dublin Brigade (1917-1921). London: Peter Davies, 1929. 1st ed. Frontis, fldg map. Grn cl (corners, spine lt worn). VG. *Patterson.* $39/£25

DALTON, EMMETT. When the Daltons Rode. GC: Doubleday, Doran, 1931. 1st ed. 15 b/w photo plts. Untrimmed. Brn pebbled cl (spine sl dknd; text sl aged, foxed), dk brn stamping. Howes D39. *Baltimore*.* $80/£51

DALTON, JOHN and THOMAS THOMSON. A System of Chemistry. Edinburgh/London/Dublin: Bell & Bradfute and E. Balfour/John Murray/Gilbert & Hodges, 1807. 3rd ed. 5 vols. 4 engr plts. New bds, calf spines, morocco labels. *Bickersteth.* $437/£280

DALTON, JOHN. History of the College of Physicians and Surgeons in the City of New York. NY, 1888. 208pp. VG. *Fye.* $100/£64

DALTON, MICHAEL. The Countrey Justice: Containing the Practice of the Justices of the Peace Out of Their Sessions.... London: Ptd by H. Sawbridge, S. Roycroft et al, 1682. Unlettered contemp calf. Very well preserved. *Boswell.* $750/£481

DALTON, O. M. Byzantine Art and Archaeology. NY, 1961. Rpt of 1911 ed. Good in dj. *Washton.* $45/£29

DALY, ELIZABETH. Any Shape or Form. London: Hammond, 1949. 1st UK ed. VG + in dj (edgeworn). *Murder By The Book.* $30/£19

DALZELL, JAMES McCORMICK. Private Dalzell, His Autobiography, Poems and Comic War Papers.... Cincinnati: Robert Clarke, 1888. 1st ed. 242,(3)pp. Good (sl insect traces; sl rubbed). *Wantagh.* $75/£48

DAM, NGUYEN CAO and TRAN CAO LINH. Vietnam: Our Beloved Land. Rutland, VT/Tokyo: Charles E. Tuttle, 1968. 1st ed. 86 photo plts. VG in pict stiff wrappers (few creases). *Cahan.* $50/£32

DAMAS, DAVID (ed). Handbook of North American Indians. Vol 5 Arctic. Washington: Smithsonian Inst, 1984. Fine. *High Latitude.* $50/£32

Dame Crump and Her Pig. NY: McLoughlin, n.d. (ca 1870). 4to. 20 unnumbered pp + 1pg list lower wrapper, 1st/last pp pasted down; 6 superb full-pg chromolithos by J. H. Howard. (Pencil name.) Full color pict stiff paper wrappers (sm chip) w/added gold (sl oxidation; edges lt soiled, sm chip). Internally Fine (lt trace offsetting). *Hobbyhorse.* $300/£192

Dame Hubbard and Her Dog. London: Dean's Rag Books, n.d. (1920s?). 8.5x6. (12)pp (sl soiled), w/sm info sheet. Loose cl. *King.* $45/£29

DAMPIER, WILLIAM. A New Voyage Round the World. London: Argonaut, 1927. #503/975. Pub's prospectus laid in. Unopened. Maroon cl (lt worn, bumped), ptd paper backstrip (replacing vellum spine). *Bohling.* $150/£96

DAMPIER, WILLIAM. Voyages and Discoveries. N. M. Penzer (ed). London: Argonaut, 1931. One of 975. 4 fldg maps. Mostly unopened. Burgundy cl, gilt, vellum spine. NF. *Parmer.* $250/£160

DANA, C. L. (ed). Contributions to Medical and Biological Research Dedicated to Sir William Osler.... NY, 1919. #35/1600. 2 vols. Plt. (Cl mkd.) *Maggs.* $133/£85

DANA, C. W. The Garden of the World. Boston: Wentworth, 1856. 396pp (1st few pp damp). Stamped bds (extrems worn). Good. *Dumont.* $135/£87

DANA, CHARLES A. Recollections of the Civil War. NY, 1898. 1st ed. Port. 296 w/index pp. (Cvrs dknd; sm spine tear.) *King.* $35/£22

DANA, CHARLES A. Recollections of the Civil War. NY, 1902. Rpt. VG + . *Pratt.* $27/£17

DANA, DANIEL. Memoirs of Eminently Pious Women. Newburyport: Angire March, 1803. 1st ed. 396pp (sigs). Contemp calf (hinges loose, spine top chipped). *Second Life.* $125/£80

DANA, EDWARD S. Dana's Manual of Mineralogy. NY: (Wm Ford), 1915. 13th ed. Grn cl, gilt. VG. *Price.* $24/£15

DANA, FREEMAN. (Pseud of Phoebe Atwood Taylor.) Murder at the New York World's Fair. NY: Random House, 1938. 1st ed. (Stamps, pen note; soiled, stained; dampstain few pp.) Dj (price-clipped; well worn; much interior tape reinforcement; soil, losses). *Metropolitan*.* $258/£165

DANA, J. Corals and Coral Islands. NY, 1872. 1st ed. Color frontis, 398pp; 3 plts, 3 maps, 2 fldg. Pict cl, gilt. (Sm tear tp repaired; sl worn), o/w Good. *Henly.* $195/£125

DANA, J. Manual of Geology. NY, 1862. Rev ed. 800pp; hand-colored fldg map. Marbled edges. Brn cl, gilt. (1/4 inch spine tear), else VG. *Price.* $37/£24

DANA, J. Manual of Mineralogy. New Haven: H.C. Peck, 1865. 2nd ed. xii,456pp. 1/4 calf. VG. *Blake.* $65/£42

DANA, J. A System of Mineralogy. NY: Wiley, 1877. 5th ed. xlviii,827,19,64pp. Contemp blue buckram. VG (lib stamp tp). *Blake.* $325/£208

DANA, JOHN COTTON. Notes on Bookbinding for Libraries. Chicago: Library Bureau, 1906. 1st ed. Fine. *Oak Knoll.* $55/£35

DANA, RICHARD H. III (ed). Richard Henry Dana, Jr. Speeches...and Letters to a Son. Boston: Houghton Mifflin, 1910. 1st ed. 5 photogravure plts; map. Blue cl, gilt. VG. BAL 4487. *Shasky.* $50/£32

DANA, RICHARD HENRY, JR. To Cuba and Back. Boston, 1859. 1st ed. Blue cl. VG. BAL 4447. *Argosy.* $125/£80

DANA, RICHARD HENRY, JR. Two Years Before the Mast. Boston/NY: Houghton Mifflin, 1911. 1st ed thus. #243/350. Frontispieces in 2 states, hand-colored and not. Extra labels tipped in. (Unrelated illus tipped to feps), o/w VG in Fair djs (tattered), Fair slipcase. Scribe's Perch*. $75/£48

DANA, RICHARD HENRY, JR. Two Years Before the Mast. Chicago: Lakeside Press, 1930. Ltd to 1000. Edward A. Wilson (illus). Gilt-stamped cl. Teg. VF (bkpl) in dec cl slipcase. Bromer. $200/£128

DANA, RICHARD HENRY, JR. Two Years Before the Mast. Chicago: Lakeside, 1930. 1st ed thus. One of 1000 unnumbered. Teg, uncut. Gilt-stamped beige cl, blue denim, gilt spine. VG + in pub's heavy tan bd slipcase. Houle. $225/£144

DANA, RICHARD HENRY, JR. Two Years Before the Mast. NY: Random House, 1936. One of 1000 ptd. Port, facs. Uncut. Suede-backed linen-finish bds. Fine in dj (sl chipped, torn, repaired). Pacific*. $58/£37

DANA, RICHARD HENRY, JR. Two Years Before the Mast.... L.A.: Ward Ritchie, 1964. 2 vols. 8 color plts. Fine set in slipcase (lt rubbed). Argonaut. $125/£80

Dance of Death. J. Coxhead, 1816. 2 ports, full-pg engr plt, 30 engrs after Hans Holbein. (Sl foxed throughout.) Contemp straight-grained calf gilt, gilt-panelled back (both joints partly cracked). Hatchwell. $156/£100

Dance of Life. (By William Combe.) London: Ackermann, 1817. 1st ed. 8vo. 2 vols. 26 hand-colored aquatint plts by Thomas Rowlandson. Red polished calf, gilt extra, dbl grn morocco labels. (Ex-libris, shelf label, bkpl, sm stamps ad leaf.) Swann*. $632/£405

Dance of Life. (By William Combe.) London: R. Ackermann, 1817. 1st ed. Hand-colored aquatint frontis, 24 plts (sl offset, sl spotted) by Thomas Rowlandson. Teg. Contemp calf (spine head, 1 label torn; upper joint split, spine stained), gilt, contrasting morocco lettering pieces. Christie's*. $281/£180

DANDY, WALTER J. Orbital Tumors Results Following the Transcranial Operative Attack. NY, 1941. 1st ed. (Ex-lib, spine label, shelfwear.) Internally VG (stamps eps). Goodrich. $350/£224

DANDY, WALTER. Benign Tumors in the Third Ventricle of the Brain.... Springfield, 1933. Near Mint. Goodrich. $295/£189

DANE, CLEMENCE. Tradition and Hugh Walpole. London: Heinemann, (1930). 1st Eng ed. NF in dj (spine rubbed, browned; sm tears). Antic Hay. $25/£16

DANESE, RENATO (intro). 14 American Photographers. Balt: Balt Museum of Art, 1974. 1st ed. VG in stiff wrappers (faded, lt soiled). Cahan. $30/£19

DANESE, RENATO (ed). American Images. NY: McGraw-Hill, 1979. (Owner stamp), else NF in dj (rubbed, scuffed). Cahan. $45/£29

DANIEL, GLYN E. The Prehistoric Chamber Tombs of England and Wales. CUP, 1950. 16 plts. (Cl spine lt faded.) Edwards. $31/£20

DANIEL, HAWTHORNE. Dorothy Stanhope—Virginian. Coward-McCann, (c. 1931). Good (cvr stained). Book Broker. $20/£13

DANIEL, HOWARD. Devils, Monsters and Nightmares. London, 1964. Good in dj (worn). Washton. $45/£29

DANIEL, J. FRANK. The Elasmobranch Fishes. Univ of CA, 1934. 3rd ed. 11 plts. Grn cl, gilt. VG in dj. Price. $95/£61

DANIELL, WILLIAM. Interesting Selections from Animated Nature with Illustrative Scenery. London: The Author, n.d. (plts dated 1809). Vol 1 (of 2). 50 aquatint plts (lt soiled; few text leaves repaired at margins). Contemp 1/2 calf (worn). Christie's*. $385/£247

DANIELL, WILLIAM. Sketches Representing the Native Tribes, Animals and Scenery of Southern Africa. London, 1820. 40 (of 46) plts (stained, foxed). Blue cl bds (bumped, dknd). Metropolitan*. $250/£160

DANIELS, GEORGE. The Art of Breguet. NY/London: Sotheby, 1975. 1st ed. Port. VG in dj (very worn). Weber. $75/£48

DANIELS, GEORGE. English and American Watches. London/NY/Toronto: Abelard-Schuman, (1967). 23 plts. Maroon bds. Dj (waterstained, soiled, worn). Weber. $40/£26

DANIELS, GEORGE. Watchmaking. (NY): Sotheby, (1981). 1st Amer ed. Blue cl. Fine in dj. Weber. $75/£48

DANIELSON, HENRY. Bibliographies of Modern Authors. London: Bookman's Journal, 1921. Facs tps. Dk cl. (Lt wear.) Cullen. $55/£35

DANNER, MRS. J. M. Sayre of Red River Valley. Sayre, OK: N.p., 1939. VG in wraps. Dumont. $50/£32

DANNETT, SYLVIA G. L. A Treasury of Civil War Humor. NY, (1963). 1st ed. VG + in VG + dj. Pratt. $35/£22

DANTE. La Divina Commedia. (London), 1928. One of 1475 numbered. Folio. 42 dbl-pg plts. Orange vellum, gilt. Swann*. $373/£239

DANTE. The Divine Comedy.... Melville Best Anderson (trans). Verona: (Officina Bodoni), 1932. One of 1500. Signed by Hans Mardersteig (ptr/designer). Patterned cl. Box (worn). Kane*. $80/£51

DARBY, WILLIAM. The Emigrant's Guide to the Western and Southwestern States and Territories. NY, 1818. Contemp 1/4 roan (extrems worn; ex-lib, spine #s, ink stamp tp). Howes D61. Swann*. $977/£626

DARBY, WILLIAM. A Tour from the City of New York, to Detroit...Made Between the 2nd of May and the 22nd of September 1818.... NY: Kirk & Mercein, 1819. 1st ed. Errata slip. 3 fldg maps, all partly colored. Orig bds, part of orig label. (Scattered foxing; backstrip chipped away.) Howes D66. Sadlon. $350/£224

DARLEY, GEORGE M. Pioneering in the San Juan. Chicago/NY/Toronto: Fleming H. Revell, 1899. 1st ed. (226)pp. Pict gray cl. VG. Lucas. $150/£96

DARLEY, HENRY. Slaves and Ivory in Abyssinia. NY: McBride, 1935. 1st ed. Frontis, 6 plts, 2 maps. VG in dj (sl torn). Worldwide. $45/£29

DARLING, F. FRASER. Wild Country. CUP, 1938. 1st ed. Dec grey cl, gilt. VG in dj. Price. $29/£19

DARLING, W. The Private Papers of a Bankrupt Bookseller. Oliver & Boyd, 1932. VG. Moss. $19/£12

DARLINGTON, C. D. and E. K. JANAKI AMMAL. Chromosome Atlas of Cultivated Plants. London, 1945. 1st ed. Brooks. $32/£21

DARLINGTON, P. J. Zoogeography: The Geographical Distribution of Animals. NY: Wiley, (1963). VG. Mikesh. $45/£29

DARLINGTON, WILLIAM. Flora Cestrica. West-Chester: For the Author, 1837. 1st ed. Color frontis map, xxiii,640pp (foxing, stains, soil). Contemp tree-calf (rubbed). Oinonen*. $140/£90

DARRACH, WILLIAM. Drawings of the Anatomy of the Groin with Anatomical Remarks. Phila, 1844. 2nd ed. 127pp; 4 litho plts. (Cl worn, foxing.) Goodrich. $75/£48

DARRAH, WILLIAM CULP. Powell of the Colorado. Princeton Univ, 1951. 1st ed. Fine (pencil sig) in pict dj (sl chipped, soiled). Argonaut. $60/£38

DARRELL, MARGERY (ed). Once Upon a Time. NY: Viking, (1972). 1st ed. Arthur Rackham (illus). Cl-backed paper-cvrd bds. VG in dj. Hermitage. $85/£54

Darton's Nursery Leading Strings. (London), n.d. (1880s?). Darton's Indestructable Elementary Children's Books. 10x7. (13)pp. Pict paper over starched cl (lg chip, worn, soiled). *King*. $35/£22

DARTON, F. J. HARVEY. Alibi Pilgrimage. London, 1936. 1st ed. (Bumped), o/w VG in dj (tears, spine browned, frayed). *Words Etc*. $39/£25

DARTON, N. H. et al. Guidebook of the Western United States: Part C. The Santa Fe Route. GPO, 1915. 42 full-pg plts, 24 fldg color maps. Good in ptd wraps. *Scribe's Perch**. $25/£16

DARTON, N. H. et al. Guidebook of the Western United States; Part C. The Santa Fe Route. Washington: GPO, 1915. Good (worn) in wraps. *Dumont*. $50/£32

DARWIN, BERNARD et al. A History of Golf in Britain. London: Cassell, (1952). 1st ed. Cl, leather spine label. VG in dj (chipped, creased, tears, lacks sm piece). *Pacific**. $230/£147

DARWIN, BERNARD and ELINOR. Mr. Tootleoo and Co. London: Faber, 1935. 1st ed. 9 1/2 x 7 1/2. 48pp. Pict bds. Good (fep replaced). *Cattermole*. $125/£80

DARWIN, BERNARD. British Golf. London, 1946. 8 color plts. Dj (sl chipped). *Edwards*. $23/£15

DARWIN, BERNARD. The Golf Courses of the British Isles. London: Duckworth, (1910). 1st ed. 64 color plts, guards. Teg. Gilt-lettered grn cl. (Foxing), else NF. *Pacific**. $863/£553

DARWIN, BERNARD. Golf: Pleasures of Life Series. London: Burke, (1954). 1st ed. Fine in VG dj (chipped). *Pacific**. $184/£118

DARWIN, BERNARD. Second Shots: Casual Talks About Golf. London: George Newnes, 1930. 1st ed. (Lt spots fr cvr), else VG. *Pacific**. $219/£140

DARWIN, CHARLES and A. R. WALLACE. Evolution by Natural Selection. Cambridge: CUP, 1958. 1st ed. Fine in Fine dj. *Mikesh*. $45/£29

DARWIN, CHARLES. Charles Darwin's Autobiography. Francis Darwin (ed). NY, 1950. 1st Amer ed. Frontis. Brn cl. (Handwritten poem fep), else VG in dj (chipped). *Price*. $22/£14

DARWIN, CHARLES. The Descent of Man and Selection in Relation to Sex. NY: D. Appleton, 1871. 1st Amer ed, 1st issue w/corrective note in vol 2. 2 vols. 409; v,436pp (lt stains couple ll). Dec cl (extrems sl worn, fore-edges sl soiled), gilt. Nice. *Shasky*. $185/£119

DARWIN, CHARLES. The Descent of Man, and Selection in Relation to Sex. London, 1899. 2nd ed, 35th thousand. Fine. Freeman 985. *Henly*. $39/£25

DARWIN, CHARLES. The Descent of Man, and Selection in Relation to Sex. Volume II. 1871. 1st ed. viii,475pp. (Cl sl stained.) *Whitehart*. $39/£25

DARWIN, CHARLES. The Descent of Man. NY: Appleton, 1871. 1st ed. 2 vols. 409; 436pp + ads. Blind-stamped dec cl. (Sm spine tear), else VG. *Mikesh*. $200/£128

DARWIN, CHARLES. The Descent of Man. London, 1901. New ed. Sound (binding dull). *Petersfield*. $23/£15

DARWIN, CHARLES. The Descent of Man. Adelaide: LEC, 1971. #1029/1500 signed by Fritz Kredel (illus). Fine in slipcase. *Hermitage*. $175/£112

DARWIN, CHARLES. The Different Forms of Flowers on Plants of the Same Species. NY: Appleton, (1896). 352pp. Teg. 1/2 leather, marbled bds. Fine. *Mikesh*. $45/£29

DARWIN, CHARLES. The Different Forms of Flowers on Plants of the Same Species. London: John Murray, 1877. 1st ed. viii,352,32pp ads (sl foxed, mostly edges). Entirely unopened. Grn cl. Virtually Mint. *Pirages*. $1,500/£962

DARWIN, CHARLES. The Effects of Cross and Self Fertilisation in the Vegetable Kingdom. London, 1876. 1st ed, w/errata slip. viii,482pp. (Sl trace of label removal fr cvr.) *Wheldon & Wesley*. $281/£180

DARWIN, CHARLES. The Effects of Cross and Self-Fertilization in the Vegetable Kingdom. London: Murray, 1876. 1st ed. 8vo. 482pp (tp sl foxed). Fine. *Argosy*. $650/£417

DARWIN, CHARLES. The Expression of the Emotions in Man and Animals. NY: Appleton, (1896). 374pp, 7 photo plts. Teg. 1/2 leather, marbled bds. VG. *Mikesh*. $30/£19

DARWIN, CHARLES. The Expression of the Emotions in Man and Animals. Murray, 1872. 1st ed. (Lacks blank fep.) *Petersfield*. $273/£175

DARWIN, CHARLES. The Expression of the Emotions in Man and Animals. NY: Appleton, 1873. 1st Amer ed, 1st issue. v,(1),374,(14 ads)pp; 7 heliotype plts (3 fldg). Dec cl. VG (sig; extrems rubbed, sl frayed). *Glaser*. $275/£176

DARWIN, CHARLES. The Formation of Vegetable Mould Through the Action of Worms.... London, 1881. 3rd thousand. vii,errata slip,326pp,2 ads. Fine. *Henly*. $70/£45

DARWIN, CHARLES. The Formation of Vegetable Mould Through the Action of Worms.... London: John Murray, 1881. 1st ed, 3rd thousand. vii,326pp (sm lib stamps text, bkpls eps). 1/2 leather (lt chipped). (Tp sl spotted), else Good. *White*. $55/£35

DARWIN, CHARLES. The Formation of Vegetable Mould, Through the Action of Worms, Etc. NY: Appleton, (1896). 326pp. Teg. 1/2 leather, marbled bds. VG + . *Mikesh*. $30/£19

DARWIN, CHARLES. Geological Observations on the Volcanic Islands and Parts of South America.... NY, 1897. 3rd ed. 648pp. 1/2 leather. VG. *Fye*. $60/£38

DARWIN, CHARLES. Journal of Researches into the Natural History and Geology of the Countries Visited During the Voyage of H.M.S. Beagle Round the World. T. Nelson, 1893. *Petersfield*. $55/£35

DARWIN, CHARLES. Journal of Researches into the Natural History and Geology of the Countries Visited During the Voyage of H.M.S. Beagle.... NY: Harper, 1846. 1st Amer ed. 2 vols. VG (foxed; spine ends chipped). *M&s*. $400/£256

DARWIN, CHARLES. Journal of Researches into the Natural History and Geology of the Countries Visited During the Voyage Round the World of H.M.S. 'Beagle'.... London: John Murray, 1890. xvi,552pp; 10 plts, 2 color fldg maps. Aeg. Full red morocco, dec gilt arms (award pasted inside cvr). *Karmiole*. $125/£80

DARWIN, CHARLES. Journal of Researches into the Natural History and Geology of the Countries Visited, Etc. London: Nelson, 1890. 1st ed. 615pp. Gilt-dec maroon cl. VG-. *Mikesh*. $60/£38

DARWIN, CHARLES. Life and Letters of Charles Darwin, Including an Autobiographical Chapter. Francis Darwin (ed). NY: Appleton, 1893. 2 vols. viii,558,(2 ads); iv,(4),562,(2 ads)pp. VG set. *Glaser*. $75/£48

DARWIN, CHARLES. The Life and Letters of.... Francis Darwin (ed). London: John Murray, 1887. 1st ed. 3 vols. Blue cl, gilt spines. VG set (bkpls). *Pacific**. $150/£96

DARWIN, CHARLES. More Letters of Charles Darwin. Francis Darwin (ed). NY, 1903. 1st Amer ed. 2 vols. 14 photo plts. Teg, uncut. Brn cl, gilt. VG. *Price*. $95/£61

DARWIN, CHARLES. On the Origin of Species.... John Murray, 1860. 2nd ed, 2nd issue, binding variant a. 5th thousand. ix,(i),502pp; fldg plt, pub's 32-pg cat dated Jan 1860 at end. Grn cl, gilt. (Ink name; slit upper joint, inner joint cracked, some sewing sl loose.) *Bickersteth*. $234/£150

DARWIN, CHARLES. On the Structure and Distribution of Coral Reefs.... London, 1890. xx,549pp, 6 ads; 6 plts. (Sm lib stamp 1/2 title.) *Henly*. $44/£28

DARWIN, CHARLES. The Origin of Species.... London, 1872. 6th ed, 11th thousand. (Name torn from blank upper portion 1/2 title, brn feps replaced.) Grn cl (worn, soiled, recased.) *Maggs*. $195/£125

DARWIN, CHARLES. The Origin of Species.... John Murray, 1891. 6th ed, 41st thousand. xxi,432pp, ad leaf. Grn cl. *Bickersteth*. $44/£28

DARWIN, CHARLES. The Origin of the Species by Means of Natural Selection.... NY, 1860. 1st US ed, 2nd issue, w/3 quotes facing tp. Fldg chart. New grn eps. Orig grn cl (rebacked retaining ptd portion of spine, edges rubbed w/bds exposed; foxed, sl pencilling). *Kane**. $120/£77

DARWIN, CHARLES. The Power of Movement in Plants. F. Darwin (ed). NY: Appleton, (1896). 592pp. Teg. 1/2 leather, marbled bds. VG + . *Mikesh*. $30/£19

DARWIN, CHARLES. The Structure and Distribution of Coral Reefs. NY: Appleton, (1896). 3rd ed. 344pp, 2 color fldg maps. Teg. 1/2 leather, marbled bds (spine rubbed). Contents Fine. *Mikesh*. $30/£19

DARWIN, CHARLES. The Variation of Animals and Plants Under Domestication. NY: Appleton, (1896). 2 vols. 473; 495pp. Teg. 1/2 leather, marbled bds. (Spine gutter split vol 1), else VG. *Mikesh*. $45/£29

DARWIN, CHARLES. The Variation of Animals and Plants Under Domestication. London, 1868. 2 vols. Vol 1 1st ed, 1st issue; vol 2 1st ed, 2nd issue. viii,141,43; viii,486pp,2 ads. (Vol 1 lacks 32pp ads; vol 2 rebacked, preserving spine, eps.) *Henly*. $281/£180

DARWIN, CHARLES. The Variation of Animals and Plants Under Domestication. London: John Murray, 1868. 1st ed, 2nd issue, w/2-line imprint and 1-line erratum in Vol 1. 2 vols. viii,411,32(ads); viii,486,(2 ads)pp. (Binding worn, corners bumped.) Internally VG set. *Glaser*. $485/£311

DARWIN, CHARLES. The Variation of Animals and Plants Under Domestication. London, 1890. 2nd ed. 7th thousand. 2 vols. Good. *Henly*. $87/£56

DARWIN, CHARLES. The Variation of Animals and Plants. London, 1885. 2nd ed, 5th thousand. 2 vols. *Wheldon & Wesley*. $117/£75

DARWIN, CHARLES. The Various Contrivances by Which Orchids Are Fertilised by Insects. London, 1888. 2nd ed, 4th thousand. xvi,300,pp + 32 ads. (Inner hinge cracked.) Unopened. *Henly*. $66/£42

DARWIN, CHARLES. The Works of Charles Darwin. NY/London: Appleton, n.d. (c 1900?). #387/1000 w/facs sig on 1/2-title. 15 vols complete. Teg. Gilt-dec dk grn cl. (Lt cl mottling), else VG + . *Mikesh*. $275/£176

DARY, DAVID. True Tales of the Old-Time Plains. NY, 1979. 1st ed. Fine in dj (price-clipped). *Baade*. $50/£32

DASENT, G. W. (trans). The Story of Burnt Njal. Edinburgh, 1861. 1st ed. 2 vols. 104,256; 14,507pp; 5 maps, 3 fldg (1 w/much tape repair); 4 plts, 1 fldg. Dec cl. Good- (foxing, hinge cracks). *Scribe's Perch**. $37/£24

DATER, JUDY. Imogen Cunningham: A Portrait. Boston: NYGS, 1979. 1st ed. NF in VG dj (closed tear fr panel). *Smith*. $55/£35

DAUDET, ALPHONSE. Jack. Laura Ensor (trans). London: J.M. Dent, 1896. 1st ed in English. 2 vols. Beige cl dec in gray-grn. NF (sl soiled, rubbed). *Sumner & Stillman*. $95/£61

DAUDET, ALPHONSE. Port Tarascon. Henry James (trans). London: Sampson Low et al, 1891. 1st Eng ed. Secondary binding of red sand-grain cl (w/o cvr illus, beveled edges, or ad cat of primary blue-gray binding). NF (rear cvr sl soiled). *Sumner & Stillman*. $125/£80

DAUDET, ALPHONSE. Port Tarascon. Henry James (trans). NY: Harper, 1891. 1st Amer ed. Dec blue cl. VG (hinges sl cracked, ink name, sl foxed). *Antic Hay*. $75/£48

DAUDET, ALPHONSE. Port Tarascon. The Last Adventures of the Illustrious Tartarin. Henry James (trans). NY: Harper, 1891. 1st ed, primary binding. Teg. Gilt/silver dec cl (spine ends sl shelfworn). VG. BAL 10592. *Reese*. $125/£80

DAUDET, ALPHONSE. Sidonie. Charlotte Haldane (trans). NY: Roy Pub, (1960). 1st Amer ed, 1st ed in English. Fine in dj (sl soiled). *Antic Hay*. $25/£16

DAUDET, ALPHONSE. Works. Boston, 1898-1900. One of 1000. 24 vols. Marbled eps; teg. 1/2 grn morocco (spines uniformly dknd), marbled bds, gilt. *Kane**. $325/£208

DAUGHERTY, JAMES. Andy and the Lion. NY: Viking, 1938. 1st ed. Signed. 8x11. 72pp. VG (rubbed). *Cattermole*. $150/£96

DAULTE, FRANCOIS. French Watercolors of the 19th Century. NY, 1970. 42 tipped-in color plts. Good in dj. *Washton*. $40/£26

DAUMAS, MAURICE. Scientific Instruments of the Seventeenth and Eighteenth Centuries and Their Makers. London: Batsford, (1972). 1st Eng ed. Mary Holbrook (trans). Black cl. VG in dj (rubbed). *Weber*. $80/£51

DAUNT, ACHILLES. The Three Trappers: A Story of Travel and Adventure in the Wilds of Canada. London: T. Nelson, 1882. 1st ed. Red cl, gilt. (Spine sl faded, lower cvr rubbed, bkpl), o/w Immaculate. *Cummins*. $75/£48

DAVENPORT, BISHOP. A New Gazetteer, or Biographical Dictionary, of North America and the West Indies.... Balt/Providence, 1832. 1st ed. Fldg hand-colored map. (Marginal foxing, fep removed). Orig calf (rubbed). VG. *Mcclintock*. $35/£22

DAVENPORT, BISHOP. A Pocket Gazeteer, or Traveller's Guide Through North America and the West Indies. Trenton/Balt: The Author/Plaskitt, 1834. 468pp, fldg color map, fldg profile plt. Orig calf (fr outer hinge opened, sl shelfwear, spine #). *Brown*. $150/£96

DAVENPORT, C. B. Experimantal Morphology. NY, 1897/9. 2 vols. xiv,280; xviii,227pp. (Ink dedication, lib stamps, #s to spines, label fr cvr), o/w VG. *Whitehart*. $39/£25

DAVENPORT, CYRIL. The Book—Its History and Development. Constable, 1907. 7 plts. Grn cl. VG. *Moss*. $31/£20

DAVENPORT, CYRIL. Cameos. London, 1900. 1st ed. 8 color plts. VG (ex-lib). *Swann**. $57/£37

DAVENPORT, CYRIL. English Embroidered Bookbindings. London: Kegan Paul, Trench, Trubner, 1899. 1st ed. xxxii,113pp; 52 plts, incl color frontis. Grn buckram (rubbed, spine yellowed). *Oak Knoll*. $225/£144

DAVENPORT, CYRIL. English Embroidered Bookbindings. Alfred Pollard (ed). London, 1899. Color frontis, 51 plts. Teg. Grn cl (lt bumped, spine sl faded, tracings of bindings inserted loose; bk label). *Maggs*. $156/£100

DAVENPORT, CYRIL. Mezzotints. London: Methuen, 1904. 1st ed. 40 engr plts. Teg, uncut. Red dec cl gilt (edges sl dknd). *Hollett*. $101/£65

DAVENPORT, CYRIL. Roger Payne: English Book-binder of the Eighteenth Century. Chicago: Caxton Club, 1929. 1st ed. One of 250 ptd. Lg 4to. Full-pg collotype frontis, 32 full-pg plts (13 Fine litho color plts, 19 in collotype), guards. Teg. Red cl, gilt. Fine in pub's bd slipcase (sl rubbed). *Cady.* $600/£385

DAVENPORT, CYRIL. Royal English Bookbindings. Seeley, 1896. 8 Fine color plts. Maroon dec cl. Good. *Moss.* $94/£60

DAVENPORT, CYRIL. Royal English Bookbindings. London/NY: Seeley/Macmillan, 1896. Frontis, 7 color plts. 1st binding: gilt-stamped blue cl. VG. *Heller.* $110/£71

DAVENPORT, CYRIL. Royal English Bookbindings. London: Seeley, 1896. 1st ed. 96pp; 8 color plts. (Cvrs faded.) *Oak Knoll.* $100/£64

DAVENPORT, GUY. The Resurrection in Cookham Churchyard. NY: Jordan Davies, 1982. One of 230 numbered, signed. Fine in Fine dj. *Beasley.* $35/£22

DAVENPORT, HOMER. Davenport's Arabians. Ft. Collins: Caballus, 1973. Ltd to 2000. VG. *October Farm.* $45/£29

DAVENPORT, JOHN. Aphrodisiacs and Anti-Aphrodisiacs. London, 1869. 1st ed. 154pp; 7 plts. 1/4 leather. Contents Fine (hinges cracked, spine lacks two 1-inch pieces). *Fye.* $150/£96

DAVENPORT, JOHN. Curiosities of Erotic Physiology. NY: Robin Hood House, 1932. 1st ed. Ltd to 675. NF. *Worldwide.* $22/£14

DAVENPORT, MONTAGUE. Under the Gridiron. London: Tinsley Bros, 1876. 1st ed. (xii),(144),(iv)pp. Pict cl (sl rubbed, sl shaken), gilt. Nice. *Ash.* $101/£65

DAVID, CITIZEN. A History of the Campaigns of General Pichegru. London, 1796. 1st Eng ed. 268pp (bkpl). Teg. 3/4 red leather (sl worn), gilt-stamped spine. *King.* $195/£125

DAVID, ELIZABETH. French Country Cooking. NY: Horizon Press, (n.d. c 1952). 1st Amer ed, from Eng sheets. (Lt wear bd bottoms), else NF in VG dj (lt chipped; some crown loss). *Between The Covers.* $125/£80

DAVID, ELIZABETH. French Country Cooking. 1951. 1st ed. VG in pict dj (chip). *Words Etc.* $86/£55

DAVID, ELIZABETH. French Provincial Cooking. London, 1960. 1st ed. Dj (sl chipped). *Edwards.* $31/£20

DAVID, JAY and ELAINE CRANE. The Black Soldier. NY: Morrow, 1971. 1st ed. (Pg edges tanned, sl stain final blank pg), else NF in NF dj. *Between The Covers.* $50/£32

DAVID, M. E. Professor David. The Life of Sir Edgeworth David. London: Edward Arnold, 1937. Map. Good (sig; cl faded, discolored). *High Latitude.* $30/£19

DAVID, ROBERT BEEBE. Finn Burnett, Frontiersman. Glendale: Clark, 1937. 1st ed. One of 1000. 8 plts. Fine (spine ends, corners lt rubbed, corner worn). *Argonaut.* $175/£112

DAVID, VILLERS. The Guardsman and Cupid's Daughter and Other Poems. (London), 1930. 1st ed. One of 500 numbered, signed by David and John Austen (illus). (Soiled, edges lt sunned; 2pp roughly opened), o/w interior VG. *Mcclintock.* $16/£10

DAVIDSON, BASIL. The Lost Cities of Africa. Boston/Toronto: Little Brown/Atlantic Monthly, 1970. Rev ed. 5 maps (2 full-pg), 20 plts. NF in dj. *Worldwide.* $22/£14

DAVIDSON, BASIL. Tir A'Mhurain: Outer Hebrides. London: Macgibbon & Kee, 1962. 1st ed. NF in dj (edgetorn, separated along spine). *Cahan.* $300/£192

DAVIDSON, BASIL. Tir A'Mhurain: Outer Hebrides. NY: Grossman, 1968. 1st US ed. (Name, stamp), else VG in dj (2 closed tears, tape-repaired). *Cahan.* $250/£160

DAVIDSON, BRUCE. Bruce Davidson: Photographs. NY: Agrinde/Summit Book, 1978. 1st ed. VG in illus stiff wrappers (sl worn). *Cahan.* $50/£32

DAVIDSON, BRUCE. East 100th Street. Cambridge, MA: Harvard Univ, 1970. 1st ed. Beige cl, mtd photo. (Name stamp), else VG in ptd clear acetate dj (chipped). *Cahan.* $325/£208

DAVIDSON, BRUCE. East 100th Street. Cambridge, MA: Harvard Univ, 1971. 2nd ptg. (Name stamp), else VG in pict stiff wrappers. *Cahan.* $100/£64

DAVIDSON, DONALD. The Tennessee. NY: Rinehart, 1946, 1948. 1st ed. 2 vols. Fine in VG djs (torn, rubbed). *Archer.* $75/£48

DAVIDSON, ELLIS A. A Practical Manual of House-Painting, Graining, Marbling and Sign-Writing. London: Crosby Lockwood, 1922. 11th imp. 9 color plts. VG. *Hollett.* $70/£45

DAVIDSON, HOMER K. Black Jack Davidson, a Cavalry Commander on the Western Frontier. Glendale, 1974. 1st ed. Fine in Fine dj. *Turpen.* $48/£31

DAVIDSON, HOMER K. Black Jack Davidson, a Cavalry Commander on the Western Frontier. Glendale: Clark, 1974. 1st ed. One of 1205. 3 color maps. VF in dj. *Argonaut.* $50/£32

DAVIDSON, HOMER K. Black Jack Davidson. Glendale, 1974. 1st ed. Fldg map. Fine in Fine dj. *Pratt.* $35/£22

DAVIDSON, JOHN. A Full and True Account of the Wonderful Mission of Earl Lavender. London: Ward & Downey, 1895. 1st ed. Frontis by Aubrey Beardsley. 2pp undated ads. Blue-gray cl. VG (Davidson photos glued to fep; spine sl dull). *Sumner & Stillman.* $195/£125

DAVIDSON, K. L. The Unheated Greenhouse. Country Life, 1907. (Margins lt browned; spine sl faded.) *Edwards.* $31/£20

DAVIDSON, PATRICIA F. and ANDREW OLIVER, JR. Ancient Greek and Roman Gold Jewelry in the Brooklyn Museum. Emma Swan Hall and Bernard V. Bothmer (eds). Brooklyn: Brooklyn Museum, 1984. (Corner bumped.) *Archaeologia.* $150/£96

DAVIDSON, THOMAS. The Parthenon Frieze and Other Essays. London, 1882. Frontis, x,(i),224pp + 32pp pub's cat (ex-lib; ink stamps; fep chipped w/loss, hinges cracked). Dec cl (lt faded, spine chipped). *Edwards.* $23/£15

DAVIE, OLIVER. Methods in the Art of Taxidermy. Phila, (1900). (Lt worn, soiled.) Dj (worn, soiled). *Freeman*.* $60/£38

DAVIE, W. GALSWORTHY and H. TANNER. Old English Doorways. Batsford, 1903. 1st ed. 70 collotype plts. Teg. (Bk label, eps sl spotted), o/w Excellent. *Cox.* $47/£30

DAVIES, A. MERVYN. Warren Hastings. London, 1935. 1st ed. Frontis port, fldg map. (Spine chipped, sl faded.) *Edwards.* $59/£38

DAVIES, ANDREW. Dirty Faxes. Methuen, 1990. 1st UK ed. Fine in dj. *Williams.* $28/£18

DAVIES, BENJAMIN. A New System of Modern Geography. Phila: J. Downing Ptr, 1813. 3rd ed. 447pp. Orig full calf. VG (foxed, spine ends, corners worn). *Mcgowan.* $150/£96

DAVIES, CHARLES. Grammar of Arithmetic. NY/Cincinnati: A.S. Barnes/H.W. Derby, 1850. 1st ed. 144pp. VG in ptd wrappers. *Brown.* $15/£10

DAVIES, D. H. About Sharks and Shark Attacks. London: Routledge, 1965. 1st ed. VG. *Mikesh.* $35/£22

DAVIES, E. W. L. Algiers in 1857. Longman et al, 1858. Sole ed. xi,163pp, 32-pg pub's cat; 4 tinted litho plts. Orange cl, gilt. (Lib stamps, sm tear upper joint.) *Bickersteth.* $148/£95

DAVIES, EDWARD. Celtic Researches, on the Origin, Traditions and Language, of the Ancient Britons. London: The Author, 1804. 1st ed. lxxiii,(i),561pp (ink notes bottom margin 1 pg); 2 plts (1 loose, fr edge sl chipped). Mod grn cl (rubbed), burgundy leather spine label (chipped). NF. *Blue Mountain.* $275/£176

DAVIES, G. CHRISTOPHER. Norfolk Broads and Rivers or the Water-Ways, Lagoons, and Decoys of East Anglia. Edinburgh/London: William Blackwood, 1883. 1st ed. (x),290pp (blank margins lt foxed); 12 photogravure plts, guards. Gilt-dec cl (sm stain; spine ends, fr hinge worn; new eps). Good. *Cahan.* $325/£208

DAVIES, GEORGE R. Collection of Old Chinese Porcelains. NY, 1913. 25 color plts. (Few text ll foxed.) *Swann*.* $115/£74

DAVIES, GERALD S. Renascence: The Sculptured Tombs of the 15th C. in Rome.... London, 1910. 1st ed. 88 plts. Gilt-stamped cl. VG. *Argosy.* $100/£64

DAVIES, HANNAH. Among Hills and Valleys in Western China. 1901. 1st ed. Frontis port, fldg map. (Feps lt browned, bkpl; joints, spine head sl rubbed, spine tail sl chipped.) *Edwards.* $86/£55

DAVIES, HENRY E. General Sheridan. NY, 1895. 1st ed. 332pp. Gilt edges. Pict cl. VG + . *Pratt.* $47/£30

DAVIES, HUGH WILLIAM. Devices of the Early Printers, 1457-1560, Their History and Development. London: Grafton, 1935. Frontis. VG (pastedowns lt foxed, ink notes, spine faded) in blue buckram case. *Heller.* $100/£64

DAVIES, HUNTER. The Beatles. The Authorised Biography. Heinemann, 1968. 1st ed. VG in dj. *Sclanders.* $19/£12

DAVIES, J. G. The Origin and Development of Early Christian Church Architecture. 1952. 1st ed. Map. Dj (sl chipped). *Edwards.* $23/£15

DAVIES, JOHN. Hindu Philosophy: The Sankhya Karika of Iswara Krishna. London: Trubner, 1881. 1st ed. 151pp. Gilt dec orange cl. VG. *Terramedia.* $60/£38

DAVIES, N. DE G. The Rock Tombs of Sheikh Said. London: Egypt Exploration Fund, 1901. 35 plts. (Bkpl.) *Archaeologia.* $125/£80

DAVIES, PHILIP. Splendours of the Raj. British Architecture in India 1660 to 1947. London: Murray, 1985. Sound in dj. *Ars Artis.* $39/£25

DAVIES, R. TREVOR. Four Centuries of Witch Beliefs. London: Methuen, 1947. 1st ptg. VG + in Good + dj. *Middle Earth.* $60/£38

DAVIES, RANDALL. Chelsea Old Church. London: Duckworth, 1904. #105/320. (Cvrs weak.) *Yudkin*.* $65/£42

DAVIES, RHYS. The Black Venus. NY: Howell, Soskin, (1946). 1st ed. NF (sm bkseller's label fr pastedown) in VG dj (chips, sm tears). *Antic Hay.* $25/£16

DAVIES, RHYS. Daisy Matthews and Three Other Tales. Golden Cockerel, 1932. 1st ed. #132/325 signed. (4),64pp + colophon; 4 Fine wood engrs by Agnes Miller Parker. Teg, others uncut. VG in tan morocco-backed patterned cl. *Cox.* $172/£110

DAVIES, RHYS. Daisy Matthews and Three Other Tales. Golden Cockerel, 1932. One of 325 numbered. Signed. Agnes Miller Parker (engrs). 1/4 tan leather, patterned cl bds. Fine. *Michael Taylor.* $211/£135

DAVIES, RHYS. The Darling of Her Heart and Other Stories. Heinemann, (1958). 1st ed. VG in dj. *Ash.* $31/£20

DAVIES, RHYS. The Red Hills. NY: Covici, 1933. 1st Amer ed. VG in dj (nicks, sm tears). *Houle.* $125/£80

DAVIES, ROBERTSON. The Diary of Samuel Marchbanks. Toronto: Clarke, Irwin, 1947. 1st ed. Signed. VG (name; extrems worn) in dj (browned, lg chips, splits). *Metropolitan*.* $402/£258

DAVIES, ROBERTSON. An Introduction to the Twenty-First Toronto Antiquarian Book Fair. (Toronto: Coach House, 1993.) 1st ed. Fine in illus wrappers. *Dermont.* $35/£22

DAVIES, ROBERTSON. A Jig for the Gypsy. Toronto: Clarke, Irwin, 1954. 1st ed. Signed. Fine in dj (sl torn, worn, internal tape). *Metropolitan*.* $316/£203

DAVIES, ROBERTSON. The Lyre of Orpheus. Canada: Macmillan, 1988. 1st ed. Signed. Fine in dj (back panel sl scratched). *Virgo.* $62/£40

DAVIES, ROBERTSON. The Lyre of Orpheus. Toronto: Macmillan, 1988. 1st ed. Signed. Fine in dj. *Captain's Bookshelf.* $125/£80

DAVIES, ROBERTSON. A Mixture of Frailties. NY: Scribner, (1951). 1st Amer ed. Fine in dj (sl used, 2 sm chips, sm tear, spine sl dknd). *Captain's Bookshelf.* $100/£64

DAVIES, ROBERTSON. The Personal Art. London: Secker & Warburg, 1961. (Mk to tp verso, sl loose; sl shelfwear), o/w Fine in dj (price-clipped, browned, lt worn). *Metropolitan*.* $327/£210

DAVIES, ROBERTSON. The Rebel Angels. London, 1982. 1st Eng ed. Very Nice in dj (price-clipped). *Clearwater.* $31/£20

DAVIES, ROBERTSON. Samuel Marchbanks' Almanack. Toronto: McClelland & Stewart, 1967. 1st ed. Signed. Fine in Fine dj (price-clipped). *Metropolitan*.* $201/£129

DAVIES, ROBERTSON. What's Bred in the Bone. NY: Viking, (1985). 1st ed. Signed 'compliments of the author' slip laid in. Fine in Fine dj. *Metropolitan*.* $57/£37

DAVIES, ROBERTSON. World of Wonders. NY: Viking, (1976). 1st Amer ed. NF in VG dj. *Hermitage.* $30/£19

DAVIES, ROBERTSON. World of Wonders. London, 1977. 1st Eng ed. Very Nice in dj. *Clearwater.* $39/£25

DAVIES, W. H. The Autobiography of a Super-Tramp. London: A.C. Fifield, 1908. 1st UK ed. VG + (few pp sl foxed, pencil name). *Williams.* $125/£80

DAVIES, W. H. Moss and Feather. London: Faber & Gwyer, 1928. #364/500 signed. William Nicholson (illus). Cream paper bds, gilt. (Spine sl mkd), else VG. *Heller.* $135/£87

DAVIES, W. H. Moss and Feather. (London: Faber & Faber, n.d.) NF in sewn pict wraps. *Antic Hay.* $25/£16

DAVIES, W. H. Nature Poems and Others. London: A.C. Fifield, 1908. 1st ed. Bkpl and sig of G.D.H. Cole. Stiff grey bds, black lettering. (Uniform browning of spine), else NF. *Vandoros.* $125/£80

DAVIES, W. H. The Poems. London, 1934. 1st ed. (Spine dknd, cvrs sl mkd), o/w VG. *Words Etc.* $12/£8

DAVIES, W. H. Poems: 1930-31. Cape, 1932. 1st ed. Dec bds. VG in dj (sl mkd). *Whiteson.* $20/£13

DAVIES, W. H. Selected Poems. London: Gregynog, 1928. One of 310. 1/4 cl. *Swann*.* $103/£66

DAVIS, ANDREW JACKSON. Tale of a Physician. Boston/NY: William White/Amer News Co, 1869. 1st ed. 325,(1),8pp. Grn cl stamped in gilt/blind. (Feps discolored; spine sl rubbed), o/w Very Nice. *Reese.* $125/£80

DAVIS, ARTHUR KYLE, JR. (ed). More Traditional Ballads of Virginia. Univ of NC, (c. 1960). VG in VG- dj. *Book Broker.* $45/£29

DAVIS, BENJAMIN J. Communist Councilman from Harlem. NY: International, (1969). 1st ed, wrapper issue. VG in pict wrappers (spine sl tanned). *Reese.* $20/£13

DAVIS, BRITTON. The Truth about Geronimo. M.M. Quaife (ed). New Haven: Yale Univ, 1929. 1st ed. Gray cl. VF in pict dj (chipped). *Argonaut.* $100/£64

DAVIS, BRITTON. The Truth About Geronimo. Milo M. Quaife (ed). Chicago: Lakeside, Christmas, 1951. Dk red cl. NF. *Sadlon.* $35/£22

DAVIS, BURKE. Jeb Stuart: The Last Cavalier. NY: Rinehart, (1957). 1st ed. VG in dj. *Lien.* $50/£32

DAVIS, BURKE. Jeb Stuart: The Last Cavalier. NY, 1957. 1st ed. Fine in dj (sl wear). *Pratt.* $37/£24

DAVIS, BURKE. Our Incredible Civil War. Holt, Rinehart & Winston, (c. 1960). 1st ed. VG in VG dj. *Book Broker.* $25/£16

DAVIS, BURKE. They Called Him Stonewall. NY, (1954). 1st ed. VG in dj (used). *King.* $35/£22

DAVIS, BURKE. To Appomattox: Nine April Days, 1865. NY: Rinehart, 1959. 1st ed. VG in dj. *Lien.* $25/£16

DAVIS, CHARLES G. The Ship Model Builder's Assistant. Salem: Marine Research Soc, 1926. 1st ed. VG in dj (faded). *Parmer.* $65/£42

DAVIS, CHARLES G. Ship Models. Salem, MA, 1929. 1st ed. Plan in rear pocket. Dec eps. Good. *Scribe's Perch*.* $35/£22

DAVIS, DEERING et al. Georgetown Houses of the Federal Period 1780-1830. Architectural Book, 1944. VG in Good dj. *Book Broker.* $25/£16

DAVIS, DEREK C. English and Irish Antique Glass. London, 1965. 2nd imp. Frontis. Dj (chipped, w/loss). *Edwards.* $47/£30

DAVIS, E. ADAMS. Of the Night Wind's Telling. Norman: Univ of OK, 1946. 1st ed. Fine in dj. *Bohling.* $25/£16

DAVIS, E. O. The First Five Years of the Railroad Era in Colorado. Golden: Sage Books, 1948. 1st ed. Signed. Good in dj (chipped). *Dumont.* $50/£32

DAVIS, ELLIS A. and EDWIN H. GROBE. The New Encyclopedia of Texas. Dallas, (ca 1926). 1st ed. 4 vols. Dec cl. *Ginsberg.* $250/£160

DAVIS, FREDERICK C. Coffins for Three. NY: DCC, 1938. 1st ed. (Name), o/w VG in dj (internal tape mends, wear). *Mordida.* $35/£22

DAVIS, FREDERICK C. Thursday's Blade. GC: DCC, 1947. 1st ed. VG in dj (short closed tears). *Mordida.* $30/£19

DAVIS, FREDERICK C. Tread Lightly Angel. GC: DCC, 1952. 1st ed. (Pp dknd), o/w VG in dj (nicks, wear). *Mordida.* $25/£16

DAVIS, GEORGE. Recollections of a Sea Wanderer's Life. NY, 1887. 1st ed. (8),408pp. Pict cl. Howes D111. *Ginsberg.* $250/£160

DAVIS, GEORGE. Recollections of a Sea Wanderer's Life. NY: A.H. Kellogg, 1887. 1st ed. (vii),408pp. Howes D111. *Lefkowicz.* $250/£160

DAVIS, H. P. Gold Rush Days in Nevada City. Nevada City: Berliner & McGinnis, 1948. One of 750 signed, cl-bound. Fldg map bound in, orig prospectus laid in. Red cl, gilt. Fine. *Harrington.* $50/£32

DAVIS, HENRY C. Painless Childbirth and Nitrous Oxide-Oxygen Analgesia. 1916. 2nd ed. Good in Good dj. *Doctor's Library.* $45/£29

DAVIS, HENRY T. Solitary Places Made Glad. Cincinnati, 1890. Frontis, 422pp; port. (Sm rubber lib stamp tp; spine label removed.) Howes D114. *Ginsberg.* $100/£64

DAVIS, J. C. BANCROFT. Mr. Fish and the Alabama Claims. Boston/NY, 1893. 1st ed. 158pp; port. (Sl foxed; back inner hinge cracked.) *Wantagh.* $20/£13

DAVIS, JANE ELIZABETH. Round About Jamestown. Hampton, (c. 1907). VG (paper cvr chipped, tape-repaired). *Book Broker.* $45/£29

DAVIS, JEFFERSON. The Rise and Fall of the Confederate Government. NY: D. Appleton, 1881. 1st ed. 2 vols. (Extrems sl worn), else VG set. Howes D120. *Mcgowan.* $275/£176

DAVIS, JOHN STAIGE. Plastic Surgery. Phila: Blakiston, (1919). 1st ed. 8vo. VG (lib bkpl, sm lib stamp tp). *Glaser.* $500/£321

DAVIS, JOHN. Travels of Four Years and a Half in the United States of America During 1798, 1799, 1800, 1801, and 1802. NY: Henry Holt, 1909. Paper spine label. VG. Howes D123. *Brown.* $25/£16

DAVIS, JOHN. Travels of John Davis in the United States of America 1798 to 1802. J.V. Cheney (ed). Boston: Bibliophile Soc, 1910. One of 487 sets ptd. 2 vols. Vellum spines (faded). *Ginsberg.* $150/£96

DAVIS, JOHN. Travels of John Davis in the United States of America, 1798 to 1802. John Vance Cheney (ed). Boston: Privately ptd, 1910. 2 vols. VG. Howes D123. *Lien.* $95/£61

DAVIS, JOHN. Travels...in the United States of America, 1798 to 1802. Boston: Bibliophile Soc, 1910. One of 487 sets. 2 vols. Howes D123. *Swann*.* $149/£96

DAVIS, JOSEPH BARNARD and JOHN THURNAM. Crania Britannica. London: Ptd for the Subscribers, 1865. 2 folio vols bound in 1. Engr frontis (repaired), tp, (3),253pp, 56 engr plts. Later blue 1/2 morocco (rebound), gilt, marbled bds, raised bands. (Foxing, browning), else Clean. *Goodrich.* $1,295/£830

DAVIS, JULIA. The Shenandoah. NY: F&R, 1945. 1st ed. Fine in VG dj. *Archer.* $35/£22

DAVIS, KATHARINE BEMENT. Factors in the Sex Life of 2200 Women. NY: Harper, 1929. 1st ed. (Name, ex-libris; fore-edge sl waterstained, not affecting text.) *Second Life.* $65/£42

DAVIS, LINDSEY. Poseidon's Gold. London: Century, 1993. 1st ed. Signed. VF in dj. *Mordida.* $50/£32

DAVIS, LINDSEY. Shadows in Bronze. London: Sidgwick & Jackson, 1990. 1st ed. Fine in dj. *Mordida.* $175/£112

DAVIS, LINDSEY. Silver Pigs. NY: Crown, 1989. 1st Amer ed. VF in dj. *Mordida.* $45/£29

DAVIS, M. D. Winslow Homer: An Annotated Bibliography of Periodical Literature. Metuchen: Scarecrow, 1975. 1st ed. VG (ex-lib). *Mikesh.* $37/£24

DAVIS, MARGO. Antigua Black. SF: Scrimshaw, 1973. 1st ed. Fine in Fine dj. *Warren.* $95/£61

DAVIS, MARGO. Antigua Black: Portrait of an Island People. SF: Scrimshaw, 1973. 1st ed. Emb cl, mtd photo. (Owner stamp), else Fine in dj. *Cahan.* $100/£64

DAVIS, NICHOLAS A. The Campaign from Texas to Maryland with the Battle of Fredericksburg. Austin, TX: Steck Co, 1961. Facs rpt. *Cullen.* $60/£38

DAVIS, NOAH. A Narrative of the Life of Rev. Noah Davis, a Colored Man. Balt: John F. Weishampel, Jr., (1859). 1st ed. 12mo. 86pp + (4)pp ads (foxing); port. Blind-stamped brn cl (worn along joints), gilt cvr title: Narrative of a Colored Man. *Petrilla.* $650/£417

DAVIS, NOAH. A Narrative of the Life of Rev. Noah Davis, a Coloured Man.... Balt: John S. Weishampel, Jr., (1859). 1st ed. Frontis port. VG+ (foxing 1st 1/2 of bk; spine ends lt worn, sl loss finish back bd). *Between The Covers.* $850/£545

DAVIS, NORBERT. The Mouse in the Mountain. NY: Morrow, 1943. 1st ed. VG (soil) in dj (sun, soil, long closed tear). *Metropolitan**. $161/£103

DAVIS, RAY J. Flora of Idaho. Provo: BYU, 1952. VG. *Brooks*. $49/£31

DAVIS, RICHARD HARDING. About Paris. NY, (1895). 1st ed. Charles Dana Gibson (illus). 219pp. Blue cl. VG. BAL 4519. *Truepenny*. $45/£29

DAVIS, RICHARD HARDING. About Paris. NY: Harper, 1895. 1st ed. Charles Dana Gibson (illus). Dec blue cl. VG- (spine sl dknd). BAL 4519. *Antic Hay*. $45/£29

DAVIS, RICHARD HARDING. Cuba in War Time. NY: R.H. Russell, 1897. 1st ed. 143pp; 24 plts. Untrimmed. Ptd bds. VG (lt wear, spine soiled). *Bohling*. $85/£54

DAVIS, RICHARD HARDING. In the Fog. NY: R.H. Russell, 1901. 1st ed. NF (lt mks; lt wear). *Beasley*. $30/£19

DAVIS, RICHARD HARDING. The Rulers of the Mediterranean. NY: Harper, 1894. x,228pp. (Sl rubbed), o/w VG. *Worldwide*. $20/£13

DAVIS, RICHARD HARDING. The Scarlet Car. NY: Scribner, 1907. 1st ed. Frederic Dorr Steele (illus). 2pp undated ads. Tan cl pict dec in red/black. VG (sl dampstain some ll; sl soiled, rubbed). *Sumner & Stillman*. $75/£48

DAVIS, RICHARD HARDING. Three Gringos in Venezuela and Central America. NY: Harper, 1896. 1st ed. (Ink name; spine lt sunned), o/w Fine. *Hermitage*. $125/£80

DAVIS, RICHARD HARDING. The West from a Car Window. NY: Harper, 1892. 1st ed. Frederic Remington (illus). Frontis. Bright blue cl pict dec in silver; 'Harpers' on spine measuring 5/8-inch across. Fine. *Sumner & Stillman*. $170/£109

DAVIS, RICHARD HARDING. The West from a Car-Window. NY: Harper, (1892). 243pp. Good. *Lien*. $30/£19

DAVIS, SAM. The First Piano in Camp. NY: Harper, (1919). 1st bk ed. Color frontis. Pict bds. (Pencil mks fr pastedown, text), o/w VG in pict dj (sl chipped). *Pacific**. $29/£19

DAVIS, SUSAN LAWRENCE. Authentic History Ku Klux Klan, 1865-1877. NY: The Author, 1924. 1st ed. Gray cl (spine faded). Good. *Archer*. $175/£112

DAVIS, TERENCE. The Architecture of John Nash. Studio, 1960. VG in dj (creased, tears). *Hadley*. $53/£34

DAVIS, TERENCE. The Architecture of John Nash. The Studio, 1960. 1st ed. Frontis port. Dj (chipped, sl torn). *Edwards*. $47/£30

DAVIS, WALTER BICKFORD and DANIEL S. DURRIE. An Illustrated History of Missouri. St. Louis/Cincinnati: A.J. Hall/Robert Clarke, 1876. Frontis, xx,639pp; 98 plts. (Spine sl faded, rubbed.) *Bohling*. $150/£96

DAVIS, WILLIAM C. (ed). The Image of War 1861-1865. GC: Doubleday, 1981-4. Ltr ptg. 6 vols. NF in VG djs. *Archer*. $200/£128

DAVIS, WILLIAM C. The Orphan Brigade. Doubleday, 1980. Fine in VG dj. *Connolly*. $25/£16

DAVIS, WILLIAM HEATH. Seventy-Five Years in California. Harold A. Small (ed). SF: John Howell, 1967. 3rd ed. Ltd to 2500. Frontis port, 19 plts (4 fldg). VF in dj. *Argonaut*. $50/£32

DAVIS, WILLIAM HEATH. Sixty Years in California. SF: A.J. Leary, 1889. 1st ed. xxii,639pp. Marbled edges. Red pebbled cl, gilt spine. (Spine sl faded), o/w Fine in later paper-cvrd slipcase. Howes D136. *Pacific**. $259/£166

DAVIS, WILLIAM M. Nimrod of the Sea: or, The American Whaleman. NY, 1874. 1st ed. 403pp. Dec cl. Howes D157. *Ginsberg*. $150/£96

DAVISON, RALPH C. Concrete Pottery and Garden Furniture. NY: Munn, 1910. (Sl soiled), else Fine. *Quest*. $50/£32

DAVY, GYPSY. The Himalayan Letters of...and Lady Ba. Cambridge, 1927. 1st ed. 4 fldg maps. Illus eps (lt browned). Illus cl (sl wear). *Edwards*. $390/£250

DAVY, HUMPHRY. Elements of Agricultural Chemistry, in a Course of Lectures for the Board of Agriculture. London, 1813. 1st ed. 10 engr plts, incl 1 fldg (foxed). Contemp 1/2 calf (rehinged). *Argosy*. $200/£128

DAVY, HUMPHRY. Elements of Agricultural Chemistry. London/Edinburgh: Longman et al/A. Constable, 1813. 1st ed. 10 engr plts, 1 fldg. Later bds (recased, sl worn, soiled). VG. *Waverly**. $143/£92

DAVY, HUMPHRY. Elements of Agricultural Chemistry. London: Longman et al, 1814. 2nd ed. 479pp; 9 fldg plts. Calf-backed bds (worn). *Second Life*. $225/£144

DAWDY, DORIS OSTRANDER. Artists of the American West. Chicago: Swallow, (1980). 3 vols. VG in djs. *Lien*. $50/£32

DAWKINS, W. B. Early Man in Britain and His Place in the Tertiary Period. London, 1880. xxiii,537pp. (Contemp ink sigs tp), o/w VG in new cl. *Whitehart*. $39/£25

DAWKINS, W. B. Early Man in Britain and His Place in the Tertiary Period. London, 1880. 537 w/index pp. All edges marbled. 3/4 leather. (Foxing; extrems rubbed), else attractive. *King*. $85/£54

DAWSON, ELMER A. Buck's Winning Hit. G&D, 1930. 5x7.5. 216pp + ads. VG+ (sl shelfworn) in dj (edgeworn). *My Bookhouse*. $100/£64

DAWSON, FIELDING. A Letter from Black Mountain. Univ of CT Library, (1974). One of 250. Fine in illus wrappers. *Dermont*. $25/£16

DAWSON, FIELDING. Man Steps into Space. (NY: Shortstop Press, 1965.) 1st ed. One of 500. NF in wrappers. *Turtle Island*. $75/£48

DAWSON, GEORGE. The Pleasures of Angling with Rod and Reel for Trout and Salmon. NY, 1876. 264pp. Gilt-stamped grn cl. Fine. *Truepenny*. $125/£80

DAWSON, KENNETH. Marsh and Mudflat. London/NY, (1931). VG (cvrs lt worn). *Truepenny*. $25/£16

DAWSON, KENNETH. Modern Salmon and Sea Trout Fishing. Country Life, 1938. 1st ed. 17 half-tone plts. VG in dj (worn). *Cox*. $23/£15

DAWSON, N. Goldsmiths' and Silversmiths' Work. NY: Putnam, 1907. Good. *Blake*. $85/£54

DAWSON, NICHOLAS. Narrative of Nicholas 'Cheyenne' Dawson....Douglas S. Watson (ed). SF: Grabhorn, 1933. One of 500. Cl-backed illus paper over bds; paper spine label. (Sl discoloration eps), else Fine. Howes D159. *Cahan*. $150/£96

DAWSON, PERCY G. et al. Early English Clocks. Suffolk: Antique Collectors' Club, (1982). 1st ed. Color frontis, 35 color plts. Fine in dj. *Weber*. $70/£45

DAWSON, W. (ed). Sir Grafton Elliot Smith, a Biographical Record. London, 1938. Dj (sl worn). *Maggs*. $28/£18

DAWSON, W. L. and L. JONES. The Birds of Ohio. Columbus, 1903. Author's ed, ltd to 1000 signed. 2 vols. 80 color plts. Orig rexine. (Spine head vol 1 sl defective.) *Wheldon & Wesley*. $148/£95

DAWSON, WARREN (ed). The Nelson Collection at Lloyd's. London, 1932. 21 plts. Navy cl, gilt. *Maggs*. $273/£175

DAWSON, WARREN. Magician and Leech, a Study in the Beginnings of Medicine.... London, 1929. 4 plts. (Sl worn.) *Maggs*. $28/£18

DAWSON, WILLIAM LEON. The Birds of California. San Diego, 1923. 'Format de Luxe.' 4 vols. Grn buckram (shelfworn). Oinonen*. $250/£160

DAWSON, WILLIAM LEON. The Birds of California. San Diego: South Moulton, 1923. 3 vols. (Spines faded, lt wear), else VG set. Dumont. $325/£208

DAWSON, WILLIAM. Medicine and Science...Historical and Rare Books from the 15th to the 20th Century. London, 1956. 1st ed. VG in wrappers. Fye. $200/£128

DAY, A. GROVE. Coronado's Quest, Discovery of the Southwestern States. Berkeley, 1940. 1st ed. 2 maps (1 fldg). Fine in Fine dj. Turpen. $50/£32

DAY, F. The Fishes of Great Britain and Ireland. London, 1880-84. 1st ed. 2 vols. 180 litho plts (sl foxed). Dk grn cl (worn, several splits in joints). Maggs. $499/£320

DAY, J. W. Coastal Adventure, a Book About Marshes and the Sea. London: Harrap, 1949. 1st ed. Fine in VG + dj. Mikesh. $27/£17

DAY, J. W. Coastal Adventure. Harrap, (1949). Dj (edges torn). Petersfield. $22/£14

DAY, JEREMIAH. An Inquiry Respecting the Self-Determining Power of the Will.... New Haven: Herrick & Noyes, 1838. 1st ed. Presentation copy, inscribed. (ii),200,(2)pp. Emb brn cl (rubbed), paper label. VG (lt foxed). Gach. $135/£87

DAY, LEWIS F. and MARY BUCKLE. Art in Needlework. Batsford, 1907. 3rd ed. Dec cl. (Sl soiled, worn), o/w VG. Whittle. $39/£25

DAY, THOMAS. Essay on the Law of Usury.... Hartford: The Ed, 1809. 3rd ed. viii,135,8,(14)pp. Unopened. Paper-backed plain bds. (Lt foxed; worn, soiled, spine eroded), o/w VG. New Hampshire*. $75/£48

DAY, W. C. Behind the Footlights. London/NY: Frederick Warne, 1885. 1st ed. Inscribed presentation copy. Frontis. Dec-gilt cl. VG. Dramatis Personae. $40/£26

DAY-LEWIS, C. Beechen Vigil and Other Poems. London: Fortune, (1925). 1st ed, 1st bk. VG in ptd grn wrappers (lt edgeworn). Argosy. $250/£160

DAY-LEWIS, C. The Buried Day. London: C&W, 1960. 1st ed. (Name), else VG in dj. Turtle Island. $35/£22

DAY-LEWIS, C. Country Comets. London, 1928. 1st ed. Fine in glassine wrapper (torn). Words Etc. $39/£25

DAY-LEWIS, C. From Feathers to Iron. Hogarth, 1931. 1st trade ed. (Bds lt soiled, spine sl browned.) Edwards. $75/£48

DAY-LEWIS, C. A Hope for Poetry. Oxford: Basil Blackwell, 1934. 1st ed. VG in dj (chipped, browned). Argosy. $50/£32

DAY-LEWIS, C. An Italian Visit. NY: Harper, (1953). 1st ed, Amer issue, bound from British sheets. (Ep gutters tanned), else NF in VG dj (sl sunned, nicked). Reese. $30/£19

DAY-LEWIS, C. Noah and the Waters. London: Hogarth, 1936. 1st ed. One of 2000. Fine (sm ink name) in dj (sl soiled). Antic Hay. $65/£42

DAY-LEWIS, C. The Otterbury Incident. Cleveland: World, 1969. 1st US ed. Edward Ardizzone (illus). 5 3/4 x 8 1/4. 176pp. Fine in dj. Cattermole. $50/£32

DAY-LEWIS, C. The Poet's Way of Knowledge. Cambridge: CUP, 1957. 1st ed. Ptd bds. Fine in dj. Antic Hay. $25/£16

DE ALARCON, PEDRO ANTONIO. The Three-Cornered Hat. NY: H. Bittner, 1944. One of 500 ptd. 8vo. 151pp; 21 hand-colored woodcuts by Fritz Kredel. Unopened. Fine in dj (sl dknd, torn, chipped). Bromer. $100/£64

DE AMICIS, EDMONDO. Constantinople. Caroline Tilton (trans). NY: Putnam, 1888. vi,326,2pp. (Sl rubbed, ex-lib, spine #), o/w VG. Worldwide. $25/£16

DE AMICIS, EDMONDO. Holland. Helen Zimmern (trans). Phila, 1894. 2 vols. 273; 275pp; fldg map. Teg. (Spines sl rubbed.) Orig cl dj (sl frayed). Edwards. $47/£30

DE ANGELI, ARTHUR C. The Empty Barn. Phila: Westminster, 1966. 1st ed. Marguerite de Angeli (illus). 6 1/2 x 9 1/2. 60pp. VG in dj. Cattermole. $40/£26

DE ANGELI, MARGUERITE. Copper-Toed Boots. NY: Doubleday Doran, 1938. 4to. Unpaginated; 8 full-pg color illus. Illus eps. Beige cl. VG in VG dj (sl chipped, rubbed). Dower. $65/£42

DE ANGELI, MARGUERITE. The Door in the Wall. Doubleday, (1949). Stated 1st ed. 8vo. 112pp; 3 color plts, incl 1 dbl-pg. Dec cvr. Good. Scribe's Perch*. $36/£23

DE ANGELI, MARGUERITE. Skippack School. NY: Doubleday, 1939. 1st ed. 8 1/2 sq. 88pp. Cl spine. VG in dj. Cattermole. $75/£48

DE ANGELI, MARGUERITE. Thee, Hannah! NY: Doubleday, 1940. 1st ed. 8 1/2 sq. 88pp. Cl spine. VG in dj. Cattermole. $60/£38

DE ANGELI, MARGUERITE. Turkey for Christmas. Westminster, 1949. 1st ed. 5x6.5. Pict bds. (Sl shelfworn), o/w VG + in dj (sl edgeworn). My Bookhouse. $50/£32

DE ANGELI, MARGUERITE. Yonie Wondernose. NY: Doubleday, 1944. 1st ed. 9 1/4 x 10 1/4. Cl spine. VG in dj. Cattermole. $75/£48

DE ARMENT, ROBERT K. Knights of the Green Cloth. Norman: Univ of OK, (1982). 1st ed. VF in pict dj. Argonaut. $35/£22

DE ARMENT, ROBERT K. Knights of the Green Cloth. Norman: Univ of OK, 1982. Fine in dj. Dumont. $30/£19

DE ASSIS, JOAQUIM MACHADO. Counselor Ayres' Memorial. Berkeley, CA: Univ of CA, 1972. 1st English trans. (Bd edges shelfworn), else NF in VG + dj (rear panel creased, loss). Lame Duck. $45/£29

DE AVILA, JUAN. The Audi Filia, or A Rich Cabinet of Spiritual Jewells. (St. Omer: English College Press), 1620. 1st ed. 4to. (xxxviii),584,(vi)pp. (Tp sl dusty, sm tear inner blank margin final gathering, partly repaired on last leaf w/o loss; sl marginal waterstain.) Good in contemp lip vellum (no eps; bkpl). Autograph of 'Maria Teresa de Jesu 1743.' Sokol. $928/£595

DE BALZAC, HONORE Old Goriot. NY: LEC, 1948. #904/1500 numbered, signed by Rene Ben Sussan (illus). 1/2 leather, marbled bds. Fine in slipcase (sl rubbed). Hermitage. $75/£48

DE BALZAC, HONORE. The Physiology of Marriage. Francis Macnamara (trans). London: Casanova Soc, 1925. Ltd to 1000. Uncut. Paper spine label. VG. Hollett. $117/£75

DE BAYE, J. The Industrial Arts of the Anglo-Saxons. T. B. Harbottle (trans). London, 1893. xii,135pp, 17 plts. Teg. Gilt-dec cl (spine sl rubbed, sl soil; bkpl). Edwards. $75/£48

DE BAZANCOURT, BARON. Secrets of the Sword. London/NY: George Bell, 1900. 1st ed in English. Teg. 3/4 grn morocco, cl, raised bands, gilt. NF. Blue Mountain. $200/£128

DE BEAUVOIR, SIMONE. Les Belles Images. NY: Putnam, (1968). 1st US ed. Fine in dj (lt wear). Antic Hay. $20/£13

DE BEAUVOIR, SIMONE. The Coming of Age. Patrick O'Brian (trans). NY: Putnam, (1972). 1st US ed. (Leaves stained), o/w VG in dj. Second Life. $45/£29

DE BEAUVOIR, SIMONE. Force of Circumstance. NY, 1965. 1st Amer ed. Fine in dj (edges lt rubbed). Polyanthos. $25/£16

DE BEAUVOIR, SIMONE. The Mandarins. Cleveland: World, (1956). One of 500 numbered, signed. Fine in slipcase (edges sl sunned). *Lenz.* $150/£96

DE BEAUVOIR, SIMONE. Must We Burn De Sade? London, 1953. 1st ed. NF (edges lt sunned) in dj (sm edge tears, edges rubbed). *Polyanthos.* $25/£16

DE BEAUVOIR, SIMONE. A Very Easy Death. Patrick O'Brian (trans). NY: Putnam, (1966). 1st Amer ed. Fine in NF dj (lt worn). *Between The Covers.* $85/£54

DE BEER, G. The Sciences Were Never at War (1689-1815). London, 1960. Dj (sl worn). *Maggs.* $34/£22

DE BERNIERES, LOUIS. Captain Corelli's Mandolin. Secker, 1994. 1st UK ed. Signed, dated. Fine in dj. *Williams.* $31/£20

DE BERNIERES, LOUIS. Labels. (London: One Horse Press, 1993.) 1st ed. One of 2000 signed. As New in ptd wrappers, wraparound band. *Jaffe.* $65/£42

DE BERNIERES, LOUIS. Senor Vivo and the Coca Lord. London, 1991. 1st Eng ed. Fine in dj (flap sl creased). *Clearwater.* $47/£30

DE BERNIERES, LOUIS. The War of Don Emmanuel's Nether Parts. NY: Morrow, 1990. 1st ed. Signed. VF in VF dj. *Unger.* $75/£48

DE BOSSCHERE, JEAN. Marthe and the Madman. Pierre Loving (trans). NY: Covici-Friede, 1928. 1st Amer ed. VG in dj (spine sunned, sm stain, tear). *Antic Hay.* $20/£13

DE BOTHEZAT, GEORGE. Back to Newton. NY: G.E. Stechert, 1936. 1st ed. Fine in dj. *Glaser.* $35/£22

DE BRAY, LYS. Fantastic Garlands. Dorset: Poole, 1982. 64 full-pg paintings. Fine in dj. *Brooks.* $25/£16

DE BREBEUF, JEAN. The Travels and Sufferings of Father Jean de Brebeuf Among the Hurons of Canada. London: Golden Cockerel, 1938. One of 300. Frontis, 2 engrs by Eric Gill. *Swann*.* $345/£221

DE BRUNHOFF, JEAN. Babar at Home. Methuen, 1938. 1st ed. Lg folio. Cl-backed pict red bds. (2 corners, some edges rubbed), o/w VG. *Words Etc.* $62/£40

DE BRUNHOFF, JEAN. Babar et le Pere Noel. NY: Random House, 1941. 1st ed. 10 1/4 x 14 1/2. 40pp. Good. *Cattermole.* $50/£32

DE BRUNHOFF, JEAN. Babar the King. NY: Random House, 1935. 4to. Pict cvr. VG in dj (chips, tears). *Metropolitan*.* $138/£88

DE BRUNHOFF, JEAN. Babar the King. Methuen, 1936. 1st ed. Lg folio. Cl-backed pict yellow bds. (Corners, some edges rubbed), o/w VG. *Words Etc.* $62/£40

DE BRUNHOFF, JEAN. Babar's Friend Zephyr. London: Methuen, 1937. 1st ed. 10 1/4 x 14 1/2. 40pp. Good. *Cattermole.* $150/£96

DE BRUNHOFF, JEAN. The Story of Babar.... NY: Smith & Hass, 1933. 1st Amer ed. Cl-backed pict bds (spine frayed, corners worn; rear hinge cracked, bkpl). Good. *Agvent.* $250/£160

DE BRUNHOFF, LAURENT. Babar's French Lesson. NY: Random, 1963. 4th ptg. 8 1/2 x 12 1/4. 28pp. Glossy bds. VG in dj. *Cattermole.* $15/£10

DE BRUNHOFF, LAURENT. Babar's Visit to Bird Island. NY: Random, 1952. 1st ed. 10 1/2 x 14 1/2. 40pp. Cl spine, pict bds. VG. *Cattermole.* $75/£48

DE BURY, RICHARD. The Philobiblon of Richard de Bury.... NY: Elston Press, 1901. #64/485. Parchment-backed bds. (Spine sl smudged), else VG. *Reese.* $45/£29

DE BURY, RICHARD. The Philobiblon. NY: Grolier Club, 1889. One of 300 sets. 3 vols. Imitation vellum, gilt. Vols 1 and 2 in contemp bd slipcases, vol 3 in mod cl slipcase. *Swann*.* $149/£96

DE BURY, RICHARD. The Philobiblon. Andrew Fleming West (trans). NY: Philip C. Duschnes, 1945. One of 600 ptd. 1/4 brn morocco. VG. *Truepenny.* $75/£48

DE CAMP, L. SPRAGUE and FLETCHER PRATT. The Carnelian Cube. NY: Gnome, (1948). 1st ed. Signed by both authors in year of pub. Dj (sm tears, lt edge-worn). *Swann*.* $115/£74

DE CAMP, L. SPRAGUE and FLETCHER PRATT. The Castle of Iron. NY: Gnome, (1950). 1st ed. Signed by De Camp. Dj. *Swann*.* $57/£37

DE CAMP, L. SPRAGUE and FLETCHER PRATT. Tales from Gavagan's Bar. Twayne, (1953). 1st ed. VG in VG dj (sl chipped). *Certo.* $40/£26

DE CAMP, L. SPRAGUE and FLETCHER PRATT. Wall of Serpents. NY: Avalon, (1960). 1st ed. Dj (lt edge-worn). *Swann*.* $69/£44

DE CAMP, L. SPRAGUE. Demons and Dinosaurs. Sauk City, WI: Arkham House, 1970. One of 500. Signed. (Fr corner tips sl bumped), o/w Fine in dj (lt soiled). *Bernard.* $300/£192

DE CAMP, L. SPRAGUE. Demons and Dinosaurs. Sauk City: Arkham House, 1970. 1st ed. Dj (sl dust-soiled). *Swann*.* $230/£147

DE CAMP, L. SPRAGUE. The Glory That Was. NY: Avalon, 1960. 1st ed. Signed. Dj (sm tear, lt rubbed). *Swann*.* $57/£37

DE CAMP, L. SPRAGUE. Lest Darkness Fall. NY: Henry Holt, (1941). 1st ed. Dj (sl chipped, sm nicks, lt coloring, 2 sm tears back panel). *Waverly*.* $231/£148

DE CAMP, L. SPRAGUE. Solomon's Stone. NY, (1957). 1st ed. Fine in VG dj (edges lt rubbed). *Mcclintock.* $45/£29

DE CAMP, L. SPRAGUE. Tales from Gavagan's Bar. Twayne, 1953. 1st ed. Fine in dj. *Madle.* $50/£32

DE CAMP, L. SPRAGUE. The Tritonian Ring. Twayne, 1953. 1st ed. VG in dj. *Madle.* $40/£26

DE CAMP, L. SPRAGUE. The Wheels of If.... Chicago: Shasta, 1948. 1st ed. Dj (sm tear, top edge sl dknd). *Kane*.* $100/£64

DE CARLE, DONALD. Clock and Watch Repairing. London: Hale, 1981. VG in dj. *Hollett.* $39/£25

DE CASSERES, BENJAMIN. When Huck Finn Went Highbrow. NY, 1934. 1st ed. Ltd to 125 numbered. Port, facs. Vellum-backed bds. (Spine sl dknd), else VG in glassine dj (defective), box (broken). *King.* $75/£48

DE CASSERES, WALTER. The Sublime Boy. NY: Seven Arts, 1926. 1st ed, 1st bk. NF in dj (worn, sm chips). *Beasley.* $50/£32

DE CHAIR, SOMERSET. The First Crusade. London: Golden Cockerel, 1945. One of 500 numbered. 1/4 vellum. *Swann*.* $103/£66

DE CHARDIN, PIERRE TEILHARD. Building the Earth. Wilkes-Barre: Dimension Book, (1965). 1st Amer ed. Fine in slipcase. *Hermitage.* $45/£29

DE CHARDIN, PIERRE TEILHARD. Letters from a Traveller. London, 1962. 1st Eng ed. 4 plts, dbl-pg map. Fine. *Henly.* $14/£9

DE CHARME, LESLIE. Elizabeth of the German Garden. London: Heinemann, 1959. Frontis. Nice in pict dj (tired). *Quest.* $35/£22

DE CLIFFORD, NORMAN FREDERICK. Egypt the Cradle of Ancient Masonry. Phila: Lincoln, 1902. 1st ed. Frontis, 49 plts. Aeg. Orig full black leather (rubbed, cvrs detached), gilt, raised bands. Internally Fine. *Blue Mountain.* $250/£160

DE COCK, LILIANE (ed). Wynn Bullock. Dobbs Ferry, NY: Morgan & Morgan, 1973. 1st ed. NF (name stamp) in illus dj. *Cahan.* $60/£38

DE COLANGE, AUGUSTE LEON. The American Dictionary of Commerce, Manufactures, Commercial Law, and Finance. Boston: Estes & Lauriat, 1880-1881. 1st ed. 2 vols. viii,1-622; 623-1142pp. Brn cl (lt worn). *Karmiole.* $125/£80

DE COLANGE, LEO (ed). Voyages and Travels: or, Scenes in Many Lands. Boston: E.W. Walker, c. 1887. Vols I and II (of 4). 52 (of 53) steel-engr plts, 6 photogravure plts. 1/2 leather, cl bds (worn; fr inner hinge vol 1 broken). *New Hampshire*.* $85/£54

DE COSTER, CHARLES. The Glorious Adventures of Tyl Ulenspiegl. Allan Ross MacDougall (trans). Haarlem: LEC, 1934. Ltd to 1500 signed by Richard Floethe (illus). Full natural linen, gilt. Fine in slipcase (sl worn). *Truepenny.* $85/£54

DE DILLMONT, THERESE. D.M.C. Library. Encyclopedia of Needlework. Alsace: Mulhouse, n.d. (ca 1910). New ed. 13 color plts. Teg. Ptd, pict cl. VG. *New Hampshire*.* $45/£29

DE DURFORT, CLAIRE. Ourika. John Fowles (trans). Austin: W. Thomas Taylor, (1971). One of 500. Signed by Fowles. 1/4 morocco, marbled paper over bds. Fine. *Lenz.* $225/£144

DE FAVRE, ABBE. Beauty's Day. H.G. Keene (trans). Vizetelly, n.d. (c1890). #509/850. Gilt/maroon dec buckram-backed bds. (Sl spotting; spine bumped, shelfwear). Good. *Tiger.* $62/£40

DE FONTENELLE, BERNARD LE BOUYER. A Plurality of Worlds. John Glanvill (trans). (London): Nonesuch, 1929. One of 1600 numbered. Limp vellum (sl soiled) over wrappers. VG. *Reese.* $65/£42

DE FONTENELLE, BERNARD. A Plurality of Worlds. London: Nonesuch, 1929. Teg. Good in vellum-like wrappers, pub's slipcase (chipped). *Karmiole.* $85/£54

DE FOREST, JOHN. History of the Indians of Connecticut from the Earliest Known Period to 1850. Hartford, CT: Hamersley, 1851. 1st ed. Fldg frontis map, xxvi,509pp; 6 plts. (Sm hole back cvr, some wrinkling.) Internally VG. Howes D216. *Oregon.* $95/£61

DE FOREST, JOHN. A Union Officer in the Reconstruction. James H. Croushore and David Morris Potter (eds). New Haven: Yale, 1948. Gray cl. VG+ in dj (edgeworn). *Bohling.* $25/£16

DE FOREST, JOHN. A Volunteer's Adventures. James H. Croushore (ed). London, 1946. 1st Eng ed, 2nd ptg. VG in dj (sl worn). *Wantagh.* $35/£22

DE FOREST, L. EFFINGHAM and ANNE L. Captain John Underhill, Gentlemen. Soldier of Fortune. NY: DeForest, 1934. 1st ed. Paper labels spine, fr cvr. *Ginsberg.* $75/£48

DE FOREST, LEE. Father of Radio. Chicago: Wilcox & Follett, 1950. 1st ed. 16 photo plts. Fine in Good+ dj. *Connolly.* $55/£35

DE FRANCESCO, GRETE. The Power of the Charlatan. Miriam Beard (trans). New Haven: Yale Univ, 1939. 1st ed in English. Frontis. VG in dj. *Glaser.* $85/£54

DE GALVEZ, BERNARDO. Instructions for Governing the Interior Provinces of New Spain 1786. Donald E. Worcester (ed). Berkeley, 1951. 1st Eng ed. #341/500. Untrimmed, unopened. VF. No dj as issued. Howes N223. *Turpen.* $195/£125

DE GASPARIN, AGENOR. The Uprising of a Great People. Mary L. Booth (trans). NY: Scribner, 1861. 1st ed in English. 263pp. (Worn), o/w Good. *Brown.* $30/£19

DE GIVRY, E. G. Picture Museum of Sorcery, Magic and Alchemy. J. Courtenay Locke (trans). New Hyde Park, NY: University Books, (1963). B/w frontis, 9 plts. Color pict eps. Black cl-backed red cl (stained), gilt. NF internally in pict slipcase (rubbed). *Blue Mountain.* $25/£16

DE GIVRY, G. Witchcraft Magic and Alchemy. London: George G. Harrap, 1931. 1st ed. 10 color plts. Black cl. Fine in dj (sl torn). *Cummins.* $200/£128

DE GIVRY, G. Witchcraft Magic and Alchemy. J. Cortenay Locke (trans). London, (1931). 1st ed. 10 color plts. Gilt-stamped black buckram (ends worn; inner fr hinge repaired). *Argosy.* $125/£80

DE GOUY, L. P. The Derrydale Cook Book of Fish and Game. NY: Derrydale, (1937). Ltd to 1250 numbered. Vol 2 only. (Lt wear.) *King.* $50/£32

DE GRAY BIRCH, WALTER and HENRY JENNER. Early Drawings and Illuminations. London, 1879. 310pp; 12 plts hors texte. (Cl sl soiled.) *Washton.* $75/£48

DE GROOT, IRENE. Landscape Etchings by the Dutch Masters of the Seventeenth Century. 1979. 250 plts (17 color). Dj (spine faded). *Edwards.* $31/£20

DE HARTOG, JAN. The Inspector. London: Hamish Hamilton, (1960). 1st ed. NF (sm abrasion fr pastedown, top edge spotted) in dj (sl soiled). *Antic Hay.* $25/£16

DE HEZETA, BRUNO. For Honor and Country, the Diary of.... Herbert K. Beals (ed). Portland, 1985. 1st ed. Frontis. Fine. *Turpen.* $55/£35

DE JONG, MEINDERT. Billy and the Unhappy Bull. NY: Harper, 1946. 1st ed. Marc Simont (illus). 5 1/2 x 8 1/4. 206pp. VG in dj. *Cattermole.* $20/£13

DE KAY, JAMES. Natural History of New York. Part I, Zoology, Volumes 3 and 4. Reptiles, Amphibians and Fishes. Albany, 1842. 2 vols. 102 plain plts. (Foxing; cl sl used.) *Wheldon & Wesley.* $312/£200

DE KAY, JAMES. Natural History of New York. Part One. Zoology. Mollusca and Crustacea. NY: Appleton, 1843. iv,(2),271; (3),70pp, 53 water color plts. (Very worn w/new rebacking saving orig spine; foxed, bottom outer corner of ll chewed in blank portion only.) *Goodrich.* $150/£96

DE KAY, JAMES. Zoology of New-York...Part V Mollusca. Albany, 1843. 271,65pp (foxed); 53 Nice full-pg color plts. (Torn, chipped, frayed.) *King.* $250/£160

DE KNIGHT, FREDA. A Date with a Dish—A Cook Book of American Negro Recipes. NY: Hermitage, (1948). 1st ed. VG in dj. *Perier.* $75/£48

DE KNIGHT, FREDA. A Date with a Dish: A Cook Book of American Negro Recipes. NY: Hermitage, 1948. 1st ptg. Good in dj (chipped). *Brown.* $25/£16

DE KOCK, CHARLES P. The Barber of Paris. NY: Quinby, (1903). Ltd to 1000. 2 vols. 19 plts, incl 2 watercolors from dwgs by John Sloan; 4 orig etchings by C. H. White and M. H. Sterne. 3/4 red leather. VG. *Argosy.* $150/£96

DE KRUIF, PAUL. Life Among the Doctors. NY, 1949. 1st ed. VG (sl worn) in Good dj. *Doctor's Library.* $45/£29

DE LA BECHE, HENRY. The Geological Observer. London, 1851. 1st ed. xxxii,846pp. Fine (neatly rebacked). *Henly.* $156/£100

DE LA CAMPA, MIGUEL. A Journal of Explorations Northward Along the Coast from Monterey in the Year 1775. John Galvin (ed). SF: John Howell-Books, 1964. 1st ed. 2 maps. Floral-patterned cl, gilt spine. Fine. *Pacific*.* $40/£26

DE LA FAILLE, J. -B. Vincent Van Gogh. Prudenvce Montagu-Pollock (trans). London: Heinemann, n.d. (c. 1932). Rev, enlgd ed. 16 color plts. VG. *Hollett.* $148/£95

DE LA FAYETTE, MME. The Death of Madame. Paris: (Harrison of Paris), 1931. One of 325 ptd. Aeg. Full vellum, gilt, sewing threads worked through spine. Pub's case (sl worn), gilt. *Book Block.* $125/£80

DE LA FONTAINE, JEAN. The Fables of Jean de la Fontaine. London: Heinemann, 1931. One of 525 signed by Stephen Gooden (illus) and Edward Marsh (trans). 2 vols. 26 engrs. Vellum. *Swann**. $316/£203

DE LA GUERRA ORD, ANGUSTIAS. Occurrences in Hispanic California. Francis Price and William H. Ellison (eds). Washington, DC: Academy of American Franciscan History, 1956. 1st ed. Frontis port. Fine. *Cahan*. $50/£32

DE LA MARE, WALTER and HAROLD JONES. This Year: Next Year. London: Faber & Faber, (1937). 1st ed, trade issue. Pict cl. VG in dj (sl tanned, lt edge-worn). *Reese*. $50/£32

DE LA MARE, WALTER. Alone. London: Faber & Gwyer, n.d. #298/350. Blair Highes-Stanton (illus). Cream paper bds. (Mkd), else VG. *Heller*. $100/£64

DE LA MARE, WALTER. A Beginning and Other Stories. London: Faber & Faber, (1955). 1st ed. Fine in dj. *Reese*. $35/£22

DE LA MARE, WALTER. Broomsticks. London: Constable, 1925. 1st ed. Sm 8vo. Dec cl. NF (sm brn spot from glue residue fep) in dj (spine sunned, lt soiled). *Antic Hay*. $45/£29

DE LA MARE, WALTER. A Child's Day. London: Constable, 1912. Carine and Will Cadby (illus). 4to. Cl-backed bds (shelfworn, soiled), pict cvr label. Internally Sound. *Oinonen**. $80/£51

DE LA MARE, WALTER. The Connoisseur and Other Stories. London: W. Collins, (1926). 1st ed. #73/250 signed. Uncut, partly unopened. VG in linen-backed cl (backstrip sl browned), morocco label. *Cox*. $39/£25

DE LA MARE, WALTER. Ding Dong Bell. London, 1924. 1st ed. VG in dj. *Truepenny*. $60/£38

DE LA MARE, WALTER. Ding Dong Bell. London: Selwyn & Blount, 1924. 1st Eng trade ed. 8vo. NF in dj. *Antic Hay*. $50/£32

DE LA MARE, WALTER. Ding Dong Bell. London: Selwyn & Blount, 1924. 1st ed. #264/300. Signed. 8vo. Uncut. 1/2 tan cl, brn bds, gilt spine. VG. *Houle*. $85/£54

DE LA MARE, WALTER. Down-Adown-Derry. London: Constable, (1922). 1st ed, trade issue. Dorothy P. Lathrop (illus). 4to. Frontis. Teg. Gilt-pict cl. *Reese*. $60/£38

DE LA MARE, WALTER. The Fleeting and Other Poems. London: Constable, (1933). 1st ed. 8vo. NF (sl faded) in white dj (spine browned, sm tear, soiled). *Antic Hay*. $75/£48

DE LA MARE, WALTER. Henry Brocken, His Travels and Adventures.... John Murray, 1904. 1st ed, 1st issue, top edge plain, lacks closing bracket after 'Ramal' on tp. Dec cl, gilt. Nice (lt mks, signs of age). *Ash*. $133/£85

DE LA MARE, WALTER. Henry Brocken. London: W. Collins, (1924). #100/250 signed. 6 plts by Marian Ellis. Unopened. VG in linen-backed bds (backstrip sl browned), morocco label. *Cox*. $39/£25

DE LA MARE, WALTER. Jack and the Beanstalk. NY: Knopf, 1959. 1st ed. Joseph Low (illus). 5 3/4 x 12 1/4. 52pp. VG. *Cattermole*. $25/£16

DE LA MARE, WALTER. Lewis Carroll. London: Faber & Faber, (1932). 1st ed, trade issue. NF in VG dj (2 edge tears mended on verso, sl dkng). *Reese*. $40/£26

DE LA MARE, WALTER. The Listeners and Other Poems. London: Constable, 1912. 1st ed. Pub's presentation blindstamp on title. Nice (sm bkpl, spine sl sunned, sm mk upper cvr). *Reese*. $100/£64

DE LA MARE, WALTER. Memoirs of a Midget. London: Collins, (1921). 1st ed, 1st issue, w/'Copyright 1921' (only) on tp verso. Signed 'Walter Dadus Pollacke.' 4pp pub's ads at end. VG in dj (chip). *Houle*. $125/£80

DE LA MARE, WALTER. Memoirs of a Midget. London: W. Collins, (1921). 1st ed. One of 210 signed. Cl-backed bds, leather spine label. (Eps lt offset, edge bumped), o/w VG. *Jaffe*. $125/£80

DE LA MARE, WALTER. Miss Jemima. Oxford: Blackwell, (1925). 1st ed. Color frontis. Dec bds (spine nick, edges tanned). VG. *Reese*. $30/£19

DE LA MARE, WALTER. News. London: Faber & Faber, 1930. #229/500 signed. Full-pg 2-color illus; dwgs by Barnett Freedman. Blue paper bds, gilt. VG. *Heller*. $85/£54

DE LA MARE, WALTER. News...with Drawings by Barnett Freedman. London: Faber & Faber, 1930. 1st ed, deluxe issue. One of 500 numbered, specially bound, signed. (Sm spine nick), else Nice. *Reese*. $50/£32

DE LA MARE, WALTER. Poems 1901 to 1918. London: Constable, (1920). 1st ed, trade issue. 2 vols. Gilt-dec cl. Fine in djs (lt used). *Reese*. $60/£38

DE LA MARE, WALTER. Poems for Children. London: Constable, (1930). 1st ed, trade issue. Gilt-dec cl. Fine in VG dj (white spine panel browned). *Reese*. $35/£22

DE LA MARE, WALTER. Poems. London, 1906. 1st ed. Nice. *Buckley*. $62/£40

DE LA MARE, WALTER. Poems. London: John Murray, 1906. 1st ed. (Sm bkpl, bkseller label), o/w VG in slipcase. *Reese*. $125/£80

DE LA MARE, WALTER. The Return. London: Edward Arnold, 1910. 1st ed, preferred 'issue' w/terminal cat. (Sm bkpl; spine, upper cvr edges soiled), else VG. *Reese*. $85/£54

DE LA MARE, WALTER. Self to Self. London: Faber & Gwyer, 1928. #404/500 signed. Blair Hughes-Stanton. Cream paper bds. (Mkd), else VG. *Heller*. $90/£58

DE LA MARE, WALTER. A Snowdrop. (London: Faber & Faber, 1929.) 1st ed. NF (sm chip) in sewn grn wraps. *Antic Hay*. $25/£16

DE LA MARE, WALTER. Stories from the Bible. Faber & Gwyer, 1929. 1st ed. Dec eps. (Faded.) Dj (chipped). *Bickersteth*. $34/£22

DE LA MARE, WALTER. Stuff and Nonsense and So On. London: Constable, 1927. 1st ed. Signed presentation. Als from Elfrida de la Mare. 8vo. (i-viii)ix-xi(xii),(1)2-110(111-112)pp. Grn cl, gilt. NF in pict dj (worn). *Vandoros*. $275/£176

DE LA MARE, WALTER. Stuff and Nonsense. London: Constable, 1927. 1st ed. Grn cl. Fine in dj (sl worn). *Appelfeld*. $35/£22

DE LA MARE, WALTER. The Sunken Garden and Other Poems. (London: Beaumont, 1917.) Ltd to 250 numbered. Tall 8vo. Cl, patterned bds. VG (browning). *Antic Hay*. $75/£48

DE LA MARE, WALTER. The Three Mulla-Mulgars. London: Selwyn & Blount, (1924). #103/260 signed. J.A. Shepherd (illus). Color frontis. Unopened. VG in canvas-backed bds, morocco label. *Cox*. $39/£25

DE LA MARE, WALTER. The Three Mulla-Mulgars. Knopf, 1919. 1st ed. Dorothy P. Lathrop (illus). 12 plts, (8 color). Blue cl, gilt. (Cl edge faded), else VG. *Certo*. $60/£38

DE LA MARE, WALTER. Told Again. Oxford, 1927. 1st trade ed. A.H. Watson (illus). 8x5.5. 320pp. (Cvrs sl worn, scratched.) *King*. $25/£16

DE LA MARE, WALTER. Told Again. Oxford: Blackwell, 1927. 1st trade ed. A. H. Watson (illus). Gilt blue buckram. (Eps tanned), else Fine. *Reese*. $65/£42

DE LA MARE, WALTER. The Traveller. London: Faber & Faber, (1946). 1st ed. 4 color lithos by John Piper. (Inscrip), else Fine in VG dj (sm chips, tears). *Reese*. $35/£22

DE LA MARE, WALTER. Winged Chariot. London: Faber & Faber, (1951). 1st ed. NF in dj (sl edge-tanned, sm stain spine). *Reese*. $30/£19

DE LA MOTTE-FOUQUE, FREIDRICH H. K. Undine. London/NY: Heinemann/Doubleday, Page, 1909. Variant binding? of 1st trade ed. 15 tipped-in color plts by Arthur Rackham. Cl-backed bds (lt worn); no pict eps. Contents, plts NF. *New Hampshire**. $60/£38

DE LA MOTTE-FOUQUE, FREIDRICH H. K. Undine. London/NY: Heinemann/Doubleday, Page, 1909. One of 1000 signed by Arthur Rackham (illus). 15 mtd color plts (1 sl damaged; 1-inch tear margin 1 leaf). Gilt-dec vellum. (Lacks fr ribbon tie), o/w VG. *New Hampshire**. $400/£256

DE LA SALLE, NICOLAS. Relation of the Discovery of the Mississippi River Written from the Narrative of.... Chicago: Caxton Club, 1898. 1st ed. One of 261 ptd. 69pp. Vellum spine. Howes L109. *Ginsberg*. $300/£192

DE LA SALLE, NICOLAS. Relation of the Discovery of the Mississippi River. Chicago: Caxton Club, 1898. One of 266. Howes L109. *Swann**. $230/£147

DE LA TORRE, LILLIAN (ed). Villainy Detected, Being a Collection of the Most Sensational True Crimes...of Britain in the Years 1660-1800. NY: Appleton-Century, 1947. *Boswell*. $45/£29

DE LA VAUGUION, M. A Compleat Body of Chirurgical Operations. 1707. 2nd ed. xxiv,456pp (sl foxed); 12 plts. Contemp calf (joints sl weak). *Whitehart*. $655/£420

DE LACY, CHARLES. The History of the Spur. The Connoisseur, n.d. 47 plts. Marbled eps. (Spotting; spine lt faded.) *Edwards*. $133/£85

DE LAGUNA, FREDERICA. Under Mount Saint Elias. Washington: Smithsonian Inst, 1972. 3 vols. VG in box. *Lien*. $100/£64

DE LANCEY, LADY FRANCES. A Week at Waterloo in 1815. London, 1906. 9 plts. Grn cl (sl stained). *Maggs*. $109/£70

DE LAND, CHARLES E. The Sioux Wars. Pierre, SD: State Hist Soc, 1930, 1934. 1st ed. 2 vols. Grn cl. NF. *Harrington*. $250/£160

DE LEEUW, HENDRIK. Flower of Joy. NY: Willey Book, 1944. 1st ed. Fine in dj (lt used; sticker tear). *Beasley*. $35/£22

DE LEON, DANIEL. Woman's Suffrage. NY: NY Labor News, (1909). 1st ed. Yellow wraps. Good (sl wear, marginalia). *Second Life*. $150/£96

DE LILLO, DON. End Zone. London: Deutsch/Wildwood House, 1973. 1st UK ed. (Sl crease fep), else Fine in dj. *Williams*. $70/£45

DE LINT, CHARLES. Westlin Wind. Eugene: Axolotl Press/Pulphouse, (1989). 1st ed. One of 300 clbound signed by De Lint and Emma Bull (intro). Fine in Fine dj. *Other Worlds*. $50/£32

DE LOCRE, ELZA. Older Than Earth. London; Fanfrolico, 1930. One of 175 numbered, signed. 18 leaves, incl blanks. Red cl-backed dec bds (bumped, soiled), gilt. NF internally. *Blue Mountain*. $45/£29

DE LOLME, JEAN LOUIS. The Constitution of England.... London: G. Kearsley, 1775. 1st Eng ed. viii,448pp. Aeg. 19th-cent calf (rebacked, extrems rubbed). *Karmiole*. $250/£160

DE LONG, EMMA. Explorer's Wife. NY, 1938. Good (ex-lib; few mks, faded). *High Latitude*. $30/£19

DE MABLEY, GABRIEL B. Remarks Concerning the Government and Laws of the United States of America. Dublin, 1785. Complete w/half-title. (Sig, sl spotting.) Orig bds (worn, spine gone). *Freeman**. $90/£58

DE MADARIAGA, SALVADOR. Hernan Cortes. Chicago: H. Regnery, 1955. Frontis. VG in dj. *Lien*. $25/£16

DE MAISTRE, XAVIER. A Journey Round My Room. NY: Hurd & Houghton, 1871. 1st ed in English. (Sm ink price fep), else VG +. *Lame Duck*. $150/£96

DE MAUPASSANT, GUY. Bel-Ami. NY: LEC, 1968. #1029/1500 signed by Bernard Lamotte (illus). (Ding to spine), else Fine in slipcase (bump). *Hermitage*. $75/£48

DE MAUPASSANT, GUY. A Woman's Life. Marjorie Laurie (trans). NY: LEC, 1952. #493/1500. VG in morocco-backed marbled bds; matching labeled slipcase. *Cox*. $55/£35

DE MILFORD, LOUIS LECLERC. Memoir or A Cursory Glance at My Different Travels and My Sojourn in the Creek Nation. Geraldine De Courcy (trans). Chicago: R.R. Donnelley/Lakeside, 1956. Map. VG. *Lien*. $20/£13

DE MILFORD, LOUIS LECLERC. Memoir or A Cursory Glance at My Different Travels and My Sojourn in the Creek Nation. John Francis McDermott (ed). Geraldine DeCourcy (trans). Chicago: Lakeside, Christmas, 1956. Dk blue cl. NF. *Sadlon*. $30/£19

DE MONTAIGNE, MICHAEL. The Essays.... Charles Cotton (trans). Alex. Murray, 1872. 2 vols. 512; (4)(513-)926pp. Maroon cl. Sound (shaken). *Cox*. $19/£12

DE MONTAIGNE, MICHAEL. The Journal of Montaigne's Travels in Italy...1580 and 1581. W. G. Waters (ed). John Murray, 1903. 3 vols. Teg, others uncut. Grn cl, gilt. VG. *Cox*. $55/£35

DE MONTEFAUCON, BERNARD. The Antiquities of Italy. London, 1725. 2nd ed. Contemp calf (rubbed, defective). *Freeman**. $100/£64

DE MORANT, GEORGE SOUILE. Chinese Love Tales. NY: Three Sirens, 1935. (Bkpl; cvrs lt soiled), o/w VG in slipcase. *Truepenny*. $25/£16

DE MORGAN, AUGUSTUS. An Essay on Probabilities.... London: Ptd for Longman and John Taylor, 1838. 1st ed. xviii,306,xl,(2 ads)pp; add'l engr tp (waterstained), 12-pg pub's cat at fr. Orig plum linen (neatly rebacked). *Burmester*. $234/£150

DE MORGAN, AUGUSTUS. On the Study and Difficulties of Mathematics. Chicago, 1902. 2nd rpt ed. Frontis port. (Bkpl remains fep; spine faded.) *Whitehart*. $39/£25

DE PALMA, A. F. Surgery of the Shoulder. Phila, 1950. 1st ed. Red cl bds (sl worn). VG. *Doctor's Library*. $75/£48

DE PAOLA, TOMIE (retold by). The Legend of the Bluebonnet. Methuen, 1983. 1st Eng ed. 4to. (32pp). Glossy pict bds. Mint. *Bookmark*. $27/£17

DE PAOLA, TOMIE. The Little Friar Who Flew. NY: Putnam, 1980. 1st ptg. Obl sm 4to. Emb pict paper-cvrd bds. Fine in VG + dj (mkd). *Book Adoption*. $40/£26

DE QUERVAIN, F. Clinical Surgical Diagnosis. NY, 1913. 1st ed in English. Good (sl worn, spine chipped, rubbed). *Doctor's Library*. $60/£38

DE QUINCEY, THOMAS. California and the Gold Mania. (SF: Colt, 1945.) Ltd to 500. Fldg b/w illus. Cl-backed dec bds, paper spine label. VF in plain grn dj. *Argonaut*. $90/£58

DE QUINCEY, THOMAS. Confessions of an English Opium-Eater. Oxford: LEC, 1930. 12 lithos by Zhenya Gay. 1/4 black canvas, marbled paper over bds. VG (sl shelfworn) in slipcase (broken). *Heller*. $250/£160

DE QUINCEY, THOMAS. Confessions of an English Opium-Eater. Richard Garnett (ed). London, 1891. xxii,275pp. Marbled eps; teg, rest uncut. Full calf, gilt, leather spine label. *Edwards*. $31/£20

DE QUINCEY, THOMAS. Confessions of an English Opium-Eater.... Boston: Ticknor, 1841. Orig bds. (Spine cracked, ends chipped.) Yudkin*. $40/£26

DE QUINCEY, THOMAS. A Diary of Thomas De Quincey. Horace A. Eaton (ed). NY: Payson & Clark, 1927. 1st ed. One of 1500 ptd. Unopened. Olive cl. (Partly sun stained), o/w VG. Cullen. $85/£54

DE QUINCEY, THOMAS. An Essay on Novels. (SF): Privately ptd, 1928. Ltd to 100 numbered. Parchment-backed marbled bds. (Spine sl soiled), o/w Very Nice in slipcase. Karmiole. $100/£64

DE QUINCEY, THOMAS. The Works. Edinburgh: A&C Black, 1862-3. 2nd ed in 15 vols; 1st ed thus. (Sl spotted), o/w NF set in recent cl, gilt. Poetry Bookshop. $312/£200

DE RAPIN, THOYRAS. The History of England as Well Ecclesiastical as Civil. London: James & John Knapton, 1728-1731. 15 vols. 29 copper engrs, 6 fldg tables, 4 fldg maps. Marbled eps. 1/2 morocco, marbled bds. Attractive set. New Hampshire*. $325/£208

DE REAUMUR, R. A. F. Reaumur's Memoirs on Steel and Iron. Anneliese Grunhaldt Sisco (trans). Chicago: Univ of Chicago, (1956). 1st ed thus. Repros of tp, 17 plts. Fine in dj. Glaser. $60/£38

DE REGNIERS, BEATRICE SCHENK. Red Riding Hood. NY: Atheneum, 1972. 1st ed. Edward Gorey (illus). 6 3/4 x 8 1/4. 44pp. Fine in dj. Cattermole. $90/£58

DE RETZ, CARDINAL. Memoirs.... London: Grolier Soc, n.d. (c. 1910). Ltd to 1000. 7 plts. Teg, others uncut. Good in contemp crimson hard-grain morocco, gilt. Cox. $55/£35

DE RICCI, S. English Collectors of Books and Manuscripts (1530-1930) and Their Marks of Ownership. NY, 1930. 1st ed, Amer issue. 8 plts. (Bk label.) Blue cl, paper spine label. Dj. Maggs. $125/£80

DE ROOS, F. FITZGERALD. Personal Narrative of Travels in the United States and Canada in 1826.... London, 1827. 3rd ed. Fldg litho frontis, (12),238pp; 11 plts, 2 maps. Bds (bkpl partly removed, spine ends sl chipped), paper label. Internally NF. Howes D268. Reese. $300/£192

DE SAINT-AUBIN, CHARLES GERMAIN. Art of the Embroiderer. Godine, 1983. (Slipcase sl worn), o/w Mint. Whittle. $47/£30

DE SAINT-EXUPERY, ANTOINE. Flight to Arras. Lewis Galantiere (trans). NY: Reynal & Hitchcock, (1942). 1st US ed in English. Bernard La Motte (illus). (Sm ink name), o/w Nice in dj (spine quite sunned). Reese. $35/£22

DE SAINT-EXUPERY, ANTOINE. Letter to a Hostage. Jacqueline Gerst (trans). London, 1950. 1st Eng ed. Very Nice in dj (sl rubbed). Clearwater. $39/£25

DE SAINT-EXUPERY, ANTOINE. The Little Prince. NY: Reynal & Hitchcock, (1943). 1st Amer ed. VG (eps, pastedowns sl dknd) in dj (sl dknd, edgewear). Captain's Bookshelf. $200/£128

DE SAINT-EXUPERY, ANTOINE. The Wisdom of the Sands. Stuart Gilbert (trans). London: Hollis & Carter, (1952). 1st British ed. NF in VG dj (sl chipped, spine tanned). Reese. $35/£22

DE SAINT-PIERRE, BERNARDIN. Paul and Virginia...with an Original Memoir of the Author. London, 1839. 30 mtd engrs (several foxed). 1/2 leather, marbled bds, gilt spine (extrems sl worn). Contents VG. New Hampshire*. $30/£19

DE SAINT-PIERRE, JAMES HENRY B. Studies of Nature. Henry Hunter (trans). Phila: Birch & Small et al, 1808. 3 vols. Frontis, 4 fldg plts. Leather (rebacked, worn, sl foxing, contents sl offset, ex-lib). Waverly*. $104/£67

DE SCHAUENSEE, R. M. The Birds of Columbia and Adjacent Areas of South and Central America. Narbeth: Livingston, (1964). 11 color, 9 b/w plts. VG + . Mikesh. $50/£32

DE SEGUR, PHILIP. History of the Expedition to Russia...1812. London, 1825. 3rd ed. 2 vols. 392; 408pp (bkpl, hinges broken, map detached, torn). Full grn calf (worn, lacks port), gilt spines, leather labels. King. $175/£112

DE SHIELDS, JAMES T. They Sat in High Places. San Antonio: Naylor, 1940. 1st ed. Fine in dj (sm hole spine fold, chips, tear). Gibbs. $85/£54

DE SMET, PIERRE-JEAN. Life, Letters and Travels of..., 1801-1873. Hiram M. Chittenden and Alfred T. Richardson (eds). NY: Harper, 1905. 4 vols. 16 maps & plts. (Bkpls removed; spine lt chipped; sm emb lib stamps each vol.) Howes C392. Ginsberg. $600/£385

DE SMET, PIERRE-JEAN. Oregon Missions and Travels Over the Rocky Mountains, in 1845-46. NY, 1847. 1/2-title, litho tp, 408,(4)pp; 13 plts, fldg map. (Lt foxed, map corner chipped w/some loss; cl soiled, spine ends worn), else VG. Howes D286. Reese. $1,250/£801

DE SMET, PIERRE-JEAN. Western Missions and Missionaries: A Series of Letters.... NY, 1863. 532pp. Later 3/4 gilt calf, marbled bds. (Neat bkpls, traces of dampstaining few ll), else NF. Howes D289. Reese. $750/£481

DE SOTO, FERDINANDO. The Discovery and Conquest of Terra Florida. London: Hakluyt Soc, 1851. 14,lxvii,200,vpp; fldg map. Mod cl. (Ex-lib.) Adelson. $60/£38

DE TERRA, HELMUT. Humboldt: The Life and Times of Alexander von Humboldt (1769-1859). NY: Knopf, 1955. 1st ed. VG in dj. Lien. $40/£26

DE THULSTRUP, A. Drawings by Thulstrup and Others. NY: E.R. Herrick, 1898. 22 color plts. (Endsheets ripped, dampstaining along plt margins, no loss; bds dampstained, chipped, soiled, spine ripped.) Metropolitan*. $201/£129

DE TIZAC, H. D'ARDENNE. Animals in Chinese Art. London: Benn Bros, 1923. Ltd to 250. 50 plts. Uncut. (Bkpl; lt scratch upper bd, sl wear spine ends.) Hollett. $351/£225

DE TOCQUEVILLE, ALEXIS. Democracy in America. NY, 1838. 1st Amer ed. (Sl foxing; spine crudely repaired, edgeworn.) Freeman*. $240/£154

DE TOCQUEVILLE, ALEXIS. Democracy in America. Parts 1 and 2. London, 1835-40. 1st complete ed in English. 4 vols. 8vo. Half-titles vols 1-2 (not called for in vols 3, 4). (Lacks map.) 1/2 morocco (extrems sl rubbed), gilt. Howes T278-79. Swann*. $4,370/£2,801

DE TOLNAY, CHARLES. The Drawings of Pieter Bruegel the Elder. NY, n.d. 96 plts. Good in dj. Washton. $90/£58

DE TUBIERES, ANNE-CLAUDE-PHILIPPE. The Coachman's Story. Eric Sutton (trans). London: Chapman & Hall, 1927. Ltd to 1000. Teg, uncut. Cl-backed patterned bds (spine lt frayed, sm nick upper bd; ex-lib, pastedown label, stamps). Hollett. $47/£30

DE UNAMUNO, MIGUEL. Mist. NY: Knopf, 1928. 1st US ed. NF (inscrip; spine gutters, bd edges lt foxed) in dj. Lame Duck. $275/£176

DE VARIGNY, CHARLES. Fourteen Years in the Sandwich Islands 1855-1868. Alfons L. Korn (trans). Honolulu: Univ of HI/Hawaiian Hist Soc, 1981. 1st Eng ed. VG in dj (lt worn). Parmer. $45/£29

DE VILLAMIL, R. Newton: The Man. London: Gordon Knox, n.d. (ca 1934). Cl over bds, photo port onlaid top cvr. (Sl warp.) Cullen. $45/£29

DE VINNE, THEODORE LOW. The Plantin-Moretus Museum. SF: Grabhorn, 1929. One of 425 numbered, this copy out of series. Hand-colored frontis, initials. Crushed morocco (backstrip faded). *Swann**. $103/£66

DE VOE, S. S. The Tinsmiths of Connecticut. Middletown, CT: Wesleyan Univ, 1968. Stated 1st ed. Paper over bds, linen spine. Good+ in dj (chipped). *Scribe's Perch**. $32/£21

DE VOLNEY, CONSTANTIN F. View of the Climate and Soil of the United States of America. London: J. Johnson, 1804. 1st Eng ed. xxiv,(4),504pp; 2 engr fldg plts, 2 engr fldg maps. Contemp calf (extrems rubbed), spine label (sl chipped). Sound. Howes V141. *Karmiole*. $275/£176

DE VOTO, BERNARD. Across the Wide Missouri. Boston: Houghton Mifflin, 1947. 1st ed. Dj (sm stain, edgewear, fore-edge soiled), slipcase. *Shasky*. $45/£29

DE VOTO, BERNARD. Across the Wide Missouri. Boston: Houghton Mifflin, 1947. 1st ed. NF in dj (sl soiled). Howes D296. *Sadlon*. $45/£29

DE VOTO, BERNARD. The Year of Decision 1846. Boston: Little, Brown, 1943. 1st ed. Pict cl. NF in dj (lt edgewear). *Sadlon*. $40/£26

DE VOTO, BERNARD. The Year of Decision. Boston, 1943. 1st ed. Fine in VG dj. *Turpen*. $40/£26

DE VRIES, HUGO. Intracellular Pangenesis, Including a Paper on Fertilization and Hybridization. C. Staurt Gager (trans). Chicago, 1910. 1st ed. VG in Good dj. *Doctor's Library*. $60/£38

DE VRIES, HUGO. Species and Varieties, Their Origin by Mutation. Chicago: Open Court, 1905. 1st ed. Later cl, contrasting spine label. Sig of S.J. Holmes. VG. *Glaser*. $285/£183

DE VRIES, LEONARD. Flowers of Delight. NY: Pantheon, 1965. 1st ed. 7 3/4 x 10 1/2. 232pp. VG in dj. *Cattermole*. $45/£29

DE VRIES, PETER. Angels Can't Do Better. NY: Coward, 1944. 1st ed. Fine in dj (lt used; sl rippling fr panel). *Beasley*. $350/£224

DE WALD, ERNEST T. Italian Painting 1200-1600. NY, 1961. Good. *Washton*. $35/£22

DE WINDT, HARRY. Through the Gold-Fields of Alaska to Bering Straits. NY: Harper, 1898. ix(3)314pp; fldg map. Dec cl. VG. *High Latitude*. $125/£80

DE WOLF, LYMAN E. Money; Its Uses and Abuses, Coinage, National Bonds.... Chicago: Pigott, 1869. 1st ed. (8),196pp. *Ginsberg*. $300/£192

DEAM, C. C. Flora of Indiana. Indianapolis, 1940. 2243 maps. *Wheldon & Wesley*. $156/£100

Dean's Rag Book: A to Z. Dean's Rag Book Co, n.d. (ca 1918). 1st ed. #190 in series. Pub's file copy. E. S. Berkeley (illus). 290x195mm. (14)pp. Pict cvr. VF. *Bookmark*. $117/£75

Dean's Rag Book: ABC and 123. Dean's Rag Book Co, n.d. (ca 1920). 1st ed. #268 in Series 3. Pub's file copy. 210x180mm. Contains ptd leaflet listing 'Rag' bk titles, announcing cat of Dolls, Toys & Plush Animals. Mint in pict wraps. *Bookmark*. $140/£90

DEAN, B. Handbook of Arms and Armor, European and Oriental Including the W.H. Riggs Collection. NY: MMA, Jan 1915. Ltd to 1000. 45 plts. VG in dec wraps. *Mikesh*. $45/£29

DEAN, C. G. T. The Royal Hospital Chelsea. Hutchinson, 1950. Add'l tipped-in plt. Scarlet cl, gilt. Fine. *Peter Taylor*. $36/£23

DEANE, DOROTHY NEWELL. Sierra Railway. Berkeley: Howell-North, 1960. 1st ed. (Eps sl offset), else Fine in pict dj. *Argonaut*. $40/£26

DEANE, SAMUEL. The New England Farmer. Worcester: Isaiah Thomas, 1797. 2nd ed, enlgd. (4)leaves, 397 (misnumbered 396) pp (foxed, soiled, sl stains). Contemp calf (worn, shaken, cvrs nearly detached). Internally Sound. *Oinonen**. $120/£77

DEARDEN, HAROLD. Medicine and Duty. London, 1928. Red cl (sl worn). *Maggs*. $47/£30

DEARDEN, S. The Gypsy Gentleman, a Study of George Borrow. London, 1939. VG. *Gretton*. $19/£12

DEARMER, PERCY. The Little Lives of the Saints. Wells Gardner, Darton, July 1904. 2nd ed. 8vo. Frontis, 131pp; 25 b/w illus by Charles Robinson. Illus eps. Dec cl (edges rubbed). VG. *Bookmark*. $23/£15

Death Valley, a Guide. Boston, 1939. 1st ed. (Ink name, date), else VG in dj (rubbed). *King*. $40/£26

Death Valley. Boston: Houghton Mifflin, 1939. 1st ed. Fldg map. Fine in Fine dj. *Book Market*. $80/£51

DEATHERAGE, CHARLES P. Steamboating on the Missouri River in the 'Sixties. (Kansas City, MO, 1924.) VG+ in ptd wraps. *Bohling*. $25/£16

DEBENHAM, FRANK (ed). The Voyage of Captain Bellingshausen to the Antarctic Seas 1819-1821. (By Thaddeus Bellingshausen.) London: Hakluyt Soc, 1945. 2 vols. VG. *High Latitude*. $600/£385

DEBO, ANGIE. Geronimo. Norman: Univ of OK, (1976). 1st ed. 3 maps. VF in pict dj. *Argonaut*. $90/£58

DEBO, ANGIE. Prairie City—The Story of an American Community. NY: Knopf, 1944. 1st ed. VG in dj (worn). *Perier*. $35/£22

Debrett's Peerage, Baronetage, Knightage, and Companionage. C. F. J. Hankinson (ed). London, 1949. Gilt dec cl (soiled, rubbed, spine sl chipped). *Edwards*. $55/£35

DEBS, EUGENE VICTOR. Walls and Bars. Chicago: Socialist Party, 1927. 1st ed. Fine in dj (chipped). *Beasley*. $125/£80

DEBUS, ALLEN (ed). Science, Medicine and Society in the Renaissance. NY, 1972. 1st ed. 2 vols. VG. *Fye*. $50/£32

DECATEUR, STEPHEN, JR. Private Affairs of George Washington. Boston, 1933. 1st ed. #66/160 signed. Paper spine label. (Bkpl; lt wear, soil.) Slipcase (defective). *Freeman**. $45/£29

DECKER, PETER (comp). Descriptive Check List (Priced) Together with Short Title Index.... NY, 1960. 1st ed. 4 vols. NF. *Turpen*. $135/£87

DECKER, ROBERT OWEN. The Whaling City: A History of New London. Chester, CT, (1976). 1st ed. Fine in dj. *Lefkowicz*. $65/£42

DEE, JOHN. The Private Diary of Dr. John Dee. James Orchard Halliwell (ed). London: Camden Soc, 1842. 1st ed. viii,102pp+33pp. (Bkpl, stamp), o/w VG+. *Middle Earth*. $800/£513

DEEPING, WARWICK. The King Behind the King. McBride, 1914. 1st ed. VG. *Madle*. $20/£13

DEFENBACH, BYRON. Idaho: The Place and Its People, A History.... Chicago: Amer Hist Soc, 1933. Emb cvrs. Fine set. *Perier*. $295/£189

DEFOE, DANIEL. Journal of the Plague Year. Bloomfield, CT: LEC, 1968. #1077/1500. Signed by Domenico Gnoli (illus). Tan burlap, heavy bds, gilt red leather label. Fine in slipcase. *Hartfield*. $85/£54

DEFOE, DANIEL. Journal of the Plague Year.... (By Daniel Defoe.) Bloomfield, CT: LEC, 1968. One of 1500 numbered, signed by Domenico Gnoli (illus). 8 color plts. Burlap cl, leather label. VG in bd slipcase. *Argosy*. $100/£64

DEFOE, DANIEL. The Life and Surprising Adventures of Robinson Crusoe. London, 1831. 2 vols. Etched frontispieces by George Cruikshank. 19th-cent 1/2 calf, gilt (vol 2 fr joint starting). *Swann**. $149/£96

DEFOE, DANIEL. Roxana. Avon, CT: LEC, 1976. One of 2000 numbered, signed by Bernd Kroeber (illus). 12 color plts. Dec cl. Mint in bd slipcase, paper spine label. *Argosy*. $125/£80

DEFOE, DANIEL. A Tour Through the Island of Great Britain.... Ptd for W. Strahan et al, 1778. 4 vols. (2 or 3 gatherings sl loose.) Orig calf, gilt spines (rubbed, sl worn at head, foot), red/grn labels. *Bickersteth*. $257/£165

DEGENER, F. SCHMIDT and H. E. VAN GELDER. Jan Steen. London: Bodley Head, 1927. 40 plts, guards. (Sm crease spine head), o/w Fine. *Europa*. $66/£42

DEGENER, OTTO. Naturalist's South Pacific Expedition: Fiji. Honolulu, 1949. VG. *Brooks*. $35/£22

DEGERING, HERMANN. Lettering. London: Ernest Benn, 1929. 1st ed. 240 facs plts. Black cl (worn, chipped, hinges split; lib stamp). *Cox*. $39/£25

DEGERING, HERMANN. Lettering. Modes of Writing in Western Europe...to the Eighteenth Century. Ernest Benn, 1965. 2nd Eng ed. 240 facs plts. VG in dj. *Cox*. $44/£28

DEIBERT, RALPH C. (comp). A History of the Third United States Cavalry. (Harrisburg, PA: Telegraph, ca 1933.) 1st ed. (Cvrs speckled), else VG. *Mcgowan*. $650/£417

DEIGHTON, LEN. ABC of French Food. London: Century, 1989. 1st UK ed. Fine in dj. *Williams*. $19/£12

DEIGHTON, LEN. Berlin Game. London, 1983. 1st ed. VG in dj. *Typographeum*. $18/£12

DEIGHTON, LEN. Berlin Game. London: Hutchinson, 1983. 1st UK ed. Fine in dj. *Williams*. $19/£12

DEIGHTON, LEN. Blitzkrieg. London: Cape, 1979. 1st UK ed. Fine in dj. *Williams*. $23/£15

DEIGHTON, LEN. Bomber. Cape, 1970. 1st UK ed. NF in dj. *Williams*. $31/£20

DEIGHTON, LEN. City of Gold. London: Century, 1992. 1st UK ed. Fine in NF dj. *Williams*. $16/£10

DEIGHTON, LEN. Declarations of War. London: Cape, 1971. 1st UK ed. Fine in dj. *Williams*. $39/£25

DEIGHTON, LEN. An Expensive Place to Die. London: Jonathan Cape, 1967. 1st ed. Fine in dj (2 sm tears, crease). *Certo*. $25/£16

DEIGHTON, LEN. Fighter. London: Cape, 1977. 1st UK ed. VG in dj. *Williams*. $16/£10

DEIGHTON, LEN. Funeral in Berlin. Cape, 1964. 1st UK ed. VG (sl bump) in dj (price-clipped). *Williams*. $44/£28

DEIGHTON, LEN. Goodbye Mickey Mouse. London: Hutchinson, 1982. 1st UK ed. Signed. VG+ in dj. *Williams*. $39/£25

DEIGHTON, LEN. The Ipcress File. Hodder, 1962. 1st ed, 1st bk. One of 4000. VG+ in dj. *Williams*. $507/£325

DEIGHTON, LEN. Len Deighton's Continental Dossier. Michael Joseph, 1968. 1st UK ed. NF in photo bds as issued. *Williams*. $39/£25

DEIGHTON, LEN. Mexico Set. London: Hutchinson, 1984. 1st UK ed. Fine in dj. *Williams*. $16/£10

DEIGHTON, LEN. Spy Hook. London: Hutchinson, 1988. 1st ed. Fine in Fine dj. *Janus*. $35/£22

DEIGHTON, LEN. Spy Sinker. London: Hutchinson, 1990. 1st ed. As New in As New dj. *Janus*. $35/£22

DEIGHTON, LEN. SS-GB. London, 1978. 1st Eng ed. Fine in dj. *Clearwater*. $23/£15

DEIGHTON, LEN. SS-GB. London: Cape, 1978. 1st UK ed. Signed. Fine in dj. *Williams*. $47/£30

DEIGHTON, LEN. Twinkle, Twinkle, Little Spy. London, 1976. 1st Eng ed. Fine in dj (price-clipped). *Clearwater*. $23/£15

DEIGHTON, LEN. Winter, A Berlin Family 1899-1945. London, 1987. 1st ed. VG in dj. *Typographeum*. $28/£18

DEIGHTON, LEN. XPD. London: Hutchinson, 1981. 1st UK ed. Fine in dj. *Williams*. $16/£10

DEKAY, JAMES A. Natural History of New York: Part I, Zoology. Albany, 1842. 2 vols. Vol I, 415pp; Vol II, 144 engrs. VG set (lt foxed; extrems worn). *Bowman*. $350/£224

DEKENS, CAMIEL. Riverman Desertman. Riverside: Press-Enterprise, (1962). Pict wrappers. *Dawson*. $20/£13

DEL CASTILLO, BERNAL DIAZ. The Discovery and Conquest of Mexico. Mexico City: LEC, 1942. #904/1500 numbered, signed by Rafael Loera Y Chavez (printer), Harry Block (ed), and Miguel Covarrubias (illus). Fine in pub's slipcase (lt worn). *Hermitage*. $250/£160

DEL MAR, A. A History of the Precious Metals from the Earliest Times to the Present. London: George Bell, 1880. 1st ed. xx,373pp. Largely unopened. Good. *Blake*. $125/£80

DEL POMAR, FELIPE COSSIO. Peruvian Colonial Art. Genaro Arbaiza (trans). NY, (1964). One of 2000 numbered. VG in dj (chipped). *Argosy*. $100/£64

DEL REY, LESTER. And Some Were Human. Phila: Prime Press, 1948. 1st ed, 1st bk. Sol Levin (illus). Fine in dj (spine faded; lt chipped). *Bromer*. $75/£48

DELABARRE, EDMUND B. Dighton Rock: A Study of the Written Rocks of New England. NY: Neale, 1928. 108 maps and plts. (Few spots spine.) *Ginsberg*. $125/£80

DELACOUR, J. The Waterfowl of the World. London, 1954-64. 1st ed. 4 vols. Very Nice in djs (heads sl frayed). *Maggs*. $320/£205

DELAFIELD, CLELIA. Mrs. Mallard's Ducklings. Boston: Lothrop, 1946. 1st ed. Leonard Weisgard (illus). 7 1/2 x 10 1/4. 32pp. VG in dj. *Cattermole*. $35/£22

DELAFIELD, E. M. Diary of a Provincial Lady. Macmillan, 1930. 1st UK ed. VG (upper hinge sl wormed) in Clean dj. *Williams*. $75/£48

DELAND, MARGARET. The Encore. Harper, 1907. 1st ed. Alice Barber Stephens (illus). Pict cl. (Soil, shelfwear), else VG. *My Bookhouse*. $20/£13

DELAND, MARGARET. The Old Garden and Other Verses. Boston, 1894. 1st ed thus, 1st bk. Walter Crane (illus). Dec cl (sl rubbed, sl faded). *Kane**. $60/£38

DELANEY, MATILDA J. SAGER. A Survivor's Recollections of the Whitman Massacre. Spokane, 1920. 1st ed. Signed presentation from Edmond S. Meany to George W. Soliday. Frontis, plt. Good in wrappers (sl worn). Howes D229. *Brown*. $150/£96

DELANEY, SHELAGH. The Lion in Love. NY: Grove, 1961. 1st ed. Fine in wrappers w/wrap-around band. *Words Etc*. $23/£15

DELANO, ALONZO. Across the Plains and Among the Diggings. NY: Wilson-Erickson, 1936. Rpt. Red cl, gilt. Fine in pict dj (chipped, sl soiled). *Pacific**. $52/£33

DELANO, ALONZO. Pen-Knife Sketches or Chips of the Old Block. SF, 1934. Rpt. Ltd to 550. Linen-backed blue/grn bds, paper title labels. Very Nice (sig). *Cady*. $60/£38

DELANY, SAMUEL R. Stars in My Pocket Like Grains of Sand. NY: Bantam, (1984). 1st ed. Fine in Fine dj. *Other Worlds*. $35/£22

DELANY, SAMUEL R. Stars in My Pocket Like Grains of Sand. NY: Bantam, (1984). 1st ed. Fine in dj (lt rubbed). *Captain's Bookshelf*. $40/£26

DELARIO, A. J. A Handbook of Roentgen and Radium Therapy. Phila, 1938. Good (ex-libris, inner hinges cracked). *Doctor's Library.* $50/£32

DELAVAN, DAVID BRYSON. Early Days of the Presbyterian Hospital in the City of New York. Privately Pub, 1926. 34 full-pg illus. VG. *Goodrich.* $125/£80

DELAVENAY, EMILE. An Introduction to Machine Translation. NY: Frederick Praeger, (1960). 1st ed. Fine in dj. *Glaser.* $60/£38

Delaware Archives. Wilmington, 1911. Vols 1-3. Later buckram. VG +. *Zubal*.* $85/£54

DELCOURT, MARIE. Hermaphrodite. Studio Books, 1961. (Bkpl.) Dj (sl chipped). *Edwards.* $23/£15

DELDERFIELD, R. F. The Avenue. NY: S&S, (1964). 1st Amer ed. (Spine wrinkled), else NF in Fine dj. *Between The Covers.* $65/£42

DELESSERT, ETIENNE. How the Mouse Was Hit on the Head by a Stone and So Discovered the World. GC: Doubleday, 1971. 4to. 32pp; 1 dbl-pg, 11 full-pg illus. Silver cl (sl soiled), purple mouse fr cvr. NF in pict dj (sl foxed). *Blue Mountain.* $35/£22

Delights for Ladies, to Adorne Their Persons, Tables, Closets, and Distillatories. (By Hugh Platt.) London: H.L. and R.T., 1628. 7th(?) ed. 95 (of 96) unnumbered leaves. Later roan (rubbed, soiled, stained, marginal fraying, sm piece torn edge of H11 affecting border). *Oinonen*.* $1,500/£962

DeLILLO, DON. Americana. Boston: Houghton Mifflin, 1971. 1st ed, 1st bk. Cl-backed bds. Fine in dj. *Jaffe.* $275/£176

DeLILLO, DON. End Zone. Boston: Houghton Mifflin, 1972. 1st ed. Black cl. NF in pict dj. *Blue Mountain.* $45/£29

DeLILLO, DON. The Names. NY: Knopf, 1982. 1st ed. Cl-backed bds. (Cvrs sl dust soiled), o/w Fine in dj. *Jaffe.* $35/£22

DeLILLO, DON. White Noise. (NY): Viking, (1985). 1st ed. Cl-backed bds. Fine in dj. *Jaffe.* $50/£32

DELL'ISOLA, FRANK. Thomas Merton: A Bibliography. NY, 1956. 1st ptg. Dj (chipped). *Freeman*.* $30/£19

DELL, ANTHONY. Isles of Greece. London, 1926. 1st ed. Teg. 2-tone cl (sl soiled). *Edwards.* $39/£25

DELL, FLOYD. The Golden Spike. NY: Farrar, (1934). 1st ed. Nice in limp dj (edge chips, mends verso). *Reese.* $35/£22

DELL, FLOYD. Homecoming, An Autobiography. NY: Farrar, (1933). 1st ed. Fine in VG dj (narrow chips spine crown). *Reese.* $85/£54

DELL, FLOYD. Intellectual Vagabondage. NY: George H. Doran, (1926). 1st ed. Fine in dj (price sticker). *Jaffe.* $125/£80

DELL, FLOYD. King Arthur's Socks and Other Village Plays. NY: Knopf, 1922. 1st ed. Fine in Fine dj (sl dknd). *Beasley.* $50/£32

DELL, FLOYD. Looking at Life. NY: Knopf, 1924. 1st ed. (Bkseller label fep), o/w Fine in dj (sl faded, rubbed). *Jaffe.* $125/£80

DELL, FLOYD. Love in Greenwich Village. NY: Doran, (1926). 1st ed. (Few spots, ink erasure eps), o/w Nice in VG dj (sm edge tears mended on verso). *Reese.* $75/£48

DELL, FLOYD. Moon-Calf. NY: Knopf, 1920. 1st ed. Good (sig, sl used). *Reese.* $30/£19

DELL, FLOYD. Souvenir. GC: Doubleday, 1929. 1st ed. Fine in NF pict dj (sm chip spine crown, sl internal mending, price-clipped). *Reese.* $125/£80

DELL, FLOYD. Souvenir. GC: Doubleday, Doran, 1929. 1st ed. VG + (spine wear) in dj (lt used, sm chip). *Beasley.* $125/£80

DELLENBAUGH, FREDERICK S. Breaking the Wilderness. NY/London: Putnam, 1905. 1st ed. Color frontis w/guard; fldg map. (Spines dull; extrems lt rubbed.) VG. *Cahan.* $150/£96

DELLENBAUGH, FREDERICK S. A Canyon Voyage. NY/London, 1908. 1st ed. Frontis. Teg. Dec cvr. (Inscrip; spine lt sunned), else NF. *Five Quail.* $175/£112

DELLENBAUGH, FREDERICK S. A Canyon Voyage. New Haven, 1926. Uncut. (Long inscrip; spine lt faded, cvrs soiled.) *King.* $35/£22

DELLENBAUGH, FREDERICK S. Fremont and '49. NY: Putnam, 1914. Blue cl (lt worn). VG (bkpl). *Parmer.* $75/£48

DELLISOLA, FRANK. Thomas Merton: A Bibliography. NY: Farrar, Straus & Cudahy, (1956). 1st ptg. Gilt-stamped brn cl. Fine in ptd pink dj. *Bromer.* $35/£22

DELMAR, VINA. Kept Woman. NY: Harcourt, 1929. 1st ed. Fine (name, address; sl discolored fr edge) in Fine dj (lt worn). *Beasley.* $35/£22

DELTEIL, LOYS and HAROLD J. L. WRIGHT. Catalogue Raisonne of the Etchings of Charles Meryon.... NY, 1924. Folio. Addenda/errata booklet laid in. Cl-backed bds. *Swann*.* $258/£165

DELVING, MICHAEL. Bored to Death. NY: Scribner, 1975. 1st ed. Fine in dj. *Mordida.* $35/£22

DELVING, MICHAEL. The Devil Finds Work. NY: Scribner, 1969. 1st ed. Fine in dj. *Mordida.* $45/£29

DEMARIS, OVID and ED REID. The Green Felt Jungle. London, 1965. 1st British ed. (Pp browned), o/w Fine in Fine dj. *Warren.* $35/£22

DEMBY, WILLIAM. The Catacombs. NY: Pantheon, (1965). 1st ed. (Corners sl bumped), else Fine in VG + dj (chip rear panel, sm nicks). *Between The Covers.* $45/£29

DEMIDOFF, E. After Wild Sheep in the Altai and Mongolia. London: Rowland Ward, 1900. 1st ed. 8vo. Fldg map. Gilt-lettered cl (sl shelfworn, shaken). *Oinonen*.* $550/£353

DEMING, THERESE O. Little Brothers of the West. NY: Frederick A. Stokes, (1902). 1st ed. Sm 4to. Color frontis, 24pp (ink inscrip, lt foxed, fr hinge cracked); 5 color plts (margins sl soiled) by Edward Willard Deming. Pict cl (bumped, heavily soiled, chipped), circular b/w illus mtd fr cvr. Fair. *Blue Mountain.* $35/£22

DEMPSEY, HUGH A. Crowfoot. Norman, 1972. 1st ed. Fine (bkpl) in dj (sl rubbed). *Baade.* $65/£42

DEMUS, OTTO. Byzantine Art and the West. NY: NY Univ, (1970). 1st ed. 272 plts (8 color). Errata laid in. Red cl (fore-edge rubbed), gilt spine. Dj. *Karmiole.* $50/£32

DEMUS, OTTO. Byzantine Art and the West. 1970. 8 color plts. Dj (sl torn, cellotape repaired). *Edwards.* $70/£45

DEMUS, OTTO. Byzantine Mosaic Decoration. London, 1953. 2nd ed. 64 plts. Good. *Washton.* $60/£38

DENBY, EDWIN. Snoring in New York. NY: Angel Hair/Adventures in Poetry, 1974. 1st trade ed. One of 750. VG in illus wraps. *Cahan.* $40/£26

DENCH, EDWARD BRADFORD. Diseases of the Ear. NY, 1898. 645pp. Grn cl bds (sl worn). VG. *Doctor's Library.* $50/£32

DENDY, WALTER C. The Book of the Nursery.... NY, 1833. 1st Amer ed. 148pp, 1 hand-colored plt. Orig cl (stained, faded). *Argosy.* $125/£80

DENDY, WALTER C. The Philosophy of Mystery. London: Longman et al, 1841. 1st ed. (iii)-xii,443,(1)pp. Emb brn cl. VG. *Gach.* $125/£80

DENHAM, DIXON and HUGH CLAPPERTON. Narrative of Travels and Discoveries in Northern and Central Africa...1822, 1823 and 1824. London: John Murray, 1826. 1st ed. 2 parts in 1 vol. 4to. 1xviii,335,(iv),269pp; fldg map, 37 plts (1 hand-colored). Mod grn 1/2 morocco, red spine label. (Scattered foxing, appreciable offsetting from plts), else VG. *Terramedia.* $1,000/£641

DENHARDT, ROBERT MOORMAN. The Horse of the Americas. Norman: Univ of OK, 1947. 1st ed. 20 plts. Tan cl. Fine in pict dj (chipped, rubbed). *Argonaut.* $45/£29

DENHARDT, ROBERT MOORMAN. The Horse of the Americas. Norman: Univ of OK, 1947. Good. *Dumont.* $55/£35

DENIS, ALBERTA JOHNSTON. Spanish Alta California. NY: Macmillan, 1927. 1st ed. Frontis. Uncut. Tan cl, gilt. (Erasure fep), o/w Fine. *Pacific*.* $58/£37

DENIS, ALBERTA JOHNSTON. Spanish Alta California. NY: Macmillan, 1927. 1st ed. (Sm emb stamp ep, sl tear tp), else Fine. *Argonaut.* $75/£48

DENISON, FREDERIC. The Battle of Groveton. Providence, RI, 1885. 1st ed. Ltd to 250. PNRISSHS Series 3, #9. 35pp. NF in ptd wrappers. *Mcgowan.* $45/£29

DENISON, MERRILL. Canada's First Bank. NY, (1966). 2 vols. Mint in box. *Argosy.* $125/£80

DENLEY, CHARLES F. Ornamental Pheasants. N.p., 1953. 1st ed. (Sl worn.) *King.* $35/£22

DENMAN, THOMAS. An Introduction to the Practice of Midwifery. Brattleborough: Wm. Fessenden, 1807. Contemp calf. VG. *Argosy.* $200/£128

DENNETT, TYLER (ed). Lincoln and the Civil War. NY, 1939. 1st ed. Frontis. (Spine dull, cvrs worn.) *King.* $30/£19

DENNING, WILLIAM F. Telescope Work for Starlight Evenings. London: Taylor & Francis, 1891. Frontis, 361pp (sm ink blot margin 2pp). Dec cl (neatly rebacked). VG. *Savona.* $78/£50

DENNIS, MICHAEL. Court and Garden. (MA): MIT, 1986. 2nd ptg. VG in dj. *Hadley.* $47/£30

DENNIS, PATRICK. Around the World with Auntie Mame. NY: HB&Co, (1958). NF in NF dj (price-clipped). *Between The Covers.* $50/£32

DENSLOW, W. W. The Pearl and the Pumpkin. Boston: Courier, 1905. 12pp. Pict wraps. *Metropolitan*.* $201/£129

DENSMORE, F. Papago Music. BAE Bulletin 90. GPO, 1929. 19 photo plts. Good. *Scribe's Perch*.* $10/£6

DENSMORE, FRANCES. Papago Music. BAE Bulletin 90. Washington: GPO, 1929. VG. *Lien.* $25/£16

DENSMORE, FRANCES. Pawnee Music. BAE Bulletin 93. Washington: GPO, 1929. VG. *Lien.* $25/£16

DENSMORE, FRANCES. Pawnee Music. BAE Bulletin 93. Washington: GPO, 1929. 1st ed. Olive cl, gilt. VG. *Parmer.* $45/£29

DENSMORE, FRANCES. Teton Sioux Music. BAE Bulletin 61. Washington: GPO, 1918. 82 plts. VG. *Perier.* $50/£32

DENT, ALAN (ed). Bernard Shaw and Mrs. Patrick Campbell: Their Correspondence. Alan Dent (ed). London: Gollancz, 1952. Fine in dj (spine sunned; sm tear, lt soil). *Antic Hay.* $20/£13

DENT, HASTINGS CHARLES. A Year in Brazil. London, 1886. xvii,444pp (lt margin browning); 10 full-pg illus, 2 fldg maps. (Cl worn, some loss at joints, spine; stained, faded.) *Edwards.* $47/£30

DENYS, F. WARD. Our Summer in the Vale of Kashmir. Washington: Bryan, 1915. 1st ed. 54 plts (8 color). (Cl sl rubbed), o/w VG. *Worldwide.* $35/£22

DER LING, PRINCESS. Two Years in the Forbidden City. London: Unwin, 1912. 17 plts. (Cl sl rubbed, soiled, spine sl frayed), o/w VG. *Worldwide.* $28/£18

DER NERSESSIAN, SIRARPIE. Armenia and the Byzantine Empire. Cambridge, MA: Harvard Univ, 1945. 1st ed. 32 plts. (Sl rubbed, ex-lib, spine #), o/w VG. *Worldwide.* $30/£19

DERANIYALAGA, P. E. P. The Tetrapod Reptiles of Ceylon. Volume I. Ceylon, 1939. (Shelfwear, stains.) *Oinonen*.* $100/£64

DERBY, J. C. Fifty Years Among Author, Books, and Publishers. NY: Carleton, 1884. 1st trade ed. 500 ptd. 739pp. Purple cl, gilt. VG. *Macdonnell.* $165/£106

DERCUM, FRANCIS. Rest: Mental Therapeutics Suggestion. Phila, 1911. Brn cl. NF. *Doctor's Library.* $75/£48

DERENNES, CHARLES. The Life of the Bat. London, 1925. 1st ed. Wood block by Daglish tipped on frontis. Tan cl, black bds. (Edgewear), else VG in dj (chipped). *Price.* $45/£29

DERLETH, AUGUST (ed). Dark Mind, Dark Heart. Sauk City: Arkham House, 1962. 1st ed. Fine in Fine dj. *Mcclintock.* $47/£30

DERLETH, AUGUST (ed). Dark of the Moon. Sauk City: Arkham House, 1947. 1st ed. VF in dj (sm tears spine). *Bromer.* $100/£64

DERLETH, AUGUST (ed). Dark of the Moon. Sauk City: Arkham House, 1947. 1st ed. (Spine head bumped, top edges bds abraded), else VG+ in NF 1st state dj (spine sl wear). *Other Worlds.* $150/£96

DERLETH, AUGUST (ed). The Night Side: Masterpieces of the Strange and Terrible. NY: Rinehart, 1947. 1st ed. NF in dj (price-clipped, spine sunned, lt edgewear). *Janus.* $35/£22

DERLETH, AUGUST (ed). Who Knocks. Rinehart, 1946. 1st ed. VG in dj (spine ends worn, chipped). *Certo.* $50/£32

DERLETH, AUGUST. The Adventure of the Unique Dickensians. Sauk City: 1968. 1st ed. Booklet. Fine in wraps. *Certo.* $35/£22

DERLETH, AUGUST. And You, Thoreau! Norfolk, CT: New Directions, (1944). 1st ed. 2 wood engrs. Fine in ptd wrappers. *Turtle Island.* $25/£16

DERLETH, AUGUST. The Casebook of Solar Pons. Arkham House, 1965. 1st ed. Fine in Fine dj. *Certo.* $85/£54

DERLETH, AUGUST. The Chronicles of Solar Pons. WI: Mycroft & Moran, 1973. 1st US ed. Ltd to 4176. Good in Good dj (wear). *Gravesend.* $35/£22

DERLETH, AUGUST. Colonel Markesan and Less Pleasant People. Sauk City: Arkham House, 1966. 1st ed. Signed. VF in dj. *Bromer.* $85/£54

DERLETH, AUGUST. Dark Things. Sauk City: Arkham House, 1971. 1st ed. VF in dj (discoloration, spine edges rubbed). *Bromer.* $100/£64

DERLETH, AUGUST. Death by Design. NY: Arcadia House, 1953. 1st ed. Fine in dj (spine lettering sl faded). *Mordida.* $50/£32

DERLETH, AUGUST. The Exploits of Solar Pons. London: Robson Books, 1975. 1st UK ed. VG+ in dj. *Williams.* $23/£15

DERLETH, AUGUST. Fire and Sleet and Candlelight. Sauk City: Arkham House, 1961. 1st ed. VF (bkpl) in dj. *Bromer.* $125/£80

DERLETH, AUGUST. H. P. L. A Memoir. Ben Abramson, 1945. 1st ed. Inscribed, signed. VG (bkpl, fr hinge cracked) in VG dj (internal tape mend). *Certo.* $50/£32

DERLETH, AUGUST. Harrigan's File. Sauk City: Arkham House, 1975. 1st ed. VF in dj (lt chipped). *Bromer.* $45/£29

DERLETH, AUGUST. House of Moonlight. Iowa City: Prairie Press, (1953). One of 550 ptd. Cl-backed dec bds. VG in dj. Truepenny. $60/£38

DERLETH, AUGUST. In Re: Sherlock Holmes. Sauk City, WI: Mycroft & Moran, 1945. 1st ed. (Edgewear, lt soiled), else VG + in dj (spine dknd, sm tear). Murder By The Book. $100/£64

DERLETH, AUGUST. Last Light. Mt. Horeb, WI: Perishable Press, (1978). Ltd to 150. 3 wood engrs by Frank Utpatel. Vellum-backed paste-paper bds, gilt-stamped spine. VF. Bromer. $375/£240

DERLETH, AUGUST. Lonesome Places. Sauk City: Arkham House, (1962). 1st ed. Fine in VG dj (lt rubbed). Mcclintock. $47/£30

DERLETH, AUGUST. Lonesome Places. Sauk City: Arkham House, 1962. 1st ed. Signed. Fine (sl offsetting from orig dj). Bromer. $110/£71

DERLETH, AUGUST. The Mask of Cthulhu. Jersey: Spearman, (1974). 1st thus. Fine in Fine dj. Other Worlds. $45/£29

DERLETH, AUGUST. The Mask of Cthulhu. Sauk City: Arkham House, 1958. 1st ed. Fine in Fine dj (sl browning). Other Worlds. $175/£112

DERLETH, AUGUST. The Memoirs of Solar Pons. Sauk City: 1951. 1st ed. NF (pg edges sl dknd) in NF dj (rear panel soiled). Certo. $100/£64

DERLETH, AUGUST. Night's Yawning Peal: A Ghostly Company. (Sauk City): Arkham House, 1952. 1st ed. (Erasure spot fep), else Fine in NF dj (spine ends worn, short closed tears). Other Worlds. $125/£80

DERLETH, AUGUST. No Future for Luana. NY: Scribner, 1945. 1st ed. Advance rev copy, slip laid in. (Pastedowns sl dknd), o/w Fine in dj. Mordida. $50/£32

DERLETH, AUGUST. Over the Edge. Sauk City: Arkham House, 1964. 1st ed. VF in dj (sl chipped). Bromer. $100/£64

DERLETH, AUGUST. The Reminiscences of Solar Pons. Arkham House, 1961. 1st ed. Fine in Fine dj. Certo. $85/£54

DERLETH, AUGUST. Sac Prairie People. Sauk City: Stanton & Lee, 1948. 1st ed. Inscribed. Dj (sl worn). Swann*. $57/£37

DERLETH, AUGUST. The Seven Who Waited. NY: Scribner, 1943. 1st ed. VG (sl soil) in dj (1-inch tear fr flap, soil, edgewear). Metropolitan*. $34/£22

DERLETH, AUGUST. The Shield of the Valiant. NY: Scribner, 1945. 1st ed. VG + in VG + dj. Bernard. $25/£16

DERLETH, AUGUST. Some Notes on H. P. Lovecraft. (Sauk City: Arkham House, 1959.) 1st ed. Wrappers. Swann*. $80/£51

DERLETH, AUGUST. Someone in the Dark. (Sauk City): Arkham House, 1941. True 1st ed. (Sm bump top edge fr cvr, lt dinges back cvr), o/w Fine in dj (spine sl worn). Levin. $350/£224

DERLETH, AUGUST. Someone in the Dark. Sauk City: 1941. Inscribed presentation to Leo Margolies (ed). NF (pg edges sl dknd) in dj (lacks piece top edge fr panel, spine). Certo. $195/£125

DERLETH, AUGUST. Someone in the Dark. Sauk City: Arkham House, 1966. 2nd ed. Fine in dj (sl sunned, soiled). Metropolitan*. $241/£154

DERLETH, AUGUST. Something Near. Sauk City, 1945. 1st ed. Fine in NF dj (sl rubbed). Mcclintock. $185/£119

DERLETH, AUGUST. Something Near. Sauk City: Arkham House, 1945. 1st ed. Fine (shelfworn) in dj (price-clipped, spine browned). Metropolitan*. $86/£55

DERLETH, AUGUST. Something Near. Sauk City: Arkham House, 1945. 1st ed. Fine (bkpl) in dj. Bromer. $150/£96

DERLETH, AUGUST. Time to Come. Farrar, 1954. 1st ed. Fine in NF dj. Madle. $35/£22

DERLETH, AUGUST. The Trail of Cthulhu. Jersey: Spearman, (1974). 1st thus. NF in dj (short closed tear). Other Worlds. $30/£19

DERLETH, AUGUST. The Trail of Cthulhu. Sauk City, WI: Arkham House, 1962. 1st ed. Fine in dj (sl wear, soil, internal mend). Antic Hay. $50/£32

DERLETH, AUGUST. The Trail of Cthulhu. Sauk City: Arkham House, 1962. 1st ed. VF in dj. Bromer. $75/£48

DERLETH, AUGUST. Travellers by Night. Sauk City: Arkham House, 1967. 1st ed. Fine in Fine white dj (fold spine edge). Other Worlds. $60/£38

DERLETH, AUGUST. Village Year. NY, (1941). 1st ed. VG. Mcclintock. $10/£6

DERLETH, AUGUST. Vincennes: Portal to the West. NJ, 1968. 1st Amer ed. Fine (spine sl sunned) in dj (sl rubbed). Polyanthos. $25/£16

DERLETH, AUGUST. The Wind Leans West. NY: Candlelight, 1969. 1st ed. New in New dj. Bernard. $25/£16

DERRY, T. K. and T. I. WILLIAMS. A Short History of Technology from the Earliest Times to A.D. 1900. London, 1960. 1st ed. Frontis. Fine. Henly. $39/£25

DERWENT, LAVINIA. Pug the Pig. Glasgow: Collins, (1946). Marjorie Anderson (illus). Collins 'Little Country Book.' 12mo. 10pp. VG in color illus wraps. Dower. $20/£13

DES MONTAIGNES, FRANCOIS. The Plains, Being a Collection of Veracious Memoranda Taken During the Expedition of Explorationn 1845.... Norman, 1972. 1st ed. Fine in NF dj (spine sl faded). Turpen. $29/£19

DESANI, G. V. Hali, A Play. (London): Saturn Press, (1950). 1st ed. 1/4 leather. (Sl rubbing edges leather spine), else NF in NF dj (sm chip, tears). Between The Covers. $150/£96

DESCHARNES, ROBERT and JEAN-FRANCOIS CHABRVU. Auguste Rodin. NY: Viking, 1967. Dj (sl discolored). Metropolitan*. $34/£22

DESCHARNES, ROBERT. The World of Salvador Dali. Atide/Crown, 1962. 1st ed. VG (corners bumped, sl shelfworn) in dj (stain, sl edgeworn). My Bookhouse. $60/£38

DESCHARNES, ROBERT. The World of Salvador Dali. Harper & Row, 1962. 1st ed. Portfolio of 52 tipped-in color plts. (Cl edges sl yellowed.) VG in VG dj. Certo. $75/£48

Description of the Early Printed Books Owned by the Grolier Club.... NY, 1895. One of 400. Uncut. Cl, calf back. (Sl worn, spine sl dknd, dried.) Oinonen*. $60/£38

Descriptive and Priced Catalogue of Books...California and the Far West...Collection of Thomas Wayne Norris.... Oakland: Holmes Book Co., 1948. One of 500 ptd at Grabhorn Press. Frontis. Red linen-backed patterned bds, paper spine label. Fine. Harrington. $175/£112

DESMARAIS, CHARLES (ed). Michael Bishop. Chicago: Chicago Center for Contemp Photography, Columbia College, 1979. 1st ed. 24 b/w, 12 color photos. (Owner stamp, sl dusty), else Fine in ptd stiff wrappers. Cahan. $20/£13

DESMOND, R. Wonders of Creation, Natural History Drawing in the British Library. London, 1986. 50 color plts. Dj. Maggs. $28/£18

Detached Dwellings. NY: Swetland, 1909. Tan cl (worn, soiled). Freeman*. $70/£45

DEUTSCH, ALBERT. The Shame of the States. NY, 1948. 1st ed. VG. Fye. $60/£38

DEUTSCH, BABETTE. Fire for the Night. NY: Cape & Smith, (1930). 1st ed. Nice (sl dusty) in dj (sl nicked). *Reese.* $60/£38

DEUTSCH, BABETTE. Potable Gold. NY, 1929. 1st Amer ed. *Polyanthos.* $20/£13

DEUTSCH, HELENE. The Psychology of Women. NY: Grune & Stratton, 1944/1945. 1st ptg. 2 vols. VG+. *Beasley.* $85/£54

DEVERAUX, ROY. Side Lights on South Africa. NY: Scribner, 1899. (viii),273pp; lg fldg color map. (Sl rubbed, soiled; ex-lib, spine sticker), o/w VG. *Worldwide.* $22/£14

DEVEREUX, GEORGE. A Study of Abortion in Primitive Societies. NY: Julian, (1955). 1st ed. VG. *Glaser.* $30/£19

DEVEREUX, GEORGE. A Study of Abortion in Primitive Societies. NY, 1955. VG in dj. *Fye.* $50/£32

DEVOE, SHIRLEY S. The Art of the Tinsmith. Schiffer, 1981. 1st ed. Red cl, gilt. Fine in dj, plastic cvr. *Whittle.* $31/£20

DEWAR, DOUGLAS. Bombay Ducks. London, 1906. 38 photo plts. Teg. Red cl (spine edge damaged, repaired), gilt. Good. *Price.* $48/£31

DEWEES, JACOB. The Great Future of America and Africa. Phila: The Author, 1854. 1st ed. (4),8-236pp. Internally Fine (spine ends chipped). *M & S.* $175/£112

DEWEES, WILLIAM POTTS. A Treatise on the Diseases of Females. Phila: Blanchard & Lea, 1831. 3rd ed. 590pp, 12 engr plts. Orig sheep (rebacked saving orig spine label). Good (foxing). *Goodrich.* $125/£80

DEWEY, EDWARD HOOKER. A New Era for Women: Health Without Drugs. Norwich, CT, 1896. 1st ed. 371pp. Gilt-tooled cl. NF. *Doctor's Library.* $65/£42

DEWEY, JOHN. Experience and Nature. Chicago: Open Court, 1925. 1st ed. NF (name, spine sl sunned). *Beasley.* $85/£54

DEWEY, THOMAS B. Death and Taxes. NY: Putnam, 1967. 1st ed. Fine in dj (spine ends, corners sl worn). *Mordida.* $35/£22

DEWEY, THOMAS B. Hue and Cry. Jefferson House, 1944. 1st ed. VG in VG dj (sm chip). *Certo.* $30/£19

DEWHURST, HENRY WILLIAM. The Natural History of the Order Cetacea, and the Oceanic Inhabitants of the Arctic Regions.... London: The Author, 1834. xx,331pp, 24 plts. Uncut, mostly unopened. Orig bds, new cl spine, orig paper label. VG. *High Latitude.* $550/£353

DEXTER, COLIN. The Dead of Jericho. London: Macmillan, 1981. 1st ed. Fine in dj. *Mordida.* $400/£256

DEXTER, COLIN. The Jewel That Was Ours. Scorpion, 1991. Ltd to 150 signed. 1/4 leather, marbled paper sides. Mint. *Martin.* $75/£48

DEXTER, COLIN. The Jewel That Was Ours. London, 1991. 1st ed. Signed. Fine in dj. *Words Etc.* $34/£22

DEXTER, COLIN. The Jewel That Was Ours. London: Macmillan, 1991. 1st ed. VF in dj. *Mordida.* $65/£42

DEXTER, COLIN. The Riddle of the Third Mile. Macmillan, 1983. 1st UK ed. Signed. NF in dj. *Williams.* $156/£100

DEXTER, COLIN. The Riddle of the Third Mile. London: Macmillan, 1983. 1st ed. Fine in dj. *Mordida.* $300/£192

DEXTER, COLIN. The Secret of Annexe 3. London: Macmillan, 1986. 1st ed. Fine in dj (sl edgewear). *Janus.* $85/£54

DEXTER, COLIN. Service of All the Dead. NY: St. Martin's, (1979). 1st ed. Fine (spine ends sl worn) in VG dj (lt soiled, worn). *Metropolitan*.* $51/£33

DEXTER, COLIN. The Silent World of Nicholas Quinn. Macmillan, 1977. 1st UK ed. Good+ (new fep, few pp sl grubby, stamp removed copyright pg; spine sl bumped, creased) in NF dj. *Williams.* $133/£85

DEXTER, COLIN. The Silent World of Nicholas Quinn. London: Macmillan, 1977. 1st ed. Signed. (Lib labels removed feps, lib stamp), o/w Fine in dj. *Mordida.* $300/£192

DEXTER, COLIN. The Way Through the Woods. Bristol: Scorpion, 1992. 1st ed. One of 150 specially bound, numbered, signed. 1/4 leather, marbled bds. VF in acetate dj. *Mordida.* $150/£96

DEXTER, PETE. Deadwood. NY: Random House, (1986). 1st ed. Fine (rmdr mk top edge) in dj (price-clipped). *Antic Hay.* $25/£16

DEXTER, PETE. God's Pocket. NY: Random, (1983). 1st ed, 1st bk. Fine in NF dj. *Robbins.* $100/£64

DEXTER, PETE. Paris Trout. NY: Random House, (1988). 1st ed. Fine in dj. *Antic Hay.* $25/£16

DEYDIER, CHRISTIAN. Chinese Bronzes. Janet Seligman (trans). NY: Rizzoli, 1980. 1st ed in English. NF in dj. *Worldwide.* $45/£29

DEYO. History of Barnstable County. NY, 1890. Brn morocco (rebound). *Eldred's*.* $99/£63

DI GRAPPA, CAROL (ed). Landscape: Theory. NY: Lustrum, 1980. 1st ed. (Owner stamp), else Fine in dj. *Cahan.* $60/£38

DI PRIMA, DIANE. Dinners and Nightmares. NY: Corinth, 1961. 1st ed. NF (name, stamp) in wraps. *Beasley.* $35/£22

DI PRIMA, DIANE. Earthsong. NY: Poets Press, 1968. 1st ed. NF (bumped) in wraps. *Beasley.* $20/£13

DIAMONSTEIN, BARBARALEE. Visions and Images. NY: Rizzoli, 1982. VG+ in wrappers. *Smith.* $40/£26

Diary of the Revolution. Hartford, 1875. 1084pp. Purple cl (shaken, worn). *Zubal*.* $35/£22

DIAZ DEL CASTILLO, BERNAL. The True History of the Conquest of Mexico. London: J. Wright, 1800. 1st ed in English. Engr frontis map (foxed, deep crease upper left, 2 edges skillfully reinforced), viii,514,(2)pp, incl errata (browned, sm stains, sl foxing, tp corner skillfully supplied). Untrimmed. Recent 1/4 calf. *Waverly*.* $187/£120

DIBDIN, MICHAEL. Rat King. NY: Bantam, 1989. 1st Amer ed. Fine in dj (sl wear, sl crease fr panel). *Mordida.* $35/£22

DIBDIN, MICHAEL. Ratking. Faber, 1988. 1st UK ed. NF in dj. *Williams.* $86/£55

DIBDIN, MICHAEL. A Rich Full Death. London: Jonathan Cape, 1986. 1st ed. Fine in Fine dj. *Metropolitan*.* $63/£40

DIBDIN, THOMAS F. The Bibliographical Decameron. London: W. Bulmer, 1817. 1st ed. 3 vols. Binder's notice (v.2), 1/2 titles, errata; separate colophon leaf vols 1, 3. Mod blue buckram. Fine (sl toning, foxing). *Waverly*.* $412/£264

DIBDIN, THOMAS F. Bibliomania. London: C&W, 1876. New, improved ed. Frontis port, xviii,63,(1),618,xxxivpp; 2 plts. Roan-backed textured cl, gilt. Fine. *Pirages.* $150/£96

DIBDIN, THOMAS F. Bibliomania: or Book-Madness; a Bibliographical Romance. C&W, 1876. New ed. xviii,618,xxivpp. Grn roan-backed cl (spine ends repaired sl crudely w/leather strips), o/w Good. *Cox.* $101/£65

DIBDIN, THOMAS F. Bibliomania; or Book Madness; A Bibliographical Romance in Six Parts. London: McCreery, Longman et al. 1811. 2nd ed. Frontis, title vignette, ix,782pp + errata (inscrip); vol II title bound in in case owner wanted to bind in 2 vols. Calf (sm scuff mks), gilt, blind-tooled inner panel, spine blind-tooled, raised bands. Attractive. *Maggs.* $265/£170

DIBDIN, THOMAS F. Introduction to the Knowledge of Rare and Valuable Editions of the Greek and Latin Classics. London: Harding & Lepard, 1827. 4th ed. 2 vols. (Cl worn, spines gone, fr cvr vol 2 detached.) Contents VG. *New Hampshire**. $75/£48

DIBDIN, THOMAS F. The Library Companion. London: Harding, Triphook & Lepard, 1824. 1st ed. li,912pp. Contemp 1/4 leather (rubbed, 2 inch crack fr joint), paper-cvrd sides. VG. *Graf.* $150/£96

DIBDIN, THOMAS F. The Library Companion. London: Harding, Triphook and Lepard & J. Major, 1824. 1st ed. Recent (not professional) 1/2 morocco, raised bands. VG (sig, old notes, sl browned, foxed). *Pirages.* $125/£80

DIBNER, BERN. Moving the Obelisks. Cambridge: MIT, (1970). 2nd ed. Lg fldg plt. VG in stiff pict wrappers. *Glaser.* $25/£16

DIBNER, BERN. Moving the Obelisks. NY: Burndy Library, 1950. 1 plt. (Pencil underlinings.) Wrappers. *Archaeologia.* $35/£22

DICK, EVERETT. Vanguards of the Frontier. NY, 1941. 1st ed. (Spine sl sunned.) *Hayman.* $25/£16

DICK, PHILIP K. The Collected Stories of Philip K. Dick. LA/Columbia, PA: 1987. 1st ed. One of 400 numbered sets. Synopsis leaflet laid in. VF in VF cl slipcase. *Mcclintock.* $300/£192

DICK, PHILIP K. Confessions of a Crap Artist. Entwistle Books, 1975. Ltd to 500. (Cvrs sl dust-mkd), else Fine in wraps. *Certo.* $50/£32

DICK, PHILIP K. The Cosmic Puppets. (London, 1986.) 1st hb ed. VG in dj. *King.* $35/£22

DICK, PHILIP K. Dr. Futurity. NY: Ace Books, (1960). 1st ed. Pict wraps (extrems worn). *King.* $35/£22

DICK, PHILIP K. Flow My Tears, the Policeman Said. Doubleday, 1974. 1st ed. NF (sm spots top edge) in dj (spine ends creased, sm closed tear). *Certo.* $75/£48

DICK, PHILIP K. Flow My Tears, the Policeman Said. Doubleday, 1974. 1st ed. Fine in NF dj. *Aronovitz.* $125/£80

DICK, PHILIP K. Flow My Tears, the Policeman Said. Doubleday, 1974. 1st ed. NF in dj. *Madle.* $185/£119

DICK, PHILIP K. Galactic Pot-Healer. Gollancz, 1971. 1st ed. Fine in dj. *Sclanders.* $62/£40

DICK, PHILIP K. The Game Players of Titan. London: White Lion, 1974. 1st hb ed. NF (top edge sl dusty) in dj. *Certo.* $115/£74

DICK, PHILIP K. Lies, Inc. Gollancz, 1984. 1st ed. Fine in dj. *Sclanders.* $23/£15

DICK, PHILIP K. The Man in the High Castle. Putnam, 1962. 1st ed. Fine in dj (torn). *Madle.* $400/£256

DICK, PHILIP K. Martian Time Slip. London: New English Library, 1976. 1st hb ed. VG (lower edge dented) in dj (sm chip, lt worn). *Certo.* $90/£58

DICK, PHILIP K. A Maze of Death. NY, 1970. 1st ed. VG in NF dj. *Warren.* $200/£128

DICK, PHILIP K. The Penultimate Truth. NY: Belmont, 1964. 1st ed. (Sm date cvr), else NF in wraps. *Associates.* $50/£32

DICK, PHILIP K. The Preserving Machine and Other Stories. Gollancz, 1971. 1st ed. Fine in dj. *Sclanders.* $62/£40

DICK, PHILIP K. Puttering About in a Small Land. Chicago: Academy, 1985. 1st ed. Fine in dj. *Sclanders.* $31/£20

DICK, PHILIP K. Time Out of Joint. Phila/NY: Lippincott, (1959). 1st hb US ed. (Sm spot fore-edge, spine sl rubbed), else NF in NF dj (spine sl tanned). *Between The Covers.* $650/£417

DICK, PHILIP K. Time Out of Joint. Lippincott, 1959. 1st ed. (Sl shelfwear spine ends), else Fine in VG dj (4 sm tears, soil rear panel, sl shelfwear). *Certo.* $250/£160

DICK, PHILIP K. Time Out of Joint. London, 1961. 1st British ed. Fine in dj. *Swann**. $126/£81

DICK, THOMAS. Practical Astronomer. NY, 1846. 1st ed. xiv,437+10pp ads. Unopened. Brn pub's cl (sl worn). *Truepenny.* $150/£96

DICK, WILLIAM B. Dick's Games of Patience; or, Solitaire with Cards. NY: Dick & Fitzgerald, (1884). New ed. (Sl foxing.) *Sadlon.* $50/£32

Dickens's Dictionary of London. London, 1888. 16 maps. (Upper joint splitting, sl browning.) Orig wrappers. *Edwards.* $23/£15

DICKENS, CHARLES and WILKIE COLLINS. The Lazy Tour of Two Idle Apprentices.... London: Chapman & Hall, 1890. 1st ed. Largely unopened. Blue-grn cl (sl rubbed). Bright. *Waverly**. $187/£120

DICKENS, CHARLES. The Adventures of Oliver Twist or The Parish Boy's Progress. Chapman & Hall, 1895. One of 500. 26 color plts by George Cruikshank. Recent 1/2 brn morocco, marbled sides, gilt. Fine. *Petersfield.* $281/£180

DICKENS, CHARLES. American Notes for General Circulation. Chapman & Hall, 1842. 2nd ed. 2 vols. viii,(2),308pp+ad leaf; viii,306pp+6pp pub's ads. Uncut. Orig cl (backstrips uniformly faded). VG (sig partly sprung). *Cox.* $172/£110

DICKENS, CHARLES. American Notes for General Circulation. London: Chapman & Hall, 1842. 1st ed, 1st issue, 1st binding. 2 vols. Orig violet brn cl, gilt. (Sl faded, rubbed), o/w NF set. Howes D316. *Macdonnell.* $850/£545

DICKENS, CHARLES. American Notes for General Circulation. London: Chapman & Hall, 1842. 1st ed, 1st issue w/o intro, contents pg numbered 'xvi.' 2 vols. Orig cl variant, w/vertical ribbing. Fine. *Bromer.* $1,500/£962

DICKENS, CHARLES. American Notes for General Circulation. London: Chapman & Hall, 1850. 1st ed thus, w/new preface dated 1850. Eps imprinted w/ads, no inserted ads. Orig grn cl, gilt extra. (Sl sunned), else Attractive. *Macdonnell.* $150/£96

DICKENS, CHARLES. American Notes for General Circulation. Avon: LEC, 1975. #417/2000 signed by Raymond F. Houlihan (illus). Fine in pub's slipcase. *Hermitage.* $85/£54

DICKENS, CHARLES. Barnaby Rudge. Chapman & Hall, 1841. 1st separate issue. Variant binding in olive grn fine diaper cl, cvrs and spine stamped in blind, cvrs w/borders, leaf and chain-like design, gilt-lettered spine. *Sotheby's**. $2,332/£1,495

DICKENS, CHARLES. The Battle of Life. London: Bradbury & Evans, 1846. 1st ed, 4th issue, w/'A Love Story' within scroll borne by Cupid on vignette tp, and no pub's imprint. VG in orig red cl (stain fr bd), gilt. *Williams.* $211/£135

DICKENS, CHARLES. The Battle of Life. London: Bradbury & Evans, 1846. 1st ed, w/usual 4th state of engr tp. Steel engr frontis, extra engr tp, (x),175pp+2 ads. Aeg. Pict red cl (spine ends chipped), gilt, blind-stamped dec frame on cvrs. NF. *Blue Mountain.* $250/£160

DICKENS, CHARLES. The Battle of Life. London: Bradbury & Evans, 1846. 1st ed. 8vo. (i-viii),(1-3)4-175(176),(1-2)pp. Aeg; yellow-coated eps. Orig crimson ribbed cl, stamped in blind/gold. (Spine ends lt rubbed), else NF. *Vandoros.* $500/£321

DICKENS, CHARLES. The Battle of Life. London: Bradbury & Evans, 1846. 1st ed. Eckel 2, Todd C2 issue. 8vo. (i-viii),(1-3)4-175(176),(1-2)pp. Aeg; yellow-coated eps. Orig crimson ribbed, blind-stamped cl; 2 cherubs stamped in gold on fr cvr and spine. (Inner hinges tender), else Fine. Vandoros. $795/£510

DICKENS, CHARLES. Bleak House. London: Bradbury & Evans, (1852-1853). 1st ed. 20 parts in 19. 8vo. 624,xvipp; frontis, title, 38 engr plts by H.K. Browne. Most ads listed by Hatton & Cleaver are present as described, incl the scarce 'The Village Pastor.' Fine in cl chemise, solander box. Bromer. $1,500/£962

DICKENS, CHARLES. Bleak House. London, 1853. 1st ed in bk form. 40 engr plts by H. K. Browne. Morocco, gilt, by Delrue. (Sl staining.) Swann*. $172/£110

DICKENS, CHARLES. Bleak House. London, 1853. 1st ed in bk form. 40 engr plts by H. K. Browne (lt foxed; lacks half-title). Later polished tan calf, gilt, by Sangorski and Sutcliffe. Swann*. $316/£203

DICKENS, CHARLES. Bleak House. London: Bradbury & Evans, 1853. 1st ed in bk form, bound up from the parts. Engr frontis, added engr title, xvi,624pp; 38 engr plts by H.K. Browne. Aeg. Brn straight-grain morocco, gilt. Fr wrapper (sl cut down) from orig part-issue bound in at fr. (Some plts sl mottled, sl dknd, bkpl, fr joint sl worn), o/w Excellent internally. Pirages. $750/£481

DICKENS, CHARLES. Bleak House. London: Bradbury & Evans, 1853. 1st ed bound from orig parts. H.K. Browne (illus). Ads as called for in Hatton & Cleaver present. Teg. Full tan polished calf, gilt, raised bands, red/grn labels. Fr/rear wrappers of orig parts bound in at rear. Fine. Appelfeld. $950/£609

DICKENS, CHARLES. Bleak House. London: Bradbury & Evans, March 1852-Sept 1853. 1st ed as issued in 20 orig monthly parts in 19 vols. 8vo. 40 etched plts by H.K. Browne ('Phiz'). W/Bleak House Advertiser in each part, 'Village Pastor' leaflet in part 15, and most of other inserted ads, slips as called for by Hatton & Cleaver. (Marginal browning to plts), o/w VG set in orig ptd wrappers (sl soiled, minor repairs) in 1/4 grn morocco fldg box. Cummins. $1,500/£962

DICKENS, CHARLES. The Chimes. London: Hodder & Stoughton, (1913). 1st Thomson ed. Hugh Thomson (illus). Red cl, gilt. (Several ll lt foxed.) Glenn. $185/£119

DICKENS, CHARLES. The Chimes. Chapman & Hall, 1845. 2nd ed. Aeg. Dec cl (rebacked, orig backstrip relaid). Good (new eps, margins soiled). Tiger. $47/£30

DICKENS, CHARLES. The Chimes. London: Chapman & Hall, 1845. 1st ed, 2nd state of engr tp. Frontis, extra engr tp, (xii),175pp (top edge of frontis, engr title, last few leaves stained; sl foxing, soil). 3/4 grn calf, marbled bds (rubbed, scuffed), raised bands, blind title to spine. VG. Blue Mountain. $150/£96

DICKENS, CHARLES. The Chimes. London: Chapman & Hall, 1845. 1st ed, 2nd state of vignette tp. 8vo. (viii),(1)2-175(176)pp. Aeg; yellow-coated eps. Orig crimson ribbed cl, stamped in blind/gold. (Frontis, tp foxed), else NF. Vandoros. $525/£337

DICKENS, CHARLES. The Chimes. London: LEC, 1931. One of 1500 numbered, signed by Arthur Rackham (illus). (Lt worn, spine sl dknd.) Slipcase (worn, 1 edge split). Oinonen*. $130/£83

DICKENS, CHARLES. The Chimes. London: LEC, 1931. One of 1500 signed by Arthur Rackham (illus). (Spine dknd.) Box (rubbed, worn). Kane*. $250/£160

DICKENS, CHARLES. A Christmas Carol in Prose. London: Chapman & Hall, 1843. 2nd ed w/corrected text and 1st ed tp. 2000 ptd. 8vo. (viii),(1)2-166(167-168)pp; 4 hand-colored steel plts by John Leech. Aeg; yellow-coated eps. Lt reddish-brn ribbed cl. Upper serif of 'D' in Dickens within gold wreath of holly leaves in center of fr cvr is broken; closest interval between blind-stamping on left margin and left extrem of wreath is sl over 12mm. NF. Vandoros. $3,900/£2,500

DICKENS, CHARLES. A Christmas Carol. London/Phila: Heinemann/Lippincott, (1915). Arthur Rackham (illus). 12 color plts, 20 b/w illus. Gilt-dec lavender cl (sl worn, spine sl dull). (Sl foxing), o/w Contents VG. New Hampshire*. $60/£38

DICKENS, CHARLES. A Christmas Carol. Phila: Lippincott, (1915). Arthur Rackham (illus). 12 color, 20 b/w illus. Gilt-dec red cl. VG. New Hampshire*. $60/£38

DICKENS, CHARLES. A Christmas Carol. Boston: Atlantic Monthly, (1920). Facs of 1st ed. 4 color plts, incl frontis. Red cl. (Lt worn, bumped), else VG. Glenn. $85/£54

DICKENS, CHARLES. A Christmas Carol. London: Chapman & Hall, 1844. 9th ed. 2pp undated ads. Orig brn cl, gilt. (Spine corners sl worn), else Fine. Sumner & Stillman. $1,275/£817

DICKENS, CHARLES. Complete Works. London: Chapman & Hall, (1871-1880). 'The Household Edition.' 22 bks in 10 vols, bound from orig parts. 22 frontispieces, 42 plts. (1 frontis loose, lacks 15 half-titles.) 3/4 red morocco, cl (sl scuffed, joints sl worn 1 vol), gilt. NF set. Blue Mountain. $950/£609

DICKENS, CHARLES. The Complete Works. NY: Lovell, Coryell, n.d. (ca 1890s). 15 vols. 8vo. 3/4 tan calf, marbled bds and eps; teg. Spines in compartments, dec tooled in gold, contrasting labels. Very Attractive set. Vandoros. $995/£638

DICKENS, CHARLES. The Cricket on the Hearth, a Fairy-Tale of Home. London: LEC, 1933. #904/1500 numbered. Hugh Thompson (illus). Full pict cl. Fine in pub's slipcase (sl worn). Hermitage. $150/£96

DICKENS, CHARLES. The Cricket on the Hearth. London: Bradbury & Evans, 1846 (i.e. 1845). 1st ed. Wood-engr frontis. Contents VG (few spots, fep cracked along hinge, 1845 sig). Gilt red cl (sl worn; waterspot fr cvr). Waverly*. $231/£148

DICKENS, CHARLES. The Cricket on the Hearth. London: Bradbury & Evans, 1846 (i.e., 1845). 1st ed. Contents VG (1845 inscrip reverse of wood-engr frontis, bkpls, sm stains). Red cl (cocked, lt soiled, worn, few stains), gilt. Waverly*. $88/£56

DICKENS, CHARLES. The Cricket on the Hearth. London, 1846. 1st ed, 2nd state of ad leaf. Add'l tp, frontis. Straight-grain crimson morocco, gilt. Swann*. $258/£165

DICKENS, CHARLES. The Cricket on the Hearth. London: Bradbury & Evans, 1846. 2nd ed. Frontis, extra engr tp, (x),174pp + 2 ads (1 sig pulled). Aeg. Pict red cl (bumped, rubbed, rear joint split, spine chipped, 2 slits), gilt. Internally Very Nice. Blue Mountain. $50/£32

DICKENS, CHARLES. The Cricket on the Hearth. London/NY: J.M. Dent/E.P. Dutton, 1905. Deluxe ed. Aeg. Full vellum, gilt. Glenn. $225/£144

DICKENS, CHARLES. The Cricket on the Hearth. A Fairy Tale of Home. London: Bradbury & Evans, 1846. 1st ed, 1st state ad leaf. 8vo. (viii),(1)2-174,(1-2)pp. Aeg; yellow-coated eps. Crimson ribbed cl, stamped in blind/gold. (Spotting few pp), else NF. Vandoros. $500/£321

DICKENS, CHARLES. The Dickens-Kolle Letters. Harry B. Smith (ed). Boston: Bibliophile Soc, 1910. One of 483. Vellum-backed bds (2 sm tears). Argosy. $85/£54

DICKENS, CHARLES. Dombey and Son. London: Bradbury & Evans, 1846-1848. 1st ed, 1st issue (p324, last line 'Capatin'; p426, line 9, first word 'if' omitted). 8vo. 40 plts (sl foxed; sl dampstained, dknd) by H. K. Browne. Contents largely VG (foxing; lacks some ads). Orig wraps (lt soiled, stained, worn; most parts rebacked, other repairs) in custom 1/2 morocco pull-off case. Waverly*. $522/£335

DICKENS, CHARLES. Dombey and Son. Bradbury & Evans, 1848. 1st ed. H.K. Browne (illus). xvi,(2),624pp, extra engr tp, frontis, 38 plts. (1st opening, several plts extensively spotted) Contemp grn 1/2 morocco (edges sl rubbed), backstrip gilt. VG. Cox. $133/£85

DICKENS, CHARLES. Dombey and Son. London, 1848. 1st ed in bk form, 2nd state of ad leaf. 40 engr plts by H. K. Browne. Morocco gilt. Swann*. $258/£165

DICKENS, CHARLES. Great Expectations. Edinburgh: LEC, 1937. 1st ed. One of 1500 signed by Gordon Ross (illus). NF (spine sl dknd) in slipcase (worn). Captain's Bookshelf. $100/£64

DICKENS, CHARLES. Hard Times. London, 1854. 1st ed. Later tan calf, gilt. Swann*. $345/£221

DICKENS, CHARLES. Hard Times. London: Bradbury & Evans, 1854. 1st ed, 1st binding. Gilt/blind-stamped grn cl (rebacked at early date, orig backstrip laid down, sm mends extrems). Good. Internally VG. Reese. $350/£224

DICKENS, CHARLES. Hard Times. London: Bradbury & Evans, 1854. 1st issue binding, w/'Price 5/-' at spine bottom. Lt olive-grn cl. Good (bds faded, professional repair). Williams. $351/£225

DICKENS, CHARLES. Hard Times. NY: LEC, 1966. One of 1500 signed by Charles Raymond (illus). 15 wash drawings (1 dbl). 1/2 cl, gilt-stamped spine title label. Ad laid in. (Name), else Fine in plastic dj, slipcase. Bohling. $45/£29

DICKENS, CHARLES. Hard Times. NY: LEC, 1966. One of 1500 numbered, signed by Charles Raymond (illus). Fine in pub's slipcase. Hermitage. $85/£54

DICKENS, CHARLES. The Haunted Man and the Ghost's Bargain. Bradbury & Evans, 1848. 1st ed, 1st issue w/fallen '1' in '166' at top of p166. Orig red emb cl, gilt title, wreath fr cvr. (19th cent inscrip; cl worn through 2 places spine hinge; lower hinge worn). Words Etc. $195/£125

DICKENS, CHARLES. The Haunted Man and the Ghost's Bargain. London: Bradbury & Evans, 1848. 1st ed. 188pp. Aeg. Red blind-stamped cl (hinges worn, spine ends frayed), gilt. Hollett. $187/£120

DICKENS, CHARLES. The Haunted Man and the Ghost's Bargain. London: Bradbury & Evans, 1848. 1st ed. 8vo. (viii),(1)2-188pp. Aeg; yellow-coated eps. Ribbed cl stamped in blind/gold. (Lt pencil notation fep), else Fine. Vandoros. $650/£417

DICKENS, CHARLES. Hunted Down. John Camden Hotten, n.d. (1870). Contemp 1/2 leather over cl. Good (ex-lib, stamp, margin soiling, several leaf edges frayed, pp77/78 supplied in facs, copy of orig upper wrapper). Tiger. $468/£300

DICKENS, CHARLES. The Life and Adventures of Martin Chuzzlewit. London, 1844. 1st ed. Frontis, extra engr tp, 38 plts (1 edge tear) by H. K. Browne. Aeg. Later full tan morocco, earlier gilt-dec leather spine preserved (chipped), new gilt-lettered leather spine labels. Kane*. $225/£144

DICKENS, CHARLES. The Life and Adventures of Martin Chuzzlewit. London, 1844. 1st ed in bk form. Engr frontis, 38 plts (foxed) by H. K. Browne. 1/2 brn polished calf, gilt. Swann*. $230/£147

DICKENS, CHARLES. The Life and Adventures of Martin Chuzzlewit. London: Chapman & Hall, 1844. 1st ed, 1st issue, bound from orig parts. Frontis, add'l engr title, 38 plts by Phiz. (Lt foxing, sl cut down, fr wrapper part #13 bound in). Aeg. Late 19th-cent full polished brn calf (scuffed), gilt, leather labels. Freeman*. $170/£109

DICKENS, CHARLES. The Life and Adventures of Martin Chuzzlewit. NY: Harper, 1844. 1st Amer ed in bk form. (vi),312pp (bottom corner 1st few ll lt dampstained; lt foxed); 14 plts by H.K. Browne (Phiz). 3/4 maroon calf, marbled bds (bumped, rubbed), gilt. VG. Blue Mountain. $95/£61

DICKENS, CHARLES. The Life and Adventures of Nicholas Nickleby. London, 1839. 1st ed in bk form, later reading at p123. Frontis; 39 engr plts by H. K. Browne. Morocco, gilt. (Lt spotted.) Swann*. $172/£110

DICKENS, CHARLES. The Life and Adventures of Nicholas Nickleby. London, 1839. 1st ed. Bound from parts, w/specimen fr wrapper incl; w/1st issue misprints pp123, 160. 8vo. Frontis port by Maclise; illus by Phiz. Full polished calf, gilt. VG. Argosy. $600/£385

DICKENS, CHARLES. The Life and Adventures of Nicholas Nickleby. London: Chapman & Hall, 1839. Full grn calf (spine starting to split, rubbing). Metropolitan*. $86/£55

DICKENS, CHARLES. The Life and Adventures of Nicholas Nickleby. London: Chapman & Hall, 1839. 1st ed, apparently bound from mixed 1st and 2nd issues of the parts. (Soiled; some stains, sm tears; margins sl trimmed; plt conditions varies, VG to Poor; few repaired tears, one very lg; some margins cropped; few plts laid down on paper.) Mod 1/2-calf over earlier grn pebble-grain cl (sl soiled), old marbled eps. Waverly*. $143/£92

DICKENS, CHARLES. The Life and Adventures of Nicholas Nickleby. London: Chapman & Hall, 1839. 1st ed. Bound from the Parts. Frontis port, illus by Phiz; w/extra illus: 2 Series, one by Peter Palette, and also ports by Onwhyn. Period style 3/4 polished calf, marbled bds, eps, red/black labels. Nice (sl worn). Hartfield. $595/£381

DICKENS, CHARLES. The Life of Our Lord. London: Associated Newspapers, 1934. 1st Eng ed. Full flexible blue leather, gilt. Fine. Macdonnell. $175/£112

DICKENS, CHARLES. Little Dorrit. London: Bradbury & Evans, 1855-1857. 1st ed, 1st issue (p326 'Rigaud'), w/all inserts and ads called for. As 1st issued, in orig 20/19 parts. 40 plts by H. K. Browne. Contents clean (lt foxing to few plts, ads; sigs; bkseller's labels). Wraps uniformly firm (spines skillfully repaired or rebacked; lt soiled, toned, frayed). Custom 1/4 leather slipcase. Waverly*. $990/£635

DICKENS, CHARLES. Little Dorrit. London, 1857. 1st ed in bk form, 1st issue. 40 engr plts by H. K. Browne. Later polished tan calf, gilt, by Sangorski and Sutcliffe. (Sl crackling top corner fr cvr.) Swann*. $316/£203

DICKENS, CHARLES. Little Dorrit. London, Bradbury & Evans, 1857. 1st ed. Engr frontis, tp, 38 plts (browned, foxed). Contemp cl (rebacked), part of orig spine laid down. Sound. Andrew Stewart. $101/£65

DICKENS, CHARLES. Little Dorrit. London: Bradbury & Evans, 1857. 1st ed. 8vo. Book the First: (v)vi-vii(viii-ix)x-xiv,(1)2-320pp; Book the Second: (321-323)324-625(626)pp. 40 illus by Phiz (incl frontis, engr tp). Olive-grn fine-diaper clw/dec blind-stamping as called for. (Uniform mellow browning of spine, lt rubbing at spine foot), else Very Nice. Vandoros. $1,750/£1,122

DICKENS, CHARLES. Master Humphrey's Clock. London: Chapman & Hall, 1840 (-1841). 1st ed. H.K. Browne and George Cattermole (illus). 3 vols. Lg 8vo. Pub's primary binding of purplish-brn bold-ribbed cl, cvrs stamped in blind, gilt-stamped clocks on each cvr w/hands indicating volume #; hair-vein marbled edges, eps. (Lt overall wear; spine head, foot rubbed, lt sunned.) D & D. $800/£513

DICKENS, CHARLES. Master Humphrey's Clock. London, 1840-1. 1st ed, bound from parts. George Cattermole and H. K. Browne (illus). 3 vols. 1/2 polished calf, marbled bds (worn, 2 spines lack pieces; lacks dedication leaf, probably discarded in binding). Kane*. $85/£54

DICKENS, CHARLES. Master Humphrey's Clock. London, 1840-1. 1st ed. George Cattermole and H. K. Browne (illus). 3 vols. Teg. Full red morocco, gilt. (Backstrips dknd, sl rubbed; orig fr cvrs, backstrips bound in at rear each vol.) Kane*. $250/£160

DICKENS, CHARLES. Master Humphrey's Clock. London: Chapman & Hall, 1840-1. 3 vols. Last 2 vols 1st issue, w/'hairline' marbled eps instead of later cafe au lait. P.(iii), l.31 has the spelling 'favorite,' possibly as always. Gathered in sixes, 1/2 titles not called for. Frontis, tissue guard each vol. (vi),306; (vi),306; vi,426pp. Marbled edges, eps. Vol 1 in old 1/2 dk red sheep, blue stippled sides, gilt spine. Vols 2 & 3 in orig ribbed puce cl. (1 frontis lacks guard; spine top sheep sl split vol 1, headband sl worn, sides sl rubbed; cl vol 2 sl worn; cvrs faded vol 3.) Text Nice. Temple. $281/£180

DICKENS, CHARLES. Master Humphrey's Clock. Chapman & Hall, 1840-1841. 1st-issue binding, w/clock device fr cvrs. 3 vols. George Cattermole and H. K. Browne (illus). Orig brn emb cl (lt wear spine extrems), elaborate gilt. Superior. Williams. $858/£550

DICKENS, CHARLES. Master Humphrey's Clock. London: Chapman & Hall, 1840-1841. 1st ed. 3 vols. George Cattermole and Hablot Browne (illus). Contents VG (lacks dedication leaf; fore-edges lt foxed). Marbled eps; teg. Early 1/2 grn morocco, marbled bds (rubbed, soiled; end wear), ribbed gilt spines. Waverly*. $132/£85

DICKENS, CHARLES. Master Humphrey's Clock. London, 1840-41. 1st ed in bk form. 3 vols. George Cattermole and H. K. Browne (illus). (Ink names, owner label; sl stained, faded, worn, sl soiled.) Swann*. $103/£66

DICKENS, CHARLES. Master Humphrey's Clock. London: Chapman & Hall, 1840-41. 1st ed, 1st binding. 3 vols. Marbled eps, edges. Orig purple cl, gilt. (Lt rubbed), else Very Nice set. Macdonnell. $750/£481

DICKENS, CHARLES. Memoirs of Joseph Grimaldi. London, 1838. 1st ed, 2nd issue, w/half-titles. 2 vols. George Cruikshank (illus). 1/2 brn levant. (Lt foxed.) Swann*. $402/£258

DICKENS, CHARLES. Mrs. Lirriper's Lodgings. London: Chapman & Hall, (1863). 1st appearance. Orig blue wrappers. Fine. Sumner & Stillman. $85/£54

DICKENS, CHARLES. The Mystery of Edwin Drood. London, 1870. 1st ed in bk form. Engr frontis, 11 plts by S. L. Fildes. 1/2 contemp polished black calf (lt rubbed; 2 bkpls), gilt. Swann*. $92/£59

DICKENS, CHARLES. The Mystery of Edwin Drood. London, 1870. 1st ed, 1st issue, w/price cancel on fr wrapper Part VI, w/cork hat slip Part II. Most ads present. 6 parts (all issued). 14 engr plts by S. L. Fildes. Orig pict wrappers (backstrips repaired, sl soiled, sm tears). Morocco case. Swann*. $402/£258

DICKENS, CHARLES. The Mystery of Edwin Drood. VT: T.P. James, 1873. 1st ed of this complete version. (Bkpl; frayed, sl shaken.) Metropolitan*. $126/£81

DICKENS, CHARLES. The Old Curiosity Shop. London: Chapman & Hall, 1841. 1st separate ed, complete in 1 vol. 8vo. Sheets measure 26x17.1cm. George Cattermole and Phiz (illus). (i-v)vi,(37)2-38,39-46,47-79,80-306pp; (1)2-223(224)pp. Yellow-coated eps. Olive grn fine-diaper cl variant or secondary binding; stamped in blind w/3-line border enclosing rectangular frame. Within frame: leaves, stems each corner, chain-like pattern of flowers. Spine stamped in blind, thick band top, bottom, 4 rectangular frames, gold lettering. (2pp carelessly opened), o/w Fine. Vandoros. $1,100/£705

DICKENS, CHARLES. The Old Curiosity Shop. Boston: Estes & Lauriat, 1895. Phiz & G. Cattermole (illus). 2 vols. Teg. 3/4 red morocco, marbled bds (extrems scuffed), gilt. Freeman*. $20/£13

DICKENS, CHARLES. Oliver Twist. London: Richard Bentley, 1838. 1st ed, 1st issue, 1st state binding (no imprint). 3 vols. 8vo. 2 ll ads, 24 etched plts by George Cruikshank (sl foxed, mostly marginal; mildly toned). Contents (foxed, stained). Orig blind-stamped cl bds (recased in orig cl; faded, worn; Vol 1 plt list reinserted on new stub). Cl clamshell case. Waverly*. $770/£494

DICKENS, CHARLES. Oliver Twist. London: Richard Bentley, 1838. 1st ed in bk form. W/fireside plt vol III; pub's name on spine. 3 vols. Etched frontis each vol, 21 etched plts by George Cruikshank, 1/2-titles 1st 2 vols. (Some plts severely browned, 1 plt w/sm marginal tear; some gatherings vols II-III badly pulled, becoming detached at inner margin; gathering H vol III bound in twice, offsetting, spotting to text, some quires cut short at gin.) Orig reddish-brn fine-diaper cl (spines, extrems faded, worn, corners bumped, block of vol III damaged, pushed out of shape), stamped in blind, spines gilt w/imprint 'London/Bentley.' Christie's*. $1,491/£956

DICKENS, CHARLES. Oliver Twist. Richard Bentley, 1839. 2nd ed. 3 vols. George Cruikshank (illus). Ad leaf vol I. Good (plts spotted; rebacked, orig backstrips relaid). Tiger. $468/£300

DICKENS, CHARLES. Our Mutual Friend. Chapman & Hall, 1864-1865. 1st ed in orig 20/19 parts. 8vo. Ads and slips; pg 13, part 10 correctly numbered; slip 'Foreign Bank Notes' present in parts 19/20. Marcus Stone (illus). Orig grn ptd wrappers (sl torn, frayed, missing few pieces from edges). 2 morocco collector's boxes. Sotheby's*. $986/£632

DICKENS, CHARLES. Our Mutual Friend. Chapman & Hall, 1865. 1st ed in bk form (though vol 1 and 1 section vol 2 have clearly been stabbed for part issue). 2 vols. xii,320; viii,309,(1)pp + ad leaf, 24-pg 12mo inserted pub's cat dated Dec. 1, 1865; 1/2 title present each vol; 40 wood-engr plts by Marcus Stone. Uncut. VG in maroon cl stamped in blind on sides, gilt on backstrip w/tickets of Virtue & Co (neatly rebacked, sl defective orig backstrips laid down). Cox. $390/£250

DICKENS, CHARLES. Our Mutual Friend. London, 1865. 1st ed. 2 vols. 40 engr plts by Marcus Stone. 36pp cat dated Jan 1865 at end vol 1. Teg. Full red morocco (lt rubbed; orig fr cvr, backstrip bound in at rear each vol), gilt. Kane*. $160/£103

DICKENS, CHARLES. Our Mutual Friend. London: Chapman & Hall, 1865. 1st bk ed. 2 vols. 40 engr plts (lt foxed) by Marcus Stone. Early lt brn calf, marbled bds (sl worn, spines rubbed; sl aged, lt foxed), black leather spine labels. 1 fr wrapper bound in. Baltimore*. $120/£77

DICKENS, CHARLES. Our Mutual Friend. London: Chapman & Hall, 1865. 1st ed. 2 vols in 1. Marcus Stone (illus). Contents clean (plts sl foxed; lacks half-titles). Marbled edges, eps. Early 1/2 grn calf, marbled bds (sl worn; joints starting, fr joint repaired), dec gilt spine. Waverly*. $198/£127

DICKENS, CHARLES. Pearl-Fishing. Auburn: Alden, Beardsley, 1854. 1st ed. Frontis port. Olive grn cl (sl worn, sl loss spine ends, corners; skillful repair lower panel; eps, prelims spotted), gilt (sl dull). *Maggs.* $312/£200

DICKENS, CHARLES. The Personal History of David Copperfield. London, 1850. 1st ed in bk form. Engr frontis, 38 plts by H. K. Browne. Contemp 1/2 polished tan calf (spine, tips rubbed), gilt. *Swann**. $258/£165

DICKENS, CHARLES. The Personal History of David Copperfield. London: Bradbury & Evans, 1850. 1st ed, apparently bound from the parts. 40 etched plts (many backed w/paper, some repaired tears; lg tear 1 plt w/stain from tape mend; foxing) by H. K. Browne. Early 1/2 calf, cl bds (rubbed). Sound (new eps; lacks 1/2-title; text lt soiled, stained, torn). *Waverly**. $165/£106

DICKENS, CHARLES. The Personal History of David Copperfield. London: Bradbury & Evans, 1850. 1st ed. Bound from parts. (i-vii)viii(ix)x-xii(xiii)xiv(xv-xvi),(1)2-624pp; 40 illus by Phiz (incl frontis, engr tp). Variant binding: olive-grn fine-diaper cl (expertly rebacked), orig spine neatly mtd (new eps, corners refurbished; lt foxing). Nice. *Vandoros.* $1,650/£1,058

DICKENS, CHARLES. The Personal History of David Copperfield. Chapman & Hall, 1866. 2 vols. Frontis, (4),266 + ad leaf; frontis, (4),249pp. Uncut. Orig grn pict bds (rubbed, extrems worn; rebacked in cl, remains of orig backstrips laid in). *Cox.* $70/£45

DICKENS, CHARLES. The Pic Nic Papers. By Various Hands. London: Henry Colburn, 1841. 1st ed, 2nd issue, w/error 'publisher young' corrected in intro. 3 vols. 12mo. Vol 1: frontis, plt by Cruikshank, 2 plts by Phiz; Vol 2: frontis, 3 plts by Phiz; Vol 3: frontis, 5 plts by Robert J. Hamerton. Uncut. Orig olive-grn cl. Attractive set (cvrs faded, stained, spines faded, sl rubbed; vol II w/new eps; plts browned, foxed). Internally Clean. *Cummins.* $1,250/£801

DICKENS, CHARLES. Pictures from Italy. London: Bradbury & Evans, 1846. 1st ed, 1st issue, w/o folios on pp (5), (270). Orig cl (sl rubbed, soiled; crown sl frayed). Contents VG. *Waverly**. $319/£204

DICKENS, CHARLES. Pictures from Italy. London: Bradbury & Evans, 1846. 1st ed, 1st issue. Samuel Palmer (illus). Orig blue cl. NF. *Captain's Bookshelf.* $350/£224

DICKENS, CHARLES. Pictures from Italy. London: Bradbury & Evans, 1846. 1st ed. Samuel Palmer (illus). 8vo. Pub's orig lt blue cl, stamped in blind, gilt letters spine. Bright. *D & D.* $690/£442

DICKENS, CHARLES. The Posthumous Papers of the Pickwick Club. London: Chapman & Hal, 1836-1837. 20 orig parts. Wrappers, all dated 1836; ads on wrappers in parts 1-11, more ads in parts 12-19. (Some wrappers detached, all present; chips, tears, fading, discoloration.) All parts contained in 1/2 leather closed slipcases. *Metropolitan**. $690/£442

DICKENS, CHARLES. The Posthumous Papers of the Pickwick Club. London, 1837. 1st bk ed. R. Seymour and Phiz (illus). (Plts heavily foxed.) 19th-cent morocco (rubbed, soiled). *Oinonen**. $90/£58

DICKENS, CHARLES. The Posthumous Papers of the Pickwick Club. London, 1837. 1st ed, later state of engr tp, later readings pp400, 432. 43 plts by R. Seymour and Phiz (H. K. Browne). Morocco, grn leather labels. (Sl spotted.) *Swann**. $92/£59

DICKENS, CHARLES. The Posthumous Papers of the Pickwick Club. London, 1837. 1st ed in bk form, later state of engr tp, later readings at p484. (Lacks half-title; expert archival repair plt 36, p484.) 43 engr plts by R. Seymour and Phiz (H. K. Browne). Polished purple calf, gilt extra. *Swann**. $161/£103

DICKENS, CHARLES. The Posthumous Papers of the Pickwick Club. London: Chapman & Hall, 1837. 1st ed. 8vo. Orig 43 plts by Seymour, Buss, Phiz (many 1st state), and 30 extra plts by T. Onwhyn. Teg; marbled eps. Contents VG (plts lt foxed, few sm marginal repairs). Bound from orig parts, fr wrapper from orig part XV bound in. Full crushed grn morocco w/lg Art Nouveau floral design (corners sl bumped), ribbed gilt spine in 6 panels (faded). *Waverly**. $550/£353

DICKENS, CHARLES. The Posthumous Papers of the Pickwick Club. London: Chapman & Hall, 1837. 1st ed. 43 illus by Seymour and Phiz, plus 2 add'l cancelled plts by Buss. Teg, silk ribbon marker. 3/4 crimson polished calf, marbled bds, eps, raised bands, leather labels. Bound by Zaehnsdorf. Most Attractive. *Hartfield.* $950/£609

DICKENS, CHARLES. The Posthumous Papers of the Pickwick Club. London: Chapman & Hall, 1838. 1st ed, later issue w/late state plts. Demy 8vo. (i-v)vi(vii)viii-ix(x-xi)xii-xiv(xv-xvi),(1)2-609(610)pp. Collated complete, w/vignette tp dated 1837, tp dated 1838. Both dates in Roman numerals. 43 plts as called for. Purplish-black fine-diaper cl stamped in blind, thick and thin rectangular frames on cvrs; spine blindstamped w/thick and thin bands, gold lettering. Very Nice (neatly rebacked, orig spine mtd; orig yellow-coated eps preserved in NF condition; contemp dated inscrip, bkpl) in dk brn lined slipcase. *Vandoros.* $3,150/£2,019

DICKENS, CHARLES. The Posthumous Papers of the Pickwick Club. London: 1910. 2 vols. 24 full-pg color plts by Cecil Aldin. Fine. *Truepenny.* $150/£96

DICKENS, CHARLES. The Posthumous Papers of the Pickwick Club. With Forty-three Illustrations by R. Seymour and Phiz. London: Chapman & Hall, 1837. 1st ed, bound from the parts. xiv,(2),609pp; w/the Buss cricket-match plt, 7 by Seymour, rest by H. K. Browne; engr tp is 'Veller' version, plts 10 and 11 in 'very uncommon' 1st state described by Hatton and Cleaver, plts 14 and 15 also early issues but correctly numbered. Contemp 1/2 calf, morocco label. Sound (sig, bkpl; plts lt browned w/some offsetting; backstrip chipped, corners bumped). *Cox.* $172/£110

DICKENS, CHARLES. The Readings of Mr. Charles Dickens, As Condensed by Himself. A Christmas Carol and Boots at the Holly-Tree Inn. Boston: Ticknor & Fields, 1868. 1st Amer of the 'Reading' ed. Frontis by S. Eytinge, Jr., 53,(iii),18pp, incl 2 tps (sigs loose in binding; few pg edges, corners chipped; sl pencil mks). Ptd gray wraps (pencil name; soil, corners lt creased, spine repaired w/white paper, paste); ads inside cvrs, on rear cvr. Good. *Blue Mountain.* $375/£240

DICKENS, CHARLES. The Short Stories of Charles Dickens. NY: LEC, 1971. #1029/1500 signed by Edward Ardizzone (illus) and Joseph Blumenthal (ptr). Fine in slipcase. *Hermitage.* $150/£96

DICKENS, CHARLES. Sketches by Boz. London, 1839. 1st ed in bk form. Frontis, engr half-title, 37 plts by George Cruikshank. Later tan calf, gilt extra. Fine. *Swann**. $373/£239

DICKENS, CHARLES. Sunday, Under Three Heads. London: J.W. Jarvis, 1884. Facs of orig 1836 tp and orig wrappers, to which new fr wrapper and 2-pg intro have been added. This copy w/o caption title p35. Early (orig?) 1/2 red sheep, grn cl bds (sl scuffs). *Waverly**. $82/£53

DICKENS, CHARLES. A Tale of Two Cities. London: Chapman & Hall, 1859. 1st ed, 2nd issue w/p213 correctly numbered. 16 plts by H. K. Browne. Aeg. Early tan calf bds (sl worn), mod gilt calf spine. Sound (lacks ads) w/orig fr wrapper from Pt 1 bound in. *Waverly**. $330/£212

DICKENS, CHARLES. A Tale of Two Cities. London: Chapman & Hall, 1859. 1st ed, 1st issue w/pg 213 mis-numbered 113. H.K. Browne (illus). (Lt spotting.) Contemp 1/2 dk blue calf, ribbed gilt-dec spine, gilt-lettered brn morocco spine label. *D & D.* $1,200/£769

DICKENS, CHARLES. A Tale of Two Cities. London: Chapman & Hall, 1859. 1st ed, 1st issue, bound from orig parts w/p213 misnumbered 113. H.K. Browne (illus). Tall 8vo. 3/4 19th cent grn morocco, gilt-paneled spine, raised bands, edges gilt. Fine. *Appelfeld.* $1,250/£801

DICKENS, CHARLES. A Tale of Two Cities. London: Chapman & Hall, 1859. 1st ed w/following issue points: pg (vii) Chapter VII in contents titled 'Monsieur the Marquis in Town' but 'Monseigneur in Town' in text; pg (vii) Chapter VIII in contents titled 'Monseigneur the Marquis in the Country' but 'Monseigneur in the Country' in text; pg (ix) 'Stryver' spelled 'Striver' in caption of plt; pg 98 appears to be a comma rather than the usual period after chapter number; pg 134, line 12 'affetcionately'; pg 166, 5 lines up 'If' correctly ptd in 'himself'; pg 213 correctly numbered 213; pg 238, line 14 triple end quotes. H.K. Browne (illus). Pub's olive grn cl, blind-stamped spine, cvrs (spine faded, cvrs unevenly faded, spine worn, some loss), gilt. Good in blue open-ended slipcase. *D & D.* $1,900/£1,218

DICKENS, CHARLES. The Unpublished Letters...to Mark Lemon. Walter Dexter (ed). London: Halton & Truscott Smith, 1927. 1st ed. One of 525 numbered. 1/2 vellum. Fine. *Argosy.* $150/£96

DICKENS, CHARLES. Works. NY: Riverside Press for Hurd and Houghton, 1871. 28 vols. 8vo. Marbled edges. 3/4 royal blue calf, marbled bds, dec gilt spine. Protective acetate djs. *Sotheby's*.* $2,870/£1,840

DICKENS, CHARLES. Works. London: Chapman & Hall, 1873-6. This ed w/imprint of Virtue & Co. on tp verso and at foot of last text pg. 30 vols. Marbled eps; teg. 1/2 polished brn calf, marbled bds (shelfworn), red/black spine labels, gilt. *Kane*.* $400/£256

DICKENS, CHARLES. Works. London: Chapman & Hall, 1890-91. 16 vols. 8vo. (Bkpl, private lib stamps.) Contemp calf (rubbed, corners worn), gilt, morocco labels. *Christie's*.* $562/£360

DICKENS, HENRY F. Memories of My Father. London, 1928. (Spine sunned), else Good. *King.* $25/£16

DICKENS, MAMIE. My Father As I Recall Him. Westminster: Roxburghe, (1896). 1st ed. 128,(ii)pp (name), 4pp cat; 10 plts, facs. Pict grn cl (lt bumped), gilt. NF. *Blue Mountain.* $95/£61

DICKESON, MONTROVILLE WILSON. The American Numismatic Manual of the Currency or Money of the Aborigines, and Colonial, State, and United States Coins.... Phila, 1860. 2nd ed. 271pp; 21 plts, port. (Sl frayed, spine sunned), else Good. *King.* $150/£96

DICKEY, CHARLEY. Backtrack. Clinton: Amwell Press, (1977). Ltd to 1000 signed by Dickey & Donald Shoffstall (illus). Full blue leather. Fine in slipcase. *Truepenny.* $50/£32

DICKEY, JAMES. Tucky the Hunter. NY: Crown, (1978). 1st ed. Marie Angel (illus). Grn cl bds, gilt-stamped spine. VF in pict dj. *Bromer.* $50/£32

DICKEY, LUTHER S. History of the Eighty-Fifth Regiment Pennsylvania Volunteer Infantry. NY, 1915. Port. VG. *Cullen.* $100/£64

DICKINSON, EDWIN. The Drawings of.... New Haven, 1963. 58 plts. Cl-backed bds. Fine in bd slipcase, pict label. *Argosy.* $125/£80

DICKINSON, EMILY. Emily Dickinson's Letters to Dr. and Mrs. Josiah Gilbert Holland. Theodora Van Wagenen Ward (ed). Cambridge: Harvard, 1951. 1st ed. Fine in dj (price-clipped, edges tanned). *Reese.* $40/£26

DICKINSON, EMILY. Further Poems of Emily Dickinson. Boston, 1929. 1st ed. Ltd to 1000. Fine. *Bond.* $125/£80

DICKINSON, EMILY. Letters of Emily Dickinson. Cleveland: World, (1951). 1st ed thus. (Pencil sig, notes), else VG in dj (lt nicked, worn). *Reese.* $25/£16

DICKINSON, EMILY. Letters of Emily Dickinson. Boston: Roberts, 1894. 1st ed, 2nd ptg, binding 4 (of 5). 2 vols in 1. Orig tan cl, paper label. Nice (sm spots). BAL 4660. *Macdonnell.* $225/£144

DICKINSON, EMILY. The Poems of Emily Dickinson, Including Variant Readings Critically Compared.... Thomas H. Johnson (ed). Cambridge: Belknap/Harvard, 1955. 1st ptg this ed. 3 vols. Fine in slipcase (edgeworn, stain to label). BAL 4701. *Reese.* $150/£96

DICKINSON, EMILY. Poems of Emily Dickinson. NY: LEC, 1952. 1st ptg. #44/1500 signed by Helen Sewall (illus). Full black morocco. VG (sl rubbed, lacks glassine dj) in brn slipcase (label frayed). BAL 4700. *Lucas.* $100/£64

DICKINSON, EMILY. Poems of Emily Dickinson. Louis Untermeyer (ed). NY: LEC, 1952. One of 1500 numbered, signed by Helen Sewell (illus). Full black pebbled morocco. Fine in slipcase. *Reese.* $75/£48

DICKINSON, EMILY. The Poems of Emily Dickinson.... Thomas H. Johnson (ed). Cambridge: Belknap, 1955. 3 vols. Gray cl (sl worn). Good in red slipcase (worn, label stained, chipped). BAL 4701. *Lucas.* $200/£128

DICKINSON, EMILY. The Single Hound. Boston: Little, Brown, 1915. 1st ed, 2nd ptg. White cl spine, white bds (sl soiled, bumped). VG. *Lucas.* $250/£160

DICKINSON, F. A. Lake Victoria to Khartoum. London/NY: Lane, 1910. Teg. Red cl, gilt. VG. *Bowman.* $250/£160

DICKINSON, H. W. Robert Fulton: Engineer and Artist. London: Bodley Head, 1913. 1st ed. *Ginsberg.* $75/£48

DICKINSON, JONATHAN. Jonathan Dickinson's Journal or, God's Protecting Providence. Evangeline Walker Andrews and Charles McLean Andrews (eds). New Haven: Yale, 1945. VG+ in dj (lt worn). *Bohling.* $20/£13

DICKINSON, MARQUIS F. (ed). John Marshall, the Tribute of Massachusetts.... Boston: Little, Brown, 1901. #398/750. Good (sl worn, stained). *Boswell.* $125/£80

DICKINSON, PETER. The Lizard in the Cup. NY, 1972. 1st Amer ed. Fine in dj (sm nick). *Polyanthos.* $25/£16

DICKINSON, PETER. The Poison Oracle. London: Hodder & Stoughton, 1974. 1st ed. Signed. NF (name) in NF dj. *Janus.* $65/£42

DICKINSON, PETER. Walking Dead. London: Hodder & Stoughton, 1977. 1st ed. Fine in NF dj. *Janus.* $35/£22

DICKINSON, RODOLPHUS. A Compilation of the Laws of Massachusetts (etc). Boston: Bradford & Read, 1810. Contemp sheep (worn). Sound. *Boswell.* $150/£96

DICKINSON, SALLY BRUCE. Confederate Leaders. Hampden-Sydney, VA, (1937). 1st ed. Errata slip. VG+. *Pratt.* $90/£58

DICKINSON, W. HOWSHIP. A Treatise on Albuminuria. NY, 1881. 2nd ed. 300pp. Brn tooled cl (sl worn). VG. *Doctor's Library.* $75/£48

DICKSON, ALBERT JEROME. Covered Wagon Days. Cleveland: Clark, 1929. 1st ed. One of 1250. Blue cl. (Sl water spotting to cvrs), else Fine. *Argonaut.* $125/£80

DICKSON, CARTER. (Pseud of John Dickson Carr.) Death in Five Boxes. NY: William Morrow, 1938. 1st ed. (Bkpl removed fr pastedown), o/w VG in dj (1/2-inch strip missing spine base, spine top chipping; edges, corners, folds worn). *Mordida*. $100/£64

DICKSON, CARTER. (Pseud of John Dickson Carr.) He Wouldn't Kill Patience. Heinemann, 1944. 1st UK ed. VG+ in Good+ dj (sl dusty, closed tears, sl spine loss). *Williams*. $70/£45

DICKSON, R. W. Practical Agriculture. London, 1814. New ed. 87 engr plts, incl 27 hand-colored. (Sl foxing, soiling.) Contemp 3/4 leather (rubbed, joints broken). Internally Sound. *Oinonen**. $375/£240

Dictionary of Modern Slang, Cant, and Vulgar Words.... (By John Camden Hotten.) London: John Camden Hotten, 1860. 2nd ed. xvi,300pp. Orig cl w/binder's ticket. Nice (sl mkd, neatly restored). *Ash*. $117/£75

DIDION, JOAN. Run River. NY, 1963. 1st ed, 1st bk. VG (foxed) in VG dj (price-clipped). *Smith*. $40/£26

DIDRON, ADOLPHE NAPOLEON. Christian Iconography. E. J. Millington (trans). 1886. 2 vols. xii,508; vii,452pp (prelims sl spotted). Marbled eps, edges. 1/2 morocco (sl worming upper bd vol 2), gilt. *Edwards*. $75/£48

DIEHL, EDITH. Bookbinding, Its Background and Technique. NY, 1946. 1st ed. 2 vols. 91 full-pg plts. Orig prospectus laid in. Full black buckram. VF in slipcase (lt worn). *Truepenny*. $250/£160

DIEHL, EDITH. Bookbinding, Its Background and Technique. NY: Rinehart, 1946. 1st ed. 2 vols. 91 plts. Black cl, gilt. VG. *Shasky*. $150/£96

DIEHL, EDITH. Bookbinding, Its Background and Technique. NY: Rinehart, 1946. 1st ed. 2 vols. 91 full-pg plts. (Inscrip.) Boxed. *Oak Knoll*. $195/£125

DIEHL, HUSTON. An Index of Icons in English Emblem Books 1500-1700. Norman/London: Univ of OK, (1986). Gray bds (bumped). Fine in pict white dj. *Blue Mountain*. $35/£22

DIENST, ALEX. Navy of the Republic of Texas 1835-45. Ft. Collins, 1987. 2nd ed. One of 150. Blind-stamped red cl. VF. No dj as issued. Howes D339. *Turpen*. $100/£64

DIETHELM, OSKAR (ed). Etiology of Chronic Alcoholism. Springfield: Charles C. Thomas, 1955. 1st ed. Fine in dj (lt used). *Beasley*. $45/£29

DIETHELM, OSKAR. Treatment in Psychiatry. Springfield, IL: Charles C. Thomas, (1955). 3rd ed. Inscribed. VG. *Gach*. $30/£19

DIETRICH, DR. The German Emigrants; or Frederick Wohlgemuth's Voyage to California.... Leopold Wray (trans). Stanford: James Ladd Delkin, 1949. Rpt. Ltd to 1000. Hand-colored frontis, 7 hand-colored plts. Dec bds. VF in ptd dj. *Argonaut*. $75/£48

DIETZ, ARTHUR ARNOLD. Mad Rush for Gold in Frozen North. L.A.: Times-Mirror, 1914. 2 photo plts. Blue dec cl (worn; bkpl removed). *Parmer*. $70/£45

DIETZ, ARTHUR ARNOLD. Mad Rush for Gold in Frozen North. L.A.: Times-Mirror, 1914. Frontis. Dec cl (Spine sl dull), else VG in dj (chipped, fragile). *High Latitude*. $80/£51

DIEULAFAIT, L. Diamonds and Precious Stones. NY: Scribner, Armstrong, 1874. xii,292pp. Fine. *Blake*. $125/£80

DIGBY, KENELM. Letters Between the Ld George Digby, and Kenelm Digby Concerning Religion. London: Humphrey Moseley, 1651. 1st ed, 'Sherborn' variant. (2),132pp. Recent full calf. Good. *Goodrich*. $175/£112

DIGBY, KENELM. Private Memoirs of Sir Kenelm Digby.... London: Saunders & Otley, 1827. 1st ed. Copper-engr frontis port, lxxxvi,(2),328pp (old engr bkpl). All edges marbled. 19th-cent 1/2 calf, marbled bds (rubbed). *Karmiole*. $125/£80

DIJKMAN, M. J. Hevea. Univ of Miami, 1951. 1st ed. Grn cl, gilt. Fine in dj. *Price*. $48/£31

DILELLO, RICHARD. The Longest Cocktail Party. An Insider's Diary of the Beatles. Chicago, 1972. 1st Amer ed. NF (name) in NF dj. *Polyanthos*. $45/£29

DILKE, CHARLES WENTWORTH. Greater Britain. London, 1868. 2 vols. (11),404; 428pp; color port vol 2, half-titles. (Lt foxed, bkpls removed, fr hinges broken, shaken; extrems worn, soiled.) *Reese*. $250/£160

DILKE, LADY. French Painters of the XVIIIth Century. London, 1899. 1st ed. 79 plts, 12 photogravures, incl frontis. VG. *Argosy*. $85/£54

DILL, SAMUEL. Roman Society in the Last Century of the Western Empire. London, 1906. 2nd ed. (1/2 title, tp heavily spotted, text somewhat so; bkpl.) Marbled eps, aeg. Full morocco (corners, spine sl rubbed), gilt, raised bands. *Edwards*. $31/£20

DILLARD, ANNIE. Encounters with Chinese Writers. Middletown, CT: Wesleyan, (1984). 1st ed. Fine in NF dj (price-clipped; 2 tears). *Between The Covers*. $65/£42

DILLARD, ANNIE. The Living. Harper Collins, (1992). 1st ltd ed of 300 numbered, signed. Fine in Fine slipcase. *Authors Of West*. $125/£80

DILLARD, ANNIE. The Living. (NY): Harper Collins, (1992). One of 300 numbered, signed. Fine in Fine slipcase. *Lenz*. $100/£64

DILLEY, A. U. Oriental Rugs and Carpets. NY: Scribner, 1931. 1st ed. 79 plts, incl 14 color. (Some plts foxed), o/w Good. *Scribe's Perch**. $50/£32

DILLON, JOHN B. The History of Indiana. Vol 1 (all pub). Indianapolis, 1843. Recent cl. (Lt foxed.) Howes D343. *Swann**. $373/£239

DILLON, RICHARD. Burnt-Out Fires, California's Modoc Indian War. Englewood Cliffs, NJ, (1973). 1st ed. Fine in dj (spine faded). *Pratt*. $30/£19

DILLON, RICHARD. Fool's Gold. NY: Coward-McCann, (1967). 1st ed. VF in dj. *Argonaut*. $30/£19

DILLON, RICHARD. Fool's Gold: The Decline and Fall of Captain John Sutter of California. NY: Coward-McCann, (1967). 1st ed. VG in dj. *Lien*. $35/£22

DILLON, RICHARD. Fool's Gold: The Decline and Fall of Captain John Sutter of California. NY: Coward-McCann, (1967). 1st ed. 16 plts. Black cl, gilt. Fine in pict dj. *Pacific**. $52/£33

DILLON, RICHARD. The Hatchet Men. The Story of the Tong Wars.... NY: Coward-McCann, (1962). 1st ed. Fine in dj (lt chipped). *Argonaut*. $45/£29

DILLON, RICHARD. Images of Chinatown. SF: Book Club of CA, 1976. 1st ed. Ltd to 450 ptd. Cl-backed dec bds. VF. *Argonaut*. $175/£112

DILLON, RICHARD. The Legend of Grizzly Adams: California's Greatest Mountain Man. NY: Coward-McCann, (1966). 1st ed. Signed. Fine in dj. *Argonaut*. $45/£29

DILLON, RICHARD. Texas Argonauts. SF: Book Club of CA, 1987. One of 450. Cl-backed bds. As New in plain dj. *Bohling*. $250/£160

DILLON, RICHARD. Wells Fargo Detective: A Biography of James B. Hume. NY: Coward-McCann, (1969). 1st ed. VF in dj. *Argonaut*. $45/£29

DIMAND, M. S. A Handbook of Muhammadan Art. NY, 1947. 2nd, rev ed. Good. *Washton*. $40/£26

DIMSDALE, THOMAS J. The Vigilantes of Montana. Helena, (1915). 4th ed. (Ink name), else VG. Howes D345. *Perier*. $70/£45

DIMSDALE, THOMAS J. The Vigilantes of Montana. Helena, MT: State Pub Co, (ca 1915). 4th ed. Fine in gilt-pict grn cl. Howes D345. *Glenn*. $85/£54

DIMSDALE, THOMAS J. The Vigilantes of Montana. Virginia City, MT, 1882. 2nd ed. Sm 4to. 241pp. Contemp dyed sheep, spine gilt. (Spine, extrems rubbed), else VG. Howes D345. Reese. $600/£385

DINES, GLEN. Overland Stage. NY: Macmillan, 1961. 1st ed. (Spine top, outer fr hinge torn.) October Farm. $30/£19

DINESEN, ISAK. Anecdotes of Destiny. NY, (1958). 1st ed. (Cvrs sl spotted), else Good in dj (sl edge-worn). King. $95/£61

DINESEN, ISAK. Last Tales. London: Putnam, (1957). 1st ed. Fine in NF dj (sm tears). Antic Hay. $50/£32

DINESEN, ISAK. Out of Africa. NY, (1938). 1st ed. VG- (eps sl soiled) in dj (lt worn, soiled). Freeman*. $60/£38

DINESEN, ISAK. Out of Africa. NY: Random House, (1938). 1st US ed. (Ep gutters browned), o/w VG in dj (spine tanned, chipped, sm internal edge mends). Reese. $60/£38

DINESEN, ISAK. Out of Africa. NY: Random House, (1938). 1st ed. Fine (owner stamp) in Fine dj (sl worn, lt browned). Metropolitan*. $287/£184

DINESEN, ISAK. Out of Africa. NY: Random House, 1938. 1st US ed. NF in VG+ dj (spine lt sunned). Lame Duck. $150/£96

DINESEN, ISAK. Seven Gothic Tales. NY: Smith & Haas, 1934. 1st Amer ed, trade issue. Gilt cl, bds. (Offset to eps), o/w VG in Good dj (sl chipped). Reese. $100/£64

DINESEN, ISAK. Seven Gothic Tales. NY: Smith & Haas, 1934. 1st ed. Fine (owner stamp) in Fine dj. Metropolitan*. $115/£74

DINESEN, ISAK. Shadows on the Grass. NY: Random House, 1961. 1st US ed. VG+ in dj (spine tanned). Lame Duck. $65/£42

DINGLE, EDWIN J. Borderlands of Eternity Embracing 'Across China on Foot.' L.A.: Privately pub, 1911. 1st ed. (Cl sl rubbed), o/w VG. Worldwide. $65/£42

DINGMAN, REED and PAUL NATVIG. Surgery of Facial Fractures. Phila, 1964. 1st ed. VG. Fye. $150/£96

DINGWALL, ERIC. Very Peculiar People: Portrait Studies in the Queer, the Abnormal and the Uncanny. New Hyde Park, NY, 1962. 1st ed. VG. Fye. $45/£29

DINNERSTEIN, LEONARD. The Leo Frank Case. Together with The Tennessean Special News Section, Sunday, March 7, 1982. Birmingham: Notable Trials Library, 1991. Aeg. 1/4 gold-stamped grn leather, cl sides. Fine. Zubal*. $40/£26

DINSMOOR, WILLIAM BELL. The Architecture of Ancient Greece. London, 1950. 3rd ed. 71 plts. (Cl sl worn.) Ars Artis. $47/£30

DINSMOOR, WILLIAM BELL. The Architecture of Ancient Greece. London: Batsford, 1950. 3rd ed. 71 plts. Good. Archaeologia. $50/£32

DINSMOOR, WILLIAM BELL. The Archons of Athens. Cambridge: Harvard Univ, 1931. Folio. 27 tables. (Corners sl bumped), o/w Fine. Archaeologia. $550/£353

DIONIS, PIERRE. A Course of Chirurgical Operations. London: J. Tonson, 1733. 2nd Eng ed. (16),496,(16)pp; 61 copper engr plts. Contemp panelled calf (fr hinge cracked). Karmiole. $350/£224

DIRINGER, DAVID. The Illuminated Book. NY/Washington: Praeger, (1967). Rev, augmented ed. VG in dj. Waverly*. $82/£53

DIRINGER, DAVID. Writing. London: Thames & Hudson, (1962). 3 maps. (Ex-lib.) Dj. Archaeologia. $45/£29

DISBROW, ALBERT. Glimpses of Chickamauga. Chicago, (1895). 1st ed. 136pp. (2 tears fep), o/w Fine. Pratt. $75/£48

DISCH, THOMAS M. 334. MacGibbon & Kee, 1972. 1st UK ed. Fine in dj. Williams. $125/£80

DISCH, THOMAS M. Camp Concentration. Rupert Hart-Davis, 1968. 1st ed. VG in VG dj (wrinkled). Certo. $55/£35

DISCH, THOMAS M. Camp Concentration. NY: Doubleday, 1969. 1st Amer ed. Signed. Dj (lt rubbed). Swann*. $46/£29

DISNEY, A. N. et al. Origin and Development of the Microscope. London: R.M.S., 1928. 30 plts. VG (cl faded, corners bumped). Savona. $148/£95

DISNEY, WALT. The Farmyard Symphony. Whitman, 1939. 5.5x5. 64pp (browned, pencil mks rep, rear hinge cracked). Pict bds (shelfworn, rubbed). VG. My Bookhouse. $45/£29

DISNEY, WALT. Mickey Mouse and the Magic Lamp. Racine, WI: Whitman, (1942). Disney Big Little Book; flip book. 4.5x3.5. 424pp. Color pict bds (extrems worn). King. $45/£29

DISNEY, WALT. Mickey Mouse Crusoe. Racine, WI: Whitman, 1936. 9.5x7. Color frontis, 70pp (spotted, dwgs crudely colored in). Color pict wraps (worn, spine chipped, splitting). King. $65/£42

DISNEY, WALT. Mickey Mouse Runs His Own Newspaper. Racine, WI: Whitman, (1937). Disney Big Little Book. 4.5x3.5. 424pp. Color pict bds (bumped, rubbed). King. $35/£22

DISNEY, WALT. Mickey Mouse Stories. Phila: David McKay, 1934. 8vo. Cl-backed pict bds (soiled, stained, sl scratched). Nice (1952 inscrip; few pp wrinkled, sl erasures). Glenn. $150/£96

DISNEY, WALT. A Mickey Mouse Story from A to Z. London: Collins Clear Type Press, n.d. Pict paper-cvrd bds (soiled, worn; stiff paper pp browned, few loose, inscrip). Metropolitan*. $86/£55

DISNEY, WALT. Mickey Mouse the Mail Pilot. Racine, WI: Whitman, 1933. Disney Big Little Book. 4x3.5. 320pp. Color pict wraps (extrems worn). King. $40/£26

DISNEY, WALT. Three Little Pigs. Disney, 1934. 1st ed. Full-color pastedowns. Color pict bds. VG. Aronovitz. $175/£112

DISNEY, WALT. Walt Disney's the Ugly Duckling. Phila: Lippincott, c. 1939. Oblong 4to. (40)pp. Pict cl. (Sig, few thumbprints, smudges; sl worn, soiled, spine faded), o/w Contents VG. New Hampshire*. $35/£22

Disowned. (By Edward Bulwer Lytton.) London, 1829. 1st ed. 4 vols. Mod bds (rebound; lt foxed, vol 4 lacks ad leaf). Kane*. $100/£64

Dispensary. A Poem in Six Canto's. (By S. Garth.) London, 1706. 6th ed. 15 leaves, 120pp (lacks frontis). Old calf (rebacked w/new eps). (Sl edgeworn), o/w VG. Whitehart. $78/£50

DISRAELI, BENJAMIN. Lothair. London: Longmans, Green, 1870. 2nd ed. 3 vols. Cancel tps. Uncut. Grn cl, gilt. Maggs. $156/£100

DISRAELI, ISAAC. Curiosities of Literature. Paris: Baudry's European Library, 1835. 3 vols. Bound w/o half-titles. Orig purple roan (backstrips faded), marbled bds. Maggs. $101/£65

DISTURNELL, JOHN. Influence of Climate in North and South America. NY: Van Nostrand, 1867. Color frontis, 334pp (fep removed); 2 fldg maps (both w/tear). Good (extrems frayed). Bohling. $85/£54

DITMARS, RAYMOND L. Reptiles of the World. NY: Macmillan, 1928. Cullen. $25/£16

DITMARS, RAYMOND L. Reptiles of the World. NY, 1944. New revised ed. Frontis. Dj (chipped w/loss). Edwards. $31/£20

DITMARS, RAYMOND L. Snakes of the World. NY, 1954. Frontis, 84 b/w plts at rear. Dj (chipped, sl faded). Edwards. $39/£25

DIX, JOHN A. Speech of General John A. Dix, President of the Mississippi and Missouri Railroad Co.... NY: W.C. Bryant, 1856. 19pp. Newly bound grn cl; gold stamping. VG (tp lt foxed; sm label removed tp). *Graf.* $100/£64

DIX, JOHN. The Life of Thomas Chatterton. Hamilton Adams, 1837. 1st ed. Frontis port (sl offset onto tp), viii,366pp (bound w/o 1/2 title). Contemp 1/2 morocco, marbled paper sides (sl rubbed). *Cox.* $101/£65

DIXEY, ANNIE COATH. The Lion Dog of Peking. London: Peter Davies, 1931. 1st ed. (Sl soiled, spine faded.) *Hollett.* $62/£40

DIXIE, FLORENCE. Across Patagonia. 1880. 1st ed. xiii,251pp. Dec eps. (Cvr sl spotted; chipped, lib label.) *Edwards.* $70/£45

DIXIE, FLORENCE. In the Land of Misfortune. London: R. Bentley, 1882. 1st ed. (Frontis, tp lt foxed, offset; rear hinge cracking) VG grn pict cl (cocked). *Waverly*.* $71/£46

DIXIE, FLORENCE. In the Land of Misfortune. London: Richard Bentley, 1882. 1st ed. Frontis, xvi,434pp (tp, final pp lt foxed); 15 engr plts. Pict cl (spine lt worn), gilt. *Maggs.* $234/£150

DIXON, C. The Bird-Life of London. London, 1909. 23 plts (7 color). *Wheldon & Wesley.* $28/£18

DIXON, EDWARD. Scenes in the Practice of a New York Surgeon. NY, 1855. 1st ed. 407pp (corners 40 leaves waterstained). *Fye.* $75/£48

DIXON, FRANKLIN W. The House on the Cliff. G&D, 1935. VG (bumped) in dj (edgeworn, sl dingy). *My Bookhouse.* $150/£96

DIXON, FRANKLIN W. The House on the Cliff. G&D, 1943. Med thick ed w/orange spine, Rogers cvr art. (Pp browned, 1943 stamped on tp; bumped), else VG in dj (edgeworn, chipped). *My Bookhouse.* $55/£35

DIXON, FRANKLIN W. The Missing Chums. G&D, 1928. 5x7.5. 214pp + ads. Med thick ed w/orange spine, Rogers cvr art. VG + (pp browned; sl shelfworn) in dj (sl edgeworn, chipped). *My Bookhouse.* $60/£38

DIXON, FRANKLIN W. The Mystery of the Chinese Junk. G&D, 1960. 1st ed. 5x7.5. 184pp. NF (sl shelfworn) in dj (sl edgeworn; name). *My Bookhouse.* $40/£26

DIXON, FRANKLIN W. The Mystery of the Desert Giant. G&D, 1961. 1st ed. 5x7.5. 182pp. Tan cl (sl shelfworn). VG + in dj (edgeworn). *My Bookhouse.* $40/£26

DIXON, FRANKLIN W. The Secret of Pirates Hill. G&D, 1956. 1st ed. 5x7.5. 213pp. VG (shelfworn) in dj (edgeworn, fold lt stained). *My Bookhouse.* $45/£29

DIXON, FRANKLIN W. The Short-Wave Mystery. G&D, 1945. Thin ed. 5x7.5. 217pp. Lists to 'Secret Panel.' (Acidic pp; bumped, sl shelfworn), else VG in dj (tear, sl edgeworn). *My Bookhouse.* $25/£16

DIXON, FRANKLIN W. What Happened at Midnight. G&D, 1931. Thick ed. 5x7.5. 213pp + ads. Brn cl (shelfworn). VG + in white spine dj (spine top lacks 3/4-inch, rear top lacks 1/4-inch), red shield. *My Bookhouse.* $70/£45

DIXON, HOMER B. Surnames. Boston: John Wilson & Son, 1855. Good (text lt foxed; rear hinge wormed; worn, soiled, ends chipped). *Waverly*.* $22/£14

DIXON, THOMAS, JR. Comrades, a Story of Social Adventure in California. NY: Doubleday, Page, 1909. 1st ed. VG. *Mcgowan.* $45/£29

DIXON, THOMAS, JR. The Fall of a Nation. NY, 1916. 1st ed. (Spine sl faded), o/w VG + . *Pratt.* $30/£19

DIXON, THOMAS, JR. The Leopard's Spots, a Romance of the White Man's Burden 1865-1900. NY: Doubleday, Page, 1902. 1st ed. VG. *Mcgowan.* $45/£29

DIXON, THOMAS, JR. The Leopard's Spots. NY: Doubleday, Page, 1902. 1st ed. Red cl dec in white. NF (sl discolored). *Sumner & Stillman.* $75/£48

DIXON, THOMAS, JR. The Traitor. NY, 1907. 1st ed. (Spine label fading), o/w VG + . *Pratt.* $30/£19

DIXON, WILLIAM HEPWORTH. Her Majesty's Tower. Harper, 1869. Fldg frontis map (torn), 263pp. VG (shelfworn). *My Bookhouse.* $20/£13

DIXON, WILLIAM HEPWORTH. Robert Blake, Admiral and General at Sea. London: Bickers, 1889. New ed. xvi,(4),300pp; 10 mtd Woodbury-type photo plts. All edges marbled. Full polished mottled calf, gilt, red calf spine label. Good. *Karmiole.* $150/£96

DIXON, WILLIAM HEPWORTH. Royal Windsor. London, 1879-80. 2nd ed. 4 vols. Fldg frontis. (Feps sl browned, lt spotting, foxing mainly to edges; vol 1 hinge cracked, few pp detached; soil, spines sl chipped.) *Edwards.* $55/£35

DIXON, WILLIAM SCARTH. Fox-Hunting in the Twentieth Century. London, 1925. 1st ed. (Sm splits upper joint, spine faded, sl staining.) *Edwards.* $31/£20

DIXON, WILLIAM SCARTH. The Hunting Year. London, 1912. 1st ed. (Feps lt browned; sl faded.) *Edwards.* $23/£15

DOBELL, C. Antony Van Leeuwenhoek and His 'Little Animals.' London: Bale/Danielsson, 1932. 32 plts. Paper-cvrd bds (lt dust-stained, sl worn). VG. *Savona.* $117/£75

DOBIE, J. FRANK (ed). Foller De Drinkin' Gou'd. Texas Folk-Lore Soc, 1928. 1st pb ed. Fine. *Authors Of West.* $35/£22

DOBIE, J. FRANK (ed). Man, Bird, and Beast. Texas Folk-Lore Soc, 1930. 1st pb ed. Fine. *Authors Of West.* $35/£22

DOBIE, J. FRANK et al. Mustangs and Cow Horses. Dallas, 1965. 2nd ed. As New in like dj. *Bond.* $100/£64

DOBIE, J. FRANK (ed). Puro Mexicano. Texas Folk-Lore Soc, 1935. 1st pb ed. Fine. *Authors Of West.* $35/£22

DOBIE, J. FRANK (ed). Southwestern Lore. Texas Folk-Lore Soc, 1931. 1st pb ed. Fine. *Authors Of West.* $35/£22

DOBIE, J. FRANK (ed). Spur-of-the-Cock. Texas Folk-Lore Soc, 1933. 1st pb ed. Fine. *Authors Of West.* $35/£22

DOBIE, J. FRANK (ed). Texas and Southwestern Lore. Texas Folk-Lore Soc, 1927. 1st hb ed. Fine. *Authors Of West.* $125/£80

DOBIE, J. FRANK. The Ben Lilly Legend. Boston: Little, Brown, 1950. 1st ed. Pict cl. Fine in NF dj. *Sadlon.* $60/£38

DOBIE, J. FRANK. The Ben Lilly Legend. London: Hammond, Hammond, 1952. 1st British ed. Fine in VG dj (corners torn, chipped). *Backman.* $62/£40

DOBIE, J. FRANK. Coronado's Children. Dallas: Southwest, 1930. 1st ed, 1st ptg. VG. *Gibbs.* $25/£16

DOBIE, J. FRANK. Coronado's Children. Dallas: Neiman-Marcus, 1980. One of 300. Frontis fldg map. Orig morocco-backed Mexican bark paper bds. Cl slipcase. *Swann*.* $316/£203

DOBIE, J. FRANK. The Flavor of Texas. Dallas: Dealey & Lowe, 1936. 1st ed. Frontis, 8 full-pg illus. Dec tan cl. VG (bkpl, foxing, dkng; cvrs lt soiled). *Argonaut.* $125/£80

DOBIE, J. FRANK. Guide to the Life and Literature of the Southwest, with a Few Observations. Univ of TX, 1943. 1st ed. Pb. Fine. *Authors Of West.* $80/£51

DOBIE, J. FRANK. Guide to the Life and Literature of the Southwest. Austin, 1943. 1st ed. Fine in Fine dj. *Turpen*. $55/£35

DOBIE, J. FRANK. The Longhorns. Boston: Little Brown, 1941. 1st ed. Color frontis. Pict cl (sm spot spine). Fine (ink name) in pict dj (worn, tape-repaired). Howes D375. *Argonaut*. $60/£38

DOBIE, J. FRANK. The Longhorns. Boston: Little, Brown, 1941. 1st trade ed. Pict cream cl. Fine in VG pict dj (2 short tears). *Blue Mountain*. $50/£32

DOBIE, J. FRANK. Lost Mines of the Old West: Coronado's Children. London: Hammond, Hammond, (1960). 1st British ed. Fine in dj. *Authors Of West*. $50/£32

DOBIE, J. FRANK. The Mexico I Like. Dallas: Univ Press, 1942. 1st ed thus. NF in dj. *Certo*. $45/£29

DOBIE, J. FRANK. The Mezcla Man. El Paso Del Norte: Carl Hertzog, 1954. Signed, inscribed. VG in wraps. *Gibbs*. $150/£96

DOBIE, J. FRANK. The Mustangs. Boston, (1952). 1st ed. VG. *Mcclintock*. $35/£22

DOBIE, J. FRANK. The Mustangs. Boston: Little, Brown, (1952). 1st ed. Pict eps. 2-tone pict cl, gilt. VG + in dj (edgewear). *Bohling*. $45/£29

DOBIE, J. FRANK. The Mustangs. Boston: Little Brown, 1952. 1st ed. VG in Good dj. *October Farm*. $65/£42

DOBIE, J. FRANK. Some Part of Myself. Boston: Little Brown, (1952). 1st ed. Grn cl. (Spine sl faded), else Fine in dj (sl chipped). *Argonaut*. $35/£22

DOBIE, J. FRANK. Tongues of the Monte. GC: Doubleday, 1935. 1st ed. Dec pict cl. *Ginsberg*. $125/£80

DOBIE, J. FRANK. The Voice of the Coyote. Boston: Little, Brown, 1949. 1st ed. Pict cl. Fine in NF dj. *Sadlon*. $55/£35

DOBLE, JOHN. John Doble's Journal and Letters from the Mines.... Charles L. Camp (ed). Denver: Old West, (1962). 1st ed. Ltd to 1000 ptd by Lawton Kennedy. Frontis, 3 fldg maps. Pict cl. VF. *Argonaut*. $90/£58

DOBLIN, ALFRED. Alexanderplatz Berlin. Eugene Jolas (trans). NY: Viking, 1931. 1st US ed. 2 vols. NF set (spines sl bleached, lt foxed) in NF djs (vol 2 spine chipped); illus pub's slipcase. *Lame Duck*. $250/£160

DOBRIN, ARNOLD. Peter Rabbit's Natural Foods Cookbook. NY: Warne, 1977. 1st ed. Beatrix Potter (illus). 6 3/4 x 7 1/2. 112pp. Fine. *Cattermole*. $40/£26

DOBSON, AUSTIN. A Bookman's Budget. London: OUP, 1917. 1st ed. One of 2000. NF (ink name, eps browning) in dj (browning, spine worn). *Antic Hay*. $50/£32

DOBSON, AUSTIN. De Libris. NY: Macmillan, 1908. 1st Amer ed. Dec red cl. VG (bkpl). *Antic Hay*. $25/£16

DOBSON, AUSTIN. Eighteenth Century Vignettes. NY, 1892. 1st Amer ed. Extra-illus w/inserted engrs. Crushed dk blue levant (joints rubbed). *Swann**. $46/£29

DOBSON, AUSTIN. Eighteenth Century Vignettes. NY: Dodd, Mead, 1892. 1st Amer ed. Ltd to 250 numbered. Dec white cl (browned, soiled). Good. *Antic Hay*. $45/£29

DOBSON, AUSTIN. Rosalba's Journal and Other Papers. London: C&W, 1915. 1st ed. One of 1000. Teg. Dec blue cl. NF. *Antic Hay*. $30/£19

DOBSON, AUSTIN. The Story of Rosina and Other Verses. London: Kegan Paul et al, 1895. 1st ed. Teg. Dec red cl. VG (sl worn, dknd). *Antic Hay*. $45/£29

DOBSON, AUSTIN. William Hogarth. NY: Dodd, Mead, 1891. 1st Amer ed, from English sheets. Extra-illus w/added engrs. Grn silk more eps. Salmon-red crushed morocco, gilt extra, inlaid corner fleurons, dec morocco doublures. *Swann**. $431/£276

DOBSON, EDWARD. Rudimentary Treatise on Masonry and Stone-Cutting. London: John Weale, 1859. 123pp, 12 fldg plts, 12pp ads in rear. Blind-stamped limp bds (extrems worn). *Cullen*. $125/£80

DOBSON, MRS. The Literary History of the Troubadours. London, 1807. 1st ed. (Faint pencil mks), o/w VG in 1/2 morocco (sl rubbed). *Poetry Bookshop*. $47/£30

DOBY, TIBOR. Discoverers of Blood Circulation from Aristotle to the Times of da Vinci and Harvey. NY, 1963. 1st ed. VG in dj. *Fye*. $75/£48

DOBY, TIBOR. Discoveries of Blood Circulation.... NY: Abelard Schuman, 1963. 1st ed. Good in dj (spine faded). *White*. $34/£22

DOBYNS, HENRY F. and ROBERT C. EULER. The Ghost Dance of 1889 Among the Pai Indians of Northwestern Arizona. Prescott: Prescott College, 1967. Gray-grn cl, black cl spine. Dj. *Dawson*. $40/£26

DOBYNS, STEPHEN. Man of Little Evils. NY: Atheneum, 1973. Fine in Fine white dj (sm spot fr panel, extrems lt dknd). *Between The Covers*. $300/£192

DOCKSTADER, FREDERICK. Indian Art in America. Greenwich: NYGS, (1962). Color frontis. Good in dj. *Archaeologia*. $95/£61

DOCKSTADER, FREDERICK. Indian Art of the Americas. NY: Heye Foundation, 1973. 1st ed. Pict bds. VG. *Oregon*. $40/£26

DOCTOROW, E. L. Billy Bathgate. NY: Random House, (1989). 1st ed. Signed. Fine in dj. *Between The Covers*. $85/£54

DOCTOROW, E. L. Billy Bathgate. NY: Random House, (1989). One of 300 numbered, signed. Fine in Fine slipcase. *Lenz*. $125/£80

DOCTOROW, E. L. Lives of the Poets. NY: Random House, (1984). 1st ed. Signed. Fine in dj (short tear rear panel). *Between The Covers*. $85/£54

DOCTOROW, E. L. Lives of the Poets. NY: Random House, (1984). One of 350 numbered, signed. Fine in Fine slipcase. *Lenz*. $125/£80

DOCTOROW, E. L. Loon Lake. NY: Random House, (1980). One of 350 numbered, signed. Fine in Fine slipcase. *Lenz*. $125/£80

DOCTOROW, E. L. Ragtime. NY, 1975. 1st ed. VG + in VG + dj. *Smith*. $15/£10

DOCTOROW, E. L. World's Fair. NY: Random House, (1985). 1st ed. Signed. Fine in dj. *Between The Covers*. $85/£54

DOCTOROW, E. L. World's Fair. NY: Random House, (1985). One of 300 numbered, signed. Fine in Fine slipcase. *Lenz*. $125/£80

Documents Relating to the Colonial History of the State of New Jersey...1631-1776. Vols 1-6, 8-10, index vol. Newark, 1880-88. 10 vols. VG (vol 1 sl stained; bindings sl dull, few spine ends chipped). *Bohling*. $100/£64

DODD, ALFRED. The Martyrdom of Francis Bacon. London: Rider, (1945). VG in dj (worn). *Turtle Island*. $60/£38

DODD, WILLIAM. Thoughts in Prison. Exeter, NH: Odiorne's Edition, 1794. 148pp. Contemp calf. (Outer hinges weak; eps chipped), else Good. *Brown*. $45/£29

DODGE, DAVID. To Catch a Thief. NY: Random House, 1952. 1st ed. (Name fep), o/w VG in dj. *Mordida*. $45/£29

DODGE, GRENVILLE M. The Battle of Atlanta and Other Campaigns, Addresses, etc. Council Bluffs, 1911. (Cvr sl worn), o/w Fine. *Pratt*. $45/£29

DODGE, ORVIL. The Heroes of Battle Rock, or the Miners Reward. Jan 1904. 1st ed. Fine in wraps. *Oregon*. $80/£51

DODGE, RICHARD IRVING. The Hunting Grounds of the Great West. London, 1877. 1st Eng ed. Map. Contemp calf (skillfully rebacked). Howes D404. *Swann**. $92/£59

DODGE, WALTER PHELPS. The Real Sir Richard Burton. London: T. Fisher Unwin, 1907. 1st ed. Inscribed. 'Vanity Fair' frontis port. Teg. Brn cl, gilt. (Bkpl, label fr cvr; lib stamp tp.) *Morrell*. $101/£65

DODGE, WILLIAM SUMNER. History of the Old Second Division, Army of the Cumberland. Chicago, 1864. (One port loose; spine worn.) Interior Good. *Mcclintock*. $45/£29

DODGSON, CAMPBELL. The Etchings of James McNeill Whistler. London, 1922. One of 200 numbered, this copy out-of-series. Sm folio. Gilt-lettered paper vellum. *Swann**. $230/£147

DODGSON, CAMPBELL. An Iconography of the Engravings of Stephen Gooden. London, 1944. One of 500 numbered. Engr frontis, signed by Gooden in pencil lower margin. 1/4 vellum. Slipcase. *Swann**. $287/£184

DODGSON, CAMPBELL. Old French Colour-Prints. London, 1924. One of 1250. 88 plts incl 24 color tipped in. (Eps sl spotted.) Teg. Japon-backed cl bds, japon label. *Edwards*. $195/£125

DODGSON, CAMPBELL. Prints in the Dotted Manner and Other Metal-Cuts of the XV Century in the Department of Prints and Drawings, British Museum. London: B.M. Trustees, 1937. Color frontis, guard, 43 plts. Grn buckram. VF. *Europa*. $250/£160

DODS, A. The Physician's Guide.... Worcester, 1821. 322pp. Orig bds. *Whitehart*. $218/£140

DODSLEY, R. (ed). Select Fables of Esop...New Edition. Phila: For Mathew Carey, 1807. Contemp sheep (very worn; sm tears, browned). *Swann**. $57/£37

DODSON, OWEN. Powerful Long Ladder. NY: Farrar, Straus, 1946. 1st ed, 1st bk. VG+ (eps lt foxed) in dj (sl loss spine head). *Lame Duck*. $125/£80

DODSON, W. C. (ed). Campaigns of Wheeler and His Cavalry, 1862-1854.... Atlanta: Hudgins, 1899. 1st ed. (24),431,78pp (new eps). Pict cl (spine, cvrs soiled). *Ginsberg*. $175/£112

DOERR, HARRIET. Stones for Ibarra. NY: Viking, 1984. 1st ed, 1st bk. Fine in Fine dj. *Unger*. $75/£48

DOHEN, DOROTHY. Women in Wonderland. NY: Sheed & Ward, (1960). 1st ed. VG (ex-libris) in dj. *Second Life*. $35/£22

DOHERTY, P. C. The Masked Man. London: Robert Hale, 1991. 1st ed. Signed. Fine in dj (rear panel lt soiling). *Janus*. $45/£29

DOHERTY, WILLIAM and DAGOBERT RUNES. Rehabilitation of the War Injured: A Symposium. NY, 1943. 1st ed. Lib binding (rebound, sl worn). VG (ex-libris). *Doctor's Library*. $75/£48

DOHRMAN, H. T. California Cult. Beacon Hill, Boston: Beacon Press, (1958). 1st ed. Fine in dj. *Argonaut*. $45/£29

DOIG, IVAN. The Sea Runners. NY: Atheneum, (1982). 1st ed. Fine in Fine dj (price-clipped). *Unger*. $150/£96

DOIG, IVAN. The Sea Runners. Atheneum, 1982. 1st ed. Rev copy, slip and promo sheet laid in. (Fr corner jammed, affecting pg corners), else Fine in Fine dj. *Authors Of West*. $30/£19

DOIG, IVAN. Winter Brothers. NY: Harcourt Brace Jovanovich, 1980. 1st ed. VG in VG dj. *Revere*. $45/£29

DOISNEAU, ROBERT. Robert Doisneau's Paris. NY: S&S, 1956. 1st Amer ed. 148 gravure plts. VG (owner stamp) in plain stiff wrappers, illus dj (chipped). *Cahan*. $85/£54

DOLE, E. J. (ed). The Flora of Vermont. Burlington, 1937. 3rd ed. Limp bds. *Wheldon & Wesley*. $50/£32

DOLL, EDGAR A. et al. Mental Deficiency Due to Birth Injuries. NY: Macmillan, 1932. 1st ed. Inscribed. Blue cl. VG. *Gach*. $35/£22

DOLLARD, JOHN. Victory over Fear. NY: Reynal & Hitchcock, (1942). 1st ed. Inscribed. Grey cl. VG. *Gach*. $75/£48

DOMAT, JEAN. The Civil Law in Its Natural Order. Luther Cushing (ed). Boston: Little, Brown, 1861. 2 vols. New speckled 1/4 calf. Good. *Boswell*. $350/£224

DOMENECH, EMANUEL H. D. Seven Years' Residence in the Great Deserts of North America.... London: Longman, 1860. 1st ed. 2 vols. (25),445; (12),(1)-46,(466)pp; lg fldg map, 59 color plts. Untrimmed. Nice. Howes D410. *Ginsberg*. $850/£545

DONAGHE, M. VIRGINIA. Picturesque Utah. Denver: Frank S. Thayer, 1888. 1st ed. 33pp. Faux snakeskin eps. Gilt-dec cl, mtd color photo. (Inner hinge cracked; sl rubbed, lt dampstain top edge rear cvr), else VG. *Cahan*. $250/£160

Donald and Pluto. N.p. (London): Collins, (1939). Disney Flip Book. 9x4. Loose instruction sheet present. Nice in color pict wraps (sl wear). *King*. $175/£112

DONALD, DAVID. Lincoln's Herndon. NY, 1948. 1st ed. VG+ in VG+ dj. *Pratt*. $25/£16

DONALD, DAVID. Lincoln's Herndon. NY, 1948. 1st ed. *Wantagh*. $35/£22

DONALDSON, ALFRED L. A History of the Adirondacks. NY: Century, 1921. 2 vols. 4 fldg maps (1 color). Good (sl foxing, 1pg browned by clipping). *Scribe's Perch**. $160/£103

DONALDSON, STEPHEN R. Forbidden Knowledge. NY: Bantam, (1991). One of 350 numbered, signed. Fine in Fine slipcase. *Lenz*. $75/£48

DONALDSON, STEPHEN R. Lord Foul's Bane. NY: Doubleday, (1977). 1st ed. Signed, inscribed on special bkpl mtd to half-title. Fine (sl rubbed) in dj (sl crimped, sm creased tear). *Waverly**. $27/£17

DONDERS, F. C. On the Anomalies of Accomodation and Refraction of the Eye. William Daniel Moore (trans). London: New Sydenham Soc, 1864. xvii,(i-errata),635pp, fldg chart. Brn cl. VG. *White*. $117/£75

DONDERS, F. C. On the Anomalies of the Refraction of the Eye. W. D. Moore (trans). New Sydenham Soc, 1864. xviii,635pp. (Spine defective, section loose.) *Whitehart*. $125/£80

DONLEAVY, J. P. De-Alfonce Tennis. London: Weidenfeld, 1984. 1st UK ed. Fine in dj. *Williams*. $23/£15

DONLEAVY, J. P. De-Alfonce Tennis. NY, 1984. 1st ed. NF in NF dj. *Smith*. $15/£10

DONLEAVY, J. P. The Destinies of Darcy Dancer, Gentleman. London: Allen Lane, 1978. 1st UK ed. Fine in dj. *Williams*. $28/£18

DONLEAVY, J. P. The Ginger Man. Paris: Olympia Press, (1955). 1st ed, 1st bk. Fine in ptd wrappers. *Reese*. $500/£321

DONLEAVY, J. P. The Ginger Man. Paris: Olympia, (1958). 1st hb ed. Signed. Grn bds, ptd labels. As New in dj. *Jaffe*. $275/£176

DONLEAVY, J. P. The Ginger Man. NY, (1965). 1st complete, unexpurgated Amer ed; 1st bk. (Ink name; ends sl worn), else VG in dj (frayed, chipped). *King*. $35/£22

DONLEAVY, J. P. Leila. Franklin Library, 1983. 1st ed. Signed on tipped in leaf. Gilt leather, bands; aeg; ribbon marker. Fine. *Beasley*. $45/£29

DONLEAVY, J. P. Meet My Maker. The Mad Molecule. London, 1965. 1st ed. Fine in dj (2 sm edge tears, rear panel lt soiled). *Polyanthos*. $25/£16

DONLEAVY, J. P. The Saddest Summer of Samuels. NY, (1966). 1st Amer ed. Signed. Fine in NF dj. *Polyanthos*. $45/£29

DONLEAVY, J. P. Schultz. London, 1980. 1st ed. NF (sl lean) in NF dj. *Smith*. $15/£10

DONLEAVY, J. P. A Singular Man. Boston: Atlantic Monthly, (1963). 1st ed. NF (lt bumped) in dj (chipped). *Hermitage*. $45/£29

DONLEAVY, J. P. A Singular Man. London: Bodley Head, 1964. 1st UK ed. NF in VG + dj (spine top reinforced to rear). *Williams*. $39/£25

DONN, J. Hortus Cantabrigiensis; or An Accented Catalogue.... London, 1845. 13th ed. xii,772pp. Good. *Henly*. $50/£32

DONNE, JOHN. The Courtier's Library, or Catalogus Librorum Aulicorum. (London): Nonesuch, 1930. One of 950 numbered. Paper-cvrd bds in style of dj affixed by eps. (Spine sunned, piece lacking.) Pub's slipcase (sl dusty). *Hermitage*. $125/£80

DONNE, JOHN. The Courtier's Library. Evelyn Mary Simpson (ed). London: Nonesuch, 1930. #565/950 ptd. Uncut. Good in paper-cvrd bds (sl rubbed), morocco label; black slipcase, gilt. *Cox*. $78/£50

DONNE, JOHN. Poems, &c...with Elegies on the Author's Death.... (London): Henry Herringman, 1669. 7th collected ed. 8vo. (4),414pp (w/errors in pagination as noted by Keynes). Contemp panelled calf. (Bound w/o 1st, final blanks; old mend to tear and fore-edge of 2D6; neatly rebacked), o/w VG-. *Reese*. $950/£609

DONNELLEY, R. R. and SONS. A Rod for the Back of the Binder. Chicago: Lakeside, 1928. 16 plts. Dec cl, leather label. *Edwards*. $78/£50

DONNELLY, IGNATIUS. The Great Cryptogram. 1888. 998pp. Full leather. VG. *Middle Earth*. $99/£63

DONNELLY, ROBERT B. Just Like the Flowers Dear. NY, 1932. #630/950 signed. 60 plts. Cl spine (faded) over color bds (tips worn). *Brooks*. $37/£24

DONOVAN, E. The Natural History of British Birds.... London: The Author, 1815. New ed. Vols III-IV bound together. 38 (of 52) Fine hand-colored plts. 3/4 leather, marbled paper-cvrd bds (coming disbound). *Metropolitan**. $460/£295

DONOVAN, RICHARD E. and JOSEPH S. F. MURDOCH. The Game of Golf and the Printed Word, 1566-1985. Endicott: Castalio, 1987. 1st trade ed. Grn cl, gilt. Mint in VF dj. *Baltimore**. $60/£38

DOOLEY, JOHN. John Dooley, Confederate Soldier, His War Journal. (Washington): Georgetown Univ, 1945. 1st ed. Fine in NF dj. *Mcgowan*. $150/£96

DOOLEY, JOHN. John Dooley, Confederate Soldier. Joseph T. Durkin (ed). Georgetown Univ, 1945. 1st ed. Good (name, card pocket fep; sl cvr spots; sl bumped). *Wantagh*. $45/£29

DOONER, P. W. Last Days of the Republic. SF: Alta CA Pub House, 1880. 1st ed. Litho frontis, 258pp (eps foxed, sl soiling), 4 plts. Brn cl, gilt vignette. *Reese*. $75/£48

DOONER, P. W. Last Days of the Republic. SF: Alta California Pub House, 1880. 1st ed. Frontis, 4 full-pg litho plts. Brick cl (lt rubbing to spine ends, corners), cvr design, gilt. Fine. *Argonaut*. $350/£224

DORAN, G. H. Chronicles of Barabbas 1884-1934. Methuen, 1935. 1st ed. Black cl. Good. *Moss*. $14/£9

DORESSE, J. Secret Book of the Egyptian Gnostics. NY, 1960. Fine in VG + dj. *Middle Earth*. $60/£38

DOREY, JACQUES. Three and the Moon. NY, 1929. One of 260 signed by Boris Artzybasheff (illus). 8 full-pg color plts. Unopened. Internally Fine in dj, slipcase (both defective). *Kane**. $150/£96

DORMENT, RICHARD. British Painting in the Philadelphia Museum of Art. Phila, 1986. Good in wraps. *Washton*. $25/£16

DORNAN, S. S. Pygmies and Bushmen of the Kalahari. London, 1925. Fldg map. (Feps lt browned; cl spine sl rubbed.) *Edwards*. $117/£75

DORNBLASER, THOMAS F. My Life-Story for Young and Old. (N.p.): The Author, 1930. 1st ed. *Ginsberg*. $125/£80

DORSEY, JOHN M. (ed). The Jefferson-Dunglison Letters. Charlottesville: Univ of VA, (1960). 1st ed. Signed presentation. Frontis port. VG. *Glaser*. $35/£22

DORSON, RICHARD M. Jonathan Draws the Long Bow. Cambridge, 1946. Frontis. VG + in dj (chipped). *Bohling*. $18/£12

DOS PASSOS, JOHN. The 42nd Parallel. NY: Harper, 1930. 1st ed. (Spine label discolored), o/w Fine in dj (lt used, sm spine chip). *Beasley*. $150/£96

DOS PASSOS, JOHN. The 42nd Parallel. NY: Harper, 1930. 1st ed. (Spine ends rubbed), else VG in NF dj (sl chipped, sm tears, flaps clipped). *Pacific**. $184/£118

DOS PASSOS, JOHN. Adventures of a Young Man. London, 1939. 1st Eng ed. (Spine, parts of cvrs faded), o/w VG. *Words Etc*. $19/£12

DOS PASSOS, JOHN. The Big Money. NY: Harcourt Brace, (1936). 1st ed. (Name), else VG in dj (spine ends sl chipped, flaps clipped). *Pacific**. $127/£81

DOS PASSOS, JOHN. Easter Island: Island of Enigma. GC: Doubleday, 1971. 1st ed. VG (glass ring fr bd) in VG dj (rubbed, tears, price-clipped). *Between The Covers*. $85/£54

DOS PASSOS, JOHN. Facing the Chair. Boston: Sacco-Vanzetti Def Comm, 1927. 1st ed. VG in wraps (chipping). *Beasley*. $60/£38

DOS PASSOS, JOHN. The Fourteenth Chronicle, Letters and Diaries of John Dos Passos. Boston: Gambit, 1973. 1st ed. NF in dj. *Hermitage*. $35/£22

DOS PASSOS, JOHN. The Head and Heart of Thomas Jefferson. GC: Doubleday, 1954. 1st ed. Inscribed presentation dated December 1953. Port. VG (no dj). *Reese*. $75/£48

DOS PASSOS, JOHN. One Man's Initiation—1917. London, (1920). 1st ed, 1st bk, 1st state: broken 'd' and the word 'flat' obliterated p35, l. 32. Blue ptd cl (lt faded). Ptd dj (1-inch break along fr flap fold, old tape repair verso rear flap). *Kane**. $275/£176

DOS PASSOS, JOHN. One Man's Initiation. London: George Allen & Unwin, 1920. 1st ed, 1st bk. One of 750. (Top edge lt dusted), else NF in dj. *Lame Duck*. $950/£609

DOS PASSOS, JOHN. The Theme Is Freedom. NY: Dodd, Mead, 1956. 1st ed. One of 3000 ptd. VG (ink name) in dj. *Antic Hay*. $45/£29

DOS PASSOS, JOHN. Tour of Duty. HMCO, 1946. 1st ed. Fine in VG dj (short tears). *Certo*. $25/£16

DOS PASSOS, JOHN. U.S.A. Boston: Houghton, Mifflin, 1946. One of 356 signed by Dos Passos and Reginald Marsh (illus). 3 vols. Teg. Creme cl over beveled bds. Fine in plain paper djs (lt soiled, torn) w/die-cut spine windows. *Waverly**. $330/£212

DOSTOEVSKI, FYODOR. Poor Folk. Lena Millman (trans). Boston: Roberts, 1894. 1st US ed. White cl-cvrd bds. (Cl soiled, worn), else VG. *Lame Duck*. $250/£160

DOSTOEVSKY, FEODOR. Crime and Punishment. NY: Thomas Y. Crowell, n.d. (1886). 1st US ed. VG + (sig) in tan cl-cvrd bds (lt shelfworn), gilt. *Lame Duck*. $850/£545

DOSTOEVSKY, FYODOR. The Brothers Karamazov. Constance Garnett (trans). NY: LEC, 1949. #214/1500 signed by Fritz Eichenberg (illlus). 2 vols. 2-tone red cl stamped in silver. Fine in pub's slipcase. *Hermitage.* $125/£80

DOSTOEVSKY, FYODOR. Buried Alive or Ten Years of Penal Servitude in Siberia. Marie van Thilo (trans). NY: Holt, 1881. 1st Amer ed. Pict cl. VG (spine cocked; extrems sl frayed; fr hinge lt cracked). *Between The Covers.* $350/£224

DOSTOEVSKY, FYODOR. The Grand Inquisitor. (London): Elkin Mathews & Marrot, 1930. 1st ed in English. #255/300 ptd. Full vellum w/blue, black geometric onlays. Fine in modern custom slipcase. *Hermitage.* $450/£288

DOSTOEVSKY, FYODOR. A Raw Youth. Constance Garnett (trans). Verona: LEC, 1967. One of 2000 numbered, signed by Fritz Eichenberg (illus). 2 vols. Fine in djs, bd slipcase. *Argosy.* $150/£96

DOSTOEVSKY, FYODOR. A Raw Youth. Constance Garnett (trans). Verona: LEC, 1974. One of 2000 numbered, signed by Fritz Eichenberg (illus). 2 vols. Fine in pub's slipcase. *Hermitage.* $125/£80

DOSTOIEVSKY, FYODOR. Poor Folk. Lena Millman (trans). Boston: Roberts Bros, 1894. 1st Amer ed. Aubrey Beardsley dec bds. VG (spine extrems lt worn, 2 sl stains rear bd). *Between The Covers.* $250/£160

DOSTOIEVSKY, FYODOR. Poor Folk. London: Elkin Matthews/John Lane, 1894. 1st ed in English. (Eps sl foxed), else VG+ in illus cl-cvrd bds (sl soiled, 2 sm stains fr bd). *Lame Duck.* $250/£160

DOSTOIEVSKY, FYODOR. Summer Impressions. (London): Calder, (1955). 1st Eng ed. NF (eps sl browned, ink name) in dj (sl worn). *Antic Hay.* $35/£22

DOTEN, ALFRED. Journals of...1849-1903. Walter Van Tilburg Clark (ed). Reno: Univ of NV, 1974. 3 vols. Fine in slipcase (edges sl split). *Bohling.* $45/£29

DOTSON, SUSAN MERLE (comp). Who's Who of the Confederacy. San Antonio: Naylor, (1966). Fine in dj. *Cullen.* $55/£35

DOTY, ROBERT (ed). Photography in America. NY: Random House, 1974. 1st ed. NF (owner stamp) in dj (rubbed). *Cahan.* $40/£26

DOTY, ROBERT. American Folk Art in Ohio Collections. Akron Art Inst, 1976. NF in NF dj. *My Bookhouse.* $30/£19

DOUBLEDAY, ABNER. Reminiscences of Forts Sumter and Moultrie. NY: Harper, 1876. 1st ed. Frontis, 184pp + 8pp ads; map. Dec cvr. Good. *Scribe's Perch*.* $42/£27

DOUBLEDAY, ROMAN. The Hemlock Avenue Mystery. Boston: Little, Brown, 1908. 1st ed. (Extrems sl worn.) *Metropolitan*.* $57/£37

DOUGHTY, ARTHUR G. and CHESTER MARTIN. The Kelsey Papers. Ottawa: Public Archives of Canada/The Public Record Office of N. Ireland, 1929. 1st ed. Frontis, fldg map. Fine in stiff ptd wrappers. *Harrington.* $100/£64

DOUGHTY, CHARLES M. The Clouds. London: Duckworth, 1912. 1st ed. (Eps tanned, edge-sizing lt flecked), o/w Nice in dj (tanned, sl chipped). *Reese.* $50/£32

DOUGHTY, CHARLES M. The Dawn in Britain. London: Duckworth, 1906. 1st ed. 6 vols. NF set (lt foxed). *Captain's Bookshelf.* $300/£192

DOUGHTY, CHARLES M. Travels in Arabia Deserta. CUP, 1888. 1st ed. 2 vols. Lg fldg map rear pocket vol 1. Gilt-pict cl. VG set (lt foxed, inner hinges vol 1 cracked; lt rubbed, sm frays). *Reese.* $1,850/£1,186

DOUGHTY, CHARLES M. Travels in Arabia Deserta. NY: Random House, 1937. 1st Amer ed thus. 2 vols. Fine set (lacks slipcase). *Captain's Bookshelf.* $150/£96

DOUGHTY, CHARLES M. Travels in Arabia Deserta. NY: Heritage, 1953. Edward Garnett (abridged by). Fine in slipcase. *Truepenny.* $30/£19

DOUGHTY, CHARLES M. Wanderings in Arabia. London, 1926. Authorized, abridged ed. (Fore-edges lt spotted), o/w Lovely in dj (sl browned). *Words Etc.* $94/£60

DOUGLAS, AMANDA M. The Old Woman Who Lived in a Shoe. Boston: William F. Gill, 1875. 1st ed. 8vo. 380pp. Grn cl (rubbed, lt worn). Good. *Lucas.* $75/£48

DOUGLAS, C. L. Cattle Kings of Texas. Dallas: Cecil Baugh, 1939. 2nd ptg. Pict cl. Fine in pict dj (chipped). Howes D434. *Argonaut.* $150/£96

DOUGLAS, DAVID. Journal Kept by David Douglas During His Travels in North America, 1823-1827.... NY, 1959. Ltd to 750 numbered. Frontis. Howes D435. *Ginsberg.* $125/£80

DOUGLAS, FREDERIC H. and D'HARNONCOURT. Indian Art of the United States. NY: MOMA, 1941. 1st ed. 123 plts (16 color). NF. *Worldwide.* $45/£29

DOUGLAS, GEORGE M. Lands Forlorn. NY: Putnam, 1914. Color frontis, fldg map. Teg. Dec cl (spine dull, sl spots). VG. *High Latitude.* $225/£144

DOUGLAS, J. Myographiae Comparatae Specimen. 1763. 2nd ed. xxxii,240pp. Contemp calf (edgeworn, bkpl). *Whitehart.* $250/£160

DOUGLAS, JAMES. Theodore Watts-Dunton: Poet, Novelist, Critic. London, 1904. 1st ed. Blue buckram, gilt. (Foxing), o/w VG. *Words Etc.* $56/£36

DOUGLAS, JOHN. Shawnee Alley Fire. NY: St. Martin's, 1987. 1st ed. Fine in dj (price-clipped). *Mordida.* $45/£29

DOUGLAS, KEITH. Alamein to Zem Zem. London: Editions Poetry, 1946. 1st Eng ed. Cl-backed bds (sl rubbed). Good (tp hinge tender, few fore-edges sl ragged, crayon price fep) in Poor dj. *Clearwater.* $62/£40

DOUGLAS, LANGTON. Leonardo da Vinci. Chicago, 1944. 57 plts. Good. *Washton.* $35/£22

DOUGLAS, MARJORY STONEMAN. Road to the Sun. NY: Rinehart, (1952). 1st ed. (Sm foxing spots bd bottoms), else Fine in VG+ dj (sm scrape-chip spine edge, lt rubbed). *Between The Covers.* $100/£64

DOUGLAS, MICHAEL. (Pseud of Michael Crichton.) Dealing, or the Berkeley-to-Boston Forty-Brick Lost Bag Blues. NY: Knopf, 1970. 1st ed. (Bds, edges sl dkng; sm binding flaw), else NF in VG dj (price-clipped; snag tear rear panel). *Between The Covers.* $125/£80

DOUGLAS, MICHAEL. (Pseud of Michael Crichton.) Dealing, or The Berkeley-to-Boston Forty-Brick Lost-Bag Blues. NY: Knopf, 1970. 1st ed. Fine in dj. *Mordida.* $75/£48

DOUGLAS, NORMAN. An Almanac. London: C&W, 1945. 1st ed. VG in dj. *Hollett.* $39/£25

DOUGLAS, NORMAN. In the Beginning. (N.p.): Privately ptd, 1927. Ltd to 700 numbered, signed. Patterned bds, leather spine label (scuffed). VG. *Antic Hay.* $85/£54

DOUGLAS, NORMAN. In the Beginning. Florence, 1927. #156/700 signed. Dec bds (spine rubbed). *Argosy.* $50/£32

DOUGLAS, NORMAN. Late Harvest. London: Lindsay Drummond, 1946. 1st ed. VG in dj. *Hollett.* $23/£15

DOUGLAS, NORMAN. London Street Games. London: St. Catherine Press, 1916. 1st ed. One of 500. Uncut edges (dusty). Good (sl foxed, mostly 1st, last pp; bds sl scratched, rubbed; lacks dj). *Virgo*. $234/£150

DOUGLAS, NORMAN. London Street Games. London: St. Catherine, 1916. One of 500. Buckram (mkd, stained). *Clearwater*. $109/£70

DOUGLAS, NORMAN. London Street Games. London: Chatto 'Dolphin Books,' 1931. Rev, enlgd ed. VF in dj. *Clearwater*. $47/£30

DOUGLAS, NORMAN. Looking Back. London: C&W, 1934. 1st general ed. Good in dj (soiled, sl frayed). *Cox*. $31/£20

DOUGLAS, NORMAN. Nerinda. Florence: Orioli, 1929. #112/475 signed. Unopened. (Name, address fep), o/w Fine in new slipcase w/orig title laid on. *Virgo*. $109/£70

DOUGLAS, NORMAN. Paneros. Florence: Privately ptd, 1930. One of 250 signed. Very Nice. *Clearwater*. $234/£150

DOUGLAS, NORMAN. Paneros: Some Words on Aphrodisiacs and the Like. London: C&W, 1931. 1st ed. #235/650 numbered. Frontis port. VG in dj (spine dknd, nicked). *Houle*. $125/£80

DOUGLAS, NORMAN. A Selection from His Work. London, 1955. 1st ed. VG in dj. *Typographeum*. $18/£12

DOUGLAS, NORMAN. Siren Land. London: Dent, 1911. 1st ed. Olive cl. Fine. *Argosy*. $275/£176

DOUGLAS, NORMAN. South Wind. LEC, 1932. One of 1000 signed by Carlotta Petrina (illus). Coarse linen. (Spine faded), o/w VF in pub's slipcase (tape-repaired, reinforced). *Pirages*. $50/£32

DOUGLAS, NORMAN. South Wind. NY: LEC, 1932. #117/1500 signed by C. Petrina (illus). VG in slipcase (broken). *Typographeum*. $65/£42

DOUGLAS, NORMAN. Summer Islands: (Ischia and Ponza). NY: The Colophon, 1931. 1st Amer ed. One of 550 numbered, signed. NF (lacks dj) in dec cl. *Captain's Bookshelf*. $75/£48

DOUGLAS, NORMAN. Summer Islands: Ischia and Ponza. Harmsworth, 1931. One of 500 numbered. Bright (name; cvrs sl mkd) in dj. *Clearwater*. $86/£55

DOUGLAS, NORMAN. Together. London: Chapman & Hall, 1923. 1st ed. (Lt spotted.) *Hollett*. $31/£20

DOUGLAS, NORMAN. Together. London: Chapman & Hall, 1923. 1st ed. One of 250 for sale signed. 2 plts. NF in dj (chafed, faded, tape-repaired, sl loss ends). *Pirages*. $90/£58

DOUGLAS, ROBERT. China. London, 1887. 2nd ed. viii,433pp; fldg map. (Margins lt browned, prelims spotted; spine sl chipped, rubbed, sm dent upper bd edge.) *Edwards*. $31/£20

DOUGLAS, ROBERT. Three Boy Scouts in Africa. NY: Putnam, 1928. 1st ed. Grn cl (spine sunned). Else VG. *Terramedia*. $75/£48

DOUGLAS, WALTER B. Manuel Lisa. Abraham P. Nasatir (ed). NY: Argosy-Antiquarian Ltd, 1964. 1st bk ed. One of 750. Gray-grn cl. Fine. *Argonaut*. $75/£48

DOUGLASS, FREDERICK. My Bondage and My Freedom.... NY/Auburn: Miller et al, 1855. 1st ed. 2 plts. (Lacks port, flyleaf, fep; sl foxed, worn.) *Agvent*. $90/£58

DOUGLASS, FREDERICK. Narrative of the Life of Frederick Douglass, an American Slave. Boston: Anti-Slavery Office, 1846. 2nd ed. Frontis port w/guard, xvi,125pp. Dec blind-emb cl, gilt spine (tips, spine ends rubbed). Good (dampstained, sl foxed). *Cahan*. $150/£96

DOUGLASS, FREDERICK. Negroes and the National War Effort. (NY: Workers Library, 1942.) 1st ed thus. Port. VG in ptd self-wraps. *Petrilla*. $40/£26

DOUGLASS, MARJORY STONEMAN. The Everglades: River of Grass. Rinehart, (c. 1947). 1st ed. VG. *Book Broker*. $25/£16

DOUKAS, JAMES N. Electric Tibet. The Rise and Fall of the San Francisco Rock Scene. North Hollywood: Dominion, 1969. 1st ed. Pb. (Lt wear.) *Beasley*. $45/£29

DOULTON, LIEUT. COL. The Fighting Cock. Aldershot, Gale & Polden, 1951. (Binding sl mkd.) *Petersfield*. $31/£20

DOW, CHARLES MASON. Anthology and Bibliography of Niagara Falls. Albany, 1921. 2 vols. 3 color plts, 40 b/w photo plts, 4 maps (1 flg). Good (Vol 1 ex-lib; cl rubbed, hinge cracks). *Scribe's Perch**. $18/£12

DOW, GEORGE F. Slave Ships and Slaving. Salem: Marine Research Soc, 1927. 1st ed. 48 plts. 2 maps. Black buckram, gilt spine title. VG. Howes D438. *Petrilla*. $75/£48

DOW, GEORGE F. Whale Ships and Whaling. Salem: Marine Research Soc, 1925. VG. *High Latitude*. $85/£54

DOW, GEORGE F. Whale Ships and Whaling. Salem: Marine Research Soc, 1925. 1st ed. (Bent corner), else VG. *Perier*. $195/£125

DOWDEN, EDWARD. Letters of Edward Dowden and His Correspondents. London: J.M. Dent, 1914. Frontis port. Grn cl. *Turtle Island*. $25/£16

DOWDEY, CLIFFORD. Experiments in Rebellion. GC, 1946. Stated 1st ed. Good in dj (chipped). *Scribe's Perch**. $25/£16

DOWDEY, CLIFFORD. The Great Plantation. NY, 1957. Berkeley Plantation ed. Fine in dj (sl worn, chipped). *Pratt*. $27/£17

DOWDEY, CLIFFORD. The Land They Fought For...1832-1865. Doubleday, (c. 1955). 1st ed. VG (top edge foxed) in VG dj (foxed). *Book Broker*. $25/£16

DOWER, KENNETH GANDAR. The Spotted Lion. Boston, 1937. 1st ed. Fldg map. (Spine faded.) *Edwards*. $31/£20

DOWNAME, JOHN. The Christian Warfare Against the Devill, World and Flesh. London: William Stansby, 1634. (Title, fr matter defective; dampstaining.) Contemp calf (rubbed, joints cracked). *Freeman**. $200/£128

DOWNES, KERRY. The Architecture of Wren. Granada, 1982. 88pp plts. VG in dj. *Hadley*. $31/£20

DOWNES, WILLIAM HOWE. John S. Sargent: His Life and Work.... London, (1926). 1st ed. Grn cl (sl wear, soil), gilt. *Freeman**. $60/£38

DOWNEY, FAIRFAX. Dogs for Defense. NY: Trustees of Dogs for Defense, (1955). Dj. *Dawson*. $35/£22

DOWNEY, FAIRFAX. Indian Fighting Army. NY, 1941. 1st ed. (Ex-lib, rubber stamps), o/w VG + . *Pratt*. $65/£42

DOWNEY, FAIRFAX. Indian Wars of the U.S. Army, 1776-1865. NY: Doubleday, 1963. 1st ed. VG in dj. *Lien*. $30/£19

DOWNEY, SUSAN B. Mesopotamian Religious Architecture: Alexander Through the Parthians. Princeton: Princeton Univ, (1988). Good in dj. *Archaeologia*. $65/£42

DOWNIE, WILLIAM. Hunting for Gold: Reminisences [sic] of Personal Experience and Research.... SF, 1893. 407pp, port. Contemp 3/4 calf, gilt cl (sl spotted, extrems rubbed; contents shaken, few sigs starting). Good. *Reese*. $375/£240

DOWNING, A. J. The Architecture of Country Houses. NY: Appleton, 1850. 1st ed. 484pp (foxed). Dec cvr (spine chipped). Good. *Scribe's Perch**. $175/£112

DOWNING, A. J. The Fruits and Fruit Trees of America. NY/London, 1846. 6th ed. 594pp + ads (foxed). Orig pub's cl, dec spine. Good. *Scribe's Perch**. $80/£51

DOWNING, A. J. A Treatise on the Theory and Practice of Landscape Gardening. NY, (1859). 8th ed, enlgd, rev. 576 w/index pp. (Worn, loose.) *King*. $75/£48

DOWNING, A. J. A Treatise on the Theory and Practice of Landscape Gardening. NY/London: Wiley & Putnam, 1844. 2nd ed. 11 (of 16) plts. (Contents lt browned; lacks spine panel, bds worn, chipped). *Waverly**. $38/£24

DOWNING, ANTOINETTE F. and VINCENT J. SCULLY, JR. The Architectural Heritage of Newport Rhode Island, 1640-1915. Cambridge, MA: Harvard Univ, 1952. 1st ed. Fldg map. Grn buckram. Good in dj. *Karmiole*. $60/£38

DOWNING, C. TOOGOOD. Neuralgia: Its Various Forms, Pathology, and Treatment. London: John Churchill, 1851. 1st ed. xvi,375,(32 ads)pp. Contemp 1/2 morocco, marbled bds (sl scuffed). VG. *Glaser*. $85/£54

DOWNS, E. C. Four Years a Scout and Spy. Zanesville, 1866. 1st ed. (Foxed, frayed.) *King*. $100/£64

DOWNS, JOSEPH. American Furniture: Queen Anne and Chippendale Periods.... NY, 1952. 1st ed. *Kane**. $85/£54

DOWNS, JOSEPH. American Furniture: Queen Anne and Chippendale.... NY: Macmillan, 1952. 1st ed. 10 color plts (top margins lt dampstained). Red-brn cl (sl shelfworn), silver stamping. Ptd dj (heavily chipped, worn). *Baltimore**. $60/£38

DOWSE, THOMAS STRETCH. The Brain and Its Diseases. Part I. London: Bailliere et al, 1879. 1st ed. (viii),144pp; 3 orig photos, 3 chromolithos. Ptd grn cl (lt shelfworn, corner stained). VG (lib bkpl, stamps to tp, other ll). *Gach*. $250/£160

DOWSON, ERNEST and ARTHUR MOORE. Adrian Rome. London: Methuen, 1899. 1st ed. (Fr inner hinge partly cracked; sl worn, spine sl torn), else Good. *Holmes*. $250/£160

DOWSON, ERNEST. The Pierrot of the Minute. Portland: Thomas B. Mosher, 1913. One of 750. Fine in slipcase (damaged). *Dramatis Personae*. $50/£32

DOWST, HENRY P. Random Notes of Boston. Boston: H.B. Humphrey, 1913. 1st ed. Teg. Pict cl, gilt. Fine. *Sadlon*. $30/£19

DOXIADIS, C. A. Architectural Space in Ancient Greece. Cambridge: MIT, (1972). Good in dj. *Archaeologia*. $95/£61

DOYLE, A. CONAN. The Adventures of Gerard. Collier, 1903. 1st US ed. VG + . *Williams*. $70/£45

DOYLE, A. CONAN. The Adventures of Gerard. London: George Newnes, n.d. (1903). 1st ed. Dk blue cl, gilt. Fine (extrems sl rubbed) in morocco-backed slipcase. *Sumner & Stillman*. $325/£208

DOYLE, A. CONAN. The Adventures of Sherlock Holmes. NY: Harper, (1892). 1st Amer ed. (Bkpl, loose pp, fr inside hinge split, peeling; spine, edges browned, frayed.) *Metropolitan**. $201/£129

DOYLE, A. CONAN. The Adventures of Sherlock Holmes. NY: Harper, (1892). 1st Amer ed, 2nd issue w/'if he had' on line 4, pg 65. 307pp. (Cl sl cocked; spine dknd, head chipped), else VG. *Mcgowan*. $300/£192

DOYLE, A. CONAN. The Adventures of Sherlock Holmes. NY: Harper, (1892). 1st Amer ed, 2nd issue. Blue/gray cl stamped in gilt/black. Very Nice (title paper separating along lower gutter, spine sl skewed; spine, bds sunned). *Hermitage*. $325/£208

DOYLE, A. CONAN. The Adventures of Sherlock Holmes. London: George Newnes, 1892. 1st ed w/floral eps (cracked); no street name on fr cvr illus. Lt blue cl dec in black/gilt. VG (spine sl dknd, extrems sl rubbed) in morocco-backed slipcase. *Sumner & Stillman*. $1,650/£1,058

DOYLE, A. CONAN. The Author's Edition of the Collected Works. John Murray, 1903 (1917). 1st ed, ltd to 1000, Eng issue w/1st vol signed, 1st gatherings reimposed to incl list of illus. 12 vols. Orig pink cl ruled, lettered in gilt. Orig lt blue djs lettered in dk blue (edgetears) w/Smith, Elder imprints at foot of spines (and fr flaps of djs) blocked over w/imprint of John Murray, colophon and djs numbered 657 in ink, correspondence to Stanley MacKenzie relating to issue points loosely inserted. *Sotheby's**. $4,664/£2,990

DOYLE, A. CONAN. The British Campaign in France and Flanders 1914. London, 1916. 1st ed. (Sl mkd), o/w VG. *Words Etc*. $23/£15

DOYLE, A. CONAN. The Case Book of Sherlock Holmes. NY: Doran, (1927). 2nd imp. Grey textured cl titled in red. Good (hinge weak; bkseller's label, price, penciled date rear ep). *Gravesend*. $35/£22

DOYLE, A. CONAN. The Case Book of Sherlock Holmes. NY: George H. Doran, (1927). 1st Amer ed, 2nd issue (in gray rather than tan cl, w/no pub's colophon on c. pg). Fine (eps unevenly browned). *Sumner & Stillman*. $135/£87

DOYLE, A. CONAN. The Case of Oscar Slater. London/NY/Toronto: Hodder & Stoughton, n.d. (1912). 1st ed. Lt gray wrappers. VF. *Sumner & Stillman*. $165/£106

DOYLE, A. CONAN. The Case-Book of Sherlock Holmes. London: John Murray, (1927). 1st ed. Rose cl. VF in Good at best dj (lg corner fr panel lacking incl some of 'Holmes,' tears, edgewear), morocco-backed slipcase. *Sumner & Stillman*. $975/£625

DOYLE, A. CONAN. The Croxley Master. NY: McClure, Phillips, 1907. 1st separate ed. Color frontis. Tan cl pict dec in black/white/grn. NF (white cvr panel sl flaked). *Sumner & Stillman*. $195/£125

DOYLE, A. CONAN. Danger! and Other Stories. London: John Murray, 1918. 1st ed, 1st issue. Rose cl. Fine in off-white dj w/brn print (1-inch spine tear, sm chips), morocco-backed slipcase. *Sumner & Stillman*. $675/£433

DOYLE, A. CONAN. A Desert Drama. Phila: Lippincott, 1898. 1st ed. 32 full-pg illus. NF in pict cvrs (spine sl faded). *Else Fine*. $65/£42

DOYLE, A. CONAN. The Doings of Raffles Haw. London/Paris/Melbourne: Cassell, 1892. 1st ed. One of 2001 ptd. 8pp undated ads. Dk blue cl. Fine in morocco-backed slipcase. *Sumner & Stillman*. $425/£272

DOYLE, A. CONAN. A Duet. Grant Richards, 1899. Pb issue of 1st ed sheets. (1-inch loss spine bottom), o/w VG. *Williams*. $70/£45

DOYLE, A. CONAN. A Duet. NY, 1899. 1st Amer ed. Fine (spine extrems, corners sl rubbed). *Polyanthos*. $60/£38

DOYLE, A. CONAN. A Duet. NY: D. Appleton, 1899. 1st Amer ed, 1st issue. One of 1350. Lists 19 (rather than 6) titles on 1/2-title verso. 8pp undated ads. Red cl dec in silver/gilt. Fine. *Sumner & Stillman*. $125/£80

DOYLE, A. CONAN. A Duet; With an Occasional Chorus. NY: D. Appleton, 1899. 1st Amer ed, 1st ptg, w/19 titles by Doyle listed opposite tp. Reportedly only 1350 of 1st ptg were produced. Dec maroon cl (spine sl faded). VG (ink name fr blank pg). *Antic Hay*. $100/£64

DOYLE, A. CONAN. The Early Christian Church and Modern Spiritualism. Westminster: Psychic Bookshop & Library, n.d. (1925). 1st ed. 12-pg pamphlet. NF in self-wrappers (sm corner chipped, short closed tear). *Sumner & Stillman*. $125/£80

DOYLE, A. CONAN. The Exploits of Brigadier Gerard. London: George Newnes, 1896. 1st ed. 8pp ads dated '10.2.96.' Red cl dec in black. NF (sm cvr mks) in morocco-backed slipcase. *Sumner & Stillman*. $375/£240

DOYLE, A. CONAN. The Exploits of Brigadier Gerard. London: Newnes, 1896. 1st UK ed. VG (few pp sl foxed). *Williams*. $148/£95

DOYLE, A. CONAN. The Firm of Girdlestone. C&W, 1890. 1st UK ed. 32-pg ad insert to rear dated Jan 1890. VG (chip top edge tp, bkpl). *Williams*. $257/£165

DOYLE, A. CONAN. The Firm of Girdlestone. London: C&W, 1890. 1st ed, 1st state (w/32pp ads dated January 1890; some copies have ads dated April). Maroon cl dec in black. NF (eps sl cracked; spine sl faded) in morocco-backed slipcase. *Sumner & Stillman*. $950/£609

DOYLE, A. CONAN. The Great Boer War. London: Smith, Elder, 1900. 1st ed. 12pp undated ads. Dk blue cl. VG (few string dents fr cvr, eps sl cracked) in morocco-backed slipcase (scuffed). *Sumner & Stillman*. $375/£240

DOYLE, A. CONAN. The Great Shadow and Beyond the City. Bristol: J.W. Arrowsmith, n.d. (1893). 1st ed, preferred state, w/'Kent & Co. Limited' so ptd at end of London pub's name tp foot and w/tp verso blank. James Greig and Paul Hardy (illus). Orange cl dec in black/blue. NF (extrems sl rubbed) in morocco-backed slipcase. *Sumner & Stillman*. $350/£224

DOYLE, A. CONAN. The Great Shadow. Bristol/London: J.W. Arrowsmith/Simpkin et al, (1893). 1st ed, later ptg. Orange cl, gilt. Good (inscrip, lt foxed, sl rubbed). *Houle*. $200/£128

DOYLE, A. CONAN. The Green Flag and Other Stories of War and Sport. London: Smith, Elder, 1900. 1st ed. Frontis. 4pp undated ads. Red cl (sl discolored) pict dec in black. VG (eps sl cracked) in morocco-backed slipcase. *Sumner & Stillman*. $225/£144

DOYLE, A. CONAN. The Guards Came Through. London: John Murray, 1919. 1st ed. One of 2033. 2pp undated ads. Red wrappers. Fine. *Sumner & Stillman*. $195/£125

DOYLE, A. CONAN. His Last Bow. NY: George H. Doran, (1917). 1st Amer ed. 'Agriculture' for 'apiculture' in preface. Salmon cl (spine sl faded, few lt damp mks). VG. *Sumner & Stillman*. $150/£96

DOYLE, A. CONAN. His Last Bow. London: John Murray, 1917. 1st (Eng) ed. 6pp undated ads. 'Agriculture' for 'apiculture' in preface. Rose cl (dull, sl shelfworn). Good (eps cracked) in morocco-backed slipcase. *Sumner & Stillman*. $195/£125

DOYLE, A. CONAN. His Last Bow. NY: Doran, 1917. 1st ed. (Soiled, frayed, spine ends clipped, hinges weak.) *Metropolitan**. $57/£37

DOYLE, A. CONAN. The Hound of the Baskervilles. George Newnes, 1902. 1st ed. 8vo. 16 illus by Sidney Paget. (Ink inscrip.) Scarlet cl (rubbed), gilt (sl faded). *Sotheby's**. $825/£529

DOYLE, A. CONAN. The Hound of the Baskervilles. London, 1902. 1st ed, 1st issue w/'you' for 'your' p13, line 3. 16 plts. (Sl browned, plt sl creased, tail sl chipped, red cl bleeding onto lower pastedown, fore-edge, margin last 15pp.) Gilt/black dec cl (spine sl rubbed, sunned, corner sl bumped.) *Edwards*. $936/£600

DOYLE, A. CONAN. The Hound of the Baskervilles. London: George Newnes, 1902. 1st ed, 1st issue, w/misprint 'you' for 'your' p13 line 3. 8vo. Pub's gilt-lettered, dec red cl (sl cocked, spine lt sunned). *D & D*. $1,100/£705

DOYLE, A. CONAN. The Hound of the Baskervilles. London: Newnes, 1902. 1st ed, 1st issue. 8vo. Frontis by Sidney Paget. Pict red cl (spine sl sunned, extrems sl rubbed). *Swann**. $977/£626

DOYLE, A. CONAN. The Hound of the Baskervilles. NY: McClure, Phillips, 1902. 2nd Amer ed. Frontis. (Sl wear.) *M & S*. $150/£96

DOYLE, A. CONAN. An Incursion into Diplomacy. London: Smith, Elder, 1906. 1st separate ed. NF in blue ptd wrappers. *Sumner & Stillman*. $165/£106

DOYLE, A. CONAN. The Land of Mist. NY: Doran, (1926). 1st Amer ed, 1st ptg. Pale grn cl lettered in dk grn. Bright (sl worn, sm smudge; rear hinge paper cracked). *Macdonnell*. $165/£106

DOYLE, A. CONAN. The Later Adventures of Sherlock Holmes. Edgar W. Smith (ed). NY: LEC, 1952. 3 vols. VG. *Argosy*. $175/£112

DOYLE, A. CONAN. The Limited Editions Sherlock Holmes. NY: LEC, 1950-1952. 1st ptgs. Ltd to 1500 numbered. 8 vols. 1/2 black linen in glassine wrappers. VG (bkpl in all but 1st vol) in 3 Good pub's slipcases. *Gravesend*. $800/£513

DOYLE, A. CONAN. The Lost World. NY: Hodder & Stoughton, (1912). 1st Amer ed. Brn cl. Fine. *Appelfeld*. $100/£64

DOYLE, A. CONAN. The Lost World. Hodder, 1912. 1st UK ed. VG (ink inscrip; lt stain fr cvr). *Williams*. $226/£145

DOYLE, A. CONAN. The Maracot Deep and Other Stories. London: John Murray, (1929). 1st ed. 10pp undated ads. Rose cl. VF in NF pict dj (nicks, sl soil), morocco-backed slipcase. *Sumner & Stillman*. $2,750/£1,763

DOYLE, A. CONAN. The Maracot Deep. GC: Doubleday Doran, 1929. 1st Amer ed. (Rubbed, extrems worn, frayed.) *Metropolitan**. $23/£15

DOYLE, A. CONAN. The Memoirs of Sherlock Holmes. Newnes, 1894. 1st UK ed. VG + (lt foxed; gold spine panels sl rubbed). *Williams*. $1,170/£750

DOYLE, A. CONAN. The Memoirs of Sherlock Holmes. London: George Newnes, 1894. 1st ed. Sidney Paget (illus). Blue cl dec in black/gilt, beveled. VG + (eps sl cracked; gilt spine panels sl rubbed) in morocco-backed slipcase. *Sumner & Stillman*. $1,650/£1,058

DOYLE, A. CONAN. The Memoirs of Sherlock Holmes. NY: Harper, Sept 1894. 'New and Revised' Amer ed (w/o 'The Adventure of the Cardboard Box'). 4pp undated ads. Lt blue cl dec in black. VG (sl cvr soil, sl wear spine ends). *Sumner & Stillman*. $95/£61

DOYLE, A. CONAN. Memories and Adventures. Hodder & Stoughton, 1924. 2nd ed. Inscribed presentation copy. 8vo. (Foxed, repairs 1st few leaves.) Orig blue cl (sl rubbed) ruled in blind, gilt-lettered. *Sotheby's**. $718/£460

DOYLE, A. CONAN. Memories and Adventures. Boston: Little, Brown, 1924. 1st US ed. VG (sl cvr wear); ink presentation fep of Constance Holland. *Gravesend*. $200/£128

DOYLE, A. CONAN. Micah Clarke. London: Longmans, Green, 1889. 1st ed. One of 1000. 2pp undated ads, 16pp ads dated June 1888 (earliest ad cat, though bk was not pub until Feb 1889). Mostly unopened. Dk blue cl, beveled. Fine in morocco-backed slipcase (sl scuffed). *Sumner & Stillman*. $1,175/£753

DOYLE, A. CONAN. Micah Clarke. NY: Harper, 1889. 1st US ed. Pb. Blue cl (rebound), grn leather label, gilt. VG (tp, dedication pg damaged, last text pg repaired). Bound w/o orig wrappers. *Williams*. $101/£65

DOYLE, A. CONAN. My Friend the Murderer, and Other Mysteries and Adventures. NY: R.F. Fenno, n.d. (wrapper dated June 15, 1895 w/pub's address as 112 Fifth Avenue). Early Amer (pirated) ed. Issued as #19 in Fenno's 'Lenox Series.' Orig lt blue wrappers ptd in dk blue, Doyle port. NF (little soil, edgewear) in morocco-backed slipcase. *Sumner & Stillman*. $650/£417

DOYLE, A. CONAN. The New Revelation. NY: Doran, (1918). 1st US ed. Brn cl. VG (ink name, date fep) in Good dj (lt wear, 1-inch piece missing backstrip). *Gravesend*. $50/£32

DOYLE, A. CONAN. An Open Letter. (London): Psychic Press, n.d. (1929). 1st ed. Self-wrapped 12-pg pamphlet. NF (sl browned). *Sumner & Stillman*. $115/£74

DOYLE, A. CONAN. The Outlook on the War. London: Daily Chronicle, (1915). 1st separate ed. 8-pg self-wrappered leaflet. VG (corner creased, short tear). *Sumner & Stillman*. $95/£61

DOYLE, A. CONAN. The Parasite. Westminster: Constable, 1894. 1st ed. Gilt-dec blue cl. NF (extrems sl rubbed) in morocco-backed slipcase. *Sumner & Stillman*. $375/£240

DOYLE, A. CONAN. Pheneas Speaks. (London): Psychic Press and Bookshop, (1927). 1st ed. Frontis photo. 3pp undated ads. Lt blue-gray wrappers. NF (sl cvr soil, ink title on spine). *Sumner & Stillman*. $175/£112

DOYLE, A. CONAN. The Poems of Arthur Conan Doyle. Collected Edition. London: John Murray, 1922. 1st ed, 1st issue. One of 1516. 2pp undated ads. Blue cl. Fine in VF dj, morocco-backed slipcase. *Sumner & Stillman*. $1,250/£801

DOYLE, A. CONAN. The Poison Belt. London/NY/Toronto: Hodder & Stoughton, (1913). 1st ed. Blue cl pict dec in black. VG (sl foxed; spine sl faded, sm mks fr cvr). *Sumner & Stillman*. $225/£144

DOYLE, A. CONAN. The Refugees. NY: Harper, 1893. 1st Amer ed. Lt blue cl (rubbed, upper hinge starting). Good. *Houle*. $125/£80

DOYLE, A. CONAN. The Refugees: A Tale of Two Continents. NY: Harper, 1893. 1st ed. Dec cvrs (worn). VG. *Else Fine*. $225/£144

DOYLE, A. CONAN. The Return of Sherlock Holmes. London: George Newnes, 1905. 1st Eng ed. Sidney Paget (illus). 4pp undated ads. Dk blue cl, flat spine. NF (extrems sl rubbed) in morocco-backed slipcase. *Sumner & Stillman*. $1,950/£1,250

DOYLE, A. CONAN. The Return of Sherlock Holmes. NY: McClure, Phillips, 1905. 1st ed. Orig black pict cl, dec in yellow/terra cotta. (Spine lettering half flaked; lt rubbed, hinge paper cracked.) *Macdonnell*. $300/£192

DOYLE, A. CONAN. The Return of Sherlock Holmes. NY: McClure, Phillips, 1905. 1st ed. Orig black pict cl, dec in yellow/terra cotta. (Spine lettering sl flaked), else Fine. *Macdonnell*. $800/£513

DOYLE, A. CONAN. Rodney Stone. London: Smith, Elder, 1896. 1st ed. 10pp pub's ads at end. Black eps, uncut. Black cl (spine sl worn, faded, rubbed), gilt. VG. *Houle*. $125/£80

DOYLE, A. CONAN. Rodney Stone. London: Smith, Elder, 1896. 1st ed. Sidney Paget (illus). 10pp undated ads. Black cl. NF (eps sl cracked) in morocco-backed slipcase. *Sumner & Stillman*. $375/£240

DOYLE, A. CONAN. Rodney Stone. NY: Appleton, 1896. 1st Amer ed. Red cl dec in silver/gold. (Tape mks ep, ink inscrip 1st blank), o/w VG. *Hermitage*. $175/£112

DOYLE, A. CONAN. Rodney Stone. NY: Appleton, 1896. 1st Amer ed. Dec red cl. Fine in dj (sl worn, 2 needless internal mends), custom slipcase. *Captain's Bookshelf*. $1,000/£641

DOYLE, A. CONAN. Rodney Stone. NY: D. Appleton, 1896. 1st Amer ed. Sidney Paget (illus). 14pp undated ads. Maroon cl dec in silver/gilt. NF (spine lettering sl rubbed). *Sumner & Stillman*. $70/£45

DOYLE, A. CONAN. Round the Fire Stories. London: Smith, Elder, 1908. 1st ed. Frontis. 4pp undated ads. Red cl, gilt cvr vignette. NF (fr cvr lt spotted) in morocco-backed slipcase. *Sumner & Stillman*. $250/£160

DOYLE, A. CONAN. Round the Red Lamp. London: Methuen, 1894. 1st ed. One of 6000 ptd. 32-pg pub's cat at end. Red cl (browned, frayed), gilt. Good. *Houle*. $175/£112

DOYLE, A. CONAN. Round the Red Lamp. London: Methuen, 1894. 1st ed. 32pp 1st state ads dated Oct 1894. Red cl. VG (spine sl faded, sm dampstain cvr fore-edge) in morocco-backed slipcase. *Sumner & Stillman*. $275/£176

DOYLE, A. CONAN. The Sign of Four. Spencer Blackett, 1890. 1st ed, 1st issue. Variant state w/'138' correctly spelled at pg (iv), 32pp ads inserted at end, misprint pg56. 8vo. Frontis by Charles Kerr. Black-coated eps. Orig dk red fine-ribbed cl blocked in black, gilt-lettered. (Cvrs sl dull, discolored, rebacked preserving most of orig spine.) *Sotheby's**. $1,345/£862

DOYLE, A. CONAN. The Sign of Four. Spencer Blackett, 1890. 1st ed, 1st issue, w/'Spencer Blackett's Standard Library' at base of spine. Variant w/'138' misprinted as '13' on contents pg (iv), misprint 'w shed' for 'wished' pg56, w/o 32pp of ads at end. Frontis by Charles Kerr. (Sig, address; pencil notes loosely inserted.) Black-coated eps. Orig dk red fine-ribbed cl blocked in black, gilt-lettered. (Sl restoration spine head, neat repair at foot.) *Sotheby's**. $3,588/£2,300

DOYLE, A. CONAN. The Sign of Four. London: Spencer Blackett, 1890. 1st ed, 1st issue (w/Spencer Blackett tp, 'Spencer Blackett's Standard Library' at spine foot). 32pp (Blackett) ads dated Oct 1890. Reads '13' rather than '138' on contents pg. Maroon cl dec in black. VG (few sm lighter-color areas near fr cvr fore-edge, few sl mks rear cvr, sl wear top 1/2-inch fr hinge, eps sl cracked) in morocco-backed slipcase. *Sumner & Stillman*. $4,750/£3,045

DOYLE, A. CONAN. The Sign of Four. Spencer Blackett, 1891. 1st ed, 2nd issue w/imprint at spine foot 'Griffith Farran & Cos Standard Library;' 8pp ads at end, '13' for '138' pg (iv). 8vo. Frontis. (Sl red staining fore-edge margin final leaves.) Dk brn coated eps. Dk red fine-ribbed cl (rubbed, rather dull) blocked in black, gilt-lettered. *Sotheby's**. $1,076/£690

DOYLE, A. CONAN. The Sign of Four. George Newnes, 1892. 1st ed, 3rd issue using Griffith Farran cvrs but w/dbl leaf inserted w/new prelims, '13' for '138' pg (iv). 8vo. Frontis. Dk brn coated eps. Dk red fine-ribbed cl blocked in black, gilt-lettered. *Sotheby's**. $1,435/£920

DOYLE, A. CONAN. Sir Nigel. Smith, Elder, 1906. 1st British ed. 8 plts. Nice (edges sl spotted, sl signs of age). *Ash*. $117/£75

DOYLE, A. CONAN. Sir Nigel. London: Smith Elder, 1906. 1st ed. Dec red cl (spine sunned), gilt. *D & D*. $65/£42

DOYLE, A. CONAN. Sir Nigel. London: Smith, Elder, 1906. 1st Eng ed. 2pp undated ads. Red cl, gilt cvr vignette. VG (minor cvr soil) in morocco-backed slipcase. *Sumner & Stillman*. $185/£119

DOYLE, A. CONAN. Sir Nigel. London: Smith, Elder, 1906. 1st UK ed. VG (fep hinge sl starting). *Williams*. $187/£120

DOYLE, A. CONAN. Sir Nigel. NY: McClure, Phillips, 1906. 1st Amer ed. Dec blue cl. VG (worn, ink name). *Antic Hay*. $30/£19

DOYLE, A. CONAN. Songs of Action. London: Smith Elder, 1898. 1st ed. viii,136pp (fep lt spotted). Untrimmed. Buckram (sl rubbed), gilt. *Hollett*. $133/£85

DOYLE, A. CONAN. Songs of Action. London: Smith, Elder, 1898. 1st ed. One of 1000. Blue cl, gilt. NF. *Sumner & Stillman*. $165/£106

DOYLE, A. CONAN. Songs of the Road. London: Smith, Elder, 1911. 1st ed. 2pp undated ads. Blue cl. Fine (sig). *Sumner & Stillman*. $145/£93

DOYLE, A. CONAN. Spiritualism and Rationalism. London: Hodder & Stoughton, n.d. (1920). 1st ed. Gray ptd wrappers. NF (sl soil). *Sumner & Stillman*. $150/£96

DOYLE, A. CONAN. The Stark Munro Letters. Longmans, 1895. 1st UK ed. 24pp ads dated July 1895 as called for. VG (few pages lt foxed). *Williams*. $195/£125

DOYLE, A. CONAN. The Stark Munro Letters. London: Longmans, Green, 1895. 1st ed. 24pp ads dated June 1895. Dk blue cl, beveled. NF (cl sl bubbled). *Sumner & Stillman*. $190/£122

DOYLE, A. CONAN. The Stark Munro Letters. NY: D. Appleton, 1895. 1st Amer ed. 6pp undated ads. 8 full-pg plts by Alice Barber Stephens. Maroon cl dec in gold/silver. Fine. *Sumner & Stillman*. $135/£87

DOYLE, A. CONAN. A Study in Scarlet. Ward, Lock & Bowden, (Nov), 1895. 3rd Eng ed. James Greig (illus). 8vo. (Sl browned, bkpl.) Orig pict stapled wrappers (edges frayed, sl soiled), upper cvr blocked, titled in red/black. Fldg brn clamshell box. *Sotheby's**. $1,076/£690

DOYLE, A. CONAN. Three of Them. London: John Murray, 1923. 1st ed. 4pp undated ads. Gray bds, red cl spine, spine label. Fine in Good dj (soiled, few tears). *Sumner & Stillman*. $75/£48

DOYLE, A. CONAN. Through the Magic Door. London: Smith, Elder, 1907. 1st ed. 6pp undated ads. Red cl, gilt cvr vignette. VG (fr cvr sl discolored) in morocco-backed slipcase. *Sumner & Stillman*. $165/£106

DOYLE, A. CONAN. Through the Magic Door. NY: McClure, 1908. 1st issue, 1st Amer ed (468 copies thus). Gilt-dec cl (spine ends sl rubbed). VG (ink name dated in year of pub). *Reese*. $85/£54

DOYLE, A. CONAN. Through the Magic Door. NY: McClure, 1908. 1st Amer ed. One of 468. Gray cl, gilt. NF (few sl mks). *Sumner & Stillman*. $195/£125

DOYLE, A. CONAN. The Tragedy of the Korosko. London: Smith Elder, 1898. 1st ed. (Hinges sl cracked), o/w NF in red cvrs, gilt. *Mordida*. $200/£128

DOYLE, A. CONAN. The Tragedy of the Korosko. London: Smith, Elder, 1898. 1st ed. xii,333(vi,ads)pp; 40 full-pg illus by Sydney Paget. Red cl, gilt. VG (joints tender). *Hollett*. $218/£140

DOYLE, A. CONAN. The Tragedy of the Korosko. London: Smith, Elder, 1898. 1st Eng ed. Sidney Paget (illus). 6pp undated ads. Black eps (cracked). Red cl, gilt vignette fr cvr. NF in morocco-backed slipcase. *Sumner & Stillman*. $325/£208

DOYLE, A. CONAN. Uncle Bernac. London: Smith, Elder, 1897. 1st ed. 8pp undated ads; 11 plts. Red cl (bubbled, sl soiled), gilt pict panel. Good (eps cracked) in morocco-backed slipcase. *Sumner & Stillman*. $115/£74

DOYLE, A. CONAN. Uncle Bernac. NY: Appleton, 1897. 1st Amer ed. Dec red cl. VG (ink name, stamp). *Antic Hay*. $35/£22

DOYLE, A. CONAN. The Valley of Fear. NY: George H. Doran, 1914. 1st Amer ed. Red cl, gilt. Fine. *D & D*. $195/£125

DOYLE, A. CONAN. The Valley of Fear. Smith, Elder, 1915. 1st ed. 8vo. Frontis by Frank Wiles. Blindstamp 'Presentation Copy' on title. Orig pink cl. *Sotheby's**. $610/£391

DOYLE, A. CONAN. The Valley of Fear. London: Smith, Elder, 1915. 1st Eng ed. Frontis, 6pp undated ads. Rose cl. NF (lt cvr soil) in morocco-backed slipcase. *Sumner & Stillman*. $575/£369

DOYLE, A. CONAN. A Visit to Three Fronts. June 1916. 1st ed. Off-white wrappers ptd in blue-gray. Fine. *Sumner & Stillman*. $165/£106

DOYLE, A. CONAN. The Vital Message. NY: George H. Doran, n.d. (1919). 1st Amer ed, 2nd issue (ending at pg 164). Gray-grn cl. Fine in NF dj (sl edgeworn). *Sumner & Stillman*. $195/£125

DOYLE, A. CONAN. The War in South Africa. London: Smith, Elder, 1902. 1st ed. VG in white wrappers (soil). *Sumner & Stillman*. $125/£80

DOYLE, A. CONAN. What Does Spiritualism Actually Teach and Stand For? London: Psychic Bookshop, n.d. (1928). 1st ed. Gray wrappers. Fine. *Sumner & Stillman*. $145/£93

DOYLE, A. CONAN. The White Company. London: Smith, Elder, 1891. 1st ed. One of 750. 3 vols. 2pp undated ads vols II and III. Orig red-brn cl dec in black. (Faint patches fr cvr from former lib labels; rear cvr 1 vol substantially dampstained, rubbed that carries to lower corner spine; few sl mks; 2 vols w/later plain eps.) Good in morocco-backed slipcase. *Sumner & Stillman*. $875/£561

DOYLE, A. CONAN. The White Company. Smith, Elder, 1897. 18th ed. Ad leaves. Pict cl (spine bumped). Good (prize plate fr pastedown, thumb mks). *Tiger*. $25/£16

DOYLE, A. CONAN. The White Company. NY, 1922. 1st ed thus. N. C. Wyeth (illus). Dec cl (sl rubbed). Contents VG. *Whiteson*. $70/£45

DOYLE, A. CONAN. The White Company. NY: Cosmopolitan Book Corp, 1922. 1st ed w/the N. C. Wyeth illus. 13 color plts. Maroon cl, pict label, gilt top. Fine. *Appelfeld*. $150/£96

DOYLE, A. CONAN. The White Company. NY: Cosmopolitan, 1922. 1st ed thus. Lg 8vo. 363pp; 16 full-pg color plts by N.C. Wyeth. Illus eps; teg. Maroon cl, gilt. VG + . *Dower*. $225/£144

DOYLE, A. CONAN. A Word of Warning. (London): Psychic Press, n.d. (1928). 1st ed. Gray wrappers. VF. *Sumner & Stillman*. $135/£87

DOYLE, ADRIAN CONAN and JOHN DICKSON CARR. The Exploits of Sherlock Holmes. London: John Murray, 1954. 1st ed. (Pg edges, eps lt spotted, bkseller stamp), o/w VG in dj (nicks, sl wear, internal tape mends). *Mordida*. $75/£48

DOYLE, ADRIAN CONAN. Micah Clarke: His Statement. Longmans, Green, 1889. Pub's cat dated June 1888. Beveled bds. Good (margin soiling, spotting, new eps; spine bumped, chipped, corners rubbed). *Tiger*. $187/£120

DOYLE, ADRIAN CONAN. The True Conan Doyle. NY: Coward-McCann, (1946). 1st Amer ed. NF in VG dj. *Turtle Island*. $65/£42

DOYLE, J. A. English in America; Virginia, Maryland, and the Carolinas. London: Longmans, 1882. 1st ed. (16),556,(24 ads)pp; fldg color map. Howes D454. *Ginsberg*. $100/£64

DOYLE, P. J. and E. W. McDIAMID (eds). The Baker Street Dozen. NY: Congdon & Weed, 1987. 1st ed. Fine in dj (sl edgewear). *Janus*. $25/£16

DOYLE, RODDY. The Commitments. Dublin: King Farouk, 1987. Orig pb. VG (ink inscrip; spine sl worn, creased). *Williams.* $234/£150

DOYLE, RODDY. The Commitments. NY, 1987. 1st Amer ed. Fine in wraps. *Warren.* $75/£48

DOYLE, RODDY. Paddy Clarke Ha Ha Ha. London: Secker & Warburg, 1993. 1st UK ed. Fine in dj. *Moorhouse.* $55/£35

DOYLE, RODDY. The Snapper. London, 1990. 1st ed. NF in dj. *Buckley.* $39/£25

Dr. Radcliffe's Life and Letters. (By W. Pittis.) A. Bettesworth et al, 1736. 4th ed. (vi),102pp, w/prelim, final ad ll. Orig calf. *Bickersteth.* $125/£80

DRABBLE, MARGARET. A Writer's Britain: Landscape in Literature. Thames & Hudson, 1979. (Inscrip, spine sl faded), else VG in dj. *Hadley.* $25/£16

DRACOPOLI, I. N. Through Jubaland to the Lorian Swamp. London, 1914. 2nd ed. 2 maps (1 fldg). (Lt browned, ink stamp fep; spine sl worn, corners sl creased.) *Edwards.* $78/£50

DRAGO, HARRY SINCLAIR. Notorious Ladies of the Frontier. NY, (1969). 1st ed. VG+ in VG+ dj. *Pratt.* $30/£19

DRAGO, HARRY SINCLAIR. Outlaws on Horseback. NY: Dodd, Mead, (1964). #45/150 signed, slipcased deluxe ed. Map. Pict eps; teg. Full red pebble-grained leather. Fine in NF orig slipcase w/pict label. *Harrington.* $175/£112

DRAGO, HARRY SINCLAIR. Red River Valley. NY: Clarkson N. Potter, (1962). 1st ed. VG in dj. *Lien.* $35/£22

DRAGO, HARRY SINCLAIR. Road Agents and Train Robbers. NY, (1973). 1st ed. Fine in Fine dj. *Pratt.* $25/£16

DRAGO, HARRY SINCLAIR. Wild, Woolly and Wicked. NY: Clarkson N. Potter, 1960. 1st ed. Good in dj. *Dumont.* $30/£19

DRAGO, HARRY SINCLAIR. Wild, Wooly, and Wicked. NY: Clarkson N. Potter, (1960). 1st ed. VG in dj. *Perier.* $32/£21

DRAKE, BENJAMIN. The Life and Adventures of Black Hawk. Cincinnati: George Conclin, 1841. 7th ed. Frontis woodcut port, 288pp; port, 6 other plts. Later calf-backed marbled bds. Good (ink name top margin port leaving traces on title). Howes D459. *Wantagh.* $125/£80

DRAKE, DANIEL and JOHN D. GODMAN. Memoir of Dr. John D. Godman and Rambles of a Naturalist. Phila, 1833. 1st ed. 152pp. Contemp calf. VG. *Argosy.* $125/£80

DRAKE, DANIEL. Pioneer Life in Kentucky, 1785-1800. Emmet F. Horine (ed). NY: Henry Schuman, 1948. Lg paper ed. Ltd to 250. *Wantagh.* $65/£42

DRAKE, DANIEL. A Systematic Treatise, Historical, Etiological, and Practical, on the Principal Diseases of the Interior Valley of North America. Cincinnati/Phila: Winthrop B. Smith/Lippincott, Grambo, 1850 (1st series)/1854 (2nd series). xvi,878pp incl tables and 19 plts; xix,(17)-985pp incl tables. (Foxing, browning, clean tear tp vol 1.) Vol 1 matching sheep (newly rebound), vol 2 orig sheep (newly rebacked, orig spine laid down). *Goodrich.* $995/£638

DRAKE, FRANCIS. The World Encompassed. Cleveland: World, 1966. Frontis map. 24-pg pamphlet. Fine in clamshell box. *Dumont.* $50/£32

DRAKE, J. MADISON. Historical Sketches of the Revolutionary and Civil Wars. NY, 1908. 1st ed. (Cvr lt worn) o/w Fine in plain plastic dj. *Pratt.* $90/£58

DRAKE, MAURICE. A History of English Glass-Painting. London: T. Werner Laurie, 1912. 1st ed. 36 mtd plts. (Sm stamp tp verso.) Orig bds (edges worn, rather soiled). *Hollett.* $101/£65

DRAKE, S. A. Old Boston Taverns and Tavern Clubs. Boston, 1917. Fldg map. Fair (water stains throughout). *Scribe's Perch*.* $16/£10

DRAKE, ST. CLAIR and HORACE R. CLAYTON. Black Metropolis. NY: Harcourt, Brace, (1945). Red cl. VG. *Petrilla.* $45/£29

DRAKE, ST. CLAIR and HORACE R. CLAYTON. Black Metropolis. NY: HB&Co, (1945). 1st ed. Errata slip tipped in. (Inscrip, spine base lt wear), else NF in VG dj (spine tanned, crown chipped, lg chip rear panel). *Between The Covers.* $135/£87

DRAKE, STILLMAN and C. D. O'MALLEY (trans). The Controversy on the Comets of 1618. Phila: Univ of PA, (1960). 1st ed thus. Frontis. NF in dj. *Glaser.* $60/£38

DRANNAN, WILLIAM F. Thirty-One Years on the Plains and in the Mountains. Chicago, 1907. (Shaken; cvrs worn.) *King.* $35/£22

DRAPER, JOHN W. History of the American Civil War. NY: Harper, (1867-1870). 1st ed. Attractive (spine ends chipped, lower corner margin vol 3 sl damped). *Waverly*.* $38/£24

DRAPER, JOHN W. History of the Conflict Between Religion and Science. NY, 1875. 1st ed. 373pp. VG. *Fye.* $75/£48

DRAPER, LYMAN COPELAND (ed). Collections.... Madison: WI State Hist Soc, 1903-1909. Vols 1-10. Blue cl (lt shelfwear, few hinges tender or cracked; bkpls). *Bohling.* $250/£160

DRAPER, LYMAN COPELAND (ed). Collections...Volume III. Madison: WI State Hist Soc, 1904. One of 2000. Port. VG+ (spine lettering dull). *Bohling.* $20/£13

DRAPER, T. The 84th Infantry Division in the Battle of Germany. NY: Viking, 1946. 1st ed. Red buckram (recased). Good. *Scribe's Perch*.* $60/£38

DRAPER, W. R. and MABEL. The Blood-Soaked Career of Bonnie Parker. Girard, KS: Haldeman-Julius, (1946). VG+ (paper dknd) in orange ptd wrapper. *Bohling.* $20/£13

DRAPER, WILLIAM R. Cub Reporter in the Old Indian Territory. Girard, KS: Haldeman-Julius, (1946). VG+ (pp dknd) in orange ptd wraps. *Bohling.* $15/£10

DRAPER, WILLIAM R. Last Government Land Lottery. Girard, KS: Haldeman-Julius, (1946). VG (pp dknd) in ptd wraps. *Bohling.* $20/£13

DRAPER, WILLIAM R. Oklahoma. Girard, KS: Haldeman-Julius, (1947). VG (pp dknd) in ptd wraps. *Bohling.* $15/£10

Drawings by Giovanni Domenico Tiepolo, the Property of the Right Hon. the Earl of Beauchamp. Sotheby's, 1965. Ptd bds. VF. *Europa.* $39/£25

DRAX, PETER. Crime to Music. NY: D. Appleton-Century, 1939. 1st Amer ed. Fine in dj (spine top frayed, corners chipped, sm tears). *Mordida.* $45/£29

DREISER, THEODORE. America Is Worth Saving. NY: Modern Age Books, (1941). 1st ed. Fine in dj (lt worn, few sm closed tears). *Hermitage.* $100/£64

DREISER, THEODORE. An American Tragedy. Cleveland/NY: World Publishing, (1948). 1st ed thus. (Lt spotting top edge stain), else NF in VG dj (chip bottom fr panel; sl rubbing). *Between The Covers.* $65/£42

DREISER, THEODORE. An American Tragedy. LEC, 1954. One of 1500. VF in pub's slipcase (sl soiled, faded). *Pirages.* $100/£64

DREISER, THEODORE. Chains. NY: Boni & Liveright, 1927. One of 440 specially bound, numbered, signed. Rice paper-cvrd bds, cl backstrip, paper label. Box (sl worn). *Beasley.* $250/£160

DREISER, THEODORE. The Financier. NY: Harper, 1912. 1st ed. Blue mottled cl (lt worn). VG. *Hermitage.* $50/£32

DREISER, THEODORE. A Gallery of Women. NY, 1929. 1st Amer ed. 2 vols. NF (fr cvr vol 1 sl rubbed) in djs (spines sunned, extrems lt chipped), box (edges chipped). *Polyanthos.* $100/£64

DREISER, THEODORE. A Gallery of Women. NY: Horace Liveright, 1929. Ltd to 560 numbered, signed sets. 2 vols. Unopened set. Cream parchment-backed dec black bds (bumped, corners chipped). Internally Fine. *Blue Mountain.* $95/£61

DREISER, THEODORE. Sister Carrie. NY: LEC, 1939. One of 1500 numbered, signed by Reginald Marsh (illus). Teg. Leather spine label. VG in bd slipcase. *Argosy.* $350/£224

DREISER, THEODORE. The Titan. NY: John Lane, 1914. 1st ed. 1st binding of blue mottled cl. VG (lt worn). *Hermitage.* $50/£32

DREISER, THEODORE. Tragic America. NY: Liveright, (1931). 1st ed. Fine in dj (spine sl faded). *Between The Covers.* $300/£192

DREPPERD, C. W. American Clocks and Clockmakers. NY: Doubleday, 1947. Stated 1st ed. Good. *Scribe's Perch*.* $30/£19

Dresden Gallery. N.p., 1864. Vol 2 only. 60 photogravure plts. Morocco (worn, defective). *Freeman*.* $25/£16

DREWITT, F. D. The Romance of the Apothecaries Garden at Chelsea. London, 1924. 2nd ed. 15 plts. (Spine faded.) *Wheldon & Wesley.* $39/£25

DREWRY, G. OVEREND. Consumption and Wasting Diseases Successfully Treated by 'Hydrated Oil'. London, (1877). 48pp. (Ex-lib.) Ptd wrappers. *Argosy.* $45/£29

DREXLER, ARTHUR. The Drawings of Frank Lloyd Wright. NY: MOMA, 1962. 1st ed. 303 plts. Gilt-emb cl. (Name; rubbed), else VG. *Cahan.* $50/£32

DREYFUS, ALFRED. Five Years of My Life. James Mortimer (trans). London: George Newnes, 1921. 1st Eng ed. 4 plts (1 edge sl worn). Pict cl (lt worn, mkd). VG (fingermks, feps spotted). *Hollett.* $133/£85

DREYFUS, JOHN. A History of the Nonesuch Press.... London, 1981. One of 950 numbered. Dj. *Swann*.* $172/£110

DRIBERG, TOM. Guy Burgess. London, 1956. 1st ed. VG in dj. *Typographeum.* $35/£22

DRIGGS, FRANK and HARRIS LEWINE. Black Beauty, White Heat. NY: Morrow, 1982. 1st ed. Fine in NF dj. *Beasley.* $150/£96

DRIGGS, HOWARD R. Mormon Trail Pathway of Pioneers Who Made the Deserts Blossom. NY: American Pioneer Trails Assoc, 1947. 1st ed. VG. *Brown.* $15/£10

DRINKER, ELIZABETH. Extracts from the Journal of Elizabeth Drinker, from 1759 to 1807, A.D. H. D. Biddle (ed). Phila: Lippincott, 1889. 423pp. Good (hinge cracks, wear, cl wrinkled). *Scribe's Perch*.* $20/£13

DRINKWATER, JOHN. Cotswold Characters. New Haven: Yale Univ, 1921. 1st ed. 5 wood engrs by Paul Nash. Brn bds. VF in dj (lt chipped). *Bromer.* $175/£112

DRINKWATER, JOHN. A History of the Late Siege of Gibraltar. London: T. Spilsbury, 1790. 4th ed. Inscribed presentation. 4to. xxiv,356pp; 10 fldg maps, plts, plans. Contemp straight-grained blue morocco, gilt, aeg. VG (lt dampstain fore-edge). *Lefkowicz.* $900/£577

DRINNON, RICHARD. Rebel in Paradise. Chicago: Univ of Chicago, 1961. 1st ed. Fine (bkpl) in Fine dj (top edge sl worn). *Beasley.* $35/£22

DRINNON, RICHARD. White Savage. The Case of John Dunn Hunter. NY: Schocken, (1972). 1st ed. Frontis, 3 maps. Fine in Fine dj. *Oregon.* $30/£19

DRINNON, RICHARD. White Savage: The Case of John Dunn Hunter. NY: Schocken, (1972). 1st ed. Fine in Fine dj. *Sadlon.* $25/£16

DRIVER, CARL S. John Sevier: Pioneer of the Old Southwest. Chapel Hill: Univ of NC, 1932. 1st ed. Frontis port. NF in dj (chipped, soiled). *Cahan.* $75/£48

DROLET, GODIAS J. and ANTHONY M. LOWELL. A Half Century's Progress Against Tuberculosis in New York City, 1900-1950. NY, 1952. 1st ed. Good in paper wrappers (worn). *Doctor's Library.* $50/£32

DROWER, MARGARET S. Flinders Petrie: A Life in Archaeology. London: Gollancz, 1985. Good in dj. *Archaeologia.* $65/£42

DROWN, WILLIAM and SOLOMON. Compendium of Agriculture, or The Farmer's Guide.... Providence, 1824. Paper-backed plain bds (spine heavily chipped, extrems sl worn), ptd spine label. (Lt foxing), o/w Contents VG. *New Hampshire*.* $40/£26

DRUCKER, PHILIP. Ceramic Sequences at Tres Zapotes, Vera Cruz, Mexico. BAE Bulletin 140. Washington: GPO, 1943. 1st ed. 65 plts. Blue wraps (worn, spotted). Internally VG. *Parmer.* $30/£19

DRUCKREY, TIMOTHY and MARNIE GILLETT. Reasoned Space. Tucson: Center for Creative Photography, Univ of AZ, 1980. 1st ed. Inscribed by Druckrey. Fine in ptd stiff wrappers. *Cahan.* $35/£22

DRUITT, HERBERT. A Manual of Costume as Illustrated by Monumental Brasses. De La More, 1906. Teg, rest uncut. (Sl rubbed, hinges tender.) *Peter Taylor.* $61/£39

DRUMMOND, JAMES. Ancient Scottish Weapons &c. Edinburgh/London: G. Waterston, 1881. One of 500 numbered. 54 chromolitho plts. 1/4 morocco (heavily worn in part, fr joint splitting; contents nearly separated from casing, some text sl foxed, short marginal tears). *Waverly*.* $357/£229

DRUMMOND, W. Memoir on the Antiquity of the Zodiacs of Esneh and Dendera. London, 1821. 1st ed. 191pp. Marbled bds. (Lt foxing, lacks 2 plts; inner hinge reinforced), o/w VG-. *Middle Earth.* $199/£128

DRUMMOND, WILLIAM. The Poems of William Drummond, of Hawthornden. London: Cochrane & M'Crone, 1833. 336pp. (Lacks fep, 1/2 title; lib label fr pastedown; cl rubbed, paper spine label removed.) *Hollett.* $47/£30

Drums and Shadows. Athens: Univ of GA, 1940. 1st ed. NF in dj (used). *Beasley.* $125/£80

DRUON, MAURICE. The Strangled Queen. London, 1956. 1st ed. VG in dj. *Words Etc.* $11/£7

DRURY, CLIFFORD M. William Anderson Scott. Glendale: Clark, 1967. 1st ed. Good in dj. *Heinoldt.* $30/£19

DRURY, CLIFFORD. Elkanah and Mary Walker, Pioneers among the Spokanes. Caldwell: Caxton, 1940. 1st ed. #261/500 signed. News clippings laid in. VG in dj (tape repaired). *Perier.* $95/£61

DRURY, CLIFFORD. Marcus and Narcissa Whitman and the Opening of Old Oregon. Glendale: A.H. Clark, 1973. 1st ed. Vol 1 signed. 2 vols. Fine set. *Perier.* $145/£93

DRURY, JOHN. Chicago in Seven Days. NY: Robert M. McBride, 1930. New, rev ed. NF in VG dj. *Sadlon.* $20/£13

DRURY, WELLS. An Editor on the Comstock Lode. Palo Alto: Pacific Books, (1948). New ed. VG + (corners bumped) in dj (lt worn). *Bohling.* $15/£10

DRYDEN, ALICE. The Arts of the Church: Church Embroidery. London: Mowbray, (1911). 1st ed. VG (name; hinges tender). *Second Life.* $35/£22

DRYDEN, JAMES. Poultry Breeding and Management. NY: OJ, 1931. Blue cl, gilt. VG. *Price.* $19/£12

DRYDEN, JOHN. Alexander's Feast. Oxford: Clarendon, 1925. Typographical facs of orig 1697 ed. One of 550. VG in marbled paper wrappers (extrems lt worn), ptd label. *Turtle Island.* $30/£19

DRYDEN, JOHN. The Dramatic Works.... Montague Summers (ed). Nonesuch, 1931. #564/750. 6 vols. Teg on the rough, others uncut, partly unopened. Grn buckram-backed marbled bds. VG (backstrips faded). *Cox.* $257/£165

DRYDEN, JOHN. Of Dramatick Poesie. London: Frederick Etchells & Hugh Macdonald, 1928. One of 580 ptd. Marbled bds, linen spine. Nice. *Appelfeld.* $125/£80

DRYDEN, JOHN. Secret Love or the Maiden-Queen. London: Henry Herringman, 1669. 2nd ed. Gilt edges. Mod 1/2 morocco, cl. *Christie's*.* $148/£95

DU BOIS, CONSTANCE GODDARD. Martha Corey: A Tale of the Salem Witchcraft. Chicago: A.C. McClurg, 1890. 1st ed. Gilt-dec cl (sl rubbed, few sm bubbles). VG (early ink name). *Reese.* $50/£32

DU BOIS, JOHN VAN DEUSEN. Campaigns in the West, 1856-1861. George P. Hammond (ed). Tucson: AZ Pioneers Hist Soc, 1949. One of 300. Lg fldg map. 1/2 red morocco, patterned bds, black leather spine label. Fine. Howes D521. *Harrington.* $350/£224

DU BOIS, W. E. B. In Battle for Peace. NY: Masses & Mainstream, 1952. 1st ed. NF (lt wear) in wraps. *Beasley.* $35/£22

DU BOIS, W. E. B. The Gift of Black Folk. Boston: Stratford, 1924. 1st ed. (Spine dknd, extrems sl worn), else VG. *Mcgowan.* $250/£160

DU BOIS, W. E. B. The Negro. NY: Holt, (1915). 1st ed. Pub as a vol in the Home University Library. (Few pg corners sl creasing; sl soiling), else NF (lacks dj). *Between The Covers.* $250/£160

DU BOIS, W. E. B. The Souls of Black Folk. Chicago: McClurg, 1903. 2nd ed. Black cl, black leather spine label, gilt. (Bkpl, pg sl torn; rebound, label sl rubbed), else NF. *Between The Covers.* $185/£119

DU BOIS, W. E. B. The Souls of Black Folk. London: Constable, 1905. 1st Eng ed. Frontis port. (Crease, sm name; lt worn), else NF. *Between The Covers.* $975/£625

DU BOIS, W. E. B. A W.E.B. Du Bois Reader. Andrew G. Paschal (ed). NY: Macmillan, (1971). 1st ed. Brn cl. VG in pict dj. *Petrilla.* $35/£22

DU BOIS, WILLIAM E. Trial of Lucretia Chapman. Phila: Mentz, 1832. 1st ed. 214,11pp. Later 1/2 morocco (worn, separate, sl foxed). VG. *Second Life.* $165/£106

DU BOIS, WILLIAM PENE. Bear Party. NY: Viking, 1951. 1st ed. 5 1/2 x 8 1/4. 48pp. Cl spine, pict bds (worn). Good. *Cattermole.* $35/£22

DU BOIS, WILLIAM PENE. Elisabeth the Cow Ghost. NY: Thomas Nelson, 1936. 1st ed. Dec yellow cl. (Extrems lt worn), else VG in pict dj. *Cummins.* $500/£321

DU BOIS, WILLIAM PENE. The Giant. NY: Viking, 1954. 1st ed. 6 1/4 x 9 1/2. 124pp. Good (lt soil) in dj. *Cattermole.* $35/£22

DU BOIS, WILLIAM PENE. Otto and the Magic Potatoes. NY: Viking, 1970. 1st ed. 7 1/2 x 10 1/4. 48pp. Pict cl. Good in dj. *Cattermole.* $45/£29

DU BOIS, WILLIAM PENE. The Three Policemen. NY: Viking, 1938. 1st ptg. Signed. 8vo. 92pp. Good. *Scribe's Perch*.* $36/£23

DU BOSE, JOHN WITHERSPOON. General Joseph Wheeler and the Army of Tennessee. NY: Neale, 1912. 1st ed. (Extrems sl rubbed), else NF. Howes D523. *Mcgowan.* $450/£288

DU BOSE, JOHN WITHERSPOON. General Joseph Wheeler and the Army of Tennessee. NY: Neale, 1912. 1st ed. (Extrems sl rubbed), else NF. Howes D523. *Mcgowan.* $450/£288

DU CANE, FLORENCE. The Canary Islands. A&C Black, 1911. 20 color plts, fldg map. (Feps lt browned; spine sl rubbed, sm scratches.) *Edwards.* $39/£25

DU CHAILLU, PAUL. In African Forest and Jungle. Scribner, 1903. 1st ed. (Name, address.) Pict cvr, gilt lettering. Good+ (wear). *Backman.* $20/£13

DU CHAILLU, PAUL. In African Forest and Jungle. NY: Scribner, 1903. 1st ed. 8vo. xii,193pp; 24 full-pg plts by Victor Perhard. Pub's cl, gilt. (Fr cvr lt faded), else Fine. *Bromer.* $100/£64

DU CHAILLU, PAUL. A Journey to Ashango-Land and Further Penetration into Equatorial Africa. NY: Appleton, 1867. 1st ed. 501pp + ads, 23 engrs, fldg map. Lib cl. NF. *Mikesh.* $65/£42

DU CHAILLU, PAUL. A Journey to Ashango-Land. London: John Murray, 1867. 1st ed. Inscribed Dec., 1871, tipped-in. Frontis: xxiv,501,32ads; fldg map. Grn 1/2 morocco, gilt, red spine label. Fine. *Terramedia.* $350/£224

DU CHAILLU, PAUL. The Land of the Midnight Sun. NY: Harper, 1882. 2 vols. 441; 474pp; color map in rear pocket vol 1. Dec cvrs. (Heads frayed, fr hinge cracked vol 1), o/w Good. *Scribe's Perch*.* $28/£18

DU CHAILLU, PAUL. The Land of the Midnight Sun. London, 1899. New ed. vii,759pp (lacks map?; text split between pp 530-1, feps lt browned; cl spine sl rubbed, sm tear). *Edwards.* $55/£35

DU CHAILLU, PAUL. Lost in the Jungle: Narrated for Young People. NY: Harper, 1869. 1st ed. Sm 8vo. 260pp. Gilt-dec cl. VG. *Mikesh.* $30/£19

DU CHAILLU, PAUL. My Apingi Kingdom. NY: Harper, 1871. 254pp; 33 engrs (9 full-pg). (Spine ends frayed), o/w VG. *Worldwide.* $45/£29

DU CHAILLU, PAUL. The Viking Age. London: Murray, 1889. 2 vols. Burgundy (sl worn), gilt. *Yudkin*.* $47/£30

DU CHAILLU, PAUL. The Viking Age. NY: Scribner, 1889. 1st ed. 2 vols. 591; 562pp. Dec cvrs. Good. *Scribe's Perch*.* $70/£45

DU MAURIER, DAPHNE. The Du Mauriers. London, 1937. 1st ed. Dj (soiled). *Typographeum.* $20/£13

DU MAURIER, DAPHNE. Frenchman's Creek. London, 1941. 1st ed. Dj. *Typographeum.* $75/£48

DU MAURIER, DAPHNE. The House on the Strand. London: Gollancz, 1969. 1st ed. VG+ in VG dj (price-clipped, extrem loss). *Lame Duck.* $125/£80

DU MAURIER, DAPHNE. The King's General. Gollancz, 1946. 1st UK ed. VG (ink inscrip) in dj (rear panel stained). *Williams.* $39/£25

DU MAURIER, DAPHNE. Kiss Me Again, Stranger. GC: Doubleday, (1953). 1st US ed. NF in NF dj (edge-worn). *Unger.* $125/£80

DU MAURIER, DAPHNE. Rebecca. Gollancz, 1938. 1st UK ed. VG (cvrs sl mkd) in dj (lt wear, uneven fading). *Williams.* $429/£275

DU MAURIER, GEORGE. A Legend of Camelot, Pictures and Poems. NY/London, 1898. Gilt edges. Dec cl (rubbed, lt stained; inscrip). *Argosy.* $50/£32

DU MAURIER, GEORGE. The Martian. NY: Harper, 1897. 1st Amer ed. Dec cl. Fine. *Antic Hay.* $85/£54

DU MAURIER, GEORGE. The Martian. London, 1898. 1st ed. Blue cl, gilt. (Spine foot torn, sl rubbed), o/w VG. *Words Etc.* $19/£12

DU MAURIER, GEORGE. Trilby. Harper, 1894. 1st US ed. VG-. *Madle*. $30/£19

DU PUIGAUDEAU, ODETTE. Barefoot Through Mauretania. 1937. 1st ed. Dj (chipped, sl soiled). *Edwards*. $59/£38

DU RU, PAUL. Journal of Paul Du Ru (Feb. 1 to May 8, 1700). Ruth L. Butler (trans). Chicago: Caxton Club, 1934. 1st ed. One of 300 ptd. Paper label spine, fr cvr. Howes D597. *Ginsberg*. $150/£96

DU TOIT, ALEX. The Geology of South Africa. London: Oliver & Boyd, 1926. 1st ed. 39 plts, fldg map. (Spine faded.) *Argosy*. $75/£48

DUANE, JAMES T. Dear Old 'K.' Boston, 1922. Lg fldg photo at rear. Good (ex-lib). *Scribe's Perch**. $20/£13

DUANE, WILLIAM. Hand Book for Infantry.... Phila: The Author, 1813. 3rd ed. (2),v,(1),112pp (browning, lt dampstaining); 11 engr plts (1 w/old tape repair, stained, 1 lacks corner piece). Orig bds (shabby, spine, fr bd detached). *Waverly**. $49/£31

DUARTE, MARGARIDA. The Legend of the Palm Tree. NY: G&D, 1940. 1st ltd ed. Paul Werneck (illus). 10 1/2 x 12 1/2. 48pp. Good in dj, remnants of grass cl slipcase. *Cattermole*. $60/£38

DuBELLET, LOUIS P. Some Prominent Virginia Families. (Lynchburg, VA, 1903-1907.) 1st ed. 4 vols. *Ginsberg*. $300/£192

DUBH, SCIAN. Ridgeway: An Historical Romance of the Fenian Invasion of Canada. Buffalo: McCarroll, 1868. 1st ed. (20),262pp. Dec cl. *Ginsberg*. $125/£80

DUBIN, ARTHUR DETMERS. Some Classic Trains. (Milwaukee): Kalmbach, (1964). Color frontis, 2 color fldg plts. Fine in dj (lt rubbed). *Bohling*. $125/£80

DUBOIS, FELIX. Timbuctoo: The Mysterious. Diana White (trans). London, 1897. 1st ed. xi,(i),377pp (feps lt browned); 11 maps and plans. (Spine chipped.) *Edwards*. $101/£65

DUBOIS, FELIX. Timbuctoo: The Mysterious. Diana White (trans). London: Heinemann, 1897. 1st ed. xii,377pp, 11 maps & plans. Mod 1/2 levant morocco, gilt. Nice (fingering, sm lib stamp). *Hollett*. $148/£95

DUBON, DAVID. Tapestries from the Samuel H. Kress Collection at the Philadelphia Museum of Art. London, 1964. 75 plts. Good. *Washton*. $50/£32

Dubuque City Directory for 1873-1874. Dubuque, 1873. Pub's cl (needs rebinding). *Swann**. $126/£81

DUBUS, ANDRE. Adultery and Other Choices. Boston: Godine, 1977. (Top edge lt foxed), else Fine in Fine dj. *Between The Covers*. $150/£96

DUBUS, ANDRE. Finding a Girl in America. Boston: Godine, (1980). Fine in Fine dj. *Between The Covers*. $100/£64

DUBUS, ANDRE. The Last Worthless Evening. Boston: Godine, (1986). 1st ed. NF in NF dj. *Pettler & Lieberman*. $45/£29

DUCANE, FLORENCE. The Flowers and Gardens of Madeira. London: A&C Black, 1926. 24 color plts. (Eps browned; spine sl soiled), else VG. *Quest*. $35/£22

DUCHARTE, PIERRE LOUIS. The Italian Comedy. NY: John Day, n.d. (1929). Color frontis. (Cl dull, foot sl dampstained.) *Dramatis Personae*. $50/£32

DUCHAUSSOIS, P. Mid Snow and Ice. NY: Kennedy, 1923. 1st US ed. 32 plts, lg fldg color map. (Ex-lib; sl rubbed), o/w VG. *Worldwide*. $18/£12

DUCHAUSSOIS, P. Mid Snow and Ice: The Apostles of the North-West. London, 1923. 1st ed. Lg fldg map. (Emb stamp tp.) Pict cl. *Ginsberg*. $85/£54

DUCHENNE, G. B. Physiology of Motion Demonstrated by Means of Electrical Stimulation and Clinical Observation.... Phila, 1949. 1st ed in English. 1/4 leather. NF. *Doctor's Library*. $250/£160

DUCHENNE, G. B. Physiology of Motion.... Phila, 1949. 1st ed in English. (Ex-lib.) 1/4 leather. *Fye*. $175/£112

DUCHENNE, G. B. Selections from the Clinical Works of Dr. Duchenne. G. V. Poore (ed). London, 1883. 1st ed. 472pp. (Port margin waterstained; ex-lib; binding dull), o/w VG. *Fye*. $150/£96

DUCKWORTH, DYCE. A Treatise on Gout. London: Charles Griffin, 1890. 1st ed. Color frontis, xvi,476pp. Red cl. *White*. $55/£35

DUCRE, BENNO. Ducre's Account of the Expulsion of the Jesuits from Lower California 1767-69. Ernest J. Burrus (ed). St. Louis, 1967. Fldg map. Fine. *Turpen*. $95/£61

DUCRET, S. German Porcelain and Faience. NY: Universe Books, (1962). 1st Amer ed. 56 tipped-in color plts, 124 photo engrs. Beige linen. Good in illus dj. *Karmiole*. $125/£80

DUCROT, NICOLAS. Andre Kertesz: Sixty Years of Photography, 1912-1972. NY: Grossman, 1972. 1st ed. 218 b/w plts. (owner stamp), else NF in Good dj. *Cahan*. $165/£106

DUDEN, GOTTFRIED. Report on a Journey to the Western States of North American.... Columbia, MO: State Hist Soc, 1980. VF in dj. *Bohling*. $18/£12

DUDIN, M. The Art of the Bookbinder and Gilder. Leeds: Elmete, 1977. 1st ed in English. One of 490. 16 plts. Gilt leather-backed cl. *Kane**. $120/£77

DUDLEY, A. T. The Great Year. Lothrop, Lee & Shepard, 1907. 1st ed. Pict cvr. VG. *Plapinger*. $35/£22

DUDLEY, ELIZABETH (ed). The Life of Mary Dudley. Phila: Kite, 1842. 2nd Amer ed. 293pp (foxed). Full leather (rear joint chipped), lettering piece. Good. *Scribe's Perch**. $20/£13

DUDLEY, ERNEST. Nightmare for Dr. Morelle. London: Robert Hale, 1960. 1st ed. Fine in dj (crease fr panel, lt soil back panel). *Mordida*. $35/£22

DUERRENMATT, FRIEDRICH. The Pledge. Richard & Clara Winston (trans). NY: Knopf, 1959. 1st ed. Fine in NF dj. *Antic Hay*. $45/£29

DUERRENMATT, FRIEDRICH. The Quarry. Greenwich, CT: NYGS, 1962. 1st ed. NF in dj. *Antic Hay*. $45/£29

DUERRENMATT, FRIEDRICH. The Visit. (Adapted by Maurice Valency.) NY: Random House, (1958). 1st ed. Fine in dj (sl soiled). *Antic Hay*. $45/£29

DUFF, E. GORDON. A Century of the English Book Trade. London: Bibliographical Soc, 1948. Uncut. Holland-backed bds. Good (lib label, stamps). *Cox*. $19/£12

DUFFERIN, LORD. Letters from High Latitudes...1856. John Murray, 1857. 3rd ed (imp). Frontis, xx,428pp + 16pp pub's cat dated Nov 1857; 10 full-pg illus, 3 fldg maps. Uncut. Blue cl (extrems lt soiled, rubbed), gilt. Sound. *Cox*. $70/£45

DUFFERIN, MARCHIONESS OF. Our Viceregal Life in India. London: Murray, 1890. 1st ed. 2 vols. Frontis, x,344; viii,346pp, color fldg map. Lib buckram (ex-lib, spine #). VG. *Worldwide*. $32/£21

DUFFEY, D. M. Hunting Hounds: The History, Training and Selection.... NY: Winch, (1974). Fine in VG dj. *Mikesh*. $20/£13

DUFFEY, MRS. E. B. No Sex in Education. Phila: Stoddart, (1874). 1st ed. 139pp + 7pp ads. Pub's cl (sl soiled, chipped, cl cut along hinge, spine head lacks top 1/2-inch cl, affecting title). *Second Life*. $150/£96

DUFFUS, R. L. Books: Their Place in a Democracy. Boston/NY, 1930. VG in dj. *Truepenny*. $25/£16

DUFFUS, R. L. L. Emmett Holt Pioneer of a Children's Century. NY: Appleton, 1940. 18 plts. (Spine lettering faded.) *Goodrich*. $70/£45

DUFFUS, R. L. The Santa Fe Trail. NY: Tudor, (March 1936, c. 1930). 16 plts. Navy cl, gilt. VG in dj (edge-worn, chipped). *Bohling.* $30/£19

DUFFUS, R. L. The Santa Fe Trail. NY, 1930. 1st ed. Frontis, map. Fine in dj (chipped). *Turpen.* $70/£45

DUFIEF, NICOLAS GOUIN. A New Universal and Pro-nouncing Dictionary of the French and English Lan-guages. Phila: T. & G. Palmer, 1810. 1st ed. 3 vols. (Foxed, browned, lt dampstain upper margins.) Full mod calf in antique style, morocco labels. *Oinonen*.* $260/£167

DUFOUR, CHARLES L. The Night the War Was Lost. GC, (1960). 1st ed. Fine in dj (wear). *Pratt.* $40/£26

DUFRESNE, FRANK. Alaska's Animals and Fishes. West Hartford, (1946). One of 475 numbered, signed by Dufresne and Bob Hines (illus). Pict cvr label. (Sl worn.) *Oinonen*.* $80/£51

DUFRESNE, FRANK. Alaska's Animals and Fishes. NY: A.S. Barnes, 1946. 1st trade ed. Grn cl. (Sticker rem-nant fep.) Dj (very worn). *Parmer.* $85/£54

DUFUR, S. M. Over the Dead Line. Burlington, VT, c. 1902. 1st ed. 2 ports. (Cvr spots.) *Wantagh.* $50/£32

DUGANNE, A. J. H. The Fighting Quakers. NY, 1866. 1st ed. Frontis, 116pp. VG (ink inscrip). *Wantagh.* $75/£48

DUGMORE, A. RADCLYFFE. Camera Adventures in the African Wilds. London: Heinemann, 1910. 1st ed. 104 plts. Red pict cl (lt rubbed). *Adelson.* $95/£61

DUGMORE, A. RADCLYFFE. Camera Adventures in the African Wilds. NY: Doubleday, Page, 1910. 1st ed. Pict cl. (Sl shaken, inner hinges repaired), o/w VG. *New Hampshire*.* $30/£19

DUGUID, JULIAN. Green Hell. NY: Century, 1931. VG. *Bowman.* $15/£10

DUHAMEL, GEORGES. News from Havre. Beatrice de Holthoir (trans). London: Dent, (1934). 1st ed thus. VG in dj (lt soiled, sm tear). *Reese.* $30/£19

DUKE, BASIL WILSON. Morgan's Cavalry. NY: Neale, 1906. 1st ed thus. VG (spine dknd). Howes D548. *Mcgowan.* $350/£224

DUKE, THOMAS S. Celebrated Criminal Cases of Amer-ica. SF: James H. Barry, 1910. Brn cl (rubbed, worn), gilt. Sound. *Boswell.* $125/£80

DUKE, WILL. (Pseud of William Campbell Gault.) Fair Prey. London: Boardman, 1958. 1st hb ed. VG + in VG dj. *Certo.* $50/£32

DUKE-ELDER, W. S. Text-Book of Ophthalmology. Vol III. St. Louis, 1941. (Cl mkd, sl worn), o/w VG. *White-hart.* $59/£38

DULAC, EDMUND. Edmund Dulac's Fairy Book. Fairy Tales of All Nations. London, (1916). One of 350 numbered, signed. 4to. 15 tipped-in color plts. Orig white buckram, gilt (fr cvr dec sl rubbed). *Swann*.* $690/£442

DULAC, EDMUND. Edmund Dulac's Picture Book. Hodder & Stoughton, n.d. (1915). 1st ed thus. 4to. 135pp; port, 19 mtd color plts. Pict dec grey-grn cl (sl faded). VG + . *Bookmark.* $86/£55

DULAC, EDMUND. A Fairy Garland. London, (1928). One of 1000 numbered, signed. 12 color plts. (Ep, prelim margins lt foxed.) 1/4 imitation vellum (spine soiled), gilt. *Swann*.* $402/£258

DULAC, EDMUND. Lyrics Pathetic and Humorous. London: Warne, 1908. 4to. 24 color plts. Pict bds (sl soiled, shelfworn), cl back. *Oinonen*.* $225/£144

DUMAS, ALEXANDRE. Camille. London: LEC, 1937. One of 1500 numbered, signed by Marie Laurencin (illus). (Spine lt soiled.) Bd slipcase. *Swann*.* $402/£258

DUMAS, ALEXANDRE. Camille. Edmund Gosse (trans). London: LEC, 1937. #904/1500 numbered, signed by Marie Laurencin (illus). Paper dj (sl chipped), pub's slipcase (sl sunned, dusty). *Hermitage.* $600/£385

DUMAS, ALEXANDRE. Marguerite de Valois. NY: LEC, 1969. #1029/1500 signed by Edy Legrand (illus). Fine in slipcase. *Hermitage.* $85/£54

DUMAS, ALEXANDRE. My Memoirs. E. M. Waller (trans). London: Methuen, 1907/09. 1st ed thus. 6 vols. Frontis each vol. Sound set in red cl, gilt. *Cox.* $55/£35

DUMAS, ALEXANDRE. The Three Musketeers. William Robson (trans). NY: LEC, 1953. Fine in bd slipcase. *Ar-gosy.* $125/£80

DUMAS, ALEXANDRE. The Wolf Leader. L. Sprague de Camp (ed). Phila, 1950. 1st ed w/Blaine illus. VG in VG dj (chip). *Mcclintock.* $65/£42

DUMBAULD, EDWARD. Thomas Jefferson, American Tourist. Univ of OK, 1946. 1st ed. VG. *Book Broker.* $35/£22

DUMMER, JER. A Defense of the New England Char-ters. London, (1765). 1st Eng ed. (Ex-lib, ink stamp tp.) Sl trimmed. Mod cl, marbled bds. Howes D554. *Freeman*.* $80/£51

DUMONT, HENRIETTA. The Lady's Oracle. Phila: Peck & Bliss, 1853. 270pp; 5 full-pg plts. Aeg. Red cl (sl worn), gilt. VG. *Second Life.* $60/£38

DUN, FINLAY. American Farming and Food. London, 1881. viii,477,(2)pp + 12pp ads. Gilt grn cl. Fine. *Reese.* $250/£160

DUNAS, JEFF. Voyeur. L.A.: Melrose, 1983. 1st ed. 53 full-pg color photos. Fine in slipcase. *Cahan.* $40/£26

DUNBAR, EDWARD E. The Romance of the Age, or the Discovery of Gold in California. NY: Appleton, 1867. 134pp + 10pp ads (lt foxing, bkpl), port, 2 engr plts. Gilt-dec blue cl bds (lt shelfwear). *Cullen.* $200/£128

DUNBAR, EDWARD E. The Romance of the Age, or The Discovery of Gold in California. NY: D. Apple-ton, 1867. 1st ed. Frontis port, 134,(10 ads)pp; 2 engr plts. Brn cl, gilt. (Rear joint cracking, lt worn), o/w Fine. *Pacific*.* $80/£51

DUNBAR, FLANDERS. Emotions and Bodily Changes: A Survey of the Literature on Psychosomatic Interrela-tionships. NY: Columbia Univ, 1935. 1st ed. Blue-grn buckram. VG in dj (lt worn). *Gach.* $100/£64

DUNBAR, M. C. Dunbar's Complete Handbook of Eti-quette. NY: Excelsior, (1884). 1st ed(?). 6pp pub's ads. Patterned eps; edges stained red. Color pict bds, dk brn cl spine. VG (rubbing, sm stains). *Houle.* $225/£144

DUNBAR, PAUL LAURENCE. Candle-Lightin' Time. NY, 1901. 1st ed. Teg. Dec cl. (Inner rear hinge cracked; cvrs rubbed, sl speckled.) *King.* $195/£125

DUNBAR, PAUL LAURENCE. The Heart of Happy Hol-low. NY: Dodd, Mead, 1904. 1st ed. (Lt wear spine ends; sm stain fore-edge), o/w NF. *Beasley.* $300/£192

DUNBAR, PAUL LAURENCE. Li'l Gal. NY: Dodd, Mead, 1904. 1st ed. Teg. Dec olive cl (spine ends lt rubbed). BAL 4951. *Petrilla.* $125/£80

DUNBAR, PAUL LAURENCE. Lyrics of Lowly Life. NY: Dodd, 1896. 1st ed, 1st issue. Frontis (guard dknd). Nice (tp offset, name). *Between The Covers.* $450/£288

DUNBAR, PAUL LAURENCE. Poems of Cabin and Field. NY: Dodd, Mead, 1899. 1st ed. Fine (bd sl stained). *Between The Covers.* $150/£96

DUNBAR, PAUL LAURENCE. Poems of Cabin and Field. NY: Dodd, Mead, 1900. 1st ed. Dec cl (sunned, sl bumped, scraped). *Metropolitan*.* $70/£45

DUNBAR, PAUL LAURENCE. Speakin' O' Christmas. NY: Dodd, Mead, 1914. 1st ed, 1st issue binding. VG (gutters, bds sl foxed; bkpl, inscrip). *Between The Covers.* $485/£311

DUNBAR, SEYMOUR. A History of Travel in America. Indianapolis: Bobbs-Merrill, 1915. 4 vols. 2 maps, 12 color plts. (Erasure vol 1 tp, stamps other tps.) Marbled paper over bds (sl shelfworn), blue leather spines. *Parmer.* $250/£160

DUNBAR-NELSON, ALICE. Give Us Each Day. Gloria T. Hull (ed). NY: Norton, (1984). 1st ed. Port. Cl-backed bds. VG in pict dj. *Petrilla.* $35/£22

DUNCAN, BOB. Buffalo Country. NY: Dutton, 1959. VG in dj. *Dumont.* $25/£16

DUNCAN, DAVID DOUGLAS. Picasso's Picassos. NY, (1962). (Ex-lib.) Dj. *Swann*.* $115/£74

DUNCAN, DAVID DOUGLAS. War Without Heroes. NY: Harper & Row, 1970. 1st ed. Fine in dj (sm tears, sm stains). *Cahan.* $135/£87

DUNCAN, DAVID DOUGLAS. Yankee Nomad. NY/Chicago/etc: Holt, Rinehart & Winston, 1967. 2nd ed. VG (bkpl). *Worldwide.* $45/£29

DUNCAN, GEORGE and BERNARD DARWIN. Present-Day Golf. NY: George H. Doran, (1921). 1st Amer ed. Grn cl, gilt spine. (Spots lower cvr), else VG-. *Pacific*.* $98/£63

DUNCAN, ISADORA. My Life. NY, 1927. Presentation ed. One of 650. 24 plts. Black cl (sl rubbed; few pp carelessly opened), leather spine label. *Kane*.* $75/£48

DUNCAN, KUNIGUNDE and D. F. NICHOLS. Mentor Graham, the Man Who Taught Lincoln. Chicago, (1944). 1st ed. Fine. *Pratt.* $15/£10

DUNCAN, P. M. British Fossil Corals. London, 1866-72. vii,iii,66,46,24,73pp; 49 plts. Fine. *Henly.* $140/£90

DUNCAN, ROBERT. Play Time Pseudo Stein. Tenth Muse, 1969. 1st Amer ed. Fine in dec wrappers. *Polyanthos.* $25/£16

DUNCAN, THOMAS D. Recollections of Thomas J. Duncan, a Confederate Soldier. Nashville: McQuiddy Print Co, 1922. 1st ed. NF in stiff ptd wrappers (sl chipped). *Mcgowan.* $350/£224

DUNDONALD, EARL OF. The Autobiography of a Seaman. London, 1860. 2nd ed. 2 vols. xv,428; xiv,488pp; 4 plans. Contemp 1/2 calf, marbled bds (sm nick spine vol I), gilt, red/black calf labels. Attractive set. *Maggs.* $187/£120

DUNGLISON, ROBLEY. General Therapeutics and Materia Medica.... Phila: Lea & Blanchard, 1843. 1st ed. 2 vols. 515,vi; (13)-489pp; 30pp pub's cat end vol 1, 6pp end vol 2. Orig full sheep (spines sl dknd, sl worn, scuffed, old stains; sl aged, foxed), black leather spine labels. *Baltimore*.* $70/£45

DUNGLISON, ROBLEY. History of Medicine from the Earliest Ages to the Commencement of the Nineteenth Century. Phila, 1872. 1st ed. 287pp. VG. *Fye.* $150/£96

DUNGLISON, ROBLEY. Human Physiology. Phila, 1846. 6th ed. 2 vols. Contemp sheep (rubbed). *Argosy.* $175/£112

DUNGLISON, ROBLEY. Medical Lexicon. Phila, 1845. 5th ed. 771pp. Full leather. VG. *Fye.* $100/£64

DUNGLISON, ROBLEY. Medical Lexicon. Phila, 1874. New ed. 1131pp. Full leather. VG. *Fye.* $100/£64

DUNGLISON, ROBLEY. Medical Lexicon: A Dictionary of Medical Science. Phila, 1860. Rev ed. 992pp. Full leather (soiled, scuffed), black spine label. VG (extrems sl worn, text foxed). *Doctor's Library.* $120/£77

DUNHAM, JACOB. Journal of Voyages. NY, 1851. Frontis port, (iii),8-243pp (lt foxing); 10 plts. Brn cl (sl worn, shaken, extrems frayed), gilt spine. Howes D567. *Bohling.* $200/£128

DUNIWAY, ABIGAIL SCOTT. David and Anna Matson. NY: S.R. Wells, 1876. 1st ed. 194pp. VG. *Perier.* $30/£19

DUNIWAY, ABIGAIL SCOTT. Path Breaking. (Portland: The Author, 1914.) 1st ed. Card laid in. VG (sl worn, inscrip). *Second Life.* $300/£192

DUNLAP, JACK. American, British and Continental Pepperbox Firearms. CA: H.J. Dunlap, 1964. Presentation copy. Pict cl gilt. VG. *Hollett.* $117/£75

DUNLAP, JANE. Exploring Inner Space. Personal Experiences Under LSD-25. Scientific Bk Club, n.d. (1962). 1st UK ed. VG in dj. *Sclanders.* $23/£15

DUNLAP, ROY F. Gunsmithing. Georgetown, SC: Small Arms Technical Pub Co, 1952. 2nd ptg (unstated). Color frontis. Lime grn buckram. Fine in NF pict dj. *Biscotti.* $45/£29

DUNLAP, WILLIAM. A History of the American Theatre. NY: J&J Harper, 1832. 1st ed. viii,420pp,64pp ads. Muslin-cvrd bds. (Textual spotting; lacks most of spine, some of paper label), else Good. Howes D571. *Brown.* $95/£61

DUNLAP, WILLIAM. History of the Rise and Progress of the Arts of Design in the United States. NY: George P. Scott, 1834. 1st ed. 2 vols. 436; viii,480pp. Textured grn cl (sl rubbed), brn bds. Very Nice set. *Karmiole.* $200/£128

DUNLAP, WILLIAM. History of the Rise and Progress of the Arts of Design in the United States. Alexander Wyckoff (ed). (NY): Bloom, (1965). New ed. 3 vols. Fine in djs (sl worn). *Waverly*.* $44/£28

DUNLAY, THOMAS W. Wolves for the Blue Soldiers: Indian Scouts...1860-1890. Lincoln: Univ of NE, 1982. 1st ed. VF in dj. *Argonaut.* $40/£26

DUNLOP, RICHARD. Great Trails of the West. Nashville: Abingdon, (1971). 1st ed. VG in dj (sl worn). *Lien.* $25/£16

DUNN, DOUGLAS. Terry Street. Faber & Faber, 1969. 1st ed, 1st bk. (Pencil notes.) Dj (chipped, sl loss upper edge, lower edges faded). *Edwards.* $23/£15

DUNN, J. Massacres of the Mountains. NY: Harper, 1886. 1st ed. ix,784pp; fldg map. Dec cl. Good+ (internal soil; worn). Howes D575. *Agvent.* $150/£96

DUNN, J. ALLEN. Buffalo Boy. G&D, 1929. 5x7.5. 224pp. (Spine top dampstained), else VG in dj (chipped, lacks lg piece, dampstained). *My Bookhouse.* $15/£10

DUNN, KATHERINE. Attic. NY: Harper, (1970). 1st ed, 1st bk. Fine in dj (sl edgewear). *Captain's Bookshelf.* $125/£80

DUNN, KATHERINE. Geek Love. London: Hamish Hamilton, (1989). 1st UK ed. Fine in Fine dj. *Other Worlds.* $30/£19

DUNN, KATHERINE. Geek Love. NY, 1989. 1st ed. NF in NF dj. *Smith.* $35/£22

DUNN, KATHERINE. Geek Love. NY: Knopf, 1989. 1st ed. Fine in Fine dj. *Other Worlds.* $45/£29

DUNN, NELL. Poor Cow. London: MacGibbon & Key, 1967. 1st UK ed. Fine in VG dj (price-clipped). *Williams.* $31/£20

DUNNE, DOMINICK. People Like Us. NY, 1988. 1st Amer ed. Signed presentation copy. NF in NF dj. *Polyanthos.* $25/£16

DUNNE, JOHN GREGORY. The Studio. NY: FSG, (1969). 1st ed. VG (name) in dj. *Turtle Island.* $25/£16

DUNNE, PETER M. Black Robes in Lower California. Berkeley/L.A.: Univ of CA, 1952. 1st ed. Fldg map. (Sl tape stains to inner cvrs), else Fine in dj. *Argonaut.* $75/£48

DUNNE, PETER M. Black Robes in Lower California. Berkeley, 1968. 1st ed. Map. Fine in VG dj. *Turpen.* $55/£35

DUNNE, PETER M. Early Jesuit Missions in Tarahumara. Berkeley, CA, 1948. 1st ed. 2 plts, fldg map. *Ginsberg.* $75/£48

DUNNE, PETER M. Early Jesuit Missions in Tarahumara. Berkeley/L.A.: Univ of CA, 1948. 1st ed. Fldg map. VG dj. *Argonaut.* $50/£32

DUNNE, PETER M. Pioneer Black Robes on the West Coast. Berkeley, 1940. 1st ed. Frontis, 2 maps. Fine in VG dj. *Turpen.* $55/£35

DUNNE, PETER M. Pioneer Black Robes on the West Coast. Berkeley/L.A.: Univ of CA, 1940. 1st ed. 2 maps. Fine in dj (fr cvr faded). *Argonaut.* $50/£32

DUNNE, PETER M. Pioneer Jesuits in Northern Mexico. Berkeley/L.A.: Univ of CA, 1944. 1st ed. Fldg map. Fine in dj. *Argonaut.* $50/£32

DUNNING, JOHN. Booked to Die. Scribner, 1992. 1st ed. (Lt stain top), else Fine in dj. *Murder By The Book.* $135/£87

DUNSANY, EDWARD PLUNKETT. The Last Revolution. Jarrolds, (1951). 1st ed. (Edges sl spotted), o/w VG in dj (sl sunned). *Ash.* $78/£50

DUNSANY, LORD. The Fourth Book of Jorkens. Sauk City: 1948. 1st ed. VG (spine gilt worn) in dj (corners chipped, spine lacks 1/2-inch). *Certo.* $30/£19

DUNSANY, LORD. The Fourth Book of Jorkens. Sauk City: Arkham House, 1948. 1st US ed. NF in dj (spine sl dknd, 1/2-inch closed tear). *Other Worlds.* $70/£45

DUNSANY, LORD. Lord Adrian. Golden Cockerel, 1933. Ltd to 325 numbered. Robert Gibbings (illus). 4to. (iv),73,(iii)pp. Red calf-backed dec grn bds (rubbed, soiled), gilt. Internally NF. *Blue Mountain.* $45/£29

DUNSANY, LORD. Lord Adrian. Golden Cockerel, 1933. Ltd to 325 numbered. Robert Gibbings (illus). Red calf-backed dec grn bds (rubbed, soiled), gilt. Internally NF. *Blue Mountain.* $45/£29

DUNSANY, LORD. The Sword of Welleran. NY: Devin Adair, 1954. 1st ed. NF (stamp fep) in VG + dj (edge-worn, smudged). *Fuller & Saunders.* $15/£10

DUNSANY, LORD. Tales of Three Hemispheres. Boston, (1919). 1st Amer ed. Fine. *Polyanthos.* $60/£38

DUNSANY, LORD. Tales of Three Hemispheres. Boston: John W. Luce, (1919). 1st Amer ed. Dec cl, bds. VG. *Antic Hay.* $75/£48

DUNSANY, LORD. Tales of War. Boston, 1918. 1st Amer ed. NF (name; spine sl sunned). *Polyanthos.* $25/£16

DUNTHORNE, GORDON. Flower and Fruit Prints of the 18th and Early 19th Centuries.... Washington, 1938. Ltd to 2500 numbered. W/color examples in facs. Teg. (Ex-lib), else VG. *King.* $250/£160

DUPIN, JACQUES. Fits and Starts. Paul Auster (trans). Living Hand, 1973. 1st ed. NF in wrappers. *Words Etc.* $55/£35

DUPIN, JACQUES. Joan Miro: Life and Work. NY, (1962). Sm folio. (Ex-lib.) Dj. *Swann*.* $201/£129

DUPIN, JACQUES. Joan Miro: Life and Work. NY: Abrams, 1962. 1st ed. 46 tipped-in color plts. Fine in dj. *Cahan.* $250/£160

DUPIN, JACQUES. Miro Engraver. Volume I, 1928-1960. NY: Rizzoli, (1989). 1st ed. 3 woodcuts. Fine in dj (lt soiled). *Hermitage.* $150/£96

DUPIN, JACQUES. Miro. NY: Abrams, (1962). 1st ed. 46 mtd color plts. Black cl. Fine in dj. *Karmiole.* $250/£160

DUPIN, JACQUES. Miro. Norbert Gutermann (trans). London: Thames & Hudson, 1962. 1st Eng ed. 46 tipped-in color illus. VG (fr hinge weak; bkpl; margins pencilled, ink notes margins cat section) in dj (edge chipped; tape repaired). *Cahan.* $85/£54

DUPIN, JACQUES. Miro. Saint Paul: Fondation Maeght, 1968. 1st ed. VG (spine, top edge sl dknd; spine wear) in self-wrappers. *Cahan.* $75/£48

DUPLAIX, GEORGES. Gaston and Josephine. NY: OUP, 1933. 1st ed. 8 3/4 x 11 1/2. 32pp. Cl spine, pict bds. VG. *Cattermole.* $125/£80

DUPONT, JACQUES and CESARE GNUDI. Gothic Painting. Geneva, 1954. 110 tipped-in color plts. *Washton.* $60/£38

DUPONT, SAMUEL FRANCIS. Samuel Francis Du Pont, A Selection from His Civil War Letters. Ithaca, NY: Cornell Univ, (1969). 1st ed. 3 vols. NF set. *Mcgowan.* $125/£80

DUPREE, A. H. Asa Gray 1810-1888. Cambridge, MA: Belkamp/Harvard, 1959. Frontis, 22 plts. VG in dj (tired). *Brooks.* $45/£29

DUPREE, A. H. Asa Gray, 1810-1888. Cambridge: Harvard, 1959. 1st ed. VG (ex-lib). *Mikesh.* $25/£16

DUPUYTREN, BARON. On Lesions of the Vascular System, Diseases of the Rectum, and Other Surgical Complaints.... F. Le Gros Clark (ed). London: Sydenham Soc, 1854. viii,378pp. (Cl faded, spine ends chipped), o/w Clean. *White.* $86/£55

DURACK, MARY and ELIZABETH. The Magic Trumpet. Melbourne: Cassell, n.d. (1945). 1st ed. 7 x 9 3/4. 44pp. Pict bds. Good. *Cattermole.* $45/£29

DURAND, E. R. An Autumn Tour in Western Persia. Westminster: Archibald Constable, 1902. 1st ed. (Foxing, sm blind lib stamp tp, bar code mk 1/2-title.) Fldg map at end; 22 plts, incl frontis. Teg. Blue cl, gilt Persian lettering, beveled edges (lib plt rear cvr). *Morrell.* $101/£65

DURAND, EDWARD. Rifle, Rod and Spear in the East. London, 1911. Pict buckram (spine faded), gilt. *Grayling.* $86/£55

DURAS, MARGUERITE. 10:30 on a Summer Night. NY: Grove, 1962. 1st US ed. NF in VG + dj. *Lame Duck.* $35/£22

DURAS, MARGUERITE. The Lover. NY: Pantheon, 1985. 1st US ed. Fine in NF dj (lt soiled). *Lame Duck.* $20/£13

DURAS, MARGUERITE. The Sea Wall. NY: Pellegrini & Cuhady, 1952. 1st US ed. NF in dj (lt worn, nicked). *Lame Duck.* $100/£64

Durer in America. Washington: Nat'l Gallery of Art, 1971. Stechow suppl inserted. Good in wraps (backstrip bottom sl torn, mended). *Washton.* $75/£48

DURER, ALBRECHT. Albrecht Durer. Sketchbook of His Journey to the Netherlands 1520-1521.... London: Elek, 1971. Emb cl. Fine in slipcase. *Europa.* $37/£24

DURET, THEODORE. Manet and the French Impressionists. Phila, 1910. 4to. 2 etchings by Renoir, 1 by Manet, 1 by Morisot. (Bkpl; joints rubbed, spine ends chipped.) *Swann*.* $1,495/£958

DURHAM, PHILIP and EVERETT L. JONES. The Negro Cowboys. NY: Dodd, Mead, 1965. 16 plts. VG. *Connolly.* $17/£11

DURLING, RICHARD. A Catalogue of Sixteenth Century Printed Books in the National Library of Medicine. Bethesda, 1967. 1st ed. VG. *Fye.* $150/£96

DURRELL, GERALD. The Overloaded Ark. NY: Viking, 1953. 1st ed, 1st bk. Fine in dj (soiled, worn). *Antic Hay.* $25/£16

DURRELL, LAWRENCE. The Alexandria Quartet. NY: Dutton, (1962). 1st Amer 1-vol ed. Fine in dj (lt rubbed, few sm tears). *Captain's Bookshelf.* $100/£64

DURRELL, LAWRENCE. The Alexandria Quartet. Justine, Balthazar, Mountolive, Clea. London: Faber & Faber, (1962). 1st 1-vol ed. One of 500 specially-bound, numbered, signed. Fine in slipcase (sl rubbed). *Captain's Bookshelf*. $750/£481

DURRELL, LAWRENCE. Bitter Lemons. London, 1957. 1st ed. VG in dj (sl browned, corners chipped). *Buckley*. $31/£20

DURRELL, LAWRENCE. The Black Book. Paris: Obelisk, (1938). 1st ed. VG (spine leaned) in wraps. *Certo*. $175/£112

DURRELL, LAWRENCE. The Black Book. NY: Dutton, 1960. 1st ed thus. NF in VG dj. *Antic Hay*. $20/£13

DURRELL, LAWRENCE. The Black Book. London: Faber, 1973. 1st UK ed. NF in dj (sl chipped, rubbed). *Virgo*. $39/£25

DURRELL, LAWRENCE. Blue Thirst. Santa Barbara, CA: Capra, 1975. One of 250 numbered, signed. Fine in Fine clear acetate dj. *Lenz*. $100/£64

DURRELL, LAWRENCE. Deus Loci. Ischia: Privately ptd, 1950. One of 200 (this not numbered), signed. 8pp. Red wrappers. (Spine sl faded), o/w VG. *Virgo*. $390/£250

DURRELL, LAWRENCE. Esprit de Corps. NY: Dutton, 1958. 1st Amer ed. NF (ink name) in dj (wear, sm tears). *Antic Hay*. $27/£17

DURRELL, LAWRENCE. The Ikons and Other Poems. NY, 1967. 1st Amer ed. Fine in dj (sm edge tear fr panel, spine sl rubbed). *Polyanthos*. $20/£13

DURRELL, LAWRENCE. A Landmark Gone. L.A.: Privately ptd, 1949. One of 125 ptd. Card wrappers (stained, chafed, tear skillfully repaired). *Clearwater*. $117/£75

DURRELL, LAWRENCE. On Seeming to Presume, Poems. London: Faber & Faber, (1948). 1st ed. Fine in dj. *Hermitage*. $40/£26

DURRELL, LAWRENCE. A Private Country. London: Faber, 1943. 1st Eng ed. Very Nice. *Clearwater*. $78/£50

DURRELL, LAWRENCE. Prospero's Cell. London, 1945. 1st Eng ed. Very Nice (spine sl faded). *Clearwater*. $39/£25

DURRELL, LAWRENCE. Prospero's Cell. London: Faber, 1945. 1st ed. (Lt mkd, faded.) *Hollett*. $23/£15

DURRELL, LAWRENCE. The Red Limbo Lingo. London: Faber, (1971). One of 200 numbered, signed. Fine in Fine slipcase. *Lenz*. $175/£112

DURRELL, LAWRENCE. Sauve Qui Peut. London: Faber & Faber, (1966). 1st ed. Fine in dj (browned, soiled, sl stained). *Antic Hay*. $35/£22

DURRELL, LAWRENCE. Sicilian Carousel. 1977. 1st ed. VG in dj (spine sl discolored). *Words Etc*. $19/£12

DURRELL, LAWRENCE. Spirit of Place. A. G. Thomas (ed). London, 1969. 1st Eng ed. Fine (name) in dj. *Clearwater*. $39/£25

DURRELL, LAWRENCE. Zero and Asylum in the Snow. Berkeley: Circle Editions, 1947. 1st trade ed. Ptd paper bds. (Lt stain rear panel and dj rear panel), else Very Nice in dj. *Turtle Island*. $65/£42

DUSS, JOHN S. The Harmonists: A Personal History. Harrisburg: PA Book Service, 1943. 1st ed. VG in dj (sl worn, soiled, spine wrapper sunned). *Brown*. $35/£22

DUSSAUCE, H. A New and Complete Treatise on the Arts of Tanning, Currying, and Leather Dressing. Phila, 1867. 2nd ed. 596 w/index pp; 212 wood engrs. (Stamped names; staining; cvrs worn, frayed.) *King*. $100/£64

Dutch Landscape. The Early Years. London: Nat'l Gallery, 1986. Good in wraps. *Washton*. $40/£26

Dutch Religious Art of the Seventeenth Century. New Haven: Yale Univ Art Gallery, 1975. Good in wraps. *Washton*. $20/£13

Dutchman's Fireside. (By James Kirke Paulding.) NY: Harper, 1831. 1st issue w/ads on rear cvr Vol 1 dated May, 1831. 2 vols. Ptd cl. VG set (sig clipped, lacks bottom corner fep, foxed). BAL 15714. *Cahan*. $100/£64

DUTTON, C. E. Geology of the High Plateaus of Utah. US Geog & Geol Surv, 1880. 1st ed. 307pp. Marbled ep, edgepapers. 1/2 leather, maroon cl, gilt, ribbed spine. (Sl dampstains few pp), else VG. *Price*. $395/£253

DUTTON, RALPH. The Age of Wren. Batsford, 1951. VG in dj. *Hadley*. $50/£32

DUTTON, RALPH. The English Country House. London: Batsford, 1935. 1st ed. Color frontis. Pict eps. (Spine dulled, ends sl worn), else VG. *Quest*. $30/£19

DUVAL, J. C. Early Times in Texas. Austin, TX: H.P.N. Gammel, c. 1892. 1st ed, 2nd issue. VG (pp browned) in ptd wrapper (sl soiled). Howes D603. *New Hampshire**. $35/£22

DUVAL, K. D. Scott and His Scotland. Frenich, Foss, Pitlochry, 1971. Wrappers. *Maggs*. $31/£20

DUVAL, MATHIAS. Artistic Anatomy. London, 1892. 6th ed. 324pp; 77 Fine woodcuts. VG. *Fye*. $60/£38

DUVALL, MARIUS. A Navy Surgeon in California 1846-47, the Journal of.... SF, 1957. 1st ed. One of 600. Frontis port. Unopened. Fine. *Turpen*. $55/£35

DUVALL, MARIUS. A Navy Surgeon in California, 1846-1847. The Journal of.... Fred Blackburn Rogers (ed). SF: John Howell-Books, 1957. 1st ed. Ltd to 600 ptd. Frontis port, 4 fldg plts. Dec maroon cl. VF. *Argonaut*. $45/£29

DUVALL, MARIUS. A Navy Surgeon in California...1846-1847. Fred Blackburn Rogers (ed). SF: John Howell, 1957. One of 600. Burgundy cl, gilt. Fine (inscrip). *Parmer*. $95/£61

DUVEEN, D. and H. KLICKSTEIN. A Bibliography of the Works of Antoine Laurent Lavoisier 1743-1794. London: Wm. Dawson & E. Weil, c 1954. VG in dj. *Blake*. $200/£128

DUVEEN, JOSEPH. Thirty Years of British Art. Studio Special Autumn Number, 1930. Color frontis, 7 color plts. Teg. (Lt soiled, spine lt faded.) *Edwards*. $31/£20

DUVOISIN, ROGER. The Christmas Cake. NY: Amer. Artists, 1941. 1st ed. 6 1/2 x 5. Pict bds. VG in dj. *Cattermole*. $35/£22

DUVOISIN, ROGER. Donkey-Donkey. Chicago: Whitman, 1933. 1st ed. 6 1/2 x 8 3/4; Pict bds. VG; no dj as issued. *Cattermole*. $45/£29

DUVOISIN, ROGER. Lonely Veronica. NY: Knopf, 1963. 1st ed. 8 1/4 x 10 1/2. 40pp. VG in dj. *Cattermole*. $35/£22

DUVOISIN, ROGER. They Put Out to Sea, the Story of the Map. NY: Knopf, 1943. 1st ed. Sm 8vo. Pict cl. NF in NF dj. *Book Adoption*. $60/£38

DUVOISIN, ROGER. Veronica and the Birthday Present. NY: Knopf, 1971. 1st ed. Sm 4to. Emb pict cl. Fine in VG + dj (blemish fr cvr, spine ends worn). *Book Adoption*. $35/£22

DUVRIES, HENRI. Surgery of the Foot. St. Louis, 1965. 2nd ed. VG. *Argosy*. $50/£32

DUYCKINCK, EVERT A. National Portrait Gallery of Eminent Americans. NY, c. 1862. 2 vols. 119 engr ports. Full leather (sl worn). Contents VG. *New Hampshire**. $120/£77

DUYCKINCK, EVERT A. National Portrait Gallery of Eminent Men and Women of Europe and America. NY, c. 1873. 2 vols. Engr tps, 119 steel-engr ports, 2 engr tps. (Lt foxing, lt dampstaining.) 1/2 leather, marbled bds. (Extrems sl worn), o/w VG. *New Hampshire**. $60/£38

DWIGHT, E. W. Memoir of Henry Obookiah, a Native of the Sandwich Islands.... NY: Amer Tract Soc, n.d. (c. 1830s). Rev ed. Engr frontis port, guard; (7),8-124pp (foxing). Leather-backed marbled bds (rubbed), gilt-lettered spine. Fine. *Argonaut*. $150/£96

DWIGHT, S. E. The Hebrew Wife. Glasgow: Gallie, 1837. 1st Glasgow ed. 148pp. Uncut. VG (wear). *Second Life*. $150/£96

DWIGHT, THEODORE. The Northern Traveller, and Northern Tour. NY: Harper, 1830. 4th ed. 444pp (sl browned, foxed, hinges lt cracked) incl extra engr tp; 19 engr maps, 9 plts. Orig black sheep, marbled bds (sl worn, scuffed, spine top chipped), gilt. Howes D607. *Baltimore**. $40/£26

DWIGHT, THEODORE. The Northern Traveller. NY: Wilder & Campbell, 1825. 214pp; 16 maps, 4 plts. Mod cl. (Foxed.) Howes D607. *Adelson*. $80/£51

DWIGHT, TIMOTHY. Travels in New England and New York. London: Wm. Baynes, 1823. 1st Eng ed. 4 vols. Port, 3 fldg maps. Full panelled calf, gilt, leather spine labels, marbled edges. Eps lt foxing, port offset), o/w Very Attractive. Howes D612. *Sadlon*. $500/£321

DWIGHT, TIMOTHY. Travels in New England and New York. B. M. Solomon (ed). Belknap/Harvard, 1969. 4 vols. Good+ in Good slipcase. *Scribe's Perch**. $80/£51

DWYER, K. R. (Pseud of Dean R. Koontz.) Dragonfly. NY: Random House, (1975). 1st ed. Fine in VG dj. *Metropolitan**. $109/£70

DWYER, K. R. (Pseud of Dean R. Koontz.) Dragonfly. NY: Random House, (1975). 1st ed. (Top edge lt bumped), else Fine in Fine dj. *Other Worlds*. $150/£96

DYAR, H. G. List of North American Leipdoptera and Key to the Literature of This Order of Insects. Washington: Smithsonian, 1902. 1st ed. NF in wraps. *Mikesh*. $37/£24

DYCE, JAMES M. Photographic Aids to Clinical Dental Practice. NY, 1948. 1st ed. Red cl (sl worn). VG. *Doctor's Library*. $50/£32

DYER, DAVID. Impressions of Prison Life in Great Britain. Albany: J. Munsell, 1868. 25pp. Ptd wraps (soiled, chipped, stamps on cvr). *Bohling*. $18/£12

DYER, G. A Restoration of the Ancient Modes of Bestowing Names on the Rivers, Hills...of Britain. Exeter, 1805. 314pp. Full calf, dec spine. Good+. *Scribe's Perch**. $36/£23

DYER, G. A Restoration of the Ancient Modes of Bestowing Names on the Rivers.... Exeter, 1805. (Contemp notes.) Contemp calf (rubbed, spine top gone). *Freeman**. $35/£22

DYER, ISADORE (ed). The American Journal of Tropical Diseases and Preventive Medicine. Washington, 1915. Good (worn). *Doctor's Library*. $50/£32

DYER, JOHN P. From Shiloh to San Juan, the Life of 'Fighting Joe' Wheeler. Baton Rouge, (1961). Rev ed. Map. VG+ in VG+ dj. *Pratt*. $65/£42

DYER, JOHN P. The Gallant Hood. Indianapolis, (1950). 1st ed. VG+. *Pratt*. $40/£26

DYER, JOHN P. The Gallant Hood. Indianapolis: Bobbs-Merrill, 1950. Stated 1st ed. VG in Good+ dj. *Scribe's Perch**. $55/£35

DYHRENFURTH, G. O. To the Third Pole. London, (1955). 1st British ed. (Bumped), else Good in dj (extrems chipped). *King*. $75/£48

DYK, WALTER. A Navaho Autobiography. NY: Viking Fund Publications in Anthropology, 1947. 1st ed. VG in stiff wraps. *Oregon*. $50/£32

DYKES, J. C. Billy the Kid: The Bibliography of a Legend. Albuquerque: Univ of NM, 1952. 2nd ptg. Ptd gray wrappers (erasure). *Dawson*. $50/£32

DYKES, J. C. Billy the Kid: The Bibliography of a Legend. Albuquerque: Univ of NM, 1952. 1st ed, 1st issue. One of 470 in wrappers (total run 500). Frontis. VF in grey ptd wrappers. *Harrington*. $150/£96

DYKES, JEFF. Fifty Great Western Illustrators. Flagstaff, 1975. 1st ed. Pict cl. NF in dj. *Baade*. $80/£51

DYKES, JEFF. Fifty Great Western Illustrators: A Bibliographic Check-List. Northland, (1975). 1st Collector's ed of 200 numbered, signed. Dk blue pict cvr; black leather shelfback, silver stamped. New in slipcase. *Authors Of West*. $200/£128

DYKES, JEFF. I Had All the Fun, Some Recollections of a Book Collector. Coll. Sta., 1978. 1st ed. Signed. Fine in stiff wraps. *Turpen*. $30/£19

DYKES, JEFF. Western High Spots: Reading and Collecting Guides. N.p.: Northland Press, (c. 1977). 1st ed. Blue buckram, silver spine title. Fine in dj. *Heller*. $75/£48

DYKES, WILLIAM R. The Genus Iris. Cambridge, 1913. 1st ed. Folio. 48 color plts. Orig 1/4 morocco (spine ends rubbed, fr cvr sl spotted, blistered), gilt. *Swann**. $690/£442

DYOTT, G. M. Silent Highways of the Jungle. NY: Putnam, 1922. 1st ed. VG+. *Mikesh*. $37/£24

E

E., A. (Pseud of George Russell.) Enchantment and Other Poems. NY: Fountain Press, 1930. 1st ed. One of 542 numbered, signed. Cl, dec bds. VG (edges sl dknd). *Reese*. $45/£29

E., A. (Pseud of George W. Russell.) The House of the Titans and Other Poems. Macmillan, 1934. 1st ed. (Sl string-mkd), o/w VG in dj. *Ash*. $47/£30

E., A. (Pseud of George W. Russell.) The House of the Titans and Other Poems. London: Macmillan, 1934. 1st Eng ed. One of 2000 ptd. Grn cl. Fine in dj (sl wear, price-clipped). *Antic Hay*. $50/£32

E., A. (Pseud of George Russell.) The House of the Titans and Other Poems. NY: Macmillan, 1934. 1st Amer ed. (Ink inscrip), else VG in dj (lt chipped). *Reese*. $20/£13

E., A. (Pseud of George Russell.) Vale and Other Poems. NY: Macmillan, 1931. 1st Amer ed. Cl, gilt labels. Fine in VG dj (sl chipped). *Reese*. $30/£19

EAGLE, J. H. Adventures of an Amateur Hunter in Africa. Boston: Chapple, 1915. 1st ed. Inscribed. Frontis. Gilt lettering; inlaid cvr photo. VG (spine lettering faded). *Backman*. $125/£80

EAGLETON, WELLS P. Brain Abscess. NY: Macmillan, 1922. (Lib stamp fr/back bds; rubbed.) *Goodrich*. $75/£48

EALAND, C. A. Insect Life. A&C Black, 1921. 50 color plts. Marbled eps. (Ink owner stamp.) Maroon morocco-backed marbled bds (rebound), blind-edged raised bands, gilt spine. *Edwards*. $70/£45

EAMES, F. E. et al. Fundamentals of Mid-Tertiary Stratigraphical Correlation. London, 1962. 17 plts, 3 fldg tables. Fine in dj. *Henly*. $33/£21

EARDLEY-WILMOT, S. The Life of an Elephant. London: Edward Arnold, 1912. 1st ed. 9 b/w photo plts. Teg. Gilt pict red cl (backstrip lt faded). Clean. *House.* $150/£96

EARL, MAUD. British Hounds and Gun-Dogs. London: Berlin Photographic, (1902). 1st ed. One of 500 numbered, signed. Elephant folio. 24 gravure plts mtd on rectos of hinged stiff ll, each signed in the print. Marbled eps; teg. Brn morocco, grn cl, raised bands, gilt. Cvrs VG (sl worn, edges scuffed, corners lt bumped; bkpl of Duchess of Bedford). *Baltimore**. $700/£449

EARL, MAUD. The Power of the Dog. London/NY/Toronto: Hodder & Stoughton, (1911). 1st ed. 20 tipped-in full-pg color plts. Vellum, gray cl (sl worn, dusted, sl bumped), gilt. Text VG (eps browned). *Baltimore**. $210/£135

EARLE, A. M. Curious Punishments of Bygone Days. Chicago: Stone, 1896. Prelims + 149pp + ads. Dec cvrs (spine faded, hinge cracks). Good. *Scribe's Perch**. $20/£13

EARLE, A. M. Sundials and Roses of Yesterday. NY, 1902. (Lacks fep; bkpl, upper hinge cracked; cl lt spotted, sl dknd.) *Edwards.* $78/£50

EARLE, A. M. Two Centuries of Costume in America. NY: Macmillan, 1903. 1st ed. 2 vols. Dec cl. NF. *Agvent.* $100/£64

EARLE, A. S. (ed). Surgery in America. Phila, 1965. 1st ed. VG. *Fye.* $50/£32

EARLE, EDWARD W. (ed). Points of View. (Rochester): Visual Studies Workshop, 1979. 1st ed. Fine in illus dj. *Cahan.* $85/£54

EARLE, JOHN. Micro-Cosmographie or a Piece of the World Discovered in Essayes and Characters. Gwendolen Murphy (ed). Waltham St. Lawrence, 1928. One of 400. Red buckram (sl soiled). Nice. *Cady.* $60/£38

EARLE, MRS. C. W. Pot-Pourri from a Surrey Garden. London, 1897. 8th ed. xii,381pp + 6 ads. (Spine faded.) *Henly.* $28/£18

EARLE, PLINY. Memoirs of Pliny Earle, M.D.... F. B. Sanborn (ed). Boston: Damrell & Upham, 1898. 1st trade ed. Frontis, xvi,409,(3)pp (bkpl removed, old lib pocket rep). Olive cl. *Gach.* $85/£54

EARLE, SWEPSON. The Chesapeake Bay Country. Balt, 1924. 2nd ed. Howes E8. *Wantagh.* $75/£48

Early American Bookbindings from the Collection of Michael Papantonio. M. NY: Pierpont Morgan Library, 1972. 62 plts. Wrappers (sl grubby; sm tear spine top). *Maggs.* $39/£25

Early American Trade Cards. (By Bella C. Landauer.) NY: Rudge, 1927. Fldg color frontis, 43 plts. *Rostenberg & Stern.* $125/£80

Early Christian and Byzantine Art. Balt: Walters Art Gallery, 1947. 121 plts. 1/4 cl. Good. *Washton.* $45/£29

Early History of the Seventh Kansas Cavalry. (By Simeon M. Fox.) (Topeka, 1910). (Marginal tears 1st ll.) Stapled self-wraps. *Wantagh.* $25/£16

EARLY, JUBAL ANDERSON. A Memoir of the Last Year of the War for Independence...1864 and 1865. Toronto: Lovell & Gibson, 1866. 1st ed. 144pp. Ptd wrappers. VG (wear along backstrip). Howes E14. *Mcgowan.* $450/£288

EARLY, JUBAL ANDERSON. A Memoir of the Last Year of the War for Independence...1864 and 1865. Lynchburg, VA: Charles W. Button, 1867. 1st Amer ed. 135,(1)pp. VG in orig ptd wrappers. Howes E14. *Mcgowan.* $175/£112

EARLY, R. H. Lieutenant General Jubal Anderson Early C.S.A. Phila: Lippincott, Nov 1912. Good. *Scribe's Perch**. $240/£154

EARNEST, E. John and William Bartram, Botanists and Explorers 1699-1777 and 1739-1823. Phila: Univ of PA, 1940. 1st ed. 2 port repros. Gilt-dec cl. NF in VG + dj. *Mikesh.* $30/£19

EARNEST, ERNEST. The American Eve in Fact and Fiction, 1775-1914. Urbana: Univ of IL, (1974). (Wrinkled eps, ex-libris.) Dj (sl stained). *Second Life.* $35/£22

EARNEST, ERNEST. Weir Mitchell, Novelist and Physician. Phila, 1950. 1st ed. Blue cl bds. VG. *Doctor's Library.* $50/£32

EAST, TERRENCE. The Story of Heart Disease. London, 1958. 1st ed. VG. *Fye.* $50/£32

EASTLAKE, C. Hints on Household Taste in Furniture, Upholstery.... Boston: Osgood, 1877. 5th Amer ed. xxxiv,304pp; 36 plts, 6 color plts, 8 color wallpaper samples. VG (old dampstains tp, few other pp; cvrs soiled). *Agvent.* $125/£80

EASTLAKE, WILLIAM. The Bamboo Bed. NY, 1969. 1st ed. NF in VG + dj. *Smith.* $20/£13

EASTLAKE, WILLIAM. A Child's Garden of Verses for the Revolution. NY: Grove Press, (1970). 1st ed. Fine in VG dj (closed tear fr panel). *Reese.* $50/£32

EASTMAN, GEORGE. Chronicles of an African Trip. Ptd for Author, 1927. 1st ed. 29 plts. Inscribed card tipped in. Teg. Paper on bds, cl spine, paper spine label. VG (spine lt soiled; bkpl; sig, date, blind stamp). *Backman.* $110/£71

EASTMAN, GEORGE. Chronicles of an African Trip. Rochester: (N.p.), 1927. 1st ed. Fine in 1/4 cl and bds, tissue dj, special box. *Smith.* $200/£128

EASTMAN, MARY H. American Aboriginal Portfolio. Phila: Lippincott, Grambo, (1853). 4to. 26 engrs incl engr tp. Gilt-dec cl. (Cvr sl worn, foxing), o/w VG. Howes E17. *New Hampshire**. $525/£337

EASTMAN, MARY H. Aunt Phillis's Cabin. Phila, 1852. 1st ed. 280,(iv) + 24pp ads. (Cl soiled; spine faded; lower spine wear). Good- (1 sig pulled). *Wantagh.* $45/£29

EASTMAN, MARY H. Dahcotah; or, Life and Legends of the Sioux Around Fort Snelling. NY: John Wiley, 1849. 1st ed. xxxii,33-268pp; 4 tinted lithos. 1/2 calf, leather labels, cl sides. (Ex-lib, rebound; stamps, text spotted), else VG. *Brown.* $300/£192

EASTMAN, MAX. Kinds of Love, Poems. NY: Scribner, 1931. 1st ed. Inscribed. (Spine faded, crown wear), else Good. *Reese.* $35/£22

EASTMAN, RALPH M. Some Famous Privateers of New England. (Boston): State Street Trust Co, 1928. Orig wraps (spine faded, chipped). *Parmer.* $29/£19

EASTMAN, W. R. and A. C. HUNT. The Parrots of Australia. Sydney: A. & R., 1966. 1st ed. 16 full-pg color plts. NF in Good dj. *Mikesh.* $60/£38

EASTON, JOHN. British Postage Stamp Design. London: Faber & Faber, 1943. 1st ed. Frontis port, 41 plts. Teg. (Eps lt spotted; spine, lower bd faded.) *Edwards.* $39/£25

EASTON, JOHN. Postage Stamps in the Making. London: Faber & Faber, 1949. 1st ed. Frontis port, 52 plts. (Edges, spine sl faded.) *Edwards.* $31/£20

EASTON, MALCOLM. Aubrey and the Dying Lady. London: Secker & Warburg, 1972. 1st UK ed. Frontis. Dj (spine chipped, lt faded). *Edwards.* $31/£20

EASTON, ROBERT. Max Brand. Norman: Univ of OK, 1970. 2nd ptg. Color frontis port, 32 plts. Fine in NF dj. *Connolly.* $30/£19

EATES, MARGOT. Paul Nash: Paintings, Drawings and Illustrations. London: Lund Humphries, 1948. Frontis, 132 plts. Blue cl over bds. VG (spine faded). *Heller.* $275/£176

EATES, MARGOT. Paul Nash: The Master of the Image, 1889-1946. London: John Murray, 1973. Orange buckram, gilt. (Sl edgeworn), else Fine in dj. *Heller.* $200/£128

EATON, ALLEN H. Handicrafts of the Southern Highlands. NY: Russell Sage, 1937. 1st ed. 112 full-pg illus (8 color). Fine in dj (sl nicked). *Second Life.* $125/£80

EATON, AMOS. A Manual of Botany for the Northern and Middle States of America. Albany: Websters & Skinners, 1822. 3rd ed. 536pp (foxing). Pebbled cl (newly rebound). Nice. *Bookcell.* $200/£128

EATON, CHARLES E. The Shadow of the Swimmer. NY: Fine Editions Press, 1951. 1st ed. (Inscrip), o/w NF in dj. *Reese.* $25/£16

EATON, DANIEL CODY. The Ferns of North America. Boston/Salem: S.E. Cassino, 1879, 1880. 2 vols. xiv,352; xxxi,285pp; 82 color lithos; b/w plt. Teg. (Extrems lt worn), else Fine. *Quest.* $375/£240

EATON, EDWARD BAILEY. Original Photographs Taken on the Battlefields During the Civil War of the United States. Hartford: The Author, 1907. 1st ed. Matthew Brady & Alexander Gardner (photos). Paper-cvrd bds, cl spine. VG. *Mcgowan.* $350/£224

EATON, ELON HOWARD. Birds of New York (Plates). State of NY, 1925. Louis Agassiz Fuertes (illus). Good+. *Books & Birds.* $65/£42

EATON, ELON HOWARD. Birds of New York. Albany: Univ of State of NY, 1910. 1st ed. 2 vols. (3 sm spots fr bds vol 2), o/w Fine. *Hermitage.* $200/£128

EATON, ELON HOWARD. Birds of New York. Albany: Univ of the State of NY, 1910. 1st ed. 2 vols. Louis Agassiz Fuertes (illus). VG. *Books & Birds.* $175/£112

EATON, ELON HOWARD. Birds of New York. Albany: Univ of State of NY, 1914. 2 vols. 106 color plts. VG (few stained edges, soil, wear). *Waverly*.* $71/£46

EATON, ELON HOWARD. Birds of New York. Univ of State of NY, State Museum, 1925. 106 color plts by Louis Agassiz Fuertes (1 sl torn). Cl portfolio. VG (lacks ties). *King.* $75/£48

EATON, JOHN. Grant, Lincoln and the Freedmen.... NY, 1907. Port. (Ex-lib), else Good. *King.* $35/£22

EATON, WALTER PRICHARD. Skyline Camps. N.p.: W.A. Wilde, (1922). Pict label. (Bumped, spine dull.) *King.* $35/£22

EAVES, CHARLES DUDLEY and C. A. HUTCHISON. Post City, Texas: C. W. Post's Colonizing Activities in West Texas. Austin: TX State Hist Assn, 1952. Frontis port. VG+ in dj. *Bohling.* $30/£19

EBAN, ABBA. An Autobiography. NY, (1977). 1st trade ed. Ltd to 500 signed. VG in slipcase. *King.* $65/£42

EBELING, WALTER. Handbook of Indian Foods and Fibers of Arid America. Berkeley: Univ of CA, (1986). 1st ed. Brn cl. Fine in pict dj. *Pacific*.* $52/£33

EBERHARD, FREDERICK G. The Secret of the Morgue. NY: MacAulay, n.d. 1st ed. Clean in dj (worn, torn). *Metropolitan*.* $23/£15

EBERHART, MIGNON G. The House on the Roof. NY: Doubleday, Doran, 1935. 1st ed. Nice in dj (bumped, chipped, edgeworn). *Metropolitan*.* $23/£15

EBERHART, RICHARD. A Bravery of Earth. London: Cape, 1930. 1st ed, 1st bk. VG (spine, bd edges dknd, top dusty) in dj (soiled, rubbed, chipped, sm tears). *Waverly*.* $38/£24

EBERLE, JOHN. A Treatise of the Materia Medica and Therapeutics. Phila, 1834. 4th ed. 2 vols. 929pp. VG (extrems sl worn, rebound). *Doctor's Library.* $200/£128

EBERLEIN, H. D. and C. HUBBARD. American Georgian Architecture. London: Pleiades Books, 1952. 1st ed. Gray cl. Good in dj. *Karmiole.* $60/£38

EBERLEIN, H. D. and C. HUBBARD. Historic Houses of George-Town and Washington City. Richmond: Deitz, 1958. 1st ed. Dec cvr. Good+ in Poor dj. *Scribe's Perch*.* $20/£13

EBERS, G. Egypt: Descriptive, Historical, and Picturesque. London, n.d. (ca 1880). 2 vols. Aeg. Gilt-pict brn cl (spine ends gone, hinges cracked). *Freeman*.* $120/£77

EBERS, GEORG. Richard Lepsius: A Biography. NY: William S. Gottsberger, 1887. Frontis, v,347pp. (Ex-lib; spine faded, soiled.) *Archaeologia.* $75/£48

EBERSTADT, EDWARD AND SONS. The Northwest Coast...Catalogue No. 119. NY, 1941. 1st ed. Orig ptd wrappers. *Ginsberg.* $35/£22

ECCLES, W. J. The Canadian Frontier. Albuquerque: Univ of NM, 1983. Good in dj (sl soiled). *Dumont.* $25/£16

ECCLESTON, ROBERT. The Mariposa Indian War, 1850-1851. C. Gregory Crampton (ed). Univ of UT, 1957. 1st ed. Frontis, fldg map. VF. *Oregon.* $90/£58

ECCLESTON, ROBERT. The Mariposa Indian War, 1850-1851. C. Gregory Crampton (ed). Salt Lake City: Univ of UT, 1957. 1st ed. Ltd to 500. Map. Rust cl, gilt. VF. *Argonaut.* $75/£48

ECHARD, MARGARET. If This Be Treason. GC: DCC, 1944. 1st ed. (Spine base sl bumped), o/w Fine in dj (price-clipped; corners, edges sl worn). *Mordida.* $35/£22

Echoes of Glory. Alexandria, (1991). 3 vols. Pict cvrs. Fine in Fine slipcase. *Pratt.* $105/£67

ECKBO, GARRETT. Urban Landscape Design. NY: McGraw-Hill, (1964). Fine in dj (worn). *Quest.* $40/£26

ECKEL, JOHN C. The First Editions of the Writings of Charles Dickens and Their Values. London, 1913. 1st ed. Ltd to 750 numbered. Port. Teg. (Bkpl, pencil notes, contents soiled, few pp loose; rubbed, rear cvr sl stained.) *King.* $175/£112

ECKENRODE, H. J. The Story of the Campaign and Siege of Yorktown. GPO, 1931. Paper cvr. VG-. *Book Broker.* $20/£13

ECKENRODE, H. J. and BRYAN CONRAD. James Longstreet. Chapel Hill: Univ of NC, 1936. 1st ed. Frontis port, 14 maps. Good. *Scribe's Perch*.* $55/£35

ECKERT, ROBERT P. Edward Thomas; a Biography and a Bibliography. 1937. 1st ed. (Foxing), o/w VG. *Words Etc.* $47/£30

ECKHARDT, GEORGE H. Pennsylvania Clocks and Clockmakers. NY: Bonanza, (1955). (Top cvr sl bumped.) Dj. *Weber.* $35/£22

ECO, UMBERTO. The Aesthetics of Chaosmos: The Middle Ages of James Joyce. Tulsa: Univ of Tulsa, (1982). 1st Amer ed. Inscribed. Fine in wrappers. *Between The Covers.* $135/£87

ECO, UMBERTO. The Bomb and the General. London, 1989. 1st ed. VG in dj. *Words Etc.* $56/£36

ECO, UMBERTO. The Bomb and the General. San Diego: Harcourt Brace Jovanovich, 1989. 1st ed. Fine in NF dj (sm tear). *Lame Duck.* $65/£42

ECO, UMBERTO. Foucault's Pendulum. William Weaver (trans). Franklin Center, PA: Franklin Library, 1989. 1st ed. Signed. Frontis. Full black leather, gilt. Fine. *Argosy.* $40/£26

ECO, UMBERTO. Foucault's Pendulum. London, 1989. 1st UK ed. Fine in Fine dj. *Smith.* $20/£13

ECO, UMBERTO. Postscript to the Name of the Rose. San Diego, (1983). 1st ed. VG in dj (sl used). *King.* $20/£13

Economy of Human Life. Complete, in Two Parts...by an Ancient Bramin.... (By Robert Dodsley.) NY: William Durell, 1793. 2 parts in one. 130pp (waterstains final ll). Contemp calf over bds (bds quite worn, chipped). *Karmiole.* $125/£80

Economy. London, 1845. 375pp. Partially unopened. Blind-emb cl (sl chipped, sl soiled), gilt. *Edwards.* $78/£50

EDDINGTON, A. The Internal Constitution of the Stars. 1926. 1st ed. (Inner hinge sl cracked; spine ends sl defective, corners sl worn), o/w VG. *Whitehart.* $55/£35

EDDINGTON, A. Relativity Theory of Protons and Electrons. Cambridge, 1936. (Fep sl grubby, damaged w/ink sig; spine ends, corners sl worn.) *Whitehart.* $133/£85

EDDINGTON, A. Stellar Movements and the Structure of the Universe. 1914. 1st ed. 4 plts. (Spine sl defective), o/w VG. *Whitehart.* $55/£35

EDDISON, E. R. The Worm Ouroboros. NY: Albert & Charles Boni, 1926. 1st US ed. Frontis. Pict eps; top edge stained blue-gray. Black cl (lt shelfworn), gilt. *Baltimore*.* $40/£26

EDDY, CLYDE. Down the World's Most Dangerous River. NY, 1929. 2nd ptg. Yellow cl (spine heavily scuffed, black mk spine base, hinges tender). Internally VG; cvrs Good. *Five Quail.* $50/£32

EDDY, MARY BAKER. Historical Sketch of Christian Science Mind-Healing. Boston, 1890. 3rd ed. 27pp. Good (tp stained) in ptd wraps (chipped). *Second Life.* $45/£29

EDE, CHARLES. The Art of the Book. London/NY: Studio, (1951). 1st ed. Grn cl. Fine in VG dj (lg seamed tear rear cvr). *House.* $80/£51

EDE, CHARLES. The Art of the Book...1939-1950. London: The Studio, (1951). 1st ed. Fine in dj (worn). *Graf.* $45/£29

EDEN, EMILY. The Semi-Attached Couple. London: Folio Soc, 1955. 1st ed thus. 7 two-color woodcuts by Dorothea Braby. (Spine sl faded.) Slipcase. *Hollett.* $39/£25

EDEN, THOMAS WATTS. A Manual of Midwifery. 1906. 26 plts. (Lt browned, pencil notes, underlinings; cl sl rubbed.) *Edwards.* $23/£15

EDGAR, IRVING I. A History of Early Jewish Physicians in the State of Michigan. NY: Philosophical Library, (1982). 1st ed. Fine in dj. *Glaser.* $35/£22

EDGAR, JOHN F. Pioneer Life in Dayton and Vicinity, 1796-1840. Dayton, 1896. Frontis port, 289pp; map, index. Good (paper cracking fr inner hinge, pp dknd; rubbed, spots back cvr). *Bohling.* $50/£32

EDGELL, GEORGE HAROLD. A History of Sienese Painting. NY, 1932. (Spine dknd, sl worn.) *Washton.* $95/£61

EDGERTON, CLYDE. The Floatplane Notebooks. Chapel Hill: Algonquin, 1988. 1st ed. Fine (rmdr dot) in dj. *Turtle Island.* $25/£16

EDGERTON, CLYDE. Raney. Chapel Hill: Algonquin, 1985. 1st ed, 1st bk. Fine in dj (price-clipped). *Captain's Bookshelf.* $250/£160

EDGEWORTH, MARIA. Harrington, a Tale; and Ormond, a Tale. London: Hunter et al, 1817. 1st ed. 3 vols. 521; 422; 352pp (tp vol professionally repaired). Contemp calf (joints worn), leather labels. Good (sig). *Second Life.* $350/£224

EDGEWORTH, MARIA. Helen, a Tale. London: Richard Bentley, 1834. 2nd ed. 3 vols. Half-titles. Teg. Later 1/2 grn morocco, marbled sides. *Maggs.* $187/£120

Ediciones Poligrafa. London: Redfern Gallery, (1979). Color pict wrappers. *Swann*.* $230/£147

EDIGER, DONALD. The Well of Sacrifice. GC: Doubleday, 1971. 1st ed. Good in dj. *Archaeologia.* $35/£22

EDITH. Somersaults and Strange Company. London: Lawrence & Wishart, 1937. 1st ed. Illus bds. VG. *Patterson.* $25/£16

EDLIN, A. A Treatise on the Art of Bread-Making. London: J. Wright, 1805. 1st ed. 5 fldg plts. Contemp 1/2 leather, marbled paper bds (hinges splitting, edges worn, lt foxing). *Metropolitan*.* $172/£110

EDLIN, H. L. British Woodland Trees. Batsford, 1945. 2nd ed. Color frontis. Dj (sl chipped). *Edwards.* $28/£18

EDLIN, H. L. British Woodland Trees. Batsford, 1949. 3rd rev ed. NF in NF dj. *Hadley.* $23/£15

EDLIN, H. L. England's Forests. Faber, 1958. VG in dj. *Hadley.* $23/£15

EDLIN, H. L. Trees, Woods and Man. London: Collins, 1970. 3rd ed. VG in dj. *Cox.* $47/£30

EDLIN, H. L. and M. NIMMO. Tree Injuries. London, 1956. VG in dj (chipped). *Brooks.* $25/£16

EDMINSTER, FRANK C. The Ruffed Grouse, Its Life Story, Ecology and Management. NY: Macmillan, 1947. 1st ptg. 56 plts. (Sl rubbed, lower corner sl affected by damp), o/w Good. *Worldwide.* $18/£12

EDMINSTER, FRANK C. The Ruffed Grouse. NY, 1947. 1st ed. 56 photo plts. Blue cl. VG in dj (chipped). *Price.* $68/£44

EDMONDS, J. M. Some Greek Love-Poems. London: Peter Davies, 1929. #77/450. Teg. (Spine sl faded, chipped.) *Edwards.* $55/£35

EDMONDS, WALTER B. In the Hands of the Senecas. Boston: Little, Brown, 1947. 1st ed. Signed. Frontis. VG in dj. *Houle.* $175/£112

EDMUNDS, JAMES. The Medical Use of Alcohol.... NY: Nat'l Temperance Soc, 1874. 1st ed. 96pp. Good (worn) in ptd wrappers. *Doctor's Library.* $35/£22

EDMUNDS, R. DAVID. The Potawatomis: Keepers of the Fire. Norman: Univ of OK, (1978). 1st ed. VG in dj. *Lien.* $40/£26

EDMUNDS, RICHARD. The Solicitor's Guide to the Practice of the Office of Pleas in His Majesty's Court of Exchequer.... London: T. Cadell et al, 1744. Contemp calf (rebacked). Good. *Boswell.* $450/£288

EDWARDES, ERNEST L. The Grandfather Clock. Altrincha: John Sherratt, (1971). 3rd ed. Color frontis, 221 plts. Navy blue leatherette. Fine in dj. *Weber.* $40/£26

EDWARDES, ERNEST L. Weight-Driven Chamber Clocks of the Middle Ages and Renaissance. Altrincha: John Sherratt, (1965). 1st ed. Frontis, 64 plts. Red cl. Fine in dj. *Weber.* $40/£26

EDWARDES, HERBERT B. A Year on the Punjab Frontier, in 1848-49. Richard Bentley, 1851. 2 vols. 2 color plts. Gilt-dec red cl (joints sl torn). Contents VG. *Petersfield.* $281/£180

EDWARDES, HERBERT B. A Year on the Punjab Frontier, in 1848-49. London, 1851. 1st ed. 2 vols. Frontis port, color frontis, xxiii,608; xiv,734pp; 3 plts (2 color), fldg panorama, facs letter, fldg map, 2 plans. Contemp black 1/2 calf, marbled bds (spines rubbed). *Maggs.* $390/£250

EDWARDS, AMELIA B. A Midsummer Ramble in the Dolomites. London: George Routledge, (1889). 2nd ed. xxiv,389pp; 9 wood engr plts. Some pp uncut. Pict blue cl. Fine. *Sotheran.* $200/£128

EDWARDS, AMELIA B. A Thousand Miles Up the Nile. London: Longmans, Green, 1877. 1st ed. xxv,732pp (up to pg vi re-stubbed); 17 plts, 1 photo litho plt, 2 color fldg maps. Teg. Dec cl (rubbed, sl cl loss, sl soiled, rebacked w/ orig split spine laid down). *Edwards.* $234/£150

EDWARDS, AMELIA B. A Thousand Miles Up the Nile. London: Routledge, 1889. 2nd ed. Pict-stamped grn cl (spine ends frayed, edges rubbed). VG. *Hermitage*. $95/£61

EDWARDS, AMELIA B. Untrodden Peaks and Unfrequented Valleys. London: Longmans, Green, 1873. 1st ed. Frontis, xxvi,385pp; 7 plts, fldg color map. Marbled edges. Recent oxblood coarse grain morocco, raised bands, orig calf label. (Tp, frontis mottled), o/w VF. *Pirages*. $250/£160

EDWARDS, AVERYL. Fanny Burney 1752-1840. Staples Press, 1948. 1st ed. Good in dj (defective). *Cox*. $16/£10

EDWARDS, B. B. Missionary Gazetteer. Boston, 1832. 25 plts (some heavily foxed). Cl (worn, soiled), handwritten paper spine label. (Lt foxed), o/w Contents VG. *New Hampshire**. $35/£22

EDWARDS, C. The History and Poetry of Finger-Rings. NY: John W. Lovell, c 1874. vii,239pp. VG. *Blake*. $150/£96

EDWARDS, CHARLES et al. Historic Houses of the United Kingdom. London: Cassell, 1892. viii, 328pp (eps lt spotted; corners sl bumped, sm split spine head). *Edwards*. $39/£25

EDWARDS, E. I. Desert Voices: A Descriptive Bibliography. L.A.: Westernlore, 1958. One of 500. 9 full-pg illus. Dj. *Dawson*. $75/£48

EDWARDS, E. I. The Enduring Desert: A Descriptive Bibliography. (L.A.): Ward Ritchie, 1969. 1st ed. Spine label. Slipcase. *Dawson*. $100/£64

EDWARDS, E. I. The Valley Whose Name Is Death. Pasadena: San Pasqual, 1940. One of 500. White-stamped cl, paper spine label (silverfishing). *Dawson*. $30/£19

EDWARDS, EDWARD. Anecdotes of Painters Who Have Resided or Been Born in England.... London: Leigh & Sotheby et al, 1808. xxxix,327pp, errata pg, 25 Fine engr port plts. Aeg. 19th cent 1/2 calf, vellum bds, gilt panelled spine, raised cords. (Few early pp browned; spine sl faded), o/w Fine. *Europa*. $101/£65

EDWARDS, EMILY. Painted Walls of Mexico. Austin: Univ of TX, (1966). 9 color plts, 3 maps. Good in dj. *Archaeologia*. $45/£29

EDWARDS, ETHEL. Carver of Tuskegee. Cincinnati: Psyche Psyche, (1971). One of 200 numbered. Fine. Issued w/o dj? *Bernard*. $40/£26

EDWARDS, G. B. The Book of Ebenezer Le Page. London, 1981. 1st ed. VG in dj. *Typographeum*. $30/£19

EDWARDS, G. W. Vanished Towers and Chimes of Flanders. Phila, 1916. 30 plts (21 color), guards. Dec cvrs, gilt. Good. *Scribe's Perch**. $34/£22

EDWARDS, GLADYS BROWN. The Arabian War Horse to Show Horse. Covina, 1973. Rev Collector's Ed. Errata sheet laid in. VG in VG dj. *October Farm*. $165/£106

EDWARDS, JENNIE. John N. Edwards: Biography, Memoirs, Reminiscences, and Recollections.... Kansas City: Jennie Edwards, 1889. 1st ed. (Sl edgeworn.) Howes E55. *Glenn*. $175/£112

EDWARDS, LEE R. et al (eds). Woman: An Issue. Boston/Toronto: Little, Brown, 1972. 1st ed. Frontis. (Owner stamp), else Fine in dj (lt worn). *Cahan*. $35/£22

EDWARDS, LEO. Andy Blake's Comet Coaster. G&D, 1928. 5x7.5. 247pp + ads. Red cl (shelfworn, bumped). VG + (lacks dj). *My Bookhouse*. $25/£16

EDWARDS, LEO. Jerry Todd and the Flying Flapdoodle. G&D, 1934. 5x7.5. 244pp. Red cl (shelfworn). VG + in dj remains. *My Bookhouse*. $40/£26

EDWARDS, LEO. Jerry Todd in the Whispering Cave. G&D, 1927. 5x7.5. 237pp. Red cl (edgeworn). Lists to #10. VG in dj (edges ragged). *My Bookhouse*. $45/£29

EDWARDS, LEO. Jerry Todd, Caveman. G&D, 1932. 1st ed. 5x7.5. 258pp + ads. Red cl (shelfworn). Last title on lists. VG + in dj (edgeworn). *My Bookhouse*. $85/£54

EDWARDS, LEO. Poppy Ott and the Freckled Goldfish. G&D, 1928. 1st ed. 5x7.5. 269pp + ads. Last title listed. VG (shelfworn, soiled) in dj (worn). *My Bookhouse*. $45/£29

EDWARDS, LEO. Poppy Ott's Pedigreed Pickles. G&D, 1927. 5x7.5. 243pp + ad. Red cl (shelfworn). Lists to #6. VG in dj (edges ragged, chipped). *My Bookhouse*. $40/£26

EDWARDS, LEO. Tuffy Bean at Funny-Bone Farm. G&D, 1931. 5x7.5. 225pp + ads. Red cl (shelfworn, finger-mkd). Lists to this title. VG in dj (chipped). *My Bookhouse*. $85/£54

EDWARDS, LIONEL. Huntsmen Past and Present. London, 1929. 1st ed. Teg. Gilt-stamped buckram. Fine. *Argosy*. $85/£54

EDWARDS, MATILDA BETHAM. A Winter with the Swallows. London, 1867. Frontis, viii,286pp + 12pp pub's cat (ppvii-viii misbound after 1st text leaf; sl foxing). Gilt-edged 1/2 cl (rebound), marbled bds, buckram spine label. *Edwards*. $70/£45

EDWARDS, MAY. The Hobo Hound. Chicago: Rand-McNally, 1947. Stated 1st ed. Suzanne Suba (illus). 'Slottie' bk, w/card of die-cut punchouts bound in at rear. Good + in Good + dj (price-clipped). *Scribe's Perch**. $30/£19

EDWARDS, PAUL. English Garden Ornament. Bell, 1965. VG in dj. *Hadley*. $25/£16

EDWARDS, RALPH and MARGARET JOURDAIN. Georgian Cabinet-Makers. Country Life, 1944. 1st ed. Frontis. Dj (ragged w/loss). *Edwards*. $47/£30

EDWARDS, RUTH DUDLEY. Corridors of Death. London: Quartet, 1981. 1st ed, 1st bk. Fine in dj. *Murder By The Book*. $35/£22

EDWARDS, SAMUEL E. The Ohio Hunter: Or A Brief Sketch of the Frontier Life of Samuel E. Edwards.... Battle Creek, MI: Review & Herald Steam Press, 1866. 1st ed. Port. (Foxing; cl lt soiled, rubbed; spine ends, corners sl frayed.) Howes E70. *Sadlon*. $650/£417

EDWARDS, SYDENHAM and R. W. DICKSON. The New Flora Britannica. London: John Stockdale, 1812. 2 vols in 1. 4to. (Inscrips.) 61 hand-colored engr plts (lt browned, lt stained, frontis torn at margin). Contemp red morocco (worn), gilt. *Christie's**. $2,983/£1,912

EDWARDS, SYDENHAM. The Botanical Register...Exotic Plants.... London: James Ridgway, 1818. 86 hand-colored engrs. Full grn emb leather (bumped, rubbed). Very Nice. *Metropolitan**. $776/£497

EDWARDS, W. A Mediaeval Scrap-Heap. London, 1930. Uncut. (Cl spine sl rubbed.) *Edwards*. $31/£20

EDWARDS, WALTER N. The Beverages We Drink. London, 1898. 1st ed. 220pp. (Browned, ink inscrip; bumped, dknd, rubbed.) *King*. $45/£29

EDWARDS, WILLIAM and BEATRICE HARRADEN. Two Health-Seekers in Southern California. Phila, 1897. 1st ed. 144pp (stamp fep, top margin ll waterstained). VG (sm spine #). *Fye*. $150/£96

EDWARDS, WILLIAM B. Civil War Guns. Harrisburg, (1962). 1st ed. (Sl water damage), o/w VG in VG dj. *Pratt*. $47/£30

EDWARDS, WILLIAM B. Civil War Guns.... Harrisburg: Stackpole Co, (1962). 1st ed. VF in pict dj (chipped). *Argonaut*. $50/£32

EDWARDS, WILLIAM J. Twenty-Five Years in the Black Belt. Boston: Cornhill, (1918). 1st ed. Frontis port. (Corners bumped), else VG. *Wantagh.* $65/£42

EDWARDS, WILLIAM SEYMOUR. Into the Yukon. Cincinnati: Robert Clarke, 1905. 2nd ed. 2 maps. Teg. (Few sigs sprung), else VG. *High Latitude.* $45/£29

EDWARDS, WILLIAM. The Early History of North Riding. London: A. Brown, 1924. Fldg map at rear. Very Nice. *Hermitage.* $85/£54

EFFINGER, GEORGE ALEC. When Gravity Fails. NY: Arbor House, (1987). 1st ed. Fine in dj. *Other Worlds.* $25/£16

EGAN, BERESFORD. Pollen. Denis Archer, (1933). 1st ed. Secondary binding: orange cl. Nice (lt mks) in acetate dj (sl torn, complete w/ptd price). *Ash.* $62/£40

EGAN, FEROL. The El Dorado Trail. NY: McGraw-Hill, (1970). Rev copy w/card laid in. Map. Red cl, gilt. Fine in pict dj. *Pacific*.* $34/£22

EGAN, HOWARD R. Pioneering the West, 1846 to 1878. Richmond, UT: Howard R. Egan Estate, 1917. Text Fine (bkpl; shelfwear to spine). Howes E76. *Cullen.* $150/£96

EGAN, PIERCE. Life in London. London: Sherwood, Neely & Jones, 1821. 1st ed, 1st issue, w/half-title. Tall 8vo. 36 hand-colored aquatint plts, 3 fldg sheets of music. Grn silk moire eps. Later crushed maroon levant, gilt extra. *Swann*.* $805/£516

EGAN, PIERCE. Life in London. London, 1822. 2nd ed. 376pp, 36 scenes. (Ink name; contents, plt margins soiled; offsetting, foxing.) Blind-stamped calf (cvrs detached). Well Used. *King.* $150/£96

EGAN, PIERCE. Sporting Anecdotes.... Sherwood, Jones, 1825. New ed. 6 engr plts (3 colored of which 1 fldg), 3 signed J. R. or R. Cruikshank. 2 ports (sl foxed). Contemp dk blue calf gilt, dec back in panels, marbled edges. *Hatchwell.* $312/£200

EGELMANN, CHARLES FREDERICK. The Farmers and Mechanics Almanac for 1848. Phila: Mentz & Rovoudt, (1847). 36pp. Fine. *Cahan.* $30/£19

EGELMANN, CHARLES FREDERICK. The Farmers and Mechanics Almanack, for 1846.... Phila: Mentz & Rovoudt, (1845). 18 leaves. VG in wrappers (short tear, rear wrapper partially detached). *Cahan.* $40/£26

EGERTON, FRANCIS. Mediterranean Sketches. London: Murray, 1843. 1st ed. vi,(i)contents,(i)blank,184pp + 4pp pub's list dated July 1842 (lt foxing title, fep). Blue ribbed blindstamped cl (sl stained), gilt spine. VG. *Morrell.* $133/£85

EGGENHOFER, NICK. Wagons, Mules and Men. NY, 1961. 1st ed. (Cvr dye lt flaking, sm edge spots, sm dampstain back cvr), o/w Fine in dj (lt chipped, worn, price-clipped). *Baade.* $150/£96

EGGLER, ALBERT. The Everest-Lhoste Adventure. London, (1957). 1st Eng ed. VG in dj (wrinkled). *King.* $45/£29

EGGLESTON, EDWARD. Queer Stories for Boys and Girls. NY: Scribner, 1884. 1st ed. Grn cl pict stamped in rust/black. Attractive (lt stain rear bd, lt wear). *Hermitage.* $75/£48

EGLE, WILLIAM HENRY (ed). Documents Relating to the Connecticut Settlement in the Wyoming Valley. Harrisburg, 1893. 792pp; 3 fldg maps. 3/4 leather, marbled bds (rebacked w/black tape, hinges nearly broken). *Bohling.* $18/£12

Egyptian Antiquities. London, 1849. 2 vols. viii,399; vi,447pp; map. (Sl browned, bkpl; sl stained, spines sl sunned.) *Edwards.* $47/£30

EHLE, JOHN. Kingstree Island. London: Hodder & Stoughton, (1959). 1st Eng ed. (Sm yellow triangle fr pastedown; sl abrasions fep), else NF in VG dj (2 tears rear panel). *Between The Covers.* $85/£54

EHLERT, LOIS. Color Zoo. NY: Lippincott, 1989. 1st ed. 9 1/4 sq. 32pp. Glossy bds. VG in dj. *Cattermole.* $25/£16

EHRLICH, J. W. (ed). Howl of the Censor. San Carlos: Nourse, (1961). 1st ed. Fine in dj (lt edgewear). *Reese.* $30/£19

EHRMANN, HERBERT B. The Untried Case. NY: Vanguard, (1960). Black cl. Fine in NF black dj (sm tear). *Blue Mountain.* $20/£13

EHWA, CARL, JR. The Books of Pipes and Tobacco. NY, (1974). 1st ptg. (Lt worn.) Dj. *Freeman*.* $10/£6

EICHENBERG, FRITZ. The Wood and the Graver. NY, (1977). Fine in dj. *Argosy.* $125/£80

EICKEMEYER, RUDOLF, JR. Down South. NY: R.H. Russell, 1900. 1st ed. Folio. Frontis. Ptd brn bds (rubbed; shaken), cl spine, lg illus mtd on cvr. Internally Attractive. BAL 7146. *Petrilla.* $325/£208

EIDE, ARTHUR HANSIN. Drums of Diomede. Hollywood, c. 1952. VG in dj. *High Latitude.* $30/£19

EIFERT, VIRGINIA S. Louis Jolliet, Explorer of Rivers. NY: Dodd, Mead, 1961. 1st ed. Fine in dj (sl edgewear). *Sadlon.* $15/£10

EINARSEN, ARTHUR S. The Pronghorn Antelope and Its Management. Washington: Wildlife Mgmt Inst, 1948. 1st ed. 2 color plts. Pict eps. Tan buckram. Fine in VG pict dj. *Biscotti.* $35/£22

EINSTEIN, ALBERT. Relativity. The Special and General Theory. Robert W. Lawson (trans). NY, 1920. 1st Amer ed. Frontis port. (Name; cl soiled.) *Argosy.* $150/£96

EINSTEIN, ALBERT. Relativity. The Special and General Theory. Robert W. Lawson (trans). NY: Henry Holt, 1920. 1st Amer ed. Frontis. (Pencil notes throughout.) Blue cl. *Karmiole.* $75/£48

EINSTEIN, M. I. D. and M. A. GOLDSTEIN. Collectors' Marks. St. Louis: Laryngogscope Press, 1918. Ltd to 300. Red cl (sl chipped, bumped). *Maggs.* $55/£35

EISEN, G. Glass: Its Origin, History, Chronology, Technic and Classification to the Sixteenth Century. NY: Rudge, 1927. #159/525. 2 vols. 10 full-pg color plts. NF in VG slipcase. *Scribe's Perch*.* $200/£128

EISEN, G. Glass: Its Origin, History, Chronology, Technic and Classification to the Sixteenth Century. NY: William Edwin Rudge, 1927. 2 vols complete. 198 plts (10 color). Orig bds (spines soiled, lower margins lt water-stained). *Archaeologia.* $375/£240

EISEN, G. Glass: Its Origin, History.... NY: Wm. E. Rudge, 1927. 1st ed. One of 525. 2 vols. 10 color plts. 1/4 cream cl. NF (institutional stamps, paperclip mks fr blanks, bkpls) in slipcase (partly soiled, split). *Waverly*.* $143/£92

EISEN, G. The Raisin Industry. SF: H.S. Crocker, 1890. 1st ed. Frontis, iii,223pp,(11pp ads), 9 plts. Maroon cl, gilt-lettered spine. (Name fep, pencil mks rep; spine faded, extrems lt worn), else Fine. *Argonaut.* $125/£80

EISENBERG, DEBORAH. Transactions in a Foreign Currency. NY: Knopf, 1986. 1st ed, 1st bk. Fine in dj (lt rubbed). *Hermitage.* $30/£19

EISENHOWER, JOHN. So Far from God. NY: Random House, (1989). 1st ed. 14 maps. *Argonaut.* $25/£16

EISENSCHIML, OTTO and E. B. LONG. As Luck Would Have It. Indianapolis, (1948). 1st ed. Fine. *Pratt.* $32/£21

EISENSCHIML, OTTO and RALPH NEWMAN. The American Iliad. Indianapolis, (1947). 1st ed. Fine in dj (worn). *Pratt.* $27/£17

EISENSCHIML, OTTO. Why the Civil War? Indianapolis, (1958). 1st ed. Signed. VG + . *Pratt.* $50/£32

EISENSCHIML, OTTO. Why the Civil War? Indianapolis: Bobbs-Merrill, (1958). 1st ed. VG in dj. *Cullen.* $25/£16

EISENSTAEDT, ALFRED. Eisenstaedt on Eisenstaedt. NY: Abbeville, 1985. 1st ed. Frontis. Fine in NF dj. *Cahan*. $40/£26

EISENSTAEDT, ALFRED. Witness to Our Time. NY: Viking, 1966. 1st ed. (Owner stamp), else VG in dj (chipped). *Cahan*. $60/£38

EISSLER, K. R. Goethe. A Psychoanalytic Study. 1775-1786. Detroit: Wayne State Univ, 1963. 1st ed. 2 vols. NF in NF slipcase. *Beasley*. $175/£112

EITNER, LORENZ. Gericault. An Album of Drawings in the Art Institute of Chicago. Chicago, 1960. 64 plts. Good. *Washton*. $50/£32

EL COMANCHO. The Old Timer's Tale. Chicago: Canterbury, 1929. VG. *Dumont*. $50/£32

El Grego to Goya. London: Nat'l Gallery, 1981. Good in wraps (sl rubbed). *Washton*. $25/£16

ELDER, J. G. History of Lewiston. Lewiston, ME, 1882. 48pp. Blue printed wraps (sl worn, chipped, stamps on cvr). *Bohling*. $50/£32

ELDER, PAUL. The Old Spanish Missions of California. SF, (1913). VG in dj (shattered). *King*. $35/£22

ELDER, PAUL. The Old Spanish Missions of California. SF: Paul Elder, (1913). 1st ed. Orig burlap-backed bds, pict cvr label. (Spine ends, corners sl bumped), o/w Fine in dj (sl chipped). *Sadlon*. $75/£48

ELDER, WILLIAM. Biography of Elisha Kent Kane. Phila: Childs & Peterson, 1858. 416pp + ads. Marbled edges. 3/4 leather, marbled paper over bds (worn, esp edges). *Parmer*. $55/£35

ELDON, MAGDALEN. Snow Bumble. London: Collins, (1951). 1st ed. 4to. Color illus eps. Color illus bds. (Edges, corners sl worn), o/w VG. *Dower*. $50/£32

Eleanor Farjeon Book. Hamilton, 1966. 1st ed. Edward Ardizzone (illus). Lg 8vo. 184pp (mks, fep renewed, bkpl mtd over lib stamp). VG in pict dj. *Bookmark*. $27/£17

ELGAR, EDWARD. My Friends Pictured Within. Novello, (n.d.). Card wrappers. *Clearwater*. $39/£25

ELIAS, S. P. The Law of Theater Tickets. SF: W.A. Hiester, 1905. Presentation copy. Well Preserved in wraps. *Boswell*. $125/£80

ELIOT, CHARLES W. (ed). Charles Eliot, Landscape Architect. Boston, 1903. Frontis, 62 full-pg illus; map rear pocket (lacks map fr pocket). Tight (paper tanning; lt shelfworn). *Brooks*. $99/£63

ELIOT, E. West Point and the Confederacy. NY: Baker, 1941. 1st ed. Good + . *Scribe's Perch**. $45/£29

ELIOT, GEORGE. (Pseud of Mary Ann Evans.) Adam Bede. Edinburgh/London: William Blackwood, 1859. 1st ed, w/pub's ads present in 3rd vol. 3 vols. Orig orange cl, gilt. (Joints split, sewing loose, spine chipped.) *Macdonnell*. $150/£96

ELIOT, GEORGE. (Pseud of Mary Ann Evans.) Daniel Deronda. William Blackwood, 1876. 4 vols. Complete w/errata slip vol 1. Marbled edges. Contemp 1/2 leather (sl rubbed), marbled bds, raised bands, leather spine labels (cracked). VG (bkpls fr pastedowns). *Tiger*. $468/£300

ELIOT, GEORGE. (Pseud of Mary Ann Evans.) Essays and Leaves from a Note-Book. Blackwood, 1884. 1st ed. (Hinges sl weak; spine dknd), o/w NF. *Poetry Bookshop*. $70/£45

ELIOT, GEORGE. (Pseud of Mary Ann Evans.) Essays and Leaves from a Note-Book. William Blackwood & Sons, 1884. 1st Eng ed. x,382pp, ad leaf. (Cl lt spotted, lower cvr discolored by damp.) Contents Fine. *Bickersteth*. $125/£80

ELIOT, GEORGE. (Pseud of Mary Ann Evans.) How Lisa Loved the King. Boston: Fields, Osgood, 1869. 1st ed. 48pp. Grn cl, gilt. (Sl pencil underlining, fr hinge starting; spine head chipped), else NF. *Blue Mountain*. $35/£22

ELIOT, GEORGE. (Pseud of Mary Ann Evans.) Impressions of Theophrastus Such. NY: Harper, 1879. 1st Amer ed. 6pp undated ads. Grn cl. Fine (fr cvr sl mottled). *Sumner & Stillman*. $80/£51

ELIOT, GEORGE. (Pseud of Mary Ann Evans.) The Legend of Jubal and Other Poems. William Blackwood, 1874. Pub's cat. Beveled bds (spine bumped, chipped, sunned; corners rubbed). Good (sl spotted). *Tiger*. $117/£75

ELIOT, GEORGE. (Pseud of Mary Ann Evans.) The Legend of Jubal. Boston: James R. Osgood, 1874. 1st Amer ed. Brn cl, gilt, beveled. NF. *Sumner & Stillman*. $95/£61

ELIOT, GEORGE. (Pseud of Mary Ann Evans.) Middlemarch: A Study of Provincial Life. William Blackwood, 1871-1872. 4 vols. Sprinkled edges. Contemp 1/2 leather (vols 1 & 2 rebacked, orig backstrips relaid; hinges, corners rubbed), marbled bds, raised bands, leather spine labels. Good (tps trimmed w/partial loss to 'rights of translation,' ink inscrip tp, bkpls fr pastedown, sl spotted). *Tiger*. $624/£400

ELIOT, GEORGE. (Pseud of Mary Ann Evans.) The Mill on the Floss. William Blackwood, 1860. 3 vols. Pub's cat vol 3. Good (margins soiled, spotted, labels fr pastedowns, sig, leaf edges frayed; spines bumped, chipped, upper hinges nicked, corners rubbed, shelfwear). *Tiger*. $468/£300

ELIOT, GEORGE. (Pseud of Mary Ann Evans.) The Mill on the Floss. (NY): LEC, 1963. One of 1500 numbered, signed by Wray Manning (illus). Fine in pub's slipcase. *Hermitage*. $75/£48

ELIOT, GEORGE. (Pseud of Mary Ann Evans.) Romola. London: Smith, Elder, 1863. 1st ed. 3 vols. Bound w/o half titles, ads; feps neatly excised. Contemp binder's cl. Good (few spots). *Reese*. $95/£61

ELIOT, GEORGE. (Pseud of Mary Ann Evans.) Scenes from Clerical Life. NY: Harper, 1858. 1st Amer ed. Uncut. VG in orig brn ptd wrappers (fr wrapper foreedge, rear corner chipped; fr joint rubbed, spine paper lacking; foxed). *Macdonnell*. $850/£545

ELIOT, GEORGE. (Pseud of Mary Ann Evans.) Silas Marner. Edinburgh: Blackwood, 1861. 1st ed, Carter's binding A. 16,(4)pp terminal cat. Brn cl stamped in blind/gilt. (Ink name, bkpl; spine sl cocked, nicked, bumped), o/w VG. *Reese*. $550/£353

ELIOT, GEORGE. (Pseud of Mary Ann Evans.) Silas Marner. NY: Harper, 1861. 1st US ed. 22pp pub's ads at rear. Lt yellow eps. Blind grn cl (worn, frayed, sl puckered), gilt (dull). Text Good (browned, old dampstain margin 1st few sigs) in recent cl-cvrd bd slipcase. *Baltimore**. $40/£26

ELIOT, GEORGE. (Pseud of Mary Ann Evans.) The Spanish Gypsy. Boston: Ticknor & Fields, 1868. 1st Amer ed. Terra cotta cl, gilt. Fine. *Macdonnell*. $85/£54

ELIOT, GEORGE. (Pseud of Mary Ann Evans.) The Spanish Gypsy. Boston: Ticknor & Fields, 1868. 1st Amer ed. Grn cl, beveled. NF. *Sumner & Stillman*. $95/£61

ELIOT, GEORGE. (Pseud of Mary Ann Evans.) The Spanish Gypsy. Edinburgh: Blackwood, 1868. 3rd ed. Aeg. Contemp crushed morocco (rubbed). *Stewart*. $47/£30

ELIOT, T. S. After Strange Gods. London: Faber & Faber, (1934). 1st ed. (Eps lt foxed), o/w VG in dj (edges tanned, nicks mended top edge). *Reese*. $75/£48

ELIOT, T. S. Animula. London, 1929. Lg paper ed, ltd to 400 numbered, signed. (Spine badly chipped, cvrs heavily soiled.) *King*. $250/£160

ELIOT, T. S. Charles Whibley. Oxford: English Assoc, 1931. 1st ed. NF in sewn ptd wraps (borders sl tanned). *Lame Duck*. $100/£64

ELIOT, T. S. The Classics and the Man of Letters. London: Oxford, 1942. 1st ed. NF in lt blue ptd wraps (spine faded). *Lame Duck*. $100/£64

ELIOT, T. S. The Cocktail Party. London, 1950. 1st ed. VG (spine bumped) in dj (corners rubbed, 2 closed tears). *Buckley.* $47/£30

ELIOT, T. S. Collected Plays. London: Faber, 1962. 1st ed thus. Fine in VG dj (sl browned). *Williams.* $31/£20

ELIOT, T. S. Collected Poems 1909-1935. London: Faber & Faber, (1936). 1st ed. One of 6000 ptd. Blue cl. (Lt rubbed), o/w Fine in dj (chipped, rubbed, price-clipped, old internal tape mend residue). *Jaffe.* $150/£96

ELIOT, T. S. Collected Poems 1909-1935. NY: Harcourt, (1936). 1st Amer ed. (Pencil sig, notes, ep gutters dknd), o/w Nice in dj (shabby). *Reese.* $45/£29

ELIOT, T. S. The Complete Poems and Plays. NY, 1952. 1st ed. VF in VG dj. *Bond.* $35/£22

ELIOT, T. S. The Confidential Clerk. Faber & Faber, (1954). 1st ed. VG in earlier (10s 6d) dj (sl nicked, torn, repaired). *Ash.* $31/£20

ELIOT, T. S. The Confidential Clerk. London, 1954. 1st issue @ 10/6d. (Sm bkpl), else VG in dj (sl faded, nicked). *Buckley.* $23/£15

ELIOT, T. S. The Confidential Clerk. London, 1954. 1st ed, 1st state. Misprint 'I hads' for 'I had' pg 7. NF (sl rubbed) in NF 1st state dj (few sm edge tears). *Polyanthos.* $40/£26

ELIOT, T. S. The Confidential Clerk. NY, 1954. 1st Amer ed. NF (spine sl rubbed) in dj (spine sunned, 2 edge tears, rubbed). *Polyanthos.* $25/£16

ELIOT, T. S. The Cultivation of Christmas Trees. London, 1954. 1st ed. Fine in Fine envelope. *Polyanthos.* $60/£38

ELIOT, T. S. The Cultivation of Christmas Trees. London: Ariel Poems, 1954. 1st Eng ed. Fine in sewn wrappers. *Clearwater.* $23/£15

ELIOT, T. S. Dante. London: Faber, (1929). 1st ed, trade issue. Pict bds. (Sl offsetting eps), o/w Fine in Good 1st dj (lt stains, sm chips, splits at folds). *Reese.* $75/£48

ELIOT, T. S. East Coker. London, 1940. 1st ed. Orig ptd wrappers. (Dusty, rubbed, string slit both fore-edges), o/w VG. *Words Etc.* $47/£30

ELIOT, T. S. The Elder Statesman. London, (1959). 1st ed. (Cvrs sl faded), else Good in dj (sl chipped, frayed). *King.* $35/£22

ELIOT, T. S. The Elder Statesman. NY, 1959. 1st Amer ed. Fine in dj (edge rubbed). *Polyanthos.* $30/£19

ELIOT, T. S. The Family Reunion. NY: Harcourt, (1939). 1st Amer ed (2500 ptd). Fine in NF dj (nick). *Reese.* $100/£64

ELIOT, T. S. The Family Reunion. London, 1939. 1st Eng ed. Very Nice in dj (sl rubbed, torn, dusty). *Clearwater.* $55/£35

ELIOT, T. S. For Lancelot Andrewes. London, (1928). 1st ed. VG in dj. *Argosy.* $275/£176

ELIOT, T. S. For Lancelot Andrewes. GC: Doubleday, 1929. 1st Amer ed (2000 ptd). (Edges lt sunned), o/w VG in dj (spine tanned). *Reese.* $135/£87

ELIOT, T. S. Four Quartets. London: Faber & Faber, 1960. #115/290 signed. 1/4 vellum spine, marbled cvrs. Fine in NF marbled slipcase. *Vandoros.* $2,975/£1,907

ELIOT, T. S. Four Quartets. Folio Soc, 1968. 1st ed. Fine in slipcase. *Words Etc.* $31/£20

ELIOT, T. S. Homage to John Dryden. London: Hogarth, 1924. 1st ed. VG (bkpl) in white wraps (aged). *Certo.* $65/£42

ELIOT, T. S. John Dryden the Poet, the Dramatist, the Critic. NY: Terence & Elsa Holliday, 1932. 1st ed, trade issue (1000 ptd). Fine in white dj (lt tanned, sl finger smudges). *Reese.* $150/£96

ELIOT, T. S. The Letters of T. S. Eliot. Vol I, 1898-1922. Valerie Eliot (ed). (London/NY): Faber/Harcourt Brace, (1988). One of 500 numbered, signed by Valerie Eliot. Fine in Fine slipcase. *Lenz.* $175/£112

ELIOT, T. S. Little Gidding. London: Faber & Faber, (1942). 1st ed. NF in sewn ptd wrappers. *Dermont.* $35/£22

ELIOT, T. S. Marina. London: Ariel Poems, (1930). 1st Eng ed. Crisp (sl creased) in sewn wrappers. *Clearwater.* $47/£30

ELIOT, T. S. Murder in the Cathedral. London: Faber & Faber, (1935). 1st Faber ed, preceded by acting ed. Fine in NF dj (sl use top edge). *Reese.* $165/£106

ELIOT, T. S. Murder in the Cathedral. NY: Harcourt, Brace, 1935. 1st ed. Rev copy, stamp fep. (Ep hinges foxed), else NF in VG dj (spine tanned, extrems worn, edgetears). *Lame Duck.* $200/£128

ELIOT, T. S. The Music of Poetry. Glasgow, 1942. One of 1000 ptd. Crisp in card wrappers. *Clearwater.* $47/£30

ELIOT, T. S. Old Possum's Book of Practical Cats. Faber & Faber, (1939). 1st ed. Yellow cl (sl worn, sl mks). Good. *Ash.* $101/£65

ELIOT, T. S. On Poetry and Poets. NY: Farrar, (1957). 1st Amer ed. Good (sl dusty; edges, eps foxed) in dj. *Reese.* $20/£13

ELIOT, T. S. Poetry and Drama. Cambridge: Harvard, 1951. 1st ed (preceding Faber ed). Fine in dj (lt creased) bearing MacLeish blurb sticker. *Reese.* $35/£22

ELIOT, T. S. The Rock. NY, 1934. 1st Amer ed. Fine in dj (sl rubbed, sl soiled, price-clipped). *Polyanthos.* $60/£38

ELIOT, T. S. The Sacred Wood, Essays on Poetry and Criticism. London: Methuen, (1920). 1st ed, 1st binding. Gilt blue cl. Good (pencil sig, notes; spine extrems rubbed). *Reese.* $85/£54

ELIOT, T. S. Selected Essays 1917-1932. NY: Harcourt, (1932). 1st Amer ed (3700 ptd). (Edges sl tanned), o/w NF in dj (spine tanned, nicks lower edge). *Reese.* $100/£64

ELIOT, T. S. A Song for Simeon. London: Faber & Gwyer, 1928. 1st ed. #217/500 lg paper copies signed. 1 color plt. Fore, bottom edges untrimmed. Stiff off-white paper bds ptd in gold fr cvr. (Spine lt browned), else Fine. *Vandoros.* $500/£321

ELIOT, T. S. Sweeney Agonistes. London: Faber & Faber, 1932. 1st ed. Good in blue bds, yellow dj (lt soiled, frayed, sm loss top margin). *Cox.* $62/£40

ELIOT, T. S. The Three Voices of Poetry. Cambridge: for National Bk League by Cambridge Univ, 1953. 1st ed. Fine in dec wrappers. *Reese.* $40/£26

ELIOT, T. S. The Undergraduate Poems of T. S. Eliot.... Cambridge: Harvard Advocate, (1949). 1st (unauthorized) ed. One of 1000 ptd. Fine in ptd wrappers. *Reese.* $125/£80

ELIOT, T. S. The Waste Land. NY: Boni & Liveright, 1922. 1st ed, 2nd issue w/'mount' p41. #665/1000 ptd. 8vo. Black stiff cl bds as issued. Fine. *Appelfeld.* $950/£609

ELIOT, T. S. The Waste Land. Hogarth, 1923. 1st Eng ed. (Inscrip, sl foxing.) Blue marbled paper bds (spine foot lacks piece, rest torn; extrems rubbed), 2nd state white paper label upper cvr w/heavy single-line rule above, below title. *Sotheby's*.* $718/£460

ELIOT, T. S. The Waste Land. A Facsimile and Transcript of the Original Drafts.... Valerie Eliot (ed). Faber & Faber, 1971. 1st ed. 61 facs plts. Fine in dj. *Cox.* $47/£30

ELIOT, T. S. The Waste Land. A Facsimile and Transcript. London: Faber & Faber, 1971. #327/500. Fine in slipcase. *Williams.* $187/£120

ELIOT, T. S. What Is a Classic? London: Faber, 1945. 1st ed. (Spine, edges faded.) *Hollett.* $39/£25

ELISOFON, E. Java Diary. London: Macmillan, 1969. 1st ed. Blind-stamped dec cl. Fine in Fine dj. *Mikesh.* $30/£19

Elizabethan Image. Painting in England 1540-1620. Roy Strong (cat). ROY. London: Tate Gallery, 1969. Good. *Washton.* $25/£16

ELKIN, STANLEY. Boswell. NY: Random House, 1964. 1st ed, 1st bk. (Bds lt spotted), else Fine in NF dj. *Lame Duck.* $150/£96

ELKINS, JOHN M. Indian Fighting on the Texas Frontier. Amarillo, 1929. Port, 3 plts. VG+ in gray wraps. *Bohling.* $100/£64

ELKINTON, JOSEPH. The Doukhobors. Phila, 1903. 1st ed. 3 maps (2 fldg). (Recased, spine sl discolored, rubbed.) *Edwards.* $55/£35

ELKINTON, JOSEPH. Selections from the Diary of Joseph S. Elkinton 1803-1905, and Correspondence. Phila: Leeds & Biddle, 1913. 1st ed. NF (ex-lib). *Archer.* $12/£8

ELLACOMBE, HENRY. In a Gloucestershire Garden. London: Edward Arnold, 1895. 1st ed. 302pp + ads; 4 plts. Gilt decs. (Spine dknd), else Fine. *Quest.* $60/£38

ELLACOMBE, HENRY. In a Gloucestershire Garden. London, 1896. 2nd ed. 302pp + 32pp pub's ads. Teg. (Worn.) *Edwards.* $25/£16

ELLACOMBE, HENRY. Plant Lore and Garden Craft of Shakespeare. London/NY: Edward Arnold, 1896. New ed. Pub's presentation copy. 383 + 32pp ads; 16 plts. Teg, uncut. Pict cl (spine relaid, hinges reinforced), gilt. Fine. *Quest.* $120/£77

ELLACOMBE, HENRY. The Plant-Love and Garden-Craft of Shakespeare. Exeter: The Author, (1878). Tp,1 f,303pp. (Cl edges sl rubbed.) *Marlborough.* $140/£90

ELLENBECKER, JOHN G. The Jayhawkers of Death Valley. Marysville, KS, 1938. Ptd wrappers. *Dawson.* $200/£128

ELLENBERGER, D. FRED (comp). History of the Basuto. London, 1912. Frontis port, fldg map, fldg table. (Fep worn w/sm hole; extrems sl rubbed, lower joint scuffed penetrating cl.) *Edwards.* $55/£35

Ellesmere Collection of Drawings by the Carracci and Other Bolognese Masters Collected by Sir Thomas Lawrence, Pt. I. Sotheby's, 1972. 7 fldg plts. Fine. *Europa.* $44/£28

ELLINGTON, CHARLES G. The Trial of U.S. Grant: The Pacific Coast Years, 1852-1854. Glendale: A.H. Clark, 1987. 1st ed. Collector's ed. Full leather. *Book Market.* $70/£45

ELLINGTON, DUKE. Music Is My Mistress. NY, 1973. 1st ed. NF in VG+ dj. *Warren.* $50/£32

ELLIOT, DANIEL GIRAUD. The Gallinaceous Game Birds of North America.... NY, 1897. xviii,220pp,(i) (margins lt browned, lib ink stamp tp), 46 plts, color chart. Color pict cl (soiled, spine sl chipped). *Edwards.* $39/£25

ELLIOT, DANIEL GIRAUD. List of Mammals from Somali-Land.... Chicago, 1897. 51pp, 39 plts (some plt folds cut too fine). Fine. *Grayling.* $55/£35

ELLIOT, DANIEL GIRAUD. North American Shore Birds. NY: Francis P. Harper, 1895. 268pp (eps foxed); 71 plts, 1 fldg diag. Dec cl. Good. *Scribe's Perch*.* $95/£61

ELLIOT, DANIEL GIRAUD. North American Shore Birds. NY: Francis P. Harper, 1897. 2nd ed. xvi,268pp, 74 plts, fldg outline. Dec cvrs. VG (lt soiled). *Backman.* $35/£22

ELLIOT, FRANCIS PERRY. The Haunted Pajamas. Bobbs-Merrill, (1911). 1st ed. VG (cl sl soiled). *Certo.* $30/£19

ELLIOT, HUGH S. R. and A. G. THACKER. Beasts and Men. London, 1909. Frontis port. (Feps browned.) Gilt illus upper bd, spine. *Edwards.* $75/£48

ELLIOT, JONATHAN. The Debates, Resolutions, and Other Proceedings, in Convention, on the Adoption of the Federal Constitution. Washington: The Editor, 1827-30. 1st ed. 4 vols. (Foxing, soil, sl stains.) Contemp calf (rubbed). Howes E98. *Oinonen*.* $400/£256

ELLIOT, ROBERT HENRY. Sclero-Corneal Trephining in the Operative Treatment of Glaucoma. NY: Hoeber, 1913. 1st Amer ed. (New eps.) *Goodrich.* $95/£61

ELLIOTT, CHARLES WYLLYS. Mysteries; or, Glimpses of the Supernatural.... NY: Harper, 1852. 1st ed. vi,(4),(11)-273,(1),(14)pp. (Lt foxing, few corners creased), o/w Very Nice. *Reese.* $85/£54

ELLIOTT, GRACE DALRYMPLE. Journal of My Life During the French Revolution. London, 1859. 1st ed. 206pp; 52 plts. Teg. Gilt-dec full grn leather. (Sl scuffed), else Nice. *King.* $300/£192

ELLIOTT, HENRY W. Report on the Seal Islands of Alaska. (Washington: GPO, 1884.) 188pp. Mod cl. *Lefkowicz.* $150/£96

ELLIOTT, JOHN MALSBURY KIRBY. Fifty Years' Fox-Hunting. London, 1900. 1st ed. (Ink inscrip.) Pict cl (dknd, spine ends chipped). *King.* $45/£29

ELLIOTT, ORRIN L. Stanford University. The First Twenty-Five Years. Stanford Univ, (1937). 1st ed. Frontis port. Grn cl, gilt lettering. Fine. *Argonaut.* $60/£38

ELLIOTT, RICHARD SMITH. Notes Taken in Sixty Years. St. Louis: R.P. Studley, 1883. Frontis port, (4),336pp. Grn cl, gilt. VG+. Howes E111. *Bohling.* $200/£128

ELLIOTT, T. J. (trans). A Medieval Bestiary. Boston: Godine, 1971. One of 1000 numbered. 4to. (56)pp; 14 wood engrs by Gillian Tyler. Cream cl-backed red cl. Internally Fine in pict dj (spine dknd, sm hole, top edge sl worn) in gray paper-cvrd slipcase (soiled, rubbed, bumped, chipped). *Blue Mountain.* $45/£29

ELLIS, ARTHUR ERSKINE. British Snails. Oxford: Clarendon, 1926. 1st ed. 14 color plts. VG. *Hollett.* $47/£30

ELLIS, C. and M. W. SWANEY. Soilless Growth of Plants. NY, 1947. 2nd ed. x,227pp; 3 color plts. Good. *Henly.* $23/£15

ELLIS, GEORGE. Bell Ranch as I Knew It. Kansas City: Lowell Press, (1973). 1st ed. Color frontis, 4 dbl-pg illus. Dk red cl, gilt lettering. (Lt spotting cvrs), else Fine in dj (sl worn, 2 sm tears). *Argonaut.* $75/£48

ELLIS, GEORGE. Modern Practical Joinery. Vol 2: Constructional Joinery. Batsford, 1921. 4th ed. Cl-backed bds. Generally Good+ (worn). *Whittle.* $39/£25

ELLIS, H. Elgin and Phigaleian Marbles. London, 1846. 2 vols. 249; viii,271pp. Partially unopened. Blind-emb cl (sl chipped, lt sunned; bkpl), gilt. *Edwards.* $47/£30

ELLIS, HAMILTON. Some Classic Locomotives. 1949. 1st ed. Dj (chipped, creased). *Edwards.* $31/£20

ELLIS, HAVELOCK. The Criminal. London: Walter Scott, 1890. 1st ed. viii,337,(7)pp; 16 plts. Ptd pebbled mauve cl (spine faded). VG. *Gach.* $100/£64

ELLIS, HAVELOCK. The Criminal. London, 1895. 2nd ed. viii,337pp + (xx) ads. (Eps sl spotted, margins lt browned; edges, joints sl rubbed.) *Edwards.* $23/£15

ELLIS, HAVELOCK. Kanga Creek. London: Golden Cockerel, 1922. 1st ed. One of 1375 ptd. Uncut, partly unopened. Buckram-backed bds, paper label. VG in ptd dj (sl soiled). *Cox.* $70/£45

ELLIS, HAVELOCK. Kanga Creek. London: Golden Cockerel, 1922. 1st ed. One of 1375. Uncut. Yellow cl-backed grn bds (edges sl faded, eps spotted). Dj (spine faded, panel torn). *Hollett.* $148/£95

ELLIS, HAVELOCK. The New Spirit. London: George Bell, 1890. 1st bk. (Sm name; spine sl worn, sm spot fr bd), else NF. *Between The Covers.* $250/£160

ELLIS, JOSEPH HENRY H. Sam Houston and Related Spiritual Forces. Houston: Concord, 1945. Unopened. VG + . *Bohling.* $28/£18

ELLIS, LEONARD BOLLES. History of New Bedford and Its Vicinity 1602-1892. Syracuse, 1892. 1st ed. 731,(5),175pp; 3 maps, 65 plts. Aeg. Orig 1/2 roan (spine sl dried, brittle). Howes E120. *Lefkowicz.* $250/£160

ELLIS, RICHARD N. General Pope and U.S. Indian Policy. Albuquerque: Univ of NM, (1970). 1st ed. Fine in dj (lt soiled). *Argonaut.* $40/£26

ELLIS, S. M. Wilkie Collins, Le Fanu and Others. London: Constable, 1931. Color frontis, 12 plts. Blue cl (sl bumped). *Maggs.* $34/£22

ELLIS, WILLIAM. Polynesian Researches, During a Residence of Nearly Six Years in the South Sea Islands. London: Fisher, Son, & Jackson, 1829. 1st ed. 2 vols. xvi,536pp (1st sig detached, sl aged, foxed, fr gutter sl wormed); viii,576pp (gutter stains); 2 maps vol 1, 8 engr ports/plts. Recent mismatched grn/maroon cl (drab, frayed, spotted), handwritten later paper spine labels. *Baltimore*.* $225/£144

ELLIS, WILLIAM. A Treatise on the Nature, Symptoms, Causes, and Treatment of Insanity.... London, 1838. 1st ed. Mod bds, leather label. VG. *Argosy.* $400/£256

ELLIS, WILLIAM. A Treatise on the Nature, Symptoms, Causes, and Treatment of Insanity.... London: Samuel Holdsworth, 1838. 1st ed. viii,344pp + inserted pub's cat. Unopened. Emb grn cl (expertly rebacked, corners shelfworn; lacks fldg frontis litho, eps lt dampstained). *Gach.* $475/£304

ELLISON, BERARD C. H.R.H. The Prince of Wales's Sport in India.... London, 1925. 1st ed. (Hinges loose, cvrs well worn, soiled.) *King.* $50/£32

ELLISON, HARLAN (ed). Dangerous Visions. NY: Doubleday, 1967. Signed, inscribed on mtd hotel stationery. (Lt worn.) Dj (lt worn, chipped). *Swann*.* $80/£51

ELLISON, HARLAN (ed). Dangerous Visions. NY: Doubleday, 1967. Signed. (Lt worn.) Dj (sl edgeworn). *Swann*.* $149/£96

ELLISON, HARLAN. Alone Against Tomorrow. NY: Macmillan, (1971). 1st ed. (Sm crease pg corner), else Fine in dj. *Between The Covers.* $45/£29

ELLISON, HARLAN. Angry Candy. Easton, (1988). Signed, ltd ed. As New in full dec leather. *Certo.* $100/£64

ELLISON, HARLAN. Angry Candy. Boston: Houghton Mifflin, 1988. 1st ed. Fine in dj. *Mordida.* $65/£42

ELLISON, HARLAN. Deathbird Stories. Harper & Row, 1975. 1st ed. Fine in Fine dj. *Certo.* $50/£32

ELLISON, HARLAN. Harlan Ellison's Watching. L.A.: Underwood Miller, 1989. 1st ed. One of 600 numbered, signed. Dj, slipcase. *Swann*.* $92/£59

ELLISON, HARLAN. The Man with Nine Lives [and] A Touch of Infinity. NY: Ace, 1960. 1st ed. 2 vols in 1. VF in wrappers. *Swann*.* $28/£18

ELLISON, HARLAN. Strange Wine. Harper & Row, 1978. Rev copy w/slip laid in. Fine in Fine dj. *Certo.* $50/£32

ELLISON, RALPH. Invisible Man. NY: Random House, (1952). 1st ed. (Spine lettering rubbed), else NF in VG dj (extrems lt rubbed, loss at crown). *Between The Covers.* $650/£417

ELLISON, RALPH. Invisible Man. NY: Random House, 1952. 1st ed. NF in VG + dj (rubbed, edgeworn, short edgetears). *Lame Duck.* $750/£481

ELLISON, RALPH. Shadow and Act. NY: Random House, (1964). 1st ed. Fine in NF dj (sm tear, sl rubbed). *Between The Covers.* $85/£54

ELLMS, CHARLES (comp). The Pirates Own Book, Or Authentic Narratives of the Lives...of the Most Celebrated Sea Robbers.... Portland: Sanborn & Carter, (ca 1837). 432pp (pub w/o frontis). Orig cl; gilt skull & crossbones on spine. Decent (cvrs lt worn; foxing). Howes E126. *Lefkowicz.* $275/£176

ELLMS, CHARLES (comp). The Pirates Own Book, or Authentic Narratives.... Salem, MA: Marine Research Soc, 1924. Facs ed. Black cl. *Appelfeld.* $85/£54

ELLMS, CHARLES (comp). The Pirates Own Book.... Salem, 1924. Facs of orig 1837 ed. Marine Research Soc Pub 4. Black cl; skull & crossbones on spine. NF. *Lefkowicz.* $125/£80

ELLROY, JAMES. The Black Dahlia. NY: Mysterious, 1987. 1st ed. VF in dj. *Mordida.* $75/£48

ELLROY, JAMES. Blood on the Moon. NY: Mysterious Press, 1984. 1st ed. Fine in dj (short closed tears). *Mordida.* $45/£29

ELLROY, JAMES. Brown's Requiem. NY: Avon, 1981. 1st ed, 1st bk. Pb orig. NF in wrappers. *Janus.* $45/£29

ELLROY, JAMES. Brown's Requiem. NY: Avon, 1981. 1st ed. Inscribed. Pb orig. VF in wrappers. *Mordida.* $150/£96

ELLROY, JAMES. Silent Terror. L.A.: Blood & Guts, 1986. #326/350 numbered, signed. Fine (sl shelfworn) in Fine dj (sl bump). *Metropolitan*.* $34/£22

ELLSBERG, EDWARD. Hell on Ice—The Saga of the Jeannette. NY: Dodd, Mead, 1938. 1st ed. VG in dj (edgeworn). *Perier.* $40/£26

ELLWANGER, H. B. The Rose. NY, 1882. 1st ed. 293pp. Grn blind-stamped cl, gilt. (Crayon mks 2 back pp, ink underlining 1 pg; edgewear), else Good. *Price.* $49/£31

ELLWOOD, T. The Book of the Settlement of Iceland. Kendal: T. Wilson, 1898. 1st ed. xxxi,245,(ii),4(subs)pp; pict tp, fldg map loosely inserted. VG. *Hollett.* $218/£140

ELMER, ROBERT P. Archery. Phila: Penn, (1939). Rev ed. White-lettered navy cl, gold-stamped medallion in center. VF in dj. *House.* $85/£54

ELMER, ROBERT P. Target Archery. NY: Knopf, 1946. 1st ed thus. Blind-stamped red cl, gilt. Fine in Fine pict dj. *Biscotti.* $55/£35

ELMES, JAMES. Memoirs of the Life and Works of Sir Christopher Wren.... London: Priestly & Weale, 1823. Engr frontis, xxxvi,532,147pp; 12 engr plts. Uncut. Later 1/2 linen, marbled bds. (Text foxing, browning), o/w Clean. *Goodrich.* $395/£253

ELMES, JAMES. Sir Christopher Wren and His Times. London: Chapman Hall, 1852. Port, xix,436pp. Sound. *Ars Artis.* $55/£35

ELSEN, ALBERT. Paul Jenkins. NY: Abrams, (1975). 1st ed. 56 tipped-in color plts. Beige cl. Good in illus dj. *Karmiole.* $85/£54

ELSENSOHN, M. ALFREDA. Pioneer Days in Idaho County. Caldwell: Caxton. 1947, 1951. 1st ed. 2 vols. (Ink name), else VG in dj (edge torn). *Perier.* $135/£87

ELSON, HENRY W. The Civil War Through the Camera. Springfield, MA: Patriot, 1912. 16 parts, complete. Each w/color frontis. Wraps (lt soil, chips). *Waverly*.* $71/£46

ELSON, ROBERT. Quack! The Portrait of an Experimentalist. Small & Maynard, (1925). 1st US ed. NF in dj. *Certo.* $40/£26

ELTON, C. Voles, Mice and Lemmings. London: OUP, 1942. 1st ed. 64 tables, 22 maps. VG. *Mikesh.* $45/£29

ELTON, CHARLES I. The Career of Columbus. London, 1892. 1st ed. Author's presentation copy. Fldg frontis map, xii,307pp + (xvi)pp pub's ads. Unopened. Newspaper cutting affixed to 1/2 title verso. (Spine sl chipped, joints sl rubbed.) *Edwards.* $39/£25

ELVILLE, E. M. English and Irish Cut Glass 1750-1950. Country Life, 1953. 1st ed. Dj (sl worn, torn, some loss). *Edwards.* $31/£20

ELWELL, NEWTON W. (comp). The Architecture, Furniture and Interiors of Maryland and Virginia During the Eighteenth Century. Boston: Geo. H. Polley, 1897. 1st ed. 63 loose collotype plts (ink stamps), laid in cl portfolio. (Few margins sl dusty, portfolio lacks cl ties), o/w VG. *Cahan.* $150/£96

ELWELL, NEWTON W. (comp). Colonial Furniture and Interiors. Boston: Geo. H. Polley, 1896. 1st ed. Folio. Laid-in orig platinum photo, 66 loose collotype plts (ink lib stamps). Laid in cl portfolio (lacks some ties). VG (few edges worn). *Cahan.* $150/£96

ELWES, HENRY JOHN. Memoirs of Travel, Sport, and Natural History. Edward G. Hawke (ed). London, 1930. 1st ed. Presentation from Ethel Elwes. Frontis port. Teg. (Sl rubbed, sl soiled, spine sl faded.) *Edwards.* $70/£45

ELWIN, MALCOLM. The Life of Llewelyn Powys. London: John Lane, (1946). 1st ed. Port. (Sl dusty), else VG in dj. *Reese.* $25/£16

ELY, ALFRED (comp). North American Big Game. NY: Scribner, 1939. (Shelfworn.) *Oinonen*.* $130/£83

ELY, ALFRED (comp). North American Big Game. NY: Scribner, 1939. (Sl worn.) Dj (chipped, frayed). *Oinonen*.* $250/£160

ELY, ALFRED (comp). North American Big Game. NY: Scribner, 1939. (Sl worn.) Dj (chipped, frayed). *Oinonen*.* $325/£208

ELY, ALFRED et al (comps). North American Big Game. NY: Scribner, 1939. 1st ed. Gilt. VG+ (pencil sig, date, dwg 1st blank pg). *Backman.* $350/£224

ELY, SIMS. The Lost Dutchman Mine. NY: William Morrow, (1957). Dj (lt worn). *Dawson.* $25/£16

EMERSON, EARL W. Black Hearts and Slow Dancing. NY: William Morrow, 1988. 1st ed. VF in dj. *Mordida.* $40/£26

EMERSON, EDWARD W. The Life and Letters of Charles Russell Lowell.... Boston, 1907. 1st ed. Inscribed. (Cvr sl worn), o/w Fine. *Pratt.* $75/£48

EMERSON, ELLEN RUSSELL. Masks, Heads, and Faces. Boston/NY, 1891. xxvi,312pp. Teg. (Upper hinge cracked; cl soiled.) *Edwards.* $62/£40

EMERSON, N. Unwritten Literature of Hawaii. BAE Bulletin 38. GPO, 1909. 14 plts. Good (cracked at p161). *Scribe's Perch*.* $22/£14

EMERSON, RALPH WALDO (ed). Parnassus. Boston: James R. Osgood, 1875. 2nd ed. Grn cl, gilt. Fine. BAL 5269. *Macdonnell.* $60/£38

EMERSON, RALPH WALDO. Compensation. East Aurora, NY: Roycrofters, 1904. 1st ed thus. Limp suede leather. NF. BAL 5467. *Antic Hay.* $25/£16

EMERSON, RALPH WALDO. English Traits. Boston: Phillips, Sampson, 1856. 1st ed, 1st ptg. Black cl, gilt. (Spine ends frayed), else Clean. BAL 5226. *Macdonnell.* $100/£64

EMERSON, RALPH WALDO. English Traits. Boston: Phillips, Sampson, 1856. 1st ed, 1st ptg. Black cl, gilt. Fine (early inscrip) in 1/2 morocco slipcase (sl rubbed) w/inner cl wrapper. BAL 5226. *Macdonnell.* $200/£128

EMERSON, RALPH WALDO. Essays. London: James Fraser, 1841. 1st Eng ed. Orig dk grn cl (crudely re-backed). BAL 5338. *Macdonnell.* $75/£48

EMERSON, RALPH WALDO. Essays. Hammersmith: Doves, 1906. Ltd to 300. Full vellum, spine gilt. (Bkpl, ink name fep), o/w Fine. *Truepenny.* $475/£304

EMERSON, RALPH WALDO. Essays.... Hammersmith, 1906. One of 300. Limp vellum. Cl slipcase. *Swann*.* $517/£331

EMERSON, RALPH WALDO. Essays: Second Series. Boston: James Munroe, 1844. 1st ed, 1st ptg, 1st binding state. Orig olive grey-grn cl, gilt. Attractive (cvr spots, faded, spine tips worn). BAL 5198. *Macdonnell.* $400/£256

EMERSON, RALPH WALDO. Fortune of the Republic. Boston: Houghton, Osgood, 1878. 1st ed. One of 504 bound in cl. Dk brn cl, gilt. NF. BAL 5278. *Macdonnell.* $165/£106

EMERSON, RALPH WALDO. Journals 1820-1876. Cambridge: Riverside, 1909-1914. #455/600. 10 vols. Brn cl (corners sl worn; bkpls in 9), paper labels (chipped). VG set. BAL 5318. *Glenn.* $600/£385

EMERSON, RALPH WALDO. Letters and Social Aims. Boston: James R. Osgood, 1876. 1st ed, 3rd ptg. Grn cl, gilt. NF. BAL 5272. *Macdonnell.* $50/£32

EMERSON, RALPH WALDO. Letters and Social Aims. Boston: James R. Osgood, 1876. 1st ed, 1st ptg. One of 5000. Grn cl, gilt. Fine. BAL 5272. *Macdonnell.* $75/£48

EMERSON, RALPH WALDO. Letters and Social Aims. Boston: James R. Osgood, 1876. 1st ed. 314pp. Chocolate brn eps. Grn 'C' cl over bds, beveled edges. (Lt wear, extrems sl rubbed), else NF. BAL 5272. *Turtle Island.* $150/£96

EMERSON, RALPH WALDO. Letters of Ralph Waldo Emerson. Ralph L. Lusk (ed). NY: Columbia Univ, 1939. 6 vols. VG. *New Hampshire*. $50/£32

EMERSON, RALPH WALDO. May-Day and Other Pieces. Boston: Ticknor & Fields, 1867. 1st ed. One of 2000 ptd. Terra cotta cl, gilt. (Chip at crown), else Fine. BAL 5250. *Macdonnell.* $100/£64

EMERSON, RALPH WALDO. May-Day and Other Pieces. London: George Routledge, 1867. 1st Eng ed. Teg. Grn cl, gilt. (Inner hinge paper cracked), else Attractive. BAL 5374. *Macdonnell.* $125/£80

EMERSON, RALPH WALDO. Miscellanies. Boston: Phillips, Sampson, 1856. 1st ed this title. One of 500 ptd. Black cl, gilt. NF. BAL 5367. *Macdonnell.* $150/£96

EMERSON, RALPH WALDO. An Oration Delivered Before the Phi Beta Kappa Society, at Cambridge, August 31, 1837. Boston, 1837. 1st ed. Later wrappers. (Lacks final blank leaf.) Cl fldg case. BAL 5183. *Swann*.* $230/£147

EMERSON, RALPH WALDO. The Riverside Edition of the Collected Works. Boston: Houghton Mifflin, 1884. 11 vols. Port. Uniform gilt blue cl. Nice set (few spine crowns rubbed). *Reese.* $125/£80

EMERSON, RALPH WALDO. Society and Solitude. Boston: Fields, Osgood, 1870. 1st ed, 1st ptg. One of 1500. Grn cl, gilt. Fine. BAL 5260. *Macdonnell.* $60/£38

EMERSON, RALPH WALDO. Success, Greatness, Immortality. Boston: James R. Osgood, 1877. 1st ed. Grn cl blocked in black/gold (spine ends rubbed, sl loss). BAL 5397. *Swann*.* $92/£59

EMERSON, RALPH WALDO. Timely Extracts from the Writings. Boston: Thomas Todd, 1921. 1st ed thus. Blue bds, label. Fine. *Macdonnell.* $15/£10

EMERSON, RALPH WALDO. Works. Boston, 1891-94. Riverside ed. 12 vols. 8vo. Frontis port. Contemp 1/2 tan calf, gilt, spines in 6 compartments, crimson morocco lettering pieces in 2. *Swann*.* $920/£590

EMERSON, WILLIAM and GEORGES GROMORT. Old Bridges of France.... NY: Amer Inst of Architects, 1925. 24 VF tipped-in repros. (Gatherings, plts loose in cl portfolio; sl worn, rear cvr detached.) *New Hampshire**. $60/£38

EMERY, JOHN. European Spoons Before 1700. London: John Donald, 1976. 1st ed. VG in dj. *Hollett*. $55/£35

EMERY, R. G. Relief Pitcher. MacRae Smith, 1953. 1st ed. VG in VG dj. *Plapinger*. $45/£29

EMETT, MARY. Anthony and Antimacassar. London: Faber, n.d. (c 1955). 1st ed. Rowland Emett (illus). 10 x 7 1/2. 32pp. Pict bds. Good in dj (worn). *Cattermole*. $20/£13

EMMETT, CHRIS. Fort Union and the Winning of the Southwest. Norman: Univ of OK, 1965. 1st ed. 7 maps. Fine in pict dj (chipped). *Argonaut*. $60/£38

EMMITT, ROBERT. The Last War Trail. Norman, (1954). 1st ed. VG+ in VG+ dj. *Pratt*. $30/£19

EMMITT, ROBERT. The Last War Trail. Norman: Univ of OK, 1954. Good in dj (sl worn). *Dumont*. $35/£22

EMMONS, EARL H. Mavericks. NY: Oswald, 1924. 1st ed. Cl-backed bds, paper labels. *Petrilla*. $30/£19

EMMONS, W. Gold Deposits of the World. NY: McGraw-Hill, c 1937. 1st ed, 3rd imp. VG. *Blake*. $150/£96

EMORY, W. H. Notes of a Military Reconnoissance, from Fort Leavenworth.... Washington: Wendell & Van Benthuysen, 1848. 2 fldg maps (sm repaired tear 1 map), 64 plts, incl 3 plans. (Foxing; lacks 1 fldg map.) Recent cl. Howes E145. *Sadlon*. $325/£208

EMORY, WILLIAM H. Lieutenant Emory Reports. Albuquerque: Univ of NM, 1951. Rpt. Facs of orig tp, 6 maps. Cl-backed dec bds, gilt. Fine in pict dj. *Pacific**. $63/£40

EMORY, WILLIAM H. Report on the United States and Mexican Boundary Survey. Austin: TX State Hist Assoc, (1987). Rpt. One of 750. 3 vols. 37 full color engrs, 4 fldg maps. Blue/tan cl. Fine in slipcase. *Bohling*. $175/£112

EMORY, WILLIAM H. Report on the United States and Mexican Boundary Survey. Vol I, Parts 1 and 2. Washington, 1857. 2 fldg maps, 12 color plts. Black emb cl. (Hinges broken.) *Yudkin**. $400/£256

EMORY, WILLIAM H. Report on the United States and Mexican Boundary Survey....Volume II (separate plt vol only). Washington, 1859. 50 color, 95 b/w plts. Old calf, black cl. (Some plts clipped, some sl foxed; worn, chipped, splits.) *Baltimore**. $90/£58

EMPSON, WILLIAM. Collected Poems. NY: Harcourt, Brace, (1949). 1st ed. Fine in NF dj (lt soiled). *Antic Hay*. $25/£16

EMPSON, WILLIAM. Milton's God. New Directions, (1961). 1st ed. VG in dj. *Argosy*. $45/£29

EMPSON, WILLIAM. Poems. London: Chatto, 1935. 1st Eng ed. Good (inscrip). *Clearwater*. $47/£30

EMPSON, WILLIAM. Seven Types of Ambiguity. Chatto, 1930. 1st ed. (Cl sl dknd, mkd), o/w VG. *Poetry Bookshop*. $44/£28

EMPSON, WILLIAM. Seven Types of Ambiguity. London, 1930. 1st ed. Dj (frayed, soiled). *Typographeum*. $85/£54

Encyclopaedia Britannica. Edinburgh: Archibald Constable, 1815. 5th ed. 20 vols. 4to. (Lt browning, ex-libris, few joints sl tender.) Marbled eps, edges. Full blind-tooled calf (corners, spines few vols sl rubbed), gilt. Attractive. *Edwards*. $1,872/£1,200

Encyclopedia Britannica...11th Edition. 1910. Handy Volume Issue. 29 vols. Full leather (some spine ends chipped, torn, all worn). VG. *New Hampshire**. $75/£48

ENDICOTT, WENDELL. Adventures in Alaska and Along the Trail. NY: Frederick A. Stokes, 1928. Grn cl. (Spine sl dknd), else Fine. *Parmer*. $125/£80

ENDO, SHUSAKU. The Sea and Poison. Michael Gallagher (trans). NY: Taplinger, 1980. 1st Amer ed. Fine in Fine dj. *Revere*. $30/£19

ENDO, SHUSAKU. Silence. Peter Owen, 1976. 1st UK ed. Fine in VG dj. *Williams*. $39/£25

ENDO, SHUSAKU. Volcano. London: Peter Owen, (1978). 1st Eng ed. Fine in NF dj. *Antic Hay*. $25/£16

ENDORE, GUY. Detour at Night. NY: S&S, 1959. 1st Amer ed. (Pp dknd, bottom edges ink-mkd), o/w VG in dj (chip, sm closed tear fr panel). *Mordida*. $45/£29

ENFIELD, J. E. Man from Packsaddle. Hollywood: House-Warven, 1951. 1st ed. VG in dj (sl worn, spine faded). *Lien*. $75/£48

ENGASS, ROBERT. The Paintings of Baciccio. University Park, 1964. Good in dj. *Washton*. $500/£321

ENGEL, CARL. The Music of the Most Ancient Nations.... London: William Reeves Bookseller, (1929). Rpt of 1864 ed. Grn cl, gilt. NF. *Blue Mountain*. $45/£29

ENGEL, CLAIRE ELAINE. A History of Mountaineering in the Alps. NY, 1950. 1st Amer ed. VG in dj (chipped). *King*. $35/£22

ENGEL, H. The Japanese House. Rutland, 1946. 167 plts. Sound. *Ars Artis*. $70/£45

ENGELBACH, R. The Problem of the Obelisks.... London: T. Fisher Unwin, (1923). (Inscrip.) Emb pict cl. *Archaeologia*. $85/£54

ENGELBACH, WILLIAM. Endocrine Medicine. Springfield, 1932. 4 vols. VG. *Argosy*. $125/£80

ENGELHARDT, GEORGE W. Philadelphia, PA: The Book of Its Bourse and Co-operating Public Bodies. 1898-99. (Phila, 1899.) (Sl internal dampstaining.) Aeg. Morocco (scuffed, sl soiled), gilt. *Freeman**. $150/£96

ENGELHARDT, ZEPHYRIN. The Franciscans in California. Harbor Springs, 1897. 1st ed. Frontis, 516pp. VG. Howes E153. *Turpen*. $195/£125

ENGELHARDT, ZEPHYRIN. The Franciscans in California. Harbor Springs, MI: Holy Childhood Indian School, 1897. 1st ed. (6),xvi,518pp; map. Textured black cl (spine faded). Howes E153. *Karmiole*. $150/£96

ENGELHARDT, ZEPHYRIN. Mission Nuestra Senora De La Soledad. Santa Barbara, 1929. 1st ed. Pb. 3 vols in 1. Frontis, map, port. VG. *Turpen*. $55/£35

ENGELHARDT, ZEPHYRIN. Mission San Carlos Borromeo (Carmelo), Father of Missions. Santa Barbara, 1934. 1st ed. Pb. Fine. *Turpen*. $35/£22

ENGELHARDT, ZEPHYRIN. The Missions and Missionaries of California. SF: James H. Barry, 1908-1916. 1st ed. 5 vols. Red cl, gilt spines. (Bkpls, letter F stamped fep each vol; some gilt faded), o/w VG. Howes E154. *Pacific**. $345/£221

ENGELHARDT, ZEPHYRIN. San Diego Mission. SF, 1920. 1st ed. Fine. *Turpen*. $60/£38

ENGELHARDT, ZEPHYRIN. San Francisco, or Mission Dolores. Chicago: Franciscan Herald, 1924. 1st ed. Fldg plan. Pict cl stamped in gilt. (Ink inscrip), else Fine. *Argonaut*. $45/£29

ENGINEERING RESEARCH ASSOCIATES. High-Speed Computing Devices. NY: McGraw-Hill, 1950. 1st ed, 5th ptg. VG (sig clipped from tp). *Glaser*. $150/£96

England and America. (By Edward G. Wakefield.) NY, 1834. (2),7,17-376pp. Early cl. (Extrems rubbed), else VG. Howes W18. *Reese*. $150/£96

England's Black Tribunal, Containing the Complete Tryal of King Charles the First.... London: Rivington, 1737. 6th ed. Engr port. Mod cl. VG. *Argosy.* $100/£64

England's Black Tribunal. London: J. Wilford, 1720. 5th ed. Mod 3/4 speckled calf. *Boswell.* $350/£224

ENGLAND, GEORGE A. Vikings of the Ice. NY: Doubleday Page, 1924. VG (sl wear). *High Latitude.* $35/£22

ENGLAND, JOHN. The Works of the Rt. Reverend John England...First Bishop of Charleston. Cleveland, 1908. 7 vols. Sound (ex-lib). *Ginsberg.* $375/£240

ENGLAND, ROBERT. The Baroque Ceiling Paintings in the Churches of Rome 1600-1750. Hildesheim, 1979. Good in wraps. *Washton.* $40/£26

ENGLEBERT, OMER. The Last of the Conquistadors. NY, 1956. 1st ed. VG+ in VG+ dj. *Turpen.* $35/£22

ENGLEBERT, OMER. The Last of the Conquistadors: Junipero Serra (1713-1784). Katherine Woods (trans). NY: Harcourt, Brace, (1956). 1st Amer ed. VG in dj. *Lien.* $35/£22

ENGLEBERT, OMER. The Last of the Conquistadors: Junipero Serra (1713-1784). NY: HBJ, (1956). 1st ed. Fine in dj (sl chipped). *Argonaut.* $35/£22

English Bards and Scotch Reviewers. (By Lord Byron.) London: James Cawthorn, (1809). 1st ed, w/half-title. Later polished grn calf by Zaehnsdorf, red morocco spine label. (Name.) *Swann*.* $287/£184

English Dance of Death. London: J. Diggens, 1815-16. 1st ed. 2 vols. Hand-colored aquatint frontispieces, 74 plts (sl offset, lt spotted) by Thomas Rowlandson. Teg. Contemp calf (spines sl rubbed, stained, upper joints vol 1 split; bkpl; gilt, contrasting morocco lettering pieces. *Christie's*.* $526/£337

English Dance of Death. (By William Combe.) London: Ackermann, 1815-1816. 1st ed in bk form. 2 vols. 8vo. 74 hand-colored aquatint plts by Thomas Rowlandson, guards. Polished crimson calf, gilt extra, dbl grn morocco labels. (Ex-libris, shelf labels, bkpl, sm stamps.) *Swann*.* $1,380/£885

English Landscape Scenery. London: Bohn, 1855. Complete w/40 guarded landscapes in mezzotint after orig designs by Constable. (Prelims, outer margins some plts lt soiled.) Contemp 1/2 red morocco, marbled bds (scuffed, edgeworn.) *Waverly*.* $495/£317

English Printers' Marks of the Fifteenth Century. (By F. C. Avis.) 1964. (Ex-lib, ink stamps, bkpl; text loose where stitched.) Dj. *Edwards.* $23/£15

ENGLISH, JAMES DOUGLASS. To the West in 1894. Indianapolis: IN Hist Soc, 1977. Port. VG+ in pict wraps. *Bohling.* $12/£8

Englishman in Paris. (By Albert Dresden Vandam.) London: Chapman & Hall, 1892. 6th ed. 2 vols. xvi,332; xvi,352pp. Dk grn eps; uncut. (Sl rubbed, mkd.) *Cox.* $44/£28

ENGVICK, WILLIAM. Lullabies and Night Songs. NY: Harper & Row, 1965. Maurice Sendak (illus). 9 1/2 x 13. 78pp. VG. *Cattermole.* $30/£19

ENNEMOSER, JOSEPH. The History of Magic. William Howitt (trans). London: Henry G. Bohn, 1854. 2 vols. Red cl over bds (worn). VG. *Old London.* $85/£54

ENNEMOSER, JOSEPH. The History of Magic. NY: University Books, 1970. 2 vols. Fine in VG djs. *Middle Earth.* $85/£54

ENOCK, C. REGINALD. Farthest West Life and Travel in the United States. NY, 1910. Frontis, color fldg map. VG. *Reese.* $75/£48

ENOS, CHRIS. Gar-Baj. Rochester: Visual Studies Workshop, 1982. 1st ed. Fine in spiral-bound stiff wrappers in blind-emb paper box (sl worn). *Cahan.* $65/£42

Enquire Within Upon Everything. London: Houlston, n.d. 825th thousand. x,(iv),412,(iv)pp. Orig cl, gilt. (Upper joint tender, sl worn.) *Hollett.* $47/£30

ENRIGHT, ELIZABETH. Christmas Tree for Lydia. NY: Rinehart, 1951. 1st ed. Sm 16mo. Pict paper-cvrd bds. NF in NF dj (spine toned). *Book Adoption.* $60/£38

ENRIGHT, ELIZABETH. Tatsinda. NY: HBJ, 1963. 1st ed. Irene Haas (illus). 6 3/4 x 8 1/2. 80pp. Fine in dj. *Cattermole.* $35/£22

ENSIGN and THAYER. Traveller's Guide Through the State of Ohio, Michigan, Indiana, Illinois, Missouri, Iowa and Wisconsin.... NY: Ensign, 1855. 33,(2)pp; lg fldg color map. Gilt-stamped pict leather (spine expertly mended). Howes E165. *Ginsberg.* $500/£321

ENTWISLE, E. A. French Scenic Wallpapers 1800-1860. Leigh-on-Sea: F. Lewis, (1972). 1st ed. Fine in pub's glassine wrapper. *Hermitage.* $150/£96

ENYEART, JAMES. Bruguiere: His Photographs and His Life. NY: Knopf, 1977. 1st ed. 109 photo-plts. (Owner stamp), else Fine in dj (sm closed tear). *Cahan.* $60/£38

Eothen, or Traces of Travel Brought Home from the East. (By Alexander William Kinglake.) London: John Ollivier, 1845. 2nd ed. xi,418pp; 2 hand-colored litho plts, incl fldg frontis. Orig cl, gilt cvr vignette. (Bkpl; spine faded, corners sl worn), else NF. *Pacific*.* $87/£56

EPICURUS. The Extant Remains of the Greek Text. Cyril Bailey (trans). NY: LEC, 1947. #904/1500 numbered, signed by Bruce Rogers. Fine in pub's slipcase. *Hermitage.* $175/£112

EPICURUS. The Extant Remains of the Greek Text. Cyril Bailey (trans). NY: LEC, 1947. One of 2000 numbered, signed by Bruce Rogers. Teg. Blind-stamped full black leather, gilt spine. VG in bd slipcase. *Argosy.* $225/£144

EPSTEIN, BARBARA LESLIE. The Politics of Domesticity. Middletown, CT: Wesleyan Univ, (1981). 1st ed. Fine (name, ex-libris) in dj. *Second Life.* $25/£16

EPSTEIN, LADY. Epstein Drawings. Cleveland, (1962). 1st ed. Color frontis. VG in dj. *Argosy.* $60/£38

ERASMUS, DESIDERIUS. Moriae Encomium, An Oration Spoken by Folly in Praise of Herself. NY: LEC, 1943. #904/1500 numbered, signed by Lynd Ward (illus). Full leather. (Sl rubbed at crown, heel), else Fine in pub's slipcase (sl rubbed). *Hermitage.* $100/£64

ERB, WILLIAM. Handbook of Electrotherapeutics. NY, 1883. 1st ed. 366pp. Red tooled cl (worn; inner fr hinge cracked). Good. *Doctor's Library.* $125/£80

ERBEN, WALTER. Joan Miro. NY: Braziller, 1959. 1st US ed. 8 tipped-in color plts. Full dec cl. Good+ in dj (tape-repaired, price-clipped). *Scribe's Perch*.* $34/£22

ERDMAN, LOULA GRACE. Save Weeping for the Night. Dodd, Mead, (1975). 1st ed. Fine in Fine dj. *Authors Of West.* $20/£13

ERDRICH, LOUISE. Love Medicine. NY: Holt, Rinehart & Winston, (1984). 1st ed. Fine in Fine dj. *Bernard.* $150/£96

ERDRICH, LOUISE. Snares. Middlebury, VT: Friends of the Library, 1987. 1st ed. One of 350. Fine in ptd wrappers. *Turtle Island.* $200/£128

ERICKSON, STEVE. Rubicon Beach. NY: Poseidon Press, (1986). 1st ed. Fine in dj (extrems sl dknd). *Between The Covers.* $45/£29

ERIKSON, ERIK HOMBURGER. Life History and the Historical Moment. NY: W.W. Norton, (1975). 1st ed. Signed. Black cl. VG in dj. *Gach.* $40/£26

ERNST, MORRIS L. and DAVID LOTH. American Sexual Behavior and the Kinsey Report. NY, 1948. 1st ed. Red cl (sl worn). VG. *Doctor's Library.* $40/£26

EROFEEV, VENEDIKT. Moscow to the End of the Line. NY: Taplinger, 1980. 1st US ed. (Ink price fep), else Fine in dj. *Lame Duck.* $20/£13

ERRINGTON, PAUL L. Muskrats and Marsh Management. Harrisburg: Stackpole/Wildlife Mgmt Inst, 1961. 1st ed. Yellow buckram. Fine in Fine pict dj. *Biscotti.* $45/£29

ERSKINE, GLADYS SHAW. Broncho Charlie. NY: Crowell, (1934). 2nd ed. Signed. 21 plts incl frontis, plus 3 maps (1 fldg); 4 photos (faded) tipped in. (Spine stained, sl musty, cocked, sl foxing.) Howes E172. *Waverly*.* $66/£42

ERSKINE, GLADYS SHAW. Broncho Charlie. London, 1935. 1st Eng ed. (Pencil sig; cvrs dull, backstrip dknd.) Text VG. Howes E171. *Baade.* $30/£19

ERSKINE, JOHN. Adam and Eve. Bobbs-Merrill, 1927. 1st ed. Fine in dj (chipped). *Madle.* $20/£13

ERSKINE, JOHN. Books and Habits from the Lectures of Lafcadio Hearn. NY, 1921. 1st US ed in bk form. (Ink stamp tp, lower pastedown; cl spine faded, paper title label sl rubbed, sm paper label spine tail.) *Edwards.* $39/£25

ERVINE, ST. JOHN. Four Irish Plays.... Dublin: Maunsel, 1914. 1st ed. Port. Linen, bds (corners bumped), paper label (nicked). Good. *Reese.* $25/£16

ERWIN, ALLEN A. The Southwest of John H. Slaughter, 1841-1922. Glendale: Clark, 1965. 1st ed. One of 2022. Red cl, gilt-lettered spine. Fine in pict dj. *Argonaut.* $125/£80

ERWITT, ELLIOT. Photographs and Anti-Photographs. Greenwich: NYGS, 1972. 1st ed. (Owner stamp, sm split spine cl), else VG in dj. *Cahan.* $85/£54

ERWITT, ELLIOT. Photographs and Anti-Photographs. Greenwich: NYGS, 1972. NF (fep crease) in NF dj. *Smith.* $150/£96

ERWITT, ELLIOT. Recent Developments. NY: S&S, 1978. 1st ed. NF in NF dj. *Smith.* $125/£80

ESAREY, LOGAN. The Indiana Home. Bloomington: IN Univ, 1953. Ltd to 1550. 1/4 red cl, dec bds. Fine. *Truepenny.* $145/£93

ESDAILE, JAMES. Hypnosis in Medicine and Surgery. NY: Julian, (1957). Rpt. VG in dj. *Glaser.* $50/£32

ESDAILE, JAMES. Mesmerism in India, and Its Practical Application in Surgery and Medicine. Chicago, 1902. Purple gilt-tooled cl bds (soiled, lt worn). VG. *Doctor's Library.* $200/£128

ESDAILE, KATHERINE A. English Monumental Sculpture Since the Renaissance. London: SPCK, 1927. 1st ed. Frontis, 33 plts hors-texte. (Pencil notes; spine sl worn), o/w Fine. *Europa.* $28/£18

ESKEW, GARNETT L. Salt: The Fifth Element. Chicago: J.G. Ferguson, 1948. 1st ed. Fine in dj (worn, torn). *Perier.* $20/£13

ESPINOSA, J. MANUEL (ed). First Expedition of De Vargas into New Mexico. Albuquerque, 1940. 1st ed. Frontis port. Untrimmed, unopened. NF in dj (faded, chipped). *Turpen.* $195/£125

ESPY, JAMES. The Philosophy of Storms. Boston: Little, Brown, 1841. 1st ed. 552pp (foxed). Orig cl (worn). *Second Life.* $300/£192

ESQUIROL, JEAN. Mental Maladies: A Treatise on Insanity. Phila: Lea & Blanchard, 1845. 1st ed in English. 496pp + inserted ads. Mod calf-backed marbled bds, leather spine label. Attractive (sl foxing). *Gach.* $1,500/£962

Essay on the Genius and Writings of Pope. (By Joseph Warton.) London: J. Dodsley, 1782. 4th ed. 2 vols. xiv,416; 424pp. Contemp tree calf (fr hinges cracked but holding, vol 1 missing one spine label). *Karmiole.* $75/£48

Essay Upon Ways and Means of Supplying the War. (By Charles Davenant.) London: Jacob Tonson, 1695. 1st ed. 1/2 title, 160pp (browning); lg fldg table. Old calf (worn, nicely rebacked), black spine label. *Karmiole.* $450/£288

Essays on the Spirit of Legislation. Newark: W. Reid, 1800. Reissue of 1st Eng trans. 479,(1),viipp (sl toned, lt foxing, ink sigs). Old calf (shabby, bds detached). *Waverly*.* $55/£35

Estelle Doheny Collection from the Edward Laurence Doheny Memorial Library...Sold on Behalf of the Archdiocese of Los Angeles. NY: Christie, Manson & Woods, 22nd Oct, 1987-19th May, 1989. 4to. 7 vols. Prospectus inserted loose. Red cl. *Maggs.* $312/£200

ESTEP, H. COLE. How Wooden Ships Are Built. Cleveland: Penton, 1918. 1st ed. *Lefkowicz.* $95/£61

ESTES, ELEANOR. The Lollipop Princess. NY: HBJ, 1967. 1st ed. 9 1/4 x 6. 32pp. VG in dj. *Cattermole.* $20/£13

ESTES, ELEANOR. The Middle Moffat. NY: HBJ, 1942. 1st ed. Louis Slobodkin (illus). 5 1/2 x 8 1/4. 317pp. Cl, pict labels. VG. *Cattermole.* $30/£19

ESTES, GEORGE. The Rawhide Railroad. Canby, OR: Clackamas County News, 1916. 1st ed. VG. Howes E199. *Perier.* $65/£42

ESTLEMAN, LOREN D. The Glass Highway. Boston: Houghton Mifflin, 1983. 1st ed. Fine in dj. *Mordida.* $45/£29

ESTLEMAN, LOREN D. Stamping Ground. NY: Doubleday, 1980. 1st ed. Inscribed. Fine in Fine dj (sl sunned). *Metropolitan*.* $28/£18

ESTREN, MARK JAMES. A History of Underground Comics. SF: Straight Arrow, 1974. 1st ed. Pb. Fine. *Beasley.* $40/£26

ESTVAN, BELA. War Pictures from the South. NY: Appleton, 1863. 1st Amer ed. viii,352pp. VG (stamps; label chipped). Howes E203. *Agvent.* $125/£80

ESTVAN, BELA. War Pictures from the South. NY, 1963. 1st Amer ed. (Sm portion spine title worn off, 1/2-inch gouge), o/w VG. *Pratt.* $75/£48

ETCHECOPAR, R. D. and FRANCOIS HUE. The Birds of North Africa. Edinburgh/London, 1967. 1st UK ed. 27 plts. (Eps lt spotted.) Dj (sl chipped, spine lt faded). *Edwards.* $101/£65

ETCHENBASTER, PIERRE. Pierre's Book. The Game of Court Tennis. George Plimpton (ed). Barre, MA, 1971. 1st ed. Orig ptd wrappers. *Cummins.* $75/£48

ETS, MARIE HALL. Mr. T. W. Anthony Woo. NY: Viking, 1951. 1st ed. 10 3/4 x 8. 54pp. Cl spine, pict bds. Good. *Cattermole.* $45/£29

ETTLINGER, LEOPOLD D. and HELEN S. Raphael. Phaidon, 1987. 1st ed. 41 color plts. Dj. *Edwards.* $39/£25

EURIPIDES. Alcestis. London: C&W, 1930. 1st ed. #16/260 signed by Richard Aldington (trans). Cl-backed dec bds. (Spine lt faded), else Fine. *Hermitage.* $125/£80

EURIPIDES. Iphigenia in Tauris. Witter Bynner (trans). NY: Mitchell Kennerley, 1915. 1st ed. Maroon cl. NF (cvr corner dampstained) in dj (lt worn, sl dampstained). *Antic Hay.* $35/£22

EURIPIDES. The Plays.... (Newtown): Gregynog, 1931. One of 500 numbered sets. 2 vols. Cl slipcases. *Swann*.* $373/£239

European Portraits 1600-1900 in the Art Institute of Chicago. Chicago: Art Inst, 1978. Good in wraps. *Washton.* $15/£10

EUSTACE, JOHN CHETWODE. A Classical Tour Through Italy. Phila: M. Carey, 1816. 1st Amer ed. 2 vols. 10 engrs (2 fldg). Lib binding (ex-lib, rubber stamps tps). *Argosy.* $250/£160

EUSTACE, ROBERT. A Human Bacillus. London: Long, 1907. 1st ed. (Internal foxing; edgeworn, stained.) *Metropolitan**. $28/£18

EUSTIS, CELESTINE. Cooking in Old Creole Days. NY: Derrydale, 1928. 2nd ed. One of 500. Photo frontis. Partially unopened. Pict bds, cl spine w/paper label. Fine (sl rubbed). *Cummins*. $275/£176

EVANS, ALBERT S. A La California. Sketches of Life in the Golden State. SF: A.L. Bancroft, 1873. 1st ed. 379pp, 25 full-pg woodcut plts. Orig 3/4 calf, marbled bds (lt rubbed), grn leather spine labels (faded). VG. *Argonaut*. $125/£80

EVANS, C. S. Cinderella. London: Heinemann, (1919). 1st trade ed. Arthur Rackham (illus). 4to. Full color tipped-in frontis, 110pp. Fine in dj. *Captain's Bookshelf*. $600/£385

EVANS, C. S. The Sleeping Beauty. London, (1920). One of 625 numbered, signed by Arthur Rackham (illus). 4to. Tipped-in color plt. Orig 1/4 imitation vellum, gilt. *Swann**. $632/£405

EVANS, CHARLES et al. American Bibliography. Chicago/Worcester, 1903-34/1955-59. 14 vols. (Several vols need rebinding.) *Swann**. $431/£276

EVANS, CHARLES. Kangchenjunga, the Untrodden Peak. London, (1956). 1st ed. (Bumped), else VG in dj (tear). *King*. $60/£38

EVANS, CHICK, JR. Chick Evans' Golf Book. Chicago: Thos. E. Wilson, (1921). 1st ed. Gilt-lettered grn cl. (Sl rubbed), else VG. *Pacific**. $92/£59

EVANS, CLEMENT A. (ed). Confederate Military History. NY: Yoseloff, (1962). 12 vols + 4to atlas in wrappers. (Shelfwear, fore-edges stained.) *Oinonen**. $100/£64

EVANS, DONALD. Ironica. NY: Nicholas L. Brown, 1919. 1st ed. Inscribed. Ptd bds. Very Nice. *Reese*. $100/£64

EVANS, DONALD. Nine Poems from a Valetudinarium. Phila: Nicholas L. Brown, 1916. 1st ed. Paper spine label (sl dknd), o/w Very Nice. *Reese*. $85/£54

EVANS, DONALD. Sonnets from the Patagonian. NY: Claire Marie, 1914. 1st ed. Paper bds (spine extrems, corners sl chipped), ptd label. Good in orig glassine (chipped). *Reese*. $85/£54

EVANS, DONALD. Two Deaths in the Bronx. Phila: Nicholas Brown, 1916. 1st ed. Bds, paper label. (Bkpl), o/w Nice. *Reese*. $75/£48

EVANS, EDWARD. British Polar Explorers. London: Collins, 1946. 2nd ptg. 8 color plts. VG. *Parmer*. $28/£18

EVANS, EDWARD. South with Scott. London, 1921. 1st ed, 4th imp. (Sl stain fr cvr), else VG. *High Latitude*. $30/£19

EVANS, EDWARD. South with Scott. London: W. Collins Sons, 1921. 1st ed, 2nd imp. Photogravure frontis port, 2 fldg maps, dbl-pg map, fldg plan. VG (cl separated from bds few places). *High Latitude*. $50/£32

EVANS, F. GAYNOR. Stress and Strain in Bones. Springfield, 1957. Black textured cl. NF in VG dj. *Doctor's Library*. $40/£26

EVANS, F. W. Shaker, Compendium of the Origin, History, Principles.... NY: Appleton, 1859. 1st ed. 189pp, sewn. (Ex-lib, lt soil, waterstain.) *Cullen*. $100/£64

EVANS, G. G. Illustrated History of the United States Mint. Phila, 1886. 'New Revised Edition.' 162pp + ads. Dec cvr. Good (spine faded). *Scribe's Perch**. $10/£6

EVANS, GEOFFREY. The Johnnies. London, 1964. Mint cl in dj. *Maggs*. $31/£20

EVANS, GEORGE BIRD. An Affair with Grouse. Old Hemlock, 1982. One of 1000 numbered, signed by Evans and Jim Rikhoff. Gilt-stamped red leatherette (lt worn). Slipcase. *Oinonen**. $140/£90

EVANS, GEORGE BIRD. The Bird Dog Book. Clinton: Amwell, (1979). One of 1000 numbered, signed by Evans and Jim Rikhoff. Full red leatherette (lt worn). Slipcase. *Oinonen**. $190/£122

EVANS, GEORGE BIRD. Opus 10: Men Who Shot and Wrote About It. Old Hemlock, 1983. One of 990 numbered. Presentation copy. Signed, inscribed. (Lt worn.) Slipcase. *Oinonen**. $200/£128

EVANS, GEORGE BIRD. Recollections of a Shooting Guest. Clinton: Amwell, (1978). One of 1000 numbered, signed by Evans, Gordon Allen (illus), and Jim Rikhoff (preface). Gilt-stamped leatherette (lt worn). Slipcase. *Oinonen**. $300/£192

EVANS, GEORGE BIRD. The Ruffed Grouse Book. Clinton: Amwell, (1977). One of 1000 numbered, signed by Evans, Jim Rikhoff (foreword), and Donald Shoffstall (illus). (Lt worn.) Slipcase. *Oinonen**. $300/£192

EVANS, GEORGE BIRD. The Upland Gunner's Book. Clinton: Amwell, (1979). One of 1000 numbered, signed by Evans, Tom Hennessey (illus), and Jim Rikhoff. Gilt-stamped leatherette (lt worn). Slipcase. *Oinonen**. $180/£115

EVANS, GEORGE BIRD. The Upland Shooting Life. NY: Knopf, 1971. Stated 1st ed. VG + (crease fep) in VG + dj. *Backman*. $35/£22

EVANS, GEORGE BIRD. The Woodcock Book. Clinton: Amwell, (1977). One of 1000 numbered, signed by Evans, Jim Rikhoff (foreword), and Donald Shoffstall (illus). This copy stamped 'Publisher's Presentation.' (Lt worn.) Slipcase. *Oinonen**. $200/£128

EVANS, GLEN L. and T. N. CAMPBELL. Indian Baskets of the Paul T. Seashore Collection. Austin: Texas Memorial Museum, 1970. 2nd ed. Pict wrappers. *Dawson*. $20/£13

EVANS, H. M. Exhibition of First Editions of Epochal Achievements in the History of Science. Berkeley, 1934. Inscribed by Jake Zeitlin. Wrappers. *Maggs*. $31/£20

EVANS, HENRY HERMAN. A Contribution Toward a Check List of Bibliographies and Reference Material. SF: Peregrine, 1950. One of 75. Inscribed twice. Wraps. *Kane**. $35/£22

EVANS, IVOR H. N. Among Primitive Peoples in Borneo. Phila, 1922. Fldg map. (Lt browning; upper bds lt dampstained.) *Edwards*. $75/£48

EVANS, JOAN. Art in Mediaeval France 987-1498. OUP, 1948. 11 plans. Blue cl (sl faded), gilt. Fine. *Peter Taylor*. $69/£44

EVANS, JOAN. English Jewellery from the Fifth Century A.D. to 1800. London, (1921). 34 plts. Teg. Gilt-dec cl. (Ex-lib, inner hinges loose), else Good. *King*. $200/£128

EVANS, JOHN. The Ancient Stone Implements, Weapons and Ornaments of Great Britain. 1897. 2nd ed. xviii,748pp; 2 fldg plts. (Spine cl rather rubbed.) *Whitehart*. $70/£45

EVANS, JOHN. The Ancient Stone Implements, Weapons, and Ornaments of Great Britain. NY: Appleton, 1872. Blind-, gilt-dec cl (extrems sl worn). Contents VG. *New Hampshire**. $40/£26

EVANS, JOHN. Halo in Blood. Bobbs Merrill, (1946). 1st ed. VG + in VG dj. *Certo*. $135/£87

EVANS, JOHN. A History of Jewellery 1100-1870. Boston: Boston Book & Art, 1970. 2nd ed. Fine in dj. *Blake*. $125/£80

EVANS, JOHN. If You Have Tears. NY: Mystery House, 1947. 1st ed. Fine in dj (sl soiled, sunned, nicked, torn). *Metropolitan**. $69/£44

EVANS, LARRY. His Own Home Town. NY: H.K. Fly, (1917). 1st ed. VG in dj. *Turtle Island*. $45/£29

EVANS, MAX. Long John Dunn of Taos. L.A.: Western-lore, (1959). 1st ed. Fine in Fine dj (sl faded). *Unger*. $150/£96

EVANS, MAX. Long John Dunn of Taos. L.A.: Western-lore, 1959. 1st ed. Blindstamped maroon cl, gilt. VF in pict dj (spine dknd). *Argonaut*. $50/£32

EVANS, MAX. The Mountain of Gold. Norman S. Berg, 1965. 1st ed. Inscribed, signed. (Spine gilt dknd), else Fine in Nice dj (price-clipped). *Authors Of West*. $60/£38

EVANS, MAX. One-Eyed Sky. Nash, (1974). 1st separate ed. Fine in dj. *Authors Of West*. $30/£19

EVANS, OLIVER. The Young Mill-Wright and Miller's Guide. Phila, 1834. 8th ed. 392pp, errata; 28 plts at rear. Full leather. Binding copy. *Scribe's Perch**. $55/£35

EVANS, PETER A. The First Hundred Years. A Descriptive Bibliography.... (N.p.: CA Hist Soc, 1971.) 1st ed. Dec tan bds. Fine. *Argonaut*. $50/£32

EVANS, POWYS. Eighty-Eight Cartoons. London, 1926. 88 plts. (Lt browned.) Cl, label upper bd. (Bds sl warped.) *Edwards*. $39/£25

EVANS, RACHEL. Home Scenes: Tavistock and Its Vicinity. Tavistock: T.W. Greenfield, 1875. 2nd ed. Albumen frontis, viii,176pp (names; fr hinge partly cracked); 7 engrs. Gilt/blind-dec cl (spine ends rubbed). VG. *Cahan*. $100/£64

EVANS, ROBLEY D. A Sailor's Log. NY: Appleton, 1901. 14 plts. Untrimmed. (Joints cracked; extrems sl rubbed.) *Hollett*. $70/£45

EVANS, WALKER. American Photographs. (NY): MOMA, (1938). 1st ed w/errata slip. 87 plts. (Spine top sl worn, label sl spotted), else VG in dj (discolored, rubbed, chipped). *King*. $150/£96

EVANS, WALKER. American Photographs. (NY): MOMA, (1938). 1st ed. Errata slip. Paper spine label. (Lt wear lower fore corners), o/w VG in Good dj (tanned, sm chips, closed tear). *Reese*. $185/£119

EVANS, WALKER. American Photographs. (NY): MOMA, (1938). 1st ed. Errata tipped in. Fine in VG dj (lt worn, sm chips, tears). *Between The Covers*. $275/£176

EVANS, WALKER. American Photographs. NY: MOMA, (1962). 2nd ed. 87 photo plts. Fine in illus dj. *Cahan*. $125/£80

EVANS, WALKER. First and Last. NY: Harper & Row, 1978. 1st ed. (Name), else VG in dj (price-clipped). *Cahan*. $125/£80

EVANS, WALKER. Many Are Called. Boston/Cambridge: Houghton Mifflin/Riverside, 1966. 1st ed. 89 full-pg b/w photos. (Name, stamp), else VG. *Cahan*. $225/£144

EVANS, WALKER. Message from the Interior. NY: Eakins, (1966). 1st ed. 12 Fine full-pg repros. NF in gray linen, ptd paper label. *Captain's Bookshelf*. $350/£224

EVANS, WALKER. Message from the Interior. NY: Eakins, 1966. 1st ed. 12 gravure plts, guards. Ptd paper label fr cvr. Fine. *Cahan*. $500/£321

EVANS-PRITCHARD, E. E. The Position of Women in Primitive Societies.... NY: Free Press, (1965). 1st ed. VG (ex-libris) in dj. *Second Life*. $35/£22

EVANS-WENTZ, W. Y. The Fairy Faith in Celtic Countries. NY: University Books, 1966. Fine in VG dj. *Middle Earth*. $60/£38

EVE, G. W. Heraldry as Art. Batsford, 1907. (Feps lt browned, ex-libris.) Teg; gilt device upper bd, spine. (Cl sl soiled, rubbed.) *Edwards*. $101/£65

EVELYN, JOHN. Diary and Correspondence of John Evelyn, F.R.S. William Bray (ed). London, 1881-7. New ed. 4 vols. Uncut, unopened in parts. Emb cl (edges sl rubbed, vol 4 spine sl dknd), gilt. *Edwards*. $55/£35

EVELYN, JOHN. Diary of John Evelyn. William Bray (ed). London, 1906. New ed. 4 vols. Frontis ports. Teg, rest uncut. Gilt spine titles. (Marginal browning; edges rubbed, spine heads sl bumped.) *Edwards*. $156/£100

EVELYN, JOHN. Diary. Austin Dobson (ed). London/NY: Macmillan, 1906. 1st trade ed thus. 3 vols. (Foxed), o/w Good. *Scribe's Perch**. $40/£26

EVELYN, JOHN. The Life of Mrs. Godolphin. William Pickering, 1848. 2nd ed. Engr frontis, (2),xviii,292pp. Uncut. Orig brn cl (neatly rebacked in buckram; no label). VG. *Cox*. $39/£25

EVELYN, JOHN. Memoires for My Grand-Son. Geoffrey Keynes (ed). Nonesuch, 1926. 1st ed. #775/1250. Unopened. Vellum stamped in blind, lettered in gold. VG in marbled paper slipcase (defective). *Cox*. $101/£65

EVELYN, JOHN. Memoirs. London: Henry Colburn, 1827. 5 vols. Nearly 200 Fine inserted engrs. 1/4 morocco. *Swann**. $460/£295

EVELYN, JOHN. Memoirs...and a Selection of His Familiar Letters. Wm. Bray (ed). H. Colburn, 1819. 2nd, best ed. 2 vols. xxviii,671; viii,336pp; 11 plts, fldg pedigree. Contemp calf (sl surface damage), gilt. Sound. *Cox*. $234/£150

EVELYN, JOHN. The Miscellaneous Writings.... William Upcott (ed). London: Henry Colburn, 1825. 1st ed. Frontis, xxvi,849pp, 3 plts (bound sl at variance from directions to binder). Leaf 257/8 appears to be in its cancelled state. Aeg. Later full polished calf, gilt extra. VG (lt foxing early/late, mended tear 1 leaf, bound w/o ads). *Reese*. $300/£192

EVELYN, JOHN. Silva; or, A Discourse of Forest-Trees.... York: J. Dodsley, 1776. 6th ed and 1st Hunter ed. 649pp; 40 Fine copper plt engrs (1 fldg), fldg table. Lovely w/new matching leather spine over marbled bds. *Captain's Bookshelf*. $500/£321

EVELYN, JOHN. Sylva; or, A Discourse of Forest-Trees.... London: Martyn, 1670. 2nd ed. Engr tp, 5 engr illus. (Marginal notations, sl spotting, few corners damaged.) Full leather (worn; bds worn off). *Metropolitan**. $258/£165

Events in Indian History. (By James Wimer.) Lancaster, 1841. 1st ed. 8 litho plts (sm tears, repaired tears; text lt dampstained). Mod 1/4 morocco. Howes W548. *Swann**. $138/£88

EVERARD, H. S. C. A History of the Royal and Ancient Golf Club: St. Andrews from 1754-1900. Edinburgh: William Blackwood, 1907. 1st ed. Teg. Gilt-lettered grn cl. (Corners bumped, spine ends shelfworn), else VG. *Pacific**. $1,150/£737

EVERARD, JOHN. In Camera. London: Robert Hale, 1957. 1st ed. (Eps, 1st, last leaves foxed; some creased tips), else VG in dj (edgeworn). *Cahan*. $75/£48

EVERETT, CHARLES P. The Adventures of a Treasure Hunter. Boston, 1951. 1st ed. (Bkpl; dj transferred to top back cvr.) Contents Fine. Dj (dampstain, chipped, torn, price-clipped). *Baade*. $25/£16

EVERETT, EDWARD. Account of the Fund for the Relief of East Tennessee. Boston: Little, Brown, 1864. 1st ed. 99pp. (Corner chipped), else NF in ptd wrappers. *Mcgowan*. $60/£38

EVERETT, EDWARD. An Address Delivered at the Consecration of the National Cemetery at Gettysburg, 19th November, 1863. Boston: Little, Brown, 1864. 56pp; 2 maps. Unopened. Stiff paper cvrs (sl worn, irregular toning). Contents NF. *Waverly**. $176/£113

EVERETT, EDWARD. The Life of George Washington. NY: Sheldon, 1860. 1st ed. VG (spine lightened, lightened spots cvrs). *Sadlon*. $20/£13

EVERETT, FRANKLIN. Memorials of the Grand River Valley. Chicago, 1878. 1st ed. 545,74pp (browned, esp eps, fr inner hinge cracked, stain lower rt corners). Leather (worn, rear cvr detached). *King*. $95/£61

EVERITT, CHARLES P. The Adventures of a Treasure Hunter. Boston, 1951. 1st ed. Good in dj. *Heinoldt*. $25/£16

EVERITT, GRAHAM. English Caricaturists and Graphic Humourists of the Nineteenth Century. London, 1886. (Sl browning; lt wear, soil.) *Freeman**. $50/£32

EVERITT, GRAHAM. English Caricaturists and Graphic Humourists of the Nineteenth Century. London, 1893. 2nd ed. xix,427pp. (Lt spotting, 1/2-title browned, hinges sl tender; sm nick lower joint, cl lt soiled, sl edgeworn.) *Edwards*. $117/£75

EVERMANN, B. and L. RADCLIFFE. The Fishes of the West Coast of Peru and the Titicaca Basin. Washington: Smithsonian Inst, 1917. 1st ed. 14 plts. (Margins sl frayed.) Unopened. Wrappers. *Maggs*. $31/£20

EVERSON, WILLIAM. Cutting the Firebreak. Swanton: Kingfisher, (1979). One of 200 ptd, signed, w/initial hand drawn. Lg folio broadside. (Soft crease across middle), else NF. *Reese*. $60/£38

EVERSON, WILLIAM. Man-Fate: The Swan Song of Brother Antoninus. NY, 1974. 1st Amer ed. Fine in Fine dj. *Polyanthos*. $25/£16

EVERSON, WILLIAM. On Printing. Peter Rutledge Koch (ed). SF: Book Club of CA, 1992. 1st ed. One of 450. Frontis port, facs broadside folded, tipped on to rep, erratum slip laid in. Spine label. Fine. *Shasky*. $100/£64

EVERTS, TRUMAN C. Thirty-Seven Days of Peril. SF, 1923. One of 500. Cl-backed paper over bds. VG. *Cahan*. $60/£38

EWALD, C. A. Lectures on Diseases of the Digestive Organs. Robert Saundby (trans). London: New Sydenham Soc, 1891/92. 2 vols. (iii),214; 217-680pp. (Ex-lib.) *White*. $47/£30

EWAN, JOSEPH (ed). William Bartram. Phila: Amer Philosophical Soc, 1968. Color frontis, 59 plts (19 color). Dj (sl wormed, sl loss upper joint, lower edge). *Edwards*. $156/£100

EWAN, JOSEPH (ed). William Bartram: Botanical and Zoological Drawings, 1756-1788. Phil: Amer Philo Soc, 1968. 1st ed. Fine in VG dj. *Archer*. $200/£128

EWAN, JOSEPH and NESTA. John Banister and His Natural History of Virginia, 1678-1692. Urbana: Univ of IL, (1970). Map. Purple cl, mtd cvr illus, gilt. Fine in dj (price-clipped). *Bohling*. $18/£12

EWBANK, JANE M. (ed). Antiquary on Horseback. Kendal: Titus Wilson, 1963. 1st ed. VG in dj (sl worn, chipped). *Hollett*. $70/£45

EWBANK, T. Hydraulic and Other Machines for Raising Water, Ancient and Modern. NY, 1864. 15th ed. viii,608pp + addenda (labels, stamp). 1/2 leather (badly rubbed, joints weak, fr cvr detached, part of spine missing). *Whitehart*. $62/£40

EWBANK, THOMAS. Life in Brazil. NY, 1856. 469pp. Brn cl, gilt. (New ep, dampstains orig ep), else VG. *Price*. $195/£125

EWERS, HANNS HEINZ. Rider of the Night. NY: John Day, 1932. 1st ed in English. VG + in dj (spine lt tanned, nicked). *Lame Duck*. $85/£54

EWERS, JOHN C. (ed). Adventures of Zenas Leonard, Fur Trader. Norman, (1959). 1st ed thus. VG in dj (sl worn). *King*. $40/£26

EWERS, JOHN C. The Blackfeet: Raiders on the Northwestern Plains. Norman: Univ of OK, (1958). 1st ed. VG in dj (sl worn). *Lien*. $50/£32

EWERS, JOHN C. Indian Life on the Upper Missouri. Norman: Univ of OK, (1968). 1st ed. VG in dj (sl worn). *Lien*. $40/£26

EWING, JULIANA. Jackanapes. SPCK, 1884. 1st ed. Randolph Caldecott (illus). Sm 4to. Frontis, 47pp. Pict bds, cl spine. (Edges sl grazed), else VG. *Bookmark*. $39/£25

EWING, JULIANA. Jackanapes. NY: OUP, 1948. 1st thus. Tasha Tudor (illus). 5 1/2 x 8. 62pp. Fine in dj. *Cattermole*. $75/£48

Excursions in the County of Surrey.... (By Thomas Cromwell.) London: Longman et al, 1821. 1st ed. iv,190pp, extra engr tp; fldg map, plan, 45 engr plts. Good (marginal spotting) in contemp full polished calf (backstrip dknd, lacks label). *Cox*. $148/£95

Exhibition of French Drawings from Clouet to Ingres. London: Wildenstein, 1934. 16 plts, guards. Good in wraps (sl soiled). *Washton*. $15/£10

Exhibition of Italian XIX Century Paintings Sponsored by the City of Florence. NY: Wildenstein, 1949. 122 plts. *Washton*. $50/£32

Exhibition of Renaissance Jewels Selected from the Collection of Martin J. Desmoni. SF: Privately ptd, 1958. 24 plts. Good in wrappers. *Washton*. $30/£19

EXLEY, FREDERICK. A Fan's Notes: A Fictional Memoir. NY: Harper, (1968). 1st ed, 1st bk. Fine in dj. *Captain's Bookshelf*. $150/£96

Exploration of the Colorado River of the West...1869, 1870, 1871, 1872.... Washington: GPO, 1875. Blue cl (sl soiled, rubbed). *Metropolitan**. $115/£74

Explorations and Field Work of the Smithsonian Institution in 1921. Washington: Smithsonian, 1922. Unopened. Good (name stamp fr wrap, chipped). *Parmer*. $30/£19

Extended Document: An Investigation of Information and Evidence in Photographs. Rochester: Internat'l Museum of Photography at George Eastman House, 1975. (Name), else VG in pict stiff wrappers (lt stain). *Cahan*. $40/£26

Eye-Witness; or, Life Scenes in the Old North State.... (By A.O.Wheeler.) Boston, 1865. 1st ed. 276pp. Orig cl (spine mended). Howes W314. *Ginsberg*. $125/£80

EYLES, DESMOND and RICHARD DENNIS. Royal Doulton Figures Produced at Burslem, ca 1890-1978. Stoke-on-Trent: Royal Doulton Tableware, 1978. 1st ed. Blue cl, gilt. Fine in VG dj. *Baltimore**. $35/£22

EYLES, DESMOND. Good Sir Toby. Doulton, 1955. 1st ed. Lg 8vo. 108pp; 123 illus. VG in 2-tone cl, glacine wrapper. *Cox*. $39/£25

EYLES, DESMOND. Royal Doulton 1815-1965. London, 1965. 1st ed. Color frontis port, 20 color plts. (Tp sl spotted, presentation letter celotaped to fep; cl sl soiled.) *Edwards*. $156/£100

EYRE, FRANK. British Children's Books in the 20th Century. NY: Dutton, 1971. 1st US ed. Fine in dj. *Cattermole*. $25/£16

EYRE, J. The Stomach and Its Difficulties. London, 1852. 2nd ed. xvi,154pp. Blind-stamped cl. (Worn, dust-stained, spine ends defective; lib stamp tp, pencil mks), o/w Good. *Whitehart*. $55/£35

EYRE, JOHN. The Christian Spectator: Being a Journey from England to Ohio. Albany: J. Munsell, 1838. 1st ed. iv,72pp; errata pasted in. Bound (w/o orig wrappers) in cl, gilt. (Residue from label on fr; bkpl, ll foxed.) Howes E252. *Cahan*. $175/£112

EYSTER, WARREN. The Goblins of Eros. NY: Random House, (1957). 1st ed. VG (red cl rubbed) in dj (sl chipped, rear panel soiled). *Blue Mountain*. $15/£10

Ezra Pound at Seventy. (Norfolk: New Directions, 1956.) 1st ed. Fine in pict wrappers. *Reese.* $20/£13

Ezra Pound: His Metric and Poetry. (By T.S. Eliot.) NY: Knopf, 1917. 1st ed. (32)pp. (Hinges sl dknd, spine sunned), o/w Fine in plain pub's dj (lt chipped). *Hermitage.* $650/£417

F

FABES, G. H. The Autobiography of a Book. London: Elzevier Press, (1926). 1st ed. Inscribed, signed. Polished black buckram stamped in gilt. (Few sm bubbles to cl), o/w Very Nice. *Reese.* $60/£38

FABES, G. H. The First Editions of A. E. Coppard, A. P. Herbert and Charles Morgan. London: Myers, 1933. Blue cl (spine faded, sl worn), gilt. *Maggs.* $31/£20

FABES, G. H. The First Editions of Ralph Hale Mottram. London: Myers, 1934. Ltd to 300. 3 plts. Blue cl. Dj (sl defective). *Maggs.* $16/£10

FABES, G. H. John Galsworthy, His First Editions. London: W. & G. Foyle, 1932. Ltd to 500 numbered. Blue cl. Dj (edges ragged). *Maggs.* $16/£10

Fable for Critics. (By J. R. Lowell.) NY: Putnam, 1848. Early copy of 2nd ed w/o '10 Park Place' address added to imprint. Slate cl, gilt. (Lt foxed, sunned), else Attractive. BAL 13064. *Macdonnell.* $45/£29

Fables of Aesop, and Others with Designs on Wood by Thomas Bewick. Newcastle: E. Walker, 1818. 1st ed. Lg paper issue w/subs receipt preceding tp. Full crimson crushed levant, gilt extra. *Swann*. $488/£313

FABOS, JULIUS GY et al. Frederick Law Olmsted, Sr. Amherst: Univ of MA, 1968. Good in dj (faded). *Brooks.* $47/£30

Facts and Falsehoods. Concerning the War on the South 1861-1865. (By Elizabeth Meriwether.) Memphis: A.R. Taylor, (1904). 1st ed. NF in ptd wrappers. Howes M535. *Mcgowan.* $125/£80

FAENSEN, HUBERT and VLADIMIR IVANOV. Early Russian Architecture. Mary Whittall (trans). 1975. 420 plts (86 color), dbl-pg chart, map. Dj. *Edwards.* $94/£60

FAENSEN, HUBERT and VLADIMIR IVANOV. Early Russian Architecture. London: Elek, 1975. Sound. *Ars Artis.* $55/£35

FAGAN, BRIAN M. The Rape of the Nile. NY: Scribner, 1975. 1st ed. VG. *Worldwide.* $30/£19

FAGAN, JAMES O. Autobiography of an Individualist. Boston/NY, 1912. Grn cl (sl scratch fr cvr), gilt. Fine. *Bohling.* $18/£12

FAGES, PEDRO. Colorado River Campaign Diary of Pedro Fages 1781-82. Herbert I. Priestly (ed). Berkeley, 1913. 1st ed. Pb. Fine. *Turpen.* $40/£26

FAHIE, J. J. A History of Wireless Telegraphy, 1838-1899. Edinburgh: William Blackwood, 1899. 1st ed. Frontis, xvii,325,32(ads)pp. VG (bkpl). *Glaser.* $175/£112

FAIFAX-BLAKEBOROUGH, J. (ed). The Hunting and Sporting Reminiscences of H.W. Selby Lowndes, M.F.H. London, 1926. Frontis port. Blind-emb cl. (Browning; spine faded, sl rubbed.) *Edwards.* $31/£20

FAIR, A. A. (Pseud of Erle Stanley Gardner.) The Count of Nine. Morrow, 1958. 1st ed. (Bds sl stained), else VG + in dj (price-clipped, lacks sm spine piece, lt rubbed). *Murder By The Book.* $27/£17

FAIR, A. A. (Pseud of Erle Stanley Gardner.) Gold Comes in Bricks. Morrow, 1940. VG in VG dj (sl creasing). *Certo.* $65/£42

FAIRBANK, JOHN KING and KWANG-CHING LIU. Modern China: A Bibliographical Guide to Chinese Works 1898-1937. Cambridge, MA, 1950. VG. *Argosy.* $125/£80

FAIRBANKS, GEORGE R. History of Florida from Its Discovery by Ponce de Leon, in 1512, to the Close of the Florida War, in 1842. Phila, 1871. 1st ed. xii,350pp. Later red buckram, gilt. (Ex-lib), o/w VG +. Howes F8. *Turpen.* $195/£125

FAIRBROTHER, NAN. The Nature of Landscape Design. London: Architectural Press, 1974. As New. *Quest.* $45/£29

FAIRBROTHER, NAN. New Lives, New Landscapes. Architectural Press, 1970. 1st ed. Dj. *Edwards.* $39/£25

FAIRCHILD, DAVID et al. The World Was My Garden. NY/London: Scribner, 1938. 1st ed. VG. *Worldwide.* $30/£19

FAIRCHILD, DAVID. The World Grows Round My Door. NY: Scribner, 1947. Fine. *Quest.* $35/£22

FAIRCHILD, JOHNSON E. (ed). Women Society and Sex. NY: Sheridan House, (1952). 1st ed. VG (ex-libris) in dj. *Second Life.* $30/£19

FAIRCHILD, LEE. Don Juan's Bouquet. NY: Edwin Hill, 1903. 1st ed. #84/500. Signed presentation. Frontis. Unopened, untrimmed. (Rubbed), o/w VG. *Worldwide.* $25/£16

FAIRCHILD, LUCIUS. California Letters of Lucius Fairchild. Joseph Schafer (ed). Madison: State Hist Soc of WI, 1931. 1st ed. VG. *Sadlon.* $30/£19

Fairhaven, Massachusetts. Fairhaven: WPA, 1939. Blue cl. (Lt rubbed), else Fine. *Bromer.* $75/£48

FAIRHOLT, FREDERICK WILLIAM. Up the Nile, and Home Again. London: Chapman & Hall, 1862. 1st ed. (xx),448pp; 20 lithotint plts. Marbled sides, edges. Contemp 1/2 calf, gilt. (Sl worn), o/w Nice. *Ash.* $195/£125

FAIRLEY, LINCOLN. Mount Tamalpais, A History. SF: Scottwall Assoc, 1987. 1st ed. Frontis. Gilt-lettered grn cl. Fine in pict dj. *Argonaut.* $45/£29

Fairy Garland. Being Fairy Tales from the Old French. London, (1928). 1st ed. One of 1000 signed by Edmund Dulac (illus). 12 color plts. Vellum-backed bds (vellum discolored; foxed). *Kane*. $225/£144

FAITHFULL, EMILY. Three Visits to America. NY: Fowler & Wells, 1884. 16pp ads. Pict cl. *Rostenberg & Stern.* $300/£192

FALCONER, THOMAS. Letters and Notes on the Texan Santa Fe Expedition 1841-1842. NY, 1930. Bd, cl backstrip. Howes F14. *Ginsberg.* $150/£96

FALCONER, THOMAS. Letters and Notes on the Texan Santa Fe Expedition 1841-1842. NY: Dauber & Pine Bookshops, 1930. Frontis. Unopened. (Age browning), else Fine. Howes F14/15. *Dumont.* $135/£87

FALCONER, WILLIAM. Mushrooms: How to Grow Them. NY: OJ, 1907. Grn cl, gilt. VG. *Price.* $24/£15

FALCONER, WILLIAM. The Shipwreck. London, 1811. Fldg map, engr dedication, 18 engr plts, 4 vignettes. (Lt foxing, offsetting, pencil underscoring.) Contemp 1/4 morocco, bds (rubbed, worn). *Freeman*. $130/£83

FALCONER, WILLIAM. The Shipwreck. London: Wm. Baynes, 1811. Fldg map, 18 plts. Full polished calf (rubbed, lt foxed). *Kane*. $140/£90

FALCONER, WILLIAM. An Universal Dictionary of the Marine. London: T. Cadell, 1784. 12 fldg engr plts (few torn, 1 frayed, soiled at margins; sl wormholing to text). Contemp calf (rubbed, joints weak). *Christie's*. $78/£50

FALEY, KATHY KELSEY. Edward Weston's Gifts to His Sister. Dayton: Dayton Art Inst, 1978. 1st ed. 16 full-pg b/w photos. (Owner stamp; corner sl crimped), else VG in pict stiff wrappers. *Cahan.* $45/£29

FALKLAND, AMELIA CARY. Chow-Chow. London: Hurst & Blackett, 1857. 1st ed. 2 vols. Color litho frontispieces, ix,326; vii,(1)errata,287,ixpp. Contemp 1/2 calf (sl rubbed). *Maggs.* $273/£175

FALKLAND, AMELIA CARY. Chow-Chow. London: Eric Partridge, 1930. (Sl soiled), o/w VG. *Worldwide.* $45/£29

FALL, BERNARD. Street Without Joy: Indochina at War, 1946-54. Harrisburg: Stackpole, (1961). 1st ed. (Sm name repeated twice), else Fine in VG+ dj (sm chips spine extrems, 2 sm tears). *Between The Covers.* $500/£321

FALSTAFF, JAKE. Alice in Justice-Land. NY: Amer Civil Liberties Union, 1937. Stapled self wraps (browned, mkd, chipped). *Boswell.* $45/£29

Family Prayer-Book. (New Haven, CT): Sidney's Press, 1823. Apparent 1st ed w/Brownell's commentary. (Foxed.) Marbled eps. Contemp full calf (partly worn, fr joint split), black leather label. *Waverly*.* $38/£24

Famous Movie Story of Walt Disney's Snow White and the Seven Dwarfs. (K.K. Publications, 1938.) Disney authorized ed. Obl 4to. 15pp. VG in pict cvrs. *Blue Mountain.* $50/£32

Famous Parks and Gardens of the World. T. Nelson & Sons, 1880. x,230pp (prelims, some margins lt spotted). Black-ruled cl, gilt device upper bd. (Rubbed w/sl cl loss, sm split upper joint.) *Edwards.* $101/£65

Famous Small Bronzes. NY: Gorham, 1928. Grn bds. Fine (hinge starting). *Metropolitan*.* $30/£19

Fanaticism. (By Isaac Taylor.) London: Holdsworth & Ball, 1833. 1st ed. viii,515pp. Blue bds, drab spine (top sl worn), ptd label. *Burmester.* $117/£75

Fanning's Illustrated Gazetteer of the United States.... NY, 1854. 1st ed or early ptg. 3/4 leather, marbled bds (spine top chipped). Interior Fine. *Mcclintock.* $35/£22

FANNING, DAVID. Narrative of Colonel David Fanning...Giving an Account of His Adventures in North Carolina, from 1775 to 1783.... (NY, 1865). #48/250. (26),86pp. New black leather spine label. Howes F26. *Ginsberg.* $250/£160

FANNING, EDMUND. Voyages and Discoveries in the South Seas, 1792-1832. Salem, MA: Marine Research Soc, 1924. 32 plts, dec eps. Blue cl (corners lt worn), gilt. VG (sl foxed). *Parmer.* $115/£74

FANNING, EDMUND. Voyages and Discoveries in the South Seas, 1792-1832. Salem: Marine Research Soc, 1924. Frontis, 31 plts. (Bkpl inner cvr; jacket fr pasted to flyleaf), else Fine. *Argonaut.* $100/£64

FANNING, PETE. Great Crimes of the West. SF: Pete Fanning, (1929). 1st ed. Frontis. Good. *Lien.* $35/£22

FANNING, PETE. Great Crimes of the West. (SF: Privately pub, 1929.) 1st ed. Port. Grn cl. Fine in VG+ dj (spine faded, soiled, edges worn). *Harrington.* $65/£42

FANON, FRANTZ. Black Skin, White Masks. NY: Grove, (1967). 1st Amer ed, 1st bk. Fine in NF dj (spine ends crinkling, sm tears rear panel). *Between The Covers.* $65/£42

FANTE, JOHN. Dreams from Bunker Hill. Santa Barbara, CA: Black Sparrow, 1982. One of 200 numbered, signed. Teal cl-backed tan/grn bds, ptd spine label. NF in acetate dj. *Blue Mountain.* $95/£61

FARADAY, MICHAEL. A Course of Six Lectures on the Chemical History of a Candle. William Crookes (ed). NY: Harper, 1861. 1st Amer ed. 223pp. Fine. *Bickersteth.* $273/£175

FARADAY, MICHAEL. The Life and Letters...By Dr. Bence Jones. London: Longmans, Green, 1870. 1st ed. 2 vols. Frontis each vol, vi,(4),427; (12),499pp, complete w/half-titles. Mod cl. VG set (frontispieces, tps dampstained). *Glaser.* $225/£144

FARAGO, LADISLAS. Abyssinia on the Eve. London: Putnam, 1935. 1st ed. (Sl rubbed), o/w VG. *Worldwide.* $22/£14

FARBER, NORMA. Where's Gomer? NY: Dutton, 1974. 1st ed. Willim Pene Du Bois (illus). 8 1/2 x 8. 32pp. Fine in dj. *Cattermole.* $30/£19

FARINA, RICHARD. Been Down So Long It Looks Like Up to Me. NY: Random House, (1966). 1st ed. Fine in NF dj (spine extrems sl worn, sm crease fr flap edge). *Between The Covers.* $175/£112

FARINA, RICHARD. Been Down So Long It Looks Like Up to Me. NY: Random House, (1966). 1st ed, 1st bk. Beautiful in dj (lt edgewear). *Captain's Bookshelf.* $250/£160

FARIS, JOHN T. Seeing the Sunny South. Phila, 1921. 1st ed. Color frontis. *Wantagh.* $45/£29

FARISH, THOMAS E. The Gold Hunters of California. Chicago: M.A. Donahue, 1904. 1st ed. Frontis. Grn pict cl, gilt. Fine (bkpl, label, rubberstamp). *Pacific*.* $195/£125

FARISH, THOMAS E. History of Arizona. Phoenix, 1915. Vols 1 through 7 only (lacks vol 8). Port. VG. Howes F37. *Reese.* $750/£481

FARJEON, B. L. The March of Fate. F.V. White, 1895. 1 vol ed. Pict bds. Good (sig; spine bumped; hinges, corners rubbed). *Tiger.* $25/£16

FARJEON, B. L. Samuel Boyd of Catchpole Square. London: Hutchinson, 1899. 1st ed. (Extrems frayed, sl soil.) *Metropolitan*.* $86/£55

FARJEON, ELEANOR. Cherrystones. Phila: Lippincott, (1942). 1st ed. 8vo. 61pp; 29 full-pg line illus by Isobel and John Morton-Sale. Red cl, gilt. (School name stamp; sl fade mk fr cvr), o/w VG. *Dower.* $45/£29

FARJEON, ELEANOR. The Children's Bells. NY: Walck, 1960. 1st ed. Peggy Fortnum (illus). 6 x 9 1/4. 212pp. VG in dj. *Cattermole.* $35/£22

FARJEON, ELEANOR. Dark World of Animals. London: Sylvan, (1945). 1st ed. Obl 4to. 31,(i)pp (fep creased); 11 wood engrs by T. Stoney. Tan cl (bumped, sl rubbed). VG. *Blue Mountain.* $45/£29

FARJEON, ELEANOR. Nursery Rhymes of London Town. Duckworth, 1916. 1st ed. Color frontis, 63,(1)pp. Good (sl mkd, corners knocked). *Cox.* $39/£25

FARJEON, ELEANOR. Nursery Rhymes of London Town. London: Duckworth, 1916. 1st Eng ed. 8vo. Color frontis, 64pp. Blue cl, gilt. (Sl foxing; spine ends rubbed), o/w VG. *Dower.* $45/£29

FARJEON, J. JEFFERSON. The 5.18 Mystery. NY: Dial, 1929. 1st Amer ed. VG in dj (internal tape mend; spine ends, corners chipped; sm closed tears). *Mordida.* $45/£29

FARJEON, J. JEFFERSON. The Judge Sums Up. Indianapolis: Bobbs-Merrill, 1942. 1st Amer ed. Fine in dj (sm closed tear, sl wear spine ends). *Mordida.* $45/£29

FARJEON, J. JEFFERSON. Seven Dead. Indianapolis: Bobbs-Merrill, 1939. 1st Amer ed. (Eps lt spotted), o/w NF in dj (spine ends sl worn, corners worn, sm closed tears.) *Mordida.* $45/£29

FARJEON, J. JEFFERSON. The Z Murders. NY: Dial, 1932. 1st Amer ed. Fine in dj (spine sl dknd, spine ends sl worn, sm closed tear). *Mordida.* $65/£42

FARLEIGH, JOHN. Engraving on Wood. Dryad, 1954. 1st ed. Pict bds. NF. *Whittle.* $31/£20

FARLEIGH, JOHN. Fifteen Craftsmen on Their Crafts. London: Sylvan, 1945. 1st ed. VG. *Hollett.* $39/£25

FARLEY, HARRIET. Happy Nights at Hazel Nook. Boston: Dayton & Wentworth, 1854. 1st ed. 256pp; 13 full-pg engr plts. Red cl (sl worn). VG. *Second Life.* $125/£80

FARLEY, JOHN. The London Art of Cookery. London: Scatcherd & Letterman, 1804. 10th ed. xxiv,366pp (lt foxed, tp soiled); 12 copper plts (lacks port). Early 1/2 roan, cl (worn, chips, sm loss of leather fr cvr; fr hinge starting), gilt. *Waverly**. $99/£63

FARLEY, WALTER. Black Stallion Mystery. NY: Random House, 1957. 1st ptg. Mal Singer (illus). Lg 12mo. VG (faded spots on spine) in VG dj (sm tears, chips). *Book Adoption*. $35/£22

FARLEY, WALTER. Black Stallion Revolts. NY: Random House, 1953. 1st ptg. Harold Eldridge (illus). Lg 12mo. NF in VG + dj (top edge rough). *Book Adoption*. $35/£22

FARLEY, WALTER. The Black Stallion's Courage. NY: Random House, 1956. 1st ed. Signed. VG in Fair dj. *October Farm*. $45/£29

FARLEY, WALTER. The Black Stallion's Filly. NY: Random House, 1952. 1st ed. VG in VG dj. *October Farm*. $35/£22

FARLEY, WALTER. The Horse-Tamer. NY: Random House, 1958. 1st ed. James Schucker (illus). 5 1/2 x 8 1/4. 175pp (browned). VG in dj. *Cattermole*. $25/£16

FARLIE, GERARD. Suspect. GC: Crime Club, 1930. Crime Club 1st ed. Great in dj (sm chips, losses, edges foxed). *Metropolitan**. $51/£33

FARMBOROUGH, FLORENCE. With the Armies of the Tsar, A Nurse at the Russion Front 1914-18. NY, (1975). 1st Amer ed. VG + in VG + dj. *Pratt*. $32/£21

FARMER, JOHN S. and W. E. HENLEY. A Dictionary of Slang and Colloquial English. London/NY, n.d. (c. 1900). 4th imp. Morocco-backed cl bds (upper edge sl soiled, faded, spine sl bumped, color retouched; lt textual spotting). *Edwards*. $56/£36

FARMER, PENELOPE. A Castle of Bone. NY: Atheneum, 1972. 1st ed. 5 1/2 x 8 1/2. 152pp. VG in dj. *Cattermole*. $20/£13

FARMER, PENELOPE. Year King. London: C&W, 1977. 1st ed. 5 1/4 x 8. 232pp. Fine in dj. *Cattermole*. $45/£29

FARMER, PHILIP JOSE. Dayworld Breakup. NY: Tor, (1990). 1st ed. (Sm corner bump), else Fine in Fine dj. *Other Worlds*. $20/£13

FARMER, PHILIP JOSE. Down in the Black Gang. NY: Science Fiction Book Club, 1971. 1st ed, 2nd issue. Signed. Dj. *Swann**. $57/£37

FARMER, PHILIP JOSE. Fire and the Night. Evanston, IL, (1962). 1st ed. Signed. Ptd wrappers. *Swann**. $57/£37

FARMER, PHILIP JOSE. Gods of River World. NY: Putnam, (1983). 1st ed. NF (sm rmdr mk) in dj. *Antic Hay*. $20/£13

FARMER, PHILIP JOSE. Lord Tyger. NY: Doubleday, 1970. 1st ed. Dj (sm tear). *Swann**. $172/£110

FARMER, PHILIP JOSE. The Lovers. Del Rey Books, 1979. 1st ed. Fine in dj. *Madle*. $20/£13

FARMER, PHILIP JOSE. A Private Cosmos. Huntington Woods, MI: Phantasia, 1981. 1st ed. One of 250 numbered, signed. VG in dj, slipcase. *King*. $35/£22

FARMER, PHILIP JOSE. River of Eternity. Huntington Woods: Phantasia, 1983. 1st ed. One of 500 signed, numbered. Fine in Fine dj in slipcase. *Other Worlds*. $75/£48

FARMER, PHILIP JOSE. Strange Relations. London: Gollancz, 1964. 1st British ed. Fine (fore-edge foxed) in dj (sl discoloration, price-clipped). *Metropolitan**. $57/£37

FARMER, PHILIP JOSE. A Woman a Day. NY: Beacon Books, (1960). 1st ed. Ptd wrappers. *Swann**. $57/£37

FARMER, SILAS. The History of Detroit and Michigan. Detroit, 1889. 2nd ed. 2 vols. 1234pp. Aeg. 1/2 leather, gilt-dec cl. (Hinges starting, rubbed, spine scuffed, stained), else Nice set. *King*. $295/£189

FARNHAM, CHARLES H. Life of Francis Parkman. Boston: Little, Brown, 1901. #192 of Deluxe Ed. Frontis port, guard. Unopened. (Bkpl; leather spine sl scuffed), else NF. *Parmer*. $75/£48

FARNHAM, ELIZA W. Life in Prairie Land. NY: Harper, 1855. Later ed. 1st bk. 408pp. Uncut. Good (sig, sm chip fep). *Second Life*. $85/£54

FARNHAM, THOMAS J. Life, Adventures, and Travels in California.... NY, 1849. Pictorial ed. Pub's gilt-pict cl. Howes F49. *Swann**. $103/£66

FARNHAM, THOMAS J. Travels in the Great Western Prairies, the Anahuac and Rocky Mountains, and in the Oregon Territory. Poughkeepsie, 1841. 1st ed. 197pp (foxing, lt dampstaining, old lib bkpl; sig loose). Contemp calf (rubbed), leather label (chipped). Good. Howes F50. *Reese*. $750/£481

FARNHAM, THOMAS J. Travels in the Great Western Prairies, the Anahuac and Rocky Mountains, and in the Oregon Territory. NY: Greeley & McElrath, 1843. 3rd ed. 112pp. Orig ptd wrappers (dknd, edges chipped; lt foxing, few corners creased, ink sig). VG in 1/2 morocco slipcase, spine gilt. Howes F50. *Reese*. $500/£321

FARNSWORTH, R. W. C. (ed). A Southern California Paradise, in the Suburbs of Los Angeles.... Pasadena: R.W.C. Farnsworth, 1883. 2nd ed (w/10pp supp, 9pp ads not in 1st ed). 142,ixpp (tp, lower margin of bk stained; short tear foremargin last few leaves), map. Ptd blue wrappers (chipped). *Dawson*. $300/£192

FAROVA, ANNA (ed). Andre Kertesz. NY: Paragraphic Books, 1966. 1st ed. 66 full-pg b/w photos. VG (owner stamp) in pict stiff wrappers. *Cahan*. $25/£16

FAROVA, ANNA (ed). Robert Capa. NY: Paragraphic Books, Grossman Pub, 1969. 1st ed. (Owner stamp), else VG in pict stiff wrappers (creased). *Cahan*. $20/£13

FAROVA, ANNA. The World of Jan Saudek. Millerton, NY: Aperture, 1983. 1st US ed. Tipped-in color illus. Illus eps. Fine in illus dj. *Cahan*. $100/£64

FARQUHAR, FRANCIS P. Books of the Colorado River and the Grand Canyon. L.A.: Dawson, 1953. 1st ed. One of 600 ptd. Red cl (sl worn), paper label. NF. *Five Quail*. $225/£144

FARQUHAR, FRANCIS P. The Grizzly Bear Hunter of California. SF, 1948. Ltd to 200. Sewn grn heavy paper wrappers. Fine in fldg grn linen protective case, gilt. *Cady*. $50/£32

FARQUHAR, FRANCIS P. History of the Sierra Nevada. Berkeley: Univ of CA, 1966. 1st ed. Color frontis, 48 plts, 5 maps. Pict cl. Fine in NF dj. *Mikesh*. $45/£29

FARQUHAR, FRANCIS P. Yosemite. The Big Trees and the High Sierra. Berkeley: Univ of CA, 1948. 1st ed. Signed. Engr on tp. VG in dj (few restored tears top edge). *Shasky*. $200/£128

FARQUHAR, FRANCIS P. and GARFIELD MERNER. Flight to the North Pole 24 August, 1949. SF: Grabhorn Press, 1950. VG in orig ptd wrapper. *High Latitude*. $25/£16

FARQUHAR, FRANCIS P. and ARISTIDES E. PHOUTRIDES. Mount Olympus. SF: Johnck & Seeger, 1929. 1st bk ed. Ltd to 950. 2 maps (1 fldg). 1/2 vellum, dec bds. Fine in slipcase (lt worn). *Argonaut*. $125/£80

FARQUHAR, GEORGE. The Complete Works of George Farquhar. Charles Stonehill (ed). Bloomsbury, 1930. Ltd to 1000. 2 vols. Blue buckram-backed lt blue Ingres paper bds (spines faded, corners sl worn), paper title labels. Nice set. *Cady*. $60/£38

FARQUHAR, GEORGE. The Recruiting Officer. London: Peter Davies, 1926. Ltd to 550 numbered. 12 color plts. Yellow vellum-backed dec bds. Fine in Fair pict dj (chipped, edges torn, lacks flaps), yellow cl chemise in VG tan calf-backed yellow cl slipcase. *Blue Mountain*. $275/£176

FARRAR, EMMIE FERGUSON and EMILEE HINES. Old Virginia Houses: The Heart of Virginia. Hale Pub, (c. 1974). 1st ed. VG in VG- dj. *Book Broker.* $35/£22

FARRAR, EMMIE FERGUSON and EMILEE HINES. Old Virginia Houses Along the Fall Line. Hastings House, (c. 1971). 1st ed. VG in VG dj. *Book Broker.* $35/£22

FARRAR, EMMIE FERGUSON. Old Virginia Houses Along the James. Hastings House, (c. 1957). 1st ed. VG- (bottom edge rubbed) in Good- dj (tape-repaired). *Book Broker.* $35/£22

FARRE, HENRY. Sky Fighters of France. Boston: Houghton Mifflin, 1919. (Bds foxed, edges worn.) Contents Fine. *Metropolitan*. $40/£26

FARRELL, HENRY. What Ever Happened to Baby Jane? NY: Rinehart, (1960). 1st ed. (Paper sl tanned), o/w Fine in black dj (lt rubbed, short closed tear spine crown). *Reese.* $60/£38

FARRELL, J. G. Troubles. NY: Knopf, 1971. 1st Amer ed. (Stain corner rear bd, jacket; sticker shadow fr panel), else Fine in dj. *Between The Covers.* $85/£54

FARRELL, JAMES T. Judith and Other Stories. NY, 1973. 1st Amer ed. Signed presentation. Fine in dj (sm tear, sl soiled). *Polyanthos.* $45/£29

FARRELL, JAMES T. The Silence of History. NY: Doubleday, 1963. 1st ed. Fine in VG dj (spine lt faded, crease back panel). *Hermitage.* $40/£26

FARREN, MICK and EDWARD BARKER. Watch Out Kids. Open Gate Bks, 1972. 1st ed. NF in dj (sm chip). *Sclanders.* $34/£22

FARRER, J. A. Literary Forgeries. London: Longmans, Green, 1907. 1st ed. (Lib label pastedown, faint stamp reverse tp, few marginal blind-stamps; sm label remnants spine base.) *Hollett.* $117/£75

FARRER, REGINALD. Alpines and Bog-Plants. London: Edward Arnold, 1908. 1st ed. 16 plts. (1/2-title repaired.) Teg, uncut. Mod 1/4 grn morocco, gilt, raised bands, marbled bds. *Hollett.* $117/£75

FARRER, REGINALD. The Dolomites. London: A&C Black, 1913. 1st ed. Pict cl. Fine. *Archer.* $150/£96

FARRER, REGINALD. The English Rock Garden. London, 1919. 1st ed. 2 vols. 102 plts. Grn cl (sl used, corners bumped). *Wheldon & Wesley.* $109/£70

FARRER, REGINALD. The English Rock Garden. London, 1928. 4th imp. 2 vols. 102 plts. (Lt browned; sl chipped, mkd.) *Edwards.* $62/£40

FARRER, REGINALD. The English Rock Garden. London, 1955. 2 vols. 107 plts. Fine in djs (spine heads chipped). *Henly.* $94/£60

FARRER, REGINALD. The Garden of Asia. London: Methuen, 1905. 2nd ed. Red cl, gilt. VG (lt foxed; sm spine stain). *Hollett.* $187/£120

FARRER, REGINALD. The Rainbow Bridge. London, 1926. 3rd imp. Map, 16 plts. Fine. *Henly.* $66/£42

FARRER, REGINALD. The Rock Garden. London, (1912). 1st ed. 8 color plts. (Fep removed.) *Wheldon & Wesley.* $28/£18

FARRERE, CLAUDE. Black Opium. NY: Nicholas L. Brown, 1929. One of 1250 numbered. NF. *Beasley.* $75/£48

FARRINGTON, S. KIP. Atlantic Game Fishing. NY, 1937. VG (cvr lt rubbed, faded). *Truepenny.* $75/£48

FARRINGTON, S. KIP. Atlantic Game Fishing. NY, 1937. 1st ed. (Ink name), else Fine. *Truepenny.* $150/£96

FARRINGTON, S. KIP. Atlantic Game Fishing. NY: Kennedy Bros, 1937. 1st ed. 7 color plts. Blue cl. VG +. *Bowman.* $175/£112

FARRIS, JOHN. Shatter. London: W.H. Allen, 1980. 1st ed. Signed, inscribed. Fine in Fine dj. *Certo.* $60/£38

FARWELL, A. F. Reminiscences of John V. Farwell by His Elder Daughter. Chicago: Fletcher, (1928). 1st ed. 2 vols. Ptd pict bds, cl spines. *Ginsberg.* $125/£80

FASS, JOHN S. Some Oriental Versions of the Turtle. (NY): Hammer Creek Press, 1952. Sm 8vo. (18)pp. Ptd in 3 colors on Japanese paper, bound Oriental-style in variant binding of grn handmade paper. Cartouche on title-label matches that on tp. VF (bkpl). *Bromer.* $125/£80

FAST, HOWARD. The Naked God. NY: Frederick A. Praeger, (1957). 1st ed. VG in dj. *Turtle Island.* $30/£19

FAST, HOWARD. Never to Forget. Book League of Jewish Peoples Fraternal Order, I.O.W., 1946. 1st ed. VG in wrappers. *Warren.* $75/£48

FAST, HOWARD. Spain and Peace. NY: Joint Anti-Fascist Refugee Committee, n.d. 1st Amer ed. Fine. *Polyanthos.* $25/£16

FAST, HOWARD. Tony and the Wonderful Door. NY: Blue Heron, 1952. 1st ed. William Vigoda (illus). (Name, 3 pg corners creased), else NF in VG dj (tear fr flap; chip rear panel). *Between The Covers.* $65/£42

Father Tuck's Annual (1906). Raphael Tuck, n.d. (1906 inscrip). 4to. 256pp; 6 color plts. Pict bds, cl spine. (Lt worn), else VG. *Bookmark.* $117/£75

FATIO, LOUISE. A Doll for Marie. NY: Whittlesey House, 1957. Probable 1st ed. Roger Duvoisin (illus). 7 1/4 x 10. Sm facs of the bk in rear pocket. Fine in dj. *Cattermole.* $75/£48

FATIO, LOUISE. The Happy Lion and the Bear. NY: Whittlesey, 1964. 1st ed. Roger Duvolsin (illus). 8 1/4 x 10 1/4. 32pp. Fine in dj. *Cattermole.* $35/£22

FATOUT, PAUL. Ambrose Bierce, the Devil's Lexicographer. Norman: Univ of OK, (1951). 1st ed. VG + in dj (edgeworn). *Bohling.* $30/£19

FAUCHER, LIDA. Bruin the Brown Bear. NY: Harper, 1937. 1st ed. Feodor Rojankovsky (illus). 9 1/4 x 10 1/2. 32pp. Cl spine, pict bds. VG. *Cattermole.* $35/£22

FAUCHER, LIDA. Pompom, the Little Red Squirrel. NY: Harper, 1937. 1st ed. Feodor Rojankovsky (illus). 9 1/4 x 10 1/2. 32pp. VG. *Cattermole.* $35/£22

FAUGHNAN, THOMAS. Stirring Incidents in the Life of a British Soldier. Picton, Ontario, 1890. 31st thousand. Frontis, xiv,537pp (lt browned). Blue/black pict cl (mkd). *Maggs.* $218/£140

FAULCONER, ALBERT and THOMAS KEYS. Foundations of Anesthesiology. Springfield, 1965. 1st ed. 2 vols. VG. *Fye.* $250/£160

FAULDING, GERTRUDE M. Nature Children; A Flower Book for Little Folks. Frowde/OUP, 1911. 1st ed. Eleanor S. March (illus). Tall 8vo. Color frontis, 104pp. Bds, pict onlay. (Bds faded, sl knocked, sl nicks ends), else VG. *Bookmark.* $94/£60

FAULK, ODIE B. Destiny Road, the Gila Trail and the Opening of the Southwest. NY, (1973). 1st ed. NF (sl bumped) in NF dj (sl soiled). *Turpen.* $35/£22

FAULK, ODIE B. The Last Years of Spanish Texas, 1778-1821. The Hague: Mouton, 1964. 1st ed. Fine in dj. *Gibbs.* $55/£35

FAULKNER, FRANK. The Theory and Practice of Modern Brewing. London, 1884. iv,283pp + xx ads; 10 plts. Emb cl (sl water-stained, bumped w/sl cl loss, spine sl chipped; bkpl remains, upper hinge tender). *Edwards.* $55/£35

FAULKNER, JOHN. Uncle Good's Girls. NY: Fawcett, (1952). 1st ed, pb orig. NF in wrappers. *Pettler & Lieberman.* $40/£26

FAULKNER, WILLIAM J. The Days When the Animals Talked. Chicago: Follett, 1977. 2nd ed. Troy Howell (illus). 6x9. 190pp. VG (ex-lib, mks). *Cattermole.* $16/£10

FAULKNER, WILLIAM. Absalom, Absalom! NY: Random House, (1936). 1st ed (correctly not stating). Fine (lacks dj). *Captain's Bookshelf.* $175/£112

FAULKNER, WILLIAM. As I Lay Dying. NY: Jonathan Cape & Harrison Smith, (1930). 1st ed, 1st issue. VG (lacks dj). *Captain's Bookshelf.* $300/£192

FAULKNER, WILLIAM. As I Lay Dying. London: C&W, 1935. 1st UK ed. (Inscrip, sm bkseller ticket fep; spine unevenly faded), else VG in dj (soiled, nicked, spine sunned). *Gekoski.* $234/£150

FAULKNER, WILLIAM. Big Woods. NY: Random House, 1955. 1st ed this collection. VF in Fine dj. *Pirages.* $150/£96

FAULKNER, WILLIAM. Doctor Martino and Other Stories. NY: Harrison Smith & Robert Haas, 1934. 1st ed this collection. (Cl spine sl faded, shadow of dj lettering), o/w Fine in dj (sm tear fr panel tape-repaired to verso, spine sl dknd, 3 sm tears to top). *Pirages.* $350/£224

FAULKNER, WILLIAM. Doctor Martino and Other Stories. NY: Harrison Smith, 1934. 1st ed, ltd issue. One of 360 numbered. Signed on tipped-in leaf. Top edge stained black. Black/red gilt-lettered cl (spine lt faded). Fine. *Kane*.* $700/£449

FAULKNER, WILLIAM. Doctor Martino and Other Stories. NY: Smith & Haas, 1934. 1st ed. VG (bkpl; sl cocked, lt soil) in dj (spine head loss, chips, soil, wear). *Metropolitan*.* $230/£147

FAULKNER, WILLIAM. Doctor Martino and Other Stories. NY: Smith & Haas, 1934. One of 360 numbered, signed. Black cl spine (sl faded). Fine w/o dj as issued. *Between The Covers.* $1,200/£769

FAULKNER, WILLIAM. A Fable. (NY): Random House, (1954). 1st ed. Fine in NF dj (spine lettering sl dknd; rubbing; tear rear panel). *Between The Covers.* $150/£96

FAULKNER, WILLIAM. A Fable. (NY): Random House, (1954). Ltd to 1000 numbered, signed. 8vo. Blue dec cl. Good in slipcase. *Karmiole.* $850/£545

FAULKNER, WILLIAM. A Fable. NY: Random House, (1954). 1st ed. VG (lt stains) in VG dj (short closed tear, tape residue, fr flap worn). *Metropolitan*.* $57/£37

FAULKNER, WILLIAM. A Fable. NY: Random House, (1954). 1st trade ed. Fine in NF dj (2 sm tears). *Pacific*.* $86/£55

FAULKNER, WILLIAM. A Fable. London, 1955. 1st ed. VG in dj (chipped, closed tear). *Buckley.* $31/£20

FAULKNER, WILLIAM. Faulkner at Nagano. Robert A. Jelliffe (ed). Tokyo: Kenkyusha Ltd, (1956). 1st ed. Fine in VG dj (internally mended tears spine crown). *Reese.* $200/£128

FAULKNER, WILLIAM. Faulkner's County. Tales of Yoknapatawpha County. London, 1955. 1st Eng ed. Very Nice (bkpl) in dj (sl torn). *Clearwater.* $70/£45

FAULKNER, WILLIAM. Go Down, Moses.... NY: Random House, 1942. 1st ed. VG (rubbed) in dj (price-clipped, head chipped). *Metropolitan*.* $258/£165

FAULKNER, WILLIAM. The Hamlet. NY: Random House, (1940). 1st ed. 8vo. Black cl. (Owner label fep), o/w Fine in dj (lt rubbed). *Jaffe.* $1,000/£641

FAULKNER, WILLIAM. The Hamlet. NY: Random House, 1940. 1st ed. One of 250 signed. 8vo. Pict tp. VF in glassine dj. *Jaffe.* $3,000/£1,923

FAULKNER, WILLIAM. Idyll in the Desert. NY, 1931. 1st ed. Ltd to 400 numbered, signed. 8vo. Dec bds, paper title label fr cvr. Nice (edges, spine sl rubbed). *Black Sun.* $750/£481

FAULKNER, WILLIAM. Intruder in the Dust. NY: Random House, (1948). 1st ed. Fine in dj. *Houle.* $350/£224

FAULKNER, WILLIAM. Intruder in the Dust. NY: Random House, 1948. 1st ed. (Sm dent fr cvr), o/w NF in NF dj (sl soiled, rubbed). *Pirages.* $175/£112

FAULKNER, WILLIAM. Knight's Gambit. NY: Random House, 1949. 1st ed. Fine in VG dj (sl creased, frayed, sm loss 1 joint top, sl soiled, mkd). *Pirages.* $125/£80

FAULKNER, WILLIAM. Light in August. Harrison Smith & Robert Haas, (1932). 3rd ptg. VG + in Very Attractive dj (sm chips spine corners, sm tears). *Certo.* $85/£54

FAULKNER, WILLIAM. Light in August. NY: Smith & Haas, (1932). 1st ed. VG in VG dj (edgeworn). *Unger.* $575/£369

FAULKNER, WILLIAM. The Mansion. NY: Random House, (1959). 1st ed. Fine in dj (sl worn). *Metropolitan*.* $115/£74

FAULKNER, WILLIAM. The Mansion. NY: Random House, 1959. 1st ed. VF in VF dj. *Pirages.* $150/£96

FAULKNER, WILLIAM. The Mansion. NY: Random House, 1959. 1st ed. One of 500 signed. VF. *Pirages.* $550/£353

FAULKNER, WILLIAM. The Mansion. Chatto, 1961. 1st UK ed. NF in dj. *Williams.* $37/£24

FAULKNER, WILLIAM. Mosquitoes. NY: Boni & Liveright, 1927. One of 3047 ptd. Sm 8vo. Blue cl. Earliest dj, ptd w/red on grn featuring a mosquito design. Fine in dj (wear, spine dkng). *Antic Hay.* $2,500/£1,603

FAULKNER, WILLIAM. New Orleans Sketches. New Brunswick, NJ: Rutgers Univ, 1958. 1st Amer ed. 1/4 maroon cl, gilt. Nice in dj (fr panel chip). *Macdonnell.* $50/£32

FAULKNER, WILLIAM. Notes on a Horsethief. Greenville, MI: Levee, (1950). 1st ed. Ltd to 975 numbered, signed. 8vo. Grn cl, silver design top cvr. *Black Sun.* $850/£545

FAULKNER, WILLIAM. Notes on a Horsethief. Greenville: Levee, 1950. 1st ed. One of 950 numbered, signed. Fine w/o slipcase, as issued. *Captain's Bookshelf.* $800/£513

FAULKNER, WILLIAM. The Portable Faulkner. Malcolm Cowley (ed). NY: Viking, 1946. 1st ed. Fine in dj (few sm tears, internal archival mend fr flap). *Captain's Bookshelf.* $125/£80

FAULKNER, WILLIAM. Pylon. London: Chatto, 1935. 1st Eng ed. Nice (inscrip) in dj (rubbed, sl mkd, chipped spine panel, tanned). *Clearwater.* $234/£150

FAULKNER, WILLIAM. Pylon. NY: Harrison Smith & Robert Haas, 1935. 1st ed. (Spine sl dull), else VG in Good 1st issue dj w/ ptg on rear panel (lacks much of rear panel, lower spine; chipped, rubbed). *Pacific*.* $52/£33

FAULKNER, WILLIAM. Pylon. NY: Smith & Haas, 1935. One of 310 numbered, signed. Bright silver bds (sl rubbed, spine sunned). Box (damaged; fore-edge panel missing). *Beasley.* $650/£417

FAULKNER, WILLIAM. The Reivers. NY: Random House, (1962). 1st ed. Fine (sl bump) in dj (rubbed, edgeworn, short closed tears). *Metropolitan*.* $43/£28

FAULKNER, WILLIAM. The Reivers. NY: Random House, (1962). 1st ed. One of 500 signed. Fine. *Bromer.* $575/£369

FAULKNER, WILLIAM. The Reivers. NY: Random House, 1962. 1st ed. (Sm crease in cl), o/w NF in dj (sl sunned). *Pirages.* $50/£32

FAULKNER, WILLIAM. The Reivers. NY: Random House, 1962. 1st ed. One of 500 signed, specially bound. VF in acetate dj. *Pirages.* $550/£353

FAULKNER, WILLIAM. Requiem for a Nun. NY: Random House, (1951). 1st ed. One of 750 specially bound, numbered, signed. (Spine sl sunned), o/w Fine (w/o dj or slipcase, as issued). *Captain's Bookshelf*. $750/£481

FAULKNER, WILLIAM. Requiem for a Nun. NY: Random House, (1951). 1st ed. One of 750 specially bound, signed, this out of series. 8vo. Cl-backed marbled bds. Fine. *Jaffe*. $850/£545

FAULKNER, WILLIAM. Sartoris. NY: Harcourt, Brace, (1929). 1st ed. One of 1998 ptd. (Spine extrems sl frayed), else NF in dj (professionally repaired, 1-inch chip, sm chips). *Captain's Bookshelf*. $1,750/£1,122

FAULKNER, WILLIAM. Sartoris. London, 1932. Later binding in brn cl (sl mkd). *Clearwater*. $55/£35

FAULKNER, WILLIAM. Soldiers' Pay. London: C&W, 1930. 1st British ed. VG in dj (browned, 1-inch split fr flap at spine, sl tape residue interior). *Metropolitan**. $690/£442

FAULKNER, WILLIAM. The Sound and the Fury. NY: Cape & Smith, (1929). 1st ed. White cl spine (bottom edges rubbed, extrems browned), b/w patterned paperbds. NF. (Lacks dj.) *Captain's Bookshelf*. $400/£256

FAULKNER, WILLIAM. The Sound and the Fury. NY: Cape, (1929). 1st ed. (Bkpls, sl dampstaining; spine dknd, ends frayed, corners through, edges worn, soiled.) *Metropolitan**. $143/£92

FAULKNER, WILLIAM. The Sound and the Fury. NY: Cape/Harrison Smith, (1929). 1st ed, 1st ptg. 1/4 cl, dec bds. (Bkpl removed fr pastedown, lib name, stamps rep), else Fine. *Macdonnell*. $275/£176

FAULKNER, WILLIAM. The Sound and the Fury. NY: Jonathan Cape & Harrison Smith, 1929. One of 1789. 8vo. Fine unblemished copy in 1st issue dj w/Humanity Uprooted by Maurice Hindus priced at $3.00. Top edges stained blue. White cl, dec paper bds. (Red portion of dj spine sl faded, lg diagonal piece missing top right portion fr panel.) *Dermont*. $6,000/£3,846

FAULKNER, WILLIAM. These Thirteen. Stories. NY: Jonathan Cape & Harrison Smith, (1931). 1st ed. NF (bkpl under fr flap) in dj (few sm chips, dknd spine). *Captain's Bookshelf*. $500/£321

FAULKNER, WILLIAM. These Thirteen. Stories. NY: Jonathan Cape & Harrison Smith, (1931). One of 299 signed. 2-tone cl (sl faded, grn stain fr cvr). *Argosy*. $1,200/£769

FAULKNER, WILLIAM. The Town. NY: Random House, (1957). 1st ed. Fine (sl shelfworn) in dj (sl worn). *Metropolitan**. $172/£110

FAULKNER, WILLIAM. The Town. NY: Random House, (1957). 1st ed, 1st issue. Fine in NF dj (short tears; sl rubbed). *Between The Covers*. $175/£112

FAULKNER, WILLIAM. The Town. NY: Random House, 1957. 1st ed. 2nd binding orange cl stamped in grn/black w/grn topstain; no date on dj flap, earliest price ($3.95) on flap. Fine in NF dj (edges rough). *Beasley*. $60/£38

FAULKNER, WILLIAM. The Town. Chatto, 1958. 1st UK ed. NF in dj (sm chip). *Williams*. $34/£22

FAULKNER, WILLIAM. The Unvanquished. NY: Random House, (1938). 1st ed. Fine (lacks dj). *Captain's Bookshelf*. $75/£48

FAULKNER, WILLIAM. The Unvanquished. NY: Random House, (1938). 1st ed. VG in dj (laid on paper backing). *Pacific**. $127/£81

FAULKNER, WILLIAM. The Unvanquished. NY: Random House, (1938). 1st ed. (Browning at pastedown, also external.) Dj (closed tears, soil, spine browned, lt stains, 1-inch split, internal reinforcements). *Metropolitan**. $287/£184

FAULKNER, WILLIAM. The Unvanquished. NY: Random House, (1938). 1st ed. Fine in VG dj (edge tear, dust soil). *Dermont*. $300/£192

FAULKNER, WILLIAM. The Unvanquished. NY: Random House, (1938). One of 250 numbered, signed. Fine (bd bottoms lt rubbing) w/o dj or slipcase as issued. *Between The Covers*. $2,500/£1,603

FAULKNER, WILLIAM. The Unvanquished. NY: Random House, (1938). 1st ed. One of 250 specially ptd, bound, signed. Edward Shenton (illus). 8vo. Cl-backed bds. VF in orig glassine dj (sl torn), custom-made cl fldg box. *Jaffe*. $3,500/£2,244

FAULKNER, WILLIAM. The Wild Palms. NY: Random House, (1939). 1st trade ed. (Rear hinge cracked, adhesion residue fr cvr, reps), else VG- in dj (chipped, sl rubbed, torn, creased). *Pacific**. $92/£59

FAULKNER, WILLIAM. The Wild Palms. NY: Penguin, (1948). 2nd Amer ed, 1st pb ed. NF in illus wrappers. *Turtle Island*. $35/£22

FAULKNER, WILLIAM. The Wild Palms. London, 1939. 1st Eng ed. Good. *Clearwater*. $70/£45

FAULKNER, WILLIAM. The Wild Palms. NY: Random House, 1939. 1st ed. VF in dj. *Pirages*. $750/£481

FAULKNER, WILLIAM. The Wishing Tree. NY: Random House, (1964). 1st ed. Ltd to 500. (Dj spine faded), else VF in slipcase. *Bromer*. $250/£160

FAULKNER, WILLIAM. The Wishing Tree. NY: Random House, (1967). One of 500 numbered. 8vo. Fine in dj (sl used), orig pub's slipcase. *Dermont*. $200/£128

FAUNCE, HILDA. Desert Wife. Boston: Little, Brown, 1934. Good in dj (sl soiled). *Dumont*. $45/£29

FAURE, GABRIEL. The Gardens of Rome. NY, 1924. Color pict bds (worn, edges frayed). *Freeman**. $30/£19

FAUST, KARL IRVING. Campaigning in the Philippines. SF: Hicks-Judd, 1899. 314,94pp. Aeg. Gold-stamped leather (spine crack, sm chip). *Dawson*. $50/£32

FAVOUR, ALPHEUS H. Old Bill Williams, Mountain Man. Chapel Hill: Univ of NC, (1936). 1st ed. Inscribed, signed, dated 1936. Fldg map. (Sl offsetting reps), else Fine in 1962 rpt dj. *Argonaut*. $150/£96

FAXON, F. W. Ephemeral Bibelots—A Bibliography of Modern Chap-Books and Their Imitators. Boston Book Co, 1903. Ptd cvrs, 1/4 cl cvrs. Good (lib stamp). *Moss*. $23/£15

FAY, CHARLES EDEY. Mary Celeste. NY: Atlantic, 1960. One of 1000. 14 plts, map. Blue cl, gilt. (Extrems sl worn), else VG. *Parmer*. $45/£29

FAY, MR. ELIZA. Original Letters from India (1779-1815).... NY: Harcourt, (1925). 1st Amer ed. Gilt cl. NF. *Reese*. $40/£26

FAYRER, JOSEPH. Recollections of My Life. London, 1900. Frontis port. (Spine chipped, extrems rubbed, sl cl loss.) *Edwards*. $47/£30

FAZZINI, RICHARD. Images for Eternity: Egyptian Art from Berkeley and Brooklyn. Brooklyn: Brooklyn Museum, 1975. Mint. *Archaeologia*. $65/£42

FEARING, CLARENCE W. Contemporary Kindred of Abraham Lincoln. Weymouth, MA, (1929). 1st ed. Frontis port. VG. *Wantagh*. $45/£29

FEARING, F. Reflex Action. Balt, 1930. Signed. (Spine spotted, dull.) *Fye*. $125/£80

FEARING, KENNETH. Angel Arms. NY: Coward-McCann, 1929. 1st ed, 1st bk. Fine in dj (lt used). *Beasley*. $175/£112

FEARING, KENNETH. The Generous Heart. NY: Harcourt Brace, 1954. 1st ed. Fine in dj (spine sl faded). *Mordida*. $95/£61

FEARON, HENRY B. Sketches of America. London, 1818. 2nd ed. xi,454pp + (8)pp ads, half-title. Untrimmed. Paper bds (edgeworn, expertly rebacked in paper), ptd paper spine label. Fine. Howes F65. *Reese.* $250/£160

FEARON, HENRY B. Sketches of America. London: Longman et al, 1818. 1st ed. Later full dk blue polished calf, leather spine label, raised bands. NF (few foxing spots). Howes F65. *Sadlon.* $275/£176

FEARON, HENRY B. Sketches of America. London: Longman, Hurst, 1818. 1st ed. vii,(1),462pp, errata; sm map. Teg; untrimmed. Later 3/4 red leather. Nice (foxed). Howes F65. *Bohling.* $200/£128

Feast of the Poets. (By Leigh Hunt.) NY: Van Winkle & Wiley, 1814. 143pp (lt stain lower portion some ll). Full leather (edges scuffed). *Bohling.* $40/£26

FEATHER, JOHN. English Book Prospectuses: An Illustrated History. Newtown/Minneapolis: Bird & Bull, 1984. One of 325 numbered w/folder of 14 facs. Prospectus laid in. 1/4 morocco. Bd slipcase. *Swann*.* $149/£96

FEATHER, LEONARD. The Encyclopedia of Jazz in the Sixties. NY: Horizon, 1966. 1st ed. Fine in dj (lt used). *Beasley.* $45/£29

FEATHER, LEONARD. Inside Be-Bop. NY: J.J. Robbins, (1949). 1st ed. Pict wrapper. (Spine faded, cvrs sl worn), o/w VG. *New Hampshire*.* $50/£32

FEATHERSTONAUGH, G. W. A Canoe Voyage Up the Minnay Sotor. London, 1847. 1st ed. 2 vols in 1. 2 maps, 2 plts. Orig cl. Howes F67. *Ginsberg.* $850/£545

FEDDEN, HENRY ROMILLY. Suicide. London, 1938. 1st Eng ed. Good. *Clearwater.* $39/£25

FEDER, NORMAN. American Indian Art. NY: Harry Abrams, (1965). 60 hand-tipped full-color plts. Fine in Fine dj. *Perier.* $195/£125

FEELINGS, MURIEL. Moja Means One. NY: Dial, 1971. 1st ed. Tom Feelings (illus). 11 3/4 x 8 3/4. 26pp. Fine in dj. *Cattermole.* $30/£19

FEHRENBACH, T. R. Comanches. The Destruction of a People. NY: Knopf, 1974. 1st ed. 6 color plts, 2 maps. (Lower corners sl jammed), else Fine in pict dj. *Argonaut.* $60/£38

FEIFFER, JULES. Carnal Knowledge. NY: FSG, (1971). 1st ed. Fine in dj. *Between The Covers.* $125/£80

FEIFFER, JULES. Harry, the Rat with Women. NY, (1963). 1st ed. VG in dj. *Argosy.* $30/£19

FEIFFER, JULES. Little Murders. NY, 1968. 1st Amer ed. Fine in dj (spine sl rubbed). *Polyanthos.* $25/£16

FEIKEMA, FEIKE. This Is the Year. Doubleday, 1947. 1st ed. Fine in VG dj (chipped). *Authors Of West.* $40/£26

FEILD, ROBERT D. The Art of Walt Disney. NY, 1942. 1st ed. (Ink inscrip.) Dj fragments. *Kane*.* $250/£160

FEILD, ROBERT D. The Art of Walt Disney. NY: Collins, 1942. 2nd ed. 8 1/4 x 11 1/4. 290pp. Good. *Cattermole.* $60/£38

FEININGER, ANDREAS. Andreas Feininger. A Retrospective. NY: ICP, 1976. 1st ed. NF in wrappers. *Smith.* $40/£26

FEININGER, ANDREAS. The Mountains of the Mind. NY: Viking, 1977. 1st ed. NF in NF- dj. *Smith.* $50/£32

FEIST, RAYMOND. Faerie Tale. Hill House, (1988). One of 500 numbered, signed by Feist, Don Maitz & Lela Dowling (illus). Fine in dj, slipcase. *Certo.* $75/£48

FEIST, RAYMOND. Magician. NY: Doubleday, 1982. 1st ed. Signed. Dj. *Swann*.* $230/£147

FELL, ALFRED. A Furness Military Chronicle. Ulverston: Kitchin, 1937. Frontis. Uncut. (Feps lt spotted; spine sl faded, sm mk.) *Hollett.* $452/£290

FELLINI, FEDERICO. Juliet of the Spirits. NY: Orion, 1965. 1st US ed. VG+ in dj (rubbed, 2-inch tear). *Lame Duck.* $35/£22

FELLINI, FEDERICO. Juliet of the Spirits. NY: Orion, 1965. 1st ed. Fine in NF dj. *Antic Hay.* $45/£29

FELLOWES, R. A Picture of Christian Philosophy. London, 1800. 3rd ed. xlviii,289,xlixpp (dust-soiled, few pp sl foxed). Paper-cvrd bds, linen spine (all worn, torn in places, binding loose). *Whitehart.* $39/£25

FELLOWES, W. D. A Visit to the Monastery of La Trappe in 1817. London, 1820. 3rd ed. 15 plts (12 hand-colored). Aeg. (Sl foxing, soiling.) Contemp straight grained morocco (warped, edges scuffed), gilt. *Freeman*.* $110/£71

FELLOWES-GORDON, IAN. The Battle for Naw Seng's Kingdom. London, 1971. Mint cl in dj. *Maggs.* $23/£15

FELLOWS, CHARLES. Travels and Researches in Asia Minor.... London: John Murray, 1852. xvi,510pp; 2 maps, 6 plts, all fldg. Gilt-pict cl (ends worn). *Adelson.* $120/£77

FELTON, MRS. American Life. Leeds, 1843. 3rd thousand. 136pp; fldg map. Contemp calf, gilt. (Hinges expertly repaired), else VG. *Reese.* $125/£80

FELTON, MRS. Life in America. Hull: Hutchinson, 1838. 1st ed. 129pp; 2-pg map. Aeg. Pub's cl (fr hinge repaired). VG (sl foxed). *Second Life.* $350/£224

FENELON, FRANCOIS DE SALIGNAC DE LA MOTHE. The Adventures of Telemachus, the Son of Ulysses.... London, 1797. 2 vols in 1. 12 engr plts. Leather (fr joint splitting). *Yudkin*.* $50/£32

FENN, JOHN (ed). Paston Letters. London, 1840. New Ed. 2 vols in 1. xxiv,200; vii,168pp (margins lt browned). Marbled eps; aeg. Full morocco (sl rubbed, upper hinge detached), emb gilt device upper bd, raised bands. *Edwards.* $70/£45

FENNER, PHYLLIS R. Cowboys, Cowboys, Cowboys. NY: Franklin Watts, (1950). 1st ed. Silver pict cl. NF in dj (sl edgeworn). *Sadlon.* $15/£10

FENOLLOSA, ERNEST. The Chinese Written Character as a Medium for Poetry. London: Stanley Nott, 1936. One of 2000 ptd. Good (sl mkd). *Clearwater.* $101/£65

FENOLLOSA, ERNEST. Epochs of Chinese and Japanese Art. NY, (1913). 2 vols. 1/4 cl (extrems worn; lt foxed). *Swann*.* $201/£129

FENTON, JAMES and JOHN FULLER. Partingtime Hall. (London): Viking/Salamander, (1987). 1st ed. Signed by Fenton. Fine in Fine dj. *Dermont.* $45/£29

FENTON, JAMES. All the Wrong Places. London, 1989. 1st Eng ed. Fine in dj. *Clearwater.* $31/£20

FENTON, JAMES. A German Requiem. Edinburgh: Salamander, 1980. 1st ed. Fine in handsewn ptd wraps. *Lame Duck.* $85/£54

FENTON, JAMES. The Memory of War. Edinburgh: Salamander, 1982. 1st ed. Signed. Red cl. Fine in Fine dj. *Dermont.* $45/£29

FENTON, NORMAN. Shell Shock and Its Aftermath. St. Louis: C.V. Mosby, 1926. 1st ed. Frontis. Panelled crimson cl. Jelliffe's bkpl, stamp. VG (lib stamp tp, spine #s). *Gach.* $75/£48

FENWICK, JOHN. Observations on the Trial of James Coigly.... London: the Author, 1798. Mod 1/4 sheep (browned, foxed). Good. *Boswell.* $350/£224

FENYO, IVAN. North Italian Drawings from the Collection of the Budapest Museum of Fine Arts. NY, 1965. 144 plts. Good in dj (worn). *Washton.* $45/£29

FERBER, EDNA. Giant. GC: Doubleday, 1952. 1st ed. VG in dj (few nicks). *Houle.* $225/£144

FERBER, EDNA. Giant. NY: Doubleday, 1952. 1st ed. (Bkseller's label fep), else Fine in dj (price-clipped, lt worn). *Hermitage.* $45/£29

FERBER, EDNA. Saratoga Trunk. GC: Doubleday Doran, 1941. 1st ed. Fine (eps sl dknd) in Fine dj (tiny tears). *Between The Covers.* $85/£54

FERBER, EDNA. Show Boat. GC: Doubleday, 1926. 1st ed. One of 201 numbered, signed. (Bkpl), else Fine in pub's slipcase. *Unger.* $400/£256

FERBER, JOHN JAMES. Travels Through Italy, in the Years 1771 and 1772. London: L. Davis, 1776. Half-title, xxxiii,377 + (2)pp ads. Contemp gold-ruled calf (wear, scuffing). *Dawson.* $200/£128

FERENCZI, SANDOR. Contributions to Psychoanalysis. Boston: Badger, 1916. 1st US ed, 1st bk. Fine. *Beasley.* $125/£80

FERGUSON, ADAM. The History of the Progress and Termination of the Roman Republic. London: Jones, 1826. Engr frontis, extra tp, viii,480pp; fldg map. Contemp 1/2 calf (sl worn, sl mks). Nice. *Ash.* $78/£50

FERGUSON, CHARLES D. California Gold Fields. Oakland, CA: Biobooks, (1948). Ltd to 750. Fldg map. Good. *Heinoldt.* $25/£16

FERGUSON, CHARLES D. The Experiences of a Forty-Niner During Thirty-Four Years of Residence in California and Australia. Frederick T. Wallace (ed). Cleveland: Williams Pub Co, 1888. 1st ed. Frontis, viii,(2),9-507pp; 2 ports. Brn cl, gilt. Fine (sl insect damage spine). *Pacific*.* $184/£118

FERGUSON, CHARLES D. The Experiences of a Forty-Niner during Thirty-Four Years' Residence in California and Australia. Cleveland, 1888. 1st ed. 507pp. (Cvrs rubbed.) *King.* $100/£64

FERGUSON, F. O. Architectural Perspective. 1891. 1st ed. 41pp; 38 fldg diags. Paper-cvrd bds (soiled, spine ends damaged). Internally VG. *Whittle.* $47/£30

FERGUSON, HENRY LEE. The English Springer Spaniel in America. NY: Derrydale, 1932. Ltd to 850. VG (spine lt rubbed). *Truepenny.* $95/£61

FERGUSON, JAMES. An Easy Introduction to Astronomy.... Phila: Benjamin Warner, 1819. 4th ed. 177,(1)pp; 7 engr fldg plts. Orig full mottled calf (expertly rebacked), morocco spine label. *Weber.* $300/£192

FERGUSON, JOHN. Bibliotheca Chemica. Glasgow: James Maclehose, 1906. 1st ed for private distribution. 2 vols. Engr frontis ports. Uncut. *Christie's*.* $281/£180

FERGUSON, JOHN. Bibliotheca Chemica. London: Derek Verschoyle, 1954. Rpt. 2 vols. Red spine labels. Dj (vol 1 only, sl scruffy). *Maggs.* $140/£90

FERGUSON, JOSEPH. Life Struggles in Rebel Prisons. Phila: Ferguson, 1865. 1st ed. 206,(24)pp; port, 4 plts. *Ginsberg.* $250/£160

FERGUSON, MUNGO. Printed Books in the Library of the Hunterian Museum.... Glasgow, 1930. 1st ed. VG. *Fye.* $150/£96

FERGUSON, ROBERT. Harpooner. Leslie Dalrymple Stair (ed). Phila: Univ of PA, 1936. VG. *High Latitude.* $45/£29

FERGUSSON, ERNA. Murder and Mystery in New Mexico. Albuquerque: Merle Armitage, (1948). Signed, inscribed. Frontis dwg by Peter Hurd. (Spine wear, lacks dj.) *Cullen.* $60/£38

FERGUSSON, ERNA. Murder and Mystery in New Mexico. NM: Merle Armitage Editions, (1948). 1st ed. Frontis. Gilt-lettered black cl. VF in pict dj. *Argonaut.* $75/£48

FERGUSSON, ERNA. Our Southwest. NY: Knopf, 1940. VG in dj (clipped, worn). *Dumont.* $45/£29

FERGUSSON, HARVEY. Grant of Kingdom. NY: Wm. Morrow, 1950. 1st ed. Fine in dj (sl edgeworn). *Sadlon.* $30/£19

FERGUSSON, HARVEY. Wolf Song. Knopf, 1927. 1st ltd ed of 100, numbered, signed. Fine (no slipcase). *Authors Of West.* $350/£224

FERGUSSON, JAMES (ed). Notes and Recollections of a Professional Life, By the Late William Fergusson. London, 1846. 248pp. VG. *Fye.* $250/£160

FERGUSSON, W. N. Adventures, Sports and Travel on the Tibetan Steppes. London, 1911. 1st ed. Teg. (Sl worn.) *Oinonen*.* $225/£144

FERLINGHETTI, LAWRENCE. Her. New Directions, (1960). 1st ed. Wraps (rubbed, soiled). *King.* $30/£19

FERLINGHETTI, LAWRENCE. The Secret Meaning of Things. (NY): New Directions, (1968). 1st ed. Signed. Fine in dj (sl wear). *Lenz.* $45/£29

FERLINGHETTI, LAWRENCE. Starting at San Francisco. New Poems. (NY): New Directions, (1961). 1st ed. Record in rear pocket w/seal intact. (Spine faded; sm sticker fr pastedown), else NF in pict bds. *Captain's Bookshelf.* $75/£48

FERMOR, PATRICK LEIGH. Mani. London, 1958. 1st UK ed. Frontis. Dj (sl worn). *Edwards.* $47/£30

FERMOR, PATRICK LEIGH. Mani. London, 1958. 1st Eng ed. Frontis. Fine in dj. *Clearwater.* $62/£40

FERMOR, PATRICK LEIGH. Roumeli. London, 1966. 1st UK ed. Dbl-pg map. Dj (sl rubbed). *Edwards.* $39/£25

FERMOR, PATRICK LEIGH. Roumeli. NY, 1966. 1st ed. VG in dj. *Typographeum.* $45/£29

FERMOR, PATRICK LEIGH. The Traveller's Tree. London, 1950. 1st Eng ed, 1st bk. Nice (foxed) in dj (sl torn). *Clearwater.* $101/£65

FERN, ALAN and JUDITH O'SULLIVAN. The Complete Prints of Leonard Baskin: A Catalogue Raisonne, 1948-1983. Boston: Little, Brown for NYGS, (1984). 1st ed. Black cl, slate bds (sl shelfworn), silver lettering. NF in pict dj (sl sunned, chipped). *Baltimore*.* $80/£51

FERNALD, CHARLES. A County Judge in Arcady. Glendale: A.H. Clarke, 1954. 1st ed. VG. *Lien.* $50/£32

FERNIE, F. Dry-Fly Fishing in Border Waters. London: A&C Black, 1912. 1st ed. VG. *Hollett.* $39/£25

FERNOW, BERTHOLD. The Ohio Valley in Colonial Days. Albany: Joel Munsell's Sons, 1890. 299pp (dknd tape repair tp), index. Untrimmed. Ptd bds, leather protective cvr added. Howes F92. *Bohling.* $45/£29

FERRALL, SIMON A. A Ramble of Six Thousand Miles Through the United States of America. London, 1832. 1st ed. (12),360,(1)pp (sm emb stamp tp). Old cl (lib spine #s). Howes F93. *Ginsberg.* $400/£256

FERREE, BARR. Fort Tryon Hall. The Residence of C. K. G. Billings, Esq. Washington Heights, NY: Privately ptd, 1910. 65 plts, guards. Teg, others uncut. Full crimson morocco (upper hinge strengthened). *Europa.* $125/£80

FERRI, ENRICO. Criminal Sociology. NY: Appleton, 1898. Later ed. Gilt-stamped leather backstrip, corners, marbled paper-cvrd bds. (Spine sl worn), o/w NF. *Beasley.* $30/£19

FERRIAR, JOHN. Medical Histories and Reflections. Volume 3. London, 1798. 1st ed. 232pp. Marbled bds (detached, lacks backstrip). *Fye.* $125/£80

FERRIDAY, PETER. Lord Grimthorpe, 1816-1905. London: John Murray, (1957). 1st ed. Grn cl. VG in dj (worn). *Weber.* $25/£16

FERRIDAY, PETER. Victorian Architecture. Cape, 1963. VG in dj. *Hadley.* $47/£30

FERRIER, D. The Functions of the Brain. 1886. 2nd ed. xxiii,498pp (few fox-mks, 1 line text underlined in ink, bkpl). Eps, edges marbled. Morocco (spine sl worn), gilt. *Whitehart.* $234/£150

FERRIER, J. P. Caravan Journeys and Wanderings in Peris, Afghanistan, Tuirkistan and Beloochistan. Murray, 1856. Thick 8vo. Map. Blind-stamped cl (dull, label removed from spine, ink stain rear cvr). *Petersfield.* $546/£350

FERRIGNO, ROBERT. Horse Latitudes. NY, 1990. 1st ed, 1st bk. Fine in Fine dj. *Smith.* $20/£13

FERRIS, JAMES CODY. The X-Bar-X Boys at the Round Up. G&D, 1927. 1st ed. 5x7.5. 212pp. Lists only to this title. VG (sl cocked, sl shelfworn) in dj (chipped, spine browned, tape-reinforced, price tag removed). *My Bookhouse.* $15/£10

FERRIS, ROBERT G. (ed). Explorers and Settlers. Washington: US Dept of the Interior, 1968. VG (spine bottom sl dented). *Lien.* $25/£16

FERRIS, ROBERT G. (ed). Founders and Frontiersmen. Washington: US Dept of the Interior, 1967. VG. *Lien.* $25/£16

FERRIS, ROBERT G. (ed). Lewis and Clark. Historic Places.... Washington: US Dept of the Interior, 1975. 1st ed. Color frontis; pict eps. Yellow cl. (Ink inscrip 1/2-title), else Fine. *Argonaut.* $50/£32

FERRIS, ROBERT G. (ed). Prospector, Cowhand, and Sodbuster. Washington: US Dept of the Interior National Park Service, 1967. 1st ed. Fine. *Book Market.* $10/£6

FERRIS, WARREN ANGUS. Life in the Rocky Mountains...Rivers Missouri, Columbia, and Colorado, 1830-1835. LeRoy R. Hafen (ed). Denver: Fred A. Rosenstock, Old West, 1983. New rev ed. Fine. Howes F100. *Lien.* $35/£22

FESTING, GABRIELLE. Strangers Within the Gates. London, 1914. 1st ed. Color frontis. Teg. Illus upper bd. (Feps lt browned; spine sl rubbed.) *Edwards.* $55/£35

Festivals in San Francisco. Stanford Univ, 1939. 1st ed. Ltd to 1000. Cl-backed pict bds (cvrs spotted, soiled). *King.* $50/£32

FETLER, JOHN. The Pike's Peak People. Caldwell: Caxton, 1966. 1st ed. Frontis. (Name), else Fine in Fine dj. *Connolly.* $30/£19

FEUCHTWANGER, LION. Paris Gazette. NY: Viking, 1940. 1st US ed. Inscribed. (Crayon price fr pastedown; shelfworn), else VG + in illus bds (lacks dj). *Lame Duck.* $175/£112

FEUCHTWANGER, LION. The Pretender. Willa & Edwin Muir (trans). NY: Viking, 1937. 1st Amer ed. VG (eps sl browned) in dj (sl edgeworn, sm tears). *Antic Hay.* $20/£13

Few Days at Nashotah. (By William Ingraham Kip.) Albany: J. Munsell, 1849. 31pp, stitched. Untrimmed, unopened. (Exterior soiled.) Howes K177. *Bohling.* $75/£48

FEWKES, JESSE W. Antiquities of the Mesa Verde National Park: Cliff Palace. BAE Bulletin 51. Washington, 1911. 35 plts. VG. *Five Quail.* $25/£16

FEWKES, JESSE W. Preliminary Report on a Visit to the Navaho National Monument, Arizona. BAE Bulletin 50. GPO, 1911. 22 plts, incl dbl-pg photo, dbl-pg map, fldg map. (Plt 1 detached but present), o/w Good-. *Scribe's Perch*.* $26/£17

FEWKES, JESSE W. Preliminary Report on a Visit to the Navaho National Monument, Arizona. BAE Bulletin 50. Washington: GPO, 1911. Fine. *Perier.* $20/£13

FFOULKES, CHARLES. Gun-Founders of England. Cambridge, 1937. *Truepenny.* $75/£48

FIALA, ANTHONY. Fighting the Polar Ice. NY: Doubleday, Doran, 1907. 2nd ed. Fldg map. Teg. (Lt wear), else VG. *High Latitude.* $110/£71

FIBBLETON, GEORGE. (Pseud of Asa Greene.) Travels in America. NY: Pearson, 1833. 1st ed. 216pp. Mod cl. Howes G376. *Ginsberg.* $200/£128

FIDLER, ISAAC. Observations on Professions, Literature, Manners...During a Residence There in 1832. NY: J&J Harper, 1833. 1st Amer ed. (Margins, parts of text stained by water; rebacked, orig cl laid down; worn, mkd, label stained.) Good. *Hermitage.* $150/£96

FIELD, EUGENE. The Immortal Little Willie. SF: Ptd by John Henry Nash, 1929. Ltd ed. Folio. 4pp, incl ptd 1st pg and colophon. Color illus top of ptd pg, text ptd black/red, gilt floral border. Marbled cl folder (bkpl on inner cvr). *Argonaut.* $75/£48

FIELD, EUGENE. A Little Book of Profitable Tales. Chicago: (Privately ptd), 1889. One of 250 numbered. Colophon leaf, signed 'John Wilson & Son' (ptr), in ink, limitation notice appears to be signed 'F' or 'T.' (viii),286,(ii)pp. Teg, others uncut. 1/2 dotted ribbed ivory cl (browned, spine sl worn), black leather spine label, gilt, blue/yellow headband, blue silk marker. Internally Fine. *Temple.* $140/£90

FIELD, EUGENE. Lullaby-Land. NY, (1897). 1st Amer ed. Teg, uncut. Pict cvrs, gilt. NF (name; spine sl sunned, cvrs sl faded). *Polyanthos.* $50/£32

FIELD, EUGENE. The Mouse and the Moonbeam. NY: William Edwin Rudge, Christmas 1919. Ltd to 250. Engr frontis. Violet cl-backed marbled bds (top edge sl dknd), gilt. Very Nice (hinges cracked). *Blue Mountain.* $75/£48

FIELD, EUGENE. Penn-Yan Bill's Wooing. N.p.: Bibliophile Soc, 1914. VG + in slipcase. *Truepenny.* $30/£19

FIELD, EUGENE. Poems of Childhood. NY: Scribner, 1904. 1st ed thus. 8 color plts by Maxfield Parrish. Pict eps; untrimmed. Black cl, gilt, lg mtd color pict label fr cvr. VG (bkpl; sl rubbed, dusty). *Baltimore*.* $140/£90

FIELD, EUGENE. Poems of Childhood. NY: Scribner, Sept 1904. 1st ed. Lg 8vo. 9 color plts (incl tp) by Maxfield Parrish. Illus eps. Cl, pict label. (1 illus cvr sheet repaired.) *Book Adoption.* $250/£160

FIELD, EUGENE. Three Poems. NY: Privately ptd, n.d. (ca 1900). #126/350. (10)pp. Deckle edges. Gilt-titled cl. (Sl rubbed tips; name ep), else NF. *Cahan.* $20/£13

FIELD, EUGENE. Verse and Prose. Henry A. Smith (ed). Boston: Bibliophile Soc, 1917. 1st ed. Japan vellum spine, corners; spine gilt. (Lt soiled, bkpl pastedown), else Fine. *Hermitage.* $75/£48

FIELD, HENRY M. Bright Skies and Dark Shadows. NY, 1890. 1st ed. Color frontis, map. VG. *Wantagh.* $50/£32

FIELD, HORACE and MICHAEL BUNNEY. English Domestic Architecture of the XVII and XVIII Centuries. 1928. New, rev ed. (Lib ink stamp; cl lt soiled.) *Edwards.* $86/£55

FIELD, JOSEPH EMERSON. Three Years in Texas. Austin, 1935. Rpt. Red cl. VG + . Howes F114. *Bohling.* $22/£14

FIELD, KATE. Pen Photographs of Charles Dickens's Readings. Boston: James R. Osgood, 1871. 1st bk ed. Grn cl, gilt. *Macdonnell.* $85/£54

FIELD, MATTHEW C. Prairie and Mountain Sketches. Kate L. Gregg and John Francis McDermott (eds). Norman: Univ of OK, (1957). 1st ed. (Sl stains 2 leaves), else Fine in dj. *Argonaut.* $40/£26

FIELD, MICHAEL. (Pseud of Katherine Bradley & Edith Cooper.) The Race of Leaves. (Hacon & Ricketts, 1901.) 1st ed. Ltd to 280. Largely unopened. Bds (corners, spine head sl rubbed), dec paper, paper label. VG. *Cox.* $211/£135

FIELD, RACHEL. An Alphabet for Boys and Girls. NY: Doubleday, 1928. 1st ed. 4 1/4 x 5 3/4. 54pp. VG. *Cattermole.* $30/£19

FIELD, RACHEL. Calico Bush. NY: Macmillan, 1931. 1st ed. Inscribed. 4 wood-engr plts. Dec cl (extrems sl worn), ptd paper label fr cvr. (Lt dampstaining bottom of fore-edge), o/w Contents VG. *New Hampshire*.* $40/£26

FIELD, RACHEL. Hitty, Her First Hundred Years. NY: Macmillan, 1929. 14th ptg. 7 x 8 3/4. 3 color plts by Dorothy P. Lathrop. VG (sl worn, discolored). *Cattermole.* $20/£13

FIELD, RICHARD S. and ROBIN JAFFEE FRANK. American Daguerreotypes. New Haven: Yale Univ Art Gallery, 1989. 1st ed. 67 plts. (Inscrip) else Fine in dj. *Cahan.* $35/£22

FIELD, SAUL and MORTON LEVITT. Bloomsday. Greenwich: NYGS, (1972). One of 250 numbered. Signed by both. Orig color engr numbered, signed by Field laid in. Fine in dj (price-clipped, spine soiled), slipcase (lt soiled, worn). *Waverly*.* $38/£24

FIELD, STEPHEN J. Personal Reminiscences of Early Days in California with Other Sketches By.... (Washington): Ptd for Friends, (1893). (6),472pp. Howes F117. *Ginsberg.* $200/£128

FIELD, THOMAS W. Essay Toward an Indian Bibliography.... Columbus: Longs, 1951. Good. *Heinoldt.* $100/£64

FIELD, THOMAS W. Pear Culture: A Manual for the Propagation...and Management of the Pear Tree. NY, 1863. 286pp. Brn cl, gilt. Good. *Price.* $65/£42

FIELDING, DAPHNE. The Duchess of Jermyn Street. Boston: Little, Brown, 1964. 1st Amer ed. VG in dj (sl soiled, spine faded, sl chipped, price-clipped). *Virgo.* $31/£20

FIELDING, GABRIEL. The Birthday King. London, 1962. 1st ed. VG in dj. *Typographeum.* $15/£10

FIELDING, GABRIEL. The Birthday King. NY: Morrow, 1963. 1st ed. Fine in dj. *Antic Hay.* $20/£13

FIELDING, HENRY. The History of Tom Jones, a Foundling. A. Millar, 1750; 1749 (vol 2). 4 vols. Vol 2, 3rd ed; others 4th eds. Contemp calf, red/blue spine labels, gilt. (Sigs heavily inked out 2 vols, some joints cracked, spine ends sl worn, vol 2 spine label renewed.) *Bickersteth.* $281/£180

FIELDING, HENRY. History of Tom Jones, a Foundling. London: J. Barker, 1786. 20th-cent 3/4 morocco, marbled bds. VG (some ll soiled, marginally repaired; hinges tender). *Sumner & Stillman.* $145/£93

FIELDING, HENRY. The History of Tom Jones, a Foundling. NY: LEC, 1952. Signed by T. M. Cleland (illus). 2 vols. Full cl, paper spine label. (Hinges reinforced), else Fine in slipcase (worn). *Truepenny.* $45/£29

FIELDING, HENRY. The History of Tom Jones. London: A. Millar, 1749. 1st ed. 6 vols. 12mo. (Sl browned, pp137-154 vol 1 sm tear 1st 2 leaves, sm dent.) 18th-cent style speckled calf (rebound, lt scratches fr bd vol 4), blind dec fillet, gilt dentelled edges, dec gilt-ruled raised bands, gilt morocco spine labels. Lacks final blanks vols 1 and 3; w/exception of these variances this copy collates exactly as Rothschild 851, w/3 cancels vol 3 (H8, H9 & H10) correctly inserted and B1 vol 4 a cancel. *Edwards.* $1,950/£1,250

FIELDING, HENRY. The Journal of a Voyage to Lisbon. London: (A. Millar), 1755. 1st published ed. 8vo. Complete w/half-title, contemp binding. Contemp calf spine (sl strengthening), 5 raised bands, red morocco label, marbled bds; all edges sprinkled. Protective slipcase w/inner chemise. 2 bkpls of Col. R.H. Isham. *Book Block.* $700/£449

FIELDING, HENRY. The Journal of a Voyage to Lisbon. London: A. Millar, 1755. 1st pub ed. Complete w/half-title. As always, pp241-276 mispaginated 193-228. Early full calf (rebacked in later calf), leather spine label. VG (sl edgeworn). *Sumner & Stillman.* $575/£369

FIELDING, HENRY. A Journey from This World to the Next. Waltham Saint Lawrence: Golden Cockerel, 1930. 1st ed thus. #206/500. 6 copper etchings by Denis Tegetmeier. Teg; uncut. Gilt-stamped beige cl (spine sl dknd), gilt-stamped red morocco spine label. VG. *Houle.* $150/£96

FIELDING, HENRY. Miscellanies. London: The Author, 1743. Vols 1-2, 1st ed; vol 3, 2nd ed. Contemp calf. (2 vols lack feps; edgeworn, joints sl cracked), o/w internally VG. *Sumner & Stillman.* $475/£304

FIELDING, HENRY. The Tragedy of Tragedies. London: J. Roberts, 1731. 1st ed, 1st ptg of 'Annotations of H. Scriblerus Secundus.' 1/2 calf, marbled bds (worn). Good (Frontis, tp, leaves sl browned; final text leaf cut close at bottom margin, final blank wanting). *Black Sun.* $250/£160

FIELDING, HENRY. Works. With an Essay on His Life and Genius by Arthur Murphy Esq. J. Johnson, 1806. New ed. 8vo. 10 vols. Port, facs vol 1. Extra-illus by addition of 2 plts vol 3 and 20 etchings by George Cruikshank vols 5-9 illustrating novels Joseph Andrews, Amelia, and Tom Jones. (Some foxing incl 1 or 2 plts, sm corner of leaf vol 6 neatly repaired.) 20th cent mottled calf gilt, dec cvrs gilt, backs panelled, gilt, aeg. Fine set. *Hatchwell.* $936/£600

FIELDING, T. H. On the Theory and Practice of Painting in Oil and Water Colours.... London: Ackerman, 1846. 4th ed. Frontis, 2 chromolithos, 9 lithos (foxed), 7 other plts. Orig cl. VG. *Argosy.* $250/£160

FIELDING, WILLIAM. Strange Superstitions and Magical Practices. 1945. VG +. *Middle Earth.* $25/£16

FIELDS, JOSEPH and JEROME CHODOROV. The Ponder Heart. NY: Random House, (1956). 1st ed. Photo frontis and title. Bds, pict onlay. NF in VG dj (longish closed tear fr panel). *Reese.* $50/£32

FIENNES, CELIA. The Journeys of.... Christopher Morris (ed). London, 1949. Rev ed. Dj (chipped). *Edwards.* $23/£15

FIFOOT, RICHARD. A Bibliography of Edith, Osbert and Sacheverell Sitwell. London, 1971. 2nd ed. NF in NF dj. *Polyanthos.* $35/£22

Fifty Years of Lawn Tennis in the United States. NY: US Lawn Tennis Assoc, 1931. 1st ed. One of 3000. Grn cl. VF. *Cummins.* $150/£96

Fifty-One Original Fables, with Morals and Ethical Index. (By Jonathan Birch.) Also a translation of Plutarch's Banquet of the Seven Sages, rev for this work. Hamilton, Adams, 1833. 1st ed. Frontis, 51 engr plts. 85 orig designs by R. Cruikshank. (Gathering sprung.) Contemp binder's cl (sl worn), leather label. Clean. *Hatchwell.* $94/£60

FIGGIS, DARRELL. The Paintings of William Blake. London: Ernest Benn, 1925. Ltd to 1150. 100 plts (5 color). Cl-backed patterned bds (sl worn), gilt. *Hollett.* $234/£150

FILKINS, C. C. The China Painters' A, B, C. Buffalo, NY: Courier, 1915. 1st ed. 8 chromolitho plts. Lib bds, orig stiff wraps bound in. Good (ex-lib). *Worldwide.* $18/£12

FILLEY, WILLIAM. Life and Adventures of William Filley, Who Was Stolen from His Home.... Chicago: Filley & Ballard, 1867. 2nd ed. 112pp; 8 plts. Orig fr pict wrapper (chipped, soiled, rear lacking; occasional fox mk, sl marginal dampstaining), else Internally VG in 1/2 gilt morocco and cl slipcase. Howes F128. *Reese.* $850/£545

Film Flashes, the Wit and Humor of a Nation in Pictures. NY: Leslie-Judge, (1916). Cl-backed bds (heavily worn, soiled). *King.* $50/£32

FINCH, HENRIE. Law or, A Discourse Thereof. London: Soc of Stationers, 1627. Mod sheep, blind-emb cvrs (sl dusty). Boswell. $650/£417

FINCHAM, HENRY W. Artists and Engravers of British and American Bookplates. London: Kegan Paul et al, 1897. 1st ed. One of 1050. Inscribed presentation copy. Frontis. Good (corners bumped, cl soiled). Reese. $85/£54

Finden's Illustrations of the Life and Works of Lord Byron. London: John Murray, 1833-4. 4th ed. 3 vols. 160 plts, incl 3 engr titles. Aeg. Full pebble-grain red morocco (soiled, worn), gilt. (Some pg, plt margins dampstained), else Contents VG. Waverly*. $385/£247

FINDEN, WILLIAM and WILLIAM HENRY BARTLETT. The Ports, Harbours, Watering-Places, and Coast Scenery of Great Britain. London: George Virtue, 1839. 2 vols. 4to. Engr frontis, 122 engr plts (lacks frontis vol 2, lt spotting, browning). Gilt edges. Contemp grn morocco (lt rubbed, stained), gilt. Christie's*. $613/£393

FINDLEY, PALMER. Priests of Lucina, the Story of Obstetrics. Boston, 1939. VG. Fye. $100/£64

Fine Old Bindings with Other Interesting Miscellanea in Edward Almack's Library. London: Blades, East & Blades, 1913. Ltd to 200. 52 plts (27 emb chromolithos). White/maroon cl (sl bumped). Good (minor offset from chromolithos). Maggs. $741/£475

FINE, RUTH E. and WILLIAM MATHESON (selected by). Printers' Choice: A Selection of American Press Books, 1968-1978. Austin: W. Thomas Taylor, 1983. One of 325 numbered. Graduated lt brn/orange/cream linen paper, paper spine label. VF. Heller. $425/£272

FINERTY, JOHN F. War-Path and Bivouac, or, The Conquest of the Sioux. Chicago: (Privately pub, 1890). 1st ed. 460pp; fldg map. Dec blue cl (rubbed, spotted, worn, corners showing), gilt. Internally Fine. Overall VG-. Howes F136. Harrington. $125/£80

FINERTY, JOHN F. War-Path and Bivouac. Milo M. Quaife (ed). Chicago: Lakeside, 1955. Teg. Fine in box. Reissue of Howes F136. Cahan. $30/£19

FINKELSTEIN, SIDNEY. Jazz: A People's Music. NY: Citadel, 1948. 1st ed. Black bds (soiled, bumped, sm spine tear). VG in Fair ptd dj (lacks spine, chipped, blurb detached from rear flap). Very Nice internally. Blue Mountain. $45/£29

FINLAY, VIRGIL. An Astrology Sketch Book. West Kingston: Grant, 1975. 1st ed. Fine in Fine dj. Other Worlds. $25/£16

FINLAYSON, ARCHIBALD W. A Trip to America. Glasgow, 1879. Inscribed. 54pp. Gilt blue cl. VG (bkpl). Reese. $200/£128

FINLAYSON, H. H. The Red Centre. Sydney, 1943. 5th ed. 52 photo plts, fldg map. Black cl, gilt. VG. Price. $27/£17

FINLEY, JAMES B. Sketches of Western Methodism. W. E. Strickland (ed). Cincinnati: The Author, 1854. 1st ed. 551pp; port. (Cl faded.) Howes F146. Ginsberg. $125/£80

FINLEY, JOHN. A Pilgrim in Palestine. NY: Scribner, 1920. Frontis, 23 plts. (Edges rubbed), o/w VG. Worldwide. $18/£12

FINLEY, M. I. and DENIS MACK SMITH. A History of Sicily. NY: Viking, 1968. 3 vols. VG in dj. Turtle Island. $135/£87

FINN, FRANK. Wild Beasts of the World. NY: Dodge, ca 1909. Probable 1st Amer ed. 2 vols. 100 color plts. (Sl foxed, hinges cracking; spines cocked, sl faded, stains, soil vol 1, sm split rear joints.) Waverly*. $77/£49

FINNEY, CHARLES G. The Circus of Dr. Lao. NY: Viking, 1935. 1st ed, 1st bk. Fine in dj (lt rubbed, few sm chips, spine dknd). Captain's Bookshelf. $150/£96

FINNEY, CHARLES G. The Circus of Dr. Lao. NY: Viking, 1935. 1st ed. Illus eps. VF in dj. Jaffe. $350/£224

FINNEY, CHARLES G. The Circus of Dr. Lao. NY: LEC, 1982. One of 2000 numbered, signed by Claire Van Vliet (illus). Dec cl, bds. VF in slipcase. Reese. $95/£61

FINNEY, CHARLES G. The Circus of Dr. Lao. NY: LEC, 1982. #1761/2000 signed by Claire Van Vliet (illus). Fine in slipcase (lt soiled). Hermitage. $125/£80

FINNEY, CHARLES G. The Circus of Dr. Lao. Viking, July 1935. 1st ed. Dec eps, cvr. Good. Scribe's Perch*. $60/£38

FINNEY, JACK. The Body Snatchers. London: Eyre & Spottiswoode, 1955. 1st British ed. VG (ep split, pp lt sunned, sm white mk fr panel) in dj (sl worn, creased, back panel sl dusty). Metropolitan*. $195/£125

FINNEY, JACK. Good Neighbor Sam. S&S, 1963. 1st ed. VG in dj. Madle. $65/£42

FINNEY, JACK. Good Neighbor Sam. NY: S&S, 1963. 1st ed. VG+ (sm stamp fr pastedown; corners sl bumped) in VG+ dj (lt nicking, sl dkng spine ends). Between The Covers. $100/£64

FINNEY, JACK. I Love Galesburg in the Springtime. NY: S&S, 1963. 1st ed. VG+ in VG dj (lt soiled, spine browned, sl chipped). Bernard. $60/£38

FINNEY, JACK. Time and Again. NY: S&S, 1970. 1st ed. (Bkpl), else NF in VG+ dj (short edgetear, lt edgewear). Lame Duck. $150/£96

FIRBANK, RONALD. The Artificial Princess. London, 1934. One of 2000 ptd. Very Nice in dj. Clearwater. $117/£75

FIRBANK, RONALD. The Complete Ronald Firbank. London: Duckworth, 1961. 1st ed thus. Fine in VG dj (sl browned). Williams. $47/£30

FIRBANK, RONALD. The Flower Beneath the Foot. NY: Brentanos, (1924). 1st Amer ed. VG (contemp inscrip, sl offsetting fep) in VG dj (lt soil, lt edgeworn). Between The Covers. $150/£96

FIRBANK, RONALD. The Flower Beneath the Foot. NY: Brentano's, 1924. 1st ed. NF (sig, date from year of pub; lacks dj). Warren. $45/£29

FIRBANK, RONALD. Inclinations. London: Grant Richards, 1916. VG (sm name stamp; sl bumped, crown lt sunned) in VG- dj (lt crown loss, spine crease, sm chips, tears). Between The Covers. $185/£119

FIRBANK, RONALD. The New Rythum and Other Pieces. London, 1962. 1st ed. Fine in Fine dj. Polyanthos. $25/£16

FIRBANK, RONALD. Odette. 1916. 1st ed. VG in wrappers (lower wrapper sl browned). Words Etc. $195/£125

FIRBANK, RONALD. Prancing Nigger. NY, (1924). 1st Amer ed. Fine (spine sl sunned, extrems sl rubbed) in dj lined w/rice paper (spine sunned, pieces missing, few chips, tears). Polyanthos. $60/£38

FIRBANK, RONALD. The Princess Zoubaroff. London: Grant Richards, 1920. One of 530 ptd. VG (sl mkd, bumped, sl worn) in dj (ragged, lacks much of spine). Clearwater. $133/£85

FIRBANK, RONALD. Santal. NY: Grove, 1955. 1st Amer ed. One of approx 500 ptd. NF in NF dj. Warren. $75/£48

FIRBANK, RONALD. Sorrow in Sunlight. London, 1924. #493/1000 numbered. Unopened. (Cvrs sl waterstained), else VG. Buckley. $55/£35

FIREBAUGH, ELLEN. The Physician's Wife and the Things That Pertain to Her Life. Phila, 1899. 186pp. VG. Fye. $60/£38

FIREBAUGH, W. C. The Inns of the Middle Ages. Chicago: Pascal Covici, 1924. One of 900 numbered. Good (edgeworn, rubbed). Agvent. $35/£22

FIREMAN, JANET R. The Spanish Royal Corps of Engineers in the Western Borderlands, Instrument of Bourbon Reform 1764-1815. Glendale, 1977. 1st ed. One of 1001. VF. No dj as issued. *Turpen.* $70/£45

FIREMAN, JANET R. The Spanish Royal Corps of Engineers in the Western Borderlands. Glendale: A.H. Clark, 1977. 1 fldg map repro. (Lt worn), else VG. *Dumont.* $85/£54

FIREMAN, JANET R. The Spanish Royal Corps of Engineers in the Western Borderlands.... Glendale: Clark, 1977. 1st ed. One of 1001. Frontis map, 13 maps and plans. Red cl. VF. *Argonaut.* $75/£48

First Garden Book, Being a Faithful Reprint...by Thomas Hyll Londyner 1563. Herrin, IL, 1939. Ltd to 266. 9 facs. Prospectus laid in. Orange/brn cl, gilt. Very Nice in dj. *Cady.* $20/£13

First Impressions of America. (By John Walter.) London, 1867. 1st ed. Inscribed. iv,131pp. Grn cl, gilt. Howes W72. *Maggs.* $273/£175

First Railroad in America. Quincy: Granite Railway Co, 1926. Dec paper over bds, plain linen spine. Good. *Scribe's Perch*.* $20/£13

First Settlers of Virginia.... (By John Davis.) NY: I. Riley, 1806. 2nd ed. Later period-style full calf, red leather spine labels, gilt. (Sm blank piece excised tp, marginal tear 1 leaf), o/w Fine. *Kane*.* $190/£122

FISCHEL, OSKAR. Raphael. Bernard Rackham (trans). 1948. 2 vols. Frontis port, 302 plts. Djs (soiled, torn, sl loss). *Edwards.* $101/£65

FISCHEL, OSKAR. Raphael. London, 1948. 2 vols. 302 plts. (Sl shelf-rubbed.) *Washton.* $50/£32

FISCHER, BRUNO. Quoth the Raven. GC: DCC, 1944. 1st ed. Fine in dj (rubbed, sl wear). *Mordida.* $45/£29

FISCHER, HANS. Puss in Boots. NY: HBJ, n.d. 1957. 8 1/2 x 11 1/4. 32pp. Pict bds. Good in dj. *Cattermole.* $25/£16

FISCHER, MARTIN. William B. Wherry: Bacteriologist. Springfield, IL, 1938. 1/2 leatherette. VG in dj, box. *Argosy.* $50/£32

FISH, ROBERT L. Schlock Homes. NY: S&S, 1966. 1st ed. Fine in dj (sl browned). *Metropolitan*.* $57/£37

FISHBEIN, MORRIS. A Bibliography of Infantile Paralysis. 1789-1944. Phila, 1946. 1st ed. VG. *Fye.* $60/£38

FISHER, A. The Art of Enamelling Upon Metal. London: Studio, 1906. 26 plts (2 color). Contents Clean; casing Good-. *Scribe's Perch*.* $90/£58

FISHER, A. K. The Hawks and Owls of the United States in Their Relation to Agriculture. Washington, 1893. 1st ed. 26 chromolithos. (Cl sl worn, shaken.) *Maggs.* $242/£155

FISHER, A. K. et al. NAF No. 7: The Death Valley Expedition: A Biological Survey of Parts of California...Part II. Washington: USDA, 1893. 1st ed. 402pp, 14 plts, 5 color maps. Uncut. Contents VG + in pict wraps (spine chipped). *Mikesh.* $45/£29

FISHER, BUD. The Mutt and Jeff Cartoons. Book 3. Boston, 1912. (Worn, soiled, warped, stained.) *King.* $65/£42

FISHER, E. A. Anglo-Saxon Towers. Newton Abbot: David & Charles, 1969. 4 maps. (Emb lib stamp tp.) Dj. *Ars Artis.* $28/£18

FISHER, ELIJAH. Elijah Fisher's Journal While in the War for Independence.... Augusta: Badger & Manley, 1880. 1st ed. Fine in orig ptd wrappers. Howes F149. *Lucas.* $80/£51

FISHER, G. P. Life of Benjamin Silliman, M.D., LL.D.... NY, 1866. 2 vols. Frontis. (Ex-lib; some sigs sprung; cvrs worn.) *Goodrich.* $95/£61

FISHER, HARRISON. Bachelor Belles. NY: Dodd, Mead, 1908. 1st ed. Gray cl, pict paper onlay fr bd stamped in gilt. (Few lt stains), else VG. *Hermitage.* $150/£96

FISHER, HENRY W. Abroad with Mark Twain and Eugene Field, Tales They Told a Fellow Correspondent. Merle Johnson (ed). NY: Nicholas L. Brown, 1922. 1st trade ed. Blue cl lettered in brn. Fine. BAL II:252. *Macdonnell.* $65/£42

FISHER, JOSEPH. The History of Landholding in England. London, 1876. 1st ed. 95pp + 43pg list. Paper spine label. (Upper hinge cracked, spine faded; lib bkpl.) *Edwards.* $47/£30

FISHER, M. F. K. The Art of Eating. Cleveland: World, (1954). 1st ed. Fine in dj (inside tape repairs). *Dermont.* $35/£22

FISHER, M. F. K. A Cordiall Water. London, 1963. 1st Eng ed. Very Nice in dj. *Clearwater.* $31/£20

FISHER, M. F. K. The Gastronomical Me. NY: Duell, Sloan & Pearce, (1943). 1st ed. (Ink inscrip), o/w VG in dj (lt worn, chip). *Hermitage.* $65/£42

FISHER, M. F. K. Here Let Us Feast. NY, 1946. 1st ed. NF in NF dj (sl shelf wear, sunning). *Warren.* $60/£38

FISHER, M. F. K. Here Let Us Feast. NY: Viking, 1946. 1st ed. NF (inscrip) in dj (price-clipped). *Turtle Island.* $50/£32

FISHER, M. F. K. Here Let Us Feast: A Book of Banquets. NY: Viking, 1946. VG (bd edges sl dknd) in VG + dj (lt edgeworn, lt dknd). *Between The Covers.* $85/£54

FISHER, M. F. K. With Bold Knife and Fork. NY: Putnam, (1969). 1st ed. Beautiful in dj (price-clipped). *Captain's Bookshelf.* $100/£64

FISHER, R. A. Contributions to Mathematical Statistics. NY: John Wiley, 1950. 1st collected ed. Frontis port. VG. *Glaser.* $150/£96

FISHER, RAYMOND H. The Russian Fur Trade, 1550-1700. Berkeley/L.A.: Univ of CA, 1943. 1st ed. Frontis, fldg map. Fine in ptd wrappers (spine, edges sl dknd). *Argonaut.* $90/£58

FISHER, STANLEY W. English Blue and White Porcelain of the 18th Century. London: Batsford, (1947). 1st ed. 45 plts (4 color). Blue cl, gilt. Good in dj. *Karmiole.* $75/£48

FISHER, T. W. Plain Talk About Insanity.... Boston: Alexander Moore, 1872. 1st ed. 98,(2)pp. Ptd mauve cl (sl shelfworn). VG. *Gach.* $125/£80

FISHER, VARDIS. Children of God. NY/London: Harper, (1939). 1st ed. 2-tone cl, gilt lettering. (Spine sl soiled), else Fine. *Argonaut.* $40/£26

FISHER, VARDIS. City of Illusion. NY: Harper, (1941). 1st ed. VG in dj (chipped, edgeworn). *Turtle Island.* $45/£29

FISHER, VARDIS. Idaho: A Guide in Word and Picture. Caxton, 1937. 1st ed. Fine in Clean dj (spine, rear panel chipped). *Authors Of West.* $200/£128

FISHER, VARDIS. Passions Spin the Plot. Caldwell/GC: Caxton/Doubleday, Doran, 1934. 1st ed. One of approx 2000. (Eps sl browned), o/w VG + in VG + color pict dj. *Bernard.* $100/£64

FISHER, VARDIS. Tale of Valor. Doubleday, 1958. 1st ed. Fine in VG dj. *Authors Of West.* $40/£26

FISHER, WILLIAM E. and ARTHUR A. A Monograph of the Works of William E. Fisher, Arthur Fisher, Architects. N.p., n.d. (ca 1925). 27 photo plts. Lettered wrappers (lt worn). *Freeman*.* $325/£208

FISHER, WILLIAM R. The Forest of Essex. London, 1887. Frontis. Cl bds (rebacked w/calf). Excellent. *Grayling.* $133/£85

FISHER, WILLIAM. New Travels Among the Indians.... Phila, 1812. 1st ed. 300pp; 2 ports at fr. Full leather. Fair. Howes F153. *Scribe's Perch*.* $200/£128

FISHMAN, ROBERT. Urban Utopias in the Twentieth Century. NY, 1977. 1st ed. (Ex-lib, ink stamps tp.) Dj (edges lt browned). *Edwards.* $31/£20

FISHWICK, MARSHALL W. Lee After the War. NY: Dodd, Mead, (1963). 1st ed. Fine in dj (lt rubbed). *Sadlon*. $15/£10

FISKE, AMOS KIDDER. The West Indies. NY/London: Putnam/Fisher Unwin, 1911. 2 fldg maps. (Sl rubbed), o/w VG. *Worldwide*. $30/£19

FISKE, DOROTHY. Academic Murder. London: Cassell, 1980. 1st ed. Fine in dj. *Mordida*. $65/£42

FISKE, ELIZABETH FRENCH. I Lived Among the Apaches. Pasadena, 1947. 1st ed. (Sm tear/crease edge tp), o/w VG in dj (sl chipped, pencil inscrip). *Baade*. $50/£32

FISKE, ELIZABETH FRENCH. I Lived Among the Apaches. (Pasadena: Trails End, 1947.) 1st ed. Signed. Fine in VG dj. *Perier*. $35/£22

FISKE, JOHN. Dutch and Quaker Colonies in America. Cambridge: Riverside, 1903. One of 250 sets. 2 vols. Cl-backed bds, ptd spine labels. VG + (spines soiled, vol 2 stained). *Bohling*. $85/£54

FISKE, JOHN. The Mississippi Valley in the Civil War. Boston, (1902). (Cvr sl worn), o/w Fine. *Pratt*. $35/£22

FISON, LORIMER and A. W. HOWITT. Kamilaroi and Kurnai, Group-Marriage and Relationship.... Melbourne, 1880. 372pp, fldg map. (Ex-lib), else Good. *King*. $75/£48

FITCH, ASA. First and Second Report on the Noxious. Albany, 1856. 336pp (upper edge many ll sl waterstained, lower joint sl wormed); 4 plts. Emb cl (sl rubbed, loss to spine ends). *Edwards*. $39/£25

FITCH, MICHAEL H. Echoes of the Civil War As I Hear Them. NY, 1905. 1st ed. Pict cvrs. Fine. *Pratt*. $115/£74

FITCH, MICHAEL H. Ranch Life and Other Sketches. Pueblo, 1914. 1st ed. One of 150 ptd. Howes F157. *Ginsberg*. $500/£321

FITCHETT, LAURA S. Beverages and Sauces of Colonial Virginia. NY: Neale, 1906. (Edgeworn, spine faded.) *Perier*. $50/£32

FITE, EMERSON D. and ARCHIBALD FREEMAN. A Book of Old Maps Delineating American History...to the Close of the Revolutionary War. Cambridge, 1926. 75 plts, incl color frontis. (Corner frayed.) *Swann**. $138/£88

FITE, GILBERT C. The Farmers' Frontier, 1865-1900. NY: Holt, Rinehart & Winston, (1966). 1st ed. VG in dj. *Lien*. $30/£19

FITHIAN, PHILIP VICKERS. Journal and Letters of Philip Vickers Fithian 1773-1774. Hunter Dickinson Farish (ed). Williamsburg, VA: Colonial Williamsburg, 1943. 2nd ptg (Oct). NF. *Sadlon*. $20/£13

FITSIMONS, F. W. The Natural History of South Africa: Mammals. London: Longmans, 1919. 1st ed. 4 vols complete. (Lt foxing), else VG + . *Mikesh*. $200/£128

FITTS, DUDLEY. More Poems from the Palatine Anthology in English Paraphrase. Norfolk: New Directions, (1941). VG in wrappers. *Graf*. $15/£10

FITZ GIBBON, CONSTANTINE. When the Kissing Had to Stop. London: Cassell, 1960. 1st ed, 1st issue (in subsequent issues reference on pg 3 to Don Juan Club was suppressed, replaced w/a cancel). Very Nice in VG dj (sm mk on spine). *Virgo*. $39/£25

FITZ-GERALD, JOHN D. Rambles in Spain. NY, 1910. 1st ed. Teg. Gilt-dec cl (sm chip upper bd). *Edwards*. $31/£20

FITZGERALD, C. P. Barbarian Beds. London/Canberra: Cresset/Australian Nat'l Univ, 1965. 1st ed. 17 plts. VG in dj (sl chipped, mkd). *Hollett*. $101/£65

FITZGERALD, ED. The Turning Point. Barnes, 1948. 1st ed. VG in Good + dj. *Plapinger*. $65/£42

FITZGERALD, EDWARD. Edward Fitzgerald and Bernard Barton. F. R. Barton (ed). Putnam, 1924. 1st ed. 2 ports. VG. *Poetry Bookshop*. $39/£25

FITZGERALD, EDWARD. Polonius: A Collection of Wise Saws and Modern Instances. Portland, ME: Thomas B. Mosher, 1901. Ltd to 450. Teg. 1/2 leather Stineman binding, dec spine, gilt, raised bands, marbled bds. Fine (bkpl, fep offsetting). *Polyanthos*. $150/£96

FITZGERALD, F. SCOTT. Afternoon of an Author. Princeton, 1957. 1st ed. Fine in dj. *Argosy*. $60/£38

FITZGERALD, F. SCOTT. All the Sad Young Men. NY, 1926. 1st ed. Grn cl. VG. *Argosy*. $175/£112

FITZGERALD, F. SCOTT. All the Sad Young Men. NY: Scribner, 1926. 1st ed. NF (bkpl; lacks dj). *Captain's Bookshelf*. $125/£80

FITZGERALD, F. SCOTT. All the Sad Young Men. NY: Scribner, 1926. 1st ed. VF in Fine dj (lt chipped). *Bromer*. $1,850/£1,186

FITZGERALD, F. SCOTT. The Beautiful and Damned. Scribner, (1922). 1st ed. VG (spine gilt dulled; lacks dj). *Certo*. $65/£42

FITZGERALD, F. SCOTT. The Beautiful and Damned. NY: Scribners, 1922. Fine in NF 2nd issue dj w/black lettering (sm nick crown). *Between The Covers*. $5,500/£3,526

FITZGERALD, F. SCOTT. Bits of Paradise. Scottie Fitzgerald Smith and Matthew J. Bruccoli (eds). London, (1973). 1st ed. Fine in dj. *Argosy*. $45/£29

FITZGERALD, F. SCOTT. Borrowed Time. Alan and Jennifer Ross (eds). (London): Grey Walls, (1951). 1st ed. (Sig.) Dj (dknd). *Argosy*. $50/£32

FITZGERALD, F. SCOTT. The Crack-Up. NY, 1945. 1st ed, 1st Eng issue w/pasted label on p2, 'This is a New Directions book distributed through the British Empire.' VG in VG dj. *Smith*. $50/£32

FITZGERALD, F. SCOTT. Flappers and Philosophers. NY: Scribner, 1920. 1st ed. NF (spine dull; lacks dj). *Captain's Bookshelf*. $175/£112

FITZGERALD, F. SCOTT. The Great Gatsby. (London): Grey Walls, (1948). 1st ed thus. Fine in NF dj (spine extrems sl rubbed). *Between The Covers*. $85/£54

FITZGERALD, F. SCOTT. The Great Gatsby. NY: Scribner, 1925. 1st ed, 1st ptg ('sick in tired' at 205.9-10). Grn cl, gilt. Fine (inscrip). *Macdonnell*. $600/£385

FITZGERALD, F. SCOTT. The Great Gatsby. (NY): LEC, 1980. One of 2000 numbered, signed by Fred Meyer (illus). Pict cl. Fine in pub's slipcase. *Hermitage*. $125/£80

FITZGERALD, F. SCOTT. The Great Gatsby. SF: Arion, 1984. One of 400 signed by Michael Graves (illus). Prospectus laid in. 1/2 cl. Cl slipcase. *Swann**. $201/£129

FITZGERALD, F. SCOTT. The Last Tycoon. Grey Walls, 1949. 1st ed. VG in pict dj (rubbed). *Words Etc.* $55/£35

FITZGERALD, F. SCOTT. The Letters of.... Andrew Turnbull (ed). NY: Scribner, (1963). 1st ed. NF (name) in VG + dj (edgeworn, chipped). *Fuller & Saunders*. $35/£22

FITZGERALD, F. SCOTT. Tales of the Jazz Age. NY: Scribner, 1922. 1st ed. (Spine dull), else NF (lacks dj). *Captain's Bookshelf*. $150/£96

FITZGERALD, F. SCOTT. Taps at Reveille. NY: Scribner, 1935. 1st ed. 8vo. Dk grn cl. Fine in dj (sl repair). *Appelfeld*. $1,750/£1,122

FITZGERALD, F. SCOTT. Tender Is the Night. London: Grey Walls, (1953). 1st Eng ed, author's final rev text. Fine (ep sl brn) in Fine wraparound dj. *Certo*. $85/£54

FITZGERALD, F. SCOTT. Tender Is the Night. London: Grey Walls, (1953). 1st Eng ed of rev version. (Eps dknd from flap offsetting), else Fine in Fine dj. *Between The Covers*. $125/£80

FITZGERALD, F. SCOTT. Tender Is the Night. (NY): LEC, (1982). One of 1500 numbered, signed by Charles Scribner III (intro) and Fred Meyer (illus). Pict cl. Fine in pub's slipcase. *Hermitage.* $125/£80

FITZGERALD, F. SCOTT. Tender Is the Night. NY: Scribner, 1934. 1st ed, 2nd state w/o 'A' on c. pg. Grn cl, gilt. (Name inked out fep), else VG. *Macdonnell.* $65/£42

FITZGERALD, F. SCOTT. Tender Is the Night. NY: Scribner, 1934. 1st ed w/dj. 8vo. Dk grn cl. Dj (reinforced w/masking tape to verso). *Appelfeld.* $1,750/£1,122

FITZGERALD, F. SCOTT. Tender Is the Night. LEC, 1982. One of 2000 signed by Fred Meyer (illus) and Charles Scribner III (intro). Frontis, 8 color plts. LEC newsletter laid in. Pict cl. Mint in tissue dj, pub's slipcase. *Pirages.* $125/£80

FITZGERALD, F. SCOTT. This Side of Paradise. NY, 1920. 1st Amer ed, 1st bk. (New eps; spine professionally mended, corners sl rubbed, fr cvr sl faded.) *Polyanthos.* $250/£160

FITZGERALD, F. SCOTT. This Side of Paradise. NY: Scribner, 1920. 1st ed, 1st bk. Grn cl. Sound. *Appelfeld.* $500/£321

FITZGERALD, FRANCES. Fire in the Lake. Boston: Little, Brown, (1972). 1st ed. VG+ in VG+ dj. *Fuller & Saunders.* $25/£16

FITZGERALD, PERCY. The Book Fancier, or The Art of Book Collecting. London: Sampson Low etc., 1886. 1st ed. 312pp. Teg. Grn cl, gilt, beveled edges. Excellent. *Hartfield.* $85/£54

FITZGERALD, PERCY. The Life of Charles Dickens as Revealed in His Writings. C&W, 1905. 2 vols. Frontis ports. Good (ink inscrip, sl spotting; spines chipped, bumped, spine head vol I repaired, corners rubbed). *Tiger.* $28/£18

FITZGERALD, PERCY. The Life of James Boswell (of Auchinleck) with an Account of His Sayings, Doings, and Writings. London: C&W, 1891. 1st ed. 2 vols. Good (ex-lib). *Reese.* $40/£26

FITZGERALD, PERCY. Picturesque London. London, 1890. Photogravure frontis, xii,303pp + (ii) (1/2 title lt browned). Teg. Dec cl (spine sl rubbed, sl mkd). *Edwards.* $55/£35

FITZGIBBON, MARY AGNES. A Veteran of 1812. Toronto/Montreal/Halifax, 1898. 2nd ed. VG. *Mcclintock.* $25/£16

FITZHUGH, BESSIE LEE. Bells Over Texas. El Paso: Texas Western Press, 1955. One of 1250 signed. Fine in VG dj. *Gibbs.* $75/£48

FITZHUGH, GEORGE. Cannibals All! Richmond, VA: A. Morris, 1857. 1st ed. 379,(4)pp. VG (spine ends chipped, corners scuffed). Howes F165. *Mcgowan.* $450/£288

FITZHUGH, PERCY KEESE. Pee-Wee Harris: As Good as His Word. G&D, 1925. 5x7.5. 219pp. Lists (on reverse of dj) to #9. VG (shelfworn, fr cvr wrinkled) in dj (chipped). *My Bookhouse.* $30/£19

FITZHUGH, PERCY KEESE. Skinny McCord. G&D, 1928. 5x7.5. 235pp + ads. VG (shelfworn, fr cvr wrinkled) in dj (ragged). *My Bookhouse.* $30/£19

FITZPATRICK, JOHN. The Merchant of Manchac.... Margaret Fisher Dalrymple (ed). Baton Rouge/London: LA State Univ, (1978). 1st ed. Frontis, 4 maps. Blue cl. Fine in dj. *Argonaut.* $60/£38

FITZPATRICK, PERCY. Jock of the Bushveld. London/NY: Longman's, 1922. Color frontis. Grn gilt pict cl. VG. *Terramedia.* $50/£32

FITZPATRICK, PERCY. South African Memories. London, 1932. Frontis port, 3 ports. (Bkpl; sl edgeworn.) *Edwards.* $39/£25

FITZSTEPHEN, WILLIAM. The Life and Death of Thomas Becket.... George Greenaway (ed). Folio Soc, 1967. 4th imp. 8 full-pg illus. 1/4 calf, bds. Fine in pub's slipcase. *Peter Taylor.* $16/£10

FLACELIERE, ROBERT. Love in Ancient Greece. James Cleugh (trans). NY: Crown, 1962. 1st ed in English. 17 plts. VG in dj (sl torn). *Worldwide.* $18/£12

FLACK, MARJORIE. Angus and the Cat. NY: Doubleday, 1932. 10 x 6 3/4. 32pp. Pict bds. VG in dj. *Cattermole.* $50/£32

FLACK, MARJORIE. The Restless Robin. Houghton Mifflin, 1937. 10x7. Blue cl. VG in dj (smudges, closed tears). *My Bookhouse.* $25/£16

FLADER, S. L. Thinking Like a Mountain. Columbia: Univ of MO, 1974. 1st ed. Pict cl. Fine in Fine dj. *Mikesh.* $35/£22

FLAGG, WILSON. Studies in the Field and Forest. Boston: Little, Brown, 1857. vi,(ii),330pp. Textured burgundy cl (rubbed, spine faded, soiled, chipped). VG. *Blue Mountain.* $45/£29

FLAGG, WILSON. The Woods and By-Ways of New England. Boston: James R. Osgood, 1872. 1st ed. xvi,442pp; 17 heliotype plts, guards. Aeg. Pict grn cl. (Fr inner hinge sl weak; spine ends worn), else VG. *Cahan.* $200/£128

FLAHERTY, FRANCES HUBBARD. Elephant Dance. NY: Scribner, 1937. 1st ed. 33 gravure illus. Gilt-emb cl. (Spine faded), o/w Fine. *Cahan.* $50/£32

FLAHERTY, ROBERT J. and FRANCIS H. My Eskimo Friends 'Nanook of the North.' NY: Doubleday, Page, 1924. 9 photogravure plts, 6 maps. Cl-backed bds (edges, corners worn, lt soiled), paper labels. Good. *High Latitude.* $125/£80

FLAKE, OTTO. The Marquis de Sade with a Postscript on Restif de la Bretonne. London: Peter Davies, 1931. Fine w/'Colonial Edition' stamp fep. *Beasley.* $65/£42

FLAMMARION, CAMILLE. Death and Its Mystery Before Death. E. S. Brooks (trans). London: T. Fisher Unwin, 1922. Fore/lower edges uncut. (Cl sl soiled.) *Edwards.* $47/£30

FLANDERS, ROBERT BRUCE. Nauvoo. Urbana: Univ of IL, 1965. 1st ed. VG in dj (sl worn). *Lien.* $35/£22

FLANNAGAN, JOHN B. Letters of.... NY, 1942. 1st ed. VG in dj (spine tear). *King.* $45/£29

FLANNER, JANET. The Cubical City. NY/London: Putnam, 1926. 1st ed. Pict eps; top edge stained red-orange. Black cl (sl rubbed, sm tear upper joint), gilt. *Baltimore*.* $65/£42

FLANNER, JANET. The Cubical City. NY/London: Putnam, 1926. 1st ed, 1st bk. 8vo. VG (sig, cvrs sl worn) in pict dj (worn, dust-soiled). *Jaffe.* $1,250/£801

FLAUBERT, GUSTAVE. Madame Bovary. NY: LEC, 1950. #904/1500 numbered, signed by Pierre Brissaud (illus). Fine in pub's slipcase (sl sunned). *Hermitage.* $125/£80

FLAXMAN, JOHN. Compositions...from the Divine Poem of Dante Alighieri. London, 1807. Obl folio. Engr add'l tps, 110 engr plts (heavily foxed). Contemp 1/4 morocco (extrems worn). *Swann*.* $172/£110

FLECKER, JAMES ELROY. The Bridge of Fire. London: Elkin Mathews, 1907. 1st Eng ed, 1st bk. Wrappers (mkd, sl faded, edges overlapping, sl torn, creased). *Clearwater.* $109/£70

FLECKER, JAMES ELROY. Forty-Two Poems. London: Dent, 1911. 1st Eng ed. (Cvrs sl mkd, spine head chafed.) *Clearwater.* $47/£30

FLECKER, JAMES ELROY. The King of Alsander. Max Goschen, 1914. 1st ed, 1st issue. Orig red (Goschen) binding. (Sl sunned, sl bruised, spine head split), o/w Excellent in what appears to be orig tissue dj (sl nicked, creased). *Ash.* $156/£100

FLECKER, JAMES ELROY. The Old Ships. Poetry Bookshop, (1915). 1st Eng ed. (Foxing.) Pict wrappers (spine foot, edges chafed). *Clearwater.* $47/£30

FLEISCHER, NAT. Gene Tunney: The Enigma of the Ring. (NY): The Ring, Inc, 1931. 1st ed. Pict red cl (spine faded, extrems rubbed; lacks fep, frontis loose). *Cummins.* $50/£32

FLEISHMANN, MAX. After Big Game in Arctic and Tropic. Cincinnati: Jennings & Graham, 1909. 1st ed. Signed, inscribed presentation. Frontis. (Inner hinges taped.) Marbled eps; teg. Lt blue cl (cvr decs sl chipped, spine dec chipped away; sm nick), gilt. *Backman.* $515/£330

FLEITMANN, LIDA L. The Horse in Art. NY, 1931. 1st ed. Teg. (Ink inscrip, inner fr hinge loose; cvr stained, dknd.) *King.* $95/£61

FLEMING, A. M. The Gun Sight Mine. Boston: Meador, (1929). Dj (folded, chip rear). *Dawson.* $300/£192

FLEMING, A. P. M. and H. J. BROCKLEHURST. A History of Engineering. London: A&C Black, 1925. 1st ed. Frontis. VG (lib spine #s, card pocket). *Glaser.* $45/£29

FLEMING, ALEXANDER (ed). Penicillin. Its Practical Application. 1946. (Cl sl mkd, lib stamp fep), o/w VG. *Whitehart.* $23/£15

FLEMING, AMALIA. A Piece of Truth. Boston: Houghton Mifflin, 1973. 1st ed. Fine (ex-libris, sig) in dj. *Second Life.* $15/£10

FLEMING, ARCHIBALD LANG. Dwellers in Arctic Night. Westminster: Soc for the Propogation of the Gospel, 1929. 2nd ed. Signed. Map. VG. *High Latitude.* $30/£19

FLEMING, HOWARD. Narrow Gauge Railways in America. Grahame Hardy and Paul Darrell (eds). Oakland, CA: G. Hardy, 1949. One of 950 signed by Hardy, Darrell & Thompson (comp). Fine in dj. *Bohling.* $65/£42

FLEMING, IAN. Casino Royale. Macmillan, 1954. 1st US ed. VG. (Lacks dj.) *Williams.* $117/£75

FLEMING, IAN. Chitty Chitty Bang Bang—A Pop-Up Book. London: Graphics Internat'l, 1968. 1st UK ed. VG in pict bds. *Williams.* $234/£150

FLEMING, IAN. The Diamond Smugglers. NY: Macmillan, 1958. 1st Amer ed. Fine (name) in dj (sl used). *Dermont.* $100/£64

FLEMING, IAN. Diamonds Are Forever. London: Cape, (1956). 1st ed. Fine in Good dj (spine chip, nicks corners). *Reese.* $275/£176

FLEMING, IAN. Diamonds Are Forever. London: Cape, (1956). Fine in Fine dj (sl rubbed, sm bkseller label fr panel). *Between The Covers.* $1,250/£801

FLEMING, IAN. Diamonds Are Forever. London: Jonathan Cape, (1956). 1st ed. Fine in dj (sl worn). *Holmes.* $1,750/£1,122

FLEMING, IAN. Diamonds Are Forever. Cape, 1956. 1st UK ed. VG+ in VG dj (2 sm closed tears, sl crease). *Williams.* $390/£250

FLEMING, IAN. Dr. No. London: Cape, 1958. 1st ed. Girl's silhouette fr cvr. Fine in dj. *Mordida.* $700/£449

FLEMING, IAN. For Your Eyes Only. London: Cape, (1960). 1st ed. Black cl stamped in gilt/white. VF in dj (sl rubbed). *Macdonnell.* $200/£128

FLEMING, IAN. For Your Eyes Only. London: Jonathan Cape, 1960. 1st ed. NF in dj. *Lame Duck.* $200/£128

FLEMING, IAN. For Your Eyes Only. NY: Viking, 1960. 1st Amer ed. Fine (name) in dj (sl used). *Dermont.* $60/£38

FLEMING, IAN. From Russia with Love. London: Cape, (1957). 1st ed. NF (w/o dj). *Reese.* $50/£32

FLEMING, IAN. From Russia with Love. London: Cape, 1957. 1st ed. Fine in dj (sl wear spine top). *Mordida.* $900/£577

FLEMING, IAN. Gilt-Edged Bonds. NY: Macmillan, 1961. 1st ed. Fine in Fine dj. *Dermont.* $35/£22

FLEMING, IAN. Goldfinger. London: Cape, (1959). 1st ed. Black cl, gilt. VF in dj (lt rubbed, aged). *Macdonnell.* $250/£160

FLEMING, IAN. Goldfinger. Macmillan, 1959. 1st US ed. Fine in Fine dj (sm closed tear to rear panel). *Certo.* $100/£64

FLEMING, IAN. Goldfinger. NY: Macmillan, 1959. 1st Amer ed. Fine in VG dj (sl sunned, soiled). *Metropolitan*.* $103/£66

FLEMING, IAN. Ian Fleming Introduces Jamaica. Morris Cargill (ed). (London): Deutsch, (1965). 1st Eng ed. Fine in dj. *Antic Hay.* $50/£32

FLEMING, IAN. The Man with the Golden Gun. (NY): NAL, (1965). 1st Amer ed. Fine in dj (sl worn). *Antic Hay.* $45/£29

FLEMING, IAN. The Man with the Golden Gun. London: Cape, (1965). 1st ed. VF in NF dj. *Macdonnell.* $75/£48

FLEMING, IAN. The Man with the Golden Gun. London: Cape, 1965. 1st UK ed. Fine in dj. *Williams.* $70/£45

FLEMING, IAN. Moonraker. London: Cape, 1955. 1st ed. (Pg edges sl dknd, few spots on eps), o/w Fine in dj (spine sl faded, back panel sl dknd). *Mordida.* $1,500/£962

FLEMING, IAN. Octopussy and the Living Daylights. London: Cape, (1966). 1st ed. Black cl stamped in silver. Fine in dj. *Macdonnell.* $40/£26

FLEMING, IAN. Octopussy and the Living Daylights. London, 1966. 1st ed. Fine in dj. *Polyanthos.* $30/£19

FLEMING, IAN. Octopussy. NY: NAL, (1966). 1st Amer ed. Black cl stamped in red/gilt. VF in Nice dj. *Macdonnell.* $30/£19

FLEMING, IAN. On Her Majesty's Secret Service. Cape, (1963). 1st ed. Dj (sl torn, sl soiled), o/w VG. *Petersfield.* $41/£26

FLEMING, IAN. On Her Majesty's Secret Service. NAL, 1963. 1st US ed. (Label fr pastedown.) VG+ in VG dj. *Certo.* $20/£13

FLEMING, IAN. On Her Majesty's Secret Service. London: Cape, 1963. 1st ed. VG in dj. *Hollett.* $78/£50

FLEMING, IAN. The Spy Who Loved Me. NY: Viking, (1962). 1st Amer ed. Pale tan cl. Fine in VG dj. *Macdonnell.* $65/£42

FLEMING, IAN. The Spy Who Loved Me. London: Cape, 1962. 1st ed. Fine in dj. *Mordida.* $150/£96

FLEMING, IAN. The Spy Who Loved Me. NY: Viking, 1962. 1st Amer ed. Fine in dj. *Mordida.* $75/£48

FLEMING, IAN. Thunderball. London: Cape, (1961). 1st ed. NF in dj (sl tanning, price-clipped). *Reese.* $65/£42

FLEMING, IAN. Thunderball. NY: Viking, 1961. 1st Amer ed. (Name), o/w Fine in VG dj (sl wear, scrape fr panel). *Mordida.* $100/£64

FLEMING, IAN. Too Hot to Handle. NY: Perma Books, 1956. 1st pb ed. NF (spine sl slanted). *Janus.* $45/£29

FLEMING, IAN. You Only Live Twice. London: Cape, (1964). 1st ed. Black cl stamped in gilt/silver. VF in NF dj. *Macdonnell.* $75/£48

FLEMING, IAN. You Only Live Twice. London: Cape, 1964. 1st ed. Fine in dj. *Mordida.* $125/£80

FLEMING, IAN. You Only Live Twice. NY, 1964. 1st Amer ed. Fine in dj (price-clipped). *Polyanthos.* $30/£19

FLEMING, JOHN A. (ed). The Ziegler Polar Expedition 1903-1905. Washington: National Geographic Soc, 1907. 3 fldg maps in pocket. Fine. *High Latitude.* $125/£80

FLEMING, LAURENCE and ALAN GORE. The English Garden. Joseph, 1980. 2nd imp. VG in dj. *Hadley.* $25/£16

FLEMING, PATRICIA L. Upper Canadian Imprints, 1801-1841. Toronto: Univ of Toronto, 1988. VG. *New Hampshire*.* $45/£29

FLEMING, SANDFORD. England and Canada. A Summer Tour Between Old and New Westminster. London, 1884. 1st ed. xi,449,32pp; fldg color map. (Spine sunned), else VG. *Reese.* $275/£176

FLEMING, W. Four Days in the Niagara Falls in North America. Manchester: Ptd by Love & Barton, 1840. 1st ed. 24pp; fldg map, steel engr view. Dk purple cl (spine faded), gilt motif. VG. *Sotheran.* $148/£95

FLETCHER, H. The Story of the Royal Horticultural Society 1804-1968. London, 1969. Dj. *Maggs.* $41/£26

FLETCHER, HAROLD. Antarctic Days with Mawson. London/Melbourne: Angus & Robertson, 1984. 1st ed. VG in VG dj. *Parmer.* $50/£32

FLETCHER, HENRY. The Perfect Politician. London, 1680. 2nd ed. Sm 8vo. Frontis port, (viii),294pp (lt browned). Early full paneled calf (rebacked at earlier date, back corners bumped), orig spine. *D & D.* $590/£378

FLETCHER, J. S. The Chestermarke Instinct. NY: Knopf, 1921. 1st Amer ed. (Pg edges spotted), o/w Fine in dj (corners chipping, folds worn, 2 sm closed tears). *Mordida.* $50/£32

FLETCHER, J. S. The Missing Chancellor. NY: Knopf, 1927. 1st Amer ed. (Pg edges spotted), o/w Fine in dj (lt soiled, corners sl worn). *Mordida.* $45/£29

FLETCHER, J. S. The Rayner-Slade Amalgamation. NY: Knopf, 1922. 1st Amer ed. (Pg edges lt spotted; cvrs sl mottled), o/w Fine in dj (lt soiled, 2 scrapes, sm closed tears). *Mordida.* $50/£32

FLETCHER, W. Y. Bookbinding in France. Seeley Service, 1894. 1st ed. 80pp; 8 Superb full-pg chromolithos, 30 engrs. Red cl (rebound), retaining orig fr wrapper, gilt. VG (lacks last text leaf). *Whittle.* $55/£35

FLIGHT, EDWARD G. The True Legend of St. Dunstan and the Devil. London: D. Bogue, (1852). 1st ed. 24pp (1st 5 ll creased, eps foxed, sm stain bottom edge last few ll). Teg. Orig ptd wraps (dknd, professionally repaired) bound into red leather (rebacked in cl), portion of leather spine mtd (rubbed, chipped, dknd), gilt. VG. *Blue Mountain.* $275/£176

FLINDERS, MATTHEW. Matthew Flinders' Narrative of His Voyage in the Schooner Francis. London: Golden Cockerel, 1946. One of 750 numbered. Gilt-pict cl. *Swann*.* $460/£295

FLINDERS, MATTHEW. Matthew Flinders' Narrative of His Voyage in the Schooner Francis: 1798. (London): Golden Cockerel, 1946. One of 750 numbered. Fine in cl as issued. *Between The Covers.* $450/£288

FLINT, AUSTIN. Handbook of Physiology for Students and Practitioners of Medicine. NY, 1905. Presentation copy. (Cl worn, 2 sm spine tears.) *Goodrich.* $125/£80

FLINT, MAURICE S. Operation Canon. London, 1949. VG in dj. *High Latitude.* $20/£13

FLINT, TIMOTHY. The History and Geography of the Mississippi Valley. Cincinnati: E.H. Flint & L.R. Lincoln, 1832. 2nd ed. 2 vols in 1. 464,276pp (foxed). Full leather (rebacked, retaining worn orig bds, spine label). Howes F200. *Bohling.* $325/£208

FLINT, TIMOTHY. The History and Geography of the Mississippi Valley. To which is appended a Condensed Physical Geography of the Atlantic United States.... Cincinnati: E.H. Flint & L.R. Lincoln, 1832. 2nd ed. 2 vols in 1. 464; 276pp (foxed). Contemp calf, leather label (scuffed). Very Sound. BAL 6125; Howes F200. *M & S.* $225/£144

FLINT, TIMOTHY. Recollections of the Last Ten Years.... Boston, 1826. Orig bds (fr cvr loose, spine cracked), paper spine label remnants. Howes F204. *Swann*.* $138/£88

FLINT, TIMOTHY. Recollections of the Last Ten Years.... Boston: Cummings, Hilliard, 1826. 1st ed. 395pp. Recent 1/2 calf (rebound), marbled bds, leather labels. (Text sl browned), else VG. Howes F204. *Brown.* $175/£112

FLINT, TIMOTHY. Recollections of the Last Ten Years.... Boston: Cummings, Hilliard, 1826. 1st ed. 2,395pp. Mod buckram, grn leather labels. (Ex-lib.) Howes F204. *Adelson.* $225/£144

FLINT, WILLIAM RUSSELL. Minxes Admonished or Beauty Reproved. London: Golden Cockerel, 1955. #163/550. Color frontis. Orig 1/4 vermilion levant morocco, gilt, morocco bds (few sm scratches). *Hollett.* $281/£180

Flora's Dictionary. Balt: Fielding Lucas Jr., (1837). Ptd bds. (Lt foxed; worn, chipped, hinges repaired.) *Freeman*.* $410/£263

FLORESCU, RADU. In Search of Frankenstein. Boston: NYGS, 1975. 1st ed. VF in VF dj. *Else Fine.* $45/£29

FLOREY, M. E. The Clinical Application of Antibiotics. Penicillin. OUP, 1952. 1st ed. Red cl (lt mkd; ex-lib). Text Clean. *White.* $70/£45

FLORIN, LAMBERT. Boot Hill. Seattle: Superior, (1966). 1st ed. Fine in Fine dj. *Book Market.* $30/£19

FLORIN, LAMBERT. Ghost Town Treasures. Seattle: Superior, (1965). 1st ed. Fine in Fine dj. *Book Market.* $30/£19

FLORIN, LAMBERT. Tales the Western Tombstones Tell. Seattle: Superior, (1967). 1st ed. NF in VG dj. *Archer.* $35/£22

FLORIN, LAMBERT. Western Ghost Towns. Seattle: Superior, (1961). 1st ed. Fine in Fine dj. *Book Market.* $30/£19

FLOWER, B. O. (ed). The Arena. Vol. IV, V. Boston: Arena, 1891, 1892. 781; 783pp. 3/4 calf (scuffed). VG. *Second Life.* $150/£96

FLOWER, M. Victorian Jewellery. NY: Duell, Sloan & Pearce, 1951. VG. *Blake.* $100/£64

Flower-Garden. London: W.S. Orr, 1838. Color frontis, tp (both tape-repaired), 515pp (sl foxing); 10 full-pg color plts. Aeg. Orig pub's cl (repaired). Good. *Scribe's Perch*.* $110/£71

FLOYD, DOLORES BOISFEUILLET. New Yamacraw and the Indian Mound Irene. Savannah: The Author, 1936. (Sl worn), else Good in wrappers. *Brown.* $12/£8

FLUCKIGER, F. and D. HANBURY. Pharmacographia. London, 1874. 1st ed. 704pp. 1/4 leather. VG. *Fye.* $200/£128

FLUGEL, J. C. The Psycho-Analytic Study of the Family. London: IPP/Allen & Unwin, 1921. 1st ed. Fine in most of dj (3-inch spine chip, fr flap detached but present). *Beasley.* $85/£54

FLUGEL, J. C. The Psychology of Clothes. London, 1950. 3rd imp. Good. *Washton.* $25/£16

FLYING OFFICER 'X.' (Pseud of H. E. Bates.) The Greatest People in the World and Other Stories. London, 1942. 1st Eng ed. Very Nice in dj (sl frayed). *Clearwater.* $47/£30

FLYING OFFICER 'X.' (Pseud of H. E. Bates.) How Sleep the Brave and Other Stories. London, 1943. 1st Eng ed. Nice in dj (rubbed). *Clearwater.* $47/£30

FLYNN, JAY. The Five Faces of Murder. NY: Avon, 1962. 1st ed. Pb orig. Unread. VF in wrappers. *Mordida.* $30/£19

FLYNN, JAY. It's Murder McHugh. NY: Avon, 1960. 1st ed. Pb orig. Unread. Fine in wrappers. *Mordida.* $30/£19

FOA, EDOUARD. After the Big Game in Central Africa. Frederick Lees (trans). London: A&C Black, 1899. 1st ed. Frontis, xxvii,330pp, 10pp ads; map. Blue gilt pict cl (recased w/new eps; frontis, tp sl stained), else VG. *Terramedia.* $350/£224

FOA, GEORGE R. The Blood Rushed to My Pockets. London: John Calder, (1957). 1st ed. Nice (bkstore stamp) in dj. *Turtle Island.* $35/£22

FOCH, FERDINAND. The Memoirs of Marshal Foch. T. Bentley Mott (trans). GC, 1931. 1st Amer ed. Pict cvr. (Cvr sl worn), o/w Fine. *Pratt.* $35/£22

FOCILLON, HENRI. The Art of the West in the Middle Ages. Jean Bony (ed). London, 1963. 2 vols. Good. *Washton.* $65/£42

FOCK, H. C. A. L. Popular Aesthetic Considerations on the Symmetry of Pleasing Proportions. F. Lowe (trans). Cambridge, 1877. 26 plts. Cl-backed bds (worn). *Argosy.* $125/£80

FOGG, WILLIAM PERRY. Letters from Japan, China, India, and Egypt. Cleveland, 1872. Signed frontis port, 11 mtd photos (yellowed). 3/4 leather (sl rubbed), gilt. *Metropolitan*.* $201/£129

FOLDA, JAROSLAV. Crusader Manuscript Illumination at Saint-Jean d'Acre. Princeton, 1976. Good. *Washton.* $80/£51

FOLEY, EDWIN. The Book of Decorative Furniture. London, n.d. (1911?). 2 vols. 100 tipped-in color plts. (1 defective plt, ex-lib, hinges cracked; cvrs worn, sm abrasion vol 2 spine.) *King.* $195/£125

FOLEY, WILLIAM E. and C. DAVID RICE. The First Chouteaus. Urbana/Chicago: Univ of IL, (1983). Fine in dj. *Bohling.* $35/£22

FOLIGNO, CESARE. The Story of Padua. London, 1910. 2 fldg plans. Teg. Gilt-dec cl (staining). *Edwards.* $19/£12

FOLKARD, RICHARD. Plant Lore, Legends and Lyrics. London: Sampson, Low, 1884. Frontis, xxiv,610,(1)pp. Dec cl. NF. *Quest.* $190/£122

FOLKES, MARTIN. Tables of English Silver and Gold Coins. London: Soc of Antiquaries, 1763. 1st ed. 3 vols. 4to. (4),162,12; 216; (134)pp. Vol 3: 67 copper engrs. Contemp mottled calf (finely rebacked). *Karmiole.* $600/£385

FOLMSBEE, BEULAH. Little History of the Horn-Book. Boston, (1942). 16mo. 58pp. VG. *Truepenny.* $25/£16

FOLSOM, CHARLES FOLLEN. Studies of Criminal Responsibility and Limited Responsibility. N.p.: Privately ptd, 1909. 1st ed. Inscribed by James Jackson Putnam. Russet cl (edgewear). *Gach.* $50/£32

FOLTZ, CHARLES S. Surgeon of the Seas. Indianapolis, (1931). 1st ed. (Cvr lt worn, spine extrems faded, chipped), o/w VG + . *Pratt.* $55/£35

FOLWELL, WILLIAM WATTS. A History of Minnesota. St. Paul: MN Hist Soc, 1921-30. Inscribed presentation, vol 1. 4 vols. Teg. Maroon cl. VG + (vol 1 spine worn). *Bohling.* $75/£48

FONBLANQUE, JOHN. A Treatise of Equity. Phila: Abr'm Small, 1820. 2nd Amer ed. 2 vols. Contemp sheep (rebacked, worn, browned). Sound. *Boswell.* $250/£160

FONDA, PETER et al. Easy Rider. NY: Signet, 1969. 1st ed. Pb orig. NF (spine crease, sl rubbed). *Sclanders.* $23/£15

FONT, PEDRO. The Complete Diary (1775-6) of.... Herbert E. Bolton (ed). Berkeley, 1933. 1st ed. Frontis, fldg map. Fine. *Turpen.* $150/£96

FONT, PEDRO. Font's Complete Diary. Herbert E. Bolton (ed). Berkeley: Univ of CA, 1931. 1st separate ed, 1st ptg. Fldg map. VF. *Argonaut.* $175/£112

FONTAINE, WILLIAM MORRIS. Contributions to the Knowledge of the Older Mesozoic Flora of Virginia. GPO, 1883. 144pp; 54 plts. Good- (ex-lib; browning, foxed; cvr torn). *Book Broker.* $150/£96

FOORD, EDWARD. Napoleon's Russian Campaign of 1812. London, 1914. Fldg plan, 2 fldg maps. Navy cl (sl worn, shaken; lt foxed; 1 plt loose). *Maggs.* $55/£35

FOOTE, ANDREW H. Africa and the American Flag. NY: D. Appleton, 1854. 390,18ads pp; map, 7 plts. (Rubbed, spine chipped.) *Adelson.* $75/£48

FOOTE, ANDREW H. Africa and the American Flag. NY: D. Appleton, 1854. 1st ed. 390pp (sm piece clipped fep; lt foxed); 8 tinted lithos. Indigo cl (bumped, rubbed, spine faded). VG. *Blue Mountain.* $75/£48

FOOTE, HENRY STUART. The Bench and Bar of the South and Southwest. St. Louis: Soule, Thomas & Wentworth, 1876. 1st ed. viii,264pp. VG (extrems worn, spine chipped). Howes F236. *Mcgowan.* $350/£224

FOOTE, HENRY STUART. Casket of Reminiscences. Washington: Chronicle, 1874. 1st ed. 498pp. VG (extrems sl worn, rear inner hinge just starting). Howes F237. *Mcgowan.* $250/£160

FOOTE, HORTON. Harrison, Texas. NY: Harcourt, Brace, (1956). 1st ed. NF in dj (sm chip). *Bernard.* $75/£48

FOOTE, JOHN TAINTOR. Change of Idols. NY: Appleton, 1935. 1st ed. VG + in VG dj (soiled). *Bowman.* $45/£29

FOOTE, MRS. HENRY GRANT. Recollections of Central America and the West Coast of Africa. London: T. Cautley Newby, 1869. 1st ed. (vi),221,(17 ads)pp. Blue cl, gilt. Fine. *Burmester.* $468/£300

FOOTE, SAMUEL. Bon-Mots of Samuel Foote and Theodore Hook. Walter Jerrold (ed). London: J.M. Dent, 1904. 3rd ed. Aubrey Beardsley (illus). Teg. Dec pale grn cl. NF. *Captain's Bookshelf.* $75/£48

FOOTE, SHELBY. The Civil War: A Narrative. NY: Random House, 1958-1974. 1st ed. 3 vols. Vol 1 signed on special tipped-in leaf. Vol 3 inscribed. Civil War motif bkpls vols 1&2. NF in djs (vol 1 sl chipped, 1.5-inch scrape spine vol 2). *Captain's Bookshelf.* $600/£385

FOOTE, SHELBY. Shiloh. NY: Dial, 1952. 1st ed. (Spine discolored), o/w Good in dj (chipped, price-clipped). *Scribe's Perch*.* $42/£27

FOOTE, SHELBY. A View of History. (N.p.): Palaemon Press, (1981). One of 100 (of 140) numbered, signed. Saddle-stitched. Fine in stiff wrapper and dj. *Between The Covers.* $150/£96

FORAKER, JOSEPH B. Notes of a Busy Life. Cincinnati: Stewart & Kidd, 1917. 3rd ed. 2 vols. Teg. NF. *Sadlon.* $25/£16

FORBES, ALEXANDER. California: A History of Upper and Lower California. Herbert Ingram Priestley (ed). SF: John Henry Nash, 1937. Rpt. Facs sig and facs letter inserted, lg fldg map at rear. Cl-backed marbled bds, ptd paper spine label. Fine. *Pacific*.* $173/£111

FORBES, ALEXANDER. Quest for a Northern Air Route. Cambridge: Harvard Univ, 1953. 2nd ptg. VG in dj. *High Latitude.* $40/£26

FORBES, ALLAN and RALPH M. EASTMAN. Taverns and Stagecoaches of New England. Boston, 1953-4. 2 vols. Color frontis. Wraps (sl loss vol 1 backstrip). *Edwards.* $23/£15

FORBES, ALLAN and RALPH M. EASTMAN. Yankee Ship Sailing Cards. Boston: State Street Trust Co, 1948/1949/1952. 1st eds. 3 vols. Fine set in stiff pict wrappers. *Argonaut.* $175/£112

FORBES, BRYAN. The Endless Game. NY: Random House, 1986. 1st Amer ed. Fine in dj. *Mordida.* $30/£19

FORBES, BRYAN. Stranger. GC: Doubleday, 1980. 1st Amer ed. Fine in dj. *Mordida.* $40/£26

FORBES, COLIN. Deadlock. London: Collins, 1988. 1st ed. Fine in dj. *Mordida.* $35/£22

FORBES, COLIN. Target Five. London: Collins, 1973. 1st ed. Fine in dj (nicks). *Mordida.* $65/£42

FORBES, E. F. Five Years in China. London: Bentley, 1848. 1st ed. Hand-colored frontis, x,405pp. Mod 1/4 morocco. Fine. *Terramedia.* $300/£192

FORBES, ESTHER. Paul Revere and the World He Lived In. Boston: Houghton Mifflin, 1942. 1st ed. (Blind-stamp), o/w Fine in dj (sl edgeworn). *Sadlon.* $15/£10

FORBES, HENRY O. A Handbook to the Primates (Lloyd's Natural History—Monkeys). London, 1896-1897. 2 vols. 286; 302pp; 49 Nice color plts & maps. Brn cl, gilt. (Edgewear), else VG. *Price.* $65/£42

FORBES, JAMES. Illustrations to Oriental Memoirs with Explanatory Notices. London: Richard Bentley, 1835. 4to. 83 engr plts (of 85 listed), 23 hand-colored (lacks frontispieces to 2 text vols, heavy browning mostly to margins of plts, lt marginal soil). Contemp 1/2 calf, marbled bds (extrems rubbed), lettering piece (sl frayed). *Christie's*.* $1,053/£675

FORBES, JAMES. Norway and Its Glaciers, Visited in 1851. Edinburgh, 1853. 1st ed. 18 color litho plts. Sl later 3/4 polished brn calf (scuffed, joints, extrems rubbed), leather labels. *Freeman*.* $200/£128

FORBES, JAMES. Travels Through the Alps of Savoy and Other Parts of the Pennine Chain.... Edinburgh, 1843. 424pp; fldg map. Teg. 3/4 leather. (Stained.) *King.* $195/£125

FORBES, MRS. A. S. C. Mission Tales in the Days of the Dons. Chicago, 1909. 1st ed. VG. *Book Market.* $30/£19

FORBUSH, EDWARD H. Birds of Massachusetts and Other New England States. Boston, 1925-1927-1929. 1st ed. 3 vols. Louis Agassiz Fuertes (illus). NF set. *New Hampshire*.* $170/£109

FORBUSH, EDWARD H. Birds of Massachusetts and Other New England States. Vol II. MA Dept of Agriculture, 1927. 1st ed. Louis Agassiz Fuertes (illus). VG-. *Books & Birds.* $75/£48

FORCE, M. F. From Fort Henry to Corinth—Campaigns of the Civil War, Vol II. NY. Undated rpt. 204pp. Fine in dj (sl worn). *Pratt.* $20/£13

FORCE, PETER (comp). Tracts and Other Papers.... Washington, 1838, 1844, 1846. 3 vols. Untrimmed. VG (vol 2 hinges chipped, vol 4 spine top chipped). Howes F247. *Bohling.* $300/£192

FORD, BORIS (ed). The Cambridge Guide to the Arts in Britain. Volume 3. Cambridge, 1989. 12 color plts. Good in dj. *Washton.* $35/£22

FORD, BORIS (ed). The Cambridge Guide to the Arts in Britain. Volume 6. Cambridge, 1990. 10 color plts. Good in dj. *Washton.* $50/£32

FORD, CHARLES HENRI (ed). A Night with Jupiter. NY: Vanguard, 1945. 1st ed. NF in VG- dj (chipped, 2 sm holes rear panel). *Lame Duck.* $100/£64

FORD, COLIN. The Cameron Collection. NY: Van Nostrand Reinhold, 1975. NF in NF dj. *Smith.* $125/£80

FORD, COREY. Where the Sea Breaks Its Back. Boston: Little, Brown, (1966). 1st ed. (Ink name), else VG in VG dj. *Perier.* $35/£22

FORD, E. B. Butterflies of the World. London, (1946). 1st ed. NF in Good+ dj. *Mikesh.* $25/£16

FORD, FORD MADOX. The English Novel. London: Constable, 1930. 1st ed. (Paper clip removed fep), o/w Fine in VG dj (spine sl dknd, sm chips). *Captain's Bookshelf.* $125/£80

FORD, FORD MADOX. The Good Soldier. London: John Lane, 1915. 1st ed. NF (sm snag spine head). *Captain's Bookshelf.* $1,250/£801

FORD, FORD MADOX. The Good Soldier. NY: Boni & Liveright, 1927. 1st ed thus. One of 300 numbered, signed. Fine (bkpl, lacks slipcase). *Captain's Bookshelf.* $650/£417

FORD, FORD MADOX. Last Post. London: Duckworth, 1928. 1st ed. (Top pg edges dusted, lt foxed), else NF in VG dj (spine tanned, 1-inch edgetears mended on verso). *Lame Duck.* $150/£96

FORD, FORD MADOX. A Man Could Stand Up. Duckworth, (1926). 1st ed. (Sl foxing), o/w Nice. *Ash.* $70/£45

FORD, FORD MADOX. A Man Could Stand Up. London: Duckworth, (1926). 1st ed. (Sl offsetting to eps), else Fine in pict dj (2 internal mends at spine extrems). *Captain's Bookshelf.* $150/£96

FORD, FORD MADOX. Mister Bosphorus and the Muses. London: Duckworth, 1923. 1st Eng ed. Paul Nash (engrs). Buckram-backed pict bds. Excellent (foxing) in dj (sl faded, frayed). *Clearwater.* $312/£200

FORD, FORD MADOX. Provence, from Minstrels to the Machine. Phila: Lippincott, 1935. 1st Amer ed. VG in dj (sl chipped). *Hermitage.* $65/£42

FORD, GERALD R. A Time to Heal. Norwalk, CT: Easton, (1987). Signed. Aeg. Full gilt-stamped red leather. VG. *King.* $150/£96

FORD, HUGH. Published in Paris. Garnstone, 1975. 1st ed. Fine in dj (price-clipped). *Poetry Bookshop.* $23/£15

FORD, HUGH. Published in Paris. NY, 1975. Very Nice in dj. *Clearwater.* $31/£20

FORD, JAMES A. Eskimo Prehistory in the Vicinity of Point Barrow, Alaska. Anthrop Papers of Amer Mus of Nat Hist, 1959. 13 plts. VG in wraps. *Perier.* $35/£22

FORD, JULIA ELLSWORTH. Snickerty Nick. NY: Moffat, Yard, 1919. 3 color plts by Arthur Rackham. (Sl worn.) Dj (sl frayed). *Oinonen*.* $375/£240

FORD, LESLIE. Siren in the Night. NY: Scribner, 1943. 1st ed. Fine in VG+ dj (spine extrems chipping, lt rubbing). *Janus.* $50/£32

FORD, LESLIE. Trial by Ambush. NY: Scribner, 1962. 1st ed. Fine in VG dj. *Janus.* $20/£13

FORD, PAUL LEICESTER (ed). New-England Primer, a Reprint of the Earliest Known Edition.... NY: Dodd, Mead, 1899. 113,77pp; facs. Cl-backed bds (corners chipped). *Bohling.* $22/£14

FORD, PAUL LEICESTER. A Checked Love Affair. NY: Dodd, Mead, 1903. 1st ed. (Ink inscrip fep), o/w Fine in dec cl (lt worn). *Hermitage.* $75/£48

FORD, PAUL LEICESTER. The Great K and A Train Robbery. NY: Dodd Mead, 1897. 1st ed, 2nd issue, w/'train' on tp. Pict cl. Pict dj (chipped). *Swann*.* $201/£129

FORD, PAUL LEICESTER. The Great K and A Train Robbery. NY: Dodd, Mead, 1897. 1st ed, 1st state w/'train' missing from tp. Frontis, 200pp. Teg. Blue pict cl. (Feps stained; cloth worn, rubbed), else Good. *Brown.* $25/£16

FORD, PAUL LEICESTER. The Great K and A Train Robbery. NY: Dodd, Mead, 1897. 1st ed, 2nd issue, w/'Train' added to tp. Blue cl pict dec in black/red. Fine (bkpl). *Sumner & Stillman*. $80/£51

FORD, PAUL LEICESTER. Monographs of the American Revolution: Thomas Jefferson. Cambridge/Boston: CUP/A.W. Elson, (1904). Ltd to 500 numbered. 2 plts. Cancelled strike of plts add'lly laid in. Unopened. Fine in natural parchment wraps. *Blue Mountain*. $75/£48

FORD, RICHARD. A Handbook for Travellers in Spain. Part I and II. London, 1890. 7th ed. 2 vols. Map rear pocket. (Vol 2 lacks fep, sl stain pastedown vol 1; spines faded.) *Edwards*. $78/£50

FORD, RICHARD. A Piece of My Heart. NY: Harper & Row, (1976). 1st ed. Fine in dj (lt worn, dknd, few sm closed spine chips). *Hermitage*. $125/£80

FORD, RICHARD. The Sportswriter. NY: Vintage Books, 1986. 1st ed. Signed. Pb orig. Fine in pict wrappers. *Captain's Bookshelf*. $100/£64

FORD, RICHARD. Wildlife. NY: Atlantic Monthly, (1990). One of 200 numbered, signed. Fine in Fine slipcase. *Lenz*. $150/£96

FORD, RICHARD. Wildlife. NY, 1990. 1st ed. Signed. Fine (corners bumped) in Fine dj. *Smith*. $25/£16

FORD, S. H. The Great Pyramid of Egypt. St. Louis, 1882. 1st ed. Signed. 208pp. VG+. *Middle Earth*. $95/£61

FORD, THOMAS. A History of Illinois from Its Commencement as a State in 1818 to 1847. Milo M. Quaife (ed). Chicago: Lakeside, Christmas, 1945. 2 vols. Dk red cl (few sm pale spots, spine head vol 2 sl rubbed). *Sadlon*. $45/£29

FORDHAM, ELIAS P. Personal Narrative of Travels in Virginia, Maryland, Pennsylvania, Ohio, Indiana, Kentucky...1817-1818. Cleveland: Clark, 1906. 1st ed. 4 plts. Howes F257. *Ginsberg*. $125/£80

FORDHAM, ELIAS P. Personal Narrative of Travels in Virginia, Maryland, Pennsylvania.... Cleveland: A.H. Clark, 1906. 1st ed. 4 plts. Howes F257. *Wantagh*. $100/£64

FORDYCE, GEORGE. Elements of the Practice of Physic. London, 1771. 3rd ed. viii,380pp. Contemp leather (rebacked). (Sm lib stamp tp, outer margin 1 text pg), o/w VG. *Whitehart*. $234/£150

FORDYCE, GEORGE. Five Dissertations on Fever. Boston, 1823. 444pp. (Ex-lib.) Orig tree calf (worn). *Argosy*. $60/£38

FOREMAN, GRANT (ed). A Pathfinder in the Southwest. Norman: Univ of OK, 1941. 1st ed. Fldg map. (Browned, spine faded.) *Dumont*. $35/£22

FOREMAN, GRANT (ed). A Traveler in Indian Territory. Cedar Rapids: Torch, 1930. Inscribed. Frontis, fldg map. Good (lt worn, foxed). *Dumont*. $175/£112

FOREMAN, GRANT. Fort Gibson: A Brief History. Norman: Univ of OK, 1943. 2nd ed. VG in illus wraps. *Cahan*. $20/£13

FOREMAN, GRANT. Pioneer Days in the Early Southwest. Cleveland, 1926. 1st ed. (Joints lt worn, spine sl discolored.) Howes F260. *Ginsberg*. $150/£96

FOREST, LEON. Divine Days. Oak Park, IL: Another Chicago Press, 1992. 1st ed. Fine in dj. *Lame Duck*. $100/£64

FORESTER, C. S. The Annie Marble in Germany. London, 1930. 1st Eng ed. Good (rep corner torn off; cvrs sl mkd, spotted). *Clearwater*. $86/£55

FORESTER, C. S. The Barbary Pirates. NY: Random House, (1953). 1st Amer ed. Charles J. Majoujian (illus). 8vo. 187,(i)pp. Red cl. NF in pict dj. *Blue Mountain*. $85/£54

FORESTER, C. S. The Barbary Pirates. London: Macdonald, 1956. 1st UK ed. VG in dj (sl edgeworn, nicked, sl loss spine bottom). *Williams*. $39/£25

FORESTER, C. S. Beat to Quarters. NY: Editions for the Armed Services, (1945). VG in wrappers (sl worn). *Turtle Island*. $15/£10

FORESTER, C. S. The Bedchamber Mystery. Toronto, 1944. Pict bds (spine sl nicked). Nice in dj (top edge lacks 2 sm pieces). *Clearwater*. $101/£65

FORESTER, C. S. The Bedchamber Mystery. Toronto: Saunders, 1944. 1st ed. Fine in dj (spine chip). *Else Fine*. $200/£128

FORESTER, C. S. The Captain from Connecticut. Michael Joseph, 1941. 1st UK ed. VG (ink name) in dj (sl loss spine extrems). *Williams*. $117/£75

FORESTER, C. S. Captain Horatio Hornblower. Boston: Little, Brown, 1939. 1st ed. N.C. Wyeth (illus). (Lt offsetting eps), else Fine in NF dj (crown lt rubbed, sm tears). *Between The Covers*. $150/£96

FORESTER, C. S. Commodore Hornblower. Little, Brown, 1945. 1st US ed. VG in dj (sl edgewear, sl repairs rear). *Williams*. $47/£30

FORESTER, C. S. The Commodore. Michael Joseph, 1945. 1st UK ed. VG (lacks dj). *Williams*. $16/£10

FORESTER, C. S. The Commodore. London: Michael Joseph, 1945. 1st UK ed. VG+ (ink name) in dj (sl edgeworn, nicks). *Williams*. $55/£35

FORESTER, C. S. The Earthly Paradise. London: Michael Joseph, 1940. 1st UK ed. Fine (ink name, address) in NF dj (sm chip) complete w/wrap-around band. *Williams*. $148/£95

FORESTER, C. S. Flying Colours. Boston: Little, Brown, (1939). 1st US ed. Signed. Fine in NF dj (nicked). *Unger*. $550/£353

FORESTER, C. S. The Good Shepherd. London: Michael Joseph, 1955. 1st UK ed. VG+ in VG dj (spine sl browned). *Williams*. $23/£15

FORESTER, C. S. The Happy Return. Michael Joseph, 1937. 1st UK ed. VG (fore-edges sl worn). *Williams*. $39/£25

FORESTER, C. S. Hornblower and the Crisis. London: Michael Joseph, 1967. 1st UK ed. Fine in dj (rear sl strengthened). *Williams*. $55/£35

FORESTER, C. S. Hornblower and the Hotspur. London: Michael Joseph, 1962. 1st ed. Fine in wrap-around pict dj (lt edgeworn). *Else Fine*. $60/£38

FORESTER, C. S. Hornblower in the West Indies. Michael Joseph, 1958. 1st UK ed. VG+ in dj (price-clipped). *Williams*. $39/£25

FORESTER, C. S. Hornblower in the West Indies. London: Michael Joseph, 1958. 1st ed. (Sm name), else Fine in dj. *Associates*. $100/£64

FORESTER, C. S. Josephine, Napoleon's Empress. London, 1925. 1st Eng ed. Good (frontis fore-edge frayed, hinges weak; cvrs sl faded, ring-mk fr bd). *Clearwater*. $78/£50

FORESTER, C. S. The Last Nine Days of the Bismarck. Boston: Little, Brown, (1959). 1st Amer ed. Fine in Fine dj (rear panel sl foxing). *Between The Covers*. $50/£32

FORESTER, C. S. Lieutenant Hornblower. London: Michael Joseph, 1952. 1st UK ed. VG in dj. *Williams*. $28/£18

FORESTER, C. S. Long Before Forty. London: Michael Joseph, 1967. 1st UK ed. Fine in VG dj (sl browned). *Williams*. $22/£14

FORESTER, C. S. Lord Hornblower. London: Michael Joseph, 1946. 1st UK ed. VG+ in Good dj (sl chipped, browned, crease fr cvr). *Williams*. $28/£18

FORESTER, C. S. Lord Hornblower. London: Michael Joseph, 1946. 1st ed. NF in dj (worn, mended internally). *Else Fine.* $95/£61

FORESTER, C. S. Lord Nelson. Indianapolis: Bobbs-Merrill, 1929. 1st ed. VG in dj (brittle, spine dknd, chips). *Else Fine.* $185/£119

FORESTER, C. S. Louis XIV, King of France and Navarre. London, 1928. 1st Eng ed. Nice. *Clearwater.* $62/£40

FORESTER, C. S. Mr. Midshipman Hornblower. Michael Joseph, (1950). 1st ed. Nice (top edge sl dusty) in dj (sl worn). *Ash.* $39/£25

FORESTER, C. S. The Naval War of 1812. London, 1957. 1st Eng ed. Fine in dj (nicked). *Clearwater.* $39/£25

FORESTER, C. S. The Naval War of 1812. London: Michael Joseph, 1957. 1st UK ed. NF. *Williams.* $16/£10

FORESTER, C. S. The Nightmare. Boston: Little, Brown, 1954. 1st ed. Fine in dj (sl used; rear panel rumpled). *Beasley.* $35/£22

FORESTER, C. S. Plain Murder. (NY: Dell, 1954). 1st Amer ed. NF (name stamp; pp browned; spine edges sl rubbed) in wrappers. *Between The Covers.* $75/£48

FORESTER, C. S. Poo-Poo and the Dragons. Joseph, 1942. 1st ed. Robert Lawson (illus). 8vo. 189pp (2 corners torn away). Dec yellow cl. (Lt dusty), else VG-. *Bookmark.* $47/£30

FORESTER, C. S. Poo-Poo and the Dragons. Boston: Little-Brown, 1942. 1st ed. (Inscrip), o/w Fine in Fine dj (spine ends sl worn). *Beasley.* $175/£112

FORESTER, C. S. A Ship of the Line. London: Michael Joseph, 1938. 1st UK ed. VG (ink name; spine unevenly faded) in dj (sm chips, lacks piece fr panel removing author's first initial, 3cm closed tear fr panel). *Williams.* $367/£235

FORESTER, C. S. The Ship. Michael Joseph, (1943). 1st ed. Nice (edges sl spotted) in dj (frayed, chipped, sl repaired). *Ash.* $39/£25

FORESTER, C. S. The Sky and the Forest. London: Michael Joseph, 1948. 1st ed. Fine in dj (lt worn). *Else Fine.* $50/£32

FORESTER, C. S. To the Indies. Boston, 1940. 1st Amer ed. Nice (sl spotted) in dj (chipped). *Clearwater.* $47/£30

FORESTER, C. S. U 97—A Play in 3 Acts. London: Bodley Head, 1931. 1st UK ed. NF (spine sl faded) in dj. *Williams.* $741/£475

FORESTER, C. S. Victor Emmanuel II and the Union of Italy. London, 1927. 1st Eng ed. Later binding, grn cl lettered in black. (Name, bkpl; spine tanned, cvrs sl mkd.) *Clearwater.* $70/£45

FORESTER, FRANK. (Pseud of Henry William Herbert.) Hitchcock Edition of Frank Forester. NY: Derrydale, 1930. Ltd to 750. 4 vols. Blue cl. (Spines rubbed), o/w Fine. *Truepenny.* $300/£192

FORESTER, FRANK. (Pseud of Henry William Herbert.) My Shooting Box. NY: Derrydale, 1941. Ltd to 250. Hand-colored frontis, tp. Fine. *Truepenny.* $250/£160

FORESTER, FRANK. (Pseud of Henry William Herbert.) The Sporting Novels of Frank Forester. NY: Derrydale, 1930. 1st Derrydale ed. #129/750. 4 vols. Blue cl w/remnants of orig black ptd labels (spine vol 1 soiled). Internally Fine. *Cummins.* $200/£128

FORESTER, FRANK. (Pseud of Henry William Herbert.) The Warwick Woodlands. NY: Derrydale, 1934. 1st Derrydale ed. #68/250. Hand-colored frontis, 6 plts. Maroon cl, gilt. Fine. *Cummins.* $175/£112

FORESTIER, J. C. N. A Notebook of Plans and Sketches. Helen Morenthau Fox (trans). NY: Scribner, 1924. 1st ed in English. Gilt cl, spine. (Fep removed), else Fine. *Quest.* $175/£112

FORGUE, NORMAN W. Poorer Richard, an Almanac Long After Franklin. Chicago: Black Cat, 1954. Ltd ed. French fold. Fine. *Bohling.* $25/£16

FORKNER, CLAUDE E. Leukemia and Allied Disorders. NY, 1938. 1st ed. VG in dj (tattered). *Doctor's Library.* $50/£32

FORMAN, SAMUEL. Narrative of a Journey Down the Ohio and Mississippi in 1789-90. Cincinnati, 1888. Wrappers. Howes F263. *Swann*.* $92/£59

FORMAN, SAMUEL. Narrative of a Journey Down the Ohio and Mississippi in 1789-90. Cincinnati: Clarke, 1888. 1st ed. 67pp. (Emb stamp tp, lacks fep.) Howes F263. *Ginsberg.* $125/£80

FORMBY, JOHN. The American Civil War. NY, 1910. 1st Amer ed. 66 maps, plans; errata slip. Good (spine worn). *Wantagh.* $45/£29

FORNANDER, ABRAHAM. Fornander Collection of Hawaiian Antiquities and Folk-Lore. Thomas G. Thrum (notes). Honolulu: Bishop Museum Press, 1916-20. 9 vols. 4to. Frontis port. Orig parts bound in cl-backed bds, orig wrappers bound in. (Wear to cvrs), else Fine set. *Argonaut.* $1,200/£769

FORNEY, JOHN W. Life and Military Career of Winfield Scott Hancock. Phila: Hubbard, (c. 1880). 504pp. Blue cl (lt shelfworn, smudged), gilt. *Bohling.* $15/£10

FORNEY, JOHN W. What I Saw in Texas. Phila: Ringwalt & Brown, 1872. 92pp; map. Wraps (lacks rear wrap, fr chipped, but encapsulated in plastic). *Dumont.* $375/£240

FORREST, ANTHONY. The Pandora Secret. NY: Hill & Wang, 1982. 1st ed. (Sm spots top edge), o/w Fine in dj. *Mordida.* $35/£22

FORREST, EARLE R. Arizona's Dark and Bloody Ground. Caldwell: Caxton, 1936. 1st ed. VG in VG dj. Howes H265. *Perier.* $175/£112

FORREST, EARLE R. Missions and Pueblos of the Old Southwest, Their Myths, Legends, Fiestas, and Ceremonies.... Cleveland, 1929. 1st trade ed. One of 1498. NF (owner note). *Turpen.* $150/£96

FORREST, EARLE R. Missions and Pueblos of the Old Southwest.... Cleveland: Clark, 1929. 1st trade ed. One of 1498. Blue cl, gilt-lettered spine. (Sl water staining rear cvr), else Fine. *Argonaut.* $125/£80

FORREST, GEORGE. The Life of Lord Clive. London, 1918. 2 vols. 12 photogravure ports, fldg map, fldg facs. Blind-emb cl (spines sl faded, rubbed). *Edwards.* $47/£30

FORRESTER, ALLEN. The City Hall, Baltimore. Balt: By Authority of the Mayor and City Council, 1877. Dbl-pg chromolitho frontis, 10 plts. (Spine sl rubbed, stained, corners sl worn.) *Waverly*.* $88/£56

FORRESTER, IZOLA. This One Mad Act. Boston, 1937. 1st ed. Fine in dj (worn). *Pratt.* $50/£32

FORSHAW, JOSEPH M. Australian Parrots. Melbourne: Landsowne, (1981). 2nd rev enlgd ed. VG + . *Mikesh.* $127/£81

FORSHAW, JOSEPH M. Australian Parrots. London, 1981. 2nd (rev) ed. Dj. *Edwards.* $39/£25

FORSHAW, JOSEPH M. Parrots of the World. Melbourne: Lansdowne, 1973. William T. Cooper (illus). Dj. *Christie's*.* $192/£123

FORSHAW, JOSEPH M. Parrots of the World. David & Charles, 1978. 2nd ed. VG in dj. *Cox.* $101/£65

FORSTER, E. M. Alexandria: A History and a Guide. Alexandria: Whitehead Morris, 1922. 1st ed. Frontis, 21 maps and plans rear pocket. (Feps lt browned, inscrip; sl discolored, spine sl rubbed.) *Edwards.* $351/£225

FORSTER, E. M. Alexandria: A History and a Guide. Alexandria: Whitehead Morris, 1938. 2nd (rev) ed. VG- (bds grubby, sl worn, spine rubbed). *Williams.* $109/£70

FORSTER, E. M. Commonplace Book. Philip Gardner (ed). Stanford Univ, 1985. 1st Amer ed. VG in dj. *Argosy.* $45/£29

FORSTER, E. M. The Development of English Prose Between 1918 and 1939. Glasgow: Jackson, 1945. 1st ed. One of 1000 ptd. NF (edges sl dknd) in ptd wrappers. *Reese.* $35/£22

FORSTER, E. M. Goldsworthy Lowes Dickinson. London: Edward Arnold, 1934. Advance state of 1st ed. VG in plain wraps (sl used). *Reese.* $150/£96

FORSTER, E. M. The Hill of Devi. London: Edward Arnold, (1953). 1st ed. NF in dj (lt used, 2 sm tears). *Antic Hay.* $75/£48

FORSTER, E. M. The Hill of Devi. NY, 1953. 1st Amer ed. Fine (spine sl rubbed) in Fine dj. *Polyanthos.* $25/£16

FORSTER, E. M. A Letter to Madam Blanchard. NY: Harcourt, Brace, (1932). NF in ptd wraps. *Antic Hay.* $25/£16

FORSTER, E. M. A Letter to Madam Blanchard. London: Hogarth, 1931. 1st ed. Orig ptd wrappers (sl soiled). *Hollett.* $39/£25

FORSTER, E. M. A Letter to Madam Blanchard. London: Hogarth, 1931. 1st ed. NF in pict wrappers (sm spot fr wrapper). *Reese.* $45/£29

FORSTER, E. M. The Life to Come and Other Stories. 1972. 1st ed. VG in dj (hinge sl torn). *Words Etc.* $25/£16

FORSTER, E. M. The Manuscripts of a Passage to India. Arnold, 1978. #961/1500. VG + in VG + dj. *Martin.* $37/£24

FORSTER, E. M. Maurice. NY: Norton, (1971). 1st Amer ed. Fine in dj. *Antic Hay.* $20/£13

FORSTER, E. M. Maurice. London: Arnold, 1971. 1st UK ed. NF in VG dj. *Williams.* $39/£25

FORSTER, E. M. Nordic Twilight. Macmillan, 1940. 1st UK ed. VG in wraps (dusty). *Williams.* $23/£15

FORSTER, E. M. A Passage to India. NY: Harcourt, Brace, (1924). 1st Amer ed. Black cl lettered in yellow. (Cvrs sl spotted, few pp roughly opened), else NF. *Macdonnell.* $100/£64

FORSTER, E. M. A Passage to India. London, 1924. 1st ed. (Contemp inscrip, tp sl foxed; spine sl rubbed, sl dull), o/w Good. *Words Etc.* $140/£90

FORSTER, E. M. Pharos and Pharillon. Hogarth, 1923. Cl-backed patterned bds w/horizontal design. Good (sl foxed; rubbed, chipped). *Clearwater.* $140/£90

FORSTER, E. M. Selected Letters. Vol I, 1879-1920. Mary Lago & P. N. Furbank (eds). Collins, 1983. 1st ed. Fine in dj. *Poetry Bookshop.* $19/£12

FORSTER, E. M. Virginia Woolf. NY: Harcourt, Brace, (1942). 1st Amer ed. Grn cl. Fine in dj. *Macdonnell.* $100/£64

FORSTER, FRANK J. Country Houses. NY: William Helburn, 1931. 183 photo plts. Purple/brn cl, gilt. (Wear, soil.) *Freeman*.* $150/£96

FORSTER, JOHN. The Life of Charles Dickens. London, 1872-74. 3 vols in 6. 8vo. Grn calf, gilt, w/Dickens bust, facs sig on cvrs, spines in 6 compartments, crimson morocco labels in 2. *Swann*.* $1,495/£958

FORSTER, JOHN. Sir John Eliot: A Biography. 1590-1632. Longman, Green, 1864. 2 vols. Steel engr frontispieces, xxx,649; xxii,766pp (tp, leaf neatly repaired). Mod binders cl. Sound (ex-lib). *Peter Taylor.* $75/£48

FORSYTH, A. R. Theory of Functions of a Complex Variable. Cambridge, 1893. 1st ed. xxii,682pp. (Spine top neatly repaired), o/w VG. *Whitehart.* $70/£45

FORSYTH, FREDERICK. The Day of the Jackal. Hutchinson, (1971). 1st ed. Nice (top edge sl spotted) in dj. *Ash.* $94/£60

FORSYTH, FREDERICK. The Day of the Jackal. Taiwan piracy, 1971. 1st ed thus. NF in NF dj. *Smith.* $15/£10

FORSYTH, FREDERICK. The Day of the Jackal. London: Hutchinson, 1971. 1st UK ed. VG in dj. *Williams.* $117/£75

FORSYTH, FREDERICK. The Devil's Alternative. London, 1979. 1st ed. VG in dj. *Typographeum.* $25/£16

FORSYTH, FREDERICK. The Devil's Alternative. London: Hutchinson, 1979. 1st ed. Fine (corner bumped) in Fine dj. *Janus.* $35/£22

FORSYTH, FREDERICK. The Dogs of War. London, 1974. 1st ed. Dj. *Typographeum.* $30/£19

FORSYTH, FREDERICK. The Fourth Protocol. London, 1984. 1st ed. VG in dj. *Typographeum.* $25/£16

FORSYTH, FREDERICK. The Fourth Protocol. SF: Brandywine, 1984. One of 600 signed. VF in dj, slipcase. *Mordida.* $75/£48

FORSYTH, FREDERICK. The Odessa File. NY: Viking, (1972). 1st ed. NF in dj (sm tears). *Antic Hay.* $25/£16

FORSYTH, FREDERICK. The Odessa File. London, 1972. 1st ed. VG in dj (sm nicks, edges sl rubbed). *Words Etc.* $19/£12

FORSYTH, FREDERICK. The Shepherd. London, 1973. 1st ed. Dj. *Typographeum.* $18/£12

FORSYTH, W. A Treatise on the Culture and Management of Fruit Trees.... London, 1824. 7th ed. Port, 13 engr plts. (Foxed; worn, cvrs off.) *Maggs.* $23/£15

FORSYTHE, JAMES. The Sporting Rifle and Its Projectiles. London, 1863. 1st ed. 3 plts (2 fldg). Uncut. Pub's cl (shelfworn). *Oinonen*.* $190/£122

FORT, CHARLES. The Outcast Manufacturers. Dodge, 1909. 1st ed. VG + . *Madle.* $75/£48

FORT, CHARLES. The Outcast Manufacturers. NY: Dodge, 1909. 1st ed, 1st bk. 1st binding; emb red stamping. VG + . *Beasley.* $100/£64

FORTESCUE, JOHN. Wellington. London, 1925. Frontis, 3 fldg maps. Blue cl. *Maggs.* $55/£35

FORTOVA-SAMALOVA, P. Egyptian Ornament. London: Allan Wingate, (1963). 1st ed. 343 color plts. White cl. Good in dec dj. *Karmiole.* $100/£64

FORTUNE, DION. Training and Work of an Initiate. London, 1955. 2nd ed. Fine in VG dj. *Middle Earth.* $35/£22

FORTUNE, ROBERT. A Residence Among the Chinese. John Murray, 1857. 1st ed. Frontis, (xvi),440pp; 5 plts. Contemp 1/2 calf (rebacked). *Bickersteth.* $226/£145

Fortunes of Nigel. (By Walter Scott.) Edinburgh: Constable/Hurst, Robinson, 1822. 1st ed. 3 vols. Half-titles. Contemp 1/2 brn calf (sl scuffed), marbled sides. *Maggs.* $172/£110

FOSKETT, DAPHNE. A Dictionary of British Miniature Painters. NY/Washington: Praeger, (1972). 1st US ed. 2 vols. 31 color, 400 b/w plts. Blue cl (sl shelfworn), gilt. VG pict djs. *Baltimore*.* $100/£64

FOSS, EDWARD. A Biographical Dictionary of the Judges of England from the Conquest to the Present Time 1066-1870. Boston: Little, Brown, 1870. (Cl worn, rebacked.) Good. *Boswell.* $250/£160

FOSSETT, FRANK. Colorado: A Historical Descriptive and Statistical Work.... Denver: Daily Tribune Steam Ptg, 1876. 1st ed. 470pp. VG (rebound). Howes F281. *Lien.* $75/£48

FOSSETT, FRANK. Colorado: Its Gold and Silver Mines, Farms and Stock Ranges, and Health and Pleasure Resorts. NY: C.G. Crawford, 1879. 540pp; fldg dwg, fldg maps. Good (cvrs spotted). Howes F281. *Lien.* $60/£38

FOSSETT, FRANK. Colorado: Its Gold and Silver Mines.... NY: C.G. Crawford, 1879. 2nd ed. vii,540pp; 3 fldg maps, 1 fldg view. Clean (shelfworn). Howes F281. *Dumont.* $100/£64

FOSSETT, FRANK. Colorado: Its Gold and Silver Mines.... NY: C.G. Crawford, 1879. vii,540pp. Good. *Blake.* $125/£80

FOSSIER, A. E. History of the Orleans Parish Medical Society, 1878-1928. (New Orleans): Privately Ptd, 1930. VG. *Argosy.* $85/£54

FOSTER, ALAN S. Goodbye Bobby Thomson, Goodbye John Wayne. S&S, 1973. 1st ed. VG+ in VG dj. *Plapinger.* $40/£26

FOSTER, J. J. Miniature Painters British and Foreign. London/NY, 1903. Author's ed. 2 vols. Frontis ports, 123 plts. (Margins sl browned.) Marbled eps. Teg, rest uncut. Cl-backed bds (fore-edge sl soiled, corner sl bumped, spine head vol 2 bumped, chipped), gilt. *Edwards.* $211/£135

FOSTER, JAMES C., JR. 20th Century Dog Breeding. San Antonio: Naylor, 1939. 1st ed. VG+. *Bowman.* $100/£64

FOSTER, JOHN. A Shakespeare Word-Book. London/NY, 1908. Teg. 2-tone cl (lower joint head sl split; stamps tp, last leaf, ex-lib, bkpl). *Edwards.* $78/£50

FOSTER, M. and J. F. GASKELL. Cerebro-Spinal Fever. CUP, 1916. 1st ed. 11 plts. Dk grn cl (top cvr sl mkd). VG. *White.* $55/£35

FOSTER, MICHAEL. Claude Bernard. London, 1899. Frontis port, xi,245pp + (ii) ads (eps, tp lt spotted). Dec gilt title upper bd, spine. (Edges sl rubbed.) *Edwards.* $39/£25

FOSTER, MRS. ARNOLD. In the Valley of the Yangtse. London, 1899. 1st ed. xii,216pp. Illus cl (lt discolored, spine faded, sl chipped). *Edwards.* $39/£25

FOSTER, SAMUEL T. One of Cleburne's Command. Norman D. Brown (ed). Austin, (1980). 1st ed. VG+ in VG+ dj. *Pratt.* $50/£32

FOSTER, THOMAS D. A Letter From the Fire. N.p. (Ottumwa, IA): Torch Press, Christmas 1949. Rpt. Inscribed by T. Henry Foster. Patterned paper over bds, cl spine. Fine. *Graf.* $38/£24

FOSTER, W. C. A Treatise on Wooden Trestle Bridges.... NY: Wiley, 1891. 160pp; 38 full-pg plts. Good (spine rubbed). *Scribe's Perch*.* $130/£83

FOSTER-MELLIAR, A. The Book of the Rose. London, 1894. 1st ed. 336pp; 29 photo plts. Teg. Red cl, gilt. (Spine sl faded), else VG. *Price.* $65/£42

FOTHERGILL, EDWARD. Five Years in the Sudan. London: Hurst & Blackett, 1910. 1st ed. 32 plts. Teg. VG (1st section working loose, sl spotted, prize label). *Hollett.* $234/£150

FOTHERGILL, G. A. Hunting, Racing, Coaching and Boxing Ballads. London, 1926. Color frontis, 16 b/w plts. (Sl spotting, feps lt browned; cl spine faded.) Dj (sl chipped, loss spine head). *Edwards.* $55/£35

FOTHERGILL, J. MILNER. The Practitioner's Handbook of Treatment. Phila, 1877. 1st ed. 575pp. Grn cl bds (extrems sl worn). VG. *Doctor's Library.* $100/£64

FOTHERGILL, SAMUEL. Discourses Delivered Extempore at Several Meeting Houses of the People Called Quakers. Phila: B. & J. Johnson, 1800. xv,(3),270pp (foxed, some gatherings sl pulled). Full calf (sl worn). *New Hampshire*.* $35/£22

FOULKES, C. H. Gas! London: William Blackwood, 1934. 1st ed. 21 plts, 7 maps, 2 graphs. (Edges spotted.) *Hollett.* $101/£65

FOURCADE, FRANCOIS. Art Treasures of the Peking Museum. NY: Abrams, n.d. (ca 1965). 1st ed. 87 color plts tipped in. NF in dj. *Worldwide.* $35/£22

Fourteen Months in American Bastiles. (By F.K. Howard.) Balt: Kelly, Hedian & Piet, 1863. 1st ed. 89pp. NF in grn ptd wrappers (spines sl worn). *Harrington.* $100/£64

FOWKE, FRANK REDE. The Bayeux Tapestry. London, 1898. ix,139pp (lt spotting); 79 plts at rear. Teg, rest uncut. (Cl soiled, faded, sl rubbed, spine sl worn.) *Edwards.* $55/£35

FOWKE, GERARD. Evolution of the Ohio River. Indianapolis, 1933. VG (name; lt stain lower corner). *Bohling.* $45/£29

FOWLE, GEORGE. Letters to Eliza from a Union Soldier, 1862-1865. Margery Greenleaf (ed). Chicago, 1970. 1st ed. VG+ in VG+ dj. *Pratt.* $30/£19

FOWLER, H. W. A Dictionary of Modern English Usage. Oxford, 1926. 1st ed. Blue cl, gilt. Nice in dj. *Hartfield.* $95/£61

FOWLER, H. W. A Dictionary of Modern English Usage. Oxford/London, 1926. 1st ed. VG (corners sl bumped, spine tips sl frayed). *M&s.* $200/£128

FOWLER, HARLAN D. Three Caravans to Yuma. Glendale: Clark, 1980. 1st ed. Ltd to 772. VF. *Argonaut.* $60/£38

FOWLER, JACOB. The Journal of Jacob Fowler Narrating an Adventure from Arkansas.... Elliott Coues (ed). NY: Harper, 1898. #790/950. Fldg frontis, xxiv,183pp; facs. Blue cl, gilt. VG. Howes F298. *Bohling.* $175/£112

FOWLER, JACOB. The Journal of Jacob Fowler Narrating an Adventure...1821-22. Elliott Coues (ed). NY: Francis P. Harper, 1898. 1st ed. One of 950. Frontis, xxiv,183pp. (Cl sl rubbed), else Good. Howes F298. *Brown.* $150/£96

FOWLER, RUSSELL. The Operating Room and the Patient. Phila, 1906. 1st ed. Pub's copy w/text notes. VG. *Fye.* $300/£192

FOWLES, JOHN et al. Steep Holm. Sherborne: Dorset, 1978. Adv pre-pub copy. Illus prospectus, rev slip laid in. NF in dj (sl rubbed, closed tear). *Moorhouse.* $70/£45

FOWLES, JOHN. A Brief History of Lyme. Lyme Regis: Friends of the Museum, 1981. 1st ed. Signed. Fine in stapled wrappers. *Between The Covers.* $85/£54

FOWLES, JOHN. Cinderella. London: Jonathan Cape, (1974). 1st ed. Sarah Beckett (illus). 4to. 32pp. Fine in dj (edges lt dknd). *Bromer.* $75/£48

FOWLES, JOHN. The Collector. Boston: Little Brown, (1963). 1st Amer ed. Signed. Fine in dj (sl extrem wear). *Between The Covers.* $250/£160

FOWLES, JOHN. The Collector. Boston: Little, Brown, (1963). 1st Amer ed, 1st bk. Fine in dj. *Hermitage.* $150/£96

FOWLES, JOHN. The Collector. Boston: Little, Brown, (1963). 1st US ed, 1st bk. Fine in Fine dj. *Unger.* $150/£96

FOWLES, JOHN. The Collector. London: Jonathan Cape, (1963). 1st ed, 1st bk. Signed. Fine in 1st issue dj (sm spot rear panel). *Captain's Bookshelf.* $750/£481

FOWLES, JOHN. The Collector. London, 1963. 1st ed. VG (spine sl bumped) in dj (dusty, rubbed). *Buckley.* $304/£195

FOWLES, JOHN. The Collector. London: Cape, 1963. 1st UK ed. NF (ink inscrip) in VG dj (price-clipped, sl browned, rubbed). *Williams.* $250/£160

FOWLES, JOHN. Daniel Martin. Boston: Little, Brown, (1977). 1st Amer ed. NF in dj. *Antic Hay.* $35/£22

FOWLES, JOHN. Daniel Martin. London: Cape, (1977). 1st ed. Signed. Fine in dj. *Between The Covers.* $150/£96

FOWLES, JOHN. The French Lieutenant's Woman. Boston: Little, Brown, (1969). 1st Amer ed. Signed. VG (sun, soil) in dj (spine ends worn, sm chips, creases, wear, sm tape interior). *Metropolitan*.* $86/£55

FOWLES, JOHN. A Maggot. Boston, 1985. 1st ed. NF in NF dj. *Smith.* $15/£10

FOWLES, JOHN. Mantissa. Boston: Little, Brown, (1982). One of 510 numbered, signed. Fine in Fine slipcase. *Lenz.* $125/£80

FOWNES, GEORGE. Elementary Chemistry: Theoretical and Practical. Blanchard & Lea, 1853. 555pp. Leather (sl worn). *Bookcell.* $50/£32

FOX, CARROLL. Insects and Disease of Man. Phila, 1925. 1st ed. Grn cl (sl worn). VG. *Doctor's Library.* $35/£22

FOX, CHARLES JAMES. Memorials and Correspondence of Charles James Fox. Lord John Russell (ed). Richard Bentley, 1853. 1st ed. 3 vols. Diapered cl, blocked in blind (spines faded). Good set. *Bickersteth.* $106/£68

FOX, EDWARD LONG. The Pathological Anatomy of the Nervous Centres. London: Smith, Elder, 1874. 1st ed. 401pp; 19 color plts. Grn cl (spine relaid). (Sl spotted), o/w VG. *White.* $39/£25

FOX, GUSTAVUS VASA. Confidential Correspondence of Gustavus Vasa Fox. Robert Means Thompson and Richard Wainwright (eds). NY: Naval History Soc, 1918/1919. 1st ed. Ltd to 1200 numbered. 2 vols. Frontis. Teg. Vellum spine, tips. Fine in pub's boxes (vol 2 box spine worn). *Cahan.* $125/£80

FOX, HELEN MORGENTHAU. Patio Gardens. NY: Macmillan, 1929. 1st ed. Good (lt water mk along fore-edge; cvrs sl soiled). *Second Life.* $25/£16

FOX, JOHN, JR. The Little Shepherd of Kingdom Come. NY, 1931. One of 512 numbered, signed by N.C. Wyeth (illus). 4to. 16 tipped-in color plts. 1/4 vellum, gilt. Pub's bd box. *Swann*.* $1,380/£885

FOX, JOHN, JR. The Little Shepherd of Kingdom Come. NY: Scribner, 1931. 1st ed thus. N.C. Wyeth (illus). 322pp. Black cl, color pict label. (Corners sl bumped), o/w VG. *Dower.* $175/£112

FOX, JOSEPH. The Natural History of the Human Teeth.... London: Thomas Cox, 1803. 1st ed. 4to. vii,(1),100,(1)pp; 13 plts. (Lib stamp tp; few plts, prelims foxed; bkpl.) Untrimmed. Bds (rebacked in cl), orig paper title label fr cvr. VG. *Glaser.* $2,500/£1,603

FOX, LORENE. Antarctic Icebreakers. NY, 1937. VG in dj (tattered). *High Latitude.* $25/£16

FOX, RALPH. Storming Heaven. London: Constable, 1928. 1st Eng ed. Good (fore-edge sl foxed). *Clearwater.* $62/£40

FOX, ROBERT and GEORGE WEISZ (eds). The Organization of Science and Technology in France 1808-1914. CUP, (1980). 1st ed. Fine in dj. *Glaser.* $45/£29

FOX, WILLIAM F. The Adirondack Black Spruce. Albany, NY, 1895. 82pp; 2 color plts, 8 b/w photo plts. Brn cl, gilt. (Edgewear), else VG. *Price.* $48/£31

FOX, WILLIAM J. (comp). Final Report on the Battlefield of Gettysburg. Albany: Ptd by J.B. Lyon, 1900. 1st ed. 3 vols. 5 fldg maps. (1 inner hinge starting each vol), else VG set. *Mcgowan.* $350/£224

FOX-DAVIES, A. C. The Mauleverer Murders. NY: John Lane, (1907). 1st Amer ed. (Bkpl; rubbed.) *Metropolitan*.* $34/£22

FOXON, DAVID. Libertine Literature in England 1660-1745. NY, 1965. 13 plts. Dj (sl rubbed). *Edwards.* $23/£15

FOY, GENERAL. History of the War in the Peninsula, Under Napoleon. London, 1829. 2nd ed. 2 vols. 8vo. Engr frontis port (crease), xii,440; xvi,638pp (sl foxing); fldg table. Mod calf-backed bds, spines in compartments. *Maggs.* $624/£400

FRACHTENBERG, LEO J. Alsea Texts and Myths. BAE Bulletin 67. Washington: GPO, 1920. *Lien.* $18/£12

FRAENKEL, MICHAEL. Bastard Death. Paris, 1946. 2nd ptg. NF in ptd dj. *Polyanthos.* $25/£16

FRAME, JANET. The Lagoon. Christchurch, New Zealand: Caxton, 1951. 1st ed, 1st bk. VG + (inner hinges sl starting, sig, address) in VG dj (chipped, extrems tape-repaired). *Lame Duck.* $1,500/£962

FRAME, JANET. Mona Minim and the Smell of the Sun. NY: Braziller, (1969). 1st ed. Robin Jacques (illus). Fine in dj. *Bernard.* $40/£26

FRAME, JANET. Snowman Snowman/The Reservoir. NY: Braziller, (1963). 1st ed. 2 vols. NF in dj, cardbd slipcase (lt worn). *Antic Hay.* $45/£29

FRAMPTON, HOLLIS. Circles of Confusion. Rochester: Visual Studies Workshop, 1983. 1st ed. 31 b/w plts. Fine in illus stiff wrappers. *Cahan.* $20/£13

FRANCE, ANATOLE. The Crime of Sylvestre Bonnard. Lafcadio Hearn (trans). NY: LEC, 1937. Ltd to 1500, signed by Sylvain Sauvage (illus). Color frontis. (Bkpl removed, offset to pastedowns; orig glassine browned), else NF in slipcase (rubbed, corners split). *Cahan.* $85/£54

FRANCE, ANATOLE. Golden Tales. NY, 1928. 1st Amer ed. Pict cvrs (sl soiled, spine sl sunned, extrems sl rubbed), gilt. NF (bkpl). *Polyanthos.* $45/£29

FRANCE, ANATOLE. Penguin Island. NY: LEC, 1947. #904/1500 numbered, signed by Malcolm Cameron (illus). 1/2 leather, dec bds. Fine in pub's slipcase. *Hermitage.* $75/£48

FRANCE, ANATOLE. The Revolt of the Angels. Mrs. Wilfrid Jackson (trans). London/NY: John Lane, Bodley Head/Dodd, Mead, (1927). Ltr ptg. ix,357pp; 12 plts by Frank C. Pape. Black cl, gilt. NF in black dj (chipped). *Blue Mountain.* $25/£16

FRANCE, ANATOLE. Thais. Robert B. Douglas (trans). London/NY: John Lane, Bodley Head/Dodd, Mead, (1926). 8vo. Frontis, (x),249pp (offsetting tp, fr hinge starting, rear hinge cracked); 11 plts by Frank C. Pape. Deckle-edged. Black cl (bumped, rubbed, rear cvr soiled). Fair. *Blue Mountain.* $20/£13

FRANCESHI, F. Santa Barbara Exotic Flora. Santa Barbara, 1895. 88pp. Wrappers (few separations on spine, sm chip fr cvr). *Dawson.* $100/£64

FRANCH, JOSE ALCINA. Pre-Columbian Art. NY: Abrams, (1983). 177 color plts. Good in dj. *Archaeologia.* $250/£160

FRANCHERE, GABRIEL. Adventure at Astoria, 1810-1814. Hoyt C. Franchere (ed). Norman: Univ of OK, (1967). Map. VG in dj. *Lien.* $35/£22

FRANCHERE, GABRIEL. Adventure at Astoria, 1810-1814. Hoyt C. Franchere (ed). Norman: Univ of OK, (1967). New ed. Dbl-pg map. Gray cl. VF in pict dj. *Argonaut.* $50/£32

FRANCHERE, GABRIEL. Narrative of a Voyage to the Northwest Coast of America in the Years 1811, 1812, 1813 and 1814. J. V. Huntington (ed). NY: Redfield, 1854. 1st Amer ed. 3 plts. Orig gilt/blind-stamped cl (expertly rebacked, orig backstrip laid on, corners rubbed, fr inner hinge cracked but tight). Howes F310. *Sadlon.* $450/£288

FRANCHERE, GABRIEL. Narrative of a Voyage to the Northwest Coast of America...1811, 1812, 1813.... NY, 1854. Frontis, 376pp (sl foxed, tanned); 2 plts, ads. (Spine sl chipped, sm nick fr joint), else VG. Howes F310. *Reese.* $450/£288

FRANCIS, DICK. Across the Board. NY: Harper, 1975. 1st ed. Fine in Fine dj. *Beasley.* $50/£32

FRANCIS, DICK. Banker. London: Michael Joseph, 1982. 1st ed. Signed. Fine in dj. *Mordida.* $85/£54

FRANCIS, DICK. Blood Sport. London: Michael Joseph, 1967. 1st Eng ed. VG in dj. *Hadley.* $101/£65

FRANCIS, DICK. Blood Sport. London: Michael Joseph, 1967. 1st ed. Fine in dj (sm scrape fr panel, short closed tear). *Mordida.* $175/£112

FRANCIS, DICK. Blood Sport. NY: Harper & Row, 1967. 1st Amer ed. Dj (price-clipped, soil, lt browned). *Metropolitan*.* $63/£40

FRANCIS, DICK. Blood Sport. NY: Harper & Row, 1968. 1st Amer ed. Fine in dj. *Mordida.* $100/£64

FRANCIS, DICK. Bolt. Michael Joseph, 1986. 1st UK ed. NF in dj. *Williams.* $16/£10

FRANCIS, DICK. Bonecrack. London: M. Joseph, 1971. 1st ed. Dj (price-clipped, sl worn). *Metropolitan*.* $40/£26

FRANCIS, DICK. Break In. Michael Joseph, 1985. 1st UK ed. NF in dj. *Williams.* $16/£10

FRANCIS, DICK. Comeback. London: Michael Joseph, 1991. 1st ed. Signed. Fine in dj. *Murder By The Book.* $50/£32

FRANCIS, DICK. Comeback. London: Michael Joseph, 1991. 1st ed. Signed. VF in dj. *Mordida.* $65/£42

FRANCIS, DICK. The Danger. London: Michael Joseph, 1983. 1st ed. Fine in dj. *Mordida.* $45/£29

FRANCIS, DICK. Dead Cert. Michael Joseph, 1962. 1st ed. (Lt crease 1 leaf.) Pub's plum cl. Orig dj (sl soiled). *Sotheby's*.* $1,345/£862

FRANCIS, DICK. Driving Force. London: Michael Joseph, 1992. 1st ed. VF in dj. *Mordida.* $50/£32

FRANCIS, DICK. The Edge. London: Michael Joseph, 1988. 1st ed. Fine in dj. *Mordida.* $45/£29

FRANCIS, DICK. Enquiry. London: M. Joseph, 1969. 1st ed. NF (sl cocked) in dj (lt edgeworn, back panel discolored). *Metropolitan*.* $57/£37

FRANCIS, DICK. Enquiry. London: Michael Joseph, 1969. 1st ed. Fine in dj (sl wear, sm scrapes rear panel). *Mordida.* $150/£96

FRANCIS, DICK. Flying Finish. London: Michael Joseph, 1966. 1st British ed. Fine (fore-edge sl foxed) in dj (nicks, edges sl dicolored price-clipped). *Metropolitan*.* $207/£133

FRANCIS, DICK. Flying Finish. London: Michael Joseph, 1966. 1st ed. Fine in dj. *Mordida.* $350/£224

FRANCIS, DICK. Flying Finish. Harper & Row, 1967. 1st US ed. (Top edge sl spotted.) NF in dj (2 short tears). *Certo.* $65/£42

FRANCIS, DICK. Forfeit. London: M. Joseph, 1968. 1st ed. Fine in dj (edgeworn, short tears, inside foxed). *Metropolitan*.* $126/£81

FRANCIS, DICK. Forfeit. London: Michael Joseph, 1968. 1st UK ed. VG in dj (stained, edgeworn, rubbed, sm tears). *Williams.* $75/£48

FRANCIS, DICK. Forfeit. NY: Harper & Row, 1969. 1st Amer ed. Fine in dj (spine faded, nick). *Mordida.* $45/£29

FRANCIS, DICK. High Stakes. London: Michael Joseph, 1975. 1st ed. Fine in dj. *Mordida.* $75/£48

FRANCIS, DICK. Hot Money. London: Michael Joseph, 1987. 1st ed. Signed. VF in dj. *Mordida.* $65/£42

FRANCIS, DICK. In the Frame. London: Michael Joseph, 1976. 1st ed. Fine in dj. *Mordida.* $75/£48

FRANCIS, DICK. Knock Down. Michael Joseph, 1974. 1st UK ed. NF in VG + dj. *Williams.* $25/£16

FRANCIS, DICK. Knock Down. London: M. Joseph, 1974. 1st ed. Inscribed. Fine in Fine dj (sl soiled). *Metropolitan*.* $149/£96

FRANCIS, DICK. Lester: The Official Biography. London: Michael Joseph, 1986. 1st ed. Fine in dj. *Mordida.* $45/£29

FRANCIS, DICK. Longshot. London: Michael Joseph, 1990. 1st ed. Fine in dj. *Mordida.* $45/£29

FRANCIS, DICK. Nerve. London: Michael Joseph, 1964. 1st ed. Fine in dj (spine sl faded, spine ends sl worn, sm closed tear). *Mordida.* $850/£545

FRANCIS, DICK. Odds Against. London: Michael Joseph, 1965. 1st ed. Fine in dj (price-clipped, closed tears, back panel lt soiled). *Mordida.* $200/£128

FRANCIS, DICK. Odds Against. Harper & Row, 1966. 1st US ed. NF in NF dj. *Certo.* $85/£54

FRANCIS, DICK. Proof. London: Michael Joseph, 1984. 1st ed. Signed. Fine in dj. *Mordida.* $85/£54

FRANCIS, DICK. Rat Race. London: Michael Joseph, 1970. 1st ed. Fine in dj (price-clipped, lt stain to spine). *Mordida.* $100/£64

FRANCIS, DICK. Rat Race. London: Michael Joseph, 1970. 1st ed. Fine in dj (lt worn, lt soiled). *Metropolitan*.* $149/£96

FRANCIS, DICK. Reflex. London: Michael Joseph, 1980. 1st ed. Fine in dj. *Mordida.* $50/£32

FRANCIS, DICK. Risk. London: Michael Joseph, 1977. 1st ed. Inscribed. Fine in dj. *Mordida.* $125/£80

FRANCIS, DICK. Slay Ride. London: M. Joseph, 1973. 1st ed. Fine (sl cocked) in Fine dj (lt discolored). *Metropolitan*.* $40/£26

FRANCIS, DICK. Slay Ride. London: Michael Joseph, 1973. 1st UK ed. Fine in dj. *Williams.* $55/£35

FRANCIS, DICK. Slay Ride. London: Michael Joseph, 1973. 1st ed. Fine in dj. *Mordida.* $75/£48

FRANCIS, DICK. Smoke Screen. Michael Joseph, 1972. 1st UK ed. Fine in VG + dj. *Williams.* $39/£25

FRANCIS, DICK. The Sport of Queens. London: Michael Joseph, 1957. 1st ed. Fine (edges sl discolored, worn, chipped, creased, 1-inch closed tear spine bottom, lt soiled). *Metropolitan*.* $253/£162

FRANCIS, DICK. Straight. London: Michael Joseph, 1989. 1st ed. Signed. Fine in dj (sl wear). *Mordida.* $50/£32

FRANCIS, DICK. Three to Show. NY: Harper, 1969. 1st ed. Fine in NF dj (sm internally mended tears, rubs). *Beasley.* $65/£42

FRANCIS, DICK. Trial Run. London: Michael Joseph, 1978. 1st ed. (Name fep), o/w Fine in dj. *Mordida.* $45/£29

FRANCIS, DICK. Twice Shy. London: Michael Joseph, 1981. 1st ed. Fine in dj. *Mordida.* $50/£32

FRANCIS, DICK. Whip Hand. London: Michael Joseph, (1979). 1st ed. Signed, dated. Fine in Fine dj. *Certo.* $50/£32

FRANCIS, DICK. Whip Hand. London: Michael Joseph, 1979. 1st ed. Fine in Fine dj. *Old London.* $35/£22

FRANCIS, DICK. Whip Hand. NY: Harper & Row, 1979. 1st US ed. Fine in Fine dj. *Old London.* $25/£16

FRANCIS, FRANCIS. A Book of Angling. London, 1867. 1st ed. 15 plts. Contemp 1/2 calf (newly rebacked; sl foxed). *Petersfield.* $431/£276

FRANCIS, FRANCIS. A Book of Angling. London: Longmans, Green, 1872. 3rd ed. 482pp + 34pp ads; 16 plts (6 color). Good- (cracks at hinges, at p289). *Scribe's Perch*.* $70/£45

FRANCIS, FRANCIS. A Book on Angling. London: Longmans, Green, 1880. 5th ed. 16 b/w plts. Partially unopened. Purple cl. (Spine sl faded, bkpl), else Fine in morocco-backed protective case. *Cummins.* $250/£160

FRANCIS, FRANCIS. A Book on Angling. Longmans, 1885. 6th ed. 6 color, 10 b/w plts (lacks frontis port). Mod 1/2 red morocco (rebound). *Petersfield.* $66/£42

FRANCIS, FRANCIS. Hot Pot. London, 1880. *Petersfield.* $50/£32

FRANCIS, GRANT R. Old English Drinking Glasses. London: Herbert Jenkins, 1926. 1st ed. 72 plts. Teg, uncut. (Owner stamp 2 prelims), o/w Fine in dj (torn, sl defective). *Hollett*. $343/£220

FRANCIS, JOHN W. Old New York. NY: W.J. Widdleton, 1866. Sig of Francis from another source tipped in. cxxxvi,400pp (paper dknd); port. Brn cl. VG. Howes F315. *Bohling*. $30/£19

FRANCIS, JOHN. A History of the English Railway. London: Longman et al, 1851. 1st ed. 2 vols. Mod smooth 1/2 calf, orange cl sides, raised bands, gilt, grn morocco dbl labels. (Sm adhesion fr pastedown each vol, 1st few leaves both vols sl dknd, frayed, few creases, sl spots), o/w internally Excellent. *Pirages*. $400/£256

FRANCK, HARRY A. The Fringe of the Moslem World.... NY: Century, 1928. 1st ed. 63 plts. (Sl rubbed), o/w VG. *Worldwide*. $28/£18

FRANCK, HARRY A. Roaming Through the West Indies. NY: Century, 1923. (Sl rubbed), o/w VG. *Worldwide*. $20/£13

FRANCK, HARRY A. Vagabonding Down the Andes. NY: Century, 1917. 1st ed. 96 plts, fldg color map. (Sl rubbed), o/w VG. *Worldwide*. $15/£10

FRANCO, JEAN and LIONEL TERRAY. At Grips with Jannu. Hugh Merrick (trans). London: Gollancz, 1967. 1st ed. 48 plts. VG in dj (fr flap replaced). *Hollett*. $70/£45

FRANE, JEFF and JACK REMS (eds). World Fantasy Convention, Seventh. (Berkeley: Seventh World Fantasy Convention, 1981.) 1st ed. One of 1000 numbered. Signed by Ray Bradbury, William F. Nolan, and Robert Bloch. Dj. *Swann**. $126/£81

Frank and the Kite. Troy, NY: Merriam & Moore, n.d. (ca 1855). 12mo. Full-pg engr frontis w/initials A.A., 12pp + 1pg list lower wrapper (penciled dedication; lt foxing; 2 sm splits internal fold, repaired); 10 VF wood engrs (by Alexander Anderson). VG in pict paper wrappers (lt soiled). *Hobbyhorse*. $150/£96

FRANK, ANNE. The Diary of a Young Girl. London: Constellation Books, 1952. 1st Eng ed. Good (spine gilt faded). *Clearwater*. $78/£50

FRANK, BRUNO. The Persians Are Coming. NY: Knopf, 1929. 1st US ed. VG (pp dknd; cl lt soiled) in VG- dj (loss upper edges). *Lame Duck*. $35/£22

FRANK, JEROME. Persuasion and Healing. Balt: Johns Hopkins, (1961). 1st ed. Inscribed. Blue cl. VG. *Gach*. $30/£19

FRANK, JEROME. Psychotherapy and the Human Predicament. NY: Schocken, (1978). 1st ed. Presentation copy. VG in dj (lt worn). *Gach*. $50/£32

FRANK, L. and F. H. HARLOW. Historic Pottery of the Pueblo Indians, 1600-1880. Boston: NYGS, (1974). 1st ed. Map. Brn cl. Fine in Fine dj. *Harrington*. $55/£35

FRANK, L. and M. HOLBROOK. Indian Silver Jewelry of the Southwest 1868-1930. Boston: NYGS, c 1978. VG in dj. *Blake*. $75/£48

FRANK, MORRY. Every Young Man's Dream. Silverback, 1984. 1st ed. Fine in VG+ dj. *Plapinger*. $65/£42

FRANK, WALDO. City Block. Darien, 1922. #968/1225. VG. *Smith*. $20/£13

FRANKEL, S. HERBERT. Capital Investment in Africa. London: OUP, 1938. 1st ed. 102 tables, fldg chart, 2 maps. Buckram (lt spine wear). *Shasky*. $37/£24

FRANKENSTEIN, ALFRED. After the Hunt. Berkeley/L.A.: Univ of CA, 1953. 1st ed. Signed presentation. Color frontis. Grn cl (sl shelfworn), white lettering. Text VG in pict dj (sl dusty, chipped, old stain). *Baltimore**. $45/£29

FRANKFORT, H. Ancient Egyptian Religion: An Interpretation. NY: Columbia Univ, 1948. 1st ed. Frontis. (Pencil underlining, sig.) Dj (tattered). *Archaeologia*. $30/£19

FRANKFORT, H. Cylinder Seals: A Documentary Essay on the Art and Religion of the Ancient Near East. London: Gregg, 1965. Rpt of 1939 ed. 47 plts. Good. *Archaeologia*. $350/£224

FRANKFURTER, FELIX. The Case of Sacco and Vanzetti, a Critical Analysis for Lawyers and Laymen. Boston: Little, Brown, 1927. 1st reissue. Usable only (cl worn). *Boswell*. $50/£32

FRANKLIN, BENJAMIN. The Art of Making Money Plenty, in Every Man's Pocket. London: Harvey & Darton, 1817. 16mo. 8 leaves. (Sl foxed, worn.) Stiff ptd wrappers. Roan-backed case. *Oinonen**. $750/£481

FRANKLIN, BENJAMIN. Autobiography of Benjamin Franklin. John Bigelow (ed). Phila/London: Lippincott/Trubner, 1868. 1st complete ed. Engr frontis port w/tissue guard, 409pp. (Sm puncture fr hinge), else VG. Howes F323. *Cahan*. $50/£32

FRANKLIN, BENJAMIN. Autobiography. Chicago: Lakeside Classic, 1903. Black cl. Good. *Scribe's Perch**. $90/£58

FRANKLIN, BENJAMIN. The Autobiography. SF: John Henry Nash, 1931. Ltd to 1500. Signed by Nash. Port. Vellum-backed marbled bds. Fine in slipcase (sl shelfworn). *Sadlon*. $200/£128

FRANKLIN, BENJAMIN. Experiments and Observations on Electricity, Made at Philadelphia in America. London: David Henry, 1769. 4th ed. 4to. iv,(2),496,(16)pp (bkpl); 7 plts (lt offsetting). Complete w/half-title (sig), ad, errata, and blanks. (Bkpl.) Mod full morocco. NF. *Glaser*. $3,000/£1,923

FRANKLIN, BENJAMIN. Memoirs of the Life and Writings of Benjamin Franklin, LL.D.... London, 1818. 572pp (foxed), 8 plts. Diced calf (cvrs detached, heavily worn), spine label (chipped). *King*. $100/£64

FRANKLIN, BENJAMIN. Memoirs. May Farrand (ed). Berkeley, 1949. Parallel text ed. Howes F323. *Ginsberg*. $75/£48

FRANKLIN, BENJAMIN. Mr. Franklin, a Selection from His Personal Letters. Leonard W. Labaree and Whitfield J. Bell, Jr. (eds). New Haven: Yale, 1956. 6 color plts. Cl-backed bds. VG (inscrip). *Bohling*. $20/£13

FRANKLIN, BENJAMIN. The Papers of Benjamin Franklin. Vol. I. L. Labaree (ed). New Haven: Yale Univ, 1959. 1st ed. Fine. *Archer*. $35/£22

FRANKLIN, BENJAMIN. Poor Richard: The Almanacks for the Years 1733-1758. Phila: LEC, 1964. One of 1500 numbered, signed by Norman Rockwell (illus). Natural cowhide, hand-marbled bds, zodiac signs stamped at spine overlap. Very Nice (spine sl rubbed) in bd slipcase (sl worn, sm cracks). *Baltimore**. $140/£90

FRANKLIN, BENJAMIN. Works of the Late.... NY: Samuel Campbell, 1794. 2 vols in 1. Port. (Sl internal repairs, spotting.) Trimmed. 19th-cent 3/4 morocco, marbled bds (scuffed). *Freeman**. $80/£51

FRANKLIN, COLIN. The Ashendene Press. Dallas, 1986. One of 750. Prospectus laid in. Linen-backed patterned bds. *Swann**. $69/£44

FRANKLIN, JOHN. Narrative of a Journey to the Shores of the Polar Sea in the Years 1819, 20, 21, and 22. Edmonton: Hurtig, 1969. Facs rpt of 1823 1st ed. 4 fldg maps in pocket. VG. *High Latitude*. $90/£58

FRANKLIN, JOHN. Narrative of a Journey to the Shores of the Polar Sea in the Years 1819, 20, 21, and 22.... London: John Murray, 1823. 1st ed. 4to. Frontis, xvi,768, 30 plts (10 color), 4 fldg maps. Leather, raised bands, gilt, leather spine label. NF (corners sl worn, sl offset from plts). *Parmer*. $1,250/£801

FRANKLIN, K. J. A Monograph on Veins. Springfield, 1937. 1st ed. VG. *Fye.* $75/£48

FRANKLIN, KENNETH J. (trans). Movement of the Heart and Blood in Animals. Oxford: Blackwell, 1957. Color frontis. Good. *Goodrich.* $35/£22

FRANTZ, JOE B. and JULIAN ERNEST CHOATE, JR. The American Cowboy: The Myth and the Reality. Univ of OK, (1955). 1st ed. Fine in dj. *Authors Of West.* $40/£26

FRANTZ, MABEL GOODE. Full Many a Name, the Story of Sam Davis Scout and Spy, C.S.A. Jackson, TN: The Author, 1961. 1st ed. NF in NF dj. *Mcgowan.* $60/£38

FRARY, I. T. Ohio: In Homespun and Calico. Richmond: Garrett & Massie, 1942. Signed. Frontis, 30 plts. Checkered cl. VG. *Cahan.* $35/£22

FRARY, I. T. Thomas Jefferson Architect and Builder. Garrett & Massie, 1931. Good+ (water-stained; spine frayed). *Book Broker.* $65/£42

FRASCONI, ANTONIO. The House That Jack Built. NY: HBJ, 1958. 1st ed. 8 1/4 x 10 1/2. 32pp. Fine in dj. *Cattermole.* $60/£38

FRASER, EDWARD. Bellerophon. London, 1909. Frontis. Pict cl, gilt. *Maggs.* $101/£65

FRASER, EDWARD. The Sailors Whom Nelson Led. London, 1913. Color frontis. Blue cl (spine faded). *Maggs.* $86/£55

FRASER, GEORGE MacDONALD. Flashman and the Dragon. London: Collins Harvill, 1985. 1st ed. (Spine sl cocked), else Fine in dj. *Lame Duck.* $65/£42

FRASER, GEORGE MacDONALD. Flashman and the Redskins. London: Collins, 1982. 1st ed. NF (bkpl) in dj. *Antic Hay.* $50/£32

FRASER, GEORGE MacDONALD. Flashman at the Charge. NY, 1973. 1st Amer ed. VG in dj (sl bumped). *King.* $35/£22

FRASER, GEORGE MacDONALD. Flashman at the Charge. NY: Knopf, 1973. 1st Amer ed. NF (bkpl) in dj (lt edgewear, sm tears, price-clipped). *Antic Hay.* $50/£32

FRASER, GEORGE MacDONALD. Flashman's Lady. (London): Barrie & Jenkins, (1977). 1st Eng ed. NF (bkpl, sig ep) in dj. *Antic Hay.* $60/£38

FRASER, GEORGE MacDONALD. Flashman's Lady. Barrie & Jenkins, 1977. 1st UK ed. VG+ in dj (spine sl faded). *Williams.* $50/£32

FRASER, GEORGE MacDONALD. Flashman. NY: World, (1969). 1st US ed. Fine in Fine dj (sl soiled). *Unger.* $125/£80

FRASER, GEORGE MacDONALD. Flashman. NY: World, 1969. 1st Amer ed. Fine in dj. *Mordida.* $100/£64

FRASER, GEORGE MacDONALD. McAuslan in the Rough. London: Barrie & Jenkins, (1974). 1st ed. (Adhesion residue eps), else VG in dj. *Pacific*.* $52/£33

FRASER, GEORGE MacDONALD. McAuslan in the Rough. London: Barrie & Jenkins, 1974. 1st UK ed. NF in VG dj (edges sl creased). *Williams.* $101/£65

FRASER, GEORGE MacDONALD. Mr. American. NY: S&S, 1980. 1st Amer ed. Fine in dj. *Mordida.* $50/£32

FRASER, GEORGE MacDONALD. The Pirates. NY: Knopf, 1984. 1st Amer ed. Fine in dj. *Mordida.* $50/£32

FRASER, GEORGE MacDONALD. The Pyrates. Collins, 1983. 1st UK ed. NF in dj. *Williams.* $28/£18

FRASER, GEORGE MacDONALD. Royal Flash. NY: Knopf, 1970. 1st US ed. VG+ (mks fep) in VG+ dj. *Other Worlds.* $20/£13

FRASER, GEORGE MacDONALD. The Steel Bonnets. London: Barrie & Jenkins, 1971. 1st ed. 19 plts, fldg plan. VG in dj (spine head sl worn). *Hollett.* $55/£35

FRASER, GEORGE MacDONALD. The Steel Bonnets. NY, 1972. 1st Amer ed. NF in NF dj. *Warren.* $35/£22

FRASER, JAMES B. An Historical and Descriptive Account of Persia. Edinburgh, 1834. 2nd ed. Fldg map. Gilt edges. Dec cl (spine ends sl worn). *Petersfield.* $28/£18

FRASER, P. M. Ptolemaic Alexandria. Oxford: Clarendon, 1972. Vol III only. Good in dj. *Archaeologia.* $50/£32

FRASER, SIMON. Simon Fraser. Letters and Journals, 1806-1808. W. Kaye Lamb (ed). Toronto: Macmillan of Canada, 1960. Black cl. VG in dj (worn, soiled). *Parmer.* $65/£42

FRAZER, JAMES GEORGE. The Golden Bough. NY: Macmillan, 1951. 3rd ed, Amer issue. 13 vols. (Bkpl and stamp each vol), o/w Fine set in NF djs (spines dknd). *Captain's Bookshelf.* $400/£256

FRAZER, JAMES GEORGE. The Golden Bough: A Study in Magic and Religion. NY: LEC, 1970. Ltd to 1500 signed by James Tewicki (illus). 2 vols. 3-piece cl. Mint in slipcase (lt worn). *Truepenny.* $175/£112

FRAZER, PERRY D. Amateur Rodmaking. NY: Macmillan, 1922. VG+. *Bowman.* $20/£13

FRAZER, PERRY D. Rodmaking for Beginners. NY: Forest & Stream, 1908. 1st ed. Photo frontis. VG. *Bowman.* $40/£26

FRAZIER, DON. Recognizing Derrydale Press Books.... (Morristown, NJ), 1983. One of 347. 22 color photo plts in rear cvr pocket (corners ripped). Full gilt-pict leather. Box. *Kane*.* $140/£90

FRAZIER, E. FRANKLIN. The Free Negro Family. Nashville: Fisk Univ, 1932. 1st ed. 2 maps. Blue cl (ex-lib, spine ends worn; whited-out stamps eps). *Petrilla.* $50/£32

FRAZIER, IAN. Dating Your Mom. NY: FSG, (1986). 1st ed, 1st bk. Signed. Fine in dj. *Between The Covers.* $85/£54

FRAZIER, IAN. Great Plains. NY: FSG, 1989. 1st ed. Fine in Fine dj. *Revere.* $30/£19

FREAR, MARY DILLINGHAM. Flowers of Hawaii. NY: Dodd, Mead, 1938. 1st ed. 30 mtd color plts. Blue cl. Good in illus slipcase (worn). *Karmiole.* $75/£48

FREDERIC, LOUIS. The Art of Southeast Asia. Temples and Sculpture. NY: Abrams, (1965). 1st ed. 44 maps and diags. White cl. Good in dj. *Karmiole.* $150/£96

FREDERICS, DIANA. Diana, A Strange Autobiography. NY: Dial, 1939. 1st ed. (Sl shelfwear), else VG. *Brown.* $30/£19

Free-Holder, or Political Essays. (By Joseph Addison.) London: D. Midwinter & J. Tonson, 1716. 1st collected ed. 400pp. Speckled calf (rebacked), gilt. (Sl foxing), o/w Very Nice. *Second Life.* $350/£224

FREE. (Pseud of Abbie Hoffman.) Revolution for the Hell of It. NY, 1968. 1st ed. Fine in Fine dj. *Warren.* $150/£96

FREE. (Pseud of Abbie Hoffman.) Revolution for the Hell of It. NY: Dial, 1968. 1st ed. NF- in wraps. *Sclanders.* $23/£15

FREECE, HANS P. The Letters of an Apostate Mormon to His Son. Elmira, NY, 1908. 2nd ed. Frontis port. Grn cl. (Ex-lib), else VG. *Five Quail.* $30/£19

FREECE, HANS P. The Letters of an Apostate Mormon to His Son. Elmira: Chemung Ptg, 1908. 2nd ed. (Sl worn, rubbed, spine sl frayed), else Good. *Brown.* $20/£13

FREECE, HANS P. The Letters of an Apostate Mormon to His Son. NY, n.d. 6th ed. 60pp. (Name; lt stain cvr.) *Zubal*.* $22/£14

FREED, LEONARD. Black in White America. NY: Grossman, 1967. 1st ed. (Owner stamp, name, spine top split), else VG in stiff wrappers. *Cahan.* $25/£16

FREEDBERG, S. J. Painting of the High Renaissance in Rome and Florence. Cambridge, MA: Harvard Univ, 1961. 2 vols. VG in djs (chipped). *Argosy*. $125/£80

FREELAND, ROBERT. The Soap Maker's Private Manual. Phila, 1876. 1st ed. Tipped-in photo frontis, 314pp. Dec full leather clasp casing (lacks rear clasp, scuffed). Good. *Scribe's Perch**. $65/£42

FREELING, NICOLAS. Gun Before Butter. London: Gollancz, 1963. 1st UK ed. Fine in VG dj (sl worn, nicked). *Williams*. $28/£18

FREELING, NICOLAS. A Long Silence. London: Hamilton, 1972. 1st UK ed. Fine in dj. *Williams*. $25/£16

FREELING, NICOLAS. Sand Castles. London: Andre Deutsch, 1989. 1st ed. Fine in Fine dj. *Janus*. $35/£22

FREELING, NICOLAS. Those in Peril. London: Andre Deutsch, 1990. 1st ed. Fine in NF dj. *Janus*. $25/£16

FREELING, NICOLAS. Tsing-Boum! London: Hamilton, 1969. 1st UK ed. VG + in VG dj (sl edgeworn, sm closed tears). *Williams*. $22/£14

FREEMAN, D. S. (ed). A Calendar of Confederate Papers. Richmond, 1908. One of 1000, out of series. (Rear hinge starting), o/w Good + . *Scribe's Perch**. $75/£48

FREEMAN, DANA. (Pseud of Phoebe Atwood Taylor.) Branbury Bog. NY: Norton, (1938). 1st ed. Fine in dj (short tears, soil, chips, perfs). *Metropolitan**. $46/£29

FREEMAN, DOUGLAS SOUTHALL (ed). Lee's Dispatches. NY: Putnam, 1915. 2nd ptg. (Head, foot bumped), o/w Good. *Scribe's Perch**. $50/£32

FREEMAN, DOUGLAS SOUTHALL. The Last Parade. Richmond, VA: Whittet & Shepperson, 1932. 1st ed. Mtd frontis, 20 leaves. VG (sl soiled). *Mcgowan*. $450/£288

FREEMAN, DOUGLAS SOUTHALL. Lee's Lieutenants. NY: Scribner, 1946. Arlington ed. 4 vols. Typed letter secretarially signed laid in w/orig envelope. (Spines dknd), else NF. Howes F349. *Mcgowan*. $275/£176

FREEMAN, DOUGLAS SOUTHALL. Lee's Lieutenants.... NY, (1946). 'Arlington Edition.' 4 vols. Blue cl (spines dknd), gilt. *Kane**. $160/£103

FREEMAN, DOUGLAS SOUTHALL. R. E. Lee: A Biography. NY: Scribner, 1936. 1st ptg of Pulitzer Prize ed w/elaborate gilt on spine not found on later ptgs. 4 vols. VG set. Howes F350. *Mcgowan*. $275/£176

FREEMAN, DOUGLAS SOUTHALL. R. E. Lee: A Biography. NY, 1945. 'The Pulitzer Prize Edition.' 4 vols. Dk blue cl, gilt. *Kane**. $150/£96

FREEMAN, DOUGLAS SOUTHALL. R. E. Lee: A Biography. NY/London: Scribner, 1947. 4 vols. NF in pub's box (sl shelfworn), paper label. *Sadlon*. $75/£48

FREEMAN, EDWARD A. Some Impressions of the United States. London: Longmans, 1883. 1st ed. (1),289,(12)pp. Dec cl. *Ginsberg*. $100/£64

FREEMAN, F. Yaradee; a Plea for Africa, in Familiar Conversations.... Phila: J. Whetham, 1836. 1st ed. 360pp. Emb blue cl (spine top worn, cvr partly stained), gilt-stamped spine. Sound. *Petrilla*. $75/£48

FREEMAN, G. DENIS and DOUGLAS COOPER. The Road to Bordeaux. London: Cresset, 1940. 1st ed. Edward Ardizzone (illus). VG. *Hollett*. $62/£40

FREEMAN, JOHN. Life of the Rev. William Kirby. London, 1852. Steel-engr port, litho letter, tinted view. Bound w/o half-title. Marbled edges. Contemp blue polished calf (sl worn), gilt spine. *Maggs*. $86/£55

FREEMAN, LEWIS R. Down the Columbia. NY, 1921. 1st ed. Good. *Heinoldt*. $25/£16

FREEMAN, LEWIS R. Down the Columbia. London, 1922. Gilt cl. (Sunned, rubbed, ex-lib, sticker remnants fr cvr, loan card rear pastedown), else Good. *Reese*. $65/£42

FREEMAN, LEWIS R. Down the Grand Canyon. NY, 1930. Blue cl. VG (spine lettering sl dull). *Five Quail*. $40/£26

FREEMAN, LEWIS R. On the Roof of the Rockies. NY, 1925. 1st ed. 63 photo plts. Dec grey cl. (Rear hinge starting), else VG. *Price*. $85/£54

FREEMAN, LEWIS R. Sea-Hounds. NY: Dodd, Mead, 1919. Blue cl. VG. *Parmer*. $45/£29

FREEMAN, LEWIS R. Waterways of Westward Wandering. NY, 1927. Blue cl (sl cvr flaws). VG (bkpl removed). *Five Quail*. $30/£19

FREEMAN, MARGARET B. The Unicorn Tapestries. NY, 1976. Good. *Washton*. $40/£26

FREEMAN, R. AUSTIN. As a Thief in the Night. Dodd, Mead, 1928. 1st US ed. Fine in dj (2 sm chips at spine fold, closed tear and browning to inner flaps, rear panel). *Certo*. $225/£144

FREEMAN, R. AUSTIN. The Cat's Eye. London: Hodder & Stoughton, (1923). 1st UK ed. Fine. *Williams*. $156/£100

FREEMAN, R. AUSTIN. A Certain Dr. Thorndyke. London: Hodder & Stoughton, (1927). 1st UK ed. VG (sm ink name; spine sl creased). *Williams*. $109/£70

FREEMAN, R. AUSTIN. A Certain Dr. Thorndyke. NY: Dodd-Mead, 1928. 1st ed. Fine. *Else Fine*. $60/£38

FREEMAN, R. AUSTIN. The Eye of Osiris. London: Hodder & Stoughton, (1911). 1st UK ed. 8pp ads inserted at rear as called for. Variant plain brn bds, gilt spine. Fine. *Williams*. $195/£125

FREEMAN, R. AUSTIN. Felo de Se? London: Hodder & Stoughton, 1937. 1st ed. (Very rubbed, spine faded, soil.) Dj (creased, worn, internal tape). *Metropolitan**. $402/£258

FREEMAN, R. AUSTIN. Felo de Se? London: Hodder & Stoughton, 1937. 1st UK ed. VG in dj (nicks strengthened to rear). *Williams*. $1,053/£675

FREEMAN, R. AUSTIN. The Jacob Street Mystery. London: Hodder & Stoughton, 1942. 1st UK ed. NF. *Williams*. $62/£40

FREEMAN, R. AUSTIN. Mr. Pottermack's Oversight. NY: Dodd Mead, 1930. 1st Amer ed. (Name, date fep), o/w Fine in dj (spine ends, back panel chipped, sm closed tears). *Mordida*. $175/£112

FREEMAN, R. AUSTIN. The Mystery of Angelina Frood. London: Hodder & Stoughton, (1924). 1st UK ed. NF (spine sl faded). *Williams*. $156/£100

FREEMAN, R. AUSTIN. Pontifex, Son and Thorndyke. NY: Dodd, Mead, 1931. 1st US ed. VG + (spine sl dull). *Williams*. $47/£30

FREEMAN, R. AUSTIN. The Shadow of the Wolf. London: Hodder & Stoughton, (1925). 1st UK ed. 'For Review' stamped to 1/2 title. (Cvrs lt stained), o/w VG + . *Williams*. $195/£125

FREEMAN, R. AUSTIN. The Surprising Experiences of Mr. Shuttlebury Cobb. London: Hodder & Stoughton, (1927). 1st UK ed. Fine in dj (rear flap creased). *Williams*. $1,170/£750

FREEMAN, R. AUSTIN. When Rogues Fall Out. Hodder, 1932. 1st UK ed. VG. *Williams*. $44/£28

FREEMAN, RICHARD A. Travels and Life in Ashanti and Jaman. NY: Stokes, 1898. 1st Amer ed. Frontis, xx,559pp; color fldg map at end. Orange gilt pict cl (spine sl dulled), else VG. *Terramedia*. $250/£160

FREEMAN, RICHARD B. The Lithographs of Ralston Crawford. (Lexington): Univ of KY, (1962). 1st ed. Cl-backed illus paper over bds. Fine in VG dj. *Cahan*. $85/£54

FREEMAN, ROLAND L. City Pavements/Country Roads. Phila: Antioch Univ, (1978). 1st ed. Fine in glossy stapled wrappers as issued (sm stain fr wrap). *Between The Covers*. $85/£54

FREEMAN, SARAH. Medals Relating to Medicine and Allied Sciences in the Numismatic Collection of the Johns Hopkins University. Balt, 1964. 1st ed. 32 plts. VG. *Fye.* $200/£128

FREEMAN, WALTER. Neuropathology. Phila: Saunders, 1933. 1st ed, 1st bk. Nice (ex-lib, bkpl removal, spine label). *Beasley.* $60/£38

FREEMAN, WALTER. Neuropathology: The Anatomical Foundation of Nervous Diseases. Phila, 1933. 1st ed. Grn cl (text foxed, inner rear hinge cracked; extrems worn). Good. *Doctor's Library.* $60/£38

FREEMAN, WALTER. Psychosurgery: Intelligence, Emotion and Social Behavior Following Prefrontal Lobotomy for Mental Disorder. Springfield, IL: Charles C. Thomas, (1950). 2nd rev, enlgd ed. 21 tables. Blue cl. VG. *Gach.* $200/£128

FREEMANTLE, ARTHUR JAMES LYON. The Freemantle Diary, Being the Journal of.... Boston: Little, Brown, (1954). Rpt of 1863 ed. NF in NF dj. Howes F361. *Mcgowan.* $35/£22

FREEMANTLE, BRIAN. Clap Hands, Here Comes Charlie. London: Jonathan Cape, 1978. 1st ed. Fine in dj (price-clipped). *Janus.* $75/£48

FREEMANTLE, BRIAN. Goodbye to an Old Friend. London: Cape, 1973. 1st ed. (Fore-edge lt spotted), o/w Fine in dj (spine faded). *Mordida.* $45/£29

FREEMANTLE, BRIAN. The Man Who Wanted Tomorrow. London: Cape, 1975. 1st ed. Fine in dj. *Mordida.* $75/£48

FREEMANTLE, BRIAN. See Charlie Run. NY: Bantam, (1987). 1st ed. Fine in NF dj. *Antic Hay.* $25/£16

FREER GALLERY OF ART. A Descriptive and Illustrative Catalogue of Chinese Bronzes.... Washington, 1946. Folio. 50 plts. *Swann*.* $92/£59

FREER, R. L. Memoirs, Extracts of Speeches, Diary of a Journey to America.... Hereford, England, 1866. 294pp; 3 photo plts. Presentation slip laid in. Gilt calf. Howes F358. *Reese.* $300/£192

FREER, R. L. Memoirs, Extracts of Speeches, Diary of a Journey to America.... Hereford, England, 1866. 1st ed. Presentation slip laid in. 294pp. Full gold-stamped leather. Howes F358. *Ginsberg.* $300/£192

FREMANTLE, ARTHUR J. Three Months in the Southern States: April-June, 1863. NY, 1864. 1st Amer ed. 309pp; port. Dec blind-stamped cl. (Bkpl, port sl foxed), else Fine. Howes F361. *Reese.* $175/£112

FREMANTLE, FRANCIS E. Impressions of a Doctor in Khaki. London, 1901. 1st ed. VG. *Argosy.* $45/£29

FREMONT, JESSIE BENTON. Mother Lode Narratives. Shirley Sargent (ed). Ashland: Lewis Osborne, 1970. 1st ed. One of 650 numbered, this being copy 'PC' (printer's copy). VF. *Argonaut.* $50/£32

FREMONT, JOHN C. Life Explorations and Public Services of John Charles Fremont. Boston: Ticknor & Fields, 1856. 1st ed. 356pp; 13 plts. (Sl foxed, ex-lib; sl rubbed, faded, spine ends frayed), o/w Good. *Worldwide.* $35/£22

FREMONT, JOHN C. Memoirs of My Life... together with A Sketch of the Life of Senator Benton...by Jessie Benton Fremont. Chicago/NY, 1887. viii,(3),xvi-xix,(1),655pp (occasional fox mk). Contemp mottled calf (rebacked), spine gilt, leather label. VG. Howes F367. *Reese.* $800/£513

FREMONT, JOHN C. Narrative of the Exploring Expedition to the Rocky Mountains in the Year 1842.... Balt: Taylor, Wilde, 1846. Wrapper says 3rd ed, tp says 2nd. Good- in wraps (wrinkles, stains). *Scribe's Perch*.* $40/£26

FREMONT, JOHN C. Narrative of the Exploring Expedition to the Rocky Mountains in the Year 1842.... NY: Appleton, 1846. 1st ed thus. iv,186pp. 1/4 morocco, marbled bds. (Lt foxed, recently rebound), o/w VG. *Worldwide.* $145/£93

FREMONT, JOHN C. Narrative of the Exploring Expedition to the Rocky Mountains, in the Year 1842, and to Oregon and North California in the Years 1843-44. London: Wiley & Putnam, 1846. 1st Eng ed. 4 plts, fldg map. (Sl foxing.) 3/4 polished calf, marbled bds (extrems rubbed), leather spine label. Howes F370. *Sadlon.* $400/£256

FREMONT, JOHN C. Report of the Exploring Expedition to the Rocky Mountains in the Year 1842, and to Oregon and North California in the Years 1843-44. Washington: Gales & Seaton, 1845. 1st ed, Senate issue. 22 plts, 5 maps incl lg fldg map rear pocket (sm repaired breaks, 6-inch tear backed w/document repair tape). Orig cl, gilt (corners, spine ends sl rubbed). Sound. Howes F370. *Sadlon.* $900/£577

FREMONT, JOHN C. Report of the Exploring Expedition to the Rocky Mountains in the Year 1842. Washington: Gales & Seaton, 1845. 4 (of 5) maps, 19 (of 22) litho plts. (Lt foxed.) Howes F370. *Swann*.* $149/£96

FREMONT, JOHN C. Report of the Exploring Expedition to the Rocky Mountains in the Year 1842.... Washington, 1845. Senate issue. 693pp; 22 plts, 5 maps (3 fldg, 1 in rear pocket). Orig cl. Good (rubbed, spine ends frayed, bumped; foxing, pocket bottom split). Howes F370. *Reese.* $1,000/£641

FREMONT, JOHN C. Report of the Exploring Expedition to the Rocky Mountains in the Year 1842.... Washington: Gales & Seaton, 1845. 1st ed, Senate issue. 8vo. 693pp; 22 plts, 5 maps (3 fldg, 1 lg map in rear pocket). (Lt spotted, pocket splitting, short tears to map; shelfworn), else VG. Howes F370. *Brown.* $650/£417

FREMONT, JOHN C. Report of the Exploring Expedition to the Rocky Mountains in the Year 1842...and to Oregon...1843-'44. Washington, 1845. 1st ed, House issue. 22 tinted litho plts, 4 (of 5?) maps, 2 fldg. Contemp 1/2 calf (edgeworn, spine rubbed, chipped). Howes F370. *Swann*.* $402/£258

French Drawings from American Collections. NY: MMA, 1959. 208 plts. Good in wrappers (sl soiled). *Washton.* $20/£13

French in Indo-China. (By Francois Garnier.) London: T. Nelson, 1884. 1st ed. 263pp, incl frontis, 32 line-engrs, map. (Lt foxing.) Blue pict cl, gilt. Externally Fine. *Morrell.* $70/£45

French Nineteenth Century Paintings, Drawings, Pastels, and Watercolors. NY: Shepherd Gallery, 1984. Good in wraps. *Washton.* $20/£13

French Painting 1774-1830. The Age of Revolution. Detroit: Detroit Inst of Arts, 1975. Good in wrappers (backstrip sl rubbed). *Washton.* $50/£32

FRENCH, B. L. Nome Nuggets. NY: Montross, Clarke & Emmons, 1901. 1st ed. Dec cl. Good. *Karmiole.* $150/£96

FRENCH, BENJAMIN BROWN. Witness to the Young Republic, A Yankee's Journal, 1828-1870. Donald B. Cole & John J. McDonough (eds). Hanover, (1989). 1st ed. VG + in VG + dj. *Pratt.* $40/£26

FRENCH, FIONA. The Blue Bird. NY: Walck, 1972. 1st US ed. 8 3/4 x 10 1/4. 36pp. Pict bds. Fine in dj. *Cattermole.* $35/£22

FRENCH, FIONA. Jack of Hearts. NY: HBJ, 1970. 1st US ed. 8 1/2 x 11 1/4. 32pp. Cl spine, pict bds. VG in dj. *Cattermole.* $50/£32

FRENCH, HERBERT (ed). An Index of Differential Diagnosis of Main Symptoms by Various Writers. NY, 1913. 1st Amer ed. VG. *Fye.* $50/£32

FRENCH, JOHN D. (ed). Frontiers in Brain Research. NY: Columbia Univ, 1962. 1st ed. VG in dj. *Argosy.* $30/£19

FRENCH, PAUL. (Pseud of Isaac Asimov.) David Starr, Space Ranger. World's Work, 1953. 1st UK ed. Fine in VG dj (few closed tears). *Williams.* $117/£75

FRENCH, PAUL. (Pseud of Isaac Asimov.) Lucky Starr and the Oceans of Venus. GC: Doubleday, 1954. 1st ed. VG (bds discolored) in dj (edgewear). *Captain's Bookshelf.* $100/£64

FRENCH, PETER. John Dee: The World of an Elizabethan Magus. London: RKP, 1972. 1st ptg. Frontis, 16 glossy plts. Fine in VG + dj. *Middle Earth.* $60/£38

FRENCH, SAMUEL G. Two Wars: An Autobiography. Nashville: Confederate Veteran, 1901. 1st ed. (Fr hinge crudely repaired, rear hinge tender), else VG in pict maroon cl. *Captain's Bookshelf.* $200/£128

FRENCH-SHELDON, MRS. M. Sultan to Sultan. London/Boston: Saxon/Arena, 1892. (Ex-lib, stamp verso tp, blind stamps prelims, tp sl tear, sl soiled.) Maroon buckram (rebound). *Grayling.* $187/£120

FRERE-COOK, GERVIS (ed). The Decorative Arts of the Mariner. London, 1966. 1st ed. Dw. *Edwards.* $55/£35

FRERICHS, F. T. A Clinical Treatise on Diseases of the Liver. C. Murchison (trans). London: New Sydenham Soc, 1860/61. 2 vols. xxvi,(i),402pp, plt, 32 woodcuts; xix,(i),584pp, 2 plts, 36 woodcuts. Brn cl (rebacked, spines relaid). Very Clean set internally. *White.* $55/£35

FRESHFIELD, DOUGLAS W. The Life of Horace Benedict de Saussure. London, 1920. 1st ed. (Inner fr hinge cracked; bumped, dull.) *King.* $95/£61

FRESHFIELD, DOUGLAS W. Round Kangchenjunga. London, 1903. 1st ed. (Ink inscrip, lt foxed, esp ends; spotted, worn.) *King.* $695/£446

FREUCHEN, PETER. Ice Floes and Flaming Water. London, 1955. 1st Eng ed. Good in dj (defective). *King.* $20/£13

FREUCHEN, PETER. The Legend of Daniel Williams. NY: Julian Messner, (1956). VG in dj (edgewear). *Perier.* $30/£19

FREUD, ANNA. The Psycho-Analytical Treatment of Children. N. Procter-Gregg (trans). London: Imago, (1946). (Sl pencilling.) Dj. *Argosy.* $50/£32

FREUD, SIGMUND. Beyond the Pleasure Principle. C.J.M. Hubback (trans). Internat'l Psycho-Analytical Press, 1922. 1st ed in English. Nice (sl mks). *Ash.* $117/£75

FREUD, SIGMUND. Civilization and Its Discontents. Joan Riviere (trans). Hogarth, 1930. 1st ed in English. 1860 ptd. Frontis port. Nice (edges sl spotted, lt worn). *Ash.* $78/£50

FREUD, SIGMUND. The Cocaine Papers. Vienna/Zurich: Dunquin, 1963. 1st ed in English. (X stamped over pub's name in 4 places), o/w Fine. *Beasley.* $125/£80

FREUD, SIGMUND. Collected Papers. NY: Basic Books, 1959. 1st US ed. 5 vols. NF (name; few spines sl scuffed). *Beasley.* $100/£64

FREUD, SIGMUND. Collected Papers. Vols 1-4. J. Riviere and Strachey (trans). NY/London, 1924-34. (Cl rubbed.) *Argosy.* $125/£80

FREUD, SIGMUND. Collected Papers. Vols 1-5. Joan Riviere and A. & J. Strachey (trans). London: Hogarth/Inst of Psychoanalysis, 1953-6. VG. *Argosy.* $150/£96

FREUD, SIGMUND. The Future of an Illusion. W. D. Robson-Scott (trans). London: Hogarth, 1928. 1st ed in English. One of 1516. Grn cl. VG. *Argosy.* $150/£96

FREUD, SIGMUND. Inhibitions, Symptoms and Anxiety. Alix Strachey (trans). Hogarth, 1936. 1st ed in English. Nice (sl worn). *Ash.* $78/£50

FREUD, SIGMUND. The Interpretation of Dreams. London: George Allen & Unwin, (1954). 1st ed. 1st separate appearance of the Strachey trans. Blue cl. VG in dj (worn). *Gach.* $85/£54

FREUD, SIGMUND. The Interpretation of Dreams. Authorized Translation of the Third Edition with Introduction by A. Brill. A.A. Brill (trans). NY: Macmillan, 1913. 1st ed in English; 1st issue w/integral tp. (xiv),510,(2)pp. Ptd straight-grained blue cl (rear joint cl bubbled, edges sl rubbed). VG +. *Gach.* $750/£481

FREUD, SIGMUND. Moses and Monotheism. NY: Knopf, 1939. Stated 1st ed. Good (pencil annotation). *Scribe's Perch*.* $30/£19

FREUD, SIGMUND. The Origins of Psycho-Analysis. London: Imago, 1954. 1st ed. Fine (owner label fep) in NF dj. *Beasley.* $65/£42

FREUD, SIGMUND. An Outline of Psychoanalysis. London: Hogarth, 1949. 1st ed in English. VG (worn). *Beasley.* $40/£26

FREUD, SIGMUND. The Problem of Anxiety. NY, 1936. 1st Amer ed. Fine in dj (few sm tears). *Polyanthos.* $45/£29

FREUD, SIGMUND. Selected Papers on Hysteria. NY: NMD, 1912. 2nd enlgd ed. Tan cl (rebound), paper spine label. Fine. *Beasley.* $85/£54

FREUD, SIGMUND. Three Contributions to the Theory of Sex. NY, 1930. 4th ed. Internally VG (ex-lib, stamps; recently rebacked). *Goodrich.* $35/£22

FREUD, SIGMUND. Wit and Its Relation to the Unconscious. NY: Moffat, Yard, 1916. 1st ed in English. VG. *Beasley.* $150/£96

FREUDENTHAL, ELSBETH E. Flight into History: The Wright Brothers and the Air Age. Norman: Univ of OK, 1949. 1st ed. Rev copy. Fine in dj (lt worn). *Hermitage.* $45/£29

FRIED, FREDERICK. Artists in Wood. NY, 1970. 1st ed. Color frontis. Dj (spine lt faded). *Edwards.* $39/£25

FRIED, FREDERICK. A Pictorial History of the Carousel. NY: Barnes, 1964. 2nd ptg. VG in Good+ dj. *October Farm.* $38/£24

FRIED, HENRY B. The Watch Repairer's Manual. NY: Van Nostrand, 1949. 1st ed. (Sl pencilling, blindstamp.) *Weber.* $17/£11

FRIEDE, JUAN and BENJAMIN KEEN (eds). Bartolome de las Casas in History. DeKalb: Northern IL Univ, 1971. Fldg map. VG in dj. *Dumont.* $40/£26

FRIEDE, REINHARD L. A Histochemical Atlas of Tissue Oxidation in the Brain Stem of the Cat. NY, 1961. Thin folio. VG. *Argosy.* $40/£26

FRIEDENWALD, HARRY. The Jews and Medicine, Essays. Balt, 1944-1946. 1st ed. 2 vols. VF. *Fye.* $250/£160

FRIEDENWALD, HARRY. The Jews and Medicine, Essays. NY, 1967. 2nd ed. 2 vols. VG. *Fye.* $75/£48

FRIEDLANDER, IRA. The Whirling Dervishes. NY: Collier Books, (1975). Pict wraps (corner creased, sm tear spine tail). Internally Fine. *Blue Mountain.* $15/£10

FRIEDLANDER, LEE and JIM DINE. Work from the Same House. London: Trigram, 1969. 1st ed. 16 full-pg b/w photos, 16 etchings. NF in ptd stiff wrappers (lt discolored, spine lt worn). *Cahan.* $85/£54

FRIEDLANDER, MAX J. Early Netherlandish Painting. Volume I. The Van Eycks-Petrus Christus. NY, 1967. 111 plts. Good. *Washton.* $325/£208

FRIEDLANDER, MAX J. Early Netherlandish Painting. Volume II. Rogier van der Weyden and the Master of Flemalle. NY, 1967. 144 pp plts. Good. *Washton.* $325/£208

FRIEDLANDER, MAX J. Early Netherlandish Painting. Volume III. Dieric Bouts and Joos van Gent. NY, 1968. 128pp plts. Good. *Washton.* $150/£96

FRIEDLANDER, MAX J. Early Netherlandish Painting. Volume IV. Hugo van der Goes. NY, 1969. Good. *Washton*. $150/£96

FRIEDLANDER, MAX J. Early Netherlandish Painting. Volume V. Geertgen tot Sint Jans and Jerome Bosch. NY, 1969. 135 plts. Good. *Washton*. $150/£96

FRIEDLANDER, MAX J. Early Netherlandish Painting. Volume XI. The Antwerp Mannerists-Adriaen Ysenbrant. NY, 1974. 207 plts. Good. *Washton*. $450/£288

FRIEDLANDER, MAX J. On Art and Connoisseurship. Tancred Borenius (trans). London: Cassirer, 1942. 1st ed. Fine in dj. *Europa*. $31/£20

FRIEDLANDER, MAX J. and JAKOB ROSENBERG. The Paintings of Lucas Cranach. Secaucus, 1978. 26 color plts. Good in dj. *Washton*. $65/£42

FRIEDLANDER, WALTER. Mannerism and Anti-Mannerism in Italian Painting. NY, 1957. Orig ed. Good. *Washton*. $35/£22

FRIEDMAN, BRUCE JAY. The Dick. NY: Knopf, 1970. 1st ed. Fine in dj. *Jaffe*. $25/£16

FRIEDMAN, BRUCE JAY. Steambath. NY: Knopf, 1971. 1st trade ed. Cl, dec bds. (Pencil erasure), else Fine in dj. *Reese*. $35/£22

FRIEDMAN, BRUCE JAY. Stern. NY: S&S, 1962. 1st ed, 1st bk. Fine in dj (lt dust-soiled). *Jaffe*. $45/£29

FRIEDMAN, I. K. Poor People. Boston: Houghton Mifflin, 1900. 1st ed. NF. *Beasley*. $150/£96

FRIEDMAN, MARTIN. The Frozen Image: Scandinavian Photography. Minneapolis/NY: Walker Art Center/Abbeville, 1982. 1st ed. (Name, blindstamp; spine, lower edge sunstruck), else NF in pict stiff wrappers. *Cahan*. $40/£26

FRIEDMAN, MARTIN. Hockney Paints the Stage. London: Arts Council, 1986. VG in pict wrappers. *Hollett*. $47/£30

FRIEDMAN, REUBEN. A History of Dematology in Philadelphia. FL, 1955. Inscribed. VG (sl worn). *Doctor's Library*. $75/£48

FRIEDMAN, REUBEN. A History of Dermatology in Philadelphia. NY, 1955. VG. *Fye*. $65/£42

FRIEDMANN, HERBERT et al. Distributional Check-List of the Birds of Mexico. Part I and II. Berkeley, CA, 1950, 1957. (Bkpl, new eps; cl sl soiled.) *Edwards*. $39/£25

FRIEDRICK, ADOLF. From the Congo to the Niger and the Nile. Phila: John Winston, 1913. 1st Amer ed. 2 vols. Color frontis, color fldg map. Blue gilt dec cl. Nice. *Terramedia*. $350/£224

FRIEL, BRIAN. The Gold in the Sea. London: Victor Golancz, 1966. 1st ed. Fine in dj. *Jaffe*. $150/£96

FRIEND, LLERENA. Sam Houston, the Great Designer. Austin: Univ of TX, 1954. 1st ed. VF in Fine dj. *Gibbs*. $60/£38

FRIES, AMOS and CLARENCE WEST. Chemical Warfare. NY, 1921. VG. *Fye*. $65/£42

FRIES, ULRICH E. From Copenhagen to Okanogan, the Autobiography of a Pioneer. Caldwell: Caxton, 1949. Red cl. 3 dj panels, trimmed, laid in. VG. *Bohling*. $20/£13

FRINK, H. W. Morbid Fears and Compulsions. NY: Moffat, Yard, 1918. 1st ed. Good+ (sig, bkpl, pocket; rubbed). *Beasley*. $75/£48

FRINK, MAURICE with CASEY BARTHELMESS. Photographer on an Army Mule. Norman: Univ of OK, 1966. 2nd ptg. (Owner stamp), else NF in dj. *Cahan*. $35/£22

FRISBIE, ROBERT DEAN. The Book of Puka-Puka. NY, 1929. 1st ed. VG. *Mcclintock*. $45/£29

FRISCH, MAX. Biography. NY: Hill & Wang, 1969. 1st US ed. NF in dj. *Lame Duck*. $35/£22

FRISCH, MAX. The Chinese Wall. NY: Hill & Wang, 1961. 1st US ed. NF in VG+ dj. *Lame Duck*. $35/£22

FRISCH, MAX. Homo Faber. Michael Bullock (trans). London/NY: Abelard-Schuman, (1959). 1st ed. Fine in dj (sl soiled, price-clipped). *Antic Hay*. $30/£19

FRISCH, MAX. Homo Faber. London: Abelard-Schuman, 1959. 1st British ed. (Sm stains top pg edge), else NF- in dj. *Lame Duck*. $65/£42

FRISCH, MAX. Three Plays. Michael Bullock (trans). London: Methuen, (1962). 1st Eng ed. NF (sm stain rep) in dj (sl worn, sm stain). *Antic Hay*. $30/£19

FRISON-ROCHE, ROGER and PIERRE TAIRRAZ. Mount Blanc and the Seven Valleys. London, (1961). 1st Eng ed. (Sm spot spine), else VG in dj. *King*. $50/£32

FRISWOLD, CARROLL. Frontier Fighters and Their Autograph Signatures. L.A.: Corral of Westerners Keepsake, 1968. Ltd to 600. Wraps. *Oregon*. $60/£38

FRITTS, CHARLES E. The Watch Adjuster's Manual. Phila: Keystone, 1912. 4th ed. Navy blue cl (worn, soiled, back cvr off). *Weber*. $30/£19

FROHMAN, CHARLES EUGENE. Rebels on Lake Erie. Columbus, OH: Ohio Hist Soc, 1965. 2nd ed. (Owner blindstamp), else NF. *Mcgowan*. $60/£38

FROISETH, JENNIE ANDERSON (ed). The Women of Mormonism. Detroit: C.G.G. Paine, 1882. 1st ed. (Foxing; sl rubbed, soiled, rear hinge cracked.) *Sadlon*. $40/£26

FROISETH, JENNIE ANDERSON (ed). The Women of Mormonism. Detroit, 1887. 416pp. VG (cl lt worn). *Benchmark*. $50/£32

From Today Painting Is Dead: The Beginnings of Photography. (London): Victoria & Albert Museum, 1975. 50 plts. VG (name, ink mks 2pp) in pict stiff wrappers. *Cahan*. $25/£16

FROST, A. B. Stuff and Nonsense. NY: Scribner, (1884). 1st ed, 1st bk. Cl-backed pict bds (soiled). Good (pp soiled). *Captain's Bookshelf*. $150/£96

FROST, A. B. Stuff and Nonsense. (London): John C. Nimmo, c. 1884. 1st Eng ed. 92pp. 1/2 cl, pict bds (wear, soil, few pencil notes). *Waverly**. $71/£46

FROST, FREDERICK. The Bamboo Whistle. Phila: McCrae, Smith, 1937. 1st ed. Dj (creases, tears, internal tape). *Metropolitan**. $57/£37

FROST, LAWRENCE A. Boy General in Bronze. Glendale: A.H. Clark, 1985. Fine in plain dj. *Bohling*. $40/£26

FROST, LAWRENCE A. The Custer Album. Seattle, (1964). 1st ed. VG in dj (sl frayed). *King*. $40/£26

FROST, LAWRENCE A. The Custer Album. Seattle: Superior, (1964). 1st ed. Good (pg bottoms sl water-stained) in dj. *Lien*. $45/£29

FROST, ROBERT. A Boy's Will. NY: Henry Holt, 1915. 1st Amer ed, 2nd state, 1st bk. 'And' at p14. Blue cl, gilt. Fine. *Macdonnell*. $200/£128

FROST, ROBERT. Collected Poems. NY: Holt, (1930). 1st trade ed. Signed, dated (1938). VG overall (cracked before frontis, fep and blank loosened; lt rubbed, sm frays, spine foxed). *Waverly**. $121/£78

FROST, ROBERT. Collected Poems. NY: Random House, 1930. 1st ed. #37/1000 signed. Teg. Tan buckram, morocco spine label. (Label lt rubbed), else VG. *Pacific**. $196/£126

FROST, ROBERT. The Complete Poems. 1951. 1st ed. NF in dj. *Words Etc*. $70/£45

FROST, ROBERT. In the Clearing. NY: Henry Holt, (1962). 1st ed. #735/1500 signed. Fine in slipcase. *Pacific**. $288/£185

FROST, ROBERT. In the Clearing. NY, 1962. 1st Amer ed. NF (name; edges sl rubbed) in NF dj (edges sl rubbed). *Polyanthos*. $35/£22

FROST, ROBERT. The Letters of Robert Frost to Louis Untermeyer. NY: Holt, (1963). 1st ed. Fine in VG dj (couple creased edge tears). *Reese.* $20/£13

FROST, ROBERT. The Lone Striker. (NY: Knopf, 1933.) 1st ed. Fine in illus sewn wrappers w/mailing envelope as issued. *Dermont.* $75/£48

FROST, ROBERT. A Masque of Mercy. NY: Henry Holt, (1947). 1st ed. #483/751 signed. 1/2 cl, bds, gilt. Fine in slipcase. *Pacific*.* $259/£166

FROST, ROBERT. A Masque of Reason. NY: Henry Holt, (1945). 1st ed. One of 800 specially-bound, numbered, signed. Fine in slipcase (worn). *Captain's Bookshelf.* $300/£192

FROST, ROBERT. Mountain Interval. NY: Henry Holt, (1916). 1st ed, 1st state w/line 6, p88 omitted, line 7 repeated. (Old notes fr pastedown), else VG in dj (spine ends rubbed, tape repair verso). *Pacific*.* $575/£369

FROST, ROBERT. Selected Letters. Lawrance Thompson (ed). Cape, 1965. 1st UK ed. Fine in dj (sl chipped, price-clipped). *Poetry Bookshop.* $31/£20

FROST, ROBERT. Selected Poems. NY: Henry Holt, (1932). Later ptg. Signed. Cl-backed bds (sl worn, soiled; name). *Waverly*.* $82/£53

FROST, ROBERT. Steeple Bush. NY: Henry Holt, 1947. 1st ed. #497/751 signed. 1/2 cl, gilt-dec bds, gilt spine. Fine in orig glassine, slipcase. *Pacific*.* $345/£221

FROST, ROBERT. A Witness Tree. NY: Ptd by Spiral Press, 1942. Ltd to 735 numbered, signed. Frontis port. Uncut. Patterned bds, gilt spine. Fine in NF box. *Polyanthos.* $250/£160

FROST, THOMAS. Circus Life and Circus Celebrities. London: C&W, 1881. New ed. (Marginalia.) Dec cl (dull, spine ends frayed). *Dramatis Personae.* $150/£96

FROST, WILLIAM and R. V. BOUGHTON. Modern Practical Brickwork. Batsford, 1954. 1st ed. (Eps lt spotted.) Dj (chipped, spine loss). *Edwards.* $39/£25

FROTHINGHAM, ALICE WILSON. Lustreware of Spain. NY, 1951. *Swann*.* $57/£37

FROUD, BRIAN. Goblins. NY: Macmillan, 1983. 1st US ed. Pop-up bk. Sm 4to. Glazed pict paper-cvrd bds. NF. *Book Adoption.* $50/£32

FROUDE, JAMES ANTHONY. The English in the West Indies. London, 1888. x,373pp + 24pp pub's cat; 9 plts. (Loss to lettering tp; sm stain upper bd, recased, spine chipped, corners bumped.) *Edwards.* $47/£30

FROUDE, JAMES ANTHONY. The English in the West Indies. London: Longmans, Green, 1888. New ed. viii,328pp; 7 full-pg wood engrs. (Frontis, fep sl browned.) Calf prize binding, spine gilt. Excellent. *Sotheran.* $231/£148

FROUDE, JAMES ANTHONY. Oceana, or England and Her Colonies. NY: Scribner, 1886. xii,396,8ads pp; 8 plts. (Lt rubbed.) *Adelson.* $50/£32

FROUDE, JAMES ANTHONY. Oceania or England and Her Colonies. London, 1886. 1st ed. xi,396pp (lt marginal browning); 8 plts. Dec eps. Early rebind in cl (spine lt sunned), morocco spine label. *Edwards.* $70/£45

FROUDE, JAMES ANTHONY. Thomas Carlyle. A History of the First Forty Years...1795-1835. Together with A History of His Life In London 1834-1881. London: Longmans, Green, 1882-84. 4 vols. 6 ports and etched plts, engr port. (Joints tender, sm stain 2 bds.) *Hollett.* $101/£65

FRY, CHRISTOPHER. The Dark Is Light Enough. NY/London: OUP, 1954. Inscribed presentation. Lt purple cl (sl bumped). NF in pict yellow dj (spine soiled). *Blue Mountain.* $75/£48

FRY, CHRISTOPHER. An Experience of Critics. London: Perpetua, 1952. 1st Eng ed. Fine in dj (lt worn, spine lt browned). *Antic Hay.* $25/£16

FRY, CHRISTOPHER. The Lady's Not for Burning. London, 1949. 1st ed. (Ink inscrip), else VG in dj (sl rubbed, sl tears). *King.* $25/£16

FRY, CHRISTOPHER. A Sleep of Prisoners. London: OUP, 1951. 1st UK ed. NF (sm bkpl) in dj. *Williams.* $28/£18

FRY, HENRY. The History of North Atlantic Steam Navigation with Some Account of Early Ships and Shipowners. London: Sampson Low, Marston, 1896. 1st ed. xiv,324pp; fldg map. 3/4 navy polished calf, gilt-panelled back, red leather lettering piece, gilt date. (Corners lt worn), o/w VG + . *House.* $180/£115

FRY, ROGER. Flemish Art. NY, 1927. 31 plts hors texte. Good in dj. *Washton.* $25/£16

FRY, ROGER. Transformations. Critical and Speculative Essays on Art. London: C&W, 1926. 1st ed. 36 plts hors-texte. Interior Fine (lt stain cvr, spine sl faded). *Europa.* $55/£35

FRYE, NORTHRUP. Fearful Symmetry: A Study of William Blake. Princeton: Princeton Univ, 1947. 1st ed, 1st bk. VG (lacks dj). *Captain's Bookshelf.* $50/£32

FRYE, W. E. After Waterloo. Salomon Reinach (ed). London, 1908. 1st ed. (Feps lt browned; fore-edge bds lt dampstained.) *Edwards.* $39/£25

FRYER, JANE EAYRE. Mary Frances Knitting and Crocheting Book. NY: John C. Winston, 1918. 1st ed. Jean Allen Boyer (illus). 7 x 9 1/2. 270pp. Good. *Cattermole.* $75/£48

FRYXELL, FRITIOF (ed). Francois Matthes and the Marks of Time. SF: Sierra Club, (1962). 1st ed. VG in dj (soiled, edgetorn). *King.* $50/£32

FUCHS, VIVIAN and EDMUND HILLARY. The Crossing of Antarctica. London, 1958. 1st ed. Ptd sticker signed by Fuchs. VG. *High Latitude.* $25/£16

FUCHS, VIVIAN and EDMUND HILLARY. The Crossing of Antarctica. Boston: Little, Brown, 1959. 1st Amer ed. Blue cl. VG in dj (worn). *Parmer.* $30/£19

FUCHSHUBER, ANNEGERT. The Wishing Hat. NY: Morrow, 1977. 1st US ed. 8 1/2 x 9 1/4. 32pp. Pict bds. Fine in dj. *Cattermole.* $25/£16

FUENTES, CARLOS. The Death of Artemio Cruz. London, 1964. 1st ed. Fine in NF dj. *Polyanthos.* $50/£32

FUENTES, CARLOS. Distant Relations. NY: Farrar, (1982, 1980). 1st Amer ed. Signed. VG in dj. *Houle.* $75/£48

FUENTES, CARLOS. The Good Conscience. NY: Ivan Obolensky, (1961). 1st ed in English. Fine in dj. *Pacific*.* $104/£67

FUENTES, CARLOS. The Hydra Head. Margaret Sayers Peden (trans). NY: FSG, (1978). 1st ed. Fine in NF dj (sm tears). *Antic Hay.* $25/£16

FUENTES, CARLOS. The Hydra Head. NY, 1978. 1st ed. NF in NF dj. *Smith.* $20/£13

FUERTES, LOUIS AGASSIZ and ALLAN BROOKS. Portraits of New England Birds. Commonwealth of MA, 1932. VG. *Books & Birds.* $100/£64

FUERTES, LOUIS AGASSIZ and WILFRED HUDSON OSBOOG. Artist and Naturalist in Ethiopia. NY: Doubleday, Doran, 1936. 1st ed. 16 full-pg color plts. Black linen. *Appelfeld.* $200/£128

FUJIMOTO, T. The Nightside of Japan. London: Laurie, 1927. 3rd imp. Color frontis, 32 plts. (Ex-lib; cl sl rubbed, soiled, lib spine sticker), o/w VG. *Worldwide.* $45/£29

FULANAIN. The Marsh Arab. Phila: Lippincott, 1928. 1st ed. Frontis, map. (Sl rubbed, soiled), o/w VG. *Worldwide.* $24/£15

FULCHER, GEORGE WILLIAMS. Life of Thomas Gainsborough.... London: Longman et al, 1856. 2nd ed. viii,248pp,60pp cat; extra engr tp, 4 plts. Uncut. VG in grn cl, gilt. *Cox*. $47/£30

FULLER, ANDREW S. The Grape Culturist. NY: D&K, 1864. 1st ed. 263pp. Dk blue cl (corners chewed, bds soiled). Good. *Archer*. $25/£16

FULLER, ANDREW S. The Grape Culturist. NY: The Author, 1864. 1st ed. 262pp + ads. Brn cl. (Faded, sl soiled), o/w Nice. *Second Life*. $125/£80

FULLER, ANDREW S. The Grape Culturist. NY: OJ, 1924. Grn cl, gilt. (Edgewear), else VG. *Price*. $34/£22

FULLER, ANDREW S. The Small Fruit Culturist. NY: OJ, 1921. Grn cl, gilt. VG. *Price*. $27/£17

FULLER, CLAUD E. and R. D. STEUART. Firearms of the Confederacy. Huntington, WV: Standard, 1944. 1st ed. 37 photo plts. Dec cvr. Good + . *Scribe's Perch**. $100/£64

FULLER, FRANCIS. Medicina Gymnastica: or, A Treatise Concerning the Power of Exercise.... London: John Matthews for Robert Knaplock, 1705. 1st ed. (xxxii),229 (i.e. 283). Contemp panelled calf (lt rubbed, corners bumped, spine ends repaired, new label). Text Very Clean. *White*. $460/£295

FULLER, JOHN. The Beautiful Inventions. Secker & Warburg, (1983). 1st ed. VG in white dj (sl browned). *Ash*. $31/£20

FULLER, R. BUCKMINSTER. And It Came to Pass—Not to Stay. NY: Macmillan, (1976). 1st ed. NF (presentation) in dj. *Turtle Island*. $30/£19

FULLER, R. BUCKMINSTER. Critical Path. NY: St. Martin's, (1981). 1st ed. One of 250 numbered, signed. Fine in slipcase. *Bohling*. $70/£45

FULLER, R. BUCKMINSTER. Ideas and Integrities. NJ, (1963). 1st Amer ed. Fine (spine sl rubbed) in dj (sl rubbed, sm chips, price-clipped). *Polyanthos*. $30/£19

FULLER, R. BUCKMINSTER. Nine Chains to the Moon. Phila: Lippincott, (1938). 1st ed, 1st bk. 2 fldg charts. Gold cl. Good in dj (sl chipped). *Karmiole*. $125/£80

FULLER, R. BUCKMINSTER. Operating Manual for Spaceship Earth. (Carbondale: Southern IL Univ, 1969). 1st ed. (Bds sl splayed), else Fine in Fine dj (sl soiling). *Between The Covers*. $85/£54

FULLER, R. BUCKMINSTER. Untitled Epic Poem on the History of Industrialization. Highlands, NC: Jonathan Williams, 1962. 1st ed. Rev copy w/ptd slip. Wrappers. NF in NF ptd acetate dj. *Dermont*. $50/£32

FULLER, ROY. Mianserin Sonnets. Edinburgh: Tragara, 1984. One of 120 numbered (of 145). Fine in wrappers. *Dermont*. $50/£32

FULLER, S. MARGARET. Literature and Art. NY: Fowlers & Wells, 1852. 2 vols in 1. viii,164,(2); 184pp. Burgundy cl (faded, sl rubbed). BAL 6502. *Karmiole*. $100/£64

FULLER, T. Pharmacopoeia Extemporanea. 1710. (xvi),443pp + index (corners creased; ink notes fep, margins). Orig calf (joints sl weak). *Whitehart*. $250/£160

FULLER, THOMAS. The Holy State and the Profane State. London: William Pickering, 1840. 1st ed thus. viii,400pp. Uncut. Orig drab cl, paper label (browned, rubbed). Sound (backstrip sl worn). *Cox*. $47/£30

FULLER, TIMOTHY. Keep Cool, Mr. Jones. Boston: Atlantic Little, Brown, 1950. 1st ed. VG- (spine stained; edgewear) in dj (chipped; rear soiled). *Murder By The Book*. $40/£26

FULLERTON, GEORGIANA. Lady-Bird. NY: Appleton, 1853. 1st ed (?). 3 vols in 1. 328pp. (Lt foxed; sl rubbed, spine ends frayed), o/w Good. *Worldwide*. $20/£13

FULLERTON, HUGH. Jimmy Kirkland of the Cascade College Team. Winston, 1915. Later ptg. VG in VG dj. *Plapinger*. $50/£32

FULOP-MILLER, HENRY. The Power and Secret of the Jesuits. NY: Viking, 1930. 95 plts. (Ink underlining; sl rubbed, soiled), o/w Good. *Worldwide*. $28/£18

FULTON, AMBROSE C. Life's Voyage: A Diary of a Sailor on Sea and Land.... NY: The Author, 1898. 1st ed. (8),555pp. Howes F413. *Ginsberg*. $300/£192

FULTON, J. D. Woman as God Made Her; the True Woman. Boston: Lee & Shepard, 1869. 1st ed. Frontis port, 262pp. Brn cl. VG. *Second Life*. $225/£144

FULTON, JAMES ALEXANDER. Peach Culture. NY: OJ, (1870). 1st ed. 190 + 14pp ads. (Pp browned; cl mottled), else VG. *Quest*. $60/£38

FULTON, JOHN (ed). Decompression Sickness. Phila: W.B. Saunders, 1951. 1st ed. Signed by E. Newton Harvey (contributor). Carbon of letter from Harvey to Fulton laid in. VG. *Glaser*. $75/£48

FULTON, JOHN. Aviation Medicine in Its Preventive Aspects, a Historical Survey. London, 1948. 1st ed. VG. *Fye*. $150/£96

FULTON, JOHN. A Bibliography of the Honourable Robert Boyle. Oxford, 1961. 2nd ed. Nice in dj (edgewear). *Goodrich*. $145/£93

FULTON, JOHN. A Bibliography of Visual Literature, 1939-1944. Washington, DC, 1945. 1st ed. VG (sl worn). *Doctor's Library*. $50/£32

FULTON, JOHN. Harvey Cushing. A Biography. London: Blackwells, 1946. London cancel title of 1st ed. (Cl lt rubbed.) Internally Fine. *Goodrich*. $65/£42

FULTON, JOHN. Harvey Cushing. A Biography. Springfield, 1946. Internally Fine (sl rubbed). *Goodrich*. $55/£35

FULTON, JOHN. Harvey Cushing. A Biography. Springfield, 1946. 1st ed. VG. *Doctor's Library*. $75/£48

FULTON, JOHN. Harvey Cushing. A Biography. Springfield: Charles C. Thomas, 1946. 1st ed, corrected 2nd ptg. Frontis port. Fine in dj (lt worn). *Glaser*. $100/£64

FULTON, JOHN. Harvey Cushing. A Biography. Springfield: Thomas, 1946. 1st ed. Nice in dj (worn). *Goodrich*. $95/£61

FULTON, JOHN. Physiology of the Nervous System. OUP, 1938. 1st ed. Plt. VG. *White*. $86/£55

FULTON, JOHN. Physiology of the Nervous System. London, 1938. 1st ed. VG. *Argosy*. $85/£54

FULTON, JOHN. Selected Readings in the History of Physiology. Springfield, 1930. 1st ed. VG. *Fye*. $100/£64

FULTON, JOHN. Selected Readings in the History of Physiology. Springfield, 1966. 2nd ed. (Ex-lib.) *Fye*. $80/£51

FULTON, JOHN. The Sign of Babinski. Springfield, 1932. 1st ed. VG in dj. *Fye*. $75/£48

FULTON, JUSTIN D. The Outlook of Freedom: or The Roman Catholic Element in American History. Cincinnati: Moore et al, 1856. 1st ed. (Fore-edge, flyleaves lt foxed, leaf w/paper loss lower margin; spine lightened.) *Sadlon*. $30/£19

FULTON, MARIANNE. Mary Ellen Mark: 25 Years. Boston: Little Brown, 1991. 1st ed. Signed by Mark. Fine in pict stiff wrappers. *Cahan*. $50/£32

FULTON, ROBERT LARDIN. Epic of the Overland. L.A.: N.A. Kovach, 1954. Reissued 1st ed. #110/275. Fldg map. Blue cl. Fine in NF dj. *Harrington*. $55/£35

FUNAROFF, S. The Spider and the Clock. NY: International, 1938. 1st ed. Fine in Fine dj. *Beasley*. $50/£32

FUNG, KWOK YING. China. NY: Henry Holt, 1943. 1st ed. 84 full-pg photos. (Owner stamp), else VG in Fair dj. *Cahan*. $50/£32

FUNKHOUSER, W. D. Ancient Life in Kentucky. Frankfort: KY Geological Survey, 1928. Frontis. (Ex-lib, inkstamps.) *Archaeologia*. $65/£42

FURER-HAIMENDORF, CHRISTOPH. The Naked Nagas. Calcutta, 1933. (Feps lt browned.) Dj (ragged). *Edwards*. $23/£15

FURLONG, CHARLES W. Let'er Buck. NY: Putnam's, 1921. 1st ed. (Ink inscrip), else VG. *Perier*. $45/£29

FURLONG, LAWRENCE. The American Coast Pilot. NY: Edmund M. Blunt, 1812. 7th ed. Old calf (edges worn, some loss; spine weak; few plts lacking or torn; foxing, loose, tears). *Metropolitan**. $86/£55

FURNEAUX, W. Life in Ponds and Streams. London: Longmans, Green, 1906. New imp. 8 color plts. Aeg. Dec cl (spine head repaired). VG. *Savona*. $23/£15

FURNISS, HARRY. P and O Sketches in Pen and Ink. London: Studio of Design & Illustrations Supply Agency, (c. 1888). 203pp. Aeg. Orig pict grn cl (rebacked in matching levant morocco; sm mk lower bd), gilt. *Hollett*. $187/£120

FURNIVALL, FREDERICK J. Captain Cox, His Ballads and Books. London: Ballad Soc, 1871. Fldg litho plt. Teg. Crimson 3/4 morocco. VG. *Argosy*. $100/£64

FURNIVALL, FREDERICK J. (ed). The Fifty Earliest English Wills in the Court of Probate, London. A.D. 1387-1439. London: Trubner, 1882. Vol 78. Later 1/4 morocco (repaired; ex-lib, bkpl). Orig wraps bound in. *Boswell*. $225/£144

FURSE, C. Elephant Island, an Antarctic Expedition. Shrewsbury, 1979. Dj (sl worn). *Maggs*. $25/£16

FURST, VIKTOR. The Architecture of Sir Christopher Wren. London, 1956. (Sm stain tp.) Dj. *Washton*. $75/£48

Fuseli Circle in Rome. New Haven: Yale Center for British Art, 1979. (Ink notes fep), o/w Very Nice in wraps. *Washton*. $25/£16

FUSS, J. D. Roman Antiquities. Oxford, 1840. xv,608pp (lt foxing, bkpl). Unopened. Blind-emb cl (spine faded). *Edwards*. $47/£30

FUSSELL, EDWIN. Frontier: American Literature and the American West. Princeton Univ, 1965. 1st ed. Fine in dj. *Authors Of West*. $40/£26

FUSSELL, G. The English Rural Labourer. Batchworth, 1949. 1st ed. 18 plts. Dj (lt soiled, sl chipped). *Edwards*. $23/£15

FUSSELL, G. The Farmer's Tools 1500-1900. London, 1952. Dj (sl worn). *Maggs*. $36/£23

FUSSELL, PAUL, JR. Theory of Prosody in Eighteenth-Century England. New London: Connecticut College, 1954. 1st ed, 1st bk. Fine (sl dknd edges; name) in wraps. *Beasley*. $40/£26

FUTRELLE, JACQUES. The High Hand. Indianapolis: Bobbs-Merrill, (1911). 1st ed. (Edges rubbed.) *Metropolitan**. $34/£22

FUTRELLE, JACQUES. My Lady's Garter. Chicago: Rand McNally, (1912). 1st ed. (Sl soiled.) Dj (very worn, loss to spine head). *Metropolitan**. $34/£22

FUTRELLE, JACQUES. The Thinking Machine. NY: Dodd Mead, 1907. 1st ed. VG in pict cl-cvrd bds. *Mordida*. $250/£160

FYLEMAN, ROSE. The Fairy Green. Methuen, 1919. 1st ed. 63,(1)pp. 2 edges uncut. Rose cl, gilt. Fine. *Cox*. $23/£15

FYLEMAN, ROSE. The Fairy Green. Methuen, 1919. 1st ed. Sm 8vo. 63pp. Dec pink cl (faded), gilt. *Bookmark*. $27/£17

G

GABA, LESTER. On Soap Culture, Concerning Its History, Technique, and Style. NY: Holt, 1935. 1st ed. VG in dj. *Worldwide*. $16/£10

GABRIEL, RALPH HENRY. Elias Boudinot, Cherokee and His America. Norman: Univ of OK, 1941. 1st ed. Frontis port, fldg map, 3 plts, fldg facs. Tan cl. Fine (top corner ll sl stained) in dj (spine sl faded). *Argonaut*. $75/£48

GABRIELSON, IRA N. (ed). The New Fisherman's Encyclopedia. Harrisburg, (1963). 1st ptg of rev 2nd ed. Fine in dj. *Truepenny*. $45/£29

GABRIELSON, IRA N. and FRANCESCA LAMONTE (eds). The Fisherman's Encyclopedia. Harrisburg, PA: Stackpole & Heck, 1950. 1st ed. 17 color plts. VG (sl rubbed). *Worldwide*. $65/£42

GABRIELSON, IRA N. and FREDERICK C. LINCOLN. Birds of Alaska. Harrisburg/Washington: Stackpole/Wildlife Mgmt Inst, 1959. VG in dj (worn). *Parmer*. $350/£224

GABRIELSON, IRA N. and FREDERICK C. LINCOLN. Birds of Alaska. Harrisburg: Stackpole/Wildlife Management Inst, 1959. 1st ed. Color frontis. VG + (eps sl spotted) in Good + dj (torn, tape-repaired, chipped). *Backman*. $125/£80

GADDA, CARLO EMILIO. That Awful Mess on Via Merulana. NY: Braziller, 1965. 1st US ed. NF in VG dj. *Lame Duck*. $45/£29

GADDIS, WILLIAM. Carpenter's Gothic. Deutsch, 1986. 1st UK ed. NF in dj. *Williams*. $19/£12

GADDIS, WILLIAM. Jr. NY: Knopf, (1975). 1st ed. Fine in NF dj (price-clipped). *Pettler & Lieberman*. $85/£54

GADDIS, WILLIAM. The Recognitions. NY: Harcourt, Brace, (1955). 1st ed. Black cl (sl rubbed), gilt. *Baltimore**. $30/£19

GADOW, HANS. Through Southern Mexico. London: Witherby, 1908. 1st ed. Fldg map. Purple cl (spine faded). *Karmiole*. $100/£64

GAG, WANDA. Millions of Cats. NY: Coward McCann, 1928. 1st ed. 9 3/4 x 6 3/4. 32pp. Pict bds. Good in dj. *Cattermole*. $250/£160

GAG, WANDA. Snippy and Snappy. NY: Coward-McCann, 1931. Oblong 8vo. Yellow illus bds (sl sun, soil). Interior Fine. *Metropolitan**. $40/£26

GAG, WANDA. Tales from Grimm. NY: Coward, (1936). 1st ed. Inscribed. NF (bkpl; lacks dj). *Captain's Bookshelf*. $250/£160

GAG, WANDA. Tales from Grimm. NY: Coward-McCann, 1936. 2nd ed. 5 1/2 x 8 1/4. 237pp. VG in dj. *Cattermole*. $50/£32

GAG, WANDA. Wanda Gag's Story Book. NY: Coward McCann, 1932. Early rpt. 9 3/4 x 6 3/4. Bound in sigs. Good (facs fep, tp; hinges repaired). *Cattermole*. $100/£64

GAIDZAKIAN, O. Illustrated Armenia and the Armenians. Boston, 1898. 1st ed. 256pp. Dec cvr. Good (hinge cracks). *Scribe's Perch**. $32/£21

GAINES, ERNEST J. Catherine Carmier. NY: Atheneum, (1964). 1st ed, 1st bk. Fine in Fine dj (price-clipped, sm closed tear). *Pettler & Lieberman*. $225/£144

GAINES, PIERCE WELCH (comp). Political Works of Concealed Authorship Relating to the United States 1789-1810, with Attributions. CT: Shoe String Press, (1972). 3rd ed. Fine in dj (price-clipped). *Heller*. $25/£16

GAIRDNER, JAMES (ed). The Paston Letters A.D. 1422-1509. London/Exeter, 1904. New Complete Library ed. 6 vols. Teg, rest uncut. (Bkpl, eps sl spotting, newspaper clippings tipped in vol 1; cl sl rubbed, spines rubbed, lt faded.) *Edwards*. $234/£150

GAITSKILL, MARY. Two Girls, Fat and Thin. London, 1991. 1st ed. Fine in Fine dj. *Smith*. $15/£10

GALASSI, PETER. Before Photography: Painting and the Invention of Photography. NY: MOMA, 1981. 82 plts (9 color). (Owner stamp), else Fine in illus stiff wrappers. *Cahan*. $25/£16

GALE, GEORGE. Upper Mississippi: or, Historical Sketches of the Mound Builders...in the North-West.... Chicago, 1867. 1st ed. 460pp; 14 plts. Howes G14. *Ginsberg*. $200/£128

GALEN. On the Natural Faculties. London, 1916. 1st ed of the Brock trans. VG. *Fye*. $100/£64

GALEN. On the Usefulness of the Parts of the Body. Margaret Tallmadge May (trans). Ithaca: Cornell Univ, (1968). 1st ed in English. 2 vols. Frontis each vol. NF in slipcase. *Glaser*. $135/£87

GALEN. A Translation of Galen's Hygiene (De Sanitate Tuenda). Robert Montraville Green (trans). Springfield: Charles C. Thomas, (1951). 1st ed in English. Fine in dj. *Glaser*. $75/£48

GALLAGHER, TESS. Instructions to the Double. Washington: Graywolf, (1976). One of 1500. Signed presentation. Fine in ptd wraps (sl soiled). *Polyanthos*. $35/£22

GALLAHER, JAMES. The Western Sketch-Book. Boston: Crocker & Brewster, 1850. Blind-emb brn cl, gilt. (Foxing, spine ends chipped), else NF. *Bohling*. $120/£77

GALLEGLY, JOSEPH. Footlights on the Border. The Hague, Netherlands: Mouton, 1962. 1st ed. Fine (pencil notes) in dj (worn). *Gibbs*. $50/£32

GALLICHAN, WALTER M. The Sterilization of the Unfit. London: T. Werner Laurie, 1929. 1st ed. Red bds. VG. *Patterson*. $39/£25

GALLICHAN, WALTER M. The Story of Seville. London, 1910. 2nd ed. Fldg plan. Teg. Gilt-dec cl (spine sl discolored; bkpl). *Edwards*. $19/£12

GALLICHAN, WALTER M. Women Under Polygamy. London, 1914. 1st ed. (Lt browned; spine lt spotted, sl soiled.) *Edwards*. $39/£25

GALLICO, PAUL. The Lonely. London, 1947. 1st ed. VG in dj (chipped). *Buckley*. $16/£10

GALLICO, PAUL. The Small Miracle. London, 1951. 1st ed. Excellent in dj. *Buckley*. $16/£10

GALLOWAY, ELIJAH. History and Progress of the Steam Engine.... London: Kelly, 1833. 863pp. Very Nice (rebound). *Bookcell*. $150/£96

GALLUP, DONALD. A Bibliography of Ezra Pound. Hart-Davis, 1963. 1st ed. Fine in untrimmed dj (top edge worn). *Poetry Bookshop*. $47/£30

GALLUP, GEORGE. A Guide to Public Opinion Polls. Princeton: Princeton Univ, 1944. 1st ed. Signed card laid in. Fine in dj. *Cummins*. $300/£192

GALLY, J. W. Sand and Big Jack Small. Chicago: Belford, Clarke, 1880. 1st ed. Frontis, 243pp. (Spine dknd, frayed, worn), else Good. *Brown*. $30/£19

Gallynipper in Yankeeland. London, 1882. viii,192pp. Pict cl (spine lt soiled), gilt bee, Uncle Sam's head. VG. *Reese*. $225/£144

GALSWORTHY, JOHN. Author and Critic. NY: House of Books, 1933. Ltd to 300 numbered. Black cl. VG in (supplied) acetate dj. *Antic Hay*. $75/£48

GALSWORTHY, JOHN. Autobiographical Letters of.... NY, 1933. 1st ed. Ltd to 150 numbered (this out of series). Port, facs. Cl-backed patterned bds (sl worn, discolored). *King*. $45/£29

GALSWORTHY, JOHN. Awakening. NY: Scribner, (1920). Inscribed. Color frontis. Brn paper-cvrd bds, gilt. VG. *Cullen*. $150/£96

GALSWORTHY, JOHN. A Commentary. London: Richards, 1930. Ltd to 275 numbered, signed. NF in dj (lt worn, internal mends). *Antic Hay*. $75/£48

GALSWORTHY, JOHN. Ex Libris. London, (1933). 1st ed. (Sl cvr wear.) Wraps. *King*. $35/£22

GALSWORTHY, JOHN. Five Tales. London: Heinemann, (1918). 1st ed. One of 5000 ptd. Grn cl. NF (eps discolored). *Antic Hay*. $45/£29

GALSWORTHY, JOHN. Flowering Wilderness. London: Heinemann, 1932. 1st ed. #128/400 signed. Unopened. Beveled bds, gilt pigskin spine. Fine. *Vandoros*. $125/£80

GALSWORTHY, JOHN. The Forest. London: Duckworth, (1924). Fine in dj. *Between The Covers*. $125/£80

GALSWORTHY, JOHN. Loyalties. London: Duckworth, (1922). (Name), else Fine in dj (sm tear). *Between The Covers*. $125/£80

GALSWORTHY, JOHN. Maid in Waiting. London: Heinemann, (1931). 1st ed. Grn cl. NF in VG dj (edgewear, tears). *Antic Hay*. $25/£16

GALSWORTHY, JOHN. A Modern Comedy. NY: Scribner, 1929. 1st US ed. Signed, inscribed. Grn cl (spine dknd, sl worn). Contents VG. *Waverly**. $33/£21

GALSWORTHY, JOHN. Moods, Songs, and Doggerels. London: Heinemann, 1912. 1st ed. One of 750 ptd. Paper spine label (worn). VG (bkpl). *Antic Hay*. $75/£48

GALSWORTHY, JOHN. A Motley. London: Heinemann, 1910. 1st ed, 1st issue. Grn buckram, gilt. NF. *Antic Hay*. $50/£32

GALSWORTHY, JOHN. Old English. London: Duckworth, (1924). 1st ed. One of 1800 bound in cl. Grn cl. VG in dj. *Antic Hay*. $25/£16

GALSWORTHY, JOHN. The Plays of John Galsworthy. London: Duckworth, 1929. 1st collected ed, ltd issue. #300/1275 signed. Teg, rest untrimmed. Grn cl, gilt spine. Fine in VG plain off-white dj. *Vandoros*. $175/£112

GALSWORTHY, JOHN. The Plays of.... London, 1929. Ltd to 1250 numbered, signed. Teg. VG in dj (heavily chipped), Nice marbled slipcase. *King*. $75/£48

GALSWORTHY, JOHN. The Silver Spoon. London: Heinemann, (1926). Lg paper ed. Ltd to 265 signed, numbered. Teg. Blue buckram cl. Fine in white dj (lt edgewear, browning). *Antic Hay*. $125/£80

GALSWORTHY, JOHN. Soames and the Flag. London: Heinemann, 1930. Ltd to 1025 signed. Teg. Full-vellum leather. VG in slipcase. *Antic Hay*. $85/£54

GALSWORTHY, JOHN. Soames and the Flag. London: Heinemann, 1930. 1st ed, ltd issue. One of 1025 ptd on laid paper, signed. Teg, rest untrimmed. Orig pigskin, gilt. Fine in NF slipcase. *Vandoros*. $125/£80

GALSWORTHY, JOHN. Swan Song. London: Heinemann, 1928. Ltd to 525 numbered, signed. (Eps sl browned.) Teg. Blue buckram cl. NF in dj (back panel creased, torn). *Antic Hay*. $85/£54

GALSWORTHY, JOHN. Two Forsyte Interludes. London: Heinemann, 1927. Ltd to 525 numbered, signed, of which 500 were for sale. Teg. Cl, marbled bds. NF in dj (sl worn, browned). *Antic Hay*. $85/£54

GALSWORTHY, JOHN. Two Forsyte Interludes. NY: Scribner, 1928. 1st ed. Paper labels. Fine, issued w/o dj. *Antic Hay*. $17/£11

GALSWORTHY, JOHN. Two Forsyte Interludes. A Silent Wooing. Passersby. London: Heinemann, 1927. 1st ed, ltd issue. One of 525 ptd on laid paper, signed. Dk blue spine, gilt, patterned bds. Fine in VG dj. *Vandoros*. $100/£64

GALT, JOHN. The Life of Lord Byron. London: Henry Colburn & Richard Bentley, 1830. 1st ed. xii,372pp; engr port, add'l engr tp (lacks series tp). 19th-cent 1/2 calf. Burmester. $140/£90

GALTON, F. Narrative of an Explorer in Tropical South Africa, Etc. in 1851, Etc. London: Ward, Lock, (1889). 2nd ed w/new map. Frontis port, 320pp + ads. Dec cl. VG. Mikesh. $60/£38

GALTON, FRANCIS. Hereditary Genius. NY, 1870. 1st Amer ed. 390pp. Recent buckram. VG. Fye. $200/£128

GALTON, FRANCIS. Hereditary Genius. London, 1892. 2nd ed. 379pp. VG. Fye. $100/£64

GAMBA, PETER. A Narrative of Lord Byron's Last Journey to Greece. Paris: A. & W. Galignani, 1825. 1st ed. xii,314pp (old waterstain last 40pp). Old 1/2 calf, mottled bds (rubbed, spine tip worn). Karmiole. $150/£96

GAMBLE, S. G. A Practical Treatise on Outbreaks of Fire. 1942. 3rd ed. Frontis plt. (Tp stamp.) Whitehart. $28/£18

Gambling World. (By Henry Vizetelly.) London: Hutchinson, 1898. 1st ed. Frontis port, viii,(ii),373,(iii)pp. Uncut. (Eps browned, foxed; scattered spotting; spine sl worn, faded.) Hollett. $117/£75

GAMETT, JAMES and STANLEY W. PAHER. Nevada Post Offices: An Illustrated History. Las Vegas: Nevada Publications, (1983). 1st ed. VF in dj. Argonaut. $45/£29

GANDEE, B. F. The Artist or, Young Ladies' Instructor in Ornamental Painting, Drawing.... Chapman & Hall, 1835. Colored engr and ptd tp; colored frontis by G. Baxter, 17 litho plts. Pub's brn cl gilt, gilt edges. Baxter's 1st work. Bright. Hatchwell. $281/£180

GANNETT, HENRY. A Gazetteer of Texas. Washington: USGS, 1904. 1st ed. VG in wraps. Gibbs. $25/£16

GANS-RUEDIN, E. Indian Carpets. Valerie Howard (trans). NY: Rizzoli, (1984). Fine in dj. Terramedia. $60/£38

GANT, S. G. Diagnosis and Treatment of Diseases of the Rectum, Anus, and Contiguous Textures. Phila, 1900. 1st ed. 16 full-pg chromolitho plts, 115 woodengrs. Gilt-tooled cl bds (sl worn). VG. Doctor's Library. $100/£64

GANZ, PAUL. The Paintings of Hans Holbein. London, 1950. 1st complete ed. 228 plts (16 color). Good. Washton. $95/£61

GARA, LARRY. Westernized Yankee, the Story of Cyrus Woodman. Madison, WI: State Hist Soc, 1956. VG+. Bohling. $15/£10

GARAVAGLIA and WORMAN. Firearms of the American West 1866-1894. Albuquerque: Univ of NM, (1985). Stated 1st ed. Good+ in Good dj. Scribe's Perch*. $29/£19

GARCES, FRANCISCO. On the Trail of a Spanish Pioneer. Elliott Coues (ed). NY: Harper, 1900. Ltd to 950. 2 vols. Uncut, partly unopened. Blue cl, gilt. (Ink name, fldg map partly detached vol 1; extrems worn, hinges cracked), o/w VG. Howes C801. Pacific*. $184/£118

GARCES, FRANCISCO. On the Trail of a Spanish Pioneer...1775-1776. Elliott Coues (ed). NY: Francis P. Harper, 1900. Ltd to 950 numbered. 2 vols. 3 maps (1 fldg). Dk blue cl. Good. Howes C801. Karmiole. $200/£128

GARCES, FRANCISCO. On the Trail of a Spanish Pioneer: The Diary and Itinerary of...1775-1776. Elliott Coues (trans). NY: Harper, 1900. 1st ed. One of 950 numbered sets. 2 vols. 3 fldg maps, 5 facs, 12 plts. Howes C801. Ginsberg. $375/£240

GARCIA LORCA, FEDERICO. Lament for the Death of a Bullfighter and Other Poems. A. L. Lloyd (trans). London/Toronto: Heinemann, 1937. 1st ed in English. Frontis port. Orange cl, gilt. NF in cream dj (spine dknd, internally reinforced). Blue Mountain. $125/£80

GARCIA LORCA, FEDERICO. Lament for the Death of a Bullfighter and Other Poems. A. L. Loyd (trans). London: Heinemann, 1937. 1st ed. Port. NF in dj (sl edge-tanned). Reese. $75/£48

GARCIA LORCA, FEDERICO. Poems. Stephen Spender and J. L. Gili (trans). London: The Dolphin, 1939. 1st Eng ed. Good (ink poem blank leaf, name; bumped). Clearwater. $31/£20

GARCIA LORCA, FEDERICO. Poems. Stephen Spender and J. L. Gili (trans). NY, 1939. 1st ed, Amer issue. Very Nice in dj. Clearwater. $55/£35

GARCIA LORCA, FEDERICO. Poems. R. M. Nadal (ed). London: The Dolphin, 1939. 1st ed. Port. Fine in dj (lt tanned, sl worn). Reese. $75/£48

GARCIA LORCA, FEDERICO. The Poet in New York and Other Poems. Rolfe Humphries (trans). NY: Norton, (1940). 1st ed. (Top edge dusty), o/w NF in dj (sl dust-soiled). Reese. $125/£80

GARCIA LORCA, FEDERICO. The Poet in New York and Other Poems. Rolfe Humphries (trans). NY: W.W. Norton, (1940). 1st ed. Orange cl (soiled). NF (sl offset ep edges) in Good pict cream dj (soiled, chipped, torn, 2 sm pieces out from bottom). Blue Mountain. $150/£96

GARCIA LORCA, FEDERICO. Three Tragedies of Federico Garcia Lorca. (NY: New Directions, 1947.) 1st ed thus. (Lt spine fading), o/w Fine in VG dj (chipped). Hermitage. $75/£48

GARCIA LORCA, FRANCISCO. In the Green Morning. Christopher Maurer (trans). NY, 1986. 1st ed. NF in NF dj. Smith. $15/£10

GARCIA MARQUEZ, GABRIEL. The Autumn of the Patriarch. G. Rabassa (trans). London, 1977. 1st ed. (Sm stain ep.) Typographeum. $25/£16

GARCIA MARQUEZ, GABRIEL. The Autumn of the Patriarch. Gregory Rabassa (trans). London, 1977. 1st Eng ed. Fine in dj. Clearwater. $62/£40

GARCIA MARQUEZ, GABRIEL. Chronicle of a Death Foretold. Gregory Rabassa (trans). NY: Knopf, 1983. 1st Amer ed. (Sticker back panel), o/w NF in dj. Hermitage. $50/£32

GARCIA MARQUEZ, GABRIEL. The General in His Labyrinth. NY: Knopf, 1990. 1st Amer ed. Fine in dj. Hermitage. $25/£16

GARCIA MARQUEZ, GABRIEL. The General in His Labyrinth. NY: Knopf, 1990. 1st Amer ed. Inscribed. Fine in Fine dj (sm bump crown). Between The Covers. $850/£545

GARCIA MARQUEZ, GABRIEL. Innocent Erendira and Other Stories. Gregory Rabassa (trans). London, 1979. 1st Eng ed. Fine (fr cvr sl chafed) in dj. Clearwater. $47/£30

GARCIA MARQUEZ, GABRIEL. Love in the Time of Cholera. NY: Knopf, 1988. 1st Amer ed. #104/350 signed. Pink/black cl in ptd glassine wrapper, slipcase. As New. Hermitage. $350/£224

GARCIA MARQUEZ, GABRIEL. Love in the Time of Cholera. Edith Grossman (trans). NY: Knopf, 1988. 1st Amer ed. One of 350 specially-bound, signed; this unnumbered. VF in ptd acetate dj, slipcase. Captain's Bookshelf. $400/£256

GARCIA MARQUEZ, GABRIEL. No One Writes to the Colonel and Other Stories. NY: Harper & Row, (1968). 1st Amer ed. Fine in dj. Pacific*. $316/£203

GARCIA MARQUEZ, GABRIEL. One Hundred Years of Solitude. NY: Harper & Row, (1970). 1st ed. VG (text lt soiled; spine sl cocked, ends sl rubbed) in 1st issue dj w/period, not exclamation pt, at end of 1st paragraph on flap (crimps, tears, sm chips). Waverly*. $253/£162

GARCIA MARQUEZ, GABRIEL. One Hundred Years of Solitude. NY: Harper & Row, (1970). 1st Amer ed. W/o series of numbers on last leaf. 2nd issue dj w/an exclamation point at the end of the 1st paragraph on fr flap. Fine (bkpl) in NF dj. Antic Hay. $500/£321

GARCIA MARQUEZ, GABRIEL. One Hundred Years of Solitude. NY: Harper, (1970). 1st ed. (Sl stain edge rear bd), else Fine in NF dj (sl rubbing spine extrems). Between The Covers. $650/£417

GARCIA MARQUEZ, GABRIEL. One Hundred Years of Solitude. Gregory Rabassa (trans). London, 1970. 1st Eng ed. Good (mk, inscrip fep; edges sl faded) in dj (rubbed, chipped). Clearwater. $78/£50

GARCIA MARQUEZ, GABRIEL. One Hundred Years of Solitude. NY, 1970. 1st Amer ed. NF in NF dj (price-clipped, w/o exclamation mark after 1st paragraph fr flap). Warren. $550/£353

GARCIA MARQUEZ, GABRIEL. One Hundred Years of Solitude. NY: Harper, 1970. 1st Amer ed, 1st state. Orig grn cl, gilt. Grn/yellow headbands; no row of #s present on last leaf verso; 'First Edition' slug present on tp verso; no ! end of 1st paragraph on dj fr flap; paper dj w/indistinct cross-hatch texture, mild gloss; $7.95 price not clipped or altered. Fine in supposed 1st issue dj. Macdonnell. $650/£417

GARCIA MARQUEZ, GABRIEL. The Story of a Shipwrecked Sailor. Randolph Hogan (trans). NY: Knopf, 1986. 1st US ed. Fine in dj. Reese. $25/£16

GARCIA, ANDREW. Tough Trip through Paradise, 1878-1879. Bennett H. Stein (ed). Boston: Houghton Mifflin, 1967. Stated 1st ptg. Map. VG + (adhesive stain fep) in Good + dj (tape repaired, edges torn). Backman. $30/£19

GARD, WAYNE. The Chisholm Trail. Norman, (1954). 1st ed. VG in dj (spine sunned). King. $35/£22

GARD, WAYNE. The Great Buffalo Hunt. NY: Knopf, 1959. 1st ed. VG in dj. Lien. $25/£16

GARD, WAYNE. The Great Buffalo Hunt. NY: Knopf, 1959. 1st ed. Fine in pict dj (sl chipped). Argonaut. $50/£32

GARD, WAYNE. Sam Bass. Boston: Houghton Mifflin, 1936. 1st ed. Frontis, 7 plts. Tan cl (sl foxing rear cvr, spine dknd). Overall VG; internally Fine in pict dj (sl chipped). Argonaut. $90/£58

Garden of the World, or the Great West...a Complete Guide to Emigrants. (By C. W. Dana.) Boston, 1856. Lib buckram. Swann*. $92/£59

GARDENHIRE, SAMUEL M. The Longarm. NY: Harper, 1906. 1st ed. (Rubbed, shaken.) Metropolitan*. $86/£55

GARDENIER, ANDREW A. (ed). Hand-Book of Ready Reference. Springfield, MA, nd. c.(1897). Frontis, x,636pp (lt browning mainly on pp facing plts); 3 color plts. Dec eps. Diced-effect cl (rebacked, orig spine laid down; worn; hinges cracked, repaired). Edwards. $39/£25

Gardens Old and New. Vol I and II John Leyland (ed). Vol III W. Avray Tipping (ed). Country Life, n.d. (ca 1900/1910). 1st ed. 3 vols. (Last few ll vol II sl cockling.) Aeg. Gilt-dec pict cl (extrems worn, hinges cracked). Quest. $485/£311

GARDHAM, JANE. The Sidmouth Letters. London, 1980. 1st Eng ed. Fine in dj. Clearwater. $31/£20

GARDINER, ALAN. Ancient Egyptian Onomestica. London: OUP, 1947. 1st ed. 3 vols. 8vo, folio. (Spines faded.) Vol 3 (sig, notes) w/plts, in dj (sl tattered). Archaeologia. $750/£481

GARDINER, ALAN. Egypt of the Pharaohs. Oxford: Clarendon, 1961. 22 plts, 3 maps. Good. Archaeologia. $55/£35

GARDINER, C. HARVEY. Naval Power in the Conquest of Mexico. Austin: Univ of TX, 1956. 1st ed. Blue cl. VG in dj. Parmer. $40/£26

GARDINER, HOWARD C. In Pursuit of the Golden Dream. Dale L. Morgan (ed). Stoughton, MA: Western Hemisphere, 1970. 1st ed, 1st issue in red cl binding. Later issues bound in blue cl. Frontis. Gilt decs. VF. Argonaut. $90/£58

GARDINER, J. and L. BRACE. Provisional List of the Plants of the Bahama Islands. Phila, 1889. Offprint. Wrappers (soiled, worn). Maggs. $28/£18

GARDINER, LINDA. Rare, Vanishing and Lost British Birds. London: J.M. Dent, 1923. 1st ed. 26 color plts. (Few leaves lt foxed; spine sl faded.) Nice. Shasky. $50/£32

GARDINER, W. A Trip to Canada and the United States. Glasgow, 1883. 32pp. Aeg. Contemp gilt limp morocco. VG. Reese. $225/£144

GARDINER, WILLIAM. The Music of Nature. Boston: J.H. Wilkins & R.B. Carter, 1838. 1st Amer ed. Color frontis, 505pp (offsetting tp, lt foxed, stain bottom edge rear ll). Brn cl (bumped, rubbed, chipped, dampstained, rebacked), gilt. Good. Blue Mountain. $175/£112

GARDNER, E. A. The Art of Greece. London: The Studio, 1925. 56 plts. (Bkpl, sig.) Archaeologia. $17/£11

GARDNER, EDMUND. Captain Edmund Gardner of Nantucket and New Bedford: His Journal and His Family. John M. Bullard (ed). New Bedford: (The Author), 1958. 1st ed. Signed by Bullard. Fine. Lefkowicz. $90/£58

GARDNER, EDMUND. The Story of Florence. London, 1905. Fldg plan. Teg. Gilt-dec cl (spine sl discolored, tail sl frayed, upper bd sl stained). Edwards. $19/£12

GARDNER, EDMUND. The Story of Siena and San Gimingnano. London, 1926. Rpt. Fldg map. Gilt-dec cl (spine sl discolored; lacks fep). Edwards. $16/£10

GARDNER, ERLE STANLEY. The Case of the Amorous Aunt. NY: William Morrow, 1963. 1st ed. Fine in Fine dj. Janus. $50/£32

GARDNER, ERLE STANLEY. The Case of the Buried Clock. Morrow, 1943. 1st ed. (Spots, abrasion 1st blank pg.) VG + in VG dj. Certo. $45/£29

GARDNER, ERLE STANLEY. The Case of the Cautious Coquette. NY: William Morrow, 1949. 1st ed. Inscribed. VG + in VG + dj. Janus. $175/£112

GARDNER, ERLE STANLEY. The Case of the Demure Defendant. London: Heinemann, 1962. 1st UK ed. VG + in VG dj (sl dusty, creased). Williams. $19/£12

GARDNER, ERLE STANLEY. The Case of the Glamorous Ghost. NY: William Morrow, 1955. 1st ed. Fine in NF dj (spine extrems worn). Janus. $50/£32

GARDNER, ERLE STANLEY. The Case of the Hesitant Hostess. London: Heinemann, 1959. 1st UK ed. VG in dj. Williams. $22/£14

GARDNER, ERLE STANLEY. The Case of the Lame Canary. NY: Morrow, 1937. 1st ed. VG (fep lt sunned, cvr sl grayed) in dj (some edges worn through). Metropolitan*. $86/£55

GARDNER, ERLE STANLEY. The Case of the Lame Canary. NY: Morrow, 1937. 1st ed. NF (sm scuff) in dj (lt worn, spine nicked, sm closed tear back panel). Metropolitan*. $345/£221

GARDNER, ERLE STANLEY. The Case of the Lucky Legs. London: Harrap, 1934. 1st UK ed. VG (bds lt mkd, edges sl foxed). Williams. $39/£25

GARDNER, ERLE STANLEY. The Case of the Nervous Accomplice. NY: William Morrow, 1955. 1st ed. Inscribed. NF in dj (sm chips). Janus. $175/£112

GARDNER, ERLE STANLEY. The Case of the Nervous Accomplice. London: Heinemann, 1961. 1st UK ed. Fine in VG dj (sl dusty, rear panel mkd). *Williams*. $19/£12

GARDNER, ERLE STANLEY. The Case of the One-Eyed Witness. NY: William Morrow, 1950. 1st ed. Inscribed. NF in dj (internally repaired closed tear). *Janus*. $190/£122

GARDNER, ERLE STANLEY. The Case of the Rolling Bones. NY: Morrow, 1939. 1st ed. Fine in dj (lt soiled, extrems worn, torn). *Metropolitan**. $345/£221

GARDNER, ERLE STANLEY. The Case of the Silent Partner. NY: Morrow, 1940. 1st ed. VG (hinges sl worn) in dj (water damaged, lt soiled, nicked, torn). *Metropolitan**. $57/£37

GARDNER, ERLE STANLEY. The Case of the Singing Skirt. NY: William Morrow, 1959. 1st ed. Fine in NF dj. *Janus*. $45/£29

GARDNER, ERLE STANLEY. The Case of the Spurious Spinster. NY: Morrow, (1961). 1st ed. Fine in dj (lt worn, sticker removed). *Hermitage*. $40/£26

GARDNER, ERLE STANLEY. The Case of the Stuttering Bishop. NY: Morrow, 1936. 1st ed. VG (ink inscrip; corners sl frayed, lt rubbed, spine lettering dknd) in dj (discolored, rubbed, nicks). *Metropolitan**. $287/£184

GARDNER, ERLE STANLEY. The Case of the Worried Waitress. NY: William Morrow, 1966. 1st ed. (Stamp fep), o/w Fine in dj. *Mordida*. $30/£19

GARDNER, ERLE STANLEY. The D.A. Draws a Circle. NY: William Morrow, 1939. 1st ed. (Lt ring stains back cvr), o/w Fine in dj (lt dampstaining back panel). *Mordida*. $235/£151

GARDNER, ERLE STANLEY. The Hidden Heart of Baja. London: Jarrolds, (1964). 1st British ed. NF in dj (worn). *Agvent*. $25/£16

GARDNER, F. B. The Carriage Painters' Illustrated Manual. NY: Fowler & Wells, 1886. Later ptg. (Cvr rubbed, worn.) Interior Clean (1 illus scribbled on). *October Farm*. $125/£80

GARDNER, JOHN and LENNIS DUNLAP. The Forms of Fiction. NY: Random House, 1962. 1st ed, 1st bk. Ptd paper over bds (orig price-sticker fr bd). VG w/o dj, as issued. *Cahan*. $75/£48

GARDNER, JOHN. The Airline Pirates. London: Hodder & Stoughton, 1970. 1st ed. Fine in dj. *Mordida*. $65/£42

GARDNER, JOHN. Amber Nine. NY: Viking, 1966. 1st US ed. Signed. Fine in Fine dj. *Old London*. $40/£26

GARDNER, JOHN. For Special Services. London, 1982. 1st ed. VG in dj (sl rubbed). *Words Etc*. $25/£16

GARDNER, JOHN. The Gawain-Poet. Lincoln: Cliff's Notes, (1967). 1st ed. Fine in wraps. *Turlington*. $100/£64

GARDNER, JOHN. Grendel. NY, 1971. 1st ed. Fine in Fine dj (price-clipped). *Mcclintock*. $95/£61

GARDNER, JOHN. Grendel. NY: Knopf, 1971. 1st ed. (Ink name, # ep), o/w Fine in dj (crease fr flap). *Reese*. $125/£80

GARDNER, JOHN. A Killer for a Song. London: Hodder & Stoughton, 1975. 1st ed. Fine in dj. *Mordida*. $65/£42

GARDNER, JOHN. The King's Indian. London: Jonathan Cape, 1975. 1st British ed. Fine in NF dj. *Lame Duck*. $65/£42

GARDNER, JOHN. Licence Renewed. London: Cape, 1981. 1st UK ed. NF in dj. *Williams*. $28/£18

GARDNER, JOHN. The Life and Times of Chaucer. NY: Knopf, 1977. 1st ed. Maroon cl. Fine in pict dj. *House*. $30/£19

GARDNER, JOHN. Mallory le Morte d'Arthur. Lincoln: Cliff's Notes, (1967). 1st ed. (Nicks), else Fine in wraps. *Turlington*. $85/£54

GARDNER, JOHN. The Resurrection. (NY): New Amer Library, (1966). 1st ed. NF in VG dj (lt soiled, internally reinforced, price-clipped). *Bernard*. $450/£288

GARDNER, JOHN. The Resurrection. NY: NAL, (1966). 1st ed. VG (emb ex-lib stamp tp) in dj (rear panel soiled, wrinkled). *Metropolitan**. $345/£221

GARDNER, JOHN. The Revenge of Moriarty. NY: Putnam, (1975). 1st US ed. Good (fore-edge lt spotted) in VG dj (sl wear). *Gravesend*. $30/£19

GARDNER, JOHN. The Sunlight Dialogues. NY, 1972. 1st ed. (Sl bumped), else Good in dj (sm tears). *King*. $35/£22

GARDNER, LEONARD. Fat City. NY, 1969. 1st Amer ed, 1st bk. Fine (spine sl rubbed) in dj (spine sl creased). *Polyanthos*. $35/£22

GARDNER, MARSHALL B. A Journey to the Earth's Interior or Have the Poles Really Been Discovered. Aurora, IL: The Author, 1920. 12 plts. VG. *High Latitude*. $75/£48

GARDNER, PERCY and FRANK BYRON JEVONS. A Manual of Greek Antiquities. NY: Scribner, 1895. xii,736pp. Burgundy cl. VG. *Turtle Island*. $60/£38

GARDNER, PERCY. The Principles of Christian Art. 1928. 1st ed. *Edwards*. $31/£20

GARDNER, RAYMOND HATFIELD. Old Wild West; Adventures of Arizona Bill. San Antonio: Naylor, 1944. Signed by B.H. Monroe (co-author). Frontis port. VG in dj (worn, quite chipped). *Bohling*. $30/£19

GARDNER-SHARP, ABBIE. History of the Spirit Lake Massacre and Captivity of Miss Abbie Gardner. Des Moines, 1885. 1st ed. 386pp. Pict cl. (Cvr sl worn), o/w Fine. *Pratt*. $115/£74

GARFIELD, BRIAN. The Hit. NY: Macmillan, 1970. 1st ed. Signed. Fine in NF dj. *Janus*. $25/£16

GARFIELD, BRIAN. Hopscotch. NY: M. Evans, 1975. 1st ed. VF in dj. *Mordida*. $45/£29

GARFIELD, BRIAN. Necessity. NY: St. Martin's/Marek, 1984. 1st ed. Signed. Fine in Fine dj. *Janus*. $25/£16

GARFIELD, BRIAN. The Romanov Succession. NY: M. Evans, 1974. 1st ed. (Name), o/w Fine in dj (spine top wear, 2 sm closed tears). *Mordida*. $25/£16

GARFIELD, BRIAN. Valley of the Shadow. GC: Doubleday, 1970. 1st ed. VF in dj. *Mordida*. $45/£29

GARFIELD, JAMES A. James A. Garfield's Diary of a Trip to Montana in 1872. Oliver W. Holmes (ed). Missoula, 1935. (Lib stamp on cvr.) *Bohling*. $25/£16

GARFIELD, JAMES A. The Wild Life of the Army. Frederick D. Williams (ed). N.p., 1964. 1st ed. Fine in Fine dj. *Pratt*. $27/£17

GARFIELD, LEON and EDWARD BLISHEN. The God Beneath the Sea. London: Longman, 1970. 1st ed. Charles Keeping (illus). 6 1/2 x 9 1/4. 168pp. VG (fr cvr sl water-mkd bottom edge) in dj. *Cattermole*. $50/£32

GARFIELD, LEON. The Wedding Ghost. NY: OUP, 1985. 1st ed. Charles Keeping (illus). 8 3/4 x 11 1/4. 32pp. Glossy bds. Fine. *Cattermole*. $50/£32

GARFIELD, VIOLA E. and LINN A. FORREST. The Wolf and the Raven. Seattle: Univ of WA, 1948. VG in dj. *High Latitude*. $27/£17

GARIS, CLEO. Missing at the Marshlands. Burt, 1934. 5.5x8. 249pp. VG (bumped, shelfworn) in dj (tattered, lacks fr flap). *My Bookhouse*. $15/£10

GARIS, HOWARD R. Buddy and His Winter Fun. Cupples & Leon, 1929. 5x7.5. 208pp. Lists 7 titles. VG (shelfworn) in dj (edges ragged). *My Bookhouse*. $15/£10

GARIS, HOWARD R. Uncle Wiggily and Baby Bunty. NY, (1920). 1st ed. Louis Wisa (illus). 8x5.5. 161pp (ink inscrip). Pict cl (sl worn, soiled). *King*. $35/£22

GARIS, HOWARD R. Uncle Wiggily in the Woods. NY: A.L. Burt, 1917. Louis Wisa (illus). Lg 12mo. Pict cl. VG. *Book Adoption*. $35/£22

GARIS, HOWARD R. Uncle Wiggily's Holidays. Racine: Whitman, (1936). Lang Campbell (illus). Sq 12mo. 33pp. Color ptd bds (rubbed). Good. *Scribe's Perch**. $15/£10

GARIS, LILIAN. The Hermit of Proud Hill. G&D, 1940. 5x7.5. 210pp. Blue pict cl (shelfworn). Last title in the series. VG+ in dj (ragged, 1-inch piece missing). *My Bookhouse*. $32/£21

GARIS, ROGER. My Father Was Uncle Wiggily. McGraw Hill, 1966. 1st ed. 5.5x8. 217pp. (Bumped), else VG+ in dj (sl edgeworn). *My Bookhouse*. $25/£16

GARITEE, JEROME R. The Republic's Private Navy. Middletown: Wesleyan Univ/Mystic Seaport, (1977). Stated 1st ed. #265/300 signed. VG in VG slipcase. *Scribe's Perch**. $32/£21

GARLAND, HAMLIN. The Captain of the Gray-Horse Troop. NY/London: Harper, (1902?). 'Sunset Edition.' Signed, inscribed in 1934. Frontis. Red cl, gilt. Cvrs Good (spine lt sunned, hinges cracked) in Fine recent leather and cl-cvrd bd slipcase w/inner cl/bd liner. *Baltimore**. $90/£58

GARLAND, HAMLIN. Main-Travelled Roads. Chicago: Herbert S. Stone, 1894. vii,251pp. Teg. Gilt dec cl. (Worn, shaken, hinges strengthened.) *Bohling*. $10/£6

GARLAND, HAMLIN. A Son of the Middle Border. NY: Macmillan, 1917. Special Autographed ed. Signed. Attractive (pencil underlining text, verso rep; cat descrip mtd to pastedown; bkpl; rubbed, stained). *Waverly**. $33/£21

GARLAND, HAMLIN. A Spoil of Office: A Story of the Modern West. Arena Press, 1892. 1st ed. Frontis photo. NF (corners bumped). *Authors Of West*. $80/£51

GARLAND, HAMLIN. Wayside Courtships. D. Appleton, 1897. 1st ed. Fine. *Authors Of West*. $80/£51

GARLAND, MADGE. The Small Garden in the City. Architectural Press, 1973. VG in dj. *Hadley*. $31/£20

GARMAN, K. E. Moving-Picture Circus.... Chicago, 1914. Moveable book. 10.5x5.5. Die-cut color pict wraps (wear, creases). *King*. $125/£80

GARMAN, R. H. Moving Picture Teddies. Chicago: Garman, 1907. 8vo. Pict cardbd cvrs. Fine. *Metropolitan**. $172/£110

GARNER, ALAN. Alan Garner's Book of British Fairy Tales. Collins, 1984. 1st ed. Lg 8vo. 160pp; 22 plts by Derek Collard. Fine in NF pict dj. *Bookmark*. $34/£22

GARNER, ALAN. Alan Garner's Fairytales of Gold. NY: Philomel, 1979. 1st ed. Michael Foreman (illus). 6 1/2 x 9 1/2. 200pp. Glossy bds. Fine in dj. *Cattermole*. $25/£16

GARNER, ALAN. A Bag of Moonshine. NY: Delacorte, 1986. 1st ed. Patrick James Lynch (illus). 7 x 9 1/2. 144pp. Fine in dj. *Cattermole*. $25/£16

GARNER, ALAN. The Breadhorse. Collins, 1975. 1st ed. Albin Trowski (illus). Tall 4to. Pict bds. NF in pict dj. *Bookmark*. $55/£35

GARNER, ALAN. Elidor. Collins, 1965. 1st ed. Charles Keeping (illus). 8vo. 160pp. VG (faded). *Bookmark*. $39/£25

GARNER, ALAN. Elidor. London: Collins, 1965. 6th ed. Charles Keeping (illus). 5.5 x 8.5. 160pp. VG in dj. *Cattermole*. $25/£16

GARNER, ALAN. The Guizer. NY: Greenwillow, 1975. 1st US ed. 6 x 9 1/4. 32pp. Cl spine. VG in dj. *Cattermole*. $30/£19

GARNER, ALAN. The Moon of Gomrath. London: Collins, 1963. 1st ed. 5 3/4 x 8 1/2. 160pp. Fine in dj. *Cattermole*. $30/£19

GARNER, ALAN. The Owl Service. Collins, 1967. 1st ed. Nice (sm tape mk fr pastedown, sl dusty) in dj (lt worn). *Ash*. $101/£65

GARNER, ALAN. The Owl Service. London: Collins, 1967. 1st Eng ed. VG in VG dj (price-clipped). *Hadley*. $109/£70

GARNER, ALAN. The Owl Service. London: Collins, 1967. 1st ed. 5 1/2 x 8 1/4. 157pp. Fine in dj. *Cattermole*. $150/£96

GARNER, ALAN. Red Shift. Collins, 1973. 1st ed. 8vo. 158pp. NF in VG pict dj (sl torn). *Bookmark*. $23/£15

GARNER, ALAN. The Weirdstone of Brisingamen. Collins, 1961. 2nd ptg, 1st bk. 8vo. 224pp. Pict map eps. VG in pict dj (defective). *Bookmark*. $39/£25

GARNER, ALAN. The Weirdstone of Brisingamen. London: Collins, 1968. 5 1/4 x 8. 224pp. Fine in dj. *Cattermole*. $30/£19

GARNER, BESS ADAMS. Windows in an Old Adobe. Pomona: Sanders, (1939). 1st ed. Ltd to 2000 signed, inscribed. *Book Market*. $40/£26

GARNER, F. H. English Delftware. London: Faber & Faber, 1948. 1st ed. Color frontis, 3 color, 96 b/w plts. (Cl sl soiled.) *Edwards*. $47/£30

GARNER, R. L. Gorillas and Chimpanzees. London: Osgood, McIlvaine, 1896. 1st ed. Frontis port, viii,(ii),271pp (prelims spotted, label removed fep); 19 plts. Uncut. Pict cl, gilt. Very Nice. *Hollett*. $117/£75

GARNER, WILLIAM ROBERT. Letters from California, 1846-1847. Donald Munro Craig (ed). Berkeley: Univ of CA, 1970. 1st ed. Frontis. Maroon cl. Fine in dj. *Argonaut*. $40/£26

GARNETT, DAVID (ed). The White-Garnett Letters. London: Cape, 1968. 1st Eng ed. VG in dj. *Hadley*. $31/£20

GARNETT, DAVID. Aspects of Love. London: C&W, 1955. 1st ed. Nice (sm ink inscrip, lt foxing) in dj (sm nicks). *Reese*. $50/£32

GARNETT, DAVID. Aspects of Love. London: Chatto, 1955. 1st UK ed. VG in dj (rear panel lt mkd). *Williams*. $70/£45

GARNETT, DAVID. Beany-Eye. London: C&W, 1935. 1st ed. Very Nice (sl foxed) in Good dj (sl chipped, browned). *Virgo*. $23/£15

GARNETT, DAVID. Beany-Eye. London: C&W, 1935. 1st ed. (Spine sunned through dj), o/w VG in dj (lt soiling rear panel). *Reese*. $60/£38

GARNETT, DAVID. The Familiar Faces. London, 1962. 1st Eng ed. Fine in dj. *Clearwater*. $31/£20

GARNETT, DAVID. The Master Cat. The Story of Puss in Boots. London, 1974. 1st Eng ed. Fine in dj (sl faded). *Clearwater*. $31/£20

GARNETT, DAVID. A Net for Venus. 1959. 1st ed. VG in dj (spine browned, sl chipped). *Words Etc*. $25/£16

GARNETT, DAVID. No Love. London: C&W, 1929. 1st Eng ed. Patterned bds. NF in dj (soil, sm tear). *Antic Hay*. $35/£22

GARNETT, DAVID. Two by Two. London: Longmans, 1963. 1st UK ed. NF in VG dj (sm closed tear rear panel). *Williams*. $23/£15

GARNETT, DAVID. War in the Air: September 1939 to May 1941. London, 1941. 1st Eng ed. Good (name; spine lettering faded) in dj (worn, strengthened). *Clearwater*. $31/£20

GARNETT, EVE. The Family from One End Street. London: Muller, 1938. 9th ed. 5 1/2 x 8 3/4. 212pp. VG in dj. *Cattermole.* $35/£22

GARNETT, LOUISE AYRES. The Merrymakers. Chicago: Rand McNally, (1918). 1st ed. 8 color plts. Blue cl, color plt on cvr. VG+ in dj (edges lt chipped, soiled). *House.* $120/£77

GARNETT, PORTER (ed). Papers of the San Francisco Committee of Vigilance of 1851. Berkeley: Univ of CA, 1910-11. 2 vols. Ptd sewn buff wraps. *Boswell.* $65/£42

GARNETT, RICHARD. English Literature: An Illustrated Record. NY: Macmillan, 1923. 4 vols. (Few stains in text; sl worn, fr hinges vols I & II cracked.) *Waverly*.* $55/£35

GARNIER, ALBERT. Scientific Billiards, Garnier's Practice Shots, with Hints to Amateurs. NY: Appleton, 1880. xiii,106 leaves color illus, pp107-109. (Fep removed, hinges broken; worn, extrems chipped.) *Bohling.* $90/£58

GARRARD, LEWIS H. Wah-To-Yah and the Taos Trail. Ralph P. Bieber (ed). Glendale, 1938. Rpt of 1850 1st ed. Fldg map. Untrimmed, unopened. VF. Howes G70. *Turpen.* $105/£67

GARRETSON, M. S. The American Bison. NY: Zoo. Soc, 1938. 1st ed. Dec eps. Gilt-dec cl. Fine in NF dj. *Mikesh.* $95/£61

GARRETT, ALBERT. A History of British Wood Engraving. London: Bloomsbury Books, 1986. Fine in dj. *Michael Taylor.* $31/£20

GARRETT, ALBERT. A History of Wood Engraving. Bloomsbury, 1978. 1st ed. NF in dj. *Words Etc.* $55/£35

GARRETT, GEORGE. The Sleeping Gypsy and Other Poems. Austin: Univ of TX, 1958. 1st ed. (Sl smudge 1/2-title), else Fine in NF dj (3 sm tears). *Between The Covers.* $85/£54

GARRETT, JULIA K. Green Flag over Texas. NY, 1939. 1st ed. NF. *Turpen.* $175/£112

GARRETT, PAT F. Authentic Story of Billy the Kid. J. Brussel (ed). NY: Atomic Books, 1946. Rpt. VG in wraps (ink blotch). *Perier.* $15/£10

GARRETT, RANDALL. Lord Darcy Investigates. NY: Ace Books, 1981. 1st ed. Pb orig. Fine. *Janus.* $35/£22

GARRETT, RANDALL. Murder and Magic. NY: Ace Books, 1979. 1st ed. Pb orig. Fine. *Janus.* $35/£22

GARRETT, RANDALL. Too Many Magicians. GC: Doubleday, 1967. 1st ed. NF (bkpl) in dj (short tears, edgewear). *Metropolitan*.* $126/£81

GARRISON, FIELDING H. and LESLIE T. MORTON. A Medical Bibliography. Grafton, 1943. 1st ed thus. Morocco-backed cl (hinges rubbed, spine head chipped). *Cox.* $55/£35

GARRISON, GEORGE P. (ed). Diplomatic Correspondence of the Republic of Texas. Washington: GPO, 1908, 1911. 1st ed. 3 vols. Blue cl (lt rubbed; sl spotting vol 3), gilt-lettered spines. Fine set. *Argonaut.* $175/£112

GARRISON, GEORGE P. (ed). Diplomatic Correspondence of the Republic of Texas. Washington: GPO, 1908-1911. 3 vols. VG. *Graf.* $75/£48

GARRISON, WILLIAM LLOYD. The Letters of... Volume V. W. Merrill (ed). Cambridge: Belknap/Harvard Univ, 1979. 1st ed. Fine in dj. *Archer.* $35/£22

GARRISON, WILLIAM LLOYD. The Letters.... Walter M. Merrill (ed). Cambridge, MA, 1971-81. 6 vols. VF in djs. *Kane*.* $55/£35

GARROD, ARCHIBALD E. Inborn Errors of Metabolism, The Croonian Lectures...June, 1908. London: Henry Frowde, 1909. 1st ed. Sm 8vo. vii,168pp (contemp bkpl, dated sig). NF (edges sl rubbed). *Glaser.* $950/£609

GARSTANG, JOHN. The Land of the Hittites. NY: Dutton, 1910. Frontis, 87 plts, 3 maps, 3 plans. (Spine sl torn.) *Archaeologia.* $85/£54

GARSTIN, CROSBIE. Samuel Kelly—An Eighteenth Century Seaman. NY: Frederick A. Stokes, 1925. 1st ed. Teg. Grn ribbed cl. (Fr pastedown, bkpl offset), else VG. *Parmer.* $60/£38

GARTNER, LLOYD P. History of the Jews of Cleveland. (Cleveland): Western Reserve Hist Soc/Jewish Theological Seminary of America, 1978. 1st ed. NF in ptd dj. *Cahan.* $30/£19

GARVER, THOMAS H. Danny Lyon: Ten Years of Photographs. (Newport Beach, CA): Newport Harbor Art Museum, 1973. Frontis. (Owner stamp), else VG in ptd stiff wrappers (sl soiled, worn). *Cahan.* $45/£29

GARVER, THOMAS H. New Photography: San Francisco and the Bay Area. SF: Fine Arts Museums of SF, 1974. 1st ed. Fine in stiff wrappers. *Cahan.* $35/£22

GARY, GEORGE. Studies in the Early History of the Fox River Valley. Oshkosh, WI: Times Pub Co, (1901). Frontis. Pict cl (worn; bkpl). *Bohling.* $50/£32

GARY, ROMAIN. The Ski Bum. NY/Evanston: Harper & Row, (1965). 1st Amer ed. NF (blue cl sl bumped, rubbed) in dj (sl soiled). *Blue Mountain.* $35/£22

GARY, ROMAIN. White Dog. NY/Cleveland: (NAL)/World, (1970). 1st Amer ed. Black/white cl. NF (sticker mks pastedowns) in dj (sl bumped, soiled; sticker rear panel). *Blue Mountain.* $50/£32

GASH, JONATHAN. Gold from Gemini. Collins, 1978. 1st UK ed. VG in dj (spine sl bumped, fep hinge professionally restored). *Williams.* $148/£95

GASH, JONATHAN. The Gondola Scam. London: CCC, 1984. 1st ed. (Pp sl dknd), o/w Fine in dj (sl wear along folds). *Mordida.* $75/£48

GASH, JONATHAN. The Great California Game. London: Century, 1991. 1st ed. VF in dj. *Mordida.* $45/£29

GASH, JONATHAN. Jade Woman. Collins, 1988. 1st UK ed. Fine in dj. *Williams.* $55/£35

GASH, JONATHAN. Jade Woman. London: CCC, 1988. 1st ed. VF in dj. *Mordida.* $65/£42

GASH, JONATHAN. The Judas Pair. London: CCC, 1977. 1st ed. Fine in dj (sl wear spine top, top edge fr panel). *Mordida.* $500/£321

GASH, JONATHAN. Moonspender. Collins, 1986. 1st UK ed. Fine in NF dj. *Williams.* $62/£40

GASH, JONATHAN. Pearlhanger. Collins, 1985. 1st UK ed. NF in dj. *Williams.* $94/£60

GASH, JONATHAN. Pearlhanger. London: CCC, 1985. 1st ed. Signed. (Name, few sm tears), o/w Fine. *Mordida.* $85/£54

GASH, JONATHAN. The Very Last Gambado. London: CCC, 1989. 1st ed. VF in dj. *Mordida.* $50/£32

GASH, JONATHAN. The Very Last Gambado. London: Collins, 1989. 1st UK ed. VG+ in dj. *Williams.* $39/£25

GASIOROWSKA, XENIA. Women in Soviet Fiction 1917-1964. Madison: Univ of WI, 1968. 1st ed. VG (ex-libris, name) in dj (sl soiled). *Second Life.* $25/£16

GASKELL, E. C. The Life of Charlotte Bronte. Smith, Elder, 1860. viii,441pp + ad leaf, ads eps. Good in orange ptd linen (lt soiled). *Cox.* $55/£35

GASKELL, P. John Baskerville, a Bibliography. Cambridge, 1959. 1st ed. W/the folded specimen sheet of Baskerville's types inside back cvr pocket. Good in dj. *Moss.* $94/£60

GASKIN, STEPHEN et al. Hey Beatnik! This Is the Farm Book. Summertown, TN: Book Pub Co, 1974. 1st ed, (2nd issue). VG+ in wraps. *Sclanders.* $31/£20

GASKINS, BILL (ed). Perspectives on Landscape. London: Arts Council of Great Britain, 1978. 1st ed. 57 b/w full-pg photos, 1 fldg. Fine in pict stiff wrappers (sl soiled). *Cahan.* $30/£19

GASQUE, JIM. Hunting and Fishing in the Great Smokies. NY: Knopf, 1948. 1st ed. Color frontis. Blind-stamped red cl, gilt. Fine in VG pict dj. *Biscotti.* $35/£22

GASQUET, ABBOT. Parish Life in Mediaeval England. London, 1906. 1st ed. 7 plts. Gilt-edged cl. (Feps lt browned, lib bkpl; spine faded, sm chip.) *Edwards.* $39/£25

GASQUET, FRANCIS AIDAN. Henry VIII and the English Monasteries. London: John Hodges, 1893-95. 2 vols. xxxii,478; vii,612pp + 4 maps. (Bkpl each vol; spines sl rubbed, joints cracked.) *Hollett.* $101/£65

GASS, PATRICK. Gass's Journal of the Lewis and Clark Expedition. Reprinted from the Original of 1811.... Chicago: A.C. McClurg, 1904. 1st ed thus. Teg. Tan cl, brn backstrip, gilt. VG (bds rubbed, lt dampstain). Howes G77. *Harrington.* $100/£64

GASS, WILLIAM H. Fiction and Figures of Life. NY: Knopf, 1970. 1st ed. Fine in dj (rear panel sl soiling). *Between The Covers.* $65/£42

GASS, WILLIAM H. Fiction and the Figures of Life. NY: Knopf, 1970. 1st ed. (Spine sl rolled), else Fine in NF dj. *Lame Duck.* $45/£29

GASS, WILLIAM H. In the Heart of the Heart of the Country and Other Stories. NY: Harper & Row, (1968). 1st ed. Fine in Fine dj. *Captain's Bookshelf.* $125/£80

GASS, WILLIAM H. Omensetter's Luck. (NY): NAL, (1966). 1st ed, 1st bk. (Sm rmdr mk bottom edge), else Fine in NF dj (sl rubbing, sm puncture). *Between The Covers.* $150/£96

GASS, WILLIAM H. Omensetter's Luck. (NY): NAL, (1966). 1st ed, 1st bk. Fine in dj (sl worn). *Captain's Bookshelf.* $200/£128

GASS, WILLIAM H. Omensetter's Luck. NY: NAL, (1966). 1st bk. VG in dj (lt rubbed, chipped). *Hermitage.* $100/£64

GASSIER, PIERRE and JULIET WILSON. Goya. His Life and Work. London, 1971. 48 tipped-in color plts. Good in dj (worn). *Washton.* $135/£87

GAST, ROSS H. Contentious Consul. L.A.: Dawson's Book Shop, 1976. 1st ed. Signed. Grn cl, gilt. NF. *Parmer.* $65/£42

GASTINEAU, HENRY. Wales Illustrated. London: Jones, n.d. Vol I only. 1/2 calf, marbled bds (worn, fr hinge cracked, lt foxing, lacks 3 leaves). *Waverly*.* $49/£31

GASTON, EDWIN W., JR. The Early Novel of the Southwest. Albuquerque: Univ of NM, 1961. 1st ed. NF in VG dj. *Connolly.* $47/£30

GATE, ETHEL MAY. Tales from the Enchanted Isles. New Haven: Yale, 1926. 1st ed. Dorothy P. Lathrop (illus). 7x10. 120pp. Fine. *Cattermole.* $30/£19

GATES, DORIS. Blue Willow. NY: Viking, 1940. 1st ed. Paul Lantz (illus). 6 1/4 x 8 3/4. 172pp. VG. *Cattermole.* $25/£16

GATES, JOSEPHINE. The Story of Live Dolls. Indianapolis: Bobbs-Merrill, 1901. 1st ed. Virginia Keep (illus). 7 1/4 x 9 3/4. 103pp. Good. *Cattermole.* $60/£38

GATES, SUSA YOUNG. John Stevens' Courtship. Salt Lake, 1909. 1st ed. Inscribed by John A. and Leah D. Widtsoe. (Spine sl mottled, fr cvr stained), o/w VG. *Benchmark.* $55/£35

GATEWOOD, WILLARD B., JR. Smoked Yankees and the Struggle for Empire. Urbana: Univ of IL, (1970). 1st ed. Fine in dj. *Between The Covers.* $85/£54

GATHMANN, HENRY. American Soaps. Chicago: Gathmann, 1893. 334pp; fldg plt. Fair (hinges weak, cvr mottled). *Scribe's Perch*.* $75/£48

GATHORNE-HARDY, A. E. Autumns in Argyleshire with Rod and Gun. London, 1900. 1st ed. 8 plts. (Cl faded, stained; foxing.) *Maggs.* $37/£24

GATHORNE-HARDY, A. E. Autumns in Argyleshire with Rod and Gun. London: Longmans, Green, 1901. 8 plts. (Eps lt browned.) Pict cl, gilt. *Hollett.* $55/£35

GATHORNE-HARDY, ROBERT. Recollections of Logan Pearsall Smith. Constable, 1949. 1st ed. Color port. Good in dj. *Cox.* $31/£20

GATHORNE-HARDY, ROBERT. Wild Flowers in Britain. London: Batsford, 1938. 1st ed. 4 color lithos. (Spine sl soiled), else VG. *Quest.* $35/£22

GATSCHET, ALBERT SAMUEL. The Karankawa Indians, the Coast People of Texas. Cambridge: Peabody Museum, 1891. Presentation copy. 103pp, map. Ptd wraps (torn, chipped). *Bohling.* $85/£54

GATTY, MRS. ALFRED. The Fairy Godmothers and Other Tales. London: George Bell, 1851. 1st ed. 8vo. Hand-tinted steel-engr frontis. Blind-dec pale pink cl, gilt. *Maggs.* $133/£85

GAUDIER-BRZESKA, HENRI. Drawings and Sculpture. London, 1965. 1st ed. VG in dj. *Words Etc.* $62/£40

GAUDIER-BRZESKA, HENRI. Drawings and Sculpture. London: Cory, Adams & Mackay, 1965. Fine in dj (tears). *Metropolitan*.* $40/£26

GAUGUIN, PAUL. The Intimate Journals. NY, 1921. Pict bds (backstrip sl dknd). *Swann*.* $172/£110

GAUGUIN, PAUL. The Intimate Journals. London: Heinemann, 1923. 1st ed. One of 530 numbered. 24 plts. VG (spine sl smudged, sl rubbed). *Waverly*.* $66/£42

GAUGUIN, PAUL. Noa Noa. Tahiti/NY, (1987). Folio. Coarse cl, color pict fr cvr label. *Swann*.* $80/£51

GAUGUIN, PAUL. Paul Gauguin's Intimate Journals. Van Wyck Brooks (trans). NY: Boni & Liveright, 1921. 1st ed in English. #830/990. 27 plts. Pict paper-cvrd bds. VG. *New Hampshire*.* $70/£45

GAULT, WILLIAM CAMPBELL. The Bad Samaritan. Toronto: Raven House, 1980. 1st ed. Pb orig. VF in wrappers. *Mordida.* $35/£22

GAULT, WILLIAM CAMPBELL. Come Die With Me. Random House, 1959. 1st ed. VG + in dj (creased tear to rear). *Certo.* $30/£19

GAULTIER, BON (ed). The Book of Ballads. London, n.d. (ca 1903). New ed. 254pp; aeg. Gilt-pict cl (inner hinges cracked; spine sl sunned). *King.* $35/£22

GAUNT, GRAHAM. (Pseud of Jonathan Gash.) The Incomer. GC: DCC, 1982. 1st Amer ed. Advance rev copy, slip laid in. Fine in dj. *Mordida.* $100/£64

GAUNT, WILLIAM and M. D. E. CLAYTON-STAMM. William De Morgan: Pre-Raphaelite Ceramics. Greenwich, CT: NYGS, 1971. 1st Amer ed. 24 color plts. Very Nice (fr cvr sl bubbled) in dj (torn, chipped, neatly repaired). *Clearwater.* $94/£60

GAUNT, WILLIAM. The Etchings of Frank Brangwyn, R.A. London, 1926. 1/4 vellum. *Swann*.* $201/£129

GAUNT, WILLIAM. Etchings of Today. C. Geoffrey Holme (ed). London: The Studio, n.d. 120 plts. Teg. (Lower corner pp7-10 sl creased, chipped; spine sl faded; sl bumped.) *Edwards.* $39/£25

GAUNT, WILLIAM. Marine Painting. London, 1975. 1st UK ed. 43 color plts. (Bkpl.) Dj. *Edwards.* $31/£20

GAUNT, WILLIAM. Rome. Geoffrey Holme (ed). The Studio, 1926. 144 plts. (Prelims sl browned.) *Edwards.* $39/£25

GAUSS, KATHLEEN McCARTHY. New American Photography. L.A.: L.A. County Museum of Art, 1985. 1st ed. 67 plts. Fine in dj (price-clipped, spine faded). *Cahan*. $45/£29

GAUTIER, THEOPHILE et al. Russia. Florence MacIntyre Tyson (trans). Phila, (1905). 2 vols. Deep blue cl, gilt. Fine in stiff blue cl djs, orig slipcase. *Truepenny*. $75/£48

GAUTIER, THEOPHILE. Mademoiselle de Maupin. A. Bessie (trans). London, 1931. VG. *Typographeum*. $35/£22

GAUTIER, THEOPHILE. Mademoiselle de Maupin. NY: LEC, 1943. #904/1000 numbered, signed by Andre Dugo (illus). 1/2 leather, dec bds. Fine in pub's slipcase (sl rubbed). *Hermitage*. $75/£48

GAVIN, C. M. Royal Yachts. London, 1932. Ltd to 1000. Full blue morocco, gilt. VG (bkpl). *Truepenny*. $300/£192

GAY, EBEN HOWARD. A Chippendale Romance. NY, 1915. One of 1000. Teg. (Bkpl, lt wear.) *Freeman**. $25/£16

GAY, JOHN. The Beggar's Opera. Paris: LEC, 1937. #904/1500 numbered, signed by Mariette Lydis (illus). Fine in pub's slipcase (lt worn). *Hermitage*. $85/£54

GAY, JOHN. Fables, with a Life of the Author and Embellished with Seventy Plates. John Stockdale, 1793. Lg 8vo. 2 vols in 1. Frontis, 2 engr tp, 67 Fine engr plts (12 by William Blake). Orig tissues. 11pp list of subs, 1pg ad for Stockdale's ed of Francis Barlow's Aesop's Fables end of vol 2. (1st engr tp cut into by binder, sl foxed, some offsetting.) Contemp diced russia gilt, gilt back, marbled edges (neatly rebacked, orig back laid down, corners rubbed). *Hatchwell*. $624/£400

GAY, JOHN. Fables, with a Life of the Author, and Embellished with a Plate to Each Fable. Ptd by Darton & Harvey et al, 1793. 2 parts in 1. Frontis, engr title, lg oval engr, 66 sm engrs on 34 leaves (tp, frontis foxed, some plts sl foxed). 2 plts signed 'G. Neagle Sculpt.' Early 19th cent mottled calf (neatly rebacked), gilt, eps renewed. *Hatchwell*. $187/£120

GAY, JOHN. Fables. London: F. & C. Rivington et al, 1793. 36 engr plts, incl frontis and tp. Mod mottled calf (fr cvr detached; lib stamps tp verso, bkpls), gilt. *Swann**. $92/£59

GAY, JOHN. Fables. London: Stockdale, 1793. 2 vols. Uncut. (Foxing, soil, sl stains, offsetting.) 1/2 morocco. *Oinonen**. $170/£109

GAY, JOHN. Fables. Barre: Imprint Soc, 1970. One of 1950 numbered, signed by Gillian Lewis Tyler (illus). Fine in pub's slipcase. *Hermitage*. $85/£54

GAY, JOHN. Poems on Several Occasions. London: J. Tonson & B. Lintot, 1720. 1st collected ed. 2 vols. Subs list; 2 plts, incl frontis. (Lt foxed, soiled; marginal tears.) Old calf bds (worn, stains), recent speckled calf spine, gilt maroon labels. Sound. *Waverly**. $132/£85

GAY, JOHN. Poems on Several Occasions. London: W. Strahan et al, 1775. Early collected ed. 2 vols. Full contemp calf, later morocco spines. (Sl edgeworn), else VG. *Sumner & Stillman*. $145/£93

GAY, JOHN. Trivia: or The Art of Walking the Streets of London. London, 1922. 16 plts. Good in Good- dj (chipped). *Scribe's Perch**. $20/£13

GEDDES, NORMAN BEL. Horizons. Boston: Little, Brown, 1932. 1st ed. Silver cl. Fine in dj. *Karmiole*. $150/£96

GEDDES, PAUL. A Special Kind of Nightmare. London: Bodley Head, 1988. 1st ed. Fine in dj. *Mordida*. $35/£22

GEE, ERNEST R. Early American Sporting Books 1734 to 1844. NY: Derrydale, 1928. Ltd to 500. Frontis, 12 plts. Tan cl spine, brn bds, paper spine/cvr labels. Good. *Karmiole*. $150/£96

GEE, HELEN. Photography of the Fifties. Tucson: Center for Creative Photography, Univ of AZ, 1983. Fine in NF dj. *Cahan*. $30/£19

GEER, ELIHU (ed). Hartford City Directory for 1862-63. Hartford, 1862. 488pp; fldg map (1/2-inch tear). Pub's cl (chipped). Good. *Scribe's Perch**. $30/£19

GEER, J. J. Beyond the Lines. Phila: J.W. Daughaday, 1863. Frontis, 285pp + (2)pp pub's ads (foxing, esp eps, 2 sigs starting). Grn cl. Good. *Lucas*. $90/£58

GEER, T. T. Fifty Years in Oregon. NY: Neale, 1912. 1st ed. NF. *Perier*. $75/£48

GEER, T. T. Fifty Years in Oregon. NY: Neale, 1916. (2nd ptg.) Frontis port. (Rubbed, soiled.) *Bohling*. $30/£19

GEER, WALTER. Campaigns of the Civil War. NY, 1926. 1st ed. Fldg maps. (Cvr sl worn), o/w Fine. *Pratt*. $110/£71

GEERLINGS, GERALD K. Metal Crafts in Architecture. NY, 1929. 2-tone cl (ex-lib, sm ink stamps, bkpl; lt soiled, spine #s), blind stamp, gilt. *Edwards*. $55/£35

GEERLINGS, GERALD K. Wrought Iron in Architecture. NY, 1929. (Sl internal soil; cl lt worn.) *Freeman**. $90/£58

GEERLINGS, GERALD K. Wrought Iron in Architecture. NY/London, 1929. 2-tone cl (ex-lib, sm ink stamps, bkpl; soiled, spine #s), blind stamp, gilt. *Edwards*. $55/£35

GEHMAN, JESSE MERCER. Smoke Over America. East Aurora, NY, 1943. 1st ed. VG (sl worn). *Doctor's Library*. $40/£26

GEIGER, MAYNARD J. (ed). Palou's Life of Fray Junipero Serra. Washington, 1955. 1st ed. Frontis. (Marginalia on 3pp Notes, 2pp text), o/w Fine. *Turpen*. $88/£56

GEIGER, VINCENT and WAKEMAN BRYARLY. Trail to California. David Morris Potter (ed). New Haven: Yale Univ, 1945. 1st ed. Frontis port, fldg map. Grn cl, gilt spine. (Sm marginal pg tear repaired w/tape; sl cvr wear), o/w Fine. *Pacific**. $58/£37

GEIKIE, A. The Ancient Volcanoes of Great Britain. London: Macmillan, 1897. 2 vols. 7 maps. Grn cl over bds (sl worn). NF. *Old London*. $350/£224

GEIKIE, A. Class-Book of Geology. London, 1903. 4th ed. (Rebacked.) *Henly*. $9/£6

GEIKIE, A. Outlines of Field Geology. London, 1882. 3rd ed. xv,222pp + 64 ads. Good. *Henly*. $8/£5

GEIKIE, A. Scenery of Scotland Viewed in Connection with Its Geology. London, 1887. 2nd ed. 2 maps (1 fldg color). Fine. *Henly*. $39/£25

GEIKIE, A. Text-Book of Geology. Macmillan, 1882. 1st ed. Fldg frontis, xi,971pp; fldg ptd sheet. VG (eps slit along inner joints). *Bickersteth*. $179/£115

GEIKIE, J. Earth Sculpture. London, 1898. xvi,320pp; 2 plts. *Wheldon & Wesley*. $47/£30

GEIKIE, J. Fragments of Earth Lore. Edinburgh, 1893. 1st ed. (vii),428pp; 6 color fldg maps. *Bickersteth*. $75/£48

GEIKIE, J. The Great Ice Age and Its Relation to the Antiquity of Man. London, 1874. xxiii,575pp + 4 ads; 16 plts and maps; map in pocket. (Rebacked preserving spine.) *Henly*. $55/£35

GEIKIE, J. Prehistoric Europe, a Geological Sketch. Edward Stanford, 1881. 1st ed. xviii,592pp (corner cut from fep) + 3 ad leaves, 5 color plts (3 fldg), maps. *Bickersteth*. $106/£68

GEIKIE, J. Prehistoric Europe, a Geological Sketch. London, 1881. 5 tinted maps and plts. (Inner joint broken; sl worn, spine cracked.) Maggs. $39/£25

GEIKIE, J. Structural and Field Geology for Students of Pure and Applied Science. London, 1940. 5th ed. 69 plts. Fine in dj. Henly. $16/£10

GEIKIE, JOHN C. (ed). Adventures in Canada. Phila: Porter & Coates, ca 1875. 408pp. Pict cvrs. Good. Lien. $40/£26

GEISERT, ARTHUR. Oink. Boston: HM, 1991. 1st ed. 8 1/2 x 7 1/4. Fine in dj. Cattermole. $30/£19

GELLER, MICHAEL. Major League Murder. NY: St. Martin's, 1988. 1st ed. Fine in dj (sl wear along folds). Mordida. $25/£16

GELLERMAN, ROBERT F. The American Reed Organ. NY: Vestal, 1973. VG in dj. Hollett. $70/£45

GELLHORN, MARTHA. Pretty Tales for Tired People. NY, 1965. 1st ed. Rev copy, slip laid in. VG+ in VG+ dj. Smith. $20/£13

GELLHORN, MARTHA. Travels with Myself and Another. NY, 1978. 1st ed. VG in VG dj. Smith. $15/£10

GELLMAN, MARC. Does God Have a Big Toe? NY: Harper & Row, 1989. 2nd ed. Oscar De Mejo (illus). 6 1/4 x 9 1/4. 88pp. Cl spine. Fine in dj. Cattermole. $16/£10

Gems from Mother Goose, Curly Locks! Curly Locks! NY: McLoughlin Bros, 1898. 10.5x8.5. (10)pp. Color stiff linen (sl staining, wear). King. $45/£29

Gems from Mother Goose. NY: McLoughlin Bros, 1899. 4to. (11)pp; 6 chromolithos. (Cvr hinge sl torn), else Nice in self-wrappers. Bromer. $75/£48

GENAUER, EMILY. Chagall at the 'Met.' NY: Metropolitan Opera Assoc, (1971). 1st ed. Folio. Tan cl, gilt. VG color pict dj, bd slipcase (sl worn). Baltimore*. $55/£35

General Atlas of the World. Chicago/NY: Rand McNally, 1907. 4 added pp of Jamestown views and letterpress. Tan ptd cl. (Broken, 1 leaf torn.) Hudson. $200/£128

General Regulations for the Army. Phila: M. Carey & Sons, 1821. 11 leaves incl half-title, 13-355pp (offset, foxed, browned, partly stained); 3 plts (1 flg), 2 fldg tables (1 loose). Calf (quite worn, rear hinge split, nearly detached, fr starting). Waverly*. $33/£21

GENET, JEAN. The Balcony. Faber, 1957. 1st UK ed. NF in dj. Williams. $23/£15

GENET, JEAN. The Blacks. London: Faber, 1960. 1st UK ed. Fine in VG dj (spine sl browned, nicked). Williams. $39/£25

GENET, JEAN. Funeral Rites. NY, 1969. 1st Amer ed. Fine in Fine dj. Polyanthos. $30/£19

GENET, JEAN. The Maids/Deathwatch. Bernard Frechtman (trans). NY: Grove, (1954). 1st ed. Fine in NF dj. Antic Hay. $45/£29

GENET, JEAN. May Day Speech. (SF): City Lights, (1970). 1st ed. (Finger mks 1 margin), o/w NF in pict wrappers. Reese. $25/£16

GENET, JEAN. Miracle of the Rose. NY: Grove, 1966. 1st Amer ed. Fine in dj (sm scratch). Polyanthos. $30/£19

GENET, JEAN. Miracle of the Rose. NY: Grove, 1966. 1st Amer ed. VG in dj. Argosy. $30/£19

GENET, JEAN. Our Lady of the Flowers. NY, (1963). 1st Amer ed. VG in dj (sl used). King. $35/£22

GENET, JEAN. The Screens, A Play in Seventeen Scenes. Bernard Frechtman (trans). NY: Grove, (1962). 1st Amer ed. Inscribed presentation copy. (Finger smudges), o/w NF in Good dj (lt soiled, sm edge tears). Reese. $650/£417

GENET, JEAN. The Screens. Bernard Frechtman (trans). NY: Grove, (1962). 1st ed. Fine in VG dj (lt worn, dknd). Antic Hay. $50/£32

GENET, JEAN. The Screens. NY, 1962. 1st Amer ed. Fine (spine sl rubbed) in dj (sl sunned, price-clipped). Polyanthos. $25/£16

GENET, JEAN. The Thief's Journal. B. Frechtman (trans). Paris: Olympia/Traveller's Companion Series, (1959). 1st ptg in TC format. Nice in ptd wrappers (NF stamp rear). Reese. $20/£13

GENET, JEAN. The Thief's Journal. B. Frechtman (trans). NY: Grove, (1964). 1st Amer ed. Fine in dj (sm tear). Antic Hay. $25/£16

GENET, JEAN. The Thief's Journal. Paris: Olympia, 1954. 1st ed in English. VG+ (spine sl tanned) in illus self-wraps (sm edgetear). Lame Duck. $85/£54

GENET, JEAN. The Thief's Journal. B. Frechtman (trans). Paris: Olympia, 1954. (Sl foxing.) Typographeum. $135/£87

GENET, JEAN. The Thief's Journal. B. Frechtman (trans). London, 1965. Dj (sl worn). Typographeum. $25/£16

GENTHE, ARNOLD (ed). Highlights and Shadows. NY: Greenberg, 1937. Spiral bound wrappers, fr panel translucent, rear bd plain. (Sl soil rear bd), else NF. Cahan. $150/£96

GENTHE, ARNOLD and WALT WHITMAN. Walt Whitman in Camden. Hadden Craftsmen, 1938. Ltd to 1100. Fine (sl rubbed). Polyanthos. $35/£22

GEOGHEGAN, EDWARD. A Commentary on the Treatment of Ruptures, Particularly in a State of Strangulation. London: Samuel Highley, 1810. 1st ed. 95pp (marginal dampstaining). Orig bds (extrems sl worn; expertly rebacked), new ptd paper label. VG. Glaser. $200/£128

George W. Bellows. NY, 1927. 1st trade ed. (Rubbed, soiled.) King. $150/£96

GEORGE, BERNARD. Edouard Boubat. M. Oberli-Turner (trans). NY: Macmillan, 1973. 1st Amer ed. 59 plts. (Owner stamp), else NF in illus dj. Cahan. $45/£29

GEORGE, ELIZABETH. A Great Deliverance. NY: Bantam, 1988. 1st ed. VF in dj. Mordida. $50/£32

GEORGE, J. N. English Guns and Rifles. Plantersville, SC, 1947. Frontis. Dj. Maggs. $117/£75

GEORGE, J. N. English Guns and Rifles. Planterville, SC: (Samworth), 1947. (Name on eps, 1 plt), o/w Good+ in Good- dj. Scribe's Perch*. $70/£45

GEORGE, J. N. English Guns and Rifles. Harrisburg: Stackpole, n.d. (1947). Rpt of Samworth ed. Frontis. VG+ (inscrip). Backman. $45/£29

GEORGE, J. N. English Pistols and Revolvers. Onslow County, NC: (Samworth), 1938. (Name), o/w VG in Fair dj (tape-repaired). Scribe's Perch*. $65/£42

GEORGE, JOHN B. Shots Fired in Anger. Plantersville: Small Arms, 1947. 1st ed. Frontis. Fine in dj (chipped). Bowman. $80/£51

GEORGE, STEFAN. Poems. Carol North Valhope and Ernst Morwitz (trans). (NY): Pantheon, (1943). 1st Amer ed. NF (lacks dj) in linen, morocco spine label. Captain's Bookshelf. $35/£22

GEORGE, W. Animals and Maps. Berkeley: Univ of CA, 1969. 1st ed. Gilt-dec cl. VG. Mikesh. $25/£16

GEORGE, W. L. Children of the Morning. NY, 1927. 1st Amer ed. NF (spine sl sunned). Polyanthos. $25/£16

Georgia: A Guide to Its Towns and Countryside. Athens: Univ of GA, 1946. 2nd ptg. Fine. Archer. $20/£13

GERARD, FRANCIS. Bare Bodkin. London: Macdonald, 1951. 1st ed. VG in dj (back panel soiled, corners worn, internal tape repair). Mordida. $35/£22

GERARD, JOHN. The Autobiography of a Hunted Priest. Philip Caraman (trans). NY: Pellegrini & Cudahay, 1952. Frontis. Good (dull, sl rubbed). *Peter Taylor.* $28/£18

GERARD, MAX (ed). Dali. NY: Abrams, (1968). 1st ed. 80 color plts, 23 gravures. Pict cl. Fine in dj (sl worn). *House.* $120/£77

GERARD, MONTAGU. Leaves from the Diaries of a Soldier and Sportsman...1865-1885. London, 1903. (Orig cl expertly restored). *Grayling.* $117/£75

GERDTS, WILLIAM H. and RUSSELL BURKE. American Still-Life Painting. NY: Praeger, (1971). 1st ed. NF in VG dj. *Waverly*.* $143/£92

GERE, CHARLOTTE. Nineteenth-Century Decoration: The Art of the Interior. NY: Abrams, (1989). 1st ed. Dk brn cl, gilt. Fine in Fine color pict dj. *Baltimore*.* $20/£13

GERE, J. A. Drawings by Raphael and His Circle from British and North American Collections. NY: Pierpont Morgan Library, 1987. 91 plts. Good in wraps. *Washton.* $30/£19

GERGEN, JOHN A. and PAUL D. MacLEAN. A Stereotaxic Atlas of the Squirrel Monkey's Brain (Saimiri Sciureus). Bethesda, (1962). Signed presentation by MacLean. VG. *Argosy.* $60/£38

GERHARD, FREDERICK. Illinois as It Is. Chicago/Phila, 1857. 1st ed. Frontis, 451pp + 5pp ads; 3 hand-colored fldg maps. pub's cl, dec spine. Good (foxing). *Scribe's Perch*.* $75/£48

GERHARD, PETER. Pirates on the West Coast of New Spain, 1575-1742. Glendale: Clark, 1960. 1st ed. One of 1546. Map. Fine. *Argonaut.* $60/£38

GERHARDI, WILLIAM. Eva's Apples. NY: Duffield, 1928. 1st ed. Fine in NF dj (sm chip). *Between The Covers.* $95/£61

GERLACH, MARTIN. Industrial Monograms. Vienna, n.d. (1881). 2nd ed. 110 plts. (Worn, crudely rebacked.) *King.* $200/£128

GERMAN, ANDREW W. Down on T Wharf. Mystic, CT: Mystic Seaport Museum, 1982. 1st ed. Full-pg b/w photo frontis, map. VG in dj. *Cahan.* $30/£19

GERMAN, EDWARD. The Just So Song Book. London: Macmillan, 1914. Dec maroon cl (extrems sl worn, upper joint cracked; lg inscrip, dwg flyleaf). *Hollett.* $39/£25

GERNSHEIM, HELMUT and ALISON. The History of Photography from the Camera Obscura to the Beginning of the Modern Era. 1969. VG in dj. *Whitehart.* $70/£45

GERNSHEIM, HELMUT and ALISON. L. J. M. Daguerre. Cleveland: World, 1956. Stated 1st US ed. Dec cvr. Good+ in dj (chipped). *Scribe's Perch*.* $30/£19

GERNSHEIM, HELMUT and ALISON (eds). Alvin Langdon Coburn, Photographer. NY: Frederick A. Praeger, 1966. 1st Amer ed. 64 full-pg gravure plts. (Bkpl), else VG in dj (scuffed, sm closed tears). *Cahan.* $75/£48

GERNSHEIM, HELMUT. The History of Photography from the Earliest Use of the Camera Obscura in the Eleventh Century up to 1914. 1955. (Spine sl discolored), o/w VG. *Whitehart.* $70/£45

GERNSHEIM, HELMUT. Incunabula of British Photographic Literature. London/Berkeley: Scolar Press, 1984. 1st ed. Fine in dj (lt rubbed). *Cahan.* $125/£80

GERNSHEIM, HELMUT. Julia Margaret Cameron: Her Life and Photographic Work. London: Gordon Fraser, 1975. 1st ptg, rev ed. (Owner stamp, ink name, yellow highlighting), o/w VG in illus stiff wrappers. *Cahan.* $30/£19

GERNSHEIM, HELMUT. Julia Margaret Cameron: Her Life and Photographic Work. NY: Aperture, 1975. NF in NF dj. *Smith.* $40/£26

GERNSHEIM, HELMUT. Julia Margaret Cameron: Her Life and Photographic Work.... London: Fountain, (1948). 1st ed. Fine in NF dj. *Reese.* $125/£80

GERNSHEIM, HELMUT. Lewis Carroll, Photographer. NY: Chanticleer, 1949. 1st ed. 64 photogravure plts. (Top edge lt spotted.) Dj (price-clipped). *Hollett.* $187/£120

GERNSHEIM, HELMUT. The Origins of Photography. NY: Thames & Hudson, 1982. 1st US ed. 191 plts. Fine in dj, pub's slipcase (lt worn). *Cahan.* $85/£54

GERRARE, WIRT. (Pseud of William Oliver Greener.) A Bibliography of Guns and Shooting. Westminster: Roxburghe, (1894). 1st ed. vii,216pp + ad leaf. Uncut. (Author's true name penned on tp by owner; shelfworn.) *Oinonen*.* $275/£176

GERRARE, WIRT. (Pseud of William Oliver Greener.) The Story of Moscow. London, 1910. 3rd ed. Fldg plan, fldg map. Teg. Gilt-dec cl (spine sl discolored). *Edwards.* $23/£15

GERRISH, THEODORE. Army Life, A Private's Reminiscences of the Civil War. Portland, ME, (1882). 1st ed. 372pp. (Cvr sl worn), o/w Fine. *Pratt.* $55/£35

Gerrit Smith and the Vigilant Association of the City of New York. NY: J. Gray, 1860. 29pp. (Spot fr cvr, lt soiled.) Ptd wraps. *Bohling.* $30/£19

GERSHWIN, GEORGE. George Gershwin's Song-Book. NY: S&S, (1941). Rev ed. Frontis port. Black over maroon paper. Good in dj. *Karmiole.* $75/£48

GERSHWIN, GEORGE. George Gershwin's Song-Book. Herman Wasserman (ed). NY: S&S, (1941). Rev ed. VG in dj (few nicks). *Houle.* $150/£96

GERSHWIN, GEORGE. Song-Book. NY, 1932. 1st trade ed. Frontis port. 1/4 suede-backed cl. Dj (defective). *Kane*.* $130/£83

GERSON, VIRGINIA. Little Dignity. NY: Routledge, (1881). Sm 4to. 64pp. Grn cl-backed pict bds (rubbed, bumped). Internally NF. *Blue Mountain.* $35/£22

GERSTACKER, FREDERICK. Western Lands and Western Waters. London: S.O. Beeton, 1864. 1st Eng ed. xii,388pp. Marbled edges, eps. Full dk blue morocco (edges lt rubbed), gilt. VG in Fine later slipcase. Howes G140. *Bohling.* $350/£224

GERSTACKER, FRIEDRICH. Scenes of Life in California. George Cosgrave (trans). SF: John Howell, (1942). 1st ed in English. Ltd to 500 ptd. Cl-backed dec bds, paper spine label. Fine (spine lt faded). *Argonaut.* $90/£58

GERSTAECKER, FREDERICK. Narrative of a Journey Round the World. NY: Harper, 1853. 1st Amer ed. xii,13-624pp. Emb blue cl, gilt spine. (Lt foxed, 1.5-inch tear 1 pg expertly repaired w/archival tape; rear cvr water-spotted, spine ends worn), o/w VG. *Pacific*.* $98/£63

GERSTAECKER, FREDERICK. Wild Sports in the Far West. Boston: Crosby, Nichols, 1859. xi,396pp; 8 tinted plts. Pict cl (spine faded). *Adelson.* $55/£35

GERSTAECKER, FREDERICK. Wild Sports in the Far West. Boston: Crosby & Nichols, 1864. Fair. Howes G142. *Lien.* $50/£32

GERSTEIN, MORDICAI. Beauty and the Beast. NY: Dutton, 1989. 1st ed. 9 3/4 x 9 1/4. 42pp. Glossy bds. Fine in dj. *Cattermole.* $25/£16

GERSTER, GEORGE. Churches in Rock. London, 1970. 68 color, 143 b/w plts. Good in dj. *Washton.* $125/£80

GERSTLEY, JAMES M. Borax Years: Some Recollections 1933-1961. L.A.: (US Borax Co), 1979. Dj. *Dawson.* $25/£16

GERTLER, MARK. Mark Gertler. Selected Letters. Noel Carrington (ed). London: Rupert Hart-Davis, 1965. 1st ed. NF (name) in dj. *Turtle Island.* $45/£29

GERVASUTTI, GIUSTO. Gervasutti's Climbs. London, 1957. Good in dj (sl worn). *King.* $45/£29

GESELL, ARNOLD et al. An Atlas of Infant Behavior. New Haven/London: Yale Univ/Humphrey Milford, OUP, 1934. 1st ed. 2 vols. 523,(1); (525)-921,(1)pp. (Lib stamps, rear pocket, spine #s.) Ptd panelled pebbled maroon fabrikoid, heavy bds, rounded backs. Jelliffe's name stamp, bkpl. *Gach.* $500/£321

GESELL, ARNOLD. Wolf Child and Human Child. NY: Harper, 1941. Stated 1st ed. 8 photo plts. Good. *Scribe's Perch*.* $22/£14

GETZ, JOHN. An Illustrated and Descriptive Catalogue of Rare Old Persian Pottery.... NY, 1908. (Ex-lib, mks removed, fr cvr creased), else Good. *King.* $60/£38

GEWEHR, WESLEY M. The Great Awakening in Virginia, 1740-1790. Durham: Duke Univ, 1930. 1st ed. Frontis, map. Unopened. NF in dj. *Cahan.* $45/£29

GHADIALI, DINSHAH P. Dinshah Naturalization Case Clearing Contested Citizenship. Malaga, NJ, 1944. 1st ed. Good (worn; cvrs soiled). *Doctor's Library.* $50/£32

GHENT, W. J. The Road to Oregon. London/NY/Toronto: Longmans, Green, 1929. 2nd ptg. Map. (Sl rubbed, gilt faded.) *Sadlon.* $15/£10

GHENT, W. J. The Road to Oregon. NY: Longmans, Green, 1929. 1st ed. VG (spine lettering faded; dj parts attached to 1/2-title, fep, frontis verso). *Lien.* $75/£48

GIACOMELLI, MARIO. Mario Giacomelli. Carmel: Friends of Photography, 1983. 1st ed. Fine in pict stiff wrappers. *Cahan.* $25/£16

GIACOMOTTI, JEANNE. French Faience. NY: Universe Books, (1963). 1st ed. 133 photo engrs, 52 mtd color plts. Beige cl. Good in illus dj. *Karmiole.* $85/£54

GIAEVER, JOHN. The White Desert. London: C&W, 1954. Fine in dj. *High Latitude.* $25/£16

GIBB, ANDREW DEWAR. The Trial of Motor Car Accident Cases. London: Sweet & Maxwell, 1938. 2nd ed. *Boswell.* $50/£32

GIBBES, JAMES GUIGARD. Who Burnt Columbia? Newberry, SC: Elbert H. Aull, 1902. 1st ed. Pamphlet bound in later cl. VG (related newspaper clippings tipped in at rear). *Mcgowan.* $150/£96

GIBBINGS, ROBERT. Coming Down the Seine. London: J.M. Dent, (1953). 1st ed. Signed. Wood engr tp. Red cl. NF (inscrip) in dj (lt rubbed). *Turtle Island.* $65/£42

GIBBINGS, ROBERT. Iorana! Boston, 1932. Cl-backed dec bds (spine faded). VG in slipcase (lt worn, tarnished). *Truepenny.* $125/£80

GIBBINGS, ROBERT. Lovely Is the Lee. London, 1945. 1st ed. (Bkpl), o/w VG in dj (chipped). *Words Etc.* $28/£18

GIBBINGS, ROBERT. Sweet Cork of Thee. London: J.M. Dent, (1951). 1st ed. Signed presentation. Wood-engr frontis. Grn cl. NF in dj. *Turtle Island.* $100/£64

GIBBINGS, ROBERT. A True Tale of Love in Tonga. Dent, 1954. 1st ed thus. VG in dj. *Words Etc.* $23/£15

GIBBINGS, ROBERT. The Wood Engravings of Robert Gibbings. Patience Empson (ed). London: Dent, 1959. 1st ed. Black cl. Fine in clear plastic dj. *Michael Taylor.* $156/£100

GIBBON, EDWARD. The Decline and Fall of the Roman Empire. Dayton, 1856. 2 vols. (Lib stamp feps, sl foxing, lt soiling.) Calf (sl worn, soiled). *Waverly*.* $22/£14

GIBBON, EDWARD. The Decline and Fall of the Roman Empire. Oxford World's Classics, 1925. 7 vols. Blue cl. VG. *Gretton.* $55/£35

GIBBON, EDWARD. The History of the Decline and Fall of the Roman Empire. London: W. Strahan & T. Cadell, 1776-88. 1st ed, 2nd state vol 1. 6 vols. 4to. Engr port vol 1 (lt foxed, offsetting to tp), 3 engr maps, all half-titles present, errata leaves vols 2-3 (lacking in vol 1). Contemp calf (rebacked; eps renewed). *Swann*.* $2,300/£1,474

GIBBON, EDWARD. The History of the Decline and Fall of the Roman Empire. London: W. Allason et al, 1817. New ed. 12 vols. Engr port, lg fldg map. Contemp 1/2 calf, marbled sides. (Spotting throughout; rubbed, few backstrips sl worn.) *Cox.* $172/£110

GIBBON, EDWARD. The History of the Decline and Fall of the Roman Empire. Cadell & Davies et al, 1820. New ed. 12 vols. 8vo. Frontis port vol 1. (Leaves browned.) Yellow eps. 19th-cent full red morocco (rebacked), gilt. *Sotheby's*.* $1,615/£1,035

GIBBON, EDWARD. The History of the Decline and Fall of the Roman Empire. London: Thomas Tegg, 1827. 11 vols. (Bkpl; lt spotted.) Marbled eps; aeg. 1/2 calf, cl bds (sl faded), raised bands, leather spine labels. *Edwards.* $273/£175

GIBBON, EDWARD. The History of the Decline and Fall of the Roman Empire. J. B. Bury (ed). London, (1909). 7 vols. 8vo. Gilt-stamped blue cl. (Spine vol 7 dull), o/w VG set. *Truepenny.* $750/£481

GIBBON, EDWARD. Miscellaneous Works. London: A. Strahan et al, 1796-(1815). 3 vols. 2 ports, 1 fldg genealogy; final errata leaf vol 2 (lacks final ad leaf vol 3). Matching diced calf, spines gilt w/red morocco labels. (All vols rebacked preserving orig spines.) *Bickersteth.* $445/£285

GIBBONS, HERBERT ADAMS. The Blackest Page of Modern History. NY, 1916. 1st ed. (Ex-lib, worn, cvrs dknd.) *King.* $35/£22

GIBBONS, KAYE. Ellen Foster. Chapel Hill, NC: Algonquin, 1987. 1st ed. Signed. Fine in dj. *Lame Duck.* $200/£128

GIBBONS, STELLA. Cold Comfort Farm. London: Folio Soc, 1977. Color frontis, 8 color plts. Dec cl. Card slipcase. *Edwards.* $23/£15

GIBBONS, STELLA. A Pink Front Door. Hodder & Stoughton, (1959). 1st ed. Nice in dj (sl spotted). *Ash.* $31/£20

GIBBS, JAMES. Pacific Graveyard. Portland, OR: OR Hist Soc, 1950. Fldg chart. (Cl sunned), else VG. *Reese.* $65/£42

GIBBS, JAMES. Rules for Drawing the Several Parts of Architecture. London: W. Innys, 1753. 3rd ed. 64 full-pg plts. Full leather, raised bands, red leather label. (Fr hinge split, rubbed; foxing, even browning.) *Metropolitan*.* $345/£221

GIBBS, JOSIAH F. Lights and Shadows of Mormonism. J.F. Gibbs: (Salt Lake Tribune, 1909). 1st ed. Good (spine faded). *Lien.* $75/£48

GIBBS, SHARON L. Greek and Roman Sundials. New Haven/London: Yale Univ, 1976. VG. *Turtle Island.* $40/£26

GIBSON, A. H. Natural Sources of Energy. Cambridge/NY: CUP/Putnam, 1913. 1st ed. Red cl (sl faded). VG. *Second Life.* $75/£48

GIBSON, A. M. The Life and Death of Colonel Albert Jennings Fountain. Norman: Univ of OK, (1965). 1st ed. 12 ports, map. Blue cl lettered in silver. VF in pict dj (lt chipped). *Argonaut.* $75/£48

GIBSON, ASHLEY. Cinnamon and Frangipanni. London, 1923. 1st ed. (Edges sl foxed; sl worn.) *Edwards.* $70/£45

GIBSON, CHARLES DANA. The Education of Mr. Pipp. NY: R.H. Russell, 1899. 1st ed. Cl-backed bds. (Fr bd sl bowed, white spine soiled), o/w Fine in pub's box (broken). *Hermitage.* $125/£80

GIBSON, CHARLES DANA. The Gibson Book. NY, 1907. 2 vols. Red cl (rubbed; hinges weak). *Argosy.* $250/£160

GIBSON, CHARLES DANA. The Gibson Book. NY: Scribner, R.H. Russell, 1907. 2 vols. Red cl; gilt design upper cvrs. Fine. *Cullen.* $275/£176

GIBSON, CHARLES R. Photography and Its Mysteries. 1925. 8 b/w plts. Color pict cl. dj (sl soiled, chipped, sl loss spine). *Edwards.* $31/£20

GIBSON, FRANK. Charles Conder, His Life and Work. London: John Lane, 1914. 1st ed. 12 color plts. Linen-backed bds (spine ends frayed, torn). Good (bkpls frontis recto, pastedown; rear hinge cracked) in newly made slipcase. *Hermitage.* $400/£256

GIBSON, GEORGE R. Journal of a Soldier Under Kearny and Doniphan 1846-47. Ralph P. Bieber (ed). Glendale, 1935. 1st ed. One of 1050. Fldg map. VF. No dj as issued. *Turpen.* $145/£93

GIBSON, GEORGE R. Journal of a Soldier Under Kearny and Doniphan, 1846-1847. Ralph P. Bieber (ed). Glendale: Clark, 1935. 1st ed. One of 1050. Fldg map. Uncut. VF in plain dj. *Argonaut.* $150/£96

GIBSON, KATHARINE. The Goldsmith of Florence. NY, 1936. Illus cl. *Edwards.* $70/£45

GIBSON, MILES. The Sandman. Heinemann, 1984. 1st UK ed. NF in dj. *Williams.* $19/£12

GIBSON, RALPH. Days at Sea. NY: Lustrum, 1974. 1st ed. (Owner stamp), else NF in pict stiff wrappers. *Cahan.* $50/£32

GIBSON, RALPH. Deja-Vu. NY: Lustrum, 1973. 1st ed. (Owner stamp), else VG in stiff wrappers. *Cahan.* $35/£22

GIBSON, RALPH. The Somnambulist. NY: Lustrum, 1973. 2nd ed. (Owner stamp, sl spine crease), else VG in pict stiff wrappers. *Cahan.* $30/£19

GIBSON, TOM. The Maori Wars. London, 1974. Dj (sl rubbed). *Edwards.* $31/£20

GIBSON, W. HAMILTON. Our Edible Toadstools and Mushrooms. NY: Harper, 1895. 1st ed. 30 color plts. Maroon dec cl, gilt top. Fine. *Appelfeld.* $125/£80

GIBSON, WALTER B. Houdini's Escapes. NY, (1930). 2nd ptg. (Cvrs sl worn, yellowed.) *King.* $25/£16

GIBSON, WILLIAM. Count Zero. London: Gollancz, 1986. 1st ed. Signed. Dj. *Swann*.* $92/£59

GIBSON, WILLIAM. Mona Lisa Overdrive. Toronto: Bantam, 1988. 1st ed. Fine in NF dj. *Lame Duck.* $45/£29

GIBSON, WILLIAM. Neuromancer. London: Gollancz, 1984. 1st hb ed. Signed. Dj. *Swann*.* $431/£276

GIBSON, WILLIAM. Our Native Orchids. NY, 1905. 58 plts. (Sl foxed, tanned; spine ends worn.) *Brooks.* $39/£25

GIBSON, WILLIAM. Young Endeavour. Springfield, 1958. 1st ed. VG. *Fye.* $80/£51

GIDAL, SONIA and TIM. My Village in Denmark. NY: Pantheon, 1963. 1st ed. VG in illus dj. *Cahan.* $40/£26

GIDAL, TIM N. Modern Photojournalism. NY: Collier Books, 1973. VG in pict stiff wrappers. *Cahan.* $20/£13

GIDDINGS, J. LOUIS. Ancient Men of the Arctic. NY: Knopf, 1967. 1st ed. VG in dj. *High Latitude.* $25/£16

GIDDINGS, JOSHUA R. The Exiles of Florida. Columbus, 1858. 1st ed. Frontis, viii,338pp; 5 plts. *Wantagh.* $125/£80

GIDDINGS, JOSHUA R. The Exiles of Florida. Columbus, OH, 1858. 1st ed. 338pp; 6 plts. Lib cl. (Ex-lib, mkd; worn.) *King.* $50/£32

GIDE, ANDRE. Amyntas. V. David (trans). London, 1958. #1100/1500. *Typographeum.* $25/£16

GIDE, ANDRE. The Counterfeiters with Journal of the Counterfeiters. Bussy & O'Brien (trans). NY: Knopf, 1951. 1st ed. NF in dj (lt edgeworn). *Antic Hay.* $35/£22

GIDE, ANDRE. Dostoevsky.... London: Dent, 1925. 1st British ed. VG in dj (tanned, internal mends). *Reese.* $35/£22

GIDE, ANDRE. Marshlands and Prometheus Misbound. George D. Painter (trans). (NY): New Directions, (1953). 1st ed. NF in dj. *Antic Hay.* $45/£29

GIDE, ANDRE. Montaigne, an Essay. London, 1929. #713/800 signed. (Cvrs sl worn, frayed.) *Typographeum.* $60/£38

GIDE, ANDRE. Montaigne. NY: Liveright, 1929. One of 500 signed. (Offsetting feps, tape residue fep hinge), else NF in dj (lacks few mid-size pieces). *Lame Duck.* $150/£96

GIDE, ANDRE. Montaigne. An Essay in Two Parts. London/NY: Blackamore/Liveright, 1929. 1st ed. One of 800 signed. Fine in NF dj (spine sunned), box (worn). *Beasley.* $200/£128

GIDE, ANDRE. Montaigne: An Essay in Two Parts. London: Blackamore, 1929. st ed. One of 800 numbered, signed. Fine in dj (spine dknd, chipped). *Captain's Bookshelf.* $100/£64

GIDE, ANDRE. Persephone. Samuel Putnam (trans). NY: Gotham Book Mart, 1949. 1st ed. One of 500 ptd. Cl-backed marbled bds. Mint. *Jaffe.* $75/£48

GIELOW, MARTHA S. Mammy's Reminiscences and Other Sketches. NY: A.S. Barnes, (1898). 2nd ed. (xiii),109pp,(4)pp letters; 12 plts. Pict cl. VG. *Petrilla.* $85/£54

GIFFEN, HELEN S. Trail-Blazing Pioneer: Colonel Joseph Ballinger Chiles. (SF): John Howell Books, 1969. 1st ed. Ptd in ltd ed. Frontis port, 6 plts. VF in pict dj. *Argonaut.* $75/£48

GIFFORD, BARRY. Letters to Proust. Buffalo, NY: White Pine, 1976. 1st ed. Fine in stapled stiff wraps. *Lame Duck.* $65/£42

GIFFORD, BARRY. Poems from Snail Hut. Santa Barbara: Christopher Books, 1978. One of 600. Fine in illus glossy wraps. *Lame Duck.* $50/£32

GIFFORD, E. W. The Kamia of Imperial Valley. Washington: BAE, 1931. Wrappers. *Dawson.* $25/£16

GIFFORD, JOHN. Gifford's English Lawyer. London: Ptd by R. MacDonald, 1828. 15th ed. Calf-backed marbled bds (joints repaired, spine chipped). Quite Sound (bkpl). *Boswell.* $150/£96

GIFFORD, JOHN. History of the Political Life of the Right Honourable William Pitt. London: T. Cadell & W. Davies, 1809. 6 vols. 2 ports. 3/4 leather, marbled bds and edges, gilt. VG (bkpls; lt shelfworn). *Bohling.* $120/£77

GIFFORD, THOMAS. The Glendower Legacy. NY: Putnam, 1978. 1st ed. Fine in dj. *Mordida.* $45/£29

GIFFORD, THOMAS. The Wind Chill Factor. NY: Putnam, 1975. 1st ed. (2 lt stains fore-edge), o/w Fine in dj. *Mordida.* $65/£42

GILBERT, ANTHONY. Death Against the Clock. NY: Random House, 1958. 1st US ed. Fine in NF dj. *Janus.* $25/£16

GILBERT, CHRISTOPHER. The Life and Work of Thomas Chippendale. London: Studio Vista/Christie's, 1978. 1st ed. 2 vols. VG in slipcase. *Hollett.* $117/£75

GILBERT, G. K. Report on the Geology of the Henry Mountains. Washington: GPO, 1880. 2nd ed. 170pp; 5 fldg plts inside back cvr. Brn cl (worn, soiled, spine dull, 2-inch cl separation fr spine gutter). Internally VG + (lib bkpl); externally Good-. *Five Quail.* $140/£90

GILBERT, HENRY. King Arthur's Knights. NY: Frederick A. Stokes, 1911. 1st ed thus. 4to. 367pp; 16 full-pg color plts by Walter Crane. Dec eps. Teg, dec edges. Gilt-dec grey cl (2 sm chips fep), o/w VG. *Dower.* $325/£208

GILBERT, JUDSON. Disease and Destiny. London, 1962. 1st ed. VG. *Fye.* $150/£96

GILBERT, MERCEDES. Aunt Sara's Wooden God. Boston: Christopher Pub House, (1938). 1st ed. Fine in VG dj (spine sl dknd, stain, sl chipped). *Between The Covers.* $750/£481

GILBERT, MICHAEL. The Empty House. London: Hodder & Stoughton, 1978. 1st ed. Fine in dj. *Mordida.* $45/£29

GILBERT, MICHAEL. The Final Throw. London: Hodder & Stoughton, 1982. 1st ed. VF in dj. *Mordida.* $35/£22

GILBERT, MICHAEL. Flash Point. London: Hodder & Stoughton, 1974. 1st ed. Fine in dj (price-clipped). *Mordida.* $45/£29

GILBERT, MICHAEL. Game Without Rules. NY: Harper & Row, 1967. 1st ed. Fine in dj (rear panel lt soiling). *Janus.* $50/£32

GILBERT, MICHAEL. Game Without Rules. NY: Harper, 1967. 1st ed. NF in NF dj. *Beasley.* $45/£29

GILBERT, MICHAEL. Trouble. London: Hodder & Stoughton, 1987. 1st ed. Fine in Fine dj. *Janus.* $35/£22

GILBERT, MICHAEL. Young Petrella. London: Hodder & Stoughton, 1988. 1st ed. Signed. Fine in Fine dj. *Janus.* $45/£29

GILBERT, W. S. The Bab Ballads. London: John Camden Hotten, 1869. 1st ed. 4pp undated ads. Dec grn cl, beveled. NF (extrems sl rubbed). *Sumner & Stillman.* $225/£144

GILBERT, W. S. The Bab Ballads. NY: C.S. Nathan, n.d. (1870s). Denoted '2nd ed,' but no doubt a piracy. Good (mks, smudges) in ptd wrappers (sm mended tear). *Reese.* $30/£19

GILBERT, W. S. Gretchen. A Play in Four Acts. London: Newman, 1879. 2nd ed, w/new 'tipped-in leaf of Dramatis Personae,' in shorter binding lettered 'Gretchen' on fr cvr. Dec cl (sl soiled, worn), beveled edges. VG. *Holmes.* $250/£160

GILBERT, W. S. The Magic Mirror. London: Alexander Strahan, 1866. 1st ed. W.S. Gilbert (illus). Pict cl (partially faded, worn), o/w Good. *Holmes.* $125/£80

GILBERT, W. S. More Bab Ballads. London: George Routledge, n.d. (1872). 1st ed. 4pp undated ads. Grn cl, gilt, beveled. VG (Nov 1872 inscrip; sl shelfworn). *Sumner & Stillman.* $135/£87

GILBERT, W. S. Savoy Operas. London: Bell, 1909. 31 full-pg color plts (1 torn) by W. Russell Flint. Good (foxing). *Scribe's Perch*.* $110/£71

GILBERT, W. S. Selected Operas: Second Series. London: Macmillan, 1930. Later ed. Marbled eps, teg. Maroon 1/2 calf, cl, spine gilt. NF (sl worn, ink presentation). *Antic Hay.* $75/£48

GILBERT, W. S. The Story of the Mikado. London: Daniel O'Connor, 1921. 1st ed. Pict cl, eps. (Lt spotted.) *Hollett.* $31/£20

GILBEY, WALTER. Animal Painters of England. London, 1900. 2 vols. Teg, rest uncut. (Upper hinge vol 1 cracked, eps lt spotted; cl soiled, spines sl bumped.) *Edwards.* $211/£135

GILBEY, WALTER. Early Carriages and Roads. London: Vinton, 1903. 1st ed. (Shelfworn, corners bumped.) *October Farm.* $68/£44

GILCHER, EDWIN. A Bibliography of George Moore. Dekalb, IL: Northern IL Univ, 1970. 1st ed. Frontis port. Fine in dj (price-clipped; lt rubbed). *Cahan.* $35/£22

GILCHRIST, ANNE and HERBERT (eds). Letters of William Michael Rossetti Concerning Whitman, Blake, and Shelley. Durham, NC: Duke Univ, 1934. 1st ed. Grn cl. Fine in NF dj. *Macdonnell.* $75/£48

GILCHRIST, DUNCAN. Montana—Land of Giant Rams. (Hamilton, MT, 1990.) One of 100 numbered, signed by Gilchrist and Dick Williams (illus). Silver-gilt leather (lt worn). Slipcase. *Oinonen*.* $60/£38

GILCHRIST, ELLEN. In the Land of Dreamy Dreams. (London): F&F, (1982). 1st UK ed. Fine in Fine dj. *Robbins.* $65/£42

GILCHRIST, ELLEN. In the Land of Dreamy Dreams. Fayetteville: Univ of AR, 1981. 1st ed, 1st bk. (Fr joint rubbed; lt soiled), else Fine in paper wraps. *Hermitage.* $100/£64

GILCHRIST, MARIE. The Story of the Great Lakes. NY: Harper, 1942. 1st ed. Cornelius DeWitt (illus). 10 1/4 x 11 1/4. 32pp. Cl spine. Fine in dj. *Cattermole.* $35/£22

GILDER, WILLIAM H. Ice-Pack and Tundra. NY: Scribner, 1883. xi,344pp; 3 maps (1 fldg). Dec cl (sl worn, mkd). VG. *High Latitude.* $125/£80

GILDER, WILLIAM H. Schwatka's Search. NY: Scribner, 1881. Frontis, xvi,316pp; 3 maps. Dec cl (sl worn, mkd). VG. *High Latitude.* $125/£80

GILES, DR. Hebrew and Christian Records. London: Trubner, 1877. 1st complete ed. 2 vols. 422; vii,(i),432pp (hinges cracked, eps offset). Gray cl (rubbed, bumped, stained, 1-inch slit spine top vol 1, paper labels rubbed away). Internally Good. *Blue Mountain.* $45/£29

GILL, B. M. Seminar for Murder. NY: Scribner, 1986. 1st US ed. Fine in Fine dj. *Janus.* $25/£16

GILL, EMLYN. Practical Dry Fly Fishing. London: Newnes, 1912. 1st British ed. Grn cl, gilt. Fine. *Bowman.* $80/£51

GILL, EMLYN. Practical Dry-Fly Fishing. NY: Scribner, 1912. 1st ed. Grn cl, gilt. Fine. *Biscotti.* $100/£64

GILL, ERIC. And Who Wants Peace? (SF: Greenwood, 1948.) One of 100. Grn bds, cl spine, ptd paper label on fr cvr. Fine (eps renewed). *Argonaut.* $175/£112

GILL, ERIC. Art-Nonsense and Other Essays. London: Cassell/Francis Walterson, 1929. Blue buckram (spine faded, sl shelfwear), gilt. VG. *Heller.* $135/£87

GILL, ERIC. Autobiography. London, 1940. 1st Eng ed. Good (inscrip; bkpl; sl bumped). *Clearwater.* $39/£25

GILL, ERIC. Autobiography. London: Jonathan Cape, 1940. 1st ed. Frontis self-port. Red cl. (Eps lt toned), o/w Fine in dj. *House.* $80/£51

GILL, ERIC. Autobiography. London: Jonathan Cape, 1940. 1st ed. Frontis self-port. Red cl bds. (Eps sl browned), else VG in dj. *Heller.* $110/£71

GILL, ERIC. Autobiography. NY, 1945. 25 gravure plts. VG in dj. *Truepenny.* $30/£19

GILL, ERIC. Clothes: An Essay upon the Nature and Significance of the Natural and Artificial Integuments.... London: Jonathan Cape, 1931. Fine (cvrs sl faded) in grn cl case, dj. *Heller.* $105/£67

GILL, ERIC. Drawings from Life. London, 1940. 1st ed. 36 full-pg plts. (Name, eps sl foxed.) *Petersfield.* $94/£60

GILL, ERIC. The Human Person and Society. London: Peace Pledge Union, 1940. 1st ed. Ptd wrappers (sl soiled, tape mk). *Cox.* $28/£18

GILL, ERIC. Letters. Walter Shewring (ed). London, 1947. 1st Eng ed. Dj (frayed). *Clearwater.* $39/£25

GILL, ERIC. Letters. Walter Shewring (ed). London: Cape, 1947. 1st ed. VG. (Lacks dj.) *Michael Taylor.* $20/£13

GILL, ERIC. Letters. Walter Shewring (ed). London: Jonathan Cape, 1947. 1st ed. 12 facs and illus. Good (lt soiled). *Cox.* $28/£18

GILL, ERIC. Money and Morals.... London: Faber & Faber, 1934. 1st ed. One of 1413. Good. *Cox.* $31/£20

GILL, ERIC. Sacred and Secular. London, 1940. 1st Eng ed. Nice (spine sl faded). *Clearwater.* $47/£30

GILL, ERIC. Social Justice and the Stations of the Cross. London: James Clarke, 1939. 1st ed. Grn bds. Good (lt foxed, inscrip). *Cox.* $39/£25

GILL, ERIC. Twenty-Five Nudes Engraved by Eric Gill. NY, (1950). 25 engrs ptd one-side only. VG in dj. *Truepenny.* $45/£29

GILL, ERIC. Unholy Trinity. J.M. Dent, 1938. 1st ed. 11 full-pg line dwgs. VG in stiff pink wrapper, matching paper slipcase (sl worn). *Cox.* $47/£30

GILL, ERIC. Work and Property. J.M. Dent, 1937. 1st ed. One of 1450 ptd. VG in maize buckram (spine head dknd). Dj (frayed, lacks sm section spine head). *Cox.* $39/£25

GILL, EVAN R. Bibliography of Eric Gill. Cassell, 1953. 1st ed. One of 1000 ptd (this unnumbered). Good (label) in buckram. *Cox.* $44/£28

GILL, EVAN R. (comp). The Inscriptional Work of Eric Gill: An Inventory. London: Cassell, (1964). 1st ed. 16 plts. Blue cl. Fine in dj (edges lt browned). *Heller.* $85/£54

GILL, WILLIAM F. The Life of Edgar Allan Poe. C&W, 1878. 3rd ed. Pub's cat dated Nov 1877. Good (sl spotted, old cellotape repairs to plts; newspaper articles, old illus pasted, laid in; spine bumped, chipped, nick upper hinge). *Tiger.* $25/£16

GILL, WILLIAM W. Life in the Southern Isles.... London, 1876. viii,270pp; 2 maps, 19 plts. Pict cl (faded, worn). *Adelson.* $50/£32

GILL, WILLIAM. Gems from the Coral Islands. London, 1856. 2 vols in 1. xv,iii,243; xvii,320pp. (Marginal notes, feps browned; rebound, spine faded.) *Edwards.* $117/£75

GILL, WILLIAM. Gems from the Coral Islands. Western Polynesia. Phila: Presbyterian Board, 1855. Frontis, vi,7-232pp. Pict cl (worn). *Adelson.* $35/£22

GILLETT, JAMES B. Six Years with the Texas Rangers 1875 to 1881. Milo M. Quaife (ed). Chicago: Lakeside Classic, 1943. Frontis port, fldg map. Teg. Dk red cl, gilt. VG. *Bohling.* $18/£12

GILLETT, JAMES B. Six Years with the Texas Rangers, 1875 to 1881. Austin: Von Boeckmann-Jones, (1921). 1st ed. 8 plts. Grn cl. Howes G177. *Ginsberg.* $250/£160

GILLETTE, WILLIAM and ARTHUR CONAN DOYLE. Sherlock Holmes: A Play. NY: Doubleday, 1977. 1st ed thus. NF in NF dj. *Gravesend.* $30/£19

GILLIAM, HAROLD. Island in Time. SF: Sierra Club, (1962). 1st ed. VG in dj (sl used). *King.* $50/£32

GILLIAT-SMITH, ERNEST. The Story of Bruges. London, 1901. Fldg plan. Teg. Gilt-dec cl (spine sl discolored; bkpl). *Edwards.* $19/£12

GILLIAT-SMITH, ERNEST. The Story of Brussels. London, 1906. Fldg plan, dbl-pg genealogy chart. Teg. Gilt-dec cl (spine, edges lt discolored; bkpl). *Edwards.* $19/£12

GILLIS, STEVE. Memories of Mark Twain and Steve Gillis. Sonora, CA: Ptd by Banner, (1924). 1st ed. Signed. Fine in grn ptd wrappers. BAL II:252. *Macdonnell.* $100/£64

GILLISPIE, CHARLES COULSTON. The Montgolfier Brothers and the Invention of Aviation, 1783-1784. Princeton Univ, 1983. 1st ed. Fine in dj. *Glaser.* $60/£38

GILLISPIE, CHARLES COULSTON. Science and Polity in France at the End of the Old Regime. Princeton Univ, 1980. 1st ed. Fine in dj. *Glaser.* $45/£29

GILLISS, J. M. The U.S. Naval Astronomical Expedition to the Southern Hemisphere, During the Years 1849-50-51-52. Washington, 1855. 2 vols. 7 maps/plans, 6 tinted litho views, 1 lg fldg panorama; 37 plts. Marbled bds, taupe 1/4 leather (scuffed). *Yudkin*.* $230/£147

GILLMORE, PARKER. Prairie Farms and Prairie Folk. Hurst & Blackett, 1872. 1st ed. 2 vols. Engr frontis each vol, 16pg pub's cat end vol 1. Mod 1/2 calf, red/grn morocco labels. (Sl foxed.) *Bickersteth.* $125/£80

GILLMORE, PARKER. Travel, War and Shipwreck. London, 1880. viii,307pp + (iv)pp pub's list (lt browned, foxed, upper hinge cracked, fep nearly detached, ex-lib bkpl). Marbled eps. Contemp marbled bds (rebacked in mod calf), calf corners (worn, loss), morocco spine label (chipped). *Edwards.* $70/£45

GILMAN, CAROLINE. Letters of Eliza Wilkinson, During the Invasion and Possession of Charlestown.... NY: Samuel Colman, 1839. 1st ed. 1/2 title, 108pp. Ptd paper label fr cvr. (Cl fading.) Howes G182. *M & S.* $150/£96

GILMAN, DANIEL. James Monroe. Boston: Houghton Mifflin, 1883. 1st ed. Teg. VG. *Archer.* $30/£19

GILMAN, DANIEL. The Launching of a University and Other Papers. NY, 1906. 1st ed. VG. *Fye.* $125/£80

GILMAN, J. J. (ed). The Art and Science of Growing Crystals. NY, 1963. Fine in dj. *Henly.* $44/£28

GILMOR, HARRY. Four Years in the Saddle. NY: Harper, 1866. 1st ed. VG. *Mcgowan.* $250/£160

GILMOUR, PAT (ed). Lasting Impressions. 1988. 1st ed. Dj. *Edwards.* $47/£30

GILPIN, LAURA. The Rio Grande, River of Destiny. NY: Duell, Sloan & Pearce, 1949. 1st ed. (Owner stamp, edges sl dknd, rubbed), else VG, dj fragments laid in. *Cahan.* $65/£42

GILPIN, SIDNEY. Sam Bough, R.S.A. London: George Bell, 1905. 1st ed. (Eps sl spotted, browned; hinges sl worn, lt scratch lower bd.) *Hollett.* $47/£30

GILPIN, WILLIAM. Observations on the River Wye. London: Ptd by A. Strahan, 1800. 5th ed. xvi,154pp + (i)pub's ads; 16 aquatint plts. Japon-backed cl (amateur rebind, sl faded, soiled, sm dent lower joint, ms title spine). *Edwards.* $140/£90

GIMBEL, R. Thomas Paine: A Bibliographical Check List of Common Sense with an Account of Its Publication. New Haven: Yale Univ, 1956. 19 facs. Blue cl. Dj. *Maggs.* $81/£52

GIMLETTE, G. H. D. A Postscript to the Records of the Indian Mutiny. London, 1920. Navy cl (sl worn). *Maggs.* $117/£75

GINSBERG, ALLEN et al. Wholly Communion, International Poetry Reading at the Royal Albert Hall, London, June 11, 1965. NY: Grove, (1965). 1st Amer ed. Rev slip laid in. NF in pict wrappers. *Reese.* $30/£19

GINSBERG, ALLEN and WILLIAM BURROUGHS. The Yage Letters. (SF): City Lights, (1963). 1st ed. One of 3000. Good in pict wrappers (sl rubbed). *Reese.* $40/£26

GINSBERG, ALLEN. Ankor Wat. London: Fulcrum, 1968. NF in VG dj. *Warren.* $35/£22

GINSBERG, ALLEN. Ankor Wat. London: Fulcrum, 1968. 1st ed. Signed. Fine in Fine dj. *Polyanthos.* $50/£32

GINSBERG, ALLEN. First Blues, Rags, Ballads and Harmonium Songs 1971-74. (NY): Full Court Press, (1975). 1st ed, clbound issue. Signed. Fine in dj. *Reese.* $35/£22

GINSBERG, ALLEN. Howl. NY: Harper & Row, (1986). 1st ed. Signed. Fine in Fine dj. *Lenz.* $75/£48

GINSBERG, ALLEN. Iron Horse. (Toronto): Coach House, 1972. 1st ed. One of 1000. Inscribed. Nice in pict wrappers (few mks). *Reese.* $35/£22

GINSBERG, ALLEN. Journals, Early Fifties, Early Sixties. Gordon Ball (ed). NY: Grove, (1977). 1st ed. Fine in dj. *Reese.* $25/£16

GINSBERG, ALLEN. New Year Blues. NY: Phoenix Bookshop, 1972. 1st ed. Fine in sewn wraps. *Warren.* $35/£22

GINSBERG, ALLEN. Planet News 1961-1967. (CA): City Lights, (1968). 1st ed. Ltd to 500 signed. Mint in slipcase (sl rubbed). *Jaffe.* $125/£80

GINSBERG, ALLEN. Planet News: 1961-1967. SF: City Lights, 1968. 1st ed. NF in wraps (sl soiled). *Associates.* $45/£29

GINSBERG, ALLEN. Reality Sandwiches. SF: City Lights, 1963. 1st ed. Signed. (Spine sl tanned), else NF in ptd wraps. *Lame Duck.* $150/£96

GINSBERG, ALLEN. Scrap Leaves. (NY: Poet's Press, 1968.) 1st ed. Ltd to 150 signed. Mint in ptd wrappers. *Jaffe.* $125/£80

GINSBERG, ALLEN. T.V. Baby Poem. (SF: Beach Bks/City Lights, 1968.) 1st this ed. NF in ptd wrappers. *Reese.* $20/£13

GINSBURG, MIRRA. The Strongest One of All. NY: Greenwillow, 1977. 1st ed. Jose Aruego & Arlane Dewey (illus). 8 1/4 x 10 1/4. 32pp. Pict bds. VG in dj. *Cattermole.* $20/£13

GIOIA, DANA. For the Birth of Christ. (N.p.): Joanne & Joseph Dermont, 1983. 1st ed. One of 500 ptd. Sm broadside. Fine. *Jaffe.* $50/£32

GIOIA, DANA. Letter to the Bahamas. Omaha, NE: Abattoir Editions, 1983. 1st ed. One of 265 ptd. Fine in wrappers. *Jaffe.* $50/£32

GIONO, JEAN. The Hussar on the Roof. London: Museum Press, 1953. 1st British ed. NF in dj (lt worn, sl soiled). *Lame Duck.* $50/£32

GIOVANNITTI, ARTURO. Arrows in the Gale.... Riverside, CT: Hillacre Bookhouse, 1914. 1st ed. VG (joint nicked). *Reese.* $60/£38

GIRAUD, J. P. The Birds of Long Island. NY: Wiley & Putnam, 1844. 1st ed. xxii,(2),398pp; 1 plt. Brn cl (spine sl chipped; corners, lower edges frayed), blind-stamped, gilt. *Karmiole.* $200/£128

GIRAUD, JANE E. The Flowers of Shakespeare. (London: Ackermann, 1846.) 29 hand-colored plts. Grn cl (faded, stained, spine ends worn, rear joint partly split). Contents VG (sl foxing). *Waverly*.* $660/£423

GIRAUDOUX, JEAN. The Madwoman of Chaillot. NY: Random House, 1947. 1st US ed. VG+ in dj (spine tanned). *Lame Duck.* $45/£29

GIRLING, F. A. English Merchants' Marks. OUP, 1964. (Bkpl.) Dj (sl chipped). *Edwards.* $23/£15

GIRODIAS, MAURICE (ed). The Olympia Reader. NY: Grove, 1965. 1st ed. NF in dj. *Associates.* $50/£32

GIROUARD, MARK. Robert Smythson and the Architecture of the Elizabethan Era. Country Life, 1966. 1st ed, 1st bk. VG in dj. *Hadley.* $47/£30

GIROUARD, MARK. Sweetness and Light. OUP, 1977. 1st ed. 8 color plts. Dj. *Edwards.* $55/£35

GIROUARD, MARK. The Victorian Country House. OUP, 1971. 1st ed. 420 plt illus, 2 maps, 35 plans, cat of houses. (Few ink lines.) Dj. *Ars Artis.* $47/£30

GIRTIN, THOMAS and DAVID LOSHAK. The Art of Thomas Girtin. London, 1954. (Edges sl foxed, spine sl sunned.) *Washton.* $150/£96

GIRTIN, THOMAS and DAVID LOSHAK. The Art of Thomas Girtin. London: A&C Black, 1954. 1st ed. Color frontis. (Edges sl faded.) Dj (sl worn). *Hollett.* $101/£65

GIRVIN, BRENDA. The Tapestry Adventure. OUP, 1925. 1st ed. Lg 8vo. Color frontis, 160pp; 11 b/w illus by H. R. Millar. Pub's leaflet laid in. Pict bds. VG. *Bookmark.* $31/£20

GISHFORD, ANTHONY. Tribute to Benjamin Britten on His Fiftieth Birthday. London: Faber & Faber, 1963. 1st ed. 10 plts. VG in dj (sl frayed). *Cox.* $47/£30

GISSING, ALGERNON. One Ash. F.V. White, 1911. 1st ed. Good in blue cl, gilt. *Cox.* $39/£25

GISSING, ALGERNON. The Scholar of Bygate. London: Hutchinson, 1897. 1st ed. 3 vols. Dec cl (sl mkd, worn), o/w Good. *Holmes.* $750/£481

GISSING, GEORGE. By the Ionian Sea. Chapman & Hall, 1905. '2nd imp of newer, cheaper ed.' Fldg map. VG in grn cl, gilt. *Cox.* $39/£25

GISSING, GEORGE. The Crown of Life. Methuen, 1899. (New fep; spine bumped, chipped, sunned, corners rubbed, cvrs mkd.) *Tiger.* $28/£18

GISSING, GEORGE. The Crown of Life. Methuen, 1899. 1st ed. (4),329pp. (Lt spotting 1st few ll), o/w Sound in contemp binder's cl. *Cox.* $39/£25

GISSING, GEORGE. The Emancipated. Richard Bentley & Son, 1890. 1st ed. 3 vols. 8vo. Orig dec paper-cvrd bds (edges rubbed), brn cl spine. *Sotheby's*.* $986/£632

GISSING, GEORGE. The House of Cobwebs and Other Stories. Archibald Constable, 1907. 3rd imp. Sound in blue cl. *Cox.* $23/£15

GISSING, GEORGE. Human Odds and Ends. Lawrence & Bullen, 1896. 1st ed. vi,308pp (sig dated 25.12.08). Uncut. Maroon ribbed cl (spine head, corners rubbed), gilt. (Pp of 2 early openings sl mkd), o/w VG. *Cox.* $70/£45

GISSING, GEORGE. Letters to Members of His Family. Algernon and Ellen Gissing (eds). London: Constable, 1927. 1st Eng ed. Good. *Clearwater.* $47/£30

GISSING, GEORGE. The Letters...to Eduard Bertz 1887-1903. Arthur C. Young (ed). London: Constable, 1961. 1st ed. VG in dj. *Cox.* $23/£15

GISSING, GEORGE. New Grub Street, a Novel. Smith, Elder, 1891. 2nd ed. 3 vols. (6),305, ad leaf; (6),316; (6),335pp. Uncut. Grn cl (backstrips uniformly faded not affecting gilt). *Cox.* $593/£380

GISSING, GEORGE. New Grub Street. London: Smith, Elder, 1891. 1st ed. 3 vols. 8vo. Grn cl. (Renewed eps), else Fine. *Appelfeld.* $1,200/£769

GISSING, GEORGE. Our Friend the Charlatan. Chapman & Hall, 1901. 1st ed. Frontis, 4 plts by Launcelot Speed. Good in blue cl (sl rubbed), gilt. *Cox.* $70/£45

GISSING, GEORGE. The Private Papers of Henry Ryecroft. Westminster: Constable, 1903. 1st Eng ed. 3 ad leaves bound in at rear. Dec grn cl (sm crack fr hinge, spine dknd). VG. *Antic Hay.* $125/£80

GISSING, GEORGE. The Town Traveller. Methuen, 1898. 2nd ed. vi,313pp + 40-pg pub's cat dated Sept. 1898. Good in red cl (backstrip faded). *Cox.* $23/£15

GISSING, GEORGE. Will Warburton. A Romance of Real Life. Archibald Constable, 1905. 1st ed. VG (backstrip faded). *Cox.* $39/£25

GIST, CHRISTOPHER. Christopher Gist's Journals. William Darlington (ed). Cleveland: A.H. Clark, 1893. 7 maps. Howes D72. *Swann*.* $201/£129

GIUDICI, DAVIDE. The Tragedy of the Italia. London: Ernest Benn, 1928. Fldg map. VG. *High Latitude.* $40/£26

GLADDEN, WASHINGTON. The Forks of the Road. NY: Macmillan, 1916. 1st ed. (Bookmark offsetting pp6-7), else Fine in dj (spine tanned). *Beasley.* $50/£32

GLADDEN, WASHINGTON. From the Hub to the Hudson. Boston: New England News, 1869. Pub's cl (sl worn). VG. *Hermitage.* $50/£32

GLADSTONE, THOMAS. The Englishman in Kansas.... NY: Miller, 1857. 1st Amer ed. lv,328pp. VG (tear spine top). *Agvent.* $100/£64

GLAESER, LUDWIG. Ludwig Mies van der Rohe. NY: MOMA, 1969. Ring-binder style bds (sl worn). *Edwards.* $234/£150

GLAISTER, G. Glossary of the Book. Allen & Unwin, 1960. 1st ed. Paper samples tipped in. (Lib bkpl, blind stamp), o/w VG. *Moss.* $94/£60

GLANVILL, JOSEPH. Saducismus Triumphatus. London, 1681-(1682). 2 parts in 1 vol. (Lacks both frontispieces, title-leaf vol 2.) Later 3/4 morocco (rubbed, soiled, sl stains). *Oinonen*.* $180/£115

GLANVILLE, S. R. K. The Egyptians. London: A&C Black, 1933. Frontis. (Sig.) Dj (tattered). *Archaeologia.* $25/£16

GLASFURD, A.I.R. Rifle and Romance in the Indian Jungle. London/NY: John Lane, Bodley Head, 1905. 1st ed. Frontis. Teg. Gilt. VG (bkpl, stamp; spotted). *Backman.* $100/£64

GLASGOW, DAVID. Watch and Clock Making. Ayrton and R. Wormell (eds). London/Paris/Melbourne: Cassell, 1891. 1st ed. xii,341,ads,(14)pp (several sigs loose, bkpl, sig, stamps, soiled). Maroon cl (soiled, hinges cracked, spine split, worn, shaken). *Weber.* $50/£32

GLASGOW, ELLEN. The Ancient Law. NY: Doubleday, Page, 1908. 1st ed, 1st ptg, w/the 3 early readings. Red cl, gilt. Nice (spine sl sunned, pencil mks in text). *Macdonnell.* $25/£16

GLASGOW, ELLEN. The Deliverance. NY: Doubleday, 1904. 1st ed. 1st issue w/smooth-grained cl. (Lt wear spine), o/w Fine. *Hermitage.* $45/£29

GLASGOW, ELLEN. Letters of Ellen Glasgow. Blair Rouse (ed). Harcourt, Brace, (c. 1958). 1st ed. VG in VG- dj. *Book Broker.* $25/£16

GLASGOW, ELLEN. The Miller of Old Church. NY: Doubleday, Page, 1911. 1st ed, 1st ptg, w/singleton tp. Grn cl, gilt. NF. *Macdonnell.* $25/£16

GLASGOW, ELLEN. The Voice of the People. NY: Doubleday, Page, 1900. 1st ed. Dec cl. (Fr cvr sl mkd), else VG. *Hermitage.* $40/£26

GLASGOW, ELLEN. The Wheel of Time. NY: Doubleday, Page, 1906. 1st ed, 1st ptg, w/the 2 early readings. Grn cl, gilt. Fine. *Macdonnell.* $25/£16

GLASS, B. et al. Forerunners of Darwin: 1745-1859. Balt, 1959. Review pasted in. Dj (sl worn). *Maggs.* $47/£30

GLASSCOCK, C. B. Big Bonanza, the Story of the Comstock Lode. Indianapolis: Bobbs-Merrill, (1931). Apparent 1st ed. Frontis port. Postcard laid in. VG+ in dj (sl frayed). *Bohling.* $30/£19

GLASSCOCK, C. B. Here's Death Valley. NY: Bobbs-Merrill, (1940). 1st ed. Fine in Fine dj. *Book Market.* $65/£42

GLASSE, HANNAH. The Art of Cookery Made Plain and Easy. W. Strahan et al, 1770. New ed (11th). (ii),vi,(xxiv),384,(24)pp. 'A Certain Cure for the Bite of a Mad Dog' at end. Contemp sheep (long ago rebacked, lower corners repaired, backstrip edges worn). VG. *Cox.* $312/£200

GLASSER, OTTO (ed). The Science of Radiology. Springfield, 1933. Fair (backstrip worn, section starting). *Fye.* $50/£32

GLASSTONE, V. Victorian and Edwardian Theatres. London: Thames & Hudson, 1975. Sound in dj. *Ars Artis.* $39/£25

GLAZEBROOK, RICHARD (ed). A Dictionary of Applied Physics. London, 1922-3. 5 vols. (Feps lt foxed; sl rubbed.) *Edwards.* $117/£75

GLAZIER, RICHARD. A Manual of Historic Ornament. Batsford, 1926. 4th ed. (Marginal pencil notes; cl lt soiled, sl worn.) *Edwards.* $31/£20

GLAZIER, WILLARD. Down the Great River. Phila: Hubbard, 1888. Frontis, 22 plts, 2 maps. Cl, beveled bds (rubbed, lt soiled) gilt/black-stamped (spine gilt sl rubbed). *Sadlon.* $20/£13

GLAZIER, WILLARD. Down the Great River. Phila: Hubbard Bros, 1891. 443,lxiiipp; fldg map. Stamped bds, gilt. *Dumont.* $45/£29

GLEASON, HENRY A. The New Britton and Brown Illustrated Flora of the Northeastern United States and Adjacent Canada. NY/London: NY Botanical Garden, 1963. 3rd ed. 3 vols complete. VG (bkpls; cl lt stained). *Cahan.* $60/£38

GLEASON, RALPH. The Jefferson Airplane and the San Francisco Sound. NY: Ballantine, 1969. 1st ed. Pb orig. VG+. *Sclanders.* $20/£13

GLEN, A. R. and N. A. C. CROFT. Under the Pole Star. London: Methuen, 1937. 1st ed. 48 plts, 18 maps (1 fldg), 4 diags. Mod 1/2 levant morocco, gilt. VG. *Hollett.* $133/£85

GLENN, CONSTANCE W. and JANE K. BLEDSOE (eds). Frederick Sommer at Seventy-Five. Long Beach, CA: CA State Univ, 1980. 1st ed. 31 full-pg b/w photos. Fine in ptd stiff wrappers. *Cahan.* $45/£29

GLENN, CONSTANCE W. and JANE K. BLEDSOE (eds). Long Beach: A Photography Survey. Long Beach: CA State Univ, 1980. (Bumped, rubbed), else VG in ptd stiff wrappers. *Cahan.* $25/£16

GLENN, THOMAS ALLEN. Some Colonial Mansions and Those Who Lived in Them. Phila: Coates, 1898-1899. 1st ed. 2 vols. 459; 503pp. Pict cl (lt soiled). Howes G208. *Ginsberg.* $175/£112

GLENN, THOMAS ALLEN. Some Colonial Mansions and Those Who Lived in Them. Phila, 1900. 1st ed. Howes G208. *Ginsberg.* $75/£48

GLICK, WILLIAM J. William Edwin Rudge. NY: Typophiles, 1984. One of 750 ptd. Fine in cl-backed dec bds. *Cox.* $31/£20

GLISAN, RODNEY. Journal of Army Life. SF: A.L. Bancroft, 1874. 1st ed. xi,511pp, 21 plts, fldg table. Gilt, black-stamped maroon cl (neatly rebacked w/new eps). Fine. Howes G209. *Argonaut.* $300/£192

GLOAG, J. Mr. Loudon's England. London, 1970. Dj (sl spotted). *Maggs.* $34/£22

GLOAG, JOHN. The Chair: Its Origins, Design and Social History. S. Brunswick/NY: A.S. Barnes, 1967. 1st US ed. Color frontis, 62 b/w plts. NF in illus dj (edges torn, few sm stains). *Cahan.* $50/£32

GLOVER, AGNES F. My Diary for 1883...to 1890. Hartford, ME, 1883-1889. 129pp. Calf spine, corners, marbled bds. VG. *Lucas.* $95/£61

GLOYNE, S. ROODHOUSE. John Hunter. Balt: Williams & Wilkins, 1950. 1st Amer ed. Color frontis port, 16 plts. VG. *Glaser.* $50/£32

GLUBB, JOHN BAGOT. Glubb Pasha's Story of the Arab Legion. London, 1948. 1st ed. (Spine lt faded), o/w VG in dj (sl creased, nicked). *Words Etc.* $39/£25

GLUBB, JOHN BAGOT. A Soldier with the Arabs. London, 1957. 2nd imp. Frontis port; 11 plts, maps and plans. Blue cl. *Maggs.* $62/£40

GLUBB, JOHN BAGOT. A Soldier with the Arabs. NY, 1957. 1st ed. Frontis port. Dj (chipped). *Edwards.* $31/£20

GLUBB, JOHN BAGOT. A Soldier with the Arabs. NY: Harper, 1957. 1st US ed. 23 plts. VG in dj (torn). *Worldwide*. $22/£14

GLUECK, NELSON. Deities and Dolphins. NY: FSG, 1965. 1st ptg. 6 plans (4 dbl-pg), 5 maps (2 dbl-pg). VG in dj. *Worldwide*. $45/£29

GLUECK, NELSON. Explorations in Eastern Palestine. New Haven: ASOR, 1935. Vol II (only). 32 plts, fldg map rear pocket. Cl-backed bds. Good. *Archaeologia*. $125/£80

GLUECK, SHELDON. War Criminals, Their Prosecution and Punishment. NY: Knopf, 1944. *Boswell*. $50/£32

GLYNN, JOSEPH. A Treatise on the Power of Water. NY: Van Nostrand, 1869. 3rd ed. 162pp + 12pp ads (pencil notes). Good- (frayed, hinge cracks). *Scribe's Perch**. $55/£35

GLYNNE, STEPHEN R. Notes on the Churches of Kent. London, 1877. xiv,351pp + 32pp pub's cat. Blind emb cl (sm scuff lower joint; bkpl). *Edwards*. $78/£50

GNUDI, MARTHA T. and J. P. WEBSTER. The Life and Times of Gaspare Tagliacozzi, Surgeon of Bologna, 1545-1599. NY: Reichner, (1950). 1st ed. One of 2100 numbered. Frontis port. Fine. *Glaser*. $200/£128

GOBAT, SAMUEL. Journal of a Three-Years' Residence in Abyssinia. London: Hatchard, 1834. 1st ed. Pub's patterned cl (spine sunned), paper spine label. Fine (bkpl). *Book Block*. $275/£176

GOBLE, PAUL. Death of the Iron Horse. Scarsdale: Bradbury, 1987. 1st ed. 10 3/4 x 8. 32pp. Cl spine. VG in dj. *Cattermole*. $20/£13

GOBLE, PAUL. Iktomi and the Boulder. NY: Orchard, 1988. 1st ed. 9x11. 32pp. Cl spine. Fine in dj. *Cattermole*. $15/£10

GODDARD, BENJAMIN. Truths for Truth-Seekers on Utah and the Mormons. SLC: Bureau of Info, n.d. ca 1919. VG (soil streaks p2, 15) in ptd wraps. *Bohling*. $35/£22

GODDARD, HENRY HERBERT. The Kallikak Family: A Study...of Feeble-Mindedness. NY, 1913. 1st ed. (Fep creased, sm tears.) Grn cl (fr bd, inner hinge cracked; extrms worn). Good. *Doctor's Library*. $35/£22

GODDEN, GEOFFREY A. Coalport and Coalbrookdale Porcelains. NY: Praeger, (1970). 1st ed. 10 color plts, 232 b/w photos. Blue cl. Good in illus dj. *Karmiole*. $75/£48

GODDEN, GEOFFREY A. Stevengraphs and Other Victorian Silk Pictures. Rutherford: Farleigh Dickinson Univ, (1971). 1st US ed. 12 color plts. Tan cl, red spine lettering. Cvrs Fine (top edge lt dusty) in pict dj (sl sunned, few sm tears). *Baltimore**. $60/£38

GODDEN, GEOFFREY A. Stevengraphs and Other Victorian Silk Pictures. NJ: Assoc Univ Presses, 1971. 1st US ed. 321 plts (12 color). VG in dj. *Hollett*. $101/£65

GODDEN, GEOFFREY A. Victorian Porcelain. London, 1961. 1st ed. 102 b/w plts. (Fep sl browned.) Dj (sl chipped). *Edwards*. $44/£28

GODDEN, GEOFFREY A. Victorian Porcelain. London: Herbert Jenkins, 1962. 102 plts. VG in dj. *Hollett*. $55/£35

GODDEN, RUMER. The Doll's House. NY: Viking, 1947. 2nd ed. Tasha Tudor (illus). 5 1/2 x 8. 136pp. Fine in dj. *Cattermole*. $25/£16

GODDEN, RUMER. The Dragon of Og. London: Macmillan, (1981). 1st Eng ed. 8vo. 61pp; 7 full-pg color illus by Pauline Baynes. Grn bds. Fine. *Dower*. $45/£29

GODDEN, RUMER. The Dragon of Og. NY: Viking, 1981. 1st US ed. Pauline Baynes (illus). 6 1/4 x 9 1/2. 60pp. Fine in dj. *Cattermole*. $20/£13

GODDEN, RUMER. The Mousewife. NY: Viking, 1951. 1st ed. Fine in Fine dj (price-clipped). *Between The Covers*. $85/£54

GODDEN, RUMER. The Mousewife. London: Macmillan, 1958. William Pene Du Bois (illus). 8vo. Unpaginated. Blue bds. VG in dj (edges sl chipped). *Dower*. $45/£29

GODDEN, RUMER. The Old Woman Who Lived in a Vinegar Bottle. NY: Viking, 1972. 1st ed. Mairi Hedderwick (illus). 8 1/2 x 10 3/4. 48pp. Pict bds. Fine in dj. *Cattermole*. $30/£19

GODDING, W. W. Two Hard Cases. Boston: Houghton, Mifflin, 1882. 1st ed. Inscribed. (ii),257,(3)pp. Ptd emb brn cl (edges rubbed, sl remnant spine label), gilt. VG (lib bkpl). *Gach*. $75/£48

GODFREY, EDWARD SETTLE. The Field Diary of Lt. Edward Settle Godfrey.... (Portland): Champoeg, 1957. One of 1000. 8 full-pg illus and maps. Illus cl. *Dawson*. $75/£48

GODFREY, EDWARD SETTLE. The Field Diary of Lt. Edward Settle Godfrey.... (Portland): Champoeg, 1957. One of 1000. Fldg pictograph, 2 fldg maps. Blue cl, pict inset on cvr (spine sl dknd). NF. *Harrington*. $80/£51

GODFREY, W. The English Staircase. London: Batsford, 1911. 83 plts. (Sl soiling.) New blind cl. *Ars Artis*. $55/£35

GODFREY, W. EARL. The Birds of Canada. Ottawa, 1966. VG in dj. *Argosy*. $75/£48

GODFREY, W. H. K. Three Months on the Continent. Waterbury, CT, 1875. Inscribed. vii,(1),180pp. (Cl discolored, edgeworn), else VG. *Reese*. $175/£112

GODINE, DAVID R. (comp). Lyric Verse, a Printer's Choice. (N.p.): David R. Godine, 1966. 1st bk of Godine Press. Ptd by Stinehour Press. Of 500, one of 280 on Curtis Tweedweave. B/c of copyright problems the book was never offered for sale. Cream paper spine, gilt title, brn marbled paper over bds. (Sm tape mk fr pastedown), o/w Fine in pub's box. *Heller*. $200/£128

GODLEE, R. J. Lord Lister. Oxford: Clarendon, 1924. 3rd ed. Frontis. VG. *Savona*. $44/£28

GODMAN, JOHN D. American Natural History. Volume I. Mastology. Phila: Carey & Lea, 1826. 1st ed. Inscribed. 3 vols. Full contemp rainbow calf (spines skillfully repaired), gilt, leather labels. *Argosy*. $250/£160

GODMAN, JOHN D. Rambles of a Naturalist. To Which Are Added...Reminiscences of a Voyage to India, by Reynell Coates. Phila, 1833. 151pp (heavily foxed). Fair (backstrip detached but present). *Scribe's Perch**. $15/£10

GODSELL, PHILIP H. Arctic Trader. Toronto, 1943. *Grayling*. $31/£20

GODSELL, PHILIP H. Arctic Trader. NY: Putnam, c. 1934. (Spine, edges faded.) Dj (sl chipped). *High Latitude*. $20/£13

GODSELL, PHILIP H. Red Hunters of the Snows. London: Robert Hale, 1938. Fldg map. VG (lacks fep, perf stamp 2 leaves). *High Latitude*. $70/£45

GODWIN, H. The Archives of the Peat Bogs. Cambridge, 1981. Dj. *Maggs*. $31/£20

GODWIN, HENRY. The English Archaeologist's Handbook. Oxford: James Parker, 1867. 1st ed. xii,276,8pp; 3 plts. Good (lt worn, string mks; notes). *Ash*. $62/£40

GODWIN, WILLIAM. Fleetwood; or, the New Man of Feeling. Alexandria: Cottom & Stewart, 1805. 1st US ed. 2 vols. Plain eps; trimmed. Orig full tree calf (worn, scuffed; browned, sl foxed, sig), crimson leather spine labels, gilt. *Baltimore**. $25/£16

GODWIN, WILLIAM. Life of Geoffrey Chaucer. London: Richard Phillips, 1804. 2nd ed. 4 vols. Frontis port. Later cl. (Spotted, stained; ex-lib), o/w VG. Poetry Bookshop. $148/£95

GOERCH, CARL. Carolina Chats. Raleigh, NC, 1944. 1st ed, 1st ptg. Inscribed. Wantagh. $35/£22

GOETHE. See VON GOETHE, J. W.

GOETZMANN, WILLIAM H. Army Exploration in the American West, 1803-1863. New Haven: Yale Univ, 1959. 1st ed. 21 maps (5 lg fldg in rear pocket). Fine in pict dj. Argonaut. $150/£96

GOFF, RICHARD D. Confederate Supply. Durham: Duke Univ, 1969. 1st ed. Fine in dj. Cahan. $40/£26

GOFFSTEIN, M. B. An Artist. Harper & Row, (1980). 1st ed. Sm 4to. 18 leaves, incl blanks; 19 color illus. Teal cl-backed white bds, gilt spine title. Fine in color pict dj. Blue Mountain. $45/£29

GOFFSTEIN, M. B. Goldie the Dollmaker. NY: FSG, 1969. 1st ed. 7x6. 55pp. VG in dj. Cattermole. $30/£19

GOFFSTEIN, M. B. A Little Schubert.... NY/Evanston/SF/London: Harper & Row, (1972). 4to. 18 leaves, incl blanks. Record laid in rear pocket. Pict lt blue bds. Fine in matching dj. Blue Mountain. $45/£29

GOFFSTEIN, M. B. My Crazy Sister. NY: Dial, (1976). 1st ed. Sm 4to. 22 leaves, incl blanks. Pict orange bds. Fine in matching dj. Blue Mountain. $45/£29

GOFFSTEIN, M. B. Natural History. NY: FSG, (1979). 1st ed. Sm 4to. 18 leaves, incl blanks; 23 color illus. Brn cl, silver spine title. Fine in color pict grn dj. Blue Mountain. $45/£29

GOFFSTEIN, M. B. Neighbors. NY/Hagerstown/SF/London: Harper & Row, (1979). 1st ed. Sm 4to. 18 leaves, incl blanks. Pict grn bds. Fine in matching pict dj. Blue Mountain. $45/£29

GOGARTY, OLIVER ST. JOHN. Mourning Becomes Mrs. Spendlove. NY: Creative Age, (1948). 1st ed. NF in VG dj. Turtle Island. $40/£26

GOGOL, NIKOLAI. Dead Souls. London: T. Fisher Unwin, 1893. 1st ed in English. VG- (inner fr hinge starting) in red cl-cvrd bds (1-inch tear spine head). Lame Duck. $175/£112

GOGOL, NIKOLAI. The Overcoat and Other Stories. Constance Garnett (trans). NY: Knopf, 1923. 1st US ed. Definitive Edition. (Spine sl rolled, tanned), else NF in VG dj (price-clipped, sl chipped, 1-inch internal piece missing spine). Lame Duck. $75/£48

GOGOL, NIKOLAI. The Overcoat. Constance Garnett (trans). Westport, CT: LEC, 1976. One of 2000 numbered, signed by Saul Field (illus). 9 full color plts. VG in bd slipcase. Argosy. $125/£80

GOGOL, NIKOLAI. Taras Bulba. Jeremiah Curtin (trans). Troy, NY: Nims & Knight, 1889. 1st US ed. Lame Duck. $150/£96

GOLD, H. L. (ed). The Sixth Galaxy Reader. GC: Doubleday, 1962. 1st ed. VG+ in NF dj. Other Worlds. $20/£13

GOLD, HERBERT. The Man Who Was Not with It. Boston: Little Brown, 1956. 1st ed. Fine in dj (crown chipped). Cahan. $30/£19

GOLD, MICHAEL. Jews Without Money. NY, (1930). 1st Amer ed. NF (names; cvrs sl rubbed). Polyanthos. $50/£32

Gold-Headed Cane. (By William Macmichael.) London: John Murray, 1827. 1st ed. Uncut. Orig bds. (Rebacked, orig spine laid down; Holland House bkpls fr bd, fr pastedown; soiled, sl worn), else Fine. Cummins. $500/£321

Gold-Tooled Bookbindings. Oxford: Bodleian Library, (1951). 1st ed. 24 b/w plts. Fine in ptd wrappers. Heller. $25/£16

GOLDBERG, JIM. Rich and Poor. NY: Random House, 1983. 1st ed. NF in pict stiff wrappers. Cahan. $35/£22

GOLDBERGER, JOSEPH. Goldberger on Pellagra. Milton Terris (ed). Baton Rouge, 1964. 1st ed. VG in dj. Fye. $50/£32

Golden Age of Naples. Art and Civilization Under the Bourbons 1734-1805. Detroit: Inst of Arts, 1981. 2 vols. Good in wrappers. Washton. $65/£42

GOLDEN, GEORGE FULLER. My Lady and Her White Rats. NY: (for) The White Rats of America, 1909. 1st ed. 52pp ads, 13pp professional cards. Dec cl (worn, sl shaken, spine faded). Dramatis Personae. $50/£32

GOLDER, FRANK A. (ed). March of the Mormon Battalion from Council Bluffs to California, Taken from the Journals of Henry Standage. NY, 1928. 1st ptg. Frontis port, map. Blind-stamped blue cl, gilt. VG+. Turpen. $65/£42

GOLDIN, JUDAH (trans). The Living Talmud. The Wisdom of the Fathers and Its Classical Commentaries. NY: LEC, 1960. One of 1500 signed by Ben-Zion (illus). VG in pub's slipcase. Hermitage. $225/£144

GOLDING, ARTHUR. A Moral Fable-Talk. SF: Arion, 1987. One of 425. Prospectus laid in. Brn leather, gilt. Swann*. $149/£96

GOLDING, HARRY (ed). Fairy Tales. Ward Lock, n.d. Early ed. (Only 3 bks had been pub'd in this series, incl this title. Ad at end of bk states 'Others are in preparation;' March 1918 inscrip.) Lg 8vo. 403pp + 4pp ads; 48 color plts incl pict eps by Margaret Tarrant. Grn cl, pict onlay. (Spine edges, corners worn), else Sound. Bookmark. $66/£42

GOLDING, LOUIS. The Camberwell Beauty. Gollancz, 1935. 1st ed. VG in dj (lt sunned). Ash. $39/£25

GOLDING, LOUIS. Poems Drunk and Drowsy. London: Centaur, (1933). 1st ed. One of 100. Inscribed in 1933. Nice in ptd wrappers. Reese. $150/£96

GOLDING, WILLIAM. The Brass Butterfly. London: Faber, (1958). 1st British ed. VG+ in VG dj. Pettler & Lieberman. $85/£54

GOLDING, WILLIAM. Close Quarters. London, 1987. 1st Eng ed. Fine in dj. Clearwater. $31/£20

GOLDING, WILLIAM. Darkness Visible. NY: FSG, (1979). 1st Amer ed. VF in dj. Antic Hay. $20/£13

GOLDING, WILLIAM. An Egyptian Journal. London: Faber, 1985. 1st UK ed. Fine in dj. Williams. $31/£20

GOLDING, WILLIAM. Fire Down Below. London: Faber, 1989. 1st UK ed. Fine in dj. Williams. $25/£16

GOLDING, WILLIAM. Free Fall. Faber, 1959. 1st UK ed. Fine in VG+ dj. Williams. $94/£60

GOLDING, WILLIAM. Free Fall. London: Faber, 1959. 1st UK ed. Signed. VG in dj (lt chipping, sl soiling). Moorhouse. $156/£100

GOLDING, WILLIAM. The Inheritors. NY: Harcourt, Brace & World, (1962). 1st Amer ed. Fine in dj (edge-rubbed; sm spine tear, crease). Hermitage. $50/£32

GOLDING, WILLIAM. The Inheritors. Faber, 1955. 1st UK ed. Fine in VG dj (sm closed tear, sm hole fr panel). Williams. $172/£110

GOLDING, WILLIAM. The Inheritors. London: Faber, 1955. 1st UK ed. Sm card w/author's sig laid in. VG in dj (lt rubbed, extrems worn, edge tears, no loss; spine sl browned). Moorhouse. $281/£180

GOLDING, WILLIAM. Lord of the Flies. NY: Coward-McCann, (1955). 1st Amer ed. VG (lt sunned, edge-worn) in dj (worn, chipped, short tears, sl loss head). Metropolitan*. $258/£165

GOLDING, WILLIAM. Lord of the Flies. Faber & Faber, 1954. 1st ed. Signed in 1954. (Sl foxing.) Red cl (sm stain upper cvr, sl cocked). Sotheby's*. $538/£345

GOLDING, WILLIAM. Lord of the Flies. Faber, 1954. 1st UK ed. NF in VG dj (spine browned, lt edgeworn, rubbed, price-clipped). *Williams.* $1,084/£695

GOLDING, WILLIAM. Lord of the Flies. Coward-McCann, 1955. 1st US ed. VG+ (lt bumped) in VG dj (sl edgewear, rubbed). *Williams.* $148/£95

GOLDING, WILLIAM. A Moving Target. NY: FSG, (1982). 1st Amer ed. Fine in dj. *Antic Hay.* $15/£10

GOLDING, WILLIAM. A Moving Target. FSG, 1982. 1st US ed. Fine in dj. *Williams.* $19/£12

GOLDING, WILLIAM. The Paper Men. London: Faber, (1984). 1st ed. Fine in dj. *Between The Covers.* $35/£22

GOLDING, WILLIAM. Pincher Martin. Faber, 1956. 1st UK ed. Fine (sm ink name) in VG dj (price-clipped). *Williams.* $187/£120

GOLDING, WILLIAM. The Pyramid. NY: Harcourt, Brace & World, (1967). 1st Amer ed. NF (eps faded) in dj (lt used). *Antic Hay.* $15/£10

GOLDING, WILLIAM. Rites of Passage. Faber, 1980. 1st UK ed. Fine in Fine dj. *Martin.* $31/£20

GOLDING, WILLIAM. Rites of Passage. London, 1980. 1st Eng ed. Very Nice in dj (closed tear). *Clearwater.* $31/£20

GOLDING, WILLIAM. The Scorpion God. Faber, 1971. 1st UK ed. Fine in dj (price-clipped). *Williams.* $39/£25

GOLDING, WILLIAM. The Spire. London: Faber & Faber, (1964). 1st Eng ed. Fine in dj (sl used, 2 stains rear panel). *Antic Hay.* $45/£29

GOLDING, WILLIAM. The Spire. NY: Harcourt, Brace & World, (1964). 1st Amer ed. Fine in NF dj (spine sl sunned). *Antic Hay.* $20/£13

GOLDING, WILLIAM. The Spire. Faber, 1964. 1st UK ed. (Sl flaw fr bd), o/w Fine in dj. *Williams.* $59/£38

GOLDING, WILLIAM. The Two Deaths of Christopher Martin. NY: Harcourt, Brace, (1956). 1st Amer ed. Fine in dj (lt rubbed, soiled). *Hermitage.* $75/£48

GOLDMAN, EMMA. Anarchism and Other Essays. NY/London: Mother Earth/A.C. Fifield, 1911. 2nd rev ed. (Eps, spine dknd.) *Zubal*.* $22/£14

GOLDMAN, EMMA. Philosophy of Atheism and the Failure of Christianity. NY: Mother Earth, 1916. 1st ed. Fine (store stamp) in wraps. *Beasley.* $175/£112

GOLDMAN, EMMA. Syndicalism. NY: Mother Earth, 1913. 1st ed. NF in wraps. *Beasley.* $175/£112

GOLDMAN, JOAN M. The School in Our Village. London: Batsford, 1957. 1st ed. Edward Ardizzone (illus). VG in dj (spine faded, price-clipped). *Hollett.* $39/£25

GOLDMAN, WILLIAM. Magic. NY: Delacorte, (1976). 1st ed. Fine in dj. *Between The Covers.* $65/£42

GOLDMAN, WILLIAM. Marathon Man. NY: Delacorte, (1974). 1st ed. Fine in dj. *Hermitage.* $30/£19

GOLDMAN, WILLIAM. Marathon Man. NY: Delacorte, 1974. 1st ed. Fine in Fine dj (sm worn spot). *Revere.* $40/£26

GOLDMAN, WILLIAM. The Princess Bride. Harcourt, Brace & Jovanovich, 1973. 1st ed. (Marginal stain to last 10 ll), else Fine in dj (inner flap panels creased). *Certo.* $225/£144

GOLDMAN, WILLIAM. The Season: A Candid Look at Broadway. NY: HBW, (1969). 1st ed. Fine in dj. *Between The Covers.* $100/£64

GOLDRING, DOUGLAS. James Elroy Flecker. NY, 1923. Amer issue of 1st ed. (Spine sl chafed, cvrs sl mkd, faded.) *Clearwater.* $39/£25

GOLDRING, DOUGLAS. The Permanent Uncle. Constable, 1912. 1st ed. Color frontis, 3 other plts. Red cl (sl mkd). *Cox.* $23/£15

GOLDSCHEIDER, LUDWIG. Roman Portraits. NY: OUP, 1940. Phaidon ed. 120 full-pg b/w plts. VG in dj (chipped). *Turtle Island.* $70/£45

GOLDSCHMIDT, RICHARD. The Mechanism and Physiology of Sex Determination. London, 1923. 1st ed in English. VG. *Fye.* $100/£64

GOLDSMID, EDMUND. A Complete Catalogue of All the Publications of the Elzevier Presses.... Edinburgh: Privately ptd, 1885-1888. One of 275. 3 vols in 4. Frontis. Uncut, unopened. VG in ptd wraps (1 spine sl chipped). *Argosy.* $150/£96

GOLDSMITH, ALFRED N. Radio Telephony. NY: Wireless, (1918). 1st ed. (Spine, back cvr water-stained), else Good. *Glaser.* $75/£48

GOLDSMITH, J. (Pseud of Sir Richard Phillips.) The Natural and Artificial Wonders of the United Kingdom. London, 1825. 1st ed. 3 vols. 360; 360; 356pp. 1/2 leather. (Cvrs rubbed), else Nice. *King.* $150/£96

GOLDSMITH, OLIVER and THOMAS PARNELL. Poems. London: W. Bulmer, 1795. 5 wood-engr plts by Thomas Bewick, guards. (Sm stain 1 divisional title.) Contemp stained calf (lt scuffed, lt rubbed), gilt (sl faded), flat back w/grn morocco lettering piece. *Christie's*.* $262/£168

GOLDSMITH, OLIVER. The Deserted Village. London: Joseph Cundall, 1855. Frontis. Aeg. (Lt foxed.) *Stewart.* $39/£25

GOLDSMITH, OLIVER. The Deserted Village. UK: Campden Glos., 1904. Ltd to 150 numbered. Color frontis by C.R. Ashbee. Pict vellum cvrs (sl soiled). Fine. *Polyanthos.* $400/£256

GOLDSMITH, OLIVER. A History of the Earth and Animated Nature, Vol I and II. London: A. Fullerton, 1851. 51 hand-colored plts. (Foxing.) 3/4 leather, marbled bds, gilt-dec spines. *Metropolitan*.* $172/£110

GOLDSMITH, OLIVER. A History of the Earth and Animated Nature. Dublin: James Williams, 1777. 8 vols. 90 b/w engrs (1 w/corner torn away). Full contemp calf. Very Nice. *Metropolitan*.* $258/£165

GOLDSMITH, OLIVER. A History of the Earth and Animated Nature. London, 1875-6. 2 vols in 6 divisions. xlvi,616; xiv,655pp; 2 add'l chromolitho tps, 2 engr ports, 30 plts, 34 chromolitho plts. Aeg. Gilt/black illus cl (sl rubbed). *Edwards.* $234/£150

GOLDSMITH, OLIVER. The Life of Richard Nash, of Bath. London: J. Newbery, 1762. 1st ed. Engr frontis port, 234pp w/errata, 4 ad ll, w/cancel leaf. Orig full calf. (Bkpl; professionally rebacked, orig spine laid down), else Nice. *Turtle Island.* $500/£321

GOLDSMITH, OLIVER. The Poems of.... Robert Aris Willmott (ed). London, n.d. (1870s?). 162pp, each w/gold rules. Aeg. Later 1/2 leather, marbled bds (rubbed, spine chipped, fr hinge broken; sl foxing). *King.* $35/£22

GOLDSMITH, OLIVER. The Roman History. London: S. Baker et al, 1775. 3rd ed. 2 vols. Contemp speckled calf. Good. *Andrew Stewart.* $94/£60

GOLDSMITH, OLIVER. The Vicar of Wakefield. London, (1929). One of 575 (of 775) numbered, signed by Arthur Rackham (illus). 12 color plts. Pict eps. Orig vellum, gilt. (Bkpl.) *Swann*.* $373/£239

GOLDSMITH, OLIVER. The Vicar of Wakefield. Phila: David McKay, (1929). One of 775 signed by Arthur Rackham (illus). 12 tipped-in color plts. Unopened. Full gilt-dec vellum. NF in orig box (broken). *New Hampshire*.* $400/£256

GOLDSMITH, OLIVER. The Vicar of Wakefield. London: F. Newberry, 1766. 1st London ed. 2 vols. 19th-cent brn polished calf (expertly rebacked, extrems worn; bkpl, marginalia). *Appelfeld.* $450/£288

GOLDSMITH, OLIVER. The Vicar of Wakefield. Hereford: Ptd by D. Walker, 1798. 1st T. Bewick illus ed. 2 vols in 1. 12mo. 224pp; 7 woodcuts. Interior VG (old bds worn, rebacked w/paper). *Bookmark.* $351/£225

GOLDSTEIN, KURT. Aftereffects of Brain Injuries in War.... NY, 1948. (Ex-lib.) *Goodrich.* $35/£22

GOLDSTONE, ADRIAN H. and JOHN R. PAYNE. John Steinbeck, a Bibliographical Catalogue of the Adrian H. Goldstone Collection. Austin: UT/HRC, (1974). 1st ed. One of 1200. Port. (Edges lt foxed), o/w NF. *Reese.* $175/£112

GOLDSTONE, ADRIAN H. and JOHN R. PAYNE. John Steinbeck: A Bibliographical Catalogue of the Adrian H. Goldstone Collection. Austin: Univ of TX, (1974). One of 1200. Frontis photo port. Fine. *Pacific*.* $316/£203

GOLDSTROM, JOHN. A Narrative History of Aviation. NY: Macmillan, 1930. 1st ed. Frontis port, 31 plts. VG (few spots cvrs) in dj (sm tear). *Glaser.* $85/£54

Golf: A Royal and Ancient Game. Edinburgh: Ptd by R&R Clark, 1875. (Ep splits; edges worn through, disbinding, cl soiled, spine tears.) *Metropolitan*.* $575/£369

GOLL, CLAIRE and MARC CHAGALL. Diary of a Horse. NY: Thomas Yoselef, 1956. 1st ed. NF in dj (price-clipped, ink-mkd price fr flap seeped through to pastedown). *Lame Duck.* $35/£22

GOMBROWICZ, WITOLD. Pornografia. NY, (1966). 1st Amer ed. (Sl spotting), else Good in dj (rubbed). *King.* $35/£22

GOMME, ALICE BERTHA. The Traditional Games of England, Scotland, and Ireland.... London, 1894-98. 2 vols. xix,433; xv,531pp. Uncut, partly unopened. (Eps lt spotted, inner hinges sprung; spine heads sl bumped.) *Edwards.* $390/£250

GONEIM, M. ZAKARIA. The Lost Pyramid. NY: Rinehart, (1956). Good in dj. *Archaeologia.* $45/£29

GOOCH, ELIZABETH SARAH VILLA-REAL. The Contrast: A Novel. Wilmington: Wilson, 1796. 1st Amer ed. Calf. *Rostenberg & Stern.* $150/£96

GOOCH, FANNY CHAMBERS. Face to Face with the Mexicans. NY: Fords, Howard & Hulbert, (1887). 1st ed. 584pp; 2 chromolithos. VG. *New Hampshire*.* $90/£58

GOOCH, R. On Some of the Most Important Diseases Peculiar to Women. London: New Sydenham Soc, 1859. lv,(i),235pp. (Ex-lib, stamps prelims; rebacked w/orig spine), o/w VG. *White.* $44/£28

GOOD, PETER P. A Materia Medica Botanica.... NY: J.K. Wellman, 1845. 1st ed. 2 vols. 97 color lithos. Lib cl. Bright. *Metropolitan*.* $517/£331

GOOD, R. A Geographical Handbook of the Dorset Flora. London, 1948. Frontis, 42 maps, 1st addendum loosely inserted. Good. *Henly.* $66/£42

GOODALL, JANE. In the Shadow of Man. Boston: Houghton, Mifflin, 1971. 1st ed. NF in dj (sl edgeworn, price-clipped). *Antic Hay.* $35/£22

GOODCHILD, GEORGE. Q33. London: Odhams, (1933). 1st ed. Fine in dj. *Mordida.* $75/£48

GOODE, GEORGE BROWN (ed). The Smithsonian Institution, 1846-1946. Washington, 1897. 1st ed. 856pp. (Ex-lib.) *Fye.* $100/£64

GOODE, GEORGE BROWN and TARLETON H. BEAN. Oceanic Ichthyology. Washington, 1895. 2 vols. xxxv,26,553; xxiii,26pp; 123 plts. (Ex-lib, ink stamps, labels, feps browned, lower hinge vol 1 cracked; rebound, orig paper wrappers bound in; accession labels, spines cracked, chipped, sl discolored; joints cracking; worn.) *Edwards.* $117/£75

GOODE, GEORGE BROWN. The Fisheries and Fishery Industries of the United States...Section V History and Methods.... Washington: GPO, 1887. 1st ed. 3 vols. xxii,808; xx,881pp; atlas xvipp, 255 plts. Sound (sl damp-damage cvrs). *Lefkowicz.* $350/£224

GOODE, WILLIAM H. Outposts of Zion; With Limnings of Mission Life. Cincinnati, 1864. 464pp. Howes G236. *Ginsberg.* $150/£96

GOODENOUGH, ERWIN R. Jewish Symbols in the Greco-Roman Period. Volume Three. Illustrations. NY, 1953. Later lib buckram. Good. *Washton.* $75/£48

GOODHUE, BERTRAM GROSVENOR. A Book of Architectural and Decorative Drawings. NY: Architectural Book Pub Co, 1924. 1/2 cl, bds (lt wear, soil). *Freeman*.* $110/£71

GOODIS, DAVID. Black Friday. NY: Lion Original, 1954. 1st ed. Pb orig. NF (pp dknd). *Janus.* $75/£48

GOODIS, DAVID. Dark Passage. NY: Julian Messner, 1946. 1st ed. VG in dj (sl shortened, spine faded, spine ends chipped, sm closed tears). *Mordida.* $75/£48

GOODISON, NICHOLAS. English Barometers 1680-1860. NY: Clarkson N. Potter, (1968). 1st ed. VG in dj. *Weber.* $75/£48

GOODMAN, JOHN B. Personal Recollections of Harvey Wood. Pasadena: Privately ptd, 1955. Ltd to 200 signed, numbered. Fine. *Book Market.* $85/£54

GOODMAN, MITCHELL. The End of It. NY: Horizon, (1961). 1st ed. NF in dj (chips). *Turtle Island.* $35/£22

GOODMAN, NATHAN G. (ed). A Franklin Miscellany: The Ingenious Dr. Franklin. Phila: Univ of PA, 1956. 3 vols. Patterned bds, cl backstrip. Fine in VG+ slipcase. *Zubal*.* $20/£13

GOODMAN, PAUL. Art and Social Nature. NY, (1946). 1st Amer ed. NF in dj (sl rubbed, nicks). *Polyanthos.* $25/£16

GOODMAN, PAUL. Art and Social Nature. (NY): Vinco, 1946. 1st ed. NF in dj. *Cahan.* $30/£19

GOODMAN, PAUL. Collected Poems. Taylor Stoehr (ed). NY: Random House, (1973). 1st ed. Fine in Fine white dj (sl extrem dkng). *Between The Covers.* $65/£42

GOODMAN, PAUL. Don Juan, or The Continuum of the Libido. Taylor Stoehr (ed). Santa Barbara, CA: Black Sparrow, 1979. One of 200 numbered, signed. Floral dec cl-backed dec bds, ptd spine label. NF in acetate dj. *Blue Mountain.* $30/£19

GOODMAN, PAUL. Homespun of Oatmeal Gray. NY, 1970. 1st Amer ed. Fine in Fine dj. *Polyanthos.* $25/£16

GOODRICH, CHARLES A. The Universal Traveler. Hartford: Robins & Smith, 1845. Frontis, 504pp.. Marbled eps. Orig emb calf (corners worn, spine leather split, gone from top/bottom edges). Good (most plts foxed, 1 w/closed tear). *Connolly.* $35/£22

GOODRICH, FRANCES LOUISA. Mountain Homespun. New Haven: Yale Univ, (April 1931). 2nd ptg. Patterned bds. VG. *New Hampshire*.* $65/£42

GOODRICH, LLOYD. Edward Hopper. NY, (1978). Obl folio. Dj. *Swann*.* $92/£59

GOODRICH, LLOYD. Edward Hopper. NY: Abrams, n.d. (Sl worn.) Dj. *Oinonen*.* $50/£32

GOODRICH, LLOYD. Raphael Soyer. NY: Abrams, (1972). 1st ed. 77 mtd color plts. Tan cl (rear cvr soiled; lt stains eps, outer edges). Illus dj. *Karmiole.* $150/£96

GOODRICH, S. G. A Pictorial History of the United States, with Notices of Other Portions of America North and South. Phila: J.H., Butler, 1875. New ed. Thick 8vo. 316pp, supplement. (Pencil scriptures rep, ink sig fep, 1 pg repaired, 1 sig partially sprung.) Grn pebble grain cl on bds (rubbed, chipped), 3/4 grn leather, gilt. Good. *Hobbyhorse.* $75/£48

GOODRICH, S. G. The Third Reader for the Use of Schools. Louisville, KY: Morton & Griswold, 1839. 12mo. vii+180pp (foxing; fore-edge chipped; lacks eps). 3/4 black leather, ptd paper on bds (heavily rubbed, chipped; worm holes to spine; bound upside down). Poor. *Hobbyhorse.* $75/£48

GOODRICH-FREER, A. In a Syrian Saddle. 1905. 1st ed. (Feps lt browned, reps wormed? w/loss; cl worn, spine chipped; pen mk.) *Edwards.* $55/£35

GOODRIDGE, CHARLES M. Narrative of a Voyage to the South Seas, and the Shipwreck of the Princess of Wales Cutter.... Exeter: W.C. Featherstone, 1841. 4th ed. Frontis, (xxix),(11)-170pp; 2 plts. Errata slip. Orig cl. VG. *High Latitude.* $195/£125

GOODSPEED, CHARLES ELIOT. Angling in America. Boston, 1939. One of 795 numbered, signed. Uncut. Newer blue cl (sl worn), orig cvr/spine label. *Oinonen*.* $110/£71

GOODSPEED, T. H. Plant Hunters in the Andes. NY, 1941. 65 plts. Good. *Henly.* $47/£30

GOODSPEED, T. H. Plant Hunters in the Andes. NY: F&R, 1941. 1st ed. VG (bumped) in VG dj (chipped). *Archer.* $90/£58

GOODSPEED, T. H. Plant Hunters in the Andes. Univ of CA, 1961. Dj (sl chipped). *Edwards.* $62/£40

GOODWIN, CARDINAL. John Charles Fremont, and Explanation of His Career. Stanford: Stanford Univ, (1930). 1st ed. Lg fldg map. Fine in dj (worn). *Argonaut.* $45/£29

GOODWIN, G. A History of Ottoman Architecture. Balt: Johns Hopkins, 1971. 4 color plts. Sound. *Ars Artis.* $70/£45

GOODWIN, GEORGE M. Russell A. Hibbs, Pioneer in Orthopedic Surgery, 1869-1932. NY, 1935. 1st ed. Fine. *Doctor's Library.* $40/£26

GOODWIN, GEORGE. Buildings and Monuments, Modern and Medieval. London, 1850. Aeg. Orig cl, gilt. (Backstrip gone, worn.) *Freeman*.* $40/£26

GOODWIN, JOHN. The Idols and the Prey: A Novel of Haiti. NY: Harper, (1953). 1st ed. Fine in dj (sl extrem wear). *Between The Covers.* $45/£29

GOODWIN, M. et al (eds). Historic New York. NY: Putnam, 1897. 1st ed. Teg. Pict cl. VG. *Archer.* $25/£16

GOODYEAR, W. A. The Coal Mines of the Western Coast of the United States. SF: A.L. Bancroft, 1877. 1st ed. 4,(2),5-153pp. Grn cl (extrems rubbed), gilt. VG. *Bohling.* $110/£71

GOODYEAR, W. A. The Coal Mines of the Western Coast of the United States. NY: John Wiley, 1879. 2nd ed. 153pp. Maroon cl (spotting to cvrs, spine sl faded), gilt lettering. NF; internally Fine. *Argonaut.* $75/£48

GOOLRICK, JOHN T. Historic Fredericksburg. Whittet & Sheperson, (c. 1922). 2nd ed. VG-. *Book Broker.* $45/£29

GORDIMER, NADINE. The Conservationist. Cape, 1974. 1st UK ed. (Sm splash mk top edge), o/w Fine in Fine dj. *Martin.* $25/£16

GORDIMER, NADINE. A Guest of Honour. NY: Viking, (1970). 1st ed. Fine in NF dj. *Hermitage.* $35/£22

GORDIMER, NADINE. Livingstone's Companions. London: Jonathan Cape, (1972). 1st ed. Fine in dj (sl used). *Dermont.* $25/£16

GORDIMER, NADINE. My Son's Story. (London): Bloomsbury, (1990). 1st ed. Signed. Fine in dj. *Between The Covers.* $150/£96

GORDIMER, NADINE. A World of Strangers. London: Gollancz, 1958. 1st UK ed. Fine in dj (lt chipped, dknd, spine stain). *Hermitage.* $45/£29

GORDON, A. C. PAGE and THOMAS NELSON. Befo' de War. NY: Scribner, 1906. Later ptg. Signed by Gordon. NF. *Old London.* $65/£42

GORDON, ANNA A. The Beautiful Life of Frances E. Willard. Chicago: Woman's Temperance Pub Assoc, (1898). 416pp. VG+. *Bohling.* $18/£12

GORDON, BENJAMIN LEE. The Romance of Medicine. Phila, 1945. 2nd ed. VG in Good dj. *Doctor's Library.* $50/£32

GORDON, C. G. Letters of.... London, 1888. xix,404pp. (Upper hinge tender, sl wear.) *Edwards.* $39/£25

GORDON, CAROLINE. Alec Maury Sportsman. NY: Scribner, 1934. 1st ed, 1st binding. Pale grn cl (Sunning, sm spots, sl discoloration rear cvr), o/w VG in dj (lt nicked, chip to spine crown). *Reese.* $200/£128

GORDON, CAROLINE. The Forest of the South. NY: Scribner, 1945. 1st ed. (Spine sl faded), o/w VG in dj (sl chipped, sm tear). *Bernard.* $175/£112

GORDON, CAROLINE. The Forest of the South. Stories. NY: Scribner, 1945. 1st ed. NF in dj (extrems lt worn, sm chip spine heel). *Captain's Bookshelf.* $175/£112

GORDON, CAROLINE. How to Read a Novel. NY: Viking, 1957. 1st ed. (Sm pencil erasure ep), else NF in dj (price-clipped, sm rubs, nicks). *Reese.* $85/£54

GORDON, CAROLINE. The Strange Children. NY: Scribner, 1951. 1st ed. NF in dj (chipped, 1/4-inch chip fr panel; bkseller's label fr flap). *Hermitage.* $75/£48

GORDON, CAROLINE. The Strange Children. NY: Scribner, 1951. 1st ed. (Name, date, place on fep), o/w VG+ in dj. *Bernard.* $100/£64

GORDON, CAROLINE. The Women on the Porch. NY: Scribner, 1944. 1st ed. VG (lt flecking) in dj (chips, old inner reinforcement). *Reese.* $85/£54

GORDON, CHARLES GEORGE. The Journals of Major-Gen C.G. Gordon, C.B. at Kartoum....Egmont A. Hake (intro). London: Kegan Paul, Trench, 1885. 1st UK ed. 416pp. Good (spine, cvr edges faded). *Gravesend.* $35/£22

GORDON, COLIN. Beyond the Looking Glass. Hodder & Stoughton, 1982. Dj. *Edwards.* $31/£20

GORDON, DUDLEY. Charles F. Lummis: Crusader in Corduroy. L.A.: Cultural Assets, 1972. Fabricoid. Dj. *Dawson.* $30/£19

GORDON, E. A. Clear Round! or Seeds of Story from Other Countries.... London: Sampson Low, Marston, 1893. 1st ed. (viii),442,32pp; 8 plts, fldg map. (Map brittle, torn, no loss; cl sl rubbed, soiled), o/w VG. *Worldwide.* $18/£12

GORDON, H. LAING. Sir James Young Simpson and Chloroform (1811-1870). London: T. Fisher Unwin, 1897. 1st ed. Frontis port, xii,233pp. Text Clean (exlib). *White.* $39/£25

GORDON, H. LAING. Sir James Young Simpson and Chloroform (1811-1870). NY, 1898. 1st ed. 233pp. VG. *Fye.* $75/£48

GORDON, JOHN B. Reminiscences of the Civil War. NY, 1903. 1st ed. Pict cl. (Cvr sl worn), o/w Fine. *Pratt.* $125/£80

GORDON, LINA DUFF. The Story of Assisi. London, 1900. 2 fldg plans. Teg. Gilt-dec cl (spine sl discolored; bkpl). *Edwards.* $19/£12

GORDON, MAURICE BEAR. Aesculapius Comes to the Colonies. Ventnor, NJ: Ventnor Pub, (1949). 1st ed. Lg fldg facs. Fine. *Glaser.* $75/£48

GORDON, NELLY KINZIE. The Fort Dearborn Massacre. Rand McNally, (1912). 1st ed. Frontis, 3 plts. Fort Dearborn postcards laid in. Fine. *Oregon.* $40/£26

GORDON, RUTH. Years Ago. NY, 1947. 1st ed. Fine in NF dj (sm tear). *Warren.* $40/£26

GORDON, SETON. Afoot in Wild Places. London: Cassell, 1937. 1st ed. 48 plts. Very Nice in dj (few sm tears neatly repaired). *Hollett.* $70/£45

GORDON, SETON. The Charm of the Hills. London: Cassell, 1914. 2nd ed. 85 plts (1 tipped in w/tape, edges sl dusty, few loose). Nice (extrems sl worn, sm mks, spots). *Hollett.* $70/£45

GORDON, SETON. A Highland Year. London: Eyre & Spottiswoode, 1944. 1st ed. Dj (defective). *Hollett.* $31/£20

GORDON, SETON. Islands of the West. London: Cassell, 1933. 1st ed. 51 plts. Very Nice (edges sl spotted). *Hollett.* $117/£75

GORDON, SETON. The Land of the Hills and the Glens. London: Cassell, 1920. 1st ed. (Joints tender.) *Hollett.* $47/£30

GORDON, W. J. Our Country's Butterflies and Moths and How to Know Them. London: Day, n.d. (1910). 33 color plts. Good (cl dust-stained). *Savona.* $22/£14

GORDON, W. J. Round About the North Pole. NY: Dutton, 1907. 64 plts, 6 maps. Teg. Dec cl. VG. *High Latitude.* $40/£26

GORDON, WILLIAM. History of the Rise, Progress, and Establishment of the Independence of the United States.... NY, 1794. 2nd Amer ed. 3 vols. (Lt foxing; lacks maps vols 1-2, all blank flyleaves.) Full calf (extrems sl worn), red leather spine labels. *New Hampshire*.* $120/£77

GORELL, LORD (ed). Characters and Observations, an 18th Century Manuscript. London, 1930. 1st ed. Marbled bds, cl spine. VG. *Gretton.* $19/£12

GORER, EDGAR and J. F. BLACKER. Chinese Porcelain and Hard Stones. London: Bernard Quaritch, 1911. 1st ed. 2 vols. 12.25 x 9.5. Cream linen (spines sl dknd, lt wear), gilt. Fine (lt foxing, mostly prelims, not affecting plts). *Hermitage.* $800/£513

GORER, RICHARD. The Development of Garden Flowers. London: Eyre & Spottiswoode, 1970. 6 color, 68 b/w plts. (Lacks fep), else VG. *Quest.* $35/£22

GORES, JOE. Final Notice. NY: Random House, (1973). 1st ed. Fine in dj (lt worn). *Hermitage.* $75/£48

GORES, JOE. Final Notice. NY: Random House, 1973. 1st ed. Signed. Fine in dj. *Mordida.* $50/£32

GORES, JOE. Gone, No Forwarding. NY: Random House, 1978. 1st ed. Fine in dj. *Mordida.* $45/£29

GOREY, EDWARD. Amphigorey Also. NY: Congdon & Weed, (1983). 1st ed. #153/250 signed. Fine in Fine dj, pub's slipcase. *Metropolitan*.* $143/£92

GOREY, EDWARD. The Black Doll. NY: Gotham Bk Mart, 1973. 1st ed. Signed. Fine in wrappers. *Lenz.* $35/£22

GOREY, EDWARD. The Broken Spoke. NY, 1976. 1st ed. NF in NF dj. *Warren.* $35/£22

GOREY, EDWARD. The Broken Spoke. NY: Dodd, Mead, 1976. 1st ed. 7 1/2 x 5 1/4. Dec paper bds. VG in dj. *Cattermole.* $100/£64

GOREY, EDWARD. The Bug Book. NY: Looking Glass Library, (1959). True 1st ed. Ltd to 600. Signed. NF (bkpl) in ptd wrappers. *Bromer.* $450/£288

GOREY, EDWARD. Dancing Cats and Neglected Murderesses. NY: Workman, 1980. 1st ed. 4 1/2 x 6 1/2. 80pp. Fine in wraps. *Cattermole.* $35/£22

GOREY, EDWARD. The Doubtful Guest. GC: Doubleday, 1957. 1st ed. Signed. Ptd bds. Fine in dj (lt soiled). *Bromer.* $350/£224

GOREY, EDWARD. The Epileptic Bicycle. NY: Dodd, Mead, (1969). Oblong 12mo. Unpaginated. Grn illus bds. VG in dj (rear cvr sl stained). *Dower.* $45/£29

GOREY, EDWARD. The Green Beads. NY: Albondocani, 1978. One of 400 numbered, signed. Fine in Fine wrappers. *Lenz.* $90/£58

GOREY, EDWARD. The Listing Attic. NY: Duell Sloan, Pierce, (1954). 1st ed. Pict bds. (Extrems sl worn), else VF in VF dj. *Bromer.* $250/£160

GOREY, EDWARD. The Other Statue. S&S, (1968). 1st ed. Fine in Fine dj. *Certo.* $35/£22

GOREY, EDWARD. The Tunnel Calamity. (NY: Putnam, 1984.) 1st ed. 8vo. 9 fldg sections. VG. *Houle.* $75/£48

GOREY, EDWARD. Unstrung Harp, or Mr. Earbrass Writes a Novel. NY: Duell Sloane, 1953. 1st ed. Pict paper-cvrd bds. NF in NF dj (spine extrems sl worn, head chipped). *Book Adoption.* $250/£160

GOREY, EDWARD. The Willowdale Handcar. Indianapolis: Bobbs-Merrill, (1962). 1st ed. Signed. Fine in wrappers. *Lenz.* $75/£48

GORGAS, JOSIAH. The Civil War Diary of General Josiah Gorgas. Frank E. Vandiver (ed). University, AL: Univ of AL, 1947. 1st ed. NF in VG dj w/ed presentation. *Mcgowan.* $175/£112

GORHAM, HARRY M. My Memories of the Comstock. L.A.: Suttonhouse, (1939). 1st ed. (Ink name), else VG in dj (edgeworn). *Perier.* $75/£48

GORHAM, MAURICE and H. McG. DUNNETT. Inside the Pub. Architectural Press, 1950. (Sl mkd), else VG. *Hadley.* $31/£20

GORHAM, MAURICE. Back to the Local. London: Percival Marshall, 1949. 1st ed. Edward Ardizzone (illus). VG in dj (spine faded, price-clipped). *Hollett.* $62/£40

GORHAM, MAURICE. The Local. 1939. 1st ed. Edward Ardizzone (color lithos). Ptd bds (head of spine nicked, lower hinge weakening). *Words Etc.* $234/£150

GORHAM, MAURICE. The Local. London, 1939. 1st ed. Edward Ardizzone (illus). Ptd bds (spine sl nicked, lower hinge weak). *Words Etc.* $172/£110

GORKI, MAXIM. Other Fires. Alexander Bakshy (trans). NY: Appleton, 1933. 1st ed. Fine (ink name) in VG dj (edgewear, chips). *Antic Hay.* $35/£22

GORKI, MAXIM. Reminiscences of Leonid Andreyev. Katherine Mansfield and S. S. Koteliansky (trans). NY: Crosby Gaige, 1928. Ltd to 400 ptd. Black cl-backed grn bds, gilt. Very Nice. *Cady.* $20/£13

GORKI, MAXIM. Reminiscences of Leonid Andreyev.... Katherine Mansfield & S.S. Koteliansky (trans). NY: Crosby Gaige, 1928. 1st ed. One of 400. Gilt cl-backed bds. (Bds sunned toward edges), o/w Nice. *Reese.* $65/£42

GORKY, MAXIM et al (eds). The White Sea Canal. London, 1935. Frontis port, sketch map. (Feps lt browned; spine sl rubbed.) *Edwards.* $39/£25

GORMAN, ED and MARTIN GREENBERG (eds). Stalkers. IL: Dark Harvest, 1989. Ltd to 750 signed by 20 authors. Fine in Fine dj, slipcase. *Metropolitan*.* $34/£22

GORMAN, HERBERT S. The Procession of Masks. Boston, 1923. Cl-backed bds (name; spine foot sl torn). *Clearwater.* $55/£35

GORMAN, HERBERT. The Scottish Queen. NY: Farrar & Rinehart, (1932). 1st US ed. VG (ex-libris). *Second Life.* $25/£16

GORMAN, WARREN. Body Image and the Image of the Brain. St. Louis: Warren H. Green, (1969). 1st ed. Inscribed. Grn cl. (Bkpl, spine label, rear pocket of Amer Psychiatric Assoc Library.) *Gach.* $30/£19

GORTON, JOHN. A General Biographical Dictionary. London: Henry Bohn, 1851. New ed. 4 vols. (Vol 3 spine top torn), o/w VG. *New Hampshire**. $50/£32

GOSLING, NIGEL. Nadar. NY: Knopf, 1976. 1st Amer ed. (Owner stamp), else Fine in pict dj. *Cahan.* $60/£38

GOSLING, PAULA. Loser's Blues. London: Macmillan, (1980). 1st ed. Fine in Fine dj (price-clipped). *Metropolitan**. $23/£15

GOSLING, WILLIAM GILBERT. The Life of Sir Humphrey Gilbert.... Constable, 1911. Frontis. Uncut. Sound (edges foxed, text sl spotted). *Peter Taylor.* $39/£25

GOSS, CLAY. Homecookin': Five Plays. Washington: Howard Univ, 1974. 1st ed, 1st bk. Fine in NF dj (sm tear, rubbed, fr panel sm scrape). *Between The Covers.* $45/£29

GOSS, N. S. History of the Birds of Kansas. Topeka, 1891. 692,(1)pp; 35 plts. (Cl sl faded, neatly refixed.) *Wheldon & Wesley.* $109/£70

GOSSE, EDMUND. The Life and Letters of John Donne.... NY/London: Dodd, Mead/Heinemann, 1899. Amer issue of British sheets. 2 vols. Good (corners rubbed, hinges sl cracking). *Reese.* $45/£29

GOSSE, EDMUND. Silhouettes. London: Heinemann, 1925. 1st ed. Brn cl, gilt. VF. *Macdonnell.* $75/£48

GOSSE, P. H. Evenings at the Microscope. London: SPCK, 1877. New ed. 422pp. Grn/gilt dec cl. VG. *Savona.* $31/£20

GOSSE, P. H. Evenings at the Microscope. NY, 1896. xii,480pp. Teg. 1/2 morocco. Fine. *Henly.* $47/£30

GOSSE, P. H. A Naturalist's Rambles on the Devonshire Coast. London, 1853. xvi,451pp (sl foxed at ends, plts); 12 color, 16 plain plts. 1/2 calf (neatly rebacked), gilt. *Henly.* $106/£68

GOSSE, P. H. A Year at the Shore. London, 1865. 3rd thousand. xii,330,2pp; 36 color plts. Good. *Henly.* $94/£60

GOSSE, P. H. A Year at the Shore. London, 1865. 1st ed. xii,330,2pp; 36 color plts. (Ends sl foxed.) *Henly.* $112/£72

GOSSE, PHILIP. The Squire of Walton Hall. London: Cassell, 1940. 1st ed. Color frontis, 9 plts, map. (Edges, eps lt spotted.) Dj (spine sl spotted). *Hollett.* $39/£25

GOTCH, J. ALFRED. Early Renaissance Architecture in England. Batsford, 1901. 87 plts. Teg. (Bkpl, plts lt browned, margins sl thumbed, 1st leaves sl waterstained, lower hinge cracked; sl worn, spine sl faded.) *Edwards.* $55/£35

GOTCH, J. ALFRED. The English Home from Charles I to George IV. London: Batsford, 1919. (Spine worn.) *Ars Artis.* $55/£35

GOTCH, J. ALFRED. Inigo Jones. London: Methuen, 1929. 31 plts. (Lib stamp spine, tp, plt corners), else Good. *Ars Artis.* $28/£18

GOTCH, J. ALFRED. Old English Houses. London: Methuen, 1925. 48 plts, 7 plans. (Spine faded.) *Ars Artis.* $23/£15

Gothic and Renaissance Art in Nuremberg 1300-1550. NY: MMA, 1986. Good in dj. *Washton.* $50/£32

GOTLIEB, C. C. and J. N. P. HUME. High-Speed Data Processing. NY: McGraw-Hill, 1958. 1st ed. Fine. *Glaser.* $75/£48

GOTTFREDSON, PETER (ed). History of Indian Depredations in Utah. (Salt Lake City: Press of Skelton, c. 1919.) 1st ed. Dec blue cl (lt shelfwear). Bright. *Cullen.* $125/£80

GOTTSHALL, FRANKLIN H. Reproducing Antique Furniture. Stobart, 1984. Pict card. (Top edge sl bruised), o/w Fine. *Whittle.* $23/£15

GOUDGE, ELIZABETH. The Little White Horse. Univ of London, 1946. 1st ed. C. Walter Hodges (illus). 8vo. 286pp; 4 color plts. (Spine faded, cvr wear), else Good + . *Bookmark.* $39/£25

GOUDY, FREDERIC W. The Alphabet, Fifteen Interpretive Designs.... NY, 1918. 1st ed. Frontis, 27 plts. (Ink name, cvrs sl rubbed, soiled), else Good. *King.* $125/£80

GOUDY, FREDERIC W. Typologia. Berkeley/L.A.: Univ of CA, 1940. 1st ed. Ltd to 300 signed. Dec eps. 1/2 leather, bds. VF in glassine dj (torn), slipcase. *Jaffe.* $250/£160

GOUGH, MARY. Travel into Yesterday. GC: Doubleday, 1954. 1st ed. 12 plts. VG in dj (sl torn). *Worldwide.* $25/£16

GOULARD. A Treatise on the Effects and Various Preparations of Lead. 1769. 1st ed. xvi,222pp + index (new eps). New calf. *Whitehart.* $218/£140

GOULD, A. A. Report on the Invertebrata of Massachusetts. W. G. Binney (ed). Boston, 1870. 2nd ed. viii,524pp; 12 plts (11 color). (Cl sl loose, spine sl defective.) *Wheldon & Wesley.* $133/£85

GOULD, CHARLES N. Covered Wagon Geologist. Norman, 1959. 1st ed. 2 fldg maps. Fine in VG + dj. *Five Quail.* $45/£29

GOULD, EMERSON W. Fifty Years on the Mississippi. Columbus, OH: Long's College Book Co, 1951. Rpt. Gilt dec cl. Fine in dj, plastic wrapper. Howes G273. *Bohling.* $60/£38

GOULD, GEORGE (ed). The American Year-Book of Medicine and Surgery. Volumes 1-4. Phila, 1896-1899. 1st eds. 4 vols. 1183; 1257; 1077; 1102pp. VG. *Fye.* $200/£128

GOULD, GEORGE M. and WALTER L. PYLE. A Cyclopedia of Practical Medicine and Surgery. Phila, 1901. Marbled eps, flysheets. 1/4 leather (worn). Good (rear cvr, flysheet detached but present). *Doctor's Library.* $50/£32

GOULD, GERALD. Monogamy. Allen & Unwin, 1918. 1st ed. Uncut. Good in ptd wrapper (lt soiled) over bds. *Cox.* $39/£25

GOULD, LAURENCE M. Cold. The Record of an Antarctic Sledge Journey. NY: Brewer, Warren & Putnam, 1931. Inscribed, signed. Color frontis. Good (few binding mks). *High Latitude.* $40/£26

GOULD, LEWIS L. and RICHARD GREFFE. Photojournalist: The Career of Jimmy Hare. Austin/London: Univ of TX, 1977. 1st ed. NF (eps lt foxed) in pict dj (fr lt foxed). *Cahan.* $40/£26

GOULD, M. E. Early American Wooden Ware. Rutland: Tuttle, 1962. 1st rev ed. Good in dj (chipped). *Scribe's Perch**. $10/£6

GOULD, MAURICE M. Alaska's Coinage Through the Years. Racine: Whitman, 1965. Rev 2nd ed. Fine. *Perier.* $35/£22

GOULD, RUPERT T. Enigmas, Another Book of Unexplained Facts. NY: University Books, (1966). 2nd ptg. 5 plts. 1/4 red cl, bds. Dj (sm tear). *Weber.* $25/£16

GOULD, RUPERT T. The Marine Chronometer, Its History and Development. London: J.D. Potter, 1923. 1st ed. Frontis port, 39 plts. Dk grn cl. (Sm hole fep, tp tissue torn; corners bumped, sl rubbed), else VG. *Weber.* $300/£192

GOULD, RUPERT. T. Oddities [and] Enigmas. London, 1928-29. 2 vols. *Wheldon & Wesley.* $78/£50

GOULLART, PETER. Land of the Lamas. NY: Dutton, 1959. 1st ed. Map. VG in dj. *Worldwide.* $30/£19

GOVE, JESSE A. The Utah Expedition 1857-1858. Concord: NH Hist Soc, 1928. Frontis port. VG+. Howes G279. *Bohling.* $75/£48

GOVE, JESSE A. The Utah Expedition, 1857-1858: Letters of Capt Jesse A. Gove.... Otis G. Hammond (ed). Concord, NH, 1928. 1st ed. Howes G279. *Ginsberg.* $125/£80

GOVER, ROBERT. The Maniac Responsible. NY: Grove, (1963). 1st ed. (Spine lt soiled), o/w Fine in dj (lt soiled, worn). *Hermitage.* $45/£29

GOVER, ROBERT. One Hundred Dollar Misunderstanding. London: Neville Spearman, 1961. 1st ed, 1st bk. Gilt cl bds. Fine in VG dj (soil rear panel). *Reese.* $85/£54

GOVER, ROBERT. One Hundred Dollar Misunderstanding. NY: Grove Press, 1962. 1st ed. Fine in djs (warp mks rear panels, tear fr panel). *Beasley.* $45/£29

GOVER, ROBERT. One Hundred Dollar Misunderstanding. NY: Grove, 1962. 1st ed. Fine in dbl djs. *Associates.* $50/£32

GOW, A. S. F. A. E. Housman. NY, 1936. 1st Amer ed. Very Nice in dj (chafed). *Clearwater.* $39/£25

GOWANLOCK, THERESA and THERESA DELANEY. Two Months in the Camp of Big Bear. Park Dale: Times Office, 1885. 1st ed. Nice (hinges neatly repaired, lt wear; gathering 6 missing, replaced by duplicate gathering 1). *Hermitage.* $75/£48

GOWANLOCK, THERESA and THERESA DELANEY. Two Months in the Camp of Big Bear. Parkdale, 1885. 136pp. Fine. *Reese.* $425/£272

GOWANLOCK, THERESA and THERESA DELANEY. Two Months in the Camp of Big Bear. Parkdale: Times Office, 1885. 1st ed. iii,130,vi+ 3pp ads (fep detached but present). Grn cl (shelfwear; sl soiling, scratches fr cvr). Good. *Brown.* $200/£128

GOWERS, WILLIAM. The Border-Land of Epilepsy. London: Churchill, 1907. 1st ed. 8vo. vi,121pp. Fine (label pasted over Churchill imprint; spine ends sl rubbed). *Glaser.* $500/£321

GOWERS, WILLIAM. Lectures on the Diagnosis of Diseases of the Brain. London, 1885. Nice (lt blistered, worn, rubbed). *Goodrich.* $395/£253

GOWIN, EMMET. Emmet Gowin: Photographs. NY: Knopf, 1976. 1st ed. 68 b/w plts. (Owner stamp), else NF in illus stiff wrappers. *Cahan.* $85/£54

GOWING, LAWRENCE. Lucian Freud. London: Thames & Hudson, 1982. 1st ed. Pict bds. VG in ptd clear plastic dj. *Hollett.* $62/£40

GOWING, T. A Soldier's Experience, or A Voice from the Ranks. Nottingham, 1899. Rev, enlgd ed. Frontis port, xvi,585pp (lt foxing tp), fldg plt. Aeg. Blue pict cl, gilt. *Maggs.* $78/£50

GOYTISOLO, JUAN. Island of Women. NY: Knopf, 1962. 1st US ed. NF in dj. *Lame Duck.* $45/£29

GOYTISOLO, JUAN. Juan the Landless. Helen R. Lane (trans). NY: Viking, (1977). 1st ed. Fine in dj. *Antic Hay.* $25/£16

GOYTISOLO, JUAN. The Party's Over. Jose Yglesias (trans). NY: Grove, (1966). 1st Amer ed. Fine in NF dj (sl soiled). *Antic Hay.* $25/£16

GRABER, RALPH (ed). The Baseball Reader. Barnes, 1951. 1st ed. VG+ in VG dj (spot). *Plapinger.* $50/£32

GRACIE, ARCHIBALD. The Truth About Chickamauga. Boston: Houghton Mifflin, 1911. Fldg map. *Cullen.* $85/£54

GRAFTON, C. W. The Rope Began to Hang the Butcher. NY: Farrar & Rinehart, 1944. 1st ed. Fine in dj (sm chip spine base, corners sl worn). *Mordida.* $100/£64

GRAFTON, SUE. A Is for Alibi. London: Macmillan, (1982). 1st ed. Signed. Fine in Fine dj. *Metropolitan*.* $212/£136

GRAFTON, SUE. B Is for Burglar. NY: Holt, Rinehart & Winston, 1985. 1st ed. VF in dj. *Mordida.* $650/£417

GRAFTON, SUE. E Is for Evidence. NY: Holt, (1988). 1st ed. Fine in Fine dj. *Metropolitan*.* $86/£55

GRAFTON, SUE. F Is for Fugitive. Macmillan, 1989. 1st UK ed. Fine in NF dj. *Williams.* $55/£35

GRAFTON, SUE. F Is for Fugitive. NY: Henry Holt, 1989. 1st ed. VF in dj. *Mordida.* $65/£42

GRAFTON, SUE. G Is for Gumshoe. NY, (1990). 1st ed. Cl-backed bds. VG in dj. *King.* $35/£22

GRAFTON, SUE. G Is for Gumshoe. NY: Henry Holt, 1990. 1st ed. VF in dj. *Mordida.* $40/£26

GRAFTON, SUE. H Is for Homicide. NY: Henry Holt, 1991. 1st ed. VF in dj. *Mordida.* $35/£22

GRAFTON, SUE. J Is for Judgement. NY, (1993). 1st ed. Cl-backed bds. VG in dj. *King.* $20/£13

GRAFTON, SUE. J is for Judgement. NY, 1993. 1st Amer ed. Signed. Mint in dj. *Polyanthos.* $35/£22

GRAFTON, SUE. J Is for Judgement. NY: Henry Holt, 1993. 1st ed. Signed. VF in dj. *Mordida.* $40/£26

GRAFTON, SUE. K Is for Killer. NY, (1994). 1st ed. Cl-backed bds. VG in dj. *King.* $17/£11

GRAFTON, SUE. Kinsey and Me. Santa Barbara: Bench Press, 1991. 1st ed. One of 300 numbered, signed. Very Fine in slipcase. *Mordida.* $350/£224

GRAHAM, ALISTAIR. Eyelids of Morning. Greenwich, CT: NYGS, 1973. 2nd ptg. 16 color plts. (Owner stamp), else NF in VG dj. *Cahan.* $50/£32

GRAHAM, ANDREW J. The Standard-Phonographic Dictionary. NY: Graham, 1863. 1st ed. 1053,(6)pp. Orig full leather (sm emb lib stamp; bkpl removed), gilt. *Ginsberg.* $125/£80

GRAHAM, ANDREW. Andrew Graham's Observations on Hudson's Bay, 1767-1791. London: Hudson's Bay Record Soc, 1969. Fldg map. VG in dj. *Lien.* $35/£22

GRAHAM, ANGUS. The Golden Grindstone. The Adventures of George M. Mitchell. Phila: Lippincott, c. 1935. Frontis. VG. *High Latitude.* $35/£22

GRAHAM, HARVEY. Eternal Eve: The Story of Gynecology. GC, NJ, 1951. 1st Amer ed. VG. *Fye.* $60/£38

GRAHAM, HENRY GREY. The Social Life of Scotland. London: A&C Black, 1909. 2nd ed. (Extrems sl rubbed, upper joint strained.) *Hollett.* $23/£15

GRAHAM, JAMES WALTER. The Palaces of Crete. Princeton, 1962. Good in dj. *Washton.* $30/£19

GRAHAM, JAMES. (Pseud of Jack Higgins.) The Wrath of God. GC: Doubleday, 1971. 1st Amer ed. Fine in dj. *Mordida.* $85/£54

GRAHAM, JOHN ALEXANDER. Babe Ruth Caught in a Snowstorm. Houghton Mifflin, 1973. 1st ed. Fine in VG dj. *Plapinger.* $60/£38

GRAHAM, MARIA. Journal of a Residence in India. Edinburgh, 1812. 1st ed. 16 plts, incl hand-colored frontis and 2 fldg plts. (Lt foxing.) Contemp 1/4 calf, marbled bds. *Freeman*.* $220/£141

GRAHAM, MARIA. Journal of a Residence in India. Edinburgh: Constable, 1813. 2nd ed. Hand-colored frontis, xii,215pp; 15 plts (2 fldg). Later 1/2 morocco, gilt. (Plts sl foxed, offsetting), else VG. *Terramedia.* $500/£321

GRAHAM, R. B. CUNNINGHAME. Bibi. London: Heinemann, 1929. Signed ltd ed. Untrimmed. (Sl mkd.) *Hollett.* $86/£55

GRAHAM, R. B. CUNNINGHAME. Charity. London, 1912. 1st ed. NF (eps sl offset; spine extrems sl rubbed). *Polyanthos.* $35/£22

GRAHAM, SHIRLEY. There Was Once a Slave...The Heroic Story of Frederick Douglass. NY: Julian Messner, (1947). 1st ed. NF (pg edges sl browned; bds sl worn) in VG dj (spine sl dknd; sm tears, nicks extrems). Between The Covers. $85/£54

GRAHAM, W. A. Custer's Battle Flags. (N.p.): Privately ptd, 1952. 1st separate ed. #102/300, signed. 2 color plts. Fine in grey ptd wrappers (worn). Harrington. $125/£80

GRAHAM, W. A. The Reno Court of Inquiry. Harrisburg, (1954). 1st ed. Fldg map. (Cvr sl worn), o/w VG + . Pratt. $65/£42

GRAHAM, W. S. Malcolm Mooney's Land. Faber, 1970. 1st ed. Fine in Fine dj. Whiteson. $20/£13

GRAHAM, W. S. The Nightfishing. London: Faber, 1955. 1st Eng ed. Very Nice (fr cvr sl faded, feps tanned) in dj. Clearwater. $78/£50

GRAHAM-SMITH, G. S. Flies in Relation to Disease. Non-Bloodsucking Flies. Cambridge, 1913. 24 plts. (Name stamp tp, fep.) Bickersteth. $28/£18

GRAHAME, KENNETH. The Golden Age. London: John Lane, (1928). 1st ed w/Ernest H. Shepard dwgs. Beige cl. Appelfeld. $50/£32

GRAHAME, KENNETH. The Golden Age. London/Chicago: John Lane/Stone & Kimball, 1895. 1st (British) ed. Inscribed attachment. Blue cl (extrems sl rubbed), gilt. Good (2 bkpls, pencil mks; inner hinge sl cracking) in 1/2 morocco slipcase (rubbed). Reese. $185/£119

GRAHAME, KENNETH. The Golden Age. London: John Lane, 1915. 1st ed. Frontis, 18 color plts. Dec grn cl. Good in dj. Karmiole. $85/£54

GRAHAME, KENNETH. The Headswoman. NY/London: John Lane, Bodley Head, 1898. 1st separate ed. (Ink name ep, spine sl tanned), else VG in pict wrappers (sm mend lower corner, fore-edge). Reese. $60/£38

GRAHAME, KENNETH. The Wind in the Willows. London: Methuen, (1908). 1st ed. 8vo. Gilt-pict blue cl (lt rubbed, spine base sl rubbed; inscrip, sig). Swann*. $1,265/£811

GRAHAME, KENNETH. The Wind in the Willows. NY: Scribner, (1908). 1st Amer ed. Pub's 1908 cat. Grn cl, gilt. (Spine, bds sunned), else Lovely. Metropolitan*. $143/£92

GRAHAME, KENNETH. The Wind in the Willows. London, (1951). 100th ed. One of 500 numbered. 4to. 12 tipped-in color plts by Arthur Rackham. Orig cream leather, gilt. Swann*. $1,265/£811

GRAHAME, KENNETH. The Wind in the Willows. NY, 1914. 8th ptg, Nov 1914. Teg. VG + in gilt-lettered cl (spine sunned). Smith. $20/£13

GRAHAME, KENNETH. The Wind in the Willows. NY: Scribner, 1925. 1st ed thus. 8vo. 351pp; 12 full-pg color illus by Nancy Barnhart. Illus eps. Blue cl, illus cvr. Fine in Good orig box (bottom corners taped). Dower. $75/£48

GRAHAME, KENNETH. The Wind in the Willows. NY: LEC, 1940. One of 2020 numbered, signed by Bruce Rogers (designer). 16 tipped-in color plts by Arthur Rackham. Teg, untrimmed, partly unopened. Tan buckram, patterned lt yellow-orange bds (lt worn, bumped, sm holes spine top, ends sl stained), gilt. Text VG (bkpl). Baltimore*. $270/£173

GRAHAME, KENNETH. The Wind in the Willows. NY: LEC, 1940. 1st ed w/Rackham's illus. Ltd to 1500 signed by Bruce Rogers (designer). 4to. Cl-backed bds. (Spine sl foxed), o/w Fine in slipcase (lt worn). Jaffe. $650/£417

GRAHAME, KENNETH. The Wind in the Willows. NY: Heritage, 1944. 11th ed. Arthur Rackham (illus). 6 1/2 x 10. 190pp. VG in slipcase. Cattermole. $30/£19

GRAHAME, KENNETH. The Wind in the Willows. NY: Viking, 1983. 1st ed. John Burningham (illus) 6 1/2 x 9 1/2. 240pp. Fine in dj. Cattermole. $40/£26

GRAINGE, WILLIAM. The Castles and Abbeys of Yorkshire. York: John Sampson, 1855. viii,382,(i)pp; 8 full-pg plts. Blind-stamped cl gilt. VG. Hollett. $94/£60

GRAN, TRYGGVE. The Norwegian with Scott. England, 1984. Fine in dj. High Latitude. $25/£16

Grand Army Blue Book, Edition of 1912. Phila, 1913. Signed by 'T.E. Blanchard, 1912, Judge Advocate.' (Cvr sl worn), o/w Fine. Pratt. $35/£22

Grand Master; or Adventures of Qui Hi? in Hindostan. (By William Combe.) London: Tegg, 1816. 1st ed, w/frontis dated Oct 1, 1815. Lacks cancel (C8). Has errata slip at end. Fldg hand-colored frontis 'map,' tp, 25 hand-colored aquatint plts, 1 sepia plt by Thomas Rowlandson. Later 1/4 calf, flamed bds (extrems lt rubbed). Swann*. $488/£313

GRAND, GORDON. Colonel Weatherford and His Friends. NY, 1933. One of 1450. Good (presentation; lt wear). Cullen. $45/£29

GRAND, GORDON. Colonel Weatherford and His Friends. NY: Derrydale, 1933. Ltd to 1450. VG. October Farm. $65/£42

GRAND, GORDON. Colonel Weatherford and His Friends. NY: Derrydale, 1933. 1st ed. One of 1450. Red cl, gilt. (Spine dull), else Fine. Cummins. $65/£42

GRAND, GORDON. Redmond C. Stewart. Foxhunter and Gentleman of Maryland. NY: Scribner, 1938. 1st ed. Grn linen bds, vellum spine. Fine. Appelfeld. $100/£64

GRAND, GORDON. Redmond C. Stewart: Foxhunter and Gentleman of Maryland. NY: Scribner, 1938. 1st Amer ed. 1/4 Japan vellum over cl (top edge, upper spine panel faded, dknd). Nice (eps dknd). Hermitage. $100/£64

GRAND, W. JOSEPH. Illustrated History of the Union Stockyards. Chicago, (1901). (Cvrs heavily soiled, stained.) King. $60/£38

Grandes Heures of Jean, Duke of Berry. NY: Braziller, (1971). 110 full-pg facs color plts. Maroon cl. Good in illus dj. Karmiole. $100/£64

Grandmamma Easy's General Tom Thumb. (By Charles Stratton.) Boston/Nashua: Brown, Bozin/N.P. Greene, n.d. (c. 1850). Lg 8vo. Color woodcut frontis. VG in dec wraps (backstrip reinforced). Dramatis Personae. $150/£96

GRANGER, BYRD H. Arizona Place Names. Tucson, 1960. Gold cl. NF. Five Quail. $55/£35

GRANGER, LEWIS. Letters of Lewis Granger. L.A.: Glen Dawson, 1959. One of 250. Facs photo tipped in. Dawson. $75/£48

GRANIT, RAGNAR. Charles Scott Sherrington. NY, 1967. 1st ed. VG in dj. Argosy. $45/£29

GRANIT, RAGNAR. Receptors and Sensory Perception. New Haven: Yale Univ, (1956). 8vo. VG in dj. Argosy. $500/£321

GRANT, BLANCHE C. (ed). Kit Carson's Own Story of His Life. Taos, NM, 1926. Frontis. VG in ptd wrappers (sm splits spine ends, sl creases). Howes C182. Cahan. $100/£64

GRANT, BLANCHE C. When Old Trails Were New, the Story of Taos. NY, 1934. 1st ed. (Spine faded), o/w VG. Turpen. $95/£61

GRANT, CHARLES L. The Soft Whisper of the Dead. West Kingston: Grant, 1982. 1st ed. Fine in NF dj. Other Worlds. $25/£16

GRANT, DOUGLAS. The Cock Lane Ghost. NY: Macmillan, 1965. 1st ed. London map eps. Frontis, 7 plts. White linen. VG in pict dj (sl worn). Hartfield. $65/£42

GRANT, GEORGE M. Ocean to Ocean. Sandford Fleming's Expedition Through Canada in 1872. Canada/London, 1873. Frontis, xiv,371pp (hole in several ll incl tp, lt foxing; fr hinge cracked). Gilt cl (worn, frayed, soiled). Sound. *Reese*. $225/£144

GRANT, JERRY V. and DOUGLAS R. ALLEN. Shaker Furniture Makers. Hanover/London: Hancock Shaker Village, 1989. 1st ed. As New in illus dj. *Cahan*. $25/£16

GRANT, JOY. Harold Monro and the Poetry Bookshop. London: Routledge/Kegan Paul, (1967). Frontis. Red bds. Fine in dj. *Heller*. $30/£19

GRANT, JULIA DENT. The Personal Memoirs of Julia Dent Grant. John Y. Simon (ed). NY, (1975). 1st ed. VG+ in dj (sl worn). *Pratt*. $32/£21

GRANT, MAURICE HAROLD. A Chronological History of the Old English Landscape Painters. London/Leigh-on-Sea, n.d./1947. 3 vols. (Vols 1 & 2 lt soiled, rubbed.) *Edwards*. $273/£175

GRANT, MAXWELL. The Living Shadow: A Detective Novel. NY: Street & Smith, (1933). 1st ed. (Fr hinge starting, spine foxed), else VG+. *Other Worlds*. $75/£48

GRANT, MAXWELL. Norgil: More Tales of Prestigitection. NY: Mysterious, 1979. 1st ed. Fine in dj (sm closed tears spine base). *Mordida*. $35/£22

GRANT, U. S. Personal Memoirs. NY: Charles Webster, 1885-1886. 1st ed. 2 vols. NF. *Beasley*. $85/£54

GRANT, U. S. Personal Memoirs. NY: Chas Webster, 1885-1886. 1st ed. 2 vols. (Sl foxing, owner stamps; sl rubbed.) *Waverly**. $77/£49

GRANT, U. S. Personal Memoirs. NY, 1885-86. 1st ed. 2 vols. 584; 647 w/index pp. Gilt-dec grn cl. (Extrems bumped, worn; cvrs rubbed), else Good. *King*. $85/£54

GRANTHAM, A. E. Hills of Blue. London, 1927. 1st ed. 19 ports. *Edwards*. $44/£28

GRANTHAM, A. E. Hills of Blue. London: Methuen, 1927. 1st ed. Frontis, 15 plts. (Cl sl rubbed, spine top sl frayed), o/w VG. *Worldwide*. $45/£29

GRANVILLE-SMITH, W. Drawings by...and Others. NY: E.R. Herrick, 1898. 22 color plts. Linen spine, dec paper bds (lt sunned). Orig box (broken). *Metropolitan**. $402/£258

GRASS, GUNTER. Dog Years. Ralph Manheim (trans). NY: Harcourt, Brace & World, (1965). 1st ed. NF in dj. *Antic Hay*. $35/£22

GRASS, GUNTER. The Flounder. Ralph Manheim (trans). London: Secker & Warburg, (1978). 1st Eng ed. Fine in NF dj. *Antic Hay*. $25/£16

GRASS, GUNTER. The Flounder. NY: LEC, 1975. Ltd to 1000 signed. 3 vols. Grey Italian bk cl, natural eelskin spines. VF in slipcase (lt soiled). *Truepenny*. $350/£224

GRASS, GUNTER. The Flounder. Ralph Manheim (trans). NY: LEC, 1985. Ltd to 1500 numbered, signed. 3 vols. Eel skin, cl. Fine in orig cl-cvrd slipcase. *Antic Hay*. $475/£304

GRASS, GUNTER. Kinderlied. Northridge, CA: Lord John, 1982. One of 300 numbered. Signed. Illus 1/4 cl, paper-cvrd bds. Fine. *Lame Duck*. $150/£96

GRASS, GUNTER. Local Anaesthetic. NY, (1969). 1st ed. Signed. VG in dj. *Argosy*. $60/£38

GRASS, GUNTER. Local Anaesthetic. NY, 1970. 1st Amer ed. NF in NF dj. *Polyanthos*. $25/£16

GRASS, GUNTER. Selected Poems. NY: Harcourt Brace & World, 1966. 1st US ed. Fine in VG- dj (price-clipped, chipped, torn). *Lame Duck*. $35/£22

GRASS, GUNTER. The Tin Drum. Ralph Manheim (trans). London: Secker & Warburg, 1962. 1st Eng ed. VG in dj. *Hadley*. $78/£50

GRASS, GUNTER. The Tin Drum. NY: Pantheon, 1962. 1st ed. (Price fep; spine lt sunned), else Fine in NF dj. *Beasley*. $45/£29

GRASS, GUNTHER. Dog Years. NY, 1965. 1st ed. VG in VG dj. *Smith*. $15/£10

GRATTEN, J. H. G. and CHARLES SINGER. Anglo-Saxon Magic and Medicine. London, 1952. 1st ed. VG. *Fye*. $125/£80

GRATWICK, WILLIAM. My, This Must Have Been a Beautiful Place When It Was Kept Up. Pavilion, NY: William Gratwick, 1965. 1st ed. Ltd to 1000 signed. (Dec labels on cl lt soiled), else Fine. *Cahan*. $50/£32

GRATWICK, WILLIAM. The Truth, Tall Tales and Blatant Lies. Rochester: Visual Studies Workshop, 1981. 1st ed. Fine in dec stiff wrappers. *Cahan*. $35/£22

GRAU, SHIRLEY ANN. The Black Prince and Other Stories. NY, 1955. 1st bk. Cl-backed bds (sl bumped, rubbed). Nice (name) in dj (torn). *Clearwater*. $39/£25

GRAU, SHIRLEY ANN. The House on Coliseum Street. NY: Knopf, 1961. 1st ed. (Ink name fep), o/w VG in dj (chipped). *Hermitage*. $35/£22

GRAVES, ALFRED P. (ed). Welsh Poetry Old and New in English Verse. London: Longmans, Green, 1912. 1st ed (2000 ptd). Grn cl stamped in black/red. (Lt soil spine), o/w VG. *Reese*. $85/£54

GRAVES, C. B. et al. Catalogue of the Flowering Plants and Ferns of Connecticut. Hartford, 1910. VG- (blind stamp) in wrappers (name). *Brooks*. $35/£22

GRAVES, C. L. The Life and Letters of Sir George Grove, C.B. London: Macmillan, 1903. Good. *Scribe's Perch**. $16/£10

GRAVES, CHARLES and HENRY LONGHURST. Candid Caddies. London: Duckworth, (1935). 1st ed. Cl-backed pict bds. (Sl soiled, pencil mustache to character fr cvr), else VG. *Pacific**. $86/£55

GRAVES, CHARLES L. Mr. Punch's History of Modern England. London: Cassell, 1921. 2 vols. (Vol 1 frontis detached but present; sl foxed.) Dec gilt-stamped cl. *Argosy*. $125/£80

GRAVES, J. A. My Seventy Years in California 1857-1927. L.A.: Times-Mirror, 1927. 1st ed. Good. *Lien*. $45/£29

GRAVES, JOHN. Goodbye to a River. NY: Knopf, (1960). 1st ed. Fine in NF dj. *Pettler & Lieberman*. $60/£38

GRAVES, JOHN. Goodbye to a River. NY: Knopf, 1960. 1st ed. Map. Good in dj. *Dumont*. $50/£32

GRAVES, KERSEY. The World's Sixteen Crucified Saviors. NY: Truth Seeker Co, 1960. 6th ed. Gray cl. Fine in VG dj (spine tail lacks piece; price-clipped). *Blue Mountain*. $25/£16

GRAVES, ROBERT (ed). The Less Familiar Nursery Rhymes. Augustan Books, (1927). 1st Eng ed. (Dusty, foxed, inscrip.) Wrappers (spine worn, sl chipped). *Clearwater*. $31/£20

GRAVES, ROBERT and SPIKE MILLIGAN. Dear Robert, Dear Spike, Correspondence. P. Scudamore (ed). Stroud, 1991. 1st ed. VG in dj. *Typographeum*. $18/£12

GRAVES, ROBERT. At the Gate. N.p. (London): Privately ptd, 1974. One of 500 numbered, signed. Fine in Fine dj. *Lenz*. $200/£128

GRAVES, ROBERT. Beyond Giving. N.p. (London): Privately ptd, 1969. One of 500 numbered, signed. Fine in Fine dj. *Lenz*. $200/£128

GRAVES, ROBERT. The Big Green Book. (N.p.): Crowell-Collier, (1962). 1st illus ed. Maurice Sendak (illus). Pict lime-grn bds. (Edge bumped), else Fine. *Bromer*. $85/£54

GRAVES, ROBERT. The Big Green Book. Crowell-Collier, 1968. 1st ed thus. Maurice Sendak (illus). Fine in Fine dj. *Certo*. $30/£19

GRAVES, ROBERT. Claudius the God. NY, 1935. 1st Amer ed. VG + in Good dj (chipped, spine lacks piece). *Warren.* $75/£48

GRAVES, ROBERT. Collected Poems. NY, 1961. 1st Amer ed. Fine (sl rubbed) in dj (spine sl sunned, 2 sm tears, few chips). *Polyanthos.* $25/£16

GRAVES, ROBERT. Colophon to Love Respelt. N.p. (London): Privately ptd, 1967. One of 350 numbered, signed. Fine in Fine dj. *Lenz.* $200/£128

GRAVES, ROBERT. The Common Asphodel. London, 1949. 1st ed. Frontis. Fine in dj. *Petersfield.* $23/£15

GRAVES, ROBERT. Contemporary Techniques of Poetry. London: Hogarth, 1925. 1st ed. Good in wrappers (foxing; cvrs soiled, faded; spine split, chipped; sm label inside back cvr). *Virgo.* $78/£50

GRAVES, ROBERT. The English Ballad. London: Benn, 1927. 1st Eng ed. (Name; spine sl faded, edgeworn, cvrs sl mkd). *Clearwater.* $39/£25

GRAVES, ROBERT. Fairies and Fusiliers. 1917. 1st ed. (Cl sl soiled, spine sl faded), o/w VG. *Words Etc.* $70/£45

GRAVES, ROBERT. The Feather Bed. Richmond: Hogarth, 1923. 1st ed. One of 250. Uncut. Dec pink bds (spine chipped, bds stained, mkd). *Macdonnell.* $75/£48

GRAVES, ROBERT. Goodby to All That. Folio Soc, 1981. 1st ed. Illus cl. Fine in slipcase. *Words Etc.* $28/£18

GRAVES, ROBERT. The Green-Sailed Vessel. N.p. (London): Privately ptd, 1971. One of 500 numbered, signed. Fine in Fine dj. *Lenz.* $200/£128

GRAVES, ROBERT. Hercules, My Shipmate. NY: Creative Age, 1945. (Spine sl soiled), else Fine in dj (lt used). *Beasley.* $35/£22

GRAVES, ROBERT. Homer's Daughter. London: Cassell, (1955). 1st ed. NF in dj (lt wear, few sm tears). *Antic Hay.* $75/£48

GRAVES, ROBERT. I, Claudius. London: Arthur Barker, 1934. 1st ed. Black cl (spine head worn). *Appelfeld.* $50/£32

GRAVES, ROBERT. The Islands of Unwisdom. NY, 1949. 1st Amer ed. Fine (spine sl rubbed) in dj (few pieces missing, sm tear, sl rubbed). *Polyanthos.* $35/£22

GRAVES, ROBERT. King Jesus. NY: Creative Age, 1946. Correct 1st ed. Fine in dj (lt used, spine sl soiled, sl faded). *Beasley.* $45/£29

GRAVES, ROBERT. Lars Porsena: Or the Future of Swearing and Improper Language. London/NY: Kegan Paul et al/E.P. Dutton, (1927). 1st ed. Glazed black paper over bds, ptd labels. VG (eps sl offset; edges foxed). *Cahan.* $35/£22

GRAVES, ROBERT. Love Respelt Again. GC: Doubleday, (1969). One of 1000 numbered, signed. Fine in Fine dj. *Lenz.* $125/£80

GRAVES, ROBERT. Love Respelt Again. NY, 1969. One of 1000 signed. Amer issue of 1st ed. Fine in dj (sl dusty). *Clearwater.* $86/£55

GRAVES, ROBERT. Mammon and the Black Goddess. London, 1965. 1st Eng ed. Bright in dj (sl tanned, foxed). *Clearwater.* $39/£25

GRAVES, ROBERT. Mock Beggar Hall. London: Hogarth, 1924. 1st ed. Most pp unopened. Ptd bds (lt wear, spine nick). NF, issued w/o dj. *Antic Hay.* $375/£240

GRAVES, ROBERT. The More Deserving Cases. (N.p.): Marlborough College, 1962. One of 400 bound in full morocco, signed. (Lt scratching rear bd), else Fine. *Between The Covers.* $150/£96

GRAVES, ROBERT. Mrs. Fisher or The Future of Humour. Kegan Paul, 1928. 1st UK ed. VG + in VG dj (sm closed tears; sl loss spine top, strengthened). *Williams.* $117/£75

GRAVES, ROBERT. My Head! My Head! NY: Knopf, 1925. 1st Amer ed. One of 500. Color dec cl (spine bumped, sm chip), ptd yellow paper labels spine, fr cvr. NF in Fair ptd dj (chipped, piece out rear flap, fr blurb detached). *Blue Mountain.* $175/£112

GRAVES, ROBERT. Occupation: Writer. London: Cassell, 1951. 1st UK ed. Fine in dj (lt worn). *Hermitage.* $65/£42

GRAVES, ROBERT. On English Poetry. Heinemann, 1922. 1st ed. (Cl sl rubbed, dknd, sl nick to fore-edge; label remains spine foot, bkpl, name.) *Poetry Bookshop.* $47/£30

GRAVES, ROBERT. Over the Brazier. Poetry Bookshop, 1916. 1st ed, 1st bk. (Foxed.) Gray paper pict wrappers (sl creased). *Sotheby's*.* $753/£483

GRAVES, ROBERT. Poems 1926-1930. London: Heinemann, 1931. One of 1000 ptd. Patterned cl. Very Bright in dj (chipped, torn). *Clearwater.* $94/£60

GRAVES, ROBERT. Poems, 1953. London: Cassell, 1953. 1st ed. One of 250 numbered, signed. Cl-backed bds (extrems sl rubbed). VG (lacks plain tissue dj). *Cahan.* $275/£176

GRAVES, ROBERT. Poems. NY: LEC, 1980. One of 2000 numbered, signed by Freeman Keith and Paul Hogarth (illus). Fine in pub's slipcase. *Hermitage.* $85/£54

GRAVES, ROBERT. Poetic Unreason and Other Studies. Cecil Palmer, 1925. 1st Eng ed. Bright (foxing). *Clearwater.* $101/£65

GRAVES, ROBERT. The Poor Boy Who Followed His Star. NY: Doubleday, 1968. 1st ed. Alice Meyer-Wallace (illus). 6 1/2 x 9 1/2. 42pp. VG in dj. *Cattermole.* $50/£32

GRAVES, ROBERT. Seventeen Poems Missing from Love Respelt. N.p. (London): Privately ptd, 1966. One of 300 numbered, signed. Fine in Fine dj. *Lenz.* $200/£128

GRAVES, ROBERT. The Siege and Fall of Troy. London: Cassell, 1962. 1st Eng ed. Walter Hodges (illus). Nice in dj. *Clearwater.* $47/£30

GRAVES, ROBERT. Ten Poems More. Paris: Hours Press, 1930. 1st ed. One of 200 signed. Pict bds, black morocco spine (extrems worn). *Appelfeld.* $200/£128

GRAVES, ROBERT. They Hanged My Sainted Billy. GC, 1957. 1st Amer ed. VG in dj (sl rubbed). *King.* $25/£16

GRAVES, ROBERT. They Hanged My Saintly Billy. GC: Doubleday, 1957. 1st Amer ed. Fine in dj (sl wear, soil). *Antic Hay.* $30/£19

GRAVES, ROBERT. Timeless Meeting. N.p. (London): Privately ptd, 1973. One of 500 numbered, signed. Fine in Fine dj. *Lenz.* $200/£128

GRAVES, ROBERT. Watch the North Wind Rise. NY, 1949. 1st Amer ed. Fine in dj. *Polyanthos.* $50/£32

GRAVES, ROBERT. Watch the North Wind Rise. NY: Creative Age, 1949. 1st ed. Signed in full on tipped-in leaf, as issued. VG (ink name, date) in dj (sl chipped). *Waverly*.* $38/£24

GRAY, A. Darwiniana: Essays and Reviews Pertaining to Darwinism. NY: Appleton, (1888). 396pp + ads. Blind-stamped dec cl. VG + (ex-lib, bkpl). *Mikesh.* $37/£24

GRAY, A. W. Bino. NY: Dutton, 1988. 1st ed. VF in dj. *Mordida.* $45/£29

GRAY, ANDREA. Ansel Adams: An American Place, 1936. (Tucson): Center for Creative Photography, Univ of AZ, 1982. 1st ed. 46 b/w plts. Fine in pict stiff wrappers. *Cahan.* $25/£16

GRAY, ANDREA. Ansel Adams: An American Place, 1936. (Tucson): Center for Creative Photography, Univ of AZ, 1982. 1st ed. inscribed. 46 b/w plts. NF in pict stiff wrappers. *Cahan.* $65/£42

GRAY, ARTHUR. A Chapter in the Early Life of Shakespeare. CUP, 1926. Map frontis, 8 plts. Uncut. 1/2 cl, paper bds (backstrip faded, corners rubbed). *Peter Taylor.* $22/£14

GRAY, ASA. The Botanical Text-Book. NY: Wiley & Putnam, 1842. 1st ed. (Foxing, dampstaining.) White paper-cvrd spine, patterned paper-cvrd bds (rebound). *Metropolitan*.* $230/£147

GRAY, ASA. Elements of Botany. NY: G&C Carvill, 1836. 1st ed. (Foxing, dampstaining.) Patterned paper-cvrd spine, white paper-cvrd bds (rebound). *Metropolitan*.* $460/£295

GRAY, ASA. First Lessons in Botany and Vegetable Physiology. Ivison & Phinney, 1857. 1st ed. 236pp. Very Nice (new eps; rebacked). *Bookcell.* $85/£54

GRAY, ASA. Manual of the Botany of the Northern United States.... NY: Putnam, 1856. 2nd ed. 14 plts. (Spine ends, corners rubbed.) *Sadlon.* $250/£160

GRAY, BASIL. The English Print. A&C Black, 1937. 1st ed. 24 collotype plts. VG in dj (rubbed). *Cox.* $31/£20

GRAY, CHARLES GLASS. Off at Sunrise—the Overland Journal of Charles Glass Gray. San Marino: Huntington Library, 1976. 1st ed. Blue cl, gilt. As New in As New dj. *Parmer.* $25/£16

GRAY, EDWARD. Leif Eriksson Discoverer of America A.D. 1003. NY: OUP, 1930. 1st Amer ed. 22 maps, plts. (Cvrs sl soiled.) *Lefkowicz.* $60/£38

GRAY, EDWARD. William Gray of Salem, Merchant. Boston/NY, 1914. 1st ed. One of 500. Paper spine label. Fine. *Lefkowicz.* $90/£58

GRAY, G. J. A Bibliography of the Works of Sir Isaac Newton. Cambridge: Bowes & Bowes, 1907. 2nd ed. Frontis. Dj (sl defective). *Maggs.* $75/£48

GRAY, HENRY. Anatomy, Descriptive and Surgical. Phila: Henry C. Lea, 1865. 2nd Amer ed. xxxii,(33)-816pp; 395 engrs. Mod cl, orig morocco spine label. VG. *Glaser.* $285/£183

GRAY, HENRY. Anatomy, Descriptive and Surgical. T. Pickering Pick (ed). Phila, 1883. New Amer from 10th Eng ed. 1023pp. (Ex-lib; rebacked, orig spine label laid down.) *Goodrich.* $50/£32

GRAY, HUGH. Letters from Canada, Written During...1806, 1807, and 1808.... London: Longman, Hurst et al, 1809. (16),406pp, 3 fldg tables, lg fldg map (expertly repaired tear). Full calf. VG (sl foxing). *Cullen.* $400/£256

GRAY, JAMES. The Illinois. NY: Farrar & Rinehart, (1940). 1st ed. Pict ep. VG + in dj (lt worn). *Bohling.* $15/£10

GRAY, JOHN CHIPMAN and JOHN CODMAN ROPES. War Letters, 1862-1865. Boston/NY: Houghton Mifflin, 1927. 1st ed. Ltd to 1275. 2 ports, tissue guards. Unopened. NF in dj (soiled, few closed tears). *Cahan.* $100/£64

GRAY, JOHN HENRY. A Journey Round the World in the Years 1875-1876-1877. London, 1879. 1st ed. xv,612pp. Blind-emb cl (spine sl faded.) *Edwards.* $117/£75

GRAY, JOHN. Poems (1931) by John Gray. (London): Sheed & Ward, 1931. 1st ed. One of 200 ptd by Rene Hague and Eric Gill, w/woodcut illus on limitation pg. Fine in ptd wrappers, glassine dj (sl torn). *Holmes.* $250/£160

GRAY, MADELINE. Margaret Sanger. NY: Richard Marek, (1979). 1st ed. Fine in dj. *Glaser.* $30/£19

GRAY, NICHOLAS STUART. The Boys. NY: Meredith, 1964. 1st US ed. Robin Adler (photos). 6 1/2 x 10. 96pp. VG in dj. *Cattermole.* $20/£13

GRAY, NICOLETTE. Nineteenth Century Ornamented Typefaces. Berkeley: Univ of CA, (1976). Rev ed. (2 leaves in facs.) Dj. *Oak Knoll.* $95/£61

GRAY, NICOLETTE. The Painted Inscriptions of David Jones. London: Gordon Fraser, 1981. 1st ed. Fine in dj. *Michael Taylor.* $55/£35

GRAY, NICOLETTE. Rossetti, Dante and Ourselves. London: Faber & Faber, 1947. Fine in dj (smudged, sl chipped) in purple cl case. *Heller.* $45/£29

GRAY, NICOLETTE. XIXth Century Ornamented Types and Title Pages. London: Faber & Faber, (1951). 2nd ed. Fine in dj (several edge tears). *Dermont.* $25/£16

GRAY, NICOLETTE. XIXth Century Ornamented Types and Title Pages. London: Faber, 1938. 1st ed. 8 halftone plts. (Bkpl, margins pencilled; lt soiled.) *Cox.* $28/£18

GRAY, PRENTISS N. North American Big Game. Bridgeport, CT: Derrydale, (1934). Obl 8vo. Pict grn wrappers (sl worn). Provided protective bd case. *Oinonen*.* $800/£513

GRAY, PRENTISS N. Records of North American Big Game. NY: Derrydale, 1932. One of 500. 4to. Gilt-stamped buckram (sl worn, sl soiled; bkpl). *Oinonen*.* $600/£385

GRAY, S. O. British Sea-Weeds. London, 1867. xxiii,312pp, 24 ads; 16 hand-colored plts. Pict cl, gilt. Good. *Henly.* $75/£48

GRAY, THOMAS N. Common Sense and the Baby: A Book for Mothers. NY, 1907. 1st ed. VG (text marginally waterstained; sl worn). *Doctor's Library.* $35/£22

GRAY, THOMAS. Elegy Written in a Country Churchyard. (London: Edward Arnold, 1900.) Ltd to 125. 8vo. 13pp. Full-pg hand-colored wood engr by George Thomson. Full vellum over bds, blind-stamped w/rose logo, motto, 'Soul is Form.' VF. *Bromer.* $550/£353

GRAY, THOMAS. Elegy Written in a Country Churchyard. London: LEC, 1938. #904/1500 numbered, signed by Agnes Miller Parker (illus). Full pict cl stamped in silver. Fine in glassine wrapper, pub's slipcase (sl mkd). *Hermitage.* $250/£160

GRAY, THOMAS. Poems and Letters. London: Chiswick, 1867. 1st ed. xvi,416pp; 4 mtd plts. Aeg. Orig calf, gilt. (Sl rubbed, foxed), o/w Beautiful. *Karmiole.* $200/£128

GRAY, THOMAS. Poems by Mr. Gray. London: J. Dodsley, 1768. New ed. Contemp calf (rebacked). VG. *Captain's Bookshelf.* $175/£112

GRAY, THOMAS. The Poems of Mr. Gray. London: H. Hughs, 1775. 2nd ed. Frontis port, 416,110pp; 1/2 title present. Old calf (rebacked, extrems rubbed, sl chipped). *Karmiole.* $175/£112

GRAY, THOMAS. The Poems of...a New Edition Adorned with Plates. S. Jones (ed). London, 1800. 6 engr plts. Aeg. Orig cross-grained black morocco. (3 inscrips, bkpl; fr outer hinge rubbed, started), o/w VG. *New Hampshire*.* $100/£64

GRAY, WOOD. The Hidden Civil War, The Story of the Copperheads. NY, 1942. 1st ed. VG + in VG + dj. *Pratt.* $30/£19

GRAY, WOOD. The Hidden Civil War. NY, 1942. 1st ed. *Wantagh.* $25/£16

GRAYDON, NELL S. Tales of Columbia. Columbia: R.L. Bryan, 1964. 1st ed. Fine in VG dj. *Connolly.* $35/£22

Great American Menagerie. NY: McLoughlin, 1889. 5 full-pg, 1 db-pg chromolitho illus. Chromolitho pict wraps (edges sl chipped). *Dramatis Personae.* $95/£61

Great Menagerie. London: Kestrel Bks, 1979. 6pp. Pict bds. *King.* $45/£29

Great Metropolis. Phelps' New York City Guide to All That Can Be Seen, and How to See It. (By Humphrey Phelps.) NY: Amer News, c. 1865. 70,(1)pp; lg fldg map, fldg view. (Cl worn.) Contents VG. *New Hampshire**. $140/£90

Great Ones of Ancient Egypt. NY: Scribner, 1930. 1st ed. 17 mtd plts. Brn cl, gilt. Fine. *Appelfeld.* $125/£80

Greatest Plague of Life. (By Augustus Septimus Mayhew.) London, n.d. (1847). 1st ed. 285pp; 12 full-pg plts by George Cruikshank. 1/2 leather, marbled bds, edges, eps. (Scuffed.) *King.* $95/£61

GREATHOUSE, CHARLES H. Ranch Life in the Old West. Hollywood: Asgard House, (1971). 1st ed. #491/1000. Fine in dj. *Perier.* $50/£32

GREBANIER, B. The Great Shakespeare Forgery. London: Heinemann, 1966. Black cl. Dj. *Maggs.* $19/£12

Greek Portrait. London: Nonesuch, 1934. One of 425 numbered. Pict silk-cvrd bds. Slipcase. *Swann**. $161/£103

GREELEY, HORACE. An Overland Journey, from New York to San Francisco, in the Summer of 1859. NY, 1860. 386pp + 10pp ads at rear (lacks rep, staining to pp not affecting text). Good-. Howes G355. *Scribe's Perch**. $50/£32

GREELY, ADOLPHUS W. Handbook of Alaska. NY: Scribner, 1909. Lg fldg map in pocket. VG. *High Latitude.* $40/£26

GREELY, ADOLPHUS W. Handbook of Alaska. NY: Scribner, 1909. 1st ed. Map rear pocket. (1/2 inch square out of spine bottom), else VG. *Perier.* $60/£38

GREELY, ADOLPHUS W. International Polar Expedition: U.S. Expedition to Lady Franklin Bay.... Washington, 1888. 2 vols. (Sl loose), else VG. *Metropolitan**. $115/£74

GREELY, ADOLPHUS W. Three Years of Arctic Service. NY: Scribner, 1886. 1st ed. 2 vols. xxv,428; xii,1l.,444pp; 43 plts. Very Nice set (sl shelfworn). *Parmer.* $325/£208

GREELY, ADOLPHUS W. Three Years of Arctic Service. An Account...of 1881-84. NY: Scribner, 1886. 1st ed. 2 vols. xxvi,428; xiv,444pp; 9 maps (several fldg, 1 in rear pocket). Silver-lettered color pict blue cl (sl worn). Clean set. *House.* $350/£224

GREELY, ADOLPHUS W. Three Years of Arctic Service...Lady Franklin Bay Expedition of 1881-84.... NY: Scribner, 1886. 1st ed. 2 vols. Lg fldg map in pocket vol 2. Pict cl (spine ends, corners sl rubbed), gilt. (Vol 2 pg edges lt dampstained), o/w Clean. *Sadlon.* $200/£128

GREELY, ADOLPHUS W. Three Years of Arctic Service: An Account of the Lady Franklin Bay Expedition of 1881-1884. NY: Scribner, 1886. 1st ed. 2 vols. Blue dec cl. (Bkpl), else VG. *Perier.* $250/£160

GREEN, ANNA KATHARINE. The Forsaken Inn. NY: Robert Bonner's Sons, (1895). 1st Amer ed. Top edges mainly unopened. NF in ptd wraps (spine mended, lt chipped). *Polyanthos.* $75/£48

GREEN, ANNA KATHERINE. The House of the Whispering Pines. NY: Putnam, 1910. 1st ed. Signed w/8-line poem. (Spine sl dull), o/w Fine. *Mordida.* $125/£80

GREEN, BEN. Biography of the Tennessee Walking Horse. Nashville, 1960. VG. *October Farm.* $65/£42

GREEN, BEN. A Thousand Miles of Mustangin'. Flagstaff: Northland, 1972. 1st ed. VG in VG dj. *October Farm.* $125/£80

GREEN, BERTHA DE VERE. A Collector's Guide to Fans. London: Muller, 1975. 1st ed. 40 color plts. VG in dj (sl creased, price-clipped). *Hollett.* $70/£45

GREEN, CHARLES O. An Incident in the Battle of Middleburg, Virginia. Providence, RI, 1911. 1st ed. Ltd to 250. PNRISSHS Series 7, #3. NF in ptd wrappers. *Mcgowan.* $45/£29

GREEN, CHARLES R. Early Days in Kansas. Olathe, KS, Jan 1913. Pict wraps (spine chipped; smoke/damp staining). *Bohling.* $45/£29

GREEN, CHARLES R. A Historical Pamphlet. (Olathe?, KS: Privately ptd), 1914. 1st ed. 2 plts. (Sl damping), else VG in orig ptd wrappers. *Mcgowan.* $175/£112

GREEN, CHARLES R. History of the Presbyterian Church, Lyndon, Kansas. (Lyndon): C.R. Green's Ptg, 1901. 2 plts. Ptd wraps (soiled, lt chipped; text pp dknd). *Bohling.* $35/£22

GREEN, CHARLES R. The Indians of Huron County, Ohio, 100 Years Ago. Lyndon, (KS), 1905. Ptd wraps (chipped, sm paper label added). *Bohling.* $20/£13

GREEN, DAVID. Gardener to Queen Anne: Henry Wise (1653-1738) and the Formal Garden. London: Geoffrey Cumberlege/OUP, 1956. 36pp b/w plts. NF in dj. *Captain's Bookshelf.* $125/£80

GREEN, DAVID. Grinling Gibbons. London, 1964. Good in dj. *Washton.* $100/£64

GREEN, FRANCES H. Biography of Mrs. Semantha Mettle. NY: Harmonial Assoc, 1853. 1st ed. Frontis port. 115pp. VG (sl worn). *Second Life.* $225/£144

GREEN, HARRY C. and MARY W. Pioneer Mothers of America. NY: Putnam, 1912. 1st ed. 3 vols. *Ginsberg.* $150/£96

GREEN, HARRY PLUNKET. Pilot, and Other Stories. Macmillan, 1916. 1st ed. Lg 8vo. 229pp; 8 color plts, 31 b/w illus by H. J. Ford. (Rubbed), else VG. *Bookmark.* $28/£18

GREEN, HENRY. Concluding. Hogarth, 1948. 1st ed. Nice in dj (chipped, strengthened). *Ash.* $70/£45

GREEN, HENRY. Doting. London, 1952. 1st ed. VG in dj (frayed). *Typographeum.* $35/£22

GREEN, HENRY. Loving. London: Hogarth, 1945. 1st Eng ed. Nice (spine sl faded, foxed). *Clearwater.* $62/£40

GREEN, HENRY. Nothing. London: Hogarth, 1950. 1st ed. Fine in dj (price-clipped). *Captain's Bookshelf.* $100/£64

GREEN, HENRY. Nothing. NY: Viking, 1950. 1st ed. NF in dj (sl worn). *Antic Hay.* $45/£29

GREEN, HENRY. Pack My Bag. A Self-Portrait. London: Hogarth, 1940. One of 1500 ptd. 1st issue. Red cl, gilt. NF (spine sl spotted). *Clearwater.* $156/£100

GREEN, HENRY. Party Going. NY: Viking, (1951). 1st ed. NF in VG dj (price-clipped). *Pettler & Lieberman.* $30/£19

GREEN, J. R. History of the English People. NY: Harper, n.d. 4 vols. 8 maps. Teg. Contemp 1/2 brn morocco, grn cl sides (lt scuffed, ends sl worn), ribbed gilt spines. *Waverly**. $38/£24

GREEN, J. R. A Short History of the English People. Mrs. J.R. Green & Miss Kate Norgate (eds). London, 1892-94. 4 vols. Uncut. 3/4 morocco (rubbed). *Oinonen**. $70/£45

GREEN, JOHNNY. Johnny Green of the Orphan Brigade. A. D. Kirwan (ed). N.p., (1956). 1st ed. Signed by Kirwan. VG+ in VG+ dj. *Pratt.* $70/£45

GREEN, JONATHAN (ed). Camera Work: A Critical Anthology. Millerton: Aperture, 1973. 1st ed. NF. *Cahan.* $100/£64

GREEN, KENSAL. Premature Epitaphs Mostly Written in Malice. Cecil Palmer, 1927. 1st ed. Ptd paper bds. VG. *Cox.* $23/£15

GREEN, MRS. J. R. Town Life in the Fifteenth Century. London, 1894. 2 vols. xvi,439; vii,476pp + (iv)pub's ads (feps lt browned, bkpl). *Edwards.* $78/£50

GREEN, PAUL. The Field God and In Abraham's Bosom. NY: McBride, 1928. Cl-backed floral bds, paper labels. VG. *Petrilla.* $25/£16

GREEN, PETER. The Sword of Pleasure. London: John Murray, 1957. 1st ed. Review copy w/pub's slip loosely inserted. Michael Ayrton (illus). (Feps sl browned, edges lt spotted.) Dj (price-clipped). *Hollett.* $39/£25

GREEN, R. The Works of John and Charles Wesley. A Bibliography. London, 1896. 1st ed. Single leaf extracted from Gooding Catalogue, Newcastle 1744 inserted loose. Blue cl (sl rubbed, sl bumped). *Maggs.* $156/£100

GREEN, RICHARD LANCELYN (ed). The Sherlock Holmes Letters. IA City: Univ of IA, (1986). 1st US ed. NF in NF dj. *Gravesend.* $30/£19

GREEN, ROBERT B. On the Arkansas Route to California in 1849. J.O. Oliphant (ed). Lewisburg, PA: Bucknell Univ, 1955. One of 350. Paper over bds, linen spine. VG in glassine dj (chipped). *Scribe's Perch*.* $42/£27

GREEN, THOMAS M. The Spanish Conspiracy.... Cincinnati, 1891. 1st ed. (Lt worn.) *Kane*.* $170/£109

GREEN, VICTOR H. (comp). The Negro Motorist Green Book. (NY: Victor H. Green, 1951.) VG in pict wraps. *Petrilla.* $250/£160

GREEN, VIVIAN H. The Swiss Alps. London, (1961). 1st ed. (Bumped), else Good in dj (worn). *King.* $25/£16

Green-House Companion.... (By J. C. Loudon.) London, 1832. 3rd ed. Hand-colored litho frontis. (Few leaves loose, margins frayed, joints cracked; ptd label defective.) *Maggs.* $47/£30

GREENAWAY, KATE. Almanack for 1883. London: Routledge, (1882). 4x3. (Lt foxing.) Gilt-dec cl bds. Attractive. *Metropolitan*.* $201/£129

GREENAWAY, KATE. Almanack for 1884. London: Routledge, (1883). 3 5/8x5 1/4. White wraps (lt soiled, sl edgeworn), gilt. *Metropolitan*.* $201/£129

GREENAWAY, KATE. Almanack for 1885. London: Routledge, (1884). 4x3. White bd (lt soiled, edgeworn), gilt, ruled lines. *Metropolitan*.* $201/£129

GREENAWAY, KATE. Almanack for 1885. London/NY: Routledge, n.d. (1884). 1st ed. 16mo. Blue ptd floral eps. Dk blue imitation morocco flexible bds (rubbed), gilt. *Oinonen*.* $80/£51

GREENAWAY, KATE. Kate Greenaway Pictures from Originals Presented by Her to John Ruskin and Other Personal Friends. London: Warne, 1921. 1st ed. Tall 4to. Port. Uncut. Gilt-lettered 2-tone cl (lt shelfworn). *Oinonen*.* $180/£115

GREENAWAY, KATE. Kate Greenaway's Alphabet. London: Routledge, n.d. Approx 2 1/2x3. Pict soft cvr (creased, loss of litho coating). *Metropolitan*.* $57/£37

GREENAWAY, KATE. Kate Greenaway's Birthday Book for Children. London: Routledge, (1880). 1st ed. Sq 16mo. 12 color plts. All edges yellow. Color-pict cl (sl worn, spotted). *Oinonen*.* $110/£71

GREENAWAY, KATE. Kate Greenaway's Book of Games. Routledge, n.d. (1889). 1st ed, 1st issue. 4to. 64pp; 24 full-pg engr plts. Cl spine, pict bds (dusty, sl rubbed, chipped). (Pencil mks 1 picture, rep), o/w Contents Clean. *Bookmark.* $179/£115

GREENAWAY, KATE. Kate Greenaway's Book of Games. London: Routledge, n.d. (1889). 1st ed. Edmund Evans (illus). Thin 4to. 64pp. Gilt-pict grn cl (worn, soiled). *Oinonen*.* $225/£144

GREENAWAY, KATE. Marigold Garden. London: Routledge, n.d. (1885). 4to. 60pp (foxed). Good-. *Scribe's Perch*.* $40/£26

GREENAWAY, KATE. Mother Goose or The Old Nursery Rhymes. London: Routledge, (1881). 2nd issue, reads 'Boys' instead of 'Boy' on last rhyme. Ed Evans (engrs). 12mo. 48pp (spotting several pp); 48 full-pg color illus. Olive eps. Cl-backed, latticed design dec bds (sl soiled, corners bumped, rear hinge sl cracked), pink cl spine. Good. *Dower.* $200/£128

GREENAWAY, KATE. Under the Window. NY: Routledge, n.d. 8vo. 64pp (foxing). Good. *Scribe's Perch*.* $29/£19

GREENAWAY, KATE. Under the Window.... NY: Routledge, n.d. (ca 1880). 1st US ed. 'End of Contents' p14; imprint of Wemple & Co., Art Lithographers, NY, on tp verso. Grn glazed pict bds (sl worn), blue cl spine. *Kane*.* $65/£42

GREENBERG, DAVID B. (comp). The Land That Our Fathers Plowed. Norman: Univ of OK, (1969). 1st ed. VG+ in dj (price-clipped). *Bohling.* $22/£14

GREENBERG, ERIC ROLFE. The Celebrant. Everest House, 1983. 1st ed. VG+ in VG+ dj. *Plapinger.* $85/£54

GREENBERG, ERIC ROLFE. The Celebrant. NY: Everest House, 1983. 1st ed, 1st bk. Fine (name) in Fine dj. *Else Fine.* $85/£54

GREENE, ALBERT G. Recollections of the Jersey Prison-Ship.... Providence: H.H. Brown, 1829. 1st ed. Engr fldg frontis, 167pp. Cl-backed marbled bds, ptd paper label (chipped). Howes D503. *M & S.* $200/£128

GREENE, FREDERICK DAVIS. Armenian Massacres. Henry Davenport Northrop (ed). Phila, 1896. xviii,512pp; fldg map. Illus cl (spine sl rubbed). *Edwards.* $55/£35

GREENE, G. A. Italian Lyrists of Today.... Elkin Mathews/John Lane. 1st ed. One of 1000 ptd. xxxi,(i),232pp + 16-pg cat. Teg, others uncut. (Sl rubbed, mkd.) *Cox.* $28/£18

GREENE, GEORGE W. Life of Nathanael Greene, Major-General in the Army of the Revolution. NY: Putnam, 1867-1871. 1st ed. 3 vols. (24),582,(2); (11),571; (9),514pp; fldg map. Contemp 1/2 calf (spines sl worn, hinge sprung). Howes G380. *Ginsberg.* $175/£112

GREENE, GRAHAM (ed). The Old School. London: Cape, (1934). 1st ed. Black cl (lt shelfworn). *Argosy.* $500/£321

GREENE, GRAHAM et al. Why Do I Write? London: Percival Marshall, 1948. 1st ed. NF in VG dj (edgetears). *Lame Duck.* $65/£42

GREENE, GRAHAM. Another Mexico. Viking, 1939. 1st US ed. One of 2000 ptd. VG in dj (sl browned, top edge lt chipped). *Williams.* $460/£295

GREENE, GRAHAM. Babbling April. Oxford: Blackwell, 1925. One of 500 ptd. *Clearwater.* $1,248/£800

GREENE, GRAHAM. The Bear Fell Free. London: Grayson & Grayson, 1935. 1st ed. Ltd to 285 signed. Fine. *Bromer.* $1,350/£865

GREENE, GRAHAM. Brighton Rock. Heinemann, 1938. 1st Eng ed. Presentation copy inscribed 'for Eric Quayle from Graham Greene.' (Lt foxing.) Red cl. *Sotheby's*.* $986/£632

GREENE, GRAHAM. Brighton Rock. NY: Viking, 1938. 1st ed. (Gutters dknd), else VG in dj (price-clipped, lt rubbed, chipped). *Hermitage.* $500/£321

GREENE, GRAHAM. Brighton Rock. NY: Viking, 1938. 1st ed. Inscribed presentation: 'For Eric Quayle—from Graham Greene Xmas 1983.' (Previous inscrip.) Black/red cl. *Sotheby's*.* $574/£368

GREENE, GRAHAM. British Dramatists. Collins, 1942. 1st UK ed. VG (ink name) in dj. *Williams.* $39/£25

GREENE, GRAHAM. British Dramatists. London, 1942. 1st Eng ed. (Sl bumped, rubbed.) Dj (sl frayed). *Clearwater.* $39/£25

GREENE, GRAHAM. Carving a Statue. Bodley Head, 1964. 1st UK ed. Fine in dj (sm closed tear). *Williams*. $62/£40

GREENE, GRAHAM. Collected Essays. London, (1969). 1st ed. Fine in dj. *Argosy*. $85/£54

GREENE, GRAHAM. Collected Essays. London, 1969. 1st ed. VG in dj (short closed tear). *Words Etc*. $28/£18

GREENE, GRAHAM. The Comedians. NY: Viking, (1966). 1st Amer ed. NF in dj (sl wear, price-clipped). *Antic Hay*. $25/£16

GREENE, GRAHAM. The Complaisant Lover. London: Heinemann, (1959). 1st ed. Fine in dj. *Hermitage*. $100/£64

GREENE, GRAHAM. Doctor Fischer of Geneva or the Bomb Party. NY: S&S, (1980). One of 500 numbered, signed. Fine in Fine slipcase. *Lenz*. $225/£144

GREENE, GRAHAM. Doctor Fischer of Geneva or The Bomb Party. Bodley Head, 1980. 1st issue, w/'leave alone' on pg 9. Fine in VG+ dj. *Williams*. $16/£10

GREENE, GRAHAM. The End of the Affair. NY: Viking, 1951. 1st ed. Tan cl. Fine in dj (lt rubbed). *Macdonnell*. $65/£42

GREENE, GRAHAM. The Great Jowett. London: Bodley Head, (1981). One of 525 numbered, signed. Fine. *Lenz*. $200/£128

GREENE, GRAHAM. A Gun for Sale. Melbourne: 'Truth' and 'Sportsman Limited,' 1944. 1st Australian ed. (Paper browned, sm dampstain lower edge some pp), else VG in wrappers. *Turtle Island*. $100/£64

GREENE, GRAHAM. How Father Quixote Became a Monsignor. L.A.: Sylvester & Orphanos, 1980. 1st Amer ed. #242/330 signed. Fine in pub's acetate dj. *Hermitage*. $125/£80

GREENE, GRAHAM. It's a Battlefield. Heinemann, (1934). 1st ed. Good (sl mks). *Ash*. $156/£100

GREENE, GRAHAM. It's a Battlefield. Doubleday Doran, 1934. 1st US ed. One of 1960 sold. VG+ in VG dj (sl browned, nicked, sl loss spine extrems, price-clipped). *Williams*. $507/£325

GREENE, GRAHAM. It's a Battlefield. Heinemann, 1934. 1st ed. Inscribed presentation. (Upper hinge repaired, sl foxed.) Black cl. *Sotheby's**. $718/£460

GREENE, GRAHAM. J'Accuse. London, 1982. 1st ed. Wraps. Fine in dj. *Polyanthos*. $25/£16

GREENE, GRAHAM. J'Accuse. London: Bodley Head, 1982. 1st ed. (Name fep), o/w VG in wrappers. *Virgo*. $16/£10

GREENE, GRAHAM. Journey Without Maps. London: Heinemann, (1936). 1st ed. Yellow cl. (Cvr edges dknd), o/w NF in dj (spine dknd, 1-inch chip spine heel, 2 sm chips). *Captain's Bookshelf*. $3,000/£1,923

GREENE, GRAHAM. Journey Without Maps. Doubleday Doran, 1936. 1st US ed. One of 2200 sold. NF in VG dj (sl stained). *Williams*. $460/£295

GREENE, GRAHAM. Journey Without Maps. Pan, 1948. 1st pb ed. (Sl dull), else Good in dec wraps. *Whiteson*. $8/£5

GREENE, GRAHAM. The Little Fire Engine. GC: Doubleday, (1973). Reissue. Edward Ardizzone (illus). Color illus bds. NF in VG dj (edges sl creased). *Bernard*. $60/£38

GREENE, GRAHAM. The Little Fire Engine. London: Bodley Head, 1973. 1st ed. Edward Ardizzone (illus). Pict bds. Mint in dj. *Hollett*. $133/£85

GREENE, GRAHAM. The Little Fire Engine. London: Max Parrish, n.d. (1950). Dorothy Craigie (illus). VG (paper browned; spine extrems rubbed) in dj (sm chips spine, corners; creased, nicked). *Gekoski*. $1,170/£750

GREENE, GRAHAM. The Little Horse Bus. London: Max Parris, 1952. Dorothy Craigie (illus). (Cvrs bowed), o/w Excellent in dj (sl chipped, torn). *Gekoski*. $468/£300

GREENE, GRAHAM. The Little Train. London: Bodley Head, (1973). 1st Eng ed. Ed Ardizzone (illus). Oblong 12mo. 47pp. Glazed color illus bds. VG. *Dower*. $50/£32

GREENE, GRAHAM. The Little Train. London: Bodley Head, 1973. 1st ed. Edward Ardizzone (illus). Pict bds. Mint in dj. *Hollett*. $133/£85

GREENE, GRAHAM. The Living Room. London: Heinemann, 1953. 1st UK ed. VG (ink name) in dj (browned, rubbed, edges strengthened to rear). *Williams*. $70/£45

GREENE, GRAHAM. Lord Rochester's Monkey. London: Bodley Head, 1974. 1st ed. VG in dj (sl bruised). *Cox*. $23/£15

GREENE, GRAHAM. The Lost Childhood. Eyre & Spottiswoode, 1951. 1st ed. Inscribed presentation. (Foxed.) Tan cl. Dj (sl foxed). *Sotheby's**. $431/£276

GREENE, GRAHAM. The Lost Childhood. London, 1951. 1st ed. (Spine sl worn), else VG in dj (sl browned, spine chipped 1cm). *Buckley*. $47/£30

GREENE, GRAHAM. The Lost Childhood. London: Eyre & Spottiswoode, 1951. 1st ed. Fine in dj (price-clipped, lt rubbed). *Hermitage*. $175/£112

GREENE, GRAHAM. The Lost Childhood. NY: Viking, 1952. 1st Amer ed. Fine in dj (lt worn, soiled; spine faded). *Hermitage*. $95/£61

GREENE, GRAHAM. The Man Within. Leipzig, (1930). Copyright ed. Vol 4917 of Tauchnitz Collection. VG in ptd wrappers (lt worn). *Argosy*. $85/£54

GREENE, GRAHAM. May We Borrow Your Husband? London: Bodley Head, (1967). Ltd to 500 numbered, signed. Cl, patterned bds. Fine in acetate dj (lacks cardbd slipcase). *Antic Hay*. $250/£160

GREENE, GRAHAM. May We Borrow Your Husband? London: Bodley Head, (1967). One of 500 numbered, signed. Fine. *Lenz*. $250/£160

GREENE, GRAHAM. May We Borrow Your Husband? and Other Comedies of the Sexual Life. NY: Viking, 1966. 1st US ed. (Erasure fep), else Fine in Fine dj. *Beasley*. $30/£19

GREENE, GRAHAM. The Ministry of Fear. NY: Viking, 1943. 1st US ed. NF in VG dj (lt wear). *Gravesend*. $450/£288

GREENE, GRAHAM. Monsieur Quixote. NY: S&S, (1982). One of 250 numbered. Fine in Fine slipcase. *Lenz*. $250/£160

GREENE, GRAHAM. Mr. Visconti...An Extract from Travels with My Aunt. London: Bodley Head, (1969). 1st ed. Edward Ardizzone (illus). Fine in wrappers. *Black Sun*. $400/£256

GREENE, GRAHAM. The Name of Action. Heinemann, 1930. 1st ed. Inscribed presentation. (Sl spotting.) Dk blue cl. *Sotheby's**. $789/£506

GREENE, GRAHAM. Nine O'Clock Stories. G. Bell, 1934. 1st ed. Inscribed presentation. Red cl. *Sotheby's**. $466/£299

GREENE, GRAHAM. Nineteen Stories. London: Heinemann, 1947. 1st UK ed. (Few pp sl creased, nick fep), else Fine in VG dj (spine browned, sl edgeworn). *Williams*. $133/£85

GREENE, GRAHAM. Nineteen Stories. NY: Viking, 1949. 1st ed. Fine (name) in dj (lt worn, sm flake chips). *Else Fine*. $175/£112

GREENE, GRAHAM. Our Man in Havana. London, 1958. 1st Eng ed. Nice in dj (sl chafed). *Clearwater*. $62/£40

GREENE, GRAHAM. Our Man in Havana. London, 1958. 1st ed. (Ink inscrip, sl bumped), else Good in dj (edgeworn). *King.* $95/£61

GREENE, GRAHAM. Our Man in Havana. NY: Viking, 1958. 1st US ed. Good in Good- dj. *Scribe's Perch*.* $34/£22

GREENE, GRAHAM. Our Man in Havana. NY: Viking, 1958. (Sm sticker mk fep), else Fine in VG dj (lt rubbed). *Between The Covers.* $65/£42

GREENE, GRAHAM. The Pleasure-Dome. John Russell Taylor (ed). London, (1972). 1st ed. VG in dj. *Argosy.* $50/£32

GREENE, GRAHAM. The Potting Shed. London: Heinemann, (1958). 1st British ed. Nice (bkpl, tape mks eps) in dj. *Reese.* $30/£19

GREENE, GRAHAM. The Power and the Glory. London: Heinemann, (1940). 1st ed. VG (sig; lacks dj). *Captain's Bookshelf.* $275/£176

GREENE, GRAHAM. The Quiet American. Heinemann, (1955). 1st ed. Good in dj (sl rubbed). *Ash.* $62/£40

GREENE, GRAHAM. The Quiet American. Heinemann, 1955. 1st ed. Inscribed presentation. (Sl foxed.) Blue cl. Dj. *Sotheby's*.* $538/£345

GREENE, GRAHAM. The Quiet American. NY: Viking, 1956. 1st ed. Fine in NF dj (shallow spine chips). *Beasley.* $45/£29

GREENE, GRAHAM. Reflections on Travels with My Aunt. NY: Firsts & Co, 1989. Signed, ltd ed. Fine in dec paper-cvrd wraps. *Metropolitan*.* $143/£92

GREENE, GRAHAM. A Sense of Reality. London, 1963. 1st Eng ed. Very Nice in dj (sl tanned, mkd, worn). *Clearwater.* $56/£36

GREENE, GRAHAM. Stamboul Train. London, 1932. 1st ed. VG (sl foxed; spine top professionally mended, cvrs sl stained). *Polyanthos.* $45/£29

GREENE, GRAHAM. Stamboul Train. London, 1932. 1st ed. (Sm mks cvr, spine crease), o/w VG. (Lacks dj.) *Buckley.* $78/£50

GREENE, GRAHAM. Stamboul Train. Sydney: 'Truth' and 'Sportman,' 1944. 1st Australian ed. (Pp browning, rear panel lt spotted), else VG in wrappers. *Turtle Island.* $100/£64

GREENE, GRAHAM. The Third Man and the Fallen Idol. London, 1950. 1st ed. (Inscrip), else VG in dj (extrems rubbed, chipped). *Buckley.* $125/£80

GREENE, GRAHAM. This Gun For Hire. GC: Doubleday, 1936. 1st ed. VG (bkpl) in VG intact dj (separated at folds; internal mends). *Unger.* $900/£577

GREENE, GRAHAM. Travels with My Aunt. Bodley Head, (1969). 1st ed. VG in dj (rubbed, mkd, foxed). *Ash.* $39/£25

GREENE, GRAHAM. Travels with My Aunt. NY: Viking, (1970). 1st ed. NF in dj. *Antic Hay.* $20/£13

GREENE, GRAHAM. Travels with My Aunt. NY, 1970. 1st ed. VG + (sig; spine sunned) in VG + dj. *Smith.* $15/£10

GREENE, GRAHAM. Ways of Escape. Toronto: Dennys, 1980. 1st ed. Very Nice (2 corners knocked) in dj. *Clearwater.* $39/£25

GREENE, GRAHAM. Yes and No and For Whom the Bell Chimes. London: Bodley Head, (1983). One of 750 numbered, signed. Fine in Fine clear acetate dj. *Lenz.* $200/£128

GREENE, MAX. The Kanzas Region: Forest, Prairie, Desert, Mountain, Vale and River. NY, 1856. 1st ed. 192,(4),(4)pp; map. (Few spine pieces missing.) Howes G383. *Ginsberg.* $400/£256

GREENE, NANCY L. Ye Olde Shaker Bells. Lexington, KY: The Author, 1930. *Cullen.* $45/£29

GREENE, WELCOME ARNOLD. Journals of...the Voyages of the Brigantine Perseverence, 1817-1820. Howard Greene and Alice E. Smith (eds). Madison: WI State Hist Soc, 1956. Port. VG +. *Bohling.* $15/£10

GREENE, WILLIAM H. Wooden Walls Among the Ice Floes. London: Hutchinson, 1933. Gilt-dec cl. (Sl worn), o/w VG. *New Hampshire*.* $70/£45

GREENER, LESLIE. The Discovery of Egypt. London: Cassell, 1966. 1st ed. (Cl sl soiled.) *Archaeologia.* $35/£22

GREENER, W. W. The Gun and Its Development. London: Cassell, 1899. 7th ed. Frontis, xvi,768,xiipp. Pict grn cl gilt (neatly recased). *Hollett.* $226/£145

GREENER, W. W. The Gun and Its Development. London: Cassell, 1910. 9th ed. Pict cl. (Edgeworn), else VG. *Bowman.* $60/£38

GREENER, WILLIAM. The Gun. London, 1835. 1st ed. 4 plts. Mod buckram (sl worn; foxed, sl soiled). *Oinonen*.* $250/£160

GREENER, WILLIAM. Gunnery in 1858. London, 1858. 1st ed. 5 plts. Mod buckram (sl worn; foxed). *Oinonen*.* $120/£77

GREENER, WILLIAM. The Science of Gunnery.... London, 1846. New ed. Mod buckram (sl worn). *Oinonen*.* $150/£96

GREENEWALT, C. H. Hummingbirds. NY: Doubleday, 1960. 70 tipped-in color plts. Good + in dj (tape-repaired, chipped). *Scribe's Perch*.* $65/£42

GREENEWALT, CRAWFORD H. Hummingbirds. GC, (1960). 1st ed. (Eps foxed; sl worn.) Dj (sl frayed, chipped). *Oinonen*.* $90/£58

GREENEWALT, CRAWFORD H. Hummingbirds. NY: For Amer Museum of Natural History, 1960. Tipped-in color frontis, 67 tipped-in color plts. Dj (lt browned, sl chipped). *Edwards.* $156/£100

GREENFIELD, ELOISE. Rosa Parks. NY: Thomas Y. Crowell, (1973). 1st ed. Eric Marlow (illus). Thin 4to. VG (corners sl bumped) in VG- dj (sl soiled, stained). *Between The Covers.* $35/£22

GREENFIELD, J. G. et al. Neuropathology. 1958. Inscribed, signed by W. Blackwood (author). (Ink sig, sm rust mk ep.) *Whitehart.* $39/£25

GREENHALGH, P. A. L. Early Greek Warfare: Horsemen and Chariots.... Cambridge: CUP, 1973. Good. *Archaeologia.* $65/£42

GREENHILL, B. Archaeology of the Boat. Middle., CT: Wesleyan, 1976. 1st ed. Fine in NF dj. *Mikesh.* $37/£24

Greenhouse Favorites. (By Shirley Hibberd.) Groombridge, n.d. (ca 1878). 310pp, 36 Fine full-pg color plts by James Andrews. Marbled edges, eps. 1/2 calf (recased), marbled bds, gilt, false raised bands. Splendid. *Quest.* $635/£407

GREENHOW, E. HEADLAM. Chronic Bronchitis. Phila, 1868. Good (ex-libris, mks). *Doctor's Library.* $60/£38

GREENHOW, ROBERT. The History of Oregon and California, and the Other Territories on the North-West Coast of North America.... NY: D. Appleton, 1845. 3rd ed. (4),xviii,(2),492,7pp; lg fldg map laid in (rubber stamp). 1/2 leather, bds (newly bound), gilt-lettered spine. Fine. Howes G389. *Argonaut.* $350/£224

GREENHOW, ROBERT. The History of Oregon and California.... NY, 1845. 3rd ed. xviii,(2),492,7pp, half-title, lg fldg map (detached; lt foxing). Internally VG (occasional fox mk; extrems worn, spine head chipped, nicks). Howes G389. *Reese.* $600/£385

GREENLEAF, STEPHEN. Death Bed. NY: Dial, 1980. 1st ed. Fine in dj. *Mordida.* $40/£26

GREENLEAF, STEPHEN. State's Evidence. NY: Dial, 1982. 1st ed. VF in dj. *Mordida.* $75/£48

GREENLEAF, STEPHEN. Toll Call. NY: Villard Books, 1987. 1st ed. Fine in Fine dj. *Janus.* $25/£16

GREENLY, A. H. A Bibliography of Father Richard's Press in Detroit. Ann Arbor: Wm. Clements Library, 1955. One of 750. Deckle edges. Cl-backed patterned bds. VG + . *Bohling.* $50/£32

GREENMAN, FREDERICK F. Wire-Tapping. Stamford, CT: Overbrook, 1938. Ltd to 600. Blue cl (lt rubbed). *Karmiole.* $75/£48

GREENOUGH, SARAH. Paul Strand: An American Vision. NY, 1990. VG in dj. *Argosy.* $125/£80

GREENSPAN, SOPHIE. Westward with Fremont. The Story of Solomon Carvalho. Phila: Jewish Pub Soc of Amer, 1969. 1st ed. Blue cl. Fine in pict dj (spine faded). *Argonaut.* $25/£16

GREENSTREET, W. J. (ed.) Isaac Newton 1642-1727. 1927. Frontis port, 25 plts. Wrappers. *Whitehart.* $28/£18

GREENWOOD, JAMES. Curiosities of Savage Life. London: S.O. Beeton, 1863. 1st ed. xiv,418pp; 9 color plts. Contemp grn 1/2 calf, cl sides, gilt, red morocco label. (Inscrip; fr cvr detached, corners sl worn, sl mkd), else Fine. *Pirages.* $150/£96

GREENWOOD, JAMES. Legends of Savage Life. London: John Camden Hotten, 1869. 2p.l.,(5)-164pp + (8)ll ads; 24 plts, added engr title (inscrip). Pict grn cl (fr joint neatly reinforced w/matching paper; sl worn, sm tears, bumped). Internally VG. *Pirages.* $200/£128

GREENWOOD, JAMES. The Purgatory of Peter the Cruel. London/NY, 1868. 164pp (few margins sl thumbed, sl spotted). Marbled edges. Mod calf-backed marbled bds (rebound), gilt. *Edwards.* $101/£65

GREENWOOD, JEREMY (comp). The Wood Engravings of John Nash. Liverpool: Wood Lea, 1987. One of 750. 1/4 cl, patterned bds. Fine in slipcase. *Michael Taylor.* $75/£48

GREENWOOD, MAJOR. Some British Pioneers of Social Medicine. London, 1948. 1st ed. VG. *Fye.* $50/£32

GREENWOOD, ROBERT (ed). California Imprints, 1833-1862: A Bibliography. Los Gatos: Talisman, 1961. 1st ed. Ltd to 750. VF in dj (sl chipped). *Argonaut.* $125/£80

GREENWOOD, ROBERT. The California Outlaw: Tiburcio Vasquez. Los Gatos: Talisman, 1960. Ptd bds (fr bottom tip bumped), cl spine. Dj (sm tears spine). *Dawson.* $50/£32

GREER, HILTON ROSS (comp). Voices of the Southwest. NY: Macmillan, 1923. 1st ed. VG + . *Bohling.* $15/£10

GREER, JOSEPH H. The Drugless Road to Perfect Health. Chicago, 1934. 1st ed. VG (sl worn) in ptd wrappers. *Doctor's Library.* $30/£19

GREGG, JOSIAH. Commerce of the Prairies. Max L. Moorhead (ed). Norman: Univ of OK, (1954). 1st ptg of new ed. 2 maps (1 fldg). VF in pict dj. *Argonaut.* $125/£80

GREGG, JOSIAH. Commerce of the Prairies: or the Journal of a Santa Fe Trader.... NY: Henry G. Langley, 1844. 1st ed, 1st issue. 2 vols. 12mo. 320; 318pp (lt foxing, primarily to frontis, tp; vol 2 lacks rep; 1 leaf, 1 plt quite spotted); 3 plts each vol; lg fldg map vol 1 (6-inch tear exerptly repaired), sm map vol 2. Orig blind and gilt-stamped brn cl (lt worn, lt rubbed), gilt vignette spines, fr cvrs. Overall VG set in gilt-lettered cl slipcase. Howes G401. *Argonaut.* $2,250/£1,442

GREGG, JOSIAH. Commerce of the Praries or the Journal of a Santa Fe Trader.... NY, 1845. 2nd ed, 1st state. 2 vols. Frontis map, xvi,320; viii,318pp; 5 plts. Orig blind-stamped brn cl, gilt. (Frontis, rep glued to bds, extrems lt worn), o/w NF. Howes G401. *Turpen.* $495/£317

GREGG, JOSIAH. Commerce of the Praries or the Journal of a Santa Fe Trader.... Univ of OK, 1941. UOK ptg. 1st ed thus. VG. *Turpen.* $20/£13

GREGG, JOSIAH. Diary and Letters of.... Norman, 1941-44. 1st ed. 2 vols. Frontis ports, 2 fldg maps. Fine. *Turpen.* $145/£93

GREGG, KATE L. (ed). The Road to Santa Fe, Journal and Diaries of Geo. Champlin Sibley and Others...1825-27. Albuquerque, 1952. 1st ed. Frontis. Fine in Fine dj. *Turpen.* $55/£35

GREGG, LEAH. Scarface Al. Girard: Haldeman-Julius, n.d. 1st ed. Fine in wraps. *Beasley.* $30/£19

GREGORY, DICK with ROBERT LIPSYTE. Nigger: An Autobiography. NY: Dutton, 1964. 1st ed. VG in dj (chip). *Petrilla.* $40/£26

GREGORY, DICK. Dick Gregory's Political Primer. James R. McGraw (ed). NY: Harper & Row, (1972). 1st ed. Full-pg port preceding each chapter. Cl-backed bds. VG in pict dj. *Petrilla.* $30/£19

GREGORY, DICK. Up from Nigger. NY: Stein & Day, (1976). 1st ed. Cl-backed bds. Fine in dj. *Sadlon.* $15/£10

GREGORY, G. The Life of Thomas Chatterton. London: G. Kearsley, 1789. 1st ed. Facs plt. Contemp calf. (Lacks 1/2 title, foxed, stained; rebacked), o/w VG. *Poetry Bookshop.* $187/£120

GREGORY, HERBERT E. The Navajo Country. Washington, 1916. 29 plts, 2 lg color fldg maps rear pocket. (Facs of orig cvrs, spine.) Overall VG + in orange wraps. *Five Quail.* $110/£71

GREGORY, HERBERT E. The San Juan Country. 1938. 26 plts. Tan stiff wraps. (Sl lib mks), o/w Fine. *Five Quail.* $95/£61

GREGORY, HORACE. The Shield of Achilles: Essays on Beliefs in Poetry. NY: Harcourt, Brace, (1944). 1st ed. Fine in dj. *Hermitage.* $35/£22

GREGORY, JACK and RENNARD STRICKLAND. Sam Houston with the Cherokees, 1829-1833. Austin: Univ of TX, (1967). Grn cl. Fine in dj (price-clipped). *Bohling.* $22/£14

GREGORY, JACKSON. The Emerald Murder Trap. NY: Scribner, 1934. 1st ed. Sharp in VG dj (price-clipped, sl soiled, spine sunned). *Metropolitan*.* $57/£37

GREGORY, JOSEPH W. Gregory's Guide for California Travellers Via the Isthmus of Panama. SF: Book Club of CA, 1949. One of 300. Map frontis, 2 facs, prospectus laid in. Fine in dj. Howes G407. *Cahan.* $65/£42

GREGORY, LADY. Irish Folk-History Plays. NY: Putnam, 1912. 1st Amer ed. Cl-backed bds. Fine. *Hermitage.* $50/£32

GREGORY, T. E. and ANNETTE HENDERSON. The Westminster Bank Through a Century. OUP, 1936. 2 vols. 2 color frontispieces, 17 plts. Compliments slip loosely inserted. Leather spine labels. Fine set in djs, slipcase (sl repaired). *Hollett.* $133/£85

GREGORY, WILLIAM K. and H. C. Raven. In Quest of Gorillas. New Bedford: Darwin, 1937. 1st ed. 110 photo plts. Grn cl, gilt. VG (ex-lib). *Price.* $35/£22

GREGSON, WILFRED. A Student's Guide to Wood Engraving. London: Batsford, 1953. (Sl spotted), o/w Fine in dj. *Michael Taylor.* $31/£20

GRENDON, STEPHEN. (Pseud of August Derleth.) Mr. George and Other Odd Persons. Sauk City: Arkham House, 1963. 1st ed. NF in dj (wear, spine browned). *Other Worlds.* $38/£24

GRENFELL, WILFRED T. Labrador Looks at the Orient. Boston: Houghton Mifflin, 1928. 1st ed. Inscribed w/dwg by author. (Sm bkpl), o/w Fine in dj (chip fr panel, lib #s spine). *Hermitage.* $100/£64

GRENIER, JEAN. Bores. NY, (1961). 8 color lithos. (Bkpl.) Color pict bds. *Swann*.* $172/£110

GRENN, ROBERT B. On the Arkansas Route to California in 1849. Oliphant J. Orin (ed). Lewisburg: Bucknell Univ, 1955. One of 350. Cl spine (lower tips bumped). *Dawson.* $60/£38

GRESHAM, WILLIAM L. The Book of Strength. NY: John Day, 1961. 1st ed. NF (lt soiling) in VG+ dj. *Beasley.* $30/£19

GRESHAM, WILLIAM L. Nightmare Alley. NY: Rinehart, (1946). 1st ed, 1st bk. (Ep gutters tanned), o/w VG in dj (sl shelfworn, creased tears). *Reese.* $45/£29

GRESHAM, WILLIAM L. Nightmare Alley. NY, 1946. 1st ed, 1st bk. NF in VG+ dj. *Warren.* $150/£96

GREVILLE, CHARLES C. F. The Greville Memoirs 1814-1860. Lytton Strachey and Roger Fulford (eds). London: Macmillan, 1938. Ltd to 630. 8 vols incl index. Frontispieces (lt spotted). Teg. Red pub's cl. *Christie's**. $315/£202

GREVILLE, CHARLES C. F. The Greville Memoirs...[and] A Journal of the Reign of Queen Victoria. Henry Reeve (ed). London: Longmans, Green, 1874-87. 1st ed. 8 vols. Marbled eps; teg. Deep purple crushed 3/4 morocco, linen sides, ochre dbl labels. Internally Fine. (Spines sl faded, sm ink mk 1 cvr.) *Pirages.* $650/£417

GREVILLE, FULKE. Sir Fulke Greville's Life of Sir Philip Sidney Etc. London/Edinburgh/NY/Toronto: Henry Frowde, at the Clarendon Press, 1907. White parchment (joints split; lt soiled; spine sl chipped), blind-dec cvrs. NF internally. *Blue Mountain.* $30/£19

GREVILLE, ROBERT FULKE. The Diaries of...Equerry to King George III. F. McKno Bladon (ed). John Lane, 1930. 1st ed. 9 plts. VG in orig buckram. *Cox.* $28/£18

GREY, WILLIAM. (Pseud of William F. White.) A Picture of Pioneer Times in California.... SF: W.M. Hinton, 1881. 1st ed. vii,677pp. Blind-emb dk brn cl (corner, spine-end wear beginning), gilt (lettering on spine dknd). VG. Howes W372. *Harrington.* $125/£80

GREY, ZANE. Arizona Ames. NY: Harper, 1932. 1st ed. Fine in dj (few edge nicks). *Unger.* $450/£288

GREY, ZANE. The Call of the Canyon. Toronto: Musson Book Co, (1924). 1st Canadian ed. Fine in Good dj (chipped). *Authors Of West.* $30/£19

GREY, ZANE. Captives of the Desert. London: Hodder & Stoughton, (1953). 1st British ed. VG (names) in dj (chipped). *Authors Of West.* $20/£13

GREY, ZANE. The Day of the Beast. NY: Harper, (1922). 1st ed. VG in VG dj (edgeworn). *Unger.* $350/£224

GREY, ZANE. The Deer Stalker. NY: Harper, 1949. 1st ed. Fine in dj (sl worn). *Else Fine.* $120/£77

GREY, ZANE. King of the Royal Mounted and the Ghost Guns of Roaring River. Racine, WI: Whitman, 1946. 1st ed. Fine in Clean dj. *Associates.* $150/£96

GREY, ZANE. The Lost Wagon Train. NY/London: Harper, 1936. 1st ed. NF in VG pict dj (quarter-size hole rear panel, spine ends chipped). *Bernard.* $175/£112

GREY, ZANE. The Maverick Queen. NY: Harper, 1950. 1st ed. Fine in VG+ dj (edge rubbed). *Unger.* $100/£64

GREY, ZANE. The Mysterious Rider. NY: Harper, (1921). 1st ed. VG (name) in VG wrap-around illus dj (edgeworn). *Unger.* $250/£160

GREY, ZANE. The Ranger and Other Stories. NY: Harper, 1960. 1st ed. Fine in dj (lt worn). *Else Fine.* $85/£54

GREY, ZANE. The Reef Girl. Harper & Row, (1977). 1st ed. NF in NF dj. *Authors Of West.* $30/£19

GREY, ZANE. Tales of Fishing Virgin Seas. NY: Harper, (c. 1925). Binding imprinted w/Grosset & Dunlap. (Cl faded, lt worn overall), o/w Contents VG. *New Hampshire**. $45/£29

GREY, ZANE. Tales of Fishing Virgin Seas. NY: Harpers, 1925. 1st ed. 4to. 112 full-pg photos. Fine in NF dj (price-clipped; 2 sm stains fr panel; short tears, rubbing extrems). *Between The Covers.* $575/£369

GREY, ZANE. Tales of Lonely Trails. NY/London: Harper, (1922). 1st ed. Untrimmed. Dk grn cl (spine dknd), gilt (faded), mtd photo repro fr cvr. Text VG (sl foxed, ink sig, note). *Baltimore**. $20/£13

GREY, ZANE. Tales of Southern Rivers. Hodder, 1924. 1st ed. *Petersfield.* $78/£50

GREY, ZANE. Tales of Southern Rivers. London: Hodder & Stoughton, 1924. 1st Eng ed. Good (sm piece torn corner tp). *Books & Birds.* $78/£50

GREY, ZANE. Tales of Swordfish and Tuna. NY: G&D, (1927). Orange cl. VG (sm split spine, ink name ep). *Truepenny.* $45/£29

GREY, ZANE. Tales of Swordfish and Tuna. NY/London: Harper, 1927. 1st ed. (Corners bumped), o/w VG in dj (worn). *New Hampshire**. $160/£103

GREY, ZANE. Tales of Tahitian Waters. NY: Harper, 1931. (Sl worn.) Dj (chipped, frayed). *Oinonen**. $120/£77

GREY, ZANE. Tales of Tahitian Waters. NY: Harper, 1931. Stated 1st ed. Pict eps. Grn buckram, gilt. NF in ptd dj. *Biscotti.* $475/£304

GREY, ZANE. Tales of the Angler's Eldorado, New Zealand. London, 1926. 1st ed. 1/2 grn morocco, gilt. *Petersfield.* $234/£150

GREY, ZANE. Tappan's Burro and Other Stories. NY: Harper, (1923). 1st ed. VG (upper edge stained, bottom edge bumped, bkseller's label fr pastedown) in dj (tear back panel; plt tipped onto fr panel). *Hermitage.* $325/£208

GREY, ZANE. Tappan's Burro. NY, (1923). 1st ed. (Bumped, lettering dull), else Good in dj (worn, edge-torn, chipped). *King.* $250/£160

GREY, ZANE. The Vanishing American. Toronto: Musson Book Co, (1925). 1st Canadian ed. Fine in VG dj. *Authors Of West.* $30/£19

GREY, ZANE. Wanderer of the Wasteland. NY: Harper, (1923). 1st ed. Fine in Fine dj, hand-made slipcase. *Book Market.* $150/£96

GREY, ZANE. Wanderer of the Wasteland. Toronto: Musson Book Co, (1923). 1st Canadian ed. Fine in VG dj. *Authors Of West.* $30/£19

GREY, ZANE. Western Union. NY: Harper, 1939. 1st ed. (3pp sm edge tears; top edge dust soiled), else Fine in pict dj. *Associates.* $200/£128

GREY, ZANE. The Young Lion Hunter. London: Nelson, n.d. Sm 8vo. 278pp, 8 halftone dwgs. Color pict cl. VG. *Mikesh.* $45/£29

GREYSMITH, BRENDA. Wallpaper. Studio Vista, 1976. Dj. *Edwards.* $62/£40

GREYSMITH, DAVID. Richard Dadd. 1973. (Bkpl.) Dj (sl faded, spine chipped). *Edwards.* $47/£30

GRIBBLE, FRANCIS. The Early Mountaineers. London, 1899. 1st ed. 338pp (lacks rep). Teg. (Rubbed, bumped.) *King.* $195/£125

GRIBBLE, LEONARD. Death Pays the Piper. London: Herbert Jenkins, 1956. 1st ed. (Lt spotting pg edges, eps), o/w Fine in dj. *Mordida.* $45/£29

GRIBBON, LENORE S. Who's Whodunit. Chapel Hill: Univ of NC, 1969. 1st ed. Pb orig. Fine (rear cvr sl soiling). *Janus.* $25/£16

GRIER, SYDNEY C. The Letters of Warren Hastings to His Wife. London, 1905. 1st ed. Frontis port, 5 plts. (Bkpl; rebound, spine sl faded.) *Edwards.* $47/£30

GRIERSON, JOHN. High Failure, Solo Along the Arctic Air Route. William Hodge, 1936. (Tp sl foxed.) Dj. *Petersfield*. $23/£15

GRIERSON, JOHN. Sir Hubert Wilkins. London, 1960. VG in dj. *High Latitude*. $25/£16

GRIESINGER, WILHELM. Mental Pathology and Therapeutics. NY: William Wood, (1882). 1st Amer ed. (ii),viii,375,(3)pp. Emb Victorian cl (crown chipped). VG. *Gach*. $150/£96

GRIEVE, MRS. M. Culinary Herbs and Condiments. NY: Harcourt, Brace, 1940. (Fr hinge cracked.) Dj (sl worn). *Quest*. $25/£16

GRIEVE, SYMINGTON. The Book of Colonsay and Oronsay. Edinburgh/London: Oliver & Boyd, 1923. 1st ed. 2 vols. Fldg map. Teg. Gilt-dec cl. (Bkpls), o/w Fine in djs (lt nicked, dust mkd). *Reese*. $125/£80

GRIFFEN, JOHN S. A Doctor Comes to California. SF: CA Hist Soc, 1943. 1st ed. Frontis port, 4 maps. Red cl. Fine. *Pacific**. $69/£44

GRIFFIN, A. H. In Mountain Lakeland. Preston: Guardian, 1963. 1st ed. VG in dj (spine head sl worn). *Hollett*. $39/£25

GRIFFIN, JOHN HOWARD. The Devil Rides Outside. Ft. Worth: Smith's Inc, 1952. 1st ed, 1st bk. Later solicited inscription; als (initialed). NF in VG dj (sl shelfworn, sm spots). *Reese*. $150/£96

GRIFFIN, JOHN HOWARD. Twelve Photographic Portraits. Greensboro: Unicorn, 1973. 1st ed. One of 1000. Fine in wraps. *Turlington*. $20/£13

GRIFFIN, JOHN S. A Doctor Comes to California. SF: CA Hist Soc, 1943. Port. (Ex-lib, bkpl removed; spine rubbed, sunned, cvrs lt soiled.) Internally VG + . *Five Quail*. $35/£22

GRIFFIN, JOHNNIE HARRY. A Man Without a Country Since Prohibition. (New Orleans: Rogers Ptg, n.d.) 1st ed. (8)pp. NF in orig ptd wrappers. *Mcgowan*. $350/£224

GRIFFIN, LEPEL HENRY. The Great Republic. NY: Scribner, 1884. 1st ed. 189pp. Uncut. *Ginsberg*. $100/£64

GRIFFIN, MARTIN I. J. Commodore John Barry 'The Father of the American Navy.' Phila: The Author, 1903. One of 600 ptd. Howes G423. *Ginsberg*. $125/£80

GRIFFIN, SUSAN. Let Them Be Said. Oakland: Mama's Press, 1973. 1st ed. NF in ptd wrappers. *Captain's Bookshelf*. $125/£80

GRIFFITH, G. W. E. My 96 Years in the Great West. L.A.: The Author, 1929. 1st ed. Frontis, addendum. Good. *Lien*. $35/£22

GRIFFITH, G. W. E. My 96 Years in the Great West: Indiana, Kansas and California. (L.A.): G.W.E. Griffith, (1929). Brn cl, gilt. VG + . *Bohling*. $30/£19

GRIFFITH, G. W. E. My 96 Years in the Great West: Indiana, Kansas and California. L.A.: The Author, 1929. 1st ed. VG. *Sadlon*. $20/£13

GRIFFITH, GEORGE. The Great Pirate Syndicate. London: F.V. White, 1899. 1st ed. Maroon cl (damp-mkd), gilt. Internally Nice. *Certo*. $85/£54

GRIFFITH, HARRISON PATILLO. Variosa. N.p., 1911. 1st ed. Inscribed. Frontis. VG (ex-libris). *Mcgowan*. $350/£224

GRIFFITH, PEGGY. The New Klondike: A Story of a Southern Baseball Training Camp. NY: Jacobsen-Hodgkinson, (1926). 1st ed. NF (pg edges yellowed; couple corners lt creased) in wrappers. *Between The Covers*. $125/£80

GRIFFITH, R. EGLESFELD. Medical Botany: or Descriptions of the More Important Plants Used in Medicine.... Phila: Lea and Blanchard, 1847. 1st ed. 704,32pp (sl foxing). Full leather (cvrs worn). NF. *Argonaut*. $750/£481

GRIFFITHS, A. B. Biographies of Scientific Men. 1912. 16 port plts. (Inner hinge sl cracked; spine ends sl defective, corners sl worn), o/w VG. *Whitehart*. $39/£25

GRIFFITHS, ARTHUR. Secrets of the Prison-House or Gaol Studies and Sketches. London: Chapman & Hall, 1894. 2 vols. Mod 3/4 crushed brn morocco. Handsome set. *Boswell*. $350/£224

GRIFFITHS, JULIA (ed). Autographs for Freedom. Auburn/Rochester: Alden, Beardsley/Wanzer, Beardsley, 1854. 1st ed. 309pp + ads. VG (cl nicked). BAL 5224. *Second Life*. $125/£80

GRIFFITHS, PHILIP JONES. Vietnam Inc. NY: Collier, 1971. 1st ed. NF in photo-illus wrappers. *Smith*. $275/£176

GRIGSON, GEOFFREY (ed). About Britain. London: Festival of Britain Office, 1951. 13 vols. Pict bds. (Piece torn from upper panel vol 10 wrapper), o/w Fine set in djs. *Hollett*. $133/£85

GRIGSON, GEOFFREY. A Dictionary of English Plant Names. London: Allen Lane, 1974. 1st ed. Gilt-dec cl. Fine in dj. *Quest*. $35/£22

GRIGSON, GEOFFREY. English Drawing from Samuel Cooper to Gwen John. Thames & Hudson, 1955. 1st ed. (Spine sl dull, fr cvr mkd), o/w VG. *Words Etc*. $23/£15

GRIGSON, GEOFFREY. The Englishman's Flora. London: Folio Soc, 1987. Facs ed. 45 woodcuts. Cl-backed marbled bds, gilt. Card slipcase. *Edwards*. $39/£25

GRIGSON, GEOFFREY. Gardenage, or the Plants of Ninhursaga. London, 1952. 1st ed. 15 plts. Dj (sl chipped). *Edwards*. $31/£20

GRIGSON, GEOFFREY. A Herbal of All Sorts. NY: Macmillan, 1959. 4 color plts. VG in dj. *Goodrich*. $30/£19

GRIGSON, GEOFFREY. Notes from an Odd Country. London, 1970. 1st ed. Dj (sl chipped). *Edwards*. $23/£15

GRIGSON, GEOFFREY. Portrait of Wessex. London, 1951. 1st ed. VG in dj (nick). *Words Etc*. $16/£10

GRIGSON, GEOFFREY. Samuel Palmer. 1947. 1st ed. Color frontis, 67 b/w plts (1 color). Dj (adhered to cl, dampstained). *Edwards*. $47/£30

GRIMBLE, AUGUSTUS. The Salmon Rivers of England and Wales. London, 1913. 2nd ed. Fldg frontis map. (Rep torn w/o loss, lt browned; sm stain upper bd, spine sl rubbed.) *Edwards*. $47/£30

GRIMBLE, AUGUSTUS. The Salmon Rivers of Scotland. London, 1902. 1-vol ed. 4 maps. Japon-backed bds. (Ex-lib, ink stamps, bkpl; feps browned; corners rubbed, sl loss.) *Edwards*. $172/£110

GRIMES, JOHN. House Ghosts. Chicago: Robert Ballou, 1924. 1st US ed. Good (fr cvr bumped, affecting lower leaves) in Good dj (worn, torn). *Gravesend*. $35/£22

GRIMES, JOHN. Institutional Care of Mental Patients in the United States. Chicago: The Author, 1934. 1st ed. (Ex-lib, pocket, bkpls), o/w Fine. *Beasley*. $35/£22

GRIMES, MARTHA. The Anodyne Necklace. Boston: Little, Brown, (1983). 1st ed. Fine in Fine dj. *Unger*. $125/£80

GRIMES, MARTHA. The Deer Leap. Boston: Little Brown, 1985. 1st ed. Fine in dj (price-clipped, inner fr flap creased). *Mordida*. $30/£19

GRIMES, MARTHA. The Man with a Load of Mischief. Boston: Little, Brown, (1981). 1st ed. Signed. Fine in Fine dj (price-clipped). *Unger*. $225/£144

GRIMES, MARTHA. The Old Fox Deceiv'd. Boston: Little, Brown, (1982). 1st ed. Fine in dj (lt worn, sl rubbed). *Metropolitan**. $23/£15

GRIMM, JACOB and WILHELM (GRIMM BROTHERS.) King Grisly-Beard. (NY): FSG, 1973. 1st ed thus. Maurice Sendak (illus). 8vo. 24pp. NF in dec bds as issued. *Hadley.* $47/£30

GRIMM, JACOB and WILHELM. (GRIMM BROTHERS.) Grimm's Fairy Tales. Margaret Hunt (trans). NY: Cupples & Leon, (1914). 1st ed. 4to. 419pp; 11 full-pg color plts by Johnny Gruelle. Maroon cl, color pict label. VG. *Dower.* $250/£160

GRIMM, JACOB and WILHELM. (GRIMM BROTHERS.) Grimm's Folk Tales. Eleanor Quarrie (trans). London: Folio Soc, 1949. 1st ed thus. George Cruikshank (illus). 8vo. 206pp. 18 hand-colored plts by Maud Johnson. VG in dj. *Hollett.* $31/£20

GRIMM, JACOB and WILHELM. (GRIMM BROTHERS.) Hansel and Gretel and Other Stories. NY, n.d. (1927). 4to. 12 tipped-in color, 10 b/w plts by Kay Nielsen. Red/black/gold pict onlay. (Spine gilt sl faded.) *Kane*.* $325/£208

GRIMM, JACOB and WILHELM. (GRIMM BROTHERS.) Household Tales. Eyre & Spottiswoode, 1946. 1st ed w/these illus. Mervyn Peake (illus). Sm 4to. 303pp; dbl-pg pict tp, 4 other color plts; 56 illus in line. Yellow cl. VG in dj (sl frayed, short tear). *Cox.* $94/£60

GRIMM, JACOB and WILHELM. (GRIMM BROTHERS.) The Juniper Tree and Other Tales from Grimm. Lore Segal (trans). NY: FSG, (1973). 1st trade ed. Maurice Sendak (illus). 2 vols. Fine in djs (spine sl dknd), slipcase. *Jaffe.* $125/£80

GRIMM, JACOB and WILHELM. (GRIMM BROTHERS.) Little Brother and Little Sister. London: Constable, (1917). 1st trade ed. This ed has same # eps, b/w dwgs as the ltd ed; lacks 1 less plt than ltd ed. Lg 4to. 250pp; 12 full-pg illus by Arthur Rackham tipped in, 43 b/w line dwgs. Illus eps. Lt grn cl, gilt. (Spine sl faded, sl bumped, 4 sm fade mks back cvr, gutter edge sl worn), o/w VG. *Dower.* $500/£321

GRIMM, JACOB and WILHELM. (GRIMM BROTHERS.) The Wolf and the Seven Kids. London: Bancroft, (1966). 8vo. 8 pop-ups, each w/moveable element. Cl-backed pict wrappers. *Glenn.* $200/£128

GRIMSLEY, DANIEL AMON. Battles in Culpeper County, Virginia, 1861-1865. Culpeper, VA: Privately Pub, 1900. 1st ed. NF in ptd wrappers. *Mcgowan.* $375/£240

GRIMWOOD, V. R. American Ship Models and How to Build Them. NY: W.W. Norton, c. 1942. Blue cl, gilt. Internally VG (inscrips) in dj (worn). *Parmer.* $55/£35

GRINNELL, GEORGE BIRD (ed). Hunting at High Altitudes. NY/London, 1913. Silver-gilt cl (shelfworn, silver partly worn away). *Oinonen*.* $40/£26

GRINNELL, GEORGE BIRD (ed). Hunting at High Altitudes. NY: Harper, 1913. 1st ed. Silver-gilt pict cl (sl worn, spine gilt partly worn away). *Oinonen*.* $50/£32

GRINNELL, GEORGE BIRD and THEODORE ROOSEVELT (eds). Trail and Camp-Fire. NY: Forest & Stream, 1897. 1st ed. Silver-gilt pict cl (sl worn, spine gilt gone; inner joint broken). *Oinonen*.* $50/£32

GRINNELL, GEORGE BIRD. American Big Game in Its Haunts. NY: Forest & Stream, 1904. 1st ed. VG. *Books & Birds.* $150/£96

GRINNELL, GEORGE BIRD. American Duck Shooting. NY, (1901). 1st ed. 10pp pub's ads, 58 ports. VG (bkpl, ink inscrip, name). *Truepenny.* $150/£96

GRINNELL, GEORGE BIRD. American Duck Shooting. NY, 1901. 8 full-pg plts; fldg plt at rear. Dec cvr. Good (spine sunned). *Scribe's Perch*.* $60/£38

GRINNELL, GEORGE BIRD. American Duck Shooting. NY, 1901. 1st ed. Foldout at rear. Grn dec cl. Good. *Scribe's Perch*.* $95/£61

GRINNELL, GEORGE BIRD. American Duck Shooting. NY: Forest & Stream, 1901. 58 ports. Red gilt-dec cl. VG. *Bowman.* $150/£96

GRINNELL, GEORGE BIRD. American Game Bird Shooting. NY: Forest & Stream, (1910). VG (spine lt soiled, inner hinges starting). *Truepenny.* $150/£96

GRINNELL, GEORGE BIRD. By Cheyenne Campfires. New Haven: Yale Univ, 1926. 1st ed. 9 b/w photo plts. Scarlet cl (sl rubbed; ink handstamp eps). *Baltimore*.* $35/£22

GRINNELL, GEORGE BIRD. The Fighting Cheyennes. Norman: Univ of OK, (1956). VG in dj (sl worn). Howes G433. *Lien.* $45/£29

GRINNELL, GEORGE BIRD. The Fighting Cheyennes. NY: Scribner, 1915. 1st ed. 3 fldg maps. Brn cl (worn), cvr vignette. (Spine-end wear beginning, rear hinge repaired.) VG. Howes G433. *Harrington.* $125/£80

GRINNELL, GEORGE BIRD. When Buffalo Ran. New Haven: Yale Univ, 1920. 1st ed. 8 b/w photo plts. Untrimmed. Pict tan bds stamped in black/grn (dknd, lt chipped, sl dusty; text lt foxed, aged, bkpl). *Baltimore*.* $35/£22

GRINNELL, ISABEL HOOPES. Greek Temples. NY: MMA, 1943. One of 1000. 54 plts. Paper-cvrd illus bds (rubbed, corners sl bumped). *Washton.* $55/£35

GRINNELL, JOSEPH. Gold Hunting in Alaska, As Told by.... Elizabeth Grinnell (ed). Elgin, IL: David C. Cook, c. 1901. Cl-backed bds. VG. *High Latitude.* $45/£29

GRINNELL, JOSHIA BUSHNELL. Men and Events of Forty Years. Boston: Lothrop, (1891). 1st ed. (16),426pp. (Fr cvr stained.) *Ginsberg.* $100/£64

GRINSELL, L. V. The Ancient Burial-Mounds of England. London, 1953. 2nd ed. 24 plts, 12 plans, diags. (Bkpl.) Dj (ragged). *Edwards.* $31/£20

GRINSELL, L. V. The Archaeology of Wessex. London, 1958. 1st ed. 15 plts, 6 maps. Dj (chipped). *Edwards.* $23/£15

GRINSPOON, LESTER. Marihuana Reconsidered. Cambridge, MA: Harvard Univ, 1971. VG + in dj. *Sclanders.* $22/£14

GRISCOM, JOHN H. Animal Mechanism and Physiology.... NY, 1839. 1st ed. 357pp. Paper-cvrd bds. Good (outer hinges cracked; extrems worn). *Doctor's Library.* $45/£29

GRISHAM, JOHN. The Chamber. NY: Doubleday, (1994). 1st ed. #227/350 numbered, signed. As New in tissue dj, slipcase. *Hermitage.* $250/£160

GRISHAM, JOHN. The Firm. NY: Doubleday, 1991. 1st ed. Fine in Fine dj. *Beasley.* $150/£96

GRISHAM, JOHN. The Pelican Brief. Doubleday, 1992. 1st US ed. Fine in NF dj. *Williams.* $47/£30

GRISHAM, JOHN. A Time to Kill. NY: Doubleday, 1993. One of 350 numbered, signed. Full leather. VF in tissue dj, slipcase. *Mordida.* $350/£224

GRISWOLD, A. B. New Orleans Guide Book. Phila: Rowley & Chew, 1873. 62pp. Fine (ink name). *Wantagh.* $125/£80

GRISWOLD, MAC. The Pleasures of the Garden. NY: Abrams, 1987. Presentation copy. *Quest.* $45/£29

GRISWOLD, RUFUS W. The Republican Court or American Society in the Days of Washington. NY, 1856. New, rev ed. 21 Fine hand-colored steel-engr plts. (Sl foxed, soiled.) Aeg. Pub's morocco (rubbed). *Oinonen*.* $100/£64

GRISWOLD, RUFUS W. The Republican Court. NY, 1859. New ed. Blind-dec leather (heavily worn, spine torn). Contents VG (inner hinges broken). *New Hampshire*.* $30/£19

GRIVAS, THEODORE. Military Governments in California, 1846-1850.... Glendale: A.H. Clark, 1963. 1st ed. 10 ports. Uncut. Blue cl, gilt spine. Plain dj. *Pacific**. $75/£48

GRIVOT, DENIS and GEORG ZARNECKI. Gislebertus, Sculptor of Autun. NY, 1961. Good in dj. *Washton*. $100/£64

GROBER, KARL. Children's Toys of Bygone Days.... London: Batsford, (1932). New ed. 309 plts. Good in dj (worn). *Agvent*. $75/£48

GRODINSKY, JULIUS. Transcontinental Railway Strategy, 1869-1893. Phila: UP Press, 1962. 1st ed. VG in dj. *Archer*. $20/£13

GROGAN, WALTER E. The 10-12 Express. London: Sisley's, n.d. 1st ed. (Sl soiled, faded.) *Metropolitan**. $34/£22

GROHMANN, WILL. Paul Klee: His Life, His Work, and His Teaching. NY: Abrams, n.d. Fine in Fine dj. *Metropolitan**. $80/£51

GROHMANN, WILL. Wassily Kandinsky. NY, (1958). Folio. (Ex-lib.) Dj. *Swann**. $92/£59

GROLLMAN, EARL A. Judaism in Sigmund Freud's World. NY: Appleton-Century, (1965). 1st ed. Presentation copy. Ochre cl. VG in dj (lt worn). *Gach*. $30/£19

GROMME, O. J. Birds of Wisconsin. Madison: Univ of WI, 1963. 1st ed. Gilt-dec cl. VG. *Mikesh*. $85/£54

GRONOW, CAPTAIN. The Reminiscences and Recollections of Captain Gronow. London, 1892. 2 vols. xxviii,353; xiv,340 + 22pp pub's cat; 33 hand-colored plts. Teg. (Eps, edges sl spotted.) Gilt/color armorial cl. *Edwards*. $195/£125

GRONOW, CAPTAIN. The Reminiscences and Recollections...1810-1860. John C. Nimmo, 1900. 2 vols. Port. Teg. Good in blue dec cl. *Cox*. $39/£25

GROOM, WINSTON and DUNCAN SPENCER. Conversations with the Enemy. NY: Putnam, (1983). 1st ed. Rev slip, flyer, photo laid in. Fine in dj. *Reese*. $30/£19

GROOM, WINSTON. As Summers Die. NY: Summit, 1980. 1st ed. (Rmdr stamp bottom edge, bd edges sl tanned) else NF in dj (edgetears). *Lame Duck*. $50/£32

GROOM, WINSTON. Forrest Gump. GC, 1986. 1st ed. Fine in dj. *Between The Covers*. $350/£224

GROOM, WINSTON. Forrest Gump. GC: Doubleday, 1986. 1st ed. Fine in dj (lt rubbed, sm tears). *Beasley*. $200/£128

GROOM, WINSTON. Forrest Gump. GC: Doubleday, 1986. 1st ed. Fine in dj (sm tear, sl rubbing). *Captain's Bookshelf*. $250/£160

GROOME, FRANCIS HINDES. Kriegspiel: The War-Game. London: Ward Lock & Bowden, 1896. 1st ed. Frontis, 380pp,12pp ads (sm chip in margin of ad leaf, no loss, sm tear margin dedication leaf, trace of clover leaf laid in). Blue cl (hinges cracked but firm), gilt spine lettering, monogram fr cvr. *Shasky*. $65/£42

GROOME, H. C. Fauquier During the Proprietorship. Richmond, 1927. 1st ed. (Bkpl removed; sm paper spine label.) *Ginsberg*. $75/£48

GROSBY, RUTH. The Mystery at Mountain View. G&D, 1940. 5x7.5. 243pp. (Pp browned; sl cocked, sl shelfworn), else VG+ in dj (edgeworn). *My Bookhouse*. $20/£13

GROSE, FRANCIS. The Antiquities of England and Wales. London: Hooper & Wigstead, n.d. New ed. 8 vols incl supplement. 4to. (Bkpl, label, lt spotting.) Contemp calf (rubbed), gilt, morocco labels. *Christie's**. $877/£562

GROSE, FRANCIS. Lexicon Balatronicum. London: Ptd for C. Chappel, 1811. 4th ed. (Disbound; lacks fldg frontis), else Internally Fine. *Cummins*. $350/£224

GROSS, HANS. Criminal Investigation, a Practical Textbook.... London: Sweet & Maxwell, 1946. 3rd ed. Blue cl, gilt. *Boswell*. $65/£42

GROSS, S. D. History of American Medical Literature From 1776 to the Present Time. Phila, 1876. 1st ed. Limp black cl (edges worn; neatly rebacked). *Maggs*. $133/£85

GROSSKURTH, PHYLLIS. John Addington Symonds, A Biography. London, 1964. 1st ed. VG in dj (sm puncture). *Typographeum*. $32/£21

GROSSMAN, JULIAN. Echo of a Distant Drum: Winslow Homer and the Civil War. Abrams, (1974). VG in VG dj. *Book Broker*. $30/£19

GROSSMAN, SID. Journey to the Cape. NY: Grove, 1959. 1st ed. 39 plts. (Owner stamp), else NF in illus wrappers, ptd glassine dj. *Cahan*. $45/£29

GROSSMANN, F. Pieter Bruegel. Complete Edition of the Paintings. London, 1973. 3rd rev ed. Good in dj. *Washton*. $65/£42

GROSVENOR, FREDRIKA. A Very Small Tale of Two Very Small Bears. NY: McLoughlin Bros, 1905. 12x9.5. (15)pp. Color pict glazed bds (worn, soiled). *King*. $75/£48

GROSVENOR, GILBERT and ALEXANDER WETMORE. The Book of Birds. Washington: Nat'l Geographic Soc, (1939). 2 vols. 950 color ports. VG in djs (sl frayed, soiled). *King*. $45/£29

GROSZ, GEORGE. 30 Drawings and Watercolors. NY: Erich S. Herrmann, 1944. 1st ed. (Text lt aged.) Wire spiral-bound gray bds (sl dusty, edgeworn). *Baltimore**. $60/£38

GROSZ, GEORGE. Ecce Homo. NY: Brussel, 1965. One of 1000. Gilt-lettered bds (sl worn). Slipcase. *Oinonen**. $70/£45

GROSZ, GEORGE. Ecce Homo. NY: Jack Brussell, 1965. 1st Amer ed. 100 uncensored dwgs (16 color) by Grosz. VG in dj (sl rubbed, soiled). *King*. $75/£48

GROSZ, GEORGE. A Little Yes and a Big No. NY, 1946. 1st ed. Dj. *Swann**. $115/£74

GROUNDS, JOHN CURETON. Trail Dust of the Southwest. Marysvale, UT: N.p., 1977. (Sl faded), else Good. *Dumont*. $75/£48

GROUT, A. J. Mosses with Hand-Lens and Microscope. NY: The Author, 1903. 1st ed. Blue cl. NF (few notes). *Archer*. $65/£42

GROUT, JOSIAH. Memoir of Gen'l. William Wallace Grout and Autobiography of Josiah Grout. Newport, VT, 1919. 1st ed. *Ginsberg*. $100/£64

GROVE, LILLY. Dancing. London: Longmans, Green, 1895. 1st ed. xvii,454,(ii)pp; 38 full-pg woodcuts. Brn pict cl, gilt. (Inscrip.) *Hollett*. $86/£55

GROVES, ERNEST R. and GLADYS HOAGLAND. Wholesome Childhood. Boston: Houghton Mifflin, 1924. 1st ed. Fine. *Second Life*. $35/£22

GRUBB, DAVIS. Shadow of My Brother. NY, 1966. 1st Amer ed. Fine in dj (sm piece missing, price-clipped). *Polyanthos*. $30/£19

GRUBB, DAVIS. The Siege of 318: Thirteen Mystical Stories. Webster Springs, WV: Back Fork, (1978). 1st ed. (Flyleaf sl rumpled), o/w Fine in VG+ dj (2 lt dampstains fr panel). *Bernard*. $25/£16

GRUBB, EUGENE H. and W. GUILFORD. The Potato. NY, 1912. 66 photo plts. Dec tan cl, gilt. VG. *Price*. $39/£25

GRUBER, FRANK. Beagle Scented Murder. Rinehart, 1946. 1st ed. (Lt wear), else NF in dj (lt rubbed, few nicks, lt soiled). *Murder By The Book*. $75/£48

GRUBER, FRANK. The Buffalo Box. Farrar & Rinehart, 1942. 1st ed. (Few pp roughly cut open; lt edgewear), else VG in dj (few chips, closed tears). *Murder By The Book*. $90/£58

GRUBER, FRANK. The Laughing Fox. NY: Farrar & Rinehart, 1940. 1st ed. Fine in dj (sm chips, price-clipped). *Else Fine.* $65/£42

GRUBER, FRANK. The Lock and the Key. NY: Rinehart, 1948. 1st ed. Fine in dj (sl worn, price-clipped). *Else Fine.* $35/£22

GRUBER, FRANK. Lonesome River. NY: Rinehart, 1957. 1st ed. (Pp tanned), else Fine in dj (spine dknd, sm chips). *Else Fine.* $35/£22

GRUBER, FRANK. The Pulp Jungle. L.A.: Sherbourne, 1967. 1st ed. (Sm name), else Fine in dj. *Associates.* $45/£29

GRUBER, FRANK. The Silver Tombstone. NY: Farrar & Rinehart, 1945. 1st ed. Fine in dj (worn). *Else Fine.* $40/£26

GRUBER, FRANK. Zane Grey, a Biography. Cleveland: World, (1970). 1st ed. Fine in Fine dj. *Book Market.* $35/£22

GRUELLE, JOHNNY. Raggedy Ann and the Golden Butterfly. NY: Johnny Gruelle, (1940). 8vo. Color pict bds (corners bumped, edgeworn). *Freeman*.* $40/£26

GRUELLE, JOHNNY. Raggedy Ann's Fairy Stories. Chicago: Donohue, (1928). Thin 8vo. Cl-backed pict bds (lt edgeworn). *Argosy.* $125/£80

GRUELLE, JOHNNY. Wooden Willie. Chicago/NY: M.A. Donahue, (1935). 8vo. Cl-backed pict bds. (Marginal crease p67; lt edgeworn), else VG. *Glenn.* $75/£48

GRUEN, JOHN. The New Bohemia. NY: Shorecrest, (1966). 1st ed. (Lt dust spotting edges), else Nice in dj (dust mks edges, spine). *Reese.* $25/£16

GRUENBERGER, FRED (ed). Computer Graphics. Washington: Thompson, 1967. 1st ed. VG in dj. *Glaser.* $60/£38

GRUNER, LEWIS. Specimens of Ornamental Art. London: Thomas M'Lean, 1850. Plt vol only. 80 litho plts incl 49 chromolithos, 8 tinted lithos. (Lib stamp tp, lt spotting, soil, 1 plt repaired, few plts w/margins neatly repaired at verso.) Contemp 1/2 calf (worn). *Christie's*.* $1,491/£956

GRUNER, O. CAMERON. A Treatise on the Canon of Medicine of Avicenna. London, 1930. 1st ed. VG. *Fye.* $200/£128

GRUSHKIN, PAUL D. The Art of Rock. NY: Abbeville, 1987. 1st ed. Fine in dj. *Sclanders.* $62/£40

GSCHWIND, H. W. Design of Digital Computers. NY: Springer-Verlag, 1967. 1st ed. NF. *Glaser.* $60/£38

GUARESCHI, GIOVANNI. The House That Nino Built. Gollancz, 1953. 1st UK ed. VG in dj (browned, lt worn, bumped). *Williams.* $19/£12

GUARESCHI, GIOVANNI. My Secret Diary. Gollancz, 1958. 1st UK ed. VG (sl stains 1/2-title) in dj (price-clipped). *Williams.* $19/£12

GUDDE, ERWIN G. 1000 California Place Names. Berkeley, 1951. 2nd ptg. VG. *Turpen.* $29/£19

GUDDE, ERWIN G. California Gold Camps. Elisabeth K. Gudde (ed). Berkeley/L.A./London: Univ of CA, (1975). 1st ed. Charcoal cl, gilt spine. Fine in pict dj. *Pacific*.* $58/£37

GUDDE, ERWIN G. California Place Names. Berkeley/L.A.: Univ of CA, (1969). 3rd, best ed. VF in dj. *Argonaut.* $50/£32

GUDDE, ERWIN G. California Place Names. Berkeley: Univ of CA, 1949. 1st ed. Good in dj (sl sunned, nicked). *Brown.* $30/£19

GUDDE, ERWIN G. Sutter's Own Story. NY: Putnam, 1936. 1st ed. Good in dj (worn). *Lien.* $25/£16

GUENON, FRANCIS. A Treatise on Milch Cows. N. P. Trist (trans). NY: Judd, (1856). 63rd thousand. 88pp. VG (cl sl worn). *Second Life.* $45/£29

GUERIN, E. J. Mountain Charley or the Adventures of Mrs. E.J. Guerin.... Norman: Univ of OK, (1968). 1st ptg of new ed. Fine in dj, plastic jacket. *Bohling.* $20/£13

GUERIN, MARCEL (ed). Edgar Germain Hilaire Degas. Oxford, 1947. Frontis port. *Edwards.* $31/£20

GUERNSEY, WILLIAM JEFFERSON. The Homoeopathic Therapeutics of Haemorrhoids. Phila: Boericke & Tafel, 1892. 2nd ed. 142pp. (Notes in index), else Good. *Goodrich.* $85/£54

GUERREIRO, FERNAO. Jahangir and the Jesuits. C. H. Payne (trans). London, 1930. Frontis port, 5 maps. *Edwards.* $31/£20

GUGGISBERG, C. A. W. Early Wildlife Photographers. NY: Taplinger, (1977). 1st US ed. Fine in illus dj. *Cahan.* $50/£32

GUHA-THAKURTA, P. The Bengali Drama. London: Routledge, 1930. 1st ed. Grn gilt cl. Fine. *Terramedia.* $50/£32

GUIART, JEAN. The Arts of the South Pacific. Anthony Christie (trans). NY: Golden Press, (1963). 1st ed. 5 maps (1 fldg). Red cl. Good in dj. *Karmiole.* $175/£112

GUICCIOLI, COUNTESS. My Recollections of Lord Byron. Richard Bentley, 1869. New ed. Frontis port. Reading Copy (shaken). *Poetry Bookshop.* $31/£20

Guide for the Pennsylvania Railroad, with an Extensive Map. Phila: T.K. & P.G. Collins, 1855. 1st ed. 40pp (fep clipped, browned); lg fldg hand-colored map at fr (folds sl worn). Orig red sheep, tan lettered bds (sl worn, dusty, spine chipped, lt stains). *Baltimore*.* $140/£90

Guide to Philadelphia, Its Public Buildings, Places of Amusement, Churches, Hotels.... Phila: John Dainty, 1868. Fldg map. (Lt wear, soil.) *Freeman*.* $90/£58

Guide to the English Lake District. London/Windermere: Simpkin, Marshall/J. Garnett, (c. 1865). 2nd ed. Color frontis, viii,123,viiipp (Garnett's ads), 4 fldg maps, 2 woodcut plts. (Upper joint tender; extrems sl worn.) *Hollett.* $94/£60

Guide to the First and Second Egyptian Rooms. London: British Museum, 1904. 2nd ed. 32 plts. (Spine chipped.) *Archaeologia.* $65/£42

Guide to the Fossil Reptiles and Fishes in the Department of Geology and Paleontology. London: Privately pub, 1896. 1st ed. 129pp. VG in wraps. *Mikesh.* $25/£16

Guide to the Preservation of Life at Sea After Shipwreck. London: Medical Research Council, 1943. 21pp pamphlet. *Goodrich.* $35/£22

Guide to the Virginia Springs. (By John Jennings Moorman.) Staunton, VA/Phila: Robert Cowan/Thomas, Cowperthwait, 1851. Fldg frontis map, (2),(xi)-xii,(13)-141pp + 11pp ads. Receipt laid in for restoration work. Nice. *Bohling.* $200/£128

GUIDO, MARGARET. The Glass Beads of the Prehistoric and Roman Periods in Britain and Ireland. London: Soc of Antiquaries, 1978. 4 color plts. VG in dj. *Turtle Island.* $55/£35

GUILLEMARD, ARTHUR G. Over Land and Sea.... London: Tinsley Bros, 1875. 1st ed. Engr frontis, extra tp, (xvi),(356),(16)pp. Dec cl (lt worn, sl shaken, sl used). Nice. *Ash.* $148/£95

GUILLEMIN, AMEDEE. The Heavens. 1878. x,436pp; 26 plts. (Spine ends defective, cl mkd, spine sl torn), o/w VG in pict bds. *Whitehart.* $39/£25

GUILLEMIN, AMEDEE. The Heavens: An Illustrated Handbook of Popular Astronomy. London: Bentley, 1868. 3rd ed. 503pp, 12 color lithos. Aeg. Morocco (sl wear). *Bookcell.* $85/£54

GUILLOU, CHARLES F. B. Oregon and California Drawings, 1841 and 1847. (SF): Book Club of CA, 1961. 1st ed. Ltd to 450 ptd. Frontis, 12 plts (3 dbl-pg), 1 dbl-pg map. Tan pict cl, gilt-lettered spine. VF. *Argonaut.* $75/£48

GUINN, J. M. A History of California and an Extended History of Los Angeles and Environs. L.A.: Hist Record, 1915. 3 Vols. Red cl bds, brn leather spines, tips; teg. (Lt edgewear.) *Dawson.* $250/£160

GUINNESS, GERALDINE. In the Far East. London/NY, (1889). 15th thousand. 192pp + 16pp index, ads. Dec cvr. Good. *Scribe's Perch*.* $22/£14

GUINNESS, MARY GERALDINE. The Story of the China Inland Mission. London: Morgan & Scott, 1893-4. 1st ed. 2 vols. xvii,(i),476,(2 ads); xi,(i),512,(2 contents),(2 ads)pp; 3 color maps (1 lg fldg), pub's apology slip vol 2. Dk blue cl (sl rubbed). *Burmester.* $133/£85

GUINOT, M. EUGENE. A Summer at Baden-Baden. London, n.d. (1853). 11x7. 299pp; 1 color map, 2 ports, 6 VG color plts, 12 views. (Spine chipped, torn; cvrs dknd.) *King.* $500/£321

GULDAHL, RALPH. Groove Your Golf: Cine-Sports Library. (Indianapolis: Internat'l Sports, 1939.) 1st ed. Flip-book. Pebbled cl. VG. *Pacific*.* $230/£147

GULICK, JOHN. Cherokees at the Crossroads. Chapel Hill, 1960. VG (name, bkpl, pencil mks) in ptd wraps. *Bohling.* $27/£17

GULLAND, W. G. Chinese Porcelain. London: Chapman and Hall, 1902. 2nd ed. 2 vols. Gilt-lettered grn cl (inner hinges starting vol 2, extrems lt worn). VG (bkpls). *Argonaut.* $175/£112

Gun at Home and Abroad: The Big Game of Asia and North America. London, 1915. #547/600. Frontis, 118 plts. Full morocco (edges chipped). Good+. *Scribe's Perch*.* $300/£192

GUNCKEL, JOHN E. Boyville, A History of Fifteen Years Work Among the Newsboys. Toledo: Toledo Newsboys' Assoc, (1905). 8vo. 219pp. Cl-cvrd bds, onlaid photo. Fine. *Cullen.* $80/£51

GUNN, ALEXANDER. Letters. NY, 1902. 1st ed. #94/500. Full morocco, gilt. (Lt chipped, lt rubbed), else VG. *Cahan.* $75/£48

GUNN, JOHN C. Gunn's Domestic Medicine, Or Poorman's Friend, in the Hours of Affliction, Pain, and Sickness. NY, 1849. 893pp, port. Full leather. (Lacks spine label.) *Fye.* $200/£128

GUNN, THOM. Mandrakes. (London): Rainbow Press, (1973). 1st ed. One of 150 signed. 1/4 vellum, bds. Mint in slipcase. *Jaffe.* $375/£240

GUNN, THOM. Moly. London: Faber & Faber, (1971). 1st ed. Fine in dj (lt soiled). *Antic Hay.* $25/£16

GUNN, THOM. Talbot Road. NY: Helikon, 1981. One of 150 numbered, signed. Fine in sewn illus wrappers. *Dermont.* $50/£32

GUNN, THOM. Touch. London: Faber & Faber, (1967). 1st ed. Fine in dj (sm tear, sl worn). *Antic Hay.* $35/£22

GUNN, THOM. Touch. Faber, 1967. 1st ed. VG in dj (sl chipped). *Whiteson.* $19/£12

GUNNISON, J. W. The Mormons; or, Latter Day Saints, in the Valley of the Great Salt Lake.... Phila, 1852. 1st ed. Frontis, 168,(27 ads)pp. (Spine lt discolored, emb lib stamps, bkpl w/inscrip.) Howes G463. *Ginsberg.* $200/£128

GUNSAULUS, HELEN C. Japanese Sword-Mounts in the Collections of the Field Museum. Chicago, 1923. 61 plts. Wrappers. *Swann*.* $92/£59

GUNTHART, LOTTE. Water Colors and Drawings. Pittsburgh, PA: Hunt Botanical Library, Carnegie-Mellon Univ, 1970. 1st ed. Ltd to 1500. VG (eps lt foxed, owner's card ep). *Cahan.* $45/£29

GUNTHER, JOHN. Eisenhower: The Man and the Symbol. NY: Harper, (1952). VG in VG- dj (long tear spine edge, chip). *Between The Covers.* $55/£35

GUNTHER, R. T. Early British Botanists and Their Gardens.... Oxford: The Author, 1922. 1st ed. 9 plts. NF. *Captain's Bookshelf.* $150/£96

GUPTILL, A. B. Haynes Guide to Yellowstone Park. St. Paul, 1902. Sm fldg map. VG in ptd wraps. *Bohling.* $45/£29

GUPTILL, ARTHUR L. Norman Rockwell. NY, 1947. 2nd ed. Newspaper clipping loosely inserted. Dj (sl browned, chipped). *Edwards.* $44/£28

GURDJIAN, E. S. and J. E. WEBSTER. Mechanisms, Diagnosis and Management of Head Injuries. Boston, 1958. 1st ed. VG. *Fye.* $100/£64

GURGANUS, ALLAN. Oldest Living Confederate Widow Tells All. NY, 1989. 1st Amer ed. Fine in Fine dj. *Polyanthos.* $45/£29

GURNEY, J. H. Rambles of a Naturalist in Egypt and Other Countries. London, (1876). vii,307pp. (Foxing at ends, sl stains; cl sl loose.) *Wheldon & Wesley.* $55/£35

GURNEY, JOSEPH JOHN. A Winter in the West Indies...Letters to Henry Clay of Kentucky. London: John Murray, 1840. xvi,282pp + 15pp ads. VG (bds faded, edgeworn). *Parmer.* $175/£112

GUROWSKI, ADAM. Diary, from March 4, 1861, to November 12, 1862. Boston, 1862. 1st ed. (Inner fr hinge cracked; spine defective.) *King.* $25/£16

GUSMAN, PIERRE. Pompeii. London, 1900. 12 color plts. (Corners rubbed w/loss, rebacked, much of orig spine laid down, tail chipped.) *Edwards.* $59/£38

GUSTAFSON, A. F. Handbook of Fertilizers. NY: OJ, 1928. 1st ed. Fine in ptd dj. *Second Life.* $40/£26

GUTCH, JOHN MATHEW (ed). A Lytell Geste of Robin Hode with Other Ancient and Modern Ballads.... London: Longman (et al], 1847. 1st ed. 2 vols. Frontispieces (sl tanned). Orig cl, gilt. VG set (hinges sl weak, sl worn). *Reese.* $125/£80

GUTERSON, DAVID. The Country Ahead of Us, the Country Behind. NY: Harper, (1989). 1st bk. Fine in Fine dj. *Unger.* $150/£96

GUTHRIE, A. B., JR. The Big Sky. NY: William Sloane, (1947). 1st ed. Fine in NF dj (sm chip corner spine base; rubbing). *Between The Covers.* $100/£64

GUTHRIE, A. B., JR. Fair Land, Fair Land. Houghton Mifflin, 1982. 1st ed. Fine in Fine dj. *Authors Of West.* $40/£26

GUTHRIE, A. B., JR. The Genuine Article. Houghton Mifflin, 1977. 1st ed. Fine in Fine dj. *Authors Of West.* $40/£26

GUTHRIE, A. B., JR. The Last Valley. Houghton Mifflin, 1975. 1st ed. Fine in Fine dj. *Authors Of West.* $40/£26

GUTHRIE, A. B., JR. These Thousand Hills. Boston: Houghton, Mifflin, 1956. 1st ed. Fine in dj (lt worn). *Else Fine.* $35/£22

GUTHRIE, A. B., JR. The Way West. NY: William Sloane, (1949). 1st ed. VG in dj (spine ends sl chipped, rubbed). *Pacific*.* $104/£67

GUTHRIE, DOUGLAS. A History of Medicine. Phila: Lippincott, (1946). 1st Amer ed. 78 plts. VG. *Glaser.* $50/£32

GUTHRIE, DOUGLAS. A History of Medicine. 1945. 1st ed. 72 plts. (Spine ends sl bumped), o/w VG. *Whitehart.* $39/£25

GUTHRIE, WILLIAM. A New Geographical, Historical, and Commercial Grammar. Phila, 1809. 1st Amer ed. Plt, 25 fldg maps. (Foxed, browned, sl frayed.) Contemp calf (rubbed). *Oinonen*.* $140/£90

GUTHRIE, WOODY. American Folksong. (NY: Moe Asch/DISC Company of Amer, 1947). 1st ed. Canvas, stiff card cvrs. NF- (sl rubbing extrems). *Between The Covers.* $750/£481

GUTMAN, JUDITH MARA. Lewis W. Hine and the American Social Conscience. NY: Walker, 1967. 1st ed. (Owner stamp), else VG. *Cahan.* $65/£42

GUTTERY, D. R. From Broad-Glass to Cut Crystal. London: Leonard Hill, 1956. 1st ed. Frontis, 68 plts. VG. *Hollett.* $133/£85

GUTTMANN, PAUL. A Handbook of Physical Diagnosis. Alex Napier (trans). London: New Sydenham Soc, 1879. xii,441pp. Brn cl (spine relaid). VG. *White.* $23/£15

GUTZLAFF, CHARLES. The Journal of Two Voyages Along the Coast of China in 1813 and 1832. NY: Haven, 1833. 1st ed. vii,332pp. Orig cl. (Foxing; rebacked, cvrs worn, sl damp-affected), o/w Good. *Worldwide.* $85/£54

GUY, ROSA. Bird at My Window. Phila/NY: Lippincott, 1966. 1st ed, 1st bk. (Top edge sl dampstain), else Fine in NF dj (crown sl nicked). *Between The Covers.* $300/£192

GUY, ROSA. Bird at My Window. Phila: Lippincott, 1966. 1st ed, 1st bk. Cl-backed bds. VG in illus dj. *Petrilla.* $75/£48

GUY, WILLIAM A. The Factors of the Unsound Mind.... London: Thos de la Rue, 1881. 1st ed. xx,232pp + inserted ads. Partly unopened. Panelled ochre cl (scratched, shelfworn, spine shellacked). VG- (textblock sl gouged). *Gach.* $175/£112

GUYE, SAMUEL and HENRI MICHEL. Time and Space: Measuring Instruments from the 15th to the 19th Century. NY: Praeger, 1971. 1st ed. 20 tipped-in color illus. Linen. VG in dj (extrems sl worn). *Weber.* $80/£51

GUYER, ELMER E. Pioneer Life in West Texas. Brownwood, TX: N.p., 1938. Fine. *Dumont.* $75/£48

GUYER, JAMES S. Pioneer Life in West Texas. Brownwood, 1938. Red cl. Fine. Howes G469. *Bohling.* $60/£38

GUYER, S. My Journey Down the Tigris. Joseph McCabe (trans). London, 1925. 1st Eng ed. 16 plts. (Spine sl rubbed, sl worn.) *Edwards.* $94/£60

GUYER, S. My Journey Down the Tigris. NY: Adelphi, 1925. Frontis, 15 plts. Dj (tattered). *Archaeologia.* $85/£54

GUZMAN, JESSIE P. (ed). Negro Year Book...1941-1946. Tuskegee, AL, 1947. Inscribed. (Sl shaken, sl worn), o/w VG. *New Hampshire*.* $30/£19

GWATHMEY, JOHN H. Legends of Virginia Courthouses. Dietz, 1933. 1st ed. Good (sig; spine insect damage). *Book Broker.* $40/£26

GWILT, J. Rudiments of Architecture, Practical and Theoretical. London: James Maynard, 1835. 2nd ed. xiv,1f,230pp, 1f ads (trace lib stamp tp verso); 6 + 11 engr plts. 1/2 cl (sl worn, spine tear repaired, gilt lib mk spine), marbled bds. *Ars Artis.* $133/£85

GWILT, J. Sciography; or, Examples of Shadows... London: Priestley & Weale, 1833. 3rd ed. 24 engr plts. (Lib stamp verso tp, verso some plts.) 1/2 leather (rubbed, gilt lib stamp spine). *Ars Artis.* $117/£75

GWYNN, STEPHEN. Captain Scott. NY: Harper, 1930. 1st Amer ed. Map. Blue cl. (Eps dknd; sm mks rear cvr, sl worn), else VG. *Parmer.* $55/£35

H

H. (Anna Holstein). Three Years in Field Hospitals of the Army of the Potomac. Phila, 1867. 1st ed. 131pp. VG. *Fye.* $375/£240

HAAK, BOB. Rembrandt. His Life, His Work, His Time. NY, n.d. (1969). Good in dj. *Washton.* $145/£93

HAAS, ERNST. In America. NY: Viking, 1975. 1st ed. NF in VG dj (2 closed tears). *Smith.* $65/£42

HAAS, IRVIN (ed). Bibliography of Modern American Presses. Chicago: Black Cat, 1935. 1st ed. One of 300. Glazed linen, ptd label fr bd. Fine. *Cahan.* $100/£64

HAAS, ROBERT BARTLETT (ed). Gertrude Stein. L.A.: Black Sparrow, 1971. Ltd to 500 hb. Pub leaflet laid in. Pict cvrs. Fine in Fine dj. *Polyanthos.* $60/£38

HABACHI, LABIB. The Obelisks of Egypt: Skyscrapers of the Past. NY: Scribner, (1977). Frontis. Good in dj (top edge lt rubbed). *Archaeologia.* $35/£22

HABENSTEIN and LAMERS. The History of American Funeral Directing. Milwaukee, 1956. 2nd ptg. 77 full-pg plts. Dec cvr. Good+. *Scribe's Perch*.* $70/£45

HABERLY, LOYD. Anne Boleyn, and Other Poems. Newtown: Gregynog, 1934. One of 300 numbered. Full brn crushed levant. *Swann*.* $201/£129

HABERSHAM, A. W. The North Pacific Surveying and Exploring Expedition.... Phila, 1857. 1st ed. 507pp (1 sig loose but present) + 4pp ads. (Spine ends somewhat worn), o/w VG. *Truepenny.* $200/£128

HABIB-AYROUT, HENRY. The Fellaheen. Cairo: R. Schindler, (1945). (Sig; spine faded.) Wrappers. *Archaeologia.* $35/£22

HABLY, W. D. Origins of Education Among Primitive Peoples. London, 1926. 1st ed. (Prelims lt browned; spine sl rubbed, sl cl loss top edge.) *Edwards.* $94/£60

HACHIYA, MICHIHIKO. Hiroshima Diary: The Journal of a Japanese Physician, August 6-September 30, 1945. Chapel Hill, NC, 1955. 1st ed in English. VG. *Fye.* $100/£64

HACKENBROCH, YVONNE. Bronzes Other Metalwork and Sculpture in the Irwin Untermeyer Collection. NY: MMA, (1962). 1st ed. Fine. *Hermitage.* $85/£54

HACKETT, CHARLES WILSON (ed). Historical Documents Relating to New Mexico, Nueva Vizcaya, and Approaches Thereto, to 1773. Washington: Carnegie Inst, 1923, 1926, 1937. 1st ed. Signed presentation vol 1. 3 vols. Map, 5 facs. Dk blue cl, gilt lettered spines (sl rubbed). Overall Fine set. *Argonaut.* $750/£481

HACKETT, CHARLES WILSON (ed). Revolt of the Pueblo Indians of New Mexico and Otermin's Attempted Reconquest, 1680-1682. Albuquerque: Univ of NM, 1970. 2nd ptg. 2 vols. Maroon cl. Uncut, unopened. Djs. *Dawson.* $100/£64

HACKETT, FRANK W. Memoir of William H. Y. Hackett. Portsmouth, NH: Privately ptd, 1879. 1st ed. #267 of sm numbered ed. (6),157pp. *Ginsberg.* $75/£48

HACKNEY, L. W. and Y. CHANG-FOO. A Study of Chinese Paintings in the Collection of Ada Small Moore. OUP, 1940. Grn cl gilt. Dj (torn). *Hatchwell.* $226/£145

HACKWOOD, FREDERICK W. Inns, Ales, and Drinking Customs of Old England. London, 1909. 1st ed. Color frontis, 40 plts. Teg. (Lt browning, lacks fep; spine faded intruding sl onto bds.) *Edwards.* $86/£55

HADDEN, J. CUTHBERT. The Operas of Wagner, Their Plots, Music and History. London, 1908. 24 color plts by Byam Shaw (1 detached). Teg. Gilt-stamped cl (sl worn, dknd). *King*. $35/£22

HADER, BERTA and ELMER. Chicken Little. NY: Macmillan Happy Hour, 1934. 5 3/4 sq. 44pp. Pict bds. Good. *Cattermole*. $30/£19

HADER, BERTA and ELMER. Little Appaloosa. NY: Macmillan, 1949. 1st ed. 8 3/4 x 10. 48pp. Fine in dj. *Cattermole*. $30/£19

HADER, BERTA and ELMER. The Mighty Hunter. NY: Macmillan, 1943. 1st ed. 8 x 10. 32pp. VG in dj. *Cattermole*. $75/£48

HADFIELD, JOHN (ed). Restoration Love Songs. Cupid Press, 1950. 1st Eng ed. Rex Whistler (dwgs). Buckram-backed Cockerell bds. Fine in orig cellophane wrapper. *Clearwater*. $101/£65

HADFIELD, JOHN. Love on a Branch Line. London: Hutchinson, 1959. 1st UK ed. VG + in dj (sl stained, sl rubbed, sl loss spine top). *Williams*. $50/£32

HADFIELD, M. (ed). The Gardener's Album. London, 1954. Inscribed by R. Gathorne-Hardy (contrib). 48 plts (24 color). (Cl sl discolored.) Dj (rubbed). *Maggs*. $47/£30

HADFIELD, M. A History of British Gardening. London, 1969. Rev ed. Dj. *Maggs*. $22/£14

HAESAERTS, PAUL. James Ensor. NY, (1959). Sm folio. Dj (torn). *Swann**. $115/£74

HAFEN, LEROY R. Broken Hand. The Life Story of Thomas Fitzpatrick.... Denver: Old West Pub Co, 1931. 1st ed. Fine. Howes H10. *Argonaut*. $375/£240

HAFEN, LEROY R. Broken Hand: The Life of Thomas Fitzpatrick.... Denver: Old West, (1973). One of 200. Signed. Dbl-pg map. Brn cl w/illus applied, in blue slipcase w/applied illus. *Dawson*. $125/£80

HAFEN, LEROY R. Colorado: The Story of a Western Commonwealth. Denver: Peerless, 1933. 1st ed. Frontis. Grn cl, gilt. VG (tips sl rubbed). *Cahan*. $75/£48

HAFEN, LEROY R. The Far West and the Rockies, Historical Series 1820-1875. Glendale, CA: A.H. Clark, 1956-61. 15 vols. Fine. *Reese*. $2,500/£1,603

HAFEN, LEROY R. (ed). The Mountain Men and the Fur Trade of the Far West. Glendale: A.H. Clark, 1965-1972. 1st ed. 10 vols, 9 3/8x6 1/4 in. Brn cl. *Dawson*. $900/£577

HAFEN, LEROY R. (ed). The Mountain Men and the Fur Trade of the Far West.... Glendale: Clark, 1964-72. 1st ed. One of approx 2000. 10 vols. Map. Brn-grey cl. VF. *Argonaut*. $1,750/£1,122

HAFEN, LEROY R. The Overland Mail, 1849-1869. Cleveland: A.H. Clark, 1926. 1st ed. Fldg map. Teg. Grn cl. Fine. Howes H11. *Harrington*. $225/£144

HAFEN, LEROY R. (ed). Pike's Peak Gold Rush Guide Books of 1859. Glendale: Clark, 1941. 1st ed. One of 1020. Fldg map. (Spine sl faded), else Fine. *Argonaut*. $125/£80

HAFEN, LEROY R. (ed). Reports from Colorado: The Wildman Letters 1859-1865. Glendale: Clark, 1961. 1st ed. Fldg map. *Ginsberg*. $75/£48

HAFEN, LEROY R. Utah Expedition 1857-1858. Glendale: A.H. Clark, 1982. 2nd ptg. Fldg map. Fine. *Bohling*. $30/£19

HAFEN, LEROY R. and ANN W. Fremont's Fourth Expedition. Glendale: Clark, 1960. 1st ed. One of 1500. Fldg map. VF. *Argonaut*. $90/£58

HAFEN, LEROY R. and ANN W. Handcarts to Zion. Glendale: A.H. Clark, 1960. Pioneers ed. Brn cl. (Sl shelfworn), else VG. *Parmer*. $47/£30

HAFEN, LEROY R. and ANN W. Old Spanish Trail. Glendale: A.H. Clark, (1960). 1st ed, 2nd ptg. Frontis, 16 plts, lg fldg map tipped to rep. Uncut. Grn cl, gilt spine. Fine. *Pacific**. $69/£44

HAFEN, LEROY R. and ANN W. Old Spanish Trail: Santa Fe to Los Angeles. Glendale: Clark, 1960. 2nd ptg. One of 506. Fldg map. VF. *Argonaut*. $90/£58

HAFEN, LEROY R. and ANN W. (eds). Handcarts to Zion: the Story of a Unique Western Migration, 1856-1860.... Glendale: Clark, 1969. 2nd ed. One of 153. Unopened. Grn cl. Fine. *Argonaut*. $45/£29

HAFEN, LEROY R. and ANN W. (eds). Journals of the Forty-Niners: Salt Lake to Los Angeles. Glendale: Clark, 1954. 1st ed. One of 1116. Frontis. Grn cl (sl worn, spine ends lt rubbed), gilt-lettered spine. NF (sig, few marginal pencil notes). *Argonaut*. $50/£32

HAFEN, LEROY R. and ANN W. (eds). Powder River Campaigns and Sawyers Expedition of 1865. Glendale: Clark, 1961. 1st ed. One of 1582. Grn cl (lt rubbed), gilt-lettered spine. Fine (bkpl inner cvr). *Argonaut*. $90/£58

HAFEN, LEROY R. and ANN W. (eds). Reports from Colorado: The Wildman Letters, 1859-1865.... Glendale: Clark, 1961. 1st ed. One of 1513. Frontis ports, 15 plts, fldg map. VF. *Argonaut*. $75/£48

HAFEN, LEROY R. and ANN W. Handcarts to Zion: The Story of a Unique Western Migration 1856-1860. Glendale: A.H. Clark, 1960. 1st ed. Fine in dj (price-clipped, sl rubbed, chipped). *Hermitage*. $85/£54

HAFEN, LEROY R. and FRANCIS MARION YOUNG. Fort Laramie and the Pageant of the West, 1834-1890. Glendale: Clark, 1938. 1st ed. (Spine sl faded.) Howes H11. *Ginsberg*. $175/£112

HAFEN, MARY ANN. Recollections of a Handcraft Pioneer of 1860.... Denver, 1938. True 1st ed. Inscribed by Leroy Hafen. Frontis. (Fr cvr sl bowed), o/w NF. *Benchmark*. $400/£256

HAFTMANN, WERNER. Marc Chagall. Heinrich Baumann and Alexis Brown (trans). NY: Abrams, 1972. 49 hand-tipped plts. Mint in dj. *Argosy*. $300/£192

HAFTMANN, WERNER. The Mind and Work of Paul Klee. NY: Praeger, 1947. 1st ed. Color frontis. VG (eps sl discolored; inscrip) in dj (worn). *Cahan*. $30/£19

HAGAN, WILLIAM T. American Indians. Univ of Chicago, (1961). 1st ed. VG in dj. *Lien*. $25/£16

HAGAN, WILLIAM T. The Sac and Fox Indians. Norman: Univ of OK, (1958). 1st ed. VG in dj (sl worn). *Lien*. $40/£26

HAGER, JEAN. Night Walker. NY: St. Martin's, 1990. 1st ed. Fine in dj. *Mordida*. $65/£42

HAGERTY, HARRY J. The Jasmine Trail. NY: Lothrop, 1936. 1st ed. Fine in VG dj (sl worn, browned). *Metropolitan**. $23/£15

HAGGAR, ARTHUR L. and LEONARD F. MILLER. Suffolk Clocks and Clockmakers. (Ramsgate: AHS, 1974.) 1st ed. Fldg map. VG in dj. *Weber*. $85/£54

HAGGAR, REGINALD G. English Country Pottery. London: Phoenix House, 1950. 1st ed. 32pp of plts. VG in dj (sl worn, chipped). *Hollett*. $62/£40

HAGGAR, REGINALD G. Staffordshire Chimney Ornaments. London, 1955. 1st ed. Color frontis; 4 color, 98 b/w plts. Als loosely inserted. (Spine lt faded.) *Edwards*. $75/£48

HAGGARD, H. RIDER and ANDREW LANG. The World's Desire. Longmans, 1890. 1st UK ed. 16-pg ad cat dated Oct 1890 as called for. VG (sl wear bottom edges, sm nick spine top). *Williams*. $101/£65

HAGGARD, H. RIDER and ANDREW LANG. The World's Desire. London: Longmans, Green, 1890. 1st ed. 16pp ads dated Oct 1890. Dk blue-black cl, beveled. NF (spine sl sunned, sm closed nick). *Sumner & Stillman*. $190/£122

HAGGARD, H. RIDER and ANDREW LANG. The Worlds' Desire. London: Longmans, Green, 1890. 1st ed. viii,316,16pp. Cl over beveled bds. Very Nice. *Hollett.* $70/£45

HAGGARD, H. RIDER. Allan and the Ice-Gods. NY: Doubleday, 1927. 1st Amer ed. (Lt rubbed.) Dj (fr panel lacks 3 pieces, spine dknd, chipped). *Swann*.* $80/£51

HAGGARD, H. RIDER. Allan Quatermain. London: Longmans, Green, 1887. 1st ed. Blue cl (spine head sl worn), beveled edges. *Appelfeld.* $150/£96

HAGGARD, H. RIDER. Allan Quatermain. Chicago, n.d. Early Amer ed. Modern Author's Library #153. VG (paper browned) in wraps. *Mcclintock.* $35/£22

HAGGARD, H. RIDER. The Ancient Allan. Cassell, 1920. 1st UK ed. Brn cl, paper inlay. VG. *Williams.* $117/£75

HAGGARD, H. RIDER. Ayesha, the Return of She. Ward Lock, 1905. 1st UK ed. Fine (edges sl foxed). *Williams.* $148/£95

HAGGARD, H. RIDER. Ayesha, The Return of She. London, 1905. 1st ed. (Foxing, fr hinge separated.) *Typographeum.* $85/£54

HAGGARD, H. RIDER. Ayesha, the Return of She. London: Ward Lock, 1905. 1st Eng ed. (Hinges cracking, cvrs sl mkd, chafed.) *Clearwater.* $62/£40

HAGGARD, H. RIDER. Ayesha, the Return of She. NY: Doubleday, Page, 1905. 1st Amer ed. (Lt overall soil, sl bubbling of cl along fr joint), o/w Very Nice. *Hermitage.* $75/£48

HAGGARD, H. RIDER. Ayesha, the Return of She. NY: Doubleday, Page, 1905. 1st Amer ed. Red cl, gilt. *Appelfeld.* $125/£80

HAGGARD, H. RIDER. Beatrice. Longmans, 1890. 1st UK ed. VG (sm spine nicks). *Williams.* $125/£80

HAGGARD, H. RIDER. Belshazzar. NY: Doubleday, 1930. 1st Amer ed. Dj (chipped, rubbed). *Swann*.* $69/£44

HAGGARD, H. RIDER. Black Heart and White Heart and Other Stories. London: Longmans, 1900. 1st UK ed. VG (fr hinge starting, ink inscrip). *Williams.* $101/£65

HAGGARD, H. RIDER. The Brethren. London/Paris/NY/Melbourne: Cassell, 1904. 1st ed. 2pp undated ads, 16pp ads dated Sept 1904. Red cl, gilt. NF (sl offset of red onto eps; lt damp mks rear cvr). *Sumner & Stillman.* $190/£122

HAGGARD, H. RIDER. The Brethren. London: Cassell, 1904. 1st UK ed. 16pp ads dated Sept 1904 as called for. NF. *Williams.* $148/£95

HAGGARD, H. RIDER. Cleopatra. London: Longmans, Green, 1889. 1st ed. Dk blue cl (sl worn). *Appelfeld.* $250/£160

HAGGARD, H. RIDER. Colonel Quaritch V.C. Longmans, 1889. 1st 1 vol ed. VG (fep hinges starting, lt foxing). *Williams.* $94/£60

HAGGARD, H. RIDER. Doctor Therne. London: Longmans, 1898. 1st UK ed. Binding variant w/rounded spine, 'Longmans' at bottom of spine. Near Mint. *Williams.* $195/£125

HAGGARD, H. RIDER. Eric Brighteyes. London: Longmans, Green, 1891. 2nd ed. xiv,318pp+24pp pub's cat. Uncut. Good (backstrip sl faded). *Cox.* $23/£15

HAGGARD, H. RIDER. A Gardener's Year. London, 1905. 2nd imp. Plan, 25 plts. Teg. (Spine faded.) *Henly.* $44/£28

HAGGARD, H. RIDER. The Ghost Kings. Cassell, 1908. 1st UK ed. VG (spine sl faded). *Williams.* $101/£65

HAGGARD, H. RIDER. Heu-Heu. London: Hutchinson, 1923. 1st UK ed. VG in dj (worn, dusty, sl chipped). *Williams.* $585/£375

HAGGARD, H. RIDER. The Holy Flower. London: Ward, Locke, 1915. 1st ed. Variant binding: 'for sale abroad' blind-stamped on rear bd. (Bkseller stamp eps; rubbed, worn, spine creased, sm tear, glass ring fr cvr, sl stained.) *Swann*.* $46/£29

HAGGARD, H. RIDER. The Ivory Child. Cassell, 1916. 1st ed. VG-. *Aronovitz.* $85/£54

HAGGARD, H. RIDER. Joan Haste. London: Longmans, 1895. 1st ed. (Worn, fr joint starting, sl bubbling.) *Swann*.* $46/£29

HAGGARD, H. RIDER. King Solomon's Mines. NY: Editions for the Armed Services, (1945). Nice in wrappers. *Turtle Island.* $15/£10

HAGGARD, H. RIDER. Maiwa's Revenge. London: Longmans, 1888. 1st ed. Black cl (lt rubbed, sl askew; foxed, ink sig). *Swann*.* $103/£66

HAGGARD, H. RIDER. Maiwa's Revenge. Chicago, n.d. Early Amer ed. Modern Author's Library #152. NF (paper sl browned) in wraps. *Mcclintock.* $35/£22

HAGGARD, H. RIDER. Marion Isle. NY: Doubleday, 1929. 1st Amer ed. (Sl worn.) Dj (chips, creases, internal cellotape mends). *Swann*.* $80/£51

HAGGARD, H. RIDER. Montezuma's Daughter. Longmans, Green, 1893. 1st ed. viii,325pp+24pp pub's cat. Good (backstrip sl faded, chipped). *Cox.* $39/£25

HAGGARD, H. RIDER. Morning Star. Longmans, Green, 1910. 1st ed. NF. *Aronovitz.* $100/£64

HAGGARD, H. RIDER. Mr. Meeson's Will. Spencer Blackett, 1888. 1st ed. 286pp+32pp pub's cat dated Oct 1888. Uncut. Good in pict cl (backstrip dull, ends repaired). *Cox.* $101/£65

HAGGARD, H. RIDER. Mr. Meeson's Will. London: Spencer Blackett, 1888. 1st UK ed. VG (sm section neatly excised from 1/2 title, bkpl; bds unevenly faded, spine sl bumped). *Williams.* $133/£85

HAGGARD, H. RIDER. Nada the Lilly. Longmans, Green, 1892. 1st ed. Frontis, xv,(i),295pp, pub's 24-pg cat dated 2/92; 22 plts. (Lt waterstain 1st text leaf, spine faded, lt stains upper cvr.) *Bickersteth.* $59/£38

HAGGARD, H. RIDER. Nada the Lily. London, 1892. 1st ed. VG. *Madle.* $200/£128

HAGGARD, H. RIDER. Our Lady of the Heavens. NY, (1908). 1st Amer ed. Variant binding: red-violet cl, gilt, girl's head blindstamped on cvr. VG. *Mcclintock.* $75/£48

HAGGARD, H. RIDER. Pearl-Maiden. Longmans, 1903. 1st UK ed. Fine. *Williams.* $148/£95

HAGGARD, H. RIDER. Pearl-Maiden. London: Longmans, 1903. 1st ed. (Ink sig; bumped, sl rubbed, sl spotted.) *Swann*.* $46/£29

HAGGARD, H. RIDER. Pearl-Maiden. NY: Longmans, Green, 1903. 1st Amer ed. 6pp undated ads. Dk blue cl, gilt. NF (spine sl dknd). *Sumner & Stillman.* $130/£83

HAGGARD, H. RIDER. Queen of the Dawn. London: Hutchinson, (1925). 1st UK ed. 48-pg cat at rear dated Spring 1925. Fine (fore-edge sl foxed) in VG dj (sl rubbed, worn, sm loss spine extrems). *Williams.* $616/£395

HAGGARD, H. RIDER. Queen of the Dawn. NY: Doubleday, Page, 1925. 1st ed. NF. *Hermitage.* $125/£80

HAGGARD, H. RIDER. Queen of the Dawn. Hutchinson, n.d. (1925). 48-pg cat at rear dated Spring 1925 as called for. VG +. *Williams.* $101/£65

HAGGARD, H. RIDER. Red Eve. Doubleday Page, 1911. 1st US ed. Color frontis. Blind-stamped brick red cl, gilt. VG. *Certo.* $65/£42

HAGGARD, H. RIDER. Regeneration. Longmans, 1910. 1st UK ed. VG (ink inscrip, foxed; sm mks bds). *Williams.* $55/£35

HAGGARD, H. RIDER. Regeneration. London: Longmans, Green, 1910. 1st ed. (Lt foxing, bds sl bowed, sunned), else VG. *Hermitage.* $45/£29

HAGGARD, H. RIDER. She. Longmans, 1887. 1st issue, w/misprint 'Godness me' line 38 pg 269. Fine (fep hinges sl starting). *Williams.* $624/£400

HAGGARD, H. RIDER. She. London: Longmans, Green, 1887. 1st ed. Blue cl, gilt. Nice. *Appelfeld.* $350/£224

HAGGARD, H. RIDER. Stella Fregelius. NY: Longmans, Green, 1903. 1st ed. 24pp undated ads. Grn-blue cl. VG (bkpl; sl rubbed). *Sumner & Stillman.* $50/£32

HAGGARD, H. RIDER. Stella Fregelius. Longmans, 1904. 1st UK ed. Fine. *Williams.* $148/£95

HAGGARD, H. RIDER. Stella Fregelius. Longmans, Green, 1904. 1st British ed. Nice (eps sl strained, sl mks, sl wear). *Ash.* $62/£40

HAGGARD, H. RIDER. Stella Fregelius. London: Longmans, 1904. 1st ed. Fine. *Swann*.* $69/£44

HAGGARD, H. RIDER. Swallow. London: Longmans, 1899. 1st UK ed. VG (sl foxed). *Williams.* $62/£40

HAGGARD, H. RIDER. Treasure of the Lake. NY: Doubleday, (1926). 1st Amer ed. (Owner stamp; sl worn.) Dj (dknd, chipped, rubbed). *Swann*.* $103/£66

HAGGARD, H. RIDER. When the World Shook. Cassell, 1919. 1st UK ed. VG (closed tear rep hinge) in Attractive pict dj (lt edgewear, 3 sm chips, no loss). *Williams.* $1,170/£750

HAGGARD, H. RIDER. When the World Shook. London, 1919. 1st ed. VG-. *Madle.* $75/£48

HAGUE, HARLAN. The Road to California. Glendale: Clark, 1978. 1st ed. One of 1048. Red cl, gilt spine. VF. *Argonaut.* $75/£48

HAGUE, WILLIAM. Life Notes; or, Fifty Years Outlook. Boston: Lee, 1888. 1st ed. (11),362pp. (Spine cl lt flecked.) *Ginsberg.* $75/£48

HAHN, GEORGE W. The Catawba Soldier of the Civil War. A Sketch of Every Soldier...Together with a Sketch of Catawba County.... Hickory, NC: Clay Printing, 1911. 1st ed. (Fr bd soiled), else VG. *Mcgowan.* $450/£288

HAID, ALAN G. Decoys of the Mississippi Flyway. Exton, PA: Schiffer, 1981. 1st ed. Brn leatherette, gilt. Orig prospectus laid in. Fine in Fine dj. *Biscotti.* $50/£32

HAIG-BROWN, RODERICK L. Return to the River: A Story of the Chinook Run. Toronto: McClelland & Stewart, (1946). 1st Canadian ed. (Name, address), else Fine in Nice dj (chipped). *Authors Of West.* $40/£26

HAIG-BROWN, RODERICK L. The Whale People. London: Collins, 1962. 1st British ed. Fine in dj. *Authors Of West.* $40/£26

HAIG-THOMAS, DAVID. Tracks in the Snow. NY: OUP, 1939. Map. Fine in dj. *High Latitude.* $50/£32

HAIGHT, ANNE LYON (ed). Hroswitha of Gandersheim, Her Life, Times, and Works and a Comprehensive Bibliography. NY: Hroswitha Club, 1965. One of 1200. Frontis. Brn cl bds, gilt spine title. Fine; issued w/o dj. *Heller.* $65/£42

HAIGHT, ANNE LYON. Banned Books. NY: Bowker, 1935. 1st ed. One of 1000 ptd. Dec spine. *Ginsberg.* $100/£64

HAIL, WILLIAM JAMES. Tseng Kuo-Fan and the Taiping Rebellion. New Haven: Yale Univ, 1927. 1st ed. Inscribed. Maroon cl. VG. *Terramedia.* $75/£48

HAILE, BERNARD. Emergence Myth According to the Hanelthnayhe or Upward-Reaching Rite. Santa Fe: Museum of Navajo Ceremonial Art, 1949. 1st ed. 13 serigraph plts. Grn cl. Fine in Fine dj. *Harrington.* $225/£144

HAIMAN, MIECISLAUS. Polish Pioneers of Virginia and Kentucky. Chicago: Polish Rom. Cath. Union, 1937. Facs. VG in red ptd wraps (spine foot frayed). *Bohling.* $15/£10

HAINAUX, RENE (ed). Stage Design Throughout the World Since 1935. NY: Theatre Arts, (1957). VG. *Dramatis Personae.* $40/£26

HAINES, ELIJAH M. The American Indian (Uh-Nish-In-Na-Ba). Chicago: Mas-sin-na'-gan, 1888. 1st ed. (Sl spotting.) Fldg map. Dec brn cl, beveled bds (wear beginning, fr hinge expertly repaired). VG. Howes H19. *Harrington.* $125/£80

HAINES, ELIJAH M. Historical and Statistical Sketches, of Lake County, Illinois. Waukegan, IL, 1852 (i.e., 1853). Sm 8vo. Fldg frontis, errata leaf. Orig white letterpress wrappers (fr joint splitting). Howes H20. *Swann*.* $1,035/£663

HAINES, FRANCIS. The Nez Perces. Norman: Univ of OK, (1955). 1st ed. VG in dj. *Lien.* $75/£48

HAINES, HERBERT. A Manual of Monumental Brasses. Oxford/London: J.H. & Jas. Parker, 1861. 1st ed. 2 vols. Color litho frontis, cclxiii,286pp+ad leaf. VG set in brn cl (rebacked, new eps), orig backstrips. *Cox.* $94/£60

HAINES, HERBERT. A Manual of Monumental Brasses.... Oxford/London: J. H. & Jas. Parker, 1861. 2 vols. Color frontis. (Head, foot of spines worn.) *Bickersteth.* $55/£35

HAINES, JOHN. Twenty Poems. (Santa Barbara): Unicorn, (1971). 1st ed. One of 485 numbered. Fine in dj (sl worn). *Turlington.* $35/£22

HAINING, PETER (ed). The Hashish Club. An Anthology of Drug Literature. Peter Owen, 1975. 2 vols. NF set. *Sclanders.* $44/£28

HAINING, PETER (ed). The Hashish Club. An Anthology of Drug Literature. Peter Owen, 1975. 1st UK ed. 2 vols. VG set in djs. *Williams.* $78/£50

HAINING, PETER (ed). The Sherlock Holmes Scrapbook. NY: Clarkson Potter, (1974). 1st US ed. VG in Good dj (wear). *Gravesend.* $30/£19

HAINING, PETER. Movable Books. London, (1979). Obl 4to. (Sl worn.) Dj (sl frayed, sl soiled, spotted). *Oinonen*.* $120/£77

HAITES, ERIK F. et al. Western River Transportation. Balt: Johns Hopkins, (1975). Dbl map. Errata slip laid in. VG (lib bkpl). *Bohling.* $20/£13

HAJEK, LUBOR and WERNER FORMAN. A Book of Chinese Art. Arnost Jappel (trans). London: Spring Books, 1966. 221 plts (20 color). NF in dj. *Worldwide.* $35/£22

HAKE, A. EGMONT. The Story of Chinese Gordon. London, 1884. 4th ed. Frontis port, 407pp; port, 2 fldg maps. (Spine faded, sl soiled, sm chip lower joint, corners rubbed w/sl cl loss.) *Edwards.* $47/£30

HALBERSTAM, DAVID. The Making of a Quagmire. NY: Random House, (1965). 1st ed. NF in NF dj (sl edgeworn, spine sl faded). *Fuller & Saunders.* $25/£16

HALBERT, HENRY S. and TIMOTHY H. BALL. The Creek War of 1813 and 1814. Chicago, 1895. 1st ed. 331,(3)pp; fldg map. (Cl faded.) Howes H28. *Ginsberg.* $375/£240

HALBERT, HENRY S. and TIMOTHY H. BALL. The Creek War of 1813 and 1814. Chicago: Donohue & Henneberry, 1895. 1st ed. 331,(3)pp; 4 plts, fldg map. VG (inner hinges starting; sl soiled). Howes H28. *Mcgowan.* $350/£224

HALDANE, A. R. B. The Drove Roads of Scotland. Edinburgh: University Press, 1968. 16 plts, fldg map in rear pocket. (Sigs.) Dj (sl edgeworn). *Hollett.* $62/£40

HALDANE, R. B. The Life of Adam Smith. London, 1887. 160,x,(xii)pp. (Feps sl browned, bkpl; cl lt soiled, spine sl chipped.) *Edwards.* $23/£15

HALDEMAN-JULIUS, MARCET and E. Violence. NY: S&S, 1929. 1st ed. (Pg edges spotted), o/w VG in dj (sl soiled). *Mordida.* $45/£29

HALDEMAN-JULIUS, MARCET. Clarence Darrow's Two Great Trials. Girard, KS: Haldeman-Julius, (1927). Ptd wraps. VG (dknd). *Bohling.* $22/£14

HALE, EDWARD E. Kanzas and Nebraska, the History, Geographical and Physical Characteristics.... Boston: Phillips, Sampson, 1854. 1st ed. Fldg map. Purple cl (spine faded, ends chipped; fep lacks piece). Very Nice. *Glenn.* $250/£160

HALE, EDWIN M. Lectures on Diseases of the Heart. NY: Boericke & Tafel, 1871. 1st ed. ix,(2),(19)-206,(3 ads)pp. Orig cl (rebacked). VG. *Glaser.* $275/£176

HALE, EDWIN M. A Systematic Treatise on Abortion. Chicago: C.S. Halsey, 1866. xiv,347pp, 2 color plts. New 1/2 calf, marbled bds. Good. *Goodrich.* $175/£112

HALE, HORATIO. An International Idiom. A Manual of...'Chinook Jargon.' London, 1890. Als mtd fep. (Bd edges worn.) *Freeman*.* $60/£38

HALE, JOHN PETER. Trans-Allegheny Pioneers. Cincinnati: Graphic Press, 1886. 1st ed. 330pp, fldg facs. Blue cl, gilt. VG+. Howes H32. *Bohling.* $125/£80

HALE, KATHLEEN. Orlando and the Three Graces. London: Murray, 1965. 1st ed. 9 x 7 1/2. 30pp. Pict bds. Fine in dj. *Cattermole.* $100/£64

HALE, KATHLEEN. Orlando's Magic Carpet. NY: Murray, 1958. 1st ed. 9 x 7 1/2. 30pp. Pict bds. Fine in dj. *Cattermole.* $100/£64

HALE, KATHLEEN. Orlando: A Seaside Holiday. London: Country Life, 1952. 1st ed. 10 1/2 x 14 1/4. 32pp. Cl spine. Good (sl worn, bumped). *Cattermole.* $150/£96

HALE, KATHLEEN. Puss in Boots. Boston: Houghton Mifflin, 1951. 1st ed. 5 1/2 x 6 3/4. 6pp. Opens to full circle w/6 scenes. VG. *Cattermole.* $200/£128

HALE, LUCRETIA P. The Peterkin Papers. Boston: James R. Osgood, 1880. 1st ed. Grn cl (spine base lt rubbed). *Swann*.* $230/£147

HALE, MATTHEW. The History of the Common Law...by Charles Runnington. London: G.G. & J. Robinson, 1794. 5th ed. 2 vols. Mod bds. Good set (some browning). *Boswell.* $650/£417

HALE, MATTHEW. History of the Pleas of the Crown...A New Edition...by George Wilson. London: T. Payne, P. Uriel, 1778. 2 vols. Contemp calf (spine ends chipped). Good set. *Boswell.* $850/£545

HALE, MRS. Flora's Interpreter. Boston: Marsh et al, 1842. 11th ed. 264pp; 2 hand-colored plts. Brn cl (spine extrems sl worn). Good. BAL 6792. *Second Life.* $45/£29

HALE, PHILIP. The Book of Live Stock Champions 1905.... St. Louis: National Farmer and Stock Grower, 1905. (Inner hinges broken; shelfworn.) *October Farm.* $65/£42

HALE, SHARRON LEE. A Tribute to Yesterday.... Santa Cruz: Valley Publishers, (1980). 1st ed. Red cl. Fine in dj. *Argonaut.* $35/£22

HALES, JOHN G. A Survey of Boston and Its Vicinity. Boston, 1821. Frontis. Orig bds (part of backstrip lacking; bk label), paper cvr label. Slipcase. *Swann*.* $316/£203

HALEY, ALEX. Roots. GC: Doubleday, 1976. 1st ed. Untrimmed. Black cl, lt brn bds (sl shelfworn), gilt. Dj (spine lt sunned, creased). *Baltimore*.* $50/£32

HALEY, ALEX. Roots. GC: Doubleday, 1976. 1st ed. Cl-backed bds. Fine in dj. *Jaffe.* $100/£64

HALEY, ALEX. Roots. GC: Doubleday, 1976. One of 500 numbered, signed. Fine in full leather. Fine slipcase. *Lenz.* $250/£160

HALEY, EARL. Revolt on the Painted Desert. Hollywood: House-Warven, 1952. Fabricoid. *Dawson.* $25/£16

HALEY, GAIL E. The Post Office Cat. NY: Scribner, 1976. 1st ed. 10 1/4 x 8 1/4. 32pp. As New in dj. *Cattermole.* $65/£42

HALEY, GAIL. The Green Man. NY: Scribner, 1979. 1st ed. 10 1/4 x 8 1/4. 32pp. Fine in dj. *Cattermole.* $60/£38

HALEY, J. EVETTS. A Bit of Bragging About a Cow. N.p.: George Autry, 1948. Signed, inscribed. Fine in wraps. *Gibbs.* $160/£103

HALEY, J. EVETTS. Charles Goodnight, Cowman and Plainsman. Boston: Houghton Mifflin, 1936. 1st ed. Signed, inscribed from 'Nita and Evetts Haley, December, 1937.' Nice dj (scrape on fr, closed tear, sl edgewear). *Gibbs.* $425/£272

HALEY, J. EVETTS. Charles Goodnight. Norman: Univ of OK, (1949). 2nd ed. Tan linen over bds. Fine in dj (worn). Howes H36. *Glenn.* $50/£32

HALEY, J. EVETTS. Charles Schreiner, General Merchandise, the Story of a Country Store. Austin, 1944. VG+ in dj (plastic protective cvr attached). *Bohling.* $125/£80

HALEY, J. EVETTS. Earl Vandale on the Trail of Texas Books. Canyon, TX: Palo Duro, 1965. 1st ed. One of 500. Port. Fine. W/o dj, as issued. *Reese.* $85/£54

HALEY, J. EVETTS. Earl Vandale on the Trail of Texas Books. Canyon, TX: Palo Duro, 1965. One of 500 ptd. Fine. *Gibbs.* $150/£96

HALEY, J. EVETTS. Focus on the Frontier. Amarillo: Shamrock Oil & Gas Corp, 1957. 1st ed. Red leatherette over bds, gilt. Fine. *Harrington.* $55/£35

HALEY, J. EVETTS. Focus on the Frontier. Amarillo: Shamrock Oil & Gas Corp, 1957. Fine. *Hermitage.* $65/£42

HALEY, J. EVETTS. George W. Littlefield, Texan. Norman: Univ of OK, 1943. 1st ed. VF in VG dj. *Gibbs.* $125/£80

HALEY, J. EVETTS. Jeff Milton, a Good Man with a Gun. Norman: Univ of OK, 1948. 1st ed, 2nd state w/index error corrected. VF in dj (spine faded). *Argonaut.* $90/£58

HALEY, J. EVETTS. Jeff Milton: A Good Man with a Gun. Norman: Univ of OK, (1953). 3rd ed. Inscribed. Fine in dj (sl rubbed, spine lightened, old tape stains). *Sadlon.* $65/£42

HALEY, J. EVETTS. Men of Fiber. El Paso: Carl Hertzog, 1963. Signed. Fine in wraps. *Gibbs.* $35/£22

HALEY, J. EVETTS. Some Southwestern Trails. El Paso, TX: Carl Hertzog, 1948. Ltd ed. Inscribed by Haley. Pict cl. (Spine sl lightened), o/w Fine in NF slipcase w/paper label. *Sadlon.* $300/£192

HALEY, J. EVETTS. Some Southwestern Trails. San Angelo, TX: San Angelo Standard-Times, 1948. Fine in wrappers. *Gibbs.* $195/£125

HALEY, J. EVETTS. The XIT Ranch of Texas and the Early Days of the Llano Estacado. Chicago: Lakeside, 1929. 1st ed. Inscribed 1983. Fine. *Gibbs.* $475/£304

HALEY, JAMES. The Buffalo War. GC: Doubleday, 1976. 1st ed. VG in dj. *Archer.* $20/£13

HALEY, NELSON COLE. Whale Hunt. NY: Ives Washburn, (1948). 1st ed. Dj (sl worn). *Lefkowicz.* $45/£29

HALEY, NELSON COLE. Whale Hunt. NY: Ives Washburn, 1948. (Spine faded), else VG. *Parmer.* $30/£19

HALFORD, FREDERIC M. Dry-Fly Fishing.... London: Vinton, 1899. Rev ed. xx,354,(i)pp; 18 plts (3 hand-colored, 1 chromolitho plan). (Sl worn, bumped.) *Hollett.* $429/£275

HALFPENNY, JOSEPH. Fragmenta Vetusta. York: J. Halfpenny, 1807. 1st ed. Etched title, 34 etchings. Desc. letterpress, 1/2-title, subs list. Old marbled bds (worn, serviceably rebacked in mod buckram). Contents VG (lt foxing to plts). *Waverly**. $154/£99

HALKETT, SAMUEL and JOHN LAING. Dictionary of Anonymous and Pseudonymous English Literature. Edinburgh/London, 1926-34. New, enlgd ed. 7 vols. Uncut. (Sl worn.) Djs (frayed, soiled). *Oinonen**. $375/£240

HALL, A. NEELY. Carpentry and Mechanics for Boys. Boston: Lothrop, Lee & Shepard, 1918. (Sl rubbed, soiled), o/w VG. *Worldwide*. $15/£10

HALL, ADAM. The Berlin Memorandum. Collins, 1965. 1st UK ed. NF in VG dj (closed tear, lt edgewear). *Williams*. $39/£25

HALL, ADAM. The Burning Shore. London: Heinemann, 1961. 1st ed. Fine in dj (price-clipped). *Else Fine*. $45/£29

HALL, ADAM. (Pseud of Elleston Trevor.) The Kobra Manifesto. London: Collins, 1976. 1st ed. Fine in dj (lt edgewear). *Janus*. $35/£22

HALL, ADAM. (Pseud of Elleston Trevor.) The Scorpion Signal. London: Collins, 1979. 1st ed. Signed. Fine in Fine dj. *Janus*. $65/£42

HALL, ADAM. (Pseud of Elleston Trevor.) The Sinkiang Executive. London: Collins, 1978. 1st ed. Signed. Fine in dj (spine top sl worn). *Mordida*. $45/£29

HALL, B. M. Life of Rev. John Clark. NY: Carlton, 1856. 1st ed. 276,(12)pp; port. (Rear joint lt worn.) Howes H45. *Ginsberg*. $300/£192

HALL, BASIL. Extracts from a Journal Written on the Coasts of Chili, Peru,...1820, 1821, 1822. Edinburgh: Constable, 1824. 3rd ed. 2 vols. 3/4 leather, marbled bds (worn; foxed). *Old London*. $140/£90

HALL, BASIL. Extracts from a Journal, Written on the Coasts of Chili, Peru, and Mexico, in the Years 1820, 1821, 1822. Edinburgh: Archibald Constable, 1824. 2nd ed. 2 vols. (iii)-xviii,372; iii-xi,288,65pp. Marbled eps. Period tan calf, gilt, raised spine bands, morocco labels. (Map foxed, 4-inch tear; bkpls; lt shelfworn), else NF. *Pacific**. $196/£126

HALL, BASIL. The Lieutenant and Commander. Bell & Daldy/Sampson Low, 1862. 1st ed. xii,382,(4)pp. (Backstrip ends sl frayed.) *Cox*. $28/£18

HALL, BASIL. Patchwork. Edward Moxon, 1841. 3 vols. Contemp 1/2 leather (corners rubbed), marbled bds, raised bands. Good (spotted). *Tiger*. $70/£45

HALL, BASIL. Travels in North America in the Years 1827 and 1828. Edinburgh: Cadell, 1829. 1st ed. 3 vols. Fldg hand-colored map, chart. Orig blue bds, tan paper spines priced 1£, 11s. 6d, (most hinges cracked; spines chipped), orig ptd paper labels. Internally Bright, Uncut. *D & D*. $490/£314

HALL, BERT L. Roundup Years. Pierre, SD: State Pub Co, (1954). 1st ed. Signed. Good in pict cl (spine tear repaired). *Lien*. $125/£80

HALL, C. R. A Scientist in the Early Republic: Samuel Lathan Mitchill 1764-1831. NY: Columbia, 1934. 1st ed. Frontis port. NF. *Mikesh*. $30/£19

HALL, CARROLL DOUGLAS. The Terry-Broderick Duel. SF: Colt, (1939). Cl-backed pict bds (edges sl rubbed), paper spine label. *Sadlon*. $45/£29

HALL, CHARLES FRANCIS. Life with the Esquimaux. London: Sampson Low, Son & Marston, 1865. Popular ed. x,547pp; 4 color plts, fldg map in pocket. Gilt-dec cl. (Lacks fep), else VG. *High Latitude*. $125/£80

HALL, CHARLES FRANCIS. Life with the Esquimaux.... London, 1865. Popular ed. Later calf (backstrip dknd, joints rubbed), gilt. *Swann**. $69/£44

HALL, CHARLES FRANCIS. Narrative of the North Polar Expedition U.S. Ship Polaris.... C. H. Davis (ed). (By Charles F. Hall.) Washington: GPO, 1876. 696pp. Good (extrems worn, lt soil). *High Latitude*. $175/£112

HALL, CHARLES FRANCIS. Narrative of the North Polar Expedition....C. H. Davis (ed). Washington: US Naval Observatory, 1876. 1st ed. Frontis, 696pp. Dec orange cl, gilt. (Frontis, tp foxed; cl rubbed, worn), else Very Nice. *Parmer*. $300/£192

HALL, CHARLES FRANCIS. Narrative of the Second Arctic Expedition. Washington, 1879. Fldg map in rear pocket. Gilt-pict cl (sl worn). *Swann**. $126/£81

HALL, DONALD. Exiles and Marriages. NY: Viking, 1955. 1st ed. Lamont Award slip tipped in. Fine in NF dj (spine sl tanned). *Reese*. $75/£48

HALL, DONALD. The Man Who Lived Alone. Boston: David Godine, (1984). 1st ed. Signed by Hall and Mary Azarian (illus). 8vo. 35pp. Mint in dj. *Bromer*. $85/£54

HALL, DONALD. Ox Cart Man. NY: Viking, (1979). 1st ed. Barbara Cooney (illus). Oblong 8vo. (40pp). Grn cl-backed bds. (Sm tear fep), o/w As New. *Dower*. $55/£35

HALL, DONALD. Riddle Rat. NY: Frederick Warne, (1977). 1st ed. Inscribed. Mort Gerberg (illus). VF in red bds, pict dj. *Bromer*. $75/£48

HALL, DONALD. The Town of Hill. Boston: Godine, (1975). 1st ed. Dec bds. Fine w/o dj as issued. *Reese*. $30/£19

HALL, E. C. Printed Books 1481-1900 in the Horticultural Society of New York. NY, 1970. Frontis. Cutting loosely inserted. *Maggs*. $42/£27

HALL, FLORENCE HOWE. Social Customs. Boston: Estes & Lauriat, (1887). 1st ed(?). Teg, uncut. Brn pict cl, gilt/white/black-stamped. VG. *Houle*. $150/£96

HALL, FLORENCE HOWE. Social Usages at Washington. NY: Harper, 1906. 1st ed. VG. *Second Life*. $35/£22

HALL, FLORENCE HOWE. Social Usages at Washington. NY: Harper, 1906. 1st ed. Uncut. Blue-gray pict cl, white-stamped. VG. *Houle*. $85/£54

HALL, G. STANLEY. Adolescence.... NY, 1931. 2 vols. VG. *Argosy*. $60/£38

HALL, HARRISON. Hall's Distiller.... Phila: John Bioren, 1813. 1st ed. Fldg copperplt frontis in expert facs, x,244pp; 1 plt. Mod 1/4 calf, marbled bds. VG (browned, stained). *Glaser*. $475/£304

HALL, HENRY MARION. The Ruffed Grouse. NY, 1946. VG. *Truepenny*. $25/£16

HALL, HENRY MARION. The Ruffed Grouse. NY: OUP, 1946. 1st ed. 9 color plts. VG in dj. *Worldwide*. $20/£13

HALL, HENRY MARION. The Ruffed Grouse. NY: OUP, 1946. 1st ed. Color frontis. VG + in VG dj (edge tears; 1-inch piece torn spine). *Backman*. $48/£31

HALL, HENRY MARION. The Ruffed Grouse. NY: Oxford, 1946. 1st ed. 8 color plts. VG. *Bowman*. $30/£19

HALL, HENRY MARION. Woodcock Ways. NY, 1946. VG. *Truepenny*. $25/£16

HALL, HENRY MARION. Woodcock Ways. NY: OUP, 1946. 1st ed. VG in Good dj. *Books & Birds*. $60/£38

HALL, J. Geology of New York. Albany, 1843. xxii,(6),638,3pp. Good. *Blake*. $185/£119

HALL, J. K. (ed). One Hundred Years of American Psychiatry. NY, 1944. VG. *Fye*. $125/£80

HALL, J. K. (ed). One Hundred Years of American Psychiatry. NY, 1947. 1st ed, 2nd ptg. (Ex-lib.) *Fye*. $75/£48

HALL, JAMES BAKER (ed). Ralph Eugene Meatyard. Millerton: Aperture, 1974. 1st ed. (Owner stamp), else Fine in dj. *Cahan.* $65/£42

HALL, JAMES W. Bones of Coral. NY: Knopf, 1991. 1st ed. Signed. VF in dj. *Mordida.* $40/£26

HALL, JAMES W. Tropical Freeze. NY: Norton, 1989. 1st ed. Signed. VF in dj. *Mordida.* $45/£29

HALL, JAMES W. Tropical Freeze. NY: W.W. Norton, 1989. 1st ed. Fine (sm corner bump) in Fine dj. *Janus.* $45/£29

HALL, JAMES W. Under Cover of Daylight. NY: W.W. Norton, 1987. 1st ed. Fine in dj. *Mordida.* $65/£42

HALL, JAMES. Legends of the West. NY: T.L. Magagnos, 1854. Frontis, 435pp, extra engr tp. Leather (simply rebound) w/title portion of orig backstrip laid down. Good reading copy. *Bohling.* $10/£6

HALL, JOHN. Staffordshire Portrait Figures. London, 1972. 1st ed. Color frontis, 60 color plts. Dj. *Edwards.* $23/£15

HALL, MANLEY P. Lectures on Ancient Philosophy. L.A.: Hall, 1929. 1st ed. NF in NF dj. *Beasley.* $85/£54

HALL, MANLY P. An Encyclopedic Outline of Masonic, Hermetic, Quabbalistic and Rosicrucian Symbolical Philosophy. SF, 1928. King Solomon ed. Ltd to 550 numbered. Teg. (Sl insect damage top margin few pp.) Vellum-backed bds (rubbed), spine label (chipped). Wooden slipcase (damaged). *King.* $495/£317

HALL, MANLY P. The Phoenix. L.A.: Philosophical Research Soc, 1956. 3rd ed. One of 1000. Signed. Grn cl. NF in dj (sl soiled). *House.* $150/£96

HALL, MARSHALL. A Descriptive, Diagnostic, and Practical Essay on Disorders of the Digestive Organs.... Keene, NH, 1823. 2nd ed. 142pp (prelims dampstained). Uncut. Orig bds (spine worn). *Goodrich.* $95/£61

HALL, MARSHALL. Essay on Disorders of the Digestive Organs and General Health. Keene, NH, 1823. 2nd ed. 192pp. Orig binding. Good. *Doctor's Library.* $150/£96

HALL, MARTIN HARWICK. Sibley's New Mexico Campaign. Austin: Univ of TX, (1960). 1st ed. NF in VG dj. *Mcgowan.* $250/£160

HALL, MARY. A Woman in the Antipodes. London, 1914. 1st ed. Pub's cat. 3 maps. Gilt-edged cl. *Edwards.* $62/£40

HALL, MAUD R. English Church Needlework. London, 1913. 2nd ed. Teg. (Bkpl, some margins sl thumbed, newspaper clippings loosely inserted; lower bds sl soiled, spine faded.) *Edwards.* $56/£36

HALL, MAX. Benjamin Franklin and Polly Baker: The History of a Literary Deception. Chapel Hill: Inst of Early Amer History and Culture, 1960. 1st ed. Frontis port. Fine in NF dj. *Cahan.* $20/£13

HALL, PERCY. Ultra-Violet Rays in the Treatment and Cure of Disease. London: Heinemann, 1924. 1st ed. (Stamp), o/w Good in blue cl. *Cox.* $28/£18

HALL, RADCLYFFE. The Master of the House. NY: Jonathan Cape/Robert Ballou, (1932). 1st Amer ed. Top edge stained black, uncut. Lt grn cl, gilt. VG in dj (lt soil). *Houle.* $225/£144

HALL, S. C. The Baronial Halls and Ancient Picturesque Edifices of England. London, 1858. 71 tinted litho plts. (Foxed, marginally affecting some plts.) Later 19th-cent brn leather (joints, extrems worn), gilt. *Swann*.* $345/£221

HALL, SHARLOT. Sharlot Hall on the Arizona Strip. C. Gregory Crampton (ed). Flagstaff, 1975. 1st ptg. Frontis, map. Grn cl. VF in pict dj (lt soiled). *Five Quail.* $35/£22

HALL, SUSAN. Gentleman of Leisure: A Year in the Life of a Pimp. NY: NAL, 1972. 1st ed. (Owner stamp), else VG in dj (lt rubbed, scuffed). *Cahan.* $35/£22

HALL, THOMAS B. Medicine on the Santa Fe Trail. (Dayton, Ohio): Morningside Bookshop, 1971. One of 1000 numbered, signed. Fldg table. Gold-stamped blue cl. *Dawson.* $35/£22

HALL, TROWBRIDGE. California Trails, Intimate Guide to the Old Missions.... NY, 1920. 1st ed. Frontis. VG. *Turpen.* $40/£26

HALL, WILLIAM. A Biography of David Cox. London: Cassell, Petter, Galpin, 1881. 1st ed. Frontis port, xv,268,viiipp. VG (bkpl). *Hollett.* $101/£65

HALL, WILLIAM. Reminiscences and Sketches, Historical and Biographical. Harrisburg, PA, 1890. vi,269pp. VG (rubbed). *Bohling.* $27/£17

HALLAM, HENRY. Introduction to the Literature of Europe in the Fifteenth, Sixteenth, and Seventeenth Centuries. Paris: Baudry's European Library, 1839. 1st Paris ed. 4 vols. Contemp 1/2 black calf, gilt spines. (Lt foxing, 2 spine crowns chipped), o/w VG. *Reese.* $75/£48

HALLE, CLIFFORD. To Menelek in a Motor Car. London: Hurst & Blackett, 1913. 1st ed. (Sl rubbed.) *Maggs.* $187/£120

HALLENBECK, CLEVE. Alvar Nunez Cabeza de Vaca. Glendale: A.H. Clark, 1940. 5 fldg maps. (Sm bkpl), else VG. *Dumont.* $95/£61

HALLENBECK, CLEVE. Alvar Nunez Cabeza de Vaca...1534-36. Glendale, 1940. 1st ed. One of 1018. 9 maps and charts. Fine. *Turpen.* $150/£96

HALLENBECK, CLEVE. Land of the Conquistadores. Caldwell, ID: Caxton, 1950. 1st ed. Fldg color map. NF in NF dj. *Sadlon.* $25/£16

HALLENBECK, CLEVE. Spanish Missions of the Old Southwest. GC, 1926. 1st ed. VG. *Turpen.* $95/£61

HALLER JOHN S., JR. and ROBIN M. The Physician and Sexuality in Victorian America. Urbana: Univ of IL, (1974). 1st ed. Fine. *Glaser.* $45/£29

HALLEY, ANNE and ALAN TRACHTENBERG. Jerome Liebling Photographs. (Amherst): Univ of MA, 1982. 1st ed. 97 full-pg b/w photos. Fine in illus dj. *Cahan.* $60/£38

HALLIDAY, BRETT. The Private Practice of Michael Shayne. NY: Holt, 1940. Fine in dj (worn, back panel soiled). *Metropolitan*.* $46/£29

HALLIDAY, F. E. Shakespeare in His Age. Duckworth, 1956. Frontis. Black cl. Fine in dj (head neatly repaired). *Peter Taylor.* $31/£20

HALLIDAY, MICHAEL. (Pseud of John Creasey.) Cunning as a Fox. London: Hodder & Stoughton, 1965. 1st ed. Fine (top edges lt soiling) in dj (rear panel lt soiled). *Janus.* $35/£22

HALLIDAY, SAMUEL B. The Lost and Found; or Life Among the Poor. NY: Phinney et al, 1860. 1st ed. Frontis port, 356pp. Contemp cl (spine dull). VG. *Second Life.* $250/£160

HALLINAN, TIMOTHY. Everything but the Squeal. NY: NAL, 1990. 1st ed. Inscribed. VF in dj. *Mordida.* $45/£29

HALLIWELL, JAMES ORCHARD. A Dictionary of Archaic and Provincial Words.... London: Reeves & Turner, 1889. 11th ed. 2 vols. xxxvi,480; (4),(481-)960pp + 16pp pub's cat. Good set (paper labels defective). *Cox.* $86/£55

HALLIWELL-PHILLIPPS, J. O. Outlines of the Life of Shakespeare. London, 1882. 2nd ed. 703pp. (Margins lt browned, 1/2 title soiled, lib ink stamp tp, last pg of text; new eps; rebacked, orig spine laid down, corners sl worn.) *Edwards.* $55/£35

HALLOCK, CHARLES. Our New Alaska. NY: Forest & Stream, 1886. 1st ed. 209pp; fldg map. Pict cvrs (wear). Good. *Lien.* $50/£32

HALLOCK, CHARLES. Our New Alaska; or, The Seward Purchase Vindicated. NY: Forest & Stream, 1886. viii(2)9-209pp; fldg map. Dec cl. VG. *High Latitude.* $40/£26

HALLOWELL, ANNA DAVIS (ed). James and Lucretia Mott: Life and Letters. Boston: Houghton Mifflin, 1884. 1st ed. (ix),566pp; 3 ports. Teg. Brn cl, gilt. VG. *Petrilla.* $35/£22

HALLOWELL, BENJAMIN. Autobiography of Benjamin Hallowell. Phila, 1883. 1st ed. (11),394pp. *Ginsberg.* $50/£32

HALPRIN, LAWRENCE. Notebooks 1959, 1971. Cambridge/London: MIT, (1972). 1st ed. Dec eps. Cl, paper inset cvr. Fine. *Quest.* $75/£48

HALPRIN, LAWRENCE. Notebooks 1959-1971. Cambridge/London: MIT, (1972). Black cl (rear cvr sl creased), spine titled in yellow; mtd ptd label fr cvr (sl soiled), mtd port rear cvr. VG. *Blue Mountain.* $95/£61

HALSELL, H. H. Cowboys and Cattleland. Dallas: Wilkinson Ptg, n.d. 3rd ed. VG in dj (sl worn). Howes H99. *Lien.* $60/£38

HALSEY, ASHLEY, JR. Illustrating for the Saturday Evening Post. Boston, (1951). VG (wear). *King.* $45/£29

HALSEY, R. T. H. The Boston Port Bill as Pictured by a Contemporary London Cartoonist. NY: Grolier Club, 1904. One of 325. Gilt-paneled calf. Dj (spine top chipped). *Swann*.* $57/£37

HALSMAN, PHILIPPE. Halsman on the Creation of Photographic Ideas. NY: A.S. Barnes, 1961. 1st ed. 39 plts. (Owner stamp), else NF in dj (rubbed). *Cahan.* $50/£32

HALSMAN, PHILIPPE. Piccoli. NY, 1953. 1st ed. Paul Julian (illus). NF in VG + dj (spine sl worn). *Warren.* $45/£29

HALSTEAD, MURAT. Fire the Salute! Kingsport, TN, 1960. Centennial ed. Ltd to 1250. Fine in plain plastic dj (2 sm tears), slipcase (worn). *Pratt.* $35/£22

HALSTED, WILLIAM. Surgical Papers by William Stewart Halsted. Balt, 1924. 1st ed. 2 vols. Contents VG (backstrips worn, spine ends torn). *Fye.* $400/£256

HAMBURGER, ROBERT. Our Portion of Hell. NY/London: Links Books, 1973. 1st ed. NF in VG dj. *Cahan.* $45/£29

HAMEL, FRANK. Human Animals. NY: University Books, 1969. Fine in VG + dj. *Middle Earth.* $45/£29

HAMERTON, PHILIP GILBERT. Landscape. London, 1885. xvi,386pp + (ii) (few margins sl thumbed); 43 plts. Uncut, partly unopened. Morocco-backed cl bds (corners sl rubbed, spine head split w/o loss), gilt. *Edwards.* $390/£250

HAMILTON, ALEXANDER. Hamilton's Itinerarium, Being a Narrative of a Journey from Annapolis, Maryland.... St. Louis, 1907. Presentation from William K. Bixby. Fldg map, 6 plts, 22 facs. 3/4 calf, cl. (Joints rubbed), else VG. Howes H125. *Reese.* $150/£96

HAMILTON, ALEXANDER. The Works of Alexander Hamilton. NY: Williams & Whiting, 1810. 1st ed. 3 vols in 1. Thick 8vo. Frontis port each vol, 7,(3),325; (2),4,368; (2),4,368pp. New 1/2 calf, marbled bds. Fine set. *M&s.* $950/£609

HAMILTON, ALICE. Industrial Poisons in the United States. NY: Macmillan, 1929. Rpt. Grn cl. VG. *Glaser.* $95/£61

HAMILTON, ANTHONY. Memoirs of Count Grammont. London: James Carpenter & Wm. Miller, 1811. 2 vols. 64 engr ports. Mod 1/2 morocco, marbled bds, gilt spines. (Foxing), o/w Contents VG. *New Hampshire*.* $80/£51

HAMILTON, BOB. Gene Autry and the Redwood Pirates. Racine, WI: Whitman, 1946. Erwin L. Hess (illus). Lg 12mo. Pict paper-cvrd bds. Fine (pp toned) in VG + dj (sl worn). *Book Adoption.* $25/£16

HAMILTON, CHARLES. Great Forgers and Famous Fakes.... NY: Crown Publishers, (1980). 1st ed. Cl-backed bds. (Name.) Dj (chipped). *Oak Knoll.* $45/£29

HAMILTON, EDWARD JOHN. The Human Mind: A Treatise in Mental Philosophy. NY: Robert Carter, 1883. 1st ed, 1st bk. Inscribed (laid-in), signed. (ii),viii,720,(2)pp. Pebbled brn cl. (Lib stamp tp), else NF. *Gach.* $100/£64

HAMILTON, EDWARD. Recollections of Fly Fishing for Salmon, Trout, and Grayling. Sampson Low, 1884. 1st ed. Teg. 1/2 brn morocco, gilt. *Petersfield.* $70/£45

HAMILTON, EDWARD. Recollections of Fly-Fishing for Salmon, Trout and Grayling.... London, 1891. 2nd ed. Mezzotint frontis, 12,190pp; vignette tp & 5 full-pg woodcut plts. Dec cvr. Good-. *Scribe's Perch*.* $27/£17

HAMILTON, ELIZABETH. Letters Addressed to the Daughter of a Nobleman. London: Cadell & Davies, 1806. 1st ed. xxxi,1-257; xiv,271pp (lacks 1/2 titles?). Contemp full calf (sl worn). VG. *Second Life.* $225/£144

HAMILTON, HENRY W. The Sioux of the Rosebud. Norman, 1971. 1st ed. Fine in dj (price-clipped). *Baade.* $60/£38

HAMILTON, J. ARNOTT. Byzantine Architecture and Decoration. London: Batsford, 1933. 1st ed. Color frontis, 71pp plts. (Spine, edges faded.) *Hollett.* $47/£30

HAMILTON, J. ARNOTT. Byzantine Architecture and Decoration. Batsford, 1956. Rev ed. VG in dj (sl creased). *Hadley.* $31/£20

HAMILTON, JAMES. The Battle of Fort Donelson. NY, (1968). 1st ed. VG + . *Pratt.* $45/£29

HAMILTON, JAMES. Outlines of Midwifery, for the Use of Students. Edinburgh: Bell & Bradfute, 1826. 1st ed. viii,239pp (lg lib stamp tp). Uncut. Recent pale brn 1/2 morocco, marbled bds. *Bickersteth.* $343/£220

HAMILTON, JAMES. Wanderings in North Africa. London: John Murray, 1856. xxv,320pp; 8 plts. (Lt rubbed.) *Adelson.* $285/£183

HAMILTON, JOSEPH GREGOIRE DE ROULHAC. Reconstruction in North Carolina. Raleigh, NC: Edwards & Broughton, (c. 1906). 1st ed. Later cl; orig wrappers bound in. (Bkpl removed, sm lib blindstamp), else VG. Howes H129. *Mcgowan.* $175/£112

HAMILTON, PATRICK. The Resources of Arizona. SF: A.L. Bancroft, 1884. 3rd ed. 414,xivpp; fldg map. (Spine dknd, ends worn, stamps), else Good. Howes H134. *Dumont.* $250/£160

HAMILTON, RICHARD VESEY (ed). The Letters and Papers of Admiral of the Fleet Sir Thos. Byam Martin, G.C.B. London: Navy Records Soc, 1898, 1901, 1903. 3 vols. 3 frontispieces, 5 tinted plts, color plan. Blue/white cl (sl grubby), gilt. *Maggs.* $117/£75

HAMILTON, SINCLAIR. Early American Book Illustrators and Wood Engravers, 1670-1870. Princeton, 1958-68. 2 vols. *Swann*.* $345/£221

HAMILTON, SINCLAIR. Early American Book Illustrators and Wood Engravers, 1670-1870. Princeton, 1968. 2 vols, w/supp. *Hatchwell.* $312/£200

HAMILTON, THOMAS M. The Young Pioneer, When Captain Tom Was a Boy. Washington: Library Press, (1932). 1st ed. *Ginsberg.* $75/£48

HAMILTON, WILLIE M. P. My Queen and I. London, 1975. 1st ed. Inscribed. Fine in Fine dj. *Smith.* $20/£13

HAMILTON-BROWNE, G. A Lost Legionary in South Africa. London, n.d. (1912). Frontis port, 11 plts. Red cl (sl mks, spine faded), gilt. *Maggs.* $156/£100

HAMLEY, EDWARD. The War in the Crimea. London, 1891. 4th ed. vi,312pp. Marbled edges. Blue calf, gilt. *Maggs.* $94/£60

HAMLIN, A. The History of Mount Mica. Bangor: The Author, 1895. 72pp; 44 chromolitho plts. (Ex libris, lib mks, lacks rep; spine ends frayed.) *Blake.* $275/£176

HAMLIN, P. G. Old Bald Head. Strasburg, VA, 1940. 3 photo plts. (Lacks tp), o/w Good. *Scribe's Perch*.* $32/£21

HAMLIN, P. G. Old Bald Head. Strasburg, VA: Shenandoah, 1940. 1st ed. Gray cl (sm dent spine). VG. *Lien.* $150/£96

HAMLIN, T. Some European Architectural Libraries— Their Methods, Equipment, Administration. Columbia Univ, 1939. VG. *Moss.* $37/£24

HAMLIN, TALBOT. Benjamin Henry Latrobe. NY, 1955. 40 plts hors texte. Good. *Washton.* $45/£29

HAMLIN, TALBOT. Greek Revival Architecture in America. London: OUP, 1944. 1st ed. Linen-backed dec bds (spine sl dknd). VG. *Hermitage.* $50/£32

HAMMACHER, A. M. The Evolution of Modern Sculpture. NY: Abrams, (1969). 1st ed. 404 plts (27 mtd color). Brn cl, gilt. Good in dj. *Karmiole.* $65/£42

HAMMACHER, A. M. Genius and Disaster: The Ten Creative Years of Vincent Van Gogh. NY: Abrams, n.d. 50 tipped-in color plts. *Metropolitan*.* $287/£184

HAMMER, WILLIAM J. Radium, and Other Radio-Active Substances. NY: D. Van Nostrand, 1903. 1st ed. Frontis. NF. *Glaser.* $150/£96

HAMMERTON, J. A. George Meredith. Edinburgh: John Grant, 1911. New ed. Frontis, 54 plts. (Inscrips, stamps), o/w VG. *Cox.* $23/£15

HAMMERTON, J. A. In the Track of R.L. Stevenson. Bristol: J.W. Arrowsmith, (1907). 1st ed. Frontis. Blue cl. *Turtle Island.* $30/£19

HAMMETT, DASHIEL. The Dain Curse. NY: Knopf, 1929. 1st ed, 1st issue, w/'dopped in' misprint p260. Yellow dec cl (sl sunned, sl mks, spotting mainly of edges). *Ash.* $351/£225

HAMMETT, DASHIELL (ed). Creeps by Night. NY, (1931). 1st ed. VG (cvr sl rubbed). *Mcclintock.* $45/£29

HAMMETT, DASHIELL. The Continental Op. NY: Random House, (1974). 1st ed. VG in dj. *Antic Hay.* $25/£16

HAMMETT, DASHIELL. The Continental OP. Dell Mapback #129, 1946. 1st ptg. (Sm chip lower edge, lt edgewear), else Bright. *Murder By The Book.* $35/£22

HAMMETT, DASHIELL. Dead Yellow Women. NY: Lawrence E. Spivak, 1947. 1st ed. Pb orig. Correct 1st ed w/25-cent price fr cvr. Fine in wrappers. *Mordida.* $150/£96

HAMMETT, DASHIELL. Hammett Homicides. Dell Mapback #223, 1948. 1st ptg. (Edge lamination peeling, lt wear), else VG +. *Murder By The Book.* $45/£29

HAMMETT, DASHIELL. The Maltese Falcon. NY: Modern Library, (1934). 1st Mod Lib ed. (Spine faded.) *Heinoldt.* $25/£16

HAMMETT, DASHIELL. The Maltese Falcon. SF: Arion, 1983. One of 400. 1/4 morocco, 'black bird' onlay on cvrs. Cl slipcase. *Swann*.* $517/£331

HAMMETT, DASHIELL. A Man Named Thin. NY: Joseph W. Freeman, 1962. 1st ed. Pb orig. (Pp sl dknd), o/w Fine in wrappers. *Mordida.* $100/£64

HAMMETT, DASHIELL. Red Harvest. NY/London: Knopf, 1929. 1st ed, 1st bk. Internally Fine (bkpl; spine sl faded, sl rolled, sl rubbed). *Pirages.* $350/£224

HAMMETT, DASHIELL. The Thin Man. NY: Knopf, 1934. 1st ed. (Spine, bd edges faded, sl rolled), else Fine. *Pirages.* $250/£160

Hammond's Modern Atlas of the World. NY, 1922. Rose red cl (sl soiled). Internally VF. *Hudson.* $110/£71

Hammond's Pictorial Atlas of the World. NY, 1912. Grn dec cl. VG. *Hudson.* $185/£119

HAMMOND, ALEX. The Book of Chessman. London: Arthur Barker, (1950). 1st ed. Signed. 61 plts. Beige cl. Good in dj (sl chipped, soiled). *Karmiole.* $50/£32

HAMMOND, GEORGE P. The Adventures of Alexander Barclay, Mountain Man. Denver: Old West, 1976. 3 maps in rear pckt. Gold-stamped brn fabricoid. Dj. *Dawson.* $50/£32

HAMMOND, GEORGE P. The Adventures of Alexander Barclay, Mountain Man. Denver: Old West, MCMLXXVI. 1st ed. Maps in pocket. VG in dj. *Lien.* $50/£32

HAMMOND, GEORGE P. The Adventures of Alexander Barclay.... Denver, 1976. 1st ed. 3 fldg maps pocket. VF in VF dj. *Turpen.* $40/£26

HAMMOND, GEORGE P. Coronado's Seven Cities. Albuquerque, 1940. 1st ed. Pb. VG. *Turpen.* $20/£13

HAMMOND, GEORGE P. Narratives of the Coronado Expedition 1540-1542. Albuquerque: Univ of NM, 1940. Red cl. (Sl rubbed), else VG. *Metropolitan*.* $57/£37

HAMMOND, GEORGE P. et al. Scientist on the Trail, Travel Letters of a Bandelier 1880-81. Berkeley, 1949. 1st ed. #260/500. Untrimmed, unopened. Fine. No dj as issued. *Turpen.* $135/£87

HAMMOND, GEORGE P. (ed). The Treaty of Guadalupe Hidalgo, February Second, 1848. Berkeley: Friends of the Bancroft Library, (1949). Facs ed. One of 500 ptd. Lg fldg facs map in separate folder. Orange/white patterned bds, white linen spine, ptd paper label. Fine. *Argonaut.* $175/£112

HAMMOND, GEORGE P. and AGAPITO REY. Don Juan de Onate: Colonizer of New Mexico 1595-1628. (Albuquerque): Univ of NM, 1953. 2 vols. Gold-stamped red cl. Uncut, unopened. Djs. *Dawson.* $250/£160

HAMMOND, ISAAC B. Reminiscences of Frontier Life. Portland, 1904. Inscribed. Port. VG in gray wraps (edges worn). Howes H142. *Bohling.* $300/£192

HAMMOND, JOHN FOX. A Surgeon's Report on Socorro, N. M. 1852. Stagecoach, 1966. One of 750. Fine in dj. *Bohling.* $30/£19

HAMMOND, JOHN MARTIN. Quaint and Historic Forts of North America. Phila/London: Lippincott, 1915. 1st ed. VG +. *Mcgowan.* $250/£160

HAMMOND, JOHN MARTIN. Quaint and Historic Forts of North America. Phila: Lippincott, 1915. 1st ed. Good in pict cl. *Lien.* $125/£80

HAMMOND, WILLIAM A. Physics and Physiology of Spiritualism. NY: D. Appleton, 1871. 1st ed. Presentation copy. 86,(2)pp. Ptd emb grn cl (rt edge fr bd gouged, joints rubbed). Good +. *Gach.* $250/£160

HAMMOND, WILLIAM A. Physics and Physiology of Spiritualism. NY: D. Appleton, 1871. 1st ed. Presentation copy. 86,(2)pp. Ptd emb grn cl (fr bd gouged, joints rubbed). Good +. *Gach.* $250/£160

HAMMOND, WILLIAM A. Sexual Impotence in the Male. NY: Bermingham, 1883. 1st ed. (ii),274,(2)pp. Beveled brn cl. VG (lt shelfworn). *Gach.* $175/£112

HAMMOND, WILLIAM A. A Treatise on Insanity in Its Medical Relations. NY: D. Appleton, 1883. 1st ed. (iv),(xiv),(8)-767,(3)pp + undated inserted ads. Pub's sheep, leather spine label. VG (stamps; edges rubbed, spine chafed). *Gach*. $225/£144

HAMMOND, WILLIAM A. A Treatise on Diseases of the Nervous System. NY, 1873. 3rd ed. 754pp. Pebbled cl. VG (extrems sl worn; sm tears spine). *Doctor's Library*. $250/£160

HAMNER, EARL. Fifty Roads to Town. Random House, (c.1953). 1st ed. VG- (edges browned, soiled, top edge faded) in Fair dj (tattered, water-stained). *Book Broker*. $75/£48

HAMNETT, NINA. Is She a Lady? London: Wingate, 1955. 1st ed. Very Nice in dj (soiled, frayed, chipped). *Virgo*. $86/£55

HAMPDEN, GORDON. Our Girls in Wartime. London: John Lane, Bodley Head, n.d. 25 full-pg illus. Pict bds (wear), cl spine. *Dawson*. $25/£16

HAMPSON, ALFRED LEETE. Emily Dickinson, a Bibliography. Northampton: Hampshire Bookshop, 1930. 1st ed. One of 50 numbered, from total ed of 500. Wrappers, ptd foil label. (Heavy offset from laid-in clipping, edges sl tanned), o/w VG. *Reese*. $35/£22

HAMPSON, JOHN. Man About the House. London, 1935. #116/285 signed. VG in dj. *Typographeum*. $45/£29

HAMSUN, KNUT. Hunger. London: Leonard Smithers, 1899. 1st ed in English. VG in illus wraps (worn, chipped). *Lame Duck*. $85/£54

HAMSUN, KNUT. Vagabonds. NY, 1930. 1st ed. Pict grn cl. VG+. *Smith*. $15/£10

HANAFORD, MRS. P. A. Field, Gunboat, Hospital and Prison. Boston: C.M. Dinsmoor, 1866. 379pp, 8pp ads. Gilt dec spine (shelfwear; shaken). *Cullen*. $50/£32

HANAYAMA, SHINSHO. The Way of Deliverance. Hideo Suzuki et al (trans). NY: Scribner, 1950. 1st ed. Frontis. (1st, last ll sl smudged; sl rubbed, smudged, spine sl frayed), o/w VG. *Worldwide*. $20/£13

HANCOCK, A. R. Reminiscences of Winfield Scott Hancock by His Wife. NY: Charles L. Webster, 1887. xiii,340pp. (Frontis, tp corners stained; rubbed.) *Zubal**. $45/£29

HANCOCK, B. F. (comp). The Law, Without the Advice of an Attorney. Norristown, 1831. (Waterstained, foxed.) 1/4 leather, bds (insect damage backstrip). *Yudkin**. $23/£15

HANCOCK, CORNELIA. South After Gettysburg. H.S. Jaquette (ed). Phila: Univ of PA, 1937. 1st ed. Map. (Spine faded.) *Wantagh*. $35/£22

HANCOCK, H. IRVING. The Square Dollar Boys Smash the Ring. Altemus, 1912. (Cvr dingy, spotted; lacks dj), else VG. *My Bookhouse*. $30/£19

HANCOCK, MRS. W. S. Reminiscences of Winfield Scott Hancock by His Wife. NY, 1887. 1st ed. Gilt edges. Leather. (Cvr sl worn), o/w Fine. *Pratt*. $85/£54

HANCOCKS, D. Animals and Architecture. London, 1971. (Sl worn.) *Maggs*. $34/£22

Hand-Book for Visitors to Oxford.... Oxford: John Henry Parker, 1847. Text reset, fldg map, w/o engr plts. Orig black morocco, gilt. *Bickersteth*. $34/£22

Hand-Book of Reference to the History, Chronology, Religion and Country of the Latter-Day Saints Including the Revelation on Celestial Marriage. Salt Lake: (A.H. Cannon), 1884. 1st ed. Inscribed by John Nicholson. 157pp. Good+ (hinges cracked, shaken, cvrs worn). *Benchmark*. $50/£32

Hand-Book of the Oneida Community. 1875. Oneida, NY: Office of the Oneida Circular, (1875). 48pp. Orig ptd wrappers. *M&s*. $65/£42

HANDASYDE. The Four Gardens. London, 1924. Color frontis, 180pp; 3 color plts tipped in. Uncut. Pict bds (worn, soiled). Internally VG. *Quest*. $30/£19

Handbook for Residents and Travellers in Shropshire and Cheshire. London: John Murray, 1896. 3rd ed. vi,156,6pp + 48pp pub's cat; 8 fldg maps and plans (1 in rear pocket). (Spine sl discolored, tail chipped.) *Edwards*. $47/£30

Handbook for Scoutmasters: A Manual of Troop Leadership. NY: Boy Scouts of America, c. 1947. 4th ed. NF in orig stiff wrappers. *Mcgowan*. $55/£35

Handbook for Travellers in Central Italy. London: John Murray, 1843. 568 w/index pp; lg fldg map in rear pocket. Full black roan. Marbled fore-edge (sl stain). (Bkpl; ink inscrip; back hinge cracked), but Good. *King*. $35/£22

Handbook for Travellers in Devon. London: John Murray, 1895. 11th ed. 291,16pp + 48pp ads; 12 maps and plans (1 in rear pocket). (Cl sl discolored, spine chipped.) *Edwards*. $47/£30

Handbook for Travellers in Durham and Northumberland. London: John Murray, 1890. New ed. xxxvi,342pp + 52pp pub's ads; 5 maps and plans (2 fldg in fr, rear pockets). (Spine discolored.) *Edwards*. $55/£35

Handbook for Travellers in France. Part I and II. London: John Murray, 1886-92. 17th & 18th eds. 2 vols. 35,422pp + 52pp ads; 32,425pp + 48pp ads; 2 maps rear pocket. (Cl vol 1 soiled, vol 2 lt faded.) *Edwards*. $62/£40

Handbook for Travellers in Japan. London: Murray, 1907. 8th ed. 29 (of 30; lacks 'key to sectional map' which should face tp) maps, plans. (Sl shaken, edges rubbed, sl soiled), o/w Good. *Worldwide*. $65/£42

Handbook for Travellers in Somerset. London: John Murray, 1899. 5th ed. 24pp ads; 8 maps and plans (3 fldg, 1 in rear pocket). (Spine sl faded.) *Edwards*. $47/£30

Handbook for Travellers in Yorkshire.... London: John Murray, 1882. 3rd ed. (lvi),vi,535pp + 52pp ads; 4 plans, fldg map rear pocket. (Spine, edges discolored.) *Edwards*. $55/£35

Handbook of Artillery Instruments. London, 1914. Good (wear, spine sunned). *King*. $40/£26

Handbook of Turning. (By Miss Gascoigne.) London, 1859. 4th ed. Port, 14 plts. (New eps.) Pink cl (rebacked, part of orig backstrip mtd.) *Maggs*. $125/£80

HANDFORTH, THOMAS. Mei Li. NY: Doubleday, 1938. 1st ed. 9 1/4 x 12 1/4. 50pp. Fine. *Cattermole*. $100/£64

HANDKE, PETER. The Goalie's Anxiety at the Penalty Kick. NY: FSG, 1972. 1st US ed. Fine in NF dj (lt worn). *Lame Duck*. $35/£22

HANDKE, PETER. Nonsense and Happiness. NY: Urizen, 1974. 1st US ed. NF in VG+ dj. *Lame Duck*. $45/£29

HANDKE, PETER. A Sorrow Beyond Dreams. Ralph Manheim (trans). NY: FSG, (1975). 1st ed. Fine in NF dj. *Antic Hay*. $25/£16

HANDKE, PETER. A Sorrow Beyond Dreams. NY: FSG, 1974. 1st ed in English. (Top edge lt foxed), else NF in VG+ dj (sl toned). *Lame Duck*. $35/£22

HANDLEY, CHARLES O. and CLYDE P. PATTON. Wild Mammals of Virginia. VA Comm. of Game & Inland Fisheries, 1947. VG-. *Book Broker*. $40/£26

HANDLEY-READ, CHARLES. The Art of Wyndham Lewis. London, (1951). Dj (chipped, soiled). *Freeman**. $50/£32

HANES, BAILEY C. Bill Doolin, Outlaw O.T. Norman: Univ of OK, (1968). 1st ed. Dec bds. Fine in pict dj. *Argonaut*. $45/£29

HANFF, HELENE. 84, Charing Cross Road. NY, 1970. 1st ed. VG+ in VG+ dj. *Warren*. $35/£22

HANFF, HELENE. 84, Charing Cross Road. Deutsch, 1971. 1st Eng ed. VG in dj (few tears). *Words Etc.* $47/£30

HANKS, O. T. History of Captain B. F. Benton's Company, Hood's Texas Brigade, 1861-1865. (Austin, TX, 1984.) 1st ed. Ltd to 300. Fine in orig ptd wrappers. *Mcgowan*. $37/£24

HANLEY, GERALD. Drinkers of Darkness. NY: Macmillan, 1955. 1st Amer ed. NF in dj (lt worn). *Antic Hay*. $20/£13

HANLEY, GERALD. The Year of the Lion. London: Collins, 1953. 1st Eng ed. NF (eps sl browned) in dj (lt worn, rear panel soiled). *Antic Hay*. $35/£22

HANLEY, J. FRANK. A Day in the Siskiyous. Indianapolis: Art Press, 1916. 1st ed. 33 color, 5 b/w plts; fldg plt laid in as issued. Pict cl, gilt fr cvr. VG. *Shasky*. $85/£54

HANLEY, JAMES. Aria and Finale. Boriswood, 1932. 1st Eng ed. Very Nice (cvr edges sl faded) in dj (chipped, torn). *Clearwater*. $70/£45

HANLEY, JAMES. Boy. London: Boriswood, 1931. #40/145 signed. Teg, rest uncut. Leather title label. (Fep lt browned, newspaper clippings loosely inserted; cl lt spotted; edges, spine browned.) *Edwards*. $140/£90

HANLEY, JAMES. The Furys. NY: Macmillan, 1935. 1st Amer ed. Nice in dj (chipped). *Turtle Island*. $75/£48

HANLEY, JAMES. The German Prisoner.... (London): The Author, (1930). 1st ed. One of 500 numbered, signed. Frontis. (Cl sl sunned), else Fine. *Reese*. $85/£54

HANLEY, JAMES. Grey Children. A Study in Humbug and Misery. London, 1937. 1st Eng ed. Very Nice in dj (sl torn, tanned). *Clearwater*. $94/£60

HANLEY, JAMES. Half an Eye. Sea Stories. London, 1937. 1st Eng ed. Very Nice in dj (sl faded, nicked, price-clipped). *Clearwater*. $101/£65

HANLEY, JAMES. The Ocean. London, 1941. 1st Eng ed. NF in dj (sl torn, spine faded, price-clipped). *Clearwater*. $70/£45

HANLEY, JAMES. Sailor's Song. London, 1943. 1st Eng ed. Bright (cvrs sl mkd) in dj (tanned). *Clearwater*. $55/£35

HANLEY, JAMES. The Secret Journey. NY: Macmillan, 1936. 1st Amer ed. Nice in dj (chipped, edgeworn). *Turtle Island*. $50/£32

HANLEY, JAMES. Stoker Bush. NY: Macmillan, 1936. 1st US ed. Fine in NF dj (few tears; sl dknd spine). *Beasley*. $50/£32

HANLEY, JAMES. Stoker Haslett, a Tale. London, 1932. Ltd to 350 numbered, signed. Teg. White cl. (Cvr fore-edge stained), else Good. *King*. $35/£22

HANLEY, JAMES. What Farrar Saw and Other Stories. (London): Andre Deutsch, (1984). 1st Eng ed. Paper-cvrd bds. Fine in dj. *Antic Hay*. $20/£13

HANLEY, TIMOTHY. A Flight of Birds. London, 1953. 1st Eng ed, 1st bk. Nice (inscrip) in dj (nicked). *Clearwater*. $31/£20

HANNA, CHARLES A. The Wilderness Trail. NY, 1911. One of 1000 sets. 2 vols. Howes H162. *Swann**. $172/£110

HANNA, PHIL TOWNSEND. The Dictionary of California Land Names. L.A.: Automobile Club of Southern CA, 1946. 1st ptg. (Ink underlining), else Good in dj (spine sl dknd). *Brown*. $15/£10

HANNA, WARREN L. The Life and Times of James Willard Schultz. Norman: Univ of OK, (1986). 1st ed. VF in pict dj. *Argonaut*. $35/£22

HANNAY, JAMES. The Life and Times of Sir Leonard Tilley. St. John, 1897. 1st ed. 400pp. (Inner hinges cracked; bottom edge ink-stained, cvrs rubbed.) *King*. $45/£29

HANNING, ROBERT and JOAN FERRANTE (trans). The Laid of Maria de France. NY, 1978. 1st ed. NF in NF dj (price-clipped). *Smith*. $20/£13

HANNON, JESSIE GOULD. The Boston-Newton Company Venture. Lincoln: Univ of NE, (1969). 1st ed. 7 plt maps. Red cl. Fine in dj. *Argonaut*. $45/£29

HANSARD, G. The Book of Archery. London: Bohn, (1845). 3rd ed. 456pp, 15 engrs, 24 full-pg dwgs. (Rebound), else VG+. *Mikesh*. $125/£80

HANSBERRY, LORRAINE. A Raisin in the Sun. NY: Random House, (1959). 1st ed. Fine in white dj (spine extrems sl worn). *Between The Covers*. $300/£192

HANSEN, GLADYS C. The Chinese in California. (Portland): Richard Abel, 1970. 1st ed. Ltd to 1000. VF. *Argonaut*. $150/£96

HANSEN, HANS JURGEN (ed). Art and the Seafarer. Faber, 1968. 1st UK ed. Dj (sl chipped). *Edwards*. $62/£40

HANSEN, JOSEPH. Death Claims. NY: Harper & Row, (1973). 1st ed. Fine in VG dj. *Metropolitan**. $46/£29

HANSEN, JOSEPH. Fadeout. NY: Harper & Row, (1970). 1st ed. Fine in VG dj. *Metropolitan**. $28/£18

HANSEN, JOSEPH. Fadeout. NY: Harper & Row, (1970). 1st ed. Fine (sl shelfworn) in VG dj (extrems worn). *Metropolitan**. $34/£22

HANSEN, JOSEPH. Troublemaker. NY, 1975. 1st ed. Fine in NF dj. *Warren*. $40/£26

HANSEN, MARCUS L. Old Fort Snelling, 1819-1858. Minneapolis: Ross & Haine, 1958. Ltd to 1500. VG in dj. *Lien*. $30/£19

HANSEN, RON. The Assassination of Jesse James by the Coward Robert Ford. NY: Knopf, 1983. Fine in dj (lt worn, label residue). *Hermitage*. $40/£26

HANSEN, THORKILD. Arabia Felix. NY/Evanston: Harper & Row, 1962. 1st ed. Dbl-pg map. VG in dj (sl torn). *Worldwide*. $35/£22

HANSEN, WOODROW JAMES. The Search for Authority in California. Oakland: Biobooks, 1960. Ltd to 750. Lg fldg map. 2-tone cl. VF. *Argonaut*. $45/£29

HANSFORD, S. Chinese Jade Carving. London: Lund Humphries, c 1950. (Ink underlining 4pp, notes 1 pg), else VG. *Blake*. $45/£29

HANSHEW, T. W. Cleek of Scotland Yard. GC: Doubleday, 1914. (Sl rubbed.) Dj (browned, spine ends worn). *Metropolitan**. $92/£59

HANSON, JOHN ARTHUR. Roman Theatre Temples. Princeton, 1959. Good in dj. *Washton*. $50/£32

HANSON, WILLIS T., JR. The Early Life of John Howard Payne.... Boston: For Bibliophile Soc, 1913. Ltd to 483. 2 vols. Orig 3/4 calf, linen (extrems rubbed, spine dknd; 1st ll vol 1 lt foxed). *Sadlon*. $30/£19

HANSSEN, HELMER. Voyages of a Modern Viking. London: Routledge, 1936. Map. Very Nice in dj (chipped). *High Latitude*. $60/£38

HAPGOOD, HUTCHINS. The Spirit of the Ghetto: Studies of the Jewish Quarter in New York. NY/London: Funk & Wagnalls, 1902. 1st ed. Jacob Epstein (illus). Pict cl. (Spine rubbed, crease fr cvr), else VG. *Pacific**. $184/£118

Happy Farm. Collins, n.d. (1953). 1st ed. 'Magic Circle' Book. Tall 4to. Moveable picture bk. 6pp; 2 circular revolving color plts. NF in pict wraps. *Bookmark*. $28/£18

Happy New Lear. Guinness, n.d. (1957). 1st ed. Illus wrappers. (Fr wrapper sl stained, outer edge sl nibbled), o/w VG. *Words Etc.* $31/£20

Happy Schooldays. Chicago: M.A. Donohue, n.d. Happy Holiday Series. Color frontis, 49 leaves (lacks eps, hinges reinforced, sl dknd, sl worming fr edge 1st leves). Blue cl-backed color pict paper-cvrd bds (rubbed, bumped, soiled, chipped). Good. *Blue Mountain.* $20/£13

HARADA, J. The Gardens of Japan. Studio, 1928. 6 color plts. Teg. Dec cl (cvr sl worn). *Ars Artis.* $55/£35

HARADA, J. The Gardens of Japan. London: The Studio, 1928. 1/2 cl. *Maggs.* $31/£20

HARBEN, WILL N. The Caruthers Affair. London: Neely, 1898. 1st ed. (Edgeworn, 2 stained corners, few spots.) *Metropolitan*.* $28/£18

HARBORD, JAMES G. Leaves from a War Diary. NY: Dodd, Mead, 1925. 1st ed. (Sig; spine extrems, tips worn, spine faded.) *Dawson.* $30/£19

HARBUTT, CHARLES and LEE JONES (eds). America in Crisis. NY: Holt, Rinehart & Winston, 1969. Fine in dj. *Cahan.* $50/£32

HARBUTT, CHARLES. Travelog. Cambridge: MIT, 1973. 1st ed. 110 photo plts. (Owner stamp, price ep), else Fine in VG dj. *Cahan.* $30/£19

HARCOURT-SMITH, SIMON. The Last of Uptake, or The Estranged Sisters. Batsford, n.d. (c. 1940). Rex Whistler (illus). Rose buckram (lt wear, sl soil), gilt. Good +. *Whittle.* $47/£30

HARCUS, WILLIAM (ed). South Australia. London, 1876. 1st ed. 8vo. xv,432,24ads pp (inscrip tp); fldg table, 66 plts. Cl (recased, spine sl faded). *Maggs.* $351/£225

HARD, WILLIAM. The Women of Tomorrow. NY: Baker, Taylor, 1911. 1st ed. VG (ex-lib, few stamps). *Second Life.* $45/£29

HARDEE, W. J. Rifle and Light Infantry Tactics. Phila, 1861. Rpt. 2 vols. 250; 232pp. Fine. *Pratt.* $40/£26

HARDEN, JOHN WILLIAM. The Devil's Tramping Ground and Other North Carolina Mystery Stories. Chapel Hill: Univ of NC, (1949). 1st ed, 2nd ptg. NF in VG dj. *Mcgowan.* $30/£19

HARDIE, MARTIN and ARTHUR K. SABIN. War Posters Issued by Belligerent and Neutral Nations 1914-1919. London: A&C Black, 1920. 1st ed. Pict-stamped grn cl. (Corners bumped, spine expertly restored), else VG. *Hermitage.* $200/£128

HARDIE, MARTIN and ARTHUR K. SABIN. War Posters. London: A&C Black, 1920. 1st ed. 80 plts (17 color). Pict cl gilt (cockled in places). *Hollett.* $148/£95

HARDIE, MARTIN. Water-Colour Painting in Britain. Dudley Snelgrove (ed). London: Batsford, 1967-68. 1st ed. 3 vols. 8 color plts. Fine in djs. *Hollett.* $273/£175

HARDIE, MARTIN. Water-Colour Painting in Britain. Vol I. The 18th Century. Dudley Snelgrove et al (eds). Batsford, 1966. 1st ed. Color frontis. Dj (sl chipped). *Edwards.* $70/£45

HARDING, A. R. Wolf and Coyote Trapping. Columbus, OH: Harding, (1937). 1st ed. Dec cl. VG +. *Agvent.* $45/£29

HARDING, GEORGE L. Charles A. Murdock, Printer and Citizen of San Francisco: An Appraisal. Berkeley: Tamalpais, 1973. 1st ed. One of 310. Frontis port. Brn cl, gilt. Orig announcement laid in. VF. *Argonaut.* $60/£38

HARDING, GEORGE L. Don Agustin V. Zamorano: Statesman...and California's First Printer. L.A.: Zamorano Club, 1934. 1st ed. Not indicated, but ltd to 325. Frontis port, lg fldg map. Card of Edward Dean Lyman laid in. (Offsetting 2 blank flyleaves), else Fine in dj (lt soiled, sl chipped). *Argonaut.* $275/£176

HARDOUIN-FUGIER, E. et al. French Flower Painters of the 19th Century, a Dictionary. London, 1989. Dj. *Maggs.* $34/£22

HARDY, ALISTER. Great Waters. NY, c. 1987. 1st US ed. VG in dj. *High Latitude.* $25/£16

HARDY, ALLISON. Kate Bender, the Kansas Murderess. Girard, KS: Haldeman-Julius, 1944. 1st ed. VG in Fine wraps (fragile, cvr loose). *Book Market.* $20/£13

HARDY, ALLISON. Kate Bender, the Kansas Murderess. Girard, KS: Haldeman-Julius, 1944. VG + (dknd paper). *Bohling.* $20/£13

HARDY, CAMPBELL. Forest Life in Acadie. London: Chapman & Hall, 1869. Color frontis, ix,371pp; 10 plts. 1/2 black morocco (lt rubbed). *Adelson.* $260/£167

HARDY, CAMPBELL. Sporting Adventures in the New World. London: Hurst & Blackett, 1855. 1st ed. 2 vols. Litho frontis in 3 colors each vol. (Lt foxed, incl frontispieces; 1 section of 4 leaves sl loose, bkpl), else Internally Fine (sl cocked, shelf labels). *Pirages.* $500/£321

HARDY, FLORENCE E. The Early Life of Thomas Hardy [with] The Later Years of Thomas Hardy. NY: Macmillan, 1928-30. 1st Amer ed. 2 vols. VG; vol 2 in dj (spine chipped). *Reese.* $65/£42

HARDY, G. A. The Complete Ironmonger. London: Ironmonger, (1895). *Freeman*.* $50/£32

HARDY, MARY. Through Cities and Prairie Lands. NY: R. Worthington, 1881. xii,338pp. Dk red cl (sl worn, faded, spots), ptd spine label. *Bohling.* $65/£42

HARDY, ROBERT WILLIAM HALE. Travels in the Interior of Mexico 1825-28. London, 1829. 1st ed. 8vo. xiv,540pp; fldg map (neatly repaired), 7 plts. Fine. *Turpen.* $995/£638

HARDY, THOMAS. Autobiography: The Early Life, 1840-1892: The Later Years, 1892-1928. Florence Emily Hardy (ed). NY, 1928-1930. 1st Amer ed. 2 vols. Very Nice (bkpl) in djs (torn, chipped). *Clearwater.* $117/£75

HARDY, THOMAS. Catalogue of the Books by and About Thomas Hardy in Dorset County Library. (Dorchester), 1973. 2nd ed. Ptd wrappers. *Clearwater.* $23/£15

HARDY, THOMAS. A Changed Man and Other Tales. NY: Harper, 1913. 1st Amer ed. Dec blue cl. VG (eps, cl sl dampstained). *Antic Hay.* $75/£48

HARDY, THOMAS. A Changed Man. 1913. 1st ed. Frontis. Grn cl, gilt. VG. *Words Etc.* $117/£75

HARDY, THOMAS. A Changed Man. London, 1913. 1st ed. Frontis. Grn cl, gilt. VG. *Words Etc.* $86/£55

HARDY, THOMAS. The Collected Letters. Vol I, 1840-1892. Richard Little Purdy and Michael Millgate (eds). Clarendon, 1978. 1st ed. Fine in dj (sl worn). *Poetry Bookshop.* $39/£25

HARDY, THOMAS. The Dynasts. Macmillan, 1910. The Complete Edition. 1st ed in 1 vol. VG. *Words Etc.* $56/£36

HARDY, THOMAS. The Dynasts. London: Macmillan, 1927. One of 525 signed. 3 vols. Engr frontis port signed in pencil by Francis Dodd. Vol 1 largely unopened. Vellum-backed patterned bds (corners of 2 vols skillfully refurbished). VF. *Pirages.* $650/£417

HARDY, THOMAS. The Dynasts. London: Macmillan, 1927. Ltd to 525 sets signed and w/etched frontis port signed by Francis Dodd (artist). 3 vols. Vellum-backed dec bds (bkpl each fr pastedown, offsetting feps). (Lt spine soiling), o/w VF set. *Hermitage.* $850/£545

HARDY, THOMAS. The Famous Tragedy of the Queen of Cornwall at Tintagel in Lyonnesse.... London: Macmillan, 1923. 1st British ed. Frontis. Teg. 3/4 brn morocco, gilt. (Offsetting to eps from morocco turn-ins), o/w Very Nice. *Reese.* $75/£48

HARDY, THOMAS. The Famous Tragedy of the Queen of Cornwall. NY: Macmillan, 1923. 1st Amer ed. One of 1200 numbered. Uncut. Cl-backed paper-cvrd bds w/paper label. VG in slipcase (worn). *Hermitage.* $85/£54

HARDY, THOMAS. Far from the Madding Crowd. London: Smith Elder, 1874. 2 vols. 12 engrs. VG (spine ends discolored) in orig grn cl (extrems minimally rubbed). *Gekoski.* $3,120/£2,000

HARDY, THOMAS. Far from the Madding Crowd. Cambridge: LEC, 1958. Ltd to 1500 numbered, signed by Miller Parker (wood engrs). Brn calf-backed patterned bds. VG in ptd patterned bd slipcase (upper edge rubbed). *Words Etc.* $211/£135

HARDY, THOMAS. Far from the Madding Crowd. Cambridge: LEC, 1958. One of 1500 numbered, signed by Agnes Miller Parker (illus). Signed add'l plt laid in. Fine in pub's slipcase. *Hermitage.* $225/£144

HARDY, THOMAS. A Group of Noble Dames. London, 1891. 1st ed. (Sl rubbed, spine sl faded), o/w VG. *Words Etc.* $70/£45

HARDY, THOMAS. The Hand of Ethelberta, a Comedy in Chapters. London: Smith, Elder, 1876. 1st ed. 2 vols. Frontispieces. Orig grn cl stamped in gilt/blind (secondary binding). Good set (lt foxed, new eps, recased, sl edgeworn, rubbed). *Reese.* $300/£192

HARDY, THOMAS. Human Shows Far Phantasies. London: Macmillan, 1925. 1st Eng ed. Many pp unopened. NF (eps foxed) in dj (edgewear). *Antic Hay.* $100/£64

HARDY, THOMAS. Human Shows Far Phantasies. London: Macmillan, 1925. 1st UK ed. VG in dj (creased). *Williams.* $117/£75

HARDY, THOMAS. Jude the Obscure. London: Osgood, McIlvaine, (1896, but preface dated 1895). 1st ed. Frontis etching, map. Grn cl, gilt top. Good. *Appelfeld.* $250/£160

HARDY, THOMAS. Jude the Obscure. London, 1896. 1st issue w/'Osgood' on spine and title. Grn cl, gilt. VG. *Words Etc.* $133/£85

HARDY, THOMAS. Jude the Obscure. London: Osgood, McIlvaine, 1896. 1st ed. (viii),(1-2)3-515(516)pp. W/map of Wessex, etching by H. Macbeth-Raeburn. Blue-grn ribbed cl, author's gilt monogram fr cvr. Fine. *Vandoros.* $395/£253

HARDY, THOMAS. Late Lyrics and Earlier.... Macmillan, 1922. 1st ed. Nice in dj (sl frayed). *Ash.* $133/£85

HARDY, THOMAS. Life's Little Ironies. London: James R. Osgood, McIlvane, (1894). 1st ed. Grn cl, gilt. NF. *Macdonnell.* $200/£128

HARDY, THOMAS. The Mayor of Casterbridge. NY: LEC, 1964. One of 1500 numbered, signed by Agnes Miller Parker (illus). 1/2 leather. VG in bd slipcase. *Argosy.* $150/£96

HARDY, THOMAS. Moments of Vision and Miscellaneous Verses. London, 1917. 1st ed. VG. *Bond.* $30/£19

HARDY, THOMAS. Moments of Vision and Miscellaneous Verses. London, 1917. 1st ed. (Inner hinge weak), o/w VG in dj (internally repaired). *Words Etc.* $86/£55

HARDY, THOMAS. Old Mrs. Chundle. NY: Crosby Gaige, 1929. #198/742. Dec bds, gilt spine. NF (spine side sl discolored). *Polyanthos.* $35/£22

HARDY, THOMAS. Our Exploits at West Poley. 1952. Ltd to 1050 numbered. Lynton Lamb (wood engrs). NF in dj. *Words Etc.* $25/£16

HARDY, THOMAS. Our Exploits at West Poley. OUP, 1952. 1st trade ed. (Sl mkd, rubbed.) *Cox.* $12/£8

HARDY, THOMAS. Our Exploits at West Poley. OUP, 1952. #766/1050. NF in dj. *Hadley.* $75/£48

HARDY, THOMAS. The Poetry of William Barnes. Tagara Press, 1979. Ltd to 95 numbered. Orig marbled paper wrappers, title label. *Black Sun.* $65/£42

HARDY, THOMAS. The Poetry of William Barnes. Tagara, 1979. Ltd to 95. Fine in marbled paper wrappers. *Words Etc.* $31/£20

HARDY, THOMAS. Selected Poems of Thomas Hardy. London: Medici Soc, 1921. 1st ed. Ltd to 1025. Frontis port. Linen-backed bds, paper spine, cvr labels. VG (bkpl). *Truepenny.* $175/£112

HARDY, THOMAS. Selected Poems. London: (Medici Soc), 1921. One of 1025. Color woodcut port of Hardy signed with Wm. Nicholson's initial 'N' and the date, 1921. Pub's holland-backed blue bds; paper cvr, spine labels (edges sl browned). Dj (spine top lacks sm piece). *Book Block.* $185/£119

HARDY, THOMAS. Song of the Soldiers. Hove, 1914. 1st ed, 1st issue. Self-wrappers; custom gilt-lettered blue cl protective sleeve. *Freeman*.* $50/£32

HARDY, THOMAS. Song of the Soldiers. Hove, (Brighton: E. Williams), 1915. 1st 'Hove' ed, 1st state, w/comma after 'September' on tp. VG in stiff brn wrappers, brn silk tie. *Houle.* $125/£80

HARDY, THOMAS. Tess of the D'Urbervilles. London: James R. Osgood, McIlvaine, (1892). 1st ed, 2nd issue. 3 vols. Gilt-dec cvrs. (Spine vol 1 sl sunned, extrems sl chipped, cvrs sl soiled), else Fine set. *Polyanthos.* $750/£481

HARDY, THOMAS. Tess of the D'Urbervilles. 1892. 1st ed, 2nd issue dated 1892. 3 vols. (Lacks fep vol I; spines sl dull, corners sl bumped), o/w VG. *Words Etc.* $702/£450

HARDY, THOMAS. Tess of the D'Urbervilles. London: Macmillan, 1926. One of 325. Signed. 41 engrs by Vivien Gribble. Top edge trimmed, others untrimmed. 1/4 vellum-backed marbled bds. NF. *Vandoros.* $1,350/£865

HARDY, THOMAS. Time's Laughingstocks. London: Macmillan, 1909. 1st UK ed. VG (spine sl faded, mkd). *Williams.* $55/£35

HARDY, THOMAS. Under the Greenwood Tree or Mellstock Quire, a Rural Painting of the Dutch School. London: Macmillan, 1940. 1st this ed. Clare Leighton (illus). (Eps sl offset from dj flaps), o/w Nice in dj (foxed, edge nicks, sm tears). *Reese.* $50/£32

HARDY, THOMAS. Under the Greenwood Tree. 1913. 1st ed. (Prelims foxed), o/w VG. *Words Etc.* $31/£20

HARDY, THOMAS. The Well-Beloved. London, 1897. 1st ed. (Spine head neatly repaired), o/w VG. *Words Etc.* $70/£45

HARDY, THOMAS. The Well-Beloved. NY: Harper, 1897. 1st Amer ed. Blue cl, gilt. Fine. *Macdonnell.* $100/£64

HARDY, THOMAS. The Well-Beloved. A Sketch of a Temperament. London: Osgood, McIlvaine, 1897. 1st ed. (iv)v-viii(ix-x),3-338(339-340)pp. Teg; fr, bottom edges rough-trimmed. Dk grn ribbed cl, fr cvr blocked in gold w/TH monogram medallion, gilt spine. Very Nice. *Vandoros.* $275/£176

HARDY, THOMAS. Winter Words. Macmillan, 1928. 1st ed. Nice (sl sunned) in dj (chipped). *Ash.* $94/£60

HARDY, THOMAS. The Woodlanders. Macmillan, 1887. 1st ed. 3 vols. 8vo. 1/2 titles each vol, ad leaf vol 1, dk brn cl. dk grn cl, cvrs (spotted) blocked in blind/black, spines gilt (sl wear). (Lib label removed from lower 1/2 each upper cvr; fore-edges upper, lower cvrs vol 2 sl discolored by damp.) *Bickersteth.* $905/£580

HARDY, THOMAS. The Woodlanders. 1896. 1st ed. VG. *Words Etc.* $62/£40

HARDY, TONEY A. No Compromise With Principle: Autobiography and Biography of William Harris Hardy. NY: (Amer Book, Stratford Press, 1946). 1st ed. Inscribed. Frontis port. (Ep creased sm spot, loss to illus). Top edge lt wrinkling, else VG in dj (worn, chipped). *Cahan.* $40/£26

HARDY, W. J. The Handwriting of the Kings and Queens of England. London, 1893. 172pp, 7 photogravure plts. Aeg. (Cl spine, corners sl rubbed.) *Edwards.* $47/£30

HARE, AMORY. Tristram and Iseult. Gaylordsville, (CT): Slide Mountain, 1930. Presentation. Uncut. (Cl stained, warped.) *Argosy.* $125/£80

HARE, AUGUSTUS. In Italy. Gavin Henderson (ed). London, 1977. Ltd to 850. Map. Red-ruled cl, gilt device. *Edwards.* $31/£20

HARE, AUGUSTUS. Walks in London. NY: Routledge, 1878. 1st Amer ed. 2 vols in 1. xxxvi,480,511pp (lt foxed, sig). Dec cl (rubbed). VG-. *Agvent.* $35/£22

HARE, CYRIL. He Should Have Died Hereafter. London: Faber & Faber, 1957. 1st ed. Fine in dj (nicks, short closed tears). *Mordida.* $45/£29

HARE, CYRIL. He Should Have Died Hereafter. 1958. 1st ed. VG in dj (sm tear spine head). *Words Etc.* $62/£40

HARE, CYRIL. When the Wind Blows. London: Faber & Faber, 1949. 1st ed. NF (edges lt foxed) in VG + dj (spine extrems chipped). *Janus.* $85/£54

HARE, RICHARD. The Art and Artists of Russia. London: Methuen, (1965). 1st ed. Fine in dj. *Hermitage.* $50/£32

HARGRAVE, CATHERINE PERRY. A History of Playing Cards and a Bibliography of Cards and Gaming. Boston, 1930. (Shelfworn.) *Oinonen*.* $110/£71

HARGRAVE, CATHERINE PERRY. A History of Playing Cards and a Bibliography of Cards and Gaming. Boston: Houghton Mifflin, 1930. (Edgewear.) *Metropolitan*.* $345/£221

HARGRAVE, CATHERINE PERRY. A History of Playing Cards, and a Bibliography of Cards and Gaming. Boston: Houghton, Mifflin, 1930. 1st ed. Maroon buckram. Fine. *Appelfeld.* $325/£208

HARGRAVE, JOHN. Summer Time Ends. Indianapolis/NY: Bobbs-Merrill, 1935. 1st ed. Nice in pict dj (sl chipped, worn). *Patterson.* $70/£45

HARGRAVE, JOSEPH JAMES. Red River. Montreal, 1871. 506pp. VG (extrems rubbed, spine faded). *Reese.* $225/£144

HARINGTON, EDWARD. A Schizzo on the Genius of Man. Bath, 1793. Inscribed. xlviii,390pp; fldg engr plt, errata pg. 19th cent cl (spine head sl worn), maroon gilt label. (Lib stamps verso tp, final pg; inscrip, newspaper cutting fep), o/w Interior Fine. *Europa.* $78/£50

HARINGTON, JOHN. Nugae Antiquae.... Thomas Park (newly arranged by). London: Vernor & Hood, 1804. 2 vols. 2 half-titles. Aeg, marbled eps. Later straight-grain red morocco, smooth spines (lt scuffed) gilt-ruled in 6 panels, single-rule framing to bds. *Waverly*.* $231/£148

HARK, ANN. The Story of the Pennsylvania Dutch. NY: Harper, 1943. 1st ed. C. H. DeWitt (illus). 10 1/4 x 11 1/4. 32pp. Cl spine, dec bds. VG. *Cattermole.* $35/£22

HARKORT, EDUARD. In Mexican Prisons, the Journal of...1832-34. College Station, 1986. 1st ed. Frontis. VF in VF dj. *Turpen.* $28/£18

HARLAN, ROBERT D. At the Sign of the Lark. (SF): Book Club of CA, 1983. 1st bk ed. One of 550. Purple cl. Fine. *Harrington.* $55/£35

HARLAND, HENRY. The Lady Paramount. London/NY: John Lane, 1902. 1st ed. 9pp undated ads. Lt grn cl. Fine. *Sumner & Stillman.* $65/£42

HARLAND, MARION. Common Sense in the Household. NY: Scribner, (1871). Rpt ed. 556pp. (Cl sl worn, faded.) *Second Life.* $40/£26

HARLING, ROBERT. The Steep Atlantick Stream. London, 1946. 1st Eng ed. (Sl faded.) Dj (sl torn, chipped). *Clearwater.* $31/£20

HARLOW, NEAL. California Conquered: War and Peace on the Pacific 1846-1850. Berkeley: Univ of CA, (1982). 1st ed. Red cl, gilt spine. Fine in pict dj. *Pacific*.* $52/£33

HARLOW, NEAL. Maps and Surveys of the Pueblo Lands of Los Angeles. L.A.: Dawson's, 1976. 1st ed. Ltd to 375 ptd. 14 plts (2 laid into rear pocket). Cl-backed dec bds, gilt-lettered spine. VF. *Argonaut.* $300/£192

HARLOW, NEAL. The Maps of San Francisco Bay from the Spanish Discovery in 1769 to the American Occupation. SF: Book Club of CA, 1950. Ltd to 375 ptd. 21 collotype facs maps on 19 plts. Dec bds, red morocco spine, gilt. Fine in orig plain brn dj. Howes H202. *Pacific*.* $575/£369

HARLOW, NEAL. The Maps of San Francisco Bay from the Spanish Discovery in 1769 to the American Occupation. SF: Book Club of CA, 1950. One of 375 ptd. Collotype facs of 21 maps on 19 plts. 1/2 red morocco, dec bds, gilt-lettered spine. (Spine ends sl rubbed), else Fine. *Pacific*.* $632/£405

HARLOW, NEAL. The Maps of San Francisco Bay from the Spanish Discovery in 1796 to the American Occupation. (SF): Book Club of CA, 1950. 1st ed. Ltd to 375. Sm folio. 19 maps (10 fldg). Orig announcement w/envelope laid in. Patterned bds, red crushed morocco backstrip, gilt spine. VF. *Argonaut.* $800/£513

HARLOW, V. T. Raleigh's Last Voyage.... London: Argonaut, 1932. One of 775 numbered. Port, 2 maps. Vellum-backed bds. *Ginsberg.* $150/£96

HARLOW, W. S. Duties of Sheriffs and Constables.... SF, 1907. 2nd ed. VG. *Pratt.* $25/£16

HARMAN, S. W. Hell on the Border. Fort Smith, (1898). 1st ed. (14),720pp; port. Orig ptd grn wraps. Howes H203. *Ginsberg.* $1,350/£865

HARMAN, S. W. Hell on the Border. Ft. Smith: Hell on the Border Pub Co, 1953. VG in stiff wraps. Howes H201. *Dumont.* $40/£26

HARMON, APPLETON MILO. Appleton Milo Harmon Goes West. Maybelle Harmon Anderson (ed). (Berkeley), 1946. Tipped-in color illus on tp. VG +. *Bohling.* $65/£42

HARMON, JACK. Texas Missions and Landmarks. N.p.: Southwest Research Inst, 1977. Ltd ed. VF in slipcase. *Gibbs.* $35/£22

HARMSWORTH, ALFRED C. Motors and Motor-Driving. London: Longmans, Green, 1902. 1st ed. Good (pict cl sl worn, sm mk spine; spotted, browned throughout). *Ash.* $195/£125

HARPER, CHARLES G. The Holyhead Road. London, 1902. 2 vols. (Rebound, sl rubbed.) *Edwards.* $133/£85

HARPER, CHARLES G. The Smugglers. Chapman & Hall, 1909. *Petersfield.* $66/£42

HARPER, CHARLES G. Stage-Coach and Mail in Days of Yore. London: Chapman & Hall, 1903. 2 vols. 63 plts. Teg, rest uncut. (Sl shaken, sl soiled, spines faded.) *Edwards.* $195/£125

HARPER, HENRY H. A Journey in Southeastern Mexico. NY: For Author, 1910. Ltd ed. Etched frontis. Parchment-like spine, gilt, grn bds. Good in slipcase (rubbed). *Karmiole.* $75/£48

HARPER, HENRY H. Letters from an Outsider to an Insider. Cedar Rapids: Privately Ptd by Torch Press, 1932. Paper over bds, imitation vellum spine. VG. *Graf.* $20/£13

HARPER, JENNIFER. City Work at Country Prices. Danbury, NH: Addison House, 1977. 1st ed. 54 full-pg plts. NF in ptd stiff wrappers, pict dj. *Cahan.* $30/£19

HARPUR, JERRY. The Gardener's Garden. Viking, 1985. (Label remains ep), else VG in dj. *Hadley.* $19/£12

HARRADEN, BEATRICE. A New Books of the Fairies. London: Griffith Farran Browne, n.d. (1897). Edith Lupton (illus). 8vo. 179pp. Aeg. Gilt-dec blue cl. VG. *Dower.* $65/£42

HARRADEN, BEATRICE. Things Will Take a Turn. Blackie, n.d. (1928 inscrip). John Bacon (illus). 8vo. Color frontis by Gordon Browne, 163pp + 32pp ads. Grn bds, pict onlay, cl spine. (Rubbed), else VG. *Bookmark.* $19/£12

HARRER, HEINRICH. The White Spider. London, 1959. 1st Eng ed. VG in dj (sl rubbed). *King.* $35/£22

Harriet and Mary: Being the Relations Between Percy Bysshe Shelley, Harriet Shelley, Mary Shelley, and Thomas Jefferson Hogg. (London): Golden Cockerel, 1944. One of 500 numbered. Frontis. 1/4 crushed morocco. *Swann*.* $103/£66

HARRINGTON, FRED HARVEY. Hanging Judge. Caldwell: Caxton, 1951. VG in dj (spine sunned). *Lien.* $50/£32

HARRINGTON, JOHN W. The Jumping Kangaroo and the Apple Butter Cat. NY: McClure, Phillips, 1900. 1st ed. 9 1/2 x 7 1/4. Orig cl-backed pict bds. (Spine head soiled), else NF in VG dj (chipped, rear flap crease torn). *Pacific*.* $127/£81

HARRINGTON, M. R. How to Build a California Adobe. L.A.: Ward Ritchie/Southwest Museum, 1948. Cl-backed bds. VG. *Truepenny.* $35/£22

HARRINGTON, MARK W. Notes on the Climate and Meteorology of Death Valley, California. Washington: Weather Bureau, 1892. 50pp. Ptd wrappers (torn, chipped). *Dawson.* $100/£64

HARRINGTON, MARK W. Notes on the Climate and Meteorology of Death Valley, California. Washington: Weather Bureau, 1892. 1st ed. 50pp. Fine (chipped). *Book Market.* $150/£96

HARRIOT, JOHN F. X. Farewell to True Bookshops. Blewbury, Oxfordshire: Rocket Press, 1987. Fine in pict wrappers. *Truepenny.* $10/£6

HARRIOTT, JOHN. Struggles Through Life.... London, 1808. 2nd ed. 2 vols. (24),375; (12),347pp; port, fldg plt. Contemp full calf (spines mended). Howes H220. *Ginsberg.* $450/£288

HARRIS, A. C. Alaska and the Klondike Gold Fields. N.p.: n.p., 1897. 566pp; 2 fldg maps. Ptd bds. (Worn, soiled), else Good. *Dumont.* $100/£64

HARRIS, ALBERT W. The Cruise of a Schooner. (Chicago): Privately ptd, (1958). 36 plts, maps. Pict cl (spine lt faded). Howes H221. *Ginsberg.* $125/£80

HARRIS, ALBERT W. The Yellow Dog. Chicago: PP, 1939. Color frontis. Blue cl. VF in orig glassine. *Bowman.* $75/£48

HARRIS, ALBERT. The Blood of the Arab. Chicago: AHC, 1941. 1st ed. VG. *October Farm.* $125/£80

HARRIS, BENJAMIN BUTLER. The Gila Trail. Norman: Univ of OK, (1960). 1st ed. VG in dj. *Lien.* $25/£16

HARRIS, BENJAMIN BUTLER. The Gila Trail. Richard H. Dillon (ed). Norman: Univ of OK, (1960). 1st ed. VF in dj. *Argonaut.* $45/£29

HARRIS, BRANSON L. Some Recollections of My Boyhood.... (Indianapolis: Privately ptd, 1908.) 1st ed. One of 100 ptd. Frontis, port. Howes H223. *Ginsberg.* $300/£192

HARRIS, C. E. Hyannis Sea Captains. (Yarmouthport, MA: Register Press), 1939. 1st ed. Port; fldg map laid in. (Sl foxed.) *Lefkowicz.* $75/£48

HARRIS, DEAN. By Path and Trail. Chicago, 1908. 1st ed. Frontis. VG. *Turpen.* $100/£64

HARRIS, ELIZABETH. The Common Press. Boston: David R. Godine, (1978). One of 2000. Folder of plans. VG in tan wrappers, brn paper bd slipcase. *Heller.* $50/£32

HARRIS, FRANK and JOHN HAMMOND. Black Beauty, White Heat. NY, 1982. 1st ed. 16-pg color insert. (Inscrip), o/w Fine in Fine dj. *Warren.* $85/£54

HARRIS, FRANK. Elder Conklin and Other Stories. London: Heinemann, 1895. 1st ed, 1st bk. 1/2 title not called for. Sage grn glazed linen, pub's mongram blocked on back cvr, gilt. (Cl sl faded, sm neat spine restorations), o/w Very Nice. *Temple.* $23/£15

HARRIS, FRANK. My Reminiscences as a Cowboy. NY: Charles Boni, 1930. VG in wraps. *Perier.* $25/£16

HARRIS, FRANK. My Reminiscences as a Cowboy. NY: Charles Boni, 1930. 1st pb ed. Dec eps. NF in pict stiff wrappers (sl soiled, stained). *Argonaut.* $45/£29

HARRIS, HENRY. California's Medical Story. SF: J.W. Stacey, 1932. 1st ed. Tan buckram, grn bds. Good in dj (sl chipped, soiled). *Karmiole.* $75/£48

HARRIS, HENRY. California's Medical Story. Springfield, 1932. 1st ed. (Ex-lib.) *Fye.* $125/£80

HARRIS, J. Sir William Chambers. Zwemmer, 1970. 2 ports, 199 plt illus, cat. Sound in dj. *Ars Artis.* $117/£75

HARRIS, J. and A. A. TAIT. Catalogue of the Drawings by Inigo Jones, John Webb and Isaac de Caus at Worcester College, Oxford. OUP, 1979. 127 plt illus. Sound in dj. *Ars Artis.* $55/£35

HARRIS, J. R. An Angler's Entomology. Collins, 1952. 1st ed. VG in dj. *Petersfield.* $55/£35

HARRIS, JAMES. Philological Inquiries in Three Parts. London, 1781. 2 vols in 1. 3 plts. Contemp full brn calf (joints, extrems rubbed; bkpls), gilt-paneled spine, leather label. *Freeman*.* $100/£64

HARRIS, JAMES. Three Treatises. London: J. Nourse, 1765. 2nd ed. 377pp + index. Mod bds. (Lacks frontis), o/w Fine. *Europa.* $97/£62

HARRIS, JOEL CHANDLER. Gabriel Tolliver. NY: McClure, Phillips, 1902. 1st ed. VG (spine sl cocked, frayed; hinges starting). *Hermitage.* $50/£32

HARRIS, JOEL CHANDLER. Nights with Uncle Remus. Boston, 1883. 1st ed. 12mo. Pub's pict cl (extrems quite rubbed; dampstained throughout in lower margin). As Is. BAL 7109. *Swann*.* $80/£51

HARRIS, JOEL CHANDLER. On the Plantation. NY: Appleton, 1892. 1st Amer ed. Port. Pict mustard yellow cl. (1892 ink inscrip, cl sl soiled, few mks), o/w Good. BAL 7124. *Reese.* $150/£96

HARRIS, JOEL CHANDLER. The Tar-Baby and Other Rhymes of Uncle Remus. NY, 1904. 1st ed. A. B. Frost and E. W. Kemble (illus). 8vo. Pub's gilt-pict cl (extrems sl worn). Nice. *Swann*.* $345/£221

HARRIS, JOEL CHANDLER. The Tar-Baby and Other Rhymes of Uncle Remus. NY: Appleton, Sept 1904. 1st ed. A.B. Frost & E.W. Kemble (illus). 8vo. 191pp (cracked at p64). Teg. Dec cvr (lt soiled). Good. *Scribe's Perch*.* $110/£71

HARRIS, JOEL CHANDLER. Uncle Remus Returns. Boston: Houghton Mifflin, Sept 1918. 1st ed. 12mo. 175pp; 8 plts, vignette tp by A.B. Frost & J.M. Conde. Dec cl (sl soiled, corner bumped, stained, fr hinge starting). Good. *Scribe's Perch*.* $70/£45

HARRIS, JOEL CHANDLER. Uncle Remus, His Songs and Sayings. NY: Appleton, 1881. 1st ed, 3rd state w/'presumptuous' spelled correctly on p9, terminal ads contain glowing reviews of this bk. Pink butterfly eps. Rust brn cl, gilt. VG (edgeworn; stamp eps). BAL 7100. *Macdonnell.* $200/£128

HARRIS, JOEL CHANDLER. Uncle Remus, His Songs and Sayings. NY: D. Appleton, 1881. 1st ed, 1st state w/'presumptuous' for 'presumptuous' last line p9. Frederick S. Church and James H. Moser (illus). 8vo. Gilt-pict brn cl. 1/4 morocco slipcase. BAL 7100. *Swann**. $1,495/£958

HARRIS, JOEL CHANDLER. Uncle Remus, His Songs and Sayings. NY: Appleton, 1896. New rev ed. A. B. Frost (illus). Teg. Dec red cl. Fine in dj (sl chipped). *Captain's Bookshelf*. $150/£96

HARRIS, JOEL CHANDLER. Uncle Remus. Mt. Vernon: Peter Pauper, (1937). One of 1100. Fritz Eichenberg (illus). 8vo. 136pp. Paper over bds, linen spine. Good. *Scribe's Perch**. $19/£12

HARRIS, JOHN. The Artists and the Country House...Britain 1540-1870. London, 1979. 26 color plts. Dj (spine sl faded). *Edwards*. $70/£45

HARRIS, JOHN. From Old Mobile to Fort Assumption. Parthenon, (1959). Frontis map. VG. *Oregon*. $30/£19

HARRIS, JOSEPH. Harris on the Pig. NY: OJ, 1883. Rev ed. Dec cl. VG (sl soiled). *Agvent*. $30/£19

HARRIS, JOSEPH. Harris on the Pig. NY: OJ, 1889. New ed. (Shelfwear), o/w VG. *October Farm*. $38/£24

HARRIS, L. J. Vitamins. In Theory and Practice. 1938. 3rd ed. 44 tables. (Fr cvr sl damaged, contemp ink sig fep; ex-lib, pencil mks.) *Whitehart*. $28/£18

HARRIS, MARK. The Southpaw. Bobbs Merrill, 1953. 1st ed. VG in Good+ dj. *Plapinger*. $200/£128

HARRIS, MARK. Trumpet to the World. NY: Reynal & Hitchcock, (1946). 1st ed, 1st bk. Fine in dj (lt soiled). *Hermitage*. $75/£48

HARRIS, ROBERT. Canals and Their Architecture. London, 1969. (1/2 title sl spotted; cl lt soiled.) *Edwards*. $50/£32

HARRIS, SARAH HOLLISTER. An Unwritten Chapter of Salt Lake, 1851-1901. NY: Privately ptd, 1901. Teg. Grn cl, gilt. Overall VG (lt rubbed, etched). Howes H231. *Bohling*. $400/£256

HARRIS, STANLEY. Old Coaching Days. London, 1882. 1st ed. viii,(iv),279pp (1st few ll reinforced to inner margin; later eps; bkpls), 12 sepia tinted litho plts. Illus cl (corners rubbed w/loss, recased, spine chipped w/sl loss). *Edwards*. $101/£65

HARRIS, THADDEUS WILLIAM. A Treatise on Some of the Insects Injurious to Vegetation. Charles L. Flint (ed). Boston: Crosby & Nichols, 1863. New ed. xi,640pp (sl aged, 1pg lacks blank corner); 8 composite engr plts w/orig hand-coloring, guards. Brn coated eps. Blind dk grn cl. Cvrs Good (joints once repaired, tender, spine ends frayed). *Baltimore**. $50/£32

HARRIS, THADDEUS. The Journal of a Tour into the Territory Northwest of the Alleghany Mountains. Boston, 1805. 8vo. 4 maps (very browned), 1 plt. Contemp tree calf (skillfully rebacked). Howes H233. *Swann**. $546/£350

HARRIS, THOMAS. Black Sunday. NY: Putnam, 1975. 1st ed. Signed. Fine in dj (price-clipped, short closed tears). *Mordida*. $300/£192

HARRIS, THOMAS. Red Dragon. NY, (1981). 1st ed. Fine in Fine dj. *Mcclintock*. $85/£54

HARRIS, THOMAS. Red Dragon. NY, 1981. 1st ed. Fine in Fine dj. *Warren*. $60/£38

HARRIS, THOMAS. Red Dragon. NY: Putnam, 1981. 1st ed. Signed. (Pg edges sl spotted), o/w Fine in dj. *Mordida*. $250/£160

HARRIS, THOMAS. Red Dragon. Bodley, 1982. 1st UK ed. Fine in Fine dj. *Martin*. $22/£14

HARRIS, THOMAS. Silence of the Lambs. NY, 1988. 1st ed. Fine in Fine dj. *Warren*. $50/£32

HARRIS, TOMAS. Goya. Engravings and Lithographs. Oxford: Cassirer, 1964. Inscribed by Willie Harris. 2 vols. Fldg plt. VF in pict djs. *Europa*. $702/£450

HARRIS, W. C. The Wild Sports of Southern Africa. London: Bohn, 1852. 5th ed. 359pp; 26 full-pg color plts; fldg map at rear. Binding copy. *Scribe's Perch**. $135/£87

HARRIS, WILLIAM RICHARD. By Path and Trail. Chicago, 1908. Gilt spine title. VG+ (spine name flaking). *Bohling*. $60/£38

HARRIS, WILLIAM RICHARD. The Catholic Church in Utah Including an Exposition of Catholic Faith.... Salt Lake, 1909. 1st ed. Presentation slip pasted fep. Frontis, map. (Cvrs sl stained, mottled), o/w VG. *Benchmark*. $125/£80

HARRISON, ADA M. Some Umbrian Cities. A&C Black, 1925. 1st ed. 24 plts. (Eps lt foxed), o/w Fine in dj. *Cox*. $31/£20

HARRISON, CARTER H. A Race with the Sun. NY: Putnam, 1889. xiii,569pp; 32 plts. Pict cl. VG. *Adelson*. $50/£32

HARRISON, CONSTANCE CARY. Woman's Handiwork in Modern Homes. (NY), 1882. 242pp (bkpl, sl foxed), 2 color lithos. Dec cl (spine frayed, fr hinge loose, worn). *King*. $65/£42

HARRISON, FRED. Hell Holes and Hangings. Clarendon, TX: Clarendon, 1968. (Sl pencil notes), else Good in dj. *Dumont*. $45/£29

HARRISON, FREDERICK. Medieval Man and His Notions. Murray, 1947. Good (faded) in dj (rubbed). *Peter Taylor*. $20/£13

HARRISON, G. B. and R. A. JONES. De Maisse. London: Nonesuch, 1931. Uncut. VG in dj. *Hollett*. $70/£45

HARRISON, HANK. The Dead Book. A Social History of the Grateful Dead. NY: Links, 1973. 1st ed 2nd ptg. Flexi-disc recording of Neal Cassady at the Straight Theatre, SF, in Sept. 1967, w/the Dead in background making 'Prankster music' incl. VG+ (inscrip, disc detached) in wrappers (lt creasing). *Sclanders*. $55/£35

HARRISON, HARRY. Two Tales and 8 Tomorrows. London: Gollancz, 1965. 1st ed. Dj. *Swann**. $57/£37

HARRISON, J. E. and D. S. MacCOLL. Greek Vase Painting. London: T. Fisher Unwin, 1894. Color frontis, 32pp; 42 plts. Orig dec cl (neatly recased). Excellent (lt spots, pencil marginalia). *Hollett*. $273/£175

HARRISON, J. M. The Birds of Kent. London: Witherby, 1953. 1st ed. 2 vols. 80 color plts. NF. *Mikesh*. $150/£96

HARRISON, JACK. Famous Saddle Horses and Distinguished Horsemen. Columbia, 1933. 1st ed. Good (pg edges rippled; sl faded, soiled). *October Farm*. $325/£208

HARRISON, JANE and HOPE MIRRLEES (trans). The Book of the Bear. London: Nonesuch, 1926. 1st ed. Orig buckram-backed Chinese paper bds (sides rubbed, corners sl worn). *Cox*. $28/£18

HARRISON, JANE ELLEN. Reminiscences of a Student's Life. London: Hogarth, 1925. 1st Eng ed. (Paper spine label creased), else VG in pub's red dec cl. *Hadley*. $62/£40

HARRISON, JIM. Farmer. NY: Viking, (1976). 1st ed. Fine in dj. *Between The Covers*. $150/£96

HARRISON, JIM. Locations. Norton, 1968. 1st ed. Fine in wrappers. *Certo*. $35/£22

HARRISON, JIM. Sundog. NY, 1984. 1st Amer ed. Fine in Fine dj. *Polyanthos*. $30/£19

HARRISON, JOHN. Essay Towards a Correct Theory of the Nervous System. Phila: Lea & Blanchard, 1844. viii-292pp (browned). Uncut, unopened. Orig bds (worn, newly rebacked). *Goodrich*. $175/£112

HARRISON, JOSEPH T. Story of the Dining Fork. Cincinnati: C.J. Krehbiel, 1927. Ltd ed. Gilt titled cl. VG+. *Bohling*. $30/£19

HARRISON, JOSEPH. The Accomplish'd Practiser in the High Court of Chancery.... By John Griffith Williams. London: A. Strahan & W. Woodfall, 1790. 7th ed. 2 vols. Later cl (dusty). Good. *Boswell.* $350/£224

HARRISON, MICHAEL. All the King's Ladies. Douglas Cliff, (1946). 1st ed. VG. *Gravesend.* $25/£16

HARRISON, MICHAEL. Dawn Express: There and Back. London: Collins, 1938. 1st UK ed. Good (foxed; cvr bowing, edges faded; dj imprint shadowed onto fr cvr) in Good dj (worn, soiled, frayed). *Gravesend.* $75/£48

HARRISON, MICHAEL. Gambler's Glory: The Story of John Law of Lauriston.... London: Rich & Cowan, (1940). 1st UK ed. VG in VG dj (lt wear). *Gravesend.* $50/£32

HARRISON, MICHAEL. Higher Things. London: Macdonald, (1945). Good (fep missing) in Good dj (worn, torn). *Gravesend.* $25/£16

HARRISON, MICHAEL. The House in Fishergate. London: Macdonald, (1946). 1st UK ed. Good (sl cocked, foxed) in Good dj (wear, fraying; price-clipped). *Gravesend.* $50/£32

HARRISON, MICHAEL. In the Footsteps of Sherlock Holmes. NY: Frederick Fell, (1960). 1st US ed. VG in VG dj (lt wear). *Gravesend.* $55/£35

HARRISON, MICHAEL. In the Footsteps of Sherlock Holmes. NY: Fell, 1960. 1st US ed. Good in Good dj. *Whiteson.* $20/£13

HARRISON, MICHAEL. In the Footsteps of Sherlock Holmes. David & Charles, 1971. Rev ed. Fine in NF dj. *Williams.* $25/£16

HARRISON, MICHAEL. Peter Cheney: Prince of Hokum. London: Neville Spearman, (1954). 1st UK ed. Good (eps discolored; foxed) in Good dj (inside discolored, price-clipped; quite worn, soiled). *Gravesend.* $50/£32

HARRISON, MICHAEL. The World of Sherlock Holmes. NY: E.P. Dutton, 1975. 1st US ed. VG (ink name fep) in VG dj (sl wear). *Gravesend.* $40/£26

HARRISON, RAY. A Season for Death. London: Quartet, 1987. 1st ed. VF in dj. *Mordida.* $30/£19

HARROD, R. F. The Life of John Maynard Keynes. London: Macmillan, 1951. 1st ed. 11 plts. VG. *Hollett.* $94/£60

HART, A. TINDAL. The Curate's Lot. London, 1970. 1st ed. 36 plts. Dj (spine lt faded). *Edwards.* $23/£15

HART, B. H. LIDDELL. The Tanks. London: Cassell, 1959. 1st ed. 2 vols. 55 maps. Excellent set (edges sl spotted) in djs. *Hollett.* $218/£140

HART, FRANK J. The Speed Boy. Lakewood House, 1938. 1st ed. VG in VG dj (sm chips). *Plapinger.* $150/£96

HART, HERBERT M. Old Forts of the Northwest. Seattle: Superior Pub Co, (1963). 1st ed. Fine in dj (lt worn). *Argonaut.* $35/£22

HART, HERBERT M. Old Forts of the Northwest. Seattle, 1963. 1st ed. VG + in dj (lt worn). *Pratt.* $35/£22

HART, HERBERT M. Old Forts of the Southwest. Seattle: Superior Pub Co, (1964). 1st ed. Fine in dj (lt worn). *Argonaut.* $35/£22

HART, HERBERT M. Old Forts of the Southwest. Seattle, (1964). 1st ed. VG + in dj (worn). *Pratt.* $35/£22

HART, HERBERT M. Pioneer Forts of the West. Seattle: Superior Pub Co, (1967). 1st ed. Fine in pict dj (lt rubbed). *Argonaut.* $35/£22

HART, JAMES D. The Private Press Ventures of Samuel Lloyd Osbourne and R.L.S.... SF: Book Club of CA, 1966. 1st ed. Ltd to 500 ptd. Frontis port; 11 facs in rear pocket, orig announcement laid in. Pict cl. Orig announcement laid in. VF. *Argonaut.* $75/£48

HART, SCOTT. The Moon Is Waning. NY: Derrydale, (1939). Ltd to 950. (Ink name; lt bumped), else Fine. *Truepenny.* $95/£61

HART, SCOTT. The Moon Is Waning. NY: Derrydale, 1939. 1st ed. #155/950. Dk blue pict cl, gilt. Fine. *Cummins.* $55/£35

HART-DAVIS, DUFF. Monarchs of the Glen. London: Cape, 1978. 1st ed. 48 plts, map. VG in dj. *Hollett.* $47/£30

HARTE, BRET. The Complete Works Collected and Revised by the Author. C&W, 1890/96. 1st collected ed (w/o the 3 vols pub'd after 1896). 9 vols. Uncut. Blue cl blocked in black/gold (vols 6-7 spines dknd, corners worn). Good. *Cox.* $156/£100

HARTE, BRET. The Complete Works.... London, 1882. 5 vols. Port. Contemp 1/2 grn morocco, gilt, spines (faded) in 6 compartments, lettered in 2. *Swann*.* $230/£147

HARTE, BRET. Echoes of the Foothills. Boston: James R. Osgood, 1875. 1st ed. (Spine, edges lightened, spotted, spine head chipped.) BAL 7278. *Sadlon.* $15/£10

HARTE, BRET. Flip and Found at Blazing Star. Boston: Houghton, Mifflin, 1882. 1st ed. (Sm bkpl, fr hinge separating), o/w VG. *Hermitage.* $75/£48

HARTE, BRET. The Luck of Roaring Camp. Boston: Fields, Osgood, 1870. 1st ed, w/o 'Brown of Calaveras.' Full brn morocco (wear, joint starting, bds sl bowed), ribbed gilt spine (dknd), wide lacy frame each bd. Contents VG. BAL 7246. *Waverly*.* $132/£85

HARTE, BRET. The Luck of Roaring Camp. Boston: James R. Osgood, 1872. 1st illus ed. Signed photo CDV of Bret Harte (torn) mtd fr pastedown. 75pp (new eps, sm tear fr edge several pp), 6 plts. Grn cl (bumped, rubbed; rebacked w/new spine, black leather label), gilt. Aeg. *Blue Mountain.* $375/£240

HARTE, BRET. The Luck of Roaring Camp. SF: Ransohoffs, 1948. Ltd to 300. 4 color plts. Violet cl-backed bds (sl rubbed), gilt, paper spine label. NF. *Blue Mountain.* $95/£61

HARTE, BRET. The Luck of Roaring Camp. SF: Ransohoffs, 1948. One of 300. 4 color plts by Malette Dean. Violet cl-backed bds (sl rubbed), gilt-lettered paper spine label. NF. *Blue Mountain.* $125/£80

HARTE, BRET. Maruja. Boston: Houghton, Mifflin, 1885. 1st ed. (Sm bkpl), o/w VG. *Hermitage.* $75/£48,

HARTE, BRET. Openings in the Old Trail. Boston/NY: Houghton, Mifflin, 1902. 1st ed, 1st ptg (w/printer's imprint on p[334] and w/only 2pp undated ads). Brn cl. Fine. *Sumner & Stillman.* $40/£26

HARTE, BRET. Poems. Boston: James R. Osgood, 1871. 1st ed, later issue (same year, but w/imprint of James R. Osgood & Co. rather than Fields, Osgood & Co.). 1 prelim pg undated ads. Grn cl, beveled. VF. *Sumner & Stillman.* $45/£29

HARTE, BRET. The Queen of the Pirate Isle. London: C&W, (1886). 1st ed. Kate Greenaway (illus). 8vo. Pict cl (sl rubbed). *Swann*.* $230/£147

HARTE, BRET. The Queen of the Pirate Isle. Boston/NY: Houghton, Mifflin, 1887 (actually 1886). 1st ed, 1st binding, states 'A.' Kate Greenaway (illus). Gilt edges; blue eps. Unbleached linen over bds, pict designs. VG (sl offsetting of plts). BAL 7338. *Cullen.* $175/£112

HARTE, BRET. The Queen of the Pirate Isle. Boston: Houghton Mifflin, 1887. 1st Amer ed, in Blanck's binding 'A.' Kate Greenaway (illus). 8vo. Aeg. Pict cl (sl soiled, worn). BAL 7338. *Oinonen*.* $90/£58

HARTE, BRET. San Francisco in 1866...Being Letters to the Springfield Republican. George R. Stewart and Edwin S. Fussell (eds). SF: Book Club of CA, 1951. One of 400 ptd. Prospectus laid in. Cl, dec bds (spine sl foxed). VG (sm bkpl). BAL 7415. *Reese.* $50/£32

HARTE, BRET. Stories in Light and Shadow. London: C. Arthur Pearson, 1898. 1st ed. 6pp undated ads. Grn cl dec in dk grn. Fine. *Sumner & Stillman.* $75/£48

HARTE, BRET. Tales of the Gold Rush. Norwalk: Heritage, 1972. Fine in Fine slipcase. *Connolly.* $20/£13

HARTE, BRET. The Wild West. (Harrison of Paris, 1930.) One of 36 (of 876). Grass-cl, embroidered spine. VF in embroidered slipcase. *Bromer.* $450/£288

HARTE, BRET. Writings. Boston/NY: Houghton Mifflin/Riverside Press Cambridge, n.d. (?1900-1914). Standard Library ed. 20 vols. (Pg carelessly opened vol XX, browned area between 2 leaves from laid-in news clipping.) Teg. Grn ribbed cl (spine ends sl rubbed, sm snag spine head vol I, sm dent spine vol XX), gilt. Very Attractive. *Sadlon.* $150/£96

HARTLEY, CECIL B. The Gentlemen's Book of Etiquette, and Manual of Politeness. Boston: J.S. Locke, 1876 (1873). Early ed. Dk brn coated eps. Dk purple dec cl, gilt/black/blind-stamped. VG (sl rubbing, corners bumped). *Houle.* $125/£80

HARTLEY, DOROTHY. Thomas Tusser. Country Life, 1931. Color frontis. (Newspaper review affixed pastedown.) Dj (sl chipped). *Edwards.* $75/£48

HARTLEY, DOROTHY. Water in England. London, 1964. 1st ed. 42 plts. Dj (sl chipped). *Edwards.* $25/£16

HARTLEY, FLORENCE. The Ladies' Book of Etiquette and Manual of Politeness. Boston: DeWolfe, Fiske, (1879). 840pp. Brn cl. Good (hinges loose). *Second Life.* $45/£29

HARTLEY, H. (ed). The Royal Society, Its Origins and Founders. London, 1960. Dj. *Maggs.* $28/£18

HARTLEY, L. P. The Brickfield. London, 1964. 1st Eng ed. Very Nice in dj. *Clearwater.* $39/£25

HARTLEY, L. P. The Collections. London, 1972. 1st Eng ed. Fine in dj. *Clearwater.* $31/£20

HARTLEY, L. P. Facial Justice. London: Hamish Hamilton, 1960. 1st ed. VG in dj. *Hollett.* $23/£15

HARTLEY, L. P. The Hireling. Hamish Hamilton, (1957). 1st ed. VG in dj. *Ash.* $39/£25

HARTLEY, L. P. The Hireling. Hamish Hamilton, 1957. 1st ed. Dj (sl torn, spine sl browned). *Edwards.* $31/£20

HARTLEY, L. P. A Perfect Woman. Hamish Hamilton, 1955. 1st ed. Dj (sl chipped). *Edwards.* $31/£20

HARTLEY, L. P. A Perfect Woman. London, 1955. 1st ed. VG in dj (sl foxed). *Words Etc.* $16/£10

HARTLEY, L. P. A Perfect Woman. London, 1955. 1st ed. Dj. *Typographeum.* $30/£19

HARTLEY, L. P. The Traveling Grave and Other Stories. Sauk City: Arkham House, 1948. 1st ed. Dj (sl browned, sl worn). *Swann*.* $69/£44

HARTLEY, L. P. The Traveling Grave. Sauk City: Arkham House, 1948. 1st ed. VG (bkpl) in dj (browned, edgeworn). *Metropolitan*.* $28/£18

HARTLEY, L. P. Two for the River. London, 1961. 1st Eng ed. Fine in dj. *Clearwater.* $39/£25

HARTMAN, JOAN M. Chinese Jade of Five Centuries. Rutland, VT/Tokyo: Tuttle, 1969. 1st ed. 55 plts (10 color). Silk cl. NF in dj, protective carbd box. *Worldwide.* $35/£22

HARTMANN, ERNEST L. The Biology of Dreaming. Springfield, IL: Charles C. Thomas, (1967). 1st ed. Ptd blue cl. VG (stamps) in dj. *Gach.* $50/£32

HARTMANN, FRANZ. The Life and Doctrines of Jacob Boehme. Boston: Occult Pub, 1891. 1st ed. x,338pp. (50pp mkd; nicely rebound), o/w VG. *Middle Earth.* $65/£42

HARTMANN, FRANZ. The Life and Doctrines of Paracelsus. London: Kegan et al, 1896. 2nd ed. xv,311pp. (Inner hinge exposed), o/w VG. *Middle Earth.* $95/£61

HARTMANN, FRANZ. The Life and the Doctrines of...Paracelsus and the Substance of His Teaching. London, 1896. 2nd ed. 311pp. Good. *Goodrich.* $65/£42

HARTMANN, FRANZ. The Life and the Doctrines of...Paracelsus. NY: Macoy, 1945. 4th ed. Nice. *Goodrich.* $30/£19

HARTMANN, R. Anthropoid Apes. London: Kegan Paul, (1904). 2nd ed. 63 engrs. Blind-stamped dec cl. VG. *Mikesh.* $37/£24

HARTMANN, SADAKICHI. Landscape and Figure Composition. NY: Baker & Taylor, 1910. Aeg. Gilt-titled cl. (Fr inner hinge sl tender; spine lettering rubbed), else VG. *Cahan.* $125/£80

HARTMANN, SADAKICHI. The Valiant Knights of Daguerre. Berkeley: Univ of CA, 1978. 1st ed. (Owner stamp), else VG in dj (edgetorn). *Cahan.* $40/£26

HARTNELL, A. P. Shop Planning and Design. N.d. (c. 1935). 47 plts. Empty pocket rear pastedown. Dj (sl chipped, lt browned). *Edwards.* $31/£20

HARTREE, D. R. Calculating Machines. Cambridge: CUP, 1947. 1st ed. 2 photo plts. Nice in orig self-wrappers (sl dusty). *Patterson.* $39/£25

HARTSHORN, CHARLES W. The New England Sheriff, Being a Digest of All the Laws of Massachusetts.... Worcester: Enos Dorr, 1855. Orig sheep. Good. *Boswell.* $250/£160

HARTSHORNE, ALBERT. Old English Drinking Glasses. London: Edward Arnold, 1897. xxiii,490pp; 67 plts (2 color). Teg. 1/2 dec japon bds (sl rubbed). *Hollett.* $273/£175

HARTT, FREDERICK et al. The Chapel of the Cardinal of Portugal 1434-1459 at San Miniato in Florence. Phila: Univ of PA, (1964). 1st ed. White cl. Good in dj. *Karmiole.* $50/£32

HARTT, FREDERICK et al. The Chapel of the Cardinal of Portugal 1434-1459 at San Miniato in Florence. Phila, 1964. 156 plts (4 color). Good in dj. *Washton.* $75/£48

HARTWIG, G. The Polar and Tropical Worlds. A.H. Guernsey (ed). Springfield, MA/Chicago: Nichols/Heron, 1876. 2 vols in 1. 811pp. Orig full morocco. (Rubbed, spine frayed, sl tear), o/w Good. *Worldwide.* $35/£22

HARTWIG, G. The Subterranean World. London, 1875. 3rd ed. xix,522pp; 3 maps, 8 plts. 1/2 red morocco. *Wheldon & Wesley.* $55/£35

Harvard Medical School, 1782-1906. Boston, 1906. 1st ed. VG. *Fye.* $100/£64

Harvey Cushing Collection of Books and Manuscripts. Schuman's, 1943. VG+. *Bookcell.* $225/£144

HARVEY, D. C. The French Regime in Prince Edward Island. New Haven: Yale, 1926. 1st ed. Paper spine label. *Ginsberg.* $75/£48

HARVEY, GERALD. (Pseud of Vance Randolph.) The Secret Lore of Witchcraft. Girard: Haldeman-Julius, 1946. 1st ed. Wraps, digest-size. Fine. *Beasley.* $40/£26

HARVEY, J. Victorian Novelists and Their Illustrators. Sidgwick & Jacksson, 1970. VG in dj. *Moss.* $47/£30

HARVEY, JOHN. English Mediaeval Architects. A Biographical Dictionary Down to 1550. London: Batsford, 1954. (Lib # verso tp; cl sl marked.) *Ars Artis.* $70/£45

HARVEY, JOHN. The Gothic World 1100-1600. London: Batsford, 1950. 295 plt illus. Sound. *Ars Artis.* $33/£21

HARVEY, JOHN. Henry Yevele c.1320 to 1400. Batsford, 1944. 1st ed. Color frontis. Dj (frayed). *Cox.* $23/£15

HARVEY, JOHN. The Perpendicular Style. Batsford, 1978. 1st ed. (Pub's file stamp), else VG in dj. *Hadley.* $31/£20

HARVEY, MRS. Our Cruise in the Claymore. London: Chapman & Hall, 1861. 1st ed. xi,(i)blank,309pp; 8 litho plts, incl frontis (plts browned, lt waterstain upper edge), engr title vignette (sm blind lib stamp). Marbled edges. Contemp grn 1/2 morocco, marbled bds (rubbed), gilt spine devices. Good. *Morrell.* $187/£120

HARVEY, W. H. The Sea-Side Book. London, 1854. 3rd ed. x,324pp (sl foxed). Aeg. Blind-emb cl (damp-stained, sl soiled, chipped, joints splitting, sl rubbed). *Edwards.* $31/£20

HARVEY, WILLIAM. The Anatomical Exercises of Dr. William Harvey. Geoffrey Keynes (ed). London: Nonesuch, (1953). 1st ed. One of 1450 ptd. Teg. Full morocco. (Offsetting ep edges; extrems sl rubbed), o/w Fine. *Jaffe.* $250/£160

HARVEY, WILLIAM. De Motu Locali Animalium, 1627. G. Whitteridge (ed). Cambridge, 1959. Ltd ed. VG in dj. *Fye.* $100/£64

HARVEY, WILLIAM. Lectures on the Whole of Anatomy. C. D. O'Malley et al (trans). Univ of CA, 1961. 1st ed thus. Color frontis port, 4 full-pg illus. 2-tone cl. Fine in dj. *Glaser.* $45/£29

HARVEY, WILLIAM. Movement of the Heart and Blood in Animals. K. J. Franklin (trans). Springfield, 1957. Ltd ed. VG in dj. *Fye.* $60/£38

HARVEY, WILLIAM. Works of William Harvey, M.D. London, 1847. 1st ed. 624pp. VG. *Fye.* $300/£192

HARVEY, WILLIAM. The Works of William Harvey, M.D. Robert Willis (trans). London: Sydenham Soc, 1847. xcvi,624pp. Orig cl (rebacked, spine relaid). Clean. *White.* $133/£85

HARWELL, RICHARD B. (ed). The Confederate Reader. NY, 1957. 1st ed. Signed. VG in dj (sl used). *King.* $30/£19

HARWELL, RICHARD B. In Tall Cotton: The 200 Most Important Confederate Books for the Reader, Researcher and Collector. Austin, 1978. 1st ed. Ltd to 750. Fine. *Mcgowan.* $350/£224

HARWELL, RICHARD B. (ed). The Union Reader. NY, 1958. 1st ed. Dj. *Wantagh.* $25/£16

HARWELL, RICHARD B. (ed). The War They Fought. NY, 1960. 1st ed. VG+ in dj (torn). *Pratt.* $35/£22

HASELDEN, R. B. Scientific Aids for the Study of Manuscripts. Oxford, 1935. 16 plts. VG in wrappers (edges sl worn). *Whitehart.* $39/£25

Hasheesh Eater. (By Fitz Hugh Ludlow.) NY: Harper, 1857. 1st ed. Black cl, gilt. (Spine worn, gilt tarnished), else Attractive. *Macdonnell.* $400/£256

HASKELL, DANIEL C. A Tentative Check-List of Early European Railway Literature, 1831-1848. Boston: Harvard, (1955). 1st ed. Fine. *Glaser.* $95/£61

HASKELL, FRANK ARETAS. The Battle of Gettysburg. Bruce Catton (ed). Boston, 1958. 1st ed. VG. *Pratt.* $30/£19

HASKINS, JAMES. Pinckney Benton Stewart Pinchback. NY: Macmillan, (1973). 1st ed. Fine in dj (sm stain spine). *Between The Covers.* $50/£32

HASKINS, JIM. Diary of a Harlem Schoolteacher. NY: Grove, (1969). 1st ed. Fine in dj (sm tear). *Between The Covers.* $45/£29

HASKINS, SAM. November Girl. NY: Madison Square, 1967. 1st ed. Fine in illus dj. *Cahan.* $85/£54

HASKOLL, W. DAVIS. The Assistant Engineer's Railway Guide in Boring. London: J. Williams, 1846-48. 2 vols. iii,136pp, 3 fldg plts, 16pp ads; iv,192,31,125-128,16pp ads, 28 plts. (Ex-lib, perf blindstamp, 1 plt vol 1 protrudes w/dknd, frayed edge; spine top torn, rear hinge cracked vol 2, sl frayed.) *Bohling.* $120/£77

HASLEM, JOHN. The Old Derby China Factory. London, 1876. Frontis, xvi,255pp (marginal ruling, notes; hinges cracked); 11 color plts. Teg. (Joints splitting, sl frayed, spine faded, chipped.) *Edwards.* $211/£135

HASLUCK, F. W. Cyzicus. Cambridge: CUP, 1910. 3 fldg maps (on 2 sheets) rear pocket. (Top bd sl discolored.) *Archaeologia.* $125/£80

HASLUCK, P. N. Lathe-Work, a Practical Treatise.... London, 1904. 8th ed. (Cl rubbed.) *Maggs.* $31/£20

HASS, JULIUS. Congenital Dislocation of the Hip. Springfield, 1951. 1st ed. Leatherette cl bds. VG. *Doctor's Library.* $50/£32

HASSALL, A. G. and W. O. HASSALL. Treasures from the Bodleian Library. London, 1976. 36 color plts. (Sm dampstain bottom of cvrs.) Internally Very Nice. *Washton.* $65/£42

HASSAUREK, F. Four Years Among Spanish-Americans. Cincinnati: R. Clarke, 1881. 3rd ed. 397pp + ads. (Lib mks inside), else VG+. *Bohling.* $12/£8

HASSE, CHARLES EWALD. An Anatomical Description of the Diseases of the Organs of Circulation and Respiration. W. E. Swaine (ed). London: Sydenham Soc, 1846. 400pp. Good. *Goodrich.* $65/£42

HASSELL, J. Memoirs of the Life of the Late George Moreland. London, 1806. Add'l engr title, 8 plts. (Lt foxing.) Contemp bds (worn, rebacked). *Freeman*.* $80/£51

HASSLER, JON. Four Miles to Pinecone. NY: Warne, 1977. 1st ed, 1st bk. Fine (bkpl) in dj (1/4-inch chip). *Else Fine.* $125/£80

HASSLER, WARREN W., JR. General George B. McClellan. Baton Rouge, (1957). 1st ed. Signed. VG in dj (edge-torn, sl spotted). *King.* $65/£42

HASTIE, T. The Only Method to Make Reading Easy. Newcastle: Emerson Charnley, 1839. 73rd ed. 12mo. Woodcut frontis, 108pp. Orig calf over bds. Good. *Karmiole.* $75/£48

Hastings Hours. (NY): Thames & Hudson, (1983). Tan cl, gilt. Fine in pub's slipcase. *Karmiole.* $65/£42

HASTINGS, JOHN. Lectures on Yellow Fever. Phila: Lindsay & Blakiston, 1848. 1st ed. (4),(17)-69pp,(6 ads). Emb cl. Fine. *Glaser.* $250/£160

HASTINGS, JOHN. The Practice of Surgery. Phila: Lindsay & Blakiston, 1850. Orig leather (edges sl rubbed). VG (lt foxed). *Yudkin*.* $85/£54

HASTINGS, LANSFORD W. The Emigrant's Guide to Oregon and California. Princeton: Princeton Univ, 1932. Facs rpt. Frontis port. Red cl, gilt. Fine. *Pacific*.* $127/£81

HASTINGS, MACDONALD. Cork in Bottle. NY: Knopf, 1954. Stated 1st Amer ed. VG in Good+ dj (chipped). *Backman.* $25/£16

HASTINGS, MACDONALD. English Sporting Guns and Accessories. London/Sydney: Ward Lock, (1969). Color frontis. Fine (name stamp) in Fine dj. *Backman.* $20/£13

HASTINGS, SALLY. Poems on Different Subjects. Lancaster, (PA): The Author, 1808. 1st ed. Full contemp calf (rubbed; some pp dampstained, lacks fr/rear blanks). *Kane*.* $120/£77

HASTINGS, SELINA. Sir Gawain and the Green Knight. NY: Lothrop, 1981. 1st US ed. Juan Wijngaard (illlus). 8 1/2 sq. 32pp. Fine (ex-lib) in dj. *Cattermole.* $15/£10

HATCH, ALDEN and FOXHALL KEENE. Full Tilt: The Sporting Memoirs of Foxhall Keene. NY: Derrydale, (1938). Ltd to 950. (Ink name), else Fine. *Truepenny.* $150/£96

HATCH, ALDEN. Remington Arms in American History. NY: Rinehart, (1956). 1st ed. VG in dj. *Lien.* $35/£22

HATCH, EVELYN M. (ed). A Selection from the Letters of Lewis Carroll to His Child-Friends. Macmillan, 1933. 1st ed. Frontis port. (Feps lt spotted.) Teg. *Edwards.* $39/£25

HATCHER, HARLAN. The Buckeye Country. NY: Kinsey, 1940. 1st ed. Good. *Archer.* $22/£14

HATCHER, ROBERT. The Pharmacopoeia and the Physician: A Series of Articles.... Chicago, 1908. 2nd ed. VG. *Fye.* $100/£64

HATCHER, WILLIAM E. The Life of J.B. Jeter, D.D. H.M. Warton, 1887. 508pp, port. Good+ (foxing; cl insect spot, fr hinge torn). *Book Broker.* $35/£22

HATFIELD, AUBREY W. Pleasures of Herbs. NY: St. Martin's, 1965. 1st Amer ed. Fine in pict dj (rubbed). *Quest.* $30/£19

HATLEM, JOHN. The War Against Germany and Italy. Washington: Dept of Army/USGPO, 1951. 1st ed. VG+ (spine sl sunned). *Archer.* $25/£16

HATTERER, LAWRENCE J. The Artist in Society. NY: Grove, (1965). 1st ed. Inscribed. Red cl. VG in dj (lt worn). *Gach.* $40/£26

HATTON, RICHARD G. The Craftsman's Plant Book. Chapman & Hall, 1909. 1st ed. Color frontis. (Sl foxing.) Teg. VG (spine sl faded, fr hinge pulled, lt wear; prize label). *Whittle.* $187/£120

HATTON, THOMAS and ARTHUR CLEAVER. A Bibliography of the Periodical Works of Charles Dickens. London, 1933. One of 750. VG. *Argosy.* $250/£160

HATTON, THOMAS and ARTHUR CLEAVER. A Bibliography of the Periodical Works of Charles Dickens. London: Chapman & Hall, 1933. One of 750. Fine (sl foxed) in textured paper dj (sl worn). *Waverly*.* $264/£169

HAUCK, A. H. R. et al. American Silver 1670-1830: The Cornelius C. Moore Collection at Providence College. Providence, 1980. 1st ed. #566/1000. NF in NF dj. *Scribe's Perch*.* $20/£13

HAUG, LEROY and GERHARD MALM. Bible of Bridle Bits. 1975. 1st ed. Ltd to 3000. Pb. VG. *October Farm.* $95/£61

HAULTAIN, ARNOLD. The Mystery of Golf. Boston: Houghton Mifflin, 1908. 1st ed. #408/440. Cl-backed dec bds, gilt spine. (Ex-lib, bkpl, emb stamp tp, stamped # contents pg, bkpls removed), else VG in Good slipcase (spine #s, lacks upper edge). *Pacific*.* $1,265/£811

HAUPTMANN, GERHART. The Island of the Great Mother. Willa & Edwin Muir (trans). NY, 1925. 1st Amer ed. Fine (sm stain corner fep, sl corner crease 3 prelim pp; 2 sm tears spine) in dj (spine sunned, sl rubbed, extrems sl chipped, few sm fold tears). *Polyanthos.* $30/£19

HAUPTMANN, GERHART. The Island of the Great Mother. NY: B.W. Huetsch, 1925. 1st US ed. (Sig), else NF in VG+ dj (spine tanned). *Lame Duck.* $65/£42

HAURANNE, ERNEST D. A Frenchman in Lincoln's America. Lakeside, 1974 & 1975. 2 vols. Good. *Heinoldt.* $35/£22

HAUSER, HEINRICH. Bitter Waters. NY: Horace Liveright, 1929. 1st in English. VG (bds sl spotted) in dj (worn). *Lame Duck.* $50/£32

HAVEL, VACLAV. The Memorandum. London: Cape, 1967. 1st British ed. (Inscrip), else NF in dj (spine faded). *Lame Duck.* $65/£42

HAVEN, GILBERT. Our Next-Door Neighbor: A Winter in Mexico. NY: Harper, 1875. 1st ed. Frontis, 468pp + 2pp pub's ads. Gilt-stamped maroon cl. Good. *Karmiole.* $75/£48

HAVERGAL, FRANCES RIDLEY. Life Chords.... London, 1880. 300pp; 12 chromolithos. Aeg. Pict cl (Cvr wear), o/w VG. *New Hampshire*.* $50/£32

HAVERKAMP-BEGEMANN, E. and ANNE-MARIE LOGAN. European Drawings and Watercolors in the Yale University Art Gallery 1500-1900. New Haven, 1970. 2 vols. Good in dj. *Washton.* $100/£64

HAVILAND, LAURA S. A Woman's Life-Work: Labors and Experiences. Cincinnati: Walden & Stowe, 1881. 1st ed. 515pp; engr port, guard. Dec purple cl (spine sl sunned). *Petrilla.* $175/£112

HAWES, HARRY. My Friend the Black Bass. NY, 1930. 1st ed. Inscribed. VF. *Bond.* $25/£16

HAWES, JOEL. Lectures Addressed to the Young Men. Hartford: Oliver Cooke et al, 1828. 2nd ed. Linen-backed bds (sl soiled). *Second Life.* $65/£42

HAWES, JOEL. Lectures to Young Men. Hartford: Belknap & Hamersley, 1836. 11th ed. Pub's cl. VG (foxed, ex-lib). *Second Life.* $45/£29

HAWKER, ROBERT STEPHEN. Stones Broken from the Rocks. C. E. Byles and E. R. Appleton (eds). Oxford: Blackwell, 1922. 1st Eng ed. Bright (name) in dj (sl torn, chafed). *Clearwater.* $70/£45

HAWKES, JOHN. The Beetle Leg. NY: New Directions, 1951. 1st ed. NF (bkpl) in dj (lt used). *Beasley.* $65/£42

HAWKES, JOHN. The Blood Oranges. NY: New Directions, 1971. 1st ed. Fine in NF dj (nicks). *Lame Duck.* $45/£29

HAWKING, STEPHEN W. A Brief History of Time: From the Big Bang to Black Holes. NY: Bantam, (1988). A copy of the earliest state of the book which was recalled by the pub. Recalled issue has silver-blue dj and lacks a contents and Hawking's dedication to his editor. As New in dj. *Between The Covers.* $300/£192

HAWKINS, FREDERICK. Annals of the French Stage from Its Origin to the Death of Racine. London: Chapman & Hall, 1884. 1st ed. 2 vols. Engr frontis ports; errata slip. Blue-grn cl. Fine. *Burmester.* $140/£90

HAWKINS, JOSEPH. A History of a Voyage to the Coast of Africa, and Travels into the Interior of That Country. Phila: The Author, 1797. 1st ed. Engr frontis, 179pp, errata. Old calf (edges worn; fr bd loose), gilt-ruled spine, leather label. *Petrilla.* $450/£288

HAWKINS, WILLIAM GEORGE. Life of John H.W. Hawkins. Boston, 1859. 1st ed. 433pp. Brn tooled cl. VG. *Doctor's Library.* $50/£32

HAWKS, ELLISON. The Microscope. NY, 1919. 1st ed. Good (extrems worn). *Doctor's Library.* $50/£32

HAWKS, FRANCIS L. A Narrative of Events Connected with the Rise and Progress of the Protestant Episcopal Church in Virginia. NY: Harper, 1836. 1st ed. 286,(2),332pp. Orig cl, paper spine label (faded). Howes H323. *Ginsberg.* $100/£64

HAWKS, FRANCIS L. Narrative of the Expedition of an American Squadron to the China Seas and Japan...1852, 1853, and 1854.... NY: Appleton, 1856. 1st 1-vol ed. vii,624pp (lt aged, foxed, lacks fep, ink owner stamp); tipped-in errata, 11 fldg engr plts, 77 b/w engr plts. Lt blue eps. Blind crimson cl (frayed, joints sl torn, worn), gilt. *Baltimore*.* $170/£109

HAWLEY, HENRY. Neo-Classicism. Cleveland Museum of Art, 1964. Good in dj (worn). *Washton.* $50/£32

HAWORTH, M. E. Road Scrapings. London: Tinsley Bros, 1882. Frontis, viii,202pp; 10 plts. Marbled eps; teg. 1/2 morocco, marbled bds (spine chipped), gilt, raised bands. *Edwards.* $133/£85

HAWORTH-BOOTH, MARK (ed). Golden Age of British Photography, 1839-1900. NY: Aperture, 1984. NF in pict stiff wrappers. *Cahan*. $30/£19

HAWTHORNE, HILDEGARDE (ed). Arabian Nights. Phila: Penn, (1928). 1st ed thus. Virginia Frances Sterrett (illus). 16 Fine color plts, guards. Pict eps. Black cl, gilt, lg color pict label fr cvr. (Spine ends lt frayed, gilt faded.) *Baltimore**. $35/£22

HAWTHORNE, HILDEGARDE. California's Missions. NY: Appleton Century, (1942). 1st ed. 48 full-pg b/w dwgs. VG in dj (sl worn). *Lien*. $18/£12

HAWTHORNE, JULIAN. Nathaniel Hawthorne and His Wife: A Biography. Cambridge: CUP, 1884. 1st ed. One of 350 numbered. 2 vols. Plain paper bds (lt chipped, rubbed, spines dknd), paper spine labels. Good set. *Captain's Bookshelf*. $75/£48

HAWTHORNE, JULIAN. Rumpty-Dudget's Tower. Stokes, 1924. George W. Hood (illus). 6x8. 72pp. Cl, pict paste-on (sl chipped). VG (bumped, pulled sl at spine). *My Bookhouse*. $45/£29

HAWTHORNE, JULIAN. Section 558 or The Fatal Letter. London: Cassell, n.d. (1888). 1st Eng ed (Amer sheets in Eng binding, w/Eng tp and ads at back imprinted '5G.7 88'). Pict bds (extrems chipped, worn; foxing). *Holmes*. $250/£160

HAWTHORNE, MRS. NATHANIEL. Notes in England and Italy. NY: Putnam, 1875. 1st illus ed. Aeg. Terra cotta cl, gilt. Nice (lt worn). *Macdonnell*. $100/£64

HAWTHORNE, NATHANIEL. The Blithedale Romance. Boston, 1852. 1st Amer ed. 288pp, cat dated July 1852. (Bkpl; ends chipped), else Good. *King*. $95/£61

HAWTHORNE, NATHANIEL. The Blithedale Romance. Boston: Ticknor, Reed & Fields, 1852. 1st Amer ed, 1st ptg. Brn cl stamped in gilt/blind. (Few leaves spotted, nicks spine toe), o/w VG. *Reese*. $125/£80

HAWTHORNE, NATHANIEL. The Blithedale Romance. Boston: Ticknor, Reed & Fields, 1852. 1st Amer ed. 288pp; ads dated April 1852. (Spine ends chipped, edges worn.) BAL 7611, binding A. *M & S*. $250/£160

HAWTHORNE, NATHANIEL. The Blithedale Romance. Boston: Ticknor, Reed & Fields, 1852. 1st ed, 1st ptg w/copyright notice opposite lines 4-6 of preface. Brn cl, gilt. Fine. BAL 7611. *Macdonnell*. $400/£256

HAWTHORNE, NATHANIEL. The Blithedale Romance. Boston: Ticknor, Reed, & Fields, 1852. 1st Amer ed. 1/2 title not called for, 288pp. Eps faced lt grn. Contemp 1/2 natural calf (sl rubbed), gilt, oil-marbled sides, matching edges, black label. Nice. *Temple*. $47/£30

HAWTHORNE, NATHANIEL. The Blithedale Romance. Chapman & Hall, 1855. 3rd ed. Marbled edges. Contemp 1/2 leather, marbled bds (rebacked, lacks spine label), orig backstrip relaid. Good (sl spotted). *Tiger*. $87/£56

HAWTHORNE, NATHANIEL. The Complete Works. Boston, 1892. Riverside ed. 13 vols. 8vo. Frontispieces. Contemp 1/2 tan calf, gilt, spines in 6 compartments, red/grn morocco lettering pieces in 2. *Swann**. $747/£479

HAWTHORNE, NATHANIEL. Doctor Grimshawe's Secret. Boston: James R. Osgood, 1883. 1st ed, 1st ptg, 1st binding w/Osgood's logo at foot. Grn pict cl, gilt. (Spine sl dknd, sl rubbed; early inscrip), else Nice. BAL 7642. *Macdonnell*. $75/£48

HAWTHORNE, NATHANIEL. The Gentle Boy: A Thrice Told Tale. Boston/NY/London, 1839. 1st separate ed w/new preface by him. Obl 4to. Engr frontis. Untrimmed. Ptd wrappers, sewn. (Lt foxed.) Superb in 1/4 morocco slipcase. BAL 7587. *Swann**. $1,955/£1,253

HAWTHORNE, NATHANIEL. The Golden Touch. (SF): Grabhorn, 1927. One of 240 ptd. Parchment-backed bds. (Parchment mottled, sl spine wear), o/w Nice. *Reese*. $100/£64

HAWTHORNE, NATHANIEL. Grandfather's Chair: A History for Youth. Boston: E.P. Peabody, 1841. 1st ed. Orig purple slate T cl, black glazed label, gilt. Nice (sl faded, fr hinge crack) in 1/4 morocco slipcase, gilt. BAL 7590. *Macdonnell*. $850/£545

HAWTHORNE, NATHANIEL. The House of the Seven Gables. Boston: Ticknor, Reed & Fields, 1851. 1st ed, 2nd ptg w/perfect type at p149. Later 3/4 tan calf, raised bands, gilt. Fine. BAL 7604. *Macdonnell*. $100/£64

HAWTHORNE, NATHANIEL. The House of the Seven Gables. Boston: Ticknor, Reed, & Fields, 1851. 1st ed, 2nd ptg w/perfect type at p149 as noted only by Clark. March cat. Brn cl, gilt. (Sl rubbed.) BAL 7604. *Macdonnell*. $500/£321

HAWTHORNE, NATHANIEL. Life of Franklin Pierce. Boston: Ticknor, Reed & Fields, 1852. 1st ed. Brn cl, gilt. (Spine chipped, frayed.) BAL 7612. *Macdonnell*. $100/£64

HAWTHORNE, NATHANIEL. The Marble Faun. Boston: Ticknor & Fields, 1860. 1st ed, 4th ptg w/the 'Conclusion' added. 2 vols. Brn cl, gilt. (Spine tips lt frayed), else Nice set. BAL 7624. *Macdonnell*. $100/£64

HAWTHORNE, NATHANIEL. Passages from the American Note-Books. Boston: Ticknor & Fields, 1868. 1st ed, 1st ptg, 1st binding. 2 vols. Orig grn cl, gilt. (Crowns frayed), else Bright. BAL 7632. *Macdonnell*. $200/£128

HAWTHORNE, NATHANIEL. Passages from the English Note-Books. Boston: Fields, Osgood, 1870. 1st ed, 1st ptg. 2 vols. Grn cl, gilt. (Bkpls removed; crown chipped), else VG. BAL 7634. *Macdonnell*. $100/£64

HAWTHORNE, NATHANIEL. Passages from the English Notebook of Nathaniel Hawthorne. London: Strahan, 1870. 2 vols. x,472,(ii)ads; 455,(ii)ads pp. Uncut. (Hinges cracked; cl sl soiled, rubbed, vol 2 sl split, spines sl bumped, sl loss.) *Edwards*. $62/£40

HAWTHORNE, NATHANIEL. Passages from the French and Italian Note-Books. Boston: James R. Osgood, 1872. 1st ed, 1st ptg, binding A (1st of 3). One of 1500 sets ptd. 2 vols. Orig grn cl, gilt. (Crown frayed), else Bright. BAL 7636. *Macdonnell*. $150/£96

HAWTHORNE, NATHANIEL. The Scarlet Letter, A Romance. Boston: Ticknor, Reed, & Fields, 1850. 3rd ed, 1st ptg. 6,307pp, ads dated November 1850. (Cvrs lt stained, spine ends chipped.) Very Sound. *M & S*. $450/£288

HAWTHORNE, NATHANIEL. The Scarlet Letter. Boston, 1850. 2nd ed, 1st ptg. Orig cl (spine ends chipped; bkpl). 1/4 morocco slipcase. BAL 7601. *Swann**. $258/£165

HAWTHORNE, NATHANIEL. The Scarlet Letter. NY: Grolier Club, 1908. One of 300. Uncut. Cl-backed bds (sl worn). Slipcase (broken). *Oinonen**. $120/£77

HAWTHORNE, NATHANIEL. The Snow-Image, a Childish Miracle. NY: James G. Gregory, 1864. 1st separate ed. Blue cl, gilt. (Text foxing, inscrip), else NF. BAL 7660. *Macdonnell*. $225/£144

HAWTHORNE, NATHANIEL. Tanglewood Tales for Boys and Girls. Boston: Ticknor, Reed & Fields, 1853. 1st Amer ed. 12mo. 336pp (no ads bound into this copy). Gilt/blind-stamped cl (spine ends chipped; rubbed). VG. BAL 7614. *M & S*. $600/£385

HAWTHORNE, NATHANIEL. Tanglewood Tales. London, (1918). One of 500 numbered, signed by Edmund Dulac (illus). 4to. 14 tipped-in color plts. Orig 1/2 vellum, gilt. *Swann**. $805/£516

HAWTHORNE, NATHANIEL. Tanglewood Tales. Phila: Penn, (1921). 1st ed thus. Virginia Frances Sterrett (illus). 9 Fine color plts. Pict eps. Navy cl, gilt, mtd color illus fr cvr.) (Ink sig, note, fep creased; sl rubbed, shelfworn.) Baltimore*. $60/£38

HAWTHORNE, NATHANIEL. Transformation: or, The Romance of Monte Beni. Leipzig: Tauchnitz, 1860. 2 vols. 92 mtd photos. Full vellum, gilt. Metropolitan*. $172/£110

HAWTHORNE, NATHANIEL. True Stories from History and Biography. Boston: Ticknor, Reed & Fields, 1851. 1st ed, 3rd ptg. Dk blue cl, spine gilt. (Sm cvr stain.) BAL 7655. Macdonnell. $150/£96

HAWTHORNE, NATHANIEL. A Wonder Book and Tanglewood Tales for Girls and Boys. NY: Duffield, 1910. 1st ed thus. Maxfield Parrish (illus). 10 Fine color plts, guards. Untrimmed, partly unopened. Navy cl (sl edgeworn, lower cvr paint-stained), gilt, lg mtd color pict label fr cvr (sm scratches). Text VG (few pp roughly opened). Baltimore*. $100/£64

HAWTHORNE, NATHANIEL. A Wonder Book. London, (1922). 24 tipped-in color plts by Arthur Rackham, guards. Dj. Swann*. $230/£147

HAWTHORNE, NATHANIEL. A Wonder Book. London, (1922). One of 600 numbered, signed by Arthur Rackham (illus). 4to. 16 mtd color plts, guards, 8 full-pg color illus. Pict eps. Swann*. $747/£479

HAWTHORNE, NATHANIEL. A Wonder Book. London: Hodder & Stoughton, (1922). One of 600 signed by Arthur Rackham (illus). 24 color plts (16 tipped in). Gilt-dec white cl (sl worn, discolored). Contents VG. New Hampshire*. $500/£321

HAWTHORNE, NATHANIEL. A Wonder-Book and Tanglewood Tales. Harrap, 1925. 1st ed thus. Gustaf Tenggren and Stephen Reid (illus). Lg 8vo. 356pp (mks); 8 color plts. Emb cl, gilt. (Tips sl worn), else VG. Bookmark. $23/£15

HAWTHORNE, NATHANIEL. A Wonder-Book for Boys and Girls. Boston, 1871. Later ed. Blind/gilt-stamped cl. VG. Mcclintock. $15/£10

HAWTHORNE, NATHANIEL. A Wonder-Book for Girls and Boys. Boston: Ticknor, Reed & Fields, 1852. 1st ed, 2nd ptg w/'lifed' corrected to 'lifted' at 21.3). Orig brn cl, gilt. (Spine chipped, frayed.) BAL 7606. Macdonnell. $350/£224

HAWTHORNE, NATHANIEL. The Works of.... Boston: Houghton Mifflin, 1882. Standard Library ed. 15 vols. Teg. 3/4 red morocco, marbled bds, gilt spine, raised bands. (Joints sl rubbed, spines sl sunned), else NF set. Pacific*. $489/£313

HAWTHORNE, NATHANIEL. The Works...the Riverside Edition. Cambridge: Riverside, 1883. 1st ed, lg paper issue. One of 250 numbered sets. 12 vols. Uncut. Cream bds, labels. (Thin crack upper joint vol 1; spine paper sl aged, sl worn.) BAL 7643. Macdonnell. $475/£304

HAWTIN, THOMAS H. Gymnastic Pyramids. OUP, 1934. 1st ed. 4 plts. (Fore-edges few leaves sl soiled; bds lt soiled, edges rubbed, spine bumped, sl surface worming.) Edwards. $31/£20

HAY, IAN. The Battle of Flanders, 1940. London: HMSO, 1941. Wrappers (dust soiled, edge chipped, no loss). Maggs. $31/£20

HAY, JOHN. The Pike County Ballads. Boston/NY, (1912). 1st ed. 48pp; 6 full-pg color plts, color tp vignette, 26 monochrome vignettes by N.C. Wyeth (illus). Full buckram w/lg color plt affixed to fr cvr (sl worn). VG. Truepenny. $95/£61

HAY, JOHN. The Pike County Ballads. Boston: Houghton Mifflin, (Oct 1912). 1st Wyeth illus ed. (Fep lt foxed; sm soil spots cvrs.) Pict label. BAL 7841. Sadlon. $100/£64

HAY, MICHAEL. Bentley, the Vintage Years. London, (1986). 1st ed. Ltd to 200 numbered, signed. Aeg. Full grn leather, raised bands. VG in slipcase. King. $250/£160

HAY, SIDNEY. Historic Lucknow. Lucknow, 1939. Dj. Petersfield. $16/£10

HAY, THOMAS ROBSON and M. R. WERNER. The Admirable Trumpeter. GC: Doubleday, Doran, 1941. 1st ed. Dumont. $35/£22

HAY, THOMAS ROBSON. Hood's Tennessee Campaign. NY, 1929. 1st ed. 4 maps. (Bkpl, few ms corrections.) Kane*. $95/£61

HAYDEN, ARTHUR. Spode and His Successors. London: Cassell, (1925). 1st ed. 24 mtd color plts, guards. Blue cl. Nice. Karmiole. $175/£112

HAYDEN, F. V. Eleventh Annual Report of the United States Geological and Geographical Survey of the Territories.... Washington: GPO, 1879. 1st ed. xxviii,720pp. (Ex-lib, spine #, stamps; worn, rubbed), else Good. Brown. $50/£32

HAYDEN, F. V. Sixth Annual Report of the U.S.G.S. of the Territories Embracing Portions of Montana, Idaho, Wyoming and Utah. Washington, 1873. xi,844pp; 5 maps, 12 plts. (Stamp tp.) Henly. $34/£22

HAYDEN, F. V. U.S. Geological and Geographical Survey of the Territories Embracing Colorado...1873. Washington: GPO, 1874. Good. Cullen. $125/£80

HAYDEN, ROBERT. Angle of Ascent: New and Selected Poems. NY: Liveright, (1975). 1st ed. (Name, 2 emb stamps), else Fine in NF dj (sm tear, lt soiled). Between The Covers. $45/£29

HAYDN, RICHARD. The Journal of Edwin Carp. NY: S&S, (1954). 1st Amer ed, 1st bk. Fine in dj (rear panel soiled). Antic Hay. $20/£13

HAYDON, A. L. The Riders of the Plains. London, 1910. Frontis, fldg map. Gilt cl (spotted, rubbed), else VG. Reese. $85/£54

HAYDON, F. STANSBURY. Aeronautics in the Union and Confederate Armies...1861. Vol I. Balt, 1941. 1st ed. 45 plts. Orig ptd wraps (soiled, sl worn). Wantagh. $250/£160

HAYES, A. A., JR. New Colorado and the Santa Fe Trail. London, 1881. Rpt of 1880 1st ed. Frontis map, 200pp. Red cl, gilt. Fine. Turpen. $45/£29

HAYES, ALBERT H. Physiology of Woman, and Her Diseases. Boston: Peabody Medical Inst, (1869). 1st ed. 345pp + ads. Grn cl (sl gnawed). VG. Second Life. $85/£54

HAYES, ARTHUR J. The Source of the Blue Nile. London, 1905. 1st ed. (Feps lt browned, hinges cracked; dampstained.) Edwards. $70/£45

HAYES, BENJAMIN. Pioneer Notes from the Diaries of Judge...1849-1875. L.A., 1929. 1st ed. Frontis. Fine. Turpen. $125/£80

HAYES, CHARLES W. Long Journey. The Story of Daniel Hayes. Portland, ME, 1876. 1st ed. #62/100. Inscribed presentation copy. 76pp. Howes H344. M & S. $325/£208

HAYES, HARRY (ed). Anthology of Plastic Surgery. Rockville, MD, 1986. 1st ed. VG. Fye. $125/£80

HAYES, HELEN ASHE. The Antietam and Its Bridges. NY/London: Putnam, 1910. Pict cl, gilt. VG (lib bkpl, other mks; rubbed). Zubal*. $45/£29

HAYES, HELEN. On Reflection, an Autobiography. NY, (1968). 1st ed. Ltd to 1000 numbered, signed. (Inner hinge cracked), else VG in slipcase. King. $60/£38

HAYES, ISAAC I. An Arctic Boat Journey in the Autumn of 1854. Boston: Brown et al, 1860. xvii,375pp, 2 fldg maps. Blind/gilt-stamped cl. (Spine sl faded), else VG. High Latitude. $100/£64

HAYES, ISAAC I. An Arctic Boat Journey. Boston: Brown, Taggard & Chase, 1860. xvii,375pp (flaws); 2 fldg maps. Brn gilt-dec cl (edges worn, chipped, spine faded). Parmer. $65/£42

HAYES, ISAAC I. The Land of Desolation. NY: Harper, 1872. 21 plts. Dec cl (sl mottled). VG. High Latitude. $70/£45

HAYES, ISAAC I. The Open Polar Sea. NY, 1867. xxiv,454pp + 6pp subs (1 leaf detached; lt margin browning); 9 plts incl 3 maps. (Spine chipped w/head loss.) Edwards. $117/£75

HAYES, ISAAC I. The Open Polar Sea. NY: Hurd & Houghton, 1867. Frontis port, xxiv,454pp; 6 plts, 3 color maps. VG. High Latitude. $85/£54

HAYES, J. GORDON. The Conquest of the South Pole. London, 1936. 2nd ed. VG (sl worn). High Latitude. $30/£19

HAYES, JESS G. Apache Vengeance: True Story of Apache Kid. Albuquerque: Univ of NM, 1954. 1st ed. Signed. Blue cl, gilt. VF in pict dj. Argonaut. $60/£38

HAYES, JOHN. Gainsborough. Paintings and Drawings. London, 1975. (Sl bumped.) Washton. $50/£32

HAYES, JOHN. Roman and Pre-Roman Glass in the Royal Ontario Museum. Toronto: Royal Ontario Museum, 1975. Good. Archaeologia. $150/£96

HAYES, JUSTIN. Therapeutic Use of Faradic and Galvanic Currents in the Electro-Thermal Bath with History of Cases. 1877. 1st ed. 111pp. (1/2 of last pg clipped), else Fine. Doctor's Library. $100/£64

HAYES, M. H. Among Horses in Russia. London, 1900. 1st ed. Teg. Gilt-illus cl (spine sl chipped, sl faded; feps lt browned). Edwards. $133/£85

HAYES, RICHARD. Irish Swordsmen of France. Dublin: M.H. Gill, 1934. 1st ed. Color frontis, 7 plts. Gilt-lettered grn cl. Fine in dj (spine dknd). Argonaut. $75/£48

HAYES, WILLIAM C. Royal Sarcophagi of the XVIII Dynasty. Princeton: Princeton Univ, 1935. Sm 4to. Frontis, 235 plts. 1/2 dk blue calf. Good. Archaeologia. $675/£433

HAYES, WILLIAM C. The Scepter of Egypt. NY/Cambridge: Harper/Harvard Univ/Metropolitan Museum of Fine Art, 1953/1959. 1st eds. 2 vols. Frontis each vol; 2 fldg maps. Gilt-stamped cl, color pict label each vol. Fine set in color pict djs (chipped). House. $180/£115

HAYGOOD, WIL. King of the Cats.... Boston/NY: Houghton Mifflin, 1993. 1st ed. Signed. New in New dj. Bernard. $40/£26

HAYNES, DRAUGHTON STITH. Field Diary of a Confederate Soldier. Darien, GA: Ashantilly, 1963. One of 400. Tipped-in frontis port. Paper over bds, ptd label. NF (sm closed tear spine end) in dj. Cahan. $100/£64

HAYNES, GIDEON. Pictures From Prison Life...Massachusetts State Prison. Boston: Lee & Shepard, 1869. 1st ed. VG (spine worn; lt pulling 1 sig). Beasley. $100/£64

HAYTER, ADRIAN. The Year of the Quiet Sun. London: Hodder & Stoughton, 1968. Fine in dj. High Latitude. $25/£16

HAYWARD, ARTHUR L. The Dickens Encyclopaedia. London: Routledge, 1924. 1st ed. (Feps, 1/2-title lt browned, spotted; very faded.) Hollett. $39/£25

HAYWARD, JOHN. English Poetry. (London): Nat'l Book League/CUP, 1950. One of 550 numbered. NF in dj (lt soiled, chips, tears). Waverly*. $187/£120

HAYWOOD, A. H. W. Through Timbuctu and Across the Sahara. London: Seeley, 1912. 1st ed. Frontis, fldg map. Red pict cl. (Few leaves foxed), else VG. Terra-media. $125/£80

HAYWOOD, GAR ANTHONY. Fear of the Dark. NY: St. Martin's, 1988. 1st ed. VF in dj. Mordida. $100/£64

HAYWOOD, GAR ANTHONY. You Can Die Trying. NY: St. Martin's, 1993. 1st ed. Signed. VF in dj. Mordida. $50/£32

HAZARD, FORRESTER. The Hex Murder. Phila: Lippincott, 1936. 1st ed. Dj (edgeworn). Metropolitan*. $51/£33

HAZARD, T. Nailer Tom's Diary. Boston: Merrymount, 1930. One of 400. Good + (sl cvr soil). Howes H368. Scribe's Perch*. $75/£48

HAZARD, THOMAS. Recollections of Olden Times. Newport, 1879. 264pp. Good (hinge cracks). Scribe's Perch*. $29/£19

HAZARD, THOMAS. Report on the Poor and Insane in Rhode-Island...1851. Providence, RI: Joseph Knowles, State Printer, 1851. 1st ed. Inscribed. Engr frontis, (120)pp. Emb black cl (Stamp tp; edges lt chipped), else Fine. Gach. $250/£160

HAZARD, WILLIS P. The Jersey, Alderney, and Guernsey Cow. Phila: Porter & Coates, 1872. 1st ed. Good + (shelfworn, spine top torn). October Farm. $68/£44

HAZELIUS, ERNEST LEWIS. The Life of John Henry Stilling. Gettysburg, 1831. 1st ed. Orig calf (spine damaged). Argosy. $200/£128

HAZELTON, JOHN ADAMS. The Hazelton Letters. Mary Geneva Bloom (ed). Stockton: College of the Pacific, 1958. Tipped in photo frontis. (Bds faded), else Fine. Parmer. $65/£42

HAZELTON, JOHN ADAMS. The Hazelton Letters: A Contribution to Western Americana. Mary Geneva Bloom (ed). Stockton: College of the Pacific, 1958. Tipped-in frontis port. Cl spine. Plain dj. Dawson. $40/£26

HAZELWOOD, SHANNON and J. W. GLEESON WHITE (eds). The Pageant. London: Henry, 1896, 1897. 2 vols (all pub'd). Orig litho port by James McNeil Whistler, orig woodcut by Lucien Pissarro. (Foxing.) Gilt-stamped cl (worn, soiled, joints frayed). Waverly*. $242/£155

HAZEN, ALLEN T. A Bibliography of Horace Walpole. New Haven: Yale Univ, 1948. 1st ed. VG in dj. Oak Knoll. $75/£48

HAZEN, ALLEN T. A Catalogue of Horace Walpole's Library. Yale Univ, 1969. 1st ed. 3 vols. Djs (spine vol 1 lt faded). Edwards. $117/£75

HAZLITT, W. C. Bibliographical Collections and Notes (1474-1700). London, 1892. 3rd series, 2nd supp. 106pp + ads. VG. Truepenny. $30/£19

HAZLITT, W. C. The Book Collector.... London: George Redway, 1904. 1st ed. Frontis. Teg. Fine. Oak Knoll. $50/£32

HAZLITT, W. C. Gleanings in Old Garden Literature. London: Elliott Stock, 1898. vii,263pp. Uncut. Gilt-dec cl, gilt medallion inset. Fine. Quest. $45/£29

HAZLITT, W. C. Mary and Charles Lamb. London: C&W, 1874. Extra-illus w/inserted Fine entrs. Purple watered silk doublures. Full crushed blue levant, gilt extra. Swann*. $460/£295

HAZLITT, W. C. (ed). A Select Collection of Old English Plays. London: Reeves & Turner, 1874-76. 4th ed. 15 vols. 8vo. Gilt edges. Contemp burgundy morocco (spines sl faded, lt spotted), gilt. Christie's*. $613/£393

HAZLITT, WILLIAM and B. R. HAYDON. Painting and the Fine Arts. Edinburgh: A&C Black, 1838. 1st ed thus. 227pp + errata (ink name effaced from pastedown). Brn cl stamped in blind/gilt (edgeworn). Reese. $50/£32

HAZLITT, WILLIAM. Conversations of James North-cote, Esq. Henry Colburn & Richard Bentley, 1830. 1st ed. Port, (iv),328pp. 1/2 grn morocco, marbled bds (sl rubbed). *Bickersteth.* $70/£45

HAZLITT, WILLIAM. Liber Amoris or the New Pygma-lion. With Additional Matter.... N.p.: Privately ptd, 1894. 1st ed thus. One of 500. (Frontis browned), o/w NF in buckram (spine sl dknd). *Captain's Bookshelf.* $60/£38

HAZLITT, WILLIAM. Selected Essays. Geoffrey Keynes (ed). Nonesuch, 1934. (Spine faded.) Dj. *Edwards.* $31/£20

HAZLITT, WILLIAM. Table Talk or Original Essays on Men and Manners. London: Henry Colburn, 1824. 2nd ed. 2 vols. 400; 401pp. 3/4 black pebbled mo-rocco, raised bands, gilt in panels, marbled bds, eps; top edges; silk ribbon markers. Fine set. *Hartfield.* $295/£189

HEAD, CHARLES FRANKLIN. Eastern and Egyptian Scenery, Ruins.... London: Smith, Elder, 1833. 3 fldg maps, 1 colored (1 torn, edge soiled), 22 mtd litho plts (spotted throughout, mainly marginal on plts, heavier on title). Orig calf-backed ptd bds (worn). *Christie's*.* $2,106/£1,350

HEAD, GEORGE. Forest Scenes and Incidents, in the Wilds of North America. London: John Murray, 1829. 1st ed. vii,362pp. New 1/2 mottled tan calf, black la-bel, marbled bds. VG. *Adelson.* $275/£176

HEAD, RICHARD and FRANCIS KIRKMAN. The Eng-lish Rogue Described in the Life of Meriton Latroon.... George Routledge, 1928. 12 plts. Buckram (backstrip faded). VG. *Cox.* $39/£25

HEAD, RICHARD and FRANCIS KIRKMAN. The Eng-lish Rogue. London, 1928. 12 plts. (Cl sl rubbed, spine head bumped.) *Edwards.* $62/£40

HEADLAM, CECIL. The Story of Chartres. London, 1902. Fldg plan. Teg. Orig gilt-dec roan. *Edwards.* $23/£15

HEADLAM, CECIL. The Story of Naples. London, 1927. Extra illus, photos affixed to verso of plts and blanks (wrinkling). Gilt-dec cl (spine sl discolored). *Edwards.* $23/£15

HEADLAM, CECIL. The Story of Oxford. London, 1907. 2 fldg plans. Teg. Gilt-dec cl (spine sl discol-ored). *Edwards.* $19/£12

HEADLAND, F. W. An Essay on the Action of Medi-cines in the System. 1855. 2nd ed. x,394pp + index (prelims lt foxed). Orig cl (rebacked). *Whitehart.* $94/£60

HEADLAND, ISAAC TAYLOR. Court Life in China. Lon-don, 1909. 1st ed. Color frontis. (Feps lt browned; dec cl lt soiled.) *Edwards.* $31/£20

HEADLAND, ISAAC TAYLOR. Court Life in China. NY: Revell, 1909. 2nd ed. Color frontis. Yellow pict cl. (Sl wear), else VG. *Terramedia.* $75/£48

HEADLEY, J. The Second War with England. NY: Scrib-ner, 1853. 1st ed. 2 vols. NF (lt foxed, ends worn). *Agvent.* $75/£48

HEADLEY, J. T. Letters from Italy. London: Wiley & Put-nam, 1845. 1st Eng ed. viii,224pp, 8-pg pub's cat. Grn blind-stamped cl (spine faded). Nice. *Burmester.* $70/£45

HEADLEY, J. T. The Life and Travels of General Grant. Phila: Hubbard, 1879. 1st ed. 251,599pp. (Inner hinges weak; sl rubbed), o/w VG. *Worldwide.* $10/£6

HEADLEY, J. T. The Second War with England. NY: Scribner, 1853. 2 vols. xiii,15-346,2ads; ix,11-328,6ads pp; 10 plts (1 fldg). Pict brn cl (ends worn). *Adelson.* $135/£87

HEAL, AMBROSE. The London Goldsmiths 1200-1800. CUP, 1935. 1st ed. 80 plts. VG in buckram, dj (sl frayed, spotted). *Cox.* $172/£110

HEAL, AMBROSE. London Tradesmen's Cards of the XVIII Century. London: Privately ptd, 1925. #55/100. Frontis, 101 plts. (Tp sl spotted, plt margins lt browned.) Vellum-backed cl bds, gilt. *Edwards.* $250/£160

HEAL, AMBROSE. London Tradesmen's Cards. NY: Scribner, 1925. Frontis, 101 plts. Dj. *Marlborough.* $140/£90

HEAL, AMBROSE. The Signboards of Old London Shops. Batsford, 1947. 1st ed. One of 250 (of 1250) specially bound. 5 plts. VG in 1/2 crimson morocco, gilt. *Cox.* $172/£110

HEALD, WELDON F. Sky Island. Princeton: D. Van Nostrand, 1967. VG in dj. *Dumont.* $20/£13

HEALY, W. J. Women of Red River. Winnipeg, 1923. 1st ed. Ltd to 1000 numbered. Pict cl (rubbed; inner hinges reglued). *King.* $50/£32

HEALY, WILLIAM. Mental Conflicts and Misconduct. Boston: Little, Brown, 1917. 1st ed. Signed. Brn cl. VG. *Gach.* $75/£48

HEANEY, SEAMUS. The Cure at Troy. London: Field Day, 1990. One of 500 numbered, signed. This copy unsigned. Fine in dj. *Williams.* $78/£50

HEANEY, SEAMUS. Death of a Naturalist. London, 1966. 1st ed, 1st bk. NF (sig) in dj (spine sl faded). *Buckley.* $328/£210

HEANEY, SEAMUS. Door into the Dark. NY: OUP, 1969. 1st Amer ed. NF in dj (2 sm edge tears). *Der-mont.* $125/£80

HEANEY, SEAMUS. Eleven Poems. (Belfast): Festival Publications, (1965?). 2nd ed, 1st bk. Lt blue-grn ptd self-wrappers. Mint. *Jaffe.* $250/£160

HEANEY, SEAMUS. Field Work. NY: FSG, (1979). 1st Amer ed. Mint in dj. *Jaffe.* $100/£64

HEANEY, SEAMUS. Field Work. London, 1979. 1st ed. Fine in dj (spine faded). *Buckley.* $47/£30

HEANEY, SEAMUS. Field Work. London: Faber, 1979. 1st UK ed. NF in dj (sl creased, spine faded). *Wil-liams.* $50/£32

HEANEY, SEAMUS. The Fire Gaze. Friends of the Cheltenham Festival, n.d. 1st Eng ed. Fine. *Clearwa-ter.* $23/£15

HEANEY, SEAMUS. The Fire i' the Flint. British Acad-emy, 1974. 1st ed. Inscribed. Fine in wrappers. *Buck-ley.* $78/£50

HEANEY, SEAMUS. The Haw Lantern. NY: Farrar Straus, (1987). One of 250 numbered, signed. Fine in Fine slipcase. *Lenz.* $150/£96

HEANEY, SEAMUS. The Haw Lantern. NY: FSG, (1987). Ltd to 250 numbered, signed. Fine in slipcase. *Antic Hay.* $125/£80

HEANEY, SEAMUS. The Haw Lantern. NY: FSG, 1987. #107/250 signed. Fine in slipcase. *Williams.* $172/£110

HEANEY, SEAMUS. The Makings of a Music. Univ of Liverpool, 1978. 1st UK ed. Fine in wraps. *Williams.* $23/£15

HEANEY, SEAMUS. North. London: Faber & Faber, (1975). 1st ed. 8vo. (Feps dknd), o/w Fine in dj, grn wraparound band. *Jaffe.* $500/£321

HEANEY, SEAMUS. Place and Displacement. London: Trustees of Dove Cottage, 1985. 1st UK ed. Fine in wraps. *Williams.* $23/£15

HEANEY, SEAMUS. Poems 1965-1975. NY: FSG, (1980). 1st ed. Fine in dj. *Jaffe.* $50/£32

HEANEY, SEAMUS. Seeing Things. London: Faber, 1991. 1st UK ed. Fine in dj. *Williams.* $19/£12

HEANEY, SEAMUS. Selected Poems 1966-1987. NY: Farrar Straus, (1990). One of 200 numbered, signed. Fine in Fine slipcase. *Lenz.* $150/£96

HEANEY, SEAMUS. Sweeney Astray. NY: Farrar Straus, (1984). One of 350 numbered, signed. Fine in Fine slipcase. *Lenz.* $150/£96

HEANEY, SEAMUS. Sweeney Astray. NY, 1984. Ltd to 350 numbered, signed. Fine in slipcase. *Buckley.* $148/£95

HEANEY, SEAMUS. The Tree Clock. Belfast: Linen Hall Library, 1990. #91/120 signed (of 870). Linen, hand-marbled sides. Fine in marbled slipcase. *Williams.* $234/£150

HEANEY, SEAMUS. Wintering Out. London: Faber & Faber, (1972). 1st ed. Mint in dj. *Jaffe.* $500/£321

HEAP, GWINN HARRIS. Central Route to the Pacific, from the Valley of the Mississippi to California. Phila: Lippincott, Grambo, 1854. 1st ed. 13 litho-tint plts. Map, not issued w/all copies, not present. (Foxed.) Recent simulated leather, blind/gilt-stamped. Howes H378. *Sadlon.* $275/£176

HEAP, GWINN HARRIS. Central Route to the Pacific...1853-1854. LeRoy R. and Ann W. Hafen (eds). Glendale: Clark, 1957. 1st ed. One of 1272. Grn cl, gilt spine. VF. Howes H378. *Argonaut.* $125/£80

HEARD, FRANKLIN FISKE. Curiosities of the Law Reporters. SF: Sumner Whitney, 1885. Rust cl (worn). Usable (underlining). *Boswell.* $50/£32

HEARD, GERALD. The Lost Cavern and Other Stories of the Fantastic. NY, (1948). 1st ed. Fine in Fine dj (sl shelfworn). *Mcclintock.* $45/£29

HEARD, GERALD. Murder by Reflection. London: Cassell, (1945). 1st ed. VG in dj (edgewear, short tears, spine ends worn). *Metropolitan*.* $23/£15

HEARD, H. F. Doppelgangers. Vanguard, (1947). 1st ed. (Fore-edge sl dusty), else NF in dj (spine ends sl worn). *Certo.* $50/£32

HEARD, H. F. The Great Fog and Other Weird Tales. NY, (1944). 1st ed. VG + in VG dj (price-clipped). *Mcclintock.* $40/£26

HEARD, H. F. The Notched Hairpin. NY: Vanguard, (1949). 1st ed. VG in dj (chipped, internal tape, short tears). *Metropolitan*.* $23/£15

HEARD, ISAAC. History of the Sioux War and Massacres of 1862 and 1863. NY: Harper, 1863. 1st ed. 354pp. Clippings attached fep. Red buckram (rebound). VG (pencil notes). Howes H378. *Lien.* $75/£48

HEARN, LAFCADIO. Creole Sketches. Houghton Mifflin, 1924. 1st ed. VG. *Certo.* $22/£14

HEARN, LAFCADIO. Editorials. Charles Woodward Hutson (ed). Boston: Houghton Mifflin, 1926. 1st ed. One of 250 'Large Paper' copies bound w/uncut edges. Beige cl over bds (corners sl rubbed), paper spine label. *Karmiole.* $100/£64

HEARN, LAFCADIO. Exotics and Retrospectives. Boston: Little Brown, 1898. Dec cl (mottled). Good-. *Scribe's Perch*.* $22/£14

HEARN, LAFCADIO. Fantastics and Other Fancies. Houghton Mifflin, 1914. 1st ed. Good +. *Certo.* $25/£16

HEARN, LAFCADIO. Fantastics and Other Fancies. Houghton Mifflin, 1914. One of 550. Good + (ring mk to cvr, corners worn). *Certo.* $45/£29

HEARN, LAFCADIO. Glimpses of Unfamiliar Japan (First Series). Leipzig, 1907. Emb device upper bd. *Edwards.* $23/£15

HEARN, LAFCADIO. Glimpses of Unfamiliar Japan (First Series). Leipzig: Tauchnitz, 1907. 1st ed thus. Fine (spine sunned) in ptd wrappers (sl dust soiled). *Polyanthos.* $25/£16

HEARN, LAFCADIO. Glimpses of Unfamiliar Japan. Boston, 1894. 1st ed, 1st ptg vol 1, state 'B,' no priority of spine imprint; 1st ed vol 2 (no later ptg this vol noted). 2 vols. Silver-dec olive cl. (Lib stamp feps), o/w Fine. BAL 7926. *Kane*.* $150/£96

HEARN, LAFCADIO. Glimpses of Unfamiliar Japan. Boston/NY: Houghton Mifflin, 1894. 1st ed. 2 vols. Teg. Black cl stamped in silver incl fr cvr, spine designs. VG (sl rubbed) in later plain bd divided slipcase (sl worn). BAL 7926. *Baltimore*.* $180/£115

HEARN, LAFCADIO. Interpretations of Literature. John Erskine (ed). London: Heinemann, 1916. 1st ed. 2 vols. Frontis port. Lib cl (label pastedowns, stamp reverse tps, marginal blind stamps), gilt. *Hollett.* $133/£85

HEARN, LAFCADIO. Japan; An Attempt at Interpretation. NY: Macmillan, 1904. 1st ed, 4th ptg. Color frontis, vi,549,(ii)pp (ads). Lt brn cl, gilt. VG. *Sotheran.* $187/£120

HEARN, LAFCADIO. Japan; An Attempt at Interpretation. NY: Macmillan, 1904. 1st ed. Teg. Brn cl, gilt. Nice. *Appelfeld.* $200/£128

HEARN, LAFCADIO. Japanese Fairy Tales. Phila: Macrae-Smith, (1931). 5 vols. 8vo. Color pict wraps and text, all ptd in Japan by T. Hasegawa, all on creped paper w/exposed silk ties. (1 cvr corner lt creased.) Near Mint. All in plain glassine sleeves (chipped), orig cl-cvrd bd folder w/bone clasps, ptd paper label upper cvr. *Baltimore*.* $600/£385

HEARN, LAFCADIO. Japanese Fairy Tales. (Tokyo: T. Hasegawa), early 1900s. 5 vols. Sm 8vo. Orig Japanese-style color pict crepe paper wrappers. Cl sleeve w/paper fr cvr label, ivory clasps (spine faded, joints partly cracked). *Swann*.* $2,185/£1,401

HEARN, LAFCADIO. The Japanese Letters of Lafcadio Hearn. Elizabeth Bisland (ed). London, 1911. Photogravure frontis, photogravure port, 4 plts. (Ex-lib, ink stamps tp recto.) Teg. Gilt-edged cl (rebacked, orig spine laid down, corners sl worn, sm spine stain from label removal). *Edwards.* $55/£35

HEARN, LAFCADIO. Kokoro, Hints and Echoes of Japanese Inner Life. Boston/NY: Houghton, Mifflin, 1896. 1st ed. Grn dec cl (sl fading around spine), gilt top. Sound. *Appelfeld.* $250/£160

HEARN, LAFCADIO. Kokoro. Boston/NY, 1896. 1st US ed. (vi),388pp. Teg. (Spine sl faded.) *Edwards.* $94/£60

HEARN, LAFCADIO. Kotto. NY: Macmillan, 1902. 1st ed, 1st issue. Teg. Brn cl, gilt. Fine. *Appelfeld.* $200/£128

HEARN, LAFCADIO. Kotto: Being Japanese Curios, with Sundry Cobwebs. NY, 1902. 1st ed, 1st issue w/tp background-design ptd upside-down. Pub's cl. VG. *Truepenny.* $300/£192

HEARN, LAFCADIO. Kotto: Being Japanese Curios, with Sundry Cobwebs. NY: Macmillan, 1902. 1st ed, 1st state. Fine in dec olive cl (spine sl dulled). BAL 7938. *Captain's Bookshelf.* $200/£128

HEARN, LAFCADIO. Kwaidan: Stories and Studies of Strange Things. Boston/NY: Houghton Mifflin, 1904. 1st ed, 2nd issue. Teg. Tan cl w/floral design, gilt. (Hinges cracked, weak, eps discolored; spine, edges sl dknd; sl rubbed.) BAL 7940. *Baltimore*.* $40/£26

HEARN, LAFCADIO. Kwaidan: Stories of Strange Things. Tokyo: Shimbi Shoin, 1932. One of 1500 ptd for LEC, signed by Yasumasa Fujita (illus). Full dec silk. Fine in fldg case. *Appelfeld.* $250/£160

HEARN, LAFCADIO. Leaves from the Diary of an Impressionist. Boston: Houghton Mifflin, 1911. 1st ed. One of 575 numbered. Gilt label. (Pencil erasure ep), o/w Nice. *Reese.* $75/£48

HEARN, LAFCADIO. Letters from The Raven. Milton Bronner (ed). NY, (1907). Good- (water staining mostly to casing, some gutters). *Scribe's Perch**. $20/£13

HEARN, LAFCADIO. Letters from the Raven. Milton Bronner (ed). NY, 1907. 1st Amer ed. Fine (name). *Polyanthos.* $60/£38

HEARN, LAFCADIO. Occidental Gleanings. Albert Mordell (ed). NY: Dodd, Mead, 1925. 1st ed. 2 vols. Top edges stained grn, untrimmed. Red cl (sl worn, spotted), paper spine labels. Texts Good in djs (partial, worn, chipped, tape remnants, stains). BAL 7990. *Baltimore**. $40/£26

HEARN, LAFCADIO. The Romance of the Milky Way and Other Studies and Stories. Boston: Houghton Mifflin, 1905. 1st ed. Dec cl. (Ink name, date; offsetting to eps from clipping; spine stamping sl rubbed), else VG. BAL 7943. *Reese.* $75/£48

HEARN, LAFCADIO. Shadowings. Little Brown, 1900. 1st ed. Pict blue cl, gilt. (Fep browned), else Fine. *Certo.* $135/£87

HEARN, LAFCADIO. Some Chinese Ghosts. Boston, 1887. 1st ed. Pub's pict cl. *Swann**. $201/£129

HEARN, LAFCADIO. Some Chinese Ghosts. Boston: Roberts Bros, 1887. 1st ed. (Text lt aged, smudged, 1 leaf torn, skillfully repaired.) Top edge stained red, floral eps. Yellow cl (spine dknd, lt frayed, sm tear, lt dusty). Issued in red, yellow, tan, and rose cl, w/no known priority...a premium has been placed on copies in yellow cl due to their scarcity. BAL 7916. *Baltimore**. $70/£45

HEARN, LAFCADIO. Two Years in the French West Indies. NY: Harper, 1923. 1st ed thus. Fine (lacks dj). *Captain's Bookshelf.* $50/£32

HEARNE, R. Aerial Warfare. London: Lane, 1909. Teg. (Sl head, backstrip tail chipping), o/w Good+. *Bookcell.* $125/£80

HEARNE, SAMUEL. A Journey from Prince Wales' Fort in Hudson's Bay to the Northern Ocean. London: Strahan & T. Cadell, 1795. Lg paper copy. Lg fldg map, 4 maps, 4 fldg plts. (Some foxing throughout.) Old calf bds, mod cl spine. *Metropolitan**. $550/£353

HEARNE, THOMAS. Reliquiae Hearnianae: The Remains of Thomas Hearne, M.A.... Philip Bliss (ed). Library of Old Authors, 1869. 2nd ed, enlgd. 3 vols. Port. (Pencil notes.) Emb cl. *Hatchwell.* $66/£42

HEARON, SHELBY. Armadillo in the Grass. NY: Knopf, 1968. 1st ed, 1st bk. Fine in dj. *Between The Covers.* $200/£128

Heart of Mabel Ware. A Romance. NY/Cincinnati: Derby, 1856. 1st ed. 411pp. (Lt foxing; sm adhesion mk spine), o/w VG. *Reese.* $50/£32

HEARTMAN, CHARLES F. The New England Primer. Issued Prior to 1830. NY, 1934. 1st Amer ed. Fine. *Polyanthos.* $75/£48

HEARTMAN, CHARLES F. and JAMES R. CANNY. Poe Bibliography. Hattiesburg, MS: Book Farm, 1940. 1st ed. Blue cl. Fine. *Macdonnell.* $200/£128

HEAT MOON, WILLIAM LEAST. Prairy Erth. Boston: Houghton Mifflin, 1991. 1st ed. VF in dj. *Associates.* $25/£16

HEATH ROBINSON, W. Hunlikely! London: Duckworth, 1916. 1st ed. (Sl dusty.) *Hollett.* $460/£295

HEATH ROBINSON, W. Railway Ribaldry. London: Great Western Railway, 1935. 1st ed. (Sl loose, feps browned, gutter sl spotted.) Orig stiff pict wrappers (extrems worn). *Hollett.* $133/£85

HEATH, AMBROSE. The Book of the Onion. London: Methuen, 1947. 2nd ed. VG in dj. *Perier.* $15/£10

HEATH, DUDLEY. Miniatures. London: Methuen, 1905. 1st ed. 42 plts (11 color). (Hinges sl rubbed.) *Hollett.* $70/£45

HEATH, F. G. The Fern World. London, 1885. 4th ed. xi,459pp; 16 plts (12 color). Pict cl (sl worn). *Henly.* $28/£18

HEATH, FRANK. Forty Million Hoofbeats. NY: David Turet, 1941. 1st ed. Signed. (Spine torn.) Interior Clean. Fair dj. *October Farm.* $45/£29

HEATH, LABAN. Infallible Counterfeit Detector. Boston: Heath, (1864). 31pp, 8 engr plts (2 color). *Marlborough.* $328/£210

HEATH, R. E. Shrubs for the Rock Garden and Alpine House. London, 1954. 32 plts. Good in dj (worn). *Henly.* $37/£24

HEATH, R. S. An Elementary Treatise on Geometrical Options. Cambridge, 1897. 2nd ed. xii,234pp. *Whitehart.* $23/£15

HEATH, ROBERT G. (ed). Studies in Schizophrenia.... Harvard Univ, 1954. VG. *Argosy.* $50/£32

HEATHER, WILLIAM. The New British Channel Pilot. London: William Heather, 1807. 4th ed. (8),104pp + 4pp ads. Ptd Trinity House notice tipped in, another laid in, both dated 1809. Mod plain wrappers. *Lefkowicz.* $100/£64

HEBARD, GRACE RAYMOND and E. A. BRININSTOOL. The Bozeman Trail. Cleveland: Clark, 1960. 2nd ptg. One of 867. 2 vols in 1. 2 fldg maps. (Spine ends lt rubbed), else Fine. Howes H382. *Argonaut.* $175/£112

HEBARD, GRACE RAYMOND and E. A. BRINSTOOL. The Bozeman Trail. Cleveland: A.H. Clark, 1922. 1st ed. 2 vols. Frontis each vol; 2 fldg maps. Teg. Red cl (soiled). VG. *House.* $300/£192

HEBARD, GRACE RAYMOND. Sacajawea. Glendale, CA: A.H. Clark, 1933. 1st ed. 20 plts, fldg map. Teg. (Water stain fr cvr, sm stain spine, rear cvr.) *Kane**. $130/£83

HEBARD, GRACE RAYMOND. Washakie. Cleveland: Clark, 1930. 1st ed. One of 1244. Frontis. Gilt spine. Fine (sm bkpl inner cvr, ink name; lower corner sl bumped). *Argonaut.* $275/£176

HEBER, REGINALD. Narrative of a Journey through the Upper Provinces of India. London: Murray, 1828. 1st ed. 2 vols. xlvii,631; v,515pp, 10 plts, fldg map. (1st few ll each vol foxed; rebound), else VG. *Terramedia.* $400/£256

HEBERDEN, M. V. Murder Makes a Racket. GC: DCC, 1942. 1st ed. Fine in dj (chips). *Mordida.* $45/£29

HEBERDEN, M. V. Vicious Pattern. GC: DCC, 1945. 1st ed. VG in dj (spine ends, corners, folds sl worn). *Mordida.* $30/£19

HEBERDEN, W. Commentaries on the History and Cure of Diseases. 1803. 2nd Eng ed. xii,514pp (lt foxed, tp edge repaired). New 1/4 blue morocco. *Whitehart.* $218/£140

HEBERDEN, W. Commentaries on the History and Cure of Diseases. 1816. 4th ed. xii,432pp (ink sigs). Old 1/2 morocco (spine worn, bds loose). *Whitehart.* $172/£110

HEBERDEN, WILLIAM. Commentaries on the History and Cure of Diseases. Boston: Wells & Lilly, 1818. 1st Amer ed, 1st ptg. xi,418pp. Orig tree calf (newly rebacked). (Text foxed), o/w VG. *Goodrich.* $295/£189

HECHT, ANTHONY. A Summoning of Stones. NY: Macmillan, 1954. 1st ed, 1st bk. Fine in dj (edges rubbed, few sm tape reinforcements at spine ends). *Dermont.* $75/£48

HECHT, ANTHONY. A Summoning of Stones. NY: Macmillan, 1954. 1st ed, 1st bk. (Sl offset to eps, tp), o/w NF in VG dj (lt frayed). *Reese.* $85/£54

HECHT, BEN and MAXWELL BODENHEIM. Cutie: A Warm Mama. Chicago: Privately ptd, 1924. One of 200. NF (edge rubbed). *Polyanthos.* $60/£38

HECHT, BEN and KENNETH SAWYER GOODMAN. The Wonder Hat: And Other One-Act Plays. NY: Appleton, 1925. 1st ed. VG in dj (sl nicked). *Houle.* $300/£192

HECHT, BEN and CHARLES MacARTHUR. The Front Page. London, 1929. 1st Eng ed. Fine in dj. *Clearwater.* $62/£40

HECHT, BEN. A Book of Miracles. NY: Viking, 1939. 1st ed. (Pastedown edges dknd), else Fine in bright dj (lt worn). *Hermitage.* $75/£48

HECHT, BEN. Charlie: The Improbable Life and Times of Charles MacArthur. NY: Harper, (1957). 1st ed. (Ink name fr pastedown), else Fine in dj (lt rubbed). *Hermitage.* $35/£22

HECHT, BEN. Erik Dorn. NY, 1921. 1st issue w/yellow lettering on cvr. VG (lacks dj). *Warren.* $75/£48

HECHT, BEN. Gaily, Gaily. NY, 1963. 1st Amer ed. Fine in dj (extrems sl rubbed). *Polyanthos.* $25/£16

HECHT, BEN. Humpty Dumpty. NY: Boni & Liveright, 1924. 1st ed. Fine (label) in dj (lt used, lt chipped). *Beasley.* $125/£80

HECHT, BEN. The Kingdom of Evil. Chicago: Pascal Covici, 1924. One of 2000 numbered. VG in supplied acetate dj. *Antic Hay.* $75/£48

HECHT, BEN. Letters from Bohemia. GC: Doubleday, 1964. 1st ed. VG in dj. *Hermitage.* $35/£22

HECHT, BEN. Miracle in the Rain. NY: Knopf, 1943. 1st ed. Gilt pink bds. VG (spine sl faded; pastedowns, eps dknd; bkpl; sm stains margins few pp) in dj (sl chipped, rear panel soiled)). *Blue Mountain.* $25/£16

HECHT, BEN. The Sensualists. NY, (1959). 1st Amer ed. NF in NF dj. *Polyanthos.* $25/£16

HECHT, BEN. The Sensualists. NY: Julian Messner, (1959). 1st ed. VF in VF dj. *Hermitage.* $50/£32

HECHT, BEN. To Quito and Back. NY, (1937). 1st Amer ed. NF (spine lt sunned, extrems sl soiled) in dj (spine extrems chipped, sm tear top fr panel, 2-inch piece missing). *Polyanthos.* $25/£16

HECKER, GENEVIEVE. Golf for Women. NY: Baker & Taylor, (1904). 1st ed. Gilt-stamped pict grn cl. (Spine ends rubbed, sm yellow spots fr cvr, authors' names rubbing off cvrs), else VG. *Pacific*.* $546/£350

HECKETHORN, CHARLES WILLIAM. The Secret Societies of All Ages and Countries. London: Richard Bentley, 1875. 1st ed. 2 vols. Grn cl (sl mkd). *Burmester.* $117/£75

HECKETHORN, CHARLES WILLIAM. The Secret Societies of All Ages and Countries. NY: New Amsterdam Book Co, 1897. New ed, rev, enlgd. 2 vols. xxvii,(i),352; xvi,350,(i)pp (hinges cracked, bottom corner last several leaves vol 1 dampstained). Burgundy cl (bumped, rubbed, cl split top fr joint vol 1), paper spine labels (chipped). Good. *Blue Mountain.* $75/£48

HEDEMANN, C. J. Catalogue of the Collection of Weapons. Honolulu: Honolulu Academy of Arts, 1928. Internally VG. Wraps (soiled). *Parmer.* $20/£13

HEDGES, PETER. What's Eating Gilbert Grape. NY, 1991. 1st ed. NF in NF dj. *Warren.* $45/£29

HEDGES, WILLIAM HAWKINS. Pike's Peak...or Busted! Herbert O. Brayer (ed). Evanston: Branding Iron, 1954. 1st ed. Ltd to 750. Frontis. VG in dj. *Lien.* $45/£29

HEDIN, SVEN. My Life as an Explorer. Alhild Huebsch (trans). NY: Boni & Liveright, 1925. 1st ed. Color frontis. (Cl sl rubbed, faded), o/w VG. *Worldwide.* $26/£17

HEDIN, SVEN. My Life as an Explorer. London: Cassell, 1926. 1st ed. Color frontis. (Sl foxed.) *Maggs.* $117/£75

HEDIN, SVEN. Through Asia. NY, 1899. 1st Amer ed. 2 vols. 1255pp. Teg. (Ex-lib, worn, loose, sl defects.) *King.* $100/£64

HEDIN, SVEN. Trans-Himalaya. London: Macmillan, 1909-1913. 1st ed. 3 vols. xxiii,436pp, 7 maps, ads; xvii,441pp, ads; xv,426pp, ads; 14 maps (4 lg fldg). Teg. Maroon gilt pict cl. (Spines sunned, spines of vols 1 & 2 frayed at corners, fr cvr one vol sl stained outer edge), else VG. *Terramedia.* $500/£321

HEDIN, SVEN. Trans-Himalaya. NY: Macmillan, 1909-1913. 1st ed. 3 vols. 8 color plts, 3 fldg plts, 14 maps (4 fldg). Teg. (Edges rubbed, all spines rebacked, exlib, spine stickers vols 1, 2), o/w VG. *Worldwide.* $250/£160

HEDIN, SVEN. Trans-Himalaya. NY: Macmillan, 1909. 2 vols. 10 maps, 388 plts. Pict cl. VG. *Adelson.* $95/£61

HEDRICK, U. P. Cyclopedia of Hardy Fruits. NY, 1922. 16 plts, 4 color. (Sl internal spotting; lt wear.) *Freeman*.* $45/£29

HEDRICK, U. P. Grapes of New York. Albany, 1908. 96 (of 101) color plts, 1 b/w plt. (Rear inner hinge broken, bottom edge dampstained; worn, soiled.) *New Hampshire*.* $110/£71

HEDRICK, U. P. A History of Horticulture in America to 1860. NY: OUP, 1950. 1st ed. Black cl. Fine in dj (lt chipped). *Argonaut.* $75/£48

HEDRICK, U. P. Manual of American Grape-Growing. NY, 1924. Rev ed. 32 photo plts. Blue dec cl, gilt. VG. *Price.* $29/£19

HEDRICK, U. P. Pears of New York. Albany, 1921. 76 (of 80) color plts, 2 b/w plts. (Lacks 1 leaf, lt foxing; sl worn.) *New Hampshire*.* $110/£71

HEG, H. C. The Civil War Letters of.... Theodore C. Blegen (ed). Northfield, MN, 1936. 1st ed. Frontis port. VG. *Wantagh.* $45/£29

HEGEL, GEORG WILHELM F. Lectures on the Philosophy of Religion. London: Kegan Paul et al, 1895. 1st Eng ed. 3 vols. Blue cl (spines dknd, sl worn, vol 3 cocked). Good+ (offsetting prelims, inking). *Waverly*.* $71/£46

HEIGES, GEORGE L. Henry William Stiegel: The Life Story of a Famous American Glass-Maker. Manheim, PA: The Author, 1937. 1st ed. Signed. Frontis. Fine in dj (sl worn). *Cahan.* $45/£29

HEILBRON, J. L. H. G. J. Moseley. The Life and Letters.... Berkeley: Univ of CA, (1974). 1st ed. Fine in dj. *Glaser.* $30/£19

HEILBRONER, R. L. The Great Economists. 1905. 2nd ed. (Heavy foxing.) *Whitehart.* $39/£25

HEILNER, VAN CAMPEN. A Book on Duck Shooting. Phila, (1939). VG. *Truepenny.* $60/£38

HEILPRIN, ANGELO. Town Geology: The Lesson of the Philadelphia Rocks. Phila, 1885. 8 plts. Dec cvr. Good- (hinge cracks). *Scribe's Perch*.* $35/£22

HEILPRIN, ANGELO. Town Geology: The Lesson of the Philadelphia Rocks. Phila: The Author, 1885. 1st ed. (4),142pp; 8 plts. Contemp morocco (edges sl rubbed). VG (sm lib stamp). *Glaser.* $75/£48

HEINE, HEINRICH. Florentine Nights. Charles G. Leland (trans). London: Methuen, (1927). This copy w/E.P. Dutton imprint on spine. 1st ed thus. Fine in VG gold dj. *Captain's Bookshelf.* $75/£48

HEINEMANN, LARRY. Close Quarters. NY: FSG, (1977). 1st ed. (Faint offsetting fep), else Fine in dj. *Between The Covers.* $150/£96

HEINEMANN, LARRY. Close Quarters. NY: FSG, 1977. 1st ed, 1st bk. Fine in dj. *Lame Duck.* $150/£96

HEINLEIN, ROBERT A. Assignment in Eternity. Reading: Fantasy Press, (1953). 1st ed. One of 500 signed, numbered. (Name stamp, cl lt spotted, spine sunned), else NF in As New dj. *Other Worlds.* $400/£256

HEINLEIN, ROBERT A. Assignment in Eternity. Reading: Fantasy, 1953. 1st ed. Dj (lt worn). Swann*. $230/£147

HEINLEIN, ROBERT A. Assignment in Eternity: Four Long Science Fiction Stories. Reading: Fantasy, (1953). 1st ed, 1st state w/Heinlein's name on spine 3mm high. Unrecorded variant binding, blue cl, gilt. Fine in dj. Captain's Bookshelf. $300/£192

HEINLEIN, ROBERT A. Between Planets. NY: Scribner, 1951. 1st ed. Dj (rubbed, 1-inch closed tear spine). Swann*. $126/£81

HEINLEIN, ROBERT A. Between Planets. NY: Scribner, 1951. (Sm rub bottom fr bd; eps lt foxed), else Fine in NF dj (lt rubbed). Between The Covers. $250/£160

HEINLEIN, ROBERT A. The Cat Who Walks Through Walls. NY: Putnam, (1985). 1st ed. One of 350 numbered, signed. Matching slipcase. Swann*. $115/£74

HEINLEIN, ROBERT A. The Cat Who Walks Through Walls. NY: Putnam, (1985). 1st ed, probable 2nd state w/corrected text p300. Signed. 1/4 cl. Dj. Swann*. $115/£74

HEINLEIN, ROBERT A. The Cat Who Walks Through Walls. NY: Putnam, 1985. 1st ed. Ltd to 350 signed. Color frontis. Fine in black cl, matching slipcase. Bromer. $185/£119

HEINLEIN, ROBERT A. The Door into Summer. NY: Doubleday, 1957. 1st ed. (Bkpl), else Fine in dj (ends sl worn, few thin scratches rear panel). Waverly*. $308/£197

HEINLEIN, ROBERT A. Farnham's Freehold. NY: Putnam, 1964. 1st ed. Fine (bkpl glued inside cvr; lower edges sl worn) in dj (sl scuffed, edge sl worn, price-clipped). Metropolitan*. $189/£121

HEINLEIN, ROBERT A. Have Space Suit—Will Travel. NY: Scribner, (1958). 1st ed. (Corner sl frayed), o/w VG+ in dj (lt soiled, top spine edge chipped). Bernard. $300/£192

HEINLEIN, ROBERT A. I Will Fear No Evil. Putnam, 1970. 1st ed. VG in dj. Madle. $95/£61

HEINLEIN, ROBERT A. Job: A Comedy of Justice. NY: Ballantine, (1984). 1st ed. One of 750 numbered, signed. Matching slipcase. Swann*. $103/£66

HEINLEIN, ROBERT A. The Man Who Sold the Moon. Chicago: Shasta Publishers, 1950. 1st ed. Fine in dj (lt worn, back panel sl frowsy). Metropolitan*. $143/£92

HEINLEIN, ROBERT A. The Man Who Sold the Moon. Chicago: Shasta Publishers, 1950. 1st ed. Signed. Fine in Fine dj. Metropolitan*. $345/£221

HEINLEIN, ROBERT A. The Man Who Sold the Moon. Chicago: Shasta, 1950. 1st ed. One of 200 reserved for subs, signed. (Fr inner hinge starting), else NF in VG+ dj (spine tanned, extrems lt worn). Lame Duck. $850/£545

HEINLEIN, ROBERT A. The Man Who Sold the Moon.... Chicago: Shasta, (1950). 1st ed. Ptd label 'Future History / 1951-2600 A.D.' affixed to ep time-line. Dj (rear panel sl dknd). Kane*. $180/£115

HEINLEIN, ROBERT A. Orphans of the Sky. London: Gollancz, 1963. 1st ed. (Lib stamp fr pastedown, edges sl dknd.) Dj. Swann*. $149/£96

HEINLEIN, ROBERT A. Podkayne of Mars. NY: Putnam, 1963. 1st ed. NF (fore-edge lt soiled, spine sl bumped) in dj (sl nicked, creased, lt discolored). Metropolitan*. $195/£125

HEINLEIN, ROBERT A. The Puppet Masters. GC: Doubleday, 1951. 1st ed. (Sl shelfworn, lt soiled.) Dj (sl frayed, worn, rear panel lt soiled). Waverly*. $165/£106

HEINLEIN, ROBERT A. The Puppet Masters. GC: Doubleday, 1951. 1st ed. (Bkpl, name, date), else Fine in dj (lt edgewear, sm tears, spine head chipping). Other Worlds. $250/£160

HEINLEIN, ROBERT A. Rocket Ship Galileo. NY: Scribner, 1947. 1st ed, 1st bk. NF (bkpl; edges sl rubbed) in NF dj (sm chips spine ends). Waverly*. $357/£229

HEINLEIN, ROBERT A. Stranger in a Strange Land. NY: Putnam, (1961). 1st ed. Fine in dj (sl soiled, rubbed). Waverly*. $550/£353

HEINLEIN, ROBERT A. Stranger in a Strange Land. NY: Putnams, (1961). 1st ed. Fine in NF dj (short tears; extrems rubbed). Between The Covers. $750/£481

HEINLEIN, ROBERT A. Time for the Stars. Scribner, 1956. 1st ed. VG in dj (chipped). Madle. $75/£48

HEINLEIN, ROBERT A. (ed). Tomorrow, the Stars. GC: Doubleday, 1952. 1st ed. NF in dj (sm tears, 2 sm spine chips). Captain's Bookshelf. $60/£38

HEINLEIN, ROBERT A. Tunnel in the Sky. NY: Scribner, (1955). 1st ed. Fine in dj (price-clipped, sm hole, sl endwear spine panel). Waverly*. $176/£113

HEINLEIN, ROBERT A. Universe. NY: Dell, (1951). VG in pict wraps. King. $45/£29

HEINLEIN, ROBERT A. Universe. NY: Dell, (1951). 1st ed. Pict wrappers. Swann*. $57/£37

HEINLEIN, ROBERT A. The Unpleasant Profession of Jonathan Hoag. Hicksville: Gnome, (1959). 1st ed. Dj (spine sl creased, rubbed). Swann*. $80/£51

HEINLEIN, ROBERT A. Waldo and Magic Inc. NY: Doubleday, 1950. 1st ed. Dj (rubbed, chipped). Swann*. $80/£51

HEINLEIN, ROBERT A. Waldo and Magic, Inc. GC, 1950. 1st ed. Dj (rear panel sl age-dknd). Kane*. $140/£90

HEINTZELMAN, SAMUEL P. Samuel P. Heintzelman's Journal, 1851-1853, Fort Yuma. Transcribed by Creola Blackwell. Yuma: Yuma County Hist Soc, 1989. Pict wrappers, spiral bound. Dawson. $45/£29

HEIZER, R. F. Archaeology of the Uyak Site, Kodiak Island, Alaska. Berkeley: Univ of CA, 1956. 1st ed. 85 plts, 29 tables. VG+ in wraps. Mikesh. $25/£16

HEIZER, ROBERT F. Aboriginal Fish Poisons. Washington: BAE, 1953. 4 photo plts. Good in grey wrappers. Price. $19/£12

HELD, JOHN, JR. Dog Stories. NY, 1930. 1st ed. VG+. Bond. $20/£13

HELD, JOHN, JR. The Saga of Frankie and Johnny. NY: Walter V. McKee, Dec 1930. 1st ed. Ltd to 2050. Red cl over red velour. Fine in slipcase (worn). Connolly. $65/£42

HELD, JOHN. Danny Decoy. NY: Barnes, (1953). 1st ed. Fine in pict cl, dj (sl worn, sm tear). Captain's Bookshelf. $60/£38

HELD, JULIUS S. Peter Paul Rubens: Selected Drawings. NY: Phaidon, n.d. 2 vols. Slipcase. Metropolitan*. $46/£29

HELD, JULIUS. Rubens. Selected Drawings. London, 1959. 2 vols. Good. Washton. $125/£80

HELLER, JOSEPH and SPEED VOGEL. No Laughing Matter. London: Cape, 1986. 1st UK ed. NF in dj. Williams. $28/£18

HELLER, JOSEPH. Catch-22. London: Cape, (1962). 1st British ed. Inscribed. VG (edges foxed) in VG dj (lt soil, spine mk, short tears). Metropolitan*. $230/£147

HELLER, JOSEPH. Catch-22. NY, 1961. 1st ed, 1st bk. VG in dj (lt edgeworn). Argosy. $500/£321

HELLER, JOSEPH. Catch-22. NY: S&S, 1961. 1st ed. NF in dj (nicks). Lame Duck. $1,000/£641

HELLER, JOSEPH. Catch-22. London, 1962. 1st Eng ed. VG in dj (sm tear spine head). Words Etc. $101/£65

HELLER, JOSEPH. Catch-22. NY: Modern Library, 1966. 1st ed thus. NF in VG+ dj. Smith. $20/£13

HELLER, JOSEPH. God Knows. Franklin Center, PA: Franklin Library, 1984. Signed ltd ed. Full gray leather, gilt. *Argosy*. $65/£42

HELLER, JOSEPH. God Knows. NY: Knopf, 1984. One of 350 numbered, signed. Fine in Fine dj, Fine slipcase. *Lenz*. $100/£64

HELLER, JOSEPH. God Knows. NY: Knopf, 1984. 1st ed. One of 350 signed. Cl-backed bds. VF in pub's slipcase. *Pirages*. $125/£80

HELLER, JOSEPH. Good as Gold. NY: S&S, (1979). One of 500 numbered, signed. Fine in Fine slipcase. *Lenz*. $100/£64

HELLER, JOSEPH. Good as Gold. NY: S&S, (1979). One of 500 specially bound, signed. Dec cl. VF in slipcase. *Reese*. $125/£80

HELLER, JOSEPH. Something Happened. NY: Knopf, 1974. One of 350 numbered, signed. Fine in Fine dj, Fine slipcase. *Lenz*. $175/£112

HELM, A. S. and J. H. MILLER. Antarctica. The Story of the New Zealand Party of the Trans-Antarctic Expedition. Wellington: R.E. Owen, 1964. VG in dj. *High Latitude*. $45/£29

HELMHOLTZ, H. L. F. Sensations of Tone. 1895. 3rd Eng ed. xvii,567pp. (Cl sl dull, spine rubbed; ex-lib w/stamps.) *Whitehart*. $125/£80

HELPRIN, MARK. A Soldier in the Great War. NY: Harcourt Brace, (1991). One of 250 numbered, signed. Fine in Fine slipcase. *Lenz*. $125/£80

HELPRIN, MARK. Winter's Tale. San Diego, 1983. 1st Amer ed. Fine (spine heel sl bumped) in NF dj. *Polyanthos*. $25/£16

HELPS, ARTHUR. The Spanish Conquest in America. NY: Harper, 1856-1868. Early rpt. 4 vols. Black cl (spine extrems sl frayed), gilt spines. *Karmiole*. $150/£96

HELVENSTON, HAROLD. Scenery. Stanford: Stanford Univ, 1931. 1st ed. Tipped-in color plt to frontis. Paper label upper cvr. VG. *Dramatis Personae*. $35/£22

HELVENSTON, HAROLD. Scenery: A Manual of Scene Design. Stanford Univ, 1931. 1st ed. Tipped-in color frontis. White over grn cl, mtd illus fr cvr. Good. *Karmiole*. $50/£32

HEMINGWAY, ERNEST (ed). Men at War. NY: Crown, (1942). 1st ed. NF in dj (creased, torn, tape-reinforced, chips). *Waverly**. $77/£49

HEMINGWAY, ERNEST. Across the River and into the Trees. London: Cape, (1950). 1st ed. (Lt soiled, rubbed, spine sl faded), else NF in dj (soft crease fr panel, sl crimping). *Waverly**. $99/£63

HEMINGWAY, ERNEST. Across the River and into the Trees. London: Jonathan Cape, (1950). 1st British ed. VG in dj (rubbed, sm tears). *Pacific**. $81/£52

HEMINGWAY, ERNEST. Across the River and into the Trees. Cape, 1950. 1st UK ed. VG in dj. *Williams*. $101/£65

HEMINGWAY, ERNEST. Across the River and into the Trees. London: Cape, 1950. 1st UK ed. Fine (ink inscrip) in VG dj (sl rubbed, sl loss spine top). *Williams*. $55/£35

HEMINGWAY, ERNEST. Across the River and into the Trees. NY: Scribner, 1950. 1st ed. Fine in 1st issue dj w/yellow spine. *Pacific**. $127/£81

HEMINGWAY, ERNEST. The Dangerous Summer. NY: Scribner, (1985). 1st ed. Rev photo, flyers laid in. Fine in dj. *Reese*. $45/£29

HEMINGWAY, ERNEST. Death in the Afternoon. London, (1932). 1st Eng ed. Frontis. Orange cl (lt rubbed). *Argosy*. $150/£96

HEMINGWAY, ERNEST. Death in the Afternoon. London: Cape, (1932). (Bottom, fore-edge foxed), o/w Fine in dj (lt soiled, rubbed). *Hermitage*. $600/£385

HEMINGWAY, ERNEST. Death in the Afternoon. Cape, 1932. 1st UK ed. NF in Good+ dj (spine top chipped, sl browned). *Williams*. $148/£95

HEMINGWAY, ERNEST. Death in the Afternoon. NY/London: Scribner, 1932. 1st ed. Color frontis. Gilt-dec cl (sl worn). Contents VG. *New Hampshire**. $160/£103

HEMINGWAY, ERNEST. Death in the Afternoon. NY: Scribner, 1932. 1st ed. Color frontis by Juan Gris. (Lt stain fep; insect damage cvrs), else VG in Fair color pict dj (lacks lg pieces). *Pacific**. $104/£67

HEMINGWAY, ERNEST. A Farewell to Arms. Cape, 1929. 1st UK ed. Good+ (spine sl stained, worn; sl dusty; lacks dj). *Williams*. $23/£15

HEMINGWAY, ERNEST. A Farewell to Arms. London: Jonathan Cape, 1929. 1st British ed. NF in VG dj (chipped, rubbed, sm tears, soil, flaps clipped). *Pacific**. $127/£81

HEMINGWAY, ERNEST. A Farewell to Arms. NY, 1929. 1st trade ed, 1st state w/o disclaimer. Good- (ex-loaning lib; p147 detached but present). *Scribe's Perch**. $150/£96

HEMINGWAY, ERNEST. A Farewell to Arms. NY: Scribner, 1929. 1st ed, 2nd state w/disclaimer present. Fine. *Macdonnell*. $85/£54

HEMINGWAY, ERNEST. A Farewell to Arms. NY: Scribner, 1929. 1st ed, 1st issue w/o disclaimer. Black cl, gold paper labels. Fine. *Appelfeld*. $150/£96

HEMINGWAY, ERNEST. A Farewell to Arms. NY: Scribner, 1929. 1st ed, 1st issue. Bookseller label at rear. Gold labels. NF. (Lacks dj.) *Captain's Bookshelf*. $175/£112

HEMINGWAY, ERNEST. A Farewell to Arms. NY: Scribner, 1929. 1st ed, 1st issue, w/o disclaimer notice p(x). Black cl; gilt paper labels cvr, spine. VG in dj (sl shelfwear, chipped, sm tears). *Pacific**. $345/£221

HEMINGWAY, ERNEST. A Farewell to Arms. NY: Scribner, 1929. 1st ed, 1st trade ptg w/o legal disclaimer on pg(x). (Hannemann A8a). Sm 8vo. Black cl, gold paper labels. In earliest dj, w/blurb on fr flap reading 'Katherine Barclay' instead of correct spelling, 'Catherine Barkley.' NF (fr label rubbed) in dj (sl rubbed, sm tears). *Antic Hay*. $800/£513

HEMINGWAY, ERNEST. A Farewell to Arms. NY: Scribner, 1929. 1st ed, 1st state w/o disclaimer. Black cl, gold labels. Fine in Nice 1st state dj (sl frayed, aged). *Macdonnell*. $850/£545

HEMINGWAY, ERNEST. A Farewell to Arms. NY: Scribner, 1929. 1st ed. One of 510 numbered, signed. Fine in pub's slipcase (professionally restored) in custom clamshell box. *Unger*. $5,400/£3,462

HEMINGWAY, ERNEST. A Farewell to Arms. NY: Scribner, 1948. 1st illus ed. NF (sig) in dj (lt chipped, soiled), orig slipcase (externally tape-mended). *Captain's Bookshelf*. $300/£192

HEMINGWAY, ERNEST. The Fifth Column and the First Forty-Nine Stories. NY: Scribner, 1938. 1st ed. Fine in VG dj (sm tear fr panel, spine head chipped, rear sl rubbed). *Pacific**. $460/£295

HEMINGWAY, ERNEST. The Fifth Column and the First Forty-Nine Stories. NY: Scribner, 1938. 1st ed. 8vo. Red cl. Very Bright in dj (sl edgewear, sm repaired edge tear). *Dermont*. $850/£545

HEMINGWAY, ERNEST. The Fifth Column and the First Forty-Nine Stories. London, 1939. 1st Eng ed. Good (sl dknd). *Clearwater*. $47/£30

HEMINGWAY, ERNEST. The Fifth Column. NY, 1940. 1st separate ed. Thin 8vo. Gray cl stamped in red. VG (sig; cl lt foxed). *Argosy*. $600/£385

HEMINGWAY, ERNEST. For Whom the Bell Tolls. London: Cape, (1941). VG (shelfworn) in dj (soil, lt worn, tight around spine edges). *Metropolitan**. $230/£147

HEMINGWAY, ERNEST. For Whom the Bell Tolls. NY: Scribner, 1940. Good in Fair 1st state dj. *Scribe's Perch**. $110/£71

HEMINGWAY, ERNEST. For Whom the Bell Tolls. NY: Scribner, 1940. 1st ed. Fine in VG 1st issue dj (1-inch tear rear panel, crease, rubbed) w/o photographer's name below Hemingway port. *Pacific**. $161/£103

HEMINGWAY, ERNEST. For Whom the Bell Tolls. NY: Scribner, 1940. 1st ed. Beige cl. Nice in dj (nicks). *Appelfeld*. $200/£128

HEMINGWAY, ERNEST. For Whom the Bell Tolls. NY: Scribner, 1940. 1st ed. Natural tan buckram. (Offsetting to eps), else Fine in VG 1st state pict black dj (sm piece out fr panel, 3 short edge tears) titled in red/white w/black/white/red/lt blue panoramic illus. *Blue Mountain*. $250/£160

HEMINGWAY, ERNEST. For Whom the Bell Tolls. NY: Scribners, 1940. 1st ed. (Sl foxing pg edges), else Fine in NF, 1st issue dj (internal repairs; short tears). *Between The Covers*. $650/£417

HEMINGWAY, ERNEST. For Whom the Bell Tolls. London, 1941. W/Book Society wrap-around band. Nice in dj (dust-mkd, sl chipped, torn). *Clearwater*. $125/£80

HEMINGWAY, ERNEST. For Whom the Bell Tolls. London: Cape, 1941. 1st Eng ed. (Feps lt browned.) *Hollett*. $23/£15

HEMINGWAY, ERNEST. For Whom the Bell Tolls. LEC, 1942. One of 1500 signed by Lynd Ward (illus). 24 litho plts (6 dbl-pg). (Spine faded), o/w VF in pub's slipcase (tape-reinforced). *Pirages*. $125/£80

HEMINGWAY, ERNEST. The Garden of Eden. NY: Scribner, 1986. 1st ed. VF in VF dj. *Revere*. $35/£22

HEMINGWAY, ERNEST. Green Hills of Africa. NY: Scribner, 1935. 1st ed. (Spine, extrems faded), else VG in dj (chipped, rubbed, faded, price-clipped). *Pacific**. $345/£221

HEMINGWAY, ERNEST. Green Hills of Africa. NY: Scribner, 1935. 1st ed. (Bds sunned, shelfworn.) Dj (spine sunned, edges worn). *Metropolitan**. $402/£258

HEMINGWAY, ERNEST. Hokum: A Play. Wellesley Hills: Sans Souci, (1978). 1st ed. One of 200 numbered. Fine in dj, slipcase. *Captain's Bookshelf*. $125/£80

HEMINGWAY, ERNEST. In Our Time. NY: Scribner, 1930. VG in dj (spine head loss, internal reinforcement; reinforced 2-inch triangular tear fr flap; worn). *Metropolitan**. $172/£110

HEMINGWAY, ERNEST. Islands in the Stream. NY: Scribner, (1970). 1st ed. Fine in dj. *Between The Covers*. $85/£54

HEMINGWAY, ERNEST. A Moveable Feast. London, (1964). 1st Eng ed. VG in dj. *Argosy*. $65/£42

HEMINGWAY, ERNEST. A Moveable Feast. NY: Scribner, (1964). 1st ed. (Edges sl dusty), o/w Fine in NF dj (sm tear). *Reese*. $50/£32

HEMINGWAY, ERNEST. A Moveable Feast. NY: Scribner, (1964). 1st ed. NF in dj. *Turtle Island*. $65/£42

HEMINGWAY, ERNEST. A Moveable Feast. London, 1964. 1st ed. VG in dj. *Typographeum*. $35/£22

HEMINGWAY, ERNEST. A Moveable Feast. NY, 1964. 1st ed. NF in NF dj (price-clipped). *Warren*. $50/£32

HEMINGWAY, ERNEST. The Nick Adams Stories. NY: Scribner, (1972). 1st ed. NF in dj (price-clipped). *Turtle Island*. $75/£48

HEMINGWAY, ERNEST. The Nick Adams Stories. NY: Scribners, (1972). 1st ed. Fine in Fine dj (price-clipped). *Between The Covers*. $125/£80

HEMINGWAY, ERNEST. The Nick Adams Stories. NY: Scribner, (1973). 1st ed. Fine (sm red dot top edge) in dj (sm tear). *Captain's Bookshelf*. $75/£48

HEMINGWAY, ERNEST. The Old Man and the Sea. London: Jonathan Cape, (1952). 1st Eng ed. (Spines sl faded), else NF in dj (rubbed, sl faded). *Pacific**. $127/£81

HEMINGWAY, ERNEST. The Old Man and the Sea. London: Jonathan Cape, (1952). 1st Eng ed. NF in pict dj (lt chipped). *Glenn*. $185/£119

HEMINGWAY, ERNEST. The Old Man and the Sea. NY, 1952. 1st ed thus. C. F. Tunnicliffe and Raymond Sheppard (illus). (Ink sig, address, date, pg ends stained), o/w NF in NF dj. *Smith*. $20/£13

HEMINGWAY, ERNEST. Selected Letters. Carlos Baker (ed). Granada, 1981. 1st UK ed. VG+ in dj (spine sl faded). *Williams*. $39/£25

HEMINGWAY, ERNEST. The Spanish Earth. Cleveland: J.B. Savage, (1938). 1st ed, 2nd issue w/plain tan eps, statement ptd on rear pastedown. One of 1000. Pict tan buckram lettered in black. (Cvrs foxed), else VG. *Pacific**. $161/£103

HEMINGWAY, ERNEST. To Have and Have Not. NY: Scribner, 1937. 1st ed. Fine in VG dj (1-inch closed tear fr panel, spine head chipped). *Pacific**. $431/£276

HEMINGWAY, ERNEST. To Have and Have Not. NY: Scribner, 1937. 1st ed. 8vo. Bright (ink inscrip, few ll roughly opened; cl sl soiled) in dj (lt shelfworn). *Waverly**. $660/£423

HEMINGWAY, ERNEST. To Have and Have Not. NY: Scribner, 1937. 1st ed. Fine (bkpl under fr flap) in dj (lt edgewear, few sm tears). *Captain's Bookshelf*. $750/£481

HEMINGWAY, ERNEST. The Torrents of Spring. NY: Scribner, 1926. 1st ed, 1st ptg. Orig dk grn cl lettered in red. (Eps offset), else VF. *Macdonnell*. $400/£256

HEMINGWAY, ERNEST. The Torrents of Spring. NY: Scribner, 1926. 1st ed. VF in dj (spine ends lt chipped). *Bromer*. $3,250/£2,083

HEMINGWAY, ERNEST. The Torrents of Spring. NY: Scribner, 1926. 1st ed. Fine in dj, chemise, 1/2 leather slipcase. *Bromer*. $4,500/£2,885

HEMINGWAY, ERNEST. Winner Take Nothing. NY: Scribner, 1933. 1st ed. Gold labels. Fine. (Lacks dj.) *Captain's Bookshelf*. $125/£80

HEMINGWAY, ERNEST. Winner Take Nothing. NY: Scribner, 1933. 1st ed. VG (lt rubbed) in dj (dknd, chipped, deep crease, few tears, sm hole spine; damping, affecting top text edge; tape repairs). *Waverly**. $187/£120

HEMINGWAY, ERNEST. Winner Take Nothing. NY: Scribner, 1933. 1st ed. Black cl, gilt paper labels. Fine in NF dj (spine ends rubbed). *Pacific**. $489/£313

HEMINGWAY, ERNEST. Winner Take Nothing. NY: Scribner, 1933. 1st ed. Gilt labels. Fine (bkpl) in VG dj (edge tears, sm mended nicks). *Reese*. $500/£321

HEMPEL, EBERHARD. Baroque Art and Architecture in Central Europe. Balt, 1965. 200 plts. Good. *Washton*. $100/£64

HENDERLY, BROOKS. The YMCA Boys on Bass Island. Cupples & Leon, 1916. VG (bumped, shelfworn, soiled; lacks dj). *My Bookhouse*. $25/£16

HENDERSON, ALICE PALMER. The Ninety First—The First at Camp Lewis. The Author, (1918). VG. *Perier*. $60/£38

HENDERSON, DAVID. Felix of the Silent Forest. NY: Poets Press, 1967. 1st ed, 1st bk. NF in wrappers as issued (edges sl faded). *Between The Covers*. $50/£32

HENDERSON, G. F. R. The Civil War, A Soldier's View. Jay Luvaas (ed). Chicago, (1958). 1st ed. VG+ in dj (lt worn). *Pratt*. $42/£27

HENDERSON, G. F. R. Stonewall Jackson and the American Civil War. London, 1898. 737pp. VG+ in VG+ dj. *Pratt*. $40/£26

HENDERSON, HELEN W. A Loiterer in New York. NY: Doran, (1917). 86 photo plts. Teg. Dec cvr (faded). Good. *Scribe's Perch**. $18/£12

HENDERSON, JOHN B. The Cruise of the Tomas Barrera. NY/London: Putnam, 1916. Fldg map. Gilt-dec blue cl. Fine. *Parmer*. $50/£32

HENDERSON, KEITH. Palm Groves and Hummingbirds. London: Ernest Benn, 1924. 1st ed. (1 plt crinkled; lt rubbed, spine lettering faded, lower bd scratched.) *Hollett*. $31/£20

HENDERSON, PERCY E. A British Officer in the Balkans. London, 1909. 1st ed. Fldg map. (Lt browned, bkpl; spine chipped, faded, corners sl worn.) *Edwards*. $55/£35

HENDERSON, PETER. Gardening for Profit. NY: OJ, 1874. 2nd ed. 264pp. Brn cl, gilt. VG. *Price*. $59/£38

HENDERSON, PETER. Practical Floriculture. NY: OJ, 1869. 1st ed. 249pp. Brn cl, gilt. (Spine title sl faint), else Good. *Price*. $44/£28

HENDERSON, PETER. Practical Floriculture. NY: OJ, 1928. New, enlgd ed. Fine in dj. *Second Life*. $35/£22

HENDERSON, PHILIP. William Morris. His Life, Work and Friends. London; Thames & Hudson, 1967. 1st ed. Floral bds. NF in NF dj. *Reese*. $40/£26

HENDERSON, ROBERT W. Early American Sport: A Check-List of Books.... NY: Barnes, 1953. 2nd ed. Text VG. (Cl lt soiled, spine toned, sm dent foreedge.) *Waverly**. $38/£24

HENDERSON, ZENNA. Pilgrimage: The Book of the People. Doubleday, 1961. 1st ed, 1st bk. Fine in NF dj (corner wear, closed tear). *Certo*. $175/£112

HENDRICKS, GORDON. Albert Bierstadt: Painter of the American West. (NY): Abrams/Amon Carter Museum of Western Art, (1973). 1st ed. 63 color plts. Brn cl. Good in dj. *Karmiole*. $175/£112

HENDRICKS, GORDON. Eadweard Muybridge. NY: Grossman, 1975. 1st ed. Frontis. VG in illus dj. *Cahan*. $125/£80

HENDRICKS, GORDON. The Life of Winslow Homer. NY: Abrams, (1979). 1st ed. 68 color plts. Cream linen stamped in blue. Fine in dj. *Karmiole*. $175/£112

HENDRICKS, GORDON. The Photographs of Thomas Eakins. NY: Grossman, 1972. 1st ed. (Owner stamp), else NF in illus dj. *Cahan*. $150/£96

HENDRY, J. F. The Bombed Happiness. London: Routledge, 1942. 1st Eng ed, 1st bk. Card wrappers (sl mkd, rubbed). *Clearwater*. $39/£25

HENDY, PHILIP. Piero Della Francesca and the Early Renaissance. NY, 1968. 101 plts (34 color). Good. *Washton*. $35/£22

HENLEY, W. E. (ed). A London Garland, Selected from Five Centuries of English Verse.... London/NY: Macmillan, 1895. Full dec vellum. VG. *New Hampshire**. $100/£64

HENLEY, W. E. (ed). Lyra Heroica, a Book of Verse for Boys. London, 1892. 1st ed. (Cl worn.) *Typographeum*. $25/£16

HENNELL, THOMAS. The Witnesses. London, (1938). 1st Eng ed. 8 full-pg dwgs. Nice in dj (dust-mkd, worn, repaired). *Clearwater*. $39/£25

HENNEPIN, LOUIS. A New Discovery of a Vast Country in America. London, 1698. 1st Eng ed, 'Ton' issue. 8vo. 2 maps, 7 plts (incl frontis). Contemp calf (skillfully rebacked). Morocco solander case. Howes H416. *Swann**. $4,370/£2,801

HENNEPIN, LOUIS. A New Discovery of a Vast Country in America.... London, 1698. Frontis, 4 plts, fldg map (calls for 2 fldg maps, 6 plts; foxing, dampstaining, repairs to map). Patterned paper-cvrd bds (rebound), white paper-cvrd spine. *Metropolitan**. $172/£110

HENREY, B. No Ordinary Gardener, Thomas Knowlton, 1691-1781. London, 1986. Dj. *Maggs*. $34/£22

HENREY, BLANCHE and W. J. BEAN. Trees and Shrubs Throughout the Year. London: Lindsay Drummond, 1945. 2nd ed. 4 color, 84 b/w plts. (Uneven cvr fade), else Fine. *Quest*. $30/£19

HENRIQUES, FERNANDO. Prostitution and Society. MacGibbon & Kee, 1962-8. 1st ed. 3 vols. 46 plts. Djs (sl chipped, spines lt faded). *Edwards*. $62/£40

HENRIQUES, ROBERT. Death by Moonlight. NY: Morrow, n.d. (ca 1935). 1st ed. 31 plts, map. (Sl rubbed, soiled), o/w VG. *Worldwide*. $24/£15

Henry Clay Payne, a Life. (Comp by William W. Wight.) Milwaukee: Burdick & Allen, 1907. Frontis port. Teg. Card, envelope of Mrs. Henry C. Payne laid in. VG + . *Bohling*. $20/£13

Henry Fuseli 1741-1825. London: Tate Gallery, 1975. Good in dj. *Washton*. $40/£26

Henry Moore. Vol 1. 1955. 1st ed. (Ex-lib, ink stamps, bkpl, cellotape mks pastedowns.) Dj (sl soiled). *Edwards*. $62/£40

Henry Moore. Vol 2. 1965. 2nd ed. (Ex-lib, ink stamps, bkpl.) Dj (sl chipped). *Edwards*. $62/£40

HENRY, ALEXANDER and DAVID THOMPSON. The Manuscript Journals of Alexander Henry...and of David Thomson.... Elliott Coues (ed). NY: Francis P. Harper, 1897. 1st ed. One of 1100. 3 vols. (28),446; (6),447-916; (6),917-1027pp; port, map on 4 fldg sheets. Mostly unopened. Dk grn cl. (Map sheets dknd), else Fine set in slipcase. Howes H419. *Parmer*. $950/£609

HENRY, ALICE. Women and the Labor Movement. NY: Doran, (1923). 1st ed. VG. *Second Life*. $65/£42

HENRY, E. R. Classification and Uses of Finger Prints. London: Routledge, 1900. 5 plts. VG. *Savona*. $47/£30

HENRY, FRANCOISE. The Book of Kells. NY, 1977. 126 color plts. (Spine base, back cvr sl stained, back hinge weak.) *Washton*. $75/£48

HENRY, FREDERICK. Captain Henry of Geauga. Cleveland: Gates, 1942. 1st ed. NF. *Archer*. $75/£48

HENRY, JOHN JOSEPH. An Accurate and Interesting Account of the Hardships and Sufferings of that Band of Heroes....1775. Lancaster: Ptd by William Greer, 1812. 1st ed. 235pp; c. slip pasted verso tp. Full contemp flamed calf w/red morocco spine label. (Hinges cracked; fr blank ep excised; rear blank eps soiled), else VG. Howes H423. *Cahan*. $375/£240

HENRY, JOHN JOSEPH. An Accurate and Interesting Account of the Hardships and Sufferings of That Band of Heroes...against Quebec in 1775. Lancaster, 1812. 1st ed. Contemp sheep. (Browned.) Howes H423. *Swann**. $287/£184

HENRY, MARGUERITE. Justin Morgan Had a Horse. Chicago: Wilcox & Follett, (1945). 1st ed. Wesley Dennis (illus). VG + in dj (sm chip). *Bernard*. $45/£29

HENRY, MARGUERITE. Justin Morgan Had a Horse. Chicago: JLG, Wilcox & Follet, 1945. Wesley Dennis (illus). 8 3/4 x 11 1/4. 88pp. VG in dj. *Cattermole*. $30/£19

HENRY, MARGUERITE. King of the Wind. Chicago: McGraw Hill, 1948. 1st ed. Wesley Dennis (illus). 7 1/4 x 8 3/4. 175pp. VG in dj. *Cattermole*. $60/£38

HENRY, MARGUERITE. Muley-Ears Nobody's Dog. Chicago: Rand McNally, 1959. 1st ed. Wesley Dennis (illus). 7 1/4 x 10 1/4. 64pp. VG in dj. *Cattermole*. $35/£22

HENRY, MARGUERITE. Stormy, Misty's Foal. Chicago: Rand McNally, 1963. 1st ed. Wesley Dennis (illus). 7 1/4 x 9 3/4. 224pp. Bds. Fine in dj. *Cattermole*. $50/£32

HENRY, O. (Pseud of William Sidney Porter.) The Complete Writings of O. Henry. GC: Doubleday, Page, 1917. One of 1050 numbered sets, signed by Doubleday, Page, and Gordon Grant (illus). 14 vols. Teg. (Few inner hinges neatly repaired), o/w Fine in parchment-backed blue bds. *Captain's Bookshelf.* $600/£385

HENRY, O. (Pseud of William Sydney Porter.) Heart of the West. NY: McClure, 1907. 1st ed. Pict cl. (Gray/grn color to pict design fr bd, spine mostly gone), o/w VG. *Hermitage.* $45/£29

HENRY, O. (Pseud of William Sydney Porter.) Letters to Lithopolis. GC: Doubleday, Page, 1922. Ltd to 427. White vegetable vellum shelfback & bds. VG (cvrs lt soil, bkpl). BAL 16303. *Antic Hay.* $50/£32

HENRY, O. (Pseud of William Sydney Porter.) O. Henryana: Seven Odds and Ends Poetry and Short Stories. GC: Doubleday, Page, 1920. Ltd to 377 numbered. White vegetable vellum shelfback, bds. NF. BAL 16302. *Antic Hay.* $75/£48

HENRY, O. (Pseud of William Sydney Porter.) Strictly Business. NY: Doubleday, Page, 1910. 1st ed. (Gutters dknd), o/w VG. *Hermitage.* $45/£29

HENRY, O. (Pseud of William Sidney Porter.) Strictly Business. NY: Doubleday, Page, 1910. 1st ed. Red cl. (Sl mk rear cvr), o/w Fine. *Sumner & Stillman.* $95/£61

HENRY, O. (Pseud of William Sidney Porter.) The Voice of the City and Other Stories. NY: LEC, 1935. 1st ed thus. One of 1500 numbered, signed by George Grosz (illus). Fine in slipcase. *Captain's Bookshelf.* $275/£176

HENRY, O. (Pseud of William Sydney Porter.) The Voice of the City and Other Stories. NY: LEC, 1935. #904/1500 numbered, signed by George Groscz (illus). Fine in tissue wrapper, pub's slipcase. *Hermitage.* $350/£224

HENRY, O. (Pseud of William Sydney Porter.) The Voice of the City. NY: McClure, 1908. 1st ed. *Hermitage.* $50/£32

HENRY, O. S. (Pseud of William Sidney Porter.) The Gentle Grafter. NY: McClurg, 1908. 1st ed, 2nd ptg, variant binding. Red cl, gilt. Spine foot stamped 'Doubleday' rather than 'McClure' or 'Doubleday Page & Co.' Good (spine frayed, hinges cracked). BAL 16276. *Macdonnell.* $20/£13

HENRY, O. S. (Pseud of William Sidney Porter.) The Hiding of Black Bill. NY: Ridgeway, 1913. 1st separate ed. Fine in pale blue ptd wrappers. BAL 16312. *Macdonnell.* $100/£64

HENRY, ROBERT SELPH. The Story of the Confederacy. Indianapolis: Bobbs-Merrill, (1931). Dull gray bds. Good. Howes H426. *Cullen.* $35/£22

HENRY, STUART. Conquering Our Great American Plains. NY, (1930). 1st ed. Fine in VG dj (lt edgewear, price-clipped). *Mcclintock.* $50/£32

HENRY, WILL. Alias Butch Cassidy. NY: Random House, 1967. 1st ed. Inscribed. Fine in Fine dj. *Unger.* $225/£144

HENRY, WILL. No Survivors. NY: Random House, (1950). 1st ed. Fine in VG + dj. *Book Market.* $175/£112

HENRY, WILL. No Survivors. NY: Random House, 1950. 1st ed. Inscribed. VG in VG dj (chipped). *Unger.* $250/£160

HENRY, WILL. Summer of the Gun. Phila: Lippincott, 1978. 1st ed. Inscribed. Fine in Fine dj (price-clipped). *Unger.* $150/£96

HENRY, WILLIAM. The Elements of Experimental Chemistry. Phila: James Webster, 1817. 1st ed. xxx,(2),656,xcvipp; 10 copper engrs, fldg table. Contemp calf (extrems sl rubbed), spine label. *Karmiole.* $100/£64

HENSHALL, J. A. Book of the Black Bass.... Cincinnati, 1889. 2nd issue of vol 1. 2 vols. Grn cl (1st vol sl spotted, both vols sl dusty), gilt. Good. *Maggs.* $140/£90

HENSLOW, T. GEOFFREY W. Gardens of Fragrance. London: Warne, 1932. Color frontis, 23 plts. Gilt-stamped cl. VG. *Quest.* $55/£35

HENSMAN, HOWARD. The Afghan War of 1879-80. London, 1881. 1st ed. Inscribed. xv,567pp + ads; 10 maps. Purple cl (sl worn). *Maggs.* $273/£175

HENSON, PAULINE. Founding a Wilderness Capital. Flagstaff: Northland, 1965. Fldg map. Good in dj (sl worn). *Dumont.* $30/£19

HENSON. Truth Stranger Than Fiction. Boston: Jewett, 1858. 1st thus. Engr frontis port, 212pp. Blind-stamped pub's cl. (Frontis foxed; head, foot chipped), o/w Good. *Scribe's Perch*.* $130/£83

HENTY, G. A. At Aboukir and Acre. Blackie, 1899. 1st ed. 8vo. 352pp + 32pp illus ads (lt spotted); 8 mono plts, 3 plans. William Rainey (illus). Olivine edges. Pict cl (extrems sl worn, spine sl faded, sl rubbed), gilt. VG. *Bookmark.* $94/£60

HENTY, G. A. At Agincourt: A Tale of the White Hoods of Paris. NY: Scribner, 1896. 1st ed. Pict grn cl. VG (faint ink name). *Antic Hay.* $85/£54

HENTY, G. A. In the Hands of the Cave Dwellers. Blackie, n.d. (Xmas 1902 inscrip). 1st ed, variant issue. Wat Miller (illus). 8vo. 174pp,32pp illus ads; 2 plts. Pict red cl (mks, wear), gilt, Indian brave on fr cvr. Good. *Bookmark.* $34/£22

HENTY, G. A. In the Heart of the Rockies. NY: Scribner, 1905. 8 full-pg illus. Red cl (lt worn, hinges tender), gilt. VG. *Five Quail.* $20/£13

HENTY, G. A. A March on London. NY: Scribner, 1897. 1st Amer ed. Pict grn cl. VG (frontis tissue guard torn). *Antic Hay.* $50/£32

HENTY, G. A. Out with Garibaldi. NY: Scribner, 1900. 1st Amer ed. Pict blue cl. VG (name stamp). *Antic Hay.* $50/£32

HENTY, G. A. (ed). Stories of Sea and Land. Ward, Lock & Bowden Ltd, n.d. Lg 8vo. 512pp (hinges strained). Pict mustard-yellow cl (mks, rubbed). Sound. *Bookmark.* $70/£45

HENTY, G. A. Through Russian Snows. NY: Scribner, 1895. 1st Amer ed. Pict blue cl. VG (ink presentation, few spots text). *Antic Hay.* $45/£29

HENTY, G. A. Through Three Campaigns. NY, 1903. 1st ed. (Inner hinges cracked; cvrs rubbed.) *King.* $75/£48

HENTY, G. A. The Treasure of the Incas. London/Glasgow/Dublin: Blackie, 1903. 1st ed. Map. Fine in grn pict cl, gilt. *Glenn.* $185/£119

HENTY, G. A. With Cochrane the Dauntless. NY: Scribner, 1896. 1st Amer ed. Dec cl. VG- (lt worn). *Antic Hay.* $45/£29

HENTY, G. A. With Cochrane the Dauntless. London, 1897. 1st British ed. 384+ ads pp (ink name, foxing, illus wrinkled). Pict cl (rubbed). *King.* $95/£61

HENTY, G. A. With Kitchener in the Soudan. London, 1903. 1st British ed. 3 maps (1 defective). Pict cl (inner hinges cracked; edge frayed; soiled, worn). *King.* $50/£32

HENTY, G. A. Yarns on the Beach. Blackie, n.d. (prize-plt dated 1905). 8vo. 160pp,16pp ads; 2 full-pg illus by J. J. Proctor. Dec cl, gilt. NF. *Bookmark.* $31/£20

HENTY, G. A. and GEORGE MANVILLE FENN et al. Courage and Conflict. Chambers, 1901. 1st ed. Lg 8vo. 416pp; 8 mono plts by W. Boucher. Pict cl, gilt. (Back cvr mkd, sl worn), else VG. *Bookmark.* $86/£55

HEPBURN, J. D. Twenty Years in Khama's Country. C. H. Lyall (ed). London: Hodder & Stoughton, 1896. 3rd ed. Frontis port, xv,397pp. Grn gilt pict cl (dulled), else VG. *Terramedia.* $125/£80

HEPBURN, KATHARINE. Me. NY: Knopf, 1991. 1st ed. As New in dj. *Jaffe*. $150/£96

HEPPENSTALL, RAYNER. The Greater Infortune. London: Peter Owen, (1960). 1st ed. (Pp corners sl creased), else Fine in NF dj (lt rubbed). *Between The Covers*. $45/£29

HEPWORTH, G. H. The Whip, Hoe, and Sword. Boston, 1864. 1st ed. 298pp. Blind-stamped cvrs, dec spine. Good (hinges weak). *Scribe's Perch**. $23/£15

HEPWORTH, JANET. Legends of the Flowers. London/Glasgow: Blackie, n.d. Gilt-dec cl. Fine. *Quest*. $40/£26

HERBER, E. C. (ed). Correspondence Between Spencer Fullerton Baird and Louis Agassiz. Washington, 1963. *Maggs*. $28/£18

HERBERT, A. P. Codd's Last Case. Methuen, 1952. 1st UK ed. VG+ in dj. *Williams*. $31/£20

HERBERT, A. P. Holy Deadlock. Methuen, 1934. 1st UK ed. NF in VG dj (spine browned). *Williams*. $28/£18

HERBERT, A. P. Holy Deadlock. London: Methuen, 1934. 1st ed. (Edges lt spotted.) Dj. *Hollett*. $47/£30

HERBERT, A. P. Mr. Pewter. London: Methuen, 1934. 1st ed. (Fore-edge spotted.) Dj (spine sl chipped). *Hollett*. $31/£20

HERBERT, A. P. Plain Jane. London: T. Fisher Unwin, 1927. 1st ed. (Feps browned.) *Hollett*. $31/£20

HERBERT, A. P. Tantivy Towers: A Light Opera in Three Acts. London: Methuen, (1931). 1st ed. NF (eps sl browned) in dj (spine browned, rear panel torn). *Antic Hay*. $25/£16

HERBERT, A. P. The Water Gipsies. London: Methuen, 1930. 1st ed, 1st issue w/#330 at bottom of last pg of ads. (Sl faded, edges spotted.) Pict red/grn dj (extrems sl worn). *Hollett*. $47/£30

HERBERT, EDWARD. The Autobiography. (Newtown): Gregynog, 1928. One of 300 numbered. *Swann**. $258/£165

HERBERT, FRANK. Chapterhouse: Dune. NY: Putnam, (1985). One of 750 numbered, signed. Fine in Fine slipcase. *Lenz*. $100/£64

HERBERT, FRANK. Chapterhouse: Dune. NY: Putnam, (1985). 1st ed. #504/750 signed. Fine in slipcase. *Hermitage*. $150/£96

HERBERT, FRANK. Dune. Phila: Chilton, (1965). 1st ed. (Name, date), else NF in NF dj (rubbing fr spine edge, wear rear upper spine corner). *Other Worlds*. $750/£481

HERBERT, FRANK. Dune. London: Gollancz, 1965. 1st UK ed. NF in VG dj (sl edgeworn). *Williams*. $226/£145

HERBERT, FRANK. Dune. Phila: Chilton, 1965. 1st ed. Blue cl. VG (top, bottom edges faded) in dj (edgeworn, sm chips, tears along edges). *Metropolitan**. $230/£147

HERBERT, FRANK. God Emperor of Dune. NY: Putnam, (1981). 1st ed. One of 750 numbered, signed. Matching slipcase. *Swann**. $103/£66

HERBERT, FRANK. Heretics of Dune. NY: Putnam, (1984). 1st Amer ed. One of 1500 numbered, signed. Matching slipcase. *Swann**. $103/£66

HERBERT, FRANK. The Santaroga Barrier. London: Rapp & Whiting, (1970). 1st Eng ed, 1st hb ed. Signed. Dj. *Swann**. $69/£44

HERBERT, FRANK. The White Plague. NY: Putnam, (1982). 1st ed. One of 500 numbered, signed. Matching slipcase. *Swann**. $57/£37

HERBERT, GEORGE. The Remains.... London: Pickering, 1841. 2nd Pickering ed. Frontis, cxxiv,244pp. Orig blue cl (sl mkd), paper label (sl rubbed). *Cox*. $23/£15

HERBERT, GEORGE. The Temple. Nonesuch, 1927. #1175/1500. Engr frontis port. Teg on the rough. Tapestry cl. *Cox*. $109/£70

HERBERT, GEORGE. The Temple. Sacred Poems and Private Ejaculations. London: George Bell, 1904. One of 370 numbered. Frontis. Gilt-dec cl. VG (edges lt foxed, later inscrip) in cl dj. *Reese*. $35/£22

HERBERT, HENRY WILLIAM. American Game in Its Seasons. NY: Scribner, 1853. 1st ed. 343pp. Gilt-stamped cl. In a box. VG (inscrip). BAL 8138. *M&s*. $125/£80

HERBERT, J. A. Illuminated Manuscripts. London: Methuen, (1911). 1st ed. 51 plts. VG (bkpl removed fr pastedown; spine worn; rear joint cracked, tender). *Waverly**. $66/£42

HERBERT, JAMES. The Fog. New English Library, 1975. 1st UK ed. NF in dj. *Williams*. $156/£100

HERBERT, JAMES. Lair. New English Library, 1979. 1st UK ed. Fine in NF dj. *Williams*. $304/£195

HERBERT, JAMES. Moon. London: New English Library, 1985. 1st UK ed. Fine in dj. *Williams*. $22/£14

HERBERT, JAMES. The Spear. N.E.L., 1978. 1st UK ed. Fine in Fine dj. *Martin*. $44/£28

HERBERT, JAMES. The Spear. London: New English Library, 1978. 1st UK ed. NF in dj. *Williams*. $50/£32

HERBERT, ROBERT BEVERLEY. Life on a Virginia Farm. Fauquier Democrat, 1968. VG in VG dj. *Book Broker*. $35/£22

HERBERTSON, AGNES GROZIER. Heroic Legends. Blackie, 1908. 1st ed. Helen Stratton (illus). Lg 8vo. 254pp (foxing); 16 color plts. Aeg. Gilt-dec cl (spine, edges dusty). VG-. *Bookmark*. $23/£15

HERBST, JOSEPHINE. Nothing Is Sacred. NY: Coward, McCann, 1928. 1st ed, 1st bk. Gilt dec cl. Bright in dj (spine ends lt used). *Reese*. $200/£128

HERCULES, FRANK. Where the Hummingbird Flies. NY: Harcourt, Brace, (1961). 1st ed, 1st bk. Signed, inscribed presentation. VG in pict dj (edges worn). *Petrilla*. $65/£42

HERD, SANDY. My Golfing Life, Told to Clyde Foster. London: Chapman & Hall, 1923. 1st ed. NF. *Pacific**. $219/£140

HERFORD, OLIVER. Happy Days. NY: Mitchell Kennerley, (1917). Color pict paper over bds. Good. *Scribe's Perch**. $20/£13

HERFORD, OLIVER. The Peter Pan Alphabet. NY: Scribner, Jan 1907. 1st ed. Pict paper over bds, linen spine. Good- (foxing, cracked in several places). *Scribe's Perch**. $28/£18

HERGE. Adventures of TinTin: Cigars of the Pharaoh. Methuen, 1971. 1st Eng ed. 4to. 62pp. Pict bds. (Graze on back; spine neatly reattached w/sellotape, sl wear), else VG. *Bookmark*. $25/£16

HERGE. The Adventures of TinTin: Destination Moon. Methuen, 1959. 1st Eng ed. 4to. 62pp. Pict bds. (Extrems worn, few sm mks), else VG. *Bookmark*. $59/£38

HERGE. The Adventures of TinTin: Explorers on the Moon. Methuen, 1959. 1st Eng ed. 4to. 62pp (hinges taped). Pict bds (worn). Good. *Bookmark*. $25/£16

HERGE. The Adventures of TinTin: Land of Black Gold. Methuen, 1972. 1st Eng ed. 4to. 62pp. Pict bds. (Tips rubbed), else NF. *Bookmark*. $44/£28

HERGESHEIMER, JOSEPH. The Bright Shawl. NY: Knopf, 1922. 1st ed. (Sl glazing bds), else Fine in NF dj (foxing). *Between The Covers*. $75/£48

HERGESHEIMER, JOSEPH. The Foolscap Rose. NY: Knopf, 1934. 1st ed. (Sl dkng gutters), else Fine in NF dj (spine sl faded; chips). *Between The Covers*. $75/£48

HERGESHEIMER, JOSEPH. The Presbyterian Child. NY, 1923. Ltd to 950. Signed, inscribed. (Cvrs lt worn.) Internally VG. *Truepenny*. $45/£29

HERGESHEIMER, JOSEPH. Sheridan, a Military Narrative. Boston/NY: Houghton Mifflin, (1931). 1st ed. NF in VG dj (sl chipped.) *Mcgowan*. $85/£54

HERING, D. W. The Lure of the Clock. NY Univ, 1932. 1st Amer ed. Brn cl, gilt. Fine. *Weber*. $30/£19

HERIOT, GEORGE. Travels Through the Canadas.... London: Richard Phillips, 1807. 27 plts, hand-colored fldg map. (Plts dknd, stamp residue reverse some plts; off-printing, paper repairs.) Patterned paper-cvrd bds (rebound), white paper-cvrd spine. *Metropolitan**. $805/£516

HERIVEL, J. The Background to Newton's Principia. Oxford, 1965. Frontis, 4 plts. *Whitehart*. $62/£40

HERLIHY, JAMES LEO. Midnight Cowboy. S&S, 1965. 1st US ed. VG (sm dampstain spine bottom) in dj (dampstained). *Williams*. $47/£30

HERLIHY, JAMES LEO. Midnight Cowboy. NY, 1965. Nice (spine sl creased, sl shelfworn) in dj. *Clearwater*. $55/£35

HERLIHY, JAMES LEO. The Sleep of Baby Filbertson and Other Stories. NY, 1959. 1st ed, 1st bk. Nice in dj. *Clearwater*. $55/£35

HERLOTS, G. A. C. The Birds of Trinidad and Tobago. London: Collins, (1965). 16 plts. VG + in VG dj. *Mikesh*. $27/£17

HERMAN, HENRY. The Crime of a Christmas Toy. London: Ward, Lock, & Bowden, n.d. Colonial ed. (Sl soiled, frayed, cocked.) *Metropolitan**. $23/£15

HERMANN, BINGER. The Louisiana Purchase and Our Title West of the Rocky Mountains.... Washington: GPO, 1900. Fldg color frontis map, plt map, 3 fldg maps, 7 plts. Gilt-lettered cl (worn). VG, internally Fine. *Argonaut*. $75/£48

HERMANN, LUKE. British Landscape Painting of the Eighteenth Century. NY, 1974. 136 plts (16 color). Good in dj. *Washton*. $85/£54

Hermit of the Forest, and the Wandering Infants. (By Richard Johnson.) Hudson, (NY): Ashbel Stoddard, 1804. 24mo. 30pp (foxed). Sewn, as issued. *M & S*. $150/£96

HERNDON, ANGELO. Let Me Live. NY: Random House, (1937). 1st ed. 4 port plts. Dedication ptd fep. Brn cl (lt soiled). Contents Clean. *Petrilla*. $40/£26

HERNDON, SARAH RAYMOND. Days on the Road Crossing the Plains in 1865. NY: Burr Ptg House, 1902. Frontis port. VG (lt rubbed). Howes H439. *Bohling*. $150/£96

HERNDON, SARAH RAYMOND. Days on the Road, Crossing the Plains in 1865. NY: Burr Printing House, 1902. 1st ed. Frontis port. (Eps, 1/2-title browned), o/w VG. Howes H439. *Second Life*. $265/£170

HERNDON, WILLIAM H. Lincoln and Ann Rutledge, and the Pioneers of New Salem. Herrin, IL: Trovillion Private Press, 1945. One of 898. Gilt-emb cl. (Sl rubbed), else VG. *Cahan*. $40/£26

HERNDON, WILLIAM H. Lincoln's Philosophy of Life. L.A.: H.E. Barker, 1933. #93/100 ptd, signed by Barker. Unopened. Ptd wraps. *Wantagh*. $45/£29

HERNDON, WILLIAM H. and JESSE WEIK. Herndon's Lincoln, The True Story of a Great Life. Chicago: Belford, Clarke, (1889). 1st ed. 3 vols. (20),199,(5); — 418,(6); —638,(4)pp. 63 plts (1 fldg). Teg. Blue cl (worn, bds rubbed, spotted, 1 hinge expertly repaired), gilt. VG +. Howes H440. *Harrington*. $300/£192

HERNDON, WILLIAM H. and JESSE WEIK. Herndon's Lincoln: The True Story of a Great Life. Chicago, (1889). 1st ed. 3 vols. 1/2 morocco (extrems worn). Cl fldg case. Howes H440. *Swann**. $258/£165

HERNDON, WILLIAM LEWIS and LARDNER GIBBON. Exploration of the Valley of the Amazon, Made Under Direction of the Navy Department. Washington, 1853, 1854. 2 vols. 31,414,iv; xi,339pp; 5 fldg maps; 52 plts (offsetting on some facing pp). Full leather (sl depository mks). Nice set. *Bohling*. $120/£77

HERR, JOHN K. and EDWARD S. WALLACE. The Story of the U.S. Cavalry, 1775-1942. Boston: Little, Brown, (1953). 1st ed. VG in dj. *Lien*. $50/£32

HERR, MICHAEL. Dispatches. NY: Knopf, 1977. 1st ed. Fine in Fine dj. *Metropolitan**. $86/£55

HERR, MICHAEL. Dispatches. NY: Knopf, 1977. 1st ed. Fine in dj. *Captain's Bookshelf*. $100/£64

HERR, MICHAEL. Dispatches. NY: Knopf, 1977. Excellent in dj (sl rubbed, creased). *Gekoski*. $172/£110

HERRICK, JAMES B. Memories of Eighty Years. Chicago, 1949. 1st ed. VG. *Doctor's Library*. $40/£26

HERRICK, JAMES. A Short History of Cardiology. Springfield, 1942. 1st ed. (Ex-lib.) *Fye*. $100/£64

HERRICK, ROBERT. The Poetical Works of Robert Herrick. Cresset, 1928. One of 750 numbered sets. 4 vols. Frontispieces. Teg. Cream parchment bds, spines gilt. (Eps lt browned), else Fine set in orig slipcase (edge split). *Michael Taylor*. $187/£120

HERRICK, ROBERT. Selections from the Poetry of.... NY, 1882. Pict beige cl (sm spot fr cvr; inner hinges cracked). 2-piece box (quite defective, broken). *Kane**. $35/£22

HERRICK, ROBERT. Some Poems. Norfolk: New Directions, n.d. (1942). Fine in wrappers. *Graf*. $10/£6

HERRIN, LAMAR. The Rio Loja Ringmaster. Viking, 1977. 1st ed. VG + in VG dj. *Plapinger*. $50/£32

HERRING, JAMES and JAMES B. LONGACRE (eds). National Portrait Gallery of Distinguished Americans. NY: Monson Bancroft, 1834-39. 1st ed. 4 vols. 3/4 leather, marbled bds, gilt spines. VG (edges scuffed; offsetting, foxing). Howes H443. *Bohling*. $150/£96

HERRIOT, JAMES. The Lord God Made Them All. NY: St. Martin's, (1981). 1st ed. Fine in NF dj. *Antic Hay*. $17/£11

HERRLINGER, ROBERT. History of Medical Illustration from Antiquity to 1600. NY, 1970. 1st ed in English. VG in slipcase. *Fye*. $150/£96

HERRLINGER, ROBERT. History of Medical Illustration from Antiquity to 1600. NY, 1970. 1st ed in English. NF in slipcase. *Doctor's Library*. $175/£112

HERRMANN, FRANK. The English as Collectors. C&W, 1972. VG in dj. *Hadley*. $101/£65

HERRON, JIM. Fifty Years on the Hoot Owl Trail. Harry E. Chrisman (ed). Chicago: Sage Books, 1969. 1st ed. Signed by Chrisman. VG in dj. *Dumont*. $45/£29

HERSEY, CARL KENNETH. The Salmantine Lanterns: Their Origins and Development. Cambridge: Harvard Univ, 1937. 1st ed. (Spine sl faded), else Fine. *Hermitage*. $75/£48

HERSEY, G. L. Alfonso II and the Artistic Renewal of Naples, 1485-1495. New Haven, 1959. Good in dj. *Washton*. $65/£42

HERSEY, G. L. Pythagorean Palaces.... Ithaca/London: Cornell Univ, (1976). Dk red cl. NF in pict dj (rubbed, chipped). *Blue Mountain*. $65/£42

HERSEY, JOHN. The Importance of Small Things. Georgetown: Rind's Press, 1831. iv,(1),228pp. Contemp 1/4 leather, marbled bds. (Ex-lib), else Good. *Brown*. $15/£10

HERSEY, JOHN. Under the Eye of the Storm. NY: Knopf, 1967. 1st ed. Mint in dj. *Jaffe*. $50/£32

HERSHOLT, JEAN (ed). Evergreen Tales. NY: (LEC), 1949. One of 2500 numbered, inscribed by Hersholt. 15 vols. 4to. VF in glassine wrapper each vol, 5 slipcases (1 w/chip). *Bromer*. $500/£321

HERTER, GEORGE L. and JACQUES P. The Truth About Hunting in Today's Africa and How to Go on Safari for $690. Waseca: Herters, 1963. 1st ed. Leopard-skin patterned cl. VF. *Bowman.* $45/£29

HERTZOG, PETER. Little Known Facts About Billy the Kid. Santa Fe: Press of the Territorian, 1963. 1st ed. VG in ptd wrappers. *Connolly.* $25/£16

HERTZOG, PETER. Little Known Facts About Billy, the Kid...1873 to 1902. Portales, NM: Press of the Territorian, 1963. 1st ed. Ptd wraps. *Bohling.* $20/£13

HERVEY, A. B. Sea Mosses. Boston: Cassino, 1881. 22,281pp; 20 color plts. Dec cvr. Good. *Scribe's Perch*.* $32/£21

HERVEY, JOHN. The American Trotter. NY: Coward McCann, 1947. 1st ed. VG in VG dj. *October Farm.* $150/£96

HERVEY, JOHN. Lady Suffolk: The Old Grey Mare of Long Island. NY: Derrydale, (1936). One of 500 numbered. Untrimmed, partly unopened. Cream/mustard paper-cvrd bds (spine dusted, dknd; edgeworn), gilt, ptd label fr cvr. Text VG (bkpl). *Baltimore*.* $30/£19

HERVEY, JOHN. Messenger, the Great Progenitor. NY: Derrydale, (1935). One of 1500 numbered. Untrimmed. Cream/mustard paper-cvrd bds (spine, edges dknd), gilt, ptd label fr cvr. Text VG (bkpl, order form mtd feps). *Baltimore*.* $30/£19

HESKE, FRANZ. German Forestry. Yale Univ, 1938. (Ex-lib, ink stamp, label remains, #.) *Edwards.* $31/£20

HESS, FJERIL. Toplofty. Macmillan, 1939. 1st ed. Ruth King (illus). 6x8.5. 304pp. VG+ in dj (sl edgeworn). *My Bookhouse.* $18/£12

HESS, HANS. Lyonel Feininger. NY, (1961). Sm folio. Dj. *Swann*.* $258/£165

HESS, JOAN. Madness in Maggody. NY: St. Martin, 1991. 1st ed. Fine in Fine dj. *Janus.* $25/£16

HESS, JOAN. Malice in Maggody: An Ozarks Murder Mystery. NY: St. Martin, 1987. 1st ed. Signed. Fine (corner bump) in Fine dj. *Janus.* $50/£32

HESS, JOAN. The Murder at the Mimosa Inn. NY: St. Martin, 1986. 1st ed. Signed. Fine in dj (spine extrems sl worn). *Janus.* $50/£32

HESS, JOAN. Roll Over and Play Dead. NY: St. Martin, 1991. 1st ed. Fine in Fine dj. *Janus.* $25/£16

HESS, JOAN. Stangled Prose. NY: St. Martin's, 1986. 1st ed. Advance rev copy, sheet laid in. VF in dj. *Mordida.* $75/£48

HESS, JOAN. Strangled Prose. NY: St. Martin, 1986. 1st ed, 1st bk. Signed. Fine in dj (spine extrems sl worn). *Janus.* $65/£42

HESSE, ERICH. Narcotics and Drug Addiction. NY: Philosophical Library, 1946. 1st ed. Fine in dj (sl used). *Beasley.* $50/£32

HESSE, HERMANN. Goldmund. Peter Owen, 1959. 1st ed. VG in dj (corner sl rubbed). *Words Etc.* $117/£75

HESSE, HERMANN. In Sight of Chaos. Stephen Hudson (trans). Zurich: Verlag Seldwyla, 1923. 1st ed. Orig ptd bds. Fine. *Macdonnell.* $200/£128

HESSE, HERMANN. Journey to the East. 1956. 1st Eng ed. VG in dj (sl torn, dusty). *Words Etc.* $70/£45

HESSE, HERMANN. Klingsor's Last Summer. London, 1971. 1st ed. Dj. *Typographeum.* $16/£10

HESSE, HERMANN. Peter Camenzind. 1961. 1st ed. NF- in dj (lower panel browned). *Words Etc.* $55/£35

HESSE, HERMANN. Steppenwolf. LEC, 1977. One of 1600 signed by Helmut Ackermann (illus). 10 plts. Prospectus, LEC newsletter laid in. Black morocco-backed gray cl bds, gilt. VF in tissue dj, pub's slipcase (sl smudged). *Pirages.* $75/£48

HESTON, ALFRED M. Heston's Hand-Book. Atlantic City, 1900. 20th century souvenir ed. 38 plts, lg fldg color map (detached). Pict bds, cl spine. Good+ (worn). *Bohling.* $60/£38

HETHERINGTON, A. L. The Pottery and Porcelain Factories of China. London: Kegan Paul, 1921. 1st ed. Fldg map. Cl-backed bds. (Few spots.) *Hollett.* $55/£35

HEUBNER, P. M. and F. W. VOGT. Perpetual Health: How to Secure a New Lease of Life by the Exercise of Will Power.... NY, 1905. 4th ed. VG (extrems sl worn). *Doctor's Library.* $40/£26

HEUER, PETER and KLAUS MAURICE. European Pendulum Clocks. West Chester: Schiffer, (1988). 1st ed. Brick-red buckram. Fine in dj. *Weber.* $60/£38

HEUSINGER, EDWARD W. Early Explorations and Mission Establishments in Texas. San Antonio: Naylor, 1936. 1st ed. VF in dj (lt damp stains spine). *Gibbs.* $85/£54

HEWETT, EDGAR L. Ancient Andean Life. Indianapolis: Bobbs-Merrill, (1939). 1st ed. Frontis. Good in dj. *Archaeologia.* $65/£42

HEWETT, EDGAR L. Ancient Life in Mexico and Central America. NY: Tudor, 1943. (Spine frayed.) *Archaeologia.* $35/£22

HEWETT, EDGAR L. Ancient Life in the American Southwest. Indianapolis, 1930. 1st ed. Blue cl. VG+ in VG dj. *Five Quail.* $45/£29

HEWETT, EDGAR L. The Chaco Canyon and Its Monuments. (Albuquerque): Univ of NM, (1936). Frontis map. Navy cl. VG. *Bohling.* $50/£32

HEWETT, EDGAR L. (ed). The Fiesta Book. Santa Fe: Archaeological Inst of America, 1925. 1st ed. 2 plts. Ptd stiff wrappers (lt edgewear), else VG. *Cahan.* $100/£64

HEWETT, EDGAR L. et al. Landmarks of New Mexico. Albuquerque, 1940. 1st ed. VG in VG dj. *Turpen.* $55/£35

HEWETT, EDGAR L. et al. Mission Monuments of New Mexico. Albuquerque, 1943. 1st ed. VG+ in VG dj. *Turpen.* $85/£54

HEWITSON, WILLIAM C. Coloured Illustrations of the Eggs of British Birds.... London: Van Voorst, 1846. 60 hand-colored plts. 3/4 leather (edges rubbed, lt browning). *Metropolitan*.* $201/£129

HEWITT, E. R. Telling on the Trout. NY: Scribner, 1930. Rev ed. Frontis. VG+ in VG dj (edges chipped, torn). *Backman.* $28/£18

HEWITT, GRAILY. Lettering: for Students and Craftsmen. Seeley Service, n.d. (c. 1930). (Sl shaky), o/w Good+ in dj (worn). *Whittle.* $39/£25

HEWITT, RANDALL H. Across the Plains and Over the Divide. NY: Broadway Pub, (1906). 3rd ed. Fldg map. Later cl, leather spine label. (Outer margin 3 leaves repaired), o/w Very Nice. Howes H457. *Sadlon.* $225/£144

HEWITT, RANDALL H. Across the Plains and Over the Divide: A Mule Train Journey from East to West in 1862.... NY, (1906). Enlgd ed. Fldg map. Orig cl. Very Nice. Howes H457. *Ginsberg.* $375/£240

HEWITT, RANDALL H. Across the Plains and Over the Divide: A Mule Train Journey...1862.... NY: Broadway, (1906). 3rd ed. 59 plts, fldg map. Grn cl, pict inset. (Names), o/w Fine. Howes H457. *Harrington.* $350/£224

HEWLETT, MAURICE. Artemision. London: Elkin Mathews, 1909. Ltd to 250. Tan buckram cl. VG. *Antic Hay.* $75/£48

HEWLETT, MAURICE. Earthwork Out of Tuscany. London, 1895. 1st bk. One of 500. (Sl rubbed, faded.) *Argosy.* $50/£32

HEWLETT, MAURICE. Love and Lucy. NY: Dodd, Mead, 1916. 1st Amer ed. Dec grn cl. Fine in dj (lt used). *Antic Hay*. $45/£29

HEWLETT, MAURICE. The Song of Renny. London: Macmillan, 1911. 1st ed. Emb blue cl. VG. *Antic Hay*. $40/£26

HEWLETT, MAURICE. Songs and Meditations. Westminster: Constable, 1896. 1st ed. Buckram cl. VG. *Antic Hay*. $45/£29

HEWLETT, MAURICE. The Village Wife's Lament. London, 1918. 1st ed. Paper label. (Sl worn, lower joint cracked.) *Hatchwell*. $16/£10

HEWLETT, MAURICE. Wiltshire Essays. London, 1921. 1st ed. Dj. *Hatchwell*. $12/£8

HEWSON, ADDINELL. Earth as a Topical Application in Surgery. Phila, 1887. 2nd ed. 309pp. VG (extrems sl worn). *Doctor's Library*. $300/£192

HEWSON, WILLIAM. The Works of William Hewson. G. Gulliver (ed). Sydenham Soc, 1846. Frontis port, xlviii,360pp (prelims foxed; joints weak). *Whitehart*. $187/£120

HEWSON, WILLIAM. The Works of.... George Gulliver (ed). London: Sydenham Soc, 1846. Engr frontis port, lvi,360pp; 8 plts. Dk grn cl (rebacked preserving spine). (Sm lib stamp tp, other pp; frontis, plts lt spotted), o/w Very Clean. *White*. $101/£65

HEYER, GEORGETTE. A Blunt Instrument. NY: Doubleday, 1938. 1st Amer ed. VG in dj (worn, soiled, creased). *Metropolitan**. $109/£70

HEYER, GEORGETTE. Death in the Stocks. London: Longman's, (1935). Inscribed. (Lt soiled, sl cocked.) *Metropolitan**. $63/£40

HEYER, GEORGETTE. Why Shoot a Butler? GC: Crime Club, 1936. 1st ed. (Bkpl; soiled.) Dj (price-clipped, internal tape). *Metropolitan**. $126/£81

HEYERDAHL, THOR. American Indians in the Pacific. London: George Allen & Unwin, 1952. 1st British ed. 90 plts, 11 maps. (Sm piece cut from fep; hinges weak; brn cl soiled, worn.) *Parmer*. $150/£96

HEYERDAHL, THOR. The Art of Easter Island. GC: Doubleday, 1975. 15 color, 320 b/w plts. (Text block base sl soiled), else NF in dj (worn). *Parmer*. $175/£112

HEYGATE, JOHN. Decent Fellows. London: Gollancz/Mundanus, 1930. 1st Eng ed, 1st bk. Good in card wrappers (foxed, dusty). *Clearwater*. $39/£25

HEYLIGER, WILLIAM. The Captain of the Nine. Appleton, 1912. 1st ed. Pict cvr. Good + . *Plapinger*. $65/£42

HEYMAN, MAX L., JR. Prudent Soldier. Glendale, 1959. 1st ed. (Cvr sl worn), o/w Fine. *Pratt*. $110/£71

HEYMAN, THERESE THAU. Mirror of California: Daguerreotypes. (Oakland, CA): Oakland Museum, 1973. 1st ed. 14 plts, 6-plt fldg panorama. VG (owner stamp) in illus stiff wrappers (sl creased, rubbed). *Cahan*. $40/£26

HEYWARD, DU BOSE. Angel. NY: Doran, (1926). 1st ed. #360 of Carolina Ed signed on tipped-in colophon. Fine (bkpl) in linen-backed bds, paper label in dj (lt chipped, internal mends). *Captain's Bookshelf*. $225/£144

HEYWARD, DU BOSE. The Half Pint Flask. NY: Farrar & Rinehart, 1929. One of 175 numbered, signed by Heyward and Joseph E. Sanford (illus). Patterned bds. NF in acetate dj. *Antic Hay*. $100/£64

HEYWARD, DU BOSE. Lost Morning. NY: Farrar & Rinehart, (1936). 1st ed. Maroon cl, gilt. Fine in Nice dj (spine faded). *Macdonnell*. $45/£29

HEYWARD, DU BOSE. Skylines and Horizons. NY, 1924. 1st Amer ed, 1st bk. Fine (name stamp, professionally mended tear; spine sl sunned, extrems sl rubbed). *Polyanthos*. $50/£32

HEYWOOD, GERALD G. P. Charles Cotton and His River. Manchester, 1928. Frontis. Blind-stamped cl (spine sl chipped, label; ex-lib, ink stamps, bkpl). *Edwards*. $94/£60

HEYWOOD, V. H. (ed). Flowering Plants of the World. NY: Mayflower, 1978. 1st US ed. VG in dj. *Archer*. $50/£32

HIAASEN, CARL and WILLIAM D. MONTALBANO. Powder Burn. NY: Atheneum, 1981. 1st ed. Fine in dj. *Mordida*. $300/£192

HIAASEN, CARL. Double Whammy. NY: Putnam, (1987). 1st ed. Signed. Fine in dj. *Between The Covers*. $100/£64

HIAASEN, CARL. Double Whammy. NY: Putnam, 1987. 1st ed. VF in dj. *Mordida*. $90/£58

HIAASEN, CARL. Native Tongue. NY: Knopf, 1991. 1st ed. Signed. VF in dj. *Mordida*. $45/£29

HIAASEN, CARL. Native Tongue. NY: Knopf, 1991. 1st ed. Fine in dj. *Lame Duck*. $45/£29

HIAASEN, CARL. Skin Tight. NY: Putnam, (1989). 1st ed. Fine in dj. *Between The Covers*. $65/£42

HIAASEN, CARL. Skin Tight. NY: Putnam, 1989. 1st ed. Signed. VF in dj. *Mordida*. $50/£32

HIAASEN, CARL. Tourist Season. NY: Putnam, (1986). 1st ed. Fine in NF dj (corner fr panel sl worn). *Bernard*. $125/£80

HIBBARD, HOWARD. Caravaggio. Thames & Hudson, 1983. 1st UK ed. (Sl worn.) *Edwards*. $39/£25

HIBBEN, FRANK C. Hunting American Bears. Phila: Lippincott, 1950. 1st ed. VG + in dj. *Bowman*. $55/£35

HIBBERD, SHIRLEY. The Amateur's Greenhouse and Conservatory. London: Groombridge, 1875. 2nd ed. (ii),272pp (lt spotted); 6 fldg color plts (sl creased). Dec cl (sl worn), gilt. Good. *Ash*. $117/£75

HIBBERD, SHIRLEY. The Floral World and Garden Guide. London: Groombridge, 1869. viii,376pp (tp loose; 1st/last few ll lt foxed, hinge broken); 12 chromolitho plts (all but 1 Clean). *Quest*. $110/£71

HIBBERD, SHIRLEY. Profitable Gardening. London: Groombridge, n.d. (1876). New ed. iv,296pp + ads. Gilt-stamped cvr. Fine. *Quest*. $40/£26

HIBBERD, SHIRLEY. The Sea Weed Collector. London: Groombridge, (1872). vii,152 + 16pp ads; 8 color plts (1 signed by A. F. Lydon). Aeg. Gilt-dec pict cvr (extrems rubbed, hinges strengthened). Attractive. *Quest*. $90/£58

HICHBORN, PHILIP. Report on European Dock-Yards. Washington, 1889. 3/4 leather (rubbed). *Oinonen**. $50/£32

HICHENS, ROBERT. Egypt and Its Monuments. NY: Century, 1908. Color frontis. Teg. Gilt-pict cl (bds sl soiled). *Archaeologia*. $85/£54

HICKEN, VICTOR. Illinois in the Civil War. Urbana, (1960). 1st ed. VG. *Pratt*. $32/£21

HICKEY, J. J. A Guide to Bird Watching. London: Oxford, 1943. 1st ed. Silver dec cl. VG. *Mikesh*. $25/£16

HICKEY, WILLIAM. Memoirs. Alfred Spencer (ed). Hurst & Blackett, 1948. 4 vols. Good set in djs (lt spotted, sl frayed). *Cox*. $39/£25

HICKMAN, WILLIAM. Brigham's Destroying Angel. NY, 1872. 1st ed. 219pp + ads; port. Later plain cl (dull). *King*. $125/£80

HIEOVER, HARRY. The Pocket and the Stud. London, 1848. Frontis, xvi,215pp + 32pp pub's cat. Contemp calf-backed cl, gilt device. (Bds lt damp-spotted, calf discolored, sl worn, sl loss to tail.) *Edwards*. $39/£25

HIGGINS, CHESTER, JR. Drums of Life. GC: Anchor/Doubleday, 1974. 1st ed. VG in pict stiff wrappers (lt rubbed, corner crease). *Cahan*. $45/£29

HIGGINS, GEORGE V. Cogan's Trade. NY: Knopf, 1974. 1st ed. Fine in NF dj. *Janus*. $25/£16

HIGGINS, GEORGE V. The Friends of Eddie Coyle. NY: Knopf, 1972. 1st ed, 1st bk. Grn cl. NF (edges sl faded) in dj. *Antic Hay*. $35/£22

HIGGINS, GODFREY. The Celtic Druids. London, 1827. 1st ed. Presentation copy. 4to. Full black calf (rebound). Fine. *Old London*. $750/£481

HIGGINS, JACK. Cold Harbour. London: Heinemann, 1990. 1st ed. VF in dj. *Mordida*. $45/£29

HIGGINS, JACK. The Last Place God Made. NY: Holt, Rinehart & Winston, 1971. 1st Amer ed. Fine in dj. *Mordida*. $65/£42

HIGGINS, JACK. Luciano's Luck. NY: Stein & Day, (1981). Fine in dj. *Between The Covers*. $45/£29

HIGGINS, JACK. Storm Warning. London: Collins, 1976. 1st ed. Inscribed. Fine in dj. *Mordida*. $75/£48

HIGGINS, R. A. Greek and Roman Jewellery. London, 1961. 1st ed. Color frontis, 67 plts (3 color). Dj (sl chipped, spine lt faded). *Edwards*. $39/£25

HIGGINSON, A. HENRY and JULIAN INGERSOLL CHAMBERLAIN. The Hunts of the United States and Canada, Their Masters, Hounds and Histories. Boston, 1908. Ltd to 500. Red cl, gilt. *Petersfield*. $47/£30

HIGGINSON, T. W. Army Life in a Black Regiment. Time-Life, 1982. As New in As New dj. *Pratt*. $30/£19

HIGGINSON, T. W. Part of a Man's Life. Boston: Houghton Mifflin, 1905. 1st ed. Maroon cl, gilt. (Few mks), else Fine. BAL 8472. *Macdonnell*. $75/£48

HIGGINSON, T. W. Women and Men. NY: Harper, 1888. 1st ed. 326pp. Pub's cl. Very Nice. BAL 8354. *Second Life*. $125/£80

HIGHAM, CHARLES. The Adventures of Conan Doyle. NY: Norton, (1976). 1st US ed. VG in VG dj (lt wear). *Gravesend*. $30/£19

HIGHSMITH, PATRICIA. Little Tales of Misogyny. 1977. 1st Eng ed. Rev slip loosely inserted. VG in dj (creased). *Words Etc*. $19/£12

HIGHSMITH, PATRICIA. Plotting and Writing Suspense Fiction. Boston: The Writer, 1966. 1st ed. NF in dj (lt worn; tear spine foot). *Beasley*. $65/£42

HIGHSMITH, PATRICIA. The Talented Mr. Ripley. London: Cresset, 1957. VG in dj (sl torn, dusty). *Gekoski*. $195/£125

HIGHTON, HUGH P. Shooting Trips in Europe and Algeria. London: Witherby, 1921. 1st ed. Brn cl. Fine in dj (torn). *Terramedia*. $150/£96

HIGHTOWER, JOHN. Pheasant Hunting. NY, 1946. Ltd to 350 w/extra color plt, signed. Cl-backed bds. VG. *Truepenny*. $300/£192

HIGHWATER, JAMAKE. I Wear the Morning Star. NY: Harper & Row, 1986. 1st ed. 6 x 9 1/4. 148pp. Cl spine. Fine in dj. *Cattermole*. $15/£10

HIJUELOS, OSCAR. The Mambo Kings Play Songs of Love. NY: FSG, (1989). 1st ed. Red cl (sl rubbed), gilt. NF in dj. *Blue Mountain*. $25/£16

HIJUELOS, OSCAR. Our House in the Last World. NY: Persea, 1983. 1st ed, 1st bk. Fine in dj. *Lame Duck*. $100/£64

HILBERT, A. and W. ACKERMANN. Principles of Mathematical Logic. Chelsea, 1950. VG. *Bookcell*. $38/£24

HILBERT, T. The Air Gun. Methuen, (1902). 1st ed. #3 in 'The Little Blue Books' series. Sm 8vo. 190pp; 4 illus by A. H. Buckland. Bkpl of Sybil Corbet. Illus blue cl. VG. *Bookmark*. $23/£15

HILDEBRAND, SAMUEL S. Autobiography of Samuel S. Hildebrand.... Jefferson City, MO, 1870. 312pp; 8 plts. (Foxed; spine ends chipped, extrems frayed), else VG. Howes H470. *Reese*. $450/£288

HILDRETH, R. The White Slave. London, 1852. 15th thousand. 302pp. Reading copy. *King*. $25/£16

HILDRETH, SAMUEL P. Contributions to the Early History of the North-West, Including the Moravian Missions in Ohio. Cincinnati: Hitchcock, (1864). 1st ed. 240pp (lacks fep). *Ginsberg*. $175/£112

HILEY, MICHAEL. Frank Sutcliffe. 1974. Frontis port, 64 b/w plts. (Bkpl.) Dj. *Edwards*. $117/£75

HILEY, MICHAEL. Frank Sutcliffe: Photographer of Whitby. Boston: Godine, 1974. 1st ed. Frontis port, 64 plts (Owner stamp), else NF in pict stiff wrappers. *Cahan*. $85/£54

HILEY, MICHAEL. Seeing Through Photographs. London: Gordon Fraser, 1983. 1st ed. VG in pict stiff wrappers. *Cahan*. $25/£16

HILEY, MICHAEL. Victorian Working Women. Boston: David R. Godine, 1980. 1st US ed. VG. *Cahan*. $30/£19

HILL, A. W. (ed). Henry Nicholson Ellacombe...a Memoir. London, 1919. (Sl crease fr cvr.) *Maggs*. $50/£32

HILL, AGNES LEONARD. The Colorado Blue Book. Denver: James R. Ives, 1892. 237pp. (Shelfwear.) *Dumont*. $175/£112

HILL, ALICE. Tales of the Colorado Pioneers. Denver: Pierson & Gardner, 1884. 319pp. VG. Howes H480. *Perier*. $95/£61

HILL, ALICE. Tales of the Colorado Pioneers. Denver: Pierson & Gardner, 1884. 1st ed. 320pp. Brn cl (lt rubbed). *Karmiole*. $125/£80

HILL, BRIAN. Julia Margaret Cameron: A Victorian Family Portrait. NY: St. Martin's, 1973. 1st US ed. 22 full-pg photos. (Owner stamp), else Fine in NF dj. *Cahan*. $45/£29

HILL, CAROL. Subsistence U.S.A. NY: Holt, Rinehart & Winston, 1973. 1st ed. Bruce Davidson (photos). (Owner stamp), else NF in illus stiff wrappers. *Cahan*. $25/£16

HILL, CECILIA. Moorish Towns in Spain. London, 1931. 1st ed. (Spine sl faded.) *Edwards*. $23/£15

HILL, D. and O. GRABAR. Islamic Architecture and Its Decoration. Faber, 1967. 2nd enlgd ed. 4 color plts. (Lib stamp tp, 2 margins), else Good. *Ars Artis*. $78/£50

HILL, FREDERICK TREVOR. Lincoln the Lawyer. NY: Century, 1906. Working copy (worn, rubbed; rear hinge cracked). *Boswell*. $75/£48

HILL, G. F. Pisanello. London, 1905. 74 plts hors texte. (Lacks fep; cl rubbed.) *Washton*. $35/£22

HILL, GEOFFREY. Somewhere Is Such a Kingdom. Boston: Houghton Mifflin, 1975. 1st ed. Fine in dj (fold sl rubbed). *Jaffe*. $150/£96

HILL, GEOFFREY. Tenebrae. (London): Deutsch, (1978). 1st ed. VF in dj. *Jaffe*. $65/£42

HILL, J. E. and J. D. SMITH. Bats: A Natural History. Adelaide: Rigby, 1984. 1st ed. Fine in Fine dj. *Mikesh*. $50/£32

HILL, JASON. The Contemplative Gardner. London: Faber & Faber, (1940). 1st ed. 22 plts by John Nash. VG (eps tanned, foxed) in dj (tanned, nicked). *Reese*. $25/£16

HILL, JASPER. The Letters of a Young Miner...1849-1852. SF: John Howell-Books, 1964. Frontis, fldg map tipped inside rear cvr. Dec bds, simulated morocco spine, ptd paper label. Fine. *Pacific**. $86/£55

HILL, JIM DAN. The Texas Navy. Chicago, 1937 (i.e., 1950). Inscribed, signed. True 1st ed, w/limitation slip indicating that 450 copies were distributed. Dj. Howes H485. *Swann**. $172/£110

HILL, JOE, JR. and OLA DAVIS HILL. In Little America with Byrd. Boston: Ginn, c. 1937. Double-pg map. Dec cl (Bkpl removed), else VG. *High Latitude*. $30/£19

HILL, JOHN H. Princess Malah. Washington: Associated Pubs, (1933). 1st ed. (Eps foxed; fr gutter 2 sm gouges), else NF in VG dj (chip rear panel, spine lt spotted). *Between The Covers.* $575/£369

HILL, JOSEPH J. The History of Warner's Ranch and Its Environs. L.A., 1927. 1st trade ed. #163/1000. Signed, inscribed. Map. (Faint dampstain feps to p3), o/w VG. No dj as issued. Howes H486. *Turpen.* $80/£51

HILL, JOSEPH J. The History of Warner's Ranch and Its Environs. L.A.: Privately ptd, 1927. 1st trade ed. One of 1300. 2 ports, 9 plts. Red buckram (lt shelfwear). Howes H486. *Parmer.* $125/£80

HILL, LORNA. The Little Dancer. Thos Nelson, 1957. 1st Amer ed. Genevieve Vaughan-Jackson (illus). 5.5x8.5. 151pp. VG (sl soiled) in dj (edgeworn). *My Bookhouse.* $14/£9

HILL, M. Bruno Liljefors: The Peerless Eye. Kingston: Allen, 1987. 1st ed. Fine in Fine dj. *Mikesh.* $125/£80

HILL, NORMAN NEWELL. History of Knox County, Ohio. Mt. Vernon, OH: A.A. Graham, 1881. Frontis map, 854pp, 2pp errata (tp repaired, lib blindstamp 4 ll); 49 ports, 22 views (3 dbl), 6 plts. 3/4 leather (recased, retaining orig bds, new backstrip). *Bohling.* $120/£77

HILL, PAUL and THOMAS COOPER (eds). Dialogue with Photography. NY: FSG, 1979. 1st ed. Fine in dj. *Cahan.* $40/£26

HILL, R. T. Geography and Geology of the Black and Grand Prairies, Texas. Washington, 1901. 5 maps in pocket, 64 plts (lacks 2 maps). New cl. Good. *Henly.* $101/£65

HILL, REGINALD. Another Death in Venice. London: Collins, 1976. 1st UK ed. VG (ink name) in Good+ dj (sl rubbed, chipped). *Williams.* $70/£45

HILL, REGINALD. An April Shroud. London: Collins, 1975. 1st UK ed. VG+ in VG dj (sl rubbed, few nicks strengthened to rear). *Williams.* $195/£125

HILL, REGINALD. Bones and Silence. London: Collins, 1990. 1st ed. Fine in NF dj (price-clipped). *Janus.* $30/£19

HILL, REGINALD. A Fairly Dangerous Thing. London: CCC, 1972. 1st ed. VG in dj (price-clipped). *Mordida.* $150/£96

HILL, REGINALD. Fell of Dark. London: Collins, 1971. 1st UK ed. VG in dj (bottom edge sl creased). *Williams.* $156/£100

HILL, REGINALD. A Killing Kindness. London: CCC, 1980. 1st ed. Fine in dj (sl wear, closed crease-tear fr panel). *Mordida.* $85/£54

HILL, REGINALD. No Man's Land. London, 1985. 1st ed. Dj. *Typographeum.* $40/£26

HILL, REGINALD. One Small Step. London: CCC, 1990. 1st ed. VF in dj. *Mordida.* $45/£29

HILL, REGINALD. Pascoe's Ghost. London: Collins, 1979. 1st UK ed. NF in dj. *Williams.* $101/£65

HILL, REGINALD. The Spy's Wife. London, 1980. 1st ed. Dj. *Typographeum.* $40/£26

HILL, REGINALD. Who Guards a Prince. London: Collins, 1982. 1st UK ed. NF in dj. *Williams.* $47/£30

HILL, ROY. 49 Poems. Manhattan, KS: AG Press, (1968). 1st ed. Gilt fabricoid. Fine in VG dj (rubbed). *Reese.* $30/£19

HILL, RUTH BEEBE. Hanta Yo. GC: Doubleday, 1979. 1st ed. VG in VG dj. *Perier.* $30/£19

HILL, RUTH BEEBE. Hanta Yo. NY: Doubleday, 1979. 1st ed. VG in dj. *Lien.* $35/£22

HILL, S. S. Travels in Peru and Mexico. London: Longman, Green, 1860. 1st ed. 2 vols. xiii,(i)blank,330; xii,312pp, 1/2-titles. (Foxed, waterstaining affecting 2nd half vol 1.) Contemp 1/2 roan, marbled bds (spine ends worn, cvrs vol 1 waterstained, paper worn away in places). *Morrell.* $250/£160

HILL, SARAH JANE FULL. Mrs. Hill's Journal—Civil War Reminiscences. Mark M. Krug (ed). Chicago: Lakeside, 1980. Fldg map. Teg. Fine. *Cahan.* $20/£13

HILL, SUSAN. The Bird of Night. Hamish Hamilton, (1972). 1st ed. Nice in dj. *Ash.* $31/£20

HILL, W. B. Experience of a Pioneer Evangelist of the Northwest. (N.p.: The Author, 1902.) 1st ed. Dec cl. *Ginsberg.* $125/£80

HILL, W. B. Experiences of a Pioneer Minister of Minnesota. Minneapolis: J.A. Folsom, 1892. 185pp. Black cl (sl worn, spotted, spine top frayed). *Bohling.* $65/£42

HILL-TOUT, C. The Native Races of the British Empire, British North America I. Toronto, 1907. Frontis. Good (lt foxed, inner hinges sl cracked; sl rubbed). *Reese.* $100/£64

HILLARY, EDMUND. High Adventure. London, 1955. 1st ed. Signed. Color frontis, 31 plts. Dj (ragged). *Edwards.* $39/£25

HILLEARY, WILLIAM M. A Webfoot Volunteer. Corvallis: OR State Univ, (1965). 1st ed. Fine in Fine dj. *Perier.* $35/£22

HILLER, L. Surgery Through the Ages: A Pictorial Chronicle. NY, 1944. 1st ed. VG. *Fye.* $75/£48

HILLERMAN, TONY and ERNIE BULOW. Words, Weather and Wolfmen. Gallup: Southwesterner/Books, 1989. 1st ed. One of 350 numbered, signed by Hillerman, Franklin and Bulow. VF in dj. *Mordida.* $125/£80

HILLERMAN, TONY. The Blessing Way. NY: Harper & Row, (1970). 1st ed, 1st bk. Cl-backed bds. (Sm piece tape rep), else NF in dj (sl scuffed, spine faded, surface lift to corner of flaps). *Waverly*.* $385/£247

HILLERMAN, TONY. The Boy Who Made Dragonfly. NY: Harper & Row, 1972. 1st ed. Laszlo Kubinyi (illus). 5 1/2 x 8 1/4. 86pp. Good (ex-lib, mks). *Cattermole.* $25/£16

HILLERMAN, TONY. Dance Hall of the Dead. London: Pluton, (1973). 1st British ed. Fine in dj (edgeworn). *Metropolitan*.* $44/£28

HILLERMAN, TONY. Dance Hall of the Dead. NY: Harper & Row, (1973). 1st ed. Cl-backed bds. Fine (lt paper clip imp prelims, fr jacket panel) in dj (sl soiled). *Waverly*.* $357/£229

HILLERMAN, TONY. The Dark Wind. Harper, 1982. 1st ed. Fine in dj. *Murder By The Book.* $125/£80

HILLERMAN, TONY. The Dark Wind. NY: Harper & Row, 1982. 1st ed. Fine in dj (sm crease inner fr flap). *Mordida.* $150/£96

HILLERMAN, TONY. The Ghostway. San Diego: Dennis McMillan, 1984. 1st ed. One of 300 numbered, signed. NF in NF dj. *Metropolitan*.* $212/£136

HILLERMAN, TONY. The Great Taos Bank Robbery. Albuquerque: Univ of NM, 1973. 1st ed. (Sm Library of Congress stamp fep), o/w Fine in dj w/2 pictures on back panel. *Mordida.* $450/£288

HILLERMAN, TONY. Talking God. NY: Harper & Row, 1989. 1st ed. VF in dj. *Mordida.* $35/£22

HILLERMAN, TONY. A Thief of Time. NY: Harper & Row, 1988. 1st ed. VF in dj. *Mordida.* $40/£26

HILLES, FREDERICK W. (ed). New Light on Dr. Johnson: Essays on the Occasion of His 250th Birthday. New Haven: Yale, 1959. 1st ed. VG. *Reese.* $30/£19

HILLIER, BEVIS. Victorian Studio Photographs. Boston: David R. Godine, 1976. NF in VG dj. *Cahan.* $35/£22

HILLIER, J. H. Catalogue of the Japanese Paintings and Prints in the Collection of Mr. and Mrs. Richard Gale. (London): Routledge & Kegan Paul, 1970. 1st ed. 2 vols. NF set in pub's slipcase (worn, stained). *Hermitage*. $150/£96

HILLIER, J. H. Japanese Prints and Drawings from the Vever Collection. (NY): Rizzoli/Sotheby, 1976. One of 2000 numbered sets. 3 vols. Fine in djs (sl edge-crimped). *Waverly**. $143/£92

HILLIER, MARY. The History of Wax Dolls. Souvenir, 1985. Dj. *Edwards*. $31/£20

HILLS, G. The Edwin J. Beinecke Collection of Robert Louis Stevenson. NY, 1939. Red cl. (Bk label.) *Maggs*. $19/£12

HILLS, JOHN WALLER. River Keeper. Bless, (1934). 1st ed. (Back faded.) *Petersfield*. $78/£50

HILLS, JOHN WALLER. A Summer on the Test. Geoffrey Bles, 1946. 3rd ed. Mod 1/2 grn morocco, marbled sides. *Petersfield*. $62/£40

HILLS, LEON C. History and Legends of Place Names in Iowa. Omaha: Omaha School Supply, 1937. (Sl worn), else Good in stiff pict wraps. *Brown*. $12/£8

HILLYARD, M. D. Peggy and the Giant's Aunt. A&C Black, 1921. 1st ed. 4to. 64pp; 9 (of 10) sepia plts. Buff bds, pict onlay. (Spine chipped), else VG. *Bookmark*. $34/£22

HILLYER, ROBERT. Poems for Music 1917-1947. NY: Knopf, 1947. 1st ed. (Pastedowns dknd), else VG in dj. *Reese*. $20/£13

HILPRECHT, H. V. Exploration in Bible Lands During the 19th Century. Edinburgh: T&T Clark, 1903. 4 fldg maps in fr, rear pockets. Teg. Gilt-pict cl. Good. *Archaeologia*. $150/£96

HILTON, EDWARD. The Tourist's Guide to Lucknow. By One of the Beleaguered Garrison. Lucknow, 1913. 8th ed. Frontis, 14 plts (1 missing from those called for), 1 extra unlisted plt, fldg plan, 2 loose plans (one, a lg fldg map of Lucknow, not called for). Cl-backed ptd cream bds (sl worn). *Maggs*. $187/£120

HILTON, GEORGE W. The Great Lakes Car Ferries. Berkeley, CA, 1962. 1st ed. VG in dj. *King*. $65/£42

HILTON, GEORGE W. and JOHN F. DUE. The Electric Interurban Railways in America. Stanford: Stanford Univ, 1960. 1st ed. Pict cl. Fine in NF dj. *Harrington*. $55/£35

HILTON, JAMES. Good-Bye, Mr. Chips. Boston, 1934. 1st Amer ed. Fine (sm date stamp; spine extrems sl rubbed) in dj (sm tear fr panel, spine sl soiled). *Polyanthos*. $150/£96

HILTON, JAMES. Good-Bye, Mr. Chips. Boston: Little Brown, 1935. Birthday ed. One of 600 numbered, signed by Hilton and H.M. Brock (illus). Fine in slipcase (sl wear, dkng). *Lenz*. $100/£64

HILTON, JAMES. Goodbye, Mr. Chips. Boston: Little, Brown, 1934. 1st ed. (Bkpl under flap), else Fine in dj. *Captain's Bookshelf*. $150/£96

HILTON, JAMES. Goodbye, Mr. Chips. NY, 1935. One of 600 numbered, signed by Hilton and H. M. Brock (illus). Vellum-backed bds. VG. *Argosy*. $65/£42

HILTON, WILLIAM HAYES. Sketches in the Southwest and Mexico 1858-1877. L.A.: Dawson's, 1963. Cl-backed bds, ptd spine label. Fine. *Bohling*. $35/£22

HIMES, CHESTER. A Case of Rape. NY: Targ Editions, (1980). One of 350 signed. Fine in Fine tissue dj. *Lenz*. $100/£64

HIMES, CHESTER. A Case of Rape. Washington: Howard Univ, (1984). 1st trade ed. Fine in Fine dj. *Murder By The Book*. $35/£22

HIMES, CHESTER. A Case of Rape. NY: Targ Editions, 1980. 1st ed. One of 350 signed. VF in dj, tissue dust wrapper. *Mordida*. $135/£87

HIMES, CHESTER. A Case of Rape. Washington: Howard Univ, 1984. 1st Amer trade ed. Fine in dj. *Between The Covers*. $75/£48

HIMES, CHESTER. Cast the First Stone. NY: Coward-McCann, (1952). 1st ed. (Fore-edge sl stain), else Fine in Fine dj. *Between The Covers*. $300/£192

HIMES, CHESTER. Cast the First Stone. NY: Coward-McCann, 1952. 1st ed. Cl-backed paper over bds. (Sl dknd top edge), else Fine in dj (lt wear spine ends; dkng rear top edge). *Cahan*. $150/£96

HIMES, CHESTER. The Crazy Kill. NY: Avon, (1959). 1st ed. VG in pict wraps. *King*. $40/£26

HIMES, CHESTER. The Heat's On. NY: Putnam, 1966. 1st ed. Fine in dj (rubbed, lt worn, tear). *Else Fine*. $85/£54

HIMES, CHESTER. Hot Day Hot Night. (NY): Dell, (1970). 1st ed w/this title. (Pg edges browned), else NF in wrappers. *Between The Covers*. $50/£32

HIMES, CHESTER. If He Hollers Let Him Go. GC: Doubleday, 1945. VG in dj (soiled, short tears, chipped; lg chip back flap). *Metropolitan**. $230/£147

HIMES, CHESTER. If He Hollers Let Him Go. GC: Doubleday, Doran, 1945. 1st ed, 1st bk. (Fore-edge, eps sl foxing), else NF in VG- dj (spine extrems lt loss, corners worn). *Between The Covers*. $375/£240

HIMES, CHESTER. Lonely Crusade. NY, 1947. 1st Amer ed. NF (bkpl; spine sl rubbed) in dj (sm edge chips, tears, lt rubbed). *Polyanthos*. $110/£71

HIMES, CHESTER. The Quality of Hurt. GC: Doubleday, 1972. 1st ed. Fine in Fine dj (lt rubbed). *Between The Covers*. $125/£80

HINCKLEY, EDITH PARKER. On the Banks of the Zanja. Claremont: Saunders, 1951. Gold-stamped orange cl. Dj (edgewear, sunning). *Dawson*. $30/£19

HIND, ARTHUR M. Catalogue of Early Italian Engravings Preserved in the Department of Prints and Drawings in the British Museum. London, 1910. 2 vols. *Swann**. $402/£258

HIND, ARTHUR M. A History of Engraving and Etching from the 15th Century to the Year 1914. London, 1923. (Sl worn.) *Oinonen**. $60/£38

HIND, ARTHUR M. A History of Engraving and Etching. Boston/NY: Houghton Mifflin, 1923. Teg. Red linen. *Appelfeld*. $100/£64

HIND, ARTHUR M. Wenceslaus Hollar. London: John Lane, Bodley Head, 1922. 1st ed. Frontis. Teg, uncut. Buckram gilt. (Fep browned), o/w Fine. *Hollett*. $187/£120

HIND, C. LEWIS. Authors and I. NY: John Lane, 1921. 1st ed. VF in VF dj (nick). *Between The Covers*. $150/£96

HIND, C. LEWIS. More Author's and I. NY: Dodd Mead, 1922. 1st ed. Fine in dj. *Between The Covers*. $150/£96

HINDE, G. J. Catalogue of the Fossil Sponges in the Geological Department of the British Museum.... London, 1883. Inscribed. viii,248pp; 38 plts. (Rebacked.) *Henly*. $94/£60

HINDLEY, CHARLES. The History of the Catnach Press. London: Charles Hindley, 1886. Paper labels fr cvr, spine. VG (sl foxed) in dj (edgeworn, foxed, soiled; tape repairs). *Waverly**. $71/£46

HINE, ALFRED. Magnestic Compasses and Magnetometers. London, 1968. (Upper hinge sl cracked.) Dj (chipped). *Edwards*. $39/£25

HINE, REGINALD L. The Cream of Curiosity. London: Routledge, 1920. 1st ed. (Lib label pastedown, stamp reverse tp, marginal blind-stamps; extrems rubbed.) *Hollett*. $47/£30

HINE, REGINALD L. Relics of an Un-Common Attorney. London: J.M. Dent, 1951. *Boswell*. $35/£22

HINES, GORDON. Alfalfa Bill, an Intimate Biography. Oklahoma City, 1932. (Name ep; upper 1/2 fr hinge cracked, spine faded.) Bohling. $15/£10

HINES, GUSTAVUS. Life on the Plains of the Pacific. Oregon: Its History, Condition and Prospects. NY, 1857. Pub's cl (backstrip faded). Howes H505. Swann*. $69/£44

HINES, H. K. Missionary History of the Pacific Northwest, Containing the Wonderful Story of Jason Lee.... Portland, (1899). 1st ed. Signed presentation. 510pp. Ginsberg. $85/£54

HINKS, ROGER. Myth and Allegory in Ancient Art. London: Warburg Inst, 1939. 32 plts hors-texte. (Interior sl spotted; spine sl soiled), o/w Fine. Europa. $94/£60

HINKSON, KATHARINE TYNAN. Cuckoo Songs. London: Elkin Mathews & John Lane, 1894. 1st ed. Ltd to 500 ptd. Fore/bottom edges untrimmed. Rose cl bds (spine faded, bumped), gilt. VG. Hermitage. $150/£96

HINMAN, C. The Printing and Proof-Reading of the First Folio of Shakespeare. OUP, 1963. 2 vols. VG set in djs. Moss. $172/£110

HINMAN, WILBUR F. Further Mishaps of Si Klegg and Shorty. WA, 1898. 448pp. (Cvr worn, few pp torn, stained.) Pratt. $15/£10

HINTON, A. HORSLEY. Practical Pictorial Photography. London: Hazell, Watson, & Viney, 1898. 1st ed. 2 parts in 1. 69; 108pp. Gilt-titled cl. Fine. Cahan. $150/£96

HINTON, PERCIVAL. Eden Phillpotts: A Bibliography of First Editions. Birmingham: Greville Worthington, 1931. Ltd to 350 numbered, signed by Phillpotts. Frontis photogravure port. White cl, brn bds, gilt spine. Fine. Karmiole. $85/£54

HINTON, S. E. The Outsiders. NY: Viking, (1967). 1st ed, 1st bk. (Ink name), else VG in Good dj (nicked, creased tears). Reese. $85/£54

Hints to Parents. Salem: Whipple & Lawrence, 1825. 1st US ed? 72pp. Good (ex-lib, bkpl) in ptd wraps (sl chipped). Second Life. $45/£29

HIPKINS, A. J. Musical Instruments Historic, Rare and Unique. London: A&C Black, 1921. Rpt of 1888 orig ed. 48 full-pg color plts. White/maroon cl (sl soiled), gilt. Karmiole. $375/£240

HIPKINS, A. J. Musical Instruments. London: A&C Black, 1921. 40 color plts. Buckram-backed cl gilt (sl mkd, upper hinge splitting, upper joint cracking). Hollett. $187/£120

HIPKISS, EDWIN J. Eighteenth-Century American Arts. Cambridge: Harvard Univ, 1941. 1st ed. Navy cl (sl shelfworn, lt bumped), gilt. Very Nice. Baltimore*. $210/£135

HIPPOCRATES. The Genuine Works of Hippocrates. Francis Adams (trans). London, 1849. 1st ed. 2 vols. 874pp + plts. (Spine chipped), o/w Fine set. Fye. $300/£192

HIPPOCRATES. The Genuine Works.... Francis Adams (trans). Balt: Williams & Wilkins, (1946). Frontis, 8 plts. Textured cl. Fine. Glaser. $75/£48

HIPPOCRATES. The Medical Works of Hippocrates. Springfield, 1950. 1st ed. VG. Fye. $75/£48

HIPPOCRATES. On Intercourse and Pregnancy. Tage Ellinger (trans). NY, 1952. 1st ed in English. VG. Fye. $100/£64

HIRSCH, AUGUST. Handbook of Geographical and Historical Pathology. Charles Creighton (trans). London: New Sydenham Soc, 1883/85/86. 3 vols. xvii,710; xii,681; xv,780pp. Brn cl (all vols rebacked, spines laid down). VG set. White. $101/£65

HIRSCH, NATHANIEL. Genius and Creative Intelligence. Cambridge, (MA): Sci-Art, 1931. 1st ed. Inscribed. Ptd panelled blue cl (edges bumped). VG. Gach. $50/£32

HIRSCH, SIDNEY M. The Fire Regained. NY: Knickerbocker Press/Putnam, 1913. 1st ed. Frontis. Gilt cl. (Sl rubbing, few lt spots to cl), o/w Very Nice. Reese. $225/£144

HIRSCHFELD, AL. Harlem as Seen by Hirschfeld. NY: Hyperion, 1941. #771/1000. 24 Good color lithos. (Soiled, bumped, spine off.) Metropolitan*. $1,400/£897

HIRSCHFELD, AL. The World of Hirschfeld. NY: Abrams, (1969). 1st ed. 32 color plts. White cl (sl dknd edges). VG in dj. Cahan. $125/£80

HIRSCHFELDER, J. O. et al (eds). The Effects of Atomic Weapons. 1950. (Sticker removal fr pastedown, fep; stamp; spine ends sl defective, lib #s, cvr sl discolored), o/w VG. Whitehart. $23/£15

HIRSCHMAN, LOUIS J. Handbook of Diseases of the Rectum. St. Louis: Mosby, 1917. 2nd ed. 4 color plts. (Notes rear pastedown, blank; text mks.) Goodrich. $35/£22

HIRST, BARTON COOKE and GEORGE A. PIERSOL. Human Monstrosities. Phila: Lea Brothers, 1891-93. 1st and only ed. 4 vols. 39 photo plts, 123 text woodcuts. (Private and institutional bkpl each vol; spine ends sl worn; vol 3 rebacked w/tape). VG set. Glaser. $1,500/£962

HIRST, STEPHEN. Life in a Narrow Place. NY, 1976. 1st ed, 2nd ptg. Yellow cl. Fine in VG dj. Five Quail. $45/£29

HISLOP, HERBERT R. Englishman's Arizona: The Ranching Letters...1876-1878. Tucson: Overland, 1965. Ltd to 510. VF. Truepenny. $125/£80

Hisperica Famina. SF: Privately ptd, 1974. One of 400 ptd by Andrew Hoyem. Cl-backed patterned bds. Swann*. $57/£37

HISSEY, JAMES JOHN. Across England in a Dog-Cart from London to St. David's and Back. Richard Bentley, 1891. 1st ed. Frontis (sm waterstain top margin), xvi,413pp + ad leaf; fldg map, 16 full-pg illus. Good (lt browned). Cox. $39/£25

HISSEY, JAMES JOHN. On Southern English Roads. Richard Bentley, 1896. 1st ed. xvi,420pp; fldg map, 16 full-pg wood engrs. Sound (speckled fading). Cox. $39/£25

HISSEY, JAMES JOHN. Through Ten English Counties. Richard Bentley, 1894. 1st ed. xvi,406pp + ad leaf; fldg map, 16 full-pg illus. Good (backstrip gilt faded). Cox. $39/£25

HISSEY, JAMES JOHN. Untravelled England. Macmillan, 1906. 1st ed. 24 plts. (Stamp rear pastedown; lt shaken.) Blue cl (worn). Cox. $23/£15

Historical Description of the Monastery and Chapel Royal of Holyroodhouse. Edinburgh, 1819. 118pp (tp browned, inner fr hinge cello-tape repaired), 8 plts, map. 1/2 leather, marbled bds (rubbed, spine top torn). King. $75/£48

History and Adventures of an Atom. (By Tobias Smollett.) London: Robinson & Roberts, 1769. 1st ed. 2 vols. Marbled eps. Sprinkled calf (worn, fr cvr vol 1 detached; bkpls), gilt by Tout; 3 labels. Internally Fine. Pirages. $300/£192

History and Description of the Baltimore and Ohio Rail Road.... (By William P. Smith.) Balt: John Murphy, 1853. 1st ed. 200pp (sl aged); lg fldg b/w litho map at frontis (sm tears), 5 engr ports (lacks that of Philip E. Thomas). Dk brn blind cl (lt worn, spine lt sunned, frayed). Baltimore*. $200/£128

History of Boone County, Missouri. St. Louis: Western Hist Co, 1882. vii,1144pp (foxing). 3/4 leather, gilt-stamped cl bds (rebacked w/new gilt-stamped leather back). VG. Bohling. $150/£96

History of Company A and the 22nd Regiment N.G.N.Y. (NY: Styles & Cash, 1901.) 1st ed. VG in ptd wrappers (chipped, corner clipped). *Mcgowan.* $175/£112

History of England.... London: John Wallis, 1800. 1st ed. 32mo. Copperplt frontis, 64pp; 31 hand-colored oval wood engrs. Bds, ptd label fr cvr. (Spine paper chipped off.) *Karmiole.* $100/£64

History of Helyas, Knight of the Swan. NY: Grolier Club, 1901. One of 325. Blind-stamped pigskin, device on cvrs, brass catches and clasps. (Spine dknd.) Orig pigskin slipcase, sleeve. *Swann*.* $201/£129

History of Jo Daviess County, Illinois, Containing a History of the Cities, Towns, Etc. Chicago: Kett, 1878. 1st ed. 845,(1)pp. Thick dec cl. *Ginsberg.* $150/£96

History of John Gilpin. NY: McLoughlin Bros, n.d. (ca 1860). 12mo. 8pp + 1pg list lower wrapper (edges lt spotted). Tp reads 'The Diverting History of John Gilpin.' 8 VF 1/2-pg hand-colored wood engrs. VG in pict pink paper wrappers (lt dusted; repaired sm split lower spine, 1pg). *Hobbyhorse.* $350/£224

History of Johnny Quae Genus, the Little Foundling of the Late Doctor Syntax. (By William Combe.) London: Ackermann, 1822. 1st ed. 24 aquatint plts by Thomas Rowlandson. (Sl foxed, browned.) 3/4 calf (rubbed). *Oinonen*.* $225/£144

History of Josephine Country, Oregon. (Grants Pass): Josephine Country Hist, 1988. VF. *Perier.* $47/£30

History of Little Goody Two-Shoes. Westport, CT, 1941. Ltd to 210. 12mo. 2 plts. Black cl-backed patterned bds, paper label. Nice. *Cady.* $15/£10

History of Medicine and Surgery and Physicians and Surgeons of Chicago. Chicago, 1922. 1st ed. (Ex-lib; spine worn.) *Fye.* $175/£112

History of Morris County...1710-1913.... NY, 1914. 2 vols. 1/2 buckram (vol 2 stained; ink names). *Kane*.* $80/£51

History of Pennsylvania Hall, Which Was Destroyed by a Mob, on the 17th of May, 1838. (Samuel Webb, ed.) Phila: Merrihew & Gunn, 1838. 200pp; 3 plts, errata slip. Good (foxed, lt stains from pressed leaves; worn, spotted). Howes W189. *Bohling.* $75/£48

History of the 127th Regiment Pennsylvania Volunteers Familiarly Known as the 'Dauphin County Regiment.' (Lebanon: Report Pub Co, 1902.) 1st ed. (Lt half ring fr bd), else Fine. *Between The Covers.* $150/£96

History of the American Mission to the Pawnee Indians. (By Sarah Tuttle.) Boston: MA Sabbath School Soc, 1838. 1st ed. Woodcut frontis, 76pp. Patterned brn cl (chipped, lt rubbed). *Karmiole.* $100/£64

History of the Azores or Western Islands. (By Thomas Ashe.) London: Sherwood, Neely & Jones, 1813. 1st ed. Engr frontis, 4 plts, 3 maps (2 fldg). (Later ll dampstained upper margin, lt spotting, staining.) Mod 1/2 calf. *Christie's*.* $262/£168

History of the Buccaneers of America.... (By Alexandre Olivier Exquemelin.) Boston/Portland: Sanborn, Carter & Bazin/Sanborn & Carter, 1856. 484pp. (Cl foxed, spine bottom loose.) *Lefkowicz.* $90/£58

History of the Children in the Wood. Hallowell: E. Goodale, 1817. 12mo. 44pp + 1pg list back cvr (title, last pg lt browned; sm hole margin p13; ink sig tp); 8 VF wood engrs. Tp reads 'The Affecting History of the Children in the Wood' and is dated 1816. Pict lt brn paper cvr. VG. *Hobbyhorse.* $90/£58

History of the Grange Movement. (By James Dabney McCabe.) Phila et al: Nat'l Pub Co, (1873). 534pp + 10pp ads. Full leather (fr hinge split, repaired). VG. *Bohling.* $20/£13

History of the Great Plague in London, in the Year 1665.... By a Citizen Who Lived the Whole Time in London. (By Daniel Defoe.) London: Renshaw & Rush, 1832. New ed. Engr frontis port, vii,311pp (prelims lt browned). Contemp 1/2 calf, marbled bds (sl rubbed, chipped), gilt, leather spine label. *Edwards.* $31/£20

History of the Holy Bible...for the Use of Children. Boston: J. White & C. Cambridge, 1790. 24mo. 96pp (piece torn from frontis, early ll frayed, foxing). Pastepaper wrapper (heavily worn). *New Hampshire*.* $325/£208

History of the Indian Wars with the First Settlers of the United States, Particularly in New-England. (By Daniel Sanders.) Montpelier, 1812. 1st ed. 16mo. Crimson morocco, gilt. *Swann*.* $862/£553

History of the Lives and Bloody Exploits of the Most Noted Pirates.... Hartford: Silas Andrus, 1836. Emb cl (worn). Usable (some margins defective). *Boswell.* $250/£160

History of the One Hundred Second Field Artillery July 1917—April 1919. Boston, 1927. Lg fldg photo frontis, 8 fldg maps. Dec cvr. Good. *Scribe's Perch*.* $20/£13

History of the Origin of the Place Names Connected with the Chicago and North Western and Chicago, St. Paul, Minneapolis and Omaha Railways. Chicago, 1908. 2nd ed. Fldg map. (Fore-edge sl bumped), else Good in wrappers (sl worn). *Brown.* $25/£16

History of the Pequot War. Cleveland: Helman-Taylor, 1897. #68 of ltd ed. xx,149pp; map. Mostly unopened. (Cl soiled), else Good +. Howes M369. *Cahan.* $100/£64

History of the Seventeenth Virginia Infantry. (By George Wise.) Balt: Kelly, Piet, 1870. 1st ed. 312pp. (Inner hinges starting; extrems sl worn), else VG. Howes W592. *Mcgowan.* $450/£288

History of the Siege of Delhi. (By W. W. Ireland.) Edinburgh, 1861. xii,332pp + ads; fldg plan. Grn cl. *Maggs.* $312/£200

History of the War...1812.... NY: John Low, 1816. 3rd ed. 336pp (browned, lacks fep). Calf (fr cvr detached). Good. *Agvent.* $25/£16

History of Whites. London: Algernon Burke, (1892). #311/500. 2 vols. 258; 259,98pp. (Prelims rubbed, foxed), o/w VG. *New Hampshire*.* $65/£42

HITCHCOCK, E. The Religion of Geology and Its Connected Sciences. Glasgow: Collins, 1865. 1st ed. Frontis dwg. 1/2 leather, cl. VG. *Mikesh.* $45/£29

HITCHCOCK, E. et al. Report of the Geology of Vermont. Claremont, NH: Claremont Mfg Co, 1861. 2 vols. viii,558,(v); 559-982pp; 38 plts. Emb cl. Good (margins dampstained vol 1, bottom edge of b/w plts vol II; extrems sl rubbed). *Blake.* $400/£256

HITCHCOCK, ENOS. Memoirs of the Bloomsgrove Family. Boston, 1790. 1st ed. 2 vols. 12mo. Full contemp calf (vol 1 rebacked, label laid down), leather labels. Very Nice set (sl chipping). *M & S.* $600/£385

HITCHCOCK, ETHAN A. Fifty Years in Camp and Field. NY: Putnam, 1909. 1st ed. (Spine sl discolored, lib stamps.) Howes H529. *Ginsberg.* $150/£96

HITCHCOCK, HENRY-RUSSELL. Early Victorian Architecture in Britain. New Haven, 1954. 1st ed. 2 vols. Djs. *Swann*.* $92/£59

HITCHCOCK, RIPLEY. Important New Etchings by American Artists. NY: Frederick A. Stokes, 1888. One of 600 of 'cloth bound' ed. 7 orig etchings. (Tp loose, edges chipped.) Gilt-dec cl (worn, soiled). *New Hampshire*.* $220/£141

HITTELL, JOHN S. Commerce and Industries of the Pacific Coast of North America. SF, 1882. 1st ed. 819pp. Full contemp calf. *Ginsberg.* $300/£192

HITTELL, JOHN S. et al. The Discovery of Gold in California. Palo Alto: Lewis Osborne, 1968. Ltd to 2100. Fine. *Argonaut*. $25/£16

HITTELL, THEODORE H. El Triunfo de la Cruz. (SF): Book Club of CA, 1977. One of 400 designed, illus, signed by Valenti Angelo. Grn bds. Fine. *Harrington*. $50/£32

HJORTSBERG, WILLIAM. Gray Matters. NY: S&S, (1971). 1st ed. Fine in dj (lt rubbed, soiled). *Hermitage*. $25/£16

HOAG, JONATHAN E. The Poetical Works of Jonathan E. Hoag. NY, 1923. Inscribed. H.P. Lovecraft (preface). VG. *Metropolitan**. $115/£74

HOAGLAND, EDWARD. Cat Man. Boston: Houghton, Mifflin, 1956. 1st ed, 1st bk. Fine in dj (lt worn). *Hermitage*. $75/£48

HOARE, J. DOUGLAS. Arctic Exploration. London, 1906. Fldg map. (Wax seal spine base), else VG. *High Latitude*. $20/£13

HOARE, RICHARD COLT. Journal of a Tour in Ireland, A.D. 1806. London: W. Miller, 1807. 1st ed. Frontis engr, (4),cix,(3,blank),(1)-336,(8,ads)pp; complete with 1/2-title (engr bkpl on inner cvr). Teg. 3/4 polished calf (corners lt rubbed), spine gilt-dec between panels, red leather label. Fine. *Argonaut*. $250/£160

HOBAN, RUSSELL. La Corona and the Tin Frog. Cape, 1979. 1st Bayley ed. Nicola Bayley (illus). 4to. Pict bds. NF. *Bookmark*. $28/£18

HOBAN, RUSSELL. The Dancing Tigers. London: Cape, 1979. 1st ed. David Gentleman (illus). 8 1/4 x 10 3/4. 32pp. Glossy bds. Fine. *Cattermole*. $50/£32

HOBAN, RUSSELL. How Tom Beat Captain Najork and His Hired Sportsmen. Cape, 1974. 1st ed. Quentin Blake (illus). Folio. (32)pp. Pict bds. VG (sl mks) in pict dj (sl worn). *Bookmark*. $27/£17

HOBAN, RUSSELL. The Mouse and His Child. Faber, 1969. 1st Eng ed. Lillian Hoban (illus). 8vo. 200pp. VG (2 ex-lib stamps, few brn mks eps) in pict dj (few brn mks). *Bookmark*. $47/£30

HOBART-HAMPDEN, AUGUSTUS CHARLES. Hobart Pasha. Horace Kephart (ed). Oyster Bay, NY, (1915). Pict eps. *Wantagh*. $75/£48

HOBBES, JOHN OLIVER. The Flute of Pan. London, 1905. 1st Eng ed. (Hinges tender.) *Clearwater*. $39/£25

HOBBES, JOHN OLIVER. The Vineyard. London, 1904. 1st Eng ed. (Fr hinge tender; spine sl faded, rubbed.) *Clearwater*. $39/£25

HOBBS, CLARENCE W. Lynn and Surroundings. Lynn, MA, 1886. 1st ed. 161pp. (Pp 3-6 starting; lt rubbed), o/w Good. *Scribe's Perch**. $16/£10

HOBBS, EDWARD W. How to Make Clipper Ship Models. Brown, Son & Ferguson, 1938. 2nd ed. 6 plts (5 fldg). (Hinges, corners sl worn), o/w VG. *Whittle*. $47/£30

HOBBS, EDWARD W. How to Make Old-Time Ship Models. Brown, Son & Ferguson, 1934. 2nd ed. 2 fldg plts (lacks 3 plts). (Sl worn), o/w VG. *Whittle*. $41/£26

HOBBS, EDWARD W. How to Make Old-Time Ship Models. Glasgow: Brown, Son & Ferguson, 1934. 2nd ed. 5 lg fldg plans in rear pocket. Good in blue cl. *Cox*. $44/£28

HOBBS, JAMES. Wild Life in the Far West: Personal Adventures of a Border Mountain Man.... Hartford: Wiley, Waterman, Eaton, 1873. 2nd ed. Color frontis. (Margins sl smudged; sl rubbed, extrems sl worn.) Howes H550. *Sadlon*. $200/£128

HOBBS, WILLIAM. Exploring About the North Pole of the Winds. NY, 1930. VG. *High Latitude*. $25/£16

HOBBS, WILLIAM. The Glacial Anticlones: The Poles of the Atmospheric Circulation. Macmillan, 1926. VG+. *Bookcell*. $50/£32

HOBDAY, E. A. P. Sketches on Service During the Indian Frontier Campaigns of 1897. London, 1898. 159pp; 57 plts, 14 ports. Aeg. Grn cl (stained, fr hinge weak), gilt. *Maggs*. $218/£140

HOBHOUSE, CHRISTOPHER (ed). Derbyshire. Architectural Press, 1935. VG in pict wraps. *Hadley*. $62/£40

HOBHOUSE, CHRISTOPHER (ed). Oxford. Batsford, 1939. 1st ed. VG in pict dj (spine browned, ends rubbed). *Words Etc*. $28/£18

HOBHOUSE, CHRISTOPHER (ed). Shell Guide to Derbyshire.... Architectural Press, 1935. 1st ed. Pict card cvrs (extrems sl worn), ring-bound. *Cox*. $55/£35

HOBLYN, RICHARD. A Dictionary of Terms Used in Medicine and the Collateral Sciences. Phila, 1865. 522pp. VG. *Fye*. $75/£48

Hobo-Camp-Fire-Tales by A-No. 1, America's Most Famous Tramp. Erie, PA: A-No. 1 Pub Co, 1911. 13th ed. Orig pict ptd wrappers (sm creases, lower cvr sl soiled). *Sadlon*. $15/£10

HOBSON, A. Cyril Connolly as a Book Collector. London: Tragara, 1983. #77/150. Fine in wrappers. *Virgo*. $31/£20

HOBSON, A. The Literature of Bookbinding. London: National Book League, 1954. Dec wrappers (edges sl soiled, sm tear lower cvr). *Maggs*. $44/£28

HOBSON, G. D. Maioli, Canevari and Others. Boston: Little, Brown, 1926. 1st US ed. 64 full-pg plts (6 color). (Offset eps.) Dj (chipped). *Oak Knoll*. $300/£192

HOBSON, R. L. Chinese Art. 1952. 2nd ed. 100 color plts. Dj (sl chipped, edge tears). *Edwards*. $117/£75

HOBSON, R. L. The Wares of the Ming Dynasty. London: Benn Bros, 1923. 1st ed. One of 27 ptd, signed. Full vellum, gilt. (Rear joint sl starting), o/w VF. *Hermitage*. $500/£321

HOBSON, R. L. Worcester Porcelain. London, 1910. Folio. (Worn, shaken.) *Swann**. $230/£147

HOBSON, RICHMOND P., JR. Grass Beyond the Mountains. Phila, 1951. 1st ed. NF (bkseller label rep) in dj (price-clipped). *Baade*. $55/£35

HOCH, AUGUST. Benign Stupors: A Study of a New Manic-Depressive Reaction Type. NY: Macmillan, 1921. 1st ed. Brn cl (shelfworn, shaken). Good. *Gach*. $50/£32

HOCHBAUM, H. ALBERT. The Canvasback on a Prairie Marsh. Washington, 1944. 1st ed. (Sl spotted, rubbed.) *King*. $35/£22

HOCHHUTH, ROLF. The Deputy. Richard and Clara Winston (trans). NY, 1964. 1st Amer ed. VG in dj. *Argosy*. $25/£16

HOCKNEY, DAVID. David Hockney: A Retrospective. CA/NY: L.A. County Museum of Art/Abrams, (1988). 235 plts, 3 fldg. Mint in dj. *Argosy*. $175/£112

HOCKNEY, DAVID. Hockney's Alphabet. Faber & Faber, 1991. 1st ed. Fine in dj. *Words Etc*. $55/£35

HODASEVICH, R. A Voice from Within the Walls of Sebastopol. London, 1856. 2nd ed. xii,252pp, 3 fldg plans (folds cellotape reinforced). Dec dk grn cl (sl worn, few mks). *Maggs*. $234/£150

HODGE, E. W. The Northern Highlands. Edinburgh: S.M.C., 1953. 3rd ed. Map. (Bds sl damped.) Dj (upper fold sl frayed). *Hollett*. $31/£20

HODGE, FREDERICK (ed). Handbook of American Indians North of Mexico, Part 1 and Part 2. BAE Bulletin 30. Washington: GPO, 1907, 1910. 2 vols. Vol 1 VG; (vol 2 heavily worn). *Perier*. $85/£54

HODGE, FREDERICK (ed). Handbook of American Indians North of Mexico. BAE Bulletin 30. Washington: GPO, 1907/1910. 2 vols. Good. *Lien*. $175/£112

HODGE, FREDERICK. Hawikuh Bonework. NY: Heye, 1920. 56 plts. VG in wraps. *Oregon*. $45/£29

HODGE, FREDERICK. Spanish Explorers in the Southern US 1528-43. NY, 1907. 1st ed. Facs, 2 maps. VG. *Turpen*. $60/£38

HODGE, HIRAM C. Arizona As It Is; or, The Coming Country. NY: Hurg & Houghton, 1877. 1st ed. 273pp. (Sig.) *Dawson*. $200/£128

HODGES, WILLIAM. Travels in India, During the Years 1780, 1781, 1782, and 1783. London: The Author, 1793. 1st ed. vi,156,(2)pp; 14 copper engr plts, lg fldg map. Contemp diced calf (spine sl rubbed, chipped, hinges worn). *Karmiole*. $450/£288

HODGSON, ADAM. A Letter to M. Jean-Baptiste Say. Liverpool, 1823. 2nd ed. 60pp. (Lacks cvrs, ends soiled, partially yellowed.) *King*. $75/£48

HODGSON, ADAM. Remarks During a Journey Through North America in the Years 1819, 1820 and 1821, in a Series of Letters. NY: Samuel Whiting, 1823. 1st ed. (1-inch loss title head, repaired tear penultimate leaf, lt foxing.) Calf (rebacked), marbled bds (extrems rubbed). Howes H560. *Sadlon*. $125/£80

HODGSON, FRED T. The Up-to-Date Hardwood Finisher. Chicago: Drake, 1904. 1st ed. (Finger mks, cl sl worn), o/w Good+. *Whittle*. $47/£30

HODGSON, RALPH. Poems. London: Macmillan, 1917. 1st ed. VG in dj (rubbed, sl chipped). *Cahan*. $50/£32

HODGSON, W. EARL. Trout Fishing. Black, 1930. 3rd ed. 7 color plts. (Sl foxed; binding sl spotted.) *Petersfield*. $19/£12

HODGSON, WILLIAM HOPE. Carnacki the Ghost-Finder. Sauk City: Mycroft, 1947. 1st Amer ed. VG (bds soiled, sunned, short tears, sm corner chip). *Metropolitan**. $51/£33

HODGSON, WILLIAM HOPE. Deep Waters. Arkham House, 1967. 1st ed. Fine in NF dj (rear panel sl dustmkd). *Certo*. $100/£64

HODGSON, WILLIAM HOPE. Deep Waters. Sauk City: Arkham House, 1967. 1st ed. VF in VF dj. *Mcclintock*. $125/£80

HODGSON, WILLIAM HOPE. The House on the Borderland. Sauk City: Arkham, 1946. 1st Amer ed. Fine in Fine dj. *Metropolitan**. $212/£136

HODGSON, WILLIAM HOPE. Out of the Storm. West Kingston, RI, 1975. 1st ed. VF in VF dj. *Mcclintock*. $65/£42

HODNETT, EDWARD. English Woodcuts 1480-1535. Oxford, 1973. 2nd ed. Good. *Washton*. $110/£71

HODSON, A. W. Trekking the Great Thirst. London, 1913. 2nd ed. (Foxing; corners sl rubbed, bumped.) *Grayling*. $78/£50

HOFER, PHILIP. Edward Lear as a Landscape Draughtsman. Cambridge: Belknap of Harvard Univ, 1967. Color frontis, 109 plts. Good in dj (torn). *Archaeologia*. $85/£54

HOFF, ARNE. Dutch Firearms. Walter A. Stryker (ed). (London): Sotheby Parke Bernet, (1978). Fine in dj. *Bohling*. $40/£26

HOFF, EBBE C. and JOHN F. FULTON. A Bibliography of Aviation Medicine. Springfield: Charles C. Thomas, 1942. 1st ed. NF. *Glaser*. $100/£64

HOFFMAN, ABBIE. Square Dancing in the Ice Age. NY: Putnam, 1982. VF in dj. *Associates*. $25/£16

HOFFMAN, ABBIE. Steal This Book. NY: Pirate Eds (distributed by Grove Press), 1971. 1st ed (w/Grove Press Black Cat logo). VG+ (spine sl creased, sl rubbed) in wraps. *Sclanders*. $70/£45

HOFFMAN, ABBIE. Woodstock Nation. A Talk-Rock Album. NY: Vintage, 1969. 1st ed. NF (sl rubbed) in wraps. *Sclanders*. $31/£20

HOFFMAN, CHARLES FENNO. A Winter in the Far West. London: Richard Bentley, 1835. 2 vols. (xii),336; (viii),340pp (bkpls). 1/2 calf (rubbed), leather labels (chipped). Howes H568. *Zubal**. $100/£64

HOFFMAN, E. T. A. The Tales of Hoffman. NY: LEC, 1943. #904/1500 numbered, signed by Hugo Steiner-Prag (illus). Fine in pub's slipcase (sl sunned). *Hermitage*. $95/£61

HOFFMANN, E. T. A. The Nutcracker. Ralph Manheim (trans). NY, (1984). 1st ed. Maurice Sendak (illus). VG in dj. *Argosy*. $60/£38

HOFFMANN, E. T. A. The Nutcracker. Natick, MA: Picture Book Studio, 1983. 1st US ed. Lisbeth Zwerger (illus). 8 1/4 x 13 1/2. 30pp. Fine in dj. *Cattermole*. $15/£10

HOFFMANN, E. T. A. The Nutcracker. London: Bodley Head, 1984. 1st ed thus. Maurice Sendak (illus). Obl 4to. Mint in dj. *Hadley*. $47/£30

HOFFMANN, E. T. A. The Nutcracker. NY: Crown, 1984. 1st ed. Maurice Sendak (illus). 10 1/4 sq. 102pp. VG in dj. *Cattermole*. $30/£19

HOFFMANN, FELIX. King Thrushbeard. NY: HBJ, 1970. 1st ed. 8 1/2 x 11 3/4. 32pp. VG in dj. *Cattermole*. $20/£13

HOFFMANN, PROFESSOR. Conjuring Tricks with Cards. Phila: David McKay, n.d. (c. 1910). Grn cl. NF. *Dramatis Personae*. $25/£16

HOFLAND, BARBARA. Ellen, the Teacher. London: J. Harris, 1822. 3rd ed. 12mo. Copper-engr frontis, 208,(4)pp; 1/2 title. Orig red calf, matted bds (extrems rubbed, spine top sl chipped). *Karmiole*. $75/£48

HOFLAND, T. C. The British Angler's Manual. London, 1848. 448pp; 22 steel-engr plts (sl foxed). Good- (hinges tender, spine chipped). *Scribe's Perch**. $70/£45

HOFMANN, HANS. Five Essays. NY: Abrams, n.d. 50 tipped-in color illus. (Bds sl spotted.) Dj (nicks). *Metropolitan**. $201/£129

HOGAN, JOHN. On the Mission in Missouri 1857-1868. Kansas City, MO, 1892. 1st ed. 221pp. Howes H573. *Ginsberg*. $150/£96

HOGAN, JOHN. On the Mission in Missouri 1857-1868. Kansas City, MO: John A. Heilmann, 1892. 1st ed. (Tp gutter repaired; spine ends, corners sl rubbed.) Howes H573. *Sadlon*. $200/£128

HOGAN, WILLIAM. The Quartzsite Trip. NY: Atheneum, 1980. 1st ed, 1st bk. Fine in dj. *Hermitage*. $40/£26

Hogarth's Rejected and Suppressed Plates.... NY: For members of the Fraternity of Odd Volumes, 1913. One of 150 ptd. 3/4 blue levant morocco over marbled bds; spine gilt. *Cullen*. $225/£144

HOGARTH, BASIL. Writing Thrillers for Profit. London: A&C Black, (1936). 1st UK ed. Good (bkpl). *Gravesend*. $50/£32

HOGARTH, D. G. The Life of Charles M. Doughty. OUP, 1928. 1st ed. Frontis port, 9 plts, fldg map. (Cl sl soiled, spine faded, intruding sl onto bds.) *Edwards*. $70/£45

HOGARTH, D. G. The Life of Charles M. Doughty. GC: Doubleday, 1929. 1st Amer issue, bound from British sheets. Port. (Sizing flecked), o/w VG, dj panels laid in. *Reese*. $50/£32

HOGARTH, PAUL. The Artist as Reporter. 1986. Dj (sl chipped). *Edwards*. $39/£25

HOGARTH, WILLIAM. The Complete Works of William Hogarth. London Ptg & Pub Co, ca 1860. 150 steel engrs. Contemp full brn morocco, gilt edges. Overall Fine (lt foxing). *Appelfeld.* $350/£224

HOGARTH, WILLIAM. The Complete Works. London, n.d. (ca 1870). (Lt foxing, sl dampstaining fr matter.) 3/4 morocco (rubbed, joints cracked). *Freeman*.* $20/£13

HOGARTH, WILLIAM. The Works. London, n.d. (ca 1870). 2 vols in 1. (Lt soiled, foxed.) 1/2 morocco (rubbed, casing detaching). *Freeman*.* $50/£32

HOGARTH, WILLIAM. Works...in a Series of Engravings...to which are added, Anecdotes...by J. Hogarth and J. Nichols. London, 1833. 2 vols. 105 (of 108) plts. (Lt foxing.) 1/2 leather, marbled bds (worn, both fr cvrs detached). *New Hampshire*.* $100/£64

HOGG, JABEZ. The Microscope. London: Illustrated London Library, 1854. 1st ed. Engr tp, 440pp; 15 plts. New cl (rebound). VG. *Savona.* $62/£40

HOGG, JABEZ. The Microscope. London: Herbert Ingram, 1855. 2nd ed. Frontis, engr tp, xvi,458pp + 6pp pub's cat + 16pp C. Baker Catalogue of Achromatic Microscopes and Photographic Apparatus; 14 plts. Good (cl faded, stained, sl worn). *Savona.* $101/£65

HOGG, JABEZ. The Microscope: Its History, Construction and Application. London: Routledge, 1867. 6th ed. 762pp. (Sl shaken), o/w VG. *Bookcell.* $75/£48

HOGG, JABEZ. The Microscope: Its History, Construction and Application. London, 1871. 8th ed. xx,762pp; 9 plts (8 color). Pict cl, gilt. Good. *Henly.* $70/£45

HOGG, JABEZ. The Microscope: Its History, Construction and Application. London, 1883. 11th ed. xx,764pp (3pp torn, repaired; lt spotted; new eps); 1 plain, 8 color plts. Pict cl, gilt. *Henly.* $59/£38

HOGG, JAMES. The Private Memoirs and Confessions of a Justified Sinner. Cresset, 1947. 1st ptg. Facs frontis. VG. *Cox.* $12/£8

HOGG, JAMES. The Shepherd's Calendar. NY/Phila: Sold by A.T. Goodrich (et al), 1829. 1st Amer ed. 2 vols. Muslin, bds, paper spine labels (sl dknd). Nice (foxing, early ink name). *Reese.* $75/£48

HOGG, JAMES. Winter Evening Tales, Collected Among the Cottagers in the South of Scotland. Edinburgh/London: Oliver & Boyd/G. & W.B. Whittaker, 1820. 1st ed. 2 vols. (Many pp vol 2 lt foxed.) 1/2 titles not called for. Orig bds, calf spines, labels. *Bickersteth.* $250/£160

HOGROGIAN, NONNY. Cinderella. NY: Greenwillow, 1981. 1st ed. 8 1/4 x 10 1/4. 32pp. 1/2 cl. Fine in dj. *Cattermole.* $20/£13

HOHMAN, ELMO PAUL. The American Whaleman. NY, 1928. 1st ed. VG + . *Lefkowicz.* $110/£71

HOHMAN, ELMO PAUL. The American Whaleman. NY: Longmans, Green, 1928. 1st ed. Fine in Poor dj. *Perier.* $90/£58

HOIG, STAN. The Humor of the American Cowboy. Caldwell, ID: Caxton, 1958. 1st ed. Fine in dj. *Sadlon.* $15/£10

HOIG, STAN. The Western Odyssey of John Simpson Smith.... Glendale, 1974. 1st ed. (Cvr sl worn), o/w Fine. *Pratt.* $40/£26

HOLBEIN, HANS. The Dances of Death.... London: (S. Gosnell), 1803. Sm 4to. 46 plts w/in separately engr borders in 4 different designs, 3 of which are copied w/sl variations from the Diepenbeke borders to W. Hollar's plts; the last plt, often lacking, called 'Petite Danse de Morts.' Contemp paneled calf; blind-dec sides, spine (rebacked much earlier), red morocco label; all edges stained red. Handsome (occasional foxing). *Book Block.* $575/£369

HOLBORN, MARK (intro). Beyond a Portrait. NY: Aperture, 1984. 1st ed. Rev slip laid in. Fine in VG dj. *Cahan.* $35/£22

HOLBROOK, J. Ten Years Among the Mail Bags. Boston: Shepard, Clark, 1856. 13 plts. Blue cl (worn, extrems chipped), gilt. *Bohling.* $20/£13

HOLBROOK, JOHN C. Recollections of a Nonagenarian of Life in New England, the Middle West, and New York.... Boston, 1897. 1st ed. 351pp. *Ginsberg.* $50/£32

HOLBROOK, MARTIN LUTHER. Hygiene of the Brain.... NY: M.L. Holbrook, (1878). Later ed. (ii),viii,(7)-293,(1)pp. Emb brn cl, gilt spine. VG. *Gach.* $35/£22

HOLBROOK, STEWART H. The Columbia. NY: Rinehart, (1956). 1st ed. VG in VG dj. *Perier.* $50/£32

HOLBROOK, STEWART H. Murder Out Yonder. NY: Macmillan, 1941. 1st ed. VG in dj. *Connolly.* $47/£30

HOLBROOK, STEWART H. The Old Post Road. NY: McGraw-Hill, (1962). 1st ptg. Dbl map. VG + (sl dent top edge) in dj. *Bohling.* $25/£16

HOLBROOK, STEWART H. Wild Bill Hickok Tames the West. NY: Random House, (1952). VG in dj. *Perier.* $20/£13

HOLDEN, GEORGE H. Canaries and Cage-Birds. NY, 1888. 2nd ed. 314pp; 8 color plts. Grn cl, gilt. (Fr hinge starting), else VG. *Price.* $95/£61

HOLDEN, HAROLD M. Noses. Cleveland, 1950. Good. *Doctor's Library.* $65/£42

HOLDEN, WILLIAM CURRY. Alkali Trails or Social and Economic Movements of the Texas Frontier, 1846-1900. Dallas: Southwest Press, 1930. 1st ed. Signed, inscribed. VG. *Gibbs.* $150/£96

HOLDER, CHARLES FREDERICK. Big Game at Sea. NY: Outing, 1908. 1st ed. Frontis. Pict blue-grn cl (lt wear to extrems). *Dawson.* $125/£80

HOLDER, CHARLES FREDERICK. Recreations of a Sportsman on the Pacific Coast. NY: Putnam, 1910. 1st ed. Teg. Grn cl, gilt. VG. *Biscotti.* $85/£54

HOLE, CHRISTINA. Haunted England. London: Batsford, 1940. 1st ed. (Lacks fep.) Dj (sl chipped). *Edwards.* $31/£20

HOLE, CHRISTINA. Witchcraft in England. London: Batsford, 1945. 1st ed. Frontis. Dj (chipped, flds worn). *Hollett.* $70/£45

HOLE, CHRISTINE. Witchcraft in England. NY: Scribner, 1947. 1st ed. NF in NF dj (worn, sm tears). *Beasley.* $35/£22

HOLE, S. REYNOLDS. A Little Tour in America. London/NY: Edward Arnold, 1895. 1st ed. Frontis photo, (vi),381pp. Contemp blue 1/2 calf, spine gilt, marbled bds, red/brn labels. Very Handsome (eps, edges, tp sl browned). *Sotheran.* $153/£98

HOLIDAY, BILLIE with WILLIAM DUFTY. Lady Sings the Blues. NY: Doubleday, 1956. 1st ed. VG (rep, last leaf stained from tape) in dj (worn). *Second Life.* $65/£42

HOLLAND, BOD, DAN, and RAY. Good Shot! A Book of Rod, Gun, and Camera. NY, 1946. VG. *Truepenny.* $45/£29

HOLLAND, J. G. The Mistress of the Manse. NY: Scribner, Armstrong, 1874. 1st Amer ed, 1st issue (w/ad on p[249] listing only 3 vols in 'Epochs of History' series) w/pub's spine imprint in 2nd state (w/comma and w/'Co.' written w/the 'o' over the period). 6pp undated ads. Grn cl. VF. *Sumner & Stillman.* $35/£22

HOLLAND, LADY. Sydney Smith. A Memoir by His Daughter. Mrs. Austin (ed). Harper, 1856. 1st Amer ed. 2 vols. xii,378; xviii,511pp. Blue cl, blind-blocked, gilt-lettered. Nice. *Cox.* $55/£35

HOLLAND, R. S. Historic Airships. Phila, (1928). Dec cvr. Good. *Scribe's Perch*.* $20/£13

HOLLAND, RAY P. My Gun Dogs. Boston/NY: Houghton Mifflin, (1929). Tan cl. (Spine lt faded), else VG. *Glenn.* $25/£16

HOLLAND, RAY P. Scattergunning. NY: Knopf, 1951. 1st ed. Color frontis. 1/2 grn cl, brn cl-cvrd bds. Fine in VG pict dj. *Biscotti.* $60/£38

HOLLAND, RAY P. Shotgunning in the Lowlands. West Hartford, VT: Countryman, (1945). Ltd to 350 signed by Holland & Lynn Bogue Hunt (illus). Grn buckram. Fine. *Truepenny.* $175/£112

HOLLAND, RAY P. Shotgunning in the Lowlands. NY: A.S. Barnes, 1945. Stated 1st ptg. Ltd to 3500. Color frontis; 7 full-pg color plts. VG+ in VG slipcase (tape repaired). *Backman.* $75/£48

HOLLAND, RAY P. Shotgunning in the Uplands. NY, (1944). 1st ed. 8 color plts. (Sl dull), else Good. *King.* $60/£38

HOLLAND, RAY P. Shotgunning in the Uplands. West Hartford, VT: Countryman, (1944). Ltd to 250 signed by Holland & Lynn Bogue Hunt (illus). Full buckram, beveled bds. Fine. *Truepenny.* $175/£112

HOLLAND, VYVYAN. Oscar Wilde and His World. NY, 1960. 1st Amer ed. Very Nice (sl bumped) in dj. *Clearwater.* $31/£20

HOLLAND, W. J. The Butterfly Book. NY: Doubleday, (1916). 48 color plts. VG+. *Mikesh.* $37/£24

HOLLAND, WILLIAM M. The Life and Political Opinions of Martin Van Buren.... Hartford: Belknap & Hammersley, 1835. 1st ed. 364pp; port. Orig full calf binding (extrem wear). (Lt foxing.) *Cullen.* $45/£29

HOLLANDER, BERNARD. The Mental Functions of the Brain.... NY/London: Putnam/Knickerbocker, 1901. 1st ed, Amer issue. (xviii),507,(3)pp; 38 plts. Ptd blue cl (crown chipped, fr cvr sl wrinkled). Jelliffe's bkpl. Good+ (lib stamp tp, whited spine #s). *Gach.* $65/£42

HOLLANDER, BERNARD. The Psychology of Misconduct, Vice and Crime. NY: Macmillan, 1924. 1st Amer ed. Panelled straight-grained brn cl (lib stamp tp, spine #s), gilt spine. Jelliffe's bkpl. *Gach.* $35/£22

HOLLANDER, JOHN. A Crackling of Thorns. Yale Univ, 1958. 1st ed, 1st bk. Black cl. Fine in dj (lt used). *Dermont.* $100/£64

HOLLELEY, DOUGLAS and JULIANA SWATKO. Far Fetched. Rochester: By the photographer at Visual Studies Workshop, 1976. (Owner stamp), o/w Fine in ptd stiff wrappers. *Cahan.* $65/£42

HOLLENBACK, FRANK R. and WILLIAM RUSSELL, JR. Pikes Peak by Rail. Denver: Sage Books, 1962. #54 ltd ed. Signed by both. Fine in dj. *Bohling.* $85/£54

HOLLEY, MARIETTA. Josiah Allen on the Woman Question. NY: Revell, (1914). 1st ed. VG. *Second Life.* $95/£61

HOLLEY, MARIETTA. Samantha on the Woman Question. NY: Revell, (1913). 1st ed. VG. *Second Life.* $95/£61

HOLLEY, O. L. (ed). The Picturesque Tourist. NY: J. Disturnell, 1844. 1st ed. Frontis, engr tp, 236pp; 5 maps (1 fldg), 6 plts and ads. Gilt-pict cl (lt spotted, rubbed). VG (lt foxed, lt stain through rear 1/3 of text). *Captain's Bookshelf.* $175/£112

HOLLIDAY, C. W. The Valley of Youth. Caldwell: Caxton, 1948. Stated 1st ed. #398/1000 signed. Color frontis. Good (spine faded). *Scribe's Perch*.* $24/£15

HOLLIDAY, JOE. Dale of the Mounted in Hong Kong. Allen, 1962. 6x8.5. 160pp. VG+ (sl shelfworn) in dj (edgeworn). *My Bookhouse.* $15/£10

HOLLIDAY, JOE. Dale of the Mounted, Dew Line Duty. Allen, 1957. 6x8.5. 159pp. VG in dj (ragged). *My Bookhouse.* $15/£10

HOLLIDAY, JOE. Dale of the Mounted, Pursuit on the St. Lawrence. Allen, 1960. 6x8.5. 160pp. VG (shelfworn) in dj (edgeworn). *My Bookhouse.* $15/£10

HOLLING, HOLLING C. Minn of the Mississippi. Boston: HM, 1951. 1st ed. 8 3/4 x 11 1/4. 86pp. Good in dj. *Cattermole.* $60/£38

HOLLING, HOLLING C. The Tree in the Trail. Boston: HM, 1942. 1st ed. 8 3/4 x 11 1/4. 56pp. VG in 1st state dj. *Cattermole.* $50/£32

HOLLINGHURST, ALAN. The Swimming-Pool Library. London: Chatto, 1988. 1st UK ed. Fine in VG+ dj (nick). *Williams.* $31/£20

HOLLINGSHEAD, MICHAEL. The Man Who Turned on the World. Blond & Briggs, 1973. 1st ed. VG in dj. *Sclanders.* $39/£25

HOLLINGWORTH, JANE. Collected Decanters. London: Studio Vista, 1980. 1st ed. VG in dj. *Hollett.* $47/£30

HOLLINSHEAD, W. HENRY. Functional Anatomy of the Limbs and Back. Phila, 1951. 1st ed. VG (sl worn). *Doctor's Library.* $45/£29

HOLLIS, A. C. The Nandi. Oxford: Clarendon, 1909. 1st ed. Fldg map (short tear), 44 plts. (Upper edge sl waterstained, foxed.) Red cl (sl rubbed, hinges broken), spine gilt. *Morrell.* $117/£75

HOLLISTER, OVANDO J. Colorado Volunteers in New Mexico, 1862. Richard Harwell (ed). Chicago: Lakeside, 1962. Signed by Harwell. Fine. Reissue of Howes H601. *Cahan.* $30/£19

HOLLMAN, C. and J. MITCHUM. Black Hawk's War. Phila: Auerbach, 1973. 1st ed. Fine in VG dj. *Archer.* $20/£13

HOLLO, ANSELM. Swirl. (Santa Barbara): Unicorn, 1971. 1st ed. Broadside. Fine. *Turlington.* $10/£6

HOLLON, W. EUGENE. The Lost Pathfinder: Zebulon Montgomery Pike. Norman: Univ of OK, (1949). 1st ed. VG in dj (worn). *Lien.* $35/£22

HOLLON, W. EUGENE. The Lost Pathfinder: Zebulon Montgomery Pike. Norman, 1949. 1st ed. Map. VG+ in VG dj. *Turpen.* $50/£32

HOLLON, W. EUGENE. The Southwest Old and New. NY, 1961. 1st ed. 2 maps. Fine in VG dj. *Turpen.* $38/£24

HOLLOWAY, B. ROSS. Satrianum. The Archaeological Investigations Conducted by Brown University in 1966 and 1967. Providence, 1970. Good in dj. *Washton.* $45/£29

HOLLOWAY, SALLY. London's Noble Fire Brigades 1833-1904. Cassell, 1973. 1st ed. (Feps sl browned.) Dj. *Edwards.* $31/£20

HOLLOWAY, W. The Effects of Excessive Parental Indulgence, Exhibited in the History of Robert Jones. NY: N.B. Holmes, 1830. 12mo. 108pp (pencil inscrip feps, sig). Ptd blue paper on bds (soiled, rubbed, chipped), 3/4 leather spine, gilt. Internally VG. *Hobbyhorse.* $90/£58

HOLM, FRITS. My Nestorian Adventure in China. NY/London: Revell, 1923. Frontis. Yellow cl. (Ex-lib.) *Terramedia.* $75/£48

HOLM, JOHN JAMES. Holm's Race Assimilation, or the Fading Leopard's Spots. Naperville, IL/Atlanta, GA: J.L. Nichols, (1910). 1st ed. Pict red cl (spine ends worn). *Petrilla.* $150/£96

HOLMAN, DAVID and BILLIE PERSONS. Buckskin and Homespun: Frontier Texas Clothing 1820-1870. Austin: Wind River, (1979). #91/450 signed by Holman. Lt tan cl bds, brn spine title. Prospectus laid in. Fine in unptd brn dj. *Heller.* $120/£77

HOLMAN, FELICE. The Witch on the Corner. W.W. Norton, 1966. 1st ed. Arnold Lobel (illus). 6x9. 90pp. VG+ (sl shelfworn) in dj (1-inch spine tear, sl edgeworn). *My Bookhouse.* $22/£14

HOLMAN, FREDERICK V. Dr. John McLoughlin, The Father of Oregon. Cleveland: A.H. Clark, 1907. Ltd to 1047. (Bkpl), else NF. *Perier.* $100/£64

HOLMAN, JOHN P. Sheep and Bear Trails. NY: Frank Walters, 1933. (Sl worn.) *Oinonen*.* $120/£77

HOLMAN, JOHN P. Sheep and Bear Trails. NY: Frank Walters, 1933. 1st ed. Signed, inscribed presentation. (Sl worn.) Dj (frayed). *Oinonen*.* $325/£208

HOLME, C. G. (ed). Decorative Art. The Studio, 1932. 6 color plts. (Ex-lib, bkpl, margins lt browned, fore-edge contents leaf reinforced, new eps; cl lt rubbed, spine faded, spine #s.) *Edwards.* $78/£50

HOLME, C. G. (ed). Decorative Art. The Studio, 1933. (Ex-lib, bkpl, ink stamps; spine lt faded, spine #s.) *Edwards.* $78/£50

HOLME, C. G. (ed). Decorative Art. The Studio, 1936. (Ex-lib, ink stamps, bkpl.) Dj (lt soiled, chipped). *Edwards.* $78/£50

HOLME, C. G. (ed). Decorative Art. The Studio, 1937. 8 color plts tipped in. Teg. (Ex-lib, bkpl, ink stamps; spine lt faded, spine #s.) *Edwards.* $78/£50

HOLME, C. G. (ed). Decorative Art. The Studio, 1940. (Tp lt spotted; cl lt soiled, spine sl faded.) *Edwards.* $62/£40

HOLME, C. G. (ed). Early English Portrait Miniatures in the Collection of the Duke of Buccleuch. The Studio, 1917. 68 plts. *Petersfield.* $44/£28

HOLME, C. G. (ed). English Water-Colour. The Studio, 1902. Frontis port, 13 photo plts, 66 color plts tipped in. Marbled eps. 1/2 morocco, cl bds (hinges reinforced; corners, spine sl rubbed), dec gilt raised spine bands. *Edwards.* $195/£125

HOLME, C. G. (ed). Industrial Architecture. London/NY: The Studio, 1935. 1st ed. (Name; tip bumped, spine faded), else VG. *Cahan.* $65/£42

HOLME, C. G. (ed). Modern Etchings Mezzotints and Dry-Points. The Studio, 1913. (Eps lt browned.) Grn cl (sl rubbed), gilt. *Edwards.* $39/£25

HOLME, C. G. (ed). Modern Etchings, Mezzotints and Dry-Points. London: Studio, 1913. Teg. Beveled bds. Good. *Scribe's Perch*.* $22/£14

HOLME, C. G. (ed). Old English Country Cottages. London, 1906. 15 color plts. New blind cl (orig fr cvr bound in). Sound. *Ars Artis.* $33/£21

HOLME, C. G. (ed). The Old Water-Colour Society 1804-1904. London: Studio, 1905. 40 color plts (one by Arthur Rackham). Gilt cl, beveled bds. VG. *Hollett.* $70/£45

HOLME, C. G. (ed). Peasant Art in Russia. The Studio, 1912. Card cvrs (loose, worn). Internally VG. *Whittle.* $55/£35

HOLME, C. G. and S. B. WAINWRIGHT (eds). Decorative Art 1930. The Studio, 1930. 6 color plts. Teg. (Margins lt browned, fore-edge 1st few ll thumbed, feps browned; cl sl faded, worn, some loss.) *Edwards.* $78/£50

HOLME, C. G. and S. B. WAINWRIGHT (eds). Decorative Art, 1925. The Studio, (1925). Color frontis. (Sl internal soil.) Blue cl (lt worn), gilt. *Freeman*.* $60/£38

HOLME, C. G. and S. B. WAINWRIGHT (eds). Decorative Art, 1927. The Studio, n.d. (c. 1927). Color frontis, 7 color plts. Mod cl (rebound), leather label. *Edwards.* $78/£50

HOLME, C. G. and S. B. WAINWRIGHT (eds). Decorative Art. The Studio, 1925. Color frontis, 7 color plts. Teg. Emb cl. (Feps lt browned; spine faded.) *Edwards.* $78/£50

HOLME, CONSTANCE. The Trumpet in the Dust. London: Mills & Boon, 1921. 1st ed. Frontis. (Margins sl browned; spine faded). *Hollett.* $39/£25

HOLME, GEOFFREY (ed). Decorative Art, 1924. The Studio, n.d. (c. 1924). Color frontis, 7 color plts. Mod cl (rebound), leather spine label. *Edwards.* $78/£50

HOLME, GEOFFREY (ed). The Norwich School. London: Studio, 1920. 80 plts. (Spine, lower edges sl faded.) *Hollett.* $55/£35

HOLME, GEOFFREY (ed). The Studio Yearbook of Decorative Art, 1924. London, (1924). Blind-stamped cl. Teg. (Spine top badly bumped), else bright in dj (chipped, soiled). *King.* $65/£42

HOLME, RATHBONE and KATHLEEN FROST (eds). Decorative Art...1955-1956. The Studio, 1955. Upper part orig dj loosely inserted. *Edwards.* $47/£30

HOLME, RATHBONE and KATHLEEN M. FROST (eds). Modern Lettering and Calligraphy. The Studio, 1954. 1st ed. Dj (sl chipped). *Edwards.* $55/£35

HOLMES, F. RATCLIFFE. Through Wildest Africa. 1925. 1st ed. (Cl dampstained.) *Edwards.* $47/£30

HOLMES, JOHN CLELLON. Go. NY: Scribner, 1952. 1st ed. Fine (name, pg edges sl soiled) in NF dj (lt rubbed). *Between The Covers.* $850/£545

HOLMES, JOHN CLELLON. The Horn. NY: Random House, (1958). 1st ed. (Offset from tape to dj flaps, feps), else VG in dj (chipped, fr cvr sl discolored). *Pacific*.* $63/£40

HOLMES, JOHN CLELLON. The Horn. NY: Random House, 1958. 1st ed. (Sm corner bump), o/w Fine in dj (lt used). *Beasley.* $60/£38

HOLMES, JOHN CLELLON. Nothing More to Declare. NY: E.P. Dutton, 1967. 1st ed. Fine in dj (lt rubbed, price-clipped). *Hermitage.* $45/£29

HOLMES, JOHN M. Colours in Interior Decoration. London/NY, 1931. 20 color plts (mainly tipped in). (Lacks fep, 1/2-title; 1 pg sl torn; cl sl soiled.) *Edwards.* $55/£35

HOLMES, KENNETH L. (ed). Covered Wagon Women. Glendale, CA/Spokane, WA, 1983-93. 11 vols. Fldg map. Fine, all as issued, 10 w/plain djs. *Bohling.* $350/£224

HOLMES, KENNETH L. (ed). Covered Wagon Women: Diaries and Letters from the Western Trails 1840-1890. Glendale: A. C. Clarke, 1983-1993. 11 vols. New. *Hermitage.* $350/£224

HOLMES, LEWIS. The Arctic Whaleman. Boston: Wentworth, 1857. 1st ed. Inscribed. 295pp + ads (1 corner torn). VG in dec grn cl (spine sl dknd, professionally recased). *Captain's Bookshelf.* $175/£112

HOLMES, LOUIS A. Fort McPherson, Nebraska (Fort Cottonwood, N.T.).... Lincoln, NE: Johnsen, (1963). #387/unspecified limitation, signed. Unopened. Blue pict bds. Fine. *Harrington.* $50/£32

HOLMES, MAURICE G. From New Spain by Sea to the Californias, 1519-1668. Glendale: Clark, 1963. 1st ed. One of 1520. Fldg map. Fine. *Argonaut.* $45/£29

HOLMES, OLIVER W. Astrea: The Balance of Illusions. Boston: Ticknor, Reed & Fields, 1850. 1st ptg, state A, binding A, w/yellow eps, inserted cat dated Oct 1850. 39pp. Ptd glazed cream-yellow paper bds. (Old cellophane tape on spine, cvrs sl worn), o/w VG. BAL 8757. *New Hampshire*.* $20/£13

HOLMES, OLIVER W. The Autocrat of the Breakfast Table.... Boston, 1858. 1st ed. 373pp. (Backstrip, corners worn.) *Fye.* $150/£96

HOLMES, OLIVER W. Border Lines of Knowledge in Some Provinces of Medical Science. Boston, 1862. 1st ed. 80pp. (Ex-lib.) *Fye.* $150/£96

HOLMES, OLIVER W. Border Lines of Knowledge in Some Provinces of Medical Science. Boston: Ticknor & Fields, 1862. 1st ed. One of 1500 ptd. 1st binding. (Cl sl spotted), o/w Very Nice. BAL 8814. *Reese.* $150/£96

HOLMES, OLIVER W. The Common Law. Boston, 1881. 1st ed. Lib buckram. (Several text ll chipped at fore-edge; lib bkpl.) Swann*. $402/£258

HOLMES, OLIVER W. Currents and Counter-Currents in Medical Science.... Boston, 1861. 1st ed. 406pp. (Few margins waterstained; spine rubbed, chipped), o/w VG. Fye. $175/£112

HOLMES, OLIVER W. A Dissertation on Acute Pericarditis. Boston: Welch Bibliophilic Soc, 1937. 1st ed. Untrimmed, partially unopened. Fine in glassine dj. Glaser. $60/£38

HOLMES, OLIVER W. Elsie Venner. London: Denny, (1883). Frontis, 362pp. Red cl, gilt. VG. White. $55/£35

HOLMES, OLIVER W. The Guardian Angel. Boston: Ticknor & Fields, 1867. 1st ed. Terra cotta cl, gilt. (Sig sl sprung), else Fine. BAL 8857. Macdonnell. $65/£42

HOLMES, OLIVER W. The Iron Gate and Other Poems. Boston/NY: Houghton, Mifflin, 1880. 1st ed, 1st ptg. Grey cl, gilt. (Sl frayed), else Fine. BAL 8949. Macdonnell. $50/£32

HOLMES, OLIVER W. Mechanism in Thought and Morals. Boston, 1871. 1st ed. 101pp. VG. Fye. $140/£90

HOLMES, OLIVER W. Medical Essays: 1842-1882. Boston, 1883. 1st ed. 445pp. Contents Fine (rubbed, spine worn). Fye. $90/£58

HOLMES, OLIVER W. A Mortal Antipathy, First Opening of the New Portfolio. Boston: Houghton, Mifflin, 1885. 1st ed. Nice (bkpl ep). Hermitage. $75/£48

HOLMES, OLIVER W. The One-Hoss Shay With Its Companion Poems. Boston, 1892. 1st Amer ed. Dec silver cvrs. Fine (inscrip). Polyanthos. $30/£19

HOLMES, OLIVER W. Over the Teacups. Boston/NY: Houghton, Mifflin, 1891. 1st ed, variant ptg, binding C. Teg. Lt grn cl, gilt. Fine. BAL 9027. Macdonnell. $35/£22

HOLMES, OLIVER W. Poems by Oliver Wendell Holmes. Boston, 1851. 286pp; Fine engr port. VG. Fye. $70/£45

HOLMES, OLIVER W. Poems. Boston: Otis, Broaders, 1836. 1st ed. One of 1000. xiv,163pp (foxing). Orig grn 'C' cl (spine ends frayed), paper label (chipped). VG-. BAL 8728. Reese. $200/£128

HOLMES, OLIVER W. Poems. Boston: Ticknor, Reed & Fields, 1849. 1st ed, 2nd ptg, binding A. Orig gray bds, label. (Spine worn, joint paper flaked.) BAL 8753. Macdonnell. $100/£64

HOLMES, OLIVER W. The Poet at the Breakfast Table. Routledge, 1872. 1st Eng ed. (ii),370pp. Contemp 1/2 calf, marbled paper sides, gold lib badges both cvrs. (Hinges cracked.) Cox. $31/£20

HOLMES, OLIVER W. The Poet at the Breakfast Table. Boston: James R. Osgood, 1872. 1st ed, 2nd state. Purple cl, gilt. (Spine faded), else VG. BAL 8881. Macdonnell. $30/£19

HOLMES, OLIVER W. Puerperal Fever as a Private Pestilence. Boston: Ticknor & Fields, 1855. 60pp. 19th-cent purple bds (faded, spine sunned). (Rubber stamp tp), else VG. Goodrich. $5,000/£3,205

HOLMES, OLIVER W. Songs in Many Keys. Boston, 1862. 1st ed. 308pp. VG. Fye. $100/£64

HOLMES, OLIVER W. Urania: A Rhymed Lesson. Boston: William Ticknor, 1846. 32pp pamphlet, sewn as issued. (Lt browning; lacks wraps.) Goodrich. $95/£61

HOLMES, OLIVER W. The Works. Boston, (1892). Standard Library ed. 13 vols. 8vo. Contemp 1/2 dk brn morocco, gilt, spines (sl faded) in 6 compartments, lettered in 2. Swann*. $747/£479

HOLMES, T. J. Cotton Mather: A Bibliography of His Works. Newton, MA: Crofton, 1974. 3 vols. VG. Scribe's Perch*. $60/£38

HOLMES, T. J. Increase Mather: His Works. Cleveland: For private distribution, 1930. Ltd to 250. Orig morocco-backed marbled bds. NF in dj, pub's slipcase. Sadlon. $75/£48

HOLMES, TIMOTHY. Sir Benjamin Collins Brodie. London, 1898. Frontis port, 256pp + (xii) pub's ads. (Edges sl rubbed.) Dec gilt title upper bd, spine. Edwards. $39/£25

HOLROYD, JAMES EDWARD (intro). Seventeen Steps to 221B. London: Allen & Unwin, (1967). 1st UK ed. Good (3-inch piece cut out of fr flyleaf) in Good dj (price-clipped). Gravesend. $50/£32

HOLT, EDWIN BISSELL. The Freudian Wish and Its Place in Ethics. NY: Henry Holt, 1915. 1st ed. Inscribed. Blue cl. VG. Gach. $75/£48

HOLT, L. EMMET. The Diseases of Infancy and Childhood. NY: Appleton, 1897. 1st ed. xvii,1117,(2 ads)pp (lib stamps tp); 7 color plts. New grn cl. VG. Glaser. $250/£160

HOLT, L. EMMETT. Diseases of Infancy and Childhood.... NY: Appleton, 1909. 5th ed. 8 color plts. (Sl rubbed), else Good. Goodrich. $25/£16

HOLT, RACKHAM. George Washington Carver. GC: Doubleday Doran, 1943. 1st ed. (Corner lt bumped), else Fine (lacks dj). Between The Covers. $50/£32

HOLT, ROSA BELLE. Rugs. Chicago, 1901. Color frontis, 30 plts (11 color). Teg, rest uncut. Color illus cl (hinges tender; sl rubbed). Edwards. $117/£75

HOLT-WHITE, W. The Crime Club. NY: MacAulay, 1910. 1st ed. (Spine ends, corners worn, sl buckling, lower edge faded.) Metropolitan*. $28/£18

HOLTBY, WINIFRED. Letters to a Friend. Alice Holtby and Jean McWilliam (eds). London: Collins, 1937. 1st ed. Frontis port. (Feps lt browned; edges sl dusty.) Hollett. $39/£25

HOLTBY, WINIFRED. Virginia Woolf. (London): Wishart, 1932. 1st ed. Port. (Top edge dusty), o/w Very Nice in dj. Reese. $45/£29

Holy Bible. Edinburgh: Adrian Watkins, 1752. (Lt browning.) Aeg. Full leather (lt wear, cracking to spine), gilt. Metropolitan*. $172/£110

Holy Bible. NY: Collins, 1814. 3rd ed. 9 engr plts, 3 maps. Unpaginated but appears complete. (Foxed, browned.) Early sheep (scuffed, gouged, crown worn.) Waverly*. $110/£71

Holy Bible. London: Nonesuch, 1963. 3 vols. Grn cl, gilt. Fine in orig acetate wrappers. Hermitage. $175/£112

HOLZWORTH, JOHN M. The Wild Grizzlies of Alaska. NY, 1930. 1st ed. (Joints sl rubbed.) Edwards. $59/£38

Home Authors and Home Artists. NY: Leavitt & Allen, ca 1870? 12 steel-engr plts. Full blind, gilt-dec leather (extrems lt worn). Contents VG. New Hampshire*. $30/£19

HOME, EVERARD. Practical Observations on the Treatment of the Diseases of the Prostate Gland. London: G.&W. Nicol, 1811. 1st ed. Complete w/half-title and appendix; xiv,280,lxxxpp, 13 full-pg copperplt engrs. Unopened. Bds, cl spine, ptd paper label. VG (bkpl; hinges cracked). Glaser. $385/£247

HOME, GORDON. The English Lakes. London: A&C Black, 1911. 1st ed. 8 color plts, map. Pict cl. VG in dj (piece missing spine top). Hollett. $23/£15

HOME, GORDON. France. London: A&C Black, 1918. 1st ed. 64 color plts, map. Dec cl (sl faded), gilt. Hollett. $101/£65

HOME, GORDON. Yorkshire Dales and Fells. London: A&C Black, 1906. 1st ed. 20 color plts. Red cl (spine faded), gilt. (Fep spotted, illuminated inscrip laid in), o/w Nice. Hollett. $70/£45

HOME, GORDON. Yorkshire Vales and Wolds. London: A&C Black, 1908. 1st ed. 20 color plts, fldg map. Dec blue cl, gilt. (Scattered foxing; extrems worn, spine label removed.) *Hollett.* $55/£35

HOME, GORDON. Yorkshire. London: A&C Black, 1908. 1st ed. 71 color plts, map. (Text spotted; spine sl dknd.) *Hollett.* $70/£45

HOMER, WILLIAM INNES. Alfred Stieglitz and the American Avant-Garde. Boston: NYGS, 1977. 1st ed. Frontis port. (Owner stamp), else Fine in dj (lt worn). *Cahan.* $75/£48

HOMER, WILLIAM INNES. A Pictorial Heritage: The Photographs of Gertrude Kasebier. (Wilmington): DE Art Museum, Univ of DE, 1979. 1st ed. Frontis, 19 full-pg photo plts. VG (owner stamp) in pict stiff wrappers (sl worn). *Cahan.* $35/£22

HOMER. The Iliad and The Odyssey of Homer. Alexander Pope (trans). Haarlem: LEC, 1931. #1089/1500 sets signed by J. van Krimpen (designer). 2 vols. Vol 1: red buckram bds; vol 2: blue buckram bds. Fine (spines faded) in yellow slipcases (very worn). *Heller.* $200/£128

HOMER. The Iliad of Homer. Maurice Hewlett (trans). London: Cressett, 1928. Ltd to 750. Teg. Vellum-backed orange cl bds, gilt. Very Nice. *Cady.* $60/£38

HOMER. The Iliad. Alexander Pope (trans). (London): Nonesuch, 1931. Ltd ed. Full brn niger morocco, raised bands, gilt top. Fine in box. *Appelfeld.* $400/£256

HOMER. The Iliad. London: Nonesuch, 1931. One of 1450. Brn niger. Fine. *Swann*.* $230/£147

HOMER. The Iliad. The Odyssey. Alexander Pope (trans). London: Nonesuch, 1931. One of 1450 numbered sets. 2 vols. Brn niger (spines dknd, cvrs spotted, discolored). Bd slipcases. *Swann*.* $316/£203

HOMER. The Iliad; The Odyssey. William Cullen Bryant (trans). Boston, (1898-99). 4 vols in 2. Teg. Contemp 3/4 tan calf, marbled bds (scuffed), gilt-paneled spines, leather labels. *Freeman*.* $50/£32

HOMER. The Odyssey of Homer. Alexander Pope (trans). Georgetown: Richard & Mallory, 1814. 2 vols. Engr frontis, tp each vol. Full leather. Good- (joints starting). *Scribe's Perch*.* $20/£13

HOMER. Odyssey. T.E. Lawrence (trans). (NY): OUP, 1940. 1st trade ed. VG in brn dec buckram. *Hadley.* $39/£25

HOMER. The Odyssey.... London, 1924. One of 530 numbered. 20 tipped-in color plts by William Russell Flint, guards. White buckram (spine sl dknd). Dj (spine chipped, fr panel separated). *Swann*.* $258/£165

HOMER. The Odyssey.... Cambridge, 1929. One of 550 numbered, signed by N.C. Wyeth (illus) and George Herbert Palmer (trans); w/o extra suite of loose plts. 15 tipped-in color plts, letter facs. (Prelims lt foxed.) 1/4 pigskin (spine dknd, rubbed). *Swann*.* $747/£479

HOMES, GEOFFREY. The Man Who Didn't Exist. NY: William Morrow, 1937. 1st ed. VG (cvrs spotted) in VG dj. *Janus.* $85/£54

HOMMEL, RUDOLF P. China at Work.... NY: Bucks County Hist Soc, (1937). 1st ed. Maroon cl, gilt cvr design, spine lettering. VF in dj (lt chipped). *Argonaut.* $150/£96

HOMSHER, LOLA M. (ed). South Pass 1868. Lincoln, 1960. 1st ed. Gilt-stamped cl, bds. NF in dj (shelf-rubbed). *Baade.* $35/£22

HONE, PHILIP. The Diary of Philip Hone 1828-1851. Allan Nevins (ed). NY: Dodd, Mead, 1927. 1st ed thus. One of 150. 2 vols. 1/2 vellum, bds. (1 spine cracked), else Good. Howes H620. *Brown.* $50/£32

HONE, PHILIP. The Diary of...1828-1851. Allan Nevins (ed). NY, 1927. 2 vols. Howes H620. *Ginsberg.* $50/£32

HONE, WILLIAM. Ancient Mysteries. London: William Reeves, n.d. 300pp (feps browned, hinges tender). Emb cl, gilt. *Edwards.* $55/£35

HONE, WILLIAM. The Political House That Jack Built. London, 1820. George Cruikshank (illus). (Foxing, lacks spine, bds detached, rubbed, bumped.) *Metropolitan*.* $57/£37

HONSINGER, WELTHY. Beyond the Moon Gate. London, 1925. 1st ed. (Feps lt browned; spine sl chipped.) *Edwards.* $23/£15

HOOD, CHARLES. A Practical Treatise upon Warming Buildings by Hot Water.... London/NY, 1897. 3rd new ed. xvi,593pp + 25pp ads. Ep ads. (Cl sl rubbed.) *Edwards.* $75/£48

HOOD, GRANT. Modern Methods in Horology. Peoria: Bradley Polytechnic Inst, 1913. Black blind-, gilt-stamped cl (extrems frayed, spine dull; ex-lib, pocket removed). *Weber.* $25/£16

HOOD, ROBIN A. (Pseud of Ernest Aris.) Just a Tiny Mite. Humphrey Milford, OUP, n.d. (1916). 1st ed. 16mo. (26pp); 6 color plts. Buff bds, pict onlay. VG. *Bookmark.* $47/£30

HOOD, ROBIN A. (Pseud of Ernest Aris.) Mother Mouse. Humphrey Milford, OUP, n.d. (1916). 1st ed. Sm 8vo. 28pp (foxed); 12 Fine color plts. Fine grn bds, pict onlay. *Bookmark.* $47/£30

HOOD, THOMAS. Memorials of Thomas Hood. Boston: Ticknor & Fields, 1860. 1st Amer ed. 2 vols. Emb brn cl (lt faded). VG (sm nameplt). *Antic Hay.* $50/£32

HOOD, THOMAS. Miss Kilmansegg and Her Precious Leg. E. Moxon Son, 1870. 1st ed. Thomas S. Seccombe (illus). Folio. ff.150. Aeg. (Rebound, w/orig cl; borders lt spotted), o/w VG. *Cox.* $55/£35

HOOD, THOMAS. The Plea of the Midsummer Fairies. London, 1827. 1st ed. Teg. 1/2 blue calf, spine gilt, leather label. Fine. *Argosy.* $300/£192

HOOD, WILLIAM. Spy Wednesday. NY: W.W. Norton, 1986. 1st ed. VF in dj. *Mordida.* $30/£19

HOOKER, JOHN. Some Reminiscences of a Long Life. Hartford: Belknap & Warfield, 1899. 1st ed. 351pp. Pub's cl. *Second Life.* $125/£80

HOOKER, JOSEPH DALTON. Himalayan Journals. London, 1893. 2nd ed. Frontis port, xxxi,574pp + (ii)pub's ads; 2 fldg maps, fldg panorama. (Feps lt browned; bkpl; spine sl rubbed.) *Edwards.* $39/£25

HOOKER, RICHARD. MASH. NY: Morrow, (1968). 1st ed. Fine in NF dj (2 sm stains rear panel). *Unger.* $225/£144

HOOKER, W. J. and G. A. W. ARNOTT. The British Flora. London, 1850. 6th ed. xlii,604pp (new eps), 24 ads; 12 plts. *Henly.* $33/£21

HOOLE, W. STANLEY. The Saga of Rube Burrow, King of American Train Robbers and His Band of Outlaws. University, AL: Confederate Pub Co, 1981. 1st ed. VG in wraps. *Gibbs.* $20/£13

HOOLE, W. STANLEY. Sam Slick in Texas. San Antonio: Naylor, 1945. 1st ed. Good in dj (wrapper sl chipped, worn, piece missing fr wrap). *Brown.* $20/£13

HOON, DUDLEY. The Adventures of Pongo the Pup, the Magic Train to Storyland. n.d. (c1940s). Brenda Sheldon (illus). Tall 8vo. Illus cl. NF in pict dj (chipped). *Bookmark.* $23/£15

HOOPER, JOHN and RODNEY. Modern Furniture and Fittings. Batsford, 1948. 1st ed. (Spine faded), else VG. *Hadley.* $39/£25

HOOPER, JOHN. Modern Cabinetwork, Furniture and Fitments. Batsford, 1952. 6th ed. 10 color, 82 monochrome plts. Blue cl, gilt. Good (lt wear, mks). *Whittle.* $47/£30

HOOPER, R. A Compendious Medical Dictionary. London: Murray & Highley, 1798. 1st ed. Unpaginated (c. 300pp). Contemp 1/2 calf, marbled bds. VG (lt foxed). *Glaser.* $250/£160

HOOPER, R. Lexicon Medicum; or Medical Dictionary.... London, 1831. 6th ed. 2 vols. viii,644; pp645-1311 (prelims sl foxed). Marbled eps, edges. 1/2 leather (rebacked) w/orig spines preserved. *Whitehart.* $140/£90

HOOTON, EARNEST ALBERT. The Indians of Pecos Pueblo. New Haven: Yale, 1930. 15 plts of skulls in pkt. Drk-grn cl (lt spotted). *Dawson.* $125/£80

HOOVER, HERBERT C. A Remedy for Disappearing Game Fishes. NY: Huntington, 1930. #68/900. Fine in glassine dj (sl torn), box (spine heel sl rubbed). *Polyanthos.* $150/£96

HOOVER, HERBERT. American Individualism. GC: Doubleday Page, 1922. 1st ed. (Spine gilt sl tarnished; fr bd top bumped), else NF in NF dj (tiny nicks; sl extrem dkng). *Between The Covers.* $85/£54

HOOVER, HERBERT. The Memoirs of Herbert Hoover. NY: Macmillan, 1951-1952. Vol 1 3rd ed; vol 2 1st ed; vol 3 1st ed. Frontis each vol. VG in djs (worn). *Graf.* $35/£22

HOPE, ANTHONY. Memories and Notes. NY: Doubleday, Doran, 1928. 1st US ed. VG. *Gravesend.* $35/£22

HOPE, ANTHONY. Memories and Notes.... Hutchinson, (1927). 1st ed. Frontis. VG. *Cox.* $31/£20

HOPE, ANTHONY. The Prisoner of Zenda. Bristol: Arrowsmith, (1894). 1st ed, w/ad leaf in 2nd state. Maroon cl (sl askew, spine sunned). *Swann*.* $92/£59

HOPE, ANTHONY. The Prisoner of Zenda. NY: LEC, (1966). One of 1500 numbered, signed by Donald Spencer (illus). 12 color plts. Leather-backed gilt-stamped cl. Mint in bd slipcase. *Argosy.* $100/£64

HOPE, ANTHONY. The Prisoner of Zenda. Bristol: Arrowsmith, 1894. 2nd issue w/18 rather than 17 titles listed as part of Arrowsmith 3/6 series after last text pg. VG (flyleaf hinges starting; spine sl faded, extrems sl rubbed). *Williams.* $117/£75

HOPE, ANTHONY. The Prisoner of Zenda. NY: Henry Holt, 1894. 1st Amer ed. (Sm engrs of Hope tipped to fr pastedown.) Teg. Red-stamped buckram. VG. *Antic Hay.* $125/£80

HOPE, ANTHONY. The Prisoner of Zenda. J.W. Arrowsmith, n.d. (1894). 1st ed. iv,5-310pp + 2pp ads. (Inner hinge cracked; faded), o/w VG. *Words Etc.* $56/£36

HOPE, ANTHONY. Quisante. London: Methuen, 1900. 1st ed, 1st issue. 48pp pub's cat at end dated Aug 1900. Fore-edges rough-trimmed, lower edges uncut. Ribbed greenish grey cl, gilt. (Eps, edges foxed), o/w Very Nice. *Temple.* $22/£14

HOPE, ANTHONY. Rupert of Hentzau. Arrowsmith, n.d. (1898). 1st UK ed. VG (bds lt stained). *Williams.* $39/£25

HOPE, ANTHONY. Rupert of Hentzau. Bristol: J.W. Arrowsmith, n.d. (1898). 1st ed. Inscribed presentation dated 1898. 385,(3)ad pp; 8 plts. Vertical ribbed cl (upper cvr mkd, backstrip faded), gilt. (Sm tear fep), o/w Good. *Cox.* $23/£15

HOPE, ANTHONY. The Secret of the Tower. NY: Appleton, 1919. 1st Amer ed. Good in dj (soil, spine head chipped). *Antic Hay.* $25/£16

HOPE, BOB. They Got Me Covered. (Hollywood, 1941.) 1st ed. VG in orig ptd wrappers (2 creases fr wrap). *Mcgowan.* $45/£29

HOPE, LAURA LEE. The Bobbsey Twins at School. G&D, 1913. 5x7.5. 216pp + ads. Grn cl, pict paste-on. Lists to #15. VG + (sl shelfworn) in dj (chipped). *My Bookhouse.* $35/£22

HOPE, LAURA LEE. The Bobbsey Twins at the County Fair. G&D, 1922. 1st ed. 5x7.5. 216pp. Cl, pict paste-on. Lists only to this title. (Bottom edge worn), else VG + in dj (sl worn, spine rubbed). *My Bookhouse.* $50/£32

HOPE, LAURA LEE. The Bobbsey Twins Treasure Hunting. G&D, 1920. Thicker ed w/paper dolls on dj rear. 5x7.5. 244pp + ads (sl browned). Grn cl (sl shelfworn). VG + in dj (3-inch closed tear, sl edge-worn). *My Bookhouse.* $20/£13

HOPE, LAURA LEE. The Story of a White Rocking Horse. G&D, 1920. 5.5x8.5. 120pp + ads. Yellow cl (sl shelfworn). Lists 12 titles. VG in dj (chipped). *My Bookhouse.* $18/£12

HOPE, THOMAS. An Historical Essay on Architecture. Murray, 1840. 3rd ed. 2 vols. xx,526, xiipp; 99plts. (Spines worn.) *Ars Artis.* $195/£125

HOPE, W. H. ST. JOHN. Heraldry for Craftsmen and Designers. NY, 1913. 1st Amer ed. Cl-backed bds. (Inner hinge broken; rubbed, spine dknd.) *King.* $35/£22

HOPE, WELBORN. Four Men Hanging. OKC, 1974. 1st ed. Fine. *Baade.* $65/£42

HOPE, WILLIAM. The Compleat Horseman (and) A Supplement of Horsemanship. London: R. Bonwick, 1717. 2nd ed. 2 parts in 1 vol. Tp,xlv,326; (323-324)contents, tp,xvi,300pp; 6 fldg plts (all rebacked; 2 sl chipped at fold w/sl loss; tp shaved at edges, sl soiled; 1 leaf sl torn; waterstaining 1st, last ll; lt browned, spotted; hinges reinforced.) Gilt-filleted edges (retipped), contemp calf bds (sympathetically re-backed in mod calf), raised bands, blind motifs, gilt spine title. *Edwards.* $546/£350

HOPKINS, ALFRED. American Country Houses of Today. NY: Architectural Book Pub Co, 1927. Gilt-lettered blue cl (sl worn, soiled). *Freeman*.* $100/£64

HOPKINS, EDWARD J. The Organ, Its History and Construction.... Robert Cocks, 1877. 3rd ed. xxxii,160,636pp; lg fldg plan (sm tear, w/o loss). Contemp (orig?) 1/2 maroon morocco, cl sides gold-blocked. VG. *Cox.* $101/£65

HOPKINS, FRANK E. The De Vinne and Marion Presses. Meriden: Columbian Club, 1936. One of 315. Cl, marbled bds. NF. *Dermont.* $35/£22

HOPKINS, GERARD MANLEY. The Correspondence of Gerard Manley Hopkins and Richard Watson Dixon. C. C. Abbott (ed). OUP, 1935. 1st Eng ed. Buckram. Very Nice (ex-lib, spine shelf-mk, stamp tp, inscrip) in dj (sl nicked, rubbed, shelf-mk). *Clearwater.* $78/£50

HOPKINS, GERARD MANLEY. The Correspondence of Gerard Manley Hopkins and Richard Watson Dixon. Claude Colleer Abbott (ed). OUP, 1935. 1st ed. (Inscrip; cl faded), o/w VG. *Poetry Bookshop.* $62/£40

HOPKINS, GERARD MANLEY. Further Letters of Gerard Manley Hopkins. Claude Colleer Abbott (ed). OUP, 1938. 1st ed. (Cl stained), o/w VG. *Poetry Bookshop.* $55/£35

HOPKINS, GERARD MANLEY. The Letters of Gerard Manley Hopkins to Robert Bridges. C.C. Abbott (ed). London: OUP, 1935. 1st ed. Port. Gilt cl. Fine in dj (spine sl tanned). *Reese.* $150/£96

HOPKINS, GERARD MANLEY. Letters to Robert Bridges. C. C. Abbott (ed). OUP, 1935. 1st Eng ed. Buckram. Very Nice (ex-lib, spine mk, stamp tp; inscrip) in dj (sl nicked, rubbed, shelf-mk). *Clearwater.* $86/£55

HOPKINS, GERARD MANLEY. The Note-Books and Papers of Gerard Manley Hopkins. Humphry House (ed). OUP, 1937. 1st Eng ed. Buckram. NF in dj (sl dusty). *Clearwater.* $133/£85

HOPKINS, GERARD MANLEY. Selected Poems. London: Nonesuch, 1954. One of 1100 numbered. Red morocco, inlaid w/purple morocco. 1/4 morocco fldg case. Swann*. $460/£295

HOPKINS, MANLEY. Hawaii: The Past, Present, and Future of Its Island Kingdom. London: Longmans, Green, 1866. 2nd ed. xxvii,523pp (lib stamps); fldg map, 7 plts. 1/2 brn calf, marbled bds. Adelson. $275/£176

HOPKINS, R. THURSTON. The Literary Landmarks of Devon and Cornwall. London, 1926. 1st ed. (2 leaves crudely opened, feps browned; spine frayed.) Edwards. $39/£25

HOPKINS, R. THURSTON. Moated Houses of England. Country Life, 1935. 1st ed. 47 half-tone plts. VG. Cox. $31/£20

HOPKINS, R. THURSTON. Old English Mills and Inns. London, 1927. 1st ed. Frontis. Spine label. (Feps lt browned; sl soiled, spine sl sunned.) Edwards. $55/£35

HOPKINS, RUFUS C. Roses and Thistles. SF: William Doxey, 1894. 1st ed. Frontis port, 480pp. Teg. Tan cl dec stamped in olive/gold. Fine in illus dj. Karmiole. $75/£48

HOPKINSON, CECIL. Collecting Golf Books 1743-1938. London: Constable, (1938). 1st ed. Orig ptd red wrappers. (Spine sl sunned, 1.5-inch tear fr joint, upper corner creased), else VG. Pacific*. $1,495/£958

HOPKINSON, TOM. Bert Hardy: Photojournalist. London: Gordon Fraser, 1975. 1st ed. 72 full-pg b/w photos. (Owner stamp), else Fine in pict stiff wrappers. Cahan. $35/£22

HOPPE, O. E. Romantic America. NY: B. Westermann, (1927). 1st Amer ed. 304 gravure plts. Screen-ptd color cl. (Owner stamp), else VG. Cahan. $85/£54

HOPPER, JAMES. Coming Back with the Spitball. Harper, 1914. 1st ed. Pict cvr (sm chip). VG+. Plapinger. $70/£45

HOPPER, NORA. Ballads in Prose. London: John Lane, 1894. 1st ed. Top edges yellow, rest uncut. Grn/yellow dec cl. Good (eps lt browned; spine sl bumped). Maggs. $101/£65

HORAN, JAMES D. Across the Cimarron. NY, (1956). 1st ed. Fine in dj (lt worn, stained). Pratt. $35/£22

HORAN, JAMES D. Confederate Agent, A Discovery in History. NY: Crown, (1954). 1st ed. VG in VG dj. Mcgowan. $35/£22

HORAN, JAMES D. Confederate Agent. NY: Crown, 1954. 1st ed. Frontis port, 14 plts. Fine in Good+ dj. Connolly. $40/£26

HORAN, JAMES D. The Life and Art of Charles Schreyvogel.... NY: Crown, (1969). 1st ed. Fine in Fine dj. Book Market. $50/£32

HORAN, JAMES D. Timothy O'Sullivan. GC: Doubleday, 1966. 1st ed. VG in dj. Lien. $50/£32

HORBLIT, HARRISON D. One Hundred Books Famous in Science. NY: Grolier Club, 1964. One of 1000 ptd. 2-tone cl. Fine in slipcase (sl rubbed). Waverly*. $385/£247

HORBLIT, HARRISON D. One Hundred Books Famous in Science. NY: Grolier Club, 1964. One of 1000. Inscribed, signed. Prospectus laid in. Slipcase. Swann*. $488/£313

HORDER, MERVYN. The Orange Carol Book. London: Constable, (1962). 1st Eng ed. Ed Ardizzone (illus). 8vo. 88pp. Color illus pict bds. W/o dj as issued. VG. Dower. $65/£42

HORE, EDWARD C. Tanganyika: Eleven Months in Central Africa. London: Edward Stanford, 1892. 2nd ed. Fldg frontis (repaired), xvi,2,306pp (tp blindstamp); 9 plts, 3 maps. Pict cl. Adelson. $225/£144

HORGAN, PAUL. The Centuries of Santa Fe. NY: E.P. Dutton, 1956. 1st ed. VG in dj. Perier. $50/£32

HORGAN, PAUL. Citizen of New Salem. NY: Farrar, Straus & Cudahy, (1961). 1st ed. NF in NF dj. Mcgowan. $15/£10

HORGAN, PAUL. Great River. NY, 1954. 2 vols. Fine in Fine dj. Turpen. $25/£16

HORGAN, PAUL. Great River: The Rio Grande in North American History. NY/Toronto: Rinehart, 1954. Trade ed. 2 vols. (Spines sl dull.) Pub's slipcase (sl shelfworn). Sadlon. $40/£26

HORGAN, PAUL. Great River: The Rio Grande.... NY: Rinehart, 1954. 1st ed. 2 vols. Map. VG in slipcase (sl worn). Lien. $50/£32

HORGAN, PAUL. The Thin Mountain Air. NY: FSG, (1977). 1st ed. Black cl, gilt. Fine in NF dj (fr flap creased). Blue Mountain. $25/£16

HORIGUCHI, SUTEMI. Tradition of Japanese Garden. Tokyo: Kokkussai Bunka Shinkokai, 1963. 2nd ed. 140 full-pg photo plts. Gilt-stamped pict cvr. Fine. Quest. $55/£35

HORLER, SYDNEY. The Curse of Doone. NY: Mystery League, 1930. 1st ed. VG in dj (lt wear, soil; few sm chips). Antic Hay. $25/£16

HORLER, SYDNEY. The Curse of Doone. NY: Mystery League, 1930. 1st Amer ed. NF (name; sm chip) in dj (spine, flap folds torn, spine extrems chipped). Polyanthos. $25/£16

HORLER, SYDNEY. The False Purple. NY: Mystery League, 1932. 1st Amer ed. NF (spine heel rubbed) in dj (torn, rubbed, 2 spine pieces missing). Polyanthos. $25/£16

HORLER, SYDNEY. Harlequin of Death. Little, Brown, 1933. 1st ed. (Bkpl, edges dusty.) VG+ in dj (few sm tears). Certo. $30/£19

HORN, MADELINE DARROUGH. Farm on the Hill. NY: Scribner, 1936. 1st ed. Grant Wood (illus). Sm 4to. (Sl worn.) Dj (frayed, chipped, sl spotted). Oinonen*. $80/£51

HORN, STANLEY F. The Army of Tennessee.... Indianapolis, (1941). 1st ed. One of 1000 signed. Frontis, 20 plts on 10 sheets, 11 maps. (Lt foxed; lt soil fr cvr, spine sl faded.) Kane*. $65/£42

HORN, STANLEY F. The Decisive Battle of Nashville. Knoxville, (1956). 1st ed. VG+ in dj (worn, faded). Pratt. $45/£29

HORN, STANLEY F. Invisible Empire. Boston, 1939. 1st ed. Wantagh. $60/£38

HORN, STANLEY F. (ed). The Robert E. Lee Reader. NY, (1949). 1st ed. VG+ in dj (wear). Pratt. $42/£27

HORN, TOM. Life of Tom Horn, Government Scout and Interpreter. Doyce B. Nunis, Jr. (ed). Chicago: Lakeside Classic, 1987. Color map. Teg. Brn cl, gilt. Fine. Bohling. $20/£13

HORNADAY, WILLIAM T. Camp-Fires in the Canadian Rockies. NY, 1906. 1st ed. 55 photo plts, 2 maps. Teg. Grey-blue cl, gilt, photo of mountain goat tipped on cvr. (Edgewear), else VG. Price. $175/£112

HORNADAY, WILLIAM T. Camp-Fires in the Canadian Rockies. NY: Scribner, 1906. 1st ed. Photo frontis. Teg. Grn binding, gilt lettering; inlaid photo cvr. VG+ (spine edge chipped). Backman. $135/£87

HORNADAY, WILLIAM T. Camp-Fires in the Canadian Rockies. London: T. Werner Laurie, 1907. 1st ed. xvii,353pp; 49 plts, 2 maps. Blue cl, dec vignette. (Sl scratch lower cvr), else Fine. Sotheran. $309/£198

HORNADAY, WILLIAM T. Camp-Fires on Desert and Lava. NY, 1908. 1st ed. 60 photo plts, 2 maps. Teg. Red cl, gilt, color plt of mountain sheep tipped on fr cvr. (Edgewear), else VG. Price. $95/£61

HORNADAY, WILLIAM T. Camp-Fires on Desert and Lava. NY: Scribner, 1908. 1st ed. Color frontis. Teg. Inlaid photo cvr. Good+ (spine edge worn, faded, soiled; name). *Backman.* $80/£51

HORNADAY, WILLIAM T. Camp-Fires on Desert and Lava. NY: Scribner, 1908. 1st ed. 2 maps, 8 color plts. Red cl, gilt, color illus mtd fr cvr. Good. *Karmiole.* $100/£64

HORNADAY, WILLIAM T. Our Vanishing Wild Life. NY Zoological Soc, 1913. (Bkpl; spine lt faded.) *Edwards.* $55/£35

HORNADAY, WILLIAM T. Taxidermy and Zoological Collecting. London, 1891. xix,362pp, 24 plts. (Spine sl chipped, rubbed.) *Edwards.* $273/£175

HORNBEIN, THOMAS F. Everest, the West Ridge. SF: Sierra Club, (1965). 1st ed. VG in dj (torn, chipped). *King.* $100/£64

HORNE, HERBERT P. The Binding of Books. London, 1894. Ltd to 150. 224pp. 1/4 paper-parchment, cl bds. VG. *Truepenny.* $325/£208

HORNELL, JAMES. Fishing in Many Waters. Cambridge, 1950. 1st ed. 37 plts. (Cl sl stained.) *Maggs.* $59/£38

HORNER, CHARLES F. The Life of James Redpath and the Development of the Modern Lyceum. NY/Newark: Barse & Hopkins, (1926). 1st ed. Moire silk cl (sm rubbed spot), paper cvr, spine labels. *Sadlon.* $20/£13

HORNER, G. R. B. Medical Topography of Brazil and Uruguay. Phila: Blakiston, 1845. 1st ed. 296pp, 4 plts. Complete w/errata slip laid in. Good (text foxed, browned; binding worn). *Glaser.* $125/£80

HORNUNG, E. W. Mr. Justice Raffles. London: Smith, Elder, 1909. 1st UK ed. VG. *Williams.* $195/£125

HORNUNG, E. W. Raffles, the Amateur Cracksman. London: Eyre & Spottiswoode, 1956. 1st Eng ed. Nice in dj (rubbed). *Clearwater.* $39/£25

HOROWITZ, MIKHAIL. Big League Poets. City Lights, 1978. 1st ed. VG+. *Plapinger.* $75/£48

HORRAX, GILBERT. Neurosurgery: An Historical Sketch. Springfield, 1952. 1st ed. (Red pencil underlinings.) *Fye.* $75/£48

HORRY, PETER and M. L. WEEMS. The Life of Gen. Francis Marion. Phila: Joseph Allen, 1854. Later ed. Frontis, 252pp, 3 plts. (Text sl stained; cl worn, soiled), else Good. Howes H650. *Brown.* $15/£10

HORSFALL, FRANK L. Diagnosis of Viral and Rickettsial Infections: Symposium Held...1948. NY, 1949. 1st ed. VG (ex-libris; sl worn). *Doctor's Library.* $45/£29

HORSFORD, EBEN NORTON. The Landfall of Leif Erikson A.D. 1000 and the Site of His Houses in Vineland. Boston, 1892. 1st ed. 148pp. Teg. (Back cvr soiled; wear.) *King.* $75/£48

HORSFORD, EBEN NORTON. The Problem of the Northmen. Boston: Houghton, Mifflin, 1890. 23pp; 3 fldg maps. (Sl worn.) *Dumont.* $65/£42

HORSLEY, J. SHELTON. Surgery of the Stomach and Small Intestine. NY: Appleton, 1926. (Cl rubbed), else Good. *Goodrich.* $65/£42

HORSLEY, J. W. Jottings from Jail, Notes and Papers on Prison Matters. London: T. Fisher Unwin, 1887. *Boswell.* $75/£48

HORWOOD, WILLIAM. Duncton Wood. Country Life, 1980. 1st UK ed. VG in dj (sm nick, lt creased). *Williams.* $86/£55

HOSIE, ALEXANDER. Three Years in Western China. London, 1897. 2nd ed. Frontis, xxvii,302pp; fldg map. (Feps lt browned, hinges tender; cl lt dampstained, spine sl rubbed.) *Edwards.* $31/£20

HOSKIN, BERYL. A History of the Santa Clara Mission Library. Oakland: Biobooks, 1961. 1st ed. Ltd to 500. 5 plts, 1 color. NF (damp mk fr cvr). *Connolly.* $45/£29

HOSKINS, FRANKLIN E. From the Nile to Nebo. Phila: Sunday School Times, 1912. 1st ed. 2plts, lg fldg map. Grn cl, gilt. VG. *House.* $45/£29

HOSKINS, NATHAN. A History of the State of Vermont.... Vergennes: Shedd, 1831. 1st ed. 316pp. Orig blue muslin-backed bds, ptd paper spine label. *Ginsberg.* $350/£224

HOSMER, JAMES K. (ed). History of the Expedition of Captains Lewis and Clark. Chicago: A.C. McClurg, 1924. 2 vols. VG (vol 2 corner bumped). Howes L317. *Lien.* $100/£64

HOSMER, JAMES K. A Short History of the Mississippi Valley. Boston/NY: Houghton Mifflin, 1902. 2nd ed. (Spine ends rubbed.) *Sadlon.* $15/£10

HOSMER, JOHN ALLEN. A Trip to the States. Edith M. Duncan (ed). Missoula: Rptd from The Frontier, 1932. Ptd wraps (sl worn, dknd, spine split). Howes H662. *Bohling.* $30/£19

HOSOE, EIKOH. Ba Ra Kei: Ordeal by Roses. NY: Aperture, 1985. 1st ed. Fine in illus dj (sm tear repaired on verso w/cellophane tape). *Cahan.* $125/£80

Hostetter's Illustrated U.S. Almanac for the Year 1895 Calculated for Boston, Pittsburgh and New Orleans. Pittsburgh: Hostetter, (1894). 36pp. Orig pict wrappers. (Upper cvr faded, edgewear, 3 corners sl chipped.) *Sadlon.* $10/£6

HOTCHKIN, S. F. Ancient and Modern Germantown, Mount Airy and Chestnut Hill. Phila, 1889. 3/4 morocco (rubbed, spine defective, hinges stressed). *Freeman*.* $20/£13

HOTTEN, JOHN CAMDEN (ed). The Original Lists of Persons of Quality.... NY: Empire State Book Co, ca 1930. Navy cl (sl spotted; bkpl removed), ptd paper spine label (lt chipped). *Baltimore*.* $20/£13

HOTZ, H. The Moral and Intellectual Diversity of Races.... Phila: Lippincott, 1856. 512pp. (Shelfwear, chipped ends.) *Cullen.* $40/£26

HOUART, V. Miniature Silver Toys. Alpine, NY, 1981. NF in NF dj, VG slipcase. *Scribe's Perch*.* $22/£14

HOUBEN, H. H. The Call of the North. London, 1932. Map. VG in dj (chipped). *High Latitude.* $25/£16

HOUCK, LOUIS (ed). The Spanish Regime in Missouri. Chicago: R.R. Donnelly, 1909. 1st ed. 2 vols. Teg. Cl, black leather labels. (Worn, rubbed, spotted), else Good. Howes H672. *Brown.* $175/£112

HOUDIN, ROBERT. The Memoirs of.... Phila: George G. Evans, 1859. 1st Amer ed. (1-inch x 1.5-inch piece cut from fep; lt wear spine extrems), else VG. *Between The Covers.* $300/£192

HOUDINI, HARRY. The Unmasking of Robert-Houdin. NY: Publishers Ptg Co, 1908. 1st ed. Index of illus loose, as issued. Pict cl (bkpl; extrems scuffed). *Dramatis Personae.* $150/£96

HOUDON, JEAN-ANTOINE. The Sculptures of Houdon. NY: Oxford, 1975. Fine in VG dj. *Metropolitan*.* $46/£29

HOUGH, EMERSON. The Law of the Land. Indianapolis, (1904). 1st ed. (Stamped bkpls ep; spine dull; fr cvr cl sl bubbled), else Good. *King.* $20/£13

HOUGH, WALTER. Antiquities of the Upper Gila and Salt River Valleys in Arizona and New Mexico. BAE Bulletin 35. Washington: GPO, 1907. (Lt soiled; extrems sl rubbed.) *Sadlon.* $20/£13

HOUGH, WALTER. Collection of Heating and Lighting Utensils in the United States National Museum. Washington: US Gov Office, 1928. 99 plts. (Ex-lib, ink stamp, label remains; rebound in lib cl.) *Edwards.* $62/£40

Houghton's Genuine Almanac. The Gentlemen's and Ladies Diary and Almanac...1808.... Keene, NH: John Prentiss, (1807). 44pp. (Pp browned; edges sl chipped.) Orig ptd wrappers. *Sadlon*. $45/£29

HOUGHTON, CLAUDE. This Was Ivor Trent. London: Heinemann, 1935. 1st ed. Inscribed. Fine in dj (spine top, corners chipped). *Mordida*. $150/£96

HOUGHTON, ELIZA P. DONNER. The Expedition of the Donner Party and Its Tragic Fate. Chicago: A.C. McClurg, 1911. 1st ed. Uncut. Brn cl, gilt. News clipping laid in. (Tear 1 pg skillfully repaired w/archival tape, 2pp browned), o/w VG. *Pacific**. $92/£59

HOUGHTON, SAMUEL G. A Trace of Desert Waters. Glendale: Clark, 1976. 1st ed. One of 1526. Fldg color map, 10 single-pg maps and charts. VF in pict dj. *Argonaut*. $50/£32

HOULT, NORAH. Violet Ryder. London: Elkin Matthews & Marron, 1930. One of 800. (Eps dknd), else Fine in VG dj (sm chip; spine dkng). *Between The Covers*. $75/£48

House That Jack Built. NY: McLoughlin Bros, 1904. Little Pig Series. 10.5x8.5. (14)pp. Color pict wraps (worn, creased, corners chipped). *King*. $45/£29

HOUSE, EDWARD J. A Hunter's Camp-Fires. NY: Harper, 1909. 1st ed. VG. *Bowman*. $85/£54

HOUSE, EDWARD M. The Intimate Papers of Colonel House. Charles Seymour (ed). Boston/NY: Houghton Mifflin, (1926). 2 vols. Teg. Red cl, gilt. (Ex-lib, shellac on spines.) *Bohling*. $12/£8

HOUSE, HOMER. Wild Flowers of New York. Albany: Univ of State of NY: 1918, 1920. 1st ed. 2 vols. 264 color plts. VG- (bumped). *Archer*. $120/£77

Household Primer. Boston: D. Lothrop, 1885. Sm 8vo. (8)ff. NF in self-wrappers. *Bromer*. $85/£54

HOUSEHOLD, GEOFFREY. The Courtesy of Death. Boston: Little, Brown, (1967). 1st Amer ed. Papercvrd bds. Fine in dj (sl worn). *Antic Hay*. $25/£16

HOUSEHOLD, GEOFFREY. The Last Two Weeks of Georges Rivac. London: Michael Joseph, 1978. 1st ed. Fine in dj. *Mordida*. $45/£29

HOUSEHOLD, GEOFFREY. Olura. London: Michael Joseph, 1965. 1st ed. (Pg edges sl dknd), o/w Fine in dj (spine sl dknd, back panel lt soiled). *Mordida*. $45/£29

HOUSEHOLD, GEOFFREY. Rogue Male. Little, Brown, 1939. 1st US ed. VG (spine sunned) in Good+ dj (corner tears, chips, internal mends). *Certo*. $65/£42

HOUSEHOLD, GEOFFREY. Summon the Bright Water. London: Michael Joseph, 1981. 1st ed. Fine in dj. *Mordida*. $45/£29

HOUSEHOLD, GEOFFREY. A Time to Kill. Boston: Little Brown, 1951. 1st ed. Fine in dj (crease fr panel, sm closed tear). *Mordida*. $45/£29

HOUSEHOLD, GEOFFREY. Watcher in the Shadows. London: Michael Joseph, 1960. 1st ed. Fine in dj. *Mordida*. $60/£38

HOUSHOLDER, BOB (ed). Grand Slam of North American Wild Sheep. Phoenix, (1974). Gilt-pict cl (lt worn). *Oinonen**. $90/£58

HOUSMAN, A. E. A Shropshire Lad. Alcuin Press, 1929. One of 325 numbered. Unopened. 1/4 linen, grey paper over bds. (Bd margins sl faded, bottom corners sl bumped), else Fine. *Michael Taylor*. $59/£38

HOUSMAN, A. E. A Shropshire Lad. NY: Heritage, 1935. 1st ed. Fldg frontis (corner creased), initialed by Edward A. Wilson (artist). Full blind-stamped pigskin, gilt-stamped spine. (Spine sunned), o/w Fine in cardboard slipcase (sunned). *Beasley*. $100/£64

HOUSMAN, A. E. Some Poems, Some Letters. London, 1937. 1st ed. (Label remains rep; faded, soiled), o/w VG in dj (sl chipped, soiled, torn). *Words Etc*. $23/£15

HOUSMAN, LAURENCE (retold by). Princess Badoura. London: Hodder & Stoughton, n.d. (1913). Edmund Dulac (illus). 4to. Gilt-dec cl (sl worn). *Oinonen**. $130/£83

HOUSMAN, LAURENCE (retold by). Stories from the Arabian Nights. London, (1907). One of 350 numbered, signed by Edmund Dulac (illus). 50 tipped-in color plts, guards. Vellum (spine, fr cvr dknd, spotted, lacks ties), gilt. *Swann**. $402/£258

HOUSMAN, LAURENCE (retold by). Stories from the Arabian Nights. London, (1907). One of 350 numbered, signed by Edmund Dulac (illus). 4to. 50 tipped-in color plts, guards. Rebound in red morocco by Zaehnsdorf, gilt. *Swann**. $862/£553

HOUSMAN, LAURENCE. The Cloak of Friendship. London, 1905. 1st ed. (Foxing, 2 leaves defective; cvrs sl mkd; lacks dj.) *Typographeum*. $30/£19

HOUSMAN, LAURENCE. The Life of H. R. H. The Duke of Flamborough. NY: Payson & Clarke, 1929. Crushed velvet cl, w/orig button on string bound in. NF (spine top worn) in dj (lt wear, browning). *Antic Hay*. $30/£19

HOUSMAN, LAURENCE. The New Hangman. London/NY: Putnam, (1930). Ltd to 250 numbered, signed. Teg. Dec blue cl. VG. *Antic Hay*. $75/£48

HOUSMAN, LAURENCE. Princess Badoura. London: Hodder & Stoughton, (1913). One of 750 signed by Edmund Dulac (illus). Pict cl. *Swann**. $690/£442

HOUSMAN, LAURENCE. Stories from the Arabian Nights. London, n.d. (1907). Edmund Dulac (illus). Pict cvrs, gilt. VG (bkpl; spine, corners lt rubbed). *Polyanthos*. $125/£80

HOUSTON, JAMES D. Between Battles. NY: Dial, 1968. Fine (sl rubbed) in Fine dj. *Between The Covers*. $65/£42

HOUSTON, PEYTON. Occasions in a World. Penland, NC: Jargon Society, 1969. 1st ed. Plain stiff wrappers. Fine in dj. *Cahan*. $25/£16

HOUSTON, ROBERT. Legacy to an Unborn Son. (Boston): Beacon, 1971. 1st ed. 128 full-pg photos. NF. *Cahan*. $45/£29

HOUSTON, SAM. The Autobiography of Sam Houston. Donald Day and H.H. Ullom (eds). Norman: Univ of OK, (1954). 1st ed. VG in dj. *Lien*. $35/£22

Houston, a History and Guide. Houston: Anson Jones, 1942. 1st ed. 2 maps. Pict cl. VG+ in dj (sl dknd, edgeworn). *Bohling*. $40/£26

HOVELL, MARK. Rats and How to Destroy Them. London, 1924. (Scuffed, spine sl chipped.) *Edwards*. $75/£48

HOVER, JOHN C. et al. Memoirs of the Miami Valley. Chicago, 1919-1920. 1st ed. 3 vols. Orig 1/2 morocco. *Ginsberg*. $175/£112

HOVEY, C. M. The Fruits of America.... NY: D. Appleton, 1853. 48 hand-colored plts. (Foxing, dampstaining throughout.) Full gilt-dec leather (rubbed, hinges weak). *Metropolitan**. $1,466/£940

HOW, DAVID. Diary of David How.... Morrisiana, NY, 1865. 1st ed. One of 250 numbered, signed by Henry G. Dawson (notes). (15),51pp. (Lacks paper label.) Howes H697. *Ginsberg*. $175/£112

HOW, LOUIS. Nursery Rhymes of New York City. NY, 1931. 8vo. 92pp, 20 wood-block illus by Ilse Bischoff. 1/4 cl, dec bds. Clean in dj (wear, stained). *Truepenny*. $45/£29

HOW, LOUIS. The Other Don Juan. NY, 1932. 1/4 cl, crimson bds, gilt. VG (bkpl). *Truepenny*. $45/£29

HOWARD, BENJAMIN C. Report of the Decision of the Supreme Court...in the Case of Dred Scott.... NY: Appleton, 1857. 1st ed. (Lt browning, 2 sm water stains, sl foxing tp.) Later brn buckram. Howes S221. *Waverly**. $253/£162

HOWARD, CLIFFORD. What Happened at Olenberg. Chicago: Reilly & Britton, (1911). 1st ed. 8vo. 11 full-pg illus by Emile A. Nelson. Color pict cl. VG in dj (chipped, nicked). *Houle.* $95/£61

HOWARD, DAVID and JOHN AYERS. China for the West. London, 1978. 2 vols. Djs, box (sl spotted). *Kane*.* $325/£208

HOWARD, E. Garden Cities of To-morrow. London: Swan, 1902. Port, 5 plts. Dec cl. Sound. *Ars Artis.* $39/£25

HOWARD, F. E. The Mediaeval Styles of the English Parish Church. Batsford, 1936. 1st ed. (Feps lt browned; edges sl rubbed.) *Edwards.* $39/£25

HOWARD, F. E. and F. H. CROSSLEY. English Church Woodwork. A Study...AD 1250-1550. London: Batsford, 1917. (Cvr sl faded.) Internally Good. *Ars Artis.* $39/£25

HOWARD, F. K. Fourteen Months in American Bastiles. Balt: Kelly, Hedian & Piet, 1863. Orig ptd wraps (spine worn). *Wantagh.* $60/£38

HOWARD, FRANK. Colour as a Means of Art.... London: Joseph Thomas, 1838. 1st ed. 206pp + 2pp ads; 18 hand-color aquatint plts, guards. Orig grn emb cl (rebacked), old spine (faded, ends repaired) laid down. (Sig), o/w Interior Fine. *Europa.* $109/£70

HOWARD, H. A. and D. L. McGRATH. War Chief Joseph. Caldwell: Caxton, (June 1958). Gilt-dec cl. Fine in VG dj. *Mikesh.* $35/£22

HOWARD, H. E. The British Warblers. London, 1907-14. 2 vols. 12 maps, 51 plain, 35 chromolitho plts. Nice in contemp 1/2 dk grn morocco (spines sl faded). *Maggs.* $741/£475

HOWARD, H. E. An Introduction to the Study of Bird Behaviour. CUP, 1929. 1st ed. 11 plts, 2 plans. (Lt browned, bkpl; spine lt discolored.) *Edwards.* $70/£45

HOWARD, H. H. The History of Virgil A. Stewart and His Adventures.... NY: Harper, 1842. (Damp stain fore-edge 1/3 of bk, overall lt soil, new spine label), o/w VG. Howes H700. *Hermitage.* $200/£128

HOWARD, H. R. History of Virgil A. Stewart, and His Adventure in Capturing and Exposing the Great 'Western Land Pirate'.... NY: Harper, 1836. 1st ed. 273,(36 ads)pp. Orig cl. (Tp mended; spine label gone, crown chipped, ex-lib mk.) Howes H700. *Ginsberg.* $250/£160

HOWARD, HAROLD P. Sacajawea. Norman: Univ of OK, (1971). 1st ed. VG in dj. *Lien.* $25/£16

HOWARD, JOHN TASKER. The Music of George Washington's Time. Washington: US George Washington Bicentennial Commission, 1932. VG in pict self-wrappers (sl soiled). *Connolly.* $22/£14

HOWARD, JOSEPH K. Strange Empire. NY: Morrow, 1952. 1st ed. VG. *Graf.* $25/£16

HOWARD, L. The Climate of London. 1833. 2nd ed. 3 vols. lxxii,348pp, 2 fldg charts; 408pp; 384pp (foxing). 1/2 calf (spine, corners very rubbed, vol 1 joints sl weak). *Whitehart.* $281/£180

HOWARD, L. H. The Insect Book. London, 1902. 13 color, 35 plain plts. (Rebacked, preserving spine.) *Henly.* $28/£18

HOWARD, L. O. History of Applied Entomology (Somewhat Anecdotal). Washington: Smithsonian, Nov. 1930. 1st ed. 51 photo port plts. Uncut. NF in wraps. *Mikesh.* $50/£32

HOWARD, LELAND O. et al. The Mosquitoes of North and Central America and the West Indies. Washington, DC: Carnegie Inst, 1912. 4 vols in 3. 150 plts. Brn cl, gilt. VG (ex-lib, spine # removed). *Price.* $145/£93

HOWARD, LEON. The Connecticut Wits. Chicago, (1943). 1st ed. *Ginsberg.* $75/£48

HOWARD, MICHAEL S. Jonathan Cape, Publisher. Cape, (1971). 1st ed. Buckram, gilt. VG in dj. *Ash.* $31/£20

HOWARD, MONTAGUE. Old London Silver. NY/London: Scribner, Oct 1903. 1st ed. 6 color plts. Full leather, new spine. Fair (ex-lib). *Scribe's Perch*.* $32/£21

HOWARD, ROBERT E. The Coming of Conan. NY: Gnome, (1954). 1st ed. (Lt rubbed.) Dj. *Swann*.* $80/£51

HOWARD, ROBERT E. Conan the Conqueror, with The Sword of Rhianon by Leigh Brackett. NY: Ace, (1953). 1st thus. (Store stamp each side), else VG- in pict wrappers. *Other Worlds.* $25/£16

HOWARD, ROBERT E. Conan the Conqueror. NY: Gnome, (1950). 1st ed. Dj. *Swann*.* $138/£88

HOWARD, ROBERT E. Conan the Conqueror.... NY: Gnome, (1950). 1st ed. Dj. *Kane*.* $95/£61

HOWARD, ROBERT E. The Dark Man and Others. Sauk City: Arkham House, (1963). 1st ed. Dj (crease fr panel, rear flap lacks sm piece). *Swann*.* $138/£88

HOWARD, ROBERT E. The Dark Man and Others. Sauk City: Arkham House, 1963. 1st ed. NF (bkpl sl removed fr pastedown) in dj (edgeworn). *Other Worlds.* $120/£77

HOWARD, ROBERT E. The Dark Man and Others. Sauk City: Arkham, 1963. 1st ed. VG in dj (rubbed, worn). *Metropolitan*.* $57/£37

HOWARD, ROBERT E. The Dark Man. Sauk City: Arkham House, 1963. 1st ed. VF in illus dj. *Bromer.* $175/£112

HOWARD, ROBERT E. The Garden of Fear and Other Stories of the Bizarre and Fantastic. L.A.: Crawford, (1945). 1st ed. Fine (bkpl) in ptd wrappers (chip). *Bromer.* $150/£96

HOWARD, ROBERT E. A Gent from Bear Creek. Donald M. Grant, 1965. 1st US ed. NF in dj (spine lt sunned). *Certo.* $50/£32

HOWARD, ROBERT E. The Grey God Passes. (Columbia: Charles Miller, 1975.) 1st separate ed. Fine in ptd wrappers. *Other Worlds.* $25/£16

HOWARD, ROBERT E. King Conan. NY: Gnome Press, (1953). 1st ed. Fine in dj. *Hermitage.* $250/£160

HOWARD, ROBERT E. King Conan. NY: Gnome, (1953). 1st ed. (Bkpl.) Dj. *Swann*.* $115/£74

HOWARD, ROBERT E. Marchers of Valhalla. Grant, 1972. 1st ed. Fine in Fine dj. *Certo.* $35/£22

HOWARD, ROBERT E. Red Shadows. RI: Grant, 1968. 1st ed. NF in NF dj (lt soiled). *Metropolitan*.* $57/£37

HOWARD, ROBERT E. Singers in the Shadows. West Kingston: Grant, 1970. 1st ed. Dj. *Swann*.* $92/£59

HOWARD, ROBERT E. Singers in the Shadows. West Kingston: Grant, 1970. 1st ed. (Spine roll), else Fine in As New dj. *Other Worlds.* $135/£87

HOWARD, ROBERT E. Skull-Face and Others. Arkham House, 1946. 1st ed. (Spine gilt sl oxidized, pg edges aged, spine tip sl bumped.) NF in Bright Hannes Bok dj (sm closed tear, rear panel sl soiled). *Certo.* $475/£304

HOWARD, ROBERT E. Skull-Face and Others. Sauk City: Arkham House, 1946. 1st ed. Fine in illus dj (edges lt chipped). *Bromer.* $500/£321

HOWARD, ROBERT E. Skull-Face and Others. Sauk City: Arkham, 1946. 1st ed. Fine in NF dj (edges, back panel lt grayed). *Metropolitan*.* $402/£258

HOWARD, ROBERT E. Skull-Face Omnibus. Jersey: Neville Spearman, (1974). 1st Eng ed. Fine in VG dj (corner wear, sm tears). *Certo.* $25/£16

HOWARD, ROBERT E. The Sword of Conan. NY: Gnome, (1952). 1st ed. (Lt rubbed.) Dj. *Swann*.* $92/£59

HOWARD, ROBERT E. and TEVIS CLYDE SMITH. Red Blades of Black Cathay. West Kingston, RI, 1971. 1st ed. One of 1000. VF. Dj (spine dknd) else Fine. *Mcclintock.* $55/£35

HOWARD, ROBERT WEST. The Great Iron Trail. NY: Putnam, 1962. Good in dj (worn). *Dumont.* $25/£16

HOWARD-BURY, C. K. Mount Everest, the Reconnaissance, 1921. NY, 1922. 1st Amer ed. (Soil), else Good in dj (cello-tape repaired, chipped). *King.* $150/£96

HOWAT, JOHN K. The Hudson River and Its Painters. NY: Viking, (1972). 1st ed. Orange buckram. Fine in dj. *House.* $60/£38

HOWBERT, ABRAHAM R. Reminiscences of the War. (Springfield, OH, 1884.) 1st ed. 388pp. VG (scuffed). *Mcgowan.* $125/£80

HOWDEN-SMITH, ARTHUR D. Grey Maiden. NY/London/Toronto: Argosy, 1929. 1st ed. VG in VG dj (nicks, spine lt soiled). *Mcclintock.* $100/£64

HOWE, BEA. Lady with Green Fingers: The Life of Jane Loudon. Country Life, 1961. NF in dj. *Hadley.* $25/£16

HOWE, G. Of the Making of CXXV Books—A Publisher's Bibliography. G. Howe, 1934. 1/4 cl. VG. *Moss.* $28/£18

HOWE, GRAHAM et al. Two Views of Manzanar. L.A.: Frederick S. Wight Art Gallery, UCLA, 1978. 1st ed. 36 full-pg b/w photos. NF. *Cahan.* $40/£26

HOWE, HENRY. Historical Collections of Ohio. Cincinnati: The State, 1904. Ltr ed. 2 vols. Dk red buckram. NF. *Archer.* $75/£48

HOWE, JAMES VIRGIL. The Modern Gunsmith. NY/London: Funk & Wagnalls, 1934. 1st ed. 2 vols. Gun-metal gray paint (sl flaked) over black cl backstrips (sl worn), grn/black gilt-flecked cl. Texts Good (eps sl aged) in orig bd slipcase (worn, edges partly broken). *Baltimore*.* $45/£29

HOWE, JAMES. The Celery Stalks at Midnight. Atheneum, 1983. 1st ed. 5.5x8.5. 111pp. NF in dj (sl worn). *My Bookhouse.* $30/£19

HOWE, JOSEPH W. Excessive Venery, Masturbation and Continence.... NY, 1887. 1st ed. 299pp. Tooled cl (inner fr hinge starting; sl worn). VG. *Doctor's Library.* $80/£51

HOWE, LOIS L. and CONSTANCE FULLER. Details from Old New England Houses. NY: Architectural Book Pub Co, 1913. 1st ed. 50 plts. 3/4 cl, bds (scuffed, worn), ptd lettering piece. VG. *House.* $150/£96

HOWE, LUCIEN. A Bibliography of Hereditary Eye Defects. Cambridge, MA, 1928. VG in wrappers. *Fye.* $40/£26

HOWE, MARK DE WOLFE (ed). Holmes-Pollock Letters, the Correspondence...1874-1932. Cambridge: Harvard Univ, 1944. 2 vols. (1st blank torn away), else Good in djs (defective). *Boswell.* $65/£42

HOWE, OCTAVIUS THORNDIKE. Argonauts of '49: History of Adventures of the Emigrant Companies from Massachusetts, 1849-1850. Cambridge: Harvard Univ, 1923. 1st ed. Frontis, 8 plts. Teg. (Sl worn), o/w NF. *Pacific*.* $35/£22

HOWE, SAMUEL G. An Historical Sketch of the Greek Revolution. NY: White, Galleher & White, 1828. 1st ed. xxxvi,452pp. Contemp calf. (Lacks fldg map, margins sl damp-stained, sl wormholes; edges rubbed), o/w Good. *Worldwide.* $65/£42

HOWELL, ARTHUR. Florida Bird Life. NY: FL Dept of Game, 1932. 1st ed. 58 color plts, 72 maps. NF. *Agvent.* $100/£64

HOWELL, H. GRADY. Going to Meet the Yankees. Jackson, (1981). 1st ed. Fine in dj (lt wear). *Pratt.* $65/£42

HOWELL, JAMES. Certain Letters of James Howell Selected...as First Published Between 1645 and 1655. NY: Wm. Rudge, 1928. One of 1000. Cl-backed bds, gilt. VG + . *Bohling.* $22/£14

HOWELL, JOHN. An Essay on the War-Galleys of the Ancients. Edinburgh: The Author, 1826. 1st ed. Fldg engr frontis, (iii),61pp; ad leaf, 10 full-pg engr plts at rear. Recent brn calf, marbled bds, gilt. (Orig pict ptd fr wrapper bound in; sm sticker fr cvr; lt foxed, rippled.) *Baltimore*.* $130/£83

HOWELLS, JOHN MEAD. Lost Examples of Colonial Architecture. NY, 1931. Ltd to 1100. 244 full-pg plts. VG (ink name ep). *Truepenny.* $85/£54

HOWELLS, JOHN MEAD. Lost Examples of Colonial Architecture. NY: William Helburn, 1931. Ltd to 1100. 244 plts. Good (shelfwear). *Cullen.* $75/£48

HOWELLS, WILLIAM COOPER. Recollections of Life in Ohio, from 1813 to 1840. Cincinnati, 1895. Frontis port. Pub's cl. Howes H734. *Swann*.* $69/£44

HOWELLS, WILLIAM DEAN. A Counterfeit Presentment. Boston, 1877. 1st ed. (Spine worn.) *Argosy.* $25/£16

HOWELLS, WILLIAM DEAN. Doctor Breen's Practice. Boston, 1881. 1st ed. Grn cl (spine rubbed). *Argosy.* $75/£48

HOWELLS, WILLIAM DEAN. Familiar Spanish Travels. NY, 1913. 1st ed. Grn cl, gilt. VG. *Argosy.* $60/£38

HOWELLS, WILLIAM DEAN. Heroines of Fiction. NY, 1901. 1st ed. 2 vols. (Bkpls.) *Argosy.* $100/£64

HOWELLS, WILLIAM DEAN. Italian Journeys. NY, 1867. 1st ed. Terra cotta cl. (Lacks fep.) *Argosy.* $50/£32

HOWELLS, WILLIAM DEAN. Literary Friends and Acquaintance. NY, 1900. 1st ed. VG. *Argosy.* $45/£29

HOWELLS, WILLIAM DEAN. Literature and Life. NY, 1902. 1st ed. VG. *Argosy.* $45/£29

HOWELLS, WILLIAM DEAN. The Rise of Silas Lapham. Boston: Ticknor, 1885. 1st ed, 1st state (ads read Works instead of Novels). Broken type at p176. Terra cotta cl, gilt. Fine. BAL 9619. *Macdonnell.* $125/£80

HOWELLS, WILLIAM DEAN. Seven English Cities. NY, 1909. 1st ed. VG. *Argosy.* $50/£32

HOWELLS, WILLIAM DEAN. Through the Eye of the Needle. NY, 1907. 1st ed. Grn cl. VG. *Argosy.* $50/£32

HOWES, EDITH. The Cradle Ship. Cassell, n.d. (1916). 8vo. 219pp (1/2-title lacks strip); 4 color plts by Florence Mary Anderson. Emb cl, oval pict onlay, gilt spine. (Spine dulled, edges rubbed), else VG. *Bookmark.* $39/£25

HOWES, P. G. The Giant Cactus Forest and Its World. NY/Boston: Duell/Little, Brown, 1954. 1st ed. 1 color plt. Dec cl. NF in VG dj. *Mikesh.* $30/£19

HOWES, WRIGHT. U.S.iana, 1650-1950. NY, 1963. (Extrems worn.) *Swann*.* $57/£37

HOWEY, M. OLDFIELD. The Encircled Serpent. NY: Arthur Richmond, 1955. Frontis, 8 plts. Black cl (rubbed; gilt title rubbed from spine). VG (sm edge stains, pencil note). *Blue Mountain.* $75/£48

HOWEY, M. OLDFIELD. The Encircled Serpent. Phila: David McKay, n.d. (ca 1925). 1st ed. Color frontis. Blue cl. Good. *Karmiole.* $150/£96

HOWITT, MARY. The Bird Cage—Merrill's Pictorial Gallery Series. Concord, NH: Merriam & Merrill, 1855. 12mo. 24pp. VG in yellow illus paper wraps. *Dower.* $45/£29

HOWITT, MARY. No Sense Like Common Sense. NY/Phila: D. Appleton, 1843. 12mo. VF full-pg copper engr frontis, 176pp (lt foxing). Blind tooled cl on bds (soiled, rubbed; spine cracked, chipped), gilt spine. Good. *Hobbyhorse.* $50/£32

HOWITT, SAMUEL. A New Work of Animals. London, 1811 (some plts watermarked 1819). 1st ed, later issue. 4to. 100 hand-colored etched plts (frontis mtd). Contemp red straight-grain morocco, gilt. *Swann**. $1,035/£663

HOWITT, WILLIAM. Homes and Haunts of the...British Poets. London, 1847. 2 vols. Extra-illus w/engr ports. (Lt foxing.) Teg. Later 3/4 blue morocco (joints, extrems scuffed), gilt, raised bands. *Freeman**. $80/£51

HOWORTH, BECKETT. Examination and Diagnosis of the Spine and Extremities. Springfield, 1962. VG (sl worn). *Doctor's Library*. $60/£38

HOWORTH, BECKETT. A Textbook of Orthopedics. Phila, 1952. 1st ed. Blue cl (sl worn). VG. *Doctor's Library*. $100/£64

HOWSE, DEREK and MICHAEL SANDERSON. The Sea Chart. NY, etc., (1973). 1st Amer ed. Fine in dj. *Lefkowicz*. $50/£32

HOWSHIP, JOHN. Practical Observations on the Symptoms...of Some of the Most Important Diseases of the Lower Intestines and Anus. 1821. 2nd ed. xvi,240pp (sl foxed). Full calf, new labels. *Whitehart*. $218/£140

HOWSHIP, JOHN. Practical Observations on the Symptoms...of Some of the Most Important Diseases of the Lower Intestines, and Anus. London: Longman et al, 1824. 3rd ed. xvi,282pp (sl browned, tp spotted, lib stamps). Mod cl. *White*. $86/£55

HOY, WILLIAM EDWIN. History of the China Mission of the Reformed Church in the United States. Phila: Board of Foreign Missions, 1914. 1st ed. VG in wraps (sl worn). *Brown*. $15/£10

HOYER, MARIA A. By the Roman Wall. London: David Nutt, 1908. 1st ed. 14 plts, 2 plans, fldg map. (Spine ends sl rubbed.) *Hollett*. $47/£30

HOYLAND, JOHN. A Historical Survey of the Customs, Habits, and Present State of the Gypsies. York: For the Author, 1816. 1st ed. 265pp,(1)leaf (foxed, sig obliterated tp). 3/4 calf (rubbed, joint broken). *Oinonen**. $90/£58

Hoyle's Games. London: Geo. R. Whittaker et al, 1826. x,512pp (spotted). Good in contemp sheep (neatly rebacked), morocco label. *Cox*. $59/£38

HOYLE, RAFAEL LARCO. Checan: Essay on Erotic Elements in Peruvian Art. Geneva, 1965. 1st ed. Ltd numbered ed. 135 mtd color plts. VG in dj. *Argosy*. $150/£96

HOYLE, RAFAEL LARCO. Checan: Essay on Erotic Elements in Peruvian Art. Geneva: Nagel, 1965. 1st ed. Ltd to 3000 numbered. Folio. 136 color plts. White cl (sl soiled), gilt. VG (eps lt foxed). *Cahan*. $125/£80

HOYLE, WILLIAM. Crime in England and Wales in the Nineteenth Century. London: Effingham, Wilson, 1876(?). Crimson cl (worn). Sound. *Boswell*. $175/£112

HOYT, HENRY FRANKLIN. Frontier Doctor. Doyce B. Nunis, Jr. (ed). Chicago: Lakeside Classic, 1979. Teg. Brn cl, gilt. Fine. *Bohling*. $16/£10

HRDLICKA, ALES. Alaska Diary 1926-1931. Lancaster, PA: Jacques Cattell, 1943. 1st ed. VG. *High Latitude*. $50/£32

HRDLICKA, ALES. The Aleution and Commander Islands and Their Inhabitants. Phila: Wistar Inst, 1945. (Spine lettering sl faded), else Very Nice. *Perier*. $250/£160

HRDLICKA, ALES. BAE Bulletin 33. Skeletal Remains Suggesting or Attributed to Early Man in North America. Washington: GPO, 1907. 1st ed. 21 plts. Unopened, untrimmed. NF in ptd wrappers. *Connolly*. $85/£54

HRDLICKA, ALES. Early Man in South America. BAE Bulletin 52. 1912. 1st ed. VG. *Oregon*. $50/£32

HRDLICKA, ALES. Melanesians and Australians and the Peopling of America. Washington: Smithsonian Inst, 1933. Uncut, unopened. Good in orig wrappers. *Goodrich*. $75/£48

HRDLICKA, ALES. Skeletal Remains Suggesting or Attributed to Early Man in North America. Washington: Smithsonian Bulletin 33, 1907. 1st ed. 21 plts. VG +. *Mikesh*. $27/£17

HRDLICKA, ALES. Tuberculosis Among Certain Indian Tribes of the United States. Washington, 1909. 22 plts. NF. *Goodrich*. $65/£42

HUBBACK, THEODORE R. To Far Western Alaska for Big Game. London: Rowland Ward, 1929. 1st ed. 8vo. 3 maps (1 lg fldg color). Pict gilt cl (spine sl sunned). *Maggs*. $468/£300

HUBBARD, ALICE. Woman's Work, Being an Inquiry and an Assumption. (East Aurora: Roycrofters, 1908.) Brn watered silk at pastedowns, untrimmed. Limp brn suede w/extended edges, brn stamping. Cvrs VG (sl rubbed; text sl aged, sm clipping mtd fr blank). *Baltimore**. $80/£51

HUBBARD, C. The Literature of British Dogs. Ponterwyd, 1949. Dj (sl frayed). *Maggs*. $37/£24

HUBBARD, ELBERT and ALICE. A Little Journey to the Yellowstone. East Aurora, NY: Roycrofters, (1915). VG in tan wraps, protective lib binder. *Bohling*. $45/£29

HUBBARD, ELBERT. Little Journeys to the Homes of English Authors: Alfred Tennyson. E. Aurora: Roycrofters, 1901. Port. Cl-backed bds, ptd label (rubbed). VG +. *Bohling*. $8/£5

HUBBARD, ELBERT. Little Journeys to the Homes of Great Business Men. East Aurora, 1909. Good in wraps. *Hayman*. $15/£10

HUBBARD, JEREMIAH. Forty Years Among the Indians. Miami: Oklahoma, 1913. 1st ed. Red cl (Rear inner hinge reinforced w/old cellophane tape), o/w VG. Howes H750. *New Hampshire**. $150/£96

HUBBARD, JOHN MILTON. Notes of a Private. St. Louis, 1913. Port. (Cvrs soiled, spotted.) *King*. $75/£48

HUBBARD, JOHN N. Sketches of Border Adventures in the Life and Times of Major Moses Van Campen.... Bath, NY: R.L. Underhill, 1842. 2nd ed. 310pp (tp repaired, hole at inner border, sm tear fr edge; some ll repaired; lt foxed; last pg dknd). Mod full tan calf (crudely rebound, edges rubbed). Good. Howes H752. *Blue Mountain*. $95/£61

HUBBARD, JOHN N. Sketches of Border Adventures in the Life and Times of Major Moses Van Campen.... Bath, NY: R.L. Underhill, 1842. 1st ed. 310pp (foxed; bkpl). Orig calf (rebacked in lighter calf, spine chipped, corners worn), red morocco spine label. Howes H752. *Karmiole*. $150/£96

HUBBARD, JOHN N. Sketches of Border Adventures in the Life and Times of Major Moses Van Campen.... John S. Minard (ed). Fillmore, NY: Jno. S. Minard, 1893. 337pp. Fair (backstrip faded). Howes H752. *Lien*. $75/£48

HUBBARD, JOHN N. Sketches of the Life and Adventures of Major Moses Van Campen, a Surviving Officer of the Army of the Revolution. Dansville, NY, 1841. 1st ed. 310pp. Full calf (hinges expertly mended). Howes H752. *Ginsberg*. $350/£224

HUBBARD, L. RON. The Kingslayer. L.A.: Fantasy, 1949. 1st ed. (Name, # to pastedown, fly.) Dj (soiled, worn). Overall Bright. *Metropolitan**. $126/£81

HUBBARD, L. RON. Slaves of Sleep. Chicago, 1948. 1st ed. Dj (sl faded). *Swann**. $80/£51

HUBBARD, L. RON. Typewriter in the Sky and Fear. NY: Gnome, (1951). 1st ed. (Bkpl, owner stamp; sl worn.) Dj (sl rubbed, soiled, internal cellotape mend). *Swann**. $69/£44

HUBBARD, L. RON. Typewriter in the Sky and Fear. Gnome Press, 1951. 1st ed. NF in VG+ dj (lt dust-soiled). *Aronovitz*. $175/£112

HUBBARD, N. T. Autobiography with Personal Reminiscences of New York City from 1798 to 1875. NY, 1875. Engr port. Good. *Heinoldt*. $45/£29

HUBBARD, W. D. Wild Animals: A White Man's Conquest of Jungle Beasts. NY: Appleton, 1926. 1st ed. Dec cl. Good+. *Mikesh*. $27/£17

HUBBELL, ALVIN. The Development of Ophthalmology in America, 1800-1870. Chicago, 1908. 1st ed. (Ex-lib.) *Fye*. $175/£112

HUBER, MORTON W. Vanishing Japan. Phila/NY: Chilton/Amphoto, 1965. 1st ed. 2-tone cl. VG in dj. *Worldwide*. $25/£16

HUBIN, ALLEN J. The Bibliography of Crime Fiction 1749-1975. Pub Inc., 1979. 1st ed. VG+. *Certo*. $40/£26

HUC and GABET. Travels in Tartary Thibet and China 1844-1846. William Hazlitt (trans). London, 1928. 2 vols. Dbl-pg map. (Cl edges lt dampstained, spines sl rubbed.) *Edwards*. $39/£25

HUDDLESTON, R. A New Edition of Toland's History of the Druids. London: James Watt, 1814. 434pp (sl foxed). Leather, marbled bds (rebound). VG. *Middle Earth*. $295/£189

HUDDLESTON, SISLEY. Back to Montparnasse. London: Harrap, 1935. 1st ed. Dec eps. Good (name fep; spine faded). *Virgo*. $23/£15

HUDSON, ARTHUR PALMER. Folksongs of Mississippi. Chapel Hill: UNC, 1936. 1st ed. Fine (inscrip) in VG dj. *Wantagh*. $65/£42

HUDSON, E. A Bibliography of the First Editions of the Works of E. OE. Somerville and Martin Ross. NY: Sporting Gallery & Bookshop, 1942. Ltd to 300 numbered, signed by Somerville. Blue cl (sl bumped; bk labels). *Maggs*. $94/£60

HUDSON, H. N. General Butler's Campaign on the Hudson. Boston: J.S. Cushing, 1883. 2nd ed. 62pp. Orig ptd wraps (sl worn). *Wantagh*. $25/£16

HUDSON, HARRY. Flynn's Flying Doctors. Melbourne: Heinemann, 1956. 1st ed. (Cvrs lt rubbed, sm spine split), o/w Good. *White*. $23/£15

HUDSON, HENRY A. The Mediaeval Woodwork of Manchester Cathedral. Manchester, 1924. 56 plts. Teg, rest uncut. (Spine faded, bds lt damp mottled; lt spotted.) *Edwards*. $133/£85

HUDSON, JEFFREY. (Pseud of Michael Crichton.) A Case of Need. NY: NAL, (1968). 1st ed. Fine in Fine white dj. *Between The Covers*. $500/£321

HUDSON, JEFFREY. (Pseud of Michael Crichton.) A Case of Need. NY: NAL, 1968. 1st ed. Fine in dj (corner bumped). *Mordida*. $150/£96

HUDSON, ROGER (ed). Coleridge Among the Lakes and Mountains. Folio Soc, 1991. Color frontis port. Pict cl bds, gilt. Card slipcase. *Edwards*. $23/£15

HUDSON, STEPHEN. (Pseud of Sydney Schiff.) Tony. London: Constable, 1924. 1st ed. Fine in Very Nice dj (sl dust-mkd). *Patterson*. $47/£30

HUDSON, THOMSON JAY. The Law of Psychic Phenomena.... London: Putnam, 1903. 8th ed. (Worn; pencilling.) Sound. *Boswell*. $65/£42

HUDSON, W. H. Afoot in England. London, 1909. 1st ed. Grn cl, gilt. (Inscrip), o/w VG. *Words Etc.* $55/£35

HUDSON, W. H. Afoot in England. London: Hutchinson, 1909. 1st ed. Teg. Dec grn cl. VG (sl wear, scuffing; bkpl). *Antic Hay*. $75/£48

HUDSON, W. H. Birds in London. London, 1898. 1st ed. Grn cl, gilt. (Spine badly faded, ends rubbed), o/w VG. *Words Etc.* $47/£30

HUDSON, W. H. Birds of La Plata. London, 1920. Ltd to 3000. 2 vols. 22 color plts. 1/2 buckram. Good. *Henly*. $156/£100

HUDSON, W. H. Birds of La Plata. London/Toronto: J.M. Dent, 1920. 1st ed. Ltd to 1500 for England, 1500 for US. 2 vols. 22 color plts. Grn cl. Good in pub's slipcase (worn), ptd paper label. *Karmiole*. $250/£160

HUDSON, W. H. Far Away and Long Ago, A History of My Early Life. Buenos Aires: LEC, 1943. #904/1500 numbered, signed by Alberto Kraft (designer) and Raul Rosarivo (illus). Cowhide binding. Fine in pub's slipcase. *Hermitage*. $175/£112

HUDSON, W. H. Far Away and Long Ago. London/Toronto: J.M. Dent, (1931). Rev ed. One of 110 lg-paper copies signed by Eric Fitch Daglish (illus) w/extra signed plt laid in. 12 full-pg wood engrs. Full vellum, sm gilt-pict leather label fr cvr. (Eps heavily foxed; sl soiled), o/w VG in marbled slipcase. *New Hampshire**. $100/£64

HUDSON, W. H. Green Mansions, A Romance of the Tropical Forest. NY: LEC, 1935. #904/1500 numbered, signed by Edward A. Wilson (illus). Cl-backed dec bds. Fine in pub's slipcase. *Hermitage*. $85/£54

HUDSON, W. H. Green Mansions: A Romance of the Tropical Forest. London: Duckworth, 1904. 1st ed, 2nd issue w/pub's device blind-stamped rear panel. (Rear hinge repaired), else Fine. *Captain's Bookshelf*. $175/£112

HUDSON, W. H. Hampshire Days. London: J.M. Dent, 1923. 1st ed. Fine (bkpl, ink name) in dj (sm chip). *Antic Hay*. $40/£26

HUDSON, W. H. Letters. Edward Garnett (ed). (London): Nonesuch, 1923. 1st ed. Ltd to 1000 numbered. Buckram. VG. *Argosy*. $75/£48

HUDSON, W. H. A Little Boy Lost. Duckworth, 1921. 1st ed. Dorothy P. Lathrop (illus). Tall 4to. 182pp (mks); 8 color, 4 b/w plts. Gilt-pict sky-blue cl. (Fading), else VG. *Bookmark*. $55/£35

HUDSON, W. H. The Naturalist in La Plata. London, 1895. 3rd ed. One of 750 ptd. x,394pp. (Lt foxed, upper hinge cracked; cl sl rubbed, lt discolored.) *Edwards*. $47/£30

HUDSON, W. H. Ralph Herne. NY, 1923. Ltd to 950. Cl-backed bds. VG in slipcase (lt worn). *Truepenny*. $75/£48

HUDSON, W. H. Ralph Herne. NY: Knopf, 1923. One of 950 ptd. 2-pg facs. Black cl-backed orange paper bds, ptd paper title label. Very Nice. *Cady*. $30/£19

HUDSON, W. H. Ralph Herne. NY: Knopf, 1923. 1st ed. Ltd to 950. Cl-backed orange paper bds (sl worn). *Shasky*. $45/£29

HUDSON, W. H. Rare, Vanishing and Lost British Birds. London, 1923. 25 color plts. (Sl foxed.) *Henly*. $44/£28

HUDSON, W. H. A Shepherd's Life. London, 1910. 1st ed. Grn cl, gilt. (Extrems rubbed), o/w VG. *Words Etc.* $117/£75

HUDSON, WILLIAM HENRY. The Famous Missions of California. NY: Dodge, (1901). 1 map, 2 color plts. Leather-backed pict bds. (Fr hinge cracked, cvrs soiled, water-stained, worn), o/w VG. *Pacific**. $23/£15

HUDSON, WILSON M. Andy Adams. Dallas: Southern Methodist Univ, 1964. 1st ed. 2-tone cl. VF in pict dj. *Argonaut*. $60/£38

HUEFFER, FORD H. MADOX. The Feather. London: T. Fisher Unwin, 1892. Frontis. (Spine sl cocked, dknd), o/w Excellent in red 1/2 morocco slipcase. *Gekoski*. $546/£350

HUEFFER, FORD MADOX. Memories and Impressions. NY: Harper, 1911. 1st Amer ed. Port. (Corners bruised), else VG. *Reese*. $50/£32

HUFELAND, OTTO. A Check List of Books, Maps, Pictures...Relating to the Counties of Westchester and Bronx. (NY: Knickerbocker), privately ptd, 1925. 1st ed. *Ginsberg.* $100/£64

HUGHES, ARTHUR. A History of Cytology. NY, 1959. 1st ed. VG. *Fye.* $50/£32

HUGHES, DOROTHY B. The Candy Kid. NY: Duell et al, 1950. 1st ed. Signed. Fine in dj (nicks, edges worn). *Mordida.* $65/£42

HUGHES, G. BERNARD. Antique Sheffield Plate. Batsford, 1970. 1st ed. 269 plts. Dj. *Edwards.* $47/£30

HUGHES, G. BERNARD. Horse Brasses. London: Country Life, 1956. 1st ed. Color frontis, 42 plts. VG in dj. *Hollett.* $31/£20

HUGHES, HENRY MARSHALL. A Clinical Introduction to the Practices of Auscultation.... Phila, 1846. 1st Amer ed. Frontis. VG. *Argosy.* $125/£80

HUGHES, JOHN T. Doniphan's Expedition.... Cincinnati, 1848. 2nd ed. 2 ports. (Hole in port, lacks 40% fldg map, pg 207-08 facs tipped in, eps sl foxed.) Contemp full calf (lt worn), gilt, morocco label. *Turpen.* $195/£125

HUGHES, JOHN T. Doniphan's Expedition.... Cincinnati, 1848. 12mo. 407pp, fldg map. VG. Howes H769. *M & S.* $500/£321

HUGHES, LANGSTON. Black Misery. NY: Eriksson, (1969). 1st ed. Fine in dj (lt edgewear, browned, sm tears). *Antic Hay.* $45/£29

HUGHES, LANGSTON. The First Book of Negroes. NY, 1952. 1st ed. NF in Good+ dj (fr panel lacks piece). *Warren.* $50/£32

HUGHES, LANGSTON. Simple Takes a Wife. NY: S&S, 1953. 1st ed. (2 names, pg edges dknd), else NF (bd delamination); w/o dj as issued. *Between The Covers.* $200/£128

HUGHES, LANGSTON. The Sweet Flypaper of Life. NY: S&S, 1955. 1st ed. (Inscrip), else VG in illus stiff wrappers (spine rubbed). *Cahan.* $100/£64

HUGHES, RICHARD B. Pioneer Years in the Black Hills. Agnes Wright Spring (ed). Glendale: Clark, 1957. 1st ed. One of 1000. Red cl. VF. *Argonaut.* $125/£80

HUGHES, RICHARD. The Fox in the Attic. London: C&W, 1961. 1st Eng ed. Fine in dj (lt edgewear, browning, sm stain rear panel). *Antic Hay.* $35/£22

HUGHES, RICHARD. The Fox in the Attic. London: C&W, 1961. 1st Eng ed. NF in dj. *Antic Hay.* $50/£32

HUGHES, RICHARD. A High Wind in Jamaica. Chatto, 1929. 1st UK ed. NF in VG dj (spine sl sunned). *Martin.* $53/£34

HUGHES, RICHARD. A High Wind in Jamaica. London, 1929. 1st ed. VG. *Typographeum.* $15/£10

HUGHES, RICHARD. The Innocent Voyage. NY: LEC, 1944. One of 1500 signed by Lynd Ward (illus). NF in dec cardboard sleeve in pub's slipcase. *Hermitage.* $100/£64

HUGHES, RICHARD. The Wooden Shepherdess. NY: Harper & Row, (1973). 1st Amer ed. Fine in dj. *Antic Hay.* $15/£10

HUGHES, RICHARD. The Wooden Shepherdess. London: C&W, 1973. 1st ed. Paper-cvrd bds. Orig wraparound band. Fine in dj. *Antic Hay.* $45/£29

HUGHES, ROBERT M. General Johnston. NY, 1897. 'Army and Navy ed.' 332pp. (Cvr sl worn), o/w Fine. *Pratt.* $65/£42

HUGHES, TED. The Burning of the Brothel. (London: Turret Books, 1966.) 1st ed. One of 300 ptd, this one out of series. Mint in plain wrappers, dj. *Jaffe.* $150/£96

HUGHES, TED. Cave Birds. London/Boston: Faber & Faber, (1978). 1st trade ed. Leonard Baskin (illus). Black cl. Fine in pict dj (sm closed tear rear panel). *Jaffe.* $75/£48

HUGHES, TED. Cave Birds. NY: Viking, (1978). 1st ed. Leonard Baskin (illus). Fine in NF dj (offsetting from sm label removed fr panel). *Antic Hay.* $20/£13

HUGHES, TED. Cave Birds. NY, 1978. 1st Amer ed. Leonard Baskin (illus). Fine in dj (2 sm tears, sm nick). *Polyanthos.* $30/£19

HUGHES, TED. The Coming of the Kings and Other Plays. London: Faber & Faber, (1970). 1st ed. One of 2000 ptd. (Lt offset eps), o/w Fine in dj. *Jaffe.* $125/£80

HUGHES, TED. Crow Wakes. (Essex): Poet & Printer, (1971). 1st ed. One of 200 ptd. Fine. *Jaffe.* $150/£96

HUGHES, TED. The Earth-Owl and Other Moon-People. Faber & Faber, (1963). 1st ed. (Inscrip), o/w Nice in dj. *Ash.* $55/£35

HUGHES, TED. The Earth-Owl and Other Moon-People. London, 1963. 1st ed. Fine in dj (nicks). *Polyanthos.* $35/£22

HUGHES, TED. Gaudete. NY, 1977. 1st Amer ed. Fine (spine top sl rubbed) in dj (sl soiled, price-clipped). *Polyanthos.* $30/£19

HUGHES, TED. The Hawk in the Rain. London: Faber & Faber, (1957). 1st ed, 1st bk. One of 2000 ptd. Fine in dj (sl chipped, spine dknd). *Jaffe.* $225/£144

HUGHES, TED. The Hawk in the Rain. NY: Harper, (1957). 1st Amer ed, 1st bk. Fine in dj. *Jaffe.* $150/£96

HUGHES, TED. Lupercal. NY, (1960). 1st Amer ed. Fine in dj (spine sl sunned). *Polyanthos.* $25/£16

HUGHES, TED. Meet My Folks! London: Faber & Faber, (1961). 1st ed. George Adamson (illus). Pict bds (sl rubbed). NF in dj. *Bromer.* $125/£80

HUGHES, TED. Moortown. Faber, 1979. 1st UK ed. Fine in dj. *Williams.* $23/£15

HUGHES, TED. Wodwo. London: Faber & Faber, (1967). 1st ed. (Lt offset eps), o/w Fine in dj (sl rubbed, spine dknd). *Jaffe.* $75/£48

HUGHES, THERLE and BERNARD. English Painted Enamels. London: Country Life, 1951. 1st ed. Color frontis, 90 plts (7 color). VG. *Hollett.* $62/£40

HUGHES, THERLE. More Small Decorative Antiques. London: Lutterworth, 1962. 1st ed. Color frontis, 3 color plts, 48 b/w plts. Dj (chipped w/loss spine head). *Edwards.* $31/£20

HUGHES, THOMAS. History of the Society of Jesus in North America, Colonial and Federal. London, 1908-10. 4 vols. *Ginsberg.* $300/£192

HUGHES, W. J. Rebellious Ranger, Rip Ford and the Old Southwest. Norman, 1964. 1st ed. Map. Fine in Fine dj. *Turpen.* $75/£48

HUGHES, WENDELL L. Reconstructive Surgery of the Eyelids. St. Louis: Mosby, 1943. 1st ed. 36 plts. Fine. *Glaser.* $250/£160

HUGO, RICHARD. Death and the Good Life. NY: St. Martin's, (1981). 1st ed. Fine in dj. *Jaffe.* $150/£96

HUGO, RICHARD. Death and the Good Life. NY: St. Martin's, 1981. 1st ed. Fine in NF dj. *Lame Duck.* $125/£80

HUGO, RICHARD. Good Luck in Cracked Italian. NY: World, (1969). Fine (top edge sl sunned) in Fine dj (sm tear). *Between The Covers.* $75/£48

HUGO, RICHARD. The Right Madness on Skye. NY: W.W. Norton, (1980). 1st ed. (Spine sl cocked), o/w Fine in dj (sm tear rear panel). *Jaffe.* $35/£22

HUGO, RICHARD. White Center. NY: W.W. Norton, (1980). 1st ed. Fine in dj. *Jaffe.* $35/£22

HUGO, VICTOR. Les Miserables. Charles Wilbour (trans). NY: Carleton, 1862. 1st Amer ed. 5 vols. Purple cl (spotted, spine extrems chipped each vol). Good set. *Captain's Bookshelf.* $500/£321

HUIE, WILLIAM BRADFORD. The Americanization of Emily. NY, 1959. 1st Amer ed. NF in NF dj. *Polyanthos.* $25/£16

HUIE, WILLIAM BRADFORD. The Klansman. NY: Delacorte, (1967). 1st ed. Cl-backed bds. Fine in dj (sl edgeworn). *Sadlon.* $25/£16

HULBERT, ARCHER BUTLER. Forty-Niners: The Chronicle of the California Trail. Boston: Little, Brown, 1931. 1st ed. 12 maps. Grn cl, gilt. Fine. *Pacific*.* $17/£11

HULBERT, ARCHER BUTLER. Historic Highways of America. Cleveland: A.H. Clark, 1902-05. 16 vols. (Extrems sl worn.) Howes H773. *Swann*.* $126/£81

HULBERT, ARCHER BUTLER. Historic Highways of America. Cleveland: A.H. Clark, 1902-05. 1st ed. 16 vols. 79 plts and maps. Gilt-lettered blue cl (lt worn, spines spotted). *Kane*.* $300/£192

HULBERT, ARCHER BUTLER. Pilots of the Republic. Chicago: McClurg, 1906. Frontis, 15 ports. Partly unopened. Teg. (Spine rubbed, dull.) *Bohling.* $25/£16

HULL, EDWARD. The Coal-Fields of Great Britain. London, 1873. 3rd ed. xxiii,499pp + 24pp pub's ads (tp lacks sm portion, bkpl), fldg map in rear pocket. *Edwards.* $70/£45

HULL, ROBERT CHARLTON. The Search for Adele Parker. (NY: Libra, 1974.) 1st ed. Inscribed. Fine in NF dj. *Sadlon.* $15/£10

HULME, F. EDWARD. Familiar Wild Flowers. London: Cassell, ca 1875. 5 vols in 2. Contemp 1/2 grn morocco (spine sunned; lt foxed). *Swann*.* $115/£74

HULME, F. EDWARD. Flower Painting in Water Colours. London, c. 1890. 2nd series. 19pp, 4 ads; 20 mtd color plts. Good. *Henly.* $70/£45

HULME, F. EDWARD. Plants, Their Natural Growth and Ornamental Treatment. London: Marcus Ward, 1874. 1st ed. Folio. 71pp + 44 full-pg chromolithos. Gilt-dec pict cl (hinges strengthened). Fine. *Quest.* $575/£369

HULME, T. E. Speculations, Essays on Humanism and the Philosophy of Art. Herbert Read (ed). NY/London: Harcourt/Kegan Paul, 1924. 1st ed, Amer issue. Frontis. (Foxing, dated receipt stamp w/1 erased, sig, pencil notes.) *Reese.* $75/£48

HULTEN, K. G. PONTUS. The Machine as Seen at the End of the Mechanical Age. NY: MOMA, (1968). 1st ed. Pict aluminum. (Outer edges sunned, fr panel scratched, rubbed), else VG. *Hermitage.* $100/£64

HULTEN, PONTUS and GERMANO CELANT. Italian Art 1900-1945. NY: Rizzoli, (1989). 1st ed. (Rmdr star stamp bottom edge), else VF in dj. *Hermitage.* $100/£64

HULTMAN, HELEN JOAN. Murder in the French Room. NY: Mystery League, 1931. 1st Amer ed. NF in dj (torn, few chips). *Polyanthos.* $25/£16

Humble Address and Ernest Appeal.... (By Josiah Tucker.) Gloucester: A. Raikes, 1775. 1st ed. W/ads. (Lacks fldg table.) 19th-cent 3/4 polished tree calf, marbled bds (cvrs detached). Howes T385. *Freeman*.* $35/£22

HUMBLEY, W. W. W. Journal of a Cavalry Officer. London, 1854. v-xii,616pp (lacks fldg map, 2 fldg plans, tp, dedication leaf; copies supplied). Contemp 1/2 calf, marbled bds (sl rubbed), gilt. *Maggs.* $156/£100

HUME, DAVID. Dialogues Concerning Natural Religion. London: (N.p.), 1779. 2nd ed. 8vo. 264pp, incl 1/2 title. Orig calf (rebacked, old eps preserved), gilt spine, red morocco label. *Bickersteth.* $702/£450

HUME, EDGAR ERSKINE. Medical Work of the Knights Hospitallers of Saint John of Jerusalem. Balt: John Hopkins, 1940. Fine. *Cullen.* $75/£48

HUME, FERGUS. The Millionaire Mystery. NY/London: F.M. Buckles/C&W, 1901. 1st ed. (Eps lt foxed), o/w VG+. *Bernard.* $75/£48

HUME, H. HAROLD. Camellias in America. Harrisburg, 1946. 49 color plts. Fabricoid. VG. *New Hampshire*.* $25/£16

HUME, JOHN F. The Abolitionists. NY: Putnam, 1905. 1st ed. Blue cl. VG. *Archer.* $50/£32

HUME, JOHN R. The Industrial Archaeology of Scotland. London: Batsford, 1977. 1st ed. VG in dj (spine faded). *Hollett.* $39/£25

HUME, MR. Observations on the Origin and Treatment of Internal and External Diseases, and Management of Children. Dublin: Fitzpatrick, 1802. xiii,(2),290pp. New 1/2 calf, raised bands. Good. *Goodrich.* $495/£317

HUME, SANDY et al. The Great West: Real/Ideal. Boulder: Dept of Fine Arts, Univ of CO, 1977. 1st ed. Mtd color postcard frontis. (Name; lt worn), else VG in pict stiff wrappers. *Cahan.* $35/£22

HUMFREY, BELINDA (ed). Recollections of the Powys Brothers. Peter Owen, 1980. 1st ed. NF in dj. *Words Etc.* $31/£20

Humourist. (By George Cruikshank.) London: Nimmo, 1892. One of 70 w/plts in both uncolored & colored states. 4 vols. 8vo. 220; 228; 224; 226pp. Navy cl, ptd spine labels. (Sl rubbing, few lt scratches rear cvr vol 1), else Fine set. *Bromer.* $750/£481

HUMPHREY, S. D. American Hand Book of the Daguerreotype. NY: S.D. Humphrey, 1858. 5th ed. xii,214pp + 5pp ads. Red cl, gilt. (Lt dampstain few blank margins; spine ends renewed), else VG. *Cahan.* $500/£321

HUMPHREY, WILLIAM. No Resting Place. NY, 1989. 1st ed. Fine in Fine dj. *Smith.* $15/£10

HUMPHREYS, ARTHUR L. Old Decorative Maps and Charts. London, 1926. 1st ed. One of 1500. 79 plts (19 color, tipped-in). Teg. (Spine sl faded.) *Edwards.* $195/£125

HUMPHREYS, ARTHUR L. Old Decorative Maps and Charts.... London/NY: Halton & Truscott Smith/Minton, Balch, 1926. 1st ed. One of 1500 numbered. 79 plts. (Spine faded), o/w Fine. *Lefkowicz.* $250/£160

HUMPHREYS, ARTHUR L. The Private Library. Hatchards, 1897. 162pp. Grn cl, teg. Good. *Moss.* $25/£16

HUMPHREYS, CHARLES. A Compendium of the Common Law in Force in Kentucky.... Lexington: William Gibbes Hunt, 1822. xi,594,(1)errata pp (age-spotted). Recent cl (rebound). *Zubal*.* $150/£96

HUMPHREYS, F. Humphreys' Homeopathic Mentor or Family Adviser in the Use of Specific Homeopathic Medicine. NY, 1895. Rev ed. 523pp. Blue gilt-tooled cl. NF. *Doctor's Library.* $40/£26

HUMPHREYS, F. M. D. Humphreys' Homeopathic Mentor or Family Adviser in the Use of Humphreys' Homeopathic Remedies. NY: Humphreys' Homeopathic Medical Co, 1915. 1st ed. Frontis port, guard. Beveled edges. Good+ (inner hinges strengthened; corners showing, spine ends worn). *Connolly.* $25/£16

HUMPHREYS, HENRY NOEL and JOHN OBADIAH WESTWOOD. British Butterflies and Their Transformations. London: William Smith, 1848. Add'l hand-colored engr title, 42 hand-colored engr plts (lt spotting). Gilt edges. Contemp grn 1/2 morocco (upper hinges broken, extrems rubbed). *Christie's*.* $491/£315

HUMPHREYS, HENRY NOEL. The Origin and Progress of the Art of Writing. London: Day, 1855. 2nd ed. 28 plts (9 color). Papier-mache binding. (Sprung sigs unevenly repaired; lower spine corner sl damaged.) Rostenberg & Stern. $475/£304

HUMPHREYS, P. W. The Practical Book of Garden Architecture. Phila/London: Lippincott, 1914. Color frontis, 125 plts. (Cl sl worn, rear cvr spotted.) Internally Good. Ars Artis. $39/£25

HUMPHREYS, PHEBE WESTCOTT. The Practical Book of Garden Architecture. Phila/London: Lippincott, 1914. Color frontis. Pict cvr. (Spine dknd), else VG. Quest. $85/£54

HUMPHRIES, SYDNEY. Oriental Carpets. A&C Black, 1910. 24 color plts. Teg. (Ex-lib, ink stamp verso tp, margins sl browned, blind stamp illus margins, bkpl, hinges cracked; cl sl soiled, spine browned, #s.) Edwards. $78/£50

Humpty Dumpty from Through the Looking Glass. Chicago: Reilly & Britton, (1908). Children's Stories That Never Grow Old Series. 7x5. 29pp, 8 full-pg color plts by John R. Neill. Color pict bds. (Spine ruined, interior soil), else Good. King. $35/£22

HUNEKER, JAMES. Old Fogy: His Musical Opinions and Grotesques. Phila: Theodore Presser, (1913). Fine in NF pict dj (sm tears, sl soil). Between The Covers. $75/£48

HUNGERFORD, EDWARD. Men of Erie. NY: Random House, (1946). 1st ed. Fine in dj (lt edgeworn). Sadlon. $15/£10

HUNGERFORD, EDWARD. The Story of the Baltimore and Ohio Railroad, 1827-1927. NY: Putnam, 1928. 1st ed. 2 vols. 4 ep maps. Teg. Blue cl, gilt. Fine. Harrington. $125/£80

HUNGERFORD, EDWARD. The Story of the Baltimore and Ohio Railroad. 1827-1927. NY/London: Putnam, 1928. 2 vols. Teg. Blue cl, gilt. NF set in djs (soiled). Parmer. $150/£96

HUNGERFORD, EDWARD. Wells Fargo: Advancing the American Frontier. NY: Random House, (1949). 1st ed. Pict cl. VG in dj (sm nicks, sl etchings). Bohling. $25/£16

HUNT, AURORA. Kirby Benedict, Frontier Federal Judge. Glendale: Clark, 1961. 1st ed. One of 1530. Frontis port. Fine in ptd dj (sl faded). Argonaut. $45/£29

HUNT, AURORA. Kirby Benedict, Frontier Federal Judge...1853-1874.... Glendale: A.H. Clark, 1961. Boswell. $35/£22

HUNT, AURORA. Kirby Benedict: Frontier Federal Judge. Glendale: Clark, 1961. 1st ed. Ginsberg. $50/£32

HUNT, AURORA. Major General James Henry Carleton, 1814-1873. Glendale: Clark, 1958. 1st ed. One of 1266. Fldg map. Fine. Argonaut. $90/£58

HUNT, AURORA. Major General James Henry Carleton. Glendale: A.H. Clark, 1958. VG. Dumont. $85/£54

HUNT, BLANCHE SEALE. Stories of Little Brown Koko. Chicago/NY: American Colortype, (1952). Dorothy Wagstaff (illus). 4to. 96pp. Illus paper over bds, linen spine. Good (fr hinge w/holes at staples). Scribe's Perch*. $16/£10

HUNT, BLANCHE SEALE. Stories of Little Brown Koko.... Chicago/NY: Amer Colortype Co, (1940). Dorothy Wagstaff (illus). 4to. 96pp. Red cl-backed color pict blue bds (bottom edge sl rubbed). NF in VG matching dj (edges creased, few short tears). Blue Mountain. $75/£48

HUNT, CHARLES HAVENS. Life of Edward Livingston. NY: D. Appleton, 1864. Grn cl (rubbed, faded). Sound. Boswell. $175/£112

HUNT, D. C. et al. Karl Bodmer's America. N.p.: Joslyn Mus/Univ of NE, 1984. 1st ed. Blind-stamped gilt-dec cl. Fine in Fine dj. Mikesh. $137/£88

HUNT, F. R. Horses and Heroes: The Story of the Horse in America for 450 Years. NY/London: Scribner, 1949. 1st ed. 23 plts. NF in Good dj. Mikesh. $25/£16

HUNT, FRAZIER and ROBERT. I Fought with Custer. NY: Scribner, 1947. 1st ed. VG in dj (tape-reinforced). Lien. $40/£26

HUNT, INEZ and WANETTA W. DRAPER. Colorado's Restless Ghosts. Denver: Sage Books, 1960. Signed. Good in dj (worn). Dumont. $25/£16

HUNT, J. ERIC. English and Welsh Crucifixes 670-1550. London: SPCK, 1956. 1st ed. Color frontis, 39 plts. VG in dj. Hollett. $47/£30

HUNT, JOHN. Pantheism and Christianity. London: Wm. Isbister, 1884. 1st ed. viii,397pp. 3/4 calf, marbled bds (rubbed, calf joints split; chipped, worn), gilt leather spine labels. NF internally. Blue Mountain. $85/£54

HUNT, LEIGH. Ballads of Robin Hood. Cedar Rapids: Privately ptd, 1922. 1st ed. One of 200 ptd at Torch. Fine in ptd wrappers. Captain's Bookshelf. $60/£38

HUNT, LEIGH. The Companion. London, 1828. 1st bk ed. Teg. Later 3/4 mustard morocco, marbled bds (sl scuffed), gilt-paneled spine, raised bands. Freeman*. $80/£51

HUNT, LEIGH. Men, Women and Books. Smith, Elder, 1870. New ed. Good (ink inscrip; bumped). Tiger. $16/£10

HUNT, LEIGH. Stories from the Italian Poets. London: Chapman & Hall, 1846. 1st ed. 2 vols. Uncut. Orig blue cl (bumped, spine ends frayed, sm tear outer hinge vol 2; inner hinges cracked, variant brn eps vol 2, sigs, lt spotted, no terminal ads). Maggs. $156/£100

HUNT, LEIGH. The Town; Its Memorable Characters and Events...St. Paul's to St. James. London: Smith, Elder, 1848. 1st ed. 2 vols. 45 wood-engrs. Uncut. Orig orange cl (spines sl dknd, frayed w/sl loss, outer hinge vol 1 starting, inner hinges vol 1 cracked). Maggs. $156/£100

HUNT, LYNN BOGUE. An Artist's Game Bag. NY: Derrydale, (1936). Ltd to 1225. 47 full-pg plts, fabrikoid cl. VG. Truepenny. $200/£128

HUNT, PETER. Murder Among the Nudists. NY: Vanguard, 1934. 1st ed. (Sl cocked), else NF- in dj (trimmed 1/4 inch). Between The Covers. $100/£64

HUNT, ROBERT. A Manual of Photography.... London, 1854. 4th ed. Litho frontis; 8-pg pub's cat, 32-pg cat bound at end. (Backstrip lacks top.) Swann*. $46/£29

HUNT, ROCKWELL. California in the Making. Caldwell: Caxton, 1953. 1st ed. Fine in Good+ dj. Connolly. $30/£19

HUNT, ROCKWELL. John Bidwell, Prince of California Pioneers. Caldwell: Caxton Ptrs, (1942). 1st ed. Signed. Frontis port. Grn cl, gilt. Fine. Pacific*. $58/£37

HUNT, ROCKWELL. Personal Sketches of California Pioneers I Have Known. Stockton: Univ of the Pacific, 1962. Ltd to 500. Signed. VG in Fine dj. Book Market. $50/£32

HUNT, T. F. Exemplars of Tudor Architecture, Adapted to Modern Habitations.... London: Longman, 1830. viii,200pp (foxing); 37 engr plts (lib stamps). Mod blind cl. Ars Artis. $195/£125

HUNT, VIOLET. The Workaday Woman. London: T. Werner Laurie, (1906). 1st Eng ed. Good (name; cvrs sl bruised). Clearwater. $78/£50

HUNT, WILSON PRICE. The Overland Diary of Wilson Price Hunt. Hoyt C. Franchere (ed). Ashland: Oregon Book Soc, 1973. Ltd to 600. Beige cl (sl soiled). *Karmiole.* $60/£38

Hunter's Tracks. NY: Appleton, 1957. 1st ed. VF in dj. *Bowman.* $45/£29

HUNTER, ALAN. Gently Where the Roads Go. London: Cassell, 1962. 1st ed. Fine in Fine dj. *Janus.* $30/£19

HUNTER, ALAN. Gently with the Ladies. London: Cassell, 1965. 1st ed. Fine in VG dj. *Janus.* $20/£13

HUNTER, ALAN. Gently with the Millions. London: Constable, 1989. 1st ed. Fine in dj. *Murder By The Book.* $40/£26

HUNTER, ALEXANDER. Culina Famulatrix Medicinae; Or, Receipts in Cookery.... York: Wilson & Spence, 1804. Frontis, 119pp, ms text tipped in fr. 1/4 roan, marbled bds. Good. *Goodrich.* $495/£317

HUNTER, ALEXANDER. The Huntsman in the South. Volume I. Virginia and North Carolina. (All published.) NY, 1908. 1st ed. Port. Pict cl (sl worn). *Oinonen*.* $390/£250

HUNTER, C. BRUCE. A Guide to Ancient Mexican Ruins. Norman: Univ of OK, (1978). 28 maps and plans. Good in dj. *Archaeologia.* $35/£22

HUNTER, DARD. Laid and Wove. Washington: GPO, 1923. 6 plts. NF in ptd wrappers (sl yellowed, sm edge tears). *Bromer.* $100/£64

HUNTER, DARD. The Literature of Papermaking 1390-1800. (Chillicothe: Mountain House Press, 1925.) One of 190 signed. Folio. Tls laid in. Unbound in 1/2 linen portfolio. Fine. *Bromer.* $3,200/£2,051

HUNTER, DARD. My Life with Paper, an Autobiography. NY: Knopf, 1958. 1st ed. (Fep lt browned), else VF in dj (spine faded, sm chip). *Bromer.* $175/£112

HUNTER, DARD. Papermaking by Hand in America. Chillicothe: Mountain House Press, 1950. 1st ed. One of 210 numbered, signed. Folio. Color frontis view, 171 mtd facs. Orig 1/2 linen, patterned bds. Morocco-backed cl fldg case. *Swann*.* $6,210/£3,981

HUNTER, DARD. Papermaking by Hand in India. NY: Pynson, 1939. Ltd to 370 numbered, signed by Hunter & Elmer Adler (pub). 4to. 85 photogravures, 27 orig paper samples. Black leather, hand-blocked India print cl, spine ptd in blue/gold. Prospectus laid in. Fine in slipcase (lt rubbed). *Karmiole.* $2,850/£1,827

HUNTER, DARD. Papermaking in Pioneer America. Phila: Univ of PA, 1952. 1st ed. 11pp plts. 1/4 cl, terra-cotta bds. (Sm edge-dents, edge lt faded back cvr), else Fine. *Bromer.* $150/£96

HUNTER, DARD. A Papermaking Pilgrimage to Japan, Korea, and China. NY: Pynson, 1936. Ltd to 375 signed by Hunter & Elmer Adler (ptr). Lg 4to. 68 photogravures, 50 orig paper samples. Black morocco, patterned paper bds. Fine in slipcase (partly tape-repaired). *Karmiole.* $4,500/£2,885

HUNTER, DARD. Papermaking Through Eighteen Centuries. NY: Rudge, 1930. Fldg frontis. Teg. Very Nice in dj (lt worn), glassine wrapper (dknd, chipped). *Bohling.* $250/£160

HUNTER, DARD. Papermaking: The History and Technique of an Ancient Craft. NY: Knopf, 1943. 1st ed. Fldg map. Fine in dj. *Oak Knoll.* $150/£96

HUNTER, DARD. Papermaking: The History and Technique of an Ancient Craft. NY: Knopf, 1947. 2nd ed. Fldg map. (Extrems lt worn), else Fine. *Bromer.* $175/£112

HUNTER, GEORGE et al. A Manual of Tropical Medicine. Phila, 1960. Mod Asia ed. 8pp color plts. NF. *Doctor's Library.* $60/£38

HUNTER, GEORGE. Reminiscences of an Old Timer. SF: H.S. Crocker, 1887. 1st ed. 454pp. Pict cl (spotted). Fair. Howes H811. *Lien.* $125/£80

HUNTER, GEORGE. Reminiscences of an Old Timer.... SF, 1887. Half-title, frontis, xxv,(1),454pp. Decent (spine sunned, rubbed, corners frayed, inner fr hinge cracked). Howes H811. *Reese.* $250/£160

HUNTER, J. A. Hunter's Tracks. NY: Appleton Century Crofts, 1957. 1st ed. Fine in VG dj. *Books & Birds.* $75/£48

HUNTER, J. A. Hunter. NY: Harper, 1952. VG in dj. *Bowman.* $20/£13

HUNTER, J. MARVIN (ed). The Trail Drivers of Texas. Nashville, TN: Cokesbury, 1925. 2nd ed, rev. 2 vols in 1. Frontis. Gilt-lettered dk blue cl (lt wear, corner sl jammed). VG (gutter of 2 leaves dknd from removed tape). Howes H816. *Argonaut.* $200/£128

HUNTER, J. MARVIN (ed). The Trail Drivers of Texas. Nashville: Cokesbury, 1925. 2nd ed. 2 vols in 1. (Sl shelfworn), else VG. Howes H816. *Brown.* $200/£128

HUNTER, J. MARVIN. The Trail Drivers of Texas. NY: Argosy-Antiquarian, 1963. One of 97 numbered, signed by Harry Sinclair Drago (intro). 2 vols. 1/2 leather, tan bds, gilt. Fine in slipcase (lt soiled). *Bohling.* $300/£192

HUNTER, JOHN D. Manners and Customs of Several Indian Tribes Located West of the Mississippi. Phila: The Author, 1823. 402pp. Contemp calf (fr cvr nearly loose). Nice. Howes H813. *M & S.* $400/£256

HUNTER, JOHN D. Memoirs of a Captivity Among the Indians of North America.... London, 1823. 1st British ed. Calf spine (worn; lacks cvrs). *Kane*.* $170/£109

HUNTER, JOHN D. Memoirs of a Captivity Among the Indians of North America.... London: Longman et al, 1823. 1st Eng ed. Port from 2nd London ed tipped in dated 1823. Orig cl-backed bds, paper spine label. (Lt foxed; spine ends, cvr edges sl rubbed.) Howes H813. *Sadlon.* $275/£176

HUNTER, JOHN D. Memoirs of a Captivity Among the Indians of North America.... London: Longman, Hurst et al, 1823. x,447pp; port. Orig bds, tan calf (rebacked). Howes H813. *Adelson.* $250/£160

HUNTER, JOHN D. Memoirs of a Captivity Among the Indians of North America.... London: Longman, Hurst et al, 1823. New ed w/port. Issue w/o 4pp prelim ads, w/'and Green' added to printer's line. ix,447pp. 1/2 leather, marbled bds, gilt-stamped spine. VG. Howes H813. *Oregon.* $450/£288

HUNTER, JOHN D. Memoirs of a Captivity Among the Indians of North America.... London: Longman, Hurst, 1824. 3rd ed. Frontis port. Later full mottled calf (expertly rebacked), raised bands, leather label. Nice. Howes H813. *Appelfeld.* $150/£96

HUNTER, JOHN. The Natural History of the Human Teeth. To which is added, A Practical Treatise on Diseases of the Teeth. London: J. Johnson, 1803. 3rd ed. 4to. (vi),246,(vii)pp; 16 plts. Recent grn 1/2 calf, marbled bds, spine gilt. (Tp, other pp spotted, lt browned), o/w VG. *White.* $1,365/£875

HUNTER, JOHN. A Treatise on the Blood, Inflammation and Gun-Shot Wounds. Phila: Webster, 1817. 1st Amer ed. (20),514pp (foxing, browning); 8 engr plts. Orig full calf (newly rebacked). *Goodrich.* $250/£160

HUNTER, JOHN. A Treatise on the Blood, Inflammation and Gunshot Wounds. London: B. Cox et al, 1812. 2nd ed. 2 vols. x,487; viii,511pp; 9 plts on 8 pp. Mod 1/2 calf, marbled bds. (Plts offset), else Clean. *White.* $491/£315

HUNTER, JOHN. A Treatise on the Blood, Inflammation, and Gun-Shot Wounds. London: Ptd by John Richardson, 1794. 4to. lxvii,575pp (lacks frontis, 1st 3 leaves w/margins silked, pg xi misbound, lt foxed); 9 plts. Contemp calf bds (extrems sl worn, rebacked), gilt, orig spine label (chipped). *Edwards.* $749/£480

HUNTER, MILTON R. Utah Indian Stories. Salt Lake City: Privately ptd, 1946. 1st ed. VG. *Oregon.* $60/£38

HUNTER, ROBERT HANCOCK. Narrative of.... Austin: Encino, 1966. Rpt. One of 640 signed by William D. Witliff (ed). Frontis port. Cl-backed pict bds. Fine in plastic wrapper. *Bohling.* $30/£19

HUNTER, ROBERT. The Links. NY: Scribner, 1926. 1st ed. Grn dec cl. VG. *Pacific*.* $748/£479

HUNTER, SAM. Isamu Nogushi. NY: Abbeville, n.d. (ca '80s). Blind-stamped cl. VG in dj. *Argosy.* $100/£64

HUNTER, W. Historical Account of Charing Cross Hospital and Medical School (Univ of London). 1914. 39 plts. (Ex-lib, few sm ink lib stamps; spine, corners worn, cl dull.) *Whitehart.* $62/£40

HUNTER, W. H. Annals of Rural Bengal. NY: Leypoldt & Holt, 1868. 2nd ed. xvi,475pp. Orange-brn gilt cl. VG. *Terramedia.* $200/£128

HUNTER, W. W. Orissa. London, 1872. 2 vols. Color frontis, 330; 219pp; fldg map fr pocket vol 1, 16 plts. (Margins lt browned; upper hinge cracked vol 1, spines faded, sl chipped.) *Edwards.* $195/£125

HUNTER, WILLIAM S. Hunter's Panoramic Guide from Niagara Falls to Quebec. Boston, 1857. Fldg panorama frontis. Pub's gilt-pict cl. *Swann*.* $115/£74

HUNTFORD, ROLAND. Scott and Amundsen. London: Hodder & Stoughton, 1979. 1st ed. VG in dj. *High Latitude.* $80/£51

HUNTINGTON, D. C. The Landscapes of Frederic Edwin Church. NY: Braziller, 1966. Stated 1st ed. 8 color plts. Good+ in Good dj. *Scribe's Perch*.* $70/£45

HUNTINGTON, DWIGHT W. Our Big Game. NY: Scribner, 1904. 1st ed. All edges stained yellow. Dec lt grn buckram. VG. *Biscotti.* $45/£29

HUNTINGTON, DWIGHT W. Our Wild Fowl and Waders. NY: Amateur Sportsman, 1910. 1st ed. 27 photo plts. Maroon cl. Fair (ex-lib, spine # removed). *Price.* $39/£25

HUNTINGTON, P. C. Masonic Light on the Abduction and Murder of William Morgan. NY: Macoy Pub & Masonic Supply Co, n.d. (1886). 2nd ed. 174pp. Silk-patterned cl, gilt. Fine. *Connolly.* $65/£42

HUNTLEY, G. HAYDN. Andrea Sansovino. Cambridge, 1935. Uncut. Good in dj. *Washton.* $195/£125

HUNTON, JOHN. John Hunton's Diary. (Fort Laramie: L.G. Flannery, 1956-1964.) One of 1500 sets. 5 vols. Fldg map vol 1. Gray-stamped brn velvet wrappers. *Dawson.* $75/£48

HURD, JOHN CODMAN. The Law of Freedom and Bondage in the United States. Boston, 1858/1862. 1st ed. Inscribed. 2 vols. 617; 800pp. (Ink names, stamps, sig, sl foxed; extrems frayed.) *King.* $250/£160

HURD-MEAD, KATE CAMPBELL. A History of Women in Medicine from the Earliest Times to the Beginning of the Nineteenth Century. Haddam, CT: Haddam Press, 1938. 1st ed. 39 plts. (Ink name, spine faded.) *Bickersteth.* $203/£130

HURD-MEAD, KATE CAMPBELL. Medical Women of America. 1933. 1st ed. (Ex-lib.) *Fye.* $150/£96

HURLEY, F. JACK. Portrait of a Decade. Baton Rouge: LSU, 1972. 1st ed. Roy Stryker (photos). NF in NF dj. *Smith.* $50/£32

HURLEY, F. JACK. Russell Lee Photographer. Dobbs Ferry: Morgan & Morgan, 1978. 1st ed. Signed. 167 b/w plts. NF (owner stamp) in wrappers (sl worn). *Cahan.* $75/£48

HURLIMANN, BETTINA. Three Centuries of Children's Books in Europe. Cleveland: World, 1968. 1st US ed. 6 3/4 x 9 3/4. 296pp. Fine in dj. *Cattermole.* $30/£19

HURRY, JAMIESON B. Imhotep: The Vizier and Physician of King Zoser and Afterwards the Egyptian God of Medicine. OUP, Humphrey Milford, 1926. 12 full-pg, 1 dbl-pg plts. (Ex-lib, plt removed fep, blind-stamps, sl pencil/ink mks.) Blue cl (bumped, stained, fr joint split), gilt. Good. *Blue Mountain.* $50/£32

HURRY, JAMIESON B. Imhotep: The Vizier and Physician of King Zoser.... London, 1928. 2nd ed. VG. *Fye.* $150/£96

HURRY, JAMIESON B. Vicious Circle in Disease. Phila, 1919. 3rd ed. Grn cl bds. VG. *Doctor's Library.* $100/£64

HURST, FANNIE. Lummox. NY: Harpers, 1923. 1st ed. Fine in NF dj (crown nicked). *Between The Covers.* $200/£128

HURST, H. E. The Nile. London, 1952. 1st ed. 16 photo plts. Blue cl, gilt. VG in dj. *Price.* $48/£31

HURST, JOHN F. Indika, the Country and the People. NY: Harper, 1891. Full red leather, gilt, raised bands. Card of Bishop Hurst. (Extrems sl worn), else Fine. *Metropolitan*.* $100/£64

HURSTON, ZORA NEALE. Seraph on the Suwanee. NY: Scribner, 1948. 1st ed. Fine (lacks dj). *Captain's Bookshelf.* $175/£112

HURSTON, ZORA NEALE. Tell My Horse. Phila/NY: Lippincott, (1938). 1st ed. NF (spine faded, foot lt rubbed; lacks dj). *Between The Covers.* $200/£128

HURSTON, ZORA NEALE. Tell My Horse. Phila: Lippincott, (1938). 1st ed. (Spine extrems sl rubbed), else NF (lacks dj). *Captain's Bookshelf.* $200/£128

HURSTON, ZORA NEALE. Tell My Horse. Phila: Lippincott, (1938). 1st ed. Fine (corners bottom edge sl rubbed) in pict dj (spine extrems, corners lt chipped). *Captain's Bookshelf.* $1,000/£641

HURTIG, BERNARD. Masterpieces of Netsuke Art. NY/Tokyo: Weatherhill, (1975). 2nd ed. Brn/off-white brocade cl, gilt. Fine in brocade/bd slipcase (sl worn). *Baltimore*.* $25/£16

HURWITZ, A. and G. DEGENSHEIN. Milestones in Modern Surgery. NY, 1958. 1st ed. VG. *Fye.* $100/£64

HUSE, CALEB. The Supplies for the Confederate Army. Boston: T.R. Marvin, 1904. 1st ed. NF in orig ptd wrappers. Howes H837. *Mcgowan.* $150/£96

HUSMANN, GEORGE. American Grape Growing and Wine Making. NY, 1880. 1st ed. (Spine dknd; lt marginal dampstaining.) *Swann*.* $92/£59

HUSSEY, CHRISTOPHER and JOHN CORNFORTH. English Country Houses Open to the Public. London: Country Life, 1964. 4th ed. Fine in Fine dj. *Quest.* $45/£29

HUSSEY, CHRISTOPHER. English Country Houses: Mid-Georgian 1760-1800. London: Country Life, 1963. 2nd ed. Teg. (Cvrs sl stained, worn.) *Ars Artis.* $117/£75

HUSSEY, CHRISTOPHER. English Gardens and Landscapes, 1700-1750. NY: Funk & Wagnalls, (1967). 1st ed. 246 b/w plts, 11 diags. Grn cl. Good in dj. *Karmiole.* $65/£42

HUSSEY, CHRISTOPHER. English Gardens and Landscapes, 1700-1750. London, 1967. Frontis (loose, sl frayed). Dj (frayed). *Maggs.* $59/£38

HUSSEY, CHRISTOPHER. The Life of Sir Edwin Lutyens. Country Life, 1950. 1st ed. Frontis port, 178 plts. (Spine sl worn, loss to tp.) *Edwards.* $156/£100

HUSSEY, CHRISTOPHER. The Life of Sir Edwin Lutyens. Country Life, 1953. Special ed. VG in dj. *Hadley.* $148/£95

HUSSEY, JOHN A. The History of Fort Vancouver and Its Physical Structure. Portland: WA State Hist Soc, n.d. (1957). One of 1000 numbered. Signed. Tipped-in color frontis, 54 plts. Dec bds, brn spine. (Spine ends sl worn), else NF. *Parmer.* $150/£96

HUSSEY, JOHN A. (ed). The Voyage of the Racoon. SF: Book Club of CA, 1958. Ltd to 400. Prospectus laid in. Black leather spine, marbled bds. Fine. *Karmiole.* $150/£96

HUSSEY, JOHN A. (ed). The Voyage of the Racoon: A 'Secret' Journal...1813-1814. SF: Book Club of CA, 1958. One of 400. 7 plts, errata slip in rhyme. Morocco-backed, gilt marbled bds. Fine. *Harrington.* $100/£64

HUSSEY, N. W. et al. The Pests of Protected Cultivation. NY, 1969. 1st Amer ed. VG in dj. *Brooks.* $35/£22

HUSTON, JOHN. Frankie and Johnny. NY, (1930). Frontis by Miguel Covarrubias. Dj (dknd, chips, edge tears). *Swann*.* $103/£66

HUSTON, PAUL GRISWOLD. Around an Old Homestead, a Book of Memories. Cincinnati: Jennings & Graham, (1906). Teg. Tan cl, gilt. Fine. *Bohling.* $20/£13

HUTCHINGS, J. M. Scenes of Wonder and Curiosity in California. SF, 1861. Pub's gilt-stamped roan (rubbed). *Swann*.* $92/£59

HUTCHINGS, J. M. Scenes of Wonder and Curiosity in California. NY/SF: A. Roman, 1870. 292,(4)pp. VG. *Zubal*.* $25/£16

HUTCHINGS, J. M. Scenes of Wonder and Curiosity in California. NY: A. Roman, 1870. 1st ed. 292pp (foxed, piece of 1 pg missing). Good. *Gibbs.* $45/£29

HUTCHINGS, J.M. In the Heart of the Sierras: The Yosemite Valley.... Yosemite Valley/Oakland: (J.M. Hutchings), 1888. 4th ptg. (4),xii,13-496pp. 29 photo-litho plts, fldg map. Aeg. Dec grn pict cl, beveled bds (spine sl dknd, extrems worn). VG+. *Harrington.* $75/£48

HUTCHINS, PATRICIA. James Joyce's Dublin. (London): Grey Walls Press, (1950). Copyright notice on slip pasted to tp verso. VG in dj (chipped). *Bohling.* $25/£16

HUTCHINS, WELLS A. Water Rights Laws in the Nineteen Western States. Washington: US Dept of Ag, 1971. Maroon buckram (sl dull, worn). Good set. *Boswell.* $350/£224

HUTCHINSON, C. ALAN. Frontier Settlement in Mexican California. Yale Univ, 1969. 1st ed. Dj (sl torn w/o loss). *Edwards.* $23/£15

HUTCHINSON, C. C. Resources of Kansas. Topeka, 1871. Frontis, 287,(1)pp; fldg map (outer fold splitting). Gilt-titled blue cl. VG+. *Bohling.* $120/£77

HUTCHINSON, H. N. Prehistoric Man and Beast. London: Smith, Elder, 1896. 1st ed. 298pp+ads, 10 full-pg halftone repros. Gilt-dec cl. VG. *Mikesh.* $45/£29

HUTCHINSON, HORACE G. Fifty Years of Golf. London: Country Life, (1919). 1st ed. Grn cl, gilt spine. (Name), else NF. *Pacific*.* $403/£258

HUTCHINSON, HORACE G. (ed). Fishing. 'Country Life' Library of Sport, 1904. 2 vols. Red cl (sl rubbed, sl damp mkd; foxed). *Petersfield.* $66/£42

HUTCHINSON, HORACE G. Golf. London: Longmans, Green, 1890. 1st ed. xiv,(464)pp. Good (dec cl sl worn; browned, spotted). *Ash.* $289/£185

HUTCHINSON, HORACE G. Golf: A Complete History of the Game.... Phila: Penn Publishing, 1901. Rev ed. Silver-stamped grn cl. (Insect damage cvrs, ends chipped, spine dknd), else VG. *Pacific*.* $109/£70

HUTCHINSON, HORACE G. Golfing. London: George Routledge, 1901. 6th ed. Frontis. Pict cl. (Name, offset eps; lt dents spine), else VG. *Pacific*.* $150/£96

HUTCHINSON, JONATHAN. Illustrations of Clinical Surgery Consisting of Plates, Photographs, Woodcuts, Diagrams, etc.... Volume 1 with Appendix and Index. London: J. & A. Churchill, 1878. Sm folio. 244pp; 39 engr plts (30 color). (Dampstaining affecting bottom 1/3 pp, plts more than text.) Orig 1/2 leather, bds (worn, headpiece repaired). *Goodrich.* $495/£317

HUTCHINSON, R. C. Elephant and Castle. London: Cassell, (1949). 1st ed. Inscribed in year of publication. NF in NF dj. *Captain's Bookshelf.* $100/£64

HUTCHINSON, THOMAS J. The Parana. London: Edward Stanford, 1868. 1st ed. Engr frontis port, xxvii,424pp (sl aged, sl foxed, smudged, sm tears feps); lg fldg map w/hand-colored highlights. Untrimmed. Blind royal blue cl (edges sl worn, hinges repaired), gilt. *Baltimore*.* $120/£77

HUTCHINSON, W. E. Byways Around San Francisco Bay. NY/Cinn.: Abingdon, 1915. 1st ed. Teg. Pict gilt cl. VG. *Mikesh.* $35/£22

HUTCHINSON, W. H. The Life and Personal Writings of Eugene Manlove Rhodes. Norman: Univ of OK, (1965). 1st ed. 2 maps. Grn-blue cl. Fine in dj (sl soiled). *Argonaut.* $60/£38

HUTCHINSON, WILLIAM T. and WILLIAM M. E. RACHAL (eds). The Papers of James Madison. Volume 4. Univ of Chicago, (c. 1965). VG in VG dj. *Book Broker.* $35/£22

HUTCHISON, ISOBEL W. Stepping Stones from Alaska to Asia. London: Blackie, (1937). 4 color plts, fldg map. VG in dj. *High Latitude.* $30/£19

HUTTON, BUD and ANDY ROONEY. The Story of the Stars and Stripes. NY: Farrar & Rinehart, (1946). 1st ed. Dj (chipped). *Dawson.* $35/£22

HUTTON, CHARLES and OLINTHUS GREGORY. A Course of Mathematics. London, 1841-3. 12th ed. 2 vols. viii,535,(i)errata; xii,548pp (sl browned, vol 1 w/several gatherings protruding to fore-edge). Partly unopened. Mod bds backed in orig cl (dampstained, spines chipped), mod paper labels. *Edwards.* $55/£35

HUTTON, EDWARD. The Cosmati. London, 1950. 64 plts. Good. *Washton.* $50/£32

HUTTON, EDWARD. The Story of Ravenna. London, 1926. Rev ed. Fldg plan. Teg. Gilt-dec cl (spine sl discolored). *Edwards.* $19/£12

HUTTON, F. W. Darwinism and Lamarckism, Old and New: Four Lectures. NY: Putnam, 1899. 1st ed. Engr frontis port, 226pp+2pp ads. VG. *Mikesh.* $60/£38

HUTTON, J. ARTHUR. Rod-Fishing for Salmon on the Wye. Fishing Gazette, 1920. Linen back. *Petersfield.* $47/£30

HUTTON, JAMES. Central Asia: From the Aryan to the Cossack. London: Tinsley, 1875. 1st ed. viii,472pp (some margins pencilled). Brn cl (spine discolored, cracked). *Terramedia.* $100/£64

HUTYRA, FRANZ and JOSEF MAREK. Special Pathology and Therapeutics of the Diseases of Domestic Animals. Chicago, 1926. 3 vols. 28 color plts. (Corners rubbed; vols 1, 3 shaken.) *Argosy.* $150/£96

HUXHAM, JOHN. A Dissertation on the Malignant, Ulcerous Sore-Throat. London: J. Hinton, 1759. 3rd ed. (4),70pp (lt browned; tp fore-edge sl chipped, no loss). Good in mod wrappers. *Glaser.* $250/£160

HUXLEY, ALDOUS. Adonis and the Alphabet. London: C&W, 1956. 1st Eng ed. Lt grn cl. NF in dj (rear panel soiled, few sm tears, spine head chipped). *Antic Hay.* $35/£22

HUXLEY, ALDOUS. Along the Road, Notes and Essays of a Tourist. NY: George H. Doran, (1925). 1st ed. One of 250 numbered, signed. Teg, uncut. Parchment, bds, leather label, gilt. VF in NF dj. *Macdonnell.* $275/£176

HUXLEY, ALDOUS. The Art of Seeing. London, 1943. 1st ed. Dj (frayed). *Typographeum.* $18/£12

HUXLEY, ALDOUS. Brave New World Revisited. NY: Harper, (1958). 1st Amer ed. NF (ink name) in VG dj (sl worn, soiled). *Antic Hay.* $20/£13

HUXLEY, ALDOUS. Brave New World. C&W, 1932. 1st ed. Good (lt foxing, spine sl creased). *Ash.* $78/£50

HUXLEY, ALDOUS. Brave New World. London, 1932. 1st ed. Excellent in Bright dj (heavily chipped spine bottom). *Buckley.* $281/£180

HUXLEY, ALDOUS. Brave New World. London: C&W, 1932. 1st ed. Blue cl, gilt. (Spine lt rubbed), else Bright. *Macdonnell.* $100/£64

HUXLEY, ALDOUS. Brave New World. (NY): LEC, 1974. One of 2000 numbered, signed by Mara McAfee (illus). *Hermitage.* $125/£80

HUXLEY, ALDOUS. Brief Candles. London, 1930. 1st ed. NF in dj (sm tear, spine sunned, sl chipped). *Polyanthos.* $45/£29

HUXLEY, ALDOUS. Brief Candles. London: C&W, 1930. 1st Eng ed. NF in dj (lt soil). *Antic Hay.* $75/£48

HUXLEY, ALDOUS. Brief Candles. NY: Fountain, 1930. 1st ed. One of 842 numbered, signed. Uncut. Black cl, gilt. Fine. *Macdonnell.* $150/£96

HUXLEY, ALDOUS. The Burning Wheel. Oxford: B.H. Blackwell, 1916. 1st ed, 1st bk. Unopened. Orig oversized wrappers (edges sl creased). Slipcase. *Sotheby's*.* $466/£299

HUXLEY, ALDOUS. The Cicadas and Other Poems. Chatto, 1931. 1st UK ed. NF in VG dj (spine, fr panel faded). *Williams.* $70/£45

HUXLEY, ALDOUS. The Cicadas and Other Poems. London: C&W, 1931. 1st Eng ed. Fine in dj (spine lt faded). *Antic Hay.* $85/£54

HUXLEY, ALDOUS. The Crows of Pearblossom. London: C&W, (1967). 1st Eng ed. Barbara Cooney (illus). Pict cl. VF in dj. *Bromer.* $75/£48

HUXLEY, ALDOUS. The Crows of Pearblossom. NY: Random House, 1967. 1st US ed. Barbara Cooney (illus). 6 3/4 x 8 1/4. 32pp. Fine in dj. *Cattermole.* $35/£22

HUXLEY, ALDOUS. The Defeat of Youth. (Oxford: B.H. Blackwell, 1918.) 1st ed. VG (spine restored, sl worn) in patterned wraps. *Antic Hay.* $175/£112

HUXLEY, ALDOUS. The Devils of Loudun. London: Folio Soc, 1986. Black illus cl. Card slipcase. *Edwards.* $31/£20

HUXLEY, ALDOUS. Do What You Will. London: C&W, 1929. 1st Eng ed. NF in dj. *Antic Hay.* $85/£54

HUXLEY, ALDOUS. The Doors of Perception. (NY): Harper, (1954). 1st ed. NF (sl dknd pastedowns) in dj (edgewear, sl stains, browning, 2-inch tear fr flap). *Antic Hay.* $45/£29

HUXLEY, ALDOUS. The Doors of Perception. NY: Harper, (1954). 1st Amer ed. (Sl crease fr bd), else Fine in NF dj (sl soiled; tear). *Between The Covers.* $125/£80

HUXLEY, ALDOUS. The Doors of Perception. London: C&W, 1954. 1st ed. Gilt cl. (Sm spot top edge), else NF in dj (sm smudge rear panel). *Reese.* $250/£160

HUXLEY, ALDOUS. Essays New and Old. London: C&W, 1926. One of 650 signed. Marbled bds (lt soiled, backstrip faded). *Cullen.* $75/£48

HUXLEY, ALDOUS. Eyeless in Gaza. NY: Harper, 1936. 1st Amer ed. VG in dj (sl worn, rubbed, tears). *Antic Hay.* $27/£17

HUXLEY, ALDOUS. The Gioconda Smile. London: C&W, 1948. 1st ed. Fine in dj (sl nicked). *Reese.* $40/£26

HUXLEY, ALDOUS. Island. London: C&W, 1962. 1st ed. NF in dj (sl worn, browned, price-clipped). *Antic Hay.* $125/£80

HUXLEY, ALDOUS. Letters of Aldous Huxley. Grover Smith (ed). London: C&W, 1969. 1st ed. NF in dj. *Turtle Island.* $65/£42

HUXLEY, ALDOUS. Little Mexican. London: Chatto, 1924. 1st ed. Signed. Fine (edges brnd) in Fine dj (2 edge tears). *Unger.* $350/£224

HUXLEY, ALDOUS. Mortal Coils. London: C&W, 1922. 1st ed. Fine in Fine paper dj (sl soiling). *Between The Covers.* $250/£160

HUXLEY, ALDOUS. Music at Night and Other Essays. Chatto, 1931. 1st UK ed. Fine in VG + dj (spine sl faded). *Williams.* $70/£45

HUXLEY, ALDOUS. Music at Night and Other Essays. NY: Fountain, 1931. One of 842 signed. Marbled bds, linen spine (sl wear), paper label. *Appelfeld.* $150/£96

HUXLEY, ALDOUS. The Olive Tree. C&W, 1936. 1st ed. (Margins lt browned.) Grn cl, gilt. Orig dj bound in. *Edwards.* $55/£35

HUXLEY, ALDOUS. On the Margin. London, 1923. 1st ed. VG in dj. *Argosy.* $50/£32

HUXLEY, ALDOUS. On the Margin. London: C&W, 1923. 1st Eng ed. VG in dj (scuffed rear panel, affecting lettering). *Antic Hay.* $50/£32

HUXLEY, ALDOUS. Point Counter Point. London: C&W, 1928. 1st Eng ed. Orange cl. Fine in white dj (lt edgewear, soil, sl stain). *Antic Hay.* $225/£144

HUXLEY, ALDOUS. Those Barren Leaves. London: C&W, 1925. 1st Eng ed. Fine in dj (sl soiled). *Antic Hay.* $85/£54

HUXLEY, ALDOUS. Time Must Have a Stop. NY: Harper, 1944. 1st Amer ed. NF in dj (sl worn, soiled; sm tears, chips). *Antic Hay.* $17/£11

HUXLEY, ALDOUS. Two Or Three Graces. London: C&W, 1926. 1st Eng ed. Blue cl. Fine in NF dj (sl soiled). *Antic Hay.* $125/£80

HUXLEY, ALDOUS. Vulgarity in Literature. London: C&W, 1930. 1st Eng ed. Pict bds. NF (eps sl browned) in dj. *Antic Hay.* $85/£54

HUXLEY, ELSPETH. A Man from Nowhere. London: C&W, 1964. 1st ed. Fine in dj (price-clipped). *Mordida.* $45/£29

HUXLEY, ELSPETH. The Mottled Lizard. London: C&W, 1962. 1st Eng ed. Fine in dj (sl wear). *Antic Hay.* $35/£22

HUXLEY, ELSPETH. The Red Rock Wilderness. NY: Morrow, 1957. 1st Amer ed. VG in dj (price-clipped). *Antic Hay.* $20/£13

HUXLEY, ELSPETH. The Walled City. Phila: Lippincott, 1949. 1st Amer ed. VG in dj (worn, soiled). *Antic Hay.* $17/£11

HUXLEY, G. L. Early Sparta. Faber, 1962. 1st ed. Dbl-pg map. Dj (browned, sl chipped). *Edwards.* $25/£16

HUXLEY, JULIAN and G. R. DE BEER. The Elements of Experimental Embryology. CUP, 1934. 1st ed. Blind-stamped gilt-dec cl. VG. *Mikesh.* $75/£48

HUXLEY, JULIAN. Africa View. London, 1931. 2nd imp. Fldg map. (Upper hinge cracked; joints splitting, edges rubbed w/cl loss.) *Edwards.* $23/£15

HUXLEY, JULIAN. Bird-Watching and Bird Behaviour. London: C&W, 1930. 1st ed. VG + . *Mikesh.* $37/£24

HUXLEY, JULIAN. Evolution. London, (1942). *Wheldon & Wesley.* $31/£20

HUXLEY, JULIAN. From an Antique Land. NY: Harper & Row, 1966. 1st ed. 55 plts (16 color), 3 maps. (Sl rubbed, soiled), o/w VG. *Worldwide.* $16/£10

HUXLEY, LEONARD. Life and Letters of Thomas Henry Huxley. London, 1900. 1st ed. 2 vols. Frontis ports. Uncut. (Feps sl spotted; cl corners sl bumped, spines lt faded.) *Edwards.* $101/£65

HUXLEY, LEONARD. Life and Letters of Thomas Henry Huxley. London: Macmillan, 1900. 2 vols. 2 frontispieces, 2 plts. (Eps spotted.) Unopened. *Andrew Stewart.* $55/£35

HUXLEY, T. H. Diary. Julian Huxley (ed). London, 1935. 1st ed. Color frontis, 12 plts, fldg map. (Corner lt dampstained, spine sl rubbed.) *Edwards.* $55/£35

HUXLEY, T. H. An Introduction to the Classification of Animals. London, 1869. 147pp. *Wheldon & Wesley.* $70/£45

HUXLEY, T. H. The Oceanic Hydrozoa. London: Ray Soc, 1859. 1st ed. 143pp, 12 full-pg engr plts. Cl-backed wraps. VG + . *Mikesh.* $237/£152

HUXLEY, T. H. On Our Knowledge of the Causes of the Phenomena of Organic Nature. London, 1863. 1st ed. 156pp. VG. *Fye.* $100/£64

HUXLEY, T. H. On the Origin of Species. NY, 1863. 1st Amer ed. 150pp + 6 ads. (Worn, inner joint cracked.) *Henly.* $70/£45

HUXLEY, T. H. On the Origin of Species. NY, 1872. 1st Amer ed. 150pp. Grn cl, gilt. VG. *Price.* $95/£61

HUYGENS, CHRISTIAAN. The Pendulum Clock. Ames: IA State Univ, (1986). 1st ed. Fine in dj. *Glaser.* $45/£29

HUYGHE, RENE. Eugene Delacroix. NY: Abrams, 1963. 56 color plts. *Metropolitan*.* $40/£26

HUYSHE, G. L. The Red River Expedition. London: Macmillan, 1871. 1st ed. Frontis, (11),(1),275,(1)pp, port. (Spine faded.) *Ginsberg.* $300/£192

HUYSMANS, J. K. La-Bas. London: Fortune, (1952). Violet cl (a variant binding), gilt. Nice in yellow dj. *Cady.* $30/£19

HYAMS, E. A History of Gardens and Gardening. London: Dent, 1971. Sound in slipcase. *Ars Artis.* $55/£35

HYAMS, EDWARD. Capability Brown and Humphry Repton. Dent, 1971. VG in dj. *Hadley.* $44/£28

HYAMS, EDWARD. Dionysis. A Social History of the Wine Vine. NY: Macmillan, (1965). Map. Fine in dj (repaired). *Quest.* $45/£29

HYAMS, EDWARD. The English Garden. London, 1964. 188 photogravure plts, 17 tipped-in color plts. (Margins sl browned.) Dj (sl browned, chipped). *Edwards.* $39/£25

HYATT, H. S. Manufacturing, Agricultural and Industrial Resources of Iowa.... Des Moines: Republican Steam Ptg House, 1872/3. 155pp (5 ads); fldg map. Good in ptd wrappers. *Dumont.* $135/£87

HYATT, STANLEY PORTAL. The Diary of a Soldier of Fortune. N.d. c.(1914). 2nd imp. Frontis port. (Inscrip; spine faded.) *Edwards.* $55/£35

HYATT, STANLEY PORTAL. The Old Transport Road. 1914. 1st ed. (1/2-title, frontis, tp affixed to inner margin; upper hinge cracked, fep affixed to pastedown, bkpl, bkpl remains ragged; cl sl wrinkled, spine chipped, lower joint partly split.) *Edwards.* $39/£25

HYDE, ALEXANDER et al. The Frozen Zone and Its Explorers. Hartford: Columbia Book Co, 1874. xv,800pp; fldg map. Dec cl. (Corners worn), else VG. *High Latitude.* $75/£48

HYDE, GEORGE E. Indians of the High Plains. Norman, (1959). 1st ed. VG in dj (edgeworn). *King.* $30/£19

HYDE, GEORGE E. A Life of George Bent, Written from His Letters. Norman, 1968. 1st ed. 11 maps. Fine in Fine dj. *Turpen.* $58/£37

HYDE, GEORGE E. A Life of George Bent. Savoie Lottinville (ed). Norman: Univ of OK, (1968). 1st ed. 24 plts. 2-tone cl. Fine in dj (lt rubbed, sl soiled). *Argonaut.* $60/£38

HYDE, GEORGE E. The Pawnee Indians. Norman: Univ of OK, (1974). 1st ptg of new ed. VF in pict dj. *Argonaut.* $40/£26

HYDE, GEORGE E. Red Cloud's Folk. Norman: Univ of OK, 1937. 1st ed. VG in dj (sl chipped). Howes H862. *Lien.* $80/£51

HYDE, GEORGE E. Spotted Tail's Folk. Norman, (1961). 1st ed. VG in dj (spine sl sunned). *King.* $35/£22

HYDE, GEORGE E. Spotted Tail's Folk. Norman: Univ of OK, (1961). 1st ed. VG in dj. *Lien.* $75/£48

HYDE, H. MONTGOMERY. Henry James at Home. Methuen, 1969. 1st ed. Inscribed presentation. Frontis port. Dj (sl chipped). *Edwards.* $31/£20

HYDE, H. MONTGOMERY. A History of Pornography. NY: FSG, (1965). 1st Amer ed. Fine in dj (lt worn). *Hermitage.* $30/£19

HYDE, H. MONTGOMERY. Solitary in the Ranks. NY, 1978. 1st ed. VG in dj. *Typographeum.* $30/£19

HYDE, JAMES WILSON. The Royal Mail. London, 1889. 3rd ed. xvi,306pp + 4pp pub's list. (Ink stamps prelims, pastedown notes; notes, spotting, recased, spine faded, sl rubbed.) *Edwards.* $70/£45

HYDE, JOHN, JR. Mormonism: Its Leaders and Designs. NY, 1857. 2nd ed. Frontis, 335pp + ads. (Lacks rep, internal crack between sigs; fr hinge cracked, worn), o/w VG. *Benchmark.* $50/£32

HYDE, PHILIP and FRANCOIS LEYDET. The Last Redwoods. SF: Sierra Club, (1963). 1st ed. VG in dj. *King.* $45/£29

HYMAN, SUSAN. Edward Lear's Birds. London, 1980. 1st UK ed. Dj. *Edwards.* $47/£30

HYMAN, SUSAN. Edward Lear's Birds. NY, 1980. VG in dj. *Argosy.* $75/£48

HYMAN, TONY. Handbook of Cigar Boxes. Arnot Art Museum, 1979. Ltd 1st ed, signed. VG + in dj (sl worn). *My Bookhouse.* $45/£29

HYNE, CUTCLIFFE. Adventures of Captain Kettle. London: C. Arthur Pearson, 1898. 1st ed. (viii),318,(ii)pp, imprint leaf, pub's inserted 16pp cat dated May 1898 at end. Mottled crimson fine grain unglazed cl, gilt. (Eps, cvrs sl mkd), o/w Very Nice. *Temple.* $28/£18

I

IBARRURI, DOLORES. They Shall Not Pass. London, 1966. 1st ed. Fine in dj. *Typographeum.* $25/£16

IBSEN, HENRIK. John Gabriel Borkman. William Archer (trans). London: Heinemann, 1897. 1st ed in English. One of 1000 ptd. Emb 'Presentation Copy' stamp tp. VG. *Dramatis Personae.* $50/£32

IBSEN, HENRIK. John Gabriel Borkman. William Archer (trans). NY: Stone & Kimball, 1897. 1st Amer ed. Teg. Pict cl. NF. *Reese.* $45/£29

IBSEN, HENRIK. Little Eyolf. William Archer (trans). Chicago: Stone & Kimball, 1895. 2nd Stone & Kimball ptg. Teg. Pict cl. NF. *Reese.* $20/£13

IBSEN, HENRIK. Peer Gynt. London: George G. Harrap, (1936). One of 460 signed by Arthur Rackham (illus). 12 mtd color plts. Some gatherings unopened. Gilt-dec vellum. VG. *New Hampshire**. $500/£321

IBSEN, HENRIK. Peer Gynt. Phila: Lippincott, n.d. (1936). Arthur Rackham (illus). 4to. (Sl worn.) Dj (frayed, edge-torn). *Oinonen**. $110/£71

IBSEN, HENRIK. Three Plays of Henrik Ibsen. NY: LEC, 1964. #417/1500 signed by Fredrik Matheson (illus). Fine in pub's slipcase. *Hermitage*. $85/£54

Idaho Lore. Caldwell: Caxton, 1939. 1st ed. (Sm bkpl), else VG. *Perier*. $80/£51

Idaho, A Guide in Word and Picture. Caldwell: Caxton, 1937. 1st ed. Lib ed. (Bkpl), else VG. *Perier*. $150/£96

Idaho: A Guide in Word and Picture. (By Vardis Fisher.) Caldwell: Caxton, 1937. 1st ed. 1st WPA title on individual states. Pict dk grn coated cl stamped in gilt/lt grn (sl flaking). Text VG. Pict dj (lt sunned, sl worn, sm tears, chips). Howes F153. *Baltimore**. $180/£115

IDEM, SEMPER. The Blue Book, a Bibliographical Attempt to Describe the Guide Books to the Houses of Ill Fame in New Orleans.... Privately ptd, 1936. Ltd ed. Navy cl, gilt title. (Inscrip; lt wear, sl scratched, spotted.) *Bohling*. $250/£160

Idiot Boy. (By Catherine Douglas Bell.) London/Edinburgh/NY: T. Nelson, n.d. (ca 1880). 16mo. Full-pg wood engr frontis, 15pp + 1pg list (lt foxing edges). Fine in dec paper wrappers. *Hobbyhorse*. $95/£61

IGLAUER, EDITH. Denison's Ice Road. NY: Dutton, 1975. VG in dj. *Parmer*. $25/£16

IGNOTUS. Golf in a Nutshell. London: Country Life, 1919. 1st ed. Fine. *Pacific**. $58/£37

ILF, ILYA and EUGENE PETROV. Little Golden America. NY: F&R, (1937). 1st Amer ed. (Fr gutter sl faded), else Fine in Fine dj (sl rubbed). *Between The Covers*. $350/£224

ILF, ILYA and EUGENE PETROV. Little Golden America. NY: Farrar & Rinehart, 1937. 1st US ed. NF in dj (sl rubbed). *Lame Duck*. $275/£176

ILIFF, FLORA GREGG. People of the Blue Water. NY, 1954. 1st ed. Map. Blue cl. Fine in VG+ dj. *Five Quail*. $25/£16

Illinois at Shiloh. (Chicago: Ptd by M.A. Donohue, 1905?). 1st ed. 2 fldg maps in pocket, 12 plts. Ptd slip laid in, 'Compliments of Capt. Timothy Slatery, commissioner Shiloh Battlefield.' (Cl sl soiled), o/w Fine. *Pirages*. $175/£112

Illinois Herb Company Almanac 1936. Chicago: IL Herb Co, (1935). (Nick.) Orig color pict wrappers. *Sadlon*. $10/£6

Illinois in 1837. (By Samuel Mitchell.) Phila, 1837. 1st ed, 2nd issue, w/'animals' spelled correctly on title. Fldg frontis map (very foxed). Later 1/4 morocco. Howes M689. *Swann**. $149/£96

Illuminated Books of the Middle Ages and the Renaissance. Balt: Walters Art Gallery, 1949. 80 plts. 1/2 cl, bds. Good. *Washton*. $40/£26

Illustrated Historical Atlas of the State of Indiana. Chicago: Baskin, Forster, (1876). 462pp (last few pp wrinkled, tp bottom margin frayed). Lib buckram (rebound). Good. *Cullen*. $550/£353

Illustrated History of North Idaho. Western Hist, 1903. Full leather. VG. *Perier*. $495/£317

Illustrations of Shakespeare. London: Sherwood et al, 1830. 1st ed. Engr frontis, ff.38, ptd rectos only. This copy interleaved w/blanks. Old tan cl spine, blue bds (soiled, corners rubbed). *Karmiole*. $100/£64

Illustrative Cloud Forms, for the Guidance of Observers in the Classification of Clouds. (Washington): Hydrographic Office, (1897). 1st ed. (3)leaves (inscrip) + plts; 16 color litho plts (1 w/marginal stain, some guards defective). Pebble-grain morocco (rubbed, sm paint spots), gilt. *Pirages*. $125/£80

Illustrators '59. NY, (1959). 1st issue. (Ink name; dj worn), else VG. *Truepenny*. $75/£48

Illustrators 14: The Fourteenth Annual of American Illustration. NY, (1973). VG in dj. *Truepenny*. $45/£29

Illustrators 24: The 24th Annual of American Illustration. NY, (1983). Fine in dj. *Truepenny*. $45/£29

Image and Imagination. Oil Sketches of the Baroque. L.A. County Museum of Art, 1968. 60 plts. Good in wrappers. *Washton*. $25/£16

Imagist Anthology 1930. NY: Covici, Friede, (1930). 1st ed. Fine in dj. *Bromer*. $400/£256

IMHOLTE, JOHN QUINN. First Volunteers. Minneapolis: Ross & Haines, 1963. 1st ed. Fine in dj. *Bohling*. $15/£10

IMLAY, GILBERT. A Topographical Description of the Western Territory of North America.... London, 1797. 3rd ed. 8vo. 4 maps (2 w/extensive repairs). Pub's sheep (fr joint starting). Howes I12. *Swann**. $690/£442

Impartial Relation of the Hail-Storm on the Fifteenth of July and the Tornado on the Second of August 1799.... (By Sherman Dewey.) Norwich: John Trumbull, 1799. 30pp (outer ll sl soiled, worn, last blank leaf detached). Stitched pamphlet. *New Hampshire**. $180/£115

Improvisations—Artists Equity Masquerade Ball 1953. NY, 1953. One of 2000 numbered. Pict stiff wraps (edges worn), spiral bound. *Swann**. $287/£184

IMRIE, DAVID. Lakeland Gamekeeper. London: Batchworth, 1949. 1st ed. VG in dj. *Hollett*. $55/£35

In Pursuit of Beauty: Americans and the Aesthetic Movement. NY: MMA, (1986). Dj. *Freeman**. $60/£38

In Quest of Truth. London: Watts, 1914. 1st ed. Gray wrappers. VG (sl worn, sl soiled). *Sumner & Stillman*. $135/£87

In the Far East.... (By William Henry Davenport Adams.) London: Thomas Nelson, 1879. 1st ed. 208pp. Pict cl, gilt. Nice (lt worn, sl mks). *Ash*. $117/£75

In the Rocky Mountains with the Indian, Bear and Wolf. Denver: Smith Brooks Ptg, 1913. VG in wraps. *Perier*. $45/£29

Incident on the Bark Columbia. (By Samuel McCorkle.) Cummington, MA: Cummington Press, (1941). 1st ed. One of 300 ptd. Fine. *Lefkowicz*. $150/£96

Incident on the Bark Columbia. (By James McCorkle.) Cummington, MA: Cummington Press, (1941). 1st ed. #172/300. Beige linen-like cl. NF. *Lucas*. $150/£96

Incident on the Bark Columbia. (By James McCorkle.) Cummington, MA: Cummington Press, (1941). Ltd to 300. Beige linen. VF. *Bromer*. $175/£112

Incidents of a Trip Through the Great Platte Valley...1866. (By Silas Seymour.) NY, 1867. 1st ed. Signed, inscribed. 129pp. Related news article tipped in at rear. Brn cl. VG+. Howes S315. *Bohling*. $300/£192

INDERWICK, JAMES. Cruise of the U.S. Brig Argus in 1813. Victor Hugo Paltsits (ed). NY: NY Public Library, 1917. Overall VG in ptd wraps (chipped, dknd). *Parmer*. $45/£29

Indian Treaties Printed by Benjamin Franklin, 1736-1762. Phila, 1938. One of 500. 2-pg aquatint map. Cl (lt bumped), leather spine labels. *Kane**. $350/£224

INGALLS, RACHEL. Mrs. Caliban. London: Faber, 1982. 1st ed. Fine in Fine dj. *Beasley*. $75/£48

INGE, WILLIAM. Bus Stop. NY: Random House, (1955). 1st ed. VG in dj. *Houle.* $150/£96

INGE, WILLIAM. The Dark at the Top of the Stairs. NY, 1958. 1st Amer ed. Fine in Fine dj. *Polyanthos.* $25/£16

INGE, WILLIAM. Natural Affection. NY, 1963. 1st Amer ed. Fine in dj (spine sl sunned, panels sl soiled). *Polyanthos.* $30/£19

INGELFINGEN, KRAFT ZU HOHENLOHE. Letters on Artillery. London, 1890. 2nd ed. 427 w/index pp; 6 fldg plts. (Ink name; bkpl removed; spine sunned; cvrs soiled.) *King.* $35/£22

INGELOW, JEAN. The Poetical Works of Jean Ingelow. NY: Crowell, 1863. 1st ed. 521pp; 6 plts. Aeg. Alligator leather. (Sl rubbed), o/w VG. *Worldwide.* $25/£16

INGELOW, JEAN. A Story of Doom and Other Poems. Longmans, Green, 1867. 1st ed. (6),296pp. VG. *Cox.* $28/£18

INGERSOLL, CHARLES JARED. Inchiquin, The Jesuits Letters.... NY: I. Riley, 1810. 1st ed. v,165pp. Orig bds, paper spine label. (Spine wear, chipping, portions missing), else Good. *Brown.* $40/£26

INGERSOLL, CHESTER. Overland to California in 1847: Letters Written...to the Editor of the Joliet Signal.... Douglas C. McMurtrie (ed). Chicago: Black Cat, 1937. 1st ed. One of 350. Dec bds. Howes I39. *Ginsberg.* $125/£80

INGERSOLL, ERNEST. The Conquest of the North. NY, (1909). 1st ed. Pict wraps (fr cvr frayed, corner chipped). *King.* $25/£16

INGERSOLL, ERNEST. Crest of the Continent. Chicago, 1885. 1st ed. Frontis, 344pp. Pict cl (lt rubbed). *Adelson.* $40/£26

INGERSOLL, ERNEST. Gold Fields of the Klondike and the Wonders of Alaska. Edgewood, c 1897. xiv,487pp (browned). Pict cl. Good (lt soiled). *Blake.* $65/£42

INGERSOLL, ERNEST. Gold Fields of the Klondike and the Wonders of Alaska.... N.p.: Edgewood, c. 1897. xiv,15-512pp. Dec cl. VG. *High Latitude.* $50/£32

INGERSOLL, L. D. Life of Horace Greeley, Founder of the New York Tribune. Chicago: Union Pub Co, 1873. Frontis port, 688pp. VG (spine faded, ends frayed). *Bohling.* $15/£10

INGERSOLL, ROBERT G. A Vindication of Thomas Paine. Peoria, IL: Saturday Evening Call, 1877. 1st ed. 25pp (i.e., 35). Good in ptd wraps (soiled, sl worn). *Wantagh.* $45/£29

INGERSOLL, ROBERT. Crimes Against Criminals. East Aurora, NY: Roycrofters, (1906). 1st ed. Hand-colored tp. Orig suede over paper-cvrd bds, leather spine label. *Glenn.* $50/£32

INGHOLT, HARALD. Gandharan Art in Pakistan. NY: Pantheon, 1957. 1st ed. Fine in Fine dj. *Metropolitan*.* $143/£92

INGLEBY, L. CRESSWELL. Oscar Wilde: Some Recollections. London: Werner Laurie, (1912). 1st Eng ed. Rebound in cl, retaining card wrappers. *Clearwater.* $39/£25

INGLIS, H. D. A Personal Narrative of a Journey Through Norway, Part of Sweden, and the Islands and States of Denmark. 1837. 4th ed. xii,335pp; fldg map. Orig blind emb cl (lt dampstained, faded, extrems sl frayed). *Edwards.* $47/£30

INGLIS, H. D. Rambles in the Footsteps of Don Quixote. London: Whittaker, 1837. 1st ed. George Cruikshank (illus). Gilt-pict grn cl. *Swann*.* $115/£74

INGLIS, JAMES GALE. Northern Michigan. Petoskey, MI, 1898. 1st ed. 167 + index, ads pp. (Corner stained; cvrs rubbed.) *King.* $75/£48

INGLIS, LADY. The Siege of Lucknow. London, 1892. viii,240pp. Contemp maroon 1/2 calf, marbled bds (rebacked, corners rubbed). *Maggs.* $172/£110

INGLIS-JONES, ELISABETH. Peacocks in Paradise. Faber, 1950. 1st ed. Color frontis. *Edwards.* $31/£20

INGLOW, JEAN. Mopsa the Fairy. NY: Macmillan, 1927 (Sept. 1927). 1st ed thus. Dugald Stewart Walker (illus). 8vo. Color frontis, 259pp. Illus eps. Blue pict cl. VG + . *Dower.* $135/£87

INGOLD, ERNEST. Tales of a Peddler. SF: Wallace Kibbee, 1942. 1st ed. Gold dec cl. VG. *Connolly.* $35/£22

INGOLDSBY, THOMAS. (Pseud of Richard Harris Barham.) The Ingoldsby Legends. London: Richard Bentley, 1864. 4to. 60 b/w illus. Gilt-dec leather. (Foxing; extrems sl rubbed), o/w Contents VG. *New Hampshire*.* $70/£45

INGOLDSBY, THOMAS. (Pseud of Richard Harris Barham.) The Ingoldsby Legends. NY: Widdleton, 1864. Later ptg. 2 vols. George Cruikshank & John Leech (illus). Grn cl. VG (sl worn, lt foxing). *Waverly*.* $33/£21

INGOLDSBY, THOMAS. (Pseud of Richard Harris Barham.) The Ingoldsby Legends. London: Bentley, 1868. George Cruikshank, John Leech and John Tenniel (illus). Contemp polished grn calf, gilt extra. *Swann*.* $126/£81

INGOLDSBY, THOMAS. (Pseud of Richard Harris Barham.) The Ingoldsby Legends. London: J.M. Dent, 1898. 12 color plts by Arthur Rackham, guards. Pict eps; teg, untrimmed. Grn cl (sl shelfworn; lt foxed aged), gilt. *Baltimore*.* $80/£51

INGOLDSBY, THOMAS. (Pseud of Richard Harris Barham.) The Ingoldsby Legends. London: J.M. Dent, 1905 (i.e., 1910). 3rd issue. 12 color plts. Gilt-dec grn cl (sl worn). *New Hampshire*.* $40/£26

INGOLDSBY, THOMAS. (Pseud of Richard Harris Barham.) The Ingoldsby Legends. London/NY: Derf/Dutton, 1907. Arthur Rackham (illus). 4to. Gilt-dec cl (spine sl dknd). *Metropolitan*.* $172/£110

INGOLDSBY, THOMAS. (Pseud of Richard Harris Barham.) The Ingoldsby Legends. London/NY: J.M. Dent/E.P. Dutton, 1907. 24 mtd color plts by Arthur Rackham. Gilt-dec cl (edges worn, soiled). *Metropolitan*.* $57/£37

INGPEN, ARTHUR ROBERT. Master Worsley's Book. London: Chiswick, 1910. 23 plts (1 fldg), 4 fldg plts (1 colored). Teg. 1/4 morocco. *Marlborough.* $211/£135

INGRAHAM, J. H. The American Lounger; or, Tales, Sketches, and Legends Gathered in Sundry Journeyings. Phila: Lea & Blanchard, 1839. 1st ed. 273pp. Contemp calf. (Sl worn, scuffed, outer hinges weak, label missing; text spotted), else Good. *Brown.* $25/£16

INGRAHAM, J. H. The Seven Knights; or, Tales of Many Lands. Boston: H.L. Williams, (1845). 1st ed. 43pp. Uncut. (Frayed.) Orig ptd fr wrap (torn). BAL 9986. *M&s.* $175/£112

INGRAHAM, JOSEPH. Joseph Ingraham's Journal of the Brigantine Hope on a Voyage to the Northwest Coast of North America 1790-92. Barre: Imprint Soc, 1971. Fine in slipcase. *Hermitage.* $125/£80

INGRAM, DALE. Practical Cases and Observations in Surgery with Remarks Highly Proper.... London: J. Clarke, 1751. xxxii,245,(iii)pp; 2 plts. Contemp full calf (skillfully rebacked, orig spine laid down). (Text lt foxed), else Clean. *Goodrich.* $595/£381

INGRAM, JOHN H. The Haunted Homes and Family Traditions of Great Britain. [and] Second Series. London: W.H. Allen, 1884. 1st ed. 2 vols. Ads dated May, Aug 1884 at end of each vol respectively. Gray-grn dec cl, silver/gilt. *Maggs.* $281/£180

INGRAM, JOHN. Flora Symbolica. London: Warne, n.d. 3 chromolitho color plts, tissue guards. Gilt/silver-dec pict cvr. Handsome (fr hinge cracked, lacks fep). Quest. $100/£64

INGSTAD, HELGE. Klondyke Bill. London: Wm. Kimber, (1955). VG. High Latitude. $15/£10

INMAN, HENRY and WILLIAM F. CODY. The Great Salt Lake Trail. NY: Macmillan, 1898. 1st ed. 529pp. Pict cl. Good. Howes I55. Lien. $75/£48

INMAN, HENRY. The Old Santa Fe Trail. NY, 1897. 2nd ptg. 493pp. (Hinges cracked), o/w VG. Howes I57. Turpen. $65/£42

INMAN, HENRY. The Old Santa Fe Trail. Topeka: Crane, 1916. Fldg map. Ptd bds. (Browned), else Good. Dumont. $75/£48

INMAN, THOMAS. Ancient Faiths and Modern. NY: J.W. Boulton, 1876. 1st ed. xx,478pp + 45pp index, 20pp cat. VG + (nicely rebound). Middle Earth. $145/£93

INMAN, THOMAS. Ancient Faiths Embodied in Ancient Names. London: The Author, 1868. 2 vols. 789; I,1028pp. VG + set (rebound). Middle Earth. $245/£157

INMAN, THOMAS. The Phenomena of Spinal Irritation and Other Functional Diseases of the Nervous System.... London: John Churchill, 1858. 1st ed. Inscribed. (xx),201,(3)pp; 6 litho plts; inserted cat dated Oct. 1857. Emb mauve cl. VG. Gach. $225/£144

INN, HENRY. Chinese Houses and Gardens. Shao Chang Lee (ed). Honolulu: Fong Inn's, 1940. Ltd to 2000 signed. This copy inscribed. Blue linen, gilt. Good. Karmiole. $100/£64

INNES, HAMMOND. The Doomed Oasis. London: Collins, 1960. 1st ed. Fine in dj. Mordida. $65/£42

INNES, HAMMOND. The Land God Gave to Cain. London: Collins, 1958. 1st ed. (Pg edges sl dknd), o/w Fine in dj. Mordida. $65/£42

INNES, MICHAEL. From London Far. London: Victor Gollancz, 1946. 1st ed. Fine in dj (spine sl dknd). Mordida. $100/£64

INNES, MICHAEL. Going It Alone. London: Victor Gollancz, 1980. 1st ed. NF in NF dj. Janus. $30/£19

INNES, MICHAEL. The Journeying Boy. 1949. 1st ed. VG in yellow dj (sl paled, lt foxing, sm tears). Words Etc. $31/£20

INNES, MICHAEL. The Journeying Boy. London: Gollancz, 1949. 1st Eng ed. VG in dj (faded, chipped). Hadley. $39/£25

INNES, MICHAEL. The Weight of the Evidence. NY: Dodd Mead, 1943. 1st Amer ed. Fine in VG dj (wear, spine nicked, rubbed). Mordida. $65/£42

INNIS, HAROLD A. The Fur Trade in Canada. New Haven: Yale Univ, 1930. 2 plts, map. Good (sl wear). High Latitude. $75/£48

INOUE, YASUSHI. The Hunting Gun. Sadamichi Yokoo and Sanford Goldstein (trans). Rutland, VT: Charles E. Tuttle, (1961). 1st ed in English. NF (owner seal tp) in dj. Turtle Island. $30/£19

Instructions for Officers and Non-commissioned Officers on Outpost and Patrol Duty, and Troops in Campaign. In Two Parts. Washington: GPO, 1863. 1st ed. 88pp (ink sigs in text; pencil sig, notes). Ptd wrappers. Fair (lacks rear wrapper, 1-1/2 inch bottom final l torn off w/loss, fr wrapper soiled, stained, oil stain 1st few ll). Lucas. $200/£128

Interest of Great Britain Considered. (By Benjamin Franklin.) London, 1761. 2nd ed. Old-style tooled brn morocco (lt browned). Maggs. $234/£150

International Competition for a New Administration Building for the Chicago Tribune, 1922. (Chicago, 1923.) 281 competition plts. (Spine ends frayed, back hinge starting.) Leather labels. Freeman*. $550/£353

International Competition for a New Administration Building for the Chicago Tribune.... (Chicago, 1923.) Sm folio. 282 plts. Coarse cl. Swann*. $1,035/£663

International Military Tribunal. Nazi Conspiracy and Agression. Washington, 1946. 1st ed. 8 vols. Ginsberg. $400/£256

INVERARITY, ROBERT BRUCE. Art of the Northwest Coast Indians. Berkeley/L.A.: Univ of CA, 1971. 4th ptg. Dec white cl. VG in dj (worn). Parmer. $50/£32

IOBST, RICHARD W. The Bloody Sixth: The Sixth North Carolina Regiment.... (Durham, NC: Christian Ptg, 1965.) 1st ed. Fldg chart. NF in stiff ptd wrappers. Mcgowan. $150/£96

IONESCO, EUGENE. Exit the King. Donald Watson (trans). NY: Grove Press, (1963). 1st Amer ed. Fine in dj. Hermitage. $35/£22

IONESCO, EUGENE. The Hermit. NY: Viking, 1974. 1st ed in English. (Inscrip), else NF in dj. Lame Duck. $25/£16

IONESCO, EUGENE. Journeys Among the Dead. Barbara Wright (trans). (NY: LEC, 1987.) Ltd to 1000 signed. 4 full-pg color lithos. Mint in stiff handmade Italian paper wrappers, matching slipcase w/crimson morocco on top/bottom edges. Truepenny. $300/£192

IONIDES, BASIL. Colour in Everyday Rooms. London/NY, 1934. 1st ed. Color frontis. Dj (sl ragged, sl loss). Edwards. $39/£25

IPSEN, D. C. Rattlesnakes and Scientists. Reading: Add.-Wes., 1970. 1st ed. Color pict bds. NF. Mikesh. $25/£16

IREDALE, TOM. Birds of Paradise and Bower Birds. London, 1950. 1st ed. 33 color plts, fldg map. (Lib ink stamps; sl marginal browning.) Mod 2-tone cl. Edwards. $133/£85

IRELAND, ALEXANDER. The Book-Lover's Enchiridion. London: Simpkin Marshall, 1888. 5th ed. (xx),(512)pp. Later 1/2 morocco. VG (sl mks, edges sl spotted, last leaf mtd). Ash. $312/£200

IRELAND, ALEXANDER. Emerson: His Life, Genius and Writings. London: Simpkin, Marshall, 1882. 2nd ed. Blue cl, label. BAL III:68. Macdonnell. $100/£64

IRELAND, M. W. (ed). The Medical Department of the U.S. Army in the World War. Washington, 1921-1929. Only ed. 17 vols. Fine set (ex-lib, sl mks). Fye. $950/£609

IRELAND, TOM. The Great Lakes—St. Lawrence Deep Waterway to the Sea. NY: Putnam, 1934. 1st ed. Fine in dj (sm tear). Archer. $35/£22

IRELAND, WILLIAM W. The Mental Affections of Children: Idiocy, Imbecility, and Insanity. Phila: P. Blakiston, 1900. 1st US ed. 21 plts. Panelled thatched blue-grn cl. Jelliffe's bkpl. Good + (fep detached, lib stamp tp, spine #s). Gach. $100/£64

IRISH, WILLIAM. (Pseud of Cornell Woolrich.) Dead Man Blues. Phila: Lippincott, 1948. 1st ed. (Name), o/w Fine in dj. Mordida. $400/£256

IRISH, WILLIAM. (Pseud of Cornell Woolrich.) Deadline at Dawn. Phila: Lippincott, 1944. 1st ed. VG in dj (spine ends chipped, frayed, fr panel crease-tear, chip, edges nicked, worn). Mordida. $125/£80

IRISH, WILLIAM. (Pseud of Cornell Woolrich.) Six Nights of Mystery. NY: Popular Library 258, 1950. 1st ed. Pb orig. NF. Beasley. $50/£32

IRISH, WILLIAM. (Pseud of Cornell Woolrich.) Waltz into Darkness. Phila: Lippincott, 1947. 1st ed. (Extrems rubbed.) Dj (soiled, short tears, ends chipped). Metropolitan*. $126/£81

IRVING, JOHN T. Indian Sketches, Taken During an Expedition to the Pawnee Tribes. London, 1835. 1st Eng ed. 2 vols. Orig bds, ptd paper spine labels. Attractive set. Howes I79. Ginsberg. $550/£353

IRVING, JOHN. The Cider House Rules. NY: Morrow, (1985). One of 795 numbered, signed. Fine in Fine slipcase. *Lenz.* $125/£80

IRVING, JOHN. The Hotel New Hampshire. NY: Dutton, (1981). One of 550 numbered, signed. Fine in full leather binding. Fine slipcase. *Lenz.* $150/£96

IRVING, JOHN. A Prayer for Owen Meany. NY: Morrow, (1989). 1st trade ed. Fine in dj. *Captain's Bookshelf.* $35/£22

IRVING, JOHN. The Water-Method Man. NY: Random House, (1972). 1st ed. Fine in NF dj (fr flap creased). *Antic Hay.* $150/£96

IRVING, JOHN. The World According to Garp. NY: Dutton, (1978). 1st ed. Fine in dj (corners sl rubbed). *Captain's Bookshelf.* $90/£58

IRVING, JOHN. The World According to Garp. NY: Dutton, (1978). 1st ed. Fine in NF dj (rubbed, sm tear). *Between The Covers.* $150/£96

IRVING, PIERRE. The Life and Letters of Washington Irving. London: Bohn, 1862-3. 1st ed. 4 vols in 2. Frontis port, 1007pp. Cl, dec bds. VG. *Mikesh.* $45/£29

IRVING, PIERRE. The Life and Letters of Washington Irving. NY: Putnam, 1862-64. 1st ed. 4 vols. Frontis ports. 1/2 calf, marbled bds (sl worn, soiled). VG. *Waverly*.* $38/£24

IRVING, R. L. G. A History of British Mountaineering. London, (1955). 1st ed. (Bumped), else Good in dj (sl used). *King.* $40/£26

IRVING, R. L. G. The Romance of Mountaineering. NY: Dutton, 1935. 1st ed. Dec cvr (rubbed, frayed). Good- (eps lt foxed). *Scribe's Perch*.* $42/£27

IRVING, WASHINGTON. The Alhambra. NY, 1892. 2 vols. xii,266; 312pp. Teg. Dec white cl. VG+ set. *Truepenny.* $75/£48

IRVING, WASHINGTON. The Alhambra. N.p.: LEC, 1969. #330/1500 signed by Lima de Freitas (illus). Fine in pub's slipcase. *Hermitage.* $85/£54

IRVING, WASHINGTON. Astoria, or Anecdotes of an Enterprise Beyond the Rocky Mountains. Phila: Carey, Lea & Blanchard, 1836. 1st ed, 1st setting. 2 vols. 285; 279,8pp; fldg map (torn, no loss). Purple bds (rebacked, orig spine laid down). Nice set (foxed). Howes I83. *Dumont.* $575/£369

IRVING, WASHINGTON. Astoria, or Anecdotes of an Enterprise Beyond the Rocky Mountains. Phila: Carey, Lea & Blanchard, 1836. 1st ed, 1st state, w/copyright notice on back of 1st tp, garbled footnote on pg 239, vol 2. 2 vols. xii,(1),14-285; viii,(1),10-279,(1)8pp (lower pg corners in vol 1 dampstained). Fldg map vol 2 (3-inch split along crease at lower edge; repaired w/acid-free document repair tape). Orig patterned grn cl (recased, eps renewed), gilt spine. Very Clean. BAL 10148. Howes I81. *Argonaut.* $750/£481

IRVING, WASHINGTON. Astoria, or Anecdotes of an Enterprise Beyond the Rocky Mountains. Phila: Carey, Lea & Blanchard, 1836. 1st ed, Blanck's 1st state, w/c. notice and imprint on tp verso vol 1, garbled footnote p239 vol 2. 2 vols. 285; 279,8pp (contemp ink sigs, lt foxed); fldg map. Patterned cl (rubbed, spines sunned). Good. BAL 10148. Howes I81. *Reese.* $900/£577

IRVING, WASHINGTON. A History of the Life and Voyages of Christopher Columbus. London: John Murray, 1828. 1st ed. 4 vols. 2 fldg maps. Later 1/2 leather, marbled bds. Good set (new eps). *King.* $300/£192

IRVING, WASHINGTON. The Journals of.... William Trent and George Hellman (eds). Boston: Bibliophile Soc, 1919. 1st ed. One of 430 ptd. Teg. Cl, bds (lt smudged). VG. BAL 10206. *Reese.* $100/£64

IRVING, WASHINGTON. Knickerbocker Papers, being Rip Van Winkle and the Legend of Sleepy Hollow. Philip Lee Warner, 1914. #624/1000 ptd. viii,53pp + colophon, ad leaves. Uncut; silk marker. Fine in linen-backed bds; ptd dj. *Cox.* $31/£20

IRVING, WASHINGTON. Knickerbocker's History of New York.... NY/London: Putnam, 1894. Van Twiller ed. 2 vols. Teg. Gilt pict cl, beveled bds. (Extrems sl rubbed), o/w Bright. *Sadlon.* $50/£32

IRVING, WASHINGTON. The Legend of Sleepy Hollow. London, (1928). One of 250 (of 375) numbered, signed by Arthur Rackham (illus). 4to. 8 mtd color plts. Color pict eps. Orig vellum, gilt. Bd slipcase. *Swann*.* $920/£590

IRVING, WASHINGTON. Life of George Washington. NY: Putnam, 1863. 'National ed.' 5 vols. 18 engr plts. 3/4 leather, marbled bds, eps, gilt. (Scuffed, shelfworn, 1 spine top torn.) *Bohling.* $30/£19

IRVING, WASHINGTON. Life of George Washington. Geo. Bell, 1878. 4 vols. Contemp 1/2 blue morocco; marbled paper sides, ends, edges. *Cox.* $70/£45

IRVING, WASHINGTON. Old Christmas. London: Macmillan, 1876. 2nd ed. Randolph Caldecott (illus). Aeg. Forest grn cl, gilt. *Glenn.* $125/£80

IRVING, WASHINGTON. Rip Van Winkle and The Legend of Sleepy Hollow. MA: Pennyroyal Editions, 1984. 1st ed. Barry Moser (illus). Pub's tan cl, orig matching slipcase. *D & D.* $110/£71

IRVING, WASHINGTON. Rip Van Winkle. London/NY: Heinemann/Doubleday, Page, 1910. 4to. 51 tipped-in color plts. Gilt-dec cl (extrems lt worn). (Exlib, bkpl, inkstamped # p.v), o/w Contents VG. *New Hampshire*.* $100/£64

IRVING, WASHINGTON. The Wild Hutsman. Boston: Bibliophile Soc, 1924. 1st ptg. Ltd to 455. Grn cl, vellum spine (lt wear). BAL 10210. *Cullen.* $85/£54

IRVING, WASHINGTON. Wolfert's Roost and Other Papers, Now First Collected. NY: Charles L. Webster, 1855. Grn cl, gilt. VG. *Metropolitan*.* $86/£55

IRVING, WASHINGTON. Wolfert's Roost and Other Papers, Now First Collected. NY: Putnam, 1855. 1st ed, 2nd issue, w/'12 Park Place.' Frontis. (Brn spot prelims.) Pict cl (spine lightened), gilt/blind-stamped. BAL 10188. *Sadlon.* $45/£29

IRVING, WASHINGTON. The Works. NY, 1881. 12 vols. Sm 8vo. Frontispieces. Contemp tan calf, gilt, spines in 6 compartments, crimson morocco lettering pieces in 2. *Swann*.* $690/£442

IRWIN, ALAN MAURICE. And Ships—And Sealing Wax. Toronto: Macmillan, 1934. 1st ed. Signed. (Cl sl rubbed, soiled), o/w VG. *Worldwide.* $25/£16

IRWIN, J. A. Hydrotherapy on Saratoga: A Treatise on Natural Mineral Waters. NY, 1892. 1st ed. 270pp. (Lib stamp tp), o/w VG. *Fye.* $60/£38

IRWIN, MABEL MacCOY. Whitman: The Poet-Liberator of Woman. NY: The Author, 1905. Ltd to 500. Frontis port (starting). Illus gray cl (bumped), gilt. VG. *Blue Mountain.* $50/£32

IRWIN, MABEL MacCOY. Whitman: The Poet-Liberator of Woman. NY: The Author, 1905. 1st ed. One of 500. Frontis port (loose). Uncut. Gray cl, gilt. VG. *Second Life.* $125/£80

IRWIN, MARGARET. Bloodstock and Other Tales. London, 1953. 1st ed this collection. Fine in NF dj (lt edgeworn). *Mcclintock.* $35/£22

IRWIN, MARJORY FELICE. The Negro in Charlottesville and Albemarle County.... Charlottesville, VA, 1929. 1st ed. NF in stiff ptd wrappers. *Mcgowan.* $75/£48

IRWIN, RICHARD B. History of the Nineteenth Army Corps. NY, 1892. 1st ed. 528pp. Gilt edge. Pict cl. (Cvr sl wear, fading), o/w VG+. *Pratt.* $150/£96

IRWIN, RICHARD B. History of the Nineteenth Army Corps. NY: Putnam, 1892. 1st ed. 528pp. Teg. Dec cvr. Good (eps foxed). *Scribe's Perch**. $65/£42

ISAACS, EDITH J. R. The Negro in the American Theatre. NY: Theatre Arts, 1947. Gray cl (bumped). VG in pict yellow dj (rubbed, soiled, sm hole at spine, few edge tears). *Blue Mountain*. $45/£29

ISAIAH. The Book of the Prophet Isaiah. (NY): LEC, 1979. One of 2000 numbered, signed by Chaim Gross (illus) & Franklin H. Littell (intro). 1/4 leather & cl. Fine in cardbd slipcase (spine spot). *Between The Covers*. $175/£112

ISE, JOHN. Sod and Stubble. NY: Wilson-Erickson, 1936. 1st ed. Signed by Alma Ise Lindley. 8 plts. VG in Good dj (chipped). *Connolly*. $60/£38

ISE, JOHN. Sod and Stubble: The Story of a Kansas Homestead. NY: Wilson-Erickson, 1936. 1st ed. (Spine ends sl rubbed.) *Sadlon*. $20/£13

ISHAM, ASA BRAINERD et al. Prisoners of War and Military Prisons, Personal Narratives of Experience in the Prisons.... Cincinnati: Lyman & Cushing, 1890. 1st ed. xii,571pp. NF. *Mcgowan*. $350/£224

ISHERWOOD, CHRISTOPHER and SWAMI PRABHAVANANDA. How to Know God. NY, 1953. 1st Amer ed. Fine (extrems sl rubbed) in Fine dj (spine sl sunned, sl edge-rubbed). *Polyanthos*. $20/£13

ISHERWOOD, CHRISTOPHER. The Berlin Stories: The Last of Mr. Norris, Goodbye to Berlin. (NY): New Directions, (1945). 1st Amer ed. NF in dj (lt rubbed). *Captain's Bookshelf*. $100/£64

ISHERWOOD, CHRISTOPHER. Christopher and His Kind 1929-39. London, 1977. 1st ed. VG in dj. *Typographeum*. $28/£18

ISHERWOOD, CHRISTOPHER. The Condor and the Cows. Methuen, 1949. 1st UK ed. (Bkpl), o/w VG + in VG dj (sl wrinkle spine). *Martin*. $34/£22

ISHERWOOD, CHRISTOPHER. The Condor and the Cows. Methuen, 1949. 1st UK ed. VG (ink name) in dj. *Williams*. $70/£45

ISHERWOOD, CHRISTOPHER. The Condor and the Cows: A South American Travel Diary. NY: Random House, (1949). 1st ed. Frontis. Fine in dj (2 sm tears). *Captain's Bookshelf*. $60/£38

ISHERWOOD, CHRISTOPHER. Down There on a Visit. London: Methuen, (1962). 1st Eng ed. Paper-cvrd bds. Fine in dj (sl wear). *Antic Hay*. $45/£29

ISHERWOOD, CHRISTOPHER. Down There on a Visit. Methuen, 1962. 1st UK ed. Fine (sm ink mk fep) in VG + dj (edges sl browned). *Williams*. $34/£22

ISHERWOOD, CHRISTOPHER. Exhumations. London: Methuen, (1966). 1st ed. NF in VG dj. *Turtle Island*. $35/£22

ISHERWOOD, CHRISTOPHER. Goodbye to Berlin. London: Hogarth, 1939. 1st Eng ed. Very Nice (spine sl tanned). *Clearwater*. $109/£70

ISHERWOOD, CHRISTOPHER. Lions and Shadows: An Education in the Twenties. Norfolk: New Directions, (1947). 1st US ed. VG + in VG + dj. *Fuller & Saunders*. $50/£32

ISHERWOOD, CHRISTOPHER. My Guru and His Disciple. NY, 1980. 1st ed. Fine in dj. *Words Etc*. $16/£10

ISHERWOOD, CHRISTOPHER. My Guru and His Disciple. NY: FSG, 1980. 1st ed. Signed. Fine in NF dj. *Metropolitan**. $86/£55

ISHERWOOD, CHRISTOPHER. People One Ought to Know. London, 1982. 1st ed. VG in dj. *Typographeum*. $20/£13

ISHERWOOD, CHRISTOPHER. Prater Violet. 1946. 1st ed. VG in dj (small chip upper panel). *Words Etc*. $39/£25

ISHERWOOD, CHRISTOPHER. Prater Violet. London, 1946. 1st ed. Dj. *Typographeum*. $50/£32

ISHERWOOD, CHRISTOPHER. Ramakrishna and His Disciple. NY, 1965. 1st ed. VG in dj. *Typographeum*. $20/£13

ISHERWOOD, CHRISTOPHER. Sally Bowles. Hogarth, 1937. 1st ed. Blue cl (sl rubbed). Contents Good. *Whiteson*. $47/£30

ISHERWOOD, CHRISTOPHER. Sally Bowles. London, 1937. 1st ed. (Spine sl dknd), o/w VG. *Words Etc*. $101/£65

ISHERWOOD, CHRISTOPHER. A Single Man. NY, 1964. 1st ed. VG in VG dj. *Smith*. $15/£10

ISHIGURO, KAZUO. A Pale View of Hills. NY: Putnam, (1982). 1st Amer ed, 1st bk. Fine in NF dj (sl crease fr flap; tear fr panel). *Between The Covers*. $185/£119

ISHIGURO, KAZUO. A Pale View of Hills. NY: Putnam, 1982. 1st US ed, 1st bk. (Name, date, sm sticker stain), else Fine in Fine dj (sm tear). *Beasley*. $125/£80

ISHIGURO, KAZUO. The Remains of the Day. London: Faber, 1989. 1st Eng ed. Fine in dj. *Hadley*. $70/£45

ISHIGURO, KAZUO. The Remains of the Day. NY: Knopf, 1989. 1st US ed. Fine in dj. *Turtle Island*. $85/£54

ISHIGURO, KAZUO. The Unconsoled. London: Faber & Faber, 1995. 1st ed. Signed. Fine in dj. *Lame Duck*. $85/£54

ISHIMOTO, SHIDZUE. East Way, West Way. NY: Farrar & Rinehart, 1936. 15 plts. (Cl sl rubbed, smudged), o/w VG. *Worldwide*. $25/£16

Italian Drawings Selected from Mid-Western Collections. St. Louis: St. Louis Art Museum, 1972. Good in wrappers. *Washton*. $25/£16

Italian Prisoners in Spain. NY: Universal Distributors, 1937. 1st ed. NF (foxing; lib label) in wraps. *Beasley*. $40/£26

IVENS, WALTER G. The Island Builders of the Pacific. London, 1930. 1st ed. 2 fldg maps. (Ex-lib, marginal ink stamps.) Morocco-backed marbled bds (warped, rebound). *Edwards*. $55/£35

IVES, BURL. Burl Ives' Tales of America. Cleveland, (1954). 1st ed. Signed, inscribed. Cl-backed bds. Dj (sl worn). *Argosy*. $45/£29

IVES, BURL. The Wayfaring Stranger's Notebook. Indianapolis, 1962. 1st Amer ed. Fine (spine top sl rubbed) in dj (sm edge tear, spine sl sunned, rubbed, nicks). *Polyanthos*. $25/£16

IVES, COLTA FELLER. Picturesque Ideas on the Flight into Egypt Etched by Giovanni Domenico Tiepolo. NY: Braziller, 1972. 27 plts. Patterned bds. VF in pict dj (sl mkd). *Europa*. $31/£20

IVES, H. E. et al. Transmission of Pictures Over Telephone Lines: A Technical Description.... (NY): Bell Telephone Laboratories, 1925. 1st ed. 'Compliments of the Author' stamped on fr wrapper. Separate envelope containing silver chloride photo. Fine. *Cahan*. $1,000/£641

IVES, JOSEPH C. Report Upon the Colorado River of the West. Washington: GPO, 1861. Senate issue. 26 plts (8 color), 2 fldg maps, 8 fldg views. (Lt foxing, dampstaining), o/w Contents VG (cl worn, spine chipped). Howes I94. *New Hampshire**. $250/£160

IVES, MORGAN. (Pseud of Marion Zimmer Bradley.) Spare Her Heaven. NY: Monarch, (1963). 1st ed. (Paper sl dknd), else Fine in wrappers as issued. *Between The Covers*. $125/£80

IVES, SARAH NOBLE. Altadena. Pasadena: Star-News Pub, (1938). Fine. *Book Market*. $100/£64

IVINS, WILLIAM M., JR. Art and Geometry. A Study in Space Intuitions. Cambridge, 1946. Good in dj (worn). *Washton*. $25/£16

J

Jack and Jill and Old Dame Gill. Banbury: J.G. Rusher, (ca 1830). 2 cvr illus after George Cruikshank. 32mo. 16pp; 13 wood engrs. 4to sheet folded to form 16-pg pamphlet in self-wrappers. Fine. *Bromer*. $75/£48

Jack and the Bean Stalk. NY: McLoughlin Bros, (1888). 10x7.5. (14)pp, 6 full-pg color illus. Color linen (very worn). *King*. $35/£22

Jack and the Beanstalk. NY: McLoughlin Bros, 1897. Kriss Kringle Series. 9x6.5. (12)pp, 4 color plts. Color pict wraps (sl wear). *King*. $30/£19

Jack the Giant Killer. NY: Blue Ribbon Books, (1933). 4to. 22 ll, incl eps; 2 full-pg illus, 1 dbl-pg color pop-up (giant's arm creased, early repair) by Harold B. Lentz. Color pict bds (bumped, soiled, rubbed, spine ends chipped). VG. *Blue Mountain*. $150/£96

Jack Welpott: The Artist as Teacher, the Teacher as Artist. SF: SF Museum of Art, 1975. 14 full-pg b/w photo plts. VG (owner blindstamp) in pict stiff wrappers. *Cahan*. $25/£16

JACK, ELLEN E. The Fate of a Fairy. Chicago: M.A. Donohue, (1910). Ephemera laid in. Good. *Hayman*. $35/£22

JACK, ROBERT L. History of the National Association for the Advancement of Colored People. Boston: Meador, (1943). 1st ed. (Paint spot bottom pg edges), else NF in VG dj (spine base lacks 3/4-inch, folds splitting). *Between The Covers*. $125/£80

JACKS, L. V. La Salle. NY: Scribner, 1931. Map. Good (browned) in dj (chipped, torn). *Dumont*. $35/£22

JACKSON, BLAIR. Grateful Dead. The Music Never Stopped. NY: Delilah, 1983. 1st ed. Fldg family tree. NF in wraps. *Sclanders*. $14/£9

JACKSON, BRUCE. Wake Up Dead Man. Cambridge: Harvard Univ, 1972. 1st ed. (Owner name stamp), else VG in pict stiff wrappers (ink name). *Cahan*. $20/£13

JACKSON, CHARLES J. English Goldsmiths and Their Marks. London: Macmillan, 1921. 2nd ed. (Sl rubbed, spine dull.) *Stewart*. $55/£35

JACKSON, CHARLES J. English Goldsmiths and Their Marks. London: Macmillan, 1921. 2nd ed. Frontis. Orig buckram. Sound (prelims frayed, inner hinges cracked; rubbed, mkd). *Cox*. $62/£40

JACKSON, CHARLES J. English Goldsmiths and Their Marks. London: Batsford, 1949. Fine in dj. *Hollett*. $86/£55

JACKSON, CHARLES T. The Buffalo Wallow. Indianapolis: Bobbs-Merrill, (1953). 1st ed. Dj (sl edge-worn). *Sadlon*. $15/£10

JACKSON, CHARLES T. Report to the House of Representatives...Vindicating the Rights of Charles T. Jackson to the Discovery of...Ether Vapor.... Washington, 1852. 1st ed. 57pp. 1/2 calf, marbled bds (rebound; orig wrappers bound in). Good. *Goodrich*. $250/£160

JACKSON, CHARLES. A Second-Hand Life. NY, 1967. 1st ed. Fine in Fine dj. *Smith*. $15/£10

JACKSON, CHEVALIER. Bronchoscopy and Esophagoscopy. Phila, 1922. New cl. (Ex-lib.) *Goodrich*. $45/£29

JACKSON, CLARENCE S. Picture Maker of the Old West, William H. Jackson. NY, 1947. Folio. Good. *Heinoldt*. $60/£38

JACKSON, CLARENCE S. Picture Maker of the Old West: William H. Jackson. NY: Scribner, 1947. 1st ed. VG in dj (sl worn). *Lien*. $60/£38

JACKSON, DONALD (ed). Letters of the Lewis and Clark Expedition, with Related Documents, 1783-1854. Urbana: Univ of IL, (1978). 2nd and best ed. 2 vols. VF in pub's slipcase. *Argonaut*. $175/£112

JACKSON, DONALD (ed). Letters of the Lewis and Clark Expedition, with Related Documents, 1783-1854. Urbana: Univ of IL, 1962. 1st ed. Map. VF in dj. *Argonaut*. $150/£96

JACKSON, DONALD (ed). Ma-Ka-Tai-She-Kia-Kiak, Black Hawk. Urbana, 1955. Pict cl. (Cvrs sl discolored), else Good. *King*. $30/£19

JACKSON, DONALD (ed). Ma-Ka-Tai-She-Kia-Kiak, Black Hawk. Urbana: Univ of IL, 1955. VG in dj (sl worn). *Lien*. $25/£16

JACKSON, DONALD. Gold Dust. NY: Knopf, 1980. 1st ed. Fine in Fine dj. *Book Market*. $35/£22

JACKSON, DONALD. Voyages of the Steamboat Yellow Stone. NY: Ticknor & Fields, 1985. 1st ed. VF. *Gibbs*. $20/£13

JACKSON, E. N. A History of Hand-Made Lace. London/NY, 1900. 1st ed. Dec cvr. Good (foxing). *Scribe's Perch**. $270/£173

JACKSON, EDGAR (ed). Three Rebels Write Home. (Franklin, VA: News Pub Co), 1955. 1st ed. Ltd to 150. VG in orig ptd wrappers w/cl backstrip. *Mcgowan*. $300/£192

JACKSON, ESTHER. Art of the Anglo-Saxon Age. A.D. 597-1066. Peterborough, 1964. Good in dj. *Washton*. $40/£26

JACKSON, FREDERICK G. The Great Frozen Land...Across the Tundras and a Sojourn Among the Samoyads. London: Macmillan, 1895. xviii,297pp (sl foxing). 3 fldg maps. Dec cl. VG. *High Latitude*. $125/£80

JACKSON, FREDERICK G. A Thousand Days in the Arctic. NY/London: Harper, 1899. 1st ed. Frontis, xxiii,940pp; 15 plts (1 fldg), 5 orig fldg maps. VG+ (wear). *Parmer*. $250/£160

JACKSON, FREDERICK G. A Thousand Days in the Arctic.... London: Harper, 1899. 2 vols. xii,551; xv,580pp. Teg. Dec cl (vol 2 spine head sl repaired; vol 1 cl sl bubbled). VG. *High Latitude*. $300/£192

JACKSON, GEORGE. Soledad Brother: The Prison Letters of George Jackson. NY: Coward-McCann, (1970). 1st ed. (Bkpl, bottom pg edges sl spotting), else Fine in NF dj (sl rubbed, lt staining inside, sm tears). *Between The Covers*. $45/£29

JACKSON, HELEN HUNT. Glimpses of California and the Missions. Boston: Little Brown, 1902. 1st ed. Brn pict cl, gilt. Fine. *Pacific**. $40/£26

JACKSON, HELEN HUNT. Glimpses of California and the Missions. Boston: Little, Brown, 1914. 25 plts. Pict cl. VG. *Adelson*. $35/£22

JACKSON, HELEN HUNT. Ramona. L.A.: LEC, 1959. One of 1500 numbered, signed by Everett Gee Jackson (illus). Multicolored buckram, ptd paper spine label. VF in slipcase. *Argonaut*. $175/£112

JACKSON, HERBERT J. European Hand Firearms of the Sixteenth, Seventeenth and Eighteenth Centuries. London: Philip Lee Warner, Chiswick Press, 1923. 1st ed. One of 550. 63 photo plts. Blue cl (sl rubbed, spine faded). Internally Fine. *Cummins*. $200/£128

JACKSON, HOLBROOK. The Anatomy of Bibliomania. London: Soncino, 1930. 1st ed. #280/1000. 2 vols. Polished buckram. (Spines sunned, no djs), o/w VG. *Reese*. $100/£64

JACKSON, HOLBROOK. The Anatomy of Bibliomania. NY, 1931. 1st Amer ed. 2 vols. Red buckram. VG set in djs (spine top vol I chipped away). *Truepenny*. $275/£176

JACKSON, HOLBROOK. The Anatomy of Bibliomania. NY: Scribner, 1932. 3rd ed, 1st 1-vol ed. (Hinge cracks), o/w Good. *Scribe's Perch*.* $50/£32

JACKSON, HOLBROOK. The Fear of Books. London: Soncino, 1932. 1st ed. Ltd to 2000 numbered. Fine in dj. *Oak Knoll.* $125/£80

JACKSON, JAMES. Letters to a Young Physician Just Entering Upon Practice. Boston, 1855. 1st ed. 344pp. Contents VG (fr bd, backstrip nearly detached). *Fye.* $100/£64

JACKSON, JON A. The Diehard. NY: Random House, 1977. 1st ed. Advance rev copy, slip laid in. (Pp sl dknd), o/w Fine in dj. *Mordida.* $150/£96

JACKSON, JOSEPH HENRY. Anybody's Gold: The Story of California's Mining Towns. NY: D. Appleton-Century, 1941. 1st ed. Signed, inscribed. Dec eps. Orange buckram, gilt. Fine in pict dj (lt worn). *Pacific*.* $81/£52

JACKSON, JOSEPH HENRY. Gold Rush Album. NY: Scribner, 1949. 1st ed. Black cl, gilt spine. Fine in slipcase w/dec labels. *Pacific*.* $29/£19

JACKSON, JOSEPH HENRY. Tintypes in Gold, Four Studies in Robbery. NY: Macmillan, 1939. 1st ed. Pict eps. Red cl. VG + in dj (edgeworn). *Bohling.* $25/£16

JACKSON, JOSEPH. American Colonial Architecture: Its Origin and Development. Phila: David McKay, (1924). 1st ed. Gilt pict grn cl. Fine in ptd dj (heavily chipped, defective). *House.* $55/£35

JACKSON, MARY ANNA. Memoirs of Stonewall Jackson by His Widow. Louisville, KY: Prentice, (1895). 2nd ed. xxiv,647pp. VG (extrems sl worn, rear inner hinge strengthened, sm tears 1 plt repaired w/tape). Howes J25. *Mcgowan.* $450/£288

JACKSON, MELVIN H. Privateers in Charleston, 1793-1796. Washington: Smithsonian, 1969. Fine. *Bohling.* $15/£10

JACKSON, MRS. F. NEVILL. A History of Hand-Made Lace. London/NY, 1900. 19 plts. (Feps sl browned, prelims sl spotted, hinges cracked; spine head sl chipped.) *Edwards.* $125/£80

JACKSON, PHIL. Take It All! How the New York Knicks Became World Champions. NY: Macmillan, (1970). 1st ed. Fine in dj. *Between The Covers.* $45/£29

JACKSON, RICHARD. A Year Is a Window. NY: Doubleday, 1963. 1st ed. Erik Blegvad (illus). 5 1/4 x 7 1/2. 28pp. Pict bds. Fine in dj. *Cattermole.* $30/£19

JACKSON, SHEILA. Ballet in England, a Book of Lithographs. London/NY: Transatlantic Arts, 1945. 10 full-pg color lithos, 7 b/w lithos. Fine in gilt-illus cl; color-litho dj (lt soiled, 2 chips). *Bromer.* $375/£240

JACKSON, SHELDON G. A British Ranchero in Old California. Glendale: Clark, 1977. One of 1008. Frontis port, map. VF. *Argonaut.* $75/£48

JACKSON, SHELDON. Twelfth Annual Report on Introduction of Domestic Reindeer into Alaska...1902. Washington: GPO, 1903. Lg fldg map, 36 b/w photos. Marbled eps, edges. 3/4 leather (spine, corners scuffed). Internally VG. *Parmer.* $95/£61

JACKSON, SHIRLEY. Famous Sally. (NY): Harlin Quist, (1966). 1st ed. Charles B. Slackman (illus). VF in dj (sl soiled, spine rubbed). *Bromer.* $95/£61

JACKSON, SHIRLEY. Famous Sally. NY: Harlin Quisp, 1966. Advance rev copy, card laid in. Charles B. Slackman (illus). Fine in dj (spine lt faded). *Lame Duck.* $175/£112

JACKSON, SHIRLEY. The Haunting of Hill House. NY: Viking, 1959. 1st ed. NF in VG dj (rubbed, lt worn). *Lame Duck.* $350/£224

JACKSON, SHIRLEY. The Haunting of Hill House. NY: Viking, 1959. 1st ed. NF (lt dampstain spine base) in VG dj (extrems sl rubbed; lt damp spots rear panel). *Between The Covers.* $500/£321

JACKSON, SHIRLEY. Life Among the Savages. NY, (1953). 1st ed. Dj (spine dknd). *Argosy.* $50/£32

JACKSON, SHIRLEY. Nine Magic Wishes. (N.p.): Crowell-Collier, (1963). Folio. Dec bds (edgeworn). VG. *Between The Covers.* $150/£96

JACKSON, SHIRLEY. Nine Magic Wishes. (N.p.): Crowell-Collier, (1963). 1st ed. Lorraine Fox (illus). VG- (sm tape repairs rep; smudges couple pp; rubbing; wear bd bottoms). *Between The Covers.* $225/£144

JACKSON, SHIRLEY. Raising Demons. NY: FSC, (1957). 1st ed. Fine in NF dj. (lt stains rear panel). *Between The Covers.* $85/£54

JACKSON, SHIRLEY. The Sundial. NY, (1958). 1st ed. Cl backed bds. VG in dj. *King.* $50/£32

JACKSON, SHIRLEY. The Sundial. NY: Farrar, (1958). 1st ed. Fine in NF dj (spine sl tanned). *Reese.* $75/£48

JACKSON, SHIRLEY. The Sundial. NY: FSC, (1958). 1st ed. Fine in Fine dj (sl rubbing). *Between The Covers.* $150/£96

JACKSON, SHIRLEY. The Sundial. NY, 1958. 1st ed. VG + in dj. *Smith.* $30/£19

JACKSON, SHIRLEY. The Witchcraft of Salem Village. NY: Random House, (1956). 1st ed. Fine in VG- dj (long tear rear panel; chips crown). *Between The Covers.* $175/£112

JACKSON, STANLEY. An Indiscreet Guide to Soho. London: Muse Arts Ltd, (1946). 1st ed. Map. Good (fr hinge cracked). *Patterson.* $39/£25

JACKSON, T. G. Gothic Architecture in France, England and Italy. CUP, 1915. 2 vols. 191 plts. 1/2 vellum, leather labels. Sound. *Ars Artis.* $94/£60

JACKSON, W. S. Notes of a Fly Fisher. London: Fishing Gazette, 1927. 1st ed. VF in VG + dj, orig slipcase (chipped). *Bowman.* $40/£26

JACKSON, W. TURRENTINE (ed). Twenty Years on the Pacific Slope. New Haven/London: Yale Univ, 1965. 1st ed. Cl-backed bds. Fine in dj (lt edgeworn). *Sadlon.* $20/£13

JACKSON, WILLIAM HENRY. The Canons of Colorado. Denver: Frank S. Thayer, (1900). 1st ed. 16 accordion-folded leaves. Tipped into gilt-titled, blind-dec cl folder, metal snap. VG (1 fold separated, few images sl creased, tp lt soiled). *Cahan.* $150/£96

JACOB, GILES. City Liberties. London: Ptd by E. & R. Nutt & R. Gosling, 1732. Mod blind panelled sheep (dusty). *Boswell.* $450/£288

JACOB, GILES. A Law Grammar, or Rudiments of the Law...(bound with) a New Law-Dictionary.... London: Ptd by Henry Lintot, 1744, 1756. 7th ed. Mod 3/4 morocco, 1st title laid down. *Boswell.* $850/£545

JACOB, HEINRICH E. Coffee, the Epic of a Commodity. NY: Viking, 1935. 1st ed. VG. *Perier.* $75/£48

JACOB, HEINRICH E. The Saga of Coffee. Eden & Cedar Paul (trans). London, 1935. 1st ed. (Spine, edges lt browned.) *Edwards.* $55/£35

JACOBI, CARL. Disclosures in Scarlet. (Sauk City): Arkham House, 1972. 1st ed. NF in dj. *Other Worlds.* $20/£13

JACOBI, CARL. Disclosures in Scarlet. Sauk City: Arkham House, 1972. 1st ed. VF in illus dj (lt discolored). *Bromer.* $50/£32

JACOBI, CARL. Revelations in Black. Sauk City: Arkham House, 1947. 1st ed. (Brn staining fep), else VG in dj (lt chipping). *Other Worlds.* $50/£32

JACOBI, CARL. Revelations in Black. Sauk City: Arkham House, 1947. 1st Amer ed. Fine in dj (spine sl rubbed). *Polyanthos.* $75/£48

JACOBI, CARL. Revelations in Black. Sauk City: Arkham, 1947. 1st ed. VG (sl shelfworn) in VG dj (short tear, ends worn). *Metropolitan**. $28/£18

JACOBI, PROFESSOR. Portfolio of Dermochromes. J. J. Pringle (trans). 1903. 2 vols. xii,82pp, 78 plts; x,98pp, 79 plts. Morocco (spine, corners sl rubbed, hinges cracked, foxed). *Whitehart*. $62/£40

JACOBS, FLORA G. A History of Dolls' Houses. Cassell, 1954. 1st ed. Grn cl, gilt. (Lacks fep), o/w Good+. *Whittle*. $23/£15

JACOBS, JOHN W. On the Way. (Germany, 1945.) Lg fldg map in rear. Calf-backed pict cl. VG. *Waverly**. $44/£28

JACOBS, LEONEBEL. Portraits of Thirty Authors. NY: Scribner, 1937. Signed, inscribed. 30 tipped-on sketches, ptd guards. Leather labels. Contents VG (spine soiled, lt spotted) in slipcase (worn). *Waverly**. $33/£21

JACOBS, W. W. At Sunwich Port. NY, 1902. 1st ed. Fine in period pict cl. *Mcclintock*. $12/£8

JACOBS, W. W. The Lady of the Barge. London, 1906. VG. *Madle*. $27/£17

JACOBS, W. W. Ship's Company. Hodder & Stoughton, (1911). 1st ed, 1st issue in earlier binding. Orig pict cl (sl mks). Nice. *Ash*. $39/£25

JACOBSON, DAN. The Beginners. London: Weidenfeld & Nicolson, 1966. 1st Eng ed. Fine in dj (spine sl faded). *Hollett*. $23/£15

JACOBY, FELIX. Atthis: The Local Chronicles of Ancient Athens. Oxford: Clarendon, 1949. Good. *Archaeologia*. $85/£54

JACOBY, H. New Architectural Drawings. London: Thames & Hudson, 1969. Sound in dj (sl frayed). *Ars Artis*. $39/£25

JACQ, CHRISTIAN. Egyptian Magic. Warminster: Aris & Phillips, (1985). Frontis. Good in dj. *Archaeologia*. $45/£29

Jacques Callot. Prints and Related Drawings. Washington: Nat'l Gallery of Art, 1975. Good in wraps. *Washton*. $125/£80

JACQUES, D. H. Hints Toward Physical Perfection. NY: Fowler & Wells, 1859. 1st ed. 244pp + 12pp pub's ads at rear (few sigs sprung, ink mks, marginal notes); 21 plts. Red cl (sl shelfworn, rubbed), gilt. *Baltimore**. $35/£22

JACQUES, DAVID. Georgian Gardens. Batsford, 1983. 1st ed. Dj. *Edwards*. $39/£25

JACQUES-GARVEY, AMY (ed). Philosophy and Opinions of Marcus Garvey. NY, 1925. 1st ed. Vol 2 only. (Name stamps; bumped, soiled.) *King*. $100/£64

JAEGER, EDMUND C. The California Deserts: A Visitor's Handbook.... Stanford: Stanford Univ, (1941). 2nd ed, 3rd ptg. Grn-stamped cl in dj (sm tear). *Dawson*. $25/£16

JAEGER, G. Problems of Nature: Researches and Discoveries. H. G. Schlichter (ed). NY: Brentano, 1897. 1st ed. 261pp, fldg map, 2 C. Darwin facs letters. VG. *Mikesh*. $95/£61

JAFFE, IRMA B. John Trumbull: Patriot-Artist of the American Revolution. Boston, 1975. VG in dj. *Argosy*. $100/£64

JAGGARD, WILLIAM. Shakespeare Bibliography. Stratford-on-Avon: Shakespeare Press, 1911. 'Handmade Edition,' one of 500, this out-of-series. Unopened, untrimmed. (Sl soiled, ep note.) *Waverly**. $55/£35

JAGGER, CEDRIC. Royal Clocks; The British Monarchy and Its Timekeepers 1300-1900. London: Robert Hale, (1983). 1st ed. Fine in dj, slipcase. *Weber*. $60/£38

JAHNN, HANS HENNY. The Ship. NY: Scribner, 1961. 1st US ed. NF in VG+ dj (worn). *Lame Duck*. $45/£29

JAHNS, PAT. The Frontier World of Doc Holiday. NY: Hastings House, (1957). 1st ed. VG in Poor dj (torn). *Perier*. $35/£22

JAHSS, BETTY and MELVIN. Inro and Other Miniature Forms of Japanese Lacquer Art. Rutland: Charles E. Tuttle, (1971). 1st ed. VF in dj. *Hermitage*. $175/£112

JAKES, JOHN. Susanna of the Alamo: A True Story. San Diego: HBJ, (1986). 1st ed. Folio. Paul Bacon (illus). Fine in dj (tear spine edge). *Between The Covers*. $85/£54

JAKOBOVITS, IMMANUEL. Jewish Medical Ethics. NY, 1967. 1st ed. VG in Good dj. *Doctor's Library*. $45/£29

James Barry. The Artist as Hero. London: Tate Gallery, 1983. Good in wraps. *Washton*. $30/£19

JAMES, A. EVERETTE. Legal Medicine, with Special Reference to Diagnostic Imaging. Balt, 1980. 1st ed. Glossy ptd bds. NF. *Doctor's Library*. $80/£51

JAMES, BUSHROD W. Alaskana or Alaska in Descriptive and Legendary Poems. Phila: Porter & Coates, 1892. 1st ed. 368pp. Good. *Perier*. $40/£26

JAMES, E. O. From Cave to Cathedral. London: Thames & Hudson, 1965. 152 plt illus. Sound in dj. *Ars Artis*. $39/£25

JAMES, EDWARD. The Next Volume. London, 1939. 2nd ed. #410/412. Signed, inscribed. Rex Whistler (illus). Good+ in Good dj. *Scribe's Perch**. $70/£45

JAMES, EDWIN. A Narrative of the Captivity and Adventures of John Tanner During Thirty Years Residence Among the Indians.... Minneapolis: Ross & Haines, 1956. Ltd to 2000. Good (lower pg edges water stained) in dj (water stained). Howes J42. *Lien*. $40/£26

JAMES, F. CYRIL. The Growth of Chicago Banks. NY, 1938. 1st ed. 2 vols. Color frontis. *Wantagh*. $65/£42

JAMES, F. L. The Wild Tribes of the Soudan. London, 1884. 2nd ed. (Cl sl rubbed, dulled.) *Grayling*. $109/£70

JAMES, F. L. The Wild Tribes of the Soudan. London, 1884. 2nd ed. xxxiv,265pp + (ii) pub's ads + 32pp pub's list; fldg map. (Feps lt browned, upper hinges cracked; bds sl mkd, lt stained, sl bubbled, spine sl rubbed, faded.) *Edwards*. $117/£75

JAMES, G. P. R. The Gipsy. London, 1835. 1st ed. 3 vols. Contemp bds, leather back, tips. VG (cvrs worn). *Black Sun*. $65/£42

JAMES, GEORGE WHARTON. Arizona, the Wonderland. Boston: Page, (1920). 3rd ptg. Pict eps, fldg color map. Teg. Brn cl (extrms sl worn), gilt, pict inset. VG+. *Harrington*. $45/£29

JAMES, GEORGE WHARTON. Arizona, the Wonderland. Boston, 1917. 1st ed. 60 plts (12 color), map. Teg. Fore-edge untrimmed. Grn cl (lt wear), gilt, color photo laid on cvr. Overall VG+. *Five Quail*. $125/£80

JAMES, GEORGE WHARTON. The Grand Canyon of Arizona—How to See It. Boston, 1910. 1st ed. Fldg map, fldg photo. Teg. Grn pict cl (sl wear, sl soil). VG. *Five Quail*. $95/£61

JAMES, GEORGE WHARTON. In and Out of the Old Missions of California. Boston, 1905. 1st ed. (Ex-lib, fr hinge starting), o/w Fine. *Turpen*. $25/£16

JAMES, GEORGE WHARTON. Indian Blankets and Their Makers. Glorietta, NM, 1973. 2nd ptg. Dec cvr. Good. *Scribe's Perch**. $43/£28

JAMES, GEORGE WHARTON. The Indians of the Painted Desert Region: Hopis, Navahoes.... Boston: Little, Brown, 1904. Pict cl (extrms lt worn). *Dawson*. $35/£22

JAMES, GEORGE WHARTON. Old Missions and Mission Indians of California. L.A.: R.R. Baumgardt, 1895. 1st ed. 124pp. 2-toned cl (sl soiled). *Dawson.* $75/£48

JAMES, GEORGE WHARTON. Reclaiming the Arid West. NY: Dodd, Mead, 1917. 1st ed. 48 plts. (Sl rubbed), o/w VG. *Worldwide.* $60/£38

JAMES, GEORGE WHARTON. The Wonders of the Colorado Desert. Boston: Little Brown, 1906. 1st ed. 2 vols. Teg. 3 maps (1 fldg). NF set (lack djs). Howes J44. *Five Quail.* $190/£122

JAMES, H. E. M. The Long White Mountain. London: Longmans, Green, 1888. Chromolitho frontis, xxiii,502pp (lt margin browning); 9 plts, fldg map (torn, no loss). Mod 1/2 morocco (rebound), marbled bds, gilt. *Edwards.* $312/£200

JAMES, HARRY C. The Men Called Master, the Cahuilla Indians. (L.A.): Westernlore, (1960). 1st ed. Ltd to 1250. Fine in dj. *Argonaut.* $45/£29

JAMES, HENRY. The Ambassadors. NY: Harper, 1903. 1st Amer ed, primary binding. Teg, uncut. Orig blue paper-cvrd bds, gilt. Nice (spine sl chafed) in VG orig blue fabric dj. BAL 10656. *Macdonnell.* $500/£321

JAMES, HENRY. The American Scene. Chapman & Hall, 1907. 1st ed. Teg, others uncut. Buckram (backstrips sl faded). Good. *Cox.* $70/£45

JAMES, HENRY. The American Scene. Chapman & Hall, 1907. Secondary binding w/single rule blocking upper cvr. Good (fore-edge spotted, closed tear 1 leaf, sig; spine bumped, chipped, corners rubbed, cvrs sunned). BAL 10663. *Tiger.* $72/£46

JAMES, HENRY. The American. Boston: James R. Osgood, 1877. 1st ed, 1st ptg, 1st binding. This copy has only the mere vestige of a period present after 'Co' on tp. Orig terra cotta cl, gilt. NF. BAL 10532. *Macdonnell.* $850/£545

JAMES, HENRY. The Awkward Age. NY: Harper, 1899. 1st Amer ed. VG (sl rubbed). *Captain's Bookshelf.* $50/£32

JAMES, HENRY. The Awkward Age. NY: Harper, 1899. 1st ed, 2nd issue, ptd on thinner paper, w/seriffed lettering in spine imprint. Dec brn cl. Nice. *Antic Hay.* $100/£64

JAMES, HENRY. The Awkward Age. NY: Harper, 1899. 1st Amer ed. BAL's bulk and binding A. One of 1000 ptd. Gilt brn cl. (Ink name, date ep; spine extrems sl rubbed), o/w Very Nice. BAL 10636. *Reese.* $125/£80

JAMES, HENRY. The Bostonians. London/NY, 1886. 2nd ed, 1st 1-vol ed. Teg. Full red morocco (newly rebound). *Argosy.* $375/£240

JAMES, HENRY. Confidence. Boston: Houghton, Osgood, 1880. 1st Amer ed. One of 1500. Primary binding w/'Houghton Osgood' rather than the later 'Houghton Mifflin' at spine foot. Brn cl, beveled. Fine (spine sl dknd). *Sumner & Stillman.* $375/£240

JAMES, HENRY. Daisy Miller: A Study. NY: Harper, (1879). 1st ed, later issue w/100 titles in prelim ads. Ptd buff wrappers (cvrs detached, sl chipped, spine portion perished; contemp sig dated May 15, 1879). *Swann*.* $230/£147

JAMES, HENRY. Daisy Miller: A Study. Cambridge: LEC, 1969. #330/1500 signed by Gustave Nebel (illus). Red morocco. Fine in pub's slipcase. *Hermitage.* $125/£80

JAMES, HENRY. English Hours. Boston: Houghton, 1905. 1st Amer trade ed. Frontis. (Corners sl bumped), o/w Fine. BAL 10661. *Reese.* $125/£80

JAMES, HENRY. English Hours. Boston: Houghton, Mifflin, 1905. 1st ed. One of 2000 ptd. Teg. Pict cl. (Sl label residue, sl rubbed), else Very Nice. BAL 10662. *Antic Hay.* $125/£80

JAMES, HENRY. English Hours. Cambridge: Riverside, 1905. 1st Amer ed. One of 400 numbered. Tipped in plts. Uncut. Orig 1/4 linen, label. NF. BAL 10662. *Macdonnell.* $350/£224

JAMES, HENRY. The Europeans. Boston: Houghton, Osgood, 1879. 1st ed, 1st ptg, 1st binding. Single-wove binder's fly at fr/rear. Orig terra cotta cl, gilt. (Spine lt frayed), else Bright. BAL 10537. *Macdonnell.* $225/£144

JAMES, HENRY. The Finer Grain. NY: Scribner, 1910. 1st ed. Teg. Gilt cl. (Spine sunned), o/w VG. BAL 10671. *Reese.* $175/£112

JAMES, HENRY. The Finer Grain. London: Methuen, n.d. (1910). 1st London ed. One of 1500. 32pp pub's cat dated September, 1910. Lt brn cl (rubbing), gilt. BAL 10681. *D & D.* $110/£71

JAMES, HENRY. French Poets and Novelists. London: Macmillan, 1878. 1st ed (1250 ptd). Good (ink date, lt foxing early and late; spine sl frayed, nicks lower joint; few bubbles, smudges to cl). *Reese.* $150/£96

JAMES, HENRY. Guy Domville. London: Rupert Hart-Davis, 1961. 1st ed. NF in dj. *Turtle Island.* $35/£22

JAMES, HENRY. Hawthorne. NY: Harper, 1880. 1st Amer ed, 1st ptg, 1st binding. Black cl stamped in red. NF. BAL 10547. *Macdonnell.* $150/£96

JAMES, HENRY. Hawthorne. John Morley (ed). London: Macmillan, 1879. 1st London ed. Black-stamped red cl, binding variant C (no priority), state A of pub's cat. Fine. BAL 10544. *D & D.* $195/£125

JAMES, HENRY. In the Cage. Chicago/NY: Herbert S. Stone, 1898. 1st Amer ed. Gray-grn cl, gilt. Fine (owner notes). *Sumner & Stillman.* $180/£115

JAMES, HENRY. The Ivory Tower. NY: Scribner, 1917. 1st Amer ed. Teg. Gilt cl. (Spine sunned, lt foxed), o/w VG. *Reese.* $75/£48

JAMES, HENRY. A Landscape Painter. NY: Scott & Seltzer, 1919. 1st ed, ltd issue. One of 250 specially bound, issued untrimmed and unopened. Blue cl, paper label (sl wear, few smudges). VG. *Reese.* $100/£64

JAMES, HENRY. The Lesson of the Master.... NY: Macmillan, 1892. 1st ed. (Eps foxed, 1892 ink name.) Dec cl (spine sl rubbed, dull). Good. *Reese.* $65/£42

JAMES, HENRY. A Little Tour in France. Boston: Houghton, Mifflin, 1900. 1st illus ed. Joseph Pennell (illus). Dk grn pict cl (tears spine head; rubbed, lt wear). Presentable. *Hermitage.* $90/£58

JAMES, HENRY. A Little Tour in France...with Illustrations by Joseph Pennell. Boston: Houghton, 1900. 1st illus ed, ordinary issue. Teg. Gilt-dec pict cl. (Pencil sig dated in year of pub), o/w NF. *Reese.* $85/£54

JAMES, HENRY. A London Life. NY, (1957). Specially bound, ltd to 100 numbered. Cl-backed bds. (Extrems sl discolored), else VG. *King.* $100/£64

JAMES, HENRY. Notes on Novelists. NY, 1914. 1st Amer ed. (Corners bumped, lt wear.) BAL 10681. *Freeman*.* $15/£10

JAMES, HENRY. The Outcry. London: Methuen, n.d. (1911). 1st ed. Pub's cat dated August, 1911. Grn cl (lt rubbing), gilt. BAL 10673. *D & D.* $110/£71

JAMES, HENRY. The Princess Casamassima. London/NY: Macmillan, 1886. 1st 1-vol ed, 1st Amer ed, 1st issue, primary binding. Orig blue-grn cl, gilt. Fine (stray cvr mks). BAL 10578. *Macdonnell.* $250/£160

JAMES, HENRY. The Private Life. NY: Harper, 1893. 1st Amer ed, primary binding state (blue-grn cl w/elaborate silver grillework fr cvr, spine). 4pp undated ads. Fine (fep sl cracked). *Sumner & Stillman.* $155/£99

JAMES, HENRY. The Private Life; Lord Beaupre; The Visits. NY: Harper, 1893. 1st US ed. 232pp + 4pp ads. Grn cl, silver dec. Good. *Scribe's Perch*.* $45/£29

JAMES, HENRY. Roderick Hudson. Boston: James R. Osgood, 1876. 1st ed, 1st ptg. One of 1572 ptd. 3rd binding w/'Houghton, Osgood' at spine foot. Orig terra cotta cl, gilt. (Spine sl rubbed), else Fine in cl box. BAL 10531. *Macdonnell.* $600/£385

JAMES, HENRY. The Sense of the Past. NY: Scribner, 1917. 1st Amer ed, secondary binding. Top edge not gilt. Brn cl. (Spine sl sunned, dust mkd), o/w VG. BAL 10698. *Reese.* $65/£42

JAMES, HENRY. A Small Boy and Others. NY, 1913. 1st ed. (Spine sl faded), o/w VG. *Words Etc.* $62/£40

JAMES, HENRY. The Soft Side. London, 1900. 1st Eng ed. *Clearwater.* $125/£80

JAMES, HENRY. The Spoils of Poynton. William Heinemann, 1897. 2nd binding, w/ tulip design fr cvr. Ad leaf. Good (spine bumped; hinges, corners rubbed). BAL 10622. *Tiger.* $172/£110

JAMES, HENRY. Tales of Three Cities. Boston: Osgood, 1884. 1st ed. NF. BAL 10569. *Captain's Bookshelf.* $125/£80

JAMES, HENRY. Theatricals: Second Series. Osgood, 1895. 1st and only ed. (2 inches fr/rear cvrs dampstained.) *Whiteson.* $55/£35

JAMES, HENRY. Transatlantic Sketches. Boston: James R. Osgood, 1875. 1st ed, 1st binding. Orig grn cl, gilt. (Spine ends lt rubbed), else Fine. BAL 10530. *Macdonnell.* $600/£385

JAMES, HENRY. Views and Reviews. Boston: Ball, 1908. 1st trade ed. Teg, uncut. Grn cl. Fine. BAL 10666. *Macdonnell.* $125/£80

JAMES, HENRY. Washington Square. NY: Harper, 1881. 1st ed. 6-pg pub's cat at rear. Lt brn coated eps. Pict grn cl (frayed, sl spotted, fr hinge cracked). Text Good (lt aged, lt foxed). BAL 10552. *Baltimore*.* $60/£38

JAMES, HENRY. Washington Square. NY: LEC, 1971. One of 1500 numbered, signed by Lawrence Beall Smith (illus). 10 plts. 1/4 morocco. Mint in bd slipcase. *Argosy.* $125/£80

JAMES, HENRY. What Maisie Knew. Chicago: Stone, 1897. 1st Amer ed. Gilt cl. Good (inner hinges cracked, mended). *Reese.* $45/£29

JAMES, HUBERT M. et al (eds). Theory of Servomechanisms. NY: McGraw-Hill, 1947. 1st ed, 2nd imp. VG. *Glaser.* $75/£48

JAMES, JAMES A. Collections of the Illinois State Historical Library, Virginia Series Vols. 3 and 4. Springfield: IL State Hist Library, 1912-1926. 2 vols. (Cl faded, shelfworn, spines dknd), else Good. *Brown.* $50/£32

JAMES, JAMES A. The First Scientific Exploration of Russian America and the Purchase of Alaska. Evanston: Northwestern Univ, 1942. (Shelf wear), else VG. *Perier.* $45/£29

JAMES, JASON W. Memories and Viewpoints. Roswell, NM: Privately ptd, 1928. Inscribed. VG. *Dumont.* $395/£253

JAMES, M. R. The Wanderings and Homes of Manuscripts. London: SPCK, 1919. Inscribed. Pict cl. *Maggs.* $28/£18

JAMES, MARQUIS. The Cherokee Strip. NY: Viking, 1945. 1st ed. Good in dj (worn). *Lien.* $20/£13

JAMES, MARQUIS. The Raven, a Biography of Sam Houston. London: Hutchinson, (1929). 1st Eng ed. VG (sm spots back cvr). *Shasky.* $60/£38

JAMES, MARQUIS. The Raven, a Biography of Sam Houston. Indianapolis, 1929. Frontis. Good +. *Turpen.* $18/£12

JAMES, MARTIN S. War Reminiscences. Providence, RI, 1911. 1st ed. Ltd to 250. PNRISSHS Series 7, #4. NF in ptd wrappers. *Mcgowan.* $45/£29

JAMES, MONTAGUE RHODES. A Descriptive Catalogue of the Manuscripts in the Library of Sidney Sussex College, Cambridge. Cambridge, 1895. (Few notes throughout in ink, red crayon; bkseller label.) Blue cl, gilt. *Maggs.* $125/£80

JAMES, MONTAGUE RHODES. Eton and Kings. London: Williams & Norgate, 1926. 1st ed. Port. Uncut. (Fore-edge spotted, tp lt foxed.) *Cox.* $39/£25

JAMES, MONTAGUE RHODES. Ghost-Stories of an Antiquary. Edward Arnold, 1905. 2nd imp. (Eps, some text lt spotted; bkpl; spine sl browned.) *Edwards.* $39/£25

JAMES, MONTAGUE RHODES. Ghost-Stories of an Antiquary. London: Edward Arnold, 1905. 2nd imp. 4 plts. (Lt foxed), o/w VG in ptd canvas. *Cox.* $39/£25

JAMES, MONTAGUE RHODES. More Ghost Stories of an Antiquary. Edward Arnold, 1912. 2nd imp. (Sl spotted, upper hinge cracked, ex-libris, feps lt browned; spine sl browned, chipped.) *Edwards.* $39/£25

JAMES, NORAH C. Sleeveless Errand. London: Scholartis, 1929. 1st ed, 1st bk. One of 450 (of 500). Fine. *Kane*.* $50/£32

JAMES, P. D. The Black Tower. NY: Scribner, 1975. 1st US ed. NF in NF dj. *Janus.* $65/£42

JAMES, P. D. Cover Her Face. Scribner, 1962. 1st US ed, 1st bk. Fine in Fine dj. *Certo.* $150/£96

JAMES, P. D. Devices and Desires. London: Faber & Faber, 1989. 1st ed. Signed. VF in dj. *Mordida.* $100/£64

JAMES, P. D. The Skull Beneath the Skin. London: Faber & Faber, 1982. 1st ed. Fine in dj. *Mordida.* $100/£64

JAMES, P. D. A Taste for Death. London: Faber & Faber, 1986. 1st ed. Fine in dj. *Mordida.* $75/£48

JAMES, P. D. A Taste for Death. NY: Knopf, 1986. 1st ed. Signed. Promo material laid in. NF (corners bumped) in dj. *Antic Hay.* $45/£29

JAMES, P. D. An Unsuitable Job for a Woman. London: Faber & Faber, 1972. 1st ed. (Sm spots top of pg edges), o/w Fine in dj. *Mordida.* $275/£176

JAMES, P. ROWLAND. The Baths of Bath in the 16th and Early 17th Centuries. London, 1938. 1st ed. Rev slip loosely inserted. VG in dj (sl torn, sl soiled). *Words Etc.* $39/£25

JAMES, PHILIP. Children's Books of Yesterday. C. Geoffrey Holme (ed). London: The Studio, 1933. 1st ed. (Last leaf damaged from coated paper ll sticking, 2 sm spots tp.) Dj. *Oak Knoll.* $75/£48

JAMES, PHILIP. Early Keyboard Instruments from Their Beginnings to the Year 1820. NY: Stokes, (1930). 1st Amer ed. 65 plts. (Cvrs worn, foxed.) *New Hampshire*.* $180/£115

JAMES, PHILIP. Early Keyboard Instruments. London: Peter Davies, 1930. 1st ed. 65 plts. (Ex-lib, bkpl fr pastedown, sm lib stamps prelims, plts, etc.) Cl-backed bds gilt (extrems sl worn). *Hollett.* $133/£85

JAMES, THOMAS. Three Years Among the Indians and Mexicans. St. Louis: MO Hist Soc, 1916. 2nd ed. #161/365. (Lt pencil notes on prelims.) Map. Teg. Blue paper-cvrd bds (sl edgewear). NF in Fine custom slipcase. Howes J49. *Harrington.* $300/£192

JAMES, THOMAS. Three Years Among the Indians and Mexicans. Milo Milton Quaife (ed). NY: Citadel, (1966). Black cl, gilt. Fine in dj (lt chipped). *Argonaut.* $50/£32

JAMES, THOMAS. Three Years Among the Indians and Mexicans. Walter B. Douglas (ed). St. Louis: MO Hist Soc, 1916. One of 365 numbered. Howes J49. *Ginsberg.* $250/£160

JAMES, W. P. Romantic Professions and Other Papers. London/NY: Elkin Mathews & John Lane/Macmillan, 1894. 1st ed. One of 450 ptd (of 663). 16pp ads (sterling) dated Jan 1894. Black cl. NF (sl shelfworn). *Sumner & Stillman.* $95/£61

JAMES, W. S. Cow-boy Life in Texas or 27 Years a Maverick. Chicago: Donohue, Henneberry, (1893). 1st ed, 1st issue. Blue cl dec stamped in black/gilt. (Lt patchiness spine), o/w Fine. Howes J51. *Hermitage.* $175/£112

JAMES, WILL. Lone Cowboy: The Story of My Life. NY: Scribner, 1930. 1st ed. (Notes to frontis verso), else Fine in VG dj (chipped, spine sl sunned). *Pacific*.* $127/£81

JAMES, WILL. Young Cowboy. NY: Scribner, 1936. 9 1/2 x 7 1/4. 72pp. Good. *Cattermole.* $60/£38

JAMES, WILLIAM F. and GEORGE H. McMURRY. History of San Jose. San Jose: San Jose Ptg Co, 1933. (Sl worn.) *Dumont.* $160/£103

JAMES, WILLIAM. Principles of Psychology. NY: Henry Holt, (c.1914). 1st ed, later issue. 2 vols. NF set. *Glaser.* $75/£48

JAMESON, MRS. The Beauties of the Court of King Charles the Second. London: Henry Colburn, 1833. 1st ed. Engr frontis, 20 engr ports. Marbled eps; aeg. Full contemp burgundy straight-grained morocco, gilt. Fine (sl rubbed). *Cummins.* $500/£321

JAMESON, MRS. Characteristics of Women. Phila: Carey, Lea, 1833. 1st US ed. 2 vols. 232; 266pp (name tps). Paper label. VG (cl sl faded). *Second Life.* $100/£64

JAMESON, MRS. Legends of the Madonna. London, 1890. New ed. lxxv,344pp. Teg. Gilt-ruled cl (spine sl chipped). *Edwards.* $31/£20

JAMESON, MRS. Winter Studies and Summer Rambles in Canada. London: Saunders & Otley, 1838. 1st ed. 3 vols. xi,(iii),315; vi,341; vi,356pp, 1/2-titles (occasional spot, some edges browned or brittle, foxing, lt waterstaining some eps). Grn cl (faded, stained, vol 3 loose), paper labels (worn). *Morrell.* $148/£95

JAMESON, R. S. A Dictionary of the English Language by Samuel Johnson and John Walker. William Pickering, 1847. 4th ed. Engr frontis, 1/2-title (grubby, mtd), 14,831pp (spotting). Uncut. Sound in orig cl (spotted, mkd; rebacked), morocco label. *Cox.* $70/£45

JAMESON, THOMAS. Essays on the Changes of the Human Body, at Its Different Ages.... London: Longman et al, 1811. 1st ed. xxviii,360pp. Contemp 1/2 calf. (Sm split rear hinge, corners rubbed), o/w VG. *White.* $133/£85

JAMIESON, ALEXANDER. A Dictionary of Mechanical Science, Arts, Manufactures and Miscellaneous Knowledge. London: Henry Fisher, 1831. Engr frontis, 69 plts. (Lt spotting.) Contemp blindstamped reversed calf. *Christie's*.* $105/£67

JAMIESON, JOHN. Bell the Cat; or, Who Destroyed the Scottish Abbeys? Stirling: Eneas Mackay, 1902. 36 plts. Teg, rest uncut. Ptd cl (title worn off spine, upper bd rubbed). Sound. *Peter Taylor.* $30/£19

JAMIESON, JOHN. Books for the Army, the Army Library Service in the Second World War. NY: Columbia Univ, (1951). 1st ed. Fine in dj. *Oak Knoll.* $75/£48

Jane's Fighting Ships, 1950-51. London: Sampson Low, Marston, 1951. (1st ad leaf sl creased, torn w/o loss; sl faded.) *Hollett.* $187/£120

Jane's Fighting Ships, 1954-55. London: Jane's Fighting Ships, 1955. (Few corners ad ll sl creased.) *Hollett.* $187/£120

JANE, CECIL (trans). A Spanish Voyage to Vancouver and the North-West Coast of America.... London: Argonaut, 1930. One of 525 numbered. Vellum-backed cl. VG. Howes G18. *High Latitude.* $275/£176

JANE, CECIL (trans). A Spanish Voyage to Vancouver and the North-West Coast of America...1792.... London: Argonaut, 1930. One of 525. 25.5x20. 5 plts, 2 fldg maps. (Bkpl; vellum dkng, cvrs sl soiled.) *Parmer.* $500/£321

JANET, PIERRE. The Major Symptoms of Hysteria: Fifteen Lectures.... NY: Macmillan, 1907. 1st ed. Blue cl (soiled, joints rubbed; lib stamp tp, spine #s). Jelliffe's bkpl. VG. *Gach.* $125/£80

JANET, PIERRE. Mental State of Hystericals: A Study of Mental Stigmata and Mental Accidents. NY/London: Putnam/Knickerbocker, 1901. 1st ed in English. Grn cl (recased, spine label removed). Jelliffe's name stamp. VG. *Gach.* $200/£128

JANET, PIERRE. Psychological Healing: A Historical and Clinical Study. NY: Macmillan, 1925. 1st US ed. 2 vols. Straight-grained brn cl (vol 2 spine sl gouged; eps lt foxed). VG. *Gach.* $250/£160

JANIS, EUGENIA PARRY and WENDY MacNEIL (eds). Photography Within the Humanities. Danbury, NH: Addison House, 1977. 1st ed. NF. *Cahan.* $50/£32

JANIS, HARRIET and SIDNEY. Picasso, the Recent Years. GC, 1947. Ltd to 350 numbered, signed by Picasso. 135 plts. 2-tone cl. (Rep soiled), else VG. *King.* $650/£417

JANOWITZ, TAMA. American Dad. NY: Putnam, 1981. 1st ed, 1st bk. VG in VG dj (worn, chip). *Revere.* $25/£16

JANSSENS, PAUL. Paleopathology: Diseases and Injuries of Prehistoric Man. London, 1970. 1st ed. (Ex-lib.) *Fye.* $75/£48

JANSSON, TOVE. The Book about Moomin, Mymble, and Little My. London: Benn, 1953. 2nd ed. 8 1/4 x 11. 24pp. Cl spine. Good. *Cattermole.* $75/£48

JANSSON, TOVE. The Dangerous Journey. London: Benn, 1978. 1st ed. 8 1/4 x 11 1/4. 32pp. Cl spine, pict bds. VG. *Cattermole.* $75/£48

JANSSON, TOVE. Finn Family Moomintroll. London: Benn, 1950. 1st ed. 5 x 7 1/2. 170pp; fldg map. VG in dj. *Cattermole.* $100/£64

JANSSON, TOVE. Moomin. London: Wingate, 1957. 1st ed. 8 3/4 x 11 1/4. 87pp. Pict bds. VG. *Cattermole.* $250/£160

JANSSON, TOVE. Tales from Moomin Valley. London: Benn, 1963. 1st ed. 5 1/2 x 8 1/2. 175pp. Bds. Good in dj (name on fr). *Cattermole.* $45/£29

JANVIER, THOMAS A. The Aztec Treasure House. Harpers, 1890. 1st ed. VG. *Certo.* $30/£19

JANVIER, THOMAS A. The Aztec Treasure-House. NY, 1890. 1st ed. Frederic Remington (illus). (Lt rubbed.) BAL 10841. *Argosy.* $100/£64

JANVIER, THOMAS A. The Aztec Treasure-Hunt. NY: Harper, 1890. 1st ed. NF in gilt-dec cl. *Captain's Bookshelf.* $50/£32

JANVIER, THOMAS A. In Old New York. NY: Harper, 1894. 1st ed. 2pp undated ads. Brn cl dec in black/gilt. Fine ('95 initials tp). *Sumner & Stillman.* $80/£51

JANVIER, THOMAS A. Legends of the City of Mexico. Harpers, 1910. 1st ed. 6 inserted plts. Dec grn cl, gilt. VG. *Certo.* $30/£19

JANVIER, THOMAS A. Legends of the City of Mexico. NY, 1910. 1st ed. NF. *Turpen.* $100/£64

JAQUES, FLORENCE PAGE. The Geese Fly High. Minneapolis: Univ of MN, 1939. 1st ed. Burgundy buckram. Fine in VG pict dj. *Biscotti.* $35/£22

JAQUET, E. and A. CHAPUIS. Technique and History of the Swiss Watch from Its Beginnings to the Present Day. Phila: High-Grade Books, 1953. 1st Amer ed. 190 plts. Magenta/pink cl. VG. *Weber.* $75/£48

JAQUET, E. and A. CHAPUIS. Technique and History of the Swiss Watch. NY: Spring Books, (1970). 2nd ed. 46 plts. Red cl. VG in dj (extrems worn). *Weber*. $50/£32

JARDINE, WILLIAM (ed). British Butterflies. Edinburgh, 1860. 246pp; 36 Nice hand-colored plts. Blue cl, gilt. VG (ex-lib, spine # removed). *Price*. $95/£61

JARDINE, WILLIAM (ed). British Fishes. Edinburgh, 1854. 424pp; 36 hand-colored plts. Blue cl, gilt. VG (ex-lib, spine # removed). *Price*. $65/£42

JARDINE, WILLIAM (ed). British Quadrupeds. Edinburgh, 1854. 309pp; 36 Nice hand-colored plts. Blue cl, gilt. VG (ex-lib, spine # removed). *Price*. $85/£54

JARDINE, WILLIAM (ed). Deer, Antelopes, Camels, Etc. Edinburgh, 1855. 229pp; 35 hand-colored plts. Blue cl, gilt. VG (ex-lib, spine # removed). *Price*. $95/£61

JARDINE, WILLIAM (ed). Entomology. London, 1860. 331pp; 38 hand-colored plts. Blue cl, gilt. VG (ex-libris, spine # removed). *Price*. $65/£42

JARDINE, WILLIAM (ed). Entomology. Volume 28. Edinburgh: Lizars, (1845). Later ed. Port, color engr tp; 36 plts (sl toned), most hand-colored. VG. *Agvent*. $100/£64

JARDINE, WILLIAM (ed). Exotic Moths. Edinburgh, 1858. 229pp; 34 hand-colored plts. Blue cl, gilt. VG (ex-lib, spine # removed). *Price*. $125/£80

JARDINE, WILLIAM (ed). Fishes of British Guiana. Edinburgh, 1860. 263pp; 34 hand-colored plts. Blue cl, gilt. VG (ex-lib, spine # removed). *Price*. $85/£54

JARDINE, WILLIAM (ed). Fishes. Edinburgh, 1853. 219pp; 33 hand-colored plts. Blue cl, gilt. VG (ex-lib, spine # removed). *Price*. $65/£42

JARDINE, WILLIAM (ed). The Flycatchers. Edinburgh, 1853. 256pp; 34 Nice hand-colored plts. Blue cl, gilt. VG (ex-lib, spine # removed). *Price*. $85/£54

JARDINE, WILLIAM (ed). Gallinaceous Birds. Edinburgh, 1860. 255pp; 29 hand-colored plts. Blue cl, gilt. VG (ex-lib, spine # removed). *Price*. $95/£61

JARDINE, WILLIAM (ed). Goats, Sheep, Oxen, Etc. Edinburgh, 1854. 264pp; 33 hand-colored plts. Blue cl, gilt. VG (ex-lib, spine # removed). *Price*. $125/£80

JARDINE, WILLIAM (ed). Ichthyology. Fishes...Volume 35. Edinburgh, (1845). Later ed. Port, 32 hand-colored plts. NF (spine frayed). *Agvent*. $150/£96

JARDINE, WILLIAM (ed). Marsupialia or Pouched Animals. Edinburgh, 1855. 323pp; 37 hand-colored plts. Blue cl, gilt. VG (ex-lib, spine # removed). *Price*. $125/£80

JARDINE, WILLIAM (ed). The Natural History of the Birds of Great Britain and Ireland, Part 1. Birds of Prey. Edinburgh: Lizars, 1828. 1st ed. 315pp, 36 hand-colored plts, engr port. (Fr bd stained), else VG. *Mikesh*. $150/£96

JARDINE, WILLIAM (ed). The Naturalist's Library. Ornithology Vol X, Flycatchers. Edinburgh: Lizars, 1838. Frontis port (loose), 31 hand-colored plts. (Spine sunned.) *Metropolitan**. $115/£74

JARDINE, WILLIAM (ed). The Naturalist's Library. Ornithology. Vol 4. Edinburgh: Lizars, 1841. 31 hand-colored plts. Contents Good (cvrs poor). *Yudkin**. $70/£45

JARDINE, WILLIAM (ed). Ornithology. Humming Birds. Part II. Volume 7. Edinburgh, (1845). Later ed. Port, 24 hand-colored plts (lacks 6; shaken, pp loose, paper label taped to spine). *Agvent*. $250/£160

JARDINE, WILLIAM (ed). Thick-Skinned Quadrupeds. Edinburgh, 1856. 248pp; 30 hand-colored plts. Blue cl, gilt. VG (ex-lib, spine # removed). *Price*. $125/£80

JARDINE, WILLIAM and PRIDEAUX JOHN SELBY. Illustrations of Ornithology. Edinburgh: W.H. Lizars, (1826). Vol 1 (of 3). Engr title, 42 plts (of 50), 28 hand-colored, 25 duplicate uncolored engr plts bound in. Contemp grn 1/2 morocco (rubbed), gilt. *Christie's**. $298/£191

JARMAN, THOMAS. A Treatise on Wills. Boston: Little, Brown, 1855. 3rd Amer ed. 2 vols. Contemp sheep (worn, joints cracking). Usable only. *Boswell*. $85/£54

JARRELL, RANDALL. The Animal Family. (NY): Pantheon Books, (1965). 1st ed. Maurice Sendak (decs). Fine in dj. *Jaffe*. $50/£32

JARRELL, RANDALL. The Animal Family. (NY): Pantheon, (1965). 1st ed. Maurice Sendak (illus). 8vo. 180pp. Blue buckram stamped in silver. (Spine, top edges lt faded), else Fine in dj. *Bromer*. $125/£80

JARRELL, RANDALL. The Animal Family. (NY): Pantheon Books, c. 1965. 1st ed. Maurice Sendak (decs). VG in dj (sl worn). *New Hampshire**. $45/£29

JARRELL, RANDALL. Blood for a Stranger. NY: Harcourt, Brace, (1942). 1st ed, 1st bk. One of 1700 ptd. Red cl. Fine in dj (sl edgeworn). *Jaffe*. $350/£224

JARRELL, RANDALL. Fly by Night. NY: FSG, (1976). 1st ed. 8vo. (viii),30,(i)pp; 6 plts (1 dbl-pg) by Maurice Sendak. Blue cl (sl spotted), silver spine title. NF in pict dj. *Blue Mountain*. $35/£22

JARRELL, RANDALL. Fly by Night. NY: FSG, 1976. 1st ed. Maurice Sendak (illus). 4 3/4 x 8 1/4. 32pp. VG in dj. *Cattermole*. $75/£48

JARRELL, RANDALL. Little Friend, Little Friend. NY: Dial, 1945. 1st ed. One of 2000 ptd. Fine in dj (chipped). *Jaffe*. $125/£80

JARRELL, RANDALL. Losses. NY: Harcourt, Brace, (1948). 1st ed. One of 1000 ptd. Black cl. Fine in dj (sl rubbed, sm closed tear rear panel). *Jaffe*. $200/£128

JARRELL, RANDALL. The Lost World. NY: Macmillan, (1965). 1st ed. Fine in dj. *Jaffe*. $50/£32

JARRELL, RANDALL. Pictures from an Institution. Faber & Faber, (1954). 1st British ed. VG in dj (lt mkd). *Ash*. $70/£45

JARRELL, RANDALL. Pictures from an Institution. NY, 1954. 1st Amer ed. Fine (name) in dj (sl torn, rubbed). *Polyanthos*. $35/£22

JARRELL, RANDALL. Pictures from an Institution. NY: Knopf, 1954. 1st ed. Fine in dj (lt edgeworn, faded). *Else Fine*. $65/£42

JARRELL, RANDALL. Poetry and the Age. NY: Knopf, 1953. 1st ed. One of 2000 ptd. Black cl. Fine in dj (sl rubbed). *Jaffe*. $125/£80

JARRELL, RANDALL. A Sad Heart at the Supermarket. NY: Atheneum, 1962. 1st ed. Fine in dj (price-clipped, sl edgeworn). *Jaffe*. $75/£48

JARRELL, RANDALL. A Sad Heart at the Supermarket. NY: Atheneum, 1962. 1st ed. Fine in NF dj (sl rubbed, sm tear). *Between The Covers*. $100/£64

JARRELL, RANDALL. Selected Poems. NY: Knopf, 1955. 1st ed. One of 2000 ptd. (Spine lt mottled), o/w Fine in dj (lt rubbed, edgeworn). *Jaffe*. $125/£80

JARRELL, RANDALL. The Seven-League Crutches. NY: Harcourt, Brace, (1951). 1st ed. One of 2000 ptd. Black cl. (Sig), o/w Fine in dj. *Jaffe*. $125/£80

JARRELL, RANDALL. Snow-White and the Seven Dwarfs. NY: FSG, 1972. 1st ed. Nancy Ekholm Burkert (illus). 9 1/4 x 12 1/4. 32pp. Fine in dj. *Cattermole*. $75/£48

JARRELL, RANDALL. The Third Book of Criticism. NY: FSG, (1969). 1st ed. Fine in dj (sl edgeworn). *Jaffe*. $50/£32

JARRY, ALFRED. King Turd. NY: Boar's Head, 1953. 1st ed. Fine in dj (lt soiled, rubbed, chip). *Hermitage*. $75/£48

JARRY, ALFRED. The Supermale. Barbara Wright (trans). NY: New Directions, 1977. 1st bk ed in English. (Text sl dknd), else NF in dj (borders dknd). *Lame Duck.* $25/£16

JARVES, JAMES J. Art-Hints. Architecture, Sculpture, and Painting. NY, 1855. xv,398pp (1 gathering loose). Tooled cl (spine top sl damaged). *Washton.* $75/£48

JARVES, JAMES J. History of the Hawaiian or Sandwich Islands.... Boston: Tappan & Dennet, 1843. 1st ed. 8vo. xx,(map),407pp; 5 full-pg plts, fldg map. Brn emb cl (expertly rehinged; wear), gilt. Fine. *Parmer.* $1,500/£962

JARVES, JAMES J. History of the Hawaiian or Sandwich Islands.... Boston: James Munroe, 1844. 2nd ed. Frontis, 407pp (lt dampstain). 3/4 brn morocco, marbled bds (sl rubbed). Good. *Lucas.* $250/£160

JARVIS, WESTON. Jottings from an Active Life. London, 1928. Frontis port. Dj (torn). *Maggs.* $109/£70

JASCHEK, C. and M. The Classification of Stars. Cambridge, 1987. (Label removed fep), o/w Good. *Whitehart.* $39/£25

JASEN, DAVID A. The Theatre of P.G. Wodehouse. London: Batsford, (1979). 1st ed. Fine in dj. *Turtle Island.* $45/£29

JASHEMSKI, W. R. The Gardens of Pompeii. NY, 1979. Sound in dj. *Ars Artis.* $70/£45

JAY, BILL. Customs and Faces: Photographs by Sir Benjamin Stone, 1838-1914. London/NY: Academy Editions/St. Martin's, 1972. 1st ed. 65 full-pg b/w plts. Fine in dj. *Cahan.* $50/£32

JAY, BILL. Robert Demachy, 1859-1936. London: Academy Editions, 1974. 1st ed. 50 b/w photo plts. (Owner stamp), else Fine in dj (sl rubbed). *Cahan.* $60/£38

JAYNE, WALTER. The Healing Gods of Ancient Civilizations. New Haven, 1925. 1st ed. VG. *Fye.* $150/£96

JEAFFRESON, JOHN. A Book About Doctors. NY, 1861. 1st Amer ed. 490pp. (Ex-lib; sections starting), else VG. *Fye.* $75/£48

JEAFFRESON, JOHN. A Book About Lawyers. NY: G.W. Carleton, 1868. (Foxing.) Russett cl, gilt. Sound. *Boswell.* $75/£48

JEAN-AUBRY, G. Joseph Conrad, Life and Letters. NY: Doubleday, Page, 1927. 1st ed. 2 vols. Teg. Blue cl, gilt. Fine set in pict djs. *Macdonnell.* $165/£106

JEAN-AUBRY, G. Joseph Conrad: Life and Letters. NY: Doubleday, Page, 1927. 1st Amer ed. 2 vols. Blue cl. NF (eps browned) in djs (edgewear; sm chip vol 2), cardbd slipcase (worn, cracked). *Antic Hay.* $75/£48

JEANS, J. H. Astronomy and Cosmogony. 1928. 1st ed. 16 plts. (Fr cvr sl discolored, cl sl wrinkled), o/w VG. *Whitehart.* $39/£25

JEANS, J. H. Astronomy and Cosmogony. CUP, 1928. 1st ed. Chart loosely inserted. (Spine chipped, faded, bumped.) *Edwards.* $62/£40

JEBB, BERTHA. A Strange Career. Wm Blackwood, 1894. 1st ed. xxxv,(i),335,(1)pp + 32-pg pub's cat. Pict cl (sl soiled, battered, lib label lower cvr). (Lacks fep), o/w Internally Good. *Cox.* $28/£18

JEBB, CAROLINE. Life and Letters of Sir Richard Claverhouse Jebb. Cambridge: CUP, 1907. Frontis port. (Bkpl.) *Turtle Island.* $40/£26

JEFFERIES, RICHARD. After London, or Wild England. London: Cassell, 1886. 2nd ed, w/ads dated 7/87. Good (binding cocked, fr hinge repaired). *Clearwater.* $39/£25

JEFFERIES, RICHARD. An English Village. Wild Life in a Southern County. Boston: Little, Brown, 1903. New Amer ed. Pict cl (corners bumped). Good (lacks fep; bkpl). *Clearwater.* $31/£20

JEFFERIES, RICHARD. Field and Hedgerow. London: Longmans, Green, 1889. 1st ed. 16pp ads dated Jun 1888. Dk olive cl florally dec in lt grn. (Sl foxed), o/w Fine. *Sumner & Stillman.* $95/£61

JEFFERIES, RICHARD. The Hills and the Vale. London: Duckworth, 1909. 1st Eng ed. Good (cvrs sl bowed, mkd). *Clearwater.* $62/£40

JEFFERIES, RICHARD. Hodge and His Masters. Henry Williamson (ed). London, 1937. 1st Eng ed. Very Nice in dj (sl rubbed). *Clearwater.* $47/£30

JEFFERIES, RICHARD. Jefferies' England; Nature Essays. 1937. 1st ed. (Inscrip), o/w VG in photo-illus dj (spine soiled, sm chip). *Words Etc.* $55/£35

JEFFERIES, RICHARD. Nature Near London. London: C&W, 1883. 1st ed. (Foxing early and late, bound w/o half-title.) Teg. 3/4 polished grn calf, gilt extra. (Spine sl sunned.) VG. *Reese.* $60/£38

JEFFERIES, RICHARD. Red Deer. London: Longmans, 1884. One of 1000 ptd. Pict cl. Good (foxing; spine mkd, worn). *Clearwater.* $156/£100

JEFFERIES, RICHARD. The Story of My Heart. London: Longman, 1883. 1st ed, primary binding. Grn cl stamped in black/gilt. Nice (2 bkpls, label removal upper bd, spine sl dknd, lt rubbed). *Reese.* $75/£48

JEFFERIES, RICHARD. The Toilers of the Field. London, 1892. 1st ed. Frontis port. Grn cl (sl soiled), paper label (sl soiled). *Hatchwell.* $101/£65

JEFFERS, ROBINSON. Be Angry at the Sun and Other Poems. NY: Random House, (1941). 1st ed. 8vo. NF. *Black Sun.* $500/£321

JEFFERS, ROBINSON. Californians. NY: Macmillan, 1916. 1st ed. Teg. Blue cl, gilt. (Bkpl; spine ends sl rubbed), else VG. *Pacific*.* $219/£140

JEFFERS, ROBINSON. Cawdor and Other Poems. NY: Horace Liveright, 1928. One of 375 specially bound, numbered, signed. Fine in VG + box. *Beasley.* $250/£160

JEFFERS, ROBINSON. Cawdor. NY: Liveright, 1928. 1st ed. Fine in Fine dj (sm chip lower fr panel, spine sl tanned). *Between The Covers.* $200/£128

JEFFERS, ROBINSON. Dear Judas and Other Poems. NY: Liveright, 1929. 1st ed. (Newsprint port inserted, offset), else Good in patchy dj (mends on verso). *Reese.* $40/£26

JEFFERS, ROBINSON. Descent to the Dead. NY: Random House, (1931). 1st ed. One of 500 signed. (Inscrip), o/w VF in slipcase. *Jaffe.* $450/£288

JEFFERS, ROBINSON. The Double Axe and Other Poems. NY: Random House, (1948). 1st ed, trade issue. VG in dj. *Reese.* $50/£32

JEFFERS, ROBINSON. The Double Axe and Other Poems. NY: Random House, (1948). 1st ed. One of unknown # signed on tipped-in leaf. Fine in NF dj (chip, part of spine sl sunned). *Turtle Island.* $400/£256

JEFFERS, ROBINSON. Give Your Heart to the Hawks and Other Poems. NY: Random House, 1933. 1st ed. Fine in dj (sm closed tear rear panel). *Jaffe.* $150/£96

JEFFERS, ROBINSON. Hungerfield and Other Poems. NY: Random House, (1954). 1st ed. Cl-backed bds. Fine in dj. *Jaffe.* $75/£48

JEFFERS, ROBINSON. The Selected Letters of Robinson Jeffers 1897-1962. Ann N. Ridgeway (ed). Balt: Johns Hopkins, (1968). 1st ed. Cl-backed bds. Fine in dj (edgeworn, sl dust-soiled). *Jaffe.* $50/£32

JEFFERS, ROBINSON. The Selected Poetry of Robinson Jeffers. NY: Random House, (1938). 1st ed. Port. Paper spine label. NF in VG dj (spine sl tanned, dust-soiled, sm tears). *Reese.* $85/£54

JEFFERS, ROBINSON. Solstice and Other Poems. NY: Random House/Grabhorn, 1935. One of 320 ptd by Grabhorn, signed. Fine in Fine dj. *Beasley.* $375/£240

JEFFERS, ROBINSON. Such Counsels You Gave to Me and Other Poems. NY: Random House, (1937). 1st ed, trade issue. Gilt cl. Fine in VG dj (spine tanned, 2 sm inner reinforcements). *Reese.* $65/£42

JEFFERS, ROBINSON. Thurso's Landing and Other Poems. NY: Liveright, (1932). 1st trade ed. Nice in dj (tanned, mends on verso). *Reese.* $50/£32

JEFFERSON, THOMAS. Jefferson's Notes on the State of Virginia. Balt: W. Pechin, 1800. (3)-194,(ii),53pp (lacks fr blanks, tp; sl browned, foxed); fldg table (partly torn). Contemp full calf (upper cvr detached, lacks spine label). Howes J78. *Baltimore*.* $80/£51

JEFFERSON, THOMAS. A Manual of Parliamentary Practice. Washington: Samuel Harrison Smith, 1801. 8vo. 103 unpaginated ll (incl tp, preface, text, 2 index ll, 3 blank ll). Contemp tree sheep (scuffed, fr cvr detached), leather label. *Freeman*.* $575/£369

JEFFERSON, THOMAS. Memoir, Correspondence, and Miscellanies, from the Papers of Thomas Jefferson. Thomas Jefferson Randolph (ed). Charlottesville: F. Carr, 1829. 1st ed, 1st ptg. 4 vols. Early full calf, black spine labels. (Lt foxed, stained, marginal tears, pencil notes.) Howes R60. *Glenn.* $400/£256

JEFFERSON, THOMAS. Notes on the State of Virginia with an Appendix. NY, 1801. 4th Amer ed. 392pp (lacks fr/rear fly, ep), port (detached, foxed), fldg map (offsetting, sl fold breaks). Calf (fr cvr detached, rear lacking). *King.* $125/£80

JEFFERSON, THOMAS. Notes on the State of Virginia. Boston: David Carlisle, 1801. 8th Amer ed. Fldg map backed w/Japanese tissue, fldg table (closed tears). (Sl browning, foxing.) Recent full gilt-panelled dk brn morocco, leather spine label. Howes J78. *Sadlon.* $750/£481

JEFFERSON, THOMAS. Notes on the State of Virginia. NY, 1801. 'Fourth American Edition.' 392pp (sl dampstaining, sig); port, fldg map (torn, repaired, sl worn, foxed), fldg table. Mid 19th-cent 1/2 morocco, cl. Howes J78. *Freeman*.* $130/£83

JEFFERSON, THOMAS. The Writings of.... Saul K. Padover (ed). Lunenburg, VT: LEC, 1967. One of 1500 numbered, signed by Lynd Ward (illlus). Cl-backed marbled bds. Mint in marbled bd slipcase. *Argosy.* $200/£128

JEFFRESS, L. A. (ed). Cerebral Mechanisms in Behavior. NY, 1951. Dj. *Whitehart.* $39/£25

JEFFRIES, EWEL. A Short Biography of John Leeth with an Account of His Life Among the Indians. Cleveland: Burrows, 1904. One of 167 numbered. Howes J86. *Ginsberg.* $125/£80

JEFFRIES, RODERIC. Police Dog. NY: Harper, 1965. 1st ed. VG in Good dj. *October Farm.* $18/£12

JEKYLL, FRANCIS. Gertrude Jekyll. London: Cape, 1934. 1st ed. VG. *Hollett.* $70/£45

JEKYLL, GERTRUDE and CHRISTOPHER HUSSEY. Garden Ornament. London: Country Life, 1927. 2nd ed. Buckram-backed cl, gilt. VG. *Hollett.* $374/£240

JEKYLL, GERTRUDE and SIDNEY R. JONES. Old English Household Life. London: Batsford, 1944-5. 2nd ed. 149 photo plts. Fine in pict dj. *Quest.* $60/£38

JEKYLL, GERTRUDE and EDWARD MAWLEY. Roses for English Gardens. London: Country Life, 1902. 1st ed. Buckram (extrems lt rubbed), gilt. *Hollett.* $75/£48

JEKYLL, GERTRUDE and LAWRENCE WEAVER. Gardens for Small Country Houses. London: Country Life, 1913. 2nd ed. Color frontis (fore-edge sl worn). Blue cl (extrems sl frayed, bumped; lib label pastedown), gilt. *Hollett.* $187/£120

JEKYLL, GERTRUDE. Colour Schemes for the Flower Garden. London, 1925. 6th ed. Color frontis. (Lt foxed; cl sl used, spine faded.) *Wheldon & Wesley.* $70/£45

JEKYLL, GERTRUDE. A Gardener's Testament. London: Country Life, 1937. 1st ed. VG. *Hollett.* $70/£45

JEKYLL, GERTRUDE. Gertrude Jekyll on Gardening. Penelope Hobhouse (ed). Nat'l Trust/Collins, 1983. NF in dj. *Hadley.* $23/£15

JEKYLL, GERTRUDE. Lilies for English Gardens. Country Life, 1901. (Feps lt browned; sl faded.) *Edwards.* $62/£40

JEKYLL, GERTRUDE. Old West Surrey. London: Longmans Green, 1904. 1st ed. Nice (sl rubbed, sm mks spine, neatly recased, new eps). *Hollett.* $187/£120

JEKYLL, GERTRUDE. Old West Surrey. London: Longmans Green, 1904. 1st ed. Buckram, gilt. Fine. *Quest.* $250/£160

JEKYLL, GERTRUDE. Wall and Water Gardens. London: Country Life, (1901). 1st ed. Buckram, gilt. (Cvrs sl mottled), else Fine. *Quest.* $110/£71

JEKYLL, GERTRUDE. Wall and Water Gardens. London, (1903). 2nd ed. 132 plts. Orig buckram. (Inscrip.) *Wheldon & Wesley.* $62/£40

JEKYLL, GERTRUDE. Wall and Water Gardens. (London): Country Life/George Newnes, (n.d. 1901). 1st ed. Inscribed. (Lt foxing), else NF. *Between The Covers.* $950/£609

JEKYLL, GERTRUDE. Wall and Water Gardens. NY, 1901. Dec spine. (Foxing), o/w Good. *Scribe's Perch*.* $75/£48

JEKYLL, GERTRUDE. Wall and Water Gardens. London, 1928. 7th ed. 190 plts. Fine in dj (worn). *Henly.* $37/£24

JEKYLL, GERTRUDE. Wall, Water and Woodland Gardens. London/NY, 1933. 8th ed. Good- (pp sl wrinkled) in Poor dj. *Scribe's Perch*.* $42/£27

JEKYLL, GERTRUDE. Wood and Garden. London: Longmans, Green, 1901. New ed, 9th imp, 1st bk. Frontis, 71 plts. Marbled eps. Teg. Contemp 1/2 leather (edges rubbed), gilt, raised bands. *Quest.* $95/£61

JEKYLL, GERTRUDE. Wood and Garden. London, 1904. 10th imp. 45 plts. Fine. *Henly.* $56/£36

JELENSKI, CONSTANTIN. Leonor Fini. (London/NY, 1968.) Color pict bds. *Swann*.* $80/£51

JELENSKI, CONSTANTIN. Leonor Fini. (NY: Olympia, 1968.) Fine in pub's cardboard slipcase (lt worn). *Hermitage.* $150/£96

JELLICOE, G. and S. The Landscape of Man. London: Thames & Hudson, 1975. 6 maps. Sound. *Ars Artis.* $39/£25

JELLICOE, G. A. Studies in Landscape Design. Vol II. OUP, 1966. 84 plts. Sound. *Ars Artis.* $33/£21

JELLICOE, VISCOUNT. The Grand Fleet 1914-1916. NY: Doran, 1919. 9 fldg plans; 4 diags in rear pocket. Good (rear hinge crack). *Scribe's Perch*.* $18/£12

JENKINS, C. FRANCIS. Radiomovies, Radiovision, Television. Washington: Jenkins Laboratories, 1929. 1st ed. Frontis port. Gilt-titled cl (lt rubbed, sl frayed, lt foxed). VG. *Cahan.* $325/£208

JENKINS, C. FRANCIS. Vision by Radio, Radio Photograms, Radio Programs. Washington: The Author, (1925). 1st ed. Fine. *Glaser.* $450/£288

JENKINS, CHARLES FRANCIS. Button Gwinnett. GC, NY, 1926. 1st ed. Ltd to 1001. Fine in dj, orig box (worn). *Wantagh.* $50/£32

JENKINS, CHARLES FRANCIS. Jefferson's Germantown Letters. Phila, 1906. #50/500. Paper spine label. (Ex-lib, lt wear.) *Freeman*.* $15/£10

JENKINS, DAN. Semi-Tough. NY: Atheneum, 1972. 1st ed. (Sl fading crown), else Fine in NF dj. *Between The Covers.* $125/£80

JENKINS, L. HADOW. General Frederick Young. 1923. Frontis port. Dk grn cl. (Fep removed, lib plt rep.) *Maggs.* $86/£55

JENKINS, THOMAS J. Six Seasons on Our Prairies and Six Weeks in Our Rockies. Louisville, KY, 1884. 1st ed. 218,(1)pp. Howes J95. *Ginsberg.* $600/£385

JENKINSON, HENRY IRWIN. Practical Guide to the English Lake District. London: Edward Stanford, 1876. 5th ed. xciii,352,44pp; fldg map fr pocket (folds reinforced w/linen), 10 further maps. Grn cl (damped, upper joint cracked, sl shaken), gilt. *Hollett.* $70/£45

JENKINSON, HENRY IRWIN. Practical Guide to the English Lake District. H. D. Rawnsley and Thomas Bakewell (eds). London: Edward Stanford, 1893. 9th ed. xi,(i),407,(v)pp; fldg map, 7 maps, 3 panoramas. Grn cl, gilt. VG. *Hollett.* $101/£65

JENKS, TUDOR. The Century World's Fair Book for Boys and Girls. NY: Century, (1893). 1st ed. 4to. Glazed pict bds. VG in matching dj (chips). *Houle.* $250/£160

JENKS, TUDOR. The Prince and the Dragons. Phila: Henry Altemus, (1905). 1st ed. 16mo. 101pp; 6 full-pg tri-color illus by John R. Neill. Dec eps. Brn dec cl. (Sl finger smudges), o/w VG. *Dower.* $75/£48

JENNER, EDWARD. An Inquiry into the Causes and Effects of the Variolae Vaccinae.... London: The Author, 1801. 3rd ed. 3 parts in 1 vol. 4to. vii,182pp (lt browned, water stained, tear pg 23, bkpl; lib stamps tp, verso plts; ink sigs tp, fep), 4 hand-colored engr plts, guards. Uncut. Lt grn bds (rebacked; worn, stained). *White.* $1,443/£925

JENNESS, DIAMOND. The Indians of Canada. Ottawa: F.A. Acland, 1932. 1st ed. VG. *High Latitude.* $50/£32

JENNESS, DIAMOND. Report of the Canadian Arctic Expedition 1913-18. Vol XVI. Material Culture of the Copper Eskimos. Ottawa: Edmond Cloutier, 1946. Color frontis. VG in ptd wrapper. *High Latitude.* $40/£26

JENNESS, JOHN S. Notes on the First Planting of New Hampshire and on the Piscataqua Patents. Portsmouth, NH: Brewster, 1878. 1st ed. 91pp; 2 maps. Orig stiff wrappers (chipped, spine mended, piece missing). Howes J98. *Ginsberg.* $125/£80

JENNETT, SEAN (trans). Beloved Son Felix. London, 1961. 1st UK ed. 9 plts. Dj (sl chipped). *Edwards.* $23/£15

JENNINGS, AL. Through the Shadows with O. Henry. NY: H. K. Fly, (1921). 1st ed. (Sm spots tp.) *Hayman.* $35/£22

JENNINGS, ARTHUR S. The Modern Painter and Decorator. Caxton, n.d. (c. 1935). 3 vols. Grained cl, gilt. (Edges sl bumped), o/w VG. *Whittle.* $55/£35

JENNINGS, HARGRAVE. The Indian Religions. London: G. Redway, 1890. xii,267pp. (20pp lt underlined; cvr stain), o/w VG. *Middle Earth.* $75/£48

JENNINGS, HARGRAVE. Phallicism: Celestial and Terrestrial, Heathen and Christian. London: G. Redway, 1884. 1st ed. xxvii,298pp. VG + . *Middle Earth.* $145/£93

JENNINGS, HARGRAVE. The Rosicrucians: Their Rites and Mysteries. London: J.C. Hotten, 1870. 1st ed. xv,339pp + 30pp cat; 300 engrs. (10 pp mkd), o/w VG. *Middle Earth.* $145/£93

JENNINGS, N. A. A Texas Ranger. Dallas: Turner, (1930). Rev ed, 3rd ptg. Blue cl, black title. VG (paper dknd; spine ends rubbed). *Bohling.* $22/£14

JENNINGS, N. A. A Texas Ranger. NY: Scribner, 1899. 1st ed. Pict cl (soiled, stained). Howes J100. *Glenn.* $135/£87

JENNINGS, N. A. A Texas Ranger. NY: Scribner, 1899. 1st ed. 321pp (lt pencil notes fep). Pict cl, cvr stamped in 5 colors. VF. Howes J100. *Harrington.* $350/£224

JENNINGS, N. A. A Texas Ranger. Ben Procter (ed). Chicago: Lakeside Classic, 1992. Frontis, color map. Teg. Brn cl, gilt. Fine. *Bohling.* $20/£13

JENNINGS, O. E. Wild Flowers of Western Pennsylvania and the Upper Ohio Basin. Pittsburgh: Univ of Pittsburgh, 1953. 1st ed. 2 vols. Folio. 200 color plts, ptd tissue guards. (Fore-edge sl dusty), else Fine set in illus djs. *Cahan.* $300/£192

JENNINGS, OSCAR. The Morphia Habit and Its Voluntary Renunciation. London/Paris: Bailliere et al/Brentano, 1909. 1st ed. Presentation copy. Ruled lavendar cl (sl staining, rubbing). VG. *Gach.* $100/£64

JENNISON, GEORGE. Noah's Cargo. London: Black, 1928. 32 photo plts. Maroon cl, gilt. (Sm spine spot), else VG. *Price.* $29/£19

JEPSON, WILLIS LINN. A Flora of California. Berkeley: Univ of CA, 1909-1914. NF in wraps, as issued. *Quest.* $45/£29

JERNIGAN, C. B. From the Prairie Schooner to a City Flat. (Brooklyn, 1926.) 1st ed. Pict cl. *Ginsberg.* $75/£48

JERNIGAN, E. W. Jewelry of Prehistoric Southwest. School of Amer Research/Univ of NM, (1978). 1st ed. Color frontis. VF in VG dj. *Oregon.* $60/£38

JEROME, CHAUNCEY. History of the American Clock Business for the Past Sixty Years.... New Haven: F.C. Dayton, 1860. 1st ed. Frontis port, 144pp. Orig black ptd wrappers (expertly rebacked, extrems lt worn, cvr creased). VG. *Weber.* $300/£192

JEROME, JEROME K. On the Stage and Off: The Brief Career of a Would-Be Actor. Leadenhall Press, n.d. (1885). 1st illus ed, 1st bk. Pub's cat. Good (ex-lib, bkpl fr pastedown, sig; spine bumped; nick). *Tiger.* $101/£65

JEROME, JEROME K. Stage-Land: Curious Habits and Customs of Its Inhabitants. C&W, 1890. 18th thousand. Good (lt spotted; spine bumped, chipped, creased; hinges, corners rubbed, cvrs sl grubby). *Tiger.* $19/£12

JEROME, JEROME K. Three Men in a Boat (To Say Nothing of the Dog). Bristol: J. Arrowsmith, 1889. 1st ed. (vi),315pp + 3pp ads, ads on pastedowns. (Ink name 1/2 title.) *Bickersteth.* $62/£40

JEROME, JEROME K. Three Men in a Boat. Arrowsmith, 1889. 1st issue, w/'Quay Street' on tp and 'J.W. Arrowsmith, Bristol' top of fr pastedown. VG. *Williams.* $273/£175

JEROME, JEROME K. Three Men On Wheels. NY: Dodd Mead, 1900. 1st Amer ed. (Offsetting eps), else Fine in NF ptd dj (chipped). *Between The Covers.* $350/£224

JEROME, OWEN FOX. (Pseud of Oscar J. Friend.) The Hand of Horror. NY, (1927). 1st ed. VG. *Mcclintock.* $40/£26

JEROME, V. J. The Negro in Hollywood Films. NY: Masses & Mainstream, (1950). 1st ed. Ptd stiff wraps (lt soiled). *Petrilla.* $40/£26

JERROLD, BLANCHARD. The Life of George Cruikshank, in Two Epochs. London: C&W, 1882. 1st ed. 2 vols. Blue-grn coated eps; untrimmed. Pict brn cl (sl worn), gilt. Text Good (lt aged, ex-lib, mks to eps, tears, holes, adhesions, bkpls). *Baltimore*.* $60/£38

JERROLD, WALTER (ed). The Big Book of Fairy Tales. NY/Boston: Caldwell, n.d. (ca 1911). Charles Robinson (illus). 4to. (Inner joints broken; sl soiled, foxed.) Gilt-pict cl (sl worn). *Oinonen*.* $90/£58

JESSE, EDWARD. Anecdotes of Dogs. London, 1867. Gilt-pict grn cl (joints, edges chipped). *Freeman*.* $40/£26

JESSE, EDWARD. An Angler's Rambles. London: Van Voorst, 1836. 1/4 leather, marbled bds. (Cvrs poor, hinge repair.) Text Good. *Yudkin*.* $47/£30

JESSE, EDWARD. Scenes and Tales of Country Life. London: John Murray, 1844. New ed. vii,399,(i)pp; 4 woodcut plts (lt browned). Contemp 1/2 morocco, marbled bds (sl worn, sl loss head). *Edwards*. $70/£45

JESSE, JOHN HENEAGE. George Selwyn and His Contemporaries. London: Richard Bentley, 1843-1844. 1st ed. 4 vols. 19th-cent 1/2 calf, marbled bds, red/grn morocco labels. Good. *Karmiole*. $125/£80

JESSE, JOHN HENEAGE. Memoirs of the Pretenders and Their Adherents. London: Geo. Bell, 1883. xii,564pp; 6 engr plts. Teg. Contemp 1/2 morocco, marbled paper sides. (Hinges rubbed.) *Cox*. $23/£15

JESSOPP, AUGUSTUS. Studies by a Recluse. London, 1892. 2nd ed. Frontis, xix,281pp (bkpl). Teg. Gilt device upper bd. *Edwards*. $39/£25

JESSUP, RICHARD. The Cincinnati Kid. Boston: Little, Brown, (1963). 1st ed. Fine in dj. *Hermitage*. $65/£42

JEVONS, W. STANLEY. The Principles of Science: A Treatise on Logic and Scientific Method. London: Macmillan, 1905. VG (lib label removed; edges lt rubbed). *Glaser*. $150/£96

JEWELL, J. GREY. Among Our Sailors. NY: Harper, 1874. 1st ed. 311pp. (Extrems rubbed.) *Lefkowicz*. $125/£80

JEWITT, LLEWELLYN. Grave-Mounds and Their Contents. London, 1870. xxiv,306pp + (ii) ads. Aeg. (Sl spotting, upper hinge cracked, glue mk from removed bkpl; cl faded, spine sl bumped.) *Edwards*. $62/£40

JEWITT, LLEWELLYNN and S. C. HALL. The Stately Homes of England. NY, ca 1880. 2 vols in 1. Gilt-dec cl. VG. *Argosy*. $85/£54

JHABVALA, RUTH PRAWER. Amrita. NY: Norton, (1956). 1st US ed, 1st bk. VG+ in VG+ dj (lt rubbed). *Fuller & Saunders*. $75/£48

JHABVALA, RUTH PRAWER. Esmond in India. London: Allen & Unwin, 1958. 1st ed. Very Nice in dj (price-clipped). *Virgo*. $125/£80

JHABVALA, RUTH PRAWER. Like Birds, Like Fishes and Other Stories. NY: Norton, 1963. 1st US ed. Inscribed. VG+ in dj (price-clipped). *Lame Duck*. $125/£80

JHABVALA, RUTH PRAWER. The Nature of Passion. London: Allen & Unwin, 1956. 1st ed. (Fr pastedown scuffed), o/w NF in dj (price-clipped). *Virgo*. $78/£50

JHABVALA, RUTH PRAWER. To Whom She Will. London: Allen & Unwin, 1955. 1st ed, 1st bk. VG in VG dj (sl spotted). *Virgo*. $148/£95

JILLSON, WILLARD ROUSE (ed). The Boone Narrative. Louisville, KY: Standard Ptg, 1932. 1st ed. Ltd to 1000. Later cl. VG. *Mcgowan*. $65/£42

JILLSON, WILLARD ROUSE. The Saint Peter Sandstone in Kentucky. Louisville, 1938. One of 300. Map. VG+ (stain spine top). *Bohling*. $25/£16

JIRASEK, ALOIS. Legends of Old Bohemia. Edith Pargeter (trans). London: Paul Hamlyn, (1963). 4to. Color frontis, 337,(2)pp; 14 color plts (1 dbl-pg), 24 b/w full-pg illus, 1 dbl-pg illus by Jiri Trnka. Red cl (sl bumped, rubbed, sm stains), gilt. VG. *Blue Mountain*. $25/£16

JOBE, BROCK and MYRNA KAYE. New England Furniture: The Colonial Era. Boston: Houghton Mifflin, 1984. 1st ed. Brn cl, gilt. VG dj. *Baltimore**. $70/£45

JOCELYN, STEPHEN PERRY. Mostly Alkali: A Biography. Caldwell: Caxton, 1953. 1st ed. Frontis. Gold-stamped blue cl. Dj. *Dawson*. $45/£29

John Fryer of the Bounty: Notes on His Career.... (By Mary Ann Gamble.) (London): Golden Cockerel, 1939. 1st ed. One of 300 signed by Owen Rutter (intro), Averil Mackenzie-Grieve (illus). Folio. (Lt foxing.) *Lefkowicz*. $650/£417

John Wanamaker: The Record of a Citizen's Celebration to Mark His Sixty Year Career as Merchant, April, 1861-April, 1921. Phila, 1921. 4 plts. Teg. Red cl, gilt. *Freeman**. $25/£16

JOHN, ELIZABETH A. H. Storms Brewed in Other Men's World, Confrontation...in the Southwest 1540-1795. College Station, 1975. 1st ed. 4 maps, 16 plts. VG+ in VG+ dj. *Turpen*. $50/£32

JOHNS, C. A. Flowers of the Field. Clarence Elliott (ed). London, 1907. (Lt browned.) Marbled eps, teg. Gilt-edged 1/2 morocco, cl bds (spine faded), gilt. *Edwards*. $47/£30

JOHNS, C. A. (ed). Gardening for Children. London: Charles Cox, (1849). 2nd ed. 12mo. Wood engr frontis by Whymper, viii,182pp (pencil sketch rep). Aeg. Blind-stamped cl (unevenly faded), gilt. (Hinge cracked), else Fine. *Quest*. $70/£45

JOHNS, HENRY T. Life with the Forty-Ninth Massachusetts Volunteers. Washington, 1890. Frontis, 435pp. (Fr cvr faded.) *Ginsberg*. $125/£80

JOHNS, ORRICK. Asphalt and Other Poems. NY, 1917. 1st Amer ed, 1st bk. Uncut. Fine (name, address; spine lt sunned) in dj (spine sunned, rubbed, lacks 3/4-inch piece; few edge chips, sl soiled). *Polyanthos*. $60/£38

JOHNS, ROWLAND. Jock, the King's Pony. NY: Dutton, 1936. Stated 1st ed. VG in Good dj. *October Farm*. $45/£29

JOHNS, W. E. Biggles Breaks the Silence. Hodder & Stoughton, (1949). 1st ed. Nice (edges sl spotted, sl mks, bumps) in dj. *Ash*. $39/£25

JOHNS, W. E. Biggles Flies North. OUP, 1938. Early ed. 8vo. Color frontis by Howard Leigh, 256pp (rep corner torn); 6 b/w illus by Will Narraway. Illus blue cl. (Mks, edges rubbed), else VG-. *Bookmark*. $39/£25

JOHNSGARD, P. A. Birds of the Great Plains: Breeding Species and Their Distribution. Lincoln: Univ of NE, 1979. 1st ed. Fine in Fine dj. *Mikesh*. $30/£19

JOHNSGARD, P. A. Diving Birds of North America. Univ of NE, 1987. 1st ed. 32 color plts. Dj (sl chipped). *Edwards*. $31/£20

Johnson Club Papers. London: T. Fisher Unwin, 1899. 1st ed. Teg. Full beige linen (sl soiled). *Appelfeld*. $85/£54

JOHNSON, A. B. The Physiology of the Senses. NY, 1856. 214pp. Tooled cl bds (sl worn). VG. *Doctor's Library*. $60/£38

JOHNSON, A. E. The Book of W. Heath Robinson. London: A&C Black, 1930. 6 color plts. Pict cl. VG. *Hollett*. $47/£30

JOHNSON, A. F. The First Century of Printing at Basle. Ernest Benn, 1926. 1st ed. 50 facs plts. Good in dec paper bds, paper label. *Cox*. $47/£30

JOHNSON, A. F. French Sixteenth Century Printing. 1928. (Ex-lib, ink stamp, bkpl, lower joint cracked; loss to bd corners, soiled.) *Edwards*. $31/£20

JOHNSON, A. F. French Sixteenth Century Printing. Stanley Morison (ed). London: Ernest Benn, 1928. 1st ed. Dec bds, paper labels. (Soiled, hinge worn.) *Oak Knoll*. $45/£29

JOHNSON, A. F. Selected Essays on Books and Printing. Percy H. Muir (ed). Amsterdam: Van Gendt, 1970. 1st ed. VG in dj (lt soiled). *Cox*. $78/£50

JOHNSON, AMANDUS. Swedish Settlements of the Delaware, 1638-1644.... (Phila), 1911. 1st ed. 2 vols. 6 maps, 88 plts. Howes J124. *Ginsberg*. $200/£128

JOHNSON, ARTHUR T. California, an Englishman's Impressions of the Golden State. London: Stanley Paul, (1913). 1st ed. Teg. Maroon cl, gilt spine. (Lacks frontis; lt foxing to leaf fore-edges), else Fine. *Argonaut*. $45/£29

JOHNSON, B. S. Albert Angelo. Constable, 1964. 1st UK ed. Fine in NF dj. *Williams.* $117/£75

JOHNSON, B. S. Trawl. London, 1966. 1st Eng ed. Nice in dj (price-clipped, chip). *Clearwater.* $55/£35

JOHNSON, B. S. The Unfortunates. London: Panther/Secker, 1969. 1st Eng ed. 27 sections in wrap-around band. Very Nice in fldg box (spine sl rubbed). *Clearwater.* $101/£65

JOHNSON, BERYL. Advanced Embroidery Techniques. Batsford, 1983. 1st ed. 4 color plts. Fine in dj (chipped). *Whittle.* $22/£14

JOHNSON, BRITA ELIZABETH. Maher-Shalal-Hash-Baz, Or Rural Life in Old Virginia. Claremont, VA, (1923). 1st ed. Fine in NF dj (extrems sl chipped). *Mcgowan.* $150/£96

JOHNSON, C. British Poisonous Plants. London, 1856. 1st ed. iv,59pp; 28 hand-colored plts. Good. *Henly.* $195/£125

JOHNSON, CHARLES and HILARY JENKINSON. English Court Hand AD 1066 to 1500. Oxford, 1915. 1st ed. 2 vols. 44 plts vol 2. Cl-backed ptd bds (sl mkd, sl rubbed). VG. *Cox.* $187/£120

JOHNSON, CHARLES EUGENE. Beaver in the Adirondacks: Its Economics and Natural History. Syracuse, 1927. 3 fldg maps. VG + in ptd wrapper. *Bohling.* $16/£10

JOHNSON, CHARLES. Being and Race: Black Writing Since 1970. Bloomington: IN Univ, (1988). 1st ed. Fine in NF dj (lt worn, sl rubbed, crown sl worn). *Between The Covers.* $85/£54

JOHNSON, CLIFTON. Hudson Maxim. NY, 1924. Sketch map. (Margins lt browned, tp sl stained.) Teg. Dj (waterstained, chipped). *Edwards.* $31/£20

JOHNSON, CUTHBERT WILLIAM. The Life of Sir Edward Coke.... London: Henry Colburn, 1837. 2 vols. Marbled eps. Later? diced morocco, extra gilt. *Boswell.* $350/£224

JOHNSON, DANIEL. Sketches of Indian Field Sports. London: Robert Jennings, 1827. 2nd enlgd ed. Engr frontis, xii,295pp; slip w/frontis descrip bound in before title; 3 engr plts. (Occasional sm stain.) Uncut. Orig pale grn bds (rebacked, edges sl rubbed, stained), paper label. VG. *Morrell.* $195/£125

JOHNSON, DENIS. Angels. NY: Knopf, 1983. 1st ed. Fine (sm rmdr mk) in dj. *Antic Hay.* $50/£32

JOHNSON, DOROTHY M. All the Buffalo Returning. Dodd, Mead, (1979). 1st ed. Fine in Fine dj. *Authors Of West.* $35/£22

JOHNSON, DOROTHY M. The Bloody Bozeman. NY, (1971). 1st ed. VG in dj (discolored). *King.* $25/£16

JOHNSON, DOROTHY M. The Bloody Bozeman. NY, (1971). 1st ed. VG + in dj (spine faded). *Pratt.* $35/£22

JOHNSON, FRANCIS R. A Critical Bibliography of the Works of Edmund Spenser Printed Before 1700. Balt: Johns Hopkins, 1935. Blue buckram, gilt. Fine. *Heller.* $35/£22

JOHNSON, FRANK M. Reminiscent Tales of a Humble Angler. Cincinnati: Kidd, 1921. 1st ed. Frontis. VF. *Bowman.* $35/£22

JOHNSON, GEORGE W. The Gardeners' Dictionary. London: Bell, 1877. 916pp. Grn cl. VG (ex-lib). *Second Life.* $45/£29

JOHNSON, GUION GRIFFIS. Ante-Bellum North Carolina. Chapel Hill: Univ of NC, 1937. 1st ed. (Sl shaken, newspaper clipping laid in.) VG. *Mcgowan.* $65/£42

JOHNSON, HANNIBAL AUGUSTUS. The Sword of Honor, from Captivity to Freedom. Providence, RI, 1903. 1st ed. Ltd to 250. PNRISSHS Series 6, #6. NF in ptd wrappers. *Mcgowan.* $45/£29

JOHNSON, HENRY LEWIS. Gutenberg and the Book of Books. NY: Rudge, 1932. One of 750. Facs leaf in separate portfolio. (Sl worn.) Orig box (worn). *Oinonen*.* $90/£58

JOHNSON, J. Getting Gold: A Practical Treatise for Prospectors, Miners, and Students. London: Charles Griffin, 1905. 4th ed. Good (pencil mks fep). *Blake.* $65/£42

JOHNSON, JACK. Jack Johnson Is a Dandy. NY: Chelsea House, 1969. 1st ed. Fine in dj (lt used). *Beasley.* $45/£29

JOHNSON, JACK. Jack Johnson—In the Ring and Out. Chicago: National Sports, 1927. 1st ed. (Fr gutters sl dknd), else Fine in NF dj (sm hole spine edge). *Between The Covers.* $250/£160

JOHNSON, JAMES WELDON (ed). Book of American Negro Poetry. NY: HB&Co, (1922). 1st ed. (Bd edges rubbed, spine label dknd), else VG (lacks dj). *Between The Covers.* $100/£64

JOHNSON, JAMES WELDON (ed). The Book of American Negro Spirituals. NY: Viking, 1935. 1st ed. VG + (bkpl; bds soiled; lacks dj). *Between The Covers.* $125/£80

JOHNSON, JOHN LIPSCOMB. Autobiographical Notes. (Boulder): Privately ptd, 1958. One of 500. 14 plts. Dj (sl chipped). *Kane*.* $50/£32

JOHNSON, JOYCE. Minor Characters. Boston: HMCo, 1983. 1st ed. Fine in Fine dj. *Fuller & Saunders.* $25/£16

JOHNSON, KENNETH. K-344 or the Indians of California vs. the United States. L.A.: Dawson's Book Shop, 1966. One of 500. Cl-backed dec bds, gilt spine. Fine. *Pacific*.* $35/£22

JOHNSON, LAURENCE. A Medical Formulary Based on the United States and British Pharmacopeias Together with Numerous French, German, and.... NY, 1881. 1st ed. 402pp. Brn tooled cl bds (worn). Good. *Doctor's Library.* $75/£48

JOHNSON, LAURENCE. A Medical Formulary Based on the United States and British Pharmacopoeias.... NY: William Wood, 1881. 1st ed. vii,402pp. Dec emb cl (spots; pencil notes). VG. *Cahan.* $35/£22

JOHNSON, LEROY and JEAN. Escape from Death Valley as Told by William L. Manly and Other '49ers. Reno: Univ of NV, 1987. 1st ed. Ltd to 500. Fine in Fine dj. *Book Market.* $52/£33

JOHNSON, LIONEL. The Art of Thomas Hardy. London: Elkin Mathews & John Lane, 1894. 1st Eng ed. (Fep replaced, half-title tear repaired w/adhesive tape; spine sl chafed.) *Clearwater.* $62/£40

JOHNSON, LIONEL. The Religious Poems of Lionel Johnson. NY/London: Macmillan/Elkin Mathews, 1916. 1st ed, Amer issue. VG (pub's advance rev perforated stamp title leaf, lt foxing, sm crack rear inner hinge). *Reese.* $55/£35

JOHNSON, MARTIN. Congorilla. 1932. 1st ed. (Spine faded.) *Edwards.* $31/£20

JOHNSON, MARTIN. Lion. NY/London: Putnam, 1929. 1st ed. 63 plts, fldg map. Illus eps. (Sl rubbed; ex-lib, spine sticker removed), o/w VG. *Worldwide.* $25/£16

JOHNSON, MARTIN. Lion. NY: Putnam, 1929. 1st ed. Fldg map. Teg. Red cl. VG + . *Bowman.* $25/£16

JOHNSON, MARY COFFIN et al. Charles F. Coffin: A Quaker Pioneer.... Richmond, IN: Nicholson, 1923. 1st ed. Signed by Coffin. *Ginsberg.* $100/£64

JOHNSON, MAURICE C. Damning Trifles. NY: Knopf, 1932. 1st ed. (Name; sl rubbed.) Dj (edgeworn, soiled, 3/4-inch loss to spine). *Metropolitan*.* $17/£11

JOHNSON, MERLE and JACOB BLANCK. American First Editions. NY: R.R. Bowker, 1942. 4th ed. VG (spine sunned, lt nicked). *Reese.* $75/£48

JOHNSON, MERLE. A Bibliography of the Works of Mark Twain. NY: Harper, 1935. 1st ed, 1st ptg. Rust brn cl, gilt. Fine in NF dj. *Macdonnell*. $225/£144

JOHNSON, OSA. Four Years in Paradise. Phila: Lippincott, 1941. 1st ed. *Maggs*. $86/£55

JOHNSON, OVERTON and WILLIAM H. WINTER. Route Across the Rocky Mountains. Princeton: Princeton Univ, 1932. 2nd ed. Tp facs, 2 plts. Red cl, gilt. Fine. *Pacific**. $138/£88

JOHNSON, OWEN. The Hummingbird. Baker & Taylor, 1910. 1st ed. Pict cvr. VG. *Plapinger*. $100/£64

JOHNSON, P. HANSFORD. On Iniquity. Macmillan, 1967. 1st ed. VG in dj. *Whiteson*. $16/£10

JOHNSON, P. HANSFORD. Thomas Wolfe. Heinemann, 1947. 1st ed. VG in dj (sl chipped). *Whiteson*. $16/£10

JOHNSON, PHILIP C. Mies van der Rohe. NY: MOMA, 1947. 1st ed. VG. *Hollett*. $117/£75

JOHNSON, R. BRIMLEY (ed). Frances Burney and the Burneys. London: Stanley Paul, (1926). 1st ed. Frontis. Fine in NF dj (sm mended tear). *Reese*. $30/£19

JOHNSON, R. BYRON. Very Far West Indeed. A Few Rough Experiences on the North-West Pacific Coast. London, 1872. 2nd ed. (8),280pp + 32pp ads. Later 1/2 calf, marbled bds, leather label. (Sl internal soil), else NF. *Reese*. $175/£112

JOHNSON, R. G. An Historical Account of the First Settlement of Salem.... Phila: Orrin Rogers, 1839. 1st ed. (Inscrip fep, sl foxing, last few leaves sl dampstained.) Recent dk grn cl. Howes J144. *Sadlon*. $100/£64

JOHNSON, RICHARD. The Blossoms of Morality. London: Ptd for J. Harris, 1828. 8th ed. viii,235pp + 4pp ads, 1/2 title present; 47 engrs by John Bewick. 1/4 leather, marbled bds. Satisfactory (new fep; sl dusty, corners rubbed, back bd creased). *Michael Taylor*. $55/£35

JOHNSON, ROBERT UNDERWOOD and CLARENCE CLOUGH BUEL (eds). Battles and Leaders of the Civil War. NY, (1884-1888). 4 vols. (Cl cvrs sl worn), but Nice. *King*. $250/£160

JOHNSON, ROBERT UNDERWOOD and CLARENCE CLOUGH BUEL (eds). Battles and Leaders of the Civil War. NY: Century, (1888). 1st ed. 4 vols. Patterned eps, glazed edges. Later gilt-stamped red cl (sl rubbed). VG. *Houle*. $325/£208

JOHNSON, ROBERT UNDERWOOD and CLARENCE CLOUGH BUELL (eds). Battles and Leaders of the Civil War. NY: Century, (1887). 1st ed. 8 vols. VG set. *Mcgowan*. $450/£288

JOHNSON, ROBERT UNDERWOOD. Remembered Yesterdays. NY: Little, Brown, 1923. 1st ed. Olive brn cl, gilt. VG. *Macdonnell*. $35/£22

JOHNSON, ROSSITER (ed). The Biographical Dictionary of America. Boston, 1906. 10 vols. Cl (worn; inner hinges cracked; ex-lib), leather spine labels. *New Hampshire**. $195/£125

JOHNSON, ROSSITER. Campfire and Battlefield. NY, (1896). Gilt-pict blue cl (lt worn). *Freeman**. $40/£26

JOHNSON, ROSSITER. A History of the War of Secession 1861-1865. NY, 1910. 5th ed. (Eps foxed.) *Wantagh*. $20/£13

JOHNSON, SAMUEL and JAMES BOSWELL. Journals of the Western Islands. Peter Levi (ed). London: Folio Soc, 1990. 1st ed thus. Fine in slipcase. *Gretton*. $27/£17

JOHNSON, SAMUEL. A Dictionary of the English Language. London: Harrison, 1786. Engr frontis port. Unpaginated. Orig silhouette (cut out and laid down) of Johnson loosely inserted. Old 1/2 calf (edges worn, upper hinge cracked), raised bands, spine label. *Hollett*. $445/£285

JOHNSON, SAMUEL. A Dictionary of the English Language. London, 1820. 2 vols. Thick 4to. Engr frontis. Contemp 1/2 calf. Fine (sigs). *Swann**. $546/£350

JOHNSON, SAMUEL. A Dictionary of the English Language. London: Offor et al, 1822. 2 vols. Wide 4to. Frontis port. (Offsetting tp, lt foxing.) 3/4 polished calf, linen bds (rebound). Handsome set. *Hartfield*. $1,650/£1,058

JOHNSON, SAMUEL. A Dictionary of the English Language. London: C. & J. Rivington/J. Scatcherd, 1824. (viii),832pp. Contemp calf (expertly restored, new eps; sl mks, spots). Good. *Ash*. $195/£125

JOHNSON, SAMUEL. A Dictionary of the English Language.... London: For many, 1785. 1st 1-vol ed, '7th ed.' (Lacks 1/2 title, engr frontis; fr blank, tp gutter stained; sl foxing.) Marbled edges, eps. Early polished calf, marbled bds (sl worn, lt scuffed), raised bands, black leather spine label (sl chipped). *Baltimore**. $525/£337

JOHNSON, SAMUEL. A Dictionary of the English Language.... London: Longman (et al), 1805. 9th ed. 4 vols. Port (foxed, verso lt discolored). 19th-cent 3/4 calf, marbled bds (1 spine sl worn). VG set (few sigs lt foxed; sl rubbed). *Reese*. $225/£144

JOHNSON, SAMUEL. The History of Rasselas, Prince of Abyssinia. Chiswick: John Sharpe, 1822. Signed by Sotheran & Co. viii,184pp (inscrip); extra engr tp, 3 plts. Teg, others uncut. Ca 1900 3/4 grn morocco, marbled paper sides, ends, gilt spine, raised bands. *Cox*. $55/£35

JOHNSON, SAMUEL. Johnsoniana; or Supplement to Boswell. London: John Murray, 1836. 1st ed. 530pp; 45 engr plts. Marbled edges. 1/2 leather (corners bumped, worn), gilt, leather spine label. *Argosy*. $250/£160

JOHNSON, SAMUEL. A Journey to the Western Islands of Scotland. London: Strahan, 1775. 1st ed. Mod calf, leather spine label. (Owner stamp tp, 3 sm ex-libris stamps at sig B.) *Swann**. $201/£129

JOHNSON, SAMUEL. A Journey to the Western Islands of Scotland. London: W. Strahan, 1775. 1st ed w/errata leaf, 2pp ads at end. Full old brn calf (spine ends worn), raised bands, red leather label. (Old sig title), else Good. *Appelfeld*. $325/£208

JOHNSON, SAMUEL. Letters.... George Birkbeck Hill (ed). Oxford, 1892. 1st ed. 2 vols. lii,423; (4),476pp; 4-pg fldg facs. Teg, others uncut. Good set in orig grn roan-backed cl (backs rubbed, sl worn). *Cox*. $101/£65

JOHNSON, SAMUEL. Mr. Johnson's Preface to His Edition of Shakespear's Plays. London: J. & R. Tonson et al, 1755. 1st separately pub'd ed. Contents VG (lacks 1/2-title). Mod 1/2 morocco signed H. Zucker (soiled, stains). Sound. *Waverly**. $132/£85

JOHNSON, SAMUEL. The Poetical Works. London: W. Osborne/T. Griffin, 1785. 1st collected ed. viii,152pp; 1/2 title present. Contemp grn stained calf (spine chipped, hinges cracked; bkpl), burgundy spine label. *Karmiole*. $300/£192

JOHNSON, SAMUEL. The Rambler.... London: P. Dodsley, R. Owen et al, 1794. 4 vols. Engr frontis each vol. Edges largely untrimmed. Early paper bds (shelfwear, sl tanning), spines gilt, red morocco labels. Very Nice set. *Reese*. $125/£80

JOHNSON, SAMUEL. Rasselas. London: Wm. Miller, 1805. 5 engrs. Full crimson crushed morocco (bumped, lt rubbed, lt worn, ex-lib). *Kane**. $60/£38

JOHNSON, STEPHEN. The History of Cardiac Surgery 1896-1955. Balt, 1970. 1st ed. VG in dj. *Fye*. $100/£64

JOHNSON, SUSANNAH. Narrative of the Captivity. Windsor, 1807. Mod morocco. (Tp fore-edge repaired.) Howes J153. *Swann**. $138/£88

JOHNSON, SWAFFORD. History of the U.S. Cavalry. Greenwich, (1985). 1st ed. Fine in Fine dj. *Pratt*. $25/£16

JOHNSON, T. BROADWOOD. Tramps Round the Mountains of the Moon and Through the Back Gate of the Congo State. Boston: Dana Estes, 1909. 1st Amer ed. Frontis, fldg map. Blue gilt pict cl (spine sunned, sl stained). *Terramedia*. $75/£48

JOHNSON, THEODORE T. Sights in the Gold Region and Scenes by the Way. NY, 1849. 1st ed. Pub's cl (joints rubbed, partly split; spine ends frayed; foxed, sig). Howes J154. *Swann**. $172/£110

JOHNSON, THEODORE T. Sights in the Gold Region and Scenes by the Way. NY: Baker & Scribner, 1849. 1st ed. Brn blind-stamped cl, gilt. (Offsetting, tear ep from clipping; rear blank torn out; spine sl worn, lower hinge lacks some cl.) Howes J154. *Glenn*. $200/£128

JOHNSON, THEODORE T. Sights in the Gold Region and Scenes by the Way. NY: Baker & Scribner, 1849. 1st ed. xii,278pp. Orig blue cl, gilt. (Lt foxed, few pp dknd; spine top skillfully repaired), o/w Fine. Howes J154. *Pacific**. $207/£133

JOHNSON, THOMAS H. Emily Dickinson, an Interpretive Biography. Cambridge: Belknap/Harvard, 1955. 1st ed. (Inscrip), o/w Very Nice in dj (edge-tanned). *Reese*. $30/£19

JOHNSON, THOMAS L. and PHILLIP C. DUNN (eds). A True Likeness. Columbia, SC/Chapel Hill: Bruccoli Clark/Algonquin Books, 1986. 1st ed, 2nd ptg. Fine in pict dj. *Cahan*. $50/£32

JOHNSON, VIRGINIA W. The Catskill Fairies. NY: Harper, (1875). 1st ed. 4to. Alfred Johnson (illus). (Spine head chipped), else Fine in brn cl, gilt. *Captain's Bookshelf*. $100/£64

JOHNSON, W. F. History of the Johnstown Flood. N.p.: Edgewood, 1889. 459pp. Good. *Scribe's Perch**. $10/£6

JOHNSON, W. F. Life of Sitting Bull and History of the Indian War of 1890-91. N.p., 1891. 1st ed. 544pp + music. Pict cl (Cvr sl worn), o/w VG +. *Pratt*. $50/£32

JOHNSON, WARREN B. From the Pacific to the Atlantic. Webster, MA, 1887. 1st ed. 369pp, port. (Spine, cvrs soiled.) *King*. $25/£16

Johnston's Detroit City Directory and Advertising Gazetteer of Michigan for 1856-7. Detroit: Ptd by Henry Barns, 1856. 352pp. Cl-backed ptd bds. (Inner hinges strengthened, offsetting to ads; cvrs soiled), o/w VG. *New Hampshire**. $180/£115

JOHNSTON, A. K. The Physical Atlas of Natural Phenomena. London, 1850. iv,122pp (sl foxed), 2 pub's ads; 25 hand-colored maps (1 dbl-pg). Aeg. Later cl. *Henly*. $156/£100

JOHNSTON, ANNIE FELLOWS. For Pierre's Sake. Page, 1934. 1st ed. 5.5x7.5. 200pp + ads. Blue pict cl (sl shelfworn). NF. *My Bookhouse*. $40/£26

JOHNSTON, CHARLES. Incidents Attending the Capture, Detention, and Ransom of Charles Johnston of Virginia. Cleveland: Burrows, 1905. Rpt of 1827 ed. Map frontis. Dec cl. Howes J158. *Ginsberg*. $125/£80

JOHNSTON, D. In Search of Swift. Dublin, 1959. 1st ed. Signed. VG in dj (torn). *Gretton*. $23/£15

JOHNSTON, D. E. et al. Roman Roads in the South-East Midlands. London, 1964. 1st ed. Frontis port. Dj. *Edwards*. $39/£25

JOHNSTON, EDWARD. Writing and Illuminating, and Lettering.... London: Sir Isaac Pitman, 1932. 17th imp. 24 plts. Good in 2-tone cl. *Cox*. $19/£12

JOHNSTON, G. A. (ed). Berkeley's Commonplace Book. Faber & Faber, 1930. 1st ed. (Eps browned; cl spine lt faded.) *Edwards*. $23/£15

JOHNSTON, GEORGE. A History of the British Zoophytes. London, 1897. 2nd ed. 2 vols. xvi,488pp; Vol 2 unpaginated; 74 plts. (Bkpl, feps vol 1 sl foxed, vol 2 sl foxed, 1st 2pp vol 2 detached; bds dampstained.) *Edwards*. $94/£60

JOHNSTON, HANK. The Railroad That Lighted Southern California. L.A.: TransAnglo, (1965). 1st ed. Fldg map. VF in dj. *Argonaut*. $40/£26

JOHNSTON, HARRY. British Central Africa. NY: Edward Arnold, 1897. xix,544pp; 6 fldg maps. Pict cl (rubbed, worn). *Adelson*. $350/£224

JOHNSTON, HARRY. The Uganda Protectorate. NY/London, Dodd, Mead/Hutchison, 1902. 1st Amer ed. 2 vols. Plt illus (48 colored), 9 fldg maps. Red gilt cl. VG. *Terramedia*. $350/£224

JOHNSTON, J. HALCRO. The Reverse Notation. London: Blackie, (1938). 1st ed. Nice in dj. *Patterson*. $39/£25

JOHNSTON, JAMES N. The Poets and Poetry of Buffalo. Buffalo, NY, 1904. Good (few pp poorly opened; sl shelfworn). *Cullen*. $50/£32

JOHNSTON, JOSEPH EGGLESTON. Narrative of Military Operations, Directed During the Late War Between the States. NY: D. Appleton, 1874. 1st ed. 602,(6)pp. (Extrems sl worn), else VG. Howes J167. *Mcgowan*. $250/£160

JOHNSTON, PRISCILLA. Edward Johnston. London: Faber & Faber, 1959. 1st ed. VG in dj (sl rubbed). *Michael Taylor*. $39/£25

JOHNSTON, R. M. Bull Run: Its Strategy and Tactics. Boston: Houghton Mifflin, Nov, 1913. 1st ed. 10 maps. Good (fr hinge crack). *Scribe's Perch**. $50/£32

JOHNSTON, W. G. Overland to California. Oakland, CA, 1948. Reissue of 1892 ed. Fldg blue map. Howes J173. *Ginsberg*. $50/£32

JOHNSTON, WILLIAM D. History of the Library of Congress. Vol. I, 1800-1864. Washington: GPO, 1904. 1st ed. VG +. *Archer*. $125/£80

JOHNSTON, WILLIAM PRESTON. The Life of Gen. Albert Sidney Johnston.... NY, 1878. 755pp. (Tp foxed, inner hinges broken; cvrs worn.) *King*. $75/£48

JOHNSTONE, G. H. Asiatic Magnolias in Cultivation. London, 1955. 14 Fine color plts, 20 plain plts, fldg map, bookmark. Buckram, gilt. (Eps sl foxed; binding spotted), o/w Fine. *Henly*. $296/£190

JOHNSTONE, JOHN. An Account of the Mode of Draining Land. London: Richard Phillips, 1801. 2nd ed. xvi,164pp (sl browned); 18 fldg plans (of 19). Orig bds (joints cracking, worn w/loss to spine, corners). *Edwards*. $133/£85

JOHNSTONE, WILLIAM GROSART and ALEXANDER CROALL. The Nature-Printed British Sea-Weeds. London: Bradbury, Evans, (1859-60). 4 vols. Engr titles, 221 plts (lt spotting; label). Contemp grn 1/2 morocco (rubbed). *Christie's**. $385/£247

JOINER, BETTY. Costumes for the Dance. NY: A.S. Barnes, 1937. 1st ed. 6 color plts. Color ptd paper illus mtd fr cvr (cl lt soiled). VG in die-cut ptd dj (lt soiled, sm tears). *Cahan*. $85/£54

JOLINE, ADRIAN H. The Diversions of a Book-Lover. NY: Harper, 1903. 1st ed. Teg. VG (paper label spine lt dknd). *Graf*. $20/£13

Jolly Jump-Ups ABC Book. Publicity Products, n.d. (ca 1950s). Lg 8vo. 6 pop-ups. Pict bds. (Spine cracked, worn), o/w Sound. *Bookmark*. $37/£24

JOLY, CHARLES JASPER. A Manual of Quaternions. London: Macmillan, 1905. 1st ed. VG (lacks fep). *Glaser*. $85/£54

JOLY, HENRI L. Legend in Japanese Art. Rutland/Tokyo, (1967). (Abraded stamp tp.) Dj (cellotaped to pastedowns). *Swann**. $92/£59

JONAS, MAURICE. Notes of an Art Collector. London: Routledge, 1907. 69 plts. Leather spine label. (Few mks.) *Hollett.* $55/£35

JONES, ABNER. Memoirs of the Life and Experience, Travels and Preaching of Abner Jones. Exeter: The Author, 1807. 108pp (dog-eared, sm margin tears, 1 leaf corner torn off w/sl loss, foxing). Stitched in plain wrapper (heavily worn, bottom inch fr cvr gone). *New Hampshire*. $60/£38

JONES, BILL. The Argonauts of Siberia. Phila: Dorrance, c. 1927. Frontis, 5 plts. Signed photo print of Jones laid in. VG. *High Latitude.* $80/£51

JONES, CHARLES C. The History of Georgia. Boston, 1883. 1st ed. 2 vols. Frontispieces (offset onto tps), 19 maps and plts (1 w/tear), fldg plan (separated along folds). (Lt rubbed, sl shaken.) *Kane*. $170/£109

JONES, CHARLES C. Military Operations in Georgia During the War Between the States. Augusta: Chronicle Job Ptg, 1893. 1st ed. 33pp. Largely uncut, unopened. Orig wraps. (Sl chipped), else Good. *Brown.* $40/£26

JONES, CHARLES REED. The Van Norton Murders. NY: Macaulay, (1931). 1st ed. (Soil, edges rubbed.) Dj (soil, edgewear, sl loss to head.) *Metropolitan*. $23/£15

JONES, DANIEL W. Forty Years Among the Indians. Salt Lake City: Juvenile Instructor Office, 1890. 400pp. Black cl, gilt spine lettering. Bright. This copy w/o port. Howes J207. *Cullen.* $150/£96

JONES, DAVID. The Anathemata. London: Faber & Faber, (1952). 1st ed. Fine in NF dj (spine sl tanned, nick). *Reese.* $200/£128

JONES, DAVID. The Anathemata.... Faber, 1952. Fine in dj (chipped, sl loss at corners, folds sl rubbed, sm tear, spine sl dknd). *Poetry Bookshop.* $172/£110

JONES, DAVID. In Parenthesis. 1937. 1st ed. (Cvrs dusty), o/w Good in dj (torn, worn). *Words Etc.* $117/£75

JONES, DAVID. In Parenthesis. Faber, 1937. 2nd imp. (Top edge sl stained; bd edges rubbed, sl stained.) Dj (rubbed, fragments lost at edges). *Poetry Bookshop.* $39/£25

JONES, DAVID. In Parenthesis. NY, 1961. 1st Amer ed. NF in dj. *Words Etc.* $101/£65

JONES, DAVID. Letters to a Friend: Aneirin Talfan Davies. Christopher Davies, 1980. VF in dj (price-clipped). *Poetry Bookshop.* $19/£12

JONES, DAVID. Letters to Vernon Watkins. Ruth Pryor (ed). Cardiff: Univ of Wales, 1976. Buckram. (2 short lines in margins, sig, place, date), o/w Fine in dj. *Poetry Bookshop.* $23/£15

JONES, DAVID. The Roman Quarry. Harman Grisewood and Rene Hague (eds). Agenda Editions, 1981. Mint in acetate dj. *Poetry Bookshop.* $47/£30

JONES, DOUGLAS C. Arrest Sitting Bull. NY: Scribner, 1977. 1st ed. Fine in Fine dj. *Connolly.* $25/£16

JONES, DOUGLAS C. Elkhorn Tavern. NY, (1980). 1st ed. Fine in Fine dj. *Pratt.* $17/£11

JONES, E. ALFRED. The Old Plate of the Cambridge Colleges. Cambridge: CUP, 1910. 1st ed. 120 photogravure plts, guards. Blue cl (neatly rebacked), gilt spine laid down. *Karmiole.* $450/£288

JONES, E. ALFRED. The Old Silver of American Churches. Letchworth: Nat'l Soc of Colonial Dames of America, 1913. 1st ed. One of 506 numbered. Thick sm folio. 145 b/w photo plts. Teg; untrimmed. Grn buckram (rubbed, sl worn, spot stains, sm dents; sm stain reps), gilt. *Baltimore*. $320/£205

JONES, FORTIER. With Serbia into Exile, an American's Adventures with the Army That Cannot Die. NY: Century, 1916. Pict cl. (Related clippings laid in, mtd on eps; name tp.) *Bohling.* $15/£10

JONES, G. ROBERT. Dr. John H. Pinkard, a Negro Medical Genius.... (Roanoke, VA: Stone Ptg), n.d. 1st ed. VG in ptd wrappers. *Mcgowan.* $75/£48

JONES, GEORGE. The Battle of Waterloo, Also of Ligny, and Quatre-Bras. London, 1817. 10th ed. 2 vols in 1. 4to. Frontis (browned), 34 etched plts (foxing, offsetting), 2 lg fldg hand-colored panoramas, 7 fldg color maps. Contemp red 1/2-morocco (extrems rubbed). *Maggs.* $663/£425

JONES, H. F. Charles Darwin and Samuel Butler, a Step Towards Reconciliation. A.C. Fifield, 1911. Wrappers (detached; pencil notes). *Maggs.* $28/£18

JONES, H. MACNAUGHTON. Practical Manual of Diseases of Women and Uterinetherapeutics, for Students. London, 1890. (4th ed.) 665pp. Red cl bds (extrems sl worn). VG. *Doctor's Library.* $75/£48

JONES, HARRY W. A Chaplain's Experience Ashore and Afloat. NY: A.G. Sherwood, (1901). *Dawson.* $25/£16

JONES, HERSCHEL. Adventures in Americana 1473-1926. Wilberforce Eames (ed). NY, 1964. Rpt. 3 vols. Facs of tp each bk. Fine. No dj as issued. *Turpen.* $95/£61

JONES, J. B. Life and Adventures of a Country Merchant. Phila: Lippincott & Grambo, 1854. 1st ed. Frontis, 396pp. Purple cl (spine faded). BAL 10999, binding A. *M & S.* $100/£64

JONES, J. F. D. A Treatise on the Process Employed by Nature in Suppressing the Hemorrhage from Divided and Punctured Arteries, and on the Use of the Ligature. Phila, 1811. 1st Amer ed. 237pp (lt waterstains, browning, sig starting); 15 wood engrs. Contemp calf (upper cvr detached). *Argosy.* $400/£256

JONES, JAMES. From Here to Eternity. NY, 1951. 1st ed, 1st bk. Fine in dj. *Argosy.* $250/£160

JONES, JAMES. From Here to Eternity. NY: Scribner, 1951. 1st ed. NF (gilt title faded) in NF dj (spine top sl chipped). *Unger.* $150/£96

JONES, JAMES. From Here to Eternity. NY: Scribner, 1951. 1st ed, 1st bk. (Bkpl, sl offsetting eps), o/w Fine in dj (lt worn). *Hermitage.* $150/£96

JONES, JAMES. From Here to Eternity. Collins, 1952. 1st UK ed. Fine in dj. *Williams.* $94/£60

JONES, JAMES. The Pistol. NY: Scribners, (1958). 1st ed. Fine (sl cocked) in Fine dj (sl rubbed). *Between The Covers.* $50/£32

JONES, JAMES. The Thin Red Line. NY, (1962). 1st ed. VG in dj. *Argosy.* $75/£48

JONES, JESSIE ORTON. Secrets. NY: Viking, 1945. 1st ed. Elizabeth Orton Jones (illus). Sm 8vo. Pict cl. VG + in VG dj (chipped). *Book Adoption.* $75/£48

JONES, JOHN BEAUCHAMP. A Rebel War Clerk's Diary at the Confederate States Capital. (Alexandria, VA: Time-Life, 1982.) Rpt of rare 1866 ed. 2 vols. Full leather. Pristine set. Howes J220. *Mcgowan.* $50/£32

JONES, JOHN PAUL. Life and Correspondence of John Paul Jones, Including His Narrative. NY, 1830. Frontis port, 555pp. (Dampstains fep, 1st few pp; expertly rebacked.) *Parmer.* $125/£80

JONES, JOHN THOMAS. Account of the War in Spain and Portugal, and in the South of France, from 1808, to 1814, Inclusive. London: T. Egerton, 1818. 1st ed. xxvi,448pp (2 leaves w/offset from maps, text sl foxed); 4 fldg maps (3 colored in part). Marbled edges. Contemp calf (recently, neatly rebacked, corners exposed, new eps), stippled, knotted gilt rules, raised bands, new morocco label. Excellent. *Pirages.* $250/£160

JONES, JOHN WILLIAM. Life and Letters of Robert E. Lee, Soldier and Man. NY/Washington: Neale, 1906. 1st ed. VG. *Mcgowan.* $175/£112

JONES, JOHN WILLIAM. Personal Reminiscences, Anecdotes and Letters of Gen. Robert E. Lee. NY, 1875. 509pp. Pict cl. VG (lacks 3 plts). *Pratt.* $75/£48

JONES, JOHN WILLIAM. Personal Reminiscences, Anecdotes, and Letters of Gen. Robert E. Lee. NY: D. Appleton, 1875. 1st ed. xvi,509,(2)pp. VG (lt worn, sl spotted). *Mcgowan.* $150/£96

JONES, JOSEPH. Letters of Joseph Jones, of Virginia, 1777-1787. W.C. Ford (ed). Washington, D.C.: Dept of State, 1889. 1st ed. Ltd to 250. 157pp. Orig ptd wraps (worn, chipped). Howes J233. *Wantagh.* $85/£54

JONES, JOSEPH. Man, Moral and Physical. Phila, 1861. 324pp. VG. *Fye.* $75/£48

JONES, KATHARINE M. Heroines of Dixie. Indianapolis, (1955). 1st ed. VG in dj (worn, sl abrasion fr cvr). *King.* $40/£26

JONES, KATHERINE M. Ladies of Richmond; Confederate Capital. Indianapolis: Bobbs-Merrill, (1962). 1st ed. NF in VG dj. *Mcgowan.* $35/£22

JONES, LEROI. Tales. NY: Grove, 1967. 1st ed. NF in dj. *Lame Duck.* $45/£29

JONES, LOUIS T. The Quakers in Iowa. Iowa City, 1914. 1st ed. *Ginsberg.* $75/£48

JONES, LOUISE SEYMOUR. The Human Side of Bookplates. L.A.: Ward Ritchie, 1951. 1st ed. Dec paper over bds; cl spine gold-stamped. Fine. *Graf.* $75/£48

JONES, NETTIE. Fish Tales. NY: Random House, (1983). 1st ed. Fine in dj (sm crown tear). *Between The Covers.* $45/£29

JONES, OWEN GLYNNE. Rock-Climbing in the English Lake District. Abraham, Keswick, 1911. 3rd ed. Frontis port, 31 collotype plts, 10 route plts. Good+ (sl pencil notes; sl shelfwear). *Scribe's Perch*.* $48/£31

JONES, OWEN. The Grammar of Ornament. London: Day & Son, 1856. 1st ed. Lg folio. Tp, 100 chromolitho plts, mostly VG. (Tearing, mostly marginal to plts; tp detached, mostly lacking; lt soiling). Orig 1/4 morocco (soiled, worn, joints partly split but holding). *Waverly*.* $1,100/£705

JONES, RAYMOND F. Renaissance. NY: Gnome, 1951. 1st ed. Fine in dj (sl worn, internal tape). *Else Fine.* $30/£19

JONES, RAYMOND F. The Toymaker. L.A.: FPCI, 1951. 1st ed. 1st priority binding. Fine in grn/white dj (sl rubbed). *Else Fine.* $125/£80

JONES, ROBERT and R. W. LOVETT. Orthopedic Surgery. NY, 1923. 1st ed. (Corners lt dampstained.) *Argosy.* $100/£64

JONES, ROBERT H. Disrupted Decades, the Civil War and Reconstruction Years. NY, (1973). 1st ed. VG+ in VG+ dj. *Pratt.* $30/£19

JONES, RUFUS M. et al. The Quakers in the American Colonies. London: Macmillan, 1911. 1st ed. Fldg map. *Ginsberg.* $100/£64

JONES, S. R. et al. The Village Homes of England. C. Holme (ed). London, 1912. 12 color plts. New blind cl (orig fr cvr bound in). Sound. *Ars Artis.* $33/£21

JONES, SYDNEY R. England South. London, 1948. 1st ed. Dj (ragged). *Edwards.* $23/£15

JONES, SYDNEY R. England West. London, 1950. 1st ed. Dj (ragged). *Edwards.* $23/£15

JONES, TERRY L. Lee's Tigers. Baton Rouge, (1987). 1st ed. VG+ in VG+ dj. *Pratt.* $35/£22

JONES, THOMAS. The Gregynog Press. Oxford, 1954. One of 750 numbered. Dj. *Swann*.* $161/£103

JONES, VERNON. Aesop's Fables. NY: Watts, 1969. Arthur Rackham (illus). 6 1/4 x 8 1/4. 222pp. Fine in dj. *Cattermole.* $15/£10

JONES, VIRGIL CARRINGTON. Eight Hours Before Richmond. NY: Henry Holt, (1957). 1st ed, 2nd ptg. NF in VG dj. *Mcgowan.* $45/£29

JONES, VIRGIL CARRINGTON. Eight Hours Before Richmond. Henry Holt, (c. 1957). 1st ptg. VG (stamp tp) in VG dj (worn). *Book Broker.* $35/£22

JONES, VIRGIL CARRINGTON. Gray Ghosts and Rebel Raiders. NY, (1956). 1st ed. VG+. *Pratt.* $42/£27

JONES, W. H. S. Malaria and Greek History...to Which Is Added the History of Greek Therapeutics and the Malaria Theory, by E. T. Withington. Manchester: Univ Press, 1909. 1st ed. Teg. VG. *Glaser.* $100/£64

JONES, WILLIAM. The History of the Life of Nader Shah, King of Persia. London: T. Cadell, 1773. lxxii,196pp. Contemp full diced calf (extrem wear), black morocco label. Good. *Cullen.* $365/£234

JONG, ERICA. Fruits and Vegetables. NY: Holt Rinehart, (1971). 1st ed, 1st bk. Signed. Fine in Fine dj. *Lenz.* $75/£48

JORDAN, D. S. (ed). Reports on Condition of Seal Life on the Pribilof Islands...from 1868 to 1895. Washington: GPO, 1898. 1st ed. (Vol 1 of 4.) 513pp, fldg map. VG+. *Mikesh.* $45/£29

JORDAN, DAVID STARR and VERNON L. KELLOGG. The Scientific Aspects of Luther Burbank's Work. SF, 1909. Frontis port, 37 half-tone plts. Cl spine, ptd paper-cvrd bds. (Frontis tissue torn), else Pristine. *Brooks.* $75/£48

JORDAN, MILDRED. I Won't, Said the King. NY: Knopf, 1945. 1st ed. Roger Duvoisin (illus). 6 1/4 x 8 1/4. 103pp. VG in dj. *Cattermole.* $50/£32

JORDAN, THOMAS and J. P. PRYOR. The Campaigns of Lieut.-Gen. N. B. Forrest and of Forrest's Cavalry. New Orleans: Blelock, 1868. 1st ed. Signed by John Watson Morton, Forrest's chief of artillery. xv,(17)-704pp. 1/2 leather, cl. VG. Howes J251. *Mcgowan.* $650/£417

Jose Clemente Orozco. NY: Delphic Studios, 1932. Signed by Orozco. (Sl worn, spine faded.) *Kane*.* $100/£64

JOSE, ARTHUR W. and HERBERT J. CARTER. The Australian Encyclopedia. Sydney: Angus, 1927. 1st ed. 2 vols. 2 color plts, map. Grn cl, gilt. *Ginsberg.* $150/£96

JOSEPHUS, FLAVIUS. The Genuine Works of Flavius Josephus, the Jewish Historian. London: D. Browne, 1755. 4 vols. Fldg map. Aeg. Full leather (dry, spine loss), gilt. *Metropolitan*.* $80/£51

JOSEPHY, ALVIN M., JR. The Nez Perce Indians and the Opening of the Northwest. Yale, 1965. 1st ed. 11 maps. Orange pict cl. Fine in Fine dj. *Oregon.* $80/£51

JOSEPHY, ALVIN M., JR. The Nez Perce Indians and the Opening of the Northwest. New Haven: Yale Univ, 1965. 1st ed. Frontis port. Fine (name) in pict dj. *Argonaut.* $95/£61

JOSEPHY, ALVIN M., JR. The Nez Perce Indians and the Opening of the Northwest. New Haven: Yale Univ, 1965. 1st ed. Color frontis. Fine in NF dj. *Connolly.* $115/£74

JOSEPHY, ALVIN M., JR. The Patriot Chiefs. NY: Viking, 1961. 1st ed. VG in dj. *Lien.* $30/£19

JOSLIN, ELLIOTT P. A Diabetic Manual for the Mutual Use of Doctor and Patient. Phila, 1929. 4th ed. Grn cl bds (sl worn). VG. *Doctor's Library.* $40/£26

JOSSELYN, AMOS PIATT. The Overland Journal of Amos Piatt Josselyn...April 2, 1849 to September 11, 1849. J. Wm. Barrett (ed). Balt: Gateway, 1978. 1st ed. Fine. *Sadlon.* $25/£16

JOURDAIN, MARGARET. The History of English Secular Embroidery. London: Kegan Paul, 1910. 1st ed. Fldg color frontis, 62 b/w plts. (Cl sl mkd, dull.) *Hollett.* $148/£95

JOURDAIN, MARGARET. Regency Furniture 1795-1820. London/NY, 1948. Rev, enlgd ed. Frontis. *Edwards.* $39/£25

JOURDAIN, MARGARET. Regency Furniture 1795-1820. London: Country Life, 1948. Rev, enlgd ed. VG in dj. *Hollett.* $117/£75

JOURDAIN, MARGARET. The Work of William Kent. London, 1948. Good in dj (worn). *Washton.* $100/£64

JOURDAIN, MARGARET. The Work of William Kent. London/NY: Country Life, 1948. 150/88 plts. Sound. *Ars Artis.* $78/£50

Journal of a Hunting Excursion to Louis Lake, 1851. Blue Mountain Lake, NY: Adirondack Mus., 1961. 1st ed. One of 1000. 43 plts of facs. (Bkpl removed), o/w VG. *Worldwide.* $30/£19

Journal of a Tour Around Hawaii. (By William Ellis.) Boston, 1825. Fldg map, 5 plts. Mod 1/4 morocco. (Dampstaining, some heavy.) *Swann*.* $115/£74

Journal of a Voyage of Discovery to the Arctic Regions.... (By Alexander Fisher.) London: Richard Phillips, n.d. (1819). viii,104pp; 3 plts, fldg map. Uncut. Mod 1/4 calf. VG. *High Latitude.* $250/£160

Journal of the Adventures of Matthew Bunn. Chicago, 1962. Facs of 1st ed. Ltd to 2000. Orig ptd wrappers. *Sadlon.* $15/£10

Journal of the Congress of the Confederate States of America, 1861-1865. Washington: GPO, 1904-05. 1st ed thus. 7 vols. Orig 1/2 leather, cl (bds detached vol 1; vol 2 later cl). Good set. *Mcgowan.* $750/£481

Journal of the Proceedings of the Hon. House of Representatives of the State of New Hampshire. Portsmouth: Melcher, 1794. Sewn gathers, w/o bds. Clean (lt dampstain rear flap). *Metropolitan*.* $57/£37

Journey to Jerusalem. (By Nathaniel Crouch.) Hartford, 1796. 1/4 sheep (worn). *Swann*.* $402/£258

Journeys into the Moon, Several Planets and the Sun. Phila: Vollmer & Haggenmacher, 1837. 1st ed. 12mo. 1/4 morocco, marbled bds (lt rubbed). *Swann*.* $690/£442

JOUTEL, HENRI. Joutel's Journal of La Salle's Last Voyage 1684-7.... Albany, 1906. Ltd to 500 numbered. Fldg map. Bds, cl spine, ptd paper labels. Howes J266. *Ginsberg.* $200/£128

JOY, EDWARD T. The Country Life Book of Clocks. London, (1967). Color frontis. VG in dj. *Weber.* $17/£11

JOYCE, JAMES. Anna Livia Plurabelle. London: Faber & Faber, 1930. 1st UK ed. 3 pieces of publicity material laid in. VG in self-wrappers (sl worn, browned). *Williams.* $55/£35

JOYCE, JAMES. The Cat and the Devil. NY: Dodd, Mead, 1964. 1st ed. Richard Erdoes (illus). 7 x 9 1/4. 48pp. Fine in dj. *Cattermole.* $100/£64

JOYCE, JAMES. Chamber Music. Boston: Cornhill, (1918). 1st US ed (unauthorized), 1st bk. (Sl rubbed, sm faded area rear cvr.) *Kane*.* $140/£90

JOYCE, JAMES. Chamber Music. Boston: Cornhill, (1918). 1st Amer ed. (Names, dates), o/w Fine (lacks orig tissue wrapper) in grn bds. *Warren.* $250/£160

JOYCE, JAMES. Chamber Music. Boston: Cornhill, n.d. 1st US ed. As New in grn cl-cvrd bds, glassine dj. *Lame Duck.* $350/£224

JOYCE, JAMES. Collected Poems of James Joyce. NY: Black Sun, 1936. Ltd ed of 750 (of 800) numbered. 12mo. Frontis port. Blue-stamped dec bds. NF (spine base sl browned) in orig glassine dj (sm chip), (supplied) acetate dj. *Antic Hay.* $750/£481

JOYCE, JAMES. Collected Poems. NY: Black Sun, 1936. 1st ed. One of 750 numbered. Frontis port. Dec parchment bds. VF in orig tissue dj (lt worn). *Jaffe.* $500/£321

JOYCE, JAMES. Dubliners. (NY): LEC, (1986). Ltd to 1000 signed by Thomas Flanagan (intro) and Robert Ballagh (illus). 6 hand-rubbed photogravures. 1/4 dk grn Nigerian Oasis goatskin, Irish linen. Mint in orig slipcase. *Truepenny.* $450/£288

JOYCE, JAMES. Exiles. London: Grant Richards, 1918. 1st British ed. Paper labels. (Sm erasure ep; spine label sl dknd, soiled; edged bumped), o/w VG. *Reese.* $325/£208

JOYCE, JAMES. Finnegan's Wake. NY: Viking, 1939. 1st Amer ed, trade issue. Very Nice (lacks dj). *Reese.* $65/£42

JOYCE, JAMES. Finnegan's Wake. NY: Viking, 1939. 1st Amer ed. Fine (lacks dj). *Captain's Bookshelf.* $100/£64

JOYCE, JAMES. Haveth Childers Everywhere. Paris/NY: Henry Babou & Jack Kahane/Fountain, 1930. One of 500 (of 685) numbered. 4to. NF (sm cracks spine head, scattered browning spine) in stiff ptd wraps (lacks glassine) w/remnants of orig slipcase. *Antic Hay.* $500/£321

JOYCE, JAMES. Haveth Childers Everywhere. Paris: Babou & Kahane, 1930. 1st ed. Pb. Wraps in wax paper, as issued. Fine in Fine wax paper, Fine slipcase (sm chips). *Beasley.* $800/£513

JOYCE, JAMES. Haveth Childers Everywhere. London: Faber & Faber, 1931. 1st UK ed. VG in self-wraps (sl dusty). *Williams.* $55/£35

JOYCE, JAMES. Letters. Volume I, Stuart Gilbert (ed); Volumes II and III, Richard Ellmann (ed). NY: Viking, (1966). New, rev ed vol 1; 1st eds vols 2-3. Fine in djs, slipcase (rubbed, edge split). *Jaffe.* $250/£160

JOYCE, JAMES. The Mime of Mick, Nick and the Maggies. The Hague/London: Servire Press/Faber & Faber, 1934. 1st ed. #206/1000. NF in orig tissue wraps. *Old London.* $500/£321

JOYCE, JAMES. A Portrait of the Artist as a Young Man. NY: B.W. Huebsch, 1916. 1st ed preceding the English. Blue cl (sm hole near head of spine, sm dk spot fr panel, patches of discoloration). VG (lacks dj). *Captain's Bookshelf.* $450/£288

JOYCE, JAMES. A Portrait of the Artist as a Young Man. Leipzig: Tauchnitz, 1930. Later ptg, w/ads dated Nov 1930. Card wrappers (foxed, dust-mkd). *Clearwater.* $39/£25

JOYCE, JAMES. A Portrait of the Artist as a Young Man. NY: LEC, 1968. One of 1500 numbered, signed by Brian Keogh (illus). 2 dbl color plts. Leather-backed bds. Announcement inserted. (Name), else Fine in plastic jacket, slipcase. *Bohling.* $75/£48

JOYCE, JAMES. A Portrait of the Artist as a Young Man. NY: LEC, 1968. One of 1500 ptd. Signed by Brian Keogh (illus). Pale grn bds, grn morocco spine, gold lettering. Fine in box. *Appelfeld.* $125/£80

JOYCE, JAMES. Stephen Hero. (NY): New Directions, (1955). 1st ed thus. Fine in dj (spine sunned, sm tear). *Antic Hay.* $45/£29

JOYCE, JAMES. Two Tales of Shem and Shaun. London: Faber & Faber, 1932. 1st UK ed. NF in VG dj (sm chips, lt edgewear). *Williams.* $140/£90

JOYCE, JAMES. Ulysses. Hamburg: Odyssey, (August 1935). 3rd imp. 2 vols. (Name 1/2 title.) Card wrappers (sl rubbed, dusty) in Poor cardbd slipcase. *Clearwater.* $109/£70

JOYCE, JAMES. Ulysses. London: Egoist, 1922. 2nd ed, 1st London ed. #1517/2000. Lg square 8vo. Teg. 1/2 lt blue morocco, ribbed gilt-dec spine, orig wraps bound in. Clean. *D & D.* $1,350/£865

JOYCE, JAMES. Ulysses. Paris: Shakespeare & Co, 1925. 7th ptg, Oct 1925. Blue wraps (cocked, spine rolled, chips, closed tears; prelims stained). *Waverly**. $38/£24

JOYCE, JAMES. Ulysses. Paris: Shakespeare & Co, 1926. 8th ptg. Contemp 3/4 calf, bds (bound w/o wrappers). Internally VG (worn). *Reese*. $100/£64

JOYCE, JAMES. Ulysses. Paris: Shakespeare & Co, 1928. 10th ptg. Blue ptd wrappers. (Upper panel badly stained, abraded sl affecting title, spine title chipped), o/w Good. *Words Etc*. $39/£25

JOYCE, JAMES. Ulysses. NY: Random House, 1934. 1st authorized Amer ed. White cl stamped in red/black. (Spine, edges foxed), o/w Nice in VG dj (sl tanned, nicked). *Reese*. $150/£96

JOYCE, JAMES. Ulysses. NY: Random House, 1934. 1st authorized Amer ed. Red/black-stamped white cl. (Hinges sl starting, spine sl tanned), o/w Good in VG dj (creased tear rear panel, sm nicks, tears). *Reese*. $175/£112

JOYCE, JAMES. Ulysses. NY: LEC, 1935. One of 1500 numbered, signed by Henri Matisse (illus). Sm folio. (Ink sig.) 1/4 morocco slipcase. *Swann**. $2,300/£1,474

JOYCE, JAMES. Ulysses. NY: LEC, 1935. 1st illus ed. Ltd to 1500 signed by Henri Matisse (illus). Lg 4to. Gilt-dec cl. Fine in slipcase (lt worn). *Jaffe*. $3,500/£2,244

JOYCE, JAMES. Ulysses. Bodley Head, 1937. 1st UK trade ed. Very Nice (inscrip) in dj (sl chafed). *Clearwater*. $156/£100

JOYCE, JAMES. Ulysses. London, 1937. 1st trade ed. Fine in dj (spine sl sunned, few sm edge tears, chips, sl rubbed). *Polyanthos*. $275/£176

JOYCE, JOHN ALEXANDER. Jewels of Memory. Washington: Gibson Bros, 1895. 1st ed. 245pp. NF. *Mcgowan*. $150/£96

JOYCE, STANISLAUS. My Brother's Keeper. NY: Viking, (1958). Ltd to 375. NF in acetate dj. *Antic Hay*. $150/£96

JOYCE, STANISLAUS. My Brother's Keeper. Richard Ellmann (ed). NY, 1958. Ltd to 375. Fine in dj (sl rubbed, sm tear). *Polyanthos*. $60/£38

JUDD, LAURA FISH. Honolulu: Sketches of Life in the Hawaiian Islands from 1828 to 1861. Dale L. Morgan (ed). Chicago: Lakeside, 1966. As New in glassine dj. *Cahan*. $20/£13

JUDGE, CYRIL BATHURST. Elizabethan Book-Pirates. Cambridge: Harvard Univ, 1934. Gilt-stamped red cl. (Pencil underlining, margin notes), else VG. *Heller*. $40/£26

JUDOVICH, BERNARD and WILLIAM BATES. Pain Syndromes: Treatment by Paravertebral Nerve Block. Phila, 1949. 3rd ed. Grn cl bds (sl worn). VG. *Doctor's Library*. $75/£48

Judy and Joyce Paper Doll Book. Akron, OH: Saalfield, (1943). 4to. 4 leaves of paper doll clothing. NF in pict wraps (sl creased). *Blue Mountain*. $50/£32

JULIEN, CARL (photos). Ninety-Six: Landmarks of South Carolina's Last Frontier Region. Columbia: Univ of SC, 1950. 1st ed. Frontis. Pict eps. VG (name). *Cahan*. $50/£32

JULLIAN, PHILIPPE. The Symbolists. Phaidon, 1973. 1st ed. Dj (sl torn). *Edwards*. $55/£35

JUNG, C. G. Flying Saucers. R.F.C. Hull (trans). London, 1959. Stated 1st ed, 1st ed in English. (Lt marginal pencil notes), o/w Good+ in Good dj. *Scribe's Perch**. $45/£29

JUNG, C. G. Psychology and Alchemy. NY, 1953. 1st ed in English. VG. *Fye*. $100/£64

JUNG, C. G. The Psychology of Dementia Praecox. A. A. Brill (trans). NY, 1936. Uncut. Internally VG in orig wrappers (frail, spine worn). *Goodrich*. $35/£22

JUNG, C. G. Studies in Word Association. NY: Moffat, Yard, 1919. 1st US ed. Fine. *Beasley*. $125/£80

JUNGER, ERNST. The Glass Bees. NY: Noonday, 1960. 1st ed in English. VG+ (pp dknd) in dj (price-clipped). *Lame Duck*. $35/£22

JUNIUS. The Letters of Junius. London: N.p., 1794. New ed. xxviii,368pp (sl red underlining). Orig calf (lt rubbed). *Karmiole*. $85/£54

JUNOD, HENRY A. Life of a South African Tribe. NY: University Books, (1962). VG in slipcase. *Terramedia*. $75/£48

JUSSIM, ESTELLE and PAUL VANDERBILT. Barbara Crane: Photographs, 1948-1980. (Tucson): Center for Creative Photography/Univ of AZ, 1981. 1st ed. (Owner stamp), else NF in pict stiff wrappers (rubbed). *Cahan*. $40/£26

JUST, ADOLPH. Return to Nature! NY, 1903. 4th ed. Vol 1 complete. Blue cl, gilt. VG. *Doctor's Library*. $45/£29

Justice for Huey P. Newton and the Black Panther Party. (By Huey P. Newton.) Oakland: Committee for Justice for Huey P. Newton, n.d. (1974). 1st ed. VG in pict stiff wraps (white spots). *Petrilla*. $25/£16

JUSTICE, DONALD. Sixteen Poems. Iowa City: Stone Wall, 1970. 1st ed. One of 250. Fine in brn ptd wrappers. *Heller*. $150/£96

K

KABOTIE, FRED. Designs from the Ancient Mimbrenos, with a Hopi Interpretation. Northland, (1982). 2nd ed. Fine. *Oregon*. $35/£22

KADARE, ISMAIL. Chronicle in Stone. NY: Meredith, 1987. 1st Amer ed. Dk blue cl (sl bumped), gilt. NF in Fine dj. *Blue Mountain*. $17/£11

KAFKA, FRANZ. America. Edwin & Willa Muir (trans). London: Routledge, 1938. 1st Eng ed. Attractive. *Clearwater*. $55/£35

KAFKA, FRANZ. Amerika. Norfolk: New Directions, 1940. 1st US ed. NF in dj (spine sl faded). *Lame Duck*. $250/£160

KAFKA, FRANZ. The Country Doctor. Vera Leslie (trans/illus). Oxford: Counterpoint, 1945. 1st separate ed. VG+ in illus wraps (soiled). *Lame Duck*. $100/£64

KAFKA, FRANZ. The Diaries of Franz Kafka. Max Brod (ed). London: Secker & Warburg, 1948. 1st Eng ed. 2 vols. NF in dj (spines dknd, sm chips). *Captain's Bookshelf*. $100/£64

KAFKA, FRANZ. A Franz Kafka Miscellany: Pre-Fascist Exile. NY: Twice a Year, 1946. 2nd ed. VG in dj (foxed). *Cahan*. $15/£10

KAFKA, FRANZ. The Great Wall of China. NY: Schocken, 1946. 1st US ed. VG+ in VG dj (spine tanned, chip, 2-inch tear foot, sm snag). *Lame Duck*. $100/£64

KAFKA, FRANZ. In the Penal Colony. Willa and Edwin Muir (trans). LEC, 1987. One of 800 signed by Michael Hafftka (illus). 4 lithos. Hand-made, hand-sewn paper binding, exposed thongs. Mint in pub's fleece-lined fldg cl box. *Pirages*. $275/£176

KAFKA, FRANZ. Metamorphosis. NY: Vanguard, (1946). 1st Amer ed of this trans by A.L. Loyd. Pict cl. Fine in VG dj (sm inner mend, sm corner chips). *Reese*. $125/£80

KAFKA, FRANZ. Metamorphosis. Willa & Edwin Muir (trans). NY: LEC, (1984). Ltd to 1500 signed by Jose Luis Cuevas (illus). Morocco-backed pastepaper bds. Monthly newsletter laid in. VF in slipcase. *Bromer*. $400/£256

KAFKA, FRANZ. The Metamorphosis. London: Parton Press, 1937. 1st ed in English. 1/4 cl, paper label upper bd. VG+ in orig clear plastic wrapper (sl worn, chipped, lacks piece fr panel bottom) w/blue-ptd price of 3/6d net on fr flap. *Williams*. $897/£575

KAFKA, FRANZ. The Trial. NY: Knopf, 1937. 1st US ed. VG in dj (fr panel sl stained). *Lame Duck*. $350/£224

KAFKA, FRANZ. The Trial. Avon: LEC, 1975. One of 2000 numbered, signed by Alan Cober (illus). Full red leather titled in gilt/blind. Fine in pub's slipcase. *Hermitage*. $175/£112

KAGAN, SOLOMON. Contributions of Early Jews to American Medicine. Boston, 1934. 1st ed. VG. *Fye*. $65/£42

KAGAN, SOLOMON. Jewish Contributions to Medicine in America from Colonial Times to the Present. Boston, 1939. 2nd ed. VG. *Fye*. $250/£160

KAHLENBERG, MARY and A. BERLANT. The Navajo Blanket. L.A. County Museum of Art, (1972). 1st ed. Fine in pict wraps. *Oregon*. $70/£45

KAHLENBERG, MARY and A. BERLANT. The Navajo Blanket. L.A.: Praeger, (1972). VG in wraps. *Perier*. $50/£32

KAHLER, HEINZ. Hagia Sophia. NY, 1967. 4 color plts, 100 b/w plts and plans. Good in dj. *Washton*. $100/£64

KAHMEN, VOLKER. Art History of Photography. Brian Tubb (trans). NY: Viking, 1974. 1st US ed. 370 b/w photo plts. Fine in NF illus dj. *Cahan*. $60/£38

KAHN, EDGAR M. (ed). From Land's End to the Ferry. SF: Black Vine Press, (1942). One of 200. Inscribed. 1/2 cl, bds. Fine. *Harrington*. $40/£26

KAHN, FRITZ. Man in Structure and Function. NY, 1943. 1st ed. 2 vols. Buckram (sl worn). VG. *Doctor's Library*. $75/£48

KAHN, HERMAN. On Thermonuclear War. Princeton, NJ: Princeton Univ, 1960. 1st ed. Brick-red cl. Fine in dj. *Karmiole*. $50/£32

KAHNWEILER, DANIEL-HENRY. Juan Gris, His Life and Work. Douglas Cooper (trans). NY: Curt Valentin, 1947. 1st ed. Tipped-in frontis, 2 tipped-in color plts. Tan cl (cvrs sl bowed). *Karmiole*. $75/£48

KAHNWEILER, DANIEL-HENRY. Juan Gris, His Life and Work. NY: Abrams, 1968. Rev ed. White-emb black cl. VF in color dj (frayed). *Europa*. $218/£140

KAHNWEILER, DANIEL-HENRY. Juan Gris, His Life and Work. Douglas Cooper (trans). NY: Abrams, 1969. Rev ed. Illus cl. NF. *Cahan*. $175/£112

KAHNWEILER, DANIEL-HENRY. The Sculptures of Picasso. London: Rodney Phillips, 1948 (1949). 1st Eng ed. Cl-backed glazed paper over bds. (Bds lt rubbed; name ep), else NF. *Cahan*. $150/£96

KAKONIS, TOM. Michigan Roll. NY: St. Martin's, 1988. 1st ed, 1st bk. VF in dj. *Mordida*. $45/£29

KALLIR, OTTO. Egon Schiele. NY: Crown, 1966. 243 plts (18 tipped-in color). Beige cl. VG in pub's slipcase. *Metropolitan*. $300/£192

KALLIR, OTTO. Grandma Moses. NY: Abrams, 1973. Fine in Fine dj. *Metropolitan*. $92/£59

KAMAL, AHMAD. Land Without Laughter. NY, 1940. 1st ed. Frontis port. Dj (chipped). *Edwards*. $31/£20

KAMES, HENRY HOME. Elements of Criticism. Boston, 1796. 1st Amer ed. 2 vols. (Foxing, vol 1 lacks fr flyleaf.) Full calf (rebacked, sl worn). *New Hampshire*. $20/£13

KAMINSKY, STUART M. Bullet for a Star. NY: St. Martin's, 1977. 1st ed. (Erasure fep), o/w Fine in dj (sl wear). *Mordida*. $100/£64

KAMINSKY, STUART M. A Cold Red Sunrise. NY: Scribner, 1988. 1st ed. Fine in dj (price-clipped). *Mordida*. $45/£29

KAMINSKY, STUART M. Exercise in Terror. NY: St. Martin's, 1985. 1st ed. VF in dj. *Mordida*. $45/£29

KAMINSKY, STUART M. The Howard Hughes Affair. NY: St. Martins, 1979. 1st ed. Fine in dj (sl worn). *Else Fine*. $50/£32

KAMINSKY, STUART M. Never Cross a Vampire. NY: St. Martin's, 1980. 1st ed. Fine in dj (closed tear). *Mordida*. $65/£42

KAMINSKY, STUART M. You Bet Your Life. NY: St. Martin, 1978. 1st ed. Fine in NF dj (few sm closed tears). *Janus*. $65/£42

KAMINSKY, STUART M. You Bet Your Life. NY: St. Martins, 1978. 1st ed. Fine in dj (sm tears). *Else Fine*. $60/£38

KAMOURASKA. The Chickenborough Chit-Chat Club. Tinsley Bros, 1877. 3 vols in 1. Good (spine bumped, chipped). *Tiger*. $47/£30

KANAGA, TILLIE (comp). History of Napa County. W. F. Wallace (ed). (Oakland: Enquirer Print, 1901.) 1st ed. Map. Gilt-lettered cl (rubbed, sl cocked). Overall VG (sl dampstain fore-edge last few leaves). *Argonaut*. $300/£192

KANAVEL, A. B. Infections of the Hand. 1925. 5th ed. (Few pp corners bent, cl sl mkd, worn, fr inner hinge cracked; ex-lib w/stamps.) *Whitehart*. $28/£18

KANAVEL, ALLEN B. Infections of the Hand. Phila: Lea & Febiger, 1921. 4th ed. Color frontis. VG (sl shelfwear). *Glaser*. $75/£48

KANDEL, LENORE. The Love Book. SF: Stolen Paper Eds, 1966. 1st ed, 2nd issue. NF in slim wraps. *Sclanders*. $39/£25

KANDINSKY, WASSILY. Concerning the Spiritual in Art 1912. NY: Wittenborn, 1947. 1st ed this revision. Frontis. VG in dec wrappers (lt dust soiled). *Reese*. $50/£32

KANE, ELISHA KENT. Arctic Explorations. Phila: Childs & Peterson, 1856. 2 vols. 2 engr tps, 18 plts, 2 fldg maps. VG overall (sl worn, bumped, ends frayed). *Waverly*. $121/£78

KANE, ELISHA KENT. Arctic Explorations. Phila, 1857. 2 vols. 464; 467pp. (Extrems chipped), else Good set. *King*. $135/£87

KANE, ELISHA KENT. Arctic Explorations. London, 1894. Fldg map. (Spine sl rubbed, faded.) *Edwards*. $39/£25

KANE, ELISHA KENT. Arctic Explorations: The Second Grinnell Expedition in Search of Sir John Franklin, 1853, '54, '55. NY, 1857. 2 vols. 2 fldg maps. (Vol 1 plts dampstained in corners; spine ends chipped, vol 1 cl worn.) *Swann*. $80/£51

KANE, ELISHA KENT. Arctic Explorations: The Second Grinnell Expedition in Search of Sir John Franklin, 1853, 54, 55. Phila, 1856. 1st ed. 2 vols. 2 frontispieces, 18 plts, 2 extra-engr tps, 3 maps (2 fldg). Blind-stamped cl (worn). *Kane*. $95/£61

KANE, ELISHA KENT. Arctic Explorations: The Second Grinnell Expedition...1853, '54, '55. Phila: (Childs & Peterson), 1856. 2 vols. Inserted engr titles w/vignettes, steel-engr port frontispieces, 18 steel-engr plts, 3 litho charts (2 fldg). Pub's dk brn grained cl, pict blind-blocked dec, gilt-stamped spine. Splendid. *Book Block*. $395/£253

KANE, ELISHA KENT. Arctic Explorations: The Second Grinnell Expedition...1853, '54, '55. Phila: Childs & Peterson, 1856. 1st ed. 2 vols. 464pp, 12 plts, port, 3 maps (1 fldg); 457pp, 8 plts, port, map, fldg diag. Marbled eps, edges. 1/2 leather, marbled paper over bds. (Prelims lt foxed; rubbed, worn.) Parmer. $250/£160

KANE, ELISHA KENT. The U.S. Grinnell Expedition in Search of Sir John Franklin. NY, 1854. Map. Pub's gilt-pict cl (rubbed, backstrip faded). Swann*. $57/£37

KANE, GRACE FRANKS. Myths and Legends of the Mackinacs and the Lake Region. Cincinnati, 1897. 1st ed. 159pp. (Ink inscrip; extrems worn.) King. $85/£54

KANE, HARNETT T. Gentlemen, Swords and Pistols. NY: Wm. Morrow, 1951. 1st ed. NF in dj (lt edgewear). Sadlon. $15/£10

KANE, HARNETT T. New Orleans Woman: A Biographical Novel of Myra Clark Gaines. NY: Doubleday, 1947. 1st ed. Inscribed. (Sm stain cvr.) Dj (sl edgeworn). Sadlon. $30/£19

KANE, PATRICIA E. 300 Years of American Seating Furniture. Boston: NYGS, 1976. 1st ed. Color frontis, 17 color plts. Dj. Edwards. $39/£25

KANE, PAUL. Wanderings of an Artist. Rutland, VT: Charles E. Tuttle, (1968). VG (lt pencilled) in dj (sl worn). Lien. $30/£19

KANN, JEROME H. California's Code Time Table.... SF: L.R. Dempster, 1902. Brn cl (worn). Sound. Boswell. $45/£29

KANNER, LEO. Folklore of the Teeth. NY, 1936. 1st ed. VG in dj (worn). Doctor's Library. $75/£48

KANSAS STATE HISTORICAL SOCIETY. Collections of Kansas State Historical Society 1911-12. Topeka, 1912. 1st ed. NF. Turpen. $55/£35

KANTOR, MACKINLEY. Diversey. NY: Coward-McCann, 1928. 1st ed, 1st bk. VG. Beasley. $35/£22

KAPPEL, A. W. and W. E. KIRBY. British and European Butterflies (Macrolepidoptera). London, n.d. (late 19th cent). 273pp, 30 color lithos. Teg. Gilt-dec cl. VG +. Mikesh. $225/£144

KAPPEL, A. W. and W. E. KIRBY. British and European Butterflies and Moths. London/NY, (1896). 1st ed. 30 full-pg color plts. Pict cl. (Cvr wear), o/w VG. New Hampshire*. $50/£32

KARAGEORGHIS, VASSOS. Salamis in Cyprus. London: Thames & Hudson, (1969). 17 color plts. Good in dj. Archaeologia. $65/£42

KARAGEORGHIS, VASSOS. Salamis. NY/St. Louis/SF: McGraw-Hill, 1969. 1st ed. 145 plts, 33 plans. (Lacks fep, dj scotch-taped to cvrs, ex-lib), o/w VG in dj (lib sticker). Worldwide. $35/£22

KARNS, HARRY J. (trans). Unknown Arizona and Sonora, 1693-1721. Tucson, AZ: AZ Silhouettes, 1954. Ltd to 1500 numbered. Map in back pocket. VG in dj. Lien. $60/£38

KAROLEVITZ, ROBERT F. Doctors of the Old West. Seattle: Superior, (1967). 1st ed. Dj (sm spine tear). Dawson. $30/£19

KARPINSKI, LOUIS C. Bibliography of Mathematical Works Printed in America Through 1850. Ann Arbor, 1940. (Shaken, spine sl faded.) Swann*. $138/£88

KARPMAN, BEN. Case Studies in the Psychopathology of Crime.... Washington: Medical Science, 1933, 1947, 1947, 1948. 1st ed. 4 vols. Color plt vol 3, vol 4. Pebbled black cl. Generally VG (pg loose vol 1; vol 4 tp creased, scotch-taped, label removed spine). Gach. $350/£224

KARPOVICH, PETER. Adventures in Artificial Respiration. NY, 1953. 1st ed. VG. Fye. $125/£80

KARR, CHARLES LEE, JR. and CAROLL ROBBINS KARR. Remington Handguns. Harrisburg, PA: Military Service, 1947. 1st ed. Fldg diag. Pict cl (rubbed). VG in dj (sl chipped). Cahan. $45/£29

KARSH, YOUSUF. Faces of Destiny, Portraits by Karsh. Chicago, (1946). 1st ed. Rev slip. (Ink inscrip; spine worn.) King. $35/£22

KARSH, YOUSUF. Faces of Our Time. Toronto, (1971). Signed, inscribed presentation. 48 full-pg ports. VG in dj (frayed). King. $100/£64

KARSH, YOUSUF. Faces of Our Time. Toronto/Buffalo: Univ of Toronto, 1972. Fine in dj (sl edgeworn). Cahan. $50/£32

KARSH, YOUSUF. In Search of Greatness. NY: Knopf, 1962. 1st ed. (Owner stamp, name), else NF in Good dj. Cahan. $25/£16

KARSHAN, DONALD. Malevich: The Graphic Work 1913-1930, a Print Catalogue Raisonne. Jerusalem, 1975. Dj. Swann*. $172/£110

KASANIN, JACOB S. (ed). Language and Thought in Schizophrenia. L.A.: Univ of CA, 1946. 1st ed. Grn cl. VG. Gach. $35/£22

KASTNER, JOSEPH. A Species of Eternity. NY, 1977. 1st ed. Dj (sl rubbed). Edwards. $39/£25

KATZ, STEVE. The Exaggerations of Peter Prince. NY: Holt, (1968). 1st ed. (Edges sl dknd), else Nice in dj (sm edge tear). Reese. $30/£19

KATZ, STEVE. Stolen Stories. NY: Fiction Collective, (1984). 1st ed. Fine in VG + dj (rubbed; short tears). Between The Covers. $45/£29

KAUFFELD, CARL. Snakes and Snake Hunting. NY, 1957. Tan cl. VG. Price. $29/£19

KAUFMAN, GEORGE S. and MARC CONNELLY. Beggar on Horseback. NY: Boni & Liveright, 1924. 1st ed. VG (name) in VG dj. Beasley. $100/£64

KAUFMAN, PAUL. Indian Lore of the Muskingum Headwaters of Ohio. N.p., (1973). 1st ed. Pict cl, gilt. Fine (issued w/o dj). Sadlon. $20/£13

KAUFMAN, PAUL. Indian Lore of the Muskingum Headwaters of Ohio. (Walnut Creek, OH, 1973.) 1st ed. Fine. Mcclintock. $25/£16

KAUFMANN, C. M. An Altarpiece of the Apocalypse from Master Bertram's Workshop in Hamburg. London: Victoria & Albert Museum, 1968. 24 plts. Good in wrappers. Washton. $25/£16

KAUFMANN, E. (ed). An American Architecture: Frank Lloyd Wright. NY: Horizon, 1955. 1st ed. Dec cvr. Good+ in dj (chipped). Scribe's Perch*. $42/£27

KAUFMANN, E. Architecture in the Age of Reason. Cambridge, 1955. Good. Washton. $50/£32

KAVAN, ANNA. A Bright Green Field. London: Peter Owen, 1958. 1st UK ed. Fine in dj (sl production flaw rear panel). Williams. $39/£25

KAVAN, ANNA. Ice, a Novel. London: Peter Owen, (1967). 1st ed. Signed, inscribed. (Owner stamp), o/w VG in black dj (edgeworn). Reese. $175/£112

KAVANAGH, DAN. (Pseud of Julian Barnes.) Duffy. Cape, (1980). 1st ed. VG in dj. Ash. $62/£40

KAVANAGH, DAN. (Pseud of Julian Barnes.) Duffy. London, 1980. 1st Eng ed, 1st bk. Fine in dj. Clearwater. $55/£35

KAVANAGH, DAN. (Pseud of Julian Barnes.) Fiddle City. London: Cape, 1981. 1st ed. Lame Duck. $350/£224

KAVANAGH, DAN. (Pseud of Julian Barnes.) Going to the Dogs. NY: Pantheon, (1987). 1st ed. Fine in dj. Antic Hay. $17/£11

KAVANAGH, MORGAN. Origin of Language and Myths. London: Sampson Low, Son, & Marston, 1871. 1st ed. 2 vols. xl,436; vi,(ii), 594pp (sm tear fr edge 1 leaf. Teg. 3/4 tan calf, marbled bds (leather split at bottom fr joint vol 1, rubbed, bumped, lacks labels), gilt spines. NF internally. Blue Mountain. $65/£42

KAY, GERTRUDE ALICE. Us Kids and the Circus. Saalfield, 1928. 6.5x8.5. Pict bds (bumped). VG (inky finger mk 1pg). *My Bookhouse*. $70/£45

KAYE-SMITH, SHEILA. Little England. London, 1918. 1st ed. NF (spine sl sunned, extrems sl rubbed). *Polyanthos*. $25/£16

KAZANTZAKIS, NIKOS. England. NY: S&S, (1965). 1st Amer ed. Tan cl-backed bds (bumped). NF in VG pict white dj (spotted, spine dknd). *Blue Mountain*. $40/£26

KAZANTZAKIS, NIKOS. Japan China. NY: S&S, 1963. 1st ed. Fine in NF dj (lt soiled, sl edgeworn). *Fuller & Saunders*. $25/£16

KAZANTZAKIS, NIKOS. Journey to the Morea. NY: S&S, 1965. 1st US ed. VG in dj. *Lame Duck*. $35/£22

KAZANTZAKIS, NIKOS. The Last Temptation. Oxford: Bruno Cassirer, 1960. 1st Eng ed. VG in VG dj (spine dknd, chipped). *Lame Duck*. $75/£48

KAZANTZAKIS, NIKOS. Report to Greco. P. A. Bien (trans). NY: S&S, (1965). 1st Amer ed. Brn cl (sl rubbed), gilt. NF in Fine dj. *Blue Mountain*. $50/£32

KAZANTZAKIS, NIKOS. Report to Greco. P. Bien (trans). NY, 1965. 1st ed. Dj (sl frayed). *Typographeum*. $22/£14

KAZANTZAKIS, NIKOS. Report to Greco. Oxford: Cassirer, 1965. 1st UK ed. VG+ (ink inscrip) in dj. *Williams*. $39/£25

KAZANTZAKIS, NIKOS. Serpent and Lily. Berkeley, CA: Univ of CA, 1980. 1st ed in English. NF in dj (lt soiled). *Lame Duck*. $25/£16

KAZANTZAKIS, NIKOS. Spain. NY: S&S, 1963. 1st US ed. VG+ in VG dj. *Lame Duck*. $35/£22

KAZANTZAKIS, NIKOS. Spain. Amy Mims (trans). NY: S&S, 1963. 1st Amer ed. Rust cl-backed lt gray bds. Fine in NF dj (sl soiled). *Blue Mountain*. $40/£26

KAZANTZAKIS, NIKOS. Three Plays: Christopher Columbus, Melissa, Kouros. Athena Gianakas Dallas (trans). NY: S&S, (1969). 1st Amer ed. Brn cl, gilt. (Rep sl soiled), else Fine in NF dj (top edges bumped, spine dknd). *Blue Mountain*. $35/£22

KAZANTZAKIS, NIKOS. Toda Raba. NY, 1964. 1st Amer ed. Fine in Fine dj. *Polyanthos*. $35/£22

KAZANTZAKIS, NIKOS. Todo Raba. Amy Mims (trans). NY: S&S, 1964. 1st Amer ed. Rust cl-backed grn bds. VG (rear bd stained) in dj (soiled, sl bumped). *Blue Mountain*. $40/£26

KEAN, ABRAM. Young and Old Ahead, a Millionaire in Seals, Being the Life History of.... London: Heath, Cranton, 1935. Inscribed 1941. 8 plts. VG. *High Latitude*. $45/£29

KEARNEY, BELLE. A Slaveholder's Daughter. St. Louis: St. Louis Christian Advocate Co, (1900). 2nd ed. Uncut. Ptd grn cl. VG. *Second Life*. $95/£61

KEARNY, THOMAS. General Philip Kearny, Battle Soldier of Five Wars. NY: Putnam, 1937. 1st ed. Frontis port. Blue cl, gilt. VF in pict dj (sl chipped). *Argonaut*. $125/£80

KEARTON, C. In the Land of the Lion. NY: McBride, 1930. 1st ed. Dec eps. VG+ in VG dj. *Mikesh*. $20/£13

KEARTON, R. A Naturalist's Pilgrimage. London, 1926. 8 plts. (Cl sl mkd.) *Maggs*. $34/£22

KEASBEY, EDWARD QUINTON. The Law of Electric Wires in Streets and Highways. Chicago: Callaghan, 1900. 2nd ed. Contemp sheep (worn, chafed). Sound. *Boswell*. $125/£80

KEATE, GEORGE. An Account of the Pelew Islands, Situated in the Western Part of the Pacific Ocean.... London: Capt. Wilson, 1789. 3rd ed. xviii,378pp; 16 plts (11 fldg), fldg map. Marbled eps. Full morocco. (Lt foxed, ex-lib; rebacked, back cvr stained, edges rubbed), o/w VG. *Worldwide*. $425/£272

KEATING, BERN. The Flamboyant Mr. Colt and His Deadly Six-Shooter. GC: Doubleday, 1978. 1st ed. Cl-backed bds, gilt-lettered spine. Fine in dj. *Argonaut*. $30/£19

KEATING, H. R. F. Murder Must Appetize. London: Lemon Tree, 1975. 1st ed. NF (sm ink letter fep) in glossy pict bds, w/o dj as issued. *Janus*. $45/£29

KEATING, WILLIAM H. Narrative of an Expedition to the Source of St. Peter's River, Lake Winnepeek, Lake of the Woods, &C.... London: Geo. B. Whittaker, 1825. 1st Eng ed. 2 vols. 8vo. xvi,458; 248,156pp; 8 plts (2 hand-colored), 3 tables, fldg map colored in outline. 19th cent calf, marbled bds (vol 1 rebacked, old backstrip laid down, inner hinges reinforced w/cl tape; spine vol 2 sl rubbed, chipped). Howes K20. *Karmiole*. $600/£385

KEATING, WILLIAM H. Narrative of an Expedition to the Source of St. Peter's River.... Minneapolis: Ross & Haines, 1959. Rpt. 2 vols in 1. Fldg map. Fine in dj. Howes K20. *Bohling*. $20/£13

KEATING, WILLIAM H. Narrative of an Expedition to the Source of the St. Peter's River.... Phila, 1824. 1st ed, w/half-titles. 2 vols. 8vo. Map (repaired, sl loss), 15 plts. Contemp tree sheep (skillfully rebacked; eps renewed). Howes K20. *Swann**. $747/£479

KEATS, JOHN. Endymion, a Poetic Romance. London: Golden Cockerel, (1943-1947). One of 500 ptd. John Buckland-Wright (engrs). Teg. Brn gilt-stamped linen bds, vellum spine. (3pp browned), o/w Fine. *Appelfeld*. $450/£288

KEATS, JOHN. Lamia, Isabella, the Eve of Saint Agnes and Other Poems. (Waltham Saint Lawrence): Golden Cockerel, 1928. One of 500 numbered. 1/4 morocco. *Swann**. $517/£331

KEATS, JOHN. The Letters. Oxford, 1948. 3rd ed. Frontis. Good. *Cox*. $23/£15

KEATS, JOHN. The Letters. M. Buxton Forman (ed). NY: Oxford, 1935. Rev ed. Partly unopened. Red buckram, paper label. Fine. *Hartfield*. $95/£61

KEATS, JOHN. The Letters. M. Buxton Forman (ed). Oxford, 1935. 2nd ed. Frontis. Good. *Cox*. $39/£25

KEATS, JOHN. Poems. John Middleton Murry (ed). Peter Nevill, 1948. 1st ed. Michael Ayrton (illus). VG in dj (few closed tears). *Words Etc*. $70/£45

KEATS, JOHN. The Poetical Works and Other Writings.... H. Buxton Forman (ed). London: Reeves & Turner, 1883. 1st ptg this ed. 4 vols. 8vo. Gilt-dec cl. (Bkpls, spines sl sunned, nicks), o/w VG. *Reese*. $550/£353

KEATS, JOHN. Unpublished Poem; to His Sister Fanny. Boston: Bibliophile Soc, 1909. Ltd to 489. Vellum-backed canvas bds. (Spine sl dknd, corners sl rubbed), o/w VG. *Words Etc*. $257/£165

KEEFE, CHARLES (ed). The American House. NY, 1924. (Sl internal soil; cl worn, soiled.) Leather labels (chipped). *Freeman**. $80/£51

KEEFE, CHARLES (ed). The American House. NY: UPC Book Co, 1924. 1st ed. 218 Fine b/w plts. NF in beige linen, ptd morocco labels. *Captain's Bookshelf*. $225/£144

KEELER, HARRY STEPHEN. 10 Hours. NY: Dutton, (1937). Dj (short closed tears, sl edgewear, soil). *Metropolitan**. $28/£18

KEELY, ROBERT and G. G. DAVIS. In Arctic Seas. Phila: Rufus C. Hartranft, 1892. 1st ed. 524pp. White dec cl (soiled). Contents VG. *New Hampshire**. $60/£38

KEEN, WILLIAM W. and J. WILLIAM WHITE. An American Textbook of Surgery. Phila: Saunders, 1896. 2nd ed. 1248pp. (Newly rebacked.) Internally VG. *Goodrich*. $95/£61

KEENE, CAROLYN. By the Light of the Study Lamp. G&D, 1934. Early thick ed w/internal illus. 5x7.5. 215pp + ads. Purple cl (bumped). Lists 4 titles. VG in dj (faded, edges ragged). *My Bookhouse.* $90/£58

KEENE, CAROLYN. The Haunted Lagoon. G&D, 1959. 5x7.5. 182pp. Greenish tweed cl (sl shelfworn). Lists to Bamboo Bird. VG + in dj (nicked, sl edgeworn). *My Bookhouse.* $25/£16

KEENE, CAROLYN. The Hidden Window Mystery. G&D, 1956. 1st ed w/18 Danas on rear flap. 5x7.5. 214pp. Blue tweed cl (sl shelfworn). VG in dj (edgeworn, top edge ragged). *My Bookhouse.* $35/£22

KEENE, CAROLYN. The Mystery of the Locked Room. G&D, 1938. 5x7.5. 218pp. Purple cl. Lists to #11. (Frontis foxed, pp browned), else VG + in dj (chipped). *My Bookhouse.* $30/£19

KEENE, CAROLYN. Nancy Drew Mystery Story: The Sign of the Twisted Candles. NY: G&D, 1933. R. H. Tandy (illus). 12mo. 217pp; 4 glossy internals; ad pg at end lists Larkspur Lane (1933) as latest in series, indicating this copy ptd in yr of pub. Orange 'glass' eps. Blue pict cl-cvrd bds, orange dec. Good + (eps lt soiled; cvr spotted). *Book Adoption.* $75/£48

KEENE, CAROLYN. The Portrait in the Sand. G&D, 1943. 5x7.5. 216pp (browned). Purple cl (sl spotted). Lists only to this title. VG + in dj (edgeworn). *My Bookhouse.* $60/£38

KEENE, CAROLYN. The Secret at the Hermitage. G&D, 1936. 1st ed. 5x7.5. 218pp. Purple cl (sl shelfworn). Lists only to this title. NF in dj (sl edgeworn). *My Bookhouse.* $250/£160

KEENE, CAROLYN. The Secret in the Old Attic. G&D, 1944. 1st ed. 5x7.5. 216pp (acidic). Blue cl (sl shelfworn). VG in dj (edgeworn, chipped). *My Bookhouse.* $55/£35

KEENE, FOXHALL and ALDEN HATCH. Full Tilt: The Sporting Memoirs. NY: Derrydale, (1938). Frontis. (Pencil note fep.) All pp except prelims blank. Blue cl. *Truepenny.* $75/£48

KEENE, J. HARRINGTON. Fly Fishing and Fly Making. NY: Forest & Stream, 1898. 3rd ed. 159pp + 16pp ads. Tipped-in materials in Fine condition. Gilt-dec gray cl. VG + (tp reinforced at gutter). *Bowman.* $150/£96

KEENE, J. HARRINGTON. The Mystery of Handwriting. Boston, 1896. 1st ed. 155pp. Pict cl (dknd, rubbed). *King.* $45/£29

Keeper's Travels in Search of His Master. (By Edward Augustus Kendall.) Phila: Johnson & Warner, 1808. Early Amer ed, ptd by Lydia Bailey. 12mo. Engr frontis, 87pp;(1)leaf. (Sl foxed.) Contemp plain bds (sl worn). Cl case provided. *Oinonen*.* $50/£32

Keeper's Travels in Search of His Master. (By Edward Augustus Kendall.) Phila: Johnson & Warner, 1808. 12mo. Full-pg copper engr frontis, vi,87pp + 2pp contents (browning, damp stain fore-edge feps). Orig plain bds (spine chipped). VG. *Hobbyhorse.* $175/£112

KEEPING, CHARLES. The Christmas Story. NY: Watts, 1969. 1st US ed. 8 1/2 x 10 1/2. 32pp. VG in dj. *Cattermole.* $35/£22

KEEPING, CHARLES. Classic Tales of the Macabre. NY: Bedrick, 1987. 1st ed. 6 1/4 x 9 1/4. 171pp. VG (ex-lib, mks) in dj. *Cattermole.* $20/£13

KEEPING, CHARLES. Inter-City. OUP, 1977. 1st ed. Folio. (32pp). Pict bds. NF w/price £2.95 ptd back cvr. *Bookmark.* $31/£20

KEEPING, CHARLES. Joseph's Yard. NY: Watts, 1969. 1st US ed. 8 1/2 x 11. 32pp. Pict cl. Fine in dj. *Cattermole.* $60/£38

KEEPING, CHARLES. Railway Passage. OUP, 1974. 1st ed. Folio. (32pp). Pict bds. Fine in dj (edgeworn). *Bookmark.* $37/£24

KEEPING, CHARLES. Richard. OUP, 1973. 1st ed. Folio. (32pp). Pict bds (edge sl rubbed). NF in pict dj. *Bookmark.* $34/£22

KEEPING, CHARLES. Richard. OUP, 1973. 1st ed. 8 1/2 x 11 1/4. 32pp. Pict bds. VG in dj. *Cattermole.* $60/£38

KEEPING, CHARLES. Sammy Streetsinger. OUP, 1985. 1st ed. 8 1/2 x 11 1/4. 36pp. Glossy bds. Fine. *Cattermole.* $40/£26

KEEPING, CHARLES. Shaun and the Cart-Horse. NY: Franklin Watts, 1966. 1st US ed. Obl sm 4to. Pict cl. Fine in VG + dj (rear lt soiled). *Book Adoption.* $50/£32

KEEPING, CHARLES. Through the Window. NY: Watts, 1970. 1st ed. 11 x 8 1/2. 32pp. VG. *Cattermole.* $45/£29

KEEPING, CHARLES. Wasteground Circus. OUP, 1975. 1st ed. Folio. (32pp). Pict bds. Fine in matching dj. *Bookmark.* $34/£22

KEEPING, CHARLES. Wasteground Circus. OUP, 1975. 1st ed. 8 1/2 x 11. 32pp. Pict bds. As New in dj. *Cattermole.* $60/£38

KEEPING, CHARLES. Willie's Fire Engine. NY: OUP, 1980. 1st ed. 9 x 12. 32pp. Glossy bds. As New. *Cattermole.* $30/£19

KEESE, JOHN (ed). The Floral Keepsake. NY: Leavitt & Allen, n.d. (ca 1854?). 30 color litho plts, incl extra pict title, frontis. (Foxing, few sigs sprung.) Pub's gilt-stamped cl (worn). *Oinonen*.* $375/£240

KEIFER, JOSEPH. Slavery and Four Years of War. NY: Putnam, 1900. 1st ed. 2 vols. Teg. NF. *Archer.* $25/£16

KEIGHTLEY, THOMAS. An Account of the Life, Opinions, and Writings of John Milton. Chapman & Hall, 1855. 1st ed. (Tp soiled), o/w Good + in later cl (soiled). *Poetry Bookshop.* $31/£20

KEILLOR, GARRISON. Leaving Home. (NY): Viking, (1987). One of 1500 numbered, signed. Fine in Fine slipcase. *Lenz.* $50/£32

KEILLOR, GARRISON. Leaving Home. Faber, 1988. 1st UK ed. NF in dj. *Williams.* $22/£14

KEILLOR, GARRISON. We Are Still Married. Franklin Center, PA: Franklin Library, 1989. 'Limited first edition,' signed. Port. Aeg. Full gilt-stamped leather. VG. *King.* $45/£29

KEIM, DE B. RANDOLPH. Sheridan's Troopers on the Border. Phila, 1870. Pub's cl (spine ends frayed). *Swann*.* $80/£51

KEIM, DE B. RANDOLPH. Sheridan's Troopers on the Border. Phila: David McKay, 1885. 2nd ed. 308pp. Ptd bds (sl worn). *Dumont.* $75/£48

KEITH, ARTHUR. Menders of the Maimed. London, 1919. 1st ed. Contents Fine (outer hinges cracked). *Fye.* $200/£128

KEITH, ELMER. Elmer Keith's Big Game Hunting. Boston, 1948. 1st ed. (Sl worn.) Dj (chipped, frayed). *Oinonen*.* $80/£51

KEITH, ELMER. Keith's Rifles for Large Game. Huntington, 1946. 1st ed. Silver-gilt black cl (sl worn). *Oinonen*.* $180/£115

KEITH, ELMER. Keith's Rifles for Large Game. Huntington: Standard, 1946. (Sl worn.) Dj (tattered). *Oinonen*.* $230/£147

KEITH, ELMER. Keith's Rifles for Large Game. Huntington: Standard, 1946. 1st ed. Frontis. Photo eps. Black cl; silver lettering, decs. VG (lt corner wear). *Backman.* $425/£272

KEITHAN, EDWARD L. Monuments in Cedar. Seattle: Superior, 1963. 1st ed. Fine in dj. *High Latitude.* $30/£19

KELEHER, WILLIAM A. The Fabulous Frontier: Twelve New Mexico Items. Santa Fe, NM: Rydal, (April 1946). 2nd ed. Inscribed. (Gilt sl dull.) Dj (sl tattered, edges chipped). *Sadlon.* $50/£32

KELEHER, WILLIAM A. Maxwell Land Grant. NY, 1942. 1st ed. Fldg map pocket. NF. No dj as issued. *Turpen.* $295/£189

KELEHER, WILLIAM A. Violence in Lincoln County. Albuquerque: Univ of NM, 1957. 1st ed. VG in dj. *Dumont.* $75/£48

KELLER, ALLAN. Scandalous Lady: The Life and Times of Madame Restell.... NY, 1981. 1st ed. VG in Good dj. *Doctor's Library.* $30/£19

KELLER, DAVID H. The Thing in the Cellar. Millheim, PA, n.d. (1940). 1st ed. Signed. Ptd wrappers. *Swann*.* $80/£51

KELLER, ELI. History of the Keller Family. Tiffin: Will H. Good, 1905. 1st ed. Grn cl (Pg ends stained), o/w VG. *Archer.* $65/£42

KELLER, GEORGE. A Trip Across the Plains and Life in California. Oakland: Biobooks, (1955). Ltd to 500. Dk brn buckram (extrems sl worn, sm dent fr cvr), gilt. Nice. Howes K 41. *Shasky.* $45/£29

KELLER, HELEN. The Story of My Life. NY: Doubleday, Page, 1903. 1st ed. VG (spine wear). *Beasley.* $50/£32

KELLETT, E. E. The Whirligig of Taste. London: Hogarth, 1929. 1st ed. (Eps browned; foxed, mostly 1st, last few pp, fore-edge), o/w VG in dj (sl soiled, faded). *Virgo.* $31/£20

KELLEY, A. M. In Vinculis; or The Prisoner of War.... NY: Blelock, 1866. Enlgd ed. 216pp. All edges tinted red. Cl, beveled edges. (Overall spotting, fading), o/w VG. Howes K27. *New Hampshire*.* $80/£51

KELLEY, PAT. River of Lost Dreams, Navigation in the Rio Grande. Lincoln, 1986. 1st ed. Fine in Fine dj. *Turpen.* $35/£22

KELLEY, ROBERT L. Gold vs. Grain. Glendale: Clark, 1959. 1st ed. One of 1265. Map. VF. *Argonaut.* $175/£112

KELLEY, WILLIAM D. Lincoln and Stanton.... NY, 1885. 8vo. Extra-illus w/88 engr ports. Blue morocco gilt extra by Zucker. *Swann*.* $517/£331

KELLNER, L. Alexander von Humboldt. London, 1963. 1st ed. Frontis port. Fine in NF dj. *Turpen.* $35/£22

KELLOGG, ELLA EATON. Science in the Kitchen. Battle Creek, (1892). (Worn, soiled, hinges starting.) *Freeman*.* $50/£32

KELLOGG, J. H. The Art of Massage.... Battle Creek, MI, (1895). 1st ed. 288pp; 45 plts. Marbled edges. (Cl faded.) *Argosy.* $50/£32

KELLOGG, J. H. Colon Hygiene.... Battle Creek, MI, 1917. Twenty-eighth Thousand. (Cvrs dknd; spine heavily worn.) *King.* $35/£22

KELLOGG, J. H. The Itinerary of a Breakfast. NY, 1920. Plum cl. VG (bkpl, ink name). *Doctor's Library.* $75/£48

KELLOGG, J. H. Rational Hydrotherapy. Phila, 1904. 2nd ed. 2-tone cl (sl worn, shaken). *Freeman*.* $20/£13

KELLOGG, LOUISE P. The British Regime in Wisconsin and the Northwest. Madison: SHSW, 1935. 10 plts. (Sl worn, spine dull.) Howes K50. *Bohling.* $60/£38

KELLOGG, LOUISE P. The British Regime in Wisconsin and the Northwest. NY: Da Capo, 1971. VG. *Lien.* $40/£26

KELLOGG, MINER K. M. K. Kellogg's Texas Journal, 1872. Austin: Univ of TX, (1967). Fldg map. VG + in dj. *Bohling.* $20/£13

KELLOGG, MINER K. M. K. Kellogg's Texas Journal, 1872. Austin: UT Press, 1967. Fldg map. Good in dj (worn). *Dumont.* $25/£16

KELLOGG, R. Mexican Tailess Amphibians in U.S. National Museum. Washington: Smithsonian, 1932. 1st ed. 1 plt. Uncut. Fine in wraps. *Mikesh.* $35/£22

KELLOGG, ROBERT H. Life and Death in Rebel Prisons. Hartford, 1865. 1st ed. 400pp. Dec pub's cl: Good + . *Scribe's Perch*.* $30/£19

Kelly's Directory of Barnet...49th Edition. London, 1937. Fldg map. Limp cvrs (sl rubbed, edges browned). *Cox.* $23/£15

KELLY, CHARLES. Salt Desert Trails. Salt Lake City: Western, 1930. 1st ed. Prospectus, clipping laid in. Textured cl, gilt emb. (Spine rubbed; name, pencil notes; cellophane tape residue affecting 3 leaves), else VG. Howes K59. *Cahan.* $135/£87

KELLY, EDWARD. The Alchemical Writings of Edward Kelly. Arthur E. Waite (trans). NY, 1970. Ltd to 500. Fine in VG dj. *Middle Earth.* $99/£63

KELLY, ERIC P. In Clean Hay. NY: Macmillan, 1953. 1st ed thus. Maud and Miska Petersham (illus). 8vo. 31pp. Color illus bds. VG in VG dj. *Dower.* $65/£42

KELLY, FANNY. Narrative of My Captivity Among the Sioux Indians. Clark and Mary Lee Spence (eds). Chicago: Lakeside Classic, 1990. Frontis port, color map. Teg. Brn cl, gilt. Fine. *Bohling.* $20/£13

KELLY, HOWARD. Medical Gynecology. NY: Appleton, 1908. 1st ed. Orig bds (newly recased saving orig spine, corners repaired). Internally Fine. *Goodrich.* $125/£80

KELLY, HOWARD. Some American Medical Botanists Commemorated.... Troy, 1914. 1st ed. (Cvr, margins waterstained.) *Fye.* $150/£96

KELLY, HUGH. Memoirs of a Magdalen. London: Harrison, 1785. 2nd ed. 2 vols in 1. 85pp. 3/4 calf. Fine. *Second Life.* $150/£96

KELLY, JAMES PAUL. Prince Izon. Chicago, 1910. 1st ed. (1 of 5 orig illus missing, frontis transposed to p274.) Color plt laid on cvr. Good + . *Five Quail.* $45/£29

KELLY, L. V. The Range Men: The Story of the Ranchers and Indians of Alberta. Toronto: William Briggs, 1913. 1st ed. 28 photo plts. Teg. Red cl (edges, extrems sl worn), gilt. Internally NF. Overall VG + . Howes K66. *Harrington.* $750/£481

KELLY, LUTHER S. Yellowstone Kelly. M. M. Quaife (ed). New Haven: Yale Univ, 1926. 1st ed. Fldg facs map. Dk navy cl, gilt. (Ink handstamp eps.) *Baltimore*.* $50/£32

KELLY, R. G. Trails, Trouts and Tigers. Charleston, WV: Privately Pub, 1961. 1st ed. VG + . *Mikesh.* $45/£29

KELLY, ROB ROY. American Wood Type 1828-1900. NY: Van Nostrand Reinhold, (1969). VG in dj. *Bohling.* $60/£38

KELLY, ROBERT. Armed Descent. (NY): Hawk's Well Press, (1961). 1st ed, 1st bk. Signed. (Ink writing fr/back cvrs), o/w Fine in glossy wrappers. *Jaffe.* $100/£64

KELLY, WALT. The Pogo Papers. NY, (1953). 1st ed. VG in wraps. *Mcclintock.* $20/£13

KELLY, WILLIAM. A Stroll Through the Diggings of California. Oakland: Biobooks, 1950. 1st CA ed. Ltd to 750. Good. *Heinoldt.* $35/£22

KELMAN, JAMES. Hardie and Baird and Other Plays. London: Secker & Warburg, 1991. 1st UK ed. Fine in dj. *Moorhouse.* $31/£20

KELNER, JOSEPH and JAMES MUNVES. The Kent State Coverup. NY: Harper & Row, 1980. 1st ed. NF in dj. *Sclanders.* $25/£16

KELSEY, CHARLES B. Diseases of the Rectum and Anus. NY, 1882. 1st ed. 299pp. Brn tooled cl (sl worn). VG. *Doctor's Library.* $100/£64

KELSEY, D. M. History of Our Wild West and Stories of Pioneer Life.... Chicago, 1901. 1st ed. VG. *Turpen.* $79/£51

KELSEY, VERA. Maria Rosa. NY: Doubleday, 1942. 1st ed. Candido Portinari (illus). 12 1/4 x 11. 36pp. VG in dj (torn, chipped). *Cattermole.* $50/£32

KELSEY, VERA. Red River Runs North. NY: Harper, (1951). 1st ed. Fine in NF dj. *Sadlon.* $15/£10

KELSEY, VERA. Red River Runs North. NY: Harper, (1951). 1st ed. VG in VG dj. *Perier.* $37/£24

KELTON, ELMER. The Day the Cowboys Quit. GC, 1971. 1st ed. Fine in dj (sl edgewear). *Baade.* $125/£80

KELTON, ELMER. The Good Old Boys. GC: Doubleday, (1978). 1st ed. Fine in Fine dj. *Unger.* $50/£32

KEMBLE, EDWARD C. A History of California Newspapers 1846-1858. Helen Harding Bretnor (ed). Los Gatos: Talisman, 1962. One of 750. Frontis, 2 views. Ptd spine label. Fine in dj. *Bohling.* $45/£29

KEMBLE, EDWARD C. A History of California Newspapers 1846-58. Los Gatos, 1962. 1st bk ed. One of 750. VF in VF dj. *Turpen.* $75/£48

KEMBLE, EDWARD C. A Kemble Reader: Stories of California, 1846-48. Fred Blackburn Rogers (ed). SF: CA Hist Soc, 1963. Ltd to 1000. Fldg illus. Orange cl. Good. *Karmiole.* $50/£32

KEMBLE, FRANCES ANNE. Journal of a Residence on a Georgian Plantation in 1838-1839. Harper, 1863. 10pp ads. Repeat of 'about' line 6, p314. Emb grn cl (backstrip lt faded, extrems sl worn). Contents Sound. Howes K70. *Yudkin*.* $125/£80

KEMBLE, FRANCES ANNE. Journal of a Residence on a Georgian Plantation in 1838-1839. John A. Scott (ed). NY, 1863. 1st US ed, 1st issue, w/'about' repeated line 6, p314. 2 vols. Emb cl (spine sl faded, sl chipped). *Kane*.* $85/£54

KEMBLE, JOHN HASKELL. The Panama Route 1848-1869. Berkeley/L.A.: Univ of CA, 1943. 1st ed. Ptd wrappers. *Lefkowicz.* $75/£48

KEMELMAN, HARRY. The Nine Mile Walk: The Nicky Welt Stories. NY: Putnam, 1967. 1st ed. Fine in dj (spine ends sl worn, 2 sm closed tears). *Mordida.* $45/£29

KEMP, PETER. The Oxford Companion to Ships and the Sea. London (etc): OUP, 1976. 1st ed. Dj. *Lefkowicz.* $60/£38

KEMPF, EDWARD JOHN. The Autonomic Functions and the Personality. NY: The Nervous & Mental Disease Pub Co, 1918. 1st ed, 1st bk. Ptd brn wrappers (loose). *Gach.* $35/£22

KEMPF, EDWARD JOHN. Psychopathology. St. Louis: C.V. Mosby, 1921. 1st ed. Panelled olive cl. VG (lt shelfwear). *Gach.* $75/£48

KENDALL, ELIZABETH. A Wayfarer in China. Cambridge: Riverside, 1913. 1st US ed. (Lt marginal browning, hinges cracked.) Teg. Dec cl (spine, corners, upper bd rubbed w/sl loss to illus). *Edwards.* $23/£15

KENDALL, GEORGE WILKINS. Letters from a Texas Sheep Ranch, Written 1860-1867 by...to Henry Stephens Randall. Urbana, 1959. 1st ed. Fine in Fine dj. *Turpen.* $45/£29

KENDALL, GEORGE WILKINS. Narrative of the Texan Santa Fe Expedition. NY, 1844. 1st ed. 2 vols. xii,405, fldg map laid in; xii,406pp (lt foxed). Red buckram (rebound, top 1/3 vol 1 dampstained). VG. Howes K75. *Turpen.* $395/£253

KENDALL, GEORGE WILKINS. Narrative of the Texan Santa Fe Expedition. Chicago: Lakeside Classic, 1929. Fldg map, facs of orig tp. Teg. Dk red cl, gilt. Ptd presentation card tipped in. Very Nice. *Bohling.* $50/£32

KENDALL, HENRY O. et al. Posture and Pain. Balt, 1952. 1st ed. VG (sl worn) in dj (worn). *Doctor's Library.* $50/£32

KENDALL, R. ELLIOTT. Beyond the Clouds. London, 1954. 2nd ed. Map. Dj (sl creased, portions replaced spine ends). *Edwards.* $23/£15

KENDRICK, T. D. Anglo-Saxon Art to A.D. 900. NY, 1972. Rpt. 104 plts. (Spine sl sunned.) *Washton.* $45/£29

KENEALLY, THOMAS. Blood Red, Sister Rose. London: Collins, 1974. 1st ed. Fine in dj (spine sl fading). *Between The Covers.* $100/£64

KENEALLY, THOMAS. Bring Larks and Heroes. NY: Viking, (1967). 1st ed. NF in dj (sl discolored). *Antic Hay.* $40/£26

KENEALLY, THOMAS. Bring Larks and Heroes. NY: Viking, (1968). 1st Amer ed. NF in dj (sm peeled portion inside flap). *Turtle Island.* $40/£26

KENEALLY, THOMAS. Confederates. NY: Harper, (1979). 1st Amer ed. Fine in dj (sm tear). *Between The Covers.* $85/£54

KENEALLY, THOMAS. A Family Madness. London: Hodder, 1985. 1st UK ed. Fine in dj. *Williams.* $23/£15

KENEALLY, THOMAS. The Fear. (Melbourne): Cassell Australia, (1965). 1st ed. Fine (spine sl rubbed) in VG + dj (sm tears, nicks, fr flap little split). *Between The Covers.* $350/£224

KENEALLY, THOMAS. Gossip from the Forest. London: Collins, 1975. 1st ed. Fine in Fine dj (price-clipped). *Between The Covers.* $125/£80

KENEALLY, THOMAS. Passenger. London: Collins, 1979. 1st UK ed. VG in dj (price-clipped). *Williams.* $39/£25

KENEALLY, THOMAS. Passenger. London: Collins, 1979. 1st ed. Fine in Fine dj (sl worn). *Between The Covers.* $100/£64

KENEALLY, THOMAS. The Playmaker. London: Hodder, 1987. 1st UK ed. Fine in dj. *Williams.* $23/£15

KENEALLY, THOMAS. Schindler's Ark. 1982. 1st ed. VG in dj (top right corner rubbed, sl loss). *Words Etc.* $101/£65

KENEALLY, THOMAS. Schindler's Ark. Hodder, 1982. 1st UK ed. Fine in Fine dj. *Martin.* $101/£65

KENEALLY, THOMAS. Schindler's Ark. London, 1982. 1st Eng ed. Fine (inscrip) in dj (price-clipped). *Clearwater.* $62/£40

KENEALLY, THOMAS. Schindler's Ark. London: Hodder, 1982. 1st UK ed. VG (ink inscrip) in dj (price-clipped). *Williams.* $86/£55

KENEALLY, THOMAS. Three Cheers for the Paraclete. (Sydney): Angus & Robertson, (1969). 1st ed. Fine in dj (2 sm rubbed spots). *Between The Covers.* $225/£144

Kenilworth. (By Walter Scott.) Edinburgh/London: Archibald Constable & John Bannantyne/Hurst, Robinson, 1821. 1st ed. 3 vols. 4pp undated ads vol 3. Orig lt blue bds, grn cl spines, ptd spine labels. Mixed issue: all 3 tps bear ptr's imprint on verso; on p119 vol 2 the 'H' of 'Here' is missing; on p338 vol 2, word 'ha-/ving' is ptd thus, which is a 1st issue point. VG set (ends sl worn, labels partly worn away, lacks 1 rep, sigs). *Sumner & Stillman.* $250/£160

KENNAN, GEORGE. Siberia and the Exile System. NY: Century, 1891. 1st ed. 2 vols. xvi,409; xii,575pp. Teg. (Edges rubbed, ex-lib), o/w VG. *Worldwide.* $35/£22

KENNAN, GEORGE. Siberia and the Exile System. NY: Century, 1891. 2 vols. xv,409; x,574pp. VG (extrems lt worn). *High Latitude.* $125/£80

KENNARD, JOSEPH SPENCER. The Italian Theatre: From Its Beginning to the Close of the Seventeenth Century. NY: William Edwin Rudge, 1932. 1st ed. Inscribed. 2 vols. Fine (sig each vol) in djs (worn, chipped). *Captain's Bookshelf.* $100/£64

KENNARD, MRS. EDWARD. Sporting Tales. London, 1896. 2nd ed. 312pp (fore-edge sl spotted). Marbled eps, teg. 1/2 morocco, cl bds, raised bands, floral design to spine. *Edwards.* $39/£25

KENNEDY, A. H. The Mink in Health and Disease. Fur Trade Journal, 1951. 1st ed. (Inner hinge sl sprung.) *Edwards.* $25/£16

KENNEDY, ELIJAH R. The Contest for California in 1861. Boston, 1912. 1st ed. Inscribed by 'the author.' VG+ in plain plastic dj. *Pratt.* $70/£45

KENNEDY, G. W. The Pioneer Camp Fire in Four Parts. Portland, OR: The Author, 1914. 1st ed. Pict cl (faded). *Ginsberg.* $100/£64

KENNEDY, JAMES H. History of the Ohio Society of New York, 1885-1905. NY: Grafton, 1906. One of 1000. Port. Teg. Red cl, gilt. NF. *Bohling.* $30/£19

KENNEDY, JOHN F. Why England Slept. London: Hutchinson, (1940). 1st British ed. 8vo. Ads dated 'Fall 1940.' Red cl. NF in dj (lt edgeworn). *Glenn.* $525/£337

KENNEDY, MARGARET. The Game and the Candle. London: Heinemann, 1928. Ltd to 525 numbered, signed. Cl, patterned bds. NF (eps discolored) in VG dj. *Antic Hay.* $45/£29

KENNEDY, MICHAEL STEPHEN (ed). The Assiniboines. Norman: Univ of OK, (1961). VG in dj (sl worn). *Lien.* $40/£26

KENNEDY, RICHARD. A Boy at the Hogarth Press. London, 1972. Trade ed. Fine in dj (closed tear). *Clearwater.* $62/£40

KENNEDY, ROBERT F. The Enemy Within. NY, 1960. 1st bk. Very Nice in dj (frayed). *Clearwater.* $39/£25

KENNEDY, RUTH W. Alesso Baldovinetti. New Haven, 1938. 4to. (Sl rubbed.) *Washton.* $650/£417

KENNEDY, RUTH W. The Renaissance Painter's Garden. Oxford, 1948. 62 plts (1 color). (Spine ends sl worn.) *Washton.* $75/£48

KENNEDY, WILLIAM R. Sporting Sketches in South America. London, 1892. 1st ed. xvi,269,(2)ads pp; fldg map, 15 plts. Uncut. Blue cl, gilt. *Maggs.* $195/£125

KENNEDY, WILLIAM SLOANE. Reminiscences of Walt Whitman. London: Alexander Gardner, 1896. 1st ed. ix,(v),190pp. Burgundy cl (bumped, title faded). NF internally. BAL 21444. *Blue Mountain.* $125/£80

KENNEDY, WILLIAM. The Ink Truck. NY: Dial, 1969. 1st ed, 1st bk. (Sm sticker removed fep), else Fine in dj (lt rubbed). *Captain's Bookshelf.* $275/£176

KENNEDY, WILLIAM. The Ink Truck. NY: Dial, 1969. 1st ed. NF in dj (spine sl faded, short tear, extrems lt worn). *Lame Duck.* $275/£176

KENNEDY, WILLIAM. Quinn's Book. (NY): Viking, (1988). One of 500 numbered, signed. Fine in Fine slipcase. *Lenz.* $100/£64

KENNEDY, WILLIAM. Quinn's Book. NY, 1988. 1st ed. One of 500 numbered, signed. Fine in Fine slipcase. *Smith.* $55/£35

KENNER, HUGH. Dublin's Joyce. Bloomington: IN Univ, 1956. 1st ed, Amer issue. Fine in dj. *Reese.* $65/£42

KENNEY, LOUIS A. Catalogue of the Rare Astronomical Books in the San Diego State University Library. San Diego, 1988. One of 1000. (Lt worn.) Slipcase (sl sunned). *Oinonen*.* $90/£58

KENNY, D. J. Illustrated Cincinnati: A Pictorial Hand-Book of the Queen City. Cincinnati, 1875. Local ads bound in at rear. (Cl spotted.) *Swann*.* $115/£74

KENRICK, JOHN. Ancient Egypt Under the Pharaohs. London: B. Fellowes, 1850. 2 vols. xiii,(iii),509pp, 4 litho plts; viii,528pp, pub's ad. (Eps, tps sl chipped.) VG set. *Blue Mountain.* $75/£48

KENRICK, JOHN. Ancient Egypt Under the Pharaohs. NY: Alden, 1883. 1st ed. 2 vols in 1. xiii,427; viii,448pp. (Lacks fep, 1 leaf torn, repaired; fr cvr spotted, nicked), o/w Good. *Worldwide.* $15/£10

KENRICK, TONY. The Only Good Body's a Dead One. NY: S&S, 1970. 1st Amer ed. Fine in dj (price-clipped, sm edge tears). *Mordida.* $45/£29

KENRICK, TONY. Two Lucky People. London: Michael Joseph, 1978. 1st ed. (Stamps fep), o/w Fine in dj. *Mordida.* $45/£29

KENT, ALEXANDER. Command a King's Ship. Hutchinson, 1973. 1st UK ed. Fine in VG+ dj (spine faded). *Williams.* $39/£25

KENT, ALEXANDER. Command a King's Ship. London: Hutchinson, 1973. 1st UK ed. VG+ in dj (price-clipped). *Williams.* $39/£25

KENT, ALEXANDER. Command a King's Ship. London: Hutchinson, 1973. 1st ed. Fine in Fine dj. *Unger.* $100/£64

KENT, ALEXANDER. The Flag Captain. Hutchinson, 1971. 1st UK ed. VG (bumped) in VG dj. *Williams.* $55/£35

KENT, ALEXANDER. Richard Bolitho, Midshipman. NY: Putnam, (1976). 1st Amer ed. (Name), else Fine in NF dj. *Between The Covers.* $35/£22

KENT, ALEXANDER. Signal—Close Action. NY: Putnam, (1974). 1st Amer ed. VG (name; sl cocked; rubbing) in VG dj (couple notes erased from flaps). *Between The Covers.* $35/£22

KENT, ALEXANDER. Signal—Close Action. Hutchinson, 1974. 1st UK ed. VG in dj. *Williams.* $34/£22

KENT, ALEXANDER. Signal—Close Action. London: Hutchinson, 1974. 1st ed. Fine in dj. *Mordida.* $65/£42

KENT, ALEXANDER. Sloop of War. Hutchinson, 1972. 1st UK ed. Fine (ink name) in VG dj (price-clipped). *Williams.* $39/£25

KENT, ALEXANDER. Success to the Brave. London: Hutchinson, 1983. 1st ed. Fine in dj. *Mordida.* $65/£42

KENT, ALEXANDER. Success to the Brave. London: Hutchinson, 1983. 1st ed. Fine in Fine dj. *Unger.* $75/£48

KENT, ALEXANDER. A Tradition of Victory. London: Hutchinson, 1981. 1st ed. Fine in dj. *Mordida.* $65/£42

KENT, HENRY W. Bibliographical Notes on One Hundred Books.... NY: Grolier Club, 1903. One of 305 ptd. Orig 1/4 vellum. (Bkpl; spine lt soiled, sl rubbed), else NF in slipcase (soiled, broken). *Waverly*.* $55/£35

KENT, J. P. C. Roman Coins. NY: Abrams, (1978). 4 maps. Fine in dj. *Archaeologia.* $175/£112

KENT, JAMES. Lectures on Homoeopathic Philosophy. Lancaster, PA, 1900. 1st ed. VG. *Fye.* $100/£64

KENT, NATHANIEL. Hints to Gentlemen of Landed Property. London: J. Dodsley, 1793. New ed. viii,286pp; 10 copper engr plts (6 fldg). Mod calf (rebound), orig marbled bds, red spine label. *Karmiole.* $300/£192

KENT, ROCKWELL. A Birthday Book. NY: Random House, 1931. One of 1850 numbered, signed. Full pict silk (edges browned, sl worn). Contents VG. *Waverly*.* $121/£78

KENT, ROCKWELL. The Bookplates and Marks of Rockwell Kent. NY: Random House, 1929. One of 1250 numbered, signed. Sm 8vo. 79pp, frenchfold. Blue cl, gilt. Fine (bkpl) in dj (sm chip, lt faded). *Bromer.* $250/£160

KENT, ROCKWELL. How I Make a Wood Cut. Pasadena: Esto, 1934. 1st ed. One of 1000 ptd. 4 full-pg woodcuts. Black bds, ptd paper label upper cvr. VG. *Houle.* $175/£112

KENT, ROCKWELL. It's Me O Lord. NY: Dodd, Mead, (1955). 1st ed. (Fep starting), else VF in dj (extrems lt worn). *Bromer.* $150/£96

KENT, ROCKWELL. N by E. NY: Random House, 1930. 1st ed. #268/900, signed. 8 full-pg plts. Top edge silver. Silver-stamped lt blue cl (spine sl faded). VG in pub's gray bd slipcase (cracking). *Houle.* $295/£189

KENT, ROCKWELL. N by E. NY: Random House, 1930. 1st ed. One of 900 signed. Frontis, title, 8 full-pg plts. VF in silver-stamped blue cl; slipcase. *Bromer.* $375/£240

KENT, ROCKWELL. Rockwellkentiana. NY: Harcourt, Brace, 1933. 1st ed (so stated). Frontis. Pict cvr. NF in dj (worn, chipped). *New Hampshire*. $60/£38

KENT, ROCKWELL. Salamina. NY, 1935. 1st Amer ed. Fine (corners sl rubbed) in variant dj (spine, rear panel sl sunned, edges sl chipped, sl rubbed, flaps torn). *Polyanthos.* $35/£22

KENT, ROCKWELL. Salamina. NY: Harcourt Brace, 1935. Good in dj (chipped). *Scribe's Perch*. $21/£13

KENT, ROCKWELL. What Is an American? (L.A.: Plantin, 1936.) 1st ed. VF in orig ptd wrappers. *Bromer.* $285/£183

KENT, ROCKWELL. Wilderness, a Journal of a Quiet Adventure in Alaska. NY: Putnam, 1920. 1st ed. Beige cl. Good. *Appelfeld.* $125/£80

KENT, W. P. The Story of Libby Prison. Chicago, n.d. Ed not stated. Broadfoot 255 dates this at 1890. 60pp + ads. Good- in ptd pict wraps (detached from text). *Scribe's Perch*. $50/£32

KENT, WILLIAM WINTHROP. The Life and Works of Baldassare Peruzzi of Siena. NY, 1925. 89 plts. (Sl shelf-rubbed.) *Washton.* $75/£48

KENT, WILLIAM. Reminiscences of Outdoor Life. SF: A.M. Robertson, 1929. 1st ed. Photo frontis, 13 full-pg plts. Cl-backed ptd bds, paper spine label. VF. *Argonaut.* $150/£96

KENTON, EDNA (ed). The Jesuit Relations and Allied Documents. NY, (1926). 2nd ptg. Howes J107. *Wantagh.* $75/£48

KENYON, FREDERIC G. Books and Readers in Ancient Greece and Rome. Oxford: Clarendon, 1951. (Sig.) Dj. *Archaeologia.* $35/£22

KENYON, FREDERIC G. (ed). Facsimiles of Biblical Manuscripts in the British Museum. London: The Trustees, 1900. 1st ed. 25 facs plts. Brn morocco back, cl. VG (sl worn). *Waverly*. $110/£71

KEPES, GYORGY (ed). Sign Image Symbol. NY: George Braziller, 1966. 1st ed. Fine in dj (lt used). *Beasley.* $75/£48

KEPPEL, HENRY. The Expedition to Borneo of H.M.S. Dido. NY, 1846. Fldg frontis map, xii,413pp + (xviii)pp pub's ads. (Browned.) Orig blind-emb bds (loss to edges, rebacked in mod calf), gilt. *Edwards.* $117/£75

KEPPEL, HENRY. A Visit to the Indian Archipelago, in H.M. Ship Meander. London, 1853. 2 vols. 301; 286pp; 7 (of 8) color plts. Fair (ex-lib). *Scribe's Perch*. $70/£45

KER, DONALD I. African Adventure. Harrisburg: Stackpole, 1957. Stated 1st ed. VG (spine foot chipped). *Backman.* $48/£31

KERBY, ROBERT L. Kirby Smith's Confederacy: The Trans-Mississippi South, 1863-1865. NY, 1972. VG + in dj (sl staining). *Pratt.* $50/£32

KERCHEVAL, SAMUEL A. A History of the Valley of Virginia. Woodstock: W.N. Grabill, 1902. 3rd ed. Good+ (foxing; spine, rear cvr insect spotted; edges browned, spotted). *Book Broker.* $85/£54

KERENYI, CHARLES. Asklepios. Archetypal Image of the Physician's Existence. NY, 1959. Good. *Washton.* $40/£26

KERNBERG, OTTO F. Borderline Conditions and Pathological Narcissism. NY: Jason Aronson, (1975). 1st ed. Dated, inscribed presentation. Ptd grey cl. VG in dj (chipped). *Gach.* $100/£64

KEROUAC, JACK. Big Sur. NY: FS&C, (1962). 1st ed. Fine in Very Nice dj (1-inch closed tear fr panel). *Captain's Bookshelf.* $150/£96

KEROUAC, JACK. Big Sur. NY: FSG, (1962). 1st ed. Black cl spine, blue paper bds. (Bkstore sticker), else Fine in NF dj (sm chips, closed tear). *Turtle Island.* $165/£106

KEROUAC, JACK. Big Sur. NY: Farrar, Straus & Cudahy, 1962. 1st ed. Fine in Fine dj. *Else Fine.* $225/£144

KEROUAC, JACK. The Dharma Bums. NY: Viking, 1958. 1st ed. Black cl. VG (corner bumped) in dj (worn, sm chips, sl rubbed). *Turtle Island.* $150/£96

KEROUAC, JACK. Doctor Sax. NY: Grove, (1959). 1st ed. NF in dj (edgeworn, lt rubbed, internal tape reinforcements). *Turtle Island.* $650/£417

KEROUAC, JACK. On the Road. (NY): Signet, (1958). 1st ptg, Sept 1958. 2pp pub's ads at end. VG in stiff color pict wrappers (nicks, creases). *Houle.* $65/£42

KEROUAC, JACK. On the Road. NY: Viking, 1957. 1st ed. Black cl. (Sl cocked, 3 spots fr panel, bkstore sticker), else NF in black dj (rubbed, short closed tear rear panel, sl glue residue showing through). *Turtle Island.* $425/£272

KEROUAC, JACK. On the Road. NY: Viking, 1957. 1st ed. NF in dj (sl edgeworn, price-clipped, rubbed crease 1 joint, lt offset rear panel). *Reese.* $1,500/£962

KEROUAC, JACK. Pomes All Sizes. SF: City Lights, (1992). 1st ed. Fine in pict wrappers. *Reese.* $10/£6

KEROUAC, JACK. Satori in Paris. NY: Grove, (1966). 1st ed. Blue cl. Fine in dj. *Turtle Island.* $200/£128

KEROUAC, JACK. Satori in Paris. NY: Grove, 1966. 1st ed. Fine in dj (sl rubbed). *Else Fine.* $175/£112

KEROUAC, JACK. The Scripture of the Golden Eternity. NY: Totem/Corinth, 1970. 2nd ed w/added intro. (Price blacked out rear panel), else NF in white stiff wrappers. *Turtle Island.* $45/£29

KEROUAC, JACK. The Subterraneans. NY: Avon Books, (1960). 3rd Avon ptg. Nice (ink name) in pict wrappers. *Reese.* $15/£10

KEROUAC, JACK. The Town and the City. NY, (1950). 1st ed, 1st bk. Advance rev copy. Ptd wraps (worn, spine chipped, bottom lacks piece; ink name). *Kane*. $350/£224

KEROUAC, JACK. Visions of Gerard. NY: Farrar, Straus, (1963). 1st ed. Black cl-backed pink/cream dec bds (top edge sl soiled). NF in pict cream dj (sl chipped, sl soiled, spine sl dknd). *Blue Mountain.* $65/£42

KEROUAC, JACK. Visions of Gerard. NY: FSG, (1963). 1st ed. Black cl spine (sl discolored), dec paper bds. NF in dj. *Turtle Island.* $175/£112

KEROUAC, JOHN. The Town and the City. NY: Harcourt, (1950). 1st ed, 1st bk. Top edge stained blue, uncut. Gilt-stamped red cl. VG (sm stain few pg edges; sl rubbed). *Houle.* $275/£176

KERR, P. A German Requiem. Viking, 1991. 1st UK ed. Mint in Mint dj. *Martin.* $19/£12

KERRANE, KEVIN and RICHARD GROSSINGER (eds). Baseball I Gave You All the Best Years of My Life. North Atlantic, 1978. 1st ed, 1st ptg. Good+. *Plapinger*. $50/£32

KERRY-NICHOLS, J. H. The King Country, or Explorations in New Zealand. NY: Scribner, 1884. 2nd ed. Frontis, xx,379pp, lg fldg map (repaired). Red cl, gilt picts. (Scattered foxing), else VG. *Terramedia*. $100/£64

KERSTING, R. (ed). The White World: Life and Adventures Within the Arctic Circle.... NY, 1902. 1st ed. Pict cl. VG. *Mikesh*. $65/£42

KERTESZ, ANDRE. Americana. NY: Mayflower Books, 1979. 1st ed. 64 full-pg b/w photos. (Owner stamp), else VG in pict stiff wrappers (hole punched in corner). *Cahan*. $30/£19

KERTESZ, ANDRE. Day of Paris. NY: Augustin, 1945. 1st ed. (Inscrip), else Fine in dj (lt worn, sm chips, tears). *Smith*. $250/£160

KERTESZ, ANDRE. Day of Paris. George Davis (ed). NY: J.J. Augustin, 1945. 1st ed. (Owner stamp, name; cl sl dusty, sm tear), else VG. *Cahan*. $175/£112

KERTESZ, ANDRE. J'Aime Paris: Photographs Since the Twenties. Nicolas Ducrot (ed). NY: Grossman, 1974. 1st ed. (Owner stamp), else Fine in VG pict dj. *Cahan*. $175/£112

KERTESZ, ANDRE. A Lifetime of Perception. NY: Abrams, 1982. 1st ed. Fine in NF dj. *Smith*. $95/£61

KERTESZ, ANDRE. On Reading. NY: Grossman, 1971. 1st ed. Fine (spine lt sunned) in dj (price-clipped). *Smith*. $50/£32

KERTESZ, ANDRE. On Reading. NY: Grossman, 1971. 1st ed. (Name stamp), else Fine in dj (sl discolored). *Cahan*. $65/£42

KERTESZ, ANDRE. Portraits. Nicolas Ducrot (ed). NY: Mayflower Books, 1979. 1st ed. 64 full-pg b/w photos. Pict stiff wrappers. (Owner stamp inside fr wrapper), else Fine. *Cahan*. $30/£19

KERTESZ, ANDRE. Washington Square. NY: Grossman, 1975. 1st ed. Pict stiff wrappers. (Sm closed tear fr wrapper, half-title), else VG. *Cahan*. $20/£13

KERY, PATRICIA FRANTZ. Great Magazine Covers of the World. NY: Abbeville, (1982). 1st ed. Fine in dj. *Hermitage*. $125/£80

KESEY, KEN. The Day After Superman Died. Northridge, CA: Lord John, 1980. One of 300 numbered, signed. Fine. *Lenz*. $125/£80

KESEY, KEN. One Flew Over the Cuckoo's Nest. NY, 1962. 1st ed. Fine in VG dj (price-clipped). *Warren*. $650/£417

KESEY, KEN. One Flew Over the Cuckoo's Nest. Four Square, 1965. 1st UK pb ed. NF-. *Sclanders*. $9/£6

KESEY, KEN. Sometimes a Great Notion. NY: Viking, (1964). 1st ed, 1st issue w/pub's seal 1/2 title. Boldly signed by Kesey. VG (spine sl creased) in dj (rubbed, sl chipping spine ends). *Hermitage*. $175/£112

KESEY, KEN. Sometimes a Great Notion. NY: Viking, (1964). 1st ed, preferred 'issue' w/logo on 1/2 title. Fine in NF dj (sl rub, price repeated in ink on inner flap). *Reese*. $200/£128

KESEY, KEN. Sometimes a Great Notion. NY: Viking, (1964). 1st ed, 1st issue. Fine in dj (lt rubbed, 2 sm tears). *Captain's Bookshelf*. $250/£160

KESEY, KEN. Sometimes a Great Notion. London, 1966. 1st Eng ed. VG in dj. *Words Etc*. $94/£60

KESSEL, JOSEPH. Kisling. NY, 1970s. Sm folio. Dj. *Swann**. $126/£81

KESSINGER, L. History of Buffalo County, Wisconsin. Alma, 1888. 656pp (fep chipped, lib mks, hinges split). Good. *Zubal**. $65/£42

KETCHUM, ROBERT GLENN and ROBERT CAHN. American Photographers and the National Parks. NY/Washington: Viking/Nat'l Park Foundation, 1981. (Name, blindstamp), else Fine in slipcase, mtd color illus. *Cahan*. $65/£42

KETTON-CREMER, R. W. The Early Life and Diaries of William Windham. London, 1930. 1st ed. Good+. *Gretton*. $47/£30

KEULEMANS, T. and J. COLDEWEY. Feathers to Brush, the Victorian Bird Artist John Gerrard Keulemans 1842-1912. Deventer, 1982. #141/500. 1/2 leather (sl stained; pinhole through fr cvr, 1st 20 leaves). *Maggs*. $41/£26

KEVORKIAN, JACK. The Story of Dissection. NY, 1959. 1st ed. VG in dj. *Fye*. $50/£32

KEY, ALEXANDER. Island Light. Indianapolis/NY: Bobbs Merrill, (1950). 1st ed. (Sl dkng fr gutter), else Fine in VG dj (sl used at ends; sm chips, rubbing). *Between The Covers*. $45/£29

KEY, TED. Hazel Rides Again. NY, 1955. Signed, inscribed. 10x7.5. 125pp. (Sl wear), else VG in dj (frayed). *King*. $35/£22

KEYES, E. D. From West Point to California. Oakland: Biobooks, (1950). Ltd ed. Good. *Heinoldt*. $25/£16

KEYES, EDWARD L. Urology. NY, 1917. Good (underlining, inner hinges starting; worn, spine faded). *Doctor's Library*. $50/£32

KEYES, EDWARD L. Urology. Diseases of the Urinary Organs.... NY, 1917. 18 plts. (Cl rubbed, lt staining.) *Goodrich*. $65/£42

KEYES, FRANCES PARKINSON. Joy Street. NY: Julian Messner, (1950). 1st ed. Fine in Fine dj (price-clipped). *Between The Covers*. $65/£42

KEYES, FRANCES PARKINSON. Steamboat Gothic. NY: Julian Messner, (1952). 1st ed. Fine in Fine dj (price-clipped). *Between The Covers*. $85/£54

KEYES, SIDNEY. The Collected Poems of Sidney Keyes. Routledge, (1945). 1st ed. (Sl bumped), o/w Nice in dj. *Ash*. $39/£25

KEYNES, GEOFFREY (ed). The Compleat Walton. Bloomsbury: Nonesuch, 1929. Ltd ed. Thomas Poulton (engrs). Full brn niger morocco (sl spotting), gilt top. Fine (bkpl). Als incl from Leslie Charteris presenting bk to Duke of Portland. *Appelfeld*. $350/£224

KEYNES, GEOFFREY and PETER DAVIDSON. A Watch of Nightingales. London, 1981. #125/400. *Typographeum*. $60/£38

KEYNES, GEOFFREY. A Bibliography of Sir Thomas Browne. Oxford, 1968. 2nd ed. VG in dj. *Fye*. $200/£128

KEYNES, GEOFFREY. A Bibliography of the Writings of Dr. William Harvey, 1578-1657. Winchester, 1989. 3rd ed. VG in dj. *Fye*. $75/£48

KEYNES, GEOFFREY. Bibliography of William Hazlitt. London, 1931. 1st ed. Ltd to 750. 4 collotype plts. Blue/gray paper bds, paper label. NF (bk label) in dj. *Cady*. $75/£48

KEYNES, GEOFFREY. Bibliography of William Hazlitt. London: Nonesuch, 1931. 1st ed. Ltd to 750. Port, 32 plts (3 collotype). Paper-backed bds (sl worn, sl stained). *Maggs*. $31/£20

KEYNES, GEOFFREY. Blake Studies. London, 1949. 1st ed. 48 plts. Grn buckram. VG. *Gretton*. $78/£50

KEYNES, GEOFFREY. Blake Studies. London: Hart-Davis, 1949. 1st ed. 48 collotype plts. Top edge cut, rest uncut. VF in dj (sl worn). *Europa*. $148/£95

KEYNES, GEOFFREY. Blake Studies. London: Rupert Hart-Davis, 1949. 1st ed. 48 plts. NF in dj (spine sl dknd, chipped). *Waverly**. $66/£42

KEYNES, GEOFFREY. Blood Transfusion. London: Henry Frowde/Hodder & Stoughton, 1922. 1st ed. Red cl (spine faded). VG (lib stamp tp). *White*. $86/£55

KEYNES, GEOFFREY. The Complete Portraiture of William and Catherine Blake. London: Trianon, 1977. Ltd to 562, this copy out-of-series. 1/4 brn oasis. Cl slipcase. *Swann**. $201/£129

KEYNES, GEOFFREY. Dr. Timothie Bright, 1550-1615. London: Wellcome Historical Medical Lib, 1962. 1st ed. Fine. *Glaser*. $65/£42

KEYNES, GEOFFREY. The Gates of Memory. Oxford, 1981. 1st ed. (Erasure mks ep.) Dj. *Typographeum*. $25/£16

KEYNES, GEOFFREY. Jane Austen, a Bibliography. London: Nonesuch, 1929. 1st ed. One of 875 ptd. Uncut. Orig bds, label, spare label at end. Fine (contemp bookseller's ticket). *Macdonnell*. $150/£96

KEYNES, GEOFFREY. Jane Austen: A Bibliography. London, Nonesuch. 1st ed. One of 875 numbered. Fine in dj (sm chips). *Captain's Bookshelf*. $175/£112

KEYNES, GEOFFREY. John Ray, a Bibliography. London, 1951. Ltd to 650. 2 cuttings w/corrections inserted. (Cl sl mkd.) *Maggs*. $44/£28

KEYNES, GEOFFREY. John Ray. A Bibliography. London: Faber & Faber, 1951. Ltd to 650. Frontis port, 3 plts. Grn cl. Dj (sl tears top edge). *Maggs*. $117/£75

KEYNES, GEOFFREY. The Library of Edward Gibbon, a Catalogue of His Books. London: Bibliographical Soc, 1950. 1st ed. Frontis port. Cl-backed gray bds. Fine. *Maggs*. $34/£22

KEYNES, GEOFFREY. The Life of William Harvey. Oxford: Clarendon, 1978. 33 plts. NF in dj. *White*. $44/£28

KEYNES, GEOFFREY. A Study of the Illuminated Books of William Blake, Poet, Printer, Prophet. NY/Paris: Orion/Trianon, (1964). 1st ed. 59 color plts. Blue cl. Fine in illus dj. *Karmiole*. $75/£48

KEYNES, GEOFFREY. A Study of the Illuminated Books of William Blake, Poet, Printer, Prophet. London: Trianon, 1964. 1st ed. One of 525 numbered, signed. 32 color plts. 1/4 red morocco, marbled bds. (Spine sl faded), else NF in slipcase (lt worn). *Waverly**. $165/£106

KEYNES, GEOFFREY. A Study of the Illuminated Books of William Blake. London/Paris: Trianon, (1964). 1st ed. One of 525. Signed. 1/4 maroon morocco, marbled bds. Box. *Kane**. $160/£103

KEYNES, GEOFFREY. William Blake: Essays in Honour of Sir Geoffrey Keynes. Morton D. Paley and Michael Phillips (eds). Oxford: Clarendon, 1973. Frontis port. Mint in dj. *Argosy*. $75/£48

KEYNES, GEOFFREY. William Pickering Publisher. London: Galahad, (1969). Rev ed. Good in dj (lt soiled). *Cox*. $47/£30

KEYNES, JOHN MAYNARD. The Collected Writings. (Cambridge): Royal Economic Soc, (1971). Tall 8vo. 28 vols (lacks vol 26). VG in djs. *Argosy*. $850/£545

KEYNES, JOHN MAYNARD. Essays in Biography. London: Macmillan, 1933. 1st ed. Very Nice (sm spine nick). *Hollett*. $148/£95

KEYNES, JOHN MAYNARD. Essays in Persuasion. Macmillan, 1931. 1st ed. Good (sl sunned, sl mks). *Ash*. $156/£100

KEYNES, JOHN MAYNARD. The General Theory of Employment Interest and Money. Macmillan, 1936. 1st ed. Nice (sl sunned, sl signs of age). *Ash*. $304/£195

KEYNES, JOHN MAYNARD. A Treatise on Probability. London: Macmillan, 1921. 1st ed. Errata. Brn cl (rubbed, bumped), gilt. VG (rear hinge starting). *Blue Mountain*. $150/£96

KEYSERLING, HERMANN. The Travel Diary of a Philosopher. J. Holroyd Reece (trans). NY: Harcourt, Brace, 1925. 1st ptg. 2 vols. Frontis. Teg. (Cl sl rubbed), o/w VG. *Worldwide*. $30/£19

KHAYYAAM, OMAR. The Original Rubaiyyat of Omar Khayyaam. GC: Doubleday, 1968. One of 500 numbered, signed by Robert Graves & Omar Ali-Shah. Fine in Fine slipcase. *Lenz*. $250/£160

KHAYYAM, OMAR. The Golden Cockerel Rubaiyat. (London): Golden Cockerel, 1938. One of 300 numbered. 1/4 sheep. Slipcase. *Swann**. $431/£276

KHAYYAM, OMAR. The Original Rubaiyat. NY: Doubleday, 1968. One of 500 signed by Robert Graves and Omar Ali-Shah (eds). Grey bds, black linen spine. Fine in box. *Appelfeld*. $125/£80

KHAYYAM, OMAR. The Rubaiyat of Omar Khayyam. Boston: Houghton, Mifflin, 1886. Probable 1st 4to ed. Elihu Vedder (illus). 53 stiff sheets tipped to linen stubs. Beveled grey cl bds (ends worn, spine soiled), gilt. *Waverly**. $49/£31

KHAYYAM, OMAR. Rubaiyat of Omar Khayyam. Edward Fitzgerald (trans). London: Hodder & Stoughton, n.d. ca 1912-13. 20 tipped-in color plts. (White cl soiled.) Contents Fine. *New Hampshire**. $80/£51

KHAYYAM, OMAR. Rubaiyat.... Edward Fitzgerald (trans). London, (1909). One of 750, this numbered '0000,' signed by Edmund Dulac (illus). 4to. 20 tipped-in color plts, guards. Orig vellum, gilt, silk ties. (Cvrs sl warped.) *Swann**. $747/£479

KHAYYAM, OMAR. Rubaiyat.... Edward Fitzgerald (trans). (Boston/NY), 1900. One of 300. Cl-backed bds (spine dknd). Bd slipcase. *Swann**. $161/£103

KIDD, JOHN. On the Adaptation of External Nature to the Physical Condition of Man. London, 1833. 1st ed. 375pp. Marbled edgepapers. 1/2 leather, marbled bds, gilt, ribbed spine. VG (ex-lib). *Price*. $145/£93

KIDDER, ALFRED VINCENT. The Artifacts of the Pecos. New Haven: Yale Univ, 1932. 1st ed. Good. *Archaeologia*. $350/£224

KIDDER, D. P. and J. C. FLETCHER. Brazil and the Brazilians. Phila: Childs & Peterson, 1857. Lg fldg map, 18 plts (2 color), sm map. (Foxed, edgeworn, sl bumped, soiled.) *Metropolitan**. $150/£96

KIDDER, TRACY. Among Schoolchildren. Boston, 1989. 1st Amer ed. Signed. Fine in Fine dj. *Polyanthos*. $35/£22

KIDSON, ROBERT. Catalogue of the Palaeozoic Plants...British Museum (Natural History). London, 1886. viii,288pp (ex-lib, labels, cardholders, hinge sl cracked; spine chipped, accession label, joints splitting). *Edwards*. $39/£25

KIEFER, MONICA. American Children Through Their Books 1700-1835. Phila: Univ of PA, 1948. 1st ed. NF. *Sadlon*. $30/£19

KIEFER, OTTO. Sexual Life in Ancient Rome. London: Routledge/Kegan Paul, 1963. 8th imp. 16 plts. Dj (sl chipped, spine lt faded). *Edwards*. $25/£16

KIEL, HANNA (ed). The Bernard Berenson Treasury. London, 1964. Good in dj. *Washton*. $35/£22

KIELLAND, ELSE CHRISTIE. Geometry in Egyptian Art. London: Alec Tiranti, 1955. Blue cl, gilt. NF in Fair pict red/tan dj (creased, soiled, edges chipped, several tears). *Blue Mountain*. $45/£29

KIERAN, JOHN. The American Sporting Scene. NY, 1941. 1st ed. Ltd to 500 numbered, signed by Kieran and Joseph W. Golinkin (illus). 2-tone cl. Good in slipcase (rubbed). *King*. $95/£61

KIERAN, JOHN. The Story of the Olympic Games 776 B.C. - 1936 A.D. NY, 1943. 5th ed. (Ex-lib, ink stamps, label, cardholder reps; cl sl soiled, spine chipped, upper joint worn, lower joint splitting.) *Edwards*. $23/£15

KIERNAN, T. J. The Irish Exiles in Australia. Dublin, 1954. 1st ed. (Ex-lib, bkpls, ink stamps tp verso.) Dj (ragged). *Edwards.* $23/£15

Kilgour Collection of Russian Literature 1750-1920. Cambridge: Harvard, 1959. (Sl worn.) Dj. *Oinonen*.* $120/£77

KILLEBREW, J. B. and HERBERT MYRICK. Tobacco Leaf. NY, 1920. (Eps lt foxed; upper bd sl creased, discolored, spine sl rubbed.) *Edwards.* $55/£35

KILLENS, JOHN OLIVER. Great Gittin' Up Morning: A Biography of Denmark Vesey. GC: Doubleday, (1972). 1st ed. Fine in dj (extrems sl dknd). *Between The Covers.* $85/£54

Killing No Murder. (By Edward Sexby.) Edinburgh: Ker, 1749. Red/black title. 1/4 calf. *Rostenberg & Stern.* $150/£96

KILLIP, CHRIS. In Flagrante. London: Secker & Warburg, (1988). 1st ed. 50 full-pg b/w photos. (1 tip sl bumped), o/w Fine in pict dj. *Cahan.* $125/£80

KILLOREN, JOHN J. Come, Blackrobe. Norman: Univ of OK, (1994). 1st ed. Frontis port, 4 maps. Black cl. VF in pict dj. *Argonaut.* $25/£16

KILNER, WILLIAM H. B. Arthur Letts. L.A.: Privately pub, 1927. 1st ed. Inscribed by Letts' granddaughter. Blue cl over bds. Fine in dj. *Parmer.* $30/£19

KILPATRICK, JUDSON and J. OWEN MOORE. The Blue and the Grey, or, War Is Hell. Christopher Morley (ed). GC: Doubleday, Doran, 1930. 1st ed. Ptd paper labels. VG in illus dj (chipped, rubbed). *Cahan.* $25/£16

KIMBALL, CHARLES P. The San Francisco City Directory. SF: Journal of Commerce, 1850 (ca 1898). 2nd rpt. 139pp. Blind/gold-stamped cl. *Dawson.* $100/£64

KIMBALL, F. Domestic Architecture of the American Colonies and of the Early Republic. NY: Scribner, 1922. (Cl sl stained.) *Ars Artis.* $55/£35

KIMMEL, STANLEY. The Mad Booths of Maryland. Indianapolis/NY, (1940). 1st ed. VG in dj (worn). *Wantagh.* $40/£26

KINCAID, J. Random Shots from a Rifleman. London, 1835. 1st ed. xii,343pp. Contemp maroon 1/2 calf, gilt. *Maggs.* $351/£225

KINCAID, ZOE. Kabuki, the Popular Stage of Japan. London: Macmillan, 1925. Black pict cl. (Sl worn), else Fine. *Terramedia.* $150/£96

KINDIG, JOE, JR. Thoughts on the Kentucky Rifle in Its Gilded Age.... Mary Ann Cresswell (ed). (Wilmington, DE): George N. Hyatt, 1960. 1st ed. Inscribed. 262 plts. Blue cl, gilt. Good in dj. *Karmiole.* $100/£64

King Albert's Book. (London: Daily Telegraph, 1914.) 16 color, 11 b/w plts. Dec cl (sl worn, sm stains fr cvr). Contents VG. *New Hampshire*.* $60/£38

KING, BLANCHE BUSEY. Under Your Feet. NY: Dodd, Mead, 1939. Inscribed. (Lib stamps.) *Zubal*.* $40/£26

KING, C. et al. Geological Exploration of the Fortieth Parallel. Washington, 1877-78. 2 vols. xi,803pp; 10 Fine chromolithos, 16 tinted plts, 12 color maps (7 fldg), 13 tables; xiii,890pp, 25 tinted plts. New cl. *Henly.* $250/£160

KING, C. DALY. Arrogant Alibi. NY: D. Appleton-Century, 1939. 1st ed. (Sl rubbed.) Dj (soiled, short tears, 2 lg chips). *Metropolitan*.* $287/£184

KING, C. DALY. Obelists Fly High. NY: Harrison Smith, 1935. 1st ed. (Cl browned.) Dj (browned, short tears, chips). *Metropolitan*.* $241/£154

KING, C. W. Antique Gems and Rings. London: Bell & Daldy, 1872. 2 vols. Gilt-illus cl over bds. VG (sl foxed; sl worn). *Old London.* $350/£224

KING, C. W. Antique Gems. London: Murray, 1860. 498pp + 32-pg pub's cat; 5 plts. New cl (rebound). VG. *Savona.* $117/£75

KING, CHARLES. Campaigning with Crook and Stories of Army Life. NY: Harper, 1890. 1st ed. ix,295pp + 8pp ads (eps, bulked edges sl foxed). Navy cl (sl rubbed, dusty), gilt. Good. *Baltimore*.* $20/£13

KING, CHARLES. Campaigning with Crook and Stories of Army Life. NY: Harper, 1890. 1st ed. Port, x,295pp + 8pp ads. (Shelfworn, edgeworn, sl bumped, cl lt spotted), else Good. *Brown.* $40/£26

KING, CHARLES. A Daughter of the Sioux. Hobart, 1903. 1st ed. Pict cvr, teg. (Snag on cvr photo; ep scuff), else Fine. *Authors Of West.* $50/£32

KING, CHARLES. A Garrison Tangle. NY, 1896. 280pp. Pict cl. (Cvr lt worn), o/w Fine. *Pratt.* $20/£13

KING, CHARLES. The Medal of Honor. NY, 1905. Pict cvr. VG + . *Pratt.* $25/£16

KING, CHARLES. Story of Fort Frayne. Chicago/NY: F. Tennyson Neely, (1895). Apparent 1st ed. Frontis port, 310pp + ads. Pict cl (worn, soiled). *Bohling.* $18/£12

KING, CHARLES. Tonio, Son of the Sierras. NY, (1906). 1st ed. Pict cl. VG. *Pratt.* $50/£32

KING, CHARLES. A Wounded Name. NY, (1898). 353pp. Pict cl. (Cvr sl worn), o/w Fine. *Pratt.* $20/£13

KING, CLARENCE. Mountaineering in the Sierra Nevada. Boston, 1872. 1st ed, 1st issue. (Stamp, sl foxed at end; spine ends worn.) Howes K148. *Swann*.* $345/£221

KING, CONSTANCE EILEEN. The Collector's History of Dolls. London/NY, 1978. 1st US ed. 38 color plts. Dj (price-clipped). *Edwards.* $55/£35

KING, CORETTA SCOTT. My Life with Martin Luther King, Jr. NY: Holt, (1969). 1st ed. Inscribed. Fine in Fine dj (sl rubbed). *Unger.* $125/£80

KING, CORETTA SCOTT. My Life with Martin Luther King, Jr. NY: Holt, Rinehart & Winston, (1969). 1st ed. VG in pict dj. *Petrilla.* $25/£16

KING, E. J. The Knights of St. John in the British Empire. London, 1934. (Lacks upper portion fep.) *Edwards.* $23/£15

KING, EDWIN. The Knights of St. John in the British Realm. London, 1967. 3rd ed. Color frontis. Dj (sl chipped). *Edwards.* $39/£25

KING, F. H. Farmers of Forty Centuries. Madison, WI: Mrs. F.H. King, 1911. 1st US ed. VG. *Second Life.* $85/£54

KING, FRANCIS. The Dividing Stream. London: Longmans, 1951. 1st ed. Nice (sig) in pict dj (sl nicked, foxed). *Patterson.* $39/£25

KING, FRANCIS. Flights. London: Hutchinson, 1973. 1st UK ed. NF in dj (sl rubbed). *Moorhouse.* $23/£15

KING, FRANCIS. The Japanese Umbrella. London: Longmans, 1964. 1st UK ed. Fine in dj. *Williams.* $25/£16

KING, FRANK. Skeezix and Pal. Chicago, (1925). 9.5x7. 105pp. Cl, color pict label. (Top right corners bumped), else Nice w/back cvr of dj present. *King.* $50/£32

KING, FRANK. Skeezix Out West. Chicago, (1928). 9.5x7. 114pp. Cl (well worn, hinges broken, shaken), color pict label. *King.* $40/£26

KING, FRANK. Terror at Staups House. NY: Watt, 1929. 1st Amer ed. Nice in dj (sunned, back panel stained). *Metropolitan*.* $17/£11

KING, HENRY C. The History of the Telescope. Cambridge, MA: Sky, 1955. 1st Amer ed. (Sig), else Fine. *Cahan.* $85/£54

KING, JAMES. Cleopatra's Needle: A History of the London Obelisk. London Religious Tract Soc, 1883. 1st ed. Fldg frontis, 128pp. Gilt-pict cl. Good. *Archaeologia.* $65/£42

KING, JESSIE M. The City of the West. London: T.N. Foulis, 1911. 1st ed. 25 tipped-in plts. Orig pict simulated parchment, gilt. (Top edges sl browned.) *Hollett.* $117/£75

KING, JOSEPH L. History of the San Francisco Stock Exchange Board. SF: King, 1910. 1st ed. Gray cl (lt rubbed, lt soiled). NF. *Argonaut.* $75/£48

KING, KENNETH M. Mission to Paradise, Story of Junipero Serra and the Missions of California. Chicago, 1956. 1st ed. Frontis port. Fine in Fine dj (sl soiled). *Turpen.* $45/£29

KING, LAWRENCE J. Weeds of the World. N. Polunin (ed). NY, 1966. 23 plts. (Tape mks eps), else Clean. *Brooks.* $72/£46

KING, LEONARD WILLIAM and H. R. H. HALL. Egypt and Western Asia in the Light of Recent Discoveries. London: SPCK, 1910. 17 plts. (Sig.) 1/2 morocco (extrems sl rubbed), 5 raised bands. *Archaeologia.* $85/£54

KING, MARIAN. Kees. NY: Harper, 1930. 1st ed. Elizabeth Enright (illus). 8 1/2 x 10 1/4. 80pp. Cl spine, pict bds. Fair. *Cattermole.* $30/£19

KING, MARTIN LUTHER. Why We Can't Wait. NY: Harper & Row, 1964. 1st ed. NF in dj. *Lame Duck.* $100/£64

KING, MOSES. King's Handbook of New York City. Boston, 1893. 2nd ed. 1008pp. Dec cl. Nice. *Bohling.* $50/£32

KING, MOSES. King's Photographic Views of New York. Boston: (American Bank Note Co), 1895. 720pp; fldg color map. (Soiled), else VG. *Bohling.* $40/£26

KING, MOSES. King's View of the New York Stock Exchange. NY, 1897. 1st ed. 96pp. Dec cvr. Good-(hinge cracks). *Scribe's Perch*.* $45/£29

KING, MOSES. Philadelphia and Notable Philadelphians. Phila, 1902. Pict grn cl, gilt. (Lt worn, soiled.) *Freeman*.* $80/£51

KING, RUFUS. The Case of the Dowager's Etchings. GC: DCC, 1944. 1st ed. Pub's bkmk fep. Fine in VG dj (spine ends chipped, wear, short closed tears). *Mordida.* $50/£32

KING, RUFUS. Murder on the Yacht. GC: DCC, 1932. 1st ed. (Spine sl faded), o/w Fine in dj. *Mordida.* $95/£61

KING, STEPHEN and PETER STRAUB. The Talisman. Viking, 1984. 1st ed. NF in dj. *Words Etc.* $39/£25

KING, STEPHEN and PETER STRAUB. The Talisman. RI: Donald Grant, 1984. Deluxe 1st ed. 2 vols. Fine in slipcase. *Metropolitan*.* $138/£88

KING, STEPHEN and PETER STRAUB. The Talisman. West Kingston: Grant, 1984. One of 1200 numbered, signed by both authors. Slipcase. *Swann*.* $345/£221

KING, STEPHEN. Carrie. GC, 1974. 1st ed, 1st bk. (Spine ends bumped), else VG in dj (edgeworn, sl frayed). *King.* $495/£317

KING, STEPHEN. Cujo. NY: Mysterious Press, (1981). 1st ed. One of 750 numbered, signed. Slipcase. *Swann*.* $287/£184

KING, STEPHEN. Cujo. NY: Mysterious, (1981). Ltd to 750 numbered, signed. Fine in clear plastic dj, slipcase. *Levin.* $350/£224

KING, STEPHEN. Cujo. Viking, 1981. 1st ed. Fine in dj. *Madle.* $50/£32

KING, STEPHEN. Cycle of the Werewolf. Michigan: Land of Enchantment, (1983). 1st ed. Fine in dj (chipped, rubbed, short tears). *Metropolitan*.* $143/£92

KING, STEPHEN. The Dark Half. Viking, 1989. 1st ed. NF in dj. *Words Etc.* $28/£18

KING, STEPHEN. The Dark Tower II: The Drawing of the Three. (West Kingston): Grant, (1987). 1st ed. (Bkpl, spine sl cocked), else Fine in dj. *Other Worlds.* $50/£32

KING, STEPHEN. The Dark Tower II: The Drawing of the Three. Grant, 1987. 1st ed. Signed. Fine in Fine dj. *Certo.* $125/£80

KING, STEPHEN. The Dark Tower III: The Wastelands. Hampton Falls, NH: Grant, (1991). 1st ed. One of 1250 numbered, signed by King and Ned Dameron (illus). Dj, slipcase. *Swann*.* $316/£203

KING, STEPHEN. The Dark Tower III: The Wastelands. Grant, 1991. 1st ed. Signed. Fine in Fine dj. *Certo.* $100/£64

KING, STEPHEN. The Dark Tower: The Gunslinger. RI: Grant, 1982. 1st ed. Fine (extrems very lt worn). *Metropolitan*.* $184/£118

KING, STEPHEN. The Dark Tower: The Gunslinger. RI: Grant, 1982. 1st ed. Fine in dj (spine, corners sl worn). *Metropolitan*.* $230/£147

KING, STEPHEN. The Dark Tower: The Gunslinger. West Kingston: Grant, 1982. 1st ed. (Owner blindstamp), else NF in dj (spine ends lt worn). *Other Worlds.* $350/£224

KING, STEPHEN. The Dark Tower: The Gunslinger. West Kingston: Grant, 1982. 1st ed. NF (leaf nicked) in dj. *Other Worlds.* $500/£321

KING, STEPHEN. Dolan's Cadillac. Northridge: Lord John, 1989. 1st ed. One of 250 numbered, signed. Morocco-backed marbled bds. *Swann*.* $230/£147

KING, STEPHEN. Dolan's Cadillac. Northridge: Lord John, 1989. One of 1000 numbered, signed. This mkd presentation copy, unnumbered. Cl-backed pict bds. *Swann*.* $230/£147

KING, STEPHEN. Dolan's Cadillac. Northridge: Lord John, 1989. 1st ed. One of 1000 numbered, signed. Cl-backed pict bds. *Swann*.* $258/£165

KING, STEPHEN. Dolan's Cadillac. Northridge: Lord John, 1989. 1st ed. Ltd to 1000 numbered, signed. Fine, w/o dj, as issued. *Levin.* $300/£192

KING, STEPHEN. Dolores Claiborne. London: BCA, (1992). True world 1st ed. W/'This edition published 1992/by BCA,' and the code 'CN6975,' and no statement of ptg on copyright pg. Fine in dj. *Levin.* $300/£192

KING, STEPHEN. The Eyes of the Dragon. Bangor, ME: Philtrum, 1984. 1st ed. One of 1000 (of 1250) numbered, signed. Cl-backed marbled bds. Pub's slipcase. *Swann*.* $488/£313

KING, STEPHEN. Gerald's Game. (NY): Viking, (1992). 'Special limited A.B.A. edition,' true 1st Amer ed. Fine in cardbd slipcase, as issued. *Levin.* $150/£96

KING, STEPHEN. My Pretty Pony. NY: Whitney Museum, 1988. 1st ed. One of 280 signed by King and Barbara Kruger (illus). Folio. Leather-backed brushed steel, digital timepiece mtd fr cvr. *Swann*.* $1,495/£958

KING, STEPHEN. Needful Things. Hodder & Stoughton, 1991. 1st ed. NF in dj. *Words Etc.* $28/£18

KING, STEPHEN. Night Shift. GC, 1978. 1st ed. Fine (name) in VG dj (lt wrinkled, sl rubbed). *Mcclintock.* $375/£240

KING, STEPHEN. Night Shift. GC: Doubleday, 1978. 1st ed. (Sl wear spine head), else NF in dj (short tears spine ends, lt 1-inch stain top of rear panel). *Other Worlds.* $450/£288

KING, STEPHEN. Pet Sematary. London: Hodder, 1983. 1st UK ed. Fine in NF dj. *Williams.* $39/£25

KING, STEPHEN. Pet Sematary. NY, 1983. 1st ed. VG in dj. *Argosy.* $75/£48

KING, STEPHEN. The Shining. Doubleday, 1977. 1st ed. VG + in dj (spine corners sl chipping). *Certo.* $95/£61

KING, STEPHEN. The Shining. Doubleday, 1977. 1st ed. Fine in dj (sl frayed). *Madle.* $225/£144

KING, STEPHEN. The Shining. GC: Doubleday, 1977. (Spine sl rubbed, rear hinge repaired), else NF in NF dj (sm crown tear). *Between The Covers.* $250/£160

KING, STEPHEN. The Shining. NY, 1977. 1st ed. VG in dj. *Argosy.* $250/£160

KING, STEPHEN. The Shining. NY: Doubleday, 1977. 1st ed. Black cl back, tan paper bds. (Prelim fore-edges lt stained, rmdr spray lower edge text block), else NF. *Waverly*.* $60/£38

KING, STEPHEN. The Stand. GC: Doubleday, 1978. 1st ed. NF in NF dj (2 sm closed tears). *Other Worlds.* $200/£128

KING, STEPHEN. The Stand. NY: Doubleday, 1978. 1st ed. Dj (sl soiled, worn). *Swann*.* $172/£110

KING, STEPHEN. Tommyknockers. Putnam, 1987. 1st US ed, 1st issue 'Permissions To Come'. Fine in Fine dj. *Martin.* $28/£18

KING, W. J. HARDING. Mysteries of the Libyan Desert. London: Seeley, Service, 1925. 1st ed. 16 plts, 2 fldg maps. (Sl rubbed, spine sl frayed, ex-lib, spine #, cancellation stamp tp, lib stamps), o/w VG. *Worldwide.* $45/£29

KING, W. ROSS. The Sportsman and Naturalist in Canada. London: Hurst & Blackett, 1866. 1st ed. 6 chromolithos. (Spine, extrems sl rubbed), o/w Fine. *Cummins.* $300/£192

KINGDON-WARD, F. Berried Treasure. London, 1954. 1st ed. Color frontis, 24 plain plts. (Margins sl foxed.) *Henly.* $28/£18

KINGDON-WARD, F. Berried Treasure. London, 1954. 1st ed. Color frontis, 24 b/w plts. Dj (torn, repaired). *Edwards.* $39/£25

KINGDON-WARD, F. Commonsense Rock Gardening. London, 1948. 1st ed. Dj (spine discolored, chipped). *Edwards.* $25/£16

KINGDON-WARD, F. Pilgrimage for Plants. NY, 1960. 1st Amer ed. VG in dj (chipped). *Brooks.* $56/£36

KINGDON-WARD, F. Plant Hunter in Manipur. London, 1952. 1st ed. Fldg map. (Cl sl dknd.) *Edwards.* $47/£30

KINGDON-WARD, F. Plant Hunting on the Edge of the World. London, 1930. Black cl (spine faded, fr joint splitting). *Maggs.* $106/£68

KINGDON-WARD, F. Return to the Irrawaddy. London: Melrose, (1956). 1st ed. Fldg map. NF in dj. *Captain's Bookshelf.* $50/£32

KINGDON-WARD, F. The Romance of Gardening. London, 1935. 1st ed. 16 plts. (Sl foxed.) *Henly.* $44/£28

KINGSFORD, WILLIAM. The Canadian Canals: Their History and Cost.... Toronto: Rollo & Adam, 1865. 1st ed. 191pp (sig, bkpl; fr hinge cracked). Brn cl (stained, rubbed). VG. *Blue Mountain.* $75/£48

KINGSLEY, CHARLES. Glaucus or The Wonders of the Shore. London, 1890. xi,245pp + 46 ads; 12 color plts. (Ends foxed.) *Henly.* $19/£12

KINGSLEY, CHARLES. The Heroes; or Greek Fairy Tales for My Children. London: J.M. Dent, 1899. 8vo. Color frontis, vi,(ii),177pp (offsetting eps); 11 b/w plts by T. H. Robinson. Teg; deckle-edged. Blue cl (bumped, top/bottom edges sl dknd), gilt. VG. *Blue Mountain.* $25/£16

KINGSLEY, CHARLES. The Heroes; or Greek Fairy Tales for My Children. London: Allen & Unwin, n.d. (ca 1910). 1st ed. George Soper (illus). 8vo. 248pp; 6 color plts. Illus grn cl stamped in blue. Good. *Karmiole.* $75/£48

KINGSLEY, CHARLES. The Heroes; or, Greek Fairy Tales for My Children. Cambridge: Macmillan, 1859. 2nd ed. xx,(iv),255,(1)pp (short tear 1 leaf, inscrip), 8 line engrs by Whymper. Aeg. Gilt cl (sl worn, damp mkd, sl shaken). *Cox.* $28/£18

KINGSLEY, CHARLES. The Heroes; or, Greek Fairy Tales for My Children. London, 1912. One of 500 numbered. 4to. 12 mtd color plts by William Russell Flint. Limp vellum, silk ties. Dj. *Swann*.* $287/£184

KINGSLEY, CHARLES. The Water Babies. Dent, 1942. 6th ptg. 8vo. 284pp; Margaret Tarrant (illus). Pict-dec bds. NF. *Bookmark.* $62/£40

KINGSLEY, CHARLES. The Water-Babies. Boston: T.O.H.P. Burnham, 1864. 1st US ed. 8vo. J. Noel Paton (illus). Lt yellow-orange coated eps; teg. Lt purple cl (spine, edges sunned, lt chipped, sm tears; lt aged, sl foxed, fr hinge cracked). *Baltimore*.* $80/£51

KINGSLEY, CHARLES. Westward Ho! NY: Scribner, 1920. 1st ed thus. 8vo. 17 color illus by N.C. Wyeth: Black cl, color pict label. VG + . *Dower.* $200/£128

KINGSLEY, CHARLES. Westward Ho! NY: LEC, 1947. #904/1500 numbered, signed by Edward A. Wilson (illus). 2 vols. Fine set in pub's slipcase. *Hermitage.* $95/£61

KINGSLEY, CHARLES. Westward Ho! The Voyages and Adventures of Sir Amyas Leigh.... Boston: Ticknor & Fields, 1855. Early Amer ed. (1st, last leaves lt foxed; spine ends chipped, corners sl rubbed.) *Sadlon.* $40/£26

KINGSLEY, FLORENCE M. Prisoners of the Sea: A Romance of the Seventeenth Century. Phila: David McKay, 1897. 1st ed. 480pp. (Sm worn spot rear cvr.) *Hayman.* $20/£13

KINGSLEY, GEORGE HENRY. Notes on Sport and Travel. 1900. Frontis port. (Spine sl chipped, faded.) *Edwards.* $55/£35

KINGSOLVER, BARBARA. The Bean Trees. NY: Harper & Row, 1988. 1st ed, 1st bk. Fine in Fine dj. *Lame Duck.* $250/£160

KINGSOLVER, BARBARA. The Bean Trees. (London: Virago, 1989.) 1st UK ed, 1st bk. One of 1250. New in New dj. *Bernard.* $100/£64

KINGSTON, MAXINE HONG. The Woman Warrior. Taiwan piracy, n.d. 1st bk. VG in VG dj. *Smith.* $20/£13

KINGSTON, W. H. G. Kidnapping in the Pacific. London/NY: Routledge, 1879. 1st ed. viii,173pp; 23 plts. (Sl foxing; edges rubbed, spine frayed, torn), o/w Good. *Worldwide.* $35/£22

KINGSTON, W. H. G. True Blue. Griffith, Farran, Okeden & Welsh, (1889). John Gilbert (illus). Lg 8vo. 440pp. Aeg. Pict cl. (Tips sl worn, sl mks), else VG + . *Bookmark.* $31/£20

KINIETZ, W. VERNON. The Indians of Western Great Lakes 1615-1760. Univ of MI, 1940. 1st ed. Frontis map. VG in VG dj. *Oregon.* $45/£29

KINLOCH, ALEXANDER A. Large Game Shooting in Thibet, the Himalayas, and Northern India. Calcutta: Thacker, Spink, 1885. Lg 4to. Frontis, vii,237pp + 16 ads, fldg color map. Olive-grn gilt pict cl. (Spine top sl chipped), else VG. *Terramedia.* $750/£481

KINNAIRD, LAWRENCE. Spain in the Mississippi Valley 1765-94. Washington, 1949. 1st ed. 3 vols. NF (tip bumped). No dj as issued. *Turpen.* $95/£61

KINNAIRD, LAWRENCE. Spain in the Mississippi Valley, 1765-94. Washington: GPO, 1949, 1946. 1st eds. 3 vols. Gilt-lettered blue cl. Fine. *Argonaut.* $175/£112

KINNELL, GALWAY. How the Alligator Missed Breakfast. Boston: Houghton Mifflin, (1982). 1st ed. Signed. Lynn Munsinger (illus). VF in pict dj. *Bromer.* $75/£48

KINNEY, TROY. The Etchings. NY, 1929. Sm folio. Cl-backed bds. *Swann**. $57/£37

KINROSS, LORD. The Kindred Spirit. London, 1959. 1st ed. Color frontis tipped in. Dj (lt soiled, chipped w/sl loss). *Edwards*. $31/£20

KINSELLA, THOMAS. Downstream. London: OUP, 1962. 1st ed. Fine in dj (worn). *Jaffe*. $65/£42

KINSELLA, THOMAS. Poems and Translations. NY: Atheneum, 1961. 1st ed. Fine in dj. *Jaffe*. $75/£48

KINSELLA, W. P. The Further Adventures of Slugger McBatt. Canada: Collins, 1988. 1st ed. Signed. Fine in Fine dj. *Plapinger*. $165/£106

KINSEY, ALFRED C. et al. Sexual Behavior in the Human Male. Phila, 1948. 1st ed. VG (sl worn). *Doctor's Library*. $50/£32

KINZIE, MRS. JOHN H. Wau-Bun, the 'Early Day' in the North-West. NY, 1856. 1st ed. 6 litho plts. Pub's cl. Nice. Howes K171. *Swann**. $345/£221

KINZIE, MRS. JOHN H. Wau-Bun, the 'Early Day' in the Northwest. NY: Derby & Jackson, 1856. 1st ed. Engr frontis, 5 plts. (Lt foxing; spine ends chipped, sm lightened spots lower cvr.) Howes K171. *Sadlon*. $250/£160

KINZIE, MRS. JOHN H. Wau-Bun, the 'Early Day' in the Northwest. Chicago: Lakeside, Christmas, 1932. (Inscrip, card remnants rep.) Dk red cl (spine ends sl rubbed, cvrs lt spotted). *Sadlon*. $20/£13

KINZIE, MRS. JOHN H. Early Day in the Northwest. London/NY et al: Sampson Low/Derby & Jackson et al, 1856. Frontis, 498pp; 6 engr plts; cat bound in. Good (ink name fep; extrems worn). Howes K171. *Wantagh*. $225/£144

KINZIE, MRS. JOHN H. Wau-Bun, the 'Early Day' in the North-West. NY: Derby & Jackson, 1856. Frontis, 498pp; 5 plts. Pict gilt-stamped spine, emb cvrs. VG. Howes K171. *Oregon*. $300/£192

KIP, LAWRENCE. Army Life on the Pacific. NY: Redfield, 1859. 1st ed. 144pp. (Cl sl crinkled, chip to spine.) Howes K172. *Ginsberg*. $325/£208

KIP, LAWRENCE. Army Life on the Pacific: A Journal of the Expedition Against the Northern Indians...1858. NY, 1859. 144pp (ink notes 1 pg). Good (cl sl dampstained, rumpled). Howes K172. *Reese*. $300/£192

KIP, WILLIAM. The Early Jesuit Missions in North America. NY, 1846. 1st ed. 2 vols in 1. 321pp + ads; fldg map. (Lt foxed; lt worn), o/w VG. Howes K176. *New Hampshire**. $70/£45

KIP, WILLIAM. Historical Scenes from the Old Jesuit Missions. NY, (1875). 1st ed. 375,(1)pp. *Ginsberg*. $100/£64

KIPLING, RUDYARD and WOLCOTT BALESTIER. The Naulahka: A Story of West and East. London: Heinemann, 1892. 1st ed. 8pp integral ads at end. Uncut, lower edges rough-trimmed. Ribbed orange-red cl, gilt. (Spine sl faded, corner sl bruised), o/w NF. *Temple*. $47/£30

KIPLING, RUDYARD. Actions and Reactions. Macmillan, 1909. 1st ed. Teg. Nice. *Ash*. $39/£25

KIPLING, RUDYARD. An Almanac of Twelve Sports. London, 1898. 1st ed. 'Library Edition.' 4to. Vellum-backed pict bds (bump; bkpl). *Swann**. $575/£369

KIPLING, RUDYARD. The Army of a Dream. London: Macmillan, 1905. 1st separate ed. VG in orig wrappers (edges sl faded). *Hollett*. $39/£25

KIPLING, RUDYARD. A Book of Words. Macmillan, 1928. 1st ed. Teg. VG in dj (lt frayed). *Ash*. $78/£50

KIPLING, RUDYARD. The Brushwood Boy. Doubleday, Page, 1907. 1st US ed. 12 color plts by F.H. Townsend. White cl (spine browned). VG. *Certo*. $45/£29

KIPLING, RUDYARD. The Butterfly That Stamped. NY: GC, 1947. 1st ed. Feodor Rojankovsky (illus). 7 x 9 1/2. 28pp. Pict bds. VG in dj. *Cattermole*. $35/£22

KIPLING, RUDYARD. Captains Courageous. NY: Century, 1897. 1st Amer ed. Teg. Dec grn cl. VG (bkpl). *Antic Hay*. $85/£54

KIPLING, RUDYARD. Captains Courageous. NY: Century, 1897. 1st Amer ed. Teg. Grn dec cl. Fine. *Appelfeld*. $100/£64

KIPLING, RUDYARD. The Cat That Walked by Himself. NY: GC, 1947. 1st ed. Feodor Rojankovsky (illus). 7 x 9 1/2. 28pp. Pict bds. VG in dj. *Cattermole*. $60/£38

KIPLING, RUDYARD. Chartres Windows. GC: Doubleday, 1925. 1st ed, ptd for US copyright purposes. VG in cream wrappers. *Reese*. $150/£96

KIPLING, RUDYARD. Collected Verse of Rudyard Kipling. Toronto: Copp-Clark, 1911. 4to. 17 mtd color plts by W. Heath Robinson. Gilt-dec cl. *Metropolitan**. $126/£81

KIPLING, RUDYARD. The Day's Work. NY: Doubleday, McClure, 1898. 1st Amer ed. Teg. Dec grn cl. NF. *Antic Hay*. $45/£29

KIPLING, RUDYARD. Debits and Credits. London, 1926. 1st ed. Fine in dj (spine sunned, sm chips, tear). *Polyanthos*. $65/£42

KIPLING, RUDYARD. Departmental Ditties, Barrack-Room Ballads and Other Verses. NY: United States Book Co, (1890). 1st ed, 1st issue, w/'lovell' at spine foot. Red cl. 1/2 calf slipcase. *Swann**. $345/£221

KIPLING, RUDYARD. Doctors. London: Macmillan, 1908. 1st ed. (Offsetting pp16-17; back cvr edges discolored), o/w VG in cl wrappers (sl rubbed). *Jaffe*. $65/£42

KIPLING, RUDYARD. The Elephant's Child. NY: GC, 1942. 1st ed. Feodor Rojankovsky (illus). 9 1/4 x 10 1/2. 32pp. Pict bds. VG in dj. *Cattermole*. $25/£16

KIPLING, RUDYARD. The Feet of the Young Men. NY: Doubleday, Page, 1920. 1st ed. #188/377 signed. (Stamp tp.) Parchment-backed bds (sl soiled, edges sl rubbed), gilt. *Shasky*. $110/£71

KIPLING, RUDYARD. The Five Nations. NY: Doubleday, Page, 1903. 1st Amer ed. Dec cl. (Ink inscrip; cvrs sl rubbed), o/w VG. *Jaffe*. $35/£22

KIPLING, RUDYARD. A Fleet in Being. London: Macmillan, 1898. 1st ed. VG in wrappers (spine chipped, edges sl rubbed). *Jaffe*. $75/£48

KIPLING, RUDYARD. France at War. London: Macmillan, 1915. 1st ed. (Fore-edge lt spotted.) Orig wrappers (spine dknd). *Hollett*. $39/£25

KIPLING, RUDYARD. France at War. London: Macmillan, 1915. 1st Eng ed. VG (sm stamp-like bkpl) in ptd wraps. *Antic Hay*. $50/£32

KIPLING, RUDYARD. The Fringes of the Fleet. London: Macmillan, 1915. 1st ed. VG in orig wrappers (spine dknd). *Hollett*. $39/£25

KIPLING, RUDYARD. From Sea to Sea. NY: Doubleday & McClure, 1899. 1st state. 2 vols. 460; 400pp. Dec cvrs (head, foot bumped). Good. BAL 299. *Scribe's Perch**. $40/£26

KIPLING, RUDYARD. How Shakespeare Came to Write the Tempest. NY: Dramatic Museum of Columbia Univ, 1916. Ltd to 333. Bds, paper labels. Fine (spine rubbed). *Polyanthos*. $35/£22

KIPLING, RUDYARD. How the Camel Got His Hump. NY: GC, 1942. 1st ed. Feodor Rojankovsky (illus). 7 x 9 1/4. 28pp. VG in dj. *Cattermole*. $20/£13

KIPLING, RUDYARD. How the Rhinoceros Got His Skin. NY: GC, 1942. 1st ed. Feodor Rojankovsky (illus). 7 x 9 1/4. 32pp. Pict bds. VG in dj. *Cattermole*. $25/£16

KIPLING, RUDYARD. Humorous Tales. Macmillan, 1931. 1st ed. Lg 8vo. Frontis, x,507pp,4pp list of author's works; 22 b/w plts by Reginald Cleaver. Red cl, gilt. Fine in dj. *Bookmark.* $50/£32

KIPLING, RUDYARD. Independence. London: Macmillan, 1923. 1st ed. Red cl. (Bkpl; cvrs lt rubbed), o/w VG. *Jaffe.* $25/£16

KIPLING, RUDYARD. The Irish Guards in the Great War. London, 1923. 1st ed. 2 vols. Teg, Pict cvrs, gilt. NF (edges sl rubbed). *Polyanthos.* $60/£38

KIPLING, RUDYARD. The Jungle Book and The Second Jungle Book. Macmillan, 1894/1895. 1st UK ed. 2 bks. (1st bk spine sl worn, bds spotted.) 2nd bk Clean (lt foxed). *Williams.* $562/£360

KIPLING, RUDYARD. Just So Stories for Little Children. London, 1902. 1st ed. 4to. Pict red cl (sm bump fr cvr; eps, half-title lt foxed). *Swann*.* $517/£331

KIPLING, RUDYARD. Kim. London: Macmillan, 1901. 1st British ed. Frontis. Teg. Gilt red cl. VG (edges sl rubbed). *Reese.* $185/£119

KIPLING, RUDYARD. Kim. London: Macmillan, 1901. 1st Eng ed. Teg. Dec red cl. VG in custom-made red leather/cl slipcase w/5 raised bands, gilt. *Antic Hay.* $275/£176

KIPLING, RUDYARD. Kim. NY: Doubleday, Page, 1901. 1st US ed. 10 plts. Teg, uncut. Grn pict cl (spine sl worn, upper joint cracked). *Hollett.* $187/£120

KIPLING, RUDYARD. Land and Sea Tales for Boys and Girls. Doubleday, Page, 1923. 1st ed. Blue cl. (Spine sunned), else VG. *Certo.* $25/£16

KIPLING, RUDYARD. Letters of Marque. Allahabad, 1891. 1st ed. Red/blue cl (sl rubbed; pub's stamp ep). Nice. *Swann*.* $161/£103

KIPLING, RUDYARD. Limits and Renewals. GC: Doubleday, Doran, 1932. 1st ed. Pict grn cl. Fine in dj (lt used, price-clipped). *Antic Hay.* $35/£22

KIPLING, RUDYARD. Limits and Renewals. London: Macmillan, 1932. 1st Eng ed. Teg. Dec red cl (sl dampstain). VG (lt foxing) in NF dj (sl browning). *Antic Hay.* $45/£29

KIPLING, RUDYARD. The New Army in Training. London: Macmillan, 1915. 1st ed. Mint in ptd wrappers, cl slipcase. *Jaffe.* $75/£48

KIPLING, RUDYARD. Out of India. NY, 1895. 1st Amer ed. Dec cvrs gilt. NF (name; spine sl sunned, extrems sl rubbed, rear cvr sl soiled). *Polyanthos.* $60/£38

KIPLING, RUDYARD. The Phantom 'Rickshaw. London/Allahabad: Sampson, Low, Marston et al/A.H. Wheeler, n.d. 1st Eng ed. VG in orig wrappers (edges sl browned, lower panel chipped, refixed). *Hollett.* $62/£40

KIPLING, RUDYARD. Poems 1886-1929. NY: Doubleday, Doran, 1930. 1st ed. #97/537 numbered, signed sets. 3 vols. Nice (sl soiled, sl shelfwear). *Metropolitan*.* $402/£258

KIPLING, RUDYARD. Puck of Pook's Hill. London, 1906. 1st ed. *Typographeum.* $30/£19

KIPLING, RUDYARD. Puck of Pook's Hill. NY, 1906. 1st ed. 4 color plts. Pict cl. NF. *New Hampshire*.* $60/£38

KIPLING, RUDYARD. Puck of Pook's Hill. NY: Doubleday, Page, 1906. 1st Amer ed, 1st w/Arthur Rackham illus. 8vo. Frontis, 3 illus. 1/4 morocco slipcase. *Swann*.* $126/£81

KIPLING, RUDYARD. Recessional. NY: M.F. Mansfield & A. Wessels, (1899). Ltd to 500. 16 leaves, incl blanks (sl offset eps); 5 plts. Pict eps. Pict cream cl (rubbed, sl dknd). Internally NF. *Blue Mountain.* $95/£61

KIPLING, RUDYARD. Rudyard Kipling's Letters from San Francisco. SF: Colt, 1949. One of 500. Cl-backed illus paper over bds; paper spine label (sl chipped). NF. *Cahan.* $85/£54

KIPLING, RUDYARD. Sea and Sussex. NY: Doubleday, Page, 1926. One of 150 ptd, signed. 4to. 24 mtd color plts by Donald Maxwell. Grey bds, vellum spine, gilt top. Fine in box (worn). *Appelfeld.* $250/£160

KIPLING, RUDYARD. Sea Warfare. London: Macmillan, 1916. 1st Eng ed. Many pp unopened. Dec blue cl (fr cvr sl spotted). VG (lt foxing, repaired tear p87). *Antic Hay.* $35/£22

KIPLING, RUDYARD. The Second Jungle Book. London, Macmillan, 1895. 1st ed. Blank before 1/2 title, integral ad leaf at end. Dk grn coated eps; aeg. Blue buckram, gilt. Nice (sl foxed; spine worn, dull). *Temple.* $70/£45

KIPLING, RUDYARD. The Second Jungle Book. London: Macmillan, 1895. 1st UK ed. VG + (foxing). *Williams.* $101/£65

KIPLING, RUDYARD. The Second Jungle Book. London: Macmillan, 1895. 1st ed. John Lockwood Kipling (illus). 8vo. Gilt-pict blue cl. *Swann*.* $161/£103

KIPLING, RUDYARD. The Second Jungle Book. NY: Century, 1895. 1st Amer ed. John Lockwood Kipling (illus). 8vo. 324pp. Teg. Dec emb apricot cl. (Rubbed), else VG. *Bookmark.* $39/£25

KIPLING, RUDYARD. Selected Works. NY: Peter Fenelon Collier, 1900. 1st ed. 3 vols. Olive grn cl. NF. *Sumner & Stillman.* $95/£61

KIPLING, RUDYARD. Selected Works. London: Macmillan, 1904-12. 15 vols. Teg. Contemp red 1/2 morocco by Hatchards (few vols sl dampstained), gilt spine compartments. *Christie's*.* $613/£393

KIPLING, RUDYARD. Soldiers Three/The Story of the Gadsbys/In Black and White. London: Macmillan, 1895. 1st rev ed. Blue cl dec in gilt. Fine (sl askew). *Sumner & Stillman.* $85/£54

KIPLING, RUDYARD. A Song of the English. London: Hodder & Stoughton, (1909). 30 tipped-in color plts by W. Heath Robinson, guards. (Spine sl dknd.) *Swann*.* $201/£129

KIPLING, RUDYARD. A Song of the English. London, n.d. (1915). 1st ed. Tipped-in color plts by W. Heath Robinson. White dec cl. (Dknd, mkd), o/w VG. *Words Etc.* $78/£50

KIPLING, RUDYARD. Songs from Books. GC: Doubleday, Page, 1912. 1st ed. Dec cl. (Bkpl; cvrs sl rubbed), o/w VG. *Jaffe.* $50/£32

KIPLING, RUDYARD. Stalky and Co. NY: Doubleday & McClure, 1899. 1st Amer ed. Teg. Dec grn cl. VG. *Antic Hay.* $50/£32

KIPLING, RUDYARD. Supplication of the Black Aberdeen. Medici Soc, 1927. Good (sl mks) in orig paper wrappers. *Tiger.* $16/£10

KIPLING, RUDYARD. They and the Brushwood Boy. London, 1925. 1st thus. *Typographeum.* $65/£42

KIPLING, RUDYARD. They and the Bushwood Boy. GC: Doubleday, 1926. 1st ed. NF in VG dj (sm chips). *Captain's Bookshelf.* $60/£38

KIPLING, RUDYARD. Traffics and Discoveries. London: Macmillan, 1904. 1st Eng ed. Teg. Dec red cl. VG (sl worn, eps lt browned). *Antic Hay.* $35/£22

KIPLING, RUDYARD. With the Night Mail. NY: Doubleday, Page, 1909. 1st Amer ed. Dec blue cl. Nice. *Antic Hay.* $175/£112

KIPLING, RUDYARD. The Years Between. GC: Doubleday, Page, 1919. 1st Amer ed. Teg. Dec grn cl. VG (sl repair fr hinge; bkpl) in dj (soiled, sm chips). *Antic Hay.* $45/£29

KIPLING, RUDYARD. The Years Between. London, 1919. 1st ed. Fine in dj. *Buckley.* $47/£30

KIPLING, RUDYARD. The Years Between. London: Methuen, 1919. 1st ed. Teg, uncut. (Spine, upper bd faded.) *Hollett.* $55/£35

KIRBY, F. O. Veterinary Medicine and Surgery in Diseases and Injuries of the Horse. NY: William Wood, 1883. 4 litho plts. Red cl (lt worn). *Freeman*.* $40/£26

KIRBY, PERCIVAL R. (ed). A Source Book on the Wreck of the Grosvenor. Cape Town, 1953. Fldg map, 2 plts. *Edwards.* $23/£15

KIRBY, SHEELAGH. The Yeats Country. Dolmen, 1962. 1st ed. NF in dj. *Words Etc.* $23/£15

KIRBY, WILLIAM and WILLIAM SPENCE. An Introduction to Entomology. Longman (et al), 1828. 5th ed. 4 vols. xxiv,513; (4),523; vi,732; (4),683,(5)pp ads; 2 ports, 30 plts (6 hand-colored). (Plts spotted, lt water-stained, except color ones, sl surface damage tp affecting 2 words), o/w Good set in contemp 1/2 calf, backstrips gilt, emb cl sides (faded). *Cox.* $117/£75

KIRBY, WILLIAM and WILLIAM SPENCE. An Introduction to Entomology. London: Longman et al, 1843. 6th ed. 2 vols. xxiii,(i),435pp + 32pp pub's cat; viii,426pp; 5 hand-colored plts. (Lt browned, 1 gathering vol 1 partly detached.) Dec eps. Blind-emb cl, gilt illus upper bds (lt stained, spines sl sunned.) *Edwards.* $117/£75

KIRBY, WILLIAM and WILLIAM SPENCE. An Introduction to Entomology. London, 1878. People's ed. xxviii,607pp. Marbled eps, edges. Full calf (worn; bkpl), gilt, morocco spine label. *Edwards.* $47/£30

KIRBY, WILLIAM. On the Power, Wisdom, and Goodness of God. London, 1835. 2nd ed. 2 vols. cv,406; viii,542pp; 20 plts. (Lt foxed, esp plts; lib ink stamp, eps detached vol 1.) Marbled eps, edges. Gilt-edged calf (sl rubbed, lib #s), 2 leather title labels. *Edwards.* $117/£75

KIRCHENHOFFER, H. (trans). The Book of Fate. PA: Personal Arts, 1927. (Few notes), o/w VG. *Middle Earth.* $35/£22

KIRCHHOFF, THEODORE. Handbook of Insanity for Practitioners and Students. NY: William Wood, 1893. 1st ed in English. (iv),vi,362,(4)pp. Ptd red cl. Good (shelfworn, fr hinge strained). *Gach.* $50/£32

KIRK, CHARLES H. History of the Fifteenth Pennsylvania Volunteer Cavalry.... Phila, 1906. 1st ed. Fldg pocket map. VG. *Wantagh.* $125/£80

KIRK, EDMUND. My Southern Friends. NY: Carleton, 1863. 1st ed. (Sl foxed, sm repaired tears margins pub's ads; rubbed, lt soiled.) *Sadlon.* $20/£13

KIRK, JOHN L. History of Fire Fighting. York: Castle Museum, 1960. Rev ed. 40 plts. VG in orig wrappers. *Hollett.* $47/£30

KIRK, ROBERT C. Twelve Months in Klondike. London: Heinemann, 1899. xii,273pp, map. VG. *High Latitude.* $135/£87

KIRK, RUSSELL. A Creature of the Twilight. NY, 1966. 1st ed. VG + in VG dj. *Mcclintock.* $14/£9

KIRK, RUSSELL. The Surly Sullen Bell. Fleet, 1962. 1st ed. NF in dj (spine ends lt worn, short tears). *Certo.* $45/£29

KIRK, RUSSELL. The Surly Sullen Bell. NY: Fleet, 1962. 1st ed. Dj (sl rubbed). *Swann*.* $46/£29

KIRKALDY, ANDRA. Fifty Years of Golf: My Memories. NY: E.P. Dutton, (1921). 1st Amer ed. Frontis. Grn cl, gilt. (Spine dull, spot fr cvr, rear cvr edge sl chewed), else VG. *Pacific*.* $104/£67

KIRKBRIDE, THOMAS. On the Construction, Organization and General Arrangements of Hospitals for the Insane. Phila/London: Lippincott, 1880. 2nd ed. Inscribed, dated Oct 1881. 8vo. (ii),(xviii),(15)-320,(2)pp; 23 plts. Mauve cl (fr hinge cracked, sl shelfwear). VG. *Gach.* $850/£545

KIRKEBY, ED. Ain't Misbehavin'. NY: Dodd, Mead, 1966. 1st ed. Fine in Fine dj (sl rubbed). *Beasley.* $45/£29

KIRKFIELD, STUART. The Fine Bamboo Fly Rod. Harrisburg: Stackpole, 1986. 1st ed. 1/2 brn simulated leather, ivory pebble-grain cl-cvrd bds. Fine in Fine pict dj. *Biscotti.* $50/£32

KIRKLAND, JOSEPH. The Chicago Massacre of 1812. Chicago: Dibble Pub, 1893. 1st ed. 218,(6)pp. Ptd wraps. VG. Howes K186. *Wantagh.* $125/£80

KIRKMAN, F. B. The British Bird Book. T.C. & E.C. Jack, 1911. 4 vols. 200 color plts. (Feps lt browned; cl rubbed, chipped, soiled.) Morocco spine labels. *Edwards.* $78/£50

KIRKMAN, F. B. and F. C. R. JOURDAIN. British Birds. London/Edinburgh, 1935. 202 color plts. (Eps lt spotted, hinges repaired; sl bumped.) *Edwards.* $39/£25

KIRKMAN, F. B. and F. C. R. JOURDAIN. British Birds. London, 1938. 202 color plts. Grn cl, gilt. (Taped tears 3 plts), else VG. *Price.* $75/£48

KIRKPATRICK, CLIFFORD. Women in Nazi Germany. London: Jarrolds, 1939. 1st ed. 15 plts. Nice. *Patterson.* $47/£30

KIRKPATRICK, J. Advice to the People in General with Regard to Their Health. 1768. 3rd Eng ed. xxxiv,620pp (foxed). Old calf (worn). *Whitehart.* $140/£90

KIRKPATRICK, JOHN E. Timothy Flint...1780-1840. NY: Burt Franklin, (1968). Rpt. Fine. *Wantagh.* $25/£16

KIRST, HANS HELLMUT. The 20th of July. J. M. Brownjohn (trans). London, 1966. VG in dj. *Typographeum.* $25/£16

KIRST, HANS HELLMUT. What Became of Gunner Asch. J. M. Brownjohn (trans). London, 1964. VG in dj (sl dknd). *Typographeum.* $28/£18

KIRSTEIN, LINCOLN et al. The Classic Ballet. NY, 1952. 1st ed. VG in dj. *Truepenny.* $45/£29

KIRSTEIN, LINCOLN. The Latin-American Collection of the Museum of Modern Art. NY, (1943). 2nd ed. Fine in dj (worn). *Truepenny.* $45/£29

KIRSTEIN, LINCOLN. Rhymes of a PFC. NY/Tokyo: New Directions/Weatherhill, (1964). 1st ed. Fine in VG dj. *Reese.* $40/£26

KIRTLAND, LUCIAN SWIFT. Samurai Trails. 1919. (Frontis partly detached; upper hinge tender; cl soiled, spine faded.) *Edwards.* $44/£28

KIRWAN. (Pseud of Nicholas Murray.) Letters to the Rt. Rev. John Hughes, Roman Catholic Bishop of New York. Phila: Presbyterian Board of Pub, n.d. ca 1851. 1st, 2nd, 3rd series bound in 1. 313pp. (Sl shelfworn), else Good. *Brown.* $15/£10

KITE, ELIZABETH S. Brigadier-General Louis Lebegue Duportail...Continental Army, 1777-1783. Balt: Johns Hopkins, 1933. Frontis. Good (paper spine label worn). *Lien.* $40/£26

KITSON, MICHAEL. The Complete Paintings of Caravaggio. NY, 1969(?). 64 color plts. Good. *Washton.* $25/£16

KITSON, SYDNEY D. The Life of John Sell Cotman. London: Faber, 1937. 1st ed. Color frontis. Teg. VG. *Hollett.* $101/£65

KITTENBERGER, KALMAN. Big Game Hunting and Collecting in East Africa, 1903-1926. NY/London: Longman's, 1929. 1st ed. Frontis, fldg map. Brn cl (sl wear), else VG. *Terramedia.* $200/£128

KITTON, FREDERIC. Charles Dickens by Pen and Pencil.... London: Frank Sabin, 1890. 1st ed. Bound from orig 18/14 parts. 2 vols. Folio. Bound from orig 18/14 parts. Teg; marbled eps. Contemp 1/2 blue morocco, marbled bds (faded, soiled, sl wear), ribbed spines in 6 panels. Orig paper wrappers, prospectus, pub's ads bound in at rear. Generally VG. *Waverly**. $605/£388

KITTON, FREDERIC. The Dickens Country. London: A&C Black, 1905. 1st ed. Grn cl, gilt. (Fep neatly excised), else Fine. *Macdonnell*. $65/£42

KLABER, DORETTA. Violets of the United States. South Brunswick, 1976. 108 color plts, 30 dwgs. Fine in dj. *Brooks*. $44/£28

KLAMKIN, CHARLES. Weather Vanes. NY: Hawthorn, 1973. 1st ed. VG in Good- dj. *October Farm*. $45/£29

KLEIN, ADRIAN BERNARD. Colour-Music: The Art of Light. London: Crosby Lockwood, 1926. 1st ed. 23 photo plts. Pub's color illus cl. (Rubbed, spine top sl chipped), else Good. *Cahan*. $150/£96

KLEIN, FREDERIC SHRIVER (ed). Just South of Gettysburg, Carroll County, Maryland in the Civil War. Westminster, MD, 1963. 1st ed. VG + in VG + dj. *Pratt*. $45/£29

KLEIN, WILLIAM. Moscow. NY: Crown, 1964. 1st ed. (Name, owner stamp), else VG in VG dj (chipped). *Cahan*. $350/£224

KLEIN, WILLIAM. New York: Life Is Good and Good for You in New York. Paris: Editions du Seuil, 1956. 1st ed. 4to. W/caption booklet. Pict eps. NF in pict dj (creases, sm edgetears). *Cahan*. $1,500/£962

KLEIN, WILLIAM. Tokyo. NY: Crown, 1964. 1st ed. Fine (sig) in dj (sl chipped). *Cahan*. $350/£224

KLINEFELTER, WALTER. Origins of Sherlock Holmes. Bloomington: Gaslight, 1983. Fine w/o dj, as issued. *Janus*. $50/£32

KLINGENDER, FRANCIS. Animals in Art and Thought to the End of the Middle Ages. Evelyn Antal and John Harthan (eds). Routledge, 1971. VG in dj. *Hadley*. $94/£60

Klondike: The Chicago Record's Book for Gold Seekers. Chicago, 1897. 555pp + ads; 8 maps, incl 4 dbl-pg. Good- (ex-lib). *Scribe's Perch**. $16/£10

KLUCKER, CHRISTIAN. Adventures of an Alpine Guide. H. E. G. Tyndale (ed). Erwin & Pleasaunce von Gaisberg (trans). 1932. 1st ed in English. Port, 15 plts. Dj. *Bickersteth*. $70/£45

KLUCKHOHN, CLYDE. Beyond the Rainbow. Boston, (1933). Signed, inscribed. Dedication leaf signed by John Grabau and 1 other. 3/4 red morocco, marbled bds, gilt. *Kane**. $70/£45

KLUTCH, M. S. Mr. 2 of Everything. NY: Coward-McCann, 1946. 1st ed. Kurt Wiese (illus). 10 x 7 1/4. Dec bds. VG in dj. *Cattermole*. $50/£32

KNAGGS, R. LAWFORD. The Inflammatory and Toxic Diseases of Bone. NY: William Wood, 1926. 1st Amer ed. VG (top 1/4 spine lt stained). *Glaser*. $60/£38

KNAPP, SAMUEL L. Tales of the Garden of Kosciusko. NY: West & Trow, 1834. 1st ed. 216pp. (Lt foxed, pencil scribbling last pg), o/w VG. *New Hampshire**. $30/£19

KNEALE, NIGEL. Tomato Cain and Other Stories. NY, 1950. 1st Amer ed, 1st bk. NF in NF dj. *Polyanthos*. $30/£19

KNECHT, EDMUND et al. A Manual of Dyeing. London, 1917. 4th ed. 2 vols. (1st, last few leaves lt stained, ex-lib, bkpls, ink stamps prelims; spines faded, chipped, #s.) *Edwards*. $55/£35

KNEELAND, GEORGE. Commercialized Prostitution in New York City. NY, 1913. 1st ed. VG. *Fye*. $50/£32

KNEISS, GILBERT H. Redwood Railways. Berkeley: Howell-North, 1956. 1st ed. 2 fldg maps in rear pocket. (Sl offsetting feps), else Fine in pict dj (sl chipped). *Argonaut*. $50/£32

KNICKERBOCKER, DIEDRICH. (Pseud of Washington Irving.) A History of New York.... NY, 1809. 1st ed. 2 vols. 12mo. Fldg plt. Contemp sheep. 1/4 morocco fldg case. Fine set. Howes I83. *Swann**. $1,725/£1,106

KNIGHT, ALANNA. Blood Line. London: Macmillan, 1989. 1st ed. Fine in dj. *Murder By The Book*. $50/£32

KNIGHT, ALANNA. Enter Second Murderer. London: Macmillan, 1988. 1st ed. (Sl spine lean), else Fine in dj. *Murder By The Book*. $55/£35

KNIGHT, ARTHUR and KIT (eds). Kerouac and the Beats. NY: Paragon House, (1988). 1st ed. Fine in dj. *Reese*. $25/£16

KNIGHT, CAPTAIN. Diary of a Pedestrian in Cashmire and Thibet. London, 1863. 1/2 red calf (rebacked; sl foxed). *Petersfield*. $101/£65

KNIGHT, CHARLES HUNTOON and W. SOHIER BRYANT. Diseases of the Nose, Throat and Ear. Phila, 1909. 2nd ed. Brn cl (sl worn). VG. *Doctor's Library*. $85/£54

KNIGHT, CHARLES. Half-Hours with the Best Authors. London: Routledge, ca 1868. 4 vols. Engr frontispieces. 1/2 polished dk purple calf, gilt, contrasting labels. (Name.) *Swann**. $115/£74

KNIGHT, CHARLES. Shadows of the Old Booksellers. London, 1865. 1st ed. 320pp. (Cvrs lt worn.) VG. *Truepenny*. $95/£61

KNIGHT, CHARLES. Shadows of the Old Booksellers. London: Bell & Daldy, 1865. (Bkpl.) *Rostenberg & Stern*. $22/£14

KNIGHT, CHARLES. William Caxton, the First English Printer: A Biography. London: Charles Knight, 1844. 1st ed. Frontis port, 240 + 8pp cat, 8pp prefatory blurb. Uncut. VG in orig blind-stamped cl, gilt; buckram slipcase. *Cox*. $55/£35

KNIGHT, CLIFFORD. The Affair of the Fainting Butler. NY: Dodd, Mead, 1943. 1st ed. ('X' on fep), o/w Fine in VG dj (spine sunned, stained). *Beasley*. $45/£29

KNIGHT, CLIFFORD. The Affair of the Golden Buzzard. NY: David McKay, 1946. 1st ed. Fine in dj (nicks, short closed tears). *Mordida*. $65/£42

KNIGHT, CLIFFORD. The Affair of the Jade Monkey. NY: Dodd Mead, 1943. 1st ed. Fine in VG dj (3/4-inch piece missing spine, chipping, short closed tears, wear). *Mordida*. $65/£42

KNIGHT, CLIFFORD. The Dark Road. NY: Dutton, 1951. 1st ed. Fine in dj (sl wear). *Mordida*. $45/£29

KNIGHT, CLIFFORD. The Yellow Cat. NY: Dutton, 1950. 1st ed. Fine in dj. *Mordida*. $50/£32

KNIGHT, DAMON. Charles Fort. NY, 1970. 1st Amer ed. Fine in dj (sl sunned, lt rubbed). *Polyanthos*. $30/£19

KNIGHT, ERIC. Portrait of a Flying Yorkshireman. Paul Rotha (ed). London: Chapman & Hall, 1952. 1st ed. Port. Fine in VG dj. *Reese*. $25/£16

KNIGHT, HENRY GALLY. The Normans in Sicily. London: John Murray, 1838. 1st ed. vii,(1),355pp,(1)ad. Marbled eps; aeg. Full tan calf, gilt, morocco label. (Name, few lt lines margins, underlines; extrems rubbed), else VG. *Cahan*. $75/£48

KNIGHT, JOHN ALDEN. Ruffed Grouse. NY, 1947. 1st ed. 5 color plts, 12 b/w plts. Maroon cl, gilt. Fine in VG dj. *Price*. $49/£31

KNIGHT, JOHN ALDEN. The Theory and Technique of Fresh Water Angling. NY: Harcourt Brace, 1940. 1st ed. 4 color plts. VG + in dj. *Bowman*. $30/£19

KNIGHT, JOHN ALDEN. The Theory and Technique of Fresh Water Angling. NY: Harcourt, Brace, 1940. 1st ed. Grn buckram, silver lettering. Fine in VG pict dj (dknd). *Biscotti*. $45/£29

KNIGHT, JOHN ALDEN. Woodcock. NY, 1944. Ltd to 275 signed by Knight and Edgar Buke (illus). Cl-backed bds (lt soiled). VG. *Truepenny*. $275/£176

KNIGHT, KATHLEEN MOORE. Terror by Twilight. GC: DCC, 1942. 1st ed. (Sm stains feps), o/w Fine in VG dj (spine frayed, folds worn, sm corner chips). *Mordida*. $45/£29

KNIGHT, KEMPSTER. The Book of the Rabbit.... London: L. Upcott Gill, 1889. 2nd ed. xvi,484pp + 2 ad ll, 14pp pub's cat at end; 9 chromolitho plts. Pict red cl (worn, frayed, sl stains, hinges split, repaired). Text Good (sl aged, dusty), plts Good (sl foxed, finger mks). *Baltimore**. $220/£141

KNIGHT, OLIVER. Following the Indian Wars. Norman: Univ of OK, (1960). 1st ed. VG in dj. *Lien*. $40/£26

KNIGHT, WILLIAM H. Hand-Book Almanac for the Pacific States...1862. SF: Bancroft, 1862. 1st ed. 191pp. (Cl soiled.) *Ginsberg*. $200/£128

KNIGHTLEY, PHILLIP and COLIN SIMPSON. The Secret Lives of Lawrence of Arabia. NY/St. Louis: McGraw-Hill, 1970. 1st US ed. (Sl rubbed), o/w VG. *Worldwide*. $22/£14

KNITTLE, RHEA MANSFIELD. Early American Glass. NY/London: Century, (1927). 1st ed. Inscribed. (Sm water spots cvrs.) *Sadlon*. $50/£32

KNOBEL, EDWARD. The Fresh-Water Fishes of New England.... Boston: Bradlee Whidden, (1896). 40pp. Orig pict blue wraps bound into brn cl (sl rubbed). Internally Fine. *Blue Mountain*. $20/£13

KNOLLYS, HENRY. Incidents in the China War of 1860. London, 1875. xiv,263pp + 62pp pub's cat; 3 fldg maps. (Lt browned; sl soiled, worn, spine sl dknd; chipped.) *Edwards*. $78/£50

KNOOP, DOUGLAS. Outlines of Railway Economics. London: Macmillan, 1913. 1st ed. (Lacks fep), o/w Good. *Cox*. $19/£12

KNOTT, GEORGE H. (ed). Trial of William Palmer. London: William Hodge, 1952. Good in dj (worn). *Boswell*. $75/£48

KNOWER, DANIEL. The Adventures of a Forty-Niner. Albany: Privately ptd by Weed-Parsons, 1894. 1st ed. 200pp. Grn cl, gilt. (Few pp sl dknd; cvr lt worn), o/w Fine. *Pacific**. $173/£111

KNOWLES and MAXIM. Real Pen Work. Pittsfield, MA, c. 1881. Ptd cl-backed bds (worn; contents sl shaken, leaves sl frayed). *New Hampshire**. $80/£51

KNOWLES, D. and J. S. ST. JOSEPH. Monastic Sites from the Air. CUP, 1952. 138 plts, cat. Sound in dj. *Ars Artis*. $39/£25

KNOWLES, JOHN A. Essays in the History of the York School of Glass-Painting. London: SPCK, 1936. 1st ed. 63 plts (2 color). (Eps lt spotted.) Buckram, gilt. Dj (spotted). *Hollett*. $117/£75

KNOX, BILL. The Cockatoo Crime. London: John Long, 1958. 1st ed. Fine in Fine dj (sl rear soil). *Murder By The Book*. $125/£80

KNOX, T. Underground or Life Below the Surface. Hartford: J.B. Burr, 1873. 1st ptg. 942pp. Dec cl. VG. *Blake*. $150/£96

KNOX, THOMAS W. The Boy Travellers in the Russian Empire. NY: Harper, 1887. Color frontis, 505pp. (Bds sl rubbed, soiled, spine sl frayed), o/w VG. *Worldwide*. $65/£42

KNOX, THOMAS W. The Boy Travellers on the Congo. London: Sampson Low, Marston, 1888. 1st London ed. Frontis, xii,355pp,(1)imprint (ink inscrip fep, lt foxing in places). Blue pict cl (sl faded, rubbed), gilt-lettered. Good. *Morrell*. $109/£70

KOBLER, JOHN. The Reluctant Surgeon. NY: Doubleday, 1960. 1st ed. VG (edges rubbed) in dj. *Glaser*. $35/£22

KOCH, ALBERT C. Journey Through a Part of the United States of North America in the Years 1844-1846. Ernst A. Stadler (ed). Carbondale: Southern IL Univ, 1972. 1st ed in English. VG in dj. Howes K234. *Brown*. $15/£10

KOCH, CHARLES R. E. (ed). History of Dental Surgery. Chicago, 1909. 1st ed. Vol 1 of 3, complete. 1/2 leather (hinges cracked, fr bd detached), gilt edges. Fair. *Doctor's Library*. $100/£64

KOCH, ROBERT. Louis C. Tiffany. NY, 1965. 2nd ptg. 2 color frontispieces. Cl-backed marbled bds (sl rubbed, fore-edge lt browned). *Edwards*. $39/£25

KOCH, ROBERT. Louis C. Tiffany: Rebel in Glass. NY, (1964). VG in dj. *Argosy*. $85/£54

KOCH, THEODORE W. (ed). Tales for Bibliophiles. Chicago: Caxton Club, 1929. Ltd to 300. Teg, others untrimmed. Cl-backed marbled bds. VG (bkpl). *Truepenny*. $60/£38

KOCHNO, BORIS. Diaghilev and the Ballets Russes. Adrienne Foulke (trans). London, 1971. 1st UK ed. Dj (sl chipped). *Edwards*. $70/£45

KOEHL, HERMANN et al. The Three Musketeers of the Air, their Conquest of the Atlantic from East to West. NY: Putnam, 1928. 1st ed. Fine in NF dj. *Hermitage*. $85/£54

KOEHLER, R. A Contribution to the Study of Ophiurans of the U.S. National Museum. Washington, 1914. 18 plts. (Ex-lib.) Wraps bound in. *Henly*. $56/£36

KOEHN, ALFRED. The Way of Japanese Flower Arrangement. 1937. 2nd ed. Mtd color frontis (loose, mkd, opening pulled). Good (rebound, retaining orig spine, label; new eps). *Whittle*. $39/£25

KOENIG, GEORGE. Beyond This Place There Be Dragons. Glendale: A.H. Clark, 1984. 1st ed. 3 fldg maps. Dj. *Dawson*. $30/£19

KOENIG, GEORGE. Beyond This Place There Be Dragons. Glendale: Clark, 1984. 1st ed. One of 968. 3 fldg maps. Red cl. VF in dj. *Argonaut*. $45/£29

KOENIG, GEORGE. Death Valley Tailings. Death Valley: Death Valley '49ers, 1986. Dj. *Dawson*. $30/£19

KOESTLER, ARTHUR. The Age of Longing. NY: Macmillan, 1951. 1st Amer ed. Fine in dj (sl worn, few sm tears). *Antic Hay*. $20/£13

KOESTLER, ARTHUR. The Ghost in the Machine. NY: Macmillan, (1968). 1st ed. NF in dj. *Antic Hay*. $25/£16

KOESTLER, ARTHUR. The Lotus and the Robot. NY: Macmillan, 1961. 1st ed. Fine in dj (sl worn). *Antic Hay*. $25/£16

KOESTLER, ARTHUR. The Roots of Coincidence. London, 1972. 1st ed. NF in dj (internally repaired). *Words Etc*. $25/£16

KOESTLER, ARTHUR. Spanish Testament. London, 1937. 1st ed. Flexible cl cvrs. VG in dj. *Typographeum*. $45/£29

KOGAN, HERMAN. Traditions and Challenges, the Story of Sidley and Austin. Chicago, 1983. Fine in slipcase. *Bohling*. $40/£26

KOHANSKY, MENDEL. The Hebrew Theatre. NY: KTAV, 1969. Color frontis. VG in dj (rubbed). *Dramatis Personae*. $25/£16

KOHL, JOHANN G. Kitchi-Gami: Wanderings Round Lake Superior. London, 1860. 1st Eng ed, w/ads. Mod grn morocco, gilt, by Bayntun-Riviere. Howes K247. Swann*. $161/£103

KOHL, SCHUYLER G. Perinatal Mortality in New York City. Cambridge: Harvard Univ, 1955. Good in dj. Goodrich. $25/£16

KOLB, EMERY. Through the Grand Canyon from Wyoming to Mexico. NY: 1915. 2nd ed, or 1st ptg of 'New edition published June, 1915.' 72 plts. Teg. (Inscrip, corner lt bumped, spine ends sl chafed), else VG+. Five Quail. $110/£71

KOLB, FRITZ. Himalaya Venture. London, (1959). 1st Eng ed. VG in dj (rubbed). King. $30/£19

KOLL, IRVIN S. Diseases of the Male Urethra, Including Impotence and Sterility. Phila, 1919. 1st ed. VG (sl worn). Doctor's Library. $75/£48

KOLLONTAI, ALEXANDRA. Red Love. NY: Seven Arts, 1927. 1st US ed. VG in VG- dj (substantial loss spine head). Lame Duck. $125/£80

KOLMER, JOHN A. Serum Diagnosis by Compliment Fixation. Phila, 1928. Good. Doctor's Library. $75/£48

KOLTUN, LILLY. City Blocks, City Spaces. Ottawa: Public Archives, 1980. 1st ed. Fldg panorama in rear pocket. NF in illus stiff wrappers. Cahan. $30/£19

KONGOW, IWAO. The Later Works of the Costume of No Play in Japan. Tokyo, 1935. Folio. 50 photo plts. Native-style patterned cl. Swann*. $115/£74

KONIGSBURG, E. L. About the B'Nai Bagels. NY: Atheneum, 1969. 1st ed. 5 3/4 x 8 1/2. 172pp. VG in dj (closed tear). Cattermole. $20/£13

KONIGSBURG, E. L. From the Mixed-Up Files of Mrs. Basil Frankweiler. NY: Atheneum, 1968. 1st ed. 5 3/4 x 8 1/2. 162pp. VG in dj. Cattermole. $75/£48

KONIGSBURG, E. L. A Proud Taste for Scarlet and Miniver. NY: Atheneum, 1973. 1st ed. 5 3/4 x 8 3/4. 201pp. Fine in dj. Cattermole. $40/£26

KONIGSBURG, E. L. Throwing Shadows. NY: Atheneum, 1979. 1st US ed. 5 1/2 x 8 1/4. 151pp. Fine in dj. Cattermole. $40/£26

KONINGSBERGER, HANS. I Know What I'm Doing. NY: S&S, (1964). 1st ed. Fine in NF dj. Antic Hay. $25/£16

KONKLE, BURTON ALVA. The Life of Chief Justice Ellis Lewis 1798-1871.... Phila: Campion, 1907. Maroon cl (sl worn), gilt. Sound. Boswell. $65/£42

KONODY, P. G. The Painter of Victorian Life. London: The Studio, 1930. Frontis. (Faded, joints splitting.) Interior VF. Europa. $44/£28

KONYOT, ARTHUR. The White Rider. (As told to William D. Reichmann.) Barrington: Hill & Dale, 1961. 1st ed. VG in Good+ dj. October Farm. $45/£29

KOONTZ, DEAN R. Beastchild. Lynbrook: Charnel House, 1992. 1st hb ed. One of 750 numbered, signed by author and artist. Fine in slipcase as issued. Other Worlds. $150/£96

KOONTZ, DEAN R. Cold Fire. NY: Putnam, 1991. 1st ed. One of 750 numbered, specially bound, signed. VF in dj, slipcase. Mordida. $250/£160

KOONTZ, DEAN R. The Eyes of Darkness. Arlington Hts.: Dark Harvest, 1989. 1st hb ed. One of 400 numbered, signed. Dj, slipcase. Swann*. $92/£59

KOONTZ, DEAN R. Hideaway. NY: Putnam, 1992. #108/800 'specially bound,' signed. NF in NF dj, VG slipcase. Scribe's Perch*. $45/£29

KOONTZ, DEAN R. The House of Thunder. Arlington Hts.: Dark Harvest, 1988. One of 550 numbered, signed by Koontz and Phil Parks (illus). Dj, slipcase. Swann*. $92/£59

KOONTZ, DEAN R. How to Write Best Selling Fiction. Cincinnati, (1972). 1st ed. (Bumped), else VG in dj (sl discolored, bumped). King. $95/£61

KOONTZ, DEAN R. Night Chills. NY: Atheneum, 1976. 1st ed. (Ink name, address), o/w Fine in dj. Hermitage. $125/£80

KOONTZ, DEAN R. Night Chills. NY: Atheneum, 1976. 1st ed. Fine in dj. Mordida. $150/£96

KOONTZ, DEAN R. Twilight Eyes. (Plymouth): Land of Enchantment, (1985). 1st trade ed. Fine in Fine dj. Other Worlds. $75/£48

KOONTZ, DEAN R. Twilight Eyes. London: W.H. Allen, 1987. 1st British ed, 1st ptg. Dj. Swann*. $69/£44

KOONTZ, DEAN R. The Vision. NY: Putnam, 1977. 1st ed. Fine in dj (sm closed tear). Mordida. $125/£80

KOONTZ, DEAN R. Whispers. NY: Putnam, (1980). One of 7000. Fine in Fine dj (sl rubbed). Between The Covers. $750/£481

KOONTZ, LOUIS KNOTT. Robert Dinwiddie.... Glendale: Clark, 1941. 1st ed. One of 1018. Teg. Blue cl. (Sl water spots to spine, rear cvr), else Fine. Argonaut. $75/£48

KOPELOFF, NICHOLAS. Man vs. Microbes. NY, 1931. VG. Fye. $50/£32

KORN, GRANINO A. and THERESA M. Electronic Analog Computers. NY: McGraw-Hill, 1952. 1st ed. Fine in dj (sl shelfworn). Glaser. $150/£96

KORN, GRANINO A. and THERESA M. Electronic Analog Computers. NY: McGraw-Hill, 1956. 2nd ed. Fine (sig clipped tp). Glaser. $85/£54

KORN, J. (ed). Boot and Shoe Production. Pitman, 1953. 1st ed. Good+ (worn). Whittle. $23/£15

KORNBLUTH, C. M. Not This August. GC: Doubleday, 1955. 1st ed. NF in dj (lt soiled, sl chipped). Bromer. $75/£48

KORNBLUTH, C. M. Takeoff. Doubleday, 1952. 1st ed. VG. Madle. $17/£11

KORTRIGHT, F. H. The Ducks, Geese and Swans of North America. Harrisburg/Washington, 1953. 7th ptg. 36 color plts. Good. Scribe's Perch*. $22/£14

KOSCHATSKY, WALTER. Albrecht Durer. NY, 1973. 32 color plts. Good in dj (worn). Washton. $75/£48

KOSINSKI, JERZY. Cockpit. London: Hutchinson, 1975. 1st UK ed. VG+ in VG dj (sm tear spine top). Williams. $23/£15

KOSINSKI, JERZY. The Painted Bird. London: W.H. Allen, 1966. 1st Eng ed. Fine in dj (dknd spine, edges). Dermont. $75/£48

KOSINSKI, JERZY. The Painted Bird. London: W.H. Allen, 1966. 1st UK ed. VG (ink name) in dj (sl edgeworn, sm hole spine). Williams. $75/£48

KOSKOWSKI, W. The Habit of Tobacco Smoking. London, 1955. (Feps lt spotted; staining from label to verso of tp intruding on tp, 1/2 tp.) Dj (chipped, browned). Edwards. $31/£20

KOSKOWSKI, W. The Habit of Tobacco Smoking. London, 1955. 1st ed. VG. Fye. $40/£26

KOSTER, J. and M. MURRAY. New Crochet and Hairpin Work. J. Calder, 1955. 1st ed. VG+ in dj (sl torn). Whittle. $28/£18

KOTELIANSKY, S. S. (ed). Anton Tchekhov. Routledge, 1927. 1st ed. Port. (Cl mkd, bumped.) Cox. $23/£15

KOTELIANSKY, S. S. (trans). New Dostoevsky Letters. London, (1929). Frontis port. Black cl-backed 'snakeskin' bds, paper title label. Very Nice in dj (sl worn). Cady. $20/£13

KOTLOWITZ, ROBERT. The Boardwalk. NY: Knopf, 1977. 1st ed. Cream cl-backed lt blue bds (sl soiled). NF (bkpl) in dj (sl chipped). Blue Mountain. $15/£10

KOTZE, D. J. (ed). Letters of the American Missionaries 1835-1838. Cape Town, 1950. Frontis port, fldg map. *Edwards.* $23/£15

KOTZWINKLE, WILLIAM. Hermes 3000. Pantheon, 1972. 1st ed. Fine in dj (flaps creased). *Certo.* $30/£19

KOUDELKA, JOSEF. Gypsies. NY: Aperture, 1975. 60 b/w plts. (Owner stamp), else NF in stiff wrappers. *Cahan.* $50/£32

KOURNAKOFF, SERGEI. What Russia Did for Victory. NY: New Century, (1945). 1st Amer ed. NF in pict wrappers. *Reese.* $20/£13

KOVIC, RON. Born on the Fourth of July. NY: McGraw-Hill, (1976). 1st ed, 1st bk. Fine in NF dj. *Pettler & Lieberman.* $80/£51

KOYAMA, FUJIO and JOHN FIGGESS. Two Thousand Years of Oriental Ceramics. NY: Abrams, (1960). 1st ed. 54 tipped-in color plts. Ochre cl. Good in dj (soiled). *Karmiole.* $150/£96

KOZLOFF, MAX. Jasper Johns. NY, (1968). Dj. *Swann*.* $431/£276

KOZLOFF, MAX. Jasper Johns. NY: Abrams, n.d. 142 plts. (Edges sl discolored.) Fine dj. *Metropolitan*.* $201/£129

KOZLOFF, MAX. Photography and Fascination. Danbury, NH: Addison House, 1979. 1st ed. Fine in dj (fr panel faded). *Cahan.* $45/£29

KRAAY, COLIN M. Greek Coins. NY: Abrams, (1966). Folio. 20 color plts, 4 maps. Good in dj. *Archaeologia.* $650/£417

KRAFT, LOUIS. Custer and the Cheyenne. El Segundo, CA: Upton, 1995. 1st ed. New in dj. *Lien.* $65/£42

KRAKEL, DEAN F. The Saga of Tom Horn: The Story of a Cattleman's War.... (Laramie, WY: Powder River Pub, 1954.) 1st ed, 2nd issue, w/changes to illus and text. B/c of threatened lawsuit, 1st issue pulled before release and certain illus excised, replaced w/other pp by tipping them in, not changing the pg count. Text on p13 and p54 was changed. (Name), else Fine in pict dj (sl chipped, 2 sm pieces missing top edge). *Argonaut.* $150/£96

KRAMER, FRITZ L. Twenty-Third Biennial Report Idaho State Historical Department, 1951-1952. N.p.: ID State Hist Dept, 1953. Good in stiff wrappers (chip, sl soiled). *Brown.* $12/£8

KRAMER, HILTON. Richard Lindner. Boston, (1975). Dj. *Swann*.* $57/£37

KRAMER, JANE. Paterfamilias, Allen Ginsberg in America. London: Gollancz, 1970. 1st British ed. Fine in VG dj (spine faded). *Reese.* $25/£16

KRAMER, SIDNEY. A History of Stone and Kimball and Herbert S. Stone and Co. Chicago: Norman W. Forgue, 1940. Ltd to 1500. Signed. Grn cl, gilt. Good. *Karmiole.* $125/£80

KRAPPE, ALEXANDER HAGGERTY. The Science of Folklore. Methuen, 1930. 1st ed. (Margins lt browned.) Dj (sl chipped). *Edwards.* $55/£35

KRASILOVSKY, PHYLLIS. Susan Sometimes. NY: Macmillan, 1962. 1st ed. Abbi Giventer (illus). 5 3/4 x 7 1/4. Pict bds. VG in dj. *Cattermole.* $30/£19

KRAUS, GEORGE. High Road to Promontory. Palo Alto: American West, (1969). 1st ed. VF in pict dj. *Argonaut.* $45/£29

KRAUS, GEORGE. High Road to Promontory: Building the Central Pacific.... Palo Alto, CA: American West, (1969). 1st ed. VG in dj (sl worn). *Lien.* $45/£29

KRAUS, HANS P. Sir Francis Drake, a Pictorial Biography. Amsterdam: N. Israel, 1970. 1st ed. Blue cl, gilt. Fine. *Pacific*.* $58/£37

KRAUS, THEODOR. Pompeii and Herculaneum: The Living Cities of the Dead. NY: Abrams, (1975). Good in dj. *Archaeologia.* $95/£61

KRAUSE, HERBERT. The Oxcart Trail. Bobbs-Merrill, (1954). 1st ltd Minnesota ed, signed. Also inscribed, signed. Fine in Fine dj. *Authors Of West.* $35/£22

KRAUSS, RUTH. The Bundle Book. NY: Harper, 1951. 1st ed. Helen Stone (illus). 9 1/4 x 8. Bds. VG in dj (few closed tears). *Cattermole.* $125/£80

KRAUSS, RUTH. The Cantilever Rainbow. NY: Pantheon, 1965. 1st ed. 6 1/2 x 8 1/2. 40pp. VG in dj. *Cattermole.* $50/£32

KRAUSS, RUTH. Charlotte and the White Horse. NY, (1955). 1st ed. Maurice Sendak (illus). Sm 8vo. Cl-backed bds (lt worn). Dj (sl soiled, spotted). *Oinonen*.* $275/£176

KRAUSS, RUTH. Charlotte and the White Horse. NY: Harper, 1955. 1st ed. Maurice Sendak (illus). 5 x 7. 20pp. Fine in dj. *Cattermole.* $250/£160

KRAUSSE, ALEXIS. China in Decay. London, 1900. Frontis port, 6 maps (3 fldg). (Feps lt browned; soil.) *Edwards.* $47/£30

KRAUTHEIMER, RICHARD. The Rome of Alexander VII 1655-1667. Princeton, 1985. Good in dj. *Washton.* $60/£38

KRAUTHEIMER, RICHARD. Rome. Profile of a City, 312-1308. Princeton, 1980. Good in dj. *Washton.* $85/£54

KRAUZ, SIGMUND. Street Types of Great American Cities. Chicago, 1896. Dec pub's cl. *Kane*.* $225/£144

KREHBIEL, HENRY EDWARD. Afro-American Folk-songs: A Study.... NY/London: G. Schirmer, 1914. 1st ed. Gilt-dec cl (extrems rubbed). VG. *Cahan.* $200/£128

KREIDER, CLAUDE M. The Bamboo Rod and How to Build It. NY: Macmillan, 1951. 1st ed. Fine in dj. *Bowman.* $125/£80

KREMERS, E. and G. URDANG. History of Pharmacy. Phila, 1951. 2nd ed. (Cl sl dull), o/w VG. *Whitehart.* $62/£40

KRESSING, HARRY. The Cook. NY: Random House, (1965). 1st ed. VG + in VG dj. *Pettler & Lieberman.* $30/£19

KRETSCHMER, ALBERT and CARL ROHRBACH. The Costumes of All Nations.... London, 1882. Extra chromolitho tp, 104 chromolitho plts. Aeg. Pebbled red cl (worn), gilt. *Kane*.* $160/£103

KREYMBORG, ALFRED. Scarlet and Mellow. NY, 1926. 1st Amer ed. Signed presentation copy, dated 1926. Dec bds. Fine (corners sl rubbed). Issued w/o dj. *Polyanthos.* $25/£16

KRICK, ROBERT KENNETH. 30th Virginia Infantry. (Lynchburg, VA: H.E. Howard, 1985.) 2nd ed. NF. *Mcgowan.* $25/£16

KRIEGER, HERBERT W. Aboriginal Indian Pottery of the Dominican Republic. Washington: GPO, 1931. 56 plts. Uncut. Good in wrappers (sl chipped). *Archaeologia.* $75/£48

KRIMS, LES. The Deerslayers. Buffalo: Self-published, 1972. 1st ed. Signed, numbered ed. 1 fldg pg of text; 23 loose photos. (Owner stamp on fr; sl rubbed), else NF in hinged box, mtd print on fr. *Cahan.* $145/£93

KRIMS, LES. Fictcryptokrimsographs. Buffalo, NY: Humpy, (1975). 1st ed. Signed. NF in pict stiff wrappers (sl soiled, early price-sticker on rear). *Cahan.* $125/£80

KRIMS, LES. The Little People of America 1971. Buffalo: Self-published, 1972. 1st ed. Signed, numbered ed. 1 fldg pg of text; 24 loose plts. (Owner stamp on fr; sl rubbed), else NF in hinged box, mtd print on fr. *Cahan.* $145/£93

KRIPPNER, STANLEY and DANIEL RUBIN (eds). Galaxies of Life. NY/London/Paris: An Interface Book (Gordon and Breach), (1973). 1st ed. Inscribed by both. VG. *Gach.* $30/£19

KRIS, ERNST. Psychoanalytic Explorations in Art. NY, 1962. Good. *Washton.* $40/£26

KRIVATSY, PETER. A Catalogue of Incunabula and Sixteenth Century Printed Books in the National Library of Medicine. First Supplement. Bethesda, 1971. Good. *Goodrich.* $75/£48

KROEBER, A. L. Handbook of the Indians of California. Washington: GPO, 1925. 1st ed. *Book Market.* $150/£96

KROEBER, A. L. Handbook of the Indians of California. BAE Bulletin 78. Washington: GPO, 1925. 1st ed. 10 maps (7 fldg); 73 illus plts. Grn cl, gilt spine. (2 sm pieces removed fep; spine gilt dull), o/w NF. Howes K268. *Pacific*.* $138/£88

KROEBER, THEODORA and ROBERT F. HEIZER. Almost Ancestors: The First Californians. SF: Sierra Club, (1968). Tan cl, gilt. Fine in pict dj. *Pacific*.* $52/£33

KROGH, AUGUST. The Anatomy and Physiology of Capillaries. NY: Hafner, 1959. Rpt. Frontis port. Fine. *Glaser.* $75/£48

KROHN, WILLIAM O. In Borneo Jungles. Indianapolis: Bobbs-Merrill, (1927). 1st ed. Blue cl, gilt. Good. *Karmiole.* $50/£32

KROHN, WILLIAM O. In Borneo Jungles. Among the Dyak Headhunters. Indianapolis: Bobbs-Merrill, 1927. 1st ed. 31 plts, dbl-pg map. (Cl sl rubbed, soiled), o/w VG. *Worldwide.* $35/£22

KROMER, TOM. Waiting for Nothing. NY: Knopf, 1935. 1st ed. Fine in dj (few sm tears). *Captain's Bookshelf.* $150/£96

KRONFELD, RUDOLPH. Histopathology of the Teeth and Surrounding Structures. London, 1945. 2nd ed. Good (inner hinges cracked; worn). *Doctor's Library.* $50/£32

KROPOTKIN, PETER. Modern Science and Anarchism. NY: Mother Earth, 1908. 1st ed. Pb. VG (sm spots on wraps). *Beasley.* $60/£38

KRUSE, G. Trunk Call. London: Elek, 1962. 1st ed. Fine in VG dj. *Mikesh.* $20/£13

KRUSI, HERMANN. Handbook of Perspective Drawing. NY: Appleton, 1874. 1st ed. 65pp. *Marlborough.* $195/£125

KRUTCH, JOSEPH WOOD. Baja California and the Geography of Hope. SF: Sierra Club, (1967). 1st ed. Fldg map. (Bumped, sl spine tear), else Good. *King.* $65/£42

KRUTCH, JOSEPH WOOD. The Desert Year. NY: Sloane, (1951/1952). 1st ed. Fine in Fine dj. *Book Market.* $25/£16

KRUTCH, JOSEPH WOOD. Herbal. Boston: Putnam, 1965. Cl spine, dec paper-backed bds. Fine. *Quest.* $60/£38

KUCK, L. E. The Art of Japanese Gardens. NY: John Davy, 1940. Color frontis, 65 plts. Sound. *Ars Artis.* $94/£60

KUGY, JULIUS. Alpine Pilgrimage. H.E.G. Tyndale (trans). 1934. 1st ed in English. Port, 20 plts. Dj. *Bickersteth.* $55/£35

KUH, CHARLOTTE. The Delivery Men. NY: MacMillan Happy Hour, 1929. 4th ptg. Kurt Wiese (illus). 5 3/4 sq. Pict bds. Good (lt soil). *Cattermole.* $50/£32

KUH, CHARLOTTE. The Fireman. NY: MacMillan Happy Hour, 1929. 2nd ed. Kurt Wiese (illus). 5 3/4 sq. Pict bds. Good. *Cattermole.* $35/£22

KUHLMAN, CHARLES. Legend into History, the Custer Mystery. Harrisburg, (1951). 1st ed. Fold-out map; table in pouch. Pict cvr. VG. *Pratt.* $135/£87

KUHN, CHARLES L. A Catalogue of German Paintings of the Middle Ages and Renaissance in American Collections. Cambridge, 1936. 80 plts. (Newly rebacked, scuffed, stained.) *Washton.* $75/£48

KUHNE, LOUIS. Neo-Naturopathy.... Butler, NJ, 1917. VG. *Argosy.* $45/£29

KUHNE, LOUIS. Neo-Naturopathy: The New Science of Healing. Butler, NJ, 1917. Amer ed. Grn cl. VG (extrems sl worn). *Doctor's Library.* $50/£32

KUHNE, LOUIS. The New Science of Healing. Leipsic, 1904. 20th Eng ed. Grn gilt-tooled cl. NF. *Doctor's Library.* $75/£48

KUHNE, LOUIS. The Science of Facial Expression. NY, 1917. 1st ed. Grn cl (sl worn). VG. *Doctor's Library.* $40/£26

KUMIN, MAXINE. The Beach Before Breakfast. NY: Putnam, 1964. 1st ed. Leonard Weisgard (illus). 10 1/4 x 8. 32pp. Fine in dj. *Cattermole.* $25/£16

KUMM, H. K. W. Khont-Hon-Nofer. London, 1910. Color frontis tipped in. Good (ex-lib, 4 stamps, lt foxing; sl rubbed). *Grayling.* $78/£50

KUMMER, FREDERIC ARNOLD. Gentleman in Hades. NY: Sears, (1930). 1st Amer ed. VG (spine rubbed) in dj (spine sunned; pieces missing, rear panel detached; sl rubbed, soiled). *Polyanthos.* $25/£16

KUMMER, FREDERIC ARNOLD. The Scarecrow Murders. NY: Dodd Mead, 1938. 1st ed. VG in dj (price-clipped, spine ends chipped, 1/2-inch piece missing fr panel, folds worn). *Mordida.* $30/£19

KUNDERA, MILAN. The Book of Laughter and Forgetting. NY: Knopf, 1980. 1st US ed. Fine in dj. *Lame Duck.* $65/£42

KUNDERA, MILAN. The Book of Laughter and Forgetting. NY: Knopf, 1980. 1st Amer ed. Fine in Fine dj (price-clipped). *Between The Covers.* $85/£54

KUNDERA, MILAN. Immortality. NY: Grove Weidenfeld, 1991. 1st US ed. One of 250 numbered, signed. Fine in cl-cvrd bds, slipcase (sl soiled). *Lame Duck.* $150/£96

KUNDERA, MILAN. The Joke. NY: Harper & Row, (1982). 1st US ed. NF in dj (lt wear, sm tears). *Antic Hay.* $35/£22

KUNDERA, MILAN. The Joke. NY, 1967. 1st Amer ed. NF in NF dj. *Warren.* $30/£19

KUNDERA, MILAN. Laughable Loves. NY: Knopf, 1974. 1st US ed. NF in dj. *Lame Duck.* $100/£64

KUNDERA, MILAN. The Unbearable Lightness of Being. NY: Harper, (1984). 1st Amer ed. (Sl bump bottom edge), else Fine in dj (sl rubbing). *Between The Covers.* $85/£54

KUNDERA, MILAN. The Unbearable Lightness of Being. NY: Harper & Row, 1984. 1st ed. Fine in dj. *Lame Duck.* $75/£48

KUNEN, JAMES SIMON. The Strawberry Statement—Notes of a College Revolutionary. NY: Random House, 1969. 1st ed. Black cl. (Sm stain corner 2pp), else Fine in dj. *Blue Mountain.* $25/£16

KUNITZ, STANLEY. Robert Lowell: Poet of Terribilita. NY: Pierpont Morgan Library, (1974). 1st ed. NF in ptd wrappers. *Captain's Bookshelf.* $35/£22

KUNSTMANN, JOSEF. The Transformation of Eros. Phila, 1965. 80 plts. Good. *Washton.* $45/£29

KUNZ, GEORGE FREDERICK and CHARLES HUGH STEVENSON. The Book of the Pearl. NY, 1908. 1st ed. (Sl soil, sl shaken.) Gilt blue cl (sl worn, soiled, hinges tender). *Freeman*.* $170/£109

KUNZ, GEORGE FREDERICK. The Curious Lore of Precious Stones. Phila, (1913). 1st ed. 49 plts (6 color). (Bkpl, tape stains eps; shaken.) *Swann*.* $69/£44

KUNZ, GEORGE FREDERICK. The Curious Lore of Precious Stones. Phila: Lippincott, 1913. Signed presentation. Partly unopened; teg. Pict cl. (2pp lt browned), else Fine. Blake. $175/£112

KUNZ, GEORGE FREDERICK. Ivory and the Elephant in Art, Archaeology, and in Science. NY, 1916. 1st ed. Inscribed, signed. (Feps browned by laid-in obit; frontis, tp foxed.) Buckram (spine dknd, worn), full-size labels. Swann*. $373/£239

KUNZ, GEORGE FREDERICK. The Magic of Jewels and Charms. Phila, 1915. 1st ed. (Cellotape stains feps; spine dknd.) Swann*. $161/£103

KUNZ, GEORGE FREDERICK. Rings for the Finger. Phila: Lippincott, 1917. 1st ed. 3 color, 108 b/w plts. VG (sl foxing to text facing plts, 1 leaf torn; rubbed, lt frayed, spine faded). Waverly*. $49/£31

KURETSKY, SUSAN DONAHUE. The Paintings of Jacob Ochtervelt (1634-1682). Montclair, 1979. Good in dj. Washton. $100/£64

KURTEN, B. The Cave Bear Story. NY: Columbia, 1976. 1st ed. NF in VG dj. Mikesh. $25/£16

KURUTZ, GARY F. Benjamin C. Truman. SF: Bk Club of CA, 1984. One of 600. Fine in dj. Black Sun. $55/£35

KURZ, RUDOLPH. Journal of Rudolph Friederich Kurz. An Account of His Experiences...During the Years 1846 to 1852. J. N. B. Hewitt (ed). Myrtis Jarrell (trans). Washington: Smithsonian Inst, 1937. BAE Bulletin 115. 1st ptg. 48 plts. Orig ptd wrappers (spine ends lt rubbed). Howes K281. Sadlon. $175/£112

KUTUMBIAH, P. Ancient Indian Medicine. Bombay: Orient Longmans, 1969. Rev ed. VG in dj. White. $28/£18

KVASNICKA, ROBERT M. and HERMAN J. VIOLA (eds). The Commissioners of Indian Affairs, 1824-1977. Lincoln: Univ of NE, (1979). 1st ed. VG in dj. Lien. $40/£26

KYNE, PETER B. The Cappy Ricks Special. NY: H.C. Kinsey, 1935. 1st ed. NF in VG dj (sl worn). Antic Hay. $25/£16

KYNE, PETER B. The Enchanted Hill. Cosmopolitan, 1924. 1st ed. (Foxed), else Fine in VG dj. Authors Of West. $40/£26

KYNE, PETER B. Never the Twain Shall Meet. Cosmopolitan, 1923. 1st ed. Fine in Fine dj. Authors Of West. $35/£22

KYNE, PETER B. The Pride of Palomar. Cosmopolitan, 1921. 1st ed. Inscribed, signed. VG in VG + dj. Authors Of West. $50/£32

KYNE, PETER B. They Also Serve. Cosmopolitan, 1927. 1st ed. Fine in Fine dj. Authors Of West. $25/£16

KYNE, PETER B. Tide of Empire. Cosmopolitan, 1928. 1st ed. Fine in VG + dj. Authors Of West. $40/£26

KYNE, PETER B. Tide of Empire. NY: Cosmopolitan, 1928. 1st ed. W. Smithson Broadhead (illus). Fine in NF dj. Unger. $150/£96

KYNNERSLEY, T. C. Pratt's Law of Highways.... London: Shaw, 1865. 10th ed. Grn cl, label (rubbed, re-lettered). Boswell. $125/£80

KYTLE, ELIZABETH. Willie Mae. NY: Knopf, 1958. 1st ed. Fine in NF dj. Sadlon. $20/£13

L

L'AMOUR, LOUIS. Bendigo Shafter. NY: Dutton, (1979). 1st ed. Fine in Fine dj (price-clipped). Unger. $100/£64

L'AMOUR, LOUIS. The Californios. NY: Dutton, 1974. 1st ed. Fine in Fine dj (price-clipped). Unger. $175/£112

L'AMOUR, LOUIS. The Californios. NY: Dutton-Saturday Review, 1974. 1st ed. Fine in Fine dj. Warren. $175/£112

L'AMOUR, LOUIS. Jubal Sackett. NY: Bantam, 1985. 1st ed. Fine in Fine dj. Else Fine. $55/£35

L'AMOUR, LOUIS. Kilkenny. NY: Ace, (1954). Pb orig. VG + (pp lt browned, spine edges rubbed). Between The Covers. $100/£64

L'AMOUR, LOUIS. Over on the Dry Side. NY: Dutton-Saturday Review, 1975. 1st ed. Fine in Fine dj. Warren. $150/£96

L'AMOUR, LOUIS. Rivers West. NY: Dutton-Saturday Review, 1975. 1st ed. Fine in Fine dj (sm flap crease). Warren. $125/£80

L'AMOUR, LOUIS. Sackett's Land. NY: Dutton, (1974). 1st ed. Fine in Fine dj. Unger. $150/£96

L'AMOUR, LOUIS. Sackett's Land. Dutton, 1974. 1st ed. Fine in VG dj. Authors Of West. $80/£51

L'AMOUR, LOUIS. Sackett's Land. NY: Dutton-Saturday Review, 1974. 1st ed. Fine in Fine dj. Warren. $150/£96

L'AMOUR, LOUIS. To the Far Blue Mountains. Dutton, (1976). 1st ed. Fine in dj. Authors Of West. $80/£51

L'AMOUR, LOUIS. To the Far Blue Mountains. NY: Dutton, 1976. 1st ed. Fine in Fine dj. Warren. $125/£80

L'ENGLE, MADELEINE. A Ring of Endless Light. NY: FSG, 1980. 1st ed. Signed. 5 1/2 x 8 1/4. 324pp. Fine in dj. Cattermole. $60/£38

L'ENGLE, MADELEINE. A Swiftly Tilting Planet. NY: FSG, 1978. 1st ed. 5 3/4 x 8 1/2. 278pp. Fine in dj. Cattermole. $30/£19

LA BRANCHE, GEORGE M. L. The Dry Fly and Fast Water. NY: Scribner, 1914. True 1st ed. Teg. Grn cl, gilt. Fine (spine sl dknd). Biscotti. $200/£128

LA BREE, BENJAMIN (ed). Camp Fires of the Confederacy. Louisville, KY: Courier-Journal Job Ptg Co, 1898. 1st ed. 560pp. Orig 1/2 leather, cl (chipped, scuffed). VG. Mcgowan. $300/£192

LA BREE, BENJAMIN. The Confederate Soldier in the Civil War, 1861-1865.... Louisville: Courier-Journal, 1895. 1st ed. Color frontis, 480pp. Rebound w/orig cl panels laid down. VG thus. Mcgowan. $300/£192

LA FARGE, JOHN. An Artist's Letters from Japan. NY, 1897. Teg. Blue cl, gilt. (Lt wear, soil.) Freeman*. $40/£26

LA FARGE, JOHN. A Report on the American Jesuits. NY: Farrar, Straus & Cudahy, 1956. 1st ed. Margaret Bourke-White (photos). NF (sig) in VG + dj. Smith. $60/£38

LA FARGE, OLIVER. As Long as the Grass Shall Grow. NY/Toronto: Alliance Book Corp, 1940. 1st ed. NF in dj (edgeworn). Cahan. $100/£64

LA FARGE, OLIVER. A Pictorial History of the American Indian. London: Deutsch, (1958). 1st British ed. VG + (name). Authors Of West. $60/£38

LA FARGE, OLIVER. Sparks Fly Upward. Boston, 1931. 1st ed. Orange cl. VG +. Smith. $20/£13

LA FARGE, PHYLLIS. The Pancake King. NY: Delacorte, 1971. 1st ed. Seymour Chwast (illus). 12 x 9 1/4. VG in dj. Cattermole. $45/£29

LA GORCE, JOHN OLIVER. The Book of Fishes. Washington: National Geographic, 1961. 3rd ptg. (Sl soiled), o/w VG. Worldwide. $18/£12

LA MAZIERE, PIERRE. The Brothel. NY: Privately ptd, 1930. One of 50 (of 750) bound in 3/4 grn morocco. Fair (extrms worn away, scuffed, spine wormed). Cullen. $60/£38

LA MOTT, ELLEN. The Opium Monopoly. NY, 1920. 1st ed. VG. *Fye.* $45/£29

LA PEROUSE, JEAN FRANCOIS. A Voyage Round the World...To Which Are Added, A Voyage from Manilla to California, by Don Antonio Maurelle. Boston, 1801. 1st Amer ed. 333pp (foxed, tanned, marginal dampstaining, contemp sig). Contemp calf (spine ends chipped; hinges broken), spine gilt, leather label (chipped). Sound. Howes L93. *Reese.* $675/£433

LA ROSA, FERNANDO. Photographs: Fernando la Rosa. Frame Series, 1978-1988. Atlanta: Nexus Contemp Art Center, 1988. 20 full-pg b/w photos. Fine in pict stiff wrappers. *Cahan.* $20/£13

LA SALLE, ROBERT. Relation of the Discoveries and Voyages...from 1679 to 1681. Chicago: Caxton Club, 1901. One of 224. Howes L110. *Swann*.* $201/£129

LA SPINA, GREYE. Invaders from the Dark. Sauk City: Arkham House, 1960. 1st ed. Dj (sl worn). *Swann*.* $69/£44

LA WALL, CHARLES. Four Thousand Years of Pharmacy. Phila, 1927. 1st ed. VG. *Fye.* $75/£48

LABARTE, JULES. Handbook of the Arts of the Middle Ages and Renaissance.... John Murray, 1855. 1st Eng ed. xxxvi,443pp (bkpl, pencil marginalia, side-lining), binder's ticket. 19th-cent 1/2 calf (rebacked, corners repaired), marbled sides, morocco label. *Cox.* $44/£28

LABRANCHE, GEORGE. The Dry Fly and Fast Water. NY: Scribner, 1914. True 1st ed w/gilt medallion on cvr. (Spine gilt sl dull), else VG. *Bowman.* $80/£51

LACKINGTON, JAMES. Memoirs of James Lackington.... Newburgh, (NY): J. Fellows, 1796. 1st Amer ed. 268pp. Contemp mottled sheep (skillfully rebacked in period style), retaining orig spine label. (Bds sl cupped), else Very Nice. *Felcone.* $400/£256

LACKINGTON, JAMES. Memoirs of the First 45 Years. London, 1792. 1/2 calf (recently rebound), spine gilt, marbled bds. *Moss.* $117/£75

LACOUR, PIERRE. The Manufacture of Liquers, Wines, and Cordials, Without the Aid of Distillation. NY: Dick & Fitzgerald, (1868). Nicely rebound. *Perier.* $45/£29

LACROIX, PAUL. Science and Literature in the Middle Ages.... London, 1878. 1st ed. 549pp. (13 chromolithos not present, do not appear to have been bound in.) *Fye.* $75/£48

LACY, ED. Go For the Body. Boardman, 1959. 1st hb ed. Fine in Fine dj. *Certo.* $50/£32

LACY, ED. Room to Swing. Harper, 1957. 1st ed. Fine in Fine dj. *Certo.* $40/£26

LACY, GEORGE. Pictures of Travel, Sport, and Adventure. London: Pearson, 1899. xvi,420pp; 30 plts. Pict cl (lt rubbed). *Adelson.* $130/£83

LADA-MOCARSKI, VALERIAN. Bibliography of Books on Alaska Published Before 1868. New Haven: Yale, 1969. 1st ed. VG in dj. *New Hampshire*.* $195/£125

LADD, ANNA M. HAGER. Our Mediterranean Cruise, by Steamer 'New England' in 1900. Chicago, 1902. Port. VG (name stamp). *Bohling.* $16/£10

LADD, WILLIAM E. and ROBERT E. GROSS. Abdominal Surgery of Infancy and Childhood. Phila: Saunders, (1947). 1st ed, 4th ptg. NF. *Glaser.* $95/£61

Ladies Calling. (By Richard Allestree.) Oxford: At the theater, 1673. 1st ed. 8vo. (xxiv),141,1,95pp (lacks fep). Contemp calf (sl worn). Good (cut edge A1). *Second Life.* $750/£481

Ladies Friend. (By Pierre Joseph Boudier de Villemert.) New Haven, (CT): Ptd by Abel Morse, 1789. 4th Amer ed. 107pp (lacks fep, final leaf pasted down). Contemp 1/4 sheep, marbled bds. Nice (bkpl). *Second Life.* $450/£288

LAENNEC, R. A Treatise on the Diseases of the Chest and on Mediate Auscultation.... NY/Phila: S&W Wood/Thomas, Cowperwaite, 1838. 4th Amer ed. 2 litho plts. (Foxed, sig tp.) Recent 1/2 calf. *Maggs.* $343/£220

LAFAYETTE, GILBERT DE MORTIER. Memoirs...Embracing Details of His Public and Private Life. NY, 1825. Contemp tree sheep (rubbed). Howes L16. *Swann*.* $258/£165

LAGERKVIST, PAR. The Dwarf. NY: Fischer, 1945. 1st ed. (Bkpl), else NF in VG + dj (sm tear, sm puncture rear). *Lame Duck.* $85/£54

LAGERKVIST, PAR. The Dwarf. NY: LB Fischer, 1945. 1st Amer ed. Fine in dj (lt worn, price-clipped). *Hermitage.* $35/£22

LAGERKVIST, PAR. The Sibyl. Naomi Walford (trans). NY: Random House, (1958). 1st ed. NF in dj. *Antic Hay.* $25/£16

LAGERKVIST, PAR. The Sibyl. NY: Random House, 1958. 1st US ed. NF in VG + dj (spine tanned). *Lame Duck.* $50/£32

LAHUE, KALTON C. and JOSEPH A. BAILEY. Glass, Brass and Chrome. Norman: Univ of OK, 1972. 1st ed. As New in dj. *Cahan.* $65/£42

LAING, JOHN. A Voyage to Spitsbergen.... Edinburgh: Adam Black, 1818. 2nd ed. (vi),165pp. Uncut. Orig bds (worn, rebacked in cl). (Rubber stamp verso tp, last leaf), else VG. *High Latitude.* $400/£256

LAING, R. D. The Facts of Life. NY: Pantheon, (1976). 1st Amer ed. Fine in dj. *Antic Hay.* $17/£11

LAING, R. D. The Politics of Experience. NY: Pantheon, 1967. 1st ed. Fine in dj (lt used, internal mend). *Beasley.* $100/£64

LALLEMAND, M. A Practical Treatise on the Causes, Symptoms and Treatment of Spermatorrhoea. Phila, 1858. 3rd Amer ed. 412pp. Tooled cl bds (sl worn). Good. *Doctor's Library.* $75/£48

LAMARTINE, A. De. Graziella. London: Nonesuch, 1929. Ltd to 1600 numbered. Patterned cl. Teg. VG in slipcase (worn). *King.* $30/£19

LAMB, CHARLES and MARY. Tales from Shakespeare. London/NY: J.M. Dent/E.P. Dutton, 1909. One of 750 signed by Arthur Rackham (illus). 13 tipped-in color plts, 2 full-pg b/w illus. (Lacks fep, reps soiled), o/w Contents VG. Gilt-dec white cl (lacks 1 of 4 ribbon ties, sl worn, soiled). *New Hampshire*.* $275/£176

LAMB, CHARLES. Elia and the Last Essays of Elia. Gregynog Press, 1929-1930. One of 285 numbered. 2 vols. Orig invoice for 5 gns. loosely inserted. Grey-grn buckram, beveled bds, spines gilt. Fine (1st blank sl rubbed) in slipcase (sl worn). *Michael Taylor.* $390/£250

LAMB, CHARLES. Elia. Essays Which Have Appeared Under That Signature in the London Magazine. London: Taylor & Hessey, 1823. 1st ed, 2nd issue w/'13, Waterloo Place' on tp and w/the 1/2-title, 6pp ads. 8vo. Uncut. Blue bds (cvrs neatly rehinged, inner hinges strengthened), orig white paper spine (worn), orig ptd paper spine label priced 9s.6d. *D & D.* $500/£321

LAMB, CHARLES. The Essays of Elia and the Last Essays of Elia. London, 1929. 24 contemp photogravure ports. Marbled eps. Teg. 1/2 calf, cl bds (edges, spine faded), gilt, raised spine bands. *Edwards.* $47/£30

LAMB, CHARLES. The Letters of Charles Lamb. Boston: Bibliophile Soc, 1905. Ltd to 470 sets. 5 vols. Uncut. (Spine dknd.) Djs (vol 1 stained) & slipcases (rubbed, some broken). *King.* $175/£112

LAMB, CHARLES. A Masque of Days, from the Last Essay of Elia. London: Cassell, 1901. 1st ed. 4to. Full color litho frontis, 41pp folded in French style; edges uncut (1 edge cut). Walter Crane (illus). Dec eps. Gilt dec tan linen on bd (edges lt rubbed). *Hobbyhorse*. $200/£128

LAMB, CHARLES. A Masque of Days. London, 1901. Walter Crane (illus). Cl-backed color pict bds (lt worn). *Swann**. $138/£88

LAMB, CHARLES. Miscellaneous Essays and Sketches. London, 1929. 24 contemp photogravure ports (sl spotting). Marbled eps. Teg. 1/2 calf, cl bds (spine, edges faded), gilt, raised bands. *Edwards*. $47/£30

LAMB, CHARLES. A Tale of Rosamund Gray and Old Blind Margaret. London: Golden Cockerel for Frank Hollings, 1928. One of 500. Frontis port. Vellum-backed grn bds, spine gilt. Very Nice. *Cady*. $50/£32

LAMB, CHARLES. The Works of Charles Lamb. NY: A.C. Armstrong, 1890-91. 6 vols. Teg. 3/4 brn morocco, marbled bds. (Spines, edges lt rubbed), o/w VG. *Holmes*. $275/£176

LAMB, HAROLD. The March of the Barbarians. NY: Doubleday, Doran, 1940. 1st ed. (Sl soiled), o/w Good. *Worldwide*. $15/£10

LAMB, HAROLD. New World Found: How North America Was Discovered and Explored. NY: Doubleday, 1955. 1st ed. Fine in dj (rubbed, edgeworn). *Sadlon*. $15/£10

LAMB, M. C. Leather Dressing. London, 1925. 3rd ed. 4pp of mtd samples. Orig cl, orig spine laid down. (Tp sl foxed; rebacked, sl rubbed.) *Edwards*. $117/£75

LAMB, M. J. History of the City of New York. NY/Chicago, 1877-80. 1st ed. 2 vols. 786; 820pp; 32 plts, 16 maps. Dec pub's cl (bumped). (Vol 2 tp starting), o/w Good. *Scribe's Perch**. $90/£58

LAMBERT, CLARA. The Story of Alaska. NY: Harper, 1940. 1st ed. C. H. DeWitt (illus). 10 1/4 x 11 1/4. 32pp. Cl spine, dec bds. VG in dj (few chips). *Cattermole*. $45/£29

LAMBERT, JOHN. Travels Through Canada, and the United States...1806, 1807, and 1808. London, 1816. 3rd ed. 2 vols. Five of the plts are colored as are 2 maps, incl Fine fldg map. Contemp calf (hinges cracked but firm). Howes L40. *M & S*. $725/£465

LAMBERT, OSMUND. Angling Literature in England. Sampson, Low, 1881. 1st ed. (10),87pp + ads. Teg, others uncut. Ptd vellum (soiled). *Cox*. $44/£28

LAMBERT, R. S. (ed). A Journey in the Tracks of the Age of Aristocracy.... Faber, 1935. 1st ed. Fldg map, 37 plts. VG in marbled cl. *Cox*. $23/£15

LAMBERT, SAMUEL M. Yankee Doctor in Paradise. NY/Boston, 1941. Port. VG. *Argosy*. $35/£22

LAMBIE, JOSEPH T. From Mine to Market. NY Univ, 1954. 1st ed. Frontis port, 15 plts. Dj (sl chipped). *Edwards*. $25/£16

Lamentations of Jeremiah. (Newtown): Gregynog, 1933 (i.e., 1934). One of 125 numbered in calf, of 250 on Japan vellum. Folio. Wood-engr calligraphic tp, 21 illus by Blair Hughes-Stanton. Orig navy calf blocked in blind. *Swann**. $2,760/£1,769

LAMMING, GEORGE. In the Castle of My Skin. NY: McGraw-Hill, 1954. 1st US ed. Good in dj (lt chipped, spine sunned). *Scribe's Perch**. $18/£12

LAMON, WARD H. The Life of Abraham Lincoln. Boston, 1872. 1st ed. Cl fldg case. Howes L46. *Swann**. $149/£96

LAMOND, HENRY. The Sea-Trout. London, 1916. 9 color, 38 plain plts (2 sm tears bottom plt 1). Unopened. Good. *Henly*. $117/£75

LAMOND, HENRY. The Sea-Trout. London: Sherratt & Hughes, 1916. 1st ed. 9 color plts. Teg. VG. *Hollett*. $234/£150

LAMONT, CORLISS (ed). The Trial of Elizabeth Gurley Flynn. NY: Horizon, (1968). 1st ed. VG (name) in dj. *Second Life*. $35/£22

LAMONT, JAMES. Seasons with the Sea-Horses. London: Hurst & Blackett, 1861. 1st ed. xii,1l.,312pp; 8 engrs, fldg map. 3/4 leather, marbled paper over bds (rubbed, hinges starting). *Parmer*. $275/£176

LAMPMAN, BEN HUR. At the End of the Car Line. Portland: Binsfort & Mort, 1942. 1st ed. Grn cl. VF in VF dj. *Biscotti*. $50/£32

LAMPMAN, BEN HUR. The Coming of the Pond Fishes. Portland: Binsford & Mort, 1946. 1st ed. VF in dj. *Bowman*. $30/£19

LAMPORT, FELICIA. Light Metres. NY: Everest House, (1980). One of 350 numbered, signed by Lamport and Edward Gorey (illus). Fine in Fine slipcase. *Lenz*. $175/£112

LAMPUGNANI, V. M. Architecture of the 20th Century in Drawings. NY: Rizzoli, 1982. Sound in dj. *Ars Artis*. $39/£25

LAMSON, J. Round Cape Horn. Bangor, ME: O.F. & W.H. Knowles, 1878. 1st ed. 156pp. Black cl, marbled bds. Fine. Howes L48. *Karmiole*. $200/£128

LAMSON, J. Round Cape Horn. Bangor: O.F. & W.H. Knowles, 1878. 1st ed. 156pp. 3/4 pebble-grained black cl, marbled bds (fr hinge tender). NF. Howes L48. *Harrington*. $175/£112

LAMSON, PAUL. The Heart Rhythms. Balt, 1921. 1st ed. VG. *Fye*. $75/£48

LANCASTER, CLAY. The Japanese Influence in America. NY, (1963). 8 color plts. Dec eps. Leather label. Fine. *Argosy*. $125/£80

LANCASTER, OSBERT. Classical Landscape. London, 1947. 1st ed. VG in dj (torn, chipped, frayed). *Words Etc*. $31/£20

LANCASTER, OSBERT. Drayneflete Revealed. London: John Murray, 1949. 1st ed. VG in dj (extrems lt worn). *Hollett*. $39/£25

LANCASTER, OSBERT. Facades and Faces. London, 1950. 1st ed. VG in dj (torn, stain, creasing). *Words Etc*. $11/£7

LANCASTER, OSBERT. Homes Sweet Homes. John Murray, (1939). 1st ed. 34 full-pg illus. Dec eps. Yellow pict cl. Dj (spine top lacks piece, foot sl defective). *Bickersteth*. $47/£30

LANCASTER, OSBERT. Homes Sweet Homes. London, 1939. 1st ed. VG in dj (sl torn, spine head chipped). *Words Etc*. $25/£16

LANCASTER, OSBERT. Sailing to Byzantium. London, 1969. 1st ed. Fine in dj. *Polyanthos*. $30/£19

LANCASTER, OSBERT. The Saracen's Head. London: John Murray, 1948. 1st ed. VG in dj (chips, tears). *Hollett*. $16/£10

LANCASTER, OSBERT. With an Eye to the Future. London: John Murray, 1967. 1st ed. VG in dj. *Hollett*. $39/£25

LANCASTER, SAMUEL C. The Columbia: America's Great Highway Through the Cascade Mountains to the Sea. Portland: J.K. Gill, 1926. 3rd ed. 26 color plts. VG. *Perier*. $45/£29

LANCEREAUX, E. A Treatise on Syphilis. Historical and Practical. G. Whitley (trans). London: New Sydenham Soc, 1868/69. 2 vols. v,405; 379pp. Brn cl (rebacked, spines relaid). (Tp vol 2 sl spotted), o/w VG set. *White*. $59/£38

LANCIANI, RODOLFO. Ancient Rome in Light of Recent Discoveries. Boston: H&M, 1888. 1st ed. xxx,329pp; 100 plts & illus. VG+. *Middle Earth*. $95/£61

LANCIANI, RODOLFO. Pagan and Christian Rome. Boston: H&M, 1892. 1st ed. x,374pp. (Back cvr stained), o/w Attractive. *Middle Earth*. $95/£61

LANCISI, G. M. Aneurysms: The Latin Text of Rome, 1745. W. C. Wright (ed). NY, 1952. 1st ed in English. VG. *Fye.* $50/£32

LANDER, SAMUEL. Our Own School Arithmetic. Greensboro, NC/Richmond, VA: Sterling, Cambell & Albright/W. Hargrave White, 1863. 223,(1)pp (browning; accession #s bottom margin preface). Ptd paper over bds (edges chipped). Good. *Cahan.* $200/£128

LANDES, DAVID S. Revolution in Time. Cambridge: Harvard Univ, 1983. 1st ed. 8 color, 28 halftone plts, map. VG in dj (worn). *Weber.* $30/£19

LANDING, JAMES E. American Essence. Kalamazoo, 1969. (Handstamp fr pastedown), else Fine in dj. *Brooks.* $25/£16

LANDOLFI, TOMMASO. Gogol's Wife. NY: New Directions, 1963. 1st ed. NF in NF dj (spine tanned). *Lame Duck.* $65/£42

LANDON, PERCEVAL. Nepal. London, 1928. 1st ed. 2 vols. Color frontispieces, 5 fldg maps, 2 fldg charts. (Ex-lib, ink stamps verso tps, maps; rebound in cl.) *Edwards.* $148/£95

LANDOR, WALTER SAVAGE. Heroic Idyls, with Additional Poems. T. Cautley Newby, 1863. 1st ed. (vii),348,ivpp. Marbled edges, eps. Recent dk blue 1/4 calf, gilt, morocco label. *Cox.* $75/£48

LANDOR, A. HENRY SAVAGE. See SAVAGE-LANDOR, A. HENRY

LANDOR, WALTER SAVAGE. Imaginary Conversations. (Verona): LEC, 1936. #904/1500 numbered, signed by Hans Mardersteig. Full dec cl. Fine in dj (spine dknd), pub's slipcase. *Hermitage.* $150/£96

LANDOR, WALTER SAVAGE. The Last Fruit Off an Old Tree. London: Edward Moxon, 1853. 1st ed. 4pp pub's ads dated Dec 1, 1846 tipped in before fep. Purple cl (faded, spine ends worn, bumped). *Maggs.* $47/£30

LANDOR, WALTER SAVAGE. The Works of Walter Savage Landor. London: Edward Moxon, 1846. Inscribed presentation. 2 vols. Frontis port. Maroon cl (upper joint vol 1 split 3 inches, inner hinge broken; sl worn, faded). *Maggs.* $140/£90

LANDSBOROUGH, D. A Popular History of British Sea-Weeds. London, 1851. 2nd ed. xvi,400pp; 2 plain, 20 color plts. (Cl neatly repaired.) *Wheldon & Wesley.* $62/£40

LANE, LYDIA S. I Married a Soldier. Phila, 1893. 1st ed. 214pp. Dec cl (spine sl faded). Howes L68. *Ginsberg.* $300/£192

LANE, MARGARET. The Magic Years of Beatrix Potter. NY: Warne, 1978. 1st US ed. As New in dj. *Cattermole.* $50/£32

LANE, RICHARD. Images from the Floating World. NY: Putnam, 1978. Fine in Fine dj. *Metropolitan*.* $46/£29

LANE, WALTER P. The Adventures and Recollections of General Walter P. Lane, a San Jacinto Veteran. Marshall, TX: News Messanger Pub Co, 1928. 2nd ed. VF. *Gibbs.* $85/£54

LANE-CLARKE, LOUISA. Folk-Lore of Guernsey and Sark, an Appendix to le Lievre's Guernsey Guide. Guernsey: Ptd by E. le Lievre, 1880. 1st ed. (8),144pp. Good in ptd wrappers (neatly detached, spine chipped). *Reese.* $75/£48

LANE-POOLE, STANLEY. Social Life in Egypt. London, n.d. (1884?). 138 w/index pp; 5 full-pg steel engrs. Aeg; dec cl (extrems frayed; outer hinges torn). *King.* $125/£80

LANES, SELMA G. The Art of Maurice Sendak. NY: Abrams, (1980). 1st ed. Obl 4to. Color pict pop-up, tipped-in facs of 'Where the Wild Horses Are.' Pict cl (lt worn). *Oinonen*.* $50/£32

LANES, SELMA G. The Art of Maurice Sendak. NY: Abrams, (1980). 1st ed. 94 color plts, orig color mechanical pop-up. (Later impressions did not incl the pop-up of Red Riding Hood and the wolf.) Color pict cl. Cvrs Fine (ink name eps) in VG clear plastic dj. *Baltimore*.* $80/£51

LANES, SELMA G. The Art of Maurice Sendak. (NY): Abrams, 1980. 1st Amer ed. 1 pop-up. Fine in dec cl, Fine pub's glassine wrap. *Hadley.* $117/£75

LANES, SELMA G. The Art of Maurice Sendak. NY: Abradale, 1980. 2nd ed. Maurice Sendak (illus). 11 1/2 x 11. 278pp. Fine in dj. *Cattermole.* $50/£32

LANG, ANDREW. Aladdin. London: Faber & Faber, (1981). 1st Eng ed. 4to. 32pp; 14 full-pg color illus by Errol Le Cain. Illus glazed bds. Fine. *Dower.* $50/£32

LANG, ANDREW. Angling Sketches. London: Longmans, Green, 1891. 1st ed. Inscribed presentation. 3 etchings. Teg. Grn cl, gilt. Fine. *Appelfeld.* $200/£128

LANG, ANDREW. The Animal Story Book. London: Longmans, Green, 1896. 1st ed. 8vo. Gilt-pict blue cl. *Swann*.* $126/£81

LANG, ANDREW. The Animal Story Book. London: Longmans, Green, 1896. 1st ed. H. F. Ford (illus). Aeg. Blue pict cl, gilt. Fine. *Macdonnell.* $200/£128

LANG, ANDREW. The Blue Fairy Book. London, 1889. 1st trade ed. 8 inserted plts. Good (fr hinge starting; spine dknd, sm tear, lt bumped). *Kane*.* $600/£385

LANG, ANDREW. Border Ballads. London: Lawrence & Bullen, 1895. Ltd to 750. 12 etched plts. (Stained, sl rubbed.) *Hollett.* $70/£45

LANG, ANDREW. The Brown Fairy Book. NY, 1904. Color frontis, 7 color plts, 22 b/w plts. Good. *Kane*.* $140/£90

LANG, ANDREW. Cock Lane and Common-Sense. London: Longmans, 1894. NF (lt bumped). *Between The Covers.* $100/£64

LANG, ANDREW. Essays in Little. NY: Scribner, 1891. 1st Amer ed. Grn cl. VG (ink presentation, feps sl foxed). *Antic Hay.* $25/£16

LANG, ANDREW. Grass of Parnassus, Rhymes Old and New. London: Longmans, Green, 1888. 1st ed. Teg. Dec grn cl. VG (ink name). *Antic Hay.* $50/£32

LANG, ANDREW. The Green Fairy Book. London, 1892. 1st trade ed. B/w frontis. Good (frontis tissue torn; spine top torn). *Kane*.* $80/£51

LANG, ANDREW. The Grey Fairy Book. Longmans, 1900. 1st ed. Henry Justice Ford (illus). Aeg. Pict cl gilt. Presentable (leaf nicked, spotting, browning, sl mks). *Ash.* $148/£95

LANG, ANDREW. The Grey Fairy Book. NY, 1900. Frontis, 31 full-pg b/w plts. Good (fr inner hinge starting, rear inner hinge open; spine dknd). *Kane*.* $80/£51

LANG, ANDREW. The Lilac Fairy Book. NY, 1910. 6 color, 20 b/w plts. Good (sl soiled, spine faded). *Kane*.* $100/£64

LANG, ANDREW. The Olive Fairy Book. NY, 1907. Color frontis, 7 color, 20 b/w plts. Good (sm spine tear). *Kane*.* $110/£71

LANG, ANDREW. The Orange Fairy Book. 1906. 1st ed. 8 color plts by H. J. Ford. Orange cl, gilt, aeg. (Inscrip, spine dull), o/w Bright. *Words Etc.* $86/£55

LANG, ANDREW. The Orange Fairy Book. NY, 1906. Color frontis, 7 color, 17 b/w plts. Good (spine faded). *Kane*.* $70/£45

LANG, ANDREW. The Pink Fairy Book. NY, 1897. Good (feps dknd, brittle; spine faded). *Kane*.* $75/£48

LANG, ANDREW. The Poetical Works. London: Longmans, Green, 1923. One of 260 numbered. 4 vols in 2. 4 frontis ports. Aeg. VG (sl rubbed). *Waverly*.* $38/£24

LANG, ANDREW. Princess Nobody. London: Longmans Green, 1884. 1st ed. Richard Doyle (illus). Lg 8vo. Glazed pict paper-cvrd bds, cl spine (edges, corners worn; juvenile coloring some illus). *Book Adoption.* $500/£321

LANG, ANDREW. The Red Book of Animal Stories. Longmans Green, 1899. 1st ed. H. J. Ford (illus). 8vo. 379pp. Aeg. Gilt-pict red cl. (Spine faded), else VG. *Bookmark.* $55/£35

LANG, ANDREW. The Red True Story Book. London: Longmans, Green, 1895. 1st ed. 8vo. Gilt-pict red cl. (Sig.) *Swann*.* $69/£44

LANG, ANDREW. The True Story Book. London: Longmans, Green, 1907. 6th imp. Blue cl, gilt. VF. *Sumner & Stillman.* $35/£22

LANG, ANDREW. The Violet Fairy Book. NY, 1901. Color frontis, 7 color, 25 b/w plts. Good (sm spine tears). *Kane*.* $110/£71

LANG, ANDREW. XXXII Ballades in Blue China. London: C. Kegan Paul, 1881. Teg, others uncut. Full blue morocco, ribbed spine, gilt-dec red morocco doublures, gilt dentelles. *D & D.* $150/£96

LANG, ANDREW. The Yellow Fairy Book. London, 1894. 1st ed. Aeg. Yellow cl, gilt. (Name, prelims foxed; sl shaken, rubbed, spine dknd), o/w VG. *Words Etc.* $70/£45

LANG, ANDREW. The Yellow Fairy Book. London, 1894. 22 inserted plts. Good (sl soiled, spine poorly cleaned). *Kane*.* $75/£48

LANG, IAIN. Background of the Blues. London: Workers' Music Assoc, 1943. 1st ed. Pb. VG. *Beasley.* $60/£38

LANG, JOHN DUNMORE. An Historical and Statistical Account of New South Wales. London: A.J. Valpy, 1837. 2nd ed. 2 vols. xii,465,ads; iv,527pp; fldg map (repair). Orig cl (spines faded, ends worn), paper labels. *Adelson.* $285/£183

LANG, JOHN. The Land of the Golden Trade. NY: Frederick A. Stokes, n.d. (ca 1910). 1st Amer ed. Untrimmed. Illus cream cl. (Eps dknd), else NF. *Connolly.* $55/£35

LANG, MRS. The All Sorts of Stories Book. 1911. 1st ed. 5 colored plts. Red cl, gilt, aeg. VG. *Words Etc.* $50/£32

LANG, MRS. The Red Book of Heroes. 1909. 1st ed. 8 color plts. Aeg. Red cl, gilt. VG. *Words Etc.* $50/£32

LANG, MRS. The Red Book of Heroes. Longmans, 1909. 1st ed. 8vo. xiv,268pp; 8 color plts, 40 b/w illus by J. Wallis Mills. Aeg; red pict eps. Gilt-pict red cl (inner hinges strained, spine ends worn, cvr dents). *Bookmark.* $23/£15

LANG, MRS. The Red Book of Heroes. Andrew Lang (ed). London, 1909. 8 color plts by A. Wallis Mills. (Bkpl; upper hinge tender; gilt illus upper bd sl rubbed, spine sl faded.) *Edwards.* $86/£55

LANGDON-DAVIES, JOHN. Behind the Spanish Barricades. London: Secker, 1936. 1st Eng ed. (Inscrip; sl mkd.) *Clearwater.* $39/£25

LANGE, DOROTHEA and PAUL TAYLOR. An American Exodus. NY: Reynal & Hitchcock, 1939. 1st ed. NF in illus dj (sl edgeworn). *Cahan.* $325/£208

LANGE, DOROTHEA and PAUL TAYLOR. An American Exodus. New Haven/London: Yale Univ, 1969. (Owner stamp, rubbed, old price sticker), else VG in stiff wrappers. *Cahan.* $25/£16

LANGE, FRED W. History of Baseball in California and Pacific Coast Leagues, 1847-1938. Oakland: The Author, 1938. 1st ed. Pict wrappers (rear cvr stained, sl intruding on last 4 leaves), else Fine. *Argonaut.* $150/£96

LANGE, JOHN. (Pseud of Michael Crichton.) Grave Descend. (NY): Signet/NAL, (1970). Pb orig. (Pg edges lt browned), else Fine in wrappers (sm scrape fr wrap). *Between The Covers.* $125/£80

LANGE, JOHN. (Pseud of Michael Crichton.) The Venom Business. World, (1969). 1st ed. Fine in NF dj (rear flap crease). *Certo.* $110/£71

LANGE, JOHN. (Pseud of Michael Crichton.) Zero Cool. (NY): Signet/NAL, (1969). Pb orig. VG (pp browned, lt spine creasing, lt worn) in wrappers. *Between The Covers.* $100/£64

LANGE, K. and M. HIRMER. Egypt: Architecture-Sculpting-Painting in Three Thousand Years. London: Phaidon, (1957). 2nd ed. 260 plts. (Owner's label.) Dj. *Archaeologia.* $85/£54

LANGFELD, WILLIAM and PHILIP BLACKBURN (comps). Washington Irving: A Bibliography. NY: Public Library, 1933. Ltd to 450 signed, corrected by Blackburn. Fine. *Book Market.* $100/£64

LANGFORD, NATHANIEL PITT. Diary of the Washburn Expedition to the Yellowstone and Firehole Rivers in the Year 1870. (Cvr title: Discovery of Yellowstone Park.) N.p.: J.E. Haynes et al, (1905). 23 plts & ports. Teg. Dk blue cl, gilt. VG (rubberstamps). *Bohling.* $175/£112

LANGFORD, NATHANIEL PITT. Vigilante Days and Ways. Chicago: A.C. McClurg, 1931. VG in dj. Howes L78. *Lien.* $25/£16

LANGLEY, BATTY OF TWICKENHAM. New Principles of Gardening.... London: A. Bettesworth & J. Bayley, 1728. 1st ed. 28 folio engrs. Mod full leather binding (lt scratches); blindstamped; red leather title piece gilt. Fine (sm silver loss; rebound). *Between The Covers.* $2,500/£1,603

LANGLEY, SAMUEL PIERPONT. Experiments in Aeronautics. Washington, 1891. 1st ed. Folio. *Swann*.* $287/£184

LANGLOTZ, ERNST. The Art of Magna Graecia: Greek Art in Southern Italy and Sicily. London: Thames & Hudson, (1965). 188 plts (20 color). Good in dj. *Archaeologia.* $150/£96

LANGTON, JANE. The Diamond in the Window. NY: Harper & Row, 1962. 1st ed. Erik Blegvad (illus). 5 3/4 x 8 1/2. 242pp. Pict cl. VG in dj. *Cattermole.* $75/£48

LANGTON, JANE. The Transcendental Murder. NY: Harper, (1964). Fine (sm sticker) in dj (sl worn). *Metro-politan*.* $74/£47

LANGTON, N. and B. The Cat in Ancient Egypt. Cambridge, 1940. 1st ed. 20 plts (incl frontis). (Corners bumped), else VG in dj (price-clipped; dknd; sl stained, edge-frayed). *King.* $75/£48

LANGWORTHY, DANIEL A. Reminiscences of a Prisoner of War and His Escape. Minneapolis: Byron, 1915. 1st ed. Inscribed presentation. Als from Ell Torrance, to whom bk was dedicated. *Ginsberg.* $200/£128

LANGWORTHY, FRANKLIN. Scenery of the Plains, Mountains and Mines. Paul C. Phillips (ed). Princeton: Princeton Univ, 1932. Rpt. 4 plts. Red cl, gilt. Fine in pict dj. *Pacific*.* $63/£40

LANHAM, URL. The Bone Hunters. NY, 1973. 1st ed. Brn cl. VF in Fine dj. *Five Quail.* $40/£26

LANHAM, URL. The Bone Hunters. NY: Columbia, 1973. 1st ed. Fine in VG dj. *Mikesh.* $20/£13

LANIER, HENRY WYSHAM. A. B. Frost, the American Sportsman's Artist. NY: Derrydale, 1933. 1st ed. One of 950. 62 plts. Tan cl (worn). Internally Fine. *Cummins.* $200/£128

LANIER, HENRY WYSHAM. A.B. Frost, the American Sportsman's Artist. NY: Derrydale, 1933. Ltd to 950 ptd. Khaki cl. *Christie's*.* $158/£101

LANIER, LEE. Golden Phantoms. NY: Comet, 1952. 1st ed. VG in dj. *Lien.* $25/£16

LANIER, SIDNEY. (ed). The Boy's King Arthur. NY: Scribner, 1942. Dk blue cl, pict cvrs (lt rubbed). *D & D.* $20/£13

LANIER, SIDNEY. The Science of English Verse. NY: Scribner, 1880. 1st ed. (Old price fr pastedown, ink names feps; spine ends frayed, corners bumped.) Acceptable. *Hermitage.* $65/£42

LANIER, STERLING E. Hiero's Journey. PA: Chilton, (1973). 1st ed. NF in dj (sl worn). *Metropolitan*.* $17/£11

LANKES, J. J. Virginia Woodcuts. Virginia Press, (c. 1930). #293/1200. Inscribed poem by Lankes. Paper parchment spine (dknd). VG (soiled, borders foxed). *Book Broker.* $250/£160

LANKESTER, MRS. E. British Ferns. London, 1890. New ed. iv,127pp (eps waterstained, ends sl foxed), 16 color plts. Pict cl. *Henly.* $22/£14

LANMAN, CHARLES. Adventures in the Wilds of North America. London: Longman, Brown et al, 1854. 1st ed. Ad eps. Brn grained cl (spine sunned, extrems lt worn; upper cvr faded, spotted), titled in blind, gilt. Orig binder's ticket. Internally Fine (bkpl). *Cummins.* $250/£160

LANMAN, CHARLES. Farthest North. NY, 1885. 1st ed. 333pp; fldg map (torn). (Stamped name; cvrs dknd, rubbed.) *King.* $150/£96

LANMAN, CHARLES. Farthest North. NY: Appleton, 1885. 1st ed. Frontis, 333pp; port, fldg map. Blue pict cl (sl worn). VG (sl foxing frontis, guard, tp). *Parmer.* $350/£224

LANMAN, CHARLES. Haw-ho-noo; or, Records of a Tourist. Phila, 1850. Later 1/4 cl (worn; eps renewed). Howes L88. *Swann*.* $103/£66

LANMAN, CHARLES. The Private Life of Daniel Webster. NY: Harper, 1852. Apparent 1st ed. (iii)-205pp; 5 plts preceding tp. Good (foxed; chipped, torn spot fr hinge). *Bohling.* $15/£10

LANMAN, CHARLES. A Summer in the Wilderness. NY/Phila: Appleton, 1847. 208pp incl prelims, 1pg ad at fr. Contemp 3/4 leather, marbled bds (sl scuffed). Overall VG (paper age-toned, lt stained). Howes L90. *Bohling.* $375/£240

LANNING, GEORGE. Wild Life in China. Shanghai: Nat'l Review Office, 1911. 1st ed. Grn gilt cl. VG. *Terramedia.* $200/£128

LANNING, JOHN TATE. Pedro de la Torre, Doctor to Conquerors. Baton Rouge, 1974. Fine in NF dj. *Turpen.* $28/£18

LANNING, JOHN TATE. Spanish Missions of Georgia. Chapel Hill, 1935. 1st ed. #290/500. Signed. Frontis, map. Fine in NF dj (2-inch tear, neatly repaired). *Turpen.* $85/£54

LANSDALE, JOE R. Act of Love. London: Kinnell, 1989. 1st hb ed. Signed. Fine in dj. *Mordida.* $65/£42

LANSDALE, JOE R. By Bizarre Hands. Shingletown: Mark V. Ziesing, 1989. 1st ed. VF in dj. *Mordida.* $65/£42

LANSDALE, JOE R. The Nightrunners. Arlington Hts.: Dark Harvest, 1987. 1st ed. One of 300 numbered, signed by Lansdale, Dean R. Koontz (intro), and Gregory Manchess (illus). Dj, slipcase. *Swann*.* $103/£66

LANSDALE, JOE R. and PAT LOBRUTTO (eds). Razored Saddles. Arlington Hts.: Dark Harvest, 1989. 1st ed. One of 600 numbered, signed by contributors. Imitation leather. Dj, slipcase. *Swann*.* $69/£44

LANSDALE, MARIA HORNOR. Scotland Historic and Romantic. Phila: Henry T. Coates, 1902. 1st ed. 2 vols. Teg, others uncut. 1/2 grn morocco, ribbed gilt-dec spines (faded to brn). *D & D.* $125/£80

LANSDOWNE, J. F. Birds of the West Coast. Boston: Houghton Mifflin, 1976, 1980. 1st eds. 2 vols. 101 color plts. NF in NF dj. *Mikesh.* $95/£61

LANSDOWNE, J. F. Birds of the West Coast. Boston: Houghton Mifflin, 1976. 1st US ed. Fine in Fine dj. *Books & Birds.* $125/£80

LANTZ, SHERLEE. Trianglepoint. NY: Viking, 1976. 1st ed. Cl-backed bds, gilt. NF in dj. *Whittle.* $28/£18

LAPE, ESTHER (ed). American Medicine: Expert Testimony Out of Court. NY, 1937. 1st ed. 2 vols. VG. *Fye.* $100/£64

LAPHAM, INCREASE A. The Antiquities of Wisconsin, As Surveyed and Described. (Washington: Smithsonian Inst, 1855.) 1st ptg. (12),96pp; fldg map, 55 litho plts. 19th-cent 1/2 brn morocco (extrems sl rubbed), marbled bds. Howes L95. *Karmiole.* $200/£128

LAPP, RUDOLPH M. Archy Lee, a California Fugitive Slave Case. SF: Book Club of CA, 1969. One of 500. *Boswell.* $150/£96

LAPP, RUDOLPH M. Blacks in Gold Rush California. New Haven/London: Yale Univ, 1977. 1st ed. Orange cl. Fine in pict dj. *Pacific*.* $35/£22

LAPP, RUDOLPH M. Blacks in Gold Rush California. New Haven: Yale Univ, 1977. 1st ed. Fine in dj. *Between The Covers.* $45/£29

LARDNER, D. Hydrostatics and Pneumatics. 1831. viii,353pp. 3/4 leather, marbled bds. (Spine bottom defective), o/w VG. *Whitehart.* $55/£35

LARDNER, RING. Bib Ballads. Chicago: P.F. Volland, (1915). 1st ed, 1st bk. One of 500. Fontaine Fox (illus). Pict brn cl, gilt lettering (sl faded). *Kane*.* $90/£58

LARDNER, RING. The Big Town. Indianapolis: Bobbs-Merrill, (1921). 1st ed. Grn cl (lt rubbed, bumped). VG. *Hermitage.* $65/£42

LARDNER, RING. The Big Town. NY, 1925. 1st Amer ed. NF (spine sl sunned, extrems sl rubbed). *Polyanthos.* $100/£64

LARDNER, RING. Lose with a Smile. NY: Scribner, 1933. 1st ed. Grn cloth. Fine in dj (sl used, spine lt rubbed). *Dermont.* $300/£192

LARDNER, RING. Treat 'em Rough: Letters from Jack the Kaiser Killer. Indianapolis: Bobbs-Merrill, (1918). 1st ed. Cvr illus laid down. Dj (tattered). *Dawson.* $75/£48

LARGE, E. C. Sugar in the Air. NY: Scribner, 1937. 1st ed. Fine in VG + dj (extrems sl rubbed, sm tears). *Between The Covers.* $100/£64

LARIAR, LAWRENCE. The Girl with the Frightened Eyes. NY: Dodd Mead, 1945. 1st ed. (Bkseller stamp fep), o/w Fine in VG dj (rubbed, sl wear, back panel soiled). *Mordida.* $35/£22

LARKIN, ELIZABETH T. (ed). Scenes in the Eventful Life of Mary W. Few Richardson. Columbus, OH, 1894. 1st ed. 266pp; port. Pict cl (fr cvr faded). *Ginsberg.* $100/£64

LARKIN, PHILIP. All What Jazz. Faber & Faber, (1970). 1st ed. VG in dj. *Ash.* $78/£50

LARKIN, PHILIP. A Girl in Winter. London, 1947. 1st ed. (Sig; spine sunned, fr cvr creased), o/w VG. *Buckley.* $62/£40

LARKIN, PHILIP. High Windows. Faber, 1974. 1st ed. Fine in dj. *Buckley.* $70/£45

LARKIN, PHILIP. High Windows. London, 1974. 1st Eng ed. Fine in dj (sl faded, creased). *Clearwater.* $78/£50

LARKIN, PHILIP. The Less Deceived. Hessle: Marvell Press, 1955. 2nd issue (w/round spine). One of 400 (of 700). 'Second Edition, January 1956' on tp verso entirely incorrect. Nice (name; cvrs sl faded) in dj (sl rubbed). *Clearwater.* $234/£150

LARKIN, PHILIP. The North Ship. Fortune, n.d. (1965). 2nd (unauthorised) ed. NF. *Sclanders*. $70/£45

LARKIN, PHILIP. The Whitsun Weddings. Faber & Faber, (1964). 1st ed. Nice (upper cvr edge sl faded) in dj. *Ash*. $117/£75

LARKIN, PHILIP. The Whitsun Weddings. Faber, 1964. 1st ed. Fine in Fine dj. *Sclanders*. $148/£95

LARKIN, THOMAS OLIVER. Chapters in the Early Life of Thomas Oliver Larkin. SF: CA Hist Soc, 1939. 1st ed. Frontis port, plt, map. Grn cl, ptd labels. Fine. *Pacific**. $46/£29

LARKIN, THOMAS OLIVER. Chapters in the Early Life of Thomas Oliver Larkin. SF: CA Hist Soc, 1939. Frontis port, map. Grn cl (Spine label faded), else NF. *Parmer*. $75/£48

LARKIN, THOMAS OLIVER. The Larkin Papers: Business and Official Correspondence of.... George P. Hammond (ed). Berkeley: Univ of CA, 1951-1964. 1st ed. One of 1000. 10 vols + index vol. Fine set in djs. *Argonaut*. $850/£545

LARPENT, GEORGE (ed). The Private Journal of Judge-Advocate Larpent. London, 1854. 3rd ed. xx,580pp. Red dec cl (sl worn). *Maggs*. $234/£150

LARPENTEUR, CHARLES. Forty Years a Fur Trader on the Upper Missouri. Elliot Coues (ed). Minneapolis: Ross & Haines, 1962. 2 vols in 1. VG in dj (sl worn). Howes C800. *Lien*. $40/£26

LARPENTEUR, CHARLES. Forty Years a Fur Trader on the Upper Missouri: The Personal Narrative of Charles Larpenteur 1833-1872. Milo M. Quaife (intro). Chicago: Lakeside, Christmas, 1933. Teg. Dk red cl. VG. *Sadlon*. $25/£16

LARRIMORE, LIDA. The Blossoming of Patricia-the-Less. Penn, 1924. 1st ed. Hattie Longstreet Price (illus). 6.5x8.5. 253pp. Cl, pict paste-on. (Inscrip; extrems worn), else VG. *My Bookhouse*. $30/£19

LARRISON, E. J. Field Guide to the Birds of King County, Washington. Seattle: Aud Soc, 1947. 1st ed. VG in wraps. *Mikesh*. $25/£16

LARSEN, HELGE and RAINEY FROELICH. Ipiutak and the Arctic Whale Hunting Culture. Anthrop Papers of Amer Mus of Nat Hist, 1948. 101 plts. VG in wraps. *Perier*. $40/£26

LARSON, J. A. Single Fingerprint System. NY/London: Appleton, 1924. 1st ed. (Bkpl; sl worn), o/w Good. *Worldwide*. $15/£10

LARSON, WILLIAM. Big Pictures, Little Pictures. Phila: Gravity Press, 1980. Fine in NF illus dj. *Cahan*. $100/£64

LARTIGUE, JACQUES HENRI. Diary of a Century. Richard Avedon (ed). NY: Viking, 1970. 1st ed. (Tip bumped), else Fine in gilt dj (lt worn). *Cahan*. $300/£192

LASERON, CHARLES F. South with Mawson. Sydney: Angus & Robertson, 1957. 2nd ed. (Spine faded), else VG. *High Latitude*. $30/£19

LASLETT, T. Timber and Timber Trees. London: Macmillan, 1894. 2nd ed. 442pp; 172 tables. Dec cl. VG. *Savona*. $28/£18

LASS, WILLIAM E. From the Missouri to the Great Salt Lake. NE State Hist Soc, 1972. 1st ed. VG in dj. *Lien*. $30/£19

LASSAIGNE, JACQUES. The Ceiling of the Paris Opera. NY: Praeger, (1966). Marc Chagall (artist). Orig color litho frontis; 'final study' illus in rear pocket. Fine in dj (lt rubbed). *Waverly**. $154/£99

LASSAIGNE, JACQUES. Drawings and Watercolors for the Ballet. NY: Tudor, 1969. English ed. Orig litho by Marc Chagall. Dj; slipcase (discolored). *Metropolitan**. $161/£103

LASSAIGNE, JACQUES. Marc Chagall, Drawings and Watercolors for the Ballet. NY: Tudor, (1969). Orig full-pg color litho. Fine in dj, slipcase (unevenly faded). *Waverly**. $198/£127

LASSAIGNE, JACQUES. Marc Chagall: Drawings and Watercolors for the Ballet. NY, (1969). Folio. Litho by Chagall. Dj (sl worn). *Swann**. $201/£129

Last 'Graphic' Pictures. Routledge, 1888. 1st ed. Randolph Caldicott (illus). Obl folio. 71pp ptd single sides (fep torn). Cl spine, pict bds (mkd, worn). Internally VG. *Bookmark*. $78/£50

Last of the Mohicans. (By James F. Cooper.) London: John Miller, 1826. 1st British ed. 3 vols. Recent calf, marbled bds, contemp style. (Bound w/o 1/2-titles, sl foxing), o/w VG. BAL 3833. *Reese*. $750/£481

Last of the Mohicans. (By James F. Cooper.) London: Raphael Tuck, n.d. (1890s). 9x4. (12)pp (ink inscrip, sm removal mk inside fr cvr). Color stiff wraps (worn, sl creases), die-cut on top and right side outlining sm Indian boy in costume. *King*. $50/£32

Late Etchings of Rembrandt. London: British Museum, Gallery of Prints & Drawings, 1969. 25 plts. Good in wraps. *Washton*. $20/£13

LATHAM, JOHN. A General History of Birds. Winchester, 1821-28. 11 vols, incl index vol. Complete, as issued. 193 hand-colored plts. (Lt foxing; all cvrs detached, well rubbed.) *New Hampshire**. $1,025/£657

LATHAM, P. M. The Collected Works of Dr. P. M. Latham. London, 1876-1878. 1st ed. 2 vols. VG. *Fye*. $225/£144

LATHAM, P. M. The Collected Works of Dr. P. M. Latham. New Sydenham Soc, 1876/8. 2 vols. Blind/gilt-stamped cl. (Lt foxed, spines sl worn), o/w VG. *Whitehart*. $55/£35

LATHAM, R. G. The Ethnology of the British Colonies and Dependencies. London: Van Voorst, 1851. 1st ed. (6),264,(2)pp. *Ginsberg*. $300/£192

LATHAM, WILFRID. The States of the River Plate. London: Longmans, Green, 1868. 2nd ed. x,381,2ads pp; fldg map. New tan cl, leather label. VG. *Adelson*. $275/£176

Lathe and Its Uses. (By J. Lukin.) London, 1874. 4th ed. 2 fldg plts. (Foxed; spine faded.) *Maggs*. $119/£76

LATHEN, EMMA. A Stitch in Time. NY: Macmillan, 1968. 1st ed. Fine in dj. *Mordida*. $65/£42

LATHERN, J. Honorable Judge Wilmot, a Biographical Sketch. Halifax: Ptd at Wesleyan Office, 1880. Dec tan cl (sl rubbed), gilt. *Boswell*. $125/£80

LATHROP, DOROTHY. Bouncing Betsy. NY: Macmillan, 1936. 1st ed. 9 1/2 x 8 1/4. 32pp. Good in dj (worn, tattered). *Cattermole*. $75/£48

LATHROP, ELISE. Historic Houses of Early America. NY: Tudor, 1927. (Lt spots cvrs.) *Sadlon*. $40/£26

LATHROP, GEORGE PARSONS. A Study of Hawthorne. Boston: James R. Osgood, 1876. 1st ed. Grn cl, gilt. (Sl rubbed, 2 bkpls), else Bright. *Macdonnell*. $100/£64

LATHROP, ROSE HAWTHORNE. Memories of Hawthorne. Boston: Houghton, Mifflin, 1897. 1st ed. 482pp. (Spot fore-edge, prelims lt foxed), else VG. *Hermitage*. $35/£22

LATIMER, JONATHAN. Red Gardens. NY: Crime Club, (1939). (Rubbed, shelfworn.) Dj (worn, ends chipped). *Metropolitan**. $63/£40

LATIMER, JONATHAN. Solomon's Vineyard. Santa Barbara: Neville, 1982. 1st Amer ed. One of 300 numbered, signed. VF w/o dj as issued. *Mordida*. $75/£48

LATIMORE, SARAH B. and GRACE C. HASKELL. Arthur Rackham, a Bibliography. L.A., 1936. One of 550 numbered. Slipcase. *Swann**. $138/£88

LATROBE, BENJAMIN H. Journal of Latrobe. NY: Appleton, 1905. 1st ed. 26 plts. Dec cl (lt soiled). Howes L126. *Ginsberg.* $125/£80

LATROBE, BENJAMIN H. Virginia Journals...1795-1798. New Haven: Yale Univ, 1977. 2 vols. VG in VG djs. *New Hampshire*.* $30/£19

LATROBE, CHRISTIAN I. Journal of a Visit to South Africa.... London: L.B. Seeley, 1821. 2nd ed. xi,580pp (lacks 1/2 title); fldg map, 4 plts. 1/2 calf, gilt, marbled bds (rubbed). *Adelson.* $285/£183

LATTA, FRANK F. Black Gold in the Joaquin. Caldwell, ID: Caxton, 1949. 1st ed. Frontis port. Gilt black cl. Fine in dj (chipped, spine dknd). *Argonaut.* $40/£26

LATTA, FRANK F. Dalton Gang Days. Santa Cruz: Bear State Books, (1976). Fine. *Bohling.* $25/£16

LATTA, FRANK F. Tailholt Tales. Santa Cruz: Bear State, (1976). 1st ed. Fine. *Book Market.* $30/£19

LATTA, ROBERT R. Reminiscences of Pioneer Life. Kansas City, MO, 1912. VG- (wear, soil). Howes L130. *Bohling.* $85/£54

LATTA, S. A. The Cholera in Cincinnati. Cincinnati, 1850. 40pp. VG in ptd wrappers. *Argosy.* $75/£48

LATTIMORE, OWEN. Inner Asian Frontiers of China. NY: Amer Geographical Soc, 1940. 1st ed. VG. *Hermitage.* $65/£42

LAU, ROBERT JULIUS. Old Babylonian Temple Records. NY: Columbia Univ, 1906. 35 plts. (Sig.) *Archaeologia.* $200/£128

LAUBIN, REGINALD and GLADYS. Indian Dances of North America. Univ of OK, (1977). 1st ed. Frontis. Fine in Fine dj. *Oregon.* $65/£42

LAUBIN, REGINALD and GLADYS. The Indian Tipi, Its History, Construction, and Use. Norman: Univ of OK, (1957). 1st ed. Inscribed, signed. Color frontis. Blue cl. Fine (sl rubbed). *Argonaut.* $75/£48

LAUBIN, REGINALD and GLADYS. The Indian Tipi: Its History, Construction and Use. Norman: Univ of OK, (Apr. 1967). VF in VG + dj. *Mikesh.* $25/£16

LAUDE, G. A. Kansas Shorthorns...1857 to 1920. Iola, KS, 1920. (Spine worn, faded; rubberstamps.) *Bohling.* $25/£16

LAUDE, G. A. Kansas Shorthorns...1857 to 1920. Iola, KS, 1920. 1st ed. Blue cl, gilt. (Spine sl sunned), else VG. *Price.* $69/£44

LAUER, JEAN-PHILIPPE. Saqqara, the Royal Cemetery of Memphis. NY: Scribner, (1976). Good in dj. *Archaeologia.* $125/£80

LAUFER, BERTHOLD. Archaic Chinese Jades Collected in China by A.W. Bahr.... NY: A.W. Bahr, 1927. 35 plts (3 color). 1/4 cl, paper over bds. Good (3 sm spots cvr). *Blake.* $250/£160

LAUFER, BERTHOLD. Jade: A Study in Chinese Archaeology and Religion. Chicago, 1912. 1st ed. 68 plts (6 color). Contemp 3/4 grn morocco. *Swann*.* $138/£88

LAUFER, BERTHOLD. Ostrich Egg-Shell Cups of Mesopotamia and the Ostrich in Ancient and Modern Times. Chicago: Field Museum of Natural History, 1926. 9 plts. Good in wrappers. *Archaeologia.* $45/£29

LAUGHLIN, CLARA E. The Work-A-Day Girl. NY: Revell, (1913). 1st ed. Fine in dj (sl nicked). *Second Life.* $65/£42

LAUGHLIN, CLARENCE JOHN. Ghosts Along the Mississippi. NY: Bonanza, 1961. 100 b/w plts. (Owner stamp), else VG in dj (rubbed). *Cahan.* $35/£22

LAUGHLIN, CLARENCE JOHN. New Orleans and Its Living Past. Boston: Houghton Mifflin, 1941. 1st ed. One of 1000 numbered, signed by Laughlin and David L. Cohn (text). 62 gravure plts. Leather spine label. (Bkpl), else NF. *Cahan.* $600/£385

LAUGHLIN, LEDLIE IRWIN. Pewter in America. Boston, 1940. 1st ed. Signed, inscribed. 2 vols. Leather spine labels (chipped, spines dknd). *Kane*.* $55/£35

LAUGHLIN, LEDLIE IRWIN. Pewter in America. Boston: Houghton Mifflin, 1940. 1st ed. 2 vols. 78 b/w photo plts. Untrimmed, partly unopened. Tan/gray buckram, spine labels. Bd slipcase (sl worn, scuffed, short cracks). *Baltimore*.* $120/£77

LAUGHTON, L. G. CARR. Old Ship Figure-Heads and Sterns. London: Halton & Truscott Smith, 1925. Ltd to 1500 numbered. 56 plts (8 mtd color). Teg. (Sm blindstamp, ink notation tp.) Blue cl, dec gilt. *Karmiole.* $250/£160

LAUMER, KEITH. Time Trap. NY: Putnam, (1970). 1st ed. Dj. *Swann*.* $172/£110

LAUNE, SEIGNIORA RUSSELL. Sand in My Eyes. Flagstaff: Northland, (1956). New ed. Northland label fep. Fine in dj (lt rubbed). *Sadlon.* $20/£13

LAURENCE, ROBERT (comp). The George Walcott Collection of Used Civil War Patriotic Covers. NY: Privately ptd, 1934. 2nd ed. NF. *Mcgowan.* $85/£54

LAURIE, DUNCAN F. Poultry Foods and Feeding. London, 1913. Blue cl, gilt. (Foxing), else VG. *Price.* $34/£22

LAURIE, JOSEPH. The Homoeopathic Domestic Medicine. London: James Leath, 1851. 6th ed. xviii,885pp. Binder's cl (lower hinge frayed; upper joint cracking), gilt. *Hollett.* $101/£65

LAURIE, THOMAS. The Whitman Controversy. Astoria: Ptd by G.W. Snyder, 1886. VG in wraps. *Perier.* $60/£38

LAUT, AGNES C. Cadillac. Indianapolis, (1931). 1st ed. VG + in VG dj. *Mcclintock.* $17/£11

LAUT, AGNES C. Cadillac. Indianapolis: Bobbs-Merrill, (1931). 1st ed. VG in dj. *Lien.* $35/£22

LAUT, AGNES C. Enchanted Trails of Glacier Park. NY: McBride, 1926. 1st ed. 32 photo plts. Blind-stamped gilt-dec cl. NF in VG dj. *Mikesh.* $30/£19

LAUT, AGNES C. The Fur Trade of America. NY: Macmillan, 1921. 1st ed. Frontis, 31 plts. Red cl, gilt spine. Fine in pict dj (lt soiled). *Argonaut.* $150/£96

LAUT, AGNES C. The Story of the Trapper. Toronto, 1902. Nice in pict cl. *Grayling.* $55/£35

LAVALLEYE, JACQUES. Bruegel and Lucas Van Leydau: Complete Engravings, Etchings, and Woodcuts. NY: Abrams, n.d. *Metropolitan*.* $28/£18

LAVATER, J. C. Aphorisms on Man. Newburyport: George Jerry Osborne, 1793. 5th Amer ed. 109,(1)pp. Contemp sheep, gilt. Very Nice (pencil mks, tanning, offsetting). *Reese.* $65/£42

LAVATER, J. C. Essays on Physiognomy.... London, 1789. 1st ed in English. 8vo. 3 vols. 241; 324; 314pp. Full leather. Fine set (2 hinges cracked). *Fye.* $950/£609

LAVENDER, DAVID. Bent's Fort. NY: Doubleday, 1954. 1st ed. Fine in NF dj. *Sadlon.* $35/£22

LAVENDER, DAVID. Bent's Fort. NY: Doubleday, 1954. 1st ed. VF in pict dj. *Argonaut.* $60/£38

LAVENDER, DAVID. Bent's Fort. NY: Doubleday, 1954. 1st ed. Signed. Fine in pict dj (sl chipped). *Argonaut.* $90/£58

LAVENDER, DAVID. Climax at Buena Vista: The American Campaigns in Northeastern Mexico, 1846-47. Phila: Lippincott, (1966). 1st ed. VG in dj. *Lien.* $30/£19

LAVENDER, DAVID. Colorado River Country. NY, 1982. 1st ed. Map. VF in Fine dj. *Five Quail.* $25/£16

LAVENDER, DAVID. The Great Persuader...Collis P. Huntington. GC: Doubleday, 1970. 1st ed. VG in dj. *Lien.* $30/£19

LAVENDER, DAVID. Let Me Be Free, the Nez Perce Tragedy. NY, (1992). 1st ed. Fine in dj (lt wear). *Pratt.* $30/£19

LAVENDER, DAVID. Nothing Seemed Impossible. Palo Alto: American West, 1975. 1st ed. Frontis port. Fine in Fine dj. *Connolly.* $50/£32

LAVENDER, DAVID. River Runners of the Grand Canyon. Tucson: GCNHA/Univ of AZ, 1985. 1st ed. Dbl-pg map. Fine in Fine slick-paper dj. *Five Quail.* $45/£29

LAVENDER, DAVID. Westward Vision: The Story of the Oregon Trail. McGraw-Hill, (1963). 1st ed. Dec cvr, eps. Fine in dj (price-clipped). *Authors Of West.* $30/£19

LAVER, JAMES. Background for Venus. NY: Knopf, 1935. 1st Amer ed. NF in VG dj (sl worn, tear, spine sunned). *Antic Hay.* $25/£16

LAVER, JAMES. French Painting and the Nineteenth Century. Batsford, 1937. 1st ed. 141 plts. VG. *Cox.* $28/£18

LAVER, JAMES. Hatchards of Piccadilly 1797-1947. Hatchards, 1947. 38 plts. Yellow cl. Fine. *Moss.* $28/£18

LAVER, JAMES. A Stitch in Time. Nonesuch, 1927. One of 1525. Fine in stiff marbled paper wrappers, orig glassine protective wrapper (browned). *Words Etc.* $59/£38

LAVERAN, A. Paludism. J. W. Martin (trans). London: New Sydenham Soc, 1893. xii,197pp; 6 plts. Brn cl. VG. *White.* $47/£30

LAVIN, IRVING. Bernini and the Crossing of Saint Peter's. NY, 1968. Good. *Washton.* $40/£26

LAVRENTJEV, ALEXANDER. Rodchenko Photography. NY: Rizzoli, 1982. 1st ed. 159 photo plts. Fine (name stamp) in dj. *Cahan.* $75/£48

Law of the State of New Jersey, Revised and Published Under the Authority of the Legislature by William Paterson. New Brunswick, 1800. (Internal dampstaining, blank corner loss fr matter, old ink inscrip.) Contemp calf (rubbed, joints cracked). *Freeman*.* $80/£51

Law of the Territories. (By Sidney George Fisher, Sr.) Phila: Ptd by C. Sherman, 1859. 1st ed. xxiv,127pp. (Sl shelfworn), else VG. *Brown.* $45/£29

LAW, JOHN. The Colonial History of Vincennes, Under the French, British and American Governments.... Vincennes, 1858. Presentation copy. 8,157pp. New cl. (Ex-lib.) Howes L152. *Ginsberg.* $150/£96

LAW, PHILIP and JOHN BECHERVAISE. Anare. Australia's Antarctic Outposts. Melbourne: OUP, 1957. VG. *High Latitude.* $40/£26

LaWALL, CHARLES. Four Thousand Years of Pharmacy. Lippincott, 1927. Presentation copy. (Backstrip dulled), o/w Good. *Bookcell.* $85/£54

LAWLER, LILLIAN B. The Dance in Ancient Greece. Middletown: Wesleyan Univ, (1965). Good in dj (torn). *Archaeologia.* $45/£29

LAWLESS, PETER (ed). The Golfer's Companion. London: J.M. Dent, (1937). 1st ed. Grn cl, gilt spine. (Sm tears rear joint), else VG. *Pacific*.* $69/£44

LAWLOR, ADRIAN. Arquebus. Melbourne, 1937. 1st ed. (Cvr browned, soiled, backstrip frayed.) *Typographeum.* $50/£32

LAWRENCE, A. SUSAN. A Letter to a Woman Munitions Worker. (London: Fabian Soc, ca 1942.) Self-wraps. Fine (sm lib stamp fr cvr). *Second Life.* $45/£29

LAWRENCE, A. W. (ed). T. E. Lawrence by His Friends. London: Cape, (1937). 1st ed. Port. Fine in dj (lt soiled, 2 sm tears, 1 mended on verso). *Reese.* $125/£80

LAWRENCE, A. W. (ed). T. E. Lawrence by His Friends. London, 1937. 1st Eng ed. VG in dj (upper edge sl discolored). *Edrich.* $62/£40

LAWRENCE, ADA and G. S. GELDER. Young Lorenzo. Florence: Orioli, 1931. #265/740. Vellum cvrs (warped). Dj. *Typographeum.* $65/£42

LAWRENCE, D. H. Assorted Articles. London: Martin Secker, 1930. 1st Eng ed. NF in VG dj (torn, chipped). *Antic Hay.* $85/£54

LAWRENCE, D. H. The Captain's Doll. NY: Thomas Seltzer, 1923. 1st Amer ed. Blue cl, gilt. Fine. *Macdonnell.* $50/£32

LAWRENCE, D. H. David: A Play. NY: Knopf, 1926. 1st Amer ed. (Bkpl), else Fine in VG dj. *Between The Covers.* $125/£80

LAWRENCE, D. H. England My England. NY: Seltzer, 1922. 1st ed. Blue cl. Fine in NF dj (inside neatly repaired) w/ads for 6 titles. *Bromer.* $650/£417

LAWRENCE, D. H. The Escaped Cock. Paris: Black Sun, 1929. 1st ed. One of 450 ptd for subs. Ptd wrappers under wax paper as issued. Nice in slipcase. *Appelfeld.* $400/£256

LAWRENCE, D. H. Etruscan Places. London, 1932. 1st Uk ed. (Sl faded, mkd, sl bumped.) *Clearwater.* $62/£40

LAWRENCE, D. H. Kangaroo. NY: Thomas Seltzer, 1923. 1st Amer ed. Blue cl. VG (eps browned). *Antic Hay.* $65/£42

LAWRENCE, D. H. Lady Chatterley's Lover. Paris: Obelisk Press, (1936). 1st ptg under Obelisk imprint. Dec stiff wrappers. (Ink name dated 1937, few creases to spine, sl tanning), else VG. *Reese.* $75/£48

LAWRENCE, D. H. The Letters. Aldous Huxley (ed). Heinemann, 1932. 1st ed. VG. *Poetry Bookshop.* $47/£30

LAWRENCE, D. H. The Lost Girl. London: Seltzer, 1921. 1st UK ed. NF. *Williams.* $23/£15

LAWRENCE, D. H. The Lost Girl. NY: Thomas Seltzer, 1921. 1st Amer ed. Blue cl. VG (sm name stamp). *Antic Hay.* $50/£32

LAWRENCE, D. H. Love Among the Haystacks. Nonesuch, 1930. #749/1600. (Sl spotting 1st, final leaves.) Uncut. Canvas-backed yellow buckram, morocco label. *Cox.* $101/£65

LAWRENCE, D. H. Love Among the Haystacks. London: Nonesuch Press, 1930. One of 1600 numbered. (Eps tanned), o/w VG in dj (spine chipped, browned). *Moorhouse.* $78/£50

LAWRENCE, D. H. The Man Who Died. (NY): Knopf, 1931. 1st Amer ed. VG in black cl. *Hadley.* $31/£20

LAWRENCE, D. H. The Man Who Died. London: Martin Secker, 1931. Ltd to 2000. Untrimmed. Orig grn buckram over beveled bds (spine, lower bd faded; label removed fep). *Hollett.* $70/£45

LAWRENCE, D. H. The Man Who Died. London: Martin Secker, 1931. 1st Eng ed. One of 2000. (Offsetting to eps.) Teg. Grn cl (spine, edges faded, pinhole on spine), gilt. NF internally. *Blue Mountain.* $125/£80

LAWRENCE, D. H. The Man Who Died. London: Heinemann, 1935. 1st illus ed. 4to. 64pp; 11 engrs by John Farleigh. NF (bkpl; lt foxing feps; corners bumped) in dj (sl dknd, sm tear). *Bromer.* $165/£106

LAWRENCE, D. H. Mornings in Mexico. Martin Secker, 1927. 1st ed. (1/2 title sl spotted.) Fore, lower edge uncut. (Spine tail sl rubbed; lacks dj.) *Edwards.* $70/£45

LAWRENCE, D. H. My Skirmish with Jolly Roger. NY: Random House, 1929. 1st ed. One of 600. Patterned eps, apologia laid in. Paper over bds, paper label. NF. *Cahan.* $150/£96

LAWRENCE, D. H. Pansies. London: Martin Secker, (1929). 1st trade ed. (Offsetting to fep.) Deckle-edged. Largely unopened. Blue cl-backed dec blue/gold bds, gilt. NF in ptd cream dj (spotted). *Blue Mountain.* $65/£42

LAWRENCE, D. H. Pansies. London: Martin Secker, (1929). 1st (definitive) ed. Fine in blue cl-backed patterned bds. *Captain's Bookshelf.* $125/£80

LAWRENCE, D. H. Pansies. Brooklyn, NY: Theo. Gaus Sons, 1929. Ltd to 1000 numbered, this copy unnumbered. Fine (spine sl rubbed). *Polyanthos.* $40/£26

LAWRENCE, D. H. The Plumed Serpent. London: Martin Secker, (1926). 1st ed. VG (eps lt foxed) in dj (worn, lg piece torn away). *Truepenny.* $150/£96

LAWRENCE, D. H. The Plumed Serpent. London: Secker, (1926). 1st ed. Brn cl, gilt. Nice (few spots). *Macdonnell.* $85/£54

LAWRENCE, D. H. The Plumed Serpent. Secker, 1926. VG (ink name). *Williams.* $39/£25

LAWRENCE, D. H. The Plumed Serpent. NY: Knopf, 1926. 1st Amer ed. Yellow pict cl (lt dusty). Nice. *Macdonnell.* $85/£54

LAWRENCE, D. H. Pornography and Obscenity. London: Faber & Faber, 1929. 1st ed. VG in orig orange wrappers. *Hollett.* $47/£30

LAWRENCE, D. H. A Propos of Lady Chatterley's Lover. London: Mandrake, 1930. 1st Eng ed. Very Nice in dj. *Clearwater.* $55/£35

LAWRENCE, D. H. The Prussian Officer and Other Stories. Duckworth, 1914. 1st ed. Earlier dk blue binding, w/the apparently earlier ads. Good (lt wear, label removed top cvr, lib label rep, sl shaken). *Ash.* $148/£95

LAWRENCE, D. H. The Rainbow. Methuen, 1915. One of 2500. VG (ink name, hinges repaired; spine sl faded). *Williams.* $663/£425

LAWRENCE, D. H. Rawdon's Roof. London: Elkin Mathews & Marrot, 1928. #83/530 numbered, signed. 8vo. Gray bds ptd in blue. Fine in dj, cl slipcase w/chemise. *Cummins.* $500/£321

LAWRENCE, D. H. Reflections on the Death of a Porcupine and Other Essays. Phila: Centaur Press, 1925. 1st ed. One of 925. Cl-backed marbled bds. VG. *New Hampshire*.* $30/£19

LAWRENCE, D. H. Sons and Lovers. Duckworth, 1913. 1st ed. Roberts' Variant (1), w/cancel title dated 1913. Good (lib label rear pastedown, creases, nicks, sl tears, flaws; sl worn, sm labels removed upper cvr). *Ash.* $390/£250

LAWRENCE, D. H. Sons and Lovers. London: Duckworth, 1913. 1st issue, w/dated tp tipped in. VG (foxed). *Williams.* $546/£350

LAWRENCE, D. H. Sons and Lovers. Avon: LEC, 1975. #849/2000 signed by Sheila Robinson (illus). Fine in slipcase. *Hermitage.* $100/£64

LAWRENCE, D. H. Tortoises. NY, 1921. Pict bds (extrems sl rubbed). Bright. *Clearwater.* $390/£250

LAWRENCE, D. H. Touch and Go. NY: Thomas Seltzer, 1920. 1st Amer ed. Pict ptd bds. NF (lacks dj). *Antic Hay.* $75/£48

LAWRENCE, D. H. Triumph of the Machine. London: Faber & Faber, 1930. 1st ed. One of 400. Grn bds. *Appelfeld.* $45/£29

LAWRENCE, D. H. Women in Love. London: Secker, 1921. 1st Eng ed. One of 1500 ptd. Good (pp acid, browned, 30 leaves sl tips; fr hinge cracked, spine sl torn). *Clearwater.* $78/£50

LAWRENCE, D. H. and M. L. SKINNER. The Boy in the Bush. NY: Seltzer, 1924. 1st Amer ed. Blue cl, gilt. Fine. *Macdonnell.* $75/£48

LAWRENCE, EDWARD A. Clover Passage. Caldwell: Caxton, 1954. 1st ed. VF in dj. *Bowman.* $25/£16

LAWRENCE, ROBERT. Primitive Psycho-Therapy and Quackery. London, 1910. 1st Eng ed. VG. *Fye.* $100/£64

LAWRENCE, T. E. The Letters of T. E. Lawrence. London, 1938. 1st Eng ed. VG in dj (sl mkd, closed tear). *Edrich.* $70/£45

LAWRENCE, T. E. The Letters of T. E. Lawrence. David Garnett (ed). London: Cape, (1938). 1st ed, earliest states pp182, 495. Port. Fine in VG dj. *Reese.* $125/£80

LAWRENCE, T. E. The Letters of T. E. Lawrence. David Garnett (ed). Cape, 1938. 1st UK ed. VG (cvrs lt faded, mkd). *Williams.* $39/£25

LAWRENCE, T. E. The Letters of T. E. Lawrence. David Garnett (ed). Doubleday, Doran, 1939. 1st Amer ed. Blue cl. Fine in dj. *Appelfeld.* $50/£32

LAWRENCE, T. E. The Letters of T. E. Lawrence. David Garnett (ed). NY: Doubleday, 1939. 1st Amer ed. 16 plts, 4 maps. VG in dj. *Cullen.* $30/£19

LAWRENCE, T. E. The Letters. London, 1938. 1st ed. Brn buckram. VG. *Words Etc.* $47/£30

LAWRENCE, T. E. The Mint. London: Cape, (1955). 1st trade ed. VG in dj (sl browned). *Houle.* $125/£80

LAWRENCE, T. E. The Mint. London: Jonathan Cape, 1955. 1st ed. Good (cl sl faded) in dj (browned). *Cox.* $31/£20

LAWRENCE, T. E. Oriental Assembly. A. W. Lawrence (ed). London: Williams & Norgate, (1939). 1st ed. Frontis. (Fore-edge sl foxed), else Fine in VF dj. *Reese.* $175/£112

LAWRENCE, T. E. Oriental Assembly. A.W. Lawrence (ed). Williams & Norgate, 1939. 1st ed. Frontis, 111 half-tone plts. Buckram. VG in dj (sl rubbed). *Cox.* $75/£48

LAWRENCE, T. E. Revolt in the Desert. NY: Dutton, (1927). 1st Amer ed. (Inscrip, foxing; top edge dusty.) Yellow pict dj (spine frayed, toned, verso foxed, short tear fr panel). *Waverly*.* $44/£28

LAWRENCE, T. E. Revolt in the Desert. London: Cape, 1927. 1st Eng trade ed. Port. Good (fr hinge sl cracked, price erasure, spine sl sunned). *Reese.* $40/£26

LAWRENCE, T. E. Revolt in the Desert. NY: Doran, 1927. 1st US ptg. Fldg map. VG. *Worldwide.* $12/£8

LAWRENCE, T. E. Secret Despatches from Arabia. London: Golden Cockerel, n.d. #959/1000. (Eps, edges sl foxed, browned.) Teg. 1/4 niger cream cl. (Soiled, spotted, lower corners bumped), o/w Good. *Virgo.* $624/£400

LAWRENCE, T. E. Seven Pillars of Wisdom. Cape, (1935). Ltd to 750 numbered. Loosely inserted are letter of authentication signed by pub's production mgr, letters, receipt relating to early sale of bk, related press cuttings. Partly unopened. Teg. Orig 1/4 pigskin gilt. VG (leaf creased, edges sl spotted, sl mks) in dj (sl chipped, browned). *Ash.* $1,552/£995

LAWRENCE, T. E. Seven Pillars of Wisdom. Cape, 1935. 1st trade ed. (Bds sl mkd), else VG in dj. *Williams.* $289/£185

LAWRENCE, T. E. Seven Pillars of Wisdom. Jonathan Cape, 1935. Ltd to 750. 8vo. 4 maps. Teg, marbled eps. Brn buckram bds, pict gilt, pigskin spine. Plain dj. *Sotheby's*.* $646/£414

LAWRENCE, T. E. Seven Pillars of Wisdom. GC, 1935. 1st pub Amer trade ed. Dj (price-clipped, sl chipped). *Freeman*.* $30/£19

LAWRENCE, T. E. Seven Pillars of Wisdom. London, 1935. 1st ed. VG. *Typographeum.* $45/£29

LAWRENCE, T. E. Seven Pillars of Wisdom. London: Cape, 1935. 1st trade ed. 4 fldg maps. Untrimmed. Orig brn buckram (lt scratches, sm mks), gilt. *Hollett.* $86/£55

LAWRENCE, T. E. Seven Pillars of Wisdom. NY: GC, 1935. 1st Amer ed. One of 750 on special paper. 4to. Frontis port. Crimson linen bds, brn pigskin spine, beveled edges. Fine in box. *Appelfeld.* $600/£385

LAWRENCE, T. E. T. E. Lawrence: Letters to E. T. Leeds. J. M. Wilson (ed). Whittington, 1988. One of 750 numbered, of which this is one of the standard ed. Ptd invitation loosely inserted. 1/4 buckram, ptd paper bds. Fine in slipcase. *Michael Taylor.* $156/£100

LAWRENCE, W. J. Those Nut-Cracking Elizabethans. Argonaut, 1935. Frontis, 7 plts of facs. Teg, rest uncut. Pict scarlet cl (faded, sl mkd, 3 sm stickers pastedown), gilt. Sound. *Peter Taylor.* $36/£23

LAWRENCE, WILLIAM H. Principles of Architectural Perspective. Boston: Mudge, 1895. Presentation copy. 42pp, errata slip, 11 fldg plts (1 torn). *Marlborough.* $179/£115

LAWRENCE, WILLIAM. Life of Amos A. Lawrence. Boston, 1888. 1st ed. Inscribed presentation from Amory A. Lawrence. (10),289pp. *Ginsberg.* $125/£80

LAWRIE, W. H. A Reference Book of English Trout Flies. London: Pelham Books, 1967. 1st ed. 14 plts (5 color). VG in dj. *Hollett.* $55/£35

Laws of Illinois, Passed at the Seventh General Assembly...on the First Monday in December, 1830.... Vandalia, IL: Blackwell, 1831. 1st ed. 217pp. Orig 1/2 calf, bds (spine worn). *Ginsberg.* $175/£112

Laws of the State of Mississippi, Passed...Dec. 1874. Jackson: Pilot, 1875. 24pp. Later buckram. VG. *Bohling.* $28/£18

Laws of the State of Mississippi, Passed...Nov. 1858. Jackson: E. Barksdale, 1859. 256pp (tp, last pg w/sm holes, scribbling, ink spots; new eps). Tan buckram (rebacked), orig calf bds (worn). *Bohling.* $18/£12

Laws of the State of New York. Vol 1 (only). NY: T. Greenleaf, 1792. iv,510pp (text dknd, sl worn; pg torn, no loss). Tree calf (lacks fr cvr, rest worn). *Bohling.* $18/£12

LAWSON, A. The Modern Farrier. Newcastle upon Tyne: Mackenzie & Dent, 1821. 1st ed. 616,viiipp; added engr tp, 9 plts. Old calf over marbled bds (rebacked). *Karmiole.* $250/£160

LAWSON, G. Diseases and Injuries of the Eye with Their Medical and Surgical Treatment. A. Lawson (ed). 1903. 6th ed. (Fr hinge cracked; sl worn.) *Whitehart.* $39/£25

LAWSON, HENRY. The Stories of Henry Lawson. Cecil Mann (ed). Sydney: Angus & Robertson, (1964). 1st ed. 3 vols. NF (stamp copyright pg) in VG djs. *Turtle Island.* $100/£64

LAWSON, J. A. Wanderings in New Guinea. London: Chapman & Hall, 1875. 1st ed. Color litho frontis, viii,263pp; fldg map at rear. Uncut. Dec cl (joints sl rubbed; sl bumped), gilt. Good. *Sotheran.* $304/£195

LAWSON, JOHN PARKER. History of Remarkable Conspiracies Connected with European History, During the Fifteenth, Sixteenth, and Seventeenth Centuries. Edinburgh: Constable, 1829. 1st ed. 2 vols. Frontispieces, 326; 320pp. Later 19th-cent full calf, red spine labels. Good. *Karmiole.* $125/£80

LAWSON, ROBERT. Ben and Me. Boston: Little, Brown, 1939. 1st ed. Pict eps. Lt brn cl. Very Nice (top edge lt dusty) in pict dj (lt sunned, chipped, sm tears). *Baltimore*.* $60/£38

LAWSON, ROBERT. The Fabulous Flight. Boston: LB, 1949. 2nd ed. 6 1/4 x 9 1/2. 152pp. VG in dj. *Cattermole.* $25/£16

LAWSON, ROBERT. The Great Wheel. NY: Viking, 1957. 1st ed. 6 1/4 x 9 1/2. 188pp. Fine in dj. *Cattermole.* $60/£38

LAWSON, ROBERT. Mr. Revere and I. Boston: Little, Brown, (1953). 1st ed. #27/500 signed. Fine in clear acetate dj, slipcase (top rear edge partly split, corner bumped). *Bernard.* $100/£64

LAWSON, TED W. Thirty Seconds over Tokyo. Robert Considine (ed). NY: Random House, 1943. 1st ed. VG in dj. *Worldwide.* $18/£12

LAWSON, WILL. Pacific Steamers. Glasgow: Brown, Son & Ferguson, 1927. 1st ed. Gilt-lettered blue cl (sl rubbed). Fine. *Argonaut.* $150/£96

LAWSON, WILLIAM J. The History of Banking. Boston: Gould & Lincoln, 1852. 1st Amer ed. viii,346pp; 2 ports. 3/4 leather (rubbed, hinges worn, partly split). *Agvent.* $75/£48

LAWTON, HARRY. Willie Boy. (Balboa Island): Paisano Press, (1960). 1st ed. Gray cl stamped in black. (Sl stain inner fr hinge), else Fine in pict dj (lt soiled). *Argonaut.* $45/£29

LAY, CHARLES DOWNING. A Garden Book for Autumn and Winter. NY: Duffield, 1924. Frontis. Gilt-dec cl (lt stained). *Quest.* $35/£22

LAY, WILLIAM and CYRUS M. HUSSEY. A Narrative of the Mutiny, on Board the Ship Globe...Jan, 1824. (NY: Abbey Press, n.d. ca 1901.) Howes L158. *Lefkowicz.* $100/£64

LAYARD, AUSTEN H. Discoveries in the Ruins of Ninevah and Bayblon. Murray, 1853. (Sm nick fr joint), o/w VG. *Petersfield.* $156/£100

LAYARD, GEORGE SOAMES. Suppressed Plates, Wood Engravings, &c. together with Other Curiosities.... London: A&C Black, 1907. 1st ed. 30 plts. Gilt-stamped cl. (Spine ends worn, some gilt loss), else VG. *Waverly*.* $44/£28

LAYARD, GEORGE SOMES. Suppressed Plates, Wood Engravings, &c. London: A&C Black, 1907. 1st ed. Frontis. Teg. Gilt pict cl. (Bkpl), o/w Very Nice. *Reese.* $85/£54

LAYARD, GEORGE SOMES. Suppressed Plates, Wood Engravings, Etc. Together with Other Curiosities...Alluring to the Collector. London, 1907. Teg. (Extrems frayed.) *King.* $50/£32

LAYCOCK, THOMAS. An Essay on Hysteria.... Phila/New Orleans: Haswell et al/Haswell, 1840. 1st Amer ed. 192pp. Mod calf-backed marbled bds, leather spine label. VG. *Gach.* $185/£119

LAYCOCK, W. F. et al. A Dictionary of Dyes, Mordants.... London, 1901. (Upper margin cut away fep, lt marginal browning; cl dknd, sl rubbed, spine chipped, lt faded.) *Edwards.* $31/£20

LAYMON, RICHARD. Resurrection Dreams. London: W.H. Allen, 1988. 1st ed. Dj. *Swann*.* $80/£51

LE BLANC, MAURICE. The Confessions of Arsene Lupin. GC: Doubleday, Page, 1913. 1st ed. Emb cvr. (Lt rubbed, soiled), else VG. *Murder By The Book.* $65/£42

LE BLANC, MAURICE. The Exploits of Arsene Lupin. NY/London, 1907. 1st Amer ed. Pict cl (spine lettering, design dulled). VG. *Mcclintock.* $30/£19

LE BLOND, MRS. AUBREY. Adventures on the Roof of the World. London: T. Fisher Unwin, 1904. 1st ed. xvi,333pp; 32 photo plts. Uncut. Pict cl (spine head sl bumped). Good (browning). *Sotheran.* $117/£75

LE BLOND, MRS. AUBREY. True Tales of Mountain Adventure. London, 1906. 3rd imp. Frontis port. (Lt margin browning also affecting eps; extrems sl worn.) *Edwards.* $75/£48

LE CARRE, JOHN. Call for the Dead. Gollancz, 1961. 1st UK ed. VG (pencil name erased fep) in 2nd imp dj (lacks sm piece spine top, sm closed tear fr panel). *Williams.* $702/£450

LE CARRE, JOHN. Call for the Dead. NY: Walker, 1962. 1st Amer ed. (Spine base sl fading), o/w Fine in dj (nick spine top, sm closed tear spine base, spine sl fading). *Mordida.* $600/£385

LE CARRE, JOHN. The Honourable Schoolboy. London: Hodder & Stoughton, 1977. 1st ed. Fine in dj (sl color restoration spine ends). *Mordida.* $85/£54

LE CARRE, JOHN. The Honourable Schoolboy. NY: Knopf, 1977. 1st Amer trade ed. Fine in dj. *Mordida.* $45/£29

LE CARRE, JOHN. The Little Drummer Girl. Hodder, 1983. 1st UK ed. NF in dj. *Williams.* $19/£12

LE CARRE, JOHN. The Little Drummer Girl. London: Hodder & Stoughton, 1983. 1st Eng ed. Fine (corner sl bumped) in NF dj (price-clipped). *Janus.* $35/£22

LE CARRE, JOHN. The Looking-Glass War. London: Heinemann, 1965. 1st ed. VG in VG dj (sl worn, sl faded). *Old London.* $75/£48

LE CARRE, JOHN. The Naive and Sentimental Lover. London, 1971. 1st Eng ed. Nice in dj (price-clipped). *Clearwater.* $31/£20

LE CARRE, JOHN. The Night Manager. Hodder, 1993. 1st UK ed. Fine in dj. *Williams.* $19/£12

LE CARRE, JOHN. The Night Manager. London: Hodder & Stoughton, 1993. 1st ed. Signed. VF in dj. *Mordida.* $150/£96

LE CARRE, JOHN. A Perfect Spy. London: Hodder & Stoughton, 1986. 1st ed. Fine in Fine dj. *Old London.* $50/£32

LE CARRE, JOHN. A Perfect Spy. London: Hodder & Stoughton, 1986. 1st ed. Signed. Fine in dj. *Mordida.* $175/£112

LE CARRE, JOHN. A Perfect Spy. NY: Knopf, 1986. 1st US ed. Fine in Fine dj. *Old London.* $15/£10

LE CARRE, JOHN. A Perfect Spy. NY: Knopf, 1986. 1st Amer ed. Signed. VF in dj. *Mordida.* $150/£96

LE CARRE, JOHN. The Russia House. Hodder, 1989. 1st UK ed. Fine in dj. *Williams.* $19/£12

LE CARRE, JOHN. The Russia House. London: Hodder & Stoughton, 1989. DeLuxe ed. 1/2 leather slipcase. *Old London.* $150/£96

LE CARRE, JOHN. The Russia House. London: London Limited Editions, 1989. One of 250 specially bound numbered, signed. VF in tissue dj. *Mordida.* $200/£128

LE CARRE, JOHN. The Russia House. NY: Knopf, 1989. 1st US ed. Fine in Fine dj. *Old London.* $20/£13

LE CARRE, JOHN. The Russia House. NY: Knopf, 1989. One of small # w/extra signed leaf tipped in. Fine in Fine dj. *Lenz.* $75/£48

LE CARRE, JOHN. The Russia House. NY: Knopf, 1989. 1st ed. Uncorrected proof copy. Fine in ptd cream wrappers. *Mordida.* $125/£80

LE CARRE, JOHN. The Secret Pilgrim. Hodder, 1991. 1st UK ed. Fine in dj. *Williams.* $19/£12

LE CARRE, JOHN. The Secret Pilgrim. London: Hodder & Stoughton, 1991. 1st Eng ed. Fine in Fine dj. *Janus.* $45/£29

LE CARRE, JOHN. The Secret Pilgrim. London: Hodder & Stoughton, 1991. 1st ed. Signed. VF in dj. *Mordida.* $125/£80

LE CARRE, JOHN. The Secret Pilgrim. NY: Knopf, 1991. 1st Amer ed. Signed. VF in dj. *Mordida.* $85/£54

LE CARRE, JOHN. A Small Town in Germany. NY: Coward-McCann, 1964. 1st Amer ed. One of 500 numbered, signed presentations. VF in acetate dj. *Mordida.* $350/£224

LE CARRE, JOHN. A Small Town in Germany. Heinemann, 1968. 1st UK ed. NF (edges sl foxed) in dj (price-clipped). *Williams.* $19/£12

LE CARRE, JOHN. Smiley's People. London: Hodder & Stoughton, 1979. Uncorrected proof. Pub's letter laid in. (Pp dknd), o/w Fine in proof dj (clsed tears spine top, spine sl faded, folds worn). *Mordida.* $200/£128

LE CARRE, JOHN. Smiley's People. Hodder, 1980. 1st UK ed. Signed. Fine in dj (spine sl faded). *Williams.* $117/£75

LE CARRE, JOHN. Smiley's People. NY: Knopf, 1980. 1st Amer trade ed. Fine in dj (price-clipped). *Mordida.* $35/£22

LE CARRE, JOHN. The Spy Who Came in from the Cold. London: Gollancz, 1963. 1st UK ed. VG in dj. *Williams.* $234/£150

LE CARRE, JOHN. The Spy Who Came in from the Cold. London: Gollancz, 1963. 1st ed. (Erasure fep), o/w NF in dj. *Mordida.* $350/£224

LE CARRE, JOHN. The Spy Who Came in from the Cold. London: Gollancz, 1963. 1st ed. VG in VG dj. *Old London.* $600/£385

LE CARRE, JOHN. The Spy Who Came in from the Cold. NY, 1963. 1st Amer ed. NF in VG+ dj (price-clipped). *Smith.* $15/£10

LE CARRE, JOHN. Tinker Tailor Soldier Spy. London, 1974. 1st Eng ed. Very Nice (top edges discolored) in dj (spine faded). *Clearwater.* $39/£25

LE CLEZIO, J. M. G. The Interrogation. NY: Atheneum, 1964. 1st US ed. VG in VG- dj (loss spine head). *Lame Duck.* $25/£16

LE CORBEAU, ADRIEN. The Forest Giant. L. H. Ross (trans). London: Cape, (1924). 1st ed. Frontis. Paper spine label. Sound (adhesive residue eps from old protector). *Reese.* $30/£19

LE CORBEAU, ADRIEN. The Forest Giant. L. H. Ross (trans). NY: Harper, 1924. 1st Amer ed. Frontis. Cl, dec bds. (Ll facing frontis foxed), o/w Nice in 2 examples of pict dj (lt chipped, snagged, outer one rubbed, dust-mkd). *Reese.* $75/£48

LE CORBEAU, ADRIEN. The Forest Giant. Adapted from the French by L. H. Ross (pseud of T. E. Lawrence). NY: Harper, 1924. (Inscrip.) Cl-backed patterned bds (sl shelfworn, sl chafed). Dj (skillfully backed w/stiff brn paper). *Clearwater.* $156/£100

LE CORBEILLER, CLARE. European and American Snuff Boxes 1730-1830. NY: Viking, (1966). 1st ed. 3 color plts. Black cl. Fine in dj. *Weber.* $45/£29

LE CORBEILLER, CLARE. European and American Snuff Boxes 1730-1830. Viking, 1966. 1st ed. Good in dj (chipped). *Scribe's Perch*.* $32/£21

LE CORBUSIER. The City of To-Morrow. Frederick Etchells (trans). London: Architectural Press, 1947. VG. *Hollett.* $47/£30

LE CORBUSIER. The City of Tomorrow and Its Planning. Frederick Etchells (trans). London: John Rodker, 1929. 1st UK ed. Frontis, fldg plan. Good. *Ars Artis.* $328/£210

LE CORBUSIER. The Modulor, and Modulor 2. P. de Francia & A. Bostock (trans). London: Faber, 1954/8. 1st ed in English of The Modulor. 2 vols. Sound. *Ars Artis.* $94/£60

LE CORBUSIER. Towards a New Architecture. Frederick Etchells (trans). 1931. Dj (spine head sl chipped). *Edwards.* $70/£45

LE COUTEUR, J. D. English Mediaeval Painted Glass. A. Hamilton Thompson (ed). London: SPCK, 1926. 1st ed. (Tp, text sl spotted; cl sl rubbed, spine head sl chipped.) *Edwards.* $39/£25

LE FANU, J. SHERIDAN. All in the Dark. London, n.d. (ca. 1880). New ed. Pict bds (spine sl worn, tips worn, cvr sl rubbed). Interior VG. *Mcclintock.* $75/£48

LE FANU, J. SHERIDAN. Checkmate. Phila: Evans, Stoddart, 1871. 1st Amer ed. Nice (sl foxing, pastedown, fly worn; lt rubbed). *Metropolitan**. $460/£295

LE FANU, J. SHERIDAN. Checkmate. London: Morning Herald Library, 1899. Rpt. Teg. 3/4 red leather (rebound), marbled bds. (Spine ends sl worn), o/w VG + . *Bernard*. $150/£96

LE FANU, J. SHERIDAN. The Evil Guest. London: Downey, n.d. (1895). 1st UK ed. March 1895 ads in rear. Teg. Dk grn/gold-dec cl (spine corner expertly repaired). Exceptional. *Bernard*. $600/£385

LE FANU, J. SHERIDAN. The Hours After Midnight.... Des Hickey (ed). London: Leslie Frewin, 1975. 1st ed. Fine in Fine dj. *Certo*. $75/£48

LE FANU, J. SHERIDAN. In a Glass Darkly. London: Peter Davies, 1929. 1st ed. Signed by Edward Ardizzone (illus), dated June 1975. (Sl mkd, rubbed.) *Hollett*. $234/£150

LE FANU, J. SHERIDAN. The Purcell Papers. Sauk City, WI, 1975. 1st ed. New in New dj. *Mcclintock*. $8/£5

LE GALLIENNE, RICHARD. Old Love Stories Retold. London, 1924. 1st Eng ed. Nice (sl chafed) in pict dj (chipped, repaired). *Clearwater*. $78/£50

LE GALLIENNE, RICHARD. Omar Repentant. NY: Mitchell Kennerley, (1908). 1st Amer ed. Teg, uncut. NF (name) in dj (lacks few edge pieces, soiled). *Polyanthos*. $25/£16

LE GALLIENNE, RICHARD. Painted Shadows. Boston: Little, Brown, 1904. 1st Amer ed. Teg. Dec cl. VG-(wear). *Antic Hay*. $25/£16

LE GALLIENNE, RICHARD. Prose Fancies. NY: Putnam, 1894. 1st Amer ed. Dec cl. VG (sl foxed) *Antic Hay*. $35/£22

LE GALLIENNE, RICHARD. The Religion of a Literary Man (Religion Scriptoris). London: Elkin Mathews & John Lane, 1893. Ltd to 250. Dec bds. VG (rubbed, eps discolored, bkpl). *Antic Hay*. $125/£80

LE GALLIENNE, RICHARD. Rudyard Kipling. London: John Lane, Bodley Head, 1900. 1st ed. Blue bds. VG (bkpl) in 1/2 red morocco dbl slipcase, gilt. *Cullen*. $100/£64

LE GRAND, LOUIS et al. The Military Hand-Book. NY: Beadle, (1862). 125pp (pencil sig). Ptd wrappers (lacks rear); crude 'cardboard' bds sewn on. VG. *Lucas*. $150/£96

LE GUIN, URSULA K. Catwings. NY: Orchard, 1988. 1st ed. S. D. Schindler (illus). 5 1/2 x 7 1/4. 40pp. Cl spine. As New in dj. *Cattermole*. $25/£16

LE GUIN, URSULA K. City of Illusions. NY, 1978. 1st ed. Fine in Fine dj. *Smith*. $25/£16

LE GUIN, URSULA K. The Dispossessed. Gollancz, 1974. 1st Eng ed. Fine in dj. *Aronovitz*. $60/£38

LE GUIN, URSULA K. Dreams Must Explain Themselves. (NY: Algol, 1975.) 1st ed. One of 1000. This copy inscribed. Pict wrappers. *Swann**. $69/£44

LE GUIN, URSULA K. The Farthest Shore. Gollancz, 1973. 1st UK ed. (Spine sl faded), o/w Fine in Fine dj. *Martin*. $53/£34

LE GUIN, URSULA K. The Farthest Shore. London, 1973. 1st Eng ed. Fine in dj. *Clearwater*. $62/£40

LE GUIN, URSULA K. The Lathe of Heaven. NY: Scribner, (1971). 1st ed. Fine in dj. *Captain's Bookshelf*. $250/£160

LE GUIN, URSULA K. The Lathe of Heaven. NY: Scribner, (1971). Fine in Fine dj. *Between The Covers*. $500/£321

LE GUIN, URSULA K. The Left Hand of Darkness. London: Macdonald, (1969). 1st British ed. (Sl askew.) Dj (lt worn, rear soiled, price-clipped). *Swann**. $46/£29

LE GUIN, URSULA K. The Left Hand of Darkness. Harper, 1980. 1st ed thus. Fine in dj. *Madle*. $25/£16

LE GUIN, URSULA K. A Wizard of Earthsea. SF: Parnassus, 1968. 1st ed. 6 1/4 x 8 3/4. 205pp. VG in dj. *Cattermole*. $65/£42

LE MARCHAND, ELIZABETH. Step in the Dark. London: Hart-Davis, MacGibbon, 1976. 1st ed. Fine in dj. *Mordida*. $45/£29

LE MAY, ALAN. The Searchers. NY: Harper, 1954. 1st ed. Fine in NF dj (lt edge-rubbed, lt soiled). *Unger*. $200/£128

LE QUEUX, WILLIAM. The Dangerous Game. NY: Macauley, 1926. 1st ed. NF in pict dj (lt worn, price-clipped). *Else Fine*. $65/£42

LE QUEUX, WILLIAM. Devil's Dice. Chicago: Rand McNally, 1897 1st Amer ed. Fine in pict cl cvrs, gilt. *Mordida*. $100/£64

LE QUEUX, WILLIAM. The Stretton Street Affair. NY: Macauley, 1922. 1st ed. Fine. *Else Fine*. $20/£13

LE QUEUX, WILLIAM. The Voice from the Void. NY: Macaulay, 1923. 1st Amer ed. Fine in dj (price-clipped). *Mordida*. $125/£80

LE VOLEUR. The Champington Mystery. London: Digby, Long, 1900. 1st ed. Inscribed (mkd over by later hand). (Loose, extrems rubbed.) *Metropolitan**. $34/£22

LEA, HENRY CHARLES. Materials Toward a History of Witchcraft. Arthur C. Howland (ed). Phila: Univ of PA, 1939. 1st ed. 3 vols. Red buckram (corners bumped), gilt spines. Attractive set. *Gach*. $350/£224

LEA, ISAAC. Contributions to Geology. Phila, 1833. 1st ed. 227pp (staining); 6 plts. Uncut. Recent cl. *M&s*. $200/£128

LEA, TOM. A Grizzly from the Coral Sea. (El Paso: Carl Hertzog, 1944). One of 295 signed. *Dawson*. $500/£321

LEA, TOM. The King Ranch. Boston: Little, Brown, (1957). 1st ed, 2nd issue, w/p507 beginning 'For Alice.' 2 vols. 2-tone buckram. Fine in slipcase (worn). *Argonaut*. $125/£80

LEA, TOM. The King Ranch. Boston: Little, Brown, (1957). 1st ed, 1st issue. Chapter heading pg 507 vol 2 changed to read Alice in later ptg. 2 vols. VG in slipcase (sl worn). *Lien*. $200/£128

LEA, TOM. The Primal Yoke. Little, Brown, (1960). 1st ed. NF in dj. *Certo*. $20/£13

LEACH, A. J. Early Day Stories, the Overland Trail Animals and Birds That Lived Here.... Norfolk, NE: Privately ptd, 1916. 1st ed. Signed. Port. Paper label. (Text lt soiled; rebound), else Good. Howes L162. *Brown*. $100/£64

LEACH, A. J. Early Day Stories. The Overland Trail.... Norfolk, NE, 1916. Very Nice in dj. Howes L162. *Reese*. $100/£64

LEACH, FRANK A. Recollections of a Newspaperman: A Record of Life and Events in California. SF: Samuel Levinson, 1917. 1st ed. 13 plts. Brn cl, gilt. VF. *Argonaut*. $50/£32

LEACH, HENRY. The Happy Golfer. London: Macmillan, 1914. 1st ed. Grn cl, gilt. (Inscrip partly over title; spine sl bumped), else NF. *Pacific**. $805/£516

LEACH, HENRY. The Spirit of the Links. London: Methuen, (1907). 1st ed. (Fr cvr extrems discolored), else VG. *Pacific**. $374/£240

LEACH, MacEDWARD. The Book of Ballads. LEC, 1967. 1st ed. #461/1500 numbered, signed. 36 hand-colored woodcuts. Cl-backed bds, dec paper label. Fine in slipcase. *Whittle*. $39/£25

LEACOCK, STEPHEN. Canada, the Foundations of Its Future. Montreal: Privately ptd, 1941. 1st ed. 2-tone cl. Bright in slipcase (frayed). *King*. $65/£42

LEACOCK, STEPHEN. Mark Twain. (London): Peter Davies, 1932. 1st ed. VG (ink name) in dj (foxed, soil, 2 sm chips). *Antic Hay*. $75/£48

LEACOCK, STEPHEN. Nonsense Novels. Montreal: Publishers' Press, 1911. 1st ed, Canadian issue, bound from British sheets. (Sm tear ep; spine gilt sl patinated), o/w VG. *Reese.* $60/£38

LEACOCK, STEPHEN. Over the Footlights and Other Fancies. London, 1923. 1st Eng ed. Very Nice in pict dj (chipped, sl torn, internally repaired). *Clearwater.* $55/£35

LEACOCK, STEPHEN. Short Circuits. London, 1928. 1st Eng ed. Nice in pict dj (chipped, sl torn). *Clearwater.* $55/£35

LEACOCK, STEPHEN. Winnowed Wisdom. NY: Dodd, Mead, 1926. 1st ed. VG in dj (edgeworn, spine browned, 2-inch tear rear panel). *Antic Hay.* $85/£54

LEACOCK, STEPHEN. Winsome Winnie and Other New Nonsense Novels. NY/London/Toronto: John Lane/S.B. Gundy, 1920. 1st ed. Signed. Good (rubbed). *Reese.* $35/£22

LEADBITTER, MIKE and NEIL SLAVEN. Blues Records 1943-1966. London/NY: Hanover/Oak, 1968. 1st ed. The Hanover book in an Oak dj. (Spine soiled), o/w Fine in dj (lt worn, lt soiled). *Beasley.* $125/£80

Leaf and Flower Pictures, and How to Make Them. NY: Randolph, 1857. 1st ed. Sq 8vo. 8 color litho plts. (Foxed; sl shelfworn, shaken.) *Oinonen**. $190/£122

LEAF, MUNRO. Gordon the Goat. NY: Lippincott, 1944. 1st ed. 6 1/4 x 8 1/4. 48pp. Good in dj. *Cattermole.* $40/£26

LEAF, MUNRO. Grammar Can Be Fun. NY: Stokes, Dec 1936. 5th ptg. 4to. 41pp. Illus cl. (Tips worn, sl mks), else VG. *Bookmark.* $23/£15

LEAR, EDWARD. A Book of Nonsense. London: Warne, n.d. (ca 1870?). 4to. (Sl adhesion few plts.) Gilt-pict cl (shelfworn). *Oinonen**. $80/£51

LEAR, EDWARD. Edward Lear's Journals. H. Van Thal (ed). NY: Coward-McCann, (1952). 1st ed. Fine in dj (lt used, price-clipped). *Antic Hay.* $25/£16

LEAR, EDWARD. Illustrations of the Family of Psittacidae, or Parrots. London/NY: Pion/Johnson Rpt, 1978. One of 530 numbered. 42 full-pg color repros. Teg. Crimson morocco, cl, raised bands, gilt. Very Nice (few ll smudged; sl edgeworn). *Baltimore**. $375/£240

LEAR, EDWARD. Journal of a Landscape Painter in Corsica. London: Robert John Bush, 1870. 1st ed. 8vo. Frontis, xvi,272pp; map, 39 plts. (Lt edgeworn.) *Maggs.* $663/£425

LEAR, EDWARD. The Jumblies. NY: Young Scott Books, (1968). 1st ed thus. Signed by Edward Gorey (illus). Fine in dj. *Bromer.* $45/£29

LEAR, EDWARD. Limericks by Lear. Cleveland: World, 1965. 1st ed. Lois Ehlert (illus). 8 3/4 x 11 3/4. Fine in dj. *Cattermole.* $50/£32

LEAR, EDWARD. The New Vestments. (Portland, ME): Chamberlain Press, (1978). Ltd to 100 signed by Sarah Chamberlain (illus); this copy also inscribed. 8vo. (6)pp, frenchfold; 2 full-pg wood engrs each signed by Chamberlain. VF in ptd wrappers. *Bromer.* $150/£96

LEAR, PETER. (Pseud of Peter Lovesey.) Goldengirl. London: Cassell, 1977. 1st UK ed. VG + in dj. *Williams.* $31/£20

LEARY, A. J. County Governments of California. SF: A.J. Leary, 1891. Contemp sheep (very rubbed, joints cracked). *Boswell.* $50/£32

LEARY, TIMOTHY. The Politics of Ecstasy. NY: College Notes & Texts, (1968). Trade pb. Inscribed. VG (lt shelfwear). *Gach.* $75/£48

LEARY, TIMOTHY. The Politics of Ecstasy. MacGibbon & Kee, 1970. 1st UK ed. VG + in dj. *Sclanders.* $31/£20

LEASOR, JAMES. The Yang Meridian. NY: Putnam, (1968). 1st Amer ed. Fine in dj (sl worn). *Antic Hay.* $20/£13

LEAUTAUD, PAUL. Journal of a Man of Letters. Geoffrey Sainsbury (trans). London: C&W, 1960. 1st Eng ed. Fine in NF dj (lt wear, soil). *Antic Hay.* $25/£16

LEAVITT, DAVID. Family Dancing. London: Viking, 1985. 1st British ed, 1st bk. Fine in Fine dj (price-clipped, pub's sticker). *Revere.* $35/£22

LEAVITT, DUDLEY. The Scholar's Almanack and Farmers Daily Register for the Year of Our Lord 1808. Exeter: Norris & Sawyer, (1807). Orig ptd wrappers, tied. (Edges sl chipped, worn.) *Sadlon.* $30/£19

LEAVITT, JOHN McDOWELL. Kings of Capital and Knights of Labor. NY, 1885. 1st ed. Tan cl, stamped in gilt/black. (Spine worn, frayed), o/w NF. *Beasley.* $125/£80

LEBEL, ROBERT. Marcel Duchamp. London: Trianon, 1959. 1st British ed. Color illus tipped on tp; 6 tipped-in color, 129 monochrome plts. (Bkpl; marginal pencil note), else VG in dj (sm spine tears). *Cahan.* $150/£96

LECHENPERG, HARALD (ed). Olympic Games 1960. NY, 1960. Gilt device upper bd. (Spine, heads chipped, faded.) *Edwards.* $47/£30

LECOMPTE, JANET. Rebellion in Rio Arriba 1837. Albuquerque, 1985. 1st ed. VF in VF dj. *Turpen.* $29/£19

LeCONTE, EMMA. When the World Ended: The Diary of Emma LeConte. Earl Schenck Miers (ed). NY: OUP, 1957. 1st ed. Fine in Fine dj. *Mcgowan.* $45/£29

LED, RICHARD. A Treatise of Captures in War. London: W. Sandy, 1759. Mod bds. (Foxing, browning), but Crisp. *Boswell.* $850/£545

LEDFORD, PRESTON LAFAYETTE. Reminiscences of the Civil War, 1861-1865. Thomasville, NC: News Print, 1909. 1st ed. VG in orig ptd wrappers (2 sm tape repairs), custom made cl clamshell box w/leather spine, antique marbled paper sides. *Mcgowan.* $1,200/£769

LEDGER, EDWARD (ed). The Era Almanack and Annual 1868-1898. (London), 1868-1898. 8 vols. Marbled edges, eps. Uniform 1/2 brown morocco, gilt. NF set. *Dramatis Personae.* $1,000/£641

LEDOUX, LOUIS V. An Essay on Japanese Prints. NY: Japan Soc, 1938. One of 1000. Cl-backed patterned bds. *Swann**. $126/£81

LEDYARD, JOHN. John Ledyard's Journey Through Russia and Siberia 1787-1788. Stephen D. Watrous (ed). Madison: Univ of WI, 1966. 1st ed. Dk blue cl. Fine in dj. *Argonaut.* $50/£32

LEE, ANNA MARIA. Memoirs of Eminent Female Writers, of All Ages and Countries. Phila: Grigg, 1827. 1st ed. Engr frontis, (7),183pp. Uncut. Muslin-backed bds, paper label. NF. *Second Life.* $235/£151

LEE, BOURKE. Death Valley Men. NY: Macmillan, 1932. 1st ed. Fine in Near Perfect dj. *Book Market.* $150/£96

LEE, BOURKE. Death Valley. NY: Macmillan, 1930. 1st ed. Frontis, 31 (of 32) full-pg plts. Gilt blue cl. (Lacks 1 plt), else VF. *Argonaut.* $45/£29

LEE, BOURKE. Death Valley. NY: Macmillan, 1930. 1st ed. Fine in Near Perfect dj. *Book Market.* $200/£128

LEE, C. The Elements of Geology. NY: Harper, 1840. 1st ed. viii,384pp. Orig gilt cl. Good (sm marginal dampstain; lt foxed). *Blake.* $125/£80

LEE, DANIEL and JOSEPH H. FROST. Ten Years in Oregon. NY: The Authors, 1844. Fldg frontis map, tp vignette, 344pp (lt foxed, tanned). Good (extrems frayed, spine sunned). Howes L197. *Reese.* $275/£176

LEE, ELIZABETH BLAIR. Wartime Washington. Virginia Jeans Laas (ed). Urbana, (1991). 1st ed. Fine in Fine dj. *Pratt*. $32/£21

LEE, FRED J. Casey Jones. Kingsport, TN: Southern Pub, 1939. 1st ed. (Sl rubbed), o/w VG. *Archer*. $35/£22

LEE, H. Observations on the Writings of Thomas Jefferson. NY, 1832. 1st ed. 2pp ads. Unopened. Orig bds, paper spine label. (Sl wear, soil.) Howes L205. *Freeman**. $220/£141

LEE, HANNAH FARNHAM. The Huguenots in France and America. Cambridge: Owen, 1843. 1st ed. 2 vols. (20),336; (6),302pp. (Spines lt worn.) Howes L201. *Ginsberg*. $150/£96

LEE, HARPER. To Kill a Mockingbird. Phila: Lippincott, (1960). 1st ed, 1st bk. NF (contemp sig) in dj (extrems rubbed, very sm chip spine head). *Captain's Bookshelf*. $2,000/£1,282

LEE, HARPER. To Kill a Mockingbird. London, 1960. 1st Eng ed. Very Nice in Poor dj. *Clearwater*. $55/£35

LEE, HERMIONE (intro). The Hogarth Letters. London: C&W, 1985. 1st ed thus. VG in dj. *Hollett*. $16/£10

LEE, JAMES. An Introduction to Botany. London: J.F. and & C. Rivington et al, 1776. 3rd ed. xxiv,352pp, (12) leaves, 377-432pp; 12 copper engr plts. Contemp speckled calf (expertly rebacked, sl mkd), raised bands, gilt, dk brn morocco label. (1 leaf w/paper fault in text area, sl foxing), o/w VF. *Pirages*. $250/£160

LEE, JAMES. An Introduction to the Science of Botany. London: F.C. & J. Rivington, 1810. 4th ed. Frontis port, xxiv,580pp; 12 hand-colored plts at rear. (Lt spotted, hinges tender, upper joint splitting.) Cl-backed marbled bds (rubbed), gilt spine. *Edwards*. $55/£35

LEE, JOHN D. A Morman Chronicle: The Diaries of...1848-1876. Robert Glass Cleland and Juanita Brooks (eds). San Marino, CA: Huntington Library, 1955. 1st ed. 2 vols. VF set in djs (spine spot 1 vol). *Argonaut*. $175/£112

LEE, JOHN D. Mormonism Unveiled. St. Louis, 1877. 1st ed. Frontis, 390pp + ad. Orig full leather (scuffed, worn). Good+ (name, lacks eps; interior hinges, spine crudely repaired w/heavy tape). *Benchmark*. $100/£64

LEE, JOHN D. Mormonism Unveiled. William W. Bishop (ed). St. Louis, 1877. 1st ed. xiv,390pp + ads (few pp loose, reaffixed w/scotch tape); 13 plts. Brn cl (shelfwear). Good+. Howes L209. *Five Quail*. $95/£61

LEE, JOHN EDWARD. Note-Book of an Amateur Geologist. London, 1881. 1st ed. Mtd photo frontis, v,90pp; 209 litho plts. Teg. Gilt device upper bd. (Spine sl rubbed; bkpl.) *Edwards*. $70/£45

LEE, MARGARET DuPONT. Virginia Ghosts. William Byrd, 1930. 1st ed. Inscribed. Grey cl (soiled), gilt. VG-. *Book Broker*. $125/£80

LEE, MARY KENDAL. ABC Picture Book. Sampson Low & Marston, n.d. (ca 1951). 4to. (40)pp. Pict bds, cl spine. (Sl mkd, edges, corners grazed), else VG. *Bookmark*. $39/£25

LEE, NELSON. Three Years Among the Comanches. Norman: Univ of OK, (1957). New ed, 1st ptg. Port. VG in dj, plastic jacket. *Bohling*. $20/£13

LEE, NORMAN. Klondike Cattle Drive. Vancouver, BC, 1968. 3rd ptg. Fldg map frontis, fldg facs. VG in dj. *High Latitude*. $20/£13

LEE, NORMAN. Klondike Cattle Drive. Vancouver, BC: Mitchell, c. 1960. Fldg map, fldg facs. VG in dj (torn). *High Latitude*. $30/£19

LEE, ROBERT E. The Wartime Papers of R. E. Lee. Clifford Dowdey and Louis H. Manarin (eds). NY, (1961). VG+. *Pratt*. $30/£19

LEE, RONALD A. The Knibb Family of Clockmakers. Surrey, 1964. Ltd to 1000. 4to. 190 plts (5 color). Navy blue cl. Fine in dj. *Weber*. $550/£353

LEE, TANITH. East of Midnight. St. Martins, 1978. 1st US ed. Fine in dj (sm tear). *Certo*. $35/£22

LEE, VERNON. (Pseud of Violet Paget.) The Golden Keys and Other Essays on the Genius Loci. London: John Lane, 1925. 1st ed. NF in dj (soiled, rubbed, frayed). *Holmes*. $50/£32

LEE, VERNON. (Pseud of Violet Paget.) Hauntings, Fantastic Stories. London: Heinemann, 1890. 1st ed. Cherry red cl dec in black/gilt. Internally Very Nice. (ink inscrip; spine, cvrs dknd, spots rear cvr, spine crown sl frayed). *Reese*. $300/£192

LEE, VERNON. (Pseud of Violet Paget.) Juvenilia: Being a Second Series of Essays on Sundry Aesthetical Questions. London: T. Fisher Unwin, 1887. 1st ed. 2 vols. Blue cl, mustard-colored cl back. (Cvrs soiled, worn), o/w Good. *Holmes*. $125/£80

LEE, VERNON. (Pseud of Violet Paget.) A Phantom Lover, a Fantastic Story. Edinburgh: Blackwood, 1886. 1st ed. VG in ptd wrappers (sm chip spine toe, upper wrapper neatly reattached at joint). VG. *Reese*. $450/£288

LEE, WAYNE C. Scotty Philips: The Man Who Saved the Buffalo. Caldwell: Caxton Printers, 1975. 1st ed. Fine in dj. *Graf*. $35/£22

LEE, WILLIAM. (Pseud of William S. Burroughs.) Junkie. NY, (1953). 1st ed, 1st bk. (Sl stained, worn, wrinkled). Pict wraps. Ace Double Books D-15. *King*. $250/£160

LEE, WILLIS T. Geologic Reconnaissance of a Part of Western Arizona. 1908. Color fldg map, foldout. (Spine repaired), o/w VG. *Five Quail*. $30/£19

LEECH, JOHN. Pictures of Life and Character. London: Bradbury & Agnew, n.d. (1843-63). 1st & 3rd series. 2 vols. Aeg. Limp cl (soil, edges worn). Contents VG. *Waverly**. $60/£38

LEECH, SAMUEL. Thirty Years from Home, or a Voice from the Main Deck. Boston, 1843. 305pp (incl frontis) + 1pg ad. Good (spine ends frayed; inscrips). Howes L224. *Reese*. $300/£192

LEECH, SAMUEL. Thirty Years from Home. NY: William Abbatt, 1909. Rpt. Unopened. VG+ in ptd wraps (sm tear). Howes L224. *Bohling*. $45/£29

LEEDS, E. T. Celtic Ornament in the British Isles Down to A.D. 700. London: Clarendon, 1933. 3 color plts. (Feps lt browned; spine faded.) *Edwards*. $47/£30

LEEDS, JOSIAH W. The Primitive Christians' Estimate of War and Self-Defense. New Vienna, OH: Peace Assoc of Friends in America, 1876. 1st ed. Frontis, 58,(6)pp. (Joints worn.) *Ginsberg*. $100/£64

LEEDS, W. H. Rudimentary Architecture for the Use of Beginners and Students. London: Virtue, 1867. 6th ed. viii,144pp (lib stamp verso tp, last pg). 1/2 leather (joints cracked, gilt lib stamp spine). *Ars Artis*. $78/£50

LEEPER, DAVID ROHRER. The Argonauts of Forty-Nine: Some Recollections of the Plains and the Diggings. Columbus: Long's College Book Store, 1950. Facs rpt. Grn cl, gilt. Fine in ptd dj. *Pacific**. $29/£19

LEES, R. J. An Astral Bridegroom. W. Rider, 1909. 1st ed. Good. *Aronovitz*. $50/£32

LEES-MILNE, JAMES (ed). The National Trust; a Record of Fifty Years' Achievement. Batsford, 1945. 1st ed. NF in dj. *Words Etc*. $23/£15

LEES-MILNE, JAMES. The Age of Adam. London: Batsford, 1947. 1st Eng ed. Bright (foxing) in dj. *Clearwater*. $39/£25

LEES-MILNE, JAMES. Baroque 1685-1715. Country Life, 1970. 1st ed. VG in dj. *Hadley*. $101/£65

LEES-MILNE, JAMES. Baroque in Italy. London: Batsford, 1959. (Cl sl worn, lib label fr cvr.) *Ars Artis.* $28/£18

LEES-MILNE, JAMES. Baroque in Italy. London: Batsford, 1959. 1st Eng ed. Very Nice in dj. *Clearwater.* $39/£25

LEES-MILNE, JAMES. English Country Houses: Baroque, 1685-1715. London: Country Life, 1970. Sound. *Ars Artis.* $55/£35

LEES-MILNE, JAMES. Midway on the Waves. Faber, 1985. 1st ed. VG in dj. *Hadley.* $19/£12

LEES-MILNE, JAMES. Midway on the Waves. London: Faber, 1985. 1st ed. VG in dj (sl soiled). *Virgo.* $23/£15

LEES-MILNE, JAMES. Roman Mornings. London, 1956. 1st Eng ed. Nice in dj (repaired, sl worn). *Clearwater.* $39/£25

LEES-MILNE, JAMES. Round the Clock. London, 1978. 1st Eng ed. Nice in dj. *Clearwater.* $23/£15

LEES-MILNE, JAMES. Saint Peter's. Dublin: Heyden, 1967. 48 color plts. Sound in dj. *Ars Artis.* $39/£25

LEES-MILNE, JAMES. Venetian Evenings. Collins, 1988. Fine in dj. *Hadley.* $23/£15

LEES-MILNE, JAMES. The World of Adam. London: Batsford, (1947). 1st ed. Color frontis. NF in dj. *Captain's Bookshelf.* $75/£48

LEESON, F. Identification of Snakes of the Gold Coast. London, 1950. 33 plts. Dj (sl worn). *Maggs.* $58/£37

LEFEBURE, MOLLY. The English Lake District. London: Batsford, 1964. 1st ed. 33 plts. VG in dj (sl worn). *Hollett.* $39/£25

LEFEBURE, VICTOR. The Riddle of the Rhine, Chemical Strategy in Peace and War. NY: Chemical Soc, 1923. 1st ed (?). 5 plts. VG (sl rubbed, faded). *Worldwide.* $10/£6

LEFFINGWELL, W. B. (ed). Shooting on Upland, Marsh and Stream. Chicago/NY: Rand McNally, 1890. 473pp + 23pp ads; 14 plts. Dec cvr, beveled bds. Good (hinges starting). *Scribe's Perch*.* $55/£35

LEGGE, ARTHUR E. J. Mutineers. London: John Lane, Bodley Head, 1898. 1st ed. (viii),342pp, blank before 1/2 title, pub's inserted 12pp cat at end, dated 1898. Ribbed navy cl, gilt. Nice (sl foxed, spine sl dull). *Temple.* $19/£12

LEGH, THOMAS. Narrative of a Journey in Egypt.... London: Murray, 1817. 2nd ed. viii,(ii),296,(1)directions to binder, w/o 1/2-title, 1 engr plt, 10 aquatint plts (3 fldg) incl frontis, fldg engr map (ink inscrip; waterstain lower frontis, tp, 1st few ll). Contemp tree calf (sl rubbed, short split spine, armorial bkpl), black label, gilt spine. Attractive. *Morrell.* $296/£190

LEGROS, L. A. and J. C. GRANT. Typographical Printing Surfaces. 1916. 1st ed. 120 full-pg plts. Blue cl (rebound), gilt. VG+. *Whittle.* $133/£85

LEHMANN, C. G. Physiological Chemistry. Cavendish Soc, 1851-4. 3 vols. Teg. Blind-emb cl, gilt dec upper bds (spines chipped, label removed). *Edwards.* $117/£75

LEHMANN, HENRY. Pre-Columbian Ceramics. NY: Viking, 1962. 32 plts (8 color). Good. *Archaeologia.* $35/£22

LEHMANN, JOHN (ed). Coming to London. London, 1957. 1st Eng ed. Nice (crayon price fep) in dj (sl nicked). *Clearwater.* $31/£20

LEHMANN, JOHN. Edward Lear and His World. London: Thames & Hudson, (1977). 1st ed. Fine in dj. *Captain's Bookshelf.* $35/£22

LEHMANN, JOHN. Edward Lear and His World. NY, 1977. Good in dj. *Washton.* $25/£16

LEHMANN, JOHN. I Am My Brother; Autobiography 2. 1960. 1st ed. VG in dj (nicks). *Words Etc.* $19/£12

LEHMANN, JOHN. The Whispering Gallery. NY: Harcourt, Brace, (1955). 1st Amer ed. NF in VG dj. *Antic Hay.* $17/£11

LEHMANN, ROSAMOND. The Echoing Grove. London: Collins, 1953. 1st ed. VG in dj (spine tanned). *Reese.* $25/£16

LEHMANN, ROSAMOND. Invitation to the Waltz. London: C&W, 1932. 1st ed. Good in dj (tanned, smudged). *Reese.* $20/£13

LEHMANN, ROSAMOND. A Letter to a Sister. London: Hogarth, 1931. 1st ed. Fine in pict wrappers. *Reese.* $40/£26

LEHMANN, ROSAMOND. A Note in Music. London: C&W, 1930. 1st ed, trade issue. Nice in dj (spine, edges tanned). *Reese.* $50/£32

LEHMANN, ROSAMOND. The Weather in the Streets. London: Collins, 1936. 1st ed. VG in dj (sl chipped). *Reese.* $30/£19

LEIBER, FRITZ. The Change War. Boston: Gregg, (1978). 1st ed. Signed. W/o dj as issued. *Swann*.* $172/£110

LEIBER, FRITZ. Conjure Wife in Witches Three. Twayne, (1952). 1st bk pub. VG in dj (sm spine chip, rear panel foxed). *Certo.* $75/£48

LEIBER, FRITZ. Gather, Darkness. Pellegrini & Cudahy, (1950). 1st ed. NF in dj (sm stain rear panel). *Certo.* $45/£29

LEIBER, FRITZ. The Green Millennium. NY: Abelard, (1953). 1st ed. Signed. Dj (lt soiled, rubbed). *Swann*.* $69/£44

LEIBER, FRITZ. The Leiber Chronicles. Arlington Hts.: Dark Harvest, 1990. 1st ed. One of 500 numbered, signed. Dj, slipcase. *Swann*.* $80/£51

LEIBER, FRITZ. Night's Black Agents. Sauk City: Arkham, 1947. 1st ed. (Shelfworn, sl worn, back flap browned.) *Metropolitan*.* $80/£51

LEIBER, FRITZ. The Wanderer. NY: Walker, (1974). 1st ed. Signed. Fine in dj (lt browned). *Metropolitan*.* $80/£51

LEIBOVITZ, ANNIE. Annie Leibovitz Photographs. NY: Rolling Stone, 1983. 1st ed. VG+ in VG+ dj. *Smith.* $60/£38

LEIGH, FELIX. London Town. London: Marcus Ward, (1883). 1st ed. Lemon edges. Cl-backed glazed pict bds (sl worn, sl shaken, loose). Nice. *Ash.* $195/£125

LEIGH, PERCIVAL (ed). Manners and Cutoms of Ye Englyshe. (London): Bradbury & Evans, (1849). Rychard Doyle (illus). Aeg. (Lt foxing.) Orig 1/4 morocco, bds (rubbed, worn, hinges repaired). *Freeman*.* $70/£45

LEIGH, RANDOLPH. Forgotten Waters. Phila, 1941. 16 photo plts. Grn cl. VG. *Price.* $34/£22

LEIGH, W. R. Frontiers of Enchantment. NY: Simon & Schuster, (1940). 53 full-pg b/w dwgs. VG+ in Fair dj. *Mikesh.* $35/£22

LEIGHLY, JOHN. California as an Island...1622-1785. SF: Book Club of CA, 1972. One of 450 ptd. 25 hinged plts. Uncut. Morocco-backed pict bds, gilt spine. Prospectus laid in. Fine. *Pacific*.* $518/£332

LEIGHTON, CLARE. Country Matters. London: Gollancz, 1937. 1st ed. Fine. *Quest.* $80/£51

LEIGHTON, CLARE. Country Matters. London: Gollancz, 1937. 1st ed. (Fore-edge sl spotted), o/w Attractive in dj (sl spotted, mkd). *Hollett.* $94/£60

LEIGHTON, CLARE. Country Matters. NY, 1937. VG in dj (sl frayed, torn, sunned). *King.* $50/£32

LEIGHTON, CLARE. Four Hedges. A Gardener's Chronicle. NY: Macmillan, 1935. 1st ed. 88 wood engrs. (Eps, cl dknd along hinge), else VG in illus dj (chipped, tape-repaired closed tear). *Cahan.* $45/£29

LEIGHTON, CLARE. Four Hedges. A Gardener's Chronicle. NY: Macmillan, 1935. 1st Amer ed. Signed. Gilt cl. (Ep gutters sl tanned; cl sl faded;) else VG in dj (edge-tanned, lt chipped). *Reese.* $75/£48

LEIGHTON, CLARE. Four Hedges. A Gardener's Chronicle. London: Gollancz, 1936. 1st cheap ed. (Sl browned, spine chipped.) VG in dj. *Michael Taylor.* $28/£18

LEIGHTON, CLARE. Growing New Roots. SF: Book Club of CA, 1976. #143/500 ptd, signed. 14 wood engr. Fine. *Graf.* $50/£32

LEIGHTON, CLARE. Southern Harvest. Gollancz, 1943. 1st ed. 4to. 124pp. (Cl faded), else VG in dj (torn, repaired). *Bookmark.* $37/£24

LEIGHTON, MARGARET. Comanche of the Seventh. NY: Ariel Books, (1957). 1st ed. VG in dj (sl worn). *Lien.* $18/£12

LEINSTER, MURRAY. Four from Planet 5. London: White Lion, 1974. 1st hb ed. NF in dj (rubbed, sm tear). *Certo.* $20/£13

LEINSTER, MURRAY. The Last Spaceship. Fell, 1949. 1st ed. Fine in dj (sl soiled). *Madle.* $50/£32

LEINSTER, MURRAY. The Last Spaceship. Frederick Fell, 1949. 1st ed. NF in dj (spine chipS). *Certo.* $35/£22

LEINSTER, MURRAY. Murder in the Family. London: John Hamilton, (1935). 1st ed. Good (spine sunned). *Certo.* $20/£13

LEINSTER, MURRAY. The Murder of the U. S. A. Crown, (1946). 1st ed. NF in dj (long closed spine tear). *Certo.* $50/£32

LEINSTER, MURRAY. Scalps. Brewer & Warren, 1930. 1st ed. Yellow cl (sl soiled). VG. *Certo.* $30/£19

LEIRIS, MICHEL. Francis Bacon. London: Phaidon, 1983. 1st Eng ed. VG in dj. *Hollett.* $70/£45

LEIRIS, MICHEL. Manhood. NY: Grossman, 1963. 1st US ed. (Sl dampstain fr bd), else VG+ in VG dj (price-clipped, sm tears). *Lame Duck.* $75/£48

LEISINGER, HERMANN. Romanesque Bronzes. Church Portals in Medieval Europe. London, 1956. 160 plts. Good. *Washton.* $60/£38

LEITH HAY, ANDREW. A Narrative of the Peninsular War. London, 1850. 4th ed. xii,451pp, 20 engr plts, fldg map. (Frontis, tp, plt foxed; few other plts sl foxed.) Full tan calf (sl worn), gilt. *Maggs.* $390/£250

LEJARD, ANDRE. The Art of the French Book from Early Manuscripts to the Present Time. London: Elek, n.d. (1947). (Sl worn.) Dj (frayed, soiled). *Oinonen*.* $40/£26

LELAND, CHARLES G. The Algonquin Legends of New England. London: Sampson Low et al, 1884. 1st Eng ed. 379pp (sl dampstain upper margin). Gray cl (rubbed, sl worn, soiled). Good. *Lucas.* $90/£58

LEM, STANISLAW. Cyberiad. NY: Seabury, 1974. 1st US ed. (Pp sl dknd), else Fine in dj. *Lame Duck.* $85/£54

LEM, STANISLAW. The Futurological Congress. NY: Seabury, 1974. 1st ed in English. Fine in NF dj (lt worn). *Lame Duck.* $50/£32

LEM, STANISLAW. Memoirs Found in a Bathtub. NY: Seabury, 1973. 1st US ed. (Lt shelfworn), else NF in dj. *Lame Duck.* $65/£42

LEM, STANISLAW. Return from the Stars. NY: Harcourt Brace Jovanovich, 1980. 1st US ed. Fine in dj. *Lame Duck.* $35/£22

LEMMON, KENNETH. The Golden Age of the Plant Hunters. NY: A.S. Barnes, 1968. 4 color, 16 b/w plts. Fine in dj. *Quest.* $55/£35

LeMOINE, J. M. The Chronicles of the St. Lawrence. Montreal, 1878. 1st ed. 380pp (eps foxed), fldg map. (Cvrs dknd, ends frayed.) *King.* $50/£32

LEMOYNE, LOUIS V. Country Residences in Europe and America. London: Fisher Unwin, 1909. Teg. (Last pg sl damaged from sticking; cl worn.) *Ars Artis.* $94/£60

LEMPRIERE, JOHN. Universal Biography. London: Cadell & Davies, 1808. 1st ed. Unpaginated. Contemp 1/2 calf, gilt-tooled, marbled bds (fr cvr neatly re-hinged w/matching calf). *Karmiole.* $250/£160

LENNARD, ERICA and ELIZABETH. Sunday. (NY: Lustrum, 1973.) 1st ed. 16 full-pg b/w photos. (Owner stamp), else VG in pict stiff wrappers. *Cahan.* $65/£42

LENNON, FLORENCE BECKER. Victoria Through the Looking-Glass. NY: S&S, 1945. 1st ed. NF in VG dj. *Turtle Island.* $40/£26

LENNON, JOHN. In His Own Write. London, 1964. 1st ed. Laminated pict bds. (Spine ends rubbed), o/w VG. *Words Etc.* $39/£25

LENNON, JOHN. A Spaniard in the Works. London, 1965. 1st ed. Laminated pict bds. (Lower corner edges scorched), o/w VG. *Words Etc.* $39/£25

LENNON, JOHN. A Spaniard in the Works. London: Cape, 1965. 1st ed. Pict bds. VG. *Hollett.* $47/£30

LENNOX, WILLIAM PITT. Coaching with Anecdotes of the Road. London: Hurst & Blackett, 1876. ix,307pp (spotted). Marbled eps; teg, rest uncut. 1/2 morocco (sl rubbed), gilt. *Edwards.* $133/£85

LENO, JOHN BEDFORD. The Art of Boot and Shoe-making, A Practical Handbook. London: Crosby, Lockwood & Son, (n.d.). *Cullen.* $25/£16

LENOX, EDWARD H. Overland to Oregon in the Tracks of Lewis and Clarke [sic]. Oakland, CA, 1904. 'Autograph copy,' unsigned as usual. Gilt-pict cl. (Owner stamp ep, marginal ink stain few ll; shelfwear), else VG. Howes L255. *Reese.* $250/£160

LENROOT, CLARA C. Long, Long Ago. (Appleton, WI), 1929. Signed. 13 plts. VG. *Bohling.* $30/£19

LENSKI, LOIS. A-Going to the Westward. NY: F.A. Stokes, 1937. 1st ed. Signed. 5 3/4 x 8. 369pp. Fine in dj. *Cattermole.* $100/£64

LENSKI, LOIS. Blue Ridge Billy. Phila: Lippincott, 1946. 1st ed. 6 3/4 x 8 3/4. 203pp. VG in dj. *Cattermole.* $50/£32

LENSKI, LOIS. Blueberry Corners. NY: Stokes, 1940. 1st ed. 6 1/2 x 9. 209pp. Good in facs dj. *Cattermole.* $60/£38

LENSKI, LOIS. The Little Fireman. NY: OUP, 1946. 1st ed. 8 1/2 x 7 1/4. Good in dj (few chips, lt soil). *Cattermole.* $60/£38

LENSKI, LOIS. The Little Sail Boat. NY: OUP, 1937. 1st ed. 7 1/4 sq. Good. *Cattermole.* $40/£26

LENSKI, LOIS. Mama Hattie's Girl. Phila: Lippincott, (1953). 1st ed. Lois Lenski Regional Story. 8vo. 182pp. VG in VG dj. *Dower.* $100/£64

LENSKI, LOIS. Mama Hattie's Girl. Phila: Lippincott, 1953. 1st ed. 6 1/2 x 8 3/4. 182pp. Good (name mkd out). *Cattermole.* $25/£16

LENSKI, LOIS. Prairie School. Phila: Lippincott, 1951. 1st ed. Lg 8vo. Pict cl. NF in VG dj (chipped). *Book Adoption.* $60/£38

LENSKI, LOIS. Texas Tomboy. Phila: Lippincott, (1950). 1st ed. Regional Series. 8vo. 180pp; 39 illus. VG in Good+ dj. *Dower.* $55/£35

LENSKI, LOIS. We Are Thy Children. NY: Crowell, 1952. 1st ed. 11x9. 32pp. Good (sl bowed) in dj. *Cattermole.* $25/£16

LENSKI, LOIS. We Live in the City. Phila: Lippincott, 1954. 1st ed. 5 3/4 x 8 1/4. 128pp. VG in dj. *Cattermole.* $35/£22

LENTZ, HAROLD. The Pop-Up Pinocchio. NY: Blue Ribbon, (1932). Sq 8vo. 4 color pop-up plts. Pict bds (shelfworn). *Oinonen*.* $200/£128

LENYGON, FRANCIS. (Pseud of M. Jourdain.) Decoration in England from 1660 to 1770. London, (1920). 2nd imp. (Inner hinges loose; worn, soiled.) *King.* $100/£64

LENYGON, FRANCIS. (Pseud of M. Jourdain.) Decoration in England from 1660 to 1770. Batsford, n.d. (c. 1914). Frontis. Teg, rest uncut. (Lt spotted, bkpl; faded.) *Edwards.* $94/£60

LENYGON, FRANCIS. (Pseud of M. Jourdain.) Furniture in England from 1660 to 1760. London, (1920). 2nd rev ed. VG. *Argosy.* $75/£48

LEON, DERRICK. Livingstones. Hogarth, 1933. 1st ed. VG in dj (sl creased). *Words Etc.* $140/£90

LEON-PORTILLA, MIGUEL. The Broken Spears. Boston: Beacon, (1962). 1st Amer ed. VG in dj. *Lien.* $30/£19

LEONARD, C. HENRI. Hair: Its Growth, Care, Diseases and Treatment. Detroit, 1880. (Wear, extrems frayed.) *Bohling.* $28/£18

LEONARD, ELIZABETH JANE and JULIA CODY GOODMAN. Buffalo Bill, King of the Old West. NY: Library Publishers, (1955). 1/2 cl. VG + in dj. *Bohling.* $18/£12

LEONARD, ELMORE. Bandits. NY: Arbor House, 1987. 1st ed. Fine in Fine dj. *Revere.* $20/£13

LEONARD, ELMORE. The Big Bounce. Gold Medal R2079, (1969). 1st ed. Pb original. VG. *Certo.* $30/£19

LEONARD, ELMORE. The Big Bounce. Greenwich: Fawcett, 1969. 1st ed. Pb orig. (Spine creases), o/w VG in wrappers. *Mordida.* $35/£22

LEONARD, ELMORE. The Big Bounce. Armchair Detective Library, 1989. 1st US hb ed. Fine in Fine dj. *Certo.* $18/£12

LEONARD, ELMORE. The Bounty Hunters. Boston, 1954. 1st ed (w/35-cent cvr price). (Ink note, pp browning, sl worn), else Nice in pict wraps. *King.* $75/£48

LEONARD, ELMORE. Cat Chaser. NY: Arbor House, 1982. 1st ed. Fine in dj. *Mordida.* $45/£29

LEONARD, ELMORE. City Primeval. NY: Arbor House, 1980. 1st ed. Fine in dj. *Mordida.* $45/£29

LEONARD, ELMORE. Escape from Five Shadows. (NY: Dell, 1957.) 1st pb ed. (Ink note), else VG in pict wraps. *King.* $15/£10

LEONARD, ELMORE. Fifty-Two Pickup. London: Secker & Warburg, 1974. 1st Eng ed. Fine in dj (sl wear corners). *Mordida.* $125/£80

LEONARD, ELMORE. Fifty-Two Pickup. London: Secker, 1974. 1st UK ed. VG + in dj (price-clipped). *Williams.* $86/£55

LEONARD, ELMORE. Fifty-Two Pickup. NY: Delacorte, 1974. 1st ed. (Lt spotting pg edges, lt scrape back cvr), o/w Fine in dj (short crease inner back flap). *Mordida.* $250/£160

LEONARD, ELMORE. Forty Lashes Less One. (NY): Bantam, (1972). 1st ed. (Ink note, sl stain), else Good in pict wraps. *King.* $25/£16

LEONARD, ELMORE. Glitz. NY: Mysterious, (1985). One of 500 numbered, signed. Fine in Fine slipcase. *Lenz.* $100/£64

LEONARD, ELMORE. Gunsights. (NY): Bantam, (1979). 1st ed. (Ink note, sl worn.) Pict wraps. *King.* $25/£16

LEONARD, ELMORE. Gunsights. NY: Bantam, 1979. 1st ed. Pb orig. VF in wrappers. *Mordida.* $65/£42

LEONARD, ELMORE. La Brava. London: Viking, 1984. 1st Eng ed. VF in dj. *Mordida.* $45/£29

LEONARD, ELMORE. The Law at Randado. (NY): Dell, (1954). 1st pb ed. (Ink note; sl spotted, worn.) Pict wraps. *King.* $15/£10

LEONARD, ELMORE. The Moonshine War. Doubleday, 1969. 1st ed. (Narrow strip lifted from rear flyleaf), else VG in VG dj. *Certo.* $135/£87

LEONARD, ELMORE. The Moonshine War. GC: Doubleday, 1969. 1st ed. Signed. Fine in dj (spine base sl worn). *Mordida.* $375/£240

LEONARD, ELMORE. Mr. Majestyk. NY: Dell, 1974. 1st ed. Pb orig. Unread. (Short crease back cvr), o/w Fine in wrappers. *Mordida.* $50/£32

LEONARD, ELMORE. Split Images. NY: Arbor House, 1981. 1st ed. VF in dj. *Mordida.* $45/£29

LEONARD, ELMORE. Swag. NY: Delacorte, (1976). 1st ed. NF in NF dj. *Metropolitan*.* $74/£47

LEONARD, ELMORE. Swag. Delacorte, 1976. 1st ed. Fine in Fine dj. *Certo.* $75/£48

LEONARD, ELMORE. Valdez Is Coming. Greenwich: Fawcett, (1970). Pb orig. (Sl spine crease), else NF. *Between The Covers.* $50/£32

LEONARD, LEVI W. The History of Dublin, N.H. Dublin, NH: Town of Dublin, 1920. 1st ed. Frontis port, 68 plts. Blue cl (sl rubbed). *Karmiole.* $100/£64

LEONARD, WILLIAM ELLERY. The Locomotive God. NY/London: Century, (1927). 1st ed. Olive cl, paper label (spine label chipped). VG. *Gach.* $50/£32

LEONARD, ZENAS. Adventures of Zenas Leonard, Fur Trader. John C. Ewers (ed). Norman: Univ of OK, (1959). 1st ed thus. VF in dj (lt rubbed). *Argonaut.* $60/£38

Leonardo da Vinci. London: Hutchinson's Children's Books, 1984. 11.5x8. 4 dbl-pg pop-ups + pull tabs; disappearing picture. Glazed pict bds. VG. *King.* $35/£22

LEONARDO, R. History of Medical Thought. NY: Froben, 1946. 16 ports. (Cl worn, label removed fr bds), o/w Good. *Goodrich.* $45/£29

LEONARDO, R. Lives of Master Surgeons. NY, 1948-49. 1st ed. 2 vols. Port. Cl and wrappers. *Maggs.* $47/£30

LEOPOLD, A. A Sand County Almanac with Other Essays on Conservation from Round River. NY: OUP, (1969). Pict cl. Fine in VG dj. *Mikesh.* $25/£16

LEOPOLD, L. B. (ed). Round River: From the Journals of Aldo Leopold. NY: OUP, 1953. 1st ed. Blind-stamped dec cl. NF in VG dj. *Mikesh.* $45/£29

LEPSIUS, RICHARD. Discoveries in Egypt, Ethiopia, and the Peninsula of Sinai in the Years 1842-1845. Kenneth R. H. Mackenzie (ed). London: R. Bentley, 1852. 1st ed. 3/4 coffee-brn morocco over blue cl sides, spine w/5 raised bands, gilt. Very Nice. *Book Block.* $475/£304

LEPSIUS, RICHARD. Letters from Egypt, Ethiopia, and the Peninsula of Sinai. London: Henry G. Bohn, 1853. Color frontis, 578pp; 2 fldg maps. Orig cl backed in new grn morocco. VG. *Adelson.* $200/£128

LERNER, ALAN JAY. Brigadoon. NY: Coward-McCann, (1947). 1st ed. Fine in dj. *Hermitage.* $125/£80

LERNER, ALAN JAY. Camelot. NY: Random House, 1961. 1st ed. NF in NF dj (sl chipped). *Unger.* $125/£80

LERNER, ALAN JAY. My Fair Lady. NY: Coward-McCann, (1956). 1st ed. Fine in dj. *Hermitage.* $125/£80

LERNER, ALAN JAY. My Fair Lady. NY: Coward-McCann, 1956. 1st ed. NF in VG dj (chip crown top). *Unger.* $125/£80

LEROUX, GASTON. The Kiss That Killed. NY: Macaulay, 1934. 1st ed. (Bkpl; soiled, shaken.) Lacks dj. *Metropolitan*.* $34/£22

LEROUX, GASTON. The Phantom of the Opera. London: Mills & Boon, (1911). 1st British ed. (Fly loose, chipped; shaken, spine rubbed, corners through.) Lacks dj. Metropolitan*. $345/£221

LEROUX, GASTON. The Phantom of the Opera. London: Mills & Boon, 1911. 1st London ed. (Corner fep clipped.) Pub's black-stamped red cl (spine lt soiling, lt loss to lettering). Cvrs Bright. D & D. $850/£545

LESAGE, ALAIN-RENE. The Adventures of Gil Blas de Santillane. Oxford: LEC, 1937. #904/1500 numbered, signed by John Austen (illus). 2 vols. Fine set in pub's dj, slipcase. Hermitage. $150/£96

LESAGE, ALAIN-RENE. The Adventures of Gil Blas. London: T. Osbourne, 1766. 3rd ed. 4 vols. Contemp full calf, raised bands, gilt, dbl labels. (Few labels wanting.) Macdonnell. $100/£64

LESKOV, NICHOLAS. The Steel Flea. NY: Harper, 1943. 1st ed. Mstislav Dobujinsky (illus). 6 1/4 x 9 1/2. 64pp. Fine in dj. Cattermole. $35/£22

LESLEY, J. P. Manual of Coal and Its Topography. Phila, 1856. 1st ed. 224pp. (New ep.) Brn cl, gilt. Good. Price. $95/£61

LESLEY, LEWIS BURT (ed). Uncle Sam's Camels. Cambridge: Harvard Univ, 1929. Frontis port, 3 plts, fldg map. Unopened. VG + in dj (worn, chipped, lt soiled). Bohling. $110/£71

LESLEY, PETER. Annual Report of the Geological Survey of Pennsylvania for 1887. Harrisburg, 1889. 13 plts, lg fldg map in pocket. (Spine gilt dull.) Sadlon. $20/£13

LESLIE, CHARLES ROBERT and TOM TAYLOR. The Life and Times of Sir Joshua Reynolds. London: John Murray, 1865. 1st ed. 4 vols. Lg 8vo. 150 extra engrs by Joshua Reynolds. Blue polished calf, gilt extra. (Bkpl.) Swann*. $977/£626

LESLIE, FRANK. Frank Leslie's Illustrated Famous Leaders and Battle Scenes.... NY: Leslie, (1896). Mod cl, orig fr cvr laid down. Contents VG (few sl tears). Waverly*. $82/£53

LESLIE, JOHN et al. Narrative of Discovery and Adventure in the Polar Seas and Regions. Edinburgh: Oliver & Boyd, 1835. 4th ed. 484pp; added engr tp, fldg map. Later 1/2 calf, marbled bds, gilt-tooled spine, red/grn morocco spine labels. Good. Karmiole. $75/£48

LESLIE, JOHN et al. Narrative of Discovery and Adventures in the Polar Seas with an Account of the Whale Fisheries. NY: J&J Harper, 1831. 1st Amer ed. 373pp + ads; fldg map. Tan muslin. (Prelims, edges, cvrs spotted.) Parmer. $125/£80

LESLIE, MISS (ed). The Gift: A Christmas and New Year's Present for 1840. Phila: Carey & Hart, (1839). 1st ed, 1st issue, w/date stamped on spine. Extra engr tp, 8 steel-engr plts (foxed), guards. Yellow coated eps; aeg. Full dk brn morocco (sl scuffed, spine sl curled, sm snag). Text Good (sl foxed). BAL 16130. Baltimore*. $100/£64

LESLIE, MISS. The Behavior Book. Phila: Hazard, 1853. 3rd ed. 336pp. (Spine top cl torn), o/w VG (ex-lib). Second Life. $65/£42

LESLIE, SHANE. The Skull of Swift. Indianapolis: Bobbs Merrill, (1928). 1st Amer ed. Frontis. Paper spine label. VG (sl foxed) in dj (lt nicked). Reese. $30/£19

LESQUEREUX, L. The Flora of the Dakota Group. Washington: US Geol Survey, 1891. 1st ed. 66 plts. (Few lib stamps; cl sl soiled, worn.) Maggs. $28/£18

LESSER, ROBERT. A Celebration of Comic Art and Memorabilia. Hawthorne Books, 1975. 1st ed. VG + in VG + dj. My Bookhouse. $30/£19

Lessing J. Rosenwald Collection, a Catalog of the Gifts of Lessing J. Rosenwald to the Library of Congress, 1943 to 1975. Washington: Library of Congress, 1977. (Spine rubbed.) Oak Knoll. $75/£48

LESSING, DORIS. African Stories. London: Michael Joseph, 1964. 1st UK ed. Fine in VG dj. Williams. $75/£48

LESSING, DORIS. Briefing for a Descent into Hell. Cape, (1971). 1st ed. (Corner sl bumped), else VG in dj. Ash. $31/£20

LESSING, DORIS. Briefing for a Descent into Hell. London: Cape, 1971. 1st ed. Fine in Fine dj. Else Fine. $50/£32

LESSING, DORIS. Briefing for a Descent into Hell. NY, 1971. 1st Amer ed. Fine in Fine dj. Polyanthos. $25/£16

LESSING, DORIS. Canopus in Argos: Archives. Documents Relating to the Sentimental Agents in the Volyen Empire. NY: Knopf, 1983. 1st ed. Fine in NF dj. Antic Hay. $20/£13

LESSING, DORIS. Canopus in Argos: Archives. The Marriages Between Zones Three, Four, and Five. NY: Knopf, 1980. 1st Amer ed. Fine (bkpl) in dj (sl worn, sm tears). Antic Hay. $20/£13

LESSING, DORIS. Canopus in Argos: Archives. The Sirian Experiments. NY: Knopf, 1981. 1st Amer ed. Fine in NF dj. Antic Hay. $20/£13

LESSING, DORIS. The Fifth Child. London: Cape, 1988. 1st UK ed. Fine in dj. Williams. $16/£10

LESSING, DORIS. Particularly Cats. NY: S&S, (1967). 1st Amer ed. Fine in Fine dj (crease). Between The Covers. $45/£29

LESSING, DORIS. Stories. NY: Knopf, 1978. 1st ed. Fine in dj. Lame Duck. $50/£32

LESSING, DORIS. The Summer Before the Dark. London: Cape, (1973). 1st Eng ed. Fine in dj (price-clipped). Antic Hay. $35/£22

LESSING, DORIS. This Was the Old Chief's Country. NY: Crowell, (n.d.). 1st Amer ed from Eng sheets. Fine (rubbing spine base) in dj (price-clipped; sl soiling). Between The Covers. $200/£128

LESSING, DORIS. Under My Skin: Autobiography to 1949. London, 1994. 1st ed. Words Etc. $31/£20

LESTER, J. C. and D. L. WILSON. Ku Klux Klan. NY/Washington: Neale, 1905. 1st ed. 9 b/w plts and ports. Olive ribbed cl, gilt. VG (ink sig). Baltimore*. $230/£147

LESTER, JOHN ERASTUS. The Yosemite, Its History, Its Scenery, Its Development. Providence, 1873. VG in wraps (fragile). Book Market. $50/£32

LESY, MICHAEL. Wisconsin Death Trip. NY: Pantheon, (1973). 1st ed, 1st bk. NF in dj (sm tears). Captain's Bookshelf. $100/£64

LETCHFORD, ALBERT. A Series of Seventy Original Illustrations to Captain Sir R.F. Burton's 'Arabian Nights'.... London: Nichols, 1897. 1st ed. xvipp; 71 plts. (Rebacked, rubbed), o/w VG. Worldwide. $125/£80

LETCHWORTH, WILLIAM PRYOR. The Insane in Foreign Countries. NY/London: Putnam/Knickerbocker, 1889. 1st ed. (ii),xii,374,(4)pp; 21 plts. Beveled grn cl (fr hinge cracked, lt shelfworn). Good. Gach. $275/£176

LETHABY, W. R. Westminster Abbey Re-Examined. 1925. 1st ed. (Margins lt browned; cl sl rubbed.) Edwards. $39/£25

Letter to a Lady, on Card-Playing on the Lord's Day. (By Robert Bolton.) London, 1748. 1st ed. 50pp, removed (sl soiled). King. $75/£48

Letters from a Farmer in Pennsylvania..... (By John Dickinson.) Boston: Ptd by Mein & Fleeming, 1768. 146,(2)pp (lower corner damped throughout, sl toning, sm spot title, sl paper loss at corner). Mod cl-backed bds (soiled, rubbed). Howes D338. Waverly*. $176/£113

Letters from the Irish Highlands of Cunnemarra. By a Family Party. London: Longman, Hurst et al, 1825. 2nd ed. xvii,414pp. 3/4 brn-grn polished calf, gilt ruled spines, gilt-lettered red leather spine label, marbled bds and edges. (Corners lt worn), else Fine. *Argonaut.* $175/£112

Letters of Fabius, in 1788...and in 1797.... (By John Dickinson.) Wilmington, 1797. 1st ed. 8vo. 4,203pp. Later plain wraps. *Kane*.* $900/£577

LETTS, MALCOLM (ed). Pero Tafur. London, 1926. 1st ed. 8 plts, fldg map. (Spine faded.) *Edwards.* $39/£25

LETTS, W. M. Songs from Leinster. London: Smith, Elder, 1913. 1st ed. Pub's presentation blindstamp. Teg. Gilt grn cl. Good. *Reese.* $20/£13

LETTSOM, J. C. Memoirs of the Life and Writings of the Late John Coakley Lettsom. T. J. Pettigrew (ed). 1817. 3 vols. Frontis port, xiv,182; viii,620; xxxvi+464pp. (Few prelims discolored; cvrs sl mkd.) *Whitehart.* $437/£280

LEUCHARS, ROBERT. A Practical Treatise on the Construction, Heating and Ventilation of Hot-Houses. Boston, 1851. 366pp. (Sm stain corner; spine defective; inner hinges loose.) *King.* $100/£64

LEUCHARS, ROBERT. A Practical Treatise on the Construction, Heating and Ventilation of Hot-Houses...Graperies, etc. NY: Saxton, 1857. 1st ed. 366pp+12pp ads (ex-lib, perf stamp tp). Blind-emb cl (rebacked; sl faded), orig spine laid down (lacks top). Good. *Europa.* $70/£45

LEVAILLANT, F. Exotic Birds: Parrots, Birds of Paradise, Toucans. NY: Viking, 1963. 1st ed. Gilt-dec cl. NF in VG dj. *Mikesh.* $95/£61

LEVEL, MAURICE. The Grip of Fear. Mitchell Kennerley, 1911. 1st ed. (Spine sunned), else VG. *Certo.* $50/£32

LEVENSON, RANDAL. In Search of the Monkey Girl. Millerton: Aperture, 1982. 1st ed. 33 full-pg b/w photos. (Name, blindstamp), else Fine in illus dj. *Cahan.* $30/£19

LEVER, CHARLES. Lord Kilgobbin. NY: Harper, 1872. 1st Amer ed. Blue cl, gilt. NF. *Macdonnell.* $100/£64

LEVER, CHARLES. Roland Cashel. NY: Harper, 1850. 1st Amer ed. Phiz (illus). Emb brn cl. VG- (sm ink name stamp, foxed; spine faded). *Antic Hay.* $45/£29

LEVER, DARCY. The Young Sea Officer's Sheet Anchor. NY: Blunt, 1858. Amer ed. Engr title, 113 engr plts, 2 fldg. (Lt dampstains, sl foxing, soiling.) Contemp tree-calf (rubbed, spine tips chipped). *Oinonen*.* $325/£208

LEVERETT, F. The Pleistocene of Northern Kentucky. Frankfort: Geo. Surv., 1929. 1st ed. Tipped-in diag. VG. *Mikesh.* $25/£16

LEVERTOV, DENISE. The Blue Rim of Memory. Huntington, NY, 1979. 1st Amer ed, 1st ptg. Ltd to 500 signed. Broadside. Fine. *Polyanthos.* $15/£10

LEVERTOV, DENISE. The Double Image. London: Cresset Press, 1946. 1st ed, 1st bk. Fine in dj. *Jaffe.* $150/£96

LEVERTOV, DENISE. Here and Now. SF: City Lights, (1957). 1st ed. (Spine lt sunned), o/w Fine in ptd wrappers. *Jaffe.* $350/£224

LEVERTOV, DENISE. Life in the Forest. (NY): New Directions, (1978). 1st ed. Cl-backed bds. Fine in dj (lt stained). *Jaffe.* $25/£16

LEVERTOV, DENISE. Life in the Forest. (NY): New Directions, (1978). One of 150 numbered, signed. Fine in Fine slipcase. *Lenz.* $125/£80

LEVERTOV, DENISE. Oblique Prayers. Jean Joubert (trans). (NY): New Directions, (1984). 1st ed. Cl-backed bds. Fine in dj. *Jaffe.* $35/£22

LEVERTOV, DENISE. Poems 1960-1967. (NY): New Directions, (1983). 1st ed. Mint in dj. *Jaffe.* $35/£22

LEVERTOV, DENISE. The Poet in the World. (NY): New Directions, (1973). 1st ed. Cl-backed bds. Fine in dj. *Jaffe.* $35/£22

LEVERTOV, DENISE. Relearning the Alphabet. NY: New Directions, (1970). 1st ed. Fine in dj. *Turtle Island.* $35/£22

LEVERTOV, DENISE. To Stay Alive. (NY): New Directions, (1971). 1st ed. One of 1154 ptd. Cl-backed bds. Fine in dj. *Jaffe.* $50/£32

LEVERTOV, DENISE. A Tree Telling of Orpheus. L.A.: Black Sparow, 1968. 1st ed. One of 250 signed. Fine in wrappers. *Jaffe.* $75/£48

LEVERTOV, DENISE. With Eyes at the Back of Our Heads. New Directions, (1959). 1st ed. Fine in dj (sl used). *Dermont.* $60/£38

LEVEY, MICHAEL. Giambattista Tiepolo. New Haven/London, 1986. Good in dj. *Washton.* $65/£42

LEVEY, MICHAEL. Painting at Court. 1971. 1st ed. 7 color plts. Pict eps. Dj (sl chipped). *Edwards.* $39/£25

LEVEY, MICHAEL. Painting in XVIII Century Venice. London, 1959. 8 color plts. Good. *Washton.* $30/£19

LEVI, CARLO. Christ Stopped at Eboli. 1948. 1st Eng ed. VG in dj (spine head sl chipped, price-clipped). *Words Etc.* $39/£25

LEVI, ELIPHAS. The History of Magic. A. E. Waite (trans). London, 1913. 1st Eng trans. VG+. *Middle Earth.* $245/£157

LEVI, ELIPHAS. The Key of the Mysteries. London: Rider, 1959. Fine in VG dj. *Middle Earth.* $95/£61

LEVI, ELIPHAS. The Mysteries of Magic. A.E. Waite (ed). London: Kegan Paul, 1897. 2nd ed. 524pp. (12pp lt mkd; rubbed), o/w VG. *Middle Earth.* $195/£125

LEVI, ELIPHAS. Transcendental Magic: Its Doctrine and Ritual. Chicago: Occult Pub, 1910. 2nd ed. (Inner hinge exposed), o/w VG+. *Middle Earth.* $145/£93

LEVI, PETER. The Light Garden of the Angel King. London, 1972. 1st Eng ed. Bruce Chatwin (illus). Very Nice in dj (sl stained, chafed). *Clearwater.* $70/£45

LEVI, PRIMO. If This Is a Man. NY: Orion, 1959. 1st ed in English. Rev copy, pub's slip laid in. (Eps sl dknd), else NF in NF dj. *Lame Duck.* $250/£160

LEVI, PRIMO. The Periodic Table. Raymond Rosenthal (trans). NY: Schocken, (1984). 1st Amer ed. Fine in dj (price-clipped, sm tear). *Captain's Bookshelf.* $75/£48

LEVI, PRIMO. The Periodic Table. London: Michael Joseph, 1985. 1st UK ed. Fine in dj. *Moorhouse.* $55/£35

LEVI, PRIMO. The Reawakening. Boston: Little, Brown, 1965. 1st US ed. NF in dj (price-clipped). *Lame Duck.* $100/£64

LEVI, PRIMO. The Truce. Stuart Woolf (trans). London, 1965. 1st Eng ed. Very Nice (foxed, mostly fore-edges) in dj. *Clearwater.* $70/£45

LEVI, WENDELL M. Pigeon. Columbia, SC, 1941. VG+ in Good dj (taped edge tears). *Books & Birds.* $125/£80

LEVIN, IRA. Rosemary's Baby. Random House, 1967. 1st ed. (Eps spotted), else Fine in Fine dj. *Certo.* $60/£38

LEVIN, IRA. The Stepford Wives. NY: Random House, 1972. 1st ed. Fine in NF dj (price-clipped). *Janus.* $45/£29

LEVIN, LOUIS and SAMUEL. Practical Benchwork for Horologists. L.A.: Horology, 1938. 1st ed. Red cl. (Owner labels, top edge foxed.) *Weber.* $50/£32

LEVINE, PHILIP. Thistles. London: Turret Bks, 1970. 1st ed. One of 100 numbered, signed. Fine in dec wrappers. *Captain's Bookshelf.* $175/£112

LEVINSON, ABRAHAM. Pioneers of Pediatrics. NY, 1936. 1st ed. VG. *Fye.* $100/£64

LEVITT, HELEN and JAMES AGEE. A Way of Seeing. NY: Viking, 1965. 1st ed. 50 photo plts. VG in illus dj (price-clipped). Cahan. $225/£144

LEVITT, HELEN. Helen Levitt: Color Photographs. El Cajon, CA: Grossmont College Gallery, 1980. 1st ed. Fine in ptd stiff wrappers. Cahan. $30/£19

LEVY, JULIEN. Arshile Gorky. NY: Abrams, n.d. (Bds sl discolored.) Transparent dj. Metropolitan*. $172/£110

LEVY, MELVIN. Gold Eagle Guy. NY: Random House, 1935. 1st ed. NF (label) in dj (lt used). Beasley. $85/£54

LEVY, MELVIN. The Last Pioneers. NY: Alfred H. King, 1934. 1st ed. Fine (lt sunned spine) in dj (chipped; 1/4 rear panel missing). Beasley. $50/£32

LEVY, MERVYN. The Drawings of L. S. Lowry. London: Jupiter Books, 1976. 1st ed. 292 plts (9 color). VG in dj. Hollett. $47/£30

LEVY, MERVYN. The Paintings of L. S. Lowry. London: Jupiter Books, 1975. 1st ed. 131 plts (31 color). VG in dj. Hollett. $47/£30

LEWIN, MICHAEL Z. Hard Line. NY: William Morrow, 1982. 1st ed. Fine in Fine dj. Janus. $25/£16

LEWIN, MICHAEL Z. Outside In. NY: Knopf, 1980. 1st ed. Fine in Fine dj. Janus. $25/£16

LEWIN, PHILIP. The Back and Its Disk Syndromes. Phila, 1955. 2nd ed. Red cl bds. VG (name stamp). Doctor's Library. $100/£64

LEWIN, PHILIP. The Foot and Ankle. Phila, 1947. 3rd ed. Grn cl. VG (text yellowed, foxed, bkpls). Doctor's Library. $50/£32

LEWIN, PHILIP. The Knee and Related Structures. Phila: Lea & Febiger, 1952. 1st ed. 2 color plts. VG. Glaser. $60/£38

LEWINSKI, JORGE. The Camera at War. London: W.H. Allen, 1978. 1st ed. Fine in illus dj (chip). Cahan. $45/£29

LEWIS, ALFRED HENRY. Confessions of a Detective. NY: Barnes, 1906. 1st ed. VG (hinges worn). Beasley. $30/£19

LEWIS, ALFRED HENRY. Wolfville Nights. NY, 1902. 1st bk, 1st issue. Frontis. NF (bkpl; spine sl sunned, extrems sl rubbed). Polyanthos. $75/£48

LEWIS, ALUN. Ha! Ha! Among the Trumpets: Poems in Transit. London: Allen & Unwin, 1945. VG. Cahan. $20/£13

LEWIS, ALUN. The Last Inspection. London, 1942. 1st Eng ed. Good (cocked, sl bumped) in dj (ragged). Clearwater. $70/£45

LEWIS, ALUN. Raider's Dawn and Other Poems. London, 1942. 1st Eng ed, 1st bk. Stiff card wrappers (sl dusty). Clearwater. $70/£45

LEWIS, BERKELEY R. Notes on Ammunition of the American Civil War 1861-1865. Washington, 1959. 1st ed. Pb. VG +. Pratt. $30/£19

LEWIS, C. DAY. See DAY-LEWIS, C.

LEWIS, C. S. The Case for Christianity. NY, 1947. 1st Amer ed. Fine in dj (price-clipped). Polyanthos. $30/£19

LEWIS, C. S. The Four Loves. London, (1960). 1st ed. VG in dj. Argosy. $75/£48

LEWIS, C. S. The Lion, the Witch, and the Wardrobe. NY: Macmillan, 1950. 1st Amer ed. (Inscrip; spine faded, bds spotted, faded). Dj (worn, 4-inch tear; few stains; sporadic loss). Waverly*. $220/£141

LEWIS, C. S. Perelandra. London: John Lane/Bodley Head, 1943. (Edges, prelims sl foxed), o/w Nice in dj (chipped, rubbed, spine head lacks few pieces, price sticker inner flap). Gekoski. $468/£300

LEWIS, C. S. Reflections on the Psalms. London: Geoffrey Bles, (1958). 1st ed. NF in NF dj. Captain's Bookshelf. $50/£32

LEWIS, C. S. The Screwtape Letters. Bles, 1942. 1st ed. (Cvrs rubbed, sl faded), o/w Decent. (Lacks dj.) Buckley. $39/£25

LEWIS, C. S. The Screwtape Letters. Geoffrey Bles, 1942. 1st UK ed. NF in VG dj (sl dusty, browned, sl loss spine ends). Williams. $390/£250

LEWIS, C. S. Till We Have Faces. Bles, 1956. 1st UK ed. VG in dj (sl edgewear). Williams. $94/£60

LEWIS, C. S. Till We Have Faces. Harcourt, Brace, 1957. 1st US ed. Fine in NF dj. Certo. $45/£29

LEWIS, CECIL. Broadcasting from Within. London: George Newnes, (1924). 1st ed. Good (spotted; spine sl creased) in dj (worn, chipped). Ash. $70/£45

LEWIS, CECIL. The Trumpet Is Mine. London: Peter Davies, (1938). 1st ed. VG (cvrs browned) in dj (price-clipped). Antic Hay. $17/£11

LEWIS, CLIFFORD M. et al. The Spanish Jesuit Mission in Virginia 1570-72. Chapel Hill, 1953. 1st ed. 15 fldg maps. Fine. Turpen. $45/£29

LEWIS, D. B. WYNDHAM. The Hooded Hawk, or The Case of Mr. Boswell. NY: Longmans, Green, 1947. 1st ed. (Sl damp fore-edge fr bd), else VG in dj (nicked). Hermitage. $25/£16

LEWIS, D. B. WYNDHAM. The Hooded Hawk. NY: Longmans, Green, 1947. 1st Amer ed. VG (pp160-161 browned) in dj (spine sunned). Antic Hay. $20/£13

LEWIS, DAVID LEVERING. When Harlem Was in Vogue. NY: Knopf, 1981. 1st ed. Fine in dj. Between The Covers. $50/£32

LEWIS, DOUGLAS. The Late Baroque Churches of Venice. NY, 1979. 150 plts. Good. Washton. $100/£64

LEWIS, ELISHA J. The American Sportsman. Phila, 1868. 3rd ed. Frontis, 510pp. (Lt browned; cl spotted, spine chipped, head repaired.) Edwards. $62/£40

LEWIS, ERNEST A. The Fremont Cannon, High Up and Far Back. Glendale: Clark, 1981. 1st ed. One of 768. VF. Argonaut. $50/£32

LEWIS, F. W. Dominoes. London: George Routledge, n.d. (ca 1912). Pict bds. Good. Cullen. $20/£13

LEWIS, FLORENCE. China Painting. London: Cassell, 1883. 1st ed. 16 chromolithos. (Foxing not affecting plts, hinges loose), o/w VG. Hermitage. $150/£96

LEWIS, GEORGE E. The Indiana Company, 1763-1798.... Glendale: Clark, 1941. 1st ed. One of 763. Teg. Blue cl. (Sl water spot fr cvr), else Fine. Argonaut. $90/£58

LEWIS, GRISELDA. A Picture History of English Pottery. Hulton Press, 1956. 1st ed. Color frontis, tipped-in color plt. (Spine head sl rubbed.) Edwards. $31/£20

LEWIS, J. C. The World of the Wild Turkey. Phila: Lippincott, 1973. 1st ed. Blind-stamped dec bds. Fine in VG + dj. Mikesh. $27/£17

LEWIS, JOHN FREDERICK. Sketches and Drawings of the Alhambra...in the Years 1833-4. London, (1835). 1st ed. 26 tinted litho plts, incl title; litho dedication/plt list. (Foxed, affecting plts.) Contemp 1/4 roan (partly faded; needs rebacking). Swann*. $2,070/£1,327

LEWIS, JOHN W. The Life, Labors, and Travels of Charles Bowles, of the Free Will Baptist Denomination. Watertown, NY: Ingalls & Stowell's Steam Press, 1852. 1st ed. (Eps, prelims, edges lt foxed), else NF in dec cl-cvrd bds (sl surface loss to corners). Lame Duck. $1,250/£801

LEWIS, LESLEY. Connoisseurs and Secret Agents in Eighteenth Century Rome. London, 1961. Good in dj (worn). Washton. $40/£26

LEWIS, LLOYD and HENRY J. SMITH. Oscar Wilde Discovers America (1882). NY: Harcourt, (1936). 1st ed. Frontis. (Frontis rumpled lower corner), o/w Very Nice in dj (foxing, spine faded). *Reese.* $35/£22

LEWIS, LLOYD. Captain Sam Grant. Boston, 1950. 1st ed. Port. (Bkpl.) *Wantagh.* $30/£19

LEWIS, LLOYD. Letters from Lloyd Lewis Showing Steps in the Research for His Biography of U.S. Grant. Boston: Little, Brown, 1950. Rev copy. Orig plain white wrappers (spine sl worn). *Sadlon.* $15/£10

LEWIS, LLOYD. Sherman, Fighting Prophet. NY, (1932). 1st ed. VG + . *Pratt.* $27/£17

LEWIS, LLOYD. Sherman, Fighting Prophet. NY, 1932. 1st ed. *Wantagh.* $30/£19

LEWIS, M. G. Ambrosio, or the Monk. London, 1798. 4th ed. 3 vols. Teg. Maroon 1/4 leather, ribbed spines, black leather labels, gilt. *Yudkin*.* $180/£115

LEWIS, M. G. The Monk. Paris, 1807. 3 vols. Aeg. Polished calf (all cvrs detached but present; vol 1 spine lacks top). *King.* $150/£96

LEWIS, M. G. The Monk: A Romance. Paris, 1807. 1st ed ptd in English in France. 3 vols in 1. Frontispieces, ad leaves at ends all vols. Blue marbled eps; teg. Contemp 3/4 red leather (sl rubbed, snag), marbled bds, gilt. *Mcclintock.* $285/£183

LEWIS, M. J. T. Temples in Roman Britain. Cambridge, 1966. 4 plts. Sound. *Ars Artis.* $55/£35

LEWIS, MERIWETHER and WILLIAM CLARK. History of the Expedition of Captains Lewis and Clark, 1804-5-6. Reprinted from the Edition of 1814. Chicago: A.C. McClurg, 1905. 3rd ed thus. 2 vols. Frontis ports. Teg. Tan cl (very rubbed, not worn through), brn cl backstrip, gilt. VG + . Internally Fine. Howes L317. *Harrington.* $100/£64

LEWIS, MERIWETHER and WILLIAM CLARK. History of the Expedition Under the Command of Captains Lewis and Clark...in 1804, 1805, 1806. NY: Harper, 1844. 2 vols. Fldg map, 5 charts, 1 plt. Orig brn cl (extrems worn, spotted, sl dampstained). *Appelfeld.* $200/£128

LEWIS, MERIWETHER and WILLIAM CLARK. Original Journals of the Lewis and Clark Expedition 1804-1806. Reuben Gold Thwaites (ed). NY, 1959. 7 text vols, map portfolio. Red cl. Fine set. *Reese.* $850/£545

LEWIS, MERIWETHER and WILLIAM CLARK. Original Journals of the Lewis and Clark Expedition, 1804-1806. Reuben Gold Thwaites (ed). NY: Arno, 1969. 8 vols, incl box of maps. Maroon buckram. (1 binding mismatched), else VG + . *Zubal*.* $140/£90

LEWIS, MERIWETHER and WILLIAM CLARK. Original Journals of the Lewis and Clark Expedition. Reuben Gold Thwaites (ed). NY: Arno Press, 1969. 8 vols, incl slipcased portfolio of fldg maps as vol 8. Buckram (sl worn). *Oinonen*.* $160/£103

LEWIS, MERIWETHER and WILLIAM CLARK. Travels to the Source of the Missouri River, and Across the American Continent to the Pacific Ocean. London, 1817. 3 vols. Lg fldg map in facs, 5 orig maps. Vol 2 only w/half-title. Mod calf (very worn). Howes L317. *Swann*.* $345/£221

LEWIS, NAOMI (ed). The Silent Playmate; A Collection of Doll Stories. Gollancz, 1979. 1st ed. Harold Jones (illus). Tall 8vo. 220pp. Fine in pict dj. *Bookmark.* $34/£22

LEWIS, NORMAN. The Changing Sky. London, 1959. 1st Eng ed. Very Nice in dj. *Clearwater.* $39/£25

LEWIS, NORMAN. Golden Earth. London, 1952. 1st Eng ed. Nice (name) in dj (sl nicked, rubbed). *Clearwater.* $39/£25

LEWIS, NORMAN. The Honoured Society. London, 1964. 1st Eng ed. Very Nice in dj. *Clearwater.* $31/£20

LEWIS, NORMAN. Sand and Sea in Arabia. London, 1938. 1st ed. (Sl discolored.) *Edwards.* $70/£45

LEWIS, NORMAN. Within the Labyrinth. London, 1950. 1st Eng ed. Very Nice in dj (sl stained, frayed). *Clearwater.* $39/£25

LEWIS, OSCAR and LEWIS FRANCIS BYINGTON. The History of San Francisco. Chicago/SF: S.J. Clarke, 1931. 1st ed. 3 vols. Fine. *Argonaut.* $250/£160

LEWIS, OSCAR. Autobiography of the West, Personal Narratives of Discovery and Settlement of the American West. NY, 1958. 1st ed. Fine in Fine dj. *Turpen.* $25/£16

LEWIS, OSCAR. High Sierra Country. NY, (1955). 1st ed. Nice in dj. *King.* $30/£19

LEWIS, OSCAR. Lola Montez, the Mid-Victorian Bad Girl in California. SF: Colt Press, (1938). 1st ed. One of 750 signed. Cl-backed dec bds. Fine (lt offsetting ep from plain dj). *Argonaut.* $75/£48

LEWIS, OSCAR. The Origin of the Celebrated Jumping Frog of Calaveras County. SF: Book Club of CA, 1931. Ltd to 250 numbered. Fldg facs pg of Sonora Herald. Grn cl-backed marbled bds, gilt. NF. *Blue Mountain.* $95/£61

LEWIS, OSCAR. Sutter's Fort: Gateway to the Gold Fields. Englewood Cliffs: Prentice-Hall, (1966). 1st ed. Signed. 48pp booklet incl; recent color photos laid in. Orange/black cl, gilt. Fine in pict dj (lt worn). *Pacific*.* $23/£15

LEWIS, PERCY WYNDHAM. The Human Age. Methuen, (1955). 1st ed. Good (spine sl creased, sl rubbed) in dj (sl foxed, browned). *Ash.* $31/£20

LEWIS, PERCY WYNDHAM. The Red Priest. London, 1956. 1st ed. NF in dj. *Buckley.* $47/£30

LEWIS, R. B. Light and Truth; Collected from the Bible and Ancient and Modern History.... Boston: Committee of Colored Gentlemen, 1844. 1st ed. NF (1st, last few ll foxed, emb stamp fep; extrems sl worn). *Between The Covers.* $850/£545

LEWIS, ROY. The Fenokee Project. London: Collins, 1971. 1st ed. Fine in dj (lt soiled). *Murder By The Book.* $45/£29

LEWIS, SINCLAIR. Arrowsmith. PA: Franklin Library, 1975. Fine in full leather. *Smith.* $20/£13

LEWIS, SINCLAIR. Babbit. NY: Harcourt, Brace, (1922). 1st ed, 1st state w/'Purdy' at 49.4. Blue cl stamped in orange. VG. *Macdonnell.* $125/£80

LEWIS, SINCLAIR. Babbitt. NY, (1922). 2nd state. VG (spine sunned). *Polyanthos.* $75/£48

LEWIS, SINCLAIR. Dodsworth. NY, 1929. 1st Amer ed. NF (spine lt sunned, extrems sl rubbed). *Polyanthos.* $40/£26

LEWIS, SINCLAIR. The God-Seeker. NY, (1949). 1st ed. VG in dj. *Argosy.* $40/£26

LEWIS, SINCLAIR. It Can't Happen Here. NY: Dramatists Play Service, (1938). 1st ed. Fine in wrappers (sl soiling). *Between The Covers.* $125/£80

LEWIS, SINCLAIR. Kingsblood Royal. NY: Random House, 1947. #389/1050. Signed. Fine in glassine, slipcase (faded). *Metropolitan*.* $69/£44

LEWIS, SINCLAIR. Main Street. NY, 1920. 1st Amer ed. NF (spine extrems, cvrs sl rubbed). *Polyanthos.* $95/£61

LEWIS, SINCLAIR. Main Street: The Story of Carol Kennicott. NY: Harcourt, Brace & Howe, 1920. 1st ed, 2nd issue. Denim-blue cl stamped in orange. (Spine sl faded, rubbed.) *Pirages.* $125/£80

LEWIS, SINCLAIR. The Prodigal Parents. NY, 1938. 1st ed. VG in dj. *Argosy.* $50/£32

LEWIS, SINCLAIR. Work of Art. GC: Doubleday, 1934. 1st ed. VG in dj (nicks). *Houle.* $150/£96

LEWIS, SINCLAIR. Work of Art. NY, 1934. 1st Amer ed. NF (spine, edges sl sunned). *Polyanthos*. $25/£16

LEWIS, SUZANNE. Art of Matthew Paris in the 'Chronica Majora.' Berkeley: Univ of CA, (1987). Fine in dj. *Truepenny*. $95/£61

LEWIS, THERESA (ed). The Semi-Detached House. Richard Bentley, 1862. New ed. Good (spine bumped, chipped, rubbed, vent upper hinge). *Tiger*. $16/£10

LEWIS, THOMAS. Clinical Disorders of the Heart Beat. NY, 1921. (5th ed). VG (sl worn). *Doctor's Library*. $60/£38

LEWIS, THOMAS. Clinical Science. London: Shaw, 1934. 1st ed. VG (cvrs sl mkd). *White*. $39/£25

LEWIS, THOMAS. Exercises in Human Physiology. London: Macmillan, 1945. Sole ed. Red cl. VG. *White*. $47/£30

LEWIS, THOMAS. Lectures on the Heart. NY, 1915. (Spine ends sl worn), o/w VG. *Whitehart*. $39/£25

LEWIS, W. S. (comp). A Guide to the Life of Horace Walpole (1717-1797).... New Haven: Yale, 1973. 1st ed. Inscribed Christmas presentation copy from Lewis. Fine in NF dj. *Reese*. $45/£29

LEWIS, W. S. (ed). Horace Walpole's Fugitive Verses. London, 1935. 1st ed. One of 500, unnumbered. Buckram, gilt. VG-. *Gretton*. $55/£35

LEWIS, WYNDHAM. America and the Cosmic Man. GC: Doubleday, 1949. 1st Amer ed. VG in dj (edgewear, sm nick). *Antic Hay*. $35/£22

LEWIS, WYNDHAM. The Apes of God. London: Arthur, 1930. Ltd to 750 numbered, signed. Natural buckram (bumped, few lt stains). VG (foxed, pastedown inner edges sl roughed). *Blue Mountain*. $285/£183

LEWIS, WYNDHAM. The Apes of God. London: Arco, 1955. 'Twenty-Fifth Anniversary Edition.' #566/1000 signed. Sound (cl faded, soiled, sl worn). *Cox*. $55/£35

LEWIS, WYNDHAM. The Art of Being Ruled. NY: Harper, 1926. 1st Amer ed. Fine in Nice dj (corners nicked, spine sl tanned, rubbed). *Patterson*. $187/£120

LEWIS, WYNDHAM. The Artist. Laidlaw & Laidlaw, 1939. 1st ed. 3 color plts incl frontis port, 6 half tones. (Fore-edge sl spotted.) Partly unopened. Dj (soiled, chipped, sl spine loss). *Edwards*. $234/£150

LEWIS, WYNDHAM. The Complete Wild Body. Bernard Lafourcade (ed). Santa Barbara: Black Sparrow, 1982. Ltd to 275 signed. Ptd bds. Fine in acetate dj. *Antic Hay*. $75/£48

LEWIS, WYNDHAM. The Demon of Progress in the Arts. Methuen, 1954. 1st ed. Fine in dj (sl rubbed). *Poetry Bookshop*. $31/£20

LEWIS, WYNDHAM. The Hitler Cult. London, 1939. 1st Eng ed. Bright (cvrs sl mkd, handled). *Clearwater*. $55/£35

LEWIS, WYNDHAM. The Hitler Cult. London, 1939. 1st Eng ed. Buckram (mkd). Dj (worn, rubbed). *Clearwater*. $195/£125

LEWIS, WYNDHAM. The Hitler Cult. London, 1939. One of 2500 ptd. Black buckram (mkd). Dj. *Clearwater*. $468/£300

LEWIS, WYNDHAM. The Jews: Are They Human? London, 1939. One of 1750 ptd. Excellent in dj (sl tanned, nicked). *Clearwater*. $624/£400

LEWIS, WYNDHAM. The Letters. W. K. Rose (ed). Methuen, 1963. 1st ed. (Cl sl mkd), o/w Fine. *Poetry Bookshop*. $31/£20

LEWIS, WYNDHAM. The Letters. W. K. Rose (ed). London, 1963. 1st Eng ed. Nice in dj (sl rubbed). *Clearwater*. $55/£35

LEWIS, WYNDHAM. Men Without Art. London, 1934. 1st Eng ed. Good (spine faded, mkd, sl nicked). *Clearwater*. $70/£45

LEWIS, WYNDHAM. The Mysterious Mr. Bull. London, 1938. Very Nice (top edges scored, sm nick) in pict dj (chipped). *Clearwater*. $242/£155

LEWIS, WYNDHAM. The Red Priest. London: Methuen, (1956). 1st ed. Fine in dj. *Captain's Bookshelf*. $100/£64

LEWIS, WYNDHAM. Time and Western Man. NY: Harcourt, (1928). 1st Amer ed. One of 1500 ptd. (Sm nick fore-edge upper cvr), o/w VG. *Reese*. $45/£29

LEWIS, WYNDHAM. Wyndham Lewis the Artist. London: Laidlaw & Laidlaw, 1939. 1st ed. NF in dj, wraparound band. *Lame Duck*. $350/£224

LEWITT-HIM. The Football's Revolt. NY: Sylvan, 1944. 9x11. 28pp. Cl spine, pict bds. VG. *Cattermole*. $125/£80

LEYDA, JAY. The Melville Log. NY: Harcourt Brace, (1951). 1st ed. 2 vols. NF in VG slipcase. *Turtle Island*. $85/£54

LEYLAND, JOHN (ed). Gardens Old and New. Country Life, n.d. 2 vols. (Lib bkpl, label remains fep vol 2.) Aeg. Illus cl (rubbed, chipped, joints splitting vol 2). *Edwards*. $211/£135

LEYMARIE, JEAN. The Jerusalem Windows. NY, (1962). Folio. 2 lithos by Marc Chagall. Dj (adhesive traces rear panel). *Swann**. $1,380/£885

LEYMARIE, JEAN. The Jerusalem Windows. NY: Braziller, 1962. Folio. 2 orig lithos by Marc Chagall. (Sl bumped, edgeworn, sl sunned.) Dj (edgeworn, short tears, clipped). *Metropolitan**. $1,092/£700

LI, CH'IAO-P'ING. The Chemical Arts of Old China. Easton, PA: Journal of Chemical Education, (1948). 1st ed in English. Pict eps. Pict cl (sm stains). NF. *Glaser*. $85/£54

LIARDET, FREDERICK. Tales of a Barrister. London: C. Edmonds, 1847. 2nd ed. 3 vols. Contemp 1/2 calf (spines rubbed, lacks labels). *Burmester*. $101/£65

LIBBY, O. G. (ed). The Arikara Narrative of the Campaign Against the Hostile Dakotas, June, 1876. Bismarck: (State Hist Soc of ND), 1920. 1st ed. Grn cl, gilt (spine lettering sl worn). NF. *Harrington*. $125/£80

LIBBY, O. G. (ed). The Arikara Narrative of the Campaign Against the Hostile Dakotas, June, 1876. Bismarck: ND Historical Collections, 1920. 1st ed. Grn cl lettered in gilt. Fine (fr blank flyleaf creased). *Argonaut*. $175/£112

LIBBY, O. G. (ed). Collections of the State Historical Society of North Dakota. Vol. 3. Bismarck, ND, 1910. (Pp browned; cvrs sl worn). *King*. $50/£32

LIBERMAN, ALEXANDER (ed). The Art and Technique of Color Photography. NY: S&S, 1951. 1st ed. (Tips rubbed), else VG. *Cahan*. $35/£22

LIBERMAN, M. M. Maggot and Worm and Eight Other Stories. West Branch, IA: Cummington, 1969. #267/300. Cream cl, ptd paper spine label. Fine in Japanese (chira) paper dj. *Heller*. $125/£80

Library of Henry M. Blackmer II. London: Sotheby's, 1989. 135 plts (49 color). Price lists inserted loose. Blue bds, picture upper cvr. *Maggs*. $78/£50

Library of Henry Myron Blackmer II. London: Sotheby's, 1989. Color frontis. Good. *Archaeologia*. $150/£96

Library Planning Bookstacks and Shelving. Jersey City, (1915). Gray cl (extrems rather worn). *Freeman**. $60/£38

LICHTEN, FRANCES. Folk Art of Rural Pennsylvania. NY: Scribner, (1946). Later ed. VG in Good+ dj. *Agvent*. $45/£29

LICHTEN, FRANCES. Folk Art of Rural Pennsylvania. London/NY: Scribner, (1946, 'A'). Good (bkpl, sl worn, lt soiled). *Bohling.* $50/£32

LICHTENSTEIN, HENRY. Travels in Southern Africa. London: Colburn, 1812. 2 vols in 1. Frontis port, 8 plts, fldg map (fold splits, reinforcements; lt browning). 3/4 leather (dry, hinges repaired), gilt. *Metropolitan**. $1,495/£958

LIDDELL, DONALD M. Chessmen. NY, (1937). 1st ed. (Sl worn.) *Oinonen**. $30/£19

LIDDELL, DONALD M. Chessmen. London: Harrap, 1938. (Lib label, few stamps; cl sl mkd, edges faded.) *Hollett.* $133/£85

LIDDELL, HENRY G. A History of Rome from the Earliest Times to the Establishment of the Empire. London: Murray, 1855. 2 vols. Calf, gilt, leather labels. Good. *Andrew Stewart.* $31/£20

LIDDELL, HENRY G. and ROBERT SCOTT. A Greek-English Lexicon Based on the German Work of Francis Passow. OUP, 1843. 1st ed. xviii,1584,(2)pp (title leaf strengthened on verso). Contemp 3/4 calf (rubbed). *Oinonen**. $100/£64

LIEBIG, JUSTUS. Professor Liebig's Complete Works on Chemistry.... Phila: Peterson, 1850. 47,135,111pp (foxed). Victorian cl. Clean. *Goodrich.* $95/£61

LIEBLING, A. J. Back Where I Came From. NY: Sheridan House, (1938). 1st ed, 1st bk. (Spine lettering lt rubbed), else NF in pict dj (spine sl faded, sl chipped, edgeworn, deeply price-clipped). *Captain's Bookshelf.* $400/£256

LIEBLING, A. J. Back Where I Came From. NY, 1938. 1st ed. VG (lacks dj). *Warren.* $50/£32

LIEBLING, A. J. Between Meals. NY, 1962. 1st ed. VG in dj (sl soiled, sm hole). *King.* $35/£22

LIEBLING, A. J. Between Meals: An Appetite for Paris. NY: S&S, 1962. 1st ed. Fine in dj. *Captain's Bookshelf.* $60/£38

LIEBLING, A. J. Chicago: The Second City. NY, 1952. 1st ed. NF in VG+ dj. *Warren.* $45/£29

LIEBLING, A. J. The Wayward Pressman. GC, 1947. 1st ed. (Ink inscrip; corners bumped), else Good in dj (defective). *King.* $25/£16

LIEBLING, A. J. The Wayward Pressman. GC, 1947. 1st ed. VG in dj. *Argosy.* $65/£42

LIEBOVITZ, DAVID. The Canvas Sky. NY: HB&Co, (1946). 1st ed. Fine in NF dj (sm nicks). *Between The Covers.* $50/£32

LIENHARD, HEINRICH. From St. Louis to Sutter's Fort, 1846. Erwin and Elisabeth Gudde (eds). Norman: Univ of OK, (1961). Grn cl. Fine in pict dj. *Pacific**. $52/£33

LIENHARD, HEINRICH. A Pioneer at Sutter's Fort, 1846-1850.... Marguerite Eyer Wilbur (ed). L.A.: Calafia Soc, 1941. 1st ed in English. Frontis, 5 plts. Two-tone cl, gilt spine. Fine. Howes L332. *Argonaut.* $175/£112

LIEPMANN, HEINZ. Poison in the Air. Lippincott, 1937. (Rear cvr sl spotted), o/w VG. *Bookcell.* $20/£13

LIETZE, ERNST. Modern Heliographic Processes. NY: D. Van Nostrand, 1888. 1st ed. One of 1000. viii,143pp+4pp ads; 10 tipped-in photos. VG in later buckram, leather spine label. *Cahan.* $400/£256

Life and Adventures of Philip Quarll.... (By Peter Longueville.) London: Joseph Thomas, 1839. 1st ed. 12mo. Frontis, viii,165,(3)pp. Brn cl (faded), gilt stamp. *Karmiole.* $85/£54

Life and Adventures, Songs, Services, and Speeches of Private Miles O'Reilly. (By Charles Graham Halpine.) NY, 1864. 1st ed. 237pp. Gilt stamped cl (ink splotches back cvr; extrems frayed). *King.* $35/£22

Life and Death of Rich Mrs. Duck, a Notorious Glutton. NY: McLoughlin Bros, 1869. 8vo. (8)ff; 8 chromolithos. Fine in pict self-wrappers. *Bromer.* $125/£80

Life and Opinions of Tristram Shandy, Gentleman. (By Laurence Sterne.) London: vols 1-3, J. Dodsley, vols 4-6, T. Beckett, 1772-73. Vols 1-2, 9th ed; vols 3-6, new ed. Contemp calf, leather labels, panelled spines, gilt. (Vol 6 lacks fep.) *Stewart.* $273/£175

Life and Remarkable Adventures of Isreal R. Potter. (By Henry Trumbell.) Providence, 1824. 1st ed. Frontis. (Internal spotting, p5/6 crudely repaired, sig.) *Freeman**. $30/£19

Life and Reminiscences of Jefferson Davis by Distinguished Men of His Time. Balt, 1890. 1st ed. 490pp. (Cvr shelfwear, spine extrems chipping), o/w Fine. *Pratt.* $90/£58

Life in a Man-of-War.... (By Henry James Mercier.) Phila: Lydia R. Bailey, 1841. 1st ed. 23.3 cm. 267pp (marginal foxing). Orig cl (joints split; back missing about 30%). *Lefkowicz.* $1,500/£962

Life in Mexico During a Residence of Two Years in That Country. (By Mme. F.E. Calderon de la Barca.) Boston: Little, Brown, 1843. 2 vols. xii,412; xi,427pp. Blind-stamped cl (Bkpl, prelims foxed, 1 hinge sl weak; frayed, spine ends sl chipped), else VG. BAL 16338. *Reese.* $325/£208

Life of Ma-Ka-Tai-Me-She-Kia-Kiak or Black Hawk, Embracing the Tradition of His Nation.... Boston: J.B. Patterson, 1834. Later ptg. Frontis port, 155pp (foxed). Tan cl-backed grn bds (quite rubbed, bumped, spine chipped, joints split, fr cvr starting). Good. Howes P120. *Blue Mountain.* $150/£96

Life of Rev. Amand Parent.... Toronto: William Briggs, (1887). 235pp. Grn bds, gilt. *Cullen.* $75/£48

Life of Robert Earl of Leicester.... (By Jebb Samuel.) London: Woodman & Lyon, 1727. Engr frontis port. Calf. *Rostenberg & Stern.* $225/£144

Life of Sir Thomas Bodley. London: Privately ptd for John Lane, Christmas 1894. Fine engr frontis port. Uncut. Heavy gray paper wrappers (worn), cl spine. Contents Excellent. *Hartfield.* $65/£42

Life of Stonewall Jackson. By a Virginian. (By John Esten Cooke.) NY, 1863. 1st ed. 305pp. (Frontis, tp foxed, ink name; spine poor, extrems frayed.) *King.* $95/£61

Life, Trial and Execution of Captain John Brown. NY, (1859). New ed. 8 plts. Orig ptd wraps (chipped, lacks corner; foxed). *Kane**. $60/£38

Life, Trial and Execution of Captain John Brown.... NY: Robert M. DeWitt, (1859). 'New ed w/additions.' 108pp; 8 plts. Orig fr ptd pict wrap. (Rem from bound vol; lacks orig spine, rear wrap.) Howes B851. *Wantagh.* $100/£64

Life, Trial and Execution of Captain John Brown.... NY: Robert M. DeWitt, (1859). New ed w/additions. 108pp; 8 full-pg illus. Pict wraps (edges chipped, soiled). Good (lt foxed). Howes B851. *Wantagh.* $150/£96

LILFORD, LORD. On Birds...Falconry and Otter Hunting.... A. Trevor-Battye (ed). London, 1903. Port. (Sl worn, shaken.) *Maggs.* $37/£24

LILLY, A. T. The Silk Industry in the United States from 1766 to 1874. NY: Jenkins & Thomas, 1882. 1st ed. 12pp. VG in ptd wrappers. *Lucas.* $60/£38

LILLY, W. An Introduction to Astrology. 1860. xiv,492,64pp; 2 fldg plts. 3/4 leather, marbled bds, edges. (Scattered foxing, cartoon clipping stuck to pg facing tp, ink sig; cvrs rubbed), o/w VG. *Whitehart.* $55/£35

LIMBECK, R. R. The Clinical Pathology of the Blood. Arthur Latham and J. Nachbar (trans). London: New Sydenham Soc, 1901. Brn cl. VG. *White.* $44/£28

Lincoln's Gettysburg Address. (NY: Hammer Creek Press, 1950.) 1st bk of Hammer Creek Press. 12mo. (6)pp. Marbled bds, gilt-stamped black morocco. VF. *Bromer.* $125/£80

LINCOLN, ABRAHAM. The Collected Works of Abraham Lincoln. Roy P. Basler (ed). New Brunswick, (1953). History Book Club Edition. 9 vols. VG + . *Pratt.* $125/£80

LINCOLN, ABRAHAM. The Collected Works of Abraham Lincoln. Roy P. Basler (ed). New Brunswick, NJ: Rutgers Univ, 1953-1955. History Bk Club ed. 9 vols. NF set. *Mcgowan.* $150/£96

LINCOLN, ABRAHAM. The Collected Works. Roy P. Basler (ed). New Brunswick, 1953-55. 9 vols, incl index. *Swann*.* $46/£29

LINCOLN, ABRAHAM. The Collected Works. Roy P. Basler (ed). New Brunswick: Rutgers Univ, 1953. 1st ed. 8 vols + index vol from 1955 set. VG. *Waverly*.* $176/£113

LINCOLN, ABRAHAM. The Life and Public Service of General Zachary Taylor. Boston/NY, 1922. #9/435. Cl-backed marbled bds, deckle edge. Pub's ptd note inserted. Fine in glassine wrapper, slipcase (edgeworn). *Bohling.* $150/£96

LINCOLN, ABRAHAM. The Life and Public Services of General Zachary Taylor. Boston/NY, 1922. 1st ed in bk form. Ltd to 435. Cl-backed bds. (Name.) *Wantagh.* $35/£22

LINCOLN, ABRAHAM. Lincoln Letters Hitherto Unpublished in the Library of Brown University and Other Providence Libraries. Providence, 1927. Frontis port, facs. Stitched sigs, not yet bound. Unopened. (1/2 title creased.) *Bohling.* $25/£16

LINCOLN, ABRAHAM. Lincoln's Last Speech in Springfield in the Campaign of 1858. Chicago: UC Press, 1925. Port. Cl-backed bds, ptd title label. VG (lt soiled). *Bohling.* $30/£19

LINCOLN, ABRAHAM. Literary Works of Abraham Lincoln. Carl Van Doren (ed). Menasha, WI: LEC, 1942. Ltd to 1500 signed by John Steuart Curry (illus). Full tan muslin, leather spine label. Fine in slipcase. *Truepenny.* $175/£112

LINCOLN, ABRAHAM. Political Debates Between Hon. Abraham Lincoln and Hon. Stephen A. Douglas.... Columbus: Follett, Foster, 1860. 1st ed, 1st issue. (Foxing, sl bumped, few stains.) *Metropolitan*.* $661/£424

LINCOLN, ABRAHAM. The Writings of Abraham Lincoln. Arthur Brooks Lapsley (ed). Putnam, Vols 1-2 (1905), vols 3-4 n.d., vols 5-7 (1906), vol 8 (1888). Constitutional ed. Brn buckram. (Vols 1-2 hinges cracked, some others starting.) *Yudkin*.* $65/£42

LINCOLN, JOSEPH C. Blowing Clear. NY/London: Appleton, 1930. 1st ed. (Sl rubbed), o/w VG. *Worldwide.* $10/£6

LINCOLN, JOSEPH C. The Postmaster. NY/London: D. Appleton, 1912. 1st ed. Red-brn cl, pict onlay. Fine. *Sumner & Stillman.* $40/£26

LINCOLN, L. (ed). Southwest Indian Silver from the Doneghy Collection. Austin: Univ of TX, 1982. 5 full-pg color plts. VG in dj (chipped). *Scribe's Perch*.* $28/£18

LIND, J. A Treatise on the Scurvy. Birmingham, 1980. Facs of 1772 3rd ed. Gilt-tooled red full leather, gilt edges. Fine. *Doctor's Library.* $100/£64

LIND, J. A Treatise on the Scurvy.... London, 1772. 3rd ed. (Browned throughout, lib stamp 1st & last pp, tear Dd6 repaired w/o loss.) Recent calf. *Maggs.* $507/£325

LIND, JAKOV. Counting My Steps. NY: Macmillan, 1969. 1st US ed. NF in VG + dj (price-clipped, chip fr panel). *Lame Duck.* $35/£22

LIND, JAKOV. Landscape in Concrete. NY: Grove, 1966. 1st US ed. NF in dj (sm hole rear flap). *Lame Duck.* $35/£22

LINDBERGH, ANNE MORROW. The Unicorn and Other Poems. (NY, 1956.) 1st ed. Ltd to 850 numbered. Teg. Parchment-backed bds. (Bkpl; spine sl dknd), else Good in slipcase (defective). *King.* $50/£32

LINDEMANN, GOTTFRIED. Prints and Drawings. Gerald Onn (trans). Phaidon, 1976. 2nd imp. Dj. *Edwards.* $39/£25

LINDER, USHER F. Reminiscences of the Early Bench and Bar of Illinois. Chicago: Chicago Legal News Co, 1879. 2nd ed. Maroon cl. (Lower edge stained), else sound. *Boswell.* $125/£80

LINDERMAN, FRANK B. American: The Life Story of a Great Indian. NY: Day, (1930). 1st ed. Dec cl (spine faded). *Ginsberg.* $75/£48

LINDERMANN, GERALD F. The River of War. Ann Arbor, (1974). 1st ed. Fine in dj (worn, sm piece torn off). *Pratt.* $22/£14

LINDGREN, ASTRID. The Tomten. NY: Coward-McCann, 1962. 1st ed. Harald Wiberg (illus). 10 1/2 x 6 3/4. 32pp. VG. *Cattermole.* $30/£19

LINDLEY, GEORGE. A Guide to the Orchard and Kitchen Garden. Longman, 1831. 16pp ads. Orig cl-backed bds (sl rubbed), paper label. Sound. *Petersfield.* $62/£40

LINDLEY, J. School Botany. London, (1880). 14th ed. viii,212pp. Fine. *Henly.* $28/£18

LINDLEY, J. and T. MOORE. The Treasury of Botany. London, 1876. New ed, w/suppl. 2 vols. 20 plts. Calf (sl rubbed; sl foxed). *Wheldon & Wesley.* $62/£40

LINDLEY, KENNETH. Seaside Architecture. London, 1973. 1st ed. Dj (sl chipped). *Edwards.* $31/£20

LINDMAN, MAJ. Flicka, Ricka, Dicka and the New Dotted Dresses. Chicago: Whitman, 1939. 5th ed. 8 1/2 x 9 1/2. 24pp. Cl w/lg fr onlay. Fine in dj. *Cattermole.* $120/£77

LINDMAN, MAJ. Snipp, Snapp, Snurr and the Big Surprise. Chicago: Albert Whitman, (1944). 4to. VG. *Dower.* $65/£42

LINDMAN, MAJ. Snipp, Snapp, Snurr and the Magic Horse. Chicago: Whitman, 1939. 8th ed. 8 1/2 x 9 1/2. 24pp. Cl w/lg fr onlay. Fine in dj. *Cattermole.* $120/£77

LINDQUIST, EMORY KEMPTON. Smoky Valley People. Lindsborg: Bethany College, 1953. Purple cl. VG in dj (worn, chipped). *Bohling.* $22/£14

LINDSAY, DAVID MOORE. Camp-Fire Reminiscences.... Boston: Dana Estes, 1912. 1st ed. Frontis. Dec cvr. VG (name, address; lt wear corners). *Backman.* $70/£45

LINDSAY, DAVID. The Violet Apple. London: Sidgwick & Jackson, (1978). 1st ed. Fine in dj (sm crease fr flap). *Between The Covers.* $100/£64

LINDSAY, JACK. The Roaring Twenties. London, 1960. 1st Eng ed. Very Nice in dj. *Clearwater.* $39/£25

LINDSAY, JACK. Storm at Sea. London: Golden Cockerel, 1935. One of 250 signed. Teg. 1/4 blue morocco, ptd cl over bds, gilt. VG (spine faded). *Heller.* $225/£144

LINDSAY, JOAN. Picnic at Hanging Rock. Melbourne: F.W. Chesire, (1967). 1st ed. (Erasure fep), else NF in NF dj (spine sl faded; sl rubbing). *Between The Covers.* $185/£119

LINDSAY, MARTIN. Those Greenland Days. Edinburgh: Wm. Blackwood, 1932. Map. Very Nice in dj. *High Latitude.* $50/£32

LINDSAY, MAUD. Little Missy. Boston: Lothrop, Lee & Shepard, (1922). 1st ed. 8 color plts. Pict eps. Pict tan cl. VG. *Petrilla.* $45/£29

LINDSAY, VACHEL. The Golden Book of Springfield. NY: MacMillan, 1920. 1st ed. Dec bds. (Head of spine chipped, fore-edge discolored), o/w VF in dj (lt edgewear). *Captain's Bookshelf.* $100/£64

LINDSAY, VACHEL. The Golden Book of Springfield. NY: Macmillan, 1920. 1st ed. Dec illus cl. Fine in dj. *Cahan.* $165/£106

LINDSEY, BESSIE. Lore of Our Land Pictured in Glass. N.p.: The Author, 1948. 2 vols. VG. *Waverly*.* $27/£17

LINDSEY, DAVID L. A Cold Mind. NY: Harper & Row, 1983. 1st ed. Fine in dj. *Mordida.* $45/£29

LINDSLEY, A. L. Sketches of an Excursion to Southern Alaska. (Portland, OR, 1881.) 1st ed. Inscribd. 73pp. Ptd wrappers (rebacked; stamp). Howes L357. *Ginsberg.* $200/£128

LINFORTH, JAMES. Route from Liverpool to Great Salt Lake Valley.... L.A.: c.1959. Fldg map. Fine in NF dj. *Benchmark.* $145/£93

LINK, MAE and HUBERT COLEMAN. Medical Support of the Army Air Forces in World War II. Washington, 1955. 1st ed. VG. *Fye.* $100/£64

LINKLATER, ERIC. The Prince in the Heather. London: Hodder & Stoughton, 1965. VG in dj (price-clipped). *Hollett.* $23/£15

LINKLATER, ERIC. Private Angelo. Privately ptd, (Christmas, 1957). Ltd to 2000. Pict eps. Fine in parchment-backed dec bds. *Cox.* $39/£25

LINKS, J. G. Canaletto and His Patrons. London: Elek, 1977. Fine in color dj. *Europa.* $31/£20

LINKS, J. G. Canaletto. Phaidon, 1982. 1st ed. 43 color plts. Dj. *Edwards.* $39/£25

LINKS, J. G. The Ruskins in Normandy. Murray, 1968. VG in dj. *Hadley.* $23/£15

LINN, JOHN J. Reminiscences of Fifty Years in Texas. NY, 1883. 1st ed. Frontis port (slip pasted over correcting title), 369pp (errata sheet pasted to p369, new eps). Blind-stamped mauve cl (extrems lt worn), gilt. VG. Howes L363. *Turpen.* $350/£224

LINN, THOMAS. The Health Resorts of Europe. NY, 1893. 1st ed. 330pp. (Bds warped.) *Fye.* $75/£48

LINN, WILLIAM ALEXANDER. The Story of the Mormons from the Date of Their Origin to the Year 1901. NY, 1923. 2nd ed. (Edgewear, hinges cracked, articles pasted in rippling pp.) Reading copy. *Benchmark.* $35/£22

LINSLEY, D. C. Morgan Horses. NY: Saxton, 1857. 1st ed. VG + . *October Farm.* $495/£317

LINTHURST, RANDOLPH. Journal of Leo Smith. Adams Press, 1976. 1st ed. Fine. *Plapinger.* $45/£29

LINTON, E. LYNN. The Lake Country. London: Smith, Elder, 1864. Map. Grn cl, gilt. (Spotting; worn, hinges cracked.) *Hollett.* $101/£65

LINTON, W. J. The History of Wood-Engraving in America. London: Geo. Bell, 1882. #698/1000, signed. viii,71pp + c.30 blank leaves. Partly unopened. Cl spine (1/2-inch tear). Heavy cardbd sides w/wood veneer (edges, corners rubbed, bumped). Acceptable. *Michael Taylor.* $86/£55

LINTON, W. J. Wood Engraving, a Manual of Instruction. London: Geo. Bell, 1884. 1st ed. One of 500. x,127pp. Brn cl, gilt. (Scattered foxing), else VG. *Michael Taylor.* $78/£50

Lion's Den. NY: McLoughlin Bros, n.d. Pop-up. Pict bds (sl worn, soiled). Pop-ups VG. *New Hampshire*.* $210/£135

LIONNI, LEO. A Color of His Own. NY: Pantheon, 1975. 1st ed. 8 x 7 3/4. 32pp. Cl spine. VG in dj. *Cattermole.* $15/£10

LIONNI, LEO. Frederick. NY: Pantheon, 1967. 9 1/4 x 11. 28pp. Fine in dj. *Cattermole.* $25/£16

LIONNI, LEO. In the Rabbitgarden. NY: Pantheon, 1975. 1st ed. 9 1/4 x 11. 32pp. Cl spine. Fine in dj. *Cattermole.* $25/£16

LIONNI, LEO. Little Blue and Little Yellow. NY: Astor, 1959. 1st ed. 8x8. 38pp. Ad bkmk laid in. VG in dj. *Cattermole.* $100/£64

LIONNI, LEO. Parallel Botany. NY: Knopf, 1977. 2nd ed. Cl spine. VG in dj. *Cattermole.* $35/£22

LIONNI, LEO. Theodore and the Talking Mushroom. NY: Pantheon, 1971. 1st ed. 9 1/4 x 11 1/4. 32pp. VG in dj. *Cattermole.* $32/£21

LIONNI, LEO. Tico and the Golden Wings. NY: Pantheon, 1964. 1st ed. 8 1/4 x 10 1/4. 32pp. Cl spine, pict bds. VG in dj. *Cattermole.* $30/£19

LIPMAN, JEAN. Calder's Universe. NY, 1976. VG in dj. *Argosy.* $125/£80

LIPPA, ERNEST M. Captive Surgeon.... NY, 1953. 1st ed. VG. *Argosy.* $30/£19

LIPPE, ASCHWIN. The Freer Indian Sculptures. Washington: Smithsonian, 1970. 1st ed. Color frontis tipped in, 55 plts, map. VG (ex-lib, fr cvr #). *Worldwide.* $50/£32

LIPPINCOTT, LOUISE. Selling Art in Georgian London. New Haven/London, 1983. Good in dj. *Washton.* $35/£22

LIPTON, LAWRENCE. The Holy Barbarians. NY, 1959. 1st ed. VG in VG + dj. *Smith.* $25/£16

LISCOMB, HARRY F. The Prince of Washington Square. NY: Stokes, 1925. 1st ed. Paper-cvrd bds. (Extrems sl worn), else NF in VG + dj (spine sl damp-stained, extrems sl nicked). *Between The Covers.* $800/£513

LISNEY, ARTHUR A. A Bibliography of British Lepidoptera 1608-1799. London, 1960. Frontis port. (Ex-lib, ink stamps, label.) Gilt illus upper bd (faded, # spine, bumped). *Edwards.* $94/£60

LISTON, ROBERT. Lectures on the Operations of Surgery, and on Diseases and Accidents Requiring Operations.... Phila: Lea & Blanchard, 1846. 1st ed thus. (4 ads),xii,(13)-565,3-32(ads)pp. Orig sheep (worn). VG. *Glaser.* $450/£288

LISTON, ROBERT. Practical Surgery. Phila: Adam Waldie, 1838. 1st Amer ed. vi,(2),374,(1 ad)pp (foxed). Orig cl, leather spine label. VG. *Glaser.* $225/£144

LITCHFIELD, F. Illustrated History of Furniture. London/NY, 1899. 4th ed. 272pp. Dec cvr. Good-. *Scribe's Perch*.* $20/£13

LITCHFIELD, F. Pottery and Porcelain. 1912. New ed. 9 color plts. Teg. (Hinges cracked.) Dj (chipped). *Edwards.* $39/£25

Literary and Historical Activities in North Carolina, 1900-1905. Raleigh, 1907. (Ex-lib; lt shelfworn.) *Bohling.* $25/£16

LITTAUER, V. S. and S. N. KOURNAKOFF. The Defense of the Forward Seat. NY: Boots & Saddles, 1934. 1st ed. (Sm spot fr cvr), o/w VG. *October Farm.* $65/£42

Little Bo-Peep. Phila: Davis, Porter & Coates, (ca 1850). Sm 8vo. (8)ff. 7 hand-colored pictures. Nice in hand-colored pict wrappers (2-inch hinge tear). *Bromer.* $125/£80

Little Bo-Peep. Edinburgh: W.P. Nimmo, n.d. (ca 1880). Marcus Ward's Royal Illuminated Nursery Stories. Obl 8vo. 6 leaves + 2pp + 1pg list; 4 full-pg chromolithos w/added gold. VG in pict stiff paper wrappers (sl soiled, sm scuff), spine stitched as pub'd. *Hobbyhorse.* $135/£87

Little Boy's Velocipede. NY: American Tract Soc, n.d. 12mo. Marbled paper bds, cl spine. (Foxing.) *Metropolitan*.* $23/£15

Little Dame Crump and Her White Pig. NY: McLoughlin, n.d. (ca 1865). 12mo. 8pp + 1pg list lower wrapper; 8 VF 1/2-pg hand-colored wood engrs. Pict yellow paper wrappers (lt spotting, wear), else VF. *Hobbyhorse*. $175/£112

Little Deserter. NY: McLoughlin, n.d. (1875). Aunt Matilda's Series. Lg 8vo. 12pp + 1pg list lower wrapper; 6 VF color plts. Perfect in pict dec stiff paper wrappers (ink sig verso upper wrapper). *Hobbyhorse*. $175/£112

Little Folks and Their Friends. Raphael Tuck, 1896. 1st ed. 4to. 80pp (few margins lt mkd); 8 color chromolitho plts. Cl spine, pict bds. (Back, edges rubbed), else VG. *Bookmark*. $62/£40

Little Frog's Lecture and Other Stories. (NY: McLoughlin Bros ca 1880-90.) 8vo. (7)ff; 6 full-pg wood-engr illus. Nice (cover extrems torn) in pict self-wrappers w/ads for McLoughlin games on back. *Bromer*. $125/£80

Little Old Woman. NY: McLoughlin Bros, n.d. Susie Sunshine Series. 12mo. 4 leaves; 7 color illus. NF in pict paper wraps. *Blue Mountain*. $45/£29

Little Orphan Annie in the Circus. NY: Cupples & Leon, (1927). Harold Gray (illus). 8.5x6.5. 86pp (some dwgs colored in by crayon). Cl-backed pict bds (sl worn). *King*. $50/£32

Little Pets, Panorama Pictures on View Within. Ernest Nister, n.d. (ca 1893). Obl lg 4to. 4 lg color pop-ups w/cl hinges. Pict bds, cl spine. (Sl worn), else VG. *Bookmark*. $585/£375

Little Red Riding Hood. London, 1988. V. Kubasta (illus). 8x10. 5 fan-folded pop-ups (3 w/minor mechanics). Glazed pict bds. VG. *King*. $25/£16

LITTLE, ANDREW G. The Grey Friars in Oxford. Oxford Hist Soc, 1892. 1st bk. xvi,369pp (edge 1 leaf opened carelessly; ex-lib, stamp, #s; eps browned, spotted). Teg, rest uncut. Blue buckram (lt bumped, rubbed, spine #). Sound. *Peter Taylor*. $75/£48

LITTLE, ARTHUR WEST. From Harlem to the Rhine. NY: Covici Friede, (1936). 1st ed. VG in VG dj. *Mcgowan*. $95/£61

LITTLE, CONSTANCE and GWENYTH. The Black Smith. NY: Crime Club, 1950. 1st ed. VG (name) in dj (bumped, creased, short tears). *Metropolitan**. $23/£15

LITTLE, E. L. et al. Common Trees of Puerto Rico and the Virgin Islands. Washington, DC, 1964-74. 2 vols. 8 maps, 710 plts. Fine. *Brooks*. $125/£80

LITTLE, RICHARD HENRY. Better Angels. NY, 1928. 1st ed. VG +. *Pratt*. $20/£13

LITTLE, RICHARD HENRY. Better Angels. NY: Minton, Balch, 1928. 1st ed. Fine in Fine dj. *Sadlon*. $20/£13

LITTLEFIELD, WILLIAM. The Whiskers of Ho Ho. NY: Lothrop, 1958. 1st ed. Vladimir Bobri (illus). 9 1/4 sq. 32pp. Fine in dj. *Cattermole*. $75/£48

LITTLEJOHN, DAVID. Dr. Johnson and Noah Webster: Two Men and Their Dictionaries. SF: Grabhorn-Hoyem, 1971. One of 500. Leafbook w/leaves from 1st eds of Johnson and Webster mtd in rear. 1/4 cl. *Swann**. $172/£110

LIVELY, PENELOPE. The Revenge of Samuel Stokes. London: Heinemann, 1981. 1st ed. 5 3/4 x 8 1/2. 122pp. 1/2 cl. Fine in dj. *Cattermole*. $45/£29

LIVELY, PENELOPE. A Stitch in Time. London: Heinemann, 1976. 1st ed. 5 1/2 x 8 3/4. 140pp. Fine in dj. *Cattermole*. $75/£48

LIVERMORE, MARY A. My Story of the War: A Woman's Narrative.... Hartford, CT: A.D. Worthington, 1890. 3rd ed. 700pp; frontis port. Dec blind-emb; gilt title, spine decs. (Sl wear spine ends, tips; foxing), else VG. *Cahan*. $65/£42

LIVERMORE, MARY A. My Story of the War: A Woman's Narrative.... Hartford, 1894. Author's cut signature tipped in. Red cl (lt worn), gilt. *Freeman**. $40/£26

Lives of Distinguished Shoemakers. Portland: Davis & Southworth, 1849. 1st ed. (Lt soiled, lt foxed.) *Kane**. $100/£64

Lives of Distinguished Shoemakers. Portland: Davis & Southworth, 1849. 1st ed. 340pp (stain from pressed flowers). Black cl (worn). Good. *Lucas*. $125/£80

Lives of the Most Remarkable Criminals Who Have Been Condemned and Executed...1720 to the Year 1735.... London: Reeves & Turner, 1873. 2 vols. 3/4 calf. Good set. *Boswell*. $350/£224

LIVESLEY, R. K. An Introduction to Automatic Digital Computers. Cambridge: CUP, 1957. 1st ed. Fine in dj. *Glaser*. $60/£38

LIVINGSTON, FLORA V. Bibliographical Data Relating to a Few of the Publications of Algernon Charles Swinburne. Cambridge, MA: Privately ptd, 1920. 1st Amer ed. Fine in wraps. *Polyanthos*. $25/£16

LIVINGSTON, MYRA COHN. What a Wonderful Bird the Frog Are. NY: HBJ, 1973. 2nd ed. 5 3/4 x 8 1/2. 192pp. Fine in dj. *Cattermole*. $20/£13

LIVINGSTON, SAMUEL. The Diagnosis and Treatment of Convulsive Disorders in Children. Springfield: Thomas, 1954. Nice in dj. *Goodrich*. $25/£16

LIVINGSTONE, DAVID and CHARLES. Narrative of an Expedition to the Zambesi and Its Tributaries. NY: Harper, 1866. 1st US ed. xxii,638pp; dbl-pg illus, fldg map. (Lt foxed; spine torn, frayed), o/w Good. *Worldwide*. $65/£42

LIVINGSTONE, DAVID. Dr. Livingstone's Cambridge Lectures.... Cambridge: Deighton Bell, 1858. 1st ed. Litho frontis port, vi,(i)blank, xxx,(ii),xciii,(i)blank, 181,(1)blank pp + 8 pub's list, 2 fldg maps. (Sl foxing frontis, map, few places; bkpls.) Blue blindstamped grained cl (rebacked), orig backstrip, gilt dec. Good. *Morrell*. $148/£95

LIVINGSTONE, DAVID. The Last Journals of David Livingstone in Central Africa. London: John Murray, 1874. 2 vols. 8vo. xvi,360; viii,346pp; 2 fldg maps. Nice older 1/2 morocco binding, w/cvrs, spines bound. VG. *Terramedia*. $500/£321

LIVINGSTONE, DAVID. The Last Journals of...in Central Africa. NY, 1875. Frontis port, 541pp + 4pp pub's ads; 20 plts, dbl-pg map, fldg map rear pocket. (Hinges tender, corners rubbed w/sl cl loss, spine chipped.) *Edwards*. $117/£75

LIVINGSTONE, DAVID. Missionary Travels and Researches in South Africa. London, 1857. 1st ed. 687pp; 25 plts, 2 fldg incl frontis, fldg map. Emb cl (hinges repaired). *Argosy*. $300/£192

LIVINGSTONE, DAVID. Missionary Travels and Researches in South Africa. London: John Murray, 1857. 1st ed. 711pp + 8pp ads (lacks pocket map; water stains to corners of fldg frontis, port). Good-. *Scribe's Perch**. $37/£24

LIVINGSTONE, DAVID. Missionary Travels and Researches in South Africa. London: John Murray, 1857. 1st ed. x + 687pp; 2 fldg maps. Contemp blue calf prize binding, spine (sl rubbed) gilt w/raised bands. VG. *Sotheran*. $281/£180

LIVINGSTONE, DAVID. Missionary Travels and Researches in South Africa. NY: Harper, 1858. 1st US ed. Engr frontis port, xxiv,732pp + 4pp ads at rear; 2 fldg maps, fldg chart. Blind dk brn cl (sl worn, spine ends sl chipped, frayed; text sl aged, foxed, ink handstamps). *Baltimore**. $75/£48

LIVINGSTONE, DAVID. Some Letters from Livingstone 1840-1872. D. Chamberlin (ed). 1940. Frontisport. (Cl sl rubbed.) *Whitehart*. $23/£15

LIVY. The History of Early Rome. Aubrey de Selincourt (trans). Verona: LEC, 1970. One of 1500 numbered, signed by Giovanni Mardersteig (ptr) and Raffaele Scorzelli (illus). Fldg map. Cl-backed bds. VG in bd slipcase. *Argosy.* $150/£96

LIVY. The History of Early Rome. Verona: LEC, 1970. #330/1500 signed by Giovanni Mardesteig (ptr) and Raffaele Scorzelli (illus). Cl over patterned bds. (Spine corner lt bumped), o/w Fine in pub's slipcase. *Hermitage.* $150/£96

LLEWELLYN, RICHARD. A Few Flowers for Shiner. NY: Macmillan, 1950. 1st ed. Paper-cvrd bds. VG (eps lt browned, ink name) in dj (sm tears). *Antic Hay.* $15/£10

LLOSA, MARIO VARGAS. See VARGOS LLOSA, MARIO

Lloyd's Register of American Yachts.... NY, 1924. 41 color plts. (Inscrip; cvrs sl soiled.) *Lefkowicz.* $100/£64

Lloyd's Register of American Yachts...1920. NY, 1920. 44 colored plts, 7pg addenda laid in. Blue cl. *Lefkowicz.* $125/£80

Lloyd's Register of American Yachts...1930. NY, 1932. 65 color plts. Blue cl. *Lefkowicz.* $100/£64

Lloyd's Register of American Yachts...1936. NY, 1936. Sailcloth. (Cvrs soiled; corrections, additions within.) *Lefkowicz.* $70/£45

Lloyd's Register of American Yachts...1937. NY, 1937. Supplement laid in. Sailcloth. (Ccvrs soiled; ms additions.) *Lefkowicz.* $70/£45

Lloyd's Register of Yachts...1908-09. London, 1908. 58 color plts. Decent (foxing within; spine spotted). *Lefkowicz.* $125/£80

LLOYD, ALBERT B. Uganda to Khartoum. London: T. Fisher Unwin, 1907. Fldg map, 80 plts. Pict red cl (lt foxed; spine faded, starting). *Adelson.* $160/£103

LLOYD, ANNE. Antiques and Amber. NY: Derrydale, 1928. 1st ed. One of 400 numbered. Cl spine, marbled papers. (Corners worn, bds lt rubbed), else VG. *Turtle Island.* $75/£48

LLOYD, BENJAMIN E. Lights and Shades in San Francisco. SF: A.L. Bancroft, 1876. 1st ed. Frontis, 523pp; 18 plts. Full sheep (newly bound), orig leather labels. Fine. Howes L404. *Argonaut.* $300/£192

LLOYD, H. ALAN. Chats on Old Clocks. London: Ernest Benn, (1951). 3rd ed. Frontis, 74 plts. Navy blue cl. VG in dj (spine ends worn). *Weber.* $12/£8

LLOYD, H. ALAN. The Collector's Dictionary of Clocks. NY: A.S. Barnes, (1964). 1st ed. Color frontis. VG in dj (extrems sl worn). *Weber.* $30/£19

LLOYD, H. ALAN. Some Outstanding Clocks Over Seven Hundred Years 1250-1950. London: Leonard Hill, 1958. 1st ed. Color frontis, 173 plts. Red cl (rubbed; stamp, few ll wrinkled). *Weber.* $55/£35

LLOYD, H. ALAN. Some Outstanding Clocks Over Seven Hundred Years, 1250-1950. London: Leonard Hill, 1958. 1st ed. Color frontis, 173 photo plts. Red cl. Good in dj (soiled). *Karmiole.* $125/£80

LLOYD, JOHN EDWARD. A History of Wales. London, 1911. 2 vols. Fldg color map. (Lt foxed, some underlining vol 2; chipped, some of dj affixed to vol 2, vol 2 bds warped, spine affixed.) *Edwards.* $70/£45

LLOYD, JOHN URI. Felix Moses the Beloved Jew of Stringtown on the Pike. The Author, (1930). Ltd to 1000. Teg. Pict cvr label. Fine in NF dj. *Sadlon.* $75/£48

LLOYD, JOHN URI. Stringtown on the Pike. NY: Dodd, Mead, 1900. 1st ed. Gray cl, inset photo fr cvr. NF. *Turtle Island.* $65/£42

LLOYD, JOHN URI. Warwick of the Knobs. NY, 1901. 1st ed. Port paste-on. *Wantagh.* $35/£22

LLOYD, N. Building Craftsmanship in Brick and Tile, and in Stone Slates. Cambridge, 1929. Sound. *Ars Artis.* $39/£25

LLOYD, N. A History of English Brickwork. London: Montgomery, 1925. 1st ed. Teg. (Sl sticking, sl damage sm area few plts.) Dec cl (corners worn, spine repaired). *Ars Artis.* $117/£75

LLOYD, N. A History of English Brickwork. London: Montgomery, 1934. New abridged ed. 140 plts. Cvr Excellent. *Ars Artis.* $78/£50

LLOYD, N. A History of the English House from Primitive Times to the Victorian Period. London: Architectural Press, 1931. (Sl tidemark top margin, damp stain inner margin last ff.) New cl. Sound. *Ars Artis.* $94/£60

LLOYD, SETON et al. Ancient Architecture: Mesopotamia, Egypt, Crete, Greece. NY: Abrams, (1974). Good in dj. *Archaeologia.* $125/£80

LLOYD, SETON. Foundations in the Dust. London/NY/Toronto: OUP, 1947. 1st ed. Fldg map. (Ink underscorings), o/w VG. *Worldwide.* $20/£13

LLOYD, VALERIE (ed). Soviet Photography. NY: Greenwich House, 1984. 1st US ed. NF in dj. *Cahan.* $75/£48

LLOYD, WILLIAM P. History of the First Regiment Pennsylvania Reserve Cavalry. Phila: King & Baird, 1864. 216pp (lt foxing). Lib binding (rebound). *Cullen.* $140/£90

LLOYD-JONES, W. Havash, Frontier Adventures in Kenya. Arrowsmith, 1925. Map. (Few pp sl foxed; backstrip faded.) *Petersfield.* $39/£25

LOBEL, ARNOLD. Fables. NY: Harper & Row, 1980. 1st ed. 8 1/4 x 10 1/2. 32pp. VG in dj. *Cattermole.* $60/£38

LOBEL, ARNOLD. On the Day Peter Stuyvesant Sailed into Town. NY: Harper, 1971. 1st ed. 10 1/4 x 9 1/2. 40pp. Cl spine, pict bds. Fine in dj. *Cattermole.* $35/£22

LOBEL, ARNOLD. A Treeful of Pigs. NY: Greenwillow, 1979. 1st ed. Anita Lobel (illus). 10 1/4 x 8 1/4. 30pp. Pict bds. Fine in dj. *Cattermole.* $25/£16

LOBENSTINE, WILLIAM C. Extracts from the Diary of William C. Lobenstine December 31, 1851-1858. Privately Ptd, 1920. Cl backstrip. Howes L410. *Ginsberg.* $150/£96

LOBO, JEROME. A Voyage to Abyssinia. Samuel Johnson (trans). London: Elliot & Kay, 1789. 2nd ed. Tall 8vo. Endleaves, all edges marbled. 19th cent 3/4 black calf, marbled sides, gilt/blind dec spine w/tan morocco title label. Nice. *Book Block.* $575/£369

LOCKE, E. W. Three Years in Camp and Hospital. Boston, 1870. 1st ed. 408pp. VG. *Fye.* $225/£144

LOCKE, JOHN. An Abridgment of Mr. Locke's Essay Concerning Human Understanding. Boston: Ptd by Manning & Loring, 1794. 1st Amer ed. 250pp (foxed, browned). Old calf (very worn, cvrs nearly loose). Sound. *M & S.* $375/£240

LOCKE, JOHN. The Conduct of the Understanding.... London: Sherwood (et al), 1812. New ed. Port. Contemp 3/4 calf, bds. VG (eps lt foxed; corners rubbed). *Reese.* $40/£26

LOCKE, JOHN. An Essay Concerning Human Understanding with Thoughts on the Conduct of the Understanding. London, 1795. 3 vols. Contemp sprinkled calf (rubbed; sig). *Argosy.* $150/£96

LOCKE, JOHN. An Essay Concerning Human Understanding. London, 1721. 8th ed. 2 vols. 372; 340pp + index (ink inscrips, feps defective), port. Old panelled calf (spines poor; hinges broken). *King.* $150/£96

LOCKE, JOHN. An Essay Concerning Human Understanding. NY: Seaman, 1824. New ed. 2 vols in 1. Lg fldg table (tape repair; sig, sl foxed). Mod cl. *Agvent.* $60/£38

LOCKE, JOHN. An Essay Concerning Humane Understanding, in Four Books. London: Awnsham & Churchill, 1695. 3rd ed. (Lacks port, title leaf frayed, torn, repaired w/loss; stained, soiled.) Old calf (neatly rebacked). *Oinonen*.* $275/£176

LOCKE, JOHN. Letters Concerning Toleration. London: A. Millar et al, 1765. (Prelims corners lt dampstained, margin notes.) New 3/4 dk brn morocco, marbled bds, leather spine label, raised bands. *Sadlon.* $375/£240

LOCKE, JOHN. The Works. London, 1722. 2nd ed. 3 vols. Port, plt. (Bkpl.) Contemp paneled calf (scuffed, joints stressed), spines gilt. *Freeman*.* $420/£269

LOCKE, WILLIAM J. The Beloved Vagabond. London: John Lane, Bodley Head, 1922. 1st illus ed. Jean Dulac (illus). 16 color plts. (1/2-title browned, sl creased; spotted.) Pict cl. *Hollett.* $23/£15

LOCKE, WILLIAM J. Perella. NY: Dodd, Mead, 1926. 1st Amer ed. Fine (ink note c. pg) in VG dj (price-clipped). *Antic Hay.* $20/£13

LOCKET, G. H. et al. British Spiders. London: Ray Soc, 1951-53-74. 1st ed. 3 vols. Color frontis, 612 maps. VG in djs. *Hollett.* $78/£50

LOCKETT, H. C. Along the Beale Trail. Windowrock, AZ: US Office of Indian Affairs, 1939. NF in brn heavy wraps. *Five Quail.* $30/£19

LOCKHART, J. G. The Life of Napoleon Bounaparte. London: Bickers, 1891. Full grn calf, ribbed gilt-dec spine, gilt dentelles, gilt-lettered red morocco spine label. *D & D.* $190/£122

LOCKHART, J. G. Memoirs of the Life of Sir Walter Scott. Edinburgh/London: Robert Cadell/John Murray, 1837-38. 1st ed. 7 vols. Port (foxed), fldg plt, errata slip; 1/2-titles bound in. 3/4 contemp vellum, marbled bds, gilt morocco labels. (Spine gilt rubbed, lt soiled), o/w VG set. *Reese.* $100/£64

LOCKLEY, FRED. Across the Plains by Prairie Schooner. Personal Narrative of B. F. Bonney.... Eugene, (n.d.). VG in stitched ptd wrappers. *Reese.* $30/£19

LOCKLEY, FRED. To Oregon by Ox-Team in '47. Portland: The Author, n.d. 16pp. (Lt dampstain margin), else Good in wrappers (lt soiled, sunned). *Brown.* $25/£16

LOCKLEY, FRED. To Oregon by Ox-Team in '47. The Story of the Coming of the Hunt Family.... Portland, (n.d.). VG in ptd wrappers. *Reese.* $25/£16

LOCKLEY, R. M. The Island Farmers. London: Witherby, 1946. 1st ed. Signed. Dj. *Hollett.* $31/£20

LOCKLEY, R. M. Letters from Skokholm. London: Dent, 1947. 1st ed. (Feps spotted.) *Hollett.* $23/£15

LOCKRIDGE, FRANCES and RICHARD. The Norths Meet Murder. NY: Stokes, 1940. 1st ed, 1st bk. NF. *Else Fine.* $45/£29

LOCKRIDGE, FRANCES and RICHARD. A Pinch of Poison. NY: Stokes, 1941. 1st ed. NF. *Else Fine.* $25/£16

LOCKRIDGE, FRANCES and RICHARD (eds). Crime for Two. Phila: Lippincott, 1955. 1st ed. Fine in NF dj (lt edgewear, 2 sm chips). *Janus.* $30/£19

LOCKRIDGE, ROSS F. A. Lincoln. NY, 1931. 1st ed. Pict cvr. Fine. *Pratt.* $17/£11

LOCKWOOD, FRANK C. The Life of Edward E. Ayer. Chicago: A.C. McClurg, 1929. 1st ed. Frontis port. Teg. Fine in orig box (worn, soiled). *Wantagh.* $75/£48

LOCKWOOD, FRANK C. Pioneer Days in Arizona from Spanish Occupation to Statehood. NY, 1932. 1st ed. VG in Good dj. Howes L417. *Turpen.* $90/£58

LOCKWOOD, FRANK C. With Padre Kino on the Trail. Tucson, 1934. 1st ed. Pb. NF. *Turpen.* $65/£42

LOCKWOOD, FRANK C. and DONALD W. PAGE. Tucson, the Old Pueblo. Phoenix, 1930. 1st ed. VG. *Turpen.* $45/£29

LOCKWOOD, JOHN H. Westfield and Its Historic Influences 1669-1917. The Author, (1922). 1st ed. Teg. (Spine sl lightened, rubbed.) *Sadlon.* $75/£48

LOCKWOOD, LUKE VINCENT. Colonial Furniture in America. NY: Scribner, 1926. 3rd ed. 2 vols. Maroon cl. Good in djs (chipped, lt soiled). *Karmiole.* $125/£80

LOCKYER, J. NORMAN. Contributions to Solar Physics. London: Macmillan, 1874. Color litho frontis, 676pp. (Cvr, backstrip worn, edge fr cvr faded), o/w Clean. *Bookcell.* $100/£64

LOCKYER, T. M. and W. L. Life and Work of Sir Norman Lockyer. London: Macmillan, 1928. 1st ed. Frontis port, 16 plts. VG. *Glaser.* $60/£38

Locomotives and Locomotive Building. (A Reproduction of Rogers Locomotive and Machine Works Illustrated Catalogue, 1886.) Berkeley: Howell-North Books, 1963. #319/1250. Brn cl, gilt. Fine. *Harrington.* $85/£54

LODGE, DAVID. How Far Can You Go? London, 1980. 1st Eng ed. Fine in dj. *Clearwater.* $47/£30

LODGE, G. E. Memoirs of an Artist Naturalist. London, 1946. 24 plts (16 color). (Cl badly stained.) *Maggs.* $45/£29

LODGE, G. E. Memoirs of an Artist Naturalist. London, 1946. 24 plts (16 color). Fine in dj. *Wheldon & Wesley.* $250/£160

LODGE, G. E. Memoirs of an Artist Naturalist. London: Gurney & Jackson, 1946. 1st ed. 24 plts (16 color). (Sl cvr stains), else VG. *Mikesh.* $137/£88

LODGE, G. E. Memoirs of an Artist Naturalist. London: Gurney & Jackson, 1946. 24 plts (10 color). Teg. VG. *Hollett.* $187/£120

LODGE, HENRY CABOT. Life and Letters of George Cabot. Boston, 1877. 1st ed. (11),615pp. Howes L421. *Ginsberg.* $125/£80

LODGE, O. J. Signalling Through Space Without Wires. (1900.) (Spine sl discolored), o/w VG. *Whitehart.* $70/£45

LODGE, R. B. Bird Hunting Through Wild Europe. NY: Appleton, 1909. 1st ed. Teg. Dec cl. VG+ (ex-lib). *Mikesh.* $37/£24

LOEB, JACQUES. The Dynamics of Living Matter. 1906. 1st ed. Lib cl. (Ex-lib, 1 sm stamp tp), o/w VG. *Whitehart.* $62/£40

LOEB, JACQUES. The Mechanistic Conception of Life: Biological Essays. Chicago: Univ of Chicago, (1912). Presentation copy. Brn straight-grained cl (few snags). VG. *Gach.* $150/£96

LOEHR, MAX. Chinese Bronze Age Weapons. Ann Arbor, (1956). Folio. Mylar dj (chipped). *Swann*.* $57/£37

LOEWINSON-LESSING, F. Tables for the Determination of the Rock-Forming Minerals. J.W. Gregory (trans). 1893. 55pp. fldg table. (Fep discolored; cl sl mkd), o/w VG. *Whitehart.* $23/£15

LOEWY, RAYMOND. Industrial Design. Woodstock, NY: Overlook Press, (1979). 1st ed. Red cl. Good in dj. *Karmiole.* $50/£32

LOFTIE, W. J. A Plea for Art in the House. London: Macmillan, 1877. 2nd ed. xi,100,(ii)pp. (Sl rubbed, mkd.) *Hollett.* $39/£25

LOFTING, HUGH. Doctor Dolittle's Caravan. NY: Frederick A. Stokes, (1926). 1st Amer ed. Pict cl, color plt mtd fr cvr. VG. *New Hampshire*.* $45/£29

LOFTING, HUGH. Doctor Doolittle's Post Office. NY, (1923). 1st ed. 8x5. 359pp (pencil inscrip). Cl w/color label. (Heavily soiled, rubbed, bumped.) *King*. $25/£16

LOFTING, HUGH. The Story of Dr. Dolittle. NY: Frederick Stokes, 1920. 1st ed, 1st bk. Fine in dj (1/4-inch chip spine head, 2-inch chip spine foot). *Captain's Bookshelf*. $600/£385

LOFTING, HUGH. The Twilight of Magic. NY: Stokes, 1930. 1st ed. Lois Lenski (illus). 5 1/2 x 8. 303pp. VG. *Cattermole*. $60/£38

LOGAN, DEBORAH. Memoir of Dr. George Logan of Stenton.... Phila, 1899. One of 250. 6 illus, tissue guards. VG. *Argosy*. $65/£42

LOGAN, RAYFORD WHITTINGHAM. The Negro and the Post-War World. Washington: Minorities Publishers, 1945. 1st ed. Gilt lettering. VG. *Petrilla*. $35/£22

LOHF, KENNETH A. (comp). The Collection of Books, Manuscripts, and Autograph Letters in the Library of Jean and Donald Stralem. NY, 1962. Frontis. Cream buckram, gilt spine. Fine in glassine dj. *Heller*. $35/£22

LOHNIS, F. Studies Upon the Life Cycles of the Bacteria. Part I. Washington, 1921. 1st ed. (Ex-lib.) *Fye*. $125/£80

LOKKE, CARL L. Klondike Saga.... Minneapolis: Norwegian-American Hist Assoc, (1965). 1st ed. 3 maps. Blue-grn cl. Fine in dj. *Argonaut*. $35/£22

LOMAX, JOHN. Songs of the Cattle Trail and Cow Camp. NY: Macmillan, 1931. Ltr ptg. VG in Good dj (chipped). *Archer*. $22/£14

LONDON, JACK. The Abysmal Brute. NY, 1913. 1st ed, 1st issue. *Swann**. $230/£147

LONDON, JACK. The Abysmal Brute. NY: Century, 1913. 1st ed. Frontis. Olive-grn cl stamped in black/yellow. (Fr hinge starting), else VG in VG dj (chipped, rubbed, tear, tape to verso). BAL 11945. *Pacific**. $288/£185

LONDON, JACK. The Acorn-Planter. NY: Macmillan, 1916. 1st ed, 1st issue. Teg. BAL Binding A: maroon cl, white cl spine. Spine imprint reads 'The\Macmillan\Company.' (Cvr lettering sl rubbed), else NF. BAL 11964. *Pacific**. $1,380/£885

LONDON, JACK. Adventure. NY: Macmillan, 1911. 1st Amer ed. Dk blue cl, pict cvr. (Rubbed, bumped), else VG. BAL 11928. *Pacific**. $184/£118

LONDON, JACK. Before Adam. Macmillan, 1907. 1st ed. NF (sl lean). *Certo*. $125/£80

LONDON, JACK. Before Adam. NY, 1907. 1st ed. Pict cl. (Ink inscrip; cvrs sl rubbed, spine dknd.) *King*. $50/£32

LONDON, JACK. Before Adam. NY: Macmillan, 1907. 1st ed. Brn pict cl. Fine. *Appelfeld*. $125/£80

LONDON, JACK. Before Adam. NY: Macmillan, 1907. 1st ed. Cream pict cl. (Eps offset), o/w Fine. BAL 11903. *Macdonnell*. $125/£80

LONDON, JACK. Before Adam. NY: Macmillan, 1907. 1st ed. Color frontis, 7 color plts, 2-pg inserted map. Lt brn buckram, lettered in red/white; cvr illus of footprints in dk brn. (Offset feps from jacket flaps) else NF in Fair dj (heavily chipped, torn, lacks pieces, fr panel detached; extremely fragile). BAL 11903. *Pacific**. $1,093/£701

LONDON, JACK. Burning Daylight. NY: Macmillan, 1910. 1st ed. Macmillan spine imprint, 3 blank ll at rear, p. (366) blank. 8 plts. Blue cl, illus cvr. (Sl shelfworn, bumped), else VG. *Pacific**. $104/£67

LONDON, JACK. The Call of the Wild. London: Heinemann, 1903. 1st British ed. Color frontis. Gilt-lettered blue/white pict cl. (Lt offset fep; sl rubbed), else VG. *Pacific**. $58/£37

LONDON, JACK. The Call of the Wild. NY, 1903. 1st ed. Pub's pict cl (lt rubbed; sig). *Swann**. $373/£239

LONDON, JACK. The Call of the Wild. NY: Macmillan, 1903. Sm ad pamphlet advertising this and other Macmillan titles laid in. (Sm name, lt corner bump), else NF (pub's name spine lt rubbed, paint for white snow on fr cvr lt rubbed). *Between The Covers*. $750/£481

LONDON, JACK. The Call of the Wild. NY: Macmillan, 1903. 1st ed. Color frontis. Philip R. Godwin and Charles Livingston Bull (illus). Teg. Vertically ribbed grn cl, gilt-lettered, pict stamped in white/black/grn/red. (Sm bump spine head), else NF in dj (spine head sl chipped, upper corners rubbed), later chemise, slipcase. BAL 11876. *Pacific**. $8,050/£5,160

LONDON, JACK. Children of the Frost. NY: Macmillan, 1902. 1st ed. Frontis, 7 plts. Blue-gray wove cl. (Spine sl sunned), else Fine. BAL 11873. *Pacific**. $316/£203

LONDON, JACK. The Cruise of the Snark. NY: Macmillan, 1911. 1st ed. (Pastedown sl soiled, pp loose, tp margins discolored, few scratches, edgeworn.) *Metropolitan**. $40/£26

LONDON, JACK. The Cruise of the Snark. NY: Macmillan, 1911. 1st ed. Color frontis. Teg. Blue-grn cl, gilt, pict cvr label. Fine. BAL 11929. *Pacific**. $460/£295

LONDON, JACK. Dutch Courage and Other Stories. NY: Macmillan, 1922. 1st ed. Frontis port, 7 plts. Red cl, gilt spine. Fine. BAL 11985. *Pacific**. $460/£295

LONDON, JACK. Dutch Courage and Other Stories. NY: Macmillan, 1922. 1st ed. Frontis port, 7 plts. Red cl, gilt spine. NF in VG dj (chipped, corners lack sm pieces, fr flap oddly clipped, soiled, 3/4-inch tear fr panel). BAL 11985. *Pacific**. $1,610/£1,032

LONDON, JACK. The Faith of Men and Other Stories. NY: Macmillan, 1904. 1st ed. Teg. Lt blue illus cl, gilt spine. Fine. BAL 11878. *Pacific**. $403/£258

LONDON, JACK. The Faith of Men. NY: Macmillan, 1904. 1st ed. Lt blue pict cl, gilt. VG. BAL 11878. *Macdonnell*. $150/£96

LONDON, JACK. The Game. London: Heinemann, 1905. 1st Eng ed. Pict blue cl, gilt. Fine. BAL 11886. *Macdonnell*. $100/£64

LONDON, JACK. The God of His Fathers and Other Stories. NY: McClure, Phillips, 1901. 1st ed. Blue cl, gilt. (Name; sl rubbed), else VG. BAL 11870. *Pacific**. $518/£332

LONDON, JACK. Hearts of Three. NY: Macmillan, 1920. 1st ed. Maroon cl, gilt. VG. BAL 11982. *Macdonnell*. $225/£144

LONDON, JACK. The House of Pride and Other Tales of Hawaii. NY: Macmillan, 1912. 1st ed. Frontis. Lt grn illus cl. Fine. BAL 11936. *Pacific**. $403/£258

LONDON, JACK. The Human Drift. NY: Macmillan, 1917. 1st ed. Frontis port. Variant binding: dk red cl, spine lettered in black. (Spine sl dull), else VG. BAL 11972. *Pacific**. $345/£221

LONDON, JACK. The Iron Heel. NY: Macmillan, 1908. 1st ed. Dk blue cl, gilt. (Fr hinge cracking; rubbed, sm bumps), else VG. BAL 11908. *Pacific**. $69/£44

LONDON, JACK. Jack London Reports. NY: Doubleday, 1970. 1st ed. Fine in dj. *Hermitage*. $75/£48

LONDON, JACK. John Barleycorn or Alcoholic Memoirs. Mills & Boon, 1914. 1st Eng ed. Frontis port. Good (spine bumped, cvrs sl warped; fore-edge spotted). BAL 11946. *Tiger*. $41/£26

LONDON, JACK. John Barleycorn. Macmillan, 1913. 1st ed. VG (spine gilt dulled, head torn). *Certo*. $65/£42

LONDON, JACK. John Barleycorn. NY: Century, 1913. 1st ed, 1st ptg w/last gathering in 6 instead of 8. Blackish-grn cl, gilt. NF (inscrip). BAL 11946. *Macdonnell.* $100/£64

LONDON, JACK. Letters from Jack London. NY: Odyssey, (1965). 1st ed. Fine in dj (lt soiled). *Hermitage.* $75/£48

LONDON, JACK. The Letters of Jack London. Earle Labor et al (eds). Stanford Univ, 1988. 1st ed. 3 vols. NF in djs. *Pacific*.* $345/£221

LONDON, JACK. The Little Lady of the Big House. NY: Macmillan, 1916. 1st ed. Color frontis. Blue cl Illus in black/cream/orange; lettered in cream/gilt. Fine in VG dj (spine head chipped, sm tears, soil). BAL 11966. *Pacific*.* $1,840/£1,179

LONDON, JACK. Lost Face. NY: Macmillan, 1910. 1st ed. Frontis, 5 plts. Dk blue cl. (Spine ends shelfworn), else Fine. BAL 11915. *Pacific*.* $173/£111

LONDON, JACK. Love of Life and Other Stories. NY: Macmillan, 1907. 1st ed. Blue cl, gilt, yellow rule border. (Sl bumped, ends lt rubbed), else NF. BAL 11904. *Pacific*.* $316/£203

LONDON, JACK. Martin Eden. NY: Macmillan, 1909. 1st ed. Blue dec cl (soiled), gilt. Good (inscrip). BAL 11912. *Macdonnell.* $100/£64

LONDON, JACK. Michael, Brother of Jerry. NY: Daily Worker, 1917. Blue cl (sl rubbed, sl bumped). *Metropolitan*.* $86/£55

LONDON, JACK. Michael, Brother of Jerry. NY: Macmillan, 1917. 1st ed. VG + (contemp sig, address, date) in cl-cvrd bds (lt shelfworn). *Lame Duck.* $150/£96

LONDON, JACK. Moon-Face and Other Stories. NY: Macmillan, 1906. 1st ed. Blue dec cl. VF (spine lettering sl flaked). BAL 10895. *Macdonnell.* $175/£112

LONDON, JACK. Moon-Face and Other Stories. NY: Macmillan, 1906. 1st ed. Teg. Blue cl, lettered in cream. Cvr, spine illus in cream, lt grn, gilt. Initials R.R in center of dec on fr cvr in lt grn, not cream, as noted by Sisson & Martens. (Spine ends sl bumped), else VG in dj (rubbed, sl chipped; spine, extrems faded). *Pacific*.* $4,888/£3,133

LONDON, JACK. The Night Born. NY: Century, 1913. 1st ed, 1st ptg, w/1 blank leaf at rear. Color frontis. Gray-blue dec cl. (Spine ends lt shelfworn), else NF. BAL 11942. *Pacific*.* $196/£126

LONDON, JACK. On the Makaloa Mat. NY: Macmillan, 1919. 1st ed. Grn-blue cl lettered in yellow, cvr illus in dk blue/yellow; spine illus in dk blue. NF in VG dj (spine ends, corners chipped, foot esp so; foot lacks sm piece, spine dknd; soiled, 1.25-inch tear fr flap crease, sm tears; flap tips clipped, still w/vol). BAL 11981. *Pacific*.* $2,300/£1,474

LONDON, JACK. The People of the Abyss. NY: Macmillan, 1903. 1st ed. Blue-gray cl stamped in black/gold. Very Nice (ink name fep; spine sl skewed, overall dulling, sl stain fr bd). *Hermitage.* $750/£481

LONDON, JACK. The Red One. NY: Macmillan, 1918. 1st ed. Frontis port. Dec brn bds. (Spine ends sl rubbed), else VG. *Pacific*.* $748/£479

LONDON, JACK. Revolution and Other Essays. NY: Macmillan, 1910. 1st ed. Maroon cl, gilt. Spine imprint: The Macmillan / Company, title & London's name on fr cvr. VG (fr hinge cracked; spine foot rubbed). BAL 11916. *Pacific*.* $431/£276

LONDON, JACK. Revolution. Chicago: Charles H. Kerr, (1909). 1st ed, later issue w/well-known 'Publisher's Note to the Hundredth-thousand.' Orig pict cream wrappers, stapled as issued. NF. BAL 11913. *Macdonnell.* $225/£144

LONDON, JACK. The Road. NY: Macmillan, 1907. 1st ed. Frontis, 47 photo plts. Teg. Lt gray cl, gilt. (Spine head lt rubbed), else Fine. BAL 11906. *Pacific*.* $345/£221

LONDON, JACK. The Scarlet Plague. NY: Macmillan, 1915. 1st ed. Frontis. Plum red cl dec in orange/yellow, lettered in orange fr cvr, gilt on spine and dj. (Spine head sl sunned), else VG in dj (1.5-inch tear fr flap crease, spine ends chipped). BAL 11960. *Pacific*.* $4,025/£2,580

LONDON, JACK. The Scarlet Plague. Macmillan, 1916. 1st ed. VG + (spine sl faded, rt cvr edge sl rubbed). *Certo.* $200/£128

LONDON, JACK. Scorn of Women, in Three Acts. NY: Macmillan, 1906. 1st ed, later issue. Teg. Maroon cl, white cl spine (soiled), fr cvr lettered in white, spine in black. Spine reads: Macmillan. VG. BAL 11898. *Pacific*.* $920/£590

LONDON, JACK. The Sea-Wolf. William Heinemann, 1904. 1st Eng ed. Pict cl (recased). Good (new eps, spotted). BAL 11882. *Tiger.* $94/£60

LONDON, JACK. The Sea-Wolf. NY: Macmillan, 1904. 1st ed. Frontis, 5 plts. Teg. Illus blue cl, white lettering. No priority of issue firmly established between bindings w/gilt-lettered spines and those lettered in white. (Spine ends rubbed), else VG. BAL 11882. *Pacific*.* $288/£185

LONDON, JACK. The Sea-Wolf. Hartford: LEC, 1960. One of 1500 ptd by The Connecticut Printers. Signed by Fletcher Martin (illus). Silk-screened linen. Fine in slipcase. *Pacific*.* $52/£33

LONDON, JACK. Smoke Bellew. NY: Century, 1912. 1st ed. Blue-gray cl pict dec in black/cream. Fine (address label rear pastedown; sl bumped). *Sumner & Stillman.* $250/£160

LONDON, JACK. Smoke Bellew. NY: Century, 1912. 1st ed. 8 plts. Illus blue-gray cl lettered in black. (Spine head lt rubbed), else NF. BAL 11939. *Pacific*.* $259/£166

LONDON, JACK. Smoke Bellew. NY: Century, 1912. 1st ed. Blue-gray cl stamped in black/gray/yellow. (Lt rubbed), o/w Fine. *Hermitage.* $300/£192

LONDON, JACK. A Son of the Sun. GC: Doubleday, Page, 1912. 1st ed. Frontis, 3 plts. Navy blue cl lettered in gray. (Spine ends rubbed, sm tear), else VG. BAL 11937. *Pacific*.* $219/£140

LONDON, JACK. The Son of the Wolf. Boston: Houghton, Mifflin, 1900. 1st ed, 1st bk. Blanck's 1st ptg, w/8 prelim ll, but no terminal blank. In earliest binding: grey cl, stamped in silver; inserted fly at end, w/spine imprint in the form Houghton/Mifflin & Co. VG (sl soiled, rubbed; sm tear fr joint). BAL 11869. *Waverly*.* $308/£197

LONDON, JACK. The Son of the Wolf: Tales of the Far North. Boston: Houghton, Mifflin, 1900. 1st ed, 1st ptg, 1st bk. Frontis. Gray cl stamped in silver. 1st issue binding w/no dots flanking ampersand in pub's name on spine. (Silver lt tarnished), o/w NF. BAL 11869. *Pacific*.* $748/£479

LONDON, JACK. The Star Rover. NY: Macmillan, 1915. 1st ed. Color frontis. Pict lt blue cl (sl rubbed, lt worn). Good (lt shaken, 1 leaf detached, partly torn). BAL 11963. *Baltimore*.* $75/£48

LONDON, JACK. The Star Rover. NY: Macmillan, 1915. 1st Amer ed. Color frontis. Sky blue cl, gilt. Fine. BAL 11963. *Pacific*.* $431/£276

LONDON, JACK. The Strength of the Strong. NY: Macmillan, 1914. 1st ed. Frontis. Blue cl lettered in white; gilt-stamped design fr cvr, spine. (Spine ends sl worn), else NF in VG dj (spine ends, corners chipped; sm tear, crease bottom fr panel, top rear panel). BAL 11955. *Pacific*.* $2,070/£1,327

LONDON, JACK. Tales of the Fish Patrol. NY: Macmillan, 1905. 1st ed. Map, 7 plts. Teg. Illus blue cl lettered in pale grn fr cvr, gilt spine. VF. BAL 11887. *Pacific**. $431/£276

LONDON, JACK. Tales of the Fish Patrol. London: Heinemann, 1906. 1st Eng ed. Blue pict cl, gilt. Fine. BAL 11887. *Macdonnell*. $100/£64

LONDON, JACK. Theft: A Play in Four Acts. NY: Macmillan, 1910. 1st ed, 1st issue, w/1 blank leaf in rear. Teg. Maroon cl, white cl spine, fr cvr lettered in white, spine in black. (Spine soiled, lower fr cvr smudged; fr cvr lettering nearly worn off, sl bleeding from maroon to rear joint, rear cvr sl faded), else VG. BAL 11919. *Pacific**. $920/£590

LONDON, JACK. The Turtles of Tasman. NY: Macmillan, 1916. 1st ed. Illus mauve cl lettered in yellow fr cvr, gilt on spine. BAL notes 7 ad pp, counting title-leaf pp as ads. (Fr cvr design lt rubbed), else NF. BAL 11968. *Pacific**. $288/£185

LONDON, JACK. The Valley of the Moon. London: Mills & Boon, (1914). 1st Eng ed. Grn cl, gilt. VF. BAL 11947. *Macdonnell*. $125/£80

LONDON, JACK. The Valley of the Moon. London: Mills & Boon, (1914). 1st Eng ed. Ad cat at rear lists London books as late as The Little Lady of the Big House (1916). 32pp undated ads. Blue cl lettered in black. VG (eps sl cracked, 1 leaf corner repaired, sm sticker removed tp). *Sumner & Stillman*. $125/£80

LONDON, JACK. The Valley of the Moon. NY: Macmillan, 1913. 1st ed. Color frontis. Illus orange cl lettered in cream fr cvr, gilt on spine. (1914 inscrip; spine ends lt rubbed), else NF. BAL 11947. *Pacific**. $518/£332

LONDON, JACK. The Valley of the Moon. London: Mills & Boon, 1914. 1st ed. (Lt browned; joints cracked, spine sl faded.) *Hollett*. $31/£20

LONDON, JACK. War of the Classes. NY: Macmillan, 1905. 1st ed. Maroon cl, gilt-stamped spine. Fine. BAL 11885. *Pacific**. $374/£240

LONDON, JACK. War of the Classes. NY: Macmillan, 1905. 1st ed. One of 2530. Maroon cl. NF (lt cvr mks, gilt sl rubbed). *Sumner & Stillman*. $395/£253

LONDON, JACK. War of the Classes. NY: Macmillan, 1905. 1st ed. (Lt foxed throughout), o/w Very Nice. *Hermitage*. $450/£288

LONDON, JACK. What Life Means to Me. Girard, KS: Haldeman-Julius, n.d. 1st Haldeman-Julius ed. Ptd blue-gray wrappers. (Edges sl dusty), else Nice. *Turtle Island*. $15/£10

LONDON, JACK. When God Laughs and Other Stories. NY: Macmillan, 1911. 1st ed. Frontis, 5 plts. Olive grn cl dec in red/lt grn, gilt-lettered. (Spine ends sl worn), else VG in VG dj (spine ends, corners chipped; sm piece lacking from head; right side fr panel lacks sm piece; sm tear upper rear panel, spine sl sunned). BAL 11926. *Pacific**. $3,738/£2,396

LONDON, JACK. White Fang. NY: Macmillan, 1906. 1st ed, 2nd issue, w/tipped-in tp. Frontis, 7 color plts. Illus blue-grn cl lettered in white fr cvr, gilt on spine. (Spine ends lt rubbed), else NF. BAL 11896. *Pacific**. $98/£63

LONG, E. B. The Saints and the Union, Utah Territory During the Civil War. Urbana: Univ of IL, (1981). 1st ed. Blue cl. Fine in dj. *Argonaut*. $45/£29

LONG, E. B. with BARBARA LONG. The Civil War Day by Day, an Almanac 1861-1865. NY, 1971. 1st ed. Fine in dj (lt worn). *Pratt*. $35/£22

LONG, ESMOND. A History of Pathology. Balt, 1928. 1st ed. VG. *Fye*. $125/£80

LONG, ESMOND. Selected Readings in Pathology from Hippocrates to Virchow. Springfield, 1929. 1st ed. (Ex-lib.) *Fye*. $80/£51

LONG, ESMOND. Selected Readings in Pathology from Hippocrates to Virchow. Springfield, 1929. 1st ed. VG. *Doctor's Library*. $125/£80

LONG, FRANK BELKNAP. The Horror from the Hills. Arkham House, 1963. Issue w/o copyright notice tipped in. VG in VG + dj. *Certo*. $50/£32

LONG, FRANK BELKNAP. The Horror from the Hills. Sauk City, WI, 1963. 1st ed, state w/copyright cancel sticker affixed to back of tp. Fine in Fine dj. *Mcclintock*. $125/£80

LONG, FRANK BELKNAP. The Hounds of Tindalos. Sauk City: Arkham, 1946. 1st ed. VG (shelfworn) in dj (browned, worn). *Metropolitan**. $51/£33

LONG, FRANK BELKNAP. The Rim of the Unknown. Sauk City: Arkham House, 1972. 1st ed. VF in dj. *Bromer*. $50/£32

LONG, GEORGE. English Inns and Road Houses. London, 1937. 1st ed. Color frontis, 136 plts. *Edwards*. $75/£48

LONG, HANIEL. Pinon Country. NY, 1941. 1st ed. Grn cl. (Cvrs sl spotted), else Good + . *Five Quail*. $15/£10

LONG, HANIEL. Pittsburgh Memoranda. Santa Fe: Writers' Editions, (1935). One of 1000 numbered, signed. Black buckram, silver stamping. Fine in Fine dj. *Dermont*. $125/£80

LONG, JOHN. Describing the Manners and Customs of the North American Indians. Cleveland: Clark, 1904. 1st ed. Facs, fldg map. Teg. Maroon cl. Good. Howes L443. *Karmiole*. $85/£54

LONG, JOHN. Voyages and Travels of an Indian Interpreter and Trader.... London, 1791. 1st ed. 4to. Engr fldg map. Contemp tree calf (fr joint cracked but cords holding), orig leather spine label. Bklabel of George Montagu. Howes L443. *Swann**. $1,495/£958

LONG, JOHN. Voyages and Travels of an Indian Interpreter and Trader.... London: The Author, 1791. 1st ed. Fitzwilliam copy w/the Earl's bkpl. Fldg map (offset), sub's list, errata leaf. Contemp full polished calf (extrems sl rubbed; eps foxed), leather spine label. Attractive. Howes L443. *Sadlon*. $2,000/£1,282

LONG, JOSEPH W. American Wild-Fowl Shooting. NY: Ford, 1874. 1st ed. (Sl worn, sl spotted, sm tear spine head.) *Oinonen**. $100/£64

LONG, JOSEPH W. American Wild-Fowl Shooting. NY: J.B. Ford, 1874. 1st ed. 285pp + ads. Grn cl, gilt. Good. *Biscotti*. $80/£51

LONG, MARGARET. The Shadow of the Arrow. Caldwell: Caxton, 1950. 2nd ed. Frontis, 24 full-pg illus, 5 maps. Pict cl in dj. *Dawson*. $30/£19

LONG, STEPHEN H. Voyage in a Six-Oared Skiff to the Falls of Saint Anthony in 1817. Phila, 1860. 1st ed. 87,(1)pp; map. Leather label. Howes L445. *Ginsberg*. $175/£112

LONG, STEPHEN H. and EDWIN JAMES. Account of an Expedition from Pittsburgh to the Rocky Mountains Under the Command of Major Stephen H. Long.... Barre, MA: Imprint Soc, 1972. Boxed. Howes J41. *Ginsberg*. $75/£48

LONG, W. G. Asses vs. Jackasses. Portland: Touchstone, 1969. 1st ed. Pict cl. VG + . *Mikesh*. $22/£14

LONGACRES, EDWARD G. From Union Stars to Top Hat. Harrisburg, (1972). 1st ed. (Cvr sl worn), o/w Fine in Fine dj. *Pratt*. $45/£29

Longfellow Collector's Handbook. (By Beverly Chew.) NY: William E. Benjamin, 1885. 1st ed. One of 250. Uncut. Orig parchment-backed bds. Nice (lt dust, rubbed). BAL VI, p367. *Macdonnell*. $100/£64

LONGFELLOW, HENRY WADSWORTH (ed). The Estray. Boston: William D. Ticknor, 1847. 1st ed. One of 1150. Glazed yellow bds, paper label. (Joints rubbed, spine ends worn.) BAL 12088. *Macdonnell*. $225/£144

LONGFELLOW, HENRY WADSWORTH. Aftermath. Routledge, 1873. 1st Eng ed. 154pp + 6pp pub's cat. Grn cl (sl worn), gilt. Sound. Cox. $23/£15

LONGFELLOW, HENRY WADSWORTH. The Courtship of Miles Standish and Other Poems. W. Kent (Late D. Bogue), 1858. 1st Eng ed. Wood engr frontis, xii,227pp + 40pp inserted pub's cat dated Jan 1858, suggesting that this might pre-date Boston ed of same year. Uncut. Good in orig cl (backstrip sl faded) blocked in blind/gold. Cox. $70/£45

LONGFELLOW, HENRY WADSWORTH. The Courtship of Miles Standish and Other Poems. Boston: Ticknor & Fields, 1858. 1st ed, 1st ptg. Ad slip. Brn cl, gilt. VG (rubbed). BAL 12122. Macdonnell. $125/£80

LONGFELLOW, HENRY WADSWORTH. Evangeline. Indianapolis, (1905). 5 full-pg color plts by Howard Chandler Christy. Dec cl (worn, loose). King. $35/£22

LONGFELLOW, HENRY WADSWORTH. Hiawatha. NY: Philomel Books, 1988. 1st ed. Keith Moseley (illus). 10.5x7.5. 6 pop-ups. Pict glazed bds. VG. King. $22/£14

LONGFELLOW, HENRY WADSWORTH. The Song of Hiawatha. Boston: Ticknor & Fields, 1855. 1st Amer ed, 1st ptg, w/points as noted by BAL 12112, w/o letter 'n' in 'one,' p279. Inscribed presentation. Ads at end dated November. (Few corners creased, sl soiling, browning.) Pub's cl (shelfworn, sl shaken, spine tips sl chipped). Oinonen*. $2,100/£1,346

LONGFELLOW, HENRY WADSWORTH. The Song of Hiawatha. Boston, 1891. 1st ed thus. One of 250. Port, 22 plts by Frederic Remington. Full gilt-pict vellum (sl dust-soiled). BAL 12720. Kane*. $300/£192

LONGFELLOW, HENRY WADSWORTH. Tales of a Wayside Inn. Boston, 1863. 1st issue, w/all points. 225pp + ads. Teg. Blind/gilt-stamped grn cl (bkpl). Bright in full grn morocco solander case (scuffed). Truepenny. $350/£224

LONGFELLOW, HENRY WADSWORTH. Tales of a Wayside Inn. Boston, 1864. 2nd ed. VF. Bond. $100/£64

LONGFELLOW, HENRY WADSWORTH. Three Books of Song. Boston: James R. Osgood, 1872. 1st ed. Terra cotta cl, gilt. Fine. BAL 12159. Macdonnell. $45/£29

LONGFELLOW, HENRY WADSWORTH. The Works of.... Boston/NY: Houghton Mifflin, 1888. Riverside ed. 11 vols. 3/4 leather, marbled paper bds (sl rubbed, few heads bumped). Metropolitan*. $230/£147

LONGFIELD, CYNTHIA. The Dragonflies of the British Isles. London: Wayside & Woodland, 1937. 1st ed. (Sl used.) Maggs. $28/£18

LONGHI, ROBERTO. Piero della Francesca. Leonard Penlock (trans). London/NY, 1930. Good. Washton. $65/£42

LONGHURST, HENRY. The Borneo Story. London, 1956. 1st ed. Frontis port. Dj (sl rubbed, faded). Edwards. $23/£15

LONGHURST, M. H. English Ivories. London: Putnam, 1926. 1st ed. 56 plts. (Fr hinge crack), o/w Good. Scribe's Perch*. $28/£18

LONGINOS MARTINEZ, JOSE. Journal of...Notes and Observations...1791-92. Leslie B. Simpson (trans). SF, 1961. 2nd ed. One of 1000. 3 fldg maps. Fine. Turpen. $85/£54

LONGMAN, E. D. and S. LOCH. Pins and Pincushions. London: Longmans, Green, 1911. 1st ed. 43 plts. (Lt foxing; cl sl rubbed, faded.) Hollett. $101/£65

LONGSTREET, HELEN D. Lee and Longstreet at High Tide: Gettysburg in the Light of the Official Records. Gainesville, GA: The Author, 1905. 2nd ed. (Spine faded, browned.) Howes L450. Ginsberg. $75/£48

LONGSTREET, JAMES. From Manassas to Appomattox.... Dallas: Dallas Publishing, 1896. 1st ed. 22,13-690pp. (Sl wear spine extrems), else VG. Howes L451. Mcgowan. $450/£288

LONGUS. Daphnis and Chloe. London, 1925. John Austen (illus). 4to. Uncut. Gilt-stamped white cl (lt worn). Oinonen*. $20/£13

LONGWELL, C. and E. S. DANA. Walks and Rides in Central Connecticut and Massachusetts. Tuttle, Taylor, 1932. VG. Bookcell. $35/£22

LONGWELL, DENNIS. Steichen: The Master Prints 1895-1914. NY: MOMA, 1978. 1st ed. 73 plts, 6 color. Fine in dj (price-clipped). Cahan. $100/£64

LONGWORTH, PHILIP. The Cossacks. Constable, 1969. Frontis, 6 maps. Fine (lacks dj), cased. Peter Taylor. $34/£22

LOOKER, S. J. The Nature Diaries and Note-Books of Richard Jefferies, Etc. Essex: Grey Walls, 1941. 1st ed. NF. Mikesh. $47/£30

Looking-Glass for the Mind; or, Intellectual Mirror. Being An Elegant Collection.... London: J. Crowder, 1794. 12mo. (6),271pp; 74 woodcut vignettes by John Bewick. 19th cent 3/4 red morocco, marbled bds. (Extrems lt rubbed), else Fine. Bromer. $350/£224

LOOMIS, ALFRED L. Lessons in Physical Diagnosis. NY, 1890. 240pp. Brn cl bds (sl worn). VG. Doctor's Library. $65/£42

LOOMIS, ANDREW. Drawing the Head and Hands. NY, (1960). 3rd ptg. (Fore-edge stained), else Good in dj (beat-up). King. $45/£29

LOOMIS, ANDREW. Figure Drawing for All Its Worth. NY, 1944. 4th ptg. (Ink name; cvrs spotted, frayed.) King. $45/£29

LOOMIS, B. F. Pictorial History of the Lassen Volcano. Anderson: Privately Pub, 1926. 1st ed. Fldg map. Pict cl. VG+. Mikesh. $25/£16

LOOMIS, CHAUNCEY. Weird and Tragic Shores. NY, 1971. Map. (Sl stain blank ep), else VG in dj. High Latitude. $20/£13

LOOMIS, HEZEKIAH. Journal of Hezekiah Loomis, Steward on the U.S. Brig 'Vixen,' Captain John Smith, U.S.N. War with Tripoli, 1804. Louis F. Middlebrook (ed). Salem, MA: Essex Inst, 1928. 1st ed. Ptd paper label. Ginsberg. $75/£48

LOOMIS, LEANDER V. Journal of the Birmingham Emigrating Company. Edgar M. Ledyard (ed). SLC, 1928. One of 1000. Fldg map. NF in dj (dknd, lt chipped). Howes L464. Bohling. $85/£54

LOOMIS, NOEL M. The Texan Santa Fe Pioneers. Norman, 1958. 1st ed. Fine in Fine dj. Turpen. $40/£26

LOOS, ANITA and JOHN EMERSON. Breaking into the Movies. Phila: Jacobs, (1921). 1st ed. Red cl. VG. Houle. $225/£144

LOOS, ANITA. But—Gentlemen Marry Brunettes. Leipzig: Tauchnitz, 1929. 1st ed. VG in wrappers (sm stain). Patterson. $23/£15

LOPEZ-REY, JOSE. A Cycle of Goya's Drawings. London, 1956. (Shelf-rubbed.) Washton. $35/£22

LOPEZ-REY, JOSE. Velazquez. A Catalogue Raisonne of His Oeuvre. London, 1963. Good in dj. Washton. $145/£93

LORAC, E. C. R. Dishonour Among Thieves. London: CCC, 1959. 1st ed. (Name), o/w VG in dj (short closed tears). Mordida. $50/£32

LORAC, E. C. R. Fell Murder. London: CCC, 1944. 1st ed. VG in dj (spine dknd, chipped, closed tears). Mordida. $45/£29

LORAC, E. C. R. People Will Talk. GC: DCC, 1958. 1st Amer ed. (Lg stamp fep), o/w Fine in dj. Mordida. $30/£19

LORAND, SANDOR. Technique of Psychoanalytic Therapy. NY: International Universities, (1946). 1st ed. Inscribed. Pebbled blue cl. VG. *Gach.* $45/£29

LORANT, STEFAN (ed). The New World: The First Pictures of America Made by John White and Jacques Lemoyne.... NY: Duell, Sloan & Pearce, (1946). 1st ed. VG in dj (sl worn). *Lien.* $40/£26

LORCA, FEDERICO GARCIA. See GARCIA LORCA, FEDERICO

Lord Bateman. NY: McLoughlin Bros, n.d. Uncle Frank's Series. 12mo. 4 leaves (sl foxed); 8 color illus. VG in pict paper wraps. *Blue Mountain.* $45/£29

LORD, ALBERT B. (ed). Russian Folk Tales. NY: LEC, 1970. #330/1500 signed by Teje Etchemendy (illus). Fine in pub's slipcase. *Hermitage.* $85/£54

LORD, ELIOT. Comstock Mining and Miners. Washington: US Geological Survey, 1883. xiv,451pp; 3 maps (2 fldg). (4-inch tear 1 map.) Brn cl bds (fr hinge starting, binding sl worn, soiled), leather spine, tips. *Dawson.* $125/£80

LORD, FRANCIS ALFRED. Uniforms of the Civil War. South Brunswick, NJ: Thomas Yoseloff, (1970). 1st ed. NF in NF dj. *Mcgowan.* $45/£29

LORD, GARLAND. Murder's Little Helper. GC: DCC, 1941. 1st ed. (Eps dknd, name), o/w VG in dj (spine faded). *Mordida.* $45/£29

LORD, JACK and JENN SHAW. Where to Sin in San Francisco. (SF: Richard F. Guggenheim), 1939. 1st ed. (Name inner cvr). VG in stiff pict wrappers, spiral bound. *Argonaut.* $35/£22

LORD, JOHN P. The Maine Townsman, or Laws for the Regulation of Towns.... Boston: Ptd by White, Lewis & Potter, 1844. Contemp sheep (few defects). *Boswell.* $150/£96

LORD, JOSEPH and HENRY. A Defense of Dr. Charles T. Jackson's Claims to the Discovery of Ether. Boston, 1848. 1st separate ed. 37pp. (Ex-lib; water-stained.) Wrappers (rear wrapper detached). *Fye.* $350/£224

LORD, MARY N. Mary Milton or the Conquests of Grace. Claremont, NH, 1876. Frontis port, viii,236pp. VG (sl etching, lt foxing). *Bohling.* $18/£12

LORDE, AUDRE. Coal. NY: Norton, (1976). 1st ed. Signed. Fine in Fine dj. *Lenz.* $45/£29

LORDE, AUDRE. The First Cities. NY: Poet's Press, 1968. 1st ed, 1st bk. NF in illus stapled wraps. *Lame Duck.* $125/£80

LORE, JOHN M. An Atlas of Head and Neck Surgery. Phila, 1962. VG (extrems lt worn). *Doctor's Library.* $125/£80

LORENZ, D. E. The New Mediterranean Traveller. NY/London/Chicago/et al: Revell, 1925. 11th rev ed. (Sl rubbed, ex-lib), o/w VG. *Worldwide.* $16/£10

LORIMER, GEORGE HORACE. The False Gods. NY: D. Appleton, 1906. 1st ed. Pict cvr. Nice. *Metropolitan*.* $40/£26

LORIMER, H. L. Homer and the Monuments. London: Macmillan, 1950. 1st ed. 32 plts. Blue cl. Good in dj (soiled). *Karmiole.* $65/£42

LORIMER, JAMES. The Institutes of Law, A Treatise of the Principles of Jurisprudence.... Edinburgh: T&T Clark, 1872. Red cl (rubbed). Sound. *Boswell.* $250/£160

LORING, ROSAMOND B. Decorated Book Papers, Being an Account of Their Designs and Fashions. Cambridge: CUP, 1952. 2nd ed. 16 plts. Black cl. Fine in dj. *House.* $50/£32

LORREQUER, HARRY (ed). Arthur O'Leary: His Wanderings.... (By Charles Lever.) Henry Colburn, 1844. 1st ed. 3 vols. 10 plts (some sl foxed) by George Cruikshank. (Lacks 1/2-titles in vols 2, 3, final errata leaf vol 3.) 1/2 dk grn morocco gilt, gilt panelled backs, teg. *Hatchwell.* $250/£160

LOSSING, B. J. Pictorial Field Book of the Revolution. NY: Harper, 1855. 2nd ed. 2 vols. Color frontis. Brn cl (sl worn). Howes L477. *Glenn.* $120/£77

LOTHROP, S. K. et al. Pre-Columbian Art. NY, 1957. Folio. Bd slipcase. *Swann*.* $287/£184

LOTHROP, S. K. Treasures of Ancient America. Geneva: Skira, 1964. 1st US ed. 145 tipped-in illus (85 are color plts), map. NF in illus dj. *Cahan.* $125/£80

LOTT, MILTON. The Last Hunt. London: Collins, (1955). 1st British ed. Fine in VG+ dj. *Authors Of West.* $20/£13

LOUBAT, ALPHONSE. The American Vine-Dressers Guide. NY: Appleton, 1872. New, revised ed. 123pp. Grn cl (sl dust-soiled). Very Nice. *Second Life.* $75/£48

LOUD, GORDON. The Megiddo Ivories. Chicago: Univ of Chicago, (1939). Folio. 63 plts. (Corner bumped.) *Archaeologia.* $750/£481

LOUDON, J. C. An Encyclopaedia of Gardening. London: Longman et al, (1834). New ed. xl,1270,ipp (bkpl, lower joint cracked). Orig cl-backed marbled bds (worn, bumped), spine label. *Hollett.* $218/£140

LOUDON, J. C. An Encyclopaedia of Gardening. London: Longman, Brown, 1859. 3 vols. Contemp 3/4 brn morocco, marbled bds, raised bands. *Appelfeld.* $250/£160

LOUDON, J. C. An Encyclopaedia of Gardening. Mrs. Loudon (ed). London, 1878. New ed. xl,1278pp (perforated stamp tp, ink stamps, sm tear tp, ex-lib; rebound, spine #). *Edwards.* $70/£45

LOUDON, J. C. The Suburban Gardener, and Villa Companion.... London: Longman, 1838. Thick 8vo. (Tp),xvi,752pp. Grn blind-stamped cl (faded). *Marlborough.* $562/£360

LOUGHEED, VICTOR. Vehicles of the Air. Chicago: Reilly & Britton, 1910. 2nd ed. Dec cvr. Good- (ex-lib). *Scribe's Perch*.* $60/£38

LOUGHEED, VICTOR. Vehicles of the Air. Chicago: Reilly & Britton, 1910. 2nd rev, enlgd ed. Gilt decs. VG (spine #s). *Glaser.* $100/£64

LOUIS, JOE. How to Box. Phila: David McKay, 1948. 1st ed. Gray bds, blue title fr cvr. Fine in dj (sl torn). *Cummins.* $100/£64

LOUIS, JOE. The Joe Louis Story. NY: Grosset & Dunlap, (1953). Rpt ed w/Fine wrap around band. Fine in dj. *Between The Covers.* $45/£29

LOUIS, P. C. A. Anatomical, Pathological and Therapeutic Researches.... Henry I. Bowditch (trans). Boston: Isaac R. Butts/Hilliard, Gray, 1836. 1st ed in English. 2 vols. xxiii,395; xi,462pp (lt foxing). Orig emb cl (extrems sl worn). VG set. *Glaser.* $385/£247

LOURIE, RICHARD (ed). The Soldier and Tsar in the Forest. NY: FSG, 1972. 1st ed. Url Shulevitz (illus). 10 1/4 x 10. 32pp. Good in dj. *Cattermole.* $15/£10

LOUSLEY, J. E. Wild Flowers of Chalk and Limestone. London, 1950. 20 maps. Fine in dj. *Brooks.* $29/£19

LOUYS, PIERRE. Aphrodite. Privately ptd, 1926. Ltd to 650 numbered. 8 full-pg plts. Teg; 3/4 blue leather, gilt-stamped spine. (Text spotting; inner hinges loose; sl worn), else attractive. *King.* $125/£80

LOUYS, PIERRE. Aphrodite. N.p., 1926. #22/600. Teg. Orig 3/4 red morocco, marbled bds (edges scuffed), gilt, raised bands. *Freeman*.* $60/£38

Love Letters of Henry VIII. Herrin, IL, 1936. Ltd to 138 signed by Violet & Hal Trovillion. White paper-backed orange bds, paper title label. Very Nice. *Cady.* $25/£16

Love Letters to the Beatles. London, 1964. 1st ed. Illus bds. VG in dj (creased, sl torn). *Words Etc.* $19/£12

LOVE, JAMES KERR. Deaf Mutism. Glasgow, 1896. 1st ed. xii,(iv),369pp (feps lt browned), 2 plts (1 fldg). *Edwards.* $86/£55

LOVECRAFT, H. P. Collected Poems. Sauk City: Arkham House, (1963). 1st ed. Dj. *Swann**. $80/£51

LOVECRAFT, H. P. Collected Poems. Sauk City, 1963. 1st ed. Fine in Fine dj (spine sl discolored). *Mcclintock*. $195/£125

LOVECRAFT, H. P. Dagon and Other Macabre Tales. Sauk City: Arkham House, 1965. 1st ed, 2nd ptg. VF in illus dj. *Bromer*. $65/£42

LOVECRAFT, H. P. The Dark Brotherhood and Other Pieces. Sauk City: Arkham House, 1966. 1st ed. One of 3500. VF in VF dj. *Kane**. $100/£64

LOVECRAFT, H. P. et al. The Dark Brotherhood and Other Pieces. Sauk City: Arkham House, 1966. 1st ed. Dj. *Swann**. $115/£74

LOVECRAFT, H. P. The Dark Brotherhood and Other Pieces. Sauk City: Arkham House, 1966. 1st ed. Black cl. Fine (bkpl) in dj. *House*. $130/£83

LOVECRAFT, H. P. The Haunter of the Dark and Other Tales of Terror. London: Gollancz, 1951. 1st ed. VG in dj (spine head chipped). *Hadley*. $106/£68

LOVECRAFT, H. P. The Horror in the Museum and Other Revisions. Sauk City: Arkham House, 1970. 1st ed. VF in dj. *Bromer*. $65/£42

LOVECRAFT, H. P. Marginalia. Sauk City: Arkham House, 1944. One of 2035. Fine in Fine dj. *Else Fine*. $450/£288

LOVECRAFT, H. P. The Outsider and Others. Sauk City: Arkham House, 1939. 1st ed. One of 1268. 8vo. Black cl, gilt. VG in dj (back cvr lt soiled). *House*. $2,200/£1,410

LOVECRAFT, H. P. Selected Letters 1911-1924. Sauk City, 1965. 1st ed. Fine in Fine dj. *Mcclintock*. $50/£32

LOVECRAFT, H. P. Selected Letters 1911-1937. Sauk City: Arkham House, 1965-76. 1st eds. 5 vols. Djs. *Swann**. $258/£165

LOVECRAFT, H. P. Selected Letters 1929-1931. Sauk City, 1971. 1st ed. Fine in Fine dj. *Mcclintock*. $200/£128

LOVECRAFT, H. P. Selected Letters. Volume I. Arkham House, 1965. 1st ed. VG+ in dj (soiled, spine ends chipped). *Certo*. $35/£22

LOVECRAFT, H. P. Selected Letters. Volume II. Arkham House, 1968. 1st ed. VG+ in dj (soiled). *Certo*. $25/£16

LOVECRAFT, H. P. The Shuttered Room and Other Pieces. Sauk City: Arkham, 1959. 1st ed. Fine in dj (edges sl sunned, soiled, extrems sl bruised). *Metropolitan**. $126/£81

LOVECRAFT, H. P. Something About Cats and Other Pieces. Sauk City: 1949. 1st ed. NF (cl finger mkd) in dj (sl frayed, sm tears spine ends). *Certo*. $125/£80

LOVECRAFT, H. P. Tales of the Cthulhu Mythos. Arkham House, 1969. 1st ed. NF in dj (rear panel sl soiled). *Certo*. $55/£35

LOVECRAFT, H. P. Three Tales of Horror. Sauk City: Arkham House, (1967). 1st ed. Dj. *Swann**. $149/£96

LOVECRAFT, H. P. Three Tales of Horror. (Sauk City, 1967.) 1st ed thus. One of 1500. Fine in Fine dj (few smudges). *Mcclintock*. $245/£157

LOVECRAFT, H. P. and AUGUST DERLETH. The Survivor and Others. Sauk City, WI, 1957. 1st ed. Fine. Dj spine dknd else Fine. *Mcclintock*. $95/£61

LOVECRAFT, H. P. and AUGUST DERLETH. The Survivor and Others. Sauk City: Arkham House, 1957. 1st ed. NF in dj (spine browning). *Other Worlds*. $125/£80

LOVECRAFT, H. P. and AUGUST DERLETH. The Watchers Out of Time and Others. Arkham House, 1974. 1st ed. Fine in NF dj (rear sl dusty, sm nicks). *Certo*. $35/£22

LOVEJOY, J. C. Memoir of Rev. Charles T. Torrey, Who Died in the Penitentiary of Maryland.... Boston: J.P. Jewett, 1847. viii,364pp (foxing; waterstains 1st 15 pp); port. Orig dk cl (worn, faded). Howes L 522. *Cullen*. $225/£144

LOVEJOY, J. C. and OWEN. Memoir of the Rev. Elijah P. Lovejoy...Who Was Murdered...Nov. 7, 1837. NY, 1838. Pub's cl (lacks backstrip). Howes L522. *Swann**. $115/£74

LOVELAND, CYRUS C. California Trail Herd. Richard H. Dillon (ed). Los Gatos: Talisman, 1961. 1st ed. One of 750. Frontis photo, facs. Red cl, paper spine label. VF in dj (spine dknd). *Argonaut*. $90/£58

LOVELL, ROBERT. Sive Panzoologicomineralogia. Oxford: Hall for Godwin, 1661. 1st ed. 2 parts in 1 vol. (48)leaves, 519pp, (1)leaf, 152pp (soiled, stained, marginal worming, early penned notes, underscoring, adhesion on title verso, new eps). Contemp calf (rebacked). *Oinonen**. $450/£288

LOVESEY, PETER. Abracadaver. London: Macmillan, 1972. 1st UK ed. VG in dj. *Williams*. $86/£55

LOVESEY, PETER. The Detective Wore Silk Drawers. Macmillan, 1971. 1st UK ed. VG in dj (sl browned, price-clipped). *Williams*. $56/£36

LOVESEY, PETER. Invitation to a Dynamite Party. London: Macmillan, 1974. 1st ed. Fine in dj. *Mordida*. $75/£48

LOVESEY, PETER. Invitation to a Dynamite Party. London: Macmillan, 1974. 1st UK ed. NF in dj. *Williams*. $75/£48

LOVESEY, PETER. Keystone. London: Macmillan, 1983. 1st ed. Fine in Fine dj. *Janus*. $45/£29

LOVESEY, PETER. Keystone. London: Macmillan, 1983. 1st ed. Inscribed. VF in dj. *Mordida*. $45/£29

LOVESEY, PETER. Rough Cider. London: Bodley Head, 1986. 1st UK ed. Fine in dj. *Williams*. $23/£15

LOVESEY, PETER. Swing, Swing Together. London: Macmillan, 1976. 1st UK ed. VG (pp sl browned). *Williams*. $78/£50

LOVESEY, PETER. Wobble to Death. London: Macmillan, 1970. 1st ed. (Pp dknd), o/w Fine in dj (sl wear). *Mordida*. $100/£64

LOVET-LORSKI, BORIS. Tribute to Woman. NY: Barnes, (1965). (Rubs, stains to bds.) *Metropolitan**. $69/£44

LOW, DAVID. Low's Autobiography. NY: S&S, 1957. 1st ed. Fine in dj. *Hermitage*. $35/£22

LOW, DAVID. With All Faults. Tehran: Amate Press, 1973. Inscribed presentation. Dj. *Rostenberg & Stern*. $25/£16

LOW, DAVID. Years of Wrath. A Cartoon History 1932-1945. Victor Gollancz, 1949. 1st ed. Good. *Cox*. $31/£20

LOW, NATHANIEL. An Astronomical Diary: Almanack, for the Year of Christian Aera 1797.... Boston, 1797. 12 leaves. Sewed wraps (very worn, cvrs frayed). *King*. $40/£26

LOWE, E. J. Ferns: British and Exotic. London, 1857-62. 8 vols. 479 color plts. Pict cl, gilt. (Sm # stamped on eps, label removed, lt foxed), o/w Good. *Henly*. $343/£220

LOWE, E. J. A Natural History of British Grasses. London: Groombridge, 1862. 2nd ed. 245pp (lt foxed); 74 woodcut plts, guards. Blind-stamped cl (spine sl faded), gilt. VG. *Hollett*. $133/£85

LOWE, E. J. A Natural History of New and Rare Ferns. London, 1865. 192pp; 72 color plts. Marbled edgepapers. Grn 1/2 leather, marbled bds, ribbed spine. (Gilt title faded, name tp), else Good. *Price*. $250/£160

LOWE, E. J. Our Native Ferns. London, 1867. 2 vols. vii,348; vii,492pp; 79 color plts. (New eps; bindings sl soiled, worn.) *Henly*. $94/£60

LOWE, P. R. A Naturalist on Desert Islands. London, 1911. Map. (1 plt loose; spine faded.) *Maggs.* $56/£36

LOWELL, G. Smaller Italian Villas and Farm-houses...and More Smaller Villas and Farmhouses. NY: Architectural Bk, 1922/20. 43x32. 2 vols. 125; 140 plts. (Cl sl worn.) Internally VG. *Ars Artis.* $546/£350

LOWELL, GUY. American Gardens. Boston: Bates & Guild, 1902. 112 photo plts. Teg, uncut. Dec cl (dulled, lt scuffed). Good (fr hinge cracked). *Quest.* $215/£138

LOWELL, JAMES RUSSELL. Anti-Slavery Papers of James Russell Lowell. Boston: Houghton Mifflin, 1902. 1st ed. One of 525 numbered. 2 vols. Dk grey bds, paper spine labels (sl dknd; spine heads sl rubbed), else Fine. *Captain's Bookshelf.* $150/£96

LOWELL, JAMES RUSSELL. Latest Literary Essays and Addresses of James Russell Lowell. Boston, 1892. 1st Amer ed. Teg. Fine (spine lt sunned, cvrs sl soiled). BAL 13223. *Polyanthos.* $30/£19

LOWELL, MARIA. The Poems of Maria Lowell. Cambridge: Riverside Press, 1907. #279/330. Frontis port. Gray paper bds, ptd paper spine label, extra spine label at rear. (Bkpl, bk label fep), o/w VF. *Heller.* $300/£192

LOWELL, ROBERT. Collected Prose. Robert Giroux (ed). NY, 1987. 1st Amer ed. Fine (blind stamp) in NF dj. *Polyanthos.* $30/£19

LOWELL, ROBERT. Day by Day. NY: FSG, (1977). 1st ed. Fine in dj. *Jaffe.* $40/£26

LOWELL, ROBERT. For the Union Dead. NY: Farrar, (1964). 1st ed. NF in dj (price-clipped, nick). *Reese.* $35/£22

LOWELL, ROBERT. For the Union Dead. NY: FSG, (1964). 1st ed. Grn cl. Fine in dj (sl edgeworn, dust-soiled). *Jaffe.* $35/£22

LOWELL, ROBERT. History. NY: FSG, (1973). 1st ed. Fine in dj. *Jaffe.* $50/£32

LOWELL, ROBERT. Life Studies. NY: Farrar, Straus & Cudahy, (1959). 1st Amer ed. Fine in dj (sl rubbed). *Jaffe.* $100/£64

LOWELL, ROBERT. Life Studies. London, 1959. 1st ed. Fine in dj (spine sunned, few sm edge chips, sm edge tear, price-clipped). *Polyanthos.* $95/£61

LOWELL, ROBERT. Life Studies. NY, 1959. 1st ed. VG in Good dj (chipped). *Bond.* $40/£26

LOWELL, ROBERT. Life Studies. NY: Farrar, Straus & Cudahy, 1959. 1st ed. VG + (top pg edges dknd) in VG dj (1-inch tear fr cvr; fr flap, verso lt foxed). *Lame Duck.* $75/£48

LOWELL, ROBERT. Lord Weary's Castle. NY: Harcourt Brace, (1946). 1st ed. Black cl. (Lt offsetting eps), o/w Fine in dj (rubbed, spine head chipped, internal tape mends). *Jaffe.* $150/£96

LOWELL, ROBERT. Lord Weary's Castle. NY: Harcourt, Brace, (1946). 1st ed. Fine in dj (2 sm edge tears). *Dermont.* $250/£160

LOWELL, ROBERT. Lord Weary's Castle. NY: Harcourt Brace, 1946. 1st ed. NF in VG dj (1-inch edgetear fr panel, spine foot tear). *Lame Duck.* $250/£160

LOWELL, ROBERT. The Mills of the Kavanaughs. NY: Harcourt, Brace, (1951). 1st ed. Black cl. Fine in dj (sl rubbed, ends worn). *Jaffe.* $100/£64

LOWELL, ROBERT. Near the Ocean. NY: FSG, (1967). 1st ed. Black cl. Fine in dj (sunned). *Jaffe.* $40/£26

LOWELL, ROBERT. Notebook 1967-68. NY: FSG, (1969). 1st ed. Fine in dj. *Jaffe.* $75/£48

LOWELL, ROBERT. The Old Glory. NY: FSG, (1965). 1st ed. Black cl. Fine in dj. *Jaffe.* $50/£32

LOWELL, ROBERT. Phaedra. London: Faber & Faber, (1963). 1st Eng ed. Grn cl. Mint in dj. *Jaffe.* $65/£42

LOWELL, ROBERT. The Voyage and Other Versions of Poems by Baudelaire. Faber & Faber, 1968. 1st ed thus. 8 color, 16 monochrome plts. Good (inscrip) in buckram, dj (sl soiled, sm piece torn from rear). *Cox.* $39/£25

LOWENFELS, WALTER (ed). In a Time of Revolution: Poems from Our Third World. NY: Random House, (1969). 1st ed. Cl-backed bds. VG in pict dj. *Petrilla.* $65/£42

LOWER, MARK A. English Surnames. John Russell Smith, 1849. 3rd ed. 2 vols. xxiv,264; vi,243pp + 12pp pub's cat. Uncut. Good set in orig blind-stamped cl (sm splits hinges). *Cox.* $39/£25

LOWER, MARK A. English Surnames. London: John Russell Smith, 1849. 2nd ed. 2 vols. Full textured leather, gilt spines. (Rubbed), o/w VG. *New Hampshire*.* $40/£26

LOWERY, WOODBURY. A Descriptive List of Maps of the Spanish Possessions. Philip Lee Phillips (ed). Washington: GPO, 1912. Port. (Cvrs badly stained affecting 1st few pp.) *King.* $195/£125

LOWERY, WOODBURY. The Spanish Settlements Within the Present Limits of US, Florida 1562-74, with Maps. NY, 1905. 1st ed. Frontis port, fldg map. (2 sm dampstains spine), o/w VG. Howes L536. *Turpen.* $125/£80

LOWMAN, ALBERT T. Printing Arts in Texas. (Austin): Roger Beacham, (1975). One of 395 signed. Pub's prospectus laid in. Cl, ptd labels. Fine. *Bohling.* $200/£128

LOWMAN, ALBERT T. Printing Arts in Texas. Austin, (1981). Rpt of 1975 1st ed. Fine in Fine dj. *Turpen.* $45/£29

LOWMAN, ALBERT T. Printing Arts in Texas. (Austin): Roger Beacham, 1975. One of 395 ptd. Fine. *Gibbs.* $175/£112

LOWNDES, I. A Modern Greek and English Lexicon.... Corfu: The Author, 1837. 1st ed. (3)leaves, lxvii,(1),671pp (lib mks). Uncut. Orig bds (shelfworn, cvr detached), paper spine label. *Oinonen*.* $325/£208

LOWNDES, WILLIAM THOMAS. The Bibliographer's Manual of English Literature.... London: Bell & Daldy, 1869. 6 vols. Teg. 3/4 morocco, marbled bds (extrems sl rubbed), spines gilt extra. VG. *Reese.* $400/£256

LOWRIE, WALTER. Art in the Early Church. NY, 1947. 150 plts. Good. *Washton.* $40/£26

LOWRY, MALCOLM. Dark as the Grave Wherein My Friend Is Laid. (NY): NAL, (1968). 1st Amer ed. Fine in dj (sl wear). *Antic Hay.* $25/£16

LOWRY, MALCOLM. Lunar Caustic. Earle Birney and Margerie Lowry (eds). London: Jonathan Cape, (1968). 1st ed. Mint in wrappers, dj. *Jaffe.* $50/£32

LOWRY, MALCOLM. October Ferry to Gabriola. NY: World, (1970). 1st Amer ed. Fine in dj (lamination wrinkled). *Antic Hay.* $25/£16

LOWRY, MALCOLM. The Selected Letters. Harvey Breit and Margerie Lowry (eds). London, 1967. 1st Eng ed. Fine in dj. *Clearwater.* $55/£35

LOWRY, MALCOLM. The Selected Letters. Harvey Breit and Margerie Lowry (eds). London: Jonathan Cape, 1967. 1st ed. One of 1500. Photo frontis. NF in dj (price-clipped). *Turtle Island.* $100/£64

LOWRY, MALCOLM. Ultramarine. Phila: Lippincott, (1962). 1st Amer ed. NF (edge lt bumped) in dj (sl worn). *Antic Hay.* $125/£80

LOWRY, MALCOLM. Ultramarine. Toronto: Clarke, Irwin, (1963). 1st Canadian ed. Fine in dj. *Dermont.* $60/£38

LOWRY, MALCOLM. Under the Volcano. NY: Reynal & Hitchcock, (1947). 1st ed. Tan cl, crimson lettering. (Ink sig; sl rubbed, dusty.) Dj (sl worn, dusty, sl chipped). Baltimore*. $90/£58

LOWRY, MALCOLM. Under the Volcano. NY: Reynal & Hitchcock, (1947). 1st ed. Fine (bkpl) in dj (lt rubbed, spine extrems sl chipped). Captain's Bookshelf. $500/£321

LOWRY, ROBERT JAMES. The Prince of Pride Starring. Cincinnati: Nat'l Genius Bks, 1959. 1st ed. One of 1000. Signed. Fine in ptd stiff wrappers. Cahan. $35/£22

LOWTH, ROBERT. The Life of William of Wykeham, Bishop of Winchester. A. Millar/R&J Dodsley, 1759. 2nd ed. Engr frontis, xxxiv,357, livpp; plt, fldg engr genealogical tree. Orig calf (rebacked, orig eps preserved). Bickersteth. $94/£60

LOWTHER, G. and W. WORTHINGTON (eds). The Encyclopedia of Practical Horticulture. North Yakima, 1914. 3 vols. 6 color plts. 1/2 black leather, grn linen. VG. Brooks. $185/£119

LOWTHER, WINIFRED E. The Old Beach Road. San Antonio: Naylor, 1973. 1st ed. Fine. Gibbs. $20/£13

LUBBOCK, BASIL. The Arctic Whalers. Glasgow: Brown et al, 1937. 1st ed. Fldg plan. VG. Dj (tattered) laid-in. High Latitude. $85/£54

LUBBOCK, BASIL. The Last of the Windjammers. Glasgow: Brown, Son & Ferguson, 1954. 4th imp. 2 vols. Blue cl, gilt. VG in djs (lt worn). Parmer. $150/£96

LUBBOCK, BASIL. The Log of the 'Cutty Sark.' Glasgow, 1924. 1st ed. Good (fr hinge loose, spine worn, sl stained). King. $45/£29

LUBSCHEZ, BEN JUDAH. Manhattan: The Magical Island. NY: Press of the Amer Inst of Architects, 1927. 1st ed. Tipped-in photo frontis. Teg. Gilt-titled black cl. VG (pencil name). Cahan. $375/£240

LUCAS, A. Ancient Egyptian Materials and Industries. London: Edward Arnold, 1926. 1st ed. Inscribed presentation. Good. Archaeologia. $95/£61

LUCAS, A. Ancient Egyptian Materials. NY: Longmans, Green, 1926. 1st ed. Inscribed. (Spine sl chipped, paper spine label removed.) Archaeologia. $75/£48

LUCAS, E. V. (ed). The Book of the Queen's Dolls' House Library. Methuen, 1924. 1st Eng ed. Ltd to 1500. 2 vols. 24 plts, 8 color. Partly unopened. 3/4 blue paper over bds, gilt linen spine, white label. Sotheby's*. $287/£184

LUCAS, E. V. A Group of Londoners. Minneapolis: Privately ptd, 1913. 1st ed. Titled bds, cl spine. Fine. Black Sun. $100/£64

LUCAS, E. V. John Constable the Painter. London: Halton & Truscott Smith, 1924. 1st ed. Teg. Good (cl sl soiled). Reese. $50/£32

LUCAS, E. V. Luck of the Year. Doran, 1923. 1st ed. VG + in VG dj (sl worn, torn). Aronovitz. $35/£22

LUCAS, F. L. (trans). The Homeric Hymn to Aphrodite. (London): Golden Cockerel, 1948. One of 750 numbered. 10 engrs by Mark Severin. In 1 of 2 standard bindings for 'ordinary' copies, as opposed to the 100 lowest numbered 'special' copies which were bound in full goatskin. Untrimmed. White vellum, grn cl, gilt. (Sl rubbed.) Baltimore*. $100/£64

LUCAS, F. L. (trans). The Homeric Hymn to Aphrodite. (London): Golden Cockerel, 1948. 1st ed thus. #389/750. 10 engrs by Mark Severin. Teg, uncut. Gilt-stamped black morocco over terracotta cl. VG. Houle. $250/£160

LUCAS, F. L. (trans). The Homeric Hymn to Aphrodite. London: Golden Cockerel, 1948. One of 750. Parchment-backed grn bds, gilt Aphrodite fr cvr. Fine. Vandoros. $295/£189

LUCAS, GEORGE A. The Diary of.... Lilian M. C. Randall (ed). Princeton Univ, 1979. 2 vols. Djs. Edwards. $55/£35

LUCAS, KEITH. The Conduction of the Nervous Impulse.... E. D. Adrian (ed). London: Longmans, Green, 1917. 1st ed. Full-pg fig. Fine. Glaser. $300/£192

LUCAS, S. E. (ed). The Catalogue of Sassoon Chinese Ivories. London: Country Life, 1950. Ltd to 250. This unnumbered, unsigned. 3 vols. Teg. Contemp full vellum, gilt. Slipcases (worn). Christie's*. $789/£506

LUCAS, WALTER A. (comp). 100 Years of Railroad Cars. NY: Simmons-Boardman, (1958). Signed. VG + in dj. Bohling. $120/£77

LUCE, EDWARD S. Keogh, Comanche and Custer. (N.p., 1939.) Privately ptd in ltd signed ed. Howes L553. Ginsberg. $500/£321

LUCHETTI, CATHY and CAROL OLWELL. Women of the West. (St. George, UT): Antelope Island, 1982. 1st ed. Plum cl, silver lettering. Fine in NF dj. Harrington. $50/£32

LUCIA, ELLIS. Klondike Kate. NY: Hastings House, (1962). 1st ed. Signed presentation. VG in VG dj. Perier. $35/£22

LUCIA, ELLIS. The Saga of Ben Holladay. NY: Hastings House, (1959). 1st ed. Gold-stamped pink bds, beige cl spine. Dj. Dawson. $30/£19

LUCK, J. VERNON. Bone and Joint Diseases. Springfield, 1950. 1st ed. Red cl bds (sl worn). Good (paper clip mks in text, underlining). Doctor's Library. $50/£32

LUCKOCK, B. Jamaica: Enslaved and Free. George Peck (ed). NY: Lane, 1846. 1st Amer ed. (4),219pp. Orig cl. Ginsberg. $150/£96

LUCRETIUS. The Nature of Things. London: J. Rodwell, 1813. 1st ed. 2 vols in 1. Frontis port. 1/2 cl (worn). Argosy. $225/£144

LUDLUM, ROBERT. The Chancellor Manuscript. NY: Dial, 1977. 1st ed. Fine in dj. Mordida. $45/£29

LUDLUM, ROBERT. The Holcroft Covenant. NY: Richard Marek, (1978). 1st ed. Black cl. NF in ptd dj. Blue Mountain. $35/£22

LUDLUM, ROBERT. The Matarese Circle. London: Granada, 1979. 1st UK ed. VG in VG dj. Old London. $30/£19

LUDLUM, ROBERT. The Matlock Paper. NY, 1973. 1st ed. VG in VG dj. Smith. $15/£10

LUDLUM, ROBERT. The Osterman Weekend. London: Hart-Davis, 1972. 1st UK ed. Good (sl soil) in Good dj (worn). Old London. $40/£26

LUDLUM, ROBERT. The Osterman Weekend. NY, 1972. 1st ed. Fine in VG + acetate dj (tear). Smith. $25/£16

LUDLUM, ROBERT. The Scarlatti Inheritance. London, 1971. 1st Eng ed, 1st bk. Very Nice (spine sl creased) in dj (sl torn). Clearwater. $62/£40

LUDOLPHUS, JOB. A New History of Ethiopia. London: S. Smith, 1682. 1st ed. Fldg table, 8 copper engrs, incl 6 fldg (lacks fldg map; few leaves foxed, upper corner title supplied). Old calf bds (worn, stained; inner hinges mostly split), later calf spine. VG. Waverly*. $220/£141

LUDWIG, A. I. Graven Images: New England Stonecarving and Its Symbols 1650-1815. Middletown, CT: Wesleyan Univ, 1966. Stated 1st ed. 256 plts, 8 maps. Ptd photo paper over bds, linen spine. Good + in Good + slipcase. Scribe's Perch*. $42/£27

LUHAN, MABEL DODGE. Edge of the Taos Desert. NY: Harcourt, (1937). 1st ed. VG in dj (worn, inner flap defective). Reese. $35/£22

LUHAN, MABEL DODGE. European Experiences. NY: Harcourt, (1935). 1st ed. Frontis port. VG in dj (nicks). Houle. $75/£48

LUHAN, MABEL DODGE. Lorenzo in Taos. NY: Knopf, 1932. 1st ed, 1st bk. One of 2000 ptd. Orange cl, gilt. Fine in VG dj (lt chipped). *Macdonnell.* $200/£128

LUHAN, MABEL DODGE. Taos and Its Artists. NY: Duell, Sloan & Pearce, (1947). 1st ed, in preferred binding w/red eps. (Binding edges sl dust mkd), o/w VG in dj (soiled, rubbed, chips, internal mends). *Reese.* $200/£128

LUHAN, MABEL DODGE. Winter in Taos. NY: Harcourt, (1935). 1st ed, 1st state w/'Angel Adams' in list of illus, cutlines for his photographs. Ansel Adams (photos). Frontis. Sound (spine tanned). *Reese.* $30/£19

LUHAN, MABEL DODGE. Winter in Taos. NY: Harcourt, Brace, (1935). 1st ed. (Cl sl mottled, sl ink spot back panel), o/w VG (lacks dj). *Hermitage.* $85/£54

LUKE, PETER. Hadrian VII. NY: Knopf, 1969. 1st ed. Fine in dj (sm tear, price-clipped). *Antic Hay.* $20/£13

LULLIES, REINHARD. Greek Sculpture. NY: Abrams, (1957). 1st ed. 264 plts (8 color). Good in dj (tattered). *Archaeologia.* $85/£54

LUMHOLTZ, CARL. Unknown Mexico. A Record of Five Years' Exploration.... NY: Scribner, 1902. 1st ed. 2 vols. Frontispieces, 15 color plts, fldg map. (Sig.) Teg. Gilt cl (several corners sl bumped). *Archaeologia.* $350/£224

LUMLEY, BRIAN. Beneath the Moors. Arkham House, 1974. 1st ed. Fine in Fine dj. *Certo.* $45/£29

LUMLEY, BRIAN. Beneath the Moors. Sauk City: Arkham House, 1974. 1st ed. One of 4000. (Sl stain rear cvr), else NF in dj (sl wear, soil). *Antic Hay.* $20/£13

LUMLEY, BRIAN. Beneath the Moors. Sauk City: Arkham House, 1974. 1st ed. Fine in Fine dj. *Other Worlds.* $35/£22

LUMLEY, BRIAN. The Caller of the Black. Arkham House, 1971. 1st ed. NF (marginal creases few pp; fore edge bumped) in NF dj. *Certo.* $50/£32

LUMLEY, BRIAN. The Caller of the Black. Sauk City: Arkham House, 1971. 1st ed, 1st bk. VG+ in NF dj (sl browned). *Other Worlds.* $50/£32

LUMMER, O. Contributions to Photographic Optics. S. P. Thompson (trans). London/NY, 1900. (Ink sig.) *Whitehart.* $55/£35

LUMMIS, CHARLES F. Mesa, Canon and Pueblo. NY: Century, (1925). 1st ed. Fine in Fine dj. *Book Market.* $75/£48

LUMMIS, CHARLES F. Some Strange Corners of Our Country. Century, 1892. 1st ed. VG. *Authors Of West.* $50/£32

LUMMIS, CHARLES F. Some Strange Corners of Our Country. NY: Century, 1892. 1st ed. Frontis, xi,270pp. Gilt/color design cl, spine. (Lt rubbed), else VG. *Cahan.* $60/£38

LUMMIS, CHARLES F. The Spanish Pioneers. Chicago, 1918. 7th ed. VG. *Turpen.* $30/£19

LUNC, M. (ed). Space Crafts Systems. 1970. Vol 1 only. (Sticker removal fep, lib stamps), o/w VG. *Whitehart.* $39/£25

LUND, DORIS HEROLD. The Paint-Box Sea. NY: McGraw-Hill, 1973. 1st ed. Symeon Shimin (illus). 8 1/4 x 10 1/4. 32pp. Fine in dj. *Cattermole.* $20/£13

LUNDELL, CYRUS L. The Vegetation of Peten. Washington, DC, 1937. 39 plts incl 3 fldg maps rear pocket. (Lib bkpl, blind stamp; sm tear rear cvr.) Wrappers. *Brooks.* $65/£42

LUNDQUIST, F. (ed). Methods of Forensic Science. 1962-1965. 4 vols. (Sticker removal fep; lib sticker, stamp, #s; spine sl defective), o/w VG. *Whitehart.* $125/£80

LUNN, ARNOLD (ed). Oxford Mountaineering Essays. London, 1912. 1st ed. (Bkpl; cvrs sl worn.) *King.* $35/£22

LUNN, ARNOLD. Matterhorn Centenary. London, (1965). 1st ed. VG in dj (sl used). *King.* $35/£22

LUNN, ARNOLD. The Swiss and Their Mountains. London, (1963). 1st ed. (Sl bumped), else VG in dj (torn, soiled). *King.* $35/£22

LURIA, ALEKSANDR ROMANOVICH. Higher Cortical Functions in Man. NY: Basic Books, 1966. 1st ed in English. Fine in dj. *Glaser.* $75/£48

LURIE, ALISON. Real People. London: Heinemann, 1970. 1st UK ed. NF in dj (sl rubbed). *Moorhouse.* $23/£15

LURIE, E. Louis Agassiz: A Life in Science. Chicago: Univ of Chicago, 1960. 1st ed. Cl, dec bds. Fine in NF dj. *Mikesh.* $45/£29

LUSTBADER, ERIC V. White Ninja. Fawcett, 1990. 1st ed. Fine in dj. *Madle.* $20/£13

LUSTBADER, ERIC V. Zero. Random House, 1988. 1st ed. Fine in dj. *Madle.* $20/£13

LUTHER, TAL. Benteen, Reno and Custer. Independence, MO: Trail Guide, March 1960. VG in wraps. *Perier.* $12/£8

LUTTIG, JOHN C. Journal of a Fur Trading Expedition on the Upper Missouri 1812-1813. Stella M. Drumm (ed). St. Louis, 1920. 1st ed. One of 365 numbered. Fldg map. (Cvrs worn, spine ends frayed.) Howes L572. *Ginsberg.* $250/£160

LUTYENS, EDWIN. The Letters of Edwin Lutyens to His Wife, Lady Emily. C. Percy and J. Ridley (eds). London: Collins, 1985. 12 ports. Sound in dj. *Ars Artis.* $39/£25

LUTZ, FRANCIS EARLE. The Prince George-Hopewell Story. Wm. Byrd, 1957. VG. *Book Broker.* $50/£32

LUTZ, HENRY FREDERICK. Egyptian Statues and Statuettes in the Museum of Anthropology of the University of California. Leipzig: J. C. Hinrichs, 1930. 42 plts. Later cl, leather labels. Good. *Archaeologia.* $650/£417

LUTZ, HENRY FREDERICK. Egyptian Tomb Steles and Offering Stones.... Leipzig: J.C. Hinrichs, 1927. 49 plts (2 color). Later cl, leather labels. Good. *Archaeologia.* $650/£417

LUTZ, JOHN. Buyer Beware. NY: Putnam, 1976. 1st ed. Fine in dj. *Mordida.* $65/£42

LUTZKER, EDYTHE. Edith Pechey-Phipson, MD. NY: Exposition, (1973). 1st ed. VG (ex-libris) in dj. *Second Life.* $25/£16

LUTZOW, COUNT. The Story of Prague. London, 1902. Fldg illus, fldg plan. (Bkpl.) Teg. Gilt-dec cl. *Edwards.* $19/£12

LUXMOORE, E. Deer Stalking. London, 1980. 1st ed. (Inch tear base tp), else Fine in dj. *Grayling.* $31/£20

LUYS, JULES. The Brain and Its Function. NY: Appleton, 1897. 327pp w/ads. Emb cl. Good. *Goodrich.* $75/£48

LUZZATI, EMANUELLE. Ali Baba and the Forty Thieves. NY: Pantheon, 1969. 1st ed. 9 1/2 x 11 1/4. 36pp. Fine in dj. *Cattermole.* $25/£16

LYALL, EDNA. (Pseud of Ada Ellen Bayly.) Won by Waiting. Hurst & Blackett, 1887. 7th ed. Marbled edges. Contemp 1/2 leather, marbled bds, raised bands, leather spine labels (sl rubbed). Good (2 gatherings proud). *Tiger.* $23/£15

LYALL, GAVIN. The Most Dangerous Game. NY: Scribner, (1963). 1st Amer ed. NF (lt stains) in dj (sl edgewear). *Antic Hay.* $25/£16

LYALL, ROBERT. The Character of the Russians, and a Detailed History of Moscow.... London: Cadell, 1823. Color frontis, 1/2-title, tp, cliv,639pp; 23plts (3 fldg), fldg plan, errata pg. Aeg. Recent 1/2 calf, marbled bds. (Ex-lib, stamps tp, plts), o/w VF. *Europa*. $624/£400

LYDEKKER, R. Catalogue of the Heads and Horns of Indian Big Game. London, 1913. Frontis port. (Ex-lib, ink stamps, feps sl spotted, labels, cardholders; edges dampstained.) *Edwards*. $39/£25

LYDEKKER, R. Game Animals of Africa. London: Rowland Ward, 1908. Frontis. Mod tan polished 1/2 morocco, maroon spine label. Fine. *Terramedia*. $400/£256

LYDEKKER, R. A Hand-Book to the British Mammalia. London, 1895. (xv),339,(i)ads pp; 32 color plts. (Upper hinge sl cracked, fep torn away.) Cl-backed marbled bds (rubbed, spine lt faded). *Edwards*. $47/£30

LYDEKKER, R. The New Natural History. NY, c. 1901. 6 vols. 1/2 leather, cl bds (worn, all spines perished). Contents VG. *New Hampshire**. $130/£83

LYDEKKER, R. The Royal Natural History. London: Warne, (1893-96). Mixed set. 6 vols. 72 color plts, 1600 engrs. Speckled edges, patterned eps all vols but 4 & 5. Pict cl, gilt. VG (2 joints sl loose). *Hollett*. $187/£120

LYELL, CHARLES. The Geological Evidences of the Antiquity of Man. Phila, 1863. 1st Amer ed. Unopened. Pub's cl (shelfworn). *Oinonen**. $130/£83

LYELL, CHARLES. The Geological Evidences of the Antiquity of Man. Phila: Geo. W. Childs, 1863. 1st Amer ed. 2 plts. (Contemp inscrips; lt soiled, ends sl worn.) *Waverly**. $60/£38

LYELL, CHARLES. The Geological Evidences of the Antiquity of Man. Phila: George W. Childs, 1863. 1st Amer ed. x,518pp; 2 plts. Blue cl, gilt. Fine (bkpl). *Karmiole*. $175/£112

LYELL, CHARLES. The Geological Evidences of the Antiquity of Man. London, 1873. 4th and last ed. xix,572pp (eps foxed); 2 plts. 1/2 calf (spine faded). *Henly*. $66/£42

LYELL, CHARLES. A Manual of Elementary Geology. London, 1855. 5th ed. Frontis, xvi, errata, 655pp + 32 ads. New cl. Good. *Henly*. $55/£35

LYELL, CHARLES. Principles of Geology. London, 1837. 5th ed. 4 vols. 16 maps, plts. (Bkpl.) Calf (skillfully rebacked, preserving spines). *Henly*. $437/£280

LYELL, CHARLES. Principles of Geology. Murray, 1850. 8th ed. (Frontis, tp lt foxed.) *Petersfield*. $39/£25

LYELL, D. D. The Hunting and Spoor of Central African Game. London, 1929. (1st few pp lt foxed; cvrs sl discolor.) *Grayling*. $351/£225

LYELL, D. D. The Hunting and Spoor of Central African Game. Phila: Lippincott, n.d. (1929). Frontis. Lt brn gilt cl. (Recased w/new eps; sl wear), else VG. *Terramedia*. $300/£192

LYELL, JAMES P. Early Book Illustration in Spain. London: Grafton, 1926. One of 500 signed. Color frontis. 2-tone linen buckram. (Sl soiled, esp white spine), else VG. *Waverly**. $132/£85

LYESKOV, NICOLAI. The Sentry and Other Stories. NY: Knopf, 1923. 1st ed. NF in dj (1-inch tear). *Lame Duck*. $100/£64

LYFTOGT, KENNETH L. From Blue Mills to Columbia, Cedar Falls and the Civil War. Ames, IA, (1993). 1st ed. Fine in Fine dj. *Pratt*. $25/£16

LYMAN, CHESTER S. Around the Horn to Sandwich Islands and California 1845-1850. New Haven: Yale Univ, 1924. 16 plts. (Lt rubbed.) *Adelson*. $65/£42

LYMAN, CHESTER S. Around the Horn to the Sandwich Islands and California 1845-1850. New Haven: Yale Univ, 1924. 16 plts. Gilt-dec black cl. *Parmer*. $125/£80

LYMAN, GEORGE D. John Marsh, Pioneer, Life Story of Trail Blazer on Six Frontiers. NY, 1934. Rpt of 1931 1st ed. Fine. Howes L578. *Turpen*. $30/£19

LYMAN, GEORGE D. John Marsh, Pioneer. NY: Scribner, 1930. 1st ed. Frontis port. *Wantagh*. $35/£22

LYMAN, GEORGE D. Ralston's Ring. NY: Scribner, 1937. 1st ed. Good (ink name). *Lien*. $40/£26

LYMAN, GEORGE D. Ralston's Ring: California Plunders the Comstock Lode. NY: Scribner, 1937. 1st ed. (Sm lightened spots cvrs.) *Sadlon*. $20/£13

LYMAN, GEORGE D. The Saga of the Comstock Lode. NY: Scribner, 1934. 1st ed. Pict eps. VG in dj. *Lien*. $35/£22

LYMAN, HENRY and FRANK WOOLNER. The Complete Book of Striped Bass Fishing. NY: Barnes, 1954. 1st ed. VG in orig ptd plastic dj. *Bowman*. $25/£16

LYMAN, HENRY. Artificial Anaesthesia and Anaesthetics. NY, 1881. 1st ed. 338pp. VG. *Fye*. $150/£96

LYMAN, HENRY. Artificial Anaesthesia and Anaesthetics. NY: Wood, 1881. 'Wood Library ed.' 338pp. Nice. *Goodrich*. $95/£61

LYMAN, THEODORE. Meade's Headquarters 1863-1865... George R. Agassiz (ed). NY, 1922. 1st ed. (Cvr sl worn), o/w VG +. *Pratt*. $65/£42

LYNCH, BOHUN. A Muster of Ghosts. London: Cecil Palmer, (1924). (Cl sl puckered), else Fine (lacks dj). *Between The Covers*. $45/£29

LYNCH, H. F. B. Armenia Travels and Studies. London, 1901. 1st ed. 2 vols. Teg. 2-tone cl (worn, dknd, ex-lib). *King*. $395/£253

LYNCH, HANNAH. Toledo. London, 1898. viii,311pp; fldg plan. Teg. Gilt-dec cl (spine sl discolored; bkpl). *Edwards*. $23/£15

LYNCH, JEREMIAH. Three Years in the Klondike. Chicago: Lakeside Classics, Christmas 1967. Map. Fine. *High Latitude*. $25/£16

LYNCH, JEREMIAH. Three Years in the Klondike. Dale L. Morgan (ed). Chicago: Lakeside, 1967. As New in box. *Cahan*. $30/£19

LYNCH, JOHN R. The Facts of Reconstruction. NY: Neale, 1913. 1st ed. NF. *Mcgowan*. $150/£96

LYNCH, LAWRENCE. Dangerous Ground; or, The Rival Detectives. Chicago: Loyd, 1885. 1st ed. (Shaken, loose, extrems worn, frayed.) *Metropolitan**. $40/£26

LYNCH, LAWRENCE. The Diamond Coterie. Chicago: Sumner, 1884. 1st ed. Pict cvr. (Frayed, sl soiled.) *Metropolitan**. $63/£40

LYNCH, LAWRENCE. The Unseen Hand. London: Ward, Lock, n.d. 1st ed. (Bumped, rubbed, soiled, shaken, foxed.) *Metropolitan**. $23/£15

LYNCH, STANISLAUS. Rhymes of an Irish Huntsman. London, 1937. 1st ed. (Sl worn.) *King*. $75/£48

LYNE, MICHAEL. A Parson's Son. London: Allen, 1974. Ltd to 750 signed. VG. *October Farm*. $150/£96

LYNK, M. V. The Black Troopers...the Negro Soldiers in the Spanish American War. Jackson, TN, 1899. 163pp (lacks eps, some pp torn; inner hinges glued; cvrs worn). *King*. $295/£189

LYNN, C. Wallpaper in America...to W W 1. NY: Norton, 1980. Stated 1st ed. Good + in dj (chipped). *Scribe's Perch**. $22/£14

LYON, DANNY. Conversations with the Dead. NY/Chicago/SF: Holt, Rinehart & Winston, 1971. 2nd ptg. (Owner stamp, sticker mk on fr, rear corner creased), else VG in illus stiff wrappers. *Cahan*. $75/£48

LYON, DANNY. Conversations with the Dead. NY/Chicago/SF: Holt, Rinehart & Winston, 1971. 1st ed. VG in illus stiff wrappers. *Cahan.* $125/£80

LYON, DANNY. The Destruction of Lower Manhattan. NY: Macmillan, 1969. 1st ed. Fine in dj (sl rubbed). *Cahan.* $225/£144

LYON, DANNY. Pictures from the New World. NY: Aperture, 1981. 1st ed. NF in pict stiff wrappers (scratch fr cvr). *Cahan.* $50/£32

LYON, G. F. Brief Narrative of an Unsuccessful Attempt to Reach Repulse Bay Through Sir Thomas Rowe's Welcome in His Majesty's Ship Gripper. London: John Murray, 1825. xvi,198(2)pp (sm lib stamp tp); 7 plts, fldg map. Uncut. Orig bds (rebacked), orig spine label preserved. VG. *High Latitude.* $240/£154

LYON, G. F. Journal of a Residence and Tour in the Republic of Mexico 1826.... London, 1828. 1st ed. 2 vols in 1. viii,323; iv,304pp (pp1-21 lt foxed). Mod grn cl spine, orig bds (tip bumped), ptd paper label. VG. *Turpen.* $195/£125

LYON, G. F. The Private Journal of Capt. G. F. Lyon.... London: John Murray, 1824. 1st ed. xiii,468pp, 7 plts, fldg map. Uncut. Papered bds, new paper spine, paper label. VG. *High Latitude.* $275/£176

LYON, HASTINGS and HERMAN BLOCK. Edward Coke, Oracle of the Law. Boston: Houghton Mifflin, 1929. Red cl (rubbed, dull). Sound. *Boswell.* $65/£42

LYONS, ARTHUR. Satan Wants You: The Cult of Devil Worship. Hart-Davis, 1971. 1st Eng ed. Fine in Fine photo dj. *Certo.* $50/£32

LYONS, ARTHUR. The Second Coming: Satanism in America. Dodd Mead, 1970. 1st ed, 1st bk. Fine in Fine dj. *Certo.* $100/£64

LYONS, NATHAN (ed). Aaron Siskind, Photographer. NY: George Eastman House, 1965. 1st ed. (Owner stamp), else VG in illus stiff wrappers. *Cahan.* $40/£26

LYONS, NATHAN. Photography in the Twentieth Century. NY: Horizon Press w/George Eastman House, 1967. 150 b/w photo plts. (Owner stamp), else NF in dj. *Cahan.* $50/£32

LYRE, PINCHBECK. (Pseud of Siegfried Sassoon.) Poems. Duckworth, 1931. 1st ed. 1000 ptd. VG in tissue dj (torn, chipped). *Ash.* $94/£60

LYSAGHT, A. M. (ed). Joseph Banks in Newfoundland and Labrador, 1766. London, 1971. Dj (sl used). *Maggs.* $50/£32

LYSAGHT, A. M. (ed). Joseph Banks in Newfoundland and Labrador, 1776. Berkeley: Univ of CA, (1971). 1st ed. Frontis port, 103 plts (12 color), 9 facs (4 fldg, 1 dbl-pg). Brn cl. Good in dj. *Karmiole.* $100/£64

LYSONS, SAMUEL. A Collection of Gloucestershire Antiquities. London, 1804. 110 engr plts. Early 1/2 calf (worn; lt foxed). *Swann*.* $115/£74

LYSONS, SAMUEL. The Model Merchant of the Middle Ages.... London: Hamilton, Adams, 1860. 1st ed. Frontis port, (2),96pp; fldg family tree. Patterned brn cl. Good. *Karmiole.* $100/£64

LYTLE, ANDREW NELSON. Bedford Forrest and His Critter Company. NY, 1931. 1st ed. (Bkpl, inner hinges cracked; bumped, sl rubbed, paper spine labels discolored.) *King.* $75/£48

LYTLE, ANDREW NELSON. Bedford Forrest. London: Eyre & Spottiswoode, 1939. 1st British ed. NF in VG dj. *Mcgowan.* $350/£224

LYTLE, ANDREW. Bedford Forrest and His Critter Company. NY: McDowell, (1960). 2nd ed, 1st bk. Fine in VG dj (2 short edge tears mended on verso; rub). *Reese.* $45/£29

LYTLE, HORACE. Point! A Book About Bird Dogs. NY: Derrydale, (1941). Ltd to 950. Red cl. VG + (tape residue eps; spine lt faded). *Truepenny.* $100/£64

LYTLE, HORACE. Point! A Book About Bird Dogs. NY: Derrydale, (1941). One of 950. Cl, gilt-emb cvr label. (Sl worn.) *Oinonen*.* $170/£109

LYTLE, THOMAS G. Harpoons and Other Whalecraft. New Bedford, MA, 1984. *Eldred's*.* $77/£49

LYTTON, DAVID. The Goddam White Man. NY, 1961. 1st Amer ed, 1st bk. NF (pg edges sl browned) in dj (edges sl rubbed). *Polyanthos.* $30/£19

M

M'BAIN, JAMES. Burns' Cottage. Glasgow: David Bryce, n.d. (1904). 1st ed. Ptd canvas, backstrip blocked in gold. VG. *Cox.* $23/£15

M'CLINTOCK, CAPT. The Voyage of the 'Fox' in the Arctic Seas. Boston: Ticknor & Fields, 1860. 1st US ed. xxiii,(1),375pp. 3 fldg maps, fldg facs. VG. *High Latitude.* $65/£42

M'COLLUM, WILLIAM. California As I Saw It: Pencillings by the Way of Its Gold and Gold Diggers!.... Dale L. Morgan (ed). Los Gatos: Talisman, 1960. 2nd ed. One of 750. Tan pict bds, red cl backstrip, paper spine label. Fine in NF dj (sl chipped). Howes M55. *Harrington.* $90/£58

M'COY, F. Contributions to British Palaeontology. London, 1854. viii,272pp, 16 pub's ads; 1 plt. (Rebacked, preserving label.) *Henly.* $44/£28

M'CRIE, THOMAS. The Life of John Knox. Edinburgh: John Ogle et al, 1813. 2nd ed. 2 vols. 2 ports. (Eps foxed.) Contemp calf, gilt. *Andrew Stewart.* $78/£50

M'GAW, JAMES FRANKLIN. Philip Seymour, or Pioneer Life in Richland County, Ohio. Mansfield: R. Brinkerhoff, 1858. 295pp (age-toned); 3 full-pg woodcuts. Later 3/4 leather. Nice. Howes M100. *Bohling.* $350/£224

M'GHEE, R. J. How We Got to Pekin. London: Bentley, 1862. 1st ed. xi,365pp, 8 plts. Mod 1/4 morocco. VG. *Terramedia.* $250/£160

M'KENNEY, THOMAS L. Memoirs Official and Personal. NY: Paine & Burgess, 1846. 1st ed. 2 vols in 1. viii,17-340; vi,136pp; color plt. (Text foxed), else Good in orig cl bds (rebacked w/new spine). Howes M130. *Brown.* $150/£96

M'KIE, JAMES. The Bibliography of Robert Burns. Kilmarnock: The Author, 1881. #248/600. Signed by ptr. (Lt spotting few ll.) Uncut. Blue paper bds (spine relined w/cl retaining orig paper spine). *D & D.* $195/£125

Ma-Ka-Tai-Me-She-Kia-Kiak; or, Black Hawk, and Scenes in the West. (By Elbert H. Smith.) NY: Edward Kearny, 1848. 1st ed. Frontis, 299pp. (Sl worn, rubbed; text lt spotted), else Good. *Brown.* $40/£26

MAAS, JEREMY. Victorian Painters. London: Cresset, 1969. 1st ed. (Margins sl browned.) Dj (spine head sl chipped). *Edwards.* $62/£40

MABERLY, J. The Print Collector. Robert Hoe (ed). NY: Dodd, Mead, 1880. Teg. Drab brn cl, gilt. *Glenn.* $150/£96

MACADAM, JOHN LOUDON. Remarks on the Present System of Road Making. London: Longman, Hurst et al, 1820. 3rd ed. 196pp. Untrimmed. Contemp bds (rebacked), paper spine label. (1st few ll foxed; bds sl shelfworn), else NF. *Glaser.* $250/£160

MACALISTER, R. A. S. The Archaeology of Ireland. London, 1928. 1st ed. 16 plts. (Feps browned; cl spine sl discolored.) *Edwards.* $39/£25

MACARTNEY, C. G. My Cricketing Days. London, 1930. 1st ed. Frontis port. (Sl spotted.) *Edwards.* $31/£20

MACAULAY, ROSE. Catchwords and Claptrap. London: Hogarth, 1962. 1st ed. (Pencil notes rep.) Paper-cvrd bds. (Pencil notes rep; faded, spine browned, edges rubbed.) Good-. *Virgo.* $39/£25

MACAULAY, ROSE. Crewe Train. W. Collins, 1926. 1st ed. (Lt spotted; bumped, spine tail sl split.) *Edwards.* $31/£20

MACAULAY, ROSE. Pleasure of Ruins. (London): Thames & Hudson, (1964). 1st ed. Folio. 160 full-pg photogravures, 12 mtd color photo plts, 29 maps and plans. Pict eps. Pict cl. VG in dj (sm abrasion rear cvr). *House.* $80/£51

MACAULAY, ROSE. The Writings of E. M. Forster. London: Hogarth, 1938. 1st ed. Blue cl. Nice. *Hartfield.* $125/£80

MACAULAY, THOMAS BABINGTON. Biographies by Lord Macaulay. Edinburgh: A&C Black, 1860. lvi,235pp (prelims sl spotted). Full tan calf (few sm scratches), gilt. *Hollett.* $70/£45

MACAULAY, THOMAS BABINGTON. The History of England. London: Longmans, Green, 1886. 2 vols. xxiv,776; (xii),820pp. Marbled edges. Contemp prize calf (sl mkd). Nice set. *Ash.* $148/£95

MACAULAY, THOMAS BABINGTON. The History of England. Boston/Cambridge: Houghton, Mifflin/Riverside Press, 1899. Lg paper ed. #212/500 ptd. 20 vols. 8vo. Frontis. 1857 als laid in. Teg. 3/4 blue morocco, bds, gilt spines. Fine set. *Cummins.* $3,750/£2,404

MACAULAY, THOMAS BABINGTON. The History of England. Lady Trevelyan (ed). London: Longman et al, 1849-61. 5 vols. Orig blind-stamped cl (spines evenly faded, vols 1-2 neatly recased). Excellent set. *Hollett.* $172/£110

MACAULEY, JAMES. Grey Hawk. London: Hodder & Stoughton, 1883. 1st UK ed. Frontis, 11 b/w engrs. Aeg. Blue/gold illus binding. (Bkpl; frontis loose), o/w VG+. *Bernard.* $25/£16

MacBETH, ANN. Embroidered and Laced Leather Work. 1930. 3rd ed. Pict cl. (Sl foxed), o/w VG in dj (worn). *Whittle.* $31/£20

MACBRIDE, MacKENZIE. Wild Lakeland. London: A&C Black, 1928. 2nd ed. 32 color plts, map. Blind-stamped cl, gilt. (Edges, 1/2-title spotted), o/w Nice. *Hollett.* $55/£35

MacBRIDE, THOMAS HUSTON. In Cabins and Sod-Houses. Iowa City: State Hist Soc, 1928. 1st ed. Port. Teg. (Extrems lt rubbed, spine sl frayed), else Good. *Brown.* $20/£13

MacCABE, FREDERIC. The Art of Ventriloquism. London: Frederic Warne, n.d. (1875). 1st ed. Pict, yellow-glazed paper bds (backstrip crudely reinforced). Clean. *Dramatis Personae.* $75/£48

MacCARTHY, DESMOND. Shaw. London, 1951. 1st ed. VG in dj (sm tears). *Words Etc.* $25/£16

MacCARTHY, FIONA. Eric Gill: A Lover's Quest for Art and God. NY: Dutton, (1989). 1st Amer ed. Black bds. Fine in dj. *Heller.* $35/£22

MACCHIAVELLI, NICOLO. Opere. Florence, 1818-21. 10 vols in 5. Port, fldg plan, fldg ms facs. Ptd on blue paper. Contemp 1/4 sheep (spines faded, ends worn, few joints starting, vol 1 fr cvr detached). *Swann*.* $115/£74

MacCLINTOCK, D. A Natural History of Zebras. NY: Scribner, 1976. 1st ed. Pict bds. Fine in VG+ dj. *Mikesh.* $30/£19

MacCURDY, EDWARD. The Notebooks of Leonardo da Vinci. Jonathan Cape, 1938. 3rd imp. 2 vols. Frontis ports. Fore/lower edges uncut. (Spines lt faded, lower bd vol 1 scratched.) *Edwards.* $70/£45

MacCURDY, JOHN T. Common Principles in Psychology and Physiology. Cambridge: CUP, 1928. 1st ed. Ruled brn cl (bumped). *Gach.* $50/£32

MacDIARMID, HUGH. The Company I've Kept. London, 1966. 1st ed. Fine (sl bumped) in Fine dj. *Polyanthos.* $25/£16

MacDIARMID, HUGH. O Wha's Been Here Afore Me, Lass. (London): Blue Moon, Christmas 1931. One of 100 numbered, signed. Folded card. (4)pp. (Sm foxmks), else Fine. *Reese.* $100/£64

MACDONALD, E. M. Col. Robert G. Ingersoll as He Is. NY: Truth Seeker, n.d. Good. *Hayman.* $15/£10

MacDONALD, GEORGE. At the Back of the North Wind. Phila/London: Lippincott, (1909). 8vo. 352pp; 12 full-color illus by Maria Kirk. Illus eps. Red illus cl. VG in VG dj. *Dower.* $125/£80

MacDONALD, GEORGE. At the Back of the North Wind. Phila, 1919. 1st Amer ed. 8 full color plts. Teg. Fine (spine extrems, 2 corners sl rubbed). *Polyanthos.* $100/£64

MacDONALD, GEORGE. At the Back of the North Wind. Phila: MacKay, 1919. 1st thus. 8vo. 342pp; 8 full-pg color plts by Jessie Willcox Smith. Pict pastedown cvr. Good (fr hinge starting). *Scribe's Perch*.* $32/£21

MacDONALD, GEORGE. Cross Purposes. London: Blackie, (ca 1905). 1st separate ed. 8vo. Color frontis by H.M. Brock, 96pp + 12pp ads. Blue cl, pict design stamped fr cvr, spine. (Spine sl dknd, corners bumped), else Fine. *Bromer.* $225/£144

MacDONALD, GEORGE. The Light Princess. NY: Crowell, 1962. 3rd ed. William Pene Du Bois (illus). 7 1/4 x 10 1/4. 48pp. Good (worn, ex-lib, mks) in dj. *Cattermole.* $20/£13

MacDONALD, GOLDEN. (Pseud of Margaret Wise Brown.) Little Lost Lamb. NY: Doubleday, 1945. Early rpt. Leonard Weisgard (illus). 9 1/4 x 10 1/4. Extra color plt for framing. VG in dj (sl chipped). *Cattermole.* $50/£32

MacDONALD, HUGH and MARY HARGREAVES. Thomas Hobbes. A Bibliography. London: Bibliographical Soc, 1952. 1st ed. Port. NF. *Reese.* $95/£61

MacDONALD, JOHN D. The Beach Girls. (Greenwich): Gold Medal/Fawcett, (1959). Pb orig. Fine in wrappers as issued. *Between The Covers.* $85/£54

MacDONALD, JOHN D. The Beach Girls. Greenwich: Fawcett, 1959. 1st ed. Pb orig. NF. *Janus.* $20/£13

MacDONALD, JOHN D. The Brass Cupcake. Greenwich, CT: Gold Medal #124, 1950. 1st ed, 1st bk. Pb orig. (Sm corner tear; lt nicks), else VG+. *Murder By The Book.* $125/£80

MacDONALD, JOHN D. Bright Orange for the Shroud. Greenwich: Fawcett, 1965. 1st ed. Pb orig. NF. *Janus.* $35/£22

MacDONALD, JOHN D. Cinnamon Skin. NY: Harper & Row, 1982. 1st ed. Inscribed. Advance rev copy w/slip, photo, flyer laid in. VF in dj. *Mordida.* $300/£192

MacDONALD, JOHN D. Condominium. Phila: Lippincott, 1977. Signed, ltd ed. VG in dj (soiled, torn). *Metropolitan*.* $34/£22

MacDONALD, JOHN D. Darker Than Amber. Lippincott, 1970. 1st US hb ed. Fine in dj (price-clipped). *Certo.* $375/£240

MacDONALD, JOHN D. A Deadly Shade of Gold. Phil/NY: Lippincott, (1974). 1st hb ed. Paper-cvrd bds. (Bd edges sl faded), else Fine in Fine black dj. *Between The Covers.* $200/£128

MacDONALD, JOHN D. A Deadly Shade of Gold. Greenwich, CT: Gold Medal #d1499, 1965. 1st ed. Pb orig. VG+ (sl worn, lt soiled). *Murder By The Book.* $17/£11

MacDONALD, JOHN D. A Deadly Shade of Gold. Phila: Lippincott, 1974. 1st Amer hb ed. Fine in dj (short closed tears). *Mordida*. $175/£112

MacDONALD, JOHN D. Deadly Welcome. London: Robert Hale, 1961. 1st hb ed. Fine in dj (lt soil back panel). *Associates*. $150/£96

MacDONALD, JOHN D. The Deep Blue Good-By. Phila: Lippincott, (1964). 1st ed. VG (name) in dj (worn). *Metropolitan**. $51/£33

MacDONALD, JOHN D. The Deep Blue Good-By. Greenwich: Fawcett, 1964. 1st ed. Pb orig. Fine (rear cvr sl soiling), unread copy. *Janus*. $65/£42

MacDONALD, JOHN D. The Dreadful Lemon Sky. Phila: Lippincott, 1974. 1st ed. Fine in dj. *Mordida*. $65/£42

MacDONALD, JOHN D. Dress Her in Indigo. Phila/NY: Lippincott, 1971. 1st hb ed. (Top edge lt foxed, price fep), else Fine in dj (sl scrape spine). *Between The Covers*. $385/£247

MacDONALD, JOHN D. The Drowner. Greenwich: Fawcett, 1963. 1st ed. Pb orig. VF in wrappers. *Mordida*. $65/£42

MacDONALD, JOHN D. The End of the Night. NY: S&S, 1960. 1st ed. NF in VG dj (price-clipped). *Metropolitan**. $103/£66

MacDONALD, JOHN D. The Girl, the Gold Watch and Everything. London: Hale, 1974. 1st hb ed. Fine in dj (price-clipped). *Certo*. $45/£29

MacDONALD, JOHN D. The Good Old Stuff. Francis M. Nevins, Jr. et al (eds). NY: Harper & Row, 1982. 1st ed. Inscribed by MacDonald and Nevins. VF in dj. *Mordida*. $175/£112

MacDONALD, JOHN D. The Green Ripper. NY: Lippincott, 1979. 1st ed. Inscribed. VF in dj (price-clipped). *Mordida*. $250/£160

MacDONALD, JOHN D. I Could Go on Singing. (Greenwich): Gold Medal/Fawcett, (1963). Pb orig. NF (pp sl browned, lt rubbed). *Between The Covers*. $75/£48

MacDONALD, JOHN D. The Long Lavender Look. London, 1972. 1st ed. VG in dj (sl chipped). *Words Etc*. $59/£38

MacDONALD, JOHN D. The Long Lavender Look. London: Robert Hale, 1972. 1st hb ed. Fine in dj (price-clipped, creases inner fr flap). *Mordida*. $45/£29

MacDONALD, JOHN D. The Long Lavender Look. Phila: Lippincott, 1972. 1st ed. Fine (sig) in dj (lt worn). *Metropolitan**. $115/£74

MacDONALD, JOHN D. The Long Lavender Look. Phila: Lippincott, 1972. 1st Amer hb ed. (Sl spotting pg edges), o/w Fine in dj (sl wear spine ends). *Mordida*. $225/£144

MacDONALD, JOHN D. Nightmare in Pink. Greenwich: Fawcett, 1964. 1st ed. Pb orig. Fine. *Janus*. $50/£32

MacDONALD, JOHN D. One Fearful Yellow Eye. Greenwich: Fawcett, 1966. 1st ed. Pb orig. NF. *Janus*. $35/£22

MacDONALD, JOHN D. One Fearful Yellow Eye. Phila: Lippincott, 1977. 1st hb ed. Fine (fore-edge lt foxed) in Fine dj. *Metropolitan**. $138/£88

MacDONALD, JOHN D. The Only Girl in the Game. (Greenwich): Gold Medal/Fawcett, (1960). Pb orig. Fine (pp sl dkng) in wrappers as issued. *Between The Covers*. $75/£48

MacDONALD, JOHN D. The Only Girl in the Game. Greenwich: Fawcett, 1960. 1st ed. Pb orig. NF (pp browning). *Janus*. $25/£16

MacDONALD, JOHN D. Please Write for Details. NY: S&S, 1959. (Sm tear 1 pg, pp yellowed), else NF in Fine dj. *Between The Covers*. $125/£80

MacDONALD, JOHN D. The Quick Red Fox. Greenwich: Fawcett, 1964. 1st ed. Pb orig. NF. *Janus*. $40/£26

MacDONALD, JOHN D. The Quick Red Fox. Phila: Lippincott, 1974. 1st Amer hb ed. Fine in dj (sm stain back panel, short closed tear). *Mordida*. $250/£160

MacDONALD, JOHN D. The Scarlet Ruse. NY: Lippincott, (1973). 1st ed. Fine in VG dj. *Metropolitan**. $57/£37

MacDONALD, JOHN D. The Scarlet Ruse. Lippincott, 1980. 1st US hb. (Pg edges sl foxed), else NF in dj. *Murder By The Book*. $90/£58

MacDONALD, JOHN D. Soft Touch. NY: Dell, 1958. 1st ed. Pb orig. Unread. Fine in wrappers. *Mordida*. $45/£29

MacDONALD, JOHN D. A Tan and Sandy Silence. London, 1973. 1st ed. NF in dj. *Words Etc*. $78/£50

MacDONALD, JOHN D. The Turquoise Lament. Phila: Lippincott, 1973. 1st ed. (Sl spotting top edge), o/w Fine in dj (price-clipped, closed tear to spine). *Mordida*. $125/£80

MacDONALD, JOHN D. Wine of the Dreamers. NY: Greenberg, (1951). 1st ed. Fine in NF dj (sm chip top fr panel, spine sl tanned). *Between The Covers*. $225/£144

MacDONALD, JOHN ROSS. (Pseud of Kenneth Millar.) The Ivory Grin. NY: Knopf, 1952. 1st ed. VG in VG dj (chipped). *Lame Duck*. $200/£128

MacDONALD, JOHN. Travels. Memoirs of an Eighteenth Century Footman (1745-1779). Routledge, 1928. 8 plts. VG. *Cox*. $28/£18

MacDONALD, PHILIP. The Crime Conductor. GC: Crime Club, (1931). 1st Amer ed. Dj (bumped, sl worn, lt chipped). *Metropolitan**. $109/£70

MacDONALD, PHILIP. Death on My Left. NY: Crime Club, (1933). 1st Amer ed. Fine (spine top sl bumped). *Polyanthos*. $30/£19

MacDONALD, PHILIP. Death on My Left. London: Crime Club, 1933. 1st ed. (Name, stamp; sl faded, cocked.) Dj (lg chips, sm losses). *Metropolitan**. $155/£99

MacDONALD, PHILIP. The Link. GC: Crime Club, 1930. 1st Amer ed. (Fr bd stained.) Dj (browned, worn). *Metropolitan**. $132/£85

MacDONALD, PHILIP. The List of Adrian Messenger. NY: Crime Club, 1959. 1st ed. VG in VG dj (price-clipped). *Metropolitan**. $126/£81

MacDONALD, PHILIP. Mystery of the Dead Police. GC: Crime Club, 1943. 1st ed. VG (edgeworn) in dj (lg chips spine ends, short tears, soil). *Metropolitan**. $51/£33

MacDONALD, PHILIP. Rope to Spare. NY: GC, 1932. 1st Amer ed. (Name; bds lt spotted.) Nice dj (creased, bumped). *Metropolitan**. $138/£88

MacDONALD, ROSS. (Pseud of Kenneth Millar.) The Barbarous Coast. NY: Knopf, 1956. 1st ed. Fine (sticker) in dj (1/2-inch closed tear, sl wrinkled, spine sl dknd, back edge sl discolored). *Metropolitan**. $287/£184

MacDONALD, ROSS. (Pseud of Kenneth Millar.) The Doomsters. London: Cassell, 1958. 1st ed. Fine in dj (worn, lt discolored rear panel). *Metropolitan**. $63/£40

MacDONALD, ROSS. (Pseud of Kenneth Millar.) The Drowning Pool. NY: Knopf, 1950. 1st ed. Soft paper-cvrd bds. Fine (edges sl dknd) in dj (sm chips, sl worn). *Else Fine*. $350/£224

MacDONALD, ROSS. (Pseud of Kenneth Millar.) Find a Victim. NY: Knopf, 1954. 1st ed. (Few pp roughly opened), o/w Bright in white dj (sm closed tears, edge crease). *Else Fine*. $600/£385

MacDONALD, ROSS. (Pseud of Kenneth Millar.) Find a Victim. NY: Knopf, 1954. 1st ed. (Few pp roughly opened, sm chips bottom few pp), else Fine in Fine white dj (sm tear fr panel, sm near-puncture fr gutter). *Between The Covers*. $600/£385

MacDONALD, ROSS. (Pseud of Kenneth Millar.) The Galton Case. NY: Knopf, 1959. 1st ed. Fine (Spine ends sl bruised, rubbed) in dj (extrems sl worn). *Metropolitan**. $310/£199

MacDONALD, ROSS. (Pseud of Kenneth Millar.) Meet Me at the Morgue. NY: Knopf, 1953. 1st ed. NF in dj (sl worn). *Else Fine*. $400/£256

MacDONALD, ROSS. (Pseud of Kenneth Millar.) The Underground Man. NY: Knopf, 1971. 1st ed. Fine in dj (spine sl fading). *Mordida*. $35/£22

MACDONALD, W. A. A Farewell to Commander Byrd. NY: Coward-McCann, 1929. 1st ed. (Spine dknd.) Dj (soiled, chipped). *Parmer*. $65/£42

MACDOUGALL, ARTHUR R. Dud Dean and His Country. NY, (1946). Ltd to 450 signed. VG. *Truepenny*. $125/£80

MacDOUGALL, J. B. The Real Mother Goose. Toronto, (1940). 1st ed. 9.5x6.5. 57pp. Uncut. Wraps. VG in glassine dj. *King*. $40/£26

MacDOWELL, SYL. Western Trout. NY: Knopf, 1948. 1st ed. Red blind-stamped cl. Fine in NF pict dj. *Biscotti*. $35/£22

MACE, ARTHUR CRUTTENDEN. Egyptian Literature. NY: MMA, 1928. Ltd to 200. Good. *Archaeologia*. $75/£48

MACEWAN, GRANT. Blazing the Old Cattle Trail. Saskatoon, 1962. 1st ptg. Pict cl. VG (stamp fep mkd out) in dj. *Baade*. $30/£19

MACEWAN, GRANT. John Ware's Cow Country. Edmonton, 1960. 1st ed. Signed. (Binding sl cocked), o/w VG in dj (worn). *Baade*. $37/£24

MACEWEN, WILLIAM. Pyogenic Infective Diseases of the Brain and Spinal Cord. Glasgow: Maclehose, 1893. xxv,354pp. Uncut. New blue cl, leather label. Internally Clean. *Goodrich*. $695/£446

MACFADDEN, BERNARD. Strengthening the Eyes.... NY: Physical Culture, 1918. 28 parts in 14 booklets, loose in cl-backed bd folder. Fldg eye chart, loose as issued. VG. *Argosy*. $50/£32

MACFADDEN, HARRY ALEXANDER. Rambles in the Far West. Hollidaysburg, PA, (1906). Gilt-titled cl (extrems rubbed, sm repaired snag spine). VG +. Howes M94. *Bohling*. $75/£48

MACFALL, HALDANE. Aubrey Beardsley. London: John Lane, Bodley Head, 1928. 1st ed. Uncut. Good in orig buckram-backed bds, paper label, spare at end. *Cox*. $70/£45

MACFALL, HALDANE. The Book of Claud Lovat Fraser. London: J.M. Dent, 1923. 1st ed. Top edge stained grn. Pub's dec bds, bright blue cl spine, orange paper label. Dj (few chips). *Book Block*. $175/£112

MacFALL, J. E. W. Buchanan's Text-Book of Forensic Medicine and Toxicology. Edinburgh: Livingstone, 1930. 9th ed. VG. *Savona*. $28/£18

MacFARLAN, ALLAN A. (ed). American Indian Legends. L.A.: LEC, 1968. One of 1500 numbered, signed by Everett Gee Jackson (illus). 1/4 sheep, ptd wood spine label. VG in bd slipcase. *Argosy*. $150/£96

MacFARLAN, ALLAN A. (ed). American Indian Legends. L.A.: LEC, 1968. #238/1500 signed by Everett Gee Jackson (artist). Wood veneer cvrd bds, spine, slipcase label; tan sheepskin backstrip. NF in NF slipcase. *Harrington*. $175/£112

MACFARLANE, A. W. Insomnia and Its Therapeutics. NY: William Wood, 1891. 1st ed. VG (name; rear bd bumped, torn). *Beasley*. $75/£48

MacGAHAN, J. A. Campaigning on the Oxus and the Fall of Khiva. NY: Harper, 1874. 1st ed. xii,438,2pp. (Ex-lib; lacks tp; edges rubbed, spine frayed, lib spine #), o/w VG. *Worldwide*. $50/£32

MacGAHAN, J. A. Campaigning on the Oxus, and the Fall of Khiva. London, 1876. 4th ed. *Petersfield*. $28/£18

MacGIBBON, D. The Architecture of Provence and the Riviera. Edinburgh: Douglas, 1888. xx,467pp. (Cl sl worn.) *Ars Artis*. $39/£25

MacGIBBON, ELMA. Leaves of Knowledge. (Spokane, 1904.) 1st ed. Dec cl. *Ginsberg*. $125/£80

MacGOWAN, J. Sidelights on Chinese Life. London: Kegan Paul et al, 1907. 1st ed. 40 plts (12 color tipped in). Teg. (Edges sl rubbed, spine frayed), o/w Good. *Worldwide*. $30/£19

MACGOWAN, KENNETH. Behind the Screen. NY, 1965. 1st ed. (Celotape mks feps.) Dj. *Edwards*. $39/£25

MacGRATH, HAROLD. The Carpet from Bagdad. Indianapolis: Bobbs-Merrill, 1911. 1st ed. VG in dj (chipped, frayed, short closed tears, folds worn). *Mordida*. $65/£42

MacGRATH, HAROLD. Parrot and Co. Indianapolis: Bobbs-Merrill, 1913. 4 color illus by Andre Castaigne. Pict paper wraps (edges creased, shaken; loose pp) in shape of parrot. *Metropolitan**. $46/£29

MACGREGOR, ALASDAIR ALPIN. A Last Voyage to St. Kilda. London: Cassell, 1931. 1st ed. 52 plts, map. (Sl mks lower bd.) *Hollett*. $70/£45

MacGREGOR, J. The Rob Roy on the Jordan, Nile, Red Sea and Gennesareth.... London, 1869. 13,474pp; 4 litho color plts. Bound in 1/2 leather. Contents Fine. *Heinoldt*. $75/£48

MacGREGOR, J. The Rob Roy on the Jordan. London, 1870. 3rd ed. xiii,474pp; 8 maps, 4 chromolitho plts. (Fore-edge discolored, spine sl chipped.) *Edwards*. $31/£20

MacGREGOR, JESSIE. Gardens of Celebrities and Celebrated Gardens in and Around London. London, n.d. c.(1918). 20 color plts, 6 pencil dwgs by author. (Lt foxed, lacks fep, lower edge ink-stained w/sl intrusion onto margins, lower bd.) Gilt-dec upper bd. (Spine sl faded.) *Edwards*. $59/£38

MACHARD, ALFRED. The Wolf Man (The Were-Wolf). London: Thornton Butterworth, (1925). Advance Review Copy. VG- (sl sunned, sm stain rear bd; lacks dj). *Between The Covers*. $85/£54

MACHEN, ARTHUR. The Anatomy of Tobacco. NY, 1926. 1st Amer ed. Yellow mustard cl, purple spine label, gilt. Fine in dj (fr panel rubbed, chip). *Mcclintock*. $85/£54

MACHEN, ARTHUR. The Angels of Mons, the Bowmen and Other Legends of the War. London: Simpkin, 1915. 1st ed. Pict blue/gray bds. VG (sm spine chip). *Houle*. $125/£80

MACHEN, ARTHUR. The Bowmen and Other Legends of the War. London: Simpki Marshall, Hamilton, 1915. 1st ed. VG (sl foxed) in cardstock cvrs. *Certo*. $55/£35

MACHEN, ARTHUR. The Canning Wonder. NY, 1926. 1st Amer ed. Yellow mustard cl, purple spine label (faded), gilt (dknd). VG. *Mcclintock*. $30/£19

MACHEN, ARTHUR. The Chronicle of Clemendy. (NY): Soc of Pantagruelists, 1923. New ed. One of 1050 signed. Parchment-backed bds (sl rubbed). *Clearwater*. $86/£55

MACHEN, ARTHUR. Dog and Duck. London: Cape, (1924). 1st trade ed of 750 numbered. Patterned bds. NF (eps browned) in dj (lib mks fr flap). *Antic Hay*. $50/£32

MACHEN, ARTHUR. Dog and Duck. NY, 1924. 1st ed. Yellow mustard cl, purple spine label (faded), gilt (dknd). VG. *Mcclintock*. $45/£29

MACHEN, ARTHUR. Dr. Stiggins: His Views and Principles. Westminster (London), 1906. 1st ed. Pict bds. (Lt edgeworn), else VG. *Mcclintock*. $295/£189

MACHEN, ARTHUR. Fantastic Tales or the Way to Attain. Carbonnek: Privately ptd, 1923. Ltd to 1050 numbered, signed. Parchment-backed bds (worn, stain fr cvr, spine dknd). *King*. $50/£32

MACHEN, ARTHUR. Far-Off Things. London: Martin Secker, (1922). 1st trade ed. VG (spine bottom faded, spotted) in dj (edgewear, tear). *Antic Hay*. $35/£22

MACHEN, ARTHUR. Far-Off Things. Knopf, 1923. 1st US ed. VG. *Certo*. $25/£16

MACHEN, ARTHUR. Far-Off Things. NY, 1923. 1st Amer ed. Yellow mustard cl (soiled), purple spine label, gilt. Good. *Mcclintock*. $15/£10

MACHEN, ARTHUR. A Few Letters from Arthur Machen. Cleveland, 1932. 1st ed. Ltd to 170 numbered. Fine in Fine dj. *Mcclintock*. $185/£119

MACHEN, ARTHUR. The Great God Pan. London: Simpkin, Marshall (et al), (1916). 1st this ed. Pict bds. VG (sm bkpl). *Reese*. $45/£29

MACHEN, ARTHUR. The Great Return. London, 1915. 1st ed. Internally Very Clean (1/4-inch chip spine top, 1-inch tear spine bottom, cvrs damaged). *Mcclintock*. $45/£29

MACHEN, ARTHUR. The Green Round. London: Benn, 1933. 1st Eng ed. (Inscrip, bkpl; smoke damage cvrs, edges.) *Clearwater*. $47/£30

MACHEN, ARTHUR. The Green Round. London, 1938. 1st ed. VG (ex-lib, date stamps, erased rubber stamp). *Mcclintock*. $20/£13

MACHEN, ARTHUR. The Green Round. Arkham House, 1968. 1st US ed. (Top edge sl dust-mkd), else Fine in dj (rear panel sl dusty). *Certo*. $60/£38

MACHEN, ARTHUR. The Green Round. Sauk City: Arkham House, 1968. 1st Amer ptg (2000 copies), offset from 1st ed. (Ink inscrip), else VG in dj (sl edgeworn). *Reese*. $25/£16

MACHEN, ARTHUR. Hieroglyphics. NY, 1913. 1st Amer ed. VG (spine sl soiled). *Mcclintock*. $95/£61

MACHEN, ARTHUR. The Hill of Dreams. Estes, 1907. 1st US ed. VG-. *Madle*. $75/£48

MACHEN, ARTHUR. Holy Terrors. Harmondsworth/Middlesex/NY, (1946). 1st ed. Penguin pb #526. VG. *Mcclintock*. $22/£14

MACHEN, ARTHUR. The House of Souls. Boston: Dana Estes, 1906. 1st ed, US issue. Pict gray cl. (Eps sl foxed), else Fine. *Certo*. $250/£160

MACHEN, ARTHUR. The London Adventure or the Art of Wandering. London: Martin Secker, (1924). 1st ed. NF (eps browned) in white dj (soil, lib mks). *Antic Hay*. $50/£32

MACHEN, ARTHUR. The London Adventure. NY, 1924. 1st Amer ed. Yellow mustard cl (soiled), purple spine label (faded). Good+. *Mcclintock*. $20/£13

MACHEN, ARTHUR. The Secret Glory. Knopf, 1922. 1st US ed. VG. *Certo*. $25/£16

MACHEN, ARTHUR. The Secret Glory. NY, 1922. 1st Amer ed. Yellow mustard cl (spotted), purple spine label, gilt. VG. *Mcclintock*. $25/£16

MACHEN, ARTHUR. The Shining Pyramid. Vincent Starrett (ed). Chicago, 1923. 1st ed. #869/875. Interior VG (cvrs dull, worn, spine label chipped). *Mcclintock*. $65/£42

MACHEN, ARTHUR. Strange Roads. London: Classic Press, 1924. Ltd to 300 numbered, signed. Vellum, bds. Fine. *Antic Hay*. $125/£80

MACHEN, ARTHUR. The Terror. NY: McBride, (1917). 1st Amer ed. VG (paper browned; spine dull). *Mcclintock*. $40/£26

MACHEN, ARTHUR. The Terror. London: Duckworth, (1927). Rev ed. Full-pg signed inscription, dated Sept 12, 1927. Fine (spine sl sunned). *Certo*. $210/£135

MACHEN, ARTHUR. Things Near and Far. London: Martin Secker, (1923). 1st trade ed. Grn cl. NF in dj (sl wear, sm internal mend). *Antic Hay*. $50/£32

MACHEN, ARTHUR. Things Near and Far. London: Secker, 1923. 1st Eng ed. Very Nice in dj (sl rubbed, nicked). *Clearwater*. $78/£50

MACHEN, ARTHUR. Things Near and Far. NY, 1923. 1st Amer ed. Yellow mustard cl, purple spine label (rubbed), gilt. VG. *Mcclintock*. $27/£17

MACHEN, ARTHUR. War and the Christian Faith. London, 1918. 1st ed. (Spine ends sl chipped.) Dj (3/4-inch chip spine bottom, top nicked, lt edgeworn). *Mcclintock*. $95/£61

MACHETANZ, FREDERICK. On Arctic Ice. NY, c. 1940. VG. *High Latitude*. $25/£16

MACHETANZ, SARA. The Howl of the Malemute. NY, 1961. 1st ed. Cl-backed bds. VG in dj. *High Latitude*. $25/£16

MACHIAVELLI, NICHOLAS. The Works of the Famous Nicolas Machiavel, Citizen and Secretary of Florence. London: John Starkey, 1675. 1st collected ed. Folio. (xl),529,(16),(5 ad leaves)pp (tp remargined inner border, final leaf w/tape repair, text lt browned). Recent 1/4 calf. Clean. *Goodrich*. $1,500/£962

MACILWAIN, GEORGE. Memoirs of John Abernethy, F.R.S. London, 1853. 1st ed. 2 vols. Port. (Cl worn, sl soiled, section sprung, BMA copy w/stamps.) *Maggs*. $94/£60

MACILWAIN, GEORGE. Memoirs of John Abernethy.... London, 1853. 1st ed. 2 vols. Engr frontis port. Mod buckram. VG. *Argosy*. $65/£42

MacINNES, C. M. The Early English Tobacco Trade. London: Kegan Paul et al, 1926. 1st ed. (Text foxing.) Brn cl. *Karmiole*. $75/£48

MacINNES, COLIN. Absolute Beginners. NY, 1960. 1st Amer ed. NF in VG+ dj. *Warren*. $45/£29

MacINNES, COLIN. City of Spades. London, 1957. 1st Eng ed. Very Nice in dj. *Clearwater*. $62/£40

MacINNES, COLIN. City of Spades. NY: Macmillan, 1958. 1st Amer ed. VG (eps sl browned, 2 sm mks fore-edge) in dj (sm chip). *Antic Hay*. $15/£10

MacINNES, COLIN. City of Spades. NY: Macmillan, 1958. 1st Amer ed. NF (eps lt browned) in dj (sl worn). *Antic Hay*. $25/£16

MacINNES, COLIN. June in Her Spring. London: MacGibbon & Kee, 1952. Advance Reading Copy w/slip laid in. (Fore-edge sl foxed), else NF in VG+ dj (spine sl tanned). *Between The Covers*. $75/£48

MacINNES, COLIN. Mr. Love and Justice. London, 1960. 1st Eng ed. Nice in dj. *Clearwater*. $39/£25

MacINNES, COLIN. Prelude to Terror. NY: Harcourt, Brace, Jovanovich, (1978). 1st Amer ed. Fine in dj. *Antic Hay*. $17/£11

MacINNES, COLIN. Three Years to Play. NY: FSG, (1970). 1st Amer ed. Fine in dj (sm tear). *Antic Hay*. $17/£11

MacINNES, COLIN. Westward to Laughter. MacGibbon & Kee, (1969). 1st ed. Nice in dj. *Ash*. $31/£20

MacINNES, COLIN. Westward to Laughter. London, 1969. 1st ed. Dj. *Typographeum*. $20/£13

MacINNES, COLIN. Westward to Laughter. London, 1969. 1st Eng ed. Fine in dj. *Clearwater*. $31/£20

MacINNES, HELEN. Agent in Place. NY: Harcourt Brace Jovanovich, 1976. 1st ed. Fine in NF dj. *Janus.* $20/£13

MacINNES, HELEN. Message from Malaga. London: Collins, 1972. 1st ed. NF in dj. *Antic Hay.* $25/£16

MACINTYRE, DUGALD. Highland Naturalist. London: Seeley Service, (1944). 2nd ed. 8 plts. (Few spots fore-edge.) *Hollett.* $23/£15

MACK, CONNIE. Connie Mack's Baseball Book. NY: Knopf, 1950. 1st ed. Signed. Related material, dj flap taped to rear pastedown. Good+ (edgeworn, sl water-flecked). *Glenn.* $200/£128

MACK, CONNIE. My 66 Years in the Big Leagues. Phila: John C. Winston, (1950). Authorized ed. VG+ in wraps (edges worn, fr cvr scratched, corner wrinkled). *Fuller & Saunders.* $25/£16

MACK, EBENEZER. The Cat-Fight. NY, 1824. 1st ed. 276pp (foxed, minor stains). New plain cl. *King.* $250/£160

MACK, EFFIE MONA. Mark Twain in Nevada. NY, 1947. 1st ed. VG in dj (sl frayed). *King.* $20/£13

MACK, G. and T. GIBSON. Architectural Details of Southern Spain. NY: William Helburn, 1928. Frontis, 149 plts. Sound. *Ars Artis.* $70/£45

MACK, GERSTLE. Toulouse-Lautrec. NY, 1949. Color frontis, 58 plts. (Spine faded.) *Hollett.* $70/£45

MACKAIL, J. W. The Life of William Morris. London/NY/Bombay, 1901. New ed. 2 vols. (Rubbed.) Internally VG. *Mcclintock.* $30/£19

MACKAIL, J. W. William Morris. An Address Delivered.... Hammersmith, 1901. One of 300. Limp vellum. *Swann*.* $138/£88

MacKAY, ALASTAIR I. Farming and Gardening in the Bible. Emmaus, PA, 1950. 1st ed. Frontis. (Spine faded), else VG in dj. *Brooks.* $37/£24

MACKAY, ALEXANDER. The Western World, or Travels in the United States in 1846-47. London: R. Bentley, 1849. 3 vols. Fldg frontis map, xix,340; iv,321; fldg frontis map, iv,374pp. (New eps.) Orig brn cl-cvrd bds (rebacked), new black cl backstrips, gilt spine labels. (Pencil mks; worn, chipped), else VG. Howes M117. *Bohling.* $250/£160

MACKAY, ALEXANDER. The Western World. Phila, 1849. 1st Amer ed. 2 vols. xii,312pp+(32)pp pub's ads; iv,(13)-316pp. (Lt foxed; spine ends chipped), else VG. Howes M117. *Reese.* $300/£192

MacKAY, ANDREW. The Complete Navigator. London, 1810. 2nd ed. 268+260pp of tables. 1/2 calf (fr cvr detached, heavily worn, soiled). *King.* $50/£32

MACKAY, CHARLES (ed). Medora Leigh. Richard Bentley, 1869. 1st ed. (Upper hinge broken; cl stained.) *Poetry Bookshop.* $31/£20

MACKAY, CHARLES. Memoirs of Extraordinary Popular Delusions. London: Richard Bentley, 1841. 1st ed. 3 vols. 5 engr plts. Teg. 3/4 brn polished calf, marbled bds, raised bands. *Appelfeld.* $325/£208

MacKAY, DOUGLAS. The Honourable Company. Toronto: Musson, 1938. 1st ed under this pub. Frontis, 47 photo plts and illus. Pict eps. Gilt blue cl. Fine (sm address label on blank leaf). *Argonaut.* $90/£58

MACKAY, GEORGE HENRY. Shooting Journal 1865-1922. Cambridge, MA: Phillips, 1929. Ltd to 300. Cl-backed marbled bds. (Fr outer hinge cracked, spine lettering faded), o/w VG. *New Hampshire*.* $75/£48

MacKAY, H. Fishes of Ontario. Toronto, 1963. 1st ed. 26 color plts. (Few stamps; cl spotted.) *Maggs.* $25/£16

MACKAY, JAMES. Nursery Antiques. London, 1976. 1st UK ed. (Sl spotting.) Dj. *Edwards.* $55/£35

MACKAYE, PERCY. Poog and the Caboose Man. NY, 1952. 1st Amer ed. Fine in NF dj (spine sl sunned). *Polyanthos.* $30/£19

MACKEN, WALTER. Seek the Fair Land. London: Macmillan, 1959. 1st UK ed. Fine in dj (sl dusty). *Williams.* $28/£18

MACKEN, WALTER. Sullivan. NY: Macmillan, 1957. 1st ed. Fine in VG dj (price-clipped). *Antic Hay.* $20/£13

MACKENZIE, ALEXANDER. Voyages from Montreal, on the River St. Laurence, Through the Continent of North America. NY, 1814. 2 vols. (Worn; lacks port plt, maps.) *Swann*.* $126/£81

MACKENZIE, ALEXANDER. Voyages from Montreal...Through the Continent of North America...in the Years 1789 and 1793. London: T. Cadell et al, 1801. 1st ed. 4to. Port, 132, 3 fldg maps, 1-412pp, errata leaf. Recent 1/2 calf (rebound), marbled bds, eps, red leather label. (Ex-lib, handstamp tp, text sl browned, insect damage some margins, maps; map coloring, archival map repairs), o/w Good. Howes M133. *Brown.* $1,500/£962

MACKENZIE, COLIN. Five Thousand Receipts. Phila, 1829. (Back matter wormed, sl loss index text, damp-staining, browning.) Contemp calf (rubbed). *Freeman*.* $80/£51

MACKENZIE, COMPTON. Extraordinary Women. London: Martin Secker, 1928. Ltd to 2000. Yellow cl. Good (eps foxed). *Antic Hay.* $35/£22

MACKENZIE, COMPTON. Kensington Rhymes. Secker, 1912. 1st ed. (Bds sl dull, sl worn.) Contents Good. *Whiteson.* $22/£14

MACKENZIE, COMPTON. The Lunatic Republic. London: C&W, 1959. 1st ed. Fine in Fine dj. *Certo.* $20/£13

MACKENZIE, COMPTON. My Life and Times: Octave Six, 1923-1930. London: C&W, 1967. 1st ed. Fine in dj (wear). *Antic Hay.* $20/£13

MACKENZIE, COMPTON. On Moral Courage. London: Collins, 1962. 1st Eng ed. Fine in dj (lt wear, sl soil, crease). *Antic Hay.* $25/£16

MACKENZIE, D. The Flooding of the Sahara. 1877. xix,287pp. (Spine sl discolored, fr cvr sl mkd), o/w VG. *Whitehart.* $39/£25

MACKENZIE, DeWITT. Men Without Guns. Phila, 1945. 137 plts. Pict cvr label. (Corners worn.) *Argosy.* $65/£42

MacKENZIE, DONALD. The Quiet Killer. Boston: Houghton, Mifflin, 1958. 1st ed. Fine in dj (sl worn, rubbed). *Antic Hay.* $17/£11

MACKENZIE, J. The History of Health and the Art of Preserving It.... Edinburgh, 1759. 2nd ed. xii,436pp. Leather. (Spine top sl chipped, bkpl), o/w VG. *Whitehart.* $281/£180

MACKENZIE, JAMES. Principles of Diagnosis and Treatment in Heart Affections. London: Henry Frowde, 1918. 4th imp. Red cl (spine faded). VG. *White.* $28/£18

MACKENZIE, MORELL. The Fatal Illness of Frederick the Noble. London: Sampson Low et al, 1888. 1st ed. 246pp. VG. *White.* $44/£28

MACKENZIE, W. M. The Mediaeval Castle in Scotland. London: Methuen, 1927. 32 plts, 19 plans. (Lib stamp tp, verso, versos of plts; gilt lib #, ref on spine), else VG. *Ars Artis.* $39/£25

MACKENZIE, W. M. Pompeii. London: A&C Black, 1910. 10 color plts (1 detached), fldg plan. (Feps lt browned.) Teg. Dec cl. *Edwards.* $39/£25

MACKENZIE, W. M. Pompeii. London: A&C Black, 1910. 1st ed. 20 color plts. (Eps lt browned; sl rubbed, spotted.) *Hollett.* $70/£45

MACKEY, MARGARET G. et al. Early California Costumes 1769-1847 and Historic Flags of California. Stanford, 1932. 1st ed. Fine. *Turpen.* $29/£19

MACKEY, SAMSON A. The Mythological Astronomy of the Ancients Demonstrated. London: Hunt & Clark, 1826. Frontis wheel, x,236pp. VG (rebound). *Middle Earth*. $245/£157

MACKIE, GEORGE. Lynton Lamb. Scolar, 1978. Dj (sl chipped). *Edwards*. $23/£15

MacKINNON, DONALD D. Memoirs of Clan Fingon. Turnbridge Wells, n.d. (ca 1882). 221pp; fldg chart. Orig cl (wear, discoloring). *Cullen*. $45/£29

MACKINTOSH, HAROLD. Early English Figure Pottery. London: Chapman & Hall, 1938. 1st ed. Signed. Color frontis, 15pp of plts. VG in dj (sl soiled, chipped). *Hollett*. $250/£160

MACKLEY, GEORGE. Wood Engravings. London: National Magazine, 1948. 1st ed. VG in dj. *Michael Taylor*. $59/£38

MACKWORTH-PRAED, C. W. and C. H. B. GRANT. Birds of Eastern and North Eastern Africa. London: Longmans, 1952. 1st ed. 53 color, 6 b/w plts. Gilt-dec cl. Fine in VG dj. *Mikesh*. $95/£61

MACKWORTH-PRAED, C. W. and C. H. B. GRANT. Birds of Eastern and North Eastern Africa. Longmans, Green, 1957/60. 2nd ed. 2 vols. 96 color plts. Buckram. Good in djs (rubbed). *Cox*. $70/£45

MACKWORTH-PRAED, C. W. and C. H. B. GRANT. Birds of the Southern Third of Africa. London, 1962-3. 1st ed. 2 vols. 76 color, 20 b/w plts. Gilt-device upper bd. (Faded.) *Edwards*. $70/£45

MACLAREN-ROSS, J. Better Than a Kick in the Pants. London: Lawson & Dunn, 1945. Very Good (foxed, rubber stamp fep; fr cvr sl mkd) in dj (torn, frayed). *Clearwater*. $86/£55

MACLAREN-ROSS, J. The Funny Bone. London: Elek Books, 1956. 1st UK ed. VG in dj (sl foxed). *Williams*. $39/£25

MACLAREN-ROSS, J. The Nine Men of Soho. London: Wingate, 1946. 1st Eng ed. Good in dj (worn). *Clearwater*. $70/£45

MACLAREN-ROSS, J. The Weeping and the Laughter. London, 1953. 1st Eng ed. Very Nice in dj (sl chafed, spine chipped). *Clearwater*. $62/£40

MacLAVERTY, BERNARD. Lamb. Cape, 1980. 1st UK ed. NF (agent stamp fep) in dj. *Williams*. $23/£15

MACLAY, ARTHUR COLLINS. A Budget of Letters from Japan. NY, 1889. 2nd ed. xii,(i),391pp + (i) pub's ads (ex-lib, bkpls, blind stamps). Dec eps. (Cl sl spotted, spine faded, rubbed.) *Edwards*. $47/£30

MACLAY, EDGAR STANTON. A History of American Privateers. NY: Appleton, 1899. *Metropolitan**. $74/£47

MACLAY, EDGAR STANTON. A History of the United States Navy from 1775 to 1893. NY: Appleton, 1894. 2 vols. 577pp + ads; 640pp. Teg. Dec cvrs, spines. Good. *Scribe's Perch**. $70/£45

MACLAY, EDGAR STANTON. A History of the United States Navy from 1775 to 1893. NY: Appleton, 1894. 1st ed. 2 vols. Teg. 3/4 dk blue morocco, marbled bds (extrems sl rubbed), gilt, raised bands. *Sadlon*. $125/£80

MACLEAN, A. D. (ed). Winter's Tales 21. London: Macmillan, 1935. 1st ed. VG in dj. *Hollett*. $23/£15

MacLEAN, ALISTAIR. Caravan to Vaccares. London: Collins, 1970. 1st UK ed. Fine in dj. *Williams*. $19/£12

MacLEAN, ALISTAIR. Force 10 from Navarone. GC, 1968. 1st ed. NF in VG+ dj. *Smith*. $15/£10

MacLEAN, ALISTAIR. The Last Frontier. London: Collins, 1959. 1st ed. Fine in dj. *Mordida*. $85/£54

MacLEAN, ALISTAIR. Night Without End. Collins, 1960. 1st UK ed. NF in dj. *Williams*. $23/£15

MacLEAN, ALISTAIR. River of Death. London: Collins, 1981. 1st ed. Fine in dj. *Mordida*. $45/£29

MACLEAN, CATHERINE MACDONALD. Dorothy Wordsworth. The Early Years. NY, 1932. 1st Amer ed. NF (spine sl sunned, top edge sl stained). *Polyanthos*. $35/£22

MacLEAN, J.P. The Mound Builders. Cincinnati: Robert Clarke, 1879. 1st ed. 233,(3)pp, fldg map bound in at rear. Dec reddish brn cl, gilt, beveled bds. Fine. *Harrington*. $100/£64

MACLEAN, NORMAN. Young Men and Fire. Chicago: Univ of Chicago, (1992). 1st ed. As New in dj. *Between The Covers*. $65/£42

MacLEISH, ARCHIBALD. Conquistador. Boston: Houghton Mifflin, 1932. 1st ed. (Eps sl tanned), else Fine in VG dj (edges tanned, nicks top edge). *Reese*. $50/£32

MacLEISH, ARCHIBALD. The Happy Marriage and Other Poems. Boston, 1924. 1st Amer ed. NF (spine sunned, edges sl rubbed). *Polyanthos*. $30/£19

MacLEISH, ARCHIBALD. J.B. A Play in Verse. Boston: Houghton Mifflin, 1958. 1st ed. (Pencil name), else Fine in NF white dj (spine tanned). *Reese*. $30/£19

MacLEISH, ARCHIBALD. Land of the Free. NY: Harcourt Brace, 1938. 1st ed. Rev copy. 88 photo plts. (Owner stamp, fr hinge loose), else VG. *Cahan*. $45/£29

MacLENNAN, HUGH. Contemporary Canadian Photography. Edmonton: Hurtig, 1984. 1st ed. Fine in illus dj. *Cahan*. $65/£42

MacLEOD, CHARLOTTE. Rest You Merry. London: CCC, 1979. 1st Eng ed. VF in dj. *Mordida*. $65/£42

MacLEOD, DAWN. Oasis of the North. London: Hutcheson, 1966. 5th imp. Fine in pict dj. *Quest*. $35/£22

MACLEOD, JOHN J. R. Diabetes: Its Pathological Physiology. London: Edward Arnold, 1913. 1st ed. Red cl. Good. *White*. $101/£65

MACLEOD, N. German Lyric Poetry. London: Hogarth, 1930. (1st eps browned; spine sl faded, rubbed), o/w VG in dj (soiled, torn, lacks sm strip top edge, base of spine). *Virgo*. $31/£20

MACLISE, JOSEPH. On Dislocations and Fractures. London: John Churchill, 1859. 1st ed. Lg folio. Unpaginated (sm lib stamp tp, few fore-edges chipped); 36 full-pg plts. Teg. New 1/2 morocco. Fine. *Glaser*. $1,500/£962

MACLISE, JOSEPH. Surgical Anatomy. Phila: Blanchard & Lea, 1851. 1st Amer ed. Folio. 3(ads),xii,9-156,4-6(ads)pp (foxed); 68 partly hand-colored plts. Orig emb gilt-dec cl (rebacked), leather spine label. VG (extrems sl worn). *Glaser*. $950/£609

MacLYSAGHT, EDWARD. Irish Families: Their Names, Arms and Origins. Dublin, 1957. Dj (lt worn, soiled). *Freeman**. $80/£51

MacMICHAEL, WILLIAM. The Gold-Headed Cane. London, 1827. 1st ed. 179pp. 1/4 leather (rebacked, spine ends sl rubbed), marbled bds. *Fye*. $600/£385

MacMICHAEL, WILLIAM. Lives of British Physicians. London, 1830. 1st ed. 341pp. Recent 1/4 leather. VG. *Fye*. $100/£64

MacMICHEAL, WILLIAM. Lives of British Physicians. London, 1830. 341pp; 4 Fine engr plts. (Bds sl rubbed, worn.) *Goodrich*. $75/£48

MACMILLAN, DONALD B. Etah and Beyond or Life Within Twelve Degrees of the Pole. Boston: Houghton Mifflin, 1927. Inscribed, signed 1932. VG. *High Latitude*. $50/£32

MACMILLAN, DONALD B. Etah and Beyond. Boston/NY: Houghton Mifflin, 1927. 1st ed. 65 plts, incl 2 maps. (sl rubbed, soiled; ex-lib, # spine), o/w VG. *Worldwide*. $25/£16

MACMILLAN, DONALD B. Four Years in the White North. NY: Harper, (1918). 1st ed. Teg. VG. *High Latitude.* $50/£32

MACMILLAN, DONALD B. Four Years in the White North. London, 1925. VG (ex-lib, sl used). *High Latitude.* $20/£13

MacMINN, EDWIN. On the Frontier with Colonel Antes; or, The Struggle for Supremacy of the Red and White Races in Pennsylvania. Camden, NJ, 1900. 1st ed. One of 1000. Dec cl. *Ginsberg.* $150/£96

MacNAGHTEN, HUGH. The Story of Catullus. London: Duckworth, 1899. 1st ed. Aeg. Full dk grn crushed levant. (Bkpl, offset eps from doublures), o/w NF. *Reese.* $60/£38

MacNEICE, LOUIS. The Dark Tower. London, 1947. 1st ed. (Eps browned; cvr sl faded), o/w VG in Bright dj (spine heavily chipped). *Buckley.* $59/£38

MacNEICE, LOUIS. Holes in the Sky. NY, 1948. 1st Amer ed. Fine in dj (spine sunned, 4 sm edge tears, sl soiled). *Polyanthos.* $30/£19

MacNEICE, LOUIS. One for the Grave. London, 1968. 1st ed. NF in dj (spine nicked). *Buckley.* $55/£35

MacNEICE, LOUIS. Plant and Phantom. Faber & Faber, (1941). 1st ed. Nice (sl foxing, sl bumped) in dj (chipped, sl torn). *Ash.* $70/£45

MacNEICE, LOUIS. The Strings Are False. London: Faber & Faber, (1965). 1st ed. Fine in dj (sl wear, soil). *Antic Hay.* $25/£16

MacNEICE, LOUIS. Ten Burnt Offerings. London: Faber, 1952. 1st UK ed. Fine in VG dj (unevenly dknd, dusty). *Williams.* $31/£20

MacNEIL, NEIL. (Pseud of W. T. Ballard.) Death Takes an Option. Greenwich, CT: Gold Medal #807, 1958. 1st ed, pb orig. (Sm crease), else Fine. *Murder By The Book.* $25/£16

MACOMB, JOHN N. Report of the Exploring Expedition from Santa Fe to Junction of Grand and Green Rivers. (Washington, 1876.) (iii)-vii,(1),152pp (lacks title leaf); 11 litho color plts, 11 b/w (lacks fldg map). Contents VG (ends worn, spine mottled). *Waverly*.* $49/£31

MACOMB, JOHN N. Report of the Exploring Expedition from Santa Fe, to...Colorado of the West. Washington: GPO, 1876. Folio. Complete w/22 plts (11 color), fldg map. 1/2 leather, marbled paper. (Attractively rebound, corner bumped, internal pencil), else Nice. *Metropolitan*.* $575/£369

MacPHAIL, IAN (comp). Hortus Botanicus. Lisle: Moreton Arboretum, 1972. One of 2000. Fine in stiff pict wraps. *Quest.* $45/£29

MACPHERSON, DAVID. Annals of Commerce. London: Nichols, 1805. 4 vols. (Ex-lib, sm ink stamps, sm piece torn away tp, 1st leaf vol 3; margins sl browned, sl spotted.) Uncut. Lib cl (rebound, spine #s), gilt. *Edwards.* $468/£300

MACPHERSON, H. A History of Fowling. Edinburgh, 1897. 1st ed. (Cl sl stained.) *Maggs.* $86/£55

MACPHERSON, H. A History of Fowling. Edinburgh: David Douglas, 1897. 1st ed. Grn cl (expertly rebacked), gilt top. (Few holograph annotations on margins), else Fine. *Appelfeld.* $125/£80

MACPHERSON, H. The Home-Life of the Golden Eagle. London, 1909. 32 mtd plts, add'l watercolor. (Text ends foxed.) Wrappers. *Henly.* $44/£28

MACPHERSON, H. et al. The Pheasant. A. E. T. Watson (ed). London: Longmans, Green, 1904. 3rd imp. Teg. Pict cl (spine sl mottled), gilt. *Hollett.* $55/£35

MACPHERSON, KENNETH. Room 12 Noon. London: Collins, (1964). 1st ed. Fine in NF dj. *Reese.* $30/£19

MACPHERSON, WILLIAM CHARLES (ed). Soldiering in India, 1764-1787. Edinburgh, 1928. Frontis, 4 plts, 5 fldg maps at rear (3 called for). Maroon cl (sl worn), gilt. *Maggs.* $109/£70

MacQUEEN, PETER. In Wildest Africa. Boston: Page, 1909. Fldg map. Lt brn pict cl (shabby). Internally VG. *Terramedia.* $50/£32

MACQUOID, PERCY and RALPH EDWARD. The Dictionary of English Furniture. London/NY, n.d. c.(1924-27). 1st eds. 3 vols. Folio. 51 color plts. Teg, marbled eps. (Margins sl browned; upper hinge vol 1 sl cracked, torn; sl edgewear, head joints vol 2 sl split.) *Edwards.* $546/£350

MACQUOID, PERCY. A History of English Furniture. London, 1938. Rpt. (Ex-lib, ink stamps, label, bkpl; rebound in lib cl, spine #s.) *Edwards.* $70/£45

MacRAE, DAVID. The Americans at Home. Edinburgh, 1870. 2 vols. xxiv,332; vi,408pp. Blue cl (rubbed; hinges cracked). Howes M184. *Reese.* $200/£128

MACROBERT, H. (ed). The Central Highlands. Edinburgh: S.M.C., 1934. 1st ed. 2 photogravures, 2 maps. VG in dj. *Hollett.* $39/£25

MACY, JESSE. Jesse Macy; An Autobiography. Katherine Macy Noyes (ed). Springfield, 1933. 1st ed. VG + (ex-lib). *Pratt.* $55/£35

MACY, OBED. The History of Nantucket...together with the Rise and Progress of the Whole Fishery. Boston, 1835. Map, litho plt. Pub's cl (spine ends frayed, fr joint starting; lacks fep). Howes M195. *Swann*.* $201/£129

MADAUS, HOWARD MICHAEL. The Battle Flags of the Confederate Army of Tennessee. Milwaukee Public Museum, 1976. 1st ed. Presentation copy. NF in stiff wrappers. *Mcgowan.* $175/£112

MADDEN, R. R. A Twelvemonth's Residence in the West Indies.... Phila, 1835. 2 vols in 1. Contemp 1/2 sheep (needs rebinding). *Swann*.* $69/£44

MADDOCK, ALFRED BEAUMONT. Practical Observations on Mental and Nervous Disorders. London: Simpkin, Marshall, 1857. 2nd ed. 4,(vi),236,(4)pp. Ptd emb red cl (lib stamps tp; shelfworn, fr cvr stained). Good + . *Gach.* $250/£160

MADDOW, BEN. Faces. 1977. 1st ed. Dj (sl faded). *Edwards.* $47/£30

MADDOW, BEN. Faces: A Narrative History of the Portrait in Photography. Boston: NYGS, 1977. 1st ed. Fine in dj (sl rubbed). *Cahan.* $150/£96

MADDOW, BEN. Let Truth Be the Prejudice. NY: Aperture, 1985. 1st ed. As New in dj. *Cahan.* $100/£64

MADDOW, BEN. The Photography of Max Yavno. Berkeley: Univ of CA, 1981. 1st ed. 85 full-pg b/w photos. (Lt crease ep), else Fine in illus dj (price-clipped). *Cahan.* $100/£64

MADDOX, JERALD C. (intro). Walker Evans: Photographs for the Farm Security Administration, 1935-1938. NY: Da Capo, 1973. 1st ed. NF in VG dj. *Cahan.* $65/£42

MADISON, J. O. Madison's Direct Shoulder Measure Vest System. NY, (1906). Port. (Lt wear.) *Freeman*.* $35/£22

MADISON, JAMES. Selections from the Private Correspondence...from 1813 to 1836. Washington: McGuire for Private Distribution, 1859. Uncut, unopened. Later 1/2 sheep. *Swann*.* $149/£96

MADOX, THOMAS. Baronia Anglica. London: Francis Gosling, 1741. 1st ed. 292,(28)pp; copper engr tp vignette. Mod calf, burgundy bds, black spine label. Good. *Karmiole.* $300/£192

MADSEN, BRIGHAM D. The Bannock of Idaho. Caldwell: Caxton, 1958. Color frontis. Good in Good dj. *Scribe's Perch*.* $27/£17

MADSEN, BRIGHAM D. The Northern Shoshoni. Caldwell: Caxton, 1980. 1st ed. VG in dj. *Lien.* $40/£26

MAETERLINCK, MAURICE. Aglavaine and Selysette. Alfred Sutro (trans). NY: Dodd, Mead, 1911. 1st Amer ed. Teg. Emb grn cl. NF. *Antic Hay.* $35/£22

MAETERLINCK, MAURICE. Monna Vanna. A.I. Du Pont Coleman (trans). NY: Harper, 1903. 1st Amer ed. VG (sl foxed, esp eps). *Antic Hay.* $35/£22

MAGEE, DAVID. Infinite Riches: The Adventures of a Rare Book Dealer. NY: Eriksson, 1973. Dj. *Rostenberg & Stern.* $25/£16

MAGEE, DAVID. Two Gentlemen from Indiana Now Resident in California. SF: Privately Ptd, 1961. 1st ed. Ltd to 250. Fine in dec ptd wrappers. *Shasky.* $55/£35

Magic Picture Book. NY: G.W. Dillingham, (1908). Flip Book. Robert H. Porteous (illus). 10x7.5. Cl (sl stain back cvr), color pict label. Overall Good (interior soil, sl margin tears). *King.* $125/£80

Magician's Own Book. NY: Dick & Fitzgerald, (1857). True 1st ed w/Edward O. Jenkins to verso tp. (Foxing.) Dec-stamped cl (dull, rubbed, extrems sl worn), spine gilt. *Dramatis Personae.* $65/£42

MAGILL, JOHN. Pioneer to the Kentucky Emigrant. Thomas D. Clark (ed). Lexington, 1942. Cl-backed patterned bds, ptd spine label. Fine. *Bohling.* $28/£18

MAGILL, MARCUS. Who Shall Hang? Phila: Lippincott, 1929. 1st Amer ed. VG in dj (price-clipped, chipped, spine faded). *Mordida.* $45/£29

MAGINN, WILLIAM. A Gallery of Illustrious Literary Characters (1830-1838). William Bates (ed). C&W, (1873). Frontis, 83 Fine plts. Contemp 1/2 dk blue hard-grained morocco gilt, gilt-panelled back, gilt edges. *Hatchwell.* $312/£200

MAGNER, D. Magner's Standard Horse and Stock Book: A Complete Pictorial Encyclopedia.... Akron: Saalfield, (1916). Gilt-pict cl. (Hinges reinforced), else VG. *Mikesh.* $75/£48

MAGNER, GENE. Trial of the Masks. Sausalito: Bern Porter, 1950. 1st ed. One of 250 numbered, signed. Fine in dj (lt used). *Reese.* $35/£22

MAGNUS, ALBERTUS. Egyptian Secrets. Chicago: Egyptian Pub, n.d. (1920s). Dec cvr. (Stain ffep), o/w VG. *Middle Earth.* $60/£38

MAGOFFIN, SUSAN SHELBY. Down the Santa Fe Trail and into Mexico. New Haven: Yale Univ, 1926. Frontis, 6 plts, fldg map. Blue cl (sl rubbed). VG (bkpl, sm sticker fr pastedown). Howes M211. *Parmer.* $125/£80

MAGOFFIN, SUSAN SHELBY. Down the Santa Fe Trail and into Mexico...1846-47. Stella M. Drumm (ed). New Haven, 1926. 1st ed. Signed by ed. VG +. Howes M211. *Turpen.* $150/£96

MAGUIRE, ROCHFORT. The Journal of...1852-1854. John Bockstoce (ed). Hakluyt Soc, 1988. 2 vols. Frontis port, 5 maps (1 fldg). Djs. *Edwards.* $39/£25

MAHAFFY, J. P. Rambles and Studies in Greece. Phila: Coates, 1900. 30 plts, fldg color map. Teg. (Sl rubbed, faded), o/w VG. *Worldwide.* $30/£19

MAHAN, A. T. The Influence of Sea Power upon History 1660-1783. London: Sampson Low, Marston, (1890, but later). Early reissue of 1890 Amer ed. xxiv,(558)pp. Contemp tree calf, contrasting labels. VG. *Ash.* $195/£125

MAHAN, A. T. The Life of Nelson. Boston: Little Brown, 1897. 1st ed. 2 vols. 454; 427pp + ads. Teg. Nelson port in gilt on cvrs. (Heads sl bumped), o/w VG. *Scribe's Perch*.* $65/£42

MAHAN, A. T. The Life of Nelson. Boston: Little, Brown, 1897. 1st ed. xxiii,2 l.,454pp, 10 ports, 10 maps & plans; xvi,2 l.,427pp, 9 ports, 10 maps & plans. Blue cl (scuffed, spine worn; internal spotting), gilt. *Parmer.* $125/£80

MAHAN, A. T. The Life of Nelson. London, 1897. 1st ed. 2 vols. xxiii,454; xvi,427pp. Blue cl, gilt. *Maggs.* $187/£120

MAHAN, A. T. Some Neglected Aspects of War. Boston: Little Brown, 1907. Inscribed. (Corners lt bumped), else Fine. *Between The Covers.* $550/£353

MAHON, DEREK. Night Crossing. London, 1968. 1st ed, 1st bk. NF in wrappers (sl rubbed). *Buckley.* $39/£25

MAHON, LORD. History of the War of the Succession in Spain. London: John Murray, 1832. 1st ed. xx,131pp, fldg map, 1/2-title. (Bookseller's label, lending lib label tipped in; corners sl bumped, spine sl chipped.) 8pp unopened prospectus sewn in fr. *Hollett.* $148/£95

MAHONING VALLEY HISTORICAL SOCIETY. Historical Collections of the Mahoning Valley. Vol 1 (all pub). Youngstown, 1876. 524pp; fldg map. (Blindstamp fep; worn, soiled.) Howes M223. *Bohling.* $35/£22

MAHOOD, RUTH I. Photographer of the Southwest, Adam Clark Vroman, 1856-1916. NY: Bonanza, (1961). 90 b/w plts. Cl-backed paper over bds. (Owner stamp), else Fine in pict dj. *Cahan.* $50/£32

MAHOOD, RUTH I. Photographer of the Southwest, Adam Clark Vroman, 1856-1916. (L.A.): Ward Ritchie, 1961. 1st ed. 90 b/w plts. (Owner stamp, names), else NF in pict stiff wrappers. *Cahan.* $40/£26

MAHR, AUGUST C. The Visit of the 'Rurik' to San Francisco in 1816. Stanford: Stanford Univ, 1932. 1st ed. Frontis, 6 plts. Red cl (spine sl faded). Overall Fine (bkpl, sm stamped # on copyright pg). *Argonaut.* $75/£48

MAHY, MARGARET. The Dragon of an Ordinary Family. NY: Franklin Watts, 1969. 1st ed. Helen Oxenbury (illus). 11 x 8 3/4. Pict cl. VG in dj. *Cattermole.* $50/£32

MAHY, MARGARET. A Lion in the Meadow. NY: Franklin Watts, 1969. 1st ed. Jenny Williams (illus). 11 x 8 3/4. Pict cl. VG. *Cattermole.* $40/£26

MAHY, MARGARET. Mrs. Discombobulous. NY: Franklin Watts, 1969. 1st ed. Jan Brychta (illus). 8 1/2 x 11 1/4. Pict cl. Fine in dj. *Cattermole.* $25/£16

MAHY, MARGARET. Pillycock's Shop. NY: Watts, 1969. 1st US ed. 8 3/4 x 11 1/4. 32pp. Fine in dj. *Cattermole.* $30/£19

MAILER, NORMAN et al. We Accuse. (Berkeley, 1965.) 1st ptg. Wrappers (lt worn, soiled). *Freeman*.* $50/£32

MAILER, NORMAN. An American Dream. London: Andre Deutsch, 1965. 1st British ed. Signed. Fine in dj. *Lame Duck.* $100/£64

MAILER, NORMAN. An American Dream. NY: Dial, 1965. 1st ed. Signed. NF in dj. *Lame Duck.* $200/£128

MAILER, NORMAN. Ancient Evenings. Boston: Little Brown, (1983). One of 350 numbered, signed. Fine in Fine slipcase. *Lenz.* $175/£112

MAILER, NORMAN. Ancient Evenings. NY: Little, Brown, (1983). Signed, ltd ed. Cl in pub's box, still sealed in plastic. *Metropolitan*.* $86/£55

MAILER, NORMAN. Armies of the Night. London: Weidenfeld & Nicolson, 1968. 1st British ed. Signed. NF in dj. *Lame Duck.* $100/£64

MAILER, NORMAN. Barbary Shore. NY, (1951). 1st Amer ed. NF in dj (edges sl rubbed). *Polyanthos.* $125/£80

MAILER, NORMAN. Barbary Shore. NY/Toronto: Rinehart, (1951). 1st ed. Fine in Fine dj. *Bernard.* $250/£160

MAILER, NORMAN. Barbary Shore. NY, 1951. 1st Amer ed. Fine (sl rubbed) in dj (sl rubbed). *Polyanthos.* $75/£48

MAILER, NORMAN. The Bullfight, A Photographic Narrative. (NY): Macmillan, (1967). 1st ed. Blind-dec maroon cl. Excellent Record in paper sleeve, box (sl worn), moulded plastic cvr (soiled, sl worn). NF in dj (short tear fr panel). *Hermitage.* $250/£160

MAILER, NORMAN. The Bullfight. NY: Macmillan, (1967). 1st ed. 91 photo plts. Burgundy bds, gilt. (Lacks record), else NF in pict white dj (soiled, sm tears). *Blue Mountain.* $75/£48

MAILER, NORMAN. Cannibals and Christians. NY: Dial, 1966. Rev copy, slip laid in. Signed. NF in dj. *Lame Duck.* $200/£128

MAILER, NORMAN. Deaths for the Ladies and Other Disasters. NY, (1962). 1st ed. VG in dj (rubbed). *Argosy.* $125/£80

MAILER, NORMAN. The Deer Park. Wingate, 1957. 1st UK ed. Fine in dj. *Williams.* $39/£25

MAILER, NORMAN. The Deer Park. London: Wingate, 1957. 1st Eng ed. VG in dj (sl chipped). *Hadley.* $39/£25

MAILER, NORMAN. Existential Errands. Boston: Little Brown, (1972). 1st ed. Signed. Fine in dj (sl rubbed). *Lenz.* $75/£48

MAILER, NORMAN. The Faith of Graffiti. NY: Praeger, 1974. One of 350 signed by Mailer and photographers Mervyn Kurlansky & Jon Naar. New in slipcase. *Bernard.* $100/£64

MAILER, NORMAN. The Fight. Boston: Little Brown, (1975). 1st ed. NF (sl scuff fr bd) in dj (sl rubbing). *Between The Covers.* $65/£42

MAILER, NORMAN. The Fight. Boston, 1975. 1st ed. NF in NF dj. *Warren.* $35/£22

MAILER, NORMAN. Huckleberry Finn, Alive at 100. (Montclair, NJ): Caliban, 1985. One of 50 numbered hb copies. Cl, paper-cvrd bds. Fine. *Between The Covers.* $150/£96

MAILER, NORMAN. Miami and the Siege of Chicago. Weidenfeld & Nicolson, 1968. 1st UK ed. NF in dj. *Sclanders.* $11/£7

MAILER, NORMAN. Miami and the Siege of Chicago. NY: World, 1968. 1st ed. Signed. (Top pg edges lt dusted), else Fine in NF dj. *Lame Duck.* $200/£128

MAILER, NORMAN. The Naked and the Dead. NY: Rinehart, (1948). 1st ed, 1st bk. Ptd bds. Fine in dj. *Bromer.* $450/£288

MAILER, NORMAN. The Naked and the Dead. NY, 1948. 1st Amer ed, 1st bk. NF (spine tips professionally repaired) in dj (spine sl sunned, few edge chips, edges sl rubbed). *Polyanthos.* $125/£80

MAILER, NORMAN. The Naked and the Dead. London, 1949. 1st Eng ed, 1st bk. Very Nice in Poor dj (chaffed, nicked, closed tear, reinforced w/tape). *Clearwater.* $62/£40

MAILER, NORMAN. Why Are We in Vietnam? NY: Putnam, (1967). 1st ed. Signed. Fine in Fine dj. *Lenz.* $75/£48

MAILING, ARTHUR (ed). When Last Seen. NY: Harper & Row, 1977. 1st ed. Fine in NF dj. *Janus.* $20/£13

MAILS, THOMAS E. The Mystic Warriors of the Plains. NY: Doubleday, (1972). 1st ed. VG in dj. *Lien.* $130/£83

MAIRET, ETHEL M. Vegetable Dyes.... St. Dominic's, 1931. 6pp ads; 5 wood engrs. Dyed fabric sample tipped in. 1/4 black cl, dec paper over bds. VG. *Michael Taylor.* $70/£45

MAIS, CHARLES. The Surprising Case of Rachel Baker, Who Prays and Preaches in Her Sleep.... NY, 1814. 2nd ed. 32pp pamphlet. (Lacks wrappers.) *Gach.* $125/£80

MAISON, K. E. Themes and Variations. 1960. 31 color plts tipped in. (Margins sl browned, bkpl; spine lt faded.) *Edwards.* $39/£25

MAITLAND, ANTONY. Idle Jack. NY: FSG, 1977. 1st US ed. 8 3/4 x 11. 28pp. Fine in dj. *Cattermole.* $30/£19

MAITLAND, EDWARD. By and By: An Historical Romance of the Future. NY/London, 1873. 1st Amer ed. Grn cl, gilt. VG (sl rubbed). *Mcclintock.* $95/£61

MAJNO, GUIDO. The Healing Hand. Cambridge: Harvard Univ, (1975). 1st ed. 15 color plts. Pict linen. Fine in dj (lt worn). *Glaser.* $75/£48

Major Jones's Courtship and Travels. (By William Tappan Thompson.) Phila: T.B. Peterson, (1848). 1st ed. Signed, dated Nov 23, 1857. 2 vols in 1. 217; 192pp. Blind-emb cl, gilt. Nice (foxed). *Bohling.* $200/£128

MAJOR, CLARENCE (ed). Black Slang. London: Routledge/Kegan Paul, (1971). 1st Eng ed. Fine in dj. *Between The Covers.* $75/£48

MAJOR, CLARENCE. All-Night Visitors. NY: Olympia, (1969). 1st ed. Fine in VG dj (price-clipped, sm chip fr panel, rubbed). *Between The Covers.* $75/£48

MAJOR, RALPH. Classic Descriptions of Disease. Springfield, 1939. 2nd ed. VG. *Fye.* $75/£48

MAJORS, ALEXANDER. Seventy Years on the Frontier. Prentiss Ingraham (ed). Minneapolis: Ross & Haines, (1965). VG in dj (sl worn). Howes M232. *Lien.* $20/£13

MAJORS, ALEXANDER. Seventy Years on the Frontier.... Prentiss Ingraham (ed). Columbus, 1950. Frontis port. VG. Howes M232. *Turpen.* $38/£24

MAKAL, MAHMUT. A Village in Anatolia. London: Vallentine, Mitchell, 1954. 1st ed. 9 plts, map. (Sl rubbed), o/w VG. *Worldwide.* $22/£14

MAKINS, GEORGE. Surgical Experiences in South Africa, 1899-1900. London, 1913. 2nd ed. (Ex-lib.) *Fye.* $175/£112

MALAMUD, BERNARD. The Natural. NY: Harcourt, Brace, (1952). 1st ed, 1st bk. VG (inscrip, sm stain to text block; egdes sl soiled) in dj (lt edgewear, soiled). *Waverly*.* $385/£247

MALAMUD, BERNARD. The Natural. Eyre & Spottiswode, 1963. 1st British ed. Fine in VG + dj. *Plapinger.* $550/£353

MALAMUD, BERNARD. Pictures of Fidelman. NY, (1969). 1st ed. VG in dj. *Argosy.* $35/£22

MALAMUD, BERNARD. Rembrandt's Hat. NY: FSG, (1973). 1st ed. VG + in VG + dj (lt soiled). *Fuller & Saunders.* $25/£16

MALAMUD, BERNARD. Two Fables. (Pawlet, VT): Banyan, (1978). One of 320 numbered, signed. Fine. *Lenz.* $150/£96

MALCOLM, HOWARD. Travels in South-Eastern Asia. Boston, 1839. 2 vols. 273; 321pp + ads; map laid in vol 2 (repairable tear). Pub's cl, dec cvrs, spines. Good. *Scribe's Perch*.* $130/£83

MALCOLM, JAMES PELLER. Anecdotes of the Manners and Customs of London During the Eighteenth Century.... To Which Is Added, A Sketch of the Domestic Architecture. London: For Longman et al, 1810. 2nd ed. 2 vols. Engr frontis each vol, 45 engrs. (New eps.) Mod 1/2 blue morocco, marbled bds, leather labels. VG. *Dramatis Personae.* $300/£192

MALCOLM, JAMES. A Compendium of Modern Husbandry...of Surrey. London: The Author, 1805. 1st ed. 3 vols. Fldg engr hand-colored map, 4 engr plts, 1 fldg (lt spotting, H3 vol II severely torn w/o loss, marginal tear I2 vol II). Sprinkled edges. Contemp calf (spines, joints worn). Christie's*. $245/£157

MALCOLM, JOHN. The Godwin Sideboard. London: CCC, 1984. 1st ed. VF in dj. Mordida. $65/£42

MALCOLM, JOHN. Whistler in the Dark. London: CCC, 1986. 1st ed. VF in dj. Mordida. $50/£32

MALCOLMSON, ANNE. The Song of Robin Hood. Boston: Houghton Mifflin, 1947. 1st ed. Signed by Virginia Lee Burton (illus). 9 1/4 x 11 1/4. 124pp. Good in dj (price-clipped, worn, chipped). Cattermole. $150/£96

MALET, HUGH POYNTZ. Lost Links in the Indian Mutiny. London: T. Cautley Newby, 1867. 1st ed. (iv),314,(ii)pp. (Neatly restored, eps rejointed; sl dknd, sm tear 1 leaf, few creases.) Good. Ash. $148/£95

MALGONKAR, MANOHAR. A Bend in the Ganges. NY: Viking, (1965). 1st Amer ed. Fine in dj (sm tear). Antic Hay. $25/£16

MALINIAK, JACQUES W. Sculpture in the Living: Rebuilding the Face and Form by Plastic Surgery. NY, 1934. Red cl bds (sl worn). VG. Doctor's Library. $75/£48

MALINOWSKI, BRONISLAW. Argonauts of the Western Pacific. London: Routledge, 1922. 1st ed. 5 maps. Blue cl (spine sl sunned). VG. Terramedia. $100/£64

MALINOWSKI, BRONISLAW. The Sexual Life of Savages in North-Western Melanesia. London: Routledge, 1929. 1st ed. 96 plts. Cl, buckram spine. (Fore-edges foxed), o/w Fine. Andrew Stewart. $62/£40

MALINOWSKI, BRONISLAW. The Sexual Life of Savages in North-Western Melanesia. NY: Halcyon House, 1929. 1st US ed. 91 plts, map, plan. (Bds sl rubbed), o/w VG. Worldwide. $40/£26

MALLESON, G. B. Lord Clive and the Establishment of the English in India. Oxford: Clarendon, 1907. 1st ed. Fldg map. (Sl rubbed, soiled; ex-lib, sticker partly removed from spine), o/w VG. Worldwide. $20/£13

MALLET, ROBERT. Great Neapolitan Earthquake of 1857. London: Chapman & Hall, 1862. 1st ed. 2 vols in 1. xxiv,431; viii,399, 8(ads)pp; 5 lg fldg color maps (2 in rear pocket). Complete w/errata slip vol 2. Mod buckram. VG (lib stamps, card pocket). Glaser. $375/£240

MALLET, ROBERT. On the Physical Conditions Involved in the Construction of Artillery. London, 1856. 238pp; 5 plts. 1/2 leather (ex-lib, mkings; rubbed). King. $200/£128

MALLET, THIERRY. Glimpses of the Barren Lands. NY: Privately ptd, Revillon Freres, 1930. 1st collected ed. Cl-backed bds (spine lt soiled). Sadlon. $20/£13

MALLETT, MARGUERITE. A White Woman Among the Masai. NY, 1923. 1st ed. Frontis port. Edwards. $47/£30

MALLOCH, P. D. Life-History and Habits of the Salmon, Sea-Trout, Trout, and Other Freshwater Fish. A&C Black, 1912. 2nd ed. 2 mtd photo illus on cvr. Good (extrems lt rubbed.) Good. Cox. $59/£38

MALLOCK, W. H. A Romance of the Nineteenth Century. London, 1881. Teg. Contemp full gilt-paneled blue polished Niger morocco (joints chipped), gilt. Freeman*. $90/£58

MALLOWAN, M. E. L. Nimrud and Its Remains. NY: Dodd, Mead, 1966. 2 vols + folder of maps and plans. 9 color plts, 8 maps. Good in dj, slipcase (worn). Archaeologia. $475/£304

MALM, W. P. Japanese Music and Musical Instruments. Tuttle, 1964. 2nd ptg. Dec cvr. Good+ in Good+ dj, Good+ slipcase. Scribe's Perch*. $16/£10

MALMQUIST, O. N. First 100 Years: A History of the Salt Lake Tribune, 1871-1971. Salt Lake City: UT State Hist Soc, (1971). 1st ed. Blue cl, gilt. VG+ in dj (worn, chipped). Bohling. $15/£10

MALONEY, T. J. (ed). U.S. Camera Annual 1936. NY: William Morrow, (1936). Spiral binding. (Lt rubbed, worn), else VG. Hermitage. $65/£42

MALONEY, T. J. (ed). U.S. Camera Annual 1939. NY: William Morrow, (1938). Spiral binding. (Lt rubbed), else VG. Hermitage. $65/£42

MALONEY, T. J. (ed). U.S. Camera Annual 1941. NY: Duel, Sloan & Pearce, 1940. 1st ed. 2 vols. Red cl, paper labels. VG (lib discard stamp feps). Hermitage. $65/£42

MALONEY, T. J. (ed). U.S. Camera Annual 1942. NY: DSP, (1941). 1st ed. VG (edgeworn) in VG dj. Agvent. $65/£42

MALONEY, T. J. (ed). U.S. Camera Annual 1958. NY: U.S. Camera, 1957. 1st ed. (Sig; cl sl dusty), else NF. Cahan. $60/£38

MALORY, THOMAS. The Birth and Acts of King Arthur, of His Noble Knights of the Round Table...Etc. London/NY: J.M. Dent, 1909. 2nd Beardsley ed, containing 10 dwgs not in 1st ed. Ltd to 500 for England, 500 for US. Aubrey Beardsley (illus). Lg 4to. Grn cl, gilt floral design, gilt top. Good. Appelfeld. $650/£417

MALORY, THOMAS. Le Morte d'Arthur. London: J.M. Dent, 1897. 4 vols. Frontis each vol. Teg. Orig limp grn leather (spine rubbed w/loss, fr hinge vol 1 starting), gilt. D & D. $125/£80

MALORY, THOMAS. Le Morte d'Arthur. Boydell, 1985. Ltd to 500. 2 vols. Aubrey Beardsley (designs). New in slipcase. Cox. $55/£35

MALORY, THOMAS. Le Morte d'Arthur. Boston, (1920?). 2 vols. 36 color plts by William Russell Flint. Djs (1 w/tear repaired on verso). Swann*. $230/£147

MALORY, THOMAS. Le Morte d'Arthur. London: LEC, 1936. One of 1500 numbered, signed by Robert Gibbings (illus). 3 vols. Cl-backed bds (sl worn). Slipcase (scuffed). Oinonen*. $70/£45

MALORY, THOMAS. Le Morte d'Arthur. London: LEC, 1936. One of 1500 numbered, signed by Robert Gibbings (illus). 3 vols. Cl-backed dec bds. VG in bd slipcase. Argosy. $150/£96

MALORY, THOMAS. Le Morte d'Arthur. London: J.M. Dent, n.d. Temple Classics ed. 4 vols. Frontis each vol. Teg. Dk blue cl, gilt. VG set. Truepenny. $60/£38

MALORY, THOMAS. Le Morte d'Arthur. London: J.M. Dent, n.d. Aubrey Beardsley (illus). Sm 4to. 12 parts in orig wraps (edges chipped, worn). Very Nice. Metropolitan*. $977/£626

MALORY, THOMAS. The Noble and Joyous Boke Entytled le Morte Darthur. Oxford: Shakespeare Head, 1933. One of 375 numbered. 2 vols. Morocco, gilt. Cl slipcases. Swann*. $632/£405

MALORY, THOMAS. Romance of King Arthur and His Knights of the Round Table. London: Macmillan, 1917. One of 500 signed by Arthur Rackham (illus). Folio. 16 mtd color plts. Mostly unopened. Gilt-dec vellum. VG in cl slipcase. New Hampshire*. $625/£401

MALOUF, DAVID. Child's Play / The Bread of Time to Come. NY: George Braziller, (1982). 1st US ed. (Sm rmdr dot bottom pg edge), else NF in NF dj. Pettler & Lieberman. $25/£16

MALOUF, DAVID. Fly Away Peter. Chatto, 1982. 1st UK ed. Martin. $19/£12

MALOUF, DAVID. Harland's Half Acre. NY, 1984. 1st ed. Fine in Fine dj. Smith. $15/£10

MALOUF, DAVID. Remembering Babylon. Chatto, 1993. 1st ed. Presentation copy. Fine in Fine dj. *Whiteson.* $31/£20

MALRAUX, ANDRE. The Metamorphosis of the Gods. GC: Doubleday, 1960. 1st Amer ed. 8 sepia illus, 4 fldg illus. Red buckram. Fine in pict dj, slipcase w/ptd label. *House.* $80/£51

MALRAUX, ANDRE. The Metamorphosis of the Gods. Stuart Gilbert (trans). London, 1960. 1st UK ed. Dj (sl rubbed). *Edwards.* $31/£20

MALRAUX, ANDRE. Saturn. An Essay on Goya. London, 1957. Good. *Washton.* $50/£32

MALRAUX, ANDRE. The Voices of Silence. GC: Doubleday, 1953. 1st Amer ed. 15 color plts. Blue cl. Fine in dj, slipcase (4-inch split bottom) w/ptd label. *House.* $90/£58

MALTBY, ISAAC. The Elements of War. Boston: Thomas Wait, 1811. 1st ed. xxiv,208pp (foxed); 17 plts. Contemp calf, red leather lettering piece. Good + . *House.* $250/£160

MALTBY, W. J. Captain Jeff; or Frontier Life in Texas with the Texas Rangers. Colorado, TX: Whipkey Ptg, 1906. 2nd issue in wraps. (Back wrap sl chipped, spine repaired), else Good. *Dumont.* $80/£51

MALTE-BRUN, CONRAD. A System of Universal Geography. Boston: S. Walker, 1828-34. 3 vols. 36 engr views, 28 engr maps, 4 tables. (Sl foxing, lt dampstaining vols 1, 3 affecting several plts.) Contemp full tree calf, red morocco labels. *Freeman*.* $100/£64

MALTE-BRUN, CONRAD. A System of Universal Geography.... Boston: Samuel Walker, 1834. 3 vols. Extra engr tps each vol. 2 fldg charts. Orig full calf (sl dusted, scuffed, worn), leather spine labels. Good (sl browned). *Baltimore*.* $170/£109

MALTHUS, T. R. An Essay on the Principle of Population. George Town: J. Milligan, 1809. 1st Amer ed. 2 vols. xvi,510,xxxiv; viii,542pp. Contemp calf (rubbed, hinges partly cracked), red gilt leather spine labels. *Karmiole.* $850/£545

MALTZ, ALBERT and GEORGE SKLAR. Peace on Earth. NY: Samuel French, 1934. 1st ed. Fine in NF dj (sm tear bottom fr panel). *Warren.* $175/£112

MALVERN, GLADYS and CORINNE. Land of Surprise. McLoughlin, 1938. 8.5x11. Pict bds (corner marred from removed price tag). Hidden pictures 'appear' when you pull back pink cellophane pg. VG (1 cellophane pg corner torn; extrems worn). *My Bookhouse.* $40/£26

MAMET, DAVID. American Buffalo. NY: Grove, (1978). 1st ed. Fine in VG dj (tears; lt wear crown). *Between The Covers.* $75/£48

Man Who Killed Hitler. Hollywood: Putnam, 1939. 1st ed. VG in dj (chipped). *Associates.* $45/£29

MANCHESTER, HERBERT. Four Centuries of Sport in America 1490-1890. NY: Derrydale, 1931. 1st ed. One of 800. Brn cl. Fine. *Cummins.* $175/£112

MANCHESTER, LESLIE CLARE. The Funeral at Egg Hill. Boston: Sherman, French, 1911. 1st ed. Teg. Pict tan cl (lt rubbed). *Petrilla.* $40/£26

MANCHESTER, WILLIAM. The City of Anger. NY: Ballantine Books, (1953). 1st ed, hb issue. (Sl shelfwear, sm snag spine.) Dj (rubbed, chipped). *Hermitage.* $45/£29

MANCHESTER, WILLIAM. The Death of a President. NY: H&R, 1967. 1st ed. Fine in NF dj. *Archer.* $20/£13

MANDELKAU, JAMIE. Buttons: The Making of a President. Open Gate Bks, 1971. 1st ed. 8pp photo insert. VG + in dj. *Sclanders.* $23/£15

MANDELSTAM, OSIP. Journey to Armenia. Clarence Brown (trans). London, 1980. 1st Eng ed. Spiral-bound card cvrs. Fine. *Clearwater.* $23/£15

MANDEVILLE, G. HENRY. Flushing, Past and Present. Flushing, L.I., 1860. 180pp; 6 sm litho views mtd in text. *Cullen.* $75/£48

MANFORD, ERASMUS. Twenty Five Years in the West. Chicago: Manford, 1867. 1st ed. 359pp. (Lt soiled, spine faded.) Howes M250. *Ginsberg.* $175/£112

MANFORD, ERASMUS. Twenty Five Years in the West. Chicago, 1875. Rev ed. 375pp; port. *Ginsberg.* $75/£48

MANGAM, WILLIAM D. The Clarks: An American Phenomenon. NY: Silver Bow, 1941. Inscribed. Fine in dj (lt rubbed, spine lightened). *Sadlon.* $225/£144

MANGEOT, SYLVIAN. The Adventures of a Manchurian. London: Travel Book Club, 1975. 1st ed. 4 maps. VG in dj. *Worldwide.* $22/£14

MANGO, CYRIL. Materials for the Study of the Mosaics of St. Sophia at Istanbul. Washington, DC, 1962. 118 plts, 4 fldg maps. Good in dj (worn). *Washton.* $125/£80

MANHOOD, H. A. Bread and Vinegar. London: White Owl, 1931. Ltd to 205 numbered, signed. Dec buckram cl. VG (top edge cl dknd) in acetate dj. *Antic Hay.* $100/£64

MANION, CLARENCE E. Law of the Air, Cases and Materials. Indianapolis: Bobbs-Merrill, 1950. Sound (sl stained). *Boswell.* $65/£42

MANKOWITZ, WOLF. A Kid for Two Farthings. London: Andre Deutsch, 1953. 1st ed. VG in dj (extrems sl worn). *Hollett.* $39/£25

MANKOWITZ, WOLF. Majollika and Company. London: Deutsch, 1955. 1st ed. Fine in Fine dj. *Else Fine.* $35/£22

MANKOWITZ, WOLF. My Old Man's Dustman. London: Deutsch, 1956. 1st ed. Fine in dj (sm chip). *Else Fine.* $35/£22

MANLY, WILLIAM L. Death Valley in '49. San Jose: Pacific Tree & Vine, 1894. 1st ed. (Spine extrems, tips sl worn.) *Dawson.* $225/£144

MANLY, WILLIAM L. Death Valley in '49. Chicago: Lakeside, 1927. Fine. *Book Market.* $50/£32

MANLY, WILLIAM L. Death Valley in '49. L.A., 1949. Centennial ed. Lg fldg map. Pict ep. Tan cl. VG in dj. *Price.* $39/£25

MANLY, WILLIAM L. Death Valley in '49. Milo Milton Quaife (ed). Chicago: Lakeside, Christmas, 1927. Dk grn cl (sm spot lower cvr). *Sadlon.* $30/£19

MANN, E. J. The Deaf and Dumb. Boston: D.K. Hitchcock, 1836. 1st ed. Frontis, xii,(13)-312pp (ex-lib, stamps tp, few ll); 2 plts. Later cl (worn). Internally Good. *Glaser.* $85/£54

MANN, HARRINGTON. The Technique of Portrait Painting. London: Seeley Service, n.d. Color frontis port, 6 color plts, 48 b/w plts. (Lt spotted.) Fore/lower edges uncut. Dj (sl chipped). *Edwards.* $47/£30

MANN, HEINRICH. The Little Town. Boston: Houghton Mifflin, 1931. 1st US ed. (Top edge foxed), else VG + in VG dj (price-clipped, 2-inch tear rear flap). *Lame Duck.* $85/£54

MANN, HEINRICH. Man of Straw. Hutchinson, 1947. 1st UK ed. Fine in VG dj. *Williams.* $55/£35

MANN, HEINRICH. The Royal Woman. NY: Macaulay, 1930. 1st US ed. NF in illus dj (price-clipped). *Lame Duck.* $100/£64

MANN, HEINRICH. Small Town Tyrant. NY: Creative Age, 1944. 1st US ed. VG in VG- dj (chipped, affecting some spine letters). *Lame Duck.* $85/£54

MANN, JACK. Grey Shapes. Bookfinger, 1970. 1st US ed. Fine, not issued in dj. *Certo.* $30/£19

MANN, JACK. Her Ways Are Death. Bookfinger, 1981. 1st US ed. Fine, not issued in dj. *Certo.* $25/£16

MANN, KATHLEEN. Peasant Costume in Europe. A&C Black, 1935-6. 2 vols. Color frontispieces, 14 color plts. (Lower edge pg 13/14 chipped w/sl loss not affecting text; spines faded, head vol 1 sl chipped.) *Edwards*. $47/£30

MANN, KATHLEEN. Peasant Costume in Europe. London: Black, 1935. Rpt. 2 vols. NF in VG dj. *Agvent*. $60/£38

MANN, KLAUS. Alexander. NY: Brewer & Warren, 1930. 1st ed. VG+ in VG dj. *Lame Duck*. $100/£64

MANN, KLAUS. Mephisto. NY: Random House, 1977. 1st ed in English. (Bump), else VG+ in VG dj (edge-torn). *Lame Duck*. $35/£22

MANN, MARGERY. California Pictorialism. SF: SF Museum of Modern Art, 1977. (Name stamp), else NF in pict stiff wrappers. *Cahan*. $35/£22

MANN, MARGERY. Imogen! Imogen Cunningham Photographs, 1910-1973. Seattle/London: Univ of WA, 1974. 1st ed. 75 full-pg b/w photos. (Owner stamp), else VG in pict stiff wrappers. *Cahan*. $40/£26

MANN, RALPH. After the Gold Rush, Society in Grass Valley and Nevada City, California, 1849-1870. Stanford Univ, 1982. 1st ed. Yellow cl. Fine in dj. *Argonaut*. $35/£22

MANN, SALLY. Second Sight: The Photographs of Sally Mann. Boston: David R. Godine, 1983. 1st ed. Fine in pict paper over stiff wrappers. *Cahan*. $100/£64

MANN, SALLY. Still Time. Clifton Forge: Alleghany Highlands Arts & Crafts Center, 1988. 15 b/w plts. Fine in wrappers. *Smith*. $30/£19

MANN, THOMAS. The Beloved Returns. NY: Knopf, 1940. 1st Amer ed. One of 375 signed. Cl-backed paper bds. VF (bk, case sl faded) in glassine dj, slipcase. *Pirages*. $375/£240

MANN, THOMAS. The Black Swan. Willard Trask (trans). NY: Knopf, 1954. 1st US ed. NF in VG+ dj (spine tanned). *Lame Duck*. $65/£42

MANN, THOMAS. Confessions of Felix Krull, Confidence Man. Denver Lindley (trans). NY: Knopf, 1955. 1st Amer ed. Fine (ink name) in dj (lt worn, tear). *Antic Hay*. $25/£16

MANN, THOMAS. Death in Venice. Kenneth Burke (trans). NY, 1972. Ltd to 1500 signed by Felix Hoffmann (illus). Color frontis wood engr. 1/4 red morocco, marbled bds. Fine in slipcase. *Truepenny*. $125/£80

MANN, THOMAS. Doctor Faustus. Lowe-Porter (trans). London, 1949. 1st ed. VG (bkpl) in dj (sl chipped, stained). *Buckley*. $47/£30

MANN, THOMAS. Early Sorrow. NY: Knopf, 1930. 1st separate Amer ed of trans by Herman G. Scheffauer. Vertically striped cl, ptd spine label. Good (eps lt foxed) in dj (shelfworn, edge-tanned, short tears). *Reese*. $35/£22

MANN, THOMAS. The Holy Sinner. H. T. Lowe-Porter (trans). NY: Knopf, 1951. 1st Amer ed. NF in dj (lt worn). *Antic Hay*. $25/£16

MANN, THOMAS. Joseph the Provider. NY: Knopf, 1944. 1st Amer ed. Fine in dj (tiny tears; rubbing). *Between The Covers*. $85/£54

MANN, THOMAS. Letters to Paul Amann: 1915-1952. Richard & Clara Winston (trans). (London): Secker & Warburg, 1961. 1st Eng ed. Fine in dj (sl soiled, sm tears). *Antic Hay*. $20/£13

MANN, THOMAS. Listen, Germany! NY: Knopf, 1943. 1st US ed. (Bkpl), else NF in VG+ dj (price-clipped). *Lame Duck*. $85/£54

MANN, THOMAS. The Magic Mountain. Secker, 1927. 1st UK ed. 2 vols. VG (bds unevenly faded, spotted). *Williams*. $117/£75

MANN, THOMAS. The Magic Mountain. NY: Knopf, 1927. 1st US ed. One of 200 signed. 2 vols. 1/4 vellum, dec paper-cvrd bds. VG set (both vols edgeworn; sl touch-ups all corners vol 2). *Lame Duck*. $1,750/£1,122

MANN, THOMAS. Mario and the Magician. London: Martin Secker, 1930. 1st British ed, 1st ed in English. (Bkpl; spine cocked), else NF in VG dj. *Lame Duck*. $150/£96

MANN, THOMAS. Nocturnes. NY: Equinox, 1934. One of 1000 numbered, signed. Lynd Ward (illus). VG (dkng, mainly spine). *Lenz*. $135/£87

MANN, THOMAS. A Sketch of My Life. Paris: Harrison, 1930. One of 695 numbered. VG+ in gray cl-cvrd bds. *Lame Duck*. $75/£48

MANN, THOMAS. This War. NY: Knopf, 1940. 1st US ed. (Dk offsetting feps), else NF in VG dj (faded). *Lame Duck*. $50/£32

MANN, THOMAS. Young Joseph. NY, 1935. 1st Amer ed. Fine in dj (spine lt sunned, sl rubbed). *Polyanthos*. $25/£16

MANNERING, GEORGE EDWARD. With Axe and Rope in New Zealand Alps. London: Longmans, Green, 1891. Frontis port, (xii),139pp, 24pp pub's cat; 17 plts, map. Burgundy cl, gilt. VG (sl faded). *Sotheran*. $413/£265

MANNICHE, LISE. Lost Tombs: A Study of Certain Eighteenth Dynasty Monuments.... London/NY: KPI, (1988). 72 plts. Good in dj. *Archaeologia*. $95/£61

MANNING, DAVID. Bull Hunter. NY: Chelsea House, 1924. 1st ed. NF in NF dj. *Unger*. $250/£160

MANNING, G. C. Manual of Ship Construction. NY: Van Nostrand, 1944. 5th ptg. Dec cvr, spine. Good. *Scribe's Perch**. $50/£32

MANNING, HARVEY. The Wild Cascades. SF: Sierra Club, (1965). 1st ed. Fldg map. VG in dj. *King*. $60/£38

MANNING, MRS. TOM. A Summer on Hudson Bay. (London), 1949. Map. VG in dj (tattered). *High Latitude*. $20/£13

MANNING, OLIVIA. A Different Face. NY: Abelard-Schuman, (1957). 1st Amer ed. Fine in NF dj (chip; sl rubbing). *Between The Covers*. $65/£42

MANNING, OLIVIA. The Dreaming Shore. London: Evans, 1950. 1st ed. (Edges sl spotted; spine ends sl faded, shelfworn), o/w VG in dj (soiled, worn, chipped, 2 one-inch tears). *Virgo*. $47/£30

MANNING, OLIVIA. The Remarkable Expedition. London: Heinemann, 1947. 1st ed. (Eps sl offset, foxed; cvrs sl rubbed), o/w VG in dj (browned, soiled, internally repaired chips). *Virgo*. $78/£50

MANNING, OLIVIA. School for Love. London: Heinemann, (1951). 1st ed. NF in VG dj (sl tanned, sm nicks, chips). *Reese*. $55/£35

MANNIX, WILLIAM FRANCIS (ed). Memoirs of Li Hung Chang. Boston/NY: Houghton Mifflin (Riverside), 1913. 1st ed. Frontis. (Cl sl rubbed, foxed), o/w Good. *Worldwide*. $18/£12

MANOHA, G. (ed). Paris. NY: Lumen, (n.d.) 1st ed. NF in spiral-bound pict wrappers. *Smith*. $50/£32

MANOS, CONSTANTINE. A Greek Portfolio. NY: Viking, 1972. 1st ed. 112 full-pg b/w photo plts. (Owner stamp), else VG in illus dj. *Cahan*. $50/£32

MANPENNY, GEORGE W. Our Indian Wards. Cincinnati, 1880. 1st ed. 436pp. New cl w/leather label. Howes M268. *Ginsberg*. $175/£112

MANSELL, COLETTE. The Collector's Guide to British Dolls. London, 1983. 1st UK ed. 20 color plts. Protected dj. *Edwards*. $47/£30

MANSFIELD, G. R. and L. BOARDMAN. Nitrate Deposits of the United States. Washington: GPO, 1932. 1st ed. 2 plts, 4 color fldg maps (1 in rear pocket). Orig stiff wraps. (Sl rubbed, faded, ex-lib), o/w VG. *Worldwide*. $25/£16

MANSFIELD, H. The Museum of History. New Haven: Mansfield, 1836. 2nd ed. 2 vols in 1. 264; 264pp; 48 engrs. (Sl foxed, dampstained.) Contemp morocco (worn, cvrs detached). *Worldwide*. $20/£13

MANSFIELD, HOWARD. Whistler. As a Critic of His Own Prints. [with] Whistler. In Belgium and Holland. NY: M. Knoedler, (1935). Ltd to 525 numbered sets. 2 vols. Brn cl over bds. Good in pub's slipcase. *Karmiole*. $85/£54

MANSFIELD, JOSEPH F. K. Mansfield on the Condition of the Western Forts 1853-54. Robert W. Frazier (ed). Norman, (1963). 1st ed. VG+ (ex-lib) in dj (lt worn). *Pratt*. $40/£26

MANSFIELD, KATHERINE. Bliss and Other Stories. London: Constable: (1920). 1st ed. Red cl lettered in black (sm snag spine crown, frayed, spots at edges). Good. *Reese*. $100/£64

MANSFIELD, KATHERINE. The Doves' Nest and Other Stories. Constable, (1923). 1st ed. (Pp lt spotted.) *Bickersteth*. $59/£38

MANSFIELD, KATHERINE. The Doves' Nest and Other Stories. London: Constable, (1923). 1st ed. Blue cl. VG in ptd dj (lt chipped). *House*. $40/£26

MANSFIELD, KATHERINE. The Doves' Nest and Other Stories. London: Constable, (1923). 1st ed. (Eps sl tanned), o/w Fine in dj (spine quite discolored). *Reese*. $225/£144

MANSFIELD, KATHERINE. Journal of Katherine Mansfield: 1914-1922. J. Middleton Murry (ed). London: Constable, 1927. 1st Eng ed. VG (eps browned, foxed) in VG dj (stained, spine browned, sm chips). *Antic Hay*. $75/£48

MANSFIELD, KATHERINE. Journal. J. Middleton Murry (ed). Constable, 1927. 1st ed. (Ink name, news cutting pasted inside fr cvr.) *Bickersteth*. $47/£30

MANSFIELD, KATHERINE. Katherine Mansfield's Letters to John Middleton Murray 1913-1922. NY: Knopf, 1951. 1st Amer ed. Fine in dj (wear). *Antic Hay*. $35/£22

MANSFIELD, KATHERINE. The Letters of Katherine Mansfield. J. Middleton Murry (ed). London: Constable, 1928. 1st ed. 2 vols. Frontis port each vol. Gray cl. VG+. *House*. $50/£32

MANSFIELD, KATHERINE. Poems. NY, 1924. 1st Amer ed. NF (sl rubbed). *Polyanthos*. $25/£16

MANSFIELD, KATHERINE. Prelude. Richmond: Hogarth, n.d. One of 300. Issue w/o design on fr wrap. Internally VG+ (cvr edges tanned, worn) in professionally restored blue wrappers, custom-made 1/4 leather, paper-cvrd clamshell box. *Lame Duck*. $950/£609

MANSFIELD, KATHERINE. Something Childish and Other Stories. Constable, (1924). 1st ed. (Ink name.) *Bickersteth*. $55/£35

MANSFIELD, KATHERINE. Something Childish and Other Stories. London: Constable, (1924). 1st ed. Blue cl. VG in ptd dj (lt soiled). *House*. $60/£38

MANSON, PATRICK. Tropical Diseases. London: Cassell, 1903. 3rd ed. 2 color plts. Grn cl. Good. *White*. $23/£15

MANTELL, G. The Journal...Covering the Years 1818-1852. E. C. Curwen (ed). London, 1940. (Sl worn.) *Maggs*. $34/£22

MANTLE, MICKEY with HERB GLUCK. The Mick. GC: Doubleday, 1985. 1st ed. Fine in Fine dj. *Glenn*. $25/£16

Manual of Neuro-Surgery Authorized by the Secretary of War. Washington: GPO, 1919. Orig leather bds (newly rebacked, fore-edges chipped). Internally VG. *Goodrich*. $275/£176

Manual of Splints and Appliances for the Treatment of Bone and Joint Injuries. Amer Red Cross, c. 1917. VG (cvrs soiled). *Doctor's Library*. $40/£26

MANUS, WILLARD. Mott the Hoople. NY: McGraw-Hill, (1966). 1st ed. (Sl nick spine head), o/w Nice in dj (sl mkd). *Ash*. $31/£20

MANVILLE, BILL. Saloon Society. NY: Duell, Sloan & Pearce, 1960. 1st ed. VG in dj (rubbed, chipped). *Cahan*. $50/£32

MANYPENNY, G. W. Our Indian Wards. Cincinnati, 1880. 436pp. Poor (ex-lib). Howes M268. *Scribe's Perch**. $65/£42

MAPPLETHORPE, ROBERT. Black Males. Amsterdam: Galerie Jurka, 1980. 1st ed. 52 photo plts. NF in ptd wrappers. *Cahan*. $75/£48

MAPPLETHORPE, ROBERT. Certain People. Pasadena: Twelvetrees, 1985. One of 5000. NF in NF dj. *Smith*. $150/£96

MAPPLETHORPE, ROBERT. Robert Mapplethorpe: Foto's/Photographs. Amsterdam: Galerie Jurka, 1979. 1st ed. Frontis, 23 full-pg b/w photos. (Tip bumped), else NF. *Cahan*. $60/£38

MARAN, RENE. Batouala. London: Cape, 1922. 1st Eng ed. One of 1050 numbered. VG- (name; spine, pp bumped; spine label edges worn; lacks dj). *Between The Covers*. $85/£54

MARBERRY, M. M. The Golden Voice: Biography of Isaac Kalloch. NY: Farrar & Straus, 1947. 1st ed. NF in dj (sl edgeworn). *Sadlon*. $30/£19

MARBURY, MARY ORVIS. Favorite Flies and Their History. Boston/NY: Houghton Mifflin, 1892. 1st ed, 2nd issue w/o date on tp. 32 color plts, 6 engrs. Gilt-dec dk grn cl (cvrs sl worn), lt grn cl spine (dull). (Inner hinges split), o/w Internally Fine. *Cummins*. $425/£272

MARCH, DAVID D. The History of Missouri. NY: Lewis Hist Pub Co, (1967). 1st ed. 4 vols. Grn cl. Fine. *Glenn*. $150/£96

MARCH, EDGAR J. British Destroyers. London, 1966. Blue cl. Dj. *Maggs*. $234/£150

MARCH, WILLIAM. Company K. London: Gollancz, 1933. 1st Eng ed. VG in pub's cl. *Hadley*. $47/£30

MARCHANT, J. B. The Marchants Avizo. Patrick McGrath (ed). Cambridge, MA: Harvard Univ, 1957. VG in orig wrappers (edges faded). *Hollett*. $55/£35

MARCUS, STEVEN. The Other Victorians: A Study of Sexuality and Pornography in Mid-19th Century England. NY, 1966. 1st ed. VG. *Fye*. $40/£26

MARCY, RANDOLPH B. Exploration of the Red River of Louisiana.... Washington: Armstrong, 1853. 65 plts (botanical plt 18 not issued). (Foxing throughout; sunned, stained.) *Metropolitan**. $189/£121

MARDERSTEIG, GIOVANNI. The Officina Bodoni. Hans Schmoller (ed). Verona: Edizioni Valdonega, 1980. 1st ed. Ltd to 1500. Fine in buckram. *Cox*. $172/£110

MARDRUS, J. C. The Queen of Sheba. E. Powys Mathers (trans). Casanova Soc, c. 1930. *Petersfield*. $16/£10

MARGOLIOUTH, D. S. Cairo, Jerusalem, and Damascus. London, 1907. 1st ed. Tipped-in color frontis, 57 color plts. (Feps lt browned, sm ink lib stamp fep.) Teg. Illus laid down upper bd. (Spine discolored, sl faded.) *Edwards*. $62/£40

MARGOTTA, ROBERTO. The Story of Medicine. NY, 1968. 1st ed. VG in dj. *Fye*. $50/£32

MARIANO, NICKY (ed). Sunset and Twilight. Iris Origo (ed). Hamish Hamilton, 1964. 1st UK ed. Frontis port. Dj (sl chipped). *Edwards.* $31/£20

MARIE, PIERRE and DR. SOUZA-LEITE. Essays on Acromegaly. London: New Sydenham Soc, 1891. vi,(ii),182,38pp (bkpl fr pastedown); 2 fldg plts. Brn cl. VG. *White.* $62/£40

MARIE, PIERRE. Lectures on Diseases of the Spinal Cord. Montagu Lubbock (trans). London: New Sydenham Soc, 1895. 240 woodcuts. Brn cl. (3 sm lib stamps tp), o/w VG. *White.* $86/£55

MARINARO, VINCENT C. A Modern Dry Fly Code. NY: Putnam, 1950. True 1st ed in gray/grn cl. VG. *Bowman.* $65/£42

MARINARO, VINCENT C. A Modern Dry Fly Code. NY: Putnam, 1950. 1st ed (2nd ptg?). Dk blue buckram. Fine in ptd dj (chipped). *Biscotti.* $95/£61

MARINATOS, SPYRIDON. Crete and Mycenae. London: Thames & Hudson, (1960). Good in dj (sl chipped, edge sl soiled). *Archaeologia.* $150/£96

MARIUS, RICHARD. The Coming of Rain. NY: Knopf, 1969. 1st ed, 1st bk. NF in dj (sm edgetear). *Lame Duck.* $85/£54

MARK, JOHN. Diary of My Trip to America and Havana. Manchester, England, (1885). vi,(2),105pp. (Contents tanned, spine chipped), else VG in orig ptd wrappers. *Reese.* $250/£160

MARK, MARY ELLEN. Falkland Road: Prostitutes of Bombay. NY: Knopf, 1981. 1st ed. (Spine top sl bumped, wrappers sl rubbed), else VG. *Cahan.* $50/£32

MARK, MARY ELLEN. Passport. (NY): Lustrum, 1974. 1st ed, 1st bk. Fine in illus stiff wrappers (sl crease). *Cahan.* $125/£80

MARK, MARY ELLEN. Ward 81. NY: S&S, 1979. 1st ed. (Rmdr mk lower edge), else Fine in pict dj. *Cahan.* $100/£64

MARKHAM, ALBERT H. The Great Frozen Sea. London: Daldy, Isbister, 1878. 1st ed. Inscribed. xx,440pp; dbl-pg color plt, 2 maps. Dec cl. VG. *High Latitude.* $450/£288

MARKHAM, ALBERT H. A Polar Reconnaissance. Being the Voyage of the 'Isbjorn'...in 1879. London: Kegan Paul, 1881. xvi,(2),361pp, 6 plts, 2 fldg maps. Dec cl (sl worn, spotted). VG. *High Latitude.* $175/£112

MARKHAM, ALBERT H. A Whaling Cruise to Baffin's Bay and the Gulf of Boothia, and an Account of the Rescue of the Crew of the Polaris. London: Sampson, Low et al, 1875. 2nd ed. xxxi,307pp, 8 plts; fldg map. Dec cl (extrems rubbed). VG. *High Latitude.* $185/£119

MARKHAM, BERYL. West with the Night. Boston/Cambridge: Houghton Mifflin/Riverside, (1942). 1st ed, later ptg. VG in dj (nicks). *Houle.* $150/£96

MARKHAM, CLEMENTS R. A Life of John Davis, the Navigator, 1550-1605.... London: Geo. Philip, 1891. 2nd ed. (viii),301pp, 4 plts, 4 fldg maps. VG. *High Latitude.* $45/£29

MARKHAM, CLEMENTS R. Peruvian Bark.... London, 1880. 550pp; 3 fldg maps. VG. *Argosy.* $125/£80

MARKHAM, CLEMENTS R. The Threshold of the Unknown Region. London: Sampson Low et al, 1875. 3rd ed. 1l ads, xvi,348pp + 40pp ads; 5 color fldg maps, 1 b/w sketch map. Purple cl (spine faded, corners bumped), gilt. *Parmer.* $175/£112

MARKHAM, EDWIN. The Man with the Hoe and Other Poems. NY: Doubleday & McClure, 1899. 1st ed. Frontis. Grn cl. Fine. *Appelfeld.* $100/£64

MARKHAM, ERNEST. The Large and Small Flowered Clematis.... A. G. L. Hellyer (rev). London: Country Life, 1951. 3rd ed. (Ink notes rep), else Fine in dj (tired). *Quest.* $40/£26

MARKHAM, ROBERT. Colonel Sun—A James Bond Adventure. Cape, 1968. 1st UK ed. VG+ (sm ink inscrip) in dj. *Williams.* $39/£25

MARKS, A. A. Manual of Artificial Limbs. NY, 1908. (Spine faded), else Fine. *Doctor's Library.* $100/£64

MARKS, JEANNETTE. Geoffrey's Window. Milton Bradley, (1921). Clara M. Burd (illus). 5x8. 236pp. VG+ in dj (ragged). *My Bookhouse.* $40/£26

MARKS, JOHN GEORGE. Life and Letters of Frederick Walker, A.R.A. London: Macmillan, 1896. 1st ed. xiii,328pp; 13 plts. (Sl fingering; joints tightened; rubbed.) *Hollett.* $101/£65

MARKS, PAULA MITCHELL. And Die in the West. NY: William Morrow, (1989). 1st ed. Brn cl-backed tan bds. Fine in dj. *Argonaut.* $30/£19

MARLETT, MELBA. Escape While I Can. GC: DCC, 1944. 1st ed. (Fr cvr lt staining), o/w Fine in dj (sm closed tears). *Mordida.* $35/£22

MARLOWE, DEREK. The Memoirs of a Venus Lackey. London: Cape, (1968). 1st ed. Fine in dj (lt worn). *Hermitage.* $45/£29

MARLOWE, GEORGE FRANCIS. Coaching Roads of Old New England. NY: Macmillan, 1945. 2nd ptg. (Corners bumped.) *October Farm.* $30/£19

MARMELSZADT, WILLARD. Musical Sons of Aesculapius. NY, 1946. 1st ed. Signed. VG in dj. *Fye.* $225/£144

MARON, MARGARET. Death in Blue Folders. GC: DCC, 1985. 1st ed. Advance rev copy w/slip laid in. VF in dj. *Mordida.* $75/£48

MARON, MARGARET. Death of a Butterfly. GC: DCC, 1984. 1st ed. Fine in dj (lt rubbed). *Mordida.* $75/£48

MARON, MARGARET. Past Imperfect. NY: DCC, 1991. 1st ed. VF in dj. *Mordida.* $65/£42

MARQUAND, JOHN P. Stopover: Tokyo. Boston: Little Brown, (1957). 1st ed. (Bkpl; erasure scrape; sl offsetting fr pastedown), else NF in NF dj (nicks, tears). *Between The Covers.* $85/£54

MARQUARDT, MARTHA. Paul Ehrlich. NY: Henry Schuman, (1951). 1st ed. Fine in dj. *Glaser.* $45/£29

MARQUEZ, GABRIEL GARCIA. See GARCIA MARQUEZ, GABRIEL

MARQUIS, DON. Archy's Life of Mehitabel. GC: Doubleday-Doran, 1933. 1st ed. Fine (name) in dj (sl worn, chipped). *Else Fine.* $90/£58

MARQUIS, DON. Archy's Life of Mehitabel. 1934. 1st ed. VG in dj (chipped). *Words Etc.* $70/£45

MARQUIS, DON. Chapters for the Orthodox. GC: Doubleday-Doran, 1934. 1st ed. Fine in pict dj (sm chips). *Else Fine.* $90/£58

MARQUIS, DON. Danny's Own Story. NY, 1912. 1st Amer ed, 1st bk. NF (spine sl rubbed). *Polyanthos.* $35/£22

MARQUIS, DON. Sun Dial Time. GC: Doubleday-Doran, 1936. 1st ed. Fine in dj (sl worn). *Else Fine.* $50/£32

MARQUIS, THOMAS. Cheyenne and Sioux. Univ of Pacific, (1973). 1st ed. VG. *Oregon.* $30/£19

MARQUIS, THOMAS. Keep the Last Bullet for Yourself. NY, (1976). 1st ed. VG+ in VG+ dj. *Pratt.* $35/£22

MARR, SCOUT. Into the Frozen South. London, 1923. 3rd ptg. Good (lt foxed, binding sl soiled). *High Latitude.* $20/£13

MARR, SCOUT. Into the Frozen South. London: Cassell, 1923. 1st ed. VG. *High Latitude.* $50/£32

MARROT, H. V. A Bibliography of the Works of John Galsworthy. London, 1928. 1st trade ed. (Foxing, extrems starting to fray.) *King.* $50/£32

MARRYAT, FRANK. Mountains and Molehills or Recollections of a Burnt Journal. NY: Harper, 1855. 1st Amer ed. xii,13-393pp. Emb black cl, gilt spine. Fine. *Pacific**. $288/£185

MARRYAT, FREDERICK. A Diary in America, with Remarks on Its Institutions. Phila, 1839. 1st Amer ed. 2 vols. 242; 228pp (lt foxed, tp clipped). Contemp cl (sl rubbed), paper labels. VG. Howes M300. *Reese.* $125/£80

MARRYAT, FREDERICK. A Diary in America, with Remarks on Its Institutions. Phila: Carey & Hart, 1839. 1st Amer ed, 1st series. 2 vols. 242; 228pp (lt foxing). Grn cl (lt wear), ptd lettering pieces (chipped). VG. *House.* $150/£96

MARRYAT, FREDERICK. Masterman Ready; or, The Wreck of the Pacific. London: Longman et al, 1841. 1st ed. 3 vols. Uncut. Orig brn cl (bumped, spines faded, sl frayed; inscrip). *Maggs.* $234/£150

MARRYAT, FREDERICK. Narrative of the Travels and Adventures of Monsieur Violet, in California, Sonora, and Western Texas. NY: Harper, 1843. 1st Amer ptg. 133,(2)pp. Early 20th cent 1/4 morocco, cl (spine sl sunned, sm chip fr wrap), orig wrappers bound in. Nice (sl spotting, lt foxing). Howes M302. *Reese.* $150/£96

MARRYAT, FREDERICK. Narrative of the Travels and Adventures of Monsieur Violet.... Leipzig, 1843. 1st ed. vi,384pp; fldg map. 3/4 cl, bds (edgeworn, spine sunned). VG (lt foxed). Howes M302. *Reese.* $125/£80

MARRYAT, FREDERICK. Newton Forster. London: Routledge, 1896. 'King's Own' ed. Marbled eps, edges. Blue 1/4 morocco leather, marbled bds. NF (bkpl, sig). *Antic Hay.* $50/£32

MARRYAT, FREDERICK. The Pirate and the Three Cutters. London: Longman et al, 1836. 19 (of 20) plts incl frontisport, engr tp (foxed; glue repairs to joints). Aeg. Straight-grained morocco (edgeworn), ribbed gilt-ruled spine (ends frayed), 2 leather labels. *Waverly**. $33/£21

MARRYAT, FREDERICK. The Privateer's-Man. London: Longman et al, 1846. 1st Eng ed. 2 vols. Dk brn cl. VG (wear, ink name). *Antic Hay.* $125/£80

MARRYAT, FREDERICK. Second Series of a Diary in America, with Remarks on Its Institutions. Phila, 1840. Later ed. 300pp. (Worn, frayed, lacks spine label; foxed), else internally VG. Howes M300. *Reese.* $150/£96

MARRYAT, FREDERICK. Valerie, an Autobiography. London: Henry Colburn, 1849. 1st ed w/half-titles. 2 vols. Teg. 3/4 brn calf, marbled bds, gilt spines (dull), raised bands, grn leather labels. Good. *Appelfeld.* $200/£128

MARRYAT, JOSEPH. A History of Pottery and Porcelain, Medieval and Modern. London: Murray, 1868. 3rd ed. 6 color plts. Dec cl (spine nick, sl shaken). NF. *Agvent.* $150/£96

MARRYAT, SAMUEL FRANCIS. Mountains and Molehills, or Recollections of a Burnt Journal. London: Longman, 1885. 1st ed. 8vo. x,(2),443,(1)pp, 8 color lithos. Contemp 3/4 calf, marbled bds (extrems lt rubbed, rear outer hinge cracked but sound). Fine. Howes M299. *Argonaut.* $650/£417

MARS, GERHARDT CORNELL. Brickwork in Italy. Chicago: Amer Face Brick Assoc, 1925. Color frontis, 320 plts, map. (Foxing, tape residue eps; lt soiled, worn.) *Waverly**. $33/£21

MARSE, JUAN. The Fallen. Boston: Little, Brown, (1976). 1st Amer ed. Fine in dj (2-inch abrasion rear panel). *Hermitage.* $35/£22

MARSH, EDWARD (ed). Georgian Poetry 1913-1915. London: Poetry Bookshop, 1915. 1st ed of 2nd in series. Teg. Gilt-slate blue bds. (Bkpl residue; lower corner bruised), else Good. *Reese.* $35/£22

MARSH, JAMES B. Four Years in the Rockies. New Castle, PA, 1884. Frontis, 262pp (dust-soiled). Orig cl (rebacked, edgeworn, soiled). Sound. Howes M306. *Reese.* $500/£321

MARSH, JOHN W. A Memoir of Allen F. Gardiner, Commander R.N. London: James Nisbet, 1857. 2nd ed. Engr frontis, iv,(1)-399pp (pencil inscrip). Blue stippled cl (sl worn), gilt. *Eldred's**. $55/£35

MARSH, NGAIO. Colour Scheme. Boston: Little Brown, 1943. 1st Amer ed. VG in dj (internal tape mends, wear, short closed tears). *Mordida.* $45/£29

MARSH, NGAIO. Night at the Vulcan. Boston: Little, Brown, 1951. 1st Amer ed. VG (spine top browned) in dj (chip spine top). *Antic Hay.* $17/£11

MARSH, NGAIO. Overture to Death. NY: Lee Furman, 1939. 1st ed. Fine in dj (sl worn). *Else Fine.* $250/£160

MARSH, NGAIO. Scales of Justice. Boston: Little, Brown, (1955). 1st Amer ed. NF in dj (spine sl sunned, sm tears, sl soil). *Antic Hay.* $20/£13

MARSH, NGAIO. Scales of Justice. Boston, 1955. 1st ed. VG (foxed) in VG dj. *Smith.* $25/£16

MARSH, NGAIO. Spinsters in Jeopardy. Boston: Little-Brown, 1953. 1st ed. NF in dj (sl worn). *Else Fine.* $45/£29

MARSH, NGAIO. Surfeit of Lampreys. Collins, 1941. 1st UK ed. VG+ in Lovely dj (top edge lt creased). *Williams.* $460/£295

MARSH, RICHARD. The Beetle. London, 1922. Rpt. VG. *Mcclintock.* $35/£22

MARSH, RICHARD. The Chase of the Ruby. London: Skeffington, 1900. 1st ed. (Rubbed, extrems frayed.) *Metropolitan**. $46/£29

MARSHALL, E. Shikar and Safari. London, 1950. (Lt wear.) Dj (torn). *Grayling.* $47/£30

MARSHALL, EDWARD C. The Ancestry of General Grant, and Their Contemporaries. NY, 1869. 1st ed. xiii,186pp. Interior Fine (fr cvr spotted, soiled). *Wantagh.* $30/£19

MARSHALL, FRANK J. My Fifty Years of Chess. NY: Horowitz & Harkness, 1942. 1st ed. #454/500 signed. Inscribed. (Rubbed, bumped, faded.) *Metropolitan**. $115/£74

MARSHALL, H. RISSIK. Coloured Worcester Porcelain of the First Period (1751-1783). Newport: Ceramic Book, 1954. 31 color plts. Teg. (Eps sl spotted.) *Edwards.* $195/£125

MARSHALL, HENRY RUTGERS. Consciousness. NY: Macmillan, 1909. 1st ed. Inscribed (pasted on). Blue cl. VG. *Gach.* $85/£54

MARSHALL, JAMES S. and CARRIE MARSHALL (comps). Pacific Voyages. Selections from Scots Magazine 1771-1808. Portland, OR: Binford & Mort, 1960. VG in dj. *High Latitude.* $20/£13

MARSHALL, JOHN A. American Bastile. Phila, 1878. 24th ed (sic). 768pp. Dec cl, gilt. (Bkpl; inner rear hinge cracked), else NF. *Wantagh.* $40/£26

MARSHALL, JOHN. The Life of George Washington. London, 1804-07. 1st Eng ed. 5 vols. 8vo. 10 maps, 6 plts. 1/2 leather. *Swann**. $1,150/£737

MARSHALL, JOHN. The Life of George Washington. Phila: Crissy, 1834. 2nd ed. 2 vols. Frontis. Leather, gilt. (Waterstained.) *Yudkin**. $30/£19

MARSHALL, JOHN. The Life of George Washington...During the War Which Established the Independence of His Country.... NY: William H. Wise, 1925. Fredericksburg ed. 5 vols. Leather spine labels. VG+ set. Howes M317. *Mcgowan.* $250/£160

MARSHALL, MRS. A. B. The Book of Ices. London: Marshall's School of Cookery, n.d. 16th thousand, rev ed. vii,79pp; 4 chromolitho plts. (Hinges rubbed.) *Hollett*. $70/£45

MARSHALL, NINA L. The Mushroom Book. NY, 1903. Color frontis, 47 plts. Teg, rest uncut. (Upper hinge cracked; cl sl soiled.) Leather spine label (sl rubbed). *Edwards*. $44/£28

MARSHALL, ORSAMUS H. The Historical Writings of the Late Orsamus H. Marshall.... Albany, NY: Munsell, 1887. 1st ed. Frontis, (24),500pp; port, map. Partial paper spine label. Howes M319. *Ginsberg*. $125/£80

MARSHALL, THOMAS M. History of the Western Boundary of the Louisiana Purchase, 1819-1841. Berkeley, CA, 1914. 1st ed. Ptd wrappers. Howes M321. *Ginsberg*. $200/£128

MARSHALL, W. E. Consider the Lilies. London, (1930). 2nd ed. 36 plts (28 color). Pict cl, gilt. Good. *Henly*. $28/£18

MARSHALL, WALTER GORE. Through America. London, 1881. xx,424,(3),32pp; 16 plts, incl frontis. Gilt-pict cl (spine sunned, extrems rubbed). Good (prelims sl foxed). *Reese*. $225/£144

MARSHALL, WILLIAM I. Acquisition of Oregon and the Long Supressed Evidence About Marcus Whitman. Seattle: Lowman & Hanford, 1911. 2 vols. Many pp uncut. Good (lt wear; spine vol 1 repaired tear). Howes M322. *Lien*. $145/£93

MARSHALL, WILLIAM I. History vs. the Whitman Saved Oregon Story.... Chicago, 1904. NF in ptd stiff wrappers. *Reese*. $75/£48

MARSHALL, WILLIAM. Yellowthread Street. NY: Holt, 1976. 1st US ed. Fine in Fine dj. *Unger*. $45/£29

MARSON, T. B. The Scotch Shorthorn. Edinburgh, 1946. (Feps lt browned.) Dj (ragged). *Edwards*. $39/£25

MARSTEN, RICHARD. (Pseud of Ed McBain.) Rocket to Luna. Phila: Winston, (1953). 1st ed. VG (spine faded) in dj (edgeworn, chip). *Metropolitan**. $207/£133

MARSTON, E. Sketches of Booksellers in Other Days. Sampson Low, 1901. 9 plts. VG in 1/4 vellum, grn bds. *Moss*. $47/£30

MARTI, WERNER H. Messenger of Destiny. (SF): John Howell, 1960. 1st ed. Ltd to 600 ptd. Frontis, 3 plts, map. Red cl, gilt. VF. *Argonaut*. $75/£48

MARTI-IBANEZ, FELIX (ed). History of American Medicine: A Symposium. NY, 1959. 1st ed. VG in wrappers. *Fye*. $45/£29

MARTIN, A. C. and F. M. UHLER. Food of Game Ducks in the U.S. and Canada. Washington: USDA, Mar. 1939. 1st ed. 153 plts, 12 tables. VG+ in wraps. *Mikesh*. $37/£24

MARTIN, AYLWIN LEE. Death on a Ferris Wheel. NY: Fawcett, 1951. 1st ed. Pb orig. VF in wrappers. *Mordida*. $35/£22

MARTIN, AYLWIN LEE. Fear Comes Calling. NY: Fawcett, 1952. 1st ed. Pb orig. VF in wrappers. *Mordida*. $35/£22

MARTIN, BENJAMIN. The Philosophical Grammar. London: J. Rivington, 1778. 18th ed. (4)ff,362pp,(3)ff; 26 fldg engr plts, fldg table. Orig full calf, raised bands, dk morocco spine label. (Early sig; rubbed, extrems worn.) *Weber*. $150/£96

MARTIN, C. Keepers of the Game. Berkeley: Univ of CA, 1978. 1st ed. NF in NF dj. *Mikesh*. $30/£19

MARTIN, C. The Saga of the Buffalo. NY: Promontory, (1973). Simulated leather. NF in VG dj. *Mikesh*. $25/£16

MARTIN, C. M. Monsters of Old Los Angeles: The Prehistoric Animals of the La Brea Tar Pits. NY: Viking, 1950. 1st ed. Pict cl. VG+ in VG dj. *Mikesh*. $20/£13

MARTIN, CHARLES and LEOPOLD. Civil Costume of England.... London: Henry Bohn, 1842. 61 hand-color plts; pict tp (sm marginal waterstains few pp); marbled eps. Mod full black morocco, red morocco spine. Special slipcase. *Cullen*. $750/£481

MARTIN, DOUGLAS D. Tombstone's Epitaph. (Albuquerque: Univ of NM, 1951.) 1st ed. Brick cl, silver lettering, dec. Fine in dj. *Argonaut*. $40/£26

MARTIN, DOUGLAS D. Yuma Crossing. Univ of NM, 1954. 1st ed. Map. Yellow cl. VG+ in dj (chipped). *Five Quail*. $30/£19

MARTIN, DOUGLAS D. Yuma Crossing. Albuquerque: Univ of NM, 1954. 1st ed. Fine in Fine dj. *Book Market*. $25/£16

MARTIN, EDWARD A. A Bibliography of Gilbert White. London, 1934. Frontis port. (Bkpl; faded, spotted.) *Edwards*. $39/£25

MARTIN, EDWARD A. Gilbert White; the Naturalist and Antiquarian of Selborne. Alcuin, 1934. 1st ed. VG in dj (short tears). *Words Etc*. $34/£22

MARTIN, EDWARD S. The Life of Joseph Hodges Choate, As Gathered Chiefly from His Letters. NY: Scribner, 1920. 2 vols. Grn cl (worn). Sound set. *Boswell*. $85/£54

MARTIN, FRANKLIN. South America from a Surgeon's Point of View. NY, 1922. 1st ed. VG. *Fye*. $50/£32

MARTIN, FREDERICK. The Life of John Clare. Macmillan, 1865. 1st ed. Good (1/2-title worn, soiled; new eps; recased, sl worn). *Poetry Bookshop*. $117/£75

MARTIN, GEORGE C. Some Texas Stream and Place Names. San Antonio: Norman Brock, 1947. Tipped-in map. VG (edges dknd) in ptd wraps. *Bohling*. $22/£14

MARTIN, GEORGE R. R. The Armageddon Rag. NY/Omaha: Poseidon/Nemo, 1983. One of 500 numbered, signed. Dj, slipcase. *Swann**. $46/£29

MARTIN, GEORGE R. R. Fevre Dream. NY: Poseidon, (1982). 1st ed. Inscribed. Dj. *Swann**. $69/£44

MARTIN, H. B. Fifty Years of American Golf. NY, 1936. Lib cl. (Ex-lib), else VG. *King*. $175/£112

MARTIN, H. B. Fifty Years of American Golf. NY: Dodd, Mead, 1936. 1st trade ed. Grn cl, gilt. (Fr cvr sl discolored), else VG. *Pacific**. $219/£140

MARTIN, H. T. Castorologia. London, 1892. Frontis, xvi,238pp. Good (ex-lib, sm stamps; cl sl worn). *Wheldon & Wesley*. $78/£50

MARTIN, JOHN RUPERT. The Farnese Gallery. Princeton, 1965. Good in dj. *Washton*. $245/£157

MARTIN, JOHN. Bibliographical Catalogue of Books Privately Printed.... London: J. & A. Arch, 1834. 1st ed. Mod gray cl, maroon leather spine label. VG (contents lt age-toned, marginal chipping) in cl slipcase. *Waverly**. $66/£42

MARTIN, LAWRENCE (intro). Washington's Map of Mount Vernon. Univ of Chicago, (c. 1932). Fldg map (facs). Paper cvr. VG (pp browned). *Book Broker*. $45/£29

MARTIN, MR. and MRS. JOHN. Feminism, Its Fallacies and Follies. NY: Dodd, Mead, 1916. 1st ed. Fine. *Second Life*. $75/£48

MARTIN, PAUL S. The Last 10,000 Years. Tucson: Univ of AZ, 1963. 1st ed. 8 tables. Cl-backed bds (tip sl worn). Nice. *Shasky*. $50/£32

MARTIN, PERCY F. Through Five Republics of South America. London: Heinemann, 1905. 1st ed. 3 lg fldg maps. Uncut. (Sl foxed, sl worn, waterstain fr bd.) *Maggs*. $140/£90

MARTIN, W. Dutch Painting of the Great Period 1650-1697. Batsford, 1951. (Margins lt browned; spine lt faded.) *Edwards*. $70/£45

MARTIN, W. A. P. Lore of Catahy, or The Intellect of China. NY: Revell, 1901. 1st ed. Orange gilt dec cl. VG. *Terramedia*. $120/£77

MARTINDALE, THOMAS. Sport Indeed. Phila, 1901. Pict cl (both hinges sprung). *Grayling*. $47/£30

MARTINDALE, THOMAS. With Gun and Guide. Phila: George W. Jacobs, 1910. 1st ed. Frontis. Dec cvr, grn cl. VG + . *Backman*. $72/£46

MARTINDELL, E. W. A Bibliography of the Works of Rudyard Kipling. John Lane, Bodley Head, 1923. New ed. One of 700 numbered. 52 plts. VG. *Moss*. $94/£60

MARTINEAU, HARRIET. Feats on the Fjord. London: J.M. Dent, 1899. 1 color plt. Blue cl over flexible bds (lt worn, fr cvr sl abraded), gilt spine. Contents VG in marbled slipcase. *New Hampshire**. $45/£29

MARTINEAU, HARRIET. Guide to Windermere. Windermere: John Garnett, n.d. (1856). 3rd ed. iii,117pp; fldg map, 5 tinted illus. Pict stiff wrappers (rubbed, rebacked, lower corner back panel defective). *Hollett*. $101/£65

MARTINEAU, HARRIET. Household Education. Phila: Lea & Blanchard, 1849. 1st Amer ed. viii,212pp + (32)pp ads (text foxed). Orig blind-stamped black cl (spine extrems frayed, old lib paper spine label). *Karmiole*. $75/£48

MARTINEAU, HARRIET. Household Education. Phila: Lea & Blanchard, 1849. 1st US ed. 212pp + ads. Pub's cl. VG (ex-lib, sl foxed). *Second Life*. $150/£96

MARTINEAU, HARRIET. Illustrations of Political Economy. No. XII. French Wines and Politics. Boston: Bowles, 1833. 1st US ed. 186pp. Pub's cl, paper label (chipped). VG. *Second Life*. $75/£48

MARTINEAU, HARRIET. Letters on Mesmerism. London: Moxon, 1845. x,65pp. Good + . *Middle Earth*. $145/£93

MARTINEAU, HARRIET. Miscellanies. Boston: Hilliard, Gray, 1836. 1st US ed. 2 vols. 352; 402pp. Contemp cl. VG set. *Second Life*. $225/£144

MARTINEAU, HARRIET. Retrospect of Western Travel. London, 1838. 1st ed. 2 vols. 276; 239pp. (Foxed; fr hinge vol 2 detached; cvrs heavily soiled, worn.) *King*. $100/£64

MARTINEAU, HARRIET. Retrospect of Western Travel. London/NY: Saunders & Otley/Harper, 1838. 1st US ed. 2 vols. 276; 239pp (tps lt foxed). Pub's cl. VG set. Howes M348. *Second Life*. $350/£224

MARTINEAU, HARRIET. Retrospect of Western Travel. NY: Harper, n.d., c1940s. VG in dj. Howes M348. *Lien*. $95/£61

MARTINEAU, HARRIET. Society in America. London, 1837. 1st ed. 3 vols. Pub's cl (worn, lib labels on fr cvrs, backstrips; hinges starting). Howes M350. *Swann**. $69/£44

MARTINEAU, HARRIET. Society in America. NY, 1837. 2 vols. xviii,395; (4),420pp. Cl, ptd paper spine labels. (Cl sl spotted), else VG. Howes M350. *Reese*. $250/£160

MARTINEAU, HARRIET. Society in America. NY: Saunders & Otley, 1837. 1st US ed. 2 vols. 395; 420pp + ads. Pub's cl, paper label. NF. Howes M350. *Second Life*. $450/£288

MARTINET, DOCTOR. The Catechism of Nature. For the Use of Children. Boston: D. West & E. Larkin, 1793. 3 3/4 x 6 1/4. 108pp. Calf-backed paper over bds. (Names; bds showing along edge, cracked), else VG. *Cahan*. $200/£128

MARTINEZ, PABLO L. History of Lower California. Mexico, DF, 1960. 1st Eng ed. One of 3100. Frontis port. Fine. *Turpen*. $70/£45

MARTINGALE. Sporting Scenes and Country Characters. London: Longman et al, 1840. 1st ed. xii,332pp + 14pp pub's Dec 1840 cat at rear. Red coated eps. Orig brn bds (chipped, worn), gilt. Text Good (few ll detached, joints cracked, starting). *Baltimore**. $30/£19

MARTYN, EDWARD. The Dream Physician. Dublin: Talbot Press, (1914). 1st ed. NF (spine extrems sl rubbed). *Polyanthos*. $25/£16

MARTYN, THOMAS. Aranei; or, A Natural History of Spiders.... London, 1793. 1st ed. 4to. (4),ii,31,(1),vii,(1),70pp, incl engr tp; 28 hand-colored engr plts (upper margin lt dampstained, lacks 2 numismatic plts). Contemp red straight-grained morocco by Samuel Welcher, w/his ticket. *Swann**. $1,840/£1,179

MARTYN, THOMAS. Flora Rustica.... London: F.P. Nodder, 1792-1794. 1st ed. Vols 1, 3-4 (of 4). 144 mostly VG engr plts (108 hand-colored; 1 w/repaired tear, 1 frayed in margin) by Frederick P. Nodder. Old mottled calf (broken; lt toned, foxed). *Waverly**. $495/£317

MARTYN, WYNDHAM. The Trent Trail. NY: Robert M. McBride, 1930. Yellow pict cl (soiled, spine sl faded, corners bumped). Very Nice. *Metropolitan**. $172/£110

MARUCCI, HORACE. The Roman Forum and the Palatine According to the Latest Discoveries. Phila, 1907. 2 fldg plans hors texte. (Cl sl rubbed.) *Washton*. $45/£29

MARVELL, ANDREW. The Works. Thomas Cooke (ed). London: T. Davies, 1772. 2 vols. x,161,(3); (8),243,(5)pp (bkpl). Contemp calf (neatly rebacked), morocco labels. *Cox*. $133/£85

MARVIN, CHARLES. Training the Trotting Horse. L. E. Macleod (ed). Franklin, PA: Marvin, 1893. 4th ed. Frontis port, xxiv,17-352pp. Good-. *Scribe's Perch**. $18/£12

MARVIN, F. S. (ed). Science and Civilization.... London: OUP, 1926. 1st ed. NF (bkpl, non-authorial presentation card laid in) in dj (sl torn). *Glaser*. $45/£29

MARX, GROUCHO and RICHARD J. ANOBILE. The Marx Bros. Scrapbook. NY, (1973). 2nd ptg. (Ex-libris blindstamp tp), else Good in dj (torn, soiled). *King*. $75/£48

MARX, GROUCHO. The Groucho Letters. NY: S&S, 1967. 1st ed. (Sig), o/w VG in dj. *Hermitage*. $35/£22

MARX, GROUCHO. The Groucho Letters: Letters from and to Groucho Marx. NY: S&S, (1967). 1st ed. Signed. Fine in dj (spine sl faded). *Captain's Bookshelf*. $300/£192

MARX, KARL and FREDERICK ENGELS. Manifesto of the Communists. NY: Schaerr & Frantz, 1883. 1st Amer ed. 28pp. Wrappers (tears, chips, vertical fold). VG in fldg clbound cvr. *Metropolitan**. $460/£295

MARX, KARL. Capital: A Critical Analysis of Capitalist Production. Samuel Moore and Edward Aveling (trans). NY: Appleton, 1889. 1st Amer issue of sheets of 2 vol 1st British ed of 1887. Lg thick 8vo. xxxi,(1),816pp. Orig mustard yellow cl. (Sm snag spine crown, recased w/orig eps laid down), o/w VG. *Reese*. $1,250/£801

Maryland Geological Survey. Balt, 1897-1911. 7 vols. Grn cl (shelfwear, hinges cracked, last vol w/staining, lib mks). *Bohling*. $60/£38

Maryland: Its Resources, Industries and Institutions. Balt, 1893. (vi),vi,504pp (hinges split, eps edgetorn, lt aged); 5 toned litho plts, 2 fldg maps at rear. Marbled eps. Yellow-orange cl (sl worn), gilt. *Baltimore**. $80/£51

MASCHIO, GERALDINE. Stigmata. Madison, WI: Penstemon, (1979). 1st ed. #40/60 signed by Maschio and K. Schallock (artist). Fine in tan wrappers. *Heller.* $50/£32

MASEFIELD, JOHN (notes). John M. Synge: A Few Personal Recollections. Churchtown, Dundrum: Cuala, 1915. One of 350 ptd. Grey bds, linen spine. Fine. *Appelfeld.* $150/£96

MASEFIELD, JOHN. A Book of Prose Selections. London, 1950. 1st ed. NF in VG + dj. *Smith.* $15/£10

MASEFIELD, JOHN. Conquer. NY: Macmillan, 1941. 1st ed. VG (eps lt browned) in dj (wear, sm tears). *Antic Hay.* $15/£10

MASEFIELD, JOHN. Easter: A Play. London: Heinemann, (1929). 1st Eng ed. NF in dj (spine faded, sm tear). *Antic Hay.* $20/£13

MASEFIELD, JOHN. End and Beginning. NY: Macmillan, 1933. 1st Amer ed. NF (fr cvr lt spotted) in dj (lt wear). *Antic Hay.* $25/£16

MASEFIELD, JOHN. Enslaved and Other Poems. NY: Macmillan, 1920. 1st Amer ed. Vellum, bds. NF in dj (spine head sl worn). *Antic Hay.* $35/£22

MASEFIELD, JOHN. The Faithful. 1915. 1st issue w/illus eps. VG in dj (spine browned). *Words Etc.* $47/£30

MASEFIELD, JOHN. The Hawbucks. London: Heinemann, (1929). 1st ed. Inscribed, signed. (Bkpl, rear inner hinge sl weak), o/w Nice in dj (chipped). *Reese.* $50/£32

MASEFIELD, JOHN. A Mainsail Haul. London: Elkin Mathews, 1905. 1st ed. Frontis; cat description tipped on fr pastedown. White-ruled grn cl (sl loss to white ruling, spine lettering). *Edwards.* $117/£75

MASEFIELD, JOHN. Minnie Maylow's Story and Other Tales and Scenes. London: Heinemann, (1931). 1st Eng ed. NF (sl browned) in Nice dj. *Antic Hay.* $25/£16

MASEFIELD, JOHN. Multitude and Solitude. London: Grant Richards, 1906. 1st ed. One of 2350. Dec grn cl. VG (spine sl discolored). *Antic Hay.* $45/£29

MASEFIELD, JOHN. Multitude and Solitude. Grant Richards, 1909. 1st ed. Grn cl w/white enamel on upper cvr. (Enamel beginning to fade, corners bumped), o/w *Words Etc.* $31/£20

MASEFIELD, JOHN. The Nine Days Wonder. NY, 1941. 1st ed. VG in VG dj. *Smith.* $20/£13

MASEFIELD, JOHN. Odtaa. Heinemann, 1926. 1st UK ed. VG + in dj (spine wear). *Williams.* $23/£15

MASEFIELD, JOHN. Philip the King. London: Heinemann, 1927. Ltd to 360 numbered, signed by Masefield and Laurence Irving (illus). 12 tipped-in illus. NF in dj (sl wear, sm tear). *Antic Hay.* $100/£64

MASEFIELD, JOHN. Right Royal. London: Heinemann, 1920. Ltd to 500 numbered, signed. Teg. Vellum, bds. NF (eps browned). *Antic Hay.* $50/£32

MASEFIELD, JOHN. Salt Water Ballads. London: Grant Richards, 1902. 1st ed, 1st issue, w/pub's imprint. Blue cl. (Bkpl.) 1/4 morocco slipcase. *Swann*.* $230/£147

MASEFIELD, JOHN. So Long to Learn. NY: Macmillan, 1952. 1st ed. Fine in dj (wear, sm chips spine, price-clipped). *Antic Hay.* $15/£10

MASEFIELD, JOHN. Some Verses to Some Germans. London: Heinemann, 1939. 1st ed. VG in orig wrappers (sl mkd). *Hollett.* $23/£15

MASEFIELD, JOHN. The Square Peg. London: Heinemann, 1937. 1st ed. (Fore-edge spotted.) Dj (chip). *Hollett.* $16/£10

MASEFIELD, JOHN. The Taking of Helen. London, 1923. 1st ed. #88/750 (of 780) signed. Teg, uncut. Vellum spine (sl sunned). Fine. *Polyanthos.* $30/£19

MASEFIELD, JOHN. The Tragedy of Nan. NY: Macmillan, 1921. New illus ed. Dec grn cl. VG. *Antic Hay.* $15/£10

MASEFIELD, JOHN. The Trial of Jesus. London, 1925. 1st ed. #98/500 (of 530) signed. Teg, uncut. Vellum spine (sl sunned). NF. *Polyanthos.* $30/£19

MASEFIELD, JOHN. Tristan and Isolt, A Play in Verse. NY, 1927. 1st Amer ed. Ltd to 350 numbered, signed. Cl-backed bds (rubbed, paper spine label chipped). *King.* $35/£22

MASEFIELD, JOHN. Tristan and Isolt. London, 1927. Ltd to 250 numbered, signed. (Fore-edge, eps sl foxed), o/w VG in dj (tanned, sl soiled). *Buckley.* $55/£35

MASLAND, FRANK E., JR. By the Rim of Time. Carlisle/Phila, PA, (1949). 1st ed. VF in red/black pict wraps. *Five Quail.* $35/£22

MASLAND, FRANK E., JR. The Goat Run. Privately ptd by Masland, 1950. Near Mint in stiff pict wraps. *Five Quail.* $25/£16

MASON, A. E. W. The Four Feathers. Smith, Elder, 1902. 1st UK ed. VG (spine sl dull). *Williams.* $70/£45

MASON, A. E. W. The Life of Francis Drake. Hodder, 1941. 1st UK ed. VG + in dj. *Williams.* $31/£20

MASON, A. E. W. No Other Tiger. NY: Doran, 1927. 1st Amer ed. Bright in dj (soil, chips, short tears, long crease). *Metropolitan*.* $11/£7

MASON, A. E. W. The Witness for the Defence. London: Hodder, 1913. 1st UK ed. VG- (ink name; spine browned, bds mkd). *Williams.* $23/£15

MASON, ANITA. The Illusionist. NY: Holt, Rinehart & Winston, (1983). 1st Amer ed. Black cl-backed red bds (sm white stains; sm tear rear bd), gilt. Internally Fine in dj (sl soiled). *Blue Mountain.* $15/£10

MASON, B. F. Through War and Peace. N.p., 1891. 113pp. (Cvr sl stained), o/w VG +. *Pratt.* $45/£29

MASON, BERNARD S. The Book of Indian-Crafts and Costumes. NY: Ronald Press, (1946). VG. *Lien.* $25/£16

MASON, BERNARD. Clock and Watchmaking in Colchester, England. London: Country Life, 1969. 1st ed. Red cl. Fine. *Weber.* $125/£80

MASON, CYRUS (intro). A History of the Holy Catholic Inquisition. Phila: Henry Perkins, 1835. (Fr bd coming detached, rubbed, bumped.) *Metropolitan*.* $115/£74

MASON, EDWARD G. Illinois in the Eighteenth Century. Chicago: Fergus Ptg Co, 1881. 70pp. Unopened. (Upper corner, few leaves sl dampstained, sm breaks, sm chips.) Orig ptd wrappers. *Sadlon.* $20/£13

MASON, JOHN. A Brief History of the Pequot War. NY: Sabin, 1869. 2nd ed. vi,ix,20pp. Wraps (edges, spine chipped; cvrs reattached, spine strengthened w/tissue). Howes M369. *Oregon.* $30/£19

MASON, JOHN. A Brief History of the Pequot War. NY: Sabin, 1869. 1/2 morocco (lt rubbed). Howes M369. *Swann*.* $201/£129

MASON, KENNETH. Abode of Snow. NY, 1955. 1st Amer ed. VG in dj (sl used). *King.* $45/£29

MASON, KENNETH. Abode of Snow: A History of Himalayan Exploration and Mountaineering. NY: Dutton, 1955. 1st Amer ed. Fine. *Terramedia.* $50/£32

MASON, OTIS TUFTON. Aboriginal American Basketry. Washington, 1904. 248 plts. Orig wrappers (very worn). *Swann*.* $69/£44

MASON, R. OSGOOD. Sketches and Impressions, Musical, Theatrical and Social (1799-1885). NY/London: Putnam, 1887. 1st ed. x,294pp. Teg. NF. *Worldwide.* $20/£13

MASON, S. Bibliography of Oscar Wilde. London: E. Grant Richards, 1907. Frontis, 8 plts. Uncut. (Ink inscrip, sl grubby, sl spotted.) *Maggs*. $78/£50

MASON, VAN WYCK. The Shanghai Bund Murders. GC: DCC, 1933. 1st ed. VG in dj (spine sl faded, frayed, chipped). *Mordida*. $65/£42

MASPERO, G. Egyptian Archaeology. NY: Putnam, 1889. xx,373pp (fep chipped, 1st few pp foxed). Teg. Gilt-pict cl. *Archaeologia*. $55/£35

MASPERO, G. History of Egypt. London: Grolier, n.d. 13 vols. Good. *Scribe's Perch**. $110/£71

MASPERO, GASTON. Egypt: Ancient Sites and Modern Scenes. NY: Appleton, 1911. Frontis, 16 plts. (Bkpl.) Teg. Gilt-pict cl (spine sl torn). *Archaeologia*. $55/£35

MASPERO, GASTON. Popular Stories of Ancient Egypt. A. S. Johns (trans). New Hyde Park, NY: University Books, 1967. VG. *Worldwide*. $30/£19

MASPERO, HENRI. China in Antiquity. Frank A. Kierman, Jr. (trans). Folkestone, Kent: Dawson, 1978. 3 dbl-pg maps. NF in dj. *Worldwide*. $24/£15

MASSACHUSETTS MEDICAL SOCIETY. A Report on Spasmodic Cholera.... Boston, 1832. 1st ed. 190pp (foxed); 3 maps (2 fldg, 1 in pocket). (Ex-lib.) Mod marbled bds. *Argosy*. $125/£80

Massachusetts Register and U.S. Calendar for the Year 1808. Boston: John West/Manning & Loring, (1807). (Foxing mainly to 1st, last leaves.) Orig wrappers (edges sl chipped, old paper traces on spine). *Sadlon*. $35/£22

Massachusetts: A Guide to Its Places and People. Boston: HM, 1937. 1st ed. Blue cl (rubbed). VG (lacks map). *Archer*. $30/£19

MASSAR, PHYLLIS DEARBORN. Presenting Stefano della Bella, Eighteenth-Century Printmaker. NY: MMA, 1971. Good in dj. *Washton*. $20/£13

MASSE, H. J. L. J. Pewter Plate. 1910. 2nd ed. 5 fldg plts. (Feps sl browned; cl lt soiled, corners, spine sl rubbed.) *Edwards*. $62/£40

MASSEE, GEORGE. Diseases of Cultivated Plants and Trees. NY, 1913. Red cl (bled onto ep edges; spine faded). Nice. *Brooks*. $29/£19

MASSERMAN, JULES H. Behavior and Neurosis. Chicago: Univ of Chicago, (1943). 1st ed. Presentation copy. Blue cl. VG in dj (chipped). *Gach*. $50/£32

MASSEY, G. BETTON. Conservative Gynecology and Electrotherapeutics. Phila, 1906. 5th ed. Red cl bds (extrems sl worn). VG. *Doctor's Library*. $125/£80

MASSEY, W. T. The Desert Campaigns. London: Constable, 1918. 1st ed. 24 plts. (Scattered spotting, lower joint cracked.) Blind-dec bd. *Hollett*. $101/£65

MASSIE, CHRIS. When My Ship Comes Home. Faber, 1959. 1st ed. 8vo. 173pp (few streaks feps, ex-lib stamp). VG in pict Edward Ardizzone dj (cvrd in lib-film, surface sl skimmed). *Bookmark*. $14/£9

MASSINGHAM, BETTY. Miss Jekyll. London: Country Life, 1966. 1st ed. Dj (sm dampstain spine tail). *Hollett*. $47/£30

MASSINGHAM, BETTY. Turn on the Fountains. London: Gollancz, 1974. Color frontis. Fine in pict dj. *Quest*. $40/£26

MASSINGHAM, H. J. Remembrance. London: Batsford, 1941. 1st ed. 48 plts. (Sl spotting.) Paul Nash dj (lt rubbed, spine sl dknd, lower hinge torn). *Hollett*. $39/£25

MASSON, CHARLES. Narrative of Various Journeys in Balochistan, Afghanistan, and the Panjab. London: Richard Bentley, 1842. 1st ed. 3 vols. 8vo. 6 litho plts (lt spotting). Orig cl (spines faded, ends scuffed). *Christie's**. $807/£517

MASSON, THOMAS L. (ed). Tom Masson's Annual for 1924. GC: Doubleday, 1924. 1st ed. VG in dj. *Houle*. $100/£64

MASTAI, M. L. D'OTRANGE. Illusion in Art. NY, 1975. 1st ed. Color frontis, 23 color plts. (Lt rubbed, spine sl faded.) *Edwards*. $39/£25

Master Henry's Walk; and the Story of Jenny Crawley. Troy, NY: Merriam & Moore, n.d. (ca 1851). Sm 8vo. Full-pg wood engr frontis, 24pp + 1pg list lower wrapper (lt damp-staining). Good in pict paper wrappers (crudely hand colored, lt soiled, ink names, spine chipped). *Hobbyhorse*. $75/£48

Master of Mary of Burgundy. NY: George Braziller, (1970). Heavy blue cl, gilt. Good in slipcase (soiled). *Karmiole*. $65/£42

MASTER, ARTHUR M. The Electrocardiogram and X-Ray Configuration of the Heart. Phila, 1939. 1st ed. VG. *Argosy*. $75/£48

MASTERMAN, WALTER S. The Baddington Horror. London: Jarrolds, 1934. 8th thousand. Nice (ep split; cvr soiled, stained) in dj (creases sl worn, nicks, edgetears). *Metropolitan**. $143/£92

Masterpieces of Erotic Photography. London: Aurum Press, 1977. 1st ed. NF in VG + dj. *Smith*. $70/£45

Masters of Seventeenth Century Dutch Genre Painting. Phila: Phila Museum of Art, 1984. 127 color plts. Good in wraps. *Washton*. $30/£19

MASTERS, EDGAR LEE. Across Spoon River. NY: Farrar & Rinehart, (1936). 1st ed. Frontis port. VG in dj (sl worn). *Wantagh*. $35/£22

MASTERS, EDGAR LEE. Illinois Poems. Prairie City, IL: James A. Decker, 1941. 1st ed. Fine in dj (sl worn). *Graf*. $35/£22

MASTERS, EDGAR LEE. Invisible Landscapes. NY, 1935. 1st ed. (Glue stains feps; cvr faded), else Good in dj (price-clipped; chipped, rubbed). *King*. $25/£16

MASTERS, EDGAR LEE. The New Spoon River. NY: Boni & Liveright, 1924. 1st ed. #143/360 numbered, signed. Uncut. Gilt-stamped Japan velllum over gray bds. VG. *Houle*. $175/£112

MASTERS, EDGAR LEE. Spoon River Anthology. London: T. Werner Laurie, (1916). 1st Eng expanded, illus ed. (Bkpl removed under flap), else Fine in dj (lt sunned, shallow chip spine head). *Captain's Bookshelf*. $75/£48

MASTERS, EDGAR LEE. Spoon River Anthology. NY: Macmillan, 1915. 1st ed, 1st issue. Blue cl, gilt. (Edges bumped, rubbed; bkpl), o/w VG in folder (faded) in slipcase (faded), blue leather spine. *Metropolitan**. $115/£74

MASTERS, J. The Compleat Indian Angler. London, 1938. 1st ed. Color frontis, 16 photo plts. (Spine partly chewed), else VG. *Mikesh*. $75/£48

MASTERS, JOHN. Fandango Rock. London, 1959. 1st ed. VG in dj (chipped). *Buckley*. $16/£10

MASTERS, JOHN. The Lotus and the Wind. London: Michael Joseph, 1953. 1st UK ed. NF in dj. *Williams*. $44/£28

MASTERS, JOHN. Nightrunners of Bengal. NY: Viking, 1951. 1st Amer ed. VG (ink name) in dj (worn). *Antic Hay*. $17/£11

MASURY, JOHN W. House-Painting, Carriage-Painting, and Graining. NY: Appleton, 1881. 1st ed. 244pp + (8) pub's ads. Brn cl (sl used), gilt. *Petrilla*. $75/£48

MATHER, COTTON. The Wonders of the Invisible World. London: 1862. xvi,292pp. VG- (ex-lib). *Middle Earth*. $95/£61

MATHER, FRED. Men I Have Fished With. NY: Forest & Stream, 1897. Signed, inscribed. 371pp (pencil notes, underlining); 9 ports. Buckram (rebound), orig gilt buckram label fr cvr, spine. *Argosy*. $60/£38

MATHER, SAMUEL. The Life of the Very Reverend and Learned Cotton Mather.... Boston: Samuel Gerrish, 1729. 1st ed. 8vo. (24),186pp. 19th cent 1/4 calf, bds (extrems rubbed, upper joint starting). Interior VG (inscrip). Howes M409. *Cummins*. $600/£385

MATHER, W. Geology of New-York. Albany: Carroll & Cook, 1843. xxxvii,652,(17)pp. VG (lt foxed; sig, stamp). *Blake*. $275/£176

MATHERS, E. POWYS (trans). The Smell of Lebanon. Talybont: Francis Waterson, 1928. Ltd to 375 signed. Cl-backed patterned bds (edges faded), gilt. *Hollett*. $39/£25

MATHERS, E. POWYS. The Book of the Thousand Nights and One Night. Folio Soc, 1958. 4 vols. Eric Fraser (illus). Vellum-backed bds (sm split spine head vol 1). Slipcase. *Edwards*. $55/£35

MATHERS, E. POWYS. Red Wise. London: Golden Cockerel, (1926). One of 500 numbered. NF (tip worn). *Certo*. $125/£80

MATHERS, E. POWYS. Red Wise. (Berkshire: Waltham Saint Lawrence), 1926. One of 500. Robert Gibbings (illus). Dec eps. Red paper over bd, cream buckram spine, gilt. VG. *Heller*. $200/£128

MATHERS, MICHAEL. Riding the Rails. Boston: Houghton Mifflin, 1974. 1st ed, 1st bk. (Name stamp), else NF in pict stiff wrappers. *Cahan*. $25/£16

MATHERS, S. L. MacGREGOR. The Kabbalah Unveiled. London: G. Redway, 1887. 1st ed. x,359pp, index + 60pp cat; 3 lg fold-outs. VG. *Middle Earth*. $195/£125

MATHERS, S. L. MacGREGOR. The Kabbalah Unveiled. London: Routledge & Kegan Paul, 1951. 2 fldg charts. NF in dj. *House*. $80/£51

MATHES, C. HODGE. Tall Tales from Old Smokey. Kingsport: Southern Pub, 1952. 1st ed. NF (name) in Fair dj. *Connolly*. $25/£16

MATHES, W. MICHAEL. Mexico on Stone: Lithography in Mexico, 1826-1900. SF: Book Club of CA, 1984. 1st ed. Ltd to 550 ptd. VF in plain buff dj (lt soiled). *Hermitage*. $150/£96

MATHES, W. MICHAEL. Spanish Approaches to the Island of California 1628-32. SF, 1975. 1st ed. One of 400. VF in plain dj, as issued. *Turpen*. $65/£42

MATHESON, RICHARD. Born of Man and Woman. Phila: Chamberlain, 1954. 1st ed, 1st bk. (Lt dampstained.) Dj (dampstained w/text loss). *Swann**. $161/£103

MATHESON, RICHARD. Collected Stories. (L.A.: Dream, 1989.) 1st ed. One of 350 advance reading copies. Ptd wrappers. As New in shrink-wrap. *Swann**. $80/£51

MATHESON, RICHARD. Collected Stories. (L.A.: Dream, 1989.) 1st ed. One of 400 numbered, signed. Slipcase. *Swann**. $172/£110

MATHESON, RICHARD. Earthbound. London: Robinson, 1989. 1st hb ed. Fine in Fine dj. *Certo*. $26/£17

MATHESON, RICHARD. Hell House. NY, (1971). 1st ed. Cl-backed bds. (Fore-edge sl spotted), else VG in dj (sl used). *King*. $150/£96

MATHESON, RICHARD. Hell House. NY: Viking, (1971). 1st ed. 1/4 cl. (Sm spots fore-edge), else NF in dj (price-clipped). *Waverly**. $77/£49

MATHESON, RICHARD. Hell House. NY: Viking, (1971). 1st ed. VG + (sl spine cock) in Fine dj. *Other Worlds*. $150/£96

MATHESON, RICHARD. Hell House. NY: Viking, 1971. 1st ed. (Top edge faded, spattered; text block sl wavy), else Nice in NF dj. *Beasley*. $85/£54

MATHESON, RICHARD. Journal of the Gun Years. Evans, 1991. 1st ed. Fine in Fine dj. *Certo*. $35/£22

MATHESON, RICHARD. Scars. L.A.: Scream Press, 1987. 1st ed. (Bds sl bowed), else Fine in Fine dj. *Other Worlds*. $35/£22

MATHEW, GERVASE. Byzantine Aesthetics. NY, 1963. 25 plts hors texte. Good in dj. *Washton*. $50/£32

MATHEWS, JOHN JOSEPH. Wah'Kon-Tah: The Osage and the White Man's Road. Norman: Univ of OK, 1932. 1st ed. VG in dj (sl worn). *Lien*. $30/£19

MATHEWS, LOIS K. The Expansion of New England...1620-1865. Boston, 1909. 1st ed. Inscribed presentation. 27 maps. Howes M416. *Ginsberg*. $100/£64

MATHEWS, MARY M. Ten Years in Nevada or, Life on the Pacific Coast. Buffalo, 1880. Frontis, 343pp. Gilt cl (extrems frayed, spine tear, corners bumped). Good. Howes M417. *Reese*. $500/£321

MATHEWS, RICHARD. The Yukon. NY, c. 1968. Map. Fine in dj. *High Latitude*. $30/£19

MATHEWS, SALLIE REYNOLDS. Interwoven: A Pioneer Chronicle. Houston: Anson Jones, 1936. 1st ed. Frontis port. Textured cl (sl worn; fr inner hinge cracked, owner stamps all edges, prelims). Dj (lacks fr flap, portion of adjoining edge, 1/2 spine; long tear fr panel; sm tears, frayed). Howes M425. *Waverly**. $176/£113

MATHEWS. Tea-Table Talk, Ennobled Actresses, and Other Miscellanies. London: Thomas Cautley Newby, 1857. 1st ed. 2 vols. Patterned cl, dec gilt spines (sunned; hinges vol II tender, spine vol II worn). Internally VG. *Dramatis Personae*. $150/£96

MATHEWSON, CHRISTY. First Base Faulkner. Dodd Mead, 1916. 1st ed. Good. *Plapinger*. $65/£42

MATHEWSON, CHRISTY. Pitcher Pollack. Dodd Mead, 1914. 1st ed. VG. *Plapinger*. $65/£42

MATHEWSON, CHRISTY. Pitching in a Pinch. Putnam, 1912. 1st ed. Frontis port. (Fr hinge started, lacks fep), else VG. *Certo*. $85/£54

MATISSE, HENRI. Jazz. NY, (1983). 1st ed thus. Dj; slipcase. *Freeman**. $45/£29

MATISSE, HENRI. Jazz. NY, (1983). Folio. *Swann**. $201/£129

MATISSE, HENRI. Jazz. NY: Braziller, (1984). 3rd ptg. Fine in dj (lt worn). *Waverly**. $44/£28

Matrix 10. Whittington Press, 1990. Fine in orig wrappers. *Michael Taylor*. $195/£125

Matrix 2. Whittington Press, (1982). Orig issue. Fine in orig wrappers. *Michael Taylor*. $390/£250

Matrix 5. Whittington, Winter 1985. One of 715. Mint in wrappers. *Words Etc*. $234/£150

Matrix 6. Whittington, 1986. Fine. *Moss*. $156/£100

Matrix 7. Whittington Press, (1987). Fine in orig wrappers. *Michael Taylor*. $211/£135

Matrix 8. Whittington, 1988. Fine. *Moss*. $140/£90

Matrix 8. (Gloucestershire), 1988. One of 100 (of 900) in deluxe binding w/separate set of broadsheets enclosed in chemise within the same slipcase. 1/4 'peach' morocco over Whittington marbled bds. VF. *Truepenny*. $450/£288

Matrix 9. Whittington Press, (1989). Fine in orig wrappers. *Michael Taylor*. $195/£125

Matrix 9. (Gloucestershire), 1989. Ltd to 925. VF in wrappers. *Truepenny*. $175/£112

Matrix 9. (Gloucestershire: Whittington), 1989. One of 925, of which this is one of 105 in deluxe binding; w/facs of Robert Gibbings's 'Letter to Collette' bound in 1/4 cl, dec bds, and encl in same slipcase. 1/4 citron morocco over Whittington marbled bds. VF in slipcase. *Truepenny*. $450/£288

Matrix 10. (Gloucestershire: Whittington), 1990. One of 925. Thin bds. Mint in chromolitho wrapper. *Truepenny*. $195/£125

Matrix 11. Whittington Press, (1991). Fine in orig wrappers. *Michael Taylor*. $179/£115

Matrix 11. Whittington, 1991. Fine. *Moss*. $140/£90

Matrix 11. (Gloucestershire: Whittington), 1991. One of 955. Pict bds. Mint in dj. *Truepenny*. $225/£144

Matrix 12. Whittington Press, (1992). Fine in orig wrappers. *Michael Taylor*. $172/£110

Matrix 12. (Gloucestershire: Whittington, 1992.) Dec bds. As New in dj. *Truepenny*. $160/£103

MATSELL, GEORGE W. Vocabulum; or, The Rogue's Lexicon. NY: George Matsell, 1859. 1st ed. Contemp dec brn cl (rebacked) w/new eps. Fine. *Cummins*. $200/£128

MATSON, DONALD D. The Treatment of Acute Craniocerebral Injuries Due to Missiles. Springfield: Thomas, 1948. VG. *Goodrich*. $45/£29

MATSUTANI, MIYOKO. The Witch's Magic Cloth. NY: Parent's, 1969. 1st ed. Yasuo Segawa (illus). 8 1/2 x 10 1/4. c32pp. Fine in dj. *Cattermole*. $25/£16

MATTERS, LEONARD. Through the Kara Sea. London: Skeffington, 1932. Map. Very Nice. *High Latitude*. $75/£48

MATTES, MERRILL J. The Great Platte River Road...Via Fort Kearny to Fort Laramie. NE State Hist Soc, 1969. 1st ed. VG in dj (sl worn). *Lien*. $55/£35

MATTES, MERRILL J. Platte River Road Narratives. Urbana/Chicago: Univ of IL, 1988. 1st ed. Dbl-pg map. 2-tone red cl, silver titles. Fine. *Pacific**. $190/£122

MATTHES, FRANCOIS E. Geologic History of the Yosemite Valley. Washington: GPO, 1930. Wraps (discolored, sm tear). *King*. $95/£61

MATTHES, FRANCOIS E. The Incomparable Valley. Berkeley, 1950. 1st ed. (Sl dent fr cvr), else Good in dj (chipped). *King*. $40/£26

MATTHES, FRANCOIS E. The Incomparable Valley. Fritiof Fryxell (ed). Berkeley/L.A.: Univ of CA, 1950. 1st ed. Frontis photo, 50 photo plts (23 by Ansel Adams). VF in pict dj. *Argonaut*. $75/£48

MATTHES, FRANCOIS E. Sequoia National Park. Berkeley, 1950. 1st ed. VG in dj (sl chipped, soiled). *King*. $40/£26

MATTHEWS, BRANDER. Bookbindings Old and New. NY, 1895. 1st Amer ed. NF (sl foxed, names; spine sunned). *Polyanthos*. $60/£38

MATTHEWS, CHARLES GEORGE and FRANCIS EDWARD LOTT. The Microscope in the Brewery and Malt-House. London, 1889. Frontis, xviii,198pp (bkpl remains fep); 21 plts, 30 woodcuts. Gilt-edged 1/2 morocco (rebound, sl soiled). *Edwards*. $195/£125

MATTHEWS, HENRY. The Diary of an Invalid.... John Murray, 1820. 2nd ed. xv,(i),515,(1),(errata)pp. Contemp 1/2 calf (edges rubbed, worn), gilt back. (Lt foxed.) *Cox*. $75/£48

MATTHEWS, HENRY. The Diary of an Invalid...1817, 1818, and 1819. London, 1820. 2nd ed. 516pp. (New eps.) Recent cl-backed bds. *Fye*. $150/£96

MATTHEWS, JOSEPH M. A Treatise on Diseases of the Rectum, Anus, and Sigmoid Flexure. NY: Appleton, 1895. Later rpt. 545pp; 6 chromolithos. Orig 1/2 calf (rubbed, worn). Internally Good. *Goodrich*. $95/£61

MATTHEWS, L. HARRISON. The Life of Mammals. NY: Universe, 1969. 1st ed. 2 vols. 54 plts. VG. *Mikesh*. $60/£38

MATTHEWS, L. HARRISON. Sea Elephant. London: MacGibbon & Kee, 1952. VG in dj. *High Latitude*. $17/£11

MATTHEWS, L. HARRISON. Wandering Albatross.... London, 1951. (Spine faded.) *Maggs*. $25/£16

MATTHEWS, WILLIAM. American Diaries; An Annotated Bibliography of American Diaries Written Prior to the Years 1861. Boston, 1969. *Ginsberg*. $50/£32

MATTHEWS, WILLIAM. American Diaries; An Annotated Bibliography...Written Prior to the Years 1861. Berkeley, 1945. 1st ed. Orig ptd wrappers. *Ginsberg*. $50/£32

MATTHEWS, WILLIAM. Modern Bookbinding Practically Considered. NY: Grolier Club, 1889. One of 300. (Bkpls, spine dknd.) *Swann**. $115/£74

MATTHIAE, PAOLO. Ebla. An Empire Rediscovered. London/Sydney/Auckland: Hodder & Stoughton, 1980. 1st Eng ed. 60 plts. NF in dj. *Worldwide*. $25/£16

MATTHIESSEN, PETER. At Play in the Fields of the Lord. NY: Random House, (1965). 1st ed. Fine in NF dj (price-clipped; short tears; sl soiling; sl spine dkng). *Between The Covers*. $250/£160

MATTHIESSEN, PETER. The Cloud Forest. NY: Viking, 1961. 1st ed. Fine in dj (lt rubbed, price-clipped). *Captain's Bookshelf*. $75/£48

MATTHIESSEN, PETER. The Great Auk Escape. London: Angus & Robertson, 1974. Correct 1st ed. William Pene du Bois (illus). (Fr outer gutter bumped), else Fine in glossy illus paper-cvrd bds. *Lame Duck*. $400/£256

MATTHIESSEN, PETER. In the Spirit of Crazy Horse. NY: Viking, (1983). 1st ed. NF in dj (sm tear). *Captain's Bookshelf*. $175/£112

MATTHIESSEN, PETER. In the Spirit of Crazy Horse. NY: Viking, 1983. 1st ed. VF in VF dj. *Else Fine*. $150/£96

MATTHIESSEN, PETER. Indian Country. NY: Viking, (1984). 1st ed. Fine in dj. *Captain's Bookshelf*. $100/£64

MATTHIESSEN, PETER. Indian Country. NY: Viking, 1984. 1st ed. NF in NF dj (sm edgetear spine foot). *Lame Duck*. $125/£80

MATTHIESSEN, PETER. Killing Mister Watson. NY: Random House, (1990). 1st ed. Blue cl-backed bds, gilt. NF in pict dj. *Blue Mountain*. $25/£16

MATTHIESSEN, PETER. Men's Lives. NY, 1986. 1st ed. Fine in Fine dj. *Warren*. $50/£32

MATTHIESSEN, PETER. Men's Lives. London, 1988. 1st Eng ed. Fine in dj. *Words Etc*. $34/£22

MATTHIESSEN, PETER. Oomingmak. NY, (1967). 1st Amer ed. Fine in Fine dj. *Polyanthos*. $35/£22

MATTHIESSEN, PETER. Oomingmak. NY: Hastings House, (1967). 1st ed. Fine in NF dj. *Pettler & Lieberman*. $45/£29

MATTHIESSEN, PETER. Oomingmak. NY, 1967. 1st ed. Signed. Fine in NF dj (sm chips spine). *Warren*. $50/£32

MATTHIESSEN, PETER. Raditzer. London: Heinemann, 1962. 1st UK ed. (Ink stamp, price fep), o/w NF in dj (price-clipped; spine tear, no loss). *Moorhouse*. $16/£10

MATTHIESSEN, PETER. Seal Pool. GC: Doubleday, (1972). 1st ed. William Pene du Bois (illus). Pict bds. Fine (sl bump bottom corner bds) in Fine dj (crown sl rubbing, price-clipped). *Between The Covers*. $350/£224

MATTHIESSEN, PETER. The Shorebirds of North America. NY: Viking, (1967). 1st ed, deluxe issue. One of 350 specially bound, signed by Matthiessen, Gardner D. Stout (ed), Robert Verity Clem (illus), and Ralph S. Palmer. Folio. Marbled eps; teg. Full calf. (Spine sl rubbed, dknd), o/w Fine in cl slipcase (lt rubbed, soiled), ptd label. *Jaffe*. $1,250/£801

MATTHIESSEN, PETER. The Shorebirds of North America. NY: Viking, 1967. 1st ed. VG+ in VG dj (chips, sm tears). *Warren*. $150/£96

MATTHIESSEN, PETER. The Snow Leopard. NY: Viking, (1978). 1st ed. (Fore-edges, top lt spotted), else Fine in dj. *Captain's Bookshelf*. $50/£32

MATTSON, HANS. Recollections, the Story of an Emigrant. St. Paul: Merrill, 1891. 314pp. Red cl (spine faded, ex-lib). *Bohling.* $25/£16

MATUZAKI, MEIZI. Angling in Japan. Board of Tourist Industry, Japanese Govt Railways, (1940). VG in wraps. *King.* $35/£22

MAUDSLEY, HENRY. Body and Mind. NY: D. Appleton, 1874. 1st rev ed, 1st Amer ptg. x,(4),(13)-275,(9)pp. Pub's ruled orange cl (lt shelfworn; lib stamp tp, rear pocket, spine #). Jelliffe's bkpl. VG. *Gach.* $85/£54

MAUDSLEY, HENRY. The Pathology of the Mind. NY, 1880. 3rd ed. 580pp. Brn cl bds (sl worn). VG. *Doctor's Library.* $125/£80

MAUDSLEY, HENRY. The Physiology and Pathology of the Mind. NY: D. Appleton, 1867. 1st US ed. (xvi),442,(8)pp. Pebbled mauve cl. Jelliffe's name stamp, bkpl. VG (lib stamp tp, rear pocket, spine #s; spine, edges faded). *Gach.* $150/£96

MAUDSLEY, HENRY. Responsibility in Mental Disease. London: Henry S. King, 1874. 1st ed. x,313pp. Red cl (sl scuffed). *White.* $59/£38

MAUDSLEY, HENRY. Responsibility in Mental Disease. NY: D. Appleton, 1878. 2nd Amer ed. x,313,(11)pp. Dec red cl (spine faded, fr hinge cracked). VG. *Gach.* $50/£32

MAUGHAM, ROBIN. Come to Dust. London, 1945. 1st Eng ed, 1st bk. Nice in dj (chipped, ragged). *Clearwater.* $47/£30

MAUGHAM, ROBIN. Conversations with Willie. NY: S&S, (1978). 1st Amer ed. Fine in dj. *Antic Hay.* $15/£10

MAUGHAM, ROBIN. Nomad. London, 1947. 1st Eng ed. Good in dj (repaired, price-clipped). *Clearwater.* $23/£15

MAUGHAM, ROBIN. Nomad. London, 1947. 1st ed. Dj (frayed). *Typographeum.* $30/£19

MAUGHAM, ROBIN. The Servant. NY: Harcourt, Brace, (1949). 1st Amer ed. NF (sm bkseller's label) in dj (sl wear, soil, tear). *Antic Hay.* $30/£19

MAUGHAM, ROBIN. The Servant. NY, 1949. 1st Amer ed. VG in dj (spine ends rubbed). *Words Etc.* $16/£10

MAUGHAM, ROBIN. The Slaves of Timbuktu. London, 1961. 1st ed. 2 maps. Dj (sl chipped). *Edwards.* $28/£18

MAUGHAM, W. SOMERSET. Ah King, Six Stories. London: Heinemann, (1933). 1st ed. (Pencil notes, bk club label rep, sl rubbed), else Good. *Reese.* $35/£22

MAUGHAM, W. SOMERSET. Ah King. London: William Heinemann, 1933. 1st ed. One of 175 specially-bound, numbered, signed. (Corner sl bumped, spine sl dknd), o/w Fine (lacks slipcase). *Captain's Bookshelf.* $175/£112

MAUGHAM, W. SOMERSET. The Bishop's Apron. Chapman & Hall, 1906. 1st Eng ed. (Joints tender; spine skillfully rebacked, orig eps.) Sound. *Clearwater.* $125/£80

MAUGHAM, W. SOMERSET. The Book Bag. Florence: G. Orioli, 1932. 1st ed. One of 725 numbered, signed. Frontis. NF in dj (sl wear). *Captain's Bookshelf.* $300/£192

MAUGHAM, W. SOMERSET. The Book-Bag. Florence: G. Orioli, 1932. #63/725 signed on frontis port. Nice (bkpl; bd edges faded, top edges dusty) in dj (age-browned, sl worn, lt soiled). *Waverly*.* $220/£141

MAUGHAM, W. SOMERSET. The Bread-Winner. London: Heinemann, (1930). 1st ed. Clbound issue. Red cl (spine sl dknd). VG. *Reese.* $75/£48

MAUGHAM, W. SOMERSET. Catalina, a Romance. London: Heinemann, (1948). 1st ed. Red cl. Fine in dj. *Appelfeld.* $50/£32

MAUGHAM, W. SOMERSET. Catalina. NY, 1948. 1st Amer ed. Fine (name stamp) in dj (edges sl rubbed, few sm nicks). *Polyanthos.* $20/£13

MAUGHAM, W. SOMERSET. Christmas Holiday. London: Heinemann, (1939). 1st ed. Fine in dj (sl dust-mkd). *Reese.* $65/£42

MAUGHAM, W. SOMERSET. The Circle: A Comedy in Three Acts. NY: Doran, (1921). 1st Amer ed. NF (eps browned, ink name) in dj (worn, sl stained). *Antic Hay.* $75/£48

MAUGHAM, W. SOMERSET. Don Fernando or Variations on Some Spanish Themes. London: Heinemann, (1935). 1st ed, trade ptg. (Sl offset feps), o/w Fine in dj (lt rubbed, mended tear top edge). *Reese.* $85/£54

MAUGHAM, W. SOMERSET. Don Fernando or Variations on Some Spanish Themes. London: Heinemann, 1935. 1st ed. Signed presentation. Smooth black cl dec blocked in gold. NF in VG pict dj. *Vandoros.* $450/£288

MAUGHAM, W. SOMERSET. Don Fernando. London, 1935. 1st ed. VG in dj (frayed). *Typographeum.* $35/£22

MAUGHAM, W. SOMERSET. East and West. GC: Doubleday, (1934). 1st US ed. NF in VG dj (gold laminate worn). *Unger.* $150/£96

MAUGHAM, W. SOMERSET. Encore. NY: Doubleday, 1952. 1st Amer ed. (Ink name), else Fine in dj (lt worn). *Hermitage.* $30/£19

MAUGHAM, W. SOMERSET. First Person Singular. London: Heinemann, (1931). 1st Eng ed. Dec blue cl. Fine in dj (soil, browned). *Antic Hay.* $85/£54

MAUGHAM, W. SOMERSET. First Person Singular. NY: Avon Book Co, (1943). 1st Avon ed. VG in ptd wrappers. *Turtle Island.* $20/£13

MAUGHAM, W. SOMERSET. Liza of Lambeth. London, 1947. Jubilee ed. #813/1000 signed. (Corners worn; lacks dj.) *Typographeum.* $75/£48

MAUGHAM, W. SOMERSET. The Magician. London: Heinemann, 1908. 1st ed. Good (sm ink, wash ex-libris offset; sl rubbed). *Reese.* $150/£96

MAUGHAM, W. SOMERSET. The Making of a Saint. T. Fisher Unwin, 1898. 1st British ed. Teg. (1 leaf lacks corner, 2 roughly opened; foxing, browning, nicks, creases, eps cracked; splashed, mkd, dull.) *Ash.* $148/£95

MAUGHAM, W. SOMERSET. The Mixture as Before. London: Heinemann, (1940). 1st ed. Fine in dj. *Reese.* $65/£42

MAUGHAM, W. SOMERSET. The Moon and Sixpence. NY: Doran, (1919). 1st Amer ed, 1st binding w/author's name misspelled on both spine and fr cvr. Orig yellow-tan cl lettered in black. NF. *Macdonnell.* $200/£128

MAUGHAM, W. SOMERSET. Of Human Bondage. GC, 1936. 1st illus ed. #594/751 signed by Maugham and Randolph Schwabs (illus). Teg. Brn buckram (lt wear), gilt. Dj (edges sl chipped); slipcase (worn, soiled). *Freeman*.* $120/£77

MAUGHAM, W. SOMERSET. Of Human Bondage. New Haven: LEC, 1938. 1st ed thus. One of 1500 numbered, signed by John Sloan (etchings). 2 vols. Fine set in slipcase (lt worn). *Captain's Bookshelf.* $500/£321

MAUGHAM, W. SOMERSET. Of Human Bondage. New Haven: LEC, 1938. #904/1500 numbered, signed by John Sloan (illus). 2 vols. Fine in pub's slipcase. *Hermitage.* $600/£385

MAUGHAM, W. SOMERSET. Points of View. London: Heinemann, (1958). 1st Eng ed. NF in dj (sl wear, browned, soil). *Antic Hay.* $35/£22

MAUGHAM, W. SOMERSET. Points of View. GC: Doubleday, 1959. 1st Amer ed. Fine in dj (price-clipped). *Antic Hay.* $20/£13

MAUGHAM, W. SOMERSET. Six Stories Written in the First Person Singular. London: Heinemann, (1931). 1st British ed. NF in VG dj (tanned, soiled, nicked). *Reese.* $125/£80

MAULDIN, BILL. Back Home. NY: Wm. Sloane, (1947). 1st ed. Cl-backed bds. Fine in dj (sl edge-worn). *Sadlon.* $15/£10

MAULDIN, BILL. Back Home. NY: William Sloane, 1947. 1st ptg. Dj. *Dawson.* $35/£22

MAULDIN, BILL. Mud, Mules, and Mountains. Italy: Stars & Stripes, 1944. Pict wrappers. *Dawson.* $100/£64

MAULDIN, BILL. A Sort of a Saga. NY: Wm. Sloane, 1949. 1st ed. VG in Fair dj (deep spine chip). *Connolly.* $25/£16

MAULDIN, BILL. This Damn Tree Leaks: A Collection of War Cartoons. Italy: Stars & Stripes, 1945. (Sig.) Pict wrappers. *Dawson.* $100/£64

MAULDIN, BILL. Up Front. NY: Henry Holt, (1945). *Dawson.* $25/£16

MAULDIN, BILL. Up Front. NY: Armed Services, 1945. Armed Services ed. Pict wrappers. *Dawson.* $40/£26

MAUNDER, E. W. The Royal Observatory. 1900. Teg. Pict cl gilt. VG. *Whitehart.* $55/£35

MAURAT, CHARLOTTE. The Brontes' Secret. Margaret Meldrum (trans). London: Constable, 1969. 1st Eng ed. 12 plts. (Corners 1st 2 ll sl creased.) Dj (price-clipped). *Hollett.* $31/£20

MAURIAC, FRANCOIS. The Mask of Innocence. G. Hopkins (trans). NY: Farrar, Straus & Young, (1953). 1st Amer ed. Fine in dj (lt rubbed, soiled, price-clipped). *Antic Hay.* $25/£16

MAURIAC, FRANCOIS. Woman of the Pharisees. G. Hopkins (trans). NY: Holt, (1946). 1st ed. Fine in dj (lt worn, soiled). *Antic Hay.* $25/£16

MAURICE, ARTHUR BARTLETT. New York in Fiction. NY: Dodd, Mead, 1901. 1st ed. Inscribed in the year of publication. Beautiful in pict cl. *Captain's Bookshelf.* $100/£64

MAURICE, FREDERICK BARTON. Robert E. Lee the Soldier. Boston/NY: Houghton Mifflin, (1925). 1st ed. VG + . *Mcgowan.* $45/£29

MAURICEAU, A. M. The Married Woman's Private Medical Companion. NY, 1850. 13,238pp. *M&s.* $250/£160

MAURICEAU, FRANCIS. The Diseases of Women with Child, and in Child-Bed.... Hugh Chamerlen (trans). London: T. Cox, J. Clarke, T. Combes, 1727. 6th ed. xliv,373,(6)pp (browned, stamp tp); 10 engr plts (stamps versos, 3 defective w/part of ptd surface lacking or edges frayed). Orig panel calf (recent rebacking in calf). *Goodrich.* $495/£317

MAUROIS, A. The Life of Sir Alexander Fleming. London: Cape, 1959. 1st Eng ed. Dec eps. VG. *Savona.* $23/£15

MAUROIS, ANDRE. The Chelsea Way. NY: James H. Heineman, (1967). 1st Amer ed. Fine in dj (lt worn). *Antic Hay.* $25/£16

MAUROIS, ANDRE. The Chelsea Way. Hamish Miles (trans). London, 1930. One of 530 numbered, signed. VG + in VG + dj. *Smith.* $55/£35

MAUROIS, ANDRE. Fatapoufs and Thinifers. NY: Holt, 1940. 1st US ed. Jean Bruller (illus). 8 1/4 x 11. 92pp. VG in dj. *Cattermole.* $150/£96

MAUROIS, ANDRE. The Quest for Proust. Gerard Hopkins (trans). Cape, 1950. 1st UK ed. VG (ink name) in dj (sl worn, nicked, mkd). *Williams.* $39/£25

MAURY, ANNE FONTAINE (ed). Intimate Virginia: A Century of Maury Travels by Land and Sea. Dietz Press, 1941. 1st ed. Port. VG in VG dj. *Book Broker.* $25/£16

MAURY, DABNEY HERNDON. Recollections of a Virginian in the Mexican, Indian, and Civil Wars. NY: Scribner, 1894. 1st ed. xi,279pp. VG (lt soiled, fr inner hinge starting; spine dknd, worn at extrems). Howes M440. *Mcgowan.* $150/£96

MAURY, MATTHEW FONTAINE. The Physical Geography of the Sea. NY: Harper, 1856. 6th ed. 348pp; 9 fldg plts and charts at rear. Pub's cl (sm chips). Good + . *Scribe's Perch*.* $40/£26

MAURY, MATTHEW FONTAINE. Physical Geography. NY: University Pub Co, 1889. Rev ed. 130pp (browned); 19 color charts, 4-pg addition on blue stock. Grn dec cl (worn). *Hudson.* $75/£48

MAWE, JOHN. The Linnaean System of Conchology. London: The Author, 1823. 1st ed. 36 hand-colored litho plts (lt spotted). Contemp calf (spine faded, extrems sl worn), gilt. *Christie's*.* $315/£202

MAWE, JOHN. Travels in the Interior of Brazil.... London: Longman et al, 1812. 1st ed. 4to. vi,366pp (lt foxing), (3 plts), (21) w/8 plts, map; marbled eps. Very Nice in full leather, mod spine. *Parmer.* $1,750/£1,122

MAWE, THOMAS and JOHN ABERCROMBIE. Every Man His Own Gardener. London: Rivington et al, 1787. 11th ed. Engr frontis (foxed), 615pp (lacks final pg, lt foxing). Later 1/2 calf, marbled bds, gilt leather label. VG. *Hartfield.* $195/£125

MAWSON, DOUGLAS. The Home of the Blizzard...the Australasian Antarctic Expedition, 1911-1914. London: Heinemann, (1915). 1st ed. 2 vols. 3 fldg maps in pocket. Silver/gilt dec cl. VF. *High Latitude.* $800/£513

MAWSON, DOUGLAS. The Home of the Blizzard...the Australasian Antarctic Expedition, 1911-1914. London: Hodder & Stoughton, (1934). Rev popular ed. 3 fldg maps. VG. *High Latitude.* $70/£45

MAWSON, THOMAS H. The Art and Craft of Garden Making. London: Batsford, 1912. 4th ed. Folio. Teg. (1/2-title sl soiled, few spots; cl sl worn, mkd, upper hinge cracking, joints cracked, head sl bumped.) *Hollett.* $273/£175

MAXFIELD, VALERIE A. The Military Decorations of the Roman Army. Berkeley/L.A.: Univ of CA, (1981). 16 plts. (Sig.) Dj. *Archaeologia.* $45/£29

MAXFIELD, VALERIE A. The Military Decorations of the Roman Army. Berkeley/L.A.: Univ of CA, 1981. 16 b/w plts. VG in dj. *Turtle Island.* $35/£22

MAXWELL, DONALD. The Landscape of Thomas Hardy. London, (1928). 1st ed. VG in dj. *Argosy.* $100/£64

MAXWELL, JAMES CLERK. An Elementary Treatise on Electricity. William Garnet (ed). Oxford: Clarendon, 1881. 1st ed. xvi,208,36(ads),(8 ads)pp; 6 plts. VG (stamp, bklabel; spine ends scuffed, frayed). *Glaser.* $300/£192

MAXWELL, MARIUS. Stalking Big Game with a Camera in Equatorial Africa. London: Medici Soc, 1924. One of 568 signed. Dbl-pg frontis, 112 half-tone plts, map. Teg. (Spine faded.) *Christie's*.* $34/£22

MAXWELL, MARIUS. Stalking Big Game with a Camera in Equatorial Africa. NY/London, n.d. (1924). Dbl-pg frontis. Grn pict cl (spine lettering faded), else VG. *Terramedia.* $75/£48

MAXWELL, STUART and ROBIN HUTCHISON. Scottish Costume 1550-1850. London: A&C Black, 1958. viii,184pp; 4 colored plts, 24 dwgs. VG in dj. *Hollett.* $39/£25

MAXWELL, W. A. Crossing the Plains Days of '57. SF: Maxwell, 1915. Good in ptd wraps (chipped, sl tears). *Scribe's Perch**. $40/£26

MAXWELL, W. H. The Life of Field-Marshall, His Grace the Duke of Wellington. London: Henry Bohn, 1857. 3 vols. Engr frontis, title each vol; 42 engr ports. Gilt pict red blind dec cl (lt soil, spine ends sl chipped). Attractive. *House*. $150/£96

MAXWELL, WILLIAM QUENTIN. Lincoln's Fifth Wheel. NY, 1956. 1st ed. Signed. VG in dj (worn, spine discolored, sm stain). *King*. $35/£22

MAXWELL, WILLIAM. Time Will Darken It. NY: Harper, 1948. 1st ed. (Spine cocked), o/w Fine in dj (price-clipped). *Jaffe*. $150/£96

MAY, BARBARA. Buckle Horse. NY: Holt, 1956. 1st ed. Paul Brown (illus). Lg 8vo. Pict cl. NF in VG dj (sl chipped). *Book Adoption*. $95/£61

MAY, E. C. 2000 Miles Through Chile. NY: Century, 1924. Dec cvr. Good- (crack at p33). *Scribe's Perch**. $32/£21

MAY, H. A. R. Memories of the Artists Rifles. London, 1929. Gray cl. *Maggs*. $117/£75

MAY, J. B. The Hawks of North America. NY, 1935. 41 plts (37 color). (Sl worn, rebacked, spine stained.) *Wheldon & Wesley*. $78/£50

MAY, J. LEWIS (trans). The Unpublished Correspondence of Honore de Balzac and Madame Zulma Carraud 1829-1850. John Lane/Bodley Head, 1937. Frontis port. Good (spine bumped, hinges, corners sl rubbed; lacks dj). *Tiger*. $16/£10

MAY, JOHN. The Hawks of North America. National Assoc of Audubon Societies, 1935. 1st ed. VG. *Books & Birds*. $50/£32

MAY, JOHN. The Hawks of North America. NY: Nat'l Assoc Audubon Soc, 1935. 1st ed. Internally VG. (Rubbed, sl soiled.) *Agvent*. $60/£38

MAY, MARGARET (trans). Galen on the Usefulness of the Parts of the Body. Ithaca, 1968. 1st ed in English. 2 vols. VG in slipcase. *Fye*. $175/£112

MAYDON, H. C. Simen. London: Witherby, 1925. 1st ed. 6 maps. (Sl foxed.) VG. *Waverly**. $143/£92

MAYER, ALFRED M. (ed). Sport with Gun and Rod in American Woods and Waters. London/NY, 1883. 1st ed. (New eps.) 1/2 leather (worn, stained, esp back cvr). *Maggs*. $50/£32

MAYER, ALFRED M. (ed). Sport with Gun and Rod in American Woods and Waters. Edinburgh: David Douglas, 1884. 1st British ed. 2 vols. 888,(ii)pp (sl aged, hinges weak vol 2, ink stamps), tipped-in errata, pub's ad leaf at rear vol 2; 12 mtd engr plts. Yellow eps, cl reinforced hinges; teg, untrimmed. Black sheep, dk purple bds (sl worn, scraped, spines lt chipped), gilt. *Baltimore**. $140/£90

MAYER, C. Trapping Wild Animals in Malay Jungles. GC, NY, 1921. 8 plts. *Wheldon & Wesley*. $39/£25

MAYER, MERCER. Liza Lou and the Yeller Belly Swamp. NY: Parents' Magazine, (1976). 1st ed. Pict bds, eps. VG in pict dj. *Petrilla*. $20/£13

MAYES, EDWARD. Lucius Q. C. Lamar...1825-1893. Nashville, 1896. 1st ed. 820pp. *Ginsberg*. $125/£80

MAYFIELD, JOHN S. (ed). Mark Twain vs. the Street Railway Co. Privately ptd, 1926. Port, facs. Fine in ptd wraps. BAL 3540. *Bohling*. $110/£71

MAYHALL, MILDRED P. The Kiowas. Norman: Univ of OK, (1962). 1st ed. VF in dj (spine faded, lt worn). *Argonaut*. $45/£29

MAYHEW, EDWARD. The Illustrated Horse Doctor. NY, 1861. 1st ed. 536pp. Brn gilt-tooled cl. VG (extrems sl worn). *Doctor's Library*. $75/£48

MAYNARD, NETTIE COLBURN. Was Abraham Lincoln a Spiritualist? Phila: Rufus C. Hartranft, 1891. 1st ed. xxiv,264pp. Red cl, gilt. NF (sig). *Cahan*. $40/£26

MAYNE, R. C. Four Years in British Columbia and Vancouver Island. London: John Murray, 1862. 1st ed. Frontis, title vignette, xi,468pp, 16 plts, 2 maps (1 fldg). 3/4 morocco (rebound), matching marbled bds, leather spine labels. Fine. *Argonaut*. $350/£224

MAYNE, WILLIAM. Antar and the Eagles. NY: Delacorte, 1990. 1st US ed. 5 3/4 x 8 1/2. 16?pp. Cl spine. As New in dj. *Cattermole*. $30/£19

MAYNE, WILLIAM. Choristers' Cake. OUP, 1956. 1st ed. Walter Hodges (illus). 5 3/4 x 8 3/4. 160pp. Fine in dj. *Cattermole*. $100/£64

MAYNE, WILLIAM. A Day Without Wind. Hamilton, 1964. 1st ed. Margery Gill (illus). 4to. 64pp. Pict bds. Fine in pict dj (sl frayed). *Bookmark*. $39/£25

MAYNE, WILLIAM. Earthfasts. Hamilton, 1966. 1st ed. 8vo. 154pp. (Ex-lib stamp back tp, fep), else Contents NF in VG + David Knight dj. *Bookmark*. $34/£22

MAYNE, WILLIAM. A Grass Rope. OUP, 1957. 1st ed. Lynton Lamb (illus). 8vo. 167pp. VG (cl sl faded) in pict dj (edgeworn). *Bookmark*. $55/£35

MAYNE, WILLIAM. The Mouldy. Cape, 1983. 1st ed. Nicola Bayley (illus). 4to. 16 color plts. Pict bds. Fine. *Bookmark*. $23/£15

MAYNE, WILLIAM. The Rolling Season. OUP, 1960. 1st ed. Christopher Brooker (illus). 8vo. 175pp. VG in pict dj (sl frayed). *Bookmark*. $34/£22

MAYNE, WILLIAM. The Rolling Season. OUP, 1960. 1st ed. Christopher Brooker (illus). 5 3/4 x 8 3/4. 175pp. VG (ex-lib, few mks) in dj. *Cattermole*. $40/£26

MAYNE, WILLIAM. Summer Visitors. OUP, 1961. 1st ed. William Stobbs (illus). 8vo. 232pp. VG + in pict dj. *Bookmark*. $31/£20

MAYNE, WILLIAM. A Swarm in May. London: OUP, 1955. 1st ed. C. Walter Hodges (illus). 5 3/4 x 8 3/4. 199pp. VG in dj. *Cattermole*. $90/£58

MAYNE, WILLIAM. The Twelve Dancers. London: Hamilton, 1962. 1st ed. Lynton Lamb (illus). 5 1/4 x 8 1/4. 142pp. Good (ex-lib, mks). *Cattermole*. $30/£19

MAYNE, WILLIAM. The World Upside Down. Cumberledge/OUP, 1954. 1st ed. Shirley Hughes (illus). 8vo. 216pp. (Spine sl faded), else VG + in pict dj (lt foxed). *Bookmark*. $39/£25

MAYNE, WILLIAM. A Year and a Day. NY: Dutton, 1976. 1st US ed. 6 1/2 x 8 1/2. 88pp. Cl spine. Fine in dj. *Cattermole*. $30/£19

MAYO, EILEEN. Shells and How They Live. NY: Pleiades, 1944. 1st ed. 10 1/2 x 7 1/2. 32pp. Good. *Cattermole*. $25/£16

MAYO, JIM. (Pseud of Louis L'Amour.) Showdown at Yellow Butte. NY: Ace, (1953). Pb orig. Ace double: bound w/Outlaw River by Bliss Lomax. NF- (lt stress mks spine, lt rubbed). *Between The Covers*. $150/£96

MAYO, JIM. (Pseud of Louis L'Amour.) Utah Blaine. NY: Ace, (1954). Pb orig. Bound w/Desert Showdown by Brad Ward. NF (lt spine crease, sl rubbed). *Between The Covers*. $125/£80

MAYO, LAWRENCE SHAW. John Endecott: A Biography. Cambridge: Harvard, 1936. 1st ed. Dj. *Ginsberg*. $100/£64

MAYOR, A. HYATT. Giovanni Battista Piranesi. NY, 1952. 129 plts. Good. *Washton*. $50/£32

MAYOR, A. HYATT. Prints and People. NY, 1971. (Sl rubbed.) *Washton*. $35/£22

MAYOR, ARCHER. Open Season. NY: Putnam, 1988. 1st ed. VF in dj. *Mordida*. $65/£42

MAYR, MAURICE and KLAUS MAURICE. The Clockwork Universe: German Clocks and Automata 1550-1650. Washington/NY: Smithsonian/Neale Watson Academic Pubs, 1980. 1st Amer ed. Fine in dj (spine top sl worn). *Weber*. $40/£26

MAYR, MAURICE and KLAUS MAURICE. The Clock-work Universe: German Clocks and Automata 1550-1650. Washington: Smithsonian, 1980. 120 full-pg plts. Good+ in Good dj. *Scribe's Perch**. $36/£23

MAYS, WILLIE with LOU SAHADI. Say Hey. NY, (1988). Signed. Cl-backed bds. Dj. *Argosy*. $125/£80

MAYS, WILLIE with JEFF HARRIS. Danger in Center-field. Argonaut, 1963. 1st ed. VG in Good+ dj. *Plapinger*. $45/£29

MAYSON, BARRY with TONY MARCO. Fallen Angel. Hell's Angel to Heaven's Saint. NY: Doubleday, 1982. 1st ed. VG+ in dj. *Sclanders*. $11/£7

MAZET, HORACE S. Wild Ivory. London: Hale, 1971. 1st ed. Fine in dj (lt chipped). *Bowman*. $35/£22

MAZYCK, ARTHUR. Guide to Charleston, Illustrated.... Charleston: Walker, Evans & Cogswell, n.d. (ca 1875). Fldg map. (Lib stamp tp.) Later calf-backed marbled bds. *Kane**. $130/£83

MAZZANOVICH, ANTON. Trailing Geronimo. Holly-wood: Anton Mazzanovich, 1931. Slip reading 'New York: Wehman Bros, (1913)' pasted over orig imprint. 3rd ed. Red cl, gilt. (Spine faded), o/w Fine. *Harrington*. $55/£35

MAZZEO, HENRY (ed). Hauntings: Tales of the Super-natural. NY, 1968. 1st ed. VG in dj (lt worn). *Truepenny*. $45/£29

McADIE, ALEXANDER. The Clouds and Fogs of San Francisco. SF: A.M. Robertson, 1912. 1st ed. Mtd color frontis, 19 mtd photo plts. Gilt dec, lettered gray bds. VF in matching ptd dj. *Argonaut*. $125/£80

McADIE, ALEXANDER. Fog. Macmillan, 1934. 52 plts. VG. *Bookcell*. $50/£32

McADIE, ALEXANDER. Principles of Aerography. London: Harrap, 1917. Good+. *Bookcell*. $40/£26

McALAVY, DON and HAROLD KILMER. High Plains History of East-Central New Mexico. N.p.: High Plains Historical Press, 1980. VG. *Dumont*. $75/£48

McALEXANDER, U. G. History of the Thirteenth United States Infantry. Regimental Press, Frank D. Gunn, 1905. Buckram (faded). VG. *Cullen*. $145/£93

McALLISTER, J. T. Virginia Militia in the Revolutionary War. McAllister, (c. 1913). VG (pp wrinkled from water damage; cl worn, rebound). *Book Broker*. $45/£29

McALMON, ROBERT. A Companion Volume. (Paris: Contact Pub Co, n.d. but 1923.) 1st ed. Good (lt foxing) in ptd wrappers (spine tanned, sl cocked, nicks). *Reese*. $200/£128

McALMON, ROBERT. McAlmon and the Lost Genera-tion. Lincoln, NE, 1962. 1st ed. (Edges, jacket dust spotted), o/w VG in dj. *Reese*. $35/£22

McANDREW, J. The Open-Air Churches of Sixteenth-Century Mexico. Harvard Univ, 1965. 5 maps. Sound in dj. *Ars Artis*. $55/£35

McATEE, W. L. (ed). The Ring-Necked Pheasant and Its Management in North America. Washington: Ameri-can Wildlife Inst, 1945. Frontis, 2 color plts. Grn pebble-grain cl, gilt. Fine in pict dj (chipped). *Biscotti*. $40/£26

McBAIN, ED. (Pseud of Evan Hunter.) Beauty and the Beast. NY: Holt et al, 1982. 1st ed. (Sm stains pg edges), o/w Fine in dj. *Mordida*. $35/£22

McBAIN, ED. (Pseud of Evan Hunter.) Give the Boys a Great Big Hand. NY: S&S, 1960. 1st ed. VG in dj (price-clipped, sl wear). *Mordida*. $75/£48

McBAIN, ED. (Pseud of Evan Hunter.) Goldilocks. NY: Arbor House, 1977. 1st ed. Fine in dj. *Mordida*. $45/£29

McBAIN, ED. (Pseud of Evan Hunter.) Guns. NY: Ran-dom House, 1976. 1st ed. (Pp sl dknd), o/w Fine in dj. *Mordida*. $45/£29

McBAIN, ED. (Pseud of Evan Hunter.) The House That Jack Built. NY: Henry Holt, 1988. 1st ed. VF in dj. *Mordida*. $30/£19

McBAIN, ED. (Pseud of Evan Hunter.) The McBain Brief. NY: Arbor House, 1982. 1st ed. Fine in Fine dj. *Janus*. $35/£22

McBAIN, ED. (Pseud of Evan Hunter.) Snow White and Rose Red. NY: Holt et al, 1985. 1st ed. VF in dj. *Mordida*. $30/£19

McBAIN, ED. (Pseud of Evan Hunter.) Til Death. NY: S&S, 1959. 1st ed. (Pp dknd), o/w VG in dj. *Mordida*. $85/£54

McBRIDE, C. A. The Modern Treatment of Alcoholism and Drug Narcotism. NY: Rebman, (1910). 1st Amer ed. (Stamps.) Ptd grey cl. *Gach*. $50/£32

McCABE, JAMES D. The Illustrated History of the Cen-tennial Exhibition. Phila, etc, (1876). Orig 3/4 calf (joints, extrems rubbed). *Freeman**. $40/£26

McCABE, JAMES D. Life and Campaigns of General Robert E. Lee. St. Louis, 1866. 1867 rpt. 717pp & ads. (Cvr wear, dampstains 1/4 fr cvr, 1st few pp), o/w VG. *Pratt*. $75/£48

McCAFFREY, ANNE. Dragondrums. NY: Ballantine, 1979. 1st ed. Inscribed. Dj. *Swann**. $138/£88

McCAFFREY, ANNE. A Time When. Nesfa Press, 1975. 1st Amer ed. One of 800 numbered, signed. NF in dj (soiled). *Metropolitan**. $23/£15

McCALEB, WALTER FLAVIUS. The Aaron Burr Conspir-acy. NY: Dodd, Mead, 1903. 1st ed. Fldg map. Grn cl (lt rubbed), paper label (lt chipped). VG. *Hermitage*. $100/£64

McCALL, GEORGE ARCHIBALD. New Mexico in 1850: A Military View. Robert W. Frazier (ed). Nor-man, (1968). 1st ed. VG+ in VG+ dj. *Pratt*. $32/£21

McCALLUM, HENRY D. and FRANCES T. The Wire That Fenced the West. Norman, 1965. 1st ed. Fine in dj (worn, price-clipped). *Baade*. $50/£32

McCAMMON, ROBERT R. Blue World: And Other Sto-ries. London: Grafton, (1989). 1st ed. Fine in Fine dj. *Other Worlds*. $90/£58

McCAMMON, ROBERT R. Mystery Walk. HRW, 1983. 1st ed. Fine in Fine dj. *Certo*. $45/£29

McCAMMON, ROBERT R. The Night Boat. London: Kinnell, 1990. 1st hb ed. Fine in dj. *Other Worlds*. $50/£32

McCANDLISH, EDWARD. The Froggies' Diving School. NY: Stoll & Edwards, 1926. 4to. 12pp; 5 full-pg color illus. Pict bds (rubbed, bumped). VG. *Blue Mountain*. $15/£10

McCANN, ANNA MARGUERITE. Roman Sarcophagi in the Metropolitan Museum of Art. NY, 1978. Good. *Washton*. $40/£26

McCARNEY, SCOTT L. Memory Loss. Rochester, NY, 1988. One of 500. Accordion-folded. Black paper-cvrd bds. Fine. *Heller*. $50/£32

McCARTHY, CHARLES HALLAN. Lincoln's Plan of Re-construction. NY: McClure, Phillips, 1901. 1st ed. VG (spine lt speckled, ends frayed; fr inner hinge starting). Howes M35. *Mcgowan*. $250/£160

McCARTHY, CHARLES R. The Lost Children of the Al-leghenies. Huntington, PA, 1888. 1st ed. 60pp. Wraps (worn, detached, chipped). *King*. $20/£13

McCARTHY, CORMAC. All the Pretty Horses. Picador, 1992. 1st UK ed. Fine in dj. *Williams*. $70/£45

McCARTHY, CORMAC. All the Pretty Horses. London, 1992. 1st ed. Fine in dj. *Buckley*. $47/£30

McCARTHY, CORMAC. All the Pretty Horses. NY: Es-quire, 1992. 1st ed. Offprint from Esquire Magazine. Fine in orig stapled self-wrappers. *Jaffe*. $100/£64

McCARTHY, CORMAC. Blood Meridian. NY: Random House, (1985). 1st ed. (Sl stain fore-edge, sm marker spot top edge), else Fine in Fine dj. *Between The Covers*. $650/£417

McCARTHY, CORMAC. Child of God. NY: Random House, (1973). 1st ed. (Sm sticker fr pastedown), else VG in dj (sm tears spine head, foot lt rubbed, price-clipped). *Pacific**. $374/£240

McCARTHY, CORMAC. Child of God. NY: Random, (1973). 1st ed. (Sm sticker fr pastedown), else NF in dj (sl wear). *Robbins*. $800/£513

McCARTHY, CORMAC. Child of God. NY, 1973. 1st ed. (Top edge lt foxed), o/w NF in NF dj (sm chip, neatly repaired sm tear). *Warren*. $450/£288

McCARTHY, CORMAC. The Crossing. NY: Knopf, 1994. Uncorrected proof. (2 corners lt bumped), o/w Fine in ptd wrappers. *Captain's Bookshelf*. $200/£128

McCARTHY, CORMAC. The Crossing. NY: Knopf, 1994. 1st ed. One of 1000 signed on tipped-in leaf. As New in dj. *Captain's Bookshelf*. $300/£192

McCARTHY, CORMAC. The Orchard Keeper. NY: Random House, (1965). 1st ed, 1st bk. Mauve bds. (Eps sl foxed; bds discolored), o/w NF in Attractive dj (price-clipped, sm tear). *Captain's Bookshelf*. $1,375/£881

McCARTHY, CORMAC. The Orchard Keeper. NY: Random, (1965). 1st ed, 1st bk. (Sig), else NF in white dj (few short closed tears, scattered soiling). *Robbins*. $1,700/£1,090

McCARTHY, CORMAC. Outer Dark. NY: Random House, (1968). 1st ed. VG (sunned, sl bumped, red 'D' stamped on flyleaf) in VG dj (short closed tears, sm triangular closed tear spine). *Metropolitan**. $546/£350

McCARTHY, CORMAC. The Stonemason. NJ, 1994. 1st Amer ed. One of 7500. Fine in Fine dj. *Polyanthos*. $45/£29

McCARTHY, CORMAC. Suttree. NY: Random House, (1979). 1st ed. NF in dj (sl edgewear, sm chip, few sm tears). *Captain's Bookshelf*. $300/£192

McCARTHY, CORMAC. Suttree. NY: Random House, (1979). (Sm bump base fr bd), else Fine in NF dj (sm tear bottom fr panel). *Between The Covers*. $850/£545

McCARTHY, CORMAC. Suttree. NY: Random, (1979). 1st ed. Fine in Fine dj. *Robbins*. $900/£577

McCARTHY, CORMAC. Suttree. NY, 1979. 1st ed. Fine in NF dj (1-inch closed tear at spine fold). *Warren*. $550/£353

McCARTHY, MARY. The Group. NY: Harcourt Brace, (1963). 1st ed. Signed. VG in dj (sl wear). *Lenz*. $75/£48

McCARTHY, MARY. The Groves of Academe. NY: Harcourt Brace, (1952). 1st ed. Signed. VG in dj (sl wear). *Lenz*. $75/£48

McCARTHY, MARY. Memories of a Catholic Girlhood. NY: Harcourt, (1957). 1st ed. (Ink sig; sm spot, nick to spine), else VG in dj. *Reese*. $40/£26

McCARTY, JOHN L. Maverick Town. Norman: Univ of OK, 1946. Inscribed. Good (bkpl) in dj (worn). *Dumont*. $45/£29

McCASLIN, R. Plain Grove. Claremont, NH: Claremont Mfg, 1884. 1st ed. 272pp. NF. *Archer*. $35/£22

McCAULEY, ELIZABETH ANNE. A.A.E. Disderi and the Carte de Visite Portrait Photograph. New Haven/London: Yale Univ, 1985. 1st ed. Frontis. (Owner blindstamp), else Fine in illus dj. *Cahan*. $35/£22

McCAULEY, LOIS B. Maryland Historical Prints, 1752 to 1889. Balt: MD Hist Soc, (1975). 1st ed. Grn buckram, gilt. Dj (sl soiled, upper flap fold ragged). *Baltimore**. $140/£90

McCLANE, A. J. The Practical Fisherman. Englewood: Prentice Hall, 1953. 1st ed. 5 color plts. Fine in VG + dj (lt chipped). *Bowman*. $120/£77

McCLARY, THOMAS C. Three Thousand Years. Reading: Fantasy, (1954). 1st ed. One of 300 w/signed, numbered leaf tipped in. Dj (sm tear). *Kane**. $40/£26

McCLEARY, G. F. On Detective Fiction and Other Things. London: Hollis & Carter, 1960. 1st ed. Fine in NF dj. *Janus*. $45/£29

McCLELLAN, GEORGE B. Manual of Bayonet Exercise Prepared for the Army of the United States. Phila: (Lippincott), 1862. 2nd ed. 24 litho plts. Blind dec cl. *Book Block*. $275/£176

McCLELLAN, GEORGE B. McClellan's Own Story. NY, 1887. 1st ed. 678pp. (Pict cvr lt worn; staining), o/w VG + . *Pratt*. $75/£48

McCLELLAN, GEORGE B. The Mexican War Diary of George B. McClellan. William Starr Myers (ed). Princeton: Princeton Univ, 1917. 1st ed. Frontis, 1 map, 2 plts. Rust cl, gilt. Good. *Karmiole*. $60/£38

McCLELLAN, GEORGE B. The Mexican War Diary of.... Princeton, 1917. 1st ed. Frontis. (Ex-lib), o/w Fine. *Turpen*. $175/£112

McCLELLAN, GEORGE B. Organization of the Army of the Potomac...from July 26, 1861 to November 7, 1862. Washington, 1864. 1st ed. 242pp. VG. *Fye*. $100/£64

McCLELLAND, NANCY. Duncan Phyfe and the English Regency 1795-1830. NY, 1939. One of 1000. 295 plts. (Fep lt browned.) 2-tone cl bds (spine lt faded), paper label (sl torn, repaired). *Edwards*. $234/£150

McCLOY, HELEN. The Further Side of Fear. NY: Dodd, Mead, 1967. 1st ed. Inscribed. VG in dj (worn). *Metropolitan**. $23/£15

McCLUNG, JOHN A. Sketches of Western Adventure. Dayton, 1836. Pub's cl (spotted; foxed). Howes M46. *Swann**. $126/£81

McCLUNG, JOHN A. Sketches of Western Adventure. Dayton, OH: L.F. Claflin, 1854. Rev, corrected. 315pp (dknd; bkpl); 3 plts. Brn cl, blind stamping, gilt spine title. Nice (ends lt frayed). *Bohling*. $85/£54

McCLURE, F. A. The Bamboos. Cambridge: Harvard Univ, 1966. 1st ed. As New. *Quest*. $65/£42

McCLURE, F. A. The Bamboos. Cambridge: Harvard, 1966. 1st ed. VG. *Archer*. $40/£26

McCLURE, F. A. Chinese Handmade Paper. Newtown: Bird & Bull, 1986. One of 325 numbered. Newspaper facs, prospectus laid in. 1/4 morocco. *Swann**. $230/£147

McCLURE, JAMES. The Caterpillar Cop. London: Gollancz, 1972. 1st British ed. NF in dj (price-clipped). *Metropolitan**. $40/£26

McCLURE, JAMES. The Caterpillar Cop. London: Victor Gollancz, 1972. 1st ed. Fine in dj. *Mordida*. $75/£48

McCLURE, JAMES. Four and Twenty Virgins. London: Victor Gollancz, 1973. 1st ed. Fine in dj. *Mordida*. $85/£54

McCLURE, MICHAEL. Little Odes and the Raptors. L.A.: Black Sparrow, 1969. 1st ed. One of 1000. NF in ptd wrappers. *Turtle Island*. $30/£19

McCLURE, MICHAEL. The Mad Cub. NY: Bantam, (1970). 1st ed. Mint in pict wrappers. *Jaffe*. $25/£16

McCLURE, S. S. My Autobiography. Valparaiso, IN: Lewis E. Myers, (1924). Special ed, 3rd ptg. Frontis port. Fine. *Pacific**. $40/£26

McCOMB, ARTHUR. The Baroque Painters of Italy. Cambridge, 1934. 1/2 cl (sl soiled). *Washton*. $85/£54

McCONAUGHY, J. W. and EDWARD SHELDON. The Boss. NY: H.K. Fly, 1911. 1st ed. VG + . *Else Fine*. $55/£35

McCONKEY, HARRIET E. BISHOP. Dakota War Whoop. Chicago: Lakeside/R.R. Donnelley, 1965. VG. *Lien.* $25/£16

McCONKEY, HARRIET E. BISHOP. Dakota War Whoop: Indian Massacres and War in Minnesota. Dale L. Morgan (ed). Chicago: Lakeside, Christmas, 1965. Dk blue cl (2 sm spots lower cvr). *Sadlon.* $20/£13

McCONNELL, H. H. Five Years a Cavalryman. Jacksboro, TX: J.H. Rogers, 1889. 1st ed. 320pp (stamp tp); ptd on pink paper. Dk grn cl (sm paper lib spine label), gilt. Howes M59. *Karmiole.* $375/£240

McCOOK, HENRY C. The Martial Graves of Our Fallen Heroes in Santiago de Cuba. Phila: George W. Jacobs, 1899. 448pp. (Hinges weak.) *Dawson.* $30/£19

McCORISON, MARCUS A. (ed). Vermont Imprints 1778-1820. Worcester, 1963. VG in dj. *King.* $60/£38

McCORKLE, JILL. The Cheer Leader. Chapel Hill, NC: Algonquin, 1984. 1st ed. NF (sl shelfworn) in dj. *Lame Duck.* $125/£80

McCORKLE, JILL. The Cheer Leader. NC: Algonquin, 1984. 1st ed, 1st bk. NF in NF dj. *Warren.* $125/£80

McCORMICK, ANDREW. The Gold Torque. Glasgow: Wm. MacLellan, 1951. 1st ed. Agnes Miller Parker (engrs). Fine in dj. *Michael Taylor.* $47/£30

McCORMICK, RICHARD C. A Visit to the Camp Before Sevastopol. NY: Appleton, 1855. Frontis map, 212pp; 7 views and plans, port. (Spine faded), else VG. *Bohling.* $40/£26

McCORMICK, ROBERT. The War Without Grant. NY, (1950). 1st ed. Fine in NF dj. *Mcclintock.* $27/£17

McCORMICK, ROBERT. The War Without Grant. NY, 1950. (Spine sl sunned), else VG. *King.* $35/£22

McCORMICK, SAMUEL JARVIS. The Rev. Samuel Peters, General History of Connecticut. NY: Appleton, 1887. Blue cl, paper label. (Edges soiled, frayed.) *Metropolitan*.* $40/£26

McCORMICK, WILFRED. The Incomplete Pitcher. Bobbs Merrill, 1967. 1st ed. Fine in VG+ dj. *Plapinger.* $60/£38

McCOY, ISAAC. History of Baptist Indian Missions. Washington: William M. Morrison, 1840. 1st ed. 611pp. Black cl (rebound). VG (ex-lib). Howes M68. *Lien.* $300/£192

McCOY, JOSEPH G. Historic Sketches of the Cattle Trade of the West and Southwest. Columbus, 1951. Facs of orig 1874 ed. Fine in dj (price-clipped). Howes M72. *Baade.* $100/£64

McCOY, JOSEPH G. Historic Sketches of the Cattle Trade of the West and Southwest. Ralph P. Bieber (ed). Glendale: Clark, 1940. Rpt of extremely rare 1st ed published in 1874. One of 924. (Spine sl jammed, faded), else Fine. Howes M72. *Argonaut.* $150/£96

McCOY, RALPH E. Freedom of the Press, an Annotated Bibliography. Carbondale: Southern IL Univ, 1968. VG in dj (sl worn). *New Hampshire*.* $40/£26

McCRACKEN, H. The Biggest Bear on Earth. Phila/NY: Stokes, 1943. 1st ed. Color frontis. NF in VG dj. *Mikesh.* $60/£38

McCRACKEN, HAROLD. The Beast That Walks Like Man. London: Oldbourne, 1957. 1st British ed. Fine in VG dj (edges chipped). *Backman.* $40/£26

McCRACKEN, HAROLD. The Charles M. Russell Book. GC: Doubleday, 1957. 1st trade ed. Lt brn cl. (Sl foxed, edges sl dusty.) *Baltimore*.* $40/£26

McCRACKEN, HAROLD. The Charles M. Russell Book. GC: Doubleday, 1957. 1st trade ed. Illus eps. 35 color illus. VG in dj (sl worn). *Lien.* $60/£38

McCRACKEN, HAROLD. The Frederic Remington Book, a Pictorial History of the West. GC: Doubleday, 1966. One of 500 numbered, signed. Tipped-in color illus, color frontis. Aeg. Full brn leather, gilt. NF in slipcase (corner bumped, edge split). *Bohling.* $350/£224

McCRACKEN, HAROLD. The Frederic Remington Book. GC: Doubleday, 1966. 1st deluxe ed. Ltd to 500 numbered, signed. Tipped-on color frontis. Aeg. Full leather, gilt spine, fr cvr. VF in cardboard slipcase w/leather label (label and slipcase w/lt scratch). *Argonaut.* $475/£304

McCRACKEN, HAROLD. Frederic Remington's Own West. Dial Press, 1960. 1st trade ed. VG in dj (rubbed). *My Bookhouse.* $25/£16

McCRACKEN, HAROLD. George Catlin and the Old Frontier. NY: Bonanza Bks, (1959). Rpt of 1959 1st ed. Cl-backed bds. Fine in dj. *Sadlon.* $30/£19

McCRACKEN, HAROLD. George Catlin and the Old Frontier. NY: Dial, 1959. 1st trade ed. Color frontis, 35 color plts. Brick red cl, gilt. Fine in VG+ dj (sl chipped; one corner, spine faded). *Harrington.* $45/£29

McCRACKEN, HAROLD. Portrait of the Old West. NY: McGraw-Hill, (1952). 1st ed. Pict cl (Ink inscrip fep), o/w Fine. *Sadlon.* $20/£13

McCRACKEN, HAROLD. Portrait of the Old West. NY: McGraw-Hill, (1952). 1st ed. 40 color plts. Grn cl. Fine in pict dj (sl worn). *House.* $80/£51

McCRAE, JOHN. In Flanders Fields and Other Poems. NY, 1919. 1st ed. VG. *Fye.* $125/£80

McCULLAGH, FRANCIS. In Franco's Spain. London, 1937. 1st Eng ed. Nice (foxed). *Clearwater.* $70/£45

McCULLERS, CARSON. The Ballad of the Sad Cafe. London, 1952. 1st Eng ed. Dj (sl torn). *Clearwater.* $62/£40

McCULLERS, CARSON. Clock Without Hands. Boston, 1961. Very Nice (spine sl chafed) in dj (sl rubbed). *Clearwater.* $70/£45

McCULLERS, CARSON. Clock Without Hands. Boston/Cambridge, MA: Houghton Mifflin/Riverside, 1961. 1st ed. Red cl (spine rubbed, sm hole rear cvr), gilt. Internally Fine in dj (sl chipped). *Blue Mountain.* $55/£35

McCULLERS, CARSON. Clock Without Hands. London: Cresset, 1961. 1st Eng ed. (Inscrip), else VG in dj. *Hadley.* $23/£15

McCULLERS, CARSON. The Heart Is a Lonely Hunter. London, 1943. 1st Eng ed. Nice (name; sl faded) in dj (nicked, chafed). *Clearwater.* $101/£65

McCULLERS, CARSON. Reflections in a Golden Eye. Boston: HMCo, 1949. 1st ed. NF (binding sl soiled) in VG+ 1st issue dj w/glassine window in fr panel (lt wrinkling, sm tears at edges). *Between The Covers.* $375/£240

McCULLERS, CARSON. The Square Root of Wonderful. Boston: Houghton Mifflin, 1958. 1st ed. Cl-backed bds. VG in dj (sl chipped). *Cahan.* $50/£32

McCULLERS, CARSON. The Square Root of Wonderful. London: Cresset, 1958. 1st ed. NF in dj (sm edge tear). *Dermont.* $50/£32

McCULLERS, CARSON. The Square Root of Wonderful. London: Cresset, 1958. 1st UK ed. VG+ in dj (rear panel sl soiled). *Bernard.* $50/£32

McCULLERS, CARSON. Sweet as a Pickle and Clean as a Pig. Boston: Houghton Mifflin, 1964. 1st ed. Rolf Gerard (illus). VF in dj. *Bromer.* $95/£61

McCULLIN, DONALD. Is Anyone Taking Any Notice? Cambridge: MIT, 1973. 1st US ed. Illus paper over bds. (Owner stamp; rubbed), else VG in matching dj. *Cahan.* $165/£106

McCULLOUGH, D. R. The Tule Elk: Its History, Behavior and Ecology. Berkeley: Univ of CA, 1969. 1st ed. 8 plts, 30 tables. VG (ex-lib). *Mikesh*. $20/£13

McCURDY, R. N. C. The Rhesus Danger. London, 1950. 1st ed. VG in ptd wrappers. *Argosy*. $45/£29

McCURDY, ROBERT M. and EDITH M. COULTER. A Bibliography of Articles Relating to Holidays. Boston, 1907. 1st ed. Orig ptd wrappers. *Ginsberg*. $35/£22

McDANIEL, RUEL. Vinegarroon, the Saga of Judge Roy Bean, 'Law West of the Pecos.' Kingsport, TN, (1936). Pict cl. Fine in glassine wrapper (chipped). *Bohling*. $15/£10

McDANIEL, RUEL. Vinegarroon, the Saga of Judge Roy Bean.... Kingsport, TN, (1936). 1st ed. Pict cvr. (Cvr sl worn), o/w Fine. *Pratt*. $30/£19

McDANIEL, RUEL. Vinegarroon. Kingsport, TN: Southern, (1936). 1st ed. VG (sticker fep) in pict cvrs. *Lien*. $25/£16

McDERMOTT, CHARLES HENRY. The Outlines of Psychometry: Psychic Life and Phantasm of the Dying. Chicago, 1926. 1st ed. VG (extrems sl worn). *Doctor's Library*. $50/£32

McDERMOTT, GERALD. Arrow to the Sun. NY: Viking, 1974. 1st ed. 11 1/4 x 9 3/4. 32pp. VG (ex-lib, mks) in dj. *Cattermole*. $8/£5

McDERMOTT, GERALD. The Knight of the Lion. NY: Four Winds, 1979. 1st ed. 8 3/4 x 10. 92pp. VG (ex-lib, few mks) in dj. *Cattermole*. $15/£10

McDERMOTT, GERALD. The Stone-Cutter. NY: Viking, 1974. 1st ed. 7 3/4 x 11. 32pp. VG in dj. *Cattermole*. $40/£26

McDERMOTT, JOHN D. Forlorn Hope. Boise, 1978. 1st ed. Map. Fine. *Pratt*. $45/£29

McDERMOTT, JOHN FRANCIS (ed). Travelers on the Western Frontier. Urbana, 1970. 1st ed. Fine in VG dj (internally reinforced). *Turpen*. $35/£22

McDERMOTT, JOHN FRANCIS. George Caleb Bingham: River Portraitist. Norman: Univ of OK, (1959). 1st ed. VG in dj. *Lien*. $85/£54

McDONALD, DONALD. Sweet Scented Flowers and Fragrant Leaves. London: Sampson Low, 1895. 1st ed. liii,136+30pp ads; 16 color chromolitho plts. Gilt-stamped cvr. Well Preserved. *Quest*. $145/£93

McDONALD, JOHN. Biographical Sketches of General Nathaniel Massie, General Duncan McArthur...Who Were Early Settlers in the Western Country. Cincinnati: The Author, 1838. 1st ed. vi,267pp. Newly bound in marbled paper over bds, calf spine, morocco spine label. VG (foxed). Howes M83. *Cahan*. $425/£272

McDONALD, JOHN. Secrets of the Great Whiskey Ring. St. Louis, 1880. 346,62pp. *Bohling*. $12/£8

McDONOUGH, MARY LOU. Poet Physicians. Springfield: Thomas, 1945. 2nd ptg. (Lt wear.) *Goodrich*. $50/£32

McDOUGALL, JOHN. In the Days of the Red River Rebellion...(1868-1872). Toronto: Briggs, 1903. 1st ed. Gilt-stamped pict cl. *Ginsberg*. $150/£96

McDOUGALL, WILLIAM. The Group Mind. CUP, 1920. 1st ed. Inscribed. Ruled ptd ochre cl. (Sm stain fr cvr), else VG. *Gach*. $85/£54

McDOWALL, R. J. S. The Control of the Circulation of the Blood. With supplemental volume. 1938/1956. *Whitehart*. $101/£65

McELROY, C. J. African Safari of an Amateur Hunter. NY: Vantage, 1961. Stated 1st ed, 1st bk. Frontis port. VG+ in VG dj (edge tears). *Backman*. $80/£51

McELROY, C. J. (ed). The Sci Record Book of Trophy Animals. Tucson, 1978. 1st ed. #732/1000. Brn padded leather, gilt. Fine. *Price*. $195/£125

McELROY, JOHN. This Was Andersonville. Roy Meredith (ed). Toledo, 1879. 1st ed. VG+ in dj (worn, spine faded). *Pratt*. $30/£19

McELROY, JOSEPH. Ship Rock. Concord, NH: Ewert, (1980). One of 226 numbered, signed. Fine. *Lenz*. $100/£64

McELROY, JOSEPH. A Smuggler's Bible. London, 1968. 1st ed, 1st bk. Signed presentation copy. Fine in dj (edges sl rubbed, top edge rear panel sl soiled, sm tear). *Polyanthos*. $50/£32

McELROY, ROBERT. Jefferson Davis. NY/London, 1937. 1st ed. 2 vols. 9 ports. Recent black buckram, gilt. Fine. *Wantagh*. $50/£32

McEWAN, IAN. The Cement Garden. Cape, 1978. 1st UK ed. Fine in dj. *Williams*. $101/£65

McEWAN, IAN. The Child in Time. London, 1987. 1st ed. Signed. Dj. *Typographeum*. $35/£22

McEWAN, IAN. First Love, Last Rites. Cape, 1975. 1st UK ed, 1st bk. NF in dj. *Williams*. $172/£110

McEWAN, IAN. First Love, Last Rites. Random House, 1975. 1st US ed. (Sm offset from price sticker to fly), else Fine in Fine dj. *Certo*. $35/£22

McEWAN, IAN. In Between the Sheets and Other Stories. NY, 1978. 1st ed. NF in NF dj (price-clipped). *Warren*. $35/£22

McFADDEN, DAVID REVERE (ed). Scandinavian Modern Design 1880-1980. NY: Cooper-Hewitt Museum, 1982. (Ex-lib, ink stamp, label remains.) Dj. *Edwards*. $39/£25

McFARLANE, K. B. Hans Memling. Edgar Wind (ed). Oxford, 1971. 153 plts. Good in dj. *Washton*. $145/£93

McFARLANE, LESLIE. Ghost of the Hardy Boys. Methuen, 1976. 1st ed. 6x9. 211pp. VG (shelfworn) in dj (edges ragged). *My Bookhouse*. $65/£42

McFEE, WILLIAM. The Life of Sir Martin Frobisher. NY: Harper, 1928. VG in dj (chipped). *High Latitude*. $27/£17

McFEE, WILLIAM. The Life of Sir Martin Frobisher. NY: Harper, 1928. 1st ed. Blue cl, gilt. NF. *Parmer*. $75/£48

McFEE, WILLIAM. North of Suez. NY, 1930. 1st ed. One of 350 signed. Buckram spine, paper label. Fine in box (worn). *Black Sun*. $50/£32

McFEE, WILLIAM. North of Suez. NY: Doubleday, Doran, 1930. 1st ed. #138/350 signed. Fine in slipcase. *Hermitage*. $175/£112

McFEE, WILLIAM. A Six-Hour Shift. NY, 1920. #144/377 signed. Vellum spine (sunned). Fine (tape traces eps, inside fr cvrs). *Polyanthos*. $25/£16

McGAHERN, JOHN. Getting Through. London: Faber, 1978. 1st UK ed. Fine in dj. *Williams*. $44/£28

McGAHERN, JOHN. The Pornographer. London: Faber, 1979. 1st UK ed. Fine in dj. *Williams*. $31/£20

McGANN, A. W. God or Gorilla. NY, 1922. 1st ed. VG. *Mikesh*. $27/£17

McGAVIN, E. CECIL. Nauvoo the Beautiful. Salt Lake, 1946. 1st ed. Inscribed. Map. (Inscrip), o/w VG+ in dj (chipped, worn). *Benchmark*. $40/£26

McGHEE, REGINALD (comp). The World of James Van Derzee: A Visual Record of Black Americans. NY: Grove, 1969. 1st ed. (Owner stamp), else NF in dj (sl worn). *Cahan*. $150/£96

McGILL, W. Caverns of Virginia. VA: UV, 1933. Good. *Blake*. $75/£48

McGILLYCUDDY, JULIA B. McGillycuddy, Agent. Stanford, 1941. 1st ed. Pict cl. (Narrow tape offset to eps), o/w NF in old, but complete, dj (extensively taped, worn). *Baade*. $75/£48

McGILLYCUDDY, JULIA B. McGillycuddy, Agent: A Biography of Dr. Valentine T. McGillycuddy. Stanford Univ, (1941). 1st ed. Tan pict cl (spine sl dknd). NF. *Harrington.* $70/£45

McGIVERN, ED. Ed McGivern's Book on Fast and Fancy Revolver Shooting and Police Training. Springfield: King-Richardson, 1938. 1st ed. Leatherette (corner sl jammed). Overall Fine (eps sl dknd). *Argonaut.* $150/£96

McGLASHAN, C.F. History of the Donner Party: A Tragedy of the Sierras. Truckee: Crowley & McGlashan, (1879). 1st ed. 8 7/8x5 3/4 inches. 193pp. Blind-emb plum cl (edgewear, corners showing), gilt-lettered spine (worn at end; sl browned). Internally Fine. Overall VG-. Howes M102. *Harrington.* $700/£449

McGONIGLE, THOMAS. In Patchogue. NY: Adrift Editions, 1984. 1st ed. Fine in stapled wraps. *Lame Duck.* $45/£29

McGOVERN, WILLIAM MONTGOMERY. Jungle Paths and Inca Ruins. London: Hutchinson, n.d. (ca 1930). 24 plts, fldg color map. (Rubbed, scuffed, frayed, cvr silverfished), o/w Good. *Worldwide.* $25/£16

McGOWAN, EDWARD. Narrative of Edward McGowan.... SF: The Author, 1857. 1st ed. 12mo. viii,(9)-240pp (lt foxing, lt staining); 8 full-pg woodcuts. Early rebinding of 1/2 red leather, black cl-cvrd bds (spine ends lt worn, some worming to cvrs). Overall NF. Howes M103. *Argonaut.* $575/£369

McGRATH, ROBERT L. Early Vermont Wall Paintings, 1790-1850. Hanover, NH: Univ Press of New England, 1972. 1st ed. Fine in dj. *Cahan.* $35/£22

McGREGOR, DION. The Dream World of Dion McGregor. (NY, 1964.) 1st ed, w/dwgs and dj by Edward Gorey. VG in dj. *King.* $20/£13

McGROARTY, JOHN S. California, Its History and Romance. L.A.: Grafton, 1911. 1st ed. Good. *Lien.* $35/£22

McGUANE, THOMAS. Keep the Change. Boston, 1989. 1st ed. Fine in NF dj. *Smith.* $20/£13

McGUANE, THOMAS. The Missouri Breaks. NY: Ballantine, 1976. 1st ed. VF in wraps. *Else Fine.* $35/£22

McGUANE, THOMAS. Ninety-Two in the Shade. NY: FSG, 1973. 1st ed. Fine in dj (sl worn). *Else Fine.* $60/£38

McGUANE, THOMAS. Panama. NY: FSG, 1978. 1st ed. Fine in Fine dj. *Else Fine.* $40/£26

McGUANE, THOMAS. The Sporting Club. NY: S&S, (1968). 1st ed, 1st bk. Fine in Fine dj. *Dermont.* $125/£80

McGUANE, THOMAS. The Sporting Club. NY: S&S, 1968. 1st ed, 1st bk. Fine (name) in dj (sm tear, edges sl dknd). *Else Fine.* $175/£112

McGUANE, THOMAS. To Skin a Cat. NY, 1986. 1st ed. Fine in Fine dj. *Smith.* $20/£13

McHENRY, LAWRENCE. Garrison's History of Neurology. Springfield, 1969. VG in dj. *Fye.* $200/£128

McILHENNY, EDWARD A. The Wild Turkey and Its Hunting. GC: Doubleday, Page, 1914. 1st ed. (Cvrs sl speckled), else VG. *Mcgowan.* $450/£288

McILRAITH, JOHN. Life of Sir John Richardson.... London: Longmans, Green, 1868. Inscribed. Frontis port, xi,280pp; plt. VG (sl worn, mkd). *High Latitude.* $140/£90

McILVANNEY, WILLIAM. The Longships in Harbour. London: Eyre & Spottiswoode, 1970. 1st ed. VG in dj (edges lt faded). *Hollett.* $47/£30

McINERNEY, JAY. Bright Lights, Big City. NY: Vintage, (1984). Signed. Pb. *Metropolitan*.* $115/£74

McINTOSH, BURR. The Little I Saw of Cuba. London: F. Tennyson Neely, (1899). 1st ed. Frontis port, 173pp. Grn cl (dknd, inner hinges cracked), dec stamped in black/silver. NF, internally Fine. *Argonaut.* $90/£58

McINTOSH, CHARLES. The Practical Gardener and Modern Horticulturalist. Vol 1 (of 2). London: Thomas Kelley, 1829. 1st ed. 555-1120 + 142pp. Contemp 1/2 calf, marbled bds (worn), gilt. Internally VG. *Quest.* $90/£58

McINTOSH, DAVID GREGG. The Campaign of Chancellorsville. Richmond, VA: Wm. Ellis Jones' Sons, 1915. 1st ed. Signed presentation. NF in ptd wrappers. *Mcgowan.* $350/£224

McINTOSH, MARIA J. Woman in America. NY: Appleton, 1850. 1st ed. 155pp. Brn cl. VG. *Second Life.* $150/£96

McINTYRE, JOHN T. Ashton-Kirk Secret Agent. Phila: Penn, 1912. 1st ed. (Spine lettering chipped), o/w VG (lacks dj). *Mordida.* $45/£29

McKAY, CLAUDE. Banana Bottom. NY: Harper, 1933. 1st ed. Dec cl, paper label. (Corner jammed, label dknd), else Good. *Reese.* $85/£54

McKAY, CLAUDE. Banjo: A Story Without a Plot. NY: Harper, 1929. 1st ed. (2 sm holes fr outer joint), o/w Fine in pict dj (4 sm chips). *Captain's Bookshelf.* $650/£417

McKAY, CLAUDE. Home to Harlem. NY: Harper, 1928. 1st ed. Good (ink insrip, smudges, edgewear) in Fine (supplied) dj w/promo sticker (sm chip). *Reese.* $450/£288

McKAY, CLAUDE. A Long Way from Home. NY: Lee Furman, (1937). 1st ed, 2nd binding. Grn cl. (Pastedowns, fore-edges cvrs discolored), o/w VG in dj (sm nicks, edge tears). *Reese.* $300/£192

McKAY, GEORGE L. Some Notes on Robert Louis Stevenson, His Finances and His Agents and Publishers. New Haven: Yale Univ Library, 1958. 1st ed. Fine in sewn ptd wrappers. *Reese.* $25/£16

McKAY, WILLIAM and W. ROBERTS. John Hoppner, R.A. London, 1909. Color frontis port, 63 plts. Teg, rest uncut. (Feps browned, margins sl thumbed, upper hinge cracked; sl soiled, rubbed.) *Edwards.* $78/£50

McKEE, IRVING. Ben-Hur Wallace. The Life of General Lew Wallace. Berkeley/L.A.: Univ of CA, 1947. 1st ed. *Wantagh.* $40/£26

McKELVEY, SUSAN DELANO. Botanical Exploration of the Trans-Mississippi West, 1790-1850. Jamaica Pain, MA, 1955. 1st ed. Fldg map in pocket. Thick cl. *Ginsberg.* $200/£128

McKENNA, JAMES A. Black Range Tales. NY: Wilson-Erickson, 1936. 1st trade ed. Black cl (sl spine end wear). VG+ in dj (chipped), mylar cvr. Howes M127. *Harrington.* $60/£38

McKENNA, ROLLIE. Portrait of Dylan. London, 1982. 1st ed. VG in dj (sl rubbed). *Words Etc.* $16/£10

McKENNEY, THOMAS and JAMES HALL. History of the Indian Tribes of North America. Kent, OH: Volair, 1978. 1st ed thus. 2 vols. Aeg. Full leather, gold decs. Beautiful set. *Perier.* $300/£192

McKENNEY, THOMAS and JAMES HALL. The Indian Tribes of North America with Biographical Sketches.... Frederick Webb Hodge (ed). Edinburgh: John Grant, 1933. New ed. 3 vols. 123 color plts, 2 fldg maps. (Rubberstamp eps, tps; eradicated spine #), o/w Fine. Howes M129. *Oregon.* $625/£401

McKENNEY, THOMAS and JAMES HALL. The Indian Tribes of North America. Edinburgh: John Grant, 1933-34. One of 200 numbered sets of the Edition-de-Luxe. 3 vols. 123 color plts. Cl, leather spine labels. *Swann*.* $431/£276

501

McKENNEY, THOMAS and JAMES HALL. The Indian Tribes of North America.... Edinburgh, 1933-4. 'Edition de Luxe,' one of 200, this copy unnumbered. 3 vols. 2 ports, 2 fldg maps, 122 plts, guards. (Tp calls for 123 plts, but only 122 are listed.) Gilt-lettered leather spine labels. Vols 2, 3 in djs (worn). *Kane*. $450/£288

McKENNY, THOMAS and JAMES HALL. History of the Indian Tribes of North America. Phila, 1848. Vol 1 (of 3). 40 hand-colored plts. (Fr matter, lower fore-edge of plts dampstained, affecting many images.) Contemp 1/2 morocco, bds (worn, backstrip gone). *Freeman**. $2,100/£1,346

McKENZIE, D. F. The Cambridge University Press, 1696-1712. Cambridge: CUP, 1966. 1st ed. Pub's presentation slip laid in. Fine in djs (sl faded). *Waverly**. $49/£31

McKENZIE, THOMAS. My Life as a Soldier. St. John, New Brunswick: J. & A. McMillan, 1898. 1st ed. Inscribed. Photo frontis, x,202pp. Red cl. Good. *Karmiole*. $75/£48

McKENZIE-GRIEVE, AVERIL. Aspects of Elba.... London, 1964. 1st ed. Dj. *Edwards*. $25/£16

McKIM, IRVING. Ben-Hur Wallace. Berkeley, 1947. 1st ed. VG + in dj (lt wear). *Pratt*. $40/£26

McKIM, W. DUNCAN. Heredity and Human Progress. NY, 1900. 1st ed. Grn cl. VG. *Doctor's Library*. $50/£32

McKINLEY, ROBIN. The Hero and the Crown. NY: Greenwillow, 1985. 1st ed. 6 1/4 x 9 1/4. 246pp. Cl spine. Fine in dj. *Cattermole*. $40/£26

McLAIN, JOHN S. Alaska and the Klondike. NY: McClure, Phillips, 1905. 1st ed. VG. *Perier*. $85/£54

McLANDBURGH, FLORENCE. The Automaton Ear and Other Sketches. Jansen, McClurg, 1876. 1st ed. (Cvr sl scuffed), else VG. *Certo*. $45/£29

McLANE, LUCY NEELY. A Piney Paradise by Monterey Bay, Pacific Grove.... SF: Lawton Kennedy, 1952. 1st ed. VF in dj (chipped). *Argonaut*. $60/£38

McLAREN, JOHN. Gardening in California. SF: A.M. Robertson, 1924. 3rd ed. Grn cl, gilt. Good in dj (chipped). *Karmiole*. $65/£42

McLAREN, JOHN. Gardening in California. SF: A.M. Robertson, 1924. 3rd ed. (Lg inscrip), else Fine. *Quest*. $70/£45

McLAREN, MORAY. Shell Guide to Scotland. London: Ebury, 1965. 1st ed. 16 color plts. Orig pict bds. VG in dj. *Hollett*. $47/£30

McLAUGHLIN, J. W. Fermentation, Infection and Immunity, a New Theory of These Processes. TX, 1892. 240pp. VG (sl worn). *Doctor's Library*. $50/£32

McLEAN, GEORGE. The Rise and Fall of Anarchy in America.... R.B. Badoux, 1888. Pict red cl (stained). *Yudkin**. $42/£27

McLEAN, RUARI (ed). Motif 6. London: Shenval, 1961. Pict bds (spine lt worn). *Hollett*. $39/£25

McLEAN, RUARI. Joseph Cundall. Private Libraries Assoc, 1976. Color frontis, 3 color plts. Dj (sl chipped). *Edwards*. $31/£20

McLENNAN, J. S. Louisbourg from Its Foundation to Its Fall 1713-1758. London: Macmillan, 1918. 1st ed. Frontis; all fldg maps, plans in rear pocket. (Rear inner hinge cracked; cl sl worn, rubbed), else Good. *Brown*. $75/£48

McLEOD, ALEXANDER. Pigtails and Gold Dust. Caldwell, ID: Caxton, 1947. 1st ed. Signed. (Sl bump), else Fine in pict dj (spine chipped). *Argonaut*. $90/£58

McLOUGHLIN, JOHN. Letters of Dr. John McLoughlin Written at Fort Vancouver 1829-1832. Burt Brown Barker (ed). Portland: Binfords & Mort, (1948). 1st ed. Fine in VG dj. *Perier*. $45/£29

McLOUGHLIN, JOHN. Letters of Dr. John McLoughlin. Burt Brown Barker (ed). Portland, OR: Binfords & Mort, (1948). 1st ed. Good in dj (worn). *Lien*. $40/£26

McLOUGHLIN, MICHAEL. Five Photographers. Lincoln: Univ of NE, Sheldon Memorial Art Gallery, 1968. 1st ed. 2 panoramas. Fine in ptd wrappers. *Cahan*. $35/£22

McMAHAN, ANNA BENNESON (ed). With Shelley in Italy. T. Fisher Unwin, 1907. Good (lt spotted; spine bumped, sunned, nick upper hinge, cvrs sunned, mks). *Tiger*. $19/£12

McMICHAEL, JOHN (ed). Circulation: Proceedings of the Harvey Tercentenary Congress. Springfield, 1958. 1st Amer ed. VG. *Fye*. $100/£64

McMILLAN, TERRY. Mama. NY: HMC, (1987). 1st ed. Fine in Fine dj (spine lt toned). *Unger*. $275/£176

McMULLEN, R. T. Orion, or How I Came to Sail Alone a 19-Ton Yacht. Charles Wilson, late Norie & Wilson, 1878. 1st ed. Frontis, xvi,192pp (labels removed fr pastedown), fldg sketch-map. Blue cl (sl rubbed, worn), gilt. Sound. *Cox*. $117/£75

McMURRAY, DONALD L. Coxey's Army. Boston: Little, Brown, 1929. 1st ed. NF. *Beasley*. $50/£32

McMURRICH, J. PLAYFAIR. Leonardo da Vinci. The Anatomist (1452-1519). Balt: Williams & Wilkins, (1930). 1st ed. Frontis port, 89 plts. Untrimmed. (Frontis, tp margins spotting; spine dull), else VG. *Glaser*. $100/£64

McMURTRIE, DOUGLAS C. A Bibliography of South Carolina Imprints, 1731-1740. Charleston: Privatley ptd, 1933. Ltd to 300. 6 facs plts. Ptd wrappers. Fine. *Cahan*. $40/£26

McMURTRIE, DOUGLAS C. The Book: The Story of Printing and Bookmaking. NY, (1943). VG. *Truepenny*. $50/£32

McMURTRIE, DOUGLAS C. Early Printing in Tennessee.... Chicago, 1933. (Spine sl faded), else VG. *Bohling*. $60/£38

McMURTRIE, DOUGLAS C. Early Printing in Wisconsin with a Bibliography of the Issues of the Press, 1833-1850. Seattle: McCaffrey, 1931. 1st ed. One of 300 ptd. Personal note from pub tipped in, signed by McCaffrey. *Ginsberg*. $300/£192

McMURTRIE, DOUGLAS C. The Golden Book. Chicago: Pascal Covici, 1927. One of 2000. Heavily dec cl. (Spine gilt sl dull), o/w Fine. *Dermont*. $35/£22

McMURTRIE, DOUGLAS C. (ed). A History of California Newspapers. NY: Plandome, 1927. Bds, cl spine, paper spine label. *Dawson*. $125/£80

McMURTRIE, DOUGLAS C. Wings for Words; The Story of Johann Gutenberg and His Invention of Printing. NY: Rand McNally, 1940. 1st ed. (Ink name, address), else VG in dj (lt worn). *Hermitage*. $35/£22

McMURTRIE, DOUGLAS C. and ALBERT ALLEN. Jotham Meeker, Pioneer Printer of Kansas. Chicago: Eyncourt, 1930. One of 650. Tipped-in frontis. Fine. *Harrington*. $85/£54

McMURTRIE, FRANCIS E. (ed). Jane's Fighting Ships 1942. London: Sampson Low, Marston, 1943. 1st ed. VG in blue cl (sl speckled, faded). *Cox*. $101/£65

McMURTRIE, FRANCIS E. (ed). Jane's Fighting Ships. 1944-45. London, 1946. Blue cl (lt mkd). *Maggs*. $250/£160

McMURTRY, LARRY. All My Friends Are Going to Be Strangers. NY, 1972. 1st ed. Signed. NF in NF dj. *Warren*. $95/£61

McMURTRY, LARRY. All My Friends Are Going to Be Strangers. NY: S&S, 1972. 1st ed. Fine in dj (sl worn). *Else Fine*. $75/£48

McMURTRY, LARRY. Anything for Billy. NY, 1988. 1st ed. Signed. Fine in Fine dj. *Warren*. $50/£32

McMURTRY, LARRY. Buffalo Girls. NY et al: S&S, (1990). 1st ed. Signed. New in New dj. *Bernard.* $50/£32

McMURTRY, LARRY. Cadillac Jack. NY, 1982. 1st ed. VG (sl cock) in NF dj. *Warren.* $35/£22

McMURTRY, LARRY. Cadillac Jack. NY: S&S, 1982. 1st ed. VF (rmdr mk) in VF dj. *Else Fine.* $60/£38

McMURTRY, LARRY. Film Flam. NY: S&S, 1987. 1st ed. Fine in dj. *Lame Duck.* $45/£29

McMURTRY, LARRY. In a Narrow Grave. Encino, (1968). Later ptg. Fine in dj (faint staining). *Certo.* $35/£22

McMURTRY, LARRY. The Last Picture Show. NY: Dial, 1966. 1st ed. Fine in dj (closed tear fr panel, sm soil mk). *Dermont.* $250/£160

McMURTRY, LARRY. The Last Picture Show. NY: Dial, 1966. 1st ed. NF in VG dj (lt soiled). *Metropolitan*.* $402/£258

McMURTRY, LARRY. Leaving Cheyenne. NY: Harper & Row, 1963. 1st ed. NF in VG dj (price-clipped, spine lt faded, 3-inch crease, crumpling fr panel). *Lame Duck.* $650/£417

McMURTRY, LARRY. Lonesome Dove. NY, (1985). 1st ed. Fine in dj. *Argosy.* $135/£87

McMURTRY, LARRY. Lonesome Dove. NY: S&S, (1985). Advance uncorrected proof. NF in yellow wraps. *Metropolitan*.* $201/£129

McMURTRY, LARRY. Lonesome Dove. NY, 1985. 1st ed. Signed. Fine in Fine dj. *Warren.* $300/£192

McMURTRY, LARRY. Lonesome Dove. NY: S&S, 1985. 1st ed. Fine in Fine dj. *Metropolitan*.* $115/£74

McMURTRY, LARRY. Lonesome Dove. NY: S&S, 1985. 1st ed. Signed. NF in dj (sm scratches rear panel). *Lame Duck.* $250/£160

McMURTRY, LARRY. Moving On. NY: S&S, 1970. 1st ed. Fine in Fine dj. *Beasley.* $100/£64

McMURTRY, LARRY. Some Can Whistle. NY: S&S, (1989). 1st ed. Signed. Fine in Fine dj. *Lenz.* $75/£48

McMURTRY, LARRY. Some Can Whistle. NY: S&S, 1989. 1st ed. VF in dj. *Turtle Island.* $35/£22

McMURTRY, LARRY. Some Can Whistle. NY: S&S, 1989. 1st ed. VF in VF dj. *Else Fine.* $35/£22

McMURTRY, LARRY. Somebody's Darling. NY: S&S, 1978. 1st ed. VF (rmdr mk) in dj. *Else Fine.* $40/£26

McMURTRY, LARRY. Terms of Endearment. NY: S&S, (1975). 1st ed. Fine (lt shelfworn) in NF dj. *Metropolitan*.* $80/£51

McMURTRY, LARRY. Terms of Endearment. NY: S&S, (1975). 1st ed. (Pp sl browned), else NF in dj. *Captain's Bookshelf.* $125/£80

McMURTRY, LARRY. Terms of Endearment. NY, 1975. 1st ed. Signed. VG+ (pp browning) in NF dj (edgeworn). *Warren.* $75/£48

McMURTRY, LARRY. Texasville. NY, 1987. 1st ed. Signed. Fine in Fine dj. *Warren.* $50/£32

McNEER, MAY. The Gold Rush. NY: Artists & Writers Guild/G & D, (1944). Lynd Ward (illus). Color pict bds (sl worn). VG. *Blue Mountain.* $25/£16

McNEER, MAY. The Story of California. NY: Harper, 1944. 1st ed. C. H. DeWitt (illus). 10 1/4 x 11 1/4. 32pp. Cl spine, dec bds. VG in dj. *Cattermole.* $45/£29

McNEIR, FOREST. Forest McNeir of Texas. San Antonio: Naylor, 1956. 1st ed. Signed. Grn cl. VG. *Archer.* $35/£22

McNICHOLS, CHARLES L. Crazy Weather. NY, 1944. Brick red cl. (Spine sl dull), else VG in pict dj. *Five Quail.* $12/£8

McNIERNEY, MICHAEL (ed). Taos 1847, the Revolt in Contemporary Accounts. Boulder, 1980. 1st ed. Pb. Fine. *Turpen.* $18/£12

McNITT, FRANK. The Indian Traders. Norman: Univ of OK, 1962. 1st ed. Red cl. (Adhesion mks from dj on bds), else VG. *Parmer.* $65/£42

McNITT, FRANK. Richard Wetherill: Anasazi. Albuquerque: Univ of NM, (1957). 1st ed. Black cl. (Fep sl dknd, sm stamp bottom fore-edge), else VF in pict dj. *Argonaut.* $150/£96

McNITT, FRANK. Richard Wetherill: Anasazi. Univ of NM, 1957. 1st ed. Map. Black cl (lt soil, wear, spine dull). Internally Fine. *Five Quail.* $55/£35

McNITT, FRANK. Richard Wetherill: Anasazi. Albuquerque: Univ of NM, 1957. VG in dj. *Dumont.* $55/£35

McPHARLIN, PAUL (ed). Puppetry 1937. Detroit: Puppeteers of America, 1937. Cl-backed bds. VG. *Dramatis Personae.* $25/£16

McPHARLIN, PAUL (comp). A Repertory of Marionette Plays. NY: Viking, 1929. 1st ed. 10 plts. Dec eps. Partially unopened. (Faded.) *Dramatis Personae.* $80/£51

McPHARLIN, PAUL. Puppets in America, 1739 to Today. Birmingham, MI: Puppetry Imprints, (1936). Ltd to 1000. Beige bds (sm cracks hinges). Dj (lt chipped). *Karmiole.* $60/£38

McPHEE, JOHN. Alaska. SF: Sierra Club, (1981). 1st ed, deluxe issue. Ltd to 500 signed by McPhee and Galen Rowell (photo). Fine in cl slipcase. *Jaffe.* $350/£224

McPHEE, JOHN. Coming into the Country. London: Hamish Hamilton, (1978). 1st UK ed. 2 maps. Fine in Fine dj. *Bernard.* $50/£32

McPHEE, JOHN. The Control of Nature. NY: FSG, (1989). 1st ed. Fine in dj. *Jaffe.* $35/£22

McPHEE, JOHN. The Crofter and the Laird. NY: FSG, (1970). 1st ed. Fine in dj. *Between The Covers.* $150/£96

McPHEE, JOHN. The Crofter and the Laird. NY: FSG, 1970. 1st ed. Fine (bkpl) in Fine dj. *Else Fine.* $125/£80

McPHEE, JOHN. The Curve of Blinding Energy. NY: FSG, (1974). 1st ed. Fine in dj. *Jaffe.* $125/£80

McPHEE, JOHN. The Deltoid Pumpkin Seed. NY: FSG, (1973). 1st ed. Cl-backed bds. Fine in dj. *Jaffe.* $60/£38

McPHEE, JOHN. Giving Good Weight. NY: FSG, (1979). 1st ed. Fine in dj (rear flaf creased). *Bernard.* $17/£11

McPHEE, JOHN. Giving Good Weight. NY: FSG, (1979). 1st ed. (Bottom edge sl bumped), o/w Fine in dj. *Jaffe.* $25/£16

McPHEE, JOHN. The Headmaster: Frank L. Boyden, of Deerfield. NY: FSG, (1966). 1st ed. Fine in dj (sm closed tear). *Jaffe.* $125/£80

McPHEE, JOHN. In Suspect Terrain. NY, (1983). 1st ed. VG in dj. *King.* $25/£16

McPHEE, JOHN. Levels of the Game. NY: FSG, (1969). 1st ed. NF in NF dj (price-clipped). *Captain's Bookshelf.* $65/£42

McPHEE, JOHN. Levels of the Game. NY: FSG, (1969). 1st ed. Fine in dj. *Jaffe.* $85/£54

McPHEE, JOHN. Levels of the Game. London: Macdonald, (1970). 1st Eng ed. Fine in dj (sl rubbed, price-clipped). *Jaffe.* $50/£32

McPHEE, JOHN. Oranges. NY: FSG, (1967). 1st ed. NF in dj (spine ends sl worn, price-clipped). *Bernard.* $60/£38

McPHEE, JOHN. Pieces of the Frame. NY: FSG, (1975). 1st ed. Fine in dj. *Jaffe.* $150/£96

McPHEE, JOHN. The Pine Barrens. NY: Farrar Straus, (1968). 1st ed. Fine in dj. *Captain's Bookshelf.* $150/£96

McPHEE, JOHN. A Roomful of Hovings. NY: FSG, (1968). 1st ed. Fine in dj. *Between The Covers.* $175/£112

McPHEE, JOHN. Table of Contents. NY: FSG, (1985). 1st ed. Mint in dj. *Jaffe.* $35/£22

McPHEE, JOHN. Wimbledon: A Celebration. NY: Viking, (1972). 1st ed. Fine in NF dj (closed tear). *Bernard.* $75/£48

McPHERSON, JAMES ALAN. Elbow Room. Boston: Atlantic/Little, Brown, 1977. 1st ed. Fine in NF dj (sl wear spine ends). *Beasley.* $85/£54

McPHERSON, JAMES ALAN. Elbow Room. Boston: Atlantic/Little, Brown, 1977. 1st ed. Signed. Fine in NF dj (extrems sl worn). *Lame Duck.* $250/£160

McPHERSON, JAMES ALAN. Hue and Cry. Boston: Atlantic/Little, Brown, 1969. 1st bk. Rev copy, slip laid in. Signed. Fine in NF dj (fr panel lt rubbed). *Lame Duck.* $450/£288

McPHERSON, JOHN G. Footprints on a Frozen Continent. London, 1975. VG in dj. *High Latitude.* $25/£16

McQUAID, JAMES (ed). An Index to American Photographic Collections. Boston: G.K. Ha., 1982. 1st ed. Fine. *Cahan.* $45/£29

McREE, PATSIE. The Kitchen and the Cotton Patch. (Dalton, GA: The Author, 1948.) 1st ed, pre-pub issue in variant binding, w/copyright data & imprint rubber-stamped rather than ptd. Signed. 26 full-pg sketches by K. Burke. Dec brn leatherette. VG. *Petrilla.* $65/£42

McREYNOLDS, EDWIN C. Oklahoma. Norman, (1954). 1st ed. VG in dj (sl worn). *King.* $30/£19

McTYEIRE, HOLLAND N. A Manual of the Discipline of the Methodist Episcopal Church, South.... Nashville: Methodist Episcopal Church, South, 1871. 263pp. (Worn, spine loss). *Brown.* $15/£10

McVAUGH, ROGERS. Edward Palmer. Norman, (1956). 1st ed. VG in dj (sl bumped). *King.* $35/£22

McWATTERS, GEORGE S. Knots Untied. Hartford: J.B. Burr & Hyde, 1871. 1st US ed. 665pp. Good. *Gravesend.* $65/£42

McWHORTER, LUCULLUS VIRGIL. The Border Settlers of Northwestern Virginia from 1768 to 1795. Hamilton, OH, 1915. Frontis, 2 plts. (Worn, rubbed, spine top bumped.) Howes M192. *Bohling.* $200/£128

McWILLIAM, CANDIDA. A Case of Knives. London, 1988. 1st Eng ed. Fine in dj. *Clearwater.* $39/£25

McWILLIAMS, CAREY. Factories in the Field. Boston: LB, 1939. 1st ed. (Dj backed w/paper, pasted to pastedowns), o/w VG in Good dj. *Archer.* $30/£19

MEAD, G. R. S. Thrice-Greatest Hermes. London: John M. Watkins, 1949. 3 vols. Grn cl. NF in djs (sl chipped). *House.* $180/£115

MEAD, RICHARD. A Discourse on the Plague. London: A. Millar & J. Brindley, 1744. 9th ed. xl,164pp. Contemp speckled calf (rebacked), gilt, raised bands. Clean. *White.* $117/£75

MEAD, RICHARD. The Medical Works. Edinburgh, 1775. New ed. Calf (rubbed, crack top fr hinge). *Argosy.* $300/£192

MEADE, GEORGE GORDON. With Meade at Gettysburg. Phila, 1930. 1st ed. (Ex-lib; spine label, cvr worn), o/w VG + . *Pratt.* $65/£42

MEADE, L. T. A Little Silver Trumpet. Hodder & Stoughton, 1909. 1st ed. 8vo. 243pp (sl foxed); 4 color plts by S. B. Pearse. Cl, arch-topped pict onlay (spine discolored, tips sl worn). *Bookmark.* $39/£25

MEADE, L. T. and ROBERT EUSTACE. The Gold Star Line. London: Ward Lock, 1899. 1st ed. (Name, pp foxed), o/w NF in pict cl cvrs, gilt. *Mordida.* $100/£64

MEADE, ROBERT DOUTHAT. Judah P. Benjamin, Confederate Statesman. NY, (1944). 4th ptg. VG + in dj (lt wear, spine faded). *Pratt.* $45/£29

MEADLEY, GEORGE WILSON. Memoirs of William Paley, DD. Edinburgh: A. Constable, 1810. 2nd ed. xv,(i),408pp (upper corner 1st few leaves waterstained); port. Contemp tree calf (corners lt worn), gilt back, dbl morocco labels. *Cox.* $47/£30

MEADOWS, PAUL. John Wesley Powell: Frontiersman of Science. Lincoln, 1952. (Cvr lt soiled), else Fine in blue wraps. *Five Quail.* $30/£19

MEAGHER, MAUDE. Fantastic Traveller. Boston: HMCo, 1931. Signed. (Sl tape shadows feps), else NF in VG + dj (sl dknd, sm chips, price-clipped). *Between The Covers.* $85/£54

MEAGHER, MAUDE. White Jade. London: Scholartis, 1930. 1st ed. Frontis. Fine (spine sl rubbed, corner sl creased) in dj (spine sunned, rubbed, torn, soiled). *Polyanthos.* $30/£19

MEAKIN, ANNETTE M. B. Woman in Transition. London: Methuen, (1907). 1st ed. VG (name, ex-lib; rear hinge tender). *Second Life.* $75/£48

MEANS, FLORENCE CRANNELL. Penny for Luck. Boston/Cambridge, Houghton Mifflin/Riverside, 1935. 1st ed. 8 full-pg illus by Paul Quinn. VG in dj. *Houle.* $75/£48

MEANY, EDMOND S. History of the State of Washington. NY: Macmillan, 1909. 1st ed. NF. *Perier.* $100/£64

MEARES, AINSLIE. A System of Medical Hypnosis. Phila/London: W.B. Saunders, (1961). 2nd ptg. Presentation copy. Ptd grey cl. VG (ex-lib, bkpl, rear pocket, spine label). *Gach.* $35/£22

MEATYARD, RALPH EUGENE. The Family Album of Lucybelle Crater. N.p.: Jargon Soc, 1974. 1st ed. NF (owner stamp) in pict stiff wrappers. *Cahan.* $50/£32

MEATYARD, RALPH EUGENE. The Family Album of Lucybelle Crater. N.p.: Jargon Soc, 1974. 1st ed. NF in dj. *Cahan.* $100/£64

MEATYARD, RALPH EUGENE. Photography '72.' Lexington, KY: Lexington Camera Club, 1972. NF in stiff wrappers. *Cahan.* $40/£26

MEAUZE, PIERRE. African Art: Sculpture. Cleveland, (1968). Fldg map. VG in dj. *Argosy.* $125/£80

MECH, L. D. The Wolf, Etc. NY: Amer Museum of Natural Hist, (1970). NF in VG dj. *Mikesh.* $30/£19

MECKLIN, J. M. The Ku Klux Klan. NY: Harcourt Brace, 1924. 1st ed. Black cl (rusty). Good. *Scribe's Perch*.* $22/£14

MECKLIN, JOHN MOFFAT. The Ku Klux Klan: A Study of the American Mind. NY, 1924. 1st ed. VG. *Wantagh.* $60/£38

Medical and Surgical Reports of the Episcopal Hospital. Phila: Wm. J. Dornan, 1913-1930. 6 vols. Tight (lt wear). *Goodrich.* $450/£288

MEDLIN, F. Centuries of Owls in Art and the Written Word. Norwalk, 1967. Dj. *Maggs.* $25/£16

MEDWORTH, FRANK. Animal Drawing. Faber & Faber, 1935. 1st ed. Dj. *Edwards.* $23/£15

MEE, HUAN. Weaving the Web. London: Ward, Lock, 1902. 1st ed. (Bumped, rubbed.) *Metropolitan*.* $28/£18

MEEK, A. S. A Naturalist in Cannibal Land. London: T. Fisher Unwin, 1913. 2nd imp. (Sl rubbed), else VG. *Goodrich.* $65/£42

MEEKER, ARTHUR. Prairie Avenue. NY: Knopf, 1949. 1st ed. Inscribed. NF in dj (sl edgeworn, rear panel rubbed). *Sadlon.* $25/£16

MEEKER, EZRA. Ox-Team Days on the Oregon Trail. Howard Driggs (ed). Yonkers-on-Hudson, NY, 1922. Later ed. Signed. Port. Pict cl. (2 bkpls, shelfwear), else VG in 1/2 morocco slipcase. *Reese.* $150/£96

MEEKER, NATHAN COOK. Life in the West. NY: Samuel R. Wells, 1868. 1st ed. 360pp + 36pp ads. (Shelfworn, edgeworn, spine dknd), else Good. *Brown.* $30/£19

MEEKS, C. L. V. Italian Architecture 1750-1914. New Haven, 1966. Good. *Washton.* $135/£87

MEEKS, C. L. V. The Railroad Station. Yale Univ, (1975). Sound. *Ars Artis.* $55/£35

MEEROPOL, ROBERT and MICHAEL. We Are Your Sons. Boston: Houghton Mifflin, 1975. 1st ed. Tan cl. NF in pict yellow dj (spine faded, sm hole at fold). *Blue Mountain.* $35/£22

MEES, C. E. KENNETH. The Photography of Coloured Objects. London: Wratten & Wainwright/Kodak House, 1909. 2nd ptg. VG in stiff paper-cvrd bds (chip). *Smith.* $35/£22

Meet the U.S. Army. (By Louis MacNeice.) London: HMSO, 1943. 1st ed. Nice in wrappers (sl dusty). *Patterson.* $47/£30

MEGQUIER, MARY JANE. Apron Full of Gold. Robert Glass Cleland (ed). San Marino, CA: Huntington Library, 1949. 1st ed. VG. *Lien.* $25/£16

MEHRING, WALTER. The Lost Library. NY: Bobbs-Merrill, 1951. 1st ed. (Top edge stained), else VG+ in VG dj (soiled, chipped). *Lame Duck.* $150/£96

MEIGGS, RUSSELL. Roman Ostia. Oxford: Clarendon, 1960. B/w frontis, 40 b/w plts. Blue cl. VG. *Turtle Island.* $80/£51

MEIGO, JOHN. Peter Hurd: The Lithographs. TX: Baker Gallery, 1969. *Metropolitan*. $57/£37

MEIGS, ARTHUR. An American Country Home. NY: Architectural Book Pub, 1925. 1st ed. Lg folio. 99 plts. Dk brn/tan cl (sl edgeworn). Text VG (owner stamp) in dj (sl chipped, sunned). *Baltimore*. $110/£71

MEIGS, ARTHUR. An American Country House. NY: Architectural Book Pub Co, 1925. Gilt-lettered 2-tone brn cl (soiled, sl warped). *Freeman*. $150/£96

MEIGS, CHARLES D. Obstetrics: The Science and the Art. Phila: Blanchard & Lea, 1852. 2nd ed. xxiii-759pp + 32pp ads. Orig sheep. (Lt foxing; rubbed, corners bumped), else Tight. *Goodrich.* $95/£61

MEIGS, CORNELIA. The Willow Whistle. NY: Macmillan, (Sept) 1931. 1st ed. 4to. Color frontis, 144pp; 10 full-pg b/w illus by E. Boyd Smith. Yellow oblong cl (sl soiled). VG. *Dower.* $45/£29

MEIGS, PEVERIL. The Dominican Mission Frontier of Lower California. Berkeley: Univ of CA, 1935. 1st ed. Fldg map. Red cl. Fine in dj (spine dknd). *Argonaut.* $125/£80

MEIJER, EMILE and JOOP SWART. The Photographic Memory. London: Quiller, 1988. 1st UK ed. Frontis. As New in dj. *Cahan.* $35/£22

MEINERTZHAGEN, D. Diary of a Black Sheep. Edinburgh, 1964. (Ms additions to index; rubbed.) *Maggs.* $66/£42

MEINERTZHAGEN, FREDERICK. The Art of the Netsuke Carver. London: Routledge & Kegan Paul, 1956. 1st ed. 20 plts. VG in dj (price-clipped). *Hollett.* $117/£75

MEINERTZHAGEN, R. Kenya Diary, 1902-1906. London, 1957. VG (ink inscrip). *Truepenny.* $75/£48

MEINERTZHAGEN, R. Nicoll's Birds of Egypt. London, 1930. 2 vols. 4to. Frontis port, 3 color fldg maps, 31 color plts, 6 photogravures. (Upper hinge vol 1 cracked, both vols sl shaken; cl sl spotted, extrems sl rubbed.) *Edwards.* $593/£380

MEIS, REINHARD. Pocket Watches. West Chester: Schiffer, (1987). 1st Eng ed. Grn cl. Fine in dj. *Weber.* $75/£48

MEISEL, LOUIS K. Photo-Realism. NY, 1981. 2nd ptg. 710 color plts. Dj. *Edwards.* $70/£45

MEISELAS, SUSAN. Carnival Strippers. NY: FSG, 1976. 1st ed. NF in illus dj. *Cahan.* $125/£80

MEISELAS, SUSAN. Nicaragua, June 1978-July 1979. Claire Rosenberg (ed). NY: Pantheon, 1981. 71 full-pg color photos. NF (name, blindstamp). *Cahan.* $40/£26

MEISS, MILLARD and EDITH W. KIRSCH. The Visconti Hours. London, 1972. 1st UK ed. Teg. Cl slipcase. *Edwards.* $101/£65

MEISS, MILLARD. French Painting in the Time of Jean de Berry. London, 1968. Good in dj. *Washton.* $150/£96

MELINE, JAMES F. Two Thousand Miles on Horseback. NY: Hurd & Houghton, 1867. 1st ed. Fldg map frontis, (10),317pp. (Sl worn, soiled, dampstained.) Howes M490. *Waverly*. $66/£42

MELINE, JAMES F. Two Thousand Miles on Horseback. NY: Hurd & Houghton, 1867. 1st ed. x,317pp; fldg map. (Ex-lib, splits to map; shelfworn, else Good. Howes M488. *Dumont.* $100/£64

MELLAND, FRANK H. In Witch-Bound Africa. 1923. 1st ed. 3 maps (1 fldg). (Lacks fep; illus cl faded, stained.) *Edwards.* $59/£38

MELLEN, IDA M. The Science and the Mystery of the Cat. NY/London, 1940. Fore-edge uncut. (Spine lt faded.) *Edwards.* $55/£35

MELLON, JAMES. African Hunter. NY, (1975). 1st ed. (Sl worn.) Dj. *Oinonen*. $130/£83

MELLOR, DAVID. Modern British Photography, 1919-39. (London): Arts Council of Great Britain, 1980. 1st ed. (Owner stamp), else NF in illus stiff wrappers (lt rubbed). *Cahan.* $20/£13

MELOY, ARTHUR S. Theatres and Motion Picture Houses. NY: Architects Supply & Publishing, (1915). Gray cl (extrems rather worn). *Freeman*. $100/£64

MELTZER, DAVID. Ragas. SF: Discovery, 1959. 1st ed. NF. *Beasley.* $35/£22

MELTZER, MILTON. Dorothea Lange: A Photographer's Life. NY: FSG, (1978). 1st ed. (Top bds lt faded.) VG dj (sm internal repair, extrems lt wear). *Between The Covers.* $50/£32

MELTZER, MILTON. Dorothea Lange: A Photographer's Life. NY: FSG, 1978. 1st ed. NF in dj. *Cahan.* $50/£32

MELVILLE, F. J. Postage Stamps in the Making....Vol 1 (all published). London, 1916. 1st ed. (Sl cockled.) 1/2 cl (sl worn). *Maggs.* $172/£110

MELVILLE, HERMAN. Battle-Pieces and Aspects of the War. NY: Harper, 1866. 1st ed. 8vo. 272pp. Blind-stamped cl, gilt. Fine in chemise, protective slipcase. *Bromer.* $1,750/£1,122

MELVILLE, HERMAN. Benito Cereno. London, 1926. Ltd to 1650. 7 full-pg hand-colored illus. Full red buckram, beveled bds. VG. *Truepenny.* $175/£112

MELVILLE, HERMAN. Benito Cereno. London, 1926. One of 1650 numbered. McKnight Kauffer (illus). Maroon buckram. VG in dj (torn, chipped, spine foot lacks piece). *Words Etc.* $273/£175

MELVILLE, HERMAN. Benito Cereno. London: Nonesuch, 1926. Ltd to 1650. 7 full-pg illus. Red buckram. (Spine sl faded), else VF in dj (chipped). *Bromer.* $150/£96

MELVILLE, HERMAN. Benito Cereno. London: Nonesuch, 1926. Ltd to 1650. E. McKnight Kauffer (illus). Uncut. Orig buckram (spine faded, bds lt faded, few dents upper bd), gilt. *Hollett.* $187/£120

MELVILLE, HERMAN. Billy Budd—Benito Cereno. NY: LEC, 1965. One of 1500 numbered, signed by Robert Shore (illus). 10 full-color plts. Mint in cl bd slipcase. *Argosy.* $125/£80

MELVILLE, HERMAN. Israel Potter: His Fifty Years of Exile. NY: Putnam, 1855. 1st ed, 1st ptg. Marbled bds, mod 1/2 morocco, gilt. Fine. BAL 13667. *Macdonnell.* $250/£160

MELVILLE, HERMAN. Israel Potter: His Fifty Years of Exile. NY: Putnam, 1855. 3rd ed. 276pp (lt lib stamp tp). Purple cl (faded). BAL 13667. *M & S.* $400/£256

MELVILLE, HERMAN. Israel Potter: His Fifty Years of Exile. NY: Putnam, 1855. 1st ed, 1st ptg. Teg. 3/4 navy blue morocco (orig blue cl cvrs, spine bound in), gilt. (Sm marginal tear 1 leaf, old bkseller description pastedown), else Very Nice. BAL 13667. *Reese.* $750/£481

MELVILLE, HERMAN. Mardi and a Voyage Thither. NY: Harper, 1849. 1st ed (no ads). 2 vols. (Foxing, ex-lib rules on pastedown, inside fr, rear bds.) Contemp 1/2 leather (sl rubbed). Nice. *Metropolitan*. $345/£221

MELVILLE, HERMAN. Moby Dick or The Whale. GC: Garden City Pub, (1937). DeLuxe ed. Rockwell Kent (illus). Blue cl, gilt stamped. NF in dj (sl worn). *Lefkowicz.* $50/£32

MELVILLE, HERMAN. Moby Dick or The Whale. NY: Random House, 1930. 1st trade ed. Rockwell Kent (illus). Silver-stamped black cl. NF (lacks dj). *Lefkowicz.* $100/£64

MELVILLE, HERMAN. Moby Dick or The Whale. London: Cresset, 1946. (Feps spotted.) Orig blue buckram, gilt. *Hollett.* $16/£10

MELVILLE, HERMAN. Moby Dick or, The Whale. (NY): Artist's Limited Ed, 1975. Ltd to 1500 signed by Jacques-Yves Cousteau (preface), Leroy Neiman (illus). Folio. Frontis, xiv,272pp. Brn morocco, gilt. VF in morocco/linen slipcase (sl soiled). *Bromer.* $1,250/£801

MELVILLE, HERMAN. Moby Dick, or The Whale. Chicago: Lakeside, 1930. 1st ed thus. One of 1000. Rockwell Kent (illus). 3 vols. Polished black buckram (edges lt rubbed, spines sunned), stamped in silver. VG (w/o slipcase). *Reese.* $2,000/£1,282

MELVILLE, HERMAN. Moby Dick. SF: Arion, (1981). One of 750. Barry Moser (illus). Prospectus laid in. Cl slipcase. *Swann*. $431/£276

MELVILLE, HERMAN. Moby Dick. SF, 1979. One of 265 numbered, signed by Barry Moser (illus) and Andrew Hoyem (ptr). Silver-lettered blue morocco (spine sl dknd). Cl slipcase. *Swann*. $3,220/£2,064

MELVILLE, HERMAN. Moby Dick; or The Whale. NY: Harper, 1851. 1st Amer ed. 8vo. Mod 1/2 blue calf (amateurish; lt foxed; portion of orig cvrs bound in at rear). BAL 13664. *Swann*. $1,955/£1,253

MELVILLE, HERMAN. Narrative of a Four Months' Residence Among the Natives of a Valley of the Marquesas Islands. London: John Murray, 1846. 1st ed, 2nd issue, w/'Pomere' on p19 line 1; half-title, map of Marquesas Islands, 285pp, 16pp pub's cat at end dated March 1846. Pub's orig blind-stamped red cl, gilt-lettered spine. VF+. BAL 13652. *D & D.* $1,950/£1,250

MELVILLE, HERMAN. Narrative of a Four Months' Residence Among the Natives.... London: J. Murray, 1846. 1st ed, 2nd issue. Contents VG (browned, tp soiled; lacks ads). Early 1/2 calf, marbled bds (spine, edges worn, joints split). *Waverly*. $176/£113

MELVILLE, HERMAN. Omoo. Boston: Dana Estes, (1892). Rpt. Blue pict cl, gilt. Attractive (spine sl rubbed). *Macdonnell.* $75/£48

MELVILLE, HERMAN. Omoo: A Narrative of Adventures in the South Seas. NY: Harper, 1847. 1st Amer ed. Map. Orig brn cl, gilt. (Spine ends expertly mended), else Attractive. BAL 13656. *Macdonnell.* $650/£417

MELVILLE, HERMAN. Pierre; or The Ambiguities. NY: Harper, 1852. 1st ed. 8vo. Gray cl (2 sm wormholes rear joint, faded; 1/3 of 1st blank excised, lt foxing). BAL 13666. *Swann*. $747/£479

MELVILLE, HERMAN. Typee. NY/London: Wiley & Putnam/J. Murray, 1846. 1st Amer ed. (Sl toned, foxed, stained.) In Blanck's 'A' binding. Orig blue cl (edges faded, worn, spine chipped, fr joint sl split). Barton Currie bkpl w/misc correspondence. Custom 1/4 morocco slipcase. *Waverly*. $550/£353

MELVILLE, HERMAN. Typee. NY: LEC, 1935. #904/1500 numbered, signed by Miguel Covarrubias (illus). Full dec tappa binding. VG in pub's slipcase (lt rubbed). *Hermitage.* $150/£96

MELVILLE, HERMAN. Typee. NY: LEC, 1935. Ltd to 1500 signed by Miguel Covarrubias (illus). Full Polynesian tapa cl (spine sl dknd). VG+ in matching slipcase (lt worn). *Truepenny.* $200/£128

MELVILLE, HERMAN. White-Jacket. NY/London: Harper/R. Bentley, 1855. Apparent 2nd Amer ed. (Lt foxed, inscrip.) Brn cl (chipped; sl worn). *Waverly*. $165/£106

MELVILLE, JOHN. Crystal Gazing. London: Nichols, 1910. New & rev ed. Nice dec cvr. VG+. *Middle Earth.* $65/£42

MELVILLE, LEWIS. The Life and Letters of William Beckford of Fonthill. London: Heinemann, 1910. 1st ed. Frontis port. Red cl (sl soiled). Nice. *Turtle Island.* $65/£42

MELVIN, JEAN S. American Glass Paperweights and Their Makers. (NY): Thomas Nelson, (1967). 1st ed. Grn cl, orange spine lettering. Fine dj, bd slipcase (lt sunned, worn). *Baltimore*. $20/£13

Memoir of Pierre Toussaint, Born a Slave in St. Domingo. (By Hannah Farnham Lee.) Boston: Crosby, Nichols, 1854. 3rd ed. (ii),124pp (tp corner torn w/o loss); engr port w/facs inscription & signature. Blind-stamped tan cl (spine covering mostly gone). *Petrilla.* $65/£42

Memoir of W. H. Harvey.... (By Lydia Fisher.) London, 1869. (Engr port corner creased; few neat repairs, rubbed.) *Maggs.* $59/£38

Memoirs of a Life, Chiefly Passed in Pennsylvania, Within the Last Sixty Years. (By Alexander Graydon.) Harrisburg, 1811. 1st ed, w/errata leaf. Contemp panelled sheep (cvrs loose). Howes G344. *Swann*. $103/£66

Memoirs of a Life, Chiefly Passed in Pennsylvania.... Harrisburg: John Wyeth, 1811. 1st ed. 378,(1)pp. Old calf (rubbed, joints sl worn, spine head chipped), leather label. VG. Howes G344. *Agvent.* $185/£119

Memoirs of an American Lady. (By Ann Grant.) London: Longman et al, 1808. 1st ed. 2 vols. 12mo. 322,ads; 344pp. Contemp 1/2 calf (rubbed). VG. Howes G303. *Second Life.* $600/£385

Memoirs of an American Lady. (By Anne Grant.) London: A.K. Newman, 1817. 2 vols in 1. 322; 344pp. VG (rebound). Howes G303. *Lien.* $85/£54

Memoirs of an Infantry Officer. (By Siegfried Sassoon.) London: Faber & Faber, (1930). 1st trade ed. VG (bkpl; spine rubbed, faded) in dj (chipped, lt stained). *Antic Hay.* $25/£16

Memoirs of Captain Rock, the Celebrated Irish Chieftain.... (By Thomas Moore.) London, 1824. 1st ed. Unopened. Orig bds, paper spine label. Custom cl slipcase, protective sleeve. *Freeman*. $80/£51

Memoirs of the Lives and Characters of the Illustrious Family of the Boyles. Dublin: J. Esdall, 1754. xxiii,268pp. 1/2 leather (rubbed, spine head frayed). *Zubal*. $20/£13

Memorial and Biographical History of Northern California.... Chicago, 1891. 4to. Frontis, 834pp. Aeg, inner gilt dentelles. Gilt-dec morocco, spine gilt. (Neat bkpl, occasional fox mk, corners sl rubbed, else Fine. *Reese.* $1,000/£641

Memorial of Charles Sumner. Boston, 1874. 1st ed. 316pp. (eps, tp sl spotted; cvr worn, sl faded), o/w VG + . *Pratt.* $22/£14

Memorial of Samuel de Champlain Who Discovered the Island of Mt. Desert, Maine, September 5, 1604. (By Samuel A. Eliot and William Adams Brown.) N.p.: Privately ptd, 1906. Tipped-in frontis. Fine in stiff paper wrappers. *Zubal*.* $24/£15

Men and Manners in America. (By Thomas Hamilton.) Edinburgh/London, 1833. 1st ed. 2 vols. (Sl rubbed, spine tops worn.) *Kane*.* $30/£19

Men and Manners in America.... (By Thomas Hamilton.) Edinburgh/London, 1833. 2 vols. (xii),393pp + ads; 402pp. Contemp patterned calf (sl edgeworn). Very Nice. Howes H138. *Reese.* $250/£160

Men of Letters of the British Isles. (By Theodore Spicer-Simson.) NY: William Rudge, 1924. One of 520. Inscribed, initialed by Rudge. 29 plts. Orig card dj, ptd spine label. *Kane*.* $70/£45

MENCKEN, H. L. The American Language. NY: Knopf, 1919. 1st ed. One of 1500 numbered. VG overall (eps lt foxed, fr hinge cracked; sl soiled, rubbed, spine lettering difficult to read). *Waverly*.* $27/£17

MENCKEN, H. L. (ed). Americana 1926. NY: Knopf, 1926. 1st ed. Good in dj (sl worn). *Hayman.* $35/£22

MENCKEN, H. L. A Carnival of Buncombe.... Malcolm Moos (ed). Balt, (1956). 1st ed. VG in dj (sl worn). *Hayman.* $35/£22

MENCKEN, H. L. Christmas Story. NY, 1946. 1st ed. VG in VG dj. *Smith.* $20/£13

MENCKEN, H. L. Christmas Story. NY: Knopf, 1946. 1st ed. Blue cl, mtd color illus fr cvr. Text VG in pict dj (price-clipped). *Baltimore*.* $20/£13

MENCKEN, H. L. The Gist of Nietzsche. Boston: John W. Luce, 1910. 1st ed. VG. *Hayman.* $125/£80

MENCKEN, H. L. A Little Book in C Major. NY: John Lane, 1916. 1st ed. VG in dj (soiled, internally repaired). *Argosy.* $45/£29

MENCKEN, H. L. Notes on Democracy. NY: Knopf, (1926). #77/235 signed. Purple/brn patterned paper over bds (edgeworn, faded, corners showing), grn cl backstrip, paper spine label (spine, spine label dknd). VG-. *Harrington.* $125/£80

MENCKEN, JOHANN BURKHARD. The Charlatanry of the Learned. NY, 1937. 1st Amer ed. Fine in dj (price-clipped). *Polyanthos.* $60/£38

MENDALL, H. L. The Ring-Necked Duck in the Northeast. Orono: Univ of ME, 1958. 1st ed. 24 plts, 24 tables. VG + in pict wraps. *Mikesh.* $25/£16

MENDELEEFF, D. The Principles of Chemistry. London: Longmans, Green, 1897. 2nd, enlgd Eng ed. 2 vols. xviii,621; (6),518,32(ads)pp; fldg table. VG (extrems lt worn, vol 2 cvrs sl bubbled). *Glaser.* $450/£288

MENDELSOHN, FELIX. Superbaby. Nash, 1969. 1st ed. VG + in VG dj. *Plapinger.* $65/£42

MENDJISKY, MAURICE. To the Memory of the Martyr Fighters of the Warsaw Ghetto. Mifa Martin (trans). (Paris: Grou-Radenez, 1964.) One of unspecified numbered. 34 (of 35) b/w gravure repros, guards. Text loose, as issued. White wraps (spine sl sunned). Contents Fine in navy/gray suede cl-cvrd bd slipcase (sl worn) w/matching fldg inner liner. *Baltimore*.* $80/£51

MENDL, ROBERT WILLIAM. The Appeal of Jazz. Philip Allan, (1927). 1st ed. (Mks, underlining; cvrs bowed, spine label sl chipped, creased), o/w Good. *Ash.* $117/£75

MENDOZA, GEORGE. Goodbye, River, Goodbye. GC: Doubleday, 1971. 1st ed. (Owner stamp), else Fine in VG dj. *Cahan.* $40/£26

MENDOZA, GEORGE. The Scarecrow Clock. NY: Holt, 1971. 1st ed. Eric Carle (illus). 9 1/4 sq. 32pp. Fine in dj. *Cattermole.* $25/£16

MENGARINI, GREGORY. Mengarini's Narrative of the Rockies; Memoirs of Old Oregon, 1841-1850, and St. Mary's Mission. Albert J. Partoll (ed). Missoula, 1938. Rpt. (Lib stamp cvr.) *Bohling.* $25/£16

MENNELL, JAMES. The Science and Art of Joint Manipulation, Vol II. NY, 1952. 1st ed. VG. *Doctor's Library.* $50/£32

MENNINGER, KARL. A Psychiatrist's World: The Selected Papers of Karl Menninger. Bernard H. Hall (ed). NY: Viking, 1959. 1st trade ed. Cream cl-backed brn cl-cvrd bds. VG in dj (chipped). *Gach.* $30/£19

MENNINGER, WILLIAM C. A Psychiatrist for a Troubled World. NY, 1967. 2 vols. Nice in slipcase. *Goodrich.* $45/£29

MENOTTI, GIAN CARLO. Amahl and the Night Visitor. NY: Whittlesey House, 1952. 1st ed. Roger Duvoisin (illus). Lg 8vo. Pict cl. NF in VG dj. *Book Adoption.* $30/£19

MENPES, DOROTHY. Venice. A&C Black, 1904. Ltd to 500 signed. 100 color plts by Mortimer Menpes. Dec white linen. (Name; sl bumped.) *Petersfield.* $187/£120

MENPES, MORTIMER and DOROTHY. Japan; A Record in Color. London: A&C Black, 1905. Blue dec cl. VG. *Terramedia.* $50/£32

MENPES, MORTIMER. Brittany. London: A&C Black, 1905. 1st ed. 75 color plts. Gilt-dec cl. (Date stamp, cancelled lib label, ep sl spotted; sl worn, spine sl faded.) *Hollett.* $101/£65

MENPES, MORTIMER. India. London: A&C Black, 1912. 2nd ed. Red pict cl. VG. *Terramedia.* $50/£32

MENPES, MORTIMER. Whistler as I Knew Him. A&C Black, 1905. 'Cheap Edition.' (2pp loose), o/w VG. *Words Etc.* $16/£10

MENUHIN, YEHUDI. Unfinished Journey. London, 1977. 1st ed. Dj. *Typographeum.* $15/£10

MERA, H. P. Pueblo Indian Embroidery. Santa Fe: W. Gannon, 1975. 1st ed. 26 plts. NF in pict wraps. *Mikesh.* $27/£17

MERCER, CAVALIE. Journal of the Waterloo Campaign Kept Throughout the Campaign of 1815. London: Peter Davies, 1927. Later ptg. VG (bkpl; shaken). *Mcgowan.* $45/£29

MERCIER, CHARLES ARTHUR. Criminal Responsibility. Oxford: Clarendon, 1905. 1st ed. Pebbled blue buckram. (Fr joint worn), else VG. *Gach.* $85/£54

MERCIER, CHARLES ARTHUR. Sanity and Insanity. London/NY: Walter Scott/Scribner, 1892. Later ptg. Frontis, (xx),(396)pp + inserted ads. Ptd emb red cl (rubbed, spine faded). Good. *Gach.* $40/£26

MEREDITH, GEORGE. Beauchamp's Career. London: Chapman & Hall, 1876. Rmdr issue of 1st ed. 3 vols in 1, bound together w/half-titles. Leaf 217/8 vol 3 is a cancel. Rmdr price (31/6) stamped in gilt on spine. Brn cl (sl soiled), gilt. Good (inner hinges cracked, mended). *Reese.* $150/£96

MEREDITH, GEORGE. The Letters of George Meredith to Alice Meynell with Annotations Thereto 1896-1907. London/SF: Nonesuch, 1923. 1st ed. #598/850. Paper-cvrd bds, cl spine. (Bumped), else NF in VG dj. *Mcgowan.* $20/£13

MEREDITH, GEORGE. Letters of George Meredith. NY: Scribner, 1912. 1st ed. 2 vols. Teg. Dec grn cl. VG (sl wear, cl spotted). *Antic Hay.* $35/£22

MEREDITH, GEORGE. Modern Love. (Stamford, CT): Overbrook, 1934. Ltd to 150. Black cl, gilt. Fine in pub's slipcase. *Karmiole.* $75/£48

MEREDITH, GEORGE. One of Our Conquerors. London: Chapman & Hall, 1891. 1st ed. 3 vols. Largely unopened. Dk blue cl stamped in black/gilt. (Lt foxed, bkpls.) Cl slipcase. *Reese.* $350/£224

MEREDITH, GEORGE. The Ordeal of Richard Feverel. London: Chapman & Hall, 1859. 1st ed. 3 vols. (Lt foxing.) Rose eps; teg. Later 1/2 red morocco, ribbed spines. *Waverly*.* $99/£63

MEREDITH, GEORGE. The Tragic Comedians. London: Chapman & Hall, 1881. 1st ed, 2nd issue, w/cancel tp. 2 vols. Olive cl stamped in gilt/black. (Spine sl rubbed), o/w NF set. *Reese.* $350/£224

MEREDITH, GEORGE. Works. London: Constable, 1909-10. 'Memorial Edition.' 25 vols (of 29). Teg. Contemp burgundy 1/2 calf (few cvrs lt stained, spines sl faded), gilt spine compartments. *Christie's*.* $315/£202

MEREDITH, ROY. Mr. Lincoln's Camera Man, Mathew B. Brady. NY: Scribner, 1946. 1st ed. Blue cl. Fine in dj. *Appelfeld.* $125/£80

MEREDITH, ROY. The World of Mathew Brady. LA, (1976). 1st ed. VG + in VG + dj. *Pratt.* $35/£22

MEREDITH, SCOTT (ed). Bar I: Roundup of Best Western Stories. London: Andrew Dakers, (1952). 1st British ed. (Edges foxed), else Fine in dj (badly chipped). *Authors Of West.* $35/£22

MEREDITH, WILLIAM. Love Letter from an Impossible Land. New Haven: Yale Univ, 1944. 1st ed. VG + in dj (spine tanned, sl loss spine head). *Lame Duck.* $75/£48

MERENESS, NEWTON D. Maryland as a Proprietary Province. NY, 1901. 1st ed. Howes M533. *Ginsberg.* $75/£48

MERFIELD, FRED G. and H. MILLER. Gorilla Hunter. NY: Farrar, Straus, (1956). 1st ed. VG. *Terramedia.* $50/£32

MERIAN, MARIA SIBYLLA. Butterflies, Beetles and Other Insects. NY, (1976). One of 1800 numbered. 2 vols. Sm folio. 129 color plts, guards. Plts loose in bd fldg case as issued. (Ex-lib.) Slipcase. *Swann*.* $115/£74

MERIMEE, PROSPER. Carmen. NY: LEC, 1941. #904/1500 numbered, signed by Jean Charlot (illus). NF in pub's slipcase (lt worn, soiled). *Hermitage.* $100/£64

MERIMEE, PROSPER. The Writings of. George Saintsbury (ed). NY, 1906. #223/1000. 8 vols. Frontispieces. Teg. 3/4 red morocco (extrems rubbed, spine ends worn), gilt. *Freeman*.* $90/£58

MERIWETHER, DAVID. My Life in the Mountains and on the Plains. Norman: Univ of OK, 1966. VG in dj. *Dumont.* $30/£19

MERIWETHER, DAVID. My Life in the Mountains and on the Plains. Robert A. Griffen (ed). Norman: Univ of OK, (1965). 1st ed. Brn cl, gilt spine. VF in pict dj (lt rubbed). *Argonaut.* $50/£32

MERK, FREDERICK. Albert Gallatin and the Oregon Problem. Cambridge: Harvard Univ, 1950. 1st ed. NF. *Archer.* $30/£19

MERLIN, OLIVIER. Fangio. Batsford, 1961. 1st Eng ed. Dj (sl chipped). *Edwards.* $31/£20

MERRIAM, C. HART. The Dawn of the World: Myths and Weird Tales Told by the Mewan Indians of California. Cleveland: A.H. Clark, 1910. 1st ed. Frontis, map. Teg. Red cl. NF. *Harrington.* $110/£71

MERRIAM, EVE. Funny Town. NY: Crowell, 1963. 1st ed. 8 x 11 1/2. 64pp. Pict cl. VG. *Cattermole.* $35/£22

MERRIAM, H. G. (ed). Way Out West. Norman: Univ of OK, (1969). 1st ed. VG (bkpl) in dj (sl worn). *Lien.* $35/£22

MERRICK, ELLIOTT. True North. NY: Scribner, 1933. 1st ed. VG (newspaper rev tipped to 1/2 title) in dj (sl chipped). *High Latitude.* $40/£26

MERRICK, HENRIETTA SANDS. Caucus-Race. NY: Putnam, 1938. 1st ed. 15 plts, 2 maps. (Cl sl rubbed, faded, spine sl nicked), o/w VG. *Worldwide.* $40/£26

MERRILL, F. and M. Among the Nudists. NY: Knopf, 1931. 3rd ptg. Good (soil). *Scribe's Perch*.* $10/£6

MERRILL, JAMES M. The Rebel Shore. Boston, (1957). 1st ed. VG + in dj (lt wear). *Pratt.* $32/£21

MERRILL, JAMES. Another August. (Boston: Impressions Workshop, 1968.) 1st ed. Ltd to 150 numbered, signed by Merrill and George Lockwood (litho). Lg broadside. Fine. *Jaffe.* $350/£224

MERRILL, JAMES. Braving the Elements. London: C&W/Hogarth, 1973. 1st ed. Fine in Fine dj. *Dermont.* $35/£22

MERRILL, JAMES. Divine Comedies. NY: Atheneum, 1976. 1st ed. Fine in NF dj. *Dermont.* $35/£22

MERRILL, JAMES. Divine Comedies. NY: Atheneum, 1976. 1st ed. Signed. Fine in Fine dj. *Lenz.* $100/£64

MERRILL, JAMES. The Fire Screen. London: C&W/Hogarth, 1970. 1st British ed. Inscribed, signed. Fine in dj. *Reese.* $50/£32

MERRILL, JAMES. Ideas, Etc. NY: Jordan Davies, (1980). #130/200 signed. Fine in ptd self-wraps. *Polyanthos.* $45/£29

MERRILL, JAMES. Marbled Paper. Salem: Charles Seluzicki, 1982. 1st ed. One of 200 signed. Fine in dec wrappers. *Captain's Bookshelf.* $175/£112

MERRILL, JAMES. Metamorphosis of 741. Pawlett: Banyan, 1977. One of 440 numbered. Signed. Fine in ptd wrappers, pub's ptd envelope. *Reese.* $85/£54

MERRILL, JAMES. Nights and Days. (London): Hogarth/C&W, 1966. 1st British ed. Fine in dj. *Reese.* $25/£16

MERRILL, JAMES. Yannina. NY: Phoenix Book Shop, 1973. 1st ed. One of 100 (of 126) numbered, signed. VF in dec wrappers. *Captain's Bookshelf.* $300/£192

MERRILL, JAMES. The Yellow Pages. Cambridge, 1974. Ltd to 800 in paper (of 850). Signed. Fine. *Polyanthos.* $35/£22

MERRILL, S. M. The Second Coming of Christ. Cincinnati: 1879. 1st ed. 288pp. VG + . *Middle Earth.* $75/£48

MERRILL, SELAH. East of the Jordan. London, 1881. xv,549,(ii)pp; fldg map. Red ruled cl (spine chipped, upper joint sl split), gilt. *Edwards.* $70/£45

MERRITT, A. The Black Wheel. NY: New Collectors' Group, 1947. 1st ed. Ltd to 1000 numbered. (Cvr lettering flaked, sl worn). *King.* $40/£26

MERRITT, A. Creep, Shadow! NY: Doubleday, 1934. 1st ed. Fine (sl mks fr cvr) in dj (sl chipped, creased, lt rubbed, discolored). *Metropolitan*.* $402/£258

MERRITT, A. The Ship of Ishtar. L.A./Toronto, c. 1924 (i.e., 1949). 1st ed w/these Virgil Finlay illus. Fine in Fine dj. *Mcclintock.* $45/£29

Merry Tales of the Three Wise Men of Gotham. (By James Kirke Paulding.) NY, 1826. 1st ed. Orig cl-backed bds (worn, remnants of spine label; browned). As Is. *Swann*.* $172/£110

MERRYMAN, RICHARD. Andrew Wyeth. Boston: Houghton Mifflin, 1968. 1st ed. Fine in Fine dj. *Book Market.* $150/£96

MERSHON, WILLIAM B. (comp). The Passenger Pigeon. NY: Outing, 1907. 1st ed. Signed. Color frontis, 8 plts (2 color). Maroon cl, gilt. VG (few creased corners). *Bohling.* $150/£96

MERSHON, WILLIAM B. Recollections of My Fifty Years Hunting and Fishing. Boston, 1923. VG. *Truepenny.* $60/£38

MERSHON, WILLIAM B. Recollections of My Fifty Years Hunting and Fishing. Boston, 1923. 1st ed. Uncut. (Lt worn.) Dj (sl frayed). *Oinonen*.* $180/£115

MERTON, HOLMES W. Descriptive Mentality from the Head, Face and Hand. Phila, (1899). 224pp. Good. *Hayman.* $20/£13

MERTON, THOMAS. The Christmas Sermons of B. I. Guerric of Igny. (Trappist): Gethsemani, (1959). 1st ed. Dec paper-cvrd bds. Fine in unptd tissue dj as issued (lt chipping top). *Between The Covers.* $150/£96

MERTON, THOMAS. Clement of Alexandria. NY: New Directions, 1962. 1st ed. Fine in wraps, dj. *Lame Duck.* $85/£54

MERTON, THOMAS. Elected Silence. London: Hollis & Carter, 1949. 1st UK ed. VG in dj (nicks). *Moorhouse.* $31/£20

MERTON, THOMAS. Exile Ends in Glory. Dublin: Clonmore & Reynolds, 1951. 1st UK ed. VG in dj (sl rubbed, faded). *Moorhouse.* $16/£10

MERTON, THOMAS. A Man in the Divided Sea. (NY: New Directions, 1946.) 1st ed. Black cl. Fine in black/gray dj. *Bromer.* $185/£119

MERTON, THOMAS. Original Child Bomb. New Directions, 1962. 1st Amer ed. One of 8000 ptd. Ptd bds (dk spot spine top). *Polyanthos.* $30/£19

MERTON, THOMAS. A Secular Journal. London: Hollis & Carter, 1959. 1st UK ed. NF in dj. *Moorhouse.* $16/£10

MERTON, THOMAS. Seeds of Contemplation. (Norfolk, CT): New Directions, (1949). 1st ed. Burlap-cvrd bds. VF in dj. *Bromer.* $300/£192

MERTON, THOMAS. The Seven Story Mountain. NY, (1948). 1st ed. 8vo. 1st state binding: white cl lettered in black. VG in 2nd state dj w/caption 'author on the left.' (1-inch chip rear panel.) *Argosy.* $600/£385

MERTON, THOMAS. The Silent Life. NY: FSC, (1957). 1st ed. Fine in NF dj (sm stain rear panel). *Between The Covers.* $100/£64

MERTON, THOMAS. St. Maedoc. N.p.: Unicorn, 1970. 1st ed. One of 300. Broadside. Fine. *Turlington.* $85/£54

MERTON, THOMAS. Thirty Poems. Norfolk, CT: New Directions, (1944). 1st ed. VG overall (eps sl browned; sm dent rear bd) in dj (partly worn, tape-mended gouge rear panel). *Waverly*.* $110/£71

MERTON, THOMAS. Thirty Poems. Norfolk: New Directions, (1944). 1st ed, 1st bk. Fine in dj (lt used, sm chip). *Captain's Bookshelf.* $300/£192

MERTON, THOMAS. Thoughts in Solitude. NY: FSC, (1958). 1st ed. Fine in VF dj (extrems sl rubbed). *Between The Covers.* $100/£64

MERTON, THOMAS. The Waters of Silence. London: Hollis & Carter, 1950. 1st ed. Frontis, 16 pp plts. (Spine lt rubbed, 2 spots upper bd.) Dj (extrems sl rubbed). *Hollett.* $39/£25

MERTON, THOMAS. What Are These Wounds. Milwaukee: Bruce Pub Co, (1950). 1st ed. (Eps dknd), else Fine in dj (lt worn, soiled). *Hermitage.* $90/£58

MERTON, THOMAS. What Is Contemplation? Holy Cross, IN: Notre Dame, 1948. 1st ed. Fine in stapled ptd salmon wraps. *Lame Duck.* $150/£96

MERYMAN, RICHARD. Andrew Wyeth. Boston, 1968. Obl folio. Dj (edge tears). *Swann*.* $46/£29

MERYMAN, RICHARD. Andrew Wyeth. Boston, 1968. 1st ed. Dj. *Kane*.* $110/£71

MESERVE, FREDERICK HILL and CARL SANDBURG. The Photographs of Abraham Lincoln. NY, (1944). Signed by Meserve. (Pastedowns discolored), o/w VG in dj (sl worn). *Hayman.* $25/£16

MESERVE, FREDERICK HILL and CARL SANDBURG. The Photographs of Abraham Lincoln. NY: Harcourt, Brace, (1944). 1st ed. 94 photos. VG. *Wantagh.* $75/£48

METCALF, EDWIN. Personal Incidents in the Early Campaigns of the Third Regiment Rhode Island Volunteers and the Tenth Army Corps. Providence, RI, 1879. 1st ed. Ltd to 250. PNRISSHS Series 1, #9. 31pp. NF in ptd wrappers. *Mcgowan.* $45/£29

METCALF, M. M. An Outline of the Theory of Organic Evolution.... NY: Macmillan, (1906). 2nd rev ed. 101 plts. VG. *Mikesh.* $25/£16

METCALF, P. James Knowles, Victorian Editor and Architect. OUP, 1980. 17 plts. Sound in dj. *Ars Artis.* $55/£35

METCALF, PAUL. Patagoni. NC: Jargon Soc, 1971. 1st Amer ed. Pict cvrs (sl sunned, soiled, sm tear rear panel). *Polyanthos.* $35/£22

METCALF, SAMUEL L. A Collection of the Most Interesting Narratives of Indian Warfare in the West.... Lexington, KY: Wm. G. Hunt, 1821. 1st ed. Contemp mottled calf (sl wormed). Very Decent (corner 1st few ll sl dampstained, lacks errata, inscrips fr pastedown, fep, tp). Howes M560. *Sadlon.* $3,250/£2,083

METCALFE, JOHN. The Feasting Dead. Sauk City: Arkham House, (1954). 1st ed. Dj. *Swann*.* $69/£44

METCALFE, JOHN. The Feasting Dead. Sauk City, 1954. 1st ed. One of 1200. Fine in Fine dj. *Mcclintock.* $150/£96

METCALFE, JOHN. The Smoking Leg and Other Stories. Doubleday Page, 1926. 1st US ed. VG (sl foxed) in dec orange cl. *Certo.* $45/£29

METCALFE, RICHARD. The Rise and Progress of Hydropathy in England and Scotland. London, 1912. Grn cl bds (worn). Good. *Doctor's Library.* $50/£32

METCALFE, SAMUEL L. Caloric: Its Mechanical, Chemical, and Vital Agencies in the Phenomena of Nature. London: Pickering, 1843. 1st ed. 2 vols. 1100pp + errata, index. Orig cl (rubbed, ex-lib), paper labels. *Argosy.* $125/£80

METCHNIKOFF, ELIE. The Nature of Man, Studies in Optimistic Philosophy. London, 1903. 1st ed in English. VG. *Fye.* $100/£64

METCHNIKOFF, ELIE. The Nature of Man. London: Heinemann, 1903. 1st ed in English. VG. *White.* $59/£38

METHVIN, J. J. Andele, or The Mexican-Kiowa Captive.... Louisville, KY, 1899. 1st ed. 184pp. (Ink name; cvrs rubbed, soiled.) *King.* $75/£48

METRAUX, ALFRED. Voodoo. NY: OUP, 1959. 1st Amer ed. NF (spine top sl sunned) in dj (sm piece missing, sm edge tear). *Polyanthos.* $35/£22

Metropolitan Grievances; Or, A Serio-Comedic Glance at Minor Mischiefs in London and Its Vicinity.... London, 1812. 1st ed. Fldg frontis by George Cruikshank, 195pp. (Bkpls, sl waterstain tp; bd hinges cracked, fr hinge very loose; spine badly chipped.) Slipcase (worn, label defective). *King.* $85/£54

METTLER, CECILIA. History of Medicine. Phila, 1947. 1st ed. VG. *Fye.* $150/£96

METZKER, RAY K. Sand Creatures. Millerton, NY: Aperture, 1979. 1st ed. NF in stiff wrappers. *Cahan.* $35/£22

METZNER, SHEILA. Objects of Desire. NY: Clarkson N. Potter, 1986. 1st ed. VG (inscrip) in VG dj. *Smith.* $75/£48

MEUWISSEN, T. J. J. H. X-Ray Atlas and Manual of Esophagus, Stomach and Duodenum. Amsterdam, 1955. VG. *Argosy*. $75/£48

MEW, JAMES. Types from Spanish Story, or the Old Manners and Customs of Castile. London: J.C. Nimmo & Bain, 1884. 37 tipped-in proof etchings. Dec cl (sl worn). Contents VG. *New Hampshire**. $25/£16

MEYER, ADOLF. The Collected Papers of Adolf Meyer. Volume IV: Mental Hygiene. Balt: Johns Hopkins Univ, 1951. 1st ed. Frontis. Blue buckram. (Bkpl, stamp feps), else VG. *Gach*. $85/£54

MEYER, ADOLF. The Commonsense Psychiatry of Dr. Adolf Meyer: Fifty-Two Selected Papers. Alfred Lief (ed). NY: McGraw-Hill, 1948. 1st trade ed. Frontis port. Brn cl. VG in dj (lt worn). *Gach*. $50/£32

MEYER, ADOLF. Psychobiology. Eunice Winters and Anna Mae Bowers (eds). Springfield: Charles C. Thomas, 1957. (Rear bd sl soiled), o/w Fine in Fine dj (spine sl dknd). *Beasley*. $60/£38

MEYER, ARTHUR. An Analysis of De Generatione Animalium of William Harvey. Stanford, 1936. 1st ed. VG in dj. *Fye*. $50/£32

MEYER, EDITH PATTERSON. Not Charity, but Justice. NY: Vanguard, 1974. 1st ed. Fine in dj. *Cahan*. $65/£42

MEYER, F. W. Rock and Water Gardens. London, (1910). *Wheldon & Wesley*. $28/£18

MEYER, F. W. Rock and Water Gardens. Country Life, n.d. c.(1910). (Lt foxed; spine lt sunned.) *Edwards*. $39/£25

MEYER, FRANZ. Marc Chagall. NY: Abrams, (1964). (Sl worn.) Dj (sl frayed). *Oinonen**. $80/£51

MEYER, FRANZ. Marc Chagall: Life and Work. NY: Abrams, (1964). 53 tipped-in color plts. VG in VG dj. *Waverly**. $44/£28

MEYER, JOHN D. A Handbook of Old Mechanical Penny Banks. Tyrone: Meyer, 1948. 1st ed. Signed. Few orig inserts laid in. Pict eps. Navy cl, pict lt blue bds (edges lt sunned, rubbed), gilt. Pict dj (sl chipped, long tears). *Baltimore**. $30/£19

MEYER, ROY W. The Village Indians of the Upper Missouri. (NE: Univ of NE, 1977). 1st ed. 5 maps. Grn cl. VF in dj. *Argonaut*. $45/£29

MEYER, WILLIAM E. The Sailor on Horseback. Providence, RI, 1912. 1st ed. Ltd to 250. PNRISSHS Series 7, #5. NF in ptd wrappers. *Mcgowan*. $45/£29

MEYEROWITZ, EVA L. R. At the Court of an African King. London: Faber & Faber, 1962. 1st ed. 16 plts. VG in dj. *Worldwide*. $18/£12

MEYEROWITZ, JOEL. Cape Light. Boston: Museum of Fine Arts/NYGS, 1978. 1st ed. 40 full-pg color photo plts. NF (owner stamp) in pict stiff wrappers. *Cahan*. $40/£26

MEYEROWITZ, JOEL. A Summer's Day. NY: Times, 1985. 1st ed. Fine in Fine dj. *Smith*. $55/£35

MEYEROWITZ, JOEL. Wild Flowers. NY: Little Brown, 1983. 1st ed. VG+ in VG+ dj. *Smith*. $35/£22

MEYNELL, ALICE. The Children. NY/London: John Lane, Bodley Head, 1897. 1st ed, Amer issue. Teg, rest uncut. Pict dec loose-woven oatmeal buckram (spine sl dknd). VG. *Maggs*. $55/£35

MEYNELL, FRANCIS. A.M. A Keepsake for the A.I.G.A. London: Francis Meynell, 1930. NF in dec stiff paper wraps (rubbed). *Blue Mountain*. $15/£10

MEYNELL, FRANCIS. My Lives. London: Bodley Head, 1971. 1st ed. VG in dj. *Cox*. $23/£15

MEYNERT, THEODOR. Psychiatry: A Clinical Treatise on Diseases of the Fore-Brain...Part I. Bernard Sachs (trans). NY/London: Putnam/Knickerbocker, 1885. 1st ed in English. (xii),285,(7)pp; color litho. Grn cl (lt stained; lib bkpl, stamp tp). Good+. *Gach*. $150/£96

MEYRICK, SAMUEL. A Critical Inquiry into Ancient Armor. London, 1824. 3 vols. 80 aquatint, 69 hand-colored plts. (Rubbed, bumped; ex-lib, stickers inside cvr, blindstamp on most pp, incl plts; sl foxing along edges.) *Metropolitan**. $603/£387

MEYRINK, GUSTAV. The Golem. Boston: Houghton Mifflin, 1928. 1st Amer ed. VG+ in VG dj (price-clipped, sm puncture). *Lame Duck*. $100/£64

MEZZROW, MEZZ and BERNARD WOLFE. Really the Blues. NY: Random House, 1946. 1st ed. NF in dj (worn, torn; chip center spine). *Beasley*. $60/£38

MICHAEL, D. J. (Pseud of Charles Einstein.) Win or Else. Lion, 1954. Pb orig. Good+. *Plapinger*. $22/£14

MICHAELS, BARBARA. (Pseud of Elizabeth Peters.) The Grey Beginning. NY: Congdon & Weed, 1984. 1st ed. Signed. VG in VG dj. *Old London*. $35/£22

MICHALOWSKI, KAZIMIERZ. Art of Ancient Egypt. NY: Abrams, (1968). 2nd ed. Good. *Archaeologia*. $225/£144

MICHALOWSKI, KAZIMIERZ. Great Sculpture of Ancient Egypt. NY: Reynal & William Morrow, 1978. 32 color plts. Good in dj. *Archaeologia*. $65/£42

MICHALS, DUANE. The Photographic Illusion. Dobbs Ferry: Alskog, 1975. 1st ed. VG in wrappers. *Smith*. $35/£22

MICHALS, DUANE. Take One and See Mt. Fujiyama and Other Stories. Rochester: Stefan Mihal Book, 1976. 1st ed. 54 full-pg b/w photos. NF in translucent ptd wrappers. *Cahan*. $100/£64

MICHAUD, JEAN-CLAUDE and ROLAND. Korea. A Jade Paradise. UK: Thames & Hudson/Vendome, 1981. 1st ed. 78 color plts. VG in dj. *Worldwide*. $40/£26

MICHAUD, JOSEPH. History of the Crusades. Phila, n.d. (ca 1880). 2 vols. 364; 360pp (sl spotted); 100 full-pg plts by Gustave Dore, tissue guards. 3/4 leather (soiled, worn, vol 1 fr hinge cracked, crudely repaired w/cl tape). *King*. $250/£160

MICHAUX, F. ANDREW. The North American Sylva. Phila, 1865. 3 vols. 184; 180; 180pp; 154 (of 156) color plts (1 loose). Aeg. 3/4 leather (ex-lib, mkd). *King*. $1,500/£962

MICHAUX, HENRI. A Barbarian in Asia. Sylvia Beach (trans). NY: New Directions, 1949. 1st ed in English. NF in VG dj (edgetorn, chipped). *Lame Duck*. $50/£32

MICHAUX, HENRI. Infinite Turbulence. London: Caldar & Boyars, 1975. 1st British ed. NF in dj. *Lame Duck*. $45/£29

MICHAUX, HENRI. Light Through Darkness. NY: Orion, 1963. 1st ed in English. VG in dj. *Sclanders*. $23/£15

MICHEAUX, OSCAR. The Masquerade. NY: Book Supply, (1947). 1st ed. (Sm stain few pg edges; sm nick spine base; lacks dj.) *Between The Covers*. $125/£80

MICHEAUX, OSCAR. The Story of Dorothy Stansfield. NY: Book Supply, 1946. 1st ed. (Crayon price fep; spine base sl worn, sl frayed), else VG (lacks dj). *Between The Covers*. $100/£64

MICHEL, EMILE. Great Masters of Landscape Painting. Phila: Lippincott, 1910. 1st ed. Blue cl, gilt. Good in dj (chipped). *Karmiole*. $100/£64

MICHEL, PAUL HENRI. The Cosmology of Giordano Bruno. R. E. W. Maddison (trans). Paris/London/Ithaca: Hermann/Methuen/Cornell Univ, (1973). Rust cl, gilt. Fine in dj. *Blue Mountain*. $50/£32

MICHELL, E. B. The Art and Practice of Hawking. London: Methuen, 1900. 1st ed. 3 photogravures. Teg. VG (lt spotted, eps lt browned; spine faded, sl dented). *Hollett*. $250/£160

MICHELSON, T. Notes on the Buffalo-Head Dance of the Thunder Gens of the Fox Indians. BAE Bulletin 87. Washington: Smithsonian, 1928. 1st ed. NF. *Mikesh*. $30/£19

MICHENER, C. D. The Social Behavior of the Bees. Cambridge: Harvard, 1974. 1st ed. VG + in VG dj. *Mikesh*. $27/£17

MICHENER, JAMES A. About Centennial. NY: Random House, (1974). 1st ed. Ltd to 3200. Dec eps. Mint in dj. *Jaffe*. $75/£48

MICHENER, JAMES A. The Bridge at Andau. NY: Random House, 1957. 1st ed. (Speckles feps, offsetting tp), o/w NF in dj (lt used). *Beasley*. $50/£32

MICHENER, JAMES A. Caravans. NY: Random House, (1963). 1st ed. Fine in dj. *Between The Covers*. $125/£80

MICHENER, JAMES A. Centennial. NY: Random House, (1974). One of 500 numbered, signed. Fine in Fine slipcase. *Lenz*. $250/£160

MICHENER, JAMES A. Chesapeake. NY: Random House, (1978). One of 500 numbered, signed. Fine in Fine slipcase. *Lenz*. $200/£128

MICHENER, JAMES A. Chesapeake. NY: Random House, (1978). 1st ed. NF in slipcase, illus label (sl rubbed). *Unger*. $250/£160

MICHENER, JAMES A. The Covenant. NY: Random House, (1980). One of 500 numbered, signed. Fine in Fine slipcase. *Lenz*. $200/£128

MICHENER, JAMES A. The Drifters. NY, 1971. 1st ed. NF in VG + dj. *Warren*. $50/£32

MICHENER, JAMES A. Facing East. NY, 1970. One of 2500 numbered, signed by Michener and Jack Levine (illus). 2 parts. Folio. Contents loose in silk folder, leather wallet as issued. Silk fldg case (sl soiled). *Swann**. $230/£147

MICHENER, JAMES A. Facing East. NY: Maecelas Press, Random House, 1970. 4 color lithos by Jack Levine. 2 parts in clamshell box. (Box sl soiled), o/w Fine set. *Metropolitan**. $115/£74

MICHENER, JAMES A. Hawaii. NY, (1959). 1st ed. One of 400. Signed. Acetate dj. *Kane**. $325/£208

MICHENER, JAMES A. Hawaii. NY: Random House, (1959). 1st ed. (Bd edges sl dknd), else Fine in Fine dj (spine, extrems sl dknd, crown lt worn, price-clipped). *Between The Covers*. $150/£96

MICHENER, JAMES A. Hawaii. NY: Random House, (1959). (Bds sl foxed), else Fine in dj (lt tanned). *Between The Covers*. $175/£112

MICHENER, JAMES A. Hawaii. NY: Random House, (1959). 1st ed. Top edge stained gray, uncut. Beige cl. VG in dj (nicks). *Houle*. $250/£160

MICHENER, JAMES A. Hawaii. NY: Random House, 1959. 1st ed. NF in dj (spine lt tanned, long creases fr flap). *Lame Duck*. $150/£96

MICHENER, JAMES A. The Hokusai Sketchbooks: Selections from the Manga. Rutland: Tuttle, (1958). 2nd ptg. Fine in dj (sm tear, price-clipped), slipcase (lt used). *Captain's Bookshelf*. $75/£48

MICHENER, JAMES A. Iberia. NY: Random House, (1968). One of 500 numbered, signed. Fine in Fine dj, slipcase. *Lenz*. $275/£176

MICHENER, JAMES A. Iberia: Spanish Travels and Reflections. NY: Random House, (1968). 1st ed. Fine in dj (sl rubbed, sm tear). *Captain's Bookshelf*. $75/£48

MICHENER, JAMES A. Japanese Prints. Rutland, VT/Tokyo: Charles E. Tuttle, (1959). 257 plts (55 color). NF in dj (sl edgeworn), slipcase (soiled, worn). *Waverly**. $77/£49

MICHENER, JAMES A. Legacy. NY: Random House, (1987). One of 500 numbered, signed. Fine in Fine slipcase. *Lenz*. $100/£64

MICHENER, JAMES A. Mexico. NY: Random House, (1992). One of 400 numbered, signed. Fine in Fine slipcase. *Lenz*. $175/£112

MICHENER, JAMES A. A Michener Miscellany, 1950-1970. NY: Random House, 1973. 1st ed. Fine in NF dj (short tear). *Beasley*. $45/£29

MICHENER, JAMES A. Poland. NY: Random House, (1983). One of 500 numbered, signed. Fine in Fine slipcase. *Lenz*. $150/£96

MICHENER, JAMES A. Poland. NY: Random House, (1983). 1st ed. Ltd to 500 specially bound, signed. Dec eps. Mint in slipcase. *Jaffe*. $175/£112

MICHENER, JAMES A. Poland. NY: Random House, 1983. 1st ed. Signed. (Sl edgewear.) Dj (creases, sm chips, short tears). *Metropolitan**. $57/£37

MICHENER, JAMES A. Sayonara. NY: Random House, (1954). 1st ed. VG (bds sl soiled; corners sl worn; sl yellowing pp edges) in dj (lamination peel). *Between The Covers*. $85/£54

MICHENER, JAMES A. Sayonara: A Japanese-American Love Story. NY: Random House, (1954). 1st ed. Fine in VF dj (laminate peeling). *Book Market*. $100/£64

MICHENER, JAMES A. The Source. NY: Random House, (1965). 1st ed. NF in dj (sl rubbing). *Between The Covers*. $50/£32

MICHENER, JAMES A. Space. NY: Random House, (1982). 1st ed. Fine in Fine dj (nick). *Unger*. $50/£32

MICHENER, JAMES A. Space. NY: Random House, (1982). One of 500 numbered, signed. Fine in Fine slipcase. *Lenz*. $150/£96

MICHENER, JAMES A. Space. NY: Random House, (1982). 1st ed. Ltd to 500 specially bound, signed. Dec eps. Mint in slipcase (lt faded). *Jaffe*. $175/£112

MICHENER, JAMES A. Sports in America. NY: Random House, 1976. 1st ed. Fine in dj. *Associates*. $50/£32

MICHENER, JAMES A. Texas. NY: Random House, (1985). 1st ed. One of 1000 specially-bound, numbered, signed. Fine in slipcase. *Captain's Bookshelf*. $200/£128

MICHENER, JAMES A. Texas. NY: Random House, (1985). One of 1000 numbered, signed. Fine in cardbd slipcase as issued. *Between The Covers*. $225/£144

MICHENER, JAMES A. Texas. Austin: Univ of TX, (1986). 1st ed thus. 2 vols. Separate blue/red cl bindings, each spine w/half a star. Fine in slipcase (sl soiled). *Waverly**. $33/£21

MICHENER, JAMES A. The Voice of Asia. NY: Random House, (1951). 1st ed. NF in dj (spine extrems worn). *Captain's Bookshelf*. $125/£80

MICHENER, JAMES A. and A. GROVE DAY. Rascals in Paradise: True Tales of High Adventure in the South Pacific. London: Secker & Warburg, (1957). 1st Eng ed. Fine in NF dj (foxing rear panel; lt stain spine). *Between The Covers*. $175/£112

MICHENER, JAMES A. and A. GROVE DAY. Rascals in Paradise: True Tales of High Adventure in the South Pacific. NY: Random House, (1957). 1st ed. Fine (sl soiling fep) in VG + dj (chipped). *Between The Covers*. $150/£96

MICHIGAN PIONEER AND HISTORICAL SOCIETY. Historical Collections...Vol 14. Lansing, 1890. viii,720pp (reps removed). Good (spine rubbed, sm hole). *Bohling*. $20/£13

MICKEL, JERE C. Footlights on the Prairie. St. Cloud: North Star, 1974. 1st ed. Pict eps. Fine in Good dj. *Connolly*. $27/£17

Mickey Mouse Story Book. Phila: David McKay, (1931). 1st ed. 8.5x6. 62pp (inner hinges broken, fr one crudely repaired). Cl (worn, soiled), color pict label. *King*. $125/£80

Mickey Mouse's Summer Vacation. Racine, WI: Whitman, 1948. 6.5x4.5. Pict bds. (Sl wear), else VG. *King.* $35/£22

MICKLE, ISAAC. A Gentleman of Much Promise. Philip English Mackey (ed). Univ of PA, 1977. 2 vols. Fine in slipcase. *Bohling.* $22/£14

MICKLE, WILLIAM ENGLISH. Well Known Confederate Veterans and Their War Records. New Orleans: Wm. E. Mickle, 1907. Letter tipped in. VG (lacks rep; cvr sl speckled). *Mcgowan.* $500/£321

MICKLE, WILLIAM JULIUS. General Paralysis of the Insane. London: H.K. Lewis, 1880. 1st ed. vi,(i),246pp + 24pp pub's cat. Maroon cl (rebacked, preserving spine). (Tp sl spotted), o/w VG. *White.* $44/£28

MICKLE, WILLIAM JULIUS. General Paralysis of the Insane. London: H.K. Lewis, 1880. 1st ed. (viii),246,(2)pp + 24-pg inserted cat dated Jan 1880. Panelled mauve cl (spine faded, corners bumped, hinges cracked; lib stamp tp, bkpl). Good. *Gach.* $150/£96

MIDDELDORF, ULRICH. Raphael's Drawings. NY, 1945. 61 plts. Good. *Washton.* $65/£42

MIDDLEBROOK, LOUIS F. Seals of Maritime New England. Salem: Essex Inst, 1926. (Bkpl; sticker fr cvr), else Very Nice. *Parmer.* $50/£32

MIDDLETON, J. HENRY. The Engraved Gems of Classical Times with a Catalogue.... Cambridge: CUP, 1891. xvi,157pp + xxxvi (appendix); 2 plts. (Bkpl.) Teg. *Archaeologia.* $125/£80

MIDDLETON, J. HENRY. The Engraved Gems of Classical Times. Cambridge: CUP, 1891. xvi,157,xxxvi,(i)pp; 2 plts in appendix. (Lib bkpl pastedown, stamp erased tp.) Black buckram gilt (sl rubbed). *Hollett.* $117/£75

MIDDLETON, RICHARD. The Ghost Ship.... Eden: Aries, 1926. One of 300 ptd. Cl, marbled bds (edgewear, spine crown pulled). Good. *Reese.* $20/£13

MIDDLETON, W. E. KNOWLES. The History of the Barometer. Balt: Johns Hopkins Univ, (1964). 1st ed. VG in dj (spine faded, corners worn, bumped). *Weber.* $175/£112

MIDDLETON, W. E. KNOWLES. A History of the Theories of Rain and Other Forms of Precipitation. NY, 1966. 1st Amer ed. VG. *Fye.* $30/£19

MIDDLETON, W. E. KNOWLES. A History of the Thermometer and Its Use in Meteorology. Balt: Johns Hopkins, (1966). 1st ed. Frontis. Pict cl. VF in dj. *Glaser.* $50/£32

MIDDLETON, W. E. KNOWLES. Invention of the Meteorological Instruments. Balt: J.H.U., (1969). 1st ed. Blue cl, pict bds. Fine in VG dj (price-clipped, spine lt sunned). *Baltimore*.* $80/£51

MIDDLETON, WILLIAM D. The Time of the Trolley. (Milwaukee): Kalmbach, (1967). 1st ed. Pict eps. Orange cl, brn cl backstrip. Fine in NF dj. *Harrington.* $60/£38

MIDGLEY, W. and A. E. V. LILLEY. A Book of Studies in Plant Form and Design. 1910. Enlgd ed. Dec cl. (Prize label, sl rubbed), o/w Good+. *Whittle.* $39/£25

MIERAS, J. P. and F. R. YERBURY. Dutch Architecture of the XXth Century. London: Benn, 1926. 100 plts. Sound. *Ars Artis.* $55/£35

MIERS, EARL SCHENCK. The General Who Marched to Hell. NY, 1951. 1st ed. VG+ in VG+ dj. *Pratt.* $35/£22

MIERS, EARL SCHENCK. The Web of Victory. NY, 1955. 1st ed. 3 maps. Fine (bkpl remains) in dj (repaired). *Wantagh.* $25/£16

MIGOT, ANDRE. Thin Edge of the World. Boston: Little, Brown, 1956. 1st Amer ed. Grey cl. VG in dj (worn). *Parmer.* $35/£22

Migratory Cotton Pickers in Arizona. Washington: GPO, 1939. Frontis photo. (Ex-lib), else Good in wraps. *Dumont.* $35/£22

MIKKELSEN, EJNAR. Lost in the Arctic...1909-1912. Heinemann, 1913. 1st ed. Lg fldg map. VG (sl rubbed). VG. *Cox.* $133/£85

MILBANK, JEREMIAH, JR. The First Century of Flight in America. Princeton, NJ: Princeton Univ, (1943). 1st ed. 24 plts. VG in dj (stained). *Glaser.* $95/£61

MILBANK, JEREMIAH, JR. The First Century of Flight in America. Princeton: Princeton Univ, (1943). 1st ed. Fine in dj (label removed from spine). *Hermitage.* $85/£54

MILBURN, GEORGE. The Hobo's Hornbook. NY: Ives Washburn, 1930. 1st ed. VG. *Perier.* $45/£29

MILBURN, WILLIAM HENRY. Rifle, Axe, and Saddle-Bags, and Other Lectures. NY: Derby & Jackson, 1857. Frontis port, 309pp (foxing, lt stain upper corner; cl faded). *Bohling.* $30/£19

MILES, A. G. A Fisherman's Breeze. NY: Brentano's, 1924. 1st ed. VG+ in VG dj. *Mikesh.* $45/£29

MILES, CHARLES. Indian and Eskimo Artifacts of North America. Chicago, 1963. Fine. *Oregon.* $40/£26

MILES, CHARLES. Indian and Eskimo Artifacts of North America. Chicago: Henry Regnery, 1963. 1st ed. 6 color plts. Grn cl. Fine in pict dj (spine dknd). *Argonaut.* $50/£32

MILES, EDMUND. An Epitome, Historical and Statistical, Descriptive of the Royal Naval Service of England. London: Ackermann, 1841. 1st ed. 8 hand-colored engr plts, 14 hand-colored wood-engr flags. (Inscrip, lt spotting.) Orig red roan-backed pict cl (corners rubbed), gilt. *Christie's*.* $315/£202

MILES, HENRY DOWNES. British Field Sports. London: Mackenzie, n.d. (ca 1860). 50 lithos (16 hand-colored). Contemp 3/4 leather (rubbed, stained; foxed; 1.5-inch tear tp repaired on verso). *Oinonen*.* $450/£288

MILES, HENRY DOWNES. Pugilistica. Edinburgh, 1906. 3 vols. (Lt water-staining upper edge of plates all vols; cl sl bubbled, afecting prelims; spines sunned, sl chipped; lower joint vol 1 split; bds sl warped.) *Edwards.* $312/£200

MILES, NELSON A. Personal Recollections and Observations of General Nelson A. Miles. Chicago/NY: Werner, 1896. 1st ed, 1st issue w/caption under frontis port reading 'General Nelson A. Miles.' vii,590pp (bkpl, name). Pict brn cl stamped in gold/silver/black. Overall Fine (lt rubbed). Howes M595. *Argonaut.* $350/£224

MILES, NELSON A. Personal Recollections and Observations of General Nelson A. Miles.... Chicago, 1896. 1st ed. 590pp, port. Pict cl (spine sl faded). Howes M595. *Ginsberg.* $150/£96

MILES, RICHARD. That Cold Day in the Park. NY: Delacorte, (1965). 1st ed, 1st bk. (Extrems rubbed), else NF in dj (sl worn). *Hermitage.* $65/£42

MILES, W. J. Modern Practical Farriery. London: William Mackenzie, n.d. (1890s). (2),538,vi,96,viipp; 48 plts. VG in contemp crimson 1/2 morocco, gilt. *Cox.* $148/£95

MILES, WILLIAM. Journal of the Sufferings and Hardships of Capt. Parker H. French's Overland Expedition to California. (NY: Cadmus Book Shop, 1916.) One of 250. Ptd wrappers. *Dawson.* $50/£32

MILHOUSE, KATHERINE. Snow over Bethlehem. NY: Scribner, 1945. 1st ed. 8vo. 98pp. VG in dj (sl rubbed). *Dower.* $35/£22

Military Exploits,...of Don Juan Martin Diez, the Empeciando.... (By Charles William Doyle.) London: Carpenter, 1823. Frontis port; viii,174pp; fldg map. Paper over bds; ptd spine label. (Rubbed; expertly rebacked; foxing), else VG. *Cahan.* $225/£144

Military Operations in Jefferson County, Virginia (and West Va.) 1861-1865. Jefferson County Camp U.C.V., 1911. Map. Stiff wraps (soiled, sl worn). *King.* $65/£42

MILIZIA, FRANCESCO. The Lives of the Celebrated Architects, Ancient and Modern.... Mrs. Edwards Cresy (trans). London: J. Taylor, 1826. 2 vols. lxxii,351; 454pp. New cl, 1/2 cl; paper labels. *Ars Artis.* $328/£210

MILIZIA, FRANCESCO. The Lives of the Celebrated Architects. Mrs. Edward Cresy (trans). London: J. Taylor, 1826. 2 vols. lxxviii,351; (iv),454pp + (i) ads. (Pencil notes, lt spotted, ink stamps; upper hinges cracked.) Marbled eps; teg, rest uncut. 1/2 calf, cl bds (fr bd vol 2 soiled; sl rubbed), leather labels. *Edwards.* $187/£120

MILL, HUGH ROBERT. The Life of Sir Ernest Shackleton. Boston: Little, Brown, 1923. 1st US ed. Map. (Spine title dull), else VG. *High Latitude.* $70/£45

MILL, HUGH ROBERT. The Siege of the South Pole. NY: Stokes, 1905. 1st US ed. Lg fldg map. Dec cl. (Map tear, no loss), else VG. *High Latitude.* $100/£64

MILL, JAMES. The History of British India. London: James Madden/Piper et al, 1858. 10 vols complete. xl,376; vi,374; viii,456; viii,412; vii,452; viii,480; xv,436; xv,436; xv,415; (index vol)(iv),86pp,(2)ads. Last 3 vols unopened. Dec blind-stamped cl. (Few vols sl pencilled; lt rubbed, few vols sl mottled, 1 spine faded), else VG set. *Cahan.* $225/£144

MILL, JOHN STUART. Autobiography. Longmans et al, 1873. 1st ed. vi,313,(3)pp, prelim blank, final ad leaf. Brn eps. VG (label, lib stamps). *Cox.* $117/£75

MILL, JOHN STUART. Autobiography. London: Longmans et al, 1873. 1st ed, 1st issue (w/o errata). vi,313,(i)pp + 2 ads (sl marginal worming). Grn cl (bumped, rubbed, spine head chipped). VG. *Blue Mountain.* $85/£54

MILL, JOHN STUART. Autobiography. London: Longmans, Green, 1873. 1st ed, 1st issue w/ad leaf, no errata. Grn cl, gilt. (Sl rubbed), else NF. *Macdonnell.* $200/£128

MILL, JOHN STUART. Autobiography. London: Longmans, Green, Reader, & Dyer, 1873. *Rostenberg & Stern.* $425/£272

MILL, JOHN STUART. The Subjection of Women. NY: Appleton, 1869. 1st Amer ed. 8vo. (Bk ticket.) *Rostenberg & Stern.* $750/£481

MILL, JOHN STUART. The Subjection of Women. NY: Appleton, 1870. 2nd US ed. 188pp. VG (spine top sl worn). *Second Life.* $150/£96

MILLAIS, J. G. Far Away Up the Nile. London, 1924. (Lt marginal foxing; binding sl faded.) *Petersfield.* $70/£45

MILLAIS, J. G. Life of Frederick C. Selous.... London: Longmans, Green, 1918. 16 plts. (Rubbed, worn.) *Adelson.* $45/£29

MILLAIS, J. G. The Natural History of British Surface-Feeding Ducks. Longmans, Green, 1902. 1st ed. #308/600. 8vo. 6 photogravures, 41 color plts. Teg. NF in 2-tone cl. *Cox.* $757/£485

MILLAIS, J. G. Newfoundland and Its Untrodden Ways. London: Longmans, 1907. 2 maps, 87 plts. Pict cl (lt rubbed). *Adelson.* $80/£51

MILLAIS, J. G. Newfoundland and Its Untrodden Ways. London: Longmans, Green, 1907. 6 photogravures, 2 maps. Teg. Dec cl. VG. *High Latitude.* $110/£71

MILLAIS, J. G. Wanderings and Memories. London, 1919. 1st ed. 15 plts. Red cl, gilt. VG. *Price.* $65/£42

MILLAIS, J. G. The Wildfowler in Scotland. London: Longmans, 1901. 1st ed. 8 photogravures, 2 color plts. Teg. 1/2 vellum, bds. VG + . *Mikesh.* $350/£224

MILLAR, H. R. On the Railway. Blackie, n.d. (ca 1918). Folio. 12 full-pg pictures on thin-card glossy ll (sl chalking last pg). Pict bds (edges chipped, sl dusty), cl spine. Bright. *Bookmark.* $47/£30

MILLAR, KENNETH. Blue City. NY, 1947. 1st ed. Fine in Fine dj. *Mcclintock.* $500/£321

MILLAR, KENNETH. Trouble Follows Me. NY: Dodd Mead, 1946. 1st ed. (Bkpl removed fep; cvrs sl mottled.) Dj (sm chips, sl worn). *Else Fine.* $1,250/£801

MILLAR, MARGARET. Experiment in Springtime. NY: Random House, 1947. 1st ed. VG + in dj (spine top lt chipping, edgewear). *Janus.* $45/£29

MILLAR, MARGARET. How Like an Angel. NY: Random House, (1962). 1st ed. Fine in NF dj (2 sl spine rubs). *Between The Covers.* $50/£32

MILLAR, MARGARET. A Stranger in My Grave. NY, (1960). 1st ed. Fine in VG dj (lt shelfworn, price-clipped). *Mcclintock.* $20/£13

MILLAR, MARGARET. A Stranger in My Grave. NY: Random House, (1960). 1st ed. NF in VG dj (short tears; lt scratched). *Between The Covers.* $45/£29

MILLAR, OLIVER. The Tudor, Stuart, and Early Georgian Pictures in the Collection of Her Majesty the Queen. London, 1963. 2 vols. 5 plts. Good. *Washton.* $90/£58

MILLAR, WILLIAM. Plastering. Batsford, 1897. xvi,604pp; 52 full-pg plts. Lib morocco-backed cl bds (rebound; spine sl rubbed, spine #s; ex-lib, ink stamps, margins lt browned, sl thumbed, bkpl), gilt. *Edwards.* $234/£150

MILLAY, EDNA ST. VINCENT. Conversation at Midnight. NY: Harper, 1937. 1st trade ed. Paper label. VG in dj. *Reese.* $30/£19

MILLAY, EDNA ST. VINCENT. Huntsman, What Quarry? NY: Harper, 1939. 1st ed stated. Full limp blue leather. VG in orig glassine wrapper, pub's box. *New Hampshire*.* $35/£22

MILLAY, EDNA ST. VINCENT. Huntsman, What Quarry? NY: Harper, 1939. One of 551 numbered, signed. VG. *Lenz.* $150/£96

MILLAY, EDNA ST. VINCENT. Make Bright the Arrows, 1940 Notebook. NY: Harper, 1940. 1st ed (one of 1550 this binding). Gilt limp blue pub's calf (spine ends lt rubbed). VG. *Reese.* $50/£32

MILLAY, EDNA ST. VINCENT. Wine from These Grapes. NY: Harper, 1934. 1st trade ed. Paper label. Fine in VG dj. *Reese.* $30/£19

MILLER, ALBERT G. History of the German Hospital of Philadelphia and Its Ex-Resident Physicians. Phila: Lippincott, 1906. 1st ed. Teg. (Pg torn; cl sl rubbed, sl shelfwear), else Good. *Brown.* $25/£16

MILLER, ARTHUR. After the Fall. NY: Viking, (1964). One of 500 signed. Fine in Fine slipcase. *Lenz.* $175/£112

MILLER, ARTHUR. Death of a Salesman. Cressett, 1949. 1st UK ed. VG + in VG dj (sl stained, spine sl faded, worn). *Williams.* $47/£30

MILLER, ARTHUR. Death of a Salesman. NY: Viking, 1949. 1st ed. (Irregularly sunned), else VG in VG dj (lt spine stain). *Pacific*.* $173/£111

MILLER, ARTHUR. Death of a Salesman. NY: Viking, 1949. 1st ed. (Name; lt stain rear bd), else NF in NF dj (lt stain; sl rubbing crown). *Between The Covers.* $300/£192

MILLER, ARTHUR. Death of a Salesman. NY: LEC, 1984. #1284/1500. Signed by Miller and Leonard Baskin (illus). Fine in slipcase. *Metropolitan*.* $69/£44

MILLER, ARTHUR. Salesman in Beijing. NY: Viking, (1984). 1st ed. Signed. Fine in Fine dj. *Lenz.* $50/£32

MILLER, BLANDINA DUDLEY. Sketch of Old Utica. (Utica, NY, 1895.) Presentation copy. 63pp. (Sl rubbed, soiled; fr hinge weak, lower 1/2 of tp loose at hinge.) *Bohling.* $20/£13

MILLER, C. W. Infant Baptism. St. Louis: Southwestern, 1872. 157pp. Text Clean (spine sunned, sl shelfwear). *Brown.* $15/£10

MILLER, C. WILLIAM. Benjamin Franklin's Philadelphia Printing, 1728-1766. Phila, 1974. Fine in dj (lt soiled, sm snag). *Bohling.* $45/£29

MILLER, DARLIS A. Soldiers and Settlers Military Supply in the Southwest 1861-1865. Albuquerque: Univ of NM, (1989). 1st ed. Fine in Fine dj. *Book Market.* $45/£29

MILLER, DAVID HUMPHREYS. Custer's Fall: The Indian Side of the Story. NY: Duell, Sloan & Pearce, (1957). 1st ed. VG in dj (sl worn). *Lien.* $50/£32

MILLER, EDGAR G., JR. American Antique Furniture. Balt: Lord Baltimore, 1937. 1st ed. 2 vols. (Paper subject tabs top margin.) Tan cl. *Karmiole.* $75/£48

MILLER, EDWARD GEE. Captain Edward Gee Miller of the 20th Wisconsin: His War 1861-1865. W. J. Lemke (ed). Fayetteville, 1960. 1st ed. Pict wraps. (Lt cvr wear, fading), o/w Fine. *Pratt.* $35/£22

MILLER, FRANCIS TREVELYAN (ed). The Photographic History of the Civil War. NY, 1911. 10 vols. Teg. Uniformly bound in blue cl, gilt. VG. *Truepenny.* $400/£256

MILLER, FRANCIS TREVELYAN (ed). The Photographic History of the Civil War. NY: Review of Reviews, 1911. 1st ed. 10 vols. Orig 1/2 leather, cl. VG set (extrems sl worn; vols 1, 7 lack sm spot of leather). *Mcgowan.* $450/£288

MILLER, HAZEN L. The Old Au Sable. Grand Rapids: Eerdmans, 1963. 1st ptg. Fine in dj. *Bowman.* $75/£48

MILLER, HENRY. Account of a Tour of the California Missions, 1856. (SF): Book Club of CA, 1952. One of 375. 19 plts. Vellum-backed patterned bds. Fine in Fine slipcase. *Harrington.* $150/£96

MILLER, HENRY. Collector's Quest. Richard Clement Wood (ed). Univ Press of VA, (1968). 1st ed. Fine in Fine dj. *Dermont.* $35/£22

MILLER, HENRY. A Devil in Paradise. NY: Signet, (1956). 1st ed. Pb orig. Fine. *Turtle Island.* $30/£19

MILLER, HENRY. First Impressions of Greece. Santa Barbara, CA: Capra, 1973. One of 250 numbered, signed. Fine. *Lenz.* $125/£80

MILLER, HENRY. Henry Miller's Book of Friends. Santa Barbara, CA: Capra, 1976. One of 250 numbered, signed. Fine. *Lenz.* $125/£80

MILLER, HENRY. Insomnia, or The Devil at Large. NY, 1974. 1st ed. VG in dj (sl chipped). *Words Etc.* $39/£25

MILLER, HENRY. Mother, China, and the World Beyond. Santa Barbara, CA: Capra, 1977. One of 250 numbered, signed. Fine. *Lenz.* $125/£80

MILLER, HENRY. On Turning Eighty. S.B.: Capra, 1972. 1st Amer ed. Fine in pict wrappers. *Polyanthos.* $20/£13

MILLER, HENRY. Order and Chaos Chez Hans Reichel. New Orleans: Loujon, (1966). One of 1399 signed. Fine in Fine dj, slipcase. *Lenz.* $100/£64

MILLER, HENRY. Reflections on the Death of Mishima. Santa Barbara: Capra, 1972. Ltd to 200 numbered, signed. Frontis port; pub's device on colophon. Brn cl-backed pict bds (bumped, sl rubbed, ink stain rear bd), ptd paper spine label. VG (bkpl removed). *Blue Mountain.* $150/£96

MILLER, HENRY. Reflections on the Maurizius Case. S.B.: Capra Press, 1974. #246/275 signed. Pict cvrs. Fine. *Polyanthos.* $60/£38

MILLER, HENRY. The Rosy Crucifixion. Book Two: Plexus. Paris: Olympia, (1953). 1st ed in English. One of 2000 numbered. 2 vols. VG in ptd wrappers (lt rubbed). *Cahan.* $150/£96

MILLER, HENRY. The Rosy Crucifixion. Book Two: Plexus. Paris: Olympia, (1953). 1st ed in English. Ltd to 2000 numbered. 2 vols. (Sl worn.) Wraps. *King.* $150/£96

MILLER, HENRY. The Smile at the Foot of the Ladder. NY, (1948). 1st ed. Fine in dj (lt edgeworn). *Argosy.* $250/£160

MILLER, HUGH. The Testimony of the Rocks. Boston: Gould & Lincoln, 1857. 1st Amer ed. (Corners, spine head sl rubbed.) *Sadlon.* $35/£22

MILLER, HUGH. The Testimony of the Rocks. London, 1858. 20th thousand. Frontis, xi,500pp. (Rebacked.) *Henly.* $23/£15

MILLER, HUGH. The Testimony of the Rocks. Edinburgh: Thomas Constable, 1860. 27th thousand. xii,454,(ii)pp. Blind-stamped cl (spine sl stained, ink shelf #s; lib labels eps), gilt. *Hollett.* $70/£45

MILLER, JAMES KNOX POLK. Road to Virginia City. Andrew F. Rolle (ed). Norman: Univ of OK, (1960). 1st ed. Dbl map. VG in dj (edgeworn). *Bohling.* $27/£17

MILLER, JOAQUIN. Songs of the Sierras. Roberts Bros, 1871. 1st ed. Teg, gilt-dec cvr. NF (rubbed). BAL 13751 (issue A, binding B). *Authors Of West.* $75/£48

MILLER, JOAQUIN. Songs of the Sierras. Boston: Roberts Bros, 1871. 1st US ed. Blanck's Issue A, based on ads at fr, in Binding B, w/wheel hub within spine imprint. 24-pg pub's cat at rear. Brn coated eps; teg. Red-brn cl (spine bottom stained, frayed; pp lt aged, sl foxed), gilt. BAL 13751. *Baltimore*.* $30/£19

MILLER, JOAQUIN. Unwritten History: Life Amongst the Modocs. Hartford, CT: American Pub Co, 1874. 1st Amer ed. Frontis port and frontis, 23 plts. Fine (rebound in cl). Howes M608. *Argonaut.* $150/£96

MILLER, JOHN G. The Black Patch War. Chapel Hill: UNC, 1936. 1st ed. VG. *Wantagh.* $45/£29

MILLER, JOHN. Description of Province and City of New York with Plans of City and Several Ports...1695. NY, 1862. Ltd to 50. 127pp; 6 plans, cat. (Rebound.) *Heinoldt.* $45/£29

MILLER, JOHN. An Illustration of the Sexual System of Linnaeus. London, 1794. Volume II. 105 hand-colored engrs, hand-colored tp. (Foxing throughout.) Paper-cvrd bds, cl spine (rebound). *Metropolitan*.* $920/£590

MILLER, JOSEPH. The Arizona Story. NY, (1952). (Spine sl dknd.) *King.* $20/£13

MILLER, K. E. (ed). The Chicago-Cook County Health Survey.... NY, 1949. 1st ed. VG. *Fye.* $40/£26

MILLER, KELLY. The Everlasting Stain. Washington: Associated Pubs, (1924). 1st ed. NF (name, crown corner sl faded) in VG- dj (internal repairs, uniform dknd, sm chips). *Between The Covers.* $250/£160

MILLER, LEO E. In the Wilds of South America. NY: Scribner, 1918. 1st ed. Color frontis, fldg map. Grn illus cl. Good. *Karmiole.* $125/£80

MILLER, MAX. The Cruise of the Cow. NY: E.P. Dutton, 1951. 1st ed. Map. Blue cl. VG in dj (worn). *Parmer.* $25/£16

MILLER, MAX. Fog and Men on Bering Sea. NY: E.P. Dutton, 1936. 1st ed. (Spine faded), else VG. *Perier.* $35/£22

MILLER, MAX. The Great Trek. NY, 1935. 1st ed. (Spine faded), else VG. *High Latitude.* $25/£16

MILLER, N. Heavenly Caves. NY: Braziller, 1982. Sound in dj. *Ars Artis.* $39/£25

MILLER, O. T. The Second Book of Birds: Bird Families. Boston/NY: Houghton Mifflin, (Jun. 1901). 2nd state. 8 color plts, 16 full-pg halftone dwgs. VG + . *Mikesh.* $20/£13

MILLER, OLIVE BEAUPRE (ed). Little Pictures of Japan. Chicago: Book House for Children, 1925. 1st ed. 4to. Katharine Sturges (illus). 191pp. (Cl sl rubbed), o/w VG. *Worldwide.* $40/£26

MILLER, OLIVE. Whisk Away on a Sunbeam. NY/Chicago: P.F. Volland, (1919). 1st ed. Nature Children Book. 4to. Unpaginated; 13 full-pg color illus. Illus eps. Grn illus bds. (Spine end sl worn), o/w VG. *Dower.* $100/£64

MILLER, RICHARD ROSCOE. Slavery and Catholicism. Durham, NC: North State, (1957). 1st ed. NF. *Mcgowan.* $45/£29

MILLER, SAMUEL M. Notes on Hospital Practice. Part I: Philadelphia Hospitals. Phila, 1885. 1st ed. 4 vols in 1. 431pp. Brn cl bds (extrems worn, margin staining fr cvr, water stain rear cvr). Good. *Doctor's Library.* $100/£64

MILLER, SUE. Inventing the Abbotts. NY: Harper & Row, 1977. 1st ed. Fine in Fine dj. *Revere.* $30/£19

MILLER, THOMAS, JR. The Cactus Air Force: The Story of the Handful of Fliers Who Saved Guadalcanal. NY, 1969. 1st ed. VG in VG dj. *Clark.* $45/£29

MILLER, W. D. The Narragansett Planters. Worcester, 1934. Good (pencil notes) in ptd wraps. *Scribe's Perch*.* $22/£14

MILLER, WARREN. The Cool World. Boston: Little, Brown, (1959). 1st ed. NF (pg edges sl soiled; crown sl sunned) in VG dj (rear panel lt foxed; sm nick extrems, lt rubbed). *Between The Covers.* $45/£29

MILLER, WARREN. The Siege of Harlem. NY: McGraw-Hill, (1964). 1st ed. Fine in VG + dj (sm chip fr panel, few sm tears, lt rubbed). *Between The Covers.* $50/£32

MILLETT, KATE. Sexual Politics. GC: Doubleday, 1970. 1st ed. Ptd rev, news clippings laid in. VG (ex-lib, name) in dj (sl water-mkd). *Second Life.* $45/£29

MILLHAUSER, STEVEN. Edwin Mullhouse. NY: Knopf, (1972). 1st ed, 1st bk. NF in VG + dj (price-clipped). *Pettler & Lieberman.* $25/£16

MILLHAUSER, STEVEN. Edwin Mullhouse. NY: Knopf, 1972. 1st ed. VG + (David Madden sig, 'loan copy' fep) in dj (price-clipped, lt worn, sm abrasion fr spine fold). *Lame Duck.* $75/£48

MILLHAUSER, STEVEN. Edwin Mullhouse: The Life and Death of an American Writer 1943-1954 by Jeffrey Cartwright. NY: Knopf, 1972. 1st ed, 1st bk. (Spot top edge), else Fine in VG + dj (long tear rear panel; soiling). *Between The Covers.* $85/£54

MILLHAUSER, STEVEN. Portrait of a Romantic. NY: Knopf, (1977). 1st ed. (Rmdr stamp bottom pg edge), else Fine in Fine dj. *Pettler & Lieberman.* $20/£13

MILLICAN, ALBERT. Travels and Adventures of an Orchid Hunter. London: Cassell, 1891. 1st ed. Chromolitho frontis. Pict blue cl, gilt. (Lt spots.) *Hollett.* $250/£160

MILLIGAN, ALICE. Poems.... Henry Mangan (ed). Dublin: Gill, 1954. 1st ed thus. Port. Ed's ans laid in. Nice (ed's corrections to text and expansions of footnotes) in oversized dj (lt used, nicked). *Reese.* $50/£32

MILLIGAN, SPIKE. A Book of Milliganimals. London, 1968. 1st ed. Fine (sm spine crease) in dj (rubbed). *Polyanthos.* $25/£16

MILLIGAN, SPIKE. Room for You Inside. London: Dobson Books, 1968. 1st UK ed. VG (sl bumped) in dj (price-clipped). *Williams.* $19/£12

MILLINGEN, J. G. Curiosities of Medical Experience. 1837. 1st ed in 2 vols. xviii,406; iv,411pp (foxed). Orig 1/2 calf (worn, torn). *Whitehart.* $218/£140

MILLINGEN, J. G. The Passions; or Mind and Matter. London: John & Daniel A. Darling, 1848. 2nd ed. (x),464pp. Emb grn cl (fr joint sl split). VG. *Gach.* $250/£160

MILLS, CHARLES. The History of the Crusades.... London: Longman et al, 1821. 2nd ed. 2 vols. xv,479; viii,416pp. Frontis in vol 1, fldg map, 4 genealogical tables (2 fldg). Contemp 3/4 brn calf (extrems sl rubbed, spines sl faded), marbled bds. Fine. *Argonaut.* $250/£160

MILLS, E. A. The Spell of the Rockies. Boston/NY: Houghton Mifflin, 1911. 1st ed. Dec eps. Color pict cl. VG + . *Mikesh.* $27/£17

MILLS, JAMES. The History of British India. London: James Madden, 1858. 5th ed. 10 vols. (Ex-lib, ink stamps, bkpl, sl wrinkled, sl browned.) Unopened. Blind-emb cl (spine sl faded, chipped, shelf labels). *Edwards.* $117/£75

MILLS, JOHN. On the Spur of the Moment. London: Hurst & Blackett, 1884. 1st ed. 3 vols. Dec grn cl (worn, dented, bumped, shaken; bkpls, inner hinge vol 1 split). *Maggs.* $156/£100

MILLS, JOHN. Stable Secrets. London: Ward & Lock, 1863. 1st ed. Frontis, 112,(1)pp; 2 etched plts. Honey-colored polished calf, gilt, red/grn morocco labels. (Bkpl, text sl dknd, sl soiled), o/w Internally Excellent. Binding Fine (sm spot fr cvr). *Pirages.* $200/£128

MILLS, W. W. Forty Years at El Paso, 1858-1898. El Paso: Carl Hertzog, 1962. Fine in VG dj. *Gibbs.* $90/£58

MILMAN, HENRY HART. Savonarola, Erasmus and Other Essays. London: John Murray, 1870. 1st ed. 500pp + ads. NF. *Captain's Bookshelf.* $75/£48

MILMINE, GEORGINE. The Life of Mary Baker G. Eddy and the History of Christian Science. Willa Cather (ed). London: Hodder & Stoughton, 1909. 1st Eng ed. Frontis port. Red cl, gilt spine. (Spine sl dull), else NF in later chemise, slipcase. *Pacific*.* $207/£133

MILN, LOUISE JORDAN. By Soochow Waters. NY: Stokes, 1929. 1st ed. (Cl sl rubbed, soiled), o/w VG. *Worldwide.* $25/£16

MILNE, A. A. A Gallery of Children. London, (1925). One of 500 numbered, signed. 4to. Color tp vignette, 12 plts by Saida. (Eps foxed.) Orig white cl, gilt. *Swann*.* $546/£350

MILNE, A. A. The House at Pooh Corner. London: Methuen, (1926). 1st ed. Ernest H. Shepard (illus). 8vo. Fine in dj (sl rubbed). *Jaffe.* $850/£545

MILNE, A. A. The House at Pooh Corner. Methuen, (1928). 1st ed. E.H. Shepard (illus). Teg. Pink pict cl gilt. (2 leaves sl nicked, sl used, faded.) *Ash.* $133/£85

MILNE, A. A. The House at Pooh Corner. London: Methuen, (1928). 1st Eng ed. E.H. Shepard (illus). 12mo. 178pp. Gilt-dec pink cl. (Sl faded, corners sl bumped), o/w VG. *Dower.* $250/£160

MILNE, A. A. The House at Pooh Corner. London: Methuen, 1928. 1st ed. Pub's gilt-dec pink cl; dj. (2 sm spots, sig fr of dj), else Fine. *D & D.* $400/£256

MILNE, A. A. The House at Pooh Corner. London: Methuen, 1928. 1st ed. Pub's gilt-dec pink cl. VF + in orig dj. *D & D.* $695/£446

MILNE, A. A. The Ivory Door. London: C&W, 1929. 1st ed. Fine in NF dj. *Antic Hay.* $85/£54

MILNE, A. A. The King's Breakfast. London, 1925. 1st ed. (Eps browned.) Dj (frayed, torn, sl soiled). *Typographeum.* $45/£29

MILNE, A. A. The King's Breakfast. London: Methuen, 1925. 1st ed. E. H. Shepard (decs). 4to. Orig pict bds, blue cl spine. (Contemp trade label fr pastedown; prelims foxed), else Fine in dj (sl foxed). *Cummins.* $150/£96

MILNE, A. A. Lovers in London. Alston Rivers, 1905. 1st UK ed, 1st bk. Contents NF (cvrs sl faded). *Martin.* $133/£85

MILNE, A. A. Michael and Mary. London: C&W, 1930. 1st ed. One of 260 signed. 8vo. Teg. Grn cl. *Appelfeld.* $125/£80

MILNE, A. A. Now We Are Six. London: Methuen, (1927). 1st Eng ed. E.H. Shepard (illus). 8vo. 103pp. Teg. Gilt-dec red cl. (Spine sl rubbed, sl bumped), o/w VG. *Dower.* $250/£160

MILNE, A. A. Now We Are Six. London: Methuen, 1927. 1st ed. E. H. Shepard (illus). 8vo. Maroon gilt-stamped cl, gilt top. Fine. *Appelfeld.* $150/£96

MILNE, A. A. Now We Are Six. London: Methuen, 1927. 1st ed. E. H. Shepard (illus). Sm 8vo. Teg. Red cl, gilt. Fine in dj (worn). *Cummins.* $450/£288

MILNE, A. A. Those Were the Days. Methuen, 1929. 1st UK ed. NF in VG dj. *Martin.* $25/£16

MILNE, A. A. Those Were the Days. London: Methuen, 1929. India Paper ed. #60/250 signed. Teg. Orig rose cl, gilt. (Fore-edges lt foxed), else Fine in dj (sl worn). *Cummins.* $375/£240

MILNE, A. A. Winnie-the-Pooh. London, (1926). 1st ed. E. H. Shepard (illus). Sm 8vo. Pict grn cl. VG in dj (spine lt rubbed). *Argosy.* $750/£481

MILNE, A. A. Winnie-the-Pooh. London: Methuen, (1926). 1st ed. Ltd to 350 ptd on handmade paper and signed by Milne and Ernest H. Shepard (illus). Cl-backed bds. Fine in dj, chemise, slipcase. *Bromer.* $7,500/£4,808

MILNE, A. A. Winnie-the-Pooh. London: Methuen, 1926. Excellent (upper bd sl bubbled). *Gekoski.* $585/£375

MILNE, A. A. The World of Christopher Robin. NY: Dutton, 1958. Rpt. E. H. Shepard (illus). 6 1/2 x 9 1/4. 235pp. Fine in dj. *Cattermole.* $25/£16

MILNER, ALFRED. England in Egypt. London: Edward Arnold, 1894. 5th ed. xxviii,448pp (fep stamp); fldg color map. (Spine label removed, shelfwear to extrems.) *Archaeologia.* $45/£29

MILNER, JOHN and OSWALD W. BRIERLY. The Cruise of the H.M.S. Galatea.... London: William H. Allen, 1869. xii,488pp; 6 plts. Aeg. Pict cl (lt rubbed). *Adelson.* $200/£128

MILNER, T. N. A Descriptive Atlas of Astronomy and of Physical and Political Geography. 1853. (1),174,11,55pp. (Few pp, maps loose; spine defective), o/w VG. *Whitehart.* $62/£40

MILNES, R. M. (ed). Life, Letters, and Literary Remains. NY: Putnam, 1848. 1st Amer ed. Orig grn cl, gilt. Fine. *Macdonnell.* $275/£176

MILOSZ, CZESLAW. The Captive Mind. NY: LEC, (1983). One of 1500 numbered, signed by Milosz and F. Kapusta (illus). Mint in box. *Argosy.* $200/£128

MILOSZ, CZESLAW. The Captive Mind. Jane Zielonko (trans). London: Secker & Warburg, 1953. 1st ed. Nice in dj (spine lt nicked). *Patterson.* $31/£20

MILOSZ, CZESLAW. The Captive Mind. London: Secker & Warburg, 1953. 1st British ed. VG in dj (chipped, tape repair to verso). *Lame Duck.* $50/£32

MILOSZ, CZESLAW. The Captive Mind. Jane Zielonko (trans). NY: Knopf, 1953. 1st ed. NF in VG dj (sm tears, spine head worn). *Antic Hay.* $50/£32

MILOSZ, CZESLAW. The Issa Valley. Louis Iribarne (trans). London: Sidgwick & Jackson, (1981). 1st ed. Fine in dj. *Antic Hay.* $45/£29

MILOSZ, CZESLAW. The Issa Valley. NY, 1981. 1st ed. Fine in Fine dj. *Smith.* $15/£10

MILOSZ, CZESLAW. The Land of Ulro. NY, 1984. 1st ed in English. NF in NF dj. *Smith.* $15/£10

MILTON, GEORGE FORT. Abraham Lincoln and the Fifth Column. NY, 1942. 1st ed. VG + in dj (worn, chipped). *Pratt.* $35/£22

MILTON, GEORGE FORT. Abraham Lincoln and the Fifth Column. NY, 1942. 1st ed. VG (few cvr spots). *Wantagh.* $45/£29

MILTON, JOHN. Comus, a Mask. (London: Edward Arnold, 1901.) Ltd to 150. 8vo. 47pp. Full-pg hand-colored wood engr by Reginald Savage. Full vellum blind-stamped w/rose logo, motto, 'Soul is Form.' VF. *Bromer.* $550/£353

MILTON, JOHN. Comus. London: Heinemann, (1921). One of 550 ptd, signed by Arthur Rackham (illus). 4to. 22 mtd color plts. Dec blue eps. Gilt-stamped bds, vellum spine (sl browning, soiling), gilt top. *Appelfeld.* $750/£481

MILTON, JOHN. Comus. NY/London: Doubleday, Page/Heinemann, (1921). 1st trade ed, Amer issue. 24 tipped-in color plts by Arthur Rackham. Pict eps. Grn cl (bumped, sm spine chip, spine dknd), gilt. NF internally. *Blue Mountain.* $150/£96

MILTON, JOHN. Comus. NY/London: Doubleday, Page/Heinemann, (1921). One of 550 signed by Arthur Rackham (illus). 24 tipped-in color plts. Partly unopened. Gilt-dec vellum-backed bds (sl worn, soiled). Contents VG. *New Hampshire*.* $375/£240

MILTON, JOHN. Four Poems. London: Gregynog, 1933. #240/250. 9 Fine wood engrs. Pub's full chestnut 'hermitage' calf (sl scrape, edges sl faded). *Hollett.* $351/£225

MILTON, JOHN. Il Penseroso and L'Allegro. NY: LEC, 1954. Ltd to 1780. Orig prospectus laid in. Full grn buckram, gilt. VF in slipcase. *Truepenny.* $95/£61

MILTON, JOHN. The Mask of Comus. London: Nonesuch, 1937. One of 950 numbered. R.H. Farrar (illus). Slipcase (edges sl faded). *Swann*.* $103/£66

MILTON, JOHN. The Mask of Comus. E. H. Visiak and Hubert J. Foss (eds). London: Nonesuch, 1937. Ltd to 950. 5 color plts. Largely unopened. VG in blind-stamped imitation parchment, gilt. *Cox.* $133/£85

MILTON, JOHN. The Mask of Comus. E.H. Visiak (ed). Nonesuch, 1937. One of 950 numbered. 5 full-pg color illus. Cream parchment-cvrd bds. Fine in slipcase (faded, mkd). *Michael Taylor.* $211/£135

MILTON, JOHN. Paradise Lost and Paradise Regain'd. London: John Baskerville for J&R Tonson, 1758. 2 vols. Vol 2 trimmed. (Foxing, age-toning, esp prelims.) Later calf (cvrs detached). *Waverly*.* $71/£46

MILTON, JOHN. Paradise Lost and Paradise Regain'd. SF: LEC, 1936. Ltd to 1500 signed by Carlotta Petrina (illus). Orig prospectus laid in. 1/4 natural Irish linen, batik bds (spine lt dknd). VG (lacks slipcase). *Truepenny.* $95/£61

MILTON, JOHN. Paradise Lost and Paradise Regain'd. SF: LEC, 1936. #904/1500 numbered, signed by Carlotta Petrina (illus). Cl-backed dec bds, paper label. Fine in pub's slipcase (cracked, worn). *Hermitage.* $100/£64

MILTON, JOHN. Paradise Lost. London: J&R Tonson & S. Draper, 1749. Vol 1 only. Frontis port, tp (both browned), 6 plts. Later calf (bds detached). *Waverly*.* $49/£31

MILTON, JOHN. Poems in English. London: Nonesuch, 1926. One of 1450 numbered. 2 vols. 1/4 imitation vellum, gilt. *Swann*.* $138/£88

MILTON, JOHN. Poems in English. London: Nonesuch, 1926. One of 1450 numbered. 2 vols. Paper vellum-backed bds (spine lt soiled, foxed, edges lt worn). Contents VG. *Waverly*.* $176/£113

MILTON, JOHN. The Poetical Works.... Springfield, MA: James R. Hutchins, 1794. 2 parts in 1 vol. Full calf (rubbed, bumped, corners through; loose pp). *Metropolitan*.* $25/£16

MILTON, JOHN. Samson Agonistes, a Dramatic Poem. (New Rochelle, NY: Elston Press, 1904.) 1/4 cl, paper bds, ptd paper spine label. Unopened. Attractive. *Heller.* $250/£160

MINAHAN, JOHN. Arthur Tress: The Dream Collector. Richmond: Westover, 1972. 1st ed. 56 b/w plts. (Name stamp), else NF in dj (rubbed). *Cahan.* $75/£48

MINER, W. H. A Book of Views of Heart's Delight Farm. Chazy, NY, 1909. Inscribed. 164pp ptd on heavy card stock, mtd on linen stubs. Flexible color pict leather (rubbed, worn, spine lacks pieces; 1st few ll loose). *Kane*.* $130/£83

Minerals and Metals. London: John W. Parker, 1847. 5th ed. Frontis, xii,255pp. Good in blue cl (spine ends sl worn). *Cox.* $34/£22

MINGUS, CHARLES. Beneath the Underdog. NY, 1971. 1st ed. NF in Fine dj (sl edgewear). *Warren.* $50/£32

MINICK, ALICE A. One Family Travels West. Boston: Meador, 1936. 1st ed. (Sl shelfwear, cl rubbed), else Good. *Brown.* $30/£19

MINNESOTA HISTORICAL SOCIETY. Collections...Volume I. St. Paul, 1872. 519pp. (1 pg lt soiled, margin torn; spine faded, ends chipped, cl split fr hinge, ex-lib.) Howes M641. *Bohling.* $40/£26

MINNIGERODE, MEADE. Some Personal Letters of Herman Melville and a Bibliography. NY: Brick Row Bookshop, 1922. 1st ed. One of 1500 ptd. Inscribed presentation. Uncut. 1/4 linen, bds, paper label. Fine. BAL 13678. *Macdonnell.* $125/£80

Minstrel Songs, Old and New. Boston: Oliver Ditson, 1882. (Fep loosening, hinges starting.) Cl-backed pict bds (edges worn). *Dramatis Personae.* $70/£45

MINTON, S. A. and M. R. Giant Reptiles. NY: Scribner, 1973. 1st ed. Fine in NF dj. *Mikesh.* $35/£22

MINTY, LEONARD. The Legal and Ethical Aspects of Medical Quackery. London, 1932. 1st ed. VG. *Fye.* $50/£32

MINTZ, LANNON. The Trail, a Bibliography of the Travelers on the Overland Trail to California, Oregon, Salt Lake City and Montana 1841-64. Albuquerque, 1987. 1st ed. VF in VF dj. *Turpen.* $55/£35

MINTZ, LANNON. The Trail, a Bibliography of the Travellers on the Overland Trail to California, Oregon...During the Years 1841-1864. Albuquerque: Univ of NM, (1987). 1st ed. Fine in Fine dj. *Book Market.* $65/£42

MIR HASSAN ALI, MRS. B. Observations on the Mussulmauns of India. London: Parbury, Allen, 1832. 1st ed. 2 vols. 395; 425pp. 3/4 calf (scuffed). VG set (vol 1 tp loose, bkpls). *Second Life.* $325/£208

MIRSKY, JEANNETTE. To the North! NY, 1934. Fldg map. (Cl very faded.) *High Latitude.* $20/£13

MISHIMA, YUKIO. After the Banquet. NY: Knopf, (1963). 1st Amer ed. (Ink name, stamp fep), o/w NF in dj (sl chipped). *Hermitage.* $60/£38

MISHIMA, YUKIO. After the Banquet. NY: Knopf, 1963. 1st Amer ed. NF in VG dj. *Turtle Island.* $35/£22

MISHIMA, YUKIO. Confessions of a Mask. (Norfolk CT): New Directions, (1958). 1st ed. (Sl wear crown), else Fine in Fine dj (spine sl tanned). *Between The Covers.* $150/£96

MISHIMA, YUKIO. Confessions of a Mask. Norfolk: New Directions, (1958). 1st ed in English. NF in dj (price-clipped). *Hermitage.* $65/£42

MISHIMA, YUKIO. The Decay of the Angel. NY: Knopf, (1974). 1st Amer ed. Fine in dj. *Turtle Island.* $55/£35

MISHIMA, YUKIO. The Decay of the Angel. NY, 1974. 1st Amer ed. (Edges dented, spine bumped), else Good. *King.* $25/£16

MISHIMA, YUKIO. Five Modern No Plays. NY: Knopf, 1957. 1st Amer ed. NF (reps sl browned, ink inscrip) in dj (edges browned, sm tears, price-clipped). *Antic Hay.* $75/£48

MISHIMA, YUKIO. Runaway Horses. NY: Knopf, (1973). 1st Amer ed. Fine in dj. *Turtle Island.* $55/£35

MISHIMA, YUKIO. Runaway Horses. NY, 1973. 1st ed. NF in NF dj. *Smith.* $20/£13

MISHIMA, YUKIO. The Sound of Waves. Meredith Weatherby (trans). NY: Knopf, 1956. 1st Amer ed. NF (owner seal tp) in VG dj. *Turtle Island.* $30/£19

MISHIMA, YUKIO. Spring Snow. NY: Knopf, (1972). 1st Amer ed. Fine in dj. *Turtle Island.* $55/£35

MISHIMA, YUKIO. Sun and Steel. (Palo Alto): Kodansha, (1970). 1st Amer ed. Fine in dj (sl chipped, price-clipped). *Captain's Bookshelf.* $125/£80

MISHIMA, YUKIO. The Temple of Dawn. NY: Knopf, (1973). 1st Amer ed. Fine in dj. *Turtle Island.* $55/£35

MISHIMA, YUKIO. The Temple of the Golden Pavilion. NY: Knopf, 1959. 1st Amer ed. Fine in NF dj (sl foxing, rubbing). *Between The Covers.* $100/£64

MISRACH, RICHARD. Telegraph 3 A.M. Berkeley: Cornucopia, 1974. 1st ed. Ltd to 3000 numbered, signed. Pict eps. Gilt-emb cl. (Owner stamp), else Fine in illus dj (sm soil mk). *Cahan.* $85/£54

MISRACH, RICHARD. Telegraph 3 A.M. Berkeley: Cornucopia, 1974. 1st bk. One of 3000. Fine in Fine dj. *Smith.* $150/£96

Miss Muffet Pop-Up. Burnley: Candlelight, ca 1950. Sm 4to. 4pp, lg center pop-up. VG in pict wraps. *Bookmark.* $31/£20

Mission Furniture: How to Make It. Parts 1, 2 and 3. Chicago: Popular Mechanics, 1909, 1910, 1912. Dec cvrs (spines faded). Good. *Scribe's Perch*.* $55/£35

Mississippi, a Guide to the Magnolia State. NY: Viking, 1938. 1st ed. Fldg pocket map. VG +. *Bohling.* $35/£22

MITCHELL, A. L. (comp). Songs of the Confederacy and Plantation Melodies. Cincinnati, OH: Geo. B. Jennings, ca 1901. 1st ed. Dec wrappers. VG. *Mcgowan.* $45/£29

MITCHELL, ALBERT. Recollections of One of the Light Brigade. Tunbridge Wells/London, n.d. (c.1885). 2nd ed. 130pp. Mod red calf. *Maggs.* $250/£160

MITCHELL, C. AINSWORTH. Mineral and Aerated Waters. London, 1913. 1st ed. (Prelims lt foxed; worn.) *Edwards.* $94/£60

MITCHELL, EDWIN VALENTINE. The Horse and Buggy Age in New England. NY: Coward McCann, 1937. 1st ed. VG. *October Farm.* $30/£19

MITCHELL, EDWIN VALENTINE. The Horse and Buggy Age in New England. NY: Coward-McCann, 1937. 1st ed. VG in dj (edge torn). *Perier.* $45/£29

MITCHELL, ELAINE ALLAN. Fort Timiskaming and the Fur Trade. Toronto: Univ of Toronto, (1977). 1st ed. Fldg map in rear pocket. VF. *Argonaut.* $45/£29

MITCHELL, GLADYS. The Dancing Druids. London: Michael Joseph, 1948. 1st ed. VG in dj (internal tape mends, chip). *Mordida.* $65/£42

MITCHELL, GLADYS. Death of a Burrowing Mole. London: Michael Joseph, 1982. 1st ed. (Pg edges sl soiled), o/w Fine in dj. *Mordida.* $45/£29

MITCHELL, GLADYS. Faintley Speaking. London: Michael Joseph, 1954. 1st ed. (Pg edges foxed), o/w Fine in dj (spine ends sl worn). *Mordida.* $65/£42

MITCHELL, H. H. and M. EDMAN. Nutrition and Climatic Stress with Particular Reference to Man. Springfield: Charles C. Thomas, 1951. 1st ed. VG (ex-lib). *White.* $23/£15

MITCHELL, J. A. Life's Fairy Tales. Stokes, 1892. 1st ed. (Rubbed), else VG-. *Aronovitz.* $30/£19

MITCHELL, JOHN D. Lost Mines and Buried Treasures Along the Old Frontier. Palm Desert: Desert Magazine, (1953). 1st ed. Dj (worn). *Dawson.* $30/£19

MITCHELL, JOHN D. Lost Mines and Buried Treasures Along the Old Frontier. Palm Desert: Desert Magazine, 1953. 1st ed. Fine in VG dj. *Book Market.* $100/£64

MITCHELL, JOHN D. Lost Mines of the Great Southwest Including Stories of Hidden Treasures. Mesa: (Privately ptd, 1933). Fine. *Book Market.* $250/£160

MITCHELL, JOHN KEARSLEY. Five Essays.... S. Weir Mitchell (ed). Phila: Lippincott, 1859. 1st ed thus. xiv,371pp. Emb cl (spine ends sl chipped). VG. *Glaser.* $400/£256

MITCHELL, JOHN M. The Herring. Edinburgh/London, 1864. Fldg chromolitho frontis, xii,372pp (lt spotting, few ll sl waterstained, hinges sl tender), 5 litho plts. Uncut. (Cl lt soiled, spine head sl bumped), gilt spine. *Edwards.* $195/£125

MITCHELL, JOHN. Organized Labor. Phila: Amer Book & Bible House, 1903. 1st ed. VG+. *Beasley.* $100/£64

MITCHELL, JOSEPH. The Bottom of the Harbor. Boston, (1959). 1st ed. (Bkpl, sm tear spine), else VG in dj (rubbed, torn). *King.* $35/£22

MITCHELL, JOSEPH. The Bottom of the Harbor. Boston: Little, Brown, (1959). 1st ed. Fine in dj (sl rubbed). *Captain's Bookshelf.* $125/£80

MITCHELL, JOSEPH. Joe Gould's Secret. NY: Viking, (1965). 1st ed. Fine in Fine dj (faint dampstain spine base). *Between The Covers.* $75/£48

MITCHELL, JOSEPH. McSorley's Wonderful Saloon. NY: Duell, Sloan & Pearce, (1943). 1st ed. Fine in dj (lt used, few sm chips). *Captain's Bookshelf.* $750/£481

MITCHELL, JOSEPH. Old Mr. Flood. NY: Duell, Sloan & Pearce, (1948). 1st ed. Signed. NF in dj (lt used, price-clipped, shallow chip spine head). *Captain's Bookshelf.* $100/£64

MITCHELL, JOSEPH. Old Mr. Flood. NY, 1948. 1st Amer ed. Signed. Fine in dj (few sm edge tears, lacks spine piece). *Polyanthos.* $45/£29

MITCHELL, LUCY M. A History of Ancient Sculpture. London: Kegan, Paul, Trench, 1883. 766pp; 6 plts. VG (lt foxed, inner hinges cracking). Not accompanied by companion vol, Selections from Ancient Sculpture. *New Hampshire*.* $10/£6

MITCHELL, LUCY SPRAGUE. The Here and Now Storybook. NY: Dutton, 1921. Rpt. Hendrik Van Loon (illus). 5 1/2 x 8 1/4. 360pp. Good in dj. *Cattermole.* $25/£16

MITCHELL, MAIRIN. The Maritime History of Russia 848-1948. London: Sidgwick & Jackson, (1949). 1st ed. *Lefkowicz.* $85/£54

MITCHELL, MARGARET. Gone with the Wind. NY: Macmillan, (1986). 1st ptg of 50th Anniversary ed. Red cl, gilt. Fine in pict slipcase. *Captain's Bookshelf.* $100/£64

MITCHELL, MARGARET. Gone with the Wind. NY: Macmillan, 1936. 1st ed, 1st ptg. VG (vertical crease length of spine). Pieces of dj laid in. *Captain's Bookshelf.* $450/£288

MITCHELL, MARGARET. Gone with the Wind. NY, 1939. 1st 2-vol ed. Ltd to 1000 numbered. Teg. 2-tone cl. VG (lacks glassine wrappers) in slipcase (scuffed). *King.* $950/£609

MITCHELL, MARGARET. Margaret Mitchell's Gone With the Wind Letters, 1936-1949. Richard Harwell (ed). Macmillan, (c. 1976). 1st ptg. VG (cvr sl spotted) in VG- dj (sm tears). *Book Broker.* $35/£22

MITCHELL, P. My Fill of Days. London, 1937. (Worn.) *Maggs.* $23/£15

MITCHELL, S. WEIR and EDWARD T. REICHERT. Researches upon the Venoms of Poisonous Serpents. Washington: Smithsonian, 1886. 1st ed. xiii,ix,186pp, 5 color plts. Fine. *Glaser.* $300/£192

MITCHELL, S. WEIR. The Autobiography of a Quack and the Case of George Dedlow. NY, 1900. 1st ed. Gilt-tooled grn cl bds. NF. *Doctor's Library.* $50/£32

MITCHELL, S. WEIR. A Diplomatic Adventure. NY: Century, 1906. 1st ed. (Spine sl skewed), o/w Fine. *Hermitage.* $45/£29

MITCHELL, S. WEIR. Fat and Blood: An Essay on the Treatment of Certain Forms of Neurasthenia and Hysteria. Phila: J.B. Lippincott, 1884. 3rd rev ed. (ii),164,(2)pp. Ptd bevel-edged grn cl. VG. *Gach.* $100/£64

MITCHELL, S. WEIR. Hugh Wynne, Free Quaker. NY, 1897. 1st ed, 1st pub format, w/unrevised text, cancel tps, etc. 2 vols. Binding B: gray cl, Orig ptd white djs (sl worn); cl slipcase. BAL 14178. *Kane*.* $275/£176

MITCHELL, S. WEIR. Hugh Wynne, Free Quaker. NY, 1899. 2nd ed. 2 vols. 306; 261pp. Gilt-tooled cl bds (sl worn). VG. *Doctor's Library.* $60/£38

MITCHELL, S. WEIR. Lectures on Diseases of the Nervous System, Especially in Women. Phila, 1885. 2nd ed. 288pp + inserted cat; 5 plts. Blind-emb grn cl. NF (sig). *Gach.* $475/£304

MITCHELL, S. WEIR. Some Recently Discovered Letters of William Harvey.... Phila, 1912. 1st ed. VG in wrappers. *Fye.* $100/£64

MITCHELL, S. WEIR. Two Lectures on the Conduct of the Medical Life. Phila, 1893. 1st ed. 51pp (very dog-eared; ex-lib). Mod marbled bds, orig bds (worn) bound in. *Argosy.* $50/£32

MITCHELL, S. WEIR. Westways: A Village Chronicle. NY: Century, 1913. 1st ed. (Bkpl), else NF. *Hermitage.* $45/£29

MITCHELL, S. WEIR. When All the Woods Are Green. NY, 1894. 1st Amer ed. Frontis port. Dec cvrs, gilt. NF (2 sm tears feps, lt foxed; spine sl sunned, extrems, corners sl rubbed). *Polyanthos.* $30/£19

MITCHELL, S. WEIR. The Works of S. Weir Mitchell. NY: Century, 1905. Author's definitive ed. 10 vols. Teg. Grn cl, leather spine labels. NF (ink name). BAL 14292. *Antic Hay.* $150/£96

MITCHELL, S. WEIR. The Youth of Washington, Told in the Form of an Autobiography. NY, 1904. 1st ed. Gilt-tooled cl bds (sl worn). VG. *Doctor's Library.* $35/£22

MITCHELL, SAMUEL AUGUSTUS. Mitchell's Ancient Atlas. Phila: E.H. Butler, 1864. 12 color maps on 8 sheets. Salmon ptd bds (few ink stains). Contents Good (pencil note 1 map). *Hudson.* $125/£80

MITCHELL, THEODORE. Bees of the Eastern United States. Vol II. (Raleigh): NC Ag Exp Sta, 1962. 1st ed. NF w/o dj as issued. *Archer.* $40/£26

MITCHELL, W. R. Highland Spring. London: Robert Hale, 1972. 1st ed. 20 plts, 2 maps. VG in dj (sl chipped). *Hollett.* $23/£15

MITCHELL, WESLEY C. Gold, Prices, and Wages Under the Greenback Standard. Berkeley, 1908. (Bkpl, ink inscrip, stamps; worn, soiled, lacks spine label(?).) *King.* $35/£22

MITCHELL, WILLIAM ANSEL. Linn County, Kansas: A History. Kansas City, 1928. 2 plts, dbl map at rear. VG+. *Bohling.* $50/£32

MITCHELL-HEDGES, F. A. Battles with Monsters of the Sea. NY: D. Appleton-Century, 1937. 1st ed. Blue buckram. NF in Good pict dj. *Biscotti.* $25/£16

MITCHISON, NAOMI. Beyond This Limit. London: Jonathan Cape, 1935. 21 full-pg illus by Wyndham Lewis. Top edge black. 1/2 black cl, silvered bds. VG (eps, fore-edge lt spotted; sl bumped). *Heller.* $250/£160

MITFORD, JOHN (ed). The Correspondence of Thomas Gray and William Mason. London, 1853. 1st ed. (3-inch split spine), else Clean. *Gretton.* $39/£25

MITFORD, JOHN (ed). The Correspondence of Walpole and the Rev. William Mason. London, 1851. 1st ed. 2 vols. 3/4 tan calf, gilt spine (dknd). *Argosy.* $125/£80

MITFORD, MARY RUSSELL. Recollections of Literary Life; or, Books, Places, and People. NY: Harper, 1852. 1st Amer ed. Grn cl, gilt. VG. *Macdonnell.* $150/£96

MITFORD, NANCY. Don't Tell Alfred. Hamish Hamilton, (1960). 1st ed. Good in dj (lt worn). *Ash.* $31/£20

MITFORD, NANCY. The Water Beetle. London: Hamish Hamilton, (1962). 1st Eng ed. NF (corner bumped) in dj (soil). *Antic Hay.* $30/£19

MITFORD, NANCY. The Water Beetle. London: Hamish Hamilton, 1962. 1st ed. Fine in dj. *Hollett.* $39/£25

MITFORD, R. C. W. To Caubul with the Cavalry Brigade. London, 1881. viii,205pp (frontis, tp, 1st plt, 1 leaf lt foxed); 6 tinted plts, fldg map. Red/black cl (badly stained), gilt. *Maggs.* $187/£120

MITFORD, WILLIAM. The History of Greece. London: T. Cadell, 1822. 10 vols. Contemp 3/4 calf, marbled bds, brn leather lettering pieces. VG (cvr scuffs). *House.* $275/£176

MITTELHOLZER, WALTER. By Airplane Towards the North Pole. Boston: Houghton Mifflin, 1925. 1st US ed. 4 maps. Good+ (spine age-dknd, titles sl chipped). *Parmer.* $125/£80

MITTELHOLZER, WALTER. By Airplane Towards the North Pole...in the Summer of 1923. London: Geo. Allen & Unwin, (1925). 2 fldg maps. VG. *High Latitude.* $70/£45

MITTERLING, PHILIP I. America in the Antarctic to 1840. Urbana, IL, c. 1959. VG. *High Latitude.* $27/£17

MITTLEMAN, J. B. Eight Stars to Victory. DC, 1948. VG (cvr soiled). *Clark.* $85/£54

MITTON, G. E. The Thames. A&C Black, 1906. 1st ed. 75 color plts, fldg map. (2 early postcards pinned to fep, bkpl, feps browned, hinges cracked; spine sl faded, rubbed.) *Edwards.* $117/£75

MIVART, ST. GEORGE. The Cat: An Introduction to the Study of Backboned Animals.... London, 1881. 1st ed. 557pp (hinges cracked). Uncut, mostly unopened. Pict cl (corners, spine ends sl worn). *Argosy.* $300/£192

MO, TIMOTHY. The Monkey King. London, 1978. 1st Eng ed, 1st bk. Fine in dj. *Clearwater.* $156/£100

MO, TIMOTHY. The Monkey King. London: Deutsch, 1978. 1st Eng ed, 1st bk. NF in dj. *Hadley.* $195/£125

MO, TIMOTHY. The Redundancy of Courage. London, 1991. 1st ed. Fine in dj. *Words Etc.* $23/£15

MO, TIMOTHY. Sour Sweet. Andre Deutsch, (1982). 1st ed, 1st issue, w/'Mandarin' dj. VG in dj. *Ash.* $117/£75

MO, TIMOTHY. Sour Sweet. London, 1982. 1st Eng ed. Black cl bds. Pict 1st state dj. *Clearwater.* $94/£60

MO, TIMOTHY. Sour Sweet. London: Deutsch, 1982. 1st Eng ed, 2nd bk in 1st issue 'chinese' dj. NF in dj. *Hadley.* $101/£65

MOCHI, UGO and T. DONALD CARTER. Hoofed Mammals of the World. NY, 1953. 1st ed. William Beach's bkpl. (Sl worn.) *Oinonen*.* $190/£122

Modern Book-bindings and Their Designers. London: Winter Number of The Studio, 1899-1900. Sm folio. 5 color plts; ads bound in at beginning/end. 1/2 cl, spine gilt (sl faded, rubbed, ex-lib w/ink #s, stamps on verso of plts), orig wrappers bound in. *Maggs.* $109/£70

Modern Masters of Etching, Number Eighteen: H. Rushbury. London/NY: Studio/Wm. E. Rudge, 1928. 12 b/w repros. Paper-cvrd bds (extrms worn), ptd label fr cvr. Contents VG. *New Hampshire*.* $25/£16

Modern Painters. By a Graduate of Oxford. (By John Ruskin.) NY, ca 1900. 5 vols. 1/2 polished blue calf; spines in 6 compartments w/gilt red floral inlays in 4, labels in 2. (Lt rubbed.) *Swann*.* $230/£147

Modern Traveller. Volume 9. Arabia. Boston: Lilly & Wait, 1831. iv,340pp; 3 plts, fldg map. (Foxed, ex-lib; rubbed, spine frayed, sl soiled), o/w Good. *Worldwide.* $45/£29

MOE, VIRGINIA. Animal Inn. Houghton Mifflin, (1946). 1st ed. Milo Winter (illus). 7x9.5. 174pp. VG (shelfworn) in dj (tattered). *My Bookhouse.* $25/£16

MOELLER, SUSAN D. Shooting War. NY: Basic Books, 1989. 1st ed. As New in pict dj. *Cahan.* $35/£22

MOFFAT, JOHN S. The Lives of Robert and Mary Moffat. NY: A.C. Armstrong, 1886. xix,484pp; 2 fldg maps, 2 mtd photos, 4 plts. Teg. Grn cl (spine ends starting). *Adelson.* $250/£160

MOGGRIDGE, J. TRAHERNE. Harvesting Ants and Trap-Door Spiders. Reeve, 1873. 12 plts. *Petersfield.* $117/£75

MOGGRIDGE, J. TRAHERNE. Harvesting Ants and Trap-Door Spiders. London, 1873. xi,156pp + 16pp pub's ads (last pg ads sl browned; hinges expertly repaired); 12 plts, incl 4 color. (Rebacked, orig spine laid down; sl rubbed, lt soiled.) *Edwards.* $133/£85

MOHOLY-NAGY, L. Vision in Motion. Chicago, 1961. 6th ptg. (Ex-lib, ink stamp, label remains, cellotape mks pastedowns.) Dj (sl ragged, faded, spine #s). *Edwards.* $62/£40

MOIR, FRED L. M. After Livingstone. 1924. 3rd ed. Frontis port. Dj (ragged w/loss). *Edwards.* $31/£20

MOKLER, ALFRED JAMES. History of Natrona County, Wyoming 1888-1922. Chicago: R.R. Donnelley, 1923. 1st ed. (Sl dampstain sl affecting bottom edge 1st 50 pp; eps, few pps browned from clippings once laid in.) Teg. Grn cl, gilt. NF. Howes M719. *Harrington.* $300/£192

MOKLER, ALFRED JAMES. Transition of the West. Chicago: R.R. Donnelley, 1927. 1st ed. Inscribed. Teg. Grn cl. (Some pp browned from clippings once laid in), o/w Fine. *Harrington.* $300/£192

MOKOENA, MAJAKATHATA. My Brother's Keeper. NY: Vantage, 1990. 1st ed, 1st bk. Inscribed. NF in dj (spine faded, lt offset to fr cvr). *Lame Duck.* $50/£32

MOLESWORTH, MRS. A Christmas Child. London: Macmillan, 1880. 1st ed. 24pp ads dated Oct 1880; 7 plts by Walter Crane. Orange cl dec in black. Fine (lt foxed; sl askew). *Sumner & Stillman.* $95/£61

MOLESWORTH, MRS. The Cuckoo Clock. London: J.M. Dent, (1954). 1st ed thus. Children's Illustrated Classic. 8vo. 165pp; 4 full-pg color illus, 20 b/w illus by E.H. Shepard. Dec cl. VG in VG dj. *Dower.* $45/£29

MOLESWORTH, MRS. The Rectory Children. London, 1889. 1st ed. Presentation. 12mo. 7 b/w illus by Walter Crane. Dec red cl. VG. *Argosy.* $100/£64

MOLINA, J. IGNATIUS. The Geographical, Natural and Civil History of Chili. Middletown, CT: I. Reilly, 1808. 1st ed in English. 2 vols. xii, fldg map, 271pp,viii,(1),306,68pp. Full contemp calf (worn, sl loss, outer hinges weak, sm label spines). Good. *Brown.* $100/£64

MOLINA, J. IGNATIUS. The Geographical, Natural and Civil History of Chili. Middletown, CT: I. Reilly, 1808. 2 vols. 8,xii,271, errata; 2,viii,306,68pp; fldg map (repair). Orig tree calf (rubbed, worn). *Adelson.* $275/£176

MOLLHAUSEN, BALDWIN. Diary of a Journey from the Mississippi to the Coasts of the Pacific. London: Longman, Brown, 1858. 1st ed in English. 2 vols. Ad leaf. Fldg map, 19 plts. Red cl stamped in blind/gilt. (Effaced name fr pastedown both vols, bkpl vol 2; sl spine restoration), o/w Bright in mod custom slipcase. Howes M713. *Hermitage*. $1,600/£1,026

MOLLIEN, GASPARD T. Travels in Africa, to the Sources of the Senegal and Gambia, in 1818. London: Richard Phillips, 1820. ix,128pp; fldg map, 4 plts. Uncut. Mod red buckram. VG. *Adelson*. $285/£183

MOLLOY, J. FITZGERALD. Court Life Below Stairs. London, 1882-3. 2nd ed. 4 vols. (1st, last few ll lt foxed.) Gilt-edged 1/2 morocco, raised bands, morocco spine labels. *Edwards*. $195/£125

MOLLOY, PAUL. A Pennant for the Kremlin. GC: Doubleday, 1964. VG (lt offsetting fep) in VG dj (sm tears). *Between The Covers*. $85/£54

MOLMENTI, POMPEO and GUSTAV LUDWIG. The Life and Works of Vittorio Carpaccio. Robert H. Hobart Cust (trans). London, 1907. 240 plts. (Eps sl spotted.) Teg, rest uncut. Dec cl (lower bd sl soiled), gilt. *Edwards*. $101/£65

MOMADAY, N. SCOTT. House Made of Dawn. NY: Harper & Row, (1968). 1st ed. Cl-backed bds. Fine in dj (closed tear). *Jaffe*. $250/£160

MONAGHAN, FRANK. French Travellers in the United States, 1765-1932. NY: NY Public Library, 1933. 1st ed. 10 plts. Gray cl, blue calf spine label, orig ptd wrapper bound in at back. Good. *Karmiole*. $65/£42

MONAGHAN, JAY (ed). The Book of the American West. NY, (1963). Stated 1st ed. (Sl foxing), o/w VG in Good dj. *Scribe's Perch**. $18/£12

MONAGHAN, JAY. Custer, The Life of General George Armstrong Custer. Boston, (1959). 1st ed. VG in dj (extrem frayed). *King*. $50/£32

MONAGHAN, JAY. Lincoln Bibliography 1839-1939. Springfield, 1943. 1st ed. 2 vols. *Ginsberg*. $100/£64

MONAGHAN, JAY. Lincoln Bibliography, 1839-1939. Springfield, IL: State Hist Library, (1945). 2 vols. Buckram. VG+. *Bohling*. $110/£71

MONAHAN, FLORENCE. Women in Crime. NY: Washburn, (1941). 1st ed. VG. *Second Life*. $30/£19

MONCKTON, C. A. W. Some Experiences of a New Guinea Resident Magistrate. London, 1921. 1st ed. Frontis port, fldg map. (Upper hinge cracked, extrems faded, sl chipped.) *Edwards*. $47/£30

MONCKTON, H. and R. HERRIES (eds). Geology in the Field: The Jubilee Volume...(1858-1908). London, 1910. 2 vols. 32 plts and maps. (Rubbed.) *Maggs*. $44/£28

MONCRIEFF, A. R. HOPE. Bonnie Scotland. London: A&C Black, 1912. 75 color plts. (Lt spotting; dec cl sl rubbed.) *Hollett*. $39/£25

MONCRIEFF, A. R. HOPE. The Heart of Scotland. London: A&C Black, 1909. 24 plts, fldg map at rear. Good-. *Scribe's Perch**. $22/£14

MONCRIEFF, A. R. HOPE. Highlands and Islands of Scotland. London: A&C Black, 1925. 2nd ed. 32 color plts, map. VG. *Hollett*. $39/£25

MONCRIEFF, A. R. HOPE. Surrey. London: A&C Black, 1906. 1st ed. 75 color plts, fldg map. Teg. Dec cl. (Lt marginal browning; spine faded, sl rubbed.) *Edwards*. $55/£35

MONCRIEFF, C. K. SCOTT (trans). The Letters of Abelard and Heloise. London, 1925. #662/750. (Something poorly removed from ep, corners crushed.) *Typographeum*. $35/£22

MONDOR, HENRI. Doctors and Medicine in the Works of Daumier. Boston, 1960. 1st ed in English. VG in dj. *Fye*. $100/£64

MONEY, A. W. et al. Guns, Ammunition and Tackle. NY: Macmillan, 1904. 1st ed. 3 color plts. Teg. Grn pict cl. (Hinges repaired), else VG+. *Bowman*. $35/£22

MONEY, A. W. et al. Guns, Ammunition and Tackle. NY: Macmillan, Sept 1904. 1st ed. 3 color plts. Teg. Dec cvr. Good. *Scribe's Perch**. $30/£19

MONEY, KEITH. The Art of Margot Fonteyn. (NY): Reynal, (1965). 1st ed. Inscribed by Fonteyn in 1968. Beige cl. Good in dj. *Karmiole*. $150/£96

MONGE, CARLOS. Acclimatization in the Andes. Balt: Johns Hopkins, 1948. 1st ed in English. Untrimmed. VG (sl rubbed). *Glaser*. $150/£96

MONGREDIEN, AUGUSTUS. Trees and Shrubs for English Plantations. John Murray, 1870. 1st ed. 388pp+24pp pub's cat; 29 engrs, 2 color plts. (Prelims foxed), else VG in dec cl. *Hadley*. $86/£55

MONGREDIEN, AUGUSTUS. Trees and Shrubs for English Plantations. London, 1870. xi,388pp (lt foxed, mainly edges), 24 ads; 2 color plts. Pict cl. *Henly*. $39/£25

MONGREDIEN, AUGUSTUS. Trees and Shrubs for English Plantations. London, 1870. Color frontis, xi,388pp. (Some pp sl loose; cl dust-stained, sl worn, rebacked w/orig spine preserved), o/w VG. *Whitehart*. $39/£25

MONIER-WILLIAMS, MONTAGU. Figure-Skating. B. Fletcher Robinson (ed). London, 1898. (xii),316pp+xxiv ads. (Eps lt browned.) *Edwards*. $55/£35

MONKHOUSE, W. COSMO. The Earlier English Water-Colour Painters. London: Seeley, 1890. xi,152pp; 14 copper engrs. Teg, uncut. (Cl sl worn.) *Hollett*. $55/£35

MONKHOUSE, W. COSMO. The Turner Gallery. Appleton, c. 1880. 40 parts in ptd wrappers (chipped, worn, all cvrs separated). 3 lg engrs each part (few w/dampstaining in margins). *New Hampshire**. $775/£497

MONKSHOOD, G. F. The Less Familiar Kipling and Kiplingana. Jarrold & Sons, 1917. Good. *Moss*. $78/£50

MONRO, A. The Anatomy of the Human Bones, Nerves and Lacteal Sac and Duct. Edinburgh, 1763. 7th ed. viii,410pp (tp sl foxed). Contemp calf (rebacked). *Whitehart*. $281/£180

MONRO, DONALD. A Treatise on Medical and Pharmaceutical Chemistry, and the Materia Medica...to Which Is Added...New Edition of the Pharmacopoeia...1788. London: T. Cadell, 1788. 1st ed. 3 vols. Fldg plt (torn). Contemp mottled calf (some hinges reinforced). *Argosy*. $350/£224

MONRO, HAROLD. The Winter Solstice. London: Faber & Gwyer, n.d. #87/500 signed. David Jones (illus). Pale blue paper bds, gilt. (Spine sl faded), else VG. *Heller*. $120/£77

MONROE, HARRIET. Valeria and Other Poems. Chicago: The Author, 1891. 1st ed, 1st bk. Subs ed. One of 300 signed. Inscribed. Teg, uncut. Gilt-lettered vellum-backed ptd silk (rubbed, worn) over bds. *Kane**. $110/£71

MONROE, JAMES. A Narrative of a Tour of Observation. Phila: Mitchell & Ames, 1818. xii,(13)-228,xxxvipp (fr hinge split, repaired w/paper tape; paper dknd, foxed). Full leather (scuffed, warped). Reading copy. Howes M725. *Bohling*. $75/£48

MONROE, JAMES. A View of the Conduct of the Executive in the Foreign Affairs of the United States.... Phila: Benj. Franklin Bache, 1797. 1st ed. Complete w/half-title. (Sl dampstaining.) 19th-cent 3/4 brn calf, gilt, leather labels, marbled bds (scuffed, extrems rubbed). Howes M727. *Freeman**. $130/£83

MONROE, JOHN ALBERT. Reminiscences of the War of the Rebellion of 1861-5. Providence, RI, 1881. 1st ed. Ltd to 250. PNRISSHS Series 2, #11. 78pp. NF in ptd wrappers. *Mcgowan.* $45/£29

MONROE, JOHN. The American Botanist, and Family Physician....Silas Gaskill (comp). Wheelock, (VT): Jonathan Morrison, 1824. 1st ed. 203pp. Old calf (rubbed). VG. *M&s.* $250/£160

MONROE, JOHN. The American Botanist. Wheelock, VT: J. Morrison, 1824. 1st ed. 203pp (browned, lt soiled, stained, damping, leaf repaired, old ms notes). Old calf (heavily worn). *Waverly*.* $104/£67

MONROE, ROBERT T. Chronic Arthritis. NY, 1939. Red cl bds. VG. *Doctor's Library.* $50/£32

MONSARRAT, NICHOLAS. The Nylon Pirates. Cassell, 1960. 1st UK ed. NF in VG dj. *Williams.* $23/£15

MONSARRAT, NICHOLAS. The Ship That Died of Shame and Other Stories. London: Cassell, (1959). 1st Eng ed. Paper-cvrd bds. NF (ink initials, spine sl cocked) in dj (sl wear). *Antic Hay.* $22/£14

MONSARRAT, NICHOLAS. The Tribe That Lost Its Head. London: Cassell, 1956. 1st ed. (Spotted.) Dj (edges sl rubbed, price-clipped). *Hollett.* $23/£15

MONTAGU, G. Ornithological Dictionary of British Birds. W.S. Orr & W. Smith, 1833. New ed. lx,592pp (lt foxed, mainly feps; hinges cracked). Partly unopened. (Cl sl soiled, sl rubbed, spine faded, chipped.) *Edwards.* $47/£30

MONTAGU, J. A. A Guide to the Study of Heraldry. London: William Pickering, 1840. 1st ed. Lg fldg hand-colored litho frontis, (4),76pp. Teg. Late 19th-cent 1/2 polished red calf, gilt. VG (bkpls). *Cox.* $148/£95

MONTBARD, G. Among the Moors. London, 1894. 281pp. (Bumped, cvrs loose, rubbed.) *King.* $65/£42

MONTBARD, G. Among the Moors. NY: Scribner, 1894. xxii,281pp; 24 plts. Gilt-pict cl (ends frayed). *Adelson.* $60/£38

MONTEIRO, MARIANA. Legends and Popular Tales of the Basque People. London: T. Fisher Unwin, 1890. Popular ed. Blue illus cl over bds. VG (inscrip, sl foxed, sl worn). *Old London.* $85/£54

MONTESQUIEU, CHARLES DE SECONDAT. The Spirit of Laws. Worcester: Isaiah Thomas, June 1802. 1st Amer ed. 2 vols. Tall 8vo. 1/4 calf. (1st 2 sigs misbound.) *Rostenberg & Stern.* $750/£481

MONTEZ, LOLA. The Arts of Beauty; or, Secrets of a Lady's Toilet. NY: Dick & Fitzgerald, (1858). 1st ed. xviii,132pp + 12pp ads (lt foxing). Brn cl (sl frayed), gilt, blindstamped. *Karmiole.* $75/£48

MONTGOMERY, CHARLES F. American Furniture: The Federal Period. NY, (1966). 1st ed. (Sl internal wrinkling.) Dj (sl worn, wrinkled). *Freeman*.* $130/£83

MONTGOMERY, FRANCES TREGO. Billy Whiskers, Jr. and His Chums. Chicago: Brewer, Barse, 1907. 1st ed. (Corners bumped), o/w NF. *Hermitage.* $65/£42

MONTGOMERY, L. M. Rilla of Ingleside. NY: Frederick Stokes, (1921). 1st ed. Frontis. Pict label. NF. *Captain's Bookshelf.* $100/£64

MONTGOMERY, LEROY J. The Negro Problem. NY: Island Press, (1950). 1st ed. NF (faint stain) in stapled wrappers. *Between The Covers.* $45/£29

MONTGOMERY, RICHARD G. Peechuck, Lorne Knight's Adventures in the Arctic. NY, 1932. 1st ed. VG; dj remains laid in. *High Latitude.* $25/£16

MONTGOMERY, RICHARD G. Peechuck. Lorne Knight's Adventures in the Arctic. NY: Dodd, Mead, 1932. 1st ed. VG in dj (tattered). *High Latitude.* $35/£22

MONTGOMERY, RICHARD G. The White-Headed Eagle: John McLoughlin.... NY: Macmillan, 1934. 1st ed. VG in dj (sl worn). *Lien.* $40/£26

MONTGOMERY, RUTHERFORD. High Country. NY: Derrydale, (1938). One of 950 numbered. Uncut, unopened. Cl, leather labels. (Sl worn.) *Oinonen*.* $70/£45

MONTGOMERY, RUTHERFORD. Kildee House. NY: Doubleday, 1949. 1st ed. Barbara Cooney (illus). 5 1/2 x 8 1/4. 209pp. VG in dj. *Cattermole.* $20/£13

MONTI, ACHILLE. The Fundamental Data of Modern Pathology. London, 1900. Ex-lib, ink stamps prelims, feps lt browned.) Blind-emb cl, gilt device. (Accession label upper bd, spine sl discolored.) *Edwards.* $23/£15

MONTMASSON, JOSEPH-MARIE. Invention and the Unconscious. NY: Harcourt, 1932. 1st ed. Fine in dj (lt worn). *Beasley.* $75/£48

MONTOLINIA, FRAY TORIBIO. Motolinia's History of the Indians of New Spain. Elizabeth Andros Foster (ed). Berkeley, CA: Cortes Soc, 1950. Ltd to 500. Gray buckram. Good. *Karmiole.* $100/£64

MONTROSS GALLERY. Henri Matisse Exhibition. NY, 1915. Wrappers (fr cvr partly faded). *Swann*.* $172/£110

MOODIE, ROY. The Antiquity of Disease. Chicago, 1923. 1st ed. VG. *Fye.* $50/£32

MOODY, ELLA (ed). Decorative Art in Modern Interiors. The Studio, 1962. (Ex-lib, ink stamp, bkpl.) Protected dj (sl chipped, spine #s). *Edwards.* $47/£30

MOODY, ELLA (ed). Decorative Art in Modern Interiors. The Studio, 1963. (Ex-lib, ink stamp, bkpl.) Protected dj (torn, sl loss, spine #s). *Edwards.* $47/£30

MOODY, ELLA (ed). Decorative Art in Modern Interiors. Studio Vista, 1965. (Ex-lib, ink stamps, bkpl.) Protected dj. *Edwards.* $47/£30

MOODY, ELLA (ed). Decorative Art in Modern Interiors. Studio Vista, 1967. (Ex-lib, ink stamps, bkpl.) Protected pict bds (spine #s). *Edwards.* $39/£25

MOODY, ELLA (ed). Decorative Art in Modern Interiors. Studio Vista, 1968. (Ex-lib, ink stamp, bkpl, label remains.) Protected pict bds (spine #s). *Edwards.* $39/£25

MOODY, ELLA (ed). Decorative Art in Modern Interiors. Studio Vista, 1971. (Ex-lib, sm ink stamp, bkpl, label remains.) Protected pict bds (spine #s). *Edwards.* $39/£25

MOODY, ELLA (ed). Decorative Art in Modern Interiors. Studio Vista, 1972. (Ex-lib, sm ink stamp, bkpl, label remains.) Protected pict bds (spine #s). *Edwards.* $39/£25

MOODY, WILLIAM. Official Records of the Union and Confederate Navies in the War of the Rebellion. Series 1, Vol. 14. Washington: GPO, 1902. 1st ed. Good (hinges tender). *Archer.* $25/£16

MOON, GRACE. Shanty Ann. NY: Stokes, 1935. 1st ed. 5 1/2 x 8 1/4. 200pp; color frontis, 4 b/w plts by Carl Moon. Good. *Cattermole.* $35/£22

MOON, WILLIAM LEAST HEAT. See HEAT MOON, WILLIAM LEAST

MOONEY, JAMES. The Ghost-Dance Religion and the Sioux Outbreak of 1890. Washington: GPO, 1896. 1st ed. 643-1136pp; 38 plts (5 maps, 1 color fldg plt). Olive grn cl, gilt decs. (Sm rubbed area spine, lower corners sl jammed), else Fine. *Argonaut.* $250/£160

MOONEY, TED. Easy Travel to Other Planets. London: Jonathan Cape, 1982. 1st British ed. Fine in dj. *Lame Duck.* $65/£42

MOOR, HENRY. A Visit to Russia in the Autumn of 1862. London: Chapman & Hall, 1863. 1st ed. vi,234pp, 32 pub's list dated April 1863, 8 sepia lithos incl frontis (sl foxing margins text, plts). Red blindstamped cl (sl rubbed, stained; spine worn, split). Internally Sound. *Morrell.* $86/£55

MOORCOCK, MICHAEL (ed). England Invaded. W. H. Allen, 1977. 1st ed. (Pp yellowing), else Fine in dj. *Certo.* $25/£16

MOORCOCK, MICHAEL. Mother London: A Novel. London: Secker & Warburg, (1988). 1st ed. Signed. Fine in dj. *Other Worlds.* $35/£22

MOORCOCK, MICHAEL. Stormbringer. London: Jenkins, (1965). 1st ed. Signed. (Ink stamp.) Dj. *Swann*.* $103/£66

MOORE, ALAN. Sailing Ships of War, 1800-1860. London, 1926. #90/1500. Color frontis, xiv,78pp, 90 plts (11 color). Blue patterned cl, gilt. *Maggs.* $312/£200

MOORE, ALISON. The Louisiana Tigers. Baton Rouge, 1961. 1st ed. Addenda laid in. VG +. *Pratt.* $85/£54

MOORE, BRIAN. Black Robe. London: Cape, 1985. Signed. Good+ in VG dj. *Scribe's Perch*.* $25/£16

MOORE, BRIAN. Catholics. Cape, 1972. 1st UK ed. (Name fep), o/w Fine in Fine dj (sm mended tear). *Martin.* $22/£14

MOORE, BRIAN. The Doctor's Wife. London: Cape, 1976. 1st UK ed. NF in dj. *Williams.* $39/£25

MOORE, BRIAN. The Feast of Lupercal. Boston: Little, Brown, (1957). 1st US ed. VG + in VG dj. *Pettler & Lieberman.* $40/£26

MOORE, BRIAN. The Mangan Inheritance. London: Cape, 1979. 1st ed. Mint in dj. *Hollett.* $39/£25

MOORE, BRIAN. The Temptation of Eileen Hughes. London: Cape, 1981. 1st UK ed. Fine in NF dj. *Williams.* $39/£25

MOORE, C. L. Black God's Shadow. Grant, 1977. One of 150 numbered, signed by Moore and Alicia Austen (illus). Fine in Fine dj, pub's drop lid box w/art plt affixed to cvr, as issued. *Certo.* $150/£96

MOORE, C. L. Shambleau and Others. NY: Gnome, (1953). 1st Amer ed. VG (folded pp; shelfworn) in dj (sl worn). *Metropolitan*.* $57/£37

MOORE, C. L. Shambleau and Others. NY: Gnome, (1953). 1st ed. Fine in Fine dj. *Mcclintock.* $175/£112

MOORE, CLEMENT. The Night Before Christmas. London, (1931). One of 275 (of 550) numbered, signed by Arthur Rackham (illus). 8vo. 4 color plts. Pict eps. Orig limp vellum, gilt. (Bkpl.) Pub's bd slipcase (cracked). *Swann*.* $1,380/£885

MOORE, CLEMENT. The Night Before Christmas. NY: G.W. Dillingham, 1902. 1st ed. W.W. Denslow (illus). Gray cl, pict pastedwns. Great (name; bds sl sunned). *Metropolitan*.* $776/£497

MOORE, EMILY E. Travelling with Thomas Story. Hertfordshire, 1947. 1st ed. (Lt browning.) Blue buckram (sl worn). *Edwards.* $47/£30

MOORE, FRANK. Women of the War. Hartford, 1866. 9 plts. (Cl sl worn.) Contents VG. *New Hampshire*.* $25/£16

MOORE, G. H. Supplementary Notes on Witchcraft in Massachusetts. MA, 1884. Inscribed. 25pp; 1 inserted fldg heliotype plt. Unopened. *Middle Earth.* $75/£48

MOORE, GEORGE (ed). Pure Poetry. London: Nonesuch, 1924. 1st ed. #888/1250. Uncut. Parchment-backed bds. (Bkpl; sl mkd, bumped), o/w VG. *Cox.* $31/£20

MOORE, GEORGE. Aphrodite in Aulis. London: Heinemann, (1930). Ltd to 1825 signed. Full vellum. NF (eps sl browned) in VG slipcase (wear, soil). *Antic Hay.* $65/£42

MOORE, GEORGE. The Apostle. London: Heinemann, 1923. One of 1030 numbered, signed. Good + (bkpl). *Certo.* $35/£22

MOORE, GEORGE. Avowals. London: Privately ptd, 1919. Ltd to 1000 signed. Uncut. Orig vellum-backed bds. VG in dj (spine lt dknd). *Hollett.* $55/£35

MOORE, GEORGE. Celibates. London: Walter Scott, 1895. 1st ed. 8pp undated ads. Red cl. Fine. *Sumner & Stillman.* $50/£32

MOORE, GEORGE. Conversations in Ebury Street. 1924. Ltd to 1030 signed. Vellum-backed bds (spine foxed). VG in dj (spine sl dknd). *Words Etc.* $47/£30

MOORE, GEORGE. Evelyn Innes. NY: D. Appleton, 1898. 1st Amer ed, primary binding: lt brn cl dec in brn/black. 10pp undated ads. NF (sl soiled). *Sumner & Stillman.* $40/£26

MOORE, GEORGE. Impressions and Opinions. London, 1891. 1st ed, 1st issue w/pub's name on backstrip, w/12pp ads at end. (Ink name eradicated half-title), o/w Fine. *Argosy.* $100/£64

MOORE, GEORGE. The Passing of the Essenes. London: Heinemann, 1930. Ltd to 775 numbered, signed. Teg. Dec white vellum. NF. *Antic Hay.* $75/£48

MOORE, GEORGE. The Pastoral Loves of Daphnis and Chloe. London: Heinemann, 1924. Ltd to 1250 numbered, signed. VG (pastedowns browned) in dj (soiled, browned, nicks, sm tears). *Antic Hay.* $35/£22

MOORE, GEORGE. The Pastoral Loves of Daphnis and Chloe.... Heinemann, 1924. 1st ed. #1077/1280 signed. 4 full-pg illus. Marbled bds, white buckram spine (sl discolored). *Bickersteth.* $55/£35

MOORE, GEORGE. Peronnick the Fool. (Mount Vernon, NY: Rudge), 1926. One of 785. Blue paper bds stencilled in red/yellow, paper title label. Very Nice. *Cady.* $30/£19

MOORE, GEORGE. Ulick and Soracha. Nonesuch, 1926. 1st ed. #597/1250 signed. Engr. Uncut. VG in buckram; parchment dj (cracked, sl chipped). *Cox.* $55/£35

MOORE, GEORGE. Ulick and Soracha. NY: Boni & Liveright, 1926. Ltd to 1250 numbered, signed. Vellum, bds. As New in dj, orig ptd cardbd shipping box. *Antic Hay.* $75/£48

MOORE, GEORGE. The Use of the Body in Relation to the Mind. NY: Harper, 1847. (Foxed; worn, bumped.) *Metropolitan*.* $50/£32

MOORE, GUY W. The Case of Mrs. Surratt. Norman, 1954. 1st ed. VG + in VG + dj. *Pratt.* $32/£21

MOORE, H. C. Omnibuses and Cabs. London, 1902. Illus cl (spine sl faded, soiled sl intruding onto bds). *Edwards.* $133/£85

MOORE, HENRY. Henry Moore's Sheep Sketchbook. London: Thames & Hudson, 1980. 1st Eng ed. VG in dj. *Hadley.* $62/£40

MOORE, HENRY. Shelter Sketch Book. London: Editions Poetry, (1945). 1st Eng ed. Very Nice (fr hinge weak) in dj (sl mkd, rubbed). *Clearwater.* $94/£60

MOORE, J. BERNARD. Skagway in Days Primeval. NY: Vantage, (1968). VG in VG dj. *Perier.* $35/£22

MOORE, J. E. S. To the Mountains of the Moon. London: Hurst & Blacket, 1901. Color frontis, 3 maps (incl lg fldg color map at end). Grn pict cl. (Fr flyleaf missing; back cvr stained, spotted), else VG. *Terramedia.* $300/£192

MOORE, J. E. S. To the Mountains of the Moon. London: Hurst & Blackett, 1901. 1st ed. Color frontis, 3 maps (2 fldg). Teg. Olive cl. Good. *Karmiole.* $275/£176

MOORE, JAMES. History of the Cooper Shop Volunteer Refreshment Saloon. Phila: Jas. B. Rodgers, 1866. 1st ed. Frontis, 212pp. Gilt-stamped cl (spine extrems worn). VG (inscrip). *Wantagh.* $75/£48

MOORE, JAMES. Kilpatrick and Our Cavalry. NY: W.J. Widdleton, 1865. 1st ed. 245,(4)pp. VG (rubbed). Howes M774. *Mcgowan.* $150/£96

MOORE, JAMES. Kilpatrick and Our Cavalry.... NY: Widdleton, 1865. 1st ed. 245,(4)pp (inscrip). Dec cl (faded). Howes M774. *Ginsberg.* $100/£64

MOORE, JAMES. A Narrative of the Campaign of the British Army in Spain.... London: J. Johnson, 1809. 3rd ed. (iii)-xix,(1),388,136pp; 2 lg fldg maps. Recent smooth calf, raised bands, red morocco spine label. (Maps sl creased, offset, 1 w/short tear), o/w Excellent. *Pirages.* $150/£96

MOORE, JOHN WHEELER (comp). Roster of North Carolina Troops in the War Between the States. Raleigh: Ashe & Gatling, 1882. 1st ed. 4 vols. (Cl rubbed, fr bd stained vol 1; recased, spine ends professionally repaired.) Good set. *Mcgowan.* $1,500/£962

MOORE, JOHN. The Diary of Sir John Moore. J. F. Maurice (ed). London, 1904. Port, 7 fldg maps. Red 1/2 morocco, marbled bds. Attractive set. *Maggs.* $195/£125

MOORE, JOHN. The Life and Letters of Edward Thomas. London, 1939. 1st ed. Brn cl. (Lt spotted), o/w VG in dj (torn, creased). *Words Etc.* $70/£45

MOORE, LUCIA et al. The Story of Eugene. NY: Stratford House, 1949. 1st ed. (Name gold-stamped fr cvr), else VG. *Perier.* $50/£32

MOORE, MARIANNE (trans). The Fables of La Fontaine. NY: Viking, 1954. One of 400 numbered, signed by Moore. Fine in slipcase (sl worn). *Lenz.* $250/£160

MOORE, MARIANNE. The Arctic Ox. London: Faber & Faber, (1964). 1st ed (1500 ptd). VG in dj (edge-tanned, nicks). *Reese.* $20/£13

MOORE, MARIANNE. The Arctic Ox. London: Faber & Faber, (1964). One of 1500. Fine in Fine dj. *Dermont.* $75/£48

MOORE, MARIANNE. Collected Poems. London: Faber & Faber, (1951). 1st ed. Errata sheet. Orange cl. Fine in dj. *House.* $100/£64

MOORE, MARIANNE. The Complete Poems of.... NY: Viking/Macmillan, (1967). 1st ed. (Edges sl dusty), else Fine in dj (edge-tanned, sm nicks). *Reese.* $20/£13

MOORE, MARIANNE. The Fables of La Fontaine. NY: Viking, 1954. Ltd to 400 numbered, signed. Frontis. Red cl, gilt. Fine in pub's slipcase. *Karmiole.* $300/£192

MOORE, MARIANNE. Like a Bulwark. NY: Viking, 1956. 1st ed. Pastel bds. NF (sig) in dj. *House.* $45/£29

MOORE, MARIANNE. Predilections. NY, 1955. 1st Amer ed. Fine in dj (lacks sm piece, few sm chips). *Polyanthos.* $30/£19

MOORE, MARIANNE. Predilections. NY: Viking, 1955. 1st ed. Nice in dj (spine tanned). *Reese.* $50/£32

MOORE, MARIANNE. Puss in Boots, the Sleeping Beauty and Cinderella. NY/London: Macmillan/Collier-Macmillan, 1963. 1st ed. 4to. ix,(i),46pp; 10 plts by Eugene Karlin. Color pict white/pink lib cl (bumped, sl soiled). VG (sl tape stains pastedowns, dj spine) in pict white dj (price-clipped, sl soiled, lt creased). *Blue Mountain.* $35/£22

MOORE, MARIANNE. Tell Me, Tell Me. NY, 1966. 1st ed. VF in Fine dj. *Bond.* $25/£16

MOORE, MARIANNE. Tell Me, Tell Me. NY, 1966. 1st Amer ed. Fine in dj (edges sl rubbed, price-clipped). *Polyanthos.* $30/£19

MOORE, MARIANNE. What Are Years. NY, 1941. 1st Amer ed. Fine in dj (sm spine edge tear, top edge sl rubbed). *Polyanthos.* $40/£26

MOORE, MARIANNE. What Are Years. NY: Macmillan, 1941. 1st ed. (Cl sl dust mkd, pastedowns tanned), o/w VG in dj (lt worn, sm spot rear panel). *Reese.* $85/£54

MOORE, N. F. Diary of a Trip from New York to the Falls of St. Anthony in 1845. Pargellis and Butler (eds). Chicago: Newberry Lib, 1946. 1st ed. 8 plts. (Sl pencil), o/w Good in Good dj (soil, date stamp). *Scribe's Perch*.* $20/£13

MOORE, N. HUDSON. The Old Clock Book. NY: Frederick A. Stokes, (1911). 1st ed. Frontis. Brn cl. *Weber.* $20/£13

MOORE, NICHOLAS. A Book for Priscilla. Cambridge, 1941. 1st Eng ed. Card wrappers (sl dusty). *Clearwater.* $39/£25

MOORE, NICHOLAS. The Glass Tower. London: Editions Poetry, 1944. 1st ed. Dec cvrs. Fine (edges sl rubbed, corner crease) in dj (spine sunned, few edge chips, price-clipped). *Polyanthos.* $30/£19

MOORE, NORMAN. The History of the Study of Medicine in the British Isles. Oxford, 1908. 1st ed. VG. *Fye.* $100/£64

MOORE, OPHA. History of Franklin County, Ohio. Topeka, 1930. 1st ed. 3 vols. *Ginsberg.* $175/£112

MOORE, RICHARD B. The Name 'Negro,' Its Origin and Its Use. NY: AfroAmerican Pub, 1960. 1st ed. VG (inscrip) in VG dj. *Warren.* $40/£26

MOORE, T. STURGE. A Brief Account of the Origin of the Eragny Press. Hammersmith: Eragny Press, 1903. One of 235. 15 wood engrs. (Offsetting feps, lg inscrip.) Floral patterned paper over bds, gray paper spine. (Lt soiled, joints, ends partly worn.) *Waverly*.* $522/£335

MOORE, THOMAS H. Henry Miller Bibliography. (Minneapolis: Henry Miller Literary Soc, 1961.) One of 1000 numbered. Fine in ptd wrappers. *Reese.* $30/£19

MOORE, THOMAS. British Wild Flowers. London, 1867. 2nd ed. xxivii,424pp; 24 hand-colored plts. (Neatly rebacked, preserving spine.) *Henly.* $47/£30

MOORE, THOMAS. Irish Melodies with an Appendix.... J. Power, 1821. xii,259pp. Full calf, gilt, grn morocco label. *Cox.* $47/£30

MOORE, THOMAS. Irish Melodies.... J. Power, Longman, Hurst, etc., 1822. 2nd ed. xii,251pp. Uncut. Orig bds. (Reinforced along hinges, backstrip w/strip of linen), o/w VG. *Cox.* $31/£20

MOORE, THOMAS. Memoirs of the Life of the Right Honourable Richard Brinsley Sheridan. London: Longman, 1825. 1st ed. xii,719pp; engr port, facs ms. (Lacks 1/2 title.) Contemp calf (rebacked), Signet Library arms on cvrs. *Burmester.* $156/£100

MOORE, THOMAS. A Popular History of British Ferns. London, (1859). 3rd ed. xvi,394pp; 22 color plts. (Cl sl used.) *Wheldon & Wesley.* $31/£20

MOORE, THOMAS. A Popular History of British Ferns.... London: Routledge, Warne & Routledge, 1859. 394pp incl index + 8pp ads; 22 full-pg color plts. (Cl stained), else VG. *Quest.* $70/£45

MOORE, TOM. Tom Moore's Diary. Cambridge: CUP, 1925. 1st ed. Grn cl. NF in dj (worn, torn, browned). *Antic Hay.* $25/£16

MOORE, WARD. Bring the Jubilee. Farrar, Straus & Young, (1953). 1st ed. VG + in dj (silverfish damage to rear panel). *Certo.* $45/£29

MOOREHEAD, ALAN. Montgomery; a Biography. London, 1946. 1st ed. VG in dj (few tears). *Words Etc.* $16/£10

MOOREHEAD, ALAN. The Villa Diana. London: Hamish Hamilton, 1951. 1st ed. Fine in dj. *Hollett.* $31/£20

MOOREHEAD, ALAN. The White Nile. London, 1960. 1st Eng ed. Very Nice in dj. *Clearwater.* $39/£25

MOOREHEAD, WARREN K. Primitive Man in Ohio. NY: Putnam, 1892. 1st ed. xv,246pp (lt foxed, aged). Dk grn-brn cl (ends frayed, sl dusty, lt stains), gilt. Baltimore*. $120/£77

MOOREHEAD, WARREN K. and MORRIS M. LEIGHTON. The Cahokia Mounds. Urbana: Univ of IL, 1923. 1st ed. Presentation from Moorehead. 21 plts (last plt separated along hinge), fldg map. Errata slip laid in. VG (lt foxed, bkpl; spine sl faded, title inked on spine) in self-wrappers. Cahan. $40/£26

MOORHEAD, JOHN J. Traumatic Surgery. Phila, 1918. 1st ed. Doctor's Library. $60/£38

MOORHEAD, JOHN J. Traumatotherapy: The Treatment of the Injured. Phila, 1931. 1st ed. Blue cl bds (sl worn). VG. Doctor's Library. $50/£32

MOORHEAD, MAX L. The Presidio, Bastion of the Spanish Borderlands. Norman: Univ of OK, (1975). 1st ed. 2 dbl-pg repros. Tan cl. VF in dj. Argonaut. $45/£29

MOORHEAD, MAX L. The Presidio. Norman, 1975. 1st ed. (Corners sl bumped), o/w Fine in dj priceclipped). Baade. $32/£21

MOORMAN, J. J. Mineral Springs of North America.... Phila: Lippincott, 1873. 1st ed. Signed presentation. Fldg frontis map, 294,(22 ads)pp; fldg colored map. Terra cotta cl (edges lt worn). NF. Glaser. $150/£96

MOORMAN, LEWIS J. Pioneer Doctor. Norman: Univ of OK, (1951). 1st ed. VG. Lien. $25/£16

MOORMAN, MADISON BERRYMAN. The Journal of Madison Berryman Moorman, 1850-1851. Irene D. Paden (ed). SF: CA Hist Soc, 1948. 1st ed. Ginsberg. $75/£48

MOORS, H. J. With Stevenson in Samoa. Boston, 1910. Frontis port. (Extrems sl rubbed.) Edwards. $47/£30

MORA, GILLES. Walker Evans: Havana, 1933. NY: Pantheon, 1989. 1st Amer ed. Frontis, 80 full-pg b/w photos. Fine in dj (rubbed, torn). Cahan. $25/£16

MORA, JO. Californios: The Saga of the Hard-Riding Vaqueros, America's First Cowboys. NY: Doubleday, 1949. 1st ed. Fine in pict dj (sl torn, soiled). Argonaut. $60/£38

MORA, JO. Trail Dust and Saddle Leather. NY: Scribner, 1946. 1st ed. Frontis. Pict eps. Tan cl, red lettering. VF in pict dj (spine faded). Argonaut. $75/£48

MORAGA, GABRIEL. The Diary of Ensign Gabriel Moraga's Expedition of Discovery in the Sacramento Valley, 1808. Donald C. Cutter (ed). (L.A.): Glen Dawson, 1957. Ltd to 300 ptd by Lawton Kennedy. Fldg map. Cl-backed bds (sm spots fr cvr). Nice. Shasky. $40/£26

MORAGA, GABRIEL. The Diary of Ensign Gabriel Moraga's Expedition of Discovery in the Sacramento Valley, 1808. Donald C. Cutter (ed). L.A.: Glen Dawson, 1957. Ltd to 300 ptd. Fldg map. Cl-backed bds, gilt. Fine. Pacific*. $40/£26

MORAN, JAMES. Stanley Morison, His Typographic Achievement. London: Lund Humphries, 1971. 1st ed. Moran's obituary laid in. Good in dj (sl frayed). Cox. $55/£35

MORAN, JIM. Sophocles the Hyena. NY: Whittlesey House, 1954. 1st ed. Roger Duvoisin (illus). 8vo. 48pp. Dec cvr. VG in dj (chipped). Scribe's Perch*. $18/£12

MORAND, PAUL. Black Magic. NY, 1929. 1st Amer ed. Cl-backed patterned bds. (Ink name; cvrs sl worn.) King. $35/£22

MORANTE, ELSA. Arturo's Island. I. Quigly (trans). London, 1959. 1st ed. Dj. Typographeum. $15/£10

MORANTE, ELSA. Arturo's Island. NY: Knopf, 1959. 1st US ed. VG+ (price stamp rep; spine sl cocked) in VG+ dj (chip). Lame Duck. $65/£42

MORASSI, ANTONIO. Art Treasures of the Medici. NY, 1963. 55 tipped-in color plts. Good. Washton. $50/£32

MORATH, INGE and DOMINIQUE AUBIER. Fiesta in Pamplona. London: Photography Magazine, 1957. 1st ed. NF in VG ptd acetate dj. Smith. $80/£51

MORATH, INGE and ARTHUR MILLER. In the Country. NY: Viking, 1977. 1st ed. Pict eps. Cl-backed paper over bds. VG in dj. Cahan. $35/£22

MORAVIA, ALBERTO. Roman Tales. NY, (1957). 1st Amer ed. NF in dj (2 sm chips, spine sl rubbed). Polyanthos. $25/£16

MORAVIA, ALBERTO. The Wayward Wife and Other Stories. NY, 1960. 1st Amer ed. NF (spine extrems sl rubbed) in dj (edge rubbed). Polyanthos. $25/£16

MORCOMBE, JOSEPH. The Life and Labors of Theodore Sutton Parvin.... Cedar Rapids: Grand Lodge of IA, (1906). Ptd presentation label fep; bkpl laid in. VG. Graf. $50/£32

MORE, CRESACRE. The Life of Sir Thomas More. London, 1828. Port. Contemp polished brn calf (extrems scuffed, spine end gone, fr cvr detached; bkpl), gilt, red morocco label. Freeman*. $40/£26

MORE, L. T. Isaac Newton. A Biography. 1934. Frontis port. VG. Whitehart. $39/£25

MORESBY, LOUIS. The Glory of Egypt. NY, (1926). 1st ed. Fine in VG dj (sl soil, edgewear). Mcclintock. $85/£54

MORETON, C. OSCAR. Old Carnations and Pinks. London: Geo. Rainbird, 1955. 1st ed. One of 3000. Blue cl, illus paper over bds (sl bumped). NF in VG- dj (back dampstained). Archer. $90/£58

MOREWOOD, SAMUEL. An Essay on the Inventions and Customs of Both Ancients and Moderns in the Use of Inebriating Liquors. London: Longman, Hurst et al, 1824. 1st ed. xi,(1),375pp (1st few ll marginally dampstained, sm skillful margin repair tp). Mod 3/4 brn morocco, gilt, marbled bds, red morocco spine labels, 5 raised bands. Glaser. $485/£311

MOREY, CHARLES RUFUS. Early Christian Art...from Antiquity to the Eighth Century. Princeton, 1942. (Cl sl soiled.) Washton. $145/£93

MOREY, CHARLES RUFUS. The Mosaics of Antioch. London, 1938. Color frontis, 24 plts. Good in dj (sl worn). Washton. $100/£64

MOREY, WALT. Gentle Ben. NY: Dutton, (1965). 1st ed. Fine (sl foxing fore-edge) in Fine dj (priceclipped). Between The Covers. $50/£32

MOREY, WALT. Gentle Ben. NY, 1965. 1st ed. VF in VG dj. Bond. $20/£13

MORFI, JUAN AUGUSTIN. History of Texas, 1673-1779. Carlos Eduardo Castaneda (trans). Albuquerque: Quivira Soc, 1935. One of 500 numbered. 2 vols. 4 plts, fldg map. Bds, vellum spine (paper label remnants; soil). Howes M792. Ginsberg. $450/£288

MORGAN, A. T. Yazoo; or, On the Picket Line of Freedom in the South. Washington, 1884. 1st ed. 512pp. (Cvr wear, staining), o/w VG+. Pratt. $125/£80

MORGAN, A. T. Yazoo; or, On the Picket Line of Freedom in the South. Washington, D.C.: The Author, 1884. 1st ed. 521pp (few sm paper tears, fr inner hinge partially cracked). Howes M795. M & S. $150/£96

MORGAN, BARBARA. Martha Graham. NY: Duell, Sloan & Pearce, 1941. 1st ed. VG. Smith. $150/£96

MORGAN, CHARLES. The Empty Room. London: Macmillan, 1941. 1st ed. Nice in dj (frayed, mends). Reese. $20/£13

MORGAN, CHARLES. The Fountain. London: Macmillan, 1932. 1st ed. Fine in VG dj (tanning, spine mks). Reese. $35/£22

MORGAN, CHARLES. Portrait in a Mirror. London: Macmillan, 1929. 1st Eng ed. Grn cl. NF in dj (spine sl browned, sm tear). *Antic Hay.* $50/£32

MORGAN, DALE and ELEANOR TOWLES HARRIS (eds). The Rocky Mountain Journals of William Marshall Anderson—The West in 1834. San Marino, 1967. 1st ed. Inscribed by Morgan, Jim Holliday; signed by Morgan, Harris, Ward Ritchie (designer). Frontis port. NF (Morgan inscrip bled onto frontis port) in dj (closed tear). *Benchmark.* $175/£112

MORGAN, DALE. Jedediah Smith, and the Opening of the West. Indianapolis: Bobbs-Merrill, (1953). 1st ed. Cl cvrs (dampstained). VG in dj. *Lien.* $50/£32

MORGAN, DAVID P. Diesels West! (Madison: Kalmbach, c. 1963.) VG+ in dj (frayed). *Bohling.* $25/£16

MORGAN, GEORGE H. Annals, Comprising Memoirs, Incidents, and Statistics of Harrisburg, from the Period of its First Settlement.... Harrisburg: Brooks, 1858. 1st ed. (2),400,(2)pp. (Joints expertly mended.) Howes M796. *Ginsberg.* $125/£80

MORGAN, H. T. The Life of Henry Bruce. (Chicago: Lakeside Press), 1934. 1st ed. Ptd paper label. VG. *Wantagh.* $45/£29

MORGAN, J. W. California Impressions...1886. David Perkins (ed). Northridge, CA: Santa Susana, 1990. Ltd to 200 numbered, signed by Perkins and Norman E. Tanis (series ed). Gray linen, dec bds, paper spine label. Good. *Karmiole.* $50/£32

MORGAN, JAMES MORRIS. Recollections of a Rebel Reefer. London, (1917). 1st Eng ed. Pict cl. (Cvr lt worn), o/w VG+. *Pratt.* $175/£112

MORGAN, JOHN HILL and MANTLE FIELDING. The Life Portraits of Washington and Their Replicas. Phila, (1931). One of 1000. Signed, inscribed presentation by Fielding. Blue cl (sl worn, soiled), gilt spine. Dj (sl dampstained), paper spine label. *Freeman*.* $130/£83

MORGAN, JOHN HILL and MANTLE FIELDING. The Life Portraits of Washington and Their Replicas. Phila: For the Subscribers, (1931). One of 1000. Uncut. Gilt-stamped buckram (sl worn; lib mks). *Oinonen*.* $110/£71

MORGAN, JOHN. A Discourse Upon the Institution of Medical Schools in America.... Balt: Johns Hopkins, 1937. Rpt of 1st ed. Ptd bds, cl spine (sm paint stain spine bottom). VG (bkpl, sigs). *Glaser.* $60/£38

MORGAN, LEWIS HENRY. The American Beaver and His Works. Phila: Lippincott, 1868. 1st ed. Inscribed. xv,(17)-330pp, fldg map, 23 plts. Emb cl (spine, cvrs faded). VG Internally. Howes M802. *Parmer.* $250/£160

MORGAN, LEWIS HENRY. The American Beaver and His Works. Phila: Lippincott, 1868. 1st ed. Inscribed, dated 1872. 8vo. 332,(2)pp; 23 litho plts, fldg map. (Bkpl.) Panelled mauve cl. *Gach.* $750/£481

MORGAN, LEWIS HENRY. The Indian Journals 1859-62. L.A. White (ed). Ann Arbor: Univ of MI, (1959). 16 color plts. VG in Fair dj (tape-repaired). *Scribe's Perch*.* $29/£19

MORGAN, LEWIS HENRY. The Indian Journals, 1859-62. Ann Arbor: Univ of MI, (1959). 1st ed. 16 color plts. Fine in NF dj. *Harrington.* $65/£42

MORGAN, LEWIS HENRY. Lewis Henry Morgan: The Indian Journals 1859-62. Leslie A. White (ed). Ann Arbor: Univ of MI, (1959). 1st ed. 16 color plts. VG in dj. *Lien.* $50/£32

MORGAN, MANIE. The New Stars. Jennie A. Morgan (ed). Antioch Press, OH, 1949. 1st ed. Inscribed by ed. Frontis. *Wantagh.* $45/£29

MORGAN, OWEN. The Light of Britannia. Cardiff/London/NY: Daniel Owen/Whittaker/J.W. Boulton, (c. 1893). Frontis port, (vi),v,(v),430,(i)pp; fldg plt. Red cl, gilt. (Few pg corners creased, hinges cracked; bumped, stained; cl split at fr joint.) VG. *Blue Mountain.* $150/£96

MORGAN, SETH. Homeboy. London, 1990. 1st ed. NF in NF dj. *Smith.* $35/£22

MORGAN, W. E. C. and F. W. COOPER. The Thatcher's Craft. Rural Industries Bureau, 1961. VG in dj. *Hadley.* $47/£30

MORGAN, WILLARD D. Photo Cartoons. Scarsdale, NY: Morgan & Morgan, 1948. VG in illus stiff wrappers (sl dknd, rubbed). *Cahan.* $30/£19

MORGAN, WILLARD D. et al. The Leica Manual. NY, 1935. 1st ed. (Inner fr hinge cracked; cvrs rubbed, dknd.) *King.* $35/£22

MORGAN, WILLIAM N. Prehistoric Architecture in the Eastern United States. Cambridge: MIT, (1980). Good in dj. *Archaeologia.* $45/£29

MORIARTY, GERALD P. (trans). The Paris Law Courts. London, 1894. viii,293pp+(ii) ads. (Spotting; upper hinge cracked; lt soiled, edges rubbed, spine discolored, head bumped, sl chipped.) *Edwards.* $55/£35

MORIER, JAMES. The Adventures of Hajji Baba of Ishpahan. C. J. Wills (ed). London, 1897. 623pp. (Rubbed, dknd), else Good. *King.* $40/£26

MORIER, JAMES. The Adventures of Hajji Baba of Ishpahan. C.J. Wills (ed). Lawrence & Billen, 1897. (Binding spotted.) *Petersfield.* $33/£21

MORISON, A. The Sensory and Motor Disorders of the Heart. London, 1914. (Several pp lt foxed, new eps, sl nick spine), o/w VG. *Whitehart.* $39/£25

MORISON, ROBERT. Plantarum Historiae Universalis Oxoniensis. Oxford: Sheldonian Theatre, 1680-99. 1st ed. Parts II and III (all pub). 1/2 title, engr port part III (?lacking in part II), 292 plts (lt browning, 1 plt frayed). 19th-cent 1/2 calf (worn, spine ends, inner hinges crudely reinforced). *Christie's*.* $613/£393

MORISON, S. English Prayer Books. CUP, 1943. 1st ed. VG in dj. *Moss.* $62/£40

MORISON, SAMUEL ELIOT. Journals and Other Documents on the Life and Voyages of Christopher Columbus. NY: LEC, 1963. One of 1500 numbered, signed by Lima de Freitas (illus). Fine in pub's slipcase (lt rubbed). *Hermitage.* $150/£96

MORISON, SAMUEL ELIOT. The Story of Mount Desert Island Maine. Boston: Little, Brown, (1960). 1st ed. Pict cl. Fine in dj (spine sl lightened). *Sadlon.* $15/£10

MORISON, STANLEY and KENNETH DAY. The Typographic Book, 1450-1935. (Chicago): Univ of Chicago, (1963). 1st US ed. Sm folio. Black buckram, gilt. Very Nice (bkpl removed) in dj (dusted, worn, old tape repairs spine top). *Baltimore*.* $80/£51

MORISON, STANLEY and HOLBROOK JACKSON. A Brief Survey of Printing History and Practice. NY, 1923. Cl-backed dec bds. VG+. *Truepenny.* $85/£54

MORISON, STANLEY. The Art of Printing. London: British Academy, 1937. 1st ed. 28 facs plts. VG in contemp cl, piece from orig wrapper as label upper cvr. *Cox.* $28/£18

MORISON, STANLEY. Four Centuries of Fine Printing. London: Ernest Benn, (1949). 2nd ed. #153/200. Teg. Full polished rust-colored leather, gilt. (Edges sl scuffed), else VG. *Bohling.* $150/£96

MORISON, STANLEY. Four Centuries of Fine Printing. NY: Farrar, Straus, (1949). 2nd ed. Blue cl. VG in dj (dknd, frayed, soiled). *Bohling.* $30/£19

MORISON, STANLEY. Four Centuries of Fine Printing. NY: Farrar, Straus, (1949). 1st Amer ptg of rev ed. Fine in VG dj (tear). *House.* $50/£32

MORISON, STANLEY. Four Centuries of Fine Printing. Ernest Benn, 1949. 2nd rev ed. 272 half-tone facs plts. VG in dj. Cox. $39/£25

MORISON, STANLEY. Four Centuries of Fine Printing. London: Ernest Benn Ltd, 1949. 2nd rev, 1st 8vo ed. Fine in VG dj (edge-nicked, lt soiled). Reese. $50/£32

MORISON, STANLEY. Fra Luca de Pacioli of Borgo S. Sepolcro. NY: Grolier Club, 1933. One of 390. Folio. Orig 1/4 vellum. Bd slipcase. Swann*. $862/£553

MORISON, STANLEY. Ichabod Dawks and His News-Letter with an Account of the Dawks Family of Booksellers and Stationers 1635-1731. Cambridge: CUP, 1931. 1st ed. One of 500. Frontis, 5 tipped-in collotype illus, 4-pg letterpress facs. Lt brn buckram, gilt. Fine in dj. Cady. $150/£96

MORISON, STANLEY. The Likeness of Thomas More. Nicolas Barker (ed). London: Burns Oates, 1963. Color frontis. Red cl, gilt. Europa. $39/£25

MORISON, STANLEY. Selected Essays on the History of Letterforms in Manuscript and Print. David McKitterick (ed). Cambridge: CUP, 1981. 2 vols. Pub's burgundy cl, gilt. Pristine in djs, matching slipcase w/ptd label on back. Book Block. $275/£176

MORISON, STANLEY. Type Designs of the Past and Present. Fleuron, 1926. 1st ed. Uncut. Spare paper label at end (browned). VG. Cox. $31/£20

MORISON, STANLEY. The Typographic Arts. Sylvan, 1949. 16 plts. VG in dj (defective). Cox. $28/£18

MORISOT, BERTHE. The Correspondence of.... Denis Rouart (ed). London, (1957). 1st ed in English. Boxed. Kane*. $60/£38

MORLAND, WILLIAM W. Diseases of the Urinary Organs. Phila: Blanchard & Lea, 1858. 1st ed. x,(19)-579pp + 32pp ads. Emb cl. VG (ex-lib). Glaser. $85/£54

MORLEY, CHRISTOPHER. The Curious Case of Kenelm Digby. N.p.: Angelica Press, Privately Ptd for Universal Coterie of Pipe Smokers, 1975. One of 500 numbered, signed by designer, illus. Pub's gift card laid in. Fine in French marbled wrappers. Robbins. $35/£22

MORLEY, CHRISTOPHER. John Mistletoe. London: Faber & Faber, 1931. 1st UK ed. Fine in dj. Williams. $39/£25

MORLEY, CHRISTOPHER. Notes on Bermuda. NY, 1931. 1st ed. VG in dj (sl used). Words Etc. $34/£22

MORLEY, CHRISTOPHER. Old Loopy. Chicago: Argus Book Shop, 1935. 1st ed. Pict moire cl stamped in silver. VG. Reese. $40/£26

MORLEY, CHRISTOPHER. Parnassus on Wheels. GC, 1917. 1st ptg. Clipped Morley sig inserted. Pict cl-backed bds (rubbed, sm tear spine top; inner joint opening, bkpl, inscrip). Kane*. $40/£26

MORLEY, CHRISTOPHER. Parnassus on Wheels. GC: Doubleday, Page, 1917. 1st ed, 1st state, w/space between the 'Y' and 'e' in 'Years' p4, line 8. Pict bds. VG. Antic Hay. $75/£48

MORLEY, CHRISTOPHER. The Powder of Sympathy. GC: Doubleday, 1923. Paper label. Fine in dj. Reese. $25/£16

MORLEY, CHRISTOPHER. Preface to 'Bartlett.' Boston, 1937. 1st ed. Cl-backed bds (rubbed). King. $22/£14

MORLEY, CHRISTOPHER. The Romany Stain.... Toronto: S.B. Gundy, 1926. 1st ed, Canadian issue, w/cancel tp, Gundy imprint on dj. Paper labels. Fine in dj (frayed, nicked). Reese. $25/£16

MORLEY, CHRISTOPHER. Swiss Family Manhattan. GC: Doubleday, Doran, 1932. 1st ed. Ltd to 250 signed. Gilt-dec grn bds, label. Good (bkpl) in glassine dj (frayed). Lucas. $150/£96

MORLEY, CHRISTOPHER. Thunder on the Left. GC: Doubleday, 1925. 1st ed. Paper labels. Fine in NF dj (nicks, tear). Reese. $30/£19

MORLEY, CHRISTOPHER. Where the Blue Begins. London/NY, (1922). 1st trade ed thus. 4 color plts by Arthur Rackham. Blue cl. (Cvr wear), o/w VG. New Hampshire*. $45/£29

MORLEY, CHRISTOPHER. Where the Blue Begins. NY, (1922). 1st Amer ed. 4 full-pg color illus by Arthur Rackham. Fine (spine sunned, extrems sl rubbed). Polyanthos. $95/£61

MORLEY, CHRISTOPHER. Where the Blue Begins. Phila: Lippincott, (1922). 1st Rackham ed. 8vo. 4 color plts by Arthur Rackham. Blue cl. Nice in dj (nicked). Appelfeld. $125/£80

MORLEY, CHRISTOPHER. Where the Blue Begins. London/NY: Heinemann/Doubleday Page, n.d. (1925). 1st trade ed. 4to. 4 color plts by Arthur Rackham. Blue-illus eps, gilt. NF (few sl mks). Bookmark. $234/£150

MORLEY, F. V. River Thames. London, 1926. 1st ed. 9 maps. Marbled eps. (Lt browned.) Mod morocco-backed morocco bds. Edwards. $70/£45

MORLEY, F. V. and J. S. HODGSON. Whaling North and South. NY: Century, c. 1926. VG in dj (frayed). High Latitude. $40/£26

MORLEY, JOHN. Death, Heaven and the Victorians. London, 1971. 1st UK ed. Dj (sl chipped). Edwards. $39/£25

MORO, CESAR. Amour a Mort. Frances LeFevre (trans). NY: TVRT, 1973. 1st ed. Fine in wraps. Beasley. $45/£29

Moron, a Tale of the Alhambra. (By John J. White.) Phila: John Grigg, 1829. 1st ed, 1st bk. 111pp. Orig blue ptd bds (lacks portions of spine, sl rubbed; sig, bkpl). Brown. $40/£26

MORPHET, RICHARD (intro). Wish You Were Here. Long Island: Emily Lowe Gallery, 1974. 1st ed. 4 Fine mtd color postcards. Good (damp-wrinkled) in illus stiff wrappers (soil). Cahan. $60/£38

MORRELL, DAVID. First Blood. Evans, 1972. 1st ed, 1st book. Signed, inscribed. Fine in Fine dj. Certo. $85/£54

MORRELL, DAVID. Testament. NY: Evans, 1975. 1st ed. Fine in dj (sl worn). Else Fine. $75/£48

MORRELL, DAVID. The Totem. NY: Evans, 1979. 1st ed. Fine in Fine dj. Else Fine. $50/£32

MORRELL, W. P. The Gold Rushes. London: A&C Black, 1940. 1st ed. 8 maps (2 fldg). Blue cl. Fine in dj (spine dknd, lt worn). Argonaut. $75/£48

MORRICE, F. L. H. The Nightless North. London, 1881. 184pp, fldg map. (Contemp rev affixed to fep, prelims lt browned; spine sl rubbed.) Edwards. $70/£45

MORRIS, B. F. Christian Life and Character of the Civil Institutions of the United States.... Phila/Cincinnati: George W. Childs/Rickey & Carroll, 1864. 831pp (lt age-spotted). VG. Zubal*. $35/£22

MORRIS, CHARLES. The Autobiography of Commodore Charles Morris, U.S. Navy.... Boston/Annapolis, 1880. 1st ed. 111pp; heliotype port. Ptd wrappers. Howes M822. Ginsberg. $150/£96

MORRIS, DAVID. Thomas Hearne and His Landscape. Reaktion, 1989. Fine in dj. Hadley. $23/£15

MORRIS, ETHELBERTA. Ameliaranne Bridesmaid. London: Geo. G. Harrap, (1946). 1st ed. 32 full-pg color illus by Susan Pearse. Illus bds. VG in VG dj. Dower. $75/£48

MORRIS, F. and E. A. EAMES. Our Wild Orchids. NY: Scribner, 1929. 1st ed. VG in dj. Archer. $75/£48

MORRIS, F. O. A History of British Butterflies. London: Geo. Bell, 1870. 72 full-pg hand-colored plts. Grn dec cl (sl wear spine). Nice. Appelfeld. $350/£224

MORRIS, F. O. A History of British Moths. London, 1896. 5th ed. 4 vols. 132 hand-colored plts. Pict gilt. Good. *Henly.* $206/£132

MORRIS, F. O. A Natural History of the Nests and Eggs of British Birds. London: George Bull, 1875. 2nd ed. 3 vols. 235 hand-colored lithos. Grn lib cl (rebound). Fine. *Metropolitan**. $747/£479

MORRIS, FRANK and E. A. EAMES. Our Wild Orchids. NY: Scribner, 1929. 130 full-pg photos. Good-. *Scribe's Perch**. $72/£46

MORRIS, GOUVERNEUR. The Diary and Letters of..., Minister of the United States to France.... Anne Cary Morris (ed). NY, 1888. 1st ed. 2 vols. Howes M826. *Ginsberg.* $75/£48

MORRIS, HENRY CURTIS. The Mining West at the Turn of the Century. Washington: Privately ptd, 1962. Fine. *Book Market.* $60/£38

MORRIS, HENRY CURTIS. The Mining West at the Turn of the Century.... C. S. Rice (ed). Washington: The Author, (1962). 1st ed. Frontis port. Rust cl. Fine. *Argonaut.* $50/£32

MORRIS, HENRY. Omnibus. (North Hills): Bird & Bull, 1967. One of 500 numbered. Prospectus, extra sample sheet laid in. 1/4 morocco. *Swann**. $138/£88

MORRIS, JAMES. Coast to Coast. London, 1956. 1st Eng ed, 1st bk. Nice (inscrip) in dj (sl frayed, torn). *Clearwater.* $62/£40

MORRIS, JAMES. The Hashemite Kings. London, 1959. 1st Eng ed. Very Nice (eps mkd w/adhesive tape stains) in dj (sl chafed). *Clearwater.* $55/£35

MORRIS, JAMES. South African Winter. London, 1958. 1st Eng ed. Very Nice (spine sl bumped) in dj (sl frayed). *Clearwater.* $39/£25

MORRIS, JOHN W. and EDWIN C. McREYNOLDS. Historical Atlas of Oklahoma. Norman: Univ of OK, (1965). 1st ed. VG + in dj (edgeworn). *Bohling.* $25/£16

MORRIS, MALCOLM. Diseases of the Skin. NY, 1911. 5th ed. 10 color, 67 b/w plts. Grn cl bds (worn; fr inner hinge cracked). Good. *Doctor's Library.* $50/£32

MORRIS, MAURICE O'CONNOR. Rambles in the Rocky Mountains. London, 1864. 1st ed. viii,264pp. Grn cl, gilt. *Maggs.* $351/£225

MORRIS, PAUL C. American Sailing Coasters of the North Atlantic. Chardon: Bloch & Osborn, 1973. Fldg dwg. Blue cl. NF. *Parmer.* $60/£38

MORRIS, ROBERT. Rural Architecture. London: The Author, 1750. Probable 1st ed. 4to. (12),8,ivpp incl subs list (engr tp sl soiled; few sm stains); 50 engr plts. Contemp calf (worn, fr bd detached). *Waverly**. $880/£564

MORRIS, WILFRID WALTER. An Angler in Arcadia. Edinburgh: Moray, 1934. 1st ed. 8 plts. VG in dj (torn, used). *Hollett.* $39/£25

MORRIS, WILLIAM GOUVERNEUR. Report Upon the Customs District, Public Services, and Resources of Alaska Territory. Washington: GPO, 1879. 163pp, fldg map. Black cl. (Dampstain bottom edge 1st 20 pp, no loss), else VG. *Perier.* $75/£48

MORRIS, WILLIAM. Architecture and History, and Westminster Abbey. (London: Chiswick, 1900.) Cl-backed bds (shelfworn, soiled). *Oinonen**. $30/£19

MORRIS, WILLIAM. The Art and Craft of Printing.... New Rochelle, NY: Elston, 1902. Ltd to 210 ptd. Frontis. Partly unopened; deckle-edged. Plain buckram-backed lt grayish blue paper-cvrd bds (stained), ptd paper spine label (sl chipped). Internally NF. *Blue Mountain.* $195/£125

MORRIS, WILLIAM. Child Christopher and Goldilind the Fair. (Hammersmith: Kelmscott, 1895.) One of 600 sets. 2 vols. Errata vol 1. Cl-backed bds (spines worn; bkpls). Cl slipcase. *Swann**. $488/£313

MORRIS, WILLIAM. The Defence of Guenevere and Other Poems. London/NY: John Lane, Bodley Head, 1904. 1st ed w/these illus. 29 plts by Jessie M. King. Teg, rest untrimmed. Pict cl, gilt. Excellent (spine sl dull, cl sl soiled). *Pirages.* $350/£224

MORRIS, WILLIAM. The Defence of Guenevere. Portland: Mosher, 1896. One of 950. Parchment over bds. Good (eps foxed; binding sl dknd). *Reese.* $30/£19

MORRIS, WILLIAM. The Doom of King Acrisius. NY: R.H. Russell, 1902. Gilt-stamped white cl (lt worn; ex-lib). *Truepenny.* $45/£29

MORRIS, WILLIAM. Gothic Architecture: A Lecture. (Hammersmith: Kelmscott, 1893.) One of 1500. Cl-backed bds. (Bkpl.) *Swann**. $402/£258

MORRIS, WILLIAM. A Note...on His Aims in Founding the Kelmscott Press. (Hammersmith): Kelmscott, (1898). One of 525. 8vo. (Bkpl.) Orig linen-backed bds. Cl slipcase. *Swann**. $632/£405

MORRIS, WILLIAM. Poems by the Way. London: Reeves & Turner, 1891. 1st trade ed, regular paper issue. Gilt polished buckram. Good (ink name, sunning). *Reese.* $35/£22

MORRIS, WILLIAM. The Story of the Glittering Plain. (Hammersmith): Kelmscott, (1894). One of 250. 4to. 23 woodcut illus by Walter Crane. Orig limp vellum, silk ties; protective paper slips for ties mtd on pastedowns. Cl slipcase. *Swann**. $2,760/£1,769

MORRIS, WILLIAM. The Wood Beyond the World. London: Lawrence & Bullen, 1895. 1st trade ed. VG (sl dk mk spine top, sl uneven fading). *Williams.* $55/£35

MORRIS, WILLIE. North Toward Home. Boston, 1967. 1st Amer ed, 1st bk. Fine in NF dj. *Polyanthos.* $50/£32

MORRIS, WRIGHT. The Field of Vision. London, 1957. 1st ed. Fine in dj (2 sm nicks, fr panel edge rubbed). *Polyanthos.* $25/£16

MORRIS, WRIGHT. The Home Place. NY: Scribner, 1948. 1st ed. Fine in dj (lt used, spine faded). *Dermont.* $125/£80

MORRIS, WRIGHT. The Inhabitants. NY: Scribner, 1946. 1st ed. 53 b/w plts. VG in dj (rubbed, chipped, tape-repaired). *Cahan.* $125/£80

MORRIS, WRIGHT. Love Affair. NY: Harper, 1972. 1st ed. 44 color plts. (Owner stamp), else NF in dj. *Cahan.* $40/£26

MORRIS, WRIGHT. Love Among the Cannibals. NY, 1957. 1st Amer ed. Fine in dj (spine sl sunned, extrems rubbed). *Polyanthos.* $25/£16

MORRIS, WRIGHT. Wright Morris: Structures and Artifacts, Photographs, 1933-1954. Lincoln: Sheldon Memorial Art Gallery, Univ of NE, Oct 21-Nov 16, 1975. 1st ed. 100 full-pg b/w photos. (Owner stamp), else VG in pict stiff wrappers. *Cahan.* $25/£16

MORRISON, ARTHUR. Green Ginger. Hutchinson, 1909. 1st ed. (Edges sl foxed), o/w VG. *Ash.* $70/£45

MORRISON, ARTHUR. Martin Hewitt. Investigator. Ward, Lock & Bowden, 1894. 1st ed. Sidney Paget (illus). Frontis. Teg. Blue pict cl, gilt. *Sotheby's**. $448/£287

MORRISON, ARTHUR. The Painters of Japan. London/Edinburgh: T.C. & E.C. Jack, 1911. 1st ed. #44/150. Black gilt cl. VG. *Terramedia.* $450/£288

MORRISON, C. (ed). Melbourne's Garden.... Melbourne, 1946. (Sl mks from adhesion.) Dj (sl frayed). *Maggs.* $19/£12

MORRISON, DON. The Face of Minneapolis. Minneapolis: Dillon, 1966. 1st ed. (Owner stamp, inscrip), else VG in dj (sl worn). *Cahan.* $35/£22

MORRISON, H. Early American Architecture, from the First Colonial Settlements to the National Period. NY: OUP, 1952. Sound. *Ars Artis.* $55/£35

MORRISON, HUGH. Preliminary Check-List of American Almanacs 1639-1800. Washington: Library of Congress, 1907. 1st ed. Good (label, stamps) in contemp lib cl. *Cox.* $39/£25

MORRISON, HUGH. Preliminary Checklist of American Almanacs 1639-1800. Washington: GPO, 1907. 1st ed. Maroon cl. VG (pencil marginalia final pg). *Archer.* $35/£22

MORRISON, JIM. The Lords and The New Creatures. NY: S&S, 1970. 1st ed. (Bkpl), else Fine in dj. *Associates.* $125/£80

MORRISON, TONI. Beloved. NY: Knopf, 1987. 1st ed. Fine in Fine dj. *Beasley.* $75/£48

MORRISON, TONI. Sula. London: Allen Lane, (1974). 1st Eng ed. Orange bds. Fine in NF dj. *Dermont.* $50/£32

MORRISON, TONI. Sula. NY: Knopf, 1974. 1st ed. (Several redundant fr fixed eps due to production flaw), else NF in dj (price-clipped, 2-inch closed tear fr panel, short tear rear panel). *Lame Duck.* $850/£545

MORROW, ELIZABETH. The Painted Pig. NY: Knopf, 1930. 1st ed. Rene d'Harnoncourt (illus). 8 1/4 x 11. 34pp. Paper bds. Good (inscrip; worn, lt soil, few stains) in dj (few chips). *Cattermole.* $150/£96

MORROW, ELIZABETH. The Rabbit's Nest. NY: Macmillan, 1940. 1st ed. 16mo. (iv),43pp; 1 full-pg illus by Howard Willard. Pict eps. Pict bds (sl bumped). NF in VG pict dj (2 sm tears, fr panel sl soiled). *Blue Mountain.* $17/£11

MORROW, JAMES. A Scientist with Perry in Japan. Allan B. Cole (ed). Chapel Hill: Univ of NC, 1947. 1st ed. *Lefkowicz.* $65/£42

MORSE, CHARLES F. Letters Written During the Civil War, 1861-1865. Boston: Privately ptd, 1898. 1st ed. Pres from Robert Morse. Frontis port, 222pp. Teg, uncut. Good (sl soiled, spine faded, extrems worn). *Wantagh.* $60/£38

MORSE, CHARLOTTE INGERSOLL. The Unknown Friends. Chicago, IL: A. Kroch & Son, 1948. 1st ed. 2 ports. Good (sl dampspots, corners bumped). *Wantagh.* $25/£16

MORSE, J. T. The Life and Letters of Oliver Wendell Holmes. Boston: Riverside, 1896. 1st ed. 2 vols. Frontispieces. (Cl sl rubbed.) *Goodrich.* $35/£22

MORSE, JEDIDIAH. The American Gazetteer. Boston: S. Hall & Thomas & Andrews, 1797. viii,(619)pp (foxed, 2 gatherings sl pulled); 6 (of 7) hand-colored maps. Full calf (sl worn). *New Hampshire*.* $180/£115

MORSE, JEDIDIAH. The American Gazetteer.... Boston: Thomas & Andrews, 1810. 3rd ed. (600)pp; 2 fldg maps. Full contemp calf, morocco spine label. (Maps foxed, rubbed), else VG. Howes B839. *Cahan.* $200/£128

MORSE, JEDIDIAH. The American Geography. London, 1792. 2nd ed. 2 engr fldg maps. (Lacks most of prelims.) Later 1/4 calf. *Swann*.* $138/£88

MORSE, JEDIDIAH. Elements of Geography, Exhibited Historically.... New Haven: H. Howe, 1825. 6th ed. 162pp; 4 engr map plts. Orig buff ptd bds. (Bkpl.) *Hudson.* $200/£128

MORSE, JOHN T., JR. Life and Letters of Oliver Wendell Holmes. London: Sampson Low et al, 1896. 1st ed. 2 vols. vi,(i),358; (iii),335pp. (Spot frontis vol 1.) Red cl (spines faded). *White.* $50/£32

MORSE, LUCIUS D. On Nasal Catarrh. Memphis: Dod, 1870. 2nd ed. 72pp. Victorian cl. Good. *Goodrich.* $35/£22

MORSE, PETER. John Sloan's Prints. New Haven, 1969. Folio. (Binding, contents dampstained upper corner.) *Swann*.* $172/£110

MORSE, PETER. John Sloan's Prints. New Haven: Yale, 1969. Fine in VG dj (chip). *Metropolitan*.* $149/£96

MORSHEAD, OWEN. Windsor Castle. Phaidon, 1951. Frontis port, 3 ports, 64 plts. (Spine lt faded.) *Edwards.* $44/£28

MORTENSEN, WILLIAM. The Model. SF: Camera Craft, 1948. 2nd ed. (Owner stamp; extrems rubbed), else VG in dj (worn). *Cahan.* $45/£29

MORTIMER, JOHN. Charade. Bodley Head, 1947. 1st Eng ed. Very Nice in Attractive dj (spine chipped). *Clearwater.* $78/£50

MORTIMER, JOHN. Charade. London: Bodley Head, 1947. 1st ed. VG. *Hollett.* $23/£15

MORTIMER, JOHN. Like Men Betrayed. Phila/NY: Lippincott, (1953). 1st Amer ed. Fine in VG dj (sm tears, lt stains rear panel, price-clipped). *Between The Covers.* $100/£64

MORTIMER, JOHN. The Narrowing Stream. London, 1954. 1st ed. VG in pict dj. *Words Etc.* $47/£30

MORTIMER, JOHN. Regina V. Rumpole. London: Allen Lane, 1981. 1st UK ed. VG+ in dj. *Williams.* $39/£25

MORTIMER, JOHN. Summer's Lease. London, 1988. 1st ed. Fine in dj. *Buckley.* $16/£10

MORTIMER, PENELOPE. A Villa in Summer. NY: HB&Co, (1954). 1st Amer ed. NF (sl offsetting from flaps) in NF dj (sl wear, sm tears, lt stain). *Between The Covers.* $85/£54

MORTIMER, RAYMOND. Channel Packet. Hogarth, 1942. 1st ed. Tls inserted. (Sl dull), else Good in dj (dull, sl torn). *Whiteson.* $23/£15

MORTIMER, RUTH. French 16th Century Books. Cambridge, 1964. 2 vols. (Sl worn.) Slipcase (scuffed). *Oinonen*.* $160/£103

MORTIMER, W. GOLDEN. Peru, History of Coca. NY: J.H. Vail, 1901. 1st ed. Frontis. Maroon cl (spine sl soiled), gilt. *Karmiole.* $350/£224

MORTIMER, W. GOLDEN. Peru, History of Coca: The Divine Plant of the Incas. NY, 1901. 1st ed. Teg. Red cl, gilt. *Kane*.* $200/£128

MORTIMER, W. GOLDEN. Peru, History of Coca: The Divine Plant of the Incas. NY, 1901. 1st ed. VG. *Fye.* $350/£224

MORTON, ANTHONY. (Pseud of John Creasy.) Books for the Baron. Duell, 1952. 1st ed. (Lt edgewear, spine lt discolored), else VG in dj (lt rubbed). *Murder By The Book.* $45/£29

MORTON, ARTHUR S. Sir George Simpson. (Portland): OR Hist Soc, 1944. (Back corner bent), else Fine in dj. *High Latitude.* $50/£32

MORTON, CAVENDISH. The Art of Theatrical Make-Up. London: A&C Black, 1909. 1st ed. Signed presentation copy. Color pict bds (spine ends, joints scuffed). *Dramatis Personae.* $50/£32

MORTON, H. V. In Search of South Africa. London, n.d. #195/500 signed. 8 color plts, map. Teg. Morocco spine label. (Spine sl faded.) Card slipcase. *Edwards.* $31/£20

MORTON, HENRY H. Genito-Urinary Diseases and Syphilis. Phila: Davis, 1903. 4 color plts. (Cl worn, sl shaken), else Good. *Goodrich.* $65/£42

MORTON, J. B. Tally-Ho! and Other Hunting Noises. London, 1924. 1st Eng ed. Cl-backed bds. Dj (sl torn, chipped). *Clearwater.* $39/£25

MORTON, JOHN WATSON. The Artillery of Nathan Bedford Forrest's Cavalry. Nashville: Publishing House of M.E. Church, South, 1909. 1st ed. Presentation by grandson of Morton. (Sl cvr speckling), else VG. *Mcgowan.* $375/£240

MORTON, LESLIE. Garrison and Morton's Medical Bibliography. London: Grafton, 1934. 2nd ed. VG. Bookcell. $65/£42

MORTON, MIRIAM. A Harvest of Russian Children's Literature. Berkeley: Univ of CA, 1967. 1st ed. 8x11. 474pp. Fine in dj. Cattermole. $24/£15

MORTON, OHLAND. Teran and Texas. Austin: TX State Hist Assoc, 1948. 1st ed. Frontis port; 3 maps (1 fldg). Red cl. NF in dj (worn, soiled). Waverly*. $82/£53

MORTON, OREN F. A History of Rockbridge County, Virginia. Staunton, VA: McClure, 1920. 1st ed. (Inner hinges strengthened; stain rear cvr.) Ginsberg. $125/£80

MORTON, RICHARD L. Colonial Virginia. Univ of NC, 1960. 2 vols. VG- (edges foxed, soiled; lacks box). Book Broker. $65/£42

MORTON, ROSALIE SLAUGHTER. A Woman Surgeon. NY, 1937. VG (sl worn) in dj (tattered). Doctor's Library. $25/£16

MORTON, SAMUEL GEORGE. Illustrations of Pulmonary Consumption.... Phila: Key & Biddle, 1834. 1st ed. 1/2-title, xiii,(1),(9)-183pp, ad slip, 12 hand-colored litho plts. Contemp sheep (rubbed), morocco spine label. Good (lib stamps, dampstaining). Glaser. $450/£288

MORTON, THOMAS G. The History of the Pennsylvania Hospital 1751-1895. Phila, 1895. 1st ed. 573pp. VG. Fye. $150/£96

MORTON, THOMAS G. The History of the Pennsylvania Hospital 1751-1895. Phila, 1897. Rev ed. 591pp. 2-tone cl. VG. Argosy. $75/£48

MORTON, VANDA. Oxford Rebels. Wolfeboro, NH: Alan Sutton, (1989). 1st ed. As New in illus dj. Cahan. $35/£22

MORTON, W. E. An Introduction to the Study of Spinning. London: Longmans, Green, 1937. VG. Savona. $39/£25

MORWOOD, W. Traveller in a Vanished Landscape. London, 1973. Dj. Maggs. $22/£14

MOSBY, HENRY S. and CHARLES O. HANDLEY. The Wild Turkey in Virginia. Comm. of Game & Inland Fisheries, 1943. VG-. Book Broker. $125/£80

MOSBY, JOHN S. Mosby's War Reminiscences. NY: Dodd Mead, (1887). 264pp. Red buckram (recased), orig dec fr, spine panels onlaid. Good. Scribe's Perch*. $35/£22

MOSBY, JOHN S. Mosby's War Reminiscences. Boston, 1887. 256pp. (Ink #s title, inside cvr; worn, chipped; spine taped.) Pict wraps. King. $75/£48

MOSBY, JOHN S. Mosby's War Reminiscences. NY: Dodd-Mead, 1898. 264pp. Good. Scribe's Perch*. $95/£61

MOSELEY, H. N. Notes by a Naturalist. London: Laurie, (n.d.). VG. Mikesh. $60/£38

MOSELEY, H. N. Notes by a Naturalist. London: John Murray, 1892. xxiv,540,4ads pp (foxed); port, fldg map. New 1/4 tan morocco. Adelson. $225/£144

MOSELEY, H. N. Notes by a Naturalist. NY/London: Putnam/John Murray, 1892. Frontis, xxiv, fldg map, 540pp + 4pp ads. Tan cl (age-dknd, worn), spine label. Parmer. $125/£80

MOSELEY, HENRY. The Mechanical Principles of Engineering and Architecture. NY: Wiley & Halsted, 1856. 1st US ed. xxi,699pp + 4pp ads at rear (lt aged). Yellow eps. Lt grn blind cl (spine sl sunned, sl spotted, snagged), gilt. Baltimore*. $25/£16

MOSELEY, J. H. Sixty Years in Congress and Twenty-Eight Out. NY: Vantage, (1960). 1st ed. 28 sm ports. (Edges yellowing.) Textured bds. Ptd dj. Petrilla. $40/£26

MOSELY, WALTER. Devil in a Blue Dress. NY: Norton, 1990. 1st ed. Signed. Fine in Fine dj. Unger. $75/£48

MOSER, J. F. The Salmon and Salmon Fisheries of Alaska.... Washington, 1902. 1st ed. 47 maps and plts. Dk blue cl (sl soiled). Maggs. $140/£90

MOSES, ANNA MARY ROBERTSON. Grandma Moses. Otto Kallir (ed). (NY): Harper, (1952). Ltd to 270 numbered, signed. 28 plts (16 color). Teg. (Bkpl.) 1/2 red morocco, dec bds, gilt spine. Slipcase. Karmiole. $400/£256

MOSKOWITZ, SAM (ed). A. Merritt: Reflections in the Moon Pool. Oswald Train, 1985. 1st ed. Fine in Fine dj. Certo. $20/£13

MOSKOWITZ, SAM (ed). The Man Who Called Himself Poe. Doubleday, 1969. 1st ed. Signed, inscribed. Fine in white dj (lt soiled). Certo. $35/£22

MOSKOWITZ, SAM (ed). When Women Rule. Walker, 1972. 1st ed. Signed, inscribed. Fine in Fine dj. Certo. $25/£16

MOSLEY, WALTER. Devil in a Blue Dress. NY: W.W. Norton, 1990. 1st ed. VF in dj. Mordida. $45/£29

MOSLEY, WALTER. A Red Death. NY: W.W. Norton, 1991. 1st ed. VF in dj. Mordida. $45/£29

MOSS, CYNTHIA. Portraits in the Wild. London, 1976. NF in dj (chipped). Grayling. $39/£25

MOSS, GEORGE H., JR. Double Exposure. Sea Bright, NJ: Ploughshare, 1971. 1st ed. (Owner stamp, lacks stereoscope), else NF in illus dj. Cahan. $50/£32

MOSS, HOWARD. Instant Lives. NY: Saturday Review/Dutton, (1974). 1st ed. Edward Gorey (illus). Lg 8vo. 84pp. Orange cl-backed bds. VG in VG dj. Dower. $55/£35

MOSS, HUGH M. Snuff Bottles of China. London: Bibelot, (1971). 1st ed. Mtd color frontis, 42 mtd color plts. Brn cl. Good in dj. Karmiole. $85/£54

MOSS, JAMES A. and HARRY S. HOWLAND. America in War with Guide to the American Battlefields in France and Belgium. Paris, (1920). Inscribed by Howland. Fldg maps in pouch. VG. Pratt. $40/£26

MOSS, JOHN H. Early Man in the Eden Valley. Phila: University Museum, 1951. (Sig.) Wrappers. Archaeologia. $45/£29

MOSSE, A. H. E. My Somali Book. London: Sampson Low, 1913. 1st ed. Frontis. Tan pict cl (sl stained, yellowed), else VG. Terramedia. $200/£128

MOSSER, MARJORIE. Good Maine Food. GC: Doubleday Doran, 1939. 1st ed. (Eps foxing), else Fine in NF dj (sl stain rear panel, sm tears, price-clipped). Between The Covers. $125/£80

MOSSMAN, ISAAC VAN DORSEY. A Pony Expressman's Recollections. Champoeg, 1955. One of 500 ptd. Tipped-in frontis port, facs fldg map. Red cl. Fine in glassine wrapper. Bohling. $35/£22

MOSSO, A. Fatigue. M. Drummond (trans). 1906. (Rubbed; joint cracked.) Whitehart. $55/£35

Most Popular Mother Goose Songs. NY: Hinds, Hayden & Eldredge, (1915). Mabel B. Hill (illus). 4to. 44pp + 2pp pub's cat (cracked, soiled, sm tears lower margins). Brn cl-backed pict bds (rubbed, bumped, soiled). Good. Blue Mountain. $30/£19

Mother Bunch, and Tom Hop O' My Thumb. London: E. Wallis, n.d. (ca 1830). 12mo. 8pp (lt browning, soiling); 8 1/2-pg hand-colored wood engrs. VG in stiff paper wrappers (spine, bottom pg corners repaired, ink sig). Hobbyhorse. $250/£160

Mother Goose, the Old Nursery Rhymes. London: Heinemann, 1948. Arthur Rackham (illus). 8vo. Aeg. Full blue leather (spine very rubbed, bds off), gilt ruling. Metropolitan*. $46/£29

Mother Goose. NY: McLoughlin Bros, (1895). 16x8. (14)pp. Color pict wraps (heavily creased, worn, soiled, sl stained); die-cut on top and right side following image of Mother Goose. *King.* $65/£42

Mother Goose. N.p.: Saalfield, (1932). F. and F. Peat (illus). 13x9.5. (14)pp. (Very worn, spine cello-tape repaired, sl staining, soil.) *King.* $35/£22

Mother Goose. NY, (1944). One of 500 numbered, signed by Tasha Tudor (illus). Sm sq 8vo. (Lt worn.) Dj (sl frayed), slipcase (sl scuffed). *Oinonen*.* $650/£417

Mother Goose. The Old Nursery Rhymes. NY: Century, (1913). 1st ed deluxe. One of 150 numbered, signed by Arthur Rackham. 4to. 13 plts. Gilt-pict white cl (quite soiled). *Swann*.* $632/£405

Mother Hubbard and Her Dog. NY: McLoughlin Bros, 1890. 8vo. (4)ff; 6 plts. (Extrems lt worn), else Nice in stiff pict self-wrappers. *Bromer.* $75/£48

MOTION, ANDREW. Dangerous Play. Edinburgh: Salamander, 1984. 1st ed. Fine in Fine dj. *Dermont.* $35/£22

MOTLEY, WILLARD. Let No Man Write My Epitaph. NY: Random House, (1958). 1st ed. Orange cl (fading in spots). Dj (edgeworn). *Petrilla.* $45/£29

Motor Guide to Golf Links About Chicago. Chicago: Capper & Capper, (1918). 1st ed. Fldg map. VG (adhesion residue 2pp, repaired tears 1pg) in pict wrappers. *Pacific*.* $920/£590

MOTT, EDWARD HAROLD. Between the Ocean and the Lakes. NY: John S. Collins, 1901. Cvr scuffed, discolored, else VG. *Perier.* $85/£54

MOTT, VALENTINE et al. Narrative of Privations and Sufferings of United States Officers and Soldiers While Prisoners of War.... Phila, 1864. 1st ed. 283pp. VG. *Fye.* $500/£321

MOTT, VALENTINE. Eulogy on the Late John W. Francis.... NY, 1861. 1st ed. Inscribed on fep. 33pp; 2 ports. (Ex-lib.) Orig flexible cl (worn, fr cvr detached). *Argosy.* $100/£64

MOTTRAM, R. H. John Crome of Norwich. London: John Lane, Bodley Head, 1931. 1st ed. 12 plts. (Fep removed; cl sl mkd.) *Hollett.* $31/£20

MOUBRAY, BONINGTON. A Practical Treatise on Breeding, Rearing and Fattening All Kinds of Domestic Poultry. London: Sherwood, Neely & Jones, 1819. 3rd ed. xii,288pp (tp, last text pg browned). Fore/lower edge uncut. Paper-backed bds (stained, chipped w/loss). *Edwards.* $133/£85

MOULD, D. D. C. POCHIN. Roads from the Isles. London: Oliver & Boyd, 1950. 1st ed. 17 plts, fldg map. Fine in dj. *Hollett.* $55/£35

MOULTON, GARY. Atlas of the Lewis and Clark Expedition. Lincoln, NE, 1983. 126 map facs. Blue cl stamped in gilt. (Sl soil), else Fine. *Reese.* $600/£385

MOULTON, J. E. (ed). Tumors in Domestic Animals. Berkeley: Univ of CA, (1978). 2nd ed. Fine in VG dj. *Mikesh.* $35/£22

MOULTON, JOSEPH W. New York 170 Years Ago. NY: Wm. G. Boggs, Dec 1843. Signed presentation by Leonine Moulton. 24pp; lg fldg print. Good (foxed; lacks orig wrappers). Howes W862. *Lucas.* $90/£58

Mount Hood, a Guide. Duell, Sloan & Pearce, 1940. Black cl. VG (spine sunned). *Bohling.* $40/£26

MOUNT, MARSHALL WARD. African Art: The Years Since 1920. Bloomington: IN Univ, (1973). 1st ed. VG in dj. *Terramedia.* $50/£32

MOUNTFORT, GUY. Portrait of a Desert. Boston: Houghton Mifflin, 1965. 1st Amer ed. VG in dj. *Worldwide.* $30/£19

Mouse and Kelley. (By Stanley Mouse and Alton Kelley.) Paper Tiger, 1979. 1st ed. NF in stiff card wraps. *Sclanders.* $28/£18

MOUTON, EUGENIE. Josephine Joseph Texas Sketches. Cincinnati: Editor Pub Co, 1900. 1st ed. (Sl shelfworn), o/w VG. *Brown.* $95/£61

MOWAT, FARLEY. And No Birds Sang. (Toronto): McClelland & Stewart, (1979). 1st Canadian ed. NF in dj (sl worn, few tears). *Antic Hay.* $27/£17

MOWAT, FARLEY. People of the Deer. Boston: Little, Brown, 1952. 1st ed, 1st bk. NF in VG dj (sm chip; price-clipped). *Antic Hay.* $75/£48

MOYES, PATRICIA. Helter-Skelter. London: MacDonald, 1969. 1st Eng ed. Fine in dj. *Mordida.* $45/£29

MOYES, PATRICIA. To Kill a Coconut. London: CCC, 1977. 1st ed. Fine in dj. *Mordida.* $45/£29

MOYNIHAN, B. G. A. Duodenal Ulcer. Phila: Saunderws, 1910. VG (lt shelfwear). *Goodrich.* $175/£112

MOZLEY, ANITA VENTURA. Eadweard Muybridge: The Stanford Years, 1872-1882. Stanford: Dept of Art, Stanford Univ, 1973. Rev ed. (Name stamp), else NF in illus stiff wrappers. *Cahan.* $30/£19

Mr. Sponge's Sporting Tour. (By R. S. Surtees.) London: Bradbury, Agnew, (ca 1860s). 1st ed, later issue. 12 hand-colored engr plts by John Leech. Marbled edges, eps. Early grn polished calf, grn pebbled cl (sl worn, scuffed; sl aged, rear hinge cracked), raised bands, gilt. *Baltimore*.* $60/£38

Mr. Sponge's Sporting Tour. (By R. S. Surtees.) London: Bradbury Agnew, n.d. 13 hand-colored plts. Illus gilt/black cl. (Sl spotting 1st, last ll; bkpl, hinges cracked; lower bd tail waterstained, red staining edges of last ll.) *Edwards.* $70/£45

MRABET, MOHAMMED. Hadidan Aharam. L.A.: Black Sparrow, Oct 1975. 1st ed. NF in ptd self-wrappers. *Turtle Island.* $35/£22

MRABET, MOHAMMED. Harmless Poisons, Blameless Sins. Paul Bowles (trans). Santa Barbara: Black Sparrow, 1976. #5/200, signed by author & trans. Fine in unptd glassine as issued. *Between The Covers.* $325/£208

MRABET, MOHAMMED. Love with a Few Hairs. Paul Bowles (ed). NY: George Braziller, (1968). 1st Amer ed. NF (name) in VG dj (chipped). *Turtle Island.* $35/£22

MRAZKOVA, DANIELA and VLADIMIR REMES. Early Soviet Photographers. John Hoole (ed). Oxford: Council of Museum of Modern Art, 1982. 1st ed. NF in pict stiff wrappers (sticker rear wrapper). *Cahan.* $35/£22

Mrs. Leicester's School. (By Mary & Charles Lamb.) London: M.J. Godwin, 1810. 3rd ed. 12mo. Engr frontis, 180pp. Pub's plain bds, later plain paper rebacking. VG (tp sl offset). Bound w/New Books for Children. 12pp. *Second Life.* $350/£224

Mrs. Leicester's School. (By Mary & Charles Lamb.) London: M.J. Godwin, 1820. 7th ed. 12mo. Engr frontis, 180pp. Contemp calf (rubbed, hinge wear). VG. *Second Life.* $225/£144

MUDD, NETTIE. The Life of Dr. Samuel A. Mudd. Marietta, GA: Continental Book, 1955. Rpt of 1906 Neale pub. VG. Howes M871. *Mcgowan.* $65/£42

MUDIE, ROBERT. The Feathered Tribes of the British Islands. London: Henry G. Bohn, 1841. 3rd ed. 2 vols. 379; 391pp; hand-colored tps, 19 plts. Aeg; marbled eps. Full morocco. (Spines badly rubbed, worn), o/w VG. *New Hampshire*.* $140/£90

MUDIE, ROBERT. The Feathered Tribes of the British Isles. London: Henry G. Bohn, 1854. 4th ed. 2 vols. xxvi,422; 440pp; 35 plts (sl spotted vol 1, margins sl waterstained). Marbled eps. 1/2 morocco, gilt raised bands (spines sl discolored). *Edwards.* $148/£95

MUELLER, HANS ALEXANDER. Woodcuts and Wood Engravings. NY: Pynson Ptrs, (1939). 1st ed. VG in dj (shabby). *Glenn.* $125/£80

MUELLER, HANS ALEXANDER. Woodcuts and Wood Engravings: How I Make Them. NY, 1939. 1st ed. Ltd to 3000. (Blind-stamped names, rubber-stamping), else Nice in dj (heavily chipped). *King.* $100/£64

MUENCH, JOYCE and JOSEPH. Along Yellowstone and Grand Teton Trails. NY, (1949). 1st ed. VG in dj (rubbed). *King.* $22/£14

MUGNIER, GEORGE FRANCOIS. Louisiana Images 1880-1920. Baton Rouge: LA State Univ, 1975. 1st ed. (Owner stamp, edges crinkled), else VG in illus stiff wrappers. *Cahan.* $30/£19

MUGNIER, GEORGE FRANCOIS. New Orleans and Bayou Country. NY: Weathervane Books, 1972. Illus eps. Cl-backed bds. (Owner stamp), else NF in dj. *Cahan.* $40/£26

MUHL, ANITA M. Automatic Writing: An Approach to the Unconscious. NY: Helix, 1963. 1st US ed. Ochre cl. VG in dj. *Gach.* $30/£19

MUIR, EDWIN. First Poems. 1925. 1st ed. Marbled bds. (Sl foxed), o/w VG. *Words Etc.* $101/£65

MUIR, JOHN (ed). Picturesque California and the Region West of the Rocky Mountains from Alaska to Mexico. NY/SF, (1887-88). 3 vols. Folio. Etched frontis vol 1. Pub's blind-, gilt-stamped morocco (rubbed; vol 1 w/puncture in fr cvr through 1st 25 ll). *Swann*.* $373/£239

MUIR, JOHN. The Cruise of the Corwin.... Boston, 1917. 1st ed. Teg. Pict label. (Sl wear, cvr soil.) *King.* $100/£64

MUIR, JOHN. Gentle Wilderness. SF: Sierra Club, (1964). 1st ed. W/illus Richard Kauffman's portfolio of 15 color prints in box (sunned). VG in dj (edgetorn). *King.* $100/£64

MUIR, JOHN. The Mountains of California. NY: Century, (1921). New enlgd ed. Gilt-pict cl. VG. *Mikesh.* $30/£19

MUIR, JOHN. Travels in Alaska. Boston, 1915. 1st ed. Color label. Teg. (Inner fr hinge cracked; lacks fep; sl stained, worn.) *King.* $45/£29

MUIR, JOHN. Travels in Alaska. Boston, 1915. 1st ed. 12 photo plts. Teg. Gray cl, color plt tipped on cvr. VG. *Price.* $195/£125

MUIR, JOHN. The Yosemite. NY: Century, 1912. 1st ed. 3 maps (1 w/sm tear). Dec cl (edges sl discolored). VG- (rear hinge cracked). BAL 14767. *Agvent.* $125/£80

MUIR, PERCY (ed). Talks on Book Collecting Delivered Under the Authority of the Antiquarian Booksellers Association. London: Cassell, 1952. 1st ed. VG in dj. *Moss.* $34/£22

MUIR, PERCY (ed). Talks on Book-Collecting.... London: Cassell, 1952. 1st ed. 14 plts. Good (backstrip faded). *Cox.* $19/£12

MUIR, PERCY. Book-Collecting as a Hobby. NY: Knopf, 1947. 1st Amer ed. VG. *Agvent.* $20/£13

MUIR, PERCY. English Children's Books 1600 to 1900. London: Batsford, 1985. 107 plts. Good in dj. *Stewart.* $23/£15

MUIR, PERCY. English Children's Books. London, 1954. 1st ed. VG in dj (nicked). *Words Etc.* $70/£45

MUIR, PERCY. Minding My Own Business. C&W, 1956. 1st ed. VG in dj. *Moss.* $39/£25

MUIR, PERCY. Points Second Series 1866-1934. Michael Sadleir (ed). London: Constable, 1934. 1st ed. Ltd to 750. 7 collotype plts, 6 facs ptd in line. Uncut. Good in vellum-backed marbled bds, glassine wrapper. *Cox.* $109/£70

MUIR, PERCY. Victorian Illustrated Books. London, (1989). Fine in dj. *Truepenny.* $45/£29

MUIR, WILLIAM. The Mameluke or Slave Dynasty of Egypt 1260-1517 A.D. London: Smith, Elder, 1896. 1st ed. Frontis, xxxii,245pp + (2) ads; fldg map, 11 plts. Maroon cl (backstrip soiled), gilt. VG. *House.* $100/£64

MUIRHEAD, JAMES F. The Land of Contrasts. Boston, 1898. viii,282pp. Dec cl. VG. *Reese.* $75/£48

MUKERJI, D. G. Gay-Neck. NY: Dutton, (1928). #229/1000 signed by Mukerji and Boris Artzybasheff (illus). 3 dbl-pg b/w illus. 1/2 art vellum. Good (sunned). *Scribe's Perch*.* $20/£13

MUKERJI, D. G. Gay-Neck; the Story of a Pigeon. NY: Dutton, (1928). Ltd to 1000. John Newbery Medal ed, signed by Mukerji and Boris Artzybasheff (illus). 8vo. xi,197pp. 3/4 white paper, dec bds. (Cvr lt soiled, faded, extrems sl rubbed), else NF. *Bromer.* $150/£96

MULDOON, G. Leopards in the Night: Man-Eaters and Cattle Raiders in Nyasaland. NY: Appleton-Century, 1955. 1st ed. Frontis map. Pict bds. VG+ in VG dj. *Mikesh.* $20/£13

MULFORD, CLARENCE E. Hopalong Cassidy. NY: G&D, 1910. 6th (listed) ed. 12mo. Red pict buckram. NF (paper toned) in VG dj (top edge ragged). *Book Adoption.* $25/£16

MULFORD, CLARENCE E. Mesquite Jenkins. GC: Doubleday, 1928. 1st ed. VG in VG dj (chipped). *Unger.* $300/£192

MULLER, EDWARD. Ancient Inscriptions in Ceylon. London: Trubner, 1883. Plt vol only. 54 plts. Grn cl. VG. *Terramedia.* $100/£64

MULLER, J. California, Land of Gold, or Stay at Home and Work Hard. SF, (1971). Tan cl, gilt. Fine. *Cady.* $40/£26

MULLER, MARCIA. Dark Star. NY: St. Martin, 1989. 1st ed. Signed. Fine in Fine dj. *Janus.* $30/£19

MULLER, W. MAX. The Bilingual Decrees of Philae. Washington, DC: Carnegie Inst, 1920. 39 plts (most fldg). Internally VG (ex-lib, sm mks). Wrappers (worn). *Washton.* $75/£48

MULLETT, CHARLES. Public Baths and Health in England, 16th-18th Century. Balt, 1946. 1st ed. VG in wrappers. *Fye.* $35/£22

MULLGARDT, LOUIS CHRISTIAN. The Architecture and Landscape Gardening of the Exposition. SF, 1915. Frontis, 95 b/w illus tipped in. Fore/lower edges uncut. (Some margins sl browned; cl lt soiled.) *Edwards.* $62/£40

MULLIN, GERALD W. Flight and Rebellion. NY: OUP, 1972. 1st ed. 3 maps. VG in dj. *Petrilla.* $25/£16

MULLINER, H. H. The Decorative Arts in England 1660-1780. Batsford, n.d. Unpaginated. Marbled eps; teg. Japon-backed marbled bds, leather labels (spine label sl faded). *Edwards.* $172/£110

MULLINER, H. H. The Decorative Arts in England, 1660-1780. London: Batsford, ca 1920. Folio. Vellum, marbled bds, black leather labels. (Spine worn, soiled, cvrs sl worn, scuffed.) Text Good (sl foxed, smudged, hinges lt cracked, bkpl). *Baltimore*.* $30/£19

MULOCK, MISS. The Little Lame Prince. Rand McNally, (1909). 1st ed thus. Lg 8vo. 121pp; 28 color pictures by Hope Dunlap (5 misptd out of register). Pict onlay, gilt. (Lt rubbed), else VG. *Bookmark.* $39/£25

MUMBY, FRANK ARTHUR (ed). Letters of Literary Men: The Nineteenth Century. Routledge, n.d. (c1890). Teg. Orig buckram (rebacked), orig backstrip relaid (sunned, rubbed). Good (sl spotted). *Tiger.* $22/£14

MUMEY, NOLIE. The Black Ram of Dinwoody Creek. Denver: Range Press, 1951. One of 325 numbered, signed. Uncut. Cl-backed bds (sl worn), pict cvr label. *Oinonen*.* $90/£58

MUMEY, NOLIE. Bloody Trails Along the Rio Grande. Denver: Old West, 1958. #344/500 signed. Tipped-in frontis, fldg map. Fine in Fine dj. *Harrington.* $110/£71

MUMEY, NOLIE. Bloody Trails Along the Rio Grande.... Denver: Old West, 1958. One of 500 signed. Frontis port, fldg map at end. Blue-stamped tan cl bds, red buckram spine. In dj. *Dawson.* $75/£48

MUMEY, NOLIE. Early Mining Laws of Buckskin Joe— 1859. Boulder, 1961. Ltd to 500 signed. Cl-backed bds. Fine. *Truepenny.* $125/£80

MUMEY, NOLIE. History and Legal Procedings of Buckskin Joe, C.I. 1859-1862. Boulder, 1961. Ltd to 500 signed. (Corners upper cvr sl bumped), o/w NF. *Baade.* $50/£32

MUMEY, NOLIE. History and Legal Proceedings of Buckskin Joe. Boulder: Johnson, 1961. 1st ed. Ltd to 500 signed. Cl-backed bds, ptd label. Fine. *Cahan.* $45/£29

MUMEY, NOLIE. The Saga of 'Auntie' Stone and Her Cabin, Elizabeth Hickok Robbins Stone (1801-1895). Boulder: Johnson, 1964. 1st ed. One of 500. Signed. Color plt. Unopened. Ptd labels. NF. *Cahan.* $75/£48

MUMEY, NOLIE. The Teton Mountains: Their History and Tradition.... Denver: Artcraft Press, 1947. 1st ed. #30/700 signed. (Spine sl skewed, paper spine label stained), o/w Fine. *Hermitage.* $150/£96

MUMEY, NOLIE. The Ute War: A History of the White River Massacre. Boulder: Johnson Pub Co, 1964. Facs rpt, ltd to 300. Fine in wrappers, fldg cl chemise. *Hermitage.* $65/£42

MUMFORD, JOHN KIMBERLY. Oriental Rugs. NY: Scribner, n.d. (ca 1915). 4th ed. 2 fldg maps, 32 plts (16 color). Dec red cl. Good. *Karmiole.* $85/£54

MUMFORD, LEWIS. American Taste. SF: Westgate, 1929. #174/500. Signed. Black cl-backed red dec bds. NF. *Harrington.* $70/£45

MUMFORD, LEWIS. The Letters of...and Frederic J. Osborn...1938-70. M. R. Hughes (ed). Bath: Adams & Dart, 1971. Sound in dj. *Ars Artis.* $33/£21

MUMFORD, LEWIS. Man as Interpreter. NY: Harcourt, Brace, 1951. 1st ed. Ltd ed as pub's New Year's Greeting. Dec paper bds. Fine in orig glassine. *Turtle Island.* $25/£16

MUMMERY, A. F. My Climbs in the Alps and Caucasus. London, 1908. 2nd ed, 4th imp. (Name eradicated fep.) Teg. (Bumped, soiled, sl worn.) *King.* $225/£144

MUMMERY, A. F. My Climbs in the Alps and Caucasus. Oxford, 1936. (Bumped), else Good in dj (soiled, edgetorn, frayed). *King.* $40/£26

MUMMERY, J. H. The Microscopic Anatomy of the Teeth. OUP, 1919. VG (sig). *Savona.* $55/£35

MUNARI, BRUNO. ABC. Cleveland: World, 1960. 1st ed. 8 1/2 x 12 1/2. 56pp. Dec cl. Good (few non-text pp torn). *Cattermole.* $35/£22

MUNARI, BRUNO. Animals for Sale. Cleveland: World, 1957. 1st US ed. 9 1/2 x 12 1/2. 12pp. Good. *Cattermole.* $75/£48

MUNARI, BRUNO. The Birthday Present. Cleveland: World, 1959. 1st US ed. 9 1/4 x 12 1/2. 24pp. Cl spine, pict bds. Good. *Cattermole.* $100/£64

MUNBY, A. N. L. Connoisseurs and Medieval Miniatures 1750-1850. Clarendon, 1972. Frontis, 16 plts. (Ex-lib, ink stamp tp verso, label remains; #s.) *Edwards.* $31/£20

MUNBY, A. N. L. The Cult of the Autograph Letter in England. London, 1962. 1st ed. Fine in dj (sl torn). *Gretton.* $39/£25

MUNBY, A. N. L. The Cult of the Autograph Letter in England. London: Athlone, 1962. 1st ed. 2-tone cl. (Name.) Dj (chipped). *Oak Knoll.* $45/£29

MUNDEN, KENNETH W. and HENRY PUTNEY BEERS. Guide to Federal Archives Relating to the Civil War. Washington: National Archives, (1963). 1st ed. NF. *Mcgowan.* $35/£22

MUNDY, GODFREY CHARLES. Our Antipodes. London: Richard Bentley, 1852. 2nd ed. 3 vols. 8vo. xii,410; viii,405; viii,431pp. Gilt-dec blue cl (edgewear, spotting, soil). Good. *Parmer.* $700/£449

MUNDY, TALBOT. Cock o' the North. Bobbs-Merrill, 1929. 1st ed. VG-. *Madle.* $35/£22

MUNDY, TALBOT. I Say Sunrise. Phila, 1949. 1st Amer ed. Good in dj (frayed, soiled). *King.* $40/£26

MUNDY, TALBOT. Jimgrim and Allah's Peace. Appleton-Century, 1936. 1st US ed. NF (name) in dj (spine sl faded, spine ends sl chipping). *Certo.* $90/£58

MUNDY, TALBOT. Jimgrim and Allah's Peace. NY: Appleton, 1936. 1st Amer ed. (2 bkpls; rubbed) in dj (nicks, triangular tear fr flap). *Metropolitan*.* $57/£37

MUNDY, TALBOT. The Lion of Petra. NY: Appleton Century, 1933. 1st ed. Fine (sl worn, top edge sl frayed) in dj (sl worn, nicked, lt sunned, soiled). *Metropolitan*.* $57/£37

MUNK, J. A. Activities of a Lifetime. L.A.: Times-Mirror, 1924. 1st ed. Inscribed w/2 als. *Dawson.* $100/£64

MUNK, J. A. Arizona Sketches. Grafton, 1905. 1st ed. Tan pict cl (worn, faded). Good (sl shaken). *Five Quail.* $75/£48

MUNK, J. A. Story of the Munk Library of Arizoniana. L.A.: Times-Mirror, 1927. 1st ed. Frontis port. Fine in patterned glassine wrapper, pub's box w/illus paper label. *Cahan.* $100/£64

MUNK, WILLIAM. The Roll of the Royal College of Physicians of London. London: By the College, 1875-1955. 2nd ed. 4 vols. Gilt-stamped blue buckram (sl worn; sig). *Oinonen*.* $90/£58

MUNKACSI. Nudes. NY: Greenberg, 1951. 1st ed. Silver-titled red cl. Fine in illus dj (2 chips). *Cahan.* $150/£96

MUNN, B. The Practical Land Drainer: A Treatise on Draining Land. NY: C.M. Saxton, 1855. 1st ed. 190pp,1 ad. Dec blind/gilt emb cl. (Foxed; crown frayed, spine faded, rear inner hinge repaired), else VG. *Cahan.* $65/£42

MUNRO, ALICE. The Beggar Maid. NY: Knopf, 1979. 1st Amer ed. NF (rear cvr sl worn) in dj (sm scuff). *Waverly*.* $22/£14

MUNRO, ALICE. Girls and Women. Toronto: McGraw-Hill Ryerson, 1971. 1st ed. NF in dj (sm edgetear). *Lame Duck.* $250/£160

MUNRO, ALICE. Lives of Girls and Women. NY: McGraw-Hill, (1971). 1st ed. Fine in dj (age-toned). *Waverly*.* $49/£31

MUNRO, ALICE. Something I've Been Meaning to Tell You. Toronto: McGraw-Hill, 1974. 1st ed. Fine in NF dj (price-clipped, lt creases rear panel). *Lame Duck.* $125/£80

MUNRO, HENRY S. Handbook of Suggestive Therapeutics, Applied Hypnotism, Psychic Science.... St. Louis: C.V. Mosby, 1911. 3rd rev ed. Frontis. Black cl, gilt spine (lt worn; lib stamps tp, several ll). *Gach.* $75/£48

MUNRO, ROBERT. Ancient Scottish Lake-Dwellings or Crannogs. Edinburgh: David Douglas, 1882. 1st ed. xx,326pp; 4 plts. (Sl worn.) *Hollett.* $133/£85

MUNRO, ROBERT. Archaeology and False Antiquities. Methuen, 1905. 1st ed. Sketch plan, 18 plts. (Lt spotted, upper hinge sl cracked; nick, spine lt faded.) *Edwards.* $39/£25

MUNRO, ROBERT. Prehistoric Scotland.... London: William Blackwood, 1899. 1st ed. xix,502,(ii)pp; 18 plts. (Spine faded, sl bumped, mkd, spotting; joints cracked.) *Hollett.* $70/£45

MUNROE, JAMES PHINNEY. A Life of Francis Amasa Walker. NY, 1923. 1st ed. (Ink name ep.) *Wantagh*. $30/£19

MUNROE, K. The Fur-Seal's Tooth: A Story of Alaskan Adventure. NY: Harper, 1894. 1st ed. 267pp, 30 full-pg halftone dwgs. Color pict cl. VG + . *Mikesh*. $27/£17

MUNSEY, CECIL. Disneyana. NY: Hawthorn, (1974). 1st ed. VG in dj (price-clipped, tape-repaired tear). *Waverly**. $38/£24

MUNSEY, CECIL. Disneyana: Walt Disney Collectibles. NY: Hawthorn Books, (1974). 1st ed. 2-tone cl. Fine in dj. *Oak Knoll*. $75/£48

MUNSEY, FRANK A. Under Fire; or, Fred Worthington's Campaign. NY: Frank A. Munsey, 1890. 1st ed. Inscribed. Pict cl (sl soiled, spine ends sl rubbed). *Sadlon*. $50/£32

MUNSTERHJELM, ERIK. Fool's Gold. London: Allen & Unwin, 1957. VG in dj. *High Latitude*. $17/£11

MUNZ, LUDWIG. Rembrandt's Etchings. London, 1952. 2 vols. 48 plts. Fine in djs (worn), slipcase. *Washton*. $350/£224

MUNZ, LUDWIG. Rembrandt's Etchings. London: Phaidon, 1952. 1st ed. 2 vols. 325 plts; frontis, 48 plts, cat. Black buckram, gilt. (Sm adhesion 1 pg vol 1; cvrs sl waterstained), o/w VF set. *Europa*. $296/£190

MURAKAMI, HARUKI. A Wild Sheep Chase. Alfred Birnbaum (trans). Tokyo: Kodansha, (1989). 1st Amer ed. Publicity postcard laid in. Fine in Fine dj. *Between The Covers*. $75/£48

MURBARGER, NELL. Ghosts of the Adobe Walls. L.A.: Westernlore, 1964. *Book Market*. $60/£38

MURBARGER, NELL. Ghosts of the Glory Trail. Palm Desert: Desert Magazine, (1956). 1st ed. Signed. Fine in Fine dj. *Book Market*. $60/£38

MURBARGER, NELL. Ghosts of the Glory Trail. L.A.: Westernlore, (1963). 5th ptg. Pict cl (spine tail bumped) in dj. *Dawson*. $30/£19

MURBARGER, NELL. Sovereigns of the Sage. Palm Desert: Desert Magazine, (1958). 1st ed. Signed. Fine in VG dj. *Book Market*. $65/£42

MURCHISON, R. Siluria. London: John Murray, 1854. 1st ed. Fldg frontis map, xvi,523pp; 37 litho plts w/explanatory ll, 2 fldg maps. Rebacked w/orig spine cl laid down. Good. *Blake*. $275/£176

MURDOCH, IRIS. The Bell. London: Chatto, 1958. 1st UK ed. VG + in VG dj (sm closed tears strengthened to rear, chip). *Williams*. $55/£35

MURDOCH, IRIS. Bruno's Dream. Chatto, 1969. 1st UK ed. Fine in NF dj (price-clipped). *Williams*. $39/£25

MURDOCH, IRIS. Bruno's Dream. London: C&W, 1969. 1st Eng ed. Paper-cvrd bds. NF in dj (rubbed, soiled, sm tears). *Antic Hay*. $30/£19

MURDOCH, IRIS. The Existentialist Political Myth. Delos Press, 1989. One of 225 numbered. Fine (wrappers over card). *Williams*. $39/£25

MURDOCH, IRIS. The Existentialist Political Myth. Delos, 1989. Ltd to 225 numbered. Fine in wraps. *Buckley*. $59/£38

MURDOCH, IRIS. A Fairly Honourable Defeat. London: C&W, 1970. 1st ed. NF in dj (price-clipped). *Turtle Island*. $55/£35

MURDOCH, IRIS. Henry and Cato. London: C&W, 1976. 1st Eng ed. Paper-cvrd bds. (Sm dent rear cvr), else Fine in dj. *Antic Hay*. $25/£16

MURDOCH, IRIS. Henry and Cato. London: C&W, 1976. 1st ed. Fine in dj (price-clipped). *Turtle Island*. $55/£35

MURDOCH, IRIS. Henry and Cato. London: Chatto, 1976. 1st UK ed. NF in dj (price-clipped). *Williams*. $37/£24

MURDOCH, IRIS. The Italian Girl. London: C&W, (1964). 1st ed. NF (name) in dj. *Turtle Island*. $65/£42

MURDOCH, IRIS. The Italian Girl. London: C&W, 1964. 1st Eng ed. Paper-cvrd bds. Fine in dj (wear, soil, sm tears). *Antic Hay*. $27/£17

MURDOCH, IRIS. The Italian Girl. London: Chatto, 1964. 1st UK ed. VG in dj (sl edgeworn, rear panel sl stained). *Williams*. $31/£20

MURDOCH, IRIS. The Nice and the Good. NY: Viking, (1968). 1st Amer ed. NF (label residue fr pastedown) in dj (sl wear, sm tears). *Antic Hay*. $15/£10

MURDOCH, IRIS. The Nice and the Good. London: C&W, 1968. 1st ed. Fine in NF dj. *Antic Hay*. $45/£29

MURDOCH, IRIS. Nuns and Soldiers. London, 1980. 1st ed. VG in dj. *Typographeum*. $28/£18

MURDOCH, IRIS. The Philosopher's Pupil. London, 1983. 1st ed. VG in dj. *Typographeum*. $40/£26

MURDOCH, IRIS. The Red and the Green. London: C&W, 1965. 1st Eng ed. Paper-cvrd bds. Fine in dj. *Antic Hay*. $40/£26

MURDOCH, IRIS. The Red and the Green. London: C&W, 1965. 1st ed. NF in dj. *Turtle Island*. $60/£38

MURDOCH, IRIS. Sartre. Romantic Rationalist. Cambridge: Bowes & Lyon, (1953). 1st ed, 1st bk. NF in VG dj (sl tanned, price-clipped). *Reese*. $145/£93

MURDOCH, IRIS. The Sea, the Sea. NY: Viking, (1978). 1st US ed. NF in VG dj (sm chip). *Turtle Island*. $25/£16

MURDOCH, IRIS. The Sea, the Sea. Chatto, 1978. 1st UK ed. Fine in Fine dj. *Martin*. $50/£32

MURDOCH, IRIS. The Sea, the Sea. London: Chatto, 1978. 1st UK ed. VG in dj (short closed tear). *Williams*. $39/£25

MURDOCH, IRIS. The Time of the Angels. London: C&W, 1966. 1st ed. NF in dj (price-clipped). *Turtle Island*. $60/£38

MURDOCH, IRIS. The Unicorn. NY: Viking, 1963. 1st US ed. NF in dj (price-clipped). *Turtle Island*. $35/£22

MURDOCH, IRIS. An Unofficial Rose. NY: Viking, (1962). 1st ed. Fine in NF dj. *Antic Hay*. $25/£16

MURDOCH, IRIS. An Unofficial Rose. Chatto, 1962. 1st UK ed. Pub's ad bkmarker laid in. Fine in VG + dj (spine sl browned). *Williams*. $37/£24

MURDOCH, JOHN et al. The English Miniature. Yale Univ, 1981. *Petersfield*. $44/£28

MURDOCH, JOHN et al. The English Miniature. New Haven/London, 1981. Good in wraps. *Washton*. $25/£16

MURDOCH, W. G. BURN. From Edinburgh to the Antarctic...1892-93. London: Longmans, Green, 1894. x,(2),364pp, 2 maps (1 fldg). Silver-dec cl (sl worn). VG. *High Latitude*. $400/£256

MURDOCH, W. G. BURN. Modern Whaling and Bear-Hunting. London: Seeley, Service, 1917. VG. *High Latitude*. $100/£64

MURDOCK, HAROLD. Earl Percy's Dinner-Table. Boston, 1907. 1st ed. #2/550. 1 tipped-in engr. (Sl rubbed), o/w VG. *Worldwide*. $15/£10

MURE, GEOFFERY. Josephine, a Fairy Thriller. London: OUP, (1937). 1st Eng ed. 8vo. Color frontis, 212pp; 8 full-pg b/w illus by H.R. Millar. Red illus cl (sl edgewear, sl bumped). VG. *Dower*. $55/£35

MURIE, MARGARET and OLAUS. Wapiti Wilderness. NY: Knopf, 1966. 1st ed. Fine in dj. *Perier*. $32/£21

MURIE, OLAUS J. The Elk of North America. Harrisburg/Washington: Stackpole/Wildlife Mgmt Inst, 1951. 1st ed. Full-color frontis, 29 photo plts. VG in Good dj. Connolly. $75/£48

MURPHY, DERVLA. Full Tilt. London, 1965. 1st Eng ed, 1st bk. Very Nice in dj. Clearwater. $31/£20

MURPHY, DERVLA. Tibetan Foothold. London, 1966. 1st Eng ed. Very Nice in dj. Clearwater. $23/£15

MURPHY, HENRY C. Anthology of New Netherland. NY: (Bradford Club), 1865. Ltd to 125 numbered. Frontis port, (4),208,(6)pp; plt, 4 facs. Contemp red morocco, marbled bds, gilt spine (rubbed). Karmiole. $100/£64

MURPHY, JOHN MORTIMER. Rambles in North-Western America from the Pacific Ocean to the Rocky Mountains.... London, 1879. Inscribed. 364pp, fldg map. Mod blue cl, leather label. VG. Reese. $225/£144

MURPHY, MICHAEL (ed). Starrett vs. Machen: A Record of Discovery and Correspondence. St. Louis: Autolycus, 1977. 1st ed. #228/500. Paper over bds, 1/4 leather spine. Mint. Graf. $50/£32

MURPHY, ROBERT CUSHMAN. Logbook for Grace. NY: Macmillan, 1947. 1st ptg. VG in dj (sl chipped). High Latitude. $25/£16

MURPHY, ROBERT CUSHMAN. Oceanic Birds of South America. Amer Museum of Natural History, 1936. 2 vols. 16 color plts, 72 plts. Edwards. $187/£120

MURPHY, SHIRLEY FORSTER (ed). Our Homes, and How to Make Them Healthy. London: Cassell, 1885. Color litho frontis, xii,948,(xvi)pp. Orig cl (rebacked in matching levant morocco), gilt. VG. Hollett. $273/£175

MURPHY, SHIRLEY ROSSEAU. Tattie's River Journey. London: Methuen, 1983. 1st ed, stated 1st ptg. Tomie de Paola (illus). Horizontal 4to. (32pp). Glossy pict bds. Mint. Bookmark. $39/£25

MURPHY, THOMAS D. British Highways and Byways from a Motor Car. Boston, 1908. 48 plts (16 color), 2 fldg maps. (Lt marginal browning.) Teg. Edwards. $39/£25

MURPHY, THOMAS D. On Sunset Highways. Boston: Page, 1915. 1st ed. Fine. Book Market. $60/£38

MURRAY, A. A Description of the Arteries of the Human Body, Reduced to Tables. Phila, 1816. xix,172pp (label, stamps; worming last few pp). Leather (rubbed, worn; ex-lib). Whitehart. $90/£58

MURRAY, ALBERT. South to a Very Old Place. NY: McGraw-Hill, (1971). 1st ed. VG in pict dj. Petrilla. $30/£19

MURRAY, ALEXANDER. Account of the Life and Writings of James Bruce of Kinnaird, Esq. F. R. S. Edinburgh: Ptd by George Ramsay, 1808. 1st ed. xiii,504pp (browning, lib bkpl); 18 plts (lacks port, 1 plt), 2 fldg maps (lt staining several plts, maps). Contemp marbled bds (rebacked, recornered in mod calf), gilt, morocco spine label. Edwards. $351/£225

MURRAY, ARCHIBALD W. Wonders in the Western Isles. London: Yates & Alexander, 1874. 4,345pp; 16 plts. Pict cl (rubbed). Adelson. $40/£26

MURRAY, CHARLES AUGUSTUS. The Prairie-Bird. London: Richard Bentley, 1844. 1st ed. 3 vols. iv,336; 352; 372pp. Marbled edges. 19th-cent blue-grn calf, marbled bds (sl rubbed). Karmiole. $300/£192

MURRAY, CHARLES B. Life Notes of Charles B. Murray. Cincninnati, 1915. Presentation copy. 8 items laid in (4 als). 3 ports. Dk grn cl, gilt. VG. Bohling. $50/£32

MURRAY, GEORGE W. A History of George W. Murray, and His Long Confinement at Andersonville, GA. Northampton, n.d. 1st ed. Orig ptd wraps. Wantagh. $85/£54

MURRAY, H. J. R. A History of Chess. Oxford, 1913. 1st ed. (Corners bumped, lt worn.) Freeman*. $40/£26

MURRAY, HENRY A. Lands of the Slave and the Free. London, 1857. 2nd ed. xxiii,480,(8)pp; 10 woodcut plts, 2 maps (1 fldg). Aeg. Blue gilt cl. VG (contemp bk label). Reese. $350/£224

MURRAY, JAMES A. The Avifauna of British India and Its Dependencies. London/Bombay, 1888. 2 vols. 8vo. xxiv,viii,xvii,838,42pp; 34 (of 37) plts (called for), incl 1 fldg; 1 plain plt (uncalled for), 2 color plts (uncalled for), 2 plain plts (called for as woodcuts). (Pg132 vol 1 w/plt facing both silked to fore-edge; pp673/4 vol 2 torn; pp293/4 vol 2 silked to leading corner; 2 color plts vol 2 repaired to fore-edge not affecting margin; lt browned; several plts crudely hand-colored.) Gilt-illus cl (spines sl chipped, sl dampstain upper joint). Edwards. $468/£300

MURRAY, JOHN OGDEN. The Immortal Six Hundred, a Story of Cruelty to Confederate Prisoners of War. Winchester, VA: Eddy Press, 1905. 1st ed. (Sl cocked), else VG. Mcgowan. $250/£160

MURRAY, KEITH A. The Modocs and Their War. Norman, (1959). 1st ed, 2nd ptg. VG in dj. King. $30/£19

MURRAY, KEITH A. The Modocs and Their War. Norman: Univ of OK, (1959). 2nd ed. Map. VG in dj (sl worn). Lien. $45/£29

MURRAY, KEITH A. The Modocs and Their War. Norman: Univ of OK, (1959). 2nd ptg. Yellow cl. Fine in pict dj. Pacific*. $58/£37

MURRAY, KEITH A. The Modocs and Their War. Norman: Univ of OK, (1959). 2nd ptg. 12 plts. Yellow cl (corner sl jammed), else Fine in pict dj. Argonaut. $60/£38

MURRAY, MARGARET A. Egyptian Religious Poetry. London: John Murray, (1949). 1st ed. Wrappers (lt chipped). Archaeologia. $50/£32

MURRAY, NICHOLAS. Notes, Historical and Biographical, Concerning Elizabeth-Town.... Elizabeth-Town, NJ: E. Sanderson, 1844. Frontis, 166pp (foxing). 1/2 leather (lt worn). Howes M919. Bohling. $85/£54

MURRAY, SIMON. Legionnaire, My Five Years in the French Foreign Legion. NY, (1978). 1st ed. Fine in Fine dj. Pratt. $20/£13

MURRAY, WILLIAM H. H. Adventures in the Wilderness. Boston: Field, Osgood, 1869. 1st ed. vi,(7)-236,(4)ads pp. Good (bkpl). Zubal*. $17/£11

MURRAY, WILLIAM H. H. Lake Champlain and Its Shores. Boston: DeWolfe, Fiske, (1890). Frontis port, v,261pp. Blue cl. VG. Bohling. $30/£19

MURRAY, WILLIAM. The Hard Knocker's Luck. NY: Viking, 1985. 1st ed. Fine in dj (price-clipped). Mordida. $30/£19

MURRAY, WILLIAM. When the Fat Man Sings. NY: Bantam, 1987. 1st ed. VF in dj. Mordida. $30/£19

MURRY, J. M. and R. E. MANTZ. The Life of Katherine Mansfield. London: Constable, 1933. 1st ed. Port. Nice (top edge discolored) in dj (spine tanned, spotted). Reese. $30/£19

MURRY, JOHN MIDDLETON. Reminiscences of D. H. Lawrence. With VG June/Aug 1930 copy of The New Adelphi magazine edited by Murry. London: Cape, (1933). 1st ed. VG (cl dknd) in white dj (soiled, spine browned). Antic Hay. $75/£48

MURRY, JOHN MIDDLETON. Wrap Me Up in My Aubusson Carpet. NY, 1924. #170/500. Fine. Polyanthos. $30/£19

MURTAGH, JOHN M. and SARA HARRIS. Who Live in Shadow. NY: McGraw-Hill, 1959. 1st ed. (Spine ends worn), o/w Fine in Fine dj. *Beasley.* $35/£22

MUSE, WILL F. The Travelog of a Muse. Cedar Rapids, IA: Privately ptd by Torch, 1927. 1st ed. Frontis. (1st 2 leaves dampstained; sl rubbed soiled, spine bottom chewed), o/w VG. *Worldwide.* $18/£12

Museum Disneianum, Being a Description of Ancient Marbles.... London, 1848-49. 3 vols in 1. 130 plts. 1/2 morocco (rubbed). *Swann*.* $258/£165

MUSGROVE, MARGARET. Ashanti to Zulu. NY: Dial, (1976). 1st ed, 1st bk. Map. VG in pict dj (lt chipped). *Petrilla.* $35/£22

MUSHIN, WILLIAM W. et al. Automatic Ventilation of the Lung. Springfield, 1959. VG (sl worn). *Doctor's Library.* $60/£38

MUSIL, ROBERT. Five Women. NY: Delacorte, 1966. 1st US ed. NF in VG+ dj (lt worn). *Lame Duck.* $85/£54

MUSIL, ROBERT. The Man Without Qualities. London: Secker & Warburg, 1953, 1954, 1960. 1st British ed. 3 vols (of 4). VG+ in VG djs (sl shallow loss, sm tears to spine extrems). *Lame Duck.* $750/£481

MUSIL, ROBERT. Tonka and Other Stories. London: Secker & Warburg, 1965. 1st ed in English. (Sm waterstains fep), else NF in VG+ dj (price-clipped). *Lame Duck.* $125/£80

MUSIL, ROBERT. Young Torless. NY: Pantheon, 1955. 1st US ed, 1st bk. VG+ in dj (price-clipped, 1-inch tear, crease). *Lame Duck.* $100/£64

MUSSOLINI, BENITO. The Cardinal's Mistress. Hiram Motherwell (trans). London: Cassell, 1929. (Inscrip; sl cocked, spine sl spotted.) *Clearwater.* $78/£50

MUTHER, RICHARD. The History of Modern Painting. London, 1895. 3 vols. Teg. 3/4 leather, marbled bds. Good. *Scribe's Perch*.* $32/£21

MUTHESIUS, STEFAN. The High Victorian Movement in Architecture 1850-1870. Routledge, 1972. VG in dj. *Hadley.* $78/£50

MUZZEY, A. B. The Young Man's Friend. Boston: James Monroe, 1838. 2nd ed. 165pp. (Text lt spotted; sl soiled, shelfwear), else Good. *Brown.* $12/£8

My 123 Pop-Up Book. Prague: Artia, (1988). 4th ed. J. Pavlin and G. Seda (illus). 8x9.5. 6 fan-folded pop-ups. Pict glazed bds. VG. *King.* $22/£14

My ABC Pop-Up Book. Prague: Artia, (1988). 4th ed. J. Pavlin and G. Seda (illus). 8x9.5. 6 fan-folded pop-ups. Pict glazed bds. VG. *King.* $22/£14

My Book of Nursery Stories. Blackie, n.d. (ca 1918). Helen Stratton, Harry B. Nielson et al (illus). 4to. (85pp) (mks, wear); 12 full-pg, 3 dbl-pg color pictures. Cl spine, pict bds. Nice. *Bookmark.* $23/£15

My Cave Life in Vicksburg.... (By Mary Loughborough.) NY: Appleton, 1864. 1st ed. 196pp (pg browned) + ads. VG (cl faded, sl worn). *Second Life.* $150/£96

My First Book. C&W, 1894. Frontis port. Pub's cat dated April 1894. Good (lt spotted, bkpl; spine bumped, rubbed, sunned, chipped; hinges, corners rubbed). *Tiger.* $62/£40

My Pretty Verse Book. London: Religious Tract Soc, n.d. (ca 1865). Sm 8vo. 32pp, 6 full-pg chromolithos. (Contemp pencil inscrip.) Color pict paper on bds. Fine in VF lt blue cvr. *Hobbyhorse.* $175/£112

MYDANS, CARL. More Than Meets the Eye. NY: Harper, 1959. 1st ed. (Owner stamp), else VG in dj (rubbed, sl soiled). *Cahan.* $35/£22

MYERS, ALLEN O. Bosses and Boodle in Ohio Politics. Cincinnati: Lyceum, 1895. 293pp; port. (Lt soiled, sm snag rear hinge.) *Bohling.* $30/£19

MYERS, BERNARD. McGraw-Hill Dictionary of Art. NY, 1969. 5 vols. VG in pub's box. *Metropolitan*.* $46/£29

MYERS, BERNARD. Mexican Painting in Our Time. NY: OUP, 1956. Color frontis. VG in dj (chipped). *Argosy.* $75/£48

MYERS, F. W. H. Human Personality and Its Survival of Bodily Death. London: Longmans, Green, 1903. Later ptg. 2 vols. Blue cl (sl stained, sm gash spine base vol 1). Good set. *Gach.* $85/£54

MYERS, F. W. H. Human Personality and Its Survival of Bodily Death. London: Longmans, Green, 1920. New imp. 2 vols. Very Nice in US issue djs (chipped). *Patterson.* $117/£75

MYERS, FRANK. Soldiering in Dakota, Among the Indians, in 1863-4-5. Pierre, SD: State Hist Soc, 1936. 2nd ed. VG in wrappers (sl soiled). Howes M929. *Cahan.* $40/£26

MYERS, FRANK. Soldiering in Dakota, Among the Indians, in 1863-4-5. (Pierre, SD, 1936.) 2nd ed. Orig ptd wraps. Howes M929. *Wantagh.* $35/£22

MYERS, GARY. The House of the Worm. Sauk City: Arkham House, 1975. 1st ed, 1st bk. Fine in Fine dj. *Other Worlds.* $15/£10

MYERS, J. C. A Tour Through the Northern and Eastern States, the Canadas and Nova Scotia. Harrisonburg: Wartmann, 1849. xvii,19-476pp. Orig mottled calf (rebacked). Howes M923. *Adelson.* $85/£54

MYERS, JOHN C. A Daily Journal of the 192d Reg't Penn'a Volunteers Commanded by Col. William B. Thomas.... Phila: Crissy & Markley, 1864. 1st ed. Port, 203pp. (Spine lt faded, sl worn), else Good. *Brown.* $50/£32

MYERS, JOHN MYERS. San Francisco's Reign of Terror. GC: Doubleday, 1966. 1st ed. VG in dj. *Lien.* $20/£13

MYERS, JOHN. The Death of the Bravos. Boston: Little, Brown, 1962. 1st ed. Good in dj. *Dumont.* $35/£22

MYERS, P. HAMILTON. The First of the Knickerbockers: A Tale of 1673. NY: Putnam, 1849. Stated '2nd ed.' (Sl foxed; spine lightened, ends fraying, lt spots cvr.) BAL 14831. *Sadlon.* $20/£13

MYERS, ROBERT MANSON (ed). The Children of Pride. New Haven, (1972). 1st ed. VG in VG dj. *Pratt.* $60/£38

MYNTER, HERMAN. Appendicitis and Its Surgical Treatment. Phila: Lippincott, 1897. 303pp. Nice. *Goodrich.* $150/£96

MYRON, R. Prehistoric Art. NY: Pitman, 1964. 1st ed. VG in color pict wraps. *Mikesh.* $15/£10

N

NABB, MAGDALEN. Death of an Englishman. London: CCC, 1981. 1st ed. Fine in dj (corner wear). *Mordida.* $65/£42

NABB, MAGDALEN. The Marshal and the Murderer. London: CCC, 1987. 1st ed. Fine in dj. *Mordida.* $45/£29

NABNEY, JANET. An Illustrated Handbook of Machine Knitting. Batsford, 1987. 1st ed. (Owner stamp tp), o/w Fine in dj. *Whittle.* $23/£15

NABOKOV, VLADIMIR. Ada. NY: McGraw-Hill, (1969). 1st ed. NF in dj (sm tear). *Antic Hay.* $25/£16

NABOKOV, VLADIMIR. The Annotated Lolita. Alfred Appel, Jr. (ed). NY: McGraw-Hill, (1970). 1st ed. NF in dj (sl worn, sm tear rear flap fold). *Antic Hay.* $25/£16

NABOKOV, VLADIMIR. The Defense. NY: Putnam, 1964. 1st English trans. Fine in VG+ dj (price-clipped, edgetears, sm internal tear). *Lame Duck.* $100/£64

NABOKOV, VLADIMIR. Despair. NY: Putnam, (1966). 1st Amer ed, 2nd issue dj w/title ptd in black on fr flap. Fine in white dj (lt wear, soil). *Antic Hay.* $85/£54

NABOKOV, VLADIMIR. Despair. London: Weidenfeld & Nicolson, 1966. 1st British ed. NF in dj (lt worn). *Lame Duck.* $100/£64

NABOKOV, VLADIMIR. The Eye. NY, 1965. 1st Amer ed. Fine in dj (sm tear). *Polyanthos.* $45/£29

NABOKOV, VLADIMIR. The Gift. Michael Scammel (trans). NY: Putnam, (1963). 1st Amer ed. NF in dj (few tears, wear). *Antic Hay.* $35/£22

NABOKOV, VLADIMIR. Glory. Dmitri Nabokov (trans). NY: McGraw-Hill, (1971). 1st Amer ed. NF in dj. *Antic Hay.* $25/£16

NABOKOV, VLADIMIR. Invitation to a Beheading. Dmitri Nabokov (trans). NY: Putnam, (1959). 1st Amer ed. Cl-backed paper bds. (Corners bumped), o/w VF in VF dj. *Pirages.* $125/£80

NABOKOV, VLADIMIR. Invitation to a Beheading. NY: Putnam, 1959. 1st ed. VF in dj (sl worn). *Else Fine.* $65/£42

NABOKOV, VLADIMIR. Laughter in the Dark. Indianapolis: Bobbs-Merrill, 1938. 1st ed, issue or state bound in orange cl. NF in dj (1-inch tear spine head). *Lame Duck.* $1,500/£962

NABOKOV, VLADIMIR. Lectures on Don Quixote. Fredson Bowers (ed). London: Weidenfeld, 1983. 1st Eng ed. NF in dj. *Hadley.* $47/£30

NABOKOV, VLADIMIR. Lolita. NY: Putnam, 1955. 1st US ed. VG in dj. *Lame Duck.* $275/£176

NABOKOV, VLADIMIR. Lolita. London, 1959. 1st ed. NF in dj (sl rubbed). *Buckley.* $39/£25

NABOKOV, VLADIMIR. Lolita. London: Weidenfeld, 1959. 1st UK ed. Fine in NF dj (sl rubbed). *Williams.* $75/£48

NABOKOV, VLADIMIR. Lolita: A Screenplay. NY: McGraw-Hill, 1974. 1st ed. NF in dj. *Lame Duck.* $100/£64

NABOKOV, VLADIMIR. Look at the Harlequins. NY: McGraw-Hill, (1974). 1st Amer ed. Fine in dj (lt used). *Antic Hay.* $20/£13

NABOKOV, VLADIMIR. Mary. Michael Glenny (trans). NY: McGraw-Hill, (1970). 1st Amer ed. Fine in dj (price-clipped). *Antic Hay.* $25/£16

NABOKOV, VLADIMIR. Mary. NY, 1970. 1st Amer ed. Fine in dj (sm scratch). *Polyanthos.* $25/£16

NABOKOV, VLADIMIR. Nabokov's Dozen. London: Heinemann, (1959). 1st Eng ed. Blue bds. Dj (spine dknd, edges sl worn). *Dermont.* $40/£26

NABOKOV, VLADIMIR. Nabokov's Dozen. GC: Doubleday, 1958. 1st ed. Fine in dj (lt used, rubbed). *Beasley.* $100/£64

NABOKOV, VLADIMIR. Nabokov's Quartet. (NY): Phaedra, 1966. 1st Amer ed. Fine in dj (sl wear, few tears). *Antic Hay.* $30/£19

NABOKOV, VLADIMIR. Poems. GC: Doubleday, 1959. 1st ed. Fine in NF dj (edges lt worn, lt browning). *Beasley.* $125/£80

NABOKOV, VLADIMIR. A Russian Beauty and Other Stories. NY, (1973). 1st ed. VG in dj. *Argosy.* $35/£22

NABOKOV, VLADIMIR. Transparent Things. NY: McGraw-Hill, (1972). 1st ed. Fine in NF dj (price-clipped). *Antic Hay.* $20/£13

NABOKOV, VLADIMIR. The Waltz Invention. (NY): Phaedra, 1966. 1st ed, in the earliest pink dj. This w/white eps. NF (top edge bumped) in dj (sm nick, tear). *Antic Hay.* $85/£54

NABOKOV, VLADIMIR. The Waltz Invention. NY: Phaedra, 1966. 1st ed. Fine in dj (lt worn). *Else Fine.* $40/£26

NABUCO, CAROLINA. The Life of Joaquin Nabuco. Stanford: Stanford Univ, 1950. Blue cl. VF in dj. *Parmer.* $35/£22

NADEAU, MAURICE. The History of Surrealism. NY: Macmillan, 1965. 1st ed. Fine in NF dj. *Beasley.* $45/£29

NADEAU, REMI. Fort Laramie and the Sioux Indians. Englewood Cliffs, NJ: Prentice-Hall, (1967). 1st ed. Black/yellow-grn cl. NF (sl dampstain lower fr edge cvr) in dj (chipped). *Argonaut.* $50/£32

NAEF, WESTON J. with JAMES N. WOOD. Era of Exploration. Buffalo/NY: Albright-Knox Art Gallery/MMA, 1975. 1st ed. 126 photo plts. (Owner stamp, sl loose), else VG in dj (worn). *Cahan.* $45/£29

NAEVE, LOWELL. The Phantasies of a Prisoner. Denver: Alan Swallow, (1958). 1st ed. Fine in dj (lt soiled). *Hermitage.* $45/£29

NAIPAUL, SHIVA. Black and White. London: Hamilton, 1980. 1st UK ed. NF (few pp sl creased) in dj (price-clipped). *Williams.* $23/£15

NAIPAUL, SHIVA. Fireflies. NY: Knopf, 1971. 1st ed, 1st bk. NF in dj. *Antic Hay.* $75/£48

NAIPAUL, SHIVA. Love and Death in a Hot Country. NY: Viking, (1984). 1st ed. Fine in dj (sm tear). *Antic Hay.* $20/£13

NAIPAUL, SHIVA. North of South: An African Journey. London: Deutsch, 1978. 1st Eng ed. VG in dj. *Hadley.* $34/£22

NAIPAUL, V. S. Among the Believers. NY: Knopf, 1981. 1st ed. NF in dj. *Antic Hay.* $25/£16

NAIPAUL, V. S. An Area of Darkness. London, 1964. 1st ed. VG (sig) in dj (edgewear, closed tear, chip). *Buckley.* $39/£25

NAIPAUL, V. S. A Bend in the River. London: Deutsch, 1979. 1st Eng ed. VG in dj. *Hadley.* $23/£15

NAIPAUL, V. S. A Bend in the River. London: Deutsch, 1979. 1st UK ed. Fine in dj. *Williams.* $39/£25

NAIPAUL, V. S. A Congo Diary. L.A.: Sylvester & Orphanos, 1980. One of 300 numbered, signed. Fine. *Lenz.* $125/£80

NAIPAUL, V. S. Finding the Centre. London: Deutsch, 1984. 1st UK ed. Fine in NF dj. *Williams.* $28/£18

NAIPAUL, V. S. A Flag on the Island. London: Deutsch, 1967. 1st UK ed. Fine in dj (nick). *Williams.* $56/£36

NAIPAUL, V. S. Guerrillas. NY, 1975. 1st Amer ed. NF in NF dj. *Polyanthos.* $25/£16

NAIPAUL, V. S. Guerrillas. NY: Knopf, 1975. 1st ed. Fine in NF dj. *Antic Hay.* $35/£22

NAIPAUL, V. S. A House for Mr. Biswas. (London): Andre Deutsch, (1961). 1st ed. (Pg edges foxed; spine bottom sl dknd), o/w Fine in dj. *Jaffe.* $650/£417

NAIPAUL, V. S. In a Free State. London: Deutsch, 1971. 1st UK ed. Fine in dj. *Williams.* $55/£35

NAIPAUL, V. S. Miguel Street. Deutsch, 1959. 1st UK ed. (Fep professionally replaced), else VG in VG dj (spine sl browned, sl loss spine ends). *Williams.* $234/£150

NAIPAUL, V. S. The Mimic Men. Deutsch, 1967. 1st UK ed. VG in dj (price-clipped). *Williams.* $50/£32

NAIPAUL, V. S. The Mimic Men. London, 1967. 1st ed. NF in dj (sl sunned). *Buckley.* $47/£30

NAIPAUL, V. S. The Suffrage of Elvira. (London): Andre Deutsch, (1958). 1st ed. (Bkseller label, sig), o/w Fine in dj (price-clipped). *Jaffe.* $850/£545

NAIPAUL, V. S. The Suffrage of Elvira. London: Deutsch, (1958). Fine in Fine dj (2 very short tears). *Between The Covers.* $1,200/£769

NAIPAUL, V. S. A Turn in the South. Franklin Center, PA: Franklin Library, 1989. 'Limited first edition,' signed. Aeg. Full gilt-stamped leather. VG. *King.* $50/£32

NAIPAUL, V. S. A Way in the World. NY: Knopf, 1994. 1st ed. Signed. Fine in Fine dj. *Lenz.* $60/£38

NAISAWALD, L. VAN LOON. Grape and Canister. NY, 1960. 1st ed. VG + in dj (lt wear, chipping). *Pratt.* $55/£35

NAITO, A. and T. NISHIKAWA. Katsura. A Princely Retreat. Tokyo: Kodansha/Phaidon, 1977. (Spine loose.) *Ars Artis.* $70/£45

NANSEN, FRIDTJOF. Adventure and Other Papers. London: Hogarth, 1927. Paper spine label. Good (sl pencil underlining; cl faded). *High Latitude.* $20/£13

NANSEN, FRIDTJOF. Adventure. Hogarth, 1927. 1st ed. Good. *Whiteson.* $23/£15

NANSEN, FRIDTJOF. Eskimo Life. London: Longmans, Green, 1893. xvi,350pp. Dec cl (dull, lt wear, sl discoloration fr bd). Good. *High Latitude.* $125/£80

NANSEN, FRIDTJOF. Farthest North, Being a Record of a Voyage of Exploration of the Ship 'Fram,' 1893-96.... NY/London: Harper, 1898. 2nd Amer ed. 2 vols. x,(4),587; x,(2),729,(1),4(ads)pp; 2 photogravures, 1 etching, 16 color plts, 4 fldg maps in cvr pockets vol 1. Teg. Gilt dec slate cl. Fine. *Argonaut.* $300/£192

NANSEN, FRIDTJOF. Farthest North. NY, 1897. 1st ed. 2 vols. 12 color plts, 4 maps in pockets. (Fr inner hinge vol 1 opening.) *Kane*.* $110/£71

NANSEN, FRIDTJOF. Farthest North. NY, 1898. 2 vols. 587; 729pp; 16 color plts, 4 maps. Teg. (Cvrs rubbed.) *King.* $125/£80

NANSEN, FRIDTJOF. Farthest North. NY: Harper, 1903. 2 vols. 120 full-pg plts (10 color). (Vol 2 cvr lt spotted), o/w VG. *New Hampshire*.* $100/£64

NANSEN, FRIDTJOF. The First Crossing of Greenland. London, 1890. 2 vols. Frontis ports, xxii,510; x,509pp + 24pp pub's list (lt browned, hinges tender); 2 fldg maps (of 5). Top edge silvered. (Rubbed, sl loss, sl chipped, discolored.) *Edwards.* $117/£75

NANSEN, FRIDTJOF. The First Crossing of Greenland.... London: Longmans, Green, 1895. New ed. Frontis, xii,452pp; map. VG. *High Latitude.* $40/£26

NANSEN, FRIDTJOF. In Northern Mists. NY: Frederick A. Stokes, 1911. 1st Amer ed. 2 vols. Tipped-in color frontis. Blue cl, gilt. (Bkpls removed vol 1), else NF set. *Parmer.* $400/£256

NANSEN, FRIDTJOF. In Northern Mists. NY: Stokes, 1911. 2 vols. Mtd color frontispieces. Dec cl. (Lower corners bruised), else Very Nice. *High Latitude.* $275/£176

NAPHEGYI, G. Ghardaia; or Ninety Days Among the B'no Mozah. NY/London: Putnam, 1871. 1st ed. Litho frontis; 348pp. Orig brn cl; gilt cvr illus. (Lt wear.) *Cullen.* $60/£38

NAPIER, L. EVERARD. Principles and Practice of Tropical Medicine. NY, 1946. VG. *Argosy.* $50/£32

NAPIER, MARK. Memoirs of John Napier of Merchiston... with a History of the Invention of Logarithms. Edinburgh/London: William Blackwood/Thomas Cadell, 1834. 1st ed. Frontis port, xvi,534pp; 13 plts (1 dbl-pg). Contemp calf (rebacked), raised bands, speckled edges. NF. *Glaser.* $450/£288

NAPIER, ROBINA (ed). Anecdotes of the Late Samuel Johnson by Mrs. Piozzi...Together with the Diary of Dr. Campbell.... George Bell, 1884. 1st ed. xiv,432pp; 4 plts. Uncut. 2-tone cl (lt soiled). Good. *Cox.* $55/£35

NAPIER, WILLIAM. English Battles and Sieges in the Peninsula. London, 1852. Frontis, vii,549pp. Dec grey cl. *Maggs.* $94/£60

NARAYAN, R. K. The Bachelor of Arts. London: Nelson, 1937. Excellent in dj (sl sunned, nicked, rubbed). *Gekoski.* $468/£300

NARAYAN, R. K. The English Teacher. London: Eyre & Spottiswoode, 1945. 1st ed. (Name fep, crease 1/2 title), o/w VG in dj (sl soiled, nicked, spine faded). *Virgo.* $117/£75

NARAYAN, R. K. The Guide. NY: Viking, 1958. 1st ed. Fine in VG dj (spine sunned). *Antic Hay.* $25/£16

NARAYAN, R. K. The Painter of Signs. NY: Viking, (1976). Uncorrected proof copy. Fine in ptd wraps. *Antic Hay.* $45/£29

NARAYAN, R. K. The Printer of Malgudi. (N.p.): MI State Univ, 1957. 1st ed. NF in dj (1-inch tear). *Hermitage.* $40/£26

NARAYAN, R. K. The Sweet-Vendor. London: Bodley Head, 1967. 1st ed. VG in dj. *Hollett.* $70/£45

NARAYAN, R. K. Waiting for the Mahatma. N.p.: MI State Univ, (1955). 1st ed. As New in dj. *Hermitage.* $45/£29

NARES, GEORGE S. Narrative of a Voyage to the Polar Sea During 1875-6.... London: Sampson, Low et al, 1878. 1st ed. 2 vols. xl,395; viii,378pp; 14 plts incl 6 mtd photos, 2 fldg maps. Uncut. VG (sl repair title margin vol 1; bindings lt worn). *High Latitude.* $650/£417

NARES, GEORGE S. Seamanship. Portsea/London: James Griffin/Longman et al, (1862). 2nd ed. Frontis, 230,(2 ads),4 ads pp; volvelle in pocket. (Neatly re-backed, preserving orig spine.) *Lefkowicz.* $200/£128

NARJOUX, FELIX. Notes and Sketches of an Architect in the North-West of Europe. London, 1876. Blue cl, gilt spine. *Freeman*.* $10/£6

Narrative of the Adventures and Sufferings of John R. Jewitt. (By Richard Alsop.) NY, ca 1815. Frontis. Pub's cl-backed pict paper over bds (quite worn). Howes A189. *Swann*.* $103/£66

Narrative of the Captivity and Sufferings of Benjamin Gilbert and His Family, Who Were Surprised by the Indians...in the Spring of 1780. Lancaster, PA, 1890. Ltd to 150. Orig ptd wrappers. Howes W80. *Sadlon.* $65/£42

Narrative of the Life of General Leslie Combs, of Kentucky.... (By Leslie Combs.) (NY, 1852.) Inscribed. Engr frontis port, 23pp (sl foxing). Mod 3/4 polished calf, cl, spine gilt. VG. Howes C640. *Reese.* $450/£288

Narrative of the Loss of the Kent East Indiamen. (By Duncan MacGregor.) Edinburgh: Waugh & Innes, 1825. 78pp. (Blindstamps 1st 2 ll, lt soil.) 2-tone bds (lacks part of backstrip, joints cracked, bds loose). *Edwards.* $55/£35

Narrative of the Most Remarkable Events Which Occurred in and Near Leipzig.... London, 1814. 6th ed. 104pp (bkpl, sl foxed); 2 fldg plans. Teg. 3/4 red leather (scuffed), gilt-stamped spines. *King.* $175/£112

NASATIR, ABRAHAM P. French Activities in California. (Palo Alto): Stanford Univ, (1945). 1st ed. VF in dj (sm tear top border). *Argonaut.* $75/£48

NASH, J. M. The Age of Rembrandt and Vermeer. Phaidon, 1973. 2nd imp. Dj. *Edwards.* $39/£25

NASH, JAY ROBERT. Bloodletters and Badmen. NY: M. Evans, (1973). 1st ed. VG in dj (sl worn). *Lien.* $85/£54

NASH, JOHN. English Garden Flowers. London: Duckworth, 1948. 1st ed. 12 full-pg color lithos. VG in dj (chipped, lt soiled). *Quest.* $45/£29

NASH, OGDEN. The Animal Garden. NY: M. Evans Co, 1965. Hilary Knight (illus). 7 x 8. Fine in dj. *Cattermole.* $50/£32

NASH, OGDEN. Collected Verse from 1929 On. London: Dent, (1961). 1st British ed. NF in dj (sl edge-dknd). Reese. $35/£22

NASH, OGDEN. Four Prominent So and So's. NY: (S&S), 1934. 1st complete ed. Otto Soglow (illus). Very Nice in pub's dec wrappers. Book Block. $130/£83

NASH, OGDEN. Good Intentions. London: J.M. Dent, 1943. 1st Eng ed. (Edges sl dknd.) Hollett. $47/£30

NASH, OGDEN. The Private Dining Room and Other New Verses. Boston: Little, Brown, (1953). 1st ed. Signed. NF in dj (sl browned, sm tear). Antic Hay. $125/£80

NASH, OGDEN. The Private Dining Room and Other New Verses. Boston, 1953. 1st Amer ed. Fine (bkpl; spine extrems sl rubbed) in dj (spine sl sunned, price-clipped). Polyanthos. $30/£19

NASH, OGDEN. The Private Dining Room. Boston, (1953). 1st ed. VG in dj (rubbed, sl chipped). King. $25/£16

NASH, PAUL. Outline: An Autobiography. London: Faber & Faber, 1949. 50 plts (2 color). Blue buckram bds. VG in dj. Heller. $125/£80

NASH, RAY. Printing as an Art. Harvard Univ, 1955. 1st ed. Tipped-in program signed by various printers. Fine in dj (reinforced). Dermont. $50/£32

NASH, WILLIAM GILES. America, the True History of Its Discovery. London: Grant Richards, 1924. Frontis. Red cl, gilt. VG (bkpl; lt soiled). Bohling. $27/£17

NASHE, THOMAS. The Unfortunate Traveller. London: John Lehmann, 1948. 1st ed. 14 full-pg lithos by Michael Ayrton. VG. Hollett. $70/£45

NASMYTH, JAMES. Engineer. Samuel Smiles (ed). John Murray, 1883. 1st ed. Mtd frontis port, xviii,(ii),456,(4)pp (lt foxing), 9 plts. Black eps (hinge cracked). Uncut. Grn cl (sl rubbed), gilt. Cox. $55/£35

NASON, E. The Life and Public Services of Henry Wilson. Boston: Lothrop, 1881. Ltr ptg. VG+. Archer. $20/£13

NATHAN, GEORGE JEAN. The House of Satan. NY, 1926. 1st ed. (Ink name, fr cvr cl bubbled), else Good in dj (rubbed, frayed). King. $35/£22

NATHAN, GEORGE JEAN. Materia Critica. NY, 1924. 1st ed. (Ink name), else VG in dj (chipped, sunned). King. $35/£22

NATHAN, GEORGE JEAN. Monks Are Monks: A Diagnostic Scherzo. NY: Knopf, 1929. 1st ed. Fine (eps sl browned) in VG dj (internal repair; sm hole spine; short tears). Between The Covers. $85/£54

NATHAN, LEONARD. The Matchmaker's Lament and Other Astonishments: Poems. Northampton, MA: Gehenna Press, 1967. #179/400. Brn paper-cvrd bds, paper spine label. (Bumped, sm dent upper hinge), o/w VG. Heller. $100/£64

NATHAN, MAUD. Once Upon a Time and Today. NY: Putnam, 1933. 1st ed. Fine in dj. Second Life. $65/£42

NATHAN, ROBERT. One More Spring. Stamford, CT: Overbrook, 1935. Ltd to 750. Teg. Golden orange cl-backed dec grn bds, paper spine label. NF (bkpl removed) in Good tan slipcase (soiled, sm split at bottom). Blue Mountain. $150/£96

NATION, CARRY A. The Use and Need of the Life of Carry A. Nation.... Eureka Springs: the Author, 1908. Rev ed. Fine. Beasley. $50/£32

National Academy of Design Exhibition Record 1826-1860. NY: NY Hist Soc, 1943. 2 vols, each signed by Maxim Karolik. VG. Waverly*. $44/£28

National Gallery of Pictures by the Great Masters. London: Jones, ca 1839. 2 vols. 114 steel-engr repros, engr tp vol 1, engr view vol 2. (Lt foxing.) Blind-dec cl (worn, faded, outer hinges split; fr hinges broken). Contents, plts VG. New Hampshire*. $100/£64

NATTES, JOHN CLAUDE. Scotia Depicta. London, 1819. 48 engr plts. (Rear blank ll wrinkled, dampstain top margin few plts; lacks orig cvrs.) New Hampshire*. $160/£103

Natural History of New York. NY: D. Appleton, 1843. Lg 4to. 5 vols. 3/4 leather (ex-lib, spine problems). Nice set in all. Metropolitan*. $1,035/£663

Nature and Her Harmonies. (Cvr title.) NY: Riker, Thorne, n.d. (ca 1854). Alfred Jacob Miller (illus). Chromolitho title, 5 chromolitho plts inserted by pub. Morocco (rubbed, fr cvrs detached, spine gone), gilt. Freeman*. $170/£109

Nature and Human Nature. (By Thomas Chandler Haliburton.) London: Hurst & Blackett, 1859. Engr frontis. Unopened. Blind-stamped purple cl, gilt. Maggs. $47/£30

NAUGHTON, BILL. Alfie. London: MacGibbon & Key, 1966. 1st UK ed. Fine in dj (sl rubbed, nicks). Williams. $86/£55

NAUMOFF, LAWRENCE. Taller Women: A Cautionary Tale. NY: HBJ, (1992). 1st ed. Fine in dj. Between The Covers. $45/£29

NAUNYN, B. A. A Treatise on Cholelithiasis. A. E. Garrod (trans). London: New Sydenham Soc, 1896. xi,197,38pp. Brn cl. VG. White. $50/£32

NAVAJO SCHOOL OF INDIAN BASKETRY. Indian Basket Weaving. L.A., 1903. 4-pg price list tipped in at p52. Burlap wraps. (Bottom edges water-stained, lacks much of spine), o/w Good. Scribe's Perch*. $24/£15

Naval Documents Related to the Quasi-War Between the United States and France Naval Operations from February 1797 to December 1801. Washington: GPO, 1935-1938. 7 vols. VG. Brown. $100/£64

NAVAL HISTORICAL FOUNDATION. Captain Raphael Semmes and the C.S.S. Alabama. (Washington: Naval Hist Foundation, 1968.) 1st ed. Fine in stiff ptd wrappers (price inked out). Mcgowan. $27/£17

NAVARI, L. Greece and the Levant. The Catalogue of the Henry Myron Blackmer Collection.... 1989. Ltd to 300. Sm folio. Frontis, 16 color plts. Grey cl. Maggs. $936/£600

Navy Scouts Paper Dolls. Chicago: Merrill, (1942). 4to. 8 leaves of paper doll clothing. Color pict wraps w/color punch-out paper dolls. NF. Blue Mountain. $85/£54

NAWRATH, ERNST ALFRED. The Glories of Hindustan. London, 1935. 1st ed. 240 plts. Dj (chipped). Edwards. $39/£25

NAYLOR, GLORIA. The Women of Brewster Place. London: H&S, (1983). 1st UK ed, 1st bk. Fine in NF dj. Robbins. $150/£96

NEAGOE, PETER. What Is Surrealism. Paris: New Review, 1932. 1st ed. (Bkpl), else VG in color ptd stiff wrappers (sl dusty). Cahan. $125/£80

NEALE, C. M. An Index to Pickwick. London: J. Hitchcock, 1897. 75pp. Unopened. Cl-backed ptd bds (worn). Maggs. $16/£10

NEALE, CHARLES MONTAGUE. An Index to Pickwick. London: The Author, 1897. (3),iv,75pp. Cl-backed bds (edgeworn, sl soiled). Bohling. $40/£26

NEALE, WALTER. Life of Ambrose Bierce. NY: Walter Neale, 1929. 1st ed. (1 illus loose, ink notes fep, bkpl; spine sl sunned, cvrs sl soiled.) King. $35/£22

Near East from Within. NY: Doubleday, Page, 1907. 65 plts, dbl-pg map. Teg. (Bkpl; sl rubbed, spine frayed), o/w VG. Worldwide. $65/£42

NEATE, W. R. Mountaineering and Its Literature—A Descriptive Bibliography...1744-1976. Cicerone, 1978. 1st ed. VG in dj (sl torn). Moss. $62/£40

NEAVERSON, E. Stratigraphical Palaeontology. London, 1955. 2nd ed. 18 plts. Fine. Henly. $44/£28

NEBEL, FREDERICK. Fifty Roads to Town. Boston: Little Brown, 1936. 1st ed. (Pg edges sl staining, bkpl; spine sl dknd), o/w VG in dj (1/2-inch piece missing spine top, corner wear, 2 sm closed tears). *Mordida*. $250/£160

NEBEL, FREDERICK. Sleepers East. Boston: Little Brown, 1933. 1st ed. Inscribed. (Owner's label copyright pg, pg edges sl spotted), o/w Fine in VG dj (spine sl dknd; spine ends, corners chipped). *Mordida*. $650/£417

Nebraska, a Guide to the Cornhusker State. NY: Viking, 1939. 1st ed. Fldg pocket map. Blue cl. Good+ (name; binding spotted). *Bohling*. $25/£16

NEEDHAM, J. and D. E. GREEN (eds). Perspectives in Biochemistry. CUP, 1939. 1st ed, rpt. Blue cl. (Spine faded), o/w VG. *White*. $55/£35

NEEDHAM, JAMES G. and J. T. LLOYD. The Life of Inland Waters. Ithaca, NY, 1937. 3rd ed. Blue cl, gilt. VG. *Price*. $39/£25

NEEDHAM, JOSEPH et al. Heavenly Clockwork. CUP, 1960. 1st ed. 21 full-pg plts. (Sunned), o/w Good+ in Good+ dj. *Scribe's Perch**. $70/£45

NEEDHAM, JOSEPH et al. Heavenly Clockwork. Cambridge: CUP, 1960. 1st ed. 69 plts. Red cl. Dj (edges worn). *Weber*. $100/£64

NEEDHAM, JOSEPH. Biochemistry and Morphogenesis. CUP, 1942. 1st ed. 35 plts (4 color). *Bickersteth*. $86/£55

NEEDHAM, VIOLET. The Boy in Red. Collins, 1948. 1st ed. Joyce Bruce (illus). 8vo. 256pp. NF in pict dj (lt frayed). *Bookmark*. $44/£28

NEEFUS, PETER J. Original Articles on Intemperance. 1890. 1st ed. 281pp. 1/4 leather marbled bds (spine dried, chipped off; extrems sl worn). Fair; internally VG. *Doctor's Library*. $150/£96

NEELY, MARK et al. The Confederate Image. Chapel Hill: Univ of NC, (1987). VG in VG dj. *Scribe's Perch**. $32/£21

NEFF, ANDREW. History of Utah: 1847-1869. Salt Lake, 1940. 1st ed. VG+ in dj (sm chip). *Benchmark*. $90/£58

NEFF, PAT M. Battles of Peace. Fort Worth: Pioneer, 1925. Port. Black cl, gilt. VG (spine dull). *Bohling*. $20/£13

Negotiations of Thomas Woolsey.... (By George Cavendish.) London: Sheares, 1641. 1st ed. 4to. Engr frontis port of Woolsey. Calf (rebacked; lib bk ticket). *Rostenberg & Stern*. $525/£337

NEIHARDT, JOHN. Black Elk Speaks. NY: William Morrow, 1932. 1st ed. Color pict tp, 14 full-pg illus. Untrimmed. Gray cl stamped in maroon (sl shelfworn). Text NF in most of pict dj (price-clipped, lacks spine bottom, fold separated, sl chipped, tear fr panel w/sl loss). *Baltimore**. $130/£83

NEIHARDT, JOHN. Collected Poems of John G. Neihardt. NY: Macmillan, 1926. 1st ed. One of 250 numbered sets, signed. 2 vols. Paper spine labels. *Ginsberg*. $250/£160

NEIHARDT, JOHN. The Splendid Wayfaring. NY: Macmillan, 1920. 1st ed. Dbl-pg map. Grn cl. Fine in NF dj (sl soiled, with sm rubberstamp reading 'Pages 12-15' on spine. *Harrington*. $110/£71

NEIL, C. LANG. Modern Conjurer and Drawing-Room Entertainer. Phila, 1902. VG. *New Hampshire**. $80/£51

NEILL, JOHN R. Lucky Bucky in Oz. Hutchinson's Books for Young People, n.d. (1945 inscrip). 1st Eng ed. Lg 4to. 128pp. Illus eps. Red cl (sl mkd). VG. *Bookmark*. $55/£35

NEILL, JOHN R. The Scalawagons of Oz. Reilly & Lee, 1941. Ltr ptg. 6.5x9. 309pp. Cl, pict paste-on (rubbed; lacks dj). VG (shelfworn). *My Bookhouse*. $90/£58

NEILL, PATRICK. The Fruit, Flower and Kitchen Garden. Edinburgh: Black, 1845. 3rd ed. xi+364pp,16pp ads. *Marlborough*. $70/£45

NEILSON, KATHERINE B. Filippino Lippi. Cambridge, 1938. Good. *Washton*. $400/£256

NEIMAN, S. I. Judah Benjamin, Mystery Man of the Confederacy. Indianapolis, (1963). 1st ed. (Cvr sl worn), o/w Fine in dj. *Pratt*. $47/£30

NEISON, ADRIAN. Practical Boat-Building for Amateurs. Chicago: Henneberry, 1901. Dec olive grn cl. Good (sig sprung; spine ends worn). *Bowman*. $30/£19

NELSON, BRUCE. Land of the Dacotahs. Minneapolis: Univ of MN, (1946). 1st ed. VG in dj (sl worn). *Lien*. $20/£13

NELSON, C. and A. BRADY (eds). Irish Gardening and Horticulture. Royal Horticultural Soc of Ireland, 1979. (Sl bumped.) Dj. *Maggs*. $47/£30

NELSON, CHARLES. The Boy Who Picked the Bullets Up. NY, 1981. 1st ed. Fine in Fine dj. *Warren*. $35/£22

NELSON, EDWARD W. Report upon the Natural History Collections Made in Alaska Between...1877 and 1881.... Washington: GPO, 1887. 337pp, 21 plts (12 color). (Spine ends frayed), else VG. *High Latitude*. $150/£96

NELSON, HAROLD HAYDEN. The Great Hypostyle Hall at Karnak. Vol. 1, Part 1: The Wall Reliefs. William J. Murnane (ed). Chicago: Oriental Inst, Univ of Chicago, 1981. 267 plts. *Archaeologia*. $125/£80

NELSON, HENRY L. The Army of the United States. NY: B.M. Whitlock, c. 1895. Unpaginated. Loose tp, 47 VF chromo plts. (Text ll for plts XLIV-XLVII not present; ex-lib, spine label, bkpl, inkstamp fep.) *New Hampshire**. $375/£240

NELSON, HUGH LAWRENCE. The Fence. NY: Rinehart, 1953. 1st ed. VG in dj (short closed tear). *Mordida*. $30/£19

NELSON, JACK and JACK BASS. The Orangeburg Massacre. NY/Cleveland: World, 1970. 1st ed. NF in VG dj. *Cahan*. $30/£19

NELSON, LORD. The Dispatches and Letters of Vice Admiral Lord Viscount Nelson. London, 1845-6. 2nd ed. 7 vols. 8vo. (Lt foxing.) Partly unopened. Dec blue cl (spines faded, vol V recased), gilt. *Maggs*. $780/£500

NELSON, MICHAEL. Knock or Ring. London: Cape, (1957). 1st ed. VG in dj (lt worn, chipped). *Hermitage*. $25/£16

NELSON, OLIVER. The Cowman's Southwest...1878-1893. Angie Debo (ed). Glendale: Clark, 1953. 1st ed. One of 1021. Red cl, gilt spine (sl water stain fr cvr, sl bumping fore-edge). NF. *Argonaut*. $100/£64

NELSON, PHILIP. Ancient Painted Glass in England 1170-1500. Methuen, 1913. 33 plts. (Lt foxed.) Scarlet cl (top upper joint worn; rubbed, sl dull). *Peter Taylor*. $33/£21

NELSON, R. H. (ed). Pyrethrum Flowers. Minneapolis, 1975. 3rd ed. VG in dj. *Brooks*. $34/£22

NELSON, RICHARD K. Hunters of the Northern Forest—Designs for Survival. Chicago: Univ of Chicago, (1973). 1st ed. Signed. VG in VG dj. *Perier*. $35/£22

NELSON, ROBERT. A Companion for the Festivals and Fasts of the Church of England. London: A. Wilson, 1819. Stereotype ed. Frontis port, xvi,388pp. Full polished speckled calf, gilt, spine label. VG. *Hollett*. $62/£40

NELSON, TRUMAN. The Old Man, John Brown at Harper's Ferry. NY, (1973). 1st ed. Fine in Fine dj. *Pratt.* $32/£21

NELSON, WILLIAM. Fishing in Eden. London: Witherby, 1922. 1st ed. Color frontis, 12 plts, map. (Corners sl frayed.) *Hollett.* $94/£60

NELSON, WILLIAM. Personal Names of Indians of New Jersey. Paterson: Paterson History Club, 1904. One of 250. (Eps sl dampstained; spine sl worn, soiled), else Good. *Brown.* $30/£19

NEMEROV, HOWARD. The Western Approaches: Poems 1973-75. Chicago: Univ of Chicago, (1975). 1st ed. Fine in dj (sm tear). *Between The Covers.* $45/£29

NERUDA, PABLO. Bestiary/Bestiario. NY: Ptd by Spiral Press, (1965). One of 3500 on Utopian paper. Fine in dj (sm tears, sm piece missing). *Polyanthos.* $30/£19

NERUDA, PABLO. The Heights of Macchu Picchu. Nathaniel Tarn (trans). NY: FSG, (1967). 1st ed. Fine in dj (lt worn, soiled). *Antic Hay.* $75/£48

NERUDA, PABLO. Twenty Poems. N.p.: Sixties Press, 1967. 1st ed. Pb. NF (edges dknd). *Beasley.* $50/£32

NERVO, AMADO. Plenitude. William F. Rice (trans). L.A., 1928. 1st ed. VG+. *Smith.* $25/£16

NESBIT, A. A Treatise on Practical Mensuration. London: Longman, Brown, 1844. 12th ed. xxiv,425,4pp. Tree calf (rebacked in calf, gilt, spine label). *Hollett.* $101/£65

NESBIT, E. The Enchanted Castle. NY: Harper, 1908. 1st Amer ed. 8vo. 297pp; 7 (of 8) b/w plts by H. R. Millar (photostat of 8th plt inserted). Pict cl. VG. *Bookmark.* $101/£65

NESBIT, E. Wet Magic. Werner Laurie, n.d. (1913). 1st ed. 8vo. vii,274pp (sl foxing, new eps, expertly recased); 13 plts by H. R. Millar (of 14, photostat of missing plt inserted; 2 plts frayed). Gilt-pict cl. (Spine rubbed, edgewear), else VG. *Bookmark.* $70/£45

NESBIT, E. and G. MANVILLE FENN. My Sea-Side Story Book. Ernest Nister, n.d. (1911). 1st ed. 4to. Mtd color chromolitho frontis, 108pp,3pp illus ads. Cl spine, pict bds. VG. *Bookmark.* $70/£45

NESBITT, L. M. Desolate Marches. London: Cape, 1935. 1st ed. VG (bkpl) in dj. *Worldwide.* $30/£19

NESBITT, L. M. Hell-Hole of Creation. NY: Knopf, 1935. 3rd ptg. 16 plts. (Sl rubbed, spine frayed), o/w VG. *Worldwide.* $15/£10

NESBITT, WILLIAM H. and PHILIP L. WRIGHT (eds). Records of North American Big Game. Alexandria, 1981. 8th ed. One of 750 numbered, signed by Nesbitt, Wright, and Jack S. Parker. Gilt-stamped leatherette (lt worn). Slipcase. *Oinonen*.* $60/£38

NESS, ELLIOT. The Untouchables. NY, 1957. 1st ed. NF in dj. *Warren.* $50/£32

NESS, F. C. Practical Dope on the .22. Harrisburg: Military Service Pub Co, 1947. 1st ed. Tan buckram, gilt. Fine (bkpl) in VG pict dj. *Biscotti.* $75/£48

NESS, F. C. Practical Dope on the Big Bores. Harrisburg: Stackpole & Heck, 1948. 1st ed. Inscribed. Lt tan buckram. Fine in ptd dj (tattered). *Biscotti.* $75/£48

NESS, F. C. Practical Dope on the Big Bores. Harrisburg: Stackpole, 1952. 2nd ptg. VG+ (name). *Backman.* $60/£38

NESS, MRS. PATRICK. Ten Thousand Miles in Two Continents. 1929. 1st ed. 2 maps. *Edwards.* $55/£35

NETTER, FRANK H. The Ciba Collection of Medical Illustrations: Volume 1 Nervous System. NY, 1957. Grn cl bds (sl worn). VG. *Doctor's Library.* $50/£32

NEU, JOHN (ed). Chemical, Medical and Pharmaceutical Books Printed before 1800 in the Collections of the University of Wisconsin Libraries. Madison/Milwaukee: Univ of WI, 1965. Fine in dj (lt soiled, rubbed; price-clipped). *Heller.* $35/£22

NEUBERG, VICTOR. The Penny Histories. NY: HBJ, 1969. 1st US ed. 4 1/4 x 6 3/4. 227pp. Fine in dj. *Cattermole.* $25/£16

NEUFELD, CHARLES. A Prisoner of the Khaleefa. London, 1899. 2nd ed. xiv,365pp; 3 maps. (1st, last leaves lt browned; spine sl worn.) *Edwards.* $78/£50

NEUGEBAUER, O. The Exact Sciences in Antiquity. Princeton: Princeton Univ, 1952. 14 plts (1 color). Good. *Archaeologia.* $65/£42

NEUGEBOREN, JAY. Sam's Legacy. Holt, Rinehart & Winston, 1974. 1st ed. Fine in VG dj. *Plapinger.* $35/£22

NEUHAUS, EUGEN. The San Diego Garden Fair. SF: Paul Elder, 1916. 1st ed. Gilt-stamped paper-cvrd bds. Fine. *Quest.* $65/£42

NEUMEYER, PETER F. and EDWARD GOREY. Why We Have Night and Day. NY: Young Scott Bks, (1970). 1st ed. Signed by Gorey. Fine in Fine dj. *Lenz.* $65/£42

NEVILL, RALPH. Light Come, Light Go. Macmillan, 1909. (Feps lt browned; corners, joints sl rubbed, spine lt faded.) *Edwards.* $101/£65

NEVILL, RALPH. Light Come, Light Go. London: Macmillan, 1909. 1st ed. 9 color, 14 b/w plts. Red cl, gilt. VG. *Cummins.* $250/£160

NEVILL, RALPH. Old English Sporting Books. The Studio, 1924. 1st ed. Teg. Red buckram (damp mkd, spine faded), gilt. VG. *Words Etc.* $94/£60

NEVILL, RALPH. Old English Sporting Books. Geoffrey Holme (ed). London: Studio, 1924. 1st ed. One of 1500, this unnumbered, out-of-series. 24 color, 83 b/w plts. Teg. Red-orange buckram, beveled bds, gilt. (Fr hinge lt cracked; lt frayed, lt sunned, worn.) *Baltimore*.* $70/£45

NEVILLE, A. W. The Red River Valley—Then and Now. Paris, TX: Hertzog, 1948. Signed by Neville and Jose Cisneros (illus). Dec eps. Fine in VG dj. *Parmer.* $150/£96

NEVILLE, HUGH. The Game Laws of England for Gamekeepers. London: Davis, 1879. Red cl (worn, faded). Sound. *Boswell.* $125/£80

NEVILLE, RALPH. English Country House Life. London, 1925. 1st ed. (Eps lt spotted.) Dj (lt soiled, chipped, repaired). *Edwards.* $31/£20

NEVINS, ALLAN. Fremont, Pathmarker of the West. NY: LG, 1955. 1st ed thus. NF in VG dj. *Archer.* $22/£14

NEVINS, ALLAN. Fremont, Pathmarker of the West. NY: D. Appleton-Century, 1939. 1st ed thus. VG in dj (sl worn). *Dumont.* $45/£29

NEVINS, ALLAN. Fremont, Pathmarker of the West. NY: D. Appleton-Century, 1939. 1st ed. 9 maps. Blue cl, gilt. VF in dj (sl chipped). *Argonaut.* $75/£48

NEVINS, ALLAN. The War for the Union 1861-65. NY: Scribner, 1959-71. Ltr ptg. 4 vols. VG+ in djs. *Archer.* $45/£29

NEVINS, ALLAN. The War for the Union. NY, 1959, 1960, 1971. 1st eds. 4 vols. Vol 1 inscribed. Fine in dj (lt worn, chipped; spine faded). *Pratt.* $95/£61

NEVINS, WINFIELD S. Witchcraft in Salem Village in 1692. Salem, MA: Salem Press Co, 1916. 5th ed. Inscribed presentation. Frontis. Pict grn cl (rubbed, bumped; hinges cracked; gilt title faded). *Blue Mountain.* $35/£22

NEVINSON, C. R. W. The Year 1918 Illustrated. London: Headley Bros, (?1919). Cl-backed bds (inscrip; sl creased). *Clearwater.* $78/£50

New American Cookery, or Female Companion. By an American Lady. NY: D.D. Smith, 1805. 1st ed. (Tp torn, sm chip; leaf repaired; toned, lt foxed, dampstained; sm tears.) Later blue buckram (lt soiled). *Waverly*.* $198/£127

New Clerk's Magazine, Containing All the Most Useful Forms.... Boston: Lilly, Wait, 1833. 2nd ed. Contemp speckled sheep (wear). Sound. *Boswell.* $150/£96

New Cries of London. NY: Mahlon Day, 1837. 18mo. 24pp (incl wrappers). Orig ptd, pict wrappers. *M & S.* $200/£128

New Cyclopedia of Botany.... Vol 1 (of 2). (By Richard Brooke.) London: Clark, (1854). 1st ed. Hand-color engr frontis, lix,(+ index bound in fr),349 + 36pp hand-colored plts. 1/2 calf, marbled bds. VG. *Quest.* $145/£93

New England Hurricane. Boston: Hale, Cushman & Flint, 1938. (Sl rubbed), o/w VG. *Worldwide.* $20/£13

New Gallery of British Art. NY: D. Appleton, n.d. 2 vols. 121 steel engrs. Full gilt-dec leather (rubbed). *Metropolitan*.* $402/£258

New Guide for Travellers Through the United States of America.... Boston: J. Haven, 1851. 20pp (loose); lg hand-colored fldg map. Gilt/blind-dec cl (sl worn). VG. *New Hampshire*.* $325/£208

New Hampshire Register and U.S. Calendar for the Year of Our Lord 1821. Concord: Hill & Moore. Pict wrappers (spine partly chipped, brown spots cvrs). *Sadlon.* $40/£26

New History of Blue Beard, Written by Black Beard.... (By Charles Perrault.) Phila: John Adams, 1804. 32mo. 31pp; 7 crude woodcuts. VF in buff wrappers. *Bromer.* $200/£128

New Orleans City Guide. Boston/Cambridge: Houghton Mifflin/Riverside, 1938. 1st ed. Lg color fldg map in rear pocket. VG in dj (nicks, sm tears). *Houle.* $150/£96

New Rupert (Annual 1954). 4to. (Price 4/6 present but competition pg removed, 4 sm tape tabs eps). Pict bds (18mm chip spine foot, few mks). *Bookmark.* $47/£30

New Rupert Book (1938 Annual). Bestall (illus). 4to. 125pp (2pp edges sl frayed, 4pp discolored, mks). Red cl spine w/black vignette, pict bds (sl rubbed, professionally recased). Attractive. *Bookmark.* $289/£185

New Spain and the Anglo-American West: Historical Contributions Presented to Herbert Eugene Bolton. (Lancaster, PA: Privately ptd, 1932.) 1st ed. One of 500 numbered. 2 vols. *Ginsberg.* $350/£224

New System of Domestic Cookery. (By Mrs. Maria Eliza Rundell.) London: John Murray, 1807. Engr frontis (larder, w/'Art of Cookery' on table cl), 9 full-pg engr plts; 3pp pub's ads at end. Orig brn bds (spine ends chipped, hinges weak; lt foxed), ptd paper spine label. VG. *Houle.* $500/£321

New York Commissioners of Fisheries, Game and Forests. First Annual Report. (Albany), c. 1896. 14 color plts. Pict cl (extrems worn, rear inner hinge broken). Contents VG. *New Hampshire*.* $220/£141

NEW YORK HISTORICAL SOCIETY. Collections...Second Series. Volume I. NY, 1841. Fldg map frontis, 486pp; port. Marbled eps; teg. 1/2 grn leather, marbled bds, gilt. (Sl worn), else VG. *Zubal*.* $70/£45

NEW YORK HISTORICAL SOCIETY. Collections...Second Series. Volume III. Part I. NY, 1857. 358,(1)pp. Marbled eps; teg. 1/2 grn leather, marbled bds, gilt. (Sl worn), else VG. *Zubal*.* $50/£32

NEW YORK MONUMENTS COMMISSION. Final Report on the Battlefield of Gettysburg. Albany, 1900. st ed. 3 vols. Pict cl. (Lacks all 5 fldg maps from pockets, several inner hinges broken, cl sl worn, dampspotted), o/w Contents VG. *New Hampshire*.* $25/£16

NEW YORK MONUMENTS COMMISSION. New York at Gettysburg. Albany: J.B. Lyon, 1900. 1st ed. 3 vols. 5 maps in pockets fr pastedown each vol. Slip tipped in vol 1, signed by Anson G. McCook. Partially unopened. (Lt soiled, sm lib # prelims. Paper spine labels. (Spine ends rubbed, fraying, traces removed spine #s.) *Sadlon.* $125/£80

New York State Commission in Lunacy, Annual Reports. Volume 2. Albany, NY: Wynkoop Hallenbeck Crawford, 1897. 2nd ptg. xiv,331,(3)pp. Ruled red cl (shelfworn). Good. *Gach.* $40/£26

New York State Commission in Lunacy, Annual Reports. Volume 8. Albany, 1897. 1st ed. xii,(1336)pp. Ruled red cl. (Fr hinge cracked), else VG. *Gach.* $75/£48

New York State Museum Report of the State Botanist. Albany: SUNY, 1901. 9 vols. 94 color plts. (External browning.) Interiors Clean. Wraps. *Metropolitan*.* $287/£184

New York Times Current History (of) the European War. NY, 1914-1919. 19 vols. Pub's dk grn cl. (Several vols dampstained), else VG. *Zubal*.* $170/£109

NEWALL, J. T. Hog Hunting in the East, and Other Sports. London: Tinsely, 1867. 1st ed. Frontis, xviii,466pp. Blue cl. (1st few pp foxed; recased; spine dull), else VG. *Terramedia.* $250/£160

NEWBERRY, CLARE TURLAY. April's Kittens. NY: Harper, 1940. 1st ed. 9 x 10 3/4. 33pp. VG (sl browning fep) in dj (price-clipped). *Cattermole.* $125/£80

NEWBERRY, CLARE TURLAY. Barkis. NY: Harper, 1938. 1st ed. 9 1/2 x 7 1/2. 32pp. Pict bds. Fine in dj. *Cattermole.* $75/£48

NEWBERRY, CLARE TURLAY. The Kittens' ABC. NY: Harper, 1946. 1st ed. 10 x 13. VG (sl rubbed). *Cattermole.* $50/£32

NEWBERRY, CLARE TURLAY. Marshmallow. NY: Harper, 1942. 1st ed. 12 x 10 1/4. Pict cl. Good (sl wear, rubbing, rep corner torn off). *Cattermole.* $75/£48

NEWBERRY, CLARE TURLAY. Pandora. NY: Harper, 1944. 1st ed. 10 x 13. Grey cl w/pastedown. VG in dj (back sl sunned). *Cattermole.* $50/£32

NEWBERRY, J. S. The Later Extinct Floras of North America. Washington: US Geol Survey, 1898. 1st ed. 68 tinted litho plts. (Few lib stamps; cl sl soiled, worn.) *Maggs.* $37/£24

NEWBERRY, J. S. The Paleozoic Fishes of North America. Washington: US Geol Survey, 1889. 1st ed. 53 plts. (Lib stamps, sm tear tp; cl dusty, sl worn.) *Maggs.* $41/£26

NEWBY, ERIC. The Last Grain Race. London, 1956. 1st Eng ed, 1st bk. Very Nice (foxed) in dj (sl nicked). *Clearwater.* $62/£40

NEWBY, ERIC. Love and War in the Apennines. London, 1971. 1st Eng ed. Nice in dj (sl torn, price-clipped). *Clearwater.* $39/£25

NEWBY, ERIC. On the Shores of the Mediterranean. London, 1984. 1st Eng ed. Signed. Fine in dj (clipped). *Clearwater.* $47/£30

NEWBY, ERIC. Slowly Down the Ganges. London, 1966. 1st Eng ed. Nice in dj (sl rubbed). *Clearwater.* $62/£40

NEWBY, ERIC. A Traveller's Life. London, 1982. 1st ed. Dw. *Edwards.* $23/£15

NEWBY, P. H. The Barbary Light. London, 1962. 1st ed. VG in dj (sl worn). *Typographeum.* $15/£10

NEWBY, P. H. One of the Founders. London: Faber, 1965. 1st Eng ed. VG in dj. *Hadley.* $23/£15

NEWBY, P. H. The Picnic at Sakkara. London, 1955. 1st ed. VG in dj. *Typographeum.* $28/£18

NEWCOMB, COVELLE. The Secret Door. Dodd, Mead, 1946. 1st ed. Addison Burbank (illus). 6x9. 162pp. VG + (sl bumped) in dj (edges ragged). *My Bookhouse.* $40/£26

NEWCOMB, PEARSON. The Alamo City. San Antonio: Standard Ptg Co, 1926. 1st ed. VG. *Gibbs.* $20/£13

NEWCOMB, REXFORD. In the Lincoln Country. Phila, 1928. 1st ed. Pict cl. VG. *Pratt.* $22/£14

NEWCOMB, REXFORD. The Old Mission Churches and Historic Houses of California. Phila: Lippincott, 1925. 1st ed. Pamphlet laid in. Teg. Blue cl, gilt. Fine in pict dj. *Pacific**. $161/£103

NEWCOMB, REXFORD. The Old Mission Churches and Historic Houses of California.... Phila: Lippincott, 1925. Color frontis. Grn cl. VG. *Yudkin**. $80/£51

NEWCOMB, REXFORD. The Spanish House for America. Phila: J.B. Lippincott, 1927. 1st ed. Frontis. Pict tan cl. *Dawson*. $125/£80

NEWCOMB, SIMON. Astronomy for Everybody. (1902.) (Spine ends sl defective), o/w VG in dj. *Whitehart*. $23/£15

NEWCOMB, SIMON. Popular Astronomy. 1883. xx,579pp. (Stickers fr pastedown, fep, stamps; spine ends sl defective, cl sl mkd), o/w VG. *Whitehart*. $39/£25

NEWCOMB, SIMON. The Reminiscences of an Astronomer. London/NY, 1903. (Sl adhesion mks to port; cl sl worn). *Maggs*. $36/£23

NEWDIGATE, BERNARD H. Michael Drayton and His Circle. Shakespeare Head & Blackwell, 1941. 1st ed. NF. *Poetry Bookshop*. $55/£35

NEWELL, H. A. Footprints in Spain. London: Methuen, 1922. 1st ed. 16 plts. (Sl rubbed, sm tears fr cvr), o/w VG. *Worldwide*. $14/£9

NEWELL, PETER. The Hole Book. NY, (1908). 1st ed. Sm 4to. Orig cl, full-size color pict fr cvr label. *Swann**. $172/£110

NEWELL, PETER. The Hole Book. NY: Harper, (1908). Later ptg. 4to. 51pp incl 24 full-pg color illus w/hole in center of each pg except last (text sl soiled, sm tear 1 pg edge, hole edges sl worn). Bds (bumped, rubbed, soiled), hole in fr bd, mtd pict label. Good. *Blue Mountain*. $45/£29

NEWELL, PETER. The Slant Book. NY: Harper, Nov 1910. Rhomboidal 7x9. Unpaginated; 22 plts (several marred by child's pencil). Good-. *Scribe's Perch**. $42/£27

NEWELL, ROBERT. Robert Newell's Memoranda. Portland: Champoeg, 1959. 1st ed. Ltd to 1000 ptd. Frontis, 2 plts, 1 fldg map. Uncut. VF. *Argonaut*. $60/£38

NEWHALL, BEAUMONT and DIANA EDKINS. William H. Jackson. Dobbs Ferry, NY: Morgan & Morgan w/Amon Carter Museum, 1974. 1st ed. 103 b/w plts. NF (name stamp) in pict dj. *Cahan*. $45/£29

NEWHALL, BEAUMONT. Daguerreotype in America. Greenwich, CT: NYGS, 1968. Rev ed. (Owner stamp, ink address), o/w VG in dj (lt rubbed, edgeworn). *Cahan*. $40/£26

NEWHALL, BEAUMONT. Dorothea Lange Looks at the American Country Woman. Ft. Worth/L.A.: Amon Carter Museum/Ward Ritchie, 1967. 1st ed. 28 b/w plts. Illus cl. Fine in dj (sl rubbed). *Cahan*. $75/£48

NEWHALL, BEAUMONT. The History of Photography. NY: MOMA, 1964. Rev, enlgd ed. Dj (ragged, some loss, cellotaped to bds). *Edwards*. $39/£25

NEWHALL, NANCY (ed). Edward Weston: Photographer. Rochester: Aperture, 1965. 1st ed. Frontis port. (Owner stamp), else VG in pict dj. *Cahan*. $50/£32

NEWHALL, NANCY (ed). Edward Weston: The Flame of Recognition. Rochester: Aperture, 1971. Frontis port. (Owner stamp), else VG in pict stiff wrappers (corner creased). *Cahan*. $25/£16

NEWHALL, NANCY (intro). A Portfolio of Sixteen Photographs by Alvin Langdon Coburn. Rochester, NY: George Eastman House, 1962. 1st ed thus. Ltd to 2000. 21-pg text booklet; 16 loose full-pg b/w photos mtd on paper sheets. Laid in cl-backed paper over bds folder. (Name stamp; pocket separated on 2 sides), else NF. *Cahan*. $100/£64

NEWHALL, NANCY. Ansel Adams. Vol 1. SF: Sierra Club, (1963). 1st ed. VG in dj. *King*. $125/£80

NEWHALL, NANCY. Ansel Adams. Volume 1. The Eloquent Light. SF: Sierra Club, 1963. 1st ed. Dj (sm tear, sl creased, sl loss spine head). *Edwards*. $133/£85

NEWLAND, CONSTANCE A. (Pseud of Thelma Moss.) My Self and I. F. Muller, 1963. 1st UK ed. VG in dj (sl worn). *Sclanders*. $16/£10

NEWMAN, ANDREA. The Cage. London, 1966. 1st Eng ed. Very Nice in dj. *Clearwater*. $39/£25

NEWMAN, ANDREA. Mirage. London, 1965. 1st Eng ed. Nice (spine sl mkd) in dj. *Clearwater*. $39/£25

NEWMAN, ARNOLD. One Mind's Eye. Boston: Godine, 1974. 1st ed. 192 full-pg b/w photos. (Owner stamp), else NF in dj. *Cahan*. $60/£38

NEWMAN, CHARLES and WILLIAM A. HENKIN, JR. (eds). Under 30. Bloomington/London: IN Univ, 1971. 3rd ptg. (Owner stamp), else NF in VG dj. *Cahan*. $25/£16

NEWMAN, FRANCES. Dead Lovers Are Faithful Lovers. NY: Boni & Liveright, 1928. 1st ed. VG in dj (lt soiled, chip). *Turlington*. $150/£96

NEWMAN, JOHN HENRY. Apologia Pro Vita Sua. London, 1864. 1st ed in bk form. 1/2 dk red leather. VG. *Argosy*. $250/£160

NEWMAN, JOHN HENRY. Apologia Pro Vita Sua. London: Longmans, Green (et al), 1864. 1st ed. Contemp 3/4 calf, bds (neatly rebacked), orig backstrip laid down. (Late 19th-cent inscrip; bumped), else Good. *Reese*. $100/£64

NEWMAN, NEIL. Famous Horses of the American Turf. NY: Derrydale, 1931, 1932, 1933. Ltd to 750. 3 vols. VG (sl shelfwear, spine ends sl worn). *October Farm*. $495/£317

NEWMAN, W. Moveable Shadows for the People. London: Dean & Son, n.d. (ca 1858). 8vo. Color pict tp, 8 moveable color litho plts. (Sl foxed, soiled.) Pict bds (scuffed, spine chipped). *Oinonen**. $900/£577

NEWMAN, W. Moveable Shadows. Second Series. London: Dean & Son, n.d. (ca 1857). 8vo. Pict tp, 8 moveable litho plts. (Sl foxed.) Pict bds (worn, broken). Internally Sound. *Oinonen**. $850/£545

NEWMARK, HARRIS. Sixty Years in Southern California, 1853-1913. Maurice H. and Marco R. Newmark (eds). Boston: Houghton Mifflin, 1930. 3rd ed. Frontis port. Red cl, gilt. (Corner sl jammed), else Fine. *Argonaut*. $125/£80

NEWMARK, MARCO R. Jottings in Southern California History. L.A.: Ward Ritchie, (1955). 1st ed. Errata slip tipped in. Cl-backed dec bds. Fine in ptd glassine dj (sl torn). *Argonaut*. $45/£29

NEWSON, THOMAS M. Thrilling Scenes Among the Indians. Chicago: Belford, 1884. 1st ed. 241pp; 8 plts. Dec cl (spine faded). Howes N127. *Ginsberg*. $125/£80

NEWSTEAD, R. et al. Guide to the Study of the Tsetse-Flies. London, 1924. 3 color, 25 plain plts, 4 maps. Fine. *Henly*. $33/£21

NEWTON, A. EDWARD. The Amenities of Book-Collecting and Kindred Affections. Boston: Little, Brown, 1937. (Sig sprung.) *Rostenberg & Stern*. $25/£16

NEWTON, A. EDWARD. Ascot. Daylesford, PA: Privately ptd, Christmas 1933. Frontis. Tied blue wrappers. Fine. *Graf*. $15/£10

NEWTON, A. EDWARD. Derby Day and Other Adventures. Boston: Little, Brown, 1934. 1st ed. Color frontis. (Spine browned), o/w VG in VG+ dj (spine sl tanned). *Bernard*. $45/£29

NEWTON, A. EDWARD. The Greatest Book in the World and Other Papers. Boston, (1925). Lg paper ed. #118/450 (of 475) signed. Teg, uncut. Fine. *Polyanthos*. $50/£32

NEWTON, A. EDWARD. The Greatest Book in the World and Other Papers. Boston: Little, Brown, 1925. 1st ed. Teg; paper-cvrd bds; cl spine. Fine (corner sl bumped). *Graf.* $35/£22

NEWTON, A. EDWARD. The Greatest Book in the World. Boston: Little, Brown, (1925). One of 470 signed. Color frontis. Grn cl, bds, ptd lettering piece. Fine in slipcase (worn). *House.* $110/£71

NEWTON, A. EDWARD. I Want! I Want! Daylesford, PA: Privately ptd, Christmas 1932. Frontis. Tied blue wrappers. Fine. *Graf.* $15/£10

NEWTON, A. EDWARD. A Magnificent Farce and Other Diversions of a Book Collector. Boston: Atlantic Monthly, (1921). 1st ed. VG. *Graf.* $35/£22

NEWTON, A. EDWARD. Staffordshire. Daylesford, PA: Privately ptd, Christmas 1935. Frontis. Tied blue wrappers. Fine. *Graf.* $15/£10

NEWTON, A. EDWARD. This Book Collecting Game. Boston, 1928. '1st imp of the 1st trade ed.' Bright in dj (piece missing). *Truepenny.* $30/£19

NEWTON, A. EDWARD. A Tourist in Spite of Himself. Boston, 1930. 1st ed. Fore-edge uncut. Pict cl (Lt spotted, feps lt browned; lt faded.) *Edwards.* $39/£25

NEWTON, ALFRED and HANS GADOW. A Dictionary of Birds. London, 1896. xii,1088pp; fldg map. Good. *Henly.* $34/£22

NEWTON, ALFRED and HANS GADOW. A Dictionary of Birds. London: A&C Black, 1896. 1st ed. 4 parts in 1 vol. xii,124,vi,1088pp; fldg map. Good in grn cl (rubbed, sl shaken). *Cox.* $39/£25

NEWTON, ERIC (ed). War Through Artists' Eyes. London, 1945. 1st Eng ed. Nice. *Clearwater.* $39/£25

NEWTON, ERIC. War Through Artists' Eyes. London: Murray, 1945. (2pp repaired), o/w Fine. *Europa.* $39/£25

NEWTON, HELMUT. White Women. NY: Stonehill, 1976. 1st ed. NF in NF dj. *Smith.* $75/£48

NEWTON, ISAAC. The Chronology of Ancient Kingdoms Amended. London: J. Tonson et al, 1728. 1st ed. xiv,(ii),376pp (browned, cracked, sl foxed); 3 fldg copper plts. Orig calf (joints recently repaired w/brn cl tape, edgeworn, lower cvr sl peeling). Bkpl, ink sig of William Kenrick. *Baltimore*.* $300/£192

NEWTON, ISAAC. The Correspondence of Isaac Newton, Volume V, 1709-1713. A. R. Hall and I. Tilling (eds). Cambridge, 1975. VF in dj. *Whitehart.* $94/£60

NEWTON, ISAAC. The Correspondence of Isaac Newton, Volume VI, 1713-1718. A. R. Hall and I. Tilling (eds). Cambridge Univ, 1976. VG + in dj. *Bookcell.* $90/£58

NEWTON, ISAAC. The Correspondence of Isaac Newton, Volume VI, 1713-1718. A. R. Hall and I. Tilling (eds). Cambridge, 1976. VF in dj. *Whitehart.* $94/£60

NEWTON, ISAAC. Opticks: Or, A Treatise of the Reflections, Refractions, Inflections and Colours of Light. William & John Innys, 1721. 3rd ed. 8vo. (viii),382pp + 8pg pub's list at end (tp sl dusty, early pp spotted, new eps); 12 fldg engr plts. Orig panelled calf (rebacked). *Bickersteth.* $1,521/£975

NEWTON, ISAAC. Papers and Letters on Natural Philosophy and Related Documents. I. Bernard Cohen (ed). Cambridge: Harvard Univ, 1958. 1st ed thus. Frontis port. Fine in dj. *Glaser.* $75/£48

NEWTON, JOSEPH FORT. Lincoln and Herndon. Cedar Rapids, IA: Torch Press, 1910. Frontis port. Teg. Grn cl, gilt. VG + . *Bohling.* $32/£21

NEWTON, JOSEPH FORT. Lincoln and Herndon. Cedar Rapids, IA: Torch, 1910. 1st ed. Teg. (Rubbed.) *King.* $35/£22

NEWTON, LILY. A Handbook of the British Seaweeds. British Museum, 1931. 1st ed. (Sl wear.) *Edwards.* $47/£30

NEXO, MARTIN ANDERSEN. Days in the Sun. NY: Coward-McCann, 1929. 1st US ed. VG (faded, lt offsetting from dj to fr bd) in dj (sl soiled, worn). *Lame Duck.* $50/£32

NIALL, IAN (ed). A Sketchbook of Birds. NY: H.R. & W., 1979. 1st ed. NF in VG dj. *Mikesh.* $30/£19

NIALL, IAN. Fresh Woods. Heinemann, 1951. 1st ed. (Bkpl.) Dj (chipped, sl loss). *Edwards.* $23/£15

NICHOLLS, W. H. Orchids of Australia. D. L. Jones & T. B. Muir (eds). Melbourne, 1969. Complete ed. Map, 476 color plts. NF in dj (sl torn). *Brooks.* $245/£157

NICHOLS, BEVERLEY (ed). A Book of Old Ballads. London: Hutchinson, 1934. 1st ed. 16 color plts. (Tp spots.) Uncut. Glassine dj (sl defective). *Hollett.* $39/£25

NICHOLS, BEVERLEY. All I Could Never Be. London: Jonathan Cape, (1949). 1st ed. NF in dj. *Turtle Island.* $35/£22

NICHOLS, BEVERLEY. Are They the Same at Home. NY, 1927. 1st ed. Signed. VG (lacks dj). *Warren.* $30/£19

NICHOLS, BEVERLEY. The Art of Flower Arrangement. London: Collins, 1967. 1st ed. Fine in dj. *Quest.* $75/£48

NICHOLS, BEVERLEY. A Thatched Roof. London: Cape, 1933. 1st ed. Fine. *Quest.* $40/£26

NICHOLS, BEVERLEY. A Village in a Valley. London: Cape, 1934. 1st ed. As New in dj. *Quest.* $50/£32

NICHOLS, CHARLES H. (ed). Arna Bontemps—Langston Hughes Letters 1925-1967. NY: Dodd, Mead, (1980). 1st ed. Fine in NF dj (sl worn). *Bernard.* $35/£22

NICHOLS, GEORGE WARD. The Story of the Great March, from the Diary of a Staff Officer. NY, 1865. 22nd ed (sic). xii,(1),(15)-408pp; fldg map. VG. *Wantagh.* $35/£22

NICHOLS, H. S. Fifty Drawings by Aubrey Beardsley. NY, 1920. 1st ed. Ltd to 500 numbered, signed by pub. 50 full-pg plts. Teg. Gilt-dec art-nouveau cl (worn, bumped, ends frayed). *King.* $350/£224

NICHOLS, J. P. Views of the Architecture of the Heavens. Edinburgh: Tait, 1838. 2nd ed. 222pp. Good. *Bookcell.* $45/£29

NICHOLS, JAMES WILSON. Now You Hear My Horn. Austin: Univ of TX, 1967. VG in dj. *Dumont.* $50/£32

NICHOLS, JOHN. American Blood. NY, 1987. 1st ed. Fine in Fine dj. *Smith.* $15/£10

NICHOLS, JOHN. Literary Anecdotes of the Eighteenth Century. London: The Author, 1812-15. 2nd ed. 9 vols. 8 engr frontis ports (1 fldg; some sl spotted or offset onto titles). 1/2 navy-blue levant morocco, gilt, raised bands, dbl spine labels in red/grn. Excellent (accession stamps back tps, marginal stamps). *Hollett.* $1,014/£650

NICHOLS, JOHN. Literary Anecdotes of the Eighteenth Century. Colin Clair (ed). Centaur, 1967. Frontis. VG in dj (frayed). *Cox.* $23/£15

NICHOLS, JOHN. The Milagro Beanfield War. NY, (1974). 1st ed. VG in Good dj (edgetorn, frayed). *King.* $150/£96

NICHOLS, JOHN. The Milagro Beanfield War. NY: Holt, Rinehart & Winston, 1974. 1st ed. Fine in NF dj (2 sm internal holes spine head). *Lame Duck.* $250/£160

NICHOLS, JOHN. The Nirvana Blues. NY, 1981. 1st ed. VG in VG dj. *Smith.* $25/£16

NICHOLS, JOHN. The Sterile Cuckoo. David McKay, (1965). 1st ed, 1st bk. (Eps foxed), else Fine in VG + dj. *Authors Of West.* $80/£51

NICHOLS, JOSEPH (comp). Condensed History of the Construction of the Union Pacific Railway. Omaha, 1892. Frontis, 192pp. Blue cl, gilt. VG. Howes N143. *Bohling.* $650/£417

NICHOLS, L. M. Impact: 10th Armored. NY, 1954. Signed. VG. *Clark.* $95/£61

NICHOLS, LESTER. Impact: The Battle Story of the 10th Armored Division. NY: Bradbury, Sayles, O'Neill, (1954). (Sl cocked, faint insect damage cvrs.) Dj (soiled, flap fold loss to insects). *Waverly*.* $38/£24

NICHOLS, PERRY. The Value of Escharotics Medicines Which Will Destroy Any Living or Fungus Tissue in the Treatment of Cancer, Lupus.... East Aurora, NY, 1933. 1st ed. Emb leatherette, color relief fr cvr. VG. *Doctor's Library.* $75/£48

NICHOLS, ROBERT. Fisbo or The Looking-Glass Loaned. London, 1934. #267/1000 signed. VF in Fine dj. *Bond.* $27/£17

NICHOLSON, ALFRED. Cimabue. Princeton, 1932. 1/2 cl, bds. *Washton.* $145/£93

NICHOLSON, B. E. and F. H. BRIGHTMAN. The Oxford Book of Flowerless Plants. London: OUP, 1966. 1st ed. 96 full-pg color plts. Near New. *Quest.* $35/£22

NICHOLSON, CLAUD. Ugly Idol, a Development. Boston/London: Roberts/John Lane, 1896. 1st Amer ed. Pale grn cl (spine ends sl rubbed). Nice (sig, ink inscrip). *Reese.* $45/£29

NICHOLSON, GEORGE (ed). The Illustrated Dictionary of Gardening. London, 1887. 7 vols. 22 color plts. Aeg. Highly dec cl. (Fr hinge vol 4 broken; cracked hinges, cvr stains), o/w Good. *Scribe's Perch*.* $46/£29

NICHOLSON, HELEN. Death in the Morning. London, 1937. 1st Eng ed. Very Nice in silvered dj. *Clearwater.* $70/£45

NICHOLSON, JAMES B. A Manual of the Art of Bookbinding. Phila: Henry Carey Baird, 1856. 1st ed. Frontis, 12 plts (some offset), 7 full-pg samples of marbled paper. Brn 1/2 morocco, marbled bds (extrems sl worn, upper hinge split), raised bands, marbled edges. *Maggs.* $858/£550

NICHOLSON, JAMES B. A Manual of the Art of Bookbinding. Phila: Henry Carey Baird, 1871. 2nd ed. 8vo. 318pp; 6 tipped-in specimens of marbled paper, 24pp pub's cat. Black cl. VG (sl worn). *Lucas.* $600/£385

NICHOLSON, JAMES B. A Manual of the Art of Bookbinding. Phila: Henry Carey Baird, 1902. Rpt. 12 plts, 7 samples of marbled paper. Pub's cat in back. Brn cl, gilt spine. Good. *Karmiole.* $275/£176

NICHOLSON, JOHN. The Tennessee Massacre and Its Causes; or, The Utah Conspiracy.... Salt Lake, 1884. 1st ed. Fine in Fine orig purple wraps. *Benchmark.* $75/£48

NICHOLSON, NORMAN. The Fire of the Lord. London: Nicholson & Watson, 1944. 1st ed. (Spine, edges faded.) *Hollett.* $55/£35

NICHOLSON, NORMAN. A Local Habitation. London: Faber, 1972. 1st ed. VG in wrappers. *Hollett.* $31/£20

NICHOLSON, NORMAN. A Match for the Devil. London: Faber, 1955. 1st ed. Fine in dj. *Hollett.* $117/£75

NICHOLSON, NORMAN. Prophesy to the Wind. London: Faber, 1950. 1st ed. (Few lt spots fep.) Dj (spine sl faded). *Hollett.* $101/£65

NICHOLSON, NORMAN. Wednesday Early Closing. London: Faber, 1975. 1st ed. Fine in dj. *Hollett.* $70/£45

NICHOLSON, PETER. The Carpenter's New Guide. London: J. Taylor, 1819. 7th ed. viii,92pp (sm piece missing tp, loss of 'ide' from 'Guide'); 84 engr plts; 12-pg cat bound in rear. 1/2 leather, marbled bds. *Ars Artis.* $148/£95

NICHOLSON, PETER. Nicholson's New Carpenter's Guide. J. Bowen (ed). London: Jones, 1831. Port, iv,xi-ipp memoir,83pp; 88 + 4 engr plts. New blind cl. *Ars Artis.* $148/£95

NICHOLSON, PETER. Nicholson's Practical Carpentry, Joinery and Cabinet-Making...Revised by Thomas Tredgold. London: Thomas Kelly, 1853. Engr port of Nicholson, engr tp (waterstains corners port, tp); viii,140pp; 110 engr plts incl engr tp; p.vii-xxxvi,36pp, 40pp extracts from building regulations. Mod blind 1/2 cl. *Ars Artis.* $148/£95

NICHOLSON, PETER. The Rudiments of Practical Perspective. London, 1822. 38 engr plts. (Lt foxed, browned.) 1/2 sheep (needs rebinding). *Swann*.* $69/£44

NICHOLSON, WILLIAM. An Almanac of Twelve Sports. London: Heinemann, 1898. 1st ed. Pict paper-cvrd bds (extrems worn, corner chip; inside hinges reinforced). *Metropolitan*.* $287/£184

NICHOLSON, WILLIAM. London Types. London: Heinemann, 1898. Pict paper-cvrd bds (edgewear, loose). Interior Fine. *Metropolitan*.* $287/£184

NICHOLSON, WILLIAM. The Navigator's Assistant. London, 1784. 1st ed. 16,222pp (last pg misnumbered 223); 4 fldg copper plts; 175pp tables. Full leather. Good (sl foxing; joints tender). *Scribe's Perch*.* $170/£109

NICKERSON, ANSEL D. A Raw Recruit's War Experiences. Providence, RI: Ptd by the Press Co, 1888. 1st ed. Frontis, viii,64pp. NF. *Mcgowan.* $175/£112

NICOL, W. The Gardener's Kalendar; or, Monthly Directory of Operations.... London, 1812. 2nd ed. xxi,646pp (lt browned, sl marginal waterstaining), 2 ads. Contemp straight-grained 1/2 morocco, gilt. *Henly.* $187/£120

NICOLAY, C. G. The Oregon Territory: A Geographical and Physical Account.... London, 1846. Half-title, frontis (lib rubberstamp), 226pp; fldg map. Mod 1/2 morocco, marbled bds, spine gilt. (Lt dust-soiled, tanned), else VG. Howes N151. *Reese.* $250/£160

NICOLAY, HELEN. The Boys' Life of Abraham Lincoln. NY: Century, (1906). 1st ed, 14th ptg. Dec cl. NF in dj (chipped). *Mcgowan.* $45/£29

NICOLAY, JOHN G. Lincoln's Secretary Goes West. Theodore C. Blegen (ed). La Crosse, WI: Sumac, 1965. Ltd to 500. Map. VG. *Lien.* $30/£19

NICOLL, W. ROBERTSON and THOMAS J. WISE. Literary Anecdotes of the Nineteenth Century. London, 1895-96. 2 vols. Port, 40 plts. (Inner joints vol 1 weak; worn, soiled, spines faded.) *Maggs.* $86/£55

NICOLLET, JOSEPH N. Joseph N. Nicollet on the Plains and Prairies. Edmund C. and Martha C. Bray (eds). St. Paul: MN Hist Soc, 1976. Fine in dj. *Bohling.* $15/£10

NICOLLET, JOSEPH N. Joseph N. Nicollet on the Plains and Prairies. Edmund C. Bray and Martha Coleman Bray (eds). St. Paul, MN: MN Hist Soc, 1976. VG in dj. *Lien.* $35/£22

NICOLSON, BENEDICT. The Treasures of the Foundling Hospital. Oxford: Clarendon, 1972. Frontis, port, 37 plts. Buckram. VF in pict dj. *Europa.* $55/£35

NICOLSON, HAROLD. Diaries and Letters 1930-39/1939-45/1945-62. Nigel Nicolson (ed). London: Collins, 1966/1967/1968. 1st eds. VG set in djs (vols 1-2 sl nicked, chipped; vol 1 has 1-inch closed tear internally tape-repaired). *Virgo.* $70/£45

NICOLSON, HAROLD. Diaries and Letters 1939-45. Collins, 1967. 1st ed. VG in dj (sl torn). *Whiteson.* $16/£10

NICOLSON, HAROLD. Helen's Tower. London, (1937). 1st ed. Fine in dj (browned). *Argosy.* $45/£29

NICOLSON, HAROLD. Marginal Comment. 1939. 1st ed. (Inscrip), o/w VG in dj (spine sl discolored). *Words Etc.* $28/£18

NIEBUHR, BARTHOLD GEORG. The Greek Heroes. London, 1910. 8vo. 4 color plts by Arthur Rackham. (Inner joint broken.) Cl (shelfworn), pict cvr label. *Oinonen*.* $30/£19

NIEDECKER, LORINE. The Collected Poems (1936-1966). Penland, NC: Jargon Soc, (1969). 1st ed. Dec wrappers. Fine in acetate dj. *Dermont.* $40/£26

NIEDIECK, PAUL. Cruises in the Bering Sea. London/NY, 1909. 1st ed. (Sl worn, discolored.) *Oinonen*.* $170/£109

NIERENDORF, KARL. Paul Klee: Paintings, Watercolors 1913 to 1939. NY, (1941). 1st ed. 2 tipped-in serigraphs, 65 monochromes. (Top of 1st few pp sl stained.) Spiral bds (chipped, stained). *King.* $95/£61

NIETZSCHE, FRIEDRICH. Thus Spake Zarathustra. Alexander Tille (trans). NY: Macmillan, 1896. 1st English trans. VG in grn cl-cvrd bds (shelfworn, spine sl soiled). *Lame Duck.* $100/£64

NIGHTINGALE, FLORENCE. Letters from Egypt. NY: Weidenfeld & Nicolson, 1987. 1st Amer ed. NF in dj. *Worldwide.* $30/£19

NIGHTINGALE, FLORENCE. Notes on Nursing: What It Is, and What It Is Not. NY: Appleton, 1860. 1st NY ed. 140,(4)pp (feps neatly excised; lt foxing early, late). Brn cl (sl soiled) stamped in gilt/blind. Good. *Reese.* $200/£128

Nightmare Abbey. (By Thomas Love Peacock.) London: T. Hookham, June 1818. 1st ed. (4),218pp (spotted, marginal soil). Later 19th-cent 1/2 calf, marbled sides (newly rebacked), morocco label, preserving orig bksellers ticket. *Cox.* $390/£250

NILES, BLAIR. The James. NY: F&R, 1939. 1st ed. Fine in VG dj (spine sunned). *Archer.* $35/£22

NILES, JOHN J. Singing Soldiers.... NY: Scribner, 1927. 1st ed. VG (ink inscrip) in dj (edgewear, sm nicks, chips). *Reese.* $125/£80

NIN, ANAIS. Children of the Albatross. NY, 1947. 1st ed. (Sl worn, soiled), else Good in dj (worn, lacks few pieces). *King.* $35/£22

NIN, ANAIS. Cities of the Interior. Denver: Alan Swallow, (1959). Omnibus ed, clbound issue, w/cancel Swallow imprint sticker and ad slip. White pict cl (lt soiled). VG. No dj, as issued. *Reese.* $35/£22

NIN, ANAIS. Preface to Henry Miller's Tropic of Cancer. NY: Lawrence R. Maxwell, (1947). 1st separate ed. Tipped-in frontis port. Stapled black wraps ptd in yellow. Fine. *Blue Mountain.* $75/£48

NIN, ANAIS. Under a Glass Bell and Other Stories. NY: E.P. Dutton, 1948. 1st trade ed. VG in dj (sl worn, sunned, tape stain to verso). *Ash.* $117/£75

NIN, ANAIS. Under a Glass Bell. NY, 1944. 1st ed. One of 300 ptd. Pict bds. Fine. *Appelfeld.* $125/£80

NIN, ANAIS. Under a Glass Bell. (NY: Gemor, 1944.) 1st ed. One of 300 ptd. Ian Hugo (engrs). Dec bds. Fine. *Appelfeld.* $150/£96

NIVEN, LARRY. Inferno. London: Wingate, 1977. 1st British ed. VG in VG dj. *Metropolitan*.* $23/£15

NIVEN, LARRY. Ringworld. NY: Holt, Rinehart & Winston, (1977). 1st US hb ed. (Rmdr mk), else Fine in dj (price-clipped). *Other Worlds.* $45/£29

NIVEN, LARRY. The World of Ptavvs. (London): MacDonald, (1966). 1st ed. (Sl soiled.) Dj (lt soiled, rubbed). *Swann*.* $230/£147

NIVEN, LARRY. World of Ptavvs. London: Macdonald, (1966). 1st British ed. VG in VG dj (rubbed, sl browned). *Metropolitan*.* $57/£37

NIXON, H. Sixteenth-Century Gold-Tooled Bookbindings in the Pierpont Morgan Library. NY: Pierpont Morgan Library, 1971. Signed. Sm folio. Wrappers. *Maggs.* $156/£100

NIXON, HERMAN CLARENCE. Forty Acres and Steel Mules. Chapel Hill: Univ of NC, 1938. 1st ed. (Names; spine dknd), else VG. *Cahan.* $100/£64

NIXON, OLIVER W. How Marcus Whitman Saved Oregon.... Chicago, 1895. 2nd ed. Frontis, 339pp. (Sl edgewear), else NF. *Reese.* $75/£48

NIXON, OLIVER W. Whitman's Ride Through Savage Lands with Sketches of Indian Life. (Winona, IL), 1905. Port. Pict cl. VG. *Reese.* $50/£32

NIXON, RICHARD. Real Peace. NY, (1983). 1st ed, private ltd ed. Signed. VG in dj (used). *King.* $150/£96

NOBBS, DAVID. The Itinerant Lodger. London: Methuen, 1965. 1st UK ed. Fine in VG dj. *Williams.* $31/£20

NOBILI, RICCARDO. The Gentle Art of Faking. 1922. Paper label (browned), spare paper label tipped in. (Sl soiled, spotted.) *Edwards.* $39/£25

Noble and Renowned History of Guy Earl of Warwick. London: W.O. for E.B., 1706. Frontis, (6),157,(3)pp (foxed, many corners broken off w/loss, early notes). Mod full blind-tooled leather (sl rubbed). *New Hampshire*.* $160/£103

NOBLE, JOHN. Notes on Strangers' Courts in the Massachusetts Bay Colony. Cambridge: CUP, 1902. Wraps (sl chipped, worn). Sound. *Boswell.* $35/£22

NOBLE, LOUIS L. After Icebergs with a Painter. NY, 1861. 1st ed. 6 tinted lithos. (Tp detached; spine ends chipped.) *Kane*.* $325/£208

NOEL, BAPTIST W. The Rebellion in America. London: Nesbet, 1863. 1st ed. (20),494,(2)pp. Howes N166. *Ginsberg.* $125/£80

NOEL, MARY. Villains Galore, the Heyday of the Popular Story Weekly. NY: Macmillan, 1954. 1st ed. Fine in dj (chipped, rubbed). *Oak Knoll.* $30/£19

NOGGLE, ANNE. Women of Photography. SF: SF Art Museum, 1975. VG in pict stiff wrappers (lt worn). *Cahan.* $50/£32

NOGUCHI, HIDEYO. Serum Diagnosis of Syphilis and the Butyric Acid Test for Syphilis. Phila: Lippincott, 1911. 2nd ed. (Lib stamp tp, text penciling), else Very Clean. *Goodrich.* $75/£48

NOLAN, E. H. Illustrated History of the War Against Russia. London, ca 1857. 2 vols. Engr tps, 65 steel-engr plts, 7 dbl-pg color maps. 1/2 leather, cl bds (sl worn, rubbed). Contents VG. *New Hampshire*.* $80/£51

NOLAN, J. BENNETT. Early Narratives of Berks County. (Reading, PA, 1927.) 8 plts. Maroon cl, gilt. VG (owner blindstamp). *Bohling.* $20/£13

NOLAN, L. E. Cavalry; Its History and Tactics. London, 1854. 2nd ed. xvi,342pp, 2 color lithos, 3 color plts, 2 plans (1 fldg). Orig 1/4 morocco (extrems rubbed). *Maggs.* $234/£150

NOLAN, WILLIAM F. The Ray Bradbury Companion. Detroit: Gale Research, 1975. 1st ed. Fine in slipcase (worn, nicked). *Other Worlds.* $100/£64

NOLTE, VINCENT. Fifty Years in Both Hemispheres; or, Reminiscences of a Merchant's Life. NY: Redfield, 1854. 1st Amer ed, 1st ed in English. (4),(22),(11)-484,(4)pp. Howes N169. *Ginsberg.* $150/£96

NOMA, SEIROKU. The Arts of Japan. John Rosenfield (trans). Tokyo/NY et al: Kodansha International, 1982. 3rd ptg. NF in dj. *Worldwide.* $45/£29

NOMAD. (Pseud of George A. Custer.) George A. Custer in Turf, Field and Farm. Brian W. Dippie (ed). Austin, (1980). 1st ed. VG + in dj (sm tear). *Pratt*. $27/£17

NOONAN, D. A. Alaska, the Land of Now. Seattle, 1923. 1st ed. Sm 8vo. Frontis photo, 146pp. Grn cl, gilt. (Gold lettering worn), else Fine. *Bromer*. $125/£80

NORBERG-SCHULZ, CHRISTIAN. Late Baroque and Rococo Architecture. NY, 1974. Good in dj. *Washton*. $100/£64

NORDAN, LEWIS. Music of the Swamp. Chapel Hill: Algonquin, 1991. 1st ed. Fine in Fine dj. *Revere*. $45/£29

NORDAU, MAX. Degeneration. London: Heinemann, 1895. 1st ed in English. 2,(xiv),560pp + inserted 24-pg cat. Straight-grained crimson cl (rubbed). *Gach*. $50/£32

NORDEN, FREDERICK LEWIS. Travels in Egypt and Nubia. London: Lockyer Davis, Charles Reymers, 1757. 1st 1-vol ed. 2 vols in 1. xl,154,232pp. Contemp calf. (Rubbed, hinges tender, spine chipped, sl scuffed), o/w VG. *Worldwide*. $350/£224

NORDENSKIOLD, OTTO and J. GUNNAR ANDERSON. Antarctica or Two Years Amongst the Ice of the South Pole. NY: Macmillan, 1905. xviii,(2),608pp, 4 color plts, 4 color maps (3 fldg). Dec cl (spine head sl chipped). VG ('discarded' stamp top fore-edges). *High Latitude*. $550/£353

NORDHEIMER, ISAAC. A Critical Grammar of the Hebrew Language. NY, 1838-41. 2 vols in 1. Fldg chart. Contemp sheep (cvrs loose). *Swann**. $92/£59

NORDHEIMER, ISAAC. A Grammatical Analysis of Selections from the Hebrew Scriptures. NY, 1838. Pub's 1/4 cl (worn), paper spine label (chipped). *Swann**. $92/£59

NORDHOFF, CHARLES and JAMES NORMAN HALL. Botany Bay. Boston: Little Brown, 1941. 1st ed (stated). Fine in Fine pict dj (sm chip spine head). *Captain's Bookshelf*. $150/£96

NORDHOFF, CHARLES and JAMES NORMAN HALL. The Bounty Trilogy. Comprising the Three Volumes.... Boston: Little, Brown, 1940. 1st ed thus. N. C. Wyeth (illus). NF (bkpl under flap) in dj (rubbed, dknd). *Captain's Bookshelf*. $125/£80

NORDHOFF, CHARLES and JAMES NORMAN HALL. Mutiny on the Bounty. Boston: Little Brown, 1932. 2nd issue w/illus eps. (Owner stamp), else NF in dj (short tear spine foot). *Lame Duck*. $200/£128

NORDHOFF, CHARLES and JAMES NORMAN HALL. Pitcairn's Island. Boston, 1934. 1st ed. Dj. *Typogrepheum*. $35/£22

NORDHOFF, CHARLES. Communistic Societies of the United States. NY, 1875. 1st ed. 439pp. Howes N177. *Ginsberg*. $175/£112

NORDHOFF, CHARLES. Whaling and Fishing. Cincinnati: Moore, Wilstach, Keys, 1856. 1st ed. 383pp (sl foxing); 3 plts. VG (spine head sl worn). *Lefkowicz*. $300/£192

NORDON, PIERRE. Conan Doyle: A Biography. NY: Holt, Rinehart & Winston, (1967). 1st US ed. VG in Good dj (few sm tears). *Gravesend*. $40/£26

NORFLEET, BARBARA P. The Champion Pig. Boston: Godine, 1979. 1st ed. (Name), else Fine in pict stiff wrappers. *Cahan*. $30/£19

NORFOLK, LAWRENCE. Lempriere's Dictionary. London: London Ltd Eds, (1991). 1st ed. One of 150 specially-bound, numbered, signed. Fine in glassine dj. *Captain's Bookshelf*. $100/£64

NORFOLK, LAWRENCE. Lempriere's Dictionary. London: Sinclair Stevenson, 1991. One of 150 numbered, signed. 1/4 cl, marbled paper-cvrd bds. Fine in glassine dj. *Lame Duck*. $250/£160

NORFOLK, LAWRENCE. Lempriere's Dictionary. London: Sinclair-Stevenson, 1991. 1st UK ed. Fine in dj. *Williams*. $31/£20

NORIE, J. W. A Complete Set of Nautical Tables.... 1935. (Ink sig; spine defective, corners worn, cl sl affected by damp.) *Whitehart*. $23/£15

NORMAN, B. M. Norman's New Orleans and Environs. New Orleans: B.M. Norman, 1845. 1st ed. Frontis, 223pp,(4)ads,12 blanks; map. VG (lt foxed; few sm spine chips expertly repaired). Howes N180. *Cahan*. $400/£256

NORMAN, C. B. Tonkin or France in the Far East. London: Chapman & Hall, 1884. 1st ed. xv,343pp; 2 fldg maps (1 w/clean tear along fold). *Maggs*. $429/£275

NORMAN, CHARLES. The Case of Ezra Pound. NY, 1948. Stiff card wrappers. *Clearwater*. $62/£40

NORMAN, CHARLES. The Case of Ezra Pound. NY: Bodley, 1948. 1st ed. (Paperclip mk to 1st several pp, lacks review slip; wraps hand soiled), else NF. *Associates*. $35/£22

NORMAN, DOROTHY. Alfred Stieglitz, an American Seer. NY: Random House, 1973. 1st ed. Fine in Fine dj. *Metropolitan**. $46/£29

NORMAN, DOROTHY. Alfred Stieglitz: An American Seer. NY: Random House, 1973. 1st ed. 77 full-pg b/w plts. (Owner stamp), else VG in dj (lt edgeworn). *Cahan*. $60/£38

NORMAN, HOWARD. Kiss in the Hotel Joseph Conrad. NY: Summit, 1989. 1st ed. Fine in dj. *Lame Duck*. $125/£80

NORMAN, WILLIAM M. A Portion of My Life...Written While a Prisoner of War on Johnson's Island, 1864. Winston-Salem, 1959. 1st ed. VG + in VG + dj. *Pratt*. $30/£19

NORMYX. (Pseud of Norman Douglas.) Unprofessional Tales. T. Fisher Unwin, 1901. 1st ed, 1st bk. 750 ptd. (Few ll roughly opened, leaf sl ink-splashed; bkpl.) White pict cl (sl soiled, discolored, spine sl dknd). Good. *Ash*. $624/£400

NORRIS, FRANK. Collected Letters. Jesse S. Crisler (ed). SF: Book Club of CA, 1986. One of 500. Patterned bds, red cl spine strip. Fine. *Harrington*. $125/£80

NORRIS, FRANK. The Letters of Frank Norris. Franklin Walker (ed). SF: Book Club of CA, 1956. Ltd to 350. Frontis port. Fine. *Polyanthos*. $65/£42

NORRIS, FRANK. McTeague. A Story of San Francisco. NY: Doubleday & McClure, 1899. 1st ed, 1st ptg, p106 ending w/'moment'. (Fr inner hinge cracked, poorly repaired; cvrs worn, spine faded, extrems rubbed.) BAL 15031. *Holmes*. $150/£96

NORRIS, FRANK. Vandover and the Brute. NY: Doubleday, Page, 1914. 1st ed. Orange-brn cl, gilt. Fine. BAL 15046. *Macdonnell*. $85/£54

NORRIS, GEORGE W. and HENRY R. M. LANDIS. Diseases of the Chest and the Principles of Physical Diagnosis. Phila, 1917. 1st ed. Grn cl bds (sl worn; spine, cvr stains). VG. *Doctor's Library*. $75/£48

NORRIS, THOMAS WAYNE. Catalogue of Books, Pamphlets and Maps Relating Directly or Indirectly to the History, Literature and Printing of California and the Far West.... Oakland, 1948. 1st ed. One of 500. Frontis. NF. *Turpen*. $150/£96

NORRIS, W. E. Miss Shafto. Richard Bentley, 1890. Rpt. Marbled edges. Contemp 1/2 leather, marbled bds. Good (sig; rebacked, corners rubbed, orig backstrip relaid). *Tiger*. $28/£18

North Carolina Form Book.... Raleigh: Turner & Hughes, 1841. 172pp. Full sheep. (Foxing, names, pencil sketch rep; rubbed, rear hinge starting, spine top chipped), else Good.. *Cahan*. $85/£54

NORTH, LUTHER. Man of the Plains. Lincoln: Univ of NE, 1961. 1st ed. Fine in dj. *Perier*. $75/£48

NORTH, LUTHER. Man of the Plains: Recollections of Luther North, 1856-1882. Donald F. Danker (ed). Lincoln: Univ of NE, 1961. 1st ed. 9 maps. Mint. *Graf.* $20/£13

NORTH, MARY REMSEN. Down the Colorado. By a Lone Girl Scout. NY/London, 1930. 1st ed. Pict eps. Orange cl. (Lt bumping, sl dampstaining), else VG. *Five Quail.* $65/£42

NORTH, S. N. D. and RALPH NORTH. Simeon North, First Official Pistol Maker of the United States. Concord, NH: Rumford, 1913. (Faded bds.) *Cullen.* $175/£112

NORTH, STERLING. Midnight and Jeremiah. John C. Winston, 1943. 1st ed. Kurt Wiese (illus). 6.5x8.5. 125pp. Pict cl. (Bkpl), else NF in dj (sl edgeworn). *My Bookhouse.* $35/£22

NORTHCOTE, JAMES. The Life of Titian. London, 1830. 2 vols. Frontis port (sl spotted, sl offset), 399; 384pp (eps lt spotted vol 2; bkpl, hinges repaired); fldg table. 1/2 calf, marbled bds (sl worn, crudely rebacked in calf), 3 (of 4) orig leather labels. *Edwards.* $94/£60

NORTHCOTE, ROSALIND. Devon, Its Moorlands, Streams, and Coasts. Exeter: C&W/James G. Commin, 1923. 50 color plts. Tan cl, gilt. VG. *Cox.* $39/£25

Northern Traveller. (By Timothy Dwight.) NY, 1828. 3rd ed. Frontis (detached), 19 maps, 11 views. (Bds worn, joints starting.) Howes D607. *Freeman*.* $90/£58

NORTON, ANDRE. The Iron Cage. Viking, 1974. 1st ed. Fine in dj. *Madle.* $35/£22

NORTON, ANDRE. Key Out of Time. Cleveland: World, (1963). 1st ed. Signed. Dj (sm tears, sl worn). *Swann*.* $80/£51

NORTON, ANDRE. Ordeal in Otherwhere. World, 1964. 1st ed. NF in dj. *Madle.* $85/£54

NORTON, ANDRE. Postmarked the Stars. NY: Harcourt, Brace & World, (1969). 1st ed. Dj (rubbed). *Swann*.* $57/£37

NORTON, ANDRE. Shadow Hawk. Harcourt, 1960. 1st ed. NF in dj (chip). *Madle.* $90/£58

NORTON, ANDRE. Star Rangers. Harcourt Brace, (1953). 1st ed. VG (name, date feps) in dj (torn, spine chips). *Certo.* $45/£29

NORTON, ANDRE. The Stars Are Ours. World, (1954). 1st ed. VG + in dj (sm creased tear, spine ends sl chipped). *Certo.* $95/£61

NORTON, ANDRE. Wizards' Worlds. Easton Press, (1989). Signed. Aeg. Maroon leather, gilt. VG. *Yudkin*.* $47/£30

NORTON, CHARLES ELIOT. A Leaf of Grass from Shady Hill. Cambridge, MA: Harvard Univ, (1928). Frontis. Grn cl, gilt. NF. *Blue Mountain.* $50/£32

NORTON, DOREEN. The Palomino Horse. L.A.: Borden, 1949. 1st ed. VG in Good dj. *October Farm.* $125/£80

NORTON, E. F. The Fight for Everest: 1924. NY, 1925. 1st Amer ed. Fldg map. (Hinges loose, cvrs sl rubbed.) *King.* $125/£80

NORTON, HERMAN. Record of Facts Concerning the Persecutions at Madeira in 1843 and 1846. NY: American Protestant Soc, 1849. 1st ed. 228pp. (Text sl spotted), else Good. *Brown.* $15/£10

NORTON, JOHN P. Elements of Scientific Agriculture. Pease, 1850. 1st ed. 208pp. (Cvrs sl scuffed), o/w Good. *Bookcell.* $75/£48

NORTON, MARY. The Borrowers Afield. NY: Harcourt Brace, 1955. 1st Amer ed. Beth and Joe Krush (illus). 8vo. 215pp. NF in pict dj. *Bookmark.* $34/£22

NORTON, MARY. The Borrowers Afield. NY: HBJ, 1955. 1st ed. Beth and Joe Krush (illus). 5 1/2 x 8 1/2. 215pp. Fine. *Cattermole.* $40/£26

NORTON, MARY. The Borrowers Afloat. Dent, 1959. 1st UK ed, w/later state dj. Diana Stanley (illus). 5.5x8. 176pp. VG (sl shelfworn) in dj (edges ragged). *My Bookhouse.* $45/£29

NORTON, MARY. The Borrowers Avenged. London: Kestrel Books, (1982). 1st Eng ed. 8vo. 285pp. Black bds. Fine. *Dower.* $35/£22

NORTON, MARY. The Borrowers. NY: Harcourt, Brace, (1953). 1st ed. Beth & Joe Krush (illus). Fine in Fine dj. *Bernard.* $75/£48

NORTON, MARY. The Borrowers. NY: Harcourt Brace, 1953. 1st Amer ed. Beth and Joe Krush (illus). 8vo. 179pp. (Spine faded), else VG + in pict dj (sl frayed). *Bookmark.* $39/£25

NORWAK, MARY. Kitchen Antiques. London, 1975. 1st UK ed. Dj. *Edwards.* $23/£15

Notes and Lectures upon Shakespeare and Some of the Old Poets and Dramatists. (By Samuel Taylor Coleridge.) London: William Pickering, 1849. 1st ed. Inscribed. 2 vols. Aeg. Full crushed grn morocco (extrems sl rubbed, spines faded to brn), gilt. Internally Fine. *Dramatis Personae.* $150/£96

Notions of the Americans: Picked Up by a Travelling Bachelor. (By James Fenimore Cooper.) London, 1828. 1st ed. 2 vols. Orig bds (very worn). Howes C750. *Swann*.* $201/£129

NOTT, J. C. and GEORGE R. GLIDDON. Types of Mankind. Phila, 1854. 1st ed. Map. (Lt foxing.) Contemp 1/2 morocco, bds. *Freeman*.* $150/£96

NOTT, J. FORTUNE. Wild Animals Photographed and Described. London, 1886. xi,568pp (sl spotted). Teg, rest uncut. (Faded, lt rubbed, sl bumped.) *Edwards.* $59/£38

NOTT, S. Voices from the Flowery Kingdom. NY: Chinese Culture Study Group of America, 1947. Good (inkstain spine; cvr lt soiled). *Blake.* $175/£112

NOTT, STANLEY CHARLES. Chinese Jade Throughout the Ages. London: Batsford, (1936). 1st ed. 39 color plts. (Sl bumped), else VG. *Cahan.* $85/£54

NOTUCTT, L. A. and G. C. LATHAM. The African and the Cinema. London, 1937. Fldg map. (Edges discolored.) *Edwards.* $31/£20

NOURSE, ALAN E. The Mercy Men. McKay, (1968). 1st ed. NF (sl dust mk edge) in dj (spine lt dusting). *Certo.* $50/£32

NOURSE, ALAN E. Psi High and Others. McKay, (1967). 1st ed. Fine in Fine dj (rub mks). *Certo.* $60/£38

NOVOTNY, FRITZ and JOHANNES DOBAI. Gustav Klimt. NY, (1968). One of 1250 numbered. (Ex-lib.) Dj. *Swann*.* $287/£184

NOVOTNY, FRITZ and JOHANNES DOBAI. Gustav Klimt. NY: Frederick A. Praeger, (1968). Ltd to 1250 numbered. 115 plts in collotype, 30 in color. Blue cl, dec gilt. Fine in illus dj, pub's slipcase. *Karmiole.* $600/£385

NOY, WILLIAM. The Principal Grounds and Maxims, with an Analysis. London: S. Sweet et al, 1821. 9th ed. Contemp 1/4 calf (rubbed). VG. *Boswell.* $350/£224

NOYCE, WILFRID. Mountains and Men. London, 1947. 1st ed. VG in dj (spine chipped). *King.* $25/£16

NOYES, ALFRED. Beyond the Desert. NY: Frederick A. Stokes, (1920). 1st Amer ed. Cl spine, paper labels. (Foxing; tips bumped, lt soiled.) *Dawson.* $50/£32

NOYES, ALFRED. The Flower of Old Japan. NY: Macmillan, 1907. 1st Amer ed. Teg. Dec grn cl (sl dampstained). VG. *Antic Hay.* $15/£10

NOYES, ALFRED. The Highwayman. OUP, 1981. 1st ed thus. Charles Keeping (illus). Folio. (32pp). Pict bds. NF. *Bookmark.* $55/£35

NOYES, ALFRED. No Other Man. NY: Stokes, 1940. 1st Amer ed. NF in dj (soil). *Antic Hay*. $20/£13

NOYES, ALFRED. Rada. NY: Stokes, (1914). 1st Amer ed. Dec grn cl. NF. *Antic Hay*. $20/£13

NOYES, ELLA. The Story of Milan. London, 1926. Rev ed. Fldg map. Teg. Gilt-dec cl. Dj (sl chipped). *Edwards*. $23/£15

NUNIS, DOYCE (ed). Los Angeles and Its Environs in the 20th Century. L.A.: Ward Ritchie, 1973. 1st ed. Fine in Fine dj. *Book Market*. $35/£22

NUNN, WILFRED. Tigris Gunboats. London, 1932. Good blue cl. *Maggs*. $109/£70

NURA. All Aboard, We Are Off. NY: Studio Publications, 1944. 1st ed. 9 1/4 x 11. 40pp. Fine. *Cattermole*. $40/£26

Nursery Rhymes. (By Anne Anderson.) Nelson, n.d. (ca 1950s). 145x184mm. Bd bk w/14 color pictures incl cvrs. VG. *Bookmark*. $16/£10

NUSBAUMER, LOUIS. Valley of Salt, Memories of Wine. George Koenig (ed). (Berkeley): Friends of the Bancroft Lib, 1967. xx + 68pp, fldg map. *Dawson*. $40/£26

NUSBAUMER, LOUIS. Valley of Salt, Memories of Wine. George Koenig (ed). Berkeley: Friends of the Bancroft Library, 1967. Map. NF. *Parmer*. $65/£42

NUSBAUMER, LOUIS. Valley of Salt, Memories of Wine: A Journal of Death Valley, 1849. George Koenig (ed). Berkeley: Friends of the Bancroft Library, 1967. 1st ed. Fine. *Book Market*. $65/£42

NUTALL, T. A Manual of Ornithology of the United States and of Canada. Boston, 1832-34. 2 vols. vi,683; vii,627pp. Orig cl. (Tp corner torn; rebacked, preserving spines), o/w Fine. *Henly*. $156/£100

NUTT, T. Humanity to Honey Bees. London, 1845. 6th ed. xxxiv,306pp; 2 fldg plts. Good (ex-lib; cl sl used, neatly repaired). *Wheldon & Wesley*. $117/£75

NUTTALL, THOMAS and F. ANDREW MICHAUX. The North American Sylva. Phila: D. Rice & A.N. Hart, 1859. 5 vols. 278 hand-colored plts. Aeg. Full leather (rubbed, bumped, hinges starting), raised bands. *Metropolitan**. $2,875/£1,843

NUTTALL, THOMAS. The North American Sylva. Phila, 1849. Vol 3 (of 3). 148pp (lt foxed); 40 full-pg hand-colored plts. Aeg. Grn morocco (extrems worn, 1-inch abrasion rear cvr), gilt, raised bands. *King*. $500/£321

NUTTING, WALLACE. The Clock Book. GC, (1935). VG. *Waverly**. $33/£21

NUTTING, WALLACE. Furniture of the Pilgrim Century, 1620-1720.... Boston, (1921). 1st ed. *Kane**. $50/£32

NUTTING, WALLACE. Furniture of the Pilgrim Century. Framingham: Old America, (1921). 1st ed. VG (sig; spine sl worn). *Agvent*. $135/£87

NUTTING, WALLACE. Furniture Treasury.... NY, 1948-9. 3 vols. (Spine lettering sl faded.) *Kane**. $60/£38

NUTTING, WALLACE. New York Beautiful. GC, 1936. 'De Luxe Edition.' Dec cvr. Good in Fair dj. *Scribe's Perch**. $35/£22

NYE, GIDEON, JR. The Morning of My Life in China.... Canton, 1873. Contents Clean in wraps (dknd). *Heinoldt*. $25/£16

NYE, THOMAS. Journal of Thomas Nye Written During a Journey Between Montreal and Chicago in 1837. Hugh McLellan (ed). Champlain, NY: Moorsfield, 1932. One of 68 numbered, signed by McLellan. VF in ptd wrapper, orig mailing envelope. *Bohling*. $50/£32

NYE, THOMAS. Two Letters of Thomas Nye Relating to a Journey from Montreal to Chicago in 1837. Hugh McLellan (ed). Champlain, NY: Moorsfield, 1931. One of 58 numbered, signed by McLellan. Correction slip. VF in ptd wrapper, orig mailing envelope. *Bohling*. $50/£32

NYE, WILBUR STURTEVANT. Here Comes the Rebels. Baton Rouge, 1965. 1st ed. (Cvr sl worn), o/w Fine in Fine dj. *Pratt*. $65/£42

NYLANDER, CARL. The Deep Well. London: George Allen & Unwin, (1969). Good in dj. *Archaeologia*. $25/£16

O

O'BRIAN, PATRICK. The Chian Wine and Other Stories. London: Collins, 1974. 1st UK ed. NF in VG+ dj (sl creased). *Williams*. $117/£75

O'BRIAN, PATRICK. Clarissa Oakes. (London): Harper Collins, (1992). 1st ed. Fine in dj. *Between The Covers*. $100/£64

O'BRIAN, PATRICK. The Commodore. London: Harper Collins, 1994. 1st UK ed. Fine in dj. *Williams*. $28/£18

O'BRIAN, PATRICK. Desolation Island. NY: Stein & Day, (1979). 1st Amer ed. Fine in NF dj (price-clipped; tear edge fr flap, crown). *Between The Covers*. $250/£160

O'BRIAN, PATRICK. Desolation Island. London: Collins, 1978. 1st UK ed. VG+ (pg edges sl dusty). *Williams*. $367/£235

O'BRIAN, PATRICK. Desolation Island. NY: Stein & Day, 1979. 1st ed. Fine in Fine dj. *Else Fine*. $250/£160

O'BRIAN, PATRICK. The Fortune of War. London: Collins, 1979. 1st ed. Proof copy. VG in orange ptd wrappers (sl dusty). *Williams*. $117/£75

O'BRIAN, PATRICK. The Fortune of War. London: Collins, 1979. 1st UK ed. VG (bds sl dusty) in dj. *Williams*. $312/£200

O'BRIAN, PATRICK. H.M.S. Surprise. (London): Collins, 1973. 1st ed. (Name eradicated pastedowns), o/w NF in dj (spine sl sunned). *Captain's Bookshelf*. $500/£321

O'BRIAN, PATRICK. H.M.S. Surprise. NY: Lippincott, 1973. 1st ed. (Tape shadows on bds.) Dj (lt worn). *Else Fine*. $175/£112

O'BRIAN, PATRICK. H.M.S. Surprise. NY: Norton, 1991. Uncorrected Proof. Fine (sl soiling) in wrappers. *Between The Covers*. $65/£42

O'BRIAN, PATRICK. The Letter of Marque. NY: Norton, 1990. 1st ed. VF in VF dj. *Else Fine*. $60/£38

O'BRIAN, PATRICK. The Mauritius Command. NY: Norton, 1977. 1st ed. Fine in Fine dj. *Else Fine*. $300/£192

O'BRIAN, PATRICK. Picasso—A Biography. London: Collins, 1976. 1st UK ed. VG (ink name) in dj. *Williams*. $75/£48

O'BRIAN, PATRICK. Picasso. NY, 1976. 1st ed. Fine in Fine dj. *Warren*. $40/£26

O'BRIAN, PATRICK. The Reverse of the Medal. London: Collins, 1986. 1st UK ed. VG+ (fep sl scuffed) in dj (spine faded). *Williams*. $195/£125

O'BRIAN, PATRICK. The Road to Samarkand. London: Hart-Davis, 1954. 1st UK ed. NF in VG dj (nicks). *Williams*. $218/£140

O'BRIAN, PATRICK. Testimonies. NY: HB&Co, (1952). 1st Amer ed. (Sm mk fep) else NF in NF dj (lt rubbed). *Between The Covers.* $650/£417

O'BRIAN, PATRICK. The Unknown Shore. London: Rupert Hart-Davis, 1959. 1st UK ed. Fine in VG dj (sm abraded patches rear panel). *Williams.* $234/£150

O'BRIAN, PATRICK. The Wine-Dark Sea. London: Harper Collins, 1993. 1st UK ed. Fine in dj. *Williams.* $75/£48

O'BRIEN, EDNA. The Lonely Girl. London: Jonathan Cape, 1962. 1st ed. Fine (spine head sunned; sl musty) in NF dj (few tears). *Beasley.* $75/£48

O'BRIEN, EDNA. A Scandalous Woman and Other Stories. NY: Harcourt, Brace, Jovanovich, (1974). 1st Amer ed. Fine in dj. *Antic Hay.* $20/£13

O'BRIEN, FLANN. The Best of Myles. NY: Walker, (1968). 1st ed. NF (2 corners sl bumped) in dj (lt soil). *Antic Hay.* $45/£29

O'BRIEN, FLANN. Further Cuttings from Cruiskeen Lawn. Kevin O'Nolan (ed). London, 1976. 1st Eng ed. Very Nice in dj. *Clearwater.* $39/£25

O'BRIEN, FLANN. The Hair of the Dogma. Kevin O'Nolan (ed). London, 1977. 1st Eng ed. Very Nice (2 corners sl knocked) in dj. *Clearwater.* $39/£25

O'BRIEN, FLANN. The Hard Life. NY: Pantheon, 1962. 1st ed. Fine in Fine dj. *Beasley.* $60/£38

O'BRIEN, FLANN. The Poor Mouth. NY: Viking, (1974). 1st Amer ed in English. Fine in dj. *Antic Hay.* $35/£22

O'BRIEN, FLANN. The Poor Mouth. NY, 1974. 1st Amer ed. Fine in dj (sm tear). *Polyanthos.* $25/£16

O'BRIEN, FLANN. The Third Policeman. NY: Walker, (1967). 1st US ed. NF (sm erasure fep) in dj (wear, soil, few tears, price-clipped). *Antic Hay.* $45/£29

O'BRIEN, HARRIET EILEEN. Lost Utopias. Fruitlands/Wayside Museums, 1947. 3rd ed. Errata slip. VG (lt wear, soil) in ptd wraps. *Bohling.* $20/£13

O'BRIEN, JACK and S. E. BILIK. Boxing by Philadelphia Jack O'Brien.... NY: Scribner, 1928. 1st ed. Brn cl. Fine. *Cummins.* $75/£48

O'BRIEN, TIM. If I Die in the Combat Zone. London: Calder & Boyars, (1973). 1st Eng ed. Fine in Fine dj. *Dermont.* $75/£48

O'BRIEN, TIM. Speaking of Courage. Santa Barbara: Neville, 1980. 1st ed. One of 300 numbered (of 326 signed). Ptd labels. Fine. *Reese.* $75/£48

O'BRYAN, AILEEN. The Dine: Origin Myths of the Navaho Indians. BAE Bulletin 163. Washington: GPO, 1956. Frontis. Grn cl, gilt. Fine. *Harrington.* $40/£26

O'BYRNE, DERMOT. (Pseud of Arnold Bax.) Wrack and Other Stories. Dublin: Talbot, 1918. 1st Eng ed. Cl-backed bds (mkd, rubbed). *Clearwater.* $55/£35

O'CASEY, SEAN. The Green Crow. NY, 1956. 1st Amer ed. Fine (spine heel sl bumped) in NF dj. *Polyanthos.* $25/£16

O'CASEY, SEAN. The Green Crow. NY, 1956. 1st ed. VG in dj (torn, chipped). *King.* $25/£16

O'CASEY, SEAN. The Green Crow. NY, 1956. 1st ed. Fine in Fine dj. *Smith.* $45/£29

O'CASEY, SEAN. The Green Crow. NY: Braziller, 1956. 1st Amer ed. NF in dj (sl wear, soil). *Antic Hay.* $20/£13

O'CASEY, SEAN. Inishfallen Fare Thee Well. London: Macmillan, 1949. 1st UK ed. Fine in VG dj. *Williams.* $39/£25

O'CASEY, SEAN. Oak Leaves and Lavender. NY: Macmillan, 1947. 1st ed. Fine in dj (sl wear). *Antic Hay.* $20/£13

O'CASEY, SEAN. Purple Dust. London: Macmillan, 1940. 1st Eng ed. NF (eps browned, ink name) in dj (browned, sm tear, sm spine chip). *Antic Hay.* $22/£14

O'CASEY, SEAN. Sunset and Evening Star. London, 1954. 1st ed. Fine in dj (spine extrems rubbed, sm nicks corners). *Polyanthos.* $30/£19

O'CASEY, SEAN. Windfalls. London: Macmillan, 1934. 1st UK ed. NF (ink inscrip) in dj (faded, sl edgeworn). *Williams.* $55/£35

O'CASEY, SEAN. Windfalls. NY: Macmillan, 1934. 1st US ed. Fine in NF dj. *Beasley.* $40/£26

O'CASEY, SEAN. Within the Gate. NY: Macmillan, 1934. 1st Amer ed. Fine in dj (spine sunned, head chipped). *Antic Hay.* $50/£32

O'CATHASAIGH, P. (SEAN O'CASEY.) The Story of the Irish Citizen Army. Dublin/London: Maunsel, 1919. 1st ed, 1st issue. Ptd gray wraps. *Kane*.* $95/£61

O'CONNOR, FLANNERY. Everything That Rises Must Converge. NY: FSG, (1965). 1st ed. (Bkstore label fep), o/w Fine in dj (lt soiled). *Hermitage.* $200/£128

O'CONNOR, FLANNERY. A Good Man Is Hard to Find. NY: NAL/Signet, (1956). 1st pb ed. VG in illus wrappers. *Turtle Island.* $25/£16

O'CONNOR, FLANNERY. Mystery and Manners: Occasional Prose. Sally and Robert Fitzgerald (eds). NY: FSG, (1969). 1st ed. Fine in dj. *Between The Covers.* $150/£96

O'CONNOR, FRANK. Domestic Relations. NY: Knopf, 1957. 1st Amer ed. NF in VG dj (wear). *Antic Hay.* $17/£11

O'CONNOR, FRANK. The Midnight Court. 1945. 1st ed. VG in dj (spine faded). *Words Etc.* $16/£10

O'CONNOR, FRANK. My Father's Son. NY: Knopf, 1969. 1st ed. Fine in NF dj (sl browned). *Antic Hay.* $25/£16

O'CONNOR, JACK. The Art of Hunting Big Game in North America. NY: Outdoor Life, 1967. 1st ed. VG+ in VG dj (chipped). *Backman.* $25/£16

O'CONNOR, JACK. The Big-Game Rifle. NY: Knopf, 1952. 1st ed. Ivory linen. Fine in VG pict dj. *Biscotti.* $140/£90

O'CONNOR, JACK. Game in the Desert. NY: Derrydale, (1939). One of 950 numbered. Color frontis. Uncut. Simulated snakeskin (sl worn). *Oinonen*.* $275/£176

O'CONNOR, JACK. Game in the Desert. NY: Derrydale, (1939). 1st ed. #234/950. Color frontis. Grn simulated snakeskin cl. Fine. *Cummins.* $500/£321

O'CONNOR, JACK. Game in the Desert. NY: Derrydale, (1939). One of 950 numbered. 4to. Color frontis. Uncut, partly unopened. Simulated snakeskin (sl worn). Glassine wrapper (chipped), orig box (worn) w/ptd label. *Oinonen*.* $750/£481

O'CONNOR, JACK. Game in the Desert. NY: Derrydale, 1939. 1st ed. #23/950. Color frontis. Partly unopened. Grn simulated snakeskin (spine dknd), gilt. VG+. *Backman.* $475/£304

O'CONNOR, JACK. Hunting in the Rockies. NY, 1947. 1st ed. (Dampstain upper blank margin; sl worn.) Dj (frayed, chipped). *Oinonen*.* $130/£83

O'CONNOR, JACK. Hunting in the Rockies. NY: Knopf, 1947. Stated 1st ed. VG (lt wear spine edges). *Backman.* $135/£87

O'CONNOR, JACK. The Hunting Rifle. NY: Winchester, 1970. 1st ed. VG+ in Fine dj. *Backman.* $25/£16

O'CONNOR, JACK. The Hunting Rifle. NY: Winchester, 1970. 1st ed. Fine in dj. *Bowman.* $30/£19

O'CONNOR, JACK. The Rifle Book. NY: Knopf, 1949. 1st ed. Ivory linen. Fine in VG pict dj. *Biscotti.* $80/£51

O'CONNOR, JACK. Sheep and Sheep Hunting. NY: Winchester, 1974. 1st ed. Photo eps. Fine in Fine dj. *Backman.* $155/£99

O'CONNOR, JOHN. A Pattern of People. London: Hutchinson, 1959. 1st ed. Fine in dj. *Michael Taylor.* $31/£20

O'CONNOR, JOHN. The Technique of Wood Engraving. London: Batsford, 1971. 1st ed. Fine in dj. *Michael Taylor.* $31/£20

O'CONNOR, RICHARD. Bat Masterson. GC: Doubleday, (1957). VG in VG dj. *Perier.* $30/£19

O'CONNOR, RICHARD. Hood: Cavalier General. NY: Prentice-Hall, 1949. Stated 1st ed. Frontis port, 9 maps. VG. *Scribe's Perch*.* $60/£38

O'CONNOR, RICHARD. Sheridan the Inevitable. Indianapolis, 1953. 1st ed. VG + in dj (spine faded). *Pratt.* $60/£38

O'CONNOR, V. C. SCOTT. The Charm of Kashmir. London: Longmans, Green, 1920. 1st ed. 16 color plts w/guards, 24 plts. Teg, others uncut. Sound (sl foxed) in cream linen (soiled, sl worn), gilt. *Cox.* $55/£35

O'CONOR, ANDREW P. Forty Years with Fighting Cocks. NY: E.W. Rogers, 1929. Frontis. VG (eps sl mkd; joints cracked, repaired). *Hollett.* $148/£95

O'DONNELL, BERNARD. The Old Bailey and Its Trials. London: Clerke & Cockeran, 1950. *Boswell.* $25/£16

O'DONNELL, ELLIOTT. The Dead Riders. London: Rider, 1952. 1st ed. (Spine lean.) VG in dj (tape stain on spine). *Certo.* $30/£19

O'DONNELL, PETER. Dead Man's Handle. London: Souvenir, 1985. 1st ed. Fine in dj. *Mordida.* $45/£29

O'DONNELL, PETER. Modesty Blaise. London: Souvenir, 1965. 1st UK ed. VG (ink name) in dj (sl edgeworn, short closed tears). *Williams.* $31/£20

O'DONNELL, PETER. Sabre-Tooth. London: Souvenir, 1966. 1st ed. Fine in dj. *Mordida.* $60/£38

O'DONNELL, PETER. The Xanadu Talisman. London: Souvenir Press, 1981. 1st ed. Fine in dj. *Mordida.* $45/£29

O'DONOVAN, EDMOND. The Merv Oasis. NY: Putnam, 1883. 1st US ed. 2 vols. xx,502; xiv,500pp,(4) ads; fldg map in rear pocket. Pub's cl, gilt. Good set (spine ends vol 1 chipped, fr hinge loose; spine ends vol 2 repaired). *Cahan.* $300/£192

O'DONOVAN, EDMOND. Merv. London, 1883. Frontis port, xi,348pp + (iv)pp pub's ads. Dec cl (spine sl rubbed). *Edwards.* $78/£50

O'FAOLAIN, EILEEN. The Shadowy Man. Longmans, 1949. 1st ed. Phoebe Llewellyn Smith (illus). Lg 8vo. 120pp (creases). Grn cl, red vignette. VG in pict dj (tattered). *Bookmark.* $28/£18

O'FAOLAIN, SEAN. Bird Alone. NY: Viking, 1936. 1st Amer ed. NF in dj (spine lt sunned, sl wear, few tears). *Antic Hay.* $27/£17

O'FAOLAIN, SEAN. Come Back to Erin. NY: Viking, 1940. 1st Amer ed. VG (eps browned) in dj. *Antic Hay.* $25/£16

O'FAOLAIN, SEAN. The Man Who Invented Sin. NY, 1948. 1st Amer ed. Fine in NF dj. *Polyanthos.* $25/£16

O'FAOLAIN, SEAN. Midsummer Night Madness and Other Stories. London, (1932). 1st ed, 1st bk. 2 vols. (Lt rubbed, spine lettering sl faded.) *Kane*.* $27/£17

O'FAOLAIN, SEAN. The Vanishing Hero. London, 1956. 1st ed. VG in dj. *Argosy.* $50/£32

O'FLAHERTY, LIAM. A Cure for Unemployment. London: E. Lahr, 1931. One of 100 numbered, signed. VG + in wraps. *Certo.* $60/£38

O'FLAHERTY, LIAM. The Fairy Goose and Two Other Stories. NY: Crosby Gaige, 1927. One of 1190. Signed. 12mo. Cl-backed bds (dknd), spine label (sl chipped). *Kane*.* $22/£14

O'FLAHERTY, LIAM. The Informer. Knopf, 1925. 1st US ed. VG + (bkpl, lacks dj). *Certo.* $45/£29

O'FLAHERTY, LIAM. Insurrection. London, 1950. 1st ed. Dj (dknd). *Typographeum.* $50/£32

O'FLAHERTY, LIAM. Land. NY: Random House, (1946). 1st Amer ed. NF in dj (sl wear, sm tear). *Antic Hay.* $20/£13

O'FLAHERTY, LIAM. Land. London, 1946. 1st ed. Fine in dj (spine sl sunned, extrems sl rubbed). *Polyanthos.* $25/£16

O'FLAHERTY, LIAM. The Puritan. London: Jonathan Cape, (1932). 1st ed. VG (bkpl, eps sl mkd) in VG dj. *Certo.* $60/£38

O'FLAHERTY, LIAM. Red Barbara and Other Stories. NY/London: Crosby Gaige/Faber & Gwyer, 1928. One of 600. Signed. VG. *Lenz.* $125/£80

O'FLAHERTY, LIAM. Return of the Brute. Mandrake Press, 1929. 1st ed. (Cvrs bowed, sl dusty.) Dj (nicked, sl torn, sl discolored.) *Ash.* $148/£95

O'FLAHERTY, LIAM. A Tourist's Guide to Ireland. London, (1929). 1st ed. Black cl-backed gold/black 'snakeskin' textured paper bds, ptd paper label. NF in ptd dj w/woodcut vignette. *Cady.* $40/£26

O'FLAHERTY, LIAM. Two Years. London, (1930). 1st ed. VG in dj (lt soiled). *Argosy.* $25/£16

O'FLAHERTY, LIAM. The Wild Swan and Other Stories. London: Joiner & Steele, n.d. One of 550 numbered, signed. VG. *Lenz.* $125/£80

O'HANLON, JOHN CANON. Irish-American History of the United States. NY: P. Murphy, 1907. 2 vols. (Dull, extrems frayed.) *Zubal*.* $70/£45

O'HANLON, REDMOND. Into the Heart of Borneo. Edinburgh, 1984. Fine in dj. *Clearwater.* $55/£35

O'HARA, FRANK. In Memory of My Feelings. Bill Berkson (ed). NY, 1967. Ltd 1st ed. 55 separate folded folio leaves. VG in 1/2 cl folder, cl slipcase. *Argosy.* $300/£192

O'HARA, JOHN. And Other Stories. NY: Random House, 1968. #156/300 signed. (Spine sl faded), else Fine in Fine slipcase. *Metropolitan*.* $201/£129

O'HARA, JOHN. The Big Laugh. NY: Random House, (1962). 1st ed. NF in dj (short closed tear). *Turtle Island.* $30/£19

O'HARA, JOHN. The Big Laugh. NY: Random House, (1962). 1st ed. Fine in dj. *Jaffe.* $45/£29

O'HARA, JOHN. The Big Laugh. Cresset, 1962. 1st UK ed. VG (stain fep) in dj (stain affecting flap, sl browned). *Williams.* $19/£12

O'HARA, JOHN. Hellbox. NY, 1947. 1st Amer ed. One of 7500 ptd. Fine in dj (extrems sl chipped, sm edge tear, price-clipped). *Polyanthos.* $30/£19

O'HARA, JOHN. Hope of Heaven. NY: Harcourt, Brace, (1938). 1st ed. Black cl, gilt. NF in dj (sm tears). *Blue Mountain.* $45/£29

O'HARA, JOHN. The Instrument. NY: Random House, (1967). One of 300 numbered, signed. Fine in Fine slipcase. *Lenz.* $150/£96

O'HARA, JOHN. The Lockwood Concern. NY: Random House, (1965). 1st ed. Mint in dj. *Jaffe.* $50/£32

O'HARA, JOHN. Pal Joey, the Libretto and Lyrics. NY: Random House, 1952. 1st ed. Fine in NF dj (faded). *Unger.* $75/£48

O'HARA, JOHN. Pal Joey. London: Cresset, 1952. 1st Eng ed. Fine (offsetting from dj flaps) in Fine dj. *Unger.* $75/£48

O'HARA, JOHN. Waiting for Winter. NY: Random House, (1966). One of 300 numbered, signed. Fine in Fine slipcase. *Lenz.* $150/£96

O'HIGGINS, HARVEY. Alias Walt Whitman. Newark, NJ: Carteret Book Club, 1930. Ltd to 200 numbered. Brn cl-backed dec bds, gilt. Fine. *Blue Mountain.* $65/£42

O'KANE, WALTER COLLINS. The Hopis. Norman, (1953). 1st ed. 2-tone cl. VG in dj (edgeworn). *King.* $35/£22

O'KEEFFE, GEORGIA. Georgia O'Keeffe: One Hundred Flowers. NY: Knopf, 1987. 1st ed. Plt list laid in. Fine in dj (lt scuffed). *Waverly*.* $44/£28

O'MALLEY, AUSTIN. The Ethics of Medical Homicide and Mutilation. NY, 1922. VG. *Fye.* $75/£48

O'MALLEY, C. D. and J. B. SAUNDERS. Leonardo da Vinci on the Human Body. NY, 1952. 1st ed. VG in dj. *Fye.* $150/£96

O'MEARA, B. E. (trans). Historical Memoirs of Napoleon. Book IX. 1815. (Complete.) London: Richard Phillips, 1820. Fldg color frontis map, xii,371,(7)pp (label removed tp); fldg chart. Teg. 1/2 red leather, cl (hinges rubbed). VG. *Bohling.* $85/£54

O'NEAL, HANK. A Vision Shared. NY: St. Martin's, 1976. 1st ed. (Owner stamp), else NF in dj (lt soiled, edgetorn). *Cahan.* $125/£80

O'NEAL, LULU RASMUSSEN. A Peculiar Piece of Desert. L.A.: Westernlore, 1957. One of 450. Dj (rubbed, 3 sm pieces missing). *Dawson.* $40/£26

O'NEALL, JOHN BELTON and JOHN A. CHAPMAN. The Annals of Newberry in Two Parts.... Newberry, SC: Aull & Houseal, 1892. 2nd ed, enlgd w/part II by Chapman. 816,viipp. (Extrems worn.) VG. Howes O93. *Mcgowan.* $285/£183

O'NEILL, CHARLES. Wild Train, the Story of the Andrews Raiders. NY: Random House, (1956). 1st ed. Signed for members of the Civil War Book Club. NF in VG dj. *Mcgowan.* $60/£38

O'NEILL, EUGENE et al. Provincetown Plays. First Series: Bound East for Cardiff.... NY: Frank Shay, 1916. 1st ed. W/orig program of NY performance of play given by The Provincetown Players. Uncut. Pict blue wrappers (sl faded); custom gilt-lettered blue solander box (worn, soiled). *Freeman*.* $150/£96

O'NEILL, EUGENE. Ah, Wilderness! NY, (1933). 1st ed. Nice in dj (sl frayed, soiled, edge-torn). *King.* $75/£48

O'NEILL, EUGENE. Ah, Wilderness! NY: LEC, 1972. One of 1500 numbered, signed by Shannon Stirnweis (illus). Fine in pub's slipcase (dusty). *Hermitage.* $100/£64

O'NEILL, EUGENE. Anna Christie. NY: Liveright, 1930. #682/775 signed. Unopened. Dec paper-cvrd bds. Fine in dj (2 tears fr flap), pub's box (worn). *Metropolitan*.* $287/£184

O'NEILL, EUGENE. Before Breakfast. NY: Frank Shay, 1916. 1st ed. One of 500. NF (sl shadow from bkpl; lt stain base) in wrappers w/fldg tray morocco slipcase. *Between The Covers.* $485/£311

O'NEILL, EUGENE. Dynamo. NY: Horace Liveright, 1929. One of 775 numbered, signed. (Bkpl removed fr pastedown, sm tear tp.) Full blue vellum (stained; top edge, spine heavily faded), gilt; white leather spine label (chipped). VG, largely unopened, in VG dec purple slipcase. *Blue Mountain.* $95/£61

O'NEILL, EUGENE. Dynamo. NY: Horace Liveright, 1929. 1st ed. Pict eps. Fine in dj. *Houle.* $150/£96

O'NEILL, EUGENE. Gold. NY: Boni & Liveright, (1920). 1st ed. (Fore-edge foxed; lt soiling top edge), else Fine in Fine dj. *Between The Covers.* $850/£545

O'NEILL, EUGENE. Gold. NY: Boni & Liveright, 1920. 1st ed. (Top edge dusted), else NF in dj (sl trimmed). *Lame Duck.* $850/£545

O'NEILL, EUGENE. The Iceman Cometh. NY, 1946. 1st ed. VG+ (sig) in dj (sl chipped). *Smith.* $45/£29

O'NEILL, EUGENE. The Iceman Cometh. NY: LEC, 1982. Ltd to 2000 numbered, signed by Leonard Baskin (illus). Orig litho by Baskin ptd on Arches paper, bound in at back. Gray bds, paper spine and cvr labels. Good in slipcase. *Karmiole.* $125/£80

O'NEILL, EUGENE. Lazarus Laughed. NY, 1927. #369/775 signed. Uncut. Vellum spine (sl sunned, sl rubbed). Fine. *Polyanthos.* $150/£96

O'NEILL, EUGENE. Marco Millions. NY, 1927. 1st Amer ed. Fine in dj (spine sunned, sl chipped, sm tear, price-clipped). *Polyanthos.* $40/£26

O'NEILL, EUGENE. A Moon for the Misbegotten. NY: Random House, (1952). 1st ed. Fine in dj (rear panel sl dusty). *Hermitage.* $50/£32

O'NEILL, EUGENE. More Stately Mansions. NY: Yale Univ, 1964. 1st ed. NF in dj (2 short tears spine head). *Lame Duck.* $45/£29

O'NEILL, EUGENE. Mourning Becomes Electra. NY: Horace Liveright, 1931. 1st ed. #79/550 signed. (Spine dknd, lt soiled.) *Metropolitan*.* $172/£110

O'NEILL, EUGENE. Mourning Becomes Electra. NY: Liveright, 1931. 1st ed. Near Perfect in dj (rear tears). *Between The Covers.* $450/£288

O'NEILL, EUGENE. The Plays of.... NY: Scribner, 1934-35. Wilderness ed. #558/770 numbered, signed sets. 12 vols. 8vo. Orange buckram, gilt. Fine. All glassine djs (except vol XII; few chipped); all slipcases. *Cummins.* $1,750/£1,122

O'NEILL, EUGENE. Strange Interlude. NY: Boni & Liveright, 1928. #570/775 signed. Gilt-lettered beveled vellum. (Soiled, cl irregularly dknd, sl spine stain), else VG in slipcase (stained). *Pacific*.* $150/£96

O'NEILL, EUGENE. Strange Interlude. NY: Boni & Liveright, 1928. One of 775 numbered, signed. Vellum over bds (sl browned). VG (bkpl) in orig cardbd slipcase (cracked, repairs). *Antic Hay.* $300/£192

O'NEILL, EUGENE. Thirst: Five One-Act Plays. Boston: Gorham, (1914). 1st ed, 1st bk. Fine (rub fr bd base) in NF white dj (foxing; price excised). *Between The Covers.* $2,000/£1,282

O'NEILL, JOHN P. (ed). Clyfford Still. MMA, 1979. VG+ in dj (sl edgeworn). *My Bookhouse.* $25/£16

O'NEILL, JOSEPH. Land Under England. NY, 1935. 1st ed. Fine in deco binding in VG dj. *Mcclintock.* $65/£42

O'NEILL, MARY. Hailstones and Halibut Bones. NY: Doubleday, 1961. 1st ed. Leonard Weisgard (illus). 6 1/2 x 9 1/2. 59pp. VG in dj (backstrip lacks bits). *Cattermole.* $25/£16

O'NEILL, R. E. (ed). History of the 20th Machine Gun Battalion. Kansas City, (1920). Good. *Hayman.* $25/£16

O'REILLY, BERNARD. Greenland, the Adjacent Seas, and the North-West Passage.... NY, 1818. 3 fldg engr maps. Uncut, largely unopened. Orig bds (worn, fr cvr detached). *Freeman*.* $90/£58

O'REILLY, JOHN BOYLE. Ethics of Boxing and Manly Sport. Boston: Ticknor, 1888. 358pp, 20pp ads. Pict bds. Good. *Cullen.* $125/£80

O'RELL, MAX. Jonathan and His Continent. NY: Cassell, (1889). ix,313pp+ads. (Lib bkpl, blindstamp, shaken.) *Bohling.* $12/£8

O'RIELLY, HENRY. Settlement in the West. Rochester, 1838. Frontis, 416pp; fldg map. Orig cl (sunned, extrems worn). Internally VG (inscrip). Howes O122. *Ginsberg.* $200/£128

O'ROURKE, FRANK. Bonus Rookie. Barnes, 1950. 1st ed. Good+. *Plapinger.* $30/£19

O'ROURKE, FRANK. The Greatest Victory and Other Baseball Stories. Barnes, 1950. 1st ed. VG+ in VG dj. *Plapinger.* $65/£42

O'SHAUGHNESSY, M. M. Hetch Hetchy, Its Origin and History. SF, 1934. 1st ed. Ltd to 1000 numbered. Color frontis, full-pg map. Dk grn cl lettered in silver. (Minor spot fr cvr), else Fine. *Argonaut.* $125/£80

O'SULLIVAN, MAURICE. Twenty Years A-Growing. London: C&W, 1933. 1st Eng ed. (Spine sl faded), else VG in dj (sl rubbed, chipped). *Hadley.* $78/£50

O'SULLIVAN, P. MICHAEL. Patriot Graves: Resistance in Ireland. Chicago: Follett, 1972. 1st ed. (Owner stamp), else NF in VG dj. *Cahan.* $40/£26

O'SULLIVAN, VINCENT. Aspects of Wilde. NY, 1936. 1st Amer ed. Nice in dj. *Clearwater.* $62/£40

Oak Openings; or, The Bee Hunter. (By James F. Cooper.) NY: Burgess, Stringer, 1848. 1st Amer ed. 2 vols bound in 1 (orig wrappers not bound in). Contemp 3/4 sheep. (Tanned, sl discolored, ink name), o/w Good. BAL 3929. *Reese.* $100/£64

OAKENFULL, J. C. Brazil in 1911. Frome/London: Butler/Tanner, Feb 1912. 3rd annual ed. Fldg frontis map. VG (corner bumped, rear cvr spotted). *Bohling.* $30/£19

OAKESHOTT, WALTER. The Artists of the Winchester Bible. London, 1945. 44 plts. Good. *Washton.* $45/£29

OAKLEY, GRAHAM. The Church Mice Adrift. NY: Atheneum, 1976. 1st US ed. 10 1/4 x 8 1/4. 34pp. Fine in dj. *Cattermole.* $25/£16

OAKLEY, GRAHAM. The Church Mouse. NY: Atheneum, 1972. 1st US ed. 10 1/4 x 8. 32pp. Fine in dj. *Cattermole.* $30/£19

OAKLY, OBADIAH. Expedition to Oregon. NY, 1914. Fine in ptd wraps. *Bohling.* $75/£48

OAKS, LYNDON. History of Garland Maine. Dover: Observer, 1912. 1st ed. Frontis port. (Tp lt foxed), else VG. *Cahan.* $65/£42

OATES, JOYCE CAROL. By the North Gate. NY: Vanguard, (1963). 1st ed, 1st bk. Fine in dj (lt edgeworn). *Jaffe.* $175/£112

OATES, JOYCE CAROL. By the North Gate. NY: Vanguard, (1963). 1st ed, 1st bk. Near Mint in dj. *Bromer.* $350/£224

OATES, JOYCE CAROL. A Garden of Earthly Delights. NY: Vanguard, 1967. 1st ed. NF in dj (sl worn, spine sl faded). *Else Fine.* $75/£48

OATES, JOYCE CAROL. The Hungry Ghosts. L.A., 1974. One of 350 numbered, signed. Fine in acetate dj. *Smith.* $35/£22

OATES, JOYCE CAROL. A Middle-Class Education. NY: Albondocani, 1980. One of 300 numbered, signed. Fine in Fine wrappers. *Lenz.* $75/£48

OATES, JOYCE CAROL. Miracle Play. L.A., 1974. One of 350 numbered, signed. Fine in acetate dj. *Smith.* $35/£22

OATES, JOYCE CAROL. Miracle Play. L.A.: Black Sparrow, 1974. One of 350 numbered, signed. Fine in Fine clear acetate dj. *Lenz.* $100/£64

OATES, JOYCE CAROL. Mysteries of Winterthurn. NY: E.P. Dutton, 1984. 1st ed. Signed. NF in dj. *Moorhouse.* $31/£20

OATES, JOYCE CAROL. The Seduction and Other Stories. Black Sparrow, 1975. One of 350 signed. Pub's comp slip laid in. Fine. *Certo.* $65/£42

OATES, JOYCE CAROL. Sentimental Education. L.A.: Sylvester & Orphanos, 1978. One of 300 numbered, signed. Fine in Fine clear acetate dj. *Lenz.* $100/£64

OATES, JOYCE CAROL. Them. Vanguard, (1969). 1st ed. Fine in NF 1st issue dj. *Certo.* $50/£32

OATES, JOYCE CAROL. The Wheel of Love and Other Stories. NY, 1970. 1st ed. NF (sig) in NF dj. *Smith.* $20/£13

OATES, JOYCE CAROL. The Wheel of Love. NY: Vanguard, 1965. 1st ed. Fine in dj (sl worn). *Else Fine.* $75/£48

OATES, JOYCE CAROL. Women in Love and Other Poems. NY: Albondocani, 1968. 1st ed. One of 150 (of 176) numbered, signed. NF in patterned wrappers. *Captain's Bookshelf.* $60/£38

OATES, JOYCE CAROL. Women Whose Lives Are Food, Men Whose Lives Are Money. LA State Univ, 1978. Fine (sl mks eps) in dj. *Williams.* $12/£8

OATES, JOYCE CAROL. Wonderland. NY: Vanguard, 1971. 1st ed. NF in NF dj. *Else Fine.* $20/£13

OATES, STEPHEN B. With Malice Towards None, The Life of Abraham Lincoln. NY, (1977). 1st ed. VG+ in dj (lt wear). *Pratt.* $35/£22

OBACH, EUGENE F. A. Cantor Lectures on Gutta Percha. London: William Trounce, 1898. 1st ed. Frontis, (3),102pp. Contemp 3/4 calf, marbled bds. VG (stains). *Glaser.* $75/£48

OBER, FREDERICK A. Camps in the Caribbees: The Adventures of a Naturalist in the Lesser Antilles. Boston: Lee & Shepard, 1880. 1st ed. 366pp, 34 engrs. Blind-stamped gilt-dec cl (hinges cracked). VG. *Mikesh.* $75/£48

OBER, FREDERICK A. Travels in Mexico and Life Among the Mexicans. Boston: Estes & Lauriat, 1885. Pict cl (extrems sl rubbed), gilt/black-stamped. *Sadlon.* $75/£48

OBERHOLSER, HARRY C. The Bird Life of Texas. Edgar B. Kincaid, Jr. (ed). Austin: Univ of TX, (1974). 1st ed. 2 vols. Folio. 36 color plts. Grn cl. Good in slipcase. *Karmiole.* $150/£96

OBERHUBER, KONRAD. Poussin. The Early Years in Rome. NY, 1988. Good in dj. *Washton.* $65/£42

OBERTH, HERMANN. The Moon Car. Willy Ley (trans). NY: Harper, (1959). 1st ed in English. Frontis, 9 full-pg figs. 2-toned cl. NF in dj. *Glaser.* $250/£160

Objects of Adornment. Five Thousand Years of Jewelry from the Walters Art Gallery, Baltimore. Balt: Walters Art Gallery, 1984. 23 color plts. Good in wrappers. *Washton.* $25/£16

OBRAZTSOV, SERGEI. The Chinese Puppet Theatre. J. T. MacDermott (trans). London: Faber & Faber, (1961). VG in pict dj. *Dramatis Personae.* $25/£16

Observations on the Act of Parliament Commonly Called the Boston Port-Bill. Boston: Edes & Gill, 1774. (Prelims sl soiled, chipped, not affecting text.) 20th-cent 3/4 brn sheep, marbled bds (extrems scuffed). Howes Q18. *Freeman*.* $220/£141

Observations on the Rev. Dr. Gannett's Sermon, Entitled 'Relation of the North to Slavery.' (By George Ticknor Curtis.) Boston: Redding, 1854. 2nd thousand. 29pp. VG in self-wraps, side-tied, unopened. *Petrilla.* $30/£19

OCH, JOSEPH. Missionary in Sonora...1755-1767. Theodore E. Treutlein (trans). SF: CA Hist Soc, 1965. 1st ed in English. 2 maps. 2-tone cl. Fine in dj. *Argonaut.* $40/£26

OCHINO, BARNARDINO. The Cases of Polygamy, Concubinage, Adultery, Divorce, Etc. London: E. Curll et al, 1732. 1st ed. lvii,1-240pp (tp trimmed, mtd). Later 1/2 leather (fr cvr separate; sl stained). *Second Life.* $200/£128

OCHSNER, ALBERT J. and RALPH L. THOMPSON. Surgery and Pathology of the Thyroid and Parathyroid Glands. St. Louis, 1910. 1st ed. VG (sl worn). *Doctor's Library.* $75/£48

ODLE, E. V. The Clockwork Man. Heinemann, 1923. 1st ed. Lt grey cl (rather soiled; lt foxed). *Cox.* $28/£18

ODUM, HOWARD W. Wings in My Feet, Black Ulysses at the Wars. Indianapolis: Bobb-Merrill, (1929). 1st ed. (Cvr edges rubbed.) *Heinoldt.* $50/£32

OE, KENZABURO. A Personal Matter. NY: Grove, 1968. 1st ed in English. Fine in Fine dj. *Polyanthos.* $35/£22

OELLRICH, INEZ. Murder Makes Us Gay. GC: DCC, 1941. 1st ed. (Bkpl removed), o/w VG in dj (spine ends chipped, frayed, corners chipped, closed tears). *Mordida.* $45/£29

Official Army Register of the Volunteer Force of the United States Army for the Years 1861, '62, '63, '64, '65. Part VI: Indiana-Illinois. Washington, 1865. 1st ed. (8),599pp; woodcut. Muslin spine. Orig ptd wrappers. *Ginsberg.* $50/£32

Official Guide to the Tarzan Clans of America. Tarzana: Tarzan Clans of America, 1939. 1st ed. 8vo. Pamphlet. VF in pict orange wrappers. *Swann*.* $690/£442

Official History of the Great War. Mesopotamia Campaign 1914-1918. London, 1923-7. 4 vols. Red cl (vol 1 spine spotted). *Maggs.* $468/£300

Official History of the Great War. Military Operations Egypt and Palestine. London, 1928-30. 5 vols. Red cl (1 spine faded). *Maggs.* $546/£350

Official History of the Great War. Military Operations. East Africa, August 1914-September 1916. London, 1941. Red cl. *Maggs.* $468/£300

Official History of the Great War. Military Operations. Gallipoli. London, 1932-36. 4 vols. Red cl. *Maggs.* $468/£300

Official History of the Great War. Military Operations. Italy, 1915-1919. London, 1949. 5 maps, 2 plts, 14 sketch plans. Red cl. *Maggs.* $390/£250

Official History of the Great War. Military Operations. Macedonia. London, 1933/35. 4 vols. Red cl (spines sl faded). *Maggs.* $468/£300

Official History of the Great War. Military Operations. Togoland and the Cameroons, 1914-1916. London, 1931. 15 maps, 37 plts. Red cl. *Maggs.* $507/£325

Official History of the Great War. The War in the Air. Oxford, 1922-37. 9 vols, incl Appendices and 2 boxes of maps (complete set). Blue cl, gilt. All text vols in djs (Maps Vol III sl faded). *Maggs.* $1,560/£1,000

Official History of the Three Hundred and Fourth Engineer Regiment...During the World War. (Phila), 1920. Blue cl (lt wear), gilt. *Freeman*.* $20/£13

Official History of the War. France and Belgium. 1914-1918. London, 1925-1947. 1st ed. 26 vols complete. Red cl (spines variably faded). *Maggs.* $3,900/£2,500

Official Records of the Union and Confederate Navies in the War of the Rebellion. Series I-Volume 12. Washington: GPO, 1901. (Spine ends, corners sl rubbed.) *Sadlon.* $20/£13

Official Records of the Union and Confederate Navies in the War of the Rebellion. Series I-Volume 23. Washington: GPO, 1910. (Fr inner hinge starting; rubbed.) *Sadlon.* $12/£8

Official Records of the Union and Confederate Navies in the War of the Rebellion. Series II-Volume I. Washington: GPO, 1921. (Sl rubbed.) *Sadlon.* $15/£10

Official Roster of the Soldiers of the State of Ohio in the War of the Rebellion. 1861-1866. Various cities, 1886-1895. 1st eds. 12 vols. (Presentation stamps; spine vol 1 loose, spine vol 10 chipped), o/w VG set in 3/4 black leather, gilt. *Mcclintock.* $595/£381

OGILVIE, WILLIAM. Early Days on the Yukon and the Story of Its Gold Finds. London: John Lane et al, 1913. VG. *High Latitude.* $95/£61

OGILVIE-GRANT, W. R. A Hand-Book to the Game-Birds. London: Edward Lloyd, 1897. 2 vols. xiv,304; xiv,316pp; 42 color plts. Cl, gilt (rebacked in matching maroon levant morocco, gilt). *Hollett.* $203/£130

OGILVIE-GRANT, W. R. A Hand-Book to the Game-Birds. R.B. Sharpe (ed). London: Lloyd, (1896-97). 2nd ed. 2 vols. 42 chromolitho plts. NF. *Mikesh.* $125/£80

OGLESBY, CATHARINE. Modern Primitive Arts of Mexico, Guatemala, and Southwest. Whittlesey House, (1939). 1st ed. VG in VG dj. *Oregon.* $45/£29

OGLESBY, RICHARD. Manuel Lisa and the Opening of the Missouri Fur Trade. Norman: Univ of OK, (1963). 1st ed. Map. VF in dj (spine faded). *Argonaut.* $60/£38

OHASHI, S. Japanese Floral Arrangement. Japan: Yamanaka, n.d. 2nd ed. 100 hand-color plts (plt 1 browned; text lt spotted). Marbled eps; teg, rest uncut. 1/2 calf, marbled bds (spine sl chipped), gilt, raised spine bands. *Edwards.* $195/£125

OKA, H. How to Wrap Five More Eggs. NY, 1978. 4th ptg. Dec paper over bds, linen spine. VG in VG dj. *Scribe's Perch*.* $30/£19

OKEY, THOMAS. The Story of Avignon. London, 1926. 2nd, rev ed. Fldg plan. Gilt-dec cl (spine, extrems discolored). *Edwards.* $19/£12

OKEY, THOMAS. The Story of Paris. London, 1925. Rev ed. Fldg plan. Gilt-dec cl (discoloring). *Edwards.* $19/£12

OKEY, THOMAS. The Story of Venice. London, 1905. 2 maps (1 fldg). Teg. Gilt-dec cl (spine, edges sl discolored, upper bd sl wrinkled). *Edwards.* $19/£12

OKRI, BEN. The Famished Road. London: Cape, 1991. 1st UK ed. Fine in dj. *Williams.* $62/£40

OKRI, BEN. Incidents at the Shrine. London: Heinemann, 1986. 1st UK ed. Fine in dj. *Williams.* $31/£20

OKRI, BEN. Stars of the New Curfew. NY: Viking, (1989). 1st US ed. VF in VF dj. *Pettler & Lieberman.* $30/£19

OKUBO, MINE. Citizen 13660. NY: Columbia Univ, 1946. 1st ed. VG in VG dj. *Perier.* $95/£61

Old Brewery, and the New Mission House at the Five Points. NY: Stringer & Townsend, 1854. 1st ed. Dec red cl (sl worn; foxing). *Agvent.* $75/£48

Old Engish Drinking Songs. Cincinnati: Byway, 1903. 1st ed thus, 2nd issue. Ltd to 350 numbered. Marbled eps. Unopened. Linen w/paste-paper over bds, paper spine label. Fine. *Cahan.* $100/£64

Old Fashioned Mother Goose. (NY): G.W. Carleton, 1879. Sq 8vo. Pict tp, 47 color litho plts, each w/fldg flap, and initialled 'W.L.S.' in the plt. Pict cl (worn, shaken, soiled, stained; splits, other paper flaws). *Oinonen*.* $140/£90

Old Nursery Stories. NY: McLoughlin Bros, (1892). 8x5.5. Unpaged. 36 full-pg color plts. Color pict bds (well worn). *King.* $65/£42

Old Villita. Writers' Project of the WPA in the State of Texas (comp). San Antonio: City of San Antonio, 1939. Glassine leaves fr, rear; dbl-pg map. Pict beige wrappers (foremargin sl bent). *Dawson.* $100/£64

Old Woman and Her Pig. NY: Sheldon, n.d. (ca 1855). Sq 12mo. 14pp + 1pg list wrapper (lt soiling edges); 7 full-pg litho color wood engrs. VG in pict stiff paper wrappers (dusted, soiled at fold; spine reinforced; pencil name). *Hobbyhorse.* $250/£160

Old York Road. (By Anne de B. Mears.) Phila, 1890. 2-tone cl (lt worn, soiled). *Freeman*.* $45/£29

OLDFIELD, ARTHUR. Practical Manual of Typography and Reference Book for Printers. E. Menken, (c. 1910). 3rd ed. Sound (hinges sl worn). *Cox.* $44/£28

OLDROYD, H. Collecting, Preserving and Studying Insects. London: Hutchinson, 1958. 1st ed. 15 plts, map. VG. *Mikesh.* $30/£19

OLDROYD, IDA SHEPARD. Marine Shells of the West Coast of North America. Stanford Univ, 1924-1927. 1st ed. 2 vols in 4. 108 plts. Fine set. *Glaser.* $200/£128

OLDROYD, OSBORN H. The Assassination of Abraham Lincoln. Washington, DC, 1901. 1st ed. (Stamped names; cvrs rubbed.) *King.* $50/£32

OLDS, IRVING S. Bits and Pieces of American History.... NY: Olds, 1951. One of 500. Beige gray cl, pict onlay, gilt. Fine. *Parmer.* $350/£224

OLERICH, HENRY. A Cityless and Countryless World. Holstein, IA: Gilmore & Olerich, 1893. 1st ed. 447pp. Red cl, gilt. (Lt bleed of cl color 1st few leaves; cl mkd), o/w NF. *Reese.* $350/£224

OLIPHANT, J. ORIN. On the Cattle Ranges of the Oregon Country. Seattle: Univ of WA, (1968). 1st ed. Fine in dj (ink inscrip fr flap). *Perier.* $60/£38

OLIPHANT, LAURENCE. Minnesota and the Far West. Edinburgh: William Blackwood, 1855. 1st ed. Tinted litho frontis, xiii,(i)list of illus, 306pp, 16 pub's list, 1/2-title, fldg map, 6 engr plts. (Foxing in places.) Brn grained, blindstamped cl (spine ends chipped, loose), gilt. Sound. Howes O64. *Morrell.* $148/£95

OLIPHANT, LAURENCE. Narrative of the Earl of Elgin's Mission to China and Japan in the Years 1857, '58, '59. Edinburgh: (Blackwood), 1859. 1st ed w/half-titles, 20 lithos, 5 fldg maps. 2 vols. Teg. 3/4 red crushed morocco, marbled sides, gilt-tooled spines, 5 raised bands. VF. *Book Block.* $750/£481

OLIPHANT, LAURENCE. The Trans-Caucasian Campaign of the Turkish Army under Omer Pasha. Edinburgh: Blackwood, 1856. 1st ed. xxvii,(i)blank, 234pp, 4 tinted lithos incl frontis, fldg map, plan. (Sl foxing 3 plts, tp, few places.) Marbled edges. Contemp calf (rebacked; hinges strengthened, sl rubbed), orig backstrip, gilt arms on cvrs, black label. Sound. *Morrell.* $218/£140

OLIPHANT, MRS. The Makers of Florence. London, 1877. 2nd ed. xviii,395pp; port. (Bkpl, hinges tender; rubbed, spine sl chipped.) *Edwards.* $39/£25

OLIPHANT, MRS. Royal Edinburgh. London: Macmillan, 1890. 1st ed. Teg. Dec grn cl (lt worn, bubbled). VG. *Antic Hay.* $45/£29

OLIVA, LEO E. Soldiers on the Santa Fe Trail. Norman, 1967. 1st ed. Fine in Good dj. *Turpen.* $37/£24

OLIVER, ANTHONY. Cover-Up. London: Heinemann, 1987. 1st ed. Fine in Fine dj. *Murder By The Book.* $45/£29

OLIVER, ANTHONY. The Victorian Staffordshire Figure. London: Heinemann, 1978. 8 color plts. VG in dj. *Hollett.* $62/£40

OLIVER, PAUL. The Story of the Blues. London: Barrie & Rockliff/Cresset, 1969. 1st ed. Fine in dj (lt used; strengthened w/rebacking). *Beasley.* $100/£64

OLIVER, PAUL. The Story of the Blues. Phila: Chilton, 1969. 1st US ed. Fine in NF dj. *Beasley.* $85/£54

OLIVER, PETER. A New Chronicle of the Complete Angler. NY/London: Paisley Press/Williams & Norgate, 1936. 1st ed. 32 plts. VG (sl worn, soiled). *Waverly*.* $60/£38

OLIVIER, EDITH. As Far as Jane's Grandmother's. London, 1928. 1st ed. Rex Whistler (illus). Frontis. Cl-backed marbled paper-cvrd sides. (Sl rubbed), o/w VG. *Words Etc.* $39/£25

OLIVIER, EDITH. Country Moods and Tenses. Batsford, 1941. 1st ed. (Inscrip), o/w VG in Whistler dj (chipped, worn, severely price-clipped). *Words Etc.* $55/£35

OLIVIER, EDITH. Country Moods and Tenses. London: Batsford, 1941. Inscribed. Good. *Clearwater.* $78/£50

OLIVIER, EDITH. Wiltshire. County Books Series, 1951. 1st ed. Fine in dj. *Words Etc.* $34/£22

OLIVIER, SYDNEY. Letters and Selected Writings. London: Allen & Unwin, (1948). 1st ed. NF in dj (edgeworn, scuffed). *Antic Hay.* $25/£16

OLMSTEAD, A. T. History of Assyria. NY: Scribner, 1923. Color frontis, 13 maps. (Bkpl.) Teg. Gilt-pict cl. *Archaeologia.* $95/£61

OLMSTEAD, A. T. History of Palestine and Syria to the Macedonian Conquest. NY: Scribner, 1931. Color frontis, 18 maps. Teg. Gilt-pict cl. *Archaeologia.* $95/£61

OLMSTEAD, FREDERICK LAW, JR. and THEODORA KIMBALL (eds). Frederick Law Olmstead, Landscape Architect, 1822-1903. [Vol. II] Central Park...1853-1895. NY: Putnam, 1928. 1st ed. Vol 2 of 3. Frontis, fldg map w/overlay map. Blue cl. Good in dj (chipped). *Karmiole.* $100/£64

OLMSTEAD, FREDERICK LAW. The Cotton Kingdom. NY: Mason Bros, 1861. 2 vols. Fldg map vol 1. (Faded, sl bumped), o/w VG. *Metropolitan*.* $86/£55

OLMSTED, FREDERICK LAW. A Journey in the Back Country. NY: Mason Bros, 1861. 2nd ed. VG. Howes O77. *Agvent.* $125/£80

OLSON, CHARLES. Archaeologist of Morning. London: Cape Goliard, 1970. 1st ed. Fine in NF dj (rear panel sl soiled, sm close tear). *Warren.* $75/£48

OLSON, CHARLES. The Distances. NY: Grove, (1960). 1st ed. VF in dec wrappers. *Dermont.* $30/£19

OLSON, CHARLES. The Maximus Poems IV, V, VI. London: Cape Goliard, 1968. 1st ed. Fine in dec wrappers (sl soiled). *Polyanthos.* $30/£19

OLSON, CHARLES. The Maximus Poems, IV, V, VI. London: Cape Goliard, 1968. 1st ed. Fine in NF dj. *Warren.* $75/£48

OLSON, CHARLES. Projective Verse. (NY: Totem Press, 1959.) 1st ed. NF (loose errata slip not present) in dec wrappers. *Reese.* $75/£48

OLSON, JAMES C. Red Cloud and the Sioux Problem. Lincoln: Univ of NE, (1965). 1st ed. VG in dj. *Lien.* $50/£32

OMAN, C. C. Catalogue of Wall-Papers. 1929. 25 plts. (Fep lt browned; sl rubbed, spine lt faded.) *Edwards.* $31/£20

OMAN, C. W. C. Wellington's Army 1809-1814. London, 1912. 8 plts. Red cl. Excellent. *Maggs.* $156/£100

OMAN, CHARLES. English Silversmiths' Work. London: Victoria & Albert Museum, 1965. Dj (sl worn, soiled). *Freeman*.* $20/£13

OMAN, CHARLES. A History of the Peninsular War. London, 1902-1930. 1st ed. 7 vols. 8vo. Red cl (lt worn; sm tears to map folds, no loss). *Maggs.* $1,872/£1,200

OMMANNEY, F. D. South Latitude. London, 1938. 2nd imp. Inscribed. VG in dj (repaired). *High Latitude.* $20/£13

Omniana, or Horae Otiosiores. (By S.T. Coleridge and Robert Southey.) London: Longman et al, 1812. 1st ed. 2 vols. Contemp full speckled calf, gilt. (Joints sl weak.) *Maggs.* $273/£175

OMWAKE, JOHN. The Conestoga Six-Horse Bell Teams, 1750-1850. Cincinnati: Ebbert & Richardson, 1930. 1st ed. Signed, inscribed. Good. Howes O85. *Cullen.* $135/£87

On the Heels of De Wet. (By L. James.) Edinburgh, 1911. 3rd imp. Pict cl (sl worn, faded). *Maggs.* $70/£45

On the Way, the Story of the 195th Field Artillery Battalion, United States Army. (Frankfurt), 1945. Cl-backed bds. (Ink name; spine defective, cvrs rubbed, loose.) *King.* $60/£38

ONDAATJE, MICHAEL. The Collected Works of Billy the Kid. London, 1981. 1st British ed. Fine in Fine dj (price-clipped). *Warren.* $40/£26

ONDAATJE, MICHAEL. The Collected Works of Billy the Kid. London: Boyars, 1981. 1st Eng ed. Fine in Fine dj. *Unger.* $100/£64

ONDAATJE, MICHAEL. In the Skin of a Lion. NY, 1987. 1st ed. Fine in Fine dj. *Smith.* $20/£13

ONDAATJE, MICHAEL. Rat Jelly and Other Poems 1963-1978. London: Marion Boyars, (1980). 1st ed. Fine in Fine dj. *Dermont.* $45/£29

One Hundred Fifty Years of Birth Control. NY: Margaret Sanger Research Bureau, (1948). 4th ptg? VG in ptd wraps (lib stamp). *Second Life.* $25/£16

ONIONS, OLIVER. The Hand of Cornelius Voyt. Hamish Hamilton, 1939. Good (new fep, fore-edge lt spotted; spine bumped, sunned; lacks dj). *Tiger.* $19/£12

Ophiolatreia. (By H. Jennings.) N.p.: Privately ptd, 1889. 103pp. Ptd paper over bds. Good-. *Scribe's Perch*.* $44/£28

OPIE, IONA and PETER (eds). The Oxford Dictionary of Nursery Rhymes. Clarendon, 1951. 1st ed. xxvii,467pp (feps sl spotted); 14 plts. (Cl sl edge-worn.) *Edwards.* $47/£30

OPIE, IONA and PETER (eds). The Oxford Nursery Rhyme Book. Oxford, 1955. 1st ed. xiv,224pp; 600 illus. VG in pict dj (sl frayed). *Cox.* $47/£30

OPIE, JOHN NEWTON. A Rebel Cavalryman with Lee, Stuart and Jackson. Chicago: W.B. Conkey, 1899. 1st ed. 336pp. VG. Howes O101. *Mcgowan.* $450/£288

OPIE, MRS. The Black Velvet Pelisse. Boston: Thomas Wells, 1815. 12mo. 32pp (pencil sig tp); full-pg wood engr; frontis/last pg pasted down. Good in ptd pink paper wrappers (lt rubbed, spine sl chipped), ptd title label laid on. *Hobbyhorse.* $100/£64

Opium Habit, with Suggestions as to the Remedy. (Horace B. Day, ed.) NY: Harper, 1868. 1st ed. (ii),335,(3)pp (sig sprung). Panelled ochre cl (shelfworn), gilt. (Also issued in grn silk & purple cl bindings.) Good. *Gach.* $275/£176

OPPE, A. P. (ed). The Drawings of William Hogarth. London, 1948. 91 plts. (Corner bumped.) *Washton.* $45/£29

OPPE, A. P. (intro). The Water-Colours of Turner, Cox and De Wint. London: Halton & Truscott Smith, 1925. 34 Fine plts tipped in, guards. (Eps foxed; prelims and fore-edge spotted.) Beveled bds. *Hollett.* $117/£75

OPPENHEIM, E. PHILLIPS. Crooks in the Sunshine. Boston: Little, Brown, 1933. 1st Amer ed. NF (sl sunned) in dj (rear panel browned). *Antic Hay.* $35/£22

OPPENHEIM, E. PHILLIPS. A Maker of History. Boston: Little, Brown, 1906. 1st Amer ed. Blue cl. NF (ink name; sl rubbed). *Antic Hay.* $25/£16

OPPENHEIM, H. Diseases of the Nervous System.... Edward E. Mayer (trans). Phila: Lippincott, 1900. 1st Amer ed. Clean (stamps tp, few ll; cl worn, recased, spine stamps). *Goodrich.* $150/£96

OPPENHEIMER, JANE M. New Aspects of John and William Hunter. NY: Henry Schuman, 1946. 1st ed. One of 1500. Frontis port, 4 plts. Fine. *Glaser.* $30/£19

OPTIC, OLIVER. (Pseud of William F. Adams.) The Blue and the Gray—On Land—At the Front. Boston, (1897). 437pp. Pict cl. (Sm stain fr cvr), o/w VG +. *Pratt.* $20/£13

OPTIC, OLIVER. (Pseud of William F. Adams.) Brave Old Salt; or Life on the Quarter Deck. Boston: Lee & Shepard, 1866. 1st ed. Inscribed card laid in. Frontis, engr tp. (Spine gilt, extrems sl rubbed.) *Sadlon.* $50/£32

OPTIC, OLIVER. (Pseud of William T. Adams.) Sea and Shore. Boston: Lee & Shepard, 1872. 1st ed. 2pp undated ads. Grn cl, gilt. NF (sm marginal stain corner 1st dozen ll; sl rubbed). *Sumner & Stillman.* $85/£54

OPTIC, OLIVER. (Pseud of William F. Adams.) Stand by the Union. Boston: Lothrop, Lee & Shepard, (1891). 1st ed. Pict cl (spine ends sl rubbed), gilt. *Sadlon.* $25/£16

ORCUTT, SAMUEL. The History of the Old Town of Derby, Connecticut 1642-1880. Springfield, MA, 1880. 844pp; 21 plts. 1/2 leather. Good (fr joint starting). Howes O102. *Scribe's Perch*.* $23/£15

ORCUTT, WILLIAM DANA. The Balance. NY: Stokes, (1922). 1st ed. Inscribed w/ptd Christmas greeting. (Bkpl; spine stained), else Nice in dj (soiled, worn, chipped, creased). *Metropolitan*.* $69/£44

ORCUTT, WILLIAM DANA. The Book in Italy During the Fifteenth and Sixteenth Centuries.... London: George G. Harrap, (1928). 1st Eng ed. One of 750 numbered. 128 plts. Vellum-backed bds (spine foxed). Dj. *Oak Knoll.* $150/£96

ORCUTT, WILLIAM DANA. The Book in Italy During the Fifteenth and Sixteenth Centuries.... NY: Harper, 1928. 1st US ed. One of 750 numbered. Sm folio. Tipped-in color frontis w/gilt, 2 tipped-in color plts, 125 b/w facs. Teg; untrimmed. Black cl, lt blue bds, gilt, ptd fr cvr paper label. (Spine sl spotted, cvrs sl dusty, handled.) *Baltimore*.* $60/£38

ORCUTT, WILLIAM DANA. The Kingdom of Books. Boston: Little, Brown, 1927. 1st ed. Presentation copy. Fine. *Oak Knoll.* $35/£22

ORCUTT, WILLIAM DANA. The Manual of Linotype Typography. Brooklyn, NY: Merganthaler Linotype, (1923). Mtd frontis. (Bkpl removed fr pastedown; lt wear, soil.) *Freeman*.* $30/£19

ORCUTT, WILLIAM DANA. Robert Cavelier. Chicago, 1904. 1st Amer ed, 1st bk. Uncut. Pict cvrs, gilt. NF (name; edges sl rubbed). *Polyanthos.* $75/£48

ORCZY, BARONESS. The Bronze Eagle: A Story of the Hundred Days. NY: Doran, 1915. 1st ed. Fine in dj (lacks lower 3rd of spine, corner; stained). *Else Fine.* $125/£80

ORCZY, BARONESS. By the Gods Beloved. London: White Lion, 1977. Reissue of 1905 ed. VF in VF dj. *Else Fine.* $30/£19

ORCZY, BARONESS. The Divine Folly. London: Hodder & Stoughton, 1937. 1st UK ed. VG (spine faded) in dj (browned, edgeworn, sl loss spine top). *Williams.* $75/£48

ORCZY, BARONESS. Eldorado. Hodder & Stoughton, (1913). 1st ed. As w/British Library copy, the tp is a cancel. Dec cl, pict onlay. VG (lt mks). *Ash.* $78/£50

ORCZY, BARONESS. The Elusive Pimpernel. London: Hutchinson, 1908. 1st UK ed. VG (ink inscrip, eps browned, rep corner chipped; bds sl worn, mkd). *Williams.* $47/£30

ORCZY, BARONESS. Flower o' the Lily. London: Hodder & Stoughton, (1918). 1st UK ed. (Fep creased), else NF in VG dj (sl edgeworn, top edge sl chipped, sm 7/- net label on spine). *Williams.* $148/£95

ORCZY, BARONESS. His Majesty's Well-Beloved. London: Hodder, (n.d.). 1st UK ed. VG (foxed) in Good dj (dusty, stained, spine sl worn). *Williams.* $133/£85

ORCZY, BARONESS. The Honourable Jim. NY: Doran, 1924. 1st ed. (Sl nibbled), else Fine in pict dj (sl worn, chipped). *Else Fine.* $90/£58

ORCZY, BARONESS. The Laughing Cavalier. London: Hodder, 1914. 1st UK ed. VG (spine top sl pushed) w/pict onlay fr cvr. *Williams.* $62/£40

ORCZY, BARONESS. Skin o' My Tooth. GC, 1928. 1st ed. Good +. *Mcclintock.* $20/£13

ORCZY, BARONESS. A Spy of Napoleon. London: Hodder & Stoughton, 1934. 1st UK ed. VG (ink name, eps damp-stained) in pict dj (sl edgeworn, rubbed). *Williams.* $156/£100

ORCZY, BARONESS. The Triumph of the Scarlet Pimpernel. London: Hodder & Stoughton, n.d. (1922). 1st UK ed. VG (sl damp-affected) in VG dj (sl damp-stained, sl edgeworn). *Williams.* $304/£195

ORDE, A. J. A Little Neighborhood Murder. NY: Doubleday, 1989. 1st ed. VF in dj. *Mordida.* $35/£22

Order of the Proceedings at the Darwin Celebration.... Cambridge, 1909. 12 plts. Ptd bds, white cl spine (sl soiled). *Maggs.* $47/£30

Ordnance Maintenance: Wrist Watches, Pocket Watches, Stop Watches and Clocks. Washington: GPO, 1945. Ptd wrappers. *Weber.* $35/£22

Oregon Trail: The Missouri River to the Pacific Ocean. NY, (1939). Color fldg map. Pict cl. VG. *Reese.* $125/£80

ORIANS, G. Blackbirds of the Americas. Seattle: Univ of WA, 1985. 1st ed. Fine in Fine dj. *Mikesh.* $25/£16

Origin of Nebraska Place Names. Lincoln: Stephenson School Supply, 1938. 1st ed. 28-pg pamphlet. VG in wrappers (sl dust-soiled). *Brown.* $15/£10

ORIGO, IRIS. Allegra. Hogarth, 1935. 1st ed. Yellow cl. (1/2 title, final blank sl browned; lt soiled.) *Cox.* $23/£15

ORIGO, IRIS. Leopardi: A Study in Solitude. London: Hamish Hamilton, (1953). 1st Eng ed. Fine (lacks dj). *Captain's Bookshelf.* $35/£22

ORIOLI, G. Adventures of a Bookseller. London: Chatto, 1938. 1st Eng, 1st trade ed. (Fore-edges foxed, cvrs sl stained.) Poor dj. *Clearwater.* $55/£35

ORIOLI, G. Adventures of a Bookseller. NY: Robert M. McBride, 1938. 1st US ed. Fine in dj. *Oak Knoll.* $85/£54

ORKIN, RUTH. A World Through My Window. NY: Harper & Row, 1978. 1st ed. Signed. Fine in Fine dj. *Smith.* $95/£61

ORLOFSKY, PATSY and MYRON. Quilts in America. NY: Mc-H, (1974). 1st ed. Fine in NF dj. *Agvent.* $175/£112

ORMOND, CLYDE. Bear! Harrisburg: Stackpole, 1961. 1st ed. Dec cl. VG+ in VG dj. *Mikesh.* $20/£13

ORMOND, CLYDE. Hunting in the Northwest. NY: Knopf, 1948. 1st ed. Blind-stamped red cl, gilt. VF in Fine pict dj. *Biscotti.* $40/£26

ORMOND, JESSE MARVIN. The Country Church in North Carolina. Durham: Duke Univ, 1931. 1st ed. Fine in dj (lt chipped). *Cahan.* $40/£26

ORMOND, RICHARD. John Singer Sargent: Paintings, Drawings, Watercolours. NY, (1970). 1st Amer ed. 32 color plts. VG in dj. *Argosy.* $300/£192

ORMSBY, WATERMAN L. The Butterfield Overland Mail. Lyle H. Wright & Josephine M. Bynum (eds). San Marino, CA, 1960. 1st ed. Fine. *Mcclintock.* $20/£13

ORMSBY, WATERMAN L. The Butterfield Overland Mail. Lyle H. Wright and Josephine M. Bynum (eds). San Marino, CA: Huntington Library, 1955. VG in dj (sl worn). *Lien.* $25/£16

ORR, J. W. Pictorial Guide to the Falls of Niagara. Buffalo: Press of Salisbury & Clapp, 1842. 232pp. (Age-spotted; rubbed, deep chip spine head.) *Zubal*.* $30/£19

ORR, MRS. SUTHERLAND. Life and Letters of Robert Browning. Boston: Houghton, Mifflin, 1891. 1st ed. 2 vols. Teg. Grn cl. Fine (bkpls). *Antic Hay.* $45/£29

ORTEGA Y GASSET, JOSE. Velazquez, Goya and the Dehumanization of Art. London: Studio Vista, 1972. (Spine top sl worn), o/w Fine in dj (frayed). *Europa.* $34/£22

ORTH, DONALD J. Dictionary of Alaska Place Names. Washington: GPO, 1971. 2nd ed. Frontis, portfolio of 12 color mod relief maps at rear. Blue pict cl. Fine. *Harrington.* $100/£64

ORTON, JOE. Crimes of Passion. London, 1967. 1st Eng ed. Very Nice in card wrappers. *Clearwater.* $39/£25

ORTON, JOE. Entertaining Mr. Sloane. London, 1964. 1st ed. (Eps sl foxed.) Dj. *Typographeum.* $65/£42

ORTON, JOE. Head to Toe. Blond, 1971. 1st UK ed. NF in dj. *Williams.* $55/£35

ORTON, RICHARD H. Records of California Men in the War of the Rebellion, 1861-1867. Sacramento: State Office, 1890. 887pp. Blind-ruled black cl. *Dawson.* $200/£128

ORWELL, GEORGE. Animal Farm. NY: Harcourt, Brace, (1946). 1st Amer ed. VG in dj (worn). *Antic Hay.* $27/£17

ORWELL, GEORGE. Animal Farm. NY: Harcourt, Brace, (1946). 1st Amer ed. Black cl. Fine in dj. *Appelfeld.* $50/£32

ORWELL, GEORGE. Animal Farm. NY, 1946. 1st ed. VG in dj. *Buckley.* $55/£35

ORWELL, GEORGE. Coming Up for Air. NY: Harcourt, Brace, (1950). 1st Amer ed. VG (spine sunned) in dj (lt soil). *Antic Hay.* $75/£48

ORWELL, GEORGE. Dickens, Dali and Others. NY, 1946. 1st Amer ed. Very Nice in dj (sl chipped). *Clearwater.* $78/£50

ORWELL, GEORGE. Down and Out in Paris and London. London: Gollancz, 1933. 1st bk. VG (lt foxed; spine faded, sm ring stain fr cvr; lacks dj). *Gekoski.* $780/£500

ORWELL, GEORGE. The English People. Collins, 1947. 1st ed. (Sl offsetting eps), o/w NF in dj (sl edgeworn). *Sclanders.* $39/£25

ORWELL, GEORGE. The English People. London: Collins, 1947. 1st ed. Pict bds. NF in dj (wear, few tears). *Antic Hay.* $65/£42

ORWELL, GEORGE. The English People. London: Collins, 1947. 1st ed. (Eps dknd), else Fine in dj. *Hermitage.* $75/£48

ORWELL, GEORGE. Homage to Catalonia. NY, (1952). 1st Amer ed. VG in dj. *Argosy.* $85/£54

ORWELL, GEORGE. James Burnham and the Managerial Revolution. London: Socialist Book Centre, 1946. 1st ed. Nice (pp browning) in wrappers (edges sl discolored). *Patterson.* $133/£85

ORWELL, GEORGE. Nineteen Eighty-Four. NY: Harcourt, (1949). 1st Amer ed. VG in blue dj (edgewear, lt chipping). *Captain's Bookshelf.* $75/£48

ORWELL, GEORGE. Nineteen Eighty-Four. London: Secker, 1949. 1st UK ed. VG+ (spine top sl faded) in VG purple dj (sl edgeworn, creased, sl loss). *Williams.* $663/£425

ORWELL, GEORGE. Nineteen Eighty-Four: The Facsimile of the Extant Manuscript. Peter Davison (ed). London/Weston: Secker & Warburg/M&S, 1984. 1st ed. VG in dj. *Cahan.* $65/£42

ORWELL, GEORGE. The Road to Wigan Pier. NY: Harcourt, Brace, (1958). 1st Amer ed. Fine in VG dj (sm bkseller label rear panel). *Hermitage.* $100/£64

ORWELL, GEORGE. The Road to Wigan Pier. London: Gollancz/Left Book Club, 1937. 1st ed, variant issue. 'Abbreviated' ed, consisting of chapters 1-7, and 32 plts. NF in limp orange cl wrappers (faint smudges). *Reese.* $450/£288

ORWELL, GEORGE. Shooting an Elephant and Other Essays. NY: Harcourt, Brace, (1950). 1st Amer ed. One of 4000 ptd. NF (eps lt browned) in dj (sm tears, sl worn). *Antic Hay*. $125/£80

ORWELL, GEORGE. Shooting an Elephant and Other Essays. Secker, 1950. 1st UK ed. VG + in VG dj (sl stained, sm closed tear, related creasing spine top, price-clipped). *Williams*. $70/£45

ORWELL, GEORGE. Shooting an Elephant and Other Essays. London, 1950. 1st ed. (Spine faded), else VG in dj (spine rubbed, rear sl spotted). *Buckley*. $70/£45

OSBORN, CAMPBELL. Let Freedom Ring. Tokyo, (1954). Fine in dj. *Hayman*. $35/£22

OSBORN, CHASE S. Andean Land (South America). Chicago: McClurg, 1909. 2 vols. Fldg color map. Mostly unopened. Pict cl, gilt, mtd cvr illus. VG + (feps removed vol 1). *Bohling*. $15/£10

OSBORN, HENRY FAIRCHILD. Fifty-Two Years of Research, Observation and Publication 1877-1929. NY: Scribner, 1930. 1st ed. Obituary laid in. NF. *Mikesh*. $65/£42

OSBORN, HENRY FAIRFIELD. Men of the Old Stone Age. NY, 1915. 1st ed. (Fep corner clipped; cvrs rubbed.) *King*. $35/£22

OSBORN, HENRY S. Plants of the Holy Land with Their Fruits and Flowers. Phila: Lippincott, 1861 (ca 1859). 1st ed. 174pp (marginal foxing); 6 color ptd plts. Brn cl (sl frayed), gilt. *Karmiole*. $200/£128

OSBORN, KEVIN. Upstate: Two Panoramic Views. Rochester: Visual Studies Workshop, 1976. 1st ed. Inscribed. 22 full-pg photos. (Sl soil on fr), else Fine in stitched ptd wrappers. *Cahan*. $60/£38

OSBORNE, D. Engraved Gems. NY: Holt, Aug 1912. 1st ed. 32 full-pg plts at rear. Buckram (recased). Good (ex-lib). *Scribe's Perch**. $38/£24

OSBORNE, DOROTHY. Letters to Sir William Temple, 1652-54. E. A. Parry (ed). NY, 1888. Extra-illus w/over 35 Fine 19th-cent steel engr ports. Aeg. Full blue morocco, gilt. VG. *Argosy*. $350/£224

OSBORNE, DUFFIELD. Engraved Gems. NY, 1912. (Shelfworn, cvr stained, inner joint strengthened.) *Oinonen**. $40/£26

OSBORNE, HAROLD. Indians of the Andes: Aymaras and Quechuas. Cambridge: Harvard Univ, 1952. 2 maps. (Bkpl.) Dj. *Archaeologia*. $45/£29

OSBORNE, JOHN. A Better Class of Person. London: Faber, 1981. 1st UK ed. Fine in dj. *Williams*. $31/£20

OSBORNE, JOHN. A Bond Honoured. London: Faber, 1966. 1st UK ed. Fine in NF dj (price-clipped). *Williams*. $28/£18

OSBORNE, JOHN. Inadmissible Evidence. NY: Grove, (1965). 1st ed. NF in dj. *Antic Hay*. $25/£16

OSBORNE, JOHN. Luther. London: Faber & Faber, (1961). 1st ed. Fine in dj. *Jaffe*. $50/£32

OSBORNE, JOHN. Luther. London: Faber, 1961. 1st UK ed. Signed by author and Albert Finney. (Cl faded), o/w VG in dj (browned, rubbed, soiled). *Moorhouse*. $78/£50

OSBORNE, JOHN. A Subject of Scandal and Concern. London: Faber, 1961. 1st UK ed. VG + in self-wraps as issued. *Williams*. $34/£22

OSBORNE, JOHN. Tom Jones. London: Faber, 1964. 1st UK ed. Fine in VG + dj (price-clipped). *Williams*. $31/£20

OSBORNE, JOHN. The World of Paul Slickey. London: Faber, 1959. 1st UK ed. Signed. (Sig fep), o/w VG in dj (sl soiled, rubbed). *Moorhouse*. $70/£45

Osbourne's Pictorial Alphabet. Osbourne, n.d. (ca 1835). 76x70mm. 28 engr cards by H. Wallis (1 trimmed 1mm shorter, glue trace back of some; sl spotting edges). Dec white/blue floral mod box, silk tassel. *Hobbyhorse*. $900/£577

OSBOURNE, KATHARINE D. Robert Louis Stevenson in California. Chicago: A.C. McClurg, 1911. 1st ed. 69 photos. Teg. Cl-backed bds, emb dec fr cvr, gilt-lettered leather spine label. Fine (bkpl; cvrs lt soiled). *Argonaut*. $75/£48

OSBOURNE, LLOYD. An Intimate Portrait of R. L. S. NY: Scribner, 1924. 1st Amer ed. Fine. *Graf*. $15/£10

OSGOOD, CORNELIUS. Winter. NY, c. 1953. 1st ed. Cl-backed bds. VG in dj (frayed). *High Latitude*. $25/£16

OSGOOD, ERNEST STAPLES. The Field Notes of Captain William Clark 1803-1805. New Haven: Yale Univ, 1964. 1st ed. Fine in dj (rubbed, chipped). *Hermitage*. $325/£208

OSLER, WILLIAM (ed). Montreal General Hospital.... Volume 1. Montreal: Dawson Bros, 1880. xxi,369pp; 9 plts (some mislabeled as belonging to vol II). Nice (bkpl, bkpocket). *Goodrich*. $595/£381

OSLER, WILLIAM. Aequanimitas and Other Addresses. Phila, 1905. 1st ed, 2nd ptg. VG. *Fye*. $150/£96

OSLER, WILLIAM. Aequanimitas and Other Addresses. London: H.K. Lewis, 1906. 2nd Eng ed. Red cl (lt soiled, spine lt faded). *Glenn*. $90/£58

OSLER, WILLIAM. Aequanimitas with Other Addresses to Medical Students, Nurse and Practitioners of Medicine. Phila: Blakiston, 1905. Edges deckled, uncut. Red cl (sl rubbed). Nice. *Goodrich*. $125/£80

OSLER, WILLIAM. Aequanimitas with Other Addresses. Phila, 1932. 3rd ed. VG. *Fye*. $35/£22

OSLER, WILLIAM. Aequanimitas. London: H.K. Lewis, 1928. 2nd ed, 8th imp. Red cl. VG in dj (section lacking). *White*. $23/£15

OSLER, WILLIAM. Aequanimitas. Phila, 1932. (3rd ed.) Portuguese copy. Grn cl bds (sl worn). VG. *Doctor's Library*. $50/£32

OSLER, WILLIAM. An Alabama Student and Other Biographical Addresses. London, 1909. 1st ed, 2nd ptg. VG. *Fye*. $125/£80

OSLER, WILLIAM. An Alabama Student and Other Biographical Addresses. London, 1909. 1st ed. VG (extrems sl worn). *Doctor's Library*. $150/£96

OSLER, WILLIAM. An Alabama Student and Other Biographical Essays. Oxford/London, NY, Toronto: Clarendon/Henry Frowde, 1908. 1st ed. Frontis. Red cl. (Section cut away fep, sig frontis verso; spine faded, 2 nicks), o/w VG. *White*. $101/£65

OSLER, WILLIAM. Bibliotheca Osleriana. Oxford, 1929. Buckram (joints repaired, lt worn). *Hatchwell*. $429/£275

OSLER, WILLIAM. Case of Obliteration of the Portal Vein (Ptlephlebitis Adhesiva). N.p., n.d. 8pp. VG in orig ptd wrappers. *Argosy*. $75/£48

OSLER, WILLIAM. The Collected Essays of Sir William Osler. John McGovern and Charles Roland (eds). Birmingham, 1985. 1st ed. 3 vols. Full leather. VG. *Fye*. $200/£128

OSLER, WILLIAM. Contributions to Medical and Biological Research Dedicated to Sir William Osler.... NY: Hoeber, 1919. Ltd to 1500. 2 vols. Frontis vol 1. (Inner hinge vol 2 split; cl sl rubbed.) *Goodrich*. $125/£80

OSLER, WILLIAM. The Evolution of Modern Medicine. New Haven, 1921. 1st ed. Contents VG (inner hinges cracked, shaken; binding rubbed). *Fye*. $125/£80

OSLER, WILLIAM. Incunabula Medica...1467-1480. Oxford, 1923. Rpt ed. 150 ltd ed facs. Fine. *Doctor's Library*. $150/£96

OSLER, WILLIAM. Modern Medicine. Its Theory and Practice.... Phila: Lea & Febriger, 1913. 2nd ed. 5 vols. Fair set (lib stamps, dampstaining, some vols shaken). *Goodrich*. $75/£48

OSLER, WILLIAM. The Principles and Practice of Medicine. Edinburgh/London: Young J. Pentland, 1892. 1st British ed, 1st state, w/misspelling 'Georgias' in Platonic inscription. Thick 8vo. xvi,(1),1079(39 ads)pp. VG (inner hinges started; corners lt shelfworn). *Glaser*. $2,400/£1,538

OSLER, WILLIAM. The Principles and Practice of Medicine. NY: Appleton, 1892. 1st ed, 2nd issue. Ads dated Sept 1892. Rich blue calf (rebound), raised bands, tooled bds. Internally VG (owner note). *Goodrich*. $795/£510

OSLER, WILLIAM. The Principles and Practice of Medicine. NY: D. Appleton, 1892. 1st ed, 1st state, w/misspelling 'Georgias' in quotation from Plato on leaf preceding table of contents, and w/2nd sequence of ads dated November, 1891. Tall, thick 8vo. xvi,(2),1079,(6 ads),(8 ads)pp. Orig 1/2 morocco (spine ends sl scuffed, frayed, corners sl bumped, fr joint just starting, few sm ink spots on fore-edge). VG. *Glaser*. $2,400/£1,538

OSLER, WILLIAM. The Principles and Practice of Medicine. NY, 1899. 3rd ed. 1/2 calf. Good (spine partially removed; soiled cl, stain to fore-edge; extrems worn). *Doctor's Library*. $150/£96

OSLER, WILLIAM. Science and Immortality. Boston, 1904. 1st ed, 1st ptg. VG. *Fye*. $125/£80

OSOFSKY, GILBERT (ed). Puttin' on Ole Massa. NY: Harper & Row, (1969). 1st ed. VG in pict dj. *Petrilla*. $25/£16

OSSENDOWSKY, FERDINAND. Man and Mystery in Asia. London: Arnold, 1924. 1st ed. Frontis port. Blue cl (sm tear spine top), else VG. *Terramedia*. $30/£19

OSSOLI, MARGARET FULLER. At Home and Abroad, or Things and Thoughts in America and Europe. Boston: Crosby, Nichols, 1856. 2nd ed. (Sl rubbed, spine lightened.) *Sadlon*. $20/£13

OSSOLI, MARGARET FULLER. Memoirs of Margaret Fuller Ossoli. Boston: Phillips, Sampson, 1852. 1st ed. 2 vols. Black cl, gilt. (Spine ends chipped), else Bright set. BAL 6501. *Macdonnell*. $100/£64

OSSOLI, MARGARET FULLER. Woman in the Nineteenth Century. Arthur B. Fuller (ed). Boston: Jewett, 1855. 1st ed thus. 428pp. VG (spine extrems worn). BAL 6503. *Second Life*. $175/£112

OSTEN, EARL. Tournament Fly and Bait Casting. NY: A.S. Barnes, 1946. 1st ed. Red buckram. Fine in pict dj (chipped). *Biscotti*. $20/£13

OSTROFF, EUGENE. Western Views and Eastern Visions. (Washington): Smithsonian Inst Traveling Exhibition Service, 1981. 1st ed. (Owner stamp, price sticker remnants), else VG in stiff wrappers, mtd photo. *Cahan*. $30/£19

OSTROGORSKI, M. The Rights of Women. London: Allen & Unwin, 1908. 2nd Eng ed. Red cl (worn). VG (leaves browned, ex-libris). *Second Life*. $95/£61

OSWALD, RICHARD. Memorandum on the Folly of Invading Virginia.... Charlottesville, VA, 1953. 1st ed. Ltd to 750. Rev copy w/prospectus. Port. Cl-backed bds. (Sl faded), else VG. *King*. $35/£22

OTIS, CHARLES AUGUSTUS, JR. Here I Am. Cleveland: Buehler Printcraft Corp, 1951. Signed. Grn cl. VG. *Bohling*. $25/£16

OTIS, CHARLES HERBERT. Michigan Trees. Ann Arbor: Regents of the Univ of MI, 1931. 9th ed. Frontis, map. NF. *Connolly*. $25/£16

OTIS, GEORGE ALEXANDER. A Report on the Excisions of the Head of the Femur for Gunshot Injury. Washington: Surgeon General's Office, Jan. 2, 1869. 1st ed. 3 full-pg engr plts. Full calf. VG. *Argosy*. $350/£224

OTIS, JAMES. Toby Tyler, or Ten Weeks with a Circus. NY: Harper, 1881. 1st ed, 1st bk. Pict lt brn cl. (Lt dampstain some pp; name), o/w VG in custom slipcase. *Bernard*. $175/£112

OTLEY, JONATHAN. A Descriptive Guide to the English Lakes. Keswick: The Author, 1842. 7th ed. viii,220pp; fldg map hand-colored in outline. Blind-stamped cl (spine, edges faded), gilt. *Hollett*. $195/£125

OTNESS, HAROLD M. Lewis Osborne in Oregon, a Personal Memoir. Portland: Twombly, (1990). 1st ed, 1st ptg. #50/150. VF. *Perier*. $30/£19

OTTLEY, WILLIAM. Collection of One Hundred and Twenty-Nine Fac-Similes of Scarce and Curious Prints.... London: Sold by Longman et al, 1828. 1st ed. Engr title, 117 India proof facs + duplicate set of 13 niello prints finished in silver (tarnishing). Early 1/2 morocco (sl worn, soiled). Sound. (Lt foxing), else Contents VG. *Waverly**. $385/£247

OTTO, WHITNEY. How to Make an American Quilt. NY, 1991. 1st Amer ed, 1st bk. Signed. Fine in Fine dj. *Polyanthos*. $45/£29

OTTO, WHITNEY. How to Make an American Quilt. NY: Villard, 1991. 1st ed, 1st bk. Fine in Fine dj. *Else Fine*. $65/£42

OTWAY, THOMAS. The Complete Works of Thomas Otway. Montague Summers (ed). Bloomsbury, 1926. Ltd to 1250. 3 vols. Brn buckram-backed tan bds, ptd paper title labels. Nice set. *Cady*. $100/£64

OTWAY, THOMAS. The Complete Works.... Montague Summers (ed). Nonesuch, 1926. 1st ed. Ltd to 1250 sets. 3 vols. Uncut, partly unopened. Buckram-backed bds, paper labels (1 lt rubbed, chipped). Good. *Cox*. $117/£75

OTWAY, THOMAS. The Works of Mr. Thomas Otway. London: C. Bathhurst et al, 1768. Port, 310,408,382pp. Full calf (rebacked in style). *Cullen*. $175/£112

OUGHTON, FREDERICK. Grinling Gibbons and the English Woodcarving Tradition. Stobart, 1979. NF in dj. *Hadley*. $39/£25

OUIMET, FRANCIS. A Game of Golf: A Book of Reminiscence. Boston: Houghton Mifflin, 1932. 1st ed. #238/550 ptd. Signed. (Spine, extrems sunned; lacks slipcase), else VG in glassine. *Pacific**. $1,265/£811

Our Bunny Pets. Ernest Nister, n.d. (ca 1900). 4to. 10 lg color pictures mtd on heavyweight card pp, cl hinges. Pict bds, cl spine (ends, corners worn, sl rubbed, mks). VG. *Bookmark*. $44/£28

Our New Friends. Scott, Foresman, 1946. Dick and Jane reader. 5.5x7.5. 191pp. Pict cl. (Interior dingy, finger mks, pencil; bumped, shelfworn), o/w VG. *My Bookhouse*. $45/£29

OURSLER, WILL and LAURENCE DWIGHT SMITH. Marijuana. The Facts. The Truth. NY: Paul S. Ericksson, 1968. 1st ed. Fine in NF dj. *Beasley*. $35/£22

OUSPENSKY, LEONID and VLADIMIR LOSSKY. The Meaning of Icons. Boston Book & Art Shop, (1969). 1st ed. 1 fldg plt, 12 color plts. Brick red cl. Fine in dj. *Karmiole*. $100/£64

OUSPENSKY, P. D. A New Model of the Universe. NY: Knopf, 1931. 1st ed. (1pg roughly opened), o/w NF. *Beasley*. $75/£48

OUSPENSKY, P. D. Strange Life of Ivan Osokin. NY: Holme, 1947. 1st US ed. (Fore-edges spotted), else VG+ in dj. *Lame Duck*. $45/£29

OUSPENSKY, P. D. Talks with a Devil. NY: Knopf, 1973. 1st ed. Fine in NF dj. *Antic Hay*. $25/£16

OUTCAULT, R. F. Buster Brown, His Dog Tige and Their Troubles. London: Chambers, n.d. (1903). 1st Eng ed. Horizontal folio. (Tp creased; plain sides, margins damp-mkd; sm tear, edge-chip.) Pict card cvrs, cl spine. (Mks, creasing), else Sound. *Bookmark.* $101/£65

OUTERBRIDGE, PAUL. Photographing in Color. NY: Random House, 1940. 1st ed. 14 tipped-in color plts. VG in dj (stained, worn), mtd color photo. *Cahan.* $275/£176

OUTLAND, CHARLES. Stagecoaching on El Camino Real...1861-1901. Glendale: A.H. Clark, 1973. 1st ed. (Ex-lib), o/w VG in VG dj. *October Farm.* $45/£29

OUTLAND, CHARLES. Stagecoaching on El Camino Real...1861-1901. Glendale: Clark, 1973. 1st ed. One of 1493. 2 maps (1 fldg). VF in pict dj. *Argonaut.* $90/£58

OUTLAW, EDWARD R., JR. Old Nag's Head. Elizabeth City, NC: The Author, 1956. Rev 2nd ptg. Map. NF in pict heavy wrappers. *Connolly.* $15/£10

Outline of the Life and Works of Col. Paul Revere. Newburyport, MA: Towle Mfg Co, (1901). Cl-backed bds, paper spine, cvr labels. (Sl abrasion cvr label), o/w NF. *Sadlon.* $30/£19

Outre-Mer; A Pilgrimage Beyond the Sea. (By Henry Wadsworth Longfellow.) NY, 1835. 1st ed thus, 2nd state vol 2. 2 vols. Inserted cat vol 1 BAL's cat 'B.' Orig coarse-grained grn cl (spine sl sunned, lt foxed). Very Nice. *Kane*.* $150/£96

OVENDEN, GRAHAM (ed). A Victorian Album. NY: Da Capo, 1975. 1st Amer ed. 119 photo plts. Fine in NF pict dj. *Cahan.* $75/£48

OVENDEN, GRAHAM. Clementina: Lady Hawarden. London/NY: Academy Editions/St. Martin's, 1974. 1st ed. 107 plts. (Neat stamp), else Fine in NF dj. *Cahan.* $50/£32

OVENDEN, GRAHAM. Hill and Adamson Photographs. London/NY: Academy Editions/St. Martin's, 1973. 1st US ed. (Owner stamp), else Fine in dj. *Cahan.* $35/£22

Overland to the Pacific. San Diego: Overland Mail Centennials, 1957-1958. Dbl map, facs insert. VG (lt soiled, label added) in pict wraps. *Bohling.* $20/£13

OVERTON, FRANK and W. DENNO. The Health Officer. Phila, 1919. 1st ed. VG. *Fye.* $100/£64

OVERTON, FRANK and W. DENNO. The Health Officer. Phila, 1919. 1st ed. Good (extrems worn, spine chipped, hinges starting). *Doctor's Library.* $100/£64

OVERTON, GRANT. Cargoes for Crusoes. NY/Boston, (1914). 1st ptg. Good. *Hayman.* $15/£10

OVID. The Art of Love. NY: LEC, 1971. One of 1500 numbered, signed by Eric Fraser (illus). 10 plts. Gilt-stamped full vellum. Mint in bd slipcase. *Argosy.* $150/£96

OVID. Metamorphoses. NY: LEC, 1958. #417/1500 signed by Hans Erni (illus) and Giovanni Mardersteig (ptr). As New in dj, pub's slipcase. *Hermitage.* $275/£176

OVID. Metamorphoses. Samuel Garth et al (trans). Verona: LEC, 1958. Ltd to 1500 signed by Hans Erni (engrs) and Giovanni Mardersteig (designer). 15 copper engrs. White linen over pale grn Italian block-ptd pastepaper bds. VF in dj, slipcase. *Truepenny.* $450/£288

OWEN, CHANDLER. Negroes and the War. (Washington): US Office of War Info, 1942. VG in pict self-wraps (center crease). *Petrilla.* $50/£32

OWEN, DAVID DALE. Report of a Geological Survey of Wisconsin, Iowa, and Minnesota.... Phila, 1852. 2 vols. 638pp; 27 full-pg plts. VG (cl faded, hinges weak). *Bohling.* $150/£96

OWEN, GUY. The Flim-Flam Man and the Apprentice Grifter. NY: Crown, (1972). Fine in VG dj (1-inch tear fr panel, sl rubbed). *Between The Covers.* $75/£48

OWEN, JOHN and EMANUEL BOWEN. Britannia Depicta or Ogilby Improv'd. London: Tho. Bowles, 1736. 4th ed. 4to. Engr title, 8pp letterpress tables, 137 leaves of engr maps. (Sm tear title, part of margin torn away.) Contemp tree calf (fr joints split, spine ends chipped, lt rubbed), gilt-dec spine. *Christie's*.* $842/£540

OWEN, JOHN. The Journals and Letters of Major John Owen, Pioneer of the Northwest 1850-1871.... Seymour Dunbar (ed). NY, 1927. #3/50. 2 vols. 2 maps, 30 plts. Orig 1/2 vellum (bkpls removed, labels removed lower spine). Howes O163. *Ginsberg.* $350/£224

OWEN, JOHN. The Journals and Letters of Major John Owen, Pioneer of the Northwest 1850-1871.... Seymour Dunbar (ed). NY: Edward Eberstadt, 1927. Ltd to 550 sets, of which 50 (incl this one) were ptd on lg paper, this set unnumbered. Inscribed by W. R. Coe. 1/2 vellum, paper bds. (Bkpl removed, spines soiled), else Fine in slipcase. Howes O163. *Reese.* $500/£321

OWEN, JOHN. The Journals and Letters of Major John Owen, Pioneer of the Northwest, 1850-1871.... Seymour Dunbar (ed). NY: Edward Eberstadt, 1927. One of 550 sets. 2 vols. 2 maps, 30 plts. VG. Howes O163. *Reese.* $250/£160

OWEN, M. Wild Geese of the World. London: Batsford, 1980. 1st ed. 8 color plts, 25 dwgs, 25 maps, 30 charts. VG+ in VG dj. *Mikesh.* $37/£24

OWEN, NARCISSA. Memoirs...1831-1901. (Washington, ca 1907.) 1st ed. Inscribed presentation. Frontis port. Grn cl. Howes O164. *Ginsberg.* $350/£224

OWEN, ORVILLE. Sir Francis Bacon's Cipher Story. Volume I. Detroit, 1893. 1st ed. 220pp. (Fr inner hinge exposed), o/w VG. *Middle Earth.* $95/£61

OWEN, THOMAS P. Revolutionary Soldiers in Alabama. Montgomery, 1911. 1st ed. Ptd wrappers. *Ginsberg.* $40/£26

OWEN, W. F. W. Narrative of Voyages to Explore the Shores of Africa, Arabia, and Madagascar. NY: Harper, 1833. 2 vols. 260; viii,240pp. (Browned, prize bkpl, prelims vol 2 creased sl affecting text.) Contemp gilt-ruled morocco (sl rubbed, spines lt faded, joints split). *Edwards.* $195/£125

OWEN, WILFRED. Collected Letters. Harold Owen and John Bell (eds). London: OUP, 1967. 1st ed. NF in VG dj. *Turtle Island.* $75/£48

OWEN, WILFRED. Poems. NY: Huebsch, (1920). 1st Amer ed. Frontis port. (Sl adhesion, surface lift fep; lt soiled, ends worn, loss lower inch of spine.) *Waverly*.* $60/£38

OWENS, BILL. Documentary Photography. Danbury, NH: Addison House, 1978. 1st ed. VG in illus stiff wrappers (lt rubbed, long scrape 1 edge). *Cahan.* $25/£16

OWENS, FRANCES E. Mrs. Owens' Cook Book. Chicago: J.B. Smiley, 1883. 372pp. VG. *Perier.* $85/£54

OXENHAM, JOHN. The Splendour of the Dawn. NY: Longmans, Green, 1930. 1st Amer ed. VG in dj (spine browned, internal reinforcements). *Antic Hay.* $15/£10

OZ, AMOS. My Michael. NY: Knopf, 1972. 1st ed. Fine in dj. *Antic Hay.* $25/£16

OZ, AMOS. Touch the Water Touch the Wind. NY: Harcourt, Brace, Jovanovich, (1973). 1st ed. Fine in dj. *Antic Hay.* $35/£22

OZICK, CYNTHIA. Trust. NY, 1966. 1st ed, 1st bk. NF (top edge lt foxed; sm ink stain bottom rear bds) in NF dj (2 mends, sl rubbing). *Warren.* $150/£96

P

PACHTER, HENRY M. Magic into Science. The Story of Paracelsus. NY: Schuman, 1951. Nice in dj (worn). *Goodrich*. $35/£22

PACHTER, HENRY M. Magic into Science: The Story of Paracelsus. NY, 1951. 1st ed. Dec paper-cvrd bds. VG in dj (tattered). *Doctor's Library*. $35/£22

PACK, REYNELL. Sebastopol Trenches and Five Months in Them. London, 1878. Dbl-pg color frontis, 212pp + 8pp ads; 2 b/w fldg plts. Dec cvr, spine. Good. *Scribe's Perch**. $34/£22

PACKARD, FRANCIS. The History of Medicine in the United States. Phila, 1901. 1st ed. VG. *Fye*. $200/£128

PACKARD, FRANCIS. Life and Times of Ambroise Pare (1510-1590). Hoeber, 1921. 1st ed. (New feps; backstrip dulled), o/w Good + . *Bookcell*. $60/£38

PACKARD, FRANCIS. Some Account of the Pennsylvania Hospital from Its First Rise to the Beginning of the Year 1938...to the Year 1956. Phila: (Pennsylvania Hospital, 1957). 2nd ptg. Fine in dj. *Glaser*. $75/£48

PACKARD, FRANCIS. Some Account of the Pennsylvania Hospital.... Phila, 1938. 1st ed. VG. *Fye*. $75/£48

PACKARD, FRANK L. Jimmie Dale and the Phantom Clue. NY: George H. Doran, 1922. 1st ed. (Name, date fep), o/w VG in dj (sm chips, nicks, edgewear). *Mordida*. $65/£42

PACKARD, RALPH C. Rifles That I Have Used and Designed. N.p.: The Author, 1939. 1st ed. Ltd ed (no limitation stated). (Sl worn.) *Oinonen**. $70/£45

PACKARD, SILAS SADLER. My Recollections of Ohio. (NY, 1890.) 26pp. Navy cl, gilt. VG (cvr edges sl etched). *Bohling*. $85/£54

PACKE, MICHAEL ST. JOHN. The Life of John Stuart Mill. London, 1954. 1st ed. Frontis port. Dj (soiled, sl chipped). *Edwards*. $47/£30

PADDOCK, B. B. History of Texas. Fort Worth and the Texas Northwest Edition. Chicago: Lewis Pub Co, 1922. 1st ed. 4 vols. VG. *Gibbs*. $475/£304

PADDOCK, JUDAH. A Narrative of the Shipwreck of the Ship Oswego, on the Coast of South Barbary. NY, 1818. Morocco. (Foxed, browned throughout.) *Swann**. $92/£59

PADEN, IRENE D. Prairie Schooner Detours. Macmillan, 1949. 1st ed. (Name), else Fine in VG dj (chipped). *Authors Of West*. $30/£19

PADEN, IRENE D. The Wake of the Prairie Schooner. NY: Macmillan, 1943. 1st ptg. (Lg bkpl), o/w VG in dj (frayed), plastic dj added. *Bohling*. $35/£22

PADEV, MICHAEL. Escape from the Balkans. Indianapolis: Bobbs-Merrill, (c. 1943). 1st Amer ed. Red cl, gilt. VG. *Shasky*. $35/£22

PADFIELD, PETER. The Titanic and the Californian. NY: John Day, (1966). 1st US ed. VG in VG dj (sl wear). *Gravesend*. $75/£48

PADGETT, LEWIS. Mutant. NY: Gnome, (1953). 1st ed. Fine + in Fine dj. *Mcclintock*. $150/£96

PAGDEN, A. R. (ed). Hernan Cortes; Letters from Mexico. NY: Grossman, 1971. Good in dj. *Archaeologia*. $35/£22

PAGE, BRUCE et al. Philby, The Spy Who Betrayed a Generation. London, 1968. 1st ed. VG in dj. *Typographeum*. $32/£21

PAGE, C. D. History of the Fourteenth Regiment, Connecticut Vol. Infantry. Meriden, 1906. 1st ed. Dec cvr. Good. *Scribe's Perch**. $140/£90

PAGE, D. Advanced Text-Book of Geology, Descriptive and Industrial. London, 1861. 3rd ed. 447pp + 16pp ads. (Spine head worn.) *Henly*. $22/£14

PAGE, ELIZABETH. Wild Horses and Gold. NY: Farrar & Rinehart, 1932. 1st ed. VG. *October Farm*. $30/£19

PAGE, JOHN LLOYD WARDEN. In Russia Without Russian. Plymouth: Bowering, 1898. 1st ed. xii,192pp; 11 plts. VG. *Hollett*. $70/£45

PAGE, ROSWELL. Thomas Nelson Page, a Memoir of a Virginia Gentleman. NY: Scribner, 1923. Frontis port. Cl-backed bds, ptd spine label. VG + (blindstamp, bkpl, sig). *Bohling*. $14/£9

PAGE, THOMAS N. The Old Gentleman of the Black Stock. NY: Scribner, 1901. 7 plts by H.C. Christy. Dec cvr, spine. Good (fr hinge weak). *Scribe's Perch**. $22/£14

PAGE, THOMAS N. Santa Claus's Partner. NY: Scribner, 1899. 1st ed. 12mo. 177pp; 8 illus by W. Glackens. Gilt-dec red emb cl (spine, corners sl bumped). VG. *Dower*. $20/£13

Pageant of Youth. Moscow/Leningrad: State Art Pub, 1939. 1st ed. Pict eps. Textured cl, blind-emb cvr vignette. (Cl lt soiled), o/w NF. *Cahan*. $850/£545

PAGET-FREDERICKS, J. Miss Pert's Christmas Tree. NY: Macmillan, 1929. 1st ed. 9 x 12. Fine in dj. *Cattermole*. $50/£32

PAHER, STANLEY W. Colorado River Ghost Towns. Las Vegas, 1976. 1st ed. Map. Fine in Fine dj w/mylar protector. *Five Quail*. $27/£17

PAIN, WILLIAM. The Practical Builder, or Workman's General Assistant. London: I. & J. Taylor, 1789. 4th ed, rev. 4to. (Lt foxing.) 83 full-pg plts. Contemp full calf (dry; hinges weak). 4-pg 2-leaf folio, 'Catalog of Modern Books on Architecture,' bound in rear. *Cullen*. $825/£529

PAIN, WILLIAM. The Practical Builder. London: I&J Taylor, 1793. 5th ed. 27x21. 9ff, 83 engr plts (1 mtd). (Sm tear tp neatly repaired.) Recent red leather. *Ars Artis*. $546/£350

PAIN, WILLIAM. The Practical House Carpenter. London: J. Taylor, 1805. 7th ed. 22x18. Tp, 2ff, 146 engr plts w/descriptive ff A-P, 30-pg price list. Contemp leather. *Ars Artis*. $585/£375

PAINE, ALBERT BIGELOW. The Lure of the Mediterranean. NY/London: Harper, 1921. (Sl rubbed, soiled), o/w VG. *Worldwide*. $18/£12

PAINE, ALBERT BIGELOW. Mark Twain, a Biography. NY: Harper, 1912. 1st ed, 1st ptg. 3 vols. Teg. Red cl, gilt. (Corner bumped), else VF set. BAL II:251. *Macdonnell*. $225/£144

PAINE, ALBERT BIGELOW. Mark Twain. NY, 1912. 1st Amer ed. 4 vols. Teg, uncut. Fine set (spines sl sunned). *Polyanthos*. $125/£80

PAINE, M. Letters on the Cholera Asphyxia. NY, 1832. Inscribed presentation. viii,160pp. (Eps foxed.) 1/2 cl (faded, bds soiled). *Whitehart*. $304/£195

PAINE, ROBERT TREAT and ALEXANDER SOPER. The Art and Architecture of Japan. Balt: Penguin, 1955. 1st ed. (Cl sl rubbed), o/w VG. *Worldwide*. $35/£22

PAINE, THOMAS. Rights of Man. London, 1791. 5th ed. (Sl soil, bkpl.) Contemp tree calf (rubbed). *Freeman**. $80/£51

PAINE, THOMAS. The Rights of Man. (NY): LEC, 1961. One of 1500 numbered, signed by Lynd Ward (illus). Fine in pub's slipcase. *Hermitage*. $165/£106

Painting in Italy in the Eighteenth Century: Rococo to Romanticism. Chicago: Art Inst, 1970. Good in wraps. *Washton*. $75/£48

Paintings by the Great Dutch Masters of the Seventeenth Century. NY: Duveen Galleries, 1942. Good in wraps. *Washton*. $15/£10

PAIRPOINT, ALFRED. Uncle Sam and His Country; or, Sketches of America in 1854-55-56. London: Simpkin, 1857. 1st ed. 346pp. (Sm emb stamp tp; lt lib #s spine.) *Ginsberg.* $375/£240

PALANQUE, J. R. et al. The Church in the Christian Roman Empire. Ernest C. Messenger (trans). London: Burns Oates & Washbourne, 1949. 2 vols. Black cl. VG. *Turtle Island.* $55/£35

PALARDDY, JEAN. The Early Furniture of French Canada. Eric McLean (trans). Toronto/NY: Macmillan/St. Martin's Press, 1965. 1st ed in English. 11 color plts. Gilt-titled red cl. NF. *Cahan.* $165/£106

PALAU I FABRE, JOSEP. Pablo Picasso: The Early Years, 1881-1907. NY: Rizzoli, (1981). VG in dj, box. *Argosy.* $125/£80

PALEY, GRACE. Enormous Changes at the Last Minute. NY: FSG, (1974). 1st ed. Mint in dj. *Jaffe.* $50/£32

PALGRAVE, FRANCIS TURNER. A Golden Treasury of Songs and Lyrics. NY, 1911. 1st Parrish ed. 8 color plts by Maxfield Parrish. Color cvr label. (Lt worn.) *Freeman*.* $85/£54

PALGRAVE, FRANCIS TURNER. A Golden Treasury of Songs and Lyrics. NY: Duffield, 1911. 1st ed thus. 8 VG color plts by Maxfield Parrish. Pict eps. Dk navy cl (sl worn, rubbed), gilt, lg mtd color pict label fr cvr. *Baltimore*.* $150/£96

PALGRAVE, WILLIAM GIFFORD. Personal Narrative of a Year's Journey Through Central and Eastern Arabia (1862-63). London: Macmillan, 1869. 5th ed. 427pp; 6 maps and plans. Full calf gilt prize binding (sl scraped, neatly recased), new spine label. *Hollett.* $117/£75

PALLADINO, L. B. Indian and White in the Northwest—A History of Catholicity in Montana, 1831-1891. Lancaster, PA: Wichersham, 1922. 2nd enlgd ed. Emb cvr. VG. Howes P40. *Perier.* $85/£54

PALLADIO, ANDREA. The Architecture of A. Palladio in Four Books.... London: The Author, 1721. 2 vols bound in 1. 215 engrs (lacks frontis, port, gathering C; soil, staining, leaves lt browned). Mod 1/2 calf. *Christie's*.* $789/£506

PALLADIO, ANDREA. The First Book of Architecture. Pr. Le Muet (trans). London: G. Sawbridge, 1708. 7th ed. 20x16. Engr frontis, 2ff, 239pp (recte 237pp i.e. no p.173/4 issued); inc 63 engr plts + 7 fldg plts (the one at pg 14 showing a continuous wall is missing the short fldg portion, 1 plt frayed at fold, worm hole in blank upper margin p.199/218 not affecting text or plt; few stains). Contemp leather (neatly rebacked). *Ars Artis.* $546/£350

PALLAS, P. S. Travels. London, 1802. 2 vols. (Foxing, offprinting to plts, 1 plt loose, vol 1 lacks plt 24, vol 2 lacks plt 23.) Mod brn cl (sl rubbed). *Metropolitan*.* $300/£192

PALLIS, MARCO. Peaks and Lamas. NY: Knopf, 1949. 3rd ed. 73 plts, 3 maps. VG. *Worldwide.* $40/£26

PALLISER, FANNY BURY. History of Lace. London, 1902. Dj (chipped, partly faded). *Swann*.* $57/£37

PALLOTTINO, MASSIMO et al. Art of the Etruscans. Thames & Hudson, 1955. Dj (sl chipped). *Edwards.* $31/£20

PALM, SWANTE. Notes of a Texas Book-Collector 1850-1899. TX Book Club, 1950. (Inscrip, sl worn, faded.) Ptd wraps. *Bohling.* $50/£32

PALMER, A. H. The Life of Joseph Wolf, Animal Painter.... London: Longmans, Green, 1895. 1st ed. Frontis photo port, 328pp; 53 b/w plts. Blue cl, gilt. (Fore-edges lt dampstained), o/w Very Bright. *Sotheran.* $418/£268

PALMER, A. H. The Life of Joseph Wolf. London: Longmans, Green, 1895. xviii,328pp; 54 plts. (Lt foxing, joints cracked; sm snag spine head.) *Hollett.* $218/£140

PALMER, B. M. The Life and Letters of James Henley Thornwell. Richmond: Whittet & Shepperson, 1875. 1st ed. Port, xi,614pp. (Cl sl spotted, worn), else Good. *Brown.* $25/£16

PALMER, B. M. The Life and Letters of James Henly Thornwell.... Richmond, 1875. xi,(i),614pp; port. (Spine faded.) *Wantagh.* $50/£32

PALMER, BROOKS. A Treasury of American Clocks. NY: Macmillan, 1967. 8th ptg. Frontis. VG in dj. *Weber.* $18/£12

PALMER, E. H. The Desert of the Exodus. Cambridge, 1871. 2 vols. Hand-color frontis (partly detached), xx,576pp (ink stamp tp, 1/2 titles); 14 litho plts (incl frontis). (Corners, joints sl rubbed, spine chipped, spine # remains.) *Edwards.* $195/£125

PALMER, E. L. Fieldbook of Natural History. NY: Whittlesey, 1949. 1st ed. Gilt-dec cl. VG +. *Mikesh.* $25/£16

PALMER, FREDERICK. Clark of the Ohio. NY: Dodd, Mead, 1929. 1st ed. Pict cl (extrems sl rubbed), gilt. *Sadlon.* $25/£16

PALMER, FREDERICK. In the Klondyke. NY: Scribner, 1899. x,(2),218pp. Dec cl. VG. *High Latitude.* $80/£51

PALMER, R. L. English Monasteries in the Middle Ages. London: Constable, 1930. (Cl sl worn.) *Ars Artis.* $47/£30

PALMER, RALPH S. (ed). Handbook of North American Birds. Vol I. New Haven: Yale Univ, 1962. 1st ed. Fine in Good dj. *Books & Birds.* $77/£49

PALMER, ROY. The Water Closet: A New History. Newton Abbot, 1973. 1st ed. VG (bkpl) in Good dj. *Doctor's Library.* $25/£16

PALMER, SAMUEL. Moral Essays on Some of the Most Curious and Significant English, Scotch and Foreign Proverbs. London: R. Bonwicke, 1710. xxxi,384,(16)pp (1st gathering attached to fr cvr, final leaf attached to rear cvr; foxed). Panelled calf (worn, spine eroded, cvrs detached). *New Hampshire*.* $35/£22

PALMER, STUART and FLETCHER FLORA. Hildegarde Withers Makes the Scene. NY: Random House, 1969. 1st ed. Fine in dj. *Mordida.* $45/£29

PALMER, STUART. Rook Takes Knight. NY: Random House, 1968. 1st ed. (Sm rmdr mk bottom pg edges), o/w Fine in dj (spine sl faded, corners worn). *Mordida.* $30/£19

PALMER, T. H. (ed). The Historical Register of the United States. Washington City: The Editor, 1814. 1st ed. 3 vols. x,164,226; (3),iii,132,351; vi,246,328pp. Contemp 3/4 red leather, marbled bds (sl rubbed), gilt-lettered spines. Fine. *Argonaut.* $500/£321

PALMER, T. S. Chronology of the Death Valley Region in California, 1849-1949. (Washington, Byron S. Adams), 1950. Wrappers. *Dawson.* $35/£22

PALMER, W. SCOTT (ed). The Confessions of Jacob Boehma. NY: Knopf, 1920. VG. *Middle Earth.* $65/£42

PALMER, WILLIAM T. The English Lakes. London: A&C Black, 1905. 1st ed. 75 color plts. (Eps lt spotted, browned, joints tender.) Teg. Dec cl (spine sl rubbed, dulled), gilt. *Hollett.* $94/£60

PALMER, WILLIAM T. In Lakeland Dells and Fells. London: C&W, 1903. 1st ed. Frontis. Teg. Gilt-pict cl (hinges sl rubbed; lt spotted, upper joint cracked, lib label pastedown, sm cutting pinned fep). *Hollett.* $31/£20

PALMER, WILLIAM T. Wanderings in the Pennines. London: Skeffington, 1951. 1st ed. VG in dj (sl worn, sm piece torn spine top). *Hollett.* $31/£20

PALMQUIST, PETER E. Carleton E. Watkins: Photographer of the American West. Albuquerque: Amon Carter Museum, 1983. 113 plts. VG in dj. *Argosy*. $75/£48

PALMQUIST, PETER E. With Nature's Children. Eureka, CA: Interface CA Corp, 1976. 1st ed. Frontis port, 17 full-pg b/w photos, map. As New in illus stiff wrappers. *Cahan*. $35/£22

PALOU, FRANCIS. Life of Ven. Padre Junipero Serra. J. Adam (trans). SF: P.E. Dougherty, 1884. 1st ed in English. Frontis port, 156pp. Dec blue cl. (1 pg corner chipped), o/w NF. *Pacific**. $58/£37

PALOU, FRANCISCO. Founding of the First California Missions Under Spiritual Guidance of the Venerable Padre Fray Junipero Serra...1769. SF, 1934. 1st ed thus. Fine in VG dj (spine sunned). *Turpen*. $85/£54

PALOU, FRANCISCO. Historical Memoirs of New California, By Fray Francisco Palou, O.F.M. Herbert E. Bolton (ed). Univ of CA, 1926. 1st ed in English. 4 vols. Blue cl (sl worn, rubbed). NF. Howes P55. *Harrington*. $375/£240

PALOU, FRANCISCO. Historical Memoirs of New California. Herbert E. Bolton (ed). Berkeley, 1926. 1st Eng ed. 4 vols. Frontis. (Ex-lib), o/w NF. Howes P55. *Turpen*. $295/£189

PALOU, FRANCISCO. Historical Memoirs of New California.... Herbert Bolton (ed). Berkeley, 1926. 1st ed in English. 4 vols. Howes P55. *Ginsberg*. $450/£288

PAMP, FREDERIC E., JR. Normandy to the Elbe, XIX Corps. N.p., n.d. (1945?). Wraps (spotted, spine frayed). *King*. $65/£42

PANASSIE, HUGUES. Hot Jazz. NY: M. Witmark, 1934. 1st ed. NF (spine sl sunned, sm tear) in dj (worn, chip). *Beasley*. $250/£160

PANCIROLI, GUIDO. The History of Many Memorable Things Lost. London: John Nicholson, 1715. 1st ed in English. 2 vols. (12),452,(12),16pp. Old calf (nicely rebacked; bkpls), red calf spine labels. *Karmiole*. $400/£256

PANCOAST, CHARLES EDWARD. A Quaker Forty-Niner. Phila: Univ of PA, 1930. 1st ed. Brn cl, gilt spine. (Spine rubbed), else VG. *Pacific**. $109/£70

PANCOAST, JOSEPH. A Treatise on Operative Surgery.... Phila: Carey & Hart, 1844. 380pp, 80 plts. Internally Fresh (lt foxing, outer marginal browning to plts). Orig cl (spine worn, hinges splitting, cvrs rubbed). *Goodrich*. $1,750/£1,122

PANCOAST, JOSEPH. A Treatise on Operative Surgery; Comprising a Description of the Various Processes of the Art, Including All the New Operations. Phila: Carey & Hart, 1844. 1st ed. 4to. 380pp + ads (sl foxed; ink top pp 131-170, not affecting text); 80 plts. Contemp cl (rebacked). *Argosy*. $1,500/£962

PANGBORN, E. A Mirror for Observers. Doubleday, 1954. 1st ed. NF in VG + dj. *Aronovitz*. $150/£96

PANKHURST, E. SYLVIA. The Suffragette Movement. London: Longmans, 1931. 1st ed. NF in dj (sl worn). *Second Life*. $150/£96

PANKHURST, E. SYLVIA. The Suffragette...1905-1911. Boston: The Woman's Journal, 1912. 3rd US ed. Very Nice. *Second Life*. $85/£54

PANNELL, WALTER. Civil War on the Range. L.A., (1943). VG + in pict wrapper. *Bohling*. $30/£19

PANOFSKY, ERWIN. The Life and Art of Albrecht Durer. Princeton, 1955. 4th ed. Good in dj. *Washton*. $65/£42

PANOFSKY, ERWIN. Problems in Titian. Phaidon, 1969. Frontis port. (Ex-lib, ink stamps.) Dj. *Edwards*. $59/£38

PANOFSKY, ERWIN. Problems in Titian. NY, 1969. Good in dj. *Washton*. $75/£48

PANOFSKY, ERWIN. Tomb Sculpture...from Ancient Egypt to Bernini. NY, 1964. Good in dj. *Washton*. $50/£32

PANSHIN, ALEXI. Farewell to Yesterday's Tomorrow. Barron (ed). Berkley/Putnam, 1975. 1st ed. Fine in Fine dj. *Certo*. $25/£16

PANTIN, W. A. Oxford Life in Oxford Archives. Oxford: Clarendon, 1972. *Bickersteth*. $23/£15

PAPAGEORGE, TOD. Walker Evans and Robert Frank: An Essay on Influence. (New Haven): Yale Univ Art Gallery, 1981. 1st ed. 50 full-pg b/w photos. (Owner stamp), else VG in pict stiff wrappers. *Cahan*. $35/£22

Papermaking, Art and Craft, an Account Derived from the Exhibition Presented in the Library of Congress...April 21, 1968. Washington: Library of Congress, 1968. (Edges lt faded), else Fine in white ptd wrappers, black protective sleeve. *Heller*. $40/£26

Papers in Illinois History and Transactions for the Year 1937. Springfield: IL State Hist Soc, 1938. 1st ed. (Sm lightened spots cvrs.) *Sadlon*. $30/£19

PAPUS. The Tarot of the Bohemians. London: Chapman & Hall, 1892. 1st Eng ed. 355pp; foldout. (Spine taped), o/w VG + . *Middle Earth*. $95/£61

PAPWORTH, WYATT. The Renaissance and Italian Styles of Architecture in Great Britain...1450-1700. Batsford, 1883. (Notes, bkpl; upper joint cracked.) 1/2 calf (rubbed; rebound, orig fr wrapper bound in). *Edwards*. $62/£40

Parables of Our Lord. NY: Appleton, 1848. Black papier mache (spine gone, hinges crudely repaired, affecting gutter of title, last leaf). *Freeman**. $80/£51

PARACELSUS. Paracelsus: Selected Writings. Jolande Jacobi (ed). NY, 1951. 1st ed in English. VG in dj. *Fye*. $100/£64

PARACELSUS. Selected Writings. Jolande Jacobi (ed). (NY, 1951.) VG. *Argosy*. $40/£26

PARCHER, MARIE LOUISE and WILL C. PARCHER. Dry Ditches. Bishop: The Authors, (1934). Ptd paper over bds. *Dawson*. $150/£96

PARDOE, MISS. The River and the Desart. Phila: Carey & Hart, 1838. 1st Amer ed. 2 vols. 18,xii,(13)-207; (4),viii,(13)-198,(2)pp (ink name each vol dated 'May 25, 1838,' foxing, browning). Orig cl (nicks), paper labels. VG. *Reese*. $85/£54

PARE, AMBROISE. Apologie and Treatise of Ambroise Pare. Geoffrey Keynes (ed). London: Falcon, 1951. (Lib stamp tp.) Dj (soiled). *White*. $31/£20

PARE, AMBROISE. The Apologie and Treatise of Ambroise Pare.... Geoffrey Keynes (ed). Chicago, 1952. 1st ed. VG. *Fye*. $50/£32

PARE, RICHARD. Photography and Architecture, 1839-1939. Montreal: Canadian Centre for Architecture, 1982. 1st ed. Frontis. Fine in dj (price-clipped). *Cahan*. $125/£80

PAREDES, AMERICO. With His Pistol in His Hand. Austin: Univ of TX, (1958). 1st ed. Fine in Fine dj. *Book Market*. $30/£19

PARETSKY, SARA. Bitter Medicine. NY: William Morrow, 1987. 1st ed. Fine in dj (2-inch closed tear fr panel). *Mordida*. $75/£48

PARETSKY, SARA. Deadlock. London: Gollancz, 1984. 1st UK ed. Fine in dj. *Williams*. $78/£50

PARETSKY, SARA. Killing Orders. NY: Morrow, 1985. 1st ed. Fine in Fine dj (sm chip rear panel). *Beasley*. $100/£64

PARGETER, EDITH. Reluctant Odyssey. London: Heinemann, 1946. 1st Eng ed. VG in VG dj (chipped, fr panel sl creased). *Hadley*. $39/£25

PARIS, J. A. The Life of Sir Humphry Davy. London, 1831. 2nd ed. 2 vols. Port, fldg facs (foxed; text margins pencilled). Contemp 1/2 calf (joints rubbed, vol 1 partly cracked; worn). *Hatchwell*. $78/£50

PARISOT, R. P. The Reminiscences of a Texas Missionary. San Antonio, 1899. 1st ed. 277,(5),(6)pp. Howes P67. *Ginsberg*. $150/£96

PARK, MUNGO. Travels in the Interior Districts of Africa: Performed in the Years 1795, 96 and 97.... London: T. Allman, n.d. (ca 1876?). 2 plts. Gilt-dec cl. VG + . *Mikesh*. $75/£48

PARK, MUNGO. Travels in the Interior of Africa.... London: A.K. Newman, 1817. Frontis, 254,2ads pp. 1/4 calf, red label. VG. *Adelson*. $125/£80

PARK, ORLANDO. Sherlock Holmes, Esq. and John H. Watson, M.D.: An Encyclopaedia of Their Affairs. (IL): Northwestern Univ, 1962. 1st US ed. VG in VG dj. *Gravesend*. $40/£26

PARKER, B. Arctic Orphans. London/Edinburgh: Chambers, n.d. (ca 1910?). N. Parker (illus). Obl 4to. Color pict bds (sl worn). *Oinonen**. $550/£353

PARKER, B. A Book of Baby Birds. Chambers, 1905. 1st ed. Tall 4to. 54pp (pencil mks); 12 half-tone plts by N. Parker. Pict bds (spine chipped, worn). Good. *Bookmark*. $86/£55

PARKER, B. Funny Bunnies. Chambers, c1907. 1st ed. Horizontal folio. (52pp); 12 color plts by N. Parker. Pict bds. (Spine paper chipped away, edges sl rubbed), else VG. *Bookmark*. $226/£145

PARKER, C. C. Compendium of Works on Archery. Phila: MacManus, 1950. One of 300. Frontis engr. NF. *Mikesh*. $75/£48

PARKER, CHARLES H. (ed). The Civil Practice Act of the State of California.... SF: H.H. Bancroft, 1863. Contemp sheep (scuffed, stained). Sound. *Boswell*. $250/£160

PARKER, DOROTHY. Not So Deep as a Well. Viking, 1936. 1st ed. (Sl dull), else VG in dj (faded, sl chipped). *Whiteson*. $31/£20

PARKER, DOROTHY. Sunset Gun. NY: Boni & Liveright, 1928. 1st trade ed. Black cl-backed tan/black dec bds (bumped; sm tear fr bd). *Blue Mountain*. $15/£10

PARKER, E. et al. Fine Angling for Coarse Fish. London, 1930. Good (fr hinge crack) in Fair dj w/pastedown photos. *Scribe's Perch**. $17/£11

PARKER, EDWARD G. Reminiscences of Rufus Choate, the Great American Advocate. NY: Mason Bros, 1860. Grn cl (sl rubbed). Sound. *Boswell*. $65/£42

PARKER, ERIC. Oddities of Natural History. London, n.d. 1st ed. VG. *Smith*. $20/£13

PARKER, FRANK. Anatomy of the San Francisco Cable Car. Stanford Univ, (1946). 1st ed. Ptd wrappers, photo mtd on fr wrapper (dust soiled). *Shasky*. $30/£19

PARKER, FRED R. Manuel Alvarez Bravo. Pasadena: Pasadena Art Museum, 1971. 1st ed. (Owner stamp), else Fine in pict stiff wrappers. *Cahan*. $50/£32

PARKER, G. The Early History of Surgery in Great Britain. London: A&C Black, 1920. 1st ed. 8 plts. Grn cl. (Sig tp), o/w VG. *White*. $44/£28

PARKER, G. H. The Elementary Nervous System. Phila/London: Lippincott, (1919). 1st ed. *Bickersteth*. $78/£50

PARKER, GILBERT. The Liar. Boston: Brown, 1899. 1st Amer ed. Dec grn cl. NF (1 pg roughly opened, chips). *Antic Hay*. $20/£13

PARKER, GILBERT. The Power and the Glory. NY: Harper, 1925. 1st Amer ed. Black cl. VG (ink presentation, sl browned) in VG dj (wear, soil, sm tears). *Antic Hay*. $35/£22

PARKER, HERBERT. Courts and Lawyers of New England. NY: Amer Hist Soc, 1931. 1st ed. 4 vols. Red/gilt spine labels. (Lt foxed; vol 2 spine spotted), o/w VG. *New Hampshire**. $45/£29

PARKER, IAN. Ivory Crisis. London, 1983. NF in dj. *Grayling*. $70/£45

PARKER, JOHN MONROE. An Aged Wanderer. (Bryan, TX: Fred White, Jr., ca 1971.) #23/500. Fine in pict wraps. *Bohling*. $25/£16

PARKER, K. T. The Drawings of Antoine Watteau. London: Batsford, 1931. Ltd to 1000. Color frontis, 100 plts hors-texte. Teg. Interior VF (sm mk cvr, spine sl dull). *Europa*. $156/£100

PARKER, K. T. The Drawings of Antoine Watteau. NY, 1932. One of 1000. 117 plts. (Rubbed, newly rebacked.) *Washton*. $85/£54

PARKER, K. T. The Drawings of Hans Holbein. Phaidon, 1945. 2nd ed. 85 plts, 6 ports. Dj (lt soiled, sl torn). *Edwards*. $39/£25

PARKER, NATHAN HOWE. Iowa as It Is in 1855. Chicago, 1855. Howes calls for only 2 plts; this copy has 9. (Lacks map.) Pub's cl. Howes P83. *Swann**. $69/£44

PARKER, NATHAN HOWE. Iowa as It Is in 1856: A Gazetteer for Citizens, and a Handbook for Immigrants. Chicago, 1856. 6 plts. (Lacks map, foxed, shaken, sl internal defects.) Red cl (sl worn, soiled). *Freeman**. $30/£19

PARKER, NATHAN HOWE. The Minnesota Handbook for 1856-7. Boston: John P. Jewett, 1857. 1st ed. Hand-colored fldg map. Orig gilt/blind-stamped cl (crudely rebacked, spine title hand-lettered). Howes P85. *Sadlon*. $125/£80

PARKER, NATHAN HOWE. The Minnesota Handbook, for 1856-7.... Boston, 1857. 1st ed. 159,(1)pp; lg fldg map. Howes P85. *Ginsberg*. $150/£96

PARKER, OLIVIA. Signs of Life. Boston: David R. Godine, 1978. 1st ed, 1st bk. 53 photo plts. Fine in dj (sl rubbed, sm closed tear). *Cahan*. $125/£80

PARKER, OLIVIA. Under the Looking Glass. Boston: NYGS, 1983. 1st ed, 1st bk. NF in VG dj (spine, edges sunned). *Smith*. $95/£61

PARKER, PERCY SPURLARK. Good Girls Don't Get Murdered. NY: Scribner, (1974). 1st ed. Fine (crown sl faded) in Fine dj (spine sl faded). *Between The Covers*. $165/£106

PARKER, ROBERT B. Ceremony. NY: Delacorte/Seymour Lawrence, 1982. 1st ed. VF in dj. *Mordida*. $45/£29

PARKER, ROBERT B. Early Autumn. NY: Delacorte/Seymour Lawrence, 1981. 1st ed. Fine in dj (sl edgewear). *Mordida*. $45/£29

PARKER, ROBERT B. God Save the Child. Boston: HMCo, 1974. Fine in Fine dj (lt wear). *Between The Covers*. $400/£256

PARKER, ROBERT B. God Save the Child. Andre Deutsch, 1975. 1st Eng ed. Fine in Fine dj. *Certo*. $50/£32

PARKER, ROBERT B. The Godwulf Manuscript. Deutsch, 1974. 1st UK ed, 1st bk. Fine (2 sm ink initials fep) in dj. *Williams*. $75/£48

PARKER, ROBERT B. The Godwulf Manuscript. Boston: Houghton Mifflin, 1974. 1st ed. VF in dj. *Mordida*. $400/£256

PARKER, ROBERT B. The Judas Goat. Boston: Houghton, Mifflin, 1978. 1st ed. Signed. Fine in Fine dj (price-clipped). *Old London*. $95/£61

PARKER, ROBERT B. Mortal Stakes. Boston: HMCo, 1975. 1st ed. (Inscrip), else Fine in NF dj (rubbing gold lettering, spine extrems). *Between The Covers*. $165/£106

PARKER, ROBERT B. Mortal Stakes. Boston: Houghton Mifflin, 1975. 1st ed. Fine in dj (corns, spine top sl worn). *Mordida*. $200/£128

PARKER, ROBERT B. Poodle Springs. London: Macdonald, 1990. 1st Eng ed. One of 250 specially bound, numbered, signed. VF in slipcase. *Mordida.* $75/£48

PARKER, ROBERT B. Promised Land. Boston: Houghton Mifflin, 1976. 1st ed. VF in dj. *Mordida.* $150/£96

PARKER, ROBERT B. Taming a Sea-Horse. London: Viking, 1986. 1st UK ed. Signed. Fine in Fine dj. *Old London.* $30/£19

PARKER, ROBERT B. Valediction. NY: Delacorte/Seymour Lawrence, 1984. 1st ed. VF in dj. *Mordida.* $35/£22

PARKER, ROBERT B. The Widening Gyre. NY: Delacorte/Seymour Lawrence, 1983. 1st ed. Inscribed. VF in dj. *Mordida.* $35/£22

PARKER, ROBERT B. Wilderness. Delacorte, 1979. 1st ed. Fine in Fine dj (sm crease). *Certo.* $45/£29

PARKER, ROBERT B. Wilderness. NY, 1979. 1st ed. NF in NF dj. *Warren.* $50/£32

PARKER, ROBERT B. Wilderness. NY: Delacorte/Seymour Lawrence, 1979. 1st ed. VF in dj. *Mordida.* $85/£54

PARKER, ROBERT B. and JOAN H. Three Weeks in Spring. Boston: Houghton Mifflin, 1978. 1st ed. Fine in dj (sl wear base of spine). *Mordida.* $85/£54

PARKER, SAMUEL. Journal of an Exploring Tour Beyond the Rocky Mountains.... Ithaca, NY: The Author, 1838. 371pp; plt, fldg map. Mod 3/4 gilt morocco, cl. (Tanning, lt foxing, contemp sig), else VG. Howes P89. *Reese.* $500/£321

PARKER, SAMUEL. Journal of an Exploring Tour Beyond the Rocky Mountains.... Ithaca, 1842. 3rd ed. Fldg map (extensive repair to verso), plt. Pub's cl (rebacked w/morocco), orig cl back retained. (Foxed.) Howes P89. *Swann*.* $92/£59

PARKER, SAMUEL. Parker's Exploring Tour Beyond the Rocky Mountains. Minneapolis: Ross & Haines, 1967. Ltd ed rpt. Fldg map laid in. VG in dj. *Dumont.* $25/£16

PARKER, WATSON. Gold in the Black Hills. Norman, 1966. 1st ed. Frontis. Fine in dj (sl worn, price-clipped). *Baade.* $50/£32

PARKER, WILLIAM H. Recollections of a Naval Officer 1841-1865. NY: Scribner, 1883. 1st ed. xv,372,(8)pp. (Sl worn), else VG. Howes P92. *Mcgowan.* $150/£96

PARKER, WILLIAM H. Recollections of a Naval Officer, 1841-1865. NY, 1883. 1st ed. (15),372,(8)pp. (Bkpl removed.) Howes P92. *Ginsberg.* $125/£80

PARKES, M. B. The Medieval Manuscripts of Keble College Oxford. London: Scolar Press, (1979). 1st ed. Rust cl, gilt. Fine in pict grn dj. *Blue Mountain.* $125/£80

PARKHILL, FORBES. The Last of the Indian Wars. N.p.: Crowell-Collier, (1961). 1st ed. Frontis photo, map. VG in dj. *Lien.* $25/£16

PARKINSON, C. NORTHCOTE (ed). Samuel Walters, Lieutenant, R.N. Liverpool Univ, 1949. 1st Eng ed. Buckram (sl mkd, bumped). Dj. *Clearwater.* $47/£30

PARKINSON, C. NORTHCOTE. The Life and Times of Horatio Hornblower. London, 1970. 1st Eng ed. Very Nice in dj (price-clipped). *Clearwater.* $39/£25

PARKINSON, C. NORTHCOTE. The Life and Times of Horatio Hornblower. London: Michael Joseph, 1970. 1st ed. VG in dj. *Hollett.* $70/£45

PARKINSON, RICHARD. The Experienced Farmer. Phila: C. Cist, 1799. 2 vols. xx,275,(276); (ii),292pp (bkpl removed). Contemp Eng 1/2 calf (worn, scraped). *Maggs.* $328/£210

PARKINSON, RICHARD. The Experienced Farmer.... London, 1807. 2 vols. 4 engr plts. Contemp English 1/2 russia; feps watermarked 1811. (Lonsdale bkpl; sl worn, 1 headcap broken.) *Maggs.* $226/£145

PARKINSON, S. A Treatise on Optics. 1870. 3rd ed. viii,352pp. (Eps crinkling, underlining in crayon; cl damp-stained.) *Whitehart.* $39/£25

PARKMAN, E. The Diary of Ebenezer Parkman...First Part...1719-1755. F. G. Wallett (ed). Worcester, 1974. 1st ed in bk form. Good+. *Scribe's Perch*.* $20/£13

PARKMAN, FRANCIS. Francis Parkman's Works. Boston: Little, Brown, 1898. New Library Ed. 12 vols. Teg. 3/4 grn morocco, marbled bds. (Spines, corners sl rubbed), o/w Good set. BAL 15506. *Holmes.* $450/£288

PARKMAN, FRANCIS. History of the Conspiracy of Pontiac, and the War of North American Tribes Against the English Colonies after Conquest of Canada. Little, Brown, 1851. xxiv,630pp; 4 maps (2 dbl-pg). 1/2 leather, gilt-stamped spine, raised bands. Howes P100. *Oregon.* $175/£112

PARKMAN, FRANCIS. History of the Conspiracy of Pontiac, and the War of the North American Indian Tribes.... Boston, 1851. 1st ed. 4 maps. Pub's cl. Howes P100. *Swann*.* $57/£37

PARKMAN, FRANCIS. History of the Conspiracy of Pontiac, and the War of the North American Tribes.... Boston: Little, Brown, 1855. Early ed. 3 maps. VG (blindstamp tp). *Agvent.* $100/£64

PARKMAN, FRANCIS. History of the Conspiracy of Pontiac. Boston: Little, Brown, 1855. xxiv,630pp; 4 maps. (Rubbed.) Howes P100. *Adelson.* $85/£54

PARKMAN, FRANCIS. The Journals of Francis Parkman. Mason Wade (ed). NY: Harper, 1947. 2 vols. VG in djs (sl worn, stained spines), slipcase (worn). *Lien.* $65/£42

PARKMAN, FRANCIS. The Oregon Trail. Boston: Little, Brown, 1894. Author's ed. Frontis, xv,381pp. Teg. (Spine ends sl frayed, sl rubbed, soiled), o/w Good. *Worldwide.* $20/£13

PARKMAN, FRANCIS. The Oregon Trail; Sketches of Prairie and Rocky-Mountain Life. Boston, 1892. Half-title, 411pp. Contemp pigskin (outer fr joint worn, spine scuffed), spine gilt (flaked). Internally VG. Howes P97. *Reese.* $500/£321

PARKMAN, FRANCIS. Vassall Morton. Boston: Phillips, Sampson, 1856. 1st ed. 414pp+6pp ads. Contemp calf-backed marbled bds (hinges cracked, rubbed). Sound. BAL 15451. *M&s.* $100/£64

PARKMAN, FRANCIS. The Works. Boston, 1902. La Salle ed. One of 500 numbered sets. Vols 1-10 (of 20). 8vo. Contemp dk grn morocco, gilt, red morocco onlay, spines in 6 compartments, lettered in 2. *Swann*.* $690/£442

PARKS, GEORGE BRUNER. Richard Hakluyt and the English Voyages. James A. Williamson (ed). NY, 1930. 2nd imp. 32 plts and charts. (Lt marginal browning.) Labels upper bd, spine. *Edwards.* $47/£30

PARKS, GORDON. A Poet and His Camera. NY: Viking/Studio Book, (1968). 1st ed. VG in pict dj (chipped). *Petrilla.* $35/£22

PARKS, JOSEPH HOWARD. General Leonidas Polk C.S.A. The Fighting Bishop. (Baton Rouge): LA State Univ, (1962). 1st ed. NF in NF dj. *Mcgowan.* $125/£80

PARKS, TIM. Family Planning. NY: Grove Weidenfeld, (1989). 1st ed. Promotional material laid in. Fine in dj. *Antic Hay.* $25/£16

PARKS, TIM. Home Thoughts. London, 1987. 1st ed. Fine in dj. *Buckley.* $16/£10

PARKS, TIM. Tongues of Flame. NY: Grove, (1985). 1st ed. Fine in dj. *Antic Hay.* $25/£16

PARKYN, ERNEST A. An Introduction to the Study of Prehistoric Art. London, 1915. 1st ed. Color frontis, 15 plts (1 color). (Spine faded.) *Edwards.* $44/£28

PARLEY, PETER (Pseud of Samuel Griswold Goodrich) (ed). The Travels, Voyages, and Adventures of Gilbert Go-Ahead. NY: J.C. Derby, 1856. 1st ed. 5pp undated ads. Blindstamped dk blue cl, gilt. NF (sm stain fr cvr, erasure fep). *Sumner & Stillman*. $225/£144

PARLEY, PETER. (Pseud of Samuel Griswold Goodrich.) Peter Parley's Tales About the Islands in the Pacific Ocean. Phila, 1841. 12mo. Frontis map, 144pp. Orig 1/2 calf, bds. (Lt foxing), else VG. *Reese*. $400/£256

PARLEY, PETER. (Pseud of Samuel Griswold Goodrich.) Peter Parley's Universal History, on the Basis of Geography. NY: Ivison, Blakeman, Taylor, 1875. New ed. 8vo. 718pp; 20 maps, 125 engrs. (Ink sig fep, repaired missing parts; new reps; few pp restored, inner folds chipped.) Brn linen on bds, 3/4 black roan, gilt (spotted, rubbed, some cl missing), else Good. *Hobby-horse*. $100/£64

PARLEY, PETER. (Pseud of Samuel Griswold Goodrich.) Popular Biography by Peter Parley. NY: Leavitt & Allen, (ca 1855). Gray cl stamped in gilt/blind (spine dull). *Hermitage*. $50/£32

PARLOA, MARIA. First Principles of Household Management and Cookery. Boston: Houghton Mifflin, 1888. New, enlgd ed. 176pp (name). Good. *Second Life*. $45/£29

PARMELIN, HELENE. Picasso: Women. Cannes and Mougins, 1954-1963. Amsterdam: Abrams, n.d. (ca 1964). (Sl worn.) Dj (sl edgeworn). *Oinonen**. $50/£32

PARNELL, THOMAS. Poetical Works. Glasgow: Andrew Foulis, 1786. 4-pg subs list. Later 1/2 calf (worn; 1st few leaves stained). *Argosy*. $125/£80

PAROLA, RENE. Optical Art. NY: Beekman House, 1969. Dj (sl faded). *Edwards*. $39/£25

PARRISH, EDWARD. A Treatise on Pharmacy. Phila, 1864. 3rd ed. 850pp (foxed; inner hinges starting). Brn tooled cl (extrems worn). Good. *Doctor's Library*. $150/£96

PARRISH, JOHN. Remarks on the Slavery of Black People.... Phila: The Author, 1806. 1st ed. Stapled w/orig? marbled paper wraps onto adhesive cl stubs in mod Gaylord pamphlet binder. VG (inscrip, ink #; damping to terminal blank, back wrapper). Howes P104. *Waverly**. $143/£92

PARRISH, LYDIA. Slave Songs of the Georgia Sea Islands. NY, 1942. 1st ed. (Sm abrasion fr cvr label, sm dent bottom edge), else VG in dj (torn, frayed). *King*. $100/£64

PARRISH, LYDIA. Slave Songs of the Georgia Sea Islands. NY: Creative Age, 1942. 1st ed. Map. Pict eps. Black cl, port mtd on cvr. NF in pict dj (worn). *Petrilla*. $200/£128

PARRY, ANN. Parry of the Arctic. London: C&W, 1963. VG in dj. *High Latitude*. $25/£16

PARRY, EDWARD. My Own Way, An Autobiography. London: Cassel, 1932. Crisp in dj (sl worn). *Boswell*. $50/£32

PARRY, JUDGE. Don-Quixote. London: Blackie, 1900. 1st ed thus. 8vo. 245pp; 11 full-pg color illus by Walter Crane. Deckled edges. Red dec cl (Fr hinge sl cracked, spine ends sl bumped), o/w VG. *Dower*. $225/£144

PARRY, WILLIAM. The Last Days of Lord Byron. London, 1825. 1st ed. 8vo. Hand-colored engr frontis, 3 hand-colored aquatint plts (lt offsetting onto facing pp); half-title. Tan calf by Root & Son, gilt. *Swann**. $402/£258

PARSON, BEAUFORT SIMS. Lefthandedness: A New Interpretation. NY: Macmillan, 1924. 1st ed. Inscribed. Straight-grained brn cl, gilt spine. VG. *Gach*. $30/£19

PARSON, EMILY ELIZABETH. Memoir of.... Boston: Little, Brown, 1880. 1st ed. 159pp. Grn cl. VG (hinges tender). *Second Life*. $135/£87

PARSONS, C. S. M. and F. H. CURL. China Mending and Restoration. London: Faber, 1963. 1st ed. 78 plts. Dj (edges rubbed, price-clipped). *Hollett*. $101/£65

PARSONS, CHARLES W. Memoir of Usher Parsons, M.D., of Providence, R.I. Providence: Hammond, Angell, 1870. 1st ed. Frontis port, viii,72pp. Later cl. Very Clean. *Lefkowicz*. $135/£87

PARSONS, EDWARD ALEXANDER. The Wonder and the Glory, Confessions of a Southern Bibliophile. NY: Thistle, 1962. 1st ed. Fine in dj. *Oak Knoll*. $135/£87

PARSONS, ELSIE CLEWS. Isleta Paintings. BAE Bulletin 181. Washington: Smithsonian Inst, 1962. 1st ed. Orange cl, gilt. Fine in NF dj. *Harrington*. $85/£54

PARSONS, FRANK ALVAH. The Psychology of Dress. GC, 1921. (Bumped, spine ends sl worn, frayed.) *Freeman**. $15/£10

PARSONS, J. A Mechanical and Critical Enquiry into the Nature of Hermaphrodites. 1741. liv,156pp (prelims sl foxed); 2 fldg charts. Contemp leather (rebacked). *Whitehart*. $437/£280

PARSONS, JOHN E. The First Winchester—The Story of the 1866 Repeating Rifle. NY: William Morrow, 1960. 2nd ed. Frontis. VG+ in VG dj (edge chips). *Backman*. $40/£26

PARSONS, JOHN E. West on the 49th Parallel. NY: Morrow, 1963. 1st ed. Good (margins lt pencilled) in dj (sl worn). *Lien*. $30/£19

PARSONS, JOHN E. and JOHN S. DU MONT. Firearms in the Custer Battle. Harrisburg: Stackpole, (1953). 1st ed. Issued in pict wrappers, this copy bound in cl. Fine. *Graf*. $60/£38

PARSONS, TALCOTT and KENNETH B. CLARK (eds). The Negro American. Boston/Cambridge: Houghton Mifflin/Riverside, 1966. 1st ed. 32 full-pg b/w photos. (Name stamp), else NF in VG dj. *Cahan*. $50/£32

PARSONS, THEOPHILUS. The Law of Contracts. Boston: Little, Brown, 1873. 6th ed. 3 vols. Contemp sheep (worn, rubbed, spine detached). *Boswell*. $50/£32

PARTINGTON, WILFRED. Forging Ahead. NY, 1939. Frontis port. Fore-edge uncut. Dj (edges, spine lt browned). *Edwards*. $70/£45

PARTINGTON, WILFRED. Forging Ahead. NY: Putnam, 1939. 1st ed. Frontis port, 11 plts. VF in NF dj. *Pirages*. $65/£42

PARTON, JAMES et al. Eminent Women of the Age. Hartford, 1871. 1st ed. 628pp. VG. *Fye*. $100/£64

PARTON, JAMES. General Butler in New Orleans. NY, 1864. 649pp. Good (spine chipped, faded). *Scribe's Perch**. $24/£15

PARTON, JAMES. Life of Andrew Jackson. NY, 1861. 2nd ptg. 3 vols. (Extrems lt worn), o/w VG. *New Hampshire**. $40/£26

PASCAL, BLAISE. Provincial Letters.... NY/Boston: J. Leavitt/Crocker & Brewster, 1828. 1st Amer ed? 319pp. Orig bds, muslin spine, paper spine label. (Text lt spotted; shelfworn, edgeworn), else VG. *Brown*. $15/£10

PASQUINO (J. Fairfax McLaughlin). The American Cyclops, the Hero of New Orleans and Spoiler of Silver Spoons. Balt: Kelly & Piet, 1868. 12 plts. Gilt-stamped grn cl. VG. *Waverly**. $77/£49

PASSAVANT, J. D. Tour of a German Artist in England, with Notices of Private Galleries, and Remarks on the State of Art. London: Saunders & Otley, 1836. 1st ed in English. 2 vols. Engr frontis port, xx,334pp, 2 plts (1 dbl fldg); 323pp, index. Contemp 1/2 calf, marbled bds (sl spotted). *Europa*. $343/£220

PASSMORE, AUGUSTINE C. Handbook of Technical Terms. 1904. (Pencil notes; tp, 1st few ll spotted; bkpl; faded.) *Edwards*. $39/£25

Passports Printed by Benjamin Franklin at His Passy Press. Ann Arbor: William L. Clements Library, 1925. One of 505. Marbled paper bds, blue cl spine, paper title label. (Lt residue from removed bkpl), o/w VG. *Heller.* $100/£64

PASTERNAK, BORIS. I Remember. David Magarshack (trans). (NY): Pantheon, (1959). 1st Amer ed. NF (sm partly erased ink name) in dj (worn, spine faded, few tears). *Antic Hay.* $25/£16

PASTEUR, L. Studies on Fermentation. F. Faulkner & D.C. Robb (trans). 1879. 1st Eng ed. xv,418pp; 12 plts. (Lt dampstaining few pp, mostly marginal), o/w VG in new cl (incorrect title, date on spine). *Whitehart.* $133/£85

PASTEUR, L. Studies on Fermentation. London: Macmillan, 1879. 1st ed in English. xv,(1),418,(2 ads)pp; 12 plts. VG (skillfully rebacked w/orig spine laid down, extrems lt worn). *Glaser.* $485/£311

PASTON, GEORGE. Old Coloured Books. London: Methuen, (1905). 1st ed. viii,48pp (lt foxed); 16 color plts. Red cl (stained), ptd paper spine label (dknd, stained). VG. *Blue Mountain.* $20/£13

PATCHEN, KENNETH. Before the Brave. NY: Random House, 1936. 1st ed, 1st bk. (Sunned spots), o/w Fine in dj (sl worn, lt chipped). *Beasley.* $175/£112

PATCHEN, KENNETH. Outlaw of the Lowest Planet. David Gascoyne (ed). London: Grey Walls, 1946. 1st Eng ed. Very Nice (bkpl, sl bumped) in dj. *Clearwater.* $78/£50

PATCHEN, KENNETH. Pictures of Life and of Death. NY: Padell, 1946. 1st ed. NF in stiff wrappers, illus dj. *Cahan.* $60/£38

PATCHEN, KENNETH. See You in the Morning. NY, (1947). 1st Amer ed. NF in dj (2 sm edge chips, 2 sm edge tears, sm rubbed area rear panel). *Polyanthos.* $30/£19

PATCHEN, KENNETH. The Teeth of the Lion. CT: New Directions, (1942). 1st Amer ed. Wraps. NF in ptd dj (spine sl sunned). *Polyanthos.* $25/£16

PATCHEN, KENNETH. The Teeth of the Lion. Norfolk: New Directions, (1942). 1st ed. (Cvrs sl sunned.) VG in wrappers. *Graf.* $20/£13

PATCHIN, FRANK GEE. The Pony Rider Boys in the Grand Canyon. Phila, (c.) 1912. 252pp + ads. Grey cl. (Spine faded, soiled), else VG. *Five Quail.* $20/£13

PATER, WALTER (retold by). The Marriage of Cupid and Psyche. NY: LEC, 1951. One of 1500 numbered, signed by Edmund Dulac (illus). Gilt-stamped vellum (lt worn). Slipcase (lt scuffed, soiled). *Oinonen*.* $100/£64

PATER, WALTER. An Imaginary Portrait. (London: Daniel, 1894.) 1st ed. One of 150. 1/2 brn polished calf; ptd blue-gray wrappers bound in. *Swann*.* $201/£129

PATER, WALTER. The Renaissance: Studies in Art and Poetry. Verona: LEC, 1976. One of 2000 numbered. 1/4 cl. Slipcase. *Swann*.* $92/£59

PATERSON, KATHERINE. The Great Gilly Hopkins. NY: Crowell, 1978. 1st ed. 6 1/4 x 9 1/2. 148pp. 1/2 cl. Fine in dj. *Cattermole.* $50/£32

PATERSON, LT. COL. A New and Accurate Description of All the Direct and Principal Cross Roads in England and Wales. London: Longman et al, 1811. 15th ed. Marbled flex leather, fold-over flap. VG. *Old London.* $200/£128

PATERSON, LT. COL. A New and Accurate Description of All the Direct and Principal Cross Roads in England and Wales.... London, 1808. 64,527pp; fldg map. 1/2 calf. VG. *Argosy.* $100/£64

PATERSON, WILLIAM. A Narrative of Four Journeys into the Country of the Hottentots and Caffraria, in the Years 1777, 1778, 1779. London: J. Johnson, 1790. 2nd ed. Fldg map (facs only, lacks 19 plts, ex-libris). Early tree calf bds (extrems sl worn, rebacked in sl sunned morocco). *Edwards.* $140/£90

PATERSON, WILLIAM. A Narrative of Four Journeys into the Country of the Hottentots and Caffraria. London: J. Johnson, 1789. Lg fldg map, 17 copper plts. (Lt foxing.) Mod lib binding. Very Nice. *Metropolitan*.* $1,265/£811

PATERSON, WILLIAM. Old Edinburgh Pedlars, Beggars and Criminals. Edinburgh: The Author, 1886. 107,(ii)pp. Uncut. VG in orig wrappers (rubbed, spine stripped). *Hollett.* $39/£25

PATMORE, COVENTRY. Faithful For Ever. Boston: Ticknor & Fields, 1861. 1st Amer ed. 16pp ads dated Dec 1860. Blindstamped brn cl. Fine (Dec 1860 inscrip). *Sumner & Stillman.* $85/£54

PATON, A. A. A History of the Egyptian Revolution.... London: Trubner, 1863. 1st ed. 8vo. 2 vols. xii,395; viii,352pp. Vol 2 uncut. (Sl soiled, shaken.) *Maggs.* $273/£175

PATON, ALAN. Tales from a Troubled Land. NY: Scribner, (1961). 1st Amer ed. NF (rep browned) in dj (wear, lt soil). *Antic Hay.* $25/£16

PATON, ALAN. Too Late the Phalarope. NY: Scribner, 1953. 1st Amer ed. Fine in dj (sl wear, sm tears, sm stain). *Antic Hay.* $20/£13

PATON, JOHN G. John G. Paton, Missionary to the New Hebrides. London: Hodder & Stoughton, 1889/1890. 4th ed, 1st part; 3rd ed, 2nd part. 2 vols. xc,375,(1); xvi,382pp,(1). Blue cl (sl wear), gilt. VG. *Parmer.* $50/£32

PATON, JOHN G. Missionary to the New Hebrides. NY: Revell, 1889. 2 vols. xvii,375; xvi,382pp; map, 14 plts. (Spines chipped.) *Adelson.* $50/£32

PATON, MARGARET WHITECROSS. Letters and Sketches from the New Hebrides. NY: A.C. Armstrong, 1895. Frontis, xiii,382pp (fep removed); color map. Grn cl (lt worn, soiled). *Bohling.* $25/£16

PATON, MARGARET WHITECROSS. Letters and Sketches from the New Hebrides. Jas. Paton (ed). London, 1905. 5th ed. (Feps lt browned; spine sl chipped, sl soil.) *Edwards.* $31/£20

PATRICK, MARSELLA RUDOLPH. Inside Lincoln's Army. David S. Sparks (ed). NY, (1964). 1st ed. VG+ in VG+ dj. *Pratt.* $40/£26

PATTEN, GILBERT. Clif Sterling, Captain of the Nine. McKay, 1910. 1st ed. Pict cvr. Fine. *Plapinger.* $65/£42

PATTEN, WILLIAM (ed). The Book of Sport. NY: J.F. Taylor, 1901. Ltd to 1500 numbered. Teg. Gray cl-backed bds (sl bumped), ptd paper label (sl creased). NF. *Blue Mountain.* $275/£176

PATTEN, WILLIAM and J. E. HOMANS. The New Encyclopedic Atlas and Gazetteer of the World.... NY: P.F. Collier, ca 1909. 3rd ed. Maroon cl (spine base dog-chewed) instead of grn. *Hudson.* $150/£96

PATTERSON, A. W. History of the Backwoods. Pittsburgh: The Author, 1843. Former Newberry Library copy. Fldg frontis map (edge repaired), x,(5)-311pp (lt foxed). Mod lib buckram. Howes P118. *Bohling.* $950/£609

PATTERSON, HARRY. Dillinger. London: Hutchinson, 1983. 1st ed. Fine in Fine dj. *Janus.* $35/£22

PATTERSON, HARRY. To Catch a King. London: Hutchinson, 1979. 1st ed. Fine in dj. *Mordida.* $45/£29

PATTERSON, J. H. In the Grip of the Nyika. NY: Macmillan, 1909. 1st ed. Map. Pict cl. VG. *Adelson.* $75/£48

PATTERSON, J. H. In the Grip of the Nyika.... NY: Macmillan, 1910. 1st Amer ed. 9 maps. Blue gilt pict cl (sl wear), else VG. *Terramedia.* $100/£64

PATTERSON, J. H. The Man-Eaters of Tsavo. London, 1907. 1st ed, 2nd issue. Map. Blue pict cl, gilt. *Maggs.* $125/£80

PATTERSON, J. H. The Man-Eaters of Tsavo. Macmillan, 1908. Frontis, map. Teg. VG. *Cox.* $31/£20

PATTERSON, J. H. The Man-Eaters of Tsavo. London: Macmillan, 1908. Frontis, map. Teg. Blue gilt pict cl. VG. *Terramedia.* $150/£96

PATTERSON, JAMES. The Midnight Club. Boston: Little Brown, 1989. 1st ed. (Mks bottom edge), o/w Fine in dj. *Mordida.* $30/£19

PATTERSON, LAWSON B. Twelve Years in the Mines of California. Cambridge: Miles, 1862. 1st ed. 108pp (bkpl removed). Howes P121. *Ginsberg.* $300/£192

PATTERSON, RHODA. ZYX. Chicago: Soc of Typographic Arts, 1989. 1st ed. 10 1/4 x 15 1/2. 60pp. Fine. *Cattermole.* $35/£22

PATTERSON, RICHARD NORTH. Escape the Night. NY: Random House, 1983. 1st ed. Advance rev copy, slip laid in. VF in dj. *Mordida.* $50/£32

PATTERSON, RICHARD NORTH. The Outside Man. Boston: Little Brown, 1981. 1st ed. Fine in dj (sm scrape spine, short closed tear). *Mordida.* $45/£29

PATTERSON, ROBERT. The Natural History of the Insects. London, 1841. Frontis port, xv,270pp+(i) ads. Emb cl (edges sl worn, discolored, chipped, spine recased; frontis, tp sl spotted, margins sl browned, new eps, ex-lib, ink stamps). *Edwards.* $70/£45

PATTIE, JAMES OHIO. Personal Narrative of James O. Pattie of Kentucky. Timothy Flint (ed). Chicago: Lakeside Classic, 1930. Teg. Dk red cl, gilt. VG+. *Bohling.* $35/£22

PATTIE, JAMES OHIO. Personal Narrative of James O. Pattie, of Kentucky.... Timothy Flint (ed). Cincinnati: Flint, 1833. 2nd ed. 300pp; 5 plts. Early 20th-cent 1/2 morocco. (3 bkpls.) BAL 6122. Howes P123. *Ginsberg.* $3,000/£1,923

PATTIE, JAMES OHIO. Personal Narrative of.... Cleveland, 1905. One of 459. Map. NF. Howes P123. *Turpen.* $125/£80

PATTISON, MARK. The Estiennes: A Biographical Essay. SF: Grabhorn, 1949. One of 390 w/3 orig leaves from Press of the Estiennes. Pristine in dj, mailing box. *Swann*.* $258/£165

PAUL, CONSTANTIN. Diagnosis and Treatment of Diseases of the Heart. NY, 1884. 1st Amer ed. 335pp. Tooled cl bds (sl worn). VG. *Doctor's Library.* $80/£51

PAUL, ELLIOT. Desperate Scenery. Random House, (1954). 1st ed. Fine in VG dj (price-clipped). *Authors Of West.* $25/£16

PAUL, ELLIOT. A Ghost Town on the Yellowstone. NY: Random House, 1948. 1st ptg. (Cl sl rubbed, spine sl faded), o/w VG. *Worldwide.* $16/£10

PAUL, RODMAN W. The California Gold Discovery. Georgetown, 1966. 1st ed. Map, port. VG. *Benchmark.* $45/£29

PAUL, RODMAN W. The California Gold Discovery. Georgetown: Talisman, 1966. One of 100 signed. Fldg panorama. Marbled bds, black fabricoid spine. Dbl slipcase (spotted, one edge stained). *Dawson.* $150/£96

PAUL, RODMAN W. California Gold: The Beginning of Mining in the Far West. Cambridge: Harvard Univ, 1947. 1st ed. Map. Uncut. Orange cl, gilt spine. Fine in pict dj. *Pacific*.* $40/£26

PAUL, RODMAN W. Mining Frontiers of the Far West. NY: Holt, Rinehart & Winston, (1963). VG in dj. *Lien.* $30/£19

PAUL, SHERMAN. Harry Callahan. NY: MOMA, 1967. 1st ed. VG (owner stamp) in pict stiff wrappers. *Cahan.* $20/£13

PAUL, WILLIAM. The Rose Garden. London: Kent, 1872. 3rd ed, issued w/o color plts. vi,(2),(vii),256pp; full-pg plt. Orig cl (spine relaid). *Quest.* $80/£51

PAUSE, WALTER. Salute the Mountains. London, (1962). 1st Eng ed. (Bumped), else VG in dj (yellowed). *King.* $40/£26

PAVIC, MILORAD. Landscape Painted with Tea. Hamilton, 1991. 1st UK ed. Inscribed. Fine in dj. *Williams.* $19/£12

PAVIERE, SYDNEY H. A Dictionary of Flower, Fruit, and Still Life Painters. Leigh-on-Sea: F. Lewis, 1962-64. 1st ed. 4 vols. 242pp of plts. Fine in djs (vol 1 lacks dj). *Hollett.* $429/£275

PAVLOV, I. P. Conditioned Reflexes and Psychiatry...Volume 2. W. Horsley Gantt (trans). NY: International, (1941). 1st ed in English. Panelled black cl. VG. *Gach.* $50/£32

PAVLOV, I. P. Conditioned Reflexes: An Investigation of...the Cerebral Cortex. G. V. Anrep (trans). (London): OUP/Humphrey Milford, 1927. 1st ed in English. Pebbled black cl. Jelliffe's name stamp, bkpl. (Lib stamp tp; spine #s artfully removed.) *Gach.* $200/£128

PAVLOV, I. P. Lectures on Conditioned Reflexes. W.H. Gantt (trans). 1928. 1st Eng ed. Frontis port. (Rebacked), orig spine laid on. *Whitehart.* $55/£35

PAVLOV, I. P. The Work of the Digestive Glands. London, 1910. 2nd Eng ed. (Extrems sl rubbed.) *Edwards.* $117/£75

PAVLOV, I. P. The Work of the Digestive Glands.... W. H. Thompson (trans). London, 1902. Pub's cat bound at end (sl red stain). (Cl sl worn, scuffed; stamp of Lister Inst 1/2-title.) *Maggs.* $59/£38

PAVY, F. W. A Treatise on Food and Dietetics. NY, 1881. 2nd ed. 402pp. Gilt-tooled cl bds (sl worn). VG. *Doctor's Library.* $65/£42

PAXSON, FREDERIC L. History of the American Frontier 1763-1893. Boston/NY, (1924). 2 dbl-pg color maps. Good. Howes P145. *Hayman.* $25/£16

PAXSON, FREDERIC L. History of the American Frontier 1763-1893. Boston, 1924. 1st ed. VG. Howes P145. *Turpen.* $65/£42

PAXTON, JAMES. Illustrations of Paley's Natural Theology. Boston, 1827. 36 litho plts. (Dampstaining, browning.) Orig cl (soiled, dampstained), paper cvr label. *Freeman*.* $30/£19

PAXTON, JUNE LE MERT. My Life on the Mojave. NY: Vantage, (1957). 1st ed. Fine in Fine dj. *Book Market.* $50/£32

PAYER, JULIUS. New Lands Within the Arctic Circle. NY: D. Appleton, 1877. Frontis, xxiv,399pp (edges spotted)+ads; 2 dbl-pg maps. Brn cl (worn, spotted), gilt. *Parmer.* $125/£80

PAYNE, ARTHUR F. Art Metalwork. Manual Arts, 1929. Rpt. Frontis. Dj (lt soiled, chipped). *Edwards.* $31/£20

PAYNE, DORIS PALMER. Captain Jack, Modoc Renegade. Portland: Binfords & Mort, (1938). 1st ed. VG in VG dj. *Oregon.* $35/£22

PAYNE, JOSEPH FRANK. English Medicine in the Anglo-Saxon Times. Oxford: Clarendon, 1904. 1st ed. 23 plts. Unopened. (Bkpl, sm stamp tp, #s tp verso, feps lt browned; label removed spine.) *Hollett.* $94/£60

PAYNE, JOSEPH FRANK. Thomas Sydenham. London, 1900. Frontis port, xvi,264pp+(iv) ads. (Margins browned; edges sl rubbed.) *Edwards.* $39/£25

PAYSON, GEORGE. (Ralph Raven, pseud.) Golden Dreams and Leaden Realities. NY: Putnam, 1853. 1st ed. Brn cl, gilt spine. (Lt foxed; lt worn, faded), o/w NF. Pacific*. $138/£88

PAZ, OCTAVIO. In the Middle of This Phrase and Other Poems. Helsinki: Eurographica, 1987. 1st ed thus. One of 350 numbered, signed, dated. Fine in ptd self-wraps. Lame Duck. $150/£96

PEACH, R. E. M. Street-Lore of Bath. London/Bath, 1893. iv ads + vi,154pp + xiv ads (pencil notes). Uncut. (Rebound in cl, spine lt faded.) Edwards. $70/£45

PEACOCK, MARY THOMAS. Circuit Rider and Those Who Followed. Chattanooga, 1957. Inscribed. Program for celebration laid in. Fldg view. VG in dj (edgeworn). Bohling. $18/£12

PEACOCK, THOMAS LOVE. Novels of Thomas Love Peacock. David Garnett (ed). Rupert Hart-Davis, 1948. 1st ed thus. (Fore-edge lt spotted; spine bumped), else Good in dj (chipped, repaired). Tiger. $23/£15

PEAKE, HAROLD and HERBERT JOHN FLEURE. Peasants and Potters. New Haven/London: Yale/Milford, Oxford, 1927. 1st ed. (Sl rubbed, ex-lib, spine #), o/w VG. Worldwide. $15/£10

PEAKE, JAMES. Rudimentary Treatise on Ship Building, for the Use of Beginners. London: John Weale, 1849. 1st ed. vi,132pp; 6 fldg plts. Flexible grn cl (spotted), paste-on cvr label. Parmer. $175/£112

PEAKE, MERVYN. Captain Slaughterboard Drops Anchor. NY: Macmillan, 1939. 1st US ed. 7 1/2 x 10 1/4. 44pp. VG in dj. Cattermole. $30/£19

PEAKE, MERVYN. The Craft of the Lead Pencil. Alan Wingate, 1946. 1st ed. Pict cl (sl worn). Good + (foxed). Whittle. $78/£50

PEAKE, MERVYN. Shapes and Sounds. London: C&W, 1941. 1st ed. NF in dj (chipped, worn). Captain's Bookshelf. $100/£64

PEAKE, MERVYN. Titus Groan. NY: Reynal & Hitchcock, (1946). 1st Amer ed. NF in VG dj (chips top edge). Reese. $75/£48

PEAKE, ORA B. The Colorado Range Cattle Industry. Glendale, CA: A.H. Clark, 1937. 1st ed. Inscribed. Frontis port; 2 fldg maps. Unopened, teg. (Cl bleached edge of rear bd; spine text dull), else NF. Cahan. $125/£80

PEAKE, ORA B. The Colorado Range Cattle Industry. Glendale: Clark, 1937. 1st ed. Ginsberg. $150/£96

PEARCE, PHILIPPA. Mrs. Cockle's Cat. Phila: Lippincott, 1961. 2nd US ed. Antony Maitland (illus). 7 1/2 x 10. 30pp. Pict bds. Good (ex-lib, mks) in dj. Cattermole. $25/£16

PEARCE, PHILIPPA. Tom's Midnight Garden. London: OUP, 1958. 5th ed. Susan Einzig (illus). 5 1/2 x 8 3/4. 229pp. VG in dj. Cattermole. $25/£16

PEARCE, RICHARD. Marooned in the Arctic. N.p. (Toronto), n.d. (1931). 5 photo plts, map. VG. High Latitude. $110/£71

PEARCE, WALTER J. Painting and Decorating. London: (Chas. Griffin), 1902. 2nd rev enlgd ed. 3 color plts. 86-pg Griffin cat dated 15/7/02. Pub's pebbled burgundy cl, blind dec, gilt spine. As New. Book Block. $225/£144

Pearl of Great Price, Being a Choice Selection from the Revelations, Translations, and Narrations of Joseph Smith.... Salt Lake, 1888. 136(+ 1)pp; fldg facs. (Fep torn, inscrip; hinges cracked, corners bumped), o/w VG. Benchmark. $75/£48

PEARL, RAYMOND and RUTH DeWITT. The Ancestry of the Long-Lived. Balt: Johns Hopkins, 1934. 1st ed. Frontis. NF. Glaser. $75/£48

PEARS, CHARLES. From the Thames to the Seine. London, 1910. 1st ed. Teg. (Text browned; spine sl dknd, sl bowed.) Edwards. $39/£25

PEARSALL, RONALD. The Worm in the Bud. (NY): Macmillan, (1969). 1st US ed. VG (ex-libris, name tp) in dj (sl worn). Second Life. $25/£16

PEARSALL, W. H. Mountains and Moorlands. London: Collins, 1950. 1st ed. 48 maps & diags. Fine in dj. Hollett. $55/£35

PEARSON, E. O. The Insect Pests of Cotton in Tropical Africa. London, 1958. 1st ed. 8 color plts. (Ex-lib, ink stamps, bkpl.) Edwards. $47/£30

PEARSON, EDMUND. Books in Black or Red. NY: Macmillan, 1923. Signed, inscribed. Paper labels. (Spine sl sunned, lower fr bd lt discolored), o/w VG. Reese. $35/£22

PEARSON, EDMUND. Dime Novels. Boston: Little, 1929. 1st ed. Ginsberg. $50/£32

PEARSON, EDMUND. Queer Books. NY: Doubleday, Doran, 1928. 1st ed. (Sl dull), else Fine. Hermitage. $35/£22

PEARSON, JIM B. The Maxwell Land Grant. Norman, 1961. 1st ed. 3 maps. Fine in Fine dj. Turpen. $58/£37

PEARSON, JOHN. An Exposition of the Creed. London: For John Williams, 1662. 2nd ed. Tp ruled in red. (4)leaves, 433pp. Mod calf in antique style (sl worn, sl soil, edge-fraying). Oinonen*. $60/£38

PEARSON, KARL. The Chances of Death and Other Studies in Evolution. London, 1897. 2 vols. (Sl faded, worn.) Maggs. $211/£135

PEARSON, R. J. Archaeology of the Ryukyu Islands. Honolulu: Univ of HI, 1969. 1st ed. 19 plts, 44 tables. Fine in NF dj. Mikesh. $25/£16

PEARSON, T. R. A Short History of a Small Place. NY: Linden/S&S, 1985. 1st ed. Signed. Fine in NF dj (sm closed tear, sl rubbing). Robbins. $75/£48

PEARY, JOSEPHINE. My Arctic Journal...with an Account of the Great White Journey Across Greenland by Robert E. Peary. NY: Contemporary Pub Co, 1894. (2),249pp; map. VG. High Latitude. $40/£26

PEARY, JOSEPHINE. The Snow Baby. London: Isbister, 1902. 4to. 84pp. Dec cl (spine ends sl worn). VG. High Latitude. $45/£29

PEARY, ROBERT E. Nearest the Pole. NY: Doubleday Page, 1907. 1st ed. 65 plts. Grn cl, gilt. (Edges worn), else VG. Parmer. $195/£125

PEARY, ROBERT E. The North Pole. NY: Stokes, 1910. 1st trade ed. Color frontis, lg fldg map (sl edgeworn), 7 color plts. Blue dec cl (spine ends sl worn). NF. Parmer. $225/£144

PEARY, ROBERT E. Northward Over the Great Ice. London: Methuen, 1898. 1st British ed. 2 vols. 521; 625pp; fldg map. (Sig, stamp.) Blue cl (shelfworn, rubbed), gilt. Parmer. $400/£256

PEASE and COLE. Complete Guide to the Gold Districts of Kansas and Nebraska.... (Denver, 1959.) Facs ed. Lg fldg map. Fine in cardbd slipcase w/ptd label. Cahan. $40/£26

PEASE, A. et al. Edmund Loder, Naturalist...a Memoir. London, 1923. Port. Review, obit inserted. (Cl sl mkd.) Maggs. $47/£30

PEASE, ALFRED E. The Book of the Lion. London: John Murray, 1913. 1st ed. Frontis w/onion skin protector. Red cl, gilt. VG (spine edges lt chipped; lt wear corner edges; name, address). Backman. $200/£128

PEASE, ARTHUR S. Vascular Flora of Coos County, New Hampshire. Boston, 1924. 2 maps, 7 photo plts. Blue cl. VG (ex-lib; spine label removed). Brooks. $34/£22

PEASE, JOHN C. and JOHN M. NILES. A Gazetteer of the States of Connecticut and Rhode Island.... Hartford: Wm. S. Marsh, 1819. 1st ed. 2 fldg maps (1 w/repaired tear). Contemp mottled calf. (Spine ends, corners sl chipped, lower joint cracked; new eps, sl foxing, browning.) Howes P166. *Sadlon.* $75/£48

PEASE, THEODORE CALVIN (ed). Collections of the Illinois State Historical Library French Series, Vols. 1-3. Springfield: IL State Hist Library, 1934-1940. 3 vols. (Ex-lib, call #s on spine, perf stamps, rubberstamps, spine lettering sl faded), else Good. *Brown.* $75/£48

PEAT, FRANK EDWIN. Christmas Carols. Saalfield, 1937. Fern Bisel Peat (illus). 9x11. 45pp. Pict bds (rubbed). VG in dj (chipped, spine top lacks 1 inch). *My Bookhouse.* $50/£32

PEATTIE, DONALD CULROSS. An Almanac for Moderns. Washington: LEC, 1938. #904/1500 numbered, signed by Asa Cheffetz (illus). NF in pub's slipcase (lt worn, dusty). *Hermitage.* $75/£48

PEATTIE, RODERICK (ed). The Friendly Mountains: Green, White and Adirondacks. NY: Vanguard, (1942). 1st ed. Pict cl. NF in dj (sl edgeworn). *Sadlon.* $20/£13

PECHEY, JOHN. The Compleat Herbal of Physical Plants. London: R. & J. Bonwick, 1707. 2nd ed. (vi),349pp i.e. 411 (pagination errors: 23-indices, 3-pub's ads). Contemp panelled calf (rebacked). Clean (repaired tear tp; new eps). *White.* $351/£225

PECK, CHARLES. Annual Report of the State Botanist of the State of New York. Albany: NY State, 1896. 1st ed. 241pp + 43 plts. Grn cl. Good. *Archer.* $125/£80

PECK, GEORGE BACHELER. A Recruit Before Petersburg. Providence, RI, 1880. 1st ed. Ltd to 250. PNRISSHS Series 2, #8. 74pp. NF in ptd wrappers. *Mcgowan.* $45/£29

PECK, GEORGE. The Life and Times.... NY: Nelson & Phillips, 1874. 1st ed. Port. Good (dampstaining). *Agvent.* $30/£19

PECK, GEORGE. Melbourne, and the Chincha Islands. NY: Scribner, 1854. Frontis, 2,v,13,294pp; map. (Rubbed, spine chipped.) *Adelson.* $200/£128

PECK, GRAHAM. Through China's Walls. Boston: Houghton Mifflin (Riverside), 1940. 1st ed. 14 plts. VG in dj (sl torn). *Worldwide.* $18/£12

PECK, JOHN M. A Gazetteer of Illinois in Three Parts. Jacksonville, IL, 1834. Sm 8vo. Contemp tree sheep. (Bkpl.) Howes P170. *Swann*.* $920/£590

PECK, MORTON E. Manual of the Higher Plants of Oregon. Portland: Binford & Mort, (1941). Signed. (Lt rubbed), else Fine. *Quest.* $45/£29

PECKHAM, HARRY. A Tour Through Holland, Dutch Brabant, the Austrian Netherlands, and Part of France. London: G. Kearsley, 1788. (vi),273,(3)pp; fldg engr map. New bds, calf spine, old style eps. *Bickersteth.* $172/£110

PECKHAM, HOWARD. Pontiac and the Indian Uprising. Princeton, 1947. 1st ed. 3 maps. Fine in dj (lower 1/4 fr flap torn off). *Oregon.* $45/£29

PEDDER, JAMES. The Farmer's Land-Measurer. NY: OJ, 1853. 1st ed. 144pp. Brn cl, gilt. VG. *Price.* $29/£19

Pedigree of King George the Third. London: T. Bensley, 1812. 34 engr ports. 1/4 tan morocco (monogram of William Sterling Maxwell on upper cvr; bkpl). *Swann*.* $115/£74

PEEL, FRED P. Shadowless Figure Portraiture. NY: Galleon Press, (1936). Spiral bound. VG. *Metropolitan*.* $28/£18

PEEL, SYDNEY. Trooper 8008 I.Y. London, 1901. 4th ed. Frontis, fldg map. (Foxing.) Red cl (sl worn), gilt. *Maggs.* $78/£50

Peep at the Esquimax or, Scenes on the Ice...By a Lady. London: H. R. Thomas, 1825. 2nd ed. 12mo. viii,58,(4)pp; 40 hand-colored text illus. Blue cl, ptd paper label. *Karmiole.* $400/£256

Peep at the World. London: Thos. Dean, n.d. (ca 1850). Dec wrappers w/bkseller's ticket. (Short split along spine; edge lt worn, faded), else VG. *Cahan.* $100/£64

PEET, BILL. Buford the Little Bighorn. Boston: Houghton Mifflin, 1967. 1st ed. 8 1/2 x 10. 46pp. Fine in dj. *Cattermole.* $50/£32

PEET, STEPHEN DENISON. The Cliff Dwellers and Pueblos. Chicago: Amer Antiquarian, 1899. Frontis, xviii,398pp; 95 plts. Gilt-emb cl (corner sl bumped; sig fep, edges). *Archaeologia.* $125/£80

PEIRCE, B. K. Life in the Woods; or The Adventures of Audubon. NY: Carlton & Porter, 1863. 18mo. Full-pg wood engr frontis, guard; 252pp + 4pp list (lt foxing throughout); 6 (of 8) full-pg wood engrs by Felter. (Trace of bkpl inside upper cvr; few sigs sprung.) Tooled grn cl on bds (rubbed, bumped), gilt. Fair. *Hobbyhorse.* $45/£29

PEIRCE, PARKER I. Antelope Bill. Minneapolis: Ross & Haines, 1962. Ltd to 550. VG in slipcase. Howes P180. *Lien.* $35/£22

PEIRSON, ERMA. The Mojave River and Its Valley. Glendale: A.H. Clark, 1970. 1st ed. Fldg map. Dj. *Dawson.* $25/£16

PEIRSON, ERMA. The Mojave River and Its Valley. Glendale: A.H. Clark, 1970. 1st ed. Fine in Fine dj. *Book Market.* $40/£26

PEIRSON, ERMA. The Mojave River and Its Valley. Glendale: A.H. Clarke, 1970. 1st ed. Fldg map. VG in dj. *Lien.* $25/£16

PELLETT, FRANK C. A Living from Bees. NY: OJ, 1946. Brn cl, gilt. VG in dj (tattered). *Price.* $22/£14

PELZER, LOUIS. The Cattleman's Frontier: A Record of the Trans-Mississippi Cattle Industry...1850-1890. Glendale: Clark, 1936. 1st ed. (Bkpl removed, sm emb lib stamp; lt white #s lower spine.) Howes P187. *Ginsberg.* $150/£96

PELZER, LOUIS. The Cattlemen's Frontier. Glendale: Clark, 1936. 1st ed. One of 1019 ptd. 6 plts. Maroon cl. VF. Howes P187. *Argonaut.* $200/£128

PENCIL, MARK. The White Sulphur Papers.... NY: S. Colman, 1839. (Foxed, pub's imprint partly masked out in ptg; black cl sl worn.) *Maggs.* $56/£36

PENDERGAST and WARE. Cigar Store Figures in American Folk Art. Chicago, 1953. Good. *Scribe's Perch*.* $32/£21

PENDLETON, LOUIS. King Tom and the Runaways. NY: D. Appleton, 1890. 1st ed. (vii),273pp; 6 plts. Dec grn cl. VG. *Petrilla.* $75/£48

PENDLETON, WILLIAM C. History of Tazewell County and Southwest Virginia, 1748-1920. W.C. Hill, 1920. Good (foxing, rear hinge torn). *Book Broker.* $85/£54

PENE DU BOIS, H. P. Four Private Libraries of New-York. NY, 1892. One of 1000 numbered; one of 800 on Holland paper. 12 plts (1 color); facs. Uncut. (Spine defective.) *Maggs.* $86/£55

PENFIELD, EDWARD (intro). Posters in Miniature. NY/London: R.H. Russell/John Lane, 1897. Pict cl (rubbed, soiled; shaken, loose in cvrs). *New Hampshire*.* $40/£26

PENFIELD, WILDER and T. C. ERICKSON. Epilepsy and Cerebral Localization. Springfield, 1941. 1st ed. (Spine frayed.) *Argosy.* $65/£42

PENFIELD, WILDER and T. C. ERICKSON. Epilepsy and Cerebral Localization. Springfield, 1941. (Cl rubbed, rear joint just starting.) Internally Clean. *Goodrich.* $95/£61

PENFIELD, WILDER and T. RASMUSSEN. The Cerebral Cortex of Man. NY: Macmillan, 1950. VG in dj (worn, chipped). *Goodrich*. $95/£61

PENFIELD, WILDER and L. ROBERTS. Speech and Brain Mechanisms. Princeton, 1959. Nice in dj. *Goodrich*. $75/£48

PENGELLY, H. A Memoir of William Pengelly, of Torquay, F.R.S., Geologist.... London, 1897. Inscribed. xi,341pp (ends sl foxed); port, 10 plts. *Henly*. $101/£65

PENHALLOW, SAMUEL. The History of the Wars of New-England with the Eastern Indians. Cincinnati, 1859. This copy w/Appendix which was not bound into all copies. (Extrems worn.) Howes P201. *Swann**. $373/£239

PENN, IRVING. Moments Preserved. NY: S&S, 1960. 1st ed. Fine (lacks dj) in VG pict slipcase. *Smith*. $275/£176

PENN, IRVING. Photographs in Platinum Metals—Images 1947-1975. NY: Marlborough Gallery, 1977. 1st ed. 29 plts. Fine in illus wrappers. *Cahan*. $35/£22

PENNANT, THOMAS. A Tour in Scotland. MDCCLXIX. London: B. White, 1772. 2nd ed. viii,331,(i)pp; 18 engr plts. Contemp calf (rebacked), gilt. *Hollett*. $250/£160

PENNELL, ELIZABETH ROBINS and JOSEPH. The Glory of Old New York. NY, 1926. One of 355 numbered, signed by Elizabeth Pennell. 24 color plts. Dj, pub's 2-piece box (lid imperfect). *Swann**. $316/£203

PENNELL, ELIZABETH ROBINS. French Cathedrals.... London, 1909. Teg. Blue cl (edgeworn, lt soiled), gilt. *Freeman**. $20/£13

PENNELL, JOSEPH. The Adventures of an Illustrator. Boston, (1925). 1st trade ed. Dj (lt worn). *Kane**. $30/£19

PENNELL, JOSEPH. The Adventures of an Illustrator. Boston: Little, Brown, 1925. 1st imp, trade ed. (Spine sl dknd), o/w VG. *New Hampshire**. $50/£32

PENNELL, JOSEPH. Etchers and Etching. London: Unwin, 1920. 1st ed. 39 plts. Good +. *Scribe's Perch**. $28/£18

PENNELL, JOSEPH. Pen Drawing and Pen Draughtsmen. Macmillan, 1897. xxxvii,470pp (few pp loose, inner joint cracking). Uncut. *Bickersteth*. $140/£90

PENNINGTON, SAMUEL H. Memoir of Joseph Parrish, M.D.... Newark, NJ: Advertiser Ptg House, 1891. 1st ed. (24)pp. Unopened. Drab grn-grey wrappers. (Cvrs detached), else Fine. *Gach*. $50/£32

Pennsylvania at Antietam. Harrisburg, 1906. Lg color fldg map (repaired). Good (fr hinge cracked). *Scribe's Perch**. $20/£13

PENNY, F. E. Southern India. London: A&C Black, Oct 1914. 1st ed. Fldg map at rear, 50 color plts. Dec cvr, spine. Good (chips to head, foot). *Scribe's Perch**. $40/£26

PENNYPACKER, MORTON. The Two Spies: Nathan Hale and Robert Townsend. Boston/NY: Houghton Mifflin, 1930. 1st ed. Ltd to 780 numbered. Port, fldg table, 5 plts. Uncut. Tan polished buckram, red leather gilt title labels. Fine. *Cady*. $30/£19

PENRITH, HOWARD OF. Theatre of Life. London: Hodder & Stoughton, 1936. 1st ed. 20 plts, map. Teg. (Few spots fore-edge), o/w Mint in dj. *Hollett*. $55/£35

PENROSE, CHARLES BINGHAM. The Rustler Business. Douglas, WY: Douglas Budget, n.d. (1959). 1st ed w/this title. VF in stiff orange wrappers ptd in black. *Argonaut*. $125/£80

PENROSE, ROLAND. Man Ray. Boston: NYGS, 1975. 1st ed. Fine in Fine dj. *Smith*. $75/£48

PENZER, N. M. Nala and Damayantii. London: A.M. Philpot, 1926. 1st ed. 10 color plts. Teg. Orig vellum-backed cl (rubbed, soiled), gilt. *Hollett*. $39/£25

PENZER, N. M. Poison-Damsels and Other Essays in Folklore and Anthropology. London: Privately ptd, 1952. VG in dj (used). *King*. $50/£32

Peoples' Almanac for 1839. Boston: S.N. Dickinson, (1838). 18 leaves; 14 full-pg woodcuts. (Few short closed tears), else NF. *Cahan*. $85/£54

PEPOON, H. S. An Annotated Flora of the Chicago Area. Chicago: Chicago Acad Sci, 1927. 1st ed. Grn cl. NF. *Archer*. $80/£51

PEPPER, D. STEPHEN. Guido Reni. NY, 1984. Good in dj. *Washton*. $95/£61

PEPPER, GEORGE WHARTON. Philadelphia Lawyer, an Autobiography. Phila: Lippincott, 1944. *Boswell*. $20/£13

PEPYS, SAMUEL. Diary and Correspondence. London: Swan Sonnenschein, 1906. 4 vols. Teg. 2-tone cl. VG. *Hollett*. $117/£75

PEPYS, SAMUEL. Diary and Correspondence.... London: Swan Sonnenschein, 1890. 4 vols. Each vol 500+pp. Red cl. (Inner hinges vol 1 cracked; sl rubbed.) *Cox*. $39/£25

PEPYS, SAMUEL. The Diary of Samuel Pepys. 1660-1669. Robert Latham and William Matthews (eds). Bell & Hyman, 1979-1983. 11 vols. Djs (sl chipped vol 5, sm dent index vol dj intruding to upper bd). *Edwards*. $351/£225

PEPYS, SAMUEL. The Diary of.... Henry B. Wheatley (ed). London: George Bell, 1893-99. One of 250. 10 vols incl suppl. (Lt spotted, dampstained.) Teg. Orig grn 1/2 morocco (spines faded), gilt spines. *Christie's**. $351/£225

PEPYS, SAMUEL. The Diary. London, 1928. 10 vols. 8vo. Frontispieces. Blue calf, gilt, spines in 6 compartments, red/citron morocco lettering pieces in 2. (Sl faded.) *Swann**. $805/£516

PEPYS, SAMUEL. The Diary...for the Year A.D. 1660-69. Henry B. Wheatley (ed). NY: LEC, 1942. One of 1500. Signed by William Sharp (illus). 1/4 cl, pict bds. (Sl edge-toned), else NF (lacks slipcase). *Waverly**. $55/£35

PEPYS, SAMUEL. Pepys' Memoirs of the Royal Navy 1679-1688. J. R. Tanner (ed). Oxford, 1906. Facs title of orig 1690 ed, lg fldg table. Uncut. Orig imitation parchment (lt soiled, rubbed). *Cox*. $28/£18

PEPYS, SAMUEL. Private Correspondence and Miscellaneous Papers of Samuel Pepys 1679-1703. J. R. Tanner (ed). G. Bell, 1926. 2 vols. Gravure frontis each vol. Teg, others uncut. Blue cl, gilt. VG. *Cox*. $55/£35

PEPYS, SAMUEL. Private Correspondence and Miscellaneous Papers of...1679-1703....J. R. Tanner (ed). London: G. Bell, 1926. 1st ed. 2 vols. Teg. Dk blue cl, gilt spines. VG set. *Reese*. $50/£32

PERCIVAL, A. BLAYNEY. A Game Ranger's Note Book. London: Nisbet, (1924). 1st ed. (Spine faded, sl frayed), else VG. *Waverly**. $88/£56

PERCIVAL, A. BLAYNEY. A Game Ranger's Note Book. London, 1927. (Spine top sl snagged), else Very Clean. *Grayling*. $117/£75

PERCIVAL, JOHN. The Roman Villa: An Historical Introduction. Berkeley: Univ of CA, (1976). Good in Fine dj. *Archaeologia*. $85/£54

PERCIVAL, JOHN. The Wheat Plant. London, 1921. 1st ed. (Feps lt browned, upper hinge sl tender; dampstained.) *Edwards*. $101/£65

PERCIVAL, ROBERT. An Account of the Cape of Good Hope. London: C & R Baldwin, 1804. (Lt foxed, tp repaired.) Full later calf. *Metropolitan**. $200/£128

PERCIVAL, T. Observations and Experiments on the Poison of Lead. 1774. viii,116pp (bkpl, prelims sl foxed). Contemp calf (rebacked). *Whitehart*. $437/£280

PERCY, J. Metallurgy. London: John Murray, 1861. 1st ptg of 1st vol. xiv,635pp. Good (new eps, lib stamp tp). *Blake.* $100/£64

PERCY, THOMAS. Reliques of Ancient English Poetry.... London: Swan Sonnenschein, 1886. 3 vols. VG. *Argosy.* $150/£96

PERCY, WALKER. Bourbon. Winston-Salem, NC: Palaemon, (1979). 1st ed. One of 200 signed. Mint in marbled wrappers, ptd label. *Jaffe.* $150/£96

PERCY, WALKER. Bourbon. (Winston-Salem, NC): Palaemon, (1981). 2nd ltd ed. One of 150 signed. Cl-backed dec bds, ptd spine label. Mint. *Jaffe.* $125/£80

PERCY, WALKER. Lost in the Cosmos. NY: FSG, (1983). One of 350 signed. Cl in pub's box, still sealed in plastic. *Metropolitan*.* $115/£74

PERCY, WALKER. The Message in the Bottle. NY: Farrar Straus, (1975). 1st ed. Signed. Fine in Fine dj. *Lenz.* $150/£96

PERCY, WALKER. The Moviegoer. NY: Knopf, 1961. 1st ed. Fair (ex-lib, pocket removed, stamps; lacks dj). *Captain's Bookshelf.* $45/£29

PERCY, WALKER. Questions They Never Asked Me. Northridge, CA: Lord John, 1979. One of 300 numbered, signed. Fine. *Lenz.* $135/£87

PERCY, WALKER. Questions They Never Asked Me. Northridge, CA: Lord John, 1979. 1st ed. One of 350 signed. Cl-backed dec bds. Mint. *Jaffe.* $150/£96

PERCY, WALKER. The Second Coming. NY: Farrar Straus, (1980). One of 450 numbered, signed. Fine in Fine slipcase. *Lenz.* $200/£128

PERCY, WALKER. The Second Coming. NY: FSG, (1980). 1st trade ed. Fine in dj. *Captain's Bookshelf.* $40/£26

PERCY, WALKER. The Thanatos Syndrome. NY: Farrar Straus, (1987). One of 250 numbered, signed. Fine in Fine slipcase. *Lenz.* $185/£119

PERDRIEL-VAISSIERES, J. Rupert Brooke's Death and Burial Based on the Log of the French Hospital Ship Dugay-Trouin. Vincent O'Sullivan (trans). (New Haven: Yale Univ, 1917.) 1st ed. One of 300 ptd. Port repro laid in. Contemp 3/4 morocco, marbled bds, orig wrappers bound in. (Lt discoloration fore-edges binder's blanks, lt offset from clippings laid in), o/w Nice. *Reese.* $125/£80

PEREC, GEORGES. Life: A User's Manual. Boston: Godine, 1987. 1st US ed. Fine in NF dj (lt worn). *Lame Duck.* $45/£29

PEREC, GEORGES. W or The Memory of Childhood. David Bellos (trans). London: Collins Harvill, 1988. 1st Eng ed. Fine in dj. *Between The Covers.* $45/£29

PEREIRA, GEORGE. Peking to Lhasa. Boston: Houghton Mifflin, 1926. 1st ed. Photogravure frontis port, 2 fldg maps (1 color). Blue cl, spine label (sunned). *Karmiole.* $75/£48

PEREIRA, J. The Elements of Materia Medica and Therapeutics. 1842. 2nd ed. 2 vols. xlii,870; xxxi,1056pp. (Rebacked; vol 2 spine sl coming away.) *Whitehart.* $94/£60

PERELMAN, S. J. The Ill Tempered Clavichord. NY: S&S, 1952. NF (sm mk fr bd) in VG dj (sm tears, lt rubbed). *Between The Covers.* $85/£54

PERELMAN, S. J. and OGDEN NASH. One Touch of Venus. Boston, 1944. 1st Amer ed. NF (spine sl chipped, corners rubbed). *Polyanthos.* $25/£16

PEREZ DE RIBAS, ANDRES. My Life Among the Savage Nations of New Spain. Tomas Antonio Robertson (trans). L.A.: Ward Ritchie, 1968. VG in dj (sl worn). *Lien.* $50/£32

PEREZ DE RIVAS, ANDRES. My Life Among the Savage Nations of New Spain. L.A., 1968. 1st Eng trans of 1645 1st ed. Map. Fine in Fine dj. *Turpen.* $45/£29

PERKIN, ROBERT L. The First Hundred Years: An Informal History of Denver and the Rocky Mountain News. GC: Doubleday, 1959. 1st ed. NF. *Sadlon.* $15/£10

PERKINS, CHARLTON B. Travels from the Grandeurs of the West to the Mysteries of the East. SF, (1909). Color frontis, fldg map; tipped-in notice. Blue cl (edge-worn), gilt. *Bohling.* $50/£32

PERKINS, D. C. The Homoeopathic Therapeutics of Rheumatism and Kindred Diseases. Phila: Boericke, 1888. 1st ed. 180pp. Pebbled cl. NF. *Glaser.* $95/£61

PERKINS, ELISHA DOUGLASS. Gold Rush Diary. Thomas D. Clark (ed). Lexington: Univ of KY, 1967. 1st ed. Frontis ports. Gold cl. Fine in pict dj. *Pacific*.* $69/£44

PERKINS, J. R. Trails, Rails and War, The Life of General G. M. Dodge. Indianapolis, (1929). 1st ed. VG +. *Pratt.* $47/£30

PERKINS, JAMES H. Annals of the West: Embracing a Concise Account of Principal Events Which Have Occurred in the Western States and Territories.... Cincinnatti: James R. Albach, 1847. 1st ed, 2nd ptg. 2 maps. Orig calf (crudely rebacked, orig spine label laid on; extrems scuffed; lib blindstamp, sl foxed). Howes P231. *Sadlon.* $40/£26

PERKINS, JOHN. To the Ends of the Earth. NY: Pantheon, 1981. 1st ed. (Mk lower edge), else Fine in NF dj. *Cahan.* $25/£16

PERKINS, LUCY FITCH. Italian Twins. Boston: Houghton Mifflin, 1920. 1st ed. Lg 8vo. Pict cl. VG. *Book Adoption.* $25/£16

PERKINS, LUCY FITCH. Mexican Twins. Boston: Houghton Mifflin, 1915. 1st (Nov 1915) ed. Lg 8vo. Pict cl. NF. *Book Adoption.* $35/£22

PERKINS, WILLIAM. Three Years in California. Dale L. Morgan and James R. Scobie (eds). Berkeley: Univ of CA, 1964. 1st ed in English. Frontis port, 2 maps. Orange buckram, gilt spine. Fine. *Pacific*.* $63/£40

PERKINS, WILLIAM. Three Years in California...1849-1852. Berkeley: Univ of CA, 1964. 1st ed. VF in pict dj. *Argonaut.* $60/£38

PERLES, ALFRED. Henry Miller in Villa Seurat. London: Village Press, 1973. 1st UK ed. NF in illus wrappers. *Williams.* $19/£12

PERLES, ALFRED. My Friend Henry Miller. London, 1956. 1st ed. NF in dj (2 closed tears). *Buckley.* $47/£30

PERLES, ALFRED. Scenes from a Floating Life. (London): Turret Bks, (1968). Ltd to 100 numbered, signed. Fine in dj. *Antic Hay.* $100/£64

PERLOT, JEAN-NICOLAS. Gold Seeker. Howard R. Lamar (ed). New Haven: Yale Univ, (1985). 1st ed in English. Red cl, gilt spine. Fine in pict dj. Howes P237. *Pacific*.* $86/£55

Perpetual Laws of the Commonwealth of Massachusetts...to the Last Wednesday in May, 1789. Boston, 1789. Contemp sheep (worn). *Swann*.* $316/£203

PERRAULT, CHARLES. Histories or Tales of Past Times. Told by Mother Goose. G. M. Gent (trans). London: Fortune Press, (1928). Ltd to 1025 numbered. 12mo. 108pp. Purple cl over bds. Fine in dj. *Karmiole.* $100/£64

PERREDES, P. London Botanic Gardens. Wellcome Chemical Research Labs, 1906. Wrappers. *Maggs.* $37/£24

PERRING, F. H. and S. M. WALTERS. Atlas of the British Flora. London, 1962. 1st ed. 1623 maps, 6 overlays in pocket. Fine in dj. *Henly.* $78/£50

PERRINS, C. M. British Tits. London: Collins, 1979. 1st ed. VG in dj (sl bruised). *Cox.* $44/£28

PERROT, GEORGES and CHARLES CHIPIEZ. A History of Art in Persia. London: Chapman & Hall, 1892. xii,508pp (sig); 12 color plts. Pict cl (sl shelfwear). Archaeologia. $200/£128

PERROT, GEORGES and CHARLES CHIPIEZ. A History of Art. Walter Armstrong (ed). London: Chapman & Hall, 1883-94. 7 works in 12 vols. 8vo. 79 plts (1 torn along folds, repaired w/cellotape). Marbled eps; teg. 1/2 morocco, cl bds, gilt, raised bands. (Ex-lib, ink stamp most tps, #s 1st contents leaf, few stamps to text; bkpls; sl rubbed, worn, faint spine #s; 3 spine heads chipped, sl loss.) Edwards. $1,092/£700

Perry Hand Book of Choice Fruits, Ornamentals, Roses.... (Rochester, n.d.) 100 full-pg chromolithos on 50 plts (uniformly bright). Contents VG (heavily flecked). Waverly*. $522/£335

PERRY, ALBERT. Tattoo. NY, 1933. 26 plts, 3 color. Pict paper spine label. Kane*. $130/£83

PERRY, ANNE. Bluegate Fields. NY: St. Martin's, 1984. 1st ed. Fine in dj. Mordida. $75/£48

PERRY, ANNE. Highgate Rise. NY: Fawcett Columbine, 1991. 1st ed. Fine in dj. Mordida. $45/£29

PERRY, ANNE. Silence in Hanover Close. London: Souvenir, 1989. 1st ed. Fine in Fine dj. Else Fine. $75/£48

PERRY, B. C. The Human Hair, and the Cutaneous Diseases Which Affect It. NY: J. Miller, 1865. 402pp; 6 plts. Good (soiled, edges snagged). Bohling. $30/£19

PERRY, BLISS. Fishing with a Worm. Boston: Houghton Mifflin, 1916. 1st ed. VF in VG dj. Bowman. $45/£29

PERRY, BLISS. The Heart of Emerson's Journals. Boston: Houghton Mifflin, 1926. 1st ed. One of 300 bound uncut. Red cl. Fine. BAL 5494. Macdonnell. $75/£48

PERRY, BLISS. Park-Street Papers. Boston/NY: Houghton Mifflin, 1908. 1st ed. Teg. Brn pict cl, gilt. Fine. Macdonnell. $50/£32

PERRY, CHARLES. The Haight-Ashbury. NY: Random House, 1984. (2nd ptg.) 16pp photo insert. NF in dj. Sclanders. $31/£20

PERRY, EDITH WEIR. Under Four Tudors.... Allen & Unwin, 1964. 4 plts. Fine in dj. Peter Taylor. $30/£19

PERRY, EVAN. Collecting Antique Metalware. London: Country Life, 1974. 1st ed. Dj (spine lt faded). Edwards. $39/£25

PERRY, FRED. Perry on Tennis. Phila: John C. Winston, (1937). 1st ed. 36 photos. Fine in NF black dj (lt rubbed). Between The Covers. $75/£48

PERRY, GEORGE SESSIONS. Texas: A World in Itself. NY: McGraw Hill, (1942). 1st ed. Signed. VG in dj (sl worn). Lien. $40/£26

PERRY, JOHN. Spinning Tops. London: Sheldon, 1929. Rev ed. Frontis. Pict cl. VG. Hollett. $39/£25

PERRY, MATTHEW C. The Japan Expedition 1852-1854. Roger Pineau (ed). Washington, 1968. 1st ed. Dj. Lefkowicz. $80/£51

PERRY, MATTHEW C. The Japan Expedition 1852-1854. Roger Pineau (ed). Washington, DC: Smithsonian, 1968. 1st ed. 49 color plts, 30 add'l plts and figs. Blue cl. Good in illus dj. Karmiole. $100/£64

PERRY, MATTHEW C. Narrative of the Expedition of an American Squadron to the China Seas and Japan. NY, 1857. 4to. 93 plts, 5 maps. Pub's blind-stamped morocco (extrems very rubbed), gilt. Swann*. $690/£442

PERRY, MATTHEW C. Narrative of the Expedition of an American Squadron to the China Seas and Japan...1852, 1853, and 1854. Washington: Nicholson, 1856. Thick 4to. Volume 1 only. 5 maps, 88 (of 89) tinted litho plts. Swann*. $402/£258

PERRY, R. The World of the Giant Panda. NY: Taplinger, 1969. 1st ed. VG+ in VG+ dj. Mikesh. $20/£13

PERRY, STELLA G. S. and A. STIRLING CALDER. The Sculpture and Mural Decorations of the Exposition. SF: Elder, 1915. (Inner joint weak), o/w Fine. Europa. $44/£28

PERRY, THOMAS. Big Fish. NY: Scribner, 1985. 1st ed. VF in dj. Mordida. $35/£22

PERRY, THOMAS. The Butcher's Boy. NY: Scribner, 1982. 1st ed. Advance rev copy w/slip laid in. VF in dj. Mordida. $250/£160

PERSE, ST. JOHN. Anabasis. T. S. Eliot (trans). London, 1930. 2nd issue. One of 1000. (Bds sl faded), else Excellent in grn dj (sl sunned, rubbed, sm piece top spine missing). Buckley. $86/£55

PERSHING, JOHN J. My Experiences in the World War. NY: Frederick A. Stokes, 1931. Ltd to 2100. Signed. 2 vols. Fine in djs, orig pub's slipcase (sl shelfworn). Sadlon. $225/£144

PERSHING, JOHN J. My Experiences in the World War. NY: Stokes, 1931. 1st ed. 2 vols. Teg. Buckram, gilt. VG+ (bkpls). Bohling. $25/£16

PERTCHIK, B. and H. Flowering Trees of the Caribbean. NY, 1951. (Cvr edges faded.) Dj (lt chipped). Brooks. $29/£19

Peter's Enquiries After Knowledge, with the Strange Things He Heard and Saw. London: Thos. Dean, n.d. (ca 1850). Dec wrappers w/bkseller's ticket. (Creases; name), else VG. Cahan. $100/£64

PETERS, CARL. The Eldorado of the Ancients. London: Pearson, 1902. Port, 2 fldg maps. (Lt rubbed.) Adelson. $85/£54

PETERS, DEWITT C. Kit Carson's Life and Adventures. Hartford, 1873. Later 3/4 calf (joints rubbed). Howes P256. Swann*. $69/£44

PETERS, DEWITT C. Kit Carson's Life and Adventures. Hartford, Dustin, Gilman, 1875. 604pp. Grn cl (spine rubbed, ends frayed, hinges strengthened), gilt. Howes P256. Bohling. $22/£14

PETERS, ELIZABETH. Die for Love. NY: Congdon & Weed, 1984. 1st ed. Signed. Fine in Fine dj. Old London. $25/£16

PETERS, ELIZABETH. Legend in Green Velvet. NY: Dodd, Mead, 1976. 1st ed. Signed. VG in VG dj. Old London. $75/£48

PETERS, ELIZABETH. The Night of Four Hundred Rabbits. NY: Dodd, Mead, 1971. 1st ed. Fine in Fine dj (spine head sl worn). Beasley. $60/£38

PETERS, ELLIS. Black Is the Colour of My True Love's Heart. London: CCC, 1967. 1st ed. Fine in dj. Mordida. $175/£112

PETERS, ELLIS. City of Gold and Shadows. London: Macmillan, 1973. 1st UK ed. Inscribed. VG in dj (sl worn; edge tears, no loss). Moorhouse. $62/£40

PETERS, ELLIS. Mourning Raga. London: Macmillan, 1969. 1st UK ed. VG+ in VG dj (sl rubbed). Williams. $31/£20

PETERS, ELLIS. Never Pick Up Hitch-Hikers! London: Macmillan, 1976. 1st ed. Fine in dj. Mordida. $125/£80

PETERS, ELLIS. A Rare Benedictine. (London, 1988.) 1st ed. Signed. (Sl bumped), else Good in dj. King. $60/£38

PETERS, ELLIS. St. Peter's Fair. NY: William Morrow, 1981. 1st Amer ed. VF in dj. Mordida. $75/£48

PETERS, FRED J. Railroads, Indian and Pioneer Prints by N. Currier and Currier and Ives. NY: Antique Bulletin, 1930. #241/500. (Bkpl, pencil marginalia.) Red cl, gilt. Bohling. $80/£51

PETERS, HARRY T. California on Stone. GC: Doubleday, Doran & Co, 1935. One of 501. 12x9. 105 plts. Black-ptd glazed linen. Dj, slipcase. Dawson. $600/£385

PETERS, HARRY T. Currier and Ives, Printmakers to the American People. NY, (1929). 1st ed. 2 vols. Slipcase. *Swann**. $460/£295

PETERS, HENRY T. Currier and Ives: Printmakers to the American People.... (NY: Arno, 1976.) Facs rpt of 1929 orig. 2 vols. *Ginsberg*. $175/£112

PETERS, HERMANN. Pictorial History of Ancient Pharmacy, with Sketches of Early Medical Practice. William Netter (trans). Chicago, 1902. 3rd ed. Pict cl. VG. *Argosy*. $150/£96

PETERSEN, CARL. Each in Its Ordered Place: A Faulkner Collector's Notebook. Ann Arbor: Ardis, (1975). 1st ed. One of 1000 signed. Dk grn coated cl, simulated leather grain, gilt. Fine in NF pict dj. *Baltimore**. $70/£45

PETERSEN, JAN. Our Street. A Chronicle Written in the Heart of Fascist Germany. Bettey Rensen (trans). London: Left Book Club, 1938. 1st ed. Orange limp cl. Nice. *Patterson*. $23/£15

PETERSEN, KAREN DANIELS. Howling Wolf: A Cheyenne Warrior's Graphic Interpretation of His People. Palo Alto, CA: American West, (1968). *Lien*. $40/£26

PETERSEN, MARCUS. The Fur Traders and Fur Bearing Animals. Buffalo, NY: Hammond, 1914. 1st ed. Map. VG. *Lien*. $60/£38

PETERSEN, WILLIAM J. Steamboating on the Upper Mississippi, the Water Way to Iowa. Iowa City, 1937. Good (reps wrinkled). Howes P263. *Scribe's Perch**. $60/£38

PETERSEN, WILLIAM J. Steamboating on the Upper Mississippi. Iowa City: State Hist Soc of IA, 1937. 1st ed. Grn cl, gilt. VG+. Howes P263. *Bohling*. $65/£42

PETERSEN, WILLIAM J. Steamboating on the Upper Mississippi. Iowa City, 1968. 2nd ed. Fine in dj. Howes P263. *Hayman*. $25/£16

PETERSEN, WILLIAM J. Steamboating on the Upper Mississippi. Iowa City, 1968. Rpt. Fine in dj. *Bohling*. $25/£16

PETERSEN, WILLIAM J. Steamboating on the Upper Mississippi. Iowa City: State Hist Soc of IA, 1968. Rpt. NF in dj. *Zubal**. $22/£14

PETERSHAM, MAUD and MISKA. Auntie. NY: Doubleday, 1932. 1st ed. 8 1/2 x 10 1/4. 64pp. Cl spine, pict bds. VG. *Cattermole*. $60/£38

PETERSHAM, MAUD and MISKA. The Peppernuts. NY: Macmillan, 1958. 1st ed. 8vo. 63pp. VG in Good++ dj. *Dower*. $45/£29

PETERSILEA, CARLYLE. Mary Anne Carew: Wife, Mother, Spirit, Angel. Chicago: Progressive Thinker, 1914. 1st ed. Inscribed. VG+. *Middle Earth*. $35/£22

PETERSON, DANIEL H. Looking-Glass: Being a True Report and Narrative of the Life, Travels, and Labors of Rev. Daniel H. Peterson, a Colored Clergyman.... NY: Wright, 1854. 1st ed. 150,(1)pp; 8 plts. Gilt-stamped pict cl. *Ginsberg*. $250/£160

PETERSON, FRANK LORIS. The Hope of the Race. Nashville, TN, (1934). 1st ed. (Ink inscrip; inner hinges broken; cvrs rubbed, soiled.) *King*. $95/£61

PETERSON, FRED W. Desert Pioneer Doctor and Experiences in Obstetrics. Calexico Chronicle, 1947. 1st ed. VG. *Book Market*. $60/£38

PETERSON, FRED W. Desert Pioneer Doctor and Experiences in Obstetrics. Calexico: Calexico Chronicle, 1947. Gold-stamped fabricoid. *Dawson*. $30/£19

PETERSON, H. L. Daggers and Fighting Knives of the Western World from the Stone Age til 1900. NY: Walker, 1968. 1st ed. VG. *Mikesh*. $25/£16

PETERSON, M. JEANNE. The Medical Profession in Mid-Victorian London. Berkeley, 1978. 1st ed. VG in dj. *Fye*. $30/£19

PETERSON, MARTIN SEVERIN. Joaquin Miller. Stanford Univ, (1937). 1st Amer ed. Frontis port. Uncut. Pict cvrs (spine sunned). Fine. Issued w/o dj. *Polyanthos*. $30/£19

PETRIE, W. M. FLINDERS (ed). A History of Egypt. London: Methuen, 1899-1924. 6 vols. 1928pp. (Sig, bkpl, notes; shelfwear, discoloration some vols.) *Archaeologia*. $275/£176

PETRIE, W. M. FLINDERS. Decorative Patterns of the Ancient World. London: BSAE, 1930. 1st ed. 88 plts. 3/4 cl. Good. *Archaeologia*. $150/£96

PETRIE, W. M. FLINDERS. Egyptian Decorative Art. London: Methuen, (1920). (Sig.) Dj (tattered). *Archaeologia*. $65/£42

PETRIE, W. M. FLINDERS. The Funeral Furniture of Egypt, with Stone and Metal Vases. Warminster: Aris & Phillips, (1977). 45 plts. Good. *Archaeologia*. $85/£54

PETRIE, W. M. FLINDERS. Glass Stamps and Weights with Ancient Weights and Measures. Warminster: Aris & Phillips, (1974). 2 vols in 1. 80 plts. (Emb stamp.) Dj. *Archaeologia*. $125/£80

PETRIE, W. M. FLINDERS. Objects of Daily Use. Warminster: Aris & Phillips, (1974). 62 plts. Good in dj. *Archaeologia*. $125/£80

PETRIE, W. M. FLINDERS. Tools and Weapons. London: British School of Archaeology in Egypt, 1917. 79 plts (stamp at plt margin; fep chipped). 3/4 cl. *Archaeologia*. $175/£112

PETRONIUS. The Satyricon. William Burnaby (trans). NY: LEC, 1964. Ltd to 1500 signed by Antonio Sotomayer (illus). 1/4 natural vellum, crimson cl. VF in slipcase (lt worn). *Truepenny*. $75/£48

PETRONIUS. The Satyricon.... NY: LEC, 1964. One of 1500 numbered, signed by Antonio Sotomayor (illus). Parchment-backed cl. VG in bd slipcase. *Argosy*. $75/£48

PETRY, ANN. The Narrows. Boston: Houghton Mifflin, 1953. 1st ed. Fine in NF dj (sl spine wear). *Beasley*. $125/£80

PETTIGREW, J. B. Design in Nature. London, 1908. 1st ed. 3 vols. (Cl sl worn, shabby, spine torn.) *Maggs*. $101/£65

PETTINGILL, O. S., JR. The American Woodcock. Boston: Boston NH Soc, Apr. 1936. 1st ed. 10 plts incl color frontis, 14 tables. (Lacks top portion rear cvr), else VG. *Mikesh*. $75/£48

PETTIS, GEORGE HENRY. The California Column.... Santa Fe, 1918. 1st ed. Pb. VG. *Pratt*. $325/£208

PETTY, ELIJAH P. Journey to Pleasant Hill. Norman D. Brown (ed). San Antonio, (1982). 1st ed. Fine in Fine dj. *Pratt*. $55/£35

PEVSNER, NIKOLAUS. The Englishness of English Art. Architectural Press, 1956. 1st ed. VG in dj. *Hadley*. $23/£15

PEVSNER, NIKOLAUS. Herefordshire. Penguin, 1963. 1st ed. VG in wraps in dj. *Hadley*. $19/£12

PEVSNER, NIKOLAUS. Middlesex. Penguin, 1951. 1st ed. VG in wraps in dj. *Hadley*. $19/£12

PEYROL, RENE. Rosa Bonheur, Her Life and Work. J. Finden Brown (trans). London: Art Journal, 1889. 32pp + 16pp ads (few spots); 3 engr plts. Aeg. Dec blue cl gilt, beveled bds (sl worn, scratched). *Hollett*. $55/£35

PEYTON, JOHN LEWIS. History of Augusta County, Virginia. Staunton, VA: Yost, 1882. 1st ed. (7),387,(7)pp. Howes P277. *Ginsberg*. $150/£96

PFANNSCHMIDT, E. Fountains and Springs. London: Harrap, 1968. Sound in dj. *Ars Artis*. $33/£21

PFEIFFER, G. S. F. The Voyages and Five Years' Captivity in Algiers.... Harrisburg, PA: Winebrenner, 1836. 1st ed. vi,398pp. (Foxed, marginally affected by damp; heavily soiled, rubbed), o/w Good. Worldwide. $30/£19

PHELPS, ELIZABETH STUART. The Gates Ajar. Boston: Fields, Osgood, 1869. 1st ed. Dedication leaf in 2nd state ('approaches' rather than 'nears'). Purple cl. VG (spine sl dknd, nicked). Sumner & Stillman. $95/£61

PHELPS, ELIZABETH STUART. Men, Women and Ghosts. Fields, Osgood, 1869. 1st ed. (Sm corner off fep.) Good + . Certo. $65/£42

PHELPS, HUMPHREY. Phelps Strangers and Citizens Guide to New York City.... NY: Phelps & Watson, (1857). 1st ed thus. Lg fldg color map (repaired splits; lower 1/2 fr joint split, gilt sl rubbed). Sadlon. $150/£96

PHELPS, WILLIAM DANE. Fremont's Private Navy, 1846 Journal of Capt.... Glendale, 1987. 1st ed. #421/500. Signed by Briton C. Busch (ed). VF in plain dj. Turpen. $30/£19

PHELPS, WILLIAM DANE. Fremont's Private Navy. The 1846 Journal of Captain William Dane Phelps. Briton Cooper Busch (ed). Glendale: Clark, 1987. 1st ed. Ltd to 500. VG. Shasky. $40/£26

PHELPS, WILLIAM LYON. A Dash at the Pole. Boston: Ball, 1909. Illus label (sm defect). VG (sl wear). High Latitude. $35/£22

PHILBY, H. ST. JOHN B. Arabian Days. London: Hale, 1948. 2nd ptg. 49 plts. (Sl foxed; sl rubbed), o/w VG. Worldwide. $120/£77

PHILBY, H. ST. JOHN B. The Empty Quarter Being a Description of the Great South Desert of Arabia.... Constable, 1933. 1st ed. 32 half-tone plts, 3 fldg maps. (Sm piece torn from fr pastedown, 2 date stamps.) Grn cl (rubbed, faded). Cox. $39/£25

PHILBY, H. ST. JOHN. B. A Pilgrim in Arabia. (London, 1943.) One of 350 numbered. Frontis port. Orig 1/4 brn niger. Morocco-edged cl slipcase. Swann*. $373/£239

PHILIP, A. P. W. On the Influence of Minute Doses of Mercury.... Washington, 1834. 1st Amer ed. 60pp. (Ex-lib.) Wrappers. Argosy. $40/£26

PHILIP, A. P. W. Treatise on Febrile Diseases.... Hartford, 1816. 2nd Amer ed. 2 vols. 1 plt vol 2. Full calf (sl worn, fr hinge vol 2 cracked). New Hampshire*. $40/£26

PHILLIPPS, E. M. and A. BOLTON. The Gardens of Italy. London, 1909. 2nd ed. Folio. Color frontis. (Cl sl stained, worn, corners stubbed.) Maggs. $117/£75

PHILLIPS and HILL (eds). Classics of the American Shooting Field. Boston: Houghton Mifflin, 1930. 1st ed. Good (water staining) in Fair dj. Scribe's Perch*. $24/£15

PHILLIPS, CATHERINE C. Jessie Benton Fremont. SF: John Henry Nash, 1935. 1st ed. Paper over bds, cl spine. VG (faded, worn). Howes P310. Parmer. $125/£80

PHILLIPS, CATHERINE C. Portsmouth Plaza: The Cradle of San Francisco. SF: Nash, 1932. 1st ed. One of 1000. 88 plts. Marbled bds, vellum spine. Boxed. Howes P311. Ginsberg. $150/£96

PHILLIPS, CHARLES E. S. (ed). Bibliography of X-Ray Literature and Research. (1896-1897.) London: 'The Electrician,' n.d.(c.1897). 1st ed. Frontis, xxxvii,(1),68pp, 32pp ads. Complete w/insert between pp xxxii and xxxiii. VG (extrems rubbed). Glaser. $475/£304

PHILLIPS, CHRISTOPHER. Steichen at War. NY: Abrams, 1981. 1st ed. Fine in dj. Cahan. $50/£32

PHILLIPS, D. RHYS. The History of the Vale of Neath. Swansea, 1925. 1st ed. 27 plts. (Pencil ruling.) Edwards. $437/£280

PHILLIPS, DONNA-LEE (ed). Eros and Photography. SF: Camerawork/NFS Press, 1977. 1st ed. (Owner stamp), else NF in pict stiff wrappers (spine lt rubbed). Cahan. $85/£54

PHILLIPS, ELLIS L. Alaska Summer 1938. Glen Head, NY: Privately ptd, 1938. One of 500 numbered. Frontis. Ptd bds. VG. High Latitude. $25/£16

PHILLIPS, G. A. Delphiniums. London, 1934. Popular ed. (Plt almost loose; browning.) Maggs. $47/£30

PHILLIPS, H. Pomarium Britannicum; An Historical and Botanical Account of Fruits Known in Great Britain. London, 1823. 3rd ed. ix,372pp; 3 hand-colored plts (sl foxed). (Bkpl of Plesch.) Straight-grained morocco (sl rubbed). Henly. $187/£120

PHILLIPS, HUGH. Mid-Georgian London. London: Collins, 1964. 1st ed. 17 color plts. VG in dj. Hollett. $133/£85

PHILLIPS, J. The Geology of Oxford and the Valley of the Thames. Oxford, 1871. Presentation copy. xxiv,523pp (pencil marginal notes), 12 pub's ads; 2 hand-colored maps, 2 hand-colored sections, 2 plain sections, 11 plts. (Rebacked, preserving spine.) Henly. $172/£110

PHILLIPS, J. B. (trans). St. Luke's Life of Christ. London: Collins, 1956. 1st ed. Dj (lt faded, edges sl chipped). Edwards. $23/£15

PHILLIPS, JAMES DUNCAN. Salem in the Seventeenth Century. Boston/NY: Houghton Mifflin, 1933. 1st ed. Frontis. VG. Worldwide. $10/£6

PHILLIPS, JAYNE ANNE. How Mickey Made It. St. Paul, MN: Bookslinger, 1981. One of 150 numbered, signed. Fine. Lenz. $150/£96

PHILLIPS, JAYNE ANNE. The Secret Country. Winston-Salem, NC: Palaemon, (1982). One of 150 numbered, signed. Fine. Lenz. $150/£96

PHILLIPS, MARY E. Tommy Tregennis. Constable, 1914. 1st ed. M. V. Wheelhouse (illus). Lg 8vo. Color pict tp, 209pp; 7 color plts. Teg. Illus cl. (Mks), else VG. Bookmark. $25/£16

PHILLIPS, P. LEE. A List of Maps of America in the Library of Congress. Washington: GPO, 1901. Interior Good (soiled, bds faded, hinges repaired). Dumont. $225/£144

PHILLIPS, PAUL C. (ed). Forty Years on the Frontier.... Glendale, CA, 1957. Rpt. 2 vols in 1. (Sl rubbed.) King. $65/£42

PHILLIPS, R. RANDAL. The Book of Bungalows. Country Life, 1922. 2nd ed. Cl-backed bds, ptd label. (One opening pulled), o/w NF. Whittle. $31/£20

PHILLIPS, R. RANDAL. Small Country Houses of To-Day. London: Country Life, 1925. 1st ed. Grn cl (sl shelfworn), gilt. VG. House. $85/£54

PHILLIPS, RAYMOND (ed). Trial of Joseph Kramer and Forty-Four Others. London, 1949. Fldg map at rear. (Lt spotted, lib bkpl; cl lt faded, rubbed, accession #.) Edwards. $47/£30

PHILLIPS, W. S. Indian Tales for Little Folks. NY: Platt & Munk, 1928. 4to. 80pp; 11 full-pg color plts. VF (inscrip) in bds w/paste-on color illus. Fr cvr of dj remains. Bromer. $125/£80

PHILLIPS-WOOLLEY, CLIVE. Big Game Shooting. London, 1894-1901. 2 vols. Dec brn cl (backs sl dull). Petersfield. $47/£30

PHILLPOTTS, EDEN. The Broom Squires. NY: Macmillan, 1932. 1st Amer ed. VG (eps browned) in dj (spine browned, head chipped). Antic Hay. $20/£13

PHILLPOTTS, EDEN. The Captain's Curio. NY: Macmillan, 1933. 1st Amer ed. Fine in dj (edges sl worn). Mordida. $45/£29

PHILLPOTTS, EDEN. A Clue from the Stars. NY: Macmillan, 1932. 1st Amer ed. Fine in dj (spine ends sl worn, corners sl chipped). Mordida. $65/£42

PHILLPOTTS, EDEN. Dark Horses. London: John Murray, 1938. 1st ed. (Edges lt spotted.) Hollett. $23/£15

PHILLPOTTS, EDEN. Dish of Apples. London/NY: Hodder & Stoughton, (1921). 1st trade ed. 3 color plts. Gray pict cl. VG in dj (worn). New Hampshire*. $50/£32

PHILLPOTTS, EDEN. A Dish of Apples. Hodder & Stoughton, n.d. (1921). 1st ed. Arthur Rackham (illus). Sm 4to. 3 tipped-in color plts, tissue guards, 7 full-pg b/w illus. 2-tone pict eps. Illus grey cl (sl rubbed, spine sl dknd). VG. Bookmark. $133/£85

PHILLPOTTS, EDEN. Flower of the Gods. NY: Macmillan, 1943. 1st ed. Fine in dj (spine ends, corners worn). Mordida. $45/£29

PHILLPOTTS, EDEN. Lycanthrope. NY, 1938. 1st ed. VG+ in VG dj (edgeworn, creased). Mcclintock. $45/£29

PHILLPOTTS, EDEN. Lycanthrope: The Mystery of Sir William Wolf. Macmillan, 1938. 1st US ed. VG in dj (trimmed, backed, stuck at flaps). Certo. $30/£19

PHILLPOTTS, EDEN. The Red Redmaynes. NY: Macmillan, 1922. 1st ed. (Soiled, stained, rubbed, shaken.) Lacks dj. Metropolitan*. $28/£18

Philosophy of Kissing, Anatomically and Physiologically Explained. NY: Robert H. Elton, 1841. 72pp. (Extrems sl worn), else Good (lacks wrappers). Brown. $75/£48

PHIN, JOHN. How to Use the Microscope. NY: Industrial Pubs, 1882. 5th ed. 238pp; 6 plts. VG. Savona. $39/£25

PHIPPS, CONSTANTINE JOHN. A Voyage Towards the North Pole Undertaken by His Majesty's Command, 1773. London: J. Nourse, 1774. 1st ed. 4to. 15 maps, plts, diags, 11 fldg tables. Old full polished calf (edgeworn, fr cvr held only by binding cords, rear hinge starting). Kane*. $800/£513

PHIPPS, CONSTANTINE JOHN. A Voyage towards the North Pole: Undertaken by His Majesty's Command, 1773. Dublin: Sleater et al, 1775. 1st 8vo ed, 1st Irish ed. viii,276pp; 11 fldg ptd tables, 1 fldg map (marginal tear, neatly repaired), 2 fldg engr plts. Contemp calf (spine extrems chipped; bottom edge, corners worn; fr outer hinge cracked but holding), red morocco spine label. Karmiole. $850/£545

PHIPPS, HOWARD. Further Interiors. Whittington, 1992. One of 235 (plus 65 specials) signed, numbered. 16 engrs (4 color). Fine in grey wrappers, slipcase. Michael Taylor. $109/£70

PHIPPS, MARY. Liza Jane and the Kinkies. NY: J.H. Sears, (1929). 1st ed. 4to. Pict eps. Black cl, pict bds. Cvrs VG (sl dusty, lt rubbed, sm abrasion rear cvr). Baltimore*. $100/£64

PHOENIX, JOHN. Phoenixiana, or Sketches and Burlesques. NY: Appleton, 1903. 1st ed thus. NF. Five Quail. $45/£29

Photography 63: An International Exhibition. (Rochester): George Eastman House, 1963. Fine in stiff wrappers. Cahan. $35/£22

Photography: Current Perspectives. (Amherst)/Rochester: MA Review/Light Impressions, 1978. 1st ed thus. 60 full-pg b/w plts. NF in pict dj. Cahan. $50/£32

Photography: Venice '79. NY: Rizzoli, 1979. Fine in dj. Cahan. $50/£32

PHYSICK, JOHN. Designs for English Sculpture 1680-1860. London: HMSO, 1969. Dj. Europa. $37/£24

PIANKOFF, ALEXANDRE. The Pyramid of Unas. Princeton: Princeton Univ, 1968. 77 plts, 2 fldg plans. (Sig; sm bkpls removed.) Dj. Archaeologia. $375/£240

PIANKOFF, ALEXANDRE. The Tomb of Ramesses VI. NY: Bollingen Foundation, (1954). 2 vols. 2 color plts; 14pp w/1 fig and 196 plts loose in portfolio as issued. Good in box. Archaeologia. $450/£288

PIATT, JOHN JAMES (ed). The Hesperian Tree, a Souvenir of the Ohio Valley. North Bend, OH, (1900). Grn cl (spine rubbed, sl dull), gilt. VG (sl foxed). Bohling. $35/£22

PICASSO, PABLO. Picasso for Vollard. Norbert Buterman (trans). NY: Abrams, (1956). 1st US ed. Blue pict cl (spine lt faded). Text VG in bd slipcase (edges sl worn). Baltimore*. $110/£71

PICASSO, PABLO. Picasso. Wilhelm Boeck and Jaime Sabartes (text). NY: Abrams, (1955). 1st ed. 2 dbl-spreads in color offset, 38 full-pg color plts. Dec cl. Fine in dj. Hermitage. $125/£80

PICASSO, PABLO. Toros y Toreros. Miguel Luis Dominguin (text). Edouard Roditi (trans). (London): Thames & Hudson, (1961). 1st ed in English, Amer version (pub by Abrams, but w/o any notation of such within the vol). Folio. Color pict white cl (spine sl dknd). Text Fine in pict bd slipcase (dusty, dknd), orig clear plastic partial wraparound gilt label w/Abrams credit. Baltimore*. $90/£58

PICHON, JEROME. The Life of Charles Henry Count Hoym, Ambassador from Saxony-Poland to France.... NY: Grolier Club, 1899. 1st ed in English. One of 300. Prospectus laid in. 1/2 morocco, cl (spine ends, corners rubbed; bkpls). Swann*. $46/£29

PICHON, JEROME. The Life of Charles Henry Count Hoym. NY: Grolier Club, 1899. One of 300. Calf, brocade cvrs (sl frayed). Rostenberg & Stern. $175/£112

PICHON, JEROME. The Life of Charles Henry Count Hoym...Eminent French Bibliophile 1694-1736. NY: Grolier, 1899. One of 303 (of 306 ptd). Orig 3/4 morocco, brocade over bds. (Sl wear, brocade extrems dknd), o/w Very Nice. Reese. $225/£144

PICHON, LEON. The New Book-Illustration in France. London, 1924. VG. Truepenny. $175/£112

PICKARD, MADGE E. and CARLYLE BULEY. The Midwest Pioneer, His Ills, Cures, and Doctors. NY: Henry Schuman, 1946. Rev ed. VG in VG dj. Perier. $35/£22

PICKARD, MADGE E. and CARLYLE BULEY. The Midwest Pioneer: His Ills, Cures, and Doctors. NY, 1946. 1st ed. VG. Fye. $45/£29

PICKARD, MADGE E. and R. CARLYLE BULEY. The Midwest Pioneer, His Ills, Cures, and Doctors. NY: Henry Schuman, 1946. 1st trade ed. Frontis. Paperboard binding. VG. Bohling. $15/£10

PICKARD, SAMUEL T. Hawthorne's First Diary. Boston, 1897. 1st Amer ed. A possible forgery and withdrawn by the editor. NF (spine sl rubbed). Polyanthos. $35/£22

PICKARD, SAMUEL T. The Life and Letters of John Greenleaf Whittier. Cambridge: Ptd at Riverside Press, 1894. 1st ed, lg paper issue. One of 400. This set designated as 'Author's copy.' 2 vols. Cl, bds (sl soiled, spines sl tanned, paper labels (tanned). VG-. BAL 22172. Reese. $60/£38

PICKERING, ERNEST. Architectural Design. NY: John Wiley, 1947. 2nd ed. (Spine sl faded.) Hollett. $62/£40

PICKERING, H. G. Angling of the Test, or True Love Under Stress. NY: Derrydale, 1936. 1st ed, 2nd issue. #219/297. Emb black cl, gilt. (Spine sl faded, sm abrasions upper cvr), else Fine. Cummins. $300/£192

PICKETT, LA SALLE CORBELL. Across My Path: Memories of People I Have Known. NY: Brentano's, 1916. 1st ed. (Ex-lib, bkpl removed; sm spine labels removed.) Ginsberg. $75/£48

PICKETT, LASALLE CORBELL. Across My Path. NY, 1916. 1st ed. VG+. Pratt. $27/£17

PICKETT, LASALLE CORBELL. What Happened to Me. NY: Brentano's, 1917. 1st ed. Inscribed. (Leaf tape-repaired, sm marginal dampstain last 20pp), else VG. Cahan. $50/£32

575

PICKETT, THOMAS E. Quest for a Lost Race. Filson Club, 1907. Unopened. Fine in ptd wrapper. *Bohling.* $40/£26

PICKWELL, GAYLE (ed). Spring Wild Flowers of the Open Field. San Jose, 1933. Color frontis. Grn cl. VG. *Brooks.* $24/£15

Pictorial and Descriptive Guide to the English Lake District. London: Ward, Locke, n.d. (c.1910). 18th ed. Lg fldg map, 3 section maps. Red cl (spine faded, sm nick; upper joint cracked). *Hollett.* $16/£10

Pictorial Views of Massachusetts. Worcester: Eonos Dorr, n.d. (1846). Sq 16mo. (Sl stained, soiled, few corners sl curled; old plain wrappers frayed, spine gone.) *Oinonen*.* $80/£51

Picture Alphabet. NY: McLoughlin Bros, n.d. 4to. (14)pp (lt soiled, corner chipped); 15 chromolitho illus. Good in color pict wraps (soiled, corners creased, sm tear bottom edge, spine chipped, resewn); pub's ads rear cvr. *Blue Mountain.* $150/£96

Picture Alphabet. (Derby: Thomas Richardson), n.d. (ca 1840). 16mo. 27pp + 1pg list on lower wrapper. Orig pict paper wrappers (soiled, spine rubbed). (Lt foxing), else VG. *Hobbyhorse.* $215/£138

PIDDINGTON, HENRY. The Sailor's Horn-Book for the Law of Storms. London: Williams & Norgate, 1869. 5th ed. xviii,(2),408pp; chart on tinted paper, 4 lg fldg charts, 2 cards in pockets each end. Morocco label. (Sl bruised, neatly rebacked.) *Cox.* $70/£45

Pied Piper of Hamlin. (Portland, OR): Chamberlain Press, 1980. Ltd to 150 signed by Sarah Chamberlain (illus); this copy also inscribed. 8vo. (16)pp; 11 wood engrs, each signed by Chamberlain. Prospectus, which shows another signed wood-engr from the bk. Marbled bds, leather spine label stamped in black. VF. *Bromer.* $250/£160

PIENKOWSKI, JAN. Haunted House. NY: E.P. Dutton, 1979. Pop-up bk. Sm 4to. Glazed pict paper-cvrd bds. NF. *Book Adoption.* $65/£42

PIERCE, ELIZA. The Letters of Eliza Pierce 1751-1775. London: Etchells & Macdonald, 1927. Ltd to 670. Frontis port. Blue buckram, gilt. Nice in ptd dj. *Cady.* $30/£19

PIERCE, FRANK CUSHMAN. A Brief History of the Lower Rio Grande Valley. Menasha, WI, 1917. 3 fldg maps. (Backstrip etched), else VG. *Bohling.* $45/£29

PIERCE, FRANK CUSHMAN. A Brief History of the Lower Rio Grande Valley. Menasha, WI: George Banta, 1917. 1st ed. 3 fldg maps. Good in wrappers (sl worn). *Brown.* $35/£22

PIERCE, GEORGE F. Incidents of Western Travel: In a Series of Letters. Nashville, 1857. 1st ed. 249pp; port. (Cl faded.) Howes P353. *Ginsberg.* $475/£304

PIERCE, GILBERT A. and WILLIAM A. WHEELER. The Dickens Dictionary. London: Chapman & Hall, 1878. 1st ed. xvi,607pp. (Eps sl spotted; extrems rubbed, spine faded.) *Hollett.* $148/£95

PIERCE, R. V. The People's Common Sense Medical Adviser in Plain English. Buffalo, 1888. 17th ed. 1008pp. Brn gilt-tooled cl (sl worn). VG. *Doctor's Library.* $50/£32

PIERCE, RICHARD and JOHN WINSLOW (eds). H.M.S. Sulphur at California, 1837 and 1839. SF: Book Club of CA, 1969. One of 450. Frontis map. Cl-backed dec bds. Fine. *Harrington.* $50/£32

PIERCY, CAROLINE. The Valley of God's Pleasure. NY: Stratford House, 1951. 1st ed. VG (sunned). *Archer.* $20/£13

PIERCY, FREDERICK HAWKINS. Route From Liverpool to Great Salt Lake Valley. Fawn M. Brodie (ed). Cambridge, MA, 1962. VG in dj (sl worn). Howes L359. *Lien.* $35/£22

PIERCY, FREDERICK HAWKINS. Route from Liverpool to Great Salt Lake Valley. Fawn M. Brodie (ed). Cambridge: Harvard, 1962. Map, tp facs. VG + in dj. Howes L359. *Bohling.* $40/£26

PIERCY, FREDERICK HAWKINS. Route from Liverpool to Great Salt Lake Valley.... L.A., 1959. Westernlore Press rpt. Fldg map. (Bkpl), o/w VG + in dj. *Benchmark.* $145/£93

PIERCY, MARGE. The Twelve-Spoked Wheel Flashing. NY: Knopf, 1978. 1st ed. Fine in dj. *Lame Duck.* $50/£32

Pierre Joseph Redoute's Roses. Ariel Press, 1954. 3rd imp. 24 plts. Near New in stiff pict cvrs, glassine protected. *Quest.* $100/£64

PIERSON, ERMA. The Mohave River and Its Valley. Glendale: A.H. Clark, 1970. 1st ed. Good in dj. *Heinoldt.* $25/£16

PIGMAN, WALTER. The Journal of Walter Griffith Pigman. Mexico, MO, 1942. 1st ed. Ltd to 200. Blue paper bd w/ptd paper label. Howes P361. *Ginsberg.* $150/£96

PIGNATTI, TERISIO. The Doges' Palace. NY, n.d. 42 color plts. Good in dj. *Washton.* $85/£54

PIGNATTI, TIRISIO. Five Centuries of Italian Painting 1300-1800 from...Sarah Campbell Blaffer Foundation. Houston, 1985. Good in wraps. *Washton.* $30/£19

PIKE, D. W. Secret Societies. London/NY/Toronto: OUP, (1939). Blue cl (bumped, rubbed). Internally NF. *Blue Mountain.* $25/£16

PIKE, WARBURTON. The Barren Ground of Northern Canada. London: Macmillan, 1892. ix,2,300pp; 2 fldg maps. (Ex-lib, spine ends frayed.) *Adelson.* $80/£51

PIKE, WARBURTON. The Barren Ground of Northern Canada. London: Macmillan, 1892. ix,(3),300pp, 2 fldg maps. VG. *High Latitude.* $140/£90

PIKE, WARBURTON. Through the Subarctic Forest. London/NY: Edward Arnold, 1896. 1st ed. xiv,(i)illus, (i)blank, 295,(1)blank pp, 32 pub's list, 1/2-title, 2 fldg maps, 13 plts. Brn pict cl. Generally Fine (lt foxing 1st, last 2 leaves, fore-edge). *Morrell.* $296/£190

PIKE, ZEBULON MONTGOMERY. The Expeditions of...to Headwaters of the Mississippi River...1805-7. Elliott Coues (ed). NY, 1895. Rpt of 1810 1st ed. #816/1150. Frontis port, 955pp; 7 Fine fldg maps in pocket. Grn cl, spine gilt. (Spine top vol 1 slit, expertly repaired, tip sl bumped, ex-lib), o/w Fine. Howes P373. *Turpen.* $595/£381

PIKE, ZEBULON MONTGOMERY. Exploratory Travels Through the Western Territories of North America. London: Longman et al, 1811. 1st Eng ed. 4to. xx,436pp; 2 maps (1 fldg, bound out of order). Partly unopened, untrimmed. VG (bds rebacked, later linen spine, extrems sl worn; sl offsetting from maps, sl ink marginalia p9). Howes P373. *Brown.* $1,750/£1,122

PILKINGTON, MATTHEW. A Dictionary of Painters from the Revival of the Art of the Present Period. London, 1810. New ed. 114 Fine steel-engr plts inserted. (Foxing, sl stains, soil.) Aeg. 3/4 morocco (rubbed, joints worn), spine gilt in 6 compartments. *Oinonen*.* $60/£38

PILKINGTON, MATTHEW. A General Dictionary of Painters. 1852. New ed. Engr frontis port (sl spotted), cxii,623pp. Emb cl (lt soiled, edges faded, sl bumped; hinges cracked, sl shaken). *Edwards.* $70/£45

PILKINGTON, STEPHEN M. With a Gun to the Hill. London: Herbert Jenkins, 1948. 1st ed. 15 plts. VG in dj. *Hollett.* $47/£30

PILLSBURY, ALBERT E. Lincoln and Slavery. Boston, 1913. 1st ed. (Eps spotted; cvrs sl worn.) *King.* $45/£29

PIM, S. The Wood and the Trees, a Biography of Augustine Henry. London, 1966. Dj. *Maggs.* $22/£14

PINCHOT, GIFFORD and H. S. GRAVES. The White Pine. NY, 1896. 1st ed. Photo frontis, 102pp. Grn cl, gilt. VG (ex-lib). *Price.* $34/£22

PINCKNEY, DARRYL. High Cotton. NY: FSG, (1992). 1st ed. Fine in Fine dj. *Unger.* $75/£48

PINCKNEY, DARRYL. High Cotton. NY: Farrar, 1992. 1st ed. Fine in Fine dj. *Beasley.* $50/£32

PINCKNEY, JAMES D. Reminiscences of Catskill. Catskill: Hall, 1868. 1st ed. 79pp. Orig gilt-stamped cl (expertly rebacked, recased). Howes P379. *Ginsberg.* $125/£80

PINCUS, ARTHUR. Terror in Cuba. NY: Workers Defense League, 1936. 1st ed. Pb. VG + . *Beasley.* $40/£26

PINCUS, GREGORY and KENNETH V. THIMANN (eds). The Hormones: Chemistry, Physiology and Applications. NY, 1948. 1st ed. 2 vols. Blue cl bds (sl worn). VG in djs (worn). *Doctor's Library.* $75/£48

PINE, GEORGE W. Beyond the West. Utica, NY, 1870. 1st ed. 444pp, 6 plts. Dec cl. Howes P382. *Ginsberg.* $300/£192

PINE, GEORGE W. Beyond the West.... Buffalo, 1873. Frontis port, 483pp. Good-. Howes P381. *Scribe's Perch*.* $22/£14

PINERO, ARTHUR WING. The Gay Lord Quex. R.H. Russell, 1900. 1st US ed. VG + in Lovely pict bds. *Williams.* $70/£45

PINERO, ARTHUR WING. The Second Mrs. Tanqueray. London: Heinemann, 1895. 1st ed. Dk grn cl-backed bds. VG (inscrip; tilted). *Maggs.* $203/£130

PINKERTON, A. F. Saved at the Scaffold or Nic Brown, the Chicago Detective. Chicago: Laird & Lee, (1888). 1st ed. (7)-161pp + ads. Pict cl. Good. *M & S.* $150/£96

PINKERTON, FRANK. Dyke Darrel, the Railroad Detective. Chicago: Laird & Lee, (1886). 1st ed. 155pp. Pict cl. *M & S.* $125/£80

PINKERTON, JAMES N. Sleep and Its Phenomena. London: Edmund Fry, 1839. 1st ed. Grn cl. VG (homemade paper labels, some partly removed). *Beasley.* $100/£64

PINKERTON, ROBERT E. The Canoe. NY: Outing Pub Co, 1916. Dec grn cl. (Sl worn, age-dknd, sm spots fore-edge), else VG. *Parmer.* $20/£13

PINKERTON, ROBERT E. The Canoe. NY: Outing, 1916. Pict cl. VG. *Bowman.* $25/£16

PINKWATER, DANIEL. The Last Guru. NY: Dodd, Mead, 1978. 1st ed. 5 3/4 x 8 1/4. 127pp. VG (ex-lib, few mks) in dj. *Cattermole.* $25/£16

PINKWATER, DANIEL. The Magic Moscow. NY: Four Winds, 1980. 1st ed. 5 3/4 x 8 1/2. 57pp. Cl spine. Fine in dj. *Cattermole.* $25/£16

PINNOCK, WILLIAM. Panorama of the Old World and the New.... Boston/Phila, 1853. 1st ed. 616pp; 22 hand-colored plts. (Reps torn, 1 text pg w/lg chip, sl loss; lt rubbed, spine faded), o/w VG. *New Hampshire*.* $130/£83

PINTARD, JOHN. Letters from John Pintard to His Daughter, Eliza Noel Pintard Davidson, 1816-1833. NY Hist Soc, 1940-41. 4 vols. (Lib mks.) *Bohling.* $35/£22

PINTER, HAROLD. The Birthday Party and Other Plays. London: Methuen, (1960). 1st ed. Fine in dj (extrems rubbed). *Captain's Bookshelf.* $125/£80

PINTER, HAROLD. The French Lieutenant's Woman. Boston: Little, Brown, (1981). One of 360 numbered, signed by Pinter & John Fowles (intro). Fine in Fine slipcase. *Lenz.* $150/£96

PINTER, HAROLD. The Homecoming. NY: Grove, 1966. 1st ed. NF in VG + dj. *Warren.* $40/£26

PINTER, HAROLD. Landscape. London: Pendragon, 1968. #1211/2000. NF. *Williams.* $28/£18

PINTER, HAROLD. Poems. Enitharmon, 1968. 1st UK ed. Erratum slip laid in. Fine in ptd wrappers. *Williams.* $47/£30

PIONEER LADIES CLUB. Reminiscences of Oregon Pioneers. Pendleton: East OR Pub Co, 1937. 1st ed. Fine. *Perier.* $125/£80

PIOZZI, HESTER LYNCH. Anecdotes of the Late Samuel Johnson During the Last Twenty Years of His Life. London: Cadell, 1786. 2nd ed. 307pp. Full polished morocco (recent rebinding), raised bands, blind fillets, gilt. Fine. *Hartfield.* $425/£272

PIOZZI, HESTER LYNCH. Observations and Reflections Made in...France, Italy, and Germany. London: A. Strahan & T. Cadell, 1789. 1st ed. 2 vols. Early full tree calf (fr cvr vol 2 detached), gilt-dec spines, gilt-lettered red morocco spine labels. Internally Bright. *D & D.* $375/£240

PIPER, MYFANWY. The Wood-Engravings of Reynolds Stone. (London): Art & Technics, 1951. 1st ed. (Bk label fep), o/w NF in dj (rubbed, several tears). *Heller.* $75/£48

PIPER, WATTY (ed). The Gateway to Storyland. NY: Platt & Munk, (1928). 1st ed. Eulalie (illus). 4to. 100pp. Beautiful in dj. *Captain's Bookshelf.* $125/£80

PIPER, WATTY. Little Folks of Other Lands. NY: Platt & Munk, 1943. 'Deluxe Edition.' 4to. Unpaginated. L.W. & H.C. Holling (illus). Pict pastedown cvr. Good + in dj (heavily chipped). *Scribe's Perch*.* $18/£12

Pirate. (By Walter Scott.) Edinburgh, 1822. 1st ed. 3 vols. Contemp 1/2 calf, gilt. (Sigs.) *Swann*.* $402/£258

PIRSIG, ROBERT M. Zen and the Art of Motorcycle Maintenance. London, 1974. 1st Eng ed. Very Nice in dj. *Clearwater.* $47/£30

PIRSIG, ROBERT M. Zen and the Art of Motorcycle Maintenance. NY, 1974. 1st Amer ed, 1st bk. Fine in dj (spine sl rubbed). *Polyanthos.* $75/£48

PIRSIG, ROBERT M. Zen and the Art of Motorcycle Maintenance. NY: Morrow, 1974. 1st ed, 1st bk. Nice (edges sl sunned) in dj. *Reese.* $55/£35

PIRSIG, ROBERT M. Zen and the Art of Motorcycle Maintenance. NY: Wm. Morrow, 1984. One of 1000 numbered, signed. Fine in Fine slipcase, bellyband (sm tear). *Revere.* $75/£48

PIRTLE, ALFRED. The Battle of Tippecanoe. Louisville, KY, 1900. 1st ed. Orig ptd wrappers bound in cl w/both wrappers bound in. NF. Howes P389. *Mcgowan.* $150/£96

PIRTLE, ALFRED. James Chenoweth. Louisville, KY, 1921. 1st ed. Signed, dated. Map. VG (lacks frontis; pencil name, address). *Wantagh.* $25/£16

PISANI. Vendeleur; Or, Animal Magnetism. London: Richard Bentley, 1836. Uncertain ed. Presentation copy. 3 vols. (ii),(x),(308); (iv),(332); (iv),348pp. Cl-backed drab bds (peeled, spines varnished, few gatherings sprung). Good. *Gach.* $150/£96

PISSARRO, CAMILLE. Letters to His Son Lucien. John Rewald (ed). NY, 1943. Very Nice in dj (sl chipped). *Clearwater.* $55/£35

PITMAN, BENN. Sir Isaac Pitman, His Life and Labors. (Cincinnati, 1902.) Presentation copy. VG. *Bohling.* $110/£71

PITMAN, C. R. S. A Game Warden Takes Stock. London, 1942. (Spine faded.) *Grayling.* $39/£25

PITT RIVERS, LT.-GEN. Excavations in Cranborne Chase.... London: Privately ptd, 1887-1898. 4 vols. Vol 1 bound in lib buckram, remainder in orig blue cl (2 backs lt worn), gilt. (Ex-lib, labels, #s, vol 4 stamps throughout.) *Hatchwell.* $429/£275

PITTENGER, WILLIAM. Daring and Suffering. Time-Life, 1982. Leather. Fine. *Pratt.* $30/£19

PITTENGER, WILLIAM. Daring and Suffering: A History of the Andrews Railroad Raid into Georgia in 1862.... NY, 1887. 416,55pp; map. Good (extrems sl worn). *Wantagh.* $85/£54

PITTER, RUTH. The Bridge. London: Cresset, 1945. 1st ed. VG in dj. *Hollett.* $23/£15

PITTER, RUTH. First Poems. Cecil Palmer, 1920. 1st Eng ed, 1st bk. (Name; chafed, scratched, sl faded.) *Clearwater.* $78/£50

PITTMAN, BEN (ed). The Trials for Treason at Indianapolis, Disclosing the Plans for Establishing a North-Western Confederacy.... Cincinnati: Moore, Wilstach & Baldwin, 1865. 1st ed. Frontis port (foxing), plt. Recent cl, gilt. Howes P394. *Sadlon.* $200/£128

PITTMAN, PHILIP. The Present State of the European Settlements on the Mississippi. Cleveland: A.H. Clark, 1906. One of 500 numbered. 8 maps on 7 fldg sheets. Internally Good. (Spine faded, rear bd repaired.) Howes P394. *Dumont.* $165/£106

PLACE, CHARLES A. Charles Bulfinch: Architect and Citizen. Boston, 1924. 1st ed. Grn cl (sl worn, soiled). *Freeman*.* $60/£38

PLACE, CHARLES A. Charles Bulfinch: Architect and Citizen. Boston: Houghton, 1925. 1st ed. 128 plts. (Spine sl faded.) *Ginsberg.* $150/£96

Plain Truth: Or a Letter to the Author of Dispassionate Thoughts on the American War. (By Joseph Galloway.) London, 1780. 1st ed. Complete w/half-title, ads. Mod cl, bds. Howes G45. *Freeman*.* $120/£77

PLANCHE, J. R. An Old Fairy Tale Told Anew. London: Routledge, c. 1865. Lg 12mo. 51pp; 19 illus engrs by Richard Doyle. Gilt-dec blue cl (sl rubbed). Good+. *Dower.* $100/£64

PLANTE, DAVID. The Ghost of Henry James. London, 1970. 1st Eng ed, 1st bk. Very Nice in dj (sl creased, rubbed). *Clearwater.* $62/£40

PLANTE, DAVID. Relatives. London, 1972. 1st Eng ed. Fine in dj (price-clipped). *Clearwater.* $47/£30

PLANTE, DAVID. Slides. London, 1971. 1st Eng ed. Fine in dj. *Clearwater.* $47/£30

PLASKITT, F. J. W. Microscopic Fresh Water Life. London: Chapman & Hall, 1926. Good. *Savona.* $28/£18

PLATH, SYLVIA. The Bed Book. NY: Harper & Row, 1976. 1st ed. Illus bds. Fine in dj. *Words Etc.* $47/£30

PLATH, SYLVIA. Child. Rougemont, 1971. One of 325. Ms facs. Cardboard cvrs. Fine in dj. *Buckley.* $86/£55

PLATH, SYLVIA. Crossing the Water. Faber & Faber, (1971). 1st ed. Nice in dj. *Ash.* $55/£35

PLATH, SYLVIA. Winter Trees. London, 1971. 1st ed. Fine in dj. *Buckley.* $47/£30

PLATH, SYLVIA. Winter Trees. NY, 1972. 1st US ed. VF in Good dj. *Bond.* $35/£22

PLATNER, SAMUEL BALL. A Topographical Dictionary of Ancient Rome. Oxford, 1929. 56 illus hors texte. (Cl sl shelfworn, sm tear top backstrip.) *Washton.* $125/£80

PLATO. Lysis, or Friendship. The Symposium. Phaedrus. Benjamin Jowett (trans). (Mt. Vernon, NY): LEC, 1968. One of 1500 numbered, signed by Eugene Karlin (illus). Vellum-backed gilt-stamped bds, gilt leather spine label. Mint in bd slipcase. *Argosy.* $125/£80

PLATO. Lysis, or Friendship: The Symposium and Phaedrus. Benjamin Jowett (trans). NY: LEC, 1968. One of 1500 numbered, signed by Eugene Karlin (illus). Fine in pub's slipcase. *Hermitage.* $125/£80

PLATO. The Republic. Benjamin Jowett (trans). NY: LEC, 1944. One of 1200 numbered, signed by Bruce Rogers and Fritz Kredel (illus). 2 vols. Teg. Morocco-backed pict bds, gilt spine. VG in bd slipcase. *Argosy.* $200/£128

PLATT, CHARLES A. Monograph of the Work of.... NY, 1913. (Internal soil; cl worn, soiled.) *Freeman*.* $100/£64

PLATT, HUGH. The Jewel House of Art and Nature. London: Bernard Alsop, 1653. 2nd ed. 4to. Contemp sheep (spine chipped; hinges reinforced w/cl tape), morocco label (chipped). *Dramatis Personae.* $950/£609

PLATT, ISAAC. Bacon Cryptograms of Shake-Speare. Boston: Small, Maynard, 1905. 1st ed. NF. *Middle Earth.* $65/£42

PLATT, ISAAC. Walt Whitman. Boston: Small, Maynard, 1904. 1st ed. Frontis port. Blue cl (bumped), gilt. NF. *Blue Mountain.* $75/£48

PLATT, WARD. The Frontier. NY: Young People's Missionary Movement, 1910. 2 fldg maps. Wraps (sl soiled, sl chipped). *Dumont.* $45/£29

PLAYER-FROWD, J. G. Six Months in California. London, 1872. 1st ed. 164,(20)pp. (Spine, fr cvr worn.) *Ginsberg.* $200/£128

PLAYFAIR, R. L. Handbook to the Mediterranean. London, 1881. xliv,512pp+66pp ads. (Fep, 1/2 title detached to lower portion; joints split, spine creased, chipped, corners rubbed.) *Edwards.* $39/£25

PLAYFAIR, R. L. and ROBERT BROWN. A Bibliography of Morocco. London, 1892. 1st ed. xviii,262pp. Contemp 1/4 vellum. *Maggs.* $156/£100

Pleader's Guide, a Didactic Poem: Containing the Conduct of a Suit at Law.... London: T. Cadell/W. Davies, Strand, 1804. 4th ed. Contemp speckled calf (worn, joints cracked). Usable. *Boswell.* $125/£80

Pleasant History of Reynard the Fox. Thomas Roscoe (trans). London: Sampson Low, 1873. A.T. Elwes & John Jellicoe (illus). 8vo. xv,136pp. (Lt mk fr cvr), else VF in 1/2 morocco, gilt. *Bromer.* $65/£42

PLEASANTS, JOSEPH E. The Cattle Drives of Joseph E. Pleasants from Baja California in 1867 and 1868. Don Meadows (ed). (L.A.): Dawson's Book Shop, 1965. One of 600. 3 tipped-in illus. Brn cl. *Dawson.* $50/£32

PLEASANTS, MRS. J. E. History of Orange County, California. L.A.: J.R. Finnell, 1931. 3 vols. Black fabricoid (fr inner hinge Vol II weak; sl wear, spotting). *Dawson.* $300/£192

PLEASANTS, SAMUEL AUGUSTUS. Fernando Wood of New York. NY: Columbia, 1948. VG (lt soiled) in ptd wraps. *Bohling.* $18/£12

PLENDERLEITH, H. J. The Conservation of Antiquities and Works of Art, Treatment, Repair and Restoration. London, 1956. 1st ed. VG. *Gretton.* $27/£17

PLENDERLEITH, H. J. The Conservation of Antiquities and Works of Art. London: OUP, 1956. Color frontis, 55 plts. Fine in color dj. *Europa.* $44/£28

PLIMPTON, GEORGE. The Curious Case of Sidd Finch. NY: Macmillan, (1987). 1st ed. NF in NF dj. *Fuller & Saunders.* $15/£10

PLIMPTON, GEORGE. The Curious Case of Sidd Finch. Macmillan, 1987. 1st ed. Signed. Fine in Fine dj. *Plapinger.* $85/£54

PLIMPTON, GEORGE. The Education of Shakespeare. London, 1933. 1st ed. Signed, inscribed, dated. VF. *Bond.* $30/£19

PLIMPTON, GEORGE. Paper Lion. NY, 1966. 1st ed. NF in VG dj. *Smith.* $15/£10

PLINY. The Epistles of Pliny. C. H. Moore (ed). Boston: Bibliophile Soc, 1925. One of 405. 3 vols. Teg. 1/4 vellum, bds. Fine in slipcases. *Reese.* $60/£38

PLOMER, HENRY R. English Printers' Ornaments. London: Grafton, 1924. Ltd to 500. Beige cl over bds. Good in dj. *Karmiole*. $175/£112

PLOMER, HENRY R. A Short History of English Printing 1476-1898. Alfred Pollard (ed). English Bookman's Library, 1900. Frontis port, 3 ports. Teg, ret uncut. (Exlib, perf/ink stamps; bkpl; ink stamps verso plts; margins lt browned, upper hinge cracked; cl lt soiled, sl rubbed, paper spine label.) *Edwards*. $39/£25

PLOMER, HENRY R. A Short History of English Printing 1476-1900. Kegan Paul, 1915. Brn cl. Good. *Moss*. $37/£24

PLOMER, HENRY R. Wynkyn de Worde and His Contemporaries. London: Grafton, 1925. (Foxing; 1/2-title, last pg index offset; sig.) 1/4 cl, paper bds, paper spine label (sl rubbed). VG. *Waverly**. $60/£38

PLOMER, WILLIAM. The Case Is Altered. London: Hogarth, 1932. 1st ed. VG in dj (sm chips, sm tear). *Hollett*. $94/£60

PLOOIJ, DANIEL. The Pilgrim Fathers from a Dutch Point of View. NY, 1932. 1st ed. *Ginsberg*. $75/£48

PLOSCOWE, MORRIS. Sex and the Law. NY: Prentice-Hall, 1951. *Boswell*. $50/£32

PLUCKNETT, FRANK. Boot and Shoe Manufacture. London, 1931. 21 plts. Dj (chipped). *Edwards*. $59/£38

PLUM, MARY. Dead Man's Secret. NY: Harper, 1931. 1st ed. Nice (sl foxing) in dj (sl tears, sm chip). *Metropolitan**. $143/£92

PLUMMER, JOHN. The Hours of Catherine of Cleves. NY, n.d. Good in slipcase. *Washton*. $65/£42

PLUMPTRE, C. E. Giordano Bruno: A Tale of the Sixteenth Century. London: Chapman & Hall, 1884. 1st ed. 2 vols. xvii,278; 292pp. Unopened. Brn cl, gilt/black. VG. *Hartfield*. $295/£189

PLUNKET, EMMELINE. Ancient Calendars and Constellations. London: J. Murray, 1903. 1st ed. 10 fldg charts, 24 plts. VG. *Middle Earth*. $95/£61

PLUNKETT, H. M. Women, Plumbers, and Doctors. NY, 1885. 1st ed. 248pp. (Ex-lib.) *Fye*. $150/£96

PLUTARCH. The Lives of the Noble Grecians and Romans. London: Nonesuch, 1929. One of 1550 sets. 5 vols. Paper spine labels (dknd, spotted). *Swann**. $138/£88

PLUTARCH. The Lives of the Noble Grecians and Romans.... NY: LEC, 1941. One of 1500 signed by W. A. Dwiggins (designer). 8 vols. (Bkpl.) 2 boxes (worn). *Kane**. $60/£38

POAGUE, WILLIAM THOMAS Gunner with Stonewall. Monroe F. Cockrell (ed). Jackson, TN, 1957. 1st ed. Fldg map. (Stamped name, extrems dknd), else VG in dj (frayed, torn). *King*. $40/£26

POCHE, EMANUEL. Bohemian Porcelain. N.p.: Artia, n.d. (ca 1955). 160 photo plts, 4pp chronological guide. Lt blue linen. Good in illus dj. *Karmiole*. $75/£48

Pocket Companion; or, Every Man His Own Lawyer.... Phila: M'Carty & Davis, 1821. 5th ed. Sheep-backed bds (worn, foxed). Decently Preserved. *Boswell*. $250/£160

Pocket Lawyer and Family Conveyancer.... Phila: Charles Bell, 1845. Morocco backed ptd bds (worn). Sound. *Boswell*. $125/£80

PODESCHI, JOHN B. Dickens and Dickensiana, a Catalogue of the Richard Gimbel Collection in the Yale University Library. New Haven: Yale Univ, 1980. 1st ed. Grn cl, label. Fine. *Macdonnell*. $200/£128

PODESCHI, JOHN B. Dickens and Dickensiana: A Catalog of The Richard Gimbel Collection.... New Haven: Yale Univ, 1980. Pub's grn cl, paper spine label. Fine. *Book Block*. $125/£80

POE, EDGAR A. The Conchologist's First Book. Phila: Haswell, Barrington, & Haswell, 1840. 2nd ed. 12 litho plts. (Pastedowns skinned, lacks rep.) Orig red roan back, ptd grn paper bds (worn, soiled). BAL 16132. *Waverly**. $60/£38

POE, EDGAR ALEN. The Poems of Edgar Allen Poe. NY: LEC, 1943. #904/1500 numbered, signed by Hugo Steiner-Prag (illus). Full leather. NF in pub's slipcase (lt worn). *Hermitage*. $175/£112

POE, EDGAR ALLAN. Anastatic Printing. Chicago: Silver Quoin, 1946. 1st ed. Ltd to 150. Deckle edges. Paper cvr label. Fine in glassine dj (sl torn). *Connolly*. $95/£61

POE, EDGAR ALLAN. The Bells and Other Poems. NY/London: Hodder & Stoughton, n.d. One of 750 signed by Edmund Dulac (illus). 4to. Uncut. Pub's full gilt-stamped leather (lt rubbed). *Oinonen**. $650/£417

POE, EDGAR ALLAN. Edgar Allan Poe Letters Till Now Unpublished.... Phila/London, 1925. 1st ed, Eng issue. One of 325 numbered. (Ex-lib, rubbed, worn.) *Mcclintock*. $45/£29

POE, EDGAR ALLAN. Fall of the House of Usher. (NY: LEC, 1985.) Ltd to 1500 signed by Raphael Soyer. Tall folio. 2 color lithos, 1 etching. Burgundy goatskin on spine, fore-edge; marbled bds. Mint in custom-made clamshell box. *Truepenny*. $575/£369

POE, EDGAR ALLAN. The Mask of the Red Death. Balt: Aquarius, 1969. One of 500 ptd, signed by Federico Castellon (lithos). Folio. 17 lithos. Black/brn linen bds. Fine in box. *Appelfeld*. $150/£96

POE, EDGAR ALLAN. The Narrative of Arthur Gordon Pym. London, 1838. 1st British ed, w/half-title. Pub's cl (ends frayed, fr joint partly torn; lt foxed, browned, sm ink stamp tp verso). *Swann**. $115/£74

POE, EDGAR ALLAN. Tales of Mystery and Imagination. London, (1935). 12 color plts by Arthur Rackham, guards. Pict eps. Dj (2 sm cellotape repairs verso). *Swann**. $488/£313

POE, EDGAR ALLAN. Tales of Mystery and Imagination. London, (1935). Ltd to 460 numbered. This copy unnumbered, for 'presentation,' signed by Arthur Rackham (illus). 4to. 12 mtd color plts, guards. Pict eps. Orig vellum, gilt. Pub's bd slipcase (worn, cracked). *Swann**. $1,380/£885

POE, EDGAR ALLAN. Tales of Mystery and Imagination. Tudor, 1933. Rpt of 1919 Harrap/Brentanos ed. Harry Clarke (illus). 8 tipped-in color plts. Fine in Fine dj (sm closed tear at spine fold). Orig drop-lid box (corners sl worn). *Certo*. $450/£288

POE, EDGAR ALLAN. Tales of Mystery and Imagination. NY: Tudor, 1933. 8 mtd color plts by Harry Clarke. Black cl, pict label. Fine in dj (worn). *Appelfeld*. $175/£112

POE, EDGAR ALLAN. Tales of Mystery and Imagination. London: George Harrap, 1935. 1st Rackham ed. One of 460 signed by Arthur Rackham (illus). 4to. Dec eps; teg. Full vellum (spine age-toned), gilt. Slipcase. *Appelfeld*. $1,500/£962

POE, EDGAR ALLAN. The Tales, Poems and Life of Edgar Allen Poe. Phila: George Barrie, n.d. (c.1900). #308/500. 6 vols. Square 8vo. 26 etchings, 5 photogravures. Teg, others uncut. 3/4 red morocco (fr cvr vol 7 neatly rehinged), ribbed gilt-dec spines. *D & D*. $950/£609

POE, EDGAR ALLAN. Tales. Chicago: Lakeside, 1930. Ltd to 1000. Teg. Black cl-backed patterned paper bds, gilt. Fine. *Cady*. $50/£32

POE, EDGAR ALLAN. The Works of Edgar Allan Poe. NY: A.C. Armstrong, (1884). 6 vols. Frontis each vol, (ii),xiv,499 (fr hinge starting); (vi),575; (iv),536; vi,571; vi,576; vi,571pp. All edges marbled. 3/4 brn calf, marbled bds (sl rubbed, scuffed, 2 spines sl stained), gilt-dec spines, gilt-lettered burgundy labels (tear 1 label). NF internally. BAL 16229. *Blue Mountain*. $150/£96

POE, EDGAR ALLAN. The Works of Edgar Allan Poe. Edmund Clarence Stedman and George Edward Woodberry (eds). NY: Scribner, 1914. 1st ed. 10 vols. Teg. Grn cl, gilt. Good in djs (sl chipped). *Karmiole*. $350/£224

POE, EDGAR ALLAN. The Works. Chicago: Stone & Kimball, 1894-95. 10 vols. Uncut. Cl, gilt-dec spines. (Sl worn, sl foxing.) *Oinonen**. $160/£103

POE, JOHN WILLIAM. The Death of Billy the Kid. Boston/NY: Houghton Mifflin, 1933. 1st ed. (Spine faded), else Fine. Howes P430. *Argonaut*. $60/£38

Poetical Sketches of Scarborough. (By John B. Papworth, et al.) London, 1813. 1st ed. 21 aquatint plts. (Sl foxing, offsetting.) Aeg. Full calf (rubbed, rebacked), orig spine (singed, corroded). Internally Clean. *Oinonen**. $200/£128

Poetry in Crystal. NY, 1963. 1st ed. As New w/o dj as issued. *Bond*. $50/£32

POGANY, WILLY. Willy Pogany's Mother Goose. NY: Nelson, (1928). Sm 4to. Gilt-pict cl (lt worn). Dj (frayed, tape-repaired tear verso). *Oinonen**. $425/£272

POGANY, WILLY. Willy Pogany's Mother Goose. NY: Nelson, 1928. 4th ed. Signed, inscribed. 7 1/4 x 9 1/4. 144pp. Teg. Gilt-stamped cl (worn, soiled). Good. *Cattermole*. $200/£128

POHANKA, BRIAN C. Nelson A. Miles, a Documentary Biography of His Military Career 1861-1903. Glendale: A.H. Clark, 1985. Fine in dj. *Bohling*. $30/£19

POHL, FREDERIK and C. M. KORNBLUTH. The Space Merchants. NY: Ballantine, (1952). 1st ed, hb issue. Inscribed, signed. (Sl shelfworn.) Dj (worn). *Swann**. $80/£51

POHL, FREDERIK and C. M. KORNBLUTH. A Town Is Drowning. NY: Ballantine, (1955). 1st ed. 8vo. Fine (poor quality paper browning) in dj (lt soil). *Antic Hay*. $600/£385

POHL, FREDERIK with JACK WILLIAMSON. Undersea City. Gnome, (1958). 1st ed. VG (pg edges, rep browned) in NF dj. *Certo*. $30/£19

POHL, FREDERIK with JACK WILLIAMSON. Undersea City. Gnome, 1958. 1st ed. VG + (pp sl yellowed) in dj. *Certo*. $25/£16

POHL, FREDERIK with JACK WILLIAMSON. Undersea Quest. Gnome, 1954. 1st ed. (Pastedowns sl yellowed.) VG + in dj (2 sm creased tears). *Certo*. $40/£26

POINT, NICOLAS. Wilderness Kingdom. Indian Life in the Rocky Mountains, 1840-1847. NY: Holt, Rinehart & Winston, (1967). 1st ed. Fine in pict dj. *Argonaut*. $75/£48

POINT, NICOLAS. Wilderness Kingdom. Indian Life in the Rocky Mountains: 1840-1847. NY: Holt, Rinehart & Winston, (1967). 1st ed. (Bkpl, ink name), else VG in VG dj. *Perier*. $45/£29

POINTER, LARRY. In Search of Butch Cassidy. Norman, (1977). 1st ed. Fine in dj (lt worn). *Pratt*. $32/£21

POLAND, JEFFERSON F. and VALERIE ALISON. The Records of the San Francisco Sexual Freedom League. London: Olympia, 1971. NF in wraps. *Sclanders*. $16/£10

POLEHAMPTON, EDWARD. The Gallery of Nature and Art. London: R. Willis, 1813. 6 vols. 100 plts. Full leather, gilt-dec bds (detached, spines split, edgeworn; foxing). *Metropolitan**. $258/£165

POLEHAMPTON, EDWARD. The Gallery of Nature and Art. London: R.N. Rose, 1821. 6 vols. 88 engrs (of 100). Uncut. Mod cl-backed bds, paper spine labels. (Lt spotting, pencil notes; rebacked; sl soiled, bumped.) *Edwards*. $156/£100

POLEY, G. HENRY. Domestic Architecture, Furniture and Ornament of England from the 14th to the 18th Century.... Boston, (1911). 1st ed. 76 plts. Atlas folio, loose as issued in tied cl folder. VG. *Argosy*. $150/£96

Political Code of the State of California.... SF: Bancroft-Whitney, 1897. Pocket ed. Contemp sheep (worn, rubbed). Usable. *Boswell*. $50/£32

POLK, JAMES K. Polk: The Diary of a President 1845-1849. Allan Nevins (ed). London/NY/Toronto: Longmans, Green, 1929. 1st 1-vol ed. Frontis, 15 plts: Fine. *Argonaut*. $90/£58

POLK, JAMES K. Polk: The Diary of a President 1845-49.... Allan Nevins (ed). NY, 1929. 1st ed. Frontis port, prospectus laid in. VG +. Howes P445. *Turpen*. $95/£61

POLKINGHORE, TREGELLES. My First Curacy: The Story of a Quiet Cornish Parish. Christian Commonwealth Pub Co, 1886. Ad leaves. Pict cl (spine bumped, sunned, sl chipped). Good. *Tiger*. $19/£12

POLLACK, JACKSON. The Last Sketchbook. NY: Johnson Reprint Corp, (1982). 1st ed. One of 525 numbered. Text pamphlet in brn ptd wraps, together w/vol bound in Japanese manner, w/40 folded sheets. Fine in Fine cl-cvrd solander box, ptd paper label. *Baltimore**. $130/£83

POLLACK, PETER. The Picture History of Photography. NY: Abrams, 1969. Rev, enlgd ed. (Owner stamp), else Fine in dj (sl rubbed). *Cahan*. $60/£38

POLLARD A. W. (ed). The Romance of King Arthur. NY: Macmillan, Oct 1917. 1st trade ed. 16 color plts by Arthur Rackham. Dec cvr, spine. Good. *Scribe's Perch**. $50/£32

POLLARD, A. W. Books in the House. Indianapolis: Bobbs-Merrill, (1904). One of 500 (of 510). (Mk on pastedown; tips lt rubbed), else VG. *Reese*. $45/£29

POLLARD, A. W. Books in the House. London, 1907. Marbled eps; teg. 1/2 straight-grained morocco, dec gilt spine. VG. *Truepenny*. $60/£38

POLLARD, A. W. Cobden-Sanderson and the Doves Press.... SF: John Henry Nash, 1929. One of 339 numbered. Vellum. 1/4 morocco slipcase. *Swann**. $373/£239

POLLARD, A. W. Early Illustrated Books. London, 1893. 1st ed. Uncut. Fine (sl rubbed, spine sunned). *Polyanthos*. $50/£32

POLLARD, A. W. Early Illustrated Books. London: Kegan Paul et al, 1893. 1st ed. xvi,256pp. Gilt buckram (spine sl faded). VG. *Reese*. $50/£32

POLLARD, A. W. Early Illustrated Books...Decoration and Illustration of Books in the 15th and 16th Centuries. Kegan Paul, Trench, Trubner, 1917. Good. *Moss*. $34/£22

POLLARD, A. W. Italian Book Illustrations Chiefly of the Fifteenth Century. Seeley, 1894. 1st ed. 80pp, 9 engr plts. Good (faded). *Cox*. $34/£22

POLLARD, A. W. (ed). The Library. A Quarterly Review of Bibliography. London: Bibliographical Soc, (1920-1927). 4th series. 7 vols. Maroon cl. VG. *House*. $150/£96

POLLARD, A. W. and G. R. REDGRAVE (comps). A Short-Title Catalogue of Books Printed in England, Scotland, and Ireland and of English Books Printed Abroad 1475-1640. London: Bernard Quaritch, 1926. 1st ed. 1/4 cl, bds. (Sl foxing; sl edgeworn, few spots lower bd), o/w VG. *Reese.* $225/£144

POLLARD, EDWARD ALFRED. The First Year of the War. Richmond, 1862. 'Corrected and Improved Edition.' 368pp. (Ink inscrip; sl staining; cvrs worn, spotted.) *King.* $150/£96

POLLARD, EDWARD ALFRED. The Lost Cause Regained. NY: Carleton, 1868. 1st ed. 214,(2)pp. Dec cl. Howes P456. *Ginsberg.* $100/£64

POLLARD, EDWARD ALFRED. Southern History of the Great Civil War in the United States. The First Year of the War. Toronto: P.R. Randall, 1863. 1st Canadian ed. 383pp. (Scuffed), else VG. Howes P449. *Mcgowan.* $150/£96

POLLARD, EDWARD ALFRED. Southern History of the War. The Second Year of the War. NY: Charles B. Richardson, 1864. 2nd Amer ed. 386pp. (Scuffed, spine top chipped), else VG. Howes P460. *Mcgowan.* $85/£54

POLLARD, EDWARD ALFRED. Southern History of the War. The Third Year of the War. NY: Charles B. Richardson, 1865. 1st ed. 391pp. (Scuffed), else NF. Howes P464. *Mcgowan.* $150/£96

POLLARD, H. B. C. A History of Firearms. London, 1926. Frontis. Red cl (sl mkd, spine faded), gilt. *Maggs.* $273/£175

POLLARD, H. B. C. and PHYLLIS BARCLAY-SMITH. British and American Game-Birds. NY, 1939. 1st Amer ed. (Ends, margins foxed), else VG. *King.* $75/£48

POLLARD, HUGH B. C. Game Birds. London/Boston/NY, 1929. VG. *Truepenny.* $95/£61

POLLARD, JOSEPHINE. The History of the United States. NY: McLoughlin, n.d. (ca 1905). 4to. 136pp (dated ink dedication fep); 6 full-pg VF chromolithos (incl frontis). Color/gilt pict linen (lt soiled; inner hinges sl cracked), gilt. VG. *Hobbyhorse.* $75/£48

POLLARD, JOSEPHINE. The Life of George Washington. In Words of One Syllable. NY: McLoughlin Bros, n.d. 4to. 120pp (eps, tp sl spotted); 7 color plts (1 loose). Color pict tan cl (bumped, sl rubbed, soiled). VG. *Blue Mountain.* $35/£22

POLLEY, JOSEPH BENJAMIN. Hood's Texas Brigade, Its Marches, Its Battles, Its Achievements. Dayton, OH: Morningside, 1976. Rpt of 1910 Neale pub. NF. *Mcgowan.* $55/£35

POLLEY, JOSEPH BENJAMIN. A Soldier's Letters to Charming Nellie. NY/Washington: Neale, 1908. 1st ed. (Top margin prelims sl damped), else NF. Howes P466. *Mcgowan.* $550/£353

POLLINI, JOHN. The Portraiture of Gaius and Lucius Caesar. NY: Fordham Univ, 1987. 42 b/w plts. Blue cl. VG. *Turtle Island.* $70/£45

POLLOCK, FREDERICK and F. W. MAITLAND. The History of English Law, Before the Time of Edward I. Cambridge: CUP, 1911. 2nd ed. 2 vols. (2 joints cracked, repaired.) *Boswell.* $150/£96

POLLOCK, THOMAS C. The Philadelphia Theater in the Eighteenth Century Together with the Day Book of the Same Period. Phila: Pan., 1933. 1st ed. Facs frontis. *Ginsberg.* $75/£48

POLSON, C. J. et al. The Disposal of the Dead. English Universities Press, 1953. 1st ed. (Eps lt spotted, few margins sl thumbed; cl sl soiled.) *Edwards.* $23/£15

POLUNIN, NICHOLAS. The Isle of Auks. London: E. Arnold, (1932). VG. *High Latitude.* $45/£29

POMERANZ, HERMAN. Medicine in the Shakespearean Plays and Dickens' Doctors. NY, 1936. 1st ed. VG. *Fye.* $100/£64

POMERANZ, HERMAN. Medicine in the Shakespearean Plays and Dickens' Doctors. NY: Powell, 1936. 1st ed. Fine in dj. *Glaser.* $75/£48

POMEROY, JESSE HARDING. Autobiography of Jesse H. Pomeroy. Boston: J.A. Cummings, c. 1875. 32pp; sm plan, 2 sm ports of author. Ptd wraps (worn, creased). *Bohling.* $120/£77

POMFRET, JOHN E. (ed). California Gold Rush Voyages, 1848-1849. San Marino, CA: Huntington Library, 1954. 1st ed. 2 maps. VG in dj. *Lien.* $30/£19

POND, MARIAM BUCKNER. Time Is Kind: The Story of the Unfortunate Fox Family. (NY): Centennial, 1947. 1st ed. Inscribed. 7 plts. Ptd dec white cl. VG in dj (torn, sl defective). *Gach.* $35/£22

POND, S. W. Two Volunteer Missionaries Among the Dakotas; or, The Story of the Labors of Samuel W. and Gideon H. Pond. Boston, (1893). 1st ed. (12),278pp. *Ginsberg.* $150/£96

PONGE, FRANCIS. The Voice of Things. NY: McGraw-Hill, 1972. 1st US ed. NF in VG+ dj (1-inch tear, crease). *Lame Duck.* $50/£32

PONSOR, Y. R. Gawain and the Green Knight. NY: Macmillan, 1979. 1st US ed. Signed. Darrell Sweet (illus). 5 3/4 x 9 1/4. 76pp. Fine in dj. *Cattermole.* $15/£10

PONTEY, WILLIAM. The Profitable Planter. London: John Harding, 1809. 3rd ed. Frontis, 232,(2)pp (lacks fep). Old calf, marbled bds (sl rubbed), black spine label. *Karmiole.* $125/£80

PONTING, HERBERT. The Great White South or With Scott in the Antarctic.... NY: McBride, 1923. 2nd US ed. VG. *High Latitude.* $40/£26

PONTING, HERBERT. The Great White South...Captain Scott's South Pole Expedition.... NY: Robert M. McBride, 1922. 1st US ed. Good (cl sl rubbed, spine title dull). *High Latitude.* $120/£77

PONTING, TOM CANDY. Life of Tom Candy Ponting. Evanston: Branding Iron, 1952. One of 500 numbered. Frontis. (Spine sl faded), else VG. Howes P469. *Dumont.* $50/£32

PONTOPPIDAN, ERICH. The Natural History of Norway. London: A. Linde, 1755. 1st ed in English. 2 parts in 1 vol. Folio. Fldg frontis map, hand-colored in outline (neat repair), xxiii,(i)contents,206; vii,(i)contents,291pp + (i)directions for plts, (xi)index (tp foxed, lt sporadic foxing, text browning, bkpl); 28 copper plts. Early polished gilt-edged calf bds (sl wear, corners repaired, sympathetically rebacked w/most of orig gilt compartmented spine laid down), spine label (chipped) laid down. *Edwards.* $1,482/£950

POOL, J. LAWRENCE. The Neurosurgical Treatment of Traumatic Paraplegia. Springfield: Thomas, 1951. NF in orig stiff morocco. *Goodrich.* $65/£42

POOLE, GEORGE AYLIFFE and J. W. HUGALL. An Historical and Descriptive Guide to York Cathedral and Its Antiquities. York, 1850. 1st ed. 38 litho plts. Gilt-paneled bds (sl worn, joints cracked). *Swann*.* $149/£96

POOLE, GEORGE AYLIFFE. A History of Ecclesiastical Architecture in England. London: Joseph Masters, 1848. 1st ed. Engr frontis, xiv,415pp (bkpl, inner hinges cracked). Uncut. Sound (backstrip ends sl worn). *Cox.* $62/£40

POOLE, MONICA. The Wood Engravings of John Farleigh. Gresham, 1985. 1st ed. Fine in dj, box. *Whittle.* $47/£30

POOLE, REGINALD STUART. The Cities of Egypt. London: Smith, Elder, 1882. xii,215pp. (Bkpl, inkstamp tp.) *Archaeologia.* $35/£22

Poor Wills Almanac, For the Year 1841.... Phila: Joseph M'Dowell, (1840). 18 leaves. (Insect staining), o/w Good. *Cahan.* $25/£16

POOR, CHARLES LANE. Men Against the Rule. NY: Derrydale, 1937. 1st ed. One of 950. Blue cl, dk blue linen spine. Fine. *Cummins.* $90/£58

POOR, HENRY V. Poor's Manual of the Railroads. NY: N.p., 1886. 76,cxxxvii,1022,69pp; 14 color maps. (Hinges cracked, shelfwear), else Good. *Dumont.* $175/£112

POORE, B. P. The Life and Public Services of Ambrose P. Burnside.... Providence, 1882. #260/300, 'Edition du Luxe.' 448,6pp. Marbled eps, aeg. Full tooled leather, dentelles. Good (joints cracked). *Scribe's Perch*.* $60/£38

POORE, H. R. Pictorial Composition. NY/London: Putnam, 1903. 14th ed. Frontis, guard. (Name stamp, lacks fep), else VG. *Cahan.* $25/£16

POORTENAAR, JAN. The Art of the Book and Its Illustration. London, 1935. 1st ed. Mtd color frontis. (Plts sl wrinkled, pastedowns sl dampstained, ex-lib, ink stamps tp, bkpl remains.) Lib morocco-backed cl (rebound, soiled, spine sl faded, mkd). *Edwards.* $59/£38

POPE AND YOUNG CLUB. Bowhunting Big Game Records of North America. Boulder: Johnson, 1975. 1st ed. Fine in VG + dj (rubbed). *Bowman.* $75/£48

POPE, A. U. Persian Architecture. London: Thames & Hudson, 1965. 404 plts (33 color). Sound in dj. *Ars Artis.* $70/£45

POPE, ALEXANDER. The Correspondence of Alexander Pope. George Sherburn (ed). Oxford: Clarendon, 1956. 1st ed. 5 vols. (Shadows from old jacket protectors on eps each vol), o/w Fine in djs. *Captain's Bookshelf.* $150/£96

POPE, ALEXANDER. Of the Use of Riches, an Epistle to the Right Honorable Allen Lord Bathurst. London: Ptd by J. Wright, 1732. 1st ed, regular paper issue (this copy w/uncorrected reading at 13:13). 20pp. Later cl, bds. Good (sm blindstamp, bkpl, sl foxed, tanned, lt discoloration 1 leaf). *Reese.* $200/£128

POPE, ALEXANDER. One Thousand Seven Hundred and Thirty-Eight. London: T. Cooper, (1738). 1st ed, Griffith's variant A w/price all in upper case. 10,(1)pp (lt foxing, edge tanning, creases in half-title). Extracted. (Sl stain lower edge.) Good. *Reese.* $250/£160

POPE, ALEXANDER. Pope's Own Miscellany. Norman Ault (ed). London: Nonesuch, 1935. Ltd to 750 numbered. Teg. (Sl worn.) *King.* $95/£61

POPE, ALEXANDER. The Works of Alexander Pope. London: J. and P. Knapton et al, 1751. 9 vols. 8vo. 24 engr plts. Contemp full calf, spines gilt (spine labels worn away; outer hinges starting; names, dates). Very Nice. *Karmiole.* $1,000/£641

POPE, DUDLEY. Ramage and the Dido. London: Secker & Warburg, 1989. 1st ed. Fine in dj. *Mordida.* $45/£29

POPE, DUDLEY. Ramage and the Drum Beat. London: W&N, 1967. 1st ed. Fine in Fine dj. *Else Fine.* $125/£80

POPE, DUDLEY. Ramage's Signal. London: Secker & Warburg, 1980. 1st ed. VF in dj. *Mordida.* $45/£29

POPE, THOMAS. A Treatise on Bridge Architecture. NY, 1811. 15 plts. Leather spine (cracks). Good- (foxing, facs tp tipped-in to replace orig). *Scribe's Perch*.* $120/£77

POPE-HENNESSY, JAMES. History under Fire. Batsford, 1941. 1st ed. VG in pict dj (upper panel torn, edges, corners rubbed). *Words Etc.* $62/£40

POPE-HENNESSY, JOHN and TERENCE HODGKINSON. The Frick Collection. An Illustrated Catalogue. Volume IV—Sculpture. NY, 1970. 15 color plts. Good in dj. *Washton.* $40/£26

POPE-HENNESSY, JOHN. The Complete Work of Paolo Uccello. NY: Phaidon, 1950. 2 color plts. VG in dj. *Argosy.* $85/£54

POPE-HENNESSY, JOHN. Giovanni di Paolo 1403-1483. NY, 1938. 32 plts. Good in dj (worn). *Washton.* $300/£192

POPE-HENNESSY, JOHN. Italian Gothic Sculpture. London, 1955. 108 plts. Buckram. Good. *Washton.* $85/£54

POPE-HENNESSY, JOHN. Italian High Renaissance and Baroque Sculpture. London, 1970. 2nd ed. 168 plts. Good in dj. *Washton.* $125/£80

POPE-HENNESSY, JOHN. The Portrait in the Renaissance. NY, 1966. 1st ed. VG in dj (sm nick). *Typographeum.* $30/£19

POPE-HENNESSY, JOHN. Renaissance Bronzes from the Samuel H. Kress Collection. London: Phaidon, 1965. 1st ed. VG in dj. *Hollett.* $70/£45

POPE-HENNESSY, UNA. Early Chinese Jades. London: Ernest Benn, 1923. 1st ed. 64 photo plts. (Scattered lt foxing.) Gilt-lettered spine. Fine in dj (lt chipped). *Argonaut.* $325/£208

POPHAM, A. E. and JOHANNES WILDE. The Italian Drawings of the XV and XVI Centuries in the Collection of Her Majesty the Queen at Windsor Castle. NY/London, 1984. Good in dj. *Washton.* $125/£80

POPOWSKI, BERT. Crow Shooting. NY: A.S. Barnes, 1946. 1st ed. Black buckram. Fine in dj (soiled). *Biscotti.* $20/£13

POPPENHEIM, MARY B. et al. The History of the United Daughters of the Confederacy. Richmond: Garrett & Massie, (1938). 1st ed. Dec cl. VG. *Cahan.* $50/£32

PORNY, MR. The Elements of Heraldry. T. Carnan & F. Newberry Jr., 1771. 2nd ed. xx,254,(51)pp + 1pg pub's ads (lt foxing); 24 plts. Mod cl (rebound). *Edwards.* $94/£60

PORTER, ARTHUR KINGSLEY. Medieval Architecture, Its Origins and Development. NY/London: Baker & Taylor/Batsford, 1919. 1st ed. 2 vols. 289 full-pg, fldg illus. Teg, rest uncut. Pale grn buckram, gilt. VG (text sl dampstained) in orig djs (lt frayed). *Peter Taylor.* $148/£95

PORTER, ARTHUR KINGSLEY. Medieval Architecture. NY/London: Batsford, 1909. 289 plts. (Cl sl worn.) *Ars Artis.* $234/£150

PORTER, CHARLES H. Statement of the Case of the People Against Elisha B. Fero. NY, 1870. (Reprint.) 48pp. VG in ptd wrappers. *Argosy.* $40/£26

PORTER, D. H. Baggage. (Toronto): Coach House, 1974. 1st ed. Ltd to 1000. Tipped-in color frontis. Faux morocco-backed cl. (Owner stamp), else Fine. *Cahan.* $65/£42

PORTER, DAVID D. The Naval History of the Civil War. NY: Sherman, 1886. 1st ed. 843pp (inner hinges starting to crack). Pict mustard/gold cl (lt rubbed). Good. *Lucas.* $135/£87

PORTER, EDWIN H. The Fall River Tragedy. Fall River: J.D. Munroe, 1893. 1st ed. 312pp (sl browned, sl dampstain margin at end). Orig grn cl (rebacked, orig spine laid down; recased, new eps). Good. *Lucas.* $400/£256

PORTER, ELIOT. Appalachian Wilderness. NY: E.P. Dutton, 1970. 1st ed. VG in pict dj. *Cahan.* $100/£64

PORTER, ELIOT. Birds of North America. NY: Dutton, 1972. 1st ed. NF in NF dj. *Smith.* $50/£32

PORTER, ELIOT. Intimate Landscapes. NY: MMA/Dutton, 1979. 1st ed, hb issue. Fine. *Smith.* $125/£80

PORTER, ELIOT. The Place No One Knew. SF: Sierra Club, (1963). 1st ed. VG in dj. *King.* $50/£32

PORTER, ELIOT. The Place No One Knew: Glen Canyon on the Colorado. David Brower (ed). SF: Sierra Club, (1963). 1st ed. Fine in pict dj (lt soiled, sl chipped). *Argonaut.* $150/£96

PORTER, GENE STRATTON. See STRATTON-PORTER, GENE

PORTER, KATHERINE ANNE. The Collected Essays and Occasional Writings. NY: Delacorte, (1970). One of 250 numbered, signed. Fine in Fine slipcase. *Lenz.* $200/£128

PORTER, KATHERINE ANNE. The Days Before. NY: Harcourt, Brace, 1952. 1st ed. Fine in dj (price-clipped). *Cahan.* $75/£48

PORTER, KATHERINE ANNE. A Defense of Circe. NY: Privately ptd, (1954). Ltd to 1700 privately ptd. Pub's greeting card laid in. Fine (sm nick). *Polyanthos.* $25/£16

PORTER, KATHERINE ANNE. Flowering Judas. Harcourt Brace, (1930). One of 600. VG (bkpl, eps sl mkd; spine lettering dulled) w/o dj, as issued. *Certo.* $85/£54

PORTER, KATHERINE ANNE. French Song-Book. (Paris/NY): Harrison of Paris, (1933). 1st ed. One of 595 numbered, signed. Unopened. Cl, bds, parchment corners. VF in dj. *Reese.* $350/£224

PORTER, KATHERINE ANNE. Hacienda. (NY): Harrison of Paris, (1934). 1st ed. One of 895 numbered. Fine in slipcase. *Captain's Bookshelf.* $100/£64

PORTER, KATHERINE ANNE. Noon Wine. Detroit: Shumans, 1937. One of 250 numbered, signed. (2 sm glue mks fep, 2 faint tape shadows rep), else Fine. *Certo.* $250/£160

PORTER, KATHERINE ANNE. Pale Horse, Pale Rider. Harcourt Brace, 1939. 1st ed. VG (bkpl, top edge spotted) in dj (spine faded, ends sl chipping). *Certo.* $45/£29

PORTER, MARTHA BYRD. Straight Down a Crooked Lane. John Marshall, 1945. 3rd ptg. Good+ (fep removed) in Fair dj (torn). *Book Broker.* $25/£16

PORTER, NOAH. Books and Reading or What Books Shall I Read and How Shall I Read Them. NY: Scribner, 1882. Rev ed. ix,434,(10)pp. Fine. *Oak Knoll.* $25/£16

PORTER, ROBERT. Report on Indians Taxed and Indians Not Taxed in the United States...1890. GPO, 1894. 1st ed. 638pp (occasional bottom margin damp-staining), 229 plts (20 color; 2 fldg), 25 maps (3 fldg). Orig black cl (recased, stained, worn), new eps. Howes D418. *Oregon.* $950/£609

PORTEUS, STANLEY D. And Blow Not the Trumpet. Palo Alto, CA: Pacific Books, (1947). 1st ed. Inscribed. Pict tan cl. VG. *Gach.* $35/£22

PORTIS, CHARLES. Norwood. NY: S&S, 1966. 1st ed. NF in VG+ dj (2 sm circular stains fr panel, flap). *Lame Duck.* $150/£96

PORTLOCK, NATHANIEL. A Voyage Round the World. Amsterdam/NY: N. Israel/Da Capo, 1968. Simulated vellum. New. *High Latitude.* $50/£32

PORTOGHESI, PAOLO. Roma Barocca. Cambridge/London, 1970. 475 gravure plts, 8 plans. Good in dj (worn). *Washton.* $275/£176

Portrait and Biographical Record of Adams County, Illinois.... Chicago: Chapman Bros, 1892. 598,(iii)pp (sl aged). Aeg. Full sheep, beveled bds (worn, scuffed), gilt. Text Good. *Baltimore*.* $45/£29

Portraits of William Harvey. London, 1913. 1st ed. (Few margins stained.) *Fye.* $100/£64

POSEY, WILLIAM and SAMUEL BROWN. The Wills Hospital of Philadelphia. Phila, 1931. 1st ed. VG. *Fye.* $125/£80

POSNER, DONALD. Annibale Carracci. London, 1971. 2 vols. 4to. 10 color plts. Good in djs. *Washton.* $925/£593

POST, CHARLES JOHNSON. The Little War of Private Post. Boston, (1960). 1st ed. VG+ in dj (worn, chipped). *Pratt.* $27/£17

POST, MELVILLE DAVISSON. The Nameless Thing. NY: Appleton, 1912. 1st ed. NF. *Else Fine.* $65/£42

POSTGATE, R. et al (eds). A Workers' History of the Great Strike. London: Plebs League, 1927. 1st ed. Pb. VG (spine chip). *Beasley.* $40/£26

POSTGATE, RAYMOND. Verdict of Twelve. DCC, 1940. 1st Amer ed, 1st bk. VG (spine sunned, ring mks rear, lt soiled, worn) in dj (corner chip, closed tear). *Murder By The Book.* $45/£29

Pot Art and Marijuana Reading Matter. Tucson, AZ: Apocrypha, 1972. 1st ptg of enlgd 2nd ed. VG+ (spine faded, sl rubbed) in wraps. *Sclanders.* $28/£18

POTE, WILLIAM, JR. Journal of Captain William Pote, Jr....May 1745-Aug. 1747. NY: Dodd, Mead, 1896. 1st ed. One of 350 ptd. 2 vols. Lg fldg map (bound separately). Tan bds, brn calf spines. Nice. *Appelfeld.* $250/£160

POTOCKI OF MONTALK, COUNT. Myself as a Printer. Wymondham, 1970. 1st ed. VG. Laid in wrappers. *Typographeum.* $45/£29

POTT, PERCIVALL. Observations on That Disorder of the Corner of the Eye, Commonly Called Fistula Lachrymalis. London: Hawes, Clark & Collins, 1769. 3rd ed. (iii),vii,67pp. Recent 1/4 calf, marbled bds. (2 sm stamps 1/2-title; whole vol lt browned), o/w Attractive. *White.* $172/£110

POTTER, AMBROSE GEORGE. A Bibliography of the Rubaiyat of Omar Khayyam Together with Kindred Matter in Prose and Verse Pertaining Thereto. London: Ingpen & Grant, 1929. #69/300. Orig bds, cl spine. (Rebacked, orig spine laid down, edges bumped), o/w VG. *Worldwide.* $350/£224

POTTER, BEATRIX. The Fairy Caravan. Phila: McKay, (1929). 1st Amer ed. 8vo. (Sl worn.) Dj (sl frayed, soiled). *Oinonen*.* $400/£256

POTTER, BEATRIX. Ginger and Pickles. Frederick Warne, 1909. 1st ed. Lg format. 52pp (2 inscrips); 10 color plts. Pict eps. Buff bds (back cvr lt faded, edges sl rubbed), pict onlay. VG+. *Bookmark.* $390/£250

POTTER, BEATRIX. The Journal of Beatrix Potter from 1881 to 1897. Leslie Linder (ed). London: Frederick Warne, 1974. 20 color plts, 8 facs, 3 genealogies (2 fldg). VG in dj. *Hollett.* $70/£45

POTTER, BEATRIX. The Pie and the Patty-Pan. Frederick Warne, 1905. 5.5x7. 52pp. Tan cl, round picture paste-on. (Sl dingy, corners bumped, spine lacks 1-1/4inches at bottom). *My Bookhouse.* $100/£64

POTTER, BEATRIX. The Pie and the Patty-Pan. Frederick Warne, ca 1906-7. Early ptg. (The 1st ptg was dated 1905 and had plain mottled lavender eps. When the dec eps were used, the cvr picture was then changed from a cat in a sm circle to Ribby sitting by the fire in a lg circle. However, cvr design of this present copy is exactly the same as the 1st ptg.) Orig lg format. 52pp. Creamy white eps dec in lavender w/pattern of ribbon streamers, bows from which han picturing pie and patty-pan. Blue-grey bds, title in fancy white lettering, white dec of bows colored onlay. (Spine sl faded), else NF. *Bookmark.* $156/£100

POTTER, BEATRIX. The Roly-Poly Pudding. NY: Warne, (1908). 1st Amer ed. 8vo. Cl (sm ink stain upper cvr, sl worn, spine lettering faded), pict cvr label. *Oinonen*.* $80/£51

POTTER, BEATRIX. The Roly-Poly Pudding. Frederick Warne, 1908. 1st ed, 2nd ptg, omitting 'All rights reserved' on tp. (1st 2 ptgs only have date on recto of tp). Frontis, pict tp, (iv),69,(1)pp; 17 color plts. Red cl (sl faded), pict onlay. *Cox.* $234/£150

POTTER, BEATRIX. The Tailor of Gloucester. London: F. Warne, 1903. 1st ed. Sm 8vo. 85pp. Maroon bds w/shaped pict inlay (extrems sl rubbed). Extremely Nice. *Hollett.* $546/£350

POTTER, BEATRIX. The Tailor of Gloucester. London: Warne, 1903. 1st pub ed. 16mo. Gray/grn bds (sl worn, lower backstrip torn), pict cvr label. *Oinonen**. $160/£103

POTTER, BEATRIX. The Tale of Jemima Puddle-Duck. London: F. Warne, 1908. 1st ed. Sm 8vo. 86pp. Pict grn bds (neatly rebacked), matching levant morocco, gilt. Very Nice. *Hollett*. $390/£250

POTTER, BEATRIX. The Tale of Little Pig Robinson. Frederick Warne, 1930. 1st ed, 1st issue of Sept 1930. Lg sq 8vo. 96pp; 6 color plts. Illus eps. Lt blue cl (backstrip faded, upper cvr sl mkd), gilt. *Cox*. $70/£45

POTTER, BEATRIX. The Tale of Little Pig Robinson. London: Frederick Warne, 1930. 1st rpt. Lg 8vo. 96pp (feps spotted); 6 color plts, 22 dwgs. (Spine faded, ink spot upper bd.) *Hollett*. $55/£35

POTTER, BEATRIX. The Tale of Mr. Jeremy Fisher. London: Frederick Warne, 1906. 1st ed. 86pp. Orig pict bds (rebacked in matching calf, gilt). VG (lt finger mks). *Hollett*. $351/£225

POTTER, BEATRIX. The Tale of Mrs. Tiggy-Winkle. London: F. Warne, 1905. 1st ed. 85pp. Pict bds (sl binding fault crease lower bd). (Almost invisibly recased), o/w Very Nice. *Hollett*. $429/£275

POTTER, BEATRIX. The Tale of Peter Rabbit. Phila: Henry Altemus, 1904. 12mo. 63pp; 31 full-pg plts. Cl-backed purple bds, ptd paper label fr cvr. (Extrems lt rubbed), else Fine. *Bromer*. $250/£160

POTTER, BEATRIX. The Tale of Pigling Bland. Frederick Warne, 1913. 1st ed. 1st, 2nd ptgs are identical; eps as Quinby pl. 12. Frontis, 93,(1)pp (name); 14 plts. Lt grn paper bds (string bruises to edges, lower cvr lt mkd), pict onlay. *Cox*. $187/£120

POTTER, BEATRIX. The Tale of Squirrel Nutkin. Frederick Warne, 1903. 1st ed. Either the 1st or 2nd ptg (Aug/Sept, 1903) which are indistinguishable. 84,(2)pp. Dk grey bds (rubbed, short splits upper hinge, fr inner hinge split but secure) lettered in white, white circular pict onlay. VG (marginal mks 2 openings). *Cox*. $343/£220

POTTER, BEATRIX. The Tale of the Little Pig Robinson. Phila: McKay, (1930). 8vo. Grn cl (sl worn), pict cvr label. *Oinonen**. $60/£38

POTTER, BEATRIX. The Tale of Timmy Tiptoes. Frederick Warne, 1911. 1st ed. 16mo. 85pp; 27 color plts. Pict eps. Dk grn bds, arch-topped pict onlay. VG+ (2 pencil captions; tips sl worn). *Bookmark*. $231/£148

POTTER, DENNIS. The Changing Forest. London: Secker & Warburg, 1962. 1st Eng ed. VG in laminated dec bds as issued. *Hadley*. $62/£40

POTTER, ELISHA A. The Early History of Narragansett. Providence, (1881). (18),423pp. Paper spine label (defective). Howes P510. *Ginsberg*. $75/£48

POTTER, JOHN MASON. 13 Desperate Days. NY, (1964). 1st ed. VG+ in dj (sl worn). *Pratt*. $37/£24

POTTER, JOHN. Archaeologia Graeca. London: A. Wilde et al, 1764. 8th ed. 2 vols. 27 engr plts (2 fldg). Contemp calf (new leather labels). Good. *Andrew Stewart*. $78/£50

POTTER, MARGARET HORTON. Istar of Babylon. NY/London, 1902. 1st ed. Gold/blue binding. VF. *Mcclintock*. $20/£13

POTTER, ROWLAND S. Methods of Making Three-Color Separation Negatives. Rochester, NY: Defender Photo Supply, n.d. (1937). Ptd wrappers. (Sm splits spine ends), else NF. *Cahan*. $30/£19

POTTER, SAMUEL O. L. Handbook of Materia Medica, Pharmacy, and Therapeutics. Phila, 1887. 1st ed. 828pp. Fair (cvrs worn, binding loose). *Doctor's Library*. $60/£38

POTTER, STEPHEN. The Complete Upmanship. London: Hart-Davis, 1970. 1st ed thus. NF (inscrip; sl flaw upper bd) in dj. *Williams*. $31/£20

POTTER, STEPHEN. One-Upmanship. London: Hart-Davis, 1952. 1st ed. VG in dj. *Hollett*. $23/£15

POTTER, STEPHEN. The Theory and Practice of Gamesmanship. Rupert Hart-Davis, (1947). 1st ed. Nice in dj (sl repaired). *Ash*. $78/£50

POTTER, STEPHEN. The Theory and Practice of Gamesmanship.... London: Hart-Davis, 1947. 1st ed. Inscribed. VG. *Cox*. $16/£10

POTTLE, FREDERICK A. et al. Index to the Private Papers of James Boswell from Malahide Castle.... London/NY: OUP, 1937. 1st ed. One of 1250 ptd. Unopened. Paper spine label. (Spine sl faded, no slipcase), o/w NF. *Reese*. $125/£80

POTTLE, FREDERICK A. James Boswell. The Earlier Years 1740-1769. Heinemann, 1966. 1st ed. Frontis, 8 plts. VG in dj. *Cox*. $19/£12

POTTLE, FREDERICK A. The Literary Career of James Boswell, Esq. Oxford: Clarendon, 1929. Frontis. Black cl, paper spine label. Dj. *Maggs*. $86/£55

POUCHER, W. A. The Backbone of England. London: Country Life, 1946. 1st ed. VG in dj (sl worn, chipped). *Hollett*. $47/£30

POUCHER, W. A. A Camera in the Cairngorms. London: Chapman & Hall, 1947. 1st ed. VG in dj (sl rubbed). *Hollett*. $39/£25

POUCHER, W. A. The Magic of Skye. London: Chapman & Hall, 1949. 1st ed. VG in dj (sl worn, lower panel sl spotted). *Hollett*. $133/£85

POUCHER, W. A. The North-Western Highlands. London: Country Life, 1954. 1st ed. Fine in dj (sl worn). *Hollett*. $70/£45

POUND, EZRA (trans). Confucian Analects. NY: Square $ Books, (1950). 1st ed. VG in ptd wrappers (lt used, spine sl sunned). *Captain's Bookshelf*. $75/£48

POUND, EZRA and JAMES LAUGHLIN. Selected Letters. NY: Norton, (1994). 1st ed. Rev flyer laid in. Fine in dj. *Reese*. $30/£19

POUND, EZRA. ABC of Reading. Routledge, 1934. 1st issue. (Top edges sl dusty), o/w NF in dj (spine sl frayed, dknd). *Poetry Bookshop*. $78/£50

POUND, EZRA. The Cantos of Ezra Pound. London: Faber & Faber, 1954. 1st UK ed. Fine in VG dj (price-clipped, short closed tear, crease fr panel). *Williams*. $101/£65

POUND, EZRA. Drafts and Fragments of Cantos CX-CXVII. NY: New Directions, (1968). 1st Amer ed. Fine in NF dj. *Polyanthos*. $25/£16

POUND, EZRA. Drafts and Fragments of Cantos CX-CXVII. (NY): New Directions, (1969). 1st ed. One of 3000 ptd. Fine in dj (sl dkng, sm nick). *Reese*. $40/£26

POUND, EZRA. Ezra Pound and Music. R. Murray Schafer (ed). (NY): New Directions, (1977). 1st ed. One of 1000. Fine in NF dj (price-clipped). *Reese*. $75/£48

POUND, EZRA. Ezra Pound Speaking. Radio Speeches of World War II. Leonard W. Doob (ed). Westport: Greenwood, (1978). 1st ed (1750 ptd). Fine. *Reese*. $60/£38

POUND, EZRA. Guide to Kulchur. Peter Owen, 1952. 1st Eng issue of new ed. (Fore-edge sl soiled), o/w VG in dj (spine dknd, top edge sl worn). *Poetry Bookshop*. $31/£20

POUND, EZRA. How to Read. London: Desmond Harmsworth, (1931). 1st ed. (Sl bump upper bd edge), o/w NF in NF dj (sm loss spine crown, sm mended tears, corner sl nicked). *Reese*. $275/£176

POUND, EZRA. Imaginary Letters. Paris: Black Sun, 1930. 1st ed. Ltd to 300. Fine in wrappers, tissue outer wrapper, slipcase (sl rubbed). *Jaffe.* $500/£321

POUND, EZRA. Impact. Essays on Ignorance and the Decline of American Civilization. Noel Stock (ed). Chicago: Regnery, 1960. 1st ed thus. Fine in dj. *Reese.* $60/£38

POUND, EZRA. An Introduction to the Economic Nature of the United States. Carmine Amore (trans). London: Peter Russell, 1950. 1st ed in English. NF in ptd cream wrappers. *Turtle Island.* $75/£48

POUND, EZRA. The Letters of Ezra Pound 1907-1941. D. D. Paige (ed). NY: Harcourt, (1950). 1st ed. Red cl. Fine in NF dj (price-clipped). *Reese.* $50/£32

POUND, EZRA. The Letters of Ezra Pound 1907-1941. D. D. Paige (ed). London: Faber & Faber, (1951). 1st British ed, 1st issue dj. (Pencil sig), else Fine in VG dj (sm spots). *Reese.* $50/£32

POUND, EZRA. Lustra. NY: Knopf, Oct 1917. 1st US trade ed. (Pencil notes rep; rear hinge crack), o/w Good. *Scribe's Perch*.* $70/£45

POUND, EZRA. Pavannes and Divigations. (Norfolk): New Directions, (1958). 1st ed. White-stamped brn cl. Fine in VG dj (sm mended tears, pub's price increase stamped on clipped flap). *Reese.* $40/£26

POUND, EZRA. Personae, the Collected Poems of.... (NY): New Directions, (1949). 1st ptg of augmented ed. Port. Gilt-stamped lt blue cl. (Dj offset to eps), o/w Very Nice in fiber dj (shallow chips top edge). *Reese.* $125/£80

POUND, EZRA. Provenca. Boston: Small, Maynard, (1910). 1st ed, 1st imp. One of about 200. Tan bds (spine sl tanned, crown sl worn). Nice (lacks dj). *Reese.* $450/£288

POURADE, RICHARD F. The Silver Dons. Volume Three. The History of San Diego. San Diego: Union-Tribune, 1963. 'Special Edition' signed by Pourade and James S. Copley. Christmas card from Copley laid in. Tan cl (spine faded). Slipcase (soiled). *Parmer.* $60/£38

POWELL, ADAM CLAYTON, JR. Marching Blacks. NY: Dial, 1945. 1st ed. VG in pict dj (torn). *Petrilla.* $45/£29

POWELL, ANTHONY. Afternoon Men. NY: Henry Holt, 1932. 1st US ed, 1st bk. VG in dj (worn, brn paper reinforcement verso). *Lame Duck.* $650/£417

POWELL, ANTHONY. At Lady Molly's. London, (1957). 1st ed. VF in dj. *Argosy.* $110/£71

POWELL, ANTHONY. At Lady Molly's. London: Heinemann, (1957). (Sm name), else Fine in NF dj (sl worn, extrems sl dknd). *Between The Covers.* $175/£112

POWELL, ANTHONY. At Lady Molly's. London: Heinemann, 1957. 1st ed. Red cl, gilt spine. NF in NF dec dj. *Vandoros.* $250/£160

POWELL, ANTHONY. Books Do Furnish a Room. London, (1971). 1st ed. VF in dj. *Argosy.* $85/£54

POWELL, ANTHONY. Books Do Furnish a Room. London, 1971. 1st ed. Fine in Fine dj. *Polyanthos.* $60/£38

POWELL, ANTHONY. Books Do Furnish a Room. London: Heinemann, 1971. 1st Eng ed. VG in dj. *Hadley.* $44/£28

POWELL, ANTHONY. A Buyer's Market. NY: Scribner, 1953. 1st US ed. NF in dj (sl chipped). *Lame Duck.* $150/£96

POWELL, ANTHONY. Casanova's Chinese Restaurant. London, (1960). 1st ed. VG in dj (lt rubbed). *Argosy.* $75/£48

POWELL, ANTHONY. Casanova's Chinese Restaurant. London, 1960. 1st ed. VG in dj (sl sunned). *Buckley.* $70/£45

POWELL, ANTHONY. From a View to a Death. London: Heinemann, 1933. 1st ed. VG + in dj (spine slanted, several tears, soil). *Lame Duck.* $6,500/£4,167

POWELL, ANTHONY. From a View to a Death. Lehmann, 1948. 1st ed thus. Dec spine. Good. *Whiteson.* $31/£20

POWELL, ANTHONY. Hearing Secret Harmonies. London, (1975). 1st ed. Fine in dj. *Argosy.* $65/£42

POWELL, ANTHONY. The Military Philosophers. London, (1968). 1st ed. VF in dj. *Argosy.* $65/£42

POWELL, ANTHONY. The Military Philosophers. London, 1968. 1st ed. Fine (spine heel sl bumped) in dj (spine sl sunned, heel sl creased, price-clipped). *Polyanthos.* $75/£48

POWELL, ANTHONY. The Soldier's Art. London, 1966. 1st ed. NF in dj. *Buckley.* $47/£30

POWELL, ANTHONY. The Soldier's Art. London: Heinemann, 1966. 1st ed. Red cl, gilt spine. Fine in Fine dec dj. *Vandoros.* $150/£96

POWELL, ANTHONY. The Soldiers Art. London, (1966). 1st ed. VG in dj. *Argosy.* $100/£64

POWELL, ANTHONY. Temporary Kings. London, (1973). 1st ed. Fine in dj. *Argosy.* $50/£32

POWELL, ANTHONY. Temporary Kings. London, 1973. 1st ed. Fine in dj. *Polyanthos.* $50/£32

POWELL, ANTHONY. The Valley of Bones. London, (1964). 1st ed. VF in dj. *Argosy.* $100/£64

POWELL, ANTHONY. Venusberg/Agent and Patients. NY: Periscope-Holliday, (1952). 1st ed. NF in dj. *Antic Hay.* $85/£54

POWELL, ANTHONY. What's Become of Waring. Boston: Little, Brown, (1963). 1st Amer ed. Paper-cvrd bds. Fine in dj (soil, sm tears). *Antic Hay.* $20/£13

POWELL, CHARLES. Bound Feet. Boston, 1938. 1st ed. Signed. VG. *Fye.* $100/£64

POWELL, DAWN. Jig Saw: A Comedy. NY: Farrar, (1934). 1st ed. VG in dj (nicks). *Houle.* $95/£61

POWELL, DONALD M. An Arizona Gathering II 1950-69. Tucson, 1973. 1st ed. Fine in Fine dj. *Turpen.* $38/£24

POWELL, DONALD M. An Arizona Gathering. Tucson: AZ Pioneers' Hist Soc, 1960. Ltd to 400. Signed. Unopened. VF in orange wraps. *Five Quail.* $50/£32

POWELL, DONALD M. An Arizona Gathering. A Bibliography...1950-59. Tucson, 1960. 1st ed. One of 400. Signed. Pb. Untrimmed, unopened. VF. *Turpen.* $60/£38

POWELL, E. ALEXANDER. Where the Strange Trails Go Down. NY: Scribner, 1921. Map, 15 plts. Mod cl. VG. *Adelson.* $25/£16

POWELL, FLORENCE LEE. In the Chinese Garden. NY: John Day, 1943. Fine in dj (worn). *Quest.* $65/£42

POWELL, FRED WILBUR. The Railroads of Mexico. Boston: Stratford, 1921. Fldg map. Black-stamped red cl (bkpl). *Dawson.* $40/£26

POWELL, H. M. T. The Santa Fe Trail to California 1849-52. Douglas S. Watson (ed). NY, 1981. Rpt of 1931 Grabhorn ltd ed of 300. #339/350. 2 fldg color maps. Full leather, raised spine bands. VF in VF slipcase. Howes P525. *Turpen.* $295/£189

POWELL, J. W. 15th Annual Report of the BAE. Washington: GPO, 1897. cxxi,366pp; 125 plts. Grn cl (shelfworn,   sunned), gilt. Internally VG (ex-lib); externally Good. *Five Quail.* $225/£144

POWELL, J. W. 18th Annual Report, Part 2. Washington: GPO, 1899. 521-997pp; 67 maps. Rebacked; new cl spine over orig leather bds. (Worn), o/w Good. *Dumont.* $150/£96

POWELL, J. W. 19th Annual Report of the BAE. Washington, 1900. 2 vols. *Kane*.* $200/£128

POWELL, J. W. 1st Annual Report of the BAE. Washington: GPO, 1881. xxv,603pp; 54 plts, map. Grn cl, gilt. (Spine repaired; map tears, separations repaired), o/w Good + . *Five Quail*. $250/£160

POWELL, J. W. 2nd Annual Report of the USGS. Washington: GPO, 1882. Later buckram. VG (ex-lib). *Waverly**. $220/£141

POWELL, J. W. 2nd Annual Report of the USGS. Washington: GPO, 1882. lv,588pp. (Worn, hinges starting), o/w Good. *Dumont*. $225/£144

POWELL, J. W. 2nd Annual Report of the USGS. Washington: GPO, 1882. 1st ed. lv,588pp; 61 plts, lg fldg map in rear pocket. Brn cl, gilt cvr design (cvrs rubbed, inner fr hinge starting), else Fine. *Argonaut*. $250/£160

POWELL, J. W. 7th Annual Report of the BAE. Washington: GPO, 1891. xliii,409pp; 27 plts (incl lg fldg map rear pocket). Grn cl, gilt. (Bds sl scuffed, corners sl bumped), else VG + . *Five Quail*. $325/£208

POWELL, J. W. 8th Annual Report of the USGS, Part 2. GPO, 1889. 8 maps. Leather. (Ex-lib, joints cracking, water staining lower corner.) *Yudkin**. $135/£87

POWELL, J. W. Canyons of the Colorado. NY, 1964. Facs of so-called Meadville (or Chatauqua) 1st ed. Rust-brn cl. VG + . Howes P527. *Five Quail*. $75/£48

POWELL, J. W. Exploration of the Colorado River of the West and Its Tributaries Explored in 1869, 1870, 1871, and 1872.... Washington: GPO, 1872. 1st ed. 4to. xi,(1),291pp; 62 plts; lg fldg map and fldg profile (fldg profile w/3-inch tear to one fold repaired) in rear pocket. Grn cl (newly bound), gilt black leather label. Fine. Howes P528. *Argonaut*. $500/£321

POWELL, J. W. Introduction to the Study of Indian Languages. Washington: GPO, 1880. 2nd ed. 2 fldg charts in rear pocket. Good (sl loose, rear joint starting, spine ends worn). *Hermitage*. $150/£96

POWELL, J. W. Report of the Lands of the Arid Region of the United States. Washington: GPO, 1879. 2nd ed. xv,(1),195pp, 3 lg color fldg maps in rear pocket (1 map w/tear to fold). Gilt spine (ends worn). VG; internally Fine (ink name). *Argonaut*. $400/£256

POWELL, J. W. Report on the Lands of the Arid Region of the United States. Washington: GPO, 1879. 2nd ed. 195pp; 3 VG fldg maps rear cvr pocket. Brn cl (sl soiled, dull). VG + . *Five Quail*. $225/£144

POWELL, LAWRENCE CLARK. Books in My Baggage, Adventures in Reading and Collecting. Cleveland: World Pub Co, (1960). 1st ed. Fine in dj. *Oak Knoll*. $40/£26

POWELL, LAWRENCE CLARK. Great Constellations. El Paso, TX: El Paso Public Library, (1977). 1st ed. Fine in ptd illus wrappers. *Turtle Island*. $30/£19

POWELL, LAWRENCE CLARK. The Little Package. Cleveland: World, (1964). 1st ed. Fine in Fine dj. *Dermont*. $35/£22

POWELL, LAWRENCE CLARK. Philosopher Pickett. Berkeley: Univ of CA, 1942. 1st ed. NF in VG dj. *Turtle Island*. $55/£35

POWELL, LAWRENCE CLARK. Where Water Flows. The Rivers of Arizona. Flagstaff, 1980. 1st ed. Ltd to 2000. NF in NF dj. *Five Quail*. $85/£54

POWELL, PETER J. Sweet Medicine. Norman: Univ of OK, (1969). 1st ed. 2 vols. VG in slipcase. *Lien*. $150/£96

POWER, C. A. LE P. Power's Guide to the Island of Madeira. London, 1927. 2nd ed. 6 fldg maps and panoramas. (Lt browning.) Illus cl. *Edwards*. $23/£15

POWER, EILEEN. The Wool Trade. OUP, 1941. 1st ed. (Eps sl spotted, bkpl.) Dj (sl browned, chipped). *Edwards*. $23/£15

POWER, ETHEL B. The Smaller American House. Boston: Little, Brown, 1927. 1st ed. Black cl, ptd paper lettering pieces. NF. *House*. $55/£35

POWER, J. C. History of Springfield, Illinois. Springfield: IL State Journal Print, 1871. 106pp; full-pg map. Orig ptd wraps (soiled; back cvr stains). Good (corners many pp curled). *Wantagh*. $150/£96

POWER, TYRONE. Impressions of America...1833, 1834, and 1835. London: R. Bentley, 1836. 1st ed. 2 vols. Frontis plt each vol, xv,440; vi,408pp; ads in fr vol 1. Partly unopened. Full leather (rebound). VG. Howes P533. *Bohling*. $150/£96

POWERS, EDWARD. War and the Weather. Delavan, WI: E. Powers, 1890. Presentation copy. 202pp. Photo port mtd inside fr cvr. Brn cl, gilt. (Sl worn.) *Bohling*. $125/£80

POWERS, J. H. History and Reminiscences of Chickasaw County, Iowa. Des Moines: Iowa Ptg Co, 1894. 1st ed. Frontis port, 332pp. (Sl edgewear, hinges cracked, lt browning.) Howes P533. *Waverly**. $44/£28

POWERS, STEPHEN. Afoot and Alone.... Hartford, CT: Columbia, 1872. 1st ed. Frontis, 327pp(3, ads); 12 engr plts. Gilt-stamped brn cl (lt wear, spotting). VG, internally Fine. Howes P537. *Argonaut*. $250/£160

POWERS, STEPHEN. Tribes of California. Berkeley: Univ of CA, (1976). 1st ed thus. Brn cl, gilt spine. Fine in pict dj. *Pacific**. $40/£26

POWERS, TIM. The Anubis Gates. London: C&W, (1985). 1st hb ed. Dj. *Swann**. $161/£103

POWERS, TIM. Dinner at Deviant's Palace. London: C&W, (1986). 1st UK, 1st trade hb ed. Fine in Fine dj. *Other Worlds*. $125/£80

POWERS, TIM. Night Moves. Axolotl, 1986. One of 100 (of 433) in blue cl in lt blue paper dj. (Dj very sl soiled), else Fine. *Certo*. $225/£144

POWERS, TIM. The Stress of Her Regard. Lynbrook: Charnel House, 1989. 1st ed. One of 500 numbered, signed by Powers, James P. Blaylock (afterword), and Dean R. Koontz (intro). Matching slipcase. *Swann**. $80/£51

POWICKE, F. M. King Henry III and the Lord Edward. Oxford: Clarendon, 1947. 2 vols. Fldg map each vol. Grn cl, gilt. VG. *Peter Taylor*. $76/£49

POWNALL, THOMAS. A Topographical Description of the Dominions of the United States of America. Pittsburgh: Univ of Pittsburgh, 1949. One of 2000. 2 lg fldg maps. (Spine sl faded), else VG. *Dumont*. $45/£29

POWYS, JOHN COWPER and LLEWELLYN. Confessions of Two Brothers. Manas, 1916. 1st ed. Blue buckram cl, paper title labels. VG (sm label partly removed rep). *Antic Hay*. $75/£48

POWYS, JOHN COWPER and LLEWELYN. Confessions of Two Brothers. Rochester, NY: Manas, 1916. Very Nice. *Clearwater*. $94/£60

POWYS, JOHN COWPER. Autobiography. NY: S&S, 1934. 1st US ed. Frontis. (Eps sl browned from glue.) Fine. *Graf*. $25/£16

POWYS, JOHN COWPER. Dorothy M. Richardson. London: Joiner & Steele, 1931. 1st ed. Fine in NF dj (lt chipping spine head, sl worn). *Beasley*. $100/£64

POWYS, JOHN COWPER. In Defence of Sensuality. NY, 1930. Very Nice in dj (sl chipped). *Clearwater*. $70/£45

POWYS, JOHN COWPER. Jobber Skald. 1935. 1st ed. (Spine, cvrs sl faded), o/w VG. *Words Etc*. $19/£12

POWYS, JOHN COWPER. Jobber Skald. Bodley Head, 1935. 1st Eng ed. Very Nice (sl faded) in dj (sl torn, dusty). *Clearwater*. $94/£60

POWYS, JOHN COWPER. Madragora. NY: G. Arnold Shaw, 1917. 1st Amer ed. NF (extrems sl rubbed). *Polyanthos.* $35/£22

POWYS, JOHN COWPER. Obstinate Cymric. Druid, 1947. 1st ed. Fine in dj (worn). *Poetry Bookshop.* $47/£30

POWYS, JOHN COWPER. Owen Glendower. London, 1941. 1st ed. Dj (frayed). *Typographeum.* $74/£47

POWYS, JOHN COWPER. The Owl, the Duck and— Miss Rowe! Miss Rowe! Chicago: William Targ, 1930. One of 250 signed. Sketched port. VG (sl dknd, soiled). *Bohling.* $100/£64

POWYS, JOHN COWPER. Powys to Knight. Cecil Woolf, 1983. 1st ed. Fine in dj. *Words Etc.* $23/£15

POWYS, JOHN COWPER. Rabelais. His Life.... Bodley Head, 1948. 1st ed. (Cl faded.) *Cox.* $16/£10

POWYS, JOHN COWPER. Suspended Judgments. NY, 1916. (Bkpl.) Cl-backed bds (chipped, rubbed, bumped, fr bd sl creased). *Clearwater.* $55/£35

POWYS, JOHN COWPER. The War and Culture. NY, 1914. (Few corners dog-eared; cl sl faded, mkd.) *Clearwater.* $94/£60

POWYS, JOHN COWPER. Wood and Stone. NY, 1915. VG (sl mkd, sl bumped). *Clearwater.* $86/£55

POWYS, JOHN COWPER. Wood and Stone. NY: G. Arnold, 1915. 1st ed. Dec blue cl. VG (bkpl, ink name). *Antic Hay.* $85/£54

POWYS, LLEWELYN. A Baker's Dozen. Herrin, IL: Trovillion Private Press, (1939). Ltd to 493 numbered, signed by Powys and Mathias Noheimer (illus). Dec cl. Fine (ink name) in slipcase (sl wear). *Antic Hay.* $125/£80

POWYS, LLEWELYN. Earth Memories. NY: W.W. Norton, (1938). 1st ed. Fine in dj (lt soiled, chip). *Hermitage.* $40/£26

POWYS, LLEWELYN. Glory of Life. London, 1938. 1st trade ed. Fine in dj (sl torn). *Clearwater.* $47/£30

POWYS, LLEWELYN. The Letters of Llewelyn Powys. Louis Wilkinson (ed). John Lane, Bodley Head, (1943). 1st ed. Nice (address label fr fly, top edge sl dusty, sl mks) in dj. *Ash.* $39/£25

POWYS, LLEWELYN. Somerset and Dorset Essays. 1957. 1st ed. VG in dj. *Words Etc.* $31/£20

POWYS, T. F. Black Bryony. London, 1923. 1st Eng ed. Fine in dj (sl tanned, handled). *Clearwater.* $101/£65

POWYS, T. F. Black Bryony. London: C&W, 1923. 1st ed. 5 woodcuts. VG in dj (nicks, sm tear). *Houle.* $95/£61

POWYS, T. F. Bottle's Path and Other Stories. London, 1946. 1st Eng ed. Very Nice (spine faded) in dj. *Clearwater.* $39/£25

POWYS, T. F. Christ in the Cupboard. London: E. Lahr, 1930. One of 500 numbered, signed. Sewn dec wrappers (sunned). *Dermont.* $35/£22

POWYS, T. F. Come and Dine and Tadnol. London, 1967. Ltd to 525 numbered, issued w/o dj. Reynolds Stone (engr). Fine. *Buckley.* $31/£20

POWYS, T. F. Kindness in a Corner. London: C&W, 1930. 1st Eng ed. VG (spine lt faded, corner bumped) in dj (wear, spine browned, lt chipped). *Antic Hay.* $35/£22

POWYS, T. F. Make Thyself Many. Grayson Books, 1935. One of 285 signed. This copy add'lly inscribed. Very Nice (glued item removed 1/2 title) in dj. *Clearwater.* $148/£95

POWYS, T. F. Mark Only. London, 1924. 1st ed. Fine (fep sl offset) in dj (spine sunned, extrems sl chipped, folds rubbed). *Polyanthos.* $30/£19

POWYS, T. F. Mark Only. London: C&W, 1924. 1st ed. (Sl dkng top/bottom edge fr bd), o/w Fine in dj, pub's translucent protective jacket. *Hermitage.* $85/£54

POWYS, T. F. Mr. Weston's Good Wine. London, 1927. One of 660 signed. Buckram (sl bubbled, spine foot sl chafed). Very Nice. *Clearwater.* $140/£90

POWYS, T. F. The Soliloquy of a Hermit. G. Arnold Shaw, 1916. 1st Eng ed. Sound (foxing, inscrip; cvrs mkd, sl chafed, handled). *Clearwater.* $156/£100

POWYS, T. F. The White Paternoster and Other Stories. London, 1930. One of 310 signed. Buckram-backed patterned bds. Fine. *Clearwater.* $109/£70

POYNTER, F. The History and Philosophy of Knowledge of the Brain and Its Functions. Springfield, 1958. NF in dj (worn). *Goodrich.* $95/£61

POYNTER, F. N. L. (ed). The Evolution of Hospitals in Britain. London: Pitman, (1964). 1st ed. NF (lib stamp) in dj. *Glaser.* $60/£38

PRABHAVANANDA, SWAMI. The Song of the Bhagavad-Gita. London, 1947. 1st ed. VG in dj (internally repaired, sm edgetears). *Words Etc.* $28/£18

Practipedics: The Science of Giving Foot Relief and Resolving the Cause.... Chicago: Amer School of Practipedics, 1946. 1st ed. Red cl bds (sl worn). VG. *Doctor's Library.* $30/£19

PRAGNELL, FESTUS. The Green Man of Graypec. NY: Greenberg, (1950). 1st ed. Multi-color dj. *Swann*.* $28/£18

PRASSEL, FRANK R. The Western Peace Officer. Norman: Univ of OK, (1972). 1st ed. (Ink inscrip), else Fine in Fine dj. *Perier.* $30/£19

PRATT, ANNE. The Flowering Plants, Grasses, Sedges and Ferns of Great Britain. London: Frederick Warne, 1899-1900. 4 vols. 319 chromolitho plts, 5 uncolored plts (some tissue guards adhered to plts). Teg. Contemp grn 1/2 morocco (spine faded), gilt. *Christie's*.* $421/£270

PRATT, ANNE. The Flowering Plants, Grasses, Sedges and Ferns of Great Britain.... London: Frederick Warne, 1899. 4 vols. 1/4 leather (chipped, worn). VG. *Zubal*.* $170/£109

PRATT, ANNE. The Flowering Plants, Grasses, Sedges, and Ferns of Great Britain.... London, n.d. (ca 1874). 6 vols. 2119pp; 318 plts (317 color). Aeg. Gilt-dec grn cl (lower tips sl worn; sl foxing). Well Preserved set. *Brooks.* $475/£304

PRATT, ANNE. The Poisonous Noxious and Suspected Plants of Our Fields and Woods. SPCK, n.d. (1857). 208pp; 43 Fine hand-color litho plts. (Inner hinge cracked; binding dulled.) *Quest.* $90/£58

PRATT, C. N. Pacific Railroad of Missouri.... (Denver, 1959.) Facs ed. Lg fldg map. Fine in ptd wrappers, cardbd slipcase w/ptd label. *Cahan.* $40/£26

PRATT, DAVIS (ed). The Photographic Eye of Ben Shahn. Cambridge: Harvard Univ, 1975. 1st ed. (Owner stamp), else NF in dj (sl edgeworn, smudge). *Cahan.* $65/£42

PRATT, JOSEPH. A Year with Osler 1896-1897. Balt, 1949. 1st ed. VG. *Fye.* $90/£58

PRATT, PARLEY P. The Autobiography of Parley Parker Pratt, One of the Twelve Apostles of the Church.... Chicago, 1888. 2nd ed. Frontis, 502pp + appendix, port. Marbled eps. Full leather (sl scuffing, edgewear, chip spine top), gilt. VG. *Benchmark.* $95/£61

PRATT, PARLEY P. Key to the Science of Theology.... Salt Lake, 1915. 7th ed. VG (name; lt edgewear). *Benchmark.* $30/£19

PRATT, PARLEY P. A Voice of Warning and Instruction to All People. Liverpool, 1854. 8th ed. 199pp (few ll chipped, pg corners folded, lt foxed, 1st few ll waterstained, lacks fep, pencil dwgs, #s reps). Orig full blind-stamped leather (lt wear, corners bumped). Overall Good +. *Benchmark.* $85/£54

PRATT, PARLEY P. A Voice of Warning and Instruction to All People.... Plano, IL: Church of Latter Day Saints, 1863. Rev ed. 256pp. 1/2 cl, marbled bds. *Ginsberg.* $375/£240

PRATT, RICHARD. The Picture Garden Book and Gardener's Assistant. NY: Howell, Soskin, 1942. 1st ed. (Owner stamp), o/w VG in dj (lt worn). *Cahan.* $50/£32

PRAZ, MARIO. Studies in Seventeenth-Century Imagery. Volume 1. London, 1939. (1 pg edge mended.) *Washton.* $90/£58

PREBLE, GEORGE H. Chronological History of the Origin and Development of Steam Navigation. Phila: Hamersly, 1883. 1st ed. (19),484,(2), errata pp. (Cl lt worn.) *Ginsberg.* $150/£96

PREEDY, GEORGE. General Crack. London: John Lane, Bodley Head, 1928. 1st ed. (Feps lt browned.) Black cl. *Hollett.* $23/£15

PREISS, LUDWIG and PAUL ROHRBACH. Palestine and Transjordania. NY: Macmillan, 1926. 1st US ed. 21 color plts (1 loose). Navy cl, gilt. (Sl rubbed.) Text VG. *Baltimore*.* $60/£38

PRENDERGAST, MAURICE. A Sketchbook of Maurice Prendergast. Mill Roseman (ed). Erie, PA: Hammermill Papers Group, 1974. 1st ed. Fine in pict dj. *Jaffe.* $125/£80

PRENDERGAST, THOMAS F. Forgotten Pioneers. SF: Trade Pressroom, 1942. 1st ed. Ltd to 1500. 6 ports. VF in dj (torn). *Argonaut.* $75/£48

PRENTICE, ANDREW. Renaissance Architecture and Ornament in Spain...1500-1560. Batsford, 1893. vii,16pp; 60 plts. Teg. (Lib ink stamps, few margins sl thumbed; sm nick upper bd.) *Edwards.* $140/£90

PRENTICE, ANDREW. Renaissance Architecture and Ornaments in Spain. London: Batsford, n.d. (ca 1900). 60 plts. (Binding broken, defective, chipped, sl soiled.) *Freeman*.* $45/£29

PRENTICE, E. PARMALEE. American Dairy Cattle. NY: Harper, 1942. 1st ed. VG in Fair dj. *October Farm.* $48/£31

PRENTICE, E. PARMALEE. The Influence of Hunger on Human History. Williamstown, MA, 1938. 1st ed. Signed. VG. *Fye.* $100/£64

PRENTIS, EDWARD. Ye Antient Buriall Place of New London, Conn. New London, 1899. 40pp; 3-panel fldg photo, 2 other photos. (Chip to foot), o/w Good. *Scribe's Perch*.* $24/£15

PRENTISS, HENRY M. The Great Polar Current. Polar Papers Delong-Nansen-Peary. NY: Stokes, 1897. (viii),153pp. Teg. VG. *High Latitude.* $45/£29

PRESCOTT, GEORGE B. History, Theory, and Practice of the Electric Telegraph. Boston: Ticknor & Fields, 1860. 1st ed. Frontis, xii,468pp. (Pebbled cl faded, dull; lib card pocket removed.) Good. *Glaser.* $100/£64

PRESCOTT, MARJORIE WIGGIN. Tales of a Sportsman's Wife: Shooting. Privately ptd, (1939). One of 150 ptd. Cl-backed marbled bds (spine sunned; sm hole p79 not affecting text). *Argosy.* $75/£48

PRESCOTT, PHILANDER. The Recollections of Philander Prescott, Frontiersman of the Old Northwest 1819-1862. Lincoln, (1966). 1st ed. Fine in dj (lt worn). *Pratt.* $20/£13

PRESCOTT, PHILANDER. The Recollections of Philander Prescott. Donald Dean Parker (ed). Lincoln: Univ of NE, (1966). 1st ed. VG in dj. *Lien.* $30/£19

PRESCOTT, WILLIAM H. History of the Conquest of Mexico with Preliminary View of Ancient Mexican Civilization, and Life of the Conqueror, Hernando Cortes. Phila, 1891. Later ptg. 3 vols. 430; 402; 448pp. Teg. Grn cl, spine gilt. Fine. *Turpen.* $100/£64

PRESCOTT, WILLIAM H. History of the Conquest of Mexico. NY, 1843. 1st Amer ed, 1st ptg. 3 vols. 4 plts, 2 dbl-pg maps. (Eps browned.) *Swann*.* $258/£165

PRESCOTT, WILLIAM H. History of the Conquest of Mexico. Phila, 1874. 3 vols. Engr frontis each vol, xxxiv, 477; 463; 522pp. Marbled edges, eps. 1/2 tan calf, marbled bds, dec gilt-paneled spines. VG. *Truepenny.* $150/£96

PRESCOTT, WILLIAM H. History of the Conquest of Mexico.... NY: Harper, 1843. 1st ed. 3 vols. Frontis port each vol, dbl-pg map vols 1 and 2, 1 facs plt. Few ll unopened. Slate grn cl, gilt. (Sl foxed, browned, esp eps), o/w internally Excellent. (Few scratches 1 cvr, 1 vol w/sm white paint flecks.) *Pirages.* $500/£321

PRESCOTT, WILLIAM H. History of the Conquest of Peru with a Preliminary View of the Civilization of the Incas. NY, 1848. 2nd ed. Frontis ports; xl,527; xix,547pp. Orig blind-stamped dk grn cl, spine gilt. (Pinhole in joint, foxed; extrems sl worn, ex-lib), o/w NF. *Turpen.* $95/£61

PRESCOTT, WILLIAM H. History of the Conquest of Peru, with a Preliminary View of the Civilization of the Incas. NY: Harper, 1847. 1st Amer ed, 1st issue w/no period after 'integrity' on line 20, pg 467 of vol 2. 2 vols. Engr frontis ports, xl,527; xx,547pp (lt foxing); map, facs. (Cl faded.) *House.* $160/£103

PRESCOTT, WILLIAM H. History of the Conquest of Peru, with a Preliminary View of the Civilization of the Incas. NY: Harper, 1847. 1st ed, 1st issue. 2 vols. 2 ports, facs plt and map. (Eps sl foxed; corners sl rubbed, edges sl lightened), o/w Nice. *Sadlon.* $275/£176

PRESCOTT, WILLIAM H. History of the Conquest of Peru. Phila: Lippincott, (1874). 2 vols. liv,1040pp; 2 plts. (Sigs.) *Archaeologia.* $45/£29

PRESCOTT, WILLIAM H. History of the Conquest of Peru. NY, 1947. 1st ed. 2 vols. 2 ports, map. (Foxing, eps discolored.) Unopened. Pub's cl. Good-. *Scribe's Perch*.* $20/£13

PRESCOTT, WILLIAM H. History of the Reign of Ferdinand and Isabella, the Catholic. Phila, 1893. 3rd ed. 3 vols. Frontis ports; 464; 455; 489pp. VG +. *Turpen.* $95/£61

PRESCOTT, WILLIAM H. History of the Reign of Ferdinand and Isabella. C. Harvey Gardiner (ed). NY: LEC, 1967. One of 1500 numbered, signed by Lima de Freitas (illus). Blind-stamped leather, gilt spine. VG in bd slipcase. *Argosy.* $125/£80

PRESCOTT, WILLIAM H. The Works. Phila/London, 1904. #102/250. 22 vols, complete. Color frontispieces. Teg, rest uncut. Spare paper title label tipped in rear each vol. (Spines lt faded.) *Edwards.* $975/£625

PRESCOTT, WILLIAM H. The Works. Wilfred Harold Munro (ed). Phila/London: Lippincott, (1904). One of 1000. 22 vols. 122 plts. Marbled eps; teg. Grn 3/4 crushed morocco (spines faded, corners worn, 3 sm snags to heads), cl sides, gilt. (3 leaves carelessly opened, 6 vols w/leaves loose or detached), o/w internally Fine. *Pirages.* $750/£481

Present State of His Majesties' Isles and Territories in America. (By Richard Blome.) London, 1687. Contemp sheep. (Lacks port, maps.) Howes B546. *Swann*.* $287/£184

Present State of the Universe.... (By John Beaumont.) London: Benj. Motte, 1701. 3rd ed. (12),159,(1); (7),35 ll, (1)pp; 12 engr plts. (Foxed, dampstained, few ll w/scissor cuts in margins.) Full panelled calf (worn, fr cvr detached). *New Hampshire*.* $120/£77

President Vanishes. (By Rex Stout.) NY, (1934). 1st ed. Fine (spine top chipped, lt shelfworn) in VG dj (chip, price-clipped). *Mcclintock.* $225/£144

PREST, WILFRED R. The Rise of the Barristers, A Social History of the English Bar 1590-1640. Oxford: Clarendon, 1986. Boswell. $75/£48

PRESTON, HUBERT (ed). Cricketers' Almanack 1948. Sporting Handbooks Ltd, 1948. 85th ed. 12 plts. Good (browning) in ptd limp linen cvrs (sl soiled, cockled along backstrip, edges sl frayed). Cox. $59/£38

PRESTON, HUBERT (ed). Cricketers' Almanack. Sporting Handbooks Ltd, 1950. 87th year. 12 plts. Good in brn cl (nick spine foot). Cox. $75/£48

PRESTON, KERRISON (ed). The Blake Collection of W. Graham Robertson. London: Faber & Faber, (1952). 1st ed. NF in dj (2 sm chips). Captain's Bookshelf. $75/£48

PRESTON, NORMAN (ed). Wisden Cricketers' Almanack 1961. London, 1961. Cl wrappers. Edwards. $23/£15

PRESTON, RUPERT. The Seventeenth-Century Marine Painters of the Netherlands. Leigh-on-Sea, 1974. Good in dj. Washton. $50/£32

PRESTON, WILLIAM. Illustrations of Masonry. Alexandria: Ptd by Cottom & Stewart, 1804. 1st Amer ed. x,11,360pp. Contemp calf, leather label. (Tp torn, sm portion missing, no loss; lacks eps; text sl browned, spotted, ink notes last pg, rear pastedown; worn, scuffed), else Good. Brown. $60/£38

PRESTON, WILLIAM. Illustrations of Masonry. Portsmouth, (NH): W & D Treadwell, 1804. 1st Amer improved ed. Full calf (rubbed, fr hinge broken, barely holding). New Hampshire*. $70/£45

PRESTWICH, A. A. Records of Parrots Bred in Captivity. The Author, 1950-52. 6 parts in 1 vol. Maggs. $55/£35

PRETORIUS, P. J. Jungle Man. NY: Dutton, 1948. 1st ed. VG+ in Good dj. Mikesh. $30/£19

Pretty Polly. (By Ernest Nister.) London: Nister, (ca 1899). 4to. (28)pp; 4 color pop-ups. Pict bds. (Sig starting, lt rubbed, inscrip), else NF. Bromer. $750/£481

PREVITE-ORTON, C. W. The Shorter Cambridge Medieval History. CUP, 1952. 2 vols. 26 maps, 27 tables. Gilt devices upper bds. (Vol 1 spine lt sunned.) Edwards. $39/£25

PREVOST, ABBE. Manon Lescaut. London, 1928. Ltd to 1850 numbered. 11 two-color full-pg plts (w/lettered tissue guards) by Alastair. (Eps foxed; spine snagged, cvrs soiled.) King. $95/£61

PRICE, ANTHONY. The '44 Vintage. Gollancz, 1978. Rev copy. (Sl cocked), o/w Fine in Fine dj. Martin. $41/£26

PRICE, ANTHONY. The Alamut Ambush. Gollancz, 1971. 1st UK ed. Fine in NF dj (sl rubbing). Martin. $86/£55

PRICE, ANTHONY. For the Good of the State. NY: Mysterious Press, (1986). 1st ed. NF in dj. Antic Hay. $15/£10

PRICE, ANTHONY. For the Good of the State. NY: Mysterious Press, (1986). Ltd to 250 numbered, signed. Fine in slipcase. Antic Hay. $45/£29

PRICE, ANTHONY. The Labyrinth Makers. London: Gollancz, 1970. 1st British ed, 1st bk. VG (sl cocked, soiled) in dj (extrems chipped, sl loss ends, heel stained). Metropolitan*. $46/£29

PRICE, ANTHONY. October Men. Gollancz, 1973. 1st UK ed. Fine in dj. Williams. $148/£95

PRICE, ANTHONY. The Old Vengeful. Gollancz, 1982. 1st UK ed. Fine in Fine dj. Martin. $28/£18

PRICE, ANTHONY. Our Man in Camelot. Gollancz, 1975. 1st UK ed. Fine in dj. Williams. $133/£85

PRICE, ANTHONY. Soldier No More. Gollancz, 1981. 1st UK ed. Fine in NF dj. Williams. $39/£25

PRICE, ANTHONY. Tomorrow's Ghost. Gollancz, 1979. 1st UK ed. Fine in Fine dj. Martin. $34/£22

PRICE, ANTHONY. War Game. Gollancz, 1976. 1st UK ed. Fine in dj. Williams. $117/£75

PRICE, CHARLES MATLACK. Posters: A Critical Study.... NY, 1913. (Spine sl dknd, gilt dull.) Swann*. $373/£239

PRICE, CHESTER B. Portraits of Ten Country Houses Designed by Delano and Aldrich. GC, 1924. 1st ed. 61 plts. (Sl internal soil.) Orig bds (lt worn, soiled, sl warped). Freeman*. $100/£64

PRICE, CLEMENT ALEXANDER. Freedom Not Far Distant. Newark: NJ Hist Soc, 1980. VG in pict dj. Petrilla. $40/£26

PRICE, DOUGHBERLY. Short Stirrups. L.A.: Westernlore, 1960. 1st ed. VG in dj (dknd, chipped). Bohling. $20/£13

PRICE, E. HOFFMAN. Far Lands Other Days. Carcosa, 1975. 1st ed. Subs copy w/art plt by George Evans affixed to fep. Signed by Price and Evans. Fine in Fine dj. Certo. $100/£64

PRICE, E. HOFFMAN. Far Lands, Other Days. Chapel Hill: Carcossa, 1975. 1st ed. Signed by Price and George Evans (illus). Dj. Swann*. $80/£51

PRICE, E. HOFFMAN. Strange Gateways. Sauk City: Arkham House, 1967. 1st ed. Fine in NF dj. Other Worlds. $60/£38

PRICE, F. G. HILTON. Old Base Metal Spoons. London: Batsford, 1908. 1st ed. 16 plts. 2 orig photos loosely inserted, 1 stamped 'Copyright British Museum.' (Eps sl spotted.) Dec cl silvered. Hollett. $117/£75

PRICE, F. G. HILTON. The Signs of Old Lombard Street. London: Field & Tuer, Leadenhall Press, (1887). 1st ed. (viii),xiv (but xxviii),112 (but 344)pp; fldg map. Good (edges sl spotted; rubbed). Ash. $117/£75

PRICE, GLENN W. Origins of the War with Mexico, the Polk-Stockton Intrigue. Austin, 1967. 1st ed. Fine in VG dj. Turpen. $45/£29

PRICE, HARRY and R. S. LAMBERT. The Haunting of Cashen's Gap. London: Methuen, 1936. 1st ed. 8 plts. VG. Hollett. $62/£40

PRICE, JULIUS M. From the Arctic Ocean to the Yellow Sea. NY: Scribner, 1892. 384pp; fldg map, 42 plts. Pict cl (lt rubbed). Adelson. $125/£80

PRICE, JULIUS M. From the Arctic Ocean to the Yellow Sea. London, 1893. Frontis port, xxiv,384pp; fldg map. (Lt foxed, bkpl removed, hinges tender.) Silver-illus cl (rubbed w/sl loss, spine chipped, sm stain spine from label removal). Edwards. $78/£50

PRICE, RALSTON. Duckie: Memoirs of a Cowboy. NY: Pageant, 1952. 1st ed. Fine. Gibbs. $27/£17

PRICE, REYNOLDS. The Annual Heron. NY: Albondocani Press, 1980. 1st ed. One of 300 numbered, signed. Fine in dec wrappers, ptd label. Reese. $50/£32

PRICE, REYNOLDS. The Foreseeable Future. NY, 1991. 1st Amer ed. Fine (spine heel sl rubbed) in Fine dj. Polyanthos. $25/£16

PRICE, REYNOLDS. A Generous Man. NY, 1966. 1st ed. Fine in Fine dj. Warren. $50/£32

PRICE, REYNOLDS. Good Hearts. NY: Atheneum, 1988. 1st ed. Rev slip laid in. Fine in dj. Reese. $30/£19

PRICE, REYNOLDS. The Laws of Ice. NY: Atheneum, 1986. 1st ed. Rev slip, flyers laid in. VF in dj. Reese. $30/£19

PRICE, REYNOLDS. A Long and Happy Life. NY: Atheneum, 1962. Advance reading copy of 1st ed, 1st bk. NF in ptd wrappers. Reese. $250/£160

PRICE, REYNOLDS. Love and Work. NY: Atheneum, 1968. 1st ed. Fine in Fine dj. *Beasley.* $40/£26

PRICE, REYNOLDS. Love and Work. NY: Atheneum, 1968. 1st ed. Fine in NF dj (price-clipped; sl rubbing). *Between The Covers.* $85/£54

PRICE, REYNOLDS. The Names and Faces of Heroes. NY: Atheneum, 1963. 1st ed. Fine in dj. *Reese.* $75/£48

PRICE, REYNOLDS. Permanent Errors. NY: Atheneum, 1970. 1st ed. Signed, inscribed. NF in dj. *Reese.* $85/£54

PRICE, REYNOLDS. Permanent Errors. NY: Atheneum, 1970. 1st ed. (Fore-edge lt foxed), else Fine in NF dj (creases fr flap, price-clipped). *Between The Covers.* $85/£54

PRICE, REYNOLDS. Private Contentment. NY: Atheneum, 1984. 1st ed. Fine in dj. *Between The Covers.* $85/£54

PRICE, REYNOLDS. Things Themselves. NY: Atheneum, 1972. 1st ed. Fine in dj (sl tear crown). *Between The Covers.* $125/£80

PRICE, RICHARD. Additional Observations on the Nature and Value of Civil Liberty.... London: T. Cadell, 1777. 1st ed. (Fr, back matter sl soiled, sl dampstaining.) Orig wrappers (chipped, soiled). Howes P538. *Freeman*.* $180/£115

PRICE, RICHARD. Bloodbrothers. Boston: Houghton Mifflin, 1976. 1st ed. Fine in dj (lt rubbed). *Jaffe.* $65/£42

PRICE, S. F. The Fern-Collector's Handbook and Herbarium. NY: Holt, (1897). 72pp. VG. *Mikesh.* $37/£24

PRICE, VINCENT and MARY. A Treasury of Great Recipes. Darlene Geis (ed). (N.p.): Ampersand, (1965). 1st ed. Pict dec eps; copper silk bkmks. Full copper leatherette. VG. *Houle.* $150/£96

PRICE-BROWN, J. Diseases of the Nose and Throat. Phila: F.A. Davis, 1900. 1st ed. 6 color plts, 9 color figs. VG (stamps). *Glaser.* $85/£54

PRICHARD, H. HESKETH. Through Trackless Labrador.... NY, 1911. (Sl rubbed), else NF. *Reese.* $125/£80

PRICHARD, JAMES C. The Natural History of Man. 1845. xvii,596pp. (Spine sl mkd, ends sl defective), o/w VG. *Whitehart.* $55/£35

PRICHARD, JAMES C. The Natural History of Man. Edwin Norris (ed). London: H. Bailliere, 1855. 4th ed. 2 vols. xxiv,343; 343-720pp, 62 plts. (Mottling cvrs, spine sl edgeworn), o/w VG. *Oregon.* $850/£545

PRICHARD, JAMES C. A Treatise on Insanity and Other Disorders Affecting the Mind. London: Sherwood et al, 1835. 1st ed. 2 inserted ad leaves dated Oct 1, 1835, xvi,483,(1)pp + 20pp inserted ads, ad for British and Foreign Medical Review dated Oct 1, 1836. (Sm puncture tp.) Contemp mauve cl (rebacked, new paper spine label, corners bumped, shelfworn). VG. *Gach.* $575/£369

PRIDEAUX, SARAH T. A Catalogue of Books Bound by S.T. Prideaux.... London, (1900). 26 plts. Linen-backed bds (spine faded; bkpl). *Swann*.* $103/£66

PRIEST, JOSIAH. American Antiquities, and Discoveries in the West. Albany, 1833. 2nd ed. 2 fldg plts. (Lt foxed.) Full calf (ends rubbed). Sound. *Yudkin*.* $175/£112

PRIEST, JOSIAH. American Antiquities, and Discoveries in the West. Albany: Hoffman & White, 1833. 3rd ed. 400pp (lt foxed); 2 engr plts (1 fldg), fldg map. Contemp mottled calf (extrems lt rubbed), red leather spine label, gilt. Howes P592. *Karmiole.* $150/£96

PRIESTLEY, HERBERT INGRAM. Franciscan Explorations in California. Lillian Estelle Fisher (ed). Glendale: Clark, 1946. 1st ed. One of 1020. (Bkpl on inner cvr, corners lt jammed), else Fine. *Argonaut.* $150/£96

PRIESTLEY, J. B. Albert Goes Through. London: Heinemann, (1933). 1st Eng ed. NF (offsetting eps) in dj (wear, soil). *Antic Hay.* $35/£22

PRIESTLEY, J. B. Albert Goes Through. Heinemann, 1933. 1st UK ed. Fine (eps sunned) in NF dj (tear, sl fading). *Martin.* $28/£18

PRIESTLEY, J. B. Angel Pavement. London: Heinemann, (1930). 1st Eng ed. Blue cl. VG (fore-edge spotted, eps sl discolored) in VG dj (wear, soil). *Antic Hay.* $50/£32

PRIESTLEY, J. B. Angel Pavement. London: Heinemann, 1930. 1st ed. Orig full blue levant morocco (spine lt faded), gilt. *Hollett.* $62/£40

PRIESTLEY, J. B. Angel Pavement. London: Heinemann, 1930. 1st ed, ltd issue. One of 1025 ptd on laid paper w/frontis port of Priestley, signed. Teg, others rough-trimmed. Tan cl, beveled bds, gilt spine. Fine. *Vandoros.* $150/£96

PRIESTLEY, J. B. Britain at War. NY/London: Harper, 1942. 1st Amer ed. Card wrappers (rubbed, chipped). *Clearwater.* $31/£20

PRIESTLEY, J. B. Delight. London: Heinemann, 1949. 1st ed. VG. *Hollett.* $23/£15

PRIESTLEY, J. B. The Doomsday Men. NY: Harper, 1938. 1st Amer ed. NF (bkpl) in VG dj (wear, soil). *Antic Hay.* $20/£13

PRIESTLEY, J. B. Johnson Over Jordan. NY: Harper, (1939). 1st Amer ed. NF in dj (lt browned, sm tear). *Antic Hay.* $25/£16

PRIESTLEY, J. B. Postscripts. London: Heinemann, 1940. 1st ed. (Fore-edge sl spotted.) *Hollett.* $19/£12

PRIESTLEY, J. B. Rain upon Godshill. London: Heinemann, 1939. 1st ed. (Extrems sl rubbed; spots.) *Hollett.* $23/£15

PRIESTLEY, J. B. The Town Major of Miraucourt. London: Heinemann, 1930. #315/525 signed. (Lt foxing.) Teg. (Cvrs sl discolored.) Fine in slipcase. *Virgo.* $31/£20

PRIESTLEY, J. B. with GERALD BULLETT. I'll Tell You Everything. London: Heinemann, (1933). 1st Eng ed. Fine in dj (sl wear, soil). *Antic Hay.* $35/£22

PRIESTLEY, RAYMOND E. Antarctic Adventure. Scott's Northern Party. London: T. Fisher Unwin, 1914. 3 fldg maps. Teg. Silver-dec cl (spine flaking). VG. *High Latitude.* $500/£321

PRIESTLY, HERBERT I. Jose de Galvez, Visitor-General of New Spain 1765-71. Berkeley, 1916. 1st ed, 1st bk. Pb. Frontis port, fldg map. VG (rubbed). *Turpen.* $125/£80

PRIME, A. C. (ed). Three Centuries of Historic Silver. Phila, 1938. #370/1000. Good. *Scribe's Perch*.* $50/£32

PRIME, E. D. G. Around the World. NY: Harper, 1872. 1st ed. Frontis, 455pp + 6pp cat. Grn cl (bumped, rubbed, private lib mk spine). VG. *Blue Mountain.* $35/£22

PRINCE, L. BRADFORD. Historical Sketches of New Mexico from the Earliest Records to the American Occupation. NY/Kansas City: Leggat/Ramsey, 1883. 1st ed. Inscribed presentation by Mary C. Prince. 327pp. (Lacks fep; cvrs lt worn.) Howes P611. *Ginsberg.* $200/£128

PRINCE, L. BRADFORD. Spanish Mission Churches of New Mexico. Cedar Rapids, 1915. 1st ed. VG. *Turpen.* $125/£80

PRINCE, L. BRADFORD. Spanish Mission Churches of New Mexico. Cedar Rapids, IA: Torch, 1915. 1st ed. Pict cl. Howes P613. *Ginsberg.* $125/£80

PRINCE, NANCY. A Narrative of the Life and Travels of Mrs. Nancy Prince. Boston: The Author, 1856. 3rd ed. 89pp. (Spine worn, fr bd sl bent), else Good. *Brown.* $100/£64

PRINGLE, JOHN. Observations on the Diseases of the Army. London, 1753. 2nd ed. Buckram. VG. *Argosy.* $350/£224

Prints of Lucas van Leyden and His Contemporaries. Washington: Nat'l Gallery of Art, 1983. Good in wraps. *Washton.* $60/£38

PRIOR, EDWARD S. The Cathedral Builders in England. London, 1905. 1st ed. 4 color plts. Teg. Gilt/blind dec cl (spine sl chipped, faded; feps lt browned). *Edwards.* $31/£20

PRIOR, MATTHEW. Poems on Several Occasions. T. Johnson, 1720. New ed. xx,456,(8)pp contents & ads (pg torn w/o loss). Contemp calf (rebacked). *Cox.* $47/£30

PRIOR, MATTHEW. Poems on Several Occasions. 1733. 5th ed. 2 vols. (xxvi),231,(iv); 259,(iii)pp. Contemp calf (sl worn, vol 1 sl water-stained). *Bickersteth.* $47/£30

PRIOR, W. D. Roses and Their Culture. London: Routledge, n.d. (1878). 1st ed. 179pp; 8 color plts. Aeg. Paper insert fr cvr. Gilt decs. (Sig loose), else Fine. *Quest.* $80/£51

PRITCHARD, A. and C. R. GORING. Microscopic Illustrations of Living Objects.... London: Whittaker, 1845. 3rd ed. 295pp; 4 plts (3 color). New eps. Red cl (rebacked), paper spine label. VG (sl worn). *Savona.* $117/£75

PRITCHARD, JAMES A. The Overland Diary of James A. Pritchard from Kentucky to California in 1849. Dale Morgan (ed). (Denver): Old West Pub Co, 1959. 1st ed. Frontis port, 3 maps (2 fldg), fldg chart in rear pocket. Uncut. VF in dj (sl chipped). *Argonaut.* $125/£80

PRITCHARD, JAMES A. The Overland Diary of...From Kentucky to California in 1849.... Dale L. Morgan (ed). Denver, 1959. 1st ed. Dj. *Wantagh.* $100/£64

PRITCHARD, JAMES B. (ed). Ancient Near Eastern Texts Relating to the Old Testament. Princeton, 1950. Good in dj. *Washton.* $65/£42

PRITCHETT, R. T. Smokiana. London, 1890. Contents VG (tp sl creased; extrems worn, soiled). *Waverly*.* $176/£113

PRITCHETT, V. S. Dead Man Leading. NY: Macmillan, 1937. 1st Amer ed. (Lt stain sm portion fore-edge, 1 pg), else NF in NF dj (lt dknd, faint spine crease). *Between The Covers.* $250/£160

PRITCHETT, V. S. On the Edge of the Cliff. London: C&W, 1980. 1st ed. VG in dj (price-clipped). *Hollett.* $23/£15

PRITCHETT, V. S. The Spanish Temper. NY: Knopf, (1954). 1st ed. VG in dj. *Antic Hay.* $20/£13

PRITZKE, HERBERT. Bedouin Doctor. London: Weidenfeld & Nicolson, 1957. 2nd imp. VG in dj (tattered). *Worldwide.* $25/£16

Private Papers of a Bankrupt Bookseller. NY: D. Appleton, 1932. 1st Amer issue, comprised of British sheets. Cl, paper spine label. Fine in dj (lt sunned). *Reese.* $45/£29

Priviledges and Practice of Parliaments in England. (London: B. Alsop & T. Fawcet), 1640. 2nd ed. (iv),46pp (lacks 1st blank; tp dusty, verso of last soiled, edges repaired, rest lt browned; marginal notes, underlinings, mod bkpl). Mod 1/4 vellum. *Sokol.* $351/£225

PROBERT, THOMAS. Lost Mines and Buried Treasures of the West. Berkeley: Univ of CA, 1977. 1st ed. Red cl. Fine in Fine dj. *Harrington.* $50/£32

Probus: or Rome in the Third Century. (By William Ware.) NY/Boston: C.S. Francis/Joseph H. Francis, 1838. 1st ed. 2 vols. Nice (inscrips, sl foxed; faded, cocked, spotted, sl worn). *Pirages.* $45/£29

Proceedings at Large on the Trial of John Donellan.... London, 1781. 152pp. 1/2 leather. VG. *Fye.* $250/£160

Proceedings of the Thirteenth Annual Re-Union of the Oregon Pioneer Association for 1885.... Salem, OR, 1886. 44pp. VG in dec wrappers. *Reese.* $125/£80

PROCKTOR, PATRICK. Self-Portrait. London, 1991. 1st ed. Dj. *Typographeum.* $20/£13

PROCTER BROS (eds). The Fishermen's Own Book.... Gloucester: Privately Pub, 1882. 1st ed. 274pp + ads. Blind-stamped gilt-dec cl. VG. *Mikesh.* $75/£48

PROCTER, GIL. Tucson, Tubac, Tumacacori, Tohell. Tucson, 1957. 2nd ed. Fine in Fine dj. *Turpen.* $20/£13

PROCTER, RICHARD W. The Barber's Shop. London/Manchester: Simpkin, Marshall/Abel Heywood, 1883. Rev, enlgd ed. xxxii,250pp; 40 etched plts. Teg. Pict cl, gilt, beveled bds (sl worn, bumped). *Hollett.* $133/£85

PROCTOR, FREDERICK TOWNE. The Frederick Towne Proctor Collection of Antique Watches and Table Clocks. Utica, NY, 1913. Ltd ed. 38 plts. Black cl, gilt. Fine. *Weber.* $375/£240

PROCTOR, GIL. People of the Moonlight. Pete Kitchen Museum, 1958. 1st ed. Ltd to 1000. Signed. Fine in VG dj. *Oregon.* $70/£45

PROCTOR, H. R. The Principles of Leather Manufacture. London, 1922. 2nd ed. (Ex-lib, bkpl; cl soiled, spine chipped, punctured.) *Edwards.* $47/£30

PROCTOR, L. B. Lives of Eminent Lawyers and Statesmen of the State of New York.... NY: S.S. Peloubet, 1892. 2 vols. Emb cl (chipped, rubbed). Clean set. *Boswell.* $175/£112

PROCTOR, RICHARD A. The Great Pyramid. London: C&W, (1883). Frontis, viii,323pp (sl ex-lib mks, bkpl); 3 plts. Gilt-pict cl (corners bumped, spine repaired). *Archaeologia.* $75/£48

PRODDOW, PENELOPE. Demeter and Persephone. NY: Doubleday, 1972. 1st ed. Barbara Cooney (illus). 8 3/4 x 11 1/4. 48pp. Pict bds. Fine in dj. *Cattermole.* $75/£48

Prodigies and Prodigals. Guinness, n.d. (1957). 1st ed. VG in illus wrappers. *Words Etc.* $31/£20

PROKOSCH, FREDERIC. The Asiatics. NY, 1935. 1st ed. Signed. *Argosy.* $30/£19

PROKOSCH, FREDERIC. The Seven Who Fled. NY, 1937. Signed. Dj. *Argosy.* $25/£16

PRONZINI, BILL and MARTIN H. GREENBERG (eds). The Ethnic Detectives: Masterpieces of Mystery Fiction. NY: Dodd, Mead, 1985. 1st ed. Hillerman's story, signed by him. Fine in dj (sl edgewear). *Janus.* $45/£29

PRONZINI, BILL and COLLIN WILCOX. Twospot. NY: Putnam, 1978. 1st ed. Signed by both. Fine in dj (sm closed tears, spine sl dknd). *Mordida.* $65/£42

PRONZINI, BILL. Bindlestiff. NY: St. Martin's, 1983. 1st ed. Signed. Fine in Fine dj. *Old London.* $40/£26

PRONZINI, BILL. Blowback. NY: Random House, 1977. 1st ed. Signed. Fine in dj. *Mordida.* $40/£26

PRONZINI, BILL. Dragonfire. NY: St. Martin's, 1982. 1st ed. Signed. Fine in dj. *Mordida.* $35/£22

PRONZINI, BILL. Games. NY: Putnam, 1976. 1st ed. Signed. VG in VG dj. *Old London.* $30/£19

PRONZINI, BILL. Gun in Cheek. NY: Coward et al, 1982. 1st ed. Signed. Fine in dj. *Mordida.* $35/£22

PRONZINI, BILL. Masques. NY: Arbor House, 1981. 1st ed. Signed. Fine in Fine dj. *Old London.* $25/£16

PRONZINI, BILL. Masques. NY: Arbor House, 1981. 1st ed. Signed. Fine in Fine dj. *Janus.* $30/£19

PRONZINI, BILL. Scattershot. NY: St. Martin, 1982. 1st ed. Signed. Fine (corner bump) in Fine dj. *Janus.* $25/£16

PROSCH, CHARLES. Reminiscences of Washington Territory. Seattle, 1904. Inscribed in pencil. Frontis port, 2 plts. Brn cl (extrems rubbed). VG. Howes P633. *Bohling.* $150/£96

Prose Quartos. NY: Random House, 1930. One of 875. Engr tp. 6 short stories bound separately in color paper wrappers, housed in slipcase. VG (spines, cvrs faded). *Heller.* $175/£112

PROSKE, BEATRICE GILMAN. Brookgreen Gardens. Brookgreen, SC: Ptd by Order of the Trustees, 1943. Fldg chart. Fine. *Quest.* $35/£22

Protocols and World Revolution. (By S.A. Nilus.) Boston: Small, Maynard, (1920). 1st Amer ed. Wraps (lacks spine panel, piece of fr/rear wrappers, lt fold creases, ink name fr wrap). *Waverly*.* $93/£60

PROUD, ROBERT. The History of Pennsylvania.... Phila, 1797-98. Complete w/port, fldg map. (Sl spotting.) Teg. Mid-19th-cent 3/4 grn morocco, gilt, marbled bds (spines faded to brn, scuffing). Howes P639. *Freeman*.* $210/£135

PROULX, E. ANNIE. Postcards. NY, 1992. 1st ed. Fine in Fine dj. *Warren.* $250/£160

PROULX, E. ANNIE. Postcards. London, 1993. 1st ed. (Corner bumped), else Fine in dj. *Buckley.* $31/£20

PROUST, MARCEL. By Way of Sainte-Beuve. Sylvia Townsend Warner (trans). London, 1958. 1st Eng ed. Nice (sl bumped) in dj. *Clearwater.* $39/£25

PROUST, MARCEL. Letters. Mina Curtiss (ed). NY, 1949. Very Nice (sl bumped) in dj (sl chipped). *Clearwater.* $55/£35

PROUST, MARCEL. The Sweet Cheat Gone. C. K. Scott Moncrieff (trans). Knopf, 1930. 1st UK ed. VG (ink name). *Williams.* $55/£35

PROUST, MARCEL. The Sweet Cheat Gone. London: Knopf, 1930. 1st British ed. VG + in VG dj (spine tanned, edgetorn). *Lame Duck.* $85/£54

PROUST, MARCEL. A Vision of Paris. Arthur D. Trottenberg (ed). NY, 1963. 1st ed. VG in dj (torn). *Argosy.* $350/£224

PROUT, SAMUEL. Hints on Light and Shadow, Composition, etc., as Applicable to Landscape Painting.... London: Ackermann, 1838. Folio. (4),16pp (inner margin 1/2 title split), 20 tinted litho plts (last few foxed). Orig cl (spine foot defective, joints, edges sl rubbed, bds faded), gilt. *Marlborough.* $234/£150

PROUT, W. On the Nature and Treatment of Stomach and Renal Diseases.... London, 1848. 5th ed. 7 plts (3 hand-colored), 1849 Churchill Cat bound at end. Black cl. (Contemp lib stamp; sl worn, rear joint splitting.) *Maggs.* $117/£75

PROVENSEN, ALICE and MARTIN. The Glorious Flight. NY: Viking, 1983. 1st ed. 10 1/2 x 8 1/2. 40pp. Pict bds. Fine in dj. *Cattermole.* $45/£29

PROVENSEN, ALICE and MARTIN. A Peaceable Kingdom. NY: Viking, 1978. 1st ed. 9 x 7 1/4. 32pp. Pict bds. Fine in dj. *Cattermole.* $45/£29

PROWELL, SANDRA WEST. By Evil Means. NY: Walker, 1993. 1st ed. VF in dj. *Mordida.* $200/£128

PROWN, JULES DAVID. John Singleton Copley. Cambridge: Harvard Univ, 1966. 1st ed. 2 vols. Fine in pub's slipcase. *Hermitage.* $125/£80

PRUCHA, FRANCIS PAUL. American Indian Policy in Crisis: Christian Reformers and the Indian, 1865-1900. Norman: Univ of OK, (1976). 1st ed. VG in dj (sl worn). *Lien.* $45/£29

PRUCHA, FRANCIS PAUL. Broadax and Bayonet. State Hist Soc of WI, (1953). VG in dj (sl worn; taped corners). *Lien.* $45/£29

PRUCHA, FRANCIS PAUL. The Great Father: The United States Government and the American Indians. Lincoln: Univ of NE, (1984). 2 vols. VG in slipcase. *Lien.* $85/£54

PRUCHA, FRANCIS PAUL. A Guide to the Military Posts of the United States, 1789-1895. Madison: State Hist Soc of WI, 1964. 1st ed. 21 maps (7 dbl-pg). Grn cl. Fine in dj (sl rubbed). *Argonaut.* $60/£38

PRUCHA, FRANCIS PAUL. Indian Peace Medals in American History. Madison: State Hist Soc of WI, 1971. 1st ed. VG in dj (sl worn). *Lien.* $45/£29

PRUCHA, FRANCIS PAUL. The Sword of the Republic: The United States Army on the Frontier, 1783-1846. London: Macmillan, (1969). 1st ed. VG in dj. *Lien.* $40/£26

PRUEN, MRS. The Provinces of Western China. 1906. 12 plts. (Sl browning; fore-edge bds sl dampstained.) *Edwards.* $78/£50

PRUSSING, EUGENE E. The Estate of George Washington, Deceased. Boston, 1927. 1st ed. (Sl foxed, spine sl dull.) *Wantagh.* $35/£22

PRUTSMAN, C. M. A Soldier's Experience in Southern Prisons. NY: Andrew H. Kellogg, 1901. Frontis port. Good (dampstains port, tp, few ll; bkpl removed; soiled, edgeworn). *Wantagh.* $50/£32

PRYNNE, J. H. Kitchen Poems. Cape Goliard, 1968. 1st Eng ed. Rev slip. Card wrappers (sl handled). *Clearwater.* $55/£35

PRYOR, MRS. ROGER A. Reminiscences of War and Peace. NY, 1904. 1st ed. Pict cl. (Spine faded, sm water stains), o/w VG. *Pratt.* $60/£38

PRYOR, PAUL. The Life of General Putnam. NY: McLoughlin, 1873. Uncle Sam's Big Picture Series. Folio. 22 unnumbered pp + 1pg list lower wrapper; 6 Superb full-pg chromolithos by (Justin H.) Howard. (Sm spots pg edges; inner hinges reinforced.) VG in pict stiff paper wrappers (sl soiled, spine rebacked). *Hobbyhorse.* $300/£192

PSALMANAZAR, GEORGE. Memoirs of.... London, 1764. Frontis port, (2),ii,364pp (dknd, sig, notes). Full leather (scuffed, bds detached). Fair. *Bohling.* $60/£38

Psalmi Poenitentiales. (Hammersmith: Kelmscott, 1894.) One of 300. Linen-backed bds (fr cvr sl spotted). Cl slipcase. *Swann*.* $546/£350

Published Writings of Henry R. Wagner Issued by the Zamorano Club.... L.A.: Ritchie, 1955. 1st ed. Ptd wrappers. *Ginsberg.* $75/£48

PUDNEY, JOHN. Beyond This Disregard. John Lane, Bodley Head, (1943). 1st ed. VG in dj. *Ash.* $31/£20

Puella Mea. (By E.E. Cummings.) (NY: Golden Eagle Press), 1923. 1st separate ptg. 8vo. (24)pp. Ptd in teal; bound in gilt-stamped bds. VF (spine sl sunned) in orig gold slipcase (lt rubbed). *Bromer.* $75/£48

PUFENDORF, BARON. Of the Law of Nature and Nations. London, 1729. (Internal dampstaining, soiling.) Mod cl. *Freeman*.* $110/£71

PUGH, P. D. GORDON. Naval Ceramics. Newport: Ceramic Bk Co, (1971). 1st ed. 13 color, 130 b/w photo plts. Royal blue cl, gilt. VG. *Baltimore*.* $60/£38

PUGIN, A. W. Fifteenth and Sixteenth Century Ornaments. Edinburgh, 1904. 4 color frontispieces, 101 plts. (Tp lt browned, lib ink stamp; cl lt soiled, spine accession #s.) *Edwards.* $75/£48

PUGIN, A. W. Gothic Architecture Selected from Various Ancient Edifices Vol I and II. Cleveland: D.B. Dansen, 1919. 2 vols. (Plts loose, pp dknd; bds bumped, stained.) *Metropolitan**. $75/£48

PUGIN, A. W. Gothic Furniture in the Style of the 15th Century. London: Ackermann, 1835. Engr tp, 24 engr plts. Ptd label fr cvr. VG (spotted, lt foxed, worn). *New Hampshire**. $150/£96

PUGIN, A. W. A Series of Ornamental Timber Gables. London, 1831. 1st ed. 13pp (lt browning, spotting), 30 litho plts. (Hinges cracked; corners, joints sl worn; spine #s.) Paper label, gilt. *Edwards*. $117/£75

PUGIN, A. W. Specimens of Gothic Architecture. London, 1821-23. 1st ed. 2 vols. xx,40,xxiii,32,34,8pp; 114 plts. (Ex-lib, ink stamp tp versos, spotted.) Uncut. Lib buckram (rebound, accession #s). *Edwards*. $234/£150

PUHARICH, ANDRIJA. The Sacred Mushroom. GC: Doubleday, 1959. 1st ed. Fine in NF dj (wear). *Beasley*. $60/£38

PUIG, MANUEL. Heartbreak Tango. NY, 1973. 1st Amer ed. NF in NF dj. *Warren*. $50/£32

PUIG, MANUEL. Pubis Angelical. London, 1987. 1st Eng ed. Fine in dj. *Clearwater*. $39/£25

PUIG, MANUEL. Tropical Night Falling. London, 1992. 1st Eng ed. Fine in dj. *Clearwater*. $39/£25

PULESTON, FRED. African Drums. NY, 1929. Color frontis port. *Edwards*. $31/£20

PULESTON, FRED. African Drums. London, 1930. VG. *Grayling*. $39/£25

PULLEN, JOHN J. A Shower of Stars. Phila/NY, 1966. 1st ed. Red cl. VG +. *Smith*. $15/£10

PULLEN, JOHN J. The Twentieth Maine. Phila, (1957). 1st ed. Review slip present. (Sm cvr stain), else VG in dj (sl frayed). *King*. $45/£29

PULOS, ARTHUR J. American Design Ethic: A History of Industrial Design. (MA): MIT, 1983. VG in dj. *Hadley*. $62/£40

PULTENEY, WILLIAM. Thoughts on the Present State of Affairs with America and the Means of Conciliation. London, 1778. 5th ed, w/Franklin's letter. Complete w/half-title. Sl trimmed. Mod cl. Howes P649. *Freeman**. $60/£38

PUPIN, MICHAEL J. (ed). South Slav Monuments. I. Serbian Orthodox Church. 1918. Color frontis, 53 plts (5 color), fldg map. Teg, rest uncut. (Tp lt spotted; cl sl soiled.) *Edwards*. $156/£100

PURCELL, POLLY JANE. Autobiography and Reminiscences of a Pioneer. Fairfield, WA: Ye Galleon Press, 1974. #37/300. Fine. *Perier*. $25/£16

PURDY, HELEN THROOP. San Francisco: As It Was—As It Is—and How to See It. SF: Paul Elder, 1912. 1st ed. Buckram spine, bds, gilt lettering, pict pastedown fr cvr. Fine in ptd dj. *Argonaut*. $90/£58

PURDY, JAMES. The Candles. NY: Nadja, 1985. One of 200 numbered, signed. Fine in Fine wrappers. *Lenz*. $75/£48

PURDY, JAMES. Eustace Chisholm and the Works. NY, 1967. 1st ed. Fine in NF dj. *Warren*. $30/£19

PURDY, JAMES. Eustace Chisolm and the Works. NY, 1967. 1st ed. NF in NF dj. *Smith*. $15/£10

PURDY, JAMES. In a Shallow Grave. NY, 1975. 1st ed. Fine in NF dj. *Warren*. $25/£16

PURDY, JAMES. The Nephew. FSC, 1960. 1st ed. Fine in NF dj. *Certo*. $35/£22

PURDY, RICHARD. Thomas Hardy, a Bibliographical Study. OUP, 1954. 1st ed. VG in dj. *Moss*. $70/£45

PURDY, RICHARD. Thomas Hardy: Catalogue of a Memorial Exhibition of First Editions, Autograph Letters and Manuscripts. Yale Univ, 1928. 1st Eng ed. Nice in ptd wrappers. *Clearwater*. $31/£20

PUSATERI, SAMUEL J. Flora of Our Sierran National Parks—Yosemite, Sequoia and Kings Canyon. Three Rivers, 1963. Signed. VG in dj (sl chipped). *Brooks*. $44/£28

PUSEY, W. The History and Epidemiology of Syphilis. Springfield, 1933. 1st ed. (Ex-lib; binding rubbed.) *Fye*. $75/£48

PUSEY, WILLIAM ALLEN. A Doctor of the 1870's and 80's. Springfield, IL, 1932. Frontis port. 1/2 cl. VG (lt soil). *Bohling*. $20/£13

PUSEY, WILLIAM ALLEN. Giants of Medicine in Pioneer Kentucky.... NY, (1938). 1st ed. Author's obituary inserted. (Rubbed.) *Argosy*. $40/£26

PUSHKIN, ALEXANDER. The Captain's Daughter. NY: LEC, 1971. #417/1500 signed by Charles Mozley (illus). Fine in pub's slipcase. *Hermitage*. $85/£54

PUSHKIN, ALEXANDER. Gabriel, a Poem in One Song. Max Eastman (trans). NY, 1929. Ltd to 750 numbered. Rockwell Kent (illus). Limp vellum. VG in slipcase (defective). *King*. $125/£80

PUSHKIN, ALEXANDER. The Golden Cockerel. NY: LEC, (1949). One of 1500 numbered, signed by Edmund Dulac (illus). Cl, fr cvr inlaid w/brass cock. Slipcase. *Swann**. $258/£165

PUSHKIN, ALEXANDER. The Golden Cockerel. NY: LEC, (1950). #1385/1500 signed by Edmund Dulac (illus). Fine in slipcase (lt edge-sunned). *Hermitage*. $225/£144

PUSHKIN, ALEXANDER. The Golden Cockerel. NY: LEC, n.d. (1949). Ltd to 1500 signed by Edmund Dulac (illus). Full plum cl, polished brass 'Golden Cockerel' affixed to fr cvr. Fine in chemise of silk-screened paper bds, in slipcase. *Truepenny*. $175/£112

Puss in Boots. NY: Blue Ribbon, (1934). C. Carey Cloud and Harold B. Lentz (illus). 9x8. 3 pop-ups. Color pict bds (ink date, sl crayon mks cvr; sl worn, soiled). *King*. $195/£125

Puss in Boots. NY: McLoughlin Bros, n.d. (1880s). 1st Amer ed. 10x7. 24 chromolitho transformation pp at center fold. (Center pp disbound.) Color pict bds (loose, extrems chipped, spine perished). *King*. $75/£48

PUTER, STEPHEN A. DOUGLAS. Looters of the Public Domain.... Portland, OR, 1908. Red cl, mtd cvr illus. (Bkpl, lib mks, spine #; worn, sm snag.) *Bohling*. $150/£96

PUTMAN, MRS. Receipt Book and Young Housekeeper's Assistant. NY, (1867). (Sl spotting; cl worn, soiled.) *Freeman**. $35/£22

PUTNAM, GEORGE GRANVILLE. Salem Vessels and Their Voyages. Salem: Essex Inst, 1924-30. 4 vols. Uncut. Pict cvr labels. (Sl worn.) *Oinonen**. $90/£58

PUTNAM, GEORGE HAVEN. Memories of My Youth 1844-1865. NY, 1914. 1st ed. (Cvr sl fading), o/w VG +. *Pratt*. $45/£29

PUTNAM, GEORGE P. Death Valley Handbook. NY, 1947. 1st ed. Brn cl. VG in dj (torn). *Price*. $27/£17

PUTNAM, JAMES JACKSON. A Memoir of Dr. James Jackson. Boston: Houghton Mifflin, 1906. 1st ed, 2nd imp. Frontis port. NF. *Glaser*. $60/£38

PUTNAM, SAMUEL (trans). Kiki's Memoirs. Paris: Black Manikin, 1930. 1st ed. One of 1000. Signed by Putnam. VG (lt tape offset 1st, last pp) in orig wraps (lt soiled, bumped, spine crease) w/publicity band (tape-mended). *Waverly**. $165/£106

PUTNAM, SAMUEL P. (ed). 400 Years of Freethought. NY: Truth Seeker, 1894. 1st ed. 874pp. VG + (sl leaned, shaken). *Beasley*. $150/£96

PUTNAM, SAMUEL. The World of Jean de Bosschere, a Monograph. (London): Fortune Press, n.d. (1931?). Ltd to 1000 numbered. Teg. (Sl rubbed.) *King*. $75/£48

PUZO, MARIO. The Dark Arena. NY: Random House, (1955). 1st ed, 1st bk. Fine in dj (sl used). *Dermont.* $35/£22

PUZO, MARIO. Inside Las Vegas. NY, 1977. 1st ed. NF in NF dj. *Warren.* $35/£22

PYLE, ERNIE. Here Is Your War. NY: Henry Holt, (1943). 1st ed. VG in dj (sl edgeworn). *Sadlon.* $30/£19

PYLE, ERNIE. Last Chapter. NY: Henry Holt, (1946). 1st ed. Fine in NF dj. *Sadlon.* $40/£26

PYLE, HOWARD. Howard Pyle's Book of Pirates. NY: Harper, 1921. (Discoloration, spine sl frayed.) *Metropolitan*.* $28/£18

PYLE, HOWARD. Howard Pyle's Book of Pirates. NY: Harper, 1921. Has the code 'D-V' on c. pg. Folio. Cl-backed bds, pict cvr label. (Few ll sl wrinkled; lt worn.) *Oinonen*.* $100/£64

PYLE, HOWARD. Jack Ballister's Fortunes. Osgood, 1897. 1st Eng ed. 8vo. xii,420pp; 14 mono plts. (Some joints shaken.) Teg. Gilt-pict cl (mks back cvr, spine sl fading). Attractive. *Bookmark.* $47/£30

PYLE, HOWARD. Men of Iron. NY/London, 1898. 328pp (bkpl, ink name fep), 21 full-pg plts. Pub's cl, stamped black/silver/gilt. VG. *Truepenny.* $35/£22

PYLE, HOWARD. Merry Adventures of Robin Hood. NY, 1925. 23 full-pg plts. Dec cl. (Bkpl, ink name fep), o/w VG. *Truepenny.* $45/£29

PYLE, HOWARD. A Modern Aladdin. NY: Harper, 1892. 1st ed. Gray cl (worn). *Appelfeld.* $100/£64

PYLE, HOWARD. Otto of the Silver Hand. Scribner, (1916). 6.5x9. 170pp. Pict cl, gilt. VG + (sl shelfworn, spine sl faded). *My Bookhouse.* $50/£32

PYLE, HOWARD. The Rose of Paradise. NY: Harper, 1888. 1st ed. Fine (sig). *Captain's Bookshelf.* $75/£48

PYLE, HOWARD. The Ruby of Kishmoor. NY, 1908. 1st Amer ed. 10 color plts. Teg, uncut. Pict cvrs, gilt. Fine (bkpl). *Polyanthos.* $100/£64

PYLE, HOWARD. The Ruby of Kishmoor. NY/London: Harper, 1908. 1st ed. 10 color plts. (Ex-lib; edges rubbed, lib # spine), o/w VG. *Worldwide.* $25/£16

PYLE, HOWARD. The Ruby of Kishmoor. NY: Harper, 1908. 1st ed, 1st issue. Teg. Lt grn dec cl, gilt. Beautiful. BAL 16412. *Captain's Bookshelf.* $75/£48

PYLE, HOWARD. The Ruby of Kishmoore. NY: Harper, 1908. 1st ed. Grn dec cl. Nice. *Appelfeld.* $150/£96

PYLE, HOWARD. The Story of King Arthur and His Knights. NY, 1903. 1st ed. Lt brn cl, stamped red/black/gilt. (Fr inner hinge cracked, ink inscrip), o/w VG. *Truepenny.* $200/£128

PYLE, HOWARD. The Story of the Grail and the Passing of Arthur. NY: Scribner, 1910. 1st ed. Fine. *Swann*.* $172/£110

PYM, ROLAND. Cinderella. Boston: Houghton Mifflin, 1950. 1st US ed. 5 3/4 x 6 3/4. 6pp. Opens to full circle w/6 sides. Good. *Cattermole.* $100/£64

PYNCHON, THOMAS. The Crying of Lot 49. Phila/NY: Lippincott, (1966). 1st ed. Fine (lt foxing bds) in Fine dj (spine extrems sl wear). *Between The Covers.* $350/£224

PYNCHON, THOMAS. Gravity's Rainbow. NY: Viking, (1973). 1st ed. Fine in Fine dj (sm crease fr flap). *Between The Covers.* $750/£481

PYNCHON, THOMAS. Gravity's Rainbow. Viking, 1973. 1st US ed. Fine in dj. *Williams.* $429/£275

PYNCHON, THOMAS. Gravity's Rainbow. NY, 1973. 1st Amer ed. Fine in Fine dj. *Polyanthos.* $400/£256

PYNCHON, THOMAS. The Secret Integration. London: Aloes Books, 1980. 1st ed. Ltd to 2500. Fine in pict wrappers. *Polyanthos.* $25/£16

PYNCHON, THOMAS. Slow Learner. Boston, 1984. 1st ed. Fine in NF dj. *Smith.* $20/£13

PYNCHON, THOMAS. Slow Learner. London, 1985. 1st Eng ed. Fine in dj. *Clearwater.* $39/£25

PYNCHON, THOMAS. V. NY: Modern Library, (1966). 1st Modern Library ed. Fine in dj (sm tears). *Jaffe.* $45/£29

PYNCHON, THOMAS. V. London: Cape, 1963. 1st British ed. Fine in dj (price-clipped, lt soiled, short tear, crease fr flap). *Metropolitan*.* $373/£239

PYNCHON, THOMAS. V. Phila: Lippincott, 1963. Advance copy. Gray wraps (sunned, bumped, short closed tear fr flap, spine bowed). *Metropolitan*.* $632/£405

Q

Q. (Pseud of Arthur Quiller-Couch.) The Splendid Spur. Cassell, 1893. Rpt. Walter Paget (illus). Pub's cat dated 5G.5-93. Good (sl spotted; spine bumped, chipped). *Tiger.* $19/£12

QUAIFE, MILO M. (ed). Army Life in Dakota. George Francis Will (trans). Chicago: Lakeside, Christmas, 1941. (Few pg corners creased.) Dk red cl (spine edges sl rubbed). *Sadlon.* $20/£13

QUAIFE, MILO M. (ed). Bark Covered House or, Back in the Woods Again. Chicago: Lakeside, Christmas, 1937. Dk red cl (rubbed, sl spotted). *Sadlon.* $15/£10

QUAIFE, MILO M. (ed). Growing Up with Southern Illinois 1820 to 1861 from the Memoirs of Daniel Jarmon Brush. Chicago: Lakeside, Christmas, 1944. Dk red cl. NF. *Sadlon.* $30/£19

QUAIFE, MILO M. (ed). The Siege of Detroit in 1763. Chicago: (Lakeside Classic), 1958. Frontis port. Blue cl, gilt. VG + . *Bohling.* $15/£10

QUAIFE, MILO M. (ed). True Picture of Emigration. Chicago: Lakeside, Christmas, 1936. Dk red cl. VG. *Sadlon.* $25/£16

QUAIFE, MILO M. The Yankees Capture York. Detroit: Wayne Univ, 1955. 1st ed. Orig wrappers (sl rubbed). *Sadlon.* $15/£10

QUAIN, J. and W. J. E. WILSON. The Viscera of the Human Body. 1840. 67pp; 32 VF full-pg plts. Contemp bds (rebacked). *Whitehart.* $437/£280

QUARLES, BENJAMIN (ed). Blacks on John Brown. Urbana: Univ of IL, (1972). 1st ed. Fine in dj (sl rubbed). *Between The Covers.* $75/£48

Quarto-Millenary. NY: LEC, 1959. One of 2250. Red cl, black leather spine, cvr ornament. Box (worn). *Kane*.* $70/£45

QUAYLE, ERIC. Old Cook Books, an Illustrated History. NY: E.P. Dutton, (1978). 1st US ed. Fine in dj. *Oak Knoll.* $75/£48

QUAYLE, ERIC. Old Cook Books—An Illustrated History. NY: E.P. Dutton, (1978). 1st ed. VG. *Perier.* $35/£22

Queen Mab's Fairy Realm. George Newnes, 1901. 1st ed. Lg 8vo. Color frontis, color pict tp, 310pp. Fairy-dec eps; aeg. Dec cl. (Joints shaken, prize-plt partly removed fep; sl rubbed, tips worn), else VG. *Bookmark.* $218/£140

Queen of Hearts. NY: McLoughlin Bros, 1891. Joyful Tales. 9.5x6. (12)pp, 8 color illus by Cogger. Color pict wraps. (Wear, center fold splitting), else Nice. *King.* $40/£26

Queen of Hearts. London: Frederick Warne, n.d. (1930s?). 9x8. 31pp, 8 full-pg color illus by Randolph Caldecott. Pict bds (sl defects, wear). *King.* $35/£22

Queen's Book of the Red Cross. London: Hodder & Stoughton, Nov 1939. Stated 1st ptg. Port, 12 plts. Good (lt foxing) in Fair dj (torn). *Scribe's Perch*. $42/£27

QUEEN, ELLERY (ed). Rogues' Gallery. Boston: Little, Brown, 1945. (Sm stamp fly; rubbed), else VG in dj (lg chips; long tears, tape repairs). *Metropolitan*. $23/£15

QUEEN, ELLERY. And on the Eighth Day. NY: Random House, 1964. 1st ed. Fine in dj (short closed tears, creases). *Mordida*. $35/£22

QUEEN, ELLERY. The Devil to Pay. NY: Frederick A. Stokes, 1938. 1st ed. VG in dj (wrinkled, chipped, frayed, folds worn, 2 sm closed tears). *Mordida*. $175/£112

QUEEN, ELLERY. The Door Between. NY: Stokes, 1936. 1st Amer ed. (Bds foxed, sl cocked.) Dj (extrems worn, short tears, loss to spine ends). *Metropolitan*. $46/£29

QUEEN, ELLERY. Double, Double. Boston: Little Brown, 1950. 1st ed. VF in dj. *Mordida*. $100/£64

QUEEN, ELLERY. The Dutch Shoe Mystery. NY: Stokes, 1931. 1st ed. (Spine sl faded, sl rubbed.) *Metropolitan*. $69/£44

QUEEN, ELLERY. A Fine and Private Place. NY: World, 1971. 1st ed. Fine in dj (short closed tear). *Mordida*. $35/£22

QUEEN, ELLERY. The Fourth Side of the Triangle. NY: Random House, 1965. 1st ed. VF in dj. *Mordida*. $40/£26

QUEEN, ELLERY. The Golden Eagle Mystery. NY: Stokes, 1942. 1st ed. Fine in dj (sl worn, strip missing). *Else Fine*. $60/£38

QUEEN, ELLERY. In the Queens' Parlor: And Other Leaves from the Editors' Notebook. NY: S&S, 1957. 1st ptg. Good (ink name fep) in Good dj (worn, tape repaired). *Gravesend*. $40/£26

QUEEN, ELLERY. Inspector Queen's Own Case. NY: S&S, 1956. 1st ed. (Pp dknd), o/w Fine in dj (2 sm closed tears). *Mordida*. $45/£29

QUEEN, ELLERY. The King Is Dead. Boston: Little Brown, 1952. 1st ed. Fine in dj (spine sl faded). *Mordida*. $65/£42

QUEEN, ELLERY. Queen's Full. NY: Random House, 1965. 1st ed. Fine in dj. *Mordida*. $40/£26

QUEEN, ELLERY. Queen's Quorum. Boston: Little, Brown, 1951. 1st ed. VG in VG dj (browned). *Metropolitan*. $63/£40

QUEEN, ELLERY. There Was an Old Woman. Little, Brown, 1943. 1st ed. VG + in VG dj. *Certo*. $30/£19

QUEENY, EDGAR M. Cheechako. NY, 1941. One of 1200. Signed, inscribed presentation. Uncut. Leather labels. (Sl worn.) Slipcase (worn). *Oinonen*. $140/£90

QUEENY, EDGAR M. Cheechako. NY: Scribner, 1941. 1st ed. Ltd to 1200. Color frontis. Teg. Paper title labels. Fine. *Backman*. $125/£80

QUEENY, EDGAR M. Cheechako: The Story of an Alaskan Bear Hunt. NY, 1941. Ltd to 1200. Inscribed, signed. VF. *Truepenny*. $175/£112

QUEENY, EDGAR M. Prairie Wings. NY: Ducks Unlimited, 1946. 1st ed. Color frontis. Dec cl. Good. *Scribe's Perch*. $60/£38

QUEENY, EDGAR M. Prairie Wings. NY: Ducks Unlimited, 1946. 1st ed. Richard Bishop (illus). Fine. *Books & Birds*. $300/£192

QUEENY, EDGAR M. Prairie Wings: Pen and Camera Flight Studies. Phila/NY: Lippincott, 1947. 2nd ptg. Color frontis. Photo eps. VG + . *Backman*. $165/£106

QUENEAU, RAYMOND. The Flight of Icarus. NY: New Directions, 1973. 1st US ed. Fine in dj. *Lame Duck*. $35/£22

QUENNELL, PETER. The Sign of the Fish. NY: Viking, (1960). 1st ed. NF in dj (rubbed). *Antic Hay*. $25/£16

QUICK, ARTHUR C. Wild Flowers of the Northern States and Canada. Chicago, 1939. 8 color plts. Good in dj. *Brooks*. $25/£16

QUICK, DOROTHY. Strange Awakening. NY, (1938). 1st ed. Fine in VG dj (lt edgeworn). *Mcclintock*. $85/£54

QUIETT, GLENN CHESNEY. Pay Dirt. NY: Appleton-Century, 1936. 1st ed. Frontis. *Dawson*. $50/£32

QUIETT, GLENN CHESNEY. Pay Dirt: A Panorama of American Gold-Rushes. NY: D. Appleton-Century, 1936. 1st ed. Brn cl, gilt. Fine. *Harrington*. $55/£35

QUILL, MONICA. (Pseud of Ralph McInerny.) Not a Blessed Thing! NY: Vanguard, 1981. 1st ed. Fine in dj (price-clipped). *Janus*. $25/£16

QUILLER-COUCH, A. Fort Amity. NY: Scribner, 1904. 1st ed. VG- (Sm hole fep, ink name). *Antic Hay*. $20/£13

QUILLER-COUCH, A. In Powder and Crinoline. London: Hodder & Stoughton, n.d. (1913). Kay Nielsen (illus). 4to. (Shelfworn, shaken, cvrs soiled, spine frayed.) Internally Sound. *Oinonen*. $130/£83

QUILLER-COUCH, A. The Mayor of Troy. NY: Scribner, 1905. 1st ed. Teg. Blue cl. VG. *Antic Hay*. $27/£17

QUILLER-COUCH, A. The Sleeping Beauty and Other Fairy Tales from the Old French. NY, n.d. (1910). 1st Amer ed. Edmund Dulac (illus). Pict cvrs, gilt. NF (spine sunned; lt rubbed). *Polyanthos*. $200/£128

QUILLER-COUCH, A. The Sleeping Beauty and Other Fairy Tales. George H. Doran, (n.d.). 1st ed. Edmund Dulac (illus). 16 tipped-in color plts. Dec red cl. VG in dj (spine split, lg chips). *Certo*. $65/£42

QUILLER-COUCH, MABEL and LILLIAN. The Treasure Book of Children's Verse. NY: Hodder & Stoughton, n.d. (ca 1920). 8vo. As New in pict ptd pub's box (sm ring stain). *New Hampshire*. $110/£71

QUIN, MALCOLM. Memoirs of a Positivist. London: George Allen & Unwin, 1924. 1st ed. Nice in dj. *Patterson*. $39/£25

QUINBY, M. Mysteries of Bee-Keeping Explained. NY/SF: C.M. Saxton, Barker/H.H. Bancroft, 1860. 8th ed. (Contents lt stained; cl soiled, worn.) *Waverly*. $33/£21

QUINCY, JOSIAH. Essays on the Soiling of Cattle. Boston: Loring, 1862. 3rd ed. 64pp. Contemp cl-backed bds. (Ex-lib.) *Second Life*. $25/£16

QUINCY, JOSIAH. Memoir of the Life of John Quincy Adams. Boston, 1859. 2nd ptg. 429pp; port. (Lt stain prelims), else VG. *Zubal*. $35/£22

QUINN, EDWARD. Max Ernst. Boston: NYGS, 1977. Stated 1st US ed. Fldg frontis. (Sl cvr soil), o/w VG in dj (chipped). *Scribe's Perch*. $85/£54

QUINN, ELISABETH. The Kewpie Primer. NY: Frederick A. Stokes, 1910. Rose O'Neill (illus). 8vo. Pict gray cl cvr. (Bumped; sm stain, sl fading rear cvr), o/w VG. *Metropolitan*. $126/£81

QUINN, SEABURY. Alien Flesh. Oswald Train, 1977. 1st ed. Signed by Steve Fabian (illus). Fine in Fine dj. *Certo*. $25/£16

QUINN, SEABURY. Is the Devil a Gentleman? Mirage, 1970. One of 1000 numbered. Fine in dj (white background sl dust-mkd). *Certo*. $60/£38

QUINN, SEABURY. The Phantom Fighter. Arkham House/Mycroft & Moran, 1966. 1st ed. Fine in dj (rear panel sl soiled). *Certo*. $60/£38

QUINN, SEABURY. The Phantom Fighter. Sauk City: M&M/(Arkham House), 1966. 1st ed. (Abrasion to edges), else VG + in dj (edgeworn, lt stained). *Other Worlds.* $50/£32

QUINN, SEABURY. The Phantom-Fighter. Sauk City, 1966. 1st ed. Fine in Fine dj. *Mcclintock.* $65/£42

QUINT, ALONZO H. The Potomac and the Rapidan. Boston, 1864. 1st ed. 407pp; fold-out map. (Cvr worn, torn, spine chipped), o/w VG. *Pratt.* $65/£42

QUINTON, CAPTAIN. The Strange Adventures of Captain Quinton. Bible House: Christian Herald, 1912. (Shelfworn, spotted.) *Parmer.* $50/£32

QUIRKE, T. T. Canoes the World Over. Urbana: Univ of IL, 1952. 1st ed. Signed presentation. Gilt-dec cl. Fine in VG + dj. *Mikesh.* $37/£24

R

RAAEN, AAGOT. Measure of My Days. Fargo, 1953. 1st ed. NF in dj (spine dknd). *Baade.* $30/£19

RABAN, JONATHAN. Arabia Through the Looking Glass. London, 1979. 1st Eng ed. Very Nice (name) in dj. *Clearwater.* $39/£25

RABAN, JONATHAN. Arabia. A Journey Through the Labyrinth. NY: S&S, 1979. 1st ed. VG in dj (sl torn). *Worldwide.* $20/£13

RABAN, JONATHAN. For Love and Money. London, 1987. 1st ed. (Lt bumped), o/w VG in dj. *Words Etc.* $23/£15

RABAN, JONATHAN. The Society of the Poem. London, 1971. 1st Eng ed. Fine in dj. *Clearwater.* $39/£25

RABAN, JONATHAN. Soft City. London, 1974. 1st Eng ed. Very Nice (inscrip) in dj. *Clearwater.* $39/£25

RABELAIS, FRANCIS. The Works of Mr. Francis Rabelais. London: Navarre Soc, (ca 1921). 2 vols. W. Heath Robinson (illus). Frontispieces. Moire texture cl, gilt. (Bkpls, lt foxed), o/w VG set in djs (tanned, frayed). *Reese.* $75/£48

RABELAIS, FRANCIS. The Works of Mr. Francis Rabelais. London: Navarre Soc, n.d. Rpt. W. Heath Robinson (illus). 2 vols. Cream cl (soil, spines dknd). Internally VG. *Mcclintock.* $40/£26

RABIER, BENJAMIN. Gideon in Africa. Methuen, 1978. 1st Eng ed. Folio. (48pp). Cl spine, pict bds. (Bds sl mkd), else VG + . *Bookmark.* $23/£15

RABINOWICZ, HARRY M. Treasures of Judaica. South Brunswick: Thomas Yoseloff, (1971). 1st ed. Fine in dj (sl spotted). *Oak Knoll.* $65/£42

RACKHAM, ARTHUR. The Arthur Rackham Fairy Book. London, (1933). One of 460 numbered, signed. 8vo. 8 tipped-in color plts. Pict eps. Orig vellum, gilt. Cl slipcase. *Swann*.* $1,035/£663

RACKHAM, ARTHUR. The Arthur Rackham Fairy Book. London: Geo. Harrap, (1933). 1st ed. One of 460 ptd on hand-made paper and signed. 8vo. 8 color plts. Teg. Full vellum, gilt. Fine. *Appelfeld.* $1,250/£801

RACKHAM, ARTHUR. Arthur Rackham's Book of Pictures. London, (1913). One of 1030 numbered, signed. 44 tipped-in color plts, guards. Later polished blue levant (spine faded) by Bayntun (Riviere), gilt. *Swann*.* $488/£313

RACKHAM, ARTHUR. Arthur Rackham's Book of Pictures. London: Heinemann, 1913. One of 1030 signed. 44 tipped-in color plts. Gilt-dec white cl (sl worn, soiled). Contents VG. *New Hampshire*.* $450/£288

RACKHAM, ARTHUR. The Land of Enchantment. London: Cassell, 1907. 1st ed. Frontis, 35 tinted illus. Gilt-pict cl (soiled, extrems worn; rep removed). *Hollett.* $117/£75

RACKHAM, ARTHUR. Mother Goose, the Old Nursery Rhymes. London: Heinemann, n.d. (ca 1913). #116/1100 (1130). Signed. 4to. xi,160pp; 14 tipped-in plts mtd on buff colored paper. Teg, others uncut. Cream buckram pict cl (spine sl dknd, cvr margins sl discolored), gilt. *Marlborough.* $1,482/£950

RACKHAM, BERNARD. The Ancient Glass of Canterbury Cathedral. London: Humphries, 1949. 1st ed. 25 color, 80 monochrome plts. Teg. Blue cl. Fine. *Hermitage.* $200/£128

RACKHAM, BERNARD. Medieval English Pottery. NY, 1949. 96 plts. Good. *Washton.* $50/£32

RADCLIFFE, GARNETT. The Flower Gang. Boston: Houghton Mifflin, 1930. 1st Amer ed. NF in dj (corners chipped, short closed tears). *Mordida.* $65/£42

RADICE, BETTY (trans). Pliny: A Self Portrait in Letters. London: Folio Soc, 1978. 9 full-pg plts. NF. *Middle Earth.* $45/£29

RADIGUET, RAYMOND. Devil in the Flesh. Kay Boyle (trans). (Washington): Black Sun, 1948. VG in dj (price-clipped, creased, chipped). *King.* $35/£22

RADIN, P. Catalogue of Mexican Pamphlets in the Sutro Collection: 1623-1888. With Supplements 1605-1887. NY: Kraus, 1971. *Ginsberg.* $75/£48

RAE, JOHN. New Adventures of 'Alice.' Chicago: Volland, (1917). 8vo. 12 color plts. Cl-backed bds, pict pastedown. As New in pub's orig cellophane wrapper, pub's orig pict ptd box. *New Hampshire*.* $255/£163

RAEBURN, C. and H. B. MILNER. Alluvial Prospecting. London: Murby, 1927. 32 plts. VG. *Savona.* $39/£25

RAFFALD, ELIZABETH. The Experienced English Housekeeper. London, 1778. Signed. 2 fldg plts (taped, repaired). Old calf (spine repaired; part of 1 pg gone). *Metropolitan*.* $172/£110

RAFFALD, ELIZABETH. The Experienced Housekeeper. London: Branbles et al, 1814. New ed. Engr frontis, 282pp (new eps); 3 fldg plts. Mod 1/2 calf, marbled bds. Nice. *Second Life.* $250/£160

RAFFETY, C. W. An Introduction to the Science of Radio-Activity. 1909. (Pastedown, fep sl discolored; spine sl defective, corners sl worn), o/w VG. *Whitehart.* $62/£40

RAGATZ, LOWELL J. A Guide for the Study of British Caribbean History, 1763-1834.... Washington, 1932. 1st ed. *Ginsberg.* $75/£48

Rail-Roads, History and Commerce of Chicago (cvr title). Chicago, 1854. 8vo. 72pp. Orig wrappers. Howes C374. *Swann*.* $632/£405

Railway Year Book for 1921. London: Railway Pub, 1921. Red ptd cl (mkd, worn). *Cox.* $31/£20

Raiment for the Lord's Service. Chicago: Art Inst of Chicago, 1975. Good in wrappers. *Washton.* $100/£64

RAINE, KATHLEEN. Blake and Tradition. NY: Bollingen/Princeton, (1968). 1st ed. 2 vols. Fine in djs, slipcase (sl sunned). *Captain's Bookshelf.* $175/£112

RAINE, KATHLEEN. Blake and Tradition. Princeton, (1968). 2 vols. Fine in box. *Argosy.* $200/£128

RAINE, KATHLEEN. The Collected Poems of Kathleen Raine. London: Hamish Hamilton, (1956). 1st ed. Fine in dj (spine browned, sm stain). *Antic Hay.* $25/£16

RAINE, KATHLEEN. The Pythoness and Other Poems. NY: Farrar, (n.d. but ca 1952). 1st Amer issue. (Edges lt foxed), else NF in dj (price-clipped). *Reese.* $30/£19

RAINE, WILLIAM MacLEOD. For Honor and Life. Houghton Mifflin, 1933. 1st ed. Fine in dj (chipped). *Authors Of West.* $25/£16

RAINEY, GEORGE. The Cherokee Strip. Enid, 1933. 1st ed. Signed. Gilt-pict cl. (Ink info verso sheet facing tp; cvrs lt worn), o/w Fine. Howes R18. *Baade.* $175/£112

RAINEY, GEORGE. The Cherokee Strip. Guthrie, OK: Co-Operative, 1933. 1st ed. Signed. Red pict cl (sm scuff top edge fr cvr, partial crack fr hinge, but firm), gilt. Nice. Howes R 18. *Shasky.* $125/£80

RAINSFORD, W. S. The Land of the Lion. NY: Doubleday, Page, 1909. 1st ed. Frontis, dbl-pg map. Dk grn cl, gilt. VG + (bkpl) *Backman.* $135/£87

Rainy Day Stories. Springfield, MA: McLoughlin Bros, n.d. 4to. 38 leaves (hinges cracked). Blue cl-backed color pict bds (bumped, chipped). VG. *Blue Mountain.* $25/£16

RAIT, ROBERT S. The Life of Field-Marshal Sir Frederic Paul Haines. London, 1911. Frontis, 2 maps (1 fldg). Blue cl (sl worn). *Maggs.* $125/£80

RALEIGH, WALTER. The Letters. Lady Raleigh (ed). Methuen, 1926. 1st ed. 2 vols. 9 plts. Uncut, partly unopened. (Cl rubbed, extrems sl worn.) *Cox.* $39/£25

RALEIGH, WALTER. The Letters. Lady Raleigh (ed). London: Methuen, 1928. 2nd ed. 2 vols. 9 plts. Uncut. Good set (backstrips faded). *Cox.* $19/£12

RALEIGH, WALTER. The Marrow of History. London: John & William Place, 1662. 2nd ed. (24),574pp (tp browned, sl trimmed). 19th-cent 1/2 brn morocco, cl (extrems sl rubbed). *Karmiole.* $175/£112

RALPH, JULIAN. Harper's Chicago and the World's Fair. NY: Harper, 1893. 1st ed. (Spine ends, corners sl rubbed.) *Sadlon.* $15/£10

RALPH, JULIAN. On Canada's Frontier. NY: Harper, 1892. 1st ed. Pict cl. (Feps not attached), o/w VG. *New Hampshire*.* $110/£71

RAM, JAMES. A Treatise on Facts as Subjects of Inquiry by a Jury. NY: Baker, Voorhis, 1873. 3rd Amer ed. Contemp sheep (worn, ex-libris). Usable. *Boswell.* $150/£96

RAMAGE, CRAUFURD TAIT. The Nooks and By-Ways of Italy. Liverpool, 1868. 1st ed. xiii,314pp. Partially unopened. (Reps lt dampstained, bkpl; cl dampstained upper portion.) *Edwards.* $39/£25

RAMAL, WALTER. (Pseud of Walter de la Mare.) Songs of Childhood. London: Longmans, 1902. 1st UK ed. VG (bkpl) in orig parchment-backed cl, specially made blue 1/2 leather slipcase. *Williams.* $772/£495

RAMBOVA, N. (ed). Mythological Papyri.... Alexandre Piankoff (trans). (NY: 1957.) 2 vols. Plts loose in cl case as issued. (Ex-lib.) *Swann*.* $149/£96

RAMIE, GEORGES. Picasso's Ceramics. Kenneth Lyons (trans). (Secaucus): Chartwell, ca 1974. Off-white coated cl (sl shelfworn). VG (1st 30pp sl rippled) in color dj (1-inch tear, chipped). *Baltimore*.* $70/£45

RAMPA, T. LOBSANG. The Third Eye. NY, 1957. 1st Amer ed. VG + in Good+ dj. *Middle Earth.* $35/£22

RAMPLING, ANNE. (Pseud of Anne Rice.) Belinda. NY: Arbor House, (1986). Adv rev copy w/slip/pub's material laid in. Signed. Fine in dj. *Between The Covers.* $150/£96

RAMPLING, ANNE. (Pseud of Anne Rice.) Exit to Eden. NY: Arbor House, (1985). 1st ed. (Sl bump corners), else Fine in dj. *Between The Covers.* $100/£64

RAMPLING, ANNE. (Pseud of Anne Rice.) Exit to Eden. NY, 1985. 1st ed. (Bottom tips sl bumped), o/w Fine in Fine dj. *Warren.* $100/£64

RAMSAY, BALCARRES D. WARDLAW. Rough Recollections of Military Service and Society. Edinburgh, 1882. Inscribed. 2 vols. xiii,294; vii,298pp. Red cl (spines faded, vol 1 fr cvr stained). *Maggs.* $156/£100

RAMSBOTHAM, FRANCIS H. The Principles and Practice of Obstetric Medicine.... Phila, 1843. 2nd US ed rev. 458pp (lacks fr flyleaf, sl foxing, marginal stain top edge 1st 300pp); 52 plts. Contemp leather. Good-. *Scribe's Perch*.* $35/£22

RAMSBOTTOM, J. Mushrooms and Toadstools. London, 1953. 1st ed. 46 color, 24 plain plts. (Spine sl faded.) *Henly.* $34/£22

RAMSBOTTOM, J. Mushrooms and Toadstools. London: Collins, 1953. 70 plts (46 color). VG. *Savona.* $28/£18

RAMSEY, DAVID. The Life of George Washington. NY, 1807. 1st ed. Port (offsetting on title, stamp on recto). Marbled edges. Contemp gilt-paneled, stamped diced brn calf (scuffed, extrems rubbed, spine ends gone). Howes R38. *Freeman*.* $70/£45

RAMSEY, FRED R. These Are My People. Detroit: Harlo, 1966. One of 600 numbered. Signed, inscribed. Fine in dj. *Gibbs.* $25/£16

RAMSEY, FREDERIC, JR. Chicago Documentary. Portrait of a Jazz Era. London: Jazz Music Books, 1944. 1st ed. Pb. VG + . *Beasley.* $75/£48

RAMSEY, STANLEY C. and J. D. HARVEY. Small Houses of the Late Georgian Period 1750-1820. 1919-23. 2 vols. Frontispieces, 200 plts. (Eps, text lt spotted vol 1, marginal pencil notes; spine, edges lt faded vol 1.) *Edwards.* $195/£125

RAMSEY, W. The Gases of the Atmosphere, the History of Their Discovery. 1902. 2nd ed. (Spine sl defective, discolored, fr cvr sl mkd), o/w VG. *Whitehart.* $28/£18

RANALD, JOSEF. How to Know People by Their Hands. NY, 1938. 1st ed. VG (sl worn). *Doctor's Library.* $40/£26

RANCK, GEORGE W. The Bivouac of the Dead. Cincinnati: Robert Clarke, 1898. 1st ed. Frontis port, 73pp; 4 plts. VG (news clipping fr pastedown, clippings rep). *Connolly.* $25/£16

Rand McNally & Co's New Imperial Atlas of the World. 1915. Red pict gilt cl (spine ends sl frayed). *Yudkin*.* $70/£45

RAND, AUSTIN. American Water and Game Birds. NY: E.P. Dutton, 1956. 1st ed. Grn cl, bds. VG in color dj. *House.* $30/£19

RAND, AYN. Atlas Shrugged. NY: Random House, (1957). 1st ed. Fine in dj (sl rubbed). *Captain's Bookshelf.* $400/£256

RAND, AYN. Atlas Shrugged. NY: Random House, 1967. 10th Anniversary ed. #77/2000 numbered, signed. Fine in acetate dj & pub's slipcase (sl faded). *Unger.* $1,500/£962

RAND, AYN. The Goal of My Writing. (NY): Nathaniel Branden Inst, (1963). 1st ed. 10pp. VG (sm spots, couple lines underlined) in tall stapled wrappers (lt soiled). *Between The Covers.* $100/£64

Rand, McNally and Company's Library Atlas of the World. Chicago/NY, ca 1895. 444pp. (4 missing of the 61pp US maps.) Maroon cl stamped in silver (shaken, loose). *Hudson.* $350/£224

Rand, McNally and Company's New Indexed Atlas of the World. Chicago, 1891. New ed. 930pp. *Hudson.* $125/£80

Rand, McNally and Company's New Popular Atlas of the World. Chicago/NY, ca 1898. 160pp (shaken, few loose ll). Grn limp cl. *Hudson.* $225/£144

Rand, McNally and Company's Unrivaled Atlas of the World. Chicago/NY, 1910. Reset tp omitting commas between 'Rand' and 'McNally.' Blue-grn cl. (Bkpl; broken, loose.) *Hudson.* $175/£112

Rand, McNally New Standard Atlas of the World. Chicago, 1890. 196+ pp. Brn cl (broken). *Hudson.* $365/£234

RANDALL, CHARLES A. (ed). Extraterrestrial Matter. N IL Univ, 1969. 1st ed. Dec black cl. Mint. *Price.* $29/£19

RANDALL, D. A. The Handwriting of God in Egypt, Sinai, and the Holy Land. Columbus, OH/NY: Randall & Aston/Sheldon, 1862. 1st ed. 2 parts in 1. 359; 355pp. Aeg. Orig emb morocco. (Lacks 1st tp; rubbed, fr cvr detached, sl shaken), o/w VG. *Worldwide.* $75/£48

RANDALL, DAVID (ed). Thirteen Author Collections of the Nineteenth Century and Five Centuries of Familiar Quotations. NY: Privately ptd, 1950. 1st ed. One of 375 ptd. 2 vols. Teg; uncut. Blue cl, gilt. VF. *Macdonnell.* $250/£160

RANDALL, J. T. The Diffraction of X-Rays and Electrons by Amorphous Solids, Liquids, and Gases. 1934. (Spine discolored), o/w VG. *Whitehart.* $23/£15

RANDALL, JAMES RYDER. Maryland, My Maryland and Other Poems. Balt: John Murphy, 1908. 1st ed. NF. *Mcgowan.* $150/£96

RANDALL, RICHARD H., JR. American Furniture in the Museum of Fine Arts, Boston. Boston: Museum of Fine Arts, (1965). 1st ed. Signed presentation. Color frontis. Brn cl, bds, gilt. Fine in orig plain glassine dj (chipped, sunned), bd slipcase (sl dusty). *Baltimore*.* $170/£109

RANDALL, THOMAS E. History of the Chippewa Valley. Eau Claire, WI: Free Press Print, 1875. 207pp + 4pp ads (pencil underlining early pp). Brn cl (rubbed, extrems frayed), gilt. Good. *Bohling.* $200/£128

RANDALL-MacIVER, DAVID. The Iron Age in Italy. Oxford: Clarendon, 1927. Frontis, 47 plts. (Sm tear spine head, corner sl bumped.) *Archaeologia.* $250/£160

RANDISI, ROBERT J. (ed). The Eyes Have It. NY: Mysterious, 1984. 1st ed. One of 250 numbered, signed by all contributors. Fine in Fine slipcase, issued w/o dj. *Janus.* $125/£80

RANDOLPH, EDMUND. Beef, Leather and Grass. Norman: Univ of OK, (1981). 1st ed. Fine in dj. *Bohling.* $22/£14

RANDOLPH, EDMUND. Hell Among the Yearlings. Chicago: Lakeside Classic, 1978. Good. *Heinoldt.* $20/£13

RANDOLPH, J. RALPH. British Travelers Among the Southern Indians, 1660-1763. Norman: Univ of OK, (1973). 1st ed. VG+ in dj. *Bohling.* $25/£16

RANDOLPH, MARY. The Virginia Housewife. Balt: Plaskitt, 1836. Stereotype ed. 180pp. Contemp calf (sl foxed). *Second Life.* $350/£224

RANDOLPH, PASCHAL BEVERLY. Eulis: The History of Love. Toledo, 1874. 1st ed. 222pp + 18pp cat. Dec cvr. VG (spine scuffed). *Middle Earth.* $95/£61

RANDOLPH, SARAH N. The Domestic Life of Thomas Jefferson. (Harvard Univ), 1939. 1st ed. Port. VG- (lt waterstain lower cvr, spine). *Book Broker.* $25/£16

RANDOLPH, VANCE (ed). An Ozark Anthology. Caldwell: Caxton, 1940. 1st ed. Fine in dj (very chipped, tear across spine center). *Beasley.* $85/£54

RANDOLPH, VANCE and GEORGE P. WILSON. Down in the Holler. Norman: Univ of OK, 1953. 1st ed. (Pencil mks), else Fine in dj (lt used). *Beasley.* $85/£54

RANDOLPH, VANCE. The ABC of Physiology. NY: Vanguard, 1927. 1st ed. Fine in Good dj (flap separated from rest of dj). *Beasley.* $40/£26

RANDOLPH, VANCE. From an Ozark Holler. NY: Vanguard, 1933. 1st ed. NF in VG dj (sm chip). *Beasley.* $125/£80

RANDOLPH, VANCE. Hedwig. NY: Vanguard, 1935. 1st ed. Fine in dj (lt used, internal mending spine head). *Beasley.* $150/£96

RANDOLPH, VANCE. A History of the Modern Christian Church. Girard: Haldeman-Julius, 1924. 1st ed. Pb. VG (ink mks). *Beasley.* $25/£16

RANDOLPH, VANCE. Modern Philosophers. Girard: Haldeman-Julius, 1924. 1st ed. Pb. VG (ink mks). *Beasley.* $25/£16

RANDOLPH, VANCE. Our Insect Enemies. Girard: Haldeman-Julius, 1925. 1st ed. Pb. Fine. *Beasley.* $35/£22

RANDOLPH, VANCE. Ozark Mountain Folks. NY: Vanguard, 1932. St. Louis ed. One of 250 numbered, signed on tipped-in leaf. NF (dkng edges, mottled spine) in dj (lt used, sm spine chip), Fine cardboard slipcase (sunned). *Beasley.* $200/£128

RANDOLPH, VANCE. Ozark Superstitions. NY: Columbia Univ, 1947. 1st ed. Fine in dj (spine head nicked, foot worn). *Beasley.* $85/£54

RANDOLPH, VANCE. The Ozarks. NY: Vanguard, 1931. 1st ed. Good+ (name, sm spine tear). *Beasley.* $60/£38

Random Recollections of a Commercial Traveller. London: Sheratt & Hughes, 1909. 7 plts. (Edges sl spotted.) Pict cl (spine sl faded), gilt. *Hollett.* $101/£65

RANKE, LEOPOLD. The Ottoman and the Spanish Empires, in the Sixteenth and Seventeenth Centuries. Phila: Lea & Blanchard, 1845. 138pp. 1/4 calf, marbled bds. (Sl foxed; recently rebound), o/w VG. *Worldwide.* $135/£87

RANKIN, EDWARD S. Indian Trails and City Streets. Montclair, NJ: Globe, 1927. 1st ed. Cl-backed bds (spine ends, corners rubbed), paper label. *Sadlon.* $15/£10

RANKIN, IAN. A Good Hanging and Other Stories. London: Century, 1992. 1st ed. VF in dj. *Mordida.* $45/£29

RANKIN, IAN. Westwind. London: Barrie & Jenkins, 1990. 1st ed. VF in dj. *Mordida.* $65/£42

RANKIN, MELINDA. Twenty Years Among the Mexicans. Cincinnati: Chase & Hall, 1875. 199pp. Brn cl, gilt. VG+. Howes R64. *Bohling.* $60/£38

RANSOM, JOHN L. Andersonville Diary, Escape and List of the Dead.... Auburn, NY, 1881. 1st ed. 304pp. Good. *Wantagh.* $75/£48

RANSOM, WILL. Private Presses and Their Books. NY: Bowker, 1929. 1st ed. One of 1200 ptd. Gilt brn cl. Good (sig, notes, bkpl). *Reese.* $100/£64

RANSOME, ARTHUR. Great Northern? London: Cape, (1947). 1st Eng ed. 8vo. 352pp. Grn cl (sl rub mk upper edge, spine ends sl bumped), gilt. VG. *Dower.* $75/£48

RANSOME, ARTHUR. The Picts and the Martyrs. London: Cape, (1943). 1st Eng ed. 8vo. 302pp. Grn cl, gilt. VG. *Dower.* $65/£42

RANSOME, ARTHUR. Secret Water. London: Cape, (1939). 1st Eng ed. 8vo. 380pp. Grn cl, gilt. VG. *Dower.* $90/£58

RAPAPORT, BENJAMIN. A Complete Guide to Collecting Antique Pipes. PA, 1979. Dj (sl chipped). *Edwards.* $31/£20

RAPELJE, GEORGE. Narrative of Excursions, Voyages, and Travels.... NY: West & Trow, 1834. 416pp; port. Orig gilt-pict cl (spine faded). Howes R65. *Adelson.* $125/£80

RAPER, ARTHUR F. Preface to Peasantry. Chapel Hill: Univ of NC, 1936. 1st ed. Buckram. VG in dj (edgeworn). *Petrilla.* $45/£29

RAPHAEL, MAX. Prehistoric Pottery and Civilization in Egypt. Washington: Bollingen, (1947). 36 plts. (Tape remnants eps.) *Archaeologia.* $125/£80

RAPHAELIAN, H. M. The Hidden Language of Symbols in Oriental Rugs. NY: Anatol Sivas, 1953. 1st ed. VG in VG dj. *New Hampshire*.* $85/£54

RASCOE, BURTON. The Dalton Brothers and Their Astounding Career of Crime. NY: Frederick Fell, 1954. 1st ed thus. VG in dj. *Perier.* $35/£22

RASKIN, JONAH (ed). The Weather Eye. NY: Union Square, 1974. NF in wraps. *Sclanders.* $31/£20

RASMUSSEN, STEEN EILER. London: The Unique City. London: Jonathan Cape, 1937. Eng rev ed. *Edwards.* $39/£25

RASPUTIN, MARIA. My Father. Cassell, (1934). 1st ed. (Edges sl spotted), o/w Nice in dj (sl sunned, soiled). *Ash.* $117/£75

RATCHFORD, FANNIE E. (ed). Letters of Thomas J. Wise to John Henry Wrenn. NY: Knopf, 1944. 1st ed. Fine in dj (few sm edge tears). *Dermont.* $75/£48

RATCLIFF, CARTER. Sittings, 1979-1980. NY: Pace Gallery, 1980. 1st ed. 40 full-pg photos. VG (owner stamp) in illus stiff wrappers. *Cahan.* $40/£26

RATCLIFFE, DOROTHY UNA. Delightsome Land. London: Eyre & Spottiswoode, 1945. 1st ed. Tinted frontis. VG. *Hollett.* $31/£20

RATCLIFFE, DOROTHY UNA. Island-of-the-Little-Years. London: Frederick Muller, 1947. 1st ed. VG in dj. *Hollett.* $23/£15

RATH, VIRGINIA. Death at Dayton's Folly. NY: Caxton House, 1939. 1st thus, 1st bk. (Top edge sl soiled), else NF in dj (sl edgeworn). *Murder By The Book.* $40/£26

RATHMELL, WILLIAM (rev). Life of the Marlows. (By George and Charles Marlow.) Ouray, CO: Ouray Herald Print, W.S. Olexa, (n.d., 1928?). 2nd ed. Stiff grey ptd wrappers, black cl backstrip. NF in custom cl slipcase, black morocco spine label. Howes M295. *Harrington.* $200/£128

RATTRAY, JEANNETTE EDWARDS. Whale Off! NY, 1956. Fine in slipcase. *High Latitude.* $25/£16

RATZELL, FRIEDRICH. The History of Mankind. A. J. Butler (ed). London: Macmillan, 1896. 3 vols. Gilt-dec blue cl over bds. NF (bkpl, sl foxed). *Old London.* $225/£144

RAUMER, FRIEDRICH LUDWIG. America and the American People. William W. Turner (trans). NY, 1846. 1st ed in English. 512pp (lt foxed, sig). Gilt cl (hinges repaired, spine ends frayed). Good. Howes R73. *Reese.* $250/£160

RAUSCHENBERG, ROBERT. Photos In + Out City Limits: Boston. West Islip, NY: ULAE, 1981. 1st ed. 45 full-pg b/w photos. As New in ptd stiff wrappers, pub's paper over bds slipcase. *Cahan.* $40/£26

RAUSCHENBERG, ROBERT. Photos In + Out City Limits: Boston. West Islip: ULAE, 1981. 1st ed. Fine in NF slipcase. *Smith.* $75/£48

RAUSCHENBERG, ROBERT. Photos In + Out City Limits: New York. West Islip, NY: ULAE, 1982. 1st ed. 70 full-pg b/w photos. As New in pub's cl slipcase. *Cahan.* $75/£48

RAVEN, SIMON. Brother Cain. London: Anthony Blond, 1959. 1st UK ed. Fine in dj. *Williams.* $55/£35

RAVEN, SIMON. The Feathers of Death. London: Anthony Blond, 1959. 1st UK ed, 1st bk. VG+ in dj. *Williams.* $56/£36

RAVENEL, MRS. ST. JULIEN. Life and Times of William Lowndes of South Carolina, 1782-1822. Boston/NY, 1901. 1st ed. Frontis port. Good (extrems sl worn). *Wantagh.* $35/£22

RAVENHILL, ALICE. The Native Tribes of British Columbia. Victoria, BC: Charles Banfield, 1938. VG. *Perier.* $47/£30

RAVENSHAW, THOMAS F. Antiente Epitaphes (from A.D. 1250 to A.D. 1800). London: (Joseph Masters), 1878. Fldg frontis. Pub's patterned cl, blind dec, gilt. Nice (lacks fep). *Book Block.* $95/£61

RAVENSTEIN, E. G. The Russians on the Amur. London: Trubner, 1861. 1st ed. xx,468pp (pencil underlining); 4 tinted litho plts. Grn cl, gilt. *Karmiole.* $200/£128

RAVILIOUS, ERIC. Country Walks. London Transport, 1936-37. 1st, 2nd & 3rd series. 3 vols. All 1st eds. VG in stiff card cvrs (chipped), djs. *Michael Taylor.* $44/£28

RAVOUX, A. Reminiscences, Memoirs and Lectures of Monsignor A. Ravoux, V. G. St. Paul, MN: Brown, Treacy, 1890. 1st ed. 223pp. Fair (spine top worn). Howes R75. *Lien.* $75/£48

RAVOUX, A. Reminiscences, Memoirs, and Lectures. St. Paul, MN, 1890. 1st ed. 223pp. (Ex-lib), else Good. *King.* $85/£54

RAWICZ, PIOTR. Blood from the Sky. NY: Harcourt, Brace & World, 1964. 1st US ed. NF in dj. *Lame Duck.* $35/£22

RAWLINGS, JAMES S. Virginia's Colonial Churches. Garrett & Massie, 1963. One of 2000. VG in VG dj. *Book Broker.* $35/£22

RAWLINGS, MARJORIE KINNAN. Cross Creek. NY: Scribner, 1942. True 1st ed. Fine in dj (uniformly spine dknd, lt rubbed, sm tear). *Between The Covers.* $125/£80

RAWLINGS, MARJORIE KINNAN. The Marjorie Rawlings Reader. Julia Scribner Bigham (ed). NY: Scribners, (1956). 1st ed. Fine (spine gilt sl rubbed) in NF dj (chip crown, spine lt rubbing). *Between The Covers.* $175/£112

RAWLINGS, MARJORIE KINNAN. The Secret River. NY: Scribner, (1955). 1st ed. Leonard Weisgard (illus). (Corner tip sl bumped), o/w NF in dj (spine ends sl rubbed, price-clipped). *Bernard.* $250/£160

RAWLINGS, MARJORIE KINNAN. The Sojourner. NY: Scribner, 1953. 1st ed. Fine (bkpl) in dj (lt worn). Else Fine. $55/£35

RAWLINGS, MARJORIE KINNAN. South Moon Under. NY: Scribner, 1933. 1st ed, 1st bk. Gilt-dec cl. Fine in dj (short closed edge tear, sl rubbing 1 corner). *Reese.* $350/£224

RAWLINGS, MARJORIE KINNAN. The Yearling. Scribner, 1939. One of 750 signed by Kinnan and N.C. Wyeth (illus). Sm 4to. Fine in orig sleeve (extrems sl browned). *Cummins.* $750/£481

RAWLINSON, A. Adventures in the Near East 1918-22. London, 1923. *Petersfield.* $34/£22

RAWLINSON, GEORGE. The Five Great Monarchies of the Ancient Eastern World. London: John Murray, 1879. 4th ed. 3 vols. Marbled eps. Period full vellum, gilt, morocco labels. (Bkpls; sl shelfworn), else Fine. *Pacific*.* $75/£48

RAWLINSON, GEORGE. The Seventh Great Oriental Monarchy.... London: Longmans, Green, 1876. 1st ed. Color litho frontis, xxi,691pp+24,(2)ad pp; fldg map. Mottled eps; teg. Mod 3/4 levant morocco, cl, gilt, raised bands. (Contents sl dknd, map w/marginal repairs), else VG. *Pacific*.* $46/£29

RAWLS, JAMES J. (ed). Dan De Quille of the Big Bonanza. SF: Bk Club of CA, 1980. Ltd to 650. Dec bds, cl back. VF in dj. *Black Sun.* $85/£54

RAWLS, WALTON. The Great Book of Currier and Ives' America. NY, (1979). 1st ed. VG in slipcase. *Argosy.* $300/£192

RAWNSLEY, H. D. Chapters at the English Lakes. Glasgow, 1913. 1st ed. (Cl sl browned.) *Edwards.* $31/£20

RAWNSLEY, H. D. Life and Nature at the English Lakes. Glasgow: James MacLehose, 1902. 2nd ed. 8 plts. Teg. (Feps spotted, browned; prize label pastedown; spine sl faded.) *Hollett.* $31/£20

RAWNSLEY, H. D. Literary Associations of the English Lakes. Glasgow, 1906. 3rd ed. 2 vols. Teg. (Lt foxing; spines chipped, sl soiling.) *Edwards*. $55/£35

RAWNSLEY, H. D. Literary Associations of the English Lakes. Glasgow: James MacLehose, 1906. 3rd ed. 2 vols. 32 plts. Uncut. Blue cl, gilt. (Feps lt browned, few spots; hinges sl rubbed.) *Hollett*. $86/£55

RAWNSLEY, H. D. Past and Present at the English Lakes. Glasgow: James MacLehose, 1916. 1st ed. 8 plts. Uncut. Red cl, gilt. (Fep removed; spine sl faded.) *Hollett*. $23/£15

RAWNSLEY, MRS. WILLINGHAM. The New Forest. A&C Black, 1904. 1st ed. 24 color plts. (Feps sl browned.) Teg. Dec cl (upped bd sl mkd, spine sl browned). *Edwards*. $47/£30

RAWNSLEY, MRS. WILLINGHAM. The New Forest. London: A&C Black, 1904. #11/100 signed. 20 color plts. VG (foxed, sl worn). *Old London*. $200/£128

RAWSON, KENNETT LONGLEY. A Boy's-Eye View of the Arctic. NY, 1926. 1st ed. Map. VG in dj. *High Latitude*. $20/£13

RAWSON, MARION NICHOLL. Little Old Mills. E.P. Dutton, (1935). 1st ed. Pict dj. *Cullen*. $45/£29

RAWSON, PHILIP. Erotic Art of India. NY: Gallery Bks, 1983. 1st ed. 40 color plts. NF in dj. *Worldwide*. $25/£16

RAWSON, PHILIP. Erotic Art of the East. NY: Putnam, 1968. 1st ed. NF in dj. *Worldwide*. $30/£19

RAWSTORNE, LAWRENCE. Gamonia: or, The Art of Preserving Game. Phila, 1930. New ed. 15 color plts. (Lt marginal browning; cl lt sunned, sm stain upper bd.) Dj (discolored, chipped, sl loss). *Edwards*. $133/£85

RAY, A. P. C. History of Chemistry in Ancient and Medieval India. 1956. VG in dj. *Whitehart*. $55/£35

RAY, C. and E. CIAMPI. The Underwater Guide to Marine Life. NY (London imprint pasted on), 1956. Dj (sl worn). *Maggs*. $181/£116

RAY, CYRIL. Merrie England. Vista, 1960. 1st ed. Tall 8vo. 208pp; 21 full-pg illus by Edward Ardizzone. Grey cl (Lt mkd), else VG. *Bookmark*. $28/£18

RAY, GORDON N. The Illustrator and the Book in England from 1790 to 1914. (NY): OUP, (1976). Color frontis, color plt. Pict eps. Blue buckram bds, gilt. Fine in glassine dj. *Heller*. $150/£96

RAY, GORDON N. The Illustrator and the Book in England from 1790 to 1914. (NY, 1976.) *Swann**. $92/£59

RAY, ISAAC. Contributions to Mental Pathology. Boston: Little, Brown, 1873. 1st ed. (ii),(viii),558,(2)pp (1st several ll creased, sl soiled). Ptd pebbled grn cl (spine varnished, corners frayed). VG. *Gach*. $385/£247

RAY, ISAAC. A Treatise on the Medical Jurisprudence of Insanity. Boston: Little, Brown, 1853. 3rd ed. xvi,(522)pp. Mod grey cl, leather spine label. (Edges of 1st leaves to 1st & last gathering reinforced), else VG. *Gach*. $450/£288

RAY, J. Further Correspondence. R. W. T. Gunther (ed). London: Ray Soc, 1928. 2 ports, 2 plts. Nice. *Wheldon & Wesley*. $94/£60

RAY, JOHN. The Wisdom of God Manifested in the Works of the Creation. William & John Innys, 1722. 8th ed. (xxiv),17-405pp, 3 ad pp. New eps. Orig panelled calf (rebacked). *Bickersteth*. $140/£90

RAY, MAN. Self-Portrait. Boston: Little, Brown, (1963). 1st ed. Fine in dj (lt worn, 3/4-inch closed tear). *Hermitage*. $75/£48

RAY, MAN. Self-Portrait. London, 1963. 1st ed. VG + in VG + dj. *Warren*. $45/£29

RAY, PETER (ed). Designers in Britain. London, 1947. Dec eps. (Ex-lib, ink stamp, labels, card holder remains; fr hinge sl tender; rear bd sl dampstained; sl bumped, joints chipped, spine # remains, rubbed.) *Edwards*. $55/£35

RAY, R. G. Aerial Photographs in Geologic Interpretation and Mapping. Washington, 1960. Fine in wrappers. *Henly*. $23/£15

RAY, ROBERT J. Murdock for Hire. NY: St. Martin's, 1987. 1st ed. Inscribed. Fine in dj. *Mordida*. $35/£22

RAYMOND and WHITCOMB. Raymond-Whitcomb Guide to Winter Travel in America 1928-1929. Boston, 1928. Dbl map. VG in ptd wraps (upper corner creased). *Bohling*. $25/£16

RAYMOND, JEAN PAUL and CHARLES RICKETTS. Oscar Wilde, Recollections. Bloomsbury: Nonesuch, 1932. One of 800 numbered, ptd. Full pict cl. Fine. *Hermitage*. $225/£144

RAYNAL, MAURICE. Modern French Painters. Ralph Roeder (trans). NY, 1934. 109 plts. *Edwards*. $39/£25

RAYNER, JOHN (ed). Towards a Dictionary of the County of Southampton Commonly Hampshire. Batsford, 1937. 1st ed. Pict card cvrs in plastic ring binding. *Cox*. $34/£22

RAYNER, RICHARD. Los Angeles Without a Map. London: Secker, 1988. 1st UK ed. Signed. Fine in dj. *Williams*. $28/£18

RAYNOLDS, W. F. Report on the Exploration of the Yellowstone River.... Washington: GPO, 1868. 1st ed. 174pp; lg fldg map (tears at folds; cl frayed, stained, bumped). *King*. $250/£160

READ, BENJAMIN M. Illustrated History of New Mexico. Santa Fe, 1912. 1st Eng ed. Purple cl, gilt. Fine in Fine dj. *Turpen*. $595/£381

READ, C. (ed). Bibliography of British History. Tudor Period 1485-1603. Oxford: Clarendon, 1959. 2nd ed. VG in dj. *Moss*. $94/£60

READ, C. RUDSTON. What I Heard, Saw, and Did at the Australian Gold Fields. London: T. & W. Boone, 1853. 1st ed. viii,327,(1)blank, 8 pub's list, lg fldg map at end, 4 tinted lithos incl frontis (lt foxing beginning, end; margins lt browned). Yellow ribbed, blind-stamped cl (sl rubbed, soiled). *Morrell*. $437/£280

READ, GEORGE H. The Last Cruise of the Saginaw. Boston/NY: Houghton Mifflin, 1912. 1st ed. Frontis port, 17 plts. Grn cl, stamped in white (lt rubbed, spine sl faded), else Fine. *Argonaut*. $50/£32

READ, GEORGE WILLIS. A Pioneer of 1850: George Willis Read, 1819-1880. Boston: Little Brown, 1927. 1st ed. Frontis port, fldg map. Blue cl, gilt spine. Fine in dj (spine faded). *Pacific**. $58/£37

READ, HELEN S. An Airplane Ride. NY: Scribner, 1928. 4th ed. Eleanor Lee (illus). 7 1/2 x 6 3/4. 38pp. VG. *Cattermole*. $25/£16

READ, HELEN S. An Engine's Story. NY: Scribner, 1928. 4th ed. Eleanor Lee (illus). 7 1/2 x 6 3/4. 38pp. VG. *Cattermole*. $25/£16

READ, HERBERT. Art and Industry. Faber & Faber, 1956. 4th ed. (Feps sl browned.) Dj (lt soiled, sl chipped). *Edwards*. $31/£20

READ, HERBERT. Art and Society. London, 1937. 1st ed. Red buckram, gilt. (Spine sl mkd, faded), o/w VG. *Words Etc*. $31/£20

READ, HERBERT. Phases of English Poetry. London: Hogarth, 1928. 1st ed. (Sm split spine head), o/w VG in dj (soiled, torn, sm chips, selotape mks). *Virgo*. $31/£20

READ, HERBERT. Poems 1914-1934. Faber & Faber, 1935. 1st ed. Rev copy. (Eps lt spotted.) Fore, lower edge uncut. Dj (sl chipped, spine faded). *Edwards*. $31/£20

READ, J. MARION. A History of the California Academy of Medicine, 1870 to 1930. SF: (CA Academy of Medicine), 1930. 1st ed. One of 957 ptd by Grabhorn Press. 18 plts. Red cl (spine sl faded, corners sl jammed), ptd paper spine label (sl chipped). Fine. *Argonaut.* $90/£58

READ, KENNETH E. The High Valley. NY: Scribner, 1965. 1st ed. 12 plts, 2 maps. (Flyleaf top clipped), o/w VG in dj. *Worldwide.* $18/£12

READ, OPIE. An Arkansas Planter. Chicago/NY: Rand, McNally, (1896). 1st ed. (Name, date on flyleaf), o/w Clean in pict gilt-lettered binding. *Bernard.* $75/£48

READ, PIERS PAUL. Alive. London, 1974. 1st ed. NF in NF dj. *Warren.* $50/£32

READ, PIERS PAUL. Game in Heaven with Tussy Marx. London, 1966. 1st ed, 1st bk. VG in dj (dusty, corners rubbed). *Buckley.* $31/£20

READ, WILLIAM A. Indian Place-Names in Alabama. Baton Rouge: LA State Univ, 1937. 1st ed. Fldg map. (Lt shelfworn), else VG. *Brown.* $20/£13

READE, CHARLES and COMPTON. Charles Reade, a Memoir. NY: Harper, 1887. 1st Amer ed. Grn cl, gilt. Fine. *Macdonnell.* $50/£32

READE, CHARLES. The Cloister and the Hearth: A Tale of the Middle Ages. C&W, 1889. New ed. Pub's cat dated April 1890. Good (sig, fore-edge spotted; spine bumped, sunned). *Tiger.* $19/£12

READE, CHARLES. The Cloister and the Hearth; or, Maid, Wife, and Widow. NY: Rudd & Carleton, 1861. 1st Amer ed. 256pp (age spotting, sm stain affects last few ll). Good. *Reese.* $50/£32

READE, CHARLES. Griffith Gaunt; or, Jealousy. Boston: Ticknor & Fields, 1866. 1st Amer ed. Good (eps foxing; spine ends worn). *Reese.* $60/£38

READE, CHARLES. Peg Woffington. Boston: Ticknor & Fields, 1855. 1st Amer ed. Bright blue cl, gilt. Attractive (sl worn). *Macdonnell.* $45/£29

READE, CHARLES. Peg Woffington. Boston: Ticknor & Fields, 1855. 1st Amer ed. 303pp + cat (margin spotting, couple sigs starting; cl sl sunned, soiled, spine toe lt fraying). *Reese.* $65/£42

READING, JOSEPH H. A Voyage Along the Western Coast or Newest Africa. Phila, 1901. (Sl internal spotting; cl worn, soiled.) *Freeman*.* $20/£13

Real Life in Ireland. London, 1829. 4th ed. 19 hand-colored plts, incl extra-engr tp. Aeg. Mod cl, 1/4 polished calf. *Kane*.* $95/£61

Real Life in London.... (By Pierce Egan.) London, 1821-2. 1st ed, 2nd issue. 2 vols. 2 frontispieces, 2 extra-engr tps, 28 plts, 2 optional plts, all hand-colored. Aeg. Full maroon morocco (vol 1 fr hinge weak, other hinges sl rubbed), gilt. *Kane*.* $150/£96

RECHY, JOHN. City of Night. NY, 1963. 1st Amer ed, 1st bk. Fine (spine extrems sl rubbed) in dj (rear panel sl soiled). *Polyanthos.* $50/£32

Record of the American Branch Association of the North Holland Herd Book. Vol 1. Dover, NJ, 1888. VG. *October Farm.* $65/£42

RECORD, SAMUEL J. and CLAYTON D. MELL. Timbers of Tropical America. New Haven: Yale Univ, 1924. 50 plts. Fine. *Brooks.* $85/£54

Records of Alaskan Big Game—1971 Edition. Anchorage: ABGTC, 1971. VF in dj. *Bowman.* $40/£26

Records of North American Big Game. NY, 1958. (Sl worn.) Dj (frayed). *Oinonen*.* $130/£83

Records. Town of Brookhaven, up to 1800. Patchogue: Office of the 'Advance,' 1880. Brn cl (quite worn). *Boswell.* $75/£48

Recreations of Christopher North. (By John Wilson.) Edinburgh/London, 1842. 1st ed. 3 vols. VG + (lt worn). *New Hampshire*.* $30/£19

RECTOR, WILLIAM GERALD. Log Transportation in the Lake State Lumber Industry, 1840-1918. Glendale, CA: A.H. Clark, 1953. Unopened. NF. *Cahan.* $45/£29

Red Rover. (By James Fenimore Cooper.) Paris, 1827. True 1st ed, w/half-titles. 3 vols. 12mo. Contemp calf (spines dknd; lt foxed, sig). BAL 3837. *Swann*.* $862/£553

RED, WILLIAM STUART. The Texas Colonists and Religion, 1821-1836. Austin: E.L. Shettles, 1924. 1st ed. (Sl worn), else Good in wraps (rubbed, soiled). *Brown.* $12/£8

Red, White, and Blue Socks. (By Aunt Fanny's Daughter.) NY: Leavitt & Allen, 1864. 1st bk in 'The Sock Stories' series. 8vo. 117pp; 3 full-pg plts. Blind-stamped dk blue cl, gilt-stamped spine title. (Spine ends lt worn), else Fine. *Bromer.* $125/£80

REDDAWAY, T. F. The Rebuilding of London After the Great Fire. Arnold, 1951. Coarse buckram. Fine in dj (sl faded, lt soiled). *Peter Taylor.* $36/£23

REDDING, M. W. Scarlet Book of Free Masonry. NY: Redding, Masonic Pubs, 1889. Color frontis, 547pp (fr hinge cracked; shaken); 3 color plts, 33 b/w plts (1 fldg). Brn cl (rubbed, bumped, fr joint split), gilt. Good. *Blue Mountain.* $75/£48

REDDING, M. WOLCOTT. Antiquities of the Orient Unveiled. NY, 1874. 1st ed. Color frontis, 541pp; 90 full-pg engrs, 3 fldg plts. Dec cvr. VG +. *Middle Earth.* $85/£54

REDDING, M. WOLCOTT. Antiquities of the Orient Unveiled. NY: Temple, 1875. 421pp; 2 color plts (1 fldg), fldg color map, 90 further plts (3 fldg). Recent buckram. VG. *Worldwide.* $65/£42

REDESDALE, LORD. Further Memories. NY: Dutton, 1917. 1st ed. 12 plts. (Cl sl rubbed, soiled), o/w VG. *Worldwide.* $35/£22

REDFORD, A. H. The History of Methodism in Kentucky (to 1832). Nashville, 1868-70. 1st ed. 2 vols. Howes R114. *Ginsberg.* $100/£64

REDGRAVE, GILBERT R. (ed). Outlines of Historic Ornament. London: Chapman & Hall, 1884. 1st British ed. xv,(1),170pp. (Cl soiled top edge upper bd), o/w VG. *Reese.* $65/£42

REDGROVE, PETER. The Collector and Other Poems. London, 1959. 1st ed, 1st bk. Fine (few sm specks lower edge fr cvr) in dj (spine sl sunned). *Polyanthos.* $60/£38

REDGROVE, PETER. An Explanation of the Two Visions. Leamington Spa: Sixth Chamber, 1985. 1st ed. #7/56 signed. Excellent in dk grn wrappers. *Vandoros.* $95/£61

REDMAN, WILLIAM. Illustrated Handbook of Information on Pewter and Sheffield Plate. 1903. Dbl frontis, incl port. Dec eps. *Edwards.* $47/£30

REDPATH, JAMES. The Public Life of Capt. John Brown. B: Thayer & Eldridge, 1860. 1st ed. 408pp; port. VG- (foxed; spine edge repaired). *Agvent.* $95/£61

REDPATH, JAMES. The Public Life of Capt. John Brown.... Boston: Thayer & Eldridge, 1860. 1st ed. Port, 408pp. (Text lt spotted; sl shelfworn, edgeworn), else Good. *Brown.* $75/£48

REDPATH, JAMES. The Roving Editor: or, Talks with Slaves in the Southern States. NY: A.B. Burdick, 1859. 1st ed. Frontis, 16,349pp, ads. Very Nice. Howes R121. *M & S.* $300/£192

REDWAY, LAWRENCE D. History of the Medical Society of the County of Westchester, 1797-1947. Westchester, 1947. 1st ed. Blue cl. VG. *Doctor's Library.* $50/£32

REED and CARNRICK. An Abstract of the Symptoms, with the Latest Dietetic and Medicinal Treatment of Various Diseased Conditions. NY, 1891. 1st ed. Good (inner fr hinge starting; worn). *Doctor's Library.* $40/£26

REED and CARNRICK. Gland Therapy. Jersey City, 1924. 1st ed. Gilt-tooled paper bds. VG. *Doctor's Library.* $50/£32

REED, ANDREW and JAMES MATHESON. A Narrative of the Visit to the American Churches by the Deputation from the Congregational Union of England and Wales. NY, 1835. 1st Amer ed. 2 vols. *Reese.* $150/£96

REED, ANDREW and JAMES MATHESON. A Narrative of the Visit to the American Churches. NY: Harper, 1835. 2 vols. 336; 363pp. (Spines faded, ends chipped), else VG. *Bohling.* $100/£64

REED, BENJAMIN M. A History of Education in New Mexico. Santa Fe, 1911. 20pp, ptd presentation slip, 4pp ad inserted. Ptd wrappers. (Lt soiled, wrinkled.) *Bohling.* $25/£16

REED, C. K. and C. A. Guide to Taxidermy. Worcester: Privately Pub, (1914). New, enlgd ed. Dec cl. VG +. *Mikesh.* $30/£19

REED, E. H. The Silver Arrow and Other Indian Romances of the Dune Country. Chicago: R. & L., 1926. 1st ed. 6 full-pg etched repros. Dec eps. VG +. *Mikesh.* $25/£16

REED, G. H. A First Book of Architecture. A&C Black, n.d. (c. 1938). Cl-backed bds. VG in dj (sl grubby, chipped, rubbed). *Words Etc.* $19/£12

REED, ISHMAEL. Yellow Back Radio Broke-Down. London: Allison & Busby, (1971). 1st Eng ed. Fine in dj (sm chip). *Dermont.* $35/£22

REED, ISHMAEL. Yellow Back Radio Broke-Down. GC: Doubleday, 1969. 1st ed. Fine in VG + dj (lt soiled). *Between The Covers.* $65/£42

REED, JOHN CALVIN. The Old and New South. NY, 1876. 1st ed. 24pp. VG in orig ptd wrappers. *Mcgowan.* $75/£48

REED, JOHN. Ten Days That Shook the World. NY, 1919. 1st ed. (Inner hinges badly cracked; cvrs rubbed.) *King.* $175/£112

REED, JOHN. Ten Days That Shook the World. NY: Boni & Liveright, 1919. 1st ed. (Manufacturing flaw rear inner hinge, sl fox mks plt margins), o/w NF. *Reese.* $300/£192

REED, JOHN. Ten Days That Shook the World. NY: Boni & Liveright, 1919. 1st ed. Pict eps. VF (sl rubbed, bumped). *Jaffe.* $500/£321

REED, JOSEPH. Tom Jones. London: Becket & De Hondt, 1769. 1st ed. Mod brn cl (w/o orig wrappers). Fine. *Sumner & Stillman.* $165/£106

REED, PARKER McCOBB. The Bench and Bar of Wisconsin. Milwaukee, 1882. 542pp, 42 ports, errata. Aeg. Gilt-titled brn cl (worn, spotted, lt etching fr cvr edge). Good. *Bohling.* $65/£42

REED, RONALD. The Nature and Making of Parchment. (Leeds), 1975. One of 450 numbered. 1/4 vellum. Glassine dj. *Swann*.* $126/£81

REED, SUE WELSH and RICHARD WALLACE. Italian Etchers of the Renaissance and Baroque. Boston: Museum of Fine Arts, (1989). Fine in pict wrappers. *Truepenny.* $35/£22

REED, THOMAS WALTER. David Crenshaw Barrow. Athens, GA: The Author, (1935). 1st ed. (Lacks fep.) *Ginsberg.* $75/£48

REED, WALT. John Clymer: An Artist's Rendezvous with the Frontier West. Flagstaff: Northland Press, (1976). 1st ed. VF in dj. *Hermitage.* $125/£80

REED, WALTER. The Propagation of Yellow Fever Based on Recent Researches. Balt, 1901. 1st ed. VG in wrappers. *Fye.* $125/£80

REED, WILLIAM. The Phantom of the Poles. NY: Walter S. Rockey, 1906. VG. *High Latitude.* $60/£38

REED, WILLIAM. The Phantom of the Poles. NY: Walter S. Rockey, 1906. Grn cl (worn, soiled, hinges weak). *Parmer.* $125/£80

REEMELIN, CHARLES. The Vine-Dresser's Manual. NY: Moore, 1858. Frontis, 103pp + ads. Pub's cl. Nice. *Second Life.* $150/£96

REEMELIN, CHARLES. The Vine-Dresser's Manual.... NY: C.M. Saxon, 1856. 1st ed. Frontis, 103pp. *M&s.* $300/£192

REES, ENNIS. Brer Rabbit and His Tricks. NY: Young Scott, 1967. 1st ed. Edward Gorey (illus). 9 3/4 x 8. 48pp. Pict bds. Fine in dj. *Cattermole.* $60/£38

REES, ENNIS. Fables from Aesop. NY: OUP, 1966. 1st US ed. J.J. Grandville (illus). 6 1/4 x 10 1/2. 210pp. Fine in dj. *Cattermole.* $15/£10

REES, ENNIS. Lions and Lobsters and Foxes and Frogs. NY: Young Scott Books, (1971). 1st ed thus. Signed by Edward Gorey (illus). Fine in dj. *Bromer.* $45/£29

REES, ENNIS. Lions and Lobsters and Foxes and Frogs. NY: Young Scott, 1971. 1st ed. Signed by Edward Gorey (illus). 9 x 8 1/4. 48pp. Pict bds. Fine in dj. *Cattermole.* $60/£38

REES, ENNIS. More of Brer Rabbit's Tricks. NY: Young Scott Books, (1968). 1st ed. Signed by Edward Gorey (illus). Fine in dj (price-clipped). *Bromer.* $45/£29

REES, ENNIS. More of Brer Rabbit's Tricks. NY: Young Scott, 1968. 1st ed. Edward Gorey (illus). 9 3/4 x 8. 46pp. Pict bds. Fine in dj. *Cattermole.* $50/£32

REES, L. E. RUUTZ. A Personal Narrative of the Siege of Lucknow. London, 1858. 2nd ed. *Petersfield.* $50/£32

REEVE, FRANK D. History of New Mexico. NY, 1961. 1st ed. 3 vols. VG. *Turpen.* $195/£125

REEVE, J. STANLEY. Red Coats in Chester County. NY, (1940). One of 570. 11 plts. 'Grosse Pointe Hunt, Club Metamora Branch, Ye Olde Timers, June 1941' gilt-stamped fr cvr. *Kane*.* $120/£77

REEVES, JAMES J. History of the Twenty-Fourth Regiment New Jersey Volunteers. Camden, NJ: S. Chew, printer, 1889. 1st ed. 45pp. NF in orig ptd wrappers. *Mcgowan.* $150/£96

REEVES, JAMES. How the Moon Began. Abelard-Schuman, 1971. 1st Amer ed. Edward Ardizzone (illus). 7x10. Pict bds. NF in dj (spine sl worn). *My Bookhouse.* $30/£19

REEVES, RICHARD STONE and PATRICK ROBINSON. Classic Lines. Birmingham: Oxmoor, 1975. 1st ed. Signed by Robinson. VG in Good dj. *October Farm.* $325/£208

REEVES, RICHARD STONE and PATRICK ROBINSON. Decade of Champions. NY: Fine Arts, 1980. 1st ed. Signed presentation copy. VG in VG dj. *October Farm.* $295/£189

REGARDIE, ISRAEL. Roll Away the Stone. MN: Llewellyn, 1968. 1st ed. Good (lacks fep; ex-lib, stamp; staining) in dj (frayed). *Sclanders.* $23/£15

Regulations and Instructions for the Cavalry Sword Exercise. London: Clowes, (1819). 2 plts (1 lg fldg); 4pp pub's list. Calf (fr hinge weak; bkpl, inscrip, sl foxed). *Rostenberg & Stern.* $140/£90

Regulations for the Army of the United States, 1861. NY: Harper, (1861). 1st ed. 457pp + 21pp appendix; 2 plts. Black cl. VG (inscrip, lt foxed, sl worn). *Lucas.* $150/£96

REICH, SHELDON. John Marin, a Stylistic Analysis and Catalogue Raisonne. Tucson, (1970). 2 vols. VG in dj, slipcase (soiled). *King.* $150/£96

REICH, SHELDON. John Marin: A Stylistic Analysis and Catalogue Raisonne. Tucson: Univ of AZ, (1970). 2 vols. Fine in VG djs (price-clipped), pub's slipcase. *Metropolitan**. $161/£103

REICH, WILHELM. The Function of the Orgasm...Volume One. Theodore P. Wolfe (trans). NY: Orgone Inst, 1942. 1st ed. Pale grn cl. VG in dj (edgeworn). *Gach*. $200/£128

REICH, WILHELM. The Mass Psychology of Fascism. NY: Orgone Inst, 1946. 3rd rev, enlgd ed. 1st ed in English. Fine (spine sl rubbed) in dj (sm chips, nicks). *Polyanthos*. $50/£32

REICH, WILHELM. The Mass Psychology of Fascism. Theodore P. Wolfe (trans). NY: Orgone Inst, 1946. 3rd rev, enlgd ed, 1st ed in English. Blue cl. VG. *Gach*. $85/£54

REICH, WILHELM. The Sexual Revolution. NY: Orgone Inst, 1945. 1st ed. Fine. *Beasley*. $65/£42

REID, ARTHUR. Reminiscences of the Revolution. Utica: Roberts Book & Job Printer, 1859. 1st ed. 31pp. Fine in ptd wrappers. Howes R164. *Cahan*. $85/£54

REID, ELIZA P. Reid's Historical Botany.... Windsor: C. Andrews, 1826. 3 vols in 1. viii-xiv,190; vi,185; vi,283pp. (Recased in cl.) Leather spine label, gilt. Fine (ex-lib, few mks). *Quest*. $165/£106

REID, FORREST. Walter de la Mare: A Critical Study. London, (1929). 1st ed. VG in dj (lt worn, browned). *Truepenny*. $45/£29

REID, HIRAM A. History of Pasadena.... Pasadena: Pasadena Hist Co, 1895. 675pp (pencil inscrip); fldg map. Gilt-stamped cl (expertly rebacked w/orig spine laid down). *Dawson*. $500/£321

REID, HUGO. The Indians of Los Angeles County. L.A.: (Arthur M. Ellis), 1926. One of 200. Inscribed by Ellis. Patterned gray bds, paper spine label (spine ends, label chipped, paper over fr joint cracked). *Dawson*. $135/£87

REID, JAMES D. The Telegraph in America. NY, 1879. 1st ed. Signed, inscribed. Engr add'l tp. (Prelims, 1 port rehinged; ex-lib; fr hinge reinforced.) *Swann**. $57/£37

REID, JOHN. Essays on Hypochondriacal and Other Nervous Affections. Phila: M. Carey, 1817. 209pp + 3pp ads. Uncut. Orig bds, later paper spine. (Tp margin repaired, text foxed, browned), o/w Clean. *Goodrich*. $495/£317

REID, L. W. The Elements of the Theory of Algebraic Numbers. NY, 1926. Rpt. (Sm ink sig fep; cl sl dull.) *Whitehart*. $55/£35

REID, MAYNE. The Boy Tar; or A Voyage in the Dark. Boston, 1860. Charles S. Keene (illus). 356pp. Blue pub's cl, gilt. VG (bkpl). *Truepenny*. $45/£29

REID, MAYNE. The Cliff-Climbers. London: Charles H. Clarke, (1864). 1st ed. 3/4 gilt-stamped tan calf, marbled bds, gilt-stamped black morocco spine label. VG (sl foxed, rubbed). *Houle*. $150/£96

REID, MAYNE. The Forest Exiles. Boston: Ticknor & Fields, 1858. 360pp; 12 plts. (Sl foxed, sl shaken; sl rubbed, scuffed, spine ends frayed), o/w VG. *Worldwide*. $25/£16

REID, STUART J. The Life and Times of Sydney Smith. Sampson Low, 1896. 4th ed. Frontis, xx,382pp. Good. *Cox*. $23/£15

REID, STUART J. A Sketch of the Life and Times of the Rev. Sydney Smith. Sampson Low et al, 1884. 1st ed. xx,409,(3)pp + 32pp cat; port, fldg facs letter. Uncut. Diced cl (sl spotted, backstrip faded), gilt. *Cox*. $55/£35

REID, WILLIAM JAMESON. Through Unexplored Asia. Boston: Dana Estes, 1899. 1st ed. 499pp; 3 fldg maps rear pocket (1 carefully restored). Teg. Grn pict cl (spine tail sl rubbed), gilt. Fine. *Sotheran*. $390/£250

REIGART, J. FRANKLIN. The Life of Robert Fulton. Phila: C.G. Henderson, 1856. 1st ed. Frontis (sl offsetting), xxvii,(29)-297pp; 26 plts (8 hand-colored), guards. Mod cl. Howes R178. *Glaser*. $150/£96

REIK, THEODOR. Ritual: Psycho-Analytic Studies. Douglas Bryan (trans). NY, 1958. New ptg. Internally Good (ex-lib; cl worn). *Goodrich*. $30/£19

REIK, THEODOR. Ritual: Psychoanalytic Studies. NY, 1946. 1st ed. VG + in VG dj. *Smith*. $20/£13

REILLY, C. H. McKim, Mead and White. NY, 1924. (Soil, wear, sl shaken.) *Freeman**. $40/£26

REILLY, HELEN. Compartment K. Random House, 1955. 1st ed. (Sl edgewear), else NF in dj (few sl nicks). *Murder By The Book*. $65/£42

REINER, IMRE. Grafika: Modern Designs for Advertising and Printing. NY, 1947. VG in dj (spine partly missing). *Truepenny*. $55/£35

REISNER, ROBERT. Graffiti. Selected Scrawls from Bathroom Walls. NY: Parallax/S&S, 1967. 1st ed. Pb. NF (sm stock # sticker fr wrap). *Beasley*. $25/£16

REITLINGER, GERALD. The Economics of Taste. London: Barrie & Rockcliff, 1961. 1st ed. 8 plts. VG in dj. *Hollett*. $47/£30

REITLINGER, H. C. Old Master Drawings. London: Constable, 1922. 1st ed. 72 collotypes. Cl-backed bds, leather spine label. VG. *Hollett*. $117/£75

RELANDER, CLICK. Drummers and Dreamers. Caldwell, 1956. 1st ed. Frontis. VF in VF dj. *Oregon*. $195/£125

RELANDER, CLICK. Drummers and Dreamers. Caldwell: Caxton, 1956. 1st ed. VG in VG dj. *Perier*. $125/£80

Religious, Social, and Political History of the Mormons. (By Charles Mackay.) NY, 1858. Pub's cl (spine ends frayed). *Swann**. $149/£96

REMARQUE, ERICH MARIA. The Night in Lisbon. Ralph Manheim (trans). NY: Harcourt, Brace & World, (1964). 1st Amer ed. Fine in dj (lt used). *Antic Hay*. $20/£13

REMARQUE, ERICH MARIA. The Road Back. London, (1931). 1st Eng ed. (Ink inscrip), else VG in dj (chipped). *King*. $35/£22

REMARQUE, ERICH MARIA. The Road Back. A. H. Wheen (trans). London: Putnam, (1931). 1st Eng ed. VG in white dj (edgeworn, sm tears, nicks, soiled). *Antic Hay*. $75/£48

REMARQUE, ERICH MARIA. Spark of Life. James Stern (trans). NY: Appleton, Century, Crofts, (1952). 1st Amer ed. NF in dj. *Antic Hay*. $30/£19

Rembrandt: Experimental Etcher. Boston: Museum of Fine Arts, 1969. Orig ed. Good in wraps (sl worn). *Washton*. $50/£32

REMINGTON, FREDERIC. Crooked Trails. NY: Harper, 1898. 1st ed. 150pp. Pict cl. Good (lt spotting back cvr). Howes R203. *Lien*. $150/£96

REMINGTON, FREDERIC. Done in the Open.... NY: P.F. Collier, 1903. Cl-backed pict bds (sl worn, soiled). Contents VG. *New Hampshire**. $50/£32

REMINGTON, FREDERIC. Frontier Sketches. Chicago: Werner Co, 1898. 1st ed. 15 plts. Pub's pict paper-cvrd beveled bds titled in black (sl soiled, joints splitting at top/bottom, corners showing). Sound. *Hermitage*. $375/£240

REMINGTON, FREDERIC. Men with the Bark On. NY, 1900. 1st ed. Pict cl (spotted, lt rubbed). *Argosy*. $200/£128

REMINGTON, FREDERIC. Pony Tracks. NY, 1895. 1st ed, 1st bk. Color pict cl. VG (bkpl, inscrip). BAL 16489. *Kane**. $225/£144

REMINGTON, FREDERIC. Stories of Peace and War. NY, 1899. 1st ed, 1st issue, w/author's name misspelled (Frederick) on fr/rear cvrs. Blue cl stamped in silver. VG. *Argosy*. $200/£128

REMINGTON, FREDERIC. Sundown Leflare. NY, 1899. 1st ed. Pict brn cl. Fine. *Argosy*. $200/£128

REMINGTON, FREDERIC. The Way of an Indian. NY: Fox Duffield, 1906. 1st ed. Red cl, pict label. VG. *Argosy*. $150/£96

Reminiscences of a Nonagenarian. Newburyport, MA, 1879. 1st ed. 336pp; 4 litho plts. VG. *Yudkin**. $55/£35

REMISE, JAC and JEAN FONDIN. The Golden Age of Toys. Edita Lausanne, (1967). 1st Amer ed. VF in dj. *Hermitage*. $100/£64

REMLAP, L. T. General U. S. Grant, His Life and Public Services. NY, 1888. 716pp. Pict cl. (Cvr lt worn), o/w Fine. *Pratt*. $45/£29

RENAN, ERNEST. The Life of Jesus. London/Paris: Trubner/M. Levy Freres, 1864. 1st ed in English. xii,311pp (lt spotted, paper peeling from inner joints). Maroon cl (faded), gilt. *Bickersteth*. $148/£95

RENARD, JULES. Carrots. G. W. Stonier (trans). London, 1946. 1st ed. Dj (frayed). *Typographeum*. $15/£10

RENAULT, MARY. The King Must Die. (NY): Pantheon, (1958). 1st ed. NF in dj (worn). *Antic Hay*. $17/£11

RENAULT, MARY. The King Must Die. London: Longmans, Green, (1958). 1st Eng ed. Fine in dj (sl wear, sm stain, price-clipped). *Antic Hay*. $45/£29

RENAULT, MARY. The King Must Die. NY: Pantheon, 1958. 1st ed. Fine in NF dj (sm tear). *Beasley*. $45/£29

RENAULT, MARY. The Mask of Apollo. (London): Longmans, (1966). 1st Eng ed. Paper-cvrd bds. NF (sm rubbed spot fep) in dj. *Antic Hay*. $20/£13

RENAULT, MARY. The Middle Mist. NY: Morrow, 1945. 1st ed. Fine in Fine dj (sl nick foot; tear rear panel). *Between The Covers*. $125/£80

RENAULT, MARY. The Persian Boy. London, 1972. 1st ed. Dj. *Typographeum*. $18/£12

RENDELL, RUTH. The Bridesmaid. London: Hutchinson, 1989. 1st ed. Signed. Fine in Fine dj. *Old London*. $50/£32

RENDELL, RUTH. The Copper Peacock and Other Stories. 1991. 1st ed. Fine in dj. *Words Etc*. $23/£15

RENDELL, RUTH. The Copper Peacock and Other Stories. London: Hutchinson, 1991. 1st ed. VF in dj. *Mordida*. $40/£26

RENDELL, RUTH. Death Notes. NY: Pantheon, 1981. 1st US ed. Signed. Fine in Fine dj. *Old London*. $35/£22

RENDELL, RUTH. A Demon in My View. London: Hutchinson, 1976. 1st ed. (Pp dknd), o/w VG in dj (chips, internal tape repair, sl color restoration). *Mordida*. $65/£42

RENDELL, RUTH. The Face of Trespass. GC: DCC, 1974. 1st Amer ed. NF (lt wear) in VG dj (lt rubbed, wrinkle fr panel). *Between The Covers*. $75/£48

RENDELL, RUTH. The Face of Trespass. London: Hutchinson, 1974. 1st UK ed. Fine in NF dj (sl rubbed). *Williams*. $117/£75

RENDELL, RUTH. The Fever Tree and Other Stories. Hutchinson, 1982. Signed. Ptd notice laid in noting this as #3/20 signed on Jan. 26, 1984. Fine in Fine dj. *Certo*. $60/£38

RENDELL, RUTH. The Fever Tree. NY: Pantheon, 1982. 1st US ed. Signed. Fine in VG dj (sl wear). *Old London*. $35/£22

RENDELL, RUTH. Going Wrong. London: Hutchinson, 1990. 1st ed. Fine in dj. *Mordida*. $40/£26

RENDELL, RUTH. Kissing the Gunner's Daughter. NY: Mysterious Press, 1992. 1st US ed. Signed. Fine in Fine dj. *Old London*. $40/£26

RENDELL, RUTH. Live Flesh. London: Hutchinson, 1966. 1st ed. Signed. Fine in Fine dj. *Old London*. $65/£42

RENDELL, RUTH. Make Death Love Me. Hutchinson, 1979. 1st UK ed. VG in dj. *Williams*. $50/£32

RENDELL, RUTH. Make Death Love Me. London: Hutchinson, 1979. 1st ed. Signed by Jessica Mann. Fine in dj. *Mordida*. $150/£96

RENDELL, RUTH. Master of the Moor. London: Hutchinson, 1982. 1st ed. Fine in dj. *Mordida*. $50/£32

RENDELL, RUTH. The New Girl Friend and Other Stories. London: Hutchinson, 1985. 1st ed. Signed. VF in dj. *Mordida*. $65/£42

RENDELL, RUTH. One Across, Two Down. London: Hutchinson, 1971. 1st ed. Fine in dj (inner fr flap creases). *Mordida*. $375/£240

RENDELL, RUTH. Some Lie and Some Die. Hutchinson, 1973. Uncorrected proof copy. VG in red ptd wraps. *Certo*. $60/£38

RENDELL, RUTH. Talking to Strange Men. London: Hutchinson, 1987. 1st ed. Fine in dj. *Mordida*. $40/£26

RENDELL, RUTH. To Fear a Painted Devil. John Long, 1965. 1st UK ed. VG (lt foxed, p14 sl damaged, eps replaced professionally) in dj. *Williams*. $304/£195

RENDELL, RUTH. The Tree of Hands. Hutchinson, (1984). 1st ed. VG in dj. *Ash*. $31/£20

RENDELL, RUTH. The Tree of Hands. Hutchinson, 1984. 1st UK ed. Fine in dj. *Williams*. $23/£15

RENDELL, RUTH. The Tree of Hands. London: Hutchinson, 1984. 1st Eng ed. Fine in dj. *Hadley*. $28/£18

RENDELL, RUTH. The Tree of Hands. London: Hutchinson, 1984. 1st ed. Fine in dj. *Mordida*. $45/£29

RENDELL, RUTH. An Unkindness of Ravens. Hutchinson, (1985). 1st ed. VG in dj. *Ash*. $31/£20

RENDELL, RUTH. An Unkindness of Ravens. London: Hutchinson, 1985. 1st ed. Fine in Fine dj. *Janus*. $45/£29

RENDELL, RUTH. The Veiled One. London: Hutchinson, 1988. 1st ed. Fine in Fine dj. *Janus*. $35/£22

RENDER, REV. DR. A Tour Through Germany.... London: T.N. Longman, 1801. 2 vols. Full leather (hinges weak, vol 2 bds detached), gilt spines. *Metropolitan**. $57/£37

RENIERS, PERCEVAL. The Springs of Virginia: Life, Love, and Death at the Waters, 1775-1900. Chapel Hill: Univ of NC, 1941. 1st ed. Fine in dj. *Cahan*. $35/£22

RENKEN, MAXINE. A Bibliography of Henry Miller 1945-1961. Denver: Alan Swallow, 1962. 1st ed. *Words Etc*. $11/£7

RENOIR, JEAN. The Notebooks of Captain Georges. Norman Denny (trans). London: Collins, 1966. 1st Eng ed. Fine in dj (sl worn). *Antic Hay*. $25/£16

RENTOUL, ANNIE R. The Little Green Road to Fairyland. A&C Black, 1922. 1st ed. 4to. 103pp (sm mks, fr hinge sl strained); 16 plts (8 color) by Ida Rentoul Outhwaite. Midnight-blue bds (sm stains label, spine top, extrems worn, sl rubbed), mtd title label, cl spine. Generally VG. *Bookmark*. $507/£325

RENWICK, GEORGE. Romantic Corsica. London, 1909. Fldg map. (Corner few ll stained; corners gilt-illus cl sl rubbed, sm stain spine tail, recased.) *Edwards*. $47/£30

RENWICK, JAMES et al. Lives of Count Rumford, Zebulon Montgomery Pike and Samuel Gorton. Boston: Little, Brown, 1855. Port. (Bkpl; spine faded.) *Bohling.* $18/£12

RENWICK, JAMES. The Elements of Mechanics. Phila: Carey & Lea, 1832. 1st ed. xxxii,508pp (foxed). Contemp sheep (hinges cracked). Good. *Glaser.* $50/£32

REPINGTON, C. The First World War 1914-1918. Boston, 1920. 1st ed. 2 vols. (Cvr sl worn), o/w Fine. *Pratt.* $40/£26

Report of the Commissioner of Patents for the Year 1857. Agriculture. Washington, 1858. Good. *Zubal*.* $10/£6

Report of the Commissioner on Indian Affairs...1888. Washington: GPO, 1889. lxxxix,888pp; lg fldg map. Full leather. Good (worn, foxed). *Dumont.* $100/£64

Report of the Committee Appointed by the Philomathean Society of the University of Pennsylvania to Translate the Inscription of the Rosetta Stone. (Phila, 1859.) 2nd ed. Gilt-pict red cl (joints, extrems frayed, sl worn, hinges starting). Cat of members; copyright slip at end. *Freeman*.* $425/£272

Report of the Cruise of the U.S. Revenue Cutter Bear...November 27, 1897 to September 13, 1898. Washington: GPO, 1899. iv,3-144pp; 48 plts incl fldg map. Blue cl (scuffed; hinges weak). *Parmer.* $120/£77

Report of the Joint Select Committee to Inquire into the Condition of Affairs in the Late Insurrectionary States. Washington: GPO, 1872. 13 vols. (Ink name, soil, ends chipped, most vols stained), else Good set. *King.* $495/£317

Report of the Mysterious Noises Heard in the House of Mr. John D. Fox, in Hydesville, Arcadia.... Shelburne Falls: J. P. Thorndyke, 1887. Re-issue. 42-pg pamphlet. (Lacks wrappers), else VG. *Brown.* $40/£26

Report of the Secretary of Agriculture, for the Year 1890. Washington, 1890. 612pp. *Wheldon & Wesley.* $31/£20

Report of the Special Committee Appointed to Investigate the Troubles in Kansas.... Washington: Cornelius Wendell, 1856. vii,1206pp (sl aged, foxed, eps stained, sl dampstain gutter 1st/last sigs). Dk brn blind cl (sl worn, sl stained), gilt. *Baltimore*.* $35/£22

Report of the Superintendent of the Coast Survey...1856. Washington, 1856. (1 chart torn but complete; spine worn, cracked, fr cvr detached.) *New Hampshire*.* $275/£176

Report of the Trial of Friends, at Steubenville, Ohio. (By Marcus T.C. Gould.) Phila: Jesper Harding, ptr, 1829. 340pp (foxed, lt stained). Untrimmed. Cl-backed bds (fr hinge cl splitting, spine foot chipped), ptd spine label. *Bohling.* $50/£32

Report on Population and Resources of Alaska at the Eleventh Census, 1890. Washington: GPO, 1893. 2 lg fldg maps. Recased in orig black cl binding. VG. *Perier.* $125/£80

Reports of Cases Determined in the Supreme Court of the State of Nevada, During the Year 1874-5. SF: Bancroft-Whitney, 1887. Contemp sheep (fr joint splitting). *Boswell.* $25/£16

Reports of the Trials of Colonel Aaron Burr.... Phila, 1808. 2 vols. 596; 539pp (foxed, tanned, tear 1pg vol 1). Full contemp leather (scuffed, scraped), lettering pieces. Casings Good-. Howes B1013. *Scribe's Perch*.* $180/£115

REPPLIER, AGNES. Essays in Miniature. NY: Chas. L. Webster, 1892. 1st ed. Dec cl. VG. *Antic Hay.* $50/£32

REPPLIER, AGNES. Junipero Serra, Pioneer Colonist of California. GC, 1933. 1st ed. (Spine sl faded), o/w VG. *Turpen.* $45/£29

Resignation. An American Novel. (By Sarah Ann Evans.) Boston: The Author, 1825. 1st ed. 2 vols. (Sl soil, foxing; errata leaf end vol 2 unevenly trimmed w/loss.) Contemp calf-backed bds (worn, 1 cvr missing, 1 cvr detached). *Oinonen*.* $70/£45

RESPIRO. The Secret of Satan. Glasgow: C.W. Pearce, 1907. Dk grn cl (sl rubbed), gilt black leather spine label. NF (tp stained, dknd, sm edge tear). *Blue Mountain.* $85/£54

Reuben Ramble's Travels Through the Counties of England. (By Samuel Clark.) London: Darton, n.d. (ca 1845). 1st bk ed, pub from the orig 5 parts. Sq 8vo. Color litho frontis, extra-pict tp, 40 litho maps. (Foxing; sl stained, soiled.) Upper cvr pub's cl stamped in blind/gilt (rebacked w/binder's tape, rear cvr provided from another bk; shelfworn, soiled). *Oinonen*.* $1,000/£641

REUBEN, SHELLY. Julian Solo. NY: Dodd Mead, 1988. 1st ed. Fine in dj (price-clipped). *Mordida.* $45/£29

REVERE, JOSEPH W. Naval Duty in California. Oakland: Biobooks, 1947. Ltd to 1000. Map. Good. *Heinoldt.* $45/£29

REVESZ, G. The Psychology of a Musical Prodigy. NY: Harcourt, 1925. 1st US ed. Fine in dj (lt chipped). *Beasley.* $85/£54

Revised Laws of Indiana...Fifteenth Session.... Indianapolis: Ptd by Douglas & Maguire, 1831. 8vo. 596pp. Full contemp calf; morocco spine label (rubbed). (Notes fep; foxing), else VG. *Cahan.* $200/£128

Revised Regulations for the Army of the United States, 1861.... Phila, n.d. (Pencil sig.) Blue cl, gilt. *Kane*.* $110/£71

Revised Report of the Select Committee Relative to the Soldiers National Cemetery, Together with the Accompanying Documents.... Harrisburg: Singerly & Myers, 1865. Engr frontis, 2 maps. (Bkpl removed, lt foxing; extrems rubbed, spine sl lightened.) *Sadlon.* $50/£32

REVOIL, BENEDICT H. The Hunter and Trapper in North America. W. H. Davenport Adams (trans). London: T. Nelson, 1874. 2nd ed in English. Engr frontis, 393pp + 6pp ads at rear (sl aged, foxed, inscrip). Dk red-brn cl (dusty), beveled bds, gilt. Howes R228. *Baltimore*.* $70/£45

REWALD, JOHN (ed). Degas. 1944. 112 plts. Newspaper clipping loosely inserted. (Margins lt browned, bkpl.) 2-tone cl (sl rubbed), gilt. *Edwards.* $140/£90

REXROTH, KENNETH. One Hundred Poems from the Chinese. NY, 1956. 1st Amer ed. NF (edges sunned, corners rubbed). *Polyanthos.* $25/£16

REXROTH, KENNETH. One Hundred Poems from the Japanese. NY: New Directions, 1955. 1st Amer ed. NF (extrems, spine sl rubbed) in acetate dj. *Polyanthos.* $30/£19

REXROTH, KENNETH. With Eye and Ear. NY: (1970). 1st Amer ed. Fine in dw. *Polyanthos.* $25/£16

REY, GUIDO. The Matterhorn. London, (1913). 3rd imp. (Ex-lib; frayed.) *King.* $65/£42

REY, GUIDO. The Matterhorn. London, 1913. 3rd imp. *Petersfield.* $50/£32

REY, MARGRET. Spotty. NY: Harper, 1945. 1st ed. H. A. Rey (illus). 8 1/4 x 10. Cl spine, pict bds. VG in dj (worn; piece missing rear). *Cattermole.* $300/£192

REYNARD, MAURICE. New Bodies for Old. Macaulay, (1923). 1st ed. VG. *Certo.* $45/£29

REYNARDSON, C. T. S. BIRCH. Down the Road or Reminiscences of a Gentleman Coachman. 1887. New ed. Litho, ptd titles, 12 litho plts. Incl Chapman & Hall's Catalogue of Books, 40pp, dated May 1887. Blue cl gilt (sl loose). *Hatchwell.* $187/£120

REYNOLDS, ANN CLOUD. Wild Goat Trails of Catalina. Avalon: Ann Cloud Reynolds, 1941. (Newspaper stain to 2pp, inside fr cvr). Ptd wood-look wrappers. *Dawson.* $50/£32

REYNOLDS, CHANG. Pioneer Circuses of the West. L.A.: Westernlore, 1966. 1st ed. Fine in pict dj. *Argonaut.* $35/£22

REYNOLDS, E. E. (ed). Book of Grey Owl—Pages from the Writings of Wa-Sha-Quon-Asin. London: Peter Davies, (1938). 1st ed. (Ink inscrip), else VG in dj (tape repaired). *Perier.* $35/£22

REYNOLDS, FRANCIS J. The New Encyclopedic Atlas and Gazetteer of the World. NY: P.F. Collier, ca 1918. Grn cl (water-spotted, ends frayed). *Hudson.* $125/£80

REYNOLDS, FRANCIS J. The New World Atlas and Gazetteer. NY: P.F. Collier, 1924. Fldg facs map. Red cl (worn). *Hudson.* $90/£58

REYNOLDS, FRANK with MICHAEL McCLURE. Freewheelin' Frank, Secretary of the Angels. NY: Grove, 1967. 1st ed. Signed by McClure. Fine in dj. *Sclanders.* $47/£30

REYNOLDS, FRANK. 666. The Hymn to Lucifer. SF: Privately ptd, 1968. NF in fldg color cvr. *Sclanders.* $55/£35

REYNOLDS, GEORGE W. M. The Mysteries of the Court of London. John Dicks, (n.d. about 1860?). 4 vols. (Lower outer corners both cvrs vols 1&2 dampstained), o/w Clean set. *Bickersteth.* $55/£35

REYNOLDS, HELEN BAKER. Gold, Rawhide and Iron. Palo Alto: Pacific Books, (1955). Blue bds. VG + in dj. *Bohling.* $15/£10

REYNOLDS, JAMES. Andrea Palladio and the Winged Device. NY, 1948. Frontis port. (Pencil underlinings, notes, bkpl; cl sl soiled, lt browned.) *Edwards.* $31/£20

REYNOLDS, JOHN. My Own Times, Embracing Also, the History of My Life. Belleville, IL, 1855. 1st ed. 1-600,xxiipp (lacks port, last pg of index). Later 1/2 leather, marbled bds. (Fr cvr detached but present), else Good. Howes R236. *Brown.* $350/£224

REYNOLDS, JOHN. The Pioneer History of Illinois. Belleville, IL, 1852. Pub's cl (defective). Howes R237. *Swann*.* $345/£221

REYNOLDS, JOHN. The Pioneer History of Illinois.... Belleville, IL: N.A. Randall, 1852. 1st ed. (1st/last ll sl foxed.) Later tan cl, red/black leather spine labels. Howes R237. *Sadlon.* $325/£208

REYNOLDS, JOHN. Sketches of the Country on the Northern Route from Belleville, Illinois, to the City of New York. Belleville, 1854. 12mo. Pub's cl (backstrip sl faded). Howes R238. *Swann*.* $1,265/£811

REYNOLDS, MACK. The Case of the Little Green Men. Phoenix, 1951. 1st ed. (Sm soil spot rear cvr), else VG in NF dj (spine head sl worn). *Aronovitz.* $85/£54

REYNOLDS, QUENTIN. The Fiction Factory. NY: Random House, (1955). 1st ed. Fine in Fine dj. *Dermont.* $35/£22

REYNOLDS, REGINALD. Og and Other Ogres. London, 1946. 1st Eng ed. Quentin Crisp (illus). Very Nice (inscrip) in dj. *Clearwater.* $39/£25

REYNOLDS-BALL, E. A. The City of the Caliphs. London: T. Fisher Unwin, 1898. 1st ed. (ix),(i)blank, 335pp, 1/2-title, 20 plts incl frontis (sm ink lib stamps versos of plts, title, recto last leaf). Teg, others uncut. White pict cl (sl soiled), gilt-lettered. VG in orig limp maroon cl pict wrapper (faded, rubbed). *Morrell.* $55/£35

REYNOLDS-BALL, E. A. Jerusalem. London, 1901. 5 fldg maps and plans. (Feps browned, hinges tender.) Dec cl (spine sl chipped). *Edwards.* $23/£15

REZANOV, NIKOLAI PETROVICH. The Rezanov Voyage to Nueva California in 1806. SF: Thomas C. Russell, 1926. 1st separate ed, 1st ed in English. #238/260. Signed by Russell. Frontis port, 4 plts, facs. Red linen-backed blue bds, paper spine label. VF in NF plain blue dj (spine, edges sunned) w/paper spine label (chip). Howes R244. *Harrington.* $200/£128

REZEK, ANTOINE IVAN. History of the Diocese of Sault Ste. Marie and Marquette. Houghton, MI, 1906-07. 2 vols. 3/4 leather, marbled bds (scuffed, chipped), gilt. Very Nice. *Bohling.* $200/£128

RHEAD, G. W. and F. A. Staffordshire Pots and Potters. London: Hutchinson, 1906. 1st ed. 4 color plts, 116 half-tones. (Few sm lib stamps.) Mod 1/2 morocco gilt. *Hollett.* $148/£95

RHEAD, LOUIS. American Trout Stream Insects. NY: Frederick A. Stokes, 1916. 1st ed. Color frontis w/onion skin protector. Grn cl; gilt. NF (sl soiled). *Backman.* $125/£80

RHEAD, LOUIS. American Trout Stream Insects. NY: Stokes, 1916. 1st ed. 5 color plts. Gilt insects on grn cl. VG + . *Bowman.* $130/£83

RHEES, W. J. James Smithson and His Bequest. Washington, 1880. 1st ed. 159pp, 8 engrs, 2 fldg plts. VG. *Mikesh.* $47/£30

RHEES, W. J. The Smithsonian Institution Documents Relative to Its Origin and History. Washington, 1901. 1st ed. 2 vols. VG. *Fye.* $100/£64

RHEES, W. J. (ed). The Smithsonian Institution. Washington, 1879. (1st leaves creased, lib stamp erased from margin.) Recent cl. *Maggs.* $31/£20

RHEIMS, MAURICE. The Flowering of Art Nouveau. NY: Abrams, (1966). 1st ed. 12 mtd color plts. Good in ptd plastic dj. *Karmiole.* $85/£54

RHEINGOLD, JOSEPH C. The Fear of Being a Woman: A Theory of Maternal Destructiveness. NY: Grune & Stratton, (1964). 1st ed. Ptd blue cl (sl faded). *Gach.* $75/£48

RHIND, A. HENRY. Thebes. London: Longman, Green, 1862. 1st ed. Color litho frontis, xx,(i)illus, (i)blank, 329,(1)imprint, 1/2-title, map colored in outline, 6 tinted lithos (some marginal foxing; bkpl). Contemp polished prize calf (joints, spine head repaired, sl rubbed), gilt spine, black label. VG. *Morrell.* $281/£180

RHIND, W. A History of the Vegetable Kingdom. Glasgow, 1857. 1st ed. Port, 40 steel-engr plts (21 hand-colored). (Few pp loose; cl worn, shabby.) *Maggs.* $48/£31

RHINE, J. B. New Frontiers of the Mind: The Story of the Duke Experiments. NY/Toronto: Farrar & Rinehart, (1937). 1st ed. Inscribed, dated 1948. 12 photo plts. (Pencil notes feps.) Ptd grey cl. VG in dj (chipped). *Gach.* $65/£42

RHOADES, NINA. The Children on the Top Floor. Boston: Lothrop, Lee & Shepard, (1904). 1st ed. Bertha G. Davidson (illus). 2pp undated ads. Brick red cl pict dec in white/black. NF (sl rubbed). *Sumner & Stillman.* $35/£22

RHODE, JOHN. Hendon's First Case. NY: Dodd, Mead, 1935. Nice in dj (bottom edge creased, inside flaps cut, tacked to interior of cvr). *Metropolitan*.* $230/£147

RHODE, JOHN. Tragedy on the Line. NY: Dodd, Mead, 1931. 1st Amer ed. Attractive in dj (lt worn). *Metropolitan*.* $258/£165

RHODE, JOHN. The Venner Crime. London: Odhams, 1933. 1st ed. VG in dj (spine ends chipped, back panel soiled, short closed tears). *Mordida.* $65/£42

Rhode-Island Almanack, for...1792. Newport: P. Edes, n.d. (24pp). Fair (pp browned, contemp marginal notes) in self-wraps. *Scribe's Perch*.* $80/£51

RHODES, EUGENE MANLOVE. Penalosa. Santa Fe, NM: Writer's Editions, (1934). 1st separate ptg. One of 500 numbered, signed. Fine in orange wrappers. *Argonaut*. $250/£160

RHODES, EUGENE MANLOVE. The Rhodes Reader, Stories of Virgins, Villains, and Varmints. W. H. Hutchinson (ed). Norman: Univ of OK, (1957). 1st collected ed. Frontis. Blue cl. Fine in dj. *Argonaut*. $60/£38

RHODES, EUGENE MANLOVE. The Rhodes Reader. Univ of OK, (1957). 1st ed. Fine in Nice dj (price-clipped). *Authors Of West*. $40/£26

RHODES, EUGENE MANLOVE. The Rhodes Reader: Stories.... Norman: Univ of OK, (1957). 1st ed. VG in dj. *Lien*. $45/£29

RHODES, HENRY A. Memoirs of a Merchant. Seattle: Metropolitan, 1952. Ltd signed ed. Fine in dj. *Perier*. $30/£19

RHODES, JOHN H. The Gettysburg Gun. Providence, RI, 1892. 1st ed. Ltd to 250. PNRISSHS Series 4, #19. 57pp. NF in ptd wrappers. *Mcgowan*. $45/£29

RHODES, JOHN. Surprising Adventures and Sufferings of John Rhodes.... NY, 1798. 250pp (lacks both fly-leaves, sm piece torn tp corner w/o loss, sl insect damage top margin early leaves, foxing). Full calf (sl worn, fr hinge cracked). Cl slipcase. *New Hampshire**. $80/£51

RHODES, MAY DAVISON. The Hired Man on Horseback. Boston: Houghton Mifflin, 1938. 1st ed. Frontis port, 3 plts. Tan cl. Fine in dj (spine faded, sl chipped). *Argonaut*. $75/£48

RHODES, R. C. Harlequin Sheridan: The Man and the Legends. Oxford: Basil Blackwell, (1933). 1st ed. Fine in dj (sm tears, spine dknd). *Captain's Bookshelf*. $60/£38

RHODES, RICHARD. The Ungodly. NY: Charterhouse, 1973. 1st ed, 1st bk. NF (sl shelfwear) in NF dj. *Warren*. $75/£48

RHYS, JEAN. Good Morning Midnight. London: Constable, 1939. 1st Eng ed. 2nd binding, grn cl lettered in black. *Clearwater*. $86/£55

RHYS, JEAN. Tigers Are Better Looking. NY, 1968. 1st ed. VG+ in VG+ dj. *Smith*. $15/£10

RIBEYROLLES, CHARLES. The Prisons of Africa, Guina, and Cayenne. Melton Mowbray, 1857. vii,9-148pp. VG. *Adelson*. $75/£48

RIBOUD, MARC. Face of North Vietnam. NY/Chicago/SF: Holt, Rinehart & Winston, 1970. 1st ed. Map. NF in illus dj (rubbed). *Cahan*. $50/£32

RICCI, CORRADO. Romanesque Architecture in Italy. NY, n.d. (ca 1925). (Cl sl soiled.) *Washton*. $60/£38

RICCI, ELISA. Old Italian Lace. London/Phila, 1913. 2 vols. (Lt dampstaining beginning vol 1.) Cl (shelfworn, sl shaken, vol 2 cvr sl stained, bowed). Internally Sound. *Oinonen**. $275/£176

RICCI, JAMES. The Development of Gynaecological Surgery and Instruments. Phila, 1949. 1st ed. VG. *Fye*. $300/£192

RICCI, JAMES. The Geneaology of Gynaecology...2000 B.C.-1800 A.D. Phila, 1950. 2nd ed. VG. *Fye*. $200/£128

RICE, A. H. and JOHN BAER STROUDT. The Shenandoah Pottery. VA Book Co, (1974 facs of 1929 ed). Good (dj affixed to cvr w/scotch tape which has stained both; ex-lib). Dj Good. *Book Broker*. $65/£42

RICE, A. L. British Oceanographic Vessels 1800-1950. London: Ray Soc, 1986. 74 plts, 20 maps. Fine in dj. *Savona*. $28/£18

RICE, ALLEN. Reminiscences of Abraham Lincoln by Distinguished Men of His Time. NY: Harper, 1909. 1st ed thus. Teg. NF. *Archer*. $17/£11

RICE, ANNE. Cry to Heaven. NY: Knopf, 1982. 1st ed. Dj. *Swann**. $80/£51

RICE, ANNE. The Feast of All Saints. NY: S&S, (1979). 1st ed. Fine (pub's stamp bottom edge) in NF dj. *Metropolitan**. $40/£26

RICE, ANNE. The Feast of All Saints. NY: S&S, (1979). 1st ed. Signed. Fine in dj. *Turtle Island*. $200/£128

RICE, ANNE. The Feast of All Saints. NY, 1979. 1st ed. NF in Fine dj. *Warren*. $95/£61

RICE, ANNE. Interview with the Vampire. NY: Knopf, 1976. 1st ed, 1st bk. Cl-backed bds. (Spine sl cocked), else NF in dj (edge-crimped, few long creases). *Waverly**. $231/£148

RICE, ANNE. Interview with the Vampire. NY: Knopf, 1976. 1st ed, 1st bk. Cl-backed bds (sl musty). Fine in bright gold foil dj (lt surface scratching, few edge crimps, lt spotting). *Waverly**. $330/£212

RICE, ANNE. The Mummy. London: C&W, (1989). 1st British ed, 1st hb ed. Fine in dj. *Swann**. $69/£44

RICE, ANNE. The Mummy. London: C&W, (1989). 1st hb ed. Fine in Fine dj (thin 2-inch scratch fr panel). *Other Worlds*. $75/£48

RICE, ANNE. The Mummy. London: C&W, (1989). 1st hb ed. Fine in Fine dj. *Other Worlds*. $95/£61

RICE, ANNE. The Queen of the Damned. NY: Knopf, 1988. 1st ed. NF (sl bowing) in Fine dj. *Other Worlds*. $40/£26

RICE, ANNE. The Queen of the Damned. NY: Knopf, 1988. Fine in Fine dj. *Between The Covers*. $55/£35

RICE, ANNE. The Queen of the Damned. Macdonald, 1989. 1st UK ed. Fine in dj. *Williams*. $28/£18

RICE, ANNE. The Tale of the Body Thief.... NY: Knopf, 1992. 1st ed. Fine in Fine dj. *Other Worlds*. $30/£19

RICE, ANNE. The Vampire Chronicles. NY: Knopf, 1990. One of unspecified # of sets, each vol signed. 3 vols. Pub's bd slipcase. *Swann**. $161/£103

RICE, ANNE. The Vampire Lestat. NY, 1985. 1st ed, 1st issue w/unstained top. VF in VF dj. *Mcclintock*. $200/£128

RICE, ANNE. The Vampire Lestat. NY: Knopf, 1985. 1st ed. Inscribed. Fine in NF dj. *Metropolitan**. $230/£147

RICE, CARL O. Injection Treatment of Hernia. Phila, 1937. 1st ed. VG. *Doctor's Library*. $50/£32

RICE, CRAIG. The Big Midget Murders. NY: S&S, 1942. 1st ed. (Eps, edges sl foxed, sm lib stamp fep), else Fine in pict dj (sl worn). *Else Fine*. $125/£80

RICE, CRAIG. The Corpse Steps Out. NY: S&S, 1940. 1st ed. VG (name) in dj (creased, rubbed, edgetears). *Metropolitan**. $57/£37

RICE, CRAIG. Knocked for a Loop. NY: S&S, 1957. 1st ed. Fine (pp lt browned) in NF dj (lt edgewear). *Janus*. $45/£29

RICE, CRAIG. Knocked for a Loop. NY: S&S, 1957. 1st ed. (Pp tanned), else Fine in dj (sl worn). *Else Fine*. $50/£32

RICE, D. TALBOT. The Beginnings of Christian Art. London, 1957. Good in dj. *Washton*. $35/£22

RICE, DAMON. Seasons Past. Praeger, 1976. 1st ed. Fine in VG+ dj. *Plapinger*. $50/£32

RICE, DAVID TALBOT. The Art of Byzantium. London, 1959. 44 tipped in color plts, 196 b/w plts. Good in dj. *Washton*. $85/£54

RICE, DAVID TALBOT. The Church of Haghia Sophia at Trebizond. Edinburgh: Russell Trust, (1968). 1st ed. 93 plts (13 tipped-in color), lg color fold-out in rear pocket. Rust cl, gilt spine. Good in dj. *Karmiole*. $75/£48

RICE, DAVID TALBOT. The Church of Hagia Sophia at Trebizond. Edinburgh Univ, 1968. Color frontis tipped in, 12 color plts tipped in, 80 plts hors-texte, lg fldg color plt rear pocket. Dec eps. VF in dec color dj. *Europa.* $117/£75

RICE, GRANTLAND and CLARE BRIGGS. The Duffer's Handbook of Golf. NY: Macmillan, 1926. 1st trade ed. Grn cl. (Sl rubbed, bump), else VG. *Pacific*.* $115/£74

RICE, HARVEY. Sketches of Western Life. Boston, 1887. 253pp. (Ex-lib; spine ends chipped, 1-inch hole in cl.) *Bohling.* $12/£8

RICE, HARVEY. Sketches of Western Life. Boston: Lee & Shepard, 1888. 2nd ed. 253pp. NF. *Cahan.* $50/£32

RICE, HOWARD C. Barthelemi Tardiveau, a French Trader in the West. Balt: Johns Hopkins, 1938. Fldg map. Cl-backed bds. VG+ in glassine (chipped), plastic wrapper. *Bohling.* $45/£29

RICE, NATHAN P. Trials of a Public Benefactor.... NY: Pudney & Russell, 1859. 1st ed. Complete w/insert noting the inscription by Jacob Bigelow. Frontis port, xx,(13)-460pp, 2 (of 3) engr plts, guards. Pebbled cl (extrems frayed, dull, traces paper spine label). Internally VG (lib stamp). *Glaser.* $95/£61

RICE, WILLIAM. Indian Game (From Quail to Tiger). London: Allen, 1884. 1st ed. iv,221pp + 6 appendix, 13 plts (12 color litho). Grn gilt pict cl. VG. *Terramedia.* $300/£192

RICH, ADRIENNE. Diving into the Wreck. NY: W.W. Norton, 1973. 1st ed. (Paper dknd), o/w Fine in dj (lt edgeworn). *Jaffe.* $75/£48

RICH, ADRIENNE. Necessities of Life, Poems 1962-1965. NY: W.W. Norton, (1966). 1st ed. Fine in dj. *Jaffe.* $75/£48

RICH, ADRIENNE. Poems: Selected and New, 1950-1974. NY: W.W. Norton, (1975). 1st ed. Fine in dj. *Jaffe.* $65/£42

RICH, E. E. Hudson's Bay Company, 1670-1870. NY: Macmillan, (1961). 1st Amer ed. 3 vols. 6 plts (2 color), 2 fldg maps. Blue cl (sl rubbed). NF. *Harrington.* $150/£96

RICH, E. E. (ed). London Correspondence Inward from Eden Colvile, 1849-52. London: Hudson's Bay Record Soc, 1956. *Lien.* $60/£38

RICH, VIRTULON. Western Life in the Stirrups. Dwight L. Smith (ed). Chicago: Caxton Club, 1965. Frontis port, dbl map. Prospectus laid in. Cl spine, marbled bds. VG+. *Bohling.* $40/£26

RICHARDS, BARTLETT, JR. and RUTH VAN ACKEREN. Bartlett Richards. NE State Hist Soc, 1980. 1st ed. VG in dj (sl worn). *Lien.* $35/£22

RICHARDS, EUGENE. Few Comforts or Surprises: The Arkansas Delta. Cambridge, MA/London: MIT Press, 1973. 1st ed. Pict paper over bds. NF in NF dj. *Cahan.* $200/£128

RICHARDS, EUGENE. Few Comforts or Surprises: The Arkansas Delta. Cambridge/London: MIT, 1973. 1st ed. Pict paper over bds. VG in dj (price-clipped, soiled). *Cahan.* $150/£96

RICHARDS, FRANK. Old Soldier Sahib. Faber, 1936. 1st ed. VG in dj (dusty, spine browned, chipped). *Words Etc.* $125/£80

RICHARDS, FRANKLIN D. A Compendium of the Faith and Doctrines of the Church.... Liverpool, 1857. 1st ed. 243pp. Orig full tooled leather, gilt. (Lacks rep, inscrip; lt worn, corners bumped), o/w VG+. *Benchmark.* $200/£128

RICHARDS, I. A. The Screens. (London): Routledge & Kegan Paul, (1960). 1st Eng ed. Fine in dj (sl wear, lt soil). *Antic Hay.* $27/£17

RICHARDS, J. M. (ed). The Bombed Buildings of Britain. London: Architectural Press, 1942. 1st Eng ed. Very Nice (spine sl faded) in dj (sl frayed, torn). *Clearwater.* $47/£30

RICHARDS, JOHN J. Rhode Island's Early Defenders and Their Successors. East Greenwich, 1937. Map. Fine. *Bohling.* $8/£5

RICHARDS, McCARTY and BULFORD. The New Ohio Penitentiary: Description of Preliminary Drawings. N.p., n.d. (ca 1920). Fldg view. Gilt-lettered flexible cl (edges worn). *Freeman*.* $100/£64

RICHARDS, RAYMOND. Old Cheshire Churches. London: Batsford, 1947. 365 plts (4 color), map. Sound. *Ars Artis.* $55/£35

RICHARDS, RAYMOND. Old Cheshire Churches. Merton, Manchester, 1973. Rev, enlgd ed. Dec throw-out map. Fine in pict dj (clipped). *Peter Taylor.* $86/£55

RICHARDS, ROBERT H. et al. A Text Book of Ore Dressing. NY, 1909. 1st ed, 6th imp. Maroon cl, gilt. (2 repaired chips back cvr), else VG. *Price.* $48/£31

RICHARDS, WALTER. Her Majesty's Army. London: J.S. Virtue, (1891). 1st ed. 376pp,(4) ads (corner pg 240 creased, no loss); color litho title, 15 color litho plts. Aeg. Gilt, black pict red cl (spine chipped, dull). VG. *House.* $250/£160

RICHARDSON, A. E. and H. D. EBERLEIN. The English Inn Past and Present. Batsford, 1925. 1st ed. Color frontis. (Feps lt browned; cl sl rubbed.) *Edwards.* $94/£60

RICHARDSON, A. E. and H. D. EBERLEIN. The English Inn: Past and Present. Batsford, 1925. VG in purple cl. *Hadley.* $70/£45

RICHARDSON, A. E. and H. D. EBERLEIN. The Smaller English House of the Later Renaissance 1660-1830. London: Helburn, 1925. (Spine torn, frayed.) *Ars Artis.* $70/£45

RICHARDSON, A. E. and H. D. EBERLEIN. The Smaller English House of the Later Renaissance, 1660-1830. NY, (1925). Grn cl, gilt. (Lt wear, soil.) *Freeman*.* $60/£38

RICHARDSON, ALBERT D. Beyond the Mississippi. Hartford: American Pub Co, 1867. Dbl-frontis map, 572pp. 3/4 leather (simply rebound). *Bohling.* $40/£26

RICHARDSON, DOROTHY M. Clear Horizon. London: J.M. Dent/Cresset, 1935. 1st ed. Fine in NF dj (spine lt struck). *Cahan.* $100/£64

RICHARDSON, DOROTHY M. Oberland. Duckworth, (1927). 1st ed. Good (sl faded) in dj (worn, sl discolored). *Ash.* $62/£40

RICHARDSON, EMELINE. The Etruscans. Univ of Chicago, 1964. 1st ed. 48 plts. Dj (sl chipped). *Edwards.* $31/£20

RICHARDSON, GEORGE. Engravings from the Works of Henry Liverseege. London: Routledge/L.C. Gent, 1875. 2nd ed. 20pp; 38 engr plts. Aeg. Dec cl (sl worn, faded), gilt. *Hollett.* $133/£85

RICHARDSON, H. D. Holiday Sports and Pastimes for Boys. London: William S. Orr, 1848. Litho frontis, vi,112,(2 ads)pp (foxed, spotted). Mod 1/2 cl, marbled bds (sl worn), gilt. *Waverly*.* $132/£85

RICHARDSON, J. M. Steamboat Lore of the Penobscot. Augusta, ME, 1944. 3rd ed. Good. *Scribe's Perch*.* $30/£19

RICHARDSON, JAMES. Travels in the Great Desert of Sahara in the Years of 1845 and 1846. London: Bentley, 1848. 1st ed. 2 vols. xxxi,440; xii,482pp; 2 (of 3) plts, fldg map. (Frontis, tp vol 1 missing, sl foxed, lib stamps few leaves; ex lib, vol 1 rebound; worn), o/w Good. *Worldwide.* $65/£42

RICHARDSON, JOHN. Arctic Searching Expedition. NY: Harper, 1852. 1st US ed. xi(2),14-516pp. Blind-stamped cl. (Spine faded), else Nice. *High Latitude.* $125/£80

RICHARDSON, JOHN. A Grammar of the Arabic Language. London, 1801. 2nd ed. (Internal spotting, bkpl.) Contemp 1/4 calf, bds (rubbed). *Freeman*.* $40/£26

RICHARDSON, JOHN. The Polar Regions. Edinburgh: A&C Black, 1861. ix(3)400pp; fldg map. Uncut. Old 1/2 morocco. (Map sl foxed), else VG. *High Latitude.* $150/£96

RICHARDSON, JOHN. The Polar Regions. Edinburgh: A&C Black, 1861. ix,1l,400pp; fldg map. Partly unopened. Blue emb cl, gilt. (Corners, spine edges sl worn), else VG. *Parmer.* $250/£160

RICHARDSON, JOHN. The War of 1812. Toronto: Musson, 1902. #22/100. 15 ports (14 color), 9 plts, 2 maps, 4 plans, 2 facs. 1/2 black morocco. VG. Howes R258. *Adelson.* $285/£183

RICHARDSON, ROBERT. Bellringer Street. London: Gollancz, 1988. 1st ed. Signed. VF in dj. *Mordida.* $65/£42

RICHARDSON, ROBERT. Sleeping in Their Blood. London: Gollancz, 1991. 1st ed. Signed. VF in dj. *Mordida.* $45/£29

RICHARDSON, RUPERT NORVAL. The Comanche Barrier to South Plains Settlement. Glendale: Clark, 1933. 1st ed. One of 1012. Frontis. Rebound in facs of orig gilt-lettered blue cl. (Ex-lib, w/sm perf initials on tp), else Fine. *Argonaut.* $350/£224

RICHARDSON, RUPERT NORVAL. The Frontier of Northwest Texas 1846-76.... Glendale, 1963. 1st ed. One of 1558. Frontis map. Top edges blue, others untrimmed. Fine. No dj as issued. *Turpen.* $125/£80

RICHARDSON, RUPERT NORVAL. The Frontier of Northwest Texas, 1846-1876. Glendale: Clark, 1963. 1st ed. One of 1558. Blue cl (2 sm spots fr cvr, lt rubbing), else Fine. *Argonaut.* $125/£80

RICHARDSON, SAMUEL. Letters from Sir Charles Grandison. London: Macmillan, 1896. 2 vols. 303; 319pp. Aeg. Black linen, gilt. Attractive set. *Hartfield.* $155/£99

RICHARDSON, WILLIS and MAY MILLER. Negro History in Thirteen Plays. Washington: Associated Publishers, 1935. 1st ed. Nice (bkpl). *Turtle Island.* $50/£32

RICHIE, DONALD (ed). The Masters' Book of Ikebana. Tokyo, 1966. Stated 1st ed. Dec silk casing. VG. *Scribe's Perch*.* $45/£29

RICHLER, MORDECAI. The Apprenticeship of Duddy Kravitz. London: Andre Deutsch, 1959. 1st ed. (Lt offsetting feps), else NF in dj (2-inch tear fr panel). *Lame Duck.* $275/£176

RICHMAN, IRVING BERDINE. California Under Spain and Mexico, 1535-1847. NY: Houghton Mifflin, 1911. 1st ed. Lg fldg chart fr cvr pocket, lg fldg map rear cvr pocket, 2 plans in color. Teg. Red cl (sl worn). NF (blind stamp tp). *Harrington.* $110/£71

RICHMAN, IRVING BERDINE. California Under Spain and Mexico, 1535-1847. NY: Houghton Mifflin, 1911. 1st ed. Lg fldg map in fr pocket, fldg chart in rear cvr pocket. Red cl (corners sl rubbed; fade mk, lt rubbing to sm spine area from removed label; lib stamp ep), gilt. Overall NF. *Argonaut.* $150/£96

RICHMOND, LEONARD. The Technique of the Poster. London, 1933. (1/2 title torn, repaired w/cellotape; cl worn.) *Swann*.* $258/£165

RICHTER, CONRAD. Early Americana and Other Stories. Knopf, 1936. 1st ed. Fine in dj (spine ends chipped). *Authors Of West.* $75/£48

RICHTER, CONRAD. The Free Man. Knopf, 1943. 1st ed. Inscribed, signed. (Eps foxed), else Fine in Fine dj. *Authors Of West.* $60/£38

RICHTER, CONRAD. The Light in the Forest. NY: Knopf, 1953. 1st ed. Dec cl. Fine in dj. *Reese.* $35/£22

RICHTER, GISELA. Archaic Greek Art.... NY: OUP, 1949. 107 plts, fldg map. Good in dj. *Archaeologia.* $95/£61

RICHTER, GISELA. Catalogue of Greek and Roman Antiquities in the Dumbarton Oaks Collection. Cambridge: Harvard Univ, 1956. 27 plts. (Spine label removed), o/w Fine in dj. *Archaeologia.* $65/£42

RICHTER, GISELA. A Handbook of Greek Art. Phaidon, 1959. 1st ed. Color frontis. Dj (sl chipped). *Edwards.* $34/£22

RICHTER, GISELA. Handbook of the Greek Collection. Cambridge: Harvard Univ, 1953. Ltd to 2000. 130 plts. Good. *Archaeologia.* $95/£61

RICHTER, GISELA. Kouroi. Phaidon, 1960. (Ex-lib, ink stamp tp verso, lib bkpl.) Dj (sl chipped, #s). *Edwards.* $133/£85

RICHTER, HANS. Dreams That Money Can Buy. NY: Films Intl, n.d. 1st ed. Fine in grn wraps ptd in black. *Beasley.* $65/£42

RICHTER, JULIUS. A History of Protestant Missions in the Near East. 1910. 1st ed. (Lt margin browning, upper hinge cracked; spine lt faded, sl rubbed.) *Edwards.* $117/£75

RICKARD, T. A. Journeys of Observation. SF: Dewey, 1907. 1st ed. 42 photo plts, 2 maps. Pict cl (extrems lt rubbed, lt soil). NF. *Argonaut.* $150/£96

RICKARD, T. A. Through the Yukon and Alaska. SF: Mining & Scientific Press, 1909. Dec cl. (White spine title sl flaked), else VG. *High Latitude.* $110/£71

RICKARD, T. A. Through the Yukon and Alaska. SF: Mining & Scientific Press, 1909. Good. *Perier.* $145/£93

RICKARDS, CONSTANTINE GEORGE. The Ruins of Mexico. Vol I. London: H.E. Shrimpton, 1910. Frontis, 259 illus tipped in. (Worming, foxing; corner bumped.) *Archaeologia.* $100/£64

RICKERT, MARGARET. Painting in Britain. The Middle Ages. Balt, 1954. 192 plts. Good. *Washton.* $60/£38

RICKERT, MARGARET. The Reconstructed Carmelite Missal. Chicago, 1952. 59 plts (3 color). (2 feps sl creased), o/w VG. *Washton.* $75/£48

RICKETSON, SHADRACH. Means of Preserving Health, and Preventing Diseases.... NY, 1806. 1st ed. 298pp + ads. Contemp sheep (joints weak). *Argosy.* $400/£256

RICKETT, HAROLD WILLIAM. Wild Flowers of the United States. Volume III, parts 1 and 2: Texas. NY, (1969). 2 vols. (Lt worn.) *Oinonen*.* $140/£90

RICKETT, HAROLD WILLIAM. Wild Flowers of the United States: Volume Four—The Southwestern States. NY: McGraw-Hill, n.d. (1970). 3 vols. Fine set (ink note tp) in box (sl worn). *Dumont.* $325/£208

RICKETTS, C. S. The Art of the Prado. Boston: Page, 1907. 1st ed thus. Teg, others uncut. (Old repair to short marginal tear), o/w VG in dec cl. *Cox.* $23/£15

RICKETTS, CHARLES. Unrecorded Histories. Secker, 1933. 1st ed. Ltd ed. Red/beige dec buckram. VG. *Whiteson.* $101/£65

RICKETTS, CHARLES. Unrecorded Histories. London: Martin Secker, 1933. Ltd to 950. Teg. Pale yellow cl dec in red. Good. *Karmiole.* $85/£54

RICKETTS, P. Notes on Assaying and Assay Schemes. NY: Art Ptg Est, 1876. 1st ed. 172pp + ads, errata slip; fldg chart. Good. *Blake.* $60/£38

RICKMAN, JOHN. Laird of the Lighthouses. London: Rickman, 1944. 1st ed. Card cvrs. NF. *Virgo.* $19/£12

RICORD, PHILIPPE. A Practical Treatise on Venereal Disorders.... Phila: Haswell et al, 1840. 38pp (foxing). Newly rebound in antique style cl. *Goodrich.* $75/£48

RIDDELL, JAMES. The Ski Runs of Austria. London, 1958. 1st ed. Dj (chipped). *Edwards.* $23/£15

RIDDELL, JOHN. The John Riddell Murder Case: A Philo Vance Parody. NY: Scribner, 1930. 1st ed. (Inscrips; pp spotted), o/w VG in dj (sl dknd). *Mordida.* $75/£48

RIDDELL, VICTOR HORSLEY. Blood Transfusion. London, 1939. 1st ed. VG. *Doctor's Library.* $60/£38

RIDDLE, GEORGE W. History of Early Days in Oregon. Riddle, OR, 1920. Port, plt. Stapled ptd wrappers. (Overlap edges chipped), else VG. *Reese.* $75/£48

RIDDLE, KENYON. Records and Maps of the Old Santa Fe Trail. Raton, 1949. 1st ed. Fldg map. Fine. *Turpen.* $48/£31

RIDDLE, KENYON. Records and Maps of the Santa Fe Trail. Stuart, FL: Southeastern Ptg Co, 1963. 8 fldg maps. Fine. *Dumont.* $25/£16

RIDDLE, MAXWELL. The Springer Spaniel. Chicago: Judy, 1939. Stated 1st ed. NF (name) in VG+ dj. *Backman.* $35/£22

RIDEING, WILLIAM H. Boys in the Mountains and on the Plains. NY: Appleton, 1882. 1st ed. viii,345pp + 6pp ads. Floral eps. Dec red cl (rear hinge sl tender, corner bumped, lt scuffed). VG. *Five Quail.* $150/£96

RIDEING, WILLIAM H. Overland Express. Ashland: Lewis Osborne, 1970. One of 650. Ad laid in. Red cl, gilt. Fine in plain dj. *Bohling.* $25/£16

RIDGE, LOLA. Dance of Fire. NY: Harrison Smith & Robert Haas, 1935. 1st ed. Black cl spine, ptd copper foil over bds. Fine in NF copper foil dj (sl edgeworn). *Turtle Island.* $50/£32

RIDGER, A. LOTON. A Wanderer's Trail. NY: Holt, 1914. Frontis port. Red cl. VG+. *Bohling.* $30/£19

RIDGWAY, J. L. Scientific Illustration. Stanford, 1938. Color frontis, 23 plts. (Sl scuffed.) *Maggs.* $34/£22

RIDING, LAURA and ROBERT GRAVES. A Pamphlet Against Anthologies. Cape, 1928. 1st ed. (Name, date; edges, prelims sl soiled; spine head sl pulled), o/w VG. *Poetry Bookshop.* $53/£34

RIDING, LAURA. Everybody's Letters. Arthur Barker, 1933. 1st Eng ed. NF in dj (sl creased, chipped). *Clearwater.* $234/£150

RIDING, LAURA. Progress of Stories. Deya/London: Seizen Press/Constable, (1935). 1st ed. Pale grn cl. (Cl sl sunned through dj), else NF in dj (spine lt tanned). *Reese.* $350/£224

RIDINGS, SAM P. The Chisholm Trail. Guthrie, 1936. 1st ed. Fldg map. (Corners sl bumped), o/w Fine in dj (soiled). Howes R281. *Baade.* $350/£224

RIDLER, ANNE. Cain. (London): Nicholson & Watson, (1945). 1st ed. VG in dj (wear, esp spine). *Antic Hay.* $25/£16

RIDLER, ANNE. The Golden Bird. London: Faber & Faber, (1951). 1st ed. NF in dj. *Antic Hay.* $25/£16

RIDPATH, JOHN CLARK. The Life and Work of James A. Garfield.... Jones Bros, 1882. 1st ed. Pict cl, gilt. (Extrems sl rubbed; fore-edge lt foxed.). *Sadlon.* $15/£10

RIDPATH, JOHN CLARK. A Popular History of the U.S. of America, from the Aboriginal Times to the Present Day.... Cincinnati: Jones Bros, (1889). Rev, enlgd ed. (Fore-edge sl foxing; extrems sl rubbed, short break top joint.) *Sadlon.* $15/£10

RIEFENSTAHL, LENI. The Last of the Nuba. NY, (1973). 1st Amer ed. VG in dj (sl stained, rubbed). *King.* $95/£61

RIGGS, STEPHEN R. Mary and I. Forty Years with the Sioux. Chicago: Holmes, (1880). 1st ed. (20),388pp; 2 ports. (Spine lt discolored.) Howes R288. *Ginsberg.* $175/£112

RIGNEY, FRANCIS J. and L. DOUGLAS SMITH. The Real Bohemia. NY: Basic Bks, 1961. 1st ed. NF in VG+ dj. *Sclanders.* $28/£18

RIIS, JACOB A. The Making of an American. NY: Macmillan, 1904. Later ptg. Good (inscrip). *Smith.* $40/£26

RIIS, JACOB A. Theodore Roosevelt, the Citizen. NY, 1904. 1st ed. VG (fr inner hinges sl weak). *Hayman.* $20/£13

RIKHOFF, JIM. Hunting the World's Mountains. Clinton: Amwell, (1984). One of 1000 numbered, signed. 2 vols. Aeg. Full leather (lt worn). Slipcase. *Oinonen*.* $100/£64

RILEY, ELIHU SAMUEL. Stonewall Jackson. A Thesaurus of Anecdotes and Incidents.... Annapolis, MD, 1920. 1st ed. Frontis of Jackson. VG (edges lt chipped, backstrip repaired w/cl, tape) in ptd wrappers. *Mcgowan.* $450/£288

RILEY, JAMES WHITCOMB. All the Year Round. Indianapolis, (1912). 1st ed. 12 color woodcuts. (Sl soiled.) *Swann*.* $258/£165

RILEY, JAMES WHITCOMB. Armazindy. Indianapolis, 1894. 1st Amer ed. Frontis. Teg. Fine. *Polyanthos.* $25/£16

RILEY, JAMES WHITCOMB. The Complete Works of James Whitcomb Riley: Including Poems and Prose Sketches.... NY: Harper & Bros, (c. 1916). Memorial ed. 10 vols. Frontis each vol. Teg; dec red cl binding. Fine. *Graf.* $75/£48

RILEY, JAMES WHITCOMB. The Flying Islands of the Night. Indianapolis, (1913). 1st ed thus. 16 tipped-in full-pg color plts (w/lettered tissue guards) by Franklin Booth. Cl-backed gilt-stamped pict bds (bumped, cvrs worn, soiled). *King.* $95/£61

RILEY, JAMES WHITCOMB. A Hoosier Romance. N.p., (1912). 1st ed. Fr cvr paste plt. VG. *Mcclintock.* $22/£14

RILEY, JAMES WHITCOMB. The Old Swimmin'-Hole and 'Leven More Poems. Indianapolis: Bowen-Merrill, 1891. 1st ed, 1st state. Teg. Binding state A, w/plt inserted opposite pg1. Grn/dk grn cl, gilt. VG. BAL 16576. *Houle.* $125/£80

RILEY, JAMES WHITCOMB. Riley Love-Lyrics. Indianapolis: Bobbs-Merrill, (1902). 1st illus ed, ltr ptg. Frontis, guard. VG (spine sl faded). *Cahan.* $50/£32

RILEY, JAMES WHITCOMB. Songs O' Cheer. Indianapolis, IN, 1905. 1st ed. VF. *Bond.* $30/£19

RILEY, JAMES. An Authentic Narrative of the Loss of the American Brig Commerce.... NY: The Author, 1817. 1st ed. Frontis port, xvi,554,xvipp, fldg map, 8 copper engr plts (foxing, soiling to text, plts). Orig calf (rubbed). *Karmiole.* $150/£96

RILEY, JAMES. An Authentic Narrative of the Loss of the American Brig Commerce.... Chillicothe, OH, 1820. Engr frontis port. (Leaf Dd2 w/partial loss along fore-edge margin, affecting about 20 words, 1 leaf w/paper loss, affecting several words.) Contemp calf. *Swann*.* $92/£59

RILEY, JAMES. An Authentic Narrative of the Loss of the American Brig Commerce.... Hartford, CT: Andrus & Judd, 1833. 271pp; 9 copper plts. Full morocco. (Lacks map, lt foxed, damp-staining; worn, fr cvr detached), o/w Good. *Worldwide.* $45/£29

RILING, RAY. Guns and Shooting, a Selected Chronological Bibliography. NY, (1951). One of 1500. Inscribed, signed. *Freeman*.* $90/£58

RILING, RAY. Guns and Shooting. NY: Greenberg, (1951). One of 1500. VG in dj (chipped). *Scribe's Perch**. $70/£45

RILKE, RAINER MARIA. The Lay of the Love and Death of Cornet Christoph Rilke. SF: Arion, 1983. One of 300. Prospectus laid in. *Swann**. $103/£66

RILKE, RAINER MARIA. The Letters of Rainer Maria Rilke and Princess Marie Von Thurn Und Taxis. Nora Wydenbruck (trans). Hogarth, 1958. 1st ed. VG. *Poetry Bookshop*. $16/£10

RILKE, RAINER MARIA. Letters to Merline: 1919-1922. Violet M. MacDonald (trans). London: Methuen, 1951. 1st Eng ed. Fine in dj (soil rear panel). *Antic Hay*. $25/£16

RILKE, RAINER MARIA. Selected Poems. C.F. MacIntyre (trans). NY: LEC, 1981. One of 2000 signed by Robert Kipniss (illus). 4 full-pg lithos. Cl-backed bds. VG (lacks slipcase). *Waverly**. $49/£31

RIMMEL, EUGENE. The Book of Perfumes. London: Chapman & Hall, 1865. 1st ed. xx,266pp + ad leaf; chromolitho. Gauffred edges. Moire silk (frayed, lt soiled), gilt. Sound. *Cox*. $133/£85

RIMMER, ALFRED. Ancient Stone Crosses of England. London, 1875. 1st ed. xii,159pp. (Extrems sl rubbed.) *Edwards*. $47/£30

RIMMER, ALFRED. Ancient Streets and Homesteads of England. London: Macmillan, 1877. 340pp (bkpl). Aeg. 1/2 grn leather, gilt. Good- (4-inch tear fr joint). *Scribe's Perch**. $20/£13

RIMMER, ROBERT H. The Harrad Experiment. L.A.: Sherbourne, (1966). 1st ed. (Corners sl bumped), else Fine in dj (lt wear). *Between The Covers*. $150/£96

RIN-CHEN, LHA-MO. We Tibetans. Phila: Lippincott, 1926. 1st Amer ed. Frontis. Mustard cl. VG. *Terramedia*. $125/£80

RINDER, EDITH WINGATE (trans). The Massacre of the Innocents and Other Tales by Belgian Writers. Chicago: Stone & Kimball, 1895. 1st ed. xii,292,(ii)pp; colophon leaf at end. Teg, others uncut. Pale grn linen, gilt. Nice. *Temple*. $34/£22

RINDER, FRANK. D.Y. Cameron: An Illustrated Catalogue of His Etched Work. Glasgow, 1912. #328/700. (Internal spotting, offsetting; lt wear.) *Freeman**. $110/£71

RINDFLEISCH, EDUARD. A Manual of Pathological Histology.... E. Buchanan Baxter (trans). London, 1872. 2 vols. xiii,464; viii,410pp (ex-lib, ink stamps tps). Mod cl (rebound). *Edwards*. $47/£30

RINEHART, MARY ROBERTS and AVERY HOPWOOD. The Bat. NY: Doran, (1926). 1st ed. Fine in NF dj (spine top sl soiled). *Between The Covers*. $225/£144

RINEHART, MARY ROBERTS. The Amazing Adventures of Letitia Carberry. Indianapolis, (1911). 1st Amer ed. NF (name; spine sl sunned, extrems sl rubbed). *Polyanthos*. $25/£16

RINEHART, MARY ROBERTS. The Circular Staircase. Indianapolis: Bobbs-Merrill, (1908). 1st US ed, 1st bk. Olive grn cl (w/staircase design in black at fr). With 'September' on copyright pg. VG. *Gravesend*. $100/£64

RINEHART, MARY ROBERTS. The Red Lamp. NY, (1925). 1st ed. VG (spine top chipped) in color emb dj (spine ends chipped, creased). *Mcclintock*. $35/£22

RINEHART, MARY ROBERTS. Temperamental People. NY: Doran, (1924). 1st ed. Fine in NF dj (few tears). *Between The Covers*. $85/£54

RINGGOLD, FAITH. Tar Beach. NY: Crown, (1988). 1st ed. 12mo. Fine in glossy bds. *Between The Covers*. $35/£22

RINHART, FLOYD and MARION. America's Affluent Age. South Brunswick/NY: A.S. Barnes, 1971. 1st ed. NF in dj (lt chipped). *Cahan*. $165/£106

RINHART, FLOYD and MARION. The American Daguerreotype. Athens: Univ of GA, 1981. 1st ed. Fine in illus dj. *Cahan*. $65/£42

RINHART, FLOYD and MARION. American Miniature Case Art. South Brunswick/NY: A.S. Barnes, 1969. 1st ed. 229 plts. VG (name stamp) in dj (chipped, worn). *Cahan*. $165/£106

RIPLEY, EDWARD HASTINGS. Vermont General, the Unusual War Experiences of Edward Hastings Ripley (1862-1865). Otto Eisenschiml (ed). NY, 1960. 1st ed. VG+ in VG+ dj. *Pratt*. $55/£35

RIPLEY, OZARD. Bass and Bass Fishing. Cincinnati, 1924. 1st ed. Tan cl. *Cullen*. $35/£22

RIPLEY, OZARK. Jist Huntin': Tales of the Forest, Field and Stream. Cincinnati, (1921). (Ink name), else Fine. *Truepenny*. $45/£29

RIPLEY, S. DILLON. Search for the Spiny Babbler. Boston: Houghton Mifflin, 1952. 1st ed. VG in dj (sl torn). *Worldwide*. $24/£15

RIPLEY, SHERMAN. Raggedy Animals. Chicago/NY: Rand McNally, (1935). Rpt. Harrison Cady (illus). 8vo. 32 leaves. Color pict grn bds (soiled, rubbed, bumped). VG. *Blue Mountain*. $65/£42

RIPPINGALE, O. H. and D. F. McMICHAEL. Queensland and Great Barrier Reef Shells. Brisbane: Jaacaranda, 1961. 1st ed. 29 color plts, map. (Bd lt soiled.) *Parmer*. $30/£19

RISHEL, C. D. (ed). The Life and Adventures of David Lewis the Robber and Counterfeiter. Newville, PA: C.D. Rishel, 1890. 1st ed thus. 84pp. (Last text pg, fr wrap stained; lacks rear wrap), o/w Good. Howes R315. *Brown*. $100/£64

RISTER, CARL COKE. Border Command. Norman, 1944. 1st ed. Fine in dj (lt wear). *Pratt*. $55/£35

RISTER, CARL COKE. Border Command: General Phil Sheridan in the West. Norman: Univ of OK, 1944. 1st ed. Good (lib blind stamp tp). *Lien*. $45/£29

RISTER, CARL COKE. Comanche Bondage, Dr. Chas. Beale's Settlement of la Villa de Dolores.... Glendale, 1955. 1st ed. One of 1063. Frontis. Good+ (numbers painted out on spine). *Turpen*. $85/£54

RISTER, CARL COKE. Comanche Bondage. Glendale: Clark, 1955. 1st ed. One of 1063. Lt blue cl. VF. *Argonaut*. $200/£128

RISTER, CARL COKE. Land Hunger. Norman, 1942. 1st ed. Fine. *Baade*. $45/£29

RISTER, CARL COKE. No Man's Land. Norman, 1948. 1st ed. Fine (sigs tp) in dj (chipped, worn). *Baade*. $65/£42

RITCH, JOHNNY. Horsefeathers. Helena, MT: The Author, (1941). 2nd ptg. Good. *Heinoldt*. $25/£16

RITCHIE, ANDREW CARNDUFF. Abstract Painting and Sculpture in America. NY: MOMA, 1951. 7 color plts. Dj (sl browned, chipped). *Edwards*. $31/£20

RITCHIE, G. S. Challenger, the Life of a Survey Ship. London, 1957. Dj (sl frayed). *Maggs*. $50/£32

RITCHIE, J. M. Concerning the Blind. Edinburgh/London, 1930. Fore/lower edge uncut. (Feps lt browned.) *Edwards*. $47/£30

RITCHIE, ROBERT WELLES. The Hell-Roarin' Forty-Niners. NY: J.H. Sears, (1928). 1st ed. 8 plts, incl frontis. Red cl. Fine in pict dj. *Pacific**. $98/£63

RITTENHOUSE, J. D. Maverick Tales. NY, 1971. 1st ed. Fine in dj (edgewear, price-clipped). *Baade*. $45/£29

RITTENHOUSE, J. D. The Story of Disturnell's Treaty Map. Santa Fe: Stagecoach, 1965. Lg fldg map. VG. *Dumont*. $75/£48

RITZ, CHARLES. A Fly Fisher's Life. NY: Henry Holt, 1959. 1st ed. 32 b/w photo plts. VG. *Argosy.* $200/£128

RITZ, CHARLES. A Fly Fisher's Life. NY: Holt, 1960. 1st Amer ed. VG+ in VG dj. *Bowman.* $75/£48

River Dove. (By John Lavicourt Anderson.) Pickering, 1847. Paper label. VG (cl sl dull). *Petersfield.* $140/£90

RIVERS, CONRAD KENT. The Still Voice of Harlem. London: Paul Breman, 1968. 1st ed. Fine in pict wrappers. *Reese.* $40/£26

RIVERS, R. H. The Life of Robert Pains, D.D., Bishop of the Methodist Episcopal Church, South. Nashville, 1884. 1st ed. 314pp. *Ginsberg.* $100/£64

RIVET, PAUL. Maya Cities. London: Paul Elek, (1973). Frontis, 10 color plts. Good in dj. *Archaeologia.* $45/£29

RIVOIRA, G. T. Roman Architecture and Its Principles of Construction Under the Empire. Oxford, 1925. Port. Sound. *Ars Artis.* $195/£125

RIVOIRA, G. T. Roman Architecture.... Oxford: Clarendon, 1925. Frontis. Good. *Archaeologia.* $250/£160

RIVOLIER, JEAN. Emperor Penguins. London: Elek Books, 1956. 1st ed in English. (Offset to eps; sl musty odor.) Lt blue cl. Dj (worn). *Parmer.* $35/£22

ROACH, ALVA C. The Prisoner of War, and How Treated. Indianapolis: Railroad City Pub House, 1865. 1st ed. 250pp. Good (rubbed, scuffed, neatly rebacked, recased.) Howes R334. *Mcgowan.* $225/£144

ROACH, ALVA C. The Prisoner of War, and How Treated. Indianapolis: Railroad, 1865. 1st ed. Howes R334. *Ginsberg.* $300/£192

ROACH, F. Cultivated Fruits of Britain, Their Origin and History. London, 1985. Dj. *Maggs.* $28/£18

ROBACK, ABRAHAM AARON. Behaviorism and Psychology. Cambridge, (MA): Univ Bookstore, 1923. 1st ed. Inscribed. Fldg chart. Crimson cl (lt stained, shelfworn). Good+. *Gach.* $65/£42

ROBACK, ABRAHAM AARON. The Psychology of Common Sense. Cambridge, (MA): Sci-Art, (1939). 1st ed. Presentation copy. Panelled grn cl, painted labels. VG. *Gach.* $65/£42

ROBB, DAVID M. The Art of the Illuminated Manuscript. A.S. Barnes, 1973. VG (text underlining, sticker; corners bumped) in dj (chipped, torn, repaired w/tape). *My Bookhouse.* $30/£19

ROBBINS, ARCHIBALD. Comprising an Account of the Loss of the Brig Commerce of Hartford.... Greenwich: Conde Nast, 1931. Ltd to 350. Signed by Earle Winslow (illus). Aeg. Dec full beige leather. VG in slipcase (worn, lt soiled). *Parmer.* $125/£80

ROBBINS, RUTH. Taliesin and King Arthur. SF: Parnassus, 1970. 1st ed. 7 x 8 1/4. 34pp. VG in dj. *Cattermole.* $20/£13

ROBBINS, TOM. Still Life with Woodpecker. NY: Bantam, 1980. 1st ed. (Fore-edge dusted), else NF in dj. *Lame Duck.* $125/£80

Robert Louis Stevenson. A Catalogue of the Henry E. Gerstley Stevenson Collection. Princeton, 1971. *Freeman*.* $30/£19

ROBERTS, B. H. A Comprehensive History of the Church of Jesus Christ of Latter-Day Saints, Century 1, Vols. 1-6. Salt Lake, 1930. 1st ed. Mis-matched index. Marginalia, mks, typed notes (glued to pg margins) of Samuel W. Taylor. VG. *Benchmark.* $350/£224

ROBERTS, CECIL. A Man Arose. NY: Macmillan, 1941. 1st ed. Signed presentation. Frontis port. Blue cl. Fine. *Antic Hay.* $45/£29

ROBERTS, DAVID. The Holy Land, Syria, Idumea, Arabia, Egypt and Nubia.... London: Day & Son, 1855-56. 6 vols in 3. 4to. 6 tinted litho titles, 242 tinted litho plts (few w/lt spotted margins), 2 engr maps. 19th-cent red 1/2 morocco, gilt. *Christie's*.* $3,334/£2,137

ROBERTS, EDWARD. With the Invader; Glimpses of the Southwest. SF: Carson, 1885. 1st ed. 156pp. Orig ptd pict wrappers. *Ginsberg.* $150/£96

ROBERTS, ELIZABETH MADOX. The Great Meadow. NY: Viking, 1930. 1st ed. Lg paper ed. Ltd to 295 numbered, signed, w/color fldg map. Grn cl. Fine in box (worn). *New Hampshire*.* $35/£22

ROBERTS, ELIZABETH MADOX. Under the Tree. NY: Huebsch, 1922. 1st ed. NF in dj (lt soiled, spine extrems sl worn). *Captain's Bookshelf.* $350/£224

ROBERTS, GEORGIA. The Toy Village. Ernest Nister, ca 1900. Katharine Greenland (illus). Obl 4to. (46pp) (2 leaf edges tattered, sm tears, chips other ll; leaf bound out of sequence; new eps). Pict bds, cl spine (recased; sl mks, grazes). Good. *Bookmark.* $257/£165

ROBERTS, H. The Dwellings of the Labouring Classes. London: By request of Soc for Improving the Condition of the Labouring Classes, (1853). 3rd ed. 65pp + 12 litho plts (1 w/tear blank margin). Dec cl. *Ars Artis.* $234/£150

ROBERTS, H. ARMSTRONG. The Farmer His Own Builder. Phila: McKay, (1918). 1st ed. Fine in NF dj. *Second Life.* $40/£26

ROBERTS, H. W. Architectural Sketching and Drawings in Perspective. 1906. 36 plts. (Sl spotted; spine sl faded.) *Edwards.* $55/£35

ROBERTS, KENNETH (comp). March to Quebec: Journals of the Members of Arnold's Expedition. GC: Doubleday Doran, 1938. 1st ed. (Sl tear top tp), else Fine in NF dj (internal repairs; soiling). *Between The Covers.* $125/£80

ROBERTS, KENNETH. The Battle of Cowpens: The Great Morale Builder. NY, 1958. 1st ed. NF in VG+ dj. *Warren.* $30/£19

ROBERTS, KENNETH. Lydia Bailey. GC: Doubleday, 1947. One of 1050 numbered, signed w/pg of ms (w/changes by author in ink) bound in. Inscribed presentation. Fine in slipcase (sl worn). *Lenz.* $200/£128

ROBERTS, KENNETH. Lydia Bailey. NY: Doubleday, 1947. 1st ed. #642/1050 numbered, signed. (Spine dknd), o/w VG in slipcase (sunned, rubbed, some seams starting). *Hermitage.* $225/£144

ROBERTS, KENNETH. Northwest Passage. GC, 1937. 1st ed. One of 1050. Signed. 2 vols. (Sl waterstain bottom edge vol 1.) Djs (soiled). *Kane*.* $95/£61

ROBERTS, KENNETH. Trending into Maine. Boston: Little Brown, 1938. One of 1075 signed by Roberts and N.C. Wyeth (illus). Glassine dj; slipcase. *Swann*.* $287/£184

ROBERTS, LES. An Infinite Number of Monkeys. NY: St. Martin's, 1987. 1st ed. Signed. Fine in dj. *Mordida.* $35/£22

ROBERTS, LORD. Forty-One Years in India from Subaltern to Commander-in-Chief. London, 1897. 22nd ed. 2 vols. Frontis, xx,511; xii,522pp. Dec blue cl (corner rubbed, rest sl bumped), gilt. *Maggs.* $94/£60

ROBERTS, LORD. Forty-One Years in India. London, 1898. 27th ed. 2 vols. xx,511; xii,522pp. Gilt 1/4 morocco. *Terramedia.* $125/£80

ROBERTS, MORLEY. The Flying Cloud. Boston: Page, 1907. 1st Amer ed. Pict brn cl. VG. *Antic Hay.* $20/£13

ROBERTS, OCTAVIA. Lincoln in Illinois. Boston: Houston, 1918. 1st ed. One of 1000. 25 plts. Pict bds, cl spine. *Ginsberg.* $75/£48

ROBERTS, OLIVER. The Great Understander. Aurora: William W. Walter, (1931). Article incl. Ribbed pict cl. *Dawson.* $125/£80

ROBERTSON, DAVID. A History of the High Constables of Edinburgh.... Edinburgh: High Constables of Edinburgh, 1924. Blue cl (sl faded), gilt. Very Nice. *Boswell.* $75/£48

ROBERTSON, ELSIE. Where the Sea-Flag Floats. Elgin, IL: David C. Cook, (1912). 1st ed. Dec cl. *Lefkowicz.* $35/£22

ROBERTSON, FRANK C. and BETH KAY HARRIS. Soapy Smith, King of the Frontier Con Men. NY: Hastings House, (1961). 1st ed. Dk red cl. Fine in dj. *Argonaut.* $45/£29

ROBERTSON, FRED L. Soldiers of Florida in the Seminole, Indian-Civil and Spanish-American Wars. (Live Oak): Board of State Institutions, 1903. 1st ed. New cl, leather label. *Ginsberg.* $300/£192

ROBERTSON, GEORGE. Chitral. London, 1899. 2nd ed. x,368pp + 40pp pub's cat; fldg map, 4 plans (1 fldg). Teg. *Edwards.* $78/£50

ROBERTSON, GEORGE. Outline of the Life of George Robertson, Written by Himself. Lexington: Transylvania Ptg & Pub, 1876. Frontis port, 209pp, errata. Good (old lib mks; extrems frayed). Howes R351. *Bohling.* $65/£42

ROBERTSON, H. R. Life on the Upper Thames. London, 1875. x,214pp (lt browned). Aeg. Contemp dec cl (dampstaining, esp lower bd). *Edwards.* $148/£95

ROBERTSON, J. DRUMMOND. The Evolution of Clockwork with a Special Selection on the Clocks of Japan.... London: Cassell, (1931). 1st ed. Frontis. Maroon cl (bumped, rubbed). VG (sig). *Weber.* $100/£64

ROBERTSON, J. M. (ed). The Philosophical Works of Francis Bacon. 1905. (Pastedowns, fep torn; fr cvr mkd, spine sl defective, corners sl worn.) *Whitehart.* $39/£25

ROBERTSON, JOHN (comp). Michigan in the War. Lansing, 1882. 2nd ed. 3/4 leather (repaired w/lib tape, exterior hinge cracks). Interior VG. *Mcclintock.* $50/£32

ROBERTSON, WILFRID. Rhodesian Rancher. London, 1935. 1st ed. (Feps lt browned.) Dj (chipped, sl loss). *Edwards.* $31/£20

ROBERTSON, WILLIAM BELL and F. WALKER. The Royal Clocks in Windsor Castle, Buckingham Palace, St. James' Palace and Hampton Court. London, 1905. 2nd ed. Fine in ptd red wrappers. *Weber.* $40/£26

ROBERTSON, WILLIAM. An Historical Disquisition Concerning the Knowledge Which the Ancients Had of India. Phila: Ptd by Wm. Young, 1792. viii,13-420pp. New 1/4 calf, red label. VG. *Adelson.* $185/£119

ROBERTSON, WILLIAM. The History of America. London: A. Strahan et al, 1792. 6th ed. 3 vols. Full contemp tree calf, gilt, gilt-dec spines, gilt-lettered grn/red morocco spine labels. *D & D.* $395/£253

ROBERTSON, WILLIAM. The History of America. Phila: Simon Probasco, 1821. 2nd Amer ed. 2 vols. Untrimmed. Orig paper bds, ptd spine labels. (Paper dknd, lt foxed; spines chipped, bds soiled, sl worn.) Howes R358. *Bohling.* $45/£29

ROBERTSON, WILLIAM. The History of the Reign of Charles V. With a View of the Progress of Society in Europe.... London: T. Cadell & W. Davies, 1802. 10th ed. 4 vols. Frontis plt. Full contemp speckled calf, gilt-dec spines, gilt-lettered black morocco spine labels. Internally Bright. *D & D.* $325/£208

ROBERTSON, WILLIAM. The History of the Reign of the Emperor Charles the Fifth. Boston, 1857. 3 vols. xviii,618; 604; 565pp. All edges, eps marbled. Contemp 1/2 calf, dec gilt spines, black/brn morocco spine labels. VG set. *Truepenny.* $175/£112

ROBESON, ESLANDA GOODE. African Journey. NY: John Day, (1945). 1st ed. Fine in Good dj (sl chipped, clean split upper flap fold). *Reese.* $45/£29

ROBINETT, P. M. Armor Command. DC, 1958. VG. *Clark.* $95/£61

Robinson Crusoe. NY: McLoughlin Bros, 1889. Robinson Crusoe Series. 10.5x8.5. (16)pp, 6 color illus. Pict color wraps (wear, sl chipping, creasing). *King.* $45/£29

Robinson Crusoe. Pantomime Toy Books. NY: McLoughlin, 1893. 4to. Shapebook. 7 full pp. Stiff paper cvr, red cl spines rt/left edges (spine sl discolored, lt dusted), else VG. *Hobbyhorse.* $300/£192

ROBINSON, A. J. Memorandum and Anecdotes of the Civil War. N.p., (1912). Port, map. (Cvrs spotted; bottom edge, back cvr stained), else Good. *King.* $45/£29

ROBINSON, ALFRED. Life in California. NY, 1969. Rpt of 1846 ed. Fine. Howes R363. *Turpen.* $95/£61

ROBINSON, ALFRED. Life in California...and a Historical Account of the Origin, Customs and Traditions of the Indians of Alta California. Oakland: Biobooks, 1947. Ltd to 750 ptd. 8 plts. Uncut. Gray/grn buckram, ptd paper spine label. (Spine lt faded), o/w Fine. *Pacific*.* $69/£44

ROBINSON, B. W. Persian Paintings in the John Rylands Library. NY: Sotheby Parke Bernet, 1980. Fine in Fine dj. *Metropolitan*.* $40/£26

ROBINSON, BEVERLEY W. With Shotgun and Rifle in North American Game Fields. NY/London: D. Appleton, 1925. 1st ed. Frontis. Gilt lettering. VG+. *Backman.* $85/£54

ROBINSON, BRADLEY. Dark Companion. London, 1948. VG in dj. *High Latitude.* $20/£13

ROBINSON, BRADLEY. Dark Companion. NY: National Travel Club, c. 1947. Photo illus rep. VG in dj. *High Latitude.* $25/£16

ROBINSON, CHARLES N. The British Tar in Fact and Fiction. London, 1911. 2nd ed. Frontis. Navy cl. *Maggs.* $70/£45

ROBINSON, CHARLES N. Old Naval Prints. London: The Studio, 1929. One of 1500 numbered. 96 plts, incl 24 tipped-on color repros. Full navy linen, beveled bds. (Lt rubbed, spine faded), else VG. *Waverly*.* $99/£63

ROBINSON, CHARLES N. Old Naval Prints/Their Artists and Engravers. London: The Studio, 1924. One of 1500. 4to. 96 plts, 24 tipped-in color plts, tissue guards. Gilt-dec blue cl. VG (lt foxing). *Parmer.* $650/£417

ROBINSON, CHARLES. The Kansas Conflict. NY: Harper, 1892. 1st ed. (Lt soil, spine edges sl worn.) *Glenn.* $125/£80

ROBINSON, CONWAY. An Account of Discoveries in the West Until 1519. Richmond, 1848. 1st ed. 491pp (bkpls, heavily foxed, sl stained, chipped). Later cl. *King.* $125/£80

ROBINSON, DEREK. Rotten With Honor. NY: Viking, 1973. 1st ed. NF in NF dj (sl edgeworn). *Fuller & Saunders.* $20/£13

ROBINSON, DOANE. A History of the Dakota or Sioux Indians. Minneapolis: Ross & Haines, 1956. VG in dj (tape-reinforced). *Lien.* $35/£22

ROBINSON, EDWIN ARLINGTON. Dionysus in Doubt: A Book of Poems. NY: Macmillan, 1925. 1st ed. Ltd to 350 signed. Unopened. Cl-backed bds, paper label. (Sm tape mks fr pastedown), o/w NF. *Cahan.* $60/£38

ROBINSON, EDWIN ARLINGTON. The Glory of the Nightingale. NY: Macmillan, 1930. One of 500 numbered, signed. Fine in Fine slipcase. *Lenz.* $200/£128

ROBINSON, EDWIN ARLINGTON. Matthias at the Door. NY: Macmillan, 1931. 1st ed. One of 500 specially bound, signed. Teg. Grn cl, spine label. (Spine sl faded), o/w Fine in slipcase (worn). *Jaffe.* $75/£48

ROBINSON, EDWIN ARLINGTON. Modred a Fragment. NY/New Haven: Princeton/Edmund Bryne Hackett/Brickrow Book Shop, 1929. 1st ed. #243/250 signed. Black cl spine, dk blue bds. Fine in dk blue slipcase (sl rubbed). *Lucas.* $65/£42

ROBINSON, EDWIN ARLINGTON. Roman Bartholow. NY: Macmillan, 1923. One of 750 numbered, signed. VG (cvrs sl dknd). *Lenz.* $150/£96

ROBINSON, EDWIN ARLINGTON. Tristram. NY: Macmillan, 1927. One of 350 numbered, signed. Fine. *Lenz.* $200/£128

ROBINSON, ERIC and DOUGLAS McKIE (eds). Partners in Science. Letters of James Watt and Joseph Black. London: Constable, (1970). 1st ed. VG in dj. *Glaser.* $30/£19

ROBINSON, FAYETTE. An Account of the Organization of the Army of the U.S. Phila, 1848. 1st ed. 2 vols. Frontis, 36 ports. Blind-stamped brn cl (sl foxed, extrems lt worn), spine gilt. VG +. Howes R365. *Turpen.* $295/£189

ROBINSON, J. B. The Serpent of Sugar Creek Colony. Phila, 1885. 128pp. Good. *Hayman.* $25/£16

ROBINSON, J. H. Silver-Knife. Boston: Wm. Spencer, 1854. 2nd ed. 168pp. Good (paper dknd, writing on ep, fr hinge cracked, sl shaken; chipped). Howes R367. *Bohling.* $350/£224

ROBINSON, JACOB S. A Journal of the Santa Fe Expedition Under Col. Doniphan. Princeton, 1932. Rpt of 1848 1st ed. VG. Howes R368. *Turpen.* $40/£26

ROBINSON, JACOB S. A Journal of the Santa Fe Expedition Under Colonel Doniphan. Princeton, 1932. Rpt. Frontis. Maroon bds, gilt. VG + (bkpl) in dj (chipped, worn). *Bohling.* $30/£19

ROBINSON, JAMES H. Journal of an Expedition 1400 Miles Up the Orinoco and 300 Up the Arauca. London: Black, Young & Young, 1822. 1st ed. 8vo. 7 aquatint plts (1 neatly hand-colored). Contemp 3/4 grn morocco, marbled bds. Fine. *Appelfeld.* $650/£417

ROBINSON, JAMES. American Arithmetick. Boston: Lincoln, 1825. 1st ed. 234,(6)pp. Contemp marbled bds, calf spine. *Ginsberg.* $150/£96

ROBINSON, JOHN BEVERLEY. Architectural Composition. NY/London, 1908. 88 b/w engrs. (Fep lt browned, reps sl spotted; bkpl; upper hinge cracked, head upper joint split w/sl loss; faded, spine sl frayed.) *Edwards.* $39/£25

ROBINSON, KIM STANLEY. Icehenge. (London): Macdonald, (1984). 1st hb ed. Signed. Dj. *Swann*.* $92/£59

ROBINSON, KIM STANLEY. The Wild Shore. (London): Macdonald, (1986). 1st hb ed, 1st bk. Signed. Dj. *Swann*.* $172/£110

ROBINSON, MARILYNNE. Housekeeping. NY: FSG, (1980). 1st ed, 1st bk. Fine in dj. *Hermitage.* $75/£48

ROBINSON, SPIDER. Mindkiller. NY: Holt, Rinehart & Winston, (1982). 1st ed. Fine in Fine dj. *Other Worlds.* $25/£16

ROBINSON, TOM. The Longcase Clock. Suffolk: Antique Collectors' Club, 1981. 1st ed. 22 color plts. Fine in dj. *Weber.* $100/£64

ROBINSON, VICTOR. An Essay of Hashish. NY, 1930. 2nd ed. VG in dj. *Fye.* $75/£48

ROBINSON, VICTOR. Pathfinders in Medicine. NY: Medical Life, 1929. 2nd ed. (Spine tear), else Good. *Goodrich.* $125/£80

ROBINSON, VICTOR. Story of Medicine. NY, ca 1931. 1st ed. VG. *Argosy.* $65/£42

ROBINSON, VICTOR. White Caps: The Story of Nursing. Phila, 1946. 1st ed. (Cvr faded.) *Fye.* $50/£32

ROBINSON, W. The English Flower Garden and Home Grounds. London, 1909. 11th ed. Recent cl. Good. *Henly.* $28/£18

ROBINSON, W. Gas and Petroleum Engines. 1902. 2nd ed. Contents VG. (ex-lib, sm stamp; spine faded, sl worn, cl irregularly colored.) *Whitehart.* $86/£55

ROBINSON, W. HEATH. See HEATH ROBINSON, W.

ROBINSON, W. W. Land in California. Berkeley/L.A.: Univ of CA, 1948. 1st ed. Gray cl. VF in pict dj (spine sl chipped). *Argonaut.* $75/£48

ROBINSON, W. W. Land in California. Berkeley: Univ of CA, 1948. 1st ed. Grey pict cl. Fine in VG dj. *Harrington.* $65/£42

ROBINSON, W. W. Land in California.... Berkeley, 1948. 1st ed. One of 2500. NF in NF dj. *Turpen.* $60/£38

ROBINSON, W. W. Maps of Los Angeles. L.A.: Dawson's Book Shop, 1966. Ltd to 380 numbered, signed. 26 full-pg facs maps, lg color map rear pocket. Gray cl (lt soiled; bkpl), red leather spine label. *Karmiole.* $300/£192

ROBINSON, WILL H. The Story of Arizona. Phoenix, AZ: Berryhill, (1919). 1st ed. Good. *Lien.* $65/£42

ROBINSON, WILLARD B. American Forts. Urbana: Univ of IL, (1977). 1st ed. VG in dj (sl worn). *Lien.* $40/£26

ROBINSON, WILLIAM F. A Certain Slant of Light. Boston: NYGS: 1980. 1st ed. (Stamp lower edge), else Fine in pict dj. *Cahan.* $30/£19

ROBINSON, WILLIAM MORRISON, JR. The Confederate Privateers. New Haven, 1928. 1st ed. VG +. *Pratt.* $85/£54

ROBINSON, WILLIAM MORRISON, JR. The Confederate Privateers. New Haven: Yale Univ, 1928. 1st ed. Sm color repro painting tipped in. VG. *Mcgowan.* $85/£54

ROBINSON, WILLIAM. The English Flower Garden. Roy Hay (ed). Murray, 1956. Rev ed. (Spine sl faded), else VG in blue cl. *Hadley.* $28/£18

ROBINSON, ZIRKLE D. The Robinson-Rosenberger Journey to the Gold Fields of California, 1849-1850. Francis Coleman Rosenberger (ed). Iowa City, (1966). Brn cl-backed patterned bds, spine gilt. Fine in dj. *Cady.* $30/£19

ROBISON, JOHN. Proofs of a Conspiracy Against All the Religions and Governments of Europe.... NY: George Forman, 1798. 4th ed. Contemp calf. (Sm repaired hole margin tp; rebacked, orig spine label laid on.) *Sadlon.* $125/£80

ROBSJOHN-GIBBINGS, T. H. and CARLTON W. PULLIN. Furniture of Classical Greece. NY: Knopf, (1963). Good in dj (torn). *Archaeologia.* $125/£80

ROCH, ANDRE. Climbs of My Youth. London, (1949). 1st Eng ed. (Sl bumped), else Good in dj (spine sunned, frayed). *King.* $30/£19

ROCH, ANDRE. Climbs of My Youth. London, 1949. 1st ed. 17 plts. Dj (sl rubbed). *Edwards.* $23/£15

ROCH, ANDRE. On Rock and Ice. London, 1947. 1st Eng ed. VG in dj (soiled, chip). *King.* $60/£38

ROCHE, HARRIET A. On Trek in the Transvaal.... London: Sampson Low et al, 1878. 1st ed. (xvi),(368),32pp. Pict cl, gilt. Nice (foxed, sl crease, sm hole 1 leaf, ms corrections, sl worn). *Ash.* $226/£145

ROCK, J. F. The Ornamental Trees of Hawaii. Honolulu, 1917. 79 photo-engrs, 2 color plts. NF in dj (sl torn). *Brooks.* $99/£63

ROCKFELLOW, JOHN A. Log of an Arizona Trail Blazer. Tucson: Acme, (1933). 1st ed. Inscribed. Dec cl (faded). Howes R392. *Ginsberg.* $100/£64

ROCKWELL, R. H. My Way of Hunting. London, 1956. Dj (frayed). *Grayling.* $39/£25

ROCKWELL, WILSON (ed). Memoirs of a Lawman. Denver: Sage Books, 1962. 1st ed. VG in dj. *Lien.* $50/£32

RODDIS, LOUIS. The Indian Wars of Minnesota. Cedar Rapids, IA: Torch, (1956). 1st ed. VG. *Lien.* $65/£42

RODDIS, LOUIS. A Short History of Nautical Medicine. NY, 1941. VG. *Fye.* $100/£64

RODDIS, LOUIS. A Short History of Nautical Medicine. NY: Hoeber, 1941. 2nd ptg. Good. *Goodrich.* $75/£48

RODMAN, SELDEN. Horace Pippin: A Negro Painter in America. NY: Quadrangle, 1947. 1st ed. 4 tipped-in color plts. Gray cl, white lettering (flaked). Good (text sl aged) in color pict dj (heavily worn, chipped, torn). *Baltimore*.* $150/£96

RODMAN, SELDEN. Portrait of the Artist as an American. NY: Harper, 1951. 1st ed. VG. *Cahan.* $40/£26

RODRIGUEZ, ANTONIO. A History of Mexican Mural Painting. NY, (1969). 1st Amer ed. VG in dj. *Argosy.* $150/£96

ROE, ALBERT S. Blake's Illustrations to the Divine Comedy. Princeton: Princeton Univ, 1953. 1st ed. NF in dj (soiled, few tears, snags). *Waverly*.* $55/£35

ROE, E. P. Barriers Burned Away. NY: Dodd, Mead, 1872. 1st ed, 1st bk, 1st issue, lacking pub's imprint at spine foot. Brn cl (sl rubbed, worn). Yellow eps. VG in brn/red cl slipcase, matching fldg chemise. BAL 16895. *Houle.* $150/£96

ROE, E. P. Play and Profit in My Garden. NY: OJ, 1873. 349pp. Dec grn cl, gilt. VG. *Price.* $59/£38

ROE, E. P. Success with Small Fruits. NY: Dodd, Mead, 1880. 1st ed. 313pp. Dec cl. VG. *Agvent.* $85/£54

ROE, FRANCIS M. Army Letters from an Officer's Wife, 1871-1888. NY, 1909. 1st ed. Pict cl (Cvr sl worn), o/w Fine. *Pratt.* $175/£112

ROE, FRANK GILBERT. The Indian and the Horse. Norman: Univ of OK, (1955). 1st ed. VG in dj (sl worn). *Lien.* $50/£32

ROE, FRED. Ancient Church Chests and Chairs. Batsford, 1929. 1st ed. (Cl edges sl soiled.) *Edwards.* $55/£35

ROE, FRED. Old Oak Furniture. Methuen, 1905. 1st ed. Color frontis. Teg, rest uncut. (Feps lt browned, upper hinge sl tender.) *Edwards.* $39/£25

ROE, MRS. FRANCIS M. Army Letters from an Officer's Wife. NY, 1909. 1st ed. 10 plts. (Emb lib stamp; sm spine label removed.) Howes R403. *Ginsberg.* $100/£64

ROEDIGER, VIRGINIA. Ceremonial Costumes of the Pueblo Indians. Univ of CA, 1941. 1st ed. 40 color plts, color map. Dec eps. VG. *Oregon.* $250/£160

ROEDING, GEORGE C. The Smyrna Fig at Home and Abroad. Fresno: (The Author), 1903. Color frontis. (Bottom inch spine perished), else VG in dec gray wrappers. *Brooks.* $65/£42

ROEHM, MARJORIE CATLIN. The Letters of George Catlin and His Family. Berkeley/L.A.: Univ of CA, 1966. 1st ed. Color frontis, 6 plts. Rust-brn cl. VF in dj. *Argonaut.* $60/£38

ROEHRENBECK, WILLIAM J. The Regiment That Saved the Capital. NY, (1961). 1st ed. (Bkpl.) *Wantagh.* $35/£22

ROEMER, PAUL. Textbook of Ophthamology, in the Form of Clinical Lectures. NY, 1912. 1st Amer ed. 3 vols. 13 color plts. Grn cl, red spine labels. NF. *Doctor's Library.* $150/£96

ROETHKE, THEODORE. The Waking. GC: Doubleday, 1953. 1st ed. Fine (bkpl) in dj (lt rubbed, sm tears). *Captain's Bookshelf.* $100/£64

ROGER-SMITH, H. Plant Hunting in Europe. Bedford, n.d. (1950). 16 plts. VG. *Brooks.* $25/£16

ROGERS, ANDREW DENNY III. Bernhard Eduard Fernow. Princeton Univ, 1951. 1st ed. VG in dj. *Perier.* $35/£22

ROGERS, BRUCE. Paragraphs on Printing. NY, 1943. VG (ink name ep). *Truepenny.* $95/£61

ROGERS, CAMERON. Trodden Glory. Santa Barbara, 1949. Ports tipped in. VG in dj. *Brooks.* $27/£17

ROGERS, DANIEL. The New-York City-Hall Recorder, for the Year(s) 1818 (and) 1819. NY, 1818-1819. 2 vols in 1. 216; 192pp. Contemp calf (cvrs worn, loose, hinges broken). *Zubal*.* $140/£90

ROGERS, FRED B. Soldiers of the Overland. SF, 1938. 1st ed. Ltd to 1000. Fldg map. (Cvr sl spotted), o/w Fine. *Pratt.* $110/£71

ROGERS, FRED B. Soldiers of the Overland. SF: Grabhorn, 1938. One of 1000. 2 fldg maps. Good (bumped, shelfworn). *Scribe's Perch*.* $40/£26

ROGERS, FRED B. Soldiers of the Overland. SF: Grabhorn, 1938. 1st ed. One of 1000 ptd. Frontis port, 21 plts from photos, lg fldg map. Cl-backed patterned bds (spine dknd, top edge sl faded), paper spine label (sl chipped). Fine. *Argonaut.* $125/£80

ROGERS, GEORGE. Memoranda of the Experience, Labors, and Travels of a Universalist Preacher.... Cincinnati, 1845. 1st ed. 400pp. Full calf. Howes R412. *Ginsberg.* $300/£192

ROGERS, H. The Geology of Pennsylvania. Vol I only. 1858. xxvii,586pp. Largely unopened. Good (spine ends worn). *Blake.* $150/£96

ROGERS, HORATIO. Personal Experiences of the Chancellorsville Campaign. Providence, RI, 1881. 1st ed. Ltd to 250. PNRISSHS Series 2, #9. 33pp. NF in ptd wrappers. *Mcgowan.* $45/£29

ROGERS, J. B. War Pictures. Chicago, 1863. 1st ed. 258pp. (Outer hinges torn, crudely taped.) *King.* $100/£64

ROGERS, JAMES E. HAROLD. The Economic Interpretation of History. NY: Putnam, 1888. 1st Amer ed. xviii,547,(3)pp. Maroon cl (sl rubbed). *Karmiole.* $75/£48

ROGERS, MARY ELIZA. Domestic Life in Palestine. London: Bell & Daldy, 1863. 2nd rev, enlgd ed. xv,(i)blank, 422pp, 1/2-title. (Sl foxing.) Contemp black 1/2 calf, marbled bds (rubbed), label gilt. *Morrell.* $55/£35

ROGERS, R. VASHON. The Law of the Road; or, Wrongs and Rights of a Traveller. SF: Sumner Whitney, 1876. Russett cl (sl soiled), gilt. Pretty. *Boswell.* $75/£48

ROGERS, ROBERT WILLIAM. A History of Ancient Persia. NY/London: Scribner, 1929. Color frontis. Teg. Gilt-pict cl. *Archaeologia.* $95/£61

ROGERS, WALTER T. Manual of Bibliography. Grevel, 1891. Emb chromolitho frontis, 172pp. Dk blue cl, gilt. Good. *Moss.* $56/£36

ROGERS, WALTER T. Manual of Bibliography. London, 1891. New ed. 213pp + ads. Grn pub's cl, gold-stamped beveled bds (spine extrems worn, joints tender). VG. *Truepenny.* $85/£54

ROGERS, WOODES. Cruising Voyage Around the World. NY, 1928. Rpt of 1712 ed. Frontis. NF. Howes R421. *Turpen.* $95/£61

ROGERSON, SIDNEY. Both Sides of the Road. Collins, 1949. 1st ed. 23 color plts. VG in dj (sl spotted). *Cox.* $47/£30

ROGET, S. R. (ed). Travel in the Last Two Centuries of Three Generations. NY: Appleton, 1922. VG (cl lt soiled, puckered). *Bohling*. $15/£10

ROGGEVEEN, JACOB. The Journal of.... Andrew Sharp (ed). OUP, 1970. 1st ed. Fldg map. Dj. *Edwards*. $31/£20

ROHAN, JACK. Yankee Arms Maker. NY: Harper, (1948). Rev ed. Frontis port, 3 plts. Tan cl. (Fr cvr bumped), else Fine in dj (soiled, chipped). *Argonaut*. $50/£32

ROHDE, E. S. A Garden of Herbs. London, (1920). 1st ed. Good. *Henly*. $37/£24

ROHDE, E. S. Herbs and Herb Gardening. London, 1936. 1st ed. 15 plts (1 color). Fine. *Henly*. $34/£22

ROHDE, E. S. The Old English Gardening Books. London, 1924. Aeg. Full grn calf, gilt. VG. *Truepenny*. $200/£128

ROHDE, E. S. The Old English Gardening Books. London: Martin Hopkinson, 1924. 1st ed. Linen, bds (sl bowed), paper labels. Good. *Reese*. $100/£64

ROHDE, E. S. The Old English Herbals. London, 1922. 18 plts (1 color). (Sl worn, scruffy.) *Maggs*. $45/£29

ROHDE, E. S. The Old English Herbals. London: Longmans, Green, 1922. 1st ed. Frontis. Dj (heavily frayed, worn) laid in. VG. *Reese*. $125/£80

ROHDE, E. S. The Old English Herbals. London: Longmans, Green, 1922. 1st ed. Color frontis, 17 plts. Fine. *Quest*. $210/£135

ROHDE, E. S. Shakespeare's Wild Flowers. London, (1935). 5 color plts. *Wheldon & Wesley*. $62/£40

ROHDE, E. S. The Story of the Garden, with a Chapter on American Gardens. London, 1932. 1st ed. 35 plts (5 color). (Cl soiled.) *Henly*. $44/£28

ROHMER, SAX. Bat Wing. NY: Burt, 1921. Rpt. (Fep excised.) Dj (sl worn, nicked). *Mcclintock*. $45/£29

ROHMER, SAX. The Emperor of America. London: Cassell, (1929). 1st Eng ed. VG (spine leaned) in Good dj (spine stains, tears, sm chips). *Certo*. $90/£58

ROHMER, SAX. Fu Manchu's Bride. D-D, 1933. 1st ed. Fine in VG dj (lt worn, torn, chipped). *Aronovitz*. $265/£170

ROHMER, SAX. The Green Eyes of Bast. NY, 1920. 1st ed. VG (sl soiled). *Mcclintock*. $17/£11

ROHMER, SAX. The Insidious Dr. Fu-Manchu. NY, 1913. 1st Amer ed. (Bkpl removed, ink name; cvrs worn, spine ends frayed.) *King*. $150/£96

ROHMER, SAX. The Mask of Fu Manchu. GC: DCC, 1932. 1st ed. Fine in pict dj (sm chips). *Else Fine*. $495/£317

ROHMER, SAX. The Return of Dr. Fu-Manchu. NY: Robert M. McBride, 1916. 1st Amer ed. Caramel cl stamped in gilt/black. Pleasing (lt wear). *Hermitage*. $125/£80

ROHMER, SAX. Shadow of Fu Manchu. GC: DCC, 1948. 1st ed. NF (pp tanned) in dj (brittle; sm chips). *Else Fine*. $90/£58

ROHMER, SAX. The Sins of Sumuru. London: Jenkins, (1950). 1st British ed. VG in VG dj. *Metropolitan**. $57/£37

ROHMER, SAX. Tales of East and West. GC: Doubleday, (1933). 1st US ed. NF in VG + dj. *Unger*. $425/£272

ROHMER, SAX. Tales of Secret Egypt. London: Methuen, (1918). 1st ed. (Presentation stamp tp; spine faded, sl rubbed.) *Metropolitan**. $28/£18

ROHN, ARTHUR H. Mug House: Mesa Verde National Park—Colorado. Washington: National Park Service, (1971). VG. *Lien*. $25/£16

ROJO, MANUEL C. Historical Notes on Lower California with Some Relative to Upper California Furnished to Bancroft Library by...1879. L.A., 1972. 1st ed. One of 500. Frontis. (9 sm checks by bibliography items), o/w Fine. *Turpen*. $45/£29

ROLAND, ARTHUR. The Management of Grass Land, Laying Down Grass.... William H. Ablett (ed). London: Chapman & Hall, 1881. 1st ed. viii,196pp; 32-pg pub's cat. Pict grn cl. Fine (lt foxed). *Burmester*. $75/£48

ROLF-WHEELER, FRANCIS. The Boy with the U.S. Survey. Boston, 1909. 1st ed. 2-tone cl. Photo laid on cvr. (Lt wear, soil), else VG + . *Five Quail*. $50/£32

ROLFE, EDWIN. Permit Me Refuge. L.A.: CA Quarterly, 1955. One of 1000 numbered. Fine in Good dj (1/2 of spine chipped). *Beasley*. $25/£16

ROLFE, EDWIN. To My Contemporaries. NY: Dynamo, 1936. 1st ed, 1st book. Good (dknd). *Beasley*. $50/£32

ROLFE, FREDERICK. Don Renato: An Ideal Content. Cecil Woolf (ed). London: C&W, 1963. 1st ed. Fine in dj. *Captain's Bookshelf*. $150/£96

ROLFE, FREDERICK. Don Tarquinio. London: C&W, 1905. 1st ed, 1st issue. Illus purple cl. (Pp sl foxed; spine faded.) *Black Sun*. $450/£288

ROLFE, FREDERICK. The Venice Letters. C. Woolf (ed). London, 1974. 1st ed. (2 ll unbound.) *Typographeum*. $45/£29

Roll of Honor. Washington, DC: GPO, 1867-1876. 1st ed. 7 vols. Complete set w/all 32 separate publications. Contemp 1/2 leather, marbled paper sides. NF set. *Mcgowan*. $1,250/£801

Roll of Honor. Names of Soldiers Who Died in Defense of the American Union Interred in the National Cemeteries.... Washington: Quartermaster Generals Office, 1865-1872. 1st ed. 27 vols (lacks vol 2). Orig ptd wrappers, several w/cl spines. *Ginsberg*. $750/£481

ROLLESTON, H. D. Diseases of the Liver, Gall-Bladder, and Bile-Ducts. Phila: Saunders, 1905. 1st Amer ed. Color frontis, 6 color plts. NF. *Glaser*. $125/£80

ROLLESTON, HUMPHRY. Cardio-Vascular Diseases Since Harvey's Discovery. Cambridge, 1928. 1st ed. VG. *Fye*. $75/£48

ROLLINS, HYDER EDWARD (ed). Tottel's Miscellany (1557-1587). Cambridge: Harvard Univ, 1928-1929. 1st ed. 2 vols. Maroon cl, gilt. Good in djs (chipped). *Karmiole*. $75/£48

Rollo's Experiments. (By Jacob Abbott.) Boston: Weeks, Jordan, 1839. 1st ed. 180pp (lt foxing) incl ads, plts. Orig blind-emb brn cl, gilt title. Nice (lt frayed, paper label remnants spine). *Bohling*. $60/£38

ROLPH, C. H. (ed). The Trial of Lady Chatterley. Privately ptd, 1961. #69/2000 signed by Allen Lane. Fine. *Poetry Bookshop*. $31/£20

ROLT-WHEELER, FRANCIS. The Book of Cowboys. Lothrop, Lee & Shepard, (1921). 1st ed. Fine in dj (badly chipped). *Authors Of West*. $40/£26

ROMAN, ALFRED. The Military Operations of General Beauregard.... NY, (1883). 1st ed. 2 vols. Frontispieces. (Bkpl removed vol 1; cvrs spotted.) *Kane**. $160/£103

ROMANES, MRS. E. The Life and Letters of George John Romanes.... London, 1898. 4th ed. 3 plts. (Sl shaken.) *Maggs*. $44/£28

ROMANOFF, PANTELEIMON. Without Cherry Blossom. L. Zarine (trans). NY: Scribner, 1932. 1st Amer ed. Fine in dj (sl worn, tear). *Antic Hay*. $30/£19

ROMBAUER, IRMA S. The Joy of Cooking. Indianapolis: Bobbs-Merrill, (1936). 1st trade ed, 3rd ptg. VG. *Perier*. $75/£48

ROMER, F. Makers of History. Hartford, CT: Colt's Patent Firearms Manufacturing Co, 1926. 1st ed. 5 plts. Errata slip tipped in. Pict bds. (Lt wear spine), else Fine. *Argonaut.* $125/£80

ROMIG, EMILY CRAIG. A Pioneer Woman in Alaska. Caldwell, ID: Caxton, 1948. 1st trade ed. Fine in dj. *High Latitude.* $45/£29

ROMINE, WILLIAM BETHEL. A Story of the Original Ku Klux Klan. Pulaski, TN: Pulaski Citizen, 1934. 2nd ed. NF in ptd wrappers. *Mcgowan.* $250/£160

ROMNEY, JOHN. Memoirs of the Life and Works of George Romney. 1830. Frontis port, xii,332pp (spotted); 22 plts. Aeg. Dec grn crushed morocco, gilt. *Edwards.* $390/£250

Ronald Searle in Perspective. London: New English Library, 1984. 1st UK ed. Dj. *Edwards.* $31/£20

RONALDS, ALFRED. The Fly-Fisher's Entomology. Longman, Orme, 1839. 2nd ed. Frontis, 19 color plts. Stamped grn cl, gilt title upper cvr. *Hatchwell.* $250/£160

RONALDS, ALFRED. The Fly-Fisher's Entomology. H.T. Sherringham (ed). London, 1921. *Petersfield.* $39/£25

RONALDS, ALFRED. The Fly-Fisher's Entomology...Trout and Grayling Fishing.... London, 1877. 8th ed. 20 hand-colored plts. (Sl soiled, sm marginal stain, sm wormhole blank margin at end.) Recent 1/4 morocco. *Maggs.* $140/£90

RONAN, PETER. Historical Sketch of the Flathead Indian Nation from the Year 1813 to 1890. Helena, MT: Journal Pub Co, (1890). 1st ed. (4),80,(2)pp, 12 plts. (Sm piece torn from fr pastedown), o/w VG. Howes R428, w/incorrect pagination. *M & S.* $300/£192

RONAN, PETER. Historical Sketch of the Flathead Indian Nation from the Year 1813 to 1890. Helena: Journal, (1890). 1st ed. 81pp. Howes R428. *Ginsberg.* $300/£192

RONEY, CUSACK. Rambles of Railways. London, 1868. 1st ed. xii,499 + xixpp (sl browning), 10 maps, diags (lacks fldg map). Blind emb cl (rubbed, sl loss, upper joint split to tail). *Edwards.* $39/£25

RONNE, FINN. Antarctic Command. Indianapolis: Bobbs-Merrill, c. 1961. Inscribed. Map. VG in dj. *High Latitude.* $30/£19

ROOD, F. S. and H. N. WEBBER. Anaesthesia and Anaesthetics. NY, 1930. 1st Amer ed. 4 b/w plts. Red tooled cl. NF. *Doctor's Library.* $75/£48

ROOSEVELT, ELEANOR. On My Own. NY: Harper, (1958). 1st ed. One of unspecified # for presentation. Signed. Blue cl (sl faded). *Karmiole.* $125/£80

ROOSEVELT, THEODORE and KERMIT. Trailing the Giant Panda. NY: Scribner, 1929. 1st ed. VG. *Books & Birds.* $75/£48

ROOSEVELT, THEODORE and GEORGE BIRD GRINNELL (eds). American Big-Game Hunting. NY: Forest & Stream, 1893. 1st ed. Silver-gilt pict cl (shelfworn). *Oinonen*.* $110/£71

ROOSEVELT, THEODORE and GEORGE BIRD GRINNELL (eds). American Big-Game Hunting. NY: Forest & Stream, 1901. Silver-gilt pict cl (sl worn). *Oinonen*.* $80/£51

ROOSEVELT, THEODORE and GEORGE BIRD GRINNELL. Hunting in Many Lands. NY: Forest & Stream, 1895. Uncut. (Sl worn.) *Oinonen*.* $180/£115

ROOSEVELT, THEODORE. African Game Trails. NY: Scribner, (1910) 1920. 2 vols. Frontis each vol. Dk blue cl, gilt; TR emb on cvr. VG+. *Backman.* $35/£22

ROOSEVELT, THEODORE. African Game Trails. NY, 1910. 1st ed. Pict cl (inner hinges loose; extrems frayed; worn). *King.* $45/£29

ROOSEVELT, THEODORE. African Game Trails. NY, 1910. (Upper hinge cracked; spine sl faded, head torn, repaired.) *Edwards.* $94/£60

ROOSEVELT, THEODORE. African Game Trails. NY: Scribner, 1910. 1st ed. Gilt-dec brn cl. VG. *Mikesh.* $75/£48

ROOSEVELT, THEODORE. African Game Trails. NY: Scribner, 1910. Frontis port. Grn gilt pict cl (sl rubbed), else VG. *Terramedia.* $100/£64

ROOSEVELT, THEODORE. African Game Trails. NY: Scribner, 1910. 1st ed. VG-. *Books & Birds.* $150/£96

ROOSEVELT, THEODORE. African Game Trails. NY: Scribner, 1910. Some pp unopened. Gilt-lettered brn cl (faded, stained). *Metropolitan*.* $172/£110

ROOSEVELT, THEODORE. The Letters of Theodore Roosevelt. Elting E. Morison (ed). Cambridge: Harvard Univ, 1951. 1st ed. 2 vols. (Spine ends dknd), o/w Fine in djs (sl worn, chipped). *Hermitage.* $95/£61

ROOSEVELT, THEODORE. Outdoor Pastimes of an American Hunter. NY: Scribner, 1905. 1st ed. Frontis port. Gilt decs. VG (weak fr inner hinge, re-glued; pencil name, date). *Backman.* $125/£80

ROOSEVELT, THEODORE. Ranch Life and the Hunting-Trail. NY: Century, 1888. 1st ed. Frederic Remington (illus). Howes binding variant 2. VG. *Books & Birds.* $120/£77

ROOSEVELT, THEODORE. Ranch Life and the Hunting-Trail. NY, 1902. (Rubbed.) *Swann*.* $57/£37

ROOSEVELT, THEODORE. The Works. NY, 1923-26. Memorial ed. One of 1050 numbered, signed by Edith Kermit Roosevelt. 24 vols. Uncut. (Sl worn.) *Oinonen*.* $475/£304

ROOSEVELT, THEODORE. Works. NY, 1923-26. Memorial ed. One of 1050. Vol 1 signed by Edith Kermit Roosevelt. 24 vols. Frontis each vol. Teg, mostly unopened. Vols 17-24 in orig boxes. Near New. *Kane*.* $500/£321

ROOT, A. I. The ABC of Bee Culture. Medina, OH: Root, 1887. (xvi),340pp. (Sl foxed, sl soiled, faded, edges rubbed, spine nick), o/w VG. *Worldwide.* $65/£42

ROOT, A. I. The ABC of Bee Culture. Medina, OH, 1895. 62nd thousand. 428pp + ads. Gilt-dec cl. (Sl shelfworn, cl chipped off some spots), o/w VG. *My Bookhouse.* $75/£48

ROOT, RALPH RODNEY and CHARLES FABENS KELLEY. Design in Landscape Gardening. NY: Century, 1914. Color frontis. Fine. *Quest.* $75/£48

ROOT, RILEY. Journal of Travels From St. Josephs to Oregon.... Oakland, CA: Biobooks, 1955. Ltd to 500. Good (name fep). Howes R436. *Lien.* $45/£29

ROOT, WAVERLY. The Paris Edition. SF: North Point, 1987. 1st ed. Fine in dj. *Turtle Island.* $30/£19

ROPER, FREEMAN C. S. Catalogue of Works on the Microscope, and of Those Referring to Microscopical Subjects. Bronxville, NY, 1865. Rpt ed. 102pp. Gilt-tooled cl. VG. *Doctor's Library.* $115/£74

ROPER, LANNING. Royal Gardens. London: Collinridge, 1953. Fine in dj. *Quest.* $40/£26

ROQUELAURE, A. N. (Pseud of Anne Rice.) Beauty's Punishment. NY, (1984). 1st ed. Dj. *Kane*.* $95/£61

ROQUELAURE, A. N. (Pseud of Anne Rice.) Beauty's Punishment. NY: Dutton, (1984). 1st ed. Signed. Fine in dj. *Between The Covers.* $300/£192

ROQUELAURE, A. N. (Pseud of Anne Rice.) Beauty's Punishment. (London): Macdonald, (1987). 1st UK ed. Fine in Fine dj. *Other Worlds.* $60/£38

ROQUELAURE, A. N. (Pseud of Anne Rice.) Beauty's Punishment. NY, 1984. 1st ed. NF in NF dj. *Warren.* $175/£112

ROQUELAURE, A. N. (Pseud of Anne Rice.) The Claiming of Sleeping Beauty. NY, (1983). 1st ed. Dj (sm tear, wrinkles). *Kane**. $100/£64

ROQUELAURE, A. N. (Pseud of Anne Rice.) The Claiming of Sleeping Beauty. NY: Dutton, (1983). 1st ed. Signed. Fine in dj. *Between The Covers*. $350/£224

ROQUELAURE, A. N. (Pseud of Anne Rice.) The Claiming of Sleeping Beauty. (London): Macdonald, (1987). 1st UK ed. Fine in Fine dj. *Other Worlds*. $60/£38

ROREM, NED. The Nantucket Diary 1973-1985. SF, 1987. 1st ed. Fine in dj. *Argosy*. $40/£26

RORKE, MELINA. Melina Rorke. 1939. 1st ed. Frontis port. Dj (sl soiled, chipped). *Edwards*. $31/£20

RORSCHACK, HERMANN. Psychodiagnostics: A Diagnostic Test Based on Perception. NY, 1942. 1st ed in English. 2 vols. VG. *Fye*. $125/£80

RORTY, JAMES. Children of the Sun and Other Poems. NY: Macmillan, 1926. 1st ed. Ptd bds. (Lt foxing), o/w Fine in dj (sl dknd). *Reese*. $60/£38

ROSAND, DAVID and MICHELANGELO MURARO. Titian and the Venetian Woodcut. 1976. Good in wraps. *Washton*. $50/£32

ROSCOE, THOMAS. The Tourist in Italy. London, 1831. 1st ed. viii,271pp (label remains frontis, bkpl, prelims lt browned); 26 engr plts. Aeg. Full morocco (rubbed, spine faded). *Edwards*. $117/£75

ROSE, A. Napoleon's Campaign in Russia Anno 1812, Medico-Historical. NY, 1913. 1st ed. Louis Roddis's bkpl. *Fye*. $125/£80

ROSE, ALFRED. Register of Erotic Books. NY: Jack Brussel, 1965. 2 vols. Good set. *Cox*. $101/£65

ROSE, BARBARA. Alexander Liberman. NY, (1981). Dj. *Swann**. $92/£59

ROSE, BERNICE. Jack Levine. NY: MOMA, 1969. *Metropolitan**. $28/£18

ROSE, FRANK. A Gringo in Latin America. Wynberg, Cape: Specialty Press of S. Africa, 1933. 1st ed. Signed. Pict cl, gilt. NF in dj (top edge chipped). *Sadlon*. $30/£19

ROSE, GEORGE. The Great Country; or, Impressions of America. London, 1868. Early calf (skilfully rebacked). *Swann**. $69/£44

ROSE, GEORGE. The Great Country; or, Impressions of America. London, 1868. xvi,416pp. (Sl foxed, later eps, fr hinge cracked; cl sl rubbed.) Good. *Reese*. $150/£96

ROSE, JOSHUA. Modern Machine Shop Practice. NY: Scribner, 1910. 3rd ed. 2 vols. 1/2 morocco (worn, joints splitting). Contents VG. *Waverly**. $242/£155

ROSE, ROBERT R. Advocates and Adversaries: The Early Life and Times of Robert R. Rose. Gene M. Gressley (ed). Chicago: Lakeside, Christmas, 1977. Dk blue cl. Fine. *Sadlon*. $20/£13

ROSE, STEWART. St. Ignatius Loyola and the Early Jesuits. NY, 1891. (Ex-lib, lower spine stained.) *Argosy*. $100/£64

ROSE, T. KIRKE. The Metallurgy of Gold. London, 1902. 4th ed. Foldout. Maroon cl, gilt. VG. *Price*. $165/£106

ROSE, VICTOR M. Ross' Texas Brigade. Louisville, KY: Courier Journal Book & Job Rooms, 1881. 1st ed. 185pp. VG. Howes R444. *Mcgowan*. $1,750/£1,122

ROSEN, GEORGE and BEATE CASPARI-ROSEN (eds). 400 Years of a Doctor's Life. NY: Schuman, (1947). 1st ed. VG. *Glaser*. $50/£32

ROSEN, GEORGE. The Reception of William Beaumont's Discovery in Europe. NY, 1942. 1st ed. VG. *Fye*. $55/£35

ROSEN, PETER. Pa-Ha-Sa-Pah, or The Black Hills of South Dakota. St. Louis: Nixon-Jones Ptg, 1895. 1st ed. 645pp. Good (ink stamp inside fr cvr, fep) in pict cl. Howes R446. *Lien*. $400/£256

ROSEN, R. D. Strike Three You're Dead. Walker, 1984. 1st ed. Fine in Fine dj. *Plapinger*. $150/£96

ROSEN, R. D. Strike Three You're Dead. NY: Walker, 1984. 1st ed. (Name, date, initials fr pastedown), o/w Fine in dj. *Mordida*. $100/£64

ROSEN, RICHARD. Fadeaway. NY: Harper & Row, 1986. 1st ed. VF in dj. *Mordida*. $35/£22

ROSENAU, HELEN. Boullee and Visionary Architecture. London/NY, 1976. *Edwards*. $31/£20

ROSENAU, HELEN. The Ideal City: Its Architectural Evolution in Europe. Methuen, 1983. 2nd ed. NF in dj. *Hadley*. $23/£15

ROSENBACH, A. S. W. An American Jewish Bibliography. (Phila): AJHS, 1926. 1st ed. (Sl worn, rear inner joint broken.) *Oinonen**. $120/£77

ROSENBACH, A. S. W. A Book Hunter's Holiday. Boston, 1936. #256/760 signed. Uncut. Fine in box (edges sl sunned, rubbed). *Polyanthos*. $125/£80

ROSENBACH, A. S. W. A Book Hunter's Holiday. Boston: Houghton, Mifflin, 1936. One of 760 numbered. Signed. (Few streak stains feps), else Fine in glassine dj (sl chipped), slipcase (worn, partly split). *Waverly**. $82/£53

ROSENBACH, A. S. W. Books and Bidders: The Adventures of a Bibliophile. Boston, 1927. Teg. VG. *Truepenny*. $45/£29

ROSENBACH, A. S. W. Early American Children's Books. Portland: Southworth, 1933. One of 585 signed, this copy not numbered. Teg, others uncut. Pict bds (rubbed), morocco back. Slipcase (scuffed, tape-repairs at edges), pict label. *Oinonen**. $160/£103

ROSENBACH, A. S. W. Early American Children's Books. NY: Kraus, 1966. 8vo. (Sl worn.) Dj (sl chipped, frayed). *Oinonen**. $70/£45

ROSENBERG, ADOLF. Leonardo Da Vinci. J. Lohse (trans). Bielefeld/Leipzig: Velhagen & Klasing, 1903. 1st ed in English. Blue cl (eps lt foxed; lt worn). Good. *Shasky*. $40/£26

ROSENBERG, FRANTZ. Big Game Shooting in British Columbia and Norway. London, 1928. 1st ed. (Upper bd lt stained.) *Edwards*. $70/£45

ROSENBERG, FRANTZ. Big Game Shooting in British Columbia and Norway. London: Martin Hopkinson, 1928. 1st ed. Photo frontis. VG (lt edgewear; name, label remnants). *Backman*. $90/£58

ROSENBERG, HAROLD. De Kooning. NY, (1974). Dj. *Swann**. $690/£442

ROSENBERG, JAKOB. Rembrandt. Cambridge, 1948. 2 vols. Good. *Washton*. $50/£32

ROSENBERG, LOUIS CONRAD. Cottages, Farmhouses and Other Minor Buildings in England of the 16th, 17th and 18th Centuries. NY: Architectural Book Pub Co, 1923. Gilt-lettered blue cl (lt worn, soiled; sl internal soil). *Freeman**. $80/£51

ROSENBERG, LOUIS CONRAD. Cottages, Farmhouses and Other Minor Buildings in England of the 16th, 17th, and 18th Centuries. NY: Architectural Book Pub Co, 1923. 1st ed. 102 plts. Blue cl, gilt. VG +. *House*. $225/£144

ROSENBERG, PIERRE. Fragonard. NY: MMA, 1988. Good in dj. *Washton*. $100/£64

ROSENBERG, SAMUEL. Naked Is the Best Disguise. Indianapolis: Bobbs-Merrill, (1974). 1st ptg. VG in VG dj (wear, soil). *Gravesend*. $20/£13

ROSENBLATT, JULIA CARLSON and FREDERIC H. SONNENSCHMIDT. Dining with Sherlock Holmes. Indianapolis: Bobbs-Merrill, 1976. 1st ed. Fine in dj (price-clipped). *Mordida*. $75/£48

ROSENBLUM, NAOMI. The Lewis W. Hine Document. Brooklyn: Brooklyn Museum, 1977. 1st ed. 16 loose photo plts, lg chronology laid in pocket of illus folder. (Owner stamp), else VG. *Cahan*. $50/£32

ROSENBLUM, ROBERT. Transformations in Late Eighteenth Century Art. Princeton, 1967. Good in dj. *Washton*. $40/£26

ROSENBLUM, WALTER. Walter Rosenblum: Photographer. Cambridge: Fogg Art Museum, 1964. Fine in ptd wrappers. *Cahan*. $25/£16

ROSENFELD, DAVID. Porcelain Figures. The Studio, 1949. (Spine lt faded.) *Edwards*. $47/£30

ROSENFELD, ISADORE. Hospitals: Integrated Design. NY: Reinhold, (1951). 2nd rev ed, 1st ptg. Inscribed. Ptd grey cl (edges sl chafed). VG. *Gach*. $50/£32

ROSENFELD, MORRIS. Songs from the Ghetto. Boston: Copeland & Day, 1898. 1st ed. (Corner fep clipped), else NF. *Beasley*. $40/£26

ROSENFELD, SYBIL. Georgian Scene Painters and Scene Painting. Cambridge, 1981. Good. *Washton*. $50/£32

ROSENSTEIN, I. G. Theory and Practice of Homoeopathy. Louisville, 1840. 1st ed. 288pp. (Ex-lib.) Marbled bds (rebacked). *Argosy*. $450/£288

ROSENTHAL, BARBARA. Clues to Myself. Rochester: Visual Studies Workshop, 1981. 1st ed. (Owner stamp), else Fine in illus stiff wrappers. *Cahan*. $40/£26

ROSENTHAL, EARL E. The Cathedral of Granada. Princeton, 1961. Good in dj. *Washton*. $125/£80

ROSENTHAL, MORITZ. A Clinical Treatise on the Diseases of the Nervous System.... L. Putzel (trans). NY: William Wood, 1879. 1st ed in English. 2 vols. ix,278; vi,284pp. Good (sl frayed). *Glaser*. $85/£54

Roses of Sharon. N.p.: Golden Cockerel, 1937. One of 125. 12 wood engrs. Grn morocco-backed maroon bds (spine faded, nick; ink inscrip). *Kane**. $60/£38

ROSETT, JOSHUA. Intercortical Systems of the Human Cerebrum.... Columbia Univ, 1933. VG. *Argosy*. $60/£38

ROSETTI, GIOANVENTURA. The Plictho.... Sidney M. Edelstein & Hector C. Borghetty (trans). Cambridge, MA: MIT, (1969). 1st ed in English. Pict eps. NF (spine sl faded) in pict slipcase. *Glaser*. $200/£128

ROSEVEARE, HENRY (ed). Markets and Merchants of the Late Seventeenth Century. OUP, 1987. Frontis, 3 maps. (Bkpl.) Dj (sl chipped). *Edwards*. $55/£35

ROSKE, RALPH and CHARLES VAN DOREN. Lincoln's Commando, The Biography of Commander W. B. Cushing, U.S.N. NY, (1957). 1st ed. VG in dj (lt chipping). *Pratt*. $37/£24

ROSS, ALAN. Blindfold Games. London, 1986. 1st Eng ed. Fine in dj. *Clearwater*. $31/£20

ROSS, ALEXANDER. Adventures of the First Settlers on the Oregon or Columbia River. Milo M. Quaife (ed). Chicago, 1923. Fldg map. Teg. Dk grn cl, gilt. VG +. *Bohling*. $40/£26

ROSS, ALEXANDER. Adventures of the First Settlers on the Oregon or Columbia River. Milo M. Quaife (ed). Chicago: Lakeside, 1925. Fldg map. Teg. Fine. Reissue of Howes R448. *Cahan*. $40/£26

ROSS, ALEXANDER. Mystagogus Poeticus, or the Muses Interpreter. London: J. Martyn et al, 1672. 5th ed. (7)leaves, 418pp, (16)leaves (soil, foxed, sl stains). Old lacquered bds (worn), calf back, tips. *Oinonen**. $170/£109

ROSS, E. DENISON (ed). The Art of Egypt Through the Ages. London: Studio, (1931). 1st ed. Blue cl. (Corners bumped, spine faded), o/w VG. *Hermitage*. $95/£61

ROSS, EDMUND G. History of the Impeachment of Andrew Johnson. Santa Fe: New Mexican Ptg Co, 1896. (iv),180pp. (Label taped to spine), else Good. Howes R453. *Dumont*. $175/£112

ROSS, J. and J. S. BURY. Peripheral Neuritis. 1893. vii,424pp (sm ink stamp tp, contents pg; inner hinges cracked, cl dust-stained, spine top sl defective). *Whitehart*. $62/£40

ROSS, JANET and NELLY ERICHSEN. The Story of Pisa. London, 1909. 2 maps (1 fldg). Teg. Gilt-dec cl (spine discolored, sl chipped, sm split upper joint head; bkpl). *Edwards*. $16/£10

ROSS, JOAN M. Post-Mortem Appearances. London, 1925. 1st ed. NF. *Doctor's Library*. $60/£38

ROSS, JOHN. Narrative of a Second Voyage in Search of a North-West Passage and of a Residence in the Arctic Regions During the Years 1829...1833.... London: A.W. Webster, 1835. Lg 4to. xxxiii,740pp; 31 plts & maps (9 plts color). Marbled eps, edges. Old full leather (extrems sl rubbed). VG. *High Latitude*. $500/£321

ROSS, JOHN. Narrative of a Second Voyage in Search of a North-West Passage and of a Residence in the Arctic Regions. London: A.W. Webster, 1835. 2 vols. (Foxing throughout.) Subscribers list, 50 plts and maps (lacks lg fldg chart). 3/4 leather, marbled bds, gilt. *Metropolitan**. $300/£192

ROSS, JOHN. Narrative of a Second Voyage in Search of a North-West Passage and of a Residence...During...1829...1833. Phila: E.L. Carey & A. Hart, 1835. 1st US ed. xxiii,456pp (sl foxing), fldg map. Uncut. Cl-backed bds, paper label. VG. *High Latitude*. $100/£64

ROSS, JOHN. A Voyage of Discovery...for the Purpose of Exploring Baffin's Bay. London, 1819. 1st ed, w/errata slip. 4to. 32 maps, charts, plts. Contemp calf (lt worn). *Swann**. $1,265/£811

ROSS, LAWRENCE SULLIVAN. Personal Civil War Letters of General Lawrence Sullivan Ross with Other Letters. Austin: (W.M. Morrison, 1994). 1st ed. Ltd to 500. As New. *Mcgowan*. $39/£25

ROSS, MARVIN (ed). Episodes from Life Among the Indians and Last Rambles. (By George Catlin.) Norman: Univ of OK, (1959). 1st ed. Color frontis. Grn cl. Fine in VG + pict dj. *House*. $85/£54

ROSS, MARVIN (ed). George Catlin: Episodes from Life Among the Indians and Last Rambles. Norman: Univ of OK, (1959). 1st ed thus. Grn cl. Fine in NF dj. Howes C240 and C242. *Harrington*. $65/£42

ROSS, SAM. The Empty Sleeve. Madison, WI, 1964. 1st ed. Signed. Fine in dj (lt worn). *Pratt*. $70/£45

ROSS, VICTOR and A. ST. L. TRIGGE. A History of the Canadian Bank of Commerce. Toronto: OUP, 1920-1934. 1st ed. 3 vols. 215 plts. Red cl, gilt. Good in djs. *Karmiole*. $125/£80

ROSS, W. The Blowpipe in Chemistry, Mineralogy, and Geology. London: Crosby Lockwood, 1889. 2nd ed. xv,214pp + ads. Good (rubbed). *Blake*. $125/£80

ROSSETTI, CHRISTINA. Called to Be Saints: The Minor Festivals Devotionally Studied. SPCK, 1895. Pub's ads. Teg. Good (spine bumped, chipped, sm vent fr hinge). *Tiger*. $94/£60

ROSSETTI, CHRISTINA. The Face of the Deep. London, 1892. 1st ed. (Sl rubbed), o/w VG. *Words Etc*. $56/£36

ROSSETTI, CHRISTINA. The Face of the Deep: A Devotional Commentary on the Apocalypse. SPCK, 1907. 5th ed. (Spine bumped), else VG. *Tiger*. $56/£36

ROSSETTI, CHRISTINA. Goblin Market. London, (1933). 1st ed deluxe. One of 410 numbered, signed by Arthur Rackham (illus). Thin 8vo. Limitation label. 4 color plts. Pict eps. Gilt-lettered limp vellum. Slipcase (joints cracked). *Swann**. $488/£313

ROSSETTI, CHRISTINA. Goblin Market. Phila: Lippincott, (1933). 1st Amer ed. 4 color plts. Red cl, color pict label mtd fr cvr. (Sm Christmas card mtd inside fr cvr), o/w Contents VG. *New Hampshire**. $50/£32

ROSSETTI, CHRISTINA. Goblin Market. Phila: Lippincott, (1933). 1st Amer ed. Thin 8vo. 4 color plts by Arthur Rackham. Maroon cl, pict label. Fine. *Appelfeld*. $125/£80

ROSSETTI, CHRISTINA. Poems. London: Gresham, (1910). Florence Harrison (illus). Teg. Grn cl over bds, gilt. VG. *Heller*. $400/£256

ROSSETTI, CHRISTINA. Poems. (Newtown, Wales): Gregynog, 1930. One of 300. Calf-backed marbled bds (spine dknd). *Kane**. $150/£96

ROSSETTI, CHRISTINA. The Poetical Works of Christina Georgina Rossetti. Macmillan, 1904. Rpt. Gilt-dec contemp 1/2 vellum over cl. (Sl thumb mkd), else VG. *Tiger*. $70/£45

ROSSETTI, CHRISTINA. Sing-Song. Routledge, 1872. Arthur Hughes (illus), Brothers Dalziel (engrs). Gilt-dec blue cl (spine ends sl rubbed; inscrip). *Petersfield*. $75/£48

ROSSETTI, CHRISTINA. Sing-Song. Routledge, 1872. 1st ed. Arthur Hughes (illus). 8vo. x,130pp + 2pp ads. New eps; aeg. Gilt-pict grn cl. (Recased, rubbed, sl mks), else VG-. *Bookmark*. $234/£150

ROSSETTI, DANTE GABRIEL. Ballads and Narrative Poems. (Hammersmith): Kelmscott, (1893). One of 310. 8vo. Orig limp vellum, silk ties. Cl slipcase. *Swann**. $1,035/£663

ROSSETTI, DANTE GABRIEL. Ballads and Narrative Poems. (Ptd by William Morris at the Kelmscott Press, 1893.) One of 310 ptd. 206x145mm. (4),227pp (contemp ink presentation dwg tipped to flyleaf). Uncut. VG in limp vellum (sl warped), silk ties (2 detached), lettered in gold. Buckram slipcase. *Cox*. $936/£600

ROSSETTI, DANTE GABRIEL. Ballads and Sonnets. Boston: Roberts, 1882. 1st Amer ed thus. Gilt/black-stamped dec cl (spine sl dknd, few flecks cl sizing). VG. *Reese*. $40/£26

ROSSETTI, DANTE GABRIEL. The Collected Works. William M. Rossetti (ed). London: Ellis & Scrutton, 1886. 2 vols. Uncut. Blue cl, gilt. (Fore-edges sl foxed), o/w Good. *Maggs*. $390/£250

ROSSETTI, DANTE GABRIEL. Hand and Soul. Hammersmith: Kelmscott, 1895. One of 300 paper copies pub in US by Way & Williams. (Contemp sig.) Full vellum (lt soiled, cvrs bowed at fore-edge). *Waverly**. $385/£247

ROSSETTI, DANTE GABRIEL. Hand and Soul. (Hammersmith: Kelmscott, 1895.) One of 525. (Bkpl.) Vellum. Cl slipcase. *Swann**. $488/£313

ROSSETTI, DANTE GABRIEL. Letters of Dante Gabriel Rossetti to His Publisher, F. S. Ellis. Oswald Doughty (ed). London: Scholartis, 1928. 1st ed. One of 560 numbered. Teg, uncut. Blue cl, gilt. Fine. *Macdonnell*. $75/£48

ROSSETTI, DANTE GABRIEL. Letters to William Allingham, 1854-1870. George Birkbeck Hill (ed). London: T. Fisher Unwin, 1897. 1st Eng ed. (Bkpl removed, label removed tp verso; sl mkd, scratched.) *Clearwater*. $109/£70

ROSSETTI, DANTE GABRIEL. Poems.... Boston: Roberts, 1882. 1st Amer ed. Gilt/black-stamped dec cl (spine sl dknd, sm nick crown). Good (corner prelims roughly opened). *Reese*. $40/£26

ROSSETTI, DANTE GABRIEL. Sonnets and Lyrical Poems. (Hammersmith): Kelmscott, (1894). One of 310. 8vo. Orig limp vellum, silk ties. Cl slipcase. *Swann**. $805/£516

ROSSI, FILIPPO. Italian Jeweled Arts. London: Thames & Hudson, (1957). 1st ed. VF in dj, pub's slipcase. *Hermitage*. $100/£64

ROSSITER, HARRIET I. Indian Legends From the Land of Al-Ay-Es-Ka. Ketchikan, 1925. (Exterior spots), else VG in wraps. *Perier*. $35/£22

ROSSKAM, EDWIN and LOUISE. Towboat River. NY: Duell, Sloan & Pearce, 1948. 1st ed. Frontis. (Name stamp; cl sl dusty), else VG in dj (chipped, worn). *Cahan*. $75/£48

ROSSKAM, EDWIN. San Francisco: West Coast Metropolis. NY/Toronto: Alliance Book Corp, (1939). 1st ed. VG in dj (chipped). *Cahan*. $50/£32

ROSSMAN, EARL. Black Sunlight. NY, 1926. Fldg map. VG (sl soil). *High Latitude*. $20/£13

ROSSNER, JUDITH. Looking for Mr. Goodbar. Cape, 1975. 1st UK ed. NF in dj. *Williams*. $23/£15

ROSTAND, EDMOND. Cyrano de Bergerac. Heinemann, 1898. 1st ed in English. Good (sl wear, sl mks). *Ash*. $117/£75

ROSTAND, EDMOND. L'Aiglon. Louis N. Parker (trans). NY: R.H. Russell, 1900. 2 vols. Teg. Blue cl, gilt (1 w/extra gilt on spine, rear cvr). NF (ink name, presentation). *Antic Hay*. $85/£54

ROSTOV, CHARLES and J. GUANYAN. Chinese Carpets. NY: Abrams, (1983). Fine in dj. *Terramedia*. $30/£19

ROSTOVTZEFF, M. Dura-Europos and Its Art. Oxford, 1938. 28 plts hors texte. Good. *Washton*. $65/£42

ROT, DITER. 246 Little Clouds. NY: Something Else, 1968. Charcoal cl. Fine in dj. *Blue Mountain*. $35/£22

ROTBERG, ROBERT I. Joseph Thomson and the Exploration of Africa. NY: OUP, 1971. 6 maps. VG in dj. *Terramedia*. $75/£48

ROTERMUND, HANS-MARTIN. Rembrandt's Drawings and Etchings for the Bible. Phila, 1969. Good in dj. *Washton*. $100/£64

ROTH, H. LING. Oriental Silverwork. London: Truslove & Hanson, 1910. 1st ed. Teg. Cl over beveled bds. (Eps sl spotted), o/w Excellent. *Hollett*. $273/£175

ROTH, PHILIP. The Anatomy Lesson. Franklin Center: Franklin Library, 1983. 1st ed thus. Signed. Fine in Franklin leather. *Captain's Bookshelf*. $50/£32

ROTH, PHILIP. Goodbye, Columbus. Boston: Houghton Mifflin, 1959. 1st ed. VG (sl frayed) in VG dj (browned, chipped, internal tape). *Metropolitan**. $230/£147

ROTH, PHILIP. My Life As a Man. Cape, 1974. 1st UK ed. NF in dj (spine sl faded, price-clipped). *Williams*. $19/£12

ROTH, PHILIP. Portnoy's Complaint. NY: Random House, (1967). One of 600 numbered, signed. Fine in Fine dj, slipcase. *Lenz*. $150/£96

ROTH, PHILIP. Portnoy's Complaint. NY: Random House, (1969). 1st ed. Ltd to 600 signed. VF in dj, slipcase. *Bromer*. $250/£160

ROTH, PHILIP. The Professor of Desire. Cape, 1978. 1st UK ed. Fine in dj. *Williams*. $19/£12

ROTH, W. E. Additional Studies of the Arts, Crafts, and Customs of the Guiana Indians.... BAE Bulletin 91. GPO, 1929. 34 plts (6 color). Good (corners bumped). *Scribe's Perch**. $70/£45

ROTHENBERG, JEROME (ed). New Young German Poets. SF: City Light/Pocket Poets 11, (1959). 1st ed. Fine in ptd wrappers. *Reese*. $50/£32

ROTHENSTEIN, JOHN. The Artists of the 1890's. NY, 1929. 1st Amer ed. (Hinges weak.) *Clearwater.* $62/£40

ROTHENSTEIN, JOHN. British Artists and the War. London: Peter Davies, 1931. 1st Eng ed. 64 plts. (Inscrip; sl handled, sl bumped.) *Clearwater.* $70/£45

ROTHENSTEIN, JOHN. Summer's Lease. London: Hamish Hamilton, 1965. 1st ed. 22 plts. Good in dj. *Cox.* $12/£8

ROTHENSTEIN, WILLIAM. Contemporaries: Portrait Drawings. 1937. 1st ed. VG in dj (faded, chipped, sl soiled). *Words Etc.* $39/£25

ROTHENSTEIN, WILLIAM. The Portrait Drawings 1889-1925. 1926. 101 collotype plts. Teg. (Ex-lib, ink stamps, margins sl thumbed, bkpl; sl rubbed, spine #s.) *Edwards.* $140/£90

ROTHSCHILD, M. and T. CLAY. Fleas, Flukes and Cuckoos. London: Collins, 1952. 4 maps, 22 dwgs. Good. *Savona.* $39/£25

ROTHWEILER, PAUL R. The Sensuous Southpaw. NY: Putnam, (1976). 1st ed. Fine in dj. *Between The Covers.* $45/£29

ROUGHEAD, WILLIAM (ed). Burke and Hare. London: William Hodge, 1948. New, enlgd general ed. Red cl, gilt. Bright. *Boswell.* $75/£48

ROUGHEAD, WILLIAM (ed). Trial of Deacon Brodie. Edinburgh: William Hodge, 1921. 3rd expanded ed. Crimson cl (faded, worn; bk club stickers). Sound. *Boswell.* $75/£48

ROUGHEAD, WILLIAM. Twelve Scots Trials. Edinburgh, William Green, 1913. 1st ed. Dk blue cl (sl rubbed), gilt, maroon eps. *Boswell.* $125/£80

ROUNDS, GLEN. Ol' Paul the Mighty Logger. NY: Holiday, 1936. 1st ed. 5 3/4 x 7 3/4. 133pp. VG in dj. *Cattermole.* $60/£38

ROURKE, CONSTANCE. Charles Sheeler, Artist in the American Tradition. NY: Harcourt, Brace, 1938. 1st ed. Red cl bds. *Metropolitan*.* $30/£19

ROUSE, JOHN E. The Criollo, Spanish Cattle in the Americas. Norman: Univ of OK, (1977). 1st ed. 7 maps. Brn cl. Fine in pict dj. *Argonaut.* $45/£29

ROUSE, JOHN E. World Cattle. Norman: Univ of OK, 1970, 1973. 1st ed. 3 vols. Fldg map in rear pocket vol 1. Red cl. Fine in slipcases. *Argonaut.* $90/£58

ROUSE, WILLIAM HENRY DENHAM. Greek Votive Offerings. Cambridge, 1902. Good. *Washton.* $40/£26

ROUSE, WILLIAM. The Doctrine of Chances. London: The Author, n.d. (1814). 1st ed. W/the 'Binomial Table' plt, 4 fldg plts, errata leaf at end. Contemp calf (rubbed, rebacked), gilt, morocco label. *Dramatis Personae.* $500/£321

ROUSSEAU, I. J. The Peninsular Journal of Major General Sir Benjamin D'Urban 1808-1817. London, 1930. Frontis port, fldg map, 2 fldg plans, facs. Blue cl. Dj. *Maggs.* $156/£100

ROUSSEAU, J. J. Confessions. London: Nonesuch, 1938. One of 800 numbered. 2 vols. Reynolds Stone (illus). Teg. Full cream morocco. VG. *Argosy.* $350/£224

ROUSSELET, LOUIS. India and Its Native Princes. NY, 1876. Aeg. Grn cl (frayed, lt worn), gilt. *Freeman*.* $50/£32

ROUT, ETTIE A. Maori Symbolism. NY/London: Harcourt, Brace/Kegan Paul, Trench, Trubner, 1926. 1st Amer ed from British sheets. 32 plts. Maroon cl (extrems lt worn), gilt. VG. *House.* $120/£77

ROWAN, ALISTAIR. Designs for Castles and Country Villas by Robert and James Adam. Phaidon, 1985. 1st ed. Dj. *Edwards.* $70/£45

ROWAN, CARL T. Go South to Sorrow. NY: Random House, (1957). 1st ed. (Rubberstamp bottom page edges), else NF in VG dj (faint stain fr panel). *Between The Covers.* $55/£35

ROWAN, JOHN J. The Emigrant and Sportsman in Canada. London, 1876. 440pp, fldg map, half-title. Largely unopened. (Sig, labels, inner fr hinge broken; edgeworn), else VG. *Reese.* $175/£112

ROWAN, JOHN J. The Emigrant and Sportsman in Canada. London, 1876. 1st ed. Fldg map. (Lt worn.) *Oinonen*.* $350/£224

ROWAN, RICHARD WILMER. The Pinkertons. Boston: Little, Brown, 1931. 1st ed. VG. *Lien.* $35/£22

ROWAN-HAMILTON, S. O. (ed). Trial of John Alexander Dickman. Edinburgh: William Hodge, 1914. Maroon cl. (Foxed, edges spotted.) Sound. *Boswell.* $50/£32

ROWELL, JOHN W. Yankee Cavalrymen. Knoxville, (1971). 1st ed. VG + in VG + dj. *Pratt.* $50/£32

ROWLAND, DANIEL B. Mannerism—Style and Mood. New Haven/London, 1964. Good in dj. *Washton.* $40/£26

ROWLAND, DUNBAR. History of Mississippi: The Heart of the South. Chicago: Clarke, 1925. 1st ed. 4 vols. Contemp 1/2 morocco. *Ginsberg.* $300/£192

ROWLAND, ERON. Varina Howell, Wife of Jefferson Davis. NY, 1927. 1st ed. (Vol I spine faded), o/w VG + set. *Pratt.* $95/£61

ROWLAND, KATE MASON. Life of George Mason 1725-1792. NY: Putnam, 1892. 2 vols. xvii,454; iii,527pp; port. Teg; vol 2 unopened. VG + (spines lt sunned). Howes R477. *Bohling.* $90/£58

ROWLAND, MRS. DUNBAR. Andrew Jackson's Campaigns Against the British.... NY, 1926. 1st ed. (Ex-lib, inner hinges cracked), else Good. *King.* $30/£19

ROWLAND, MRS. DUNBAR (ed). Life, Letters and Papers of William Dunbar.... Jackson, MS, 1930. 1st ed. (Few spine flecks), o/w VG. *Wantagh.* $35/£22

ROWLAND, MRS. DUNBAR. Andrew Jackson's Campaigns Against the British. NY, 1926. 2nd ed, 1st trade ed. (Bkpl, stamp.) *Wantagh.* $50/£32

ROWLANDS, WALTER. Curious Old Gravestones in and About Boston. Boston, 1924. 1st ed. Portfolio w/50 loose b/w plts. Cl-backed bds, ptd label, string ties. (Extrems lt rubbed), else VG. *Cahan.* $125/£80

ROWLANDSON, THOMAS. The Tour of Doctor Syntax Through London, or the Pleasures and Miseries of the Metropolis. London: J. Johnson, 1820. 1st ed. Frontis, iv,(2),319pp; 20 hand-colored aquatint plts, added title. Untrimmed. Mod 1/2 vellum, bds. (Some plts out of order, sl foxing, offsetting), o/w NF. *Goodrich.* $495/£317

ROWLEY, J. Taxidermy and Museum Exhibition. NY: Appleton, 1925. 1st ed. 19 plts. Gilt-dec cl. VG. *Mikesh.* $40/£26

ROWNTREE, LEONARD. Amid Masters of Twentieth Century Medicine. Springfield, 1958. 1st ed. (Ex-lib.) *Fye.* $50/£32

ROWSE, A. L. West-Country Stories. Macmillan, 1945. 1st UK ed. VG + in VG dj. *Williams.* $39/£25

ROWSON, SUSANNA. Charlotte Temple. Phila: Mathew Carey, 1809. 8th Amer ed. 2 vols in 1. Port, 137pp. Contemp calf. (Sl scuffed, worn, spinel label lacks portion), else Good. *Brown.* $50/£32

Royal Gallery of British Art. (By Edward and William Finden.) London: J. Hogarth, (ca 1850). 42 (of 48) engr repros. Dec cl. (Some ll, plts loose, edges frayed; heavily worn, cvrs detached, spine gone.) *New Hampshire*.* $170/£109

Royal Punch and Judy. London: Dean & Son, n.d. (c. 1870). Tall 8vo. 8 color-ptd movable pp (closed tear 1 pg, neatly repaired. Color pict bds (rear cvr rubbed, closed tear head of cvr), cl spine. VG (lt wear, soil). *Dramatis Personae.* $1,000/£641

ROYALL, WILLIAM L. A History of Virginia Banks and Banking Prior to the Civil War. NY/Washington: Neale, 1907. 1st ed. (Sl soiled, worn.) *Wantagh.* $75/£48

ROYALL, WILLIAM L. Some Reminiscences. Neale, 1909. Good (foxing, ex-lib; cvr faded, hinges broken). *Book Broker.* $125/£80

ROYCE, JOSIAH. The Basic Writings of.... John J. McDermott (ed); with: The Letters of Josiah Royce. John Clendenning (ed). Chicago: Univ of Chicago, (1969-1970). 1st collected ed. 3 vols. Frontis port each vol. Blue cl. Fine in djs. *Argonaut.* $125/£80

ROYCE, JOSIAH. The Conception of Immortality. Boston: Houghton Mifflin, 1900. 1st ed. NF (spine lt soiled, sl sunned). *Beasley.* $75/£48

ROYCE, JOSIAH. The Spirit of Modern Philosophy. Boston: Houghton Mifflin, 1892. 1st ed. NF (spine label removed). *Beasley.* $60/£38

ROYCE, SARAH. A Frontier Lady. New Haven: Yale Univ, 1932. 1st ed. Map. Grey cl. Fine in dj (spine dknd, losses not affecting title, at spine ends; corner chipped). *Harrington.* $70/£45

ROYCE, SARAH. A Frontier Lady: Recollections of the Gold Rush and Early California. Ralph Henry Gabriel (ed). New Haven: Yale Univ, 1932. 1st ed. Map. Gray cl. Fine. *Pacific*.* $109/£70

ROYDE-SMITH, NAOMI. The Tortoiseshell Cat. Constable, 1925. 1st ed, 1st bk. (Prelims sl spotted.) *Bickersteth.* $31/£20

ROYER, FRANCHON. The Franciscans Came First. NJ, 1951. 1st ed. VG in dj (chipped). *Turpen.* $30/£19

ROYIDIS, EMMANUEL. Pope Joan. Lawrence Durrell (trans). London, 1954. 1st Eng ed. Very Bright in dj (sl torn). *Clearwater.* $39/£25

ROZIER, FIRMIN. History of the Early Settlement of the Mississippi Valley. St. Louis, 1890. Frontis port, 337pp. (Tip bumped), o/w Fine. Howes R488. *Turpen.* $95/£61

ROZIER, FIRMIN. Rozier's History of the Early Settlement of the Mississippi Valley. St. Louis: G.A. Pierrot, 1890. 337pp (pencil mks) incl frontis port, 13 plts. Grn cl (rebacked, new backstrip, worn), gilt. Howes R488. *Bohling.* $75/£48

RUARK, ROBERT. Horn of the Hunter. GC: Doubleday, 1953. Stated 1st ed. Fine in dj (lt chipped). *Bowman.* $150/£96

RUARK, ROBERT. The Old Man and the Boy. NY: Holt, (1957). Stated 1st ed. Good in dj (chipped). *Scribe's Perch*.* $42/£27

RUARK, ROBERT. The Old Man's Boy Grows Older. NY: Holt, Rinehart & Winston, 1961. Stated 1st ed. VG+ (bkpl) in VG dj (lt soiled, corner chipped). *Backman.* $65/£42

RUARK, ROBERT. On Hunting Big Game Use Enough Gun. NY: NAL, 1966. Stated 1st ptg. VG+ in VG dj (edges torn). *Backman.* $36/£23

Rubaiyat of Omar Khayyam. SF: Johnck, Kibbee, 1926. Signed, inscribed by Lawrence A. Patterson (illus). 8 b/w plts. Paper parchment bds (soiled, rubbed, fr joint sl cracked; sl damping lower spine, sl affecting contents). *Waverly*.* $33/£21

RUBENS, PETER PAUL. The Letters of Peter Paul Rubens. Ruth Saunders Magurn (ed). Cambridge, 1971. 2nd ed. 20 plts. Good. *Washton.* $40/£26

RUBIN, JERRY. Growing (Up) at Thirty-Seven. NY: M. Evans, 1976. 1st ed. NF- in dj. *Sclanders.* $19/£12

RUBIN, JERRY. We Are Everywhere. NY: Harper & Row, 1971. 1st ed. Fine in dj. *Associates.* $65/£42

RUBIN, WILLIAM (ed). Primitivism in 20th Century Art. NY: MOMA, (1984). Djs. *Freeman*.* $55/£35

RUBY, JAMES S. (ed). Blue and Gray. Washington, (1961). 1st ed. VG in dj (lt chipping). *Pratt.* $45/£29

RUCK, BERTA. The Pearl Thief. NY: Dodd Mead, 1926. 1st ed. VG in dj (chipped, 2-inch piece missing fr panel, folds worn, closed tears). *Mordida.* $35/£22

RUD, ANTHONY. The Stuffed Men. NY: Macaulay, 1935. 1st ed. VG (sl frayed) in dj (edgewear, short tears, creases, spine tear, chips). *Metropolitan*.* $34/£22

RUDDOCK, MARGOT. The Lemon Tree. London: Dent, 1937. 1st ed. (Ex-lib, ink lib #s spine, stamps.) *Hollett.* $23/£15

RUDORFF, R. The Dracula Archives. Arbor House, 1971. 1st ed. Fine in VG+ dj. *Aronovitz.* $55/£35

RUDY, CHARLES. The Cathedrals of Northern Spain. London, 1906. 1st ed. Frontis. Dec cl (hinge tender). *Edwards.* $23/£15

RUEDEMANN, RUDOLF. Graptolites of New York. Albany: NYS Museum, 1904, 1908. 2 vols. (Ex-lib; shelfworn, soiled.) *Bohling.* $27/£17

RUELL, PATRICK. (Pseud of Reginald Hill.) The Long Kill. London: Methuen, 1986. 1st ed. Fine in dj. *Mordida.* $45/£29

RUFFNER, E. H. Lines of Communication Between Colorado and New Mexico. Washington: GPO, 1878. 37pp; 3 fldg maps. Leather. (Rebound, worn, browned) else Good. *Dumont.* $275/£176

RUHEMANN, HELMUT. The Cleaning of Paintings. NY: Praeger, 1968. Color frontis, 95 plts. Fine in color dj. *Europa.* $109/£70

RUHEMANN, HELMUT. The Cleaning of Paintings. London, 1969. Good. *Washton.* $90/£58

RUHMER, EBERHARD. Tura. Phaidon, 1958. Complete ed. 104 plts (6 color). Dj (sl rubbed). *Edwards.* $62/£40

RUHRAH, JOHN. Pediatrics of the Past. NY, 1925. 1st ed. (Backstrip dull.) *Fye.* $300/£192

RUKEYSER, MURIEL. 29 Poems. London, 1972. 1st ed. Fine in dj (price-clipped). *Polyanthos.* $25/£16

RUKEYSER, MURIEL. Body of Waking. NY, 1958. 1st Amer ed. Fine in dj (2 sm tears lower fr panel, spine sl rubbed). *Polyanthos.* $25/£16

RUKEYSER, MURIEL. The Green Wave. NY, 1948. 1st Amer ed. Fine in dj (edges sl chipped). *Polyanthos.* $25/£16

RUKEYSER, MURIEL. The Life of Poetry. NY, 1949. 1st Amer ed. Fine in NF dj (spine sl sunned). *Polyanthos.* $25/£16

RUKEYSER, MURIEL. The Orgy. London, 1966. 1st ed. Fine (spine extrems sl rubbed) in dj (spine top sl rubbed). *Polyanthos.* $25/£16

RUKEYSER, MURIEL. The Speed of Darkness. NY, 1968. 1st Amer ed. Fine in dj (edges sl rubbed). *Polyanthos.* $25/£16

RUKEYSER, MURIEL. Theory of Flight. New Haven: Yale Univ, 1935. 1st ed, 1st bk. NF in VG dj (rubbed, spine sl faded). *Captain's Bookshelf.* $175/£112

RUKEYSER, MURIEL. U.S. 1. NY: Covici Friede, 1938. 1st ed. VG in Good dj. *Warren.* $50/£32

RUMBOLD, RICHARD. Little Victims. London: Fortune, 1933. 1st Eng ed, 1st bk. Fine in dj (sl nicked). *Clearwater.* $78/£50

RUMPLE, JETHRO. A History of Rowan County, North Carolina, Containing Sketches of Prominent Families and Distiguished Men.... Salisbury, NC: Elizabeth Maxwell Steele Chapter, D.A.R., (1929). 3rd ed. NF. *Mcgowan.* $85/£54

RUNES, DAGOBERT. The Selected Writings of Benjamin Rush. NY, 1947. 1st ed. VG. *Fye.* $50/£32

RUNYON, DAMON. In Our Town. NY, (1946). 1st Amer ed. Fine (sl crease fr cvr) in dj (spine extrems sl rubbed, sm closed tear rear panel). *Polyanthos.* $30/£19

RUNYON, DAMON. Money from Home. NY: Frederick A. Stokes, 1935. 1st ed. Nice (sl mks, sl dusty) in dj (chipped, sl discolored). *Ash.* $195/£125

RUNYON, DAMON. More Than Somewhat. London, 1937. 1st ed. (Sl dust-soiled, crease fr panel), o/w VG. *Words Etc.* $12/£8

RUNYON, DAMON. Runyon a la Carte. London: Constable, 1946. 1st UK ed. Fine in NF dj. *Williams.* $55/£35

RUNYON, DAMON. Runyon from First to Last. London: Constable, 1954. 1st Eng ed. Nice (corner knocked) in dj (sl chipped, mkd). *Clearwater.* $39/£25

Rupert and Tigerlily's Magic. Purnell, 1974. 1st ed. Obl sm 4to. 6 color pictures (3 are pop-ups). Pict bds. VG (few sm creases). *Bookmark.* $23/£15

RUSCHA, EDWARD. Crackers. Hollywood: Heavy Industry Publications, 1969. 1st ed. NF in plain stiff wrappers, ptd dj (sl dusty). *Cahan.* $150/£96

RUSCHA, EDWARD. Crackers. Hollywood: Heavy Industry Publications, 1969. 1st ed. Fine in stiff paper wrappers in Fine dj. *Smith.* $225/£144

RUSCHA, EDWARD. Every Building on the Sunset Strip. L.A.: Self-published, 1966. 1st ed. Fldg panorama. Fine in stiff white wrappers (lt mk fr cvr) in silver paper-cvrd slipcase (sl rubbed). *Cahan.* $200/£128

RUSCHENBERGER, W. S. W. First Book of Natural History, Elements of Entomology, Etc. Phila, 1845. 1st ed. 121pp + ads. 1/4 leather, bds. Good +. *Mikesh.* $30/£19

RUSH, BENJAMIN. Medical Inquiries and Observations Upon the Diseases of the Mind. Phila: Kimber & Richardson, 1812. 1st ed, 2nd issue (actually ptg) w/sig H reset so that Section VIII begins on p62. (368),(4)pp (new eps). Orig calf (rebacked, bds scraped). Very Clean. *Gach.* $1,250/£801

RUSH, BENJAMIN. Medical Inquiries and Observations Upon the Diseases of the Mind. Phila: John Grigg, 1830. 4th ed. 365,(3)pp (sig cut from tp). Contemp sheep (lacks leather spine label, rear bd detached). Internally Very Clean. *Gach.* $250/£160

RUSH, BENJAMIN. Medical Inquiries and Observations Upon the Diseases of the Mind. Phila, 1835. 5th ed. 8vo. 365pp + ads. Full sheep (edges rubbed; foxed), else Fine. *Argosy.* $500/£321

RUSH, BENJAMIN. Medical Inquiries and Observations. Phila: Thomas Dobson, 1796. 1st ed. xi,258pp (sl browned, ink sigs, ink handstamps). Early tree calf, leather spine label, gilt. Cvrs VG (sl worn, scuffed, old repair upper joint). *Baltimore*.* $220/£141

RUSH, BENJAMIN. The Works of Thomas Sydenham, M.D. on Acute and Chronic Diseases.... Phila, 1815. 1st ed. 513 + pp (foxed). Full leather (hinges cracked; extrems worn). Good. *Doctor's Library.* $300/£192

RUSH, JOHN. A Pioneer's Reminiscences. Omaha, 1928. Frontis port. VG (sl dull, spine ends rubbed). *Bohling.* $30/£19

RUSHDIE, SALMAN. Haroun and the Sea of Stories. NY/London: Granta/Viking, 1990. 1st ed. 6 x 8 1/2. 219pp. 1/2 cl. Fine in dj. *Cattermole.* $45/£29

RUSHDIE, SALMAN. Shame. NY: Knopf, 1983. 1st Amer ed. Fine in dj. *Cahan.* $20/£13

RUSHTON, CHARLES. Furnace for a Foe. London, 1957. 1st ed. VG in dj. *Madle.* $30/£19

RUSINOW, IRVING. A Camera Report on El Cerrito. (Washington): Bureau of Agricultural Economics, Jan 1942. NF in ptd stiff wrappers. *Cahan.* $85/£54

RUSKIN, ARTHUR. Classics in Arterial Hypertension. Springfield, 1956. 1st ed. VG. *Fye.* $125/£80

RUSKIN, JOHN (ed). Dame Wiggins of Lee, and Her Seven Wonderful Cats. Sunnyside, Oppington, 1885. Kate Greenaway (illus). 12mo. Later 1/2 morocco (extrems worn; ex-lib, ink stamps). *Swann*.* $230/£147

RUSKIN, JOHN. Ariadne Florentina. Orpington, Kent: G. Allen, 1873-1876. 1st ed. Orig 7 parts. 17 plts (2 w/pencil notes, 2 others detached, sl frayed in margins). Contents VG (sigs) in wraps (soil, stains, wear, esp spines). *Waverly*.* $77/£49

RUSKIN, JOHN. The Brantwood Diary of John Ruskin. Helen Gill Viljoen (ed). Yale Univ, 1971. 1st ed. Ephemera loosely inserted. VG in dj. *Hollett.* $117/£75

RUSKIN, JOHN. The Crown of Wild Olive. NY, 1866. 1st Amer ed. 127pp. (Bkpl; cvrs discolored, rubbed.) *King.* $20/£13

RUSKIN, JOHN. The Elements Perspective Arranged for the Use of Schools.... Smith, Elder, 1859. 1st ed. xii,144pp, 24-pg pub's cat. (Lower cvr spotted.) *Bickersteth.* $47/£30

RUSKIN, JOHN. The Harbours of England. London: E. Gambart, 1856. 12 engr plts. (Bkpl, lt spotting.) Gilt edges. Contemp morocco (extrems rubbed), gilt. *Christie's*.* $351/£225

RUSKIN, JOHN. John Ruskin's Letters to Francesca and Memoirs of the Alexanders. Lucia Gray Swett (ed). Boston: Lothrop, Lee & Shepard, (1931). 1st Amer ed. Frontis port, 12 b/w plts. (Bkpl, stamps verso tp), else Nice. *Turtle Island.* $45/£29

RUSKIN, JOHN. The King of the Golden River. London, (1932). One of 570 numbered, signed by Arthur Rackham (illus). 4 color plts. Pict eps. Orig limp vellum, gilt. Cl slipcase. *Swann*.* $287/£184

RUSKIN, JOHN. The King of the Golden River. London: George Harrap, (1932). 1st trade ed. 8vo. 4 plts by Arthur Rackham. VG in dj (lt soiled, closed tears, sm chip). *Waverly*.* $77/£49

RUSKIN, JOHN. The King of the Golden River. London: George Harrap, (1932). #79/550 signed by Arthur Rackham (illus). 8vo. 4 color plts. Pict eps. Flexible parchment cvrs, gilt. (Frontis unbound halfway from bottom; exterior foxed), o/w VG in pub's slipcase. *Metropolitan*.* $575/£369

RUSKIN, JOHN. The King of the Golden River. London: Harrap, 1932. One of 570 ptd, signed by Arthur Rackham (illus). Tall 8vo. 4 color plts. Gilt-stamped vellum, gilt top. Fine in box (worn). *Appelfeld.* $600/£385

RUSKIN, JOHN. Lectures on Art. Oxford: Clarendon, 1870. 1st ed. (i),189,12pp. (Bkpl; spine faded.) *Hollett.* $133/£85

RUSKIN, JOHN. Letters Addressed to a College Friend During the Years 1840-1845. NY/London: Macmillan, 1894. 1st ed. (Sl ex-libris mks spine, inside rear cvr.) *Turtle Island.* $35/£22

RUSKIN, JOHN. Letters to M.G. and H.G. NY/London, 1903. Teg. NF (sl rubbed). *Polyanthos.* $35/£22

RUSKIN, JOHN. Letters to M.G. and H.G. NY/London: Harper, 1903. 1st ed. Photo frontis. (Spine lt sunned, sl ex-libris mks), else VG. *Turtle Island.* $30/£19

RUSKIN, JOHN. Notes on the Construction of Sheepfolds. London, 1851. 1st ed. 50pp + 1pg ads (title soiled, sl chipped). Sewed wraps. *King.* $100/£64

RUSKIN, JOHN. The Seven Lamps of Architecture. Smith, Elder, 1849. 1st ed. viii,(iv),205pp, 16-pg pub's cat; 13 plts. Orig emb cl (rebacked), orig eps. *Bickersteth.* $133/£85

RUSKIN, JOHN. The Stones of Venice. Sunnyside, Orpington: George Allen, 1893. 5th ed. 3 vols. 53 plts. (Lt soil, ends sl worn, sm stains 1 bd edge.) VG overall. *Waverly*.* $60/£38

RUSKIN, JOHN. Time and Tide, by Weare and Tyne. London: Smith Elder, 1867. 1st ed. viii,199pp. Limp cl, gilt. (Joints strengthened.) *Hollett.* $101/£65

RUSKIN, JOHN. Unto This Last. Chicago, 1888. 1st Amer ed. Fine. *Polyanthos.* $30/£19

RUSS, JOANNA. Picnic on Paradise. London: Macdonald, (1969). 1st British, 1st hb ed. (Bumped.) Dj (lt worn, rear stained). *Swann*.* $69/£44

RUSS, JOANNA. The Zanzibar Cat. Sauk City: Arkham House, (1983). 1st ed. NF in dj (spine corner lt wear). *Other Worlds.* $65/£42

RUSS, JOANNA. The Zanzibar Cat. (Sauk City, 1983.) 1st ed. VF in VF dj. *Mcclintock.* $45/£29

RUSSELL, BERTRAND and JOHN COWPER POWYS. Is Modern Marriage a Failure? UK: Warren House, 1983. 1st ed. Ltd to 200. Fine in Fine dj. *Polyanthos.* $25/£16

RUSSELL, BERTRAND. The Analysis of Matter. NY: Harcourt, Brace, 1927. 1st Amer ed. NF. *Glaser.* $75/£48

RUSSELL, BERTRAND. The Autobiography of Bertrand Russell. 1872-1967. London, 1967-9. 1st ed. 3 vols. (Lt faded; lacks djs.) *Edwards.* $39/£25

RUSSELL, BERTRAND. The Conquest of Happiness. 1930. 1st ed. VG in dj (spine sl browned). *Words Etc.* $25/£16

RUSSELL, BERTRAND. Education for Democracy. London: Assoc for Education in Citizenship No. 4, n.d. 1st ed. NF in ptd wraps (sl sunned). *Polyanthos.* $20/£13

RUSSELL, BERTRAND. The Impact of Science on Society. NY, 1951. 1st ed. (Sm tear bottom edge 1st few pp), else VG in dj (sl chipped, dknd). *King.* $35/£22

RUSSELL, BERTRAND. Nightmares of Eminent Persons and Other Stories. NY: S&S, 1954. 1st ed. Fine in dj (sl worn). *Beasley.* $30/£19

RUSSELL, BERTRAND. The Principles of Mathematics. CUP, 1903. 1st ed. 8vo. xxix,534pp. Navy cl. (Bkpl, inscrip; backstrip lt frayed, remnant paper spine label). VG. *Glaser.* $1,200/£769

RUSSELL, BERTRAND. Satan in the Suburbs and Other Stories. NY: S&S, 1953. 1st Amer ed. Fine in dj (sl wear). *Antic Hay.* $20/£13

RUSSELL, BERTRAND. Satan in the Suburbs and Other Stories. NY: S&S, 1953. 1st ed. Fine in dj (lt used). *Beasley.* $25/£16

RUSSELL, C. E. M. Bullet and Shot in Indian Forest, Plain and Hill. London, 1900. 2nd ed. Gilt-pict cl (sl worn; foxed). *Oinonen*.* $225/£144

RUSSELL, CARL P. Firearms, Traps and Tools of the Mountain Men. NY: Knopf, 1967. Stated 1st ed. Good + in Good dj. *Scribe's Perch*.* $26/£17

RUSSELL, CARL P. One Hundred Years in Yosemite. Stanford, CA: Stanford Univ, 1931. 1st ed. (Cvr sl speckled), else VG. *Mcgowan.* $250/£160

RUSSELL, DAN. Working Terriers. London: Batchworth, 1948. 1st ed. VG (sl shelfwear). *October Farm.* $35/£22

RUSSELL, DON (ed). Trails of the Iron Horse. NY: Doubleday, 1975. 1st ed. Fine in Fine dj. *Book Market.* $35/£22

RUSSELL, DON. Custer's Last, or, The Battle of the Little Big Horn in Picturesque Perspective.... (Ft. Worth: Amon Carter Museum, 1968.) 1st ed. Purple cl. NF in VG + dj (sl losses rear panel). *Harrington.* $65/£42

RUSSELL, DON. The Lives and Legends of Buffalo Bill. Norman: Univ of OK, (1960). 1st ed. VG in dj. *Perier.* $60/£38

RUSSELL, ERIC FRANK. Dreadful Sanctuary. Reading: Fantasy, 1951. 1st ed. One of 350 w/signed, numbered leaf tipped in. Dj (lt chipped, rear flap partly separated at fold). *Kane*.* $55/£35

RUSSELL, F. E. and P. R. SAUNDERS (eds). Animal Toxins: A Collection of Papers.... Oxford: Pergamon, 1967. 1st ed. VG + . *Mikesh.* $75/£48

RUSSELL, H. N. et al. Astronomy. A Revision of Young's Manual.... 1945. Rev ed. 2 vols. (Bkpls, ink sigs.) *Whitehart.* $39/£25

RUSSELL, I. C. Geological History of Lake Lahontan. Washington, 1885. xiv,288pp; 19 maps (1 fldg in pocket), 18 plts. *Henly.* $66/£42

RUSSELL, I. C. Lakes of North America. Boston: Ginn, 1895. x,125pp. (Foxed), else Good. *Dumont.* $35/£22

RUSSELL, J. RUTHERFORD. The History and Heroes of the Art of Medicine. London, 1861. 1st ed. 491pp. Contents Fine (fr bd detached). *Fye.* $65/£42

RUSSELL, J. RUTHERFORD. The History and Heroes of the Art of Medicine. London: John Murray, 1861. 1st ed. 492pp. Dec cl (sl rubbed, spine dknd; joints cracking, 1 section working loose). *Hollett.* $70/£45

RUSSELL, JOHN ANDREW. The Germanic Influence in the Making of Michigan. Univ of Detroit, 1927. 1st ed. Teg. 3/4 leather (sl worn). *King.* $75/£48

RUSSELL, JOHN. English Farming. London, 1941. 1st Eng ed. Excellent in dj. *Edrich.* $25/£16

RUSSELL, JOHN. Letters from a Young Painter Abroad to His Friends in England. London: W. Russel, 1750. 2nd ed. Lg paper copy. 2 vols. 8vo. (Tps),viii + 287pp,2 ff.; xii,395pp,4 ff., 13 engr plts (12 fldg). Sprinkled calf (mod repairs, rebacking both vols). *Marlborough.* $749/£480

RUSSELL, JOHN. The Life of William Lord Russell; with Some Account of the Times in Which He Lived. London: Longman et al, 1819. 1st ed. Frontis port, (i-vii)viii-xi(xii-xiii)xiv-xvi,(1)2-271(272),(273-277)278-329(330)pp. 9 appendices. 1/4 morocco, gilt spine, marbled bds. Very Nice. *Vandoros.* $225/£144

RUSSELL, OSBORNE. Journal of a Trapper. (Boise: Syms-York), 1921. 2nd ed. (Bkpl), else VG. *Hermitage.* $175/£112

RUSSELL, R. A Dissertation on the Use of Sea-Water in the Diseases of the Glands. 1752. 1st Eng ed. Frontis, xii,204pp (prelims dampstained). *Whitehart.* $281/£180

RUSSELL, RAY. Incubus. Morrow, 1976. 1st ed. Fine in Fine dj. *Certo.* $75/£48

RUSSELL, ROSS. Bird Lives! The High Life and Hard Times of Charlie (Yardbird) Parker. NY: Charterhouse, 1973. 1st ed. NF in NF dj (spine sl wrinkled, sl sunned). *Beasley.* $100/£64

RUSSELL, RUTHERFURD. The History and Heroes of the Art of Medicine. London: John Murray, 1861. 1st ed. 491pp (pp390-455 chipped margins, no loss). Partly unopened. Blind-stamped cl, gilt spine (repaired). *Argosy.* $35/£22

RUSSELL, SCOTT. Mountain Prospect. 1946. 1st ed. 46 plts. (Sm spike mk through lower cvr, final 20 pp.) *Bickersteth.* $31/£20

RUSSELL, THOMAS C. (ed). The Shirley Letters from California Mines 1851-52. SF: Thos. C. Russell, 1922. One of 250 ptd, signed. 8 hand-colored illus. Brn bds, linen spine, paper label, gilt top. Fine. *Appelfeld.* $300/£192

RUSSELL, THOMAS H. Pictures from the Wonderful Wizard of Oz.... Chicago: George W. Oglivie, (ca 1903). 8vo. 22 Bright color plts by W.W. Denslow. Cl-backed pict wrappers (creasing, few chips). Very Nice. *Metropolitan*.* $287/£184

RUSSELL, W. CLARK et al. The British Seas. London, 1894. 1st ed. xi,279pp. Marbled eps, edges. Full tree calf (sl rubbed; bkpl), gilt, leather spine label. *Edwards.* $44/£28

RUSSELL, W. CLARK. The Phantom Death and Other Stories. London: C&W, 1895. 1st ed. Dec cl (sl soiled, worn; inner hinges partly cracked). *Holmes.* $125/£80

RUSSELL, W. CLARK. The Yarn of Old Harbour Town. London: T. Fisher Unwin, 1905. 1st ed. Frontis. Pict cl. (Foxing, lt wear), o/w VG. *Holmes.* $125/£80

RUSSELL, W. CLARK. The Yarn of Old Harbour Town. London: T. Fisher Unwin, 1905. 1st ed. Lt grn pict dec cl. Fine (lt foxed). *Sumner & Stillman.* $195/£125

RUSSELL, WILLIAM HOWARD. A Visit to Chile and the Nitrate Fields of Tarapaca.... London: J.S. Virtue, 1890. 1st ed. Frontis, xii,374pp, 1/2-title, 2 fldg maps, 19 plts (foxing throughout). Blue cl (stained, extrms rubbed, hinges cracking), gilt lettering. *Morrell.* $234/£150

RUSSO, DOROTHY R. and THELMA L. SULLIVAN. Bibliographical Studies of Seven Authors of Crawfordsville, Indiana. Indianapolis, 1952. 1st ed. VG. *Argosy.* $60/£38

RUSSO, RICHARD. The Risk Pool. NY: Random House, (1988). 1st ed. Fine in dj. *Hermitage.* $45/£29

RUSSOW, K. E. Bruno Liljefors. Stockholm, 1929. One of 1000 numbered. 3/4 morocco (orig fr wrapper bound in; lt rubbed). *Oinonen*.* $160/£103

RUST, BRIAN. Jazz Records 1897-1942. London: Storyville, 1970. Rev ed. 2 vols. Red cl, gilt. VG. *Beasley.* $175/£112

RUTGERS, A. Birds of Australia. London, 1967. John Gould (lithos). 160 color plts. Fine in dj. *Henly.* $56/£36

RUTGERS, A. Birds of Europe. London, 1966. John Gould (lithos). 160 color plts. Fine in dj. *Henly.* $59/£38

RUTGERS, A. Birds of South America. London, 1972. 1st UK ed. John Gould (illus). (Pastedowns, cl sl waterstained.) Dj (sl soiled, chipped, tape-repaired). *Edwards.* $39/£25

RUTH, KENT. Great Day in the West. Norman: Univ of OK, (1963). 1st ed. VG in dj. *Lien.* $30/£19

RUTLEDGE, ARCHIBALD. An American Hunter. NY, 1937. (Ink name), else VG +. *Truepenny.* $45/£29

RUTLEDGE, ARCHIBALD. My Colonel and His Lady. Indianapolis: Bobbs Merrill, 1937. 1st ed. Fine in VG dj (chipped). *Bowman.* $50/£32

RUTTER, FRANK. The British Empire Panels Designed for the House of Lords by Frank Brangwyn, R.A. Benfleet: Lewis, 1933. Fldg color frontis, 51 plts horstexte. Fine in ptd dj. *Europa.* $101/£65

RUTTLEDGE, HUGH. Everest 1933. London: Hodder & Stoughton, 1934. 1st ed. 59 plts, 3 diags, 4 fldg maps. VG in dj (chip). *Hollett.* $148/£95

RUXTON, GEORGE F. Adventures in Mexico and the Rocky Mountains (1846-47). London, 1849. 332pp. VG (writing in margins; rebacked). Howes R553. *Turpen.* $95/£61

RUXTON, GEORGE F. Adventures in Mexico and the Rocky Mountains. London, 1847. viii,332pp. (Lt foxed; cl soiled, extrms worn, sl frayed, soiled, spine sunned, rear joint splitting.) Sound. Howes R553. *Reese.* $200/£128

RUXTON, GEORGE F. Adventures in Mexico and the Rocky Mountains. NY, 1848. 1st Amer ed. 312pp + ads. Teg. Orig ptd wrappers bound into 3/4 gilt morocco, cl. (Private lib notes, stamps; sl rubbed), else VG. Howes R553. *Reese.* $250/£160

RUXTON, GEORGE F. Adventures in Mexico and the Rocky Mountains. NY: Harper, 1848. 1st Amer ed. 312pp in 2 parts (1st few leaves part 2 waterstained; lt foxing throughout). Ad broadsheet of Toronto bkseller bound in Part Two. Ptd wraps (soiled, chipped, lacks backstrip). Howes R553. *Cullen.* $150/£96

RUXTON, GEORGE F. Life in the Far West. Edinburgh/London, 1849. xvi,312pp. Mod 3/4 polished calf, cl, spine gilt, leather label. VG. Howes R554. *Reese.* $250/£160

RUXTON, GEORGE F. Life in the Far West. Edinburgh/London: William Blackwood, 1849. 1st ed. 12mo. xvi,312pp. Blind-stamped red cl (lt rubbed, sl soiled), gilt-lettered spine. Overall NF (inner hinges sl cracked; bkpl inner cvr) in cl slipcase. Howes 554. *Argonaut.* $500/£321

RUXTON, GEORGE F. Life in the Far West. NY, 1849. 1st Amer ed. 235pp + ads. (Lt foxed, eps sl soiled; spine toe frayed), else VG. Howes R554. *Reese.* $300/£192

RUXTON, GEORGE F. Life in the Far West. Norman, 1951. 1st ed thus. Fine in Fine dj. Howes R557. *Turpen.* $38/£24

RYALL, E. C. Operative Cystoscopy. 1925. 115 plts. (Ink inscrip, lib stamp; inner hinges, few sections cracked; spine cl split, sm nicks, worn.) *Whitehart.* $62/£40

RYAN, ALAN. Cast a Cold Eye. Niles: Dark Harvest, 1984. 1st ed, trade issue. Inscribed. Fine in Fine dj. *Other Worlds.* $45/£29

RYAN, KATE. Old Boston Museum Days. Boston: Little Brown, 1915. 1st ed. 16 plts. Teg. (Sl rubbed, ex-lib), o/w VG. *Worldwide.* $15/£10

RYAN, LEE W. French Travelers in the Southeastern United States 1775-1800. Bloomington, Inc, 1939. VG (ink sig, pencil notes). *Reese.* $35/£22

RYAN, R. J. The Third Fleet Convicts. Aust., 1983. *Edwards.* $23/£15

RYAN, THOMAS. Recollections of an Old Musician. NY: Dutten, 1899. 1st ed. (16),274pp. Dec cl. *Ginsberg.* $100/£64

RYAN, VICTOR A. Some Geographic and Economic Aspects of the Cork Oak. Balt, 1948. 10 fldg color maps, 7 b/w plts. VG (lib bkpl, blind stamp tp). *Brooks.* $29/£19

RYAN, W. M. Shamrock and Cactus. San Antonio/Houston: Southern Literary Institute, 1936. 1st ed. (Lt foxing). NF in pict stiff wrappers (repaired chipping spine head, edges sl dknd). *Argonaut.* $50/£32

RYAN, W. P. Literary London, Its Lights and Comedies. London: The Author, 1898. 1st ed. (Sl spotted.) Uncut. Dk blue cl (sl scuffed), gilt. *Maggs.* $70/£45

RYDBERG, P. A. Flora of Colorado. Fort Collins, 1906. Map. Grn cl (sm snag backstrip, tip worn). *Brooks.* $49/£31

RYDBERG, VIKTOR. The Magic of the Middle Ages. A. H. Edgren (trans). NY: Holt, 1879. 1st ed in English. 231pp. VG (2-inch spine cut). *Middle Earth.* $95/£61

RYDELL, CARL. Adventures of Carl Rydell. Elmer Green (ed). London: Edward Arnold, 1924. Map. (Name), else VG. *High Latitude.* $40/£26

RYDER, DAVIS WARREN. Memories of the Mendocino Coast. SF: Privately ptd, 1948. 1st ed. VG. *Perier.* $45/£29

RYDER, JOHN. Printing for Pleasure. 1955. 1st ed. (Lacks fep.) Dj (sl chipped, price-clipped). *Edwards.* $16/£10

RYDER, JONATHAN. (Pseud of Robert Ludlum.) The Cry of the Halidon. NY: Delacorte, 1974. 1st ed. Fine in dj (sl wear). *Mordida.* $45/£29

RYDER, JONATHAN. (Pseud of Robert Ludlum.) Trevayne. NY: Delacorte, 1973. 1st ed. NF (sl spine dulling; soiling bottom edge) in NF dj. *Beasley.* $100/£64

RYE, E. C. British Beetles. London, 1866. 1st ed. xv,280,16pp ads; 16 hand-colored plts. (Spine sl faded, worn.) *Henly.* $75/£48

RYE, EDGAR. The Quirt and the Spur, Vanishing Shadows of the Texas Frontier. Chicago: W.B. Conkey, 1909. 1st ed. Frontis. Good (tp starting to pull from binding; cl dusty, corners worn). *Gibbs.* $250/£160

RYE, REGINALD ARTHUR and MURIEL SINTON QUINN. Historical and Armorial Bookbindings Exhibited in the University Library. (London): Univ of London, 1937. 11 plts. (Sm lib stamp tp, p41), o/w VG in ptd wrappers (soiled). *Heller.* $35/£22

RYE, WALTER (ed). The Norfolk Antiquarian Miscellany. Second Series. Norwich: Gibbs & Waller, 1906, 1907, 1908. 1st ed. Ltd to 100. 3 vols. Fldg chart. Cl spine, stiff ptd bds. Good (spines very worn). *Lucas.* $125/£80

RYMILL, JOHN. Southern Lights. London, 1939. Traveler's Book Club ed. Fldg map. (Lt dust soil), else VG. *High Latitude.* $25/£16

RYMILL, JOHN. Southern Lights...the British Graham Land Expedition 1934-1937. London: C&W, 1938. 1st ed. 81 plts, 8 maps (3 fldg). (New fep), else VG. *High Latitude.* $140/£90

RYNNING, THOMAS. Gun Notches. NY: Frederick A. Stokes, 1931. 1st ed. Mustard cl ptd in black. VF. *Argonaut.* $125/£80

RYUS, WILLIAM B. The Second William Penn. Kansas City: Frank T. Riley, 1913. Frontis. Fine in ptd wraps. *Parmer.* $35/£22

RYUS, WILLIAM H. Old Santa Fe Trail. KC, 1913. 1st ed. Pb. VG+. *Turpen.* $38/£24

RYUS, WILLIAM H. The Second William Penn. Kansas City, MO: Frank T. Riley, (1913). Fine in ptd wraps. *Bohling.* $20/£13

RYUS, WILLIAM H. The Second William Penn. Kansas City: Frank T. Riley, (1913). 1st ed. (Prelims sl foxed; spine ends sl chipped.) Orig pict ptd wrappers. Howes R888. *Sadlon.* $30/£19

RYWELL, MARTIN. Samuel Colt, a Man and an Epoch. Harriman, TN: Pioneer Press, (1952-55). 2nd ed. Frontis port. Brn cl. Fine in dj (worn, lacks portion at bottom rear edge). *Argonaut.* $35/£22

S

S., R. L. (Robert Louis Stevenson.) Pan's Pipes. (Boston: Riverside), 1910. #164/550. Bruce Rogers (decs). Uncut. Red bds (backstrip rubbed; bk label), gilt. *Cox.* $55/£35

SAARINEN, ALINE (ed). Eero Saarinen on His Work. Yale Univ, 1962. 1/2 canvas. Sound. *Ars Artis.* $70/£45

SABARTES, JAIME. Picasso: Toreros. NY/Monte Carlo, (1961). 4 litho plts. Dj. *Swann*.* $488/£313

SABARTES, JAIME. Toreros. NY: Braziller, 1961. 4 orig lithos (1 w/short closed tear at margin) by Pablo Picasso. Fine in dj (chips). *Metropolitan*.* $373/£239

SABATINI, RAFAEL. The Carolinian. Boston: HMC, (1925). 1st US ed. Fine in VG dj (chipped). *Unger.* $225/£144

SABATINI, RAFAEL. Fortune's Fool. Boston: HMC, (1923). 1st US ed. NF in VG dj (tape-repaired). *Unger.* $225/£144

SABATINI, RAFAEL. The Fortunes of Captain Blood. Boston: HMC, (1936). 1st US ed. NF in VG dj (sl chipped). *Unger.* $225/£144

SABATINI, RAFAEL. The Lost King. London: Hutchinson, (1937). 1st UK ed. Fine in VG dj (few closed tears, sm hole spine top). *Williams.* $62/£40

SABATINI, RAFAEL. Master-At-Arms. Boston: HMC, 1940. 1st US ed. Fine in Fine dj (spine top bump). *Unger.* $175/£112

SABATINI, RAFAEL. Mistress Wilding. Boston: HMC, (1924). 1st US ed. NF in VG dj (closed tear rear panel). *Unger.* $225/£144

SABATINI, RAFAEL. Mistress Wilding. Boston: HMC, 1924. 1st Amer ed. (Spine sl faded), else Fine in VG dj (lt chipping, tears). *Between The Covers.* $135/£87

SABATINI, RAFAEL. The Nuptials of Corbal. Boston: Houghton Mifflin, 1927. 1st ed. Pict eps. (Edges rubbed), o/w Fine in dj (chipped, sl rubbed). *Jaffe.* $100/£64

SABATINI, RAFAEL. Saint Martin's Summer. Boston: HMC, (1924). 1st US ed. NF in NF dj (sl rubbed). *Unger.* $225/£144

SABATINI, RAFAEL. Scaramouche the King-Maker. Boston: HMC, (1931). 1st US ed. NF in NF dj (edge-worn). *Unger.* $225/£144

SABATINI, RAFAEL. The Writings of.... Boston & NY/Cambridge: Houghton Mifflin/Riverside Press, 1924. #704/750 signed. 34 vols. Linen spines, paper-cvrd bds. (Some vols water-damaged, spines faded), o/w Very Nice set. *Metropolitan*.* $126/£81

SABBAH, HASSAN I. Leaves of Grass. A Compendium of Marijuana. Brighton: Unicorn Bookshop, 1971. VG+ in wraps. *Sclanders.* $23/£15

SABIN, EDWIN L. Building the Pacific Railway. Phila: Lippincott, 1919. 1st ed. Frontis, fldg map. Maroon cl, gilt. (Lt rubbed), else Fine. *Argonaut.* $100/£64

SABIN, EDWIN L. Wild Men of the Wild West. NY: Thomas Y. Crowell, (1929). 1st ed. Frontis, 18 plts. Dec stamped tan cl (lt rubbed, corner sl jammed). Overall Fine. Howes S2. *Argonaut.* $75/£48

SABINE, EDWARD (ed). North Georgia Gazette and Winter Chronicle. (By William Edward Parry.) London: John Murray, 1821. xii,132pp. Uncut. Bds (worn), later cl (rebacked), paper label. Internally Fine. *High Latitude.* $350/£224

SABINE, LORENZO. Notes on Duels and Dueling. Boston, 1855. 1st ed. (Corners bumped, sl warped, lt wear.) *Freeman*.* $40/£26

Sable Cloud: A Southern Tale, with Northern Comments. (By Nehemiah Adams.) Boston: Ticknor & Fields, 1861. 1st ed. 275,(2)pp. (Sigs sl pulled.) *Wantagh.* $75/£48

SACHS, ALBIE. Jail Diary of Albie Sachs. London: Harvill, 1966. *Boswell.* $65/£42

SACHS, ERNEST. The Care of the Neurosurgical Patient Before, During, and After Operation. St. Louis: Mosby, 1945. NF. *Goodrich.* $75/£48

SACHS, ERNEST. The Diagnosis and Treatment of Brain Tumors. St. Louis: Mosby, 1931. (Spine lettering faded), else Good. *Goodrich.* $65/£42

SACKETT, S. P. Mother, Nurse and Infant. NY, 1889. 387pp. Brn cl bds (sl worn). Good. *Doctor's Library.* $75/£48

SACKVILLE-WEST, EDWARD. And So to Bed. London: Phoenix House, 1947. 1st ed. (New fep; edges faded.) Dj (lt worn, price-clipped). *Hollett.* $39/£25

SACKVILLE-WEST, EDWARD. Piano Quintet. London: Heinemann, 1925. 1st ed, 1st bk. Gilt blue cl. (Edges, eps foxed), o/w Very Nice in white dj (lt edge used, dust soiled). *Reese.* $250/£160

SACKVILLE-WEST, EDWARD. The Rescue. London: Secker & Warburg, 1945. 1st unltd ed. 6 color plts. (Edges lt spotted.) Dj (top edge torn). *Hollett.* $27/£17

SACKVILLE-WEST, EDWARD. Thomas De Quincey. New Haven: Yale Univ, 1936. 1st US ed. 6 plts. (Sm spine label removed.) *Hollett.* $70/£45

SACKVILLE-WEST, VITA. Constantinople. London: Privately Ptd, Complete Press, 1915. 1st ed. NF in ptd wrappers, sewn. *Reese.* $350/£224

SACKVILLE-WEST, VITA. The Dark Island. Hogarth, 1934. 1st Eng ed. VG. *Clearwater.* $47/£30

SACKVILLE-WEST, VITA. Devil at Westease. NY, 1947. Very Nice (name) in dj (torn, chipped, repaired). *Clearwater.* $94/£60

SACKVILLE-WEST, VITA. In Your Garden. London: Michael Joseph, 1951. 2nd ed. Fine. *Quest.* $65/£42

SACKVILLE-WEST, VITA. Invitation to Cast Out Care. (London: Faber & Faber, n.d.) 1st ed. NF in sewn ptd yellow wraps. *Antic Hay.* $35/£22

SACKVILLE-WEST, VITA. Knole. London: Country Life, 1950. Fine in wraps. *Quest.* $65/£42

SACKVILLE-WEST, VITA. The Land. London: Heinemann, 1926. 1st ed, trade issue. Cl, paper label. Fine in dj (sl tanned, sm mended nick spine crown). *Reese.* $100/£64

SACKVILLE-WEST, VITA. Pepita. Hogarth, 1937. 1st Eng ed. Good in Poor dj (repaired). *Clearwater.* $62/£40

SACKVILLE-WEST, VITA. Seducers in Ecuador. Hogarth, 1924. One of 1500 ptd. VF in dj (sl chafed, mkd, neatly repaired). *Clearwater.* $351/£225

SACKVILLE-WEST, VITA. Sissinghurst. London: Hogarth, 1931. 1st ed. One of 500 numbered, signed. Ptd bds. (Spine crown sl bumped), o/w Very Nice. *Reese.* $400/£256

SADLEIR, MICHAEL. Blessington-d'Orsay. Folio Soc, 1983. 12 color plts. VG in silk-backed dec bds. *Cox.* $12/£8

SADLEIR, MICHAEL. Daumier; the Man and the Artist. London: Halton & Truscott, 1924. One of 700. (Bkpl.) *Argosy.* $125/£80

SADLEIR, MICHAEL. The Evolution of Publishers' Binding Styles, 1770-1900. London: Constable, 1930. 1st ed. Ltd to 500. Parchment-backed marbled paper-cvrd bds. (Spine yellowing.) *Oak Knoll.* $300/£192

SADLEIR, MICHAEL. Excursions in Victorian Bibliography. London: Chaundy & Cox, 1922. 1st ed. Errata. (Bkpl, sl rubbed), o/w Good. *Reese.* $85/£54

SADLEIR, MICHAEL. Excursions in Victorian Bibliography. London: Chaundy, 1922. Blue cl (bumped). *Maggs.* $39/£25

SADLEIR, MICHAEL. Forlorn Sunset. Constable, (1947). 1st ed. Frontis. VG in dj. *Ash.* $31/£20

SADLEIR, MICHAEL. Forlorn Sunset. London: Constable, 1947. 1st ed. Frontis. Maroon cl. Fine in dj (sl red stain rear cvr). *Maggs.* $31/£20

SADLEIR, MICHAEL. XIX Century Fiction. Cambridge: CUP, 1951. One of 1025 ptd. 2 vols. Maroon cl (bumped, sl rubbed). *Maggs.* $468/£300

SAFFARZADAH, TAHEREH. The Red Umbrella. (Iowa City: Windhover Press, 1969.) One of 320. Copper engr on red paper tipped in on tp. Gray ptd wrappers sewn in Japanese style. NF. *Heller.* $35/£22

SAFFORD, WILLIAM H. The Life of Harman Blennerhassett. Chillicothe, O(hio), 1850. 1st ed. Litho frontis, 239pp. Howes S13. *M & S.* $125/£80

SAFFORD, WILLIAM H. The Life of Harman Blennerhassett. Chillicothe, OH: Ely et al, 1850. 1st ed. Frontis, 240pp. Contemp calf over purple cl, leather label fr cvr. Good. Howes S13. *Karmiole.* $200/£128

SAFFORD, WILLIAM H. The Life of Harman Blennerhassett. Chillicothe, OH: Ely, Allen & Looker, 1850. 1st ed. Frontis, 239pp. VG (rebacked w/orig eps, backstrip upside-down). Howes S12. *Agvent.* $200/£128

SAFFRON, ROBERT. The Demon Device by Sir Arthur Conan Doyle as Communicated to Robert Saffron. NY: Putnam, (1979). 1st US ed. NF in VG dj (sl wear). *Gravesend.* $25/£16

SAFRONI-MIDDLETON, A. Sailor and Beachcomber. London: Grant Richards, 1915. 1st ed. 24 plts. *Lefkowicz.* $90/£58

SAGAN, FRANCOISE. Aimez-Vous Brahms. Peter Wiles (trans). NY: Dutton, 1960. 1st Amer ed. NF in dj (lt worn, price-clipped). *Antic Hay.* $20/£13

SAGAN, FRANCOISE. Bonjour Tristesse. NY: Dutton, 1955. 1st US ed. Contemp news clipping laid in. (Offsetting fep), else VG + in dj. *Lame Duck.* $45/£29

SAGAN, FRANCOISE. A Certain Smile. Irene Ash (trans). London: John Murray, (1956). 1st Eng ed. Paper-cvrd bds. NF in dj. *Antic Hay.* $35/£22

SAGAN, FRANCOISE. Those Without Shadows. Frances Frenaye (trans). NY: Dutton, 1957. 1st Amer ed. Fine in dj (sl worn, lt dampstain fr cvr). *Antic Hay.* $20/£13

SAGATOO, MARY A. Wah Sash Kah Moqua; or, Thirty Years Among the Indians. (By Mary A. Sagatoo.) Boston: C. White, 1897. Frontis port, 140pp. (Binding sl faded, soiled, etched.) Interior VG. Howes S14. *Bohling.* $400/£256

SAGE, JOHN H. et al. Birds of Connecticut. Hartford: State Geological & Natural Hist Survey, 1913. (Ex-lib, lib binding.) *Books & Birds.* $60/£38

SAGE, PETER. Katinka's Travels to the Himalaya and 'Fox'.... John Bale & Danielsson, n.d. (1926). 1st ed. Margaret Tempest (illus). 4to. (85pp.) Pict cream bds. (Mellowed to deeper cream on back, spine ends lt worn), else VG + in dj (repaired). *Bookmark.* $55/£35

SAGE, RUFUS B. Rufus B. Sage: His Letters and Papers, 1836-1847.... Glendale: Clark, 1956. 1st ed. Vol 1: one of 1250; vol 2: one of 1257. Uncut. Grn cl, gilt-lettered spines. VF. *Argonaut.* $300/£192

SAGGS, H. W. F. The Greatness That Was Babylon. NY: Hawthorn Books, (1962). (Spine, bds sl discolored.) Dj (tattered). *Archaeologia.* $45/£29

Sagittarius: His Book. NY: The Typophiles, 1951. One of 640. Fine. *Heller.* $40/£26

SAID, HAMED (ed). Contemporary Art in Egypt. N.p.: Ministry of Culture & Nat'l Guidance, 1964. 1st ed. 22 tipped-in color plts. Beige cl (2 corners rubbed). Illus dj. *Karmiole.* $75/£48

SAINSBURY, HARRINGTON. Drugs and the Drug Habit. London: Methuen, (1909). 1st ed. Untrimmed. VG (extrems sl worn, fr hinge started). *Glaser.* $125/£80

SAINT-GAUDENS, HOMER. The American Artist and His Times. NY, 1941. Color frontis. (Bkpl.) Dj. *Argosy.* $100/£64

SAINT-SIMON, DUC DE. Historical Memoirs of the Duc de Saint-Simon. Lucy Norton (ed). London, 1967. 2 vols. *Petersfield.* $28/£18

SAINT-SIMON, DUC DE. Memoirs. K.P. Wormeley (trans). Boston, 1899. 4 vols. Good (hinge cracks). *Scribe's Perch*.* $32/£21

SAINT-SIMON, DUKE OF. The Memoirs of the...on the Reign of Louis XIV and the Regency. Bayle St. John (trans). London, 1889. 4th ed. 3 vols. 1/2-titles present. Partly unopened; teg; marbled eps. 1/2 calf, marbled bds, morocco spine labels. (Vol 1 spine rubbed w/sl loss; vol 1 joints starting to crack.) *Edwards.* $133/£85

SAINTSBURY, GEORGE (ed). The Heptameron of the Tales of Margaret, Queen of Navarre. Navarre Soc, 1922. 5 vols. VG in djs (sl rubbed). *Gretton.* $59/£38

SAINTSBURY, GEORGE. A History of Criticism and Literary Taste in Europe. Edinburgh: William Blackwood, 1922. 4th ed. 3 vols. (Pencil notes vol 1), else Clean. *Turtle Island.* $80/£51

SAKI. (Pseud of H. H. Munro.) The Chronicles of Clovis. Bodley Head, 1912. 1st UK ed. 18pp ads at rear. VG (lt sm tape-removal mks eps). *Williams.* $195/£125

SAKI. (Pseud of H. H. Munro.) Reginald and Reginald in Russia. 1921. 1st ed. VG. *Words Etc.* $14/£9

SAKI. (Pseud of H.H. Munro.) Reginald in Russia. Methuen, (1910). 1st ed, 1st issue, lettered in gilt upper cvr. Nice (text sl browned, sl wear). *Ash.* $117/£75

SAKI. (Pseud of H. H. Munro.) The Square Egg and Other Sketches. London, 1924. 1st Eng ed. (Spine sl faded.) *Clearwater.* $70/£45

SAKI. (Pseud of H. H. Munro.) The Toys of Peace and Other Papers. London, 1919. 1st Eng ed. VG (fep creased, rear hinge cracked), dj fr panel laid in. *Clearwater.* $86/£55

SAKI. (Pseud of H. H. Munro.) The Toys of Peace. Bodley Head, 1919. 1st UK ed. VG (sl faded patch fr panel). *Williams.* $62/£40

SALA, GEORGE AUGUSTUS. America Revisited. London, 1886. Later ed. Frontis, xii,548pp. Gilt-pict cl (worn, inner hinges cracked). Sound. *Reese.* $75/£48

SALA, GEORGE AUGUSTUS. Charles Dickens. Routledge, n.d. (1870). Good (sl spotted; re-spined) in orig pict wrappers. *Tiger.* $28/£18

SALA, GEORGE AUGUSTUS. William Hogarth. London: Smith, Elder, 1866. 1st ed. (ii),318,(ii)pp (sm lib label pastedown, stamp tp verso, marginal blindstamps). Orig dec cl, beveled bds (sl worn, neatly recased). *Hollett.* $101/£65

Salad for the Solitary. (By Frederick Saunders.) Richard Bentley, 1853. 1st ed. (2),iv,(2),284,(4)pp, pub's flier tipped in fr, cat at end. Yellow eps, uncut. Silk finish marbled cl, gilt. *Cox.* $47/£30

SALAMAN, MALCOLM C. The New Woodcut. London: The Studio Special Spring Number, 1930. (1st 4pp torn, damaged; scattered foxing.) VG in wrappers. *Michael Taylor.* $47/£30

SALAMAN, MALCOLM C. The Old Engravers of England. London, 1907. (Lt spotted; sl rubbed.) *Edwards.* $31/£20

SALAMAN, MALCOLM C. Woodcut of Today at Home and Abroad. London: The Studio, 1927. (Bkpl, prelims browned, foxed), o/w VG. *Truepenny.* $75/£48

SALE, EDITH TUNIS (ed). Historic Gardens of Virginia. William Byrd, 1930. VG (hinges weak). *Book Broker.* $65/£42

SALE, EDITH TUNIS. Interiors of Virginia Houses of Colonial Times. Wm. Byrd, 1927. Ltd ed. (Cvr worn, lettering rubbed, rear hinge torn; edges soiled, foxed.) *Book Broker.* $45/£29

SALE, EDITH TUNIS. Interiors of Virginia Houses of Colonial Times: From the Beginnings of Virginia to the Revolution. Richmond: William Byrd, 1927. 1st ed. (Names; spine lettering rubbed), else Fine in dj (chipped, torn). Howes S49. *Cahan.* $125/£80

SALE, EDITH TUNIS. Old Time Belles and Cavaliers. Phila: Lippincott, 1912. 1st ed. Color frontis, 60 plts. Grn cl, gilt. (1st sig partly loose.) Howes S51. *Bohling.* $30/£19

SALE, GEORGE (trans). The Koran. London: Geo. B. Whittaker (et al), 1825. 2 vols. xvi,248,256; iv,523pp; fldg map, table, plt. 3/4 contemp calf (extrems worn, upper joints broken), gilt. *Reese.* $60/£38

SALE, RICHARD. Benefit Performance. NY: S&S, 1946. 1st ed. Fine in dj. *Mordida.* $65/£42

SALE, RICHARD. Passing Strange. NY: S&S, 1942. 1st Amer ed. VG in VG dj (ends chipped, lt browned). *Metropolitan*.* $28/£18

SALINGER, J. D. The Catcher in the Rye. London, 1951. 1st ed. Fine in Good dj (price-clipped). *Buckley.* $140/£90

SALINGER, J. D. The Complete Uncollected Short Stories of J. D. Salinger. N.p., n.d. (1974). 1st issue of pirated collection w/vol 1 in stapled wraps, vol 2 perfect bound. 2 vols. Fine in Clean wrappers. *Robbins.* $700/£449

SALINGER, J. D. Franny and Zooey. Boston: Little, Brown, (1961). 1st ed. Fine in dj (lt foxed, price-clipped). *Reese.* $35/£22

SALINGER, J. D. Franny and Zooey. Boston, 1961. 1st ed. VG in VG dj. *Warren.* $60/£38

SALINGER, J. D. Nine Stories. Boston: Little Brown, (1953). 1st ed. VG (offsetting fep; spine lettering sl rubbed) in VG dj (lt edgeworn, rubbed esp rear panel). *Between The Covers.* $650/£417

SALINGER, J. D. Nine Stories. Boston: Little, Brown, (1953). 1st ed. One of 4995. NF in VG dj (spine ends sl worn; flaps, inside foxed). *Bernard.* $850/£545

SALINGER, J. D. Raise High the Roof Beam, Carpenters and Seymour an Introduction. Boston, 1959. 1st ed, 3rd issue. VG+ in VG dj. *Warren.* $35/£22

SALINGER, J. D. Raise High the Roof Beam, Carpenters and Seymour, an Introduction. London: Heinemann, (1963). 1st Eng ed. (Fore-edge, eps foxed), else Fine in Fine dj (sl foxing rear panel). *Between The Covers.* $75/£48

SALISBURY, ALBERT and JANE. Two Captains West, an Historical Tour of the Lewis and Clark Trail. Seattle: Superior Pub Co, (1950). 1st ed. VG+ in dj (chipped). *Bohling.* $27/£17

SALISBURY, FRANK B. The Flowering Process. Oxford, 1963. Color frontis. Fine in dj (torn). *Brooks.* $21/£13

SALISBURY, J. H. The Relation of Alimentation and Disease. NY: J.H. Vail, 1888. 1st ed. xi,332pp; 19 plts. Dec cl. VG. *Glaser.* $85/£54

SALM-SALM, FELIX. Ten Years of My Life. NY: Worthington, 1877. 1st ed. 384pp. Dec cl. *Ginsberg.* $175/£112

SALMON, C. E. Flora of Surrey. London, 1931. 2 color maps, 9 plts. Fine. *Henly.* $66/£42

SALMON, J. T. New Zealand Flowers and Plants in Colour. Wellington/Auckland: A.H. & A.W. Reed, 1963. 1st ed. Frontis map. (Crack inner hinge, corner bumped, spine ends dknd), else VG in dj (edgeworn). *Cahan.* $30/£19

SALMON, THOMAS. New Geographical and Historical Grammar. Edinburgh: Willison & Darling, 1771. 14th ed. xii,(2),7-603,(13)pp (foxed, last few ll dampstained, worm holes bottom margin); 21 (of 22) fldg maps, 2 plts. Full calf (sl worn, fr hinge cracked, rear hinge starting). *New Hampshire*.* $270/£173

SALMONS, C. H. The Burlington Strike. C. H. Frisbie (ed). Aurora, IL: Bunnell & Ward, 1889. 480pp. Good. *Lien.* $25/£16

SALMONS, C. H. The Burlington Strike...the Great Dynamite Conspiracy...Forty Seven Years on a Locomotive.... Aurora, IL: Bunnell & Ward, 1889. 1st ed. (Inner hinges cracked; 1/2-inch break spine head, sl rubbed.) *Sadlon.* $25/£16

SALPOINTE, J. B. Soldiers of the Cross. Albuquerque, 1967. 1st ed. Fine in Fine dj. *Turpen.* $80/£51

SALTEN, FELIX. Bambi's Children: The Story of a Forest Family. Barthold Fles (trans). Indianapolis: Bobbs-Merrill, (1939). 1st Amer ed. Erna Pinner (illus). 8vo. NF (lt erasure, sm ink name) in dj (sl worn, lt browned). *Antic Hay.* $35/£22

SALTEN, FELIX. Fifteen Rabbits. NY: S&S, 1930. 1st ed. VG in self-wraps. *Antic Hay*. $25/£16

SALTEN, FELIX. A Forest World. Paul R. Milton & S. J. Greenburger (trans). Indianapolis: Bobbs-Merrill, (1942). 1st ed. Bob Kuhn (illus). 8vo. Grn cl. NF (lt dampstain rear cvr) in VG dj (edgeworn, sm tears, price-clipped). *Antic Hay*. $75/£48

SALTER, JAMES. The Arm of Flesh. NY: Harper, (1961). 1st ed. (Name), else Fine in VG + dj (2 sm chips, sl rubbing extrems). *Between The Covers*. $450/£288

SALTER, JAMES. Light Years. NY: Random House, (1975). 1st ed. Paper-cvrd bds. (Edges bds fading, spine base lt foxed), else Fine in Fine dj. *Between The Covers*. $75/£48

SALTER, JAMES. Solo Faces. Boston: Little Brown, 1979. 1st ed. (Short rmdr line bottom edge), else Fine in NF dj (lt rubbed). *Between The Covers*. $45/£29

SALTER, WILLIAM. The Life of James W. Grimes. NY, 1876. 1st ed. 398pp. (Sl internal spotting; lt cvr wear), o/w Fine. *Pratt*. $40/£26

SALVERTE, EUSEBE. The Philosophy of Magic. NY: Harper, 1862. 1st English trans. 2 vols. 332; 315pp. Dec cvr, spine. VG + set. *Middle Earth*. $245/£157

SALZMAN, L. F. Building in England Down to 1540. OUP, 1952. 1st ed. VG. *Hadley*. $140/£90

SAMPSON, JOHN. XXI Welsh Gypsy Folk-Tales. Newtown: Gregynog, 1933. One of 250 numbered. 4to. 8 wood-engr illus by Agnes Miller Parker. Later(?) black morocco, gilt-blocked lettering. Cl fldg case. *Swann**. $747/£479

SAMPSON, WILLIAM. Memoirs of William Sampson.... NY: The Author, 1807. 1st ed. xii,446pp (scattered foxing, lacks last pg). Brn leather (sl rubbed). VG. Howes S61. *Argonaut*. $150/£96

SAMSON, JACK. The Bear Book. Clinton: Amwell Press, (1979). Ltd to 1000 signed by Samson & Al Barker (illus). Leatherette. VF in slipcase. *Truepenny*. $85/£54

SAMUELS, EDWARD. Ornithology and Oology of New England. Boston: Nichols & Noyes, 1867. 1st ed. Good. *Books & Birds*. $150/£96

SAMUELS, EDWARD. Ornithology and Oology of New England. Boston, 1868. 587pp. Grn cl, gilt. (Spine sl chipped), else VG. *Price*. $265/£170

SAMUELSON, JAMES. The Earthworm and the Common Housefly. London: John Van Voorst, 1858. 8vo. Pub's ad leaf, 16-pg indexed cat inserted; 8 full-pg engr plts. Pub's dk grn grained cl, gilt. Spine stamped, w/series title: 'Samuelson's Humble Creatures.' As New. *Book Block*. $195/£125

SANBORN, FRANK. Recollections of Seventy Years. Boston: Richard Badger, Gorham Press, 1909. 1st ed. 2 vols. Grn cl, gilt. (Sigs, pencil mks; spines sl sunned.) *Macdonnell*. $165/£106

SANCHEZ, NELLIE VAN DE GRIFT. Spanish and Indian Place Names of California. SF: A.M. Robertson, 1914. 1st ed. (Lt underlining), o/w Good in dj (worn, battered). *Brown*. $15/£10

SANCHEZ, THOMAS. Rabbit Boss. London: Secker & Warburg, 1974. 1st Eng ed, 1st bk. VG in dj (price-clipped, sl rubbed). *Hadley*. $55/£35

SAND, GEORGE. Convent Life of George Sand. Maria Ellery MacKaye (trans). Boston: Roberts, 1893. 1st Amer ed. Dec cl. VG (eps browned; worn, discolored). *Antic Hay*. $40/£26

SAND, GEORGE. Winter in Majorca. Robert Graves (trans). Mallorca: Valldemosa Edition, (1956). 1st ed. VG (edgewear, sm tears) in ptd wraps. *Antic Hay*. $35/£22

SAND, GEORGE. Winter in Majorca. Robert Graves (trans). London: Cassell, 1956. 1st ed. VG in dj. *Hollett*. $31/£20

SAND, MAURICE. The History of Harlinquinade. Phila: Lippincott, 1915. 1st Amer ed. 2 vols. 16 hand-colored plts. Teg. (Cl dusty, repaired sm tear rear joint, hinges starting.) *Dramatis Personae*. $150/£96

SANDBERG, CARL. Always the Young Strangers. NY, (1953). 1st ed. One of 600 (500 for sale). Signed. *Kane**. $90/£58

SANDBERG, WALT. The Turn in the Trail. Clinton: Amwell Press, (1980). Ltd to 1000 signed. Full leather. VF in slipcase. *Truepenny*. $50/£32

SANDBERG-VAVALA, EVELYN. Sienese Studies. The Development of the School of Painting in Siena. Florence, 1953. Good. *Washton*. $75/£48

SANDBERG-VAVALA, EVELYN. Uffizi Studies. The Development of the Florentine School of Painting. Florence, 1948. (Cl sl worn.) *Washton*. $65/£42

SANDBURG, CARL. Abraham Lincoln: The Prairie Years and the War Years. NY, 1954. 1st ed of the 1 vol abridgement of the 6 vol set. VG + in dj (2 sm pieces torn away). *Pratt*. $25/£16

SANDBURG, CARL. Abraham Lincoln: The Prairie Years. NY: Harcourt, Brace, (1926). 1st trade ed. 2 vols. VG. *Pacific**. $35/£22

SANDBURG, CARL. Abraham Lincoln: The Prairie Years. NY, (1929). 1 vol abridged ed. VG + in VG + dj. *Pratt*. $20/£13

SANDBURG, CARL. Abraham Lincoln: The War Years. NY, (1939). One of 525 numbered, signed sets. 4 vols. Cl, leather spine labels (1 chipped). Bd slipcase. *Swann**. $488/£313

SANDBURG, CARL. Abraham Lincoln: The War Years. NY: Harcourt, (1939). 1st trade ed. 4 vols. Nice set in slipcase (sl worn, cracked). *Reese*. $75/£48

SANDBURG, CARL. Abraham Lincoln: the War Years. NY: Harcourt, Brace & World, (1939). 1st trade ed. 4 vols. (Fr inner hinge vol 1 cracking), else VG + set in orig plain white djs. Howes S82. *Mcgowan*. $150/£96

SANDBURG, CARL. Abraham Lincoln: The War Years. NY: Harcourt, Brace & World, (1939). 1st trade ed. 4 vols. (Fr inner hinge vol 1 cracked), else VG + in orig plain white djs. Howes S82. *Mcgowan*. $150/£96

SANDBURG, CARL. Abraham Lincoln: The War Years. NY: Harcourt, Brace, (1939). 1st ed. #392/525 signed. 4 vols. Teg. Gilt-lettered cl, morocco spine labels. Fine in slipcase. *Pacific**. $403/£258

SANDBURG, CARL. Abraham Lincoln: The War Years. NY: HB, 1939. Ltr ptg. 4 vols. Fine. *Archer*. $50/£32

SANDBURG, CARL. Always the Young Strangers. NY: Harcourt, Brace, (1953). 1st ed. #66/600 signed. Paper spine label. Fine in slipcase (extrems sunned). *Pacific**. $69/£44

SANDBURG, CARL. Always the Young Strangers. NY: Harcourt, Brace, (1953). 1st ed, 1st ptg. #230/600 numbered, signed. VG (ptd spine label soiled). *Wantagh*. $125/£80

SANDBURG, CARL. Always the Young Strangers. NY, 1953. 1st ed. Signed. Fine in VG dj. *Bond*. $50/£32

SANDBURG, CARL. The American Songbag. NY: Harcourt, Brace, (1927). 1st ed. NF in VG + dj (sl chipped, price-clipped). *Bernard*. $125/£80

SANDBURG, CARL. The Chicago Race Riots. NY: Harcourt, 1919. 1st ed. Wraps (heavy chipping, affecting title). *Beasley*. $100/£64

SANDBURG, CARL. The Sandburg Range. NY, 1957. 1st ed. VG + in VG + dj. *Smith*. $20/£13

SANDER, AUGUST. Men Without Masks. Greenwich, CT: NYGS, 1973. 1st US ed. Mtd frontis port. Fine in dj (2 sm closed tears). *Cahan*. $275/£176

SANDER, ELLEN. Trips: Rock Life in the Sixties. NY: Scribner, 1973. 1st ed. VG in dj (worn). *Sclanders*. $25/£16

SANDERS, ALVIN HOWARD. At the Sign of the Stock Yard Inn.... Chicago: Breeders Gazette Print, 1915. Frontis. Orig wrappers (spine sl dknd, worn, sl soiled), else Good. *Brown.* $40/£26

SANDERS, GEORGE. Crime on My Hands. Simon, 1944. 1st ed, 1st bk. NF in dj (lacks spine piece, sm nick). *Murder By The Book.* $45/£29

SANDERS, JOHN. Memoirs on the Military Resources of the Valley of the Ohio.... Pittsburgh: Whitney, Dumars & Wright, 1845. 1st ed. 19pp (sm tear repaired upper margin all leaves). Mod 3/4 calf, marbled bds, gilt-stamped spine label. Overall Very Nice. Howes S86. *Bohling.* $225/£144

SANDERS, MARTHA. Alexander and the Magic Mouse. NY: American Heritage, 1969. 1st ed. Philippe Fix (illus). 8 3/4 x 10 1/2. 44pp. Pict bds. VG in dj. *Cattermole.* $45/£29

SANDERS, SUE. Our Common Herd. NY: GC Pub Co, 1939. 1st ed. Fine in dj. *Gibbs.* $30/£19

SANDERS, W. B. Half-Timbered Houses and Carved Oak Furniture of the 16th and 17th Centuries. London, 1894. x,51pp, 30 plts. Sound. *Ars Artis.* $70/£45

SANDERS, W. FRANKLIN. (Pseud of Charles Willeford.) Whip Hand. CT: Gold Medal Books, 1961. 1st ed. Pb orig. VG+ in wraps. *Warren.* $125/£80

SANDERSON, E. DWIGHT. Insect Pests of Farm, Garden and Orchard. NY/London: Wiley/Chapman & Hall, 1921. 2nd ed. (Sl rubbed, soiled), o/w VG. *Worldwide.* $15/£10

SANDERSON, GEORGE P. Thirteen Years Among the Wild Beasts of India. London: Wm. Allen, 1879. 2nd ed. Color frontis, xviii,387pp; 23 plts. Pict grn cl (rubbed). *Adelson.* $285/£183

SANDERSON, GEORGE P. Thirteen Years Among the Wild Beasts of India.... London, 1882. 3rd ed. Hand-colored frontis (loose). Gilt-pict cl (sl worn, sl shaken). *Oinonen*.* $150/£96

SANDFORD, JOHN. Eyes of Prey. NY: Putnam, 1991. 1st ed. VF in dj. *Mordida.* $45/£29

SANDFORD, JOHN. Rules of Prey. NY: Putnam, 1989. 1st ed. VF in dj. *Mordida.* $75/£48

SANDFORD, JOHN. Shadow Prey. NY: Putnam, 1990. 1st ed. VF in dj. *Mordida.* $45/£29

SANDOZ, MARI. Cheyenne Autumn. London: Eyre & Spottiswoode, (1966). 1st British ed. VG in VG dj. *Perier.* $50/£32

SANDOZ, MARI. Old Jules Country. NY: Hastings House, 1965. #142/250 signed, bound in 1/2 grn morocco. Fldg map. Fine. *Bohling.* $175/£112

SANDOZ, MAURICE. Fantastic Memories. NY: Doubleday, Doran, 1944. 1st ed. Salvador Dali (illus). (Bkpl, blindstamp fep), o/w VG in dj (chipped, short tape repair). *Hermitage.* $85/£54

SANDOZ, MAURICE. The Maze. NY, 1945. 1st ed. Salvador Dali (illus). NF in VG dj (price-clipped). *Warren.* $50/£32

SANDOZ, MAURICE. On the Verge. GC: Doubleday, 1950. 1st ed. Salvador Dali (illus) VG in dj (price-clipped, tape-strengthened). *Hermitage.* $85/£54

SANDS, LEDYARD. The Bird, The Gun and The Dog. NY, 1939. 1st ed. VF. *Bond.* $50/£32

SANDWEIS, MARTHA A. Masterwork of American Photography. Birmingham: Oxmoor House, 1982. 1st ed. Fine in Fine dj. *Smith.* $65/£42

SANDWELL, A. H. Planes over Canada. London: Thomas Nelson & Sons, 1938. VG in dj (torn). *High Latitude.* $35/£22

SANDYS, EDWIN and T. S. VAN DYKE. Upland Game Birds. NY: Macmillan, 1902. 1st ed. (Fore-edge bumped), else VG. *Bowman.* $45/£29

SANFORD, JOHN. The Winters of That Country. Santa Barbara, CA: Black Sparrow, 1984. One of 200 numbered, signed. Lt blue cl-backed dec bds, ptd spine label. NF in acetate dj. *Blue Mountain.* $30/£19

SANFORD, MOLLIE DORSEY. Mollie. The Journal of...in Nebraska and Colorado Territories 1857-1866. Lincoln, 1959. 1st ed. Rev copy. (Sl bumped), o/w Fine in dj (price-clipped). *Baade.* $45/£29

SANFORD, PAUL. Sioux Arrows and Bullets. Naylor, (1969). 1st ed. VF in Fine dj. *Oregon.* $22/£14

SANGER, MARGARET. My Fight for Birth Control. NY: F&R, (1932). (Sm name stamp), else NF in NF dj (sm chip, lt rubbed). *Between The Covers.* $150/£96

SANGER, MARGARET. My Fight for Birth Control. London: Faber, 1932. 1st ed. Nice. *Patterson.* $39/£25

SANGER, WILLIAM. The History of Prostitution. NY: Harper, 1858. 1st ed. Inscribed. 685,(1)pp. Emb Victorian cl (new eps; rebacked, orig spine laid down; edges worn, margins soiled). Good. *Gach.* $175/£112

SANGER, WILLIAM. The History of Prostitution: Its Extent, Causes and Effects Throughout the World. NY, 1858. 1st ed. (Outer hinges cracked, spine chipped), o/w VG. *Fye.* $150/£96

SANGSTER, CHARLES. Hesperus and Other Poems and Lyrics. Montreal/Kingston: John Lovell/John Creighton, 1860. 1st ed. NF (bottom few pp sl dampstained; spine lettering sl rubbed). *Between The Covers.* $125/£80

Sanitary Commission of the United States Army: A Succinct Narrative of Its Works and Purposes. NY, 1864. 1st ed. 318pp. 1/2 leather. (Lib stamp tp), o/w Fine. *Fye.* $350/£224

SANSOM, ARTHUR ERNEST. Chloroform: Its Action and Administration. Phila: Lindsay & Blakiston, 1866. 1st Amer ed. Purple cl (faded, lt frayed). *Karmiole.* $150/£96

SANSOM, WILLIAM. Fireman Flower and Other Stories. NY: Vanguard, n.d. (1944). 1st Amer ed, 1st bk. NF in dj (rubbed, sl chipped). *Hermitage.* $50/£32

SANSOM, WILLIAM. Lord Love Us. London: Hogarth, 1954. 1st Eng ed. Paper-cvrd bds. Fine in dj (price-clipped). *Antic Hay.* $35/£22

SANSOM, WILLIAM. The Loving Eye. London: Hogarth, 1956. 1st Eng ed. Paper-cvrd bds. Fine in dj (sl soil). *Antic Hay.* $35/£22

Santa Gertrudis Breeders International Recorded Herds 1953. (Kingsville, TX: Santa Gertrudis Breeders International, 1954-66.) 1st ed. Vol 1 signed by Robert J. Kleberg, president of King Ranch. 3 vols. Maroon cl, gilt. Good. *Karmiole.* $300/£192

SANTA MARIA, VICENTE. The First Spanish Entry into San Francisco Bay, 1775. John Galvin (ed). SF: John Howell-Books, 1971. Ltd to 5000 ptd. 4 maps. Blue cl, gilt. Fine in ptd dj (spine sl sunned). *Pacific*.* $92/£59

SANTAYANA, GEORGE. Interpretations of Poetry and Religion. NY, 1900. 1st ed. (Lt rubbed.) *Argosy.* $50/£32

SANTAYANA, GEORGE. The Middle Span. London: Constable, 1947. 1st ed. VG. *Hollett.* $19/£12

SANTAYANA, GEORGE. Poems. NY, 1923. 1st Amer ed. Errata slip. NF in dj (spine sunned, edge pieces missing, sl soiled, price-clipped). *Polyanthos.* $25/£16

SANTAYANA, GEORGE. The Works of George Santayana. NY: Scribner, 1940. One of 940 signed. 15 vols. Teg, rest untrimmed. 1/4 cl, blue paper-cvrd bds, paper labels. (Spines, edges sl discolored, few vols sl warped.) *Zubal*.* $240/£154

SANTEE, ROSS. Apache Land. NY/London, 1947. 1st ed. VG+. *Mcclintock.* $25/£16

SANTEE, ROSS. Cowboy. Cosmopolitan Book Corp, 1928. 1st ed. Pict cvr. VG. *Authors Of West.* $40/£26

SANTINI, PIERO. The Forward Impulse. NY: Huntington, 1936. Ltd to 950. VG. *October Farm*. $65/£42

SAPPER. (Pseud of H. C. McNeile.) Jim Maitland. Hodder & Stoughton, n.d. (1923). 1st ed. Diagonal grain orange cl. (Sl edge foxing), o/w Fine. *Cox*. $31/£20

Saratoga Illustrated; the Visitor's Guide.... NY: Taintor Bros., Merrill, 1882. Rpt. 2 fldg maps. Wrappers (sl worn). *Maggs*. $31/£20

SARBER, MARY A. Photographs from the Border. El Paso: El Paso Public Library Assoc, 1977. 1st ed. 100 full-pg b/w photos. NF (owner stamp). *Cahan*. $150/£96

SARGANT, WILLIAM. Battle for the Mind. London: Heinemann, 1957. 1st ed, rpt. Good in dj. *White*. $19/£12

SARGANT, WILLIAM. Robert Owen, and His Social Philosophy. London: Smith, Elder, 1860. 1st ed. xxiv,446,2(ads)pp. Plum cl (neatly rebacked). *Burmester*. $117/£75

SARGANT, WILLIAM. The Unquiet Mind. London: Heinemann, 1967. 1st ed. Good in dj. *White*. $28/£18

SARGENT, DANIEL. All the Day Long. NY/Toronto: Longmans, Green, 1941. 1st ed. VG in dj. *Worldwide*. $25/£16

SARGENT, EPES. Arctic Adventure by Sea and Land.... Boston, 1857. 480pp (several gatherings loose); fldg map (torn w/o loss). Good (faded, sl worn). *High Latitude*. $25/£16

SARGENT, WINTHROP (ed). The History of an Expedition Against Fort Du Quesne in 1755. Phila, 1856. 10 maps and plts. Later cl. *Swann**. $115/£74

SARIANIDI, VICTOR. The Golden Hoard of Bactria. NY: Abrams, (1985). Fine. *Terramedia*. $30/£19

SAROYAN, WILLIAM. The Daring Young Man on the Flying Trapeze. London, 1934. 1st ed. Good. (Lacks dj.) *Buckley*. $47/£30

SAROYAN, WILLIAM. The Laughing Matter. NY, 1953. 1st Amer ed. NF in NF dj. *Polyanthos*. $25/£16

SAROYAN, WILLIAM. Letters from 74 Rue Taitbout. NY, 1969. 1st ed. NF in NF dj. *Smith*. $20/£13

SAROYAN, WILLIAM. Places Where I've Done Time. NY, (1972). 1st Amer ed. Fine in Fine dj. *Polyanthos*. $25/£16

SAROYAN, WILLIAM. The Tooth and My Father. GC: Doubleday, (1974). 1st ed. Suzanne Verrier (illus). Fine in NF dj (spine edge sl worn). *Bernard*. $30/£19

SAROYAN, WILLIAM. Two Short Paris Summertime Plays of 1974. Northridge: Santa Susana Press, 1979. Ltd to 326 numbered, signed. Cl over illus bds, paper spine label. Fine. *Karmiole*. $60/£38

SARTAIN, JOHN. The Reminiscences of a Very Old Man 1808-1897. NY: Appleton, 1899. 1st ed. 14,297pp (cracked at hinges, at p113); 20 plts. Teg. Dec cl (ex-lib, label removed spine, frayed, chipped). Good-. *Scribe's Perch**. $24/£15

SARTON, GEORGE. A History of Science, Hellenistic Science and Culture in the Last Three Centuries B.C. 1959. VG in new cl. *Whitehart*. $39/£25

SARTON, GEORGE. A History of Science. 1953-1959. 2 vols. (Spine sl mkd, discolored), o/w VG. *Whitehart*. $62/£40

SARTON, GEORGE. A History of Science. Harvard Univ, 1959. 2 vols. VG. *Bookcell*. $75/£48

SARTON, GEORGE. Introduction to the History of Science. Volume II from Rabbi Ben Ezra to Roger Bacon. Balt: Williams & Wilkins, 1931. 2 vols. VG in djs (sl worn). *Goodrich*. $150/£96

SARTON, MAY. The Fur Person. NY, (1957). 1st Amer ed. Fine (fep sl offset) in dj (rear panel sl soiled). *Polyanthos*. $25/£16

SARTON, MAY. The Poet and the Donkey. NY, (1969). 1st ed. VG. *Argosy*. $30/£19

SARTON, MAY. Punch's Secret. NY: Harper, 1974. 1st ed. Howard Knotts (illus). 7 1/4 x 9 1/4. 30pp. Pict bds. Fine in dj. *Cattermole*. $75/£48

SARTON, MAY. A Reckoning. NY: Norton, 1978. 1st ed. Fine (name) in dj (sl worn). *Else Fine*. $40/£26

SARTRE, JEAN-PAUL. The Age of Reason. Eric Sutton (trans). NY: Knopf, 1947. 1st Amer ed. (Owner label), o/w Nice in Good dj (nicked, lt soiled). *Reese*. $30/£19

SARTRE, JEAN-PAUL. Anti-Semite and Jew. George Becker (trans). (NY): Schocken, (1948). 1st Amer ed of this trans. NF in NF dj (top edge tanned). *Reese*. $35/£22

SARTRE, JEAN-PAUL. The Chips Are Down. Louis Varese (trans). NY: Lear, (1948). 1st Amer ed of this trans. Fine in dj (lt rubbed, edges lt sunned). *Reese*. $45/£29

SARTRE, JEAN-PAUL. Five Plays. Frankin Center: Franklin Library, 1978. 1st ed thus. Signed. Fine in Franklin leather. *Captain's Bookshelf*. $350/£224

SARTRE, JEAN-PAUL. Five Plays. Franklin Center, PA: Franklin Library, 1978. Ltd to unspecified #, signed. Fine in pub's full dec leather. *Lame Duck*. $250/£160

SARTRE, JEAN-PAUL. In the Mesh. Mervyn Savill (trans). London: Andrew Dakers, (1954). 1st ed. Fine in dj (sl worn, sm tear). *Antic Hay*. $75/£48

SARTRE, JEAN-PAUL. Lucifer and the Lord. London, 1952. 1st ed. Dj. *Typographeum*. $25/£16

SARTRE, JEAN-PAUL. The Reprieve. Eric Sutton (trans). London: Hamish Hamilton, (c. 1948). (Fep edges lt browned.) Dj (price-clipped) by Michael Ayrton. *Hollett*. $55/£35

SARTRE, JEAN-PAUL. The Reprieve. Eric Sutton (trans). NY: Knopf, 1947. 1st Amer ed. Fine in VG dj. *Reese*. $35/£22

SARTRE, JEAN-PAUL. A Theater of Situations. (NY): Pantheon, (1976). Uncorrected proof copy. Fine in ptd wraps. *Antic Hay*. $75/£48

SARTRE, JEAN-PAUL. Three Plays. NY: Knopf, 1949. 1st ed. Fine in NF dj (lt edgeworn). *Reese*. $45/£29

SARTRE, JEAN-PAUL. Troubled Sleep. NY: Knopf, 1951. 1st US ed. VG+ in VG dj (sl rubbed). *Williams*. $39/£25

SARZANO, FRANCES. Sir John Tenniel. NY: Pellegrini & Cudahy, n.d. Nice in dj. *Turtle Island*. $35/£22

SASAKI, HIROSHI (ed). The Modern Japanese House: Inside and Outside. Tokyo: Japan Pub, 1970. 1st ed. 7 color plts. Fine in NF dj. *Cahan*. $75/£48

SASEK, M. This Is Historic Britain. NY: Macmillan, 1974. 1st ed. 9 x 12 1/2. 60pp. VG in dj. *Cattermole*. $24/£15

Saskatchewan Journals and Correspondence: Edmonton House 1795-1800. Chesterfield House, 1800-1802. Vol XXVI. London: Hudson's Bay Record Soc, 1967. Fldg map. VG in dj. *Lien*. $45/£29

SASSOON, SIEGFRIED. The Heart's Journey. NY/London, 1927. Ltd to 590, signed. Cl-backed bds. VG. *Truepenny*. $375/£240

SASSOON, SIEGFRIED. Memoirs of an Infantry Officer. London, 1930. 1st Eng ed. Nice (foxing, stamp; spine sl sunned) in dj (sl frayed, dusty). *Clearwater*. $55/£35

SASSOON, SIEGFRIED. Memoirs of an Infantry Officer. London, 1930. One of 750 signed. Blue buckram (spine, top edges faded, fr cvr sl scratched; name). *Clearwater*. $156/£100

SASSOON, SIEGFRIED. Memoirs of an Infantry Officer. London: Faber, 1930. 1st ed. (Sl offsetting eps, name; prelims, fore-edge sl spotted; cvrs faded around edges, spine), o/w Good in dj (soiled, spotted, browned, sl nicked, chipped, pieces missing spine ends). *Virgo*. $39/£25

SASSOON, SIEGFRIED. The Old Century and Seven More Years. London, 1938. 1st Eng ed. Very Bright in dj. *Clearwater*. $78/£50

SASSOON, SIEGFRIED. The Old Century. London: Faber, 1938. 1st UK ed. (Bkpl fr pastedown; staining top edge), o/w VG in dj (sl worn; spine lt worn). *Moorhouse*. $39/£25

SASSOON, SIEGFRIED. The Path to Peace. Worcester, 1960. One of 500. Patterned bds, vellum spine. Fine. *Appelfeld*. $300/£192

SASSOON, SIEGFRIED. Satirical Poems. London: Heinemann, 1926. 1st ed. (Lower pg edges foxed), else NF in VG+ dj (spine lt tanned). *Lame Duck*. $650/£417

SASSOON, SIEGFRIED. Sherston's Progress. London: Faber, 1936. 1st UK ed. NF in dj (sl nicked, soiled). *Moorhouse*. $55/£35

SASSOON, SIEGFRIED. Siegfried's Journey 1916-1920. London: Faber, 1945. 1st ed. Frontis port. VG. *Hollett*. $23/£15

SASSOON, SIEGFRIED. To My Mother. Ariel Poems, (1928). 1st Eng ed. Wrappers (spine splitting). *Clearwater*. $39/£25

SASSOON, SIEGFRIED. To My Mother. London: Faber & Gwyer, 1928. 1st ed. VG in sewn paper wraps. *Antic Hay*. $35/£22

SASSOON, SIEGFRIED. Vigils. London: Heinemann, 1935. 1st ed. (Bkpl, note pasted fep; spine sl faded.) *Hollett*. $23/£15

SASSOON, SIEGFRIED. The War Poems. London: Heinemann, 1919. 1st ed. Paper labels (lt chipped, browned; spine faded). *Hollett*. $218/£140

Satanstoe; or, The Littlepage Manuscripts. (By James Fenimore Cooper.) NY: Burgess, Stringer, 1845. 1st Amer ed. 2 vols in 1. Later leather-backed lib binding (shabby; dampstained, foxed). BAL 3915. *New Hampshire**. $25/£16

SATTERTHWAIT, WALTER. At Ease with the Dead. NY: St. Martin's, 1990. 1st ed. VF in dj. *Mordida*. $100/£64

SATTERTHWAIT, WALTER. Miss Lizzie. NY: St. Martin's, 1989. 1st ed. Fine in dj (two 1-inch closed tears). *Mordida*. $150/£96

SAUER, CARL O. et al. Starved Rock State Park and Its Environs. (IL): Geog Soc, 1918. 1st ed. Fldg map in pocket. Grn cl, gilt. VG. *Price*. $29/£19

SAUER, JULIA. Fog Magic. NY: Viking, 1943. 1st ed. 5 1/2 x 8 1/2. 107pp. Dj, eps, cvr illus by Lynd Ward. Dec cl. VG (sl browning rep from review laid in) in dj (sl chips). *Cattermole*. $45/£29

SAUNDERS, ANN. Narrative of the Shipwreck and Sufferings of Miss Ann Saunders.... Providence, (RI): Z.S. Crossman, 1827. 1st ed. 38pp (foxed, emb stamp tp). Old binder. *M&s*. $275/£176

SAUNDERS, CHARLES FRANCIS. Finding the Worth While in the Southwest. NY, 1918. Map. Grn cl. Fine in Good+ dj. *Five Quail*. $35/£22

SAUNDERS, CHARLES FRANCIS. The Indians of the Terraced Houses. NY: Putnam, 1912. 1st ed. 51 full-pg photo illus. (Fr hinge weak, sl worn, rev glued in at rear.) *Dawson*. $50/£32

SAUNDERS, CHARLES FRANCIS. The Southern Sierras of California. Boston: Houghton, 1923. 1st ed. Fine. *Book Market*. $60/£38

SAUNDERS, HENRY S. (comp). Parodies on Walt Whitman. NY: Amer Library Service, 1923. 1st ed. (Bkpl), else VG. *Cahan*. $50/£32

SAUNDERS, J. B. and C. D. O'MALLEY. Vesalius. The Illustrations from His Works.... NY, 1950. 2nd ptg. Good in dj. *Goodrich*. $75/£48

SAUNDERS, LOUISE. The Knave of Hearts. Racine, (1925). Maxfield Parrish (illus). Folio. Pict spiral-bound wrappers (worn, soiled, sl edge tears). *Oinonen**. $270/£173

SAUNDERS, LOUISE. The Knave of Hearts. Racine: Artists & Writers Guild, (1925). 2nd ed. Maxfield Parrish (illus). Spiral-bound pict card wraps. Fine. *Kane**. $425/£272

SAUNDERS, LOUISE. The Knave of Hearts. NY, 1925. Maxfield Parrish (illus). 4to. Orig black cl, full-size color pict fr cvr label. Pub's 2-piece box, cl fldg case. Excellent. *Swann**. $2,185/£1,401

SAUNDERS, LOUISE. The Knave of Hearts. NY: Scribner, 1925. 1st ed. Sm folio. 46pp, 10 full-pg color plts by Maxfield Parrish. Pict paper label. Fine. *Bromer*. $2,000/£1,282

SAUNDERS, RICHARD. Poor Richard: The Almanacks for the Years 1733-1758. Phila: LEC, 1964. #304/1500 ptd signed by Norman Rockwell (illus). 1/4 suede, marbled bds. VF in pub's slipcase. *Hermitage*. $350/£224

SAUNIER, CLAUDIUS. The Watchmakers' Hand-Book. London/NY: J. Tripplin/L.H. Keller, 1881. 1st ed in English. xiii,482pp (bkpl); 14 fldg plts. Grn cl (worn, hinges broken). *Weber*. $50/£32

SAUTER, J. A. Among the Brahmins and Pariahs. Bernard Miall (trans). London, 1924. 1st ed. *Edwards*. $23/£15

SAVAGE, ALMA H. Dogsled Apostles. NY: Sheed & Ward, 1942. (Bkpl), else VG. *Perier*. $22/£14

SAVAGE, G. C. Ophthalmic Myology. Nashville: The Author, 1911. 2nd ed. 6 full-pg illus. Emb cl (sl soiled). VG (lower margin 1st few ll lt stained). *Glaser*. $85/£54

SAVAGE, G. C. Ophthalmic Neuro-Myology. Nashville: The Author, (1905). 1st ed. 39 full-pg illus. Emb cl (spine, corners lt worn). VG. *Glaser*. $125/£80

SAVAGE, GEORGE. 18th-Century English Porcelain. London: Rockcliff, 1952. 1st ed. Color frontis, 112 plts. (Edges sl spotted.) Dj. *Hollett*. $55/£35

SAVAGE, GEORGE. English Pottery and Porcelain. NY: Universe Books, (1961). 1st Amer ed. 56 tipped-in color plts, 128 photo engrs. Beige linen. Good in dj (few tears). *Karmiole*. $125/£80

SAVAGE, GEORGE. French Decorative Art 1638-1793. Allen Lane, 1969. 113 photo plts. VG in dj. *Hadley*. $34/£22

SAVAGE, HENRY. The Surgery, Surgical Pathology and Surgical Anatomy of the Female Pelvic Organs.... NY: Wood, 1880. 3rd ed. 129pp + 60pp Wood Lib cat; 32 woodcuts. Good. *Goodrich*. $75/£48

SAVAGE, RICHARD. The Works of Richard Savage, Esq. London: T. Evans, 1777. New ed. 2 vols. cxvi,185,(2); vi,279,(3)pp, half-titles. Contemp flame calf, gilt, leather labels. Attractive set (inscrip; hinges worn). *Hartfield*. $295/£189

SAVAGE-LANDOR, A. HENRY. Across Coveted Lands. NY: Scribner, 1903. Probable 1st Amer ed. 2 vols. 124 plts, 2 fldg maps. Teg. Dec cl (sl worn, soiled; lt foxing.) *Waverly**. $60/£38

SAVAGE-LANDOR, A. HENRY. Across Unknown South America. 1913. 1st ed. 2 vols. Frontis port, 2 fldg maps, 8 color plts. (Spines, joints sl rubbed.) *Edwards*. $133/£85

SAVAGE-LANDOR, A. HENRY. Across Widest Africa. London: Hurst & Blackett, 1907. 2 vols. Fldg map. Blue cl (rubbed; lt foxed). *Adelson.* $260/£167

SAVAGE-LANDOR, A. HENRY. Across Widest Africa. NY: Scribner, 1907. 1st ed. 2 vols. Teg. (Lt foxed, last text leaf torn w/o loss, lacks fldg map; rubbed, spine faded, cvrs sl silverfished), o/w VG. *Worldwide.* $95/£61

SAVAGE-LANDOR, A. HENRY. China and the Allies. London: Heinemann, 1901. 2 vols. 8 maps, 53 plts. Mod dk blue cl, red leather labels. VG. *Adelson.* $285/£183

SAVAGE-LANDOR, A. HENRY. The Gems of the East. NY: Macmillan, 1904. 1st US ed. 2 vols. 49 plts. Teg. (Lacks map; cl sl rubbed), o/w VG. *Worldwide.* $65/£42

SAVAGE-LANDOR, A. HENRY. In the Forbidden Land. London: Heinemann, 1898. 1st ed. 2 vols. xx,320; xvi,(264)pp; fldg map. Partly unopened. Dec cl (sl rubbed, sl mks). Nice set. *Ash.* $312/£200

SAVAGE-LANDOR, A. HENRY. In the Forbidden Land. London: Heinemann, 1899. Frontis, xxviii,508pp; lg fldg map. Good (sl spotted) in dec cl. *Cox.* $70/£45

SAVAGE-LANDOR, A. HENRY. In the Forbidden Land. NY: Harper, 1899. 2 vols. xviii,307; xiv,250pp; fldg map, 8 color plts. Pict cl (lt rubbed). *Adelson.* $200/£128

SAVAGE-LANDOR, A. HENRY. In the Forbidden Land. London, 1909. Frontis port, fldg map. (Upper hinge cracked, extrems rubbed, spine head frayed.) *Edwards.* $75/£48

SAVARY, CLAUDE ETIENNE. Letters on Greece.... Dublin: L. White et al, 1788. (4),407,(8)pp. Full calf (sl worn, fr hinge cracked). (Lt foxed), o/w Contents VG. *New Hampshire*.* $90/£58

SAVILL, THOMAS D. Clinical Lectures on Neurasthenia. London: Henry J. Glaisher, 1899. 1st ed. (xvi),144pp. (Lib stamp tp, spine #s.) Ptd maroon cl. Jelliffe's name stamp, bkpl. *Gach.* $85/£54

SAVILL, THOMAS D. Lectures on Hysteria and Allied Vaso-Motor Conditions. NY/London: William Wood/Henry J. Glaisher, 1909. 1st Amer ed. 11 halftones. (Lib stamp tp, spine #s.) Ptd panelled blue cl. Jelliffe's name stamp, bkpl. *Gach.* $75/£48

SAVILLE, MALCOLM. Strangers at Witchend. Newnes, 1970. 1st ed. 8vo. 192pp; dbl-spread pict map. NF (inscrip) in pict dj. *Bookmark.* $34/£22

SAVILLE, MALCOLM. Wings Over Witchend. Newnes, 1956. 1st ed. 8vo. 247pp. Pict map eps. VG in pict dj (worn). *Bookmark.* $34/£22

SAVORY, ISABEL. In the Tail of the Peacock. 1903. Frontis port. (Lacks rep, fep detached, upper hinge cracked; spine lt faded.) *Edwards.* $55/£35

SAVORY, ISABEL. A Sportswoman in India. London: Hutchinson, 1900. 1st ed. Frontis. Contemp dec gilt full morocco. VG. *Terramedia.* $300/£192

SAVORY, T. H. Spiders, Men and Scorpions. London, 1961. Dj. *Maggs.* $23/£15

SAWTELL, CLEMENT CLEVELAND. Captain Nash Decost and the Liverpool Packets. Mystic: Marine Historical Assoc, 1955. (Bkpl remnants inside fr cvr), else VG in orig grn ptd wraps (faded). *Parmer.* $20/£13

SAWYER, ALVAH L. A History of the Northern Peninsula of Michigan. Chicago, 1911. 1st ed. 3 vols. 1/2 leather, cl. (Ep edges discolored; cvrs worn, vol 1 outer hinge cracked w/spine tear, other hinges starting, spines chipped, sl soil), else Good. *King.* $295/£189

SAWYER, CHARLES J. and F. J. HARVEY DARTON. English Books 1475-1900. London, 1927. 1st ed. One of 2000. 2 vols. 1/2 morocco by Sangorski & Sutcliffe. *Swann*.* $149/£96

SAWYER, CHARLES J. and F. J. HARVEY DARTON. English Books 1475-1900. Westminster, 1927. One of 2000. 2 vols. Uncut. (Sl worn.) Djs (sl frayed). *Oinonen*.* $65/£42

SAWYER, CHARLES J. and F. J. HARVEY DARTON. English Books 1475-1900. Westminster/NY: Chas J. Sawyer/Dutton, 1927. One of 2000. 2 vols. Teg. (Sl soiled, worn; spines faded; few pencil notes.) *Waverly*.* $71/£46

SAWYER, CHARLES J. and F. J. HARVEY DARTON. English Books, 1475-1900. Westminster/NY, 1927. 2 vols. Teg. Red buckram. VG. *Truepenny.* $150/£96

SAWYER, FRANK. Keeper of the Stream. Country Book Club, 1954. Frontis. Mod 1/2 grn morocco, marbled sides. *Petersfield.* $62/£40

SAWYER, FREDERIC W. The Merchant's and Shipmaster's Guide.... Boston: Benjamin Loring, 1843. 3rd ed. 2 plts (1 fldg). Full sheep (stained). Sound (ex-lib). *Boswell.* $275/£176

SAWYER, LORENZO. Way Sketches, Containing Incidents of Travel Across the Plains...in 1850. NY: Edward Eberstadt, 1926. 1st ed. Ltd to 385. Frontis. Cl-backed bds, gilt. (Spine crown pulled, rear bd lt soiled), else VG. Howes S133. *Cahan.* $125/£80

SAWYER, LORENZO. Way Sketches. NY: Eberstadt, 1926. 1st ed. Ltd to 385. 1/2 cl over bds. Howes S133. *Ginsberg.* $175/£112

SAWYER, RUTH. The Christmas Anna Angel. NY: Viking, 1944. 1st ed. Kate Seredy (illus). 8vo. 48pp. VG in VG dj. *Dower.* $50/£32

SAXE, JOHN GODFREY. The Masquerade and Other Poems. Boston, 1866. 1st Amer ed. Fine (bkpl; spine extrems sl rubbed, sm chip). *Polyanthos.* $40/£26

SAXL, F. English Sculptures of the Twelfth Century. Hanns Swaarzenski (ed). Boston, n.d. (ca 1954). 100 plts. Good in dj. *Washton.* $100/£64

SAXON, ISABELLE. Five Years Within the Golden Gate. London, 1868. (10),315pp. (Lib stamps.) *Ginsberg.* $175/£112

SAXON, LYLE. Fabulous New Orleans. NY/London: Appleton-Century, 1939. 1st Suydam illus ed. Signed. (Spine head sl rubbed). Pict label. Dj (lt chipped, edgeworn). *Sadlon.* $20/£13

SAY, JEAN-BAPTISTE. A Treatise on Political Economy. Phila, 1827. 3rd Amer ed. 455pp (ink inscrip, foxed). Full speckled calf. (Sl cvr stain, spine tips worn), else Attractive. *King.* $85/£54

SAYCE, A. H. Social Life Among the Assyrians and Babylonians. Oxford: Religious Tract Soc, 1893. 127pp. Good. *Archaeologia.* $25/£16

SAYERS, DOROTHY L. Busman's Honeymoon. NY: Harcourt, Brace, (1937). 1st US ed. VG+ in VG dj (spine sl faded, edgewear). *Bernard.* $250/£160

SAYERS, DOROTHY L. Busman's Honeymoon. Gollancz, 1937. 1st UK ed. VG+ in dj (lt browned, stained). *Williams.* $195/£125

SAYERS, DOROTHY L. The Devil to Pay. Canterbury, 1939. 1st Eng ed. Card wrappers (sl dusty). *Clearwater.* $39/£25

SAYERS, DOROTHY L. The Devil to Pay. London: Gollancz, 1939. 1st ed. VG in dj (chipped). *Argosy.* $65/£42

SAYERS, DOROTHY L. The Five Red Herrings. Gollancz, 1931. 1st ed. (Spine sl creased, lower hinge sl split, sl shaken, sl mks.) *Ash.* $62/£40

SAYERS, DOROTHY L. Gaudy Night. London: Gollancz, 1935. 1st ed. (Inscrip), o/w Fine in dj (lt soiled, spine sl faded). *Mordida.* $700/£449

SAYERS, DOROTHY L. Gaudy Night. London: Gollancz, 1935. (Bkpl, edges spotted), o/w Excellent in dj (sl rubbed, nicked, spine faded). *Gekoski.* $780/£500

SAYERS, DOROTHY L. Gaudy Night. Gollancz, 1936. 1st UK ed. NF (lt foxed, bkpl) in VG dj (sl dusty, sm nicks). *Williams*. $507/£325

SAYERS, DOROTHY L. Gaudy Night. NY: Harcourt Brace, 1936. 1st Amer ed. VG in dj (spine ends, corners chipped; creases, closed tears; folds worn). *Mordida*. $95/£61

SAYERS, DOROTHY L. In the Teeth of the Evidence. Gollancz, 1939. 1st UK ed. Fine in VG dj (spine faded, lt edgewear, nicked). *Williams*. $390/£250

SAYERS, DOROTHY L. Lord Peter. NY: Harper & Row, 1972. 1st ed. Fine in dj. *Mordida*. $65/£42

SAYERS, DOROTHY L. The Man Born to Be King. London: Gollancz, 1943. 1st ed. (Typed label affixed to fep.) *Hollett*. $16/£10

SAYERS, DOROTHY L. (ed). The Omnibus of Crime. NY: Payson & Clarke, 1929. 1st Amer ed. Fine in dj. *Mordida*. $300/£192

SAYERS, DOROTHY L. Suspicious Characters. NY: Modern Age, (1937). Rpt ed. (Paper browning, sl cocked), else VG in ptd wrappers. *Turtle Island*. $15/£10

SAYERS, DOROTHY L. Unpopular Opinions. Gollancz, 1946. 1st UK ed. Fine in VG dj (spine lt faded). *Williams*. $34/£22

SAYERS, DOROTHY L. The Zeal of Thy House. Harcourt, Brace, (1937). 1st ed. Fine in Poor dj. *Authors Of West*. $50/£32

SAYERS, DOROTHY L. The Zeal of Thy House. London: Gollancz, 1937. 1st ed. VG in dj (chipped, torn). *Argosy*. $65/£42

SAYERS, MICHAEL and ALBERT E. KAHN. Sabotage! The Secret War Against America. NY: Metro, 1943. '1944 ed-brand new disclosures!' Orig ptd wrappers (sm edge tear). *Sadlon*. $20/£13

SAYLES, JOHN. The Anarchists' Convention. Boston: Little-Brown, 1979. 1st ed. Fine in dj (price-clipped). *Else Fine*. $70/£45

SAYLES, JOHN. Pride of the Bimbos. Boston: Atlantic-Little, Brown, (1975). 1st ed, 1st bk. Fine (sl spine slant) in Fine dj (spine sl faded). *Between The Covers*. $225/£144

SAYLES, JOHN. Pride of the Bimbos. Little, Brown, 1975. 1st ed. Fine in VG dj (1/2-inch chip). *Plapinger*. $110/£71

SAYLES, JOHN. Pride of the Bimbos. Boston: Little-Brown, 1975. 1st ed, 1st bk. Signed. Fine in dj (sl worn). *Else Fine*. $225/£144

SAYLES, JOHN. Union Dues. Boston, 1977. 1st ed. Fine (sl lean) in Fine dj. *Smith*. $30/£19

SCAMUZZI, ERNESTO. Egyptian Art in the Egyptian Museum of Turin. NY: Abrams, (1965). 1st ed. 115 mtd plts. Fine in dj. *Hermitage*. $150/£96

SCAMUZZI, ERNESTO. Egyptian Art in the Egyptian Museum of Turin. NY: Abrams, (1965). 115 plts (6 w/gold, 38 color). Good in dj. *Archaeologia*. $200/£128

SCARBOROUGH, ELIZABETH A. The Healer's War. NY: Foundation/Doubleday, (1988). 1st ed. Fine in Fine dj. *Other Worlds*. $50/£32

SCARRON, PAUL. Whole Comical Works of Monsr. Scarron. London: S. & J. Sprint et al, 1700. (8),120,145-359; 158; 64pp; engr tp, 3 plts. Mod 1/2 leather, marbled bds (sl worn). (Lt foxed), o/w Contents VG. *New Hampshire**. $35/£22

SCARRY, PATRICIA. The Jeremy Mouse Book. NY: Amer Heritage Press, 1969. Presumed 1st ed. Hilary Knight (illus). 10 x 11 1/4. 64pp. Pict bds. VG. *Cattermole*. $35/£22

SCEARCE, STANLEY. Northern Lights to Fields of Gold. Caldwell, ID: Caxton, 1939. Signed. VG. *High Latitude*. $35/£22

Scenes in Foreign Lands. Phila: W.A. Leary, n.d. (ca 1870). Sq 12mo. 156pp, 17 full-pg wood engrs. Grn tooled cl on bds (spine sl rubbed), gilt. Fine. *Hobbyhorse*. $95/£61

SCHAACK, MICHAEL. Anarchy and Anarchists. Chicago: F. Schulte, 1889. 1st ed. Nice bds (both hinges going; fep chipped, detached). *Beasley*. $125/£80

SCHAEFER, HERWIN. Nineteenth Century Modern. NY, 1970. 1st ed. Dj (lt rubbed, spine sl faded). *Edwards*. $39/£25

SCHAEFER, JACK. The Great Endurance Horse Race: 600 Miles on a Single Mount, 1908.... Stagecoach Press, (1963). 1st ltd ed of 750. Brochure laid in; rev copy, slip laid in. Fine in Fine dj. *Authors Of West*. $200/£128

SCHAEFFER, C. W. Early History of the Lutheran Church in America. Phila: Lutheran Board of Pub, 1857. 143pp (foxing, bkpl). Brn cl (backstrip ends chipped), gilt. *Bohling*. $35/£22

SCHAEFFER, J. PARSONS. The Nose, Paranasal Sinuses, Nasolacrimal Passageways, and Olfactory Organ in Man. Phila, 1920. Red cl bds (extrems sl worn, inner hinges cracked). VG. *Doctor's Library*. $150/£96

SCHAEFFER, SUSAN FROMBERG. The Red, White and Blue Poem. Denver: Ally Press, 1975. One of 250 (of 276) in handsewn blue ptd wraps. *Lame Duck*. $35/£22

SCHAFER, JOSEPH (ed). Memoirs of Jeremiah Curtin. Madison: State Hist Soc of WI, 1940. 1st ed. (Margin ink notes; shelfwear, lt dust soiled), else Good. *Brown*. $15/£10

SCHALDACH, WILLIAM J. Coverts and Casts. NY, (1943). 1st ptg. Signed, inscribed. VG in dj (worn). *Truepenny*. $125/£80

SCHALDACH, WILLIAM J. Coverts and Casts. NY: A.S. Barnes, 1943. Stated 1st ptg. Color frontis, 4 color plts. Gilt decs. VG (gilt worn). *Backman*. $30/£19

SCHAPIRO, MEYER. Romanesque Art. NY, 1977. Good in dj. *Washton*. $35/£22

SCHARDT, HERMANN. Paris 1900: Masterworks of French Poster Art. NY, (1970). Folio. 72 tipped-in color plts. (Ex-lib.) Dj (sl worn). *Swann**. $80/£51

SCHARF, E. E. Famous Saddle Horses. Louisville, KY, 1932. 1st ed. Emb cvr. VG (sl wear). *Bond*. $45/£29

SCHARF, GEORGE. Notes on the Authentic Portraits of Mary Queen of Scots. 1903. 33 plts. Teg, rest uncut. Full japon, gilt. (Feps lt browned, bkpl removed; sl soiled.) *Edwards*. $86/£55

SCHARF, J. THOMAS. History of Baltimore City and County, from the Earliest Period to the Present Day. Phila: Louis H. Evarts, 1881. 1st ed. 947pp; hand-colored 2-pg map at fr. Aeg; cl reinforced hinges. Orig brn sheep, cl, beveled bds, gilt. Good (fr hinge split, lt aged, dusty; scuffed, worn). Howes S142. *Baltimore**. $90/£58

SCHARF, J. THOMAS. History of Maryland from the Earliest Period to the Present Day. Hatboro, PA: Tradition Press, 1967. Facs rpt of 1879 ed. 4 vols. NF. *Sadlon*. $50/£32

SCHARF, J. THOMAS. History of the Confederate States Navy from Its Organization to the Surrender of Its Last Vessel. NY, 1887. Lg 8vo. Frontis port, 824pp, 42 plts. Gilt-stamped cl, illus on cvr. (Sl bump to spine w/tear repaired, inner hinges tender), else VG. Howes S147. *Reese*. $500/£321

SCHAU, MICHAEL. J. C. Leyendecker. NY: Watson-Guptill, (1974). 1st ed. Fine in dj. *Hermitage*. $250/£160

SCHAU, MICHAEL. J. C. Leyendecker. Watson-Guptill, 1974. 1st ptg. 64 full-color plts. VG + in dj (sl worn). *My Bookhouse*. $200/£128

SCHAUBECK, RICHARD (trans). Fortunia. A Tale by Mme d'Aulnoy. NY: Frank Hallman, 1974. One of 300. Signed by Schaubeck and Maurice Sendak (illus). Fine in ptd, string-tied self wrappers. *Cahan.* $100/£64

SCHAUINGER, J. HERMAN. Cathedrals in the Wilderness. Milwaukee: Bruce Pub, (1952). Frontis port. VG+ in dj (dknd, chipped). *Bohling.* $12/£8

SCHAUMANN, AUGUST LUDOLF FRIEDRICH. On the Road with Wellington. Anthony M. Ludovici (ed). London, 1924. 20 color plts. Blue cl (sl worn). *Maggs.* $195/£125

SCHEIDIG, WALTHER. Weimar Crafts of the Bauhaus, 1919-1924. NY: Reinhold, (1964). 1st Amer ed. VG (lt rubbed) in dj (spine ends torn w/loss). *Waverly*.* $88/£56

SCHELL, HERBERT S. History of South Dakota. Lincoln: Univ of NE, 1969. 1st ed. VG in dj. *Lien.* $35/£22

SCHELLEN, A. Artificial Insemination in the Human. NY, 1957. 1st ed. Grn cl. VG in dj (worn). *Doctor's Library.* $45/£29

SCHERF, MARGARET. The Gun in Daniel Webster's Bust. GC: DCC, 1949. 1st ed. VG+ in dj (edgeworn). *Else Fine.* $35/£22

SCHERING CORPORATION. Female/Male Sex Hormone Therapy. 1941, 42. 1st ed. 3 vol boxed set in ptd wrappers. VG. *Doctor's Library.* $60/£38

SCHEVILL, FERDINAND. Karl Bitter. Univ of Chicago, 1917. Association copy. Frontis port, 40 plts. (Ex-lib, ink stamp, label, cardholder remains, sl spotting; spine head sl chipped, corners bumped.) *Edwards.* $47/£30

SCHIAVO, GIOVANNI. Antonio Meucci, Inventor of the Telephone. NY: Vigo, (1958). 1st ed. Frontis port, 60 facs. NF. *Glaser.* $25/£16

SCHILLER, BARBARA. The Kitchen Knight. NY: Holt Rinehart, 1965. 1st ed. Nonny Hogrogian (illus). 6 3/4 x 8 1/2. 64pp. VG in dj. *Cattermole.* $25/£16

SCHILLER, FRIEDRICH. William Tell. Zurich: LEC, 1951. #904/1500 numbered, signed by Charles Hug (illus). Fine in pub's slipcase. *Hermitage.* $75/£48

SCHILLING, EDMUND. Drawings of the Holbein Family. London: Faber, 1937. 56 plts. (Spine top chipped), o/w Fine. *Europa.* $22/£14

SCHILLINGS, C. G. In Wildest Africa. London: Hutchinson, 1907. 1st ed in English. 2 vols. Partly unopened; teg. Pict cl (sl bumped, sl shaken; eps sl cracked). VG. *Ash.* $195/£125

SCHILLINGS, C. G. With Flashlight and Rifle. Frederick Whyte (trans). London: Hutchinson, 1906. 1st ed. 2 vols. Pict grn cl, gilt. Very Nice set (eps sl spotted). *Hollett.* $187/£120

SCHLEY, FRANK. American Partridge and Pheasant Shooting. Frederick: Baughman Bros, 1877. 1st ed. 222pp; 8 Fine engr plts. Gilt-pict grn cl. (Lt edgeworn), else VG+. *Bowman.* $120/£77

SCHLEY, WINFIELD S. and J. R. SOLEY. The Rescue of Greely. NY: Scribner, 1885. vii,277pp, 14 plts, 5 fldg maps. Good (cl sl spotted, worn). *High Latitude.* $85/£54

SCHLIEMANN, HENRY. Ilios: The City and Country of the Trojans. London: John Murray, 1880. 1st Eng ed. Frontis (fldg panorama), xvi,800pp; 6 fldg plans, fldg map. Teg. Gilt-pict cl. (Sm tear top bd), o/w Fine. *Archaeologia.* $650/£417

SCHLIEMANN, HENRY. Mycenae. NY: Scribner, Armstrong, 1878. 1st US ed. lxviii,384pp (sm marginal tears to several pp, contemp sig tp); 25 plts (4 color), 8 plans. Teg. Blue gilt-pict cl (sm spine tears). *Archaeologia.* $300/£192

SCHLIEMANN, HENRY. Tiryns: The Prehistoric Palace of the Kings of Tiryns. London: John Murray, 1886. lxiv,385pp; 24 chromolitho plts, map, 4 plans. (Bkpl removed, sig.) Teg. Gilt-pict cl (extrems worn, spine soiled, chipped). *Archaeologia.* $250/£160

SCHMIDT, ARNO. The Egghead Republic. London: Marion Boyars, 1979. 1st ed in English. Fine in dj. *Lame Duck.* $45/£29

SCHMIDT, EVAMARIA. The Great Altar of Pergamon. London: Peter Owen, (1965). 72 plts, map. Good in dj (chipped). *Archaeologia.* $85/£54

SCHMIDT, EVAMARIA. The Great Altar of Pergamon. London: Peter Owen, 1965. Map, 71 full-pg b/w plts. VG in dj. *Turtle Island.* $50/£32

SCHMIDT-NIELSEN, KNUT. Desert Animals. Clarendon Press, 1964. 8 plts. Dj (sl rubbed). *Edwards.* $39/£25

SCHMITT, MARTIN. General George Crook. Norman: Univ of OK, 1946. 1st ed. NF in VG dj. *Agvent.* $60/£38

SCHMOLLER, HANS et al. Chinese Decorated Papers. Newtown: Bird & Bull, 1987. One of 325 numbered. Prospectus laid in. 1/4 morocco. *Swann*.* $172/£110

SCHMOLLER, HANS. Mr. Gladstone's Washi. Newtown: Bird & Bull, 1984. One of 500 numbered, w/extra suite of plts. Prospectus laid in. 1/4 morocco. Bd slipcase. *Swann*.* $201/£129

SCHMUTZLER, ROBERT. Art Nouveau. NY: Abrams, (1962). 1st ed. 12 mtd color plts. Burgundy cl, gilt. Good in dj. *Karmiole.* $100/£64

SCHNEE, EMIL. Diabetes: Its Cause and Permanent Cure.... Phila, 1889. 215pp. Grn cl. Good (bkpl; fr inner hinge cracked). *Doctor's Library.* $65/£42

SCHNEEBAUM, TOBIAS. Keep the River on Your Right. NY: Grove, (1969). 1st ed. NF in dj. *Turtle Island.* $30/£19

SCHNEIDER, PIERRE. Matisse. NY: Rizzoli, (1984). (Lt worn.) Dj. *Oinonen*.* $60/£38

SCHNELL, DONALD E. Carnivorous Plants of the United States and Canada. Winston-Salem: John F. Blair, 1976. 1st ed. Fine in VG dj. *Connolly.* $30/£19

SCHNESSEL, S. MICHAEL. Jessie Willcox Smith. London, 1977. 1st ed. Dj. *Edwards.* $47/£30

SCHOENBERG, WILFRED P. Jesuit Mission Presses in the Pacific Northwest. (Portland): Champoeg Press, 1957. 1st ed. Ltd to 804. Frontis, tipped-in facs. Uncut. VF. *Argonaut.* $90/£58

SCHOENBERG, WILFRED P. Jesuit Mission Presses in the Pacific Northwest. (Portland): Champoeg, 1957. One of 804 ptd w/insert. Frontis port tipped in, plt, 8 facs. Unopened. Red cl (lt scratch back cvr), gilt. VG+. *Bohling.* $50/£32

SCHOENBERG, WILFRED P. Jesuit Mission Presses in the Pacific Northwest. (Portland, OR): Champoeg Press, 1957. One of 804, ptd by Lawton Kennedy w/his als laid in. Fine. *Truepenny.* $85/£54

SCHOENBERG, WILFRED P. Jesuit Mission Presses in the Pacific Northwest. Portland: Champoeg, 1957. One of 804. Frontis. *Ginsberg.* $75/£48

SCHOENER, ALLON (ed). Harlem on My Mind. NY: Random House, 1968. 1st ed. Cl-backed illus bds. (Owner stamp), else VG in dj (lt rubbed). *Cahan.* $75/£48

SCHOEPF, JOHANN DAVID. Travels in the Confederation (1783-1784). Alfred J. Morrison (ed). Phila, 1911. 1st ed in English. 2 vols. Howes S176. *Ginsberg.* $275/£176

SCHOEPF, JOHANN DAVID. Travels in the Confederation (1783-1784). Alfred J. Morrison (ed). Phila: William J. Campbell, 1911. 1st ed in English. 2 vols. Port, 2 facs. (Sl shelfwear, edgewear), else VG. Howes S176. *Brown.* $50/£32

SCHOLEFIELD, EDMUND O. Tiger Rookie. World, 1966. 1st ed. VG in VG dj. *Plapinger.* $40/£26

SCHOLZ, JACKSON. Base Burglar. Morrow, 1955. 1st ed. VG+ in VG dj. *Plapinger.* $50/£32

SCHOLZ, JACKSON. Batter Up. Morrow, 1946. 1st ed. VG in VG dj (sm mk). *Plapinger.* $45/£29

SCHONBERGER, ARNO et al. The Rococo Age. NY, 1960. Good in dj. *Washton.* $45/£29

School-Life at Winchester College. (By Robert Blackford Mansfield.) London, 1870. 243pp + (iv)pp pub's ads (lt browning, soil, blind lib stamp fep); 7 color plts, plan. Gilt-illus cl (lt soiled; rebacked, much of orig spine laid down). *Edwards.* $94/£60

SCHOOLCRAFT, HENRY R. Historical and Statistical Information Respecting the History, Condition, and Prospects of the Indian Tribes of the United States. Vol I only. Phila, (1851). 1st ed. xviii,13-568pp, 75 plts. VG (sig, leather bkpl). Howes S183. *Oregon.* $750/£481

SCHOOLCRAFT, HENRY R. Journal of a Tour into the Interior of Missouri and Arkansaw.... London: Richard Phillips, 1821. 102pp; fldg map. Mod bds, paper label. VG. Howes S185. *Adelson.* $425/£272

SCHOOLCRAFT, HENRY R. Narrative Journal of Travels Through the Northwestern Regions of the United States...in the Year 1820. Albany: Hosford, 1821. 1st ed. Extra engr frontis, 419,(4)pp; 7 plts, fldg map (sm tape-repaired tear), errata slip mtd on rep. Contemp mottled sheep, red leather spine label. Lovely (pp dknd, lt foxed; lt wear). Howes S187. *Bohling.* $950/£609

SCHOOLCRAFT, HENRY R. Narrative of an Expedition Through the Upper Mississippi to Itasca Lake.... NY: Harper, 1834. 1st ed. vi,7-308pp; 5 maps (2 fldg). Mod cl, leather label. VG. Howes S187. *Adelson.* $425/£272

SCHOOLCRAFT, HENRY R. Narrative of an Expedition Through the Upper Mississippi to Itasca Lake...in 1832. NY, 1834. 1st ed. (2),308pp; 5 maps (2 lg fldg). Mod 1/2 calf. Howes S187. *Ginsberg.* $500/£321

SCHOOLCRAFT, HENRY R. Narrative of an Expedition Through Upper Mississippi to Itasca Lake.... NY: Harper, 1834. 1st ed. 308pp, 5 maps, 2 fldg errata. (Ex-lib, sm paper spine label, label remnants verso fep; lacks reps, sm dampspot lower edge 1st few leaves.) Internally VG. Howes S187. *Oregon.* $390/£250

SCHOOLCRAFT, HENRY R. Notes on the Iroquois. Albany, 1847. 498pp; 2 color plts. Teg. Later 3/4 leather. (Name on tp poorly eradicated affecting top margin of frontis, fr hinges starting to split, worn), else Nice. *King.* $395/£253

SCHOOLCRAFT, HENRY R. A View of the Lead Mines of Missouri. NY: Charles Wiley, 1819. 1st ed. Copper-engr frontis, 2 add'l copper-engr plts. Marbled eps, edges. Period full brn calf, gilt, raised bands, black morocco spine label (edges chipped). (Fr joint cracked almost through, old repairs to spine, lt wear, dampstain rear cvr, lt intruding to latter 1/3 of contents.) VG-. Howes S194. *Harrington.* $425/£272

SCHOOLCRAFT, MRS. HENRY R. The Black Gauntlet: A Tale of Plantation Life in South Carolina. Phila: Lippincott, 1860. 1st ed. x,11-569pp. (Cl sl spotted, spine lettering faded), else Good. *Brown.* $40/£26

SCHOOLING, WILLIAM. The Hudson's Bay Company 1670-1920. London: Hudson's Bay, 1920. 1st ed. Facs fldg map. (Cvr worn.) Contents VG. *New Hampshire*.* $70/£45

SCHOONOVER, CORTLAND. Frank Schoonover: Illustrator of the North American Frontier. NY: Watson-Guptill, (1976). 1st ed. 48 color plts. Mint in dj. *Graf.* $35/£22

SCHOONOVER, T. J. The Life and Times of Gen. John A. Sutter. Sacramento: Press of Bullock-Carpenter Ptg Co, 1907. Rev, enlgd ed. Errata slip tipped in. Yellow cl (lt soiled). Carl I. Wheat's copy, pencil name. Howes S196. *Karmiole.* $85/£54

SCHOPENHAUER, ARTHUR. The Basis of Morality. Arthur Brodrick Bullock (trans). London: Swan Sonnenschein, 1903. 1st ed in English. Red cl. Inserted slip at tp from publisher George Allen, who bought c. from Sonnenschein. *Swann*.* $69/£44

SCHOULER, W. A History of Massachusetts in the Civil War. Boston, 1868. 1st ed. Engr frontis, 670pp. Good. *Scribe's Perch*.* $30/£19

SCHRADER, FRANK CHARLES. A Reconnaissance in Northern Alaska Across the Rocky Mountains...1901. Washington: GPO, 1904. 16 plts, incl 4 maps (2 fldg). Black cl spine, hand-lettered spine label. (Eps aged; sl chipped, soiled), else VG. *Parmer.* $165/£106

SCHRAM, CONSTANCE W. Olaf Lofoten Fisherman. London/NY: Longmans, Green, 1929. 1st ed. 8vo. 187pp; 9 tri-color illus by Marjorie Flack. Illus eps. Blue illus cl. VG in Good dj. *Dower.* $25/£16

SCHREIBEIS, CHARLES D. Pioneer Education in the Pacific Northwest (1789-1847). Portland: Metropolitan, n.d.(1930s?). Ptd spine label. VG (fep removed, stamp). *Bohling.* $20/£13

SCHREIBER, CHARLOTTE. Fans and Fan Leaves. London: John Murray, 1888. 161 litho plts. (Text lt thumb-soiled, lib stamps plt versos.) Gilt edges. Contemp vellum (scuffed, lt soiled, rubbed), gilt. *Christie's*.* $1,053/£675

SCHREIBER, CHARLOTTE. Lady Charlotte Schreiber's Journals. London/NY: John Lane, 1911. 2 vols. Dec cl (sl worn). Contents VG. *New Hampshire*.* $45/£29

SCHREIBER, HERMANN and GEORG. Vanished Cities. Richard and Clara Winston (trans). NY: Knopf, 1957. 1st ed. VG (rubbed, ex-lib, spine sticker). *Worldwide.* $15/£10

SCHREIBER, MARTIN H. Last of a Breed. Austin, 1982. 1st trade ed. VG- (cvr edges fading, sl abrasion top fr cvr) in dj (sl worn). *Baade.* $45/£29

SCHREINER, OLIVE. Woman and Labor. NY: Stokes, 1911. 1st ed. NF (name; mild spots spine). *Beasley.* $65/£42

SCHREINER, SAMUEL A., JR. The Trials of Mrs. Lincoln. NY, (1987). 1st ed. As New in As New dj. *Pratt.* $20/£13

SCHREYER, ALICE. East-West: Hand Papermaking Traditions and Innovations. Newark: Univ of DE Library, 1988. One of 300. VF in wrappers. *Truepenny.* $45/£29

SCHROEDER, ALBERT H. and DAN S. MATSON. A Colony on the Move. Santa Fe: School of Amer Research, 1965. VG in dj. *Dumont.* $30/£19

SCHROEDER, BINETTE. Lupinchen. NY: Delacorte, (1970). 1st Amer ed. 4to. 32pp (pastedowns sl dknd); 4 dbl-pg, 10 full-pg illus. Purple cl (stained). VG in pict dj (spotted, sl soiled, price-clipped). *Blue Mountain.* $25/£16

SCHUCHHARDT, C. Schliemann's Excavations. London: Macmillan, 1891. 363pp + ads. Good (casing repaired). *Scribe's Perch*.* $70/£45

SCHULBERG, BUDD. Everything That Moves. Robson Books, 1981. 1st UK ed. Fine in dj. *Williams.* $19/£12

SCHULBERG, BUDD. The Harder They Fall. NY: Random House, (1947). 1st ed. Inscribed. Black cl. Dj (worn). *Appelfeld.* $65/£42

SCHULBERG, BUDD. The Harder They Fall. NY: Random House, (1947). 1st ed. Stunning in dj (sm tear). *Captain's Bookshelf.* $125/£80

SCHULBERG, BUDD. Waterfront. NY: Random House, (1955). 1st ed. Fine in dj (lt worn). *Hermitage.* $40/£26

SCHULIAN, D. M. and F. E. SOMMER. A Catalogue of Incunbula and Manuscripts in the Army Medical Library. NY, 1948. Nice. *Goodrich.* $75/£48

SCHULLER, ARTHUR. Roentgen Diagnosis of Diseases of the Head. Fred F. Stocking (trans). St. Louis: Mosby, 1918. Good. *Goodrich.* $95/£61

SCHULLIAN, DOROTHY (ed). The Baglivi Correspondence from the Library of Sir William Osler. Cornell Univ, 1974. *Edwards.* $55/£35

SCHULLIAN, DOROTHY (ed). The Baglivi Correspondence from the Library of Sir William Osler. Ithaca, 1974. 1st ed. VG. *Fye.* $40/£26

SCHULLIAN, DOROTHY and MAX SCHOEN. Music and Medicine. NY, 1948. 1st ed. NF in Good dj. *Doctor's Library.* $95/£61

SCHULLIAN, DOROTHY and MAX SCHOEN. Music and Medicine. NY, 1948. 1st ed. VG. *Fye.* $95/£61

SCHULLIAN, DOROTHY and FRANCIS SOMMER. A Catalogue of Incunabula and Manuscripts in the Army Medical Library. NY, 1950. 1st ed. VG. *Fye.* $90/£58

SCHULTE, PAUL. The Flying Priest over the Arctic. NY: Harper, c. 1940. 1st ed. Fine in dj (chipped). *High Latitude.* $20/£13

SCHULTHESS, EMIL. Soviet Union. NY: Harper & Row, 1971. 1st US ed. (Owner stamp), else Fine in dj (sl edgeworn). *Cahan.* $50/£32

SCHULTZ, CARL H. The Mineral Water Controversy, Artificial or Natural? NY: Sackett & Rankin, 1882. Wrappers (faded). *Maggs.* $19/£12

SCHULTZ, GERARD. Early History of the Northern Ozarks. Jefferson City: Midland Ptg Co, (1937). Presentation copy. Tipped-in view. VG (sl faded, soiled). *Bohling.* $50/£32

SCHULTZ, JAMES WILLARD. On the Warpath. Boston, 1914. 1st ed. VG (cvr wear). *Pratt.* $75/£48

SCHULTZ, JAMES WILLARD. William Jackson, Indian Scout. Boston: Houghton Mifflin, 1926. 1st ed. 4 plts. Brn cl. (Feps adhering to pastedown; extrems sl worn, sl rubbed), o/w VG. Howes S204. *Harrington.* $125/£80

SCHULTZ, JOHN. No One Was Killed...Convention Week, Chicago—August 1968. Chicago: Big Table Bks, 1969. 1st ed. (Bds sl damp-affected), o/w NF- in dj. *Sclanders.* $16/£10

SCHULTZ, PAUL L. The 85th Infantry Division in World War II. Washington: Infantry Journal Press, 1979 rprnt. *Cullen.* $35/£22

SCHULZ, BRUNO. Letters and Drawings of. NY, (1988). 1st ed. NF in dj. *Freeman*.* $20/£13

SCHULZ, BRUNO. The Street of Crocodiles. NY: Walker, 1963. 1st US ed. NF in VG dj (chip). *Lame Duck.* $75/£48

SCHULZ, CHARLES. Peanuts. Rinehart, 1952. 1st ed. VG in wraps. *Madle.* $15/£10

SCHULZ, CHARLES. You Can't Win, Charlie Brown. NY: Holt, Rinehart & Winston, 1962. 1st ed. NF in wraps. *Associates.* $15/£10

SCHULZ, ELLEN D. Cactus Culture. NY: OJ, 1932. 1st ed. 23 photo plts. Blue cl, gilt. VG. *Price.* $29/£19

SCHULZ, JUERGEN. Venetian Painted Ceilings of the Renaissance. Univ of CA, 1968. 151 b/w plts. Dj (sl rubbed). *Edwards.* $94/£60

SCHULZ, JUERGEN. Venetian Painted Ceilings of the Renaissance. Berkeley: Univ of CA, 1968. 1st ed. Grn cl. Good in dj. *Karmiole.* $85/£54

SCHURE, EDOUARD. The Great Initiates. London: W. Rider, 1920. Rpt. 2 vols. (Cvr lt faded), o/w VG +. *Middle Earth.* $95/£61

SCHURZ, CARL. Abraham Lincoln, a Biographical Essay. Boston/NY: Houghton Mifflin, 1907. One of 1040. 1/2 cl, gilt-stamped morocco spine label, medallion port fr cvr. Partly unopened. VG (lt edgewear). *Bohling.* $40/£26

SCHUTZ, JOHN A. Thomas Pownall, British Defender of American Liberty. Glendale, CA: A.H. Clark, 1952. Frontis port, facs. Blue cl, gilt. Fine. *Bohling.* $30/£19

SCHUYLER, JAMES. Alfred and Guinevere. NY: Harcourt Brace, (1958). 1st ed, 1st bk. Inscribed. Fine in Fine dj. *Lenz.* $400/£256

SCHWANN, T. H. Microscopical Researches into the Accordance in the Structure and Growth of Animals and Plants. H. Smith (trans). Sydenham Soc, 1847. xx,268pp; 4 plts. (Rebacked, spine laid down.) *Whitehart.* $195/£125

SCHWARTZ, CHARLES W. The Ecology of the Prairie Chicken in Missouri. Columbia: Univ of MO, 1945. 1st ed. 26 tables. VG (sig) in wraps. *Mikesh.* $37/£24

SCHWARTZ, CHARLES W. The Prairie Chicken in Missouri. N.p.: Conservation Commission, State of MO, 1944. 1st ptg, unpaginated. Color photo frontis. Dec eps. Emb leatherette cvr; gilt lettering. VG + in VG dj (piece cut out). *Backman.* $80/£51

SCHWARTZ, DELMORE. In Dreams Begin Responsibilities. Norfolk, CT: New Directions, 1938. 1st ed, 1st bk. One of 1000. Black cl, gilt. NF. *Cahan.* $75/£48

SCHWARTZ, DELMORE. Shenandoah. Norfolk, CT: New Directions, (1941). 1st ed. Fine in wrappers, dj. *Jaffe.* $75/£48

SCHWARTZ, DELMORE. Shenandoah. Norfolk: New Directions, (1941). 1st ed. (Spine edge faded.) VG in wrappers. *Graf.* $35/£22

SCHWARTZ, DELMORE. Successful Love and Other Stories. NY: Corinth, 1961. 1st ed. Fine in dj (edgeworn). *Jaffe.* $100/£64

SCHWARTZ, DELMORE. Summer Knowledge. GC: Doubleday, 1959. 1st ed. Fine in dj (lt rubbed). *Jaffe.* $75/£48

SCHWARTZ, DELMORE. The World Is a Wedding and Other Stories. NY: New Directions, 1948. 1st ed. NF in dj (nick). *Lame Duck.* $150/£96

SCHWARTZ, DELMORE. The World Is a Wedding. New Directions, (1948). 1st ed. VG in dj. *Argosy.* $100/£64

SCHWARTZ, DELMORE. The World Is a Wedding. John Lehmann, 1949. 1st UK ed. VG in dj. *Williams.* $70/£45

SCHWARTZ, H. The Book Collecting Racket...Part 3. Milwaukee: Casanova, 1936. Ptd cvrs. (2-line note rear cvr), o/w VG. *Moss.* $25/£16

SCHWARTZ, JACOB. The Writings of A. E. Coppard, A Bibliography.... London: Ulysses Bkshop, 1931. 1st ed. Out of series copy, numbered '00' and designated for review, in addition to 650 signed. Paper label. VG- (bkpl; bds lt dust soiled). *Reese.* $35/£22

SCHWARTZ, JACOB. The Writings of A. E. Coppard, A Bibliography.... London: Ulysses Bookshop, 1931. One of 650 signed by Coppard. Cl-backed bds. Very Nice (eps tanned). *Clearwater.* $78/£50

SCHWARTZ, SELWYN S. The Poet in Blue Minor. Prairie City: Decker Press, 1942. 1st ed. One of 400. Inscribed. Blue cl. (Smudge on spine, no dj), o/w VG. *Reese.* $35/£22

SCHWARTZ, SELWYN S. Preface to Maturity. Prairie City: Press of James A. Decker, (1944). 1st ed. Inscribed. Fine (no dj). *Reese.* $35/£22

SCHWATKA, FREDERICK. Report of a Military Reconnaissance in Alaska, Made in 1883. Washington: GPO, 1885. 1st ed. 121pp, 38 engrs, 20 lg fldg maps. Brn cl (lt worn, stained), gilt-lettered spine. VG; internally Fine. *Argonaut.* $125/£80

SCHWEINFURTH, GEORG. The Heart of Africa. NY: Harper, 1874. 1st Amer ed. 2 vols. xvi,559; x,521pp,6pp ads; fldg map. Maroon gilt pict cl (lib labels removed from spines, spine top sl frayed), else VG. *Terramedia*. $250/£160

SCHWEITZER, ALBERT. On the Edge of the Primeval Forest and More from the Primeval Forest. London: A&C Black, 1948. 1st collected ed. Good. *White*. $39/£25

SCHWEITZER, ALBERT. The Psychiatric Study of Jesus: Exposition and Criticism. Boston: Beacon, 1948. 1st ed in English. Black cl. VG in dj (worn). *Gach*. $37/£24

SCHWIEN, EDWIN E. Combat Intelligence: Its Acquisition and Transmission. Washington, DC: Infantry Journal, 1936. 1st ed. 19 fldg plans and maps. Grn cl (spine ends faded), gilt. NF in Good pict dj (chipped, short tears). *Blue Mountain*. $75/£48

SCHWING, NED. The Winchester Model 42. (Iola, 1990.) Gilt-stamped leatherette (lt worn), pict cvr label. *Oinonen**. $60/£38

SCIASCIA, LEONARDO. The Council of Egypt. NY: Knopf, 1966. 1st ed. VG + in VG dj. *Lame Duck*. $65/£42

SCIDMORE, ELIZA RUHAMAH. Appleton's Guide-Book to Alaska and the Northwest Coast. NY, 1897. Pict cl. *Swann**. $57/£37

SCIFFMAN, JACK. Uptown: The Story of Harlem's Apollo Theatre. NY: Cowles, (1971). 1st ed. Fine in NF dj (lt rubbed, sm tear rear panel). *Between The Covers*. $45/£29

SCOBEE, BARRY. Old Fort Davis. San Antonio, (1947). 1st ed. Good in dj (torn). *Heinoldt*. $25/£16

SCOBEE, BARRY. Old Fort Davis. San Antonio: Naylor, 1947. 1st ed. VG. *Gibbs*. $25/£16

SCOBEE, BARRY. The Steer Branded Murder. Fort Davis, TX: Barry Scobee, (1952). Ptd orange wrappers. *Dawson*. $40/£26

SCOFFERN, J. et al. The Useful Metals and Their Alloys. London: Houlston & Wright, 1866. 4th ed. xvi,654pp + ads; 4 plts. Emb cl. VG (ex-libris). *Blake*. $125/£80

SCOLLARD, CLINTON. The Epic of Golf. Boston, 1923. 1st ed. Cl-backed ptd bds (extrems frayed, spine sunned, stained, dknd). *King*. $95/£61

SCOLLARD, CLINTON. The Epic of Golf. Boston: Houghton Mifflin, 1923. 1st ed. Cl-backed dec bds. Fine in VG dj (ends chipped). *Pacific**. $184/£118

SCORESBY, WILLIAM. Journal of a Voyage to Australia and Round the World, for Magnetical Research. London: Longman, Green et al, 1859. xlviii,315pp; port (water-stained), fldg map (lt foxed), errata. 1/2 tan calf, marbled bds. *Adelson*. $285/£183

SCORESBY, WILLIAM. Journal of a Voyage to the Northern Whale Fishery...Made in the Summer of 1822.... Whitby: Caedmon, 1980. Fine in dj. *High Latitude*. $40/£26

SCOTT, EDWARD B. The Saga of the Sandwich Islands. (Lake Tahoe, NV: Sierra-Tahoe, 1968.) 1st ed. Inscribed presentation. Fldg map. Cream buckram, gilt. Good. *Karmiole*. $100/£64

SCOTT, EDWIN J. Random Recollections of a Long Life: 1806 to 1876. Columbia, SC: Calvo, 1884. 1st ed. (6),216pp. Howes S220. *Ginsberg*. $175/£112

SCOTT, EVELYN. Background in Tennessee. NY: McBride, 1937. 1st ed. (Sunned), o/w Fine in NF dj (top edgewear). *Beasley*. $100/£64

SCOTT, EVELYN. The Wave. NY: Cape & Smith, 1929. 1st ed. Fine (spine sunned) in dj (lt used, spine dknd). *Beasley*. $100/£64

SCOTT, EVERETT. Third Base Thatcher. Dodd Mead, 1923. 1st ed. VG. *Plapinger*. $70/£45

SCOTT, G. Grouse Land and the Fringe of the Moor. London: Witherby, 1937. 1st ed. Frontis dwg. VG +. *Mikesh*. $30/£19

SCOTT, HUGH LENOX. Some Memories of a Soldier. NY, 1928. 1st ed. (Spine top faded.) *Ginsberg*. $150/£96

SCOTT, J. M. Gino Watkins. London: Hodder & Stoughton, 1935. Color frontis. Teg. VG. *High Latitude*. $40/£26

SCOTT, J. M. The Land That God Gave to Cain...H. G. Watkins' Expedition to Labrador, 1928-29. London: C&W, 1933. Fldg map. VG. *High Latitude*. $55/£35

SCOTT, JAMES K. P. The Story of the Battles at Gettysburg. Harrisburg, 1927. (Eps discolored, lt foxing), o/w Good in dj (foxed, chipped). *Scribe's Perch**. $24/£15

SCOTT, JOB. Journal of the Life, Travels, and Gospel Labours of That Faithful Servant and Minister of Christ, Job Scott. NY: Isaac Collins, 1797. 1st ed. xiv,360pp (dknd, foxed, hinges reinforced). Full leather (hinges split, edgeworn). Good. Howes S228. *Bohling*. $100/£64

SCOTT, JOHN. Paris Revisited, in 1815, by Way of Brussels. 1816. 3rd ed. (iv) pub ads + viii,405pp. (Edges sl spotted, orig bds detached, lacks much of backstrip.) *Edwards*. $39/£25

SCOTT, JOHN. Paris Revisited, in 1815, by Way of Brussels. London, 1817. 4th ed. 405pp (bkpl). Full blind-stamped patterned calf (extrems worn). *King*. $150/£96

SCOTT, JOHN. Partisan Life with Colonel John S. Mosby. NY, 1867. 1st ed. (Cvrs heavily worn, soiled.) Interior Good. *Mcclintock*. $85/£54

SCOTT, JOHN. A Visit to Paris in 1814.... London: Longman et al, 1815. xxiii,338,lxxipp. Contemp gilt-ruled speckled calf (crudely rebacked in morocco, extrems rubbed; lt foxed, bkpl). *Edwards*. $62/£40

SCOTT, LIEUT. GEN. Memoirs of Lieut. General Scott, LL.D. NY: Sheldon, 1864. 1st ed. 2 vols. Frontis, 653pp. Fair (spines chipped, worn). Howes S242. *Lien*. $150/£96

SCOTT, LOUISE. The Gods Are Close. (Lincoln, MA): Penmaen, (1977). Inscribed. Mottled blue paper bds, paper title label, dk blue cl spine, gilt title. Prospectus laid in. Fine. *Heller*. $60/£38

SCOTT, MARION and GERALD STRINE. Montpelier. NY: Scribner, 1976. 1st ed. VG in Good + dj. *October Farm*. $95/£61

SCOTT, MARY M. M. Abbotsford: The Personal Relics and Antiquarian Treasures of Sir Walter Scott. London: A&C Black, 1893. 25 color plts + frontis. Contents VG (partly stained, offsetting eps). *Waverly**. $22/£14

SCOTT, MARY M. M. Abbotsford: The Personal Relics and Antiquarian Treasures of Sir Walter Scott. London: A&C Black, 1893. 16,66pp; 25 VG tissue-guarded chromolitho plts. Dec cvr. Good (spine chipped). *Scribe's Perch**. $50/£32

SCOTT, NANCY N. A Memoir of Hugh Lawson White.... Phila, 1856. (10),455pp; port. (Rubber stamp tp.) Howes S238. *Ginsberg*. $100/£64

SCOTT, P. The Eye of the Wind: An Autobiography. London: Hodder & Stoughton, (Jul. 1961). Dec eps. Fine in NF dj. *Mikesh*. $30/£19

SCOTT, PAUL. The Bender. London: Secker & Warburg, (1963). 1st ed. (Name), else NF in VG- dj (extrems sl used; sm spine hole; dkng). *Between The Covers*. $85/£54

SCOTT, PAUL. The Day of the Scorpion. London: Heinemann, 1968. 1st ed. (Edges spotted, sl offsetting to eps, name), o/w VG in dj (soiled, chipped; closed, internally repaired tears). *Virgo*. $86/£55

SCOTT, PAUL. The Jewel in the Crown. London, 1966. 1st ed. Dj (frayed, chipped). *Typographeum*. $75/£48

SCOTT, PAUL. Johnnie Sahib. London: Eyre & Spottiswoode, 1952. 1st UK ed. VG (foxed, sl bumped) in dj (spine top sl worn, rear panel browned). *Williams*. $109/£70

SCOTT, PAUL. Staying On. Heinemann, 1977. 1st UK ed. Fine in Fine dj. *Martin*. $66/£42

SCOTT, PAUL. Staying On. NY: Morrow, 1977. 1st ed. Fine in dj. *Antic Hay*. $20/£13

SCOTT, PETER. Wild Geese and Eskimos. Country Life, 1951. 1st ed. Color frontis. (Prelims sl browned.) Dj (chipped). *Edwards*. $25/£16

SCOTT, QUINTA. The Eads Bridge. Columbia: Univ of MO, 1979. Inscribed. Signed by Scott and Howard S. Miller (historical appraisal). VG+ in dj. *Bohling*. $45/£29

SCOTT, R. L. Between the Elephant's Eyes. London, 1955. Nice in dj. *Grayling*. $31/£20

SCOTT, ROBERT F. Scott's Last Expedition. London: Smith, Elder, 1913. 2 vols. Photograv frontispieces, 6 orig photogravure sketches, 18 color plts, 2 fldg maps. Erratum. Acceptable (sl foxed; cvrs worn). *Parmer*. $250/£160

SCOTT, ROBERT F. Scott's Last Expedition. London: Smith, Elder, 1913. 2nd ed. 2 vols. Photogravure frontispieces, 18 color plts. Teg. Blue ribbed cl, gilt. Fine set. *Hollett*. $250/£160

SCOTT, ROBERT F. The Voyage of the 'Discovery.' London: Smith, Elder, 1905. 1st ed. 2 vols. 2 fldg maps in pockets. Teg. (Spine head vol 1 repaired), else VG. *High Latitude*. $425/£272

SCOTT, ROBERT F. The Voyage of the Discovery. NY: Scribner, 1905. 2 vols. (Few pp carelessly opened, lt foxing.) Gilt-dec cl (edgewear, sl loose). *Metropolitan**. $287/£184

SCOTT, ROBERT L. Between the Elephant's Eyes! NY: Dodd, Mead, 1954. 1st ed. Fine in VG dj (edge sl chipped). *Backman*. $20/£13

SCOTT, SUTHERLAND. The Influenza Mystery. London: Paul, n.d. VG (soil, lt wear, edges chipped). *Metropolitan**. $11/£7

SCOTT, W. W. A History of Orange County.... Everett Waddy, 1907. 1st ed. Good+ (binding weak). *Book Broker*. $125/£80

SCOTT, WALTER (trans). The Chase, and William and Helen. Edinburgh, 1796. 1st ed, 1st bk. (6),41pp (accession stamp tp verso, bkpl; related matter mtd on pastedowns). Contemp marbled bds, later vellum back. *Swann**. $373/£239

SCOTT, WALTER. Familiar Letters of Sir Walter Scott. Edinburgh: David Douglas, 1894. 1st ed. 2 vols. Emb brn cl. VG (eps browned, bkpl). *Antic Hay*. $75/£48

SCOTT, WALTER. Ivanhoe. NY/Chicago/SF: Rand McNally, (1938). Later ed. Black cl, pict pastedown. Fine in dj (lt worn). *Glenn*. $65/£42

SCOTT, WALTER. Ivanhoe. Edinburgh: A. Constable, 1820. 1st ed w/mixed issue points. 3 vols. Author's ad vol 1; lacks 2 half-titles vol 1, 3, and 1 fly-title vol 3, and pub's cat vol 3. (Contents lt soiled.) Later 1/2 calf, marbled bds (worn, joints cracked). *Waverly**. $66/£42

SCOTT, WALTER. Kenilworth. (Burlington, VT): LEC, 1966. One of 1500 numbered, signed by Clarke Hutton (illus). Brocade cl. VG in bd slipcase. *Argosy*. $100/£64

SCOTT, WALTER. Kenilworth; A Romance. Edinburgh: Constable, 1821. 1st ed, w/all 3 half-titles. 3 vols. Marbled bds, contemp 3/4 brn calf. VG (owner labels). *Macdonnell*. $125/£80

SCOTT, WALTER. The Lady of the Lake. Boston: Little, Brown, 1853. Steel-engr title, frontis, 375pp. (Extrms lt worn), else Fine in pub's blind-, gilt-stamped blue cl. *Bromer*. $150/£96

SCOTT, WALTER. The Lady of the Lake. Bobbs-Merrill, 1910. 4to. 12 full-pg color plts by Howard Chandler Christy. Dec grn cl. Fine in dj (torn, chipped). *Metropolitan**. $172/£110

SCOTT, WALTER. Letters on Demonology and Witchcraft, Addressed to J. G. Lockhart, Esq. London, 1830. 1st ed. Sm 8vo. Engr frontis, extra-illus w/12 etched plts by George Cruikshank separately issued for this work, all in 3 states (colored and uncolored on wove paper, and uncolored on India paper). Red levant, gilt. Morocco-edged cl slipcase. *Swann**. $1,092/£700

SCOTT, WALTER. Letters on Demonology and Witchcraft. London: John Murray, 1830. 1st ed. Engr frontis (lt browned), ix,402pp. Old 1/2 calf (rebacked, new eps), gilt. *Hollett*. $133/£85

SCOTT, WALTER. Letters on Demonology and Witchcraft. NY: J.J. Harper, 1830. 1st Amer ed. Engr frontis. Drab bds, linen spine, paper label. Sound (wear). *Appelfeld*. $200/£128

SCOTT, WALTER. Letters on Demonology and Witchcraft. London: John Murray, 1831. 2nd ed. Engr frontis (lt browned), ix,396(ii)pp. Full black calf (rebacked), gilt, bds blind-ruled, center patterned panel. *Hollett*. $78/£50

SCOTT, WALTER. The Life of Napoleon Buonaparte. London/Edinburgh: Longman, Rees, Orme et al/Cadell, 1827. 1st ed. 9 vols. Complete w/half-titles, errata slips, etc. 19th-cent cl, gilt. Nice set (sl mkd, used). *Ash*. $390/£250

SCOTT, WALTER. The Life of Napoleon Buonaparte. Phila: Carey, Lea & Carey, 1827. 1st Amer ed. 3 vols. Frontis port. Uncut. (Foxed.) Pub's blue bds, purple cl spine (faded), orig ptd spine labels. *D & D*. $450/£288

SCOTT, WALTER. The Life of Napoleon Buonaparte. Exeter: Williams, 1842. 2 vols. 494; 414pp+appendix. Full black leather. Good (sl chips). *Scribe's Perch**. $38/£24

SCOTT, WALTER. Marmion. Edinburgh, 1808. 4th ed. (xii),377,cxxviiipp. Aeg. (Spotting; sl rubbed, upper joint sl split.) *Edwards*. $31/£20

SCOTT, WALTER. Memoirs of John Dryden. Paris: A. & W. Galignani, 1826. 2 vols bound together. x,277; (4),219pp (water stain across corner 1st few gatherings, sl spotted). Later 19th-cent cl. *Cox*. $23/£15

SCOTT, WALTER. The Poetical Works. Edinburgh, 1857. 746,(ii)pp (lt spotted, upper hinge sl cracked). Aeg. Morocco-backed varnished Cameron tartan bds (sl rubbed). *Edwards*. $47/£30

SCOTT, WALTER. Waverley Novels. London, 1897. Victoria ed. 25 vols. Sm 8vo. Frontispieces. Contemp tan calf, gilt, spines in 6 compartments, red/citron morocco lettering pieces in 2. *Swann**. $747/£479

SCOTT, WALTER. Waverley. LEC, 1961. #418/1500 signed by Robert Ball (illus). Tan leather. Slipcase. *Yudkin**. $80/£51

SCOTT, WILLIAM. A History of Land Mammals in the Western Hemisphere. NY, 1913. 1st ed. Teg. Blue cl, gilt. (Edgewear), else VG. *Price*. $59/£38

SCOTT, WILLIAM. Lessons in Elocution. Boston: Isaiah Thomas, 1814. 407pp; 4 plts. Contemp calf (worn). Good+. *Zubal**. $20/£13

SCOTT, WILLIAM. The Riviera. A&C Black, 1907. 75 color plts, fldg sketch map. Teg. Dec cl. (Feps browned, upper hinge tender; sm stains, spine faded, rubbed). *Edwards*. $39/£25

SCOTT-GILES, C. W. The Wimsey Family. London: Gollancz, 1977. 1st UK ed. NF in dj. *Williams*. $39/£25

SCOTT-JAMES, ANNE. The Cottage Garden. Allen Lane, 1981. 1st ed. NF in dj. *Hadley*. $23/£15

SCOTT-MONCRIEFF, GEORGE. The Beauty of Scotland in Colour. London: Batsford, 1965. 1st ed. 32 full-pg color plts. VG in dj (edges sl worn). *Hollett.* $31/£20

SCOTT-MONCRIEFF, GEORGE. Edinburgh. London: Batsford, 1947. 1st ed. (Few spots title, fore-edge.) Dj (price-clipped). *Hollett.* $23/£15

Scouring of the White Horse. (By Thomas Hughes.) Cambridge/London: Macmillan, 1859. 244pp (margin p79 repaired, lacks rep). 1/2 leather, dec spine. Good-. *Scribe's Perch*.* $38/£24

SCOVELL, E. J. The River Steamer. London: Cresset, 1956. 1st ed. VG in dj (browned, torn). *Antic Hay.* $20/£13

SCRANTON, ROBERT LORENTZ. Greek Walls. Cambridge: Harvard Univ, 1941. Later 3/4 calf. (Erasure verso tp), o/w Fine. *Archaeologia.* $450/£288

SCRIBNER, HARVEY. My Mysterious Clients. Cincinnati: Robert Clarke, 1900. 1st ed. Inscribed to Charles Scribner. (Spine dknd), o/w Fine in pict cl-cvrd bds. *Mordida.* $125/£80

SCRIPPS, JOHN LOCKE. The First Published Life of Abraham Lincoln, Written in the Year MDCCCLX. (Detroit): Cranbrook Press, 1900. #55/245. Frontis port. 3/4 vellum (rubbed, sl discolored). Tls from H.E. Barker laid in. VG. Howes S247. *Bohling.* $450/£288

SCRIVNER, BOB. No More Buffalo. Kansas City: Lowell, (1982). 1st ed. VF in VF dj. *Oregon.* $50/£32

SCROPE, G. P. The Geology and Extinct Volcanos of Central France. London, 1858. 2nd ed. xvii,258pp (lib stamp recto, verso tp); 17 plts, 2 fldg color maps. Calf (extrems worn, rebacked). *Henly.* $112/£72

SCROPE, W. The Art of Deer Stalking. London, 1897. Fine in 1/2 vellum. *Grayling.* $94/£60

SCROPE, W. Days and Nights in the Tweed.... Murray, 1854. 2nd ed. (Cl rubbed.) *Petersfield.* $343/£220

SCUDDER, SAMUEL HUBBARD. The Butterflies of the Eastern U.S. and Canada. Cambridge, 1889. 3 vols. 3 frontispieces, 89 plts, 4 maps (3 fldg). Lib cl (lt worn). *Kane*.* $160/£103

SCULL, E. MARSHALL. Hunting in the Arctic and Alaska. Phila, 1915. 1st ed. 11 maps. (Spine sl rubbed.) *Edwards.* $70/£45

SCULLY, JULIA. Disfarmer: The Heber Springs Portraits 1939-1946. Danbury, NH: Addison House, 1976. 1st ed. NF in pict dj (edgeworn). *Cahan.* $145/£93

SCULLY, VINCENT. The Earth, the Temple and the Gods. Yale Univ, 1962. 1st ed. VG (sl shelfworn) in dj (edgeworn). *My Bookhouse.* $45/£29

SCULLY, VINCENT. Pueblo Architecture of the Southwest. Austin, (1971). 1st ed. VG in dj (price-clipped). *King.* $45/£29

SCULLY, VINCENT. The Shingle Style. Yale Univ, (1965). Sound in dj. *Ars Artis.* $47/£30

SEABURY, SAMUEL. Letters of a Westchester Farmer (1774-1775). White Plains, NY, 1930. *Ginsberg.* $35/£22

SEABURY, SAMUEL. Letters of a Westchester Farmer (1774-1775). Clarence H. Vance (ed). White Plains, NY: Westchester Co Hist Soc, 1930. Frontis port, facs. Fine in plain dj. *Bohling.* $20/£13

SEABY, ALLEN W. British Ponies. London: A&C Black, 1936. 83 dwgs. (Feps lt browned.) Dj (sl spotted). *Edwards.* $39/£25

SEAGLE, BLANDINA. At the End of the Santa Fe Trail. (Columbus: Columbian Press, 1932.) (Ink inscrip), else VG. *Perier.* $40/£26

SEAGO, EDWARD. Caravan. London: Collins, 1937. 1st ed. Very Nice in dj (top edges chipped). *Hollett.* $148/£95

SEAGRAVE, GORDON S. My Hospital in the Hills. NY: Norton, 1955. 1st ed. Signed. Plan. (Cl sl rubbed), o/w VG. *Worldwide.* $20/£13

SEALE, BOBBY. Seize the Time. NY: Random House, (1970). 1st ed. Fine in dj (few sm tears). *Captain's Bookshelf.* $50/£32

SEALE, BOBBY. Seize the Time. NY, 1970. 1st ed. NF in NF dj (lacks sm piece). *Warren.* $45/£29

SEALSFIELD, CHARLES. The Cabin Book; or, National Characteristics. London: Ingram, Cooke, 1852. 8 plts, ads. (Inscrip.) *Rostenberg & Stern.* $250/£160

Search for the Western Sea. The Story of the Exploration of North-Western America. (By Lawrence J. Burpee.) NY, 1908. 1st Amer ed. Frontis. (Map neatly mtd, contents sl tanned.) Gilt cl (expertly recased). VG. Howes B1006. *Reese.* $125/£80

SEARLE, RONALD. Merry England, Etc. NY: Knopf, 1957. 1st Amer ed. Fine in dj. *Hermitage.* $45/£29

SEARLE, S. A. Environment and Plant Life. London, 1973. 48 plts, 14 tables. Fine in dj. *Brooks.* $29/£19

SEARS, JOSEPH HAMBLEN. Tennessee Printers 1791-1945. Kingsport, TN: Privately ptd, n.d. 1st Amer ed. NF. *Polyanthos.* $25/£16

SEAVER, GEORGE. Scott of the Antarctic. London: John Murray, 1940. 1st ed. (Spine faded), else VG. *High Latitude.* $30/£19

SEAVER, JAMES E. Deh-He-Wa-Mis; or A Narrative of the Life of Mary Jemison.... Batavia, NY: William Seaver, 1844. 3rd ed. 192pp. Contemp leather (sl rubbed, sl foxed). VG. *Second Life.* $225/£144

SEAVER, JAMES E. Life of Mary Jemison. Buffalo, 1877. Pub's cl (joints splitting). Howes S263. *Swann*.* $138/£88

SEAVER, TOM and HERB REZNICOW. Beanball: Murder at the World Series. NY: Morrow, (1989). Fine in Fine dj (sm scuff). *Between The Covers.* $45/£29

SECKEL, DIETRICH. The Art of Buddhism. NY et al: Greystone, 1968. Rev ed. VG in dj. *Worldwide.* $40/£26

Secret History of the Court and Cabinet of St. Cloud. London: John Murray, 1806. 1st ed. 3 vols. Uncut. Later 1/2 black morocco. (Foxed, binder's eps browned.) *Maggs.* $226/£145

Secret Instructions of the Jesuits. Phila: F.C. Wilson, 1844. 72pp. VG (rebound). *Middle Earth.* $145/£93

Secret Memoirs of the Courts of Europe from the 16th to the 19th Century. Phila: George Barrie & Sons, n.d. (c. 1900?). Imperial Ed. #413/1000 w/photogravures on Japan vellum. 24 vols. Teg. 3/4 red morocco (spines, corners sl rubbed). VG. *Holmes.* $850/£545

Secret Societies of the Middle Ages. London, 1848. xi,408pp. (Lt browned, pp29-32 detached, bkpl; spine sl sunned.) *Edwards.* $23/£15

Secret Springs of Dublin Song. Dublin: Talbot, 1918. One of 500 numbered. (Surface lift from tape removal fep.) Beveled bds (spine lt rubbed). *Waverly*.* $66/£42

SECRETAN, JAMES H. E. Out West. Ottawa: Esdale, 1910. 1st ed. Dec cl. *Ginsberg.* $100/£64

SEDELMAYR, JACOBO. Jacobo Sedelmayr: Missionary, Frontiersman, Explorer in Arizona and Sonora. N.p.: AZ Pioneers' Historical Soc, 1955. One of 600. Tipped-in photo frontis, fldg map. Fine in dj. *Cahan.* $75/£48

SEDWICK, W. T. Acoma, the Sky City. Cambridge: Harvard, (1927). 39 photo plts. Cl, dec bds. VG. *Mikesh.* $25/£16

SEEBOHM, FREDERIC. The English Village Community Examined in Its Relations to the Manorial and Tribal Systems.... Longmans, Green, 1896. Rptd from 4th ed. xxii,464pp + 32-pg cat; 3 plts, 11 maps or plans. VG (bkpl). *Cox.* $47/£30

SEEBOHN, HENRY. Siberia in Asia. London: John Murray, 1882. xviii,304pp, fldg map. VG (Sl soiled). *High Latitude*. $60/£38

SEELEY, L. B. (ed). Horace Walpole and His World, Select Passages from His Letters. London, 1884. 1st ed. 296pp. (Respined.) New title label. *Gretton*. $23/£15

SEEMAN, BERTHOLD. Viti: An Account of a Government Mission...1860-61. Cambridge: Macmillan, 1862. xv,447,24ads pp; map, 4 tinted plts. Grn cl (rubbed; lt foxed, 1/2-inch lib perf stamp tp). *Adelson*. $250/£160

SEEMULLER, ANNE M. CRANE. Reginald Archer. Boston: Osgood, 1871. 1st ed. 386pp. (Rear inner hinge mended), o/w VG-. *Reese*. $45/£29

SEFERIS, GEORGE. Three Secret Poems. Cambridge: Harvard Univ, 1969. 1st ed. (Spot fore-edge), else Fine in Fine dj (price-clipped). *Between The Covers*. $50/£32

SEGAL, LORE and RANDALL JARRELL. Juniper Tree. NY: FSG, 1973. 1st ed. 2 vols. Maurice Sendak (illus). 5 3/4 x 7. 332pp. VG in dj, box. *Cattermole*. $90/£58

SEGALE, BLANDINA. At the End of the Santa Fe Trail. Milwaukee: Bruce, 1948. Frontis. Good. *Dumont*. $35/£22

SEGHERS, ANNA. The Revolt of the Fishermen. London: Elkin Matthews & Marrot, 1929. 1st British ed. (Offsetting eps), else VG+ in dj (spine tanned). *Lame Duck*. $85/£54

SEIDLITZ, W. History of Japanese Color Prints. Phila: Lippincott, 1920. 16 color plts. Grn gilt pict cl. VG. *Terramedia*. $200/£128

SEITZ, DON C. Braxton Bragg: General of the Confedercy. Columbia, SC: State Co, 1924. 1st ed. VG (ink name fr cvr). *Lien*. $200/£128

SEITZ, DON C. Surface Japan. NY: Harper, 1911. 1st ed. Pict cl, bds. VG. *Terramedia*. $100/£64

SELBY, HUBERT, JR. Last Exit to Brooklyn. NY: Grove Press, (1964). 1st ed. Fine in dj (lt soiled). *Hermitage*. $75/£48

SELBY, HUBERT, JR. Last Exit to Brooklyn. NY: Grove, (1964). 1st ed, 1st bk. Signed. Fine in Fine dj. *Lenz*. $100/£64

SELDEN, GEORGE. The Old Meadow. NY: FSG, (1987). 1st ed. Fine in NF dj (spine lt rubbed). *Between The Covers*. $35/£22

SELDEN, JOHN. Table Talk. London: Joseph White, 1786. Crimson morocco (stained, rebacked). *Boswell*. $350/£224

SELDEN, JOHN. Table Talk. London: Joseph White, 1786. Crimson morocco (stained, rebacked). Pretty. *Boswell*. $350/£224

SELDEN, JOHN. The Table-Talk. London: John Russell Smith, 1856. Aeg. Full crushed brn morocco. *Boswell*. $250/£160

SELDEN, JOHN. Titles of Honor. London: John Leigh, 1672. 3rd ed. Contemp mottled calf (joints cracking). Fresh. *Boswell*. $450/£288

SELDES, GEORGE. Witch Hunt: The Technique and Profits of Redbaiting. NY: Modern Age Books, 1940. 1st ed. (Eps, jacket flaps foxed), o/w VG in pict dj. *Reese*. $40/£26

Select Collection of English Songs, in Three Volumes. London, 1783. 3 vols. Leather (worn, vol 3 cvrs detached). *Yudkin**. $120/£77

Select Collection of Valuable and Curious Arts.... (By Rufus Porter.) Concord, (NH): Rufus Porter, 1826. 3rd ed. Frontis, viii,(9)-132pp. Orig marbled paper over bds, cl tips & spine. (Rear hinge starting, rubbed, sl worn), else VG. *Cahan*. $450/£288

Selection of the Patriotic Addresses, to the President of the United States..... (William Austin, ed.) Boston, 1798. Complete w/subs list. (Tp sl browned, lt chipping.) Late 19th-cent 3/4 tan calf, gilt-paneled spine, leather label. *Freeman**. $30/£19

SELER, E. et al. Mexican and Central American Antiquities, Calendar Sytems, and History. BAE Bulletin 28. GPO, 1904. 49 plts (3 color). Good (fr hinge weak). *Scribe's Perch**. $30/£19

SELETZ, EMIL. Surgery of the Peripheral Nerves. Springfield: Thomas, 1951. VG in dj. *Goodrich*. $75/£48

Self-Interpreting Bible. John Brown (trans). NY: Ptd by Hodge & Campbell, 1792. (Browned, sl foxed, notes, fr joint split, rear joint starting.) 18 plts incl frontis and map (1 plt w/long tear repaired, backed). Full calf (worn). *Waverly**. $121/£78

SELFRIDGE, THOMAS O., JR. Memoirs of Thomas O. Selfridge, Jr., Rear Admiral, U.S.N. NY: Putnam, 1924. 1st ed. *Ginsberg*. $75/£48

SELLERS, CHARLES COLEMAN. Benjamin Franklin Portraiture. New Haven/London: Yale Univ, 1962. *Cullen*. $75/£48

SELOUS, EDMUND. The Bird Watcher in the Shetlands. London/NY, 1905. Teg, rest uncut. (Tp, frontis spotted, feps browned; upper bd dampstained, spine sl bumped.) *Edwards*. $55/£35

SELOUS, FREDERICK C. African Nature Notes and Reminiscences. London: Macmillan, 1908. 1st ed, 2nd issue. 13 plts. (Spine ends lt worn.) *Adelson*. $285/£183

SELOUS, FREDERICK C. A Hunter's Wanderings in Africa. London, 1893. 3rd ed. 19 full-pg illus. (Binding sl dull.) *Petersfield*. $187/£120

SELOUS, FREDERICK C. A Hunter's Wanderings in Africa.... London: Macmillan, 1919. 5th ed. Fldg map, 17 plts. (Lt rubbed.) *Adelson*. $185/£119

SELOUS, FREDERICK C. Recent Hunting Trips in British North America. London, 1907. 1st ed. (Sl worn.) *Oinonen**. $160/£103

SELOUS, FREDERICK C. Sport and Travel East and West. London: Longmans, 1900. 1st ed. Frontis. Grn gilt pict cl. VG. *Terramedia*. $200/£128

SELOUS, FREDERICK C. Sunshine and Storm in Rhodesia. London: Rowland Ward, 1896. 2nd ed. xxvii,2,290,10ads pp; fldg map, 9 plts. Tan cl (rubbed, spine dknd). *Adelson*. $315/£202

SELOUS, FREDERICK C. Travel and Adventure in South-East Africa. London: Rowland Ward, 1893. 1st ed. Map. Pict tan cl (cvrs worn), gilt. Internally NF (inner fr hinge cracked, inscrip). *Cummins*. $250/£160

SELOUS, FREDERICK C. and H. BRYDEN. Travel and Big Game. London: Longman's, 1897. 1st ed. 195pp; 6 plts. Grn gilt pict cl. VG. *Terramedia*. $200/£128

SELPH, HENRY ROBERT (ed). As They Saw Forrest. Jackson, TN, 1956. Off-print map of 'The Military Campaigns of Nathan Bedford Forrest.' VG in dj (sl frayed). *King*. $45/£29

SELWAY, N. C. The Regency Road. London: Faber & Faber, 1957. 1st ed. VG in VG dj. *October Farm*. $245/£157

SELWYN, FRANCIS. Sergeant Verity and the Blood Royal. London: Andre Deutsch, 1979. 1st ed. Fine in dj. *Mordida*. $45/£29

SELYE, HANS. The Stress of Life. London: Longmans, Green, 1957. 1st British ed. Good in dj (lt chipped). *White*. $23/£15

SEMBACH, KLAUS-JURGEN. Style 1930. NY: Universe, 1971. 1st US ed. 8 color, 118 b/w plts. (Owner stamp ep), else VG in dj (sl discolored). *Cahan*. $25/£16

SEMMES, JOHN E. John H. B. Latrobe and His Times, 1803-1891. Balt, (1917). 1st ed. Color frontis. *Ginsberg.* $125/£80

SEMMES, JOHN E. John H. B. Latrobe and His Times, 1803-1891. Balt: Norman, Remington Co, (1917). 1st ed. 39 plts, 19 in color. Ptd slip laid in. *Kane*. $60/£38

SEMMES, RAPHAEL. The Campaign of General Scott, in the Valley of Mexico. Cincinnati, 1852. Fldg frontis map, 367,(9)pp. Howes S288. *Ginsberg.* $250/£160

SEMON, RICHARD. In the Australian Bush and on the Coast of the Coral Sea. London: Macmillan, 1899. 1st ed. xv,552pp; 4 fldg color maps (scattered foxing, appreciable on 1 map). Grn gilt cl. VG. *Terramedia.* $400/£256

SEMPLE, R. H. (trans). Memoirs on Diphtheria from the Writings of Brettonneau, Guersant, Trousseau, Bouchut, Empis and Daviot. London: New Sydenham Soc, 1859. 407pp. VG. *White.* $55/£35

SENAC, JEAN. Treatise on the Hidden Nature and Treatment of Intermitting and Remitting Fevers. Charles Caldwell (trans). Phila: Kimber, Conrad, 1805. 1st ed in English. 1/2 calf (hinges mended). *Argosy.* $350/£224

SENDAK, MAURICE. Dear Mili. NY: Harper & Row, 1988. 1st US ed. Signed. 10 x 9 1/4. 40pp. Fine in dj. *Cattermole.* $50/£32

SENDAK, MAURICE. Hector Protector and As I Went Over the Water. NY, (1965). 1st ed. Oblong 8vo. VG in dj. *Argosy.* $50/£32

SENDAK, MAURICE. Higglety Pigglety Pop! Harper & Row, (1967). 1st ed. Sq 8vo. 69pp; 34 full-pg illus, dbl-pg spread, 6 w/text, tail picture. Color pict onlay. Fine in pict dj (sm scotch-taped tear, sm nicks). *Bookmark.* $78/£50

SENDAK, MAURICE. In the Night Kitchen. London: Bodley Head, 1971. 1st Eng ed. 4to. 40pp. NF in dec bds in dj (sl rubbed). *Hadley.* $78/£50

SENDAK, MAURICE. Outside Over There. NY: Harper & Row, 1981. 1st ed. 10 1/4 x 9 1/4. 40pp. Fine in dj. *Cattermole.* $35/£22

SENDAK, MAURICE. Really Rosie. NY: Harper Row, 1975. 1st ed. 10 3/4 x 8 3/4. 64pp. VG (lt foxed) in wraps. *Cattermole.* $50/£32

SENDAK, MAURICE. Very Far Away. NY: Harper, 1957. 1st ed. Fine in VG dj (sm chips spine ends). *Beasley.* $150/£96

SENDAK, MAURICE. We Are All in the Dumps with Jack and Guy. (NY, 1993.) 1st ed. Oblong 4to. VG in dj. *Argosy.* $40/£26

SENDER, RAMON. Counter-Attack in Spain. Peter Chalmers Mitchell (trans). Boston, 1937. 1st Amer ed. Fine. *Clearwater.* $47/£30

SENDER, RAMON. Dark Wedding. Eleanor Clark (trans). London: Grey Walls, 1948. (Name; sl spotted.) Dj. *Clearwater.* $31/£20

SENDER, RAMON. Earmarked for Hell. London: Wishart, 1934. 1st Eng ed. Good (spine sl faded, bumped, bk club blindstamp fr cvr). *Clearwater.* $39/£25

SENDREY, ALFRED. Bibliography of Jewish Music. NY: CUP, 1951. 1st ed. Signed presentation. Blue-gray cl. Good in dj (soiled). *Karmiole.* $75/£48

SENEFELDER, ALOIS. A Complete Course of Lithography. London: R. Ackermann, 1819. 14 litho plts (1 partly colored). (Mild browning to a few of the plts, 2 sm dampstains on 2 plts). Contemp 1/2 calf, spine gilt, raised bands, Cassidy arms in top compartment, marbled bds (sl torn, rubbed, bumped, ends chipped; bkpl). VG. *Maggs.* $1,326/£850

SENEFELDER, ALOIS. Invention of Lithography. NY: Fuchs & Lang, 1911. Tipped-in frontis, plt. Good (cl dampstained, soiled); interior VG+. *Bohling.* $35/£22

SENG, R. A. and J. V. GILMOUR. Brink's, The Money Movers. (Chicago): Lakeside Press, R.R. Donnelley & Sons, (1959). 1st ed. Fine. *Wantagh.* $25/£16

SENN, NICHOLAS. Intestinal Surgery. Chicago: W.T. Keener, 1889. vi,269pp. Early cl, leather label. (Pp lt browned, bkpl), else VG. *Goodrich.* $175/£112

SENN, NICHOLAS. Principles of Surgery. Phila: Davis, 1890. xiii,611pp. (Top tp torn away w/loss of 'Surgery'; fr joint, 1st sig loose; cl worn.) *Goodrich.* $75/£48

SEPHARIAL. The Kabala of Numbers. London: Rider, 1920. New ed. 2 vols. VG+. *Middle Earth.* $95/£61

SEREDY, KATE. The Chestry Oak. Viking, 1948. 1st ed. 6x8.5. 236pp. (Name blacked out fep; sl shelfworn), else VG+ in dj (spine chipped). *My Bookhouse.* $35/£22

SEREDY, KATE. The Chestry Oak. NY: Viking, 1948. 1st ed. Signed. 5 3/4 x 8 3/4. 65pp. VG. *Cattermole.* $45/£29

SEREDY, KATE. Gypsy. NY: Viking, 1951. 1st ed. 8 1/2 x 11 1/2. 63pp. Fine in dj. *Cattermole.* $50/£32

SEREDY, KATE. A Tree for Peter. NY: Viking, 1941. 1st ed. 7 x 9 3/4. 102pp. Good in dj. *Cattermole.* $50/£32

SERLING, ROD. Patterns. S&S, 1957. 1st ed. (Sm name label fly), else NF in dj (spine fold torn). *Certo.* $65/£42

SERRAILLIER, IAN. The Tale of Three Landlubbers. NY: Coward-McCann, 1971. 1st US ed. Raymond Briggs (illus). 7 3/4 x 10 1/4. 32pp. Pict cl. Fine in dj. *Cattermole.* $25/£16

SERVICE, ROBERT W. Ballads of a Cheechako. Toronto: William Briggs, 1909. 1st ed. Dec blue cl. VG (foxed, ink name). *Antic Hay.* $75/£48

SERVICE, ROBERT W. Ballads of a Cheechako. Toronto: William Briggs, 1909. 1st ed. (Inscrip, sm cutting fep.) Teg, uncut. Pict cl, gilt. Dj (piece torn from spine, hinges rubbed). *Hollett.* $133/£85

SERVICE, ROBERT W. More Collected Verse. London: Ernest Benn, 1979. VG. *Hollett.* $47/£30

SERVICE, ROBERT W. Rhymes of a Red Cross Man. Toronto: William Briggs, 1916. 1st ed. (Ink dates, pencil name, address; sl dull), o/w Fine. *Hermitage.* $125/£80

SERVICE, ROBERT W. Rhymes of a Rolling Stone. Toronto: William Briggs, 1912. 1st ed. Teg. Dec olive cl (rubbed). VG. *Antic Hay.* $65/£42

SETH, VIKRAM. A Suitable Boy. Phoenix House, 1993. 1st UK ed. Mint in Mint dj. *Martin.* $44/£28

SETON, ERNEST THOMPSON. Animal Heroes. London, 1911. 3rd imp. Blind-emb cl (sunned; fep lt browned). *Edwards.* $23/£15

SETON, ERNEST THOMPSON. Animals, Tracks and Hunter Signs. NY: Doubleday, 1958. 1st ed. 54 full-pg b/w plts. Silver pict cl. Fine in VG dj. *Mikesh.* $35/£22

SETON, ERNEST THOMPSON. The Arctic Prairies. NY: Scribner, 1912. 2nd imp. Teg. Dec cl. VG. *High Latitude.* $65/£42

SETON, ERNEST THOMPSON. The Arctic Prairies: A Canoe Journey of 2,000 Miles.... NY: Scribner, 1911. 1st ed. Blind-stamped dec cl. NF. *Mikesh.* $137/£88

SETON, ERNEST THOMPSON. The Forester's Manual. GC: Doubleday, Page, 1912. 1st ed. Tp cancel. (Spine faded, lt soil), o/w VG. *Hermitage.* $150/£96

SETON, ERNEST THOMPSON. Lives of the Hunted. NY: Scribner, 1901. 1st ed. NF (lt spine dkng; offsetting few pp from inserted clippings). *Beasley.* $85/£54

SETON, ERNEST THOMPSON. Lives of the Hunted. London, 1903. 3rd imp. Illus cl (sl soil, lt sunned). *Edwards*. $23/£15

SETON, ERNEST THOMPSON. Two Little Savages. Doubleday, Page, 1903. 1st ed. 6x8. 542pp. Grn cl, gilt. (Spine dknd, pulled, corners bumped), o/w VG. *My Bookhouse*. $50/£32

SETON, GRACE THOMPSON. Yes, Lady Saheb. NY/London: Harper, 1925. 1st ed. (Cl sl rubbed, soiled), o/w VG. *Worldwide*. $35/£22

SETON-KARR, H. W. Bear-Hunting in the White Mountains. London: Chapman & Hall, 1891. 1st ed. Fldg map. Pict fr cvr. VG (sl soiled, rubbed, spine sl dull). *Waverly**. $88/£56

SETON-THOMPSON, ERNEST. The Biography of a Grizzly. NY: Century, (Apr. 1902). 12 full-pg half-tones. Blind-stamped dec cl. VG. *Mikesh*. $30/£19

SETON-THOMPSON, ERNEST. The Biography of a Silver-Fox. NY, 1909. 1st ed. Dec cl (rubbed; spine dknd; lettering flaked). *King*. $25/£16

Sette of Odd Volumes. Year-Boke No. 30. Sette of Odd Volumes, 1935. Ltd to 133. Unopened. Japon, gilt. *Cox*. $16/£10

SETTLE, MARY LEE. Fight Night on a Sweet Saturday. NY: Viking, 1964. 1st ed. Fine in dj. *Cahan*. $75/£48

SETTLE, MARY LEE. O Beulah Land. NY: Viking, 1956. 1st ed. Signed. Fine in dj (lt edgewear, sm chip). *Captain's Bookshelf*. $100/£64

SETTLE, RAYMOND W. (ed). The March of the Mounted Riflemen. Glendale, CA, 1940. Frontis. Teg; partly unopened. (Sig; cl spotted), else NF. *Reese*. $125/£80

SETTLE, RAYMOND W. (ed). The March of the Mounted Riflemen. Glendale: A.H. Clark, 1940. 1st ed. One of 1007. Uncut. VF. *Perier*. $150/£96

SETTLE, RAYMOND W. (ed). The March of the Mounted Riflemen. Glendale: Clark, 1940. 1st ed. One of 1007. Frontis port, 20 full-pg illus, fldg map in rear. Teg. Dk blue cl, gilt-lettered spine. (Lower corners sl bumped), else Fine. *Argonaut*. $175/£112

SETTLE, RAYMOND W. and MARY (eds). Overland Days to Montana in 1865. Glendale: A.H. Clark, 1971. Fldg map. Red cl. Fine. *Bohling*. $37/£24

SETTLE, RAYMOND W. and MARY. War Drums and Wagon Wheels. Lincoln: Univ of NE, (1966). 1st ed. VG in dj. *Lien*. $35/£22

SETTLE, RAYMOND W. and MARY (eds). Overland Days to Montana in 1865—The Diary of Sarah Raymond and Journal of Dr. Waid Howard. Glendale: A.H. Clark, 1971. One of 1605. VG. *Perier*. $35/£22

SETTLE, RAYMOND W. and MARY (eds). Overland Days to Montana in 1865. Glendale: Clark, 1971. 1st ed. Fldg map. Good. *Heinoldt*. $25/£16

SEUSS, DR. (Pseud of Theodore Seuss Geisel.) The 500 Hats of Bartholomew Cubbins. NY: Vanguard, (1938). 1st ed. 4to. Cl-backed bds (sl shelfworn, vertical crease fr cvr; eps lt stained). Dj (chipped, lt soiled, closed tears). *Waverly**. $605/£388

SEUSS, DR. (Pseud of Theodore Seuss Geisel.) The Cat in the Hat Comes Back. NY: Random House, (1958). 1st ed. VG (short tear pastedown) in dj (sl worn, 2-inch tear bottom fr flap, internal tape). *Metropolitan**. $258/£165

SEUSS, DR. (Pseud of Theodore Seuss Geisel.) The Cat in the Hat. NY: Random House, 1957. 1st ed. Dr. Seuss Christmas Card of kangaroo w/Santa in pouch incl. Excellent (shelfwear, short closed tears). *Metropolitan**. $833/£534

SEUSS, DR. (Pseud of Theodore Seuss Geisel.) Dr. Seuss's Sleep Book. NY: Random House, (1962). 1st ed. NF (bkpl) in dj (soil, bumps, lt worn). *Metropolitan**. $373/£239

SEUSS, DR. (Pseud of Theodore Seuss Geisel.) Happy Birthday to You! NY: Random House, (1959). 1st ed. Fine (bkpl, sm owner's emb; sl shelfworn) in dj (sl rubbed). *Metropolitan**. $603/£387

SEUSS, DR. (Pseud of Theodore Seuss Geisel.) Horton Hears a Who! NY: Random House, (1954). 1st ed. Nice (lt bumped, rubbed) in dj (rubbed, bumped, soil, bottom fr flap creased). *Metropolitan**. $488/£313

SEUSS, DR. (Pseud of Theodore Seuss Geisel.) How the Grinch Stole Christmas. NY: Random House, (1957). 1st ed. (Jeffrey Bergman's childhood name penned in; bumped, extrems rubbed.) Dj (creases, tears, loss to head/heel). *Metropolitan**. $632/£405

SEUSS, DR. (Pseud of Theodore Seuss Geisel.) I Had Trouble in Getting to Solla Sollew. NY: Random House, (1965). 1st ed. Glazed pict bds. Dj (soil, wear). *Metropolitan**. $172/£110

SEUSS, DR. (Pseud of Theodore Seuss Geisel.) If I Ran the Circus. NY: Random, 1956. 1st ed. 8 1/4 x 11 1/4. Glossy bds. VG in dj. *Cattermole*. $450/£288

SEUSS, DR. (Pseud of Theodore Seuss Geisel.) On Beyond Zebra! NY: Random House, (1950). 1st ed. Glazed pict bds. (Shelfworn.) Dj (soil, lt wear). *Metropolitan**. $431/£276

SEUSS, DR. (Pseud of Theodore Seuss Geisel.) The Seven Lady Godivas. NY: Random House, (1939). 1st ed. Die-cut 'Godiva Book Mark' incl. Fine (inscrip) in VG dj (chip, browning, short tears, sl worn). *Metropolitan**. $258/£165

SEUSS, DR. (Pseud of Theodore Seuss Geisel.) The Seven Lady Godivas. NY: Random House, (1987). One of 300 signed. Cl in pub's box, still sealed in plastic. *Metropolitan**. $230/£147

SEUSS, DR. (Pseud of Theodore Seuss Geisel.) This Is Ann.... GPO, 1944. Dr. Seuss (illus). 16 leaf pamphlet. (2 binder holes punched through at spine, lt browned.) *Metropolitan**. $948/£608

SEUSS, DR. (Pseud of Theodore Seuss Geisel.) You're Only Old Once. NY: Random House, (1986). Signed, ltd ed. Cl in pub's slipcase, still sealed in plastic. *Metropolitan**. $201/£129

Seven Little Sisters Who Live on the Round Ball That Floats in the Air. (By Jane Andrews.) Boston: Ticknor & Fields, 1861. 1st ed, 1st bk. (xi),127pp. Extra engr tp, 8 plts. Olive grn cl (stained, bumped, spine chipped, extrems, spine dknd), gilt. VG. *Blue Mountain*. $95/£61

Seven Voyages of Sinbad the Sailor. NY: Holiday House, 1939. Ltd ed. Philip Reed (illus). 4 3/4 x 6 1/2. 72pp. VG in dj, marbled paper slipcase. *Cattermole*. $30/£19

SEWALL, JOHN S. The Logbook of the Captain's Clerk: Adventures in the China Seas. Bangor, ME, 1905. Pict cl (spine faded; lacks fep). *Ginsberg*. $100/£64

SEWALL, SAMUEL. Diary of Samuel Sewall 1674-1729. Boston, 1878-82. 3 vols. Howes S305. *Ginsberg*. $175/£112

SEWARD, A. C. (ed). Darwin and Modern Science. Cambridge, 1909. 1st ed. VG. *Fye*. $100/£64

SEWARD, A. C. A Summer in Greenland. CUP, 1922. 29 photo plts, map. Cl-backed bds. VG (ex-lib). *High Latitude*. $30/£19

SEWARD, A. C. A Summer in Greenland. CUP, 1922. 1st ed. 29 plts, 2 maps. Pict bds. VG. *Mikesh*. $37/£24

SEWARD, ANNA. Memoirs of the Life of Dr. Darwin. London: J. Johnson, 1804. 1st ed. Uncut. (Foxed, spotted), o/w VG in orig bds (corners worn; later backstrip, label). *Poetry Bookshop*. $203/£130

SEWARD, FREDERICK W. Reminiscences of a War-Time Statesman and Diplomat 1830-1915. NY/London, 1916. 1st ed. Frontis port. *Wantagh*. $35/£22

SEWARD, GEORGE F. Chinese Immigration, in Its Social and Economical Aspects. NY: Scribner, 1881. 1st ed. Author's presentation slip pasted on tp. (15),421pp. Dec cl (spine spotted). *Ginsberg.* $125/£80

SEWARD, WILLIAM H. William H. Seward's Travels Around the World. O. R. Seward (ed). NY: Appleton, 1873. 1st ed. Frontis (foxed), 730pp + ads; fldg map at rear. 1/2 leather, dec spine, marbled bds, edges. Good- (fr hinge crack). *Scribe's Perch**. $38/£24

SEWARD, WILLIAM H. William H. Seward's Travels Around the World. Olive Risley Seward (ed). NY: Appleton, 1873. Frontis port, xii,730pp; fldg map. (Fr hinge cracked, ex-lib, chipped.) *Bohling.* $18/£12

SEWELL, BROCARD. Footnote to the Nineties. London, 1968. 1st Eng ed. Fine in dj. *Clearwater.* $39/£25

SEXTON, R. W. Spanish Influence on American Architecture and Decoration. NY, (1927). Tan cl (sl worn, soiled). *Freeman**. $120/£77

SEXTON, R. W. Spanish Influence on American Architecture and Decoration. NY: Brentano's, (1927). 1st ed. Orange-lettered brn cl. VG (surface soil). *House.* $200/£128

SEYBERT, ADAM. Statistical Annals: Embracing...the United States of America. Phila, 1818. (Sl soil, lt foxing.) Uncut. Orig bds (fr cvr gone). *Freeman**. $30/£19

SEYD, ERNEST. California and Its Resources. London, 1858. (4),168pp, 1 leaf ads; 18 Fine full-pg plts, 2 fldg maps (1 Mint, 1 torn along folds). Black pub's cl (spine worn, joints starting), gilt. Internally VF (joints tender). Howes S310. *Truepenny.* $450/£288

SEYMOUR, DAVID. David Seymour—'Chim.' NY: Paragraphicbooks, 1966. 1st ed. 64 b/w plts. (Owner stamp), else VG in pict stiff wrappers. *Cahan.* $25/£16

SEYMOUR, E. S. Sketches of Minnesota. NY: Harper, 1850. 1st ed. Lg fldg frontis map (tape-repaired), 282pp + 6pp ads (text foxed). Black cl (spine extrems frayed). Howes S313. *Karmiole.* $200/£128

SEYMOUR, FLORA. A Bookfellow Anthology: 1932. Cedar Rapids, IA: Torch, 1932. One of 600 ptd. VF. *Bond.* $16/£10

SEYMOUR, FREDERICK. Up Hill and Down Dale in Ancient Etruria. NY: Appleton, 1910. Frontis, 11 plts, map. Gilt-pict cl (spine sl faded). *Archaeologia.* $85/£54

SEYMOUR, M. HOBART. Mornings Among the Jesuits at Rome. NY: Harper, 1849. 1st ed. 237pp. (Ink underlining, sl foxed; sl rubbed, spine ends sl frayed), o/w VG. *Worldwide.* $25/£16

SEYMOUR-SMITH, MARTIN. All Devils Fading. (Palma de Mallorca): Divers Press, 1953. 1st ed. VG in dec wrappers (tanned, sl mkd). *Reese.* $45/£29

SHAARA, MICHAEL. The Killer Angels. NY: David McKay, 1974. 1st ed. VG (spine creased) in dj (lt edgewear, 2 sm tears). *Captain's Bookshelf.* $500/£321

SHACKFORD, JAMES A. David Crockett, Man and Legend. Chapel Hill, 1956. 1st ed. Frontis. (Margin checks pp3-5), o/w NF. *Turpen.* $95/£61

SHACKLEFORD, WILLIAM YANCEY. (Pseud of Vance Randolph.) Buffalo Bill Cody. Girard: Haldeman-Julius, 1944. 1st ed. Wraps, digest-size. Fine. *Beasley.* $35/£22

SHACKLETON, E. H. The Heart of the Antarctic. London: Heinemann, 1909. 1st ed. 2 vols. Photogravure frontispieces, 3 fldg maps & fldg panorama in pocket. Teg. Dec cl. VG. *High Latitude.* $450/£288

SHACKLETON, E. H. The Heart of the Antarctic. London: Heinemann, 1909. 2 vols. (Eps renewed, edges foxed.) 3 fldg maps, photo panorama. Blue cl (scuffed, worn), silver titles, decs. *Parmer.* $650/£417

SHACKLETON, E. H. The Heart of the Antarctic. London: Heinemann, 1909. 1st ed. Inscribed. 2 vols. Photogravure frontis each vol, 203 plts (12 color), 3 fldg maps and panorama loose in rear pocket vol 2. Errata slip vol 2. Blue cl (sl faded; spines, joints repaired), silver vignettes upper cvrs. Excellent. *Morrell.* $780/£500

SHACKLETON, E. H. Shackleton in the Antarctic. London, 1923. Fep map. VG. *High Latitude.* $25/£16

SHACKLETON, E. H. South. The Story of Shackleton's Last Expedition 1914-1917. NY: Macmillan, 1926. 2nd ptg of US 'new and cheaper ed,' 1st pub in 1920. Fldg map. VG. *High Latitude.* $32/£21

SHACKLETON, EDWARD. Arctic Journeys. London: Hodder & Stoughton, 1936. 1st ed. 5 maps and diags. Mod 1/2 levant morocco, gilt. VG. *Hollett.* $148/£95

SHACKLETON, EDWARD. Arctic Journeys. NY, n.d. (1938). (Lacks fep, sl dust soil), else VG. *High Latitude.* $30/£19

SHADDUCK, LOUISE. Andy Little—Idaho Sheep King. Caldwell: Caxton, 1990. 1st ed. Fine in VG dj. *Perier.* $35/£22

Shadow of the War: A Story of the South in Reconstruction Times. (By Stephen T. Robinson.) Chicago: Jansen, McClurg, 1884. 1st ed. 378 + (iv)pp ads. VG. *Wantagh.* $65/£42

SHADOW. Midnight Scenes and Social Photographs. Glasgow: Thomas Murray, 1858. 1st ed. Engr frontis (edges browned) by George Cruikshank, 145pp + (5) ads (lt foxed). Illus paper over bds, new paper spine (rubbed). Fair. *Cahan.* $350/£224

SHADWELL, LIEUT. GEN. The Life of Colin Campbell, Lord Clyde. London, 1881. 2 vols. Frontis, xviii,458; xi,489pp; 14 maps and plans. Red morocco. *Maggs.* $234/£150

SHADWELL, THOMAS. Complete Works.... Montague Summers (ed). London: Fortune, 1927. One of 1200. 5 vols. Frontis port vol 1, frontispieces vols 2, 3, 4, ms facs vol 5. Uncut, unopened. (Sl foxed.) *Kane**. $60/£38

SHAFFER, PETER. Amadeus. London, 1980. 1st ed. Fine in Fine dj. *Warren.* $50/£32

SHAFFER, PETER. Equus. London: Deutsch, (1973). True 1st ed. Fine in Fine dj. *Between The Covers.* $175/£112

SHAFFER, PETER. Five Finger Exercise. H. Hamilton, 1958. 1st UK ed. (Sl sticky patch), o/w VG + in VG dj. *Martin.* $19/£12

SHAFFER, PETER. The Private Ear/The Public Eye. NY: Stein & Day, (1964). 1st ed. Fine in NF dj. *Antic Hay.* $45/£29

SHAFFER, PETER. The Royal Hunt of the Sun. NY: Stein & Day, (1965). 1st Amer ed. Fine in dj (sl wear). *Antic Hay.* $25/£16

SHAHN, BEN. The Complete Graphic Works. Kenneth W. Prescott (text). (NY): Quadrangle/NY Times Book Co, (1973). 1st ed. VG in dj. *Hermitage.* $125/£80

SHAHN, BEN. Love and Joy About Letters. NY, 1963. 1st Amer ed. Fine in slipcase (edges, sm spot rubbed). *Polyanthos.* $75/£48

SHAHN, BERNARDA BRYSON. Ben Shahn. NY: Abrams, (1972). 1st ed. (Fep sl soiled, creased), o/w Fine in dj. *Hermitage.* $275/£176

SHAHN, BERNARDA BRYSON. Ben Shahn. NY, n.d. (1972). 1st ed. Pub's letter, 1959 exhibition list present. Good in dj (sl used, stained). *King.* $350/£224

SHAHN, BERNARDA BRYSON. Ben Shahn. NY: Abrams, n.d. (1972). VG in dj. *Argosy.* $350/£224

Shake-speares [sic] Sonnets. Tercentenary Edition. (Hammersmith, Doves Press), 1909. One of 250 ptd on paper. (Pastedown lt bubbled), else Fine in full limp vellum. *Bromer.* $450/£288

SHAKESPEARE, EDWARD O. Report on Cholera in Europe and India. Washington, 1890. xxv,945pp. Lib buckram (soiled). *Bohling*. $28/£18

SHAKESPEARE, WILLIAM. As You Like It. London: Hodder & Stoughton, n.d. (1909). Hugh Thomson (illus). (Sl soiled, foxed; sl shelfworn.) *Oinonen**. $80/£51

SHAKESPEARE, WILLIAM. The Comedies, Histories and Tragedies of William Shakespeare. (With the two volumes of poems.) Herbert Farejon (ed). NY: LEC, 1939-1940, 1941. #904/1500 numbered. 39 vols. Gilt-stamped buckram-backed dec bds. VF. Slipcase for the 2 vols poems (sl rubbed); tissue wrappers torn but present most vols. *Hermitage*. $1,750/£1,122

SHAKESPEARE, WILLIAM. The Comedies...Histories and Poems...Tragedies of William Shakespeare. London: Henry Frowde/OUP, 1911. Text of the Oxford ed. 3 vols. 8vo. 3 frontispieces. Teg, marbled eps. 1/2 tan calf, gilt spine w/raised bands tooled in compartments, gilt-lettered morocco labels. NF set (ink inscrip vol 1; lt spine wear). *Heritage*. $350/£224

SHAKESPEARE, WILLIAM. The Comedies...Histories and Poems...Tragedies of William Shakespeare. London: Henry Frowde/OUP, 1912. 3 vols. Full vellum. (Bkpl; cvrs sl soiled), o/w Fine set. *Heritage*. $150/£96

SHAKESPEARE, WILLIAM. The Complete Works of William Shakespeare. London: Nonesuch, 1953. 4 vols. Cl-backed marbled bds. Fine set in VG box. *Polyanthos*. $150/£96

SHAKESPEARE, WILLIAM. The Complete Works of.... London: Nonesuch, 1953. Coronation ed. 4 vols. Reynolds Stone (illus). Faux marbled cl (sl dull, sl worn). *King*. $195/£125

SHAKESPEARE, WILLIAM. The Family Shakspeare, in Eight Volumes. London: Longman et al, 1827. 5th ed. 8 vols. 8vo. Contemp calf, marbled bds, spines w/raised bands, gilt/blindtooled in compartments. Edges sprinkled red. (Sl cvr wear, ink stamp), o/w Fine set. *Heritage*. $950/£609

SHAKESPEARE, WILLIAM. The First Folio of Shakespeare. NY: W.W. Norton, 1968. 1st ed thus. Red morocco-backed red cl. As New in box (sl faded). *Kane**. $55/£35

SHAKESPEARE, WILLIAM. The First Folio of Shakespeare. NY: W.W. Norton, 1968. Facs ed of 1623 1st folio. 1/2 red gilt morocco over red cl. Fine in slipcase (sl soiled). *Karmiole*. $150/£96

SHAKESPEARE, WILLIAM. The First Part of Henry the Fourth. SF: Grabhorn, 1961. One of 180. Cl, dec bds. (Spine label sl rubbed), else Fine. *Reese*. $275/£176

SHAKESPEARE, WILLIAM. Hamlet. (NY: LEC, 1933.) Ltd to 1500 signed by Eric Gill (illus). 5 lg wood engrs. Full tan English pigskin. Fine in slipcase (lt faded). *Truepenny*. $450/£288

SHAKESPEARE, WILLIAM. The Life of King Henry V. NY: LEC, 1951. #904/1500 numbered. Fritz Kredel (illus). Fine in pub's slipcase (sl dusty). *Hermitage*. $100/£64

SHAKESPEARE, WILLIAM. The Merry Wives of Windsor. London, 1910. One of 350 numbered, signed by Hugh Thomson (illus). 40 tipped-in color plts, guards. (Eps foxed.) Vellum gilt, silk ties. Cl slipcase. *Swann**. $345/£221

SHAKESPEARE, WILLIAM. The Merry Wives of Windsor. London: Heinemann, 1910. Hugh Thomson (illus). Gilt-pict cl. (Sl worn, sl foxed.) *Oinonen**. $70/£45

SHAKESPEARE, WILLIAM. A Midsummer Night's Dream. London/NY: Heinemann/Doubleday, March 1911. 2nd imp. 4to. 40 mtd plts by Arthur Rackham. Gilt-dec cl (spine dknd, sl frayed, few short tears). *Metropolitan**. $172/£110

SHAKESPEARE, WILLIAM. A Midsummer-Night's Dream. London, 1908. One of 1000 numbered, signed by Arthur Rackham (illus). 4to. 40 tipped-in color plts, guards. Red morocco, gilt. Cl slipcase. *Swann**. $920/£590

SHAKESPEARE, WILLIAM. Midsummer-Night's Dream. London/NY: Heinemann/Doubleday, Page, 1908. 40 tipped-in color plts. Gilt-dec tan cl (sl worn). Contents VG. *New Hampshire**. $185/£119

SHAKESPEARE, WILLIAM. The Plays and Poems of Shakspeare. A.J. Valpy (ed). London: A.J. Valpy, 1832-1834. 15 vols. Sm 8vo. Teg, marbled eps. 1/2 red morocco, marbled bds, gilt spine w/raised bands tooled in compartments. NF set (bkpls, eps sl browning). *Heritage*. $750/£481

SHAKESPEARE, WILLIAM. The Plays and Poems of Shakspeare. A.J. Valpy (ed). London: A.J. Valpy, 1833. 14 (of 15) vols. Sm 8vo. Teg, marbled eps. 1/2 grn morocco over cl, gilt spines w/raised bands tooled in compartments. Fine set (spines uniformly dknd). *Heritage*. $650/£417

SHAKESPEARE, WILLIAM. The Plays and Poems. A.J. Valpy (ed). London: Henry G. Bohn, 1848. 15 vols. Engr frontis each vol. (Some margins dampstained, sl dust-soiled.) Contemp grn diced morocco (spines faded, rubbed), spines gilt w/morocco lettering pieces (lacks 1). *Christie's**. $262/£168

SHAKESPEARE, WILLIAM. Plays and Poems. Edmond Malone (ed). London, 1790. 1st Malone ed. 11 vols. Engr port. Old 1/2 calf, marbled bds (rubbed, outer hinges cracked, some cvrs detached). *Kane**. $180/£115

SHAKESPEARE, WILLIAM. The Plays of Shakespeare. Howard Staunton (ed). London: George Routledge, 1858-1860. 3 vols. 8vo. John Gilbert (illus). Brothers Dalziel (engrs). Marbled edges, eps. Contemp calf (sl scuffed), gilt single-rule border, gilt spine w/raised bands tooled in compartments, bd edges, turn-ins tooled in blind. VG set (bkpls). *Heritage*. $750/£481

SHAKESPEARE, WILLIAM. The Plays of William Shakespeare. Charles & Mary Cowden Clarke (eds). London: Cassell Petter & Galpin, (1864-1868). 3 vols. H.C. Selous (illus). Lg 4to. Aeg. Contemp 1/2 morocco, gilt/blindstamped spine w/raised bands. (Sl foxing), o/w Fine set. *Heritage*. $450/£288

SHAKESPEARE, WILLIAM. The Plays. Isaac Reed (ed). London/Weybridge: J. Nichols et al, 1813. 6th ed. 21 vols. Engr frontis port. (Lacks 1/2 titles, 1st tp sl offset, some plts spotted, bkpl.) Marbled edges. Contemp diced calf (joints, spines sl rubbed, spine head vol 21 chipped), gilt. *Christie's**. $1,315/£843

SHAKESPEARE, WILLIAM. The Plays.... George Stevens & Alex Chalmers (eds). For F.C & J. Rivington etc., 1805. Lg paper copy. 10 vols. 8vo. (Plts sl spotted, bkpls.) Aeg. 19th-cent calf (rubbed), gilt. *Sotheby's**. $2,691/£1,725

SHAKESPEARE, WILLIAM. The Poems. (Hammersmith): Kelmscott, (1893). One of 500. 8vo. Orig limp vellum, silk ties. Cl slipcase. *Swann**. $747/£479

SHAKESPEARE, WILLIAM. Shakespeare's Comedy of the Tempest. London, n.d. (1908). One of 500. 4to. 40 tipped-in color plts by Edmund Dulac, ptd tissue guards. Gilt-dec vellum, silk ties. Box (worn). *Kane**. $1,000/£641

SHAKESPEARE, WILLIAM. Shakespeare's Comedy of the Tempest. NY/London: Hodder & Stoughton, n.d. (ca 1908). Edmund Dulac (illus). Pict cl (sl worn). *Oinonen**. $80/£51

SHAKESPEARE, WILLIAM. Shakespeare. The First Collected Edition of the Dramatic Works of.... London: Day & Son, 1866. Exact facsimile of First Folio, 1623. Gilt/blindstamped brn cl (corners, spine extrems rubbed). Overall VG (foxing 1st, last few ll). *Heritage*. $450/£288

SHAKESPEARE, WILLIAM. The Tempest. London, (1908). One of 500 numbered, signed by Edmund Dulac (illus). 4to. 40 mtd color plts, guards. Orig vellum, gilt, silk ties (1 detached; contemp owner stamp, inscrips; prelims lt foxed). Bd slipcase (edgeworn). *Swann**. $1,035/£663

SHAKESPEARE, WILLIAM. The Tempest. London, (1926). One of 520 numbered, signed by Arthur Rackham (illus), w/add'l color plt not found in trade ed. 4to. 21 tipped-in color plts. Orig 1/4 imitation vellum, gilt. Dj (spine dknd, ends sl worn). *Swann**. $1,380/£885

SHAKESPEARE, WILLIAM. The Tempest. NY/London: Doubleday, Page/Heinemann, (1926). Trade ed. 20 tipped-in color plts. (Bkpl removed fr pastedown), o/w Contents VG. (Extrems sl worn.) *New Hampshire**. $110/£71

SHAKESPEARE, WILLIAM. The Tempest. SF: Grabhorn, 1951. One of 160. Prospectus laid in. Linen, dec bds. (Corner bumped, lt sunning, spine ends sl frayed), o/w VG. *Reese*. $250/£160

SHAKESPEARE, WILLIAM. The Tragedie of Julius Caesar. SF: Grabhorn, 1954. One of 180 ptd. Illus prospectus laid in. 1/2 morocco, dec bds (spine lt sunned). VG (label removal mk pastedown). *Reese*. $300/£192

SHAKESPEARE, WILLIAM. The Tragedie of Macbeth. SF: Grabhorn, 1952. One of 180. Prospectus laid in. 1/2 morocco, dec bds (1 bd sl sunned). VG (offsetting to eps). *Reese*. $275/£176

SHAKESPEARE, WILLIAM. The Tragedie of Othello, the Moore of Venice. SF: Grabhorn, 1956. One of 185 ptd. Fldg prospectus laid in. 1/2 morocco, dec bds. (Spine sl rubbed), o/w NF. *Reese*. $375/£240

SHAKESPEARE, WILLIAM. Twelfth Night. London, (1908). One of 350 numbered, signed by W. Heath Robinson (illus). 40 tipped-in color plts, guards. Vellum, gilt, silk ties. Cl slipcase. *Swann**. $690/£442

SHAKESPEARE, WILLIAM. Venus and Adonis. London, 1930. One of 440 numbered, signed by Monroe Wheeler (designer). 1/4 dyed vellum. *Swann**. $115/£74

SHAKESPEARE, WILLIAM. The Works of Shakspeare Revised from the Best Authorities. London: Blackie, 1886. 6 vols. 4to. Pict dec brn cl stamped in gilt/grn/black (cvrs sl worn, spines sl cocked). VG (lt foxing). *Heritage*. $250/£160

SHAKESPEARE, WILLIAM. Works. London: Charles Knight, (1838-1843). Pictorial ed. 8 vols. (Lt spotted, upper margin few ll stained, inscrip.) Contemp calf (spines, cvrs lt rubbed), gilt, contrasting morocco labels. *Christie's**. $351/£225

SHAKESPEARE, WILLIAM. Works. London: John Bell, 1788. 20 vols. 12mo. New marbled eps. Old full calf (rubbed, rebacked in dec later leather), red/black leather labels. *Kane**. $600/£385

SHAKESPEARE, WILLIAM. Works. London: Charles Knight, 1843. Cabinet ed. 11 vols. Gilt edges. Contemp grn morocco (spines faded, sl rubbed; lt spotted), gilt. *Christie's**. $140/£90

SHAKESPEARE, WILLIAM. The Works. London, 1891. 9 vols. 8vo. Contemp tree calf (rebacked w/tan calf), flat spines divided by false bands into 6 compartments, red/grn morocco lettering pieces in 2, gilt. *Swann**. $690/£442

SHAKESPEARE, WILLIAM. The Works. Phila: Lippincott, ca 1900. 20 vols. 1/2 blue morocco, gilt. (Few vols lt rubbed.) *Swann**. $488/£313

SHAMES, LAURENCE. Scavenger Reef. NY: S&S, (1994). Adv rev copy w/slip, pub's material laid in. As New in dj. *Between The Covers*. $45/£29

SHAND, P. MORTON. Modern Theatres and Cinemas. Batsford, 1930. (Feps lt foxed, upper hinge sl cracked, cl browned.) *Edwards*. $75/£48

SHANGE, NTOZAKE. From Okra to Greens. St. Paul: Coffee House, 1984. 1st ed. Fine in dj. *Lame Duck*. $100/£64

SHANGE, NTOZAKE. Mellissa and Smith. (West Branch, IA: Toothpaste Press, 1976.) One of 300 signed. Fine. *Lenz*. $75/£48

SHANKAR, RAVI. My Music My Life. NY: S&S, 1968. 1st ed. Fine in lg wraps. *Associates*. $35/£22

SHANKS, EDWARD. The Universal War and the Universal State. London: Dropmore, 1946. #304/550. Gilt cvrs. Contents Fine (sl rubbed, soiled). *Polyanthos*. $35/£22

SHAPIRO, DAVID. Jasper Johns. Drawings 1954-1984. Christopher Sweet (ed). NY: Abrams, (1984). 50 color plts, 1 fldg. Stamped cl. Mint in dj. *Argosy*. $350/£224

SHAPIRO, HARVEY. The Eye. Denver: Alan Swallow, (1953). 1st ed, 1st bk. Ptd bds. (Spine rubbed, faded), o/w Fine. *Cahan*. $30/£19

SHAPIRO, KARL. Beyond Criticism. Univ of NE, (1953). 1st Amer ed. Fine in dj (sl chipped, spine sunned). *Polyanthos*. $25/£16

SHAPIRO, M. The Screaming Eagles: The 101st Airborne. NY, 1976. VG. *Clark*. $35/£22

SHAPLEY, HARLOW. Flights from Chaos. NY: Whittlesey House, 1930. 2nd ptg. Signed. (Student award mtd fr pastedown, upper gutter margin sl damped; mkd, smudged, rubbed, ends frayed), else VG. *Waverly**. $33/£21

SHARMAN, JULIAN. A Cursory History of Swearing. London, 1884. vii,199pp + 14pp ads,(Lt spotting; cl lt soiled, 2 sm nicks spine.) *Edwards*. $47/£30

SHARP, C. MARTIN. D. H.: An Outline of de Havilland History. London: Faber & Faber, 1960. VG in dj (scuffed). *Bookcell*. $30/£19

SHARP, DENNIS. Modern Architecture and Expressionism. Longmans, 1966. VG in dj. *Hadley*. $53/£34

SHARP, MARGERY. Miss Bianca in the Orient. Little, Brown, 1970. 1st ed. Eric Blegvad (illus). 5x8. 144pp. VG + (sl shelfworn) in dj (sl edgeworn, spine faded). *My Bookhouse*. $45/£29

SHARP, MARGERY. Miss Bianca in the Salt Mines. Little, Brown, 1966. 1st ed. Garth Williams (illus). 5x8. 148pp (some pp thumbed, last few sl crumpled). VG (sl shelfworn) in dj (edgeworn). *My Bookhouse*. $45/£29

SHARP, MARGERY. The Turret. Little, Brown, 1963. 1st ed. Garth Williams (illus). 5x8. 138pp. VG (sl shelfworn) in dj (price-clipped, chipped, sl rubbed). *My Bookhouse*. $75/£48

SHARP, SAMUEL. A Critical Enquiry into the Present State of Surgery. J. & R. Tonson, 1761. 4th ed. (viii),314,(5)pp (water stain margin 1st 2 sigs). New eps. Orig calf (rebacked), old spine label. *Bickersteth*. $172/£110

SHARP, SAMUEL. A Treatise on the Operations of Surgery, with a Description...of the Instruments Used.... London: J. & R. Tonson, 1758. 7th ed. Tp,(A2-A8),liv,234pp (lt spotting, margins lt browned, thumbed; 1 pg torn, repaired; upper hinge cracked); 14 plts (1 torn, repaired). Full gilt-edged calf (corners sl worn, fore-edge sl bumped, spine chipped w/sl loss), raised bands, leather spine label. *Edwards*. $273/£175

SHARP, WILLIAM. Dante Gabriel Rossetti: A Record and a Study. London, 1882. Frontis, viii,432pp (inscrip, bkpl, photo glued to ep as envelope for postcard, spotted, fr joint starting). Blue buckram over bds, gilt. VG. *Heller*. $100/£64

SHARPE, P. B. The Rifle in America. NY: Funk & Wagnalls, (1947). 2nd ed. Silver-lettered patterned bds. NF in color dj (sl wear). *House*. $75/£48

SHARPE, P. B. The Rifle in America. NY: Morrow, 1943. 2nd ptg. Dec cvr, spine. Good + . *Scribe's Perch**. $60/£38

SHARPE, P. B. The Rifle in America. NY, 1953. 3rd ed. Dec cvr. Good+ in dj (chipped). *Scribe's Perch**. $30/£19

SHARPE, SAMUEL. Egyptian Mythology and Egyptian Christianity, with Their Influence on the Opinions of Modern Christendom. London: John Russell Smith, 1863. 1st ed. xii,116pp, 4-pg cat (sl damage fr edge 1st few leaves, top corner last few). Blue cl (spine ends chipped; stained), gilt spine title. VG. *Blue Mountain*. $55/£35

SHARPE, TOM. Blott on the Landscape. London, 1975. 1st Eng ed. Very Nice (sm dent rear cvr) in dj (price-clipped). *Clearwater*. $47/£30

SHARPE, TOM. Blott on the Landscape. London, 1975. 1st Eng ed. Fine in dj. *Clearwater*. $78/£50

SHARPE, TOM. Indecent Exposure. Secker, 1973. 1st UK ed. Signed. NF in dj (price-clipped). *Williams*. $234/£150

SHARPE, TOM. Wilt on High. Secker & Warburg, 1984. 1st UK ed. NF in 1st state Red Ranch dj. *Williams*. $25/£16

SHARPE, TOM. Wilt on High. London: Secker & Warburg, 1984. 1st ed. Fine in dj. *Lame Duck*. $50/£32

SHATTUCK, ROGER. The Banquet Years. London: Faber & Faber, (1959). 1st Eng ed, 1st bk. NF in dj (sm chip, tears). *Captain's Bookshelf*. $60/£38

SHAW, ANNA HOWARD. The Story of a Pioneer. NY: Harper, (1915). 1st ed. Red cl (spine faded). VG. *Second Life*. $30/£19

SHAW, G. General Zoology. Vol I, Part 1 and Vol II, Part 1 (Mammalia); Vol III, Parts 1 and 2 (Amphibia). London, 1800-2. 4 vols. (A complete set contains 14 vols, each in 2 parts, pub from 1800 to 1826.) 1/2 leather, marbled bds (lt wear), gilt spines. Contents VG. *New Hampshire*. $425/£272

SHAW, G. and E. NODDER. The Naturalist's Miscellany. London: Elizabeth Nodder & Son, 1813. Vol 24. 8vo. 44 Fine hand-colored engrs. 3/4 leather, marbled paper-cvrd bds (soiled, rubbed, bumped, chipped). *Metropolitan**. $575/£369

SHAW, GEORGE BERNARD (ed). Fabian Essays in Socialism. Fabian Society, 1889. 1st ed. Frontis, vii,233pp. Uncut. Illus cl (sl soiled, spine sl bumped). *Edwards*. $55/£35

SHAW, GEORGE BERNARD. Androcles and the Lion, Overruled, Pygmalion. London: Constable, 1916. 1st British ed. (Bkpl), o/w NF in dj (nicks, sm tears). *Reese*. $125/£80

SHAW, GEORGE BERNARD. Back to Methuselah. NY: LEC, 1939. #904/1500 numbered, signed by John Farleigh (illus). Fine in pub's slipcase (sl sunned). *Hermitage*. $85/£54

SHAW, GEORGE BERNARD. Bernard Shaw and Mrs. Patrick Campbell: Their Correspondence. Alan Dent (ed). London, 1952. 1st ed. VG in dj (dknd, stained). *King*. $35/£22

SHAW, GEORGE BERNARD. Cashel Byron's Profession. London: Modern, 1886. 1st ed, variant state. (Wraps detached, sl soiled, spine chipped.) Internally VG in ptd wrappers. *Reese*. $250/£160

SHAW, GEORGE BERNARD. The Collected Works of Bernard Shaw. NY: Wm. H. Wise, 1930. Ayot St. Lawrence ed. #1614/1790. 30 vols. 8vo. Teg, others uncut. Pub's 1/4 white cl, blue bds, gilt-lettered blue paper spine labels. *D & D*. $750/£481

SHAW, GEORGE BERNARD. How to Settle the Irish Question. Dublin: Talbot, (1917). 1st ed, 1st issue in blue wraps. Fine in custom cl slipcase. *Antic Hay*. $125/£80

SHAW, GEORGE BERNARD. The Intelligent Woman's Guide to Socialism and Capitalism. London: Constable, 1928. 1st ed, 1st state w/'were' for 'was' on pg 442, line 5. Teg. Lt grn dec cl, gilt. Fine in pict dj (internally reinforced). *Blue Mountain*. $185/£119

SHAW, GEORGE BERNARD. The Intelligent Woman's Guide to Socialism and Capitalism. NY, 1928. 1st Amer ed. VG in dj (worn). *Truepenny*. $75/£48

SHAW, GEORGE BERNARD. Is Free Trade Alive or Dead? London: George Standring, 1906. Excellent in wrappers (sm dk strip upper cvr). *Gekoski*. $312/£200

SHAW, GEORGE BERNARD. Misalliance, The Dark Lady of the Sonnets, Fanny's First Play. London: Constable, 1914. 1st ed. Teg, uncut. Lt grn cl, gilt. VF in dj (spine nicks). *Macdonnell*. $75/£48

SHAW, GEORGE BERNARD. Passion Play, a Dramatic Fragment 1878. Jerald E. Bringle (ed). London: Bertram Rota, 1971. 1st ed. One of 100 (#320/350). Cream cl spine, paper title label, blue patterned paste paper bds. (Bkpl fr pastedown), o/w Fine in blue slipcase w/cream cl trim. *Heller*. $200/£128

SHAW, GEORGE BERNARD. Saint Joan. London: Constable, 1924. 1st ed. (Ink name dated 1924), o/w NF in dj (nicked), slipcase. *Reese*. $100/£64

SHAW, GEORGE BERNARD. Shaw Gives Himself Away. (Newtown): Gregynog, 1939. One of 275 numbered. Wood-engr frontis port. Orig dk grn oasis w/abstract design, orange morocco onlays. *Swann**. $373/£239

SHAW, GEORGE BERNARD. Sixteen Self-Sketches. Constable, 1949. 1st UK ed. VG (sl mks fr cvr). *Williams*. $23/£15

SHAW, GEORGE BERNARD. To a Young Actress: The Letters of Bernard Shaw to Molly Tompkins. Peter Tompkins (ed). NY, 1960. 1st ed. As New in dj. *Bond*. $25/£16

SHAW, GEORGE BERNARD. An Unfinished Novel. Stanley Weintraub (ed). London/NY: Constable/Dodd, (1958). 1st ed. One of 950 (of 1025). Cl, Cockerell style bds. Fine in acetate dj (tears). *Reese*. $45/£29

SHAW, GEORGE BERNARD. The Works. London: Constable, 1930-34. Ltd to 1025. 33 vols. Teg. Turquoise cl, gilt. *Christie's**. $385/£247

SHAW, HENRY. The Decorative Arts, Ecclesiastical and Civil, of the Middle Ages. London: William Pickering, 1851. 41 b/w chromolitho plts. (Lt foxing, bkpl.) Later 19th-cent 3/4 morocco (joints, extrems rubbed). *Freeman**. $190/£122

SHAW, HENRY. Dresses and Decorations of the Middle Ages. London: Wm. Pickering, 1843. 2 vols. 94 plts. Buckram (rebound). *Kane**. $375/£240

SHAW, HENRY. The Hand Book of Medieval Alphabets and Devices. Bohn, 1856. 36 Fine plts. Blue cl. Good. *Moss*. $187/£120

SHAW, HENRY. The Handbook of Mediaeval Alphabets and Devices. Wm. Pickering, 1853. 1st ed. 8pp; 37 plts, 1 extra to those called for, on fabric hinges. Blue cl (rebound), gilt. (Foxing mainly to margins), o/w VG. *Whittle*. $94/£60

SHAW, IRWIN. Paris/Magnum: Photographs 1935-1981. Millerton, NY: Aperture Book, 1981. 1st ed. Fine in pict dj. *Cahan*. $50/£32

SHAW, JOSEPH T. Danger Ahead. NY: Mohawk Press, (1932). 1st ed. (Sl soiling fore-edge), else Fine in NF dj (sm chip spine label). *Between The Covers*. $350/£224

SHAW, JOSEPH T. Danger Ahead. NY: Mohawk, 1932. 1st ed. Dj (soiled, torn, lg chip). *Metropolitan**. $92/£59

SHAW, L. H. DE VISME et al. Wild-Fowl. A. E. T. Watson (ed). London: Longmans, Green, 1905. 1st ed. Pict cl, gilt. VG. *Hollett.* $70/£45

SHAW, REUBEN COLE. Across the Plains in Forty-Nine. Chicago: Donnelley, 1948. Frontis port, facs. Maroon cl, gilt. VF. *Argonaut.* $40/£26

SHAW, REUBEN COLE. Across the Plains in Forty-Nine. Milo M. Quaife (ed). Chicago: Lakeside Classic, 1948. Frontis port, map. Teg. Dk red cl, gilt. VG+ (spine sl faded). *Bohling.* $20/£13

SHAW, RICHARD NORMAN. Architectural Sketches from the Continent. Day & Son, 1858. 1st ed. Pict tp, (12)pp (fep, few margins sl soiled), 100 litho plts. Aeg. Tan calf-backed grn cl (newly rebound), morocco label, vellum tips. *Cox.* $257/£165

SHAW, SAM. Guttersnipe. London: Sampson Low, (1947). 1st ed. Nice. *Patterson.* $47/£30

SHAW-SPARROW, WALTER (ed). Women Painters of the World. Hodder & Stoughton, 1905. 7 facs plts, 34 photogravures, 4 duplex plts. Teg. (Lt browned; cl lt soiled.) *Edwards.* $55/£35

SHAW-SPARROW, WALTER (ed). Women Painters of the World. London: Hodder & Stoughton, 1905. Vellum bds, gilt. (Eps dknd, foxed; bds foxed), else VG. *Metropolitan*.* $70/£45

SHAW-SPARROW, WALTER. Angling in British Art. London: John Lane, Bodley Head, 1923. 1st ed. Uncut. (Flyleaves lt browned; spine sl damped.) *Hollett.* $148/£95

SHAW-SPARROW, WALTER. A Book of Bridges. London: John Lane, Bodley Head, 1915. 1st ed. 36 color plts. Teg. Pict cl (sl worn; eps lt spotted). *Hollett.* $101/£65

SHAW-SPARROW, WALTER. A Book of British Etching from Francis Barlow to Francis Seymour Haden. London: John Lane, 1926. 1st ed. Partly unopened. VG in orig buckram. *Cox.* $94/£60

SHAW-SPARROW, WALTER. British Sporting Artists. London: John Lane, Bodley Head, 1922. 1st ed. 27 color plts. (Few spots, flyleaves browned; lower hinge top worn.) *Hollett.* $250/£160

SHAY, FRANK. The Bibliography of Walt Whitman. NY: Friedman's, 1920. One of 500 numbered. Frontis. Paper label spine, fr cvr. *Ginsberg.* $75/£48

SHAY, FRANK. Judge Lynch. NY, 1938. 1st ed. *Wantagh.* $25/£16

SHEA, JOHN GILMARY. Bibliography of Hennepin's Works. NY: Shea, 1880. 1st ed. Ltd to 100. 13pp. Sewn as issued. *Ginsberg.* $50/£32

SHEA, JOHN GILMARY. Discovery and Exploration of the Mississippi Valley. NY: Redfield, 1853. 2nd ptg. Frontis facs, lxxx,267,(1)pp + 4pp ads (foxed); fldg map. Brn cl (sl worn, rear cvr puckered). Howes S357. *Bohling.* $135/£87

SHEA, JOHN GILMARY. Discovery and Exploration of the Mississippi Valley.... Albany, 1903. 2nd ed. One of 500. Paper labels spine, fr cvr. Howes S357. *Ginsberg.* $150/£96

SHEA, JOHN GILMARY. Early Voyages Up and Down the Mississippi. (Albany, 1902.) One of 500 numbered of the facs of the 1861 ed. Howes S358. *Swann*.* $161/£103

SHEAHAN and UPTON. The Great Conflagration. Chicago: Union, 1871. Fldg map. (Foxed.) Grn cl, gilt. VG. *Yudkin*.* $35/£22

SHEAHAN and UPTON. The Great Conflagration. Chicago, etc. 1871. 458pp + ads; fldg map. Dec pub's cl. Good- (fr hinge crack). *Scribe's Perch*.* $24/£15

SHEAR, JACK. Four Marines and Other Portraits. Pasadena: Twelvetrees, 1985. One of 2000. NF in dj (lacks slipcase). *Smith.* $125/£80

SHEARMAN, JOHN. The Early Italian Pictures in the Collection Her Majesty the Queen. Cambridge, 1983. Good in dj. *Washton.* $125/£80

SHECKLEY, ROBERT. Immortality Delivered. NY, (1958). 1st ed. Dj. *Swann*.* $69/£44

SHECKLEY, ROBERT. Mindswap. Delacorte, 1966. 1st ed. Fine in dj (sl soiled, 2 sm tears). *Certo.* $35/£22

SHECKLEY, ROBERT. Untouched by Human Hands. Michael Joseph, 1955. 1st Eng ed, 1st bk. Fine in dj (price-clipped, soiled). *Certo.* $40/£26

SHEED, WILFRID. The Hack. London: Cassell, (1963). 1st Eng ed. Fine in dj (sl wear). *Hermitage.* $35/£22

SHEEHAN, PERLEY POORE. The Abyss of Wonders. Polaris, 1953. One of 1500 numbered. NF in thin cardbd dj (fr fold splitting). *Certo.* $60/£38

SHELDON, CHARLES. The Wilderness of Denali. NY: Scribner, 1930. 1st ed. Fldg map. Uncut. Gilt-stamped grn cl (sl worn). *Oinonen*.* $190/£122

SHELDON, CHARLES. The Wilderness of the North Pacific Coast Islands. NY, 1912. 1st ed. Teg; uncut. Gilt-pict grn cl (shelfworn). *Oinonen*.* $130/£83

SHELDON, CHARLES. The Wilderness of the North Pacific Coast Islands. NY: Scribner, 1912. 1st ed. Fldg map. Teg. Dk grn cl, gilt lettering, decs. VG (edges, corners chipped; bkpl). *Backman.* $200/£128

SHELDON, CHARLES. The Wilderness of the North Pacific Coast Islands. NY: Scribner, 1912. 1st ed. Grn cl, gilt. Fine. *Cummins.* $250/£160

SHELDON, CHARLES. The Wilderness of the North Pacific Coast Islands. NY: Scribner, 1912. 1st ed. 45 plts, 5 maps (1 fldg). Dk grn cl, gilt. (Sm mks on cvr), else NF. *Parmer.* $250/£160

SHELDON, CHARLES. The Wilderness of the North Pacific Islands. NY: Scribner, 1912. 1st ed. Untrimmed. Grn cl, gilt. (Pencil note, ink handstamps.) *Baltimore*.* $90/£58

SHELDON, CHARLES. The Wilderness of the Upper Yukon. NY, 1911. 1st ed. Uncut. Gilt-pict cl (sl worn). *Oinonen*.* $200/£128

SHELDON, CHARLES. The Wilderness of the Upper Yukon. NY: Scribner, 1919. 2nd ed. Color frontis. VG. *High Latitude.* $95/£61

SHELDON, FREDERICK. The Minstrelsy of the English Border. London: Longman, 1847. 1st ed. Orig cl stamped in gilt/blind. (Narrow splits joint extrems, sm bkpl), o/w Fine. *Reese.* $50/£32

SHELDON, FREDERICK. The Minstrelsy of the English Border. London: Longman, Brown, et al, 1847. 1st ed. 432pp. Teg. Gilt-stamped brn leather, marbled paper-cvrd bds. (Spine sl worn), o/w NF. *Beasley.* $125/£80

SHELDON, H. HORTON and EDGAR NORMAN GRISEWOOD. Television. NY: D. Van Nostrand, (1930). 1st ed, 2nd ptg. Color plt. VG (cl sl soiled, worn). *Glaser.* $150/£96

SHELDON, HAROLD P. Tranquility Revisited. NY: Derrydale, (1940). One of 485. 7 color plts, extra engr tp. Gilt red cl. *Kane*.* $75/£48

SHELDON, HAROLD P. Tranquility Revisited. NY: Derrydale, (1940). Ltd to 485. Unopened. Fine. *Truepenny.* $200/£128

SHELDON, HAROLD P. Tranquility: Tales of Sport with the Gun. NY: Derrydale, 1936. 1st ed. #618/950. 5 plts. Red cl, gilt. (Spine sl worn, scratched), else Fine. *Cummins.* $150/£96

SHELDON, STEWART. Gleanings by the Way, from '36 to '89.... Topeka, KS, 1890. 1st ed. 262pp. (Nicks.) Howes S377. *Ginsberg.* $200/£128

SHELDON, WILLIAM H. Atlas of Men.... NY: Harper, 1954. 1st ed. Cl-backed russet bds (bumped). VG. *Gach.* $150/£96

SHELDON, WILLIAM H. The Varieties of Temperament: A Psychology of Constitutional Differences. NY/London: Harper, 1942. 1st ed. Thatched blue cl, gilt spine. NF. *Gach.* $45/£29

SHELDON, WILLIAM. History of the Heathen Gods, and Heroes of Antiquity. Worcester: Isaiah Thomas, 1810. 1st ed. Frontis, 214pp; 28 full-pg woodcut illus. (Lacks 2pp of index and fr bd; text lt browned), else Good. *Brown.* $50/£32

SHELLEY, FRANCES. The Diary of Frances Lady Shelley 1787-1817. Richard Edgcumbe (ed). John Murray, 1912. Rpt. Good (ink inscrip, fore-edge spotted; spine bumped, sunned). *Tiger.* $19/£12

SHELLEY, MARY W. The Annotated Frankenstein. Clarkson N. Potter, 1977. Fine in Fine dj. *Certo.* $65/£42

SHELLEY, MARY W. Frankenstein, or The Modern Prometheus. Harrison Smith & Robert Haas, (1934). 1st ed thus. Lynd Ward (engrs). (Spine aged; lacks slipcase), else VG. *Certo.* $85/£54

SHELLEY, MARY W. Frankenstein, or the Modern Prometheus. NY: Harrison Smith, 1934. 1st ed w/Lynd Ward engrs. White linen, patterned bds. *Appelfeld.* $100/£64

SHELLEY, MARY W. Frankenstein. NY: Dodd, Mead, (1983). One of 500 numbered, signed. This copy out-of-series but signed by King and Berni Wrightson (illus). (Bumped.) Slipcase. *Swann*.* $172/£110

SHELLEY, MARY W. Frankenstein. Halifax: Milner & Sowerby, 1865. 319,(1)pp. Yellow eps. Red cl, pict backstrip (faded), gilt title. *Cox.* $39/£25

SHELLEY, MARY W. Frankenstein. NY: LEC, 1934. #904/1500 numbered, signed by Everett Henry (illus). 1/2 leather, dec cl. Fine in pub's slipcase. *Hermitage.* $250/£160

SHELLEY, MARY W. Mary Shelley's Journal. Frederick L. Jones (ed). Norman: Univ of OK, 1947. 1st ed thus. (2 stamps), else Fine (lacks dj). *Captain's Bookshelf.* $45/£29

SHELLEY, MARY W. My Best Mary: Selected Letters of Mary Shelley. Muriel Spark and Derek Stanford (eds). London: Wingate, 1953. 1st Eng ed. VG in VG dj (price-clipped). *Hadley.* $94/£60

SHELLEY, MARY W. Rambles in Germany and Italy 1840-43. London: Moxon, 1844. 1st ed. Bound w/o 1/2-titles. Mod marble bds, leather labels. Very Nice (sm lib stamp). *Second Life.* $350/£224

SHELLEY, MARY W. Rambles in Germany and Italy in 1840, 1842 and 1843. Edward Moxon, 1844. 2 vols. Pub's ads. Orig cl. Good (sl spotted; spines bumped, sl chipped, nick upper hinge vol I, spine labels rubbed, sl chipped). *Tiger.* $562/£360

SHELLEY, MARY. Frankenstein. NY: G&D, (1931). Red cl. VG (sl soiled, bumped) in dj (torn, chipped, creased, soiled, loss). *Metropolitan*.* $350/£224

SHELLEY, MARY. Frankenstein. NY, 1934. Lynd Ward (engrs). 1/2 cl, pict bds. VG (bkpl) in slipcase (sl worn, soiled). *Truepenny.* $250/£160

SHELLEY, PERCY BYSSHE. Alastor, or The Spirit of Solitude and Other Poems. Bertram Dobell (ed). London: Shelley Soc, 1886. Facs of 1816 1st ed. Blue ptd bds. Fine (sl rubbed). *Macdonnell.* $100/£64

SHELLEY, PERCY BYSSHE. Hellas: A Lyrical Drama. London: C. & J. Ollier, 1822. 1st ed. (Sm marginal tear 1/2-title, terminal leaf; bkpl.) Full brn morocco (fr cvr edges sl dknd), ribbed spine, 4 panels floriated in gilt, cvrs bordered in gilt. Teg, others untrimmed. Custom slipcase (sl stained). *Waverly*.* $715/£458

SHELLEY, PERCY BYSSHE. Letters from Percy Bysshe Shelley to Elizabeth Hitchener. London: Bertram Dobell, 1908. 1st ed. Lg paper copy. (Foxed), o/w NF. *Poetry Bookshop.* $117/£75

SHELLEY, PERCY BYSSHE. The Poems of Percy Bysshe Shelley. Stephen Spender (ed). Cambridge: LEC, 1971. One of 1500 nmbered, signed by Richard Shirley Smith (illus). Fine in pub's slipcase. *Hermitage.* $100/£64

SHELLEY, PERCY BYSSHE. The Poems.... London/NY: Vale Press/John Lane, 1901-02. Ltd to 310. 3 vols. (Bkpl removed, erasure mks 1/2 titles; 1st leaves vol 1 offset from newspaper ad mtd to fr pastedown.) Cream buckram (soiled), gilt. Internally Very Nice. *Blue Mountain.* $375/£240

SHELLEY, PERCY BYSSHE. The Poetical Works of Percy Bysshe Shelley. Edited by Mrs. Shelley. London: Edward Moxon, 1839. 1st authorized ed. 4 vols. 8vo. Frontis port, (i-vii)viii-xvi(xvii-xviii), (1-3)4-373, (374)375-380(381-382); (vii),(1-3)4-7(8)-337(338), (339)340-347(348),(1)2-4; (i-v)vi-viii,(1-3)4-314(315-316); (i-v)vi-viii,(1-3)4-361(362),(1)-2pp. Teg. Bound by Root in full sprinkled calf, ornate gilt. Very Attractive. *Vandoros.* $1,500/£962

SHELLEY, PERCY BYSSHE. The Poetical Works. (Hammersmith, 1895.) Ltd to 250. 3 vols. 8vo. 399; 412; 421pp; engr dbl-pg title vol I. Limp vellum w/o ties, as issued. VF. *Bromer.* $2,750/£1,763

SHELSWELL-WHITE (ed). A Guide to Zanzibar. Zanzibar: Government Printer, 1949. 3rd ed. 3 maps and plans at end (1 fldg). Red wrappers (spine sl rubbed). *Morrell.* $23/£15

SHELTON, RICHARD. Journal of Return. SF: Kayak, 1969. One of 1000. Fine in illus stapled wraps. *Lame Duck.* $65/£42

SHEPARD, ERNEST H. Drawn from Memory. London: Methuen, 1957. 1st ed. Frontis. VG in pict dj (frayed). *Cox.* $31/£20

SHEPARD, LESLIE. The History of Street Literature. David & Charles, 1973. 1st ed. VG in dj. *Cox.* $19/£12

SHEPARD, LUCIUS. Green Eyes. London: C&W, (1986). 1st hb ed, 1st bk. Dj. *Swann*.* $69/£44

SHEPARD, LUCIUS. Green Eyes. London: C&W, (1986). 1st ed. Signed. Fine in dj. *Swann*.* $80/£51

SHEPARD, ODELL. A Lonely Flute. Boston: Houghton Mifflin, 1917. 1st ed. Inscribed. Teg. NF. *Reese.* $50/£32

SHEPARD, ODELL. The Lore of the Unicorn. London: Allen & Unwin, (1930). 1st British ed. Signed, extensive annotations. Frontis. (Eps foxed), o/w Very Nice. *Reese.* $250/£160

SHEPARD, THOMAS H. and JAMES ELMES. Metropolitan Improvements; or, London in the Nineteenth Century. London, 1827. Engr tp, 82 plts (heavily foxed), plan. Contemp 1/2 red straight-grain morocco (rejointed). *Swann*.* $201/£129

SHEPHERD, JANE BUSHNELL. My Old New Haven and Other Memories Briefly Told. New Haven: Tuttle et al, 1932. 1st ed. NF in dj (few chips). *Sadlon.* $15/£10

SHEPHERD, MICHAEL. (Pseud of Robert Ludlum.) The Road to Gandolfo. NY: Dial, 1975. 1st ed. Fine w/3 different djs. *Mordida.* $85/£54

SHEPHERD, R. H. The Bibliography of Swinburne. London: George Redway, 1884. 1st ed. Ltd to 250. Blue 1/2 calf (worn, tears), gilt, red morocco spine label; orig wrappers bound in. *Maggs.* $28/£18

SHEPHERD, W. J. A Personal Narrative of the Outbreak and Massacre at Cawnpore, During the Sepoy Revolt of 1857. Lucknow, 1894. 4th ed. v,213pp,xxxv, 6 plts, 4 plans (1 fldg). Red cl (spine faded). *Maggs.* $250/£160

SHEPP, DANIEL B. Story of One Hundred Years. Phila: Globe Bible Pub Co, 1900. 1st ed. Fldg frontis. Pict cl. VG. *Connolly.* $40/£26

SHEPPARD, EDGAR. The Old Royal Palace of Whitehall. London: Longmans, 1902. 6 photogravure plts, fldg plan, map in slip pocket. Teg. (Bottom edge some pp stained, name, inscrip.) Sound. *Europa.* $37/£24

SHEPPARD, ERIC WILLIAM. Bedford Forrest, The Confederacy's Greatest Cavalryman. NY, 1930. (Sl worn; soiled 1/2 title; spine sl discolored.) Remnants of dj present. *King.* $150/£96

SHEPPARD, FRANCIS. London 1808-1870. Univ of CA, 1971. 1st ed. Dj (torn w/o loss). *Edwards.* $39/£25

SHEPPARD, LUCIUS. Green Eyes. C&W, 1986. 1st Eng, 1st hb ed. Fine in Fine dj. *Certo.* $90/£58

SHEPPARD, T. (ed). Handbook to Hull and the East Ring of Yorkshire. London, 1922. (Ex-lib, bkpl, ink stamps tp, verso; cl dknd, sm spine label.) *Edwards.* $28/£18

SHEPPARD, TAD. Pack and Paddock. NY: Derrydale, 1938. Ltd to 950. VG (cvr lt soiled) in slipcase. *October Farm.* $125/£80

SHEPPARD, WILLIAM ARTHUR. Red Shirts Remembered, Southern Brigadiers of the Reconstruction Period. Atlanta, 1940. 1st ed. Inscribed. VG + . *Pratt.* $95/£61

SHEPPARD, WILLIAM. The Touch-Stone of Common Assurances.... London: W. Strahan & W. Woodfall, 1784. 5th ed. Mod 1/4 leather, buckram. Good. *Boswell.* $350/£224

SHEPPE, WALTER (ed). First Man West: Alexander Mackenzie's Journal...1793. Berkeley: Univ of CA, (1962). VG in dj. *Lien.* $35/£22

SHERATON, THOMAS. The Cabinet-Maker and Upholsterer's Drawing-Book. NY, 1946. Facs of 3rd London 1802 ed. 122 copper plts. 2-tone cl (sl bumped), dec gilt spine (sl rubbed). *Edwards.* $140/£90

SHERBORN, CHARLES DAVIES. Sketch of the Life and Work of Charles William Sherborn. London, 1912. One of 525. 6 plts. Uncut. Cl-backed bds. VG. *Argosy.* $150/£96

SHERER, CAROLINE. How Much He Remembered: The Life of John Calvin Sherer 1852-1949. (Privately ptd), 1952. Signed. VG. *Book Market.* $25/£16

SHERER, JOHN. Classic Lands of Europe. London Ptg & Pub, n.d. 2 vols. 151 steel-engr views. Gilt-dec leather (extrems rubbed). Contents VG. *New Hampshire**. $300/£192

SHERER, LORRAINE M. The Clan System of the Fort Mojave Indians. L.A.: Hist Soc of Southern CA, 1965. One of 300. *Dawson.* $35/£22

SHERIDAN, ALAN. Vacation. London: Blake Editions, (1972). 1st ed. Fine in dj (sm tears). *Antic Hay.* $25/£16

SHERIDAN, PHILIP HENRY. Personal Memoirs of P. H. Sheridan, General United States Army. NY: Charles L. Webster, 1888. 1st ed. 2 vols. Shoulder strap ed in orig 1/2 morocco, cl. NF. *Mcgowan.* $250/£160

SHERIDAN, PHILIP HENRY. Personal Memoirs. NY: Webster, 1888. 1st ed. 2 vols. (Dec cvrs mottled), o/w Good. *Scribe's Perch**. $50/£32

SHERIDAN, RICHARD BRINSLEY. The Plays and Poems of Richard Brinsley Sheridan. R. C. Rhodes (ed). Oxford: Basil Blackwell, 1928. 1st ed. 3 vols. NF set in djs (lt chipped, spines dknd). *Captain's Bookshelf.* $175/£112

SHERIDAN, RICHARD BRINSLEY. The Rivals. London, LEC, 1953. Ltd to 1500 signed by Rene Ben Sussan (illus). Full yellow buckram, gilt. VG. *Truepenny.* $60/£38

SHERIDAN, RICHARD BRINSLEY. The Rivals: A Comedy. London: LEC, 1953. One of 1500 numbered, signed by Rene Ben Sussan (illus). 12 hand-colored engrs, guards. VG in bd slipcase. *Argosy.* $125/£80

SHERIDAN, RICHARD BRINSLEY. The School for Scandal, A Comedy. Oxford: LEC, 1934. #904/1500 numbered, signed by Rene Ben Sussan (illus). Full dec paper-cvrd bds, card liner. Fine in pub's slipcase. *Hermitage.* $125/£80

SHERIDAN, RICHARD BRINSLEY. The School for Scandal. London, (1911). One of 350 numbered, signed by Hugh Thomson (illus). 25 tipped-in color plts. Gilt-blocked vellum, silk ties. Cl slipcase. *Swann**. $316/£203

SHERIDAN, RICHARD BRINSLEY. The School for Scandal. Oxford: Shakespeare Head, 1930. One of 475. Paper vellum, dec bds. *Swann**. $126/£81

SHERIDAN, RICHARD BRINSLEY. The Works of the Late Right Honourable Richard Brinsley Sheridan. London: John Murray, 1821. 1st ed. 2 vols. xiv,398; 408pp. Marbled edges. 19th-cent calf (rubbed), marbled bds. *Karmiole.* $125/£80

SHERIDAN, THOMAS A.M. A General Dictionary of the English Language.... Dublin: D. Graisberry, 1784. 1st Dublin ed. Unpaginated. Orig full calf, morocco label (worn; cracked hinges; lacks blank fly). (Lt waterstain back pp.) *Cullen.* $150/£96

SHERMAN, CINDY. Cindy Sherman. NY: Pantheon, 1984. 1st ed. (Mk lower edge, old price sticker remnants), o/w VG in pict stiff wrappers. *Cahan.* $25/£16

SHERMAN, CLAIRE RICHTER. The Portraits of Charles V of France (1338-1380). NY: NY Univ, 1969. 74 plts. (Cvr sl faded), o/w Fine. *Europa.* $55/£35

SHERMAN, JOHN. Recollections of Forty Years in the House, Senate and Cabinet. Chicago, 1895. 1st ed. 2 vols. 1239pp. Pict cl. (Cvr lt worn), o/w Fine. *Pratt.* $75/£48

SHERMAN, JOHN. Recollections of Forty Years in the House, Senate and Cabinet. Chicago: Werner, 1895/1896. Ltr 1-vol ptg. Gilt-pict bds. VG + . *Archer.* $35/£22

SHERMAN, MONTAGUE et al. Football. Badminton Library, 1899. (Sl dull.) *Petersfield.* $39/£25

SHERMAN, NANCY. Gwendolyn the Miracle Hen. NY: S&S, 1961. 1st ed. Edward Sorel (illus). 10 1/4 x 7 1/4. 32pp. Pict bds. VG. *Cattermole.* $40/£26

SHERMAN, STUART C. The Voice of the Whaleman with an Account of the Nicholson Whaling Collection. Providence: Providence Public Library, 1965. 1st ed. Fine in dj (3/4-inch chip spine). *Hermitage.* $80/£51

SHERMAN, W. T. Memoirs of Gen. William T. Sherman, Written by Himself...Also a Personal Tribute and Critique of the Memoirs, by Hon. James G. Blaine. NY: Charles L. Webster, 1891. 4th ed. 2 vols. Grn cl w/shoulder strap insignia on spine. VG set. *Mcgowan.* $150/£96

SHERMAN, W. T. Personal Memoirs. NY, 1892. 4th ed. 2 vols. 455pp + ads; 604pp. Good (engrs lack guards). *Scribe's Perch**. $75/£48

SHERMAN, W. T. The Sherman Letters. R.S. Thorndike (ed). NY: Scribner, 1894. 1st ed. Frontis (heavily foxed), 398pp. Good. *Scribe's Perch**. $35/£22

SHERMAN, WILLIAM L. Forced Labor in 16th-Century Central America. Lincoln, (1979). 1st ed. Fine in Fine dj. *Turpen.* $28/£18

SHERRARD, O. E. A Life of Lord St. Vincent. London, 1933. 2 ports. Blue cl (sl soiled; sm lib stamp 1st leaf, 4 names rep). *Maggs.* $55/£35

SHERRILL, CHARLES HITCHCOCK. A Stained Glass Tour in Italy. 1913. 1st ed. Fldg map. (Blind lib stamp fep, feps sl browned.) Teg, rest uncut. *Edwards.* $47/£30

SHERRILL, CHARLES HITCHCOCK. Stained Glass Tours in France. London/NY, 1908. 16 plts. Pict cl (spine sl browned; bkpl). *Edwards.* $39/£25

SHERRILL, CHARLES HITCHCOCK. Stained Glass Tours in Germany, Austria and the Rhine Lands. London/NY, 1917. 1st ed. Color frontis, 2 maps. (Tp, text lt spotted, blind lib stamp fep; cl lt soiled, sm split upper joint.) *Edwards.* $41/£26

SHERRILL, CHARLES HITCHCOCK. Stained Glass Tours in Spain and Flanders. 1924. 1st ed. Color frontis, 2 maps. (Lt spotting.) *Edwards.* $39/£25

SHERRINGTON, CHARLES. The Endeavour of Jean Fernel. Cambridge, 1946. 1st ed. VG. *Fye.* $75/£48

SHERRINGTON, CHARLES. The Integrative Action of the Nervous System. London, 1911. 1st UK ed, w/London cancel title. (Cl sl faded.) Internally Fine. *Goodrich.* $495/£317

SHERRINGTON, CHARLES. The Integrative Action of the Nervous System. Cambridge: CUP, 1947. 2nd ed. Frontis port. VG in dj (sl torn). *White.* $50/£32

SHERRINGTON, CHARLES. Man on His Nature. Cambridge, 1951. 2nd ed. VG. *Fye.* $50/£32

SHERRINGTON, CHARLES. Selected Writings of Sir Charles Sherrington. D. Denny-Brown (ed). NY, 1940. 1st Amer ed. VG. *Fye.* $250/£160

SHERRINGTON, CHARLES. Selected Writings. D. Denny-Brown (ed). NY, 1940. 1st ed. Frontis port. (Spine rubbed.) *Argosy.* $150/£96

SHERRINGTON, CREED et al. Reflex Activity of the Spinal Cord. London, 1932. Good (ex-lib; mks). *Goodrich.* $75/£48

SHERRINGTON, CREED et al. Reflex Activity of the Spinal Cord. London, 1938. 2nd ptg. Internally Fine (cl sl sunned). *Goodrich.* $75/£48

SHERWOOD, HENRY HALL. The Motive Power of Organic Life and Magnetic Phenomena of Terrestrial and Planetary Motions.... NY: H.A. Chapin, 1841. 196pp. Orig brn bds (scuffed, extrems worn; shaken). *Cullen.* $175/£112

SHERWOOD, ISAAC R. Memories of the War. Toledo, OH, 1923. 1st ed. Signed, inscribed presentation. (Title spotted; spine worn, soiled, back cvr w/row of sm slices.) *King.* $95/£61

SHERWOOD, MARTYN. The Voyage of the Tai-Mo-Shan. London: Geoffrey Bles, n.d. (1935). 1st ed. Frontis, 15 plts (ptd recto/verso). Blue cl lettered in white. VG. *Morrell.* $12/£8

SHERWOOD, MERRIAM and ELMER MANTZ. The Road to Cathay. NY: Macmillan, 1928. 1st ed. 3 color fldg maps. (Fep clipped; lib cl sl rubbed, spine #), o/w VG. *Worldwide.* $18/£12

SHERWOOD, MRS. JOHN. Manners and Social Usages. NY: Harper, 1888 (1884). New, enlgd ed. Frontis, 4pp pub's ads. Floral patterned eps; teg. Dk blue cl, gilt/silver/green-stamped. VG. *Houle.* $125/£80

SHERWOOD, ROBERT. The Petrified Forest. NY: Scribner, 1935. 1st ed. VG+ (spine sl rolled) in dj (1-inch tear rear spine fold). *Lame Duck.* $150/£96

SHERWOOD, ROBERT. The Petrified Forest. NY: Scribners, 1935. 1st ed. Fine in VG dj (price-clipped; nicks; lt rubbing extrems). *Between The Covers.* $250/£160

SHESTACK, ALAN. The Complete Engravings of Martin Schongauer. NY, 1969. (Pencil notes reps), o/w VG in wraps. *Washton.* $50/£32

SHEW, MRS. M. L. Water-Cure for Ladies. NY: Wiley & Putnam, 1844. 1st ed. 156pp (sl foxed); 2 full-pg lithos. Maroon cl (heavily stained, spine faded, paper label rubbed from spine). Internally Very Nice. *Blue Mountain.* $50/£32

SHIEL, M. P. Cold Steel. Vanguard, 1929. Rev text, 1st ed thus. Binding variant of charcoal gray cl. (Spine sunned), else VG. *Certo.* $30/£19

SHIEL, M. P. The Purple Cloud. London: C&W, 1901. 1st ed. (Lacks rep, 1st, last pp of pub's cat.) Teg. Grn pict cl (bottom edge of bds, spine ends worn; spine aged, dknd), gilt. Good+. *Certo.* $325/£208

SHIEL, M. P. The Purple Cloud. World, 1946. VG in dj. *Madle.* $12/£8

SHIEL, M. P. Science, Life and Literature. London, 1950. 1st ed. NF in dj (sm edge tear). *Polyanthos.* $25/£16

SHIEL, M. P. Shapes in the Fire. London, 1896. 1st ed. Uncut. Pict cl. VG. *Argosy.* $250/£160

SHIEL, M. P. This Knot of Life. London: Everett, n.d. 1st ed. Red cl. VG. *Argosy.* $50/£32

SHIEL, M. P. The Weird o'It. London: Grant Richards, 1902. 1st ed. Pict cl. (Hinges starting.) *Argosy.* $50/£32

SHIEL, M. P. Xelucha and Others. Sauk City: Arkham House, 1975. 1st ed. Fine in Fine dj. *Other Worlds.* $15/£10

SHIEL, M. P. Xelucha and Others. Sauk City: Arkham House, 1975. 1st Amer ed. Fine in Fine dj. *Polyanthos.* $25/£16

SHIELDS, G. O. (ed). The Big Game of North America.... Chicago/NY: Rand McNally, 1890. 1st ed. Brn cl, gilt. Fine. *Appelfeld.* $150/£96

SHIELDS, ROBERT. My Travels: Visits to Lands Far and Near. Winnipeg, 1907. 1st ed. Pict dec cl (rear cvr lt worn). *Ginsberg.* $125/£80

SHILLABER, B. P. Rhymes with Reason and Without. Boston: Abel Tompkins & B.B. Mussey, 1853. 1st ed, 1st bk. Engr frontis, 336pp. Blind-stamped brn cl. VG. BAL 17536. *New Hampshire*.* $20/£13

SHIMER, FLORENCE. Twelve Poems. (Hingham, MA: Press of Little Red Hen, c1950.) 1st ed. Plain paper bds. NF in dj, wrap-around ptd label. *Heller.* $50/£32

SHIMER, R. H. Squaw Point. NY: Harper & Row, 1972. 1st ed. Fine in dj (sm scrape fr panel). *Mordida.* $45/£29

SHIPHERD, JACOB R. History of the Oberlin-Wellington Rescue.... Boston, 1859. 1st ed. (8),280pp. (Spine worn, faded.) Howes S419. *Ginsberg.* $125/£80

SHIPTON, E. E. Nanda Devi. London, (1936). 1st ed. (Used.) *King.* $85/£54

SHIRAKAWA, YOSHIKAZU. Himalayas. NY, (1971). 1st ed. VG in dj, cl Japanese-style case. *King.* $150/£96

SHIRAS, GEORGE. Hunting Wild Life with Camera and Flashlight. Nat Geog Soc, 1935. 1st ed. 2 vols. Blue cl, gilt. VG. *Price.* $39/£25

SHIRK, DAVID. The Cattle Drives of David Shirk, from Texas to the Idaho Mines, 1871 and 1873.... Martin F. Schmitt (ed). (Portland): Champoeg, 1956. 1st ed. Ltd to 750 ptd. 2 plts (1 mtd). Uncut. Pict gl, gilt-lettered spine. VF. *Argonaut.* $125/£80

SHIRK, DAVID. The Cattle Drives of David Shirk...1871 and 1873. Martin F. Schmitt (ed). (Portland): Champoeg, 1956. One of 750. Frontis, mtd facs port. (Browning to 2pp.) Pict beige cl, partially unopened (marginal dkng to cvrs, eps). *Dawson.* $75/£48

SHIRLEY, GLENN. Buckskin and Spurs. NY, (1958). 1st ed. VG+ in dj (sm piece torn from spine). *Pratt.* $35/£22

SHIRLEY, GLENN. Law West of Fort Smith; A History of Frontier Justice in the Indian Territory, 1834-1896. NY: Holt, (1957). 1st ed. VG in dj (shabby). *Bohling.* $22/£14

SHIRLEY, GLENN. Toughest of Them All. (Albuquerque: Univ of NM, 1953.) Black cl. Fine in dj (price-clipped). *Bohling.* $20/£13

SHIRLEY, J. W. (ed). Thomas Harriot, Renaissance Scientist. Oxford, 1974. Dj. *Maggs.* $31/£20

SHIRLEY, JOHN M. The Early Jurisprudence of New Hampshire. Concord: Republican Press Assoc, 1885. 103 pp. Ptd wraps (worn, chipped). *Boswell.* $65/£42

SHISHIDO, MISAKO. The Folk Toys of Japan. Tokyo/Rutland, VT: Japan Publications, (1963). 1st ed. 16 full color, 32 b/w illus. Japanese Kasuri-cl over bds. Fine in Fine dj. *Glenn.* $75/£48

SHIVERS, LOUISE. Here to Get My Baby Out of Jail. NY: Random House, (1983). 1st ed. Signed. (Sm name), else Fine in Fine dj (sm tear rear panel). *Between The Covers.* $50/£32

SHOCK, NATHAN. A Classified Bibliography of Gerontology and Geriatrics. Stanford, 1951. 1st ed. VG in dj. *Fye.* $125/£80

SHOEMAKER, HENRY. North Pennsylvania Minstrelsy. Altoona: Times Trib, 1923. 2nd ed. Good in wraps. *Archer.* $25/£16

SHOEMAKER, J. V. Heredity, Health, and Personal Beauty. Phila, 1890. 1st ed. 422pp. Gilt-tooled grn cl. VG (inner fr hinge cracked; sl worn). *Doctor's Library.* $150/£96

SHOEMAKER, JAMES S. Small-Fruit Culture. Phila, 1934. Grn cl, gilt. (Few pencillings), else VG. *Price.* $22/£14

SHOLOKHOV, MIKHAIL. Harvest on the Don. H. C. Stevens (trans). NY: Knopf, 1961. 1st Amer ed. Fine in VG dj (spine head worn). *Antic Hay.* $25/£16

SHOOK, CHARLES. The True Origin of Mormon Polygamy. Cincinnati, 1914. 2nd ed. VG- (name; cvrs stained, damaged). *Benchmark.* $60/£38

SHORE, HENRY N. Smuggling Days and Smuggling Ways. London, 1892. Map frontis, 287pp (sl spotted). Mod cl (rebound), gilt. *Edwards.* $39/£25

SHORE, STEPHEN. The Gardens at Giverny. Millerton, NY: Aperture, 1983. 1st ed. 40 full-pg color photos. Fine in illus dj (chip). *Cahan.* $40/£26

SHORE, STEPHEN. Uncommon Places. Millerton, NY: Aperture, 1982. 1st ed. 49 full-pg color photos. Fine in VG dj. *Cahan.* $45/£29

SHORE, W. TEIGNMOUTH (ed). Crime and Its Detection. London, 1932. 2 vols. (Bkpl; spines lt faded.) *Edwards.* $39/£25

Short Advice to the Counties of New-York. (By Isaac Wilkins.) NY, 1774. (Sl internal soil.) Aeg. Late 19th-cent polished blue calf (extrems scuffed), gilt. *Freeman*.* $160/£103

Short Biography of John Leeth, with an Account of His Life Among the Indians. Cleveland: Burrows Bros, 1904. One of 267 ptd. Gilt top. Maroon cl, gilt. Fine. *Appelfeld.* $75/£48

Short Introduction to English Grammar. (By Robert Lowth.) A. Millar et al, 1767. New ed. xv,205,(i)pp, ad leaf. (Ink name.) Orig calf (rebacked), orig eps. *Bickersteth.* $117/£75

SHORT, C. W. and R. STANLEY-BROWN. Public Buildings. (Washington), 1939. 1st ed. (Ink inscrip, soil), else Good in dj (laminated, incomplete). *King.* $100/£64

SHORTER, A. H. Paper Making in the British Isles. David & Charles, 1971. 1st ed. 16 plts. VG in dj. *Cox.* $23/£15

SHORTER, ALAN W. The Egyptian Gods. London: Kegan Paul et al, 1937. 1st ed. Frontis, 3 b/w plts. (Rubbed), o/w VG. *Worldwide.* $25/£16

SHORTER, CLEMENT. The Brontes: Life and Letters. NY: Scribner, 1909. 1st Amer ed. 2 vols. Maroon buckram (fr hinge vol 1 repaired, lt rubbed, spines sunned). VG set. *Hermitage.* $150/£96

SHORTRIDGE, G. C. The Mammals of South-West Africa. London: Heinemann, 1934. 1st ed. 2 vols. Blind-stamped gilt-dec cl. Fine in VG+ dj. *Mikesh.* $175/£112

SHOTEN, KADOKAWA (ed). A Pictorial Encyclopedia of the Oriental Arts: China. NY: Crown, (1969). 1st ed. 2 vols. VF in pub's pict slipcase. *Hermitage.* $85/£54

SHRADY, JOHN. The College of Physicians and Surgeons New York.... NY: Lewis, 1903. 1st ed. 2 vols. 207 full-pg ports. Orig 1/2 morocco (spines sl worn, joints starting), gilt, bds. Internally Fine. *Goodrich.* $395/£253

SHRINER, CHARLES A. (comp). The Birds of New Jersey. Commission of the State of NJ, 1897. 212pp (bkpl, upper hinge cracked; cl sl soiled, spine rubbed, label removed). *Edwards.* $39/£25

SHRIVER, HARRY C. (ed). Justice Oliver Wendell Holmes, His Book Notices and Uncollected Letters and Papers. NY: Central Book Co, 1936. Good (faded) in dj (worn, chipped). *Boswell.* $65/£42

SHUBNIKOV, A. V. and N. N. SHEFTAL (eds). Growth of Crystals. Vol 3. NY, 1962. Good in dj. *Henly.* $33/£21

SHUCK, OSCAR T. Bench and Bar in California.... SF: Occident Ptg House, 1887. Part 1; notice of Part 2 tipped in. Blue cl, gilt (sl rubbed). Good. *Boswell.* $75/£48

SHUCK, OSCAR T. (ed). Eloquence of the Far West, No. I, Masterpieces of E.D. Baker. SF: the Editor, 1899. Later(?) black cl (worn). Sound. *Boswell.* $75/£48

SHUFELDT, ROBERT W. Reports of Explorations and Surveys, to Ascertain the Practicability of a Ship Canal.... Washington, 1872. 11 litho plts, 19 lg fldg maps, 1 full-pg map. (Pp stained top corner; torn, stained, disbinding.) *Metropolitan*.* $57/£37

SHUFFREY, L. A. The English Fireplace. Batsford, n.d. (c. 1912). 130 collotype plts. (Lt spotting; cl sl soiled, spine sl bumped.) *Edwards.* $195/£125

SHULEVITZ, URI. The Moon in My Room. NY: Harper & Row, 1963. 1st ed. 7 1/4 x 9. 32pp. Pict cl. Fine in dj. *Cattermole.* $75/£48

SHUMAKER, WAYNE. The Occult Sciences in the Renaissance.... Berkeley/L.A./London: Univ of CA, (1973). Gray cl. NF (bottom edge pp stained) in pict dj (soiled, chipped, spine dknd, price-clipped). *Blue Mountain.* $45/£29

SHUMATE, ALBERT. The Life of George Henry Goddard. Berkeley: Friends of the Bancroft Library, 1969. Fldg map in rear pocket. (Edgeworn), else VG in wraps. *Dumont.* $35/£22

SHUMAY, NINA PAUL. Your Desert and Mine. L.A.: Westernlore, 1960. 1st ed. Fine in Fine dj. *Book Market.* $45/£29

SHURE, DAVID S. Hester Bateman, Queen of English Silversmiths. GC: Doubleday, (1959). 1st ed. 86 plts. Beige linen. Good in dj. *Karmiole.* $60/£38

SHURE, DAVID S. Hester Bateman: Queen of the English Silversmiths. NY: Doubleday, (1959). 1st Amer ed. 87 photo plts. Fine in dj (lt worn). *Hermitage.* $85/£54

SHUTE, D. K. A First Book in Organic Evolution. Chicago: Open Court, 1899. 1st ed. 285pp + ads, 12 plts. VG+. *Mikesh.* $27/£17

SHUTE, NEVIL. Beyond the Black Stump. London, (1956). 1st ed. Good in dj (chipped, edgetorn). *King.* $65/£42

SHUTE, NEVIL. In the Wet. London, (1953). 1st ed. Good in dj (spine chipped). *King*. $65/£42

SHUTE, NEVIL. In the Wet. London: Heinemann, 1953. 1st UK ed. Fine in dj. *Williams*. $23/£15

SHUTE, NEVIL. An Old Captivity. NY: Morrow, (1959). 1st Amer Ed. Rev copy w/inserted rev slip. NF in dj (soil, sm tear). *Antic Hay*. $45/£29

SHUTE, NEVIL. On the Beach. 1957. 1st ed. VG in dj (hinges rubbed, sm tears). *Words Etc*. $31/£20

SHUTE, NEVIL. On the Beach. Heinemann, 1957. 1st UK ed. Fine in VG dj. *Williams*. $23/£15

SHUTE, NEVIL. On the Beach. London, 1957. 1st Eng ed. (Spine edge sl mkd, fr hinge tender.) Dj (sl chafed). *Clearwater*. $47/£30

SHUTE, NEVIL. Pastoral. NY, 1944. 1st ed. Fine (sl chipped) in Fine dj. *Smith*. $20/£13

SHUTE, NEVIL. The Rainbow and the Rose. London: Heinemann, (1958). 1st Eng ed. Fine in dj (wear, rubbed, lt soil). *Antic Hay*. $35/£22

SHUTE, NEVIL. The Rainbow and the Rose. London, 1958. 1st ed. VG in dj (few edge chips, edges sl rubbed). *Polyanthos*. $25/£16

SHUTE, NEVIL. The Rainbow and the Rose. NY: Morrow, 1958. 1st Amer ed. NF in dj (wear, sl browned, soil). *Antic Hay*. $20/£13

SHUTE, NEVIL. Requiem for a Wren. London, (1955). 1st ed. Good in dj (price-clipped, chipped, worn). *King*. $50/£32

SHUTE, NEVIL. Round the Bend. NY: William Morrow, 1951. 1st Amer ed. NF in dj (sl rubbed). *Cahan*. $20/£13

SHUTE, NEVIL. Slide Rule—The Autobiography of an Engineer. Heinemann, 1954. 1st UK ed. NF in dj. *Williams*. $55/£35

SHUTE, NEVIL. A Town Like Alice. London: Heinemann, 1950. 1st UK ed. VG+ in dj (edgeworn, few closed tears, sl loss spine top). *Williams*. $25/£16

SHUTE, NEVIL. Trustee from the Toolroom. NY: Morrow, 1960. 1st Amer ed. VG in dj (browned). *Antic Hay*. $15/£10

SHUTES, MILTON H. Lincoln and California. Stanford: Stanford Univ, (1943). 1st ed. Frontis port. Brn cl. Fine. *Argonaut*. $60/£38

SHY, G. M. et al. External Collimation Detection of Intracranial Neoplasia with Unstable Nuclides. Edinburgh/London, 1958. VG. *Argosy*. $60/£38

SIBLEY, JOHN LANGDON. History of the Town of Union...to the Middle of the Nineteenth Century. Boston: Mussey, 1851. Presentation copy. Frontis port, (ix,3),540pp. Nice (uneven dkng of paper; spine top chipped). Howes S446. *Bohling*. $120/£77

SIBSON, THOMAS. Illustrations of Master Humphrey's Clock.... London: Robert Tyas, 1842. 70 plts, extra engr tp. Orig cl (worn, fr hinge open). *Kane**. $160/£103

SICHEL, JULES. Spectacles: Their Uses and Abuses.... Henry W. Williams (trans). Boston, 1850. (Foxed; spine chipped.) *Argosy*. $175/£112

SIDDONS, HENRY. Practical Illustrations of Rhetorical Gesture and Action, Adapted to the English Drama from a Work by M. Engle. London, 1807. (Lt foxing, bkpl.) Complete, sl trimmed. Later 19th-cent 1/2 calf, marbled bds (rebacked). *Freeman**. $150/£96

SIDIS, BORIS. Psychopathological Researches: Studies in Mental Dissociation. NY: G.E. Stechert, 1902. 1st ed. 10 fldg plts, each w/explanatory leaf. Beveled ochre buckram. (Fep creased), else VG. *Gach*. $125/£80

SIDNEY, EDWIN. The Life of the Rev. Rowland Hill, A.M. London: Baldwin & Cradock, 1835. 3rd ed. Frontis port, xx,458pp (prelims lt browned, bkpl). Marbled eps. Early gilt-edged diced calf (sl worn), gilt, leather spine label. *Edwards*. $55/£35

SIDNEY, MARGARET. Five Little Peppers and How They Grew. Boston, (1880). 1st ed, 1st bk, 1st state, w/'said Polly' p231, '&' in pub's monogram fr cvr stamped in gilt. Dec pub's cl (sl shelfworn). *Kane**. $300/£192

SIDNEY, PHILIP. Astrophel and Stella. Mona Wilson (ed). Nonesuch, 1931. Ltd to 725. VG in dec paper-cvrd bds, paper label, card folder, slipcase. *Cox*. $62/£40

SIDNEY, PHILIP. Astrophel and Stella. Mona Wilson (ed). (London): Nonesuch, 1931. One of 485 ptd. Patterned wrappers. Fine in folder, box. *Appelfeld*. $100/£64

SIDNEY, PHILIP. The Countess of Pembroke's Arcadia. London: Lloyd for Du-Gard, 1662. 11th ed. New eps. Old calf. Excellent. *Argosy*. $450/£288

SIDNEY, PHILIP. The Countess of Pembroke's Arcadia. London: George Calvert, 1674. 13th ed. Folio. (32),624,(26)pp, port. Full brn polished calf, cvrs panelled, gilt, by Riviere. (Bkpl, some pg #s cropped; fr hinge just beginning to crack), else Fine. *Felcone*. $450/£288

SIDNEY, PHILIP. The Miscellaneous Works. London, 1893. One of 500. (x),380pp (margins lt browned, bkpl; sl rubbed). *Edwards*. $39/£25

SIDNEY, PHILIP. Shepheardes Calender. London: Cresset Press, 1930. One of 350 numbered. Frontis. (Old mtg stains, residue to eps.) 1/4 cl, silk bds (sl soiled, rubbed, corners sl frayed). *Waverly**. $77/£49

SIDNEY, RICHARD CHASE. A Brief Memoir of the Life of...Algernon Sidney.... London: James Bohn, 1835. Brn cl (worn, joints repaired). Usable only. *Boswell*. $125/£80

SIDNEY, SAMUEL. The Three Colonies of Australia. NY: C.M. Saxton, 1860. xvi,17-408pp; 10 plts. (Lt foxed, rubbed.) *Adelson*. $45/£29

SIEBERT, WILBUR H. Loyalists in East Florida, 1774 to 1785. Deland: FL Hist Soc, 1929. 1st ed. One of 350 ptd. 2 vols. 6 maps and plts. (Bkpls removed.) Howes S449. *Ginsberg*. $300/£192

SIEBERT, WILBUR H. The Underground Railroad.... NY, 1898. 1st ed. Fldg map. (Rear cvr lt soiled.) *Kane**. $190/£122

SIEGEL, RUDOLPH E. Galen's System of Physiology and Medicine. Basel: Karger, 1968. 1st ed. Fine in dj. *Glaser*. $75/£48

Siegfried and The Twilight of the Gods. London/NY: William Heinemann/Doubleday Page, 1911. 1st ed, US issue. Arthur Rackham (illus). 30 tipped-in plts, tissue guards. Grn cl spine (dull), paper-cvrd bds, gilt. VG+. *Certo*. $225/£144

SIEVERS, ED. People in My Corner. (Santa Monica, CA: Ed Sievers, 1973.) 1st ed. (Name stamp), else VG in pict stiff wrappers. *Cahan*. $35/£22

SIGAUD, LOUIS A. Belle Boyd, Confederate Spy. Richmond, (1945). 2nd ed. VG. *Pratt*. $27/£17

SIGERIST, HENRY. American Medicine. NY, 1934. 1st ed in English. VG. *Fye*. $95/£61

SIGERIST, HENRY. The Great Doctors. NY, 1933. 1st ed in English. VG. *Fye*. $100/£64

SIGERIST, HENRY. A History of Medicine. Volume 2. NY, 1961. 1st ed. VG. *Fye*. $75/£48

SIGERIST, HENRY. Man and Medicine: An Introduction to Medical Knowledge. NY, 1932. 1st ed. VG (extrems sl worn). *Doctor's Library*. $75/£48

SIGERIST, HENRY. Man and Medicine: An Introduction to Medical Knowledge. NY, 1932. 1st ed in English. VG. *Fye*. $75/£48

SIGOURNEY, L. H. Letters to Young Ladies. NY: Harper, 1854. 16th ed. 295pp. Patterned cl (sl worn). VG. *Second Life*. $65/£42

SIGSBEE, CHARLES D. The Maine: An Account of Her Destruction in Havana Harbor. NY: Century, 1899. xiv,270pp. Pict cl. *Dawson*. $35/£22

SILBER, MARK. The Family Album. (Boston): David R. Godine, 1973. 1st ed. (Owner stamp), else Fine in NF dj. *Cahan*. $30/£19

SILKO, LESLIE MARMON. Almanac of the Dead. NY: S&S, (1991). 1st ed. Fine in Fine dj. *Fuller & Saunders*. $25/£16

SILLIMAN, B. A Fatal Case of Poisoning. NY, ca 1875. 10pp. VG in ptd wrappers (mended). *Argosy*. $35/£22

SILLITOE, ALAN. The Death of William Posters. NY: Knopf, 1965. 1st ed. NF in dj. *Antic Hay*. $20/£13

SILLITOE, ALAN. Saturday Night and Sunday Morning. NY: Knopf, (1958). 1st Amer ed. NF in dj (sm closed tear, chips). *Turtle Island*. $30/£19

SILLITOE, ALAN. A Start in Life. NY: Scribner, (1970). 1st Amer ed. NF (sm stain rep) in dj. *Antic Hay*. $15/£10

SILONE, IGNAZIO. Mr. Aristotle. NY, 1935. 1st Amer ed. Fine in dj (spine sl sunned, sm nick). *Polyanthos*. $25/£16

SILTZER, FRANK. The Story of British Sporting Prints. NY, 1925. (Pencil notes, inner hinge cracked; spine sl sunned, worn), else Good. *King*. $125/£80

SILTZER, FRANK. The Story of British Sporting Prints. London: Halton & Truscott Smith, 1929. Ltd to 1000. 8 tipped-in color plts. Grn cl, gilt. NF. *Biscotti*. $225/£144

Silver Fairy Book. Hutchinson, ca 1898. 3rd ed. H. R. Millar (illus). Lg 8vo. 312pp (sl foxed; joints shaken). Midnight-blue cl, gilt. VG. *Bookmark*. $62/£40

SILVER, WALLACE W. Oxcart Days. (New Richmond, WI: Leader Pub Co, n.d. (early 1900s.) Pb. Good (spine chipped). *Lien*. $35/£22

SILVERBERG, ROBERT. Sailing to Byzantium. SF: Underwood-Miller, 1985. 1st ed. Fine in dj. *Antic Hay*. $25/£16

SILVERBERG, ROBERT. Tom O'Bedlam. NY: Donald I. Fine, (1985). 1st ed. Blue cl-backed pale tan bds, gilt. NF (sl spotted; fr bd sl soiled) in dj (rear panel sl soiled). *Blue Mountain*. $20/£13

SILVERMAN, JONATHAN. For the World to See: The Life of Margaret Bourke-White. NY: Viking/Studio, 1983. 1st ed. VG (inscrip) in VG dj. *Smith*. $65/£42

SIMAK, CLIFFORD. City. 1954. 1st ed. NF in dj. *Words Etc*. $39/£25

SIMAK, CLIFFORD. Strangers in the Universe. S&S, 1956. 1st ed. VG in dj (chipped). *Madle*. $25/£16

SIMAK, CLIFFORD. They Walked Like Men. Doubleday, 1962. 1st ed. Fine in VG+ dj (sm chip). *Aronovitz*. $60/£38

SIMAK, CLIFFORD. Why Call Them Back from Heaven. Doubleday, 1967. 1st ed. VG+ in NF dj. *Aronovitz*. $50/£32

SIME, D. Rabies. Its Place Amongst Germ-Diseases and Its Origin in the Animal Kingdom. Cambridge, 1903. (Few lib stamps throughout; ex-lib w/perf mk tp, stamps, bkpl; rebacked.) *Whitehart*. $62/£40

SIMENON, GEORGES. Big Bob. London: Hamilton, 1969. 1st UK ed. Fine in NF dj (sm nicks). *Williams*. $28/£18

SIMENON, GEORGES. Chit of a Girl. London: Routledge & Kegan Paul, 1949. 1st Eng ed. Fine in dj (nicks). *Mordida*. $85/£54

SIMENON, GEORGES. The Family Life. NY: Harcourt, Brace, Jovanovich, (1978). 1st Amer ed. Fine in 2 djs. *Antic Hay*. $25/£16

SIMENON, GEORGES. The Family Life. Hamilton, 1978. 1st UK ed. NF in VG dj. *Williams*. $23/£15

SIMENON, GEORGES. The Fate of the Malous. London: Hamilton, 1962. 1st UK ed. Fine in NF dj (price-clipped, rear panel sl stained). *Williams*. $28/£18

SIMENON, GEORGES. The First-Born. NY: Reynal & Hitchcock, 1947. 1st ed. Fine (tape shadow fr flap; rep pasted down) in NF dj. *Beasley*. $30/£19

SIMENON, GEORGES. Four Days in a Lifetime. Hamilton, 1977. 1st UK ed. Fine in dj. *Williams*. $23/£15

SIMENON, GEORGES. The Girl in His Past. Hamilton, 1976. 1st UK ed. Fine in dj. *Williams*. $23/£15

SIMENON, GEORGES. Havoc by Accident. London: Routledge, 1943. 1st UK ed. VG in dj (sl edgeworn, sl chipped). *Williams*. $62/£40

SIMENON, GEORGES. Letter to My Mother. Ralph Manheim (trans). London: Hamish Hamilton, (1976). 1st Eng ed. Fine in NF dj. *Antic Hay*. $20/£13

SIMENON, GEORGES. Magnet of Doom. London: Routledge & Kegan Paul, 1948. 1st UK ed. VG+ in dj (spine lt stained, sm nicks). *Williams*. $70/£45

SIMENON, GEORGES. Maigret Afraid. Hamilton, 1961. 1st UK ed. VG in dj (sl edgewear, sm closed tears). *Williams*. $25/£16

SIMENON, GEORGES. Maigret and the Apparition. NY: Harcourt, Brace, Jovanovich, (1976). 1st Amer ed. Fine in dj. *Antic Hay*. $20/£13

SIMENON, GEORGES. Maigret and the Black Sheep. Helen Thomson (trans). NY: Harcourt, Brace, Jovanovich, (1976). 1st Amer ed. Fine in dj. *Antic Hay*. $25/£16

SIMENON, GEORGES. Maigret and the Burglar's Wife. Hamilton, 1955. 1st UK ed. VG in dj (sl rubbed). *Williams*. $31/£20

SIMENON, GEORGES. Maigret and the Coroner. London: Hamish Hamilton, 1980. 1st Eng ed. Fine in dj (price-clipped). *Mordida*. $35/£22

SIMENON, GEORGES. Maigret and the Hotel Majestic. Hamilton, 1977. 1st UK ed. Fine in dj (price-clipped). *Williams*. $25/£16

SIMENON, GEORGES. Maigret and the Madwoman. London: Hamish Hamilton, 1972. 1st Eng ed. Fine in dj. *Mordida*. $45/£29

SIMENON, GEORGES. Maigret and the Millionaires. Jean Stewart (trans). NY: Harcourt, Brace, Jovanovich, (1974). 1st Amer ed. Fine in NF dj. *Antic Hay*. $25/£16

SIMENON, GEORGES. Maigret and the Nahour Case. Hamilton, 1967. 1st UK ed. VG in dj (sl nicked, rubbed). *Williams*. $23/£15

SIMENON, GEORGES. Maigret and the Spinster. Hamilton, 1977. 1st UK ed. Fine in dj (price-clipped). *Williams*. $25/£16

SIMENON, GEORGES. Maigret and the Spinster. London: Hamish Hamilton, 1977. 1st Eng ed. Fine in dj. *Mordida*. $45/£29

SIMENON, GEORGES. Maigret and the Toy Village. London: Hamilton, 1978. 1st UK ed. VG+ in dj (price-clipped). *Williams*. $28/£18

SIMENON, GEORGES. Maigret Goes to School. London: Hamilton, 1957. 1st UK ed. VG in dj. *Williams*. $39/£25

SIMENON, GEORGES. Maigret in Exile. London: Hamilton, 1978. 1st UK ed. VG+ in dj. *Williams*. $28/£18

SIMENON, GEORGES. Maigret in New York. Hamilton, 1979. 1st UK ed. NF in dj (price-clipped). *Williams*. $23/£15

SIMENON, GEORGES. Maigret Loses His Temper. London: Hamish Hamilton, 1965. 1st Eng ed. Fine in dj. *Mordida*. $65/£42

SIMENON, GEORGES. A Maigret Omnibus. Hamilton, 1962. 1st ed thus. NF (sl crease fep) in VG dj (sl grubby). *Williams*. $47/£30

SIMENON, GEORGES. Maigret Rents a Room. GC: DCC, 1961. 1st Amer ed. Advance rev copy, slip laid in. VF in dj. *Mordida*. $65/£42

SIMENON, GEORGES. Maigret Victorious. Hamilton, 1975. 1st UK ed. NF in dj. *Williams*. $28/£18

SIMENON, GEORGES. Maigret's Christmas. London: Hamilton, 1976. 1st UK ed. NF in dj. *Williams*. $25/£16

SIMENON, GEORGES. Maigret's Failure. Daphne Woodward (trans). London: Hamish Hamilton, 1962. 1st Eng ed. Dj (sl rubbed). *Cox*. $23/£15

SIMENON, GEORGES. Maigret's Pickpocket. Hamilton, 1968. 1st UK ed. Fine (ink inscrip) in VG dj (sm edge nicks). *Williams*. $22/£14

SIMENON, GEORGES. Maigret's Revolver. London: Hamish Hamilton, 1956. 1st Eng ed. (Inked-out name fep), o/w Fine in dj (sl wear). *Mordida*. $45/£29

SIMENON, GEORGES. Monsieur Monde Vanishes. London: Hamilton, 1967. 1st UK ed. NF in VG dj (sl nicked, price-clipped). *Williams*. $25/£16

SIMENON, GEORGES. The Neighbours. London: Hamish Hamilton, 1968. 1st Eng ed. Fine in dj (price-clipped, spine ends sl worn). *Mordida*. $40/£26

SIMENON, GEORGES. The Others. Hamilton, 1975. 1st UK ed. NF in dj. *Williams*. $23/£15

SIMENON, GEORGES. The Others. London: Hamilton, 1975. 1st UK ed. Fine in NF dj (price-clipped). *Williams*. $22/£14

SIMENON, GEORGES. The Others. Alastair Hamilton (trans). London: Hamish Hamilton, 1975. 1st ed. NF in dj. *Antic Hay*. $25/£16

SIMENON, GEORGES. The Premier. Hamilton, 1961. 1st UK ed. VG in dj. *Williams*. $19/£12

SIMENON, GEORGES. The Reckoning. Hamilton, 1984. 1st UK ed. Fine in dj (price-clipped). *Williams*. $22/£14

SIMENON, GEORGES. The Rich Man. Hamilton, 1971. 1st UK ed. Fine in dj. *Williams*. $23/£15

SIMENON, GEORGES. The Sacrifice. London: Hamilton, 1956. 1st UK ed. Fine in NF dj. *Williams*. $44/£28

SIMENON, GEORGES. The Snow Was Black. NY: Prentice Hall, (1950). 1st ed. Inscribed, signed, dated 1950. Black cl. Fine in dj (nicked). *Appelfeld*. $200/£128

SIMENON, GEORGES. The Son. London: Hamish Hamilton, 1958. 1st Eng ed. Fine in dj. *Mordida*. $75/£48

SIMENON, GEORGES. Teddy Bear. Hamilton, 1971. 1st UK ed. NF in dj (price-clipped). *Williams*. $25/£16

SIMENON, GEORGES. Three Beds in Manhattan. GC: Doubleday, 1964. 1st Amer ed. (Owner stamp), else NF in dj. *Hermitage*. $35/£22

SIMENON, GEORGES. The Train. Hamilton, 1964. 1st UK ed. VG in dj. *Williams*. $28/£18

SIMENON, GEORGES. The Train. Robert Baldick (trans). London: Hamish Hamilton, 1964. 1st Eng ed. VG in dj. *Cox*. $23/£15

SIMENON, GEORGES. Versus Inspector Maigret. GC: DCC, 1960. 1st Amer ed. Fine in dj. *Mordida*. $65/£42

SIMENON, GEORGES. Violent Ends. London: Hamish Hamilton, 1954. 1st ed. VG in dj (sl dknd). *Mordida*. $35/£22

SIMEON, CORNWALL. Stray Notes on Fishing and Natural History. Cambridge: Macmillan, 1860. Frontis. Grn pebble-grained cl. *Petersfield*. $25/£16

SIMKIN, COLIN. Currier and Ives' America. NY: Crown, 1952. (Lt worn, soiled.) Dj (worn, chipped). *Freeman**. $25/£16

SIMMONDS, W. H. The Practical Grocer. Gresham Pub Co, 1904. 4 vols. Color frontispieces. (Lt spotted.) Pict cl (lt soiled, rubbed). *Edwards*. $55/£35

SIMMONS, ALBERT DIXON. Wing Shots. NY: Derrydale, (1936). Ltd to 950. 82 full-pg photo plts. Fine. *Truepenny*. $75/£48

SIMMONS, DAN. Carrion Comfort. Arlington Hts.: Dark Harvest, 1989. 1st ed. One of 450 numbered, signed. Dj, slipcase. *Swann**. $149/£96

SIMMONS, DAN. Children of the Night. Northridge: Lord John, (1992). One of 500 numbered, signed. Slipcase. *Swann**. $92/£59

SIMMONS, DAN. The Fall of Hyperion. NY: Doubleday, (1990). 1st ed. Dj. *Swann**. $57/£37

SIMMONS, DAN. The Hollow Man. Northridge: Lord John, 1992. One of 500 numbered, signed. Cl-backed dec bds. Slipcase. *Swann**. $92/£59

SIMMONS, DAN. Hyperion. NY: Doubleday, (1989). 1st ed. Dj. *Swann**. $172/£110

SIMMONS, J. C. The History of Southern Methodism on the Pacific Coast. Nashville: Southern Methodist Pub House, 1886. 1st ed. Frontis port, 454pp. Gilt-lettered spine. (Spine ends, corners sl rubbed), else Fine. *Argonaut*. $125/£80

SIMMONS, JAMES S. et al. Global Epidemiology. Phila: Lippincott, (1944-51). 1st ed. 2 vols. VG (bkpl, blindstamp vol 2; sig vol 1) in dj (sl frayed). *Glaser*. $85/£54

SIMMONS, MARC. The Little Lion of the Southwest. Chicago, (1973). 1st ed. (Mks tp from removed bkpl), o/w VG+ in dj (sl chipped). *Pratt*. $35/£22

SIMMONS, SAMUEL. Elements of Anatomy and the Animal Economy. London: Wilie, 1775. 1st ed. xii,396pp (lt pencilling), errata leaf, 3 engr plts. Old 1/4 calf (worn). *Goodrich*. $75/£48

SIMMS, ERIC. British Thrushes. London: Collins, 1978. 1st ed. VG in dj (sl dknd). *Cox*. $31/£20

SIMMS, JEPTHA R. Trappers of New York.... Albany: J. Munsell, 1860. 3rd ed. Frontis, 3 plts. Emb grn cl (faded, worn). (Frontis, tp loose), o/w Internally NF. *Cummins*. $40/£26

SIMMS, JOSEPH PATTERSON and CHARLES WILLING. Old Philadelphia Colonial Details. NY: Architectural Book Pub Co, 1914. 55 plts. 2-tone cl (lt worn, soiled). *Freeman**. $180/£115

SIMMS, WILLIAM GILMORE. The Life of the Chevalier Bayard. NY: Harper, 1847. 1st ed. Frontis, 401pp. Full red leather, gilt. (Sl internal foxing), else NF. BAL 18107. *Turtle Island*. $150/£96

SIMON, ANDRE. The Art of Good Livings...together with A Gastronomic Vocabulary and a Wine Dictionary. London, 1929. 1st ed. *Petersfield*. $14/£9

SIMON, CLAUDE. The Palace. Richard Howard (trans). NY: Braziller, 1963. 1st ed in English. (Sig), else Fine in dj. *Lame Duck*. $45/£29

SIMON, HERBERT. Song and Words. Boston, (1973). (Bumped), else Good in dj (defective). *King*. $40/£26

SIMON, JOHN. General Pathology as Conducive to the Establishment of Rational Principles for the Diagnosis and Treatment of Disease...1850. Phila, 1852. 1st Amer ed. Inscribed. VG. *Argosy*. $200/£128

SIMON, NEIL. The Odd Couple. NY: Random House, (1966). 1st ed. Fine in dj (lt rubbing bottom fr panel). *Between The Covers*. $185/£119

SIMON, OLIVER. Printer and Playground. London: Faber & Faber, (1956). 1st ed. Fine in NF dj. *Dermont.* $35/£22

SIMOND, L. Journal of a Tour and Residence in Great Britain, During the Years 1810 and 1811. Edinburgh, 1817. 2nd ed. 2 vols. 5 etched plts, fldg chart. Uncut. Contemp 1/2 morocco. *Argosy.* $200/£128

SIMOND, L. Switzerland. London, 1823. 2nd ed. 2 vols. vii,(ii)520; (vi),500pp (spotting, ex-libris, tp vol 1 neatly repaired, no loss); dbl-pg plt. Marbled eps, edges. 1/2 vellum, marbled bds (sl rubbed, spines lt spotted), leather labels. *Edwards.* $195/£125

SIMONSON, LEE. The Stage Is Set. NY: Harcourt, Brace, (1932). 1st ed. (Bkpl; cl sl soiled, spine sunned.) *Dramatis Personae.* $45/£29

SIMPSON, CHARLES. Animal and Bird Painting, the Outlook and Technique of the Artist. Batsford, 1939. *Maggs.* $37/£24

SIMPSON, CHARLES. Animal and Bird Painting. Batsford, 1939. 1st ed. Dj (chipped). *Edwards.* $23/£15

SIMPSON, CHARLES. Emily Bronte. Country Life, 1929. Good (sl spotted, sig fep; spine bumped, sunned). *Tiger.* $37/£24

SIMPSON, GEORGE. Narrative of a Journey Round the World, During the Years 1841 and 1842. London, 1847. 2 vols. Frontis port, xi,(1),438,24pp, fldg map; vii,(1),469pp. (Bkpls each vol; spines sunned, extrems sl frayed), else VG. Howes S495. *Reese.* $900/£577

SIMPSON, GEORGE. Narrative of a Voyage to California Ports in 1841-42, Together with Voyages to Sitka.... SF: Thomas C. Russell, 1930. #38/250. 2 steel-engr ports. Uncut. Ptd spine label. Fine in plain dj w/ptd spine label. *Pacific*.* $196/£126

SIMPSON, JAMES. Report and Map of the Route from Fort Smith, Arkansas to Santa Fe, New Mexico, Made by.... Washington: SED12, 1850. 1st ed. 25pp (foxed); 4 fldg maps (2 mended). 1/2 morocco. Howes S500. *Ginsberg.* $350/£224

SIMPSON, JEFFREY. The Way Life Was. NY/Washington: Praeger, 1974. 1st ed. VG (owner stamp) in dj. *Cahan.* $75/£48

SIMPSON, PAIGE SHOAF and JERRY H. Torn Land. (J.P. Bell, 1970.) 1st ptg. Map. Good (lacks fep) in Poor dj (torn). *Book Broker.* $35/£22

SIMPSON, THOMAS. Select Exercises for Young...in the Mathematics. London: J. Nourse, 1752. 1st ed. White paper-cvrd bds, spine, leather label. (Rebound; pp dknd; lib stamp, some of title rubbed out on tp, tp rebacked, few tears.) *Metropolitan*.* $115/£74

SIMPSON, W. D. Castle from the Air. London: Country Life, 1949. 112 plts. Sound. *Ars Artis.* $33/£21

SIMPSON, WILLIAM. Meeting the Sun. Boston: Estes & Lauriat, 1877. 413pp; 48 plts. (Rubbed.) *Adelson.* $65/£42

SIMS, GEORGE. Sleep No More. London: Gollancz, 1966. 1st ed. (Spine top sl bumped), o/w Fine in dj (sl torn). *Jaffe.* $100/£64

SIMSON, O. VON. The Gothic Cathedral. The Origins of Gothic Architecture and the Medieval Concept of Order. London: RKP, 1956. 44 plts (3 color), fldg chart. Sound. *Ars Artis.* $47/£30

SIMSON, ROBERT. The Elements of Euclid. Edinburgh: J. Nourse & J. Balfour, 1775. 5th ed. vii,520pp (sm piece torn from margin E1); 3 fldg engr plts. Old polished calf (sl rubbed, bumped), gilt. *Hollett.* $148/£95

SINCLAIR, IAIN. White Chappell, Scarlet Tracings. Uppingham: Goldmark, 1987. 1st trade ed. Signed. Fine in dj. *Lame Duck.* $100/£64

SINCLAIR, IAN. The Kodak Mantra Diaries, October 1966 to June 1971. (London): Albion Village, Oct 1971. 1st ed. Fine in spiralbound stiff pict wrappers. *Reese.* $25/£16

SINCLAIR, JO. The Changelings. NY: McGraw-Hill, 1955. 1st ed. VG + in dj (price-clipped). *Lame Duck.* $100/£64

SINCLAIR, MAY. Tales Told by Simpson. Macmillan, 1930. (Spine sunned), else VG. *Certo.* $30/£19

SINCLAIR, UPTON. Between Two Worlds. NY: Viking Press, 1941. 1st ed. (Sl bump spine base; name stamp), else NF in VG + dj. *Between The Covers.* $150/£96

SINCLAIR, UPTON. The Jungle. Toronto: McLeod & Allen, (ca 1906). 1st Canadian issue, bound from Amer sheets. Pict cl (spine stamping sl rubbed). Nice (bkseller's label rear pastedown, foxing, edges lt discolored). *Reese.* $75/£48

SINCLAIR, UPTON. The Jungle. Balt: LEC, 1965. One of T500 numbered, signed by Sinclair and Fletcher Martin (illus). Leather-backed bds. VG in slipcase. *Argosy.* $100/£64

SINCLAIR, UPTON. Mammonart. CA, 1925. One of 4000. NF (name; spine sl sunned, extrems sl rubbed). *Polyanthos.* $30/£19

SINCLAIR, UPTON. One Clear Call. NY: Viking, 1948. 1st ed. Fine (sl crimp few pg edges) in NF dj (lt rubbed; spine sl faded). *Between The Covers.* $100/£64

SINCLAIR, UPTON. Sylvia's Marriage. Pasadena/Long Beach, 1928. 2nd ed. VG + (sm corner chip). *Beasley.* $25/£16

SINCLAIR, UPTON. A World to Win. Monrovia: The Author, 1946. 1st ed. Fine in dj (sl used, tears, sm chips at spine folds). *Beasley.* $25/£16

SINEL, JOSEPH. A Book of American Trade-Marks and Devices. NY: Knopf, 1924. 1st ed. #1171/2000. Pict cl-backed bds. VG. *New Hampshire*.* $90/£58

SINEL, JOSEPH. A Book of American Trade-Marks and Devices. NY: Knopf, 1924. Ltd to 2050 numbered. French-fold pp. VF in dj, box (partly broken). *Oak Knoll.* $125/£80

SINEL, JOSEPH. A Book of American Trade-Marks and Devices. NY: Knopf, 1924. 1st ed. #848/2050. French-fld pp. VG in cl-backed dec bds; dj (repaired, lt soiled). *Cox.* $148/£95

Sing a Song of Sixpence. NY: McLoughlin Bros, (ca 1890). 8vo. (6)ff. VF in pict self-wrappers. *Bromer.* $50/£32

SINGER, CHARLES et al. A History of Technology, Vol. 5, the Late 19th Century Background. Oxford: OUP, 1958. 44 plts. Clean (new backstrip, paper label; ex-lib). *Bookcell.* $25/£16

SINGER, CHARLES et al. A History of Technology, Vol. 4, the Industrial Revolution 1750 to 1850. OUP, 1958. 48 plts. VF in dj. *Bookcell.* $55/£35

SINGER, CHARLES. From Magic to Science. 1928. (2 illus loose), o/w VG. *Whitehart.* $55/£35

SINGER, CHARLES. From Magic to Science. London, 1928. 14 color plts. (Sl faded, worn.) *Maggs.* $50/£32

SINGER, CHARLES. From Magic to Science. London, 1928. 1st ed. VG. *Fye.* $125/£80

SINGER, CHARLES. A History of Biology to About the Year 1900. 1959. VG in dj. *Whitehart.* $55/£35

SINGER, CHARLES. A Short History of Medicine. Oxford, 1928. 1st ed. 1/2 leather w/raised bands. VF. *Fye.* $100/£64

SINGER, CHARLES. A Short History of Medicine. Oxford, 1962. 2nd ed. 21 plts. (Label removed fep, sm ink lib stamp tp, verso.) Dj. *Whitehart.* $55/£35

SINGER, CHARLES. A Short History of Science to the Nineteenth Century. Oxford, 1941. (Sl stained.) *Maggs.* $25/£16

SINGER, CHARLES. Vesalius on the Human Brain. London: Wellcome, 1952. NF in dj. *Goodrich.* $125/£80

SINGER, I. J. The Brothers Ashkenazi. NY: Knopf, 1936. 1st US ed. VG in VG dj (spine tanned). *Lame Duck.* $150/£96

SINGER, I. J. Of a World That Is No More: A Tender Memoir. NY: Vanguard, (1970). 1st ed. Fine in dj (sl soiled). *Between The Covers.* $125/£80

SINGER, ISAAC BASHEVIS. The Death of Methuselah. NY: Farrar, 1988. One of 250 specially bound, numbered, signed. Fine in Fine slipcase. *Beasley.* $100/£64

SINGER, ISAAC BASHEVIS. A Friend of Kafka. NY: FSG, (1970). 1st ed. Inscribed. Fine in dj (lt soiled). *Metropolitan*.* $86/£55

SINGER, ISAAC BASHEVIS. An Isaac Bashevis Singer Reader. NY: FSG, (1971). 1st ed. Fine in dj. *Jaffe.* $75/£48

SINGER, ISAAC BASHEVIS. A Little Boy in Search of God. GC: Doubleday, (1976). 1st ed. Inscribed. Fine in Fine dj. *Metropolitan*.* $258/£165

SINGER, ISAAC BASHEVIS. Magician of Lublin. Elaine Gottlieb and Joseph Singer (trans). NY: LEC, 1984. Ltd to 1500 signed by author and Larry Rivers (illus). 1/4 dk blue Nigerian Oasis goatskin, natural Polish linen. Mint in slipcase (lt worn). *Truepenny.* $450/£288

SINGER, ISAAC BASHEVIS. Mazel and Shlimazel. NY: FSG, 1967. 1st ed. Margot Zemach (illus). 11 x 9 1/4. 48pp. Fine in dj. *Cattermole.* $25/£16

SINGER, ISAAC BASHEVIS. Of a World That Is No More. NY: Vanguard, 1970. 1st ed. Fine in NF dj. *Lame Duck.* $125/£80

SINGER, ISAAC BASHEVIS. Satan in Goray. NY: Noonday, 1955. 1st ed. Fine in dj. *Hermitage.* $200/£128

SINGER, ISAAC BASHEVIS. A Tale of Three Wishes. NY: FSG, (1976). 1st ed. Irene Lieblich (illus). Fine in dj. *Between The Covers.* $65/£42

SINGER, ISAAC BASHEVIS. Why Noah Chose the Dove. NY: FSG, 1974. 1st ed. Eric Carle (illus). 8 1/2 x 11 1/4. VG in dj. *Cattermole.* $60/£38

SINGER, ISAAC BASHEVIS. Zlateh the Goat. NY: Harper & Row, 1966. Signed. Maurice Sendak (illus). Fine in NF dj (price-clipped). *Metropolitan*.* $258/£165

SINGER, JACOB. Taboo in the Hebrew Scriptures. Chicago/London: Open Court, 1928. 1st ed. Frontis. Panelled crimson cl, gilt. Jelliffe's name stamp, bkpl. Good (text tide-mkg, lib stamp tp; call #s, fr bd sl dampstained) in dj (fr dampstained). *Gach.* $35/£22

SINGH, J. A. L. and ROBERT M. ZINGG. Wolf-Children and Feral Man. Harper, 1942. 1st ed. VG + (sl musty). *Beasley.* $45/£29

SINGH, MADANJEET. Himalayan Art. NY: Macmillan/UNESCO, 1971. 1st ptg. VG. *Worldwide.* $45/£29

SINGLETON, ESTHER. The Furniture of Our Forefathers. NY: Doubleday, 1906. Rpt. 2 vols. VG. *Agvent.* $60/£38

SINGLETON, FRANK. Lancashire and the Pennines. London: Batsford, 1952. 1st ed. Color frontis. VG. *Hollett.* $19/£12

SINGLETON, WILLIAM HENRY. Contraband of War. Laurel F. & Joel A. Vlock (eds). NY, (1970). 1st ed. Fine in dj (lt wear). *Pratt.* $30/£19

SINKER, ROBERT. A Catalogue of the Fifteenth-Century Printed Books in the Library of Trinity College, Cambridge. Cambridge/London: Bell, 1876. 1st ed. x,(2),173,(1),(2),68-104pp. Forest grn cl. (Spine extrems lt worn), o/w VG. *Reese.* $85/£54

Sir Ysambrace. (Hammersmith: Kelmscott, 1897.) One of 350. Linen-backed bds (backstrip spotted). Cl slipcase. *Swann*.* $575/£369

SIREN, OSVALD. Early Chinese Paintings from A.W. Bahr Collection. Chiswick, 1938. One of 750. 27 plts. Teg. Black buckram, gilt. (Rep sl torn at fore-edge; cvrs sl soiled.) *Hatchwell.* $226/£145

SIREN, OSVALD. Early Chinese Paintings: A.W. Bahr Collection. London: Chiswick, 1938. 1st ed. Ltd to 750. 25 full-pg tipped-in plts incl 12 color. Teg. Gilt-lettered black cl. VF. *Argonaut.* $250/£160

SIREN, OSVALD. Giotto and Some of His Followers. Cambridge, 1917. 2 vols. 220 plts. (Rebacked, sl rubbed.) *Washton.* $175/£112

SIREN, OSVALD. A History of Early Chinese Painting. London, (1933). One of 525 numbered. 2 vols. VG (ex-lib). *Swann*.* $287/£184

SISKIND, AARON. Aaron Siskind: Photographs. NY: Horizon, 1959. 1st ed. Silver/black emb cl. NF in dj (edgeworn). *Cahan.* $125/£80

SISSON, EDGAR. One Hundred Red Days.... New Haven, 1931. 1st ed. (Bkpl, sl cvr wear.) *King.* $37/£24

Sister Lucy's Recreations. Tales for the Young. Phila: James K. Simon, 1848. Later ed. 16mo. Frontis, 144pp; 8 color illus. (Worn, rubbed), else Good. *Brown.* $25/£16

SITGREAVES, LORENZO. Report of an Expedition Down the Zuni and Colorado Rivers. Washington: Armstrong, 1853. SED 59. 23 tinted litho view plts, 53 other plts. (Tp fore-edge margin excised w/o loss; lacks map.) Early 1/2 morocco. *Swann*.* $149/£96

SITGREAVES, LORENZO. Report of an Expedition Down the Zuni and Colorado Rivers. Washington, 1853. Senate Exec Doc 59. 1st ed. 78 litho plts and views. (Foxing, shelfwear.) Howes S521. *Oinonen*.* $225/£144

SITGREAVES, LORENZO. Report of an Expedition Down the Zuni and Colorado Rivers. Washington: Beverly Tucker, Senate Printer, 1854. 2nd ptg. 79 plts, map (sm fold separations, tape-repaired tear; some pp foxing, stamp). Emb purple cl (spine sunned), gilt. Superb. Howes S521. *Five Quail.* $525/£337

SITWELL, EDITH (ed). Wheels, an Anthology of Verse. Oxford: Blackwell, 1916. 1st ed. Uncut. Yellow ptd bds, 1/4 yellow cl. Nice (sl rubbed, few mks). *Macdonnell.* $100/£64

SITWELL, EDITH (ed). Wheels, Sixth Cycle. London: C.W. Daniel, (1921). 1st ed. Color pict bds, 1/4 cl, label. (Label chipped), else VG. *Macdonnell.* $25/£16

SITWELL, EDITH. The Canticle of the Rose. Poems 1917-1949. NY: Vanguard, (1949). 1st Amer ed. (Spine gilding sl patinated), o/w NF in dj. *Reese.* $35/£22

SITWELL, EDITH. The Collected Poems of Edith Sitwell. London/Boston: Duckworth/Houghton Mifflin, 1930. 1st ed, ltd issue. One of 320 numbered, signed, specially ptd and bound. Port, errata slip. Pale yellow cl. NF. *Reese.* $185/£119

SITWELL, EDITH. English Eccentrics. NY: Vanguard, (1957). 1st Amer ed. Fine in NF dj. *Hermitage.* $25/£16

SITWELL, EDITH. English Eccentrics. NY: Vanguard, (1957). 1st Amer ed. NF in dj (chipped). *Turtle Island.* $30/£19

SITWELL, EDITH. Gardeners and Astronomers. London: Macmillan, 1953. 1st ed. (Feps sl browned.) Dj. *Hollett.* $23/£15

SITWELL, EDITH. Green Song and Other Poems. London: Macmillan, 1944. 1st ed. NF in dj (few smudges). *Reese.* $25/£16

SITWELL, EDITH. Green Song and Other Poems. London: Macmillan, 1944. 1st ed. (Edges faded.) Dj. *Hollett*. $78/£50

SITWELL, EDITH. Music and Ceremonies. NY: Vanguard, (1963). 1st Amer ed. NF in dj (sl wear, price-clipped). *Antic Hay*. $27/£17

SITWELL, EDITH. The Outcasts. London: Macmillan, 1962. 1st ed. Errata slip loosely inserted. VG in dj. *Hollett*. $23/£15

SITWELL, EDITH. The Outcasts. London: Macmillan, 1962. 1st ed. Dec bds. Fine in NF dj. *Reese*. $25/£16

SITWELL, EDITH. Rustic Elegies. London: Duckworth, 1927. 1st ed. Frontis port. (Lt damped.) *Hollett*. $31/£20

SITWELL, EDITH. The Song of the Cold. NY: Vanguard, (1948). 1st ed. NF in dj. *Reese*. $25/£16

SITWELL, GEORGE. On the Making of Gardens. NY/London, 1951. 16 plts. Good in dj (worn). *Washton*. $35/£22

SITWELL, N. H. H. Roman Roads of Europe. NY: St. Martin's, (1981). Good in dj. *Archaeologia*. $85/£54

SITWELL, OSBERT. The Collected Satires and Poems of Osbert Sitwell. London: Duckworth, 1933. One of 110 numbered, signed on handmade paper. Unopened. Buckram. NF. *Dermont*. $75/£48

SITWELL, OSBERT. Collected Stories. London: Duckworth/Macmillan, 1953. 1st ed. VG in dj. *Hollett*. $47/£30

SITWELL, OSBERT. Collected Stories. NY, 1953. 1st ed. VG in dj (sl torn). *Words Etc*. $23/£15

SITWELL, OSBERT. Escape with Me. NY: Harrison-Hilton Books, 1940. 1st Amer ed. VF in dj (spine smudge). *Hermitage*. $40/£26

SITWELL, OSBERT. The Four Continents. London: Macmillan, 1954. 1st ed. 24 plts. VG in dj. *Hollett*. $39/£25

SITWELL, OSBERT. Great Morning. (London): Macmillan, (1948). 1st Eng ed. Fine in dj (lt used, sm tears). *Antic Hay*. $35/£22

SITWELL, OSBERT. Who Killed Cock Robin? Daniel, 1921. 1st issue. Stiff card cvrs. (Fore-edge sl foxed), o/w NF in dj. *Poetry Bookshop*. $39/£25

SITWELL, SACHEVERELL et al. Fine Bird Books, 1700-1900. London, 1953. 1st ed. *Metropolitan**. $250/£160

SITWELL, SACHEVERELL et al. Fine Bird Books, 1700-1900. London, 1953. Folio. (Lib bkpl.) Orig 1/2 cl. *Swann**. $632/£405

SITWELL, SACHEVERELL and WILFRID BLUNT. Great Flower Books 1700-1900. London, 1956. 36 plts (20 color). Illus eps. 1/2 cl, marbled bds (corners creased). Dj (ragged). *Edwards*. $499/£320

SITWELL, SACHEVERELL. Arabesque and Honeycomb. NY: Random House, (1958). 1st Amer ed. VG (ink name, date) in dj (price-clipped, lt rubbed). *Hermitage*. $25/£16

SITWELL, SACHEVERELL. Arabesque and Honeycombe. London, 1957. 1st ed. (Prelims sl foxed), o/w Fine in dj. *Petersfield*. $23/£15

SITWELL, SACHEVERELL. British Architects and Craftsmen. Batsford, 1948. Color frontis. VG in pict dj. *Cox*. $23/£15

SITWELL, SACHEVERELL. Cupid and the Jacaranda. London: Macmillan, 1952. 1st ed. Fine in dj. *Hermitage*. $50/£32

SITWELL, SACHEVERELL. The Gothick North. London: John Lehmann, 1950. 1st ed thus. Fine in dj (spine sl dknd, price-clipped). *Captain's Bookshelf*. $45/£29

SITWELL, SACHEVERELL. The Homing of the Winds. London: Faber, 1942. 1st UK ed. Fine in dj (short closed tear). *Williams*. $19/£12

SITWELL, SACHEVERELL. The Hundred and One Harlequins. London: Grant Richards, 1922. 1st ed. Lavender cl, paper label. Fine in dj (nicked). *Appelfeld*. $75/£48

SITWELL, SACHEVERELL. The Hunters and the Hunted. London: Macmillan, 1947. 1st ed. 16 plts. VG. *Hollett*. $23/£15

SITWELL, SACHEVERELL. The Hunters and the Hunted. London: Macmillan, 1947. 1st ed. VG in dj. *Turtle Island*. $30/£19

SITWELL, SACHEVERELL. The Hunters and the Hunted. NY, 1948. 1st Amer ed. Fine in dj (few sm tears, sl rubbed). *Polyanthos*. $25/£16

SITWELL, SACHEVERELL. Journey to the Ends of Time. Volume 1, Lost in the Dark Wood. NY: Random House, (1959). 1st Amer ed. (Ink stamp), else Fine in NF dj. *Hermitage*. $30/£19

SITWELL, SACHEVERELL. Journey to the Ends of Time. Volume One: Lost in the Dark Wood. London: Cassell, (1959). 1st ed. One of 3041 ptd. VG (sig, foxed; lt dampstain rear cvr) in dj (wear, interior stain, price-clipped). *Antic Hay*. $50/£32

SITWELL, SACHEVERELL. Liszt. Boston, 1934. 1st Amer ed. Fine in dj (spine sunned, sm piece missing, torn; sl rubbed). *Polyanthos*. $35/£22

SITWELL, SACHEVERELL. Monks, Nuns, and Monasteries. NY: Holt, Rinehart, & Winston, (1965). 1st US ed. 8 color plts. VG (bkpl) in dj. *Turtle Island*. $35/£22

SITWELL, SACHEVERELL. Morning, Noon and Night in London. London, 1948. 1st Eng ed. Very Nice in dj. *Clearwater*. $39/£25

SITWELL, SACHEVERELL. Portugal and Madeira. London, 1954. 1st ed. Dj (sl torn). *Hatchwell*. $23/£15

SITWELL, SACHEVERELL. Portugal and Madeira. London: Batsford, 1954. 1st ed. NF in dj (sm spine tear, extrems sl rubbed, price-clipped). *Polyanthos*. $25/£16

SITWELL, SACHEVERELL. Spain. 1950. 1st ed. VG in dj (closed tears). *Words Etc*. $23/£15

SITWELL, SACHEVERELL. Splendours and Miseries. London: Faber & Faber, (1943). 1st ed. Yellow cl. VG in dj (edges browned, sl chipped). *Turtle Island*. $35/£22

SITWELL, SACHEVERELL. Splendours and Miseries. London: Faber, 1946. 16 plts. VG in dj. *Hollett*. $23/£15

SITWELL, SACHEVERELL. Tropical Birds from Plates by John Gould. London: Batsford, 1948. 1st ed. 16 full-pg color repros. VG+ in VG+ dj. *Mikesh*. $35/£22

SITWELL, SACHEVERELL. Truffle Hunt. London: Hale, 1953. 1st ed. 30 plts. (Eps lt spotted; sl faded, sm mk upper bd.) Dj (spine faded, edges chipped, worn). *Hollett*. $47/£30

SITWELL, SACHEVERELL. Two Poems, Ten Songs. London: Duckworth, 1929. 1st ed, ltd issue. One of 275 numbered, signed. Cl, dec bds. (Corners bumped), else VG. *Reese*. $35/£22

Six Months in the Ranks. (By Eustace Grenville Murray.) London: Smith, Elder, 1881. 1st ed. iv,362pp (lib stamps tp, text leaves; hinges cracked). Maroon cl. *Burmester*. $78/£50

Six Photographers: An Exhibition of Contemporary Photography. Urbana: Univ of IL, 1961. 6 full-pg b/w photos. (Owner stamp), else NF in stiff wrappers. *Cahan*. $30/£19

Sixteenth Century Italian Drawings from the Collection of Janos Scholz. Washington: Nat'l Gallery of Art, 1973. 113 plts. Good. *Washton*. $25/£16

SIZE, NICHOLAS. The Secret Valley. London: Warne, n.d. 4th ed. Map frontis. Uncut. VG in dj (spotted). *Hollett*. $23/£15

SKAAR, GRACE. Nothing but Cats, Cats, Cats. NY: Wm. R. Scott, 1947. 1st ed. 9 1/4 x 8. 20pp. Pict bds, plastic comb binding. VG. *Cattermole*. $65/£42

SKAAR, GRACE. A Very Little Dog. NY: Scott, 1949. 1st ed. 9x8. 12pp. Pict bds. VG. *Cattermole*. $50/£32

SKARSTEN, M. O. George Drouillard, Hunter and Interpreter for Lewis and Clark and Fur Trader, 1807-1810. Clark, 1964. 1st ed. 2 fldg maps. Fine. *Oregon*. $100/£64

SKEAT, WALTER W. An Etymological Dictionary of the English Language. Oxford: Clarendon, 1882. 1st ed. (ii),xxviii,(i),799pp. Cl bds, morocco spine, gilt. *Bickersteth*. $94/£60

SKEAT, WALTER W. An Etymological Dictionary of the English Language. Oxford: Clarendon, 1882. 1st ed. xxviii,799pp. Pub's cl (shelfworn). *Oinonen**. $100/£64

SKEAT, WALTER W. An Etymological Dictionary of the English Language. Oxford, 1898. 3rd ed. xxxiv,844pp. 1/2 morocco, grained cl sides. VG. *Cox*. $70/£45

SKELTON, CHRISTOPHER (comp). The Engraved Bookplates of Eric Gill 1908-1940. Private Libraries Assoc, 1986. 1st ed. One of 400 (of 1000). Red cl. Fine in dj. *Heller*. $55/£35

SKELTON, CHRISTOPHER (comp). The Engraved Bookplates of Eric Gill 1908-1940. Pinner: Private Libraries Assoc, 1986. 1st ed. One of 400 (of 1000). Red cl. Fine in dj. *House*. $50/£32

SKELTON, CHRISTOPHER. The Engravings of Eric Gill. Wellingborough: Skelton, 1983. One of 1350. Blind-stamped buckram bds. VF in slipcase. *Michael Taylor*. $390/£250

SKELTON, R. A. Decorative Printed Maps of the 15th to 18th Centuries. London: Staples, (1952). 84 full-pg plts. Fine in dj (hole fr cvr, spotted). *Oak Knoll*. $125/£80

Sketch of the Life and Public Services of William Henry Harrison. NY: NY Express, 1839. 32pp, stitched. (Lt dknd, foxed, edgeworn.) Howes J20. *Bohling*. $25/£16

Sketches and Incidents; or, A Budget from the Saddle-Bags of a Superannuated Itinerant. (By Abel Stevens.) NY: Carleton, (1843). 1st ed. 363,(4)pp (lacks fep). Orig cl. Howes S952. *Ginsberg*. $125/£80

Sketches of History, Life, and Manners, in the United States. (By Anne Royall.) New Haven, 1826. Frontis. 19th-cent 1/2 sheep (worn). Howes R485. *Swann**. $230/£147

SKINNER, E. M. The Modern Organ. NY, 1917. Paper over bds, linen spine. Good. *Scribe's Perch**. $20/£13

SKINNER, H. B. The Family Doctor, or Guide to Health...with 71 Valuable Recipes. Boston: The Author, 1844. 1st ed. 54pp. VG in orig ptd wrappers. *Argosy*. $50/£32

SKINNER, HENRY. The Origin of Medical Terms. Balt, 1949. 1st ed. (Underlining few ll), o/w Fine. *Fye*. $125/£80

SKINNER, MILTON P. and JOHN WARREN. A Guide to the Winter Birds of the North Carolina Sandhills. Albany, 1928. 13 color plts. (Cl lt dampstained.) *Edwards*. $31/£20

SKINNER, W. E. Mind Reading. Boston: A.B. Courtney, 1896. VG in self wraps, sewn. *Dramatis Personae*. $25/£16

SKINNER, W. E. (comp). The Wizard's Manual. NY: W.S. Trigg, 1892. 1st ed. Pulp paper (lt browned). VG in stapled pict grn wraps (upper joint chipped). *Dramatis Personae*. $50/£32

SKREBNESKI, VICTOR. Skrebneski Portraits: A Matter of Record. NY: Doubleday, 1978. 1st ed. 64 b/w plts. VG in dj (dknd strip fr panel). *Cahan*. $75/£48

SKREBNESKI, VICTOR. Skrebneski. NY: Ridge Press, 1969. 1st ed. (Name stamp), else Fine in ptd stiff wrappers, pub's slipcase (2 sides broken). *Cahan*. $150/£96

SKUES, G. E. M. Itchen Memories. Jenkins, (1951). 1st ed. Fine in dj. *Petersfield*. $62/£40

SKUES, G. E. M. Minor Tactics of a Chalk Stream. London, 1924. 3rd ed. (Fore-edges sl foxed), o/w VG in dj. *Petersfield*. $59/£38

SKUES, G. E. M. Nymph Fishing for Chalk Stream Trout. 1939. 1st ed. Color frontis, 2 plts. (Prelims lt browned.) Dj (chipped). *Edwards*. $70/£45

SKUES, G. E. M. Nymph Fishing for Chalk Stream Trout. London, 1939. 1st ed. Color frontis. Fine in dj. *Petersfield*. $125/£80

SKUES, G. E. M. The Way of a Trout With a Fly. London, 1935. 3rd ed. 1/2 grn morocco. *Petersfield*. $90/£58

SKVORECKY, JOSEF. The Engineer of Human Souls. NY: Knopf, 1984. 1st US ed. NF in VG+ dj (nick). *Lame Duck*. $35/£22

SKVORECKY, JOSEF. The Engineer of Human Souls. NY: Knopf, 1984. 1st Amer ed. Signed. Fine in dj (sl rubbed). *Between The Covers*. $85/£54

SKVORECKY, JOSEF. The Republic of Whores. (NJ): Ecco Press, (1971). 1st ed. Fine in dj. *Antic Hay*. $20/£13

SKVORECKY, JOSEF. Sins for Father Knox. London: Faber, 1989. 1st UK ed. Fine in dj. *Williams*. $28/£18

SLACK, J. H. Practical Trout Culture. NY: Woodward/OJ, 1872. 1st ed. 143pp. 4-pg pub's ad tipped-in after intro. Brn cl, gilt spine. VG. *Bowman*. $30/£19

SLADE, DANIEL. Diphtheria: Its Nature and Treatment with an Account of the History of Its Prevalance.... Phila, 1864. 1st ed. 166pp. VG. *Fye*. $75/£48

SLADEK, JOHN T. The Reproductive System. London, 1968. 1st Eng ed, 1st bk. NF (sl bumped) in dj (sl rubbed). *Clearwater*. $78/£50

SLADEN, DOUGLAS. Queer Things About Japan. London: Tremarne, 1904. 2nd imp. Color frontis. Maroon gilt pict cl. VG. *Terramedia*. $75/£48

SLADEN, DOUGLAS. Sicily. London, 1908. 2nd ed. Fldg map, table. (Lt browned; spine faded, lt spotted.) *Edwards*. $31/£20

SLAFTER, EDMUND F. Sir William Alexander and American Colonization. Boston: Prince Soc, 1873. One of 160. Frontis port, x,283pp; fldg map (1-inch tear). 3/4 red leather (lib name spine foot, scuffed). Howes S539. *Bohling*. $85/£54

SLATER, J. H. How to Collect Books. London, 1905. 1st ed. Fine. *Truepenny*. $45/£29

SLATER, J. H. Robert Louis Stevenson. London: G. Bell, 1914. Brn cl (rubbed, bumped). *Maggs*. $44/£28

SLATER, J. H. The Romance of Book-Collecting. NY: Frances P. Harper, 1898. 1st US ed. (iv),168pp. Fine. *Oak Knoll*. $45/£29

SLATIN PASHA, RUDOLF C. Fire and Sword in the Sudan. F.R. Wingate (trans). London, 1896. 2nd ed. Frontis port, xviii,636pp (upper hinge tender)+ 32pp pub's cat; fldg plan, fldg map. Teg. Illus cl (spine lt sunned, chipped, sm dent fore-edge), gilt. *Edwards*. $94/£60

Slave Laws of Jamaica. London: James Ridgway, 1828. (i-xiii),1pg contents,(1-263)pp. Partly unopened. Old paper-cvrd bds. (Spine chipped, edges curled.) *Metropolitan**. $225/£144

SLAVIN, NEAL. Portugal. NY: Lustrum, 1971. 1st ed, 1st bk. 32 b/w plts. (Owner stamp), else NF in pict stiff wrappers. *Cahan*. $35/£22

SLAVIN, NEAL. When Two or More Are Gathered Together. NY: FSG, 1976. 1st ed. 65 color plts. NF (owner stamp) in Fine dj. *Cahan*. $35/£22

SLEATOR, WILLIAM. The Angry Moon. Boston: Little Brown, 1970. 1st ed. Blair Lent (illus). 9 1/2 x 8 1/4. 48pp. VG in dj. *Cattermole.* $80/£51

Sleeping Beauty. NY: McLoughlin Bros, n.d. (1880s). 1st Amer ed. 10x7. 24 chromolitho transformation pp at center fold. (Adhesion to center pp.) Color pict bds (loose, extrems chipped, spine perished). *King.* $75/£48

SLEIGH, BERNARD. Wood Engraving Since Eighteen-Ninety. London: Pitman, 1932. 1st ed. VG (lacks dj). *Michael Taylor.* $59/£38

SLESINGER, TESS. Time, the Present. NY: S&S, 1935. 1st ed. (Sunned), o/w NF in VG dj (chips, tears). *Beasley.* $40/£26

SLIJPER, E. J. Whales. A.J. Pomerans (trans). Ithaca: Cornell Univ, (1979). 2nd rev ed. Fine in Fine dj. *Mikesh.* $55/£35

SLIJPER, E. J. Whales: The Biology of the Cetaceans. A.J. Pomerans (trans). NY: Basic, 1962. 1st ed. Rev laid in. Cl, dec bds. Fine in VG + dj. *Mikesh.* $47/£30

SLIVE, SEYMOUR. Frans Hals. London, 1970-1974. 3 vols. Color frontis; 352 plts vol 2. Good in djs. *Washton.* $500/£321

SLOAN, JOHN. John Sloan's New York Scene. Bruce St. John (ed). NY: Harper & Row, (1965). 1st ed. Fine in dj (lt chipped, soiled). *Hermitage.* $45/£29

SLOAN, SAMUEL. Sloan's Homestead Architecture.... Phila: J.P. Lippincott, 1861. 1st ed. 355pp. Sound (cl soiled). *M&s.* $450/£288

SLOANE, HANS. An Account of a Most Efficacious Medicine for Soreness, Weakness, and Several Other Distempers of the Eyes. Dublin: James Hoey, 1762. 4th ed. (i),17(47-54)pp (lt marginal browning). Later bds. *White.* $273/£175

SLOANE, JOSEPH C. French Painting Between the Past and the Present. Princeton, 1951. Good in dj. *Washton.* $150/£96

SLOCOMBE, GEORGE. The Dangerous Sea. NY: Macmillan, 1937. 1st ed. (Sl rubbed), o/w VG. *Worldwide.* $22/£14

SLOCUM, FRANK. Classic Baseball Cards. NY, (1987). 1st ed. (Sl worn.) Dj. *Oinonen*.* $70/£45

SMALE, M. and J. F. COLYER. Diseases and Injuries of the Teeth Including Pathology and Treatment. 1893. xiii,423pp (sl foxed, few pp coming loose; spine worn, cl mkd, joint cracked). *Whitehart.* $39/£25

SMALL, JOHN W. Scottish Architectural Details. Gibbings, 1901. #65/100. 65 engr plts. VG. *Hadley.* $106/£68

SMALL, TUNSTALL and CHRISTOPHER WOODBRIDGE. Architectural Turned Woodwork of the 16th, 17th, and 18th Centuries. London/NY: Architectural Press/William Helburn, (ca 1930). 1st ed. 1 folded folio sheet; 20 b/w plts. Loose as issued. VG in lt grn portfolio, grn cl ties (mostly faded). *Houle.* $150/£96

SMALL, TUNSTALL and CHRISTOPHER WOODBRIDGE. English Brickwork Details 1450-1750. Architectural Press, n.d. 20 plts. Unbound as issued, card case w/ties. (Sl faded.) *Edwards.* $55/£35

SMALL, TUNSTALL and CHRISTOPHER WOODBRIDGE. Houses of the Wren and Early Georgian Periods. London: Archit. Press, 1928. (Hole in spine, cvr spotted.) Internally Good. *Ars Artis.* $70/£45

SMALL, TUNSTALL and CHRISTOPHER WOODBRIDGE. Mouldings of the Wren and Georgian Periods. Architectural Press, n.d. 20 plts. Unbound as issued. Card slipcase (worn) w/ties. *Edwards.* $47/£30

Smaller House: Being Selected Examples of the Latest Practice in Modern English Domestic Architecture. London: Architectural Press, 1924. 1st ed. Cream cl (lt soiled, worn), bds (skinned). VG. *House.* $150/£96

SMALLEY, EUGENE V. History of the Northern Pacific Railroad. NY, 1883. xxiv,437pp; fldg profile, fldg map in rear pocket. VG (lt shelfworn, spine ends lt frayed). Howes S561. *Bohling.* $150/£96

SMART, CHRISTOPHER. The Collected Poems. Norman Callan (ed). London: Routledge, 1949. 1st ed. 2 vols. Good. *Cox.* $47/£30

SMART, ELIZABETH. By Grand Central Station I Sat Down and Wept. London: Editions Poetry, 1945. 1st Eng ed. (Sl faded.) *Clearwater.* $39/£25

SMART, HAWLEY. The Great Tontine. Volumes 1-3. London: Chapman, 1881. 1st ed. Inscribed. (Spines dknd, extrems frayed.) *Metropolitan*.* $63/£40

SMART, JOHN. A Handbook for the Identification of Insects of Medical Importance. London: British Museum, 1948. 2nd ed. Color frontis, 12 plts. Errata slip laid in. VG. *Glaser.* $75/£48

SMEATON, JOHN. John Smeaton's Diary...from the Original MS in the Library of Trinity House, London. Leamington Spa: Newcomen Soc, 1938. 1st ed. Frontis port, fldg map, facs plt. Teg. Orig 1/2 vellum, linen bds. Fine. *Glaser.* $100/£64

SMEATON, OLIPHANT. The Story of Edinburgh. London, 1905. Fldg map. Gilt-dec cl (sl shaken; spine sl discolored, lt soiling upper bd due to label removal). *Edwards.* $16/£10

SMEDLEY, HAROLD HINSDILL. Presenting Fly Patterns and Their Origins. Muskegon: Westshore, 1943. 1st ed. Errata slip tipped in. VG + (mks fr pastedown) in VG dj (sm pieces torn corners). *Backman.* $100/£64

SMEDLEY, R. C. History of the Underground Railroad in Chester and the Neighboring Counties of Pennsylvania. Lancaster: Ptd at the Office of The Journal, 1883. 1st ed. xxiv,25-407pp. (Cl worn, rubbed, soiled, spine chipped), else Good. *Brown.* $95/£61

SMEJKAL, FRANTISEK. Surrealist Drawings. London: Octopus Books, (1974). Fine in dj (lt worn, soiled). *Hermitage.* $65/£42

SMELLIE, WILLIAM. The Philosophy of Natural History. Edinburgh: Heirs of Charles Elliot et al, 1790-1799. 1st ed. 2 vols. 4to. xiii,547; xii,515pp (few margins stained). Contemp calf (sl worn, vol 1 lacks spine label). VG. *Glaser.* $485/£311

SMELLIE, WILLIAM. Set of Anatomical Tables, with Explanations, and an Abridgement, of the Practice of Midwifery. London, 1754. 1st ed. Atlas folio. 39 Splendid copper plts. Later 1/4 calf, boxed (sl soiled, stained). *Argosy.* $7,500/£4,803

SMILES, SAMUEL. George Moore, Merchant and Philanthropist. London: Routledge, 1878. 2nd ed. xv,530,6pp; etched port. Cl over beveled bds. VG (scattered spotting; spine sl faded). *Hollett.* $86/£55

SMILES, SAMUEL. Robert Dick, Baker, of Thurso, Geologist and Botanist. NY: Harper, 1879. 1st US ed. Frontis port, 436pp. Good (fr hinge starting). *Scribe's Perch*.* $40/£26

SMILEY, JANE. The Age of Grief. NY: Knopf, (1987). 1st ed, 1st bk. Fine in Fine dj. *Unger.* $125/£80

SMILEY, JANE. The Age of Grief. NY, 1987. 1st ed. NF in NF dj. *Warren.* $75/£48

SMILEY, JANE. At Paradise Gate. NY: S&S, (1981). Signed. Fine in Fine dj (lt wear). *Between The Covers.* $250/£160

SMILEY, JANE. Catskill Crafts. NY, 1988. 1st ed. Fine in Fine dj. *Warren.* $40/£26

SMILEY, JANE. Catskill Crafts. Artisans of the Catskill Mountains. NY: Crown, 1988. 1st ed. Fine in Fine dj. *Beasley.* $40/£26

SMILEY, JANE. Ordinary Love and Good Will. NY: Knopf, 1989. 1st ed. Fine in dj. *Lame Duck.* $75/£48

SMILEY, JANE. A Thousand Acres. NY: Knopf, 1991. 1st ed. Fine in Fine dj. *Lame Duck.* $100/£64

SMILLIE, WILSON. Public Health Administration in the United States. NY, 1935. 1st ed. VG. *Fye.* $50/£32

SMILLIE, WILSON. Public Health, Its Promise for the Future...1607-1914. NY, 1955. 1st ed. VG. *Fye.* $75/£48

SMITH, A. DONALDSON. Through Unknown African Countries. London/NY: Edward Arnold, 1897. 1st ed. xvi,471pp + ads; 6 fldg maps. Grey gilt pict cl (recased w/new eps). VG. *Terramedia.* $300/£192

SMITH, A. DUNCAN (ed). Trial of Madeleine Smith. London: Sweet & Maxwell, 1905. Grn cl, gilt. Sound (worn). *Boswell.* $125/£80

SMITH, AARON. The Atrocities of the Pirates. (Berkshire: Golden Cockerel, 1929.) One of 500 ptd. Eric Ravilious (engrs). Red bds, linen spine, gilt top. (Sl wear.) *Appelfeld.* $150/£96

SMITH, ABBOTTS. The Hay-Fever, Hay-Asthma, or Summer-Catarrh. London, 1868. 6th ed. 74pp + vi ads. Emb limp cl (spine, edges faded; bd edges sl water-stained), gilt title. *Edwards.* $23/£15

SMITH, ADAM B. Studies in the Anatomy and Surgery of the Nose and Ear. NY, 1918. 1st ed. Inscribed. 51 photo plts. NF. *Doctor's Library.* $125/£80

SMITH, ADAM. Essays on Philosophical Subjects. To Which Is Prefixed, an Account of the Life and Writings...by Dugald Stewart. London/Edinburgh: T. Cadell & W. Davies/W. Creech, 1795. 1st ed. xcv,244pp (tp on paper stub w/dknd edges, sl aged, new eps, blanks). Recent brn calf, old leather-cvrd bds (edges sl worn), leather spine labels. *Baltimore*.* $1,200/£769

SMITH, ADAM. An Inquiry into the Nature and Causes of the Wealth of Nations. Phila: Dobson, 1789-1796-1789. 1st Amer eds of vols I, III. 3 vols. 8vo. Orig uniform calf (scuffed; sigs vols I, II). *Rostenberg & Stern.* $1,400/£897

SMITH, ADAM. An Inquiry into the Nature and Causes of the Wealth of Nations. London: A. Strahan & T. Cadell, 1791. 6th ed. 3 vols. 19th-cent binder's cl (vol 1 recently rebacked, other spine ends sl frayed). (Bound w/o half-titles, sl foxed), o/w Good set. *Reese.* $250/£160

SMITH, ADAM. An Inquiry into the Nature and Causes of the Wealth of Nations. London: A. Strahan & T. Cadell, 1793. 7th ed. 3 vols. (Lt aged, few ll lt damp-stained, ink monogram at tps.) Plain eps, marbled edges. Recent soft dk brn calf, marbled bds (sl rubbed), raised bands, red/black leather spine labels. *Baltimore*.* $200/£128

SMITH, ADAM. An Inquiry into the Nature and Causes of the Wealth of Nations. London: A. Strahan, T. Cadell, 1793. 7th ed. 3 vols. (Lt browned). Contemp tree calf (sl worn, sl loss extrems, bd repaired, rebacked), gilt-ruled raised bands, orig title labels, new morocco vol # labels. *Edwards.* $585/£375

SMITH, ADAM. An Inquiry into the Nature and Causes of the Wealth of Nations. London: for many, 1819. 3 vols. Pub's orig blue bds (outer hinges rubbed), white paper spines (heads 2 spines rubbed w/loss), orig ptd paper spine labels. Fine set. *D & D.* $750/£481

SMITH, ADAM. An Inquiry into the Nature and Causes of the Wealth of Nations. London, 1863. New ed. Frontis, lxvi,669pp. (Hinges tender, rubbed, sl cl loss.) *Edwards.* $117/£75

SMITH, ALBERT. A Month at Constantinople. London: David Bogue, 1850. 1st ed. Hand-colored frontis, (2),xii,236pp (sm strip of brn reinforcing paper along tp inner edge). Aeg. Later full plum morocco, gilt. *Karmiole.* $125/£80

SMITH, ALEXANDER. Dreamthorp. Strahan, 1863. 1st ed. viii,296pp, pub's cat. Grn ribbed cl, blocked in blind/gilt, spine gilt. Fine. *Bickersteth.* $86/£55

SMITH, ALFRED E. Up to Now. NY: Viking, 1929. Stated 1st ptg. #907/1485. Signed. Paper over bds, gilt vellum spine (cracks). Good-. *Scribe's Perch*.* $20/£13

SMITH, ALICE R. HUGER and D. E. HUGER. The Dwelling Houses of Charleston. Phila: Lippincott, 1917. 1st ed. 1000 ptd, many destroyed by fire. Very Nice (bkpl) in dec cl. Howes S571. *Captain's Bookshelf.* $200/£128

SMITH, ALSON J. Men Against the Mountains. Jedediah Smith and the South West Expedition of 1826-1829. NY: John Day, (1965). 1st ed. Fine in pict dj. *Argonaut.* $50/£32

SMITH, AMANDA. An Autobiography. Chicago: Meyer & Brother, 1893. 1st ed. Frontis port. Fine. *Between The Covers.* $350/£224

SMITH, AMANDA. An Autobiography...Mrs. Amanda Smith, the Colored Evangelist.... Chicago: Meyer & Bro, 1893. 1st ed. 506pp; engr port, guard; 25 plts. Gilt-pict maroon cl. VG. *Petrilla.* $125/£80

SMITH, BENJAMIN T. Private Smith's Journal Recollections of the Late War. Chicago: Lakeside, 1963. 1st ed. (Eps sl stained), else VG. *Mcgowan.* $45/£29

SMITH, BRADLEY. Japan, a History in Art. NY: S&S, 1964. One of 500 signed. Silk brocade, gilt. Fine. *Cullen.* $150/£96

SMITH, BRADLEY. Japan: A History in Art. Gemini, 1964. 1st ed. Inscribed. Fine. *Whittle.* $39/£25

SMITH, CHARLES EDWARD. From the Deep of the Sea. London: A&C Black, 1922. Fldg map. Dec cl. (Lacks fep), else VG. *High Latitude.* $40/£26

SMITH, CHARLES JOHN. Historical and Literary Curiosities. London, 1875. 100 plts. 1/2 straight-grained morocco. VG. *Argosy.* $125/£80

SMITH, CHARLES M. From Andersonville to Freedom. Providence, RI, 1894. 1st ed. Ltd to 250. PNRISSHS Series 5, #3. 74pp. NF in ptd wrappers. *Mcgowan.* $45/£29

SMITH, CHARLES V. L. Electronic Digital Computers. NY: McGraw-Hill, 1959. 1st ed. NF. *Glaser.* $85/£54

SMITH, CLARK ASHTON. The Abominations of Yondo. Sauk City, 1960. 1st ed. VG in VF dj. *Mcclintock.* $125/£80

SMITH, CLARK ASHTON. The Black Book of Clark Ashton Smith. Donald Sydney-Fryer and R. A. Hoffman (eds). Sauk City, (1979). 1st ed. Pb. Fine. *Mcclintock.* $35/£22

SMITH, CLARK ASHTON. The Dark Chateau: And Other Poems. Sauk City: Arkham House, 1951. 1st ed. One of 563 ptd. NF in As New dj. *Other Worlds.* $650/£417

SMITH, CLARK ASHTON. Genius Loci and Other Tales. Sauk City, WI: Arkham House, 1948. One of 3047. NF in dj (lt soiled). *Bernard.* $150/£96

SMITH, CLARK ASHTON. Genius Loci and Other Tales. Sauk City: Arkham House, 1948. 1st ed. Dj. *Swann*.* $115/£74

SMITH, CLARK ASHTON. Genius Loci and Other Tales. Sauk City: Arkham House, 1948. 1st ed. Fine in NF dj (sl dkng). *Other Worlds.* $200/£128

SMITH, CLARK ASHTON. Grotesques and Fantastiques. Gerry de la Ree, 1973. 1st ed. Fine in wraps. *Certo.* $35/£22

SMITH, CLARK ASHTON. Klarkash-Ton and Monstro Ligriv. Gerry de la Ree, 1974. One of 500 numbered. (1st, last pp lt foxed.) NF in wraps. *Certo.* $30/£19

SMITH, CLARK ASHTON. Lost Worlds. London: Spearman, (1971). 1st thus. Fine in dj (price-clipped, lt edgeworn). *Other Worlds.* $45/£29

SMITH, CLARK ASHTON. Lost Worlds. Sauk City: 1944. 1st ed. NF in dj (price-clipped, rear panel edges, spine faded). *Certo.* $235/£151

SMITH, CLARK ASHTON. Other Dimensions. Arkham House, 1970. 1st ed. Fine in Fine dj. Certo. $65/£42

SMITH, CLARK ASHTON. Other Dimensions. Sauk City: Arkham House, 1970. 1st ed. One of 3000. VF in VF dj. Kane*. $80/£51

SMITH, CLARK ASHTON. Out of Space and Time. London: Neville Spearman, (1971). 1st Eng ed. Fine in NF dj (sl corner wear). Certo. $40/£26

SMITH, CLARK ASHTON. Poems in Prose. Sauk City: Arkham, 1964. 1st ed. Fine (sl shelfwear) in dj (spine browned). Metropolitan*. $115/£74

SMITH, CLARK ASHTON. Selected Poems. Sauk City: Arkham House, 1971. 1st ed. Dj. Swann*. $80/£51

SMITH, CLARK ASHTON. Spells and Philtres. Sauk City: Arkham House, 1958. 1st ed. One of 519. Fine in NF dj (spine browned). Other Worlds. $525/£337

SMITH, CLARK ASHTON. Tales of Science and Sorcery. Sauk City: Arkham House, 1964. 1st ed. VG + in NF dj. Other Worlds. $90/£58

SMITH, CLEVELAND H. and GERTRUDE R. TAYLOR. United States Service Symbols. NY, 1942. 1st ed. Pict cvr. Fine. Pratt. $32/£21

SMITH, CORNELIUS C., JR. Emilio Kosterlitzky, Eagle of Sonora and the Southwest Border. Glendale, 1970. 1st ed. VG + . Pratt. $50/£32

SMITH, CYRIL STANLEY (ed). Sources for the History of the Science of Steel, 1532-1786. Cambridge: MIT, (1968). 1st ed. 9 plts. Fine in dj. Glaser. $65/£42

SMITH, D. and R. EASTON. California Condor, Vanishing American, Etc. Charl./S.B.: McNally, 1964. 1st ed. Dec cl. NF in NF dj. Mikesh. $30/£19

SMITH, DAMA MARGARET. I Married a Ranger. Stanford, 1931. 1st ed. (Sl faded), else VG in dj (tattered). Five Quail. $25/£16

SMITH, DAVE. In the House of the Judge. NY, 1983. 1st Amer ed. Fine in dj (sl rubbed). Polyanthos. $25/£16

SMITH, DAVID E. and JOHN LUCE. Love Needs Care. Boston: Little, Brown, 1971. 1st ed. VG in dj. Sclanders. $31/£20

SMITH, DAVID EUGENE and YOSHIO MIKAMI. A History of Japanese Mathematics. Chicago: Open Court, 1914. 1st ed. Fine. Glaser. $95/£61

SMITH, DAVID EUGENE. Rara Arithmetica. Boston/London, 1908. Unopened. VG. Truepenny. $175/£112

SMITH, DAVID EUGENE. Rara Arithmetica. Boston: Ginn, 1908. 1st ed. 9 plts. Paper label. VG. Glaser. $200/£128

SMITH, DAVID. Victorian Maps of the British Isles. Batsford, 1985. 1st ed. 8 color plts. Dj. Edwards. $39/£25

SMITH, DE COST. Martyrs of the Oblong and Little Nine. Caldwell, 1948. 1st ed. Dec cl. NF in dj (price-clipped). Baade. $40/£26

SMITH, DE COST. Martyrs of the Oblong and Little Nine. Caldwell, ID: Caxton, 1948. 1st ed. Ltd to 1000. Many pp unopened. VG in dj. Lien. $75/£48

SMITH, DENNIS. Firehouse. GC: Doubleday, 1977. 1st ed. Fine in illus dj. Cahan. $35/£22

SMITH, DODIE. The Starlight Barking. London: Heinemann, 1967. 1st ed. Anne and Janet Grahame-Johnstone (illus). 5 3/4 x 8 1/2. 145pp. Fine in dj. Cattermole. $45/£29

SMITH, DONALD L. The Twenty-Fourth Michigan of the Iron Brigade. Harrisburg, (1962). 1st ed. Good in dj. King. $50/£32

SMITH, DONALD L. The Twenty-Fourth Michigan of the Iron Brigade. Harrisburg, PA, (1962). 1st ed. Fine in Fine dj. Mcclintock. $45/£29

SMITH, DWIGHT L. (ed). John D. Young and the Colorado Gold Rush. Chicago: Lakeside Classic, 1969. 1st ed. Map. Blue cl. Fine. Parmer. $40/£26

SMITH, DWIGHT L. (ed). John D. Young and the Colorado Gold Rush. Chicago: Lakeside, 1969. Fine. Cahan. $20/£13

SMITH, DWIGHT L. (ed). John D. Young and the Colorado Gold Rush. Chicago: Lakeside, Christmas, 1969. Dk blue cl. Fine. Sadlon. $25/£16

SMITH, E. On the Wasting Diseases of Infants and Children. 1870. 2nd ed. xxiii,309pp. (Sm ink sig half-title, few fox-mks; rebound w/orig spine laid on.) Whitehart. $62/£40

SMITH, E. BALDWIN. Architectural Symbolism of Imperial Rome and the Middle Ages. Princeton, 1956. Good in dj. Washton. $125/£80

SMITH, E. BALDWIN. Egyptian Architecture as Cultural Expression. NY: Appleton-Century, 1938. 77 plts. (Lt ex-lib mks; front edge rubbed.) Archaeologia. $95/£61

SMITH, E. C. A Short History of Naval and Marine Engineering. Cambridge, 1937. 16 plts. (Cl sl stained), o/w VG. Whitehart. $39/£25

SMITH, EDGAR W. (ed). Profile by Gaslight: An Irregular Reader.... NY: S&S, 1944. 2nd ptg, April 1944, stated. VG in Good dj (backstrip faded, 1-inch piece missing). This ed w/Wolff eps. Gravesend. $65/£42

SMITH, EDMUND BANKS. Governors Island. NY, 1923. Inserted photo. (Sm tear spine crown, sl worn, sm stains.) Wantagh. $35/£22

SMITH, EDMUND W. The One-Eyed Poacher of Privilege. NY: Derrydale, (1941). Ltd to 750 signed. Additionally signed, inscribed. VG. Truepenny. $150/£96

SMITH, EDMUND W. Tall Tales and Short. NY, (1938). One of 950. 10 plts. Kane*. $80/£51

SMITH, EDMUND W. Tall Tales and Short. NY: Derrydale, (1938). Ltd to 950. Fine. Truepenny. $125/£80

SMITH, EDMUND W. A Tomato Can Chronicle and Other Stories of Fishing and Shooting. NY: Derrydale, (1937). Ltd to 950. VG. Truepenny. $100/£64

SMITH, EDMUND W. A Tomato Can Chronicle. NY, (1937). One of 950. 6 plts. Kane*. $50/£32

SMITH, EDWARD E. Children of the Lens. Fantasy, 1954. 1st binding of gilt-lettered blue cl. NF in dj (sm tears rear panel, spine ends sl worn). Certo. $90/£58

SMITH, EDWARD E. First Lensman. Fantasy, 1950. 1st ed. VG (pastedowns browned) in dj (rear panel soiled, chip). Certo. $35/£22

SMITH, EDWARD E. Galactic Patrol. Fantasy, 1950. 1st ed. NF in NF dj. Certo. $75/£48

SMITH, EDWARD E. Galactic Patrol. Reading: Fantasy, 1950. 1st ed. Dj (chipped, rubbed). Swann*. $161/£103

SMITH, EDWARD E. Gray Lensman. Fantasy, 1951. 1st ed. NF (pastedowns sl browned) in early dj w/3 titles on rear and $3.00 overptd price (sm tears, rear panel soiled). Certo. $60/£38

SMITH, EDWARD E. Gray Lensman. Gnome Press, 1951. 1st Gnome ed. NF in NF dj. Aronovitz. $30/£19

SMITH, EDWARD E. The Lensman Series. Reading, PA: Fantasy Press, 1948-1954. 1st ed, 1st issue bindings and djs. 6 vols (complete). NF (few edges, 1 spine soiled) in djs (few chipped ends, some rubbed, creased). Waverly*. $385/£247

SMITH, EDWARD E. Second Stage Lensmen. Fantasy Press, 1953. 1st ed. Fine in dj. Aronovitz. $95/£61

SMITH, EDWARD E. Skylark of Valeron. Fantasy, 1949. 1st ed. NF (eps sl browned) in dj (rear panel soiled). Certo. $60/£38

SMITH, EDWARD E. Subspace Explorers. Canaveral, 1965. 1st ed. Fine in dj. Madle. $45/£29

SMITH, ELIAS. The American Physician, and Family Assistant. Boston: R. True, 1837. 4th ed. Frontis port, 274pp. Full contemp calf, leather label. (Inner fr hinge weak.) M&s. $150/£96

SMITH, ELIZABETH OAKES. Selections from the Autobiography of.... Mary Alice Wyman (ed). Lewiston, ME, (1924). Slip bound in. Grn cl (lt spots), gilt. VG. Bohling. $30/£19

SMITH, EMORY EVANS. The Golden Poppy. Palo Alto, CA: (SF News Co), 1902. 1st ed. Color frontis. Dec grn cl, gilt. Good. Karmiole. $60/£38

SMITH, F. HOPKINSON. Charcoals of New and Old New York. GC: Doubleday-Page, 1912. 23 tipped-in b/w plts. Mostly unopened. Cl-backed bds. VG. New Hampshire*. $40/£26

SMITH, FAY et al. Father Kino in Arizona. Phoenix, 1966. 1st ed. Fldg map. VF. No dj as issued. Turpen. $45/£29

SMITH, FREDERICK H. Rocks, Minerals and Stocks. Chicago: Railway Review, 1882. 234pp + ads. (Lt worn.) Dawson. $75/£48

SMITH, G. C. MOORE. The Life of John Colborne, Field-Marshal Lord Seaton. London, 1903. Maroon cl (spotted). Maggs. $125/£80

SMITH, G. ELLIOT and WARREN DAWSON. Egyptian Mummies. NY: Dial, 1924. 1st Amer ed. Teg. Blue cl. Appelfeld. $125/£80

SMITH, G. GREGORY (ed). Elizabethan Critical Essays. Clarendon, 1904. 1st ed. 2 vols. (Name, label on pastedown; cl sl mkd), o/w NF. Poetry Bookshop. $94/£60

SMITH, G. M. Crytogamic Botany. NY, 1938. 2 vols. viii,545; vii,380pp. Buckram. Good. Henly. $39/£25

SMITH, G. W. and C. JUDAH. Life in the North During the Civil War. Albuquerque: Univ of NM, 1966. 1st ed. Fine in Good dj (rubbed, torn). Archer. $20/£13

SMITH, GEORGE A. The Illustrated History of Rome. Phila, 1884. 52 steel-engr plts. (Sl foxing.) Orig morocco (rubbed). Freeman*. $110/£71

SMITH, GEORGE A. The Rise, Progress and Travels of the Church.... Liverpool, 1873. 3rd ed. 70pp (2 names, tp corners chipped). VG- in wraps (separated, chipped). Benchmark. $60/£38

SMITH, GEORGE A. The Rise, Progress, and Travels of the Church of Jesus Christ of Latter-Day Saints. Salt Lake City, 1872. 2nd ed. 71pp. Wraps (cvrs sl rubbed, soiled, lt rubber stamp). King. $125/£80

SMITH, GEORGE W. History of Illinois and Her People. Chicago: American Hist., 1927. 1st ed. 6 vols. Ginsberg. $300/£192

SMITH, GEORGE. Assyrian Discoveries. NY: Scribner, Armstrong, 1875. 4th ed. xviii,461,12pp; fldg illus, 4 full-pg illus. (Rubbed, spine tears), o/w VG. Worldwide. $75/£48

SMITH, GEORGE. Assyrian Discoveries...on the Site of Nineveh, During 1873 and 1874. NY: Scribner, Armstrong, 1875. 1st Amer ed. Frontis fldg map. Gilt-stamped grn cl. (Bump), else VG. Pacific*. $81/£52

SMITH, GEORGE. The Cabinet-Maker and Upholsterer's Guide. London: Jones, 1826. Add'l engr title, 147 engr plts (of 153), 2 hand-colored. (Trimmed, spotted, browned.) Contemp olive 1/2 morocco (extrems rubbed), red morocco spine label. Christie's*. $509/£326

SMITH, GOLDWIN. A Letter to a Whig Member of the Southern Independence Association. London: Macmillan, 1864. 1st ed. 76pp. NF in cl wrappers. Mcgowan. $150/£96

SMITH, GUSTAVUS WOODSON. Confederate War Papers, Fairfax Court House, New Orleans, Seven Pines, Richmond and North Carolina. NY: Atlantic, 1884. 1st ed. 381pp. VG. Howes S599. Mcgowan. $250/£160

SMITH, H. Formulae Medica Mentorum. 1772. xxxviii,164pp. Old calf (corners worn). Whitehart. $281/£180

SMITH, H. CLIFFORD. Buckingham Palace. London: Country Life, (1930). Frontis port, 351 monochrome, 3 color plts. Deckled edges. VF in dj (sm repair). Europa. $148/£95

SMITH, H. CLIFFORD. The Panelled Rooms. IV. London: HMSO, 1915. 15 plts. (Bds sl mkd.) Hollett. $70/£45

SMITH, H. M. Handbook of Amphibians and Reptiles of Kansas. Lawrence: Univ of KS, Sept 1950. 1st ed. Map. VG in color pict wraps. Mikesh. $37/£24

SMITH, H. M. Handbook of Lizards. Ithaca: Comstock, (1949). 41 maps. NF in VG dj. Mikesh. $45/£29

SMITH, HARRY B. A Sentimental Library. N.p.: Privately ptd, 1914. Orig 1/4 vellum. (Spine sl toned, bumped), else Fine in dj (tape-reinforced) and slipcase (soiled, broken). Waverly*. $66/£42

SMITH, HARRY WORCESTER. Life and Sport in Aiken. NY: Derrydale, 1935. Ltd to 950. VG+ in Good dj. October Farm. $165/£106

SMITH, HOMER W. Studies in the Physiology of the Kidney. Lawrence: Univ of KS, 1939. 1st ed. Fldg plt. VG. Glaser. $60/£38

SMITH, HUGH. Letters to Married Ladies. NY: Bliss et al, 1827. 281pp. Uncut. Linen-backed bds (worn), paper label. Good (foxed). Second Life. $250/£160

SMITH, IRA and H. ALLEN. Low and Inside: A Book of Baseball Anecdotes, Oddities and Curiosities. GC: Doubleday, 1949. 1st ed. VG in VG dj (edgeworn). Fuller & Saunders. $15/£10

SMITH, J. CALVIN. The Illustrated Hand-Book, a New Guide for Travelers Through the United States of America.... NY: Sherman & Smith, 1848. 234pp; map hand-colored in outline. (Dampstain lower corner 1st few leaves, map w/few fold breaks; cl rubbed), o/w VG-. Howes S614. New Hampshire*. $300/£192

SMITH, J. CALVIN. The Western Tourist and Emigrant's Guide, with a Compendium Gazetteer.... NY: Colton, 1847. 119,(6)pp; lg fldg color map. Orig cl. Howes S615. Ginsberg. $575/£369

SMITH, J. E. An Introduction to Physiological and Systematical Botany. London, 1826. 5th ed. xxi,435pp; 15 hand-colored plts. 1/2 calf. Fine. Henly. $94/£60

SMITH, J. E. A Sketch of a Tour on the Continent. London, 1793. 3 vols. Bkpl of Thomas Lennard. Contemp tree calf (spines sl worn, scuffed), gilt. Maggs. $203/£130

SMITH, J. M. POWIS. The Origin and History of Hebrew Law. Chicago: Univ of Chicago, (1931). Good in dj (tattered). Archaeologia. $45/£29

SMITH, JAMES EDWARD. English Botany; or, Coloured Figures of British Plants, Vol. XXXV. London: R. Taylor, 1813. 64 (of 72) hand-colored engrs by James Sowerby. Full leather (fr bd off). Interior Clean. Metropolitan*. $201/£129

SMITH, JAMES EDWARD. The English Flora. London: Longman et al, 1828. 2nd ed. 4 vols. xlvi,371; viii,470; viii,512; viii,360pp + 2 ad leaves vols 2 and 4. Good set (spotted) in late 19th-cent vellum-backed bds, morocco labels. Cox. $133/£85

SMITH, JAMES EDWARD. A Grammar of Botany.... NY: James V. Seaman, 1822. 1st Amer ed. 281pp; 21 full-pg litho plts. Plain bds, muslin back (warped, lacks paper label; lt waterstaining throughout). M&s. $300/£192

SMITH, JAMES R. Springs and Wells of Manhattan and the Bronx at the End of the Nineteenth Century. NY Hist Soc, 1938. Binder's cl. Maggs. $25/£16

SMITH, JAMES. An Account of the Remarkable Occurrences in the Life and Travels of Colonel James Smith...in the Years 1755, '56, '57, '58, and '59. Phila, 1831. 2nd ed. 18mo. Orig roan-backed lettered bds (rubbed). Slipcase. Howes S606. *Swann**. $1,035/£663

SMITH, JANET ADAM (ed). Henry James and Robert Louis Stevenson. London: Rupert Hart-Davis, 1948. 1st ed. NF in dj. *Turtle Island*. $35/£22

SMITH, JOHN THOMAS. The Cries of London. London, 1842. 1st ed. 4to. Engr frontis port, 30 hand-colored etched plts. Tan calf (rebacked; bk label), orig backstrip, gilt. *Swann**. $546/£350

SMITH, JOHN. The Congewoi Correspondence. Charles de Boos (ed). Sydney: E.R. Cole, 1874. 3/4 leather (rubbed, bumped, soiled; foxing, name). *Metropolitan**. $115/£74

SMITH, JOHN. The Generall Historie of Virginia, New England and the Summer Isles. Glasgow: James MacLehose, 1907. Ltd to 1000 sets. 2 vols. 3 fldg maps. Largely unopened. (Stamp; tip lt bumped), else VG. *Cahan*. $100/£64

SMITH, JOHN. The Generall Historie of Virginia, New-England and the Summer Isles. Cleveland: World, (1966). Full vellum yapped, w/ties. NF in cl box (sl soiled, lt foxed). *Waverly**. $44/£28

SMITH, JOHN. A Hebrew Grammar, Without Points. Boston, 1803. Contemp 1/4 speckled sheep. (Bkpl.) *Swann**. $126/£81

SMITH, JOHN. Historie of Virginia, New England and the Summer Isles. Bibliotheca Americana Facsimile Ed, 1966. Vellum, ties at fore-edge. Boxed w/pub's descriptive pamphlet. Fine in box. *Old London*. $150/£96

SMITH, JOHN. Newes from the New-World Wherin May Be Seene...the Beastes of the Field, the Fish, and Fowl.... L. Wright (ed). Huntington Lib, Ward Ritchie, 1946. #352/1000. Blue bds. VG. *Price*. $29/£19

SMITH, JOHN. Travels and Works of Captain John Smith...1580-1631. Edward Arber (ed). Edinburgh: John Grant, 1910. 2 vols. 2 ports, 4 fldg maps. 1/2 cl (spines faded, bds sl worn). *Parmer*. $150/£96

SMITH, JOHN. Travels and Works of Captain John Smith...1580-1631. Edward Arber (ed). Edinburgh: John Grant, 1910. 2 vols. 2 ports, 6 fldg maps & plts. Partially unopened. Dk burgundy, gilt. NF. *Parmer*. $250/£160

SMITH, JOSEPH F. Blood Atonement and the Origin of Plural Marriage: A Discussion. Salt Lake, 1905. 1st ed. (Sl waterstained; lacks wraps, glue residue), o/w VG. *Benchmark*. $25/£16

SMITH, JOSEPH F. (comp). Life of Joseph F. Smith, Sixth President of the Church of Jesus Christ of Latter-Day Saints. Salt Lake City: Deseret News, 1938. 1st ed. (Ex-lib, rubberstamp, fr inner hinge cracked), o/w Good. *Brown*. $25/£16

SMITH, JOSEPH H. (ed). Colonial Justice in Western Massachusetts (1639-1702).... Cambridge: Harvard Univ, 1961. *Boswell*. $65/£42

SMITH, JOSEPH, JR. (trans). The Book of Mormon. Lamoni, IA: Reorganized Church, 1874. 12,545pp. Orig roan (rubbed). *M & S*. $150/£96

SMITH, JOSEPH, JR. The Holy Scriptures, Translated and Corrected by the Spirit of Revelation. Phila, 1867. 917(O.T.)+286(N.T.)pp (writing rep, tp chipping, names). Orig full calf (edges, spine worn, corners bumped). VG. *Benchmark*. $350/£224

SMITH, JOSEPH. Old Redstone; Or, Historical Sketches of Western Presbyterianism.... Phila, 1854. 1st ed. 459pp. Howes S621. *Ginsberg*. $125/£80

SMITH, JOSEPH. The Pearl of Great Price. Salt Lake City: Deseret News, 1888. iv,136pp (sm rubber stamp on flyleaf; marginal ink notations). 3 facs (2 fldg). Gilt red cl (lt spotting to fr cvr), else Fine. *Argonaut*. $125/£80

SMITH, JOSHUA TOULMAN. The Discovery of America by the Northmen in the Tenth Century. Boston, 1839. 1st ed. 364pp incl chart, 2 fldg maps. (Foxed, cvrs worn), o/w VG. Howes S633. *New Hampshire**. $80/£51

SMITH, JULIE. New Orleans Mourning. NY: St. Martin's, 1990. 1st ed. Signed. VF in dj. *Mordida*. $65/£42

SMITH, JUSTIN H. Annexation of Texas. NY: Barnes & Noble, 1941. VG+ in dj (lt soiled). Howes S634. *Bohling*. $125/£80

SMITH, JUSTIN H. Our Struggle for the Fourteenth Colony: Canada and the American Revolution. NY: Putnam, 1907. 1st ed. 2 vols. 2 frontispieces. Dec cl. Howes S635. *Ginsberg*. $150/£96

SMITH, JUSTIN H. The Troubadours at Home. NY/London: Putnam/Knickerbocker, 1899. 2 vols. (Lt pencil in margins; sl worn, shaken.) *Waverly**. $22/£14

SMITH, L. WALDEN. Saddles Up. San Antonio, TX: Naylor, 1937. 1st ed. VG in dj. *Lien*. $45/£29

SMITH, LAWRENCE B. American Game Preserve Shooting. NY, (1933). VG (sm nick spine). *Truepenny*. $45/£29

SMITH, LINELL. And Miles to Go. Boston: Little Brown, 1967. 1st ed. VG in Good+ dj. *October Farm*. $45/£29

SMITH, LOGAN PEARSALL. Afterthoughts. London: Constable, 1931. 1st ed. (Edges sl spotted.) Dj (lt spotted). *Hollett*. $19/£12

SMITH, LOGAN PEARSALL. More Trivia. London: Constable, 1922. 1st ed. (Eps lt browned.) Uncut. Dj (torn, defective). *Hollett*. $23/£15

SMITH, LOGAN PEARSALL. Trivia. London: Chiswick, 1902. One of 300 ptd. Canvas-backed bds (stained, mkd, edges sl chafed). *Clearwater*. $78/£50

SMITH, M. The British Amphibians and Reptiles. London: Collins, (1954). Rev ed. 16 color, 16 b/w plts. Fine in VG+ dj. *Mikesh*. $30/£19

SMITH, M. A Geographical View of the Province of Upper Canada. Trenton: Moore & Lake, 1813. 3rd ed. Woodcut frontis, 117pp. Calf-backed marbled bds. (Frontis torn, 1st few ll dampstained, lt foxed; rubbed, worn), else Good. Howes S642. *Cahan*. $125/£80

SMITH, MARIAN W. The Puyallup-Nisqually. NY: Columbia Univ, 1940. 1st ed. (Bkpl), else Fine. *Perier*. $85/£54

SMITH, MARTIN CRUZ. Nightwing. London: Deutsch, 1977. 1st UK ed. Fine in dj. *Williams*. $28/£18

SMITH, MATTHEW HALE. Counsels Addressed to Young Ladies and Young Men, Young Married Persons and Young Parents...April, 1846. Boston: Tappan, Whittemore & Mason, 1850. 6th ed. Frontis facs. Aeg. Gilt/blind-stamped dk brn cl (rubbing). Good. *Houle*. $125/£80

SMITH, MOSES. History of the Adventures and Sufferings of.... Albany, 1814. 1st ed. 2 plts. (Internal spotting.) Contemp sheep (joints, extrems rubbed). *Freeman**. $35/£22

SMITH, MR. and MRS. The Long Slide. NY: Atheneum, 1977. 1st US ed. 11x9. 24pp. Fine in dj. *Cattermole*. $30/£19

SMITH, NAOMI ROYDE. The Idol and the Shrine. London, 1949. 1st ed. NF in NF dj (spine sl sunned). *Polyanthos*. $25/£16

SMITH, NORA ARCHIBALD. Boys and Girls of Bookland. Phila: McKay, (1923). Tall 4to. 11 color plts by Jessie Willcox Smith. Bds (lt worn), pict cvr label. Dj (frayed, edgeworn). *Oinonen**. $130/£83

SMITH, O. H. Early Indiana Trials and Sketches. Cincinnati: Moore, Wilstach, Keys, 1858. (Foxing; emb cl faded.) Sound. *Boswell.* $175/£112

SMITH, O. W. The Book of the Pike. Cincinnati: Stewart Kidd, (1922). Good. *Cullen.* $50/£32

SMITH, PATRICIA R. Effanbee. KY, 1983. Color pict bds (lt faded). *Edwards.* $39/£25

SMITH, ROBERT. The Universal Directory, for Taking Alive and Destroying Rats.... London: J. Walker, 1812. 4th ed. 12mo. 7 copper-engr plts. Mod 1/4 calf, bds (new eps). *Cummins.* $500/£321

SMITH, S. J. (ed). Rowland Ward's Sportsman's Handbook to Collecting and Preserving Trophies and Specimens.... San Antonio: R. Ward, 1988. (12th ed.) Fine in NF dj. *Mikesh.* $27/£17

SMITH, SOL. Theatrical Management in the West and South for Thirty Years. NY: Harper, 1868. 1st ed. Port. (Cl sunned.) Howes S672. *Dramatis Personae.* $100/£64

SMITH, STEVIE. A Good Time Was Had by All. Cape, (1937). 1st ed. VG in VG dj (lower panel sl browned). *Ash.* $289/£185

SMITH, STEVIE. Novel on Yellow Paper. NY: Morrow, 1937. 1st ed, 1st bk. Paper-cvrd bds. VG (eps discolored) in dj (worn, rubbed, sm chips). *Antic Hay.* $150/£96

SMITH, STEVIE. Over the Frontier. Cape, (1938). 1st ed. Good (sm mk top edge, sl spotted) in dj (worn, browned). *Ash.* $133/£85

SMITH, STEVIE. Selected Poems. London: Longmans, 1962. 1st Eng ed. NF in NF dj (spine head rubbed). *Hadley.* $62/£40

SMITH, SYDNEY. Mostly Murder. NY, (1959). 1st ed. Fine in NF dj. *Mcclintock.* $20/£13

SMITH, SYDNEY. Mostly Murder. NY, 1959. VG in dj. *Argosy.* $35/£22

SMITH, SYDNEY. Sermons Preached at St. Paul's Cathedral, the Foundling Hospital, and Several Churches in London. Longman, Brown et al, 1846. 1st ed. xii,429,(1)pp. Marbled eps, edges. Contemp russia (upper hinge weak, partly split), gilt backstrip. *Cox.* $31/£20

SMITH, T. C. From the Memories of Men. Brownwood, TX, (1954). VG + in ptd wraps. *Bohling.* $15/£10

SMITH, T. C. From the Memories of Men. Brownwood, TX: T.C. Smith, 1954. 1st ed. Fine in wraps. *Gibbs.* $25/£16

SMITH, THORNE. The Passionate Witch. Doubleday Doran, 1941. 1st ed. Fine in dj (deeply price-clipped). *Certo.* $75/£48

SMITH, W. HAMBLIN. The Psychology of the Criminal. NY: Robert M. McBride, 1923. 1st US ed. NF. *Beasley.* $45/£29

SMITH, W. ROBERTSON. Kinship and Marriage in Early Arabia. Cambridge, 1885. 1st ed. xiv,322pp (lib stamp tp, not affecting text). Contemp 1/2 morocco, gilt. *Maggs.* $351/£225

SMITH, WALKER C. The Everett Massacre. Chicago: IWW, 1918. 1st ed. Fine. *Beasley.* $85/£54

SMITH, WALLACE. Garden of the Sun. L.A.: Lymanhouse, (1939). 1st ed. Fine (spine faded) in dj (sl chipped). *Argonaut.* $275/£176

SMITH, WALLACE. Oregon Sketches. NY, 1925. Frontis. (Offsetting few pp), else VG in dj (chipped). *Reese.* $35/£22

SMITH, WEBSTER. The Farnese Hours. NY: George Braziller, (1976). Frontis. Brn felt, dec blindstamped. Good in slipcase. *Karmiole.* $65/£42

SMITH, WILLARD K. Bowery Murder. GC: Crime Club, 1929. 1st ed. Fine in dj (heel sl worn), wraparound ad intact. *Metropolitan*.* $97/£62

SMITH, WILLIAM B. On Wheels and How I Came There. NY: Hunt & Eaton, (1892). 1st ed. 338pp. NF. *Mcgowan.* $250/£160

SMITH, WILLIAM B. On Wheels and How I Came There. NY: Hunt & Eaton, 1893. 2nd ed. 338pp. (Cl rubbed.) VG. *Mcgowan.* $200/£128

SMITH, WILLIAM E. and OPHIA D. A Buckeye Titan. Cincinnati: Hist and Philosophical Soc, 1953. 1st ed. (Spine ends sl rubbed.) Dj (sl chipped). *Sadlon.* $30/£19

SMITH, WILLIAM GARDNER. South Street. NY: Farrar, Straus & Young, 1954. 1st ed. VG in dj (price-clipped, sl dusty, few sm chips). *Cahan.* $50/£32

SMITH, WILLIAM HENRY. The St. Clair Papers: The Life and Public Services of Arthur St. Clair.... Cincinnati: Clarke, 1882. 1st ed. 2 vols. Map, 2 ports. Howes S26. *Ginsberg.* $200/£128

SMITH, WILLIAM JAY. The Spectra Hoax. Middleton, CT: Wesleyan Univ, (1961). 1st ed. VG in dj. *Graf.* $28/£18

SMITH, WILLIAM STEVENSON. A History of Egyptian Sculpture and Painting in the Old Kingdom. London: OUP, (1949). 2nd ed. 62 plts (2 color). (Spine foot sl bumped.) *Archaeologia.* $475/£304

SMITH, WILLIAM. A Dictionary of Greek and Roman Antiquities. NY: Harper, 1843. 1st Amer ed. 1124pp (lt foxed). VG (backstrip partly peeled). *Agvent.* $50/£32

SMITH, WILLIAM. The History of the Province of New York.... London: J. Almon, 1776. 2nd ed. viii,160,(12),161-256,(12),257-334pp. Recent 1/2 leather (rebound), label, marbled bds. (Text lt spotted, browned), else VG. Howes S703. *Brown.* $350/£224

SMITH, WILLIAM. A Yorkshireman's Trip to the United States and Canada. London, 1892. 1st ed. (16),317,(3)pp. Dec cl. Howes S701. *Ginsberg.* $150/£96

SMITHER, HARRIET (ed). Journals of the Fourth Congress of the Republic of Texas 1839-1840.... Austin: TX State Library, (1929). 3 vols. Nice set in ptd wrappers. *Bohling.* $70/£45

SMITHERMAN, GENEVA. Talkin and Testifyin. Boston: HMCo, 1977. 1st ed. Fine in dj. *Between The Covers.* $65/£42

SMITHERS, JACK. The Early Life and Vicissitudes of Jack Smithers. Martin Secker, 1939. VG. *Moss.* $31/£20

SMOLAN, RICK. A Day in the Life of Australia. NY: Abrams, 1982. 1st ed. Fine in Fine dj. *Smith.* $65/£42

SMOLLETT, TOBIAS. The Adventures of Peregrine Pickle. London: R. Baldwin, 1776. 2nd ed. 4 vols. Contemp plain calf, gilt. VG. *Macdonnell.* $100/£64

SMOLLETT, TOBIAS. The Adventures of Sir Launcelot Greaves. London: Harrison, 1787. Early ed. 2 vols in 1. 4 steel-engr plts. Contemp 1/2 calf, patterned bds. Good (fr hinge split, soiled, foxed). *Sumner & Stillman.* $75/£48

SMOLLETT, TOBIAS. The Expedition of Humphrey Clinker. London: W. Johnston & B. Collins, 1771. 2nd ed. 3 vols. Contemp calf, labels, gilt. Fine set (sm spine chips). *Macdonnell.* $150/£96

SMOLLETT, TOBIAS. The Expedition of Humphrey Clinker. NY: Harper, 1836. 1st Amer ed. George Cruikshank (illus). Blind-stamped blue-grn cl. VG (ends sl worn, cl discolored). *Sumner & Stillman.* $165/£106

SMOLLETT, TOBIAS. Memoirs of a Lady of Quality. London: P. Davies, 1925. One of 500 numbered (of 550). 1/4 vellum, patterned bds (soiled, worn, lower joints split). Contents VG. *Waverly*.* $33/£21

SMOLLETT, TOBIAS. The Miscellaneous Works. Edinburgh: Mundell, Doig & Stevenson, 1806. 3rd ed. 6 vols. Marbled bds, contemp 3/4 calf, gilt. (Sl rubbed.) *Macdonnell.* $400/£256

SMOLLETT, TOBIAS. Travels Through France and Italy. London: R. Baldwin, 1778. 2 vols. 291;290pp (edges eps, prelims browned), 2 half-titles. Old full sheep (sl rubbed, heads of spine sl frayed), gilt. VG set. *Hollett.* $218/£140

SMOLLETT, TOBIAS. Works. George Saintsbury (ed). Navarre Soc, n.d. (1925). 12 vols. 12 engr frontispieces by George Cruikshank. Neatly bound in 1/2 dk grn morocco gilt, gilt-panelled backs (uniformly faded to dk brn), teg. *Hatchwell.* $468/£300

SMUCKER, ISAAC. History of the Welsh Settlements in Licking County, Ohio. Newark, OH, 1869. 22pp. (Lib stamps tp.) Yellow ptd wraps (worn, soiled, reinforced, stapled in plain protective cvr). *Bohling.* $65/£42

SMUCKER, SAMUEL. The Life of Col. John Charles Fremont.... NY: Miller, Orton & Mulligan, 1856. 1st ed. 493pp (lacks feps, part of last pg). Brn cl (sunned, worn). Good-. *Archer.* $15/£10

SMUCKER, SAMUEL. The Life of Dr. Elisha Kent Kane and of Other Distinguished Americans.... Phila, n.d. 1870s (?). Frontis port. VG (lt worn). *High Latitude.* $25/£16

SMULLYAN, RAYMOND. Alice in Puzzleland. NY: Morrow, 1982. 1st ed. Greer Fitting (illus). 6 3/4 x 9 1/2. 182pp. Cl spine. VG in dj. *Cattermole.* $35/£22

SMYTH, C. PIAZZI. Our Inheritance in the Great Pyramid. London, 1864. Photo frontis, xvi,400pp; color map, 17 plts. (Lt soil, 1 contents leaf chipped, bkpl; spine chipped, sl surface wear, rubbed.) *Edwards.* $47/£30

SMYTH, HENRY D. Atomic Energy for Military Purposes. Princeton Univ, 1945. 1st public ed. Fine (bkpl) in dj (sm lib numbers spine). *Hermitage.* $150/£96

SMYTH, HENRY D. A General Account of the Development of Methods of Using Atomic Energy for Military Purposes...1940-1945. Washington: GPO, 1945. 1st public ed. 8vo. Beautiful in orig ptd wrappers, fldg 1/4 morocco box. *Cummins.* $750/£481

SMYTH, JAMES CARMICHEAL. The Effect of the Nitrous Vapour in Preventing and Destroying Contagion...Jail or Hospital Fever.... Phila: Dobson, 1799. 174pp (foxed, tp corner shaved affecting single letter, tp stamp), fldg table. Early sheep (rebacked). *Goodrich.* $125/£80

SMYTHE, F. S. Edward Whymper. London, (1940). 1st ed. Map. (Rep toned; dent fr cvr, spine sunned.) *King.* $75/£48

SMYTHE, F. S. Kamet Conquered. London, 1932. 1st ed. Fldg map. (Edges foxed; rubbed.) *King.* $75/£48

SMYTHE, F. S. Mountaineering Holiday. London, (1940). 1st ed. (Cvrs dknd.) *King.* $40/£26

SMYTHE, F. S. Mountains in Colour.... London: Max Parrish, 1949. 1st ed. Good in dj (frayed). *Cox.* $39/£25

SMYTHE, F. S. Snow on the Hills. London: A&C Black, 1946. 1st ed. 47 plts. (Sl faded.) *Hollett.* $62/£40

SMYTHE, WILLIAM E. The Conquest of Arid America. NY: Macmillan, 1905. Rev ed. 31 full-pg illus. (Rear inner hinge starting.) *Dawson.* $75/£48

SMYTHIES, BERTRAM E. The Birds of Burma. Edinburgh/London, 1953. 2nd rev ed. 31 color plts, fldg map at rear. Fore/lower edge uncut. (Cl sl dampstained.) Dj (price-clipped, sl chipped). *Edwards.* $172/£110

SMYTHIES, BERTRAM E. The Birds of Burma. London, 1953. 2nd ed. Fldg map, 31 color plts. (Sm tear margin 1 leaf.) Dj (sl worn). *Maggs.* $70/£45

SMYTHIES, E. A. Big Game Shooting in Nepal. Calcutta: Thacker, Spink, 1942. 43 plts (11 color), 2 color fldg maps. VG. *Hollett.* $148/£95

SMYTHIES, OLIVE. Ten Thousand Miles on Elephants. London, 1961. 1st ed. 16 plts. Dj (chipped). *Edwards.* $25/£16

SNAFFLE. The Roedeer. (By Robert Dunkin.) Southampton: Ashford, 1987. One of 200 numbered, signed by Neil McReddie (illus) and Colin McKelvie (intro). 3/4 morocco (lt worn). Slipcase. *Oinonen*.* $50/£32

SNAILHAM, RICHARD. The Blue Nile Revealed. London: C&W, 1970. 1st ed. VG in dj (sl torn). *Worldwide.* $20/£13

SNELLING, WILLIAM. Tales of the Northwest. Univ of MN, 1936. Rpt. Ltd to 1000 numbered. VG. Howes S738. *Oregon.* $35/£22

SNODGRASS, ANTHONY. Early Greek Armour and Weapons from the End of the Bronze Age to 600 B.C. Edinburgh: Edinburgh Univ, (1964). 37 plts. Fine in dj. *Archaeologia.* $150/£96

SNODGRASS, W. D. Autumn Variations. NY: Nadja, (1990). One of 100 numbered, signed. Fine in wrappers. *Dermont.* $75/£48

SNODGRASS, W. D. The Boy Made of Meat. Ewert, 1983. One of 115 numbered, signed by Snodgrass & Gillian Tyler (engrs). Fine in sewn wrappers. *Dermont.* $60/£38

SNODGRASS, W. D. Six Troubador Songs. Providence: Burning Deck, (1977). One of 500. Fine in ptd wrappers. *Dermont.* $35/£22

Snow White. Murrays, (1977). 1st Eng ed. All-Action Treasure Hour Pop-Up Book. Obl 4to. V. Kubasta (illus). 6 lg color pop-ups, some w/moveable parts. Pict bds. VG. *Bookmark.* $44/£28

Snow White. London, 1988. V. Kubasta (illus). 8x10. 5 fan-folded pop-ups (4 w/minor mechanics). Glazed pict bds. VG. *King.* $35/£22

SNOW, C. P. The Conscience of the Rich. Macmillan, 1958. 1st ed. Good in dj (lt worn). *Ash.* $47/£30

SNOW, C. P. Corridors of Power. Macmillan, 1964. 1st UK ed. VG + in dj (sl rubbed). *Williams.* $14/£9

SNOW, C. P. Last Things. NY: Scribner, (1970). 1st Amer ed. Fine in dj. *Antic Hay.* $20/£13

SNOW, C. P. The Light and the Dark. Faber & Faber, (1947). 1st ed. Nice in dj (chipped). *Ash.* $101/£65

SNOW, C. P. The Masters. Macmillan, 1951. 1st ed. (Edges sl dusty, spotted), o/w Nice in dj (worn, browned). *Ash.* $70/£45

SNOW, C. P. The New Men. London, 1954. 1st Eng ed. Nice in dj (sl mkd, frayed). *Clearwater.* $39/£25

SNOW, C. P. Science and Government. Cambridge, 1961. 1st ed. NF. *Smith.* $15/£10

SNOW, C. P. Strangers and Brothers. Faber & Faber, 1940. 1st UK ed. NF (lacks dj). *Williams.* $117/£75

SNOW, E. R. Pirates and Buccaneers of the Atlantic Coast. Boston: Yankee, 1944. Stated 1st ed. Good in dj (chipped). *Scribe's Perch*.* $40/£26

SNOW, EDGAR. Red Star Over China. Gollancz, Left Book Club, 1937. 1st ed. Orange limp cl. *Hatchwell.* $70/£45

SNOW, JACK. The Magical Mimics in Oz. Chicago: Reilly & Lee, (1946). Frank Kramer (illus). Lg 8vo. Illus eps. Pict plt mtd to fr bd. (Cl, tp sm stains.) Pict dj (extensively tape-mended w/dk stains, loss; bkseller's label). *Waverly*.* $88/£56

SNOW, JACK. The Magical Mimics in Oz. Chicago: Reilly & Lee, (1946). 1st ed, 1st state. Frank Kramer (illus). 4to. 242pp (fr hinge strained). Pict eps ptd in grn on pale yellow. Gray cl, pict onlay. (Back cvr mkd, spine ends, corner worn), else VG-. *Bookmark.* $117/£75

SNOW, JOHN. Snow on Cholera. NY/London, Commonwealth Fund/Humphrey Milford, OUP, 1936. Frontis port, 2 fldg maps (1 color). Brn cl, gilt. (Ink owner stamp), else Fine in dj (sl worn). *Cady.* $30/£19

SNOW, WILLIAM PARKER. Southern Generals, Their Lives and Campaigns. NY, 1866. 2nd ptg. (Binding worn, spine cl torn.) Interior Good. *Mcclintock.* $50/£32

Snow-Drop; A Collection of Nursery Rhymes by the Authors of Original Poems. New Haven: S. Babcock, 1841. Nice (foxed throughout) in wrappers (spine tear). *Hermitage.* $45/£29

SNOWDEN, FRANK M., JR. Blacks in Antiquity: Ethiopians in the Greco-Roman Experience. Cambridge: Harvard Univ, 1970. Good in dj (tattered). *Archaeologia.* $65/£42

SNOWDEN, RICHARD. The History of North and South America, from Its Discovery to the Death of General Washington. Phila: Johnson & Warner, 1815. 1st ed. 2 vols in one. 168; 132pp (some browning); 2 fldg engr maps. Old calf (rebacked), black spine label. *Karmiole.* $150/£96

SNOWDEN, YATES. Marching with Sherman. Columbia, 1929. Wraps (sl faded). *King.* $50/£32

SNOWMAN, A. KENNETH. The Art of Carl Faberge. London: Faber, 1953. 1st ed. 27 color plts. VG in dj. *Hollett.* $86/£55

SNOWMAN, A. KENNETH. The Art of Carl Faberge. Boston, n.d. (ca 1962). 2nd ed. (Lt worn.) Dj (sl edgeworn, soiled). *Freeman*.* $30/£19

SNYDER, ANNE E. The Civil War from a Southern Stand-Point. Nashville, TN: Pub House of M.E. Church, 1891. 1st rev ed. 360pp. VG (sl rubbed, scuffed). *Mcgowan.* $45/£29

SNYDER, GARY. The Old Ways. SF: City Lights, 1977. 1st Amer ed. Fine in pict wraps. *Polyanthos.* $20/£13

SNYDER, GARY. A Range of Poetry. London: Fulcrum, (1966). 1st ed. NF in dj (rear panel torn). *Dermont.* $75/£48

SNYDER, JOEL. American Frontiers. Millerton, NY: Aperture, 1981. 1st ed. NF in dj (rubbed, chipped). *Cahan.* $65/£42

SNYDER, JOEL. American Frontiers: The Photographs of Timothy H. O'Sullivan, 1867-1874. Millerton, NY: Aperture, 1981. 1st ed. (Owner stamp), else Fine in dj (rubbed). *Cahan.* $65/£42

SNYDER, LAURENCE H. Blood Grouping in Relation to Clinical and Legal Medicine. Balt, 1929. 1st ed. VG. *Doctor's Library.* $65/£42

SOBIESKI, JOHN. The Life-Story and Personal Reminiscences of Col. John Sobieski. L.A.: L.G. Sobieski, (1907). 2nd ed. Pict cl. VG. *Mcgowan.* $150/£96

SOBIESZEK, ROBERT A. Masterpieces of Photography from the George Eastman House Collections. NY: Abbeville, 1985. 1st ed. Fine in illus dj (sl faded). *Cahan.* $100/£64

SOBRIERE, SAMUEL. A Voyage to England. London: J. Woodward, 1709. 1st Eng ed. (12),xx,190pp; fldg engr plt. Contemp panelled calf (nicely rebacked), red morocco spine label. *Karmiole.* $375/£240

Social Evil. NY: Putnam, 1902. 1st ed. VG (ex-lib). *Second Life.* $45/£29

Social Manual for San Francisco and Oakland. SF: City Pub Co, 1884. 1st ed. 296pp. Blue cl, gilt. (Spine ends, corners sl rubbed; name), else Fine. *Argonaut.* $90/£58

SOCIETY OF ANTIQUARIES. Vetusta Monumenta. London, 1789. Vol II only. 56 engr plts (7 dbl-pg), incl added view not listed in table of plts. Full mod gilt-dec leather. VG (lacks blank fep, lt dampstaining early leaves, lt foxing). *New Hampshire*.* $290/£186

SODERHOLTZ, E. E. (comp). Colonial Architecture and Furniture. Boston: Geo. H. Polley, 1895. 1st ed. Folio. 60 loose collotype plts (ink lib stamps). Laid in cl portfolio (lacks ties). VG. *Cahan.* $150/£96

SOLC, VACLAV. Swords and Daggers of Indonesia. London, n.d. (1970). Pict cl (sl rubbed), sword clasp. *King.* $40/£26

SOLEY, JAMES RUSSELL. The Blockade and the Cruisers. NY: Scribner, 1883. 1st ed. (x),257,(1 blank, 4 ads)pp; fldg map. VG. *Lefkowicz.* $65/£42

SOLLAS, W. J. Ancient Hunters and Their Modern Representatives. NY: Macmillan, (1924). 3rd rev ed. 2 fldg plts. VG. *Mikesh.* $30/£19

SOLLY, N. NEAL. Memoir of the Life of David Cox. London, 1875. Frontis port, 339 pp. Buckram, beveled bds, gilt. (Sm tear upper cvr neatly repaired, rebacked w/orig faded spine laid down), o/w Fine. *Europa.* $90/£58

SOLOGUB, FYODOR. The Petty Demon. NY: Random House, 1962. 1st US ed. VG+ (dampstain fr pastedown, fore-edge lt foxed) in dj. *Lame Duck.* $35/£22

SOLOMITA, STEPHEN. Bad to the Bone. NY: Putnam, 1991. 1st ed. Fine in dj. *Mordida.* $30/£19

SOLOMON, HARRY C. and MAIDA HERMAN. Syphilis of the Innocent: A Study of the Social Effects.... Washington: US Interdepartmental Social Hygiene Board, 1922. 1st ed. Grn cl (fr bd sl stained). Jelliffe's name stamp. VG. *Gach.* $85/£54

SOLON, M. L. A Brief History of Old English Porcelain and Its Manufactories. London/Derby, 1903. #76/1250. 20 color, 50 illus b/w plts. 2-tone cl. (Sl spotting, margins lt browned, hinges cracked; worn, spine faded.) *Edwards.* $39/£25

SOLON, M. L. A Brief History of Old English Porcelain and Its Manufactories.... Bemrose, 1903. 1st ed. #1020/1250. 20 color, 74 b/w plts. Teg, others uncut. 2-tone cl (rubbed, soiled). Sound. *Cox.* $39/£25

SOLON, M. L. A History and Description of Italian Majolica. London: Cassell, 1907. 1st ed. 24 color, 49 b/w plts. Red cl. (Overall soil, spine abrasion), o/w VG. *Hermitage.* $85/£54

SOLON, M. L. A History and Description of Italian Majolica. London: Cassell, 1907. 1st ed. 23 color, 49 plain plts. (Cl sl rubbed, bumped.) *Hollett.* $94/£60

SOLZHENITSYN, ALEXANDER. August 1914. Michael Glenny (trans). NY: FSG, (1972). 1st Amer ed. Fine in NF dj. *Antic Hay.* $30/£19

SOLZHENITSYN, ALEXANDER. Cancer Ward. N. Bethell and D. Burg (trans). London, 1968. 1st ed. Dj (frayed, taped). *Typographeum.* $25/£16

SOLZHENITSYN, ALEXANDER. Cancer Ward. Part One. Nicholas Bethell & David Burg (trans). London: Bodley Head, (1968). 1st Eng ed. Paper-cvrd bds. Fine in dj (lt used). *Antic Hay.* $45/£29

SOLZHENITSYN, ALEXANDER. The First Circle. Michael Guybon (trans). London: Collins & Harvill, (1968). 1st Eng ed. NF in dj. *Antic Hay.* $30/£19

SOLZHENITSYN, ALEXANDER. The Gulag Archipelago: 1918-1956. T. P. Whitney (trans). NY: Harper & Row, (1973). 1st Amer ed. Fine in NF dj. *Antic Hay.* $45/£29

SOLZHENITSYN, ALEXANDER. Lenin in Zurich. NY: FSG, 1976. 1st ed in English. Fine in NF dj (lt worn). *Lame Duck.* $45/£29

SOLZHENITSYN, ALEXANDER. One Day in the Life of Ivan Denisovich. NY: Dutton, 1963. 1st US ed. NF in VG dj. *Lame Duck.* $75/£48

SOLZHENITSYN, ALEXANDER. One Day in the Life of Ivan Denisovitch. Ralph Parker (trans). London: Gollancz, 1963. 1st Eng ed. (Tape mks eps.) Dj. *Hollett.* $47/£30

Some British Ballads. London, (1919). One of 575 numbered, signed by Arthur Rackham (illus). 4to. 16 tipped-in color plts, guards. Later navy morocco, gilt by Zaehnsdorf. *Swann**. $805/£516

Some British Ballads. NY: Dodd, Mead, (1919). 1st Amer ed. 16 tipped-in color plts. Gilt-dec cl (extrems lt worn). Contents VG. *New Hampshire**. $120/£77

Some Early American Hunters. NY: Derrydale, 1928. Ltd to 375. Hand-colored frontis. Internally VG (joints starting, spine missing sm pieces). *Truepenny*. $125/£80

Some Notes on America. (By W. H. Alger.) (Plymouth, England, 1884.) 101pp. VG. *Reese*. $150/£96

Some Pictures of Greater Norfolk. J.G. mcCrorey, 1906. VG- (spine faded, torn). *Book Broker*. $45/£29

SOMERS, JOHN. Judgment of Whole Kingdoms and Nations. Newport: Solomon Southwick, 1774. 12th ed. 156pp (lt foxed, outer leaves soiled, piece torn tp w/loss). Stitched pamphlet. *New Hampshire**. $50/£32

SOMERVELL, T. HOWARD. After Everest. London, 1936. 1st ed. Color frontis, 2 maps (1 fldg). (Spine sl faded, chipped.) *Edwards*. $47/£30

SOMERVILE, WILLIAM. The Chance: A Poem. NY: Doubleday, Doran, 1929. One of 375 numbered. Unopened. Contents VG. (Cl lt soiled, toned; few spots, lt rubbed.) *Waverly**. $22/£14

SOMERVILLE and ROSS. In Mr. Knox's Country. London: Longmans, 1915. 1st UK ed. VG (ink name; cvrs sl mkd). *Williams*. $39/£25

SOMERVILLE, MARY. Physical Geography. London: John Murray, 1858. 4th ed. xii,546pp; 32-pg pub's cat, engr port (foxed). Maroon cl (rubbed, sm tears spine ends). *Burmester*. $70/£45

SOMMER, F. Man and Beast in Africa. London: Jenkins, 1954. 1st ed. VG in Fair dj. *Mikesh*. $35/£22

SOMMER, FREDERICK. The Mistress of This World Has No Name. Denver: Denver Art Museum, (1988). 1st ed. 55 full-pg photos. Fine in illus stiff wrappers. *Cahan*. $40/£26

SOMMER, FREDERICK. The Poetic Logic of Art and Aesthetics. (Stockton, NJ: Carolingian Press, 1972.) (Owner stamp), else Fine in ptd stiff wrappers. *Cahan*. $75/£48

SOMMERVILLE, M. Engraved Gems. Phila: Drexel Biddle, c 1901. (Inner hinges starting; spine sl chipped), else Good. *Blake*. $100/£64

SONDHEIM, STEPHEN. Sunday in the Park with George. NY: Dodd, Mead, (1986). 1st ed. One of 250 numbered, signed by Sondheim and James Lapine. Fine in pub's slipcase. *Unger*. $250/£160

SONDHEIM, STEPHEN. Sweeney Todd, the Demon Barber of Fleet Street. NY: Dodd, Mead, (1979). 1st ed. Fine (bkstore stamp fep) in Fine dj. *Unger*. $50/£32

SONDLEY, F. A. History of Buncombe County, North Carolina. Asheville, NC: Advocate, 1930. 1st ed. 2 vols. Black morocco; gilt spine titles; bible corners. (Extrems rubbed; inner hinges reinforced w/tape; lt foxing eps of vol 1; name vol 2), else VG. *Cahan*. $200/£128

Songs, by the Ettrick Shepherd. (By James Hogg.) NY: William Stoddart, 1832. 'First American edition.' xii,311pp (foxing, fep neatly excised). Orig cl (soiled, spine chipped), leather label. Sound. *Reese*. $30/£19

SONNICHSEN, C. L. Billy King's Tombstone.... Caldwell, ID: Caxton, 1951. 3rd ptg. Pict cl. NF in dj (sm chip). *Sadlon*. $40/£26

SONNINI, C. S. Travels in Upper and Lower Egypt. London: J. Debrett, 1800. 1st 4to ed. Frontis, xl,730,14pp; fldg map, 27 plts. Recent morocco. (Lacks 1/2 title, 3 plts sl torn, repaired; sl foxed), o/w VG. *Worldwide*. $850/£545

SONO, TEL. The Japanese Reformer, an Autobiography. NY: Ptd by Hunt & Eaton, 1892. Inscribed in Japanese, English. Frontis. Blue cl. (Fep detached), else Good. *Boswell*. $225/£144

SONTAG, SUSAN. On Photography. NY, 1977. 1st ed. Fine in NF dj. *Warren*. $35/£22

SOPHIAN, ABRAHAM. Epedemic Cerebral Spinal Menengitis. St. Louis, 1913. 1st ed. Good (sl stain fr cvr). *Doctor's Library*. $50/£32

SOPWITH, T. A Treatise on Isometrical Drawing. London: John Weald, 1834. 1st ed. xxvi,239pp; 34 copperplt engrs. Recent grn cl. Good (ex-libris; foxed). *Blake*. $175/£112

SORELL, WALTER. The Duality of Vision. 1970. 1st ed. 23 color plts, 126 b/w plts. Dj (sl rubbed). *Edwards*. $39/£25

SORENSON, ALFRED. The Story of Omaha from the Pioneer Days to the Present Time. Omaha, 1923. 3rd ed. Fine. *Hermitage*. $75/£48

SORGE, ERNEST. With Plane, Boat and Camera in Greenland...Dr. Fanck Greenland Expedition. London: Hurst & Blackett, 1935. Fldg panoramic frontis. VG. *High Latitude*. $60/£38

SORIN, SCOTA. (Pseud of Edna W.S. Troop.) Blackbird, a Story of Mackinac Island. (Detroit: Citator, 1907.) Frontis, 2 plts. Dec cl. Nice in glassine wrapper (chipped, sl etching fr hinge). *Bohling*. $30/£19

SORREL, G. M. Recollections of a Confederate Staff Officer. NY: Neale, 1905. 1st ed. NF (spine sl dknd). Howes S767. *Mcgowan*. $375/£240

SORREL, G. M. Recollections of a Confederate Staff Officer. NY: Neale, 1917. 2nd ed. Frontis port. Good. *Scribe's Perch**. $70/£45

SORRENTINO, GILBERT. Black and White. Totem, (1964). 1st ed. Fine in illus wrappers (sm crease rear cvr). *Dermont*. $25/£16

SORRENTINO, GILBERT. Imaginative Qualities of Actual Things. Pantheon, (1971). 1st ed. NF in NF dj. *Dermont*. $20/£13

SORRENTINO, GILBERT. Mulligan Stew. NY: Grove, 1979. 1st ed, 1st ptg. (Text dknd), else NF in dj (price-clipped). *Lame Duck*. $150/£96

SORRENTINO, GILBERT. The Perfect Fiction. NY: Norton, 1968. 1st ed. Fine in dj (lt rubbed, tiny tears). *Beasley*. $30/£19

Sorrows of an Anglo-Indian Life, by a Sufferer. (By Robert Needham Cust.) London: Elliot Stock, 1889. 1st ed. Presentation copy. 86pp (lib label pastedown, stamp reverse tp, marginal blind stamps), 8 wood engrs. (Sm label spine base.) *Hollett*. $47/£30

SOSEY, FRANK H. Robert Devoy, a Tale of the Palmyra Massacre. (Palmyra, MO: Sosey Bros, 1903.) 1st ed. (Cl sl rubbed), else VG. *Mcgowan*. $350/£224

SOULE, FRANK et al. The Annals of San Francisco.... Palo Alto: Lewis Osborne, 1968. Rpt. Ltd to 960. Gilt-lettered red cl. Fine. *Argonaut*. $160/£103

SOULIE, BERNARD. Japanese Erotism. NY: Crescent Bks, 1981. 1st ed. NF in dj (sl wrinkled). *Worldwide*. $35/£22

SOUTH, R. The Butterflies of the British Isles. London: Wayside & Woodland, 1906. 1st ed. Blue cl (scuffed, worn), gilt. *Maggs*. $31/£20

SOUTH, R. The Moths of the British Isles, 2 vols; The Caterpillars of British Moths, 2 vols. London: Wayside & Woodland, 1939-33-48. 4 vols. Rpts of the 1st 2 vols. VG in djs. *Maggs*. $56/£36

South-Sea Bubbles. (Comp by George R. Herbert and George H. Kingsley.) NY: D. Appleton, 1872. 1st Amer ed. (298),(ii)pp. Dec cl (lt worn, lt spotted, browned). Nice. *Ash.* $148/£95

SOUTHARD, ELMER ERNEST and MARY C. JARRETT. The Kingdom of Evils.... NY: Macmillan, 1922. 1st ed. Ruled crimson cl. (Fr hinge taped, spine #s blotted out), else Good+. *Gach.* $50/£32

SOUTHARD, ELMER ERNEST. Shell-Shock and Other Neuropsychiatric Problems...from the War Literature 1914-1918. Boston: W.M. Leonard, 1919. 1st ed. Inscribed. 3 half-tones. Brn buckram, painted spine labels. (Stamp tp; bkpl; shelfworn, spine #s.) Good. *Gach.* $175/£112

SOUTHERN, EILEEN. The Music of Black Americans. NY: Norton, 1971. 1st ed. (Bkpl), o/w Fine in dj (2 sm tears). *Between The Covers.* $85/£54

SOUTHERN, H. N. The Handbook of British Mammals. London, 1964. 1st ed. 32 plts. Good. *Henly.* $37/£24

SOUTHERN, TERRY et al. Pardon Me, Sir, But Is My Eye Hurting Your Elbow? NY: Bernard Geis, (1968). 1st ed. Fine in dj (lt smudged, sm tear). *Reese.* $30/£19

SOUTHERN, TERRY and MASON HOFFENBERG. Candy. NY: Putnams, (1964). 1st unexpurgated Amer ed, 1st hb ed. (Sl foxing 1/2-title), else NF in NF dj (2 short tears rear panel). *Between The Covers.* $150/£96

SOUTHERN, TERRY and MASON HOFFENBERG. Candy. Bernard Geis, 1968. 1st UK ed. VG+ in dj. *Sclanders.* $12/£8

SOUTHERN, TERRY. Blue Movie. NY, 1970. 1st Amer ed. Fine (spine extrems sl rubbed) in dj (sm tear). *Polyanthos.* $25/£16

SOUTHERN, TERRY. Flash and Filigree. NY, (1958). 1st Amer ed, 1st bk. VG in dj (sm edge tears, sl edgewear). *King.* $50/£32

SOUTHERN, TERRY. The Magic Christian. London, 1959. 1st Eng ed. Very Nice in dj (sl rubbed, mkd). *Clearwater.* $62/£40

SOUTHEY, ROBERT. Journal of a Tour in Scotland in 1819. London: John Murray, 1929. 1st ed. 2 plts. VG. *Hollett.* $47/£30

SOUTHWARD, JOHN. Practical Printing. London: J.M. Powell, 1887. xvi,2,715+12pp ads; fldg plan. (Corner upper cvr creased), o/w Sound in grn cl. *Cox.* $70/£45

SOUTHWORTH, ALVAN. Four Thousand Miles of African Travel. NY/London: Baker, Pratt/Sampson, Low, 1875. 1st ed. Frontis, xi,381pp; fldg map. Grn cl (sl wear), else VG. *Terramedia.* $150/£96

SOWERBY, A. DE C. A Naturalist's Holiday by the Sea. London, 1923. *Wheldon & Wesley.* $23/£15

SOWERBY, E. MILLICENT. Rare People and Rare Books. London, (1967). 1st ed. VG in dj. *Truepenny.* $75/£48

SOWERBY, G. B. A Conchological Manual. London: Henry G. Bohn, 1846. 3rd ed. Hand-colored frontis, vi,(i),313pp; 2 fldg tables, 26 hand-colored plts. Orig blind-stamped cl (recased; new eps; tp, some tissues sl spotted), gilt. *Hollett.* $218/£140

SOWERBY, JAMES and JAMES EDWARD SMITH. English Botany; or, Coloured Figures of British Plants. John T. Boswell Syme (ed). London: C.E. Sowerby, (1832-)1854. Vols I-VII only (of 12). Vol 1: 2nd ed; Vols 2-7: 3rd ed. 8vo. Contemp grn 1/2 morocco, marbled bds (spines faded, extrms rubbed). *Christie's*.* $613/£393

SOWERBY, JAMES and JAMES EDWARD SMITH. English Botany; or, Coloured Figures of British Plants. John T. Boswell Syme (ed). London: Robert Hardwicke, 1863-86. 3rd ed. Vols I-XII. 4to. (Sl spotting, some plts detached.) Contemp 1/2 roan (very worn, few cvrs detached or lacking). *Christie's*.* $842/£540

SOWERBY, JAMES. English Botany; or, Coloured Figures of British Plants.... London: J. Davis, 1797. Vol VI only. 123 hand-colored plts. (Lt foxing.) Full leather, gilt. *Metropolitan*.* $402/£258

SOWERBY, JAMES. English Botany; or, Coloured Figures of British Plants.... London: J. Davis, 1800. Vol IX only. 136 hand-colored plts. (Lt foxing.) Full leather, gilt. *Metropolitan*.* $373/£239

SOWERBY, JAMES. English Botany; or, Coloured Figures of British Plants.... London: J. Davis, 1801. Vol XII only. 80 hand-colored plts. (Sl foxing.) Full leather, gilt. *Metropolitan*.* $287/£184

SOWERBY, JOHN E. British Wild Flowers. London: John Van Voorst, 1882. Reissue. Frontis, lii,186pp (presentation tp, note pasted fep). This ed w/9 added color plts. Aeg. 1/2 calf (rebound), orig bds, gilt, raised bands. *Quest.* $425/£272

SOWERBY, JOHN E. British Wild Flowers. London, 1890. lii,186pp; 90 Fine hand-colored, 2 plain plts. (Refixed in case.) *Henly.* $179/£115

SOWERBY, JOHN E. Ferns of Great Britain. London, 1855. 49 hand-colored engr plts complete. Very Nice in full leather, gilt spines. *Metropolitan*.* $201/£129

SOWLES, LYLE K. Prairie Ducks. Washington/Harrisburg: Wildlife Management Inst/Stackpole, 1955. Stated 1st ed. Frontis. NF (name stamp) in VG dj (edge chipped). *Backman.* $55/£35

SOYER, NICOLAS. Soyer's Paper-Bag Cookery. London: Andrew Melrose, 1911. 1st ed. Port. Red cl (sl mkd). Internally Fine. *Cox.* $28/£18

SOYINKA, WOLE. A Shuttle in the Crypt. NY: Hill & Wang, (1972). 1st Amer ed. Fine in dj (sm crease fr flap). *Between The Covers.* $75/£48

SOZINSKEY, THOMAS. Medical Symbolism in Connection with Historical Studies in the Arts of Healing and Hygiene. Phila, 1891. 1st ed. 171pp. VG. *Fye.* $150/£96

SPALDING, C. SUMNER. Peter Cooper: A Critical Bibliography.... NY, 1941. 1st ed. Orig ptd wrappers. *Ginsberg.* $25/£16

SPALDING, J. L. The Life of the Most Rev. M. J. Spalding, D.D., Archbishop of Baltimore. NY, 1873. 1st ed. 468,(11)pp; port. Recent buckram, gilt. (Lt foxed; margin 1 leaf repaired), o/w VG. *Wantagh.* $50/£32

Spanish Pictures, Drawn with Pen and Pencil. London, ca 1880. Gilt edges. Gilt-pict cl (worn). *Argosy.* $85/£54

SPARGO, JOHN. Anthony Haswell. Printer-Patriot-Ballader. Rutland: Tuttle, 1925. One of 300 numbered, signed. Uncut. 3/4 morocco (rubbed). *Oinonen*.* $120/£77

SPARGO, JOHN. Juridical Folklore in England, Illustrated by the Cucking-Stool. Durham: Duke Univ, 1944. 1st ed. Fine in illus dj. *Cahan.* $30/£19

SPARK, MURIEL and DEREK STANFORD (eds). Tribute to Wordsworth. London: Wingate, 1950. 1st Eng ed. VG in dj (rubbed, foxed). *Hadley.* $94/£60

SPARK, MURIEL. Collected Poems. London, 1967. 1st Eng ed. Fine in dj. *Clearwater.* $39/£25

SPARK, MURIEL. The Comforters. Macmillan, 1957. 1st UK ed. NF (sm ink name) in VG dj (lt spine wear, sm chips). *Williams.* $234/£150

SPARK, MURIEL. The Driver's Seat. Macmillan, 1970. 1st UK ed. Fine in VG+ dj. *Williams.* $23/£15

SPARK, MURIEL. The Driver's Seat. London: Macmillan, 1970. 1st Eng ed. VG in dj. *Hadley.* $23/£15

SPARK, MURIEL. The Fanfarlo and Other Verse. Aldington: Hand & Flower Press, 1952. 1st ed. NF in handsewn wraps (spine lt faded). *Lame Duck.* $200/£128

SPARK, MURIEL. The Fanfarlo and Other Verse. Aldington: Hand & Flower, 1952. 1st ed. Wraps. Fine. *Beasley*. $60/£38

SPARK, MURIEL. The Girls of Slender Means. Macmillan, 1963. 1st ed. (Lt foxing, mainly edges, spine sl creased), o/w Nice in dj (sl sunned). *Ash*. $62/£40

SPARK, MURIEL. The Girls of Slender Means. London, 1963. 1st Eng ed. Fine in dj. *Clearwater*. $39/£25

SPARK, MURIEL. The Go-Away Bird and Other Stories. Phila: Lippincott, 1960. 1st Amer ed. Fine in dj (wear, soil, sm tear, spine sunned). *Antic Hay*. $35/£22

SPARK, MURIEL. The Go-Away Bird with Other Stories. London: Macmillan, 1958. 1st Eng ed. VG in dj. *Hadley*. $78/£50

SPARK, MURIEL. The Hothouse by the East River. NY: Viking, (1973). 1st Amer ed. Fine in dj. *Antic Hay*. $20/£13

SPARK, MURIEL. John Masefield. London: Nevill, 1953. 1st Eng ed. VG in dj (chipped, closed tear, sm mk fr panel). *Hadley*. $101/£65

SPARK, MURIEL. The Mandelbaum Gate. Macmillan, 1965. 1st UK ed. VG in dj (price-clipped). *Williams*. $23/£15

SPARK, MURIEL. The Mandelbaum Gate. NY: Knopf, 1965. 1st ed. Fine in NF dj (sl soil). *Antic Hay*. $20/£13

SPARK, MURIEL. Memento Mori. London: Macmillan, 1959. 1st Eng ed. VG in VG dj (rear panel mkd). *Hadley*. $117/£75

SPARK, MURIEL. The Prime of Miss Jean Brodie. London: Macmillan, 1961. 1st Eng ed. VG in dj (creased). *Hadley*. $70/£45

SPARK, MURIEL. The Prime of Miss Jean Brodie. London: Macmillan, 1961. Uncorrected proof. VG in ptd wrappers. *Williams*. $70/£45

SPARK, MURIEL. The Public Image. London: Macmillan, 1968. 1st Eng ed. VG in dj. *Hadley*. $31/£20

SPARK, MURIEL. Voices at Play. London: Macmillan, 1961. 1st UK ed. NF in dj. *Williams*. $23/£15

SPARK, MURIEL. Voices at Play. Phila: Lippincott, 1962. 1st Amer ed. NF in dj. *Antic Hay*. $25/£16

SPARKS, J. and J. SOPER. Owls: Their Natural and Unnatural History. NY: Taplinger, 1970. 1st ed. Color frontis. Blind-stamped gilt-dec cl. Fine in VG + dj. *Mikesh*. $25/£16

SPARKS, JARED. The Life of John Ledyard, the American Traveller. Cambridge, 1829. 2nd ed. Half-title, xi,(1),310pp (foxed, few sigs starting). Cl-backed bds (spotted, worn, rubbed), leather label. Decent. Howes S818. *Reese*. $225/£144

SPARKS, W. H. The Memories of Fifty Years. Phila, 1870. 1st ed. 489pp. Howes S819. *Ginsberg*. $100/£64

SPARLING, H. HALLIDAY. The Kelmscott Press and William Morris Master Craftsman. Macmillan, 1924. 1st ed. 18 plts. 1/4 cl. Near Mint. *Moss*. $140/£90

SPARRMAN, ANDERS. A Voyage Round the World with Captain James Cook in H.M.S. Resolution. London: Golden Cockerel, 1944. One of 350. Gilt-pict buckram. *Swann**. $575/£369

SPARROW, GERALD. Gordon: Mandarin and Pasha. London: Jarrolds, 1962. 1st ed. VG in dj. *Worldwide*. $20/£13

SPARROW, JOHN. Visible Words. Cambridge, 1969. 1st ed. Good in dj (frayed). *Cox*. $31/£20

SPARROW, W. J. Count Rumford of Woburn, Mass. Crowell, 1964. VG + in dj. *Bookcell*. $20/£13

SPARROW, WALTER SHAW. See SHAW-SPARROW, WALTER

SPAULDING, EDWARD SELDEN. The Quails. NY: Macmillan, 1949. Stated 1st ptg. Color frontis; 6 full-pg color plts. VG + (inscrip) in VG dj (sm pieces torn from edges, spine; few closed edge tears). *Backman*. $75/£48

SPAULDING, KENNETH A. On the Oregon Trail: Robert Stuart's Journey...(1812-1813). Norman: Univ of OK, (1953). 1st ed. Map. VG in dj (sl worn). *Lien*. $45/£29

SPEAR, CHARLES (ed). Voices from Prison. Boston: The Author, 1849. 3rd ed. Frontis, 302pp. (Spine loss, bds rubbed), else Good. *Brown*. $15/£10

SPEAR, DOROTHEA. Bibliography of American Directories Through 1860. Worcester: American Antiquarian Soc, 1961. 1st ed. VG (spine sl faded, rubbed). *Waverly**. $66/£42

SPEAR, RICHARD E. Caravaggio and His Followers. Cleveland: Cleveland Museum of Art, 1971. (Ink notes.) *Washton*. $55/£35

SPEAR, RICHARD E. Domenichino. New Haven/London, 1982. 2 vols. 4to. 8 color plts. Good. *Washton*. $550/£353

SPEAR, T. G. P. The Nabobs, a Study of the Social Life of the English in Eighteenth Century India. OUP, 1932. *Petersfield*. $23/£15

SPEAR, VICTOR I. Vermont, a Glimpse of Its Scenery and Industries. Montpelier: State Board of Ag, 1893. 64pp. Gilt-emb wraps (worn, soiled, ends torn). *Bohling*. $35/£22

Spearhead in the West 1941-45. (Frankfurt, 1945.) VG in dj (sl frayed). *King*. $85/£54

SPEARS, JOHN R. Illustrated Sketches of Death Valley and Other Borax Deserts of the Pacific Coast. NY: Rand McNally, 1892. 1st ed. 226pp(6, ads), 56 photo plts, map. Fine in ptd yellow wrappers. *Argonaut*. $450/£288

SPEARS, JOHN R. Illustrated Sketches of Death Valley. Chicago, 1892. 1st ed. 226pp. (Obit affixed to rear inside cvr, paint spot fr cvr, sl rubbed.) *King*. $195/£125

SPEARS, JOHN R. The Story of the New England Whalers. NY: Macmillan, 1908. 10 plts. Dec cl. VG. *High Latitude*. $40/£26

SPEARS, JOHN R. The Story of the New England Whalers. NY: Macmillan, 1908. 10 plts. Pict cl. VG. *Adelson*. $40/£26

Spectator. (By Richard Steele.) London: J. & R. Tonson, 1739 (1738 vols 4, 8). 12th ed. 8 vols. Contemp panelled calf (spine ends sl worn; vol 2 lacks fep). *Bickersteth*. $70/£45

SPECTORSKY, A. C. (ed). The Book of the Sea. NY: Appleton-Century-Crofts, (1954). 1st ed. VG + in clear acetate dj. *Bernard*. $125/£80

SPEED, JOHN G. The Horse in America. NY, 1905. 1st ed. Teg. Red cl, gilt. VG. *Price*. $48/£31

SPEEDY, TOM. The Natural History of Sport in Scotland with Rod and Gun. London: William Blackwood, 1920. 1st ed. Inscribed presentation copy. Frontis port. VG. *Hollett*. $117/£75

SPEIGHT, HARRY. Romantic Richmondshire. London: Elliot Stock, 1897. 1st ed. 521pp; fldg map. Pict cl (spine faded, hinges sl rubbed), gilt. *Hollett*. $101/£65

SPEKE, JOHN HANNING. Journal of the Discovery of the Source of the Nile. London, 1863. 1st ed. Engr frontis port, xxxi,658pp + (xxxiv) pub's ads (fep, frontis, tp chipped; sl browning); 25 plts, map (lacks map in rear pocket). Cl (rebacked), much of orig spine laid down, gilt. *Edwards*. $234/£150

SPEKE, JOHN HANNING. Journal of the Discovery of the Source of the Nile. Edinburgh/London: Blackwood, 1864. 2nd ed. xxxi,658pp,38pp ads; lg fldg colored map in pocket. Brn gilt pict cl (recased, sl wear), else VG. *Terramedia*. $350/£224

SPEKE, JOHN HANNING. Journal of the Discovery of the Source of the Nile. NY, 1864. 1st Amer ed. 590pp; map. 3/4 leather. (Ink name; inner fr hinge cracked; cvrs worn; spine chipped, 1 spine label defective.) *King.* $75/£48

SPELLEN, J. N. The Vestry Clerk and Parish Officer. London: Shaw, 1853-55. 4 separate works. Contemp ptd bds (joints cracking). Sound. *Boswell.* $225/£144

SPELMAN, W. W. R. Lowestoft China. Norwich: Jarrold, 1905. Ltd to 500. Color frontis, 97 plts. Teg. Gilt cl, beveled bds. VG. *Hollett.* $203/£130

SPENCE, BASIL. Phoenix at Coventry. The Building of a Cathedral. Geoffrey Bles, 1962. Deluxe ed. #258/500 signed. 45 plts (11 color). VG in buckram, glacine wrapper, slipcase. *Cox.* $55/£35

SPENCE, CLARK C. British Investments and the American Mining Frontier, 1860-1901. Ithaca, NY: Amer Hist Assoc, Cornell Univ, (1958). 1st ed. Blue cl. Fine in dj (spine dknd). *Argonaut.* $45/£29

SPENCE, J. Lectures on Surgery. 1875-6. 2nd ed. 2 vols. xxxiv,469; xxvii,471-1152pp; 58 color plts. (Vol I tp foxed, sm split fr inner hinge, cl worn; vol II rebacked w/orig spine laid on), o/w VG set. *Whitehart.* $90/£58

SPENCE, JOSEPH. Observations, Anecdotes, and Characters. London: John Murray, 1820. 1st ed. (Ink notes tp, verso; blank prelim rucked), o/w VG in 19th-cent 1/2 morocco (rubbed). *Poetry Bookshop.* $70/£45

SPENCE, JOSEPH. A Parallel in the Manner of Plutarch. Strawberry Hill, 1758. 1st ed. One of 700. 104pp (lt foxed). Uncut. Contemp 1/2 calf (spine top chipped, fr joint cracked). *Swann*.* $230/£147

SPENCE, LEWIS. An Encyclopaedia of Occultism. New Hyde Park, NY: University Books, 1960. Rpt. 23 plts. Bds, cl spine. VG in protective cardbd slipcase. *Worldwide.* $25/£16

SPENCE, LEWIS. Legends and Romances of Spain. NY: F. Stokes, (1920). 1st ed. 16 color plts. (Back hinge exposed), o/w VG. *Middle Earth.* $55/£35

SPENCE, LEWIS. Myth and Ritual in Dance, Game, and Rhyme. London, 1947. 1st ed. (Eps lt spotted; spine sl rubbed, faded.) *Edwards.* $31/£20

SPENCE, LEWIS. Myths and Legends of Babylonia and Assyria. D. Nickerson, (1911). #508/1000 sets. 45 plts. VG +. *Middle Earth.* $48/£31

SPENCE, LEWIS. Myths and Legends of the North American Indians. London: George G. Harrap, 1916. Map. (Prelims foxed.) Grn cl (worn, soiled). *Parmer.* $75/£48

SPENCE, MARY LEE and DONALD JACKSON (eds). The Expeditions of John Charles Fremont. Volume 2, The Bear Flag Revolt and the Court-Martial. Urbana, (1973). 1st ed. Fine in Fine dj. *Pratt.* $35/£22

SPENCER, BALDWIN. Wanderings in Wild Australia. London: Macmillan, 1928. 1st ed. 2 vols. 590 photo plts (16 color), 4 fldg maps. Teg. Grn cl. Good in djs (chipped). *Karmiole.* $375/£240

SPENCER, BELLA Z. Tried and True or Love and Loyalty. Springfield, MA, 1866. 1st ed. 349pp. (Cvr lt worn), o/w Fine. *Pratt.* $45/£29

SPENCER, ELIZABETH. The Light in the Piazza. NY: McGraw-Hill, (1960). 1st ed. Fine in dj. *Reese.* $35/£22

SPENCER, HERBERT. The Visible Word. Royal College of Art, 1968. 1st ed. VG in glassine wrapper. *Cox.* $28/£18

SPENCER, J. A. History of the United States. NY: Johnson, Fry, (c. 1858). 3 vols. Aeg. 1/2 leather. Binder's ticket all vols. (Some engrs foxed, bkpls; rubbed.) *New Hampshire*.* $60/£38

SPENCER, OLIVER. Narrative...of His Captivity Among the Mohawk Indians.... London, 1854. 3rd ed. Pub's cl. Howes S835. *Swann*.* $115/£74

SPENCER, PATRICIA. The Egyptian Temple. London: Kegan Paul, 1984. Good in dj. *Archaeologia.* $95/£61

SPENCER, ROBERT F. The North Alaskan Eskimo. BAE Bulletin 171. Washington: GPO, 1959. Olive cl. VG. *Parmer.* $45/£29

SPENCER, SCOTT. Last Night at the Brain Thieves Ball. Boston: Houghton Mifflin, 1973. 1st ed, 1st bk. NF in dj. *Lame Duck.* $65/£42

SPENCER, SCOTT. Preservation Hall. NY, 1976. 1st Amer ed. Fine in Fine dj. *Polyanthos.* $25/£16

SPENCER, THEODORE. The Paradox in the Circle. CT: New Directions, (1941). 1st Amer ed, 1st bk. Wraps. Fine in dj (spine sl sunned, price-clipped). *Polyanthos.* $25/£16

SPENCER, W. T. Forty Years in My Bookshop. Constable, 1923. 9 plts. Good. *Moss.* $34/£22

SPENCER, W. T. Forty Years in My Bookshop. Thomas Moult (ed). London, 1923. 1st ed. Teg, uncut. Fine (sl rubbed). *Polyanthos.* $60/£38

SPENDER, HAROLD. Through the High Pyrenees. 1898. 1st ed. xii,365pp; 31 plts, 5 maps. (Cl slit lower joint.) *Bickersteth.* $94/£60

SPENDER, STEPHEN and JOHN LEHMANN (eds). Poems for Spain. Hogarth, 1939. 1st ed. Red cl, yellow title. (Spine sl faded, cvrs sl mkd), o/w VG. *Words Etc.* $78/£50

SPENDER, STEPHEN. European Witness. NY, 1946. 1st Amer ed, signed. VG + in VG dj. *Warren.* $85/£54

SPENDER, STEPHEN. The New Realism. London: Hogarth, 1939. Signed. Hogarth Sixpenny Pamphlets. Number 2. NF in sewn wraps. *Warren.* $150/£96

SPENDER, STEPHEN. Poems. NY: Random House, 1934. 1st ed. NF in dj (lt tanned, sl smudges, inner mend spine toe). *Reese.* $75/£48

SPENDER, STEPHEN. Ruins and Visions. NY: Random House, (1942). 1st Amer ed. Fine in dj (wear, price-clipped). *Antic Hay.* $50/£32

SPENDER, STEPHEN. Selected Poems. Faber, 1940. 1st ed. Yellow bds. (Name, sl grubby), o/w VG in green dj (spine, edges browned). *Words Etc.* $19/£12

SPENDER, STEPHEN. Selected Poems. London, 1940. 1st ed. Fine in dj (spine sunned, price-clipped). *Polyanthos.* $25/£16

SPENDER, STEPHEN. The Still Center. London: Faber, (1939). 1st ed. VG- (eps sl foxed) in dj (dknd, nicked). *Reese.* $35/£22

SPENDER, STEPHEN. Vienna. NY: Random House, 1935. 1st Amer ed. Fine in NF dj. *Reese.* $50/£32

SPENSER, EDMUND. Epithalamion. (London: Edward Arnold, 1901.) Ltd to 150. 8vo. 22pp. Full-pg hand-colored wood engr by Reginald Savage. Full vellum, blind-stamped w/rose logo, motto, 'Soul is Form.' VF. *Bromer.* $550/£353

SPERISEN, F. J. The Art of the Lapidary. Milwaukee: Bruce, 1953. 2nd ptg. Color frontis. VG. *Savona.* $62/£40

SPEWACK, SAMUEL and BELLA. Kiss Me Kate. NY: Knopf, 1953. 1st ed. Fine in dj. *Hermitage.* $125/£80

SPICER, BART. Black Sheep, Run. NY: Dodd Mead, 1951. 1st ed. VG in dj. *Mordida.* $45/£29

SPICER, BART. Exit, Running. NY: Dodd Mead, 1959. 1st ed. (Spine sl dknd), o/w Fine in dj. *Mordida.* $45/£29

SPICER, EDWARD H. Cycles of Conquest...1533-1960. Tucson: Univ of AZ, (1962). 1st ed. Signed. 20 maps. Beige cl. Good in dj (chipped). *Karmiole.* $75/£48

SPICER, WILLIAM ARNOLD. The High School Boys of the Tenth R.I. Regiment, with a Roll of Teachers and Students of the Providence High School.... Providence, RI, 1882. 1st ed. Ltd to 250. PNRISSHS Series 2, #13. 83pp. NF in ptd wrappers. *Mcgowan.* $45/£29

SPIEGELBERG, FLORA. Princess Goldenhair and the Wonderful Flowers. World Syndicate, 1932. Milo Winter (illus). 6.5x9. 176pp. Cl, pict paste-on. VG (shelfworn, cvr spotted). *My Bookhouse*. $40/£26

SPIEGELMAN, ART. Maus. NY: Pantheon, 1986. 1st ed. Signed w/dwg. NF in illus self wraps (extrems lt worn). *Lame Duck*. $200/£128

SPIELMANN, M. H. The History of Punch. Cassell, 1895. 1st ed. Lg paper copy. 592pp. 1/2 morocco (worn, hinge partly split). *Moss*. $22/£14

SPIELMANN, M. H. and G. S. LAYARD. Kate Greenaway. London, 1905. 1st ed. Kate Greenaway (illus). Teg. Dec cl (sunned, stain; rear inner hinge taped). *King*. $100/£64

SPIELMANN, M. H. and G. S. LAYARD. Kate Greenaway. London: A&C Black, 1905. 2nd, corrected, imp of 1st ed. Frontis. Gilt-dec cl. (Spine faded), o/w VG. *Reese*. $45/£29

SPIELMANN, M. H. and G. S. LAYARD. Kate Greenaway. London: A&C Black, 1910. Color frontis tipped in, 14 color plts tipped in at rear. (Fore-edge tp sl torn, no loss, lt spotting.) Color illus mtd on upper bd. *Edwards*. $39/£25

SPIER, PETER. The Erie Canal. London: World's Work, 1971. 1st ed. 10 1/2 x 8 1/4. 32pp. Pict bds. Fine in dj. *Cattermole*. $25/£16

SPIER, PETER. The Legend of New Amsterdam. NY: Doubleday, 1979. 1st ed. 10 1/2 x 8 1/4. 24pp. Pict bds. Fine in dj. *Cattermole*. $45/£29

SPIER, PETER. London Bridge Is Falling Down! NY: Doubleday, 1967. 1st ed. 9 1/4 x 7 1/2. 42pp. Fine in dj. *Cattermole*. $35/£22

SPIER, PETER. Rain. NY: Doubleday, 1982. 1st ed. 10 1/4 x 10 1/2. 36pp. Fine in dj. *Cattermole*. $35/£22

SPIERS, R. PHENE. Architectural Drawing. 1887. Dbl-pg color frontis, 24 plts, 6 woodcuts. (Prelims, tp sl spotted; hinges tender, cl lt soiled, rubbed.) *Edwards*. $101/£65

SPIES, WERNER. The Return of La Belle Jardiniere: Max Ernst, 1950-1970. NY: Harry N. Abrams, (1971). 1st US ed. 37 color plts. Yellow cl w/sm emblem. Fine. *Cahan*. $85/£54

SPIES, WERNER. Victor Vasarely. NY: Abrams, 1971. Dj. *Metropolitan**. $46/£29

SPILLANE, MICKEY. Bloody Sunrise. NY: Dutton, 1965. 1st ed. Fine in dj. *Mordida*. $50/£32

SPILLANE, MICKEY. The Body Lovers. NY: Dutton, 1967. 1st ed. Fine in dj. *Mordida*. $50/£32

SPILLANE, MICKEY. Day of the Guns. NY: Dutton, 1964. 1st ed. Fine in dj (sl wear). *Mordida*. $50/£32

SPILLANE, MICKEY. The Girl Hunters. NY: Dutton, 1962. Stated 1st ed. Good in dj (chipped). *Scribe's Perch**. $15/£10

SPILLANE, MICKEY. I, the Jury. NY: Dutton, 1947. 1st ed, 1st bk. (Name, address on flyleaf; rear pastedown, ep foxed; corner bumped), o/w VG + in VG dj (spine corners chipped, edgeworn). *Bernard*. $375/£240

SPILLANE, MICKEY. The Killing Man. Franklin Center, PA: Franklin Library, 1989. 'Limited first edition,' signed. Aeg. Full red gilt-stamped pict leather. VG. *King*. $45/£29

SPILLANE, MICKEY. The Last Cop Out. NY: Dutton, 1973. 1st ed. Fine in dj. *Mordida*. $50/£32

SPILLER, BRIAN. Victorian Public Houses. David & Charles, 1972. VG in dj. *Hadley*. $23/£15

SPILLER, BURTON L. Firelight. NY: Derrydale, (1937). Ltd to 950. Unopened. (Corner lt bumped), else Fine. *Truepenny*. $150/£96

SPILLER, BURTON L. Firelight. NY: Derrydale, (1937). One of 950 numbered. 9 plts. Uncut, unopened. Gilt-stamped cl (sl worn), color pict vignette. *Oinonen**. $190/£122

SPILLER, BURTON L. Grouse Feathers. NY: Derrydale, (1935). Ltd to 950. Unopened. (Ink inscrip ep), else Fine. *Truepenny*. $150/£96

SPILLER, BURTON L. Grouse Feathers. NY: Derrydale, (1935). One of 950 numbered. 9 plts. Uncut. Gilt-stamped cl (shelfworn), color pict vignette. *Oinonen**. $200/£128

SPILLER, BURTON L. Grouse Feathers. NY: Derrydale, (1935). 1st ed. #894/950. Maroon cl, gilt. Vignette inset fr cvr. (Spine dull), else Fine. *Cummins*. $250/£160

SPILLER, BURTON L. More Grouse Feathers. NY, (1938). One of 950. 8 plts. Circular onlay fr cvr. (Sm stain top margin 1st blank ll.) *Kane**. $70/£45

SPILLER, BURTON L. More Grouse Feathers. NY: Derrydale, (1938). One of 950 numbered. Uncut. Gilt-stamped cl (shelfworn), pict cvr vignette. *Oinonen**. $225/£144

SPILLER, BURTON L. More Grouse Feathers. NY: Derrydale, (1938). Ltd to 950. Pict cl. VG. *Truepenny*. $175/£112

SPILLER, BURTON L. Thoroughbred. NY, (1936). One of 950. 9 plts. (Spine lt rubbed.) *Kane**. $95/£61

SPILLER, BURTON L. Thoroughbred. NY: Derrydale, (1936). One of 950 numbered. Uncut. Pict blue cl (sl worn). *Oinonen**. $160/£103

SPILLER, BURTON L. Thoroughbred. NY: Derrydale, (1936). Ltd to 950. VG. *Truepenny*. $200/£128

SPILSBURY, WILLIAM HOLDEN. Lincoln's Inn, Its Ancient and Modern Buildings.... London: Reeves & Turner, 1873. 2nd ed. Blue cl (wear, fading, mkings). Sound. *Boswell*. $175/£112

SPINAGE, C. A. The Book of the Giraffe. Collins, 1968. 3 maps. Dj. *Edwards*. $31/£20

SPINETO, MARQUIS. Lectures on the Elements of Hieroglyphics and Egyptian Antiquities. London: C.J.G. & F. Rivington, 1829. 1st ed. xx,493,(iii)pp; 11 litho plts, incl 1 fldg. Mod grn cl (soiled; new eps). VG (ex-lib w/stamps tp, last plt). *Blue Mountain*. $175/£112

SPITTA, E. J. Microscopy. London: Murray, 1907. Frontis, 468pp; 16 plts. New cl. VG. *Savona*. $62/£40

SPIVAK, JOHN. The Medical Trust Unmasked. NY, 1929. 1st ed. VG. *Fye*. $75/£48

SPIVEY, RICHARD L. Maria. Flagstaff: Northland, 1979. 1st ed. NF in dj (lt rubbed). *Waverly**. $44/£28

SPLAN, JOHN. Life with the Trotters. Chicago: White, 1889. 1st ed. VG (shelfwear). *October Farm*. $45/£29

SPLAWN, A. J. Ka-Mi-Akin the Last Hero of the Yakimas. Portland: Binfords & Mort, 1944. 2nd ed. (Ink name), else VG in dj. Howes S838. *Perier*. $62/£40

Splendid Century. French Art 1600-1715. NY: MMA, 1960. Good in wraps. *Washton*. $35/£22

SPOERRI, JAMES FULLER. Catalog of a Collection of the Works of James Joyce. Chicago, 1948. Card wrappers (sl dusty). *Clearwater*. $39/£25

SPOFFORD, HARRIET. New-England Legends.... Boston: James R. Osgood, 1871. 1st ed, clbound issue. Gilt blue cl (lt rubbed, spine ends sl worn). VG. BAL 18452. *Reese*. $55/£35

SPOONER, SHEARJASHUB. A Biographical and Critical Dictionary of Painters.... NY: Putnam, 1853. 1131pp; 24 plts. (Spine ends worn, rear outer hinge covering split), o/w VG. *New Hampshire**. $85/£54

SPOONER, Z. H. (comp). Poems of the Pilgrims. Boston: A. Williams, 1882. 1st ed. (iv),99pp; 6 mtd albumen photos. Aeg. Later floral patterned silk over bds, gilt-stamped morocco spine. (Few ll lt dampstained), else VG. *Cahan*. $225/£144

SPOONER, Z. H. (comp). Poems of the Pilgrims. Boston: Cupples, Upham, 1886. (iv),99pp; 6 mtd silver photos. Aeg. Fine. *Cahan.* $200/£128

Sport and Work on the Nepaul Frontier. London: Macmillan, 1878. 1st ed. Frontis, xii,361pp + 31 ads. Grn gilt cl. (Several pp opened carelessly, w/sm loss of text on 1 pg in table of contents), else VG. *Terramedia.* $125/£80

Sporting Anecdotes. London: J. Cundee, (frontis dated 1807). 2nd ed. Frontis; 5pp ads. Teg, untrimmed. Full tree calf, ribbed gilt-tooled spine (dknd, joints sl rubbed), brn morocco label. Contents VG (few ll creased). *Waverly*.* $104/£67

Sportsman's Companion, or, An Essay on Shooting by a Gentleman. Harrisburg, 1948. Rpt of orig 1883 ed. Fine. *Truepenny.* $45/£29

Sportsman's Companion. NY: Ernest R. Gee, 1930. Ltd to 200. Orig pale blue bds (rebacked w/natural buckram). *Truepenny.* $125/£80

Sportsman's Dictionary, or the Gentleman's Companion for Town and Country. London: Robinson, 1792. 4th ed. Unpaginated (lt uniform foxing). Frontis, 12 other Fine full-pg engrs. Fine 3/4 polished morocco (recently rebound), raised bands, marbled bds, black leather title, gilt. Handsome. *Hartfield.* $495/£317

SPRAGUE, MARSHALL. A Gallery of Dudes. Boston: Little Brown, 1966. 1st ed. VG in dj. *Dumont.* $30/£19

SPRAGUE, MARSHALL. Massacre, the Tragedy at White River. Little Brown, (1957). 1st ed. Fine in VG dj. *Oregon.* $35/£22

SPRAGUE, MARSHALL. Massacre, the Tragedy of White River. Boston, (1957). 1st ed. VG + in dj (worn). *Pratt.* $25/£16

SPRAT, THOMAS. The History of the Royal Society of London. London, 1722. 3rd ed. Engr frontis, (16),438pp (bkpl); 2 fldg plts. Full leather (weak joints), dec spine, lettering piece (worn). *Scribe's Perch*.* $70/£45

SPREAIGHT, ROBERT. The Life of Eric Gill. London, 1966. 1st ed. Frontis port, dec eps. Dj (edges, spine lt browned). *Edwards.* $31/£20

SPRIGGS, A. O. Anatomy for Embalmers. Springfield/Toronto: Champion, 1934. Stated 1st ed. (Cl rubbed 3 inches at fore-edge), o/w Good. *Scribe's Perch*.* $65/£42

SPRIGGS, A. O. Champion Textbook on Embalming. Springfield, OH, 1933. 1st ed. VG (extrems sl worn). *Doctor's Library.* $100/£64

SPRIGGS, A. O. Restorative Art. Springfield/Toronto: Champion, 1934. Stated 1st ed. (Head bumped), o/w VG. *Scribe's Perch*.* $50/£32

SPRIGGS, A. O. Textbook on Embalming. Springfield/Toronto: Champion, 1933. Stated 1st ed. Good + (sl pencil note 1 pg). *Scribe's Perch*.* $60/£38

Spring and Summer in Lapland. (By Horace William Wheelwright.) London: Groombridge, 1871. 2nd ed. viii,407pp; 6 plts. Pale grn cl, spine gilt. (Joints lt rubbed), o/w Bright. *Sotheran.* $231/£148

SPRING, AGNES WRIGHT. Caspar Collins. NY: Columbia Univ, 1927. 1st ed. Good. *Lien.* $75/£48

SPRING, AGNES WRIGHT. Caspar Collins: The Life and Exploits of an Indian Fighter of the Sixties. NY: Columbia Univ, 1927. 1st ed. Brn cl. Fine in dj (soiled, spine dknd). *Harrington.* $80/£51

SPRING, AGNES WRIGHT. Casper Collins, The Life and Exploits of an Indian Fighter in the Sixties. NY, 1927. 1st ed. VG + in dj (2 sm pieces torn away). *Pratt.* $70/£45

SPRING, AGNES WRIGHT. The Cheyenne and Black Hills Stage and Express Routes. Glendale: A.H. Clark, 1949. 1st ed. Fldg map. Unopened. Red cl. Fine. *Harrington.* $135/£87

SPRING, AGNES WRIGHT. The Cheyenne and Black Hills Stage and Express Routes. Glendale: Clark, 1949. 1st ed. One of 1258. Fldg map, 17 plts. Uncut. (Spine sl faded), else Fine. *Argonaut.* $200/£128

SPRING, JAMES W. Boston and the Parker House. Boston: Privately ptd by Whipple, 1927. 1st ed. (Ink underlining), o/w VG. *Worldwide.* $18/£12

SPRINGER, CHARLES. Soldiering in Sioux Country: 1865. Benjamin Cooling (ed). San Diego, 1971. 1st ed. VG in VG dj. *Oregon.* $50/£32

SPRINGER, JOHN S. Forest Life and Forest Trees. NY: Harper, 1851. 1st ed. Frontis, 259pp (foxed, 1 leaf edge torn, few pencil mks); 8 plts. Pict red cl (bumped, rubbed, stained, 2 slits along fr joint, spine tear, chipped). Fair. *Blue Mountain.* $65/£42

SPROUL, KATHLEEN. The Birthday Sproul. NY: Dutton, (1932). 1st ed. VG (edgewear, lt soil). *Metropolitan*.* $28/£18

SPRUNT, ALEXANDER and E. B. CHAMBERLAIN. South Carolina Bird Life. Columbia: Univ of SC, (1977). 2nd ed, rev w/supp. 35 color plts. White buckram, gilt. VG + in color dj. *House.* $50/£32

SPRUNT, ALEXANDER and E. B. CHAMBERLAIN. South Carolina Bird Life. Columbia: Univ of SC, 1949. 1st ed. VG. *Mikesh.* $75/£48

SPRUNT, ALEXANDER. An Album of Southern Birds. Austin: Univ of TX, 1953. 1st ed. Color frontis. Blindstamped silver dec cl. Fine in VG slipcase. *Mikesh.* $30/£19

SPRUNT, JAMES. Chronicles of the Cape Fear River, 1660-1916. Raleigh: Edwards & Broughton, 1916. 2nd ed. 1/2 morocco (spine end chip). VG. Howes S859. *Cahan.* $285/£183

SPURR, GEORGE G. The Land of Gold: A Tale of '49. Boston: A. Williams, 1881. 1st ed. Signed. (Worn.) *Lien.* $40/£26

SPURR, JOSIAH EDWARD. Through the Yukon Gold Diggings. Boston: Eastern, 1900. Frontis. Dec cl. VG. *High Latitude.* $160/£103

SPURZHEIM, JOHANN GASPAR. Observations on the Deranged Manifestations of the Mind; or, Insanity. Boston: Marsh et al, 1833. 1st Amer ed. viii,260pp (stamp tp; gatherings smudged, sl mildewed, old lib stamp); 4 lithos. Mod cl-backed marbled bds, paper spine label. Good. *Gach.* $250/£160

SQUIER, EPHRAIM G. Notes on Central America. NY: Harper, 1855. 1st ed. xvi,17-397pp; 4 fldg maps, fldg plan, 9 plts. Brn cl (lt rubbed). *Adelson.* $185/£119

SQUIER, EPHRAIM G. Peru. NY: Harper, 1877. xx,599pp; map, 14 plts. Pict cl (rubbed; ex-lib). *Adelson.* $185/£119

SQUIER, EPHRAIM G. Travels in Central America, Particularly in Nicaragua. NY: D. Appleton, 1853. 1st ed. 2 vols. Lg 8vo. xxii,(2),424; 452pp; 26 plts (1 fldg), 9 maps, 60 wood engrs. Grn cl (lt rubbing), gilt. *Karmiole.* $600/£385

SQUIERS, GRANVILLE. Secret Hiding Places. London, 1934. 1st ed. Dj (chipped, creased, some loss). *Edwards.* $39/£25

SQUIRE, J. C. The Grub Street Nights Entertainments. London: Hodder, (1924). 1st UK ed. VG in dj (sl grubby, worn, chipped). *Williams.* $86/£55

ST. AUBYN-BRISBANE, F. If Stones Could Speak. London: Alexander-Ouseley, 1929. 1st ed. (Upper bd marked.) *Hollett.* $101/£65

ST. CLAIR, GEORGE. Creation Records Discovered in Egypt. London: David Nutt, 1898. 1st ed. xii,492pp (bkpl, name). Blue cl (bumped, spine dknd, rubbed), gilt. VG. *Blue Mountain*. $50/£32

ST. JAMES, IAN. The Balfour Conspiracy. London: Heinemann, 1981. 1st ed. Pub's slip laid in. Fine in dj. *Mordida*. $45/£29

ST. JOHN, CHARLES. Natural History and Sport in Moray. London, 1863. 1st illus ed. Frontis (corner creased). (Sm section cut from top tp; spine sl frayed.) *Grayling*. $78/£50

ST. JOHN, CHARLES. Natural History and Sport in Moray. Edinburgh, 1882. 2nd ed. Frontis (guard detached but present), 50,342pp. Dec eps. Good. *Scribe's Perch**. $95/£61

ST. JOHN, CHARLES. A Tour in Sutherlandshire. London, 1884. 2nd ed. 2 vols. (Cl lt faded, rubbed.) Contents Very Clean. *Grayling*. $101/£65

ST. JOHN, JUDITH. The Osborne Collection of Early Children's Books, 1566-1910. Toronto: Toronto Public Library, (1975). 3rd rev ed. 2 vols. Grn cl, gilt. *Baltimore**. $100/£64

ST. JOHN, P. Sea of Ice, or The Arctic Adventures. Boston: Mayhew & Baker, 1859. 1st Amer ed. 7 plts. VG. *Agvent*. $45/£29

ST. REYMONT, LADISLAS. The Peasants. London: Jarrolds, 1925. 1st eds; vol 1 in 2nd imp. 4 vols. Black cl, gilt. Fine set (few spots fore-edges). *Hollett*. $117/£75

STABLEFORD, BRIAN. The Paradox Game. London, 1976. 1st ed. Signed. Fine in dj. *Madle*. $30/£19

STACKPOLE, EDOUARD. The Sea Hunters: The Great Age of Whaling. Phila, 1953. 1st ed. VF in Good dj. *Bond*. $18/£12

STACKPOLE, EDWARD J. From Cedar Mountain to Antietam, August-September 1862. Harrisburg, (1959). 1st ed. 466pp. Fine in dj (wear, chipping). *Pratt*. $40/£26

STACKPOLE, EDWARD J. Sheridan in the Shenendoah. Harrisburg, 1961. 1st ed. VG + in dj (lt worn, sm tear). *Pratt*. $40/£26

STACPOOLE, H. DE VERE. Goblin Market, A Romance of To-Day.... NY: Doran, (1927). 1st Amer ed. (Bkpl), o/w Very Nice in dj (sticker removal scar spine). *Reese*. $20/£13

STACTON, D. A Ride on a Tiger, the Curious Travels of Victor Jacquemont. London, 1954. (Sl foxed.) Dj (frayed). *Maggs*. $19/£12

STACTON, DAVID. On a Balcony. NY, 1959. 1st Amer ed. Fine (spine extrems sl rubbed) in dj (spine sl sunned, extrems sl rubbed, sm tear). *Polyanthos*. $25/£16

STACY-JUDD, ROBERT B. Kabah: Adventures in the Jungles of Yucatan. Hollywood: House-Warren, 1951. Signed presentation. Dec grn cl. Good in dj (chipped). *Karmiole*. $60/£38

STADLING, J. Through Siberia.... F. H. H. Guillemard (ed). Westminster: Archibald Constable, 1901. Map. Dec cl (evidence of spine #). VG (rubber stamp title, new eps). *High Latitude*. $120/£77

STAEL-HOLSTEIN, ANNE LOUISE. Memoirs of the Private Life of My Father.... London, 1818. 1st Eng ed. 416pp (bkpl). Full gilt/blind-stamped leather (sl worn). *King*. $250/£160

STAFFORD, DAVID W. In Defense of the Flag. Corry, PA: Plain-Dealer Print, 1909. 1st ed. VG in ptd wrappers (sl chipped). *Mcgowan*. $85/£54

STAFFORD, JEAN. Bad Characters. NY, 1964. 1st Amer ed. Fine in dj (price-clipped). *Polyanthos*. $25/£16

STAFFORD, JEAN. The Collected Stories of Jean Stafford. NY: FSG, (1969). 1st ed. Fine (sl fading bd edges) in Fine dj (sl dknd extrems). *Between The Covers*. $100/£64

STAFFORD, JEAN. Elephi the Cat with the High IQ. NY: Farrar, 1962. 1st ed. Fine in Fine dj. *Beasley*. $65/£42

STAFFORD, WILLIAM. Around You, Your House and a Catechism. UK: Sceptre Press, 1979. 1st ed. #79/150. Signed presentation. Fine in ptd wraps. *Polyanthos*. $35/£22

STAGGE, JONATHAN. Turn of the Table. GC: DCC, 1940. 1st ed. (Inscrip), o/w Fine in VG dj (1/2-inch piece missing spine top, long closed tear fr panel, nicks). *Mordida*. $65/£42

STAIR, J. L. The Lightning Book. Chicago: Curtis Lighting, (1930). (Lt wear, soil.) *Freeman**. $60/£38

STAMER, WILLIAM. The Gentleman Emigrant. London, 1874. 2 vols. (8),306; (6),285pp + (2),15,(1)pp ads. (Edgeworn, lg dampstain fr cvr vol 2, old lib bkpls.) Internally VG. Howes S868. *Reese*. $300/£192

STAMM, CLAUS. The Dumplings and the Demons. NY: Viking, 1964. Kazue Mizamura (illus). 6 3/4 x 8 3/4. 48pp. Fine in dj. *Cattermole*. $30/£19

STAMM, CLAUS. Three Strong Women. NY: Viking, 1962. 1st ed. Kazue Mizamura (illus). 3/4 x 9. 32pp. Fine in dj. *Cattermole*. $45/£29

STAMP, T. and C. William Scoresby: Arctic Scientist. Caedmon, 1975. 1st ed. Port engr. Fine in VG + dj. *Mikesh*. $35/£22

STAMPP, KENNETH M. The Imperiled Union. NY, 1960. 1st ed. Fine in Fine dj. *Pratt*. $32/£21

STANARD, MARY NEWTON. The Dreamer: The Life Story of Edgar Allan Poe. Bell, 1909. 1st ed. VG-. *Book Broker*. $45/£29

STANARD, MARY NEWTON. Richmond, Its People and Its Story. Phila, 1923. 1st ed. Pict cl. VG + . *Pratt*. $50/£32

STANARD, MARY NEWTON. The Story of Virginia's First Century. Lippincott, 1928. 1st ed. Good + . *Book Broker*. $25/£16

STANARD, MARY S. Colonial Virginia, Its People and Customs. Phila/London, 1917. 'Limited Edition.' Pict cl (sl worn). Contents VG. Howes S869. *New Hampshire**. $35/£22

STANDIFORD, LES. Spill. NY: Atlantic Monthly, 1991. 1st ed. VF in dj. *Mordida*. $35/£22

STANDING BEAR, LUTHER. My People the Sioux. E. A. Brininstool (ed). Boston: Houghton Mifflin, 1928. 1st ed. Orange dec cl (spine sl faded). NF. *Harrington*. $65/£42

STANDISH, BURT L. Crossed Signals. Barse, 1928. 1st ed. Good + . *Plapinger*. $110/£71

STANDS IN TIMBER, JOHN and MARGOT LIBERTY. Cheyenne Memories. New Haven: Yale Univ, 1967. 1st ed. VG in dj. *Lien*. $50/£32

STANFIELD, CLARKSON. Stanfield's Coast Scenery. London: Smith, Elder, 1836. 1st ed. viii,128pp (lt browned); extra engr tp, 39 b/w engr plts (sl foxed), guards. Yellow eps; aeg. Orig full dk brn morocco (sl worn, scuffed), gilt. *Baltimore**. $140/£90

Stanford's London Atlas of Universal Geography. London, 1904. 3rd ed. 1/2 calf, cl (sl rubbed). Internally Clean. *Gretton*. $133/£85

STANFORD, ALFRED. Navigator; The Story of Nathaniel Bowditch. Morrow, 1927. VG. *Bookcell*. $20/£13

STANFORD, JANE KINDERLY. A Lady's Gift, or Woman As She Ought to Be. Phila: Carey Lea & Blanchard, 1836. 1st Amer ed. 232pp (marginal stains, lacks fep). Later 19th-cent burgundy cl (lt rubbed). *Karmiole*. $75/£48

STANGER, FRANK M. et al. Who Discovered the Golden Gate? San Mateo, 1969. 1st ed. #138/1500. Unopened, untrimmed. Fine. *Turpen.* $40/£26

STANHOPE, PHILIP HENRY. Notes of Conversations with the Duke of Wellington, 1831-1851. London, 1889. 3rd ed. xvi,341pp. Red cl (sl worn). *Maggs.* $156/£100

STANLEY, ARTHUR PENRHYN. Sinai and Palestine. London, 1889. New ed. lviii,560pp; 7 color maps (4 fldg). Marbled eps, aeg. Contemp blind-tooled calf, morocco spine label. *Edwards.* $47/£30

STANLEY, CHARLES HENRY. The Chess Player's Instructor: Or, Guide to Beginners. NY: Robert M. De Witt, (1859). 72pp (lt foxed, 2 leaves loose, pencil mks, top edge of rear blank torn out). Limp grn cl (rubbed, soiled), gilt. *Blue Mountain.* $125/£80

STANLEY, EDWARD. Before and After Waterloo. Jane H. Adeane & Maud Grenfell (eds). London, 1907. 1st ed. Teg. 3/4 leather, marbled bds, eps. (Bkpl, sl worn.) *King.* $150/£96

STANLEY, EDWARD. A Treatise on Diseases of the Bones. Phila, 1849. 310pp (foxed). Tooled cl bds. Good. *Doctor's Library.* $165/£106

STANLEY, EDWIN. Rambles in Wonderland. NY, 1883. 179pp; 12 plts, fldg map. Grn cl, gilt. (Edgewear, map taped on back), else Good. Howes S880. *Price.* $95/£61

STANLEY, FATHER. Fort Bascom, Comanche-Kiowa Barrier. N.p., (1961). 1st ed. Signed. Fine in dj (spine lt faded). *Pratt.* $105/£67

STANLEY, FATHER. Fort Stanton. N.p., (1964). 1st ed. Ltd to 500. Signed. Fine in dj (spine lt faded). *Pratt.* $105/£67

STANLEY, FATHER. Railroads of the Texas Panhandle. Borger, TX: Hess, 1976. 1st ed. Fine in dj. *Gibbs.* $85/£54

STANLEY, FRANK. Grant That Maxwell Bought. (Denver, 1952.) 1st ed. One of 250 numbered, signed. Fldg map in rear pocket. Howes C892. *Ginsberg.* $600/£385

STANLEY, GEORGE F. G. Mapping the Frontier. Seattle, 1970. 1st Amer ed. Fine in dj (sl rubbed, price-clipped). *Baade.* $50/£32

STANLEY, HENRY M. The Autobiography of Sir Henry Morton Stanley, G.C.B. Dorothy Stanley (ed). London, 1909. 1st UK ed. Frontis port, 15 plts, fldg map. (Ex-lib, ink stamps, upper hinge cracked, inner margin feps stuck to pastedown; cl rubbed.) *Edwards.* $31/£20

STANLEY, HENRY M. Autobiography. Boston: Houghton Mifflin, Oct 1909. 1st US ed. 16 full-pg guarded photogravures; lg fldg color map at rear. Teg. Dec cvr, spine. Good+ (sl chips). *Scribe's Perch*.* $47/£30

STANLEY, HENRY M. The Congo and the Founding of Its Free State. NY: Harper, 1885. 1st Amer ed. 2 vols. 2 fldg maps in cvr pockets. Grn pict cl (ends worn; hinges weak). *Argosy.* $250/£160

STANLEY, HENRY M. The Congo and the Founding of Its Free State. NY: Harper, 1885. 2 vols. xxvii,528; x,483,12ads pp; 5 maps, 44 plts. Pict cl (rubbed). *Adelson.* $285/£183

STANLEY, HENRY M. The Congo and the Founding of Its Free State. NY: Harper, 1885. 1st ed. 2 vols. xxvii,528; x,483pp,12ads; fldg maps in pockets. Pict grn cl, gilt. VG. *Terramedia.* $300/£192

STANLEY, HENRY M. How I Found Livingstone. London: Sampson Low et al, 1872. 1st ed. Frontis port, xxiii+736pp; 6 maps (3 fldg), 27 full-pg wood engr illus. Later 1/2 calf, marbled bds, spine gilt, raised bands. (Frontis, prelims sl dampstained, sm repairs maps), o/w Good. *Sotheran.* $304/£195

STANLEY, HENRY M. In Darkest Africa. NY, 1890. 2 vols. 3 fldg maps in rear pockets each vol. Pict cl (extrems sl worn). Contents VG. *New Hampshire*.* $70/£45

STANLEY, HENRY M. In Darkest Africa. NY: Scribner, 1890. 1st ed. 2 vols. xiv,547; xvi,540pp; 3 fldg maps, 46 plts. Grn pict cl (lt rubbed). *Adelson.* $200/£128

STANLEY, HENRY M. In Darkest Africa. NY: Scribner, 1891. 1st US trade ed, 2nd issue. 2 vols. Lg fldg map rear pocket each vol. Brn coated eps. Grn cl (sl rubbed, worn), gilt. *Baltimore*.* $80/£51

STANLEY, HENRY M. My Dark Companions. London: Sampson Low, 1893. 1st ed. Aeg. Pict cl, gilt. Very Nice (sl shaken). *Hollett.* $218/£140

STANLEY, HENRY M. Through the Dark Continent. NY: Harper, 1878. 1st ed. 2 vols. Engr frontis ports, lg fldg map rear pocket each vol. Marbled edges, eps. Pub's dk brn morocco, marbled bds (edges sl worn, sl scuffed; sl aged), raised bands, gilt. *Baltimore*.* $170/£109

STANLEY, HENRY M. Through the Dark Continent. NY: Harper, 1879. 2 vols. 9 (of 10) maps, incl 1 fldg in rep pocket vol 2. Pict emb grn cl, gilt. (Lacks fldg map which should be in ep pocket vol 1; eps vol 2 damaged, reglued; fr joint vol 2 splitting; rubbed, worn), else Good. *Pacific*.* $115/£74

STANLEY, HENRY M. Through the Dark Continent. NY: Harper, 1879. 2 vols. xiv,522; ix,566+ads; 10 maps (incl 2 lg fldg maps in end pockets). Grn gilt pict cl (sl worn), else VG. *Terramedia.* $300/£192

STANLEY, HENRY M. Through the Dark Continent. London: George Newnes, 1899. 2nd fully illus, rev ed. 2 vols. xxxii,400; xi,(i)blank, 419pp, 1/2-titles, frontis each vol, 32 plts, 6 maps vol 1 (1 fldg). Contemp black 1/4 calf (spine ends worn), gilt. Good (fldg map, occasional leaf sl foxed). *Morrell.* $156/£100

STANLEY, LOUIS T. Collecting Staffordshire Pottery. Doubleday, 1963. 1st ed. VG (shelfworn) in dj (edgeworn, price-clipped). *My Bookhouse.* $25/£16

STANLEY, LOUIS T. Collecting Staffordshire Pottery. London, 1963. 4 color plts. Dj (sl chipped, spine head loss). *Edwards.* $78/£50

STANNUS, MRS. GRAYDON. Old Irish Glass. London: Connoisseur, 1921. 60 plts. VG. *Hollett.* $133/£85

STANSBURY, CHARLES FREDERICK. The Lake of the Great Dismal Swamp. A&C Boni, 1925 (c. 1924). VG- (newsclips glued to rep). *Book Broker.* $50/£32

STANSKY, PETER and WILLIAM ABRAHAMS. Journey to the Frontier. London: Constable, (1966). 1st ed. NF in VG dj. *Turtle Island.* $50/£32

STANTON, CAREY. An Island Memoir. L.A.: Zamorano Club, 1984. One of 350. Brn cl, gilt. Fine. *Parmer.* $50/£32

STANTON, ELIZABETH CADY. Address to the Legislature of New-York, Adopted by the State Woman's Rights Convention. Albany: Weed, Parsons, 1854. Yellow ptd wraps (dampstained). *Metropolitan*.* $46/£29

STANTON, ELIZABETH CADY. Eighty Years and More...1815-1897. NY, 1898. 1st ed. 474pp. VG (bkpl removed fep; cvrs sl dust-speckled). *Second Life.* $90/£58

STANTON, P. B. The Gothic Revival and American Church Architecture. Johns Hopkins, 1968. 120 plts. 1/2 cl. Sound. *Ars Artis.* $47/£30

STANTON, ROBERT BREWSTER. Down the Colorado. Dwight L. Smith (ed). Norman, OK, 1965. 1st ed. Black cl. (Sm tape mk rep), else Fine in VG dj. *Five Quail.* $55/£35

STAPLEDON, OLAF. The Flames. London, 1947. 1st ed. VG in dj (chipped). *Madle.* $35/£22

STAPLEDON, OLAF. The Flames. London: Secker & Warburg, 1947. 1st ed. VG in dj (spine faded, sm chip spine head). *Certo.* $40/£26

STAPLEDON, OLAF. Last Men in London. London: Methuen, 1932. 1st ed. (Lt rubbed, few spots.) *Hollett.* $55/£35

STAPLEDON, OLAF. Odd John. London: Methuen, 1935. 1st ed. (Prelims, fore-edge lt spotted; hinges rubbed.) *Hollett.* $47/£30

STAPLES, THOMAS S. Reconstruction in Arkansas, 1862-1874. NY: Columbia, 1923. 1st ed. Contemp cl w/orig ptd wrappers bound in at end. (Ex-lib.) Howes S890. *Ginsberg.* $125/£80

STARBUCK, ALEXANDER. History of the American Whale Fishery from Its Earliest Inception to the Year 1876. Washington: SMD107, 1878. 1st ed. (9),768pp; 6 plts. Orig full calf, leather spine labels. Very Nice. Howes S892. *Ginsberg.* $600/£385

STARBUCK, ALEXANDER. History of the American Whale Fishery...to the Year 1876. NY: Argosy-Antiquarian, 1964. Facs rpt of 1878 ed. One of 750. 2 vols. Frontis port, 6 plts. VG. *High Latitude.* $125/£80

STARK, FREYA. The Arab Island: The Middle East 1939-1943. NY: Knopf, 1945. 1st US ed. 32 plts, engr tp, map. (Sl rubbed), o/w VG. *Worldwide.* $18/£12

STARK, FREYA. Baghdad Sketches. Baghdad: Times, 1932. 1st ed, 1st bk. VG (eps, prelims, edges browned, sl spotted; cvrs sl soiled, corners sl rubbed; spine faded, title label chipped, browned). *Virgo.* $546/£350

STARK, FREYA. Baghdad Sketches. NY: Dutton, 1938. 1st ed. 42 plts, dbl-pg map. (Bkpl; sl rubbed), o/w VG. *Worldwide.* $30/£19

STARK, FREYA. Beyond Euphrates. London, 1951. 1st ed. Dbl-pg map. (Sl warped.) *Edwards.* $23/£15

STARK, FREYA. Beyond Eurprates, Autobiography, 1928-33. London, 1951. 1st ed. Map. Fine in dj (sl torn). *Petersfield.* $28/£18

STARK, FREYA. Dust in the Lion's Paw: Autobiography 1939-1946. London: John Murray, (1961). (Bkpl; corner bumped.) Dj. *Archaeologia.* $35/£22

STARK, FREYA. The Lycian Shore. London, 1956. 1st ed. Fine in dj (sl torn). *Petersfield.* $28/£18

STARK, FREYA. The Lycian Shore. London, 1956. 1st Eng ed. Very Nice in dj. *Clearwater.* $44/£28

STARK, FREYA. The Lycian Shore. NY: Harcourt, Brace, 1956. 1st ed. Fldg map. (Sl rubbed, soiled), o/w VG. *Worldwide.* $22/£14

STARK, FREYA. The Minaret of Djam. London, 1970. 1st ed. Map. Fine in dj. *Petersfield.* $22/£14

STARK, FREYA. Over the Rim of the World. Caroline Moorehead (ed). London, 1988. 1st ed. Dj. *Edwards.* $23/£15

STARK, FREYA. Perseus in the Wind. London, 1948. 1st ed. Dj (sl foxed). *Petersfield.* $28/£18

STARK, FREYA. Turkey: A Sketch of Turkish History. London: Thames & Hudson, 1971. 1st Eng ed. NF in dj. *Hadley.* $70/£45

STARK, FREYA. The Valleys of the Assassins and Other Persian Travels. London, 1934. 1st ed. Frontis port, 6 maps. (Cl discoloring.) *Edwards.* $31/£20

STARK, JAMES H. Stark's History and Guide to Barbados and the Caribbee Islands. Boston/Barbados: Photo-Electrotype Co/Bowen, (1893). Frontis, (vii),221,(xv)pp (hinges cracked); fldg map (sm tear). Pict brn cl (bumped, rubbed), gilt. Good. *Blue Mountain.* $45/£29

STARK, JAMES H. Stark's History and Guide to the Bahama Islands. Boston: Photo-Electrotype, (1891). 1st ed. (xii),(244),(xii)pp. Pict cl. (Eps cracking, spines sl dknd), o/w Nice. *Ash.* $156/£100

STARK, JAMES H. Stark's History and Guide to the Bahama Islands.... Boston: Stark, (1891). 243pp + 18pp ads; fldg chart, 2 fldg maps, 2 other maps. Dec cvr, spine. Good. *Scribe's Perch*.* $34/£22

STARK, RICHARD. (Pseud of Donald Westlake.) The Handle. London: Allison & Busby, 1985. 1st UK ed. Signed. Fine in Fine dj. *Old London.* $25/£16

STARK, RICHARD. (Pseud of Donald Westlake.) The Man with the Getaway Face. London: Allison & Busby, 1984. 1st UK ed. Signed. Fine in Fine dj. *Old London.* $25/£16

STARKEY, LLEWELLYN H. (ed). The Diamond Fields of Brazil. NY, 1904. Map. (Sl pencil underlining; cvrs sl faded), else Good in wraps. *King.* $22/£14

STARKEY, MARION L. The Congregational Way. GC: Doubleday, 1966. 1st ed. VG in dj (sl worn). *Lien.* $30/£19

STARR, F. RATCHFORD. Farm Echoes. NY: OJ, 1886. 110pp. Blue dec cl, gilt. VG. *Price.* $65/£42

STARR, JOHN W., JR. Lincoln and the Railroads. NY: Dodd, Mead, 1927. 1st ed. (Bkpl, tape removal fr pastedown; spine sl faded, cvr lt soiled.) *Glenn.* $35/£22

STARR, STEPHEN Z. The Union Cavalry in the Civil War. Baton Rouge, 1979-1985. 3 vols. Vols 1, 3 1st eds; vol 2, 2nd ed. VG in VG djs. *Scribe's Perch*.* $100/£64

STARRETT, VINCENT (ed). 221B: Studies in Sherlock Holmes by Various Hands. NY: Macmillan, 1940. 1st US ed. Errata slip. Good (cvr wear). *Gravesend.* $80/£51

STARRETT, VINCENT (ed). 221B: Studies in Sherlock Holmes by Various Hands. NY: Macmillan, 1940. 1st US ed. Errata slip. VG in Good dj (sm stain fr; inner panel trimmed). *Gravesend.* $150/£96

STARRETT, VINCENT and AMES WILLIAMS. Bibliography of Stephen Crane. Glendale: John Valentine, 1949. 1st ed. Inscribed presentation from Valentine. 1/4 cl. Prospectus, unused order form laid in. VF in dj. *Macdonnell.* $100/£64

STARRETT, VINCENT. Autolycus in Limbo. NY: Dutton, 1943. 1st ed. VG in dj (worn). *Graf.* $37/£24

STARRETT, VINCENT. Book Column. Chicago: Caxton Club, 1958. 1st ed. One of 350. Mint in acetate dj. *Graf.* $70/£45

STARRETT, VINCENT. Bookman's Holiday, the Private Satisfactions of an Incurable Collector. NY: Random House, (1942). 1st ed. Fine in dj. *Oak Knoll.* $60/£38

STARRETT, VINCENT. Bookman's Holiday. NY, (1942). 1st ed. VG. *Mcclintock.* $35/£22

STARRETT, VINCENT. Books Alive. NY: Random House, 1940. 1st US ed. Good (spine, fore-edge discoloration). *Gravesend.* $30/£19

STARRETT, VINCENT. Books and Bipeds. NY: Argus Books, (1947). 1st ed. Fine in dj (chipped). *Oak Knoll.* $65/£42

STARRETT, VINCENT. Born in a Bookshop: Chapters from the Chicago Renascence. Norman: Univ of OK, (1965). 1st US ed. VG in VG dj (lt wear). *Gravesend.* $55/£35

STARRETT, VINCENT. Ebony Flame. Chicago, (1922). 1st ed. Ltd to 350 numbered, signed. Cl-backed pict bds (ends frayed, sl rubbed; sl bent). *King.* $65/£42

STARRETT, VINCENT. Et Cetera, a Collector's Scrap-Book. Chicago: Pascal Covici, 1924. 1st ed. One of 625 numbered. Teg, uncut. Orig linen-backed bds. Fine in dj (creased). BAL 4100-A. *Macdonnell.* $150/£96

STARRETT, VINCENT. Oriental Encounters. Chicago: Normandie House, 1938. 1st ed. Ltd to 249. Signed. VG. *Gravesend.* $60/£38

STARRETT, VINCENT. Oriental Encounters. Chicago: Normandie House, 1938. 1st ed. Signed, inscribed. Orange cl over bds. NF (bkpl) in custom case. *Old London*. $125/£80

STARRETT, VINCENT. Penny Wise and Book Foolish. NY: Covici Friede, 1929. 1st ed. One of 275 for sale signed. Frontis, 15 plts. Teg, rest untrimmed; largely unopened. Gilt-dec paper-cvrd bds. VF in orig glassine dj (torn, repaired), pub's slipcase (worn). *Pirages*. $150/£96

STARRETT, VINCENT. The Quick and the Dead. Sauk City, 1965. 1st ed. Fine in Fine dj. *Mcclintock*. $100/£64

STARRETT, VINCENT. The Quick and the Dead. Sauk City: Arkham House, 1965. 1st ed. Dj. *Swann**. $80/£51

Stars and Stripes in Rebeldom.... (William C. Bates, ed.) Boston: T.O.H.P. Burnham, 1862. 1st ed, '2nd thousand.' 137pp + (6)pp pub's ads (lacks rep, lt marginal dampstain rear of bk). Grn cl. Good. *Lucas*. $125/£80

State Prisoner, a Tale of the French Regency. (By Mary Louisa Boyle.) London: Saunders & Otley, 1837. 1st ed. 2 vols. 302; 304pp. Calf-backed bds. VG. *Second Life*. $200/£128

Statistics of Madison and Dane County, Wisconsin. Madison: David Atwood, Printer, 1853. 16pp; 3 engrs. Self wrapper w/engr on fr cvr. *New Hampshire**. $120/£77

STAURT, FRANCIS. The White Hare. Collins, 1936. 1st Eng ed. Bright (spine lettering sl chipped) in dj (edge sl stained) w/wrap-around band. *Clearwater*. $101/£65

STEAD, CHRISTINA. Dark Places of the Heart. NY: Holt, Rinehart, Winston, (1966). 1st ed. NF in dj. *Antic Hay*. $30/£19

STEAD, CHRISTINA. The Little Hotel. NY: HRW, (1973). NF in dj. *Between The Covers*. $50/£32

STEAD, CHRISTINA. A Little Tea, a Little Chat. NY: HB&Co, (1948). 1st ed. (Paper edges sl browned), else Fine in NF dj (long scratch fr panel, chip rear panel). *Between The Covers*. $125/£80

STEAD, CHRISTINA. The People with Dogs. Boston, 1952. 1st Amer ed. VG in dj (lt worn). *Argosy*. $75/£48

STEAD, CHRISTINA. The People with Dogs. Boston: Little Brown, 1952. 1st ed. Fine in VG dj (spine sl tanned, chip top fr panel). *Between The Covers*. $85/£54

STEAD, ESTELLE W. My Father. NY: George H. Doran, (1913). 15 plts. Maroon cl, gilt. VG (lacks frontis; foxed, fr hinge cracked, rear hinge starting; bumped, soiled). *Blue Mountain*. $25/£16

STEADMAN, RALPH. America. Fantagraphics Books, (1989). One of 500 signed. VG in dj. *Argosy*. $75/£48

STEADMAN, RALPH. Still Life with Raspberry or The Bumper Book of Steadman. Rapp & Whiting, 1969. 1st ed. VG in dj (torn, internally repaired). *Words Etc*. $78/£50

STEALINGWORTH, SLIM. Tom Wesselmann. NY: Abbeville, (1980). 1st ed. Inscribed by artist. 2 fldg illus. Pict label on cvr. Mint in mylar wrappers. *Argosy*. $350/£224

STEARN, WILLIAM T. The Australian Flower Paintings of Ferdinand Bauer.... London: Basilisk, 1976. One of 515 numbered. Folio. 25 mtd color plts, dbl-pg map. Prospectus laid in. Orig 1/4 morocco. Cl fldg case. *Swann**. $373/£239

STEARNS, E. J. Notes on Uncle Tom's Cabin. Phila: Lippincott, Grambo, 1853. 2nd ed. 314pp + ads. (Bkpl, text heavily spotted; cl sl shelfworn, spine lt sunned), o/w Good. *Brown*. $100/£64

STEBBING, E. P. The Diary of a Sportsman Naturalist in India. London: J. Lane, 1920. 1st ed. VG. *Mikesh*. $75/£48

STEBBING, HILARY. Maggie the Streamlined Taxi. London: Transatlantic Arts, 1943. 1st ed. 7 1/4 x 10. 24pp. Pict bds. VG in dj. *Cattermole*. $50/£32

STEBBINS, GILES B. Upwards of Seventy Years. NY: US Book Co, (1890). 1st ed. 308pp (sl dampstain lower corner). Brn cl. VG. *Lucas*. $95/£61

STEBBINS, R. C. Amphibians and Reptiles of Western North America. NY, (1954). 104 plts. Dec cl. VG + in Good + dj. *Mikesh*. $35/£22

STECK, FRANCIS BORGIA. The Jolliet-Marquette Expedition, 1673. Washington, DC: Catholic Univ of America, 1927. 1st ed. Ptd wraps. Good (extrems worn; cvr stains). *Wantagh*. $50/£32

STECKMESSER, KENT LADD. The Western Hero in History and Legend. Norman, (1965). 1st ed. VG + in dj (chipped, stained). *Pratt*. $40/£26

STEDMAN, E. C. Edgar Allan Poe. Cedar Rapids, IA: Privately ptd, 1909. Ltd to 200. Frontis port. Grn cl, gilt. *Maggs*. $31/£20

STEDMAN, J. G. Narrative of a Five Years Expedition Against the Revolted Negroes of Surinam. Barre, MA: Imprint Soc, 1971. #89/1950. Fine in box. *Metropolitan**. $100/£64

STEDMAN, J. G. Narrative of a Five Years' Expedition Against the Revolted Negroes of Surinam. Barre: Imprint Soc, 1971. #107/1950 numbered, signed by Rudolf van Lier (intro). 2 vols. 3 fldg maps, fldg plt. Cl-backed French marbled paper-cvrd bds, paper labels. Fine set in pub's slipcase. *Hermitage*. $150/£96

STEDMAN, J. G. Narrative of a Five Years' Expedition Against the Revolted Negroes of Surinam...1772 to 1777. Barre, MA: Imprint Soc, 1971. One of 1950. 2 vols. 80 engrs. Cl-backed marbled bds, ptd spine labels. Fine in slipcase. *Bohling*. $60/£38

STEED, NEVILLE. Chipped. London: Weidenfeld & Nicolson, 1988. 1st ed. Fine in dj. *Murder By The Book*. $45/£29

STEED, NEVILLE. Clockwork. London: Weidenfeld & Nicolson, 1989. 1st ed. Fine in dj. *Murder By The Book*. $45/£29

STEEGMAN, JOHN. The Artist and the Country House. Country Life, 1949. 1st ed. (Inscrip), else NF in dj. *Hadley*. $55/£35

STEEL, FLORA ANNIE (retold by). English Fairy Tales. NY: Macmillan, 1918. 1st trade ed. 16 color plts. (Spine faded, worn.) Contents, plts VG. *New Hampshire**. $90/£58

STEEL, J. H. A Treatise on the Diseases of the Ox. 1881. xxii,498pp; 2 plts. (Joint cracked.) *Whitehart*. $39/£25

STEEL, JOHN H. An Analysis of the Congress Spring, with Practical Remarks on Its Medical Properties. Saratoga Springs, 1854. 35pp. Gilt-tooled cl. Good (binding loose, spine chipped, extrems worn; bkpl). *Doctor's Library*. $75/£48

STEEL, JOHN H. An Analysis of the Congress Spring.... NY: William W. Rose, 1856. Rpt. Frontis view. Black cl (sl string-mkd). *Maggs*. $28/£18

STEEL, JOHN H. An Analysis of the Mineral Waters of Saratoga and Ballston.... Saratoga Springs: G. M. Davison, 1838. 2nd ed. Contemp figured purple cl (sl worn), floral design. *Maggs*. $62/£40

STEELE, JAMES W. Frontier Army Sketches. Chicago: Jansen, 1883. 329,(6)pp. Pict dec cl. Howes S922. *Ginsberg*. $100/£64

STEELE, JAMES W. Rand, McNally and Co.'s New Guide to the Pacific Coast. Santa Fe Route. Chicago: Rand, McNally, 1890. 212pp + 6pp ads (stamp 1 ad). *Dawson*. $100/£64

STEELE, JAMES. Old Californian Days. Chicago: Belford-Clark, 1889. 1st ed. 227pp. Good. *Lien.* $40/£26

STEELE, JOHN. Across the Plains in 1850. Joseph Schafer (ed). Chicago: Caxton Club, 1930. Ltd to 350 ptd. Frontis, port, 5 plts, fldg map. Teg; unopened. Red cl-backed 'gold stenciled' brn cl bds, spine gilt. Fine in in pub's tan paperbd slipcase. Howes S923. *Cady.* $100/£64

STEELE, JOHN. Across the Plains in 1850. Joseph Schafer (ed). Chicago: Caxton, 1930. 1st ed. One of 350 ptd. Fldg map. (Bkpl.) Boxed. Howes S923. *Ginsberg.* $250/£160

STEELE, MATTHEW FORNEY. American Campaigns. Washington, 1909. 2 vols. VG. *Pratt.* $65/£42

STEELE, R. The Earliest English Music Printing...to the Close of the 16th Century. Bibliographical Soc, 1903. Uncut. Clean in ptd paper cvrs (worn). *Moss.* $47/£30

STEELE, ROBERT W. and MARY DAVIES. Early Dayton...1796-1896. Dayton: Shuey, 1896. 1st ed. 247pp; 3 maps. Pict cl. *Ginsberg.* $100/£64

STEELE, THOMAS S. A Voyage to Viking-Land. Boston, (1896). 22,194pp + 3pp ads; fldg map. Good (fr hinge starting). *Scribe's Perch*.* $30/£19

STEEPLE, E. W. et al. Island of Skye. Edinburgh: S.M.C., 1935. 1st ed. Fldg map in rear pocket. (Few mks, pencil notes; label fr pastedown; worn, faded.) *Hollett.* $31/£20

STEERS, J. A. The Coastline of England and Wales. London, 1948. 2nd imp. 117 plts (2 color). Good in dj. *Henly.* $44/£28

STEEVENS, CHARLES. Reminiscences of My Military Life from 1795 to 1818. Nathaniel Steevens (ed). Winchester, 1878. Frontis port, 124pp,ix (appendix). Aeg. Red cl (spotting), gilt. *Maggs.* $234/£150

STEFANSSON, VILHJALMUR. The Adventure of Wrangel Island.... NY: Macmillan, 1925. Fldg map. Good (extrems sl rubbed). *High Latitude.* $45/£29

STEFANSSON, VILHJALMUR. Arctic Manual. NY, 1944. 1st ed. Good (ex-lib). *High Latitude.* $25/£16

STEFANSSON, VILHJALMUR. Arctic Manual. NY: Macmillan, 1944. 1st ed. VG (sl worn). *High Latitude.* $60/£38

STEFANSSON, VILHJALMUR. Arctic Manual. NY: Macmillan, 1953. VG in VG dj. *Perier.* $35/£22

STEFANSSON, VILHJALMUR. The Friendly Arctic. NY: Macmillan, 1953. New ed. Signed, inscribed. 2 fldg maps in pocket. VG. *High Latitude.* $45/£29

STEFANSSON, VILHJALMUR. My Life with the Eskimo. NY: Macmillan, 1913. 1st ed, 1st bk. 2 fldg maps. Dec cl. VG. *High Latitude.* $95/£61

STEFANSSON, VILHJALMUR. My Life with the Eskimo. NY: Macmillan, 1921. 2 fldg maps. Blue cl. Fine. *Appelfeld.* $50/£32

STEFANSSON, VILHJALMUR. The Three Voyages of Martin Frobisher in Search of a Passage to Cathay and India by the North-West, A.D. 1576-8.... Amsterdam/NY: N. Israel/De Capo, 1971. Facs rpt. 2 vols in 1. As New. *High Latitude.* $75/£48

STEGNER, WALLACE (ed). This Is Dinosaur. NY: Knopf, 1955. 1st ed. Blue/ochre cvrs (sl wear). VG+ in Good dj (chips, pieces missing). *Five Quail.* $75/£48

STEGNER, WALLACE. All the Little Live Things. NY: Viking, (1967). (Fore-edge lt spotted), else VF in dj. *Captain's Bookshelf.* $125/£80

STEGNER, WALLACE. Angle of Repose. GC: Doubleday, 1971. 1st ed. (Bkpl), else NF in dj (sm tear). *Pacific*.* $184/£118

STEGNER, WALLACE. The Gathering of Zion. NY, 1964. 1st ed. Fine in NF dj. *Warren.* $85/£54

STEGNER, WALLACE. A Shooting Star. Viking, 1961. 1st ed. NF in dj. *Authors Of West.* $60/£38

STEGNER, WALLACE. The Uneasy Chair: A Biography of Bernard DeVoto. Doubleday, 1974. 1st ed. Rev copy, slip laid in. Fine in VG dj. *Authors Of West.* $75/£48

STEGNER, WALLACE. Wolf Willow. NY: Viking, (1962). 1st ed. (Inscrip), else Fine in dj (lt used, sm tears, price-clipped). *Captain's Bookshelf.* $60/£38

STEICHEN, EDWARD (comp). US Navy War Photographs: Pearl Harbor to Tokyo Harbor. NY: US Camera, (c 1946). 1st ed. VG in ptd wrappers (rubbed, few creases). *Cahan.* $40/£26

STEICHEN, EDWARD. The Blue Ghosts. NY: Harcourt, Brace, 1947. 1st ed. Blue cl. VG. *Smith.* $75/£48

STEICHEN, EDWARD. A Life in Photography. NY: Doubleday, 1963. (Owner stamp, fep lt foxed), else NF in VG dj. *Cahan.* $50/£32

STEICHEN, EDWARD. A Life in Photography. NY: Doubleday, 1963. 1st ed. VG in VG dj (price-clipped, sl tape repair). *Smith.* $125/£80

STEIG, WILLIAM. The Bad Speller. NY: Windmill, 1970. 1st ed. 7x7. Dec cl. Fine in dj. *Cattermole.* $45/£29

STEIG, WILLIAM. The Rejected Lovers. NY, (1951). 1st Amer ed. Uncut. Dec cvrs. Fine (inscrip; spine sl sunned, extrems sl rubbed). *Polyanthos.* $25/£16

STEIN, AUREL. On Alexander's Track to the Indus. London: Macmillan, 1929. 1st ed. 2 fldg maps. Teg. Gilt-dec cl. (Corners, spine sl worn; scattered foxing), else Very Nice. *Argonaut.* $425/£272

STEIN, AUREL. On Ancient Central-Asian Tracks. Jeannette Mirsky (ed). NY: Pantheon, 1964. 1st ed. Dbl-pg map. VG in dj (sl torn). *Worldwide.* $45/£29

STEIN, DAVID LEWIS. Living the Revolution: The Yippies in Chicago. Indianapolis: Bobbs-Merrill, 1969. 1st ed. NF in dj (sl rubbed, sl spine wear, price-clipped). *Sclanders.* $23/£15

STEIN, GERTRUDE and LEON M. SOLOMON. Motor Automatism. NY: Phoenix Book Shop, 1969. One of 500. 1st ed. Ptd blue wraps. NF. *Blue Mountain.* $25/£16

STEIN, GERTRUDE. An Acquaintance with Description. London: Seizin, 1929. 1st ed. Ltd to 225 numbered, signed. Oyster-white linen, gilt-lettered spine. (Sm, very faint stain fr cvr), else Fine. *Argonaut.* $450/£288

STEIN, GERTRUDE. Alphabets and Birthdays. New Haven: Yale, 1957. 1st ed (1500 ptd). Nice (lt dust spotting) in dj. *Reese.* $85/£54

STEIN, GERTRUDE. The Autobiography of Alice B. Toklas. NY: Harcourt, Brace, (1933). 1st ed. Blue cl (sl water stain fr/back panels), silver motif. VG in dj (creased, chip, sl water stain). *Hermitage.* $150/£96

STEIN, GERTRUDE. The Autobiography of Alice B. Toklas. London: Bodley Head, 1933. 1st Eng ed. VG in dj (sl creased). *Hadley.* $179/£115

STEIN, GERTRUDE. Blood on the Dining-Room Floor. Banyan, (1948). One of 600 numbered. 1st ed. (Top corner 1 pg stained.) Red cl-backed marbled bds (edges rubbed, spine faded), gilt. NF in blue slipcase (stained). *Blue Mountain.* $75/£48

STEIN, GERTRUDE. Blood on the Dining-Room Floor. Banyan, (1948). 1st ed. Ltd to 626 numbered. Cl-backed marbled bds (sl worn) in slipcase (sl used). *King.* $175/£112

STEIN, GERTRUDE. Brewsie and Willie. NY: Random House, (1946). 1st ed. (Top edge dusty), else VG in Good dj. *Reese.* $25/£16

STEIN, GERTRUDE. Brewsie and Willie. NY: Random House, 1946. 1st ed. Fine (eps sl discolored) in NF dj (sl soiled). *Pirages.* $50/£32

STEIN, GERTRUDE. Composition as Explanation. London: Hogarth, 1926. 1st Eng ed. (Cvrs tanned, sl chafed.) Clearwater. $62/£40

STEIN, GERTRUDE. An Elucidation. N.p.: Transition, April 1927. 1st separate publication. NF in wraps (pulling away from spine staple). Beasley. $125/£80

STEIN, GERTRUDE. Everybody's Autobiography. NY: Random House, (1937). 1st ed. VG (spine, eps, pg edges sunned; lacks dj). Hermitage. $60/£38

STEIN, GERTRUDE. Everybody's Autobiography. London, 1938. 1st Eng ed. Very Nice (cvrs sl spotted) in dj (dust-mkd). Clearwater. $78/£50

STEIN, GERTRUDE. Four Saints in Three Acts. NY: Random House, 1934. 1st ed. (Eps tanned from clippings), o/w Nice in dj (spine tanned, chip, closed edge tears). Reese. $60/£38

STEIN, GERTRUDE. The Gertrude Stein First Reader and Three Plays. Dublin/London: Maurice Fridberg, (1946). 1st Eng ed. Pict eps. Yellow cl-backed lt gray bds (bumped, soiled). VG in pink pict dj (edges chipped, sm tears). Blue Mountain. $60/£38

STEIN, GERTRUDE. The Gertrude Stein First Reader and Three Plays. Dublin: Maurice Fridberg, (1946). 1st ed. NF in NF dj (price-clipped). Captain's Bookshelf. $125/£80

STEIN, GERTRUDE. The Gertrude Stein First Reader and Three Plays. Boston: Houghton Mifflin, 1948. 1st Amer ed, expanded. NF in dj. Turtle Island. $65/£42

STEIN, GERTRUDE. How to Write. Paris: Plain Edition, (1931). 1st ed (1000 ptd). Ptd label. (Eps sl foxed, label sl dknd), o/w VF. Reese. $250/£160

STEIN, GERTRUDE. In Savoy, or Yes Is for a Very Young Man. London: Pushkin, 1946. 1st Eng ed. Card wrappers (bkseller label inner flap; inscrip). Clearwater. $47/£30

STEIN, GERTRUDE. Lectures in America. NY: Random House, (1935). 1st ed. (Edges sl soiled), else NF in dj (sl toned, soiled, sm tears, lt stains rear panel). Waverly*. $99/£63

STEIN, GERTRUDE. Lectures in America. NY: Random House, (1935). 1st ed. Van Vechten frontis port. NF (fep creased) in VG dj. Turtle Island. $150/£96

STEIN, GERTRUDE. Operas and Plays. Paris: Plain Edition, (1932). 1st ed. One of 500. Stiff tan paper wraps. (Spine water-spotted, sl dknd), else VG in slipcase (sl soiled, rubbed). Waverly*. $143/£92

STEIN, GERTRUDE. Paris France. London: Batsford, 1940. 1st Eng ed. (Foxed; sl faded.) Dj. Clearwater. $47/£30

STEIN, GERTRUDE. Paris France. NY: Scribner, 1940. 2nd US ed. Blue cl. NF in dj, ptd wrap-around band. Turtle Island. $75/£48

STEIN, GERTRUDE. Picasso. Batsford, 1938. 1st ed. VG in dj (short tears, sl rubbed). Words Etc. $55/£35

STEIN, GERTRUDE. Portraits of 3 Painters: Cezanne, Matisse, Picasso. (Boston: Catherine Cakouros, 1954.) 1st separate ed(?). 3 sm repros tipped in. (Pastedowns beginning to detach, few ink mks), else NF in wrappers. Bromer. $50/£32

STEIN, GERTRUDE. Things As They Are. Pawlet, VT: Banyan, (1950). One of 516 numbered. 1st ed. Lt tan cl (edge fr cvr stained, rear cvr spotted), ptd tan paper spine label (rubbed, dknd). NF internally. Issued w/o dj. Blue Mountain. $75/£48

STEIN, GERTRUDE. Three Lives. NY: Modern Library, (1933). 1st Modern Library ed, w/new intro. One of 5000 ptd. Flexible cl stamped in gilt. Fine in Nice dj (spine tanned). Reese. $50/£32

STEIN, GERTRUDE. Three Lives. NY: Grafton, 1909. 1st ed. Nice (extrems rubbed, rubbed spot rear bd). Metropolitan*. $805/£516

STEIN, GERTRUDE. Three Lives. Stories of the Good Anna, Melanctha and the Gentle Lena. NY: Grafton, 1909. 1st ed, 1st bk. One of 700 (of 1000). Gilt blue cl (sm bubbles). VG- (ink initials fep, edges of text block sl tanned). Reese. $1,000/£641

STEIN, GERTRUDE. Useful Knowledge. London: John Lane, (1929). 1st Eng ed. Very Nice (top edges damp-stained). Clearwater. $62/£40

STEIN, GERTRUDE. Wars I Have Seen. NY: Random House, (1945). 1st ed. NF (news clipping offset 2pp) in dj. Turtle Island. $75/£48

STEIN, GERTRUDE. Wars I Have Seen. London, 1945. 1st ed. (Top edge fr cvr sl faded.) Dj. Typographeum. $65/£42

STEIN, M. AUREL. Ruins of Desert Cathay, Personal Narrative of Explorations in Central Asia and Westernmost China. London, 1912. 2 vols. Teg. (Cvrs soiled, worn.) King. $175/£112

STEINBECK, JOHN and EDWARD F. RICKETTS. Sea of Cortez. NY, 1941. 1st ed. VG in dj (lt edgeworn). Argosy. $450/£288

STEINBECK, JOHN and EDWARD F. RICKETTS. Sea of Cortez. NY: Viking, 1941. Grn cl. (Rear hinge cracked, edges soiled, offset from laid-in clipping; portion of dj.) Parmer. $250/£160

STEINBECK, JOHN. Bombs Away: The Story of a Bomber Team. NY: Viking, 1942. 1st ed. VG in dj (chipped, rubbed). Pacific*. $86/£55

STEINBECK, JOHN. Bombs Away: The Story of a Bomber Team. NY: Viking, 1942. 1st ed. VG in illus dj (extrems worn). Cahan. $135/£87

STEINBECK, JOHN. Burning Bright. NY, 1950. 1st ed. NF in NF dj. Warren. $125/£80

STEINBECK, JOHN. Burning Bright. NY: Viking, 1950. 1st ed. NF in VG dj (lt soiled, sm chip). Bernard. $100/£64

STEINBECK, JOHN. Cannery Row. NY: Viking, 1945. 1st ed, 2nd state binding. Yellow cl lined in blue. NF in VG dj (spine chipped). Pacific*. $161/£103

STEINBECK, JOHN. Cup of Gold. NY, (1936). 1st ed, 2nd issue; 1st bk. One of approx 900 rmdr copies w/new prelims, preface, binding, dj. Gilt-lettered maroon cl. Dj (spine top lacks piece w/loss; lt worn). Kane*. $225/£144

STEINBECK, JOHN. Cup of Gold. NY: Covici Friede, (1936). 2nd ed. (Ink sig, eps sl discolored.) Top edge stained blue, untrimmed. Navy cl, gilt. Pict dj (spine sl sunned, sl chipped, sl dusty). Sun Dial Press variant of dj for 1st ed, 2nd issue, produced from orig design, w/o any imprint blacked out on spine nor any mention of 'Of Mice and Men.' Fr flap does not incl ptd price, text on rear flap is for Sun Dial ed of 'It Can't Happen Here' by Sinclair Lewis, and 4 other pub's titles are described on rear panel. Bk bears no indication that it was issued by Sun Dial Press. Baltimore*. $100/£64

STEINBECK, JOHN. Cup of Gold. NY: Robert M. McBride, 1929. 1st ed, 1st issue, 1st bk, w/McBride imprint & pub'd August 1929. Yellow cl lettered in black. Fine in VG dj (spine ends, extrems sl rubbed; spine, joints sunned; flap tips clipped). Pacific*. $14,950/£9,583

STEINBECK, JOHN. East of Eden. NY, 1952. 1st Amer ed. NF (sm stain rear cvr, spine extrems sl rubbed) in dj (sl rubbed, spine crease). Polyanthos. $125/£80

STEINBECK, JOHN. East of Eden. NY, 1952. One of 1500 signed. (Lt worn.) Slipcase (scuffed). Oinonen*. $450/£288

STEINBECK, JOHN. The Forgotten Village. NY, 1941. 1st ed. Fine in NF dj (spine lacks sm piece, edges sl worn). Warren. $95/£61

STEINBECK, JOHN. The Forgotten Village. NY: Viking, 1947. 1st ed. Beautiful in Brilliant dj. *Cummins*. $400/£256

STEINBECK, JOHN. The Grapes of Wrath. London: Heinemann, (1939). 1st British ed. Fine in Fine dj. *Authors Of West*. $350/£224

STEINBECK, JOHN. The Grapes of Wrath. London: Heinemann, (1939). 1st Eng ed. VG in dj (chipped, rubbed). *Pacific**. $374/£240

STEINBECK, JOHN. The Grapes of Wrath. NY: Viking, (1939). 1st ed. Beige pict cl. Fine in dj (2.5-inch tear upper left fr and spine, sl loss; sl extrem wear, top edge trimmed, cutting into 'The' on spine). *Metropolitan**. $230/£147

STEINBECK, JOHN. The Grapes of Wrath. NY: Viking, (1939). 1st ed. NF in dj (spine dknd, spine extrems sl chipped). *Captain's Bookshelf*. $850/£545

STEINBECK, JOHN. The Grapes of Wrath. NY: Viking, (1939). 1st ed. Fine in VG dj (spine ends, corners lt rubbed; head sl chipped), later box. *Pacific**. $920/£590

STEINBECK, JOHN. The Grapes of Wrath. NY: Viking, 1939. 1st ed. Fine in NF dj (spine sl dknd, ends sl frayed). *Reese*. $1,250/£801

STEINBECK, JOHN. The Grapes of Wrath. NY: LEC, 1940. #781/1146 signed by Thomas Hart Benton (illus). 2 vols. 1/2 rawhide, grass cl, silver-stamped spines. (Insect damage to cl edges, rawhide), else VG. *Pacific**. $288/£185

STEINBECK, JOHN. In Dubious Battle. NY: Covici Friede, (1936). VG (lt sunned, lt shelfworn) in dj (sm chips to head, lt edgeworn, lt sun, stains to spine). *Metropolitan**. $690/£442

STEINBECK, JOHN. Journal of a Novel. NY, (1969). 1st trade ed. 2-tone cl. Good in dj (edge-worn). *King*. $40/£26

STEINBECK, JOHN. Journal of a Novel. NY: Viking, (1969). 1st ed. Fine in dj. *Captain's Bookshelf*. $75/£48

STEINBECK, JOHN. Journal of a Novel. Heinemann, 1970. 1st Eng ed. Fine in dj (sl dull). *Whiteson*. $20/£13

STEINBECK, JOHN. Letters to Elizabeth. Florian J. Shasky and Susan F. Riggs (eds). SF: Book Club of CA, 1978. One of 500. Facs letter. 1/2 cl, bds, paper spine label. Fine in ptd dj. *Pacific**. $109/£70

STEINBECK, JOHN. The Log from the Sea of Cortez. NY: Viking, 1951. 1st ed. Fine in dj (2 sm tears, spine sl faded). *Captain's Bookshelf*. $200/£128

STEINBECK, JOHN. The Long Valley. NY: Viking, 1938. 1st ed. VG (spine, outer joints dknd) in dj (rubbed, spine dknd). *Captain's Bookshelf*. $250/£160

STEINBECK, JOHN. The Long Valley. NY: Viking, 1938. 1st ed. Linen, cl. Fine in NF dj (spine sl dknd, sm nicks, rubs at extrems). *Reese*. $300/£192

STEINBECK, JOHN. The Moon Is Down. London: Heinemann, 1942. 1st Eng ed. VG in dj. *Hadley*. $39/£25

STEINBECK, JOHN. The Moon Is Down. NY: Viking, 1942. 1st ed, 1st issue w/o ptr's name on c. pg; w/lg period between 'talk' and 'this' on p112, line 11. Fine in rough-textured 1st state dj. *Pacific**. $115/£74

STEINBECK, JOHN. The Moon Is Down. NY: Viking, 1942. 1st ed, 1st issue. This copy incl main 1st issue points w/lg period between words 'talk' and 'this' on pg 112, no printer's notice on copyright pg and w/dj having rough texture. Blue cl stamped in blind on fr cvr and silver on spine. Fine in pict dj (extrems lt rubbed, rear w/1-inch tear at top edge). *Argonaut*. $150/£96

STEINBECK, JOHN. The Moon Is Down. NY: Viking, 1942. One of 700 bound in paper for distribution to bksellers. (Edges rubbed, lt soil.) Custom slipcase. *Metropolitan**. $172/£110

STEINBECK, JOHN. Of Mice and Men. London: Heinemann, (1937). 1st British ed. (Sunned, sl cocked), else Solid in dj (soiled, foxed, very browned) with yellow ad strip intact. *Metropolitan**. $517/£331

STEINBECK, JOHN. Of Mice and Men. NY: Covici Friede, (1937). 1st play ed. Fine in VG dj (short closed tears, chip rear flap). *Metropolitan**. $488/£313

STEINBECK, JOHN. Of Mice and Men. NY: Covici Friede, (1937). 1st ed. Inscribed. Fine in bright dj (short closed tear, sl soil). *Metropolitan**. $2,875/£1,843

STEINBECK, JOHN. Of Mice and Men. Heinemann, 1937. 1st UK ed. VG- (spine sl faded, tilted) in Good dj (piece missing spine top, affecting title; sl loss spine bottom, corners). *Martin*. $37/£24

STEINBECK, JOHN. Once There Was a War. NY: Viking, 1958. 1st ed. VF in dj. *Metropolitan**. $258/£165

STEINBECK, JOHN. The Red Pony. NY: Viking, (1962). 4th ptg. Inscribed. NF in dj (rubbed, sunned, chip rear flap). *Metropolitan**. $862/£553

STEINBECK, JOHN. The Red Pony. NY: Covici-Friede, 1937. 1st ed. One of 699 signed. Fore-edge, tail edge untrimmed. Pict cl. VF in pub's slipcase (sl rubbed) w/penned # on spine. *Pirages*. $800/£513

STEINBECK, JOHN. The Red Pony. NY: Covici-Friede, 1937. 1st ed. #577/699 signed. 8vo. Beige cl, red pony stamped on upper cvr. Fine in orig slipcase. *Cummins*. $1,000/£641

STEINBECK, JOHN. A Russian Journal. NY: Viking, 1948. 1st ed. Robert Capa (photos). (Owner stamp, rear hinge starting), else VG w/dj fragments. *Cahan*. $30/£19

STEINBECK, JOHN. A Russian Journal. NY: Viking, 1948. 1st ed. VG + in VG dj (3 chips). *Bernard*. $65/£42

STEINBECK, JOHN. A Russian Journal. NY: Viking, 1948. 1st ed. Fine in dj (sl sunned, short tears, long crease fr flap). *Metropolitan**. $172/£110

STEINBECK, JOHN. The Short Novels of John Steinbeck. NY: Viking, 1953. 1st ed. Fine in dj (tear rear panel). *Between The Covers*. $250/£160

STEINBECK, JOHN. The Short Reign of Pippin IV. NY: Viking, 1957. 1st ed. VG + in dj (sm chip). *Bernard*. $50/£32

STEINBECK, JOHN. Sweet Thursday. Heinemann, (1954). 1st British ed. (Lt mks top edge), o/w Nice in dj (sl worn). *Ash*. $62/£40

STEINBECK, JOHN. Sweet Thursday. NY, 1951. 1st ed. NF in VG + dj (price-clipped, sl edgewear, few sm closed tears). *Warren*. $75/£48

STEINBECK, JOHN. Sweet Thursday. Heinemann, 1954. 1st UK ed. Fine in VG dj (sm closed tear). *Williams*. $47/£30

STEINBECK, JOHN. Sweet Thursday. NY, 1954. 1st ed. Fine in dj. *Argosy*. $75/£48

STEINBECK, JOHN. To a God Unknown. NY: Ballou, (1933). 1st ed. VG (spine sunned, esp ends) in dj (few chips, short tears; chip, worn at head; back flap browned). *Metropolitan**. $776/£497

STEINBECK, JOHN. Tortilla Flat. NY: Viking, (1947). 1st illus ed. Peggy Worthington (illus). 8vo. Mint in dj. *Cummins*. $500/£321

STEINBECK, JOHN. Travels with Charley. NY: Viking, 1964. Signed. VG in dj (price-clipped). *Metropolitan**. $345/£221

STEINBECK, JOHN. Vanderbilt Clinic. NY: Presbyterian Hospital, 1947. 12-pg pamphlet in black photographic wraps (sl soiled, worn). *Metropolitan**. $287/£184

STEINBECK, JOHN. The Wayward Bus. NY: Viking, 1947. 1st ed. (Shelfwear), else Fine in dj (short tear rear flap, sl soil). *Metropolitan**. $115/£74

STEINBECK, JOHN. The Winter of Our Discontent. Heinemann, (1961). 1st British ed. Good (edges sl spotted) in dj. *Ash*. $31/£20

STEINBERG, S. H. (ed). Cassell's Encyclopaedia of Literature. London: Cassell, 1953. 2 vols. Blue cl (spines sl faded, upper hinges splitting). *Maggs*. $31/£20

STEINBERG, SAUL. All in Line. London: Penguin, 1945. 1st ed. (Spine faded, edges worn.) *Hollett*. $23/£15

STEINBERG, SAUL. The Inspector. NY, (1973). 1st ed. Fine in dj. *Argosy*. $40/£26

STEINBERG, SAUL. The Labyrinth. NY: Harper, 1960. 1st ed. VG in dj (lt spotted, sm repair). *Hollett*. $55/£35

STEINBERG, SAUL. The New World. NY, (1965). 1st ed. VG in dj. *Argosy*. $60/£38

STEINBERG, SAUL. The Passport. NY, (1954). 1st ed. Fine in dj. *Argosy*. $60/£38

STEINBOCK, R. TED. Paleopathological Diagnosis and Interpretation.... Springfield, 1976. VG. *Fye*. $150/£96

STEINBRUNNER, CHRIS et al. Detectionary: A Biographical Dictionary of the Leading Characters.... Loch Haven: Hammermill, 1971. 1st ed. Pb orig. Inscribed. Ltd ed of unspecified #. NF. *Janus*. $85/£54

STEINBRUNNER, CHRIS and NORMAN MICHAELS. The Films of Sherlock Holmes. NJ: Citadel, (1978). 1st US ed. VG in VG dj (lt wear). *Gravesend*. $45/£29

STEINDLER, ARTHUR. Orthopedic Operations: Indications, Techniques and End Results. Balt, 1940. 1st ed. Good (extrems worn, spine top torn). *Doctor's Library*. $100/£64

STEINER, A. RALPH. Dartmouth. Brooklyn: The Author, 1922. 1st ed, 1st bk. 24 collotype plts. Cl-backed bds (bottom edge chipped). NF (name). *Cahan*. $400/£256

STEINER, JORG. The Bear Who Wanted to Be a Bear. NY: Atheneum, 1977. 1st US ed. Jorg Muller (illus). 10x10. 32pp. Glossy bds. Fine in dj. *Cattermole*. $50/£32

STEINMETZ, ANDREW. Japan and Her People. London: Routledge et al, 1859. 1st ed. Frontis, xii,(4),448pp + 32pp ads; 34 wood engrs. (Frontis, tp sl foxed; rear inner hinge cracked.) Patterned blue cl, gilt. *Karmiole*. $150/£96

Steinway Collection of Paintings by American Artists Together with Prose Portraits of the Great Composers.... Steinway & Sons, 1919. 1st ed. Ltd to 5000 numbered. 12 tipped-in color plts. Imitation vellum self-back w/brn Japan paper bd sides. VG. BAL 9917. *New Hampshire**. $112/£72

STEJNEGER, L. and T. BARBOUR. A Check List of North American Amphibians and Reptiles. Cambridge: Harvard, (1939). 4th ed. VG. *Mikesh*. $30/£19

STEKEL, WILHELM. Impotence in the Male: The Psychic Disorders.... Oswald H. Boltz (trans). NY: Liveright, (1927). 1st ed in English. 2 vols. Fine in djs. *Gach*. $50/£32

STENDHAL. (Pseud of Marie-Henri Beyle.) Red and Black. NY: George H. Richmond, 1898. 1st ed in English. 2 vols. (Vol 1 eps lt foxed; sm smudges fr bd vol 2), else NF set in red cl-cvrd bds. *Lame Duck*. $450/£288

STENHOUSE, T. B. H. The Rocky Mountain Saints: A Full and Complete History of the Mormons.... NY: D. Appleton, 1873. 1st ed. Frontis port, xxiv,761pp; 18 plts, 3 maps, 5 facs. 3/4 dk grn morocco (newly bound); marbled bds, edges, gilt-lettered spine. (Lt dampstaining last few leaves), else Fine. *Argonaut*. $350/£224

STENHOUSE, T. B. H. Tell It All. Hartford, 1875. 3rd ed. Frontis, 623pp (ink notes fep). Good (shaken, cvr mottled, stained). *Benchmark*. $40/£26

STENSIO, E. A. The Cephalaspids of Great Britain. British Museum, 1932. 66 plts. Fine. *Henly*. $75/£48

STEP, EDWARD. Favourite Flowers of Garden and Greenhouse. London: Frederick Warne, 1896 (-1897). 1st ed. 4 vols. 8vo. Color frontis each vol, 312 color litho plts (3 detached, few tender, pencil scribbling some versos, lt spotting). Teg. Contemp 1/2 morocco (worn). *Christie's**. $1,315/£843

STEP, EDWARD. Shell Life. London, 1945. 25 color, 7 plain plts. *Henly*. $19/£12

STEP, EDWARD. Shell Life. London: Warne, 1945. VG in dj (sl tear upper fold). *Hollett*. $47/£30

STEPHEN, JAMES FITZJAMES. A Digest of the Law of Evidence. London: Macmillan, 1905. 7th ed. Russet cl (worn), gilt. Sound. *Boswell*. $60/£38

STEPHEN, LESLIE. History of English Thought in the Eighteenth Century. London, 1902. 3rd ed. 2 vols. (Pencil notes.) *Hatchwell*. $31/£20

STEPHEN, LESLIE. The Science of Ethics. London: Smith, Elder, 1882. 1st ed. xxviii,462,(vi)pp. (Lib label, eps sl cracked), o/w VG. *Ash*. $94/£60

STEPHEN, LESLIE. Studies of a Biographer. London, 1898-1902. 1st ed. 4 vols. Presentation slip. Buckram. Good+. *Gretton*. $55/£35

STEPHEN, O. L. Sir Victor Brooke, Sportsman and Naturalist. London, 1894. (Spine dull, spot fr cvr.) *Maggs*. $31/£20

STEPHENS, H. MORSE and HERBERT E. BOLTON (eds). The Pacific Ocean in History...1915. NY, 1917. 1st ed. NF. *Turpen*. $95/£61

STEPHENS, HENRY. The Book of the Farm. London, 1908. 5th ed. 3 vols. 68 plts. Marbled eps. Morocco-backed bds (faded; bkpl, feps lt foxed). *Edwards*. $117/£75

STEPHENS, HENRY. The Book of the Farm.... London, 1844. 1st ed. 3 vols. xix,670; iii,728; vi,729-1407pp; 33 engr plts (vol 1 plts waterstained). Orig bds, new 1/2 calf. *Henly*. $281/£180

STEPHENS, IAN. Horned Moon. London: C&W, 1953. 2nd ed. 44 plts (12 color), 4 maps. (Cl sl rubbed), o/w VG. *Worldwide*. $18/£12

STEPHENS, J. W. W. Blackwater Fever. Liverpool, 1937. Frontis. Internally VG (cl rubbed). *Goodrich*. $75/£48

STEPHENS, J. W. W. Blackwater Fever. London, 1937. 1st ed. VG. *Fye*. $90/£58

STEPHENS, J. W. W. Blackwater Fever. London: Univ Press of Liverpool/Hodder & Stoughton, 1937. 1st ed. Frontis port, plt. VG in dj (soiled). *White*. $28/£18

STEPHENS, JAMES. The Crock of Gold. London, 1912. 1st ed, 1st issue binding w/gilt fleurs-de-lis w/in a gilt oval design on fr cvr. Grn linen, gilt. Chemise of cl over bds; matching 1/4 grn morocco slipcase. *Truepenny*. $200/£128

STEPHENS, JAMES. The Crock of Gold. NY: Macmillan, 1931. 8vo. Color frontis, x,227,(1)pp (sm tear 2 contents pp, 1 corner creased, pencil note fep); 11 color plts by Thomas Mackenzie. Grn cl (sl rubbed, bumped, spine sl faded), gilt. VG. *Blue Mountain*. $25/£16

STEPHENS, JAMES. The Hill of Vision. Dublin, 1912. 1st ed. 1/4 linen, grn bds (spine dknd, extrems lt worn). VG. *Truepenny*. $75/£48

STEPHENS, JAMES. Reincarnations. London, 1918. 1st ed. VG in dj (worn, spine top partly missing). *Truepenny*. $75/£48

STEPHENS, JAMES. The Rocky Road to Dublin. NY: Macmillan, 1915. 1st Amer ed. VG (sm crack rear cvr). *Antic Hay*. $35/£22

STEPHENS, JAMES. Songs from the Clay. NY, 1915. 1st Amer ed. NF (spine sunned, edge rubbed, cvrs dknd, sl rubbed). *Polyanthos*. $20/£13

STEPHENS, JAMES. Strict Joy. London, 1931. 1st ed. Unopened. Dec 3-piece cl. (Eps sl browned; lacks dj), o/w VG. *Truepenny*. $35/£22

STEPHENS, JAMES. Themes and Variations. (NY): Fountain, 1930. #825/850. Signed. Fine in grn bds, gilt. *Williams*. $75/£48

STEPHENS, JAMES. Themes and Variations. NY: Fountain, 1930. Ltd to 892 numbered, signed. Grn cl. Fine in slipcase. *Antic Hay*. $85/£54

STEPHENS, JOHN L. Incidents of Travel in Central America, Chiapas, and Yucatan. NY, 1841. 1st ed. 2 vols. 8vo. viii,424; x,474pp; fldg map and plan; 41 plts (2 dbl). Mod 1/2 calf, gilt. *Maggs*. $585/£375

STEPHENS, JOHN L. Incidents of Travel in Central America, Chiapas, and Yucatan. NY: Harper, 1841. 1st ed. 2 vols. Frontis, viii,9-424pp, fldg map; frontis, vii,2,7-474pp. Gilt dec cl (spine ends chipped, lt rubbed; foxing). VG set. *Cahan*. $350/£224

STEPHENS, JOHN L. Incidents of Travel in Yucatan. London, 1843. 1st ed. 2 vols. 8vo. xii,9-459; xvi,9-478pp; fldg map, 2 panoramas, 75 plts and vignettes. Contemp mottled calf (rebacked, edgeworn), gilt. *Maggs*. $663/£425

STEPHENS, JOHN L. Incidents of Travel in Yucatan. NY, 1843. 1st Amer ed. 2 vols. Map. Mod 1/4 calf. (Frontis backed w/paper; foxed, browned throughout.) *Swann**. $103/£66

STEPHENS, JOHN L. Incidents of Travel in Yucatan. NY: Harper, 1848. 2 vols. 120 plts, incl 2 fldg views, fldg map. (Lt foxed.) Pub's blind-stamped calf (shabby, fr bd vol 2 detached). *Waverly**. $143/£92

STEPHENS, JOHN L. Incidents of Travel in Yucatan. NY, 1856. 2 vols. 2 frontispieces; xii,459; xvi,478pp; fldg map (sm tear neatly repaired), 2 fldg plts (1 plt neatly repaired), 74 full-pg engrs. Orig marbled eps, matching marbled edges. Fine (ex-lib; rebound). *Turpen*. $395/£253

STEPHENS, L. DOW. Life Sketches of a Jayhawker of '49. (N.p.), 1916. 1st ed. 6 photo plts. VG in ptd wrappers (lt edgewear). *Shasky*. $50/£32

STEPHENSEN, P. R. The Antichrist of Nietzsche. London: Fanfrolico, n.d. #378/550. (Interior dampstains, rubbed, binding stains.) 3/4 leather (soiled, bumped). *Metropolitan**. $368/£236

STEPHENSON, ISAAC. Recollections of a Long Life, 1829-1915. Chicago: Privately ptd, 1915. 1st ed. Signed. Frontis port. Teg. Blue cl. Good. Howes S948. *Karmiole*. $85/£54

STEPHENSON, MILL. A List of Monumental Brasses in the British Isles. With Appendix.... Headley Bros, 1926/1938. 1st ed. 2 vols. Blue cl (rubbed). Sound. *Cox*. $70/£45

STEPHENSON, T. A. The British Sea Anemones. Ray Soc, 1928, 1935. 2 vols. 33 color plts. (Lower hinge vol 2 cracked.) Emb cl (faded, joints vol 2 splitting, vol 1 spine sl chipped), gilt. *Edwards*. $133/£85

STEPHENSON, TERRY E. The Shadows of Old Saddleback. (Santa Ana): Fine Arts Press, 1948. 2nd ed. 9 plts. Tan/red cl. Good. *Karmiole*. $75/£48

STERN, BERNHARD. The Scented Garden. NY: American Ethnological Press, 1934. #327/600. Good-. *Scribe's Perch**. $20/£13

STERN, MADELEINE B. The Pantarch: A Biography of Stephen Pearl Andrews. Austin: Univ of TX, 1968. Dj. *Rostenberg & Stern*. $40/£26

STERN, MADELEINE B. Purple Passage, the Life of Mrs. Frank Leslie. Norman, (OK, 1953). 2nd ed. VG (ex-libris) in dj (red bled). *Second Life*. $20/£13

STERN, MADELINE B. Sherlock Holmes: Rare-Book Collector. NY: Schulte, (1953). 1st US ed. VG in pict wrappers. *Gravesend*. $30/£19

STERN, NORTON B. California Jewish History, a Descriptive Bibliography. Glendale: A.H. Clark, 1967. 1st ed. Blue cl. Fine. *Harrington*. $60/£38

STERN, NORTON B. California Jewish History, a Descriptive Bibliography. Glendale: Clark, 1967. 1st ed. One of 1180. Lt blue cl, gilt-lettered spine (ends, corners sl rubbed). Fine. *Argonaut*. $75/£48

STERN, NORTON B. Mannie's Crowd. Glendale: Clark, 1970. 1st ed. One of 983. Frontis port. Blue cl, gilt. Fine in dj. *Argonaut*. $45/£29

STERN, PHILIP VAN DOREN. An End to Valor. Boston, 1958. 1st ed. Signed. VG in dj (frayed, soiled, torn). *King*. $40/£26

STERN, THEODORE. The Rubber-Ball Games of the Americas. NY: J. J. Augustin, (c. 1949). Frontis, 7 maps. Good. *Archaeologia*. $65/£42

STERNBERG, THOMAS. The Dialect and Folk-Lore of Northamptonshire. London/Northampton: John Russell Smith (et al), 1851. 1st ed. Blind-stamped cl (chipped). Sound. *Reese*. $60/£38

STERNE, LAURENCE. Letters of the Late Rev. Mr. Laurence Sterne. London: T. Becket, 1775. 1st ed. 3 vols. 1/2 title, engr frontis vol 1. (18th-cent bkpl, sig each vol; 1st, last few ll discolored from turn-ins, trivial spots.) Fine contemp smooth calf (minor mks), gilt spine, red morocco spine labels. *Pirages*. $850/£545

STERNE, LAURENCE. The Life and Opinions of Tristam Shandy Gentleman. Chicago, 1895. 1st ed thus. 2 vols. Teg, uncut. Fine (bkpls, few pp prelims lt foxed; spines sunned). *Polyanthos*. $75/£48

STERNE, LAURENCE. The Life and Opinions of Tristram Shandy. SF, 1988. One of 400 signed by John Baldessari (illus). Orig 1/2 calf. Accompanied by vol of repros of photo-collages, booklet of commentary, prospectus. Bd slipcase. *Swann**. $345/£221

STERNE, LAURENCE. A Sentimental Journey Through France and Italy. NY: J.W. Bouton, 1884. 12 full-pg photogravure illus. Black morocco; orig multi-colored stiff wrappers bound in. *Swann**. $230/£147

STERNE, LAURENCE. A Sentimental Journey Through France and Italy. Golden Cockerel, 1928. One of 500. 6 copper-engr plts. Bkpl reading: 'Exhibition copy of a Golden Cockerel Press Book: Waltham Saint Lawrence, Berkshire.' Teg, rest untrimmed. Gilt-titled buckram. VF in dj (spine faded, sl chipped, frayed). *Pirages*. $325/£208

STERNE, LAURENCE. The Works of Laurence Stern. With a Life of the Author. London: for many, 1803. 4 vols. Frontis port vol 1. Full contemp marbled calf (rebacked), ribbed gilt-dec spine, gilt-lettered red/grn morocco spine labels. *D & D*. $295/£189

STETSON, CHARLOTTE PERKINS. The Yellow Wall Paper. Boston: Small, Maynard, 1899. (Corners, very short portion rear gutter lt worn), else Fine in dec paper-cvrd bds. *Between The Covers*. $2,750/£1,763

STETSON, JAMES B. Narrative of My Experiences in the Earthquake and Fire at San Francisco. (Palo Alto: Lewis Osborne, 1969.) 2nd ptg of 1906 ed. Ltd to 1400 numbered. Port, map. Red cl, gilt. VF. *Argonaut*. $45/£29

STETTLER, MICHAEL. Swiss Stained Glass of the Fourteenth Century. Batsford, 1949. 16 tipped-in plts. Good (few heavy freckles pg edges) in wrappered card cvrs (tops browning). *Peter Taylor.* $20/£13

STEVEN, CAMPBELL. The Island Hills. London: Hurst & Blackett, 1955. 1st ed. 35 plts, 9 maps. VG in dj (sl chipped). *Hollett.* $39/£25

STEVENS, EDWARD F. The American Hospital of the Twentieth Century. NY, 1921. Rev ed. Inscribed. VG (extrems sl worn). *Doctor's Library.* $75/£48

STEVENS, FLORENCE CARRINGTON. Uncle Roderick's Philosophy. Lynchburg, VA: J.P. Bell, (1911). 1st ed. Frontis. VG in stiff brn wraps, photo illus on cvr, side-tied as issued. *Petrilla.* $50/£32

STEVENS, FRANCIS. (Pseud of Gertrude Barrows Bennett.) Heads of Cerebus. Reading: Polaris, 1952. 1st ed. One of 1500 numbered. This copy inscribed by Lin Carter. Dj, slipcase (rubbed). *Swann*.* $46/£29

STEVENS, GEORGE THOMAS. Three Years in the Sixth Corps. NY: D. Van Nostrand, 1867. 2nd ed. xii,441pp. (Extrems sl worn), else VG. *Mcgowan.* $150/£96

STEVENS, HENRY. Recollections of Mr. James Lenox of New York and the Formation of His Library. London, 1886. 1st ed. 211pp. (Ink name, frontis detached, inner hinges cracked; cvrs rubbed.) *King.* $50/£32

STEVENS, JOHN D. An Account of the Construction, and Embellishment of Old Time Ships. Toronto: The Author, 1949. One of 500 numbered. 43 plts. Fine in stiff wrappers, spiral bound. *Lefkowicz.* $250/£160

STEVENS, JOHN F. An Engineer's Recollections. Rptd from Engineering News-Record, 1935. Ptd bds. (Spine foot chipped, top 2-1/2 inches of backstrip gone), else VG-. *Bohling.* $30/£19

STEVENS, LAURA. Account of the Life and Character of Samuel Wesley Stevens. N.p., 1908. Suede-backed bds. VG +. *Bohling.* $20/£13

STEVENS, LEVERETT C. A Forlorn Hope. Providence, RI, 1903. 1st ed. Ltd to 250. PNRISSHS Series 6, #1. NF in ptd wrappers. *Mcgowan.* $45/£29

STEVENS, LEWIS TOWNSEND. The History of Cape May County, New Jersey.... Cape May, 1897. 479pp. (Ink, stamped name; cvrs stained.) *King.* $75/£48

STEVENS, SHANE. Dead City. NY, 1973. 1st ed. NF in NF dj (2-inch closed tear back panel). *Warren.* $35/£22

STEVENS, WALLACE. The Auroras of Autumn. NY: Knopf, 1950. 1st ed. Fine in dj (price-clipped, lt spotted spine base). *Jaffe.* $350/£224

STEVENS, WALLACE. The Auroras of Autumn. NY: Knopf, 1950. 1st ed. VF in orig dj (extrems lt browned). *Bromer.* $350/£224

STEVENS, WALLACE. The Collected Poems. NY: Knopf, 1954. 1st ed. One of 2500 ptd. (Name), o/w Fine in dj (lt rubbed, spine faded). *Jaffe.* $350/£224

STEVENS, WALLACE. Letters of Wallace Stevens. Holly Stevens (ed). NY: Knopf, 1966. 1st ed. Dec eps. Fine in dj (sl edgeworn). *Jaffe.* $200/£128

STEVENS, WALLACE. Poems...Selected and with an Introduction by Helen Vendler. SF: Arion, 1985. One of 300 numbered. Signed frontis etching by Jasper Johns. Prospectus laid in. 1/2 morocco. Morocco-edged cl slipcase. *Swann*.* $2,185/£1,401

STEVENS, WALLACE. Two or Three Ideas. (N.p.): Univ of MA/CEA Critic, Oct 1951. 1st ed. VG in ptd self wrappers (upper corner, fore-edge creased, lt dust dkng top edge). *Reese.* $275/£176

STEVENS, WALTER B. A Reporter's Lincoln. St. Louis, MO: Hist Soc, 1916. #347/600. Cl spine, bds w/ptd label. (Edgeworn, spine label chipped), else VG. *Bohling.* $65/£42

STEVENS, WALTER B. The World's Fair...Saint Louis, 1904. St. Louis: Thompson, (c. 1903). (Hinges weak, spine ends chipped.) *Bohling.* $60/£38

STEVENSON, ADLAI. The Speeches of Adlai Stevenson. NY: Random House, (1952). 1st ed. Paper wraps. (Sl edgewear, rear cover lt soiled), o/w VG +. *Bernard.* $40/£26

STEVENSON, AUGUSTA. Booker T. Washington. Indianapolis/NY: Bobbs-Merrill, (1950). 1st ed. Fine in dj. *Between The Covers.* $50/£32

STEVENSON, D. Light Houses. 1864. 120pp. (Spine, fr cvr sl discolored, ends sl defective), o/w VG. *Whitehart.* $62/£40

STEVENSON, DAVID. Life of Robert Stevenson, Civil Engineer. Edinburgh/London & NY: A&C Black/Spon, 1878. Mtd engr frontis port, 12,283pp; engr plt, 11 litho plts. Good. *Scribe's Perch*.* $105/£67

STEVENSON, J. B. (ed). The Species of Rhododendron. London, 1947. 2nd ed. Blue cl, gilt. VG. *Price.* $95/£61

STEVENSON, ROBERT LOUIS and LLOYD OSBORNE. The Ebb-Tide. Heinemann, 1894. 1st ed. (viii),237,(3)pp + pub's 20-pg list. Uncut; ads unopened. Gold metallic finish cl, upper cvr pict blocked in black. (Backstrip dknd, sides dust-stained), o/w VG. *Cox.* $31/£20

STEVENSON, ROBERT LOUIS and LLOYD OSBOURNE. The Ebb-Tide. London: Heinemann, (1894). 1st Eng ed, 1st issue, w/20pp ads at rear. Dec gold cl. VG (bkpl, fep browned, soil). *Antic Hay.* $85/£54

STEVENSON, ROBERT LOUIS and LLOYD OSBOURNE. The Ebb-Tide. Heinemann, 1894. 1st ed. (8),237pp + 20pp pub's cat. Good in pict gold cl (extrems lt rubbed, backstrip dknd). Good. *Cox.* $44/£28

STEVENSON, ROBERT LOUIS with LLOYD OSBOURNE. The Ebb-Tide. Chicago: Stone & Kimball, 1894. 1st Amer ed. Teg. Dec grn cl (spine dknd). VG- (stain few pp, inner margins few prelims). *Antic Hay.* $45/£29

STEVENSON, ROBERT LOUIS with LLOYD OSBOURNE. The Wrecker. London: Cassell, 1892. 1st ed. Dec blue cl. VG (eps discolored, sm tears rep). *Antic Hay.* $85/£54

STEVENSON, ROBERT LOUIS and LLOYD OSBOURNE. The Wrong Box. Scribner, 1889. 1st ed. VG (cvr lt soiled, spine sunned). *Certo.* $55/£35

STEVENSON, ROBERT LOUIS. Ballads. London: C&W, 1890. 1st ed. Teg. Blue cl. NF (eps lt dknd). *Antic Hay.* $85/£54

STEVENSON, ROBERT LOUIS. The Black Arrow. London, 1888. 1st ed. (Spine faded, sl shaken, corners rubbed), o/w VG. *Words Etc.* $55/£35

STEVENSON, ROBERT LOUIS. Catriona, a Sequel to Kidnapped. London: Cassell, 1893. 1st ed. Blue cl. Fine. *Appelfeld.* $125/£80

STEVENSON, ROBERT LOUIS. Catriona—A Sequel to 'Kidnapped'.... London: Cassell, 1893. 1st UK ed. 371pp + 16pp ads. Bkpl of Julian Wolff laid in. Blue cl. VG (cvrs lt worn; ink name, date fep). *Gravesend.* $175/£112

STEVENSON, ROBERT LOUIS. A Child's Garden of Verses. London, 1885. 1st ed, 1st ptg. One of 1000. Sm 8vo. Orig blue cl (spine ends, corners sl rubbed; eps browned). 1/4 morocco fldg case. *Swann*.* $920/£590

STEVENSON, ROBERT LOUIS. A Child's Garden of Verses. Bodley Head, 1896. 3rd ed. Charles Robinson (illus). 8vo. xiv,139pp + 18pp ads dated 1895. Aeg. Gilt-pict holly-grn cl. NF. *Bookmark.* $70/£45

STEVENSON, ROBERT LOUIS. A Child's Garden of Verses. Phila: Henry Altemus, 1902. 8vo. Frontis, 162pp + 16pp ads; 3 full-pg color plts. Dec ptd linen on bd (lt spotted), else VG. Hobbyhorse. $70/£45

STEVENSON, ROBERT LOUIS. A Child's Garden of Verses. NY: Scribner, 1917. Jessie Willcox Smith (illus). Pict fr cvr (sl rubbed, corners frayed through). Nice (interior soil). Metropolitan*. $40/£26

STEVENSON, ROBERT LOUIS. A Child's Garden of Verses. NY: Heritage Press, 1944. Roger Duvoisin (illus). 4to. 112pp. Dec eps. Pict pastedown cvr. Good+ in Good+ dj (price-clipped). Scribe's Perch*. $20/£13

STEVENSON, ROBERT LOUIS. A Child's Garden of Verses. NY: OUP, 1947. 1st OUP ed. Tasha Tudor (illus). Fine in VG dj. Bond. $35/£22

STEVENSON, ROBERT LOUIS. A Child's Garden of Verses. Bodley Head, n.d. (1915 inscrip). Lg tall 8vo. 154pp; 8 color plts by Charles Robinson. Pict eps (sl foxed). Teg. Pict cl, gilt. (Few joints sl shaken; extrems worn), else VG. Bookmark. $117/£75

STEVENSON, ROBERT LOUIS. Confessions of a Unionist. Cambridge, MA: Privately Ptd, 1921. Ptd wraps w/folded sheets of text loosely inserted. VG. Antic Hay. $75/£48

STEVENSON, ROBERT LOUIS. Fables. NY: Scribner, 1896. 1st separate ed. Teg. Dec grn cl. VG (dampstained, few spots cvrs). VG. Antic Hay. $45/£29

STEVENSON, ROBERT LOUIS. Fables. NY: Ptd by Chiswick Press, 1914. 1st ed thus. Teg, uncut. Dec cvrs, gilt. NF (spine extrems, corners sl rubbed). Polyanthos. $50/£32

STEVENSON, ROBERT LOUIS. Fables. NY: Scribner, 1914. 20 b/w plts by E. R. Herman. Teg. Red cl (bumped, soiled), gilt. VG (hinge starting). Blue Mountain. $95/£61

STEVENSON, ROBERT LOUIS. Familiar Studies of Men and Books. London: C&W, 1882. 1st ed. One of 1000. 32pp ads dated Nov 1881. Olive grn cl dec in brn/black. (Few ll sl foxed), else Fine. Sumner & Stillman. $425/£272

STEVENSON, ROBERT LOUIS. An Inland Voyage. Boston: Roberts, 1883. 1st Amer ed. (Frontis foxed, fep pasted down, sig; sl shaken.) Grn cl (soiled, rubbed, sl frayed). Waverly*. $93/£60

STEVENSON, ROBERT LOUIS. Island Nights' Entertainment.... London, 1893. 1st Eng ed, 1st issue w/price correction on list of works. (Name stamp, sl cocked.) Kane*. $80/£51

STEVENSON, ROBERT LOUIS. Island Nights' Entertainments. London/Paris/Melbourne: Cassell, 1893. 1st Eng ed. 16pp ads dated Mar 1893. Price on prelim ad leaf raised by hand. Blue-gray cl pict dec in gilt. VF. Sumner & Stillman. $225/£144

STEVENSON, ROBERT LOUIS. Island Nights' Entertainments. London: Cassell, 1893. 1st ed, 1st issue w/price for this title corrected by hand. xi,277,(16)pp ads; color sketch map. Dec eps. Gilt pict blue cl (extrems lt rubbed, corners lt worn). VG (bkpl). House. $250/£160

STEVENSON, ROBERT LOUIS. Island Nights' Entertainments. London: Cassell, 1893. 1st ed. Illus blue cl, gilt. Lovely. Black Sun. $275/£176

STEVENSON, ROBERT LOUIS. Jolly Jump-Ups, a Child's Garden of Verses. Springfield, MA: McLoughlin Bros, 1944. Obl sm 4to. Geraldine Clyne (illus). Pop-up bk. Pict paper-cvrd bds (spine repaired but complete). VG. Book Adoption. $75/£48

STEVENSON, ROBERT LOUIS. Kidnapped. London: Cassell, 1886. 1st issue, bound in brn cl, w/ads dated 5.G.4.86. NF (sl cup-mks fr cvr). Williams. $546/£350

STEVENSON, ROBERT LOUIS. Kidnapped. NY: Scribner, 1913. 1st Wyeth ed. N. C. Wyeth (illus). Teg, others uncut. Gilt-lettered black cl (lt worn), pict label. Oinonen*. $170/£109

STEVENSON, ROBERT LOUIS. Kidnapped. NY: Scribner, 1933. Later ptg. Color tp, 12,239pp + ad; fldg map; 9 color plts by N.C. Wyeth. Pict pastedown cvr. Good. Scribe's Perch*. $38/£24

STEVENSON, ROBERT LOUIS. The Letters to His Family and Friends. Sidney Colvin (ed). London: Methuen, 1900. 1st ed. 2 vols. 2 ports, fldg facs. Teg, uncut. Paper spine labels. (Inscrips fep; rubbed, scratched.) Hollett. $101/£65

STEVENSON, ROBERT LOUIS. The Letters. Sidney Colvin (ed). NY, 1911. New ed. 4 vols. Frontis ports. Teg, rest uncut. (Sm hole pierced upper bd vol 4 through margins to p103; spines lt faded.) Edwards. $117/£75

STEVENSON, ROBERT LOUIS. The Letters.... Sidney Colvin (ed). London: Methuen, 1913. 4th ed. 4 vols. Good set in red cl, gilt. Cox. $31/£20

STEVENSON, ROBERT LOUIS. The Master of Ballantrae. London: Cassell, 1889. 1st ed. Red dec cl (sl wear). Appelfeld. $250/£160

STEVENSON, ROBERT LOUIS. The Master of Ballantrae. London: Cassell, 1889. 1st ed. viii,332 (xx,ads,dated 07.89). Red pict cl (sl soiled, spine sl faded), gilt. Hollett. $273/£175

STEVENSON, ROBERT LOUIS. The Master of Ballantrae. NY: LEC, 1965. One of 1500 numbered, signed by Lynd Ward (illus). Full plaid cl, gilt leather spine label. VG in bd slipcase. Argosy. $125/£80

STEVENSON, ROBERT LOUIS. Memories and Portraits. London: C&W, 1887. 1st ed. Dk blue cl, beveled. Fine (eps foxed). Sumner & Stillman. $115/£74

STEVENSON, ROBERT LOUIS. The Merry Men and Other Fables. London: C&W, 1887. 1st ed. Blue dec cl. Nice. Appelfeld. $200/£128

STEVENSON, ROBERT LOUIS. The Merry Men and Other Tales and Fables. London: C&W, 1887. 1st UK ed. VG (lacks half-title) in orig dec bds. Williams. $148/£95

STEVENSON, ROBERT LOUIS. A Mountain Town in France. London: John Lane, 1896. 1st ed. Teg. 3/4 red morocco (rebacked), raised bands. Orig ptd wrappers bound in. Appelfeld. $150/£96

STEVENSON, ROBERT LOUIS. The New Arabian Nights. Avon: LEC, 1976. One of 2000 numbered, signed by Clarke Hutton (illus). Fine in pub's slipcase. Hermitage. $85/£54

STEVENSON, ROBERT LOUIS. Pan's Pipes. (Boston, 1910.) 1st separate ed. Ltd to 550 numbered. (Lacks fep; worn, dknd.) King. $25/£16

STEVENSON, ROBERT LOUIS. Poems...Hitherto Unpublished.... Boston: Bibliophile Soc, 1921. 1st ed, regular issue. One of 450 ptd. Port. Parchment, cl. (Wrinkle fr pastedown), else Fine in slipcase. Reese. $75/£48

STEVENSON, ROBERT LOUIS. R.L.S. to J.M. Barrie. A Vailima Portrait. SF: Book Club of CA, 1962. Ltd to 475 ptd. 4 full-pg sketches, facs. Brn cl, dec bds, paper spine label. Karmiole. $60/£38

STEVENSON, ROBERT LOUIS. The Silverado Squatters. Ashland, OR: Lewis Osborne, 1972. Ltd to 500 numbered, ptd. Cl-backed bds. VF. Argonaut. $90/£58

STEVENSON, ROBERT LOUIS. St. Ives. NY: Scribner, 1897. 1st Amer ed. Brn cl, gilt. Appelfeld. $100/£64

STEVENSON, ROBERT LOUIS. St. Ives. Heinemann, 1898. 1st British ed. In the presumed 1st issue binding, w/pub's windmill device on lower cvr. Nice (2 leaves creased, sl nicks, sl wear). Ash. $62/£40

STEVENSON, ROBERT LOUIS. St. Ives. Being the Adventures of a French Prisoner in England. NY: Scribner, 1897. 1st Amer ed. Dec brn cl. VG. *Antic Hay.* $75/£48

STEVENSON, ROBERT LOUIS. St. Ives. Being the Adventures of a French Prisoner in England. London, 1898. 1st ed. Uncut. NF (sl rubbed). *Polyanthos.* $45/£29

STEVENSON, ROBERT LOUIS. St. Ives. Being the Adventures of a French Prisoner in England. London: Heinemann, 1898. 1st Eng ed. Dec cl. VG (wear, ink name). *Antic Hay.* $75/£48

STEVENSON, ROBERT LOUIS. A Stevenson Medley. London: C&W, 1899. 1st ed. One of 300 signed by pub. Facs tipped in. 1/2 morocco, blue cl, gilt. Fine. *Macdonnell.* $200/£128

STEVENSON, ROBERT LOUIS. A Stevenson Medley. London: C&W, 1899. 1st separate ed. One of 300. The John Spoor copy. Dk blue cl, dk blue morocco spine. Fine (bkpl) in clamshell case. *Sumner & Stillman.* $525/£337

STEVENSON, ROBERT LOUIS. Stevenson's Workshop with Twenty-Nine Ms. Facsimiles. William P. Trent (ed). Boston: Bibliophile Soc, 1921. Ltd to 450. 29 full-pg photos. 1/4 vellum, cl bds. VG (sl soil) in slipcase, box. *Cullen.* $125/£80

STEVENSON, ROBERT LOUIS. Stevenson's Workshop.... W. P. Trent (ed). Boston: Bibliophile Soc, 1921. 1st ed. One of 450. Frontis. Parchment, cl. (Lt foxed), else Very Nice in slipcase. *Reese.* $60/£38

STEVENSON, ROBERT LOUIS. The Strange Case of Dr. Jekyll and Mr. Hyde and Other Stories. NY: Editions for the Armed Services, (1945). Good in wrappers (bumped, sm stain, foxing). *Turtle Island.* $15/£10

STEVENSON, ROBERT LOUIS. The Strange Case of Dr. Jekyll and Mr. Hyde. NY: Scribner, 1886. Correct 1st ed. 8vo. Grn cl over bds (extrems worn). VG. *Old London.* $600/£385

STEVENSON, ROBERT LOUIS. Travels with a Donkey in the Cevennes. Boston: Roberts Bros, 1879. 1st Amer ed. Frontis by Walter Crane. 16pp undated ads, 4pp ads dated Spring 1879. Terra-cotta cl dec in black/gilt. NF (sl rubbed, sm mks). *Sumner & Stillman.* $375/£240

STEVENSON, ROBERT LOUIS. Travels with a Donkey. NY: LEC, (1957). One of 1500 numbered, signed by Roger Duvoisin (illus). Fine in pub's slipcase (scuffed). *Hermitage.* $45/£29

STEVENSON, ROBERT LOUIS. Treasure Island. Cassell, 1883. 1st ed. 8vo. viii,292pp (pg 83 lacks numeral 8; pg 127 has the 7 from different font; 'dead man's chest' pp 2, 7 w/o capitals; lacks 'a' line 6 pg 63; 'worse' instead of 'worst' appears line 3 pg 197), 8pp ads at end dated 5R-1083, map facing tp, black eps. Orig blue cl (spine dknd, cvrs spotted, marked; sm holes both joints, head, foot of spine), spine gilt. This copy has points of 2nd & 3rd issues, but blue cvr of 1st issue. All 4 issues count as 1st ed. *Bickersteth.* $601/£385

STEVENSON, ROBERT LOUIS. Treasure Island. Boston, 1884. 1st Amer, 1st illus ed. (Fep removed, 2 reps torn.) Pub's cl (shelfworn, sl shaken). *Oinonen*.* $160/£103

STEVENSON, ROBERT LOUIS. Treasure Island. Boston: Roberts Bros, 1884. 1st Amer ed. Turquoise cl, gilt. Attractive (lt rubbed). *Macdonnell.* $850/£545

STEVENSON, ROBERT LOUIS. Treasure Island. Boston: Roberts Bros, 1884. 1st Amer ed, 1st issue (w/'rain' for 'vain' on last line p40). 4 plts by F. T. Merrill. 4pp undated ads. Brn cl dec in black. VG (eps sl cracked, sl shelfworn, lt splash mks). *Sumner & Stillman.* $1,450/£929

STEVENSON, ROBERT LOUIS. Treasure Island. Franklin Center, PA: Franklin Library, 1975. N. C. Wyeth (illus). Satin eps, ribbon marker; aeg. Gilt-worked full blue morocco. Fine. *Antic Hay.* $50/£32

STEVENSON, ROBERT LOUIS. Underwoods. NY: Scribner, 1887. 1st Amer ed. Lt brn bds, brn cl spine. NF (sl worn). *Sumner & Stillman.* $195/£125

STEVENSON, ROBERT LOUIS. Weir of Hermiston. London: C&W, 1896. 1st Eng ed, w/March ads. Teg. Dec blue cl. VG. *Antic Hay.* $75/£48

STEVENSON, ROBERT LOUIS. Weir of Hermiston. London: C&W, 1896. 1st ed, 1st issue w/March ads. Blue cl, gilt. Fine (bkpl). *Macdonnell.* $100/£64

STEVENSON, ROBERT LOUIS. Weir of Hermiston. London: C&W, 1896. 1st ed. Blue cl, beveled edges, gilt top. Fine. *Appelfeld.* $150/£96

STEVENSON, ROBERT LOUIS. When the Devil Was Well. NY: Rosenbach, 1921. Frontis port. Glassine dj. *Swann*.* $149/£96

STEVENSON, ROBERT LOUIS. When the Devil Was Well.... Boston: Bibliophile Soc, 1921. 1st ed, regular issue. One of 450 ptd. Port, facs. Parchment, cl. (Sl foxed), else Nice in slipcase. *Reese.* $65/£42

STEVENSON, ROBERT LOUIS. The Works of.... London, 1922-23. Vailima ed. #62/1060. 26 vols. Frontispieces. Teg. Blue cl (bumped, lt worn, soiled), gilt. *Freeman*.* $220/£141

STEVENSON, ROBERT LOUIS. The Works.... London, 1906. Pentland ed. One of 1550 numbered sets. 20 vols. 8vo. Frontispieces. Contemp brn calf, gilt-panelled spines, red/black morocco lettering pieces. *Swann*.* $1,955/£1,253

STEVENSON, ROBERT LOUIS. A Lowden Sabbath Morn. London: C&W, 1898. 1st ed. 127pp. Teg. (Spotted; bkpl.) *Hollett.* $55/£35

STEVENSON, ROBERT LOUIS. Memories. London: T.N. Foulis, 1912. 1st ed. 25 tipped-in photos. VG in orig wrappers, dj. *Hollett.* $23/£15

STEVENSON, SETH WILLIAM. A Dictionary of Roman Coins. C. Roach Smith and Frederic W. Madden (eds). London: B.A. Seaby, 1964. Facs ed. VG in dj (sl torn, creased). *Hollett.* $62/£40

STEVENSON, THOMAS. Lighthouse Construction and Illumination. London: E. & F.N. Spon, 1881. 3/4 levant, marbled bds (rebound), paper label. VG (inscrip). *Old London.* $45/£29

STEVENSON, W. B. Detective Fiction. Cambridge: National Book League, 1958. 1st publication. NF. *Janus.* $35/£22

STEVENSON, WILLIAM G. Thirteen Months in the Rebel Army. NY, 1862. 1st ed. Frontis, 232pp + 8pp ads. (Rebound.) *Heinoldt.* $35/£22

STEWARD, JULIAN H. Ancient Caves of the Great Salt Lake Region. BAE Bulletin 116. Washington: Smithsonian, 1937. 8 plts, map. Good in wrappers. *Archaeologia.* $35/£22

STEWARD, JULIAN H. (ed). Handbook of South American Indians, Vol 2: The Andean Civilizations. Washington: GPO, 1946. 11 maps. (Label fep; extrems worn, sm tear to spine.) *Archaeologia.* $85/£54

STEWARD, JULIAN H. (ed). Handbook of South American Indians. Washington: GPO, 1946. 7 vols. Grn cl over bds. NF. *Old London.* $450/£288

STEWART, BASIL. Subjects Portrayed in Japanese Colour-Prints. London, 1922. 1/4 cl. (1926 sig, foxed; rear cvr abraded.) *Swann*.* $201/£129

STEWART, BASIL. Subjects Portrayed in Japanese Colour-Prints. London: Kegan Paul et al, 1922. Buff linen spine, paper-cvrd bds (bumped, rubbed, soiled). *Metropolitan*.* $201/£129

STEWART, CHARLES. A Treatise on the Law of Scotland Relating to Rights of Fishing. Edinburgh: T&T Clark, 1869. Mod 1/4 grn cl over bds. Sound. *Boswell.* $225/£144

STEWART, DONALD OGDEN. Mr. and Mrs. Haddock in Paris, France. NY: Harper, 1926. 1st ed. NF (couple pp uncut) in VG dj (few sm chips, tears extrems; rear top flap clipped). *Between The Covers.* $85/£54

STEWART, DUGALD. Elements of the Philosophy of the Human Mind. Brattleborough, VT: William Fessenden, 1808. 3rd Amer ed. viii,(9)-496pp. Contemp calf. (Sm mend rep), o/w VG. *Reese.* $45/£29

STEWART, EDGAR I. Custer's Luck. Norman: Univ of OK, (1955). 1st ed. VG in dj. *Lien.* $75/£48

STEWART, GEORGE R. The California Trail. McGraw-Hill, (1962). 1st ed. Pict eps. Fine in dj (price-clipped). *Authors Of West.* $35/£22

STEWART, GEORGE R. John Phoenix, Esq., The Veritable Squibob. NY: Henry Holt, (1937). 1st ed. Frontis port, 19 plts. VF in pict dj. *Argonaut.* $60/£38

STEWART, GEORGE R. Ordeal by Hunger: The Story of the Donner Party. NY: Henry Holt, (1936). 1st ed. Signed, dated 3/26/36. 5 maps. Blue cl, gilt. Fine. *Pacific*.* $80/£51

STEWART, GEORGE R. Ordeal by Hunger: The Story of the Donner Party. Boston: Houghton Mifflin, 1960. 2nd ed. 5 maps. Gray cl, silver titles. News clipping laid in. Fine in pict dj. *Pacific*.* $23/£15

STEWART, GEORGE R. Pickett's Charge. Boston, 1959. 1st ed. (Cvr sl worn), o/w VG +. *Pratt.* $35/£22

STEWART, GEORGE R. Pickett's Charge: A Microhistory of the Final Attack at Gettysburg, July 3, 1863. Boston: Houghton Mifflin, 1959. 1st ed. VG in VG dj. *Mcgowan.* $65/£42

STEWART, MARY. The Way to Wonderland. NY: Dodd Mead, (1917). 1st ed, 1st issue. Sm 4to. 194pp; 6 full-pg color illus by Jessie Wilcox Smith. Color illus eps. Brn cl, gilt, color pict label. VG (hinge sl cracked). *Dower.* $250/£160

STEWART, ROBERT E., JR. and M. F. Adolph Sutro: A Biography. Berkeley: Howell-North, 1962. 1st ed. VF in pict dj. *Argonaut.* $60/£38

STEWART, ROBERT LAIRD. Sheldon Jackson. NY: Fleming H. Revell, c. 1908. 1st ed. 28 plts. VG. *High Latitude.* $50/£32

STEWART, ROBERT. The American Farmer's Horse Book. Richmond: Nat'l Pub Co, 1867. 1st ed. 600pp (old stain corner many pp). Full mod leather. VG. *Agvent.* $75/£48

STEWART, WILLIAM H. The Spirit of the South. NY/Washington: Neale, 1908. Good (faded, shelfwear). *Cullen.* $50/£32

STEWART, WILLIAM M. Reminiscences of Senator William M. Stewart of Nevada. NY/Washington: Neale, 1908. 1st ed. NF in dj (sl chipped). Howes S994. *Mcgowan.* $250/£160

STICKLEY, GUSTAV. Craftsman Homes. NY: Craftsman Pub Co, (1909). 2nd ed. Coarse grained linen stamped in brn. Pleasing (hinges cracked, corners bumped, lt soil). *Hermitage.* $225/£144

STICKLEY, GUSTAV. Craftsman Homes. NY: Craftsman, (1909). Gray cl (lt worn, soiled). *Freeman*.* $240/£154

STIEB, ERNST W. Drug Adulteration. Madison: Univ of WI, 1966. 1st ed. 10 plts. Fine in dj. *Glaser.* $60/£38

STIGAND, C. H. The Game of British East Africa. London: Horace Cox, 1913. 2nd ed. Lg 4to. Grn gilt pict cl (sl warped), else Nice. *Terramedia.* $500/£321

STIGAND, C. H. Hunting the Elephant in Africa. NY, 1913. 1st ed. (Sl worn, stained.) *Oinonen*.* $180/£115

STILES, EZRA. The Literary Diary...1769-1795. F. B. Dexter (ed). NY: Scribner, 1901. 1st ed. 3 vols. Full cl, Yale seal on cvrs in gilt, beveled bds. (Heads worn, fr hinge vol 3 cracked), o/w Good. Howes S1000. *Scribe's Perch*.* $160/£103

STILES, ROBERT. Four Years Under Marse Robert. NY: Neale, 1903. 2nd ed. (Fr inner hinge broken; cvrs soiled, spotted.) *King.* $50/£32

STILL, ANDREW T. The Autobiography of Andrew T. Still: With a History of the Discovery and Development of the Science of Osteopathy. Kirksville: The Author, 1897. 1st ed. Fine. *Hermitage.* $50/£32

STILL, GEORGE F. Common Disorders and Diseases of Childhood. London: Henry Frowde, 1909. 1st ed. Red cl. (Spine ends lt bumped), o/w VG. *White.* $117/£75

STILL, JAMES. Hounds on the Mountain. NY: Viking, 1937. 1st ed, 1st bk. One of 750 numbered. VG in dj (sm chips). *Captain's Bookshelf.* $125/£80

STILL, PETER and VINA. The Kidnapped and the Ransomed. Phila: Jewish Pub Soc, 1970. 1st ed thus. 4 plts. Yellow cl. VG in ptd dj. *Petrilla.* $45/£29

STILL, WILLIAM. The Underground Rail Road. Phila: Porter & Coates, 1872. 1st ed. NF (fr hinge tender, sm tears spine extrems). *Between The Covers.* $500/£321

STILL, WILLIAM. The Underground Rail Road.... Phila, 1872. Frontis, 23 plts. (Sm mk fr cvr.) *Kane*.* $150/£96

STILLMAN, J. D. B. The Horse in Motion as Shown by Instantaneous Photography. Boston: James R. Osgood, 1882. 1st ed. Thick 4to. 127pp; 9 chromolithos, 5 full-pg heliotype plts, 93 other plts, all guards present. Brn cl stamped in black/gilt; teg. Fine (minor streaking outer rear cvr; inner fr hinge sl weak). *Argonaut.* $750/£481

STILLWELL, MARGARET BINGHAM. Incunabula and Americana 1450-1800. NY: Columbia Univ, 1931. 1st ed. VG in dj (defective). *Waverly*.* $60/£38

STILWELL, HART. Fishing in Mexico. NY: Knopf, 1948. 1st ed. Color frontis. Red blind-stamped cl, gilt. Fine in pict dj (chipped). *Biscotti.* $35/£22

STILWELL, HART. Hunting and Fishing in Texas. NY: Knopf, 1946. Stated 1st ed. 6 color plts. Good (prelims lt foxed). *Scribe's Perch*.* $16/£10

STIMSON, A. L. History of the Express Business.... NY: Baker & Godwin, 1881. Later ed. Frontis port, 11 plts. Full emb leather (rebacked), gilt train fr cvr. Howes S1008. *Glenn.* $250/£160

STIMSON, H. K. From the Stage Coach to the Pulpit. T. W. Greene (ed). St. Louis: R.A. Campbell, 1874. Frontis port, 427pp; plt. (Worn, spine ends frayed, fr hinge cracked.) *Bohling.* $40/£26

STINE, J. H. History of the Army of the Potomac. Phila, (1893). 2nd ed. (Cvr lt worn), o/w Fine. *Pratt.* $95/£61

STIPP, G. W. John Bradford's Historical &c. Notes on Kentucky from the Western Miscellany. SF: Grabhorn, 1932. Ltd to 500. Fldg map frontis. Illus paper over bds. Fine. Howes S1011. *Cahan.* $150/£96

STIPP, G. W. John Bradford's Historical &c. Notes on Kentucky.... SF: Grabhorn Press, 1932. Fldg frontis map. Unopened. Ad for series laid in. Bds w/map, gilt stamping. VG + in plain dj (dknd). Howes S1011. *Bohling.* $85/£54

STIRLING, A. M. W. William De Morgan and His Wife. NY, 1922. 1st Amer ed. VG (sl scratched, bumped, chafed). *Clearwater.* $47/£30

STIRLING, JAMES. Letters from the Slave States. London, 1857. 1st ed. Frontis map, viii,374pp. Grn cl, gilt. (Spine lt sunned), o/w Fine. Howes S1012. *Maggs.* $429/£275

STIRLING, MATTHEW W. Stone Monuments of Southern Mexico. BAE Bulletin 138. Washington: Smithsonian, 1943. Good in wrappers. *Archaeologia.* $45/£29

STIRLING, W. F. Safety Last. London, 1953. 9 plts. Fine in dj (faded, chipped). *Maggs.* $47/£30

STIX, HUGH et al. The Shell. NY, 1988. 1st ed. Fine in Fine dj. *Smith.* $25/£16

STOBART, T. Tiger Trail. London: Davis-Poy, 1975. 1st ed. Fine in Fine dj. *Mikesh.* $30/£19

STOBO, ROBERT. Memoirs of Major Robert Stobo, of the Virginia Regiment. Pittsburgh: J. Davidson, 1854. 2nd ed, 1st Amer ptg. (6 incl fr.),(9)-92pp; fldg plan. Good (lib mks, sm release label, paper dknd; spine ends chipped). Howes S1015. *Bohling.* $200/£128

STOCK, DENNIS. James Dean Revisited. Middlesex/NY: Penguin, 1978. 1st ed. VG in illus stiff wrappers (lt rubbed). *Cahan.* $25/£16

STOCK, DENNIS. Jazz Street. GC: Doubleday, 1960. 1st ed. (Sl creases 2 leaves), else VG. *Cahan.* $125/£80

STOCKER, HARRY E. Moravian Customs. Bethlehem: Times Pub Co, 1919. 2nd ed. VG. *Agvent.* $35/£22

STOCKLEY, C. H. Stalking in the Himalayas and Northern India. London, 1936. (Fep sl stained; cl sl rubbed.) *Grayling.* $101/£65

STOCKTON, FRANK. The Adventures of Captain Horn. London: Cassell, 1895. 1st British ed. Black cl, gilt. (Sl foxed, bkpl, sm crack rear inner hinge), o/w Very Nice. BAL 18920. *Reese.* $65/£42

STOCKTON, FRANK. Afield and Afloat. Scribner, 1900. 1st ed. VG + . *Certo.* $45/£29

STOCKTON, FRANK. Afield and Afloat. London: Cassell, 1901. 1st British ed. Frontis. Pict tan cl. Good (few marginal snags; spine, edges lt foxed). BAL 18938. *Reese.* $55/£35

STOCKTON, FRANK. The Bee-Man of Orn. NY: Holt, 1964. 1st ed. Maurice Sendak (illus). 7 3/4 x 8 1/4. 48pp. VG in dj. *Cattermole.* $100/£64

STOCKTON, FRANK. A Bicycle of Cathay. London/NY: Harper, 1900. 1st ed, English issue. Grn cl. VG (rear inner hinge cracking, spine sl faded). BAL 18939. *Reese.* $65/£42

STOCKTON, FRANK. The Griffin and the Minor Canon. NY: Holt, 1963. 1st ed. Maurice Sendak (illus). 7 3/4 x 8 1/4. 56pp. VG in dj (3-inch tape-stained tear on fr). *Cattermole.* $90/£58

STOCKTON, FRANK. The House of Martha. London: Osgood, McIlvaine, 1891. 1st British ed. (Bkpl, edges lt foxed, rear inner hinge sl cracked), else Good. BAL 18907. *Reese.* $40/£26

STOCKTON, FRANK. The Lady or the Tiger? NY: Scribner, 1885. 1st ed. Pict cl (lt rubbed). *Swann*.* $126/£81

STOCKTON, FRANK. Mrs. Cliff's Yacht. London: Cassell, 1896. 1st British ed. Frontis. Grn cl, gilt. (Bkpl), else NF. BAL 18923. *Reese.* $85/£54

STOCKTON, FRANK. Rudder Grange. NY: Scribner, 1879. 1st ed, 2nd issue (w/1st ad pg concerning 'Old Creole Days,' last ad pg describing this work). 6pp undated ads. Brn cl dec in black/gilt. (Extrems sl rubbed), o/w Fine. *Sumner & Stillman.* $60/£38

STOCKTON, FRANK. Rudder Grange. NY: Scribner, 1879. 1st ed, 1st issue (w/tp dated, w/1st ad pg concerning Frances Hodgson Burnett). Signed card tipped to fr pastedown. 6pp undated ads. Grn cl dec in black/gilt. VF. *Sumner & Stillman.* $115/£74

STOCKWELL, GLENN. Fly Reels of the House of Hardy. London: A&C Black, 1978. 1st ed. Color frontis. VG in dj. *Hollett.* $62/£40

STOCQUELER, J. H. The Life of Field Marshall, the Duke of Wellington. London: Ingram, Cooke, 1852. 2 vols. xii,385; xii,401pp. Full polished calf, densely gilt backs, dbl red lettering pieces. (Gilt backs dull), o/w VG. *House.* $200/£128

STODDARD, WHITNEY S. The West Portals of Saint-Denis and Chartres. Cambridge, 1952. 38 plts loose as issued. Good in slipcase (worn). *Washton.* $90/£58

STODDARD, WILLIAM O. Two Arrows: A Story of Red and White. NY, 1886. 16mo. Pict cl (lt worn, soiled). *Freeman*.* $30/£19

STODDART, THOMAS TOD. The Angler's Companion to the Rivers and Lochs of Scotland. Blackwood, 1847. 1st ed. (Title, frontis foxed.) Full calf. *Petersfield.* $117/£75

STOKER, BRAM. Dracula. NY: LEC, 1965. Ltd to 1500, signed by Felix Hoffman (engrs). Emb black cl. Fine in carbd slipcase (lt wear, few cracks, sm stain). *Antic Hay.* $125/£80

STOKER, BRAM. Dracula. NY: LEC, 1965. One of 1500 numbered, signed by Felix Hoffmann (illus). Buckram-backed blind-stamped cl, gilt spine. VG in red bd slipcase, paper spine label. *Argosy.* $175/£112

STOKER, BRAM. The Jewel of Seven Stars. NY: Harper, 1904. 1st Amer ed. (Sl internal soil, inner fr hinge starting; rubbed, heel frayed.) *Metropolitan*.* $34/£22

STOKER, BRAM. The Lair of the White Worm. London: Foulsham, (1925). Mayflower lib rpt ed. Purple cl spine (sunned). VG. *Certo.* $35/£22

STOKER, BRAM. The Lair of the White Worm. London: William Rider, 1911. 1st ed. 6 full-pg plts. (1/2 title foxed.) Pub's red cl, gilt. VF. *D & D.* $395/£253

STOKER, BRAM. Personal Reminiscences of Henry Irving. NY: Macmillan, 1906. 1st Amer ed. 2 vols. Frontis port vol 1. Teg, uncut. Gilt/blind-stamped dk red cl. VG in djs. *Houle.* $225/£144

STOKES, I. N. PHELPS and DANIEL C. HASKELL. American Historical Prints. NY, 1933. *Swann*.* $126/£81

STOKES, RICHARD L. Paul Bunyan. NY: Putnam, 1932. 1st ed. VG in dj. *Perier.* $17/£11

STOKES, THOMAS. The Savannah. NY: Rinehart, 1951. 1st ed. Fine in VG dj (spine sunned). *Archer.* $40/£26

STOKES, WILLIAM. Diseases of the Heart and Aorta. Phila: Lindsay & Blakiston, 1855. 1st Amer ed, 2nd ptg. xvi,(17)-710pp (tp lt soiled, lib stamps, lt foxed). New cl. VG. *Glaser.* $225/£144

STOKES, WILLIAM. A Treatise on the Diagnosis and Treatment of Diseases of the Chest. Part I. London: New Sydenham Soc, 1882. Frontis port, lv,596pp. Orig cl (rebacked, majority of spine laid down). Clean. *White.* $70/£45

STOLOFF, CAROLYN. Stepping Out. Santa Barbara: Unicorn, 1971. 1st ed, cl issue. Fine in dj. *Turlington.* $20/£13

STOMMEL, HENRY. Lost Islands. Univ of British Columbia, 1984. 1st ed. Fldg chart in rear pocket. Dj. *Edwards.* $37/£24

STONE, ALBERT H. and J. HAMMOND REED (eds). Historic Lushan. Hankow, 1921. 80 plts, fldg map. (Lt browned; corner sl rubbed w/sl cl loss, spine sl faded, sl rubbed.) *Edwards.* $390/£250

STONE, BARTON W. Biography of Eld. Barton Warren Stone. Cincinnati, 1847. 1st ed. (8),404,(4)pp; port. Full contemp calf, leather spine label. Howes S1029. *Ginsberg.* $275/£176

STONE, BUENA COBB. Fort Klamath, Frontier Post in Oregon, 1863-1890. TX: Royal Pub Co, (1964). 1st ed. Gilt-lettered blue cl. Fine in pict dj (spine dknd). *Argonaut.* $45/£29

STONE, CHARLES J. Cradle-Land of Arts and Creeds or Nothing New Under the Sun. London: Sampson Low et al, 1880. xx,(ii),419pp + 32-pg cat. Burgundy cl (bumped, rubbed), gilt spine title. VG. *Blue Mountain.* $95/£61

STONE, CHRISTOPHER. Eton Painted by E.D. Brinton. London: A&C Black, 1909. 1st ed. 20 color plts, fldg plan at end. Teg. (Eps browned, fore-edge spotted; corner knocked.) *Cox.* $55/£35

STONE, E. H. The Stones of Stonehenge. London, 1924. (Sl worn.) *Hatchwell.* $47/£30

STONE, I. F. This Is Israel. NY: Boni & Gaer, (1949). 2nd ptg. VG (owner stamp) in pict stiff wrappers (rubbed). *Cahan.* $20/£13

STONE, I. F. This Is Israel. NY: Boni & Gaer, 1948. 1st ed. (Spine sl worn), else Fine in dj (sl chipped). *Cahan.* $60/£38

STONE, IRVING. Men to Match My Mountains. GC: Doubleday, 1956. Signed, ltd 1st ed. Leatherette. Fine. *Perier.* $125/£80

STONE, IRVING. Men to Match My Mountains. NY: Doubleday, 1956. Far West ed. Signed, ltd ed. Full dec leatherette. Fine in acetate dj (lt scuffed). *Waverly*.* $55/£35

STONE, JAMES S. Woods and Dales of Derbyshire. Phila, 1894. Frontis port, 180pp + (ii) pub's ads. Teg. (Marginal dust-soiling; sm split lower joint, spine head w/loss across upper bd, sl dkng.) *Edwards.* $44/£28

STONE, KATE. Brokenburn; the Journal of Kate Stone, 1861-1868. Baton Rouge: LA State Univ, (1955). 1st ed. VG in VG dj. *Mcgowan.* $65/£42

STONE, LAWRENCE. Sculpture in Britain. The Middle Ages. Harmondsworth, 1972. 2nd ed. 192 plts. Good. *Washton.* $65/£42

STONE, RAYMOND. Tommy Tiptop and His Baseball Nine. Graham & Matlack, 1912. 1st ed. Pict cvr. Good +. *Plapinger.* $200/£128

STONE, REYNOLDS. Reynolds Stone Engravings. VT: Stephen Greene, 1977. 1st US ed. Fine in dj. *Michael Taylor.* $90/£58

STONE, REYNOLDS. The Wood Engravings of Gwen Raverat. London: Faber & Faber, 1959. VG (lacks dj). *Michael Taylor.* $75/£48

STONE, REYNOLDS. Wood Engravings of Thomas Bewick. London: Rupert Hart-Davis, 1953. Ltd to 1000 signed. Maroon buckram, gilt. VG in dj (worn). *Heller.* $375/£240

STONE, ROBERT. Children of Light. London: Deutsch, 1986. True 1st ed. One of 4500. Fine in dj. *Lame Duck.* $125/£80

STONE, ROBERT. Dog Soldiers. Boston: HMCo, 1974. 1st ed. Fine in Fine dj. *Dermont.* $100/£64

STONE, W. The Birds of Eastern Pennsylvania and New Jersey. Phila, 1894. 1st ed. Frontis port, 185pp, fldg map. (Pencil underlining), else NF. *Mikesh.* $45/£29

STONE, WILBUR FISK (ed). History of Colorado. Chicago: Clarke, 1918. 3 vols. Marbled edges. Red cl, beveled bds. Good +. *Scribe's Perch*.* $70/£45

STONE, WILBUR FISK (ed). History of Colorado. Chicago: S.J. Clarke, 1918. 1st ed. 3 vols. Good. *Lien.* $260/£167

STONE, WILLIAM A. The Tale of a Plain Man. Phila: John C. Winston, 1918. 2nd ed. Crimson cl (rubbed). Sound. *Boswell.* $35/£22

STONE, WILLIAM L. History of New York City. NY, 1872. 658pp + 136pp appendix; 20 steel, 85 wood engrs. Binding copy. *Scribe's Perch*.* $48/£31

STONE, WILLIAM L. (trans). Letters and Journals Relating to the War of the American Revolution and the Capture of German Troops at Saratoga. Albany: Joel Munsell, 1867. Ltd to 250. 235pp; 3 plts. (Worn, faded.) Howes R284. *Cullen.* $150/£96

STONE, WILLIAM L. (trans). Letters of Brunswick and Hessian Officers During the American Revolution. Albany: Munsell, 1891. Frontis port, 258pp + 10pp index + errata; 1 plt. 1/2 morocco, gilt spine, marbled bds. Good. Howes S1037. *Scribe's Perch*.* $90/£58

STONE, WILLIAM L. The Life and Times of Red-Jacket, or Sa-Go-Ye-Wat-Ha. NY/London: Wiley/Putnam, 1841. 1st ed. xi,484pp (sl aged, foxed, lib handstamp tp margin); 3 steel-engr plts + extra illus tp. Orig dk brn blind cl (sl stains). Howes S1038. *Baltimore*.* $130/£83

STONE, WILLIAM L. (trans). Memoirs and Letters and Journals of Major General Riedesel During His Residence in America. Albany: Joel Munsell, 1868. 2 vols. 306; 284pp; 3 plts. Generally Good (faded, shelfworn). *Cullen.* $225/£144

STONE, WILLIAM L. Poetry and History of Wyoming.... Albany: J. Munsell, 1864. 3rd ed. xxiii,406pp (foxed, pencil mks, blindstamp). Untrimmed. VG +. *Bohling.* $27/£17

STONE, WILLIAM L. Reminiscences of Saratoga and Ballston. NY, 1875. 1st ed. 451pp + 4pp ads. Contents Clean (cvr worn, mottled). *Heinoldt.* $25/£16

STONE, WILLIAM L. Reminiscences of Saratoga. NY, 1880. (Sl browned; sl worn.) *Maggs.* $47/£30

STONE, WILLIAM. Pepe Was the Saddest Bird. NY: Knopf, 1944. 1st ed. Nicolas Mordvinoff (illus). 7 x 9 1/4. Pict paper bds. VG in dj (chipped). *Cattermole.* $60/£38

STONE, ZACHARY. (Pseud of Ken Follett.) Paper Money. London: CCC, 1977. 1st ed. VF in dj. *Mordida.* $150/£96

STONEBRAKER, JOSEPH R. A Rebel of '61. NY/Albany: Wynkoop Hallenbeck Crawford, 1899. 1st ed. 39 plts, fldg table. (Contents lt smudged, sl marginal damping at rear, crack before title, sl damage frontis gutter margin; soiled, stained, ends worn.) *Waverly*.* $286/£183

STONECYPHER, A. L. A Day with Royalty: B.C. 475. Omaha, NE, (1901). 1st ed. Lg fldg plt. Bound in coarse burlap, stitch binding. Good. *Cullen.* $75/£48

STONG, PHIL. Honk the Moose. NY: Dodd, Mead, 1935. Kurt Wiese (illus). 8 1/4 x 10 1/4. 80pp. Cl spine. VG. *Cattermole.* $75/£48

STOOKEY, BYRON. Surgical and Mechanical Treatment of Peripheral Nerves. Phila: Saunders, 1922. 2 color plts. (Cl sl rubbed.) Internally Good. *Goodrich.* $195/£125

STOPES, MARIE. Birth Control Today. London: John Bale, 1934. 1st ed. Nice in dj. *Patterson.* $39/£25

STOPPARD, TOM. Rosencrantz and Guildenstern Are Dead. Faber & Faber, (1967). 1st ed. Nice in orig wraps (sl mkd). *Ash.* $78/£50

STOPPARD, TOM. Rosencrantz and Guildenstern Are Dead. London, 1967. 1st Eng ed. Very Nice in card wrappers. *Clearwater.* $101/£65

STORER, D. H. Reports on the Fishes, Reptiles and Birds of Massachusetts. Boston: State Zoo. Comm., 1839. 1st ed. 426pp, 4 plts. (Sl foxing), else VG in orig wraps. *Mikesh.* $95/£61

STOREY, DAVID. Flight into Camden. London: Longmans, 1960. 1st ed. VG in dj. *Hollett.* $117/£75

STOREY, DAVID. A Temporary Life. London: Allen Lane, 1973. 1st ed. VG in dj (price-clipped). *Hollett.* $47/£30

STOREY, HARRY. Hunting and Shooting in Ceylon. London, 1907. 2nd ed. Map. (Cvrs lt mkd.) Contents Good. *Grayling.* $101/£65

STOREY, HARRY. Hunting and Shooting in Ceylon. London: Longman's, 1907. 2nd ed. Frontis, lg fldg color map. Blue pict cl, gilt. (Lt dampstain top of ll; sl warped), else VG. *Terramedia.* $50/£32

STOREY, MOORFIELD and MARCIAL P. LICHAUCO. The Conquest of the Philippines by the United States 1898-1925. NY, 1926. 2nd ptg. Unopened. (Cvr lt worn), o/w Fine. *Pratt.* $20/£13

STOREY, SAMUEL. To the Golden Land: Sketches of a Trip to Southern California. London, 1889. 1st ed. 101pp; map. Pict cl (joints lt worn). *Ginsberg.* $150/£96

STORM, COLTON. A Catalogue of the Everett D. Graff Collection of Western Americana. Chicago, 1968. 1st ed. Fine in Fine orig glassine over dj. *Turpen.* $48/£31

STORM, COLTON. A Catalogue of the Everett D. Graff Collection of Western Americana. Chicago, 1968. 1st ed. Dj. *Ginsberg.* $50/£32

STORME, PETER. The Thing in the Brook. NY: S&S, 1937. Nice (fore-edge foxed; corners bumped) in dj (worn along seam, sm nicks). *Metropolitan*.* $57/£37

Story of British Prisoners. A. Conan Doyle (preface). London: Central Committee for Nat'l Patriotic Organizations, n.d. (1915). 1st ed. Lt brn wrappers. VG (sl creased). *Sumner & Stillman.* $125/£80

Story of Little Black Sambo. Animated Edition. GC: GC Publishing, (1933). 8vo. (60)pp; 27 full-pg color images by Kurt Wiese (incl 4 movables). Yellow cl, pict paper label. Fine. *Bromer.* $550/£353

Story of Little Red Riding Hood. NY: McLoughlin Bros, (1880?). 10.5x8. (14)pp (fr wrap, 1st pg torn 1/2 way). Color pict wraps (worn). *King.* $40/£26

Story of Little Red Riding Hood. NY: McLoughlin, n.d. (ca 1865). Miss Merryheart's Series. 8vo. 8pp + 1pg lower wrapper (lt spotting pg edges); 8 3/4-pg wood engrs colored w/pochoir process. Pict blue paper wrappers (sm chip), linen stitched spine as published. *Hobbyhorse.* $225/£144

Story of Robin Hood. NY: McLoughlin Bros, n.d. (ca 1890s?). New Wonder Story Series No. 29. 9x7. (10)pp, 4 full-pg color plts. Color pict wraps (spine splitting, worn, sm adhesion mk fr cvr). *King.* $35/£22

Story of the Seventh Kansas. (By Simeon M. Fox.) (Topeka, 1902). Self-wraps. *Wantagh.* $30/£19

STOTTER, JAMES. Beauty Unmasked. NY, 1936. 1st ed. VG. *Fye.* $45/£29

STOTZ, CHARLES MORSE. The Early Architecture of Western Pennsylvania. NY: William Helburn, 1936. 1st ed. One of 1000 nmbered. Fldg map at rear. (Eps lt foxed), o/w Fine. *Captain's Bookshelf.* $150/£96

STOUT, DAVID. Carolina Skeletons. NY: Mysterious, 1988. 1st ed. Signed. VF in dj. *Mordida.* $45/£29

STOUT, GEORGE L. The Care of Pictures. Columbia Univ, 1948. 24 plts. (Margins lt browned, bkpl.) *Edwards.* $23/£15

STOUT, HOSEA. On the Mormon Frontier...1844-1861. Juanita Brooks (ed). Salt Lake, 1964. 1st ed. 2 vols. Frontis, port, map. VG in djs. *Benchmark.* $125/£80

STOUT, REX (ed). The Illustrious Dunderheads. NY, 1942. 2nd ptg. VG in dj (ends sl chipped). *Mcclintock.* $27/£17

STOUT, REX (ed). The Illustrious Dunderheads. NY: Knopf, 1942. 1st ed. VF in VF dj. *Else Fine.* $100/£64

STOUT, REX. The Broken Vase. NY: Farrar & Rinehart, 1941. 1st ed. Fine in pict dj (sl worn). *Else Fine.* $550/£353

STOUT, REX. Champagne for One. NY: Viking, 1958. 1st ed. Fine in dj (sl worn, price-clipped). *Else Fine.* $95/£61

STOUT, REX. Corsage. Bloomington: James A. Rock, 1977. 1st ed. One of 1500 numbered. Fine in wrappers. *Mordida.* $100/£64

STOUT, REX. Crime and Again. Collins, 1959. 1st UK ed. NF in dj. *Williams.* $39/£25

STOUT, REX. Death of a Doxy. NY, (1966). 1st ed. Fine in NF dj. *Mcclintock.* $45/£29

STOUT, REX. Death of a Doxy. NY: Viking, 1966. 1st ed. (Sl soiled under die cut dj hole), o/w Fine in Fine dj (sm tear rear flap fold). *Beasley.* $45/£29

STOUT, REX. Death of a Dude. NY: Viking, 1969. 1st ed. Fine in dj. *Mordida.* $75/£48

STOUT, REX. The Final Deduction. NY: Viking, 1961. 1st ed. Fine in dj (spine sl faded, sl wear). *Mordida.* $75/£48

STOUT, REX. Gambit. London: Crime Club, 1962. 1st Eng ed. VG in dj (lt worn, browned, sm nicks). *Hollett.* $31/£20

STOUT, REX. If Death Ever Slept. Viking, 1957. 1st ed. VG+ in VG dj. *Certo.* $25/£16

STOUT, REX. If Death Ever Slept. London: Collins, 1958. 1st UK ed. VG (ink inscrip) in dj (sl edgeworn, short closed tears, rear panel browned). *Williams.* $28/£18

STOUT, REX. In the Best Families. Viking, 1950. 1st ed. VG+ in VG dj. *Certo.* $30/£19

STOUT, REX. In the Best Families. NY: Viking, 1950. 1st ed. VG+ in dj (sl worn, spine lt faded). *Else Fine.* $115/£74

STOUT, REX. The Mother Hunt. NY: Viking, 1963. 1st ed. Fine in dj. *Mordida.* $125/£80

STOUT, REX. Please Pass the Guilt. NY: Viking, 1973. 1st ed. Fine in dj (sm closed tear). *Mordida.* $50/£32

STOUT, REX. A Right to Die. NY: Viking, 1964. 1st ed. Fine in dj. *Mordida.* $100/£64

STOUT, REX. The Second Confession. NY: Viking, 1949. 1st ed. Good in dj (edges weak, extrems chipped, loss to ends). *Metropolitan*.* $28/£18

STOUT, REX. The Silent Speaker. Viking, 1946. 1st ed. VG in dj (lg spine chips, lacks 1-inch at foot). *Certo.* $30/£19

STOUT, REX. Some Buried Caesar. NY/Toronto, (1939). 1st ed. VG in dj (worn, chipped). *Mcclintock.* $195/£125

STOUT, REX. Some Buried Caesar. NY: Viking, 1939. 1st ed. NF in dj (sl worn). *Else Fine.* $1,500/£962

STOUT, REX. Where There's a Will. NY: Rinehart, 1940. 1st ed. VG (lib stamp fep; lt worn, rubbed) in dj (tears, sl worn). *Else Fine.* $1,400/£897

STOUT, TOM. Montana, Its Story and Biography. Chicago: Amer Hist Soc, 1921. 3 vols. VG. *Perier.* $425/£272

STOVES, J. L. Fibre Microscopy. London: National Trade Press, 1957. VG. *Savona.* $39/£25

STOW, MRS. J. W. Probate Confiscation. Unjust Laws Which Govern Women. (Boston): The Author, 1879. 4th ed. Gilt-, blind-dec cl. VG. *New Hampshire*.* $60/£38

STOWE, HARRIET BEECHER. Dred: A Tale of the Great Dismal Swamp. Boston, 1856. 1st ed. 2 vols. (Spine ends chipped, some gatherings sl pulled), o/w Good. *New Hampshire*.* $25/£16

STOWE, HARRIET BEECHER. Dred: A Tale of the Great Dismal Swamp. Boston: Phillips, Sampson, 1856. 1st ed. 2 vols. (Foxed; sl cocked, bumped, sl frayed.) *Metropolitan*.* $150/£96

STOWE, HARRIET BEECHER. Dred: A Tale of the Great Dismal Swamp. Boston: Phillips, Sampson, 1856. 1st ed. 2 vols. Brn cl stamped w/blind floral panel design fr/rear bds, titled in gilt. (1/8-inch piece missing spine head vol 1; lt rubbed), o/w Fine. *Hermitage*. $300/£192

STOWE, HARRIET BEECHER. A Key to Uncle Tom's Cabin. London: Clarke, Beeton/Thomas Bosworth, (1853). 2nd Eng ed. viii,504pp. Blind-stamped grn cl, gilt. VG. *Hollett*. $101/£65

STOWE, HARRIET BEECHER. A Key to Uncle Tom's Cabin. Boston: John P. Jewett, 1853. 1st ed. 262,(2)pp. (Sm spine repair, extrems worn), else VG. *Mcgowan*. $250/£160

STOWE, HARRIET BEECHER. Men of Our Times. Hartford, etc., 1868. (Lt foxing.) Grn cl (lt worn). *Freeman**. $30/£19

STOWE, HARRIET BEECHER. Men of Our Times. Hartford: Hartford Pub, 1868. 1st ed, 1st state w/Frederick Douglass' name incorrectly spelled on tp. Grn cl, gilt. Fine. BAL 19449. *Macdonnell*. $125/£80

STOWE, HARRIET BEECHER. Pink and White Tyranny. Boston: Roberts Bros, 1871. 1st ed. 4 prelim pp undated ads + 8pp ads dated Summer 1871. Blue cl. Fine. *Sumner & Stillman*. $135/£87

STOWE, HARRIET BEECHER. Uncle Tom's Cabin. London: John Cassell/Ludgate Hill, 1852. 1st Eng bk ed. George Cruikshank (illus). (iii)-xxiii,(1),391,(1)pp. 3/4 leather, marbled paper sides. VG+ (extrems sl worn). BAL 19343. *Mcgowan*. $650/£417

STOWE, HARRIET BEECHER. Uncle Tom's Cabin; or, Life Among the Lowly. Boston: John P. Jewett, 1852. 1st ed, binding B. 2 vols. 3 plts inserted each vol. (Several sigs sprung, some gatherings loose, spotting, staining throughout.) Orig brn cl (heavily rubbed, worn), gilt pict vignette fr cvrs. BAL 19343. *New Hampshire**. $325/£208

STRACHEY, JOHN. The Strangled Cry. London: Bodley Head, (1962). 1st Eng ed. Fine (fep lt browned) in dj (sm tear). *Antic Hay*. $25/£16

STRACHEY, LADY (ed). Memoirs of a Highland Lady. London: John Murray, 1928. (Spine faded.) *Hollett*. $23/£15

STRACHEY, LYTTON. Elizabeth and Essex. Chatto, 1928. 1st UK ed. Good+ (bds sl foxed, stained). *Williams*. $23/£15

STRACHEY, LYTTON. Elizabeth and Essex. NY/London: Crosby Gaige/C&W, 1928. 1st ed. One of 1060 numbered, signed. Port. Gilt cl, bds. VF in glassine dj (chipped). *Reese*. $75/£48

STRACHEY, LYTTON. Portraits in Miniature. Chatto, 1931. 1st UK ed. VG (bkpl) in dj (worn, browned). *Williams*. $28/£18

STRACHEY, LYTTON. Queen Victoria. London: C&W, 1921. 1st ed. 9 plts. Uncut. Paper spine label (sl marked). *Hollett*. $55/£35

STRACHEY, WILLIAM. The Histoire of Travell into Virginia Britania. Louis B. Wright and Virginia Freund (eds). London: Hakluyt Soc, 1953. Frontis, 3 fldg maps. Partly unopened. (Sl rubbed), o/w VG. *Worldwide*. $50/£32

STRAIN, ISAAC G. Cordillera and Pampa, Mountain and Plain. NY: Moore, 1853. 1st ed. 295,(1)pp. Dec cl (few stains fr cvr). *Ginsberg*. $300/£192

STRAND, MARK. The Monument. NY: Ecco, (1978). 1st ed. Fine in NF dj. *Robbins*. $30/£19

STRAND, MARK. The Sargeantville Notebook. Providence: Burning Deck, (1973). 1st ed. One of 400 numbered. Fine in ptd wrappers. *Captain's Bookshelf*. $60/£38

STRAND, MARK. William Bailey. NY, 1987. Good in dj. *Washton*. $25/£16

STRAND, PAUL. Ghana: An African Portrait. Millerton, NY: Aperture, 1976. 1st ed. Map. Pict eps. (Owner stamp), else NF in illus dj (spine top sl worn). *Cahan*. $85/£54

STRAND, PAUL. Living Egypt. London: MacGibbon & Kee, 1969. 1st Eng ed. (Owner stamp), else VG in dj (worn, tape-repaired). *Cahan*. $250/£160

STRAND, PAUL. The Mexican Portfolio. NY: Da Capo, 1967. 2nd ed. Ltd to 1000 numbered, signed. 20 photogravures. Cl portfolio. Fine in slipcase. *Cahan*. $2,250/£1,442

STRAND, PAUL. Paul Strand: A Retrospective Monograph, the Years 1915-1968. Millerton, NY: Aperture, 1972. 1st trade ed. 2 vols. (Owner stamp), else Fine in NF djs. *Cahan*. $250/£160

STRANG, MRS. HERBERT (ed). Snowball Time. London: Humphrey Milford, (1923). 1st ed thus. 4to. Frontis, (32pp) unpaginated; 2 color plts by Anne Anderson. Grey bds, color pict label. Good+. *Dower*. $45/£29

STRANG, WILLIAM. The Earth Fiend: A Ballad. London: John Lane, 1892. One of 150 numbered, signed by Strang and F. Goulding (ptr). 11 etched plts. (Rubbed, rebacked.) *Swann**. $172/£110

STRANGE, EDWARD. The Colour-Prints of Hiroshige. London: Cassell, 1925. Color frontis, 52 plts, 16 color. Pict eps. Cream dec cl gilt (sl soiled, sm tear rear hinge, repaired; fep, 1/2 title foxed). *Hollett*. $218/£140

Stranger's Guide to Baltimore.... Balt: Murphy, 1852. 80pp+15pp ads (lt aged); VG fldg map at fr, 11 b/w plts. Blind lt brn cl, ptd paper bds, gilt. Cvrs VG (lt frayed, edgeworn). *Baltimore**. $90/£58

STRAPAROLA, G. F. The Most Delectable Nights.... Paris: Charles Carrington, 1906. #774/1000. 2 vols. Clean. *Scribe's Perch**. $30/£19

STRATTON, ALFRED WILLIAM. Letters from India. London, 1908. 1st ed. Frontis port, 10 plts. (Fr, rear leaves foxed; spine faded, soiled, upper jt creased.) *Edwards*. $55/£35

STRATTON, ARTHUR. Elements of Form and Design in Classic Architecture. London: Batsford, 1925. 100 plts. (Cl sl worn.) *Ars Artis*. $47/£30

STRATTON, ARTHUR. The English Interior. London: Batsford, (1920). 115pp plts. Parchment-backed cl, gilt. VG. *Hollett*. $187/£120

STRATTON, GEORGE. Theophrastus and the Greek Physiological Psychology Before Aristotle. London, 1917. 1st ed. (Spine head worn.) *Fye*. $75/£48

STRATTON, ROYAL. Captivity of the Oatman Girls. NY: Carlton & Porter, 1859. 3rd ed. 21st thousand. Map. Good+ (foxed; spine frayed, cl spotted). Howes S1068. *Agvent*. $125/£80

STRATTON, ROYAL. Life Among the Indians or the Captivity of the Oatman Girls Among the Apache and Mohave Indians. Grabhorn, 1935. Ltd to 550. Frontis. (Corner wear), o/w VG. Howes S1068. *Oregon*. $150/£96

STRATTON-PORTER, GENE. The Fire Bird. GC, 1922. 1st ed. Gordon Grant (illus). Dec bds, cl back. (Sl worn.) *Oinonen**. $120/£77

STRATTON-PORTER, GENE. Laddie. NY, 1913. 1st Amer ed. 4 color plts. NF (name, bkpl; spine sl sunned, sl rubbed, sm nick, sl soiled). *Polyanthos*. $35/£22

STRATTON-PORTER, GENE. Laddie: A True Blue Story. GC: Doubleday Page, 1913. 1st ed. Good. *Hayman*. $35/£22

STRATTON-PORTER, GENE. The Song of the Cardinal. Indianapolis: Bobbs-Merrill, (1903). 1st ed, 1st bk. 17 plts. (Early inscrip mtd to pastedown; faded, rubbed, esp spine, crown sl frayed), else VG. *Waverly**. $55/£35

STRATTON-PORTER, GENE. Song of the Cardinal. London: Hodder & Stoughton, 1913. 1st Eng ed. NF. *Books & Birds.* $65/£42

STRAUB, PETER. Floating Dragon. NY: Putnam, (1983). 1st trade ed. NF in Fine dj (sm tear). *Other Worlds.* $25/£16

STRAUB, PETER. Floating Dragon. SF/Columbia: Underwood Miller, 1982. 1st ed. One of 500 numbered, signed by Straub and Leo and Diane Dillon (dj art). This copy out-of-series, stamped 'presentation copy.' Dj. *Swann*.* $57/£37

STRAUB, PETER. Ghost Story. NY: Coward McCann & Geoghegan, (1979). 1st ed. Dj. *Swann*.* $46/£29

STRAUB, PETER. Julia. Jonathan Cape, 1976. 1st Eng ed. Fine in Fine dj. *Certo.* $50/£32

STRAUB, PETER. Mrs. God. Hampton Falls: Grant, (1991). 1st separate ed. One of 600 signed by Straub and Richard Berry (artist). Fine in slipcase as issued. *Other Worlds.* $75/£48

STRAUS, R. The Unspeakable Curll. London: Chapman & Hall, 1927. Ltd to 535. Inscribed. Frontis, 31 plts. Teg. Dk blue buckram. Generally Good (later ink notes). *Maggs.* $112/£72

STRAUS, R. and R. DENT. John Baskerville—A Memoir. Cambridge, 1907. One of 300 numbered. 14 plts. Teg. (Hinge split), o/w VG. *Moss.* $94/£60

STRAUS, RALPH (ed). Tricks of the Town: Eighteenth Century Diversions. London: Chapman & Hall, 1927. 1st ed. One of 1000. Teg, uncut. Red/natural buckram, gilt. Fine in dj. *Hartfield.* $95/£61

STRAUS, RALPH. Carriages and Coaches. 1912. 1st ed. *Edwards.* $195/£125

STRAUSS, WALTER L. Chiaroscuro. NY: NYGS, 1973. 1st ed. 177 plts. VG in dj (sl chipped). *Hollett.* $234/£150

STREATFIELD, F. N. Reminiscences of an Old'un. London, 1911. (Lt rubbing.) *Grayling.* $23/£15

STREATFIELD, NOEL. Dennis the Dragon. J.M. Dent, 1939. 1st ed. Ruth Streatfeild (illus). 8vo. 32pp. (Ex-lib, stamp tp, sl fingermks, feps pasted together partly cracking 1st joint), else Sound. Illus cl in pict dj (worn). *Bookmark.* $23/£15

STREATFIELD, NOEL. On Tour. NY: Watts, 1965. 1st ed. 6 1/4 x 9 1/2. 168pp. VG in dj. *Cattermole.* $35/£22

STREET, A. G. Feather Bedding. London, 1954. 1st ed. Dj (torn). *Hatchwell.* $16/£10

STREET, A. G. Hitler's Whistle. London, 1943. 1st ed. (Faded.) *Hatchwell.* $16/£10

STREET, A. G. Shameful Harvest. London, 1952. 1st ed. (Faded.) *Hatchwell.* $12/£8

STREET, G. E. Brick and Marble in the Middle Ages. London, 1874. 2nd ed. xxvi,415pp; 65 plts. (Spine torn.) *Ars Artis.* $33/£21

STREET, JULIAN. Table Topics. NY: Knopf, 1959. 1st ed. VG in dj. *Perier.* $25/£16

STREETER, E. Precious Stones and Gems. London: George Bell, 1892. 5th ed. xii,355 + 13pp ads; 15 color plts. Contemp 1/2 calf. Clean (spine ends worn; hinges strengthened). *Blake.* $250/£160

STREETER, THOMAS W. Bibliography of Texas, 1795-1845. Cambridge: Harvard, 1955-60. 1st ed. Ltd to 600 sets. 5 vols. Dj. *Ginsberg.* $1,250/£801

STREETER, THOMAS W. Bibliography of Texas, 1795-1845. Part I. Texas Imprints. Volume 1, 1817-1838. Cambridge: Harvard Univ, 1955. VG (ex-lib). *Gibbs.* $45/£29

STREETER, THOMAS W. See also Celebrated Collection of Americana...

Streetwalker. NY, 1960. 1st ed. VG in VG dj. *Smith.* $15/£10

STRIBLING, ROBERT MACKEY. Gettysburg Campaign and Campaigns of 1864 and 1865 in Virginia. Petersburg, VA: Franklin, 1905. 1st ed. VG (sl rubbed). *Mcgowan.* $150/£96

STRIBLING, T. S. Strange Moon. GC: Doubleday, 1929. 1st ed. Fine in VG dj (dknd, spine top chipping). *Mordida.* $45/£29

STRICKER, S. (ed). Manual of Human and Comparative Histology. London, 1870-73. 3 vols. Blind-emb cl, gilt device. (Ex-lib, ink stamps feps vol 1, bkpls vols 2-3; lt foxed, feps lt browned; upper hinges vols 2-3 sl cracked; spines chipped, corners rubbed, upper joint vol 3 splitting.) *Edwards.* $70/£45

STRICKER, S. (ed). Manual of Human and Comparative Histology. Henry Power (trans). London: New Sydenham Soc, 1870/72. 2 vols (of 3). xvi,xxxvii,600; xviii,555pp. Brn cl. *White.* $31/£20

STRICKLAND, AGNES. Lives of the Queens of England. London, 1885. 8 vols. 8vo. Contemp 1/2 tan calf, gilt, spines in 6 compartments, red morocco lettering pieces in 2. *Swann*.* $546/£350

STRICKLAND, MAJOR. Twenty-Seven Years in Canada West. Agnes Strickland (ed). Edmonton, 1970. New ed. Spine labels. *Edwards.* $31/£20

Strictures on Female Education. (By John Bennett.) Norwich, (CT): Ebenezer Bushnell, (1792). 1st US ed. 133pp (lacks fep, sl foxed, stained). Contemp leather-backed bds. VG. *Second Life.* $325/£208

STRIEBER, WHITLEY. The Wolfen. Morrow, 1978. 1st ed. Fine in dj. *Madle.* $65/£42

STRIKER, RANDY. (Pseud of Randy Wayne White.) The Deadlier Sex. NY: NAL, 1981. 1st ed. Pb orig. VG in wrappers. *Mordida.* $25/£16

STRIKER, RANDY. (Pseud of Randy Wayne White.) Key West Connection. NY: NAL, 1981. 1st ed. Pb orig. (Bksllr's stamp bottom pg edges), o/w Fine in wrappers. *Mordida.* $35/£22

STRINDBERG, AUGUST. The Son of a Servant. Claud Field (trans). William Rider, 1913. 1st ed in English. Nice (edges sl spotted, sl mks, sl shaken). *Ash.* $62/£40

STRINGER, ARTHUR. The Prairie Wife. Toronto, (1915). 1st Canadian ed. Nice in dj (foxed, sl torn). *King.* $50/£32

STRINGER, GEORGE EYRE. New Hall Porcelain. London: Salisbury Square, (1949). 1st ed. Color frontis. Blue-gray cl. Good in dj. *Karmiole.* $50/£32

STROBRIDGE, IDAH MEACHAM. In Miner's Mirage Land. L.A., 1904. One of 1000 signed. Wrappers (tear, edges crumpled). *Dawson.* $75/£48

STROBRIDGE, IDAH MEACHAM. The Loom of the Desert. L.A., 1907. Wrappers (edges crumpled). *Dawson.* $100/£64

STROMMENGER, EVA. 5000 Years of the Art of Mesopotamia. NY: Abrams, (1964). 324 plts (44 color). Good. *Archaeologia.* $250/£160

STRONG, A. B. The American Flora or History of Plants and Wild Flowers. NY: Green & Spencer, 1845-1852. 4 vols. 143 hand-colored plts (lacks some). Red gilt leather (worn, rubbed, bds off; foxed, dampstained). *Metropolitan*.* $862/£553

STRONG, CHARLES J. and L. S. Strong's Book of Designs. Chicago, 1917. 'New and Enlarged Edition.' (Spine worn, cvrs loose, bumped.) *King.* $60/£38

STRONG, DONALD and DAVID BROWN (eds). Roman Crafts. London, 1976. 1st ed. 18 color plts. Dj. *Edwards.* $39/£25

STRONG, EDWARD W. Procedures and Metaphysics. Berkeley: Univ of CA, 1936. 1st ed. Fine in dj (sl tattered). *Glaser.* $60/£38

691

STRONG, GEORGE TEMPLETON. Diary 1835-1875. Nevins and Thomas (eds). NY: Macmillan, 1952. Stated 1st ptg. 4 vols. Good in Fair dec slipcase. *Scribe's Perch*. $26/£17

STRONG, HENRY W. My Frontier Days and Indian Fights on the Plains of Texas. N.p. (Dallas), n.d. (1926). Signed pict of Strong laid in. VG in pict wraps. *Perier*. $80/£51

STRONG, L. A. G. Dr. Quicksilver 1660-1742. London, 1955. 1st ed. Dj (ragged, repaired). *Edwards*. $31/£20

STRONG, L. A. G. Northern Light. London: Gollancz, 1930. Ltd to 275 signed. (Eps sl browned, spotted.) Teg, uncut. *Hollett*. $39/£25

STRONG, L. A. G. (ed). Sixteen Portraits of People Whose Houses Have Been Preserved by the National Trust. London: Naldrett Press, 1951. 1st ed. Fine in dj. *Michael Taylor*. $23/£15

STRONG, L. A. G. (ed). Sixteen Portraits. London: Naldrett, 1951. 1st ed. 16 full-pg illus. (Feps browned.) Dj. *Hollett*. $47/£30

STRONG, REUBEN MYRON. A Bibliography of Birds. Chicago: Field Museum, 1939-59. 4 vols. Ptd wrappers (shelfworn). *Oinonen**. $90/£58

STRONG, RICHARD P. (ed). The African Republic of Liberia and the Belgian Congo.... Cambridge: Harvard Univ, 1930. 1st ed. 2 vols. Crimson buckram (sl worn, corner frayed, sl scuffed; pp sl rippled), gilt. *Baltimore**. $100/£64

STRONG, ROY et al. The Destruction of the Country House. Thames & Hudson, 1974. VG in ptd wraps. *Hadley*. $47/£30

STRONG, SUSAN DE LANCEY VAN RENSSELAER. Fort Crailo, the Greenbush Manor House. N.p., 1898. 31pp (pencil underlinings). Cl, retaining orig ptd wraps. Leather spine label (scuffed). VG. *Bohling*. $18/£12

STRONG, THOMAS. Cathlamet on the Columbia. Binford & Mort, 1930. Color frontis. Fine in Fine dj. *Oregon*. $12/£8

STRONG, W. E. A Trip to the Yellowstone National Park in July, August, and September, 1875. Norman: Univ of OK, 1968. 1st ptg of New ed. Fine in VG + dj. *Backman*. $30/£19

STRONG, WILLIAM E. Canadian River Hunt. Norman, 1960. Ltd to 1050. Fldg map. Cl, pict bds. NF in orig slipcase (sl worn). *Baade*. $75/£48

STROOTMAN, RALPH E. History of the 363d Infantry. Washington, (1947). 1st ed. (Sl rubbed.) *King*. $65/£42

STROOTMAN, RALPH E. History of the 363rd Infantry Regiment. DC, 1947. VG. *Clark*. $75/£48

STROUD, D. Capability Brown. London, 1957. 2nd ed. Dj. *Maggs*. $37/£24

STROUD, D. Humphrey Repton. London, 1962. 1st ed. Dj. *Maggs*. $25/£16

STROYER, JACOB. My Life in the South. Salem: Salem Observer, 1889. New, enlgd ed. 83pp. Wrappers. (Worn, lt stained, sl chipped), o/w Good. *Brown*. $100/£64

STRUGATSKY, ARKADY and BORIS. Roadside Picnic. London: Gollancz, 1978. 1st British ed. (Bkpl), else Fine in dj. *Lame Duck*. $45/£29

STRUTT, J. W. Scientific Papers. Volume II 1881-1887. Cambridge, 1900. (Lt foxing, bkpl; nick spine top.) *Whitehart*. $62/£40

STRUTT, J. W. The Theory of Sound. Macmillan, 1926. 2 vols. VG + . *Bookcell*. $60/£38

STRUVE, CHRISTIAN AUGUSTUS. Asthenology: or, the Art of Preserving Feeble Life.... William Johnston (trans). London, 1801. 1st ed in English. Contemp 1/2 calf. VG. *Argosy*. $300/£192

STRYKER, ROY EMERSON and NANCY WOOD. In This Proud Land. Greenwich: NYGS, 1973. 1st ed. (Owner stamp), else Fine in illus dj (sl edgeworn). *Cahan*. $100/£64

STRYKER, ROY EMERSON and NANCY WOOD. In This Proud Land. Greenwich: NYGS, 1975. 1st wrapper ed. (Name), else Fine in pict stiff wrappers. *Cahan*. $50/£32

STRYPE, JOHN. Annals of the Reformation and Establishment of Religion.... Vol I only (of 4). London: Tho. Edlin, 1725. 2nd ed. (28),631,103pp. Panelled calf (worn, cvrs detached). (Some leaves loose), o/w Contents VG. *New Hampshire**. $30/£19

STUART, ALEXANDER HUGH HOLMES. A Narrative of the Leading Incidents of the Organization of the First Popular Movement in Virginia in 1865.... Richmond, VA, 1888. 1st ed. 72pp. NF in orig ptd wrappers. *Mcgowan*. $75/£48

STUART, C. M. VILLIERS. Gardens of the Great Mughals. A&C Black, 1913. 1st ed. 40 color plts. Dec blue cl. *Petersfield*. $78/£50

STUART, CHARLES. A Memoir of Granville Sharp.... NY: American Anti-Slavery Soc, 1836. Emb cl (faded), gilt. Good. *Boswell*. $225/£144

STUART, CHARLES. The Naval Dry Docks of the United States. NY/London: D. Van Nostrand/Trubner, 1870. 4th ed. (4),113,(1 blank),84pp (owner stamps, bkpl); 24 engr plts. *Lefkowicz*. $300/£192

STUART, FRANCIS. Try the Sky. London: Gollancz, 1933. 1st Eng ed. Very Nice in dj. *Clearwater*. $78/£50

STUART, JAMES. Three Years in North America. Edinburgh, 1833. 3rd ed. 2 vols. Fldg map. Pub's 1/4 cl (joints weak; sig), orig paper spine labels (browned). Howes S1099. *Swann**. $126/£81

STUART, JAMES. Three Years in North America. Edinburgh, 1833. 3rd ed. 2 vols. xii,525; viii,544pp; fldg map, half-titles. 3/4 calf (peeling), marbled bds, leather labels. Howes S1099. *Reese*. $275/£176

STUART, JAMES. Three Years in North America. NY: Harper, 1833. 1st US ed. 2 vols. xii,334; vii,337pp (foxing, sm pieces cut from tps). Red cl (rebound),gilt. VG. Howes S1099. *Graf*. $65/£42

STUART, JESSE. Head o' W-Hollow. NY: Dutton, 1936. 1st ed. Fine in dj (lt rubbed, closed tear, chip). *Else Fine*. $375/£240

STUART, JESSE. Save Every Lamb. NY: McGraw-Hill, 1964. 1st ed. Fine in Fine dj. *Else Fine*. $35/£22

STUART, MOSES. A Grammar of the Hebrew Language. Andover, 1831. Pub's cl-backed bds (worn). *Swann**. $80/£51

STUART, MOSES. A Hebrew Chrestomathy. Andover, 1829. Pub's cl-backed bds (quite worn). *Swann**. $69/£44

STUART, MOSES. A Hebrew Grammar with a Praxis.... Andover, 1823. New ed. Early 1/2 sheep (cvrs loose; ex-lib). *Swann**. $57/£37

STUART, MOSES. A Hebrew Grammar Without the Points. Andover, 1813. Early 1/2 calf. *Swann**. $126/£81

STUART, ROBERT. Caledonia Romana. Edinburgh: Sutherland & Knox, 1852. 2nd ed. xviii,(2),9-372pp; 16 litho plts, 5 fldg engr maps. Brn cl (soiled, spine sl frayed). *Karmiole*. $150/£96

STUART, ROBERT. Discovery of the Oregon Trail...To Which Is Added: An Account of the Tonquin's Voyage and of Events at Fort Astoria.... Philip Ashton Rollins (ed). NY: Edward Eberstadt, (1935). Port. NF. Howes S1103. *Reese*. $150/£96

STUBBE, WOLF. History of Modern Graphic Art. Richard Waterhouse (trans). 1963. 40 color plts. *Edwards*. $70/£45

STUBBLEBINE, JAMES H. Guido da Siena. Princeton, 1964. Good in dj. *Washton.* $225/£144

STUBBS, CHARLES W. The Story of Cambridge. London, 1905. 2 fldg plans. Teg. Gilt-dec cl (discoloring). *Edwards.* $19/£12

STUBBS, LAURA. Stevenson's Shrine. London: De la More, 1903. 1st ed. 20 plts, fldg map. Teg, uncut. Dec cl (stained), gilt. *Hollett.* $101/£65

STUBBS, LUCAS PETER. A Guide to Pawnbroking, Being the Statutes Regulating Pawns and Pawnbrokers. London: Routledge, 1866. Clean (cl worn, binding strained). *Boswell.* $150/£96

STUBBS, ROBERT. Photographer Thomas Eakins. Phila: Olympia Galleries, 1981. 1st ed. Fine in pict stiff wrappers. *Cahan.* $30/£19

STUCK, HUDSON. Voyages on the Yukon and Its Tributaries. NY: Scribner, 1917. 1st ed. 2 fldg maps. (Few pp roughly opened, ink handstamp eps.) Untrimmed, partly unopened. Blue-gray cl (lt bumped, sm stain lower cvr), gilt. *Baltimore*.* $60/£38

STUDER, JACOB H. The Birds of North America. Columbus, OH: Jacob H. Studer, 1878. 1st ed. 2 vols bound in 1. Sm folio. 119 color plts by Theodore Jasper (1st few lt foxed). Aeg. (Vertical crease 2 blank eps.) Pub's full brn morocco, ribbed gilt-dec spine, gilt dentelles, gilt bird dec fr cvr. *D & D.* $1,200/£769

STUDER, JACOB H. The Birds of North America.... NY, 1895. 119 full-pg color plts. Aeg. Full pub's calf (worn, rubbed, cvrs detached, portions of spine gone). *Kane*.* $325/£208

STUKELEY, WILLIAM. Abury, a Temple of the British Druids.... London: The Author, 1743. Folio. 40 Fine engr plts (3 fldg). Contemp calf (worn, bds rubbed, joints cracked). Internally Clean. *Hatchwell.* $757/£485

STURGE, JOSEPH. A Visit to the United States in 1841. London, 1842. 1st ed. viii,192,cxxiipp. (Spine extrems chipped, old spine repair), else VG. *Mcgowan.* $165/£106

STURGEON, THEODORE. The Dreaming Jewels. Greenberg, (1950). 1st ed. Fine in NF dj (spine sl dknd, rear panel soiled). *Certo.* $45/£29

STURGEON, THEODORE. The Dreaming Jewels. Greenberg, 1950. 1st ed. NF in VG + dj. *Aronovitz.* $45/£29

STURGEON, THEODORE. More Than Human. NY: Farrar, Straus, (1953). 1st ed. Dj (lt rubbed). *Swann*.* $161/£103

STURGEON, THEODORE. A Touch of Strange. GC: Doubleday, 1958. VG in dj (soiled, worn). *Metropolitan*.* $57/£37

STURGEON, THEODORE. A Way Home. NY: Funk & Wagnalls, 1955. 1st ed. Signed. VG (bumped, soiled, worn). *Metropolitan*.* $115/£74

STURGEON, THEODORE. Without Sorcery. Prime, 1948. 1st ed, 1st bk. Fine in NF dj (fr panel sl rubbed). *Certo.* $50/£32

STURGEON, THEODORE. Without Sorcery. (Phila), 1948. 1st ed, 1st bk. Fine in VG dj (lt shelfwear, spine lt faded). *Mcclintock.* $75/£48

STURGIS, RUSSELL. A Dictionary of Architecture and Building. NY/London, 1901-02. 3 vols. (Ex-lib, ink stamps, blind stamps, bkpls; margins lt browned.) Lib morocco-backed cl bds (rebound; soiled, spine #s). *Edwards.* $133/£85

STURGIS, WILLIAM BAYARD. New Lines for Flyfishers. NY, (1936). Ltd to 950. Frontis. (Spine rubbed, dknd.) *King.* $95/£61

STURHAHN, JOAN. Carvalho. Merrick, NY: Richwood, 1976. 1st ed. Frontis port. VG (lt pencil mks, notes) in dj. *Cahan.* $60/£38

STURT, GEORGE. The Journals of George Sturt. Geoffrey Grigson (ed). Cresset Press, (1941). (Edges sl dusty, spotted), o/w Nice in dj (sl nicked, dusty). *Ash.* $39/£25

STURT, GEORGE. A Small Boy in the Sixties. Cambridge, 1932. Good in dj (sl frayed, soiled). *Cox.* $9/£6

STUTFIELD, HUGH E. M. and J. NORMAN COLLIE. Climbs and Exploration in the Canadian Rockies. Longmans, 1903. *Petersfield.* $34/£22

STUTLER, BOYD B. Glory, Glory, Hallelujah! Cincinnati, (1960). 1st ed. Fine in plain plastic dj (wear). *Pratt.* $45/£29

STUTZENBERGER, ALBERT. American Historical Spoons. Rutland: Charles E. Tuttle, (1971). 63 b/w photo plts. Red cl, gilt. Fine in Fine pict dj, orig bd shipping box, ptd label. *Baltimore*.* $20/£13

STYRON, WILLIAM. Against Fear. (Winston Salem): Palaemon, (1981). 1st ed. One of 300 signed. Fine in ptd wrappers. *Captain's Bookshelf.* $75/£48

STYRON, WILLIAM. Against Fear. N.p.: Palaemon, (1981). One of 300 signed. Fine in wrappers. *Lenz.* $90/£58

STYRON, WILLIAM. Against Fear. NC: Palaemon, 1981. Ltd to 300 signed. Additionally signed. Fine in ptd wraps. *Polyanthos.* $75/£48

STYRON, WILLIAM. The Confessions of Nat Turner. NY: Random House, (1967). One of 500 numbered, signed. Fine in Fine slipcase. *Lenz.* $225/£144

STYRON, WILLIAM. The Confessions of Nat Turner. London: Cape, (1968). 1st UK ed. Fine in dj. *Hermitage.* $60/£38

STYRON, WILLIAM. The Message of Auschwitz. (Blacksburg): Press de la Warr, 1979. 1st ed. One of 200 (of 226) numbered, signed. Fine in dec wrappers. *Captain's Bookshelf.* $100/£64

STYRON, WILLIAM. The Message of Auschwitz. (Blacksburg, VA): Press de la Warr, 1979. One of 200 numbered, signed. Fine in Fine wrappers, dj. *Lenz.* $100/£64

STYRON, WILLIAM. Sophie's Choice. NY: Random House, (1979). One of 500 numbered, signed. Fine in Fine slipcase. *Lenz.* $175/£112

STYRON, WILLIAM. Sophie's Choice. Cape, 1979. 1st UK ed. VG in dj. *Williams.* $28/£18

STYRON, WILLIAM. This Quiet Dust and Other Writings. London: Cape, (1983). 1st Eng ed. Fine in dj. *Between The Covers.* $45/£29

STYRON, WILLIAM. This Quiet Dust. NY: Random House, (1982). One of 250 numbered, signed. Fine in Fine slipcase. *Lenz.* $150/£96

SUBA, SUSANNA. Spots by Suba. NY: E.P. Dutton, (1944). 64pp, incl 49 full-pg b/w illus. Lt tan cl (sl soiled, 2 sm red stains fr cvr), paper spine label titled in holograph. Internally NF. *Blue Mountain.* $15/£10

SUCKOW, RUTH. The Folks. Farrar & Rinehart, (1934). 1st ed. Fine in dj (chipped). *Authors Of West.* $30/£19

SUDEK, JOSEF. Sudek. NY: Clarkson N. Potter, 1978. 1st ed. Fine in Fine dj. *Smith.* $250/£160

SUDELL, RICHARD. Landscape Gardening. Ward Lock, 1933. 8 color plts. VG in grn cl. *Hadley.* $39/£25

SUDWORTH, GEORGE B. Nomenclature of the Arborescent Flora of the United States. Washington, DC, 1897. viii,419pp. 1/2 cl, marbled bds. (Lt shelfwear), else VG + . *Brooks.* $65/£42

SUGDEN, ALAN VICTOR and JOHN LUDLAM EDMONDSON. A History of English Wallpaper 1509-1914. London: Batsford, (1925). Presentation signed by both. 70 mtd color plts. Teg. Full vellum, gilt. *Christie's*.* $421/£270

SUGDEN, EDWARD BURTENSHAW. A Series of Letters to a Man of Property.... London: Reed & Hunter, 1815. 3rd ed. Uncut. Orig bds. Very Desirable. *Boswell.* $250/£160

SUGRANES, EUGENE. The Old San Gabriel Mission. San Gabriel, 1909. 1st ed. Pb. Frontis. VG. *Turpen.* $35/£22

SULLIVAN, CONSTANCE (ed). Legacy of Light. NY: Knopf, 1987. 1st ed. Fine in Fine dj. *Smith.* $125/£80

SULLIVAN, CONSTANCE (ed). Nude: Photographs 1850-1980. NY: Harper & Row, 1980. 1st ed. VG + in VG + dj. *Smith.* $100/£64

SULLIVAN, CONSTANCE (ed). Nude: Photographs 1850-1980. NY: Harper & Row, 1980. 1st ed. 134 photo plts. Cl-backed paper over bds. Fine in NF dj. *Cahan.* $150/£96

SULLIVAN, EDMUND J. The Art of Illustration. London: Chapman & Hall, 1921. 1st ed. Untrimmed. (Marginal notes.) *Hollett.* $55/£35

SULLIVAN, EDWARD. The Bungalow and the Tent. London: Richard Bentley, 1854. 1st ed. xi,(i)blank, (13)-311pp, 1/2-title (lib stamp, bkpl feps). Brn blind-stamped cl (sm mk spine; hinges cracked, sl loose), but Sound. VG internally. *Morrell.* $125/£80

SULLIVAN, LOUIS H. The Autobiography of an Idea. NY: Press of the Amer Inst of Architects, 1924. 1st ed. VG + in dj. *Houle.* $175/£112

SULLIVAN, LOUIS H. Kindergarten Chats on Architecture, Education and Democracy. Claude F. Bragdon (ed). (Washington, D.C.): SCARAB Fraternity Press, 1934. 1st ed. Frontis port, 5 plts. Orange cl stamped in blue (sl soiled). Dj. *Karmiole.* $275/£176

SULLIVAN, MAURICE S. Jedediah Smith: Trader and Trailbreaker. NY: Press of the Pioneers, 1936. 1st ed. Red cl, gilt. Fine. *Harrington.* $95/£61

SULLIVAN, NEIL and EVELYN S. STEWART. Now Is the Time. Bloomington, IN: IN Univ, 1969. 1st ed. Fine in NF dj. *Lame Duck.* $45/£29

SULLIVAN, REGINALD NOEL. Somewhere in France. (SF): Ptd for private circulation, 1917. Mtd frontis port. VG in wraps w/ptd label (presentation; lib label, bkpl added). *Bohling.* $30/£19

SULTAN, LARRY and MIKE MANDEL. Evidence. N.p.: Self-published, (1977). 1st ed. 59 full-pg b/w photos. Fine. *Cahan.* $50/£32

SULZBERGER, CYRUS. The Resistentialists. NY, 1962. 1st ed. NF in NF dj. *Warren.* $250/£160

SUMACH, ALEXANDER. A Treasury of Hashish. Toronto: Stoneworks, 1976. 1st ptg. Fine in wraps. *Sclanders.* $34/£22

SUMMERHAYES, MARTHA. Vanished Arizona: Recollections of My Army Life. Phila: Lippincott, 1908. 1st ed. Frontis. Unopened. (Stamp, bkpl; extrems sl rubbed), o/w VG. Howes S1132. *Cahan.* $125/£80

SUMMERHAYES, MARTHA. Vanished Arizona: Recollections of My Army Life. Milo M. Quaife (ed). Chicago: Lakeside, 1939. Frontis port, fldg map, 11 illus w/tissue guards. Teg. VG (bkpl). Reissue of Howes S1132. *Cahan.* $30/£19

SUMMERS, MONTAGUE (ed). Covent Garden Drollery. London: Fortune, 1927. 1st ed thus. One of 575 numbered. Frontis. Fine in NF dj (sm pinholes rear panel). *Reese.* $85/£54

SUMMERS, MONTAGUE (ed). Malleus Maleficarum. London: John Rodker, 1928. One of 1275, this unnumbered. All edges uncut. Tan cl, gilt device upper cvr, red parchment paper spine (corners bumped, cvrs sl soiled). Internally Fine. *Cummins.* $300/£192

SUMMERS, MONTAGUE. A Bibliography of the Restoration Drama. London: Fortune, n.d. Black cl, gilt. Dj. *Maggs.* $62/£40

SUMMERS, MONTAGUE. The Gothic Quest, a History of the Gothic Novel. London: Fortune, (1938). 1st ed. Ltd to 950 numbered. (Name.) *Oak Knoll.* $65/£42

SUMMERS, MONTAGUE. The Gothic Quest. London: Fortune, n.d. One of 910 numbered. VG (joints rubbed, spine sunned). *Beasley.* $125/£80

SUMMERS, MONTAGUE. The Vampire, His Kith and Kin. London: Kegan Paul (et al), 1928. 1st ed. Frontis. Good (lt foxed, cl lt soiled). *Reese.* $55/£35

SUMNER, CHARLES. The Barbarism of Slavery. Washington, 1860. 1st ed. 32pp. (Foxing), else VG in orig self-wraps. *Mcgowan.* $150/£96

SUMNER, CHARLES. White Slavery in the Barbary States. Boston: John P. Jewett, 1853. 1st ed. Brn cl over bds (worn). VG. *Old London.* $85/£54

SUMNER, CHARLES. The Works. Boston, 1870. Vol 1 signed. 15 vols. Port vol 1. Contemp 1/2 olive calf, gilt, spines in 5 compartments, red/citron morocco lettering pieces in 2. (Vol 1 fr cvr detached.) *Swann*.* $345/£221

SUMNER, G. C. et al. John Albert Monroe, a Memorial. Providence, RI, 1892. 1st ed. Ltd to 250. PNRISSHS Series 4, #18. 50pp. NF in ptd wrappers. *Mcgowan.* $45/£29

SUMNER, WILLIAM G. A History of American Currency.... NY: Henry Holt, 1874. 1st ed. iv,391pp (sl aged, fore-edge few ll sl worn). Dk brn coated eps. Red-brn cl (lt bubbled), gilt. *Baltimore*.* $60/£38

SUNDER, JOHN E. Bill Sublette, Mountain Man. Norman: Univ of OK, (1959). 1st ed. Fine in pict dj. *Argonaut.* $90/£58

SUNDER, JOHN E. The Fur Trade on the Upper Missouri, 1840-1865. Norman: Univ of OK, 1965. Good in dj (sl worn). *Dumont.* $45/£29

SUNDER, JOHN E. Joshua Pilcher, Fur Trader and Indian Agent. Norman: Univ of OK, (1968). 1st ed. 3 maps. Fine in pict dj (tear). *Argonaut.* $45/£29

SUNDER, JOHN E. Joshua Pilcher. Norman: Univ of OK, (1968). 1st ed. VG in dj (sl worn). *Lien.* $30/£19

SUNDERLAND, EDWIN S. S. Abraham Lincoln and the Illinois Central Railroad. NY: Privately ptd (Princeton Univ), 1955. 1st ed. Port. *Wantagh.* $50/£32

SUNDERLAND, LA ROY. Anti-Slavery Manual.... NY: Piercy & Reed, 1837. 1st ed. (Lib ticket fr pastedown, sl foxed; spine label lacks piece.) *Kane*.* $120/£77

SUNTER, G. H. Adventures of a Trepang Fisher. London: Hurst, 1937. 1st ed. VG. *Mikesh.* $50/£32

SUREN, HANS. Man and Sunlight. Slough, 1927. Orange cl. VG. *Doctor's Library.* $40/£26

SURFACE, H. A. (ed). The Serpents of Pennsylvania. Harrisburg: Dept of Ag, Sept 1906. 1st ed. 42 plts. (Heavily chipped), else VG. *Mikesh.* $60/£38

SURTEES, R. S. Hillington Hall. (By Robert Smith Surtees.) London: John C. Nimmo, 1888. 1st ed thus. 12 hand-colored plts. 3/4 red morocco, marbled bds (rebacked, scuffed). *Freeman*.* $160/£103

SURTEES, R. S. Jorrocks's Jaunts and Jollities. London: Kegan Paul et al, (1901). 3rd ed. 31 engr plts (incl frontis, added engr tp). Grn cl. Good. *Karmiole.* $125/£80

SURTEES, R. S. Young Tom Hall. Edinburgh/London: William Blackwood, 1926. Pict red cl. (Edges bumped), o/w VG. *Metropolitan*.* $28/£18

SUSKIND, PATRICK. Perfume. NY: Knopf, 1986. 1st ed. Fine (rmdr mk) in dj. *Antic Hay.* $15/£10

SUTCLIFF, ROBERT. Travels in Some Parts of North America, in the Years 1804, 1805, and 1806. York: Peacock for Alexander, 1811. 1st ed. Engr frontis, 5 full-pg plts. Calf (rebacked). Howes S1145. *Rostenberg & Stern.* $250/£160

SUTCLIFF, ROBERT. Travels in Some Parts of North America, in the Years 1804, 1805, and 1806. Phila: Kite, 1812. 1st Amer ed. Frontis view, ix,289pp (dknd, worn, few notes, label inside fr cvr). Full leather (worn, bds bowed). Howes S1145. *Bohling.* $30/£19

SUTCLIFF, ROSEMARY. Dawn Wind. London: OUP, 1961. 1st ed. Charles Keeping (illus). 5 3/4 x 8 3/4. 241pp. Fine in dj. *Cattermole.* $45/£29

SUTCLIFF, ROSEMARY. The Flowers of Adonis. Hodder & Stoughton, 1969. 1st ed. Lg 8vo. 383pp. VG + in pict dj (lt frayed). *Bookmark.* $27/£17

SUTCLIFF, ROSEMARY. Knight's Fee. NY: Walck, 1960. 1st US ed. Charles Keeping (illus). 5 1/2 x 8 3/4. 242pp. VG in dj. *Cattermole.* $25/£16

SUTCLIFF, ROSEMARY. The Shield Ring. London: OUP, 1956. 1st ed. C. Walter Hodges (illus). 5 3/4 x 8 3/4. 215pp. VG in dj. *Cattermole.* $35/£22

SUTCLIFF, ROSEMARY. Sword at Sunset. Hodder & Stoughton, 1963. 1st ed. Lg 8vo. 480pp, dbl-pg maps on eps. VG in pict dj (repaired). *Bookmark.* $28/£18

SUTHERLAND, CAPTAIN. A Tour up the Straits, from Gibraltar to Constantinople. The Author, 1790. 2nd ed, corrected. xlvii,372pp (lt waterstain on title, few leaves). Orig calf (lacks label). *Bickersteth.* $75/£48

SUTHERLAND, DOUGLAS. The Yellow Earl. London: Cassell, 1965. Very Nice in dj (sm edge tear, price-clipped). *Hollett.* $44/£28

SUTHERLAND, GILBERT D. (ed). An Encyclopaedia of the Arts, Manufactures, and Commerce of the United Kingdom. London, 1897. Frontis port, 488pp (tp lt browned, ex-lib, sm ink stamps, fore-edge p146 reinforced). 1/2 lib morocco (rebound, rubbed, spine #s), gilt. *Edwards.* $234/£150

SUTHERLAND, J. G. At Sea with Joseph Conrad. London, 1922. One of 1250. Very Nice in dj (torn, brittle). *Clearwater.* $70/£45

SUTHERLAND, JAMES. The Adventures of an Elephant Hunter. London, 1912. 1st ed, 1st issue. 8vo. Pict cl (recased), gilt. Good. *Maggs.* $585/£375

SUTHERLAND, JAMES. The Adventures of an Elephant Hunter. London: Macmillan, 1912. 1st ed. 8vo. Frontis. Blue gilt pict cl (recased, sl wear), else VG. *Terramedia.* $750/£481

SUTHERLAND, L. W. Aces and Kings. London, (1936). 1st Eng ed. Good (spine faded, creased, cvrs sl mkd). *Clearwater.* $55/£35

SUTHERLAND, R. Q. and R. L. WILSON. The Book of Colt Firearms. Kansas City, (1971). Deluxe ed. One of 500 numbered. Signed, inscribed presentation by both. Gilt-stamped leather (lt worn). Slipcase. *Oinonen*.* $275/£176

SUTHERLAND, R. Q. and R. L. WILSON. The Book of Colt Firearms. Kansas City: Sutherland, (1971). (Lt worn.) Dj (frayed). *Oinonen*.* $150/£96

SUTLEY, ZACK T. The Last Frontier. NY: Macmillan, 1930. 1st ed. Fldg map. (Sl shelfwear, portion dj laid down fr pastedown), else VG. *Brown.* $35/£22

SUTLEY, ZACK T. The Last Frontier. NY: Macmillan, 1930. 1st ed. Fldg map. Red-brn cl. (Sl wear ends, corners sl jammed), else Fine. *Argonaut.* $45/£29

SUTLEY, ZACK T. The Last Frontier. NY: Macmillan, 1930. 1st ed. Fldg map. Good (spine head lt worn). *Lien.* $45/£29

SUTPHEN, W. G. VAN T. The Golfer's Alphabet. NY: Harper, 1899. 1st ed. Cl-backed pict bds. (Extrems rubbed), else VG. *Pacific*.* $460/£295

SUTTER, JOHN A. New Helvetia Diary: A Record of Events...from September 9, 1845, to May 25, 1848. SF: Grabhorn, 1939. One of 950 ptd. 2 color plts, facs pg from diary, map. Patterned bds, linen backstrip, paper spine label. (Sl corner wear), o/w Fine. Howes S1155. *Harrington.* $115/£74

SUTTON, DENYS and ANN CLEMENTS. An Italian Sketchbook by Richard Wilson, R.A. London, 1968. 2 parts. 58 plts. Good in slipcase. *Washton.* $65/£42

SUTTON, DENYS. Christie's Since the War, 1945-1958.... London: Christie, Manson & Woods, (1959). 5 color, 185 b/w plts. Red cl, gilt. Fine in white dj (lt soiled). *Heller.* $45/£29

SUTTON, DENYS. French Drawings of the Eighteenth Century. London, 1949. 65 plts (2 color). Good. *Washton.* $25/£16

SUTTON, DENYS. Nocturne: The Art of James McNeill Whistler. London: Country Life, 1963. Frontis. Blue cl over bds, gilt. Fine (edges faded). *Heller.* $70/£45

SUTTON, FRED. Hands Up! Indianapolis: Bobbs-Merrill, (1927). 1st ed. Pict cl. Fair. *Lien.* $25/£16

SUTTON, GEORGE M. The Birds of Florida.... Balt, 1925. Ltd ed. 76 full-pg color plts, fldg map, dwg. *Kane*.* $140/£90

SUTTON, R. L. Tiger Trails in Southern Asia. St. Louis: Mosby, 1926. 1st ed. Gilt-dec cl. (Dampstained), else Good + . *Mikesh.* $30/£19

SUTTON, ROBERT. A Complete Guide to Landlords, Tenants, and Lodgers.... London: J. Stratford, 1802. 4th ed. Mod cl. Untrimmed. Clean. *Boswell.* $250/£160

SUTTON, WALTER. The Western Book Trade: Cincinnati as a Nineteenth-Century Publishing and Book-Trade Center. Columbus: Ohio Historical Soc, 1961. Dj. *Rostenberg & Stern.* $45/£29

SUYIN, HAN. From One China to the Other. NY, (1956). 1st ed. Henri Cartier-Bresson (photos). Good in dj (badly chipped). *King.* $95/£61

SVEVO, ITALO. A Life. London: Secker & Warburg, 1963. 1st Eng ed. VG + in VG dj (chipped). *Lame Duck.* $65/£42

SVOBODA, ANTONIN. Computing Mechanisms and Linkages. Hubert M. James (ed). NY: McGraw-Hill, 1948. 1st ed. Complete w/fldg monogram back cvr sleeve. VG (cvrs spotted). *Glaser.* $200/£128

SVYATOSLAVICH, IGOR. Slovo, a Polku Igoreve. Moscow: Academia, 1934. Folio. 10 Fine mtd color plts. (Lt worn.) Lg dec labels both cvrs. Orig box (broken). Fine. *Oinonen*.* $375/£240

SWAAN, W. The Late Middle Ages. London, 1977. 1st UK ed. (Eps lt spotted.) Dj (sl chipped). *Edwards.* $39/£25

SWADESH, FRANCES L. 20,000 Years of History, a New Mexico Bibliography. Santa Fe, 1973. 1st ed. Pb. Fine. *Turpen.* $45/£29

SWAINSON, W. Exotic Conchology. R.T. Abbott (ed). Princeton: Van Nost., (1968). One of 2000. Facs rpt of 1834 1st ed. 47 full-pg color plts. Aeg. Fine. *Mikesh.* $30/£19

SWAINSOPN, C. A Handbook of Weather Folklore...in Various Languages. Edinburgh: Blackwood, 1873. 275pp. Good + (newly rebacked). *Bookcell.* $45/£29

SWALLOW, ALAN (ed). 1955 Brand Book Being Volume Eleven of the Denver Posse of the Westerners. CO: Westerners, 1956. #407/500. Illus textured cl. (Eps sl offset), else Fine in dj (chipped, stained). *Cahan.* $60/£38

SWAN, ABRAHAM. The British Architect. London: The Author, sold Th. Meighan, 1750. 2nd ed. viii (incl tp),20pp; 59 ex 60 engr plts (5 containing ptd text) (lacks plt 59). Blind-panelled sheep (worn). *Ars Artis.* $390/£250

SWAN, JOSEPH. Delineations of the Brain in Relation to Voluntary Motion. London: Bradbury & Evans, 1864. 4to. iv,65pp (tp stained, sm rubber stain); 18 engr plts. Later 1/4 cl, marbled bds. Internally Clean. *Goodrich.* $895/£574

SWAN, JOSEPH. Illustrations of the Comparative Anatomy of the Nervous System. London: Bradbury & Evans, 1864. 2nd ed. Lg 4to. 250pp; 35 engr plts. Orig cl (rebacked), orig spine. (Pp49-52 frayed outer edge, lt foxing), else Clean. *Goodrich.* $595/£381

SWANBERG, W. A. Sickles the Incredible. NY, 1956. 1st ed. VG. *Wantagh.* $25/£16

SWANN, ALFRED J. Fighting the Slave-Hunters in Central Africa. London, 1910. 1st ed. 32 photo plts. Blue pict cl (bumped), gilt. *Maggs.* $507/£325

SWANN, BRIAN. Unreal Estate. West Branch, IA, 1982. Ltd to 1000. Fine in ptd wrappers. *Truepenny.* $15/£10

SWANTON, JOHN R. Early History of the Creek Indians and Their Neighbors. BAE Bulletin 73. GPO, 1922. 10 fldg maps at rear. Fair. *Scribe's Perch*.* $30/£19

SWANTON, JOHN R. Haida Texts and Myths Skidegate Dialect. BAE Bulletin 29. Washington: GPO, 1905. (Lt soiled; extrems lt rubbed.) *Sadlon.* $25/£16

SWANTON, JOHN R. Haida Texts and Myths: Skidegate Dialect. BAE Bulletin 29. Washington: GPO, 1905. Good. *Lien.* $25/£16

SWANTON, JOHN R. The Indian Tribes of North America. BAE Bulletin 145. Washington: GPO, 1953. 1st ed. 4 lg fldg maps. (Ink notes, mks; sl rubbed), o/w VG. *Worldwide.* $45/£29

SWANTON, JOHN R. Indian Tribes of the Lower Mississippi Valley and Adjacent Coast of the Gulf of Mexico. BAE Bulletin 43. 1911. 1st ed. Frontis, fldg color map, 31 plts. (Rubberstamp # ep, tp), o/w VG. *Oregon.* $45/£29

SWANTON, JOHN R. Tlingit Myths and Texts. BAE Bulletin 39. Washington: GPO, 1909. Good. *Lien.* $25/£16

SWANWICK, BETTY. Beauty and the Burglar. London, 1958. 1st Eng ed. Very Nice in dj (rubbed, sl torn). *Clearwater.* $39/£25

SWANWICK, BETTY. The Cross Purpose. London: Editions Poetry, 1945. 1st Eng ed. Nice in dj (sl torn). *Clearwater.* $47/£30

SWANWICK, BETTY. Hoodwinked. London, 1957. 1st Eng ed. Very Nice in dj (rubbed, sl torn). *Clearwater.* $39/£25

SWARTH, H. S. A Distributional List of the Birds of Arizona. Joseph Grinnell (ed). Hollywood, CA: Cooper Ornithological Club, 1914. Map. Untrimmed. VF (name on cvr) in gray stiff wraps. *Five Quail.* $35/£22

SWARTH, H. S. Report on a Collection of Birds and Mammals from Vancouver Island. Berkeley: Univ of CA, Feb 1912. 1st ed. 4 plts. (Ink notes, spine repaired), else VG in wraps. *Mikesh.* $45/£29

SWAYNE, GEORGE C. Lake Victoria. Edinburgh: William Blackwood, 1868. 1st ed. Engr frontis, vii,(iii),342pp + 20 pub's list, 1/2-title, 7 plts, fldg map (torn, repaired); occasional leaf soiled, spotted). Orig blue cl (well rebacked), orig backstrip. Good. *Morrell.* $70/£45

SWEENEY, JAMES JOHNSON (ed). Three Young Rats and Other Rhymes. NY: Curt Valentin, 1944. 1st ed. Ltd to 700, this copy not numbered. 85 dwgs by Alexander Calder. Cl-backed pict yellow paper bds (edges sl soiled, sl bumped). *Shasky.* $175/£112

SWEET, HENRY. The Oldest English Texts. London: Early English Text Soc, 1885. 668pp (sl soiled). Lib binding (rebound). *Cullen.* $50/£32

SWEET, R. Hortus Britannicus, or A Catalogue of All the Plants Indigenous...of Great Britain. London, (c 1833). 3rd ed. xx,799pp. 1/2 morocco (sl rubbed). *Henly.* $56/£36

SWEETSER, WILLIAM. A Treatise on Consumption. Boston: T.H. Carter, 1836. 1st ed. 254pp. Emb cl, leather label. (Sl shelfworn, edgeworn), else VG. *Brown.* $100/£64

SWICHKOW, LOUIS J. and LLOYD P. GARTNER. The History of the Jews of Milwaukee. Phila: Jewish Pub Soc of America, 1963. 1st ed. VG + in dj. *Bohling.* $25/£16

SWIFT, GRAHAM. Learning to Swim and Other Stories. London Magazine Editions, 1982. 1st ed. VG in dj (sm repaired nick). *Words Etc.* $70/£45

SWIFT, GRAHAM. Out of This World. Viking, 1988. 1st UK ed. Fine in dj. *Williams.* $19/£12

SWIFT, GRAHAM. Shuttlecock. Allen Lane, 1981. 1st UK ed. NF in dj. *Williams.* $187/£120

SWIFT, GRAHAM. The Sweetshop Owner. London: Allen Lane, 1980. 1st UK ed, 1st bk. (Spine lt bumped), o/w NF in dj (sl soiling lower flap). *Moorhouse.* $234/£150

SWIFT, H. G. A History of Postal Agitation from Fifty Years Ago Till the Present Day.... C. Arthur Pearson, 1900. (Foxed, eps browned; backstrip worn.) *Peter Taylor.* $31/£20

SWIFT, HILDEGARDE. Little Blacknose: The Story of a Pioneer. NY: HB, (1929). 1st ed. Lynd Ward (illus). Largely unopened. NF (inscrips). *Agvent.* $75/£48

SWIFT, JONATHAN. The Correspondence of Jonathan Swift.... Harold Williams (ed). Oxford: Clarendon Press, 1963. 3 vols. NF in djs. *Reese.* $125/£80

SWIFT, JONATHAN. Gulliver's Travels. London, 1909. 1st trade ed. 12 color plts by Arthur Rackham. Pict eps. 1/2 purple calf (extrems sl worn), gilt. *Swann*.* $103/£66

SWIFT, JONATHAN. Gulliver's Travels. London, 1909. One of 750 numbered, signed by Arthur Rackham (illus). 13 tipped-in color plts, guards. Cream buckram (lt soiled, spine dknd, lettering rubbed; bkpl), gilt, silk ties. *Swann*.* $632/£405

SWIFT, JONATHAN. Gulliver's Travels. London/NY, 1909. 26 + 291pp; 12 color plts by Arthur Rackham. Full dec cl. (Eps discolored, cracked at p1, 128; spine faded, bds warped), o/w Good + . *Scribe's Perch*.* $50/£32

SWIFT, JONATHAN. Gulliver's Travels. London/NY: J.M. Dent/E.P. Dutton, 1909. #569/750 signed. 4to. 13 mtd color plts by Arthur Rackham. White buckram (soiled, edges worn, lacks ties). *Metropolitan*.* $373/£239

SWIFT, JONATHAN. Gulliver's Travels. London: J.M. Dent, 1909. 1st ed w/Arthur Rackham illus. 12 color plts. Gilt-stamped maroon cl. Nice. *Appelfeld.* $150/£96

SWIFT, JONATHAN. Gulliver's Travels. Franklin Center, PA: Franklin Library, 1977. Satin eps, ribbon marker; aeg. Gilt-worked grn full morocco. Fine. *Antic Hay.* $50/£32

SWIFT, JONATHAN. Gulliver's Travels. Harold Williams (ed). London: First Edition Club, 1926. 12 full-pg facs. Teg. Black buckram, gilt. Very Nice. *Cady.* $60/£38

SWIFT, JONATHAN. The History of the Four Last Years of the Queen. London: A. Millar, 1758. 1st ed. xvi,392pp. Contemp calf (spine sl rubbed). Nice. *Karmiole.* $275/£176

SWIFT, JONATHAN. Travels into Several Remote Nations of the World, by Lemuel Gulliver. London: Golden Cockerel, 1925. One of 450. 2 vols. *Swann*.* $460/£295

SWIFT, JONATHAN. The Works. Edinburgh: Constable, 1814. 8vo. 19 vols. Engr frontis port. Old speckled bds, brn morocco spines, corners (worn). *Appelfeld.* $850/£545

SWIFT, ZEPHANIAH. A Digest of the Laws of the State of Connecticut. New Haven: S. Converse, 1822-23. Contemp sheep (rubbed; foxed). Sound. *Boswell.* $650/£417

SWIGGETT, S. A. The Bright Side of Prison Life. Balt, 1897. Frontis port, 254pp; roster. (Extrems sl worn; inner fr hinge starting.) *Wantagh.* $125/£80

SWINBURNE, ALGERNON CHARLES. Atalanta in Calydon. London: Edward Moxon, 1865. 1st ed. Uncut. Cream cl, heavy beveled bds, gilt. (New eps; grubby, recased.) *Maggs.* $289/£185

SWINBURNE, ALGERNON CHARLES. Ballads of the English Border. William A. MacInnes (ed). London, 1925. 1st Eng ed. (Foxed.) Dj (sl mkd). *Clearwater.* $39/£25

SWINBURNE, ALGERNON CHARLES. Bothwell: A Tragedy. London: C&W, 1874. 1st ed. (Fr inner hinge cracked along ep fold; cvrs sl dknd, worn), else Good. *Holmes.* $50/£32

SWINBURNE, ALGERNON CHARLES. Erechtheus: A Tragedy. London: C&W, 1876. 1st ed. Blue-grn cl (sl worn), gilt. Good. *Maggs.* $39/£25

SWINBURNE, ALGERNON CHARLES. Laus Veneris. London, 1948. Ltd to 750. 11 wood engrs. Teg. Maroon buckram-backed marbled bds, spine gilt. (Top edge bds sl browned), else Nice. *Cady.* $85/£54

SWINBURNE, ALGERNON CHARLES. Lesbia Brandon. London: Falcon, 1952. 1st Eng ed. Nice (spine sl faded) in dj. *Clearwater.* $39/£25

SWINBURNE, ALGERNON CHARLES. Locrine. A Tragedy. London: C&W, 1887. 1st ed. Good. *Holmes.* $50/£32

SWINBURNE, ALGERNON CHARLES. Mary Stuart. London: Chatto, 1881. 1st ed. Pub's 32pg cat dated Nov 1881 at end. Gilt-stamped dk grn cl. VG. *Houle.* $165/£106

SWINBURNE, ALGERNON CHARLES. Ode to Mazzini.... Boston, 1913. 1st ed. Ltd to 477. Uncut. As New in dbl protective slipcase (worn). *Bond.* $50/£32

SWINBURNE, ALGERNON CHARLES. Poems and Ballads. Second Series. London: C&W, 1878. 1st ed. Dec dk blue-grn cl. NF (sl rubbed). *Antic Hay.* $75/£48

SWINBURNE, ALGERNON CHARLES. The Poems. C&W, 1912. 5th imp. 6 vols. (Feps sl browned.) Teg, rest uncut. *Edwards.* $55/£35

SWINBURNE, ALGERNON CHARLES. Selected Poems of Swinburne. NY, 1928. 1st Amer ed. Harry Clarke (illus). Fine. *Mcclintock.* $150/£96

SWINBURNE, ALGERNON CHARLES. The Sisters. C&W, 1892. 1st ed. (ii),x,107,(1)pp + pub's 32-pg list dated Jan. '92. Uncut. (Sig; corners knocked.) *Cox.* $31/£20

SWINBURNE, ALGERNON CHARLES. A Song of Italy. John Camden Hotten, 1867. 1st ed. 66pp + 16pp ads at end (inscrip). Aeg. Contemp 1/2 maroon morocco. *Cox.* $34/£22

SWINBURNE, ALGERNON CHARLES. A Song of Italy. London: John Camden Hotten, 1867. 1st ed. 66pp + (8)leaves ads. Grn cl (ends sl worn). NF (sl foxed). *Pirages.* $65/£42

SWINBURNE, ALGERNON CHARLES. A Song of Italy. London: John Camden Hotten, 1867. Blue cl (sl bump edge fr bd, sl mottled). NF. *Between The Covers.* $150/£96

SWINBURNE, ALGERNON CHARLES. A Song of Italy. London: John Camden Hotten, 1867. 1st ed w/8pp ads in fr, 16pp ads at end. Blue cl (extrems sl worn). *Appelfeld.* $150/£96

SWINBURNE, ALGERNON CHARLES. A Song of Italy. London: John Camden Hotten, 1867. 1st ed. Gilt-stamped blue cl. VG (sl foxed). *Houle.* $150/£96

SWINBURNE, ALGERNON CHARLES. Songs of Two Nations. London: C&W, 1875. 1st ed. One of 1000. 32pp ads dated Oct 1887. Dk blue-grn cl, gilt. (Sm mk rear cvr), o/w Fine. *Sumner & Stillman.* $95/£61

SWINBURNE, ALGERNON CHARLES. The Springtide of Life. NY: Doubleday, 1926. 8 color plts by Arthur Rackham. Grn cl. Fine. *Appelfeld.* $125/£80

SWINBURNE, ALGERNON CHARLES. The Springtide of Life: Poems of Childhood. London, 1918. 1st ed. Arthur Rackham (illus). (Gathering weak; spine top rubbed, sl frayed), o/w VG. *Words Etc.* $133/£85

SWINBURNE, J. Population and the Social Problem. London: George Allen & Unwin, 1924. 1st ed. Nice. *Patterson.* $39/£25

SWINDLER, MARY HAMILTON. Ancient Painting, from the Earliest Times to the Period of Christian Art. New Haven: Yale Univ, 1929. 1st ed. 16 plts (1 color). Gray cl. Good in dj (chipped). *Karmiole.* $150/£96

Swingboat Story Book. Blackie, (1935). Rosa Petherick and H.R. Millar et al (illus). 4to. Cl spine, pict bds. (Dusty), else VG. *Bookmark.* $23/£15

SWINGLE, CALVIN F. (ed). Modern American Railway Practice. Chicago: Nat'l Inst of Practical Mechanics, (1908). 10 vols. 3/4 brn leather, cl (rubbed, bumped, vol 3 spine mostly lacking, 2 vols w/piece chipped from spines, bottom of 3 vols dampstained, 1 w/cvr warped; 2 fldg plts torn at folds). Overall VG; 3 vols Fair. *Blue Mountain.* $150/£96

SWINNERTON, FRANK. A Brood of Ducklings. GC: Doubleday, Doran, 1928. 1st Amer ed. NF in dj (edgewear, spine lt chipped, sunned). *Antic Hay.* $20/£13

SWINNERTON, FRANK. The Georgian Literary Scene. London: Hutchinson, 1938. Rev ed. (Pg edges browned, top edges dusty), o/w VG in VG dj (soiled, browned). *Virgo.* $11/£7

SWINNERTON, FRANK. Sketch of a Sinner. GC: Doubleday, Doran, 1929. 1st ed. NF in VG dj (rubbed, spotted, chip). *Antic Hay.* $25/£16

SWINNERTON, FRANK. Tokefield Papers. NY: Doran, (1927). 1st Amer ed. Fine in dj (wear, sm nicks). *Antic Hay.* $25/£16

SWINNERTON, FRANK. Tokefield Papers. London: Martin Secker, 1927. 1st ed. NF (spine top lt bumped) in dj (spine browned, worn, sm tear). *Antic Hay.* $45/£29

SWINSON, ARTHUR. Frederick Sander: The Orchid King. London: Hodder & Stoughton, 1970. 1st UK ed. 19 color, 19 b/w plts. Dj (sl faded). *Edwards.* $31/£20

SWINTON, GEORGE. Eskimo Sculpture. Toronto/Montreal, 1965. (Margins lt browned.) Dj (sl chipped). *Edwards.* $39/£25

SWINTON, GEORGE. Sculpture of the Eskimo. Greenwich, CT: NYGS, (1972). 1st ed. Gray cl. Good in dj. *Karmiole.* $65/£42

SWINTON, WILLIAM. The Twelve Decisive Battles of the Civil War. NY, 1867. 1st ed. (Cvr sl worn), o/w VG + . *Pratt.* $45/£29

SWISHER, JACOB A. The Iowa Department of the Grand Army of the Republic. Iowa City, 1936. 1st ed. *Wantagh.* $30/£19

Switzerland, Its Mountains and Valleys. NY: Scribner & Welford, 1879. 418 illus. (Several leaves sl pulled, fore-edges sl frayed, fr inner hinge broken.) Gilt-dec leather (extrems rubbed). *New Hampshire**. $80/£51

SWOPE, JOHN. Camera over Hollywood. NY: Random House, (1939). 1st ed. 110 photo plts. (Inscrip fep.) Blue cl stamped in white. *Karmiole*. $100/£64

SWYNNERTON, C. F. M. The Tsetse Flies of East Africa. London, 1936. 22 photo plts, 7 maps. Orig wraps, protected w/brn paper. *Grayling*. $109/£70

SYDENHAM, THOMAS. The Entire Works of Dr. Thomas Sydenham. J. Swan (ed). 1753. 3rd ed. xxvi,672pp + index (ep edges browned). Leather (spine rubbed, torn, joints weak). *Whitehart*. $390/£250

SYDENHAM, THOMAS. The Entire Works of Dr. Thomas Sydenham. J. Swan (ed). 1769. 5th ed. xliii,686pp. 1/2 leather (rebound), marbled bds. *Whitehart*. $281/£180

SYDENHAM, THOMAS. Opera Universa. London, 1705. 3rd ed. Tp,(A3-C4),529pp + (Mm2-Nn2) index (1 pg soiled, 1 pg corner torn away; ex-lib). Mod 1/2 morocco (nicely rebound), marbled bds, gilt. *Edwards*. $156/£100

SYDENHAM, THOMAS. The Whole Works of That Excellent Practical Physician, Dr. Thomas Sydenham. J. Pechey (ed). 1740. 11th ed. xvi,448pp (eps sl foxed, fep cut). Old full calf (spine worn, joints sl loose). *Whitehart*. $140/£90

SYDENHAM, THOMAS. The Whole Works of That Excellent Practical Physician, Dr. Thomas Sydenham.... London: W. Feales et al, 1734. 10th ed. xvi,448pp (old faded waterstain lower margin). Mod pastepaper bds, leather spine label. *Karmiole*. $150/£96

SYDENHAM, THOMAS. The Works of Thomas Sydenham, M.D. R. G. Latham (trans). London: Sydenham Soc, 1848/50. 2 vols. cvi,276; 395pp (stamp tps, lt browned; new eps). Orig grn cl (recased). *White*. $117/£75

SYDENHAM, THOMAS. The Works of Thomas Sydenham, M.D., on Acute and Chronic Diseases.... Phila, 1809. 473pp + index. Contemp sheep (worn, cvrs detached). *Argosy*. $150/£96

SYDENHAM, THOMAS. The Works of Thomas Sydenham. R. G. Latham (ed). Sydenham Soc, 1848. 2 vols. 276; 359pp. (Rebacked, spines laid down.) *Whitehart*. $218/£140

SYDENHAM, THOMAS. The Works.... R. G. Latham (trans). London: Sydenham Soc, 1848-50. 1st ed. 2 vols. Grn cl (scuffed) by Westley's, w/their ticket. *Maggs*. $117/£75

SYDENHAM, THOMAS. Works...Translated from the Latin Edition of Dr. Greenhill, With a Life of the Author by R.G. Latham. London: Sydenham Society, 1848-50. 1st ed thus. 2 vols. cvi,276; vii,395pp (marginal pencil mks). Good set (vol 1 rebacked, orig spine laid down; Vol 2 spine extrems rubbed). *Glaser*. $225/£144

SYDNEY, ANGERNON. Discourses Concerning Government. London, 1763. Port. (Internal dampstaining.) Contemp calf (rubbed, worn, rebacked). *Freeman**. $70/£45

SYKES, CHRISTOPHER. Character and Situation. NY, 1950. 1st Amer ed. Very Nice in dj (sl nicked, mkd). *Clearwater*. $39/£25

SYKES, CHRISTOPHER. Private Palaces. London, 1985. 20 color plts. Good in dj. *Washton*. $25/£16

SYKES, ELLA C. Through Persia on a Side-Saddle. 1901. 1st ed. 8 plts, fldg map. (Cl dampstained.) *Edwards*. $86/£55

SYKES, GODFREY. The Colorado Delta. Balt: Carnegie Inst of Washington, 1937. 1st ed. Fine. *Book Market*. $60/£38

SYKES, GODFREY. The Colorado Delta. N.p.: Carnegie Inst of Washington/Amer Geographical Soc of NY, 1937. 1st ed. Color fldg map. (Tips bumped.) *Dawson*. $75/£48

SYKES, GODFREY. A Westerly Trend. Tucson: AZ Pioneers' Hist Soc, 1944. Pict cl in dj. *Dawson*. $40/£26

SYLVIA, STEPHEN W. and MICHAEL J. O'DONNELL. Civil War Canteens. Orange, VA, 1983. 1st ed. Pict wraps. VG. *Pratt*. $27/£17

SYLVIA, STEPHEN W. and MICHAEL J. O'DONNELL. The Illustrated History of American Civil War Relics. Orange, VA: Moss, (1978). 1st ed. NF in NF dj. *Mcgowan*. $40/£26

SYME, JAMES. On Diseases of the Rectum. Edinburgh: A&C Black, 1838. 1st ed. vi,138pp (lacks fep). Orig bds, cl spine (some erosion). Good. *Glaser*. $85/£54

SYME, JAMES. The Principles of Surgery. Edinburgh: John Carfrae, 1837. 2nd ed. xix,460pp. Contemp 1/2 sheep, marbled bds. (Lt foxing; joints starting), else Good set. *Goodrich*. $275/£176

SYMINGTON, J. ALEXANDER. Some Unpublished Letters of Walter Scott. Oxford: Basil Blackwell, 1932. 1st ed. 14 plts, 4 facs. Prospectus, compliments slip signed by editor loosely inserted. Uncut. Fine in dj. *Hollett*. $117/£75

SYMINGTON, JOHN. In a Bengal Jungle. Univ of NC, 1935. Grn cl, gilt. (Ink underlining 4 pp), else VG. *Price*. $45/£29

SYMONDS, ARTHUR. The Art of Aubrey Beardsley. NY: Modern Library, (1918). 64 full-pg plts. Flexible grn cl (corners lt scuffed). VG. *Truepenny*. $35/£22

SYMONDS, JOHN ADDINGTON with MARGARET SYMONDS. Our Life in the Swiss Highlands. London: A&C Black, 1892. 1st ed. Dk grn cl. NF (sl wear). *Antic Hay*. $75/£48

SYMONDS, JOHN ADDINGTON. Animi Figura. London: Smith, Elder, 1882. 1st ed. Dec cl. NF (ink name, sl wear). *Antic Hay*. $100/£64

SYMONDS, JOHN ADDINGTON. In the Key of Blue. London/NY: Elkin Mathews & John Lane/Macmillan, 1893. 1st ed. Marbled eps; teg, uncut. 3/4 dk morocco, dk blue bds, gilt. VG. *Houle*. $150/£96

SYMONDS, JOHN ADDINGTON. The Life of Michelangelo Buonarroti.... London, 1893. 1st ed. 2 vols. 2 frontispieces, 50 plts. (Sl worn, 1 spine chipped.) *Kane**. $45/£29

SYMONDS, JOHN ADDINGTON. Percy Bysshe Shelley. NY: Harper, 1879. 1st ed, 1st ptg. Black cl. (Crown rubbed), else Fine. *Macdonnell*. $65/£42

SYMONDS, JOHN ADDINGTON. Walt Whitman, A Study. London, 1893. 1st ed. VG. *Typographeum*. $75/£48

SYMONDS, JOHN ADDINGTON. Walt Whitman. A Study. John C. Nimmo, 1893. 1st ed in 2nd ed case (spine base dated 1896). Teg. Good (sl spotted; spine bumped). *Tiger*. $31/£20

SYMONDS, JOHN ADDINGTON. Webster and Tourneur. London: Vizetelly, 1888. 1st ed. Frontis photogravure. Tan cl eps, white silk bkmk; teg. 3/4 brn morocco, tan cl, gilt. VG. *Houle*. $275/£176

SYMONDS, JOHN. The Stuffed Dog. Dent, 1967. 1st ed. Edward Ardizzone (illus). 8vo. 60pp (fingermks). Dec bds. VG in pict dj (rubbed). *Bookmark*. $39/£25

SYMONDS, MARY and LOUISA PREECE. Needlework Through the Ages. London: Hodder & Stoughton, 1928. 1st ed. 103 plts. Teg. VF in dec vellum-backed linen. *Captain's Bookshelf*. $500/£321

SYMONDS, R. W. A Book of English Clocks. London: Penguin, (1950). Rev ed. 64 plts. Ptd bds. VG in dj (worn). *Weber*. $10/£6

SYMONDS, R. W. A History of English Clocks. London/NY: King Penguin, 1947. 1st ed. 72 plts. (Sl rubbed, spine repaired), o/w VG. *Worldwide.* $15/£10

SYMONDS, R. W. Masterpieces of English Furniture and Clocks. London: Batsford, 1940. Ltd to 750. 8 color plts. VG. *Hollett.* $273/£175

SYMONDS, R. W. Thomas Tompion: His Life and Work. London: Batsford, (1951). 1st ed. 272 plts (2 fldg, 4 color). Blue cl. VG in dj (head taped, back torn, corner bumped). *Weber.* $100/£64

SYMONDS, R. W. Thomas Tompion: His Life and Work. London: Batsford, (1951). 1st, deluxe ed. Ltd to 350. This copy out-of-series, not signed or numbered. Color frontis, 2 fldg facs. 1/2 red morocco, gilt. Good in red cl slipcase. *Karmiole.* $350/£224

SYMONDS, R. W. Thomas Tompion: His Life and Work. London, (1969). 2 fldg illus. VG in dj. *Argosy.* $100/£64

SYMONS, A. J. A. et al. The Nonesuch Century. London: Nonesuch, 1934. One of 750. 100 tipped-in examples. Buckram (spine lt sunned). *Swann*.* $287/£184

SYMONS, A. J. A. The Quest for Corvo. London, 1934. 1st Eng ed. Nice. *Clearwater.* $47/£30

SYMONS, A. J. A. The Quest for Corvo. London, 1934. 1st ed. Fine (lower edges sl rubbed) in VG dj (spine sunned, extrems lt rubbed, 2 sm chips, 2 sm edge nicks). *Polyanthos.* $50/£32

SYMONS, A. J. A. The Quest for Corvo. Folio Soc, 1952. 1st ed. Cl-backed patterned bds. (Corners sl rubbed), else VG. *Words Etc.* $19/£12

SYMONS, A. J. A. The Quest for Corvo. London: Folio Society, 1952. Buckram-backed patterned bds. Fine (name) in dj (frayed). *Clearwater.* $47/£30

SYMONS, ARTHUR. Confessions: A Study in Pathology. NY: Fountain, 1930. Ltd to 542 numbered, signed. Teg. Dec red cl. NF. *Antic Hay.* $100/£64

SYMONS, ARTHUR. From Catullus: Chiefly Concerning Lesbia. London: Martin Secker, 1924. Ltd to 200 numbered, signed. Teg. Gilt-worked cl. VG (ink presentation, sl wear). *Antic Hay.* $175/£112

SYMONS, ARTHUR. London Nights. London: Smithers, 1896. One of 500. (Name; bumped, fr cvr holes twice, sl chafed.) *Clearwater.* $62/£40

SYMONS, ARTHUR. Notes on Joseph Conrad. London: Myers, 1926. 1st ed. One of 250 numbered, signed. 1/4 linen, bds, ptd label. Dj. *Swann*.* $149/£96

SYMONS, ARTHUR. Tristan and Iseult. NY: Brentano's, (1917). 1st ed. Teg. Dec blue cl. VG (bkpl, wear). *Antic Hay.* $27/£17

SYMONS, ARTHUR. William Blake. A Biography. Constable, 1907. 1st Eng ed. Buckram (sl handled). Very Nice (bkpl, tp hinge cracked). *Clearwater.* $70/£45

SYMONS, JULIAN. A. J. A. Symons: His Life and Speculations. Eyre & Spottiswoode, 1950. 1st ed. (Sm ink spot), o/w Good in dj. *Moss.* $31/£20

SYMONS, JULIAN. A. J. A. Symons: His Life and Speculations. London: Eyre & Spottiswoode, 1950. 1st ed. 8 plts. (Cl sl mkd.) *Cox.* $28/£18

SYMONS, JULIAN. A. J. A. Symons: His Life and Speculations. London: Eyre & Spottiswoode, 1950. 1st UK ed. VG in dj. *Williams.* $47/£30

SYMONS, JULIAN. Agatha Christie: The Art of Her Crimes. The Paintings of Tom Adams. NY: Everest House, 1981. 1st US ed. Fine in NF dj. *Janus.* $30/£19

SYMONS, JULIAN. The Kentish Manor Murders. NY: Viking, 1988. 1st US ed. Fine in Fine dj. *Janus.* $20/£13

SYMONS, JULIAN. The Thirties, a Dream Revolved. London: Cresset, 1960. 1st ed. Port. (Sm ink name), else NF in VG dj. *Reese.* $25/£16

SYMONS, JULIAN. A Three-Pipe Problem. NY: Harper & Row, (1975). 1st US ed. NF in NF dj (sl wear). *Gravesend.* $30/£19

SYMONS, JULIAN. A Three-Pipe Problem. Collins, 1975. 1st UK ed. VG in dj. *Williams.* $39/£25

SYMONS, KATHARINE E. et al. Alfred Edward Housman. Bromsgrove, 1936. One of 500. Good + . *Poetry Bookshop.* $31/£20

SYMONS, THOMAS W. Report on an Examination of the Upper Columbia River. Washington: GPO, 1882. 135pp; 26 maps, incl 1 fldg. (Fr hinge starting, sm tear fldg map, extrems worn.) *Dumont.* $75/£48

SYNGE, J. M. The Playboy of the Western World. Boston: Luce, 1911. 1st Amer ed. Gilt wrapper over bds. (Closed tears top joint wrapper), o/w Nice. *Reese.* $55/£35

SYNGE, J. M. The Tinker's Wedding. Boston: John W. Luce, 1911. 1st Amer ed. Paper vellum, bds (spine browned). VG. *Antic Hay.* $17/£11

Synopsis of the Military Career of Gen. Joseph Wheeler, Commander of the Cavalry Corps Army of the West. NY, 1865. 1st ed. 77pp. NF in ptd wrappers. *Mcgowan.* $250/£160

SYRETT, NETTA. Six Fairy Plays for Children. London/NY: Jane Lane/Bodley Head, 1904. 1st ed. (Sig unevenly opened.) Color pict cl. *Dramatis Personae.* $40/£26

SZARKOWSKI, JOHN (ed). E.J. Bellocq: Storyville Portraits. NY: MOMA, 1970. 1st ed. 34 full-pg b/w plts. (Owner stamp), else VG in dj (rubbed, edgetorn). *Cahan.* $85/£54

SZARKOWSKI, JOHN (ed). From the Picture Press. NY: MOMA, (1973). 1st ed. VG (name stamp) in pict stiff wrappers. *Cahan.* $25/£16

SZARKOWSKI, JOHN and MARIA MORRIS HAMBOURG. The Work of Atget. NY: MOMA, 1981/1982/1983/1985. 1st ed. 4 vols. 120 plts; 116 plts; 120 plts; 116 plts. Fine in pict djs. *Cahan.* $400/£256

SZARKOWSKI, JOHN and SHOJI YAMAGISHI (eds). New Japanese Photography. NY: MOMA, 1974. 1st ed. (Owner stamp), else Fine in pict dj. *Cahan.* $45/£29

SZARKOWSKI, JOHN. The Face of Minnesota. Minneapolis: Univ of MN, 1958. 1st ed. Illus cl. (Owner stamp), else VG in dj (stained, edgeworn). *Cahan.* $40/£26

SZARKOWSKI, JOHN. Irving Penn. NY: MOMA, 1984. 1st ed. 156 plts (21 color). Fine in Fine dj. *Smith.* $125/£80

SZARKOWSKI, JOHN. Mirrors and Windows. NY: MOMA, (1978). 2nd ptg. 127 plts. NF in illus stiff wrappers. *Cahan.* $20/£13

SZARKOWSKI, JOHN. Walker Evans. NY: MOMA, 1974. (Owner stamp, inscrip, eps lt foxed), else VG in dj (rubbed). *Cahan.* $25/£16

SZARKOWSKI, JOHN. William Eggleston's Guide. NY: MOMA, 1976. 1st ed. 47 color plts. Faux leather, mtd color plt on cvr. Fine, w/o dj as issued. *Cahan.* $125/£80

SZYK, ARTHUR. The New Order. NY, (1941). (Lt wear, soil.) Dj (soiled, chipped). *Freeman*.* $90/£58

SZYK, ARTHUR. The New Order. NY: Putnam, 1941. 1st ed. 38 full-pg caricatures. NF in color-illus dj (sl dusty, sl chipped). *Cahan.* $150/£96

T

Table of the Post Offices in the United States on the Thirty-First of January, 1842. Washington: J. & G.S. Gideon, Printers, 1842. 1st ed. 240pp. Cl over stiff ptd wrappers (soiled). *Karmiole.* $125/£80

TAFFT, HENRY SPURR. Reminiscences of the Signal Service in the Civil War. Providence, RI, 1899. 1st ed. Ltd to 250. PNRISSHS Series 5, #9. 41pp. NF in ptd wrappers. *Mcgowan.* $45/£29

TAFT, ROBERT. Artists and Illustrators of the Old West, 1850-1900. NY, 1953. 1st ed. VG in dj (quite chipped), protective plastic jacket. *Bohling.* $60/£38

TAFT, ROBERT. Artists and Illustrators of the Old West: 1850-1900. NY: Scribner, 1953. 1st ed. VG in VG dj. *Perier.* $50/£32

TAILLANDIER, YVON. Indelible Miro. NY: Tudor, (1972). 1st ed. 2 lithos pulled by hand. Fine in NF dj, pub's slipcase. *Hermitage.* $200/£128

TAINE, JOHN. The Crystal Horde. Fantasy, 1952. 1st ed. Fine in Fine dj. *Certo.* $35/£22

TAINE, JOHN. The Crystal Horde. Reading, PA: Fantasy, 1952. 1st ed. Fine in Fine full color dj. *Mcclintock.* $50/£32

TAINE, JOHN. The Crystal Horde. Reading: Fantasy Press, 1952. 1st ed. One of 300 signed, numbered. NF in Fine dj. *Other Worlds.* $125/£80

TAINE, JOHN. The Forbidden Garden. Fantasy, 1947. 1st ed. NF (eps sl dknd) in NF dj. *Certo.* $35/£22

TAINE, JOHN. The Forbidden Garden. Reading: Fantasy, 1947. 1st ed. One of 500 numbered, signed. Dj (sl worn, sm tears, sl internal cellotape mends). *Swann*.* $57/£37

TAINE, JOHN. Seeds of Life. Fantasy, 1951. 1st ed. VG (2 tape ghosts eps) in dj (top, bottom edges trimmed). *Certo.* $20/£13

TAIT, JAMES. Tait's Seamanship.... Glasgow: James Brown, 1913. 9th ed. 4 color plts. Cl-backed ptd bds (rubbed). Sound. *Cox.* $23/£15

TAKA-TSUKASA, NOBUSUKE. The Birds of Nippon. Tokyo: Maruzen, 1967. (Sl worn.) *Oinonen*.* $180/£115

TALBOT, C. H. and E. A. HAMMOND. The Medical Practitioners in Medieval England.... London, 1965. 1st ed. VG. *Fye.* $75/£48

TALBOT, FREDERICK A. Motor-Cars and Their Story. London: Cassell, 1912. 1st ed. Color frontis, 84 plts. Teg. Maroon cl, dec-stamped in gilt/white. (Spine ends lt rubbed), else Fine. *Argonaut.* $250/£160

TALBOT, FREDERICK A. Practical Cinematography and Its Applications. Phila: Lippincott, 1913. 1st Amer ed. Frontis, 62 plts. VG. *Glaser.* $85/£54

TALBOT, WILLIAM HENRY FOX. The Pencil of Nature. NY: Da Capo, 1969. 1st ed thus. Facs of 1844-1846 orig ltd ed. 24 tipped-in plts. Gilt-emb cl. (Owner stamp), else NF in dj (long closed tear rear panel, sl edgeworn). *Cahan.* $185/£119

TALBOT-BOOTH, E. C. Waterline Ship Models. NY/London: Appleton-Century, 1937. Good. *Scribe's Perch*.* $28/£18

Tale of a Tub. (By Jonathan Swift.) London: John Nutt, 1710. 5th ed. (xxxii),344pp, 8 engr plts. Orig calf (both joints cracked at top), spine gilt (most rubbed off; lacks spine label). Good. *Bickersteth.* $343/£220

Tale of a Tub. (By Jonathan Swift.) London: John Nutt, 1710. 5th ed. Engr frontis, (32),344pp (few sl foxmarks, smudges), 7 plts. Contemp mottled calf (neatly rebacked in plain tan calf). VG. *Reese.* $750/£481

Tale of a Tub. (By Jonathan Swift.) Dublin: Ptd by G. Faulkner, 1769. Early Dublin ed. Contemp full calf (rebacked, orig spine laid down). VG (spine label rubbed). *Sumner & Stillman.* $80/£51

Tale of a Tub...to Which Is Added an Account of a Battel Between the Antient and Modern Books in St. James's Library.... (By Jonathan Swift.) London: John Nutt, 1710. 5th ed. (32),344pp; 8 plts. Full gilt-dec polished calf. (Lt foxed; sl worn, soiled), o/w Contents VG. *New Hampshire*.* $210/£135

Tale of Emperor Coustans and of Over Sea. (Hammersmith: Kelmscott, 1894.) One of 525. Cl-backed bds. *Swann*.* $460/£295

Tales from Catland, for Little Kittens. By an Old Tabby. London: Grant & Griffith, 1851. Harrison Weir (illus). 8vo. (Pink spots to frontis; name; sunned, frayed, spine loss.) *Metropolitan*.* $28/£18

Tales from the Arabian Nights. Ward Lock, 1920. 1st ed thus. Lg 8vo. 340pp,4pp ads; 48 color plts by A. E. Jackson incl pict eps. Cl w/pict onlay. (Hinges strained, mks, sl bowed), else VG. *Bookmark.* $27/£17

Tales of the Early Days As Told to Mirandy. Hollywood: Oxford, (1938). 1st ed. Signed by Mirandy Giles. Pict cl. *Ginsberg.* $75/£48

Tales of the Puritans. (By Delia Salter Bacon.) New Haven: A.H. Maltby, 1831. 1st ed, 1st bk. 3/4 calf, bds. (Foxed, sm chips gutter of 1st 2 leaves), else Good. BAL 554. *Reese.* $40/£26

TALESE, GAY. The Bridge. NY: Harper & Row, 1964. 1st ed. Bruce Davidson (photos). (Owner stamp), else VG in illus dj. *Cahan.* $40/£26

TALESE, GAY. New York: A Serendipiter's Journey. NY, (1961). Stated 1st ed. Good in dj. *Hayman.* $15/£10

TALFOURD, THOMAS NOON. The Letters of Charles Lamb, with a Sketch of His Life. London: Edward Moxon, 1837. 1st ed. 2 vols. x,335; (iv),338pp. Contemp dk grn mottled calf (spines lt rubbed, faded), gilt. Nice set (inscrips). *Burmester.* $140/£90

TALLENT, ELIZABETH. In Constant Flight. NY: Knopf, 1983. 1st ed, 1st bk. Fine in Fine dj. *Revere.* $35/£22

TALLEY, MANSFIELD KIRBY. Portrait Painting in England. Paul Mellon Centre for Studies in British Art, 1971. 42 plts. Good. *Washton.* $145/£93

TALLIS, JOHN. Tallis's History and Description of the Crystal Palace.... London, (1851). 3 vols. Contemp red leather (cvrs detached or starting; ex-lib), gilt. *Swann*.* $402/£258

TALLMADGE, BENJAMIN. Memoir of Colonel Benjamin Tallmadge. NY: Gilliss, 1904. One of 350 ptd. Vellum-backed bds. Howes T17. *Ginsberg.* $150/£96

TALMADGE, MARIAN and IRIS GILMORE. Barney Ford, Black Baron. NY: Dodd, Mead, (1973). 1st ed. Fine in NF dj. *Between The Covers.* $45/£29

TALMAGE, JAMES E. The Great Apostasy: Considered in the Light of Scriptural and Secular History. Salt Lake, 1909. 1st ed. (Name, notes; spine sl faded, sl edgewear), o/w VG. *Benchmark.* $35/£22

TAMURA, T. SUYOSHI. Art of Landscape Garden in Japan. Tokyo, 1935. 147 plts. Dec bds. Sound in box. *Ars Artis.* $94/£60

TAN, AMY. The Kitchen God's Wife. NY, 1991. 1st ed. Fine in Fine dj. *Warren.* $25/£16

TANDRUP, HARALD. Reluctant Prophet. A. G. Chater (trans). NY: Knopf, 1939. 1st Amer ed. VG (ink name, eps browned) in dj. *Antic Hay.* $22/£14

TANNER, H. S. Atlas of the United States.... Phila, 1835. 25 dbl-pg hand-colored maps (3 separated at center fold, others starting, 1 w/brn spots; feps, tps waterstained; 3pp ads at rear detached). Orig marbled bds (scuffed), 1/4 leather. *Yudkin*.* $2,600/£1,667

TANNER, HEATHER. Wiltshire Village. 1939. 1st ed. VG in dj (repaired tear upper panel). *Words Etc.* $195/£125

TANNER, HENRY, JR. English Interior Woodwork of the XVI, XVII and XVIII Centuries. London: Batsford, 1902. 50 plts. (Spine frayed, rear cvr faded, shabby.) Internally Good. *Ars Artis.* $94/£60

TANNER, JOHN. The Hidden Treasures of the Art of Physick. London: George Sawbridge, 1659. Sm 8vo. (16),543,(25)pp (text browned, foxed; tears margins pp5-12 w/loss, remargined w/blank paper; lacks pp13-14, 209-212). Old calf (recently rebacked), raised bands. *Goodrich.* $695/£446

TANNER, T. H. The Practice of Medicine. 1875. 7th ed. 2 vols. xviii,642; (v),675pp. (Spines worn, faded, cl rubbed; vol 1 pg edges dusty, joint cracked.) *Whitehart.* $39/£25

TANNER, WILLIAM. The Book of Bond or Every Man His Own 007. London: Cape, 1965. 1st Eng ed. VG in dj (price-clipped). *Hadley.* $34/£22

TANSELLE, G. THOMAS. Guide to the Study of United States Imprints. Cambridge, 1971. 1st ed. 2 vols. *Swann*.* $69/£44

TANSLEY, A. G. The British Isles and Their Vegetation. London, 1939. 1st ed. 163 plts. Fine. *Henly.* $101/£65

TAPIE, VICTOR L. The Age of Grandeur. Baroque Art and Architecture. NY, 1966. 2nd ed. Good in wrappers (sl rubbed). *Washton.* $25/£16

TAPLEY, HARRIET S. Salem Imprints, 1768-1825. Salem, MA: Esse, 1927. 1st ed. *Ginsberg.* $150/£96

TAPPLY, WILLIAM G. Dead Meat. NY: Scribner, 1987. 1st ed. VF in dj. *Mordida.* $45/£29

TAPPLY, WILLIAM G. Dead Winter. NY: Delacorte, 1989. 1st ed. Advance rev copy w/sheet & photo laid in. VF in dj. *Mordida.* $30/£19

TAPPLY, WILLIAM G. The Marine Corpse. NY: Scribner, 1986. 1st ed. VF in dj. *Mordida.* $45/£29

TAPPLY, WILLIAM G. The Vulgar Boatman. NY: Scribner, 1987. 1st ed. VF in dj. *Mordida.* $30/£19

TARAVAL, SIGISMUNDO. Indian Uprising in Lower California, 1734-1737. Marguerite Eyer Wilbur (trans). L.A.: Quivera Soc, 1931. One of 665. Vellum-backed bds. Unopened. VG+ (bkpl removed) in plain dj (dknd, lt chipped). *Bohling.* $120/£77

TARBELL, ARTHUR WILSON. Cape Cod Ahoy! Boston: Little Brown, 1934. New, rev ed. 16 plts. (Sl rubbed, spine sl weak), o/w VG. *Worldwide.* $15/£10

TARDUCCI, FRANCESCO. John and Sebastian Cabot. Henry F. Brownson (trans). Detroit, 1893. Frontis, x,409,viii ads; map. Navy cl, gilt. VG. Howes T36. *Bohling.* $35/£22

TARG, WILLIAM (ed). Bibliophile in the Nursery. Cleveland, (1957). 1st Amer ed. Fldg frontis. NF in dj (sm spine piece missing). *Polyanthos.* $60/£38

TARG, WILLIAM (ed). Bouillabaisse for Bibliophiles. Cleveland: World, (1955). 1st ed. NF in NF dj. *Dermont.* $50/£32

TARG, WILLIAM (ed). Bouillabaisse for Bibliophiles. Cleveland, 1955. 1st Amer ed. Signed presentation. Fine (spine extrems sl rubbed). *Polyanthos.* $50/£32

TARG, WILLIAM (ed). Carrousel for Bibliophiles. NY: Duschnes, 1947. 1st Amer ed. Signed presentation. Uncut. Fine (fr cvr edge soiled). *Polyanthos.* $40/£26

TARG, WILLIAM. Abacus Now: Footnotes to Indecent Pleasure and Observations on Fine Book Printing.... NY: Targ Editions, 1984. One of 200 ptd. Signed by author and each of 3 printers. Black cl spine, red paper bds. Fine. *Heller.* $150/£96

TARG, WILLIAM. The Making of the Bruce Rogers World Bible. Cleveland/NY, 1949. (Spine faded.) Slipcase (worn). *Edwards.* $31/£20

TARKINGTON, BOOTH. Claire Ambler. NY: Doubleday, Doran, 1928. 1st ed. Beautiful in pict dj (sm tears). *Captain's Bookshelf.* $100/£64

TARKINGTON, BOOTH. The Conquest of Canaan. NY: Harper, 1905. 1st ed. Red cl. Fine in VG dj (sl chipped). *Macdonnell.* $165/£106

TARKINGTON, BOOTH. The Gentleman from Indiana. NY: Doubleday McClure, 1899. 1st ed, 1st bk. NF (bkpl, name; sl rubbing). *Between The Covers.* $150/£96

TARKINGTON, BOOTH. Penrod Jashber. GC: Doubleday, Doran, 1929. 1st ed. VG in dj (nicks). *Houle.* $200/£128

TARKINGTON, BOOTH. Penrod. NY: Doubleday & Page, 1914. 1st ed, 1st binding: mesh cl, measuring 1.25 inches across cvrs, 2nd state w/'sense' correctly spelled at 19.3up. Lt blue pict cl lettered in white. Fine. *Macdonnell.* $100/£64

TARKINGTON, BOOTH. Presenting Lily Mars. GC: Doubleday, Doran, 1933. 1st ed. Pub's business reply card laid in. Fine in NF dj (sm chip). *Associates.* $150/£96

TARKINGTON, BOOTH. Some Old Portraits. NY, 1939. 1st trade ed. (Sl sunned, sl rubbed, sm chip.) *Polyanthos.* $30/£19

TARKINGTON, BOOTH. The Two Vanrevels. NY, 1902. 1st ed. Pict cl. VG. *Argosy.* $25/£16

TARKINGTON, BOOTH. Wanton Mally. GC, 1932. 1st ed. (Ink inscrip; eps sl discolored), else VG in dj (heavily spotted, rubbed). *King.* $50/£32

TARLETON, BANASTRE. A History of the Campaigns of 1780 and 1781 in the Southern Provinces of North America. London: T. Cadell, 1787. 1st ed. 4to. viii,518pp (no prelims before tp, or ll after last text pg); 5 maps (3 fldg w/lib perfs just into image), all w/brief hand-coloring. Contents largely VG (ex-lib w/perfs tp, pp 63-64; lt dampstain lower gutter tp, several pp; few sm stains; map w/closed tear and old, professional repair). Rebound in lib buckram (rubbed). Howes T37. *Waverly*.* $660/£423

TARLING, N. The Burthen, the Risk, and the Glory, a Biography of Sir James Brooke. London, 1982. 1st ed. VG. *Gretton.* $19/£12

TARR, RALPH S. The Yakutat Bay Region, Alaska. US Geol Surv, 1909. 1st ed. 37 photo plts, color fldg maps. Grn cl (nicely rebound). VG. *Price.* $125/£80

TARTT, DONNA. The Secret History. NY, 1992. 1st ed, 1st bk. Fine in Fine dj. *Smith.* $35/£22

TASKER, JOE. Savage Arena. London: Methuen, 1985. 1st ed. 24pp plts, 8 maps, 6 diags. Fine in dj (price-clipped). Fine. *Hollett.* $70/£45

TATE, ALLEN. Collected Poems 1919-1976. NY: FSG, (1977). 1st ed. Fine in dj. *Jaffe.* $45/£29

TATE, ALLEN. Jefferson Davis: His Rise and Fall. Minton, Balch, 1929. 1st ed. Port. Good (spine frayed, cvr spotted, binding broken). *Book Broker.* $35/£22

TATE, ALLEN. On the Limits of Poetry. NY: Swallow Press/William Morrow, 1948. 1st ed. Fine in dj (edge-worn). *Jaffe.* $50/£32

TATE, ALLEN. Poems: 1928-1931. NY: Scribner, 1932. 1st ed. Signed. (Spine faded), o/w Fine. *Jaffe.* $175/£112

TATE, ALLEN. Selected Poems. NY: Scribner, 1937. 1st ed. Cl-backed bds. (Lt offsetting eps, bkseller label fep), o/w VG in dj (sl rubbed, chipped, worn). *Jaffe.* $100/£64

TATE, ALLEN. The Swimmers and Other Selected Poems. NY: Scribner, (1970). 1st ed. Fine in dj. *Jaffe.* $45/£29

TATE, ALLEN. The Vigil of Venus. (Cummington, MA): Cummington Press, (1943). 1st ed. One of 435 ptd. Mint in glassine dj (chipped, worn). *Jaffe.* $50/£32

TATE, JAMES. Nobody Goes to Visit the Insane Anymore. (Santa Barbara): Unicorn, 1971. 1st ed. One of 300. Broadside. Fine. *Turlington.* $50/£32

TATE, JAMES. The Torches. Santa Barbara: Unicorn, 1971. 2nd ed, cl issue. VG (cl soiled). *Turlington.* $25/£16

Tatler; or, Lucugrations of Isaac Bickerstaff, Esq. (By Richard Steele.) London: J&R Tonson, 1764. 4 vols. 4 engr frontispieces. Full contemp calf, leather labels. VG. *Argosy.* $375/£240

TATUM, GEORGE B. Penn's Great Town. Phila: Univ of PA, (1961). 1st ed. NF in dj (chip). *House.* $90/£58

TATUM, LAWRIE. Our Red Brothers and the Peace Policy of President Ulysses S. Grant. Phila, 1899. 1st ed. 366pp. Howes T42. *Ginsberg.* $225/£144

TAUNTON, ETHELRED L. The History of the Jesuits in England, 1580-1773. London: Methuen, 1901. 1st ed. 11 plts. (Ink underlining; sl rubbed, soiled), o/w VG. *Worldwide.* $20/£13

Tavern Anecdotes. (By William West.) London, 1825. Hand-colored fldg frontis, add'l title, port. (Soil, dampstaining.) Contemp bds (worn, joints split). *Freeman*.* $30/£19

TAVERNER, ERIC. Fly-Tying for Salmon. Seeley Service, (1942). 1st ed. Fine in dj. *Petersfield.* $39/£25

TAVERNER, ERIC. Trout Fishing from All Angles. Lonsdale Library, 1929. 1st ed. Mod 1/2 red calf. *Petersfield.* $62/£40

TAWNEY, R. H. Land and Labour in China. London, 1937. 2nd imp. Dbl-pg map. (Feps lt browned, bkpl.) Dj (chipped). *Edwards.* $23/£15

TAYLOE, EDWARD T. Mexico 1825-28, the Journal and Correspondence of Edward Thornton Tayloe. C. H. Gardiner (ed). Chapel Hill, 1959. 1st ed. Fine in Fine dj. *Turpen.* $65/£42

TAYLOR, ALFRED SWAINE. On Poisons in Relation to Medical Jurisprudence and Medicine. Phila: Henry C. Lea, 1875. 3rd ed. Contemp(?) sheep. (Portions of 4 letters on tp effaced, spine abraded), else Sound. *Boswell.* $125/£80

TAYLOR, BASIL. Stubbs. NY, 1971. 138 plts (16 color). (Fep corner clipped w/sm loss.) Dj. *Washton.* $50/£32

TAYLOR, BASIL. Stubbs. Phaidon, 1975. 2nd ed. 16 color plts. (Lg inscrip.) Dj (sl chipped). *Edwards.* $31/£20

TAYLOR, BAYARD (ed). Picturesque Europe. NY, (1875). Add'l engr titles, 41 steel-engr views. (Lt foxing throughout.) Aeg. 3/4 orig morocco (joints, extrems rubbed), gilt. *Freeman*.* $75/£48

TAYLOR, BAYARD (ed). Picturesque Europe. NY: D. Appleton, (1875-79). 3 vols. 63 steel-engr plts, incl tps. Aeg. Contents VG (dampstains vol 2, nearly broken rear hinge). Full blind-, gilt-stamped morocco (extrems worn, soiled). *Waverly*.* $275/£176

TAYLOR, BAYARD (ed). Picturesque Europe: A Delineation by Pen and Pencil.... NY: Appleton, c. 1875-79. 3 vols. 60 steel-engr views, 3 engr tps. Full blind-, gilt-dec leather (scuffed, worn). Contents VG. *New Hampshire*.* $190/£122

TAYLOR, BAYARD. Eldorado, or Adventures in the Path of Empire. London: Henry G. Bohn, 1850. 1st Eng ed. 2 vols. (4),188; iv,189-360pp. Aeg. 3/4 morocco, brn cl (handsomely rebound). *Karmiole.* $250/£160

TAYLOR, BAYARD. The Lands of the Saracen. NY: Putnam, 1867. Frontis, 451pp; 1 plt. (Sl rubbed, spine sl frayed), o/w VG. *Worldwide.* $35/£22

TAYLOR, BAYARD. Life and Letters of Bayard Taylor. Marie Hansen-Taylor and Horace E. Scudder (eds). Boston: Houghton, 1884. 1st ed. 2 vols. (6),414; (6),415-784,(4)pp. *Ginsberg.* $75/£48

TAYLOR, BAYARD. Poems of Home and Travel. Boston: Ticknor & Fields, 1855. 1st ed. One of 1000. 12pp ads dated Nov 1855. Blindstamped brn cl. Fine. *Sumner & Stillman.* $50/£32

TAYLOR, BENJAMIN F. Between the Gates. Chicago: S.C. Griggs, 1878. 1st ed. Frontis, 292,(8)pp. Grn cl, gilt-lettered spine (ends, corners lt worn). Fine (ink name). *Argonaut.* $60/£38

TAYLOR, BENJAMIN F. Theophilus Trent. Chicago: S.C. Griggs, 1887. viii,250pp (soiled). Brn cl, gilt. Good+ (worn). *Bohling.* $12/£8

TAYLOR, C. R. H. A Pacific Bibliography. Oxford: Clarendon, 1965. 2nd ed. Fldg map. Fine in dj (spine sunned). *Pacific*.* $81/£52

TAYLOR, COLEY. Mark Twain's Margins on Thackeray's Swift. NY: Gotham House, 1935. 1st ed. One of 1000 numbered. Label. Fine. BAL 3703. *Macdonnell.* $45/£29

TAYLOR, DEEMS. Walt Disney's Fantasia. NY, 1940. 1st Amer ed. VG. *Polyanthos.* $200/£128

TAYLOR, E. G. R. and M. W. RICHEY. The Geometrical Seaman. London: Inst of Navigation, 1962. 1st ed. Blue bds. Fine. *Weber.* $100/£64

TAYLOR, E. H. Operative Surgery. 1914. (Eps sl foxed), o/w VG. *Whitehart.* $55/£35

TAYLOR, EDWARD SAMUEL (ed). The History of Playing Cards.... London: John Camden Hotten, 1865. 1st ed. Color frontis, tp vignette, xiv,529,(16,6,10 ads)pp (several leaves w/clean tears; lt spotted); 47 plts (1 etched). Partly unopened. Red pict cl, gilt. *Burmester.* $390/£250

TAYLOR, ELIZABETH. At Mrs. Lippincote's. London, 1945. 1st Eng ed, 1st bk. Good (sl faded) in dj (chafed, spine defective). *Clearwater.* $133/£85

TAYLOR, ELIZABETH. Palladian. London, 1946. 1st Eng ed. Good (cvrs sl mkd, bumped) in dj (sl rubbed). *Clearwater.* $94/£60

TAYLOR, ELIZABETH. Palladian. London, 1946. 1st Eng ed. Very Nice in dj (sl nicked). *Clearwater.* $140/£90

TAYLOR, ELIZABETH. A View of the Harbour. London, 1947. 1st Eng ed. Good (spine sl faded, cvrs sl mkd) in dj remnants. *Clearwater.* $55/£35

TAYLOR, F. S. A History of Industrial Chemistry. 1957. 22 plts. VG. *Whitehart.* $55/£35

TAYLOR, G. Old London Gardens. London: Batsford, 1953. 43 plts. (Cl sl spotted.) *Ars Artis.* $28/£18

TAYLOR, G. Some Nineteenth Century Gardeners. London, 1951. Dj (sl worn). *Maggs.* $22/£14

TAYLOR, G. The Victorian Flower Garden. London, 1952. Color dj (sl worn, defective). *Maggs.* $20/£13

TAYLOR, G. L. and E. CRESY. Architectural Antiquities of Rome.... London: Lockwood, 1874. New ed. Frontis, xii,79pp; 130 plts. 1/2 leather (spotted). Internally Good. *Ars Artis.* $234/£150

TAYLOR, GEORGE H. Health by Exercise. NY, 1881. 408pp. Brn cl (sl worn). VG. *Doctor's Library.* $60/£38

TAYLOR, GRIFFITH. With Scott: The Silver Lining. London: Smith Elder, 1916. 1st British ed. 2 fldg maps, 44 plts. Grn cl (bumped, sl worn), penguin-dec cvr. NF. *Parmer.* $1,500/£962

TAYLOR, H. M. and JOAN. Anglo-Saxon Architecture. London, 1965, 1984. 3 vols. Good. *Washton.* $450/£288

TAYLOR, H. M. and JOAN. Anglo-Saxon Architecture. CUP, 1965/78. 3 vols. Sound in dj. *Ars Artis.* $390/£250

TAYLOR, H. V. The Apples of England. London, 1948. 3rd ed. 36 color plts. (Sl spotting; spine lt faded.) *Edwards.* $39/£25

TAYLOR, H. V. The Apples of England. London, 1948. 3rd ed. Inscribed. 2 plain, 36 color plts. Fine in dj. *Henly.* $50/£32

TAYLOR, H. V. The Plums of England. London, 1949. 32 color plts. (Eps, some text lt spotted.) Dj (torn, crudely repaired.) *Edwards.* $31/£20

TAYLOR, ISAAC. Ancient Christianity and the Doctrines of the Oxford Tracts for the Times. H.G. Bohn, 1844. 4th ed. 2 vols. xii,550; xlviii,510,142pp (supp and index). Marbled eps, edges. Full brn calf (backstrip head vol I sl rubbed), gilt, dbl morocco labels. *Cox.* $86/£55

TAYLOR, ISAAC. Character Essential to Success in Life. London, 1820. 2nd ed. Color engr frontis, xii,176pp. Contemp calf (lt rubbed), gilt spine, leather label. *Oinonen*.* $50/£32

TAYLOR, ISAAC. The Mine. London: John Harris, 1834. 5th ed. Sq 12mo. Full-pg engr frontis, 224pp + 6pp list; 16 perfect plts. (Dated ink dedication fep.) Grn cl, red roan gilt spine. VF. *Hobbyhorse.* $150/£96

TAYLOR, ISAAC. Scenes in America, for Little Tarry-at-Home Travellers. J. Harris, 1822. 2nd ed. 8vo. 120pp,4pp ads; fldg map, 26 (of 28) plts dated March 1821. Maroon roan spine, illus bds (rubbed, mks, wear). Good. *Bookmark.* $94/£60

TAYLOR, J. H. Taylor on Golf: Impressions, Comments and Hints. London: Hutchinson, 1902. 1st ed. Frontis. Dec gilt-lettered grn cl w/golf clubs forming 'T.' (1 plt detached), else Fine. *Pacific*.* $748/£479

TAYLOR, J. J. The Physician as a Business Man.... Phila, 1892. 1st ed. 143pp. (Ex-lib; owner notes.) *Fye.* $125/£80

TAYLOR, JAMES WICKES. A Choice Nook of Memory, the Diary of a Cincinnati Law Clerk 1842-1844. James Taylor Dunn (ed). Columbus: OH State Archaeological & Hist Soc, 1950. Sound in ptd wraps (sl worn). *Boswell.* $45/£29

TAYLOR, JAMES. The Great Historic Families of Scotland. London, n.d., ca 1890. 6 vols. Blue cl (soil). Good + . *Zubal*.* $150/£96

TAYLOR, JANE and ANN. Little Ann and Other Poems. Routledge, n.d. (1882). 1st ed, 1st issue. Kate Greenaway (illus). Sm 4to. 64pp (sl foxing). All edges blue. Bright yellow eps (narrow grazes). Grn cl spine, corners; glazed pict bds. VG (lt mkd). *Bookmark.* $148/£95

TAYLOR, JEFFERYS. Old English Sayings. London, 1827. Frontis, 147pp. Orig bds, cl back, paper label (torn; joints worn). *Argosy.* $125/£80

TAYLOR, JEREMY. The Rule and Exercises of Holy Living.... Phila: Wm Woodward, 1810. 1st Amer ed. Calf. VG. *Argosy.* $100/£64

TAYLOR, JOHN. African Rifles and Cartridges. Harrisburg: Stackpole, (1948). (Sl worn.) Dj (frayed, sl chipped). *Oinonen*.* $120/£77

TAYLOR, JOHN. Maneaters and Marauders. NY, (1960). 1st ed. (Sl worn.) Dj. *Oinonen*.* $160/£103

TAYLOR, KATHERINE AMES. Lights and Shadows of Yosemite. SF: H.S. Crocker, 1926. VG (sl nicks). *Smith.* $75/£48

TAYLOR, L. Hunting Big Game in North Western North America. (Portsmouth, OH): L. Taylor, 1915. Gilt-pict cl (shelfworn). *Oinonen*.* $475/£304

TAYLOR, LONN. New Mexican Furniture, 1600-1940. Museum of NM, (1987). Fine in dj. *Bohling.* $35/£22

TAYLOR, MILDRED. Mississippi Bridge. NY: Dial, 1990. 1st ed. Max Ginsburg (illus). 6 3/4 x 8 3/4. 62pp. Fine in dj. *Cattermole.* $24/£15

TAYLOR, MILDRED. Roll of Thunder, Hear My Cry. NY: Dial, 1976. 1st ed. Jerry Pinkney (illus). 5 3/4 x 8 1/4. 276pp. VG in dj. *Cattermole.* $35/£22

TAYLOR, MORRIS F. First Mail West, Stagecoach Lines on Santa Fe Trail. Albuquerque: Univ of NM, (1971). 1st ed. Map. VF in pict dj. *Argonaut.* $60/£38

TAYLOR, MRS. BASIL. Japanese Gardens. NY, 1912. 28 mtd color plts. Cvr gilt label. (Bumped, lt worn.) *Freeman*.* $50/£32

TAYLOR, PETER. Happy Families Are All Alike. NY: McDowell, Obolensky, (1959). 1st ed. Fine in VG dj (shelfworn, nicks). *Reese.* $50/£32

TAYLOR, PETER. A Long Fourth and Other Stories. NY: Harcourt, Brace, (1948). 1st ed, 1st bk. (Sm stain fep), o/w Fine in dj (lt dust-soiled, spine faded). *Jaffe.* $350/£224

TAYLOR, PETER. A Woman of Means. NY: Harcourt, Brace, (1950). 1st ed. Signed. (Place, date on flyleaf), o/w VG + in dj (spine ends sl worn). *Bernard.* $225/£144

TAYLOR, PHOEBE ATWOOD. 3 Plots for Asey Mayo. NY: Norton, 1942. 1st ed. Fine in dj (sl worn, price-clipped). *Else Fine.* $125/£80

TAYLOR, PHOEBE ATWOOD. The Cape Cod Mystery. Indianapolis: Bobbs, 1931. 1st ed. (Lt wear, spine lt dknd), else VG + . *Murder By The Book.* $100/£64

TAYLOR, PHOEBE ATWOOD. The Crimson Patch. NY: Norton, 1936. 1st ed. (Sl wear), else NF in homemade acetate dj. *Murder By The Book.* $40/£26

TAYLOR, ROBERT W. A Clinical Atlas of Venereal and Skin Diseases.... Phila: Lea, 1889. 2 vols. Sm folio. 22,(2),19-(172); (173)-427pp; 58 chromolitho plts. Orig 3/4 morocco, cl (bds worn, scuffed, joints weak, rear joint vol 2 coming detached). *Goodrich.* $595/£381

TAYLOR, SAMUEL W. Nightfall at Nauvoo. NY: Macmillan, (1975). 1st ed. VG in dj. *Lien.* $35/£22

TAYLOR, TOM (ed). The Autobiography and Memoirs of Benjamin Robert Haydon (1786-1846). 1926. New ed. 2 vols. Fore/lower edges uncut. Dj (lt soiled, sl chipped). *Edwards.* $47/£30

TAYLOR, W. General Lee: His Campaigns in Virginia. Norfolk: Nussbaum, 1906. 1st ed. Good (spine faded). *Scribe's Perch*.* $150/£96

TAYLOR, ZACHARY. Letters of...from the Battle-Fields of the Mexican War. Rochester, 1970. Rpt of 1908 ed. Frontis port. Fine. No dj as issued. Howes T78. *Turpen.* $45/£29

Tea Planter's Vade Mecum.... Calcutta: Tea Gazette, (1885). 1st ed. (Sl marginal worming, date erased tp.) 1/2 roan (worn, stained). *Maggs.* $140/£90

TEALE, THOMAS PRIDGIN. A Treatise on Neuralgic Diseases Dependent upon Irritation of the Spinal Marrow and Ganglia of the Sympathetic Nerve. Phila: Carey & Hart, 1830. Teale's 1st pub work, 1 of 2 Amer eds pub in 1830, the year after the orig Eng ed. iv,120pp (foxed). Untrimmed. Orig bds (rebacked). VG. *Glaser.* $250/£160

TEBBEL, JOHN. A History of Book Publishing in the United States...1630-1940. NY/London: Bowker, 1972-78. Vols 1-3 (of 4). VG (sl worn). *Waverly*.* $77/£49

Technics and Creativity. NY: MMA, (1971). Jasper Johns litho and apparatus. Orig wrapper, plastic box. *Freeman*.* $100/£64

TEE-VAN, JOHN (ed). Fishes of the Western North Atlantic. New Haven: Sears Foundation for Marine Research, 1948-1963. 3 vols. (Cl rubbed.) *Argosy.* $150/£96

TEGNER, H. The White Foxes of Gorenletch. NY: Morrow, 1954. 1st ed. NF in NF dj. *Mikesh.* $20/£13

TEICHMANN, EMIL. A Journey to Alaska in the Year 1868: Being a Diary.... Oskar Teichmann (ed). NY: Argosy-Antiquarian, 1963. 1st ed thus, ltd to 750. Fine. *Perier.* $85/£54

TEIGNMOUTH, LORD and CHARLES G. HARPER. The Smugglers. London, 1923. 1st ed. 2 vols. Navy cl (sl worn), gilt. *Maggs*. $109/£70

TEMPERLEY, H. W. V. History of Serbia. London, 1917. 3 maps. *Hatchwell*. $23/£15

TEMPLE, R. C. The Thirty-Seven Nats. London: W. Griggs, 1906. Chromolitho tp. Red cl (rubbed, bumped, soiled). *Metropolitan**. $345/£221

TEMPLE, WILLIAM. An Introduction to the History of England.... London: Richard Simpson, 1699. 2nd ed. (8),318,2pp. Teg. 19th-cent red calf, marbled bds (extrems sl rubbed). *Karmiole*. $175/£112

TEMPLETON, FREDERIC E. X-Ray Examination of the Stomach. Chicago, (1944). VG. *Argosy*. $45/£29

TEMPLETON, WILLIAM. The Engineer's Common-Place Book.... London, 1839. 1st ed. Fldg frontis, 3 fldg plts. Orig cl (spine, top sl faded), ptd paper label fr cvr. *Kane**. $45/£29

Ten Little Negro Boys. NY: Charles E. Graham, (ca 1880). 8vo. (6)ff. Very Nice (inscrip; extrems lt worn) in color self-wrappers. *Bromer*. $375/£240

TENDLER, STEWART and DAVID MAY. The Brotherhood of Eternal Love. Panther, 1984. Pb orig. Inscribed by May. 16pp photo insert. NF. *Sclanders*. $31/£20

TENDRYAKOV, VLADIMIR. Three, Seven, Ace and Other Stories. D. Alger, O. Stevens & P. Falla (trans). London: Harvill, 1973. 1st Eng ed. Paper-cvrd bds. Fine in dj (soil). *Antic Hay*. $25/£16

TENNANT, ELEONORA. Spanish Journey. London, 1936. 1st Eng ed. Good (cvrs sl spotted) in dj (sl nicked). *Clearwater*. $39/£25

TENNESON, JOYCE. Joyce Tenneson: Photographs. Boston: David Godine, 1984. 1st ed. Fine in NF dj. *Cahan*. $85/£54

TENNYSON, ALFRED. Enoch Arden. Boston, 1864. 1st Amer ed. 204pp (few bumped at fore-edge). (Staining; spine ends frayed; fr cvr sl bent.) *King*. $35/£22

TENNYSON, ALFRED. Gareth and Lynette. London, 1872. 1st ed. Full pub's morocco. VG. *Argosy*. $60/£38

TENNYSON, ALFRED. Idylls of the King. Boston: Ticknor & Fields, 1859. 1st Amer ed, w/July 1859 ads. Brn cl, gilt. Nice (lt worn). *Macdonnell*. $50/£32

TENNYSON, ALFRED. The Life and Works. London: Macmillan, 1898-99. Edition-de-Luxe. 12 vols. Frontis each vol (spotting). Uncut. Grn cl (spines faded), gilt. *Christie's**. $281/£180

TENNYSON, ALFRED. Maud, a Monodrama. (Hammersmith): Kelmscott, (1893). One of 500. 1st state of pp16, 19, 26, 69, w/ptr's errors uncorrected. 8vo. Orig limp vellum (spotted), silk ties. Orig bd slipcase. *Swann**. $690/£442

TENNYSON, ALFRED. Maud, a Monodrama. Kelmscott Press, 1893. One of 500 (+ 5 on vellum). (xiv),69,(7)pp. Partly unopened. Vellum, ribbon ties, spine gilt. VG. *Michael Taylor*. $702/£450

TENNYSON, ALFRED. Maud, and Other Poems. Edward Moxon, 1855. Pub's ads dated May 1856. Good (bkpl; rebacked, orig backstrip relaid). *Tiger*. $39/£25

TENNYSON, ALFRED. Maud, and Other Poems. London: Edward Moxon, 1855. 1st ed. Ads dated July 1855. Grn cl (extrems sl faded). Fine. *Appelfeld*. $125/£80

TENNYSON, ALFRED. Seven Poems and Two Translations. Hammersmith, 1902. Ltd to 325 ptd in red/black. (Top of rear cvr sl faded), else VF in full limp vellum. *Bromer*. $350/£224

TENNYSON, ALFRED. The Works of Alfred Lord Tennyson. London: Macmillan, 1889. 12 vols. 8vo. Teg, others uncut. Full grn morocco, ribbed gilt-lettered spines (uniformly faded to brn), gilt dentelles. *D & D*. $700/£449

TENNYSON, ALFRED. The Works. London, 1872. 6 vols. Port vol 1. Contemp tree calf, gilt, spines (sl faded) in 6 compartments, red/grn morocco lettering pieces in 2. *Swann**. $460/£295

TENNYSON, ALFRED. The Works. Kegan Paul, 1883. Cabinet ed. 13 vols. Aeg. Full morocco (vol 1 spine sl rubbed), gilt. Presentation box (worn, lid detached). *Edwards*. $117/£75

TEONGE, HENRY. The Diary of Henry Teonge, Chaplain on Board His Majesty's Ships Assistance, Bristol, and Royal Oak: Ano 1675 to 1679. London: Charles Knight, 1825. 1st ed. Fldg facs, 2 tps, xviii,1/2-title,327pp (verso tp repaired), marbled eps. Mod 3/4 maroon goat, marbled paper over bds. *Parmer*. $200/£128

TEONGE, HENRY. The Diary of Henry Teonge, Chaplain on Board His Majesty's Ships.... NY/London: Harper, 1927. Red cl, gilt. (Worn.) *Parmer*. $50/£32

TERHUNE, A. P. The Dog Book. Akron: Saalfield, 1932. 1st ed. 12 full-pg color repros. Color pict bds. VG in Good dj. *Mikesh*. $37/£24

TERHUNE, A. P. My Friend the Dog. Harper, 1926. 1st ed. 6.5x9. 317pp (few edgetears, hinges cracking); 11 tipped-in plts by Marguerite Kirmse. Grn cl, pict paste-on. Good+ (shelfworn, corner badly bumped). *My Bookhouse*. $75/£48

TERRAY, LIONEL. The Borders of the Impossible. GC, 1964. 1st Amer ed. VG in dj. *King*. $75/£48

TERRELL, JOHN UPTON. Black Robe: The Life of Pierre-Jean DeSmet.... GC: Doubleday, 1964. 1st ed. VG (margins pencilled) in dj. *Lien*. $35/£22

TERRELL, JOHN UPTON. Journey into Darkness, Cabeza de Vaca's Expedition Across North America, 1528-36. London, 1964. 1st British ed. Map. Fine in Fine dj. *Turpen*. $40/£26

TERRELL, JOHN UPTON. Journey Into Darkness. NY: William Morrow, 1962. 1st ed. VG in dj. *Lien*. $35/£22

TERRELL, JOHN UPTON. Pueblos, Gods and Spaniards. NY, 1973. 1st ed. Fine in Fine dj. *Turpen*. $30/£19

TERRINGTON, WILLIAM. Cooling Cups and Dainty Drinks. London: Routledge, 1869. 1st ed. (xvi),(224),(16)pp. Good (owner stamps cvrs, tp verso; lacks 1 ad leaf; sl worn, sl mkd, creased). *Ash*. $78/£50

TERRY, ELLEN and BERNARD SHAW. A Correspondence. Christopher St. John (ed). NY: Fountain, 1931. 1st ed. #643/3000 ptd. Teg, others uncut. VG in grn buckram (backstrip faded), slipcase (worn). *Cox*. $28/£18

TERRY, ELLEN. The Story of My Life. London: Hutchinson, 1908. Special ed, ltd to 250 numbered, signed. 8 photogravure plts. Teg. White cl (sl soiled), gilt. *Karmiole*. $200/£128

TERRY, M. D. Old Inns of Connecticut. Hartford, 1937. 1st ed. #523/1000 signed. Leather spine. Good (lt cvr soil, fr hinge tender). *Scribe's Perch**. $28/£18

TESNOHLIDEK, RUDOLF. The Cunning Little Vixen. London: Bodley Head, 1986. 1st ed thus. Maurice Sendak (illus). 4to. 187pp. Fine in dj. *Hadley*. $39/£25

TESSER, TOM. Muldoon's Baseball Club in Philadelphia. NY: Frank Tousey, June 7, 1890. Pict wraps. (Sl browned), else Fine. *Waverly**. $66/£42

TESSIER, THOMAS. How We Died. (Dublin): New Writers', (1970). One of 200 numbered, signed. Fine in ptd sewn wrappers. *Dermont*. $100/£64

TESSIER, THOMAS. The Nightwalker. Atheneum, 1980. 1st US ed. Fine in Fine dj. *Certo*. $85/£54

TESSIMOND, A. S. J. The Walls of Glass. London, 1934. 1st Eng ed, 1st bk. Nice (sl faded). *Clearwater*. $47/£30

TESTE, A. The Homoeopathic Materia Medica. Phila, 1854. 1st ed in English. 634pp. 1/2 leather. VG. *Fye*. $100/£64

Tewkesbury's Who's Who in Alaska and Alaska Business Index. Vol 1947 I. Juneau, 1947. Fldg map. Good (ex-lib, fr hinge weak). *Zubal**. $30/£19

THACHER, JAMES. American Medical Practice.... Boston, 1817. 1st ed. 744pp. Full orig sheep. Clean (lt rubbing, foxing). *Goodrich*. $125/£80

THACHER, JAMES. An Essay on Demonology, Ghost and Apparitions, and Popular Superstitions. Boston: Carter & Hendee, 1831. 1st ed. v,234pp. (Sl hole fep, sl spotted; sl rubbed, spine faded, ends sl frayed, edges torn, rubbed, sl bumped), o/w VG. *Worldwide*. $125/£80

THACHER, JAMES. An Essay on Demonology. Boston, 1831. 234pp. Teg. 3/4 leather, marbled bds, eps. Good (extrems rubbed, hinges starting). *Scribe's Perch**. $90/£58

THACHER, JAMES. A Military Journal During the American Revolutionary War, from 1775 to 1783.... Boston: Richardson & Lord, 1827. 2nd ed. viii,487pp. Uncut. Later rich gilt sprinkled calf (joints sl weak). Internally Fine. Howes T149. *Goodrich*. $175/£112

THACKERAY, WILLIAM MAKEPEACE. A Collection of Letters of Thackeray: 1847-1855. NY: Scribner, 1887. 1st ed. Teg. Gilt-worked grn cl. VG (ink name). *Antic Hay*. $75/£48

THACKERAY, WILLIAM MAKEPEACE. Doctor Birch and His Young Friends. London: Chapman & Hall, 1849. 1st ed. Orig pink pict bds ptd in blue. Nice (rubbed, sl faded). *Macdonnell*. $150/£96

THACKERAY, WILLIAM MAKEPEACE. Early and Late Papers, Hitherto Uncollected. James T. Fields (ed). Boston: Ticknor & Fields, 1867. 1st ed. 1/2-title. Emb grn cl. VG. *Antic Hay*. $75/£48

THACKERAY, WILLIAM MAKEPEACE. English Humourists. NY: Harper, 1853. 1st Amer ed. Bright red T-cl emb w/ribbon pattern. Attractive (lt rubbed). *Macdonnell*. $100/£64

THACKERAY, WILLIAM MAKEPEACE. The Four Georges: Sketches of Manners, Morals, Court, and Town Life. London, 1861. 1st Eng ed in bk form, 1st issue. 2 plts. (Half-title, tp foxed.) Pub's 16-pg cat at end dated Nov 1861. *Swann**. $103/£66

THACKERAY, WILLIAM MAKEPEACE. The History of Pendennis. London: Bradbury & Evans, 1849. 1st ed bound from orig parts. 2 vols. Marbled eps; ribbon markers. 3/4 black morocco leather. (Lt foxing), else NF set. *Turtle Island*. $225/£144

THACKERAY, WILLIAM MAKEPEACE. The History of Pendennis. NY: Harper, 1850. 2 vols. 392; iv,372pp. (Sl foxed, rubbed, spine ends frayed), o/w Good. *Worldwide*. $30/£19

THACKERAY, WILLIAM MAKEPEACE. The Letters and Private Papers of William Makepeace Thackeray. Gordon N. Ray (ed). Cambridge: Harvard Univ, 1946. 1st ed. 4 vols. Red cl. NF in djs (stained, chips, tears). *Antic Hay*. $150/£96

THACKERAY, WILLIAM MAKEPEACE. The Memoirs of Barry Lyndon. NY: Lovell, 1880. 751pp. (Sl rubbed), o/w VG. *Worldwide*. $20/£13

THACKERAY, WILLIAM MAKEPEACE. Mr. Brown's Letters to a Young Man About Town. Cambridge: Riverside, 1901. Ltd to 500. Unopened. Cl-backed marbled bds. VG. *Truepenny*. $55/£35

THACKERAY, WILLIAM MAKEPEACE. The Newcomes. London: Bradbury & Evans, 1853-1855. 1st ed. As 1st issued in orig 24/23 parts. 2 engr tps, 46 plts (sl creasing, dampstains; contents dkng); all ads. Orig wraps (skillfully rebacked, lt soiled, stains) in custom red morocco pull-off case. *Waverly**. $209/£134

THACKERAY, WILLIAM MAKEPEACE. The Newcomes. Memoirs of a Most Respectable Family. London: Bradbury & Evans, 1854-1855. 1st ed in bk form. 2 vols. viii,380; viii,375pp (sl foxing); engr title, frontis each volume, 44 plts. Contemp 1/2 calf (extrems lt rubbed, wear), marbled bds, gilt, leather lettering pieces. VG set. *House*. $275/£176

THACKERAY, WILLIAM MAKEPEACE. The Orphan of Pimlico, and Other Sketches, Fragments and Drawings. London: Smith, Elder, 1876. 1st ed. 4to. 100 leaves, incl eps. Orig grn leather-backed gray bds (spine sl rubbed, bds soiled). VG. *Blue Mountain*. $45/£29

THACKERAY, WILLIAM MAKEPEACE. Sketches and Travels in London. London: Bradbury & Evans, 1856. 1st ed. iv,176pp. Later 1/2 morocco, orig wraps bound in. Good (sm tear 1 leaf, margins creased, chipped). *Ash*. $148/£95

THACKERAY, WILLIAM MAKEPEACE. Vanity Fair. London, 1848. 1st ed in bk form, 1st issue. 40 etched plts, incl frontis, add'l tp. Mod navy levant (spine dknd, fr joint rubbed), gilt. Cl slipcase. *Swann**. $402/£258

THACKERAY, WILLIAM MAKEPEACE. The Works of.... NY: Scribner, 1903-4. 1st ed thus (Kensington). 32 vols. 8vo. Teg, uncut. Full dk grn cl (spines sl faded), gilt. VG. *Houle*. $750/£481

THACKERAY, WILLIAM MAKEPEACE. The Works. London: Smith, Elder, 1869-1886. 1st ed, 'The Library Edition.' 24 vols. Uncut. Emb grn cl, gilt. (Lt rubbed, hinge paper sl cracked), else Attractive. *Macdonnell*. $375/£240

THACKERAY, WILLIAM MAKEPEACE. Works. NY, 1884. 11 vols. Contemp 1/2 calf, gilt, spines in 6 compartments, red/black morocco lettering pieces in 2. *Swann**. $431/£276

Thackerayana: Notes and Anecdotes. C&W, n.d. (1881). New ed. Color frontis, pub's cat dated March 1881. Pict cl. Good (spotting, sig; spine bumped, corners rubbed). *Tiger*. $55/£35

THARP, BENJAMIN C. Texas Range Grasses. Austin, 1952. 5 maps (4 fldg), 25 full-pg dwgs. (Corners sl bumped), else VG in dj (chipped). *Brooks*. $25/£16

THATCHER, B. B. Indian Biography. NY: Harper, 1839. 1st ed. 2 vols in 1. Port. Teg. Later 19th cent 3/4 blue morocco, marbled bds. (Extrems sl scuffed, worn), else Nice. *Brown*. $75/£48

THAYER, EMMA H. Wild Flowers of Colorado. NY: Cassell, 1885. 54pp; 24 color plts. Aeg. Ptd bds (extrems sl worn, sm repaired spine tear). *Dumont*. $195/£125

THAYER, EMMA H. Wild Flowers of the Pacific Coast. NY: Cassell, (1887). 1st ed. 64pp (sl foxed, few pp w/residue from once-inserted dried flowers); 24 chromolitho plts (sl foxed), guards. Floral patterned eps; aeg. Pict mustard cl (sl worn, lt dusty). *Baltimore**. $140/£90

THAYER, EMMA H. Wild Flowers of the Pacific Coast. NY, 1887. 64pp; 24 chromolithos. Floral eps; aeg. Color pict cl, gilt (dull). *Brooks*. $165/£106

THAYER, EMMA H. Wild Flowers of the Rocky Mountains. NY: Cassell, (1889). 24 chromolitho plts. Pict cl (spine, fr cvr soiled, worn). Contents VG (stain lower margin some leaves, incl 5 plts). *Waverly**. $88/£56

THAYER, JAMES BRADLEY. A Western Journey With Mr. Emerson. Shirley Sargent (ed). Bk Club of CA, 1980. Ltd to 600. Dec bds, cl spine. Fine in dj. *Black Sun*. $55/£35

THAYER, W. Marvels of the New West. Norwich, CT: Henry Bill, 1888. xxxvi,715pp. Pict cl. Good. *Blake.* $75/£48

THAYER, WILLIAM M. The Pioneer Boy, and How He Became President. Boston: Walker, Wise, 1863. xiv,310pp. Emb cl (sl worn), gilt illus. Good (sm stain eps, presentation, sigs sl loose). Howes T153. *Cahan.* $25/£16

THEOBALD, FRED V. The Plant Lice or Aphididae of Great Britain. London, 1926. 3 vols. (Ex-lib, ink stamps, labels, upper hinge vol 1 cracked, accession labels to faded spines.) *Edwards.* $86/£55

THEROUX, ALEXANDER. The Great Wheadle Tragedy. (Boston): Godine, (1975). 1st ed. Fine in dj (lt rubbed). *Captain's Bookshelf.* $50/£32

THEROUX, ALEXANDER. Master Snickup's Cloak. NY: Harper & Row, (1979). 1st Amer ed. 4to. Fine in dj (price-clipped). *Turtle Island.* $30/£19

THEROUX, ALEXANDER. Master Snickup's Cloak. NY: Harper, (1979). 1st Amer ed. Signed. Fine in dj. *Captain's Bookshelf.* $75/£48

THEROUX, ALEXANDER. Master Snickup's Cloak. Harper & Row, 1979. 1st US ed. Brian Froud (illus). 4to. (30pp). Pict bds. Fine in pict dj. *Bookmark.* $22/£14

THEROUX, ALEXANDER. Master Snickup's Cloak. NY: Harper & Row, 1979. 1st ed. Fine in dj. *Lame Duck.* $85/£54

THEROUX, PAUL. Chicago Loop. Hamilton, 1990. 1st UK ed. Fine in dj. *Williams.* $19/£12

THEROUX, PAUL. Chicago Loop. NY, 1990. 1st Amer ed. Signed. Fine in Fine dj. *Polyanthos.* $30/£19

THEROUX, PAUL. The Consul's File. London: Hamish Hamilton, 1977. 1st UK ed. NF in dj. *Moorhouse.* $23/£15

THEROUX, PAUL. Doctor Slaughter. Hamish Hamilton, (1984). 1st ed. VG in dj. *Ash.* $31/£20

THEROUX, PAUL. Doctor Slaughter. Hamilton, 1984. 1st UK ed. Fine in dj. *Williams.* $23/£15

THEROUX, PAUL. Fong and the Indians. Boston: Houghton Mifflin, 1968. 1st ed. Fine in dj. *Lame Duck.* $175/£112

THEROUX, PAUL. Fong and the Indians. London, 1976. 1st ed. Fine in dj. *Buckley.* $55/£35

THEROUX, PAUL. Girls at Play. Boston: Houghton Mifflin, 1969. 1st ed. Fine in dj. *Hermitage.* $150/£96

THEROUX, PAUL. Girls at Play. London, 1969. 1st ed. (Spine rubbed), else NF in VG dj (creased, spine nicked). *Buckley.* $234/£150

THEROUX, PAUL. The Great Railway Bazaar. Hamilton, 1975. 1st UK ed. VG (spine sl creased) in dj. *Williams.* $62/£40

THEROUX, PAUL. The Great Railway Bazaar. London, 1975. 1st Eng ed. Very Nice in dj. *Clearwater.* $86/£55

THEROUX, PAUL. The Happy Isles of Oceania. NY, 1992. 1st Amer ed. Signed. Fine in Fine dj. *Polyanthos.* $35/£22

THEROUX, PAUL. Jungle Lovers. Boston: Houghton Mifflin, 1971. 1st ed. NF in VG + dj (sm bluish stain spine). *Lame Duck.* $125/£80

THEROUX, PAUL. The Kingdom by the Sea. London, 1983. 1st ed. Dj. *Typographeum.* $28/£18

THEROUX, PAUL. London Snow. (Salisbury, England): Michael Russell, (1979). One of 450 numbered, signed by Theroux & John Lawrence (engrs). Fine in Fine tissue dj. *Lenz.* $135/£87

THEROUX, PAUL. London Snow. Michael Russell, 1979. Ltd to 450 signed by Theroux and John Lawrence (illus). Patterned cl, gilt. Fine in glassine wrapper. *Words Etc.* $101/£65

THEROUX, PAUL. The Mosquito Coast. (Boston): Houghton Mifflin, 1982. #315/350 signed. David Frampton (illus). (Sm mk spine head, fep), else NF in slipcase. *Hadley.* $125/£80

THEROUX, PAUL. The Mosquito Coast. Boston: Houghton Mifflin, 1982. One of 350 numbered, signed. Fine in Fine slipcase. *Lenz.* $125/£80

THEROUX, PAUL. Saint Jack. Bodley Head, 1973. 1st UK ed. NF (ink inscrip) in VG + dj (spine lettering sl faded). *Williams.* $195/£125

THEROUX, PAUL. Saint Jack. Houghton Mifflin, 1973. 1st US ed. Fine in Fine dj. *Martin.* $44/£28

THEROUX, PAUL. Saint Jack. Boston: Houghton Mifflin, 1973. 1st ed. Signed. Fine in Fine dj. *Lenz.* $125/£80

THEROUX, PAUL. Saint Jack. Boston: Houghton, Mifflin, 1973. 1st ed. Fine in NF dj (price-clipped). *Antic Hay.* $35/£22

THEROUX, PAUL. Waldo. Boston: Houghton Mifflin, 1967. 1st ed, 1st bk. Good (mks, signs of use) in dj (sl rubbed). *Ash.* $101/£65

THEROUX, PAUL. Waldo. Boston: Houghton Mifflin, 1967. 1st ed. Fine in dj ptd w/white lettering (3/4-inch closed tear spine; lt worn). *Hermitage.* $125/£80

THEROUX, PAUL. World's End and Other Stories. London, 1980. 1st Eng ed. Fine in dj (clipped). *Clearwater.* $31/£20

THESIGER, WILFRED. Arabian Sands. London: Longmans, 1959. 1st Eng ed. VG in VG dj (creased). *Hadley.* $70/£45

THESIGER, WILFRED. Arabian Sands. NY: Dutton, 1959. 1st ed. Fldg map. (Sl rubbed, soiled), o/w VG. *Worldwide.* $28/£18

THESIGER, WILFRED. Desert Marsh and Mountain. London, 1979. Fine (inscrip) in dj. *Clearwater.* $55/£35

They Still Draw Pictures. NY: Spanish Child Welfare Assoc. of America, 1938. 1st Amer ed. Fine in pict spiral wrappers. *Polyanthos.* $25/£16

THINKER, THEODORE. First Lessons in Botany. NY: A.S. Barnes, 1851. 12mo. 141pp (1st/last few ll stained). *Quest.* $40/£26

THIRKELL, ANGELA. Grateful Sparrow and Other Tales. London: Hamish Hamilton, 1935. 1st ed. Ludwig Richter (illus). Lg 8vo. Pict cl, pict label. NF in VG dj (chipped). *Book Adoption.* $30/£19

THIRKELL, ANGELA. Marling Hall. NY: Knopf, 1942. 1st ed. Fine in dj (soil, sm stains rear panel). *Antic Hay.* $27/£17

THISSELL, G. W. Crossing the Plains in '49. Oakland, CA, 1903. 1st ed. Grn emb pict cl. Howes T160. *Ginsberg.* $450/£288

THOMA, KURT H. Oral Roentgenology.... Boston, 1922. VG. *Argosy.* $125/£80

THOMA, KURT H. Traumatic Surgery of the Jaws, Including First-Aid Treatment. St. Louis, 1942. 1st ed. Blue cl. NF. *Doctor's Library.* $50/£32

Thomas F. Flannery, Jr., Collection. Medieval and Later Works of Art. London: Sotheby's, Sale Dec. 1/2, 1983. W/estimate list, price list. Good in dj. *Washton.* $60/£38

THOMAS, ABEL C. Autobiography of Abel Thomas. Boston: J.M. Usher, 1852. 2nd thousand. 408pp; engr port, guard. Aeg. Gilt-dec blue cl. VG. *Petrilla.* $75/£48

THOMAS, BENJAMIN F. Portrait for Posterity.... New Brunswick: Rutgers Univ, 1947. 1st ed. VG. *Graf.* $20/£13

THOMAS, CAITLIN. Leftover Life to Kill. London, 1957. 1st ed. VG in dj (sl worn, torn). *King.* $25/£16

THOMAS, CHARLES W. Ice Is Where You Find It. Indianapolis/NY: Bobbs-Merrill, 1951. Blue cl. VG in dj (worn). *Parmer*. $35/£22

THOMAS, D. M. The White Hotel. NY: Viking, (1981). 1st ed. Signed. Fine in Fine dj. *Lenz*. $85/£54

THOMAS, D. M. The White Hotel. NY, 1981. 1st ed. Signed. Fine in Fine dj. *Warren*. $95/£61

THOMAS, DAVIS and KARIN RONNEFELDT (eds). People of the First Man: Life Among the Plains Indians.... NY: E.P. Dutton, (1976). 1st ed. Karl Bodmer (watercolors). VG in dj. *Lien*. $175/£112

THOMAS, DYLAN. Adventures in the Skin Trade. London, 1955. 1st ed. VG in dj (chip upper panel). *Words Etc*. $39/£25

THOMAS, DYLAN. Adventures in the Skin Trade. London, 1955. 1st Eng ed. Very Nice (name) in dj (sl torn). *Clearwater*. $47/£30

THOMAS, DYLAN. The Beach of Falesa. NY: Stein & Day, (1963). 1st Amer ed. Fine (ink name) in NF dj. *Antic Hay*. $20/£13

THOMAS, DYLAN. Conversation About Christmas. (NY): New Directions, 1954. 1st separate ed. Contents Fine in wraps. (lt soiled, sm crease). *Waverly**. $33/£21

THOMAS, DYLAN. Conversation About Christmas. (NY): New Directions, 1954. One of 2000 ptd. VG in ptd wraps (soiled). *Antic Hay*. $85/£54

THOMAS, DYLAN. Deaths and Entrances. J.M. Dent, 1946. 1st ed. Good (inscrip) in dj (frayed, piece torn from upper wrapper). *Cox*. $101/£65

THOMAS, DYLAN. The Doctor and the Devils. London, 1953. 1st ed. VG in dj (2 chips). *Words Etc*. $44/£28

THOMAS, DYLAN. The Doctor and the Devils. Macmillan, n.d. (c1980). VG in pict paper wrappers. *Tiger*. $19/£12

THOMAS, DYLAN. In Country Sleep and Other Poems. (NY): New Directions, (1952). 1st ed, trade issue. Association copy. Port. (Sig, bump), o/w Fine in dj (sl worn, nicked). *Reese*. $175/£112

THOMAS, DYLAN. Letters to Vernon Watkins. London: J.M. Dent/Faber & Faber, (1957). 1st Eng ed. Grn cl. Fine in NF dj (sm tear). *Antic Hay*. $50/£32

THOMAS, DYLAN. Letters to Vernon Watkins. V. W. (ed). NY: New Directions, (1957). 1st Amer ed. Fine in dj (spine extrems sl rubbed, price-clipped). *Polyanthos*. $25/£16

THOMAS, DYLAN. Letters to Vernon Watkins. Vernon Watkins (ed). London: J.M. Dent/Faber & Faber, (1957). 1st ed. Frontis. Fine in dj (sl worn). *Graf*. $20/£13

THOMAS, DYLAN. The Map of Love. London 1939. 1st Eng ed. Very Nice (foxed) in dj (sl nicked). *Clearwater*. $234/£150

THOMAS, DYLAN. A Prospect of the Sea and Other Stories and Prose Writings. London: J.M. Dent, (1955). 1st ed. NF in dj (sm tear). *Antic Hay*. $75/£48

THOMAS, DYLAN. Quite Early One Morning. London: Dent, (1954). 1st ed, 1st issue w/full stop after 'sailors' on pp3, 11. Fine in dj (sl rubbed, short tear). *Waverly**. $71/£46

THOMAS, DYLAN. Selected Letters. Constantine Fitzgibbon (ed). Dent, 1966. 1st ed. NF in VG dj. *Poetry Bookshop*. $47/£30

THOMAS, DYLAN. The World I Breathe. Norfolk, CT: New Directions, (1939). 1st ed. One of 700. Sm 4to. Binding w/1 star on each side of Thomas's name imprinted on spine. Bright in dj (spine sl toned, sm tears). *Waverly**. $660/£423

THOMAS, DYLAN. The World I Breathe. Norfolk, CT: New Directions, (1939). 1st ed. One of 700. This copy signed, dated, inscribed. Sm 4to. One star on either side of author's name on spine (others have 5 stars). VG (fep sl foxed; lt rubbed, soiled, spine gilt dull). *Waverly**. $1,980/£1,269

THOMAS, E. S. Reminiscences of the Last Sixty-Five Years, Commencing with the Battle of Lexington. Hartford, 1840. 2 vols. 300; 300pp (2 paper stocks used, 1 dknd, foxed). Orig cl. Clean (extrems chipped). Howes T164. *Bohling*. $85/£54

THOMAS, EDWARD (ed). British Country Life in Spring and Summer; Autumn and Winter. London, 1909. 2 vols. Illus cl (spine sl rubbed). *Edwards*. $86/£55

THOMAS, EDWARD. Algernon Charles Swinburne. London, 1912. 1st ed. (Prelims lt foxed; lt stain fr panel, corner sl bumped), o/w VG. *Words Etc*. $117/£75

THOMAS, EDWARD. The Childhood of...a Fragment of Autobiography. London: Faber & Faber, (1938). 1st ed. Good (eps sl foxed) in dj (nicked, tanned). *Reese*. $20/£13

THOMAS, EDWARD. The Country. Batsford, 1913. 1st ed. (Spine lt faded), o/w VG. *Words Etc*. $70/£45

THOMAS, EDWARD. Four Letters to Frederick Evans. (Edinburgh): Tragara, 1978. #62/150. Fine in wraps in dj. *Hadley*. $28/£18

THOMAS, EDWARD. Lafcadio Hearn. London, 1912. 1st Eng ed. Nice (spine sl rubbed). *Clearwater*. $47/£30

THOMAS, EDWARD. The Last Sheaf. Cape, 1928. 1st ed. Fine in dj (sl chipped, spine dknd). *Poetry Bookshop*. $125/£80

THOMAS, EDWARD. A Literary Pilgrim in England. London, 1917. 1st ed. Blue cl. (Spine faded, cvrs sl mkd), o/w VG. *Words Etc*. $94/£60

THOMAS, EDWARD. Maurice Maeterlinck. NY, 1911. 1st Amer ed. VG (rubber stamp fep; spine rubbed). *Clearwater*. $62/£40

THOMAS, EDWARD. Oxford. Black, 1903. 1st ed. Blue cl, gilt. (Spine sl browned; 1/2 fep cut away, name crudely erased), o/w VG. *Words Etc*. $47/£30

THOMAS, EDWARD. Richard Jefferies. His Life and Work. Boston: Little, Brown, 1909. 1st Amer ed. (2 visiting-cards pasted in as bkpls; cvrs mkd, mottled, corners knocked.) *Clearwater*. $39/£25

THOMAS, EDWARD. Rose Acre Papers. London, 1910. 1st ed. Grn cl, gilt. (Bkpl removed; spine sl dull), o/w VG. *Words Etc*. $78/£50

THOMAS, EDWARD. A Selection of Letters to Edward Garnett. Tragara, 1981. #172/175. Fine in wrappers. *Poetry Bookshop*. $37/£24

THOMAS, ELLA GERTRUDE CLANTON. The Secret Eye, The Journal of Ella Gertrude Clanton Thomas 1848-1889. Virginia Ingraham Burr (ed). Chapel Hill, (1990). 1st ed. As New in As New dj. *Pratt*. $32/£21

THOMAS, F. W. Low and I. London, 1923. 1st Eng ed. Pict bds. Dj (sl torn, dusty). *Clearwater*. $62/£40

THOMAS, GWYN. Venus and the Voters. Boston: Little, Brown, 1948. 1st ed. Fine in dj (lt soil). *Antic Hay*. $30/£19

THOMAS, HENRY WALTER. History of the Doles-Cook Brigade Army of Northern Virginia, C.S.A.... Atlanta, GA: Franklin, 1903. 1st ed. VG+ (bkpl, sm lib stamp tp). *Mcgowan*. $450/£288

THOMAS, HYLTON. The Drawings of Giovanni Battista Piranesi. NY, 1954. 80 plts. Good in dj (worn). *Washton*. $40/£26

THOMAS, ISAIAH. The History of Printing in America. Worcester: The Author, June, 1810. 1st ed. 2 vols. 8vo. 487;576pp, 3 facs (1 fldg), 2 plts (1 fldg). (Bkpl, 1846 signed note vol 2.) Contemp marbled bds (new calf spines, corners). (Tps sl foxed), else Fine. *M & S.* $1,750/£1,122

THOMAS, J. Journeys among the Gentle Japs. London: Sampson Low, 1897. 1st ed. Frontis, x,266pp + 30 ads, fldg map. Grn cl. (Sl wear), else VG. *Terramedia.* $80/£51

THOMAS, JAMES A. A Pioneer Tobacco Merchant in the Orient. Durham: Duke Univ, 1928. 1st ed. Frontis, tissue guard. Unopened. Fine in dj (lt chipped). *Cahan.* $50/£32

THOMAS, LEWIS. The Lives of a Cell. NY: Viking, 1973. 1st ed. NF in dj (1-inch tear fr panel, tape-repaired verso). *Lame Duck.* $150/£96

THOMAS, LOWELL. The Silent War in Tibet. GC: Doubleday, 1959. 1st ed. VG. *Worldwide.* $22/£14

THOMAS, LOWELL. With Lawrence in Arabia. GC: GC, 1924. 1st ed. 15 plts. (Sl rubbed), o/w VG. *Worldwide.* $14/£9

THOMAS, OLDFIELD. Catalogue of the Marsupialia and Monotremata in the Collection of the British Museum (Natural History). London, 1888. xiii,401pp (ex-lib, tp lt browned, labels, cardholders); 28 lithos (4 color). Partly unopened. (Lower bd lt faded, spine chipped, accession label, 2 sm holes lower joint.) *Edwards.* $117/£75

THOMAS, R. Interesting and Authentic Narratives of the Most Remarkable Shipwrecks.... Hartford, 1852. 359pp. (Spine torn, chipped.) *King.* $35/£22

THOMAS, R. S. Poetry for Supper. London, 1958. 1st Eng ed. Very Nice (name) in dj. *Clearwater.* $70/£45

THOMAS, R. S. Poetry for Supper. London: Rupert Hart-Davis, 1958. 1st Eng ed. (Inscrip), else VG in dec bds in dj. *Hadley.* $55/£35

THOMAS, R. S. Song at the Year's Turning. London, 1955. 1st Eng ed. Fine (inscrip) in dj. *Clearwater.* $94/£60

THOMAS, ROSS. The Backup Men. London: Hodder & Stoughton, 1971. 1st UK ed. Fine (one-line copyright oblit) in Fine dj. *Beasley.* $45/£29

THOMAS, ROSS. The Backup Men. NY: William Morrow, 1971. 1st ed. Fine in dj. *Mordida.* $135/£87

THOMAS, ROSS. Cast a Yellow Shadow. NY: William Morrow, 1967. 1st ed. Fine in dj. *Mordida.* $200/£128

THOMAS, ROSS. The Eighth Dwarf. NY: S&S, 1979. 1st ed. Fine in dj. *Mordida.* $40/£26

THOMAS, ROSS. The Porkchoppers. NY: William Morrow, 1972. 1st ed. VF in dj. *Mordida.* $85/£54

THOMAS, ROSS. The Seersucker Whipsaw. NY: William Morrow, 1967. 1st ed. Fine in dj (short closed tear). *Mordida.* $450/£288

THOMAS, ROSS. The Seersucker Whipsaw. London: Hodder & Stoughton, 1968. 1st British ed. Fine in dj (lt worn). *Else Fine.* $225/£144

THOMAS, ROSS. The Singapore Wink. NY: Morrow, 1969. 1st ed. Fine in Fine dj. *Else Fine.* $300/£192

THOMAS, ROSS. Spies, Thumbsuckers, etc. Northridge: Lord John, 1989. 1st ed. One of 300 numbered, signed. VF w/o dj as issued. *Mordida.* $75/£48

THOMAS, T. GAILLARD. A Practical Treatise on Diseases of Women. Phila, 1880. 806pp. (Spine faded), else VG. *Doctor's Library.* $50/£32

THOMAS, THOMAS EBENEZER. Correspondence of Thomas Ebenezer Thomas...Relating to the Anti-Slavery Conflict in Ohio.... N.p., 1909. 1st ed. VG. *Mcgowan.* $150/£96

THOMAS, THOMAS EBENEZER. Correspondence of...Mainly Relating to the Anti-Slavery Conflict on Ohio, Especially in the Presbyterian Church. The Author's son, 1909. 2 ports. Gilt-titled cl. VG (bkpl; sl soiled). *Bohling.* $30/£19

THOMAS, THOMAS MORGAN. Eleven Years in Central South Africa. London: John Snow, n.d. (1872). 1st ed. Line-engr frontis, xi,(i)blank, 418pp, fldg map (tear repaired), port, 30 plts. Dec brn cl (recased, hinges strengthened, ends sl rubbed). Excellent. *Morrell.* $250/£160

THOMAS, VERLIN. The Successful Physician. 1923. 1st ed. VG. *Fye.* $75/£48

THOMAS, WILBUR. General James 'Pete' Longstreet, 'Lee's Old War Horse', Scapegoat for Gettysburg. Parsons, WV, 1979. VG + in VG + dj. *Pratt.* $70/£45

THOMAS, WILLIAM H. The Gold Hunter's Adventures or, Life in Australia. Chicago: Donnelley, Lloyd, 1883. 564pp + ads. Emb grn cl (shelfwear, spine splitting; fr hinge weak). *Parmer.* $55/£35

THOMAS, WILLIAM S. Hunting Big Game. Knickerbocker, 1906. 1st ed. Teg. Illus laid down upper bd. (Bkpl; spine sl chipped.) *Edwards.* $62/£40

THOMAS, WILLIAM S. Trails and Tramps in Alaska and Newfoundland. NY/London: Putnam, 1913. 1st ed. Brn cl (edge bumped, spine tips worn), gilt. VG. *Parmer.* $125/£80

THOMAS, WILLIAM S. Trails and Tramps in Alaska and Newfoundland. NY: Putnam, 1913. Teg. Dec cl. (Sl stain lower cvr), else VG. *High Latitude.* $45/£29

THOMAS, WILLIAM S. Trails and Tramps in Alaska and Newfoundland. NY: Putnam, 1913. Paste label. VG. *Adelson.* $55/£35

THOMASON, DAVID. Handy Book of the Flower-Garden. Edinburgh/London, 1876. 3rd ed. xv,426pp; 8 fldg plts at rear. (Sl spotted, upper hinge tender; spine lt soiled, rubbed.) *Edwards.* $39/£25

THOMASON, JOHN W., JR. Lone Star Preacher. NY, 1941. 1st ed. VG + in dj (lt worn). *Pratt.* $60/£38

THOME, JAMES A. and J. HORACE KIMBALL. Emancipation in the West Indies. NY: Amer Anti-Slavery Soc, 1839. 2nd ed. Fldg frontis map, xx,412pp. (Sl foxed; sl rubbed, soiled, spine sl frayed), o/w Good. *Worldwide.* $95/£61

THOMES, W. H. The Bushrangers. Boston, 1865. 480pp. Dec spine. Good. *Scribe's Perch*.* $30/£19

THOMES, W. H. On Land and Sea, or California in the Years 1843, '44 and '45. Boston: DeWolfe, Fiske, 1884. 1st ed. (2),iv,5-351pp. Pict blue cl, gilt. (Sm stain feps; extrems lt worn), o/w Fine. *Pacific*.* $546/£350

THOMPSON, C. J. S. The Hand of Destiny. London: Rider, (1932). 1st ed. VG. *Glaser.* $50/£32

THOMPSON, C. J. S. Mysteries of History with Accounts of Some Remarkable Characters and Charlatans. Phila: Lippincott, 1928. 1st Amer ed. With the W. L. Necker bkpl. VG. *Glaser.* $50/£32

THOMPSON, C. J. S. The Mystery and Lore of Monsters.... NY, 1931. 1st Amer ed. VG. *Fye.* $100/£64

THOMPSON, CLARA MILDRED. Reconstruction in Georgia: Economic, Social, Political 1865-1872. NY: Columbia, 1915. 1st ed. New cl w/leather label. Howes T189. *Ginsberg.* $125/£80

THOMPSON, DANIEL P. The Green Mountain Boys. London: J. Cunningham, 1840. 1st Eng ed. 136pp (old bkseller's descrip taped to inner margin tp). Bottom margin p33 imprinted 'The Novel Newspaper, No. 109.' Lib binder. *M & S.* $250/£160

THOMPSON, DANIEL V. The Materials of Medieval Painting. New Haven, 1936. (Cl sl soiled.) *Washton.* $50/£32

THOMPSON, DEBORAH. Coptic Textiles in the Brooklyn Museum. Brooklyn: Brooklyn Museum, (1971). 16 color plts. Good. *Archaeologia*. $150/£96

THOMPSON, EDMUND. Maps of Connecticut...1801-1860. Windham, CT, 1942. #30/250. 1 fldg plt. Good (sl foxing). *Scribe's Perch**. $30/£19

THOMPSON, EDWIN PORTER. History of the Orphan Brigade. (Dayton, OH: Morningside, 1973.) Facs rpt of the scarce 1898 ed. VG. Howes T193. *Mcgowan*. $65/£42

THOMPSON, ELBERT A. and LAWRENCE S. Fine Binding in America, the Story of the Club Bindery. (Urbana, IL): Beta Phi Mu, 1956. 1st ed. Chapbook. Brn paper bds, title, relief illus fr cvr. NF; issued w/o ptd dj. *Heller*. $85/£54

THOMPSON, FRANCIS. Saint Ignatius Loyola. John H. Pollen (ed). London: Burns & Oates, 1913. 1st ed. (Sl rubbed), o/w VG. *Worldwide*. $18/£12

THOMPSON, FREDERICK DIODATI. In the Track of the Sun, Readings from the Diary of a Globe Trotter. NY: Appleton, 1893. 1st ed. viii,226pp; 78 plts (1 tinted). Teg. (Cl sl rubbed, soiled, spine frayed), o/w VG. *Worldwide*. $35/£22

THOMPSON, GEORGE G. Bat Masterson; The Dodge City Years. Topeka, KS, 1943. 1st ed. VG in stapled wraps. *Mcclintock*. $45/£29

THOMPSON, GEORGE. Prison Life and Reflections. Oberlin, 1847. 1st ed. 417pp. (Text browned, cl rebound), else Good. *King*. $195/£125

THOMPSON, GEORGE. Prison Life and Reflections; or, A Narrative...of...Work, Burr and Thompson...for Attempting to Aid Some Slaves to Liberty. Hartford: A. Work, 1849. 3rd ed. Fine (name, sm tear rep; 1st, last pp foxed; cl flaking in spots). *Between The Covers*. $225/£144

THOMPSON, GEORGE. Travels and Adventures in Southern Africa.... London, 1827. 2nd ed. 2 vols. Map. (Foxing, staining.) Orig bds (new spines). Good. *Metropolitan**. $862/£553

THOMPSON, GILBERT. The Engineer Battalion in the Civil War. Washington, DC: Press of the Engineer School, 1910. 1st ed. NF in ptd wrappers. *Mcgowan*. $175/£112

THOMPSON, H. C. Sweet Potato Production and Handling. NY: OJ, 1929. 1st ed. Fine in pict dj. *Second Life*. $45/£29

THOMPSON, H. P. Alpine Plants of Europe Together with Cultural Hints. London, (1911). 64 color plts, fldg map. (Text foxed.) Pict cl, gilt. Dj. *Henly*. $25/£16

THOMPSON, HAROLD W. (ed). The Last of the Logan. Ithaca, NY: Cornell Univ, 1941. Frontis. VG in dj. *High Latitude*. $45/£29

THOMPSON, HENRY T. Ousting the Carpetbagger from South Carolina. Columbia: R.L. Bryan, 1927. 2nd ed. (Shelfworn, edgeworn, rubbed), else Good. *Brown*. $25/£16

THOMPSON, HENRY. The Motor-Car. London, 1902. 1st ed. (Paper spine label rubbed, fr hinge loose; soiled, sm tear.) *King*. $150/£96

THOMPSON, HUNTER S. Fear and Loathing in Las Vegas. NY: Random House, (1971). 1st ed. (Bd edges sl faded), else Fine in VG dj (sl dampstained). *Between The Covers*. $185/£119

THOMPSON, HUNTER S. Fear and Loathing in Las Vegas. NY: Random House, (1971). 1st ed. Fine in Fine dj (top edge sl toned). *Unger*. $250/£160

THOMPSON, HUNTER S. Fear and Loathing on the Campaign Trail '72. SF: Straight Arrow, (1973). VG (spine bottom sl bumped) in VG+ 1st issue dj w/white border around author photo (price-clipped; rubbing; short tears). *Between The Covers*. $250/£160

THOMPSON, HUNTER S. Fear and Loathing: On the Campaign Trail '72. SF: Straight Arrow, (1973). 1st ed. Fine in NF dj (sticker removed fr panel, nicked). *Unger*. $125/£80

THOMPSON, HUNTER S. Generation of Swine. NY, 1988. 1st Amer ed. Fine in Fine dj. *Polyanthos*. $25/£16

THOMPSON, HUNTER S. Screwjack. Santa Barbara: Neville, 1991. One of 300 numbered (of 326), signed. Gilt stamped cl. Fine. *Between The Covers*. $150/£96

THOMPSON, HUNTER S. and RALPH STEADMAN. The Curse of Lono. NY: Bantam, 1983. 1st ed. NF in glossy illus wraps. *Lame Duck*. $85/£54

THOMPSON, I. OWEN. Adventures and Day Dreams. Long Beach, 1913. 1st ed. 20 full-pg photo illus. (Lt worn.) *Dawson*. $60/£38

THOMPSON, J. MAURICE. The Witchery of Archery. Robert P. Elmer (ed). Pinehurst, NC: Archers Co, 1928. Brn pict cl. VF. *Biscotti*. $110/£71

THOMPSON, JIM. Child of Rage. NY: Lancer, 1972. 1st ed. Pb orig. Unread. Fine in wrappers. *Mordida*. $200/£128

THOMPSON, JIM. Child of Rage. L.A.: Blood & Guts, 1991. One of 500 numbered, signed by Gerald Petievich (intro). VF in dj, slipcase. *Mordida*. $150/£96

THOMPSON, JIM. The Getaway. NY: Signet New American Library, 1959. 1st ed. Pb orig. NF (spine title ptd sl off-center; name, date tp). *Janus*. $50/£32

THOMPSON, JIM. The Getaway. London: W.H. Allen, 1972. 1st hb ed. Fine in dj (short closed tear). *Mordida*. $150/£96

THOMPSON, JIM. The Grifters. Evanston: Regency Books, 1963. 1st ed. Pb orig. (Bottom pg edges sl stained), o/w VF in wrappers. *Mordida*. $250/£160

THOMPSON, JIM. Ironside. NY: Popular Library, (1967). 1st ed. VG (pp dknd; few pg corners creased) in wrappers. *Between The Covers*. $150/£96

THOMPSON, JIM. Ironside. NY: Popular Library, 1967. 1st ed. Pb orig. (Bookseller's stamp bottom pg edges), o/w Fine in wrappers. *Mordida*. $45/£29

THOMPSON, JIM. Nothing But a Man. NY: Popular, (1970). Pb orig. (Pp sl dknd, sl rubbed), else Fine. *Between The Covers*. $100/£64

THOMPSON, JIM. The Nothing Man. (NY): Dell, (1954). 1st ed. Pict wraps (sl worn). *King*. $175/£112

THOMPSON, JIM. The Nothing Man. NY: Dell, (1954). 1st ed, pg orig. Fine in illus wrappers. *Pettler & Lieberman*. $100/£64

THOMPSON, JIM. Recoil. NY: Lion Books, (1953). 1st ed, pb orig. (Spine slanting), else Good in wrappers. *Pettler & Lieberman*. $30/£19

THOMPSON, JIM. The Undefeated. NY: Popular Library, (1969). 1st ed. VG+ (pp dknd; few pg corners bent) in wrappers (sl edge dkng). *Between The Covers*. $100/£64

THOMPSON, JOSIAH. Six Seconds in Dallas. NY, 1967. Very Nice (inscrip) in dj (sl chafed, mkd). *Clearwater*. $55/£35

THOMPSON, KAY. Eloise at Christmastime. NY: Random House, (1958). 1st ed. Hilary Knight (illus). (Sm sticker removed fep, name in ptd gift card), o/w Fine in dj (lt used). *Captain's Bookshelf*. $200/£128

THOMPSON, KAY. Miss Pooky Peckinpaugh. NY: Harper & Row, 1970. 1st ed. Fine in white dj (sm tears). *Else Fine*. $125/£80

THOMPSON, MAURICE (ed). The Boys' Book of Sports and Outdoor Life. NY: Century, 1886. 1st ed. xiv,(ii),352pp (few ll soiled, 3 sl chipped, half-title sl torn at inner edge). Pict tan cl (bumped, rubbed, soiled, hinges weak), gilt. VG. BAL 20008. *Blue Mountain.* $65/£42

THOMPSON, MAURICE. The Witchery of Archery: A Complete Manual of Archery. NY, 1878. Frontis (sl offset), (x),259pp. (Margins lt browned; spine tail chipped, sl loss.) *Edwards.* $70/£45

THOMPSON, P. William Butterfield. Routledge, Kegan Paul, 1971. 25 color plt illus, cat. (Lib stamp verso tp), else Good in dj (wear, sl frayed). *Ars Artis.* $94/£60

THOMPSON, PETER. Peter Thompson's Narrative of the Little Bighorn Campaign, 1876. Glendale: Clark, 1974. 1st ed. One of 1033. Fldg map. NF (extrems lt rubbed; sl spot to spine; eps replaced). *Argonaut.* $75/£48

THOMPSON, R. L. Glimpses of Medical Europe. Phila, 1908. 1st ed. VG. *Fye.* $75/£48

THOMPSON, R. W. The Footprints of the Jesuits. NY/Boston: Crowell, 1894. 1st ed. Frontis, 509pp. (Sl rubbed), o/w VG. *Worldwide.* $20/£13

THOMPSON, RICHARD A. Crossing the Border with the 4th Cavalry. Waco, TX: Texian Press, 1986. 1st ed. VF in dj. *Gibbs.* $20/£13

THOMPSON, ROBERT. The Gardener's Assistant. London: Blaikie, (1859). 1st ed. xv,774pp; 12 hand-color plts. Gilt-dec cl. (Sm ink stain edge few leaves), else Fine. *Quest.* $410/£263

THOMPSON, ROBERT. The Gardener's Assistant. London: Gresham, 1900. 5 vols. 14 color plts. (Spotting.) Dec cl (extrems sl worn), gilt. VG. *Hollett.* $148/£95

THOMPSON, RUTH PLUMLY. Captain Salt in Oz. Chicago, (1936). 1st ed. John R. Neill (illus). 8vo. Orig cl, full-size color pict fr cvr label (lower corner cvrs lt discolored). 1st issue dj (sl chipped) listing this as last of 29 titles. *Swann*.* $258/£165

THOMPSON, RUTH PLUMLY. The Giant Horse of Oz. Reilly & Lee, (1933). Brn cl. Good +. *Scribe's Perch*.* $45/£29

THOMPSON, RUTH PLUMLY. The Lost King of Oz. Reilly & Lee, 1925. 1st ed. 12 color plts (3 detached but present). Blue cl. Good-. *Scribe's Perch*.* $70/£45

THOMPSON, RUTH PLUMLY. Ojo in Oz. Reilly & Lee, 1933. 1st ed. 12 full-pg color plts. Blue-gray cl. Good (fr hinge crack). *Scribe's Perch*.* $100/£64

THOMPSON, RUTH PLUMLY. The Yellow Knight of Oz. Reilly & Lee, 1930. 1st ed. 12 color plts. Orange-brn cl (rear bd mottled). Good. *Scribe's Perch*.* $90/£58

THOMPSON, SILVANUS P. Dynamo-Electric Machinery. 1896. 5th ed. x,835pp; 19 fldg plts. (Faint ink name fr cvr), o/w VG. *Whitehart.* $62/£40

THOMPSON, SILVANUS P. The Life of William Thomson, Baron Kelvin of Largs. London: Macmillan, 1910. 1st ed. 2 vols. Frontis port each vol, 14 plts. Teg, untrimmed. VG set (tp vol 1 torn; spine #s removed). *Glaser.* $150/£96

THOMPSON, SLASON. Way Back When: Recollections of an Octogenarian...1849-1929. Chicago: Kroch, 1931. 1st ed. 1/2 cl. *Ginsberg.* $100/£64

THOMPSON, T. Hearts. DeBakey and Cooley, Surgeons Extraordinary. London: Michael Joseph, 1972. 1st ed. Good in dj. *White.* $19/£12

THOMPSON, W. H. Cornwall, a Survey of Its Coast, Moors, and Valleys.... London, 1930. (Sl soiled.) *Hatchwell.* $39/£25

THOMPSON, WADDY. Recollections of Mexico. NY, 1846. 1st ed. '3rd ed' on spine. Orig blind-stamped brn cl, gilt. (Lacks 1/3 of last rep, foxing; extrems worn), o/w VG. *Turpen.* $195/£125

THOMPSON, WILLIAM. Reminiscences of a Pioneer. SF, 1912. VG +. *Bohling.* $40/£26

THOMPSON, WILLIAM. Reminiscences of a Pioneer. SF, 1912. 1st ed. Frontis, 4 plts. Blue cl. (Lt rubbed), else Fine. *Argonaut.* $45/£29

THOMPSON, WINFIELD M. et al. The Yacht 'America.' Boston: Charles E. Lauriat, 1925. 1st ed. Frontis, 1 fldg illus. Blue cl, gilt. Fine. *Karmiole.* $60/£38

THOMS, HERBERT. Classical Contributions to Obstetrics and Gynecology. Springfield: Charles C. Thomas, (1935). 1st ed. VG (spine lt faded). *Glaser.* $100/£64

THOMS, HERBERT. Classical Contributions to Obstetrics and Gynecology. Springfield: Charles C. Thomas, 1935. 1st ed. VG in dj (spine dknd). *White.* $50/£32

THOMSON, A. L. Britain's Birds and Their Nests. London, 1910. 132 color plts. Pict cl (rebacked, preserving spine; sl foxing), gilt. *Henly.* $50/£32

THOMSON, ALEXANDER. The Family Physician. NY: Ptd by James Oram, 1802. 1st Amer ed. (xii),(13)-526pp + 2pp ads (lacks fep, foxed). Contemp tree calf (bds detached). *Waverly*.* $88/£56

THOMSON, C. WYVILLE. The Voyage of the 'Challenger.' London, 1877. 2 vols. xv,424; xiv,396pp, 4 ads; port, 43 plts (39 fldg). Pict cl (rebacked, preserving spines), gilt. *Henly.* $273/£175

THOMSON, C. WYVILLE. The Voyage of the 'Challenger.' NY: Harper, 1878. 2 vols. xx,17-391; viii,9-340pp. VG. *High Latitude.* $200/£128

THOMSON, D. C. Life and Labours of Hablot Knight Brown, 'Phiz.' NY: Scribner & Welford, 1885. #74/250. 245pp; 35 full-pg plts. Dec cvr (edges chipped), new leather spine. Contents VG. *Scribe's Perch*.* $30/£19

THOMSON, D. C. The Water Colour Drawings of Thomas Bewick. London, n.d. 31 tipped-in color plts on 28 leaves. Card portfolio (worn) as issued. *Edwards.* $31/£20

THOMSON, DUNCAN. The Life and Art of George Jamesone. OUP, 1974. 1st ed. Color frontis port, 126 plts. (Ex-lib, mks verso tp, sm label, label removed, sl loss fep.) Dj. *Edwards.* $44/£28

THOMSON, ELIZABETH H. Harvey Cushing: Surgeon, Author, Artist. NY: Henry Schuman, 1950. 1st ed. Frontis port, 12 plts. Fine in dj. *Glaser.* $60/£38

THOMSON, JAMES. The City of Dreadful Night and Other Poems. London: Reeves & Turner & Bertram Dobel, 1888. 2nd ed. (8),184pp. Uncut. (Eps lt foxed, lower hinge sl worn.) *Cox.* $31/£20

THOMSON, JAMES. The Seasons. Newburyport: Proprietor of the Boston Book Store, (1790). 5th Amer ed ('First American Edition' falsely appears on tp). 238pp. Contemp mottled calf (1-inch chip rear hinge). *Karmiole.* $100/£64

THOMSON, JAMES. The Seasons. London: A. Millar, 1758. Engr tp vignette, 2 p.l., 209pp (bkpl, sl spotted); 4 plts (lt offset). Very Nice contemp calf (2 corners sl worn), gilt, raised bands, red morocco label. *Pirages.* $150/£96

THOMSON, JAMES. The Seasons. London: T. Chapman, 1795. Frontis, engr tp, xiv,233pp (lt foxed, early leaves lt dampstained); 4 plts. Gilt-dec black morocco, red spine label. (Lt worn.) *New Hampshire*.* $80/£51

THOMSON, JAMES. The Seasons. London: Nonesuch, 1927. One of 1500 w/5 copper-plt engrs colored by pochoir at Curwen Press. In addition, one sm engr on tp. 8vo. Gilt-stamped deep-blue morocco by Riviere and Son. Fine in blue cl slipcase. *Bromer.* $750/£481

THOMSON, JOHN. Report of Observations Made in the British Military Hospitals in Belgium, After the Battle of Waterloo.... Edinburgh: Blackwood, 1816. Sole ed. viii,281pp. Mod 1/2 calf, marbled bds. (Few pp lt spotted), o/w Handsome. *White.* $343/£220

THOMSON, JOSEPH. Mungo Park and the Niger. London: George Philip, 1890. 1st ed. 338pp; 8 color maps. Gilt edges. Full calf, prize binding, gilt. VG. *Cullen.* $110/£71

THOMSON, MOLLY B. Jack and the Beanstalk. Collins 'Kiddie Kut,' n.d. (ca 1940s). Shape bk. 242x184mm. (18pp). VG in pict wraps. *Bookmark.* $34/£22

THOMSON, MRS. A. T. Memoirs of the Court of Henry the Eighth. London: Longman, Rees, 1826. 1st ed. 2 vols. Engr frontis port, xi,503; viii,619pp (scattered foxing, lib labels pastedowns, stamps tps). Uncut. Library cl, gilt. Good set. *Hollett.* $101/£65

THOMSON, R. B. The Coldest Place on Earth. Wellington, 1969. (Name), else VG in dj. *High Latitude.* $20/£13

THOMSON, RICHARD. Seurat. Phaidon, 1985. 1st ed. 60 color plts. (Lower margin pg 99/100 torn; bumped, upper bd sl dented.) Dj (mkd). *Edwards.* $39/£25

THOMSON, S. J. The Real Indian People. London: William Blackwood, 1914. 1st ed. Engr frontis, xiii,345pp + (ii) pub's cat. Grn cl (sl rubbed), spine gilt. Good. *Sotheran.* $200/£128

THOMSON, SAMUEL. New Guide to Health or Botanic Family Physician.... Boston: J.Q. Adams, 1835. 1st ed. Engr frontis. (Foxing, dampstaining.) Patterned paper-cvrd, white paper-cvrd bds (rebound). *Metropolitan*.* $115/£74

THOMSON, SAMUEL. New Guide to Health; or Botanic Family Physician.... Boston, 1835. 1st(?) Boston ed. 2 parts in 1 vol. Engr frontis, 223; 163pp (foxing, dampstaining). Pattern paper bds (rebound). *Goodrich.* $150/£96

THOMSON, SPENCER. Health Resorts of Britain. London, 1860. Fldg frontis map (torn), xii,330pp (lt marginal browning). Blind-emb cl (sl soil, recased w/sl loss to spine ends, surface splits to joints). *Edwards.* $62/£40

THOMSON, THOMAS. History of the Royal Society from Its Institution to the End of the Eighteenth Century. London: Robert Baldwin, 1812. 552,xcipp. Uncut. Handsome full gilt morocco, raised bands. (Lt foxing, bkpl), else NF. *Goodrich.* $495/£317

THOMSON, W. G. A History of Tapestry from the Earliest Times Until the Present Day. London: Hodder & Stoughton, 1906. 1st ed. Dec cl gilt (sl rubbed). Very Nice (upper joint tender, few spots). *Hollett.* $187/£120

THOMSON, WILLIAM M. The Land and the Book. 1883. 3 vols. 3 fldg maps, dbl-pg map. Dec cl (sl spotting upper bd vol 3, spines sl rubbed; bkpls). *Edwards.* $273/£175

THORBURN, ARCHIBALD. British Birds. Longmans, Green, 1925. 4 vols. 192 color plts. VG (backstrips uniformly faded). *Cox.* $148/£95

THORBURN, ARCHIBALD. British Birds. London, 1925. New ed. 4 vols. 192 color plts. (Lacks fep vol 1, feps lt browned vols 1 and 3; spines faded, sl chipped, vol 2 joints mkd, bds sl faded.) *Edwards.* $140/£90

THORBURN, ARCHIBALD. British Mammals. London, 1920-21. 4to. 2 vols in 1. vii,84; vi,105pp; 50 Fine color plts. (Sl waterstain top edge), o/w Fine in dj (worn). *Henly.* $546/£350

THORBURN, ARCHIBALD. Game Birds and Wild-Fowl of Great Britain and Ireland. London: Longmans & Green, 1923. 1st ed. 30 chromolitho plts. Teg. Orig pub's cl (sl rubbed). *Christie's*.* $736/£472

THORBURN, ARCHIBALD. A Naturalist's Sketchbook. London, 1919. 1st ed. 60 plts (24 color). (Sl foxed; cl sl worn, mkd.) *Maggs.* $312/£200

THOREAU, HENRY DAVID. Autumn. Boston: Houghton, Mifflin, 1892. 1st ed. Grn cl, gilt. VG. BAL 20130. *Macdonnell.* $150/£96

THOREAU, HENRY DAVID. Cape Cod. Boston: Ticknor & Fields, 1865. 1st ed. (4),252pp + 24-pg pub's cat at end w/ptd list of Tho. Sound (cl lt spotted, worn). *M & S.* $250/£160

THOREAU, HENRY DAVID. Cape Cod. Boston: Ticknor & Fields, 1865. 1st ed, 1st ptg of 2000. 8vo. (viii)252,24pp. Binding variant 2 (no priority), w/24-pg pub's cat dated Dec, 1864 at end. Fine (spine extrems lt faded, chipped, clipping remains pasted ep). BAL 20115. *Bromer.* $500/£321

THOREAU, HENRY DAVID. Cape Cod. Boston, 1896. 1st ed thus. 2 vols. Teg. Gilt-pict cl (Spines faded), o/w VG. BAL 20191. *New Hampshire*.* $80/£51

THOREAU, HENRY DAVID. Cape Cod. Boston: Houghton Mifflin, 1896. 1st ed thus. 2 vols. Grn cl (partly faded, esp spines; eps foxed). *Waverly*.* $82/£53

THOREAU, HENRY DAVID. Cape Cod. Portland, ME: LEC, 1968. One of 1500 numbered, signed by R. J. Holden (illus). Pict buckram. Mint in bd slipcase. *Argosy.* $125/£80

THOREAU, HENRY DAVID. Early Spring in Massachusetts. Boston: Houghton Mifflin, 1881. 1st ed. Grn cl, gilt. VG. BAL 20123. *Macdonnell.* $150/£96

THOREAU, HENRY DAVID. Early Spring in Massachusetts. H.G.O. Blake (ed). Boston: Houghton Mifflin, 1881. 1st ed. One of 1018 ptd. Teg. Gilt grn cl (few sm flecks). VG. BAL 20123. *Reese.* $125/£80

THOREAU, HENRY DAVID. Excursions. Boston: Ticknor & Fields, 1863. 1st ed. One of 1558. 1 prelim pg undated ads. 'Sawtooth' grain blue-grn cl, gilt. VG (sig; sl shelfworn, spine gilt tarnished). *Sumner & Stillman.* $475/£304

THOREAU, HENRY DAVID. Excursions. Boston: Ticknor & Fields, 1863. 1st ed. 8vo. Frontis port. Pub's grn horizontal grained cl, cvrs blind-stamped, gilt-lettered spine (sl rubbing head, foot spine). *D & D.* $750/£481

THOREAU, HENRY DAVID. The First and Last Journeys of Thoreau.... Franklin Benjamin Sanborn (ed). Boston: Bibliophile Soc, 1915. 1st ed. One of 489 ptd. 2 vols. Port, 3 facs of mss. 3/4 brn calf, grey bds. Fine in box. *Appelfeld.* $250/£160

THOREAU, HENRY DAVID. Letters to Various Persons. Ralph Waldo Emerson (ed). Boston: Ticknor & Fields, 1865. 1st ed, 1st ptg, binding A. Dk grn cl, gilt. Fine. BAL 5246, 20116. *Macdonnell.* $800/£513

THOREAU, HENRY DAVID. The Maine Woods. Boston: Ticknor & Fields, 1864. 1st ed. One of 1450. Purple 'Z' cl (spine faded, sl shelfworn, sm discolorings rear cvr; inscrips dated 9 June 1864). *Sumner & Stillman.* $475/£304

THOREAU, HENRY DAVID. Men of Concord. Boston, 1936. 10 color plts by N.C. Wyeth. (Bumped, worn.) *Freeman*.* $40/£26

THOREAU, HENRY DAVID. Sir Walter Raleigh. Boston: Bibliophile Soc, 1905. 1st ed. Ltd to 489. Uncut. 3/4 brn morocco, gilt. Box (sl rubbed, nicks). BAL 20142-form A. *Macdonnell.* $250/£160

THOREAU, HENRY DAVID. Transmigration of the Seven Brahmans. NY: William Rudge, 1932. 1st trade ed. One of 1000. 1/4 cl, gilt. Fine in dj (chipped). BAL 20155-form 2. *Macdonnell.* $125/£80

THOREAU, HENRY DAVID. Transmigration of the Seven Brahmans. A. Christy (ed). NY: Rudge, 1932. One of 1200. Fine in VG+ dj. *Mikesh.* $65/£42

THOREAU, HENRY DAVID. Unpublished Poems by Bryant and Thoreau. Boston: Bibliophile Soc, 1907. 1st ed. One of 470 ptd. Uncut. Vegetable vellum bds, gilt. (Crown sl nicked), else Fine. BAL 1805, 20146. *Macdonnell.* $150/£96

THOREAU, HENRY DAVID. Walden, or Life in the Woods. Boston, 1854. 1st ed. (Tp mtd at gutter; lacks map, ads.) 1/2 morocco. BAL 20106. *Swann*.* $287/£184

THOREAU, HENRY DAVID. Walden, or Life in the Woods. Boston: Ticknor & Fields, 1854. 1st ed. 8vo. Inserted map w/Chandler & Bro imprint, ads dated April 1854. Pub's 'A' binding of brn cl, gilt-lettered spine (head, foot worn w/loss). BAL 20117. *D & D.* $4,500/£2,885

THOREAU, HENRY DAVID. Walden, or Life in the Woods. Boston: Fields, Osgood, 1869. 1st ed, 8th ptg. 357pp (plan of Walden missing, appears to have never been bound in). Purple cl (sl worn). VG. *Lucas.* $300/£192

THOREAU, HENRY DAVID. Walden, or Life in the Woods. Chicago: Lakeside, 1930. One of 1000 ptd. Unopened. Cl, dec bds. (Sl offsetting to spine), o/w Very Nice in glassine dj (spine chipped) w/paper flaps, slipcase (lt dust-soiled). *Reese.* $150/£96

THOREAU, HENRY DAVID. Walden, or Life in the Woods. Boston: LEC, 1936. Ltd to 1500 signed by Edward Steichen (photos). 8vo. Cl-backed dec bds. (Spine ends sl worn), else Fine in slipcase. *Bromer.* $750/£481

THOREAU, HENRY DAVID. Walking. Riverside, 1914. 1st separate ed. #247/550 ptd. Uncut. Good in linen-backed bds (sl rubbed; sig, pencil inscrip). *Cox.* $47/£30

THOREAU, HENRY DAVID. Winter. Boston: Houghton Mifflin, 1888. 1st ed. Teg. Grn cl, gilt. VG. BAL 20129. *Macdonnell.* $150/£96

THOREAU, HENRY DAVID. A Yankee in Canada. Boston: Ticknor & Fields, 1866. 1st ed. Pub's grn horizontal grained cl, cvrs blind-stamped, gilt-lettered spine (sl rubbing head, foot spine). *D & D.* $400/£256

THOREK, MAX. The Face in Health and Disease. Phila: F.A. Davis, 1946. 1st ed. Pict cl (spine sl dull). NF. *Glaser.* $250/£160

THORINGTON, J. MONROE. A Survey of Early American Ascents in the Alps in the Nineteenth Century. (NY): American Alpine Club, 1943. (Sl worn.) *King.* $95/£61

THORN, C. JORDAN. Handbook of Old Pottery and Porcelain Marks. NY, 1947. 1st ed. VG in VG dj. *Smith.* $40/£26

THORNBER, JOHN J. and F. BONKER. The Fantastic Clan. NY, 1932. 1st ed. Color frontis, 32 photo plts. Brn cl, gilt. VG in dj. *Price.* $39/£25

THORNBROUGH, EMMA LOU. Indiana in the Civil War Era: 1850-1880. IN Hist Bur. & Hist Soc, 1965. Paper cvr. VG. *Book Broker.* $25/£16

THORNBROUGH, GAYLE (ed). Letter Book of the Indian Agency at Fort Wayne 1809-1815. IN Hist Soc, 1961. 1st ed. Fine in wraps. *Oregon.* $15/£10

THORNBURG, NEWTON. Cutter and Bone. Boston: Little Brown, 1976. 1st ed. Fine in dj (spine dknd). *Mordida.* $35/£22

THORNDIKE, EDWARD L. The Psychology of Wants, Interests, and Attitudes. NY: D. Appleton-Century, (1935). 1st ed. Inscribed. Black cl (joints worn). *Gach.* $85/£54

THORNDIKE, RUSSELL. The Master of the Macabre. London: Rich & Cowan, (1946). 1st ed. VG in VG dj. *Certo.* $60/£38

THORNE, EDWARD and HENRY W. FROHNE. Decorative Draperies and Upholstery. Grand Rapids, MI: Dean-Hicks, 1929. 1st ed. 74 Fine color plts. Linen cl. Good in dj (chipped). *Karmiole.* $150/£96

THORNE, R. T. On the Progress of Preventive Medicine During the Victorian Era. London, 1888. 1st ed. 63pp. VG. *Fye.* $75/£48

THORNTON, EDWARD. The History of the British Empire in India. London, 1841-6. 6 vols. xvi,574; xvi,576; viii,575; xi,586, 6 fldg maps; xi,728; x,549pp. Black dec cl. *Maggs.* $429/£275

THORNTON, JOHN and CAROLE REEVES. Medical Book Illustration. Cambridge, 1983. Inscribed. Frontis; 55 plts. Dj (sl worn). *Whitehart.* $39/£25

THORNTON, JOHN and CAROLE REEVES. Medical Book Illustration: A Short History. NY, 1983. 1st ed. 55 plts. VG in dj. *Fye.* $75/£48

THORNTON, JOHN. Medical Books, Libraries and Collectors.... London, 1949. 1st ed. (Spine spotted.) *Fye.* $50/£32

THORNTON, JOHN. Medical Books, Libraries and Collectors: A Study of Bibliography...in Relation to the Medical.... London, 1949. 1st ed. Red cl (outer hinges cracked; extrems worn). Good; internally VG. *Doctor's Library.* $125/£80

THORNTON, PETER. Seventeenth-Century Interior Decoration in England, France and Holland. Yale Univ, 1979. Corrected ed. NF in dj. *Hadley.* $62/£40

Thoroughbred Sires and Dams. Lexington: Blood-Horse, 1947-52. 5 vols. Full leather, gilt, blindstamping. NF. *Waverly*.* $77/£49

THORP, JOSEPH. Eric Gill. NY/London: Jonathan Cape & Harrison Smith/Jonathan Cape, 1929. Frontis, 38 plts. Black buckram, gilt. VG (bkpl; sl bumped). *Heller.* $200/£128

THORP, N. HOWARD. Pardner of the Wind: Story of the Southwestern Cowboy. Caxton, 1945. 1st ed. VG. *Authors Of West.* $50/£32

THORP, RAYMOND W. Bowie Knife. Albuquerque: Univ of NM, 1948. 1st ed. Fine in VG + dj. *Backman.* $65/£42

THORP, RAYMOND W. Spirit Gun of the West. Glendale: A.H. Clark, 1957. VG. *Bohling.* $35/£22

THORP, RAYMOND W. Spirit Gun of the West. Glendale: A.H. Clark, 1957. 1st ed. Unopened. Red cl. NF. *Harrington.* $55/£35

THORP, RAYMOND W. Spirit Gun of the West. Glendale: Clark, 1957. 1st ed. One of 1006. VF in dj. *Argonaut.* $60/£38

THORPE, ADAM. Mornings in the Baltic. Secker, 1988. 1st UK ed, 1st bk. Card cvrs. Fine in dj. *Williams.* $28/£18

THORPE, MAJOR. Scenes in Arkansaw. Phila: Peterson, (1858). Rpt. 16 plts. VG (lt foxed). *Agvent.* $60/£38

THOYTS, E. E. How to Decipher and Study Old Documents. London: Elliot Stock, 1893. 11 plts. Grn cl (bumped, upper hinge split), gilt lettering. *Maggs.* $23/£15

THOYTS, E. E. How to Decipher and Study Old Documents. London: Elliot Stock, 1893. Illus grn cl over bds (sl worn). VG. *Old London.* $75/£48

THRALE, HESTER LYNCH. Anecdotes of the Late Samuel Johnson, LL.D. During the Last Twenty Years of His Life. Dublin: Moncrieffe et al, 1786. 1st Dublin ed. viii,306,(2)pp. Contemp calf (spine chipped, hinges cracked). *Karmiole.* $275/£176

THRAPP, DAN L. The Conquest of Apacheria. Norman: Univ of OK, (1976). 1st ed. VF in dj. *Argonaut.* $60/£38

THRASHER, HALSEY. The Hunter and Trapper. NY: OJ, 1868. 1st ed. 91pp + ads. Brn cl. VG. *Bowman.* $75/£48

Three Bears. London: Frederick Warne, n.d. (ca 1900). Aunt Louisa's Home Toy Books Series 2. 10x7. (10)pp, 4 full-pg color plts. Pict bds (sl cvr stain, sl chip, wear, soil). *King.* $45/£29

Three Weeks in Palestine and Lebanon. London: John Parker, 1833. 2nd ed. viii,153pp + (vi)pub's ads; 11 plts. Marbled eps. Contemp prize calf (upper joint cracked, sl worn), gilt, remains of spine label. *Edwards.* $31/£20

Three Years with the Duke, or Wellington in Private Life. (By William Pitt Lennox.) London, 1853. 2nd ed. 272pp. Dec red cl (rebacked in red morocco). *Maggs.* $133/£85

THRELFALL, R. E. 100 Years of Phosphorus Making 1851-1951. 1951. Frontis port. (Pg edges sl spotty; spine sl defective, fr cvr sl discolored), o/w VG. *Whitehart.* $39/£25

THRESH, J. C. et al. The Examination of Waters and Water Supplies. London: Churchill, 1933. 4th ed. 36 plts. VG. *Savona.* $39/£25

THROBALD, JOHN and LILLIAN. Arizona Territory Post Offices and Postmasters. Phoenix, 1961. 1st ed. VG. *Turpen.* $25/£16

Through the Picture Frame. S&S, (1944). 1st ed. Little Golden Book. 7x7.5. Pict bds. (Sm tears at hinges; bumped, rubbed), else VG + in dj (edges ragged, spine lacks 3/4-inch piece). *My Bookhouse.* $50/£32

Through the Ranks to a Commission. (By John Edward Acland Troyte.) London: Macmillan, 1881. 1st ed. xiv,311pp; 24-pg pub's cat. (Sm lib stamp tp, text leaves). Red cl. *Burmester.* $70/£45

THRUM, THOMAS G. The Hawaiian Almanac and Annual for 1901.... Honolulu: Hawaiian Gazette, 1900. 27th issue. Ptd wrappers (sl soiled). *Lefkowicz.* $100/£64

THRUM, THOMAS G. The Hawaiian Almanac and Annual for 1921. Honolulu: The Author, 1920. Buckram (soiled; paper browned, ex-lib). *Parmer.* $60/£38

THRUM, THOMAS G. Hawaiian Folk Tales. Chicago: A.C. McClurg, 1907. 1st ed. Teg. Brn dec cl, black titles. (Sm spots cvr, spine ends sl worn), else VG. *Parmer.* $185/£119

THRUPP, JOHN. The Anglo-Saxon Home. London: Longman, Green, 1862. 1st ed. Presentation copy, inscribed. ix,410pp (scattered spotting, margins pencilled, bkpl). *Hollett.* $55/£35

THUBRON, COLIN. A Cruel Madness. London, 1984. 1st Eng ed. Fine in dj (sl stained). *Clearwater.* $31/£20

THUBRON, COLIN. Emperor. Heinemann, 1978. 1st UK ed. NF in dj. *Williams.* $56/£36

THUDICHUM, J. L. W. The Spirit of Cookery. London/NY: Frederick Warne, 1895. 1st Amer ed. Grn cl titled in gilt/black. Fine (bkpl). *Hermitage.* $150/£96

THURBER, FRANCIS. Coffee. NY: Amer Groc Publ Assoc, 1886. 13th ed. 416pp. Pict bds. NF. *Archer.* $50/£32

THURBER, FRANCIS. Coffee: From Plantation to Cup. NY: Amer Grocer Pub Assoc, 1881. 1st ed. xv,416pp; 23 tables, 2 plts. (Upper hinge cracked.) Black illus cl (edges rubbed, lt soiled), gilt. *Edwards.* $117/£75

THURBER, JAMES. Further Fables for Our Time. London: Hamish Hamilton, 1956. 1st Eng ed. VG in dj. *Hollett.* $19/£12

THURBER, JAMES. Lanterns and Lances. NY: Harper, 1961. 1st ed. (Sig, pastedowns lt foxed), else VG in dj. *Cahan.* $20/£13

THURBER, JAMES. Many Moons. St. Joseph, MI: Ptd by A.M. & R.W. Roe, 1958. Inscribed by Philip Reed (illus). 22 color woodcuts. Dec blue cl, gilt spine title. NF. *Blue Mountain.* $95/£61

THURBER, JAMES. Many Moons. NY: HBJ, 1967. Louis Slobodkin (illus). 8 3/4 x 10. 48pp. VG in dj. *Cattermole.* $25/£16

THURBER, JAMES. Men, Women and Dogs: A Book of Drawings. NY: HB&Co, (1943). Fine in VG dj (sl chips, tears). *Between The Covers.* $150/£96

THURBER, JAMES. My World—And Welcome to It. London: Hamish Hamilton, 1942. 1st ed. (Spine lettering faded.) *Hollett.* $23/£15

THURBER, JAMES. The Thurber Carnival. NY, 1957. 1st Modern Library ed. VG in VG dj (price-clipped). *Smith.* $20/£13

THURBER, JAMES. Thurber Country. Hamilton, 1953. 1st UK ed. VG (sm label removal mk, edges sl foxed) in dj (sl foxed, price-clipped). *Williams.* $39/£25

THURBER, JAMES. Thurber's Dogs. NY: S&S, 1955. Fine in Fine dj (sm tear rear panel). *Between The Covers.* $100/£64

THURBER, JAMES. The Wonderful O. NY: S&S, (1957). 1st ed. Fine in dj (sl rubbed). *Captain's Bookshelf.* $60/£38

THURBER, JAMES. The Wonderful O. NY: S&S, (1957). 1st ed. Marc Simont (illus). Fine in pict dj. *Bromer.* $75/£48

THURNE, J. M. W. Liber Fluviorum; or, River Scenery of France. London: Bohn, 1853. Engr title, 61 Fine steel-engr plts. (Sl foxing, soiling.) Gilt-stamped cl (shelfworn, spine tips frayed, inner joints broken). *Oinonen*.* $180/£115

THURSTON, CARL. Wildflowers of Southern California. Pasadena, 1936. Limp blue cl. VG. *Brooks.* $35/£22

THWAITES, REUBEN GOLD (ed). Collections.... Madison: WI State Hist Soc, 1902-1911. Vols 16-20. Navy cl, gilt spine titles. (Bkpl each vol, tender or cracked hinges last 3 vols.) *Bohling.* $200/£128

THWAITES, REUBEN GOLD (ed). Early Western Journals, 1748-1765. Cleveland: Clark, 1904. 1st ed. Frontis. Teg. Maroon cl. Good. *Karmiole.* $85/£54

THWAITES, REUBEN GOLD (ed). Early Western Travels. Cleveland: A.H. Clark, 1904-07. One of 750 numbered sets. 32 vols, incl Bodmer Atlas. 8vo w/folio Atlas. Pub's cl. Howes T255. *Swann*.* $3,680/£2,359

THWAITES, REUBEN GOLD (ed). Early Western Travels. Cleveland: A.H. Clark, 1904-7. 32 vols (incl 2 vols of index, folio atlas). Teg. Maroon cl, gilt-lettered spines. VG set (sl wear). Howes B695. *Reese.* $7,500/£4,808

THWAITES, REUBEN GOLD (ed). Early Western Travels. Vol. X. Cleveland, OH: A.H. Clark, 1904. 3 facs, 2 fldg maps. Teg. *Wantagh.* $75/£48

THWAITES, REUBEN GOLD (ed). I. Voyages of Tilly Buttrick, Jr. II. A Pedestrious Tour of Four Thousand Miles...1818. (By Estwick Evans.) Cleveland, OH: A.H. Clark, 1904. Port. Good (cvr dampspots; tps sl spotted). *Wantagh.* $65/£42

THWAITES, REUBEN GOLD (ed). I. Voyages, Travels, and Discoveries of Tilly Buttrick, Jr. (1812-1819). II. A Pedestrious Tour of Four Thousand Miles.... (By Estwick Evans.) Cleveland: Clark, 1904. 1st ed. Maroon cl (lt rubbed). *Karmiole.* $75/£48

THWAITES, REUBEN GOLD (ed). The Jesuit Relations and Allied Documents. Cleveland, OH, 1896-1901. 1st ed. Ltd to 750 numbered sets. 73 vols; w/1959 vol of Corrections & Addenda, 74 vols. Good (ex-lib; scattered marginal dampstains; last 6 vols w/cl faded, dampstains). Howes J107. *Wantagh.* $3,000/£1,923

THWAITES, REUBEN GOLD (ed). Voyages and Travels of an Indian Interpreter and Trader. Cleveland: A.H. Clark, 1904. Fldg map. (Lt worn, scratch fr bd), else VG. *Dumont.* $85/£54

TIBBLES, THOMAS. Buckskin and Blanket Days. GC: Doubleday, 1957. 1st ed. VG in dj (sl worn). *Lien.* $25/£16

TIBBLES, THOMAS. Buckskins and Blanket Days, Memoirs of a Friend of the Indians. Doubleday, 1957. Fine in VG dj. *Oregon.* $25/£16

TICE, GEORGE. Lincoln. New Brunswick, NJ: Rutgers Univ, 1984. 1st ed. Fine in illus dj. *Cahan.* $40/£26

TICE, JOHN H. Over the Plains, on the Mountains. St. Louis, 1872. 2 tps, 262,ivpp + 2pp ads. (Backstrip torn, chipped, middle portion missing; fr hinge weak), o/w Nice. *Bohling.* $200/£128

TICKNOR, GEORGE. Life, Letters, and Journals of George Ticknor. Boston: Osgood, 1877. 6th ed. 2 vols. Frontis ports. Good (ex-lib; soiled, chipped, hinges cracked). *Bohling.* $12/£8

TIDD, WILLIAM. The Practice of the Courts of King's Bench and Common Pleas. Phila: Robert H. Small, 1840. 3rd Amer ed. 2 vols. Contemp sheep (joint cracked). Usable. *Boswell.* $125/£80

TIDYMAN, ERNEST. Shaft. NY: Macmillan, 1970. 1st ed. Signed. Fine in dj. *Mordida.* $75/£48

TIETZE, HANS. European Master Drawings in the United States. NY, 1947. 160 plts. Good in dj (worn). *Washton.* $50/£32

TIETZE, HANS. Tintoretto. The Paintings and Drawings. London, 1948. Good. *Washton.* $75/£48

TIFFANY, L. H. Algae: The Grass of Many Waters. Spring./Balt: Thomas, 1938. 1st ed. 41 plts. VG. *Mikesh.* $15/£10

TIFFT, WILTON. Ellis Island. NY: W.W. Norton, 1971. 1st ed. VG in dj (rubbed). *Cahan.* $45/£29

TILGHMAN, ZOE A. Marshal of the Last Frontier. Glendale: Clark, 1940. 1st ed. One of 1050. Fldg map. Blue cl, gilt-lettered spine. Fine. *Argonaut.* $200/£128

TILGHMAN, ZOE A. Marshal of the Last Frontier. Glendale: Clark, 1964. Rev ed. One of 903. Map. Red cl, gilt-lettered spine. Fine. *Argonaut.* $90/£58

TILGHMAN, ZOE A. Outlaw Days, a True History of Early-Day Oklahoma Characters. (OK City): Harlow, 1926. VG in pict wrappers. *Bohling.* $40/£26

TILLINGHAST, PARDON ELISHA. Reminiscences of Service with the Twelfth Rhode Island Volunteers and a Memorial of Col. George H. Browne. Providence, RI, 1885. 1st ed. Ltd to 250. PNRISSHS Series 3, #15. 53pp. NF in ptd wrappers. *Mcgowan.* $45/£29

TILLOTSON, G. H. R. The Rajput Palaces. New Haven/London: Yale Univ, 1987. Map. Sound in dj. *Ars Artis.* $62/£40

TILLOTSON, M. R. and FRANK J. TAYLOR. Grand Canyon Country. Stanford, 1929. 1st ed. Pict cvrs (lt wear). *Five Quail.* $20/£13

TILNEY, F. C. The Principles of Photographic Pictorialism. Boston: Amer Photographic Pub, 1930. 1st ed. 80 b/w photo plts. VG in dj (foxed, lt edgeworn). *Cahan.* $75/£48

TILTMAN, R. F. Television Really Explained. (1952). 2 dbl-sided plts. (Pg edges sl discolored), o/w VG. *Whitehart.* $39/£25

TILTON, ALICE. (Pseud of Phoebe Atwood Taylor.) Dead Ernest. NY: Norton, 1944. 1st ed. Fine in dj (sl worn). *Else Fine.* $45/£29

TILTON, GEORGE FRED. Cap'n George Fred Himself. NY, 1929. Dec cl. VG. *High Latitude.* $25/£16

TILTON, THEODORE. The Two Hungry Kittens. NY: Tibbals & Whiting, 1866. Henry L. Stephens (illus). 8vo. 8ff. Nice (lt soil, tape traces spine) in blue/gold pict wrappers. *Bromer.* $175/£112

TIMBS, JOHN. A Century of Anecdote from 1760 to 1860. London: F. Warne, n.d. (1873). xxxi,597pp + pub's 10pp cat. *Cox.* $28/£18

TIMBS, JOHN. English Eccentrics and Eccentricities. London: C&W, 1898. New ed. Hand-colored frontis, xvi,578pp + 32pp pub's ads (tp, ads sl browned). Uncut, unopened in parts. *Edwards.* $55/£35

TIMBS, JOHN. Historic Ninepins. London: Lockwood, 1869. 1st ed. Frontis, xii,348pp. Blind-panelled cl (extrems rubbed), gilt. *Hollett.* $55/£35

TIMLIN, WILLIAM. The Ship That Sailed to Mars. London, (1923). 1st ed. 48 color plts. 1/4 imitation vellum (spine dknd), gilt. VG (ex-lib, spine label, accession # tp verso). *Swann*.* $977/£626

TIMPERLEY, C. H. A Dictionary of Printers and Printing with the Progress of Literature, Ancient and Modern. London: H. Johnson, 1939. 11 plts (lib stamps verso). 1/2 calf (rebacked, sl worn), gilt. *Maggs.* $203/£130

TING, WALASSE. Hot and Sour Soup. N.p.: Sam Francis Foundation, (1969). One of 1050 numbered. 22 color lithos. Contents loose as issued. Wrappers. Slipcase. *Swann*.* $201/£129

TINKER, C. B. (ed). Dr. Johnson and Fanny Burney, Being the Johnsonian Passages from the Works of Mme. D'Arblay. NY: Moffat, Yard, 1911. 1st ed. Port. Good (spine crown sl frayed). *Reese.* $20/£13

TINKER, E. L. Lafcadio Hearn's American Days. NY: Dodd, Mead, 1924. 2nd ed. Good (rear hinge crack). *Scribe's Perch*.* $10/£6

TINNEY, J. Compendious Treatise of Anatomy, Adapted to the Arts of Designing, Painting, and Sculpture. London: Laurie & Whittle, 1808. 8 legend leaves; 10 engr plts. Orig marbled bds, new cl spine. (Text wear), else Good. *Goodrich.* $195/£125

TINSLEY, HENRY C. Observations of a Retired Veteran. Staunton, VA, 1904. 1st ed. Paper labels. (Rear joint worn.) *Ginsberg.* $125/£80

Tiny Tots ABC Book [and] Tiny Tot's Story Book. Kenosha, WI: Abbott, n.d. 2 vols in 1. Obl 8vo. 28 leaves, incl 2 sets of cvrs (3 leaves detached). Spiral-bound pict black bds (rubbed). VG. *Blue Mountain.* $85/£54

TIPPER, H. The Growth and Influence of Music in Relation to Civilization. London, 1898. 1st ed. 224pp. VG+. *Middle Earth.* $45/£29

TIPPING, H. AVRAY. English Gardens. London, 1925. Aeg. (Spine sl faded), o/w Fine. *Henly.* $226/£145

TIPPING, H. AVRAY. English Homes. London: Country Life, 1920-1927. 1st eds. Folio. 7 vols (of 8: lacks 2nd vol of Period IV—vol 6 overall). Aeg. Blue cl (few spines lt faded), gilt. Very Nice set. *House.* $1,400/£897

TIPPING, H. AVRAY. English Homes. London: George Newnes, 1921-1929. 6 vols (of 9). 4 vols 1st eds, 2 vols 2nd eds. (Rubbed, spines faded, bumped.) *Christie's*.* $613/£393

TIPPING, H. AVRAY. English Homes. Period II, Vol I: Early Tudor 1485-1558. London: Country Life, 1929. 2nd ed. Sound. *Ars Artis.* $234/£150

TIPPING, H. AVRAY. English Homes. Periods 1-6. London, 1921-1926. 6 vols. 16 x 10.5'. Aeg. 2-tone cl (soiled, rubbed; spines heavily worn). *King.* $850/£545

TISSANDIER, GASTON and HENRY FRITH. Marvels of Earth, Air, and Water. London: Ward, Lock, (ca 1880). 129pp. Full calf prize binding (extrem wear). Kelfe Brothers signed binding. *Cullen.* $75/£48

TISSOT, M. Onanism: or, A Treatise upon the Disorders Produced by Masturbation: or, The Dangerous Effects of Secret and Excessive Venery. A. Hume (trans). London: Richardson & Urquart, 1781. 5th ed. xii,183pp. Contemp tree sheep (rebacked, spine laid down). (Few pp lt spotted), o/w VG. White. $172/£110

TITMARSH, M. A. (Pseud of W. M. Thackeray.) Mrs. Perkins's Ball. Chapman & Hall, n.d. (1847). Fldg illus. Marbled edges. Later 1/2 leather, marbled bds. VG (lt spotted). Tiger. $140/£90

TITMARSH, M. A. (Pseud of W. M. Thackeray.) Our Street. Chapman & Hall, 1848. Ad leaf. Aeg. Orig glazed bds (rubbed), later buckram spine. Good (sl spotting). Tiger. $125/£80

TITON, JEFF TODD. Early Downhome Blues. Urbana: Univ of IL, (1977). 1st ed. Sleeve w/record in rear. (Name), else Fine in VG + dj (sm chips). Between The Covers. $65/£42

TITUS, EDNA BROWN (ed). Union List of Serials in Libraries of the United States and Canada. NY: Wilson, 1965. 3rd ed. 5 vols. Buckram (shelfworn, ex-lib). Oinonen*. $140/£90

TITUS, WILLIAM A. Echoes from Old Eden. Fond du Lac, 1948. VG in ptd wraps. Bohling. $20/£13

TIXIER, VICTOR. Tixier's Travels on the Osage Prairies. John Francis McDermott (ed). Albert Salvan (trans). Norman: Univ of OK, 1940. 1st ed. VG in dj. Howes T276. Lien. $45/£29

TJADER, RICHARD. The Big Game of Africa. NY/London: Appleton, 1910. 1st ed. Frontis, fldg map. Grn gilt cl. (Sl waterstain bottom of leaves), else VG. Terramedia. $150/£96

Tobacco, Its Culture and Manufacture. London, 1936. 2nd ed. (Tp sl spotted; sl bumped.) Edwards. $23/£15

TOBE, JOHN H. Hunza. Emmaus, PA: Rodale Bks, 1960. 1st ed. Illus eps. VG in dj (sl torn). Worldwide. $35/£22

TODD, F. S. Waterfowl: Ducks, Geese and Swans of the World. San Diego: Sea World, 1979. #1280/1500 signed. Gilt-dec full leather. VF in VG + slipcase. Mikesh. $175/£112

TODD, HELEN. A Man Named Grant. Boston, 1940. 1st ed. Fine in dj (worn). Pratt. $32/£21

TODD, ROBERT BENTLEY and WILLIAM BOWMAN. The Physiological Anatomy and Physiology of Man. Phila, 1857. (1st ed.) Full leather (worn, chipped). Good. Doctor's Library. $80/£51

TODD, RUTHVEN. Tracks in the Snow. London, 1946. (Spine paint flaking.) Washton. $35/£22

TODD, RUTHVEN. Until Now. Fortune, (1942). 1st Eng ed. Very Nice (bkpl) in dj (sl stained, rubbed). Clearwater. $62/£40

TODD, SERENO EDWARDS. The Apple Culturist. NY: Harper, 1871. 1st ed. 334pp + ads. Grn cl (chip, rubbed). Good. Second Life. $75/£48

TODD, WILLIAM B. Suppressed Commentaries on the Wiseian Forgeries. Austin: Humanities Research Center, Univ of TX, (c1969). 1st ed. One of 750 ptd. 1 fold-out. Black cl, ptd label. NF. Heller. $35/£22

TODHUNTER, JOHN. Sounds and Sweet Airs. London: Elkin Mathews, 1905 (1904). 1st ed. Uncut. Orig ptd wrappers. (Sl browned; sm piece missing spine head.) Cox. $23/£15

TOEPPERWEIN, HERMAN. Rebel in Blue. NY, 1963. 1st ed. Fine in dj (sl worn). Pratt. $30/£19

Toilet. (By Stacey Grimaldi.) London: (Rock Bros & Payne), n.d. Signed on lower turn-in: Sangorski & Sutcliffe. This copy undated. 9 hand-colored plts w/all flaps present. 12mo. Aeg. Full blue crushed morocco du cap (fr cvr, spine lt sunned), gilt. Book Block. $1,250/£801

TOKLAS, ALICE B. Aromas and Flavors of Past and Present. NY, 1958. 1st Amer ed. NF (edges sl rubbed) in dj (spine sl soiled, extrems sl chipped, sm tear). Polyanthos. $30/£19

TOKLAS, ALICE B. Aromas and Flavours Past and Present. London, 1959. 1st Eng ed. Very Nice (name; sl bumped) in dj (sl nicked, mkd). Clearwater. $47/£30

TOKLAS, ALICE B. What Is Remembered. NY: Holt, Rinehart & Winston, (1963). 1st ed. NF (news clipping offset feps) in dj. Turtle Island. $45/£29

TOKLAS, ALICE B. What Is Remembered. London, 1963. 1st Eng ed. Very Nice in dj (neatly repaired). Clearwater. $55/£35

TOLD, SILAS. The Life of Mr. Silas Told Written by Himself. London: Epworth, 1954. Reissue. Engr frontis. Boswell. $50/£32

TOLKIEN, J. R. R. The Adventures of Tom Bombadil. London, 1962. 1st ed. Dj (sl frayed). Typographeum. $60/£38

TOLKIEN, J. R. R. The Annotated Hobbit. Boston: Houghton, Mifflin, 1988. 1st ed. NF in dj. Antic Hay. $35/£22

TOLKIEN, J. R. R. Farmer Giles of Ham. Boston: Houghton Mifflin, 1950. 1st US ed. Pauline Baynes (illus). 5 1/4 x 8. 80pp. Good in dj (chipped, few stains). Cattermole. $100/£64

TOLKIEN, J. R. R. The Father Christmas Letters. Boston: HM, 1976. 1st ed. 8 3/4 x 11. 48pp. Fine in dj. Cattermole. $60/£38

TOLKIEN, J. R. R. The Fellowship of the Ring. Allen & Unwin, 1955. 4th imp of 1st ed. Lg 8vo. 423pp; full-pg map, fldg pict map. VG + in dj (lt worn). Bookmark. $109/£70

TOLKIEN, J. R. R. The Return of the King. H-M, 1956. 1st Amer ed. NF in NF dj (spine head chip, price-clipped). Aronovitz. $275/£176

TOLKIEN, J. R. R. The Return of the King. Allen & Unwin, 1963. 10th imp of 1st ed. Lg 8vo. 416pp; lg fldg pict map. (Edges lt rubbed), else VG + in dj (frayed). Bookmark. $70/£45

TOLKIEN, J. R. R. The Silmarillion. London: George Allen & Unwin, (1977). 1st Eng ed. Fine in dj. Antic Hay. $45/£29

TOLKIEN, J. R. R. The Silmarillion. Boston: Houghton, Mifflin, 1977. 1st Amer ed, 1st issue, w/perfect type p299 and w/'Father' for Farmer Giles p(3). Fine in NF dj. Antic Hay. $20/£13

TOLKIEN, J. R. R. The Silmarillion. Christopher Tolkien (ed). Allen & Unwin, 1977. 5th imp of 1st ed. Lg 8vo. 365pp; lg fldg pict map. Fine in dj. Bookmark. $28/£18

TOLKIEN, J. R. R. Tree and Leaf. George Allen & Unwin, 1964. 1st ed. Fine in dj (spine sl faded, closed tear at spine fold). Certo. $150/£96

TOLKIEN, J. R. R. Tree and Leaf. London, 1964. 1st Eng ed. Fine in dj (sl faded). Clearwater. $78/£50

TOLKIEN, J. R. R. Tree and Leaf. Riverside: Houghton Mifflin, 1965. 1st Amer ed. NF in NF dj (lt browned). Metropolitan*. $69/£44

TOLKIEN, J. R. R. and E. V. GORDON. Sir Gawain and the Green Knight. Oxford: OUP, 1967. 2nd ed. 5 3/4 x 8 3/4. 232pp. VG in dj. Cattermole. $25/£16

TOLLER, ERNST. Brockenbrow. A Tragedy.... Vera Mendel (trans). Nonesuch, (1926). 1st Eng ed. Georg Grosz (illus). 6 litho plts. Uncut. Good in mottled dec bds (overlapping edge at spine head chipped away), paper label. Cox. $101/£65

TOLLIVER, ARTHUR S. (Pseud of Vance Randolph.) The Wild Adventures of Davy Crockett. Girard, KS: Haldeman-Julius, (1944). VG in ptd wraps. Bohling. $22/£14

TOLLIVER, ARTHUR S. (Pseud of Vance Randolph.) The Wild Adventures of Davy Crockett. Girard: Haldeman-Julius, 1944. 1st ed. Pb. Good (fr wrap present but detached). *Beasley.* $25/£16

TOLMAN, NEWTON F. The Search for General Miles. NY, (1968). 1st ed. Fine in Fine dj. *Pratt.* $32/£21

TOLSTOI, A. K. The Terrible Czar. H. Clare Filmore (trans). Sampson, Low, Marston, 1892. 2nd ed. 2 vols. Good (spines bumped, nick vol II head). *Tiger.* $94/£60

TOLSTOI, LEO. The Journal of Leo Tolstoi (First Volume—1895-1899). Rose Strunsky (trans). NY: Knopf, 1917. 1st ed in English. (Bkpls), o/w Fine. *Hermitage.* $45/£29

TOLSTOI, LEO. The Kreutzer Sonata. Benj. R. Tucker (trans). Boston: Benj. R. Tucker, 1890. 1st ed in English. (Sm spot fr cvr, lt rubbing), o/w Fine. *Hermitage.* $100/£64

TOLSTOI, LYOF N. Anna Karenina. Thomas Y. Crowell, 1886. 1st US ed, 1st ed in English. 1st issue binding: lt grn dec in blue/orange/gold. VG (bkpl, fr hinge sl starting). *Williams.* $585/£375

TOLSTOY, LEO. Anna Karenina. Nathan Haskell Dole (trans). NY: Thomas Crowell, (1886). 1st Amer ed. Tan cl, gilt. (Fr hinge paper cracked, cvr soiled), else VG. *Macdonnell.* $150/£96

TOLSTOY, LEO. The Awakening. NY: Street & Smith, 1900. 1st US ed. VG+ in illus cl-cvrd bds. *Lame Duck.* $85/£54

TOLSTOY, LEO. The Devil. NY: Harper, 1926. 1st US ed. (Surface loss bd edges), else VG+ in dj (spine tanned, internal tear). *Lame Duck.* $65/£42

TOLSTOY, LEO. The Invaders. Nathan Haskell Dole (trans). NY: Thomas Y. Crowell, (1887). 1st Amer ed. Dec brn cl. VG (sl dampstain edge, corners). *Antic Hay.* $85/£54

TOLSTOY, LEO. The Law of Love and the Law of Violence. Mary K. Tolstoy (trans). NY: Rudolph Field, (1948). 1st ed in English. Fine in dj (sl worn, sm tear). *Antic Hay.* $35/£22

TOLSTOY, LEO. Life Is Worth Living. NY: Charles L. Webster, 1892. 1st Amer ed. Grn cl, gilt. Nice (lt rubbed). *Macdonnell.* $75/£48

TOLSTOY, LEO. My Confession. NY: Thomas Crowell, (1887). 1st Amer ed. Pale grn cl, gilt. VG. *Macdonnell.* $85/£54

TOLSTOY, LEO. My Religion. Huntington Smith (trans). NY: Crowell, (1885). 1st Amer ed. Dec cl. Good (worn). *Antic Hay.* $35/£22

TOLSTOY, LEO. The Old Devil and the Three Little Devils. NY: Webster, 1891. 1st US ed. (Pg edges sl insect-damaged), else VG in illus pub's cl. *Lame Duck.* $150/£96

TOLSTOY, LEO. A Russian Proprietor. Nathan Haskell Dole (trans). NY: Thomas Crowell, 1887. 1st Amer ed. Grn cl, gilt. (Spine lt worn), else Fine. *Macdonnell.* $100/£64

TOLSTOY, LEO. Tolstoy's Letters. 1828-1910. R. F. Christian (ed). Athlone, 1978. 2 vols. 23 plts. Djs (spines lt faded). *Edwards.* $31/£20

TOLZMANN, DON HEINRICH (comp). German Americana: A Bibliography. Metuchen, NJ: Scarecrow, (1975). Brn cl, gilt. Fine, w/o dj as issued. *Heller.* $35/£22

Tom the Piper's Son. Blackie, n.d. 4to. (32)pp; 12 color plts by Frank Adams. Pict bds, cl spine. VG. *Bookmark.* $23/£15

TOMBLESON, WILLIAM and WILLIAM GRAY FEARNSIDE. Eighty Picturesque Views on the Thames and Medway. London, (1834). 4,84pp (lacks tp, fep detached but present); panoramic map (age stains), 79 plts (sl foxing). Good (bumps). *Scribe's Perch*.* $160/£103

TOME, PHILIP. Pioneer Life; or, Thirty Years a Hunter. Buffalo: The Author, 1854. 1st ed. 12mo. Frontis, viii,9-238pp. Orig cl-cvrd bds. (Rebacked, recased w/recent cl spine; text lt spotted, inner margin lt dampstained, new eps), else Good. Howes T288. *Brown.* $1,000/£641

TOMES, J. A System of Dental Surgery. 1906. 5th ed. (Joint sl cracked, spine sl worn, stained.) *Whitehart.* $39/£25

TOMKINSON, G. A Select Bibliography of the Principal Modern Presses, Public and Private in Great Britain and Ireland. First Editions Club, 1928. 1/4 cl. VG. *Moss.* $109/£70

TOMLINE, GEORGE. Memoirs of the Life of the Right Honourable William Pitt. John Murray, 1821. 2nd ed. 3 vols. Marbled eps. 1/2 calf, marbled bds, raised bands. (Bkpl, lt foxing throughout; upper bd, feps vol 1 detached; spines sl chipped, discolored; joints cracked, splitting; sl rubbed.) *Edwards.* $133/£85

TOMLINSON, CHARLES (ed). Cyclopaedia of Useful Arts.... London/NY, 1854. 2 vols. 832; 1052pp. 1/2 morocco, marbled bds (rubbed, vol 2 lacks fr cvr). Contents VG. *New Hampshire*.* $80/£51

TOMLINSON, H. M. All Our Yesterdays. London, 1930. #904/1025 signed. *Typographeum.* $65/£42

TOMLINSON, H. M. All Our Yesterdays. NY, 1930. #211/329 (of 350) signed. Uncut, partly unopened. Paper label (sl rubbed). Fine (bkpl; spine sunned, corners sl rubbed). *Polyanthos.* $35/£22

TOMLINSON, H. M. All Our Yesterdays. NY: Harper, 1930. 1st Amer ed. NF in VG dj (sm chips). *Antic Hay.* $25/£16

TOMLINSON, H. M. Illusion: 1915. Heinemann, 1929. 1st ed. #212/525 signed. Teg, others uncut, partly unopened. Buckram-backed batik bds. *Cox.* $23/£15

TOMLINSON, H. M. The Sea and the Jungle. London, (1930). 16 wood engrs by Clare Leighton. VG. *Truepenny.* $30/£19

TOMLINSON, H. M. The Sea and the Jungle. London, 1930. 1st ed. Uncut, partly unopened. Fine (spine sl sunned). *Polyanthos.* $75/£48

TOMLINSON, H. M. The Sea and the Jungle. London: Duckworth, 1930. 1st ed thus. 7 full-pg woodcuts. Cl-backed dec bds (few spots). *Hollett.* $39/£25

TOMLINSON, H. M. The Snows of Helicon. London: Heinemann, (1933). 1st Eng ed. NF in dj (wear). *Antic Hay.* $30/£19

TOMLINSON, H. M. Thomas Hardy. NY: Crosby Gaige, 1929. 1st ed. #692/761. Litho frontis signed by Tomlinson and Zhenya Gay (artist). Uncut. Good in russet cl (corners bumped). *Cox.* $55/£35

TOMLINSON, H. M. Thomas Hardy. NY: Crosby Gaige, 1929. Ltd to 761 numbered, signed by Tomlinson & Zhenya Gay (artist). Litho frontis port. Fine in acetate dj. *Antic Hay.* $125/£80

TOMLINSON, H. M. Waiting for Daylight. London: Cassell, 1922. 1st ed. Purple cl. VG in dj (wear, tears, sm chips). *Antic Hay.* $50/£32

TOMLINSON, JULIETTE (ed). The Paintings and the Journal of Joseph Whiting Stock. CT: Wesleyan Univ, 1976. Frontis port. Fine in color dj. *Europa.* $23/£15

TOMORY, PETER. The Life and Art of Henry Fuseli. NY/WA, 1972. 13 color plts. Good. *Washton.* $95/£61

TOMOVIC, RAJKO and WALTER J. KARPLUS. High-Speed Analog Computers. NY: Wiley, (1962). 1st ed. NF (stamp) in dj (sl worn). Glaser. $85/£54

TOMPKINS, E. P. and J. LEE DAVIS. The Natural Bridge and Its Historical Surroundings. Natural Bridge, 1939. Color frontis. VG- (photo taped to fep). Book Broker. $35/£22

TOMPKINS, FRANK. Chasing Villa. Harrisburg, 1934. 1st ed. Pict cvr. VG +. Pratt. $100/£64

TONELLI, EDITH A. and JOHN GOSSAGE (eds). Louis Faurer: Photographs from Philadelphia and New York, 1937-1973. College Park: Art Gallery, Univ of MD, March 10-April 23, 1981. 1st ed. 1 color, 35 b/w photos. (Name stamp), else Fine in pict stiff wrappers. Cahan. $25/£16

TONER, J. M. The Medical Men of the Revolution.... Phila: Collins, 1876. 1st ed. 1/4 cl (sm hole spine head, sm stain fr bd). Goodrich. $145/£93

Tony Sarg's Treasure Book, Rip van Winkle, Alice in Wonderland and Treasure Island. NY: B.F. Jay, 1942. 11.5x9.5x3. (22)pp (ink inscrip, sl worn), 3 mechanical movements (lacks 1). Box (reinforced), color pict label (soiled). King. $250/£160

Tony Sarg's Treasure Book. NY: B.F. Jay, 1942. Folio. 5 mechanicals. Mechanical diarama fr cvr, inside back bd. (Crayon name, sl exterior wear.) Metropolitan*. $230/£147

TOOLEY, R. V. Some English Books with Coloured Plates, Their Points, Collations and Values. London: Ingpen & Grant, 1935. 1st ed. Teg, rest uncut. Polished buckram (rubbed, spotted). Oak Knoll. $100/£64

TOOLEY, R. V. and CHARLES BRICKER. Landmarks of Mapmaking. Amsterdam: Elsevier, 1968. VG in dj (edgeworn, tape repairs verso). Pacific*. $104/£67

TOOLEY, R. V. and CHARLES BRICKER. Landmarks of Mapmaking. NY, 1976. 14 fldg maps. VG in dj. Argosy. $200/£128

TOOMBS, SAMUEL. New Jersey Troops in the Gettysburg Campaign from June 5 to July 32, 1863. Orange, NJ, 1888. 1st ed. 406pp. VG. Pratt. $75/£48

TOOMER, JEAN. Essentials. Chicago: Private Ed, 1931. 1st ed. One of 1000 numbered; this copy unnumbered. Black cl, ptd labels. (Sl dkng gutter fr pastedown), else Fine in dj. Cahan. $650/£417

TOOMEY, DANIEL CARROLL. The Civil War in Maryland. Balt: Toomey Press, (1983). 1st ed. Fine in NF dj. Mcgowan. $25/£16

TOPLISS, HELEN. Tom Roberts 1856-1931: A Catalogue Raisonne. Melbourne: Oxford, (1985). 2 vols. Fine in Fine djs. Metropolitan*. $172/£110

TOPONCE, ALEXANDER. Reminiscences of Alexander Toponce, Pioneer, 1839-1923. (Ogden, VT: Katie Toponce, 1923.) 1st ed. 14 photo plts. (Inner hinges reinforced w/paper tape.) Burgundy fabricoid. Karmiole. $100/£64

Topsy. NY: McLoughlin Bros, n.d. 9x4. (12)pp. Stiff color wraps (sl wear, creases); die-cut on top and right side outlining black girl in straw hat holding a basket and watermelon slice. King. $95/£61

TORKINGTON, RICHARD. Ye Oldest Diarie of Englysshe Travell...of Sir Richard Torkington to Jerusalem in 1517. W. J. Loftie (ed). Field & Tuer, n.d. (1884). 1st ed. (8),xxxviii,72,(8)pp. Paper sides, imitation parchment wrapper (backstrip sl defective). Cox. $39/£25

TORRES, ELIAS L. Twenty Episodes in the Life of Pancho Villa. Austin: Encino, 1973. Brn cl. Dj. Dawson. $50/£32

TORREY, JOHN. A Flora of the State of New York. Vol 1 only. Albany, 1843. 484pp; 72 plts. Orig brn blind-stamped cl, gilt. (Some plts foxed, ex-lib; spine chips repaired), else Good. Price. $175/£112

TORREY, JOHN. A Flora of the State of New-York. Albany, 1843. Vol 1 only. 484pp; 72 full-pg color plts. (Plts sl spotted, 1 torn, 1 stained), else Good. King. $350/£224

TORREY, RAYMOND H. New York Walk Book. NY: American Geographical Soc, 1923. (2nd ptg.) 8 maps. VG (personal lib mks; sl soiled). Bohling. $28/£18

TORRINGTON, JOHN BYNG. The Torrington Diaries. C. Bruyn Andrews (ed). London, 1934-6. 1st eds. 3 vols. Frontis ports. (Spines faded, extrems frayed.) Edwards. $62/£40

TORY, GEOFFROY. Champ Fleury. NY: Grolier, 1927. One of 390. Teg. Vellum spine, gilt title, tan paste paper w/fleur-de-lis. Fine (neat bk label fep) in dj (few repaired tears, mks). Heller. $750/£481

TOTH, KARL. Woman and Rococo in France. Roger Abingdon (trans). Phila, 1931. Color frontis port, 111 plts. (Upper hinge cracked, feps lt browned.) Partially unopened. Dj (ragged). Edwards. $47/£30

TOULOUSE-LAUTREC, HENRI DE. Unpublished Correspondence of Henri de Toulouse-Lautrec. Lucien Goldschmidt and Herbert Schimmel (eds). London: Phaidon, 1969. Fldg chart. Fine in color dj. Europa. $23/£15

Tour of Doctor Syntax.... (By Wm. Combe.) London, (1815), 1820, (1821). Vol 1: 6th ed; vols 2-3: 1st ed. 3 vols. 84 hand-colored plts by Thomas Rowlandson. Full polished calf (rubbed, vol 3 cvrs detached), gilt. Kane*. $400/£256

Tour of H.R.H. the Prince of Wales through British America and the United States by a British Canadian. (By Henry James Morgan.) Montreal, 1860. 1st ed. 271pp, port. (Ink name, foxing; staining, spine ends frayed.) King. $45/£29

Tour on the Prairies. (By Washington Irving.) Phila: Carey, Lea & Blanchard, 1835. 1st Amer ed, 1st state. 274pp,24pp ads. (Lt foxing, fep removed; (spine label rubbed, lettering no longer legible), else Nice. Howes I86. Bohling. $200/£128

Tour through England: Described in a Series of Letters from a Young Gentleman to His Sister. T.H. (rev). London: William Darton, 1821. 4th ed w/additions. 12mo. iv+212pp; 6 perfect full-pg copper engrs (incl frontis). Red roan spine (lt rubbed), marbled paper on bds (scuffed, sm label inside upper cvr). VG. Hobbyhorse. $150/£96

TOURGEE, ALBION W. The Story of a Thousand. Buffalo, 1896. 1st ed. VG (fr hinge cracked). Mcclintock. $125/£80

TOURGEE, ALBION. A Fool's Errand...Part II. The Invisible Empire. NY: Fords, Howard & Hulbert, 1880. 1st ed thus. 521pp + ads. Pict brn cl (sl rubbed). NF. Archer. $20/£13

Tourist's Guide to the English Lakes. London: T. Nelson, n.d. (c.1870). 61pp; map, 12 chromolitho plts. (Few spots.) Very Attractive. Hollett. $101/£65

Tourist, or Pocket Manual for Travellers on the Hudson River, the Western Canal and Stage Road to Niagara Falls. (By Robert J. Vandewater.) NY: Harper, 1835. 4th ed. Long fldg frontis map (fold tear), 106pp. Cl, ptd label. VG (lt worn, foxed). Howes V28. Bohling. $175/£112

TOURNEY, LEONARD. Low Treason. NY: Dutton, 1982. 1st ed. VF in dj. Mordida. $35/£22

TOURNIER, MICHEL. The Erl-King. London: Collins, 1972. 1st British ed. NF in dj (price-clipped). Lame Duck. $50/£32

TOURNIER, MICHEL. The Fetishist. Barbara Wright (trans). GC: Doubleday, 1984. 1st ed. New in New dj. Bernard. $15/£10

TOURNIER, MICHEL. Friday and Robinson. NY: Knopf, 1972. 1st US ed. (Rmdr stamp bottom edge), else NF in dj (1-inch tear, creases). Lame Duck. $65/£42

TOURNIER, MICHEL. The Ogre. GC: Doubleday, 1972. 1st US ed. Fine in dj. *Lame Duck*. $45/£29

TOUSEY, THOMAS G. Military History of Carlisle and Carlisle Barracks. Richmond: Dietz, 1939. 1st ed. Fldg chart. Fine in illus dj. *Cahan*. $45/£29

TOVEY, DUNCAN C. (ed). Letters and Relics in Great Part Hitherto Unpublished. Cambridge, 1890. 1st ed. xvi,312pp. Sound (backstrip faded). *Cox*. $39/£25

TOWLE, NANCY. Vicissitudes Illustrated, in the Experience of Nancy Towle in Europe and America. Charleston: The Author, 1832. 1st ed. Frontis, 294pp. Recent 1/2 calf, marbled bds. (Sl browned, spotted; rebound), else VG. Howes T312. *Brown*. $400/£256

TOWLE, VIRGINIA ROWE. Vigilante Woman. South Brunswick: A.S. Barnes, (1966). 1st ed. Dk blue cl. Fine in dj. *Argonaut*. $40/£26

TOWLER, J. The Silver Sunbeam. NY: E. & H.T. Anthony, 1879. 9th ed. Mtd silver print frontis, xvi,(i),599,(13),(30)pp. Gilt/blind-dec cl. (Sm text stains; spine ends worn, cl rubbed, stained), o/w Good. *Cahan*. $225/£144

TOWNDROW, KENNETH R. Works of Alfred Stevens, Sculptor, Painter, Designer, in the Tate Gallery. London: Tate, 1950. 27 plts. Fine in dj. *Europa*. $28/£18

TOWNE, ROBERT D. The Teddy Bears at School. Chicago, (1907). J.R. Bray (illus). 7x5. (12)pp (ink name). Pict bds (worn, spine chipped). *King*. $60/£38

TOWNE, ROBERT D. The Teddy Bears in a Smashup. Chicago, (1907). J.R. Bray (illus). 7x5. (12)pp (ink name). Pict bds (spine badly chipped). *King*. $50/£32

TOWNE, ROBERT D. Teddy Bears on a Lark. Chicago, (1907). J.R. Bray (illus). 7x5. (12)pp. Pict bds (sm pieces of cello-tape spine, extrems worn). *King*. $60/£38

TOWNE, ROBERT D. The Teddy Bears on a Toboggan. Chicago, (1907). J.R. Bray (illus). 7x5. (12)pp. Pict bds (wear, spine cello-tape repaired). *King*. $60/£38

TOWNE, STUART. Death Out of Thin Air. NY: Coward McCann, 1940. 1st ed. (Fly, pastedown stained; sl loose, bumped.) Dj (edgewear, creases, chips). *Metropolitan**. $109/£70

TOWNSEND, CHARLES WENDELL (ed). Captain Cartwright and His Labrador Journal. Boston, 1911. 1st ed thus. Map. (Back cvr stained.) *New Hampshire**. $50/£32

TOWNSEND, E. D. The California Diary of Gen. E. D. Townsend. Malcolm Edwards (ed). Ward Ritchie, (1970). VG in slipcase. *Lien*. $35/£22

TOWNSEND, E. D. The California Diary of General E. D. Townsend. Malcolm Edwards (ed). Ward Ritchie, 1970. Port. Black cl, gilt. Fine in pub's slipcase. *Cady*. $25/£16

TOWNSEND, GEORGE. Campaigns of a Non-Combatant, and His Romaunt Abroad During the War. (Alexandria, VA: Time-Life Books, 1982.) Orig full leather. Fine. *Mcgowan*. $15/£10

TOWNSEND, GEORGE. Journal of a Tour in Italy in 1850.... Francis & John Rivington, 1850. 1st ed. xii,300pp (lt spotted). Good in contemp 1/2 rose calf, backstrip gilt (lacks top 20mm), morocco label. *Cox*. $70/£45

TOWNSEND, JOHN K. Narrative of a Journey Across the Rocky Mountains to the Columbia River.... Phila: Henry Perkins, 1839. (Dampstained, foxed; spine split, faded, edgeworn.) *Metropolitan**. $200/£128

TOWNSEND, JOHN T. The Code of Procedure, of the State of New York. NY: John S. Voorhies, 1857. 5th ed. Mod 1/4 calf (browning). Attractive. *Boswell*. $150/£96

TOWNSHEND, CHAUNCY HARE. Facts in Mesmerism, or Animal Magnetism. Boston: Charles C. Little & James Brown, 1841. 1st US ed. xi,539pp (hinges split, lacks fr blanks, ink sig, bkpl, ink # prelim margin). Orig brn blind cl (sunned, lt frayed, ex-lib spine label), gilt. *Baltimore**. $25/£16

TOWNSHEND, R. B. Last Memories of a Tenderfoot. London: John Lane/Bodley Head, 1926. 1st ed. (Cl sl faded), else VG. *Cahan*. $60/£38

TOY, BARBARA. The Way of the Chariots. London: John Murray, 1964. 1st ed. Map. (Eps stained), o/w VG in dj. *Worldwide*. $18/£12

TOYNBEE, J. M. C. Death and Burial in the Roman World. Ithaca: Cornell Univ, (1971). Good in dj (torn). *Archaeologia*. $65/£42

TOYNBEE, PHILIP. The Barricades. London, 1943. 1st Eng ed. Good in dj remnant. *Clearwater*. $31/£20

TOYNBEE, PHILIP. Pantaloon. NY: Harper, 1961. 1st ed, Amer issue. Fine in NF dj. *Reese*. $40/£26

TRACE, MARGARET A. Block Building. Springfield, MA: Milton Bradley, (1928). 4to. Frontis, xiii,221,(3)pp (shaken), incl 102pp of illus. Blue cl (stained, rubbed, bumped, spine faded), gilt (faded). Fair. *Blue Mountain*. $28/£18

TRACHTENBERG, JOSHUA. Jewish Magic and Superstitions. NY, 1939. 1st ed. (Sm cut spine top), o/w VG +. *Middle Earth*. $145/£93

TRACY, LOUIS. The Pelham Affair. NY: Clode, (1923). 1st Amer ed. Nice in dj (chipped, soiled). *Metropolitan**. $28/£18

Tragedy of Tragedies. (By Henry Fielding.) London: J. Watts, 1751. 4th ed. Marbled eps. 3/4 brn morocco, marbled bds. VG (fr joint tender). *Sumner & Stillman*. $175/£112

TRAGER, PHILIP. Echoes of Silence. (Danbury, CT): Scroll, 1972. 1st ed. Ltd to 1000 numbered. 12 full-pg b/w photos. Cl, ptd label. (Owner stamp; sl bumped), else NF. *Cahan*. $65/£42

Tragi-Comic History of the Burial of Cock Robin. Phila: Benjamin Warner, 1821. 16mo. Frontis (as fr pastedown), 8 engr plts. Orig plain pink bds. (Browned throughout; edges worn.) *Oinonen**. $90/£58

TRAILL, H. D. and S. J. MANN. Social England. NY/London, 1901-04. 6 vols. (Cl sl rubbed.) *Argosy*. $250/£160

TRAIN, ARTHUR. The Prisoner at the Bar, Sidelights on the Administration of Criminal Justice. NY: Scribner, 1924. *Boswell*. $35/£22

Traits of American Indian Life and Character, By a Fur Trader. (By Peter Skeene Ogden.) SF: Grabhorn, 1933. One of 500 (unstated). 6 plts. Brn paper-cvrd bds, black cl spine strip; paper spine, cvr labels. NF. *Harrington*. $125/£80

TRALBAUT, MARC EDO. Vincent Van Gogh. NY: Viking, 1969. *Metropolitan**. $34/£22

Transactions of the Eighth Annual Re-Union of the Oregon Pioneer Association; for 1880.... Salem, OR, 1881. 64pp. Orig ptd wrappers bound into later bds. VG. *Reese*. $125/£80

Transactions of the Forty-Second Annual Reunion of the Oregon Pioneer Association.... Portland, OR, 1917. Frontis. VG in ptd wrappers. *Reese*. $40/£26

Transactions of the Seventh Annual Re-Union of the Oregon Pioneer Association; for 1879.... Salem, OR, 1880. 63pp. VG (few creases) in ptd wrappers. *Reese*. $150/£96

Transactions of the Third Annual Re-union of the Oregon Pioneer Association. Salem: E.M. Waite, 1876. 88pp. VG in paper wrappers (frayed). *Zubal**. $25/£16

Transactions of the Woolhope Naturalists' Field Club. 1895, 1896, 1897. Hereford, 1898. 14 plts and maps. Blind-ruled cl, gilt. *Edwards.* $47/£30

TRAPP, MARIA AUGUSTA. The Story of the Trapp Family Singers. Phila/NY: Lippincott, (1951). Later imp of 1st ed but signed by multitude of Trapp family members incl author on fep. (Ink name; dj panel affixed to pastedown), else Good. *Reese.* $35/£22

TRAPROCK, WALTER E. (Pseud of Don Marquis.) My Northern Exposure. NY: Putnam, 1922. Dec eps. Good. *Scribe's Perch*.* $14/£9

TRAUB, HAMILTON P. The Amaryllis Manual. NY, 1958. Color frontis. VG. *Brooks.* $47/£30

TRAUBEL, HORACE. With Walt Whitman in Camden April 8-September 14, 1889. Gertrude Traubel (ed). Carbondale: SIU, (1964). 1st ed. Port. Teg. VF in dj. *Reese.* $35/£22

Traveller's Steamboat and Railroad Guide to the Hudson River.... NY: Gaylord Watson, 1871. 50pp; 2 maps (1 hand-colored). Orig wraps. Good (soiled, worn). *Waverly*.* $71/£46

TRAVEN, B. The Carreta. Hill & Wang, (1970). 1st US ed. VG + in dj. *Certo.* $25/£16

TRAVEN, B. The Carreta. NY, 1970. 1st Amer ed. NF in NF dj. *Warren.* $60/£38

TRAVEN, B. The Creation of the Sun and the Moon. NY, 1968. 1st Amer ed. Fine in Fine dj. *Warren.* $70/£45

TRAVEN, B. The Night Visitor and Other Stories. NY, 1966. 1st Amer ed. Fine in NF dj. *Warren.* $85/£54

TRAVEN, B. The Rebellion of the Hanged. NY: Knopf, 1952. 1st US ed. (Bkpl), else NF in illus dj (dampstain verso rear). *Lame Duck.* $125/£80

TRAVERS, J. Starting from Scratch: Our Island for Ocelots. NY: Taplinger, 1975. 1st ed. Fine in Fine dj. *Mikesh.* $20/£13

TRAVERS, J. WADSWORTH. From Coast to Coast via the Old Spanish Trail. San Diego: Travers, 1929. VG in wraps. *Gibbs.* $10/£6

TRAVERS, MORRIS W. The Discovery of the Rare Gasses. London, 1928. Frontis. (Eps lt spotted; spine faded, sl chipped.) *Edwards.* $47/£30

TRAVERS, P. L. Friend Monkey. London: Collins, 1972. 1st ed. Fine in NF dj (price-clipped). *Antic Hay.* $25/£16

TRAVERS, P. L. Mary Poppins in the Park. NY: Harcourt, Brace, (1952). 1st US ed. Mary Shepard (illus). NF in VG dj (spine corner chipped). *Bernard.* $40/£26

TRAVERS, P. L. Mary Poppins in the Park. NY: HBJ, 1952. 1st ed. Mary Shepard (illus). 5 x 7 1/2. 235pp. Fine in dj. *Cattermole.* $45/£29

TRAVERS, P. L. Mary Poppins. NY: Reynal & Hitchcock, (1934). 1st Amer ed. 8vo. 27 b/w illus by Mary Shepard. VG (eps sl browned; nicks, spine chip) in dj. *Houle.* $350/£224

TRAVERS, ROSALIND. Letters from Finland August, 1908-March, 1909. London, 1911. Fldg map. (Feps lt browned; spine sl chipped.) *Edwards.* $47/£30

TRAVIS, N. J. and E. J. COCKS. The Tincal Trail. London: Harrap, (1984). Dj. *Dawson.* $25/£16

TRAVIS, WALTER J. Practical Golf. NY: Harper, 1903. New, rev ed. Dec grn cl, gilt. (Eps sl foxed; ends sl rubbed), else VG. *Pacific*.* $150/£96

TRAYLOR, SAMUEL W. Out of the Southwest, a Texas Boy. (Allentown, PA, 1936.) Presentation copy. Red/black cl. VG + . *Bohling.* $22/£14

TREADWELL, EDWARD F. The Cattle King. NY: Macmillan, 1931. 1st ed. Frontis port. Tan cl. Fine in dec dj. Howes T336. *Argonaut.* $125/£80

TREASE, G. E. Pharmacy in History. London: Bailliere, Tindall & Cox, 1964. VG in dj. *Savona.* $31/£20

TREASE, GEOFFREY. The Unsleeping Sword. London: Martin Lawrence, 1934. 1st ed. Pb. Fine. *Beasley.* $45/£29

Treasure Land: A Story. (By J. George Hilzinger.) Tucson: Arizona Advancement, 1897. 1st ed. Vol I (all pub). 160,(1)pp (2pp detached, 1 dog-eared). Grn cl (shaken, hinges cracked, extrems worn, cuts on spine), gilt. Good. *Harrington.* $150/£96

Treatise on the Construction and Manufacture of Ordnance in the British Service.... (By John F. Owen.) London, 1879. 446pp (ink names), 20 plts, 2 fldg charts. (Cvrs dknd, rubbed.) *King.* $65/£42

Treatise on the Police of the Metropolis. (By Patrick Colquhoun.) London: C. Dilly, 1797. 4th ed. xxx,(6),440,xxviiipp; fldg chart. Old calf (nicely rebacked), red morocco label. *Karmiole.* $225/£144

TREDGOLD, THOMAS. Elementary Principles of Carpentry. London, 1820. 22 plts. (Ink sig.) Contemp bds (worn, rebacked), mod cl. *Freeman*.* $110/£71

TREECE, HENRY. Invitation and Warning. London: Faber, 1942. 1st ed. VG in dj (sl faded). *Hollett.* $28/£18

TREGARTHEN, ENYS. The Doll Who Came Alive. NY: John Day, 1942. 1st ed. 8vo. 77pp; 11 full-pg illus by Nora Unwin. Dec beige cl. VG in VG dj. *Dower.* $50/£32

TREGO, FRANK H. Boulevarded Old Trails in the Great Southwest. NY, 1929. Red cl. (Sm spine tear), o/w VG + . *Five Quail.* $50/£32

TREMAIN, HENRY EDWIN. Last Hours of Sheridan's Cavalry. NY: Bonnell et al, 1904. 1st ed. Pub's prospectus laid in. VG. *Mcgowan.* $150/£96

TREMAIN, ROSE. The Cupboard. Macdonald, (1981). 1st ed. VG in dj. *Ash.* $39/£25

TREMAINE, MARIE. Early Printing in Canada.... Toronto: Golden Dog, 1934. 1st ed. Contemp plain wrappers (mended). *Ginsberg.* $50/£32

TRENHOLM, VIRGINIA COLE and MAURINE CARLEY. The Shoshonis. Norman: Univ of OK, (1964). 1st ed. VG in dj (sl worn). *Lien.* $45/£29

TRENTON and HOULIHAN. Native Americans. Five Centuries of Changing Images. Abrams, (1989). 1st ed. VF in VF dj. *Oregon.* $45/£29

TRESS, ARTHUR. Shadow. NY: Avon, 1975. 1st ed. 94 full-pg b/w photos. (Owner stamp), else Fine in pict stiff wrappers. *Cahan.* $40/£26

TRESS, ARTHUR. Shadow. NY: Avon, 1975. 1st ed. Signed and w/Tress's photo credit stamp. VG + in wraps as issued. *Smith.* $125/£80

TRESS, ARTHUR. Theater of the Mind. Dobbs Ferry: Morgan & Morgan, 1976. 1st ed. Stamped w/Tress's photo credit stamp. VG + in wraps as issued. *Smith.* $125/£80

TRESSELT, ALVIN and NANCY CLEAVER. The Legend of the Willow Plate. NY: Parents, 1968. 1st ed. Joseph Low (illus). 10 1/4 x 7 1/2. 44pp. Fine in dj. *Cattermole.* $32/£21

TREVANIAN. (Pseud of Rodney W. Whitaker.) The Eiger Sanction. NY: Crown, 1972. 1st ed. Fine in dj (crease fep, 2 sm closed tears). *Mordida.* $75/£48

TREVANIAN. (Pseud of Rodney W. Whitaker.) The Eiger Sanction. NY: Crown, 1972. 1st ed, 1st bk. NF in NF dj. *Else Fine.* $95/£61

TREVANIAN. The Loo Sanction. NY: Crown, 1973. 1st ed. Fine in dj (2 sm closed tears). *Mordida.* $45/£29

TREVANIAN. (Pseud of Rodney W. Whitaker.) The Loo Sanction. London: Heinemann, 1974. 1st ed. Fine in Fine dj. *Else Fine.* $30/£19

TREVELYAN, JULIAN. Indigo Days. London: MacGibbon & Kee, 1957. 1st ed. Frontis port. VG in dj. *Hollett.* $31/£20

TREVELYAN, RALEIGH. The Shadow of Vesuvius, Pompeii AD 79. London: Folio Soc, 1976. Color frontis. Pict 1/2 cl. Good. *Archaeologia.* $25/£16

TREVES, FREDERICK. The Cradle of the Deep. London: Murray, 1925. 32 plts, 4 maps. (Sl foxed; sl rubbed, spine sl frayed), o/w VG. *Worldwide.* $15/£10

TREVOR, ELLESTON. Deep Wood. Gerald Swann, 1945. 1st ed. David Williams (illus). 8vo. 160pp. (Spine, edges faded), else VG. *Bookmark.* $27/£17

TREVOR, ELLESTON. The Flight of the Phoenix. London, 1964. 1st Eng ed. Fine in dj. *Clearwater.* $31/£20

TREVOR, ELLESTON. The Wizard of the Wood. Falcon, 1948. 1st ed. 8vo. 135pp; 6 color plts by Leslie Atkinson. VG in pict dj (sl worn). *Bookmark.* $31/£20

TREVOR, WILLIAM. Angels at the Ritz and Other Stories. London, 1975. 1st Eng ed. Fine in dj. *Clearwater.* $70/£45

TREVOR, WILLIAM. Angels at the Ritz. London: Bodley Head, 1975. 1st ed. NF in dj. *Lame Duck.* $100/£64

TREVOR, WILLIAM. The Ballroom of Romance. NY: Viking, 1972. 1st US ed. Fine in dj. *Lame Duck.* $100/£64

TREVOR, WILLIAM. Beyond the Pale. London: Bodley Head, 1981. 1st ed. Fine in dj. *Lame Duck.* $65/£42

TREVOR, WILLIAM. The Children of Dynmouth. London: Bodley Head, 1976. 1st UK ed. Fine in dj. *Williams.* $55/£35

TREVOR, WILLIAM. The Children of Dynmouth. London: Bodley Head, 1976. 1st ed. Fine in dj. *Lame Duck.* $65/£42

TREVOR, WILLIAM. Elizabeth Alone. NY: Viking, (1974). 1st US ed. Fine in NF dj. *Pettler & Lieberman.* $30/£19

TREVOR, WILLIAM. Elizabeth Alone. London, 1973. 1st Eng ed. Very Nice in dj. *Clearwater.* $70/£45

TREVOR, WILLIAM. Fools of Fortune. NY: Viking, (1983). 1st ed. Fine in NF dj. *Antic Hay.* $25/£16

TREVOR, WILLIAM. Lovers of Their Time and Other Stories. London, 1978. 1st Eng ed. NF (spine sl creased) in dj. *Clearwater.* $55/£35

TREVOR, WILLIAM. Lovers of Their Time. London: Bodley Head, 1978. 1st ed. Fine in dj (price-clipped). *Lame Duck.* $75/£48

TREVOR, WILLIAM. Miss Gomez and the Brethren. London: Bodley Head, 1971. 1st UK ed. NF in dj. *Williams.* $55/£35

TREVOR, WILLIAM. Mrs. Eckdorf at O'Neill's Hotel. London, 1969. 1st Eng ed. Fine in dj. *Clearwater.* $70/£45

TREVOR, WILLIAM. Mrs. Eckdorf in O'Neill's Hotel. London: Bodley Head, (1969). 1st ed. Fine in dj. *Captain's Bookshelf.* $150/£96

TREVOR, WILLIAM. Mrs. Eckdorf in O'Neill's Hotel. Bodley Head, 1969. 1st UK ed. NF in dj (sm closed tear, spine bottom sl bumped). *Williams.* $62/£40

TREVOR-BATTYE, AUBYN. Ice-Bound on Kolguev. Westminster: Archibald Constable, 1895. 3rd ed. 453pp. Grn cl (lt soiled). *Parmer.* $100/£64

TREVOR-BATTYE, AUBYN. Ice-Bound on Kolguev: A Chapter in the Exploration of Arctic Europe to Which Is Added a Record of the Natural History of the Island. Westminster: Constable, 1895. 1st ed. 458pp, 3 color fldg maps. Teg. (Sl spine end wear), else VG. *Mikesh.* $137/£88

Trial of Margaret Lyndsay by the Author of Lights and Shadows. (By John Wilson.) Exeter, NH: Tyler & Conner, 1827. 235pp. Contemp calf. (Sl foxed, sl rubbed), o/w VG. *Worldwide.* $45/£29

Trial of the Twelve Spanish Pirates of the Schooner Panda, a Guinea Slaver.... Boston: Lemuel Gulliver, 1834. 48pp (some missing). Wrappers (very worn, torn, stitched up, some loss, stained). *Metropolitan*.* $40/£26

Trials of the Major War Criminals Before the International Military Tribunal, Nuremburg, Nov. 14, 1945-Oct. 1946. Nuremberg, 1947-1949. English language ed. 42 vols. Blue cl. *Ginsberg.* $1,250/£801

Trials of Thomas Hardy, John Horne Tooke, and John Thelwell, for High Treason. London: Allen & West, 1794. 392pp. 1/2 calf (hinges repaired). *Argosy.* $250/£160

Tribute to Jim Lowell. Cleveland: Ghost Press, 1967. 1st ed. (Wraps loosening), o/w NF. *Beasley.* $100/£64

Tributes to Graham Greene OM, CH, 1904-1991 at the Memorial Requiem Mass at Westminster Cathedral. Reinhardt Books, 1992. Ltd to 300. Fine in wraps. *Williams.* $47/£30

TRICOT, XAVIER. James Ensor: Catalogue Raisonne of the Paintings. London, (1992). 2 vols. Djs, cl slipcase. *Swann*.* $126/£81

TRIGGS, H. I. Formal Gardens in England and Scotland. London: Batsford, 1902. 72 plts. 3/4 leather (rubbed, worn, bumped, nicked, cl soiled). Internally Fine. *Metropolitan*.* $275/£176

TRIGGS, H. I. Garden Craft in Europe. London: Batsford, 1913. 15 plts. Author dedication. Sound. *Ars Artis.* $164/£105

TRIMBLE, WILLIAM J. The Mining Advance into the Inland Empire. Madison: Univ of WI, 1914. 1st ed. Map. (Spine dknd), else Fine in ptd lt grn wrappers. *Argonaut.* $150/£96

TRIMMER, MRS. The History of the Robins for the Instruction of Children on Their Treatment of Animals. London: Griffith & Farran, 1869. iv,141pp + 6pp ads. Dec grn cl bds (rubbed, soiled; inner, outer margins cracked; shaken). *Michael Taylor.* $23/£15

TRIPLETT, FRANK. Conquering the Wilderness; or New Pictorial History.... NY: N.D. Thompson, 1883. 1st ed. 716pp. Fair (rebacked using orig spine). *Lien.* $125/£80

TRIPP, C. E. Ace High. SF: Book Club of CA, 1948. Ltd to 500 ptd. Red cl-backed bds (sl rubbed, sm cut fr bd), ptd paper spine label (chipped). NF. *Blue Mountain.* $65/£42

TRIPP, WILLIAM HENRY. There Goes Flukes. New Bedford, 1938. Good (sl soil, mks). *High Latitude.* $30/£19

TRISTRAM, E. W. English Wall Painting of the Fourteenth Century. Routledge, 1955. 65 plts. (Rear bd mkd), else VG in dj. *Hadley.* $122/£78

TRISTRAM, H. B. The Land of Moab. London, 1873. xvi,408pp (ex-lib, ink stamp verso tp, bkpl pastedown); fldg map. Dec cl (corners rubbed w/sl loss, spine head sl chipped). *Edwards.* $62/£40

TRISTRAM, W. OUTRAM. Moated Houses. London, 1910. 1st ed. Teg, rest uncut. (Lt spotted, upper hinge cracked; cl sl stained.) *Edwards.* $47/£30

TRIVICK, HENRY. The Craft and Design of Monumental Brasses. London/NY: John Baker/Humanities Press, (1969). 1st ed. Black cl, gilt. Fine in dj. *House.* $100/£64

TROLLOPE, ANTHONY (ed). British Sports and Pastimes 1868. London/NY: Virtue, 1868. 1st ed, 1st issue. Grn cl stamped in blind/gilt. (Sl rubbed, sm spots), o/w Very Nice. *Reese.* $225/£144

TROLLOPE, ANTHONY. The American Senator. London: C&W, 1878. New ed. Contemp 1/2 brn morocco, ribbed gilt-dec spine. *D & D.* $95/£61

TROLLOPE, ANTHONY. An Autobiography. Edinburgh: Blackwood, 1883. 1st ed. 2 vols. Port. Brn eps. Red cl stamped in gilt/black. (Ink name, spines sunned, streaks of flecking 1 cvr), o/w Very Nice set. *Reese.* $400/£256

TROLLOPE, ANTHONY. Ayala's Angel. London: Chapman & Hall, 1881. 1st ed. 3 vols. Teg. Later 1/2 maroon morocco (scuffed; spotted throughout), gilt. *Maggs.* $936/£600

TROLLOPE, ANTHONY. Barchester Towers. NY, 1945. #795/1000 signed by Donald McKay (illus). Teg. Fine. *Polyanthos.* $35/£22

TROLLOPE, ANTHONY. The Barsetshire Novels. London: G. Bell, 1926-27. 8 vols. Teg. Contemp blue 1/2 calf, gilt. (Hinges weak.) *Christie's*.* $122/£78

TROLLOPE, ANTHONY. The Belton Estate. London: Chapman & Hall, 1866. 3rd ed. 3 vols. 19th-cent 3/4 gilt calf. Good set (chipped, bumped). *Reese.* $55/£35

TROLLOPE, ANTHONY. The Claverings. London: Smith, Elder, 1878. New ed. Contemp 1/2 brn morocco, ribbed gilt-dec spine. *D & D.* $95/£61

TROLLOPE, ANTHONY. Cousin Henry. London: Chapman & Hall, 1881. 2nd ed. A 'yellowback' vol in Select Library of Fiction, priced at 2 shillings each; lurid bds. 355pp + 8pp ads. Contents VG (wear). *Hartfield.* $265/£170

TROLLOPE, ANTHONY. Dr. Thorne. NY: Harper, 1858. 1st Amer ed. 520pp + ads. (Cl worn.) *Hartfield.* $245/£157

TROLLOPE, ANTHONY. Dr. Wortle's School. London: Chapman & Hall, 1881. 1st ed. 2 vols. Half-titles. (Prelims, 1st 2 gatherings vol 1, prelims vol 2 foxed, other lt foxing; joints sl worn.) Teg. Later 1/2 maroon morocco, gilt. *Maggs.* $546/£350

TROLLOPE, ANTHONY. The Eustace Diamonds. Chapman & Hall, 1873. New ed. Frontis. Good (sl spotted; spine bumped). *Tiger.* $47/£30

TROLLOPE, ANTHONY. An Eye for an Eye. Chapman & Hall, 1879. 1st 1-vol ed. Frontis. Good (sl cocked; spine bumped, chipped, corners rubbed). *Tiger.* $117/£75

TROLLOPE, ANTHONY. An Eye for an Eye. London: Ward, Lock, 1881. New ed. Contemp 1/2 brn morocco, ribbed gilt-dec spine. *D & D.* $85/£54

TROLLOPE, ANTHONY. Is He Popenjoy? Chapman & Hall, 1878. 3 vols. (Spotting, tanning; bound w/o 1/2-titles; later eps; rebacked, orig backstrips relaid; shelfwear, corners rubbed, labels removed upper cvrs.) Sadlier 49. *Tiger.* $515/£330

TROLLOPE, ANTHONY. Is He Popenjoy? Chapman & Hall, 1878. 1st ed. 3 vols. 8vo. Pub's ads end of vol 2. (Tear from outer margin to center of pg leaf B8 vol 1, fep vol 3 missing lg piece, vol 1 recased w/new eps.) Orig reddish-brn silk-grained cl (spine ends, corners rubbed) dec in black/gilt. *Sotheby's*.* $861/£552

TROLLOPE, ANTHONY. John Caldigate. Chapman & Hall, 1879. 3 vols. (Sl spotted; later eps; vol I rebacked, orig backstrip relaid; shelfwear, corners rubbed, labels removed upper cvrs.) Sadlier 55. *Tiger.* $569/£365

TROLLOPE, ANTHONY. John Caldigate. London: Chapman & Hall, 1879. 1st ed. 3 vols. 8vo. Half-titles. (Lt foxed, mainly prelims, final ll.) Teg. Later 1/2 maroon morocco, gilt. *Maggs.* $858/£550

TROLLOPE, ANTHONY. The Kellys and the O'Kellys. Chapman & Hall, 1861. 4th ed. (Sl spotted; edges several ll frayed; rebacked, orig backstrip relaid, corners rubbed.) *Tiger.* $47/£30

TROLLOPE, ANTHONY. The Last Chronicle of Barset. London: Smith, Elder, 1866-1867. 1st ed. 8vo. 32 parts. Dec ptd red/white/blue wrappers (sl archival repair 3 spines). Most slips, ads called for by Sadleir present, incl those in part XVI and XXXII. Cl fldg box. *Swann*.* $2,185/£1,401

TROLLOPE, ANTHONY. A Letter from Anthony Trollope Describing a Visit to California in 1875. SF: Colt, 1946. Ltd to 500. Cl-backed dec bds. VF in grn dj. *Argonaut.* $90/£58

TROLLOPE, ANTHONY. The Life of Cicero. London: Chapman & Hall, 1880. 1st ed. 2 vols. Half-titles. (Foxed, mostly fore-edges.) Teg. Later 1/2 maroon morocco, gilt. *Maggs.* $312/£200

TROLLOPE, ANTHONY. The Life of Cicero. London: Chapman & Hall, 1880. 1st ed, Sadleir's primary binding, w/spine stamped in plain caps. 2 vols. Plum brn cl, gilt. (Vol 1 hinges sl cracking), o/w VG set. *Reese.* $450/£288

TROLLOPE, ANTHONY. The Life of Cicero. London: Chapman & Hall, 1880. 1st ed, 1st issue. 2 vols. Uncut, unopened; black eps. Maroon cl (spines sl faded, corners touched), gilt; pub's imprint on spine in uniform-sized capitals. *Maggs.* $1,014/£650

TROLLOPE, ANTHONY. Mary Gresley and Other Stories. Folio Soc, 1951. 1st ed thus. Joan Hassall (engrs). Fine in dj. *Michael Taylor.* $39/£25

TROLLOPE, ANTHONY. New Zealand. London: Chapman & Hall, 1874. 1st separate ed. Fldg frontis map (repaired). (Title-hinge weakening; cl chafed, extrems sl bumped.) *Clearwater.* $70/£45

TROLLOPE, ANTHONY. New Zealand. London: Chapman & Hall, 1875. New ed. 'Yellowback' vol. 166pp, pub's ads to prelims, lg fldg color map. Pict cvrs (worn). *Hartfield.* $195/£125

TROLLOPE, ANTHONY. North America. London, 1862. 2 vols. viii,467; viii,494pp; fldg map. Later cl. (Vol 1 prelims chipped; skillfully rebacked), o/w VG. *Reese.* $250/£160

TROLLOPE, ANTHONY. North America. NY: Harper, 1862. 1st actual Amer ed (pirated ed, preceeding authorized Harper's ed by a few days). 8vo. 623pp + 4pp ads, appendices. Brn cl (skillfully rebacked), blind dec, gilt title (faded). *Hartfield.* $395/£253

TROLLOPE, ANTHONY. Orley Farm. London: Chapman & Hall, 1862. 1st ed in bk form, Sadleir's issue 4 vol 1, mixed 2nd & 3rd issues vol 2. 2 vols. Orig brn-purple cl, gilt. (Lt foxed, rubbed, recased w/new eps), else Good set. *Reese.* $125/£80

TROLLOPE, ANTHONY. Phineas Finn. London: Virtue, 1869. 1st ed. 2 vols in 1. Frontis. 3/4 contemp pebbled morocco, gilt. (Lt foxed), o/w VG. *Reese.* $200/£128

TROLLOPE, ANTHONY. Phineas Redux. London: Chapman & Hall, 1874. 1st ed. 2 vols. Half-titles. Contemp 3/4 calf, gilt labels, marbled bds. (Lt foxed, rubbed, spines sunned), o/w VG set. *Reese.* $225/£144

TROLLOPE, ANTHONY. The Prime Minister. London: Ward, Lock, 1881. New ed. Contemp 1/2 brn morocco, ribbed gilt-dec spine. *D & D.* $85/£54

TROLLOPE, ANTHONY. Rachel Ray. London: Chapman & Hall, 1868. So-called 'tenth edition.' 347pp. Victorian 3/4 olive grn polished calf, gilt extra, marbled bds. Nice. *Hartfield.* $195/£125

TROLLOPE, ANTHONY. Ralph the Heir. London: Hurst & Blackett, 1871. 1st ed. 3 vols. Half-titles. Teg. Later 1/2 maroon morocco, gilt. VG (fore-edges foxed; joints sl worn). *Maggs.* $858/£550

TROLLOPE, ANTHONY. Sir Harry Hotspur of Humblethwaite. Macmillan, 1871. 1st Macmillan ed, issued in August 1871, ptd from same type (as Eng ed), but w/new titles, cut down to 'Globe 8vo' as a cheap ed. 2000 ptd. vii,(i),323pp. Grn cl (rebacked, retaining orig backstrip; new feps), gilt spine. Good. *Cox.* $70/£45

TROLLOPE, ANTHONY. The Small House at Allington. London: Smith, Elder, 1864. 1st ed. 2 vols. (iv),(1)2-312; (iv),(1)2-316pp; w/18 illus by J. E. Millais; w/'hobbledehoya' on p33 and mispagination p70, found only in some copies of Vol 1. Grey chocolate eps w/black ptd ads on fr/rear pastedowns. Top edges uncut, others trimmed. Grn patterned cl blocked in blind, gold. NF (ink sig both feps). *Vandoros.* $2,475/£1,587

TROLLOPE, ANTHONY. The Three Clerks. London: R. Bentley, 1858. 1st ed. 3 vols. Complete as issued, w/o 1/2-titles or ads; w/terminal blanks vols 2, 3. (Stains, creasing, vol 3 terminal leaf margin repaired; bkpls.) Marbled eps; teg. Later 1/2 brn morocco, tan linen sides, ribbed spines in 6 panels (spines sl scuffed, faded; cocked), 2 grn leather labels. *Waverly*.* $385/£247

TROLLOPE, ANTHONY. Travelling Sketches. London: Chapman & Hall, 1866. 1st ed, later issue. Uncut, unopened. Orig red cl. Variant, w/neither blocking on spine nor pub's cat. (Spine faded), o/w VG. *Maggs.* $312/£200

TROLLOPE, ANTHONY. The Two Heroines of Plumplington. NY: OUP, 1954. 1st ed, Amer issue. VG in dj. *Reese.* $40/£26

TROLLOPE, ANTHONY. The Vicar of Bullhampton. London: Bradbury & Evans, 1870. 1st ed. 8vo. Half-title. Teg. Later 1/2 maroon morocco (joints, spine ends sl worn; foxed), gilt. *Maggs.* $577/£370

TROLLOPE, ANTHONY. The Vicar of Bullhampton. London: Bradbury, Evans, 1870. 1st ed in bk form. Brn cl (worn, bubbled, lt foxed, mkd). *Reese.* $150/£96

TROLLOPE, ANTHONY. The Warden. London: Longman et al, 1855. 1st ed. Sadleir's 3rd binding, w/grain of cl running vertically up the bk, ads dated Oct 1858. VG (contemp ink name dated 1857; spine sl bumped, lettering dull). *Williams.* $1,084/£695

TROLLOPE, ANTHONY. The Way We Live Now. NY: Harper, 1875. 1st Amer ed. 408pp + 8pp ads at back, 4 at fr. Brick-red cl (edges frayed, worn; lt rubbed). Sound. *Hermitage.* $125/£80

TROLLOPE, ANTHONY. The West Indies and the Spanish Main. NY: Harper, 1860. 1st Amer ed. (385)(8 ads)pp. Pub's dk brn cl, gilt spine (worn, w/sl loss, worming). Good. *D & D.* $400/£256

TROLLOPE, FRANCES. The Barnabys in America; or, Adventures of the Widow Wedded. London: Henry Colburn, 1843. 1st ed. 3 vols. 9 engrs (heavily foxed; lt foxing elsewhere). Leather-backed cl (worn, waterspotted; fr inner hinge vol 1 cracked), gilt spines. *New Hampshire*.* $90/£58

TROLLOPE, FRANCES. Domestic Manners of the Americans. Whittaker, Treacher, 1832. Vol I 2nd ed, vol II 3rd ed. 2 vols. Ribbon markers. Contemp 1/2 leather, marbled bds (hinges, corners rubbed), raised bands, leather spine labels (1 chipped). Good (sl spotted). Sadlier 3218. *Tiger.* $242/£155

TROLLOPE, FRANCES. Domestic Manners of the Americans. London, 1832. 1st ed. 2 vols. 24 litho plts. Early 1/2 calf (backstrip dknd). Howes T357. *Swann*.* $316/£203

TROLLOPE, FRANCES. Domestic Manners of the Americans. NY, 1832. 1st Amer ed. ix,(1),(3)-(8),(25)-325pp (sl foxed); 8 litho plts. Mod 1/2 red morocco, red cl. VG. Howes T357. *Reese.* $225/£144

TROLLOPE, FRANCES. The Life and Adventures of Jonathan Jefferson Whitlaw; or Scenes on the Mississippi. London: Richard Bentley, 1836. 1st ed. 3 vols. Engr frontis each vol. Contemp bds (rebacked in mod cl). Sound (bound w/o 1/2-titles, ads, prelim blank 1st vol; clippings pasted in 1st vol; plts foxed, offset, marginally nicked; plt 3rd vol bound out of order). *Reese.* $200/£128

TROLLOPE, FRANCES. One Fault. Baudry's European Library, 1840. Contemp cl (spine bumped, chipped, nick upper hinge). Good (lt spotted, sl cocked). *Tiger.* $112/£72

TROLLOPE, FRANCES. One Fault. Paris: Baudry's European Library, 1840. (4),385pp (edges browned). Contemp binder's cl (differentially faded by damp). Sound. *Cox.* $55/£35

TROLLOPE, FRANCES. Paris and the Parisians in 1835. London: Richard Bentley, 1836. 2 vols. Bound w/o half-titles. Contemp lt sprinkled calf (cracked), black/red leather labels, gilt coronet over initial 'P' each bd. *Maggs.* $133/£85

TROLLOPE, THOMAS ADOLPHUS. A Decade of Italian Women. London: Chapman & Hall, 1859. 1st ed. 2 vols. Tall 8vo. Frontis, 410; 451pp, w/appendix, notes, index. Teg. 3/4 brn crushed morocco, linen bds, eps, gilt titling, raised bands. Fine set. *Hartfield.* $295/£189

TROLLOPE, WILLIAM. A History of the Royal Foundation of Christ's Hospital.... William Pickering, 1834. 1st ed. xvi,358,(2),cxviii (appendix & addenda),(10)index,8pp pub's cat dated Oct 1833 tipped in at front; 10 engr plts. Uncut, partly unopened. (Lt spotted, stamps), o/w Good in blue cl (sl rubbed, cockled, mod cl reback). *Cox.* $211/£135

TROMHOLT, SOPHUS. Under the Rays of the Aurora Borealis. Carl Sievers (ed). London: Sampson Low, Marston, 1885. 1st ed. 2 vols. xv,(i)blank,288,(2); x,306pp, color litho frontis each vol, fldg map vol 2, 21 plts. Grn cl. (1 frontis loose; lt foxing few ll; sl rubbed.) Good. *Morrell.* $250/£160

TROTTER, THOMAS. A View of the Nervous Temperament.... NY: Wright et al, 1808. 1st Amer ed. 338,(2)pp. Contemp calf. (Lt foxed; fr bd detached), else Clean. *Gach.* $495/£317

TROUGHTON, ELLIS. Furred Animals of Australia. Sydney/London: Angus & Robertson, 1946. 3rd ed. 25 color plts. Grn cl (Shelfworn), else VG. *Parmer.* $30/£19

TROUP, J. ROSE. With Stanley's Rear Column. London, 1890. 2nd ed. Frontis port, x,(ii),361pp + 40pp pub's cat; 13 plts, fldg map. (1st, last few leaves lt foxed; sl rubbed.) *Edwards.* $133/£85

TROUT, KILGORE. (Pseud of Philip Jose Farmer.) Venus on the Half-Shell. NY: Dell, 1975. 1st ed. Fine in wraps. *Else Fine.* $20/£13

TROUTMAN, PHILIP. Albrecht Durer. London, 1971. (Cl sl soiled.) *Washton.* $35/£22

TROVILLION, HAL. Faces and Places Remembered. Herrin, IL, 1956. Ltd to 530 signed. Fine in glassine (torn). *Agvent.* $35/£22

TROWBRIDGE, J. T. The South: A Tour of Its Battlefields and Ruined Cities. Hartford, 1868. 1st ed. 590pp. (Ex-lib; sm spine tear, spine gilt gone), o/w VG + . *Pratt.* $90/£58

TROWBRIDGE, LUTHER STEPHEN. The Operations of the Cavalry in the Gettysburg Campaign. Detroit: Ostler, 1888. 1st ed. 17pp. VG in ptd wrappers. *Mcgowan.* $85/£54

TROWBRIDGE, M. E. D. Pioneer Days: The Life-Story of Gershom and Elizabeth Day. Phila: Amer Baptist Pub Soc, 1895. 1st ed. 160pp. Good. *Lien.* $50/£32

TROYTE, CHARLES A. W. Change Ringing. London: Wells Gardner, Darton, (1880). 4th ed. xii,(2),190pp; 3 litho plts. Good (hinges rubbed). Cox. $28/£18

TRUBNER, N. Trubner's Bibliographical Guide to American Literature. London: Trubner, 1859. 2nd updated version. Inscribed. Roan-backed bds (spine missing). Maggs. $47/£30

TRUESDALE, JOHN. The Blue Coats and How They Lived, Fought and Died for the Union. Phila, (1867). 1st ed. 510pp. (Tape mended; cvr worn, stained) o/w VG. Pratt. $40/£26

TRUESDELL, S. R. The Rifle. Harrisburg: Military Service Pub Co, 1947. 1st ed. Grn buckram, gilt. Fie in NF pict dj. Biscotti. $175/£112

TRUETA, J. Treatment of War Wounds and Fractures. NY: Hoeber, (c.1939). 1st Amer ed. NF. Glaser. $85/£54

TRUETA, JOSEP. The Principles and Practice of War Surgery with Reference to the Biological Method of the Treatment of War Wounds and Fractures. St. Louis: Mosby, 1943. (Rubbed.) Goodrich. $75/£48

TRULOCK, ALICE RAINS. In the Hands of Providence. Chapel Hill, (1992). 1st ed. Fine in Fine dj. Pratt. $32/£21

TRUMAN, BEN C. Occidental Sketches. SF: SF News, 1881. 1st ed. Inscribed. 212,(4)pp + 12pp ads (hinges starting). Patterned purple cl (spine faded, extrems frayed), gilt. Howes T365. Karmiole. $200/£128

TRUMBO, DALTON. Additional Dialogue, Letters of Dalton Trumbo 1942-1962. NY: M. Evans, (1970). 1st ed. VG in dj. Hermitage. $25/£16

TRUMBO, DALTON. Johnny Got His Gun. Lippincott, (1939). 2nd ptg before pub. VG in dj (chipped). Certo. $65/£42

TRUMBULL, G. Names and Portraits of Birds Which Interest Gunners. NY, 1888. 1st ed. 221pp. Gilt-dec cl. VG. Mikesh. $55/£35

TRUMBULL, H. CLAY. The Captured Scout of the Army of the James. Boston: Nichols & Noyes, 1869. 60pp. (Cl bubbled), else VG. Cullen. $65/£42

TRUMBULL, H. CLAY. War Memories of an Army Chaplain. NY, 1898. 1st ed. x,421pp. Wantagh. $45/£29

TRUMBULL, H. CLAY. War Memories of an Army Chaplain. NY, 1898. 1st ed. 421pp. (Spine faded), o/w VG+ in pict wraps. Pratt. $65/£42

TRUMBULL, J. HAMMOND (ed). The True-Blue Laws of Connecticut and New Haven and the False Blue-Laws Invented by the Rev. Samuel Peters. Hartford: American Pub Co, 1876. Blue cl (browning, worn), gilt. Fresh. Boswell. $65/£42

TRUMBULL, JOHN. Autobiography, Reminiscences and Letters of John Trumbull from 1756 to 1841. NY/New Haven, Wiley & Putnam/B.L. Hamlen, 1841. Signed. xvi,439pp; 21 plts, 2 fldg maps. Orig cl (rebacked). Adelson. $285/£183

TRUSLER, JOHN. Hogarth Moralized. Sold by S. Hooper...and Mrs Hogarth..., 1768. 1st ed of 1st attempt at a complete collection of Hogarth's engrs. Trusler's 1st bk for children. 8vo. Engr, ptd tps; frontis, 75 text engrs. (Sl spotted, stained, sm tear inner margin 3 leaves.) As in all other copies of this ed, sigs G and H ptd on thinner paper than rest of bk. Contemp calf (neatly rebacked, corners rubbed). Hatchwell. $780/£500

TRUSS, SELDON. Turmoil at Brede. NY: Mystery League, 1931. 1st Amer ed. NF in dj (sl rubbed, 2-inch spine piece missing). Polyanthos. $25/£16

TRUTH, SOJOURNER. Narrative of Sojourner Truth. Battle Creek: The Author, 1878. Port, 320pp. (Spine sunned, shelfworn, edgeworn), o/w VG. Brown. $75/£48

TRYON, THOMAS. Some Memoirs of the Life of Mr. Tho. Tryon, Late of London, Merchant. London: T. Sowle, 1705. 1st ed. Sm 8vo. Fldg copper-engr frontis port, 34,18,35-128,(4)pp (browned, foxed, 2 final ll as expert facs). Contemp calf (rebacked). VG. Glaser. $850/£545

TRYON, WARREN S. and WILLIAM CHARVAT. The Cost Books of Ticknor and Fields and Their Predecessors, 1832-1858. NY: Bibliographical Soc of America, 1949. 1st ed. Orig tan buckram, gilt. Mint. Macdonnell. $60/£38

TRYON, WARREN S. and WILLIAM CHARVAT. The Cost Books of Ticknor and Fields and Their Predecessors: 1832-1858. NY: Bibliographical Soc of Amer, 1949. Frontis. Brn cl, gilt spine. Fine; no dj as issued. Heller. $45/£29

TRYPANIS, C. A. The Elegies of a Glass Adonis. NY: Chilmark, 1967. One of 450 signed. Prospectus laid in. Dk grn paper bds. Fine in glassine dj. Heller. $150/£96

TSCHICHOLD, JON. Designing Books. NY: Schultz, ca 1950. 1st ed in English. Unopened. Dec paper over bds (ends bumped, sl worn, rear joint sl cracked). Bright in dj (unevenly dknd, chipped; tape repairs). Waverly*. $154/£99

TSCHIFFELY, A. F. The Tale of Two Horses. NY: S&S, 1935. 1st ed. VG. October Farm. $40/£26

TSCHIFFELY, A. F. Tschiffely's Ride. NY: S&S, 1933. 1st US ed. VG in Good dj. October Farm. $45/£29

TUCKER, ANNE (ed). In Sequence. Target III: Photographic Sequences from the Target Collection.... Houston: Museum of Fine Arts, 1982. 1st ed. 2 fldg photo sequences. (Rep loose), else NF in pict stiff wrappers. Cahan. $25/£16

TUCKER, ANNE (ed). The Woman's Eye. NY: Knopf, 1973. 1st ed. NF in pict stiff wrappers. Cahan. $25/£16

TUCKER, EPHRAIM W. Five Months in Labrador and Newfoundland, During the Summer of 1838. Concord, (NH): Israel S. Boyd & William White, 1839. 1st ed. 156pp, half-title. (Lt foxed, cvrs worn), o/w VG. New Hampshire*. $350/£224

TUCKER, GEORGE. The Life of Thomas Jefferson, Third President of the United States.... London: Charles Knight, 1837. 1st ed. 2 vols. Frontis port. Marbled edges. Period tan calf, gilt spines, grn morocco spine labels. (Spine heads rubbed), else VG. Pacific*. $161/£103

TUCKER, WILSON. The Chinese Doll. Rinehart, 1946. 1st ed, 1st bk. VG in VG dj. Certo. $30/£19

TUCKERMAN, HENRY T. Artist-Life: Or Sketches of American Painters. NY/Phila: D. Appleton/Geo. S. Appleton, 1847. 1st ed. 237pp. (Few dk spots fr hinge, foxed), else VG. Cahan. $185/£119

TUCKWELL, W. Reminiscences of a Radical Parson. Cassell, 1905. Port. Teg. (Upper cvr sl sprung, spotted, rubbed; pub's slip pasted over imprint tp.) Bickersteth. $23/£15

TUDOR, TASHA. And It Was So. Phila: Westminster, (1958). 1st ed. 8vo. VG in illus paper wraps. Dower. $65/£42

TUDOR, TASHA. Around the Year. NY: Walck, (1957). 1st ed. Signed. (Sl worn.) Dj. Oinonen*. $140/£90

TUDOR, TASHA. Corgiville Fair. NY: Thomas Crowell, (1971). 1st ed. Sm oblong 4to. VG in VG dj (sl edgewear, sl loss bottom spine end). Dower. $65/£42

TUDOR, TASHA. Corgiville Fair. NY: T.Y. Crowell, 1971. 1st ed. Obl sm 4to. Pict cl (bottom edge faded). NF in VG+ dj (sm tear rear). Book Adoption. $200/£128

TUDOR, TASHA. The Doll's Christmas. NY: Henry Z. Walck, (1950). Sq 12mo. Unpaginated. Illus eps. Red cl. NF in NF dj. Dower. $85/£54

TUDOR, TASHA. Snow Before Christmas. NY: OUP, 1941. 1st ed. 16mo. VG. *Dower*. $175/£112

TUDOR, TASHA. Take Joy! The Tasha Tudor Christmas Book. NY: World, 1966. 1st ed. 11 1/4 x 8 3/4. 159pp. Fine in VG dj. *Cattermole*. $45/£29

TUDOR, TASHA. The White Goose. London/NY: OUP, (1943). 1st ed. 16mo. Grey cl (spine, corners sl worn, sl bumped). *Dower*. $200/£128

TUDOR, TASHA. Wings from the Wind. Phila: Lippincott, 1964. 1st ed. 7 1/2 x 9 3/4. 120pp. Fine in VG dj. *Cattermole*. $60/£38

TUER, ANDREW W. Bartolozzi and His Works.... London: Leadenhall, (1881?). 2 vols. (Ex-lib; shaken, spines dknd.) *Swann**. $80/£51

TUER, ANDREW W. Forgotten Children's Books. London: Leadenhall, 1898-99. 1st ed. Frontis. (Fep loose w/2 ads from Leadenhall tipped on.) Pict gilt blue cl. *Swann**. $46/£29

TUER, ANDREW W. History of the Horn Book. London: Leadenhall, 1896. 1st ed. 2 vols. 4to. Frontispieces, 7 horn-bks in pockets. Full vellum, gilt. *Rostenberg & Stern*. $975/£625

TUER, ANDREW W. Pages and Pictures from Forgotten Children's Books. London: Leadenhall, 1898-99. 1st ed. 8vo. Blue gilt-stamped cl, gilt top. Fine. *Appelfeld*. $150/£96

TUGGLE, W. O. Shem, Ham and Japheth. Univ of GA, (1973). 1st ed. 2 maps on 1 fldg sheet laid in. VF in VF dj. *Oregon*. $25/£16

TUKE, DANIEL HACK. Sleep-Walking and Hypnotism. London: J&A Churchill, 1884. 1st ed, 1st issue. Inscribed. (viii),119,(5)pp + inserted ads. Pebbled brn cl. (Edges snagged), else VG. *Gach*. $250/£160

TULL, JETHRO. The Horse-Hoeing Husbandry. London: Cobbett, 1829. Later ptg. 436pp. Orig cl. VG. *Second Life*. $175/£112

TULLIDGE, EDWARD W. Life of Joseph the Prophet. NY, 1878. 1st ed. 545pp. VG- (tp, ports, feps loose, ink notes fep, fr hinge tender, rear hinge cracked; worn, rear cvr lt stained, spine sl faded). *Benchmark*. $300/£192

TULLY, JIM. Beggars of Life. London: C&W, 1925. 1st ed. (Stamp fep, sl spotted; spine faded.) *Hollett*. $23/£15

TUMBLETY, FRANCIS. A Few Passages in the Life of Dr. Francis Tumblety.... Cincinnati, 1866. 82pp (text stains). Orig ptd pict wraps (loose, chipped, spine worn, sl soiled). Howes T413. *Wantagh*. $65/£42

TUNIS, JOHN R. Rookie of the Year. Harcourt Brace, 1944. 1st ed. VG in VG dj. *Plapinger*. $50/£32

TUNIS, JOHN R. Schoolboy Johnson. Morrow, 1958. 1st ed. VG in Good+ dj. *Plapinger*. $60/£38

TUNIS, JOHN R. Young Razzle. Morrow, 1949. 1st ed. VG+ in VG dj. *Plapinger*. $50/£32

TUNNICLIFFE, C. F. Bird Portraiture. The Studio, 1945. 1st ed. 16 color plts. Grn cl. Good in dj (lt spotted, repaired), which incorporates a color plt not in bk. *Cox*. $39/£25

TUNNICLIFFE, C. F. My Country Book. London, 1942. 1st ed. (Rear cvr sl mkd), o/w VG. *Words Etc*. $31/£20

TUNNICLIFFE, C. F. and SIDNEY ROGERSON. Our Bird Book. Collins, 1949. VG in dj (sl spotted). *Cox*. $47/£30

TUPPER, MARTIN FARQUHAR. Ballads for the Times. A. Hall, Virtue, 1853. 4th ed. Frontis, extra engr tp, vii,(i),477,(3)pp + 32-pg list, yellow eps. Uncut. *Cox*. $39/£25

TURBERVILLE, A. S. (ed). Johnson's England. Clarendon, 1933. 2 vols. Frontis ports. (Newspaper clippings loosely inserted.) Djs (sl soiled, chipped). *Edwards*. $86/£55

TURBERVILLE, A. S. (ed). Johnson's England. Oxford, 1933. 1st ed. 2 vols. Good set (backstrips sl faded). *Cox*. $70/£45

TURBEVILLE, DEBORAH. Unseen Versailles. GC: Doubleday, 1981. 1st ed. Signed. Fine in Fine dj. *Smith*. $200/£128

TURBEVILLE, DEBORAH. Wallflowers. NY: Congreve, 1978. 1st ed. NF in VG+ dj. *Smith*. $80/£51

TURBEVILLE, DEBORAH. Wallflowers. NY: Congreve, 1978. 1st ed. Ptd paper over bds. VG in pict dj (sl soiled). *Cahan*. $85/£54

TURCK, HERMANN. The Man of Genius. London: A&C Black, 1914. 1st Eng ed. VG (spine sl worn). *Patterson*. $55/£35

TURGENEV, IVAN. Russian Life in the Interior, or The Experiences of a Sportsman. Edinburgh: A&C Black, 1855. 1st Eng ed. Presentation copy 'with the publisher's compliments, Jan 1, 1855.' Gilt-pict cl (lt bumped). *Swann**. $488/£313

TURKLE, BRINTON. Thy Friend, Obadiah. NY: Viking, 1969. 1st ed. 9 x 7, 38pp. Fine in dj. *Cattermole*. $40/£26

TURNBULL, ALEXANDER. Investigation into the Remarkable Medicinal Effects Resulting from the External Application of Veratria. Washington, 1834. 1st Amer ed. 46pp. VG in wrappers. *Argosy*. $45/£29

TURNBULL, COLIN M. The Mountain People. NY: S&S, 1972. 1st ed. 10 plts. VG in dj. *Worldwide*. $16/£10

Turner's Companion. Phila: Henry Carey Baird, 1867. Half-title, 135,ads,24pp; 14 plts. Maroon blind-stmped cl (ends, corners sl worn). *Weber*. $125/£80

TURNER, ALBERT (ed). The Attainment of Womanly Beauty of Form and Features. NY: Health-Culture Co, 1904. 4th ed. Gilt-stamped platinum cl (sl rubbing, corners lt bumped), silver-stamped design on upper cvr. VG. *Houle*. $150/£96

TURNER, ALBERT (ed). The Attainment of Womanly Beauty. NY, 1900. Pict cl (lt worn, soiled), gilt. *Freeman**. $20/£13

TURNER, CHARLES W. Chessie's Road. Richmond: Garrett & Massie, 1956. Frontis, 19 plts (1 fldg). Navy cl, gilt. VG+ in dj (chipped). *Bohling*. $30/£19

TURNER, DAWSON and LEWIS WESTON DILLWYN. The Botanist's Guide Through England and Wales. Ptd by Phillips & Fardon, 1805. 2 vols. xvi,363; 439pp (lt foxed, mainly prelims). Marbled eps, edges. Contemp gilt-ruled calf bds (rebacked in mod calf, sl surface loss), dec gilt, raised bands, spine labels. *Edwards*. $273/£175

TURNER, FREDERICK. Australian Grasses. Vol 1. Sydney, 1895. xxxviii,63pp;51 full-pg engrs. Gilt-dec cvrs, beveled edges. (Spine head neatly repaired, shelf/corner worn.) Clean. *Brooks*. $57/£37

TURNER, GEORGE EDGAR. Victory Rode the Rails. Indianapolis, (1953). 1st ed. (Sl soiled, worn.) *King*. $60/£38

TURNER, GERARD. Collecting Microscopes. London: Studio Vista, 1981. 1st ed. VG in dj. *Hollett*. $47/£30

TURNER, HENRY S. The Original Journals of...with Stephen Watts Kearny to New Mexico and California 1846. Norman, 1966. 1st ed. Map. Fine in Fine dj. *Turpen*. $75/£48

TURNER, J. M. W. Collected Correspondence. John Gage (ed). Oxford, 1980. Port. Dj. *Hatchwell*. $23/£15

TURNER, J. M. W. John Ruskin. Notes on His Collection of Drawings. London: Fine Art Soc, 1878. 188pp, 35 plts, guards, dbl-pg map. Teg, rest uncut. Morocco-backed cl bds (spine rubbed). *Europa*. $75/£48

TURNER, J. M. W. The Rivers of France: The Loire. London: J. McCormick, ca 1837. Engr pict tp, 39 steel-engr plts, guards. (Sl aged, few plts sl foxed.) Early black morocco, marbled bds (upper cvr detached, sl scuffed), raised bands, gilt. *Baltimore**. $140/£90

TURNER, J. M. W. Turner's Annual Tour, 1833. London: Longman, 1833. 1st ed. 21 steel-engr plts. Very Handsome. *Sotheran*. $304/£195

TURNER, J. M. W. and THOMAS GIRTIN. River Scenery. London: W.B. Cooke, 1827. 18 mezzotints (2 foxed, sl waterstains sl affecting 12 plts). Bds (scuffed), 1/4 morocco (backstrip ripped). *Yudkin**. $500/£321

TURNER, J. V. Below the Clock. NY: Appleton-Century, 1936. 1st Amer ed. (Name, address), o/w VG in dj (sm chip back panel; spine sl worn). *Mordida*. $35/£22

TURNER, JOHN. Pioneers of the West: A True Narrative. Cincinnati: Jennings, 1903. 1st ed. Howes T424. *Ginsberg*. $150/£96

TURNER, JONATHAN B. Mormonism in All Ages. NY, (1842). 304,ivpp. (Lacks fep, scattered foxing; backstrip starting), else VG. *Reese*. $475/£304

TURNER, JULIA. Human Psychology as Seen Through the Dream. London: Kegan Paul et al, 1924. 1st ed. Ruled grn cl. VG. *Gach*. $40/£26

TURNER, KATHARINE C. Red Men Calling on the Great White Father. Norman: Univ of OK, (1951). 1st ed. Map. VG in dj. *Lien*. $30/£19

TURNER, LORENZO DOW. Africanisms in the Gullah Dialect. Chicago: Univ of Chicago, (1949). 1st ed. 2 maps. VG in ptd dj. *Petrilla*. $75/£48

TURNER, LYNN W. William Plumer of New Hampshire 1759-1850. Chapel Hill: Inst of Early Amer Hist & Culture, (1962). Port. Fine in plain dj. *Bohling*. $15/£10

TURNER, NICOLAS. Florentine Drawings of the Sixteenth Century. London: British Museum, 1986. Good in wraps (sl creased, sl soiled). *Washton*. $20/£13

TURNER, RICHARD. New Introduction to Book Keeping.... Boston: I. Thomas & E.T. Andrews, 1794. 1st Amer ed. 24,(3),9 (i.e. 18),(3)pp (foxed, last few ll dampstained). Incl sample ledger. Leather-backed marbled bds (sl worn). *New Hampshire**. $160/£103

TURNER, S. Siberia: A Record of Travel, Climbing and Exploration. Phila: G.W. Jacobs, 1905. 1st ed. 2 maps. Teg. Blind-stamped gilt-dec cl. (Spine dknd), else VG. *Mikesh*. $137/£88

TURNER, T. HUDSON. Some Account of Domestic Architecture in England.... London, 1859. 4 vols. Vol 1 is 2nd ed, London, 1877, uniformly bound w/others. Blue cl. VG. *Argosy*. $300/£192

TUROW, SCOTT. One L. NY, 1977. 1st ed, 1st bk. Fine in NF dj. *Warren*. $200/£128

TUROW, SCOTT. Presumed Innocent. NY: FSG, 1987. 1st ed. Fine in dj. *Mordida*. $45/£29

TURPIE, DAVID. Sketches of My Own Times. Indianapolis, (1903). 1st ed. (Sm dampspot fr cvr), o/w Good. Howes T430. *Hayman*. $35/£22

TURRILL, CHARLES B. California Notes. SF: Edward Bosqui, 1876. 1st ed. xiii,(1),2-232pp, 2 maps. (Cvrs lt worn, trace of cracking at inner margins of few sigs.) Sound. *Shasky*. $100/£64

TURRILL, W. B. Joseph Dalton Hooker: Botanist, Explorer and Administrator. London: Nelson, 1963. 1st ed. 25 plts, 3 maps. Fine in VG dj. *Mikesh*. $30/£19

TURSKA, KRYSTYNA. The Woodcutter's Duck. NY: Macmillan, 1972. 1st US ed. 9 x 11 1/4. 32pp. Pict bds. Fine in dj. *Cattermole*. $35/£22

TURZAK, CHARLES. Abraham Lincoln: Biography in Woodcuts. (Chicago: n.p., 1933.) 1st ed. #248/1500 numbered, signed. 36 woodcuts. Unopened. VG in stiff cream cl wrappers, pub's beige/black box, lid w/sm woodcut port label. *Houle*. $275/£176

TUSSER, THOMAS. Five Hundred Points of Good Husbandry. Lackington, Allen, 1812. New ed. 36,xl,338pp + ad leaf. Uncut. VG in orig bds (rubbed, hinges split), paper label (rubbed). VG. *Cox*. $133/£85

TUSSER, THOMAS. Five Hundred Points of Good Husbandry. London, 1812. 34,xl,337pp, add'l dec title (pp323-38 sl dampstained, sl marginal dampstaining, bkpl; spine chipped, cl sl worn, faded, upper joint split). *Edwards*. $156/£100

TUSSER, THOMAS. Five Hundred Points of Good Husbandry.... E.V. Lucas (ed). London: James Tregaskis, 1931. 1st this ed. One of 500. Dec tp. Full calf. (Bkpl; spine lt rubbed), else NF. *Reese*. $250/£160

TUSSEY, A. EDGAR. Principles or Guides for a Better Selection or Classification of Consumptives Amenable to High Altitude Treatment. Phila, 1896. 1st ed. 144pp. VG (fr inner hinge starting; cvrs faded, sl worn). *Doctor's Library*. $90/£58

TUTT, J. W. British Moths. London, 1902. 12 color plts. (Piece cut from 1/2 title; 1/2 title, frontis verso mkd w/glue; cl used.) *Wheldon & Wesley*. $31/£20

TUTTLE, CHARLES R. Alaska. Seattle, 1914. Map. VG. *High Latitude*. $25/£16

TUTTLE, CHARLES R. The Centennial Northwest. Madison: Inter-State Book Co, 1876. 656pp; 24 plts. Grn cl, gilt. Nice (stain lower corner). *Bohling*. $60/£38

TUTTLE, CHARLES R. New Centennial History of the State of Kansas. Madison, WI/Lawrence, KS: Inter-State Book Co., 1876. 708pp. Gilt-stamped blue cl (rubbed, soiled, rear hinge frayed). *Bohling*. $85/£54

TUTTLE, DANIEL SYLVESTER. Reminiscences of a Missionary Bishop. NY, (1906). 2 ports. Teg. Gilt-stamped cl. VG (name; spine faded, fore-edge soiled). *Bohling*. $45/£29

TUTTLE, FRANCIS. Report of the Cruise of the U.S. Revenue Cutter Bear...for the Relief of the Whalers in the Arctic Ocean.... Washington: GPO, 1899. iv,144pp; 48 plts, lg fldg map. VG. *High Latitude*. $100/£64

TUTTLE, JAMES P. A Treatise on Diseases of the Anus, Rectum, and Pelvic Colon. NY: Appleton, 1902. 1st ed. 8 color plts. VG (fr hinge cracked). *Glaser*. $60/£38

TUTTON, A. E. H. Crystallography and Practical Crystal Measurement. 1911. (Cl sl mkd), o/w VG. *Whitehart*. $39/£25

TUTTON, A. E. H. Crystals. London: Kegan Paul et al, 1911. VG. *Savona*. $28/£18

TUTUOLA, AMOS. My Life in the Bush of Ghosts. NY: Grove, 1954. 1st US ed. (Name), o/w Fine in dj (lt used). *Beasley*. $40/£26

TUTUOLA, AMOS. The Palm-Wine Drinkard and His Dead Palm-Wine Tapster in the Deads' Town. London, 1952. 1st ed, 1st bk. Fine (spine lt sunned) in dj (spine lt sunned, 2 nicks). *Polyanthos*. $45/£29

TWAIN, MARK and CHARLES DUDLEY WARNER. The Gilded Age. Hartford: American Pub Co, 1874. 1st ed, mixed issue. Frontis, xvi,(17)-574pp + (3) ad leaves; fldg plt. Gilt-dec cl (fr hinge neatly reinforced w/matching paper, sl worn). Internally Very Nice (sl discolored). BAL 3357. *Pirages*. $175/£112

TWAIN, MARK. The £1,000,000 Bank-Note and Other New Stories. NY: Charles L. Webster, 1893. 1st ed. 260pp + 9pp ads. Pict cl (sl worn, soiled). Contents VG. BAL 3436. *New Hampshire**. $75/£48

TWAIN, MARK. 1601 or A Fireside Conversation in Ye Time of Queen Elizabeth. N.p.: Privately ptd, 1934. Ltd to 250. NF (traces removed scotch tape feps, inside cvrs; spine sl sunned, extrems sl rubbed). *Polyanthos.* $30/£19

TWAIN, MARK. 1601 or Conversation at the Social Fireside as It Was in the Time of the Tudors. Chicago: Black Cat, 1936. One of 300 ptd. Frontis. (Spine sl sunned), else VG. *Reese.* $45/£29

TWAIN, MARK. 1601, A Fireside Conversation. N.p., n.d. #9/125 ptd for subs. NF (edge crease). *Polyanthos.* $35/£22

TWAIN, MARK. 1601. NY: Golden Hind, 1933. 1st Amer ed. Frontis port. Fine (name). *Polyanthos.* $30/£19

TWAIN, MARK. The Adventures of Huckleberry Finn. London: C&W, 1884. True 1st ed, 1st issue. Dec red cl-cvrd bds (extrems restored). *Lame Duck.* $1,750/£1,122

TWAIN, MARK. Adventures of Huckleberry Finn. NY: Charles L. Webster, 1885. 1st ed, early states. Frontis port 1st state. Tp, p283 are cancels (earliest states for cl copies); pp13 ('88'), 57 ('with the was') are in earliest state; p155 (last 5 a larger font) is in the 3rd state; p155 occurs randomly in all 3 states independent of other 4 signs of set of 1st ptg sheets. Orig grn cl (spine foot frayed, lt rubbed; Christmas 1885 inscrip), gilt. Tight. BAL 3415. *Macdonnell.* $1,000/£641

TWAIN, MARK. Adventures of Huckleberry Finn. NY: Charles L. Webster, 1885. 1st ed, 1st issue containing all 1st state points: plt 283 on a stub; pg 9 w/illus captioned 'Him and Another Man' listed pg 88 rather than pg 87 where it appears; pg 57 w/'with the was' in 11th line from bottom (later corrected to 'with the saw'); pg 143 w/defective 'b' in 'body' in line 7 and 'Co' in upper right hand corner of illus; tp conjugate with (1)7 and bears copyright date 1884; pg 155 w/second 5 missing. 8vo. Pub's black/gilt dec grn cl. Clean and Bright. BAL 3415. *D & D.* $4,500/£2,885

TWAIN, MARK. Adventures of Huckleberry Finn. NY: Charles Webster, 1885. 1st Amer ed, early issue, state 2 of tp (cancel), illus listed as at p88, 1st state reading on p57, p283 a cancel, p155 in 3rd state, port in 1st state. Lg 8vo. Gilt-pict grn cl (rubbed, sl loss spine extrems; owner shelf #s fr pastedown). BAL 3415. *Swann*.* $1,150/£737

TWAIN, MARK. Adventures of Huckleberry Finn. NY: Webster, 1885. 1st ed, 1st issue. (Edgewear 1st few pp, fr hinges splitting; soiled, bumped, ends frayed w/splits, shaken.) *Metropolitan*.* $201/£129

TWAIN, MARK. Adventures of Huckleberry Finn. NY: Webster, 1885. 1st ed, early issue, w/title leaf a cancel; 'Him and another man' listed as at p88; 'with the was' at p57; p283 leaf is a conjugate; final '5' lacking p155, etc. Frontis port in Blanck's state 1. Pict grn cl. (Sl soiled, foxed, stained; shelfworn, spine tips neatly restored.) *Oinonen*.* $600/£385

TWAIN, MARK. Adventures of Huckleberry Finn....E.W. Kemble (illus). NY: Charles L. Webster, 1885. 1st ed, early state. Tp is a cancel (BAL 2); pg [13]: the illus captioned 'Him and another Man' is listed as appearing on p. 88 (BAL 1); pg 57: eleventh line from bottom reads—'...with the was...' (BAL 1); pg 283: leaf is a conjugate, w/corrected engr of Silas Phelp (BAL 4); pg 155: final five larger than 1st five (BAL 3); pg 161 has no signature mk; final leaf is a blank; port frontis: scarf is visible, 'Heliotype Printing Company' imprint, in black (BAL 1). 8vo. Grn pict cl stamped in black/gold. Good (lt foxing; wear to extrems) in slipcase. BAL 3415. *Cummins.* $1,250/£801

TWAIN, MARK. The Adventures of Tom Sawyer. Hartford, CT/Chicago/Cincinnati/SF: American Pub Co/A. Roman, 1876. 1st ed, 2nd ptg. Sq 8vo. Frontis, xvi,[(17)-274pp]+ (i) + (iv) pub's ads. (Sl shaken, upper hinge sprung, fep sl creased, sl torn, ex-libris.) 3 blanks before 1/2 title, verso of 1/2 title, recto of frontis blank, 4pp ads dated Dec 1st 1876. Gilt/black dec cl (corners rubbed, spine sl dknd, chipped, sl loss). Morocco-backed cl fall-down box, gilt. *Edwards.* $780/£500

TWAIN, MARK. The Adventures of Tom Sawyer. Hartford: Amer Pub Co, 1876. 1st Amer ed, 2nd ptg, issue 'A.' Gilt-stamped blue cl (lt rubbed, sl loss to tips, spine extrems; tape mks on pastedowns, eps; bkpl). BAL 3369. *Swann*.* $488/£313

TWAIN, MARK. The Adventures of Tom Sawyer. Hartford: Amer Pub Co, 1876. 1st Amer ed, BAL's 2nd ptg, issue C (no priority as to issue established). 4pp ads. (Short marginal tears few leaves, short marginal tear half-title/frontis leaf repaired, scattered soil.) 8vo. Blue dec cl, plain edges. (Rebacked w/morocco, orig spine laid down, corners reinforced w/morocco, lt soil.) Good in slipcase. BAL 3369. *Cummins.* $1,750/£1,122

TWAIN, MARK. The Adventures of Tom Sawyer. Hartford: Amer Pub Co, 1876. 1st Amer ed, BAL 3rd ptg. 4pp of ads. 8vo. (Sl soil few pp; inscrip, bkpl upper pastedown.) Brn sprinkled edges, pink eps. Pub's sheep, black morocco spine label, gilt. Internally VG (upper joint repaired, lt wear) in slipcase. BAL 3369. *Cummins.* $2,250/£1,442

TWAIN, MARK. The Adventures of Tom Sawyer. Hartford: American Pub Co, 1876. 1st ed, 2nd ptg, issue B on wove paper. Frontis (fore-edge chipped in margin). VG recased in orig binding, corners sl worn). BAL 3369. *Captain's Bookshelf.* $500/£321

TWAIN, MARK. The Adventures of Tom Sawyer. Hartford: American Pub Co, 1876. 1st ed, 3rd ptg. Orig blue dec cl, gilt. Good (spine ends, corners frayed; rubbed, hinge paper cracked). BAL 3369. *Macdonnell.* $600/£385

TWAIN, MARK. The Adventures of Tom Sawyer. Toronto: Belford Brows, 1876. 1st Canadian ed. Illus brn cl over bds (extrems worn). VG. *Old London.* $650/£417

TWAIN, MARK. The Adventures of Tom Sawyer. Cambridge: (LEC), 1939. #995/1500. Signed by Thomas Hart Benton (illus). (Sl internal soil; lt worn; lacks slipcase.) Paper spine label. *Freeman*.* $50/£32

TWAIN, MARK. The American Claimant. C&W, 1892. 1st ed. 8vo. Frontis, 258pp,32pp ads dated May 1892. 80 illus by Dan Beard & Hal Hurst. Illus red cl (sl bubbled). VG. *Bookmark.* $133/£85

TWAIN, MARK. The American Claimant. London: C&W, 1892. 1st British ed. 8vo. Ads dated May 1892. Pub's gilt, black-stamped red cl. (Sl cocked, lt overall wear), else Fine. *D & D.* $125/£80

TWAIN, MARK. The American Claimant. NY: Charles L. Webster, 1892. 1st ed. Olive grn cl, gilt. Good (sl worn, dull). BAL 3434. *Macdonnell.* $35/£22

TWAIN, MARK. The American Claimant. NY: Charles L. Webster, 1892. 1st ed. xv,277pp. Pict grey-grn cl (sl soiled, extrems sl worn), gilt. BAL 3434. *Shasky.* $115/£74

TWAIN, MARK. The American Claimant. NY: Charles L. Webster, 1892. 1st ed. Frontis. Gilt-pict cl (tips sl rubbed). VG. BAL 3434. *Reese.* $125/£80

TWAIN, MARK. The American Claimant. NY: Webster, 1892. 1st ed. Dan Beard (illus). Grn dec cl as issued. Fine. *Appelfeld.* $150/£96

TWAIN, MARK. The Celebrated Jumping Frog of Calaveras County, and Other Sketches. John Paul (ed). NY: Webb, 1867. 1st ed, later state, w/broken type as specified by Blanck, and w/ad leaf before title removed (but clearly once having been present); frog on fr cvr at lower left. Gilt-pict brn cl. (Foxing; shelfworn, spine edges torn, sl shaken.) BAL 3310. Oinonen*. $400/£256

TWAIN, MARK. A Champagne Cocktail and a Catastrophe. (NY: Privately ptd, 1930.) 1st ed, 1st ptg. Orig peach paper self-wrappers, stapled. Mint. BAL 3551. Macdonnell. $100/£64

TWAIN, MARK. A Connecticut Yankee in King Arthur's Court. NY, 1889. 1st US ed, earliest state w/'S' ornament in caption of picture p(59). Blue-gray patterned eps. (Sm tear lower margin frontis; spine ends worn, corners sl bumped.) BAL 3429. Kane*. $160/£103

TWAIN, MARK. A Connecticut Yankee in King Arthur's Court. NY, 1889. 1st US ed, earliest state, w/'S' ornament picture caption p(59). Lt grn floral design eps. (1890 ink sig, 1/4-inch marginal tear Table of Contents, rear inner hinge re-glued; spine ends sl worn, corners sl bumped.) BAL 3429. Kane*. $275/£176

TWAIN, MARK. A Connecticut Yankee in King Arthur's Court. NY: Charles L. Webster, 1889. 1st ed. (Lt spotting.) Grn dec cl (bumped, rubbed, frayed, worn). Metropolitan*. $115/£74

TWAIN, MARK. A Connecticut Yankee in King Arthur's Court. Toronto: Rose, 1890. 1st Canadian ed. Perfect type at p72, no 1/2 title or frontis; S-ornament present p59. Dk olive grn pict cl, darker than Amer ed, fr cvr stamping dk blue, not grey-blue used on Amer ed. VG (joint tears expertly repaired). BAL 3429. Macdonnell. $200/£128

TWAIN, MARK. A Connecticut Yankee in King Arthur's Court. NY: LEC, 1949. One of 1500 numbered, signed by Honore Guilbeau (illus). Cl-backed gold bds. VG in gold slipcase. Argosy. $100/£64

TWAIN, MARK. A Dog's Tale. (London): Nat'l Anti-Vivisection Soc, (1904). 1st ed. Orig buff ptd wrappers. Fine. BAL 3479. Macdonnell. $450/£288

TWAIN, MARK. A Double Barrelled Detective Story. NY, 1902. 1st ed. Pict eps, mixed state. Red cl. VG. BAL 3471. Argosy. $125/£80

TWAIN, MARK. A Double Barrelled Detective Story. NY: Harper, 1902. 1st ed. Teg. Gilt-stamped maroon cl. Fine. Appelfeld. $125/£80

TWAIN, MARK. A Double Barrelled Detective Story. NY: Harper, 1902. 1st ed. Orig red cl as issued w/quotation from Twain ptd in gilt on fr cvr; gilt top. Nice. Appelfeld. $150/£96

TWAIN, MARK. Editorial Wild Oats. NY/London: Harper, 1905. 7 plts. (Tp margin lt browned; faded, bumped, sl chipped; lacks dj.) Edwards. $39/£25

TWAIN, MARK. Eve's Diary. London/NY, 1906. 1st ed. Dj (sm tears, nicks, some tears w/early crude closures on verso). BAL 3489. Swann*. $373/£239

TWAIN, MARK. Extract from Captain Stormfield's Visit to Heaven. NY: Harper, 1909. 1st ed. Sheets bulk 5/8-inch (no priority between copies w/different sheet bulks: 5/8-inch, 9/16-inch, 1/2-inch). Red pict cl. VG. BAL 3511. Macdonnell. $75/£48

TWAIN, MARK. Extract from Captain Stormfield's Visit to Heaven. NY: Harper, 1909. 1st ed. Sheets bulk 1/2-inch (no priority between copies w/different sheet bulks: 5/8-inch, 9/16-inch, 1/2-inch). Red pict cl. NF (white lettering 99% intact). BAL 3511. Macdonnell. $100/£64

TWAIN, MARK. Extract from Captain Stormfield's Visit to Heaven. NY: Harper, 1909. 1st ed. Sheets bulk 5/8 inch. Pict red cl. NF (spine lettering sl rubbed). BAL 3511. Antic Hay. $125/£80

TWAIN, MARK. Extracts from Adam's Diary. NY: Harper, (1904). 1st ed, later issue, but w/'Published April, 1904' on tp verso as in 1st ptg. Red pict cl. VF. BAL 3480. Macdonnell. $50/£32

TWAIN, MARK. Following the Equator. Hartford: American Pub Co, 1897. 1st ed. (Few short tears 1st few leaves; rubbed, shaken.) Metropolitan*. $86/£55

TWAIN, MARK. Following the Equator. Hartford: American Pub Co, 1897. 1st ed, single imprint. Pict blue cl, gilt. (Foot sl frayed), else VG. BAL 3451. Macdonnell. $125/£80

TWAIN, MARK. Following the Equator.... Hartford, 1897. 1st ed. (Owner stamp, prelims foxed; rubbed.) BAL 3451. Kane*. $55/£35

TWAIN, MARK. A Horse's Tale. NY: Harper, 1907. 1st ed. Pict red cl. NF. BAL 3500. Antic Hay. $150/£96

TWAIN, MARK. Huckleberry Finn. Paul Elek, 1948. 1st ed thus. Edward Burra (illus). Tall 8vo. 307pp. Dbl-spread pict eps. Pale blue cl. (Spine, edges faded), else VG, interior NF. Bookmark. $55/£35

TWAIN, MARK. An Inglorious Peace Is Better Than a Dishonorable War! Berkeley: Wheeler Action Committee, (1970). 1st ed. Orig orange pict wrappers. Macdonnell. $50/£32

TWAIN, MARK. The Innocents Abroad. Hartford: Amer Pub Co, 1869. 1st ed, 3rd issue ads p(654). Brn cl stamped in blind/gilt (lt rubbed; ends, corners frayed, worn; early inscrip, later ribbon marker skillfully inserted). BAL 3316. Waverly*. $66/£42

TWAIN, MARK. The Innocents Abroad. London: John Camden Hotten, n.d. (1870). 1st Eng ed. 6 prelim pp undated ads, 22pp ads dated 1872. Grn cl. NF (marginal damage due to careless opening of ll, sl foxing, newspaper clipping affixed to rear pastedown). Sumner & Stillman. $425/£272

TWAIN, MARK. The Jumping Frog in English, Then in French, Then Clawed Back into a Civilized Language Once More. NY: Harper, 1903. 1st separate ed. Red pict cl. VG. BAL 3477. Macdonnell. $75/£48

TWAIN, MARK. The L1,000,000 Bank Note. NY: Webster, 1893. 1st ed. (Sl soil), else Solid. Metropolitan*. $115/£74

TWAIN, MARK. Letters from the Sandwich Islands. SF: Grabhorn, 1937. Ltd to 550. Brn cl, grn bds, paper spine label. Good. Karmiole. $100/£64

TWAIN, MARK. Life on the Mississippi. Boston, 1883. 1st ed, 1st state, intermediate A, w/Twain head in flames p441, 'St. Charles Hotel' p443. (Frontis nearly detached, rear inner hinge cracking.) BAL 3411. Kane*. $375/£240

TWAIN, MARK. Life on the Mississippi. Boston: James R. Osgood, 1883. 1st ed, later issue, 'St. Charles Hotel' p443. (Endsheets split.) Gilt-dec cl (frayed, disbinding). Metropolitan*. $69/£44

TWAIN, MARK. Life on the Mississippi. Boston: James R. Osgood, 1883. 1st ed, 2nd intermediate issue: no illus p441; caption of illus p443 reading, 'The St. Louis Hotel.' Pict brn cl (worn). Good. BAL 3411. Waverly*. $77/£49

TWAIN, MARK. Life on the Mississippi. London, 1883. 1st issue (ads for March). (Blank eps foxed; spine, 2 corners sl bumped, sm damp mk rear cvr), o/w VG. Buckley. $203/£130

TWAIN, MARK. Life on the Mississippi. London: C&W, 1883. 1st ed. Later copy, w/pub's inserted ads dated Oct 1886. Red cl (spine sl faded, extrems eroded), gilt. BAL 3410. Argosy. $250/£160

TWAIN, MARK. Life on the Mississippi. London: C&W, 1883. 1st British ed, 1st issue. (Fore-edge lt foxed), else NF in illus red cl-cvrd bds. Lame Duck. $900/£577

TWAIN, MARK. Life on the Mississippi. NY: Charles Webster, 1888. 1st ed, 1st ptg, intermediate state A, w/illus of Twain's head in flames at p441, but reads 'St. Charles Hotel' at p443. Orig pict brn cl, gilt. Fine. BAL 3411. *Macdonnell.* $650/£417

TWAIN, MARK. Life on the Mississippi. Willis Wager (ed). NY: LEC, 1944. One of 1200 ptd, signed by Thomas Hart Benton (illus). Leather-backed pict cl. Fine in pub's cl clamshell case. *Argosy.* $450/£288

TWAIN, MARK. Life on the Mississippi. Willis Wager (ed). Norwalk: Heritage, 1972. 1st ed. Thomas Hart Benton (illus). Fine in Fine slipcase. *Connolly.* $20/£13

TWAIN, MARK. The Man That Corrupted Hadleyburg. NY: Harper, 1900. 1st ed, 1st state. Orig red cl, gilt. (Spine sl sunned), else Fine. BAL 3459. *Macdonnell.* $300/£192

TWAIN, MARK. Mark Twain in Eruption. Bernard De Voto (ed). NY: Harper, (1940). 1st ed, 1st ptg. (Eps foxed), o/w Fine. BAL 3564. *Glenn.* $55/£35

TWAIN, MARK. Mark Twain's (Burlesque) Autobiography and First Romance. NY: Sheldeon, (1871). 1st ed. Maroon cl as issued. Fine. *Appelfeld.* $250/£160

TWAIN, MARK. Mark Twain's (Burlesque) Autobiography and First Romance. NY: Sheldon, (1871). 1st ed, 2nd state. 47pp, ad. Grn cl (bumped), gilt. NF. BAL 3326. *Blue Mountain.* $45/£29

TWAIN, MARK. Mark Twain's (Burlesque) Autobiography and First Romance. NY: Sheldon, (1871). 1st ed, 1st issue. Grn cl. (Contemp bkseller's ticket, early childish pencil scribbling.) BAL 3326. *Swann*.* $161/£103

TWAIN, MARK. Mark Twain's Autobiography. NY/London: Harper, 1924. 1st ed. 2 vols. Frontis port each vol. (Sl dampstain last few ll vol 1, bkpls), o/w internally Fine in djs (faded, soiled, tape-repaired). BAL 3537. *Pirages.* $60/£38

TWAIN, MARK. Mark Twain's Autobiography. NY: Harper, 1924. Stated 1st ed. 2 vols. Good. *Scribe's Perch*.* $70/£45

TWAIN, MARK. Mark Twain's Jumping Frog. Girard, KS: Haldeman-Julius, n.d. 1st Haldeman-Julius ed. (Edges browned), else Nice in ptd blue wrappers. *Turtle Island.* $15/£10

TWAIN, MARK. Mark Twain's Letters. Albert Bigelow Paine (ed). NY: Harper, (1917). 1st trade ed, 1st ptg, in pub's regular trade binding. 2 vols. Teg, untrimmed. Orig red cl, gilt, spines blocked in gold. NF. BAL 3525. *Macdonnell.* $100/£64

TWAIN, MARK. Mark Twain's Mysterious Stranger Manuscripts. William M. Gibson (ed). Univ of CA, 1969. 1st Amer ed. Fine in dj (spine sl sunned, top sl frayed, price-clipped). *Polyanthos.* $30/£19

TWAIN, MARK. Mark Twain's Mysterious Stranger Manuscripts. William M. Gibson (ed). Berkeley/L.A.: Univ of CA, 1969. 1st ed. Lt gray cl. NF (sm stains fr cvr; fr edge lt spotted) in VG dj (sl soiled, price-clipped). *Blue Mountain.* $35/£22

TWAIN, MARK. Mark Twain, the Writings of...Author's National Edition. NY: Harper, (c. 1911). 25 vols. VG. *New Hampshire*.* $90/£58

TWAIN, MARK. The Million Pound Bank-Note, and Other New Stories. London: C&W, 1893. 1st Eng ed, w/March 1893 terminal cat. Orig red pict cl, gilt. NF. BAL 3436. *Macdonnell.* $200/£128

TWAIN, MARK. More Tramps Abroad. London: C&W, 1897. 1st British ed. 8vo. Ads dated Sep. 1897. Teg. Pub's gilt, blind-stamped maroon cl. (Fr inner hinge starting; lt overall wear), else Fine. *D & D.* $125/£80

TWAIN, MARK. More Tramps Abroad. London: C&W, 1897. 1st Eng ed, 1st issue. (Lt scattered foxing 1/2-title), else Fine. *Between The Covers.* $350/£224

TWAIN, MARK. More Tramps Abroad. London: Chatto, 1897. 1st UK ed of 'Following the Equator.' 32pp cat dated Sept 1897. VG (few pp lt foxed). *Williams.* $125/£80

TWAIN, MARK. The Mysterious Stranger and Other Stories. NY/London: Harper, 1922. 1st ed, 1st ptg, binding A. Orig red cl, gilt. (Spine gilt oxidized, rear hinge paper cracked), else Fresh. BAL 3534. *Macdonnell.* $100/£64

TWAIN, MARK. The Notorious Jumping Frog and Other Stories. NY: LEC, 1970. One of 1500 numbered, signed by Joseph Low (illus). (Spine faded.) Bd slipcase. *Argosy.* $125/£80

TWAIN, MARK. The Prince and the Pauper. Montreal: Dawson Bros, 1881. Cancel tp imprinted 'Author's Canadian Edition.' (Lt foxing), o/w Contents VG. (Extrems sl worn.) BAL 3397. *New Hampshire*.* $200/£128

TWAIN, MARK. The Prince and the Pauper. Boston: James R. Osgood, 1882. 1st ed. Grn dec cl (rubbed, frayed, sl shaken). *Metropolitan*.* $115/£74

TWAIN, MARK. The Prince and the Pauper. Boston: James R. Osgood, 1882. 1st ed. Newspaper article tipped to fep (some offset). Gilt/blind-tooled grn cl. (Lt handling), else Fine. *D & D.* $490/£314

TWAIN, MARK. The Prince and the Pauper. NY: Winston, 1937. 1st ed. Robert Lawson (illus). 6 1/2 x 8 1/2. 274pp. VG in dj. *Cattermole.* $45/£29

TWAIN, MARK. The Prince and the Pauper. Westerham: LEC, 1964. One of 1500 numbered, signed by Clarke Hutton (illus). Color frontis, 11 color plts. Royal blue velvet-backed tan cl, ptd spine label. Fine in slipcase (sl soiled), ptd spine label. *Argonaut.* $175/£112

TWAIN, MARK. Pudd'nhead Wilson. London: C&W, 1894. 1st ed, w/pub's cat dated Sept 1894. Red cl (sl soiled, spine cocked; sl dknd; joints sl frayed). Text VG (rear inside hinge cracked; later ribbon marker skillfully inserted). BAL 3441. *Waverly*.* $99/£63

TWAIN, MARK. Pudd'nhead Wilson. With Pudd'nhead Wilson's Calendar. Avon, CT: LEC, 1974. One of 2000 numbered, signed by John Groth (illus). 7 color plts. Lithographed buckram, gilt-lettered leather spine label. Marbled paper wrappers, ptd paper cvr label. Fine set in slipcase w/ptd paper label. *Argonaut.* $150/£96

TWAIN, MARK. Rambling Notes of an Idle Excursion. Toronto: Rose-Belford, 1878. 1st ed, 1st ptg this title. Orig purple cl, gilt. VG (spine sunned, lt rubbed). BAL 3619. *Macdonnell.* $225/£144

TWAIN, MARK. Roughing It. Hartford: American Pub Co, 1872. 1st ed. 3/4 leather, gilt-dec spine. Fine (new eps). *Metropolitan*.* $115/£74

TWAIN, MARK. Roughing It. Hartford: American Publishing, 1872. 1st Amer ed. 2 frontispieces, 591,(1)pp; 6 inserted plts. State B of p243, lacking word 'he' in line 20; ad on p(592). Gilt-dec cl (lt worn, spine dull). Contents VG. Full imprint same as BAL 3337. *New Hampshire*.* $70/£45

TWAIN, MARK. The Stolen White Elephant. Boston: James E. Osgood, 1882. 1st Amer ed. 306pp + 12pp pub's cat. Pict beige cl (sl worn). Good. BAL 3404. *Lucas.* $60/£38

TWAIN, MARK. Tom Sawyer Abroad. NY: Charles L. Webster, 1894. 1st ed. Orig white pict cl (rubbed, soiled; scribbling eps), gilt. BAL 3440. *Macdonnell.* $125/£80

TWAIN, MARK. The Tragedy of Pudd'nhead Wilson. Hartford, 1894. 1st ed. Frontis port. Pub's cl. (Notes feps.) Nice. BAL 3442. *Swann*.* $287/£184

TWAIN, MARK. A Tramp Abroad. Hartford/London: American Pub Co/C&W, 1880. 1st ed, 2nd issue. xvi,(17)-631,(1)pp. Later 1/2 morocco, cl sides, raised bands, gilt. Internally Excellent (owner stamp; sl worn, faded) in mod slipcase (repaired). BAL 3386. *Pirages*. $225/£144

TWAIN, MARK. A Tramp Abroad. Hartford: Amer Pub Co, 1880. (Ex-libris, hinge interior exposed.) Marbled eps, edges. 3/4 brn leather. *Metropolitan**. $75/£48

TWAIN, MARK. Travels at Home. NY: Harper, 1910. 1st ed. Port, 7 plts. Dec grn cl (sl soiled, faded; bkpls). BAL 3673. *Agvent*. $100/£64

TWAIN, MARK. Travels in History...Selected from the Works of Mark Twain by C.N. Kendall.... NY: Harper, 1910. 1st ed thus. Orig red cl stamped in brn. Fine. BAL 3674. *Macdonnell*. $100/£64

TWAIN, MARK. What Is Man? Watts, 1910. Good (fore-edge sl spotted, spine bumped). *Tiger*. $55/£35

TWAIN, MARK. What Is Man? London, 1910. 1st ed. (Rubbed; sl cvr spotting; sig loose.) *King*. $125/£80

TWAIN, MARK. The Writings of Mark Twain; The Definitive Edition. NY: Gabriel Wells, 1922. Ltd to 1024 sets signed by Clemens and 'Mark Twain.' 35 vols. 8vo. Bound-in addendum. Cl-backed bds, ptd paper spine labels. Partially unopened. Fine (bkpl each vol; uniform sl spine dkng; few vols lt rubbed). *Bromer*. $3,750/£2,404

TWAIN, MARK. The Writings. NY, (1899-1907). Hillcrest ed. 25 vols. 8vo. Contemp 1/4 brn morocco, flat spines gilt. *Swann**. $1,035/£663

TWAMLEY, LOUISA ANNE. The Romance of Nature; or, The Flower-Seasons Illustrated. London: Charles Tilt, 1836. 2nd ed. Add'l hand-colored engr tp, 27 hand-colored engr plts (tp, few plts spotted). Gilt edges. Orig grn morocco (spine, extrems rubbed), gilt. *Christie's**. $245/£157

Twelve Hours on the Wreck; or, The Stranding of the Sheffield. (By Benjamin C. Butler.) NY: T.C. Butler, 1844. 1st ed. 72pp. Orig ptd bds (rehinged, cvrs rubbed). *Lefkowicz*. $125/£80

Twentieth Century Peerless Atlas and Gazetteer of All Lands. Springfield, OH: Crowell, ca 1903. Photogravure tp. Maroon pebbled bds (broken, lacks fep). Internally Good. *Hudson*. $160/£103

Twenty-Seventh Indiana Volunteer Infantry in the War of the Rebellion, 1861 to 1865.... (By Edmund Randolph Brown.) (Monticello, IN: Privately Pub, 1899.) 1st ed. 640,(2)pp. (Ex-libris.) Later buckram. Very Nice. *Mcgowan*. $250/£160

TWINING, E. W. The Art and Craft of Stained Glass. 1928. 1st ed. 10 full-pg color plts. Black gilt-dec blue cl (worn). Good+. *Whittle*. $86/£55

TWITCHELL, RALPH EMERSON. The Leading Facts of New Mexican History. Cedar Rapids: Torch, 1911-17. 5 vols. Pub's variant cl (lt worn). Howes T448. *Dumont*. $1,500/£962

TWITCHELL, RALPH EMERSON. Old Santa Fe. Santa Fe, 1925. Subs ed. #383/1000. Frontis. (Extrems sl worn), o/w Fine. *Turpen*. $125/£80

TWITCHELL, RALPH EMERSON. Spanish Archives of New Mexico. Cedar Rapids, 1914. 1st ed. 2 vols. VG. Howes T445. *Turpen*. $750/£481

TWITCHETT, JOHN. Derby Porcelain. London, 1980. 1st ed. 81 color plts. Dj. *Edwards*. $70/£45

TWITE, M. L. The World's Racing Cars. London: MacDonald, (1964). 1st ed. Grn cl, gilt. Good. *Shasky*. $45/£29

TWITTY, V. C. Of Scientists and Salamanders. SF: Freeman, 1966. 1st ed. Color frontis. Dec cl. Fine in Fine dj. *Mikesh*. $35/£22

Two by Two, Noah's Ark Book. NY: Sam'l Gabriel Sons, 1924. 4to. 12pp (edges dknd, lt foxed, soiled, sm tears 2pp). B/w pict eps. Stapled color pict wraps (soiled, creased, rear spotted, spine split). Good. *Blue Mountain*. $25/£16

Two Letters, Addressed to a British Merchant.... (By John Bowles.) London, 1796. 1st ed. (2)leaves, 83pp. 19th-cent 3/4 morocco (rubbed, spine head chipped, sl soil). *Oinonen**. $60/£38

TYAS, ROBERT. Flowers and Heraldry. London: Houlston & Wright, 1851. xiv,(1),238pp; 24 hand-color plts by James Andrews. Aeg. (Rear hinge cracked), else Well Preserved. *Quest*. $325/£208

TYERMAN, DANIEL and GEORGE BENNETT. Journal of Voyages and Travels...in the South Sea Islands, China, India...1821-1829. James Montgomery (comp). London: Frederick Westley & A.H. Davis, 1831. 1st ed. 2 vols. xxiv,566; viii,568pp; 2 frontis ports, 12 plts. Antique style calf-backed marbled bds; uncut. Very Attractive (sm lib stamps title versos). *Lefkowicz*. $850/£545

TYLER, ANNE. The Clock Winder. NY: Knopf, 1972. 1st ed. VG+ (offsetting from tape to portion of pastedowns) in dj (tape residue verso). *Lame Duck*. $650/£417

TYLER, ANNE. The Clock Winder. NY: Knopf, 1972. 1st ed. Fine (bds edges sl sunned) in VG dj (spine lt dknd, fr panel wrinkling, sm tear bottom fr panel). *Between The Covers*. $750/£481

TYLER, ANNE. If Morning Ever Comes. NY: Knopf, 1964. 1st ed. (Bd edges sl faded), else NF in VG+ dj (spine extrems lt worn, fr flap fold splitting). *Lame Duck*. $950/£609

TYLER, ANNE. If Morning Ever Comes. NY: Knopf, 1964. 1st ed, 1st bk. (Thin fade line fr panel), else Beautiful in Beautiful dj (price-clipped). *Captain's Bookshelf*. $1,500/£962

TYLER, ANNE. If Morning Ever Comes. London: C&W, 1965. 1st Eng ed, 1st bk. Fine in Fine dj (lt scuffing spine). *Between The Covers*. $850/£545

TYLER, ANNE. Searching for Caleb. London: C&W, 1976. 1st UK ed. (Ink inscrip fep), o/w NF in dj (price-clipped). *Moorhouse*. $55/£35

TYLER, ANNE. The Tin Can Tree. London, 1966. 1st ed. VG (flyleaf erasure) in dj (chipped, closed tear). *Buckley*. $70/£45

TYLER, ANNE. The Tin Can Tree. London: Macmillan, 1966. 1st British ed. (Sig, spine sl bumped), else NF in NF dj (extrems lt worn). *Lame Duck*. $200/£128

TYLER, DANIEL. A Concise History of the Mormon Battalion in the Mexican War, 1846-1847. (Salt Lake City), 1881. 1st ed. (4),376pp (new eps). Full orig leather (spine repaired). Howes T447. *Ginsberg*. $350/£224

TYLER, HAMILTON A. Pueblo Gods and Myths. Norman, OK, 1964. 1st ed. VF. *Five Quail*. $30/£19

TYLER, RON. Visions of America. 1983. 57 color plts, map. Dj. *Edwards*. $31/£20

TYMMS, W. R. and M. D. WYATT. The Art of Illuminating as Practised in Europe from the Earliest Times. London: Day & Son, 1860. 1st ed. Aeg. Orig cl (rebacked), orig cl spine strip. (Bkpl, fr hinge starting), else VG. *Pacific**. $69/£44

TYNDALE, WALTER. An Artist in Italy. London: Hodder & Stoughton, (1913). 1st ed. 26 tipped-in color plts, guards. VG in dec cl, gilt. *Cox*. $28/£18

TYNDALE, WALTER. Below the Cataracts. London/Phila: Heinemann/Lippincott, 1907. 1st ed. 60 color plts. (Sl rubbed), o/w VG. *Worldwide*. $65/£42

TYNDALE, WALTER. Below the Cataracts. London: Heinemann, 1907. 60 color plts. (Bkpl.) Pict cl (spine faded). *Archaeologia*. $95/£61

TYNDALL, JOHN. Essays on the Floating Matter of the Air in Relation to Putrefaction and Infection. 1883. 2nd ed. xix,338pp (contemp ink sig, ink notes feps). Blind-stamped cl (spine ends sl worn). *Whitehart.* $94/£60

TYNDALL, JOHN. Essays on the Floating-Matter of the Air in Relation to Putrefaction and Infection. NY: Appleton, 1882. 1st Amer ed. xix,338,(4 ads)pp. Dec emb cl. NF. *Glaser.* $235/£151

TYNDALL, JOHN. The Forms of Water in Clouds and Rivers, Ice and Glaciers. Appleton, 1877. 196pp. (New eps), o/w VG + . *Bookcell.* $40/£26

TYRRELL, FREDERICK. Practical Work on the Diseases of the Eye.... London, 1840. 1st ed. 2 vols. 1 b/w, 8 color plts. Leather-backed marbled bds (lt worn). Contents VG. *New Hampshire*.* $120/£77

TYRRELL, J. W. Across the Sub-Arctics of Canada.... Toronto: Wm. Briggs, 1897. vi,(7)-280pp, fldg map. Teg. Old 1/2 calf (sl rubbed). VG. *High Latitude.* $130/£83

TYRWHITT, R. ST. JOHN. A Handbook of Pictorial Art. Oxford: Clarendon, 1868. 1st ed. Mtd chromolitho frontis, xi,(5),480pp; 3 chromolitho plts, 2 mtd albumens, 2 salt paper prints. Blind-stamped morocco. (Bkpl, blindstamp, 1st few ll foxed; rubbed), else VG. *Cahan.* $275/£176

TYSON, JAMES L. Diary of a Physician in California. NY, 1850. 92pp. (1/2-inch missing corners 1st 2 leaves, corners 10 leaves wrinkled; fr wrapper foxed.) *Fye.* $300/£192

TYSON, JAMES L. Diary of a Physician in California. Oakland: Biobooks, 1955. One of 500. (Spine lettering rubbed), else NF. *Cahan.* $35/£22

TYTLER, SARAH and J. L. WATSON. The Songstresses of Scotland. London: Strahan, 1871. 1st ed. 2 vols. Blind-dec cl, gilt. (Top edges dusty; spines dknd, rubbed; ends worn), o/w VG. *Poetry Bookshop.* $133/£85

U

U.S. AMERICAN BATTLE MONUMENTS COMMISSION. 1st Division, Summary of Operations in the World War. Washington: Amer Battle Monuments Commission, 1944. 7 fldg pocket maps. VG in cl-cvrd folder. *Bohling.* $30/£19

U. S. GEOLOGICAL SURVEY. See USGS

U.S. Geological and Geographical Survey. Contributions to North American Ethnology. (Washington), 1879-1894. 1st ed. Vol 1-9, vol 8 not pub. *Ginsberg.* $750/£481

UDELL, JOHN. Journal Kept During a Trip Across the Plains. L.A., 1946. VG + . *Bohling.* $30/£19

UDELL, JOHN. Journal Kept During a Trip Across the Plains...in 1859. L.A., 1946. Ltd to 750. Facs tp. Brn cl, gilt. VF. Howes U3, U4. *Five Quail.* $40/£26

UELSMANN, JERRY N. Jerry N. Uelsmann: Silver Meditations. NY: Morgan & Morgan Monograph, 1977. 2nd ptg. 146 b/w plts. (Owner stamp), else VG in pict stiff wrappers. *Cahan.* $25/£16

ULLMAN, JAMES RAMSEY. Down the Colorado with Major Powell. Boston: Houghton Mifflin, 1960. 1st ed. (Name, inscrip.) Grn pict cl. Fine in VG + full-color dj. *Five Quail.* $25/£16

ULLMAN, VICTOR. Look to the North Star: A Life of William King. Boston: Beacon Press, (1969). 1st ed. Inscribed presentation. Map. Cl-backed bds. VG in ptd dj. *Petrilla.* $40/£26

ULLOM, JUDITH. Folklore of the North American Indians. Washington, 1969. 1st ed. (2 tips lt bumped), o/w NF. *Turpen.* $25/£16

ULMANN, DORIS. A Book of Portraits of the Faculty of the Medical Department of the Johns Hopkins University Baltimore. Balt, 1922. 1st ed. Folio. 36 ports. Untrimmed. Fine. *Fye.* $750/£481

Uncle Philip's Conversations with the Children About the Whale Fishery and Polar Seas. (By Francis Lister Hawks.) NY: Harper, 1854-60. 2 vols. 209; 210pp. (Vol 1 lacks blank fep; spine ends chipped.) *Lefkowicz.* $135/£87

Uncle Sam's Large Almanac, for 1839.... Phila: Wm. W. Walker, (1838). 18 leaves. VG (closed tear rear wrapper; corners creased) in wrappers. *Cahan.* $45/£29

UNDERHILL, FRANCIS T. Driving for Pleasure, or, The Harness Stable and Its Appointments. NY: D. Appleton, 1897. 1st ed. xi,158pp, 124 plts. 3/4 tan leather (extrems, spine ends sl rubbed), suede leather-cvrd bds, gilt-stamped cvr whip design, gilt lettering. Fine. *Argonaut.* $250/£160

UNDERHILL, RUTH M. The Navajos. Norman, (1956). Rev ed (1967). VG + (cvr sl worn). *Pratt.* $27/£17

UNDERHILL, RUTH M. The Navajos. Norman: Univ of OK, (1956). 1st ed. Fine in VG dj. *Perier.* $50/£32

UNDERHILL, RUTH M. People of the Crimson Evening. US Indian Service, (1951). 1st ed. VG in wraps. *Oregon.* $35/£22

UNDERHILL, RUTH M. Red Man's Religion. Chicago: Univ of Chicago, (1965). 1st ed. VG in dj. *Lien.* $60/£38

UNDERHILL, SAMUEL. Underhill on Mesmerism, with Criticisms on Its Opposers.... Chicago: The Author, 1868. 1st ed. 271,(1)pp. *Ginsberg.* $300/£192

UNDERWOOD, LAMAR. The Bobwhite Quail Book. Clinton: Amwell Press, 1980. Ltd to 1000 signed by Underwood & Donald Shoffstall (illus). Full grn leather. VF in slipcase. *Truepenny.* $95/£61

UNDERWOOD, LAMAR. The Bobwhite Quail Book. Clinton: Amwell, 1980. One of 1000 numbered, signed by Underwood, Donald Shoffstall (illus) and Jim Rikhoff. Gilt-stamped leatherette (lt worn). Slipcase. *Oinonen*.* $70/£45

UNDERWOOD, MICHAEL. A Treatise on the Diseases of Children, with General Directions for the Management of Infants from Birth.... Phila, 1793. 1st Amer ed. 402pp (tp, preface in facs). 1/4 navy cl (rebound), marbled bds, leather label, gilt bands. Good. *Doctor's Library.* $235/£151

UNDERWOOD, MICHAEL. A Treatise on the Diseases of Children.... London: Callow & Wilson et al, 1827. 8th ed. xxxii,636pp (lib stamps eps, sig tp). Contemp 1/2 calf (rubbed, joints starting to split). Text Very Clean. *White.* $101/£65

UNDERWOOD, TIM and CHUCK MILLER (eds). Fear Itself: The Horror Fiction of Stephen King. SF: Underwood-Miller, 1982. 1st trade ed. Fine in dj. *Captain's Bookshelf.* $75/£48

UNGERER, TOMI. Emile. NY, (1960). 1st ed. Cl-backed pict bds. VG. *Argosy.* $75/£48

United States Practical Receipt Book.... Phila: Lindsay & Blakiston, (1844). 1st ed. 2pp pub's ad at fr. Orig gilt/blind-stamped purple cl (rubbed, faded, stained). Good + . *Houle.* $300/£192

Universal Atlas. NY: Dodd, Mead, 1894. 86 dbl-pg color maps (1 fldg). Red cl (fr hinge torn). *Hudson.* $150/£96

UNSCHULD, PAUL. Medicine in China: A History of Pharmaceutics. Berkeley, 1986. 1st ed. VG. *Fye.* $65/£42

UNSWORTH, BARRY. The Big Day. NY: Mason/Charter, 1977. 1st US ed. Fine in dj. *Lame Duck.* $75/£48

UNSWORTH, BARRY. The Hide. London: Gollancz, 1970. 1st ed. (Sm dampstain bottom pg edges), else NF in dj. *Lame Duck.* $100/£64

UNSWORTH, BARRY. Pascali's Island. London, 1980. 1st Eng ed. Rev slip. Fine in dj. *Clearwater.* $62/£40

UNSWORTH, BARRY. Stone Virgin. London, 1985. 1st Eng ed. Very Nice in dj. *Clearwater.* $39/£25

UNSWORTH, BARRY. Stone Virgin. Boston: Houghton Mifflin, 1986. 1st Amer ed. Ochre cl-backed lt tan bds (bumped, spine rubbed, fr bd sl soiled). Internally Fine in dj (sl rubbed, chipped). *Blue Mountain.* $20/£13

UNTERECKER, JOHN. Voyager: A Life of Hart Crane. NY: FSG, (1969). 1st ed. Vermillion cl, gilt. NF in dj (back panel sl soiled). *Blue Mountain.* $30/£19

UNTERMEYER, LOUIS. Aesop's Fables. NY: Golden, 1965. 1st ed. Alice & Martin Provensen (illus). 10 1/2 x 12 1/4. 88pp. Glossy bds. VG in dj. *Cattermole.* $20/£13

Unwritten History of Slavery Autobiographical Account of Negro Ex-Slaves. Nashville: Social Science Inst, Fisk Univ, 1945. 1st ed. (Tp torn, repaired w/archival tape, ex-lib, fr wrap detached but present), else Good. *Brown.* $125/£80

UPDIKE, JOHN. Assorted Prose. NY: Knopf, 1965. 1st ed. Signed leaf tipped-in. Fine in dj (sl soiled, toned). *Waverly*.* $110/£71

UPDIKE, JOHN. Bech Is Back. NY: Knopf, 1982. One of 500 numbered, signed. Fine in Fine dj, slipcase. *Lenz.* $125/£80

UPDIKE, JOHN. Bech Is Back. NY: Knopf, 1982. One of 500 numbered, signed. Fine in dj, pub's slipcase. *Lame Duck.* $150/£96

UPDIKE, JOHN. Bech: A Book. Deutsch, 1970. 1st UK ed. Fine in NF dj (spine sl faded). *Williams.* $23/£15

UPDIKE, JOHN. Bech: A Book. NY: Knopf, 1970. One of 500 numbered, signed. Fine in Fine dj, slipcase. *Waverly*.* $71/£46

UPDIKE, JOHN. Bech: A Book. NY: Knopf, 1970. One of 500 numbered, signed. Fine in Fine dj, slipcase. *Lenz.* $125/£80

UPDIKE, JOHN. The Beloved. Northridge, CA: Lord John, 1982. One of 300 numbered, signed. Fine. *Lenz.* $125/£80

UPDIKE, JOHN. Bottom's Dream adapted from William Shakespeare's A Midsummer Night's Dream. NY: Knopf, (1969). 1st ed. Warren Chappell (illus). VF in pict dj (lt chipped). *Bromer.* $95/£61

UPDIKE, JOHN. Bottom's Dream. NY: Knopf, (1969). 1st ed. Signed. Fine in Fine dj. *Lenz.* $200/£128

UPDIKE, JOHN. Brazil. NY, 1994. 1st Amer ed. Signed presentation, dated 1994. Fine in Fine dj. *Polyanthos.* $40/£26

UPDIKE, JOHN. Buchanan Dying. NY, 1974. 1st ed. NF in NF dj. *Warren.* $75/£48

UPDIKE, JOHN. The Carpentered Hen and Other Tame Creatures. NY: Harper, 1958. 1st ed. VG (inscrip) in 1st state dj (price-clipped, browned). *Metropolitan*.* $287/£184

UPDIKE, JOHN. The Carpentered Hen. NY: Harper, (1958). 1st ed. (Sl shelf-rubbed), else Fine in 1st issue dj w/mention of 2 children (price-clipped, lt soiled). *Waverly*.* $253/£162

UPDIKE, JOHN. The Centaur. NY, 1963. 1st ed. Cl-backed bds. VG in dj (sl discolored, sl edgetorn). *King.* $125/£80

UPDIKE, JOHN. The Coup. NY: Knopf, 1978. One of 350 numbered, signed. Fine in Fine dj, slipcase. *Lenz.* $175/£112

UPDIKE, JOHN. The Coup. Deutsch, 1979. 1st UK ed. NF in dj (price-clipped). *Williams.* $16/£10

UPDIKE, JOHN. Couples. London: Andre Deutsch, 1968. 1st Eng ed. VG in dj. *Hollett.* $23/£15

UPDIKE, JOHN. Couples. NY, 1968. 1st ed. Fine in Fine dj. *Smith.* $20/£13

UPDIKE, JOHN. A Good Place. N.p.: Aloe Editions, 1973. One of 100 numbered, signed. Fine in sewn olive grn self-wraps. *Lame Duck.* $250/£160

UPDIKE, JOHN. Hawthorne's Creed. NY: Targ Editions, (1981). Ltd to 250 signed. Fine in Fine dj. *Polyanthos.* $100/£64

UPDIKE, JOHN. Hoping for a Hoopoe. Gollancz, 1959. 1st UK ed. Fine in dj (sl mk fr panel). *Williams.* $75/£48

UPDIKE, JOHN. The Magic Flute. NY: Knopf, (1962). Obl 4to. Lib binding, pict bds (lt rubbed). Fine; no dj as issued. *Between The Covers.* $850/£545

UPDIKE, JOHN. Marry Me. NY: Knopf, 1976. One of 300 numbered, signed. Fine in Fine dj, slipcase. *Lenz.* $175/£112

UPDIKE, JOHN. Midpoint and Other Poems. NY: Knopf, 1969. One of 350 numbered, signed. Fine in Find dj, slipcase. *Waverly*.* $82/£53

UPDIKE, JOHN. A Month of Sundays. NY: Knopf, 1975. One of 450 numbered, signed, specially bound. Fine in dj, pub's slipcase. *Dermont.* $125/£80

UPDIKE, JOHN. A Month of Sundays. NY: Knopf, 1975. One of 450 numbered, signed. Fine in Fine dj, slipcase. *Lenz.* $150/£96

UPDIKE, JOHN. A Month of Sundays. NY: Knopf, 1975. #2/250 numbered, signed. Fine in dj & slipcase. *Between The Covers.* $175/£112

UPDIKE, JOHN. Museums and Women and Other Stories. NY: Knopf, 1972. One of 350 numbered, signed. Fine in Fine dj, slipcase. *Lenz.* $200/£128

UPDIKE, JOHN. An Oddly Lovely Day Alone. Richmond: Waves, 1979. 1st ed. One of 250 signed (of 276). Broadside. Fine. *Cahan.* $85/£54

UPDIKE, JOHN. Picked-Up Pieces. NY: Knopf, 1975. One of 250 numbered, signed. Fine in Fine dj, slipcase. *Lenz.* $275/£176

UPDIKE, JOHN. Pigeon Feathers and Other Stories. NY: Knopf, 1962. 1st ed. 1/4 cl. NF in white dj (sl soiled, crimped, toned). *Waverly*.* $49/£31

UPDIKE, JOHN. The Poorhouse Fair. NY: Knopf, (1959). 1st ed. VG in VG dj (short tears, few creases, lt worn). *Metropolitan*.* $143/£92

UPDIKE, JOHN. Problems and Other Stories. NY: Knopf, 1979. One of 350 numbered, signed. Fine in Fine dj, slipcase. *Lenz.* $175/£112

UPDIKE, JOHN. Rabbit at Rest. NY, 1990. 1st ed. Fine in dj. *Argosy.* $30/£19

UPDIKE, JOHN. Rabbit Is Rich. NY: Knopf, 1981. One of 350 numbered, signed. Fine in Fine dj, slipcase. *Lenz.* $275/£176

UPDIKE, JOHN. Rabbit Redux. NY, 1971. 1st ed. Fine in Fine dj. *Smith.* $20/£13

UPDIKE, JOHN. Rabbit Redux. NY: Knopf, 1971. One of 350 numbered, signed. Fine in acetate dj, slipcase. *Waverly*.* $104/£67

UPDIKE, JOHN. Rabbit Redux. Deutsch, 1972. 1st UK ed. Fine in dj. *Williams.* $31/£20

UPDIKE, JOHN. Rabbit, Run. NY: Knopf, 1960. 1st ed. Cl-backed bds. (Edges sl soiled), else NF in dj (lt soiled, few sm tears, chip, stain from 4-inch mend, now removed). *Waverly*.* $110/£71

UPDIKE, JOHN. Rabbit, Run. NY: Knopf, 1960. 1st ed. Fine in dj (sl rubbed, price-clipped). *Between The Covers.* $550/£353

UPDIKE, JOHN. The Same Door. NY: Knopf, 1959. 1st ed. NF in VG dj (worn, sl chipped). *Captain's Bookshelf.* $125/£80

UPDIKE, JOHN. The Same Door. NY: Knopf, 1959. Fine in NF dj (lt rubbed, internal repair). *Between The Covers.* $250/£160

UPDIKE, JOHN. Talk from the Fifties. Northridge, CA: Lord John, 1979. One of 300 numbered, signed. Fine. *Lenz.* $125/£80

UPDIKE, JOHN. Talk from the Fifties. Northridge: Lord John Press, 1979. 1st ed. Ltd to 300 signed. Cl-backed patterned bds. VF. *Bromer.* $125/£80

UPDIKE, JOHN. Talk from the Fifties. Northridge: Lord John, 1979. One of 300 numbered, signed. Cl, paper-cvrd bds. Fine. *Between The Covers.* $150/£96

UPDIKE, JOHN. Telephone Poles and Other Poems. NY: Knopf, 1963. 1st ed. Fine in dj (2 sm tears). *Between The Covers.* $125/£80

UPDIKE, JOHN. Telephone Poles and Other Poems. London, 1964. 1st Eng ed. As New. *Bond.* $65/£42

UPDIKE, JOHN. Three Illuminations in the Life of an American Author. Targ Editions, 1979. One of 350 numbered, signed. As New in tissue dj as issued. *Dermont.* $75/£48

UPDIKE, JOHN. Three Texts from Early Ipswich. Ipswich, MA: 17th Cent Day Comm of the Town of Ipswich, 1968. 1st ed. Signed. Fine in wrappers. *Lenz.* $150/£96

UPDIKE, JOHN. Tossing and Turning. NY, 1977. 1st ed. VG in dj. *Argosy.* $45/£29

UPDIKE, JOHN. Warm Wine. NY: Albondocandi, 1973. One of 250 (of 276) numbered, signed. Fine in handsewn French marbled paper self-wraps. *Lame Duck.* $125/£80

UPDIKE, JOHN. Warm Wine. NY: Albondocani, 1973. 1st ed. One of 250 (of 276) numbered, signed. Ptd label. Fine in marbled wrappers. *Reese.* $85/£54

UPDIKE, JOHN. Warm Wine. NY: Albondocani, 1973. One of 250 numbered, signed. Fine in Fine wrappers. *Lenz.* $175/£112

UPDIKE, JOHN. The Witches of Eastwick. NY: Franklin Library, 1984. 1st ed. Signed. VF in gilt dec leather. *Else Fine.* $75/£48

UPDIKE, JOHN. The Witches of Eastwick. NY: Knopf, 1984. 1st ed. Ltd to 350 signed. VF in dec slipcase. *Bromer.* $175/£112

UPFIELD, ARTHUR W. The Battling Prophet. London: Heinemann, 1956. 1st ed. Fine in dj (price-clipped, wear). *Mordida.* $85/£54

UPFIELD, ARTHUR W. The Body at Madman's Bend. GC: DCC, 1963. 1st ed. (Stain on fore-edge), o/w VG in Fine dj (sl wear spine ends). *Mordida.* $40/£26

UPFIELD, ARTHUR W. Bony and the Black Virgin. London: Heinemann, 1959. 1st ed. Fine in dj (price-clipped, sl wear). *Mordida.* $65/£42

UPFIELD, ARTHUR W. The Bushman Who Came Back. NY, 1957. 1st ed. VG in dj (creased, chipped). *Words Etc.* $62/£40

UPFIELD, ARTHUR W. The Lake Frome Monster. London: Heinemann, 1966. 1st ed. Fine in dj (rubbed). *Mordida.* $65/£42

UPFIELD, ARTHUR W. Madman's Bend. 1963. 1st ed. (Name), o/w VG in dj (corners, spine torn). *Words Etc.* $19/£12

UPFIELD, ARTHUR W. Man of Two Tribes. 1956. 1st ed. VG in dj. *Words Etc.* $62/£40

UPFIELD, ARTHUR W. Man of Two Tribes. London: Heinemann, 1956. 1st Eng ed. VG in dj (sl creased, closed tears). *Hadley.* $55/£35

UPFIELD, ARTHUR W. The Mountains Have a Secret. GC: DCC, 1948. 1st ed. VG in dj (chip, closed tears, wear). *Mordida.* $45/£29

UPFIELD, ARTHUR W. Murder Must Wait. GC: DCC, 1953. 1st ed. (Pp dknd), o/w VG in dj (spine faded). *Mordida.* $45/£29

UPFIELD, ARTHUR W. The New Shoe. NY, 1951. 1st ed. VG in dj (spine creased). *Words Etc.* $62/£40

UPFIELD, ARTHUR W. The Sands of Windee. Sydney: Angus & Robertson, 1958. 1st Australian ed. VG in dj (short closed tears, wear). *Mordida.* $45/£29

UPFIELD, ARTHUR W. Venom House. GC: DCC, 1952. 1st ed. VG in dj (spine faded, short closed tears). *Mordida.* $45/£29

UPFIELD, ARTHUR W. The White Savage. GC: DCC, 1961. 1st ed. Fine in dj (price-clipped). *Mordida.* $45/£29

Upland Game Bird Shooting in America. NY: Derrydale, 1930. One of 850. 64 plts (5 in color). Uncut. Gilt-pict cl (sl worn, spine sl scuffed, stained). *Oinonen*.* $375/£240

UPSON, THEODORE FRELINGHUYSEN. With Sherman to the Sea. Bloomington: IN Univ, (1958). 1st ed thus. VG in VG dj. *Mcgowan.* $65/£42

UPWARD, EDWARD. The Railway Accident and Other Stories. London, 1969. 1st Eng ed. Very Nice in dj. *Clearwater.* $47/£30

URIS, LEON. The Angry Hills. NY: Random House, (1955). 1st ed. Fine (sl rubbing spine base) in dj. *Between The Covers.* $350/£224

URIS, LEON. Exodus. GC: Doubleday, (1958). 1st ed. Signed. VG+ in VG+ dj (sl worn). *Unger.* $225/£144

URQUHART, BERYL L. The Camellia. (Vol 1). Sussex: L. Urquhart Press, (1957). 1st ed. 20 color plts. 1/2 cl (faded). VG (sl foxing outer paper edges). *Waverly*.* $132/£85

URWIN, GREGORY J. W. Custer Victorious. Rutherford, (1983). 1st ed. Fine in dj (lt worn). *Pratt.* $30/£19

USBORNE, RICHARD. Wodehouse at Work. London, (1961). 1st ed. Fine in VG dj. *Mcclintock.* $45/£29

USGS. 12th Annual Report...Part II—Irrigation. Washington: GPO, 1892. xviii,576pp. (Sl shaken), else Good. *Dumont.* $75/£48

USGS. 16th Annual Report...Part II—Economic. Washington: GPO, 1895. xix,598pp (ex-lib, stamps, hinges starting); fldg map. Full leather. *Dumont.* $75/£48

USGS. Guidebook of the Western United States; Part B. The Overland Route. Washington: GPO, 1916. Good (worn) in wraps. *Dumont.* $50/£32

USHERWOOD, STEPHEN. The Great Enterprise. Folio Soc, 1978. Pict eps. Coarse buckram, gilt medallion. Fine in plain dj. *Peter Taylor.* $20/£13

USTINOV, PETER. Add a Dash of Pity. London, 1959. 1st ed. Dj (sl frayed). *Typographeum.* $25/£16

USTINOV, PETER. The Love of Four Colonels. NY: Dramatists Play Service, (1953). 1st Amer ed. NF in dj (edgeworn, chip, price-clipped). *Antic Hay.* $20/£13

Utah's Greatest Man Hunt. The True Story of the Hunt for Lopez, by an Eye Witness. (Salt Lake City: Bertrand E. Gallagher, 1913.) 1st ed. Fine (fr leaf separating from staples) in pict red wrappers (spine sl faded). *Argonaut.* $150/£96

UTLEY, GEORGE B. The Life and Times of Thomas John Claggett. Chicago: Lakeside, 1913. 1st ed. Frontis port. *Wantagh.* $35/£22

UTLEY, ROBERT M. Custer Battlefield National Monument—Montana. Washington: Natl Park Service, 1969. Pb. Good. *Lien.* $15/£10

UTLEY, ROBERT M. Frontier Regulars, the United States Army and the Indians, 1866-1890. NY, (1973). 1st ed. Inscribed. VG+ in VG+ dj. *Pratt.* $75/£48

UTLEY, ROBERT M. Frontiersmen in Blue. NY: Macmillan, (1967). 1st ed. VG in dj. *Lien.* $50/£32

UTLEY, ROBERT M. High Noon in Lincoln, Violence on the Western Frontier. Albuquerque: Univ of NM, (1987). 1st ed. Cl-backed tan bds. VF in pict dj. *Argonaut.* $40/£26

UTLEY, ROBERT M. The Last Days of the Sioux Nation. New Haven: Yale Univ, 1963. 1st ed. 20pp photos. VG in dj. *Lien.* $50/£32

UTTLEY, ALISON. Buckinghamshire. Robert Hale, 1950. 1st ed. 8vo. 415pp; 49 photo plts, fldg map. Illus cl. (Rubbed), else VG + in remains of pict dj. *Bookmark.* $39/£25

UTTLEY, ALISON. John Barleycorn. Faber, 1948. 1st ed. Philip Hepworth (illus). 8vo. 184pp. (Cl sl mkd, rubbed), else VG. *Bookmark.* $23/£15

UTTLEY, ALISON. Little Grey Rabbit Goes to the Sea. Collins, 1955. 2nd imp. Margaret Tempest (illus). 8vo. 80pp. Pict bds. NF in pict dj. *Bookmark.* $23/£15

UTTLEY, ALISON. Little Grey Rabbit's Party. London: Collins, (1936). 8vo. 112pp; 25 color plts by Margaret Tempest. (Lt rubbed, bumped), else NF. *Bromer.* $125/£80

UTTLEY, ALISON. Recipes from an Old Farmhouse. Cookery Book Club, 1968. 1st ed thus. Pauline Baynes (illus). 8vo. 132pp. Fine in pict dj (sl worn). *Bookmark.* $31/£20

UTTLEY, ALISON. Snug and Serena Meet a Queen. Heinemann, 1950. 1st ed. Katherine Wigglesworth (illus). 8vo. 71pp. Pict bds. (Edges rubbed), else VG + in pict dj (edges lt chipped). *Bookmark.* $55/£35

UTTLEY, ALISON. Toad's Castle. Heinemann, 1951. 1st ed. Katherine Wigglesworth (illus). 8vo. 71pp. Pict bds. VG + in pict dj (lt dusty, 2 pieces torn away). *Bookmark.* $47/£30

UYEHARA, GEORGE ETSUJIRO. The Political Development of Japan, 1867-1909. London: Constable, 1910. 1st ed. Maroon cl. VG. *Terramedia.* $50/£32

UZANNE, OCTAVE. French Bookbinders of the Eighteenth Century. Mabel McIlvaine (trans). Chicago: Caxton Club, 1904. One of 252 ptd. Mostly unopened. Cl-backed bds (lt bumped), ptd spine label (etched). VG (foxing). *Bohling.* $350/£224

V

VACHELL, HORACE ANNESLEY. Life and Sport on the Pacific Slope. London: Hodder & Stoughton, 1900. 1st ed. Gilt-titled grn cl (etching, lt wear). *Bohling.* $90/£58

VACHSS, ANDREW. Flood. NY, 1985. 1st Amer ed, 1st bk. Fine (spine sl rubbed) in dj. *Polyanthos.* $35/£22

VACHSS, ANDREW. Strega. NY: Knopf, 1987. 1st ed. Inscribed. Fine in Fine dj. *Beasley.* $50/£32

VAIL, R. W. G. The Voice of the Old Frontier. Phila, 1949. 1st ed. (Cvr spots), o/w VG. *Wantagh.* $50/£32

VAIL, R. W. G. The Voice of the Old Frontier. Phila: Univ of PA, 1949. 1st ed. Good. *Heinoldt.* $40/£26

VAIL, R. W. G. The Voice of the Old Frontier. Phila: Univ of PA, 1949. (Eps browned), else Fine w/o dj. *Heller.* $50/£32

VALENTINE, DAVID T. A Compilation of the Existing Ferry Leases and Railroad Grants. NY, 1866. 503pp. Fair (lower 1/2 backstrip gone, binding worn, rear hinge broken). *Bohling.* $30/£19

VALENTINE, DAVID T. Manual of Corporation of the City of New York (1841-1870). 28 vols. Complete set (no vol issued 1867). VG (1 vol lacks spine, some splits, wear). *Metropolitan*.* $3,335/£2,138

VALENTINE, DEBORAH. A Collector of Photographs. London: Gollancz, 1989. 1st hb ed. Fine in dj. *Mordida.* $45/£29

VALENTINER, W. R. Gothic and Renaissance Sculptures in the Collection of the Los Angeles County Museum. L.A., 1951. Good in wrappers (sl rubbed). *Washton.* $35/£22

VALENTINER, W. R. Studies of Italian Renaissance Sculpture. London: Phaidon Press, 1950. 1st ed. Blue cl. Good in illus dj (chipped). *Karmiole.* $85/£54

VALERY, PAUL. Introduction to the Method of Leonardo da Vinci. Thomas McGreevy (trans). London: John Rodker, 1929. 1st ed. #229/875 numbered. Cl-backed patterned bds. VG in dj (lt soiled, chipped). *New Hampshire*.* $40/£26

VALIN, JONATHAN. Dead Letter. NY: Dodd Mead, 1981. 1st ed. Fine in dj (fr panel sl rubbed). *Mordida.* $35/£22

VALIN, JONATHAN. Final Notice. NY: Dodd Mead, 1980. 1st ed. (Name, initials fep), o/w Fine in dj. *Mordida.* $85/£54

VALIN, JONATHAN. The Lime Pit. NY: Dodd Mead, (1980). 1st bk. Fine in Fine dj (sm scratch fr panel). *Between The Covers.* $100/£64

VALIN, JONATHAN. The Lime Pit. NY: Dodd-Mead, 1980. 1st ed, 1st bk. Fine in Fine dj. *Else Fine.* $65/£42

VALIN, JONATHAN. Natural Causes. NY: Congdon & Weed, 1983. 1st ed. Fine in dj (sm closed tear, spine base sl worn). *Mordida.* $30/£19

VALLANCE, AYMER. English Church Screens. Batsford, 1936. (Inscrip), else VG in dec grn cl. *Hadley.* $78/£50

VALLANCE, AYMER. Greater English Church Screens. London: Batsford, 1947. 1st ed. Color frontis. VG in dj. *Hollett.* $70/£45

VALLANCE, AYMER. The Old Colleges of Oxford. London: Batsford, 1912. Teg. Dec cl (corners sl frayed, sl shaken). Good. *Ars Artis.* $148/£95

VALLANCE, AYMER. Old Crosses and Lychgates. 1920. (Eps spotted, bkpl; spine sl discolored.) *Edwards.* $70/£45

VALLIER, DORA. Henri Rousseau. NY: Abrams, (1962). 1st ed. Color frontis, 29 mtd color plts, 161 add'l plts and repros. Grn cl stamped in yellow. Good in dj. *Karmiole.* $100/£64

VAMBERY, ARMINIUS. Sketches of Central Asia. London: Wm. H. Allen, 1868. 1st ed. viii,444pp (lt marginal soil). Good in contemp calf (rebacked), morocco label. Bound w/o 1/2 title. *Cox.* $187/£120

VAMBERY, ARMINIUS. Travels in Central Asia.... London: John Murray, 1864. 1st ed. Frontis, xviii,443pp; 11 wood-engr plts (lacks fldg map). Sound (lt marginal soil) in contemp 1/2 calf, marbled sides (rebacked), morocco label. *Cox.* $101/£65

VAN ALLSBURG, CHRIS. The Wretched Stone. (Boston): Houghton Mifflin, 1991. 1st ed. 28pp. Fine in dj. *Hadley.* $31/£20

VAN ANTWERP, WILLIAM C. A Collector's Comment on His First Editions of the Works of Sir Walter Scott. SF: Gelber, Lilienthal, 1932. One of 400 ptd. Uncut. Cl-backed bds, ptd paper labels. Fine. *Argosy.* $200/£128

VAN BUREN, A. DE PUY. Jottings of a Year's Sojourn in the South. Battle Creek, MI, 1859. 1st ed. Signed 'The Author.' 320pp. (Spine extrems worn.) Howes V15. *Wantagh.* $375/£240

VAN BUREN, E. DOUGLAS. Clay Figurines of Babylonia and Assyria. New Haven: Yale Univ, 1930. 68 plts. (Sig.) *Archaeologia*. $350/£224

VAN BUTCHELL, S. J. Facts and Observations Relative to a Successful Mode of Treating Piles, Fistula.... Henry Renshaw, 1847. 10th ed. (iv),iv,192,(8)pp (2 prelim ll repaired in inner margin). Blind-stamped cl, gilt (backstrip faded, upper cvr lt mkd). *Cox*. $47/£30

VAN CHOATE, S. F. Ocean Telegraphing: Adaption of New Principles for The Successful Working of Submarine Cables. Cambridge: Riverside, 1865. Wraps, mtd photo on fr. (Some edges dog-eared.) *Metropolitan**. $86/£55

VAN CLEVE, CHARLOTTE OUISCONSIN. Three Score Years and Ten. Minneapolis: Harrison & Smith, 1888. 1st ed, 2nd state w/copyright notice tp verso, not on ptd slip. Port, 176pp. (Sides rubbed, worn, scuffed), else Good. Howes V21. *Brown*. $65/£42

VAN DE WATER, FREDERIC F. Glory-Hunter: A Life of General Custer. Indianapolis: Bobbs-Merrill, (1934). Good (pencil underlining; spine dknd). Howes V27. *Lien*. $50/£32

VAN DE WETERING, JANWILLEM. A Glimpse of Nothingness. Boston: HMCo., 1975. 1st ed. Fine in Fine dj. *Dermont*. $50/£32

VAN DE WETERING, JANWILLEM. The Maine Massacre. Boston: HMCo, 1979. 1st ed. Rev copy, slip laid in. Fine in dj (single sm edge tear). *Dermont*. $50/£32

VAN DER ELSKEN, ED. Sweet Life. NY: Abrams, n.d. (Ep stamp), else NF in dj. *Cahan*. $135/£87

VAN DER KOLK, JACOB L. C. SCHROEDER. On the Minute Structure and Functions of the Spinal Cord and Medulla Oblongata.... William Daniel Moore (trans). London: New Sydenham Soc, 1859. 1st ed in English. (xiv),292pp; 10 plts. Emb brn cl. (Expertly re-backed, corners worn), o/w VG. *Gach*. $175/£112

VAN DER POST, LAURENS. A Far-Off Place. London: Hogarth, 1974. 1st UK ed. Fine in dj (spine sl faded). *Williams*. $23/£15

VAN DER POST, LAURENS. The Hunter and the Whale. London, 1967. 1st ed. VG in dj. *Typographeum*. $22/£14

VAN DER POST, LAURENS. The Night of the New Moon. London: Hogarth, 1970. 1st UK ed. VG+ in dj. *Williams*. $28/£18

VAN DER POST, LAURENS. The Seed and the Sower. NY, 1963. 1st Amer ed. Fine (spine sl sunned, extrems sl rubbed) in dj (spine sunned, sm nick). *Polyanthos*. $25/£16

VAN DER POST, LAURENS. Venture to the Interior. NY, 1951. 1st Amer ed. Fine in dj (4 sm tears, sl rubbed). *Polyanthos*. $25/£16

VAN DER STRAETEN, E. The History of the Violin. London, 1933. 1st ed. 2 vols. 48 plts. *Edwards*. $234/£150

VAN DER ZEE, JACOB. The Hollanders of Iowa. Iowa City, 1912. 1st ed. *Ginsberg*. $75/£48

VAN DERSAL, W. R. Native Woody Plants of the U.S. Washington: USDA, Jun. 1938. 1st ed. 44 photo plts, 2 lg fldg pocket maps. VG. *Mikesh*. $25/£16

VAN DERVOOT, J. W. The Water World. NY, 1884. 512pp. Illus cl (rear bd sl scratched). *Edwards*. $44/£28

VAN DINE, S. S. The Bishop Murder Case. NY: Scribner, 1929. 1st ed. Fine in VG dj (chipping, spine rubbed). *Mordida*. $100/£64

VAN DINE, S. S. The Bishop Murder Case. NY: Scribner, 1929. 1st ed. Fine in dj (sl worn). *Else Fine*. $245/£157

VAN DINE, S. S. The Casino Murder Case. NY: Scribner, 1934. 1st ed. Fine in VG dj (inner flaps sl trimmed w/o loss, sl wear). *Mordida*. $150/£96

VAN DINE, S. S. The Garden Murder Case. NY: Scribner, 1935. 1st ed. (Sl rubbed.) Dj (edges, extrems worn). *Metropolitan**. $212/£136

VAN DINE, S. S. The Green Murder Case. NY: Scribner, 1928. 1st ed. Has only 1928 date on copyright pg. (Pg edges dknd, spotted), o/w VG in dj (spine dknd, 1/4-inch piece missing fr panel, closed tears). *Mordida*. $85/£54

VAN DINE, S. S. The Scarab Murder Case. NY: Scribner, 1930. 1st ed. NF. *Else Fine*. $45/£29

VAN DYKE, HENRY (ed). A Creelful of Fishing Stories. NY/London, 1932. 1st ed. VG (cvr lt spotted). *Truepenny*. $45/£29

VAN DYKE, HENRY. Camp-Fires and Guide-Posts. NY: Scribner, 1921. 1st dec ed. Partially unopened. Blue pict cl. Fine w/remnants of dj. *Cummins*. $20/£13

VAN DYKE, HENRY. The Travel Diary of an Angler. NY, 1929. One of 750. Engr frontis signed by Boyer, 5 plts. (Cvrs sl age-dknd.) *Kane**. $70/£45

VAN DYKE, HENRY. The Travel Diary of an Angler. NY: Derrydale, 1929. 1st ed. Ltd to 750. Orig paper-cvrd bds, cl spine. VG. *Mcgowan*. $125/£80

VAN DYKE, JOHN C. The Desert: Further Studies in Natural Appearances. Scribner, 1901. 1st ed. Frontis. (Bkpl; # removed from spine), else VG. *Authors Of West*. $25/£16

VAN DYKE, JOHN C. The Rembrandt Drawings and Etchings. NY, 1927. One of 1200. (Cl sl rubbed.) Internally VG. *Washton*. $50/£32

VAN DYKE, T. S. The Still-Hunter. NY, 1883. 1st ed. 390pp + 6pp ads. Dec cvr, spine, beveled bds. (Fr hinge starting), o/w Good+. *Scribe's Perch**. $37/£24

VAN DYKE, T. S. The Still-Hunter. NY: Macmillan, 1927. 1st illus ed. 27 full-pg halftone dwgs. Blind-stamped gilt-dec cl. VG. *Mikesh*. $45/£29

VAN DYKE, THEODORE. The Still-Hunter. NY: Fords, 1883. 390pp. Grn cl, gilt. (2 sm spine holes, edgewear), else VG. *Price*. $65/£42

VAN EVERY, EDWARD. Sins of New York. NY, 1930. (Cl sl faded.) *Edwards*. $47/£30

VAN GIESON, JUDITH. The Other Side of Death. NY: Harper Collins, 1991. 1st ed. VF in dj. *Mordida*. $65/£42

VAN GIESON, JUDITH. Raptor. Harper, 1990. 1st ed. Signed. Fine in dj. *Murder By The Book*. $125/£80

VAN GIESON, JUDITH. Raptor. NY: Harper & Row, 1990. 1st ed. Advance rev copy w/slip laid in. VF in dj. *Mordida*. $100/£64

VAN GINDERTAEL, ROGER. Ensor. Vivienne Menkes (trans). Studio Vista, 1975. 1st ed. Dj (sl chipped). *Edwards*. $55/£35

VAN GOGH, VINCENT. The Complete Letters of.... Greenwich: NYGS, (1958). 1st trade ed. 3 vols. Tipped-in color frontis each vol. Dk brn cl, gilt. Nice set (spines, top edges sl dusty) in orig pict bd slipcase (broken, partial). *Baltimore**. $80/£51

VAN GOGH, VINCENT. The Complete Letters. Greenwich, (1958). 3 vols. (Lt worn; lacks slipcase.) *Swann**. $201/£129

VAN GRUISEN, N. L., JR. A Holiday in Iceland. London, 1879. 1st ed. 8vo. vii,98pp; 5 photo plts. Excellent orig cl, gilt. *Maggs*. $429/£275

VAN GULIK, ROBERT. The Chinese Lake Murders. Michael Joseph, 1960. 1st UK ed. Fine in VG dj (lt edgewear). *Williams*. $56/£36

VAN GULIK, ROBERT. The Chinese Nail Murders. NY: Harper & Row, (1961). 1st US ed. NF in dj (spine sl tanned). *Reese*. $50/£32

VAN GULIK, ROBERT. The Given Day. Kuala Lumpur: Art Printing Works, 1964. 1st ed. Fine in stiff cardboard wrappers. *Mordida*. $600/£385

VAN GULIK, ROBERT. The Haunted Monastery. Art Printing Works, 1961. 1st ed. One of 2000. (Bkpl; sl soiled.) *Metropolitan**. $172/£110

VAN GULIK, ROBERT. Judge Dee at Work. NY, (1967). 1st ed. VF in dj (lt rubbed). *Mcclintock*. $65/£42

VAN GULIK, ROBERT. Necklace and Calabash. London: Heinemann, 1967. 1st UK ed. VG + in VG dj (sl rubbed, ink prices flap, fep). *Williams*. $44/£28

VAN GULIK, ROBERT. Necklace and Calabash: A Chinese Detective Story. London: Heinemann, 1967. 1st ed in English. Fine in VG + dj (price-clipped, rubbing, 2 closed tears). *Janus*. $50/£32

VAN GULIK, ROBERT. The Phantom of the Temple. NY, (1966). 1st ed. (Old bkstore stamp tp), else VF in NF dj (sl shelfworn). *Mcclintock*. $45/£29

VAN GULIK, ROBERT. Poets and Murder. London: Heinemann, 1968. 1st UK ed. NF in VG dj (sl rubbed). *Williams*. $50/£32

VAN HISE, C. and C. LEITH. The Geology of the Lake Superior Region. Washington: US Geol Survey, 1911. 1st ed. 49 maps and plts. (Lib stamps; cl sl soiled, worn.) *Maggs*. $31/£20

VAN HORNE, THOMAS. History of the Cumberland. Atlas vol only. Cincinnati: R. Clarke, 1875. 1st ed. 22 maps. Red cl. Good. *Archer*. $125/£80

VAN LAREN, A. J. Cactus. Scott E. Haselton (ed). L.A.: Abbey San Encino, 1935. One of 1500. Color frontis, 133 color illus tipped in. Red-ptd linen (bottom tips sl bumped). *Dawson*. $250/£160

VAN LAREN, A. J. Succulents Other Than Cacti. L.A.: Abbey San Encino, 1934. One of 1000. Color frontis, 135 color illus tipped in. (Tips 2 leaves creased, rep lt browned.) Pict bds (extrems lt worn). *Dawson*. $250/£160

VAN LAWICK, H. Among Predators and Prey: A Photographer's Reflections on African Wildlife. SF: S.C., 1986. 1st ed. Fine in Fine dj. *Mikesh*. $35/£22

VAN LOAN, CHARLES E. Fore! NY: Doran, (1918). 1st ed. Dj (lt soiled, rubbed). *Waverly**. $55/£35

VAN LOAN, CHARLES. Score By Innings. Doran, 1919. 1st ed. VG in Good dj. *Plapinger*. $60/£38

VAN LOON, HENDRIK WILLEM. Thomas Jefferson. NY: Dodd, Mead, 1943. 1st ed. NF in dj (lt soiled, sl edgeworn, sm chip). *Captain's Bookshelf*. $75/£48

VAN LOON, HENDRIK. History with a Match. NY: David MacKay, 1917. 1st ed. 7 3/4 x 10. 126pp. Cl, pict onlay. Good. *Cattermole*. $75/£48

VAN LOON, HENDRIK. The Story of Wilbur the Hat. NY: Boni & Liveright, 1925. 1st ed. 7 1/2 x 10. 112pp. Fair. *Cattermole*. $90/£58

VAN MANEN, J. and C. W. LEADBEATER. Some Occult Experiences. India, 1913. VG. *Middle Earth*. $22/£14

VAN NOSTRAND, JEANNE. A Pictorial and Narrative History of Monterey, Adobe Capital of California, 1770-1847. SF: CA Hist Soc, 1968. 1st ed. Pict eps. Red cl, gilt spine. Fine in pict dj. *Pacific**. $58/£37

VAN PELT, DANIEL. Leslie's History of the Greater New York. NY: Arkell, (1898). 2 vols. 554; 539pp. Marbled eps. 1/2 morocco, marbled bds (extrems rubbed). *Cullen*. $150/£96

VAN RENSSELAER, MRS. JOHN KING. The Devil's Picture-Books. NY: Dodd, Mead, 1880. 1st ed. 207pp; 24 chromo plts. Dec cvr. (Spine tapped, inner hinge exposed; spine sl worn), o/w VG-. *Middle Earth*. $295/£189

VAN RENSSELAER, MRS. JOHN KING. The Devil's Picture-Books, a History of Playing Cards. NY, 1895. 207pp (bkpl; cvrs dknd, sl worn). *King*. $85/£54

VAN RENSSELAER, SOLOMON. A Narrative of the Affair of Queenstown. NY: Leavitt, Lord, 1836. viii,9-41,2,95,22ads pp; fldg map. Orig cl, paper label. VG. Howes V40. *Adelson*. $200/£128

VAN RENSSELEAR, SOLOMON. A Narrative of the Affair of Queenstown: In the War of 1812. NY: Leavitt, 1836. 1st ed. 41,95,(4),(9),(3),6pp; fldg map. Orig cl bds. Howes V40. *Ginsberg*. $175/£112

VAN ROOYEN, C. E. and A. J. RHODES. Virus Diseases of Man. London: OUP, 1940. 1st ed. 5 color plts, tissue guards. (Ex-lib.) Buckram (bumped, worn; hinge weak), paper spine label. *Argosy*. $75/£48

VAN TASSEL, CHARLES SUMNER. Story of the Maumee Valley, Toledo and the Sandusky Region. Chicago: S.J. Clarke, 1929. 2 vols (vols 1 & 2 of 4). Grn cl. VG + . *Bohling*. $85/£54

VAN VECHTEN, CARL. Music After the Great War and Other Studies. NY: Schirmer, 1915. 1st ed. Cl (sl dknd, spine crown sl worn), paper labels. VG (w/o dj). *Reese*. $100/£64

VAN VECHTEN, CARL. Parties: Scenes from Contemporary New York Life. NY: Knopf, 1930. Ltd to 250 numbered, signed. Deckle-edged; top edge silver. Lt grn-yellow vellum (rubbed, sl soiled, rear bd creased). NF internally (2 leaves roughly opened). *Blue Mountain*. $55/£35

VAN VECHTEN, CARL. Spider Boy. NY: Knopf, 1928. 1st trade ed. Top edge stained dk blue, untrimmed. Pink cl (sl shelfworn), gilt. Pict dj (sl chipped, sm tears). *Baltimore**. $50/£32

VAN VOGT, A. E. The Book of Ptath. Reading: Fantasy, 1947. 1st ed. Signed on adhesive label on frontis recto. (Lt rubbed.) Dj (lt worn, soiled). *Swann**. $57/£37

VAN VOGT, A. E. Destination: Universe! Eyre & Spottiswoode, 1953. 1st UK ed. Pub's rev slip laid in. NF in VG dj (lt wear spine top, sl stained, sm pinhole fr flap). *Williams*. $47/£30

VAN VOGT, A. E. Empire of the Atom. SFBC, 1957. VF in dj. *Madle*. $35/£22

VAN VOGT, A. E. Masters of Time. Fantasy, 1950. 1st ed. NF (pastedowns browned) in dj (sm creased tear spine fold). *Certo*. $30/£19

VAN VOGT, A. E. Masters of Time. Reading: Fantasy Press, 1950. 1st ed. One of 500 signed, numbered. (Spine cocked, soiled, brn staining pastedown corners), else VG + in As New dj. *Other Worlds*. $90/£58

VAN VOGT, A. E. Masters of Time. Reading: Fantasy, 1950. 1st ed. Dj. *Swann**. $57/£37

VAN VOGT, A. E. The Mind Cage. NY: S&S, 1957. 1st ed. Inscribed by Van Vogt and his wife. Dj (lt rubbed). *Swann**. $57/£37

VAN VOGT, A. E. The Mixed Men. NY: Gnome, (1952). 1st ed. (Name.) Dj. *Swann**. $69/£44

VAN VOGT, A. E. Slan. Sauk City, 1946. 1st ed. Fine in VG dj (spine sl dknd, soiled). *Mcclintock*. $175/£112

VAN VOGT, A. E. Slan. Sauk City: Arkham House, 1946. 1st ed. Dj (spine faded, sl abraded). *Swann**. $92/£59

VAN VOGT, A. E. The War Against the Rull. NY: S&S, 1959. 1st ed. VG + in dj (edgewear, spine sl faded, ends sl chipped). *Other Worlds*. $30/£19

VAN VOGT, A. E. The Weapon Makers. Greenberg, 1952. 1st ed. Fine in dj. *Madle*. $70/£45

VANBRUGH, JOHN. The Complete Works of John Vanbrugh. Bonamy Dobree and Geoffrey Webb (eds). Bloomsbury, 1927. Ltd to 1300. 4 vols. Blue buckrambacked blue bds, gilt, ptd paper title labels. (Spines evenly toned), else Very Nice set. *Cady*. $150/£96

VANCE, JACK. The Dragon Master. London: Dobson, 1965. 1st British, 1st hb ed. Dj. *Swann**. $103/£66

VANCE, JACK. The Dying Earth. SF: Underwood Miller, 1976. 1st hb ed. Signed. Dj (sm tear, chip). *Swann**. $126/£81

VANCE, JACK. The Eyes of the Overworld. Gregg, 1977. 1st hb ed. Fine, not issued in dj. *Certo*. $100/£64

VANCE, JACK. The Languages of Pao. NY: Avalon, (1958). 1st ed. Dj (pin hole rear, sl dust-soiled). *Swann**. $126/£81

VANCE, JACK. The Man in the Cage. NY: Random House, (1960). 1st ed. (Worn.) Dj (worn, sl faded). *Swann**. $80/£51

VANCE, JACK. The Man in the Cage. SF/Columbia, Underwood-Miller, 1983. 1st ed thus. Fine in Fine dj. *Other Worlds*. $25/£16

VANCE, JACK. The Space Pirate. Toby, (1953). 1st ed. NF in wraps. *Certo*. $45/£29

VANCE, JACK. Star King. SF, 1981. 1st Amer hb ed. Ltd to 175 numbered, signed. Frontis. VG. *King*. $30/£19

VANCE, JACK. To Live Forever. NY: Ballantine, (1956). 1st ed. 8vo. Fine in NF dj (sl soil). *Antic Hay*. $500/£321

VANCE, JOHN HOLBROOK. The Fox Valley Murders. NY: Bobbs-Merrill, 1966. 1st ed. Signed. Fine in Fine dj. *Old London*. $250/£160

VANCE, JOHN HOLBROOK. The Man in the Cage. Random House, 1960. 1st ed. Fine in NF dj. *Certo*. $100/£64

VANCE, JOHN HOLBROOK. The Man in the Cage. NY: Random House, 1960. 1st ed. Signed. Fine in VG dj (sl wear). *Old London*. $250/£160

VANDERPOEL, E. N. Chronicles of a Pioneer School from 1792 to 1833.... Cambridge, MA, 1903. 65 plts. (Hinges starting), o/w Good + . *Scribe's Perch**. $16/£10

VANDERWELL, ANTHONY and CHARLES COLES. Game and the English Landscape. NY: Viking/Studio, 1980. 1st ed. VG in VG dj. *October Farm*. $45/£29

VANDIVER, FRANK E. Their Tattered Flags. NY, (1970). 1st ed. VG + (ex-lib) in VG + dj. *Pratt*. $30/£19

VANDIVER, FRANK. Jubal's Raid. NY, (1960). 1st ed. VG + in dj (lt worn). *Pratt*. $45/£29

VANUXEM, L. Geology of New York. Albany, 1842. 307pp. Good (rubbed; sl foxed). *Blake*. $85/£54

VANUXEM, L. Geology of New York. Part III. Albany, 1842. 306pp, errata leaf. (Neatly rebacked, preserving spine.) *Henly*. $47/£30

VARDON, HARRY. The Complete Golfer. NY: McClure, Phillips, 1907. 1st ed. Frontis port. Gilt-lettered grn cl. (Insect damage spine, fr cvr), else VG. *Pacific**. $98/£63

VARESCHI, V. and E. KRAUSE. Mountains in Flower. London, 1942. 2nd imp. Color frontis, 70 plts. (Bkpl.) Dj. *Henly*. $28/£18

VARGAS LLOSA, MARIO. Aunt Julia and the Scriptwriter. London: Faber, 1982. 1st UK ed. NF in dj. *Williams*. $50/£32

VARGAS LLOSA, MARIO. The Green House. NY, 1968. 1st Amer ed. Fine (spine heel sl rubbed) in dj (few sm edge chips, edge tears, sl rubbed). *Polyanthos*. $30/£19

VARGAS LLOSA, MARIO. The Real Life of Alejandro Mayta. NY: FSG, (1986). 1st Amer ed. Fine in dj. *Hermitage*. $25/£16

VARGAS LLOSA, MARIO. The War of the End of the World. NY: FSG, (1984). 1st ed. Fine in dj (price-clipped). *Between The Covers*. $35/£22

VARLEY, JOHN. The Ophiuchi Hotline. Dial, 1977. 1st ed, 1st bk. Fine in NF dj (1/2-inch closed tear fr panel). *Certo*. $40/£26

VARLEY, JOHN. The Ophiuchi Hotline. NY: Dial, 1977. 1st ed, 1st bk. Fine in dj (sm tear, sm crease). *Antic Hay*. $50/£32

VARNER, JOHN and JEANNETTE (trans). The Florida of the Inca: A History of the Adelantado. Austin: Univ of TX, 1951. VG in dj. *Lien*. $35/£22

VASARI, GIORGIO. The Great Masters. Michael Sonino (ed). Gaston du C. de Vere (trans). NY, 1986. 120 color plts. Dj. *Edwards*. $70/£45

VASEY, GEORGE. Report of the Investigation of the Grasses of the Arid Districts of Kansas, Nebraska, and Colorado. Washington, 1886. 19pp; 13 plts. Good in wraps. *Hayman*. $15/£10

VASSAL, GABRIELLE M. In and Around Yunnan Fou. London: Heinemann, 1922. 1st ed. (Sl stained, stamp on bds.) *Maggs*. $117/£75

VASSILIKOS, VASSILIS. Z. NY: Farrar Straus, (1968). 1st US ed. NF in NF dj (price-clipped). *Pettler & Lieberman*. $25/£16

VAUCAIRE, MICHEL. Paul du Chaillu: Gorilla Hunter. Emily Pepper Watts (trans). NY/London: Harper, 1930. Stated 1st ed. Color frontis. Dec cl, paper spine label (chipped). VG (bkpl). *Backman*. $35/£22

VAUGHAN, HENRY HALFORD. New Readings and New Renderings of Shakespeare's Tragedies. London, 1886. 2nd ed. 3 vols. VG. *Argosy*. $100/£64

VAUGHAN, JOHN. The English Guide Book. London: David & Charles, 1974. 1st ed. VG. *Cox*. $19/£12

VAUGHAN, T. W. Recent Madreporaria of the Hawaiian Islands and Laysan. Washington, 1907. 96 plts. (Lacks tp; sm lib stamp ep.) Buckram. Wraps bound in. *Henly*. $37/£24

VAUGHAN, WILLIAM. German Romantic Painting. Yale Univ, 1980. 32 color plts. (Bkpl.) Dj. *Edwards*. $47/£30

VAUGHN, J. W. The Battle of Platte Bridge. Norman: Univ of OK, (1963). 1st ed. VG in dj (sl worn). *Lien*. $45/£29

VAUGHN, J. W. Indian Fights. Norman, (1966). 1st ed. VG + in dj (2 sm pieces torn away). *Pratt*. $75/£48

VAUGHN, J. W. The Reynolds Campaign on Powder River. Norman: Univ of OK, (1961). 1st ed. Brn cl (Bkpl), o/w Fine in NF dj (sl chipped). *Harrington*. $70/£45

VAUGHN, J. W. With Crook at the Rosebud. Harrisburg, PA: Stackpole, (1956). 1st ed. VG in dj. *Lien*. $60/£38

VAUGHN, J. W. With Crook at the Rosebud. Harrisburg: Stackpole, (1956). 1st ed. NF (bkpl) in NF dj (sl worn). *Harrington*. $65/£42

VAUGHN, ROBERT. Only Victims. A Study of Show Business Blacklisting. NY: Putnam, 1972. 1st ed. Fine in NF dj (lt spine wear). *Beasley*. $50/£32

VAUGHTER, JOHN B. Prison Life in Dixie, Giving a Short History of the Inhuman and Barbarous Treatment of Our Soldiers...To Which Is Added the Speech of Gen. J. A. Garfield...Oct. 3, 1879. Chicago: Central Book Concern, 1880. 1st ed. 209pp. (Extrems worn.) VG. *Mcgowan*. $85/£54

VEALE, E. Busy Brownies. N.p.: Hubbard, (1896). Palmer Cox (illus). 9x6. (16)pp. Color pict wraps (corners off fr cvr, sl staining); back wrap has ad for Cheney's Listerated Tooth Powder. *King*. $75/£48

VEBLEN, ELLEN ROLFE. The Goosenbury Pilgrims. Boston: Lothrop, 1902. 8vo. (viii),196pp (offsetting eps). Partly unopened; deckle-edged. Blue cl-backed bluish gray bds (bumped, edges dknd, sm stains). VG in Fair dj (fr panel creased, sm hole, chip, tear, spine lacks bottom). *Blue Mountain*. $45/£29

VEBLEN, THORSTEIN. The Instinct of Workmanship and the State of the Industrial Arts. NY: Macmillan, 1914. 1st Amer ed. (2-inch abrasion rear bd), else Fine. *Hermitage*. $75/£48

VEECH, JAMES. The Monongahela of Old. Pittsburgh, 1858-1892. (ii),(17)-259pp. 3/4 black leather. (Lt foxed; spine top chipped), else VG + . *Bohling*. $200/£128

VEEDER, BORDEN. Pediatric Profiles. St. Louis, 1957. 1st ed. (Lib stamp fep), o/w Fine. *Fye*. $50/£32

VEEDER, BORDEN. Pediatric Profiles. St. Louis: Mosby, 1957. 1st bk ed. VG. *Glaser*. $75/£48

VEITCH, J. Memoir of Sir William Hamilton, Bart. Edinburgh, 1869. Litho port. (Rubbed.) *Maggs*. $41/£26

VEITH, ILZA. Huang Ti Nei Ching Su Wen. Balt, 1949. 1st ed. VG. *Fye*. $125/£80

VELIKOVSKY, IMMANUEL. Worlds in Collision. NY: Macmillan, 1950. 1st ed. Fine in dj (lt rubbed). *Between The Covers*. $100/£64

VENABLE, WILLIAM HENRY. Beginnings of Literary Culture in the Ohio Valley. Cincinnati: R. Clarke, 1891. xv,519pp, index. Good + (sm bkpl, taped-in greeting, pencil mks; rubbed, extrems frayed, rear hinge cracked). Howes V67. *Bohling*. $120/£77

VENNING, MARY ANNE. A Geographical Present. London: Darton, Harvey & Darton, 1818. 2nd ed. 144pp; 60 hand-colored plts. Contemp roan-backed bds. (Sl foxed, soiled; shelfworn, spine tips sl chipped.) Internally Sound. *Oinonen**. $80/£51

VENTURI, LIONELLO. Italian Painters of Today. (NY): Universe Books, (1959). 1st ed. 66 mtd color plts. Black/white cl. Good in dj. Cardboard slipcase. *Karmiole*. $65/£42

VENTURI, LIONELLO. Marc Chagall. NY, (1945). Ltd to 1500 numbered. 2 tipped-in color plts, 64 full-pg plts. Paper over bds. VG in dj (worn). *King*. $100/£64

VER PLANCK, WILLIAM E. Salt in California. SF: Division of Mines, 1958. 1st ed. 2 fldg maps in rear pocket. Yellow cl. Fine. *Argonaut*. $50/£32

VERCEL, ROGER. Tides of Mont St. Michel. Warre Bradley (trans). NY: Random House, (1938). 1st Amer ed. NF in dj (sl worn). *Antic Hay*. $27/£17

VERCHERES, THOMAS. War on the Detroit. Milo M. Quaife (ed). Chicago: (Lakeside Classic), 1940. Frontis view, 2 maps (1 fldg). Dk red cl, gilt. VG + . Howes F288. *Bohling*. $22/£14

VERCHERES, THOMAS. War on the Detroit. Milo M. Quaife (ed). Chicago: Lakeside, Christmas, 1940. Dk red cl (pale spot lower cvr). *Sadlon*. $25/£16

VEREY, DAVID. Mid-Wales. Faber, 1960. 1st ed, 1st issue w/John Piper designed wrapper. NF in dj (sl rubbed). *Hadley*. $55/£35

VEREY, DAVID. Shell Guide to Wiltshire. London, 1956. (Lt worn, loose.) *Hatchwell*. $12/£8

VERGA, GIOVANNI. The House by the Medlar-Tree. NY: Harper, 1890. 1st ed in English. (Eps lt foxed), else NF. *Lame Duck*. $275/£176

VERHOEFF, MARY. The Kentucky River Navigation. Louisville: John P. Morton, 1917. 3 maps (2 fldg). 3/4 straight-grained morocco, marbled bds (soil, wear, joints tender; ex-lib   w/perf stamp tp affecting author's name, ink   stamp). Orig fr stiff wrap bound in at rear. *Waverly**. $44/£28

VERMES, GEZA (trans). The Dead Sea Scrolls. Westerham: LEC, 1966. #39/1500 signed by Shraga Weil (illus). Fine in slipcase (1 side unevenly faded). *Hermitage*. $225/£144

VERMONT, E. DE V. (ed). America Heraldica. NY, c. 1886. #467 of unstated limitation. 17 color plts. Gilt-dec leather (worn, cvrs detached). Contents VG. *New Hampshire**. $90/£58

VERNE, JULES. The Archipelago on Fire. Sampson Low et al, 1886. 49 (of 50) plts. Pub's cat dated Oct. 1885. (Marginal soiling, spotting.) Aeg. Orig pict cl (rebacked; orig backstrip relaid; corners rubbed). *Tiger*. $51/£33

VERNE, JULES. Around the World in Eighty Days. Boston: Osgood, 1873. 1873 on tp and tp verso. Red edges. Dec grn cl, gilt. (Joints frayed; bumped), o/w Good. *Scribe's Perch**. $65/£42

VERNE, JULES. From the Earth to the Moon and Around the Moon. NY: LEC, 1970. #417/1500 signed by Robert Shore (illus). 2 vols. Fine in pub's slipcase. *Hermitage*. $135/£87

VERNE, JULES. From the Earth to the Moon.... Louis Mercier & Eleanor E. King (trans). NY: Scribner, Armstrong, 1874. 1st ed in English. 8vo. 80 full-pg illus. Pub's brn pebble-grained cl (spine sl rubbed) stamped in black/gilt w/spaceship design. Binder's ticket 'Geo. W. Alexander New-York' rear pastedown. Beautiful. *D & D*. $1,500/£962

VERNE, JULES. The Fur Country. Boston: James R. Osgood, 1874. 1st Amer ed. 334pp. Grn pict cl (fr inner hinge broken; sl shelfwear). Bright. *Cullen*. $45/£29

VERNE, JULES. A Journey to the Center of the Earth. NY: LEC, 1966. One of 1500 numbered, signed by Edward A. Wilson (illus). Mint in bd slipcase. *Argosy*. $125/£80

VERNE, JULES. Michael Strogoff, the Courier of the Czar. Scribner, Armstrong, 1877. 1st Amer ed. Gilt/black-stamped cl. VG- (lt worn). *Aronovitz*. $250/£160

VERNE, JULES. Michael Strogoff: A Courier of the Czar. NY/London: Scribner, (1927). 1st ed thus. 4to. vi,(ii),397pp (sm red stains 5pp, sl stains); 9 color plts by N. C. Wyeth. Pict eps. Black cl (bumped, sl stained), color pict label fr cvr, gilt. VG. *Blue Mountain*. $45/£29

VERNE, JULES. The Mysterious Island. NY: Scribner, 1919. 2nd ptg. 8vo. 439pp; 14 color plts, vignette tp, color pict pastedown cvr, dec eps by N.C. Wyeth. (Hinges tender, cvr spots), o/w Good. *Scribe's Perch**. $20/£13

VERNEY, FRANCES. Florence Nightingale's Pet Owl, Athena. SF: Grabhorn-Hoyem, 1970. One of 300. Prospectus laid in. *Swann**. $92/£59

VERNEY, GEORGE HOPE. Four-Handed Chess. London/NY, n.d. c.(1881). Frontis, 32pp. (Cl lt soiled, spine sl bumped.) *Edwards*. $23/£15

VERNON, JOSEPH S. Along the Old Trail. Cimmaron, KS: Tucker-Vernon, 1910. (Rebacked), else VG. Howes V77. *Dumont*. $85/£54

VERNON, PAUL E. Morocco from a Motor. London: A&C Black, 1927. 48 full-pg color illus, fldg map. Pict cl (spine extrems, tips worn). *Dawson*. $50/£32

VERRILL, A. HYATT. The Real Story of the Pirate. Appleton, 1923. 1st ed. VG. *Madle*. $50/£32

VERRILL, A. HYATT. The Real Story of the Whaler. NY, 1923. VG. *High Latitude*. $25/£16

VERTUE, GEORGE. The Heads of the Kings of England...also...The Monuments of the Kings of England. London: For James, John & Paul Knapton, 1736. 1st ed. 2 engr frontis ports, 62 plts (40 ports, 22 monuments), extra illus w/4 maps (2 w/margins repaired), 8 leaves of tables (2 fldg, 6 cut-down, mtd to size), 10 plts of ports (all cut down, mtd to size). 19th-cent 1/2 russia (extrems rubbed, spine ends chipped, joints split; bkpl), gilt. *Christie's**. $562/£360

VERVE (ed). Moods and Movements in Art. NY, (1959). Folio. Color pict bds. Dj (sl frayed). *Swann**. $2,070/£1,327

VERY, JONES. Essays and Poems. Ralph Waldo Emerson (ed). Boston: Little Brown, 1839. 1st ed. Brn cl, label. (Lt foxed; bottom 2 inches spine gone, label chipped), else VG. BAL 5188. *Macdonnell*. $125/£80

VESEY-FITZGERALD, BRIAN et al (eds). Game Fish of the World. NY, n.d., ca 1949. Fine. *Truepenny*. $20/£13

VESTAL, STANLEY. Dobe Walls. Boston: Houghton Mifflin, 1929. 1st ed. Pale grn cl lettered in blue, top edges stained blue. Fine (ink name). *Argonaut*. $50/£32

VESTAL, STANLEY. Dodge City. Queen of Cowtowns. (London): Peter Nevill, (1955). 1st British ed. (Spine lt rubbed), else Fine in dj (sl chipped). *Argonaut*. $35/£22

VESTAL, STANLEY. Joe Meek, the Merry Mountain Man. Caldwell, 1952. 2nd ptg. VG+ in dj (lt worn). *Pratt*. $40/£26

VESTAL, STANLEY. Joe Meek, the Merry Mountain Man; A Biography. Caldwell, 1952. Port. Pict cl. NF in dj (sl chipped, worn). *Reese*. $150/£96

VESTAL, STANLEY. Joe Meek. Caldwell: Caxton, 1952. 1st ed. Blue cl lettered in silver. (Sl faded), else Fine in pict dj (chipped, sm piece lacking). *Argonaut*. $100/£64

VESTAL, STANLEY. Kit Carson; the Happy Warrior of the Old West. Boston: Houghton Mifflin, 1928. (Name stamp), else VG in dj. *Dumont*. $30/£19

VESTAL, STANLEY. The Missouri. NY: Farrar & Rinehart, (1945). 1st ed. Fine (sl spot rear cvr) in dj (sl chipped, spine faded). *Argonaut*. $50/£32

VESTAL, STANLEY. New Sources of Indian History, 1850-1891. Norman: Univ of OK, 1934. 1st ed. Frontis port, 12 plts. Lt blue cl. VG (faded, sl worn; owner stamp eps); Internally Fine. *Argonaut*. $150/£96

VESTAL, STANLEY. The Old Santa Fe Trail. Boston: Houghton Mifflin, 1939. 1st ed. (Sl dkng cvr edges), else Fine in dj (lt chipped). *Argonaut*. $75/£48

VESTAL, STANLEY. Queen of Cowtowns, Dodge City. NY: Harper, (1952). 1st ed, 1st state w/illus facing p21 captioned 'Pavillion model.' Fine in dj (chipped). *Argonaut*. $50/£32

VESTAL, STANLEY. Revolt on the Border. Boston: Houghton Mifflin, 1938. 1st ed. Dec salmon cl. Fine in dj (lt worn, 4x1-inch piece torn from bottom). *Argonaut*. $45/£29

VESTAL, STANLEY. Sitting Bull, Champion of the Sioux. Boston, 1932. 1st ed. VG+. *Pratt*. $60/£38

VESTAL, STANLEY. Sitting Bull, Champion of the Sioux. Boston/NY: Houghton Mifflin, 1932. 1st ed. Maroon cl, gilt. Fine in dj (sl chipped). *Argonaut*. $125/£80

VESTAL, STANLEY. Sitting Bull. Norman, (1957). 1st ed thus. VG in dj (lt worn). *King*. $35/£22

VESTAL, STANLEY. Wagons Southwest, Story of the Old Trail to Santa Fe. NY, 1946. 1st ed. Pb. VG. *Turpen*. $35/£22

VESTAL, STANLEY. Wagons Southwest. NY: Amer Pioneer Trails Assoc, 1946. 1st ed w/this title. Dbl-pg map. NF in wrappers, saddle stitched, color illus fr wrapper. *Argonaut*. $45/£29

VESTAL, STANLEY. Warpath and Council Fire. NY: Random House, (1948). 1st ed. Frontis. Gilt-lettered grn cl. Fine in dj. *Argonaut*. $75/£48

VESTAL, STANLEY. Warpath and Council Fire: The Plains Indians' Struggle...1851-1891. NY: Random House, (1948). 1st ed. VG in dj (sl worn). *Lien*. $65/£42

VESTAL, STANLEY. Warpath. Boston/NY: Houghton Mifflin, 1934. 1st ed. Frontis port, 10 photo plts. Gray cl ptd in red (lt soiled, spine foot sl jammed). Fine. *Argonaut*. $100/£64

VICARION, PALMIRO. Book of Limericks. Paris: Olympia, 1955. 1st ed. Fine in fragile cardbd cvrs, dj (few sl edge tears). *Associates*. $30/£19

VICKERS, ROY. Double Image. London: Herbert Jenkins, 1955. 1st ed. Fine in dj (nicks, short closed tears). *Mordida*. $75/£48

VICKERY, W. F. Advanced Gunsmithing. Plantersville: Small Arms, 1944. VG in dj (lt chipped). *Bowman*. $45/£29

VIDAL, GORE. The City and the Pillar. NY: E.P. Dutton, 1948. 1st ed. Fine in dj (sl faded). *Associates*. $150/£96

VIDAL, GORE. Creation. NY: Random House, (1981). One of 500 numbered, signed. Fine in Fine slipcase. *Lenz*. $100/£64

VIDAL, GORE. Duluth. London, 1983. Fine in Fine dj. *Smith*. $20/£13

VIDAL, GORE. An Evening With Richard Nixon. NY, 1972. 1st Amer ed. Fine in Fine dj. *Polyanthos*. $25/£16

VIDAL, GORE. The Judgement of Paris. NY, 1952. 1st Amer ed. NF (spine heel sl bumped, 2 lower corners sl rubbed) in dj (spine extrems, flap flds sl chipped, rubbed). *Polyanthos*. $60/£38

VIDAL, GORE. The Judgment of Paris. NY: Dutton, 1952. 1st ed. Signed. (Name, date on flyleaf), o/w NF in dj (rear panel lt soiled). *Bernard*. $150/£96

VIDAL, GORE. Lincoln. NY: Random House, (1984). One of 350 numbered, signed. Fine in Fine slipcase. *Lenz*. $125/£80

VIDAL, GORE. Lincoln. NY, 1984. #252/350 signed. Fine in Fine box. *Polyanthos*. $100/£64

VIDAL, GORE. Messiah. NY, 1954. 1st Amer ed. Fine (spine extrems sl rubbed) in dj (extrems, sl chipped; spine, flap flds rubbed, piece missing, inside of spine reinforced w/selotape). *Polyanthos*. $30/£19

VIDAL, GORE. Myron. Heinemann, 1975. 1st UK ed. Fine in dj (price-clipped). *Williams*. $23/£15

VIDAL, GORE. Rocking the Boat. Boston, 1962. 1st Amer ed. NF (edges sl rubbed, sm offsetting mk) in dj (spine extrems sl rubbed, flap flds sunned, rear panel sl soiled). *Polyanthos*. $75/£48

VIDAL, GORE. Visit to a Small Planet and Other Television Plays. Boston, 1956. 1st Amer ed. Fine (name, offsetting fr fep; spine extrems sl rubbed) in dj (rubbed, few sm chips, sl soiled). *Polyanthos*. $45/£29

VIELE, MRS. Following the Drum. NY, 1858. 1st ed, 1st issue. 256,(7),(1)-4pp. (Joints worn, spine chipped.) Howes V92. *Ginsberg*. $250/£160

VIELE, MRS. Following the Drum; a Glimpse of Frontier Life. NY: Rudd & Carleton, 1858. 256,(8),4pp. Stamped bds (faded, worn). Good. Howes V92. *Dumont*. $275/£176

VIETZEN, RAYMOND. Indians of the Lake Erie Basin or Lost Nations. Waho, NE: Ludi Ptg, 1965. 1st ed. Good (ex-lib) in dj (spine sticker stain). *Archer*. $35/£22

VIEUX, MOUSTACHE. That Good Old Time. NY: Hurd & Houghton, 1867. 1st ed. Frontis map, 6 full-pg plts after Winslow Homer, 2 other engr plts after another. Lt yellow coated eps. Plum cl, gilt. (Lt spotted, sunned, lacks fep.) Text Good (lt aged, bkseller ink handstamp 1st text pg). *Baltimore*. $60/£38

View of South America and Mexico, Comprising Their History.... NY: Huntington, June 1826. 2 vols in 1. Hand-colored frontis, 204; 239pp. Contemp calf. (Foxed; worn, hinges cracked), o/w Good. *Worldwide*. $45/£29

View of South America and Mexico.... NY: H. Huntington, 1825. 2 vols in 1. Frontis port, iv,223,242pp (lt foxed). Orig full calf (corners worn), gilt. *Cullen*. $250/£160

Vigilance Committee of 1856. By a Pioneer California Journalist. (By James O'Meara.) SF: James H. Barry, 1887. 1st ed w/1887 date on tp and 1890 date on cvr. (Name on tp). Fine in ptd wrappers. *Argonaut.* $90/£58

VILA, VICENTE. Diary of...Portola Expedition of 1769-70. Berkeley, 1911. 1st ed. Pb. Frontis. Fine. *Turpen.* $45/£29

VILAPLANA, RUIZ. Burgos Justice. W. Horsfall Carter (trans). London, 1938. 1st Eng ed. Nice (spine faded). *Clearwater.* $47/£30

VILES, EDWARD and F. J. FURNIVALL (eds). The Rogues and Vagabonds of Shakespeare's Youth. New Shakespeare Soc, 1880. xxx,112pp. Uncut. (Ink stamp tp, last leaf, ex-lib, hinges sl tender; spine sl discolored, head chipped w/loss.) *Edwards.* $55/£35

VILIMKOVA, M. Egyptian Jewelry. London: Paul Hamlyn, (1969). 1st ed. Fine in dj, bd slipcase. *Hermitage.* $75/£48

VILIMKOVA, M. Egyptian Ornament. London: Allen Wingate, (1963). Good in dj. *Archaeologia.* $95/£61

VILIMKOVA, M. Roman Art in Africa. London: Paul Hamlyn, 1963. 114 full-pg b/w plts, fldg list of illus. Blue cl. VG. *Turtle Island.* $45/£29

Village Orphan. London: Longman & Rees, n.d. (ca 1800). 12mo. (2) leaves; 140pp. 19th-cent 3/4 calf (rubbed). *Oinonen*.* $80/£51

Villette. (By Charlotte Bronte.) Smith, Elder, 1857. 3rd ed. iv,478pp + 5pp ads, ads on eps. Good in orange ptd linen (backstrip faded, lt soiled). *Cox.* $55/£35

VILLIERS, ALAN. To the Frozen South. Hobart: Davies Bros, 1924. 1st ed, 1st ptg; 1st bk. Cl-backed ptd bds. *Maggs.* $507/£325

VILLIERS, ELIZABETH. The Mascot Book. London, 1929. Rpt. VG (cvr stain). *Middle Earth.* $45/£29

VILLON, FRANCOIS. The Lyrical Poems of Francois Villon. NY: LEC, 1979. One of 2000 numbered, signed by Stephen Harvard (designer). Fine in slipcase. *Between The Covers.* $100/£64

VILLON, FRANCOIS. The Testaments. John Heron Lepper (trans). London: Casanova Soc, 1924. One of 775 numbered, privately ptd. Deckle-edged. Cream cl-backed gray bds (cl spotted, bds bumped, chipped), gilt. Internally Fine in orig glassine. *Blue Mountain.* $20/£13

VINCENT, FRANK, JR. Through and Through the Tropics.... NY: Harper, 1876. xvi,304pp. Dk grn cl (lt rubbed). *Adelson.* $65/£42

VINE, BARBARA. (Pseud of Ruth Rendell.) A Dark-Adapted Eye. London: Viking, 1986. 1st ed. Signed. Fine in Fine dj. *Old London.* $40/£26

VINE, BARBARA. (Pseud of Ruth Rendell.) A Dark-Adapted Eye. NY: Bantam, 1986. 1st US ed. VG in VG dj. *Old London.* $35/£22

VINE, BARBARA. (Pseud of Ruth Rendell.) Gallowglass. London: Viking, 1990. 1st ed. Signed. Fine in Fine dj. *Old London.* $40/£26

VINES, SHERARD. The Course of English Classicism. London: Hogarth, 1930. 1st ed. VG (eps browned, bkpl) in dj (sl soiled, 1-inch piece missing top corner, chips). *Virgo.* $31/£20

VIOLA, HERMAN J. The Indian Legacy of Charles Bird King. NY: Smithsonian/Doubleday, (1976). 1st ed. Fine in VG dj. *Perier.* $35/£22

Violinist's Guide. Chicago: Violinist Pub Co, (1924). Grn cl (heavily soiled). *King.* $40/£26

VIPONT, ELFRIDA (comp). Bless This Day. Collins, 1958. 1st ed. Harold Jones (illus). 4to. 96pp. Pict bds. VG+ in pict dj (sl worn). *Bookmark.* $47/£30

VIRGIL. The Aeneid. John Dryden (trans). NY: LEC, 1944. One of 1100 numbered, signed by Carlotta Petrina (illus). (Sm bkpl ep), else Fine in tissue dj, pub's drop-lid box. *Hermitage.* $125/£80

VIRGIL. The Eclogues of Virgil. C.S. Calverley (trans). NY: LEC, 1960. Ltd to 1500, signed by Vertes (artist). Illus Shiki silk, cl spine. (Bkpl), else Fine in pub's slipcase (sl soiled). *Cahan.* $100/£64

Virginia Highway Historical Markers. Shenandoah Pub House, 1930. 1st issue. Paper cvrs (torn). Good (rear pp bent). *Book Broker.* $25/£16

Virginia Highway Historical Markers. Strasburg: Shenandoah Pub House, 1931. 2nd of 2 issues. VG in pict wraps. *Bohling.* $25/£16

VISHNIAC, ROMAN. A Vanished World. NY, 1983. 1st ed. VG in dj. *Argosy.* $150/£96

VISHNY, MICHELE. Mordecai Ardon. NY: Abrams, (1973). 1st ed. Mtd frontis, 50 color plts. Blue linen. Fine in dj. *Karmiole.* $100/£64

VISIAK, E. H. The Haunted Island. London: Peter Lunn, 1946. 1st ed thus. Jack Matthews (illus). NF in dj. *Certo.* $60/£38

Visit to the States. A Reprint of Letters from the Special Correspondent of the Times. London, 1887. (4),428pp. VG. *Reese.* $200/£128

VISNIAC, ROMAN. A Vanished World. NY: FSG, 1983. 1st ed. Fine in Fine dj. *Smith.* $125/£80

VISSCHER, WILLIAM L. A Thrilling and Truthful History of the Pony Express. Chicago: Charles T. Powner, 1946. Brn cl, gilt. VG+. *Bohling.* $25/£16

VISSCHER, WILLIAM L. A Thrilling and Truthful History of the Pony Express.... Chicago: Rand, McNally, (1908). 1st ed. Pict cvrs. Good. *Lien.* $35/£22

VISSER, H. F. E. Asiatic Art. NY: 7 Art Books Soc, 1952. (Spine frayed, bumped, rubbed.) Interior clean. *Metropolitan*.* $46/£29

VITRUVIUS. The Ten Books on Architecture. Morris Hicky Morgan (trans). Cambridge: Harvard Univ, 1914 (tp date: 1926). Some plts hors texte. (Cl sl rubbed.) *Washton.* $150/£96

VITTORINI, ELIO. The Red Carnation. NY: New Directions, 1952. 1st ed in English. VG+ in dj. *Lame Duck.* $45/£29

VITZETELLY, HENRY. The Wines of the World Characterized and Classed. London: Ward, Lock, & Taylor, 1875. 200pp. Internally Nice in orig color ptd stiff wrappers (discolored, edges frayed, chip, worn). *Goodrich.* $150/£96

VIVIAN, HERBERT. Abyssinia: Through the Lion-Land to the Court of the Lion of Judah. London: Arthur Pearson, 1901. 1st ed. Frontis, 2 fldg maps. Red gilt cl (bold trace of lib label removed from spine), else VG. *Terramedia.* $150/£96

VIVIAN, JULIA. A Cavalier in Texas. San Antonio, 1953. 1st ed. NF in VG dj. *Turpen.* $28/£18

Vivisection. The Royal Society for the Prevention of Cruelty to Animals and the Royal Commission. London: Smith, Elder, 1876. Emb cl (worn), gilt. Sound. *Boswell.* $225/£144

VIZETELLY, HENRY. A History of Champagne with Notes on the Other Sparkling Wines of France. Henry Sotheran, 1882. 1st ed. xii,263,(4)pp appendix + 7pp ads; fldg map, 6 full-pg plts. Aeg. (Prelims, edges sl spotted), o/w VG (hinges sl rubbed). *Cox.* $257/£165

VLIET, R. G. Solitude. NY: HBJ, (1977). 1st ed. Fine in dj (2 short internally repaired tears). *Between The Covers.* $125/£80

VOGE, HERVEY (ed). A Climber's Guide to the High Sierra. SF, 1954. 1st ed. VG in dj (rubbed). *King.* $50/£32

VOGEL, LISE. The Column of Antoninus Pius. Cambridge: Harvard Univ, 1973. Good. *Archaeologia*. $45/£29

Voice from America to England. (By Calvin Colton.) London, 1839. 1st ed, w/ads dated Feb 1839. Orig bds, paper spine label. Howes C620. *Swann**. $431/£276

VOLLMANN, WILLIAM T. The Ice-Shirt. Deutsch, 1990. 1st UK ed. One of 1250. Fine in dj. *Williams*. $125/£80

VOLLMANN, WILLIAM T. Thirteen Stories and Thirteen Epitaphs. London: Andre Deutsch, 1991. 1st ed. (Sl rough fore-edge 1st few pp), o/w Fine in Fine dj. *Beasley*. $100/£64

VOLLMANN, WILLIAM T. Thirteen Stories and Thirteen Epitaphs. London: Deutsch, 1991. One of 1000 ptd. Fine in dj. *Moorhouse*. $117/£75

VOLTAIRE, FRANCOIS MARIE AROUET DE. Memoirs of the Life of Voltaire. London: Robinson, 1784. 1st Eng trans. (Name tp margin.) Calf. *Rostenberg & Stern*. $175/£112

VOLTAIRE, JEAN FRANCOIS MARIE. Candide. NY: Random House, 1928. One of 1470 signed by Rockwell Kent (illus). Gilt-pict buckram (rubbed). *Swann**. $80/£51

VOLTAIRE, JEAN FRANCOIS MARIE. Candide. NY: Random House, 1928. Ltd ed signed by Rockwell Kent (illus). Beige gilt-stamped linen (spine dknd). *Appelfeld*. $200/£128

VON BASSERMANN-JORDAN, ERNST and H. BERTELE. The Book of Old Clocks and Watches. NY: Crown, (1964). 1st ed in English. 20 color plts. (Stamp.) Dj (badly worn). *Weber*. $75/£48

VON BOEHN, MAX. Dolls and Puppets. Josephine Nicoll (trans). London: Harrap, 1932. 1st ed. 30 color plts. (Spine sl faded.) *Hollett*. $117/£75

VON BRAUN, WERNHER with FREDERICK I. ORDWAY III. History of Rocketry and Space Travel. NY: Crowell, (1966). 1st ed. Pict leather. Fine. *Antic Hay*. $50/£32

VON DODERER, HEIMITO. The Demons. Richard & Clara Winston (trans). NY: Knopf, (1961). 1st Amer ed. NF in djs, orig ptd cardbd slipcase (sl worn). *Antic Hay*. $25/£16

VON ECKARTSHUSEN, KARL. The Cloud upon the Sanctuary. Isabel De Steiger (trans). London: Rider, 1909. Dec cvr. VG+. *Middle Earth*. $75/£48

VON GOETHE, J. W. Faust. John Anster (trans). NY: Dingwall-Rock, (1925). One of 1000 numbered of Amer issue (of 2000) signed by Harry Clarke (illus). 8 color, 13 b/w plts. Color pict eps; teg, untrimmed. Vellum-backed lt gray bds, gilt. VF in dj (sl worn, sunned, chipped, torn), plain bd slipcase (worn, broken). *Baltimore**. $370/£237

VON GOETHE, J. W. Faust. NY, n.d. 1st Amer ed. #43/1000 signed by Harry Clarke (illus). 22 full-pg illus. 1/2 vellum, grey paper-cvrd bds, gilt. *Mcclintock*. $350/£224

VON GOETHE, J. W. Faust: A Tragedy. NY, (1930). Ltd to 501 signed by Alice Raphael (trans). Frontis signed in pencil by Lynd Ward (illus). 6 tipped-in woodengrs. Unopened. 1/4 cl, Art-Deco style air-brushed bds. (Spine lt faded.) o/w Fine in matching slipcase. *Truepenny*. $200/£128

VON GOETHE, J. W. Faust: A Tragedy. Alice Raphael (trans). NY: LEC, 1932. Ltd to 1500 signed by Rene Clarke (illus). Full purple cl, gilt. VG in dj (lt worn). *Truepenny*. $85/£54

VON GOETHE, J. W. Italian Journey (1786-1788). W. H. Auden and Elizabeth Mayer (trans). NY: Pantheon Books, 1962. Ltd to 2500. Patterned cl. Good in dj, cardbd slipcase. *Karmiole*. $125/£80

VON GOETHE, J. W. The Story of Reynard the Fox. Thomas James Arnold (trans). NY: LEC, 1954. Ltd to 1500 signed by Fritz Eichenberg (illus). 4to. 248pp. (Spine sl dknd), else VF in cl-backed patterned bds, slipcase. *Bromer*. $100/£64

VON GRIMMELSHAUSEN, JOHANN. The Adventures of Simplicissimus. John P. Spielman (trans). NY: LEC, 1981. One of 2000 numbered, signed by Fritz Eichenberg (illus). 18 engrs, 2 facs tps. Blind-stamped cl. Mint in bd slipcase. *Argosy*. $150/£96

VON HAGEN, V. W. Ecuador and the Galapagos Islands. Norman: Univ of OK, 1949. 1st ed. 3 maps. Fine in VG dj. *Mikesh*. $37/£24

VON HAGEN, V. W. Ecuador the Unknown. NY: OUP, 1940. 1st ed. Fine in Good+ dj. *Mikesh*. $47/£30

VON HAGEN, V. W. Frederick Catherwood, Archt. NY: OUP, 1950. Frontis, 25 plts. (Bkpl removed.) Dj (torn). *Archaeologia*. $45/£29

VON HAGEN, V. W. South America Called Them, Explorations of the Great Naturalists. NY, 1955. 3rd ed. Wrappers. *Maggs*. $22/£14

VON HELMHOLTZ-PHELAN, ANNA A. The Social Philosophy of William Morris. Durham: Duke Univ, 1927. 1st ed. Frontis port. Unopened. Cl-backed paper, bds, ptd labels. Fine in dj (lt worn). *Cahan*. $65/£42

VON HUBL, ARTHUR FREIHERRN. Three-Colour Photography. Henry Oscar Klein (trans). London: Percy Lund, Humphries, 1915. 2nd Eng ed. Gilt-titled red cl. (Sl faded), else NF. *Cahan*. $100/£64

VON PUCKLER-MUSKAU, PRINZ. Hints on Landscape Gardening. Boston/NY: Houghton & Mifflin, 1917. 39 plts, 2 pocket maps. Orig cl spine, paper-cvrd bds (edges, corners sl worn). *Marlborough*. $304/£195

VON SACHER-MASOCH, LEOPOLD. Venus in Furs. NY: Sylvan, 1947. 1st general trade ed in America. Fine in VG dj (chips, sm loss fr panel). *Warren*. $25/£16

VON SCHILLER, J. C. FRIEDRICH. The Visionary. NY: E. Ferrett, 1845. 1st ed in English. VG in wraps (spine dknd, sig fr cvr, loss spine extrems, edgeworn). *Lame Duck*. $275/£176

VON SEIDLITZ, W. A History of Japanese Colour-Prints. Heinemann, 1920. 2nd ed. Color frontis, 15 color plts. (Ex-lib, sm ink stamps, bkpl, few margins sl thumbed; spine sl bumped, spine #s.) *Edwards*. $75/£48

VON SIMPSON, OTTO. Sacred Fortress. Chicago, 1948. 48 plts. (Cl sl spotted.) *Washton*. $50/£32

VON WRANGELL, FERDINAND. Narrative of an Expedition to the Polar Sea, in the Years 1820...1823. Edward Sabine (ed). London: James Madden, 1840. cxxxvii,413pp; lg fldg map (linen backed). Old 1/2 leather (nicely rebacked). Good. *High Latitude*. $800/£513

VON ZIEMSSEN, HUGO (ed). Acute Infectious Diseases. NY, 1874. 1st ed in English. 2 vols. 708; 751pp. Full leather. VG. *Fye*. $125/£80

VON ZITTEL, KARL ALFRED. History of Geology and Palaeontology to the End of the 19th Century. Weinheim: J. Cramer, 1962. Rpt of 1st ed in English. Fine. *Glaser*. $45/£29

VONNEGUT, KURT. Bluebeard. NY: Delacorte, (1987). One of 500 numbered, signed. Fine in Fine slipcase. *Lenz*. $150/£96

VONNEGUT, KURT. Canary in a Cat House. Gold Medal, 1961. 1st ed. Pb orig. Fine (cvr corner sl creased). *Certo*. $125/£80

VONNEGUT, KURT. Fates Worse Than Death. Bertrand Russell Peace Foundation, 1982. 1st UK ed. Pamphlet. Fine. *Williams*. $19/£12

VONNEGUT, KURT. God Bless You, Mr. Rosewater, or Pearls Before Swine. Cape, 1965. 1st Eng ed. NF in VG dj (lt worn, torn). *Aronovitz.* $125/£80

VONNEGUT, KURT. Jailbird. (NY): Delacorte, (1979). One of 500 numbered, signed. Fine in Fine slipcase. *Lenz.* $150/£96

VONNEGUT, KURT. Jailbird. NY: Delacorte, 1979. 1st trade ed. NF in VG+ dj (fr flap lt creased). *Lame Duck.* $35/£22

VONNEGUT, KURT. Nothing Is Lost Save Honor. Jackson: Nouveau Press, 1984. 1st ed. #83/300 signed. VF. *Hermitage.* $150/£96

VONNEGUT, KURT. Palm Sunday. NY: Delacorte, (1981). One of 500 numbered, signed. Fine in Fine slipcase. *Lenz.* $150/£96

VONNEGUT, KURT. Palm Sunday. NY, 1981. 1st Amer ed. Fine in dj (sm nick). *Polyanthos.* $25/£16

VONNEGUT, KURT. The Sirens of Titan. NY: Dell, 1959. 1st ptg. VG+ in illus wraps (spine lt creased). *Lame Duck.* $75/£48

VONNEGUT, KURT. Slaughterhouse Five. Cape, 1970. 1st UK ed. NF in VG dj (spine sl faded). *Williams.* $148/£95

VONNEGUT, KURT. Sun, Moon, Star. Harper & Row, (1980). 1st ed. Ivan Chermayeff (illus). Fine in dj. *Certo.* $45/£29

VONNEGUT, KURT. Welcome to the Monkey House. Delacorte, (1968). 1st ed. NF in dj (dust soiled, spine base sl frayed). *Certo.* $225/£144

VONNEGUT, MARK. The Eden Express. NY, 1975. 1st ed. VG in VG dj. *Smith.* $15/£10

VOSBURGH, LANIER et al. The Thoroughbred Types 1900-1925. NY: Privately ptd, 1926. (Cvr spotted.) Interior Clean. *October Farm.* $95/£61

Votes and Proceedings of the House of Representatives of the Province of Pennsylvania.... Phila: B. Franklin, 1754. (Tp torn, repaired, mtd, affecting text; verso cvrd over. Sl dampstained, ink notes.) Later wrappers; custom slipcase, protective sleeve. *Freeman*.* $350/£224

Voyage Round the World. (By Charles Clerke.) London, 1776. 4th ed. Frontis, (iv),170,(2)pp; 2 plts. Contemp calf (expertly rebacked). *Maggs.* $195/£125

Voyages, Dangerous Adventures, and Imminent Escapes of Capt. Richard Falconer.... (By William R. Chetwood.) London, 1734. 4th ed. Mod lib buckram. Howes C356. *Swann.* $69/£44

Voyages, Dangerous Adventures, and Imminent Escapes of Capt. Richard Falconer.... (By William R. Chetwood.) London, 1764. 5th ed. Frontis. Contemp sheep (fr cvr loose). Howes C356. *Swann*.* $138/£88

VRIESEN, GUSTAV and MAX LONDAHL. Robert Delaunay: Light and Color. NY: Abrams, 1967. 16 tipped-in color plts. Fine in Fine dj. *Metropolitan*.* $28/£18

VULLIAMY, C. E. James Boswell. Geoffrey Bles, 1932. 1st ed. Frontis. (Cl lt rubbed.) *Cox.* $12/£8

W

W., E. B. (E. B. White.) The Lady Is Cold. NY, 1929. 1st ed, 1st bk, 2nd issue binding. (Lt rubbed.) *Kane*.* $45/£29

W., G. A Rich Store-House: or, Treasury for the Diseased. London: John Clowes, 1650. 8th ed. 4to. (22),274pp. Contemp sheep. (Rebacked, corners restored; text browning), else Very Nice. *Goodrich.* $895/£574

WADDEL, L. AUSTINE. Lhasa and Its Mysteries. NY: Dutton, 1906. 3rd, cheaper ed. Color frontis, 8 maps and plans (3 lg fldg). Tan/maroon pict cl. (Sl wear), else VG. *Terramedia.* $200/£128

WADDINGTON, RICHARD. Salmon Fishing: Philosophy and Practice. Faber, 1949. 1st ed. 18 plts incl color frontis. Grey bds, red leather backstrip. *Petersfield.* $59/£38

WADE, ALAN. (Pseud of Jack Vance.) Isle of Peril. Mystery House, (1957). 1st ed. (Lib stamps.) Dj (eps stuck), mylar cvr, sm label fr panel. *Certo.* $75/£48

WADE, H. T. With Boat and Gun in the Yangtze Valley. Shanghai: Privately Pub, (1910). 2nd ed. VG. *Mikesh.* $175/£112

WADE, HENRY. Diplomat's Folly. NY: Macmillan, 1952. 1st Amer ed. VG in dj (spine sl faded, sm chip back panel, sm closed tears). *Mordida.* $40/£26

WADE, HENRY. Policeman's Lot. London: Constable, (1933). 1st ed. (Rubbed, soiled.) Bright dj (edges, spine ends chipped, short tears). *Metropolitan*.* $977/£626

WADE, HOUSTON. Notes and Fragments of the Mier Expedition. La Grange, TX: La Grange Journal, 1936. 1st ed. Signed. Good (notes; corners bumped, worn). *Gibbs.* $130/£83

WADE, JOHN DONALD. Augustus Baldwin Longstreet. M. Thomas Inge (ed). Athens: Univ of GA, 1969. 1st ed. Frontis port. Fine. *Connolly.* $35/£22

WADE, W. M. Walks in Oxford. London, 1817. 1st 1 vol ed. Tp,ded.[a],preface(a2-[a6]),liv,276,(265-388),[ii],index,(NN-[NN5]). 1/2 title present. Lg fldg map, 13 engr plts. (Lt browned.) Contemp calf bds (worn, rubbed, rebacked in mod calf), leather label, gilt. *Edwards.* $312/£200

WAETZOLDT, W. Durer and His Times. Phaidon, 1955. VG. *Moss.* $56/£36

WAGNER, ARTHUR L. and J. D. JERROLD KELLEY. United States Army and Navy. Akron, 1899. 43 chromo plts. (Long tear tp, sm marginal tears.) Pict cl (extrems worn). *New Hampshire*.* $325/£208

WAGNER, GLENDOLIN DAMON. Old Neutriment. Boston: Ruth Hill, (1934). 1st ed. Signed. VG. Howes W5. *Lien.* $170/£109

WAGNER, GLENDOLIN DAMON. Old Neutriment. Boston: Ruth Hill, 1934. 1st ed. (Bkpl, lt foxed), else VG. Howes W5. *Cahan.* $85/£54

WAGNER, HENRY R. Bullion to Books. L.A.: Zamorano Club, 1942. Frontis port. Dj (2 chips). *Dawson.* $250/£160

WAGNER, HENRY R. California Voyages, 1539-1541: Translation of Original Documents. SF: John Howell, 1925. Inscribed. Gilt-stamped cl. *Dawson.* $350/£224

WAGNER, HENRY R. Cartography of the Northwest Coast of America to 1800. Berkeley, 1937. 1st ed. 2 vols. (Sm dampstain), o/w Fine in Fine dj. Howes W7. *Turpen.* $395/£253

WAGNER, HENRY R. Juan Rodriguez Cabrillo, Discoverer of the Coast of California. SF: CA Hist Soc, 1941. 1st ed. Ltd to 750. Presentation inscription signed by Lawton Kennedy (ptr) and Harold Seeger (topography). Cl-backed bds, paper spine label. (Off-setting feps), else Fine. *Argonaut.* $150/£96

WAGNER, HENRY R. Juan Rodriguez Cabrillo, Discoverer of the Coast of California. SF: CA Hist Soc, 1941. Ltd to 750. Color frontis. Beige linen, grn patterned bds, paper spine label. Good. *Karmiole.* $150/£96

WAGNER, HENRY R. The Life and Writings of Bartolome de las Casas. Albuquerque, (1967). 1st ed. VF in VF dj. *Turpen*. $95/£61

WAGNER, HENRY R. Peter Pond, Fur Trader and Explorer. (New Haven): Yale Univ Library, 1955. One of 500. 3 fldg maps in separate folder. Cl spine. Slipcase. *Dawson*. $125/£80

WAGNER, HENRY R. The Plains and the Rockies. SF: John Howell, 1921. 2nd issue. Tan cl spine, gray bds (corners lt chafed). *Karmiole*. $175/£112

WAGNER, HENRY R. The Plains and the Rockies. SF: John Howell, 1921. 1st ed, 2nd issue. One of 350 (not stated). Inscribed. Cl-backed bds (hinge cracked nearly through; corners bumped, showing, spine dknd), paper spine label (chipped, sm losses 2 corners). Good-. *Harrington*. $225/£144

WAGNER, HENRY R. The Plains and the Rockies. Charles L. Camp (rev). SF: Grabhorn, 1937. 2nd ed. One of 600. Facs of tps. Red cl (corner bumped), leather spine label (faded). NF. *Harrington*. $135/£87

WAGNER, HENRY R. The Plains and the Rockies. SF: Grabhorn, 1937. One of 600. NF (bkpl, # stamped on 2pp). *Bohling*. $150/£96

WAGNER, HENRY R. The Plains and the Rockies. Columbus, 1953. 3rd ed. Good. *Heinoldt*. $125/£80

WAGNER, HENRY R. The Plains and the Rockies. Columbus, OH, 1953. 3rd ed. (Sl rubbed, soiled.) *King*. $100/£64

WAGNER, HENRY R. The Plains and the Rockies. SF, 1982. 4th ed. Fine. *Turpen*. $150/£96

WAGNER, HENRY R. The Plains and the Rockies. Robert H. Becker (ed). SF: John Howell, 1982. 4th ed. *Swann**. $103/£66

WAGNER, HENRY R. The Plains and the Rockies. Robert H. Becker (ed). SF: John Howell, 1982. 4th ed. Fine. *Bohling*. $125/£80

WAGNER, HENRY R. The Rise of Fernando Cortes. L.A., 1944. 1st ed. Ltd to 300. Frontis port. Mod gray cl. (New eps; 1-inch tear cvr expertly repaired), o/w Fine. *Turpen*. $395/£253

WAGNER, HENRY R. Sir Francis Drake's Voyage Around the World. SF: John Howell, 1926. 1st ed. Frontis port. Blue cl. (Internal soil; spine sl faded), else VG. Howes W9. *Parmer*. $250/£160

WAGNER, HENRY R. Sir Francis Drake's Voyage Around the World.... SF: John Howell, 1926. 1st ed. Frontis port, 4 plts, 7 fldg maps. Unopened. Red cl, gilt spine. NF. Howes W9. *Harrington*. $200/£128

WAGNER, HENRY R. Sir Francis Drake's Voyage Around the World: Its Aims and Achievements. SF: John Howell, 1926. One of 100 w/special binding, extra illus. Inscribed. 13 ports, maps, 19 extra pp illus. Prospectus laid in. Leather spine (sunned), tips. *Dawson*. $500/£321

WAGNER, HENRY R. Sir Francis Drake's Voyage Around the World: Its Aims, and Achievements. SF, 1926. 1st ed. Howes W9. *Ginsberg*. $250/£160

WAGNER, HENRY R. Spanish Voyages to the Northwest Coast of America in the Sixteenth Century. SF: CA Hist Soc, 1929. 20 plts. Blue cl, gilt. (Corners sl bumped), else NF. *Parmer*. $425/£272

WAGNER, KARL EDWARD (ed). Horrorstory Volume Five. Novato/Lancaster: Underwood Miller, 1989. One of 350 numbered, signed by Wagner and 32 contributors. Morocco. Dj, cl fldg case. *Swann**. $46/£29

WAGNER, LEOPOLD. London Inns and Taverns. London, 1924. 1st ed. (Spine sl chipped, dknd.) *Edwards*. $31/£20

WAGNER, RICHARD. Parsifal, or The Legend of the Holy Grail Retold from Ancient Sources. London: Harrap, n.d. 4to. 16 tipped-in color plts, 8 full-pg color illus by Willy Pogany. Red 1/2 morocco, cl bds. (Fr cvr sl faded), o/w VG. *New Hampshire**. $90/£58

WAGNER, RICHARD. Tale of Lohengrin, Knight of the Swan. London: Harrap, n.d. 4to. 8 color plts by Willy Pogany. Blue 1/2 morocco, cl bds, gilt spines. VG. *New Hampshire**. $120/£77

WAGNER, RICHARD. Tannhauser. NY: Brentano's, ca 1920. 12 mtd color plts by Willy Pogany. Black cl, gilt. Fine. *Appelfeld*. $200/£128

WAGNER, RICHARD. Tannhauser. London: George C. Harrap, n.d. 4to. 22 tipped-in plts (12 color) by Willy Pogany. Grn 1/2 morocco, cl bds. VG. *New Hampshire**. $120/£77

WAGONER, J. J. History of the Cattle Industry in Southern Arizona, 1540-1940. Tucson: Univ of AZ, 1952. Pb. VG. *Lien*. $30/£19

WAGSTAFF, A. E. Life of David S. Terry. SF, 1892. 1st ed. 526pp. Howes W14. *Ginsberg*. $300/£192

WAGSTAFF, BLANCHE SHOEMAKER. Bob: The Spaniel. The True Story of a Springer. NY: G. Howard Watt, 1927. 1st ed. Photo frontis. 3 als laid in envelope mtd on rear pastedown. Tan cl (worn, soiled), black lettering. (Fep excised), else Internally Fine. *Cummins*. $100/£64

WAGSTAFFE, R. and J. H. FIDLER (eds). The Preservation of Natural History Specimens: 1. Invertebrates. London: Witherby, (1957). VG (ex-lib) in Good+ dj. *Mikesh*. $25/£16

WAHL, JAN. The Norman Rockwell Storybook. NY, (1969). 1st ed. Signed by Rockwell. Folio. Bds (sl worn). Dj (torn, frayed). *Oinonen**. $160/£103

WAHL, PAUL and DON TOPPEL. The Gatling Gun. NY, (1965). 1st ed. Fine in Fine dj. *Pratt*. $75/£48

WAHLENBERG, ANNA. Old Swedish Fairy Tales. Antoinette De Coursey Patterson (trans). NY: Hampton, (1925). Jeanette Berkowitz (illus). 8vo. 296pp; 6 color plts. VF in red cl, illus paste-on. *Bromer*. $100/£64

WAHLOO, PER. The Thirty-First Floor. Joan Tate (trans). NY: Knopf, 1967. 1st Amer ed. Fine in dj. *Antic Hay*. $25/£16

WAHLOO, PETER. The Steel Spring. NY: Delacorte, 1970. 1st ed. Fine in dj (lt worn). *Else Fine*. $35/£22

WAIN, JOHN. Preliminary Essays. London: Macmillan, 1957. 1st ed. (Stamp fep.) Dj (edges, spine browned, sm lib #s spine). *Hollett*. $47/£30

WAINWRIGHT, A. Fellwanderer. Kendal: Westmorland Gazette, 1966. 1st ed. Signed. VG in dj (sl creased, torn). *Hollett*. $117/£75

WAINWRIGHT, A. The Northern Highlands. Kendal: Westmorland Gazette, (1974). 1st ed. VG in dj (lt spotted; lower panel sl creased, chipped). *Hollett*. $62/£40

WAINWRIGHT, A. Old Roads of Eastern Lakeland. Kendal: Westmorland Gazette, 1985. 1st ed. Signed. VG in stiff pict wrappers. *Hollett*. $47/£30

WAINWRIGHT, A. Scottish Mountain Drawings. Kendal: Westmorland Gazette, 1975. 1st ed. Vol 2. VG in dj. *Hollett*. $70/£45

WAINWRIGHT, A. Wainwright on the Pennine Way. London: Michael Joseph, 1985. 1st ed. Signed. VG in dj. *Hollett*. $55/£35

WAINWRIGHT, ALEXANDER. Robert Louis Stevenson, a Catalogue of the Henry E. Gerstley Collection.... Princeton, NJ: Princeton Univ Library, 1971. 1st ed. Brn cl, gilt. Fine. *Macdonnell*. $60/£38

WAINWRIGHT, JOHN. All Through the Night. London: Macmillan, 1985. 1st ed. (Date stamped on fep), o/w Fine in dj. *Mordida*. $30/£19

WAINWRIGHT, JOHN. The Medical Knowledge of William Shakespeare with Explanatory Notes. NY, 1915. 1st ed, 4th ptg. VG. *Fye.* $150/£96

WAINWRIGHT, JOHN. Portrait in Shadows. London: Macmillan, 1986. 1st ed. (Date stamped on fep), o/w Fine in dj. *Mordida.* $30/£19

WAITE, ARTHUR. Azoth: or The Star in the East. London: Theosophical Pub, 1893. 1st ed. xv,239pp. (Cvr wear, inner hinge exposed, spots top edge), o/w VG. *Middle Earth.* $195/£125

WAITE, ARTHUR EDWARD. The Hermetic and Alchemical Writings of Paracelsus. NY: University Books, 1967. Rpt. #168/500 sets. Fine set in box. *Middle Earth.* $295/£189

WAITE, ARTHUR EDWARD. The Hermetic and Alchemical Writings of...Paracelsus the Great. NY, (1967). Facs of London 1894 ed. #2/1000. 2 vols. Full cl, dec spines. (Chemical stains cvrs), o/w Good + . *Scribe's Perch*.* $90/£58

WAITE, ARTHUR EDWARD. The Hermetic Museum. London: John M. Watkins, 1953. One of 250. 2 vols. Black cl, gilt. NF in dj (vol 1 lacks dj). *House.* $200/£128

WAITE, ARTHUR EDWARD. The Holy Kabbalah. London: Williams & Norgate, (1929). 4 plts. Red cl (worn, 2-inch tear fr joint, shaken; pencil underlining 1st chapter). *House.* $100/£64

WAITE, ARTHUR EDWARD. The Mysteries of Magic. London: Kegan Paul et al, 1897. 2nd ed. xvi,524pp. Blue cl, gilt. Good. *Karmiole.* $75/£48

WAITE, ARTHUR EDWARD. The Pictorial Key to the Tarot. London: Rider, 1911. 1st ed. VG + . *Middle Earth.* $195/£125

WAITE, ARTHUR EDWARD. Strange Houses of Sleep. London, 1906. Ltd to 250 numbered, signed. Teg. Full gilt-stamped vellum (warped; cvrs, top edge stained; bkpl). *King.* $250/£160

WAITE, ARTHUR EDWARD. Studies in Mysticism. Hodder & Stoughton, 1906. (Sl spotted, feps browned, upper hinge cracked; cl sl soiled, spine lt faded.) *Edwards.* $62/£40

WAITE, ARTHUR EDWARD. The Turba Philosophorum. London: W. Rider, 1914. 1st ed. VG + . *Middle Earth.* $195/£125

WAITLEY, DOUGLAS. Roads of Destiny. Washington: Luce, 1970. 1st ed. VG. *Archer.* $20/£13

WAITZ, JULIA ELLEN. The Journal of Julia Le Grand, New Orleans, 1862-1863. Richmond: Everett Waddey, 1911. 1st ed. (Cvrs sl soiled), else VG + . *Mcgowan.* $150/£96

WAKEFIELD, E. and R. W. G. DENNIS. Common British Fungi. London, 1950. 1st ed. 111 color plts. Good in dj. *Henly.* $37/£24

WAKEFIELD, H. R. The Clock Strikes Twelve. Sauk City: Arkham House, 1946. 1st US ed. (Inscrip, name), else VG + in NF dj. *Other Worlds.* $60/£38

WAKEFIELD, H. R. The Clock Strikes Twelve. Sauk City: Arkham House, 1946. 1st ed. (Sm patch of lt discoloration fr cvr), else Fine in illus dj. *Bromer.* $75/£48

WAKEFIELD, H. R. Old Man's Beard. London: Geoffrey Bles, (1929). 1st ed. Reading copy (fr bd edge damaged). *Certo.* $30/£19

WAKEFIELD, H. R. Strayers from Sheol. Sauk City: Arkham House, 1961. 1st ed. (Bkpls, ink date), else NF in dj (badly browned). *Other Worlds.* $45/£29

WAKEFIELD, H. R. Strayers from Sheol. Sauk City: Arkham House, 1961. 1st ed. NF in dj (sl browned). *Other Worlds.* $60/£38

WAKEFIELD, H. R. They Return at Evening. Appleton, 1928. 1st US ed. Good (spine frayed, gilt dull) in VG dj. *Certo.* $30/£19

WAKEFIELD, HUGH. Victorian Pottery. London, 1962. 1st ed. 99 plts. Dj (sl chipped). *Edwards.* $44/£28

WAKEFIELD, PRISCILLA. Excursions in North America.... London, 1810. 2nd ed. Fldg map. Contemp sheep (worn). *Swann*.* $92/£59

WAKEFIELD, W. The Happy Valley. London, 1879. 1st ed. xii,300pp (wrinkled); 8 tinted plts (dampstained), fldg map. Dec cl (lower bd, spine badly dampstained). *Edwards.* $55/£35

WAKEMAN, EDGAR. The Log of an Ancient Mariner. SF: A.L. Bancroft, 1878. 378pp + 4pp ads. (Owner stamp partly removed tp; cvrs faded, worn.) Howes W23. *Parmer.* $150/£96

WAKOSKI, DIANE. Cap of Darkness. Santa Barbara, CA: Black Sparrow, 1980. One of 250 numbered, signed. Yellow cl-backed dec bds, ptd spine label. Fine in acetate dj. *Blue Mountain.* $45/£29

WAKOSKI, DIANE. Overnight Projects with Wood. Madison, WI: Red Ozier, 1977. One of 170 numbered, signed. Fine in Kosmicpaper wraps. *Lame Duck.* $100/£64

WAKOSKI, DIANE. The Ring. Black Sparrow, 1977. One of 140 numbered, signed. Cl, dec bds. Fine in acetate dj. *Dermont.* $65/£42

WAKOSKI, DIANE. Saturn's Rings. NY: Targ Editions, 1982. Ltd to 250 signed. Burgundy cl-backed pict gray bds, gilt. Fine. *Blue Mountain.* $45/£29

Walam Olum or Red Score. Indianapolis: IN Hist Soc, 1954. 1st ed. Frontis port. VG. *Cahan.* $85/£54

WALCOTT, DEREK et al. 15 Poems for William Shakespeare. Stratford-upon-Avon: Trustees and Guardians of Shakespeare's Birthplace, 1964. One of 100 numbered. NF in pub's faux vellum. *Lame Duck.* $100/£64

WALCOTT, DEREK. Another Life. NY: Farrar, (1973). 1st US ed. Fine in NF dj (nicked). *Reese.* $40/£26

WALCOTT, DEREK. The Arkansas Testament. NY: FSG, (1987). 1st ed. Fine in dj. *Antic Hay.* $45/£29

WALCOTT, DEREK. Selected Poems. NY: Farrar, 1964. 1st ed. Fine in Fine dj (sm rubs, lt dusting rear panel). *Beasley.* $85/£54

WALCOTT, MARY VAUX. North American Wild Flowers. Washington: Smithsonian, 1925. 5 vols in portfolios. (Portfolio extrems sl defective), else VG + . *Zubal*.* $220/£141

WALDEN, ARTHUR T. A Dog Puncher on the Yukon. NY: Houghton Mifflin, 1928. 1st ed. VG in Poor dj (torn). *Perier.* $40/£26

WALDEN, HOWARD T. Big Stony. NY: Derrydale, (1940). Ltd to 550. Pict cl. VG. *Truepenny.* $150/£96

WALDEN, HOWARD T. Upstream and Down. NY: Derrydale, (1938). Ltd to 950. Dec pict cl. Unopened. Fine (cvr stamping rubbed). *Truepenny.* $150/£96

WALDEN, HOWARD T., II. Upstream and Down. NY: Derrydale, (1938). 1st ed. #629/950. VG. *Mcgowan.* $150/£96

WALDMAN, ANNE. Fast Speaking Woman. Detroit: Red Hanrahan, 1974. #103/500. Signed presentation. Fine in ptd wraps (edges sl rubbed). *Polyanthos.* $25/£16

WALDMAN, DIANE. Mark Rothko. NY: Abrams, 1978. 198 plts. VG + in dj. *Metropolitan*.* $86/£55

WALDO, S. PUTNAM. Memoirs of Andrew Jackson.... Hartford/Berlin: Silas Andrus/Frederick Hinsdale, 1818. 1st ed, 3rd ptg. 316pp (few sigs sprung, browned, sl foxed). Old full calf (worn), black leather spine label. Text Good. *Baltimore*.* $35/£22

WALDO, S. PUTNAM. The Tour of James Monroe.... Hartford: Silas Andrus, 1819. Frontis port. Teg. 3/4 maroon morocco, gilt, raised bands. Nice. Howes W29. *Appelfeld.* $100/£64

WALDRON, MALCOLM. Snow Man. Boston: Houghton Mifflin, 1931. VG. *High Latitude.* $35/£22

WALDSTEIN, CHARLES and LEONARD SHOO-BRIDGE. Herculaneum; Past, Present and Future. London: Macmillan, 1908. Color frontis. Dec pub's cl. VG. *Turtle Island.* $100/£64

WALES, GEORGE C. Etchings and Lithographs of American Ships. Boston, 1927. Signed etching, litho by Wales. 1/4 cl. Dj (spine chipped). *Swann*.* $230/£147

WALEY, ARTHUR (trans). The Lady Who Loved Insects. London: Blackamore, 1929. One of 550. Rough silk. Slipcase. *Swann*.* $126/£81

WALEY, ARTHUR (trans). The Lady Who Loved Insects. London: Blackamore, 1929. 1st ed. #60/500 (of 550). 4 drypoints. Teg, uncut. Tan cl, gilt. Fine in pub's slipcase. *Houle.* $150/£96

WALEY, ARTHUR. The Life and Times of Po Chu-I. Allen & Unwin, 1949. 1st ed. (Underlining, Chinese transliterations in margins, inscrip; cl soiled), o/w Good+. *Poetry Bookshop.* $16/£10

WALEY, ARTHUR. More Translations from the Chinese. NY: Knopf, 1937. Bds, cl spine. (Edges rubbed; lib spine #), o/w VG. *Worldwide.* $18/£12

WALEY, ARTHUR. Zen Buddhism and Its Relation to Art. 1922. 1st ed. VG in yellow wrappers (edges browned, crease). *Words Etc.* $62/£40

Walker Evans at Work. NY: Harper, (1982). Fine in NF dj (sm tears). *Between The Covers.* $85/£54

WALKER, A. BARCLAY. The Cruise of the Esquimaux (Steam Whaler) to Davis Straits and Baffin Bay April-October, 1899. Liverpool: Liverpool Ptg & Stationery Co, 1909. Frontis, fldg map. Good (lt stain fr cvr, stain affecting last several ll). *High Latitude.* $125/£80

WALKER, ALICE. Good Night, Willie Lee, I'll See You in the Morning. NY: Dial, (1979). 1st ed. Fine in dj. *Captain's Bookshelf.* $350/£224

WALKER, ALICE. Her Blue Body Everything We Know. NY: Harcourt Brace, (1991). 1st ed. Signed. Fine in Fine dj. *Lenz.* $65/£42

WALKER, ALICE. Horses Make a Landscape Look More Beautiful. San Diego, 1984. 1st Amer ed. NF (edges lt sunned) in dj (price-clipped). *Polyanthos.* $25/£16

WALKER, ALICE. In Love and Trouble. NY: Harcourt, (1973). 1st ed. Fine in dj. *Captain's Bookshelf.* $450/£288

WALKER, ALICE. In Search of Our Mothers' Gardens. San Diego/NY/London: HBJ, (1983). 1st ed. Signed. (Inscrip), o/w NF in dj (price-clipped). *Bernard.* $100/£64

WALKER, ALICE. In Search of Our Mothers' Gardens. NY: Harcourt, 1983. 1st ed. Fine in dj (sm tears). *Else Fine.* $65/£42

WALKER, ALICE. Meridian. London: Andre Deutsch, (1976). 1st British ed. Fine in Fine dj. *Pettler & Lieberman.* $75/£48

WALKER, ALICE. The Third Life of Grange Copeland. NY: Harcourt, (1970). 1st ed. (Corners sl bumped), o/w Fine in dj. *Captain's Bookshelf.* $225/£144

WALKER, ALICE. The Third Life of Grange Copeland. NY: Harcourt Brace Jovanovich, 1970. 1st ed. Fine in dj (sm spot, price-clipped). *Else Fine.* $250/£160

WALKER, C. B. The Mississippi Valley, and Prehistoric Events. Burlington, IA, 1880. 784pp; 4 tinted plts (2 are maps). Black cl (rebound), gilt. Good. *Bohling.* $75/£48

WALKER, C. E. The Essentials of Cytology.... London, 1907. 3 fldg plts, 4 figs in rear pocket. (Sl shaken.) *Maggs.* $20/£13

WALKER, CHARLES RUMFORD. Steel. The Diary of a Furnace Worker. Boston: Atlantic Monthly, 1922. 1st ed. NF. *Beasley.* $30/£19

WALKER, DAVID H. Pioneers of Prosperity. SF: (The Author), 1895. 1st ed. 191,(5)pp. Gilt-lettered grn cl (extrems rubbed), else Fine. *Argonaut.* $50/£32

WALKER, DUNCAN S. (ed). Celebration of the One Hundredth Anniversary of the Laying of the Corner Stone of the Capitol of the United States. Washington: GPO, 1896. 152pp. (Rubbed, soiled.) *King.* $35/£22

WALKER, EGBERT. Flora of Okinawa and the Southern Ryukyu Islands. Washington: Smithsonian Inst Press, 1976. 1st ed. Fine in NF dj. *Archer.* $45/£29

WALKER, FRANCIS A. General Hancock. NY, 1898. Army and Navy ed. 332pp. (Cvr worn), o/w Fine. *Pratt.* $30/£19

WALKER, FRANKLIN. San Francisco's Literary Frontier. Knopf, (1939). 1st ed. Fine in VG dj (chipped). *Authors Of West.* $40/£26

WALKER, FRANKLIN. San Francisco's Literary Frontier. NY: Knopf, 1939. 1st ed. VF in dj (spine ends lt chipped). *Argonaut.* $60/£38

WALKER, FRANKLIN. The Seacoast of Bohemia. Santa Barbara: Peregrine Smith, 1973. New, enlgd ed. 2-tone cl, gilt-lettered spine. Fine. *Argonaut.* $45/£29

WALKER, G. GOOLD. The Honourable Artillery Company 1537-1926. John Lane, 1926. 4 color, 40 monochrome plts. Dj (soiled, sl torn). *Bickersteth.* $37/£24

WALKER, GEORGE. Chess Made Easy. Balt: Bayly & Burns, 1837. 1st Amer ed. Frontis, 94pp (dampstain top margin). Purple cl-cvrd bds (faded, soiled, fr hinge tearing). *New Hampshire*.* $65/£42

WALKER, HENRY J. Jesse James, 'The Outlaw.' (Des Moines, 1961.) 'Volume 1' all pub. Signed. Orange cl. VG in dj (frayed). *Bohling.* $30/£19

WALKER, HOVENDEN. The Walker Expedition to Quebec, 1771. Gerald S. Graham (ed). Toronto: Champlain Soc, 1953. One of 550 numbered. Howes W39. *Ginsberg.* $275/£176

WALKER, J. A Rhyming Dictionary.... 1819. 3rd ed. 2 vols. xxiii,(i),347; (i),348pp. Contemp 1/2 calf. *Bickersteth.* $59/£38

WALKER, J. HUBERT. Walking in the Alps. Edinburgh, (1951). 1st ed. (Sl bumped), else VG in dj (torn). *King.* $35/£22

WALKER, JAMES B. Experiences of Pioneer Life in the Early Settlements of the West. Chicago: Sumner, 1881. 1st ed. 310pp. *Ginsberg.* $300/£192

WALKER, JOHN. Bellini and Titian at Ferrara. London, 1956. Good. *Washton.* $50/£32

WALKER, JOHN. The Life of John Walker. J. Epps (ed). London, 1831. viii,342pp. (Spine, bds worn, spine top defective, bkpl fep), o/w Good. *Whitehart.* $47/£30

WALKER, MARGARET. For My People. New Haven: Yale Univ, 1942. 1st ed, 2nd ptg, 1st bk. VG in dj (lt edgewear). *Petrilla.* $75/£48

WALKER, MARY E. Hit. NY: American News, (1871). 1st ed. 177pp. (Sl soiled, ex-lib, bkpls; fr hinge tender.) *Second Life.* $225/£144

WALKER, R. The Flora of Oxfordshire, and Its Contiguous Counties.... Oxford, 1833. cxxxv,338pp; fldg table, 12 plts. (Neatly rebacked, preserving spine.) *Henly.* $106/£68

WALKER, R. A. (ed). The Best of Beardsley. Spring Books, n.d. (c. 1960). Frontis port, 134 plts. (Margin 1 plt sl torn, repaired w/tape, margins lt browned; dec cl lt soiled, spine sl browned.) *Edwards.* $39/£25

WALKER, RICHARD. Memoirs of Medicine. London: J. Johnson, 1799. 1/2 title, xvi,258pp (lib stamp tp). Contemp 1/2 calf, marbled bds (spine repaired). *Goodrich.* $295/£189

WALKER, RICHARD. Still-Water Angling. Macgibbon & Kee, 1953. 1st ed. Fine in dj. *Petersfield.* $39/£25

WALKER, ROBERT SPARKS. Torchlights to the Cherokees: The Brainerd Mission. NY: Macmillan, 1931. 1st ed. 3 plts (1 fldg). (Spine faded.) *Ginsberg.* $75/£48

WALKER, THOMAS. Aristology or The Art of Dining. Cambridge, 1965. Ltd to 500. 10 full-pg dwgs. Olive/terra cotta patterned paper bds. Fine. *Cady.* $50/£32

WALKER, THOMAS. The Art of Dining. Cayme Press, 1928. One of 600. Teg. Paper-cvrd bds (lt soiled), grn buckram-backed spine, gilt. Fine. *Heller.* $90/£58

WALKER, THOMAS. Journal of an Exploration in the Spring of the Year 1750. Boston, 1888. 69pp (pinholes blank portion of tp). Ptd bds (rubbed). Good (spine worn). Howes W43. *Wantagh.* $175/£112

WALKER, WALTER. A Dime to Dance By. NY: Harper & Row, 1983. 1st ed. Fine in dj. *Mordida.* $45/£29

WALKER, WINSLOW M. The Troyville Mounds, Catahoula Parish, La. BAE Bulletin 113. Washington: Smithsonian, 1936. 16 plts. Good in stiff wrappers. *Archaeologia.* $35/£22

WALKINSHAW, LAWRENCE. Cranes of the World. NY: Winchester, 1973. 1st ed. VG (ex-lib) in dj. *Worldwide.* $35/£22

WALL, A. H. Artistic Landscape Photography. Bradford/London: Percy Lund, Country Press/Memorial Hall, (c 1896?). Frontis, 171pp + (4) ads. Cl-backed marbled paper over bds, paper spine label. (Edges lt rubbed), else VG. *Cahan.* $125/£80

WALLACE, A. R. Contributions to the Theory of Natural Selection. NY: Macmillan, (1871). 2nd ed. 384pp. Good+ (ex-lib). *Mikesh.* $60/£38

WALLACE, A. R. Contributions to the Theory of Natural Selection. London: Macmillan, 1870. 1st ed. 384pp + 43pp ads. (Bkpl, 2 sm holes spine), else VG+. *Mikesh.* $250/£160

WALLACE, A. R. Contributions to the Theory of Natural Selection. London: MacMillan, 1870. 1st ed. xvi,384pp + 40pp ads dated Jan. 1870. Grn cl, gilt (inner hinges starting). *Karmiole.* $350/£224

WALLACE, A. R. Darwinism. London: Macmillan, (1912). 3rd ed. Frontis port, 494pp + 2pp ads, color fldg map. Blind-stamped gilt-dec cl. VG+. *Mikesh.* $150/£96

WALLACE, A. R. Darwinism. London: Macmillan, (Oct 1889). 3rd ptg. Frontis port, 494pp + 2pp ads, color fldg map. VG. *Mikesh.* $150/£96

WALLACE, A. R. Darwinism. London: Macmillan, 1889. 1st ed. Frontis port, 494pp + 2pp ads, color fldg map. VG+. *Mikesh.* $250/£160

WALLACE, A. R. Darwinism. London, 1890. Rpt. Frontis port (marginal foxing), xvi,494pp + 2pp pub's ads, fldg map. *Edwards.* $62/£40

WALLACE, A. R. Darwinism. London: Macmillan, 1890. 2nd ed. Frontis port, xvi,494pp, fldg map. Grn cl. (Ex-lib, stamps prelims), o/w Clean. *White.* $47/£30

WALLACE, A. R. Island Life or Phenomena and Causes of Insular Faunas and Floras. London: Macmillan, 1892. 563pp; 3 maps. Grn cl. VG. *Adelson.* $80/£51

WALLACE, A. R. Island Life. London, 1911. 3rd rev ed. xx,563pp; color map. Nice. *Wheldon & Wesley.* $125/£80

WALLACE, A. R. The Malay Archipelago. NY, 1869. 1st US ed. 2 fldg maps, 8 inserted plts. Caspar Whitney's sig. (Spine faded, ends lt worn.) *Kane*.* $250/£160

WALLACE, A. R. The Malay Archipelago. NY: Harper, 1869. 1st ed. Fldg frontis map, 638pp + 2pp ads. Mod cl. (Pg edge stains), else VG. *Mikesh.* $95/£61

WALLACE, A. R. The Malay Archipelago. NY: Harper, 1869. 1st Amer ed. 2 litho maps, 8 plts. Purple cl (sl worn, spine badly faded). *Maggs.* $117/£75

WALLACE, A. R. A Narrative of Travels on the Amazon and Rio Negro with an Account of the Native Tribes, etc. London: Ward, Lock, (1889). New ed. Frontis port map, 363pp, 15 full-pg engrs. Dec cl. VG. *Mikesh.* $60/£38

WALLACE, A. R. Natural Selection and Tropical Nature. London, 1895. New ed. xii,492pp. (Inner hinges cracked; cl sl worn.) *Henly.* $66/£42

WALLACE, A. R. Tropical Nature and Other Essays. 1878. 1st ed. xiii,356pp. (Spine sl defective, fr cvr sl mkd, corners sl worn, inner hinges sl cracked), o/w VG. *Whitehart.* $62/£40

WALLACE, A. R. Tropical Nature, and Other Essays. London: Macmillan, 1878. 1st ed. xiii,(3),356pp,(1 ad)pp. Fine. *Glaser.* $285/£183

WALLACE, A. R. The World of Life. London, 1910. 1st ed. Teg. (Prelims lt foxed, hinges cracked; cl sl soiled, spine faded, sl worn, chipped, rubbed.) *Edwards.* $62/£40

WALLACE, ADAM. Parson of the Islands; A Biography of the Rev. Joshua Thomas.... Balt, 1906. Port. Dec cl (cvrs, spine stained). *Ginsberg.* $75/£48

WALLACE, BRENTON G. and FREDERIC G. WARNER. The Works of Wallace and Warner, Philadelphia. Phila, 1930. 1st ed. (Sl internal soil, creasing.) 1/4 cl, bds (worn, spine torn, frayed). *Freeman*.* $90/£58

WALLACE, D. MACKENZIE. Egypt and the Egyptian Question. London: Macmillan, 1883. 1st ed. xi,521pp. (Rubbed, soiled, spine sl chipped, ex-lib, spine sticker removed), o/w VG. *Worldwide.* $45/£29

WALLACE, DILLON. The Long Labrador Trail. NY: Outing Press, 1907. 1st ed. 2 fldg maps. (Rep lacks sm piece; illus cl sl shelfworn.) *Parmer.* $50/£32

WALLACE, DILLON. The Long Labrador Trail. NY: Outing, 1907. 1st ed. Signed, dated Jan, 1910. 2 color plts, 2 fldg maps. Dec cl. VG (sigs). *High Latitude.* $55/£35

WALLACE, DILLON. The Long Labrador Trail. Chicago: McClurg, 1911. Pict blue cl (ends frayed), gilt. *Yudkin*.* $18/£12

WALLACE, DILLON. The Lure of the Labrador Wild. NY: Fleming H. Revell, 1905. 16 plts. Pict cl. VG. *Adelson.* $45/£29

WALLACE, EDGAR. The Crimson Circle. GC: DCC, 1929. 1st Amer ed. Fine in dj (spine ends nicked, sm closed tears). *Mordida.* $100/£64

WALLACE, EDGAR. The Double. GC: DCC, 1928. 1st Amer ed. (Name), o/w Fine in VG dj (lg internal tape mends; 1-inch spine piece, long top edge, fr flap pieces missing). *Mordida.* $45/£29

WALLACE, EDGAR. The Flying Squad. GC: DCC, 1929. 1st Amer ed. (Pg edges spotted), o/w VG in dj (3/4-inch piece missing spine top, corners chipped, folds worn). *Mordida.* $65/£42

WALLACE, EDGAR. The Fourth Plague. GC: DCC, 1930. 1st Amer ed. NF in dj (spine dknd, crease fr panel, sm nicks). *Mordida.* $100/£64

WALLACE, EDGAR. The Hand of Power. NY: Mystery League, 1930. 1st US ed. NF in dj (sm closed tears). *Janus.* $50/£32

WALLACE, EDGAR. The Man Who Changed His Name. Samuel French, 1929. 1st ed. VG in wrappers (spine sl browned). *Words Etc.* $16/£10

WALLACE, EDGAR. Unofficial Despatches. London: Hutchinson, n.d. (1901). 1st ptg, w/title in gold on fr cvr. VG (ink name; bds sl mkd, dull). *Williams.* $117/£75

WALLACE, ELIZABETH. Mark Twain and the Happy Island. Chicago: McClurg, 1914. 2nd ed. Pict tan cl. VG (lt rubbed, few mks). BAL II:251. *Macdonnell.* $15/£10

WALLACE, ERNEST and E. ADAMSON HOEBEL. The Comanches. Norman: Univ of OK, (1952). 1st ed. Good in pict cl. *Lien.* $45/£29

WALLACE, ERNEST and E. ADAMSON HOEBEL. The Comanches. Norman: Univ of OK, (1954). 2nd ptg. VG in dj. *Perier.* $30/£19

WALLACE, FREDERICK T. Men and Events of Half a Century. Cleveland: Evangelical Assn, 1882. iv,363pp, index. Good+ (sl worn, soiled). *Bohling.* $30/£19

WALLACE, HAROLD FRANK. The Big Game of Central and Western China.... London: John Murray, 1913. 1st ed. Frontis, map. Teg. Orange cl, black lettering, decs. VG+ (sl soiled; sig). *Backman.* $250/£160

WALLACE, HENRY. Uncle Henry's Own Story of His Life, Personal Reminiscences. Des Moines: Wallace, 1917. Signed by John P. Wallace. Vol 1 (of 3). (Owner rubberstamp.) Howes W52. *Bohling.* $30/£19

WALLACE, IRVING. The Fabulous Originals. NY: Knopf, 1955. 1st ed, 1st bk. NF (inscrip) in VG+ dj (spine sm closed tear). *Janus.* $30/£19

WALLACE, JOHN. Carpetbag Rule in Florida. Jacksonville, FL, 1888. 444pp. *Wantagh.* $30/£19

WALLACE, JOSEPH. History of Illinois and Louisiana under the French Rule.... Cincinnati: Clark, 1893. (10),433pp. (Joints lt worn.) Howes W55. *Ginsberg.* $150/£96

WALLACE, LEW. Ben-Hur, a Tale of the Christ. NY: Harper, (1880). 1st ed, later issue, w/early form of dedication: to 'the wife of my youth.' 2nd state binding: orig grey-grn beveled cl, gilt. (Lt rubbed.) BAL 20798. *Macdonnell.* $75/£48

WALLACE, LEW. The Prince of India. Harper, 1893. 1st ed. Signed. 2 vols. VG. *Madle.* $100/£64

WALLACE, PAUL A. W. (ed). Thirty Thousand Miles with John Heckewelder. Pittsburgh: Univ of Pittsburgh, (1958). Fldg maps. VG in dj (sl worn). Howes H390, 391, 392. *Lien.* $45/£29

WALLACE, PHILIP B. Colonial Churches and Meeting Houses. NY: Architectural Book Pub, (1931). 1st ed. Blue cl, gilt. Cvrs VG (sl worn; ink handstamp fep). *Baltimore*.* $35/£22

WALLACE, PHILIP B. Colonial Ironwork in Old Philadelphia. NY: Architectural Book, (1930). 1st ed. Blue cl. NF. *House.* $180/£115

WALLACE, SUSAN. The Land of the Pueblos. NY: Alden, 1888. 285pp; 12 plts. Brn cl, gilt. Nice (inscrip, name stamp). *Bohling.* $45/£29

WALLACE, SUSAN. The Land of the Pueblos. NY: Alden, 1888. 1st ed. 285pp. Dec cl. NF. *Agvent.* $100/£64

WALLANT, EDWARD. The Human Season. London, 1965. 1st Eng ed, 1st bk. VG in dj. *Argosy.* $85/£54

WALLANT, EDWARD. The Tenants of Moonbloom. NY, 1963. 1st Amer ed. Fine in dj (spine sl sunned, sl chipped, sm tear). *Polyanthos.* $25/£16

WALLER, EDMUND. The Works in Verse and Prose. J. & R. Tonson, 1758. (xvi),272pp (bkpl); port. Contemp calf (backstrip worn, hinges cracked), gilt, raised bands, morocco label. *Cox.* $31/£20

WALLER, ROBERT JAMES. The Bridges of Madison County. NY: Warner, (1992). 1st ed. Fine in Fine dj. *Unger.* $175/£112

WALLIS, HELEN (ed). Carteret's Voyage Round the World 1766-1769. London: Hakluyt Soc, 1965. 2 vols. Fine. *High Latitude.* $30/£19

WALPOLE, F. Four Years in the Pacific...1844 to 1848. London, 1850. 2nd ed. 2 vols. Engr frontispieces, 432; 415pp. Good (hinge cracks). *Scribe's Perch*.* $230/£147

WALPOLE, HORACE. The Castle of Otranto. London: (Jones & Co), 1825. 12mo. Pub's smooth pinkish cl w/ptd paper spine label reading Diamond Classics across top and w/price, 1s. 6d. at bottom. Ptd title preceded by engr frontis of Walpole and engr title, identifying this as University Edition. 4pp pub's ads at rear. VF. *Book Block.* $175/£112

WALPOLE, HORACE. The Correspondence. Vols 13 and 14. W. S. Lewis (ed). Yale, 1970. 2 vols in 1. 12 plts. VG in blue cl. *Cox.* $47/£30

WALPOLE, HORACE. Horace Walpole's Correspondence with the Rev. William Cole. W. S. Lewis (ed). London, 1937. Vols 1-2 of the Yale Edition. 1st ed thus. VG. *Gretton.* $62/£40

WALPOLE, HORACE. Horace Walpole's Correspondence. Vols 1 and 2: Correspondence with the Rev. William Cole, 1762-1782. W. S. Lewis et al (eds). New Haven: Yale Univ, 1937-1973. 15 illus. Dk blue buckram, gilt. VG. *Hartfield.* $150/£96

WALPOLE, HORACE. Journal of the Printing-Office at Strawberry Hill. (N.p.): Constable/Houghton Mifflin, 1923. One of 650. Frontis photogravure port. Calf-backed tan bds (spine sl scuffed), black leather lettering piece. Internally Fine in slipcase (worn, chipped). *House.* $135/£87

WALPOLE, HORACE. Journal of the Reign of King George the Third from the Year 1771 to 1783. Dr. Doran (ed). The Last Journals of Horace Walpole (spine titles). Richard Bentley, 1859. 2 vols. Frontis-ports. Good (sl spotting, bkpls; vol 1 rebacked, orig backstrip relaid; spines chipped). *Tiger.* $47/£30

WALPOLE, HORACE. Letters of Horace Walpole. W. S. Lewis (ed). Folio Soc, 1951. VG in dj (sl torn). *Gretton.* $23/£15

WALPOLE, HORACE. Letters to the Countess of Ossory. London: A.L. Humphreys, 1903. 3 vols. Paper cvrs w/spare title labels. VG. *Gretton.* $62/£40

WALPOLE, HORACE. Letters to the Countess of Ossory. London: Arthur L. Humphreys, 1903. 1st ed. 3 vols. 1/4 red morocco (rebound; marginalia, pencil notes reps). *Swann*.* $138/£88

WALPOLE, HORACE. The Letters. Peter Cunningham (ed). Richard Bentley, 1886. 1st ed thus. 9 vols. Good (lt spotted, bkpls; spines bumped, chipped; sunned, corners rubbed). *Tiger.* $140/£90

WALPOLE, HORACE. The Letters. Peter Cunningham (ed). London: Richard Bentley, 1886. 9 vols. Each vol 500+pp; 39 plts. Uncut. (1st, last ll each vol foxed), o/w Good set (backstrips faded, vol 5 neatly rebacked retaining backstrip, bumped, sl worn). *Cox.* $148/£95

WALPOLE, HORACE. Letters. Peter Cunningham (ed). (Edinburgh): Grant, 1906. 9 vols. 64 full-pg steel engrs. Teg; many pp uncut. VG set in dec blue cl. *Hadley.* $234/£150

WALPOLE, HORACE. The Letters. Peter Cunningham (ed). Edinburgh, 1906. 9 vols. 64 steel-engr ports. Red cl. VG. *Gretton.* $211/£135

WALPOLE, HORACE. The Letters. Peter Cunningham (ed). Edinburgh: John Grant, 1906. 9 vols. Gilt-dec cl. VG set. *New Hampshire*.* $30/£19

WALPOLE, HORACE. Memoirs of the Last Ten Years of the Reign of George the Second. John Murray, 1822. 2 vols. Folio. Contemp full leather (rebacked, orig backstrips relaid), leather spine labels. Good (lt spotted). *Tiger.* $546/£350

WALPOLE, HORACE. Memoirs of the Reign of King George the Third. G. F. Russell Barker (ed). London, 1894. #543/740. 4 vols. 16 ports. (Lt marginal browning; spines faded, sl rubbed.) *Edwards.* $117/£75

WALPOLE, HORACE. Private Correspondence of.... Rodwell & Martin, 1820. 4 vols. Frontis port. (Lt foxing throughout, mainly prelims, rear pp; bkpls.) Orig 1/2 calf (sl surface loss), filleted edges, marbled bds (sl worn, spines discolored, worn), raised bands, title labels (sl chipped, vol 1 partially detached, vol 4 detached). *Edwards*. $133/£85

WALPOLE, HORACE. Selected Letters of Horace Walpole. W. S. Lewis (ed). New Haven: Yale, 1973. 1st ed. Inscribed by Lewis. Port. Fine in VG dj. *Reese*. $35/£22

WALPOLE, HORACE. The Works of Horatio Walpole.... London: G.G. & J. Robinson & J. Edwards, 1798. 1st collected ed, 1st issue. 5 vols. Full contemp diced russia (spines rubbed, fr hinge cracked vol 1). Sound. Internally Clean. *Gretton*. $593/£380

WALPOLE, HUGH. Anthony Trollope. London: Macmillan, 1928. 1st ed. Inscribed, signed. Excellent (bkpl) in Fine dj; chemise w/gold-lettered label, spine. *Vandoros*. $175/£112

WALPOLE, HUGH. The Blind Man's House. GC: Doubleday, Doran, 1941. 1st Amer ed. VG (ink name, eps browned) in dj (spine top worn, sm tears, soil). *Antic Hay*. $20/£13

WALPOLE, HUGH. The Blind Man's House. London: Macmillan, 1941. 1st Eng ed. Emb cl. NF (eps browned, sm ink stamp fep) in VG dj (spine lt browned). *Antic Hay*. $35/£22

WALPOLE, HUGH. Captain Nicholas. NY: Doubleday, Doran, 1934. 1st US ed. NF in dj (sm chips). *Turtle Island*. $35/£22

WALPOLE, HUGH. The Fortress. London: Macmillan, 1931. One of 350 signed lg paper copies. Extending pedigree, fldg map. Cl-backed blue bds, spine label. VG. *Hollett*. $133/£85

WALPOLE, HUGH. Hans Frost. NY: Doubleday, Doran, 1929. 1st US ed. Pict eps. (Few spots prelims.) Dj (neat repairs reverse). *Hollett*. $11/£7

WALPOLE, HUGH. The Inquisitor. London: Macmillan, 1935. 1st English ed. VG (lt browned, spine top worn). *Antic Hay*. $30/£19

WALPOLE, HUGH. John Cornelius. London: Macmillan, 1937. Ltd to 175 signed. VG (bd edges worn) in acetate dj. *Antic Hay*. $50/£32

WALPOLE, HUGH. Mr. Huffam: A Christmas Story. Cleveland: Privately Ptd by Roger Williams, 1938. One of 200. Paper over bds. Fine. *Graf*. $20/£13

WALPOLE, HUGH. The Old Ladies. London: Macmillan, 1924. 1st ed. (Cl sl rubbed, bumped.) *Hollett*. $16/£10

WALPOLE, HUGH. Portrait of a Man with Red Hair. NY: Doran, (1925). 1st trade ed. NF in dj (sm chips). *Antic Hay*. $20/£13

WALPOLE, HUGH. Portrait of a Man with Red Hair. NY: Doran, (1925). Ltd to 250 numbered, signed. Vellum, bds. Fine in dj (browned, tear, nick), slipcase. *Antic Hay*. $85/£54

WALPOLE, HUGH. Portrait of a Man with Red Hair. London: Macmillan, 1925. 1st ed. Signed. (Sm nick spine top.) *Hollett*. $23/£15

WALPOLE, JOSEPH A. The Diamond Pinheads. Gaus, 1966. 1st ed. VG (spotting fr cvr). *Plapinger*. $125/£80

WALSH, HENRY COLLINS. The Last Cruise of the Miranda. NY: Transatlantic, 1896. 232pp. 2-color cl (lt worn). Clean. *High Latitude*. $65/£42

WALSH, J. H. and E. HARVEY. The Horse in the Stable and the Field, with The American Trotting Horse, Etc. Phila: Coates, (n.d.) ca 1882. 505pp, 8 full-pg engrs. Blind-stamped gilt-dec cl. (Hinges cracked), else VG. *Mikesh*. $60/£38

WALSH, RICHARD. The Writings of Christopher Gadsden, 1746-1805. Columbia, SC: Univ of SC, 1966. 1st ed. Frontis port. VG (edges lt rubbed) in dj (price-clipped; lt worn). *Cahan*. $35/£22

WALSH, ROBERT. An Appeal from the Judgments of Great Britain Respecting the United States of America. Phila, 1819. 2nd ed, w/addition of errata slip. Contemp tree sheep (worn). Howes W67. *Swann**. $201/£129

WALSH, ROBERT. Narrative of a Journey from Constantinople to England. Phila: Carey, Lea & Carey, 1828. 1st US ed. iv,270pp (sl browned, foxed, fr hinge cracked). Untrimmed. Orig brn muslin, blue-gray bds (sl worn, spine sl curved), paper spine label. *Baltimore**. $25/£16

WALSINGHAM, LORD and RALPH PAYNE-GALLWEY. Shooting. London: Longmans, Green, 1887. 2nd ed. xiii,358pp. Pict brn cl (sl worn; lower joint cracked), gilt. *Hollett*. $55/£35

WALSINGHAM, LORD and RALPH PAYNE-GALLWEY. Shooting. Moor and Marsh. London: Longmans, 1887. 2nd ed. xiv,348pp (1st, last ll sl spotted.) Teg, others uncut. Good in deluxe 1/2 blue roan, gilt, sides w/speckled fading. *Cox*. $39/£25

WALSINGHAM, LORD. Shooting: Moor and Marsh [and] Shooting: Field and Covert. London: Longmans, Green: The Badminton Library, 1886. One of 250 lg paper copies. 2 vols. Uncut. Full brn calf, red/black morocco lettering pieces. (Cvrs sl rubbed; lt foxing), else NF set. *Cummins*. $250/£160

Walt Disney's Living Desert. NY: S&S, (1954). 1st ed. Fine. *Book Market*. $30/£19

Walt Disney's Living Desert. NY: S&S, n.d. 92 color illus tipped in. Photo illus bds, cl spine. *Dawson*. $75/£48

Walt Disney's Story of Clarabelle Cow. Whitman, 1938. 5.5x5. 90pp (browned). Pict bds (sl shelfworn, rubbed). VG + . *My Bookhouse*. $40/£26

Walt Disney's Story of Minnie Mouse. Whitman, 1938. 5.5x5. 92pp (browned, hinges cracking). Pict bds (rubbed, sl worn, 1-inch strip spine top torn away). VG. *My Bookhouse*. $50/£32

Walt Disney's Thumper. G&D, 1942. 7x8. Pict bds. (Bumped), else VG + in dj (chipped, sm tear). *My Bookhouse*. $35/£22

WALTER, ELLERY. The World on One Leg. NY, 1928. 3rd imp. Presentation copy. Frontis port, map. Illus eps. *Edwards*. $23/£15

WALTER, RICHARD. Anson's Voyage Round the World. London: Martin Hopkinson, 1928. 44 plts, 4 fldg maps. Cl-backed bds. VG. *Adelson*. $120/£77

WALTERS ART GALLERY. The History of Bookbinding 525-1950 A.D. Balt, 1957. 106 plts. Buckram (bumped, ex-lib w/shelf mk). *Maggs*. $140/£90

WALTERS, HENRY. Incunabula Typographica.... Leo Olschki (ed). Balt, 1906. Deckled-edge rag paper. Full 15th-cent style leather, fleur-de-lys tooling. Good. *Goodrich*. $225/£144

WALTERS, L. D. Tombstone's Yesterday. Tucson: Acme, 1928. 1st bk ed. Orange-brn cl, vignette on spine. (Wear beginning at spine ends), o/w NF. Howes W73. *Harrington*. $125/£80

WALTERS, L. D. The Years at the Spring. NY: Brentano, (1920). 1st Amer ed. 24 full-pg plts (12 color). (Cvr soiled.) Contents VG. *New Hampshire**. $70/£45

WALTERS, THOMAS. Nudes of the '20s and '30s. London/NY: Academy Editions/St. Martin's, 1976. 1st ed. Frontis. Fine in pict stiff wrappers. *Cahan*. $30/£19

WALTON, CLYDE C. (ed). Private Smith's Journal. Chicago: Lakeside, Christmas, 1963. Dk blue cl. NF. *Sadlon*. $25/£16

WALTON, EVANGELINE. Witch House. Sauk City: Arkham House, (1945). 1st ed. Dj. *Swann**. $92/£59

WALTON, G. E. The Mineral Springs of the United States and Canada.... NY, 1892. 3rd ed. 4 maps. (Browned, sm tears blank margins; sl worn.) *Maggs*. $20/£13

WALTON, IZAAK. Compleat Angler, or Contemplative Man's Recreation...In Two Parts...with the Lives of the Authors.... John Hawkins (ed). London: John, Francis and Charles Rivington, 1784. 4th Hawkins ed. 14 engr copperplts. Contemp calf (rebacked), red spine label. Fine in cl slipcase w/leather spine label. *Cummins*. $300/£192

WALTON, IZAAK. The Compleat Angler, or, The Contemplative Man's Recreation. (Cambridge): Riverside, 1909. One of 440 numbered. Untrimmed. Brn bds, ptd paper spine label; extra ptd label tipped in at rear. VG (upper joint lt cracked, spine sl rubbed) in plain bd slipcase (worn, scuffed, lacks 1 side). *Baltimore**. $90/£58

WALTON, IZAAK. The Compleat Angler. London: Geo. Harrap, (1931). One of 775 numbered, signed by Arthur Rackham (illus). 12 full-pg color plts, ptd guards. (Limitation leaf lt foxed.) Partly unopened. Full vellum (lt soiled), gilt. Pub's slipcase (rubbed, stained). *Waverly**. $357/£229

WALTON, IZAAK. The Compleat Angler. Phila: David McKay, (1931). 1st Amer ed. Arthur Rackham (illus). 12 color plts. Blind-, gilt-dec cl (extrems lt worn). Contents VG. *New Hampshire**. $120/£77

WALTON, IZAAK. The Compleat Angler. London: R. Marriot, 1661. 3rd ed. 12mo. 10 copperplt engrs. Marbled eps; all edges red. Contents clean (margins narrow, tp mostly supplied in facs; few repairs, supplied corners; sl foxed, few stains). Later speckled calf (joints, corners sl worn; fr joint tender), ribbed spine in 6 compartments. *Waverly**. $1,210/£776

WALTON, IZAAK. The Compleat Angler. London: H. Kent, 1750. 1st Moses Browne ed. 6 copperplt engrs by Burgh. Contents VG (lt soiled, foxed; sig, mostly erased). Old calf (worn, fr bd almost detached), red/grn labels. *Waverly**. $88/£56

WALTON, IZAAK. The Compleat Angler. London: R. & H. Causton, 1772. 3rd Moses Browne ed. 10 copperplt engrs (offset). Contents VG (margins narrow; sl toned, lt sig). All edges stained yellow. Old calf bds (edges dknd, worn), later calf backing, orig spine laid down. *Waverly**. $165/£106

WALTON, IZAAK. The Compleat Angler. London: S. Bagster, 1810. Bagster's 'Facsimile' ed. Facs tp, 6 silver engrs, 2 full-pg plts. Contents VG (lt foxed; tps, ads toned; sig, bkpl), later calf spine, corners. *Waverly**. $77/£49

WALTON, IZAAK. The Compleat Angler. London: William Pickering, 1826. xxv,325,(iv)pp; 2 engr ports (sl browned). Orig blind-stamped cl (spine sl faded, neatly recased), gilt. *Hollett*. $101/£65

WALTON, IZAAK. The Compleat Angler. London: George Harrap, 1931. One of 775 signed by Arthur Rackham (illus). Color frontis, 11 color plts. Teg, rest untrimmed; partly unopened. Vellum-cvrd bds, gilt. VF in pub's numbered slipcase w/paper spine label. *Pirages*. $1,600/£1,026

WALTON, IZAAK. The Compleat Angler. Phila: David McKay, n.d. 1st Amer ed. 12 color plts by Arthur Rackham. Grn cl, gilt top. VF in dj. *Appelfeld*. $200/£128

WALTON, IZAAK. The Compleat Angler. Richard Le Gallienne (ed). London: John Lane, Apr 1896-Apr 1897. 1st Le Gallienne ed. As issued in orig 13 monthly parts. 2 ports by Edmund H. New. Unopened. Good in orig wraps (6 spines reinforced w/Japanese tissue; few edges chipped, torn, repaired; toning). Custom 1/4 morocco drop-back case. *Waverly**. $198/£127

WALTON, IZAAK. The Compleat Angler: or, Contemplative Man's Recreation.... Moses Browne (ed). Henry Kent, 1750. 7th ed. 1st Moses Browne ed. 6 copperplt engrs, 1 pg music, 15 woodcuts. Contemp calf. (Worn, fr cvr detached, bkpl), o/w NF in cl slipcase. *Cummins*. $325/£208

WALTON, IZAAK. The Complete Angler. London: Samuel Bagster, 1808. 7th ed. Full calf, gilt motif. Fine. *Metropolitan**. $201/£129

WALTON, IZAAK. The Complete Angler. London: J. Major, 1823. 1st Major ed. Lg paper copy (trimmed). 14 inserted copper plt engrs. Teg; marbled eps. Early tan calf bds (dknd, worn, rebacked in calf), preserving most of orig ribbed gilt spine. *Waverly**. $49/£31

WALTON, IZAAK. The Complete Angler. London: Wm Pickering, 1836. 1st Nicolas ed. 2 vols. (Foxed, esp plts; inner hinge vol 1 broken.) Aeg. Full grn morocco (joints, corners worn; faded, soiled), ribbed spine, gilt. *Waverly**. $319/£204

WALTON, IZAAK. The Complete Angler. London: Sampson Low et al, 1888. 1st Marston ed. One of 500 numbered, signed by R.B. Marson (ed). 2 vols. 54 plts. 2-tone cl (lt worn, mkd), white spines (soiled, toned, vol 2 extensively split). *Waverly**. $357/£229

WALTON, IZAAK. The Complete Angler. Boston: Little Brown, 1891. 3rd Lowell ed. 2 vols. 465pp; 2 ports. Teg. Navy cl, gilt Walton cipher fr cvrs. Fine set. *Bowman*. $75/£48

WALTON, IZAAK. The Complete Angler. Phila: David McKay, n.d. (1931). 1st Amer ed. 12 color plts by Arthur Rackham. Teg; pict eps. Pict grn cl. VG (sl worn). *Waverly**. $71/£46

WALTON, IZAAK. The Complete Angler. 'Ephemera' (Edward Fitzgibbon), ed. London: Routledge, Warnes & Routledge, 1859. Frontis, xii,313,(7)pp; extra engr tp, facs, 3 plts. (1st, last leasts lt spotted), o/w Good in blind-dec grn cl, backstrip gilt. *Cox*. $44/£28

WALTON, IZAAK. The Complete Angler. Edward Jesse (ed). London: Bohn, 1861. 2nd Jesse ed. 2 engr port plts. (Foxed, esp plts.) Marbled eps, edges. Full grn calf (dknd, rubbed, chip, bumped), ribbed spine, red gilt-lettered label. *Waverly**. $82/£53

WALTON, IZAAK. The Complete Angler. Ephemera (Edward Fitzgibbon, ed). London: Ingram, Cooke, 1853. 1st Ephemera ed. Contents VG (marginal stains prelims). Teg. 1/2 red morocco, marbled bds (corner lt bumped, worn), ribbed spine. *Waverly**. $165/£106

WALTON, IZAAK. The Complete Angler. R. B. Marston (ed). London: Sampson Low et al, 1888. Lea & Dover (1st Marston) ed. One of 500 numbered demy 4to, signed by Marston. 2 vols. 54 photogravures. Grn cl bds, white linen spine (sl toned, soiled, short tears, corner wear). *Waverly**. $385/£247

WALTON, IZAAK. The Complete Angler. Richard Le Gallienne (ed). London/NY: John Lane, 1897. 1st Le Gallienne ed. 2 photogravure ports, 51 full-pg woodcuts. Untrimmed. Pub's tan cl stamped in dk grn (lt soiled, worn). Contents VG. *Waverly**. $60/£38

WALTON, IZAAK. The Complete Angler.... London: J. Major, 1835. 3rd ed by Major. 416pp; 15 plts (incl add'l copperplt of Wharton). Gilt-dec full calf. VG. *Lucas*. $300/£192

WALTON, JOSEPH S. Conrad Weiser and the Indian Policy of Colonial Pennsylvania. Phila: George W. Jacobs, 1900. 1st ed. Teg, mostly unopened. Pict cl (spine rubbed). VG. Howes W78. *Cahan*. $85/£54

WALTON, ROBERT. Random Recollections of the Midland Circuit. London: The Author, 1869. Russet cl (worn, rubbed), gilt. Sound. *Boswell.* $150/£96

WALTON, THOMAS H. Coal Mining. Phila/London, 1885. 16,(9)-175pp; 24 full-pg plts. Good- (2-inch tear fr joint). *Scribe's Perch*. $34/£22

WALTON, WILLIAM. World's Columbian Exposition MDCCCXCIII. Art and Architecture. Phila, (1893). Folio. 2 vols. (Some tissue guards foxed.) Pub's leather (joints rubbed), gilt. *Swann*. $115/£74

WAMBAUGH, JOSEPH. The Black Marble. NY: Delacorte, 1978. 1st ed. Inscribed. VG in VG dj (sl soil). *Old London.* $30/£19

WAMBAUGH, JOSEPH. The Blue Knight. Boston: Atlantic, Little, Brown, 1972. 1st ed. Inscribed. VG in VG dj (sl soil). *Old London.* $25/£16

WAMBAUGH, JOSEPH. The Glitter Dome. NY: Morrow, 1981. 1st ed. Inscribed. Fine in Fine dj. *Old London.* $20/£13

WAMBAUGH, JOSEPH. Lines and Shadows. NY: Morrow, 1984. 1st ed. Inscribed. Fine in Fine dj. *Old London.* $25/£16

WANDREI, DONALD. Dark Odyssey. Webb, (1931). One of 400 numbered. Signed. VG (name, 6 sm ink mks) in Fine ptd foil dj. *Certo.* $125/£80

WANDREI, DONALD. Ecstasy and Other Poems. Recluse, 1928. 1st bk, ltd to 322. Wandrei estate bkpl laid in. Fine in tissue dj as issued. *Certo.* $275/£176

WANDREI, DONALD. The Eye and the Finger. (Sauk City): Arkham House, 1944. 1st ed. Howard Wandrei (illus). VF in pict dj. *Bromer.* $200/£128

WANDREI, DONALD. Poems for Midnight. Sauk City: Arkham House, 1964. 1st ed. Signed. Dj (spine sl faded). *Swann*. $126/£81

WANDREI, DONALD. Strange Harvest. Sauk City: Arkham House, 1965. 1st ed. Fine in NF dj. *Other Worlds.* $65/£42

WANDREI, DONALD. The Web of Easter Island. Sauk City: Arkham House, 1948. 1st ed. VF in pict dj. *Bromer.* $100/£64

WANG, CHI KAO. Dissolution of the British Parliament, 1832-1931. NY: Columbia Univ, 1934. *Boswell.* $45/£29

WANLEY, HUMFREY. The Diary of Humfrey Wanley 1715-1726. C. E. and Ruth C. Wright (eds). London: Bibliographical Soc, 1966. 1st ed. 2 vols. Port, facs. Gilt blue cl. Fine. *Reese.* $50/£32

War Flowers, Reminiscences of Four Years' Campaigning. (By John Alcee Augustin), (New Orleans), 1865. Inscribed. 103pp + errata. Contemp 1/2 calf, marbled bds, spine gilt. VG (extrems sl worn). *Reese.* $450/£288

War Flowers, Reminiscences of Four Years' Campaigning. (By John Alcee Augustin.) (New Orleans: Hinton, Printer, 1865.) 1st ed. 103,(1)pp. Orig marbled paper bds, leather spine. NF. *Mcgowan.* $450/£288

War Medicine: A Periodical Containing Original Contributions, News and Abstracts of Articles...Volume 1. Chicago, 1941. 1st ed. (1 corner fr bd chewed.) *Fye.* $100/£64

WARBASSE, JAMES. Medical Sociology: A Series of Observations.... NY, 1909. 1st ed. VG. *Fye.* $100/£64

WARBURTON, A. F. Trial of the Officers and Crew of the Privateer Savannah, on the Charge of Piracy.... NY: Baker & Godwin, 1862. 1st ed. xxii,385pp. Teg. VG. *Wantagh.* $100/£64

WARD, ARTEMUS (ed). The Grocer's Encyclopedia.... NY, 1911. 1st ed. (Heavily rubbed, soiled.) *King.* $65/£42

WARD, CHARLES WILLIS. The American Carnation. NY: De La Mere, 1903. 1st ed. 4 color, 108 b/w plts. Good (rubbed). *Second Life.* $40/£26

WARD, CYRIL. Royal Gardens. London: Longmans, Green, 1912. 32 full-pg guarded plts, 5 pen dwgs. (Fr hinge starting), o/w Good. *Scribe's Perch*. $60/£38

WARD, EVELYN D. The Children of Bladensfield. NY: Viking, 1978. 1st ed. Fine in NF dj (lt edgeworn). *Lame Duck.* $85/£54

WARD, FRANCES ELIZABETH. Frankie's Journal. N.p.: Ptd by Westernlore, (1960). Ltd to 300. Pb. VG. *Lien.* $20/£13

WARD, FRANK. The Lakes of Wales. London, 1931. 1st ed. (Lt browned; fore-edge of bds lt dampstained.) *Edwards.* $94/£60

WARD, H. G. Mexico in 1827. London, 1828. 1st ed. 2 vols. 13 plts, 1 fldg map (of 2; loose). 1/2 leather, marbled bds (rubbed, vol 1 lacks spine, cvrs detached). *Kane*. $110/£71

WARD, HERBERT. Five Years with the Congo Cannibals. NY: Robert Bonner's Sons, 1890. 1st Amer ed. Frontis port, 308pp; 2 maps. Teg. Blue gilt pict cl. VG. *Terramedia.* $300/£192

WARD, HERBERT. A Voice from the Congo. NY: Scribner, 1910. 1st ed. Frontis. Grn gilt cl (sl wear), else VG. *Terramedia.* $100/£64

WARD, HUMPHRY and W. ROBERTS. Romney: A Biographical and Critical Essay. London, 1904. One of 350 numbered. 2 vols. Pub's 1/4 leather (spine ends worn), gilt. *Swann*. $172/£110

WARD, J. Romano-British Buildings and Earthworks. London: Methuen, 1911. Map. (Spine faded.) *Ars Artis.* $39/£25

WARD, JAMES. Historic Ornament. Chapman & Hall, 1897. 2 vols. 409; 411pp. VG set in dec grn cl. *Hadley.* $70/£45

WARD, JAMES. The Principles of Ornament. George Aichison (ed). Chapman & Hall, 1892. xvi,139pp + (iv)ads. (Sl rubbed.) *Edwards.* $31/£20

WARD, JOHN. Farmers' Almanac, for the Year 1828.... Phila: M'Carty & Davis, (1827). 18 leaves. Fine. *Cahan.* $35/£22

WARD, LESTER. Young Ward's Diary. NY, (1935). 1st ed. (Spine faded), o/w VG. *Pratt.* $60/£38

WARD, LYND and GRANVILLE HICKS. One of Us. The Story of John Reed. NY: Equinox Coop, 1935. One of 1500. Fine in NF dj (signs of coating). *Beasley.* $150/£96

WARD, LYND. The Biggest Bear. USA: Houghton Mifflin, (1952). 1st ed. 4to. 85pp; 43 full-pg monotint illus, pict tp. Illus cl. Fine in pict dj w/foil prize medal. *Bookmark.* $47/£30

WARD, LYND. God's Man: A Novel in Woodcuts. NY, (1929). 1st ed. 1/4 cl, pict bds. (Sm tear bottom tp, no loss; lt scuffed.) *Truepenny.* $125/£80

WARD, LYND. Madman's Drum. NY, (1930). 1st ed. 1/4 cl, dec bds. VG. *Truepenny.* $125/£80

WARD, LYND. Madman's Drum. Jonathan Cape & Harrison Smith, 1930. 1st ed. Lynd Ward (illus). Superb in dj (sm tear). *Certo.* $350/£224

WARD, LYND. Madman's Drum. London/Toronto: Jonathan Cape, 1930. 1st ed. 128 woodcut plts. Untrimmed. Cl-backed pict paper bds, paper spine label. (Sl faded, label dknd), o/w Fine. *Pirages.* $125/£80

WARD, LYND. Madman's Drum. NY, 1930. 1st ed. VG. *Smith.* $75/£48

WARD, MRS. HUMPHRY. Helbeck of Bannisdale. Smith, Elder, 1898. Ad leaves. Good (bkpl remains fr pastedown, lt spotted, inner hinges cracked; spine bumped, sl chipped, corners rubbed). *Tiger.* $39/£25

WARD, NED. The London-Spy. London: Casanova, 1924. #222/1000. Frontis port. (Feps lt spotted.) Uncut. Cl-backed bds (edges lt faded), paper spine label. *Edwards.* $62/£40

WARD, ROBERT. The Fallacies of Teetotalism. London, 1872. xx,415pp. Unopened in parts. (Spotted, lower fep torn w/sl loss, bkpl; hinges cracked; edges, spine faded; lower joint starting to split; spine sl chipped.) *Edwards*. $62/£40

WARD, ROLAND. The Price Guide to the Models of W. H. Goss. 1975. Color frontis, 3 color plts. Price list loosely inserted. Dj. *Edwards*. $31/£20

WARD, ROWLAND. Record of Big Game. J. G. Dollman and J. B. Burlace (eds). London, 1928. 9th ed. Buckram (soiled). *Argosy*. $250/£160

WARD, ROWLAND. Records of Big Game. 1907. 5th ed. Frontis port. Dec eps (repaired). Mod cl (rebound), gilt. *Edwards*. $140/£90

WARD, ROWLAND. Records of Big Game. London, 1907. 5th ed. (Spine faded, cvrs lt mkd.) Contents Excellent. *Grayling*. $156/£100

WARD, ROWLAND. Records of Big Game. London, 1910. 6th ed. (Cl sl rubbed.) Contents VG. *Grayling*. $156/£100

WARD, ROWLAND. Records of Big Game. London, 1922. 8th ed. Good (recased in orig cl). *Grayling*. $218/£140

WARD, ROWLAND. Records of Big Game. London, 1928. 9th ed. Buckram (sl rubbed, faded). VG. *Grayling*. $390/£250

WARD, W. H. The Architecture of the Renaissance in France, 1495-1830.... London: Batsford, 1926. 2nd ed. 2 vols. Sound. *Ars Artis*. $94/£60

WARD-JACKSON, C. H. and DENIS E. HARVEY. The English Gypsy Caravan. NY, 1973. 1st ed. Color frontis. Dj. *Edwards*. $23/£15

WARDE, FREDERIC. Bruce Rogers Designer of Books. Cambridge: Harvard Univ, 1925. 1st ed. Incl is typed 2-pg letter from Houghton Mifflin relating to Riverside Press eds. Ptd spine label. VG (sl worn). *Whittle*. $70/£45

WARDE, FREDERIC. Bruce Rogers: Designer of Books. Cambridge: Harvard Univ, 1925. 1st ed. VG (sl soiled, worn). *Waverly**. $44/£28

WARDEN, WILLIAM. Letters from Saint Helena. London: R. Ackermann, (1816). 1st ed. Engr frontis port, viii,215pp; fldg facs, engr plt. Contemp full calf (hinges tender, sl worn, lacks spine label). *Hollett*. $234/£150

WARDEN, WILLIAM. Letters Written on Board His Majesty's Ship 'The Northumberland'.... London: R. Ackermann, 1816. 3rd ed. Port, fldg plt (both sl foxed). Uncut. Orig bds. *Andrew Stewart*. $70/£45

WARDER, JOHN A. Hedges and Evergreens. NY, 1858. vii,(2),(13-)291pp (foxing), 12 plts. Emb cl (spine ends, corners worn). *Brooks*. $65/£42

WARDLAW, GEORGIA DICKINSON. The Old and the Quaint in Virginia. Dietz, 1939. 1st ed. VG in Good dj. *Book Broker*. $25/£16

WARDNER, JIM. Jim Wardner, Idaho. NY, 1900. Port. Internally Very Nice (cl soiled). *Reese*. $150/£96

WARE, EUGENE F. The Indian War of 1864. NY: St. Martin's, (1960). VG in dj. *Lien*. $35/£22

WARE, EUGENE F. The Indian War of 1864. Topeka, 1911-1960 rpt. 1st ed thus. VG in dj (faded spine). *Pratt*. $40/£26

WARE, ISAAC. Designs of Inigo Jones and Others. (1731.) 1st ed. Lg 8vo. Engr tp, 2pp list of plts, 53 engr plts (5 fldg). (Lacks outer 1/2 fldg plt 46/47; sl soiled.) Mod 1/2 red morocco, gilt back. *Hatchwell*. $546/£350

WARE, JOHN. Discourses on Medical Education and on the Medical Profession. Boston, 1847. 113pp. Sewn as issued. (Tp sl dusty), else Good. *Goodrich*. $75/£48

WARE, JOSEPH. The Emigrant's Guide to California. Princeton: Princeton Univ, 1932. Tp facs, plt, fldg facs map tipped to rep. Red cl, gilt. Fine. Howes W104. *Pacific**. $127/£81

WAREING, E. VINCENT. Rapallo's Mountain Shrine. London, 1930. (Lt browned.) *Edwards*. $31/£20

WARFIELD, J. D. The Founders of Anne Arundel and Howard Counties, Maryland. Balt: Koh & Pollock, 1905. 1st ed. VG (spine dull). Howes W106. *Captain's Bookshelf*. $100/£64

WARHOL, ANDY. Andy Warhol's Exposures. NY, (1979). 1st ed. VG in dj. *Argosy*. $150/£96

WARHOL, ANDY. Andy Warhol's Index (Book). NY: Random House, 1967. 1st ed. Pop-up. Cl-backed illus paper over bds, 3-D pict laminated sheet mtd on fr cvr. (Balloon fused to opposite pg; edges sl discolored, sl scuffed), else NF. *Cahan*. $550/£353

WARHOL, ANDY. Andy Warhol. Boston Book & Art, 1970. 3rd ed. VG+ in dec wraps. *Metropolitan**. $100/£64

WARHOL, ANDY. His Early Works 1947-1959. Andreas Brown (comp). NY: Gotham Book Mart Gallery, 1971. VG in wraps (sl faded, soiled). *Waverly**. $27/£17

WARING, EDWARD. Bibliotheca Therapeutica or Bibliography of Therapeutics.... London, 1878. 1st ed. 2 vols. 934pp. VG. *Fye*. $250/£160

WARING, GERALD A. Springs of California. Washington: Dept of the Interior, 1915. 10 plts. (Lacks pocket of 3 maps; spine worn.) Ptd wrappers. *Dawson*. $35/£22

WARING, GUY. My Pioneer Past. Boston: Bruce Humphries, (1936). Frontis. Unopened. (Foxing to pp facing plts; gilt dull), else VG+. *Bohling*. $50/£32

WARING, J. B. (ed). Art Treasures of the United Kingdom.... London: Day & Son, 1858. Chromolitho tp, 100 chromolitho plts (1 w/sm marginal tear, few mounts cracked). Marbled eps; aeg. Full morocco (lt rubbed), gilt. *Kane**. $325/£208

WARING, JANET. Early American Wall Stencils, Their Origin, History and Use. NY: William R. Scott, 1937. Tipped-in color frontis, 6 tipped-in color plts. Color stencil plt mtd on front. (Eps lt foxed; spine ends worn), else VG in dj (spine soiled, ends chipped). *Cahan*. $100/£64

WARLOCK, PETER (ed). Songs of the Gardens. Nonesuch, 1925. #632/875 ptd. (Bkpl, sl dusty, rear panel mkd), else VG in vellum-backed bds. *Hadley*. $62/£40

WARMAN, CY. Snow on the Headlight. A Story of the Great Burlington Strike. NY: Appleton, 1899. 1st ed. Dec bds. (Lt spine wear), o/w Fine. *Beasley*. $75/£48

WARNER, ELISHA. The History of Spanish Fork. Spanish Fork, 1930. 1st ed. (Sl damage), o/w VG. *Benchmark*. $50/£32

WARNER, L. J. Mammal Photography and Observation, a Practical Field Guide. London: Academic, 1978. 1st ed. Fine in VG dj. *Mikesh*. $35/£22

WARNER, LANGDON. The Long Old Road in China. NY, 1926. 3 maps. Gilt-edged cl-backed bds (fading), 2 labels. *Edwards*. $78/£50

WARNER, MARINA. The Dragon Empress. NY: Macmillan, 1972. 1st US ed. NF in dj. *Worldwide*. $30/£19

WARNER, REX. The Cult of Power Essays. London: John Lane, Bodley Head, (1946). 1st ed. (Sm bkseller's stamp ep), o/w Nice in Good dj (sm chips, spine dknd). *Reese*. $25/£16

WARNER, REX. Escapade. 1953. 1st ed. VG in dj (spine sl browned). *Words Etc*. $23/£15

WARNER, REX. The Vengeance of the Gods. London: MacGibbon & Kee, 1954. 1st ed. VG in dj (fraying, sl discoloration). *Reese*. $35/£22

WARNER, REX. Views of Attica and Its Surroundings. Lehmann, 1950. 1st Eng ed. Good in dj (frayed, price-clipped). *Clearwater.* $23/£15

WARNER, RICHARD. A Tour through the Northern Counties of England. Bath: R. Crutwell, 1802. 1st ed. 2 vols. iv,316; iv,300pp; 2 tinted plts, 2 maps. 2 titles w/engr vignettes. Old half calf (sl worn, spine head repaired), gilt. *Hollett.* $343/£220

WARNER, SYLVIA TOWNSEND (ed). The Portrait of a Tortoise Extracted from the Journals and Letters of Gilbert White. London: C&W, 1946. 1st ed. Port. Fine in NF dj. *Reese.* $30/£19

WARNER, SYLVIA TOWNSEND. After the Death of Don Juan. London: C&W, 1938. 1st ed. Fine in dj (spine sl tanned, sm edge tears). *Reese.* $60/£38

WARNER, SYLVIA TOWNSEND. Boxwood. C&W, 1960. 1st trade ed. 21 engrs by Reynolds Stone. (Eps browned), else VG in dj. *Michael Taylor.* $28/£18

WARNER, SYLVIA TOWNSEND. Elinor Barley. (London): Cresset Press, 1930. 1st ed. One of 350 numbered, signed. Parchment-backed marbled bds. (Top edge of bds, spine sl dknd), o/w NF. *Reese.* $125/£80

WARNER, SYLVIA TOWNSEND. Mr. Fortune's Maggot. Harmondsworth: Penguin Books, (1948). 1st Penguin ed. VG in ptd wrappers. *Reese.* $10/£6

WARNER, SYLVIA TOWNSEND. Mr. Fortune's Maggot. NY, 1927. Signed. Cl-backed bds (sl worn). *Argosy.* $40/£26

WARNER, SYLVIA TOWNSEND. The Salutation. London: C&W, 1932. 1st ed. Gilt-dec cl. (Spine sunned through dj), else Nice in white dj (spine tanned). *Reese.* $55/£35

WARREN, ARTHUR. The Charles Whittinghams Printers. NY: Grolier Club, 1896. One of 385. Uncut, unopened. (Sl worn, foxed.) Bds, leather back, tips. Slipcase (scuffed, soiled). *Oinonen*.* $50/£32

WARREN, B. H. Report on the Birds of Pennsylvania. Harrisburg, (1890). 2nd rev, enlgd ed. 434pp, 100 full-pg color plts. (Rebacked), else VG. *Mikesh.* $75/£48

WARREN, B. H. Report on the Birds of Pennsylvania. Harrisburg, 1890. 2nd ed. 99 chromolithos. Mod binding. *Yudkin*.* $220/£141

WARREN, C. E. T. and JAMES BENSON. Above Us the Waves. London, 1953. Grn cl (spine faded). *Maggs.* $39/£25

WARREN, CHARLES. Jacobin and Junto or Early American Politics as Viewed in the Diary of Dr. Nathaniel Ames, 1758-1822. Cambridge: Harvard Univ, 1931. 1st ed. VG. *Bohling.* $25/£16

WARREN, ELIZA SPALDING. Memoirs of the West, the Spaldings. (Portland, ca 1916.) Port. VG (sl dampstaining). Howes W117. *Reese.* $125/£80

WARREN, ELIZA SPALDING. Memoirs of the West. Portland: (Marsh Ptg, 1916). 1st ed. VF. Howes W 117. *Perier.* $125/£80

WARREN, HENRY. Notes upon Notes. London: R. Ackermann, 1832. 7 hand-colored plts. Ptd wrappers (sl worn, soiled, spine repaired; lacks letterpress title). *Oinonen*.* $50/£32

WARREN, INA (ed). The Doctor's Window: Poems by the Doctor, for the Doctor and About the Doctor. Buffalo, 1898. 1st ed. 288pp; 2 plts (lacks 3). *Fye.* $75/£48

WARREN, J. LEICESTER. A Guide to the Study of Bookplates. London: John Pearson, 1880. 1st ed. iii,228pp (ex-lib, marginal blind stamps, accession stamp tp verso); 16 plts. Cl (worn, frayed, split), paper spine label (rubbed). *Hollett.* $70/£45

WARREN, JOHN C. A Comparative View of the Sensoral and Nervous System of Man and Animal. Boston: Joseph W. Ingraham, 1822. 159pp (foxed, browned); 7 plts. Orig sugar bds (newly rebacked; worn). *Goodrich.* $595/£381

WARREN, LOUIS A. Lincoln's Youth, Indiana Years, Seven to Twenty-One, 1816-1830. NY, (1959). (Cvr lt worn), o/w VG+ in VG+ dj. *Pratt.* $22/£14

WARREN, ROBERT PENN. All the King's Men. London: Eyre & Spottiswode, (1948). 1st Eng ed in red, 2nd state dj. NF in VG dj (rubbing; lt nicking extrems; tear rear panel). *Between The Covers.* $165/£106

WARREN, ROBERT PENN. All the King's Men. London: Eyre & Spottiswoode, (1948). 1st Eng ed, 1st imp. Black cloth, gilt. Blue/white dj (chips, edge tears). *Dermont.* $125/£80

WARREN, ROBERT PENN. All the King's Men. London, 1948. 1st Eng ed. Nice (inscrip, corner sl bumped) in dj (sl rubbed, price-clipped). *Clearwater.* $62/£40

WARREN, ROBERT PENN. All the King's Men. (NY: LEC, 1990.) Ltd to 600 signed by Warren and Hank O'Neal (illus). 2 vols. 4to. 10 full-pg photogravures. 1/4 black Nigerian Oasis goatskin, natural linen bds. VF in black Italian cotton slipcase lined w/ultrasuede. *Truepenny.* $975/£625

WARREN, ROBERT PENN. Audubon: A Vision. NY: Random House, (1969). One of 300 numbered, signed. Fine in Fine dj, slipcase. *Lenz.* $125/£80

WARREN, ROBERT PENN. Band of Angels. NY: Random House, (1955). 1st ed. (Spine dknd), o/w Fine. *Jaffe.* $65/£42

WARREN, ROBERT PENN. Being Here: Poetry 1977-1980. NY: Random House, (1980). One of 250 numbered, signed. Fine in Fine slipcase. *Lenz.* $125/£80

WARREN, ROBERT PENN. Brother to Dragons. (NY): Random House, (1953). 1st ed. (Offsetting feps from clipping), else VG in dj (lt soiled). *Reese.* $35/£22

WARREN, ROBERT PENN. The Cave. London, 1959. 1st ed. Fine in dj (2 sm tears, price-clipped). *Polyanthos.* $30/£19

WARREN, ROBERT PENN. Chief Joseph of the Nez Perce. NY, (1983). 1st ed. Deluxe ed. Ltd to 250 specially bound, signed. Fine in slipcase. *Truepenny.* $135/£87

WARREN, ROBERT PENN. Chief Joseph of the Nez Perce. NY: Random House, (1983). One of 250 numbered, signed. Fine in Fine slipcase. *Lenz.* $125/£80

WARREN, ROBERT PENN. Flood. NY: Random House, (1964). Fine in Fine dj (price-clipped). *Between The Covers.* $75/£48

WARREN, ROBERT PENN. How Texas Won Her Freedom. San Jacinto Monument, TX: San Jacinto Museum of History, 1959. 2nd ptg. Fine in wraps. *Gibbs.* $10/£6

WARREN, ROBERT PENN. Jefferson Davis Gets His Citizenship Back. Lexington, 1980. 1st ed. Fine in Fine dj. *Smith.* $20/£13

WARREN, ROBERT PENN. John Brown. NY, 1929. 1st ed, 1st bk. (Ink note 1 margin, early ll lt foxed.) *Kane*.* $80/£51

WARREN, ROBERT PENN. John Brown. NY, 1929. 1st ed, 1st bk. 9 plts. *Kane*.* $110/£71

WARREN, ROBERT PENN. John Brown. NY: Payson & Clarke, 1929. 1st ed, 1st bk. NF (lt wear). *Between The Covers.* $250/£160

WARREN, ROBERT PENN. Meet Me in the Green Glen. NY: Random House, (1971). One of 300 numbered, signed. Fine in Fine slipcase. *Lenz.* $150/£96

WARREN, ROBERT PENN. A Place to Come To. NY: Random House, (1977). One of 350 numbered, signed. Fine in Fine slipcase. *Lenz.* $150/£96

WARREN, ROBERT PENN. Selected Essays. NY: Random House, 1958. 1st ed. NF in VG dj. *Cahan.* $50/£32

WARREN, ROBERT PENN. Who Speaks for the Negro? NY: Random House, (1965). 1st ed. Red cl. VG in ptd dj. *Petrilla.* $50/£32

WARREN, ROBERT PENN. Wilderness. NY, (1961). 1st ed. VG in dj (sl worn, sunned). *King.* $35/£22

WARREN, ROBERT PENN. World Enough and Time. NY: Random House, (1950). 1st ed. Fine in dj (lt foxed, rubbed, price-clipped). *Jaffe.* $45/£29

WARREN, SAMUEL. Miscellanies, Critical, Imaginative, and Juridical. Edinburgh: William Blackwood, 1855. Contemp 3/4 blue morocco (sl rubbed). Nice. *Boswell.* $250/£160

WARREN, WILLIAM W. History of the Ojibway Nation. Minneapolis: Ross & Haines, 1957. Ltd to 1500 numbered. VG in dj (sl worn). *Lien.* $35/£22

WARRY, G. TAYLOR. The Game Laws of England, with an Appendix of the Statutes.... London: Stevens, 1896. Grn cl (rubbed), gilt. Sound. *Boswell.* $150/£96

WASHBURN, CEPHAS. Reminiscences of the Indians. Richmond: Presbyterian Committee of Publication, 1869. 1st ed. 236pp. (Few pp chipped edges; worn, faded, poorly rebacked), else Good. Howes W127. *Brown.* $250/£160

WASHBURN, EMORY. Extinction of Villenage and Slavery in England, with Somerset's Case. Boston: Ptd by John Wilson, 1864. Presentation copy. Later cl-backed bds. (Ex-lib.) *Boswell.* $85/£54

WASHBURN, EMORY. Historical Sketches of the Town of Leicester, Massachusetts.... Boston, 1860. 467pp; fldg map. Brn cl (worn). Good (fr joint starting, sl lib mks). *Zubal*.* $20/£13

WASHBURN, EMORY. Lectures on the Study and Practice of the Law. Boston: Little, Brown, 1871. Brn cl (rubbed, chipped, faded). Usable. *Boswell.* $125/£80

WASHBURN, EMORY. A Manual of Criminal Law.... Marshall D. Ewell (ed). Chicago: Callaghan, 1878. Contemp sheep (worn, rubbed). Good. *Boswell.* $125/£80

WASHBURN, JOSIE. The Underworld Sewer. Omaha: Washburn, 1909. Frontis port. Red cl. VG (wear). *Bohling.* $22/£14

WASHBURNE, ELIHU BENJAMIN. Sketch of Edward Coles...and of the Slavery Struggle of 1823-4. Chicago, 1882. 1st ed. Presentation from E. Coles. 253,(2)pp. NF. *Mcgowan.* $125/£80

WASHINGTON, BOOKER T. The Man Farthest Down. GC: Doubleday, Page, 1912. 1st ed. NF (sm tear spine; lacks dj). *Between The Covers.* $200/£128

WASHINGTON, BOOKER T. Putting the Most into Life. NY: Crowell, (1906). 1st ed. (Offsetting fep), else Fine in VG ptd dj (spine lacks bottom inch, sl crown loss, long tear fr panel professionally repaired). *Between The Covers.* $850/£545

WASHINGTON, BOOKER T. The Story of My Life and Work. Toronto: Nichols, (1901). 50th thousand. Dec cl. VG (rear hinge cracked). *Agvent.* $60/£38

WASHINGTON, BOOKER T. Up from Slavery. NY, 1901. 1st ed. Frontis port. (Lt shelfworn.) *Kane*.* $85/£54

WASHINGTON, BOOKER T. Up from Slavery. NY: Doubleday, Page, 1901. 1st ed. NF (lt bumps bd edges, sig sl sprung). *Between The Covers.* $300/£192

WASHINGTON, BOOKER T. Up from Slavery. NY: LEC, 1970. One of 1500 numbered, signed by Denver Gillen (illus). 14 color plts. 3/4 cl, gilt leather spine label. Mint in bd slipcase. *Argosy.* $175/£112

WASHINGTON, GEORGE. The Journal of.... NY: Rptd for Joseph Sabin, 1865. Ltd to 200. 46pp; map. Unopened. NF in wraps. Howes W134. *Wantagh.* $100/£64

WASHINGTON, GEORGE. Writings. J. C. Fitzpatrick (ed). Washington, 1931-44. 1st ed. 39 vols. *Ginsberg.* $1,250/£801

WASHINGTON, M. BUNCH. The Art of Romare Bearden. NY: Abrams, n.d. (Ex-lib; shaken.) *Swann*.* $149/£96

Washington: City and Capital. Washington: WPA, 1937. 1st ed, 1st ptg. 2 lg fldg maps in cvr pocket. Black cl (lt worn, soiled). *Freeman*.* $30/£19

WASSON, R. GORDON. Soma: Divine Mushroom of Immortality. NY, (1968). One of 680 numbered. Folio. 24 plts, 3 maps, fldg table. Orig 1/4 morocco. Cl slipcase. *Swann*.* $402/£258

WASSON, VALENTINA PAVLOVNA and R. GORDON. Mushrooms, Russia and History. NY, (1957). One of 510 numbered. 2 vols. Uncut. (Sl worn.) Slipcase (soiled, stained). *Oinonen*.* $750/£481

WASSON, VALENTINA PAVLOVNA and R. GORDON. Mushrooms, Russia, and History. NY, (1957). One of 510 numbered. 2 vols. Folio. 82 plts, fldg table in rear pocket vol 2. Orig linen. Cl slipcase. *Swann*.* $1,092/£700

WATERER, JOHN W. Leather and Craftsmanship. London: Faber, 1950. 1st ed. 32pp plts. (Spine faded, lt mkd.) *Hollett.* $62/£40

WATERFIELD, MARGARET. Corners of Grey Old Gardens. London: T.N. Foulis, 1914. 1st ed. Gilt-dec pict cvr. Mint in like dj. *Quest.* $150/£96

WATERFIELD, R. (ed). Dear David, Dear Graham. Oxford: Alembic Press w/Amate Press, 1989. One of 250 numbered. 2 tipped-in photos. Fine. *Moss.* $109/£70

WATERHOUSE, BENJAMIN. An Essay on Junius and His Letters...1763 to 1785. Boston, 1831. 1st ed. 449pp (lt foxed). Uncut. Partly unopened. Contemp cl-backed bds. *Argosy.* $300/£192

WATERHOUSE, ELLIS. Italian Baroque Painting. London, 1962. Good. *Washton.* $40/£26

WATERHOUSE, ELLIS. Painting in Britain 1530 to 1790. Balt, 1962. 2nd ed. 194 plts. Good. *Washton.* $50/£32

WATERHOUSE, ELLIS. Roman Baroque Painting. London, 1976. Good in dj. *Washton.* $150/£96

WATERHOUSE, KEITH. Billy Liar on the Moon. London: Michael Joseph, 1975. 1st UK ed. Fine in dj. *Williams.* $28/£18

WATERHOUSE, KEITH. Billy Liar. Michael Joseph, 1959. 1st UK ed. Signed. VG in dj (rear panel sl stained, spine sl faded, sm closed tear). *Williams.* $172/£110

WATERHOUSE, KEITH. Billy Liar. London, 1959. 1st ed. Fine (spine heel sl creased) in dj (sl chipped). *Polyanthos.* $60/£38

WATERHOUSE, P. et al. Sir Christopher Wren, 1632-1723. Architectural Press, 1923. 1/2 cl (rubbed). *Ars Artis.* $39/£25

WATERMAN, LEROY. Royal Correspondence of the Assyriad Empire. Ann Arbor: Univ of MI, 1930-36. 4 vols. 4to. (Pencil notes.) Grn cl (corners bumped). *Archaeologia.* $1,250/£801

WATERMAN, T. T. The Early Architecture of North Carolina. Chapel Hill: Univ of NC, 1947. 2nd ed. Folio. (Sl musty), else Fine in pub's slipcase (lt rubbed). *Cahan.* $185/£119

WATERMAN, T. T. The Mansions of Virginia, 1706-1776. Chapel Hill: Univ of NC, n.d. (1946). Map loosely inserted. *Ars Artis.* $39/£25

WATERS, DAVID W. The Art of Navigation in England in Elizabethan and Early Stuart Times. New Haven: Yale Univ, 1958. 1st Amer ed. 87 plts. Fine. *Lefkowicz.* $200/£128

WATERS, FRANK. The Colorado. NY, 1946. 1st ed. Red cl. Fine in VG+ dj. *Five Quail.* $45/£29

WATERS, FRANK. The Colorado. NY: Rinehart, 1946. 1st ed. (Bumped), o/w Fine in VG dj (spine sunned). *Archer.* $40/£26

WATERS, FRANK. The Dust Within the Rock. Liveright, (1940). 1st ed. Fine. *Authors Of West.* $90/£58

WATERS, FRANK. The Man Who Killed the Deer. Denver: Sage, (1942). 3rd ed. Signed presentation. NF in VG dj. *Mikesh.* $35/£22

WATERS, FRANK. The Yogi of Cockroach Court. NY: Rinehart, 1947. 1st ed. Red bds. Fine in dj (few sm edge tears, sl dust soiling). *Dermont.* $200/£128

WATERS, L. L. Steel Trails to Santa Fe. Lawrence, KS, 1950. 1st ed. 4 plts. VG+ in dj (chunk torn from rear panel). *Bohling.* $45/£29

WATERS, L. L. Steel Trails to Santa Fe. Lawrence: Univ of KS, 1950. 1st ed. VG. *Archer.* $35/£22

WATERS, L. L. Steel Trails to Santa Fe. Lawrence: Univ of KS, 1950. 1st ed. VG in dj (sl worn). *Lien.* $45/£29

WATERTON, CHARLES. Letters of Charles Waterton. R. Irwin (ed). London, 1955. Dj (sl rubbed). *Maggs.* $28/£18

WATERTON, CHARLES. Wanderings in South America, the North-West of the United States, and the Antilles. London, 1828. 2nd ed. Frontis (blank corner stained), vii,(1),341pp. 3/4 leather (sl scuffed, chipped), gilt. Howes W158. *Bohling.* $110/£71

WATERTON, CHARLES. Wanderings in South America, the North-West of the United States, and the Antilles. London: B. Fellowes, 1828. 2nd ed. Engr frontis, vii,(1),341pp. Uncut. Orig grn linen bds (faded, sunned, fr joint starting). *Goodrich.* $595/£381

WATERTON, CHARLES. Wanderings in South America, the North-West of the United States, and the Antilles. J. G. Wood (ed). Macmillan, 1880. New ed. Marbled edges. Contemp full leather prize binding (rubbed; upper hinge starting, shelfwear), raised bands, leather spine label. Good (prize label fr pastedown). *Tiger.* $39/£25

WATERTON, CHARLES. Wanderings in South America, the U.S. and the Antilles. London: Blackie, (1894). 208pp + 31pp ads. VG. *Mikesh.* $35/£22

WATKIN, DAVID. The English Vision. Murray, 1982. Fine in dj. *Hadley.* $101/£65

WATKIN, DAVID. Thomas Hope 1769-1831. John Murray, 1968. 101 plts. *Edwards.* $31/£20

WATKINS, ALFRED. The Old Straight Track. London, 1948. 4th ed. Fldg map. (Spine faded, sl spotted.) *Edwards.* $31/£20

WATKINS, JOHN G. Hypnotherapy of the War Neuroses: A Clinical Psychologist's Casebook. NY: Ronald Press, (1949). 1st ed. Red cl. VG. *Gach.* $75/£48

WATKINS, NICHOLAS. Matisse. Phaidon, 1984. 1st ed. 97 color plts. Dj. *Edwards.* $39/£25

WATROUS, GEORGE R. et al. The History of Winchester Firearms 1866-1975. (NY, 1975.) 4th ed. Ltd to 1000 signed by co-authors. VF in slipcase. *Truepenny.* $65/£42

WATSON, A. An Illustrated Catalog of the Neotropic Arctiinae Types in the U.S. National Museum. Part I. Washington: Smithsonian, 1971. 1st ed. 252 plts. NF (ex-lib) in wraps. *Mikesh.* $25/£16

WATSON, CLYDE. Father Fox's Pennyrhymes. NY: Crowell, 1971. 1st ed. Wendy Watson (illus). 8 1/4 x 9 1/4. 58pp. Fine in dj. *Cattermole.* $20/£13

WATSON, E. P. A Manual of the Hand Lathe. Phila, 1874. 2nd ed. 3 plts. (Fr joint nibbled.) *Maggs.* $66/£42

WATSON, ELMO SCOTT. The Professor Goes West. Bloomington, IL, 1954. 1st ed. Grn cl, gilt. NF. *Five Quail.* $35/£22

WATSON, ERNEST W. Forty Illustrators and How They Work. NY, 1946. 1st ed. VG. (Extrems worn), else VG. *King.* $40/£26

WATSON, F. J. B. Louis XVI Furniture. NY, 1960. Good in dj. *Washton.* $445/£285

WATSON, F. J. B. The Wrightsman Collection. NY: MMA, 1966. 4 vols. Red cl. Fine in 2 slipcases. *Metropolitan**. $1,150/£737

WATSON, FREDERICK. Hunting Pie. NY: Derrydale, 1931. Ltd to 750. (Cvr lt soiled), o/w VG. *October Farm.* $125/£80

WATSON, JAMES D. The Double Helix. London, 1968. 3rd imp. Good in dj. *Henly.* $19/£12

WATSON, JAMES D. The Double Helix. London: Weidenfeld & Nicolson, 1968. 1st ed. VG (inscrip fep). *White.* $39/£25

WATSON, JAMES D. The Double Helix. NY: Atheneum, 1968. 1st ed. Fine in Fine dj (sm edge tear). *Unger.* $200/£128

WATSON, JOHN B. Psychology: From the Standpoint of a Behaviorist. Phila: Lippincott, (1919). 1st ed. (Ink name; lt wear), else VG. *Hermitage.* $100/£64

WATSON, JOHN F. Annals of Philadelphia and Pennsylvania in the Olden Time. Phila: Leary, Stuart, 1927. 3 vols. (Bkpl each vol, lt wear spine ends vol 2), o/w Very Clean set. *Hermitage.* $150/£96

WATSON, JOHN SELBY. Biographies of John Wilkes and William Cobbett. Edinburgh/London: William Blackwood, 1870. 1st ed. x,(iv),407pp; 2 engr ports. Tan cl (old paper lib label spine foot). *Burmester.* $39/£25

WATSON, JOHN. The Medical Profession in Ancient Times...November 7, 1855. NY: Baker & Godwin, 1856. 1st ed. xii,(9)-222,(1 errata)pp (some foxing). Cl back (soiled). Good in stiff ptd wraps. *Glaser.* $150/£96

WATSON, MARGARET G. Silver Theatre...1850 to 1864. Glendale: Clark, 1964. 1st ed. One of 2053. Fldg map. VF in dj. *Argonaut.* $45/£29

WATSON, RICHARD. Bitters Bottles. NY: Nelson, (1965). 1st ed. Dec eps. Good+ in dj (chipped). *Scribe's Perch**. $22/£14

WATSON, RICHARD. Bitters Bottles. NY, 1965. Fine. *Doctor's Library.* $50/£32

WATSON, ROBERT. Louise Reignier: The Communion of Crime and Criminals. London: Smith, Ainslie, n.d. (1895). 1st ed. 1/2-tone frontis, tissue guard, (xii),227,(i)pp. Dec eps. Salmon pink flecked w/pale pink linen-effect buckram, pict blocked and lettered navy fr cvr, gilt. VF. *Temple.* $55/£35

WATSON, S. et al. U.S. Geological Exploration of the 40th Parallel: The Botany. Washington, DC, 1871. 525pp + 40 full-pg engrs, fldg map. (Cl joints splitting, extrems worn.) Contents VG. *Brooks.* $169/£108

WATSON, S. H. (comp). A Folio of Old Songs. (Waxahachie, TX): Texas Division, U.D.C., 1912. 1st ed. NF. *Mcgowan.* $150/£96

WATSON, THOMAS. Lectures on the Principles and Practice of Physic. Phila, 1848. (3rd ed.) 1040pp (foxed; ex-libris). Full leather (bds scuffed, hinges starting). Good. *Doctor's Library.* $75/£48

WATSON, W. C. Portuguese Architecture. London: Constable, 1908. Color frontis. Sound. *Ars Artis.* $117/£75

WATSON, W. J. Bridge Architecture. NY: William Helburn, 1927. 199 plts. (Sm stain last ff.) 1/2 cl. *Ars Artis.* $78/£50

WATSON, W. L. History of Jamestown on Conanicut Island. Providence, 1949. 1st ed. 2 fldg maps laid in. Good in Good dj. *Scribe's Perch*.* $37/£24

WATSON, WILLIAM. The Adventures of a Blockade Runner. London: T. Fisher Unwin, 1892. 1st ed. xiii,324,(3)pp. Dec cl. (Spine sl dknd, extrems scuffed), else VG. *Mcgowan.* $250/£160

WATSON-JONES, REGINALD. Fractures and Joint Injuries. Balt, 1952. 4th ed. Blue cl bds. NF. *Doctor's Library.* $50/£32

WATTS, ALAN W. An Outline of Zen Buddhism. Golden Vista, 1932. 1st ed. Fine in yellow wrappers. *Words Etc.* $117/£75

WATTS, JOHN. Letter Book of John Watts, Merchant and Councillor of New York, Jan. 1, 1762-Dec. 22, 1765. NY Hist Soc, 1928. Grn cl, gilt. VG. *Bohling.* $18/£12

WATTS, MINOR. Americaville. NY: Olympia, 1969. 1st ed. Fine in dj (lt rubbed). *Associates.* $75/£48

WATTS, RALPH L. Vegetable Forcing. NY: OJ, 1924. Grn cl, gilt. VG. *Price.* $24/£15

WAUGH, ALEC. The Mule on the Minaret. London: Cassell, (1965). 1st Eng ed. Paper-cvrd bds. NF in dj (sl wear, few internal repairs). *Antic Hay.* $27/£17

WAUGH, ALEC. My Brother Evelyn and Other Portraits. NY: FSG, (1967). 1st ed. NF in dj (sl wear). *Antic Hay.* $20/£13

WAUGH, ALEC. My Brother Evelyn and Other Profiles. Cassell, (1967). 1st ed. (Edges sl spotted), o/w nice in dj (sl sunned). *Ash.* $31/£20

WAUGH, ALEC. No Quarter. London, 1932. 1st Eng ed. Very Nice in dj (sl mkd, nicked). *Clearwater.* $56/£36

WAUGH, EVELYN. A Bachelor Abroad. NY: Jonathan Cape, 1930. 1st US ed. NF (sl spine wear) in dj (sl worn, spine sl chipped). *Beasley.* $400/£256

WAUGH, EVELYN. Basil Seal Rides Again. Boston: Little Brown, 1963. Ltd to 1000 signed. Buckram, gilt. VG in acetate wrapper (back panel sl torn). *Words Etc.* $257/£165

WAUGH, EVELYN. Black Mischief. Chapman & Hall, 1932. 1st UK ed. VG (spine sl dull). *Williams.* $39/£25

WAUGH, EVELYN. Black Mischief. London, 1932. 1st Eng ed. (Bkpl; spine sl chafed.) *Clearwater.* $78/£50

WAUGH, EVELYN. Black Mischief. London: Chapman & Hall, 1932. 1st UK ed. Fine in VG dj (top edge sl worn, spine sl browned). *Williams.* $616/£395

WAUGH, EVELYN. Brideshead Revisited.... Chapman & Hall, 1945. 1st ed. Nice in dj (worn, repaired). *Ash.* $312/£200

WAUGH, EVELYN. Decline and Fall. London: Chapman & Hall, 1928. 1st issue w/'Martin Gaythorn-Brodie' and 'Kevin Saunderson' on pp168-169. (Lt foxed; spine cocked), o/w Excellent in dj (sl rubbed, chipped, spine faded). Labels on spine, upper cvr intact. *Gekoski.* $5,460/£3,500

WAUGH, EVELYN. Diaries. M. Davie (ed). Boston, 1976. 1st ed. Dj. *Typographeum.* $18/£12

WAUGH, EVELYN. A Handful of Dust. London: Chapman & Hall, 1934. Excellent (sl cocked) in VG dj (rubbed, torn, nicked; few sm chips missing from extrems and internally reinforced w/tape). *Gekoski.* $1,716/£1,100

WAUGH, EVELYN. Helena. Boston, 1950. 1st Amer ed. Fine in dj (spine extrems sl rubbed, price-clipped). *Polyanthos.* $45/£29

WAUGH, EVELYN. Labels. Duckworth, 1930. 1st UK ed. VG (sl faded, chip spine top) in dj (sl dusty, sm tears, chips). *Williams.* $468/£300

WAUGH, EVELYN. Letters. Mark Amory (ed). London, 1980. 1st Eng ed. Very Nice in dj. *Clearwater.* $31/£20

WAUGH, EVELYN. A Little Order, a Selection from His Journalism. Donat Gallagher (ed). London, 1977. 1st ed. VG in dj. *Gretton.* $19/£12

WAUGH, EVELYN. A Little Order. Boston: Little, Brown, (1977). 1st ed. NF in dj (sm tear). *Antic Hay.* $25/£16

WAUGH, EVELYN. A Little Order. London, 1977. 1st ed. (Cl sl damp mkd), o/w VG in dj. *Words Etc.* $19/£12

WAUGH, EVELYN. Love Among the Ruins. Chapman & Hall, 1953. 1st UK ed. NF (tear p47) in VG+ dj. *Williams.* $47/£30

WAUGH, EVELYN. Love Among the Ruins. London, 1953. 1st Eng ed. Nice in dj. *Clearwater.* $47/£30

WAUGH, EVELYN. The Loved One. Boston: Little, Brown, (1948). 1st Amer ed. NF in dj (price-clipped). *Turtle Island.* $45/£29

WAUGH, EVELYN. The Loved One. Chapman & Hall, 1948. 1st UK ed. Fine (ink name; lacks dj). *Williams.* $16/£10

WAUGH, EVELYN. The Loved One. An Anglo-American Tragedy. London, (1948). 1st Eng ed. Bright in dj. *Clearwater.* $55/£35

WAUGH, EVELYN. Men at Arms. London, 1952. 1st ed. (Spine faded, dull), o/w VG. *Words Etc.* $11/£7

WAUGH, EVELYN. Mr. Loveday's Little Outing and Other Sad Stories. London, 1936. 1st Eng ed. Frontis. (Inscrip; sl bumped.) *Clearwater.* $195/£125

WAUGH, EVELYN. Ninety-Two Days. 1934. 1st ed. VG. *Words Etc.* $148/£95

WAUGH, EVELYN. Officers and Gentlemen. Boston: Little Brown, (1955). 1st Amer ed. Fine in VG+ dj (sl tanned). *Between The Covers.* $75/£48

WAUGH, EVELYN. Officers and Gentlemen. Chapman & Hall, 1955. 1st UK ed. NF in VG dj (sl foxed, price-clipped). *Williams.* $56/£36

WAUGH, EVELYN. Officers and Gentlemen. London, 1955. 1st Eng ed. Nice (fore-edges foxed; binding sl cocked) in dj (nicked, mkd). *Clearwater.* $62/£40

WAUGH, EVELYN. The Ordeal of Gilbert Pinfold. Boston, (1957). 1st Amer ed. VG in dj (sl used). *King.* $15/£10

WAUGH, EVELYN. The Ordeal of Gilbert Pinfold. London, 1957. 1st ed. NF in dj (lt rubbed). *Buckley.* $31/£20

WAUGH, EVELYN. Put Out More Flags. Chapman & Hall, 1942. 1st UK ed. VG+ (lacks dj). *Williams.* $47/£30

WAUGH, EVELYN. Put Out More Flags. London: Chapman & Hall, 1942. 1st UK ed. VG in dj (chipped, esp spine top). *Williams.* $226/£145

WAUGH, EVELYN. Ronald Knox. Chapman & Hall, 1959. 1st UK ed. Fine in VG dj. *Williams.* $39/£25

WAUGH, EVELYN. Scoop. Chapman & Hall, 1933. 1st ed. (Sl rubbed; lacks dj.) *Edwards.* $86/£55

WAUGH, EVELYN. Scott-King's Modern Europe. Chapman & Hall, 1947. 1st UK ed. VG (sl tear upper bd) in dj (foxed, rubbed, sm closed tears). *Williams.* $23/£15

WAUGH, EVELYN. Tactical Exercise. Boston: Little, Brown, (1954). 1st ed. NF in dj (sl wear, sm abrasion rear panel). *Antic Hay.* $75/£48

WAUGH, EVELYN. A Tourist in Africa. Chapman & Hall, 1960. 1st ed. Dj (sl soiled, chipped). *Edwards.* $39/£25

WAUGH, EVELYN. A Tourist in Africa. London, 1960. 1st Eng ed. Very Nice in dj (sl dusty). *Clearwater.* $39/£25

WAUGH, EVELYN. Unconditional Surrender. Chapman & Hall, 1961. 1st UK ed. NF in VG dj (spine sl faded). *Williams.* $31/£20

WAUGH, EVELYN. Unconditional Surrender. London: Chapman & Hall, 1961. 1st UK ed. Fine in dj (spine foot lt rubbed). *Moorhouse.* $70/£45

WAUGH, EVELYN. Waugh in Abyssinia. London: Longman, 1936. 1st ed. VG (sm bkpl, edge sl foxed). Dj (damaged w/sm pieces missing top of fr panel, spine top sl soiled, rubbed; ptg inside flap sl scuffed). *Virgo.* $468/£300

WAUGH, EVELYN. Wine in Peace and War. Saccone & Speed, 1947. 1st UK ed. Rex Whistler (illus). VG (sl bruise spine) in illus bds. *Williams.* $117/£75

WAUGH, F. A. The American Apple Orchard. NY: OJ, 1911. Grn cl, gilt. VG. *Price.* $29/£19

WAUGH, F. A. The American Peach Orchard. NY: OJ, 1913. 1st ed. Grn cl. VG. *Price.* $39/£25

WAUGH, FREDERICK J. The Clan of Munes. NY: Scribner, 1916. 4to. Cl-dec bds (edgewear, stains, scratches; inside sl loose). *Metropolitan*.* $109/£70

WAUTERS, A. J. Stanley's Emin Pasha Expedition. London, 1890. 1st ed. Frontis port, xvii,378pp + (xxx) pub's list; 32 plts, fldg map. (Ex-libris; spine sl rubbed.) *Edwards.* $133/£85

WAUTERS, A. J. Stanley's Emin Pasha Expedition.... London: John C. Nimmo, 1890. 1st ed. Engr frontis port, xvii,(i)blank,378pp, (31)pub's list, fldg map, 32 plts. Brn cl (lib plt, label removed upper cvr), gilt vignette. VG. *Morrell.* $78/£50

WAUTON, CHARLES A. N. Troutfisher's Entomology. London, 1930. *Petersfield.* $22/£14

Waverley Gallery of the Principal Female Characters in Sir Walter Scott's Romances. NY: Appleton, 1860. 230pp. Gilt-dec leather. (Sl rubbed, sm chip spine; lt foxing), o/w Contents VG. *New Hampshire*.* $55/£35

WAX, MARVIN. Mystique of the Missions: Photographic Impressions by Marvin Wax. Palo Alto: American West, 1974. 1st ed. Leatherette-backed cl, gilt spine. Fine in slipcase. *Pacific*.* $29/£19

WAXELL, SVEN. The American Expedition. London: William Hodge, 1952. 1st UK ed. Blue/grn cl (worn). *Parmer.* $55/£35

WAY, THOMAS E. Sgt. Fred Platten's Ten Years on the Trail of the Redskins. Williams, AZ, 1963. 2nd ed. VG+ in pict wraps. *Pratt.* $37/£24

WAY, THOMAS R. and FREDERIC CHAPMAN. Ancient Royal Palaces in and near London. London/NY, 1902. 1st ed. One of 400 numbered, initialed by Way (illus). 24 litho plts, guards; add'l color engrs of Waterloo Place tipped in by former owner. Uncut. Purple dec buckram. VG. *Argosy.* $125/£80

WEAD, FRANK. Gales, Ice and Men. NY: Dodd, Mead, 1937. Color frontis. VG in dj. *High Latitude.* $35/£22

WEALE, B. L. PUTNAM. Indiscreet Letters from Peking, Being the Notes of an Eye-Witness...the Real Story of the Siege...in 1900.... NY: Dodd, Mead, 1907. 1st ed. Frontis. (Sm spine tear), o/w Good. *Worldwide.* $12/£8

WEATHERFORD, MARK. Bannock-Piute War. The Campaign and Battles. Corvallis, OR, 1959. 2nd ptg. Signed. VG in wraps. *Oregon.* $55/£35

WEATHERFORD, WILLIS DUKE. Negro Life in the South, Present Conditions and Needs. NY, 1911. 2nd ed. VG. *Mcgowan.* $37/£24

WEATHERLY, F. E. Peeps into Fairyland. London: Nister, n.d. 8vo. (Loss to tp corner, some illus w/tears, losses; binding damaged, worn.) *Metropolitan*.* $28/£18

WEATHERLY, F. E. Punch and Judy and Some of Their Friends. London: Marcus Ward, n.d. (c. 1885). 1st ed. Sm 4to. 12 color illus. (Sl offsetting.) Cl-backed pict bds (extrems sl worn; sl shaken). *Dramatis Personae.* $100/£64

WEATHERLY, LIONEL. The Supernatural? London, 1891. xv,273pp. VG. *Middle Earth.* $60/£38

WEATHERWAX, PAUL. Indian Corn in Old America. NY, 1954. 1st ed. Color frontis. Blue cl. VG in dj (chipped). *Price.* $45/£29

WEAVER, LAWRENCE. Cottages. Country Life, 1926. 3rd ed. Frontis. (Feps lt browned.) Dj (chipped, spine browned). *Edwards.* $59/£38

WEAVER, LAWRENCE. High Wycombe Furniture. Fanfare Press, 1929. 46 plts. (Sl foxing, few openings pulled, cvrs sl mkd, soiled), o/w VG. *Whittle.* $39/£25

WEAVER, LAWRENCE. Houses and Gardens by E.L. Lutyens. London: Country Life, 1914. Deluxe ed. Color frontis, guard. Teg. Contemp 3/4 brn morocco, gilt. VG. *Hollett.* $374/£240

WEAVER, LAWRENCE. Houses and Gardens by Sir Edwin Lutyens. London: Country Life, 1925. Teg. Red cl, gilt. (Lt wear, soil.) *Freeman*.* $190/£122

WEAVER, LAWRENCE. Lutyens Houses and Gardens. 1921. 1st ed. Cl-backed bds, gilt (sl worn; opening sl pulled). VG. *Whittle.* $62/£40

WEAVER, LAWRENCE. Memorials and Monuments. 1915. (Feps lt browned, lt spotting; lt soiled, sl bumped.) *Edwards.* $78/£50

WEAVER, LAWRENCE. Small Country Houses of Today. Country Life, 1910. VG in grn cl. *Hadley.* $55/£35

WEAVER, LAWRENCE. Small Country Houses of Today. Country Life, 1922. Vols 1 & 2 only (of 3). Vol 1, 3rd ed; vol 2, 2nd ed, rev. Grn cl, gilt. (Vol 1 spine repaired, chipped, vol 2 faded), o/w VG. *Whittle.* $133/£85

WEAVER, LAWRENCE. Small Country Houses. London, 1914. Color frontis tipped in. New marbled eps; teg. Modern cl (rebound, lt faded; bkpl), leather label. *Edwards.* $78/£50

WEAVER, WILLIAM D. (ed). Catalogue of the Wheeler Gift of Books...in the Library of the American Institute of Electrical Engineers. NY: Amer Inst of Electrical Engineers, 1909. 1st ed. 2 vols. 113 plts. VG set (sl rubbed, soiled, vol 1 rebacked w/orig backstrip laid down). *Glaser.* $450/£288

WEBB, A. P. Bibliography of the Works of Thomas Hardy 1865-1915. London: Frank Hollings, 1916. VG. *New Hampshire*.* $30/£19

WEBB, BEATRICE. The Diary of.... Norman & Jeanne MacKenzie (ed). Cambridge: Harvard Univ/Belknap, 1982, 1983, 1984. 1st ed. 3 vols. Fine (ex-libris, name tp) in dj. *Second Life.* $65/£42

WEBB, CHARLES. The Graduate. (NY): NAL, (1963). 1st ed, 1st bk. NF in VG dj (2 spine chips, closed tear, edgewear). *Fuller & Saunders.* $60/£38

WEBB, EDITH BUCKLAND. Indian Life at the Old Missions. L.A.: Warren F. Lewis, (1952). 1st ed. Orange cl, gilt. Fine in pict dj. *Pacific*.* $104/£67

WEBB, EDITH BUCKLAND. Indian Life at the Old Missions. L.A.: Warren F. Lewis, 1952. 1st ed. 52 plts. Gilt-lettered dec terra cotta cl. VF in dj. *Argonaut.* $175/£112

WEBB, GEOFFREY. Architecture in Britain: The Middle Ages. Penguin, 1956. 1st ed. VG+ in dj (chipped). *Whittle.* $39/£25

WEBB, JAMES JOSIAH. Adventures in the Santa Fe Trade 1844-47. Ralph P. Bieber (ed). Glendale, 1931. 1st ed. One of 1252. Frontis port, fldg map. VF. No dj as issued. *Turpen.* $150/£96

WEBB, JAMES JOSIAH. Adventures in the Santa Fe Trade, 1844-1847. Glendale: A. H. Clark, 1931. Photo frontis, fldg map. Dk red cl. *Dawson.* $100/£64

WEBB, JAMES JOSIAH. Adventures in the Santa Fe Trade, 1844-1847. Ralph P. Bieber (ed). Glendale: Clark, 1931. 1st ed. One of 1252. Teg. Red cl. VF. *Argonaut.* $175/£112

WEBB, M. I. Michael Rysbrack. Country Life, 1954. 1st ed. Dj (sl chipped, spine lt faded). *Edwards.* $62/£40

WEBB, MARION ST. JOHN. The House Fairies. Modern Art Society, n.d. ca 1925. Margaret Tarrant (illus). 12mo. 40pp; 6 tipped-in color plts. Grey bds, pict onlay. (Spine ends sl worn, sl dusty), else VG. *Bookmark.* $90/£58

WEBB, MARY. The Chinese Lion. London: Rota, 1937. 1st ed. One of 350 numbered. Cl, batik bds, cl label. (Eps lt foxing), o/w Fine in slipcase (sl soiled). *Reese.* $40/£26

WEBB, MRS. J. B. Naomi or The Last Days of Jerusalem. London: Routledge, 1872. 16 laid-in photos. 3/4 leather (rubbed, corners through, shaken). *Metropolitan*. $50/£32

WEBB, PETER. The Erotic Arts. Secker & Warburg, 1980. Rpt. Dj. *Edwards.* $39/£25

WEBB, PETER. The Erotic Arts. London: Secker & Warburg, 1980. VG in dj. *Hollett.* $55/£35

WEBB, SAMUEL et al (comps). Records of North American Big Game. NY: Scribner, 1952. Color frontis. (Sl worn.) Dj (tattered). *Oinonen*. $180/£115

WEBB, THOMAS H. Information for Kanzas Immigrants. Boston: A. Mudge, 1855. 3rd ed. 24pp (foxing, ink stain last 2 ll), stitched w/o wraps as issued. (Worn, wrinkled.) Howes W191. *Bohling.* $65/£42

WEBB, TODD. Georgia O'Keeffe: The Artist's Landscape. Pasadena: Twelvetrees, 1984. 1st ed. 39 full-pg sheet-fed photogravures. Fine in cl slipcase, mtd photo illus on fr. *Cahan.* $125/£80

WEBB, WALTER PRESCOTT. The Great Frontier. Boston, 1952. 1st ed. Dj. *Ginsberg.* $75/£48

WEBB, WALTER PRESCOTT. The Great Frontier. Boston: Houghton Mifflin, 1952. 1st ed. Fine (bkpl) in dj (sl chipped). *Argonaut.* $60/£38

WEBB, WALTER PRESCOTT. The Great Plains. Boston, 1931. 1st ed, 1st issue. Fine in VG dj. Howes W193. *Turpen.* $175/£112

WEBB, WALTER PRESCOTT. History as High Adventure. E.C. Barksdale (ed). Austin: Pemberton, 1969. One of 350. 1/2 morocco. Fine in slipcase. *Bohling.* $60/£38

WEBB, WALTER PRESCOTT. An Honest Preface and Other Essays. Boston: Houghton Mifflin, 1959. 1st ed. (Sm spot lower edge), o/w Fine in dj. *Gibbs.* $10/£6

WEBB, WALTER PRESCOTT. The Texas Rangers. Boston/NY: Houghton Mifflin, 1935. 1st ed. Frontis. Promo material laid in. (Spine rubbed, faded, rear dampstained), else Good. Howes W194. *Cahan.* $75/£48

WEBB, WALTER PRESCOTT. The Texas Rangers. Boston: Houghton Mifflin, 1935. 1st ed. Good (cvr sunned, stained). Howes W194. *Scribe's Perch*. $40/£26

WEBB, WALTER PRESCOTT. The Texas Rangers. Boston: Houghton Mifflin, 1935. 1st trade ed. Red cl. VG (fep expertly replaced). Howes W194. *House.* $100/£64

WEBB, WALTER PRESCOTT. The Texas Rangers. Boston: Houghton Mifflin, 1935. 1st ed, w/date on tp and caption error p565. Red cl. Fine (name; spine sl faded, ink spot). Howes W194. *Argonaut.* $175/£112

WEBB, WILLIAM and ROBERT A. WEINSTEIN. Dwellers at the Source: Southwestern Indian Photographs of A. C. Vroman, 1895-1904. NY: Grossman, 1973. 1st ed. 173 plts. (Owner stamp), else Fine in VG dj. *Cahan.* $100/£64

WEBBER and NEVINS. Old Naumkeag. Salem/Boston, 1877. 1st ed. 312pp + 7pp ads (cracked at p168). Grn cl, paper spine label (chipped). Good. *Scribe's Perch*. $36/£23

WEBBER, CHARLES W. Old Hicks the Guide; or, Adventures in the Camanche Country in Search of a Gold Mine. NY, 1848. 1st ed. 356pp. Orig cl (inner hinge strengthened; spine sl faded). Howes W198. *Ginsberg.* $300/£192

WEBBER, WINSLOW L. Books about Books, a Bio-Bibliography for Collectors. Boston: Hale, Cushman & Flint, 1937. 1st ed. Cream cl bds. VG in dj (internally repaired, torn, missing pieces). *Heller.* $55/£35

WEBER, CARL J. Thomas Hardy in Maine. ME: Southworth-Anthoensen, 1942. Ltd to 425. Parchment-backed bds. NF. *Words Etc.* $70/£45

WEBER, CARL J. A Thousand and One Fore-Edge Paintings. Waterville, ME: Colby College, 1949. 1st ed. Ltd to 1000 ptd. VF in buckram, dj. *Bromer.* $475/£304

WEBER, DAVID J. (ed). The Extranjeros. Santa Fe: Stagecoach Press, (1967). 1st ed. One of 600. Fine in dj. *Bohling.* $40/£26

WEBER, DAVID J. The Taos Trappers, the Fur Trade in the Far Southwest 1540-1846. Norman, 1971. 1st ptg. 3 maps. (Ex-lib), o/w VG+ in VG+ dj. *Turpen.* $35/£22

WEBER, DAVID J. The Taos Trappers...1540-1846. Norman: Univ of OK, (1971). VG in dj. *Lien.* $40/£26

WEBER, FRANCIS J. Prominent Visitors to the California Missions (1786-1842). L.A.: Dawson's Book Shop, 1991. One of 500 ptd. Beige cl, gilt spine. Fine in pict dj. *Pacific*. $23/£15

WEBER, JOHN PAUL. The German War Artists. Columbia, SC, 1979. Very Nice in dj. *Clearwater.* $78/£50

WEBER, MAX. Cubist Poems. London: Elkin Mathews, 1914. 1st ed, 1st bk. Blue cl (spine extrems lt rubbed), gilt cvr illus. *Karmiole.* $250/£160

WEBER, WILHELM. A History of Lithography. NY, (1966). Fine (inscrip) in dj (sl torn). *Argosy.* $125/£80

WEBERMAN, A. J. My Life in Garbology. NY: Stonehill, 1980. 1st ed. Fine in Fine dj. *Warren.* $75/£48

WEBSTER, A. D. Webster's Practical Forestry. London: Rider, n.d. (c 1904). 3rd ed. Dec cl. VG. *Savona.* $28/£18

WEBSTER, GEORGE and LINVILLE J. HALL. The Journal of a Trip Around the Horn.... Ashland: Lewis Osborne, 1970. #113/650 ptd. Fine in plain pub's dj. *Hermitage.* $75/£48

WEBSTER, H. Primitive Secret Societies. NY, 1908. VG+ (ex-lib). *Middle Earth.* $48/£31

WEBSTER, HENRY KITCHELL. The Sky-Man. NY: Century, 1910. VG (ink letters fep; spine lettering worn). *Between The Covers.* $85/£54

WEBSTER, JOHN. The Duchess of Malfi. London: Sylvan, 1945. 1st trade ed. Michael Ayrton (illus). Teg, uncut, partly unopened. (Spine sl faded.) *Hollett.* $148/£95

WEBSTER, KIMBALL. The Gold Seekers of '49. Manchester, NH, 1917. 16 plts and ports. (Internal lib mks, owner statements; spine faded.) *Bohling.* $85/£54

WEBSTER, NOAH. An American Dictionary of the English Language. NY: S. Converse, 1828. 1st ed. 2 vols. Typed note mtd fep each vol stating that this set was property of G. & C. Merriam Co. Engr frontis port vol 1. Orig full suede calf (spines recased in brn calf, most of orig spines laid down; sl worn, scuffed; sl browned, foxed, hinges w/later cl tape reinforcements), orig/later leather spine labels. Texts VG. *Baltimore**. $3,000/£1,923

WEBSTER, NOAH. The American Spelling Book.... Phila: Jacob Johnson, 1805. Johnson's 4th rev imp. 168pp (lacks eps, tears, scribbles, aged, few pp stained); 8 woodcuts. Leather-backed bds (crudely stitched). Good. *Agvent*. $125/£80

WEBSTER, NOAH. A Compendious Dictionary of the English Language. Hartford, 1806. 1st ed. Contemp sheep (backstrip crudely reinforced w/cl tape). *Swann**. $172/£110

WEBSTER, NOAH. The Elementary Spelling Book. New Brunswick: John Terhune, 1840. Linen-backed blue/gray bds. Untrimmed. (Fr joint cracking), o/w Clean. *Hermitage*. $100/£64

WEBSTER, SAMUEL C. Mark Twain, Business Man. Boston: Little, Brown, 1946. 1st ed. Fine in VG dj. BAL 3573. *Macdonnell*. $35/£22

WECHSLER, HERMAN J. Great Prints and Printmakers. NY: Leon Amiel, n.d. (c. 1970). 100 plts (16 color). Dj. *Edwards*. $39/£25

WECTER, DIXON. Sam Clemens of Hannibal. Boston: Houghton, Mifflin, 1952. 1st ed, 1st ptg. Fine in NF dj (spine sl faded). *Macdonnell*. $35/£22

WEDGE, F. J. N. (comp). Brown's Flags and Funnels of British and Foreign Steamship Companies. Glasgow, (1951). (5th ed.) Errata. Blue cl, gilt title. VG + . *Bohling*. $35/£22

WEDGWOOD, BARBARA and HENSLEIGH. The Wedgwood Circle 1730-1897. Canada: Collier Macmillan, 1980. 1st ed. Frontis. Dj (edges sl torn). *Edwards*. $31/£20

WEDGWOOD, C. V. The Great Rebellion. London, 1958. Maroon cl. *Maggs*. $39/£25

WEDGWOOD, JOSIAH. The Selected Letters of Josiah Wedgwood. Ann Finer and George Savage (eds). London, 1965. 14 plts hors texte. (Cl sl soiled.) *Washton*. $50/£32

WEDGWOOD, JOSIAH. The Selected Letters of Josiah Wedgwood. Ann Finer and George Savage (eds). London: Cory, Adams & Mackay, 1965. 1st ed. 15 plts (2 color). (Lt pencil marginal lining.) Dj (sl soiled). *Hollett*. $55/£35

WEDGWOOD, JOSIAH. Staffordshire Pottery and Its History. London: Sampson Low, Marston, n.d. (Sl rubbed.) *Edwards*. $39/£25

WEDMORE, FREDERICK. Etching in England. London: George Bell, 1895. 1st ed. xiv,185pp (eps spotted); 50 plts. Dec bds (sl rubbed). *Hollett*. $94/£60

WEED, W. The Copper Mines of the World. London: Hill, 1908. 1st ed, 2nd imp. VG. *Blake*. $150/£96

WEED, W. Geology and Ore Deposits of the Butte District, Montana. Washington: US Geol Survey, 1912. 1st ed. 41 plts. (Few lib stamps; cl sl worn.) *Maggs*. $28/£18

WEEDEN, HOWARD. Songs of the Old South. NY: Doubleday, Page, 1900. 1st ed. 7 color ports. Color plt mtd fr cvr. (Worn, water spotting, fr inner hinge broken.) *New Hampshire**. $40/£26

WEEGEE. (Pseud of Arthur Fellig.) Creative Photography. London: Ward Lock, 1964. Fine in VG dj. *Metropolitan**. $75/£48

WEEGEE. (Pseud of Arthur Fellig.) Naked City. Essential Books, 1945. (Bumped), else VG + in dj (edgeworn, chipped, soiled, rubbed, sm piece stuck to cvr). *My Bookhouse*. $175/£112

WEEGEE. (Pseud of Arthur Fellig.) Naked City. NY: Essential Books, 1945. 1st ed. Pict eps. VG (owner stamp, bkpl). *Cahan*. $100/£64

WEEGEE. (Pseud of Arthur Fellig.) Naked Hollywood. Mel Harris (text). NY: Pellegrini & Cudahy, 1953. 1st ed. Yellow cl. (Owner stamp, lower edge lt rubbed), else VG in dj (chipped). *Cahan*. $100/£64

WEEGEE. (Pseud of Arthur Fellig.) Weegee's People. NY, (1946). 1st ed. (Spine faded, spotted, cvrs discolored.) *King*. $50/£32

WEEGEE. (Pseud of Arthur Fellig.) Weegee's People. NY: Essential Books/Duell, Sloan & Pearce, (1946). 1st ed. VG + in dj (spine sl worn). *Bernard*. $100/£64

WEEGEE. (Pseud of Arthur Fellig.) Weegee. Louis Stettner (ed). NY: Knopf, 1977. 1st ed. Fine in NF + dj. *Smith*. $65/£42

Week-End Book. Nonesuch, 1928. India paper ed. Mottled limp blue leather. (Creased, spine dknd, rear cvr sl pitted), o/w VG. *Words Etc*. $23/£15

Week-End Book. London: Nonesuch, 1928. New ed. This edw/revisions, additions; includes for the 1st time 13 full-pg colored illus, dec eps by Albert Rutherston. Limp blue mottled leather. Fine. *Michael Taylor*. $47/£30

WEEKLEY, W. M. Twenty Years on Horseback or Itinerating in West Virginia. Dayton, VA, 1924. Frontis port. VG (inscrip, lt rubbed, soiled). *Bohling*. $30/£19

WEEKS, ALVIN G. Massasoit of the Wampanoags. (Fall River, MA: The Author), 1920. 1st ed. Frontis port, plt. Gilt-lettered orange cl. Fine. *Argonaut*. $25/£16

WEEKS, DELLA JERMAN. Legends of the War. Boston: Mudge, 1863. 1st ed, author's ed ptd for private circulation. 63pp, engr port. (Crown lacks sm piece.) *Ginsberg*. $125/£80

WEEKS, DONALD (ed). Frederick Rolfe and the Times, 4-12 February 1901. Edinburgh: Tragara, 1977. 1st ed. One of 175 numbered. Fine in ptd wrappers. *Turtle Island*. $50/£32

WEEKS, DONALD. Two Friends. Edinburgh: Tragara, 1978. 1st ed. One of 125. Fine in ptd wrappers. *Turtle Island*. $50/£32

WEEKS, JOHN H. Among Congo Cannibals. Phila, 1913. 1st ed. Fldg map. (Margins lt browned, ex-lib, bkpl, hinges taped; rebacked, much of orig faded spine laid down.) *Edwards*. $94/£60

WEEKS, ROBERT P. King Strang. Ann Arbor, 1971. (Ink mk), o/w VG in wraps. *Benchmark*. $20/£13

WEEKS, STEPHEN B. Southern Quakers and Slavery. Balt: Johns Hopkins, 1896. 1st ed. xiv,400pp; lg fldg map. Unopened. (Edges lt stained; extrems rubbed; bkpl removed fr pastedown; pg torn, creased; lt staining), else VG. *Cahan*. $100/£64

WEES, FRANCES SHELLEY. The Maestro Murders. NY: Mystery League, 1931. 1st Amer ed. NF in dj (tears, pieces missing). *Polyanthos*. $25/£16

WEESNER, THEODORE. The Car Thief. NY: Random House, 1972. 1st ed. NF in dj. *Lame Duck*. $45/£29

WEGG-PROSSER, F. R. Galileo and His Judges. London: Chapman & Hall, 1889. 1st ed. vi,170,40(ads)pp. Untrimmed. NF (lib bkpl). *Glaser*. $85/£54

WEICHMANN, LOUIS J. A True History of the Assassination of Abraham Lincoln and of the Conspiracy of 1865. Floyd E. Risvold (ed). NY: Knopf, 1975. 1st ed. VG in dj (worn). *Graf*. $25/£16

WEIDENSALL, JEAN. The Mentality of the Criminal Woman. Balt, 1916. 1st ed. Grn cl (sl worn). VG. *Doctor's Library*. $50/£32

WEIDMAN, GREGORY R. Furniture in Maryland, 1740-1940. Balt: MD Hist Soc, (1984). 1st ed. Signed presentation. Pict eps. Black cl, silver spine lettering. Fine in NF dj. *Baltimore**. $100/£64

WEIGALL, ARTHUR. Ancient Egyptian Works of Art. London: T. Fisher Unwin, 1924. 1st ed. Maroon cl. Fine. *Appelfeld.* $100/£64

WEIGALL, ARTHUR. Travels in the Upper Egyptian Deserts. London, 1909. 1st ed. Frontis, 33 plts. Dec cl (spine sl faded, rubbed; sl textual browning). *Edwards.* $39/£25

WEIGERT, EDITH. The Courage to Love. New Haven/London: Yale Univ, 1970. 1st ed. Inscribed. Blue-grey cl, painted spine label. VG in dj. *Gach.* $50/£32

WEIL, GUNTHER M. et al (eds). The Psychedelic Reader. New Hyde Park, NY: University Books, 1965. 1st ed. (Pg edges sl soiled; faint moisture mk cvrs), else NF in dj (rubbed). *Associates.* $45/£29

WEILER, MILTON C. Classic Shorebird Decoys: A Portfolio of Paintings by Milton C. Weiler. Text by William J. Mackey, Jr. NY: Winchester, 1971. #404/975 numbered, signed. 24 full color plts in fr inner pocket. Tan bds, gilt, brn leatherette spine. Mint in substantial slipcase. *Cummins.* $450/£288

WEINBERGER, BERNHARD WOLF. An Introduction to the History of Dentistry.... Volume I. St. Louis: C.V. Mosby, 1948. 1st ed. VG. *Glaser.* $125/£80

WEINER, MARGERY (trans). The Art of Cuisine: Henri de Toulouse-Lautrec and Maurice Joyant. London: Michael Joseph, 1966. Frontis. White/red checkered cl bds. Fine in dj, slipcase. *Heller.* $95/£61

WEINGLASS, D. H. Prints and Engraved Illustrations by and After Henry Fuseli. Aldershot, 1994. Good in dj. *Washton.* $65/£42

WEINMANN, JOSEPH P. and HARRY SICHER. Bones and Bones: Fundamentals of Bone Biology. St. Louis, 1947. 1st ed. Red cl. VG (bkpl 1/2-title). *Doctor's Library.* $50/£32

WEINSTEIN, SOL. Loxfinger. NY: Pocket Books, (1965). 1st ed. VG+ in pict wrappers. *Other Worlds.* $10/£6

WEIR, ROBERT et al. Riding and Polo. Badminton Library, 1901. (Binding sl dull.) *Petersfield.* $39/£25

WEIR, WILLIAM. Sixty Years in Canada.... Montreal: Lovell, 1903. 1st ed. Port. (Hinges cracked, spine dull.) *Ginsberg.* $125/£80

WEISBORD, ALBERT. The Conquest of Power. NY: Covici-Friede, 1937. 1st ed. 2 vols. Fine (sl sunned spines) in djs (lt used). *Beasley.* $150/£96

WEISE, ARTHUR JAMES. The City of Troy and Its Vicinity. Troy: Green, 1886. 1st ed. Dbl-pg map frontis, (4),376,errata,4pp. (Cl faded.) *Ginsberg.* $75/£48

WEISGARD, LEONARD. Cinderella. NY: Garden City, 1938. 1st ed. 8 1/2 x 10 1/4. 32pp. Cl spine, pict bds. VG in dj. *Cattermole.* $45/£29

WEISMANN, AUGUST. The Germ-Plasm. NY: Scribner, 1893. 1st ed in English, Amer issue. xxiii,477pp. VG (spine sl chipped, lib #s spine). *Glaser.* $135/£87

WEISMANN, ELIZABETH WILDER. Mexico in Sculpture 1521-1821. Cambridge, 1950. (Ink underlinings; cl backstrip sl worn.) *Washton.* $40/£26

WEISS, HARRY B. and GRACE M. ZIEGLER. Thomas Say, Early American Naturalist. Springfield: Charles C. Thomas, 1931. 1st ed. Fine in dj (sl shelfworn). *Glaser.* $65/£42

WEISS, MARGARET R. (ed). Ben Shahn, Photographer. NY: Da Capo, 1973. 1st ed. 81 full-pg plts. (Owner stamp; spine faded), else VG. *Cahan.* $50/£32

WEISS, PETER. Exile. A Novel. E. B. Garside et al (trans). NY: Delacorte, (1968). 1st US ed. Cl, pict bds. Fine in dj. *Reese.* $30/£19

WEISS, RENEE KAROL. The Bird from the Sea. NY: Crowell, 1970. 1st ed. Ed Young (illus). 10 3/4 x 8. 26pp. Fine in dj. *Cattermole.* $35/£22

WEISS, SAMUEL. Diseases of the Liver, Gall Bladder, Ducts and Pancreas.... NY, 1935. 1st ed. 6 plts. VG. *Argosy.* $60/£38

WEISSE, FRANZ. The Art of Marbling. North Hills: Bird & Bull, 1980. One of 300 numbered. Prospectus laid in. 1/4 morocco. *Swann*.* $287/£184

WEITZMANN, KURT et al. The Icon. NY, 1982. Good in dj. *Washton.* $90/£58

WEITZMANN, KURT and MARGARET ENGLISH FRAZER. Age of Spirituality...Third to Seventh Century. NY: MMA, 1977. (Not exhibition cat.) Good in wrappers. *Washton.* $15/£10

WEITZMANN, KURT. Ancient Book Illumination. Cambridge, 1959. 64 plts. Good in dj. *Washton.* $125/£80

WEITZMANN, KURT. Greek Mythology in Byzantine Art. Princeton, 1951. 60 plts. Good. *Washton.* $250/£160

WEITZMANN, KURT. Illustrations in Roll and Codex. Princeton, 1947. Good. *Washton.* $85/£54

WEITZMANN, KURT. The Joshua Roll. Princeton, 1948. 32 plts. Good. *Washton.* $250/£160

WEITZMANN, KURT. Late Antique and Early Christian Book Illumination. NY: Braziller, 1977. Stated 1st ptg. 48 full-pg color plts. NF in Good+ dj. *Scribe's Perch*.* $36/£23

WELCH, ANTHONY. Artists for the Shah. New Haven, CT/London: Yale Univ, 1976. 1st ed. 84 plts. VG in dj. *Worldwide.* $45/£29

WELCH, CHARLES A. History of the Big Horn Basin. Salt Lake, 1940. 1st ed. Inscribed. VG+. *Benchmark.* $150/£96

WELCH, D'ALTE A. A Bibliography of American Children's Books Printed Prior to 1821. Barre Publishers & AAS, 1972. (Sl worn.) *Oinonen*.* $50/£32

WELCH, DENTON. The Denton Welch Journals. Jocelyn Brooke (ed). Hamish Hamilton, 1952. 1st ed. NF in dj (spine sl rubbed). *Sclanders.* $28/£18

WELCH, DENTON. Denton Welch: A Selection from His Published Works. Jocelyn Brooke (ed). Chapman & Hall, 1963. 1st ed. Fine in dj. *Sclanders.* $23/£15

WELCH, DENTON. Extracts from His Published Works. J. Brooke (ed). London, 1963. 1st ed. Dj (sl soiled). *Typographeum.* $35/£22

WELCH, DENTON. I Left My Grandfather's House. James Campbell, 1958. One of 150. Illus bds. NF (sl worn). *Sclanders.* $125/£80

WELCH, DENTON. In Youth Is Pleasure. Routledge, 1944. 1st ed. VG in dj (sl loss spine ends). *Sclanders.* $78/£50

WELCH, DENTON. In Youth Is Pleasure. Vision, 1950. (Cl mkd), o/w VG. *Words Etc.* $19/£12

WELCH, DENTON. A Last Sheaf. John Lehmann, 1951. 1st ed. (Top/bottom edges sl spotted), o/w NF in dj. *Sclanders.* $47/£30

WELCH, DENTON. A Voice Through a Cloud. John Lehmann, 1950. 1st ed. VG in dj (spine head sl nicked). *Words Etc.* $34/£22

WELCH, DENTON. A Voice Through a Cloud. John Lehmann, 1950. 1st ed. NF in dj (sl worn). *Sclanders.* $78/£50

WELCH, DENTON. A Voice Through a Cloud. Readers Union, 1951. 2nd ed. NF in dj. *Sclanders.* $16/£10

WELCH, H. J. Dwarf Conifers. London, 1966. Color frontis, 20 plts. Good in dj. *Brooks.* $49/£31

WELCH, JAMES. Fools Crow. Viking, (1986). 1st ed. Fine in Fine dj. *Authors Of West.* $35/£22

WELCH, JAMES. Winter in the Blood. NY: Harper & Row, (1974). 1st ed. Fine in Fine dj (price-clipped). *Dermont.* $100/£64

WELCH, JAMES. Winter in the Blood. NY: Harper, 1974. 1st ed. Signed. Fine in Fine dj. *Unger.* $150/£96

WELCH, MICHAEL IRENE. Vodka and Roses. West Branch, IA, 1978. Ltd to 550. Fine in pict wrappers. *Truepenny.* $12/£8

WELCH, O. Knights Templars' Tactics and Drill...in the Burial Service of the Orders of Masonic Knighthood. NY, 1872. 215pp; 5 plts. Dec cvr. Good + . *Scribe's Perch*. $55/£35

WELCH, SAMUEL M. Home History. Buffalo, 1891. Frontis port, xiv, 423pp (penciling, bkpl). Maroon cl (edgeworn, shaken), gilt. *Bohling.* $60/£38

WELCH, WILLIAM HENRY. Contributions to the Science of Medicine Dedicated by His Pupils on the Twenty-Fifth Anniversary of His Doctorate. Balt: Hopkins, 1900. Uncut, unopened. (Marginal dampstaining lower corner; cl sl rubbed, stained), o/w Clean. *Goodrich.* $125/£80

WELD, ISAAC. Travels Through the States of North America.... London, 1799. 2nd ed. 2 vols. 16 maps and plts. (Lacks ad leaves.) Mod 3/4 morocco, gilt. Howes W235. *Swann*. $373/£239

WELDON, FAY. Remember Me. Hodder, 1976. 1st UK ed. Signed, inscribed. NF in dj. *Williams.* $34/£22

WELDON, L. B. Hard Lying. Eastern Mediterranean 1914-1919. London, 1926. 2nd ed. 16 plts, fldg map. Grn cl. *Maggs.* $47/£30

WELKER, R. Birds and Men. Cambridge, MA, 1955. (1st leaves sl creased.) Dj (ragged). *Maggs.* $36/£23

WELLER, ALLEN STUART. Francesco di Giorgio, 1439-1501. Chicago, 1943. Good. *Washton.* $275/£176

WELLER, CHARLES E. Yesterday: A Chronicle of Early Life in the West. Indianapolis: The Author, 1921. 1st ed. Port. (Cvrs spotted, spine lettering faded), else Good. *Brown.* $25/£16

WELLES, C. M. Three Years' Wanderings of a Connecticut Yankee in South America, Africa, Australia, and California.... NY: Amer Subscription, 1859. 1st ed. 358pp; 10 plts. NF (spine ends sl worn). Howes W239. *Agvent.* $200/£128

WELLES, ORSON. Mr. Arkadin. NY: Crowell, (1956). Fine in VG + dj (sm spot, sm tear, sl rubbed). *Between The Covers.* $75/£48

WELLES, ORSON. Mr. Arkadin. NY, 1956. 1st ed. (Sm stain fr cvr.) Dj (sm tears). *Typographeum.* $35/£22

WELLES, WINIFRED. The Lost Landscape: Some Memories of a Family and a Town in Connecticut 1659-1906. NY: Henry Holt, (1946). 1st ed. Cl-backed dec bds. Fine in dj (sl edgewear). *Sadlon.* $15/£10

WELLESLEY, DOROTHY. Genesis, an Impression.... London: Heinemann, 1926. 1st ed. Cl, batik bds. NF in dj (sl tanned, smudge fr panel). *Reese.* $75/£48

WELLESLEY, DOROTHY. Lost Lane. London: Heinemann, 1925. 1st ed. Signed. (Inscrip, offsetting eps), o/w Very Nice in dj (tanned, sm nick). *Reese.* $50/£32

WELLESLEY, DOROTHY. Lost Planet and Other Poems. London: Hogarth, 1942. 1st ed. Orange cl (sm areas of spine faded), gilt. VG in VG dj (edges faded, sm chip). *Virgo.* $23/£15

WELLESLEY, DOROTHY. Matrix. London: Hogarth, 1928. 1st ed. One of 500. Dec bds. (Edges sl tanned), else Nice. *Reese.* $100/£64

WELLMAN, MANLY WADE. Giants from Eternity. NY: Avalon, (1959). 1st ed. Dj. *Swann*. $57/£37

WELLMAN, MANLY WADE. Island in the Sky. NY: Avalon, 1961. 1st ed. Dj (lt worn). *Swann*. $57/£37

WELLMAN, MANLY WADE. Lonely Vigils. Carcosa, 1981. Subscriber issue w/artplate signed by Wellman & George Evans (illus) affixed fep. Fine in Fine dj. *Certo.* $100/£64

WELLMAN, MANLY WADE. The Lost and the Lurking. GC, 1981. 1st ed. VG in dj. *King.* $20/£13

WELLMAN, MANLY WADE. The Valley So Low. Dbly, 1987. 1st ed. Fine in Fine dj. *Certo.* $75/£48

WELLMAN, MANLY WADE. Who Fears the Devil. Arkham House, 1963. 1st ed. Inscribed, signed. NF in dj (spine ends sl worn). *Certo.* $250/£160

WELLMAN, MANLY WADE. Who Fears the Devil? Sauk City: Arkham House, 1963. 1st ed. Fine in As New dj (mailing fold fr spine edge). *Other Worlds.* $225/£144

WELLMAN, PAUL. Death in the Desert. NY: Macmillan, 1935. 1st ed. Fldg map. Good. *Lien.* $40/£26

WELLMAN, PAUL. Death on Horseback. Phila/NY, 1947. 1st ed. VG. *Mcclintock.* $20/£13

WELLMAN, PAUL. Glory, God and Gold. GC, 1954. 1st ed. 8 maps. VG. *Turpen.* $12/£8

WELLS, CAROLYN. Idle Idyls. NY: Dodd, Mead, 1900. 1st ed. Grn cl pict dec in black. VF. *Sumner & Stillman.* $95/£61

WELLS, EMMELINE B. Musings and Memories. Salt Lake, 1896. 1st ed. Inscribed. Frontis port, 304pp. Full dec leather (sl worn, spine top nearly chipped away, corners worn). VG-. *Benchmark.* $100/£64

WELLS, ERIC F. V. Lions Wild and Friendly. 1933. 1st ed. (Feps lt browned.) *Edwards.* $23/£15

WELLS, GARDNER. East of Gibraltar. NY, 1924. 1st ed. (Lt margin browning.) Teg. *Edwards.* $55/£35

WELLS, H. G. '42 to '44. London: Secker & Warburg, 1944. 1st ed. VG. *Hollett.* $31/£20

WELLS, H. G. The Adventures of Tommy. London: Amalgamated Press, (1928). #1205 of ltd, numbered Deluxe Ed. VG in stapled ptd wraps (sm tears, crease fr cvr). *Antic Hay.* $125/£80

WELLS, H. G. The Adventures of Tommy. London: Harrap, (1929). 1st ed, 1st issue w/narrow cl backstrip, gold dj. (Lt rubbed), else Fine in dj (chipped). *Bromer.* $175/£112

WELLS, H. G. The Adventures of Tommy. London: Harrap, 1929. 1st UK ed. VG + in dj (grubby, chipped, torn). *Williams.* $62/£40

WELLS, H. G. The Adventures of Tommy. NY: Stokes, 1929. 4to. Cl, pict cvr label. (Sl worn.) *Oinonen*. $40/£26

WELLS, H. G. All Aboard for Ararat. NY, 1941. 1st Amer ed. (Corners bumped; extrems frayed), else Good in dj (chipped, stained, faded). *King.* $35/£22

WELLS, H. G. Ann Veronica. NY: Harper, 1909. 1st Amer ed. Dec blue-grn cl. NF. *Antic Hay.* $85/£54

WELLS, H. G. The Autocracy of Mr. Parham. Heinemann, 1930. 1st UK ed. Fine (ink name) in VG 'Low' dj (spine sl faded, chip, sm closed tears, related creasing). *Williams.* $70/£45

WELLS, H. G. The Autocracy of Mr. Parham. London: Heinemann, 1930. 1st ed. (Prelims, fore-edge lt spotted.) Dj (sm tears, chips). *Hollett.* $39/£25

WELLS, H. G. The Autocracy of Mr. Parham. London: William Heinemann, 1930. 1st ed. Red cl. (Lt rubbing), else Fine. *D & D.* $35/£22

WELLS, H. G. Bealby: A Holiday. NY: Macmillan, 1915. 1st ed. Red cl. VG (spine sl dull). *Antic Hay.* $50/£32

WELLS, H. G. Brynhild. NY: Scribner, 1937. 1st Amer ed. VG (lt dampstain cvrs) in dj (edgewear, lt stains). *Antic Hay.* $45/£29

WELLS, H. G. Certain Personal Matters. London: T. Fisher Unwin, 1901. 1st pb ed. Illus wrappers (creased, spine tail chipped). *Patterson.* $31/£20

WELLS, H. G. Experiment in Autobiography. London: Victor Gollancz & Cresset, 1934. 1st ed. 2 vols. Pub's orange cl. (Spines sl sunned), else Fine. *D & D.* $35/£22

WELLS, H. G. The First Men in the Moon. London: George Newnes, 1901. 1st Eng ed. 1st binding gold-stamped dk blue cl. Good (1 plt loose). *Certo.* $165/£106

WELLS, H. G. The First Men in the Moon. London: George Newnes, 1901. 1st ed, 2nd issue in the blue cl. 12 illus. Pub's stamped blue cl (lt rubbing). VG. *D & D.* $600/£385

WELLS, H. G. The First Men in the Moon. London: Newnes, 1901. 1st ed, 3rd binding state. (Sm mk fr cvr, lacks fep), else VG in dec blue cl. *Hadley.* $187/£120

WELLS, H. G. et al. The Great State, Essays in Construction.... London/NY: Harper, 1912. 1st ed. Gilt/black-stamped red cl. VG. *Reese.* $30/£19

WELLS, H. G. The Happy Turning. London: Heinemann, 1945. 1st ed. VG. *Hollett.* $23/£15

WELLS, H. G. The History of Mr. Polly. London: Thomas Nelson, (1910). 1st ed. Grn cl. VG (sl spine loss). *Antic Hay.* $75/£48

WELLS, H. G. The Holy Terror. London: Michael Joseph, 1939. 1st UK ed. VG in dj (sl edgeworn). *Williams.* $39/£25

WELLS, H. G. The Invisible Man. Pearson, 1897. 1st UK ed. NF (sm blind-stamped address fep; spine sl dulled). *Williams.* $1,170/£750

WELLS, H. G. The Invisible Man. NY/London: Edward Arnold, 1897. 1st Amer ed. Orange cl dec in red. VG (spine sl dknd, sl edgeworn). *Sumner & Stillman.* $750/£481

WELLS, H. G. The Invisible Man. NY: Edward Arnold, 1897. 1st Amer ed. Medium orange cl. (Marginal loss 2 leaves; worn, sl discolored), else Solid. *Certo.* $350/£224

WELLS, H. G. The Invisible Man. NY: LEC, 1967. #417/1500 signed by Charles Mozley (illus). Fine in slipcase. *Hermitage.* $100/£64

WELLS, H. G. The Island of Doctor Moreau, a Possibility. NY: Stone & Kimball, 1896. 1st Amer ed. Blue cl, gilt top. Fine. *Appelfeld.* $150/£96

WELLS, H. G. The Island of Doctor Moreau. London: William Heinemann, 1896. 1st ed. Pub's red/yellow cl, stamped in black/red. VF +. *D & D.* $1,200/£769

WELLS, H. G. The King Who Was a King. London: Ernest Benn, (1929). 1st ed. (Lt foxing prelims), o/w VG in VG dj (chipping, dkng to spine; 1-inch closed tear). *Hermitage.* $75/£48

WELLS, H. G. Kipps. The Story of a Simple Soul. London: Macmillan's Colonial Library, 1905. 1st ed. Blue cl, gilt. Very Nice. *Patterson.* $62/£40

WELLS, H. G. Meanwhile. NY: Doran, (1927). 1st Amer ed. VG (ink name, eps lt browned) in dj (worn, torn, rubbed). *Antic Hay.* $20/£13

WELLS, H. G. Meanwhile. London: Ernest Benn, 1927. 1st ed. (Lt rubbed, mkd, spotted.) *Hollett.* $23/£15

WELLS, H. G. Mr. Blettsworthy on Rampole Island. GC: Doubleday, Doran, 1928. 1st Amer ed. Blue cl. VG in dj (edgewear, sm tears, nicks). *Antic Hay.* $75/£48

WELLS, H. G. Mr. Blettsworthy on Rampole Island. London: Ernest Benn, 1928. 1st ed. Brn cl. Nice. *Turtle Island.* $30/£19

WELLS, H. G. New Worlds for Old. NY: Macmillan, 1908. 1st Amer ed. Dec red cl. VG. *Antic Hay.* $50/£32

WELLS, H. G. The Research Magnificent. Macmillan, 1915. 1st ed. 8pp inserted pub's ads. Grn cl, gilt. *Bickersteth.* $39/£25

WELLS, H. G. The Research Magnificent. London: Macmillan, 1915. 1st ed. (Few spots.) *Hollett.* $23/£15

WELLS, H. G. The Science of Life. NY: Doubleday, Doran, 1931. 1st ed. #407/750 numbered, signed. 4 vols. (Lt shelfwear.) *Metropolitan*.* $230/£147

WELLS, H. G. The Science of Life. NY: Doubleday, Doran, 1931. 1st ed. #375/750 numbered, signed. 4 vols. (Paper labels, spine sl dknd, lt shelfwear.) *Metropolitan*.* $230/£147

WELLS, H. G. The Time Machine. NY: Random House, 1931. Ltd to 1200. 7 full-pg color plts. VF in patterned bds, slipcase (sl soiled). *Bromer.* $150/£96

WELLS, H. G. The Time Machine: An Invention. London: Heinemann, 1895. 1st Eng ed. Coarse wove cl (soiled, spine dknd). VG (scattered foxing eps). *Captain's Bookshelf.* $1,000/£641

WELLS, H. G. Tono-Bungay. London: Macmillan, 1909. 1st ed. 8pp ads dated Jan 1909. Blindstamped grn cl, gilt. NF (extrems sl rubbed). *Sumner & Stillman.* $170/£109

WELLS, H. G. Tono-Bungay. LEC, 1960. One of 1500 signed by Lynton Lamb (illus). Prospectus, LEC newsletter laid in. Dk grn cl. VF in pub's slipcase (sl faded). *Pirages.* $50/£32

WELLS, H. G. The War in the Air. Bell, 1908. 1st issue bk in dj (priced at 6/=), white lettered in blue on spine, fr panel. Fr panel reproduces frontis illus, but in color rather than b/w. NF (sl professional restoration) in VG + dj. *Williams.* $4,290/£2,750

WELLS, H. G. The War in the Air. London: Bell, 1908. 1st issue, in blue bds lettered in gold. NF (hinges sl cracked). *Williams.* $195/£125

WELLS, H. G. The War of the Worlds. London: Heinemann, 1898. 1st UK ed. 16pp ads dated Autumn 1897 inserted to rear. VG (contemp pencil name, date). *Williams.* $975/£625

WELLS, H. G. The War of the Worlds. London: William Heinemann, 1898. 1st ed, 2nd issue w/the white pastedowns, eps (scattered foxing, offsetting to eps). Pub's gray cl (lt soiling). VG. *D & D.* $900/£577

WELLS, H. G. The War of the Worlds. Pocket Books, 1953. 1st trade pb ed. VG + in wraps (lt soiled). *Aronovitz.* $12/£8

WELLS, H. G. When the Sleeper Wakes. NY: Harper, 1899. 1st Amer ed. Pict cl (sl rubbed). *Swann*.* $69/£44

WELLS, H. G. When the Sleeper Wakes. NY: Harper, 1899. 1st Amer ed. Pict cl. VG (sm stains text, lt rubbed). *Antic Hay.* $75/£48

WELLS, H. G. The Work, Wealth and Happiness of Mankind. GC, 1931. 1st ed. One of 250 signed. 2 vols. (Spine labels dknd.) *Kane*.* $90/£58

WELLS, H. G. The Work, Wealth and Happiness of Mankind. Heinemann, 1932. 1st UK ed. NF (card pasted to fep) in dj (chipped, dknd). *Williams.* $23/£15

WELLS, H. G. The World of William Clissold. NY: George H. Doran, (1926). 1st Amer ed. 2 vols. (Bkpls), else Fine in djs (sl chipped, faded). *Hermitage.* $50/£32

WELLS, H. G. The World of William Clissold. Ernest Benn, 1926. 1st ed. 3 vols. (Vol 3 cvr sl spotted.) Djs (chipped, torn). *Bickersteth.* $55/£35

WELLS, H. G. The World Set Free. London: Macmillan, 1914. 1st ed. 2 + 8pp undated ads. Blindstamped olive grn cl. NF (sl askew). *Sumner & Stillman.* $175/£112

WELLS, J. S. A Treatise on the Diseases of the Eye.... London, 1873. 3rd ed. 6 chromolithos. (Stamps; cl faded, repaired.) *Maggs.* $70/£45

WELLS, ROLLA. Episodes of My Life. St. Louis, 1933. 1st ed. Inscribed presentation. Bds, blue leather spine. Howes W254. *Ginsberg*. $125/£80

WELLS, ROSEMARY. Morris's Disappearing Bag. NY: Dial, 1975. 1st ed. 6 x 7 3/4. 32pp. Fine in dj. *Cattermole*. $30/£19

WELLS, THEODORE. Narrative of the Life and Adventures of Capt. Theodore Wells, of Wells, ME.... Biddeford: John E. Butler, 1874. 1st ed. 204pp. Orange cl (sl soiled; bkpl), gilt. *Karmiole*. $125/£80

WELLS, WILLIAM V. Explorations and Adventures in Honduras.... NY: Harper, 1857. 1st ed. Frontis, 588pp; lg fldg map. Brn cl, gilt. Very Nice (bkpl). *Karmiole*. $200/£128

WELLSTOOD, F. C. Catalogue of the Books, Manuscripts, Works of Art, Antiquities and Relics Exhibited in Shakespeare's Birthplace. Stratford-upon-Avon, 1925. Cl-backed ptd bds, gilt. (Cl rubbed.) *Maggs*. $16/£10

WELSH, JAMES. A White Baby. NY: Frederick A. Stokes, 1895. 1st ed. Frontis, 190pp. VG. *Brown*. $30/£19

WELSH, STANLEY L. et al. Common Utah Plants. Provo, 1965. 2nd ed. VG. *Brooks*. $24/£15

WELTMER, SIDNEY A. The Healing Hand. Nevada, MO, 1922. Rev ed. VG (extrems sl worn). *Doctor's Library*. $50/£32

WELTY, EUDORA. The Bride of the Innisfallen and Other Stories. London, 1955. 1st Eng ed. Very Nice (sm stain back cvr edge) in dj (chafed). *Clearwater*. $86/£55

WELTY, EUDORA. The Bride of the Innisfallen. NY: Harcourt, Brace, (1955). 1st ed, 1st ptg, 2nd issue w/cancelled tp listing 5 c. dates. Dj (lt stain, chips). *Macdonnell*. $100/£64

WELTY, EUDORA. Eudora. Jackson: MS Dept of Archives and History, 1984. 1st ed. VG in wraps (rubbed). *Turlington*. $35/£22

WELTY, EUDORA. The Eye of the Story: Selected Essays and Reviews. NY: Random House, (1977). 1st ed. One of 300 specially-bound, signed. Fine in slipcase. *Captain's Bookshelf*. $275/£176

WELTY, EUDORA. One Time, One Place. NY: Random House, (1971). 1st ed. One of 300 signed. Fine (lacks slipcase). *Jaffe*. $175/£112

WELTY, EUDORA. One Time, One Place. NY: Random House, (1971). 1st ed. One of 350 numbered, signed. Orig white linen, gilt. VF in box. *Macdonnell*. $450/£288

WELTY, EUDORA. One Time, One Place. NY: Random House, 1971. 1st ed. (Lt scuffing bottom edge), else NF in dj (price-clipped). *Cahan*. $75/£48

WELTY, EUDORA. One Writer's Beginnings. Harvard Univ, 1984. 1st ed. Signed. New in New dj. *Dermont*. $100/£64

WELTY, EUDORA. One Writer's Beginnings. Cambridge: Harvard, 1984. 1st ed. Autographed bkpl laid in. Fine in Fine dj. *Metropolitan**. $57/£37

WELTY, EUDORA. The Optimist's Daughter. NY: Random House, (1972). One of 300 numbered, signed. Maroon cl. Fine in pub's slipcase (bumped, cracked). *Dermont*. $250/£160

WELTY, EUDORA. The Optimist's Daughter. London, 1973. 1st Eng ed. Fine in dj. *Clearwater*. $31/£20

WELTY, EUDORA. A Pageant of Birds. NY: Albondocani, 1974. 1st ed. One of 300 signed. Mint in wrappers. *Jaffe*. $225/£144

WELTY, EUDORA. A Pageant of Birds. NY: Albondocani, 1974. One of 300 numbered, signed. Fine in Fine wrappers. *Lenz*. $250/£160

WELTY, EUDORA. The Ponder Heart. NY: Harcourt, Brace, 1954. 1st ed. Cl-backed paper bds. VF in Excellent dj (sl soiled, frayed, tape on verso). *Pirages*. $65/£42

WELTY, EUDORA. The Shoe Bird. NY: Harcourt, Brace & World, (1964). 1st ed. Beth Krush (illus). Fine in NF dj. *Bernard*. $150/£96

WELTY, EUDORA. The Wide Net. NY: Harcourt, Brace, (1943). 1st ed, 1st ptg. Blue cl lettered in white. (Sm spots), else Fine. *Macdonnell*. $150/£96

WENDLER, OTTO BERNHARD. Soldiers' Women. NY: Harper, 1930. 1st US ed. (Top edge lt foxed), else NF in illus dj. *Lame Duck*. $75/£48

WENDT, EDMUND CHARLES (ed). Treatise on Asiatic Cholera. NY: Wood, ca 1885. 403pp; 17 wood engrs, 8 maps (1 fldg). VG. *Argosy*. $60/£38

WENKAM, ROBERT. Kauai and the Park Country of Hawaii. SF: Sierra Club, (1967). 1st ed. VG in dj. *King*. $50/£32

WENTWORTH, LADY. The Authentic Arabian Horse and His Descendants. London: George Allen & Unwin, 1945. 1st ed. 265 b/w plts, 26 color plts. (Spine lt faded.) *Edwards*. $437/£280

WENTWORTH, M. P. (ed). Forged in Strong Fires: The Early Life...of John Edward Dalton. Caldwell, ID: Caxton, 1948. 1st ed. Ltd to 1000, signed. Some pp uncut. VG in dj. *Lien*. $75/£48

WENTZ, ROBY (comp). Western Printing. L.A., 1975. One of 300. Fine. *Turpen*. $75/£48

WERDERMANN, E. Brazil and Its Columnar Cacti. Pasadena, 1942. 1st ed. Red cl, gilt. VG. *Price*. $44/£28

Were You There When They Crucified My Lord. Cambridge: Harvard Univ, 1944. 1st ed. 39 full-pg plts by Allan Rohan Crite (illus). Black cl, silver lettering. Pict dj (chipped). *Petrilla*. $75/£48

WERFEL, FRANZ. The Song of Bernadette. London, 1942. 1st ed. VG in dj (sl torn). *Typographeum*. $15/£10

WERLICH, ROBERT. Beast Butler. Washington: Quaker, 1962. 1st ed. Fine in VG dj. *Archer*. $25/£16

WERNER, ALFRED. Degas Pastels. 1969. 32 color plts. Dj. *Edwards*. $31/£20

WERNER, DONALD L. (ed). Light and Lens. Yonkers, NY: Hudson River Museum, (1973). 1st ed. (Owner stamp), else NF in pict stiff wrappers. *Cahan*. $40/£26

WERNER, HERMAN. On the Western Frontier with the United States Cavalry Fifty Years Ago. N.p. (Akron, OH: privately ptd, 1934.) Port. VG+ in ptd wraps. Howes W259. *Bohling*. $100/£64

WERNER, JANE. Big Golden Book of Elves and Fairies. NY: Golden, 1951. 6th ed. Garth Williams (illus). 10x13. 76pp. Glossy bds. VG. *Cattermole*. $75/£48

WERNER, M. R. Tammany Hall. Doubleday, 1928. Stated 1st ed. Good (shelfworn, head, foot frayed). *Scribe's Perch**. $10/£6

WERSBA, BARBARA. Amanda Dreaming. NY: Atheneum, 1973. 1st ed. Mercer Mayer (illus). 8 1/2 x 10. 32pp. Fine in dj. *Cattermole*. $40/£26

WERSTEIN, IRVING. Kearny the Magnificent, Story of General Philip Kearny 1815-1862. NY, 1962. 1st ed. 248pp. Fine in Fine dj. *Turpen*. $55/£35

WERTENBAKER, THOMAS JEFFERSON. Father Knickerbocker's Rebels. NY/London: Scribner, 1948. 1st ed. Pict cl. (Lower cvr edges lt foxed), o/w Fine in dj (spine lt soiled, edgeworn). *Sadlon*. $15/£10

WERTHAM, FREDRIC. The Brain as an Organ. NY: Macmillan, 1934. 1st ed. 166 plts. Fine. *Glaser*. $75/£48

WERTHAM, FREDRIC. The Brain as an Organ: Its Post-mortem Study.... NY: Macmillan, 1934. 1st ed. 166 plts on 118pp. Ruled black cl, gilt spine. Jelliffe's name stamp, bkpl. VG (lib stamp tp) in dj (edgetorn, spine #). *Gach.* $75/£48

WERTHAM, FREDRIC. Dark Legend: A Study in Murder. NY: Duell Sloan & Pearce, (1941). 1st ed. Inscribed presentation card laid-in. Black cl. VG. *Gach.* $37/£24

WESCHER, HERTA. Collage. NY: Abrams, (ca 1979). Dj. *Freeman*.* $30/£19

WESCOTT, GLENWAY. A Calendar of Saints for Unbelievers. Paris: Harrison of Paris, 1932. One of 695 numbered, signed. Black buckram. Glassine dj; slipcase. *Swann*.* $172/£110

WESLEY, JOHN. An Extract of the Life of Madam Guion. London: Ptd by R. Hawes, 1776. 230pp (lt marginal browning, sl thumbing). Mod cl-backed bds (rebound), gilt. *Edwards.* $86/£55

WESLEY, MARY. Harnessing Peacocks. London: Macmillan, 1985. 1st UK ed. Signed. Fine in dj. *Moorhouse.* $23/£15

West of Alfred Jacob Miller, (1837). (By Alfred Jacob Miller.) Norman: Univ of OK, (1951). 1st ed. Good in dj (worn). *Lien.* $65/£42

WEST, CHARLES. Lectures on the Diseases of Infancy and Childhood. London, 1859. 4th ed. 755pp. (Rebacked, bds rubbed.) *Fye.* $100/£64

WEST, CHARLES. Lectures on the Diseases of Women. 1858. xvi,672pp. Orig cl (rebacked), orig spine preserved. *Whitehart.* $140/£90

WEST, CHARLES. On Some Disorders of the Nervous System in Childhood.... Phila: Lea, 1871. 1st Amer ed. (5),131pp. Internally Clean (stamp tp; spine sl worn, joints just starting). *Goodrich.* $135/£87

WEST, DON. Clods of Southern Earth. NY: Boni & Gaer, 1946. 1st ed. Pb. VG + . *Beasley.* $30/£19

WEST, HERBERT FAULKNER. The Mind on the Wing. NY: Coward-McCann, (1947). 1st ed. Fine in dj. *Dermont.* $35/£22

WEST, J. W. Sketches of Our Mountain Pioneers. Lynchburg: West, (1939). 1st ed. *Ginsberg.* $100/£64

WEST, JOHN. The Substance of a Journal During a Residence at the Red River Colony, British North America. London: Seely, 1827. 2nd ed. 3 plts, fldg map. 3/4 leather (dry, chipped, hinge repairs), cl. *Metropolitan*.* $218/£140

WEST, LEOTI L. The Wide Northwest. Spokane, 1927. Frontis port. Maroon cl. VG. *Bohling.* $18/£12

WEST, NATHANAEL. A Cool Million. Neville Spearman, (1954). 1st British ed. Nice in dj (sunned). *Ash.* $78/£50

WEST, NATHANAEL. The Day of the Locust. London: Grey Walls, (1951). 1st Eng ed. NF in dj. *Captain's Bookshelf.* $100/£64

WEST, NATHANAEL. Miss Lonelyhearts. Grey Walls Press, (1949). 1st British ed. Blue variant binding. VG in dj (lt worn). *Ash.* $101/£65

WEST, NATHANIEL. The Ancestry, Life and Times of Hon. Henry Hastings Sibley, LL.D. Saint Paul, 1889. 1st ed. 596pp. (Cvr sl worn, lt staining), o/w Fine. *Pratt.* $75/£48

WEST, PAUL. Alley Jaggers. London: Hutchinson, (1966). 1st ed. Fine in NF dj (lt soiling, rubbing extrems. *Between The Covers.* $85/£54

WEST, PAUL. Alley Jaggers. NY: Harper & Row, (1966). 1st ed. (Ink name, date, place), o/w Fine in dj (lt soiled, rubbed). *Hermitage.* $75/£48

WEST, PAUL. I, Said the Sparrow. London: Hutchinson, 1963. 1st ed. VG in dj. *Hollett.* $19/£12

WEST, RAY B., JR. (ed). Kingdom of the Saints. NY: Viking, 1957. 1st ed. VG in dj. *Lien.* $30/£19

WEST, REBECCA. The Fountain Overflows. NY: Viking, 1956. 1st Amer ed. Fine in dj (edgewear, price-clipped). *Antic Hay.* $20/£13

WEST, REBECCA. Henry James. NY: Holt, (1916). 1st ed, Amer ptg, 1st bk. Port. Red cl, gilt. Fine (lacks dj). *Reese.* $50/£32

WEST, REBECCA. The Modern 'Rake's Progress.' London: Hutchinson, (1934). 1st ed. 4to. 128pp; 12 dbl-pg color plts (sl foxed) by David Low. Blue cl-backed dec bds (bumped), gilt. VG. *Blue Mountain.* $35/£22

WEST, REBECCA. The Thinking Reed. London: Hutchinson, (1936). 1st ed. Inscribed, signed. NF in dj (sl edgewear, creased snag rear panel). *Reese.* $200/£128

WEST, RICHARD S., JR. Gideon Welles, Lincoln's Navy Department. Indianapolis, 1945. 1st ed. VG in dj (worn, chipped). *Pratt.* $35/£22

WEST, RICHARD S., JR. Gideon Welles. Indianapolis/NY, (1943). 1st ed. VG (ex-lib). *Mcclintock.* $25/£16

WEST, RICHARD S., JR. Lincoln's Scapegoat General. Boston, 1965. 1st ed, 1st ptg. Frontis. Dj. *Wantagh.* $30/£19

WEST, THOMAS. The Antiquities of Furness. Ulverston: George Ashburner, 1805. (xxii),426,(vi)pp; engr map, 5 aquatint plts, 3 hand-color plans, 2 engr plts. (Fore-edge 1 leaf soiled, corner torn away; ptd backstrip sl defective), o/w Good. *Hollett.* $187/£120

WEST, WALLACE. The Bird of Time. Hicksville: Gnome Press, (1959). 1st ed. (Waterstaining to bds and dj), else NF in dj. *Other Worlds.* $20/£13

WESTCOTT, GLENWAY. Twelve Fables of Aesop. (NY: MOMA, 1954.) Ltd to 975 signed by Westcott, Antonio Frasconi (illus), & Joseph Blumenthal (ptr). Fine in cl-backed illus bds, slipcase. *Bromer.* $250/£160

WESTCOTT, T. Centennial Portfolio. Phila, 1876. 10pp fr matter, 52 chromolithos. Dec cvr. Good. *Scribe's Perch*.* $110/£71

WESTENDORF, WOLFHART. Painting, Sculpture, and Architecture of Ancient Egypt. NY: Abrams, (1968). (Bkpl, emb stamp; corner bumped.) Dj. *Archaeologia.* $65/£42

WESTERMANN, WILLIAM LINN. Upon Slavery in Ptolemaic Egypt. NY: Columbia Univ, 1929. Frontis. Uncut. (Bkpl; extrems worn.) *Archaeologia.* $65/£42

Western Illuminated Manuscripts. John Carter Brown Library, Sale May 18, 1981. London: Sotheby's, 1981. Good. *Washton.* $30/£19

Westerners Brand Book 1946. Virgil Peterson (ed). Denver: Denver Posse, 1947. Ltd to 500. VG. *Perier.* $65/£42

Westerners Brand Book 1953. Brand Book #9. Denver: The Westerners, 1954. One of 500. Brn cl (spine sl smudged). NF. *Harrington.* $75/£48

Westerners Brand Book, Los Angeles Corral, 1948. (L.A.: Westerners, 1949). One of 400. Dbl-pg color plt, 2 fldg maps. Pict eps. Black/white/red pict cl, beveled bds (rubbed, edgewear). VG + . *Harrington.* $85/£54

Westerners Brand Book, Los Angeles Corral, 1949. (Los Angeles Westerners, 1950.) Ltd to 400. VG in dj. *Lien.* $200/£128

Westerners Brand Book. Los Angeles Corral, 1948. 1st ed. Ltd to 400. Fldg map. VG in dj. *Lien.* $100/£64

WESTERVELT, FRANCES A. (ed). History of Bergen County...1630-1923.... NY, 1923. 3 vols. 1/2 buckram. *Kane*.* $60/£38

WESTERVELT, LEONIDAS. The Circus in Literature. NY: Privately ptd, 1931. One of 300 numbered. Uncut, unopened. (Sl worn, sl cvr stains.) *Oinonen*.* $50/£32

WESTFALL, MARTY. The Handbook of Doll Repair and Restoration. London, 1981. 1st UK ed. 18 color plts. Dj. *Edwards.* $39/£25

WESTLAKE, DONALD E. The Curious Facts Preceding My Execution. NY: Random House, 1968. 1st ed. Fine in dj (short closed tears, sl wear). *Mordida.* $40/£26

WESTLAKE, DONALD E. Good Behavior. NY: Mysterious Press, 1985. 1st ed. Signed. Fine in Fine dj. *Old London.* $20/£13

WESTLAKE, DONALD E. High Adventure. NY: Mysterious Press, 1985. 1st ed. Signed. Fine in Fine dj. *Old London.* $20/£13

WESTLAKE, DONALD E. Under an English Heaven. Hodder, 1973. 1st UK ed. Fine in NF dj. *Williams.* $23/£15

WESTMACOTT, CHARLES. Points of Misery. London: S. Jones, 1823. 1st ed. 10 wood-engr plts, incl frontis. (Lt marginal foxing to plts; textual toning, offsetting.) 20 designs by Robert Cruikshank. Teg; marbled eps. Full burnt orange morocco (sl soiled), ribbed spine; orig wraps bound in. *Waverly*.* $110/£71

WESTMACOTT, MARY. (Pseud of Agatha Christie.) Giant's Bread. GC: Doubleday, Doran, 1930. 1st US ed. VG + (lacks dj). *Janus.* $45/£29

WESTMORELAND, MARIA J. Clifford Troup: A Georgia Story. NY: G.W. Carleton, 1873. 1st ed. 338pp + 4pp ads. (Cl sl worn, rubbed), else VG. *Brown.* $30/£19

WESTON, BRETT. (intro). Brett Weston: Photographs. Nancy Newhall (intro). Fort Worth: Amon Carter Museum, 1966. 1st ed. (Owner stamp; rubbed), else NF in stiff wrappers. *Cahan.* $35/£22

WESTON, CHARIS WILSON and EDWARD WESTON. California and the West. NY: Duell, Sloan & Pearce, 1940. 1st ed. (Owner stamp, offsetting half-title, fep; lt rubbed), else VG in dj (rubbed, chipped, torn). *Cahan.* $100/£64

WESTON, EDWARD. My Camera on Point Lobos. Yosemite Nat'l Park: Virginia Adams, 1950. 1st ed. 30 glossy photos. Black bds, spiral binding. Very Nice. *Karmiole.* $300/£192

WESTOVER, WENDELL. Suicide Battalions. NY, 1929. 1st ed. Map. (Inner hinges cracked; heavily rubbed, spine lettering gone.) *King.* $45/£29

WESTROPP, M. S. DUDLEY. Irish Glass. Herbert Jenkins, n.d. (1920). 1st ed. 40 plts. VG. *Cox.* $94/£60

Westward Ho. (By James Kirke Paulding.) NY: Harper, 1832. 1st ed, 1st issue, binding a. 2 vols. Ptd cl. VG set (tp sig clipped; foxed). BAL 15715. *Cahan.* $150/£96

WESTWOOD, THOMAS and THOMAS SATCHELL. Bibliotheca Piscatoria. London: T. Westwood, 1883. 397pp + ads. Grn cl, gilt. VG. *Biscotti.* $150/£96

WETHERILL, CHARLES M. Report on the Chemical Analysis of the White Sulphur Water of the Artesian Well of Lafayette, Ind.... Lafayette: Luse & Wilson, 1858. Inscribed. Wrappers (sl worn). *Maggs.* $25/£16

WETMORE, ALEXANDER. The Birds of the Republic of Panama. Washington, 1965-84. 4 vols. (Sl worn, lt dampstains vol 1.) 3 vols w/djs. *Oinonen*.* $50/£32

WETMORE, ALEXANDER. The Birds of the Republic of Panama. Washington, 1965-84. 4 vols. Color frontispieces. Vol 3 in orig cl. Vols 1, 2, 4 in djs (sm tear vol 4). *Edwards.* $195/£125

WETMORE, ALPHONSO. Gazetteer of the State of Missouri.... St. Louis, 1837. Frontis, 382pp (foxed, scattered marginal dampstaining, bkpl). Orig cl, ptd paper spine label (dknd, rubbed). Sound (cl sunned, extrems frayed, spine head chipped). Howes W296. *Reese.* $600/£385

WETZEL, CHARLES M. Trout Flies. Harrisburg: Stackpole, 1955. 1st ed. VF in VG + gold-tone dj. *Bowman.* $150/£96

WHALEN, PHILIP. Memoirs of an Interglacial Age. SF: Auerhahn, 1960. 1st ed. Pb. Fine. *Beasley.* $45/£29

WHALL, W. B. Sea Songs and Shanties. Glasgow: Brown, Son & Ferguson, 1927. 6th ed. Grn cl (sl faded, worn; bkpl). VG. *Parmer.* $150/£96

WHARTON, ANNE HOLLINGSWORTH. Heirlooms in Miniature. Phila: Lippincott, 1898. 4th ed. 259pp. Marbled eps. 1/2 morocco, marbled bds. (Rubbed.) Contents VG. *New Hampshire*.* $60/£38

WHARTON, DAVID B. The Alaska Gold Rush. Bloomington: IN Univ, (1972). 1st ed. (Ink name), else VG in dj. *Perier.* $35/£22

WHARTON, EDITH (ed). The Book of the Homeless. NY: Scribner, 1916. 1st ed, trade issue. Good (ink inscrip, corners bruised, general use). *Reese.* $35/£22

WHARTON, EDITH. The Age of Innocence. LEC, 1973. One of 2000 signed by Lawrence Beall Smith (illus). 12 color plts. Prospectus laid in. Buckram spine, cotton sides woven in floral pattern. VF in tissue dj, pub's slipcase. *Pirages.* $60/£38

WHARTON, EDITH. The Age of Innocence. NY: LEC, 1973. One of 2000 numbered, signed by Lawrence Beall Smith (illus). Fine in pub's slipcase. *Hermitage.* $125/£80

WHARTON, EDITH. Ethan Frome. NY: Scribner, 1911. 1st ed, 1st issue. Red cl, gilt (lt wear). *Shasky.* $50/£32

WHARTON, EDITH. Ethan Frome. NY: Scribner, 1922. Ltd to 2000 designed by Bruce Rogers. VG (ink presentation, fr hinge sl cracked; bds sl worn). *Antic Hay.* $75/£48

WHARTON, EDITH. The House of Mirth. NY: Scribner, 1905. 1st ed, 1st issue w/Scribner seal on tp verso. Teg, uncut. Red cl, gilt. NF. *Macdonnell.* $100/£64

WHARTON, EDITH. The House of Mirth. NY: LEC, 1975. One of 1500 numbered, signed by Lily Harmon (illus). Fine in slipcase. *Hermitage.* $85/£54

WHARTON, EDITH. Italian Villas and Their Gardens. NY: Century, 1904. 1st ed. Maxfield Parrish (illus). Teg, uncut. Gilt-dec pict cl. Bright. *Quest.* $310/£199

WHARTON, EDITH. Italian Villas and Their Gardens. NY: Century, 1920. 15 color, 11 b/w plts by Maxfield Parrish, 19 photo plts. Pict grn cl (rubbed, bumped, spine dknd), gilt. VG (lt dampstain fr edge 1st few leaves). *Blue Mountain.* $125/£80

WHARTON, EDITH. Madame De Tremes. NY: Scribner, 1907. 1st ed. VG (glue spot fr pastedown; spine extrems sl rubbing). *Between The Covers.* $150/£96

WHARTON, EDITH. The Touchstone. NY: Scribner, 1900. 1st ed. Teg, uncut. Orig grey bds, gilt. (Sl foxed), else Nice. *Macdonnell.* $250/£160

WHARTON, W. J. L. A Short History of H.M.S. 'Victory.' Portsmouth: Griffin, 1872. 3rd thousand. Frontis, 47pp, 3 plts. Mod cl-backed bds. *Maggs.* $133/£85

WHEAT, CARL I. Mapping the American West, 1540-1857. Worcester: Amer Antiquarian Soc, 1954. Inscribed. 2 als. *Dawson.* $100/£64

WHEAT, CARL I. The Maps of the California Gold Region, 1848-1857. SF: Grabhorn, 1942. 1st ed. One of 300. 14 1/2x9 1/2 inches. 26 facs maps (10 color, 17 fldg). Brn cl-backed tan linen bds, paper spine label. Fine. Howes W312. *Harrington.* $1,700/£1,090

WHEAT, CARL I. (ed). Pictorial Humor of the Gold Rush. SF: Book Club of CA, 1953. One of 950 unnumbered sets. 12 numbers, each 4pp + inserted loose repro. Very Nice in lt blue cl slipcase (sl dusty) w/matching liner (bkpl), leather spine labels (lettering flaking). *Baltimore*.* $30/£19

WHEAT, CARL I. The Pioneer Press of California. Oakland: Biobooks, 1948. 1st ed. One of 450 ptd. Marbled bds (soiled; bkpl clumsily removed), cl spine. *Ginsberg.* $200/£128

WHEAT, CARL I. (ed). The Shirley Letters from the California Mines 1851-1852. NY: Knopf, 1961. VG in dj. *Blake.* $30/£19

WHEAT, CARL I. Trailing the Forty-Niners Through Death Valley. SF, 1939. Fldg map, addendum slip laid in. Wrappers. *Dawson.* $35/£22

WHEATLEY, DENNIS. Bill for the Use of a Body. Hutchinson, 1964. 1st ed. Inscribed. Dj (sl chipped). *Edwards.* $23/£15

WHEATLEY, DENNIS. Curtain of Fear. Hutchinson, 1953. 1st UK ed. VG + in dj (sl edgewear). *Williams.* $16/£10

WHEATLEY, DENNIS. Dangerous Inheritance. London: Hutchinson, (1965). 1st ed. Fine in NF dj. *Antic Hay.* $25/£16

WHEATLEY, DENNIS. Dangerous Inheritance. Hutchinson, 1965. 1st ed. Inscribed. Dj. *Edwards.* $23/£15

WHEATLEY, DENNIS. Desperate Measures. London, 1974. 1st ed. Fine in dj (sl frayed). *Madle.* $25/£16

WHEATLEY, DENNIS. The Devil Rides Out. Hutchinson, 1934. 1st ed. Inscribed. (Lt browned, upper hinge cracked; cl soiled, sl stain, bumped, 2 sm splits spine.) *Edwards.* $25/£16

WHEATLEY, DENNIS. File on Bolitho Blane. Morrow, (1936). 1st US ed. VG + . *Certo.* $30/£19

WHEATLEY, DENNIS. Herewith the Clues! London, 1939. 1st ed. Dossier format, clues all present. Wrappers. (Yapped edges sl frayed, worn), o/w VG. *Words Etc.* $47/£30

WHEATLEY, DENNIS. The Mallinsay Massacre. London, 1938. 1st ed. Dossier format, clues all present. Wrappers. (Yapped edges creased, torn), o/w VG. *Words Etc.* $47/£30

WHEATLEY, DENNIS. The Memoirs 1897-1977. London, 1977, 1978, 1979. 1st ed. 3 vols. Fine in djs. *Gretton.* $31/£20

WHEATLEY, DENNIS. Murder Off Miami. London: Crime Book Soc, (1936). 1st ed. Dossier in orig ribbon-tied ptd card cvrs (sl dusty, creased). *Cox.* $39/£25

WHEATLEY, DENNIS. The Rising Storm. Hutchinson, 1949. 1st UK ed. Fine in VG dj (sm closed tear). *Williams.* $28/£18

WHEATLEY, DENNIS. Stranger Than Fiction. Hutchinson, 1959. 1st UK ed. Inscribed. VG + . *Williams.* $23/£15

WHEATLEY, DENNIS. The Sword of Fate. Hutchinson, 1941. 1st UK ed. Inscribed. NF in VG dj (tape repairs rear). *Williams.* $125/£80

WHEATLEY, DENNIS. They Found Atlantis. Hutchinson, 1936. 1st UK ed. Inscribed. VG + (sl damage spine top). *Williams.* $44/£28

WHEATLEY, DENNIS. To the Devil—A Daughter. Heinemann, 1953. 1st UK ed. VG + in VG dj (sl edgeworn, rubbed). *Williams.* $28/£18

WHEATLEY, DENNIS. Unholy Crusade. Hutchinson, 1967. 1st UK ed. Inscribed. Fine in NF dj. *Williams.* $34/£22

WHEATLEY, DENNIS. The Wanton Princess. Hutchinson, 1966. 1st UK ed. Inscribed. NF in dj. *Williams.* $31/£20

WHEATLEY, DENNIS. Who Killed Robert Prentice? London, 1936. 1st ed. Dossier format, clues all present. Wrappers. (Yapped edges creased, sl torn), o/w VG. *Words Etc.* $47/£30

WHEATLEY, HENRY B. The Story of London. London, 1909. 3rd ed. Color fldg frontis plan, fldg plan. Teg. Gilt-dec cl (spine sl faded). *Edwards.* $19/£12

WHEATLEY, WILKINS W. Square Ruggers Before the Wind.... NY, 1939. 1st ed. Diags in rear pocket. VG. *King.* $30/£19

WHEELER, A. O. The Selkirk Range. Ottawa, 1905. 2 vols. Maps in vol 2, loose as issued. Brn cl (lt worn), gilt. *Freeman*.* $150/£96

WHEELER, EDWARD S. Scheyichbi and the Strand; or, Early Days Along the Delaware.... Phila, 1876. 1st ed. 116pp; 12 plts. *Ginsberg.* $50/£32

WHEELER, H. A. (comp). A Short Catalogue of Books Printed in England and English Books Printed Abroad Before 1641 in the Library of Wadham College Oxford. London: Longmans, Green, 1929. 1st ed. Gilt polished buckram. NF in dj. *Reese.* $50/£32

WHEELER, HOMER W. The Frontier Trail or From Cowboy to Colonel. L.A.: Times-Mirror, 1923. 1st ed. Signed. Good in pict cl. Howes W322. *Lien.* $80/£51

WHEELER, JOHN MARTIN. The Collected Papers of John Martin Wheeler, M.D. on Ophthalmic Subjects. NY, 1939. 1st ed. Paper frontis label. Grn cl. VG (inner hinges starting; name; sl worn). *Doctor's Library.* $50/£32

WHEELER, MONROE (ed). Britain at War. NY: MOMA, 1941. Pict bds (sl shelfworn). Dj (sl chipped, stained). *Clearwater.* $39/£25

WHEELER, MORTIMER and KATHERINE M. RICHARDSON. Hill-Forts of Northern France. Oxford, 1957. 50 plts. (Corner sl bumped, lower bd lt dampstained.) *Edwards.* $31/£20

WHEILDON, W. Curiosities of History: Boston September 17th, 1630-1880. Boston: Lee & Shepard, 1880. 1st ed. 143pp; map, fldg facs. NF (fep detached; spine ends lt worn). *Agvent.* $75/£48

WHELEN, TOWNSEND and BRADFORD ANGIER. Mister Rifleman. L.A.: Peterson, (1965). VG + in VG + dj. *Backman.* $65/£42

WHELEN, TOWNSEND. Hunting Big Game. Harrisburg: Military Service Pub Co, 1946. 2 vols. Red cl, gilt. Fine in Fine djs. *Biscotti.* $185/£119

WHELEN, TOWNSEND. Hunting Big Game: Volume II—In the Americas. Harrisburg: Military Service, 1946. 1st ed. Gilt lettering, decs. VG + in VG dj (corners, back edge torn). *Backman.* $70/£45

WHELEN, TOWNSEND. The Hunting Rifle. Harrisburg: Stackpole, 1940. Good. *Scribe's Perch*.* $25/£16

WHELEN, TOWNSEND. The Hunting Rifle. Harrisburg: Stackpole, 1940. 1st ed. VG + . *Bowman.* $40/£26

WHELEN, TOWNSEND. The Hunting Rifle. Harrisburg: Stackpole & Heck, Jan 1950. 2nd ptg. Frontis. VG + (name). *Backman.* $38/£24

WHETHAM, J. W. BODDAM. Across Central America. London, 1877. 1st ed. Frontis, xii,353pp. Contemp cl (edges stained), gilt. *Maggs.* $273/£175

WHIGHAM, H. J. How to Play Golf. Chicago: Herbert S. Stone, 1897. 1st ed. Blue cl lettered in yellow. (Upper corner prelim clipped, sm tear half-title), else NF. *Pacific*.* $259/£166

WHINNEY, MARGARET. Sculpture in Britain 1530 to 1830. Balt, 1964. 192 plts. Good in dj (sl worn). *Washton.* $75/£48

WHIPPLE, AMIEL W. et al. Report Upon the Indian Tribes. Washington, 1855. 127pp; 8 tinted litho plts. Later cl (spotted). *Swann*.* $92/£59

WHIPPLE, LEANDER EDMUND. The Philosophy of Mental Healing: A Practical Exposition of Natural Restorative Power. NY, 1893. 1st ed. 234pp. Gilt-tooled cl (worn). Good. *Doctor's Library.* $50/£32

WHIPPLE, SIDNEY B. (ed). The Trial of Bruno Hauptman. Birmingham: Notable Trials Library, 1989. Aeg. 1/4 gold-stamped black leather, cl sides. Fine. *Zubal**. $20/£13

WHISTLER, JAMES McNEILL. Eden Versus Whistler. Paris, 1899. 1st ed. 79pp. Ochre cl-backed bds, gilt. VF. *Europa*. $86/£55

WHISTLER, JAMES McNEILL. The Gentle Art of Making Enemies. London, (1890). 1st authorized ed. Inscribed w/butterfly. 1/4 cl (sl repair fr joint). Fldg case. *Swann**. $230/£147

WHISTLER, JAMES McNEILL. The Gentle Art of Making Enemies. NY: Frederick Stokes, 1890. 1st unauthorized Amer ed. 2pp ads. Uncut. Orig gray paper wraps. Cl folder, 1/2 red morocco slipcase, ribbed gilt-lettered spine. *D & D*. $200/£128

WHISTLER, JAMES McNEILL. The Gentle Art of Making Enemies. Sheridan Ford (ed). NY: Frederick Stokes, 1890. True 1st ed. Ptd stiff gray wrappers (joints partly cracked). Slipcase. *Swann**. $373/£239

WHISTLER, JAMES McNEILL. Ten O'Clock. Portland: Mosher Press, 1920. One of 450 on handmade paper. Fine gravure frontis port, full-pg etching. Uncut. Full tan polished calf, gilt, butterfly insignia fr cvr. VG. *Hartfield*. $65/£42

WHISTLER, LAURENCE. Armed October. Codben-Sanderson, 1932. Rex Whistler (illus). (Lt spotted.) Dj (sl soiled, rubbed, sl chipped). *Edwards*. $47/£30

WHISTLER, LAURENCE. Engraved Glass 1952-58. Rupert Hart-Davis, 1959. Frontis, 88 plts. Teg. Dj. *Edwards*. $75/£48

WHISTLER, LAURENCE. The Initials in the Heart. London: Rupert Hart-Davis, 1964. 2nd imp. Blue cl. Dj. *Maggs*. $23/£15

WHISTLER, LAURENCE. Pictures on Glass Engraved by Laurence Whistler. Ipswich: Cupid, 1972. Ltd to 1400 numbered, signed. Frontis, 80 plts. Black buckram, gilt. Dec pict slipcase. *Europa*. $87/£56

WHISTLER, LAURENCE. Rex Whistler 1905-1944: His Life and Drawings. Shenval Press, 1948. 1st ed. Frontis, dec tp. Good+ (lt worn). *Whittle*. $31/£20

WHISTLER, LAURENCE. Rex Whistler. 1905-1944. London, 1948. 1st ed. (Lacks dj.) *Edwards*. $31/£20

WHISTLER, LAURENCE. Scenes and Signs on Glass. Cupid, 1985. #377/1200 signed. Frontis, 80 plts. Dj. *Edwards*. $47/£30

WHISTLER, REX. The Konigsmark Drawings. London, 1952. One of 1000 numbered. 11 mtd plts. VG. *Argosy*. $150/£96

WHISTLER, REX. Rex Whistler: The Konigsmark Drawings. London: Richards, 1952. #97/1000. Mtd facs, 10 mtd plts hors-texte. Red buckram, gilt. Brilliant in cl slipcase. *Europa*. $148/£95

WHITAKER, CHARLES HARRIS (ed). Bertram Grosvenor Goodhue: Architect and Master of Many Arts. NY: Amer Inst of Architects, 1925. 273 b/w plts. Gilt-lettered 2-tone cl (lt worn, soiled). *Freeman**. $170/£109

WHITAKER, FESS. History of Corporal Fess Whitaker. Louisville, KY, 1918. 1st ed. (Soiled.) *Wantagh*. $65/£42

WHITAKER, FESS. History of Corporal Fess Whitaker. (Louisville, 1918.) Grn cl, gilt title. VG. *Bohling*. $50/£32

WHITAKER, HADDON (ed). Wisden Cricketers' Almanack 1940. London, 1940. Cl wrappers (corners curling, backstrip worn, sm splits upper joint, sl loss by fraying at tail). *Edwards*. $125/£80

WHITAKER, MARY SCRIMZEOUR. Albert Hastings: A Novel. NY: Blelock, 1868. 1st ed. xii,13-461pp. (Cl spotted), else Good. *Brown*. $30/£19

WHITBY, A. Bird Pictures. London: G. Allen, 1901. 1st ed. Color pict bds. Good+. *Mikesh*. $45/£29

White Kitten. Valentine's 'Dolly Series' Book Toy. n.d. (ca 1918). Shape bk. 190x120mm. 16pp. Pict wraps (sl chipped, worn). VG-. *Bookmark*. $55/£35

White Mountain Guide Book. (By S.C. Eastman.) Concord, 1876. 13th ed. 232pp + ads; fldg map at fr. Dec cvr. Good-. *Scribe's Perch**. $10/£6

WHITE, ANDREW DICKSON. A History of the Warfare of Science with Theology. NY: Appleton, 1919. 2 vols. (Lt cvr spots vol 1; inner hinge reinforced vol 2), o/w VG set. *Middle Earth*. $60/£38

WHITE, CHARLES. A Treatise on the Management of Pregnant and Lying in Women.... Worcester, MA: Isaiah Thomas, 1793. 1st Amer ed. 8vo. (2),vii-xvi,17-328pp, 2 plts as called for (foxed). (Marginal tear leaf S8; foxing; sig.) Orig sheep (sl rubbed, scuffed), red morocco spine label. VG. *Glaser*. $650/£417

WHITE, CHRISTOPHER. Rembrandt as an Etcher. London, 1969. 2 vols. Good in djs. *Washton*. $175/£112

WHITE, E. B. Charlotte's Web. NY: Harper, (1952). 1st ed. Garth Williams (illus). NF in dj (sm chips, tears, spine sl sunned). *Captain's Bookshelf*. $350/£224

WHITE, E. B. Charlotte's Web. NY: Harper, (1952). 1st ed. Fine in Fine dj. *Metropolitan**. $747/£479

WHITE, E. B. Every Day Is Sunday. NY: Harper, 1934. 1st ed. Dec cl (sl dkng, lt rubbing edges). VG in Good dj (rather tanned, sm chips to extrems). *Reese*. $250/£160

WHITE, E. B. One Man's Meat. NY: Harper, (1942). 1st ed. VG in Fine dj. *Reese*. $125/£80

WHITE, E. B. Stuart Little. NY/London: Harper, (1945). 1st ed. Garth Jones (illus). Beige cl. Fine in dj (relined). *Appelfeld*. $100/£64

WHITE, E. B. Stuart Little. NY: Harper, (1945). 1st ed. Garth Williams (illus). Pict cl. VG in dj (extrems sl tanned; chip, tear spine crown). *Reese*. $125/£80

WHITE, E. B. Stuart Little. NY: Harper, 1945. 1st ed. 8vo. Garth Williams (illus). Illus cl (Bkpl), else NF in color illus dj (price-clipped, few sm tears, sm chips). *Cahan*. $125/£80

WHITE, E. B. The White Flag.... Boston: Houghton Mifflin, 1946. 1st ed. VG in dj (lt tanned, short edge tear). *Reese*. $40/£26

WHITE, E. E. Service on the Indian Reservations. Little Rock: Diploma Press, 1893. 1st ed. 336pp. Pub's cl. Good. *Scribe's Perch**. $600/£385

WHITE, E. L. A Popular Essay on the Disorder Familiarly Termed a Cold.... Phila: Bradford & Insheep et al, 1808. 1st Amer ed. (4),xxviii,248pp; add'l 1/2 title for Stuart's 'Annotations.' Uncut. Old marbled bds (rubbed; reinforced w/plain tan linen spine). *Karmiole*. $500/£321

WHITE, E. V. The First Iron-Clad Naval Engagement in the World. J.S. Ogilvie, (c. 1908). Paper cvrs (chipped). VG-. *Book Broker*. $35/£22

WHITE, E. W. Stravinsky's Sacrifice to Apollo. Hogarth, 1930. 1st ed. (Sl dull), else Good. *Whiteson*. $34/£22

WHITE, EDGAR. The Rising. NY: Boyars, (1988). 1st ed. (Pg edges sl dknd), else Fine in dj. *Between The Covers*. $45/£29

WHITE, EDGAR. Underground: Four Plays. NY: Morrow, 1970. 1st ed, 1st bk. Fine in dj. *Between The Covers*. $65/£42

WHITE, EDMUND. Nocturnes for the King of Naples. NY: St. Martin's, (1978). 1st ed. Inscribed w/short note. Cl-backed bds. Fine in dj. *Jaffe*. $100/£64

WHITE, EDMUND. Nocturnes for the King of Naples. NY: St. Martin's, 1978. 1st ed. (Sig), else Fine in NF dj (sl worn). *Lame Duck*. $65/£42

WHITE, ERNEST W. Cameos from Silver-Land.... London: Van Voorst, 1881. 2 vols. xv,436; xv,527pp; fldg map. (Ex-lib.) Adelson. $85/£54

WHITE, FREDERICK. The Spicklefisherman and Others. NY: Derrydale, (1928). Ltd to 775. VG (cvrs lt worn, soiled; spine chipped). Truepenny. $75/£48

WHITE, FREDERICK. The Spicklefisherman and Others. NY: Derrydale, 1928. Ltd to 775. Orig marbled paper bds, vellum spine (dknd). VG. Mcgowan. $125/£80

WHITE, GEORGE FRANCIS. Views in India, Chiefly Among the Himalaya Mountains. Emma Roberts (ed). London: Fisher, n.d. (ca 1838). Extra pict title, 36 Fine steel-engr plts (some loose). Pub's morocco (worn, broken, stains, marginal fraying). Oinonen*. $100/£64

WHITE, GEORGE. Historical Collections of Georgia. NY: Pudney, 1854. 1st ed. (14),688pp; 22 plts. Contemp 1/2 morocco. Howes W353. Ginsberg. $350/£224

WHITE, GEORGE. Statistics of the State of Georgia.... Savannah: W. Thorne Williams, 1849. 1st ed. 624,77pp; hand-colored fldg map. (Lt foxed, 8-inch clean tear to map), o/w VG. Howes W354. New Hampshire*. $270/£173

WHITE, GERALD T. Formative Years in the Far West. NY: Appleton-Century-Crofts, (1962). 1st ed. 5 maps, fldg table. Red cl. Fine in dj (sl chipped). Argonaut. $40/£26

WHITE, GILBERT. Gilbert White's Journals. W. Johnson (ed). NY: Taplinger, 1970. 1st ed. VG + . Mikesh. $30/£19

WHITE, GILBERT. The Natural History and Antiquities of Selborne, in the County of Southampton. London: B. White, 1789. 1st ed. 4to. Fldg engr frontis (short tear), 6 engr plts, 1 fldg. Contemp 1/2 calf, marbled bds (worn). Christie's*. $736/£472

WHITE, GILBERT. The Natural History and Antiquities of Selborne, in the County of Southampton. London, 1884. 3rd Harting ed. xxii,568pp. Pict cl (sl worn, soiled). Henly. $66/£42

WHITE, GILBERT. The Natural History and Antiquities of Selborne. London, 1833. New ed. 8vo. Grn silk endleaves. Black morocco gilt by Kelly & Sons, w/inlaid vari-colored morocco doublures. 1/4 black morocco fldg case. Swann*. $517/£331

WHITE, GILBERT. The Natural History and Antiquities of Selborne. London: J. & A. Arch et al, 1837. Bennett ed. xxiii,640pp (2 sm lib stamps, label remains tp verso). Mod 1/2 grn levant morocco, gilt. Handsome. Hollett. $187/£120

WHITE, GILBERT. The Natural History and Antiquities of Selborne. Buckland, 1887. New ed. Frontis, xxix,480pp, 32 ads. Pict cl, gilt. Good. Henly. $33/£21

WHITE, GILBERT. The Natural History and Antiquities of Selborne. London, 1890. 8th ed thus. xxii,568pp (marginal browning, tp spotted). Aeg. Gilt-illus cl (dknd, spine rubbed). Edwards. $47/£30

WHITE, GILBERT. The Natural History and Antiquities of Selborne. London, 1911. 24 color plts. (Feps lt browned, bkpl.) Gilt-illus cl (spine chipped, sm tear). Edwards. $47/£30

WHITE, GILBERT. The Natural History and Antiquities of Selbourne. London: Swan Sonnenschein, n.d. (c. 1915). xxii,568pp. Contemp grn polished calf (sm splits in hinges), gilt, prize label, gilt badge. Sound. Cox. $44/£28

WHITE, GILBERT. The Natural History of Selborne. Whittaker, Treacher, 1833. New ed. vii,440pp (lt foxing); 18 hand-color plts. Marbled eps, edges. Contemp calf (extrems sl worn), gilt. Edwards. $78/£50

WHITE, GILBERT. The Natural History of Selborne. London, 1888. Frontis, xxiv,416pp + 24 pub's ads; 40 hand-colored plts. (Rebacked.) Henly. $55/£35

WHITE, GILBERT. The Natural History of Selborne. (NY): LEC, 1972. #691/1500 signed by John Nash (illus). (Sm mk spine), else NF in VG slipcase. Hadley. $234/£150

WHITE, GILBERT. The Natural History of Selborne. Ipswich: LEC, 1972. One of 1500 numbered, signed by John Nash (illus). 16 lithos. Leather-backed bds, gilt spine. Mint in bd slipcase. Argosy. $150/£96

WHITE, GILBERT. The Natural History of Selborne. E.M. Nicholson (ed). London: Thornton Butterworth, (1929). 1st ed thus, trade issue. Port, 16 tipped-in wood engrs. Nice in dj (spine tanned, nicks, smudges). Reese. $50/£32

WHITE, GILBERT. The Natural History of Selborne. Grant Allen (ed). London, 1900. 2 ports. Later cl. Good. Henly. $44/£28

WHITE, GILBERT. The Natural History of Selborne. Grant Allen (ed). London, 1900. Frontis port. (1st, last few ll spotted; cl discolored, sl bubbled, spine dknd, sl chipped.) Edwards. $55/£35

WHITE, GILBERT. The Natural History of Selborne...to Which Are Added the Naturalist's Calendar.... London: J. & A. Arch et al, 1822. New ed. 2 vols. 4 plts (1 hand-colored). Orig polished calf (neatly rebacked, inner hinges, 1 outer hinge starting), spines extra gilt. New Hampshire*. $120/£77

WHITE, GILBERT. The Natural History of Selborne...to Which Are Added, The Naturalist's Calendar.... London: J. & A. Arch, 1822. 2 vols. Frontis, plt each vol. viii,351; 364pp (lt foxed). 19th-cent moire cl, leather labels. VG. Reese. $50/£32

WHITE, GILBERT. A Naturalist's Calendar with Observations.... London, 1795. 1st ed. iv-170,vpp (sl spotted), ad, hand-colored plt. Later polished calf, gilt. Henly. $231/£148

WHITE, GILBERT. Thirty Years in Tropical Australia. London, 1924. Reissue. Edwards. $31/£20

WHITE, GILBERT. The Writings of Gilbert White of Selborne. London: Nonesuch, 1938. One of 850 numbered. Eric Ravillious (illus). 2 vols. Gilt-pict cl. Swann*. $805/£516

WHITE, GLEESON. English Illustration. The Sixties: 1855-70. Westminster: Constable, 1897. 1st ed. Gilt cl (worn, soiled). Contents VG. Waverly*. $55/£35

WHITE, GWEN. Toys, Dolls, Automata Marks and Labels. Batsford, 1975. 1st ed. Dj (spine faded). Edwards. $39/£25

WHITE, HENRY ALEXANDER. Robert E. Lee and the Southern Confederacy 1807-1870KL. NY, 1897-1910 rpt. (Sm tear spine top), o/w VG. Pratt. $90/£58

WHITE, HENRY KIRK. The Remains.... Longman, Hurst, 1819 2 vols, w/vol 3, 1822. 8th ed; 1st ed of vol 3. Frontis, vi,336; frontis, vi,316; xix,(i),185,(3)pp. Marbled eps. Full maroon diced calf, gilt. Cox. $94/£60

WHITE, HENRY KIRKE. History of the Union Pacific Railway. Chicago: Univ of Chicago, 1895. iii,129pp, index; 14 charts (2 fldg). Grn cl (sl rubbed), gilt. VG. Bohling. $85/£54

WHITE, JACK. Easier Golf. London: Methuen, (1924). 1st ed. Grn cl, gilt spine. (Soil), else VG. Pacific*. $63/£40

WHITE, JAMES. Sketches of the Christian Life and Public Labors of William Miller.... Battle Creek, MI: Seventh Day Adventist, 1875. 1st ed. 416pp; port. Ginsberg. $250/£160

WHITE, JOHN. The Birth and Rebirth of Pictorial Space. NY, 1958. 64 plts. Good. Washton. $50/£32

WHITE, JOHN. Sketches from America. London: Sampson, 1870. 1st ed. (8),373,(16 ads)pp. (Stain fr cvr, spine faded.) Howes W358. Ginsberg. $375/£240

WHITE, K. D. Roman Farming. Ithaca: Cornell Univ, (1970). 81 plts. Good in dj. *Archaeologia.* $95/£61

WHITE, LAZARUS and EDMUND ASTLEY PRENTIS. Cofferdams. NY: Columbia Univ, 1940. 1st ed. Fine. *Graf.* $38/£24

WHITE, LESLIE A. Pioneers in American Anthropology. The Bandelier-Morgan Letters, 1873-1883. Albuquerque: Univ of NM, 1940. 1st ed. #119/400. 2 vols. Maroon cl lettered in gilt. VF in ptd djs (spines dknd). *Argonaut.* $200/£128

WHITE, LESLIE A. Pioneers in American Anthropology: The Bandelier-Morgan Letters, 1873-1883. Albuquerque: Univ of NM, 1940. 1st ed. One of 400 numbered. 2 vols. Unopened. (Frontispieces lt foxed), else NF set in djs (lt soiled). *Cahan.* $175/£112

WHITE, LIONEL. Death Takes the Bus. NY: Gold Medal, (1957). 1st ed, pb orig. NF in wrappers. *Pettler & Lieberman.* $20/£13

WHITE, LIONEL. Too Young to Die. NY: Gold Medal, (1958). 1st ed, pb orig. NF in illus wrappers. *Pettler & Lieberman.* $20/£13

WHITE, MARGARET E. (ed). A Sketch of Chester Harding, Artist, Drawn by His Own Hand. Boston, 1929. 'New Edition.' Teg. (Bkpl, lacks fep), else VG in slipcase (worn, broken). *King.* $75/£48

WHITE, MARGARET E. (ed). A Sketch of Chester Harding, Artist. Boston, 1929. Red cl. Fine. *Argosy.* $125/£80

WHITE, MINOR. Minor White: Rites and Passages. Millerton, NY: Aperture, 1978. 1st ed. (Owner stamp), else Fine in dj (sl rubbed). *Cahan.* $50/£32

WHITE, MINOR. Mirrors, Messages, Manifestations. NY: Aperture, 1969. 1st ed. Incl 9-pg Comments booklet in pocket mtd at rear; promo flyer laid in. (Sl bumped), else NF in dj (2 sm closed tears repaired on verso). *Cahan.* $250/£160

WHITE, NANCY and JOHN ESTEN. Style in Motion. NY: Clarkson N. Potter, 1979. 1st ed. 150 b/w plts. (Inscrip), else Fine in dj. *Cahan.* $75/£48

WHITE, PATRICK. The Cockatoos. London: Cape, 1974. 1st ed. (Sl bumped), o/w VG in VG dj. *Virgo.* $39/£25

WHITE, PATRICK. A Fringe of Leaves. London: Cape, (1976). 1st Eng ed. Paper-cvrd bds. Fine (label removed pastedown) in dj. *Antic Hay.* $25/£16

WHITE, PATRICK. Happy Valley. Harrap, 1939. 1st Eng ed. VG (top, fore-edges sl stained, foxed; cvrs mkd, dusty). *Clearwater.* $234/£150

WHITE, PATRICK. The Solid Mandala. 1966. 1st ed. NF in dj. *Words Etc.* $28/£18

WHITE, PATRICK. The Tree of Man. London, 1956. 1st Eng ed. Bright (cvrs sl mkd, handled) in dj (sl rubbed, price-clipped). *Clearwater.* $62/£40

WHITE, PATRICK. The Twyborn Affair. London: Cape, (1979). 1st Eng ed. Paper-cvrd bds. Fine (label removed pastedown) in dj. *Antic Hay.* $25/£16

WHITE, PATRICK. The Twyborn Affair. NY, (1980). 1st Amer ed. Cl-backed bds. VG in dj (sl used). *King.* $20/£13

WHITE, PATRICK. The Twyborn Affair. London, 1979. 1st Eng ed. Very Nice (binding cocked) in dj (sl rubbed). *Clearwater.* $23/£15

WHITE, PHILIP L. Beekmantown, New York, Forest Frontier to Farm Community. Austin: Univ of TX, (1979). 2 dbl maps. Fine in dj. *Bohling.* $15/£10

WHITE, PHILO. Philo White's Narrative of a Cruise in the Pacific, 1841-1843. Charles L. Camp (ed). Denver: Old West, (1965). Ltd to 1000. Port. Grn cl, gilt. Pub's prospectus laid in. Fine. *Pacific*.* $29/£19

WHITE, PHILO. Philo White's Narrative of a Cruize in the Pacific to South America and California...1841-1843. Charles L. Camp (ed). Denver: Old West, (1965). One of 1000. VG. *Bohling.* $50/£32

WHITE, RANDY WAYNE. Batfishing in the Rainforest. NY: Lyons & Burford, 1991. 1st ed. VF in dj. *Mordida.* $65/£42

WHITE, RAY B. The Trail of the Desert Sun. Zarephath, NJ: Pillar of Fire, 1931. Frontis port, 8 plts. (Rubbed, fr cvr spotted.) *Bohling.* $25/£16

WHITE, STEWART EDWARD. African Camp Fires. London, 1914. 1st ed. (Last leaf, rep detached, prize bkpl; rubbed, sl loss.) *Edwards.* $31/£20

WHITE, STEWART EDWARD. Gold. GC: Doubleday, 1913. 1st ed, 1st issue w/no illus in the bio of the author at the rear of the vol. Yellow pict cl (spine dulled). Good. *Cullen.* $20/£13

WHITE, STEWART EDWARD. The Land of Footprints. GC/NY: Doubleday, 1912. 1st ed. Dk grn pict cl (spine sl rubbed), else VG. *Terramedia.* $50/£32

WHITE, T. H. Burke's Steerage. London, 1938. 1st ed. VG in dj (chipped). *Words Etc.* $47/£30

WHITE, T. H. Burke's Steerage. London: Collins, 1938. 1st UK ed. VG in dj (dusty, short closed tears). *Williams.* $70/£45

WHITE, T. H. The Elephant and the Kangaroo. London, 1948. 1st Eng ed. Bright (musty; cvrs sl discolored) in dj (faded). *Clearwater.* $39/£25

WHITE, T. H. The Elephant and the Kangaroo. London: Cape, 1948. 1st UK ed. VG in dj (spine sl faded). *Williams.* $39/£25

WHITE, T. H. England Have My Bones. NY: Macmillan, 1936. 1st Amer ed. Pict black cl. Fine in dj (wear, sm chips). *Antic Hay.* $75/£48

WHITE, T. H. The Godstone and the Blackymor. NY: Putnam, (1959). 1st Amer ed. Edward Ardizzone (illus). VG in dj (sl soiled). *Hermitage.* $35/£22

WHITE, T. H. The Godstone and the Blackymor. NY: Putnam, (1959). 1st ed. Fine in dj (sl wear). *Antic Hay.* $35/£22

WHITE, T. H. The Godstone and the Blackymor. London: Cape, 1959. 1st Eng ed. Edward Ardizzone (illus). VG in dj (sl rubbed). *Hadley.* $55/£35

WHITE, T. H. The Ill-Made Knight. Collins, 1941. 1st ed. 8vo. 296pp. Interior VG. (Spine faded.) *Bookmark.* $47/£30

WHITE, T. H. Mistress Masham's Repose. London: Cape, (1947). 1st ed. Good (edges tanned) in dj (spine, edges tanned). *Reese.* $45/£29

WHITE, T. H. The Once and Future King. NY: Putnam, (1958). 1st ed. NF in dj (wear, spine sl faded, sm chips, tears). *Antic Hay.* $45/£29

WHITE, T. H. The Scandal Monger. NY: Putnam, (1952). 1st Amer ed, ptd from Eng sheets. Fine in dj (soil, browned, sm chips). *Antic Hay.* $25/£16

WHITE, T. H. The Sword in the Stone. Collins, 1938. 1st UK ed. VG (sl stain fr cvr) in Good dj (top edge chipped). *Williams.* $273/£175

WHITE, T. H. The Sword in the Stone. London: Collins, 1938. 1st Eng ed. Nice (foxed; sl bumped) in dj (frayed, lacks spine head). *Clearwater.* $187/£120

WHITE, T. H. The Sword in the Stone. NY: Putnam, 1939. 1st ed. Blue cl (spine lt soiled), gilt. *D & D.* $75/£48

WHITE, T. H. The Sword in the Stone. NY: Putnam, 1939. 1st ed. (Sl bump.) VG dj (edges rubbed, short tears). *Metropolitan*.* $172/£110

WHITE, T. H. The Witch in the Wood. Putnam, 1939. 1st ed. VG in dj (frayed). *Madle.* $50/£32

WHITE, W. BERTRAM. The Miracle of Haworth. London: Univ of London, 1937. 1st ed. 17 plts. VG. *Hollett.* $47/£30

WHITE, WILLIAM. The African Preacher. Phila: Presbyterian Board of Publication, 1849. 1st ed. Brn cl over bds. VG. *Old London.* $65/£42

WHITE, WILLIAM. The Pale Blonde of Sands Street. Viking, 1946. 1st ed. VG in dj (frayed). *Madle.* $20/£13

WHITECAR, WILLIAM B., JR. Four Years Aboard the Whaleship. Phila/London, 1860. 413pp (water damage throughout, incl cvr, which is wrinkled). *Scribe's Perch*.* $110/£71

WHITEHEAD, ALFRED NORTH and B. RUSSELL. Principia Mathematica. Vols I, II and III. Cambridge, 1968. 2nd ed. 3 vols. (Ex-lib, ink stamps feps, tp versos), o/w VG in djs. *Whitehart.* $281/£180

WHITEHEAD, ALFRED NORTH. Symbolism. CUP, 1928. 1st ed. (Feps lt browned, tp sl spotted, ex-libris, pencil underlining; spine sl discolored, sm ink spot to tail.) *Edwards.* $31/£20

WHITEHEAD, CHARLES E. Camp-Fires of the Everglades. NY, 1897. 16 plts. Uncut. (Rear inner joint opening; sl rubbed.) *Kane*.* $75/£48

WHITEHEAD, HENRY S. West India Lights. Sauk City: Arkham House, 1946. 1st ed. NF in dj (browned, price-clipped, short closed tear). *Other Worlds.* $75/£48

WHITEHEAD, HENRY S. West India Lights. Sauk City, 1948. 1st ed. Fine in Fine dj. *Mcclintock.* $125/£80

WHITEHEAD, J. This Solemn Mockery—The Art of Literary Forgery. Arlington, 1973. 1st ed. Good in dj. *Moss.* $25/£16

WHITEHEAD, JOHN. Exploration of Mount Kina Balu, North Borneo. London: Gurney & Jackson, 1893. 1st ed. (Sl toning, prelims foxed.) 32 plts (14 hand-colored). Pict gilt-stamped cl (soiled, worn, esp spine, joints torn, fr hinge cracked). *Waverly*.* $1,045/£670

WHITEHEAD, THOMAS. Virginia: A Hand-Book Giving Its History, Climate, and Mineral Wealth.... Everett Waddey, 1897. 341pp. (Paper cvr removed), o/w VG. *Book Broker.* $50/£32

WHITEHEAD, THOMAS. Virginia: A Hand-Book. Richmond: Waddey, 1893. 357pp; 6 plts. Internally VG in ptd wraps (fr wrap detached, chipped, lacks rear wrap). *Bohling.* $20/£13

WHITEHOUSE, EULA. Texas Flowers in Natural Colors. Austin: Privately pub, 1936. Color frontis, map. (Spine head sl frayed.) *Brooks.* $29/£19

WHITEHOUSE, F. R. B. Table Games of Georgian and Victorian Days. London, 1951. (Sl worn.) Slipcase (scuffed). *Oinonen*.* $100/£64

WHITELAW, ALEX (ed). The Book of Scottish Ballads. Glascow: Blackie, 1851. 1st ed. Marbled edges. 1/4 bound in brn, gilt-stamped leather, marbled paper-cvrd bds, raised bands. Very Handsome. *Beasley.* $75/£48

WHITELOCKE. A Journal of the Swedish Ambassy, in the Years 1653 and 1654. London: Becket & P.A. de Hondt, 1772. 2 vols. 1/2 morocco (rubbed, hinges reinforced). *Argosy.* $200/£128

WHITER, LEONARD. Spode. London: Barrie & Jenkins, 1970. 1st ed. 9 color plts. VG in dj. *Hollett.* $156/£100

WHITESITT, SHEILA and R. MOORE. A Memoir of the Indian War. The Reminiscences of Ezra M. Hamilton. Ashland, OR: Tree Stump Press, 1987. 1st ed. One of 250 ptd. 2 maps (1 dbl-pg). Fine. *Oregon.* $12/£8

WHITFIELD, RODERICK. In Pursuit of Antiquity. Tuttle, 1969. 1st ed. Map, color plt. NF in dj (sl frayed). *Worldwide.* $30/£19

WHITFORD, WILLIAM CLARKE. Colorado Volunteers in the Civil War....1861. Denver, 1906. 1st ed. Pict wraps. (Sm repaired tear fr cvr), o/w VG. *Pratt.* $160/£103

WHITIN, E. STAGG. Penal Servitude. NY: National Comm on Prison Labor, 1912. 1st ed. Inscribed. 12 half-tones. Ptd ruled crimson cl. VG. *Gach.* $50/£32

WHITING, F. B. Grit, Grief and Gold. Seattle: Peacock, 1933. 1st ed. Good (sl warped). *Perier.* $45/£29

WHITING, GERTRUDE. Tools and Toys of Stitchery. NY: Columbia Univ, 1928. Inscribed. Gilt-dec cl. Nice. *Metropolitan*.* $57/£37

WHITING, SAMUEL. The Connecticut Town-Officer.... Danbury: Ptd by Nathaniel L. Skinner, 1814. Contemp sheep (sl rubbed). Very Nice. *Boswell.* $225/£144

WHITING, WILLIAM. Memoir of Rev. Samuel Whiting D.D. Boston: Ptd by Rand, 1872. 3/4 leather, gilt-dec bds. VG. *Metropolitan*.* $63/£40

WHITLAW, C. A Treatise on the Causes and Effects of Inflammation, Fever, Cancer, Scrofula, and Nervous Affections. 1831. xxxii,304pp (tp, eps foxed). Contemp linen-cvrd bds (worn). *Whitehart.* $140/£90

WHITMAN, ALFRED. The Print-Collector's Handbook. George Bell, 1903. Teg, rest uncut. 2-tone cl (lt soiled, rubbed, sl bumped; spotted, feps browned, reps spotted, fr hinge tender). *Edwards.* $39/£25

WHITMAN, GEORGE WASHINGTON. Civil War Letters of.... Jerome M. Loving (ed). Durham, NC: Duke Univ, 1975. Fine in dj. *Bohling.* $12/£8

WHITMAN, ROYAL. A Treatise on Orthopedic Surgery. Phila, 1907. 3rd ed. 554 engrs. Fair (binding shaken). *Doctor's Library.* $100/£64

WHITMAN, WALT. Autobiographia or The Story of Life. Arthur Stedman (ed). NY: Charles L. Webster, 1892. 1st ed, 1st issue of this collection. Frontis, 205pp (fep creased, sm tear corner 1 leaf), 7pp cat. Grn cl (edges lt rubbed), gilt. NF. BAL 21639. *Blue Mountain.* $75/£48

WHITMAN, WALT. Good-By My Fancy. Phila: David McKay, 1891. 1st ed, Later Large Paper Issue. Grn cl, gilt top. Mostly unopened. VF. *Appelfeld.* $300/£192

WHITMAN, WALT. Hymn on the Death of President Lincoln. (London: Edward Arnold, 1900.) Ltd to 125. 8vo. Frontis by C.R. Ashbee; 18pp. Full vellum, blind-stamped w/rose logo, motto, 'Soul is Form.' VF. *Bromer.* $650/£417

WHITMAN, WALT. Leaves of Grass, Comprising All the Poems Written by...Following the Arrangement of the Edition of 1891-'2. NY: Random House, 1930. One of 400 numbered. 1/2 morocco, wooden bds (upper joint neatly mended, couple rubs to bds, spine sl dknd, bump spine toe). VG. *Reese.* $950/£609

WHITMAN, WALT. Leaves of Grass. Boston: Thayer & Eldridge, (1860-61). Meets all points for 1st Boston ed. Tinted frontis. Dec cvrs w/butterfly landing on finger on spine. Good- (loose sig; rear bd detached but present). *Scribe's Perch*.* $110/£71

WHITMAN, WALT. Leaves of Grass. Brooklyn, NY, 1856. 2nd ed. Doheny copy. Orig grn cl (recased), spine laid down, gilt (dull). VG (sl foxing) in 1/4 grn morocco slipcase. *Captain's Bookshelf.* $1,750/£1,122

WHITMAN, WALT. Leaves of Grass. Phila: David McKay, 1891-2. 1st ed, 2nd issue (clbound) of the 'Deathbed' ed. Teg. Grn cl (sl rubbed, fr hinge tender). VG. *Captain's Bookshelf.* $400/£256

WHITMAN, WALT. Leaves of Grass. Phila: David McKay, 1891-92. 9th ed. Untrimmed. (Extrems sl rubbed.) *Hollett.* $117/£75

WHITMAN, WALT. Leaves of Grass. NY: Grabhorn, 1930. One of 400. Valenti Angelo (illus). Morocco-backed wooden bds. *Swann*.* $1,725/£1,106

WHITMAN, WALT. Leaves of Grass. NY: LEC, 1942. One of 1500 signed by Edward Weston (photos). 2 vols. 50 photo plts. Illus bds, leather labels. (Sl bumped; labels, extrems rubbed), else NF in slipcase (rubbed). *Cahan*. $850/£545

WHITMAN, WALT. Leaves of Grass. NY/London: Paddington, 1976. 50 full-pg plts. Fine in dj. *Cahan*. $125/£80

WHITMAN, WALT. Leaves of Grass. Ernest Rhys (intro). London: Walter Scott, 1886. 1st ed thus. Frontis port,xxxix,(i),318pp,2ads. Pict brn cl (bumped), gilt. VG (ep edges torn, fr hinge cracked). *Blue Mountain*. $75/£48

WHITMAN, WALT. Leaves of Grass.... NY: Facs Text Soc/Columbia Univ, 1939. 1st ptg. Inscribed by Clifton Joseph Furness (intro). 2 related separates by Furness inscribed, laid in. VG. *Reese*. $60/£38

WHITMAN, WALT. Pictures. NY/London: June House/Faber & Gwyer, 1927. 1st ed. Ltd to 700. Cream bds (rubbed, bumped, lacks spine). Internally NF. *Blue Mountain*. $75/£48

WHITMAN, WALT. Specimen Days and Collect. Phila: David McKay, 1882-83. 1st ed, 2nd issue. 374pp (owner mk largely erased from title; cl sl soiled, dknd, corners bumped). *Cox*. $75/£48

WHITMAN, WALT. Specimen Days and Collect. Phila: David McKay, 1882-83. 1st ed, 2nd ptg. Yellow tan cl, gilt. (Cl sl smudged), o/w VG. BAL 21627. *Reese*. $125/£80

WHITMAN, WALT. Walt Whitman's Diary in Canada. William Sloane Kennedy (ed). Boston: Small, Maynard, 1904. 1st ed. Ltd to 500. Frontis port; pub's device on tp. Natural parchment-backed grn paper-cvrd bds (spine dknd), parchment tips, gilt. NF. *Blue Mountain*. $225/£144

WHITMAN, WALT. The Wound Dresser. Richard Bucke (ed). London: Bodley, 1949. Re-issue ed. Photo frontis. NF (news clipping offset feps) in dj. *Turtle Island*. $30/£19

WHITMAN, WALT. The Wound Dresser. Richard Maurice Bucke (ed). Boston, 1898. 1st ed. Tipped-in title. Teg. (1940 news article glued to feps, inner hinges cracked; worn, spotted, esp spine, spine ends frayed.) *King*. $65/£42

WHITNEY, CASPAR et al. Musk-Ox, Bison, Sheep and Goat. NY, 1904. 1st ed. 25 plts. Dec grn cl. (Sm cl puncture), else VG. *Price*. $59/£38

WHITNEY, CASPAR et al. Musk-Ox, Bison, Sheep and Goat. NY: Macmillan, 1904. 1st trade ed. Frontis. Dec cvr. *Backman*. $100/£64

WHITNEY, CASPAR. On Snow-Shoes to the Barren Grounds. NY: Harper, 1896. x,324pp. Teg. Dec cl. VG (new eps). *High Latitude*. $125/£80

WHITNEY, HARRY. Hunting with the Eskimos.... NY, 1911. Teg. (Cvrs sl soiled), else Nice. *King*. $50/£32

WHITNEY, HENRY C. Life on the Circuit with Lincoln. Boston, (1892). 1st ed. 8vo. Cl fldg case. Howes W386. *Swann**. $517/£331

WHITNEY, ORSON F. Saturday Night Thoughts: A Series of Dissertations on Spiritual, Historical, and Philosophical Themes. Salt Lake, 1921. 1st ed. (Names, bkpl; sl cocked, cvr sl worn), o/w VG. *Benchmark*. $25/£16

WHITNEY, THOMAS P. Vasilisa the Beautiful. NY: Macmillan, 1970. 1st ed. Nonny Hogrogian (illus). 8 1/4 x 9 3/4. 32pp. VG in dj. *Cattermole*. $16/£10

WHITSITT, WILLIAM H. The Life and Times of Judge Caleb Wallace. Louisville: John P. Morton, 1888. Folio. (viii),151pp. Unopened. Good in ptd wrappers (chipped). *Cahan*. $50/£32

WHITT, JANE CHAPMAN. Elephants and Quaker Guns. Vantage Press, (c. 1966). 1st ed. VG in Good dj. *Book Broker*. $25/£16

WHITTAKER, E. T. and G. ROBINSON. The Calculus of Observations. London: Blackie, 1937. 2nd ed. Good (nicely rebound, new eps). *Bookcell*. $65/£42

WHITTEMORE, THOMAS. The Mosaics of Haghia Sophia at Istanbul. Oxford, 1942. 39 plts, 2 color. Errata sheet inserted. Good in wrappers. *Washton*. $60/£38

WHITTICK, A. European Architecture in the 20th Century. Aylesbury: Leonard Hill, 1974. Sound in dj (torn). *Ars Artis*. $94/£60

WHITTIER, JOHN GREENLEAF. Snow-Bound. Boston/NY: Houghton, Mifflin, 1892. 1st ed thus w/new preface. One of 250. Frontis port, vii,(iii),43pp; 9 plts. Teg. Full natural vellum, gilt. Fine. *Blue Mountain*. $185/£119

WHITTIER, JOHN GREENLEAF. Snow-Bound: A Winter Idyl. NY: LEC, 1930. One of 1500 numbered, signed by Carl Purington Rollins (ptr). Untrimmed. Watered navy cl, dec ribbed lt blue cl, silver spine lettering. NF in orig plain parchment-style dj, blue bd slipcase (sl dusty, rubbed). *Baltimore**. $20/£13

WHITTIER, JOHN GREENLEAF. The Tent on the Beach and Other Poems. Boston: Ticknor & Fields, 1867. 1st imp, earliest state, w/perfect 'N' p172. Earliest binding w/single line borders: purple bds, gilt. (Spine lt sunned, extrems lt worn.) *Revere*. $95/£61

WHITTINGTON, HARRY. A Ticket to Hell. Greenwich: Fawcett, 1959. 1st ed. Pb orig. Unread. VF in wrappers. *Mordida*. $40/£26

WHITTINGTON, HARRY. Vengeance Is the Spur. NY/London: Abelard Schuman, 1960. 1st ed. VF in VF dj. *Else Fine*. $75/£48

WHITTINGTON, HARRY. Wild Lonesome. NY: Ballantine, 1965. 1st ed. Pb orig. Unread. VF in wrappers. *Mordida*. $45/£29

WHITTLE, TYLER. Some Ancient Gentlemen. NY, 1966. Color frontis. Yellow cl. VG + in dj. *Brooks*. $25/£16

WHITTLEBOT, HERNIA. (Pseud of Noel Coward.) Chelsea Buns by Hernia Whittlebot. Hutchinson, (1925). 1st ed. Cl-backed patterned bds (sl wear, fore-edges sl discolored). Good (sl foxed). *Ash*. $70/£45

Whole Family. (By W. D. Howells et al.) NY: Harper, 1908. 1st ed, 1st ptg, 1st binding. Orig blue cl, gilt. Fine. BAL 9790, 10607. *Macdonnell*. $125/£80

WHYMPER, EDWARD. Scrambles Amongst the Alps in the Years 1860-69. John Murray, 1871. 1st ed, 4th thousand. xviii,(ii),432pp (eps, 1/2 title, tp lt spotted); 23 plts, 5 fldg maps (clean tears repaired, w/o loss). Grn cl (recased, preserving orig eps; sl defective spine top repaired), gilt. *Bickersteth*. $226/£145

WHYMPER, EDWARD. Scrambles Amongst the Alps in the Years 1860-69. Phila, 1873. (Worn, sl soiled.) *Freeman**. $40/£26

WHYMPER, EDWARD. Scrambles Amongst the Alps. H. E. G. Tyndale (ed). 1936. 6th ed. Frontis port, 5 fldg maps. (Cl lt dampspotted.) *Edwards*. $55/£35

WHYMPER, EDWARD. Travels Amongst the Great Andes of the Equator. 1892. 1st ed. xxiv,456pp (fep, pastedown crudely repaired; sl shaken); 20 plts, 4 maps (3 fldg). (Cl mkd, spine rubbed, faded, perforated hole.) *Edwards*. $70/£45

WHYMPER, EDWARD. Travels Amongst the Great Andes of the Equator. London: John Murray, 1892. 1st ed. xxiv,456pp; 20 plts, 4 maps (1 in rear pocket). Aeg. Beveled bds (sl rubbed; joints tender). *Hollett*. $226/£145

WHYMPER, EDWARD. Travels Amongst the Great Andes of the Equator. London: Murray, 1892. 1st ed. xxiv,456pp; 4 maps (3 fldg). Teg. 3/4 morocco. (Lacks eps, hinges cracked, ex-lib; lib sticker spine, worn), o/w Good. *Worldwide*. $45/£29

WHYMPER, EDWARD. Travels Amongst the Great Andes of the Equator. NY: Scribner, 1892. 1st US (?) ed. xxv,456pp (lt aged, fr hinge repaired); 3 maps, add'l fldg map in rear pocket. Untrimmed; teg. Grn pict cl, beveled bds (sl worn, rubbed), gilt. *Baltimore*. $60/£38

WHYMPER, FREDERICK. Travel and Adventure in the Territory of Alaska.... NY: Harper, n.d. (1869?). Identical to 1st US ed of 1869, incl binding, but w/o the date on tp- possibly a reissue. xviii,(2),21-353pp, fldg map. Dec cl. VG + . *High Latitude*. $100/£64

WHYTT, ROBERT. Observations on the Nature, Causes, and Cure of Those Disorders Which Have Been Commonly Called Nervous, Hypochondriac, or Hysteric. Edinburgh/London: T. Becket/J. Balfour/P.A. De Hondt, 1765. 2nd ed. viii,(vi),520pp (tp browned; prelims, text lt spotted, browned; sm lib stamp recto, verso tp; name fep). Recent full leather, orig label. *White*. $725/£465

WHYTT, ROBERT. Observations on the Nature, Causes, and Cure of...Nervous Hypochondriac, or Hysteric.... London/Edinburgh: T. Becket & P.A. De Hondt/J. Balfour, 1765. 2nd corrected ed. (xiv),520,(2)pp. Contemp calf, leather spine label (joints repaired). VG. *Gach*. $1,000/£641

WIBORG, FRANK B. Printing Ink. NY: Harper, 1926. 1st ed. Black cl (rubbed, sl scuffed), dbl-ptd lettering pieces. VG. *House*. $60/£38

WICKERSHAM, JAMES. A Bibliography of Alaskan Literature 1724-1924. Cordova, AK: Alaska Agricultural College and School of Mines, 1927. 1st and only ed. Blue cl (extrems lt rubbed). Fine. *Argonaut*. $200/£128

WICKERSHAM, JAMES. Old Yukon Tales—Trails and Trials. Washington: Washington Law Bk Co, 1938. Map. VG. *High Latitude*. $40/£26

WICKERSHAM, JAMES. Old Yukon Tales—Trails and Trials. Washington: Washington Law Book, 1938. 1st ed. NF in dj (lt rubbed). *Sadlon*. $75/£48

WICKHAM, ANNA. The Man with a Hammer. London, 1916. 1st Eng ed. (1 leaf lacks corner.) *Clearwater*. $70/£45

WICKHAM, J. D. C. Records by Spade and Terrier. Bath, n.d. Fldg frontis, xxi,438,(ii)pp; 23 plts. (Ex-libris, feps sl browned.) *Edwards*. $31/£20

WICKHOFF, FRANZ. Roman Art. Mrs. S. Arthur Strong (ed). London/NY, 1900. 14 plts. (Eps, text spotted.) Uncut. *Edwards*. $86/£55

WICKHOFF, FRANZ. Roman Art: Some of Its Principles and Their Application to Early Christian Painting. London: Heinemann, 1900. Frontis, 13 plts. Good. *Archaeologia*. $150/£96

WICKSTEED, JOSEPH H. Blake's Vision of the Book of Job.... J.M. Dent, 1910. 1st ed. 22 plts. Teg. (Spine faded, fore-edges sl discolored, cvrs lt sprung.) Contents Fine. *Bickersteth*. $94/£60

WIDE, ANDERS. Hand-Book of Medical and Orthopedic Gymnastics. NY, 1909. 4th ed. Grn cl bds (sl worn). VG. *Doctor's Library*. $50/£32

WIDEMAN, JOHN EDGAR. Hurry Home. NY, (1970). 1st ed. Fine in dj (sl wear). *Between The Covers*. $175/£112

WIDEMAN, JOHN EDGAR. Hurry Home. NY, 1970. 1st ed. NF in VG + dj (2 sm tears, 1 internally strengthened w/tape). *Warren*. $95/£61

WIDEMAN, JOHN EDGAR. Hurry Home. NY: Harcourt, Brace, World, 1972. 1st ed. (1 pg corner creased; lt shelfworn), else NF in VG + dj (short edgetears, sl rubbed). *Lame Duck*. $65/£42

WIDEMAN, JOHN EDGAR. The Lynchers. NY: HBJ, (1973). 1st ed. (Sm creases pg edges), else Fine in dj. *Between The Covers*. $100/£64

WIDNEY, JOSEPH. Life and Its Problems as Viewed by a Blind Man at the Age of Ninety-Six. Hollywood: Joseph P. Widney, (1938?). Frontis port. *Dawson*. $40/£26

WIEBE, RUDY. Peace Shall Destroy Many. McClelland & Stewart, (1962). 1st Canadian ed. Signed. Fine in Fine dj. *Authors Of West*. $40/£26

WIEDEMANN, ALFRED. Religion of the Ancient Egyptians. London: H. Grevel, 1897. 1st ed. xvi,324pp + 16pp cat (marginal ink mks 1 pg). Teg. Black cl (fr joint slit, sl stained, spine ends chipped), gilt. VG. *Blue Mountain*. $65/£42

WIELAND, G. R. The Cerro Cuadrado Petrified Forest. Washington: Carnegie, Apr. 1935. 1st ed. 33 plts. VG. *Mikesh*. $65/£42

WIENER, MEYER and BENNETT Y. ALVIS. Surgery of the Eye. Phila: W.B. Saunders, 1939. 1st ed. Fine. *Glaser*. $45/£29

WIENER, NORBERT. Cybernetics, or Control and Communication in the Animal and the Machine. NY: John Wiley, (1948). 1st ed. Red cl. Fine in dj (sm chip head, 1-inch chip lower rear panel). *Cummins*. $300/£192

WIENER, NORBERT. The Human Use of Human Beings. Boston: Houghton, Mifflin, 1950. 1st ed. Signed. Grey cl. Review slip laid in. (Spine sl soiled), o/w Fine in dj. *Cummins*. $300/£192

WIENERS, JOHN. Ace of Pentacles. NY: James F. Carr & Robert A. Wilson, 1964. 1st ed. Stiff paper wraps. (Fr cvr edge sl nicked, binding lt soiled), o/w VG. *Bernard*. $15/£10

WIENERS, JOHN. Pressed Wafer. Buffalo: Gallery Upstairs, 1967. One of 1000. Pb. Fine. *Beasley*. $25/£16

WIESE, CARL. Expedition to East-Central Africa, 1888-1891. Harry W. Langsworthy (ed). Univ of OK, (1983). 1st ed in English. 5 maps. Orange cl. Fine in dj. *Terramedia*. $75/£48

WIESE, KURT. The Chinese Ink Stick. NY: Doubleday, 1929. 1st ed. 6 x 8 1/4. 199pp. VG in dj (chipped). *Cattermole*. $50/£32

WIESE, KURT. Karoo, the Kangaroo. NY: Coward-McCann, 1929. 1st ed, 1st bk. 7 x 9 1/2. Cl w/pict pastedown. Good. *Cattermole*. $40/£26

WIESE, KURT. Liang and Lo. NY: Doubleday, 1930. 1st ed. 9 1/2 x 7 1/4. Cl spine, pict bds. Fair (rubbed). *Cattermole*. $75/£48

WIESE, KURT. You Can Write Chinese. NY: Viking, 1945. 1st ed. 10 1/2 x 8. Cl spine, pict bds. VG (hinges weak) in dj. *Cattermole*. $100/£64

WIESEL, ELIE. The Accident. Anne Borchardt (trans). NY: Hill & Wang, (1962). 1st ed. NF in white dj (sl worn, soiled). *Antic Hay*. $45/£29

WIESEL, ELIE. The Golem. Anne Borchardt (trans). NY: Summit Books, (1983). 1st ed. One of 250 specially bound, signed by Wiesel and Mark Podwal (illus). Pict eps. Mint in slipcase. *Jaffe*. $125/£80

WIESEL, ELIE. The Oath. Marion Wiesel (trans). NY: Random House, (1973). 1st Amer ed. Fine in dj. *Antic Hay*. $20/£13

WIESEL, ELIE. The Oath. M. Wiesel (trans). NY, 1973. 1st ed. Dj. *Typographeum*. $10/£6

WIESEL, ELIE. Twilight. NY: Summit, (1988). One of 250 numbered, signed. Fine in Fine slipcase. *Lenz*. $100/£64

WIGGIN, KATE DOUGLAS and NORA A. SMITH. The Arabia Nights. NY, 1944. 9 full-pg color plts by Maxfield Parrish. Pict label. (Bumped, sl worn.) *King*. $65/£42

WIGGINTON, A. et al. Frederick Rolfe and Others. St. Alberts, 1961. Ltd to 400 numbered. Excellent in wraps. *Edrich*. $28/£18

WIGHT, J. A. Brick Building in England from the Middle Ages to 1550. London: Baker, 1972. 75 plt illus, 20 maps & dwgs. Sound in dj. *Ars Artis*. $33/£21

WIGHT, SAMUEL F. Adventures in California and Nicaragua in Rhyme. Boston: Mudge, 1860. (Spine ends clipped, corners worn.) *Metropolitan**. $34/£22

WILBUR, RICHARD. The Beautiful Changes and Other Poems. NY: Reynal & Hitchcock, (1947). 1st ed, 1st bk. One of 750 ptd. Good (sm sticker mk ep; lt discoloration lower cvrs) in dj (shelfwear, few spots, price-clipped). *Reese*. $125/£80

WILCOCKS, A. An Essay on the Tides: Theory of the Two Forces. Phila, 1855. Author ink dedication. 71pp. (Spine worn.) *Whitehart*. $39/£25

WILCOCKS, J. C. The Sea-Fisherman, or Fishing Pilotage. (St. Peter Port), Guernsey: The Author, (1865). 1st ed. Red cl (sl worn, repaired), orig oval ptd label (sl defective) tipped in. *Maggs*. $56/£36

WILCOX, COLLIN. Doctor, Lawyer. NY: Random House, 1977. 1st ed. Signed. NF in NF dj. *Janus*. $35/£22

WILCOX, COLLIN. Night Games. NY: Mysterious Press, 1986. 1st ed. VF in dj. *Mordida*. $25/£16

WILCOX, COLLIN. The Third Degree. NY: Dodd Mead, 1968. 1st ed. (Inscrip), o/w VG in dj (sl wear). *Mordida*. $35/£22

WILCOX, COLLIN. The Watcher. NY: Random House, 1978. 1st ed. Fine in dj. *Mordida*. $35/£22

WILCOX, JAMES. Modern Baptists. GC: Doubleday, 1983. 1st ed. NF in NF dj (sl dknd). *Fuller & Saunders*. $20/£13

WILCOX, MARRION (ed). Harper's History of the War in the Philippines. NY, 1900. (Extrems, spine worn.) *Freeman**. $30/£19

WILD, FRANK. Shackleton's Last Voyage. London, 1923. 1st ed. 8vo. Color frontis, 100 plts. VG pict cl, gilt. *Maggs*. $585/£375

WILDE, JOHN. 44 Wilde 1944. Mt. Horeb: Perishable Press, 1984. One of 200 signed, dated. 14 images offset in 3 colors, 9 runs. 14 sigs of French-folded Mohawk vellum cream, hand-sewn on thin ribbons. Prospectus laid in. Fine. *Heller*. $125/£80

WILDE, OSCAR. The Ballad of Reading Gaol. NY: LEC, 1937. #904/1500 numbered, signed by Zhenya Gay (illus). Full leather. NF in pub's slipcase. *Hermitage*. $100/£64

WILDE, OSCAR. Epigrams of Oscar Wilde. Girard, KS: Haldeman-Julius, n.d. Nice in ptd blue wrappers (sl soiled). *Turtle Island*. $10/£6

WILDE, OSCAR. The Fisherman and His Soul. (NY): Farrar & Rinehart, (1929). Signed, inscribed by Alan Devoe. 15 plts. (Spine faded), else VG. *Waverly**. $55/£35

WILDE, OSCAR. The Fisherman and His Soul. SF, 1939. One of 200. Bds, silk. NF. *Smith*. $125/£80

WILDE, OSCAR. The Happy Prince. London: Duckworth, (1913). 1st Eng ed. 4to. 12 color illus by Charles Robinson tipped in, lettered tissue guards. Line illus eps. Teg. Gilt-dec purple cl. (Fep tanned, spine sl faded), o/w VG. *Dower*. $525/£337

WILDE, OSCAR. Lady Windermere's Fan: A Play About a Good Woman. Paris: (Leonard Smithers), 1903. One of 250 numbered. Pirated ed. NF in mauve cl. *Captain's Bookshelf*. $175/£112

WILDE, OSCAR. The Letters [with] More Letters. Rupert Hart-Davis (ed). London, 1962/1985. 2 vols. Vol 1 is corrected 2nd imp. (Vol 1 tp hinge cracked; dj frayed.) Vol 2 Fine in dj. *Clearwater*. $101/£65

WILDE, OSCAR. The Letters. Rupert Hart-Davis (ed). (NY): Harcourt, Brace & World, 1962. 1st ed. VG in dj. *Hadley*. $75/£48

WILDE, OSCAR. The Letters. Rupert Hart-Davis (ed). London, 1962. 1st ed. Buckram. VG in dj (torn). *Gretton*. $70/£45

WILDE, OSCAR. The Portrait of Mr. W. H. Greenwich, CT: Literary Collector, 1905. Ltd to 275 numbered. Unopened. Gray paper bds, paper labels. Fine in plain dj. *Karmiole*. $75/£48

WILDE, OSCAR. Salome, A Tragedy in One Act. NY, (1927). 1st Vassos ed. Ltd to 500 numbered, signed by John Vassos (artist). 13 full-pg illus. (Foxing, ink inscrip, lower margin stained throughout; black bds stained, sl worn.) *King*. $100/£64

WILDE, OSCAR. Salome. Boston, 1912. (Faded.) *Clearwater*. $47/£30

WILDE, OSCAR. Salome. A Tragedy in One Act. SF: Grabhorn, 1927. One of 195. Frontis dwg signed in pencil by Valenti Angelo. Special binding. Brick-red morocco, black-lettered spine, blind pict device fr cvr. NF. *Vandoros*. $475/£304

WILDE, OSCAR. Sixteen Letters from Oscar Wilde. John Rothenstein (ed). NY, 1930. One of 515. Nice (inscrip; spine faded, lacks slipcase). *Clearwater*. $70/£45

WILDE, OSCAR. The Sphinx. London, 1920. One of 1000. Alastair (illus). Gilt-pict cl. *Swann**. $460/£295

WILDE, OSCAR. The Writings of Oscar Wilde. NY: Gabriel Wells, 1925. #503/575. 12 vols. Orig bds, paper spine labels. Fine in djs w/paper spine labels (sl worn, 1 label supplied in facs). *Holmes*. $650/£417

WILDE, OSCAR. The Young King and Other Stories. Folio Soc, n.d. (1953). John Gaastra (engrs). 1/4 maroon buckram, patterned paper bds. (Eps spotted), else VG in matching dj. *Michael Taylor*. $34/£22

WILDE, WILLIAM R. The Beauties of the Boyne, and Its Tributary, the Blackwater. Dublin, 1850. 2nd ed. 324pp (ink name, bkpl), 2 fldg maps. (Fr hinge loose, extrems rubbed.) *King*. $35/£22

WILDEBLOOD, PETER. Against the Law. NY: Julian Messner, 1959. Grn cl (worn, spotted). Sound. *Boswell*. $65/£42

WILDENSTEIN, GEORGES. Chardin. NY: NYGS, (1969). Rev, enlgd ed. 59 full-pg color plts. (Sm stain top edge), else NF in pict dj (lt worn). *Captain's Bookshelf*. $400/£256

WILDENSTEIN, GEORGES. Ingres. Phaidon, 1956. 2nd ed. Tipped-in color frontis, 7 tipped-in color plts. (Ink notes fep; spine faded.) *Edwards*. $117/£75

WILDENSTEIN, GEORGES. The Paintings of Fragonard. London, 1960. Complete ed. 16 tipped-in color plts. (Sm stain spine bottom), o/w VF in slipcase (worn). *Washton*. $275/£176

WILDER SMITH, A. E. The Drug Users. Wheaton, IL: Harold Shaw, 1969. 1st ed. NF in dj. *Sclanders*. $39/£25

WILDER, F. L. How to Identify Old Prints. London, 1969. 1st ed. 105 plts. Dj (sl loss spine head). *Edwards*. $31/£20

WILDER, MITCHELL A. Santos: The Religious Folk Art of New Mexico. Colorado Springs: Taylor Museum, 1943. 1st ed. 64 full-pg b/w plts. VG (cl sl faded along spine, edges; inscrip ep). *Cahan*. $125/£80

WILDER, THORNTON. The Angel That Troubled the Waters and Other Plays. NY: Coward McCann, 1928. Ltd to 775 numbered, signed. Frontis port. Blue paper-cvrd bds (spine chip). VG. *Blue Mountain*. $75/£48

WILDER, THORNTON. The Bridge of San Luis Rey. NY: A&C Boni, 1927. VG (dampstain top edge, binding lt soiled) in VG + dj (sm nicks, tears). *Between The Covers*. $250/£160

WILDER, THORNTON. The Bridge of San Luis Rey. NY: Albert & Charles Boni, 1929. Ltd to 1100 signed by Rockwell Kent (illus). Pict grn cl (soiled, rubbed), brn leather spine label (chipped). VG. *Blue Mountain*. $95/£61

WILDER, THORNTON. The Bridge of San Luis Rey. NY: Albert & Charles Boni, 1929. #809/1100 signed by Wilder and Rockwell Kent (illus). Morocco spine label. (Soiled, spine sl dknd), else NF in slipcase (sunned). *Pacific**. $196/£126

WILDER, THORNTON. The Cabala. London: Longmans, 1926. 1st British ed, 1st bk. (Fore-edge sl foxed), o/w Nice in dj (spine tanned, extrems worn). *Reese*. $175/£112

WILDER, THORNTON. The Eighth Day. NY: Harper & Row, (1967). 1st ed. #489/500 signed. Paper spine label. Fine in slipcase. *Pacific**. $46/£29

WILDER, THORNTON. The Skin of Our Teeth. NY: Harper, 1942. 1st pub ed (4000 copies). Ptd labels. (Ep gutters tanned), o/w VG in dj (sl tanned, nicked). *Reese*. $85/£54

WILDWOOD, WARREN. Thrilling Adventures Among the Early Settlers. Phila: Potter, 1863. Engr frontis, 384pp. (Faded, extrems frayed, shaken, spots.) *Bohling*. $30/£19

WILENTZ, ELIAS (ed). The Beat Scene. NY: Corinth, 1960. 1st ed. Pict wrappers. *Reese*. $35/£22

WILEY, BELL IRVIN. The Life of Johhny Reb. Indianapolis, (1943). 1st ed. VG in dj (used). *King*. $35/£22

WILEY, BELL IRVIN. The Road to Appomattox. Memphis, TN, (1956). 1st ed. VG in dj. *King*. $35/£22

WILEY, BELL IRVIN. The Road to Appomattox. Memphis, 1956. 1st ed. VG (inscrip) in dj (chipping). *Pratt*. $50/£32

WILGUS, WILLIAM J. Railway Interrelations of the United States and Canada. New Haven: Yale, 1937. 1st ed. Inscribed presentation. Fldg map. *Ginsberg*. $75/£48

WILHELM, STEVE. Cavalcade of Hooves and Horns. San Antonio: Naylor, 1958. 1st ed. Signed. (Shelfwear), else Good in dj (chipped, worn). *Brown*. $20/£13

WILKES, CHARLES. Columbia River to the Sacramento. Oakland: Biobooks, 1958. One of 600. VG. Howes W414. *Cahan*. $50/£32

WILKES, CHARLES. Narrative of the United States Exploring Expedition. Phila: Lea & Blanchard, 1845. 2nd trade ed. 5 vols. Lg 8vo. Gilt-dec cl. Good (rubbed, foxed). Howes W414. *Reese*. $1,250/£801

WILKES, CHARLES. Narrative of the United States Exploring Expedition. During the Years 1838, 1839, 1840, 1841, 1842. Phila: Stereotyped by J. Fagan; ptd by C. Sherman, 1849. 5 vols. Lg 8vo. lx,434; xv,476; xv,438; xvi,539; xv,558pp (occasional sl blemish); 64 engr plts, 12 fldg maps. Orig law calf, gilt-panelled backs (sl rubbed), dbl black leather lettering pieces. Sound. Howes W414. *House*. $1,500/£962

WILKES, M. V. Automatic Digital Computers. NY: John Wiley, (1956). 1st Amer ed. 9 plts (1 fldg). NF. *Glaser*. $250/£160

WILKIE, FRANC B. Davenport Past and Present. Davenport: Luse, Lane, 1858. 1st ed. Dbl-pg frontis, 333pp + errata. Blind-stamped brn cl, gilt spine. (Lib gift bkpl; corners worn, spine extrems chipped), else Very Clean. *Hermitage*. $165/£106

WILKINS, ETHNE. The Rose-Garden Game. NY, 1969. (Ex-lib.) *Washton*. $45/£29

WILKINS, G. H. Undiscovered Australia...1923-25. NY, 1929. 1st Amer ed. 46 photo plts, lg fldg map. Red cl. VG in dj (torn). *Price*. $75/£48

WILKINS, GEORGE H. Flying the Arctic. NY/London: Putnam, 1928. 1st ed. 31 plts. VG. *Worldwide*. $22/£14

WILKINS, HUBERT. Under the North Pole. N.p.: Brewer Warren & Putnam, c. 1931. Map. VG. *High Latitude*. $50/£32

WILKINS, HUBERT. Under the North Pole. London, n.d. c.(1931). 1st ed. Frontis port, map. (Blindstamp to flyleaf, ink stamp 1/2 title; label removed upper bd, rebacked, much of orig spine laid down.) *Edwards*. $39/£25

WILKINS, MALCOLM B. (ed). The Physiology of Plant Growth and Development. NY, 1969. VG in dj. *Brooks*. $39/£25

WILKINS, MARY ELLEN. The Portion of Labor. NY: Harper, 1901. 1st ed, 1st ptg w/pub's ads at rear. Dec blue cl. VG. BAL 6366. *Antic Hay*. $45/£29

WILKINS, THURMAN. Clarence King. NY, 1958. 1st ed. Black cl. (Cvr lt worn, sm tear spine head), else VG. *Five Quail*. $20/£13

WILKINS, VAUGHAN. After Bath, or, The Remarkable Case of the Flying Hat. Cape, 1945. 1st ed. Audrey Pilkington (illus). 8vo. 308pp. (Spine, edges faded), else VG in pict dj (tattered). *Bookmark*. $47/£30

WILKINS, W. A. The Cleverdale Mystery; or, The Machine and Its Wheels. NY: Fords, Howard & Hulbert, 1882. 1st ed. Dec fr cvr (extrems frayed, sl rubbed). *Metropolitan**. $28/£18

WILKINS, W. H. The Romance of Isabel Lady Burton. London: Hutchinson, 1897. 2 vols. xvi,374; viii,375-778pp; 43 plts. (Rubbed.) *Adelson*. $135/£87

WILKINS, W. H. The Romance of Isabel Lady Burton. NY, 1897. 2 vols. Frontis port, xv,778pp. Teg. (Feps affixed to pastedowns, bkpl; spines sl chipped, joints sl worn.) *Edwards*. $94/£60

WILKINS-FREEMAN, MARY E. Collected Ghost Stories. Sauk City: Arkham House, 1974. 1st ed. VF in dj. *Bromer*. $65/£42

WILKINSON, GEORGE THEODORE. An Authentic History of the Cato-Street Conspiracy. London: Thomas Kelly, (1820). 1st ed. viii,(ii),(i, paged 'v'),(ii),6-434pp (tp browned); engr port, 7 engr plts, w/add'l plt (trimmed) not called for. Contemp marbled bds, new calf spine. *Burmester*. $90/£58

WILKINSON, J. G. On Colour and on the Necessity for a General Diffusion of Taste Among All Classes.... London: Murray, 1858. ix,408pp, 8 chromolithos. (Cl sl worn.) *Ars Artis*. $133/£85

WILKINSON, J. GARDENER. The Egyptians in the Time of the Pharohs. London, 1857. 2 color plts. (Fep defective.) Gilt-pict cl (worn). *Freeman**. $60/£38

WILKINSON, J. GARDINER. A Popular Account of the Ancient Egyptians. London: John Murray, 1854. Rev, abridged ed. 2 vols in 1. xxvi,857pp, 1 plt. Later 1/2 calf, 5 raised bands, leather labels. Good. *Archaeologia*. $95/£61

WILKINSON, J. GARDNER. The Manners and Customs of the Ancient Egyptians. London: John Murray, 1878. New ed. 3 vols. xxx,510; xxii,515; xi,528pp; 9 color plts (fr edge 1 fldg plt worn). Full tree calf (bumped, joints split, cvr starting, spine missing sm piece), gilt-dec spines, raised bands, gilt-lettered leather labels. Internally NF set. *Blue Mountain*. $185/£119

WILKINSON, JEMIMA. Memoir of.... Bath, NY: Underhill, 1844. 1st ed. Frontis port, 288pp. Orig calf (sl worn). VG (sl foxed). *Second Life*. $400/£256

WILKINSON, WILLIAM. Practical Weaving: Volume 1. Nelson: Coulton, 1915. Frontis. VG. *Hollett*. $47/£30

WILL and NICOLAS. Billy the Kid. (By William Lipkind and Nicolas Mordvinoff.) NY: HBW, 1961. 1st ed. 8 1/2 x 11 1/4. Pict bds. Fine in dj. *Cattermole*. $35/£22

WILL and NICOLAS. The Boy and the Forest. (By William Lipkind and Nicolas Mordvinoff.) NY: HBW, 1964. 1st ed. 7 3/4 x 10 1/4. Fine in dj. *Cattermole.* $40/£26

WILLANS, GEOFFREY. Whizz for Atomms. Max Parrish, 1956. 1st ed. Ronald Searle (illus). 8vo. 104pp. VG in pict dj (sl worn). *Bookmark.* $28/£18

WILLARD, D. E. The Story of the Prairies, or the Landscape Geology of North Dakota. Kalamazoo: Ihling, (1919). 8th ed. Fldg map. Gilt-dec cl. (Heavily rubbed), else Good. *Mikesh.* $15/£10

WILLARD, FRANCES. A Wheel Within a Wheel. Chicago: Woman's Temperance, (1898). 1st ed. 75pp. VG (cl sl soiled). *Second Life.* $125/£80

WILLARD, FRANCES. Woman and Temperance.... Hartford, 1884. 4th ed. 654pp; Fine engr port. VG. *Fye.* $75/£48

WILLARD, NANCY. The Mountains of Quilt. NY: HBJ, 1987. 1st ed. Tomie de Paola (illus). 8 1/2 x 11. 32pp. Fine in dj. *Cattermole.* $15/£10

WILLARD, T. A. The City of the Sacred Well. NY, 1926. 1st ed. Frontis port. (Sm tear tp, lt browning, bkpl; sl wrinkling, spine sl rubbed.) *Edwards.* $31/£20

WILLARD, THEODORE A. The Lost Empires of the Itzaes and Mayas. Glendale: Clark, 1933. 1st ed. One of 1006. Teg. Blue cl. VF. *Argonaut.* $150/£96

WILLEFORD, CHARLES. Everybody's Metamorphosis. (Miami Beach): Dennis McMillan, 1988. 1st ed. One of 400 numbered, signed. Dj. *Swann*.* $69/£44

WILLEFORD, CHARLES. A Guide for the Undehemorrhoided. Boynton Beach: Star Pub, 1977. 1st ed. Signed. Fine in dj (lt soiled, nicked). *Mordida.* $150/£96

WILLEFORD, CHARLES. The Machine in Ward Eleven. NY: Belmont Books, 1963. 1st ed. Pb orig. (Pp dknd, fr cvrs sl creased), o/w NF in wrappers. *Mordida.* $45/£29

WILLEFORD, CHARLES. Miami Blues. NY: St. Martin's, 1984. 1st ed. (Fep corner clipped), o/w Fine in dj (spine, fr panel sl faded). *Mordida.* $75/£48

WILLEFORD, CHARLES. Miami Blues. London: Macdonald, 1985. 1st Eng ed. Fine in dj. *Mordida.* $65/£42

WILLEFORD, CHARLES. New Forms of Ugly. (Miami Beach): Dennis McMillan, 1987. 1st ed. One of 350 numbered, signed. Dj. *Swann*.* $69/£44

WILLEFORD, CHARLES. New Forms of Ugly. Miami Beach: Dennis McMillan, 1987. 1st ed. One of 350 numbered, signed. VF in dj. *Mordida.* $150/£96

WILLEFORD, CHARLES. New Hope for the Dead. NY: St. Martin's, (1985). 1st ed. Fine in dj (sunned, price-clipped). *Hermitage.* $50/£32

WILLEFORD, CHARLES. No Experience Necessary. Chicago: Newsstand Library, 1962. 1st ed. Pb orig. (Spine ends sl worn, sm corner crease back cvr), o/w Fine in wrappers. *Mordida.* $200/£128

WILLEFORD, CHARLES. Off the Wall. Montclair, NJ: Pegasus Rex, (1980). Fine in dj. *Between The Covers.* $125/£80

WILLEFORD, CHARLES. Off the Wall. Montclair: Pegasus Rex Press, 1980. 1st ed. Inscribed. (Lt spotting on edges), o/w Fine in dj. *Mordida.* $175/£112

WILLEFORD, CHARLES. Off the Wall. Montclair: Pegasus Rex, 1980. 1st ed. NF in NF dj. *Janus.* $125/£80

WILLEFORD, CHARLES. Understudy for Love. Chicago: Newsstand Library, 1961. 1st ed. Pb orig. (Bottom pg edges sl stained), o/w Fine in wrappers. *Mordida.* $200/£128

WILLEFORD, CHARLES. The Way We Die Now. Hastings-On-Hudson: Ultramarine, 1988. 1st ed. One of 99 numbered, signed, bound in 1/2 leather. VF w/o dj as issued. *Mordida.* $150/£96

WILLEFORD, CHARLES. The Way We Die Now. NY: Random House, 1988. 1st ed. VF in dj. *Mordida.* $35/£22

WILLEFORD, CHARLES. The Way We Die Now. London, 1989. 1st ed. Fine in Fine dj. *Smith.* $20/£13

WILLEFORD, CHARLES. The Woman Chaser. Chicago: Newstand Library Magenta Books, 1960. 1st ed. Pb orig. Unread. Fine. *Warren.* $150/£96

WILLETT, EDWARD. Cats Cradle. NY: R. Worthington, (1881). Charles Kendrick (illus). 4to. 60pp (rep lacks corner). Grn cl-backed pict bds (sl rubbed, piece off rear cvr). VG. *Blue Mountain.* $35/£22

William and Mary and Their House. NY: Pierpont Morgan Library, 1979. Good in wraps (sl rubbed). *Washton.* $20/£13

William Blake 1757-1827. A Descriptive Catalogue.... Phila: Phila Museum of Arts, 1939. 1st ed. Port. Pict wrappers (sl tanned, soiled). Internally Very Nice. *Reese.* $45/£29

William Blake 1757-1827: A Descriptive Catalogue of an Exhibition of the Works of William Blake.... Phila: Phila Museum of Art, 1939. 1st ed. (Sl stained), o/w Fine in new professionally made wrappers around the old. *Hermitage.* $85/£54

WILLIAM OF MALMESBURY. The History of the Kings of England and the Modern History. John Sharpe (trans). London, 1815. 1st ed in English. One of 50. 1/2 title, 610pp + index, subs list. Uncut. Mod 1/2 cl. Fine. *Argosy.* $275/£176

WILLIAM, FATHER. Three Days on the Ohio River. NY: Carlton & Porter, (1854). 60pp + 8pp ads (1st sig started; dknd, browned). Brn cl (faded, spotted, lt worn), gilt. Howes W444. *Bohling.* $225/£144

WILLIAMS, A. BRYAN. Game Trails in British Columbia. NY, 1925. 1st Amer ed. (Sl shelfworn, shaken.) *Oinonen*.* $70/£45

WILLIAMS, A. BRYAN. Game Trails in British Columbia. NY: Scribner, 1925. 1st Amer ed. Frontis. Gilt lettering. VG + (name, date). *Backman.* $175/£112

WILLIAMS, ALBERT. A Pioneer Pastorate and Times Embodying Contemporary Local Transactions and Events. SF: Wallace & Hassett, 1879. 1st ed. Signed, inscribed presentation. Engr frontis port, xiv,(2),240pp. Grn cl stamped in black/gold. (Lt wear), else Fine. *Argonaut.* $60/£38

WILLIAMS, ALFRED B. Hampton and His Red Shirts, South Carolina's Deliverance in 1876. Charleston: Walker, Evans, & Cogswell, (1935). 1st rev ed. VG. *Mcgowan.* $75/£48

WILLIAMS, ALFRED B. Hampton and His Red Shirts. Charleston, (1935). *Wantagh.* $45/£29

WILLIAMS, ALFRED. Folk-Songs of the Upper Thames. London, 1923. 1st ed. (Back sl faded.) *Hatchwell.* $47/£30

WILLIAMS, ALFRED. Round About the Upper Thames. London, 1922. 1st ed. Map. (Back faded.) *Hatchwell.* $39/£25

WILLIAMS, ALFRED. A Wiltshire Village. London, 1912. (Author's obituaries inserted; lacks fep; cl sl worn.) *Hatchwell.* $39/£25

WILLIAMS, ALONZO. The Investment of Fort Pulaski. Providence, RI, 1887. 1st ed. Ltd to 250. PNRISSHS Series 3, #20. 59pp. NF in ptd wrappers. *Mcgowan.* $45/£29

WILLIAMS, ALPHEUSE S. From the Cannon's Mouth. Milo N. Quaife (ed). Detroit, 1959. 1st ed. VG + in VG + dj. *Pratt.* $45/£29

WILLIAMS, ARTHUR (ed). Birds of the Cleveland Region. Cleveland: Cleve. Museum Nat. Hist, 1950. 1st ed. Grn cl. NF. *Archer.* $25/£16

WILLIAMS, B. S. The Orchid-Grower's Manual, Containing Descriptions.... London, 1877. 5th ed. xi,336pp, 24 trade ads; fldg color plt, 33 plain plts (19 dbl-pg). (Rebacked, preserving spine; cl sl soiled.) *Henly.* $66/£42

WILLIAMS, BEN AMES. The Happy End. NY: Derrydale, 1939. #223/1250. Linen spine, blue cl-cvrd bds (top edge, side, spine sl discolored). *Metropolitan*.* $57/£37

WILLIAMS, C. J. B. Principles of Medicine. 1843. xxxvi,390pp. Orig emb cl (sl cracked back hinge), color eps (ink sig blocked out in ink). *Whitehart.* $140/£90

WILLIAMS, C. T. The Climate of the South of France and Its Varieties Most Suitable for Invalids. 1867. viii,90pp. (Eps, spine spotted; joints sl weak.) *Whitehart.* $39/£25

WILLIAMS, CHARLES H. Last Tour of Duty at the Siege of Charleston. Providence, 1882. 1st ed. Ltd to 250. PNRISSHS Series 2, #16. 29pp. NF in ptd wrappers. *Mcgowan.* $45/£29

WILLIAMS, CHARLES. Dead Calm. NY: Viking, (1963). 1st ed. Fine in dj (sl rubbed). *Between The Covers.* $150/£96

WILLIAMS, CHARLES. He Came Down from Heaven and the Forgiveness of Sins. London: Faber & Faber, (1950). 1st ed. Nice in dj (sl tanned, 2 edge tears mended on verso). *Reese.* $35/£22

WILLIAMS, CHARLES. The Sailcloth Shroud. NY: Viking, 1960. 1st ed. VG in dj (spine faded, worn; back panel soiled). *Mordida.* $45/£29

WILLIAMS, CHARLES. The Sailcloth Shroud. NY: Viking, 1960. 1st ed. White cl spine. (Stamp; spine sl foxed), else Fine in dj (spine sl sunned). *Between The Covers.* $150/£96

WILLIAMS, CHARLES. Shadows of Ecstasy. London: Gollancz, 1933. 1st ed. VG (inscrip, lt offsetting feps; foxing feps, pg edges) in dj (spine dknd, lt worn). *Lame Duck.* $275/£176

WILLIAMS, CHARLES. Thomas Cranmer of Canterbury. OUP, 1936. 1st Eng ed. Nice in dj (chipped, rubbed). *Clearwater.* $47/£30

WILLIAMS, CHARLES. Thomas Cranmer of Canterbury. Canterbury, 1936. 1st Eng ed. Card wrappers. (Name; dust-mkd, spine sl worn.) *Clearwater.* $78/£50

WILLIAMS, CHAUNCEY P. Lone Elk, Life Story of Bill Williams.... Denver, 1935. 1st ed. One of 500. Pb. 2 vols. Fine. Howes W449. *Turpen.* $150/£96

WILLIAMS, CLARENCE. Gulf Coast Blues. NY: Clarence Williams Music, 1923. (Sl wear), else VG in pict self-wrappers. *Cahan.* $35/£22

WILLIAMS, CLAYTON W. Texas' Last Frontier. Ernest Wallace (ed). College Station, TX: Texas A&M Univ, 1982. 1st ed. Fine in dj. *Gibbs.* $35/£22

WILLIAMS, D. E. The Life and Correspondence of Sir Thomas Lawrence. London: Henry Colburn & Richard Bentley, 1831. 2 vols. Full leather, gilt. *Metropolitan*.* $75/£48

WILLIAMS, DAVID. Too Quick Despairer. A Life of Arthur Hugh Clough. London: Hart-Davis, 1969. 1st ed. VG in dj. *Cox.* $12/£8

WILLIAMS, DAVID. Treasure in Roubles. London: Macmillan, 1986. 1st ed. VF in dj. *Mordida.* $45/£29

WILLIAMS, DAVID. Unholy Writ. London: CCC, 1976. 1st ed. Fine in dj. *Mordida.* $45/£29

WILLIAMS, DOROTHY HUNT. Historic Virginia Gardens. Univ of VA, (c. 1975). 1st ed. VG. *Book Broker.* $75/£48

WILLIAMS, E. Walks and Talks with Fellman. Burnley: John R. Ainsworth, 1951. 1st ed. VG in dj (sl dusty). *Hollett.* $44/£28

WILLIAMS, EDWARD. The Doctor in Court. Balt, 1930. VG. *Fye.* $45/£29

WILLIAMS, EDWARD. The Walled City: A Story of the Criminal Insane. NY/London: Funk & Wagnalls, 1913. 1st ed. 15 plts. Emb beveled brn cl (rubbed). *Gach.* $35/£22

WILLIAMS, GARDNER F. The Diamond Mines of South Africa. NY: Macmillan, 1902. 1st ed. Fldg map, 30 plts (5 color). (Lt rubbed.) *Adelson.* $200/£128

WILLIAMS, GARDNER F. The Diamond Mines of South Africa. NY, 1905. 2 vols. (Inner hinges loose.) Aeg. 3/4 leather (spines, extrems chipped). *King.* $250/£160

WILLIAMS, GARDNER F. The Diamond Mines of South Africa. NY, 1906. 2 vols. 28 plts (3 color), 15 maps (4 color). Uncut, largely unopened. Recent 1/2 morocco. Fine. *Henly.* $343/£220

WILLIAMS, GEORGE. Bullet and Shell. War as the Soldiers Saw It.... NY, 1882. 1st ed. 454pp. VG. *Fye.* $150/£96

WILLIAMS, H. NOEL. The Life and Letters of Admiral Sir Charles Napier. London, 1917. Frontis port. Blue cl (spine faded). *Maggs.* $101/£65

WILLIAMS, HAROLD. Book Clubs and Printing Societies of Great Britain. London: First Edition Club, 1929. Ltd to 750 ptd. Dec cl. VG. *Truepenny.* $85/£54

WILLIAMS, HENRY S. The History of the Art of Writing. London/NY, (1902). 3 (of 4) vols. 3/4 red leather. (Ex-lib, scuffed, plt margins perf, mks), else Good. *King.* $195/£125

WILLIAMS, HENRY S. Luther Burbank: His Life and Work. NY: Hearst's International Library Co, 1915. 8 color plts, 32 half-tone plts. (1/4-inch nick fr cvr.) *Brooks.* $45/£29

WILLIAMS, I. A. Points in Eighteenth Century Verse. London, 1934. Ltd to 500. 4 collotype plts, 9 facs. Uncut. Vellum-look paper-backed marbled bds (sl bumped, sl chipped), gilt. *Maggs.* $109/£70

WILLIAMS, IOLO. Early English Watercolours. The Connoisseur, 1952. 1st ed. Color frontis, 200 plts. (Upper hinge cracked, sl shaken; cl edges sl faded.) Dj (worn, torn, some loss). *Edwards.* $86/£55

WILLIAMS, IOLO. Early English Watercolours. London: Connoisseur, 1952. 1st ed. Color frontis, 200 plts. VG in dj. *Hollett.* $203/£130

WILLIAMS, J. L. The Land of Sleepy Hollow and the Home of Washington Irving. NY: Putnam, 1887. #160/600. Dec pict pastedown cvr. (Head, foot bumped; rear cvr stained), o/w Good+. *Scribe's Perch*.* $38/£24

WILLIAMS, JAMES H. Blow the Man Down! NY: Dutton, 1959. 1st ed. VG in illus dj. *Petrilla.* $25/£16

WILLIAMS, JAMES. Seventy-Five Years on the Border. Kansas City: Standard Ptg, 1912. VG+. *Bohling.* $30/£19

WILLIAMS, JAY. Stage Left. NY: Scribner, 1974. 1st ed. Fine in Fine dj. *Beasley.* $30/£19

WILLIAMS, JOHN A. and CHARLES F. HARRIS (eds). Amistad 1: Writings on Black History and Culture. NY: Random House, (1970). 1st ed. Fine in dj. *Between The Covers.* $55/£35

WILLIAMS, JOHN. A Narrative of Missionary Enterprises in the South Sea Islands. London: John Snow, 1839. Color frontis, xx,506pp; fldg map, 5 plts. Aeg. Blind-stamped red morocco (rubbed). *Adelson.* $275/£176

WILLIAMS, JONATHAN et al. I Shall Save One Land Unvisited. Frankfort, KY: Gnomon Press, 1978. 1st ed. NF in illus stiff wrappers. *Cahan.* $45/£29

WILLIAMS, JONATHAN (ed). Madeira and Toasts for Basil Bunting's 75th Birthday. Jargon, 1977. One of 1250. Fine in wraps. *Poetry Bookshop.* $19/£12

WILLIAMS, JONATHAN. Blues and Roots Rue and Bluets. NY, 1971. 1st Amer ed. Pict bds. Fine in glassine dj (sl torn, 2 pieces missing). *Polyanthos.* $35/£22

WILLIAMS, KENNETH POWERS. Lincoln Finds a General; A Military Study of the Civil War. NY: Macmillan, 1949-1959. 1st ptg vols 1-3, 5; 2nd ptg vol 4. Inscribed presentation. VG set. *Mcgowan.* $150/£96

WILLIAMS, L. A. Road Transport in Cumbria in the Nineteenth Century. London: Allen & Unwin, 1975. 1st ed. VG in dj. *Hollett.* $39/£25

WILLIAMS, LIEUT. COL. The Life and Times of the Late Duke of Wellington. London/NY: London Ptg & Pub Co, n.d. (c. 1850?). 2 vols. Frontispieces, xxiv,344; 408pp. Contemp 1/2 calf, marbled bds (sl worn). *Maggs.* $351/£225

WILLIAMS, MARTIN. Where's the Melody? NY: Pantheon, 1966. 1st ed. Fine in NF dj (few pen indents rear panel). *Beasley.* $45/£29

WILLIAMS, MARY FLOYD. History of the San Francisco Committee of Vigilance of 1851. Berkeley: Univ of CA, 1921. 1st ed. Blue cl (sl worn, rubbed). NF. *Harrington.* $100/£64

WILLIAMS, NEVILLE. Contraband Cargoes. London, 1959. 1st ed. Dj (chipped, sl loss). *Edwards.* $31/£20

WILLIAMS, PAUL R. The Small Home of Tomorrow. Hollywood: Murray & Gee, 1945. Grn-stamped lt grn cl (tips bumped). *Dawson.* $100/£64

WILLIAMS, R. WELLS. The Middle Kingdom. NY, 1898. 2 vols. Map. (Fr cvr 1 vol sl loose.) *Petersfield.* $133/£85

WILLIAMS, RALPH D. The Honorable Peter White. Cleveland: Penton Publishing, (1905). Photo inset cvr. Fine. *Perier.* $50/£32

WILLIAMS, RAYMOND. People of the Black Mountains. C&W, 1989-90. 1st ed. 2 vols. Djs. *Edwards.* $39/£25

WILLIAMS, ROBERT F. Youth of Shakespeare. Henry Colburn, 1839. 3 vols. Pub's ad ll vols I, III. Cl-backed bds. Good (ex-lib, labels fr pastedowns, stamps tps, edges several ll frayed; rebacked, orig backstrips relaid). *Tiger.* $94/£60

WILLIAMS, ROBERT R. and TOM D. SPIES. Vitamin B1 (Thiamin) and Its Use in Medicine. NY, 1938. 1st ed. VG (extrems sl worn). *Doctor's Library.* $65/£42

WILLIAMS, S. WELLS. The Middle Kingdom. A Survey...of the Chinese Empire and Its Inhabitants. NY: Scribner, 1883. Rev ed. 2 vols. Fldg frontis each vol (1 color), xxv,836; xii,775pp; fldg map in pocket. Blue cl, gilt. VG + . *House.* $250/£160

WILLIAMS, SAMUEL. The Natural and Civil History of Vermont. Walpole, 1794. 1st ed. Engr fldg map. (Sm portion upper margin excised then restored, loss of 1 letter.) Contemp tree sheep. Howes W478. *Swann*.* $138/£88

WILLIAMS, SAMUEL. The Natural and Civil History of Vermont. Burlington: Samuel Mills, 1809. 2nd ed. 2 vols. 514,errata; 488pp (lt foxed); lg fldg map. Mod 1/2 tan calf, red labels. Howes W478. *Adelson.* $225/£144

WILLIAMS, SAMUEL. The Natural and Civil History of Vermont.... Burlington, 1809. 2nd ed. 2 vols. Early calf (skillfully rebacked; lt foxed, lacks map, bk labels), orig backs. Howes W478. *Swann*.* $57/£37

WILLIAMS, STEPHEN W. American Medical Biography.... Greenfield, 1845. 664pp, 9 engrs. Victorian emb cl (worn). *Goodrich.* $175/£112

WILLIAMS, SYDNEY B. Antique Blue and White Spode. London: Batsford, 1945. (Eps sl spotted.) *Hollett.* $62/£40

WILLIAMS, T. HARRY. Hayes of the Twenty-Third. NY, 1965. 1st ed. VG in VG dj. *Mcclintock.* $42/£27

WILLIAMS, T. HARRY. Lincoln and His Generals. NY, (1952). 1st ed. Fine. *Pratt.* $35/£22

WILLIAMS, TENNESSEE. Cat on a Hot Tin Roof. NY: New Directions, (1955). 1st ed. (Bkpl partially removed fr pastedown), 1 plt. Tan cl. NF in VG dj (top edge sl chipped). *Blue Mountain.* $125/£80

WILLIAMS, TENNESSEE. The Glass Menagerie. NY: Random House, (1945). 1st ed. Rust cl (rear dampstained), gilt. VG in ptd dj (chipped, dampstained). *Blue Mountain.* $125/£80

WILLIAMS, TENNESSEE. The Glass Menagerie. NY: Random House, (1945). 1st ed. Fine in dj (lt rubbed, spine sl faded). *Captain's Bookshelf.* $300/£192

WILLIAMS, TENNESSEE. The Knightly Quest and Other Stories. New Directions, (1966). 1st ed. Fine in dj (sl dust-mkd). *Certo.* $30/£19

WILLIAMS, TENNESSEE. The Knightly Quest and Other Stories. NY, 1966. 1st ed. VG in VG dj. *Smith.* $25/£16

WILLIAMS, TENNESSEE. The Knightly Quest. (NY): New Directions, (1966). 1st ed in bk form. Signed. Fine in white dj (edges sl dknd). *Reese.* $250/£160

WILLIAMS, TENNESSEE. The Milk Train Doesn't Stop Here Anymore. (NY): New Directions, 1964. 1st ed, 2nd (1st pub) state, w/pp19-22 as cancels. Signed. Fine in dj. *Reese.* $150/£96

WILLIAMS, TENNESSEE. Moise and the World of Reason. NY, (1975). 1st ed. Fine in dj. *Argosy.* $30/£19

WILLIAMS, TENNESSEE. Moise and the World of Reason. NY: S&S, (1975). 1st trade ed. Black cl. Fine in dj. *Blue Mountain.* $25/£16

WILLIAMS, TENNESSEE. Moise and the World of Reason. NY: S&S, (1975). One of 350 numbered, signed. Fine in full leather. *Lenz.* $250/£160

WILLIAMS, TENNESSEE. One Arm and Other Stories. (NY): New Directions, (1948). 1st ed. One of 1500 ptd. 1/2 cl, dec bds. NF in VG slipcase (irregularly sunned), paper cvr label. *Pacific*.* $92/£59

WILLIAMS, TENNESSEE. The Roman Spring of Mrs. Stone. (NY): New Directions, (1950). 1st ed. Fine in dj (lt rubbed, chipped, short closed tear). *Hermitage.* $65/£42

WILLIAMS, TENNESSEE. Steps Must Be Gentle. NY: Targ Editions, (1980). 1st ed. One of 350 signed. Lt gray-blue cl-backed bds, gilt. Fine in tissue dj. *Blue Mountain.* $150/£96

WILLIAMS, TENNESSEE. A Streetcar Named Desire. (NY): New Directions, (1947). 1st ed. Dec pink/white/black cl. VG (sunned) in dj (sunned, sm pieces missing upper panel, esp rear; flaps clipped). *Pacific*.* $288/£185

WILLIAMS, TENNESSEE. A Streetcar Named Desire. NY: LEC, 1982. One of 2000 numbered, signed by Al Hirschfeld (illus). Litho frontis; newsletter laid in. 1/4 calf, dec cl over bds. Fine in slipcase. *Reese.* $175/£112

WILLIAMS, TENNESSEE. Sweet Bird of Youth. London: Secker & Warburg, 1959. 1st Eng ed. Fine in Fine dj. *Dermont.* $35/£22

WILLIAMS, TENNESSEE. The Two-Character Play. (NY): New Directions, (1969). One of 350 numbered, signed. Fine in Fine slipcase. *Lenz.* $350/£224

WILLIAMS, URSULA MORAY. Grandpapa's Folly and the Woodworm-Bookworm. C&W, 1974. 1st ed. Faith Jaques (illus). 10 3/4 x 8 3/4. 32pp. Fine in dj. *Cattermole.* $45/£29

WILLIAMS, VALENTINE. The Fox Prowls. Boston: Houghton-Mifflin, 1939. 1st ed. VF in pict dj (sl worn). *Else Fine.* $40/£26

WILLIAMS, VALENTINE. The Spider's Touch. Boston: Houghton Mifflin, 1936. 1st Amer ed. VG in dj (spine ends frayed, closed tears, chips). *Mordida.* $45/£29

WILLIAMS, VALENTINE. The Yellow Streak. Boston, 1922. 1st ed. Fine in pict dj (sm chips, lt worn). *Else Fine.* $85/£54

WILLIAMS, VERA. The Great Watermelon Birthday. NY: Greenwillow, 1980. 1st ed, 1st bk. 8 1/4 x 7 1/4. Pict bds. As New in dj. *Cattermole.* $60/£38

WILLIAMS, VERA. Three Days on a River in a Red Canoe. NY: Greenwillow, 1981. 1st ed. 8 1/4 x 7 1/2. 32pp. Pict bds. Fine in dj. *Cattermole.* $50/£32

WILLIAMS, WALTER (ed). A History of Northeast Missouri. Chicago: Lewis Pub Co, 1913. 3 vols. Frontis, 127 ports. 3/4 leather (scuffed, peeling). *Bohling.* $120/£77

WILLIAMS, WAYNE C. A Rail Splitter for President. Denver: Univ of Denver, 1951. 1st ed. VG in dj. *Cahan.* $25/£16

WILLIAMS, WILLIAM CARLOS. The Build-Up. NY: Random House, (1952). 1st ed. NF in dj (lt chipped). *Hermitage.* $50/£32

WILLIAMS, WILLIAM CARLOS. Dear Ez: Letters from William Carlos Williams to Ezra Pound. Bloomington: Friends of the Lilly Library, 1985. 1st ed. Fine in Fine dj. *Beasley.* $60/£38

WILLIAMS, WILLIAM CARLOS. In the Money. (London): MacGibbon & Kee, (1965). 1st British ed. One of 2000. (Top edge dusty), else Nice in dj (lt sunned, sm edge nick). *Reese.* $45/£29

WILLIAMS, WILLIAM CARLOS. In the Money. London, 1966. 1st ed. Fine in dj (spine sl sunned, price-slipped). *Polyanthos.* $60/£38

WILLIAMS, WILLIAM CARLOS. Paterson (Book Five). (NY): New Directions, 1958. 1st ed. Deckle-edged. Gray cl (soiled, spotted), gilt. Internally Fine. *Blue Mountain.* $25/£16

WILLIAMS, WILLIAM CARLOS. Paterson (Books 1-5). (NY): New Directions, (1946-1958). 1st ed. 1st 4 parts ltd to 1000; 5th ltd to 3000. 5 vols. VG in djs (worn, soiled). *Jaffe.* $1,250/£801

WILLIAMS, WILLIAM CARLOS. Paterson. NY: New Directions, (1958). 1st Amer ed. Fine in Fine dj. *Polyanthos.* $75/£48

WILLIAMS, WILLIAM CARLOS. Spring and All. N.p.: Contact Pub, n.d. (1923). VG in wrappers (dknd, spine ends sl chipped). *Gekoski.* $624/£400

WILLIAMS, WILLIAM CARLOS. A Voyage to Pagany. NY: Macaulay, 1928. 1st ed. VF in dj (sm edge tears). *Dermont.* $350/£224

WILLIAMS, WILLIAM. Journal of the Life, Travels, and Gospel Labours, of William Williams, Dec. Cincinnati: Lodge et al, 1828. 1st ed. 272pp. Contemp full calf. (Foxing, staining; 2 sm hinge chips), else VG. Howes W490. *Cahan.* $250/£160

WILLIAMS-ELLIS, A. H.M.S. Beagle in South America, Etc. London: Watts, Oct 1930. 1st ed. 9 engr photos. Blind-stamped dec cl. Fine in VG dj. *Mikesh.* $60/£38

WILLIAMS-ELLIS, C. and A. The Pleasures of Architecture. Jonathan Cape, 1924. 1st ed. Frontis. Fore, lower edge uncut. Cl-backed bds, paper spine label (sl browned). *Edwards.* $31/£20

WILLIAMS-ELLIS, CLOUGH and A. The Tank Corps. London, n.d. (1919). Brn cl (fr hinge weak). *Maggs.* $62/£40

WILLIAMSON, G. H. Road in the Sky: Archaeology Explaining Pre-Inca Legends and Myths. London: Spearman, 1950. 1st ed. Fine in Fine dj. *Mikesh.* $35/£22

WILLIAMSON, GEORGE C. Bryan's Dictionary of Painters and Engravers. London, 1925-7. 5 vols. Teg. 2-tone cl (soiled, corners rubbed w/sl cl loss; hinges tender, sl shaken). *Edwards.* $156/£100

WILLIAMSON, HAROLD F. and ARNOLD R. DAUM. The American Petroleum Industry. Evanston: Northwestern Univ, 1959/1963. 2 vols. VG. *Dumont.* $100/£64

WILLIAMSON, HAROLD. Winchester, the Gun That Won the West. Washington: Combat Forces, 1952. 1st ed. Cl spine. VG (ex-lib). *Worldwide.* $25/£16

WILLIAMSON, HAROLD. Winchester: The Gun That Won the West. NY/London, (1963). VG. *Truepenny.* $45/£29

WILLIAMSON, HENRY. The Beautiful Years. London, 1921. Ltd to 750. (Prelims lt foxed; spine sl rubbed.) *Edrich.* $117/£75

WILLIAMSON, HENRY. A Clear Water Stream. Faber & Faber, (1958). 1st ed. VG (bkpl) in dj (sl scuffed, nicked). *Ash.* $55/£35

WILLIAMSON, HENRY. A Clear Water Stream. London, 1958. VG in dj. *Edrich.* $39/£25

WILLIAMSON, HENRY. Dandelion Days. London, 1922. Ltd to 600. (Prelims sl foxed; spine edge sl rubbed), o/w VG. *Edrich.* $187/£120

WILLIAMSON, HENRY. The Dark Lantern. London, 1951. 1st Eng ed. VG in dj (sl chipped). *Edrich.* $70/£45

WILLIAMSON, HENRY. Devon Holiday. London, 1935. 1st Eng ed. VG in VG dj. *Edrich.* $62/£40

WILLIAMSON, HENRY. The Dream of Fair Women. London, 1924. Ltd to 750. Superior (spine edges sl rubbed). *Edrich.* $156/£100

WILLIAMSON, HENRY. The Dream of Fair Women. London: Collins, 1924. 1st Eng ed. One of 750 ptd. VG. *Clearwater.* $234/£150

WILLIAMSON, HENRY. The Gale of the World. London, 1969. The scarce 1st ptg which was withdrawn due to numerous errors. Red ink line drawn through tp (to prevent sale), red ink annotations in text indicating errors. *Edrich.* $390/£250

WILLIAMSON, HENRY. Genius of Friendship. London, 1941. 1st ed. VG in dj (sl soiled, faded). *Typographeum.* $85/£54

WILLIAMSON, HENRY. Genius of Friendship: T.E. Lawrence. London, 1941. Variant binding: chocolate-brn cl. Very Nice (fr cvr sl spotted) in dj (sl faded). *Clearwater.* $94/£60

WILLIAMSON, HENRY. Goodbye West Country. London, 1937. Only Eng ed. (Bkpl, name.) Dj (sl frayed). *Edrich.* $70/£45

WILLIAMSON, HENRY. How Dear Is Life. London, 1954. 1st Eng ed. VG in dj (spine sl rubbed). *Edrich.* $55/£35

WILLIAMSON, HENRY. It Was the Nightingale. London: Macdonald, 1962. 1st Eng ed. 357pp + 3pp ad for other titles in Chronicles sequence. VG in VG dj (price-clipped). *Hadley.* $47/£30

WILLIAMSON, HENRY. The Linhay on the Downs. Woburn Books, 1929. Ltd to 530 numbered, signed. Fine in dj. *Edrich.* $62/£40

WILLIAMSON, HENRY. On Foot in Devon. London, 1933. 1st Eng ed. NF in pict dj (sl torn). *Edrich.* $55/£35

WILLIAMSON, HENRY. The Pathway. London, 1928. 1st Eng ed. VG in dj (sm closed tear). *Edrich.* $62/£40

WILLIAMSON, HENRY. The Patriot's Progress. NY: E.P. Dutton, (1930). 1st Amer ed. VG in dj (chipped, torn). *Hermitage.* $35/£22

WILLIAMSON, HENRY. The Patriot's Progress. London, 1930. 1st ed. Dj (sl soiled, nicked). *Typographeum.* $45/£29

WILLIAMSON, HENRY. The Peregrine's Saga. London, 1923. One of 600 ptd. VG in VG dj. *Edrich.* $218/£140

WILLIAMSON, HENRY. The Phasian Bird. Faber, 1948. 1st UK ed. Fine in VG dj. *Williams*. $23/£15

WILLIAMSON, HENRY. The Power of the Dead. Macdonald, (1963). 1st ed. Nice in dj. *Ash*. $62/£40

WILLIAMSON, HENRY. Salar the Salmon. London, 1936. 1st Eng ed. (Bkpl.) Dj. *Edrich*. $234/£150

WILLIAMSON, HENRY. A Solitary War. London: Macdonald, 1966. 1st Eng ed. 374pp + 4pp ad for other titles in the sequence. VG in VG dj (price-clipped). *Hadley*. $39/£25

WILLIAMSON, HENRY. The Star-Born. London, 1933. 1st issue. Teg. VG in later dj (badly torn, internally strengthened). *Edrich*. $47/£30

WILLIAMSON, HENRY. The Story of a Norfolk Farm. London, 1941. 2nd imp. VG in dj. *Gretton*. $27/£17

WILLIAMSON, HENRY. The Story of a Norfolk Farm. London, 1941. 1st Eng ed. VG in dj (spine head chipped). *Edrich*. $78/£50

WILLIAMSON, HENRY. Tales of a Devon Village. London, 1945. 1st Eng ed. VG in VG dj. *Edrich*. $25/£16

WILLIAMSON, HENRY. Tarka the Otter. Chiswick, 1927. 1st unltd ed. VG in dj. *Edrich*. $101/£65

WILLIAMSON, HENRY. Tarka the Otter. London, 1930. Tauchnitz ed. 1st issue w/ads dated March 1930. VG in orig wraps. *Edrich*. $19/£12

WILLIAMSON, HENRY. The Wet Flanders Plain. London: Beaumont, (1929). One of 320 numbered. Holland-backed patterned bds. NF (no dj, as issued). *Clearwater*. $140/£90

WILLIAMSON, HENRY. The Wet Flanders Plain. NY, 1929. 1st Amer ed. (Name; rear cvr sl mkd.) Dj. *Clearwater*. $117/£75

WILLIAMSON, HENRY. The Wild Red Deer of Exmoor. London, 1931. 1st ordinary ed. (Bds sl rubbed), o/w VG in dj (stained, nicked). *Edrich*. $39/£25

WILLIAMSON, HENRY. Young Phillip Maddison. London, 1953. 1st Eng ed. VG in dj (sl chipped). *Edrich*. $55/£35

WILLIAMSON, HUGH. Methods of Book Design. London: OUP, 1956. 1st ed. Fine in Fine dj. *Dermont*. $50/£32

WILLIAMSON, HUGH. Observations of the Climate in Different Parts of America.... NY: Swords, 1811. (Foxing, stamps to tp.) 3/4 leather (worn), marbled paper bds. *Metropolitan**. $258/£165

WILLIAMSON, JACK. The Humanoid Touch. Holt, 1980. 1st ed. Signed. Fine in dj. *Madle*. $40/£26

WILLIAMSON, JACK. The Legion of Space. Reading: Fantasy, 1947. 1st ed. Signed. (Sl worn, soiled.) Dj (lt rubbed). *Swann**. $57/£37

WILLIAMSON, JACK. The Legion of Time. Reading: Fantasy, 1952. 1st ed. One of 350 w/signed, inscribed, numbered leaf tipped in. Dj (chip, sm tear). *Kane**. $80/£51

WILLIAMSON, JACK. Seetee Ship. Gnome, 1951. 1st ed. Fine in NF dj. *Certo*. $75/£48

WILLIAMSON, JACK. Seetee Shock. S&S, 1950. 1st ed. NF in Nice dj (spine sl chipped, sm rubbed spot). *Certo*. $50/£32

WILLIAMSON, JAMES J. Mosby's Rangers. NY: Sturgis & Walton, 1909. 2nd ed. (Inner hinges repaired), else VG. Howes W498. *Mcgowan*. $350/£224

WILLIAMSON, W. C. Reminiscences of a Yorkshire Naturalist. London, 1896. 1st ed. (Cl sl worn, spotted.) *Maggs*. $28/£18

WILLIS, N. P. et al. Mountain, Lake, and River. Boston: Estes & Lauriat, 1884. 96pp (lacks blank fep; frontis, tp loose; fr inner hinge broken). Dec cl (sl worn). *New Hampshire**. $100/£64

WILLIS, THOMAS. The Anatomy of the Brain and Nerves. William Feindel (ed). Montreal: McGill Univ, 1965. Tercentenary ed. Ltd to 2000 sets. 2 vols. (Spines, box lt soiled). Internally Fine in slipcase. *Goodrich*. $250/£160

WILLISON, GEORGE F. Here They Dug the Gold. NY: Reynal & Hitchcock, (1946). 1st ed. Good. *Lien*. $35/£22

WILLISON, GEORGE F. Saints and Strangers. London: Heinemann, 1966. 1st ed. NF in dj. *Worldwide*. $10/£6

WILLISTON, SAMUEL. A Selection of Cases on the Law of Contracts. Boston: Little, Brown, 1922. 2nd ed. Buckram. (Notes; rubbed), else Sound. *Boswell*. $35/£22

WILLIUS, FREDRICK and THOMAS KEYS. Cardiac Classics: A Collection of Classic Works in the Heart.... St. Louis, 1941. 1st ed. VG. *Fye*. $100/£64

WILLKIE, WENDELL L. One World. NY: LEC, 1944. One of 1500 signed. Pict eps. Pigskin-backed illus bds (spine ends sl rubbed). VG in orig glassine wrapper (sl chipped), cl clamshell box (faded). *Cahan*. $60/£38

WILLOCK, COLIN. Landscape with Solitary Figure. London: Longmans Green, 1966. 1st ed. VG (corner crease several pp) in VG dj. *Backman*. $20/£13

WILLOUGHBY, VERA. A Vision of Greece. London: Phillip, Allan, 1925. #322/500. 14 plts. Deckled pp. 3/4 cl, textured paper. (Inscrip.) *Metropolitan**. $75/£48

WILLS, CECIL M. The Clue of the Lost Hour. London: Hodder & Stoughton, 1949. 1st ed. inscribed. VG in dj (tattered, long tear, spine loss, soil). *Metropolitan**. $23/£15

WILLS, CECIL M. Defeat of a Detective. London: Hodder & Stoughton, (1936). 1st ed. Inscribed. Good in dj (2 tears, sm chips). *Metropolitan**. $63/£40

WILLS, CHARLES WRIGHT. Army Life of an Illinois Soldier.... Washington: Globe Ptg, 1906. 1st ed. Presentation copy. VG +. *Mcgowan*. $250/£160

WILLSBERGER, JOHANN. Clocks and Watches: 600 Years of the World's Most Beautiful Timepieces. Renee Vera Cafiero (trans). NY: Dial, 1975. 1st ed in English. Brn cl. Fine in dj. *Weber*. $35/£22

WILLSON, BECKLES. The Life of Lord Strathcona and Mount Royal. Boston: Houghton, Mifflin, (1915). 2 vols. VG. *Perier*. $65/£42

WILLSON, JAMES L. and CHARLES ROBB. The Metals in Canada. Montreal: Dawson, 1861. 1st ed. 80pp, fldg table at rear. Ptd wrappers. *Ginsberg*. $300/£192

WILLY, COLETTE. Barks and Purrs. NY: Desmond FitzGerald, 1913. 1st US ed. VG + in cl-cvrd bds. *Lame Duck*. $150/£96

WILMERDING, JOHN. Winslow Homer. NY: Praeger, (1972). 1st ed. 50 color plts. Blue cl. Fine in pict dj. *House*. $45/£29

WILMOTT, ELLEN. The Genus Rosa. London: John Murray, 1914. Folio. 25 orig parts bound in 2 vols, orig wraps bound at rear. 132 color litho plts (few w/sl adherence to guards). 3/4 leather. Handsome. *Metropolitan**. $1,955/£1,253

WILSON, A. N. A Bottle in the Smoke. NY: Viking, 1990. 1st Amer ed. Fine (rmdr mk top edge) in Fine dj. *Revere*. $25/£16

WILSON, A. N. The Laird of Abbotsford: A View of Sir Walter Scott. Oxford, 1980. 1st ed. Dj. *Typographeum*. $25/£16

WILSON, A. N. Love Unknown. London, 1986. 1st ed. Dj. *Typographeum*. $25/£16

WILSON, A. N. Wise Virgin. Secker, 1982. 1st UK ed. NF (fep sl scuffed) in dj. *Williams*. $23/£15

WILSON, ADRIAN. The Design of Books. NY/London, (1967). 1st ed. VG in dj. *Truepenny.* $75/£48

WILSON, ALBERT. Education, Personality and Crime.... London: Greening, 1908. 1st ed. Panelled red cl. Good+ (lib stamps). *Gach.* $45/£29

WILSON, ANGUS. Anglo-Saxon Attitudes. NY: Viking, 1956. 1st Amer ed. NF in VG dj (soil, wear). *Antic Hay.* $17/£11

WILSON, ANGUS. A Bit Off the Map. London: Secker, 1957. 1st UK ed. Fine in dj. *Williams.* $39/£25

WILSON, ANGUS. For Whom the Cloche Tolls. London, 1953. 1st Eng ed. Pict bds. Very Nice in Poor dj. *Clearwater.* $47/£30

WILSON, ANGUS. Hemlock and After. Secker & Warburg, 1952. 1st ed. Nice in dj (sl worn). *Ash.* $39/£25

WILSON, ANGUS. The Mulberry Bush. London: Secker, 1956. 1st UK ed. NF in dj (sl scuffed). *Williams.* $39/£25

WILSON, ANGUS. The Old Men at the Zoo. London: Secker & Warburg, (1961). 1st ed. NF in dj (spine browned, soil, price-clipped). *Antic Hay.* $25/£16

WILSON, ANGUS. The Old Men at the Zoo. London: Secker & Warburg, (1961). 1st ed. NF in VG dj. *Turtle Island.* $30/£19

WILSON, ANGUS. Such Darling Dodos and Other Stories. Secker & Warburg, 1950. 1st ed. VG in dj. *Ash.* $94/£60

WILSON, ANGUS. Such Darling Dodos and Other Stories. London: Secker & Warburg, 1950. 1st ed. NF (eps sl browned) in dj (spine browned). *Antic Hay.* $35/£22

WILSON, ANGUS. Such Darling Dodos and Other Stories. London: Secker & Warburg, 1950. 1st ed. (Sl offset eps), else NF in dj (spine sl tanned). *Turtle Island.* $75/£48

WILSON, ANGUS. Tempo. (London): Studio Vista, (1964). 1st ed. NF in dj. *Turtle Island.* $30/£19

WILSON, ANGUS. The Wild Garden or Speaking of Writing. Secker, 1963. 1st UK ed. Fine in VG dj (rubbed, sl spine abrasion). *Williams.* $23/£15

WILSON, CAROL GREEN. Alice Eastwood's Wonderland. SF, 1955. Ltd to 2000. Signed. Frontis port. Fine. *Quest.* $40/£26

WILSON, CHARIS and EDWARD WESTON. The Cats of Wildcat Hill. NY: Duell, Sloan & Pearce, 1947. 1st ed. Fine. *Cahan.* $175/£112

WILSON, CHARIS. Edward Weston Nudes. Millerton, NY: Aperture, 1977. 1st ed. (Sl bump), else NF in dj (rubbed, lt chipped). *Cahan.* $65/£42

WILSON, CHARLES H. The Wanderer in America. Thirsk, 1822. 2nd ed. Letterpress bds (rebacked w/cl). Howes W517. *Swann*.* $57/£37

WILSON, CHARLES H., SR. Education for Negroes in Mississippi Since 1910. Newton: Crofton, 1974. Frontis; 65 full-pg ports, views from photos. Blue cl, gilt spine title. VG. *Petrilla.* $75/£48

WILSON, CHARLES WILLIAM. Picturesque Palestine, Sinai and Egypt. NY: Appleton, (1881-1883). 1st US ed. 2 vols. 2 maps, 40 steel-engr plts, guards. Aeg. Brn morocco, maroon pebbled cl (upper cvr vol 2 detached, worn, scuffed, ends chipped, few joints cracked; lt foxed, aged), gilt. *Baltimore*.* $210/£135

WILSON, COLIN. Adrift in Soho. Boston, 1961. 1st Amer ed. VG in dj (sl frayed, dknd; price-clipped). *King.* $20/£13

WILSON, COLIN. The Age of Defeat. London, 1959. 1st Eng ed. Very Nice in dj (sl rubbed). *Clearwater.* $39/£25

WILSON, COLIN. The Occult. NY, 1971. 1st ed. VG in dj. *Typographeum.* $25/£16

WILSON, COLIN. The Philosopher's Stone. NY: Crown, (1969). 1st Amer ed. Black cl. Fine in NF dj (sl bumped). *Blue Mountain.* $35/£22

WILSON, COLIN. Religion and the Rebel. London, 1957. 1st Eng ed. Very Nice (sl bumped) in dj. *Clearwater.* $47/£30

WILSON, COLIN. Ritual in the Dark. Boston: Houghton Mifflin, 1960. 1st Amer ed. Fine in NF dj (sm nicks extrems). *Reese.* $60/£38

WILSON, COLIN. Ritual in the Dark. London, 1960. 1st ed. Fine in dj (spine sl sunned, few sm chips). *Polyanthos.* $50/£32

WILSON, COLIN. The Space Vampires. NY: Random House, (1976). 1st ed. VG+ (sl twisted, sm sticker fr pastedown, rmdr stamp lower edges) in VG+ dj (sl dknd). *Fuller & Saunders.* $25/£16

WILSON, D. The Life of Jane McCrea, With an Account of Burgoyne's Expedition in 1777. NY: Baker & Godwin, 1853. 1st ed. 155pp+1pg ads. (Shelf wear, spine lt sunned, sm spots fr cvr), else Good. *Brown.* $95/£61

WILSON, DANIEL. Memorials of Edinburgh in the Olden Time. Edinburgh: A&C Black, 1891. 2nd ed. 2 vols. Steel-engr frontispieces, xxiv,282,(2); xiv,316pp; fldg map. Brn cl (lt frayed). *Karmiole.* $125/£80

WILSON, DOROTHY CLARKE. Ten Fingers of God. NY, (1965). 1st ed. VG. *Argosy.* $45/£29

WILSON, EDMUND. Axel's Castle. NY: Scribner, 1931. 1st ed. Blue cl, paper label. Fine in dj (spine tanned, sm chip). *Turtle Island.* $85/£54

WILSON, EDMUND. The Bit Between My Teeth. W.H. Allen, (1965). 1st ed. London issue of Amer sheets. VG in dj (lt rubbed, sunned). *Ash.* $31/£20

WILSON, EDMUND. The Bit Between My Teeth. NY, 1965. 1st Amer ed. Fine in dj (spine extrems sl rubbed, 2 sm tears). *Polyanthos.* $35/£22

WILSON, EDMUND. Corrections and Comments. Iowa City: Windhover, 1976. One of 175. Paste-paper bds. Fine. *Dermont.* $100/£64

WILSON, EDMUND. The Devils and Canon Barham. NY, 1973. 1st Amer ed. Fine in dj (spine sl sunned, extrems sl rubbed). *Polyanthos.* $25/£16

WILSON, EDMUND. The Duke of Palermo and Other Plays, with an Open Letter to Mike Nichols. NY: FSG, (1969). 1st ed. Fine in dj. *Between The Covers.* $75/£48

WILSON, EDMUND. Europe Without Baedeker. NY, 1966. 1st rev ed. Fine in dj (few nicks, spine heel sl rubbed). *Polyanthos.* $25/£16

WILSON, EDMUND. Patriotic Gore. NY: OUP, 1962. 1st ed. NF (trace of name fep) in dj. *Turtle Island.* $45/£29

WILSON, EDMUND. A Piece of My Mind. NY, 1956. 1st Amer ed. NF in dj (sl soiled). *Polyanthos.* $25/£16

WILSON, EDMUND. A Piece of My Mind. NY: Farrar, 1956. 1st ed. Fine in dj (lt used, scuffed). *Beasley.* $30/£19

WILSON, EDMUND. A Pience of My Mind. London: W.H. Allen, 1957. 1st British ed. VG in dj. *Cahan.* $25/£16

WILSON, EDMUND. The Rats of Rutland Range. (NY): Gotham Book Mart, (1974). One of 100 numbered, signed by Edward Gorey (illus). Fine in Fine slipcase. *Lenz.* $225/£144

WILSON, EDMUND. The Scrolls from the Dead Sea. London: W.H. Allen, 1955. Good in dj (tattered). *Archaeologia.* $25/£16

WILSON, EDMUND. The Thirties. NY, 1980. 1st Amer ed. Fine (blindstamp) in dj (spine lt sunned, price-clipped). *Polyanthos.* $25/£16

WILSON, EDMUND. This Room and This Gin and These Sandwiches. NY, 1937. 1st Amer ed. Pict wraps. Fine (spine top sl rubbed). *Polyanthos.* $200/£128

WILSON, EDMUND. The Triple Thinkers. NY: Harcourt Brace, 1938. 1st ed. VG+ in VG- dj (price-clipped, edgetears). *Lame Duck.* $175/£112

WILSON, EDMUND. The Triple Thinkers: Twelve Essays on Literary Subjects. London: John Lehmann, 1952. 1st ed thus. VG in dj (sl dusty). *Cahan.* $25/£16

WILSON, EDMUND. A Window on Russia. NY, 1972. 1st Amer ed. Fine in Fine dj. *Polyanthos.* $25/£16

WILSON, EDWARD A. The Pirate's Treasure or The Strange Adventures of Jack Adams on the Spanish Main. NY/Joliet/Boston: P.F. Volland, 1926. 11th ed. 8vo. 92pp + 1pg ad. Color pict paper on bd (rubbed, sm portion spine top missing); pict eps. Good. *Hobbyhorse.* $55/£35

WILSON, EDWARD A. The Pirate's Treasure, or The Strange Adventures of Jack Adams on the Spanish Main. P.F. Volland, (1926). 1st ed. Tall 8vo. (92pp). Pict charts eps. Pict bds (lt mks, edgewear). *Bookmark.* $23/£15

WILSON, EDWARD L. Wilson's Quarter Century in Photograpy. NY: Edward L. Wilson, 1887. 1st ed. 528pp + ads. (Spine #, sl rubbed), else NF. *Cahan.* $200/£128

WILSON, EDWARD. Diary of the 'Discovery' Expedition. Ann Savours (ed). London: Blandford, 1966. 1st ed. Fldg map. Blue cl over bds, gilt. (Eps spotted), else VG in dj (stained). *Parmer.* $135/£87

WILSON, ELIJAH NICHOLAS. Among the Shoshones. Salt Lake, 1910. 2nd ed. Frontis, port. (Closed tear 1 leaf; edgeworn, fr hinge cracked), o/w VG. *Benchmark.* $115/£74

WILSON, ERASMUS. Hufeland's Art of Prolonging Life. Phila, 1870. 298pp. Grn cl bds (sl worn). VG. *Doctor's Library.* $75/£48

WILSON, ERNEST H. Aristocrats of the Garden. Boston: Stratford, 1932. 1st ed thus. 2 vols. Teg. NF in VG djs. *Archer.* $60/£38

WILSON, ERNEST H. China: Mother of Gardens. Boston: Stratford, 1929. 1st ed. Teg. (Bkpl), else NF. *Archer.* $400/£256

WILSON, ERNEST H. More Aristocrats of the Garden. Boston: Stratford, 1928. 1st ed. Teg. VG+ in dj (chipped, damp-stained). *Archer.* $40/£26

WILSON, ERNEST H. A Naturalist in Western China. NY: Doubleday, Page, 1914. 2nd ptg. 2 vols. Fldg map. (Ex-lib, stamp tp; spine # neatly cvrd), o/w VG. *Archer.* $400/£256

WILSON, ERNEST H. Plant Hunting. Boston: Stratford, 1927. 1st ed. 2 vols. (Spines sl rubbed), o/w Fine. *Archer.* $265/£170

WILSON, F. PAUL. The Keep. NY: William Morrow, 1981. 1st hb ed. (Pencilled note; spine sl cocked), o/w NF in dj. *Levin.* $75/£48

WILSON, F. PAUL. Reborn. Arlington Hts: Dark Harvest, 1990. 1st ed, trade state. Fine in dj. *Levin.* $30/£19

WILSON, FRANCIS. John Wilkes Booth, Fact and Fiction of Lincoln's Assassination. Boston, (1929). VG+ in dj (worn, torn, spine top torn away). *Pratt.* $42/£27

WILSON, G. F. A Bibliography of the Writings of W. H. Hudson. London: Bookman's Journal, 1922. Uncut. Black cl (sl bumped; pencil notes). *Maggs.* $28/£18

WILSON, G. F. A Bibliography of the Writings of W. H. Hudson. London: Bookman's Journal, 1922. 1st ed. Good. *Shasky.* $40/£26

WILSON, GAHAN. America. S&S, 1985. 1st ed. Fine in Fine dj. *Certo.* $25/£16

WILSON, GEORGE B. Alcohol and the Nation...the Liquor Problem in the United Kingdom from 1800-1935. London, 1940. 1st ed. Grn cl. Good in dj (worn). *Doctor's Library.* $40/£26

WILSON, H. W. Ironclads in Action. Boston/London, 1896. 1st ed. 2 vols. xxxvi,357; xvi,374pp. VG. *Wantagh.* $150/£96

WILSON, HELENA CALISTA and ELSIE REED MITCHELL. Vagabonding at Fifty from Siberia to Turkestan. NY: Coward, McCann, 1929. 1st ed. Frontis map. (Edges sl affected by dampness; sl rubbed, faded), o/w Good. *Worldwide.* $16/£10

WILSON, IRIS HIGBIE. William Wolfskill 1798-1866.... Glendale, 1965. 1st ed, 1st bk. One of 2010. Frontis port, 4 maps and plts. VF. *Turpen.* $75/£48

WILSON, IRIS HIGBIE. William Wolfskill, 1798-1866. Glendale: Clark, 1965. 1st ed. One of 2010. (Spine ends, corners sl rubbed). Fine. *Argonaut.* $75/£48

WILSON, J. G. and JOHN FISKE (eds). Appleton's Cyclopaedia of American Biography. NY: Appleton, 1888. 1st ed. 6 vols. 1/2 calf, marbled bds (rubbed, sl worn). Internally Fine. *Agvent.* $300/£192

WILSON, JAMES G. Thackeray in the United States. 1852-3, 1855-6. NY, 1904. 2 vols. Frontis each vol. 2-tone cl, gilt spines. VG. *Reese.* $175/£112

WILSON, JAMES HARRISON. Under the Old Flag, Recollections of Military Operations.... NY: D. Appleton, 1912. 1st ed. 2 vols. VG set. *Mcgowan.* $275/£176

WILSON, JAMES. An Easy Introduction to the Knowledge of the Hebrew Language. Phila, 1812. Contemp tree sheep. *Swann*.* $103/£66

WILSON, JOHN A. Adventures of Alf. Wilson. Toledo: Blade, 1880. 1st ed. 237pp. Gold-stamped cl. *Ginsberg.* $350/£224

WILSON, JOHN L. Battles of America by Sea and Land. Vol III: The Great Civil War. NY, c. 1878. 976pp (lt foxing), 34 engr ports (several creased). 1/2 leather, cl bds (rubbed, fr cvr dampstained). *New Hampshire*.* $20/£13

WILSON, JOYCE LANCASTER (ed). The Work and Play of Adrian Wilson. Austin: Thomas Taylor, 1983. 1st ed. One of 325. 1/4 morocco. *Swann*.* $201/£129

WILSON, MARGARET. The Able McLaughlins. NY: Harper, (1923). VG (sm spot fr bd, top edge bumped; lacks dj). *Between The Covers.* $65/£42

WILSON, MICHAEL I. Organ Cases of Western Europe. London: C. Hurst, (1979). 1st ed. 264 plts. Grn cl, gilt spine. Fine in dj. *Karmiole.* $60/£38

WILSON, MONA. The Life of William Blake. Nonesuch, 1927. #572/1480. 24 plts. Vellum-backed marbled bds (sl worn, spine sl discolored). *Edwards.* $140/£90

WILSON, MONA. The Life of William Blake. Nonesuch, 1927. #930/1480. Uncut. 1/4 vellum (edges sl rubbed). VG. *Poetry Bookshop.* $148/£95

WILSON, MONA. The Life of William Blake. London: Nonesuch, 1927. One of 1480. 24 plts. Partly unopened. Vellum-backed marbled bds (rubbed, spine dknd). *Kane*.* $60/£38

WILSON, MONA. The Life of William Blake. London: Nonesuch, 1927. 1st ed. #28/1480. Frontis port. 1/4 vellum, marbled bds. (Bkpl; bump), else VG. *Pacific*.* $98/£63

WILSON, NEILL C. Silver Stampede. NY: Macmillan, 1937. 1st ed. VF in VF dj. *Book Market.* $75/£48

WILSON, R. L. Colt Pistols 1836-1976. Dallas: Jackson Arms, (1976). Gilt-stamped leatherette (lt worn), lg metallic medallion inset fr cvr. Slipcase. *Oinonen*.* $130/£83

WILSON, R. L. Colt. An American Legend. NY: Abbeville, (1985). Deluxe ed, specially bound, signed.
Full leather (lt worn) stamped in silver/gold, sm colt
coin inset fr cvr. Oinonen*. $140/£90

WILSON, ROBERT A. Gertrude Stein: A Bibliography.
NY: Phoenix Bookshop, 1974. Red cl, as issued. Fine.
Turtle Island. $45/£29

WILSON, ROBERT FORREST. Crusader in Crinoline.
The Life of Harriet Beecher Stowe. Phila: Lippincott,
(1941). 1st ed. 30 plts. NF in VG dj. Mcgowan.
$45/£29

WILSON, RUFUS ROCKWELL with OTILIE ERICKSON
WILSON. New York in Literature: the Story Told....
Elmira, NY: Primavera, 1947. 1st ed, 1st ptg of trade
ed of 2550. Fine in dj. Cahan. $25/£16

WILSON, RUFUS ROCKWELL. Rambles in Colonial By-
ways. Phila, 1901. Teg. Contemp 3/4 blue polished
Niger morocco, gilt, marbled bds (extrems scuffed, lt
worn). Freeman*. $70/£45

WILSON, S. A. K. Neurology. Balt: Williams & Wilkins,
1940. 1st Amer ed. 2 vols. 16 plts. (Sl dull), else VG.
Glaser. $250/£160

WILSON, S. A. K. Neurology. A. Ninian Bruce (ed).
1940. 1st ed. 2 vols. New binder's cl. Whitehart.
$234/£150

WILSON, SAMUEL. The Kentucky English Grammar....
Lexington: Daniel Bradford, 1806. 3rd ed. 97pp. Orig
fr bd (lacks back cvr, spine mostly perished). Wantagh. $350/£224

WILSON, SUZANNE COLTON (comp). Column South.
Flagstaff, 1960. 1st ed. VG+ in VG+ dj. Pratt.
$80/£51

WILSON, THOMAS L. Sufferings Endured for a Free
Government; or, A History of the Cruelties and Atrocities of the Rebellion. Washington: The Author, 1864.
1st ed. x,300pp. Grn cl (ends, corners worn; sl faded).
VG. Argonaut. $90/£58

WILSON, THOMAS. Transatlantic Sketches. Montreal,
1860. Inscribed presentation. 179pp, errata slip.
Good (ex-lib, stamps, bkpl, shaken, few sigs starting;
extrems frayed). Reese. $150/£96

WILSON, WILLIAM B. Few Acts and Actors in the Tragedy of the Civil War in the United States. Phila: The
Author, 1892. 1st ed. 114pp. Dec cl. Ginsberg.
$100/£64

WILSON, WILLIAM. A Borderland Confederate. F. Summers (ed). Pittsburgh, (1962). 1st ed. Fine in dj (lt
worn). Pratt. $45/£29

WILSON, WILLIAM. A Borderland Confederate. F. Summers (ed). Pittsburgh: UP Press, 1962. 1st ed. Fine in
NF dj (price-clipped). Archer. $35/£22

WILSON, WILLIAM. The Wabash. NY: F&R, 1940. Ltr
ptg. NF in NF dj (sl rubbed). Archer. $30/£19

WILSON, WOODROW. George Washington. NY,
1897. 1st Amer ed. Teg, uncut. Dec cvrs, gilt. Fine
(spine sunned, sl soiled, rear cvr sl soiled). Polyanthos. $60/£38

WILSON, WOODROW. Mere Literature. Boston,
1893. #259/550. Uncut. NF (spine sl rubbed). Polyanthos. $35/£22

WILSTACH, PAUL. Tidewater Maryland. Indianapolis,
(1931). 1st ed. VG (few leaves foxed). Wantagh.
$45/£29

WILSTACH, PAUL. Tidewater Virginia. Indianapolis,
(1929). 1st ed. One of 259 signed. Fldg map. Cl-
backed bds. VG (sl foxed) in orig cl dj. Wantagh.
$75/£48

WILTON, ANDREW. British Watercolours 1750 to
1850. Phaidon, 1977. 1st ed. 58 color plts. Dj (sl repaired). Edwards. $39/£25

WILTON, G. W. Fingerprints: History, Law and Romance. 1938. 8 plts. Whitehart. $39/£25

WILTSEY, NORMAN B. Brave Warriors. Caldwell,
1963. 2nd ptg. VG in dj (worn). Pratt. $17/£11

WIMSATT, W. A. Biology of Bats. NY/London: Academic, 1970. 1st ed. 3 vols. Fine. Mikesh. $250/£160

WINANS, WALTER. The Sporting Rifle. NY, 1908. 1st
ed. Teg; uncut. Gilt-pict cl (sl worn, sl spotted). Oinonen*. $180/£115

WINCHELL, ALEXANDER. Preadamites; or A Demonstration of the Existence of Men Before Adam. Chicago, 1881. 3rd ed. Frontis, xxvi,500pp, fldg map.
(Worn, hinges cracked, sm snag backstrip.) Bohling.
$20/£13

WINCKEL, FRANZ. Diseases of Women. J.H. Williamson (trans). Phila: P. Blakiston, 1887. 1st ed in English. xxix,674pp + 16pg pub's cat. Bickersteth.
$62/£40

WIND, EDGAR. Bellini's Feast of the Gods. Cambridge, 1948. 74 plts. (Rubbed.) Internally VG.
Washton. $45/£29

WIND, HERBERT W. The Story of American Golf. NY:
Farrar, Straus, 1948. 1st ed. VG (sl soiled) in dj (worn;
tears, some loss; dampstaining). Waverly*. $44/£28

WIND, HERBERT W. The World of P. G. Wodehouse.
NY: Praeger, (1971). 1st ed. Fine in dj. Turtle Island.
$55/£35

Wind-and-Wing, or Le Feu-Follet. (By James Fenimore
Cooper.) Phila: Lee & Blanchard, 1842. 1st Amer ed.
2 vols in 1. 1/2 leather (shabby). BAL 3901. New
Hampshire*. $50/£32

WINDHAM, CHARLES ASH. The Crimean Diary and
Letters of Sir Charles Ash Windham, K.C.B. London,
1897. Frontis, xi,272pp. Maroon dec cl (very faded),
gilt. Maggs. $156/£100

WINDHAM, DONALD (ed). E. M. Forster's Letters to
Donald Windham. Verona: Sandy Campbell, 1972.
One of 300. Signed. Fine in wrappers. Lenz. $100/£64

WINDLE, BERTRAM C. A. Remains of the Prehistoric
Age in England. London, 1909. 2nd ed. (Lib bkpl;
spine lt sunned.) Edwards. $39/£25

WINDLE, ERNEST. Windle's History of Santa Catalina
Island (and Guide). Avalon: Catalina Islander, 1931.
1st ed. Canvas-backed map tipped in at rear. Pict
wrappers (2 lt creases). Dawson. $125/£80

WINES, FREDERIC. The Liquor Problem in Its Legisla-
tive Aspects.... Boston, 1897. 1st ed. 342pp. VG. Fye.
$75/£48

WINGFIELD, R. D. Frost at Christmas. London: Constable, 1989. 1st ed. VF in dj. Mordida. $45/£29

WINKLES, B. French Cathedrals.... London, 1837. Engr
add'l tp, 49 plts. (Lt foxed, affecting some plts; fr
hinge cracked.) Orig cl (rebacked w/buckram).
Swann*. $69/£44

WINLOCK, H. E. et al. The Monastery of Epiphanius.
NY: MMA, 1926. Ltd to 500. 2 vols. Folio. 35 plts; 17
plts. Teg. 1/2 calf (rubbed, spine sl chipped). Archaeologia. $650/£417

WINOGRAND, GARRY. The Animals. NY: MOMA,
1969. 1st ed, 1st bk. (Owner stamp, old sticker residue), else NF in pict stiff wrappers. Cahan. $75/£48

WINOGRAND, GARRY. Garry Winogrand. El Cajon,
CA: Grossmont College Gallery, 1976. 1st ed. 40 full-
pg b/w photos. Fine in pict stiff wrappers (lt rubbed).
Cahan. $45/£29

WINOGRAND, GARRY. Public Relations. NY: MOMA,
1977. 1st ed. 75 plts. Fine in illus wrappers. Cahan.
$60/£38

WINOGRAND, GARRY. Women Are Beautiful. NY:
Light Gallery, 1975. 1st ed. Silver-emb cl. Fine in pict
dj (price-clipped). Cahan. $150/£96

WINSHIP, GEORGE PARKER. The Cambridge Press,
1638-1692. Phila, 1945. Rev slip. NF in dj (dknd, lt
chipped). Bohling. $45/£29

WINSLOW, DON. A Cool Breeze on the Underground. NY: St. Martin's, (1991). 1st ed. Fine in Fine dj. *Unger.* $100/£64

WINSLOW, DON. A Cool Breeze on the Underground. NY: St. Martin's, 1991. 1st ed. VF in dj. *Mordida.* $75/£48

WINSLOW, FORBES. The Anatomy of Suicide. London: Henry Renshaw, 1840. 1st ed. Frontis, (xvi),(340)pp. Emb brn cl (spine, joints chipped, cvrs bumped, rubbed; bkpl, stamp). Good. *Gach.* $275/£176

WINSLOW, FORBES. The Plea of Insanity in Criminal Cases. London: Henry Renshaw, 1848. 1st ed. Presentation copy. viii,78,(2)pp (marginal pencilling). Emb ptd grn cl (fr bd detached, sl edgewear). Good. *Gach.* $250/£160

WINSLOW, HORATIO and LESLIE QUIRK. Into Thin Air. GC: Crime Club, 1949. 1st Amer ed. VG (bkpl) in dj (browned, chipped, short tears). *Metropolitan*.* $126/£81

WINSLOW, L. FORBES. Man Humanity. NY: Mansfield, 1898. Frontis, xviii,451pp; 15 plts. (Cl worn.) Internally Good. *Goodrich.* $145/£93

WINSLOW, MIRON. Memoir of Mrs. Harriet L. Winslow.... NY: Amer Tract Soc, 1840. Frontis, 480pp. 1/4 calf (hinges worn). *Adelson.* $40/£26

WINSLOW, W. H. Cruising and Blockading. Pittsburgh, 1885. Inscribed. 207pp (sm emb lib stamp). *Ginsberg.* $150/£96

WINSOR, JUSTIN. Narrative and Critical History of America. Boston, 1889. One of 550 numbered sets of lg paper ed. 8 vols. Later cl. *Swann*.* $230/£147

Winter in the West. (By Charles Fenno Hoffman.) NY: Harper, 1835. 1st ed, 1st bk. 2 vols. (4),337; (4),346pp (lt foxing). VG (sl faded, rubbed, sl shaken). BAL 8521. Howes H568. *M & S.* $200/£128

WINTER, GEORGE. Journals and Indian Paintings of George Winter, 1837-1839. Indianapolis: IN Hist Soc, 1948. 1st ed. Dec blue/grey cl. Fine. *Harrington.* $60/£38

WINTER, GEORGE. The Journals and Indian Paintings...1837-1839. Indianapolis, 1948. Sm folio. *Swann*.* $57/£37

WINTER, J. A. A Doctor's Report on Dianetics Theory and Therapy. NY, 1951. 1st ed. VG (extrems sl worn). *Doctor's Library.* $50/£32

WINTER, WILLIAM (intro). The American Stage of Today. NY, 1910. Cl-backed bds (ex-lib, heavily worn, ends frayed). *King.* $95/£61

WINTERICH, JOHN T. Books and the Man. NY: Greenberg, 1929. 1st ed. Frontis, 14 plts. Fine in Excellent dj (sl faded, torn), pub's slipcase (cvrd w/contact paper). *Pirages.* $35/£22

WINTERICH, JOHN T. Collector's Choice. NY: Greenberg, 1928. 1st ed. (Inscrip.) NF dj (sl loss spine top). *Pirages.* $50/£32

WINTERICH, JOHN T. Early American Books and Printing. Boston: Houghton Mifflin, 1935. 1st ed. 8 plts. Good in dj. *Cox.* $31/£20

WINTERICH, JOHN T. Twenty-Three Books and the Stories Behind Them. Berkeley: Book Arts Club of Univ of CA, 1938. 1st ed. One of 750. Nice in VG dj. *Turtle Island.* $40/£26

WINTERNITZ, EMANUEL. Musical Autographs. Princeton, 1955. Dj (lt worn). *Freeman*.* $50/£32

WINTERNITZ, EMANUEL. Musical Instruments and Their Symbolism in Western Art. New Haven/London, 1979. 2nd ed. 96 plts. Good in dj. *Washton.* $45/£29

WINTERNITZ, M. C. et al. The Pathology of Influenza. New Haven: Yale Univ, 1920. 1st ed. 57 full-pg plts. Orig cl (rebacked w/tape). Good (ex-lib). *Glaser.* $100/£64

WINTERS, YVOR. The Giant Weapon. NY: Poets of the Year, (1943). 1st Amer ed. Wraps. Fine in dj (spine tear). *Polyanthos.* $25/£16

WINTERSON, JEANETTE. Boating for Beginners. London: Methuen, 1985. 1st UK ed. Fine in dj. *Moorhouse.* $117/£75

WINTERSON, JEANETTE. The Passion. Bloomsbury, 1987. 1st UK ed. Fine in dj. *Williams.* $86/£55

WINTERSON, JEANETTE. Sexing the Cherry. NY: Atlantic Monthly, (1989). 1st Amer ed. Fine in Fine dj. *Dermont.* $25/£16

WINTHER, OSCAR O. The Old Oregon Country. Bloomington, IN: IN Univ, (1950). 1st ed, 1st issue. Frontis. Fine in tan ptd wrappers. *Argonaut.* $150/£96

WINTHER, OSCAR O. The Transportation Frontier. NY: Holt, Rinehart & Winston, (1964). 1st ed. VG in dj. *Lien.* $30/£19

WINTHER, OSCAR O. The Transportation Frontier. NY: Holt, Rinehart & Winston, 1964. VG in dj. *Dumont.* $25/£16

WINTHROP, JOHN. The History of New England from 1630 to 1649. James Savage (notes). Boston: Little, Brown, 1853. Inscribed by Savage to Luther S. Cushing. 2 vols. Engr frontis port, (2),xx,514; 504pp. Patterned blue-grn cl. Very Nice (frontis, tps lt foxed). *Karmiole.* $100/£64

WINTHROP, ROBERT C. Reminiscences of Foreign Travel, a Fragment of Autobiography. Privately ptd, 1894. 104pp (rubberstamp ep, tp). VG. *Bohling.* $15/£10

WINTHROP, THEODORE. The Canoe and the Saddle. Boston: Ticknor & Fields, (1863). 5th ed. 375pp. Blind-stamped dec cl. VG+. *Mikesh.* $37/£24

WINTHROP, THEODORE. The Canoe and the Saddle. Boston: Ticknor & Fields, 1863. 1st ed. 375pp. Fair (spine ends chipped). Howes W584. *Lien.* $35/£22

WINTHROP, THEODORE. The Canoe and the Saddle. Boston: Ticknor & Fields, 1863. 1st ed. Purple cl. (Faded), else NF. *Cummins.* $60/£38

WINTHROP, THEODORE. The Canoe and the Saddle. Boston: Ticknor & Fields, 1863. 375pp. (Lt rubbed.) Howes W584. *Adelson.* $75/£48

WINTHROP, THEODORE. The Canoe and the Saddle. Edinburgh: William Paterson, 1883. 1st ed. (iv),266,16 (ads). (Upper joint tender, presentation label pastedown; extrems sl rubbed.) *Hollett.* $70/£45

WINTHROP, THEODORE. Life in the Open Air, and Other Papers. Boston: Ticknor & Fields, 1863. vi,374pp; port, plt. (Ends chipped.) *Adelson.* $60/£38

WINWAR, FRANCES. The Life of the Heart: George Sand and Her Times. Hamish Hamilton, 1946. (Spine bumped), else Good in dj (chipped, sm pieces missing). *Tiger.* $19/£12

WIRT, MRS. E. W. Flora's Dictionary. Balt: Lucas Bros, (1855). Color pict title, 8 Fine color litho plts. (Issues of this work appear w/varying numbers of plts, up to a full complement of 58.) Pub's gilt-pict cl (shelfworn, sl foxing, soil). Internally Sound. *Oinonen*.* $225/£144

WIRT, WILLIAM. The Letters of a British Spy. NY: Harper, 1856. 10th ed. Frontis port, 260pp. Nice (foxed, bkpl removed). *Bohling.* $18/£12

WIRT, WILLIAM. The Letters of the British Spy. NY: Harper, 1856. Frontis port, 260pp. Dec pub's cl (spine faded). Good. Howes W585. *Scribe's Perch*.* $28/£18

WIRT, WILLIAM. Sketches of the Life and Character of Patrick Henry. Phila: J. Webster, 1818. 2nd ed. Frontis port, xv,427,xiipp (lt stain upper corner 1st few leaves, blindstamp tp). Full leather (scuffed, worn, spine defect). Howes W586. *Bohling.* $18/£12

WISE, HERBERT and PHYLLIS (eds). Great Tales of Terror and the Supernatural. Random House, 1944. 1st ed. Good+ in dj (worn, lacks spine). *Madle.* $13/£8

WISE, JENNINGS C. The Red Man in the New World Drama. Washington: W.F. Robertson, 1931. 1st ed. Red cl, gilt. Fine. *Appelfeld.* $100/£64

WISE, JENNINGS CROPPER. The Long Arm of Lee. Lynchburg, 1959. VG in dj (spine faded). *Pratt.* $60/£38

WISE, JENNINGS CROPPER. The Military History of the Virginia Military Institute from 1839 to 1865. Lynchburg, VA, 1915. 16 plts. Untrimmed, unopened. Mod cl, gilt-stamped leather spine label. Fine. *Bohling.* $125/£80

WISE, KELLY (ed). The Photographers' Choice: A Book of Portfolios and Critical Opinion. Danbury, NH: Addison House, 1975. 1st ed. (Name, pencil notes, underlining), else VG in illus stiff wrappers. *Cahan.* $45/£29

WISE, KELLY. Lotte Jacobi. Danbury, NH: Addison House, 1978. 1st ed. (Owner stamp), else NF in fragmented dj. *Cahan.* $60/£38

WISE, LIEUT. Los Gringos: or, An Inside View of Mexico and California with Wanderings.... NY, 1849. 1st ed. 453pp. Orig blind-stamped grn cl, gilt. (Lt foxing), o/w VG+. *Turpen.* $175/£112

WISE, THOMAS J. A Bibliography of the Writings in Verse and Prose of George Gordon Noel.... London: Dawsons, 1963. Rpt. 2 vols. 2 frontis ports. Blue cl. Djs (sl chipped). *Maggs.* $78/£50

WISE, THOMAS J. A Conrad Library. London: Ptd for Private Circulation only, 1928. Ltd to 180. 70 photo plts. Teg. Red buckram, gilt, beveled edges. (Lt foxing; spine sl faded, trace of tiny bubble on back cvr.) *Shasky.* $235/£151

WISE, THOMAS J. and W. ROBERTSON NICOLL. Literary Anecdotes of the Nineteenth Century. London/NY: Hodder & Stoughton/Dodd, Mead, 1895-6. 1st ed. 2 vols. Teg, uncut. Pink cl, gilt. VG (vol 2 sl frayed, hinge papers cracked). *Macdonnell.* $300/£192

WISE-BROWN, MARGARET. The Little Fur Family. NY: Harper, (1946). 1st enlgd ed. Garth Williams (illus). 8vo. Blue cl. VG in Good++ + dj (sl chipped, sm repaired tear, sl dknd). *Dower.* $55/£35

WISKEMANN, ELIZABETH. Germany's Eastern Neighbours. OUP, 1956. Frontis map, pull-out map. Black cl, gilt. Fine in dj (spine lt browned). *Peter Taylor.* $42/£27

WISLIZENUS, FREDERICK A. A Journey to the Rocky Mountains in 1839. St. Louis, 1912. 1st ed in English. #146/500. Fldg map. 1/2 blue cl, lt blue bds (extrems sl worn, corner bumped). Fine. Howes W596. *Turpen.* $225/£144

WISLIZENUS, FREDERICK A. A Journey to the Rocky Mountains in the Year 1839. St. Louis, 1912. One of 500 numbered, signed 'Missouri Historical Society' (pub). Fldg map, port. Cl-backed bds (extrems worn, inner hinge cracked). VG. Howes W596. *Reese.* $225/£144

WISLIZENUS, FREDERICK A. A Journey to the Rocky Mountains in the Year 1839. St. Louis: MO Hist Soc, 1912. #138/500. Frontis port, fldg map. Teg. Cl-backed bds (edgewear, soil). Good (lt dampstain some leaves). Howes W596. *Bohling.* $160/£103

WISTAR, ISAAC JONES. Autobiography of Isaac Jones Wistar 1827-1905. NY/London, 1937. 1st trade ed. Frontis port, fldg map. Pencil sig, sm rubber stamp of Carl I. Wheat. NF. *Mcclintock.* $50/£32

WISTER, OWEN. The Dragon of Wantley. Phila, 1892. 1st ed. Pict cl. (Fep corner repaired), o/w Fine. *Argosy.* $175/£112

WISTER, OWEN. How Doth the Simple Spelling Bee. NY, 1907. 1st ed. Pict cl (lt rubbed). *Argosy.* $75/£48

WISTER, OWEN. Indispensable Information for Infants. NY, 1921. 1st ed. Red cl. VG. *Argosy.* $50/£32

WISTER, OWEN. The Jimmyjohn Boss. NY, 1900. 1st ed. Red cl, gilt, pict label. VG. *Argosy.* $100/£64

WISTER, OWEN. A Journey in Search of Christmas. NY, 1904. 1st ed. Red pict cl. VG. *Argosy.* $125/£80

WISTER, OWEN. Lady Baltimore. NY/London: Macmillan, 1906. 1st ed. One of 200 ptd on Japan vellum. This copy not numbered, but w/inscribed signed presentation. Frontis, 12 plts. Vegetable vellum spine. Internally Fine (lt edgewear, soil). *M & S.* $100/£64

WISTER, OWEN. Members of the Family. NY, 1911. 1st ed. Pict tan cl. VG. *Argosy.* $50/£32

WISTER, OWEN. Neighbors Henceforth. NY, 1922. 1st ed. Red cl, paper label. VG. *Argosy.* $45/£29

With General Sheridan in Lee's Last Campaign. (By Frederic Cushman Newhall.) Phila: Lippincott, 1866. 1st ed. Frontis, 235pp; fldg map. (Extrems scuffed), else VG. Howes N116. *Mcgowan.* $150/£96

WITHERBY, H. F. Bird Hunting on the White Nile. London: Office of 'Knowledge,' 1902. 1st ed. Pict cl (sl rubbed; eps sl spotted). *Hollett.* $101/£65

WITHERBY, H. F. et al. The Handbook of British Birds. London: H.F. & G. Witherby, 1938-41. 1st ed. 5 vols. 157 color plts. VG set in djs. *Hollett.* $234/£150

WITHERBY, H. F. et al. The Handbook of British Birds. London, 1943-45. 5 vols. Vols 1-2: 2nd imp; vols 3-5: 3rd imp. 156 plts. Good in djs. *Henly.* $148/£95

WITHERS, ALEXANDER S. (ed). Chronicles of Border Warfare. Clarksburg, VA: Joseph Israel, 1831. 1st ed. 320,(2)pp, ad leaf, 4-pg content list inserted at back. Contemp calf. (Tp sl soiled), o/w Nice. Howes W601. *Karmiole.* $375/£240

WITHERS, CARL. A Rocket in My Pocket. Bodley Head, 1969. 1st Eng ed. Susanne Suba (illus). 8vo. 214pp. Fine in pict dj (frayed). *Bookmark.* $23/£15

WITHERSPOON, JOHN. Dominion of Providence Over the Passions of Men. Phila: R. Aitken, 1776. 8vo. (4),78,(1)pp (foxed, lg piece torn last leaf, no loss). Untrimmed. Stitched pamphlet. *New Hampshire*.* $775/£497

WITHERSPOON, JOHN. A Sermon Preached at Princeton...May 17,1776.... Phila: R. Aitken, 1776. 8vo. 3/4 leather, marbled paper-cvrd bds (exterior foxing). *Metropolitan*.* $517/£331

WITHERSPOON, JOHN. The Works.... Phila, 1802. 2nd ed. 4 vols. Contemp tree sheep (worn). *Swann*.* $517/£331

WITTEN, JAMES W. Report on the Agriculture Prospects...of Alaska. Washington: GPO, 1904. 28 plts. (Heavily spotted cvrs), else VG. *Perier.* $75/£48

WITTGENSTEIN, LUDWIG. Remarks on the Foundations of Mathematics. Anscombe (trans). Oxford: Basil Blackwell, 1956. 1st ed. VG in dj (browned, worn). *Ash.* $156/£100

WITTGENSTEIN, LUDWIG. Tractatus Logico-Philosophicus. Bertrand Russell (intro). Kegan Paul, Trench, Trubner, 1922. 1st ed in English. Good (sl wear spine ends, few mks). *Ash.* $460/£295

WITTHUS, RUTHERFORD W. Blickensderfer: Images of the West. (Boulder): Cordillera, 1986. 1st ed. Ltd to 2000. 64 full-pg plts. Fine in illus dj. *Cahan.* $45/£29

WITTKE, CARL. Tambo and Bones: A History of the American Minstrel Stage. Durham: Duke Univ, 1930. 1st ed. Illus cl. NF in matching dj. *Cahan.* $60/£38

WITTKOWER, RUDOLF and MARGOT. Born Under Saturn. London, 1963. Fine in dj (spine sl faded). *Europa.* $59/£38

WITTKOWER, RUDOLF and MARGOT. Born Under Saturn. NY, 1963. Good in dj. *Washton.* $75/£48

WITTKOWER, RUDOLF. Gian Lorenzo Bernini. London, 1966. 2nd ed. 126 plts. Good in dj. *Washton.* $90/£58

WITTKOWER, RUDOLF. Palladio and Palladianism. NY, 1974. Good in dj. *Washton.* $75/£48

WITWER, H. C. The Leather Pushers. NY: Putnam, 1921. 1st ed. (Clipping pasted to fep), else Fine in white dj (lt soiled, sm nicks, tears, 2 sl stains rear panel). *Between The Covers.* $150/£96

WIXOM, WILLIAM D. Renaissance Bronzes from Ohio Collections. Cleveland Museum of Art, 1975. Good in wraps (sl rubbed). *Washton.* $50/£32

WIZINSKI, SY. Charles Manson: Love Letters to a Secret Disciple. Terre Haute, IN: Moonmad, 1976. 1st ed. NF in dj (sl rubbed, score mks). *Sclanders.* $28/£18

WODARCH, CHARLES. An Introduction to the Study of Conchology. London: Longman, Hurst, Rees et al, 1820. 1st ed. xxiv,(124),(ii)pp; 4 hand-colored plts. Orig bds (rubbed, sl split). Good. *Ash.* $117/£75

WODEHOUSE, P. G. America, I Like You. NY: S&S, 1956. 1st ed. Fine in VG dj (lt worn, sm tears). *Between The Covers.* $75/£48

WODEHOUSE, P. G. America, I Like You. NY: S&S, 1956. 1st ed. 2-tone bds. Fine in dj. *Appelfeld.* $85/£54

WODEHOUSE, P. G. Bertie Wooster Sees It Through. NY: S&S, 1955. 1st Amer ed. 1st ptg, 2nd state. Grey-blue cl spine, grey-blue stiff bds, gold/brn lettering. (Sm ink inscrip, sig), else Fine in NF pict dj. *Vandoros.* $150/£96

WODEHOUSE, P. G. Big Money. Herbert Jenkins, (1931). 1st British ed. Orange cl. Nice (sl mks). *Ash.* $78/£50

WODEHOUSE, P. G. Big Money. London: Herbert Jenkins, 1931. 1st ed. (Feps spotted; sl faded), o/w Excellent. *Hollett.* $101/£65

WODEHOUSE, P. G. Bill the Conqueror. NY, (1924). 1st Amer ed. (Sm label rep; spine sl dknd, extrems frayed.) *King.* $75/£48

WODEHOUSE, P. G. Bill the Conqueror. NY: George H. Doran, (1924). 1st Amer ed. (Lt soil), o/w Fine. *Hermitage.* $125/£80

WODEHOUSE, P. G. Bill the Conqueror. London, 1924. 1st issue w/cat dated 9/24. (Edges sl foxed), o/w Nice. *Buckley.* $62/£40

WODEHOUSE, P. G. The Brinkmanship of Galahad Threepwood. NY: S&S, (1964). 1st ed. Cl-backed pict bds. VG in dj. *Ash.* $78/£50

WODEHOUSE, P. G. The Brinkmanship of Galahad Threepwood. (NY): S&S, 1964. 1st US ed. VG in dj. *Hadley.* $55/£35

WODEHOUSE, P. G. Carry On, Jeeves. London: Herbert Jenkins, 1925. 1st ed. Grn pict cl, black lettering. Fine (lacks dj). *Vandoros.* $285/£183

WODEHOUSE, P. G. Cocktail Time. London: Herbert Jenkins, 1958. 1st ed. VG in dj (sl edgeworn). *Hollett.* $70/£45

WODEHOUSE, P. G. The Code of the Woosters. Herbert Jenkins, 1938. 1st ed. (Feps, margins lt browned; spine lt discolored, bumped, sm split.) *Edwards.* $47/£30

WODEHOUSE, P. G. The Code of the Woosters. NY, 1938. 1st ed. NF in dec cl. *Smith.* $25/£16

WODEHOUSE, P. G. The Coming of Bill. London, 1920. 1st ed. (Eps sl browned; spine sunned, cloth bubbled), o/w Okay. *Buckley.* $47/£30

WODEHOUSE, P. G. The Crime Wave at Blandings. GC, 1937. 1st ed. Grn pict cl. VG + (lt soiled). *Smith.* $25/£16

WODEHOUSE, P. G. A Damsel in Distress. London: Herbert Jenkins, (c. 1930). 12th ptg. Orange cl (rubbed, soiled; lib label fr flyleaf, fr dj panel laid down pastedown). *Hollett.* $16/£10

WODEHOUSE, P. G. Do Butlers Burgle Banks? Herbert Jenkins, (1968). 1st British ed. Nice (edges sl discolored) in dj (sl spotted). *Ash.* $62/£40

WODEHOUSE, P. G. Do Butlers Burgle Banks? London, 1968. 1st ed. VG in NF dj. *Smith.* $25/£16

WODEHOUSE, P. G. Do Butlers Burgle Banks? London: Herbert Jenkins, 1968. 1st Eng ed. Grn buckram, silver spine lettering. Fine in Fine pict dj. *Vandoros.* $150/£96

WODEHOUSE, P. G. Doctor Sally. London: Methuen, 1933. 3rd ed. Blue cl (lt soiled, sm tear). *Hollett.* $19/£12

WODEHOUSE, P. G. Enter Psmith. London: A&C Black, 1935. 1st ed. (Spine faded, rubbed.) *Hollett.* $117/£75

WODEHOUSE, P. G. A Few Quick Ones. London: Herbert Jenkins, (1959). 1st ed, 2nd issue. VG in dj (lt rubbed). *Hermitage.* $45/£29

WODEHOUSE, P. G. Full Moon. London: Herbert Jenkins, (1947). 1st British ed. Orange cl. Fine in pict dj. *Glenn.* $150/£96

WODEHOUSE, P. G. Full Moon. London: Herbert Jenkins, (1948). 1st Eng ed. Orange cl, black lettering, spine device. Fine in NF pict dj. *Vandoros.* $250/£160

WODEHOUSE, P. G. Full Moon. London, n.d. (1947). 1st Eng ed. (Reps foxed; spine sl sunned, corners lt bumped.) *King.* $25/£16

WODEHOUSE, P. G. Galahad at Blandings. London: Herbert Jenkins, 1965. 1st Eng ed. Red cl, gilt spine. Fine in Fine pict dj. *Vandoros.* $155/£99

WODEHOUSE, P. G. Golf Without Tears. NY: Doran, (1924). 1st US ed. Color pict eps; untrimmed. Lt grn cl, dk grn lettering. (Fr hinge lt cracked, rear hinge severely cracked; sl dusty.) *Baltimore*.* $70/£45

WODEHOUSE, P. G. Golf Without Tears. NY, 1924. Rpt. Black cl, orange lettering. VG-. *Smith.* $30/£19

WODEHOUSE, P. G. Good Morning Bill. A Three Act Comedy. London: Methuen, 1928. 1st ed. Lt blue cl, black lettering. Fine (lacks dj). *Vandoros.* $195/£125

WODEHOUSE, P. G. Good Morning, Bill. London, 1928. 1st ed. Nice (few pp sl foxed; spine sl bumped). *Buckley.* $47/£30

WODEHOUSE, P. G. He Rather Enjoyed It. NY, 1925. Rpt. NF in dec cl. *Smith.* $25/£16

WODEHOUSE, P. G. The Heart of a Goof. London: Herbert Jenkins, (1927). 4th ptg. Dec orange cl (mkd, stained; pastedown edges dampstained, feps lt browned, spotted). *Hollett.* $70/£45

WODEHOUSE, P. G. Heavy Weather. London: Herbert Jenkins, (1935). 2nd ptg. VG in dj (lt worn, top edge defective). *Hollett.* $39/£25

WODEHOUSE, P. G. Heavy Weather. Boston, 1933. 1st ed. Black cl, bds, red lettering. VG. *Smith.* $35/£22

WODEHOUSE, P. G. Heavy Weather. Boston: Little Brown, 1933. 1st ed. 8vo. Black cl, red lettering, decs. Excellent in NF pict dj. *Vandoros.* $895/£574

WODEHOUSE, P. G. The Ice in the Bedroom. S&S, 1961. 1st ed. NF in VG dj. *Certo.* $25/£16

WODEHOUSE, P. G. The Ice in the Bedroom. NY: S&S, 1961. 1st ed. Inscribed, signed. Black cl spine, black bds w/white/yellow/red lettering. Fine in VG + pict dj (3 short closed tears). *Vandoros*. $375/£240

WODEHOUSE, P. G. If I Were You. London, 1931. 1st ed. Nice. *Buckley*. $39/£25

WODEHOUSE, P. G. Indiscretions of Archie. London: Herbert Jenkins, (ca 1930?). 10th ptg. (Sl soiled, spine faded; lt creased, label fep; ex-lib, upper dj panel laid down on pastedown.) *Hollett*. $31/£20

WODEHOUSE, P. G. Indiscretions of Archie. London: Herbert Jenkins, (late 1930s). 12th ptg. Orange cl, black lettering, pub's device spine; single line frame, black lettering fr cvr. Fine in VG + pict dj. *Vandoros*. $225/£144

WODEHOUSE, P. G. The Inimitable Jeeves. London: Herbert Jenkins, 1923. 1st ed. Lt grn pict cl, dk grn lettering, dwg. (Spine lt rubbed; lacks dj), else NF. *Vandoros*. $275/£176

WODEHOUSE, P. G. Jeeves in the Offing. Herbert Jenkins, (1960). 1st British ed, 1st issue, w/fly-title erroneously giving the name of Wodehouse's previous book, 'A Few Quick Ones.' Nice in dj (sl worn, nicked). *Ash*. $117/£75

WODEHOUSE, P. G. Jeeves. NY, 1923. Rpt. NF in dec cl. *Smith*. $25/£16

WODEHOUSE, P. G. Laughing Gas. London, 1936. 1st ed. (Spine sl faded), o/w VG. *Buckley*. $23/£15

WODEHOUSE, P. G. Leave It to Psmith. NY: Doran, (1924). 1st US ed, w/pub's design on c. pg. Blue cl, black lettering. (Lt aged, sl shaken; lt edgeworn, sl rubbed.) Pict dj (sl worn, torn, chipped, neatly repaired on verso). *Baltimore**. $70/£45

WODEHOUSE, P. G. The Little Nugget. London: Methuen, 1929. 13th ed. Blue cl (dampstained). Dj (soiled, chipped). *Hollett*. $31/£20

WODEHOUSE, P. G. Lord Emsworth and Others. London, 1937. 1st ed. (Eps sl browned), o/w VG. *Buckley*. $47/£30

WODEHOUSE, P. G. Lord Emsworth and Others. London: Herbert Jenkins, 1937. 1st ed. Bright red cl, gilt. Very Nice (edges spotted). *Hollett*. $39/£25

WODEHOUSE, P. G. Louder and Funnier. London: Faber & Faber, 1932. Later issue, bound from same sheets as 1st issue, in grn cl. Excellent (spine sl soiled) in dj (sl rubbed, soiled). *Gekoski*. $390/£250

WODEHOUSE, P. G. The Luck of the Bodkins. Boston, 1936. 1st ed. NF in dec grn cl. *Smith*. $30/£19

WODEHOUSE, P. G. The Man Upstairs. London: Methuen, 1927. 12th ed. (Bds dampstained.) Dj (spine chipped, soiled). *Hollett*. $39/£25

WODEHOUSE, P. G. The Man with Two Left Feet. London: Methuen, 1924. 7th ed. (Eps lt mkd; lower bd dampstained.) Dj (worn, torn). *Hollett*. $70/£45

WODEHOUSE, P. G. Meet Mr. Mulliner. Herbert Jenkins, (1927). 1st ed. Nice (edges sl spotted). *Ash*. $117/£75

WODEHOUSE, P. G. Meet Mr. Mulliner. London: Herbert Jenkins, n.d. 3rd ptg. Orange cl (few mks; prelims, ads foxed). *Hollett*. $39/£25

WODEHOUSE, P. G. Money for Nothing. London: Herbert Jenkins, (1928). 2nd ptg. Orange cl (lt mkd; feps browned, edges lt dusty, mkd). *Hollett*. $31/£20

WODEHOUSE, P. G. Money in the Bank. Doubleday Doran, 1942. 1st Amer ed. VG in dj (spine faded). *Hadley*. $211/£135

WODEHOUSE, P. G. Money in the Bank. GC, 1942. 1st ed. NF in dec cl. *Smith*. $25/£16

WODEHOUSE, P. G. Mr. Mulliner Speaking. London: Herbert Jenkins, (1929). 1st ed. Orange cl. (Spotted, esp 1st, last leaves; sl faded, rubbed.) *Cox*. $28/£18

WODEHOUSE, P. G. Much Obliged Jeeves. London: Barrie & Jenkins, 1971. 1st Eng ed. Blue cl, gilt spine. Fine in Fine dj (price-clipped). *Vandoros*. $150/£96

WODEHOUSE, P. G. Mulliner Nights. Doubleday Doran, 1933. Stated 1st ed. Dec spine. (Fr flap dj pasted to fep), o/w Good-. *Scribe's Perch**. $20/£13

WODEHOUSE, P. G. Nothing but Wodehouse. Ogden Nash (ed). GC, 1932. 1st ed. VG-. *Smith*. $20/£13

WODEHOUSE, P. G. Piccadilly Jim. London: Herbert Jenkins, (c. 1929). 15th ptg. Grn cl (extrems sl rubbed; fore-edge lt spotted). *Hollett*. $31/£20

WODEHOUSE, P. G. Pigs Have Wings. GC: Doubleday, 1952. 1st ed. Advance rev copy, pub's slip laid in. Gray bds, white spine lettering. NF in pict dj (spine sunned, sl edgeworn). *Baltimore**. $60/£38

WODEHOUSE, P. G. The Prince and Betty. NY: W.J. Watt, (1912). 1st ed. Black cl, pict insets. (Sl cocked, sl mottling, spine gilt dull), else Very Nice. *Turtle Island*. $200/£128

WODEHOUSE, P. G. Psmith in the City. London: A&C Black, 1950. 14th rpt. Grn cvr, red spine lettering. Fine in NF pict dj. *Vandoros*. $125/£80

WODEHOUSE, P. G. Quick Service. London: Herbert Jenkins, 1940. 1st ed, 1st reissue. Orange cl, gilt. (Sig.) *Hollett*. $86/£55

WODEHOUSE, P. G. The Return of Jeeves. NY, 1954. 1st Amer ed. NF (sl cock) in VG dj (sl edgewear, spine sl rubbed). *Warren*. $95/£61

WODEHOUSE, P. G. The Return of Jeeves. NY: S&S, 1954. 1st ed. Fine in dj (lt worn). *Hermitage*. $200/£128

WODEHOUSE, P. G. Right Ho, Jeeves. London, 1934. 1st ed. (Sig; spine bumped, cvrs sl soiled), else VG. *Buckley*. $47/£30

WODEHOUSE, P. G. Sam the Sudden. London, 1925. 1st ed. (Edges foxed), else VG. *Buckley*. $47/£30

WODEHOUSE, P. G. Spring Fever. London: Herbert Jenkins, (1948). 1st Eng ed. Orange cl, black lettering, pub's device on spine. Fine in Fine pict dj. *Vandoros*. $250/£160

WODEHOUSE, P. G. Spring Fever. GC: Doubleday, 1948. 1st ed. Reddish-brn cl, white lettering, flowers down spine. Fine in Fine dj. *Vandoros*. $275/£176

WODEHOUSE, P. G. Summer Lightning. London: Herbert Jenkins, (1931). 2nd ptg. Orange cl. Excellent (feps lt browned). *Hollett*. $47/£30

WODEHOUSE, P. G. Summer Moonshine. London: Herbert Jenkins, (1949). 4th Eng ed. Orange cl, black lettering. NF in NF dj; spine price listing 5/ net. *Vandoros*. $125/£80

WODEHOUSE, P. G. Thank You, Jeeves! Boston: Little, Brown, 1934. 1st Amer ed. Good (spine sl sunned, top edge sl spotted). *Ash*. $78/£50

WODEHOUSE, P. G. Three Men and a Maid. NY, 1922. Rpt. NF in grn cl. *Smith*. $25/£16

WODEHOUSE, P. G. Ukridge. London, 1924. 1st ed. (Sl bumped), else VG. *Buckley*. $55/£35

WODEHOUSE, P. G. Uncle Dynamite. London: Herbert Jenkins, (1948). 1st ed. (Top edge spotted; spine faded.) Dj (hinges worn, spine soiled, defective). *Hollett*. $70/£45

WODEHOUSE, P. G. Very Good, Jeeves. (Toronto): McClelland & Stewart, 1930. 1st Canadian ed. 312pp. VG in red cl. *Hadley*. $55/£35

WODEHOUSE, P. G. Very Good, Jeeves. GC, 1930. Ltr ptg. VG. *Smith*. $35/£22

WODEHOUSE, P. G. Very Good, Jeeves. GC, 1930. 1st ed. (Cvrs worn, soiled.) *King*. $65/£42

WODEHOUSE, P. G. The World of Psmith. London: Barrie & Jenkins, 1974. 1st ed. Fine (bkpl) in Fine dj (price-clipped). *Vandoros*. $100/£64

WODEHOUSE, P. G. Young Men in Spats. London, 1936. 1st ed. (Eps foxed; spine faded, cvrs sl soiled), o/w VG. *Buckley.* $39/£25

WODEHOUSE, P. G. Yours, Plum. Letters. F. Donaldson (ed). London, 1990. 1st ed. Dj. *Typographeum.* $25/£16

WODEHOUSE, P. G. and GUY BOLTON. Bring on the Girls! NY, 1953. 1st ed. VG in dj. *Argosy.* $75/£48

WODEHOUSE, P. G. and GUY BOLTON. Bring on the Girls. NY: S&S, 1953. 1st ed. NF in dj. *Turtle Island.* $50/£32

WODEHOUSE, P. G. and IAN HAY. A Damsel in Distress. London: Samuel French, 1930. 1st Eng ed, 1st issue. 89pp + 2pp ads. VG in blue lettered wraps. *Hadley.* $78/£50

WOIWODE, LARRY. What I'm Going to Do, I Think. NY: FSG, (1969). 1st ed, 1st bk. Fine in dj (lt worn, chip). *Hermitage.* $45/£29

WOIWODE, LARRY. What I'm Going to Do, I Think. NY: FSG, (1969). 1st ed, 1st bk. VF in dj (sm tear rear panel). *Dermont.* $75/£48

WOJCIECHOWSKA, MAIA. Shadow of a Bull. NY: Atheneum, 1964. 1st ed. Alvin Smith (illus). 5 3/4 x 8 1/2. 187pp. Good in dj. *Cattermole.* $45/£29

WOJCIECHOWSKA, MAIA. Through the Broken Mirror with Alice. NY: HBJ, 1972. 1st ed. 5 1/2 x 8 1/2. 126pp. As New in dj. *Cattermole.* $15/£10

Wolf Hunting in Lower Brittany. London, 1875. (Cl sl rubbed.) *Grayling.* $117/£75

WOLF, A. A History of Science, Technology and Philosophy. 1968. 2nd ed. 2 vols. VG in djs. *Whitehart.* $55/£35

WOLF, EDWIN II with JOHN F. FLEMING. Rosenbach, a Biography. Cleveland/NY: World, 1960. 1st ed. Dj. *Rostenberg & Stern.* $65/£42

WOLF, EDWIN. The Dispersal of the Library of William Byrd of Westover. Amer Antiq. Soc, 1958. Paper cvr (sm tears). VG-. *Book Broker.* $35/£22

WOLF, GARY. Who Censored Roger Rabbit? NY: St. Martin's, (1981). 1st ed. (Sl rubbing corners), else Fine in NF dj (extrems sl rubbed). *Between The Covers.* $150/£96

WOLF, GARY. Who Censored Roger Rabbit? NY: St. Martin's, 1981. 1st ed. (Rmdr mk lower edge), else Fine in Fine dj. *Old London.* $135/£87

WOLF, SIMON. The American Jew as Patriot, Soldier and Citizen. Phila/NY: Levytype/Brentano's, 1895. 1st ed. Text VG (text block separated from casing, pp edges soiled, foxed; rubbed). *Waverly*.* $71/£46

WOLF, STEWART and HAROLD G. WOLFF. Human Gastric Function. NY: OUP, (1943). 1st ed. Color frontis, 4 full-pg plts. VG (lib stamp tp). *Glaser.* $100/£64

WOLFE, BERNARD. Limbo. NY: Random House, (1952). 1st ed. (Damp adhesion fore-edge bds, mirrored on dj), o/w Attractive in dj. *Reese.* $30/£19

WOLFE, BERNARD. Limbo. R-H, 1952. 1st ed. VG+ in VG dj (lt wear, tear, flaking). *Aronovitz.* $38/£24

WOLFE, HUMBERT (intro). The Life of Percy Bysshe Shelley. London, 1933. 2 vols. 16 photogravure ports and views. (Vol 2 lt spotted; cl lt soiled.) *Edwards.* $47/£30

WOLFE, HUMBERT. The Craft of Verse. Oxford Poetry Essay. NY: Crosby Gaige, 1928. 1st ed. One of 395 numbered, signed. Dec cl, paper label. (Spine sl sunned), else Very Nice. *Reese.* $40/£26

WOLFE, HUMBERT. Dialogues and Monologues. London: Gollancz, 1928. 1st ed. VG in dj (browned, lt chipped). *Antic Hay.* $27/£17

WOLFE, HUMBERT. Homage to Meleager. NY: Fountain, 1930. #209/450 signed. 1/2 leather, gilt. NF (sl rubbed). *Polyanthos.* $50/£32

WOLFE, HUMBERT. Notes on English Verse Satire. London: Hogarth, 1929. 1st ed. (Sig, eps, fore-edge sl foxed; spine sl faded), else VG in dj (soiled, chipped, spine faded, 2 closed tears top edge). *Virgo.* $31/£20

WOLFE, N. B. Startling Facts in Modern Spiritualism. Cincinnati, 1883. 1st ed. 25 plts. Gilt decs. (Back cvr spots), o/w VG+. *Middle Earth.* $95/£61

WOLFE, RICHARD J. Jacob Bigelow's American Medical Botany, 1817-1821. North Hills, PA: Bird & Bull, 1979. One of 300. 1 color, 1 plain plt. Leatherbacked flowered bds, gilt. *Kane*.* $200/£128

WOLFE, RICHARD J. Secular Music in America 1801-1825. NY, 1964. 1st ed. 3 vols. (Lt worn.) *Oinonen*.* $150/£96

WOLFE, RICHARD J. (ed). Three Early Essays on Paper Marbling, 1642-1765. Newtown: Bird & Bull, 1987. One of 310 numbered. Prospectus laid in. 1/4 morocco. *Swann*.* $103/£66

WOLFE, RICHARD J. and PAUL McKENNA. Louis Herman Kinder and Fine Bookbinding in America. Newtown: Bird & Bull, 1985. One of 325 numbered. Prospectus laid in. 1/4 morocco. *Swann*.* $258/£165

WOLFE, THOMAS. The Correspondence of Thomas Wolfe and Homer Andrew Watt. NY: NY Univ, 1954. 1st Amer ed. NF in NF dj. *Polyanthos.* $25/£16

WOLFE, THOMAS. The Hills Beyond. NY: New Avon Library, (1944). 1st pb ed. Ptd wrappers (fore-edge sl discolored). *Turtle Island.* $15/£10

WOLFE, THOMAS. The Letters of Thomas Wolfe. Elizabeth Nowell (ed). NY, (1956). 1st Amer ed. NF in dj (spine sl sunned, few sm nicks). *Polyanthos.* $25/£16

WOLFE, THOMAS. Look Homeward Angel. NY: Scribner, 1947. 1st illus ed. 12 plts. 2 newspaper cuttings laid in. Lt gray cl, gilt. NF (eps offsetting; sl bumped) in VG dj (chipped, chip top edge). *Blue Mountain.* $35/£22

WOLFE, THOMAS. Look Homeward, Angel. NY: Editions for the Armed Services, (1944-1945?). NF in illus stiff wrappers. *Turtle Island.* $40/£26

WOLFE, THOMAS. The Story of a Novel. NY/London: Scribner, 1936. 1st ed. Lt brick-red cl, gilt. Fine in VG dj (sl soiled, chipped). *Blue Mountain.* $50/£32

WOLFE, THOMAS. The Web and the Rock. NY: Harper, 1939. 1st ed. Gilt cl. VG in dj (sl nicked, chipped, smudge). *Reese.* $85/£54

WOLFE, TOM. The Electric Kool-Aid Acid Test. NY: Farrar, (1968). 1st ed. Fine in dj (price-clipped, nick, top edge sl sunned). *Reese.* $150/£96

WOLFE, TOM. From Bauhaus to Our House. NY, (1981). 1st ed. VG in dj. *Argosy.* $35/£22

WOLFE, TOM. From Bauhaus to Our House. NY: Farrar Straus, (1981). One of 350 numbered, signed. Fine in Fine slipcase. *Lenz.* $150/£96

WOLFE, TOM. Mauve Gloves and Madmen, Clutter and Vine. NY, 1976. 1st Amer ed. Fine in Fine dj (price-clipped). *Polyanthos.* $30/£19

WOLFE, TOM. The Pump House Gang. NY, 1968. 1st Amer ed. Fine (spine extrems sl rubbed, sm name) in Fine dj. *Polyanthos.* $35/£22

WOLFE, TOM. Radical Chic and Mau-Mauing the Flak Catchers. NY: FSG, (1970). 1st ed. Fine in dj. *Jaffe.* $65/£42

WOLFE, TOM. Radical Chic and Mau-Mauing the Flak Catchers. NY, 1970. 1st Amer ed. Fine in dj (spine top sl rubbed). *Polyanthos.* $30/£19

WOLFF, JULIAN. A Ramble in Bohemia. NY: Privately Ptd, (1957). 1st US ed. 4 leaves. This copy has stamp affixed. VG in ptd wrappers. *Gravesend.* $40/£26

WOLFF, TOBIAS. The Other Miller. Derry, NH/Ridgewood, NJ: Babcock & Koontz, 1986. #I of 40 (of 240) numbered I to XL, signed by Wolff and Gaylord Schanilec (illus). Fine in 1/4 cl, paper-cvrd bds. *Lame Duck.* $275/£176

WOLFF, TOBIAS. Ugly Rumors. London: George Allen & Unwin, (1975). 1st ed, 1st bk. Signed, inscribed, dated. (Sl edgeworn), else NF in dj. *Waverly*.* $467/£299

WOLFF, TOBIAS. Ugly Rumors. London: George Allen & Unwin, 1975. 1st ed, 1st bk. Fine (spine sl slanted) in dj. *Lame Duck.* $850/£545

WOLFF, WERNER. Island of Death. NY: J.J. Augustin, (1948). 1st ed. 20 plts. VG in dj. *Cullen.* $100/£64

WOLHUTER, H. Memories of a Game Ranger. London, 1953. (Spine sl faded.) *Grayling.* $23/£15

WOLITZER, HILMA. Ending. NY, 1974. 1st ed, 1st bk. NF in NF dj. *Warren.* $35/£22

WOLKERS, JAN. Turkish Delight. NY: Delacorte, 1974. 1st US ed. Fine in dj. *Lame Duck.* $45/£29

WOLLE, MURIEL. The Bonanza Trail. Bloomington: IN Univ, 1953. 1st ed. VG in Good dj. *Archer.* $22/£14

WOLLE, MURIEL. The Bonanza Trail: Ghost Towns and Mining Camps of the West. Bloomington: IN Univ, 1953. 1st ed. Pict eps. Orange cl. Fine in NF dj. *Harrington.* $40/£26

WOLLHEIM, DONALD A. (ed). The Portable Novels of Science. NY, (1945). 1st ed. VG. *Mcclintock.* $10/£6

WOLLIN, NILS G. Modern Swedish Arts and Crafts in Pictures. NY: Scribner, (1931). Yellow cl. (Spine head, foot reinforced, ex-lib), else Fine. *Metropolitan*.* $97/£62

WOLLSTONECRAFT, MARY. Letters Written During a Short Residence in Sweden, Norway and Denmark. J. Johnson, 1796. Contemp marbled bds, later leather spine, corners. Good (sm ink spot tp, sl spotting). *Tiger.* $858/£550

WOLLSTONECRAFT, MARY. Letters Written During a Short Residence.... London: J. Johnson, 1796. 1st ed. 8vo. (iv),262,ivpp + ad leaf. Contemp mottled calf (neatly rebacked), leather label. (Tp resized, 1840 inscrip, emb stamp rolled out, sl dknd), else Excellent. *Second Life.* $1,500/£962

WOLLSTONECRAFT, MARY. Original Stories from Real Life. London: J. Johnson, 1791. 1st ed thus. 8vo. 3pp ads at end. 6 plts by William Blake. Contemp full leather (rebacked in later leather; corners, edges professionally restored in leather), red leather spine label lettered in gilt. *Kane*.* $1,500/£962

WOLLSTONECRAFT, MARY. Vindication of the Rights of Woman. Boston: Thomas & Andrews, 1792. 340pp. Full calf (sl worn, hinges cracked). (Lt foxed), o/w Contents VG. *New Hampshire*.* $300/£192

WOLTERS, R. A. The Labrador Retriever: The History, the People. L.A.: Petersen, 1981. One of 300 signed. Silk bkmk. NF. *Mikesh.* $150/£96

WOMACK, BOB. The Echo of Hoofbeats. Shelbyville, 1973. 1st ed. VG in VG dj. *October Farm.* $185/£119

Wonder Book of Freaks and Animals in the Barnum and Bailey Greatest Show on Earth. 1898-9. London: Walter Hill, n.d. (c. 1898). Sm 4to. 44pp. VG in color pict wraps. *Dramatis Personae.* $200/£128

WONG QUINCEY, J. Chinese Hunter. London, (1939). NF. *Grayling.* $187/£120

WOOD, CASEY A. and F. MARJORIE FYFE (eds). The Art of Falconry. Stanford, CA: Stanford Univ, 1943. 1st ed. Grn cl, gilt device fr cvr. (Cvrs sl rubbed), else Fine. *Cummins.* $200/£128

WOOD, FERGUS J. (ed). The Prince William Sound, Alaska, Earthquake of 1964 and After Shocks. Washington: US Dept of Commerce, 1966-1969. 4 vols. (Ink name), else VG. *Perier.* $97/£62

WOOD, FREDERIC J. Turnpikes of New England and Evolution of the Same Through England, Virginia, and Maryland. Boston: Marshall Jones, 1919. 1st ptg. Buckram (faded, dull, esp spine). Good. *Bohling.* $40/£26

WOOD, J. E. R. (ed). Detour. (London), 1946. Cl-backed bds (stained, frayed, spine dull). *King.* $85/£54

WOOD, J. G. Common British Beetles. London: Routledge, n.d. (c 1870). 175pp; 12 color plts (1 foxed). Aeg. Dec cl (sl faded). VG. *Savona.* $47/£30

WOOD, J. G. Common Objects of the Microscope. London: Routledge, Warne, Routledge, 1861. 1st ed. 188pp + 8pp Baker cat. Blind-stamped cl. VG. *Savona.* $47/£30

WOOD, J. G. Common Objects of the Microscope. London: Routledge, 1902. 3rd ed. 14 plts (12 color). Teg. Good (inscrip). *Savona.* $19/£12

WOOD, J. G. Homes Without Hands. London, 1875. xix,632pp (feps lt browned). Marbled eps, edges. Contemp gilt-ruled calf (worn), morocco spine label (rubbed). *Edwards.* $70/£45

WOOD, J. G. Nature's Teachings. London, 1907. Frontis. Pict cl, gilt. (Edges sl foxed), o/w Fine. *Henly.* $25/£16

WOOD, J. G. Nature's Teachings. London: Virtue, n.d. (c 1890). New, rev ed. Frontis (top corner neatly repaired), 433pp. New eps. Gilt-dec cl (spine ends, hinges neatly repaired; sl worn). Good. *Savona.* $39/£25

WOOD, JOSEPH R. Tablet Manufacture: Its History, Pharmacy and Practice. Phila, 1904. 1st ed. Red cl (sl worn). VG. *Doctor's Library.* $65/£42

WOOD, JOSEPH TURNEY. The Puering, Bating and Drenching of Skins. London/NY, 1912. (Ads browned, plt sl torn, no loss; cl spine sl rubbed, lower bd sl water stained.) *Edwards.* $55/£35

WOOD, MARGARET. The English Mediaeval House. 1981. Rpt. Frontis, 60pp 1/2 tone plts, 32pp engrs. Dj. *Edwards.* $39/£25

WOOD, MRS. HENRY. Dene Hollow. Richard Bentley, 1879. Rpt. Frontis. Good (sl spotted; spine bumped). *Tiger.* $22/£14

WOOD, MRS. HENRY. Mildred Arkell. Tinsley Bros, 1865. 1st ed. 3 vols. (4),327; (4),334; (4),334pp (no 1/2-titles, margin tears, sl blemishes). Contemp 1/2 crimson roan, marbled sides (rubbed). Sound. *Cox.* $70/£45

WOOD, N. A. The Birds of Michigan. Ann Arbor, 1951. 16 plts. Mod 1/4 morocco. Good (few lib stamps). *Wheldon & Wesley.* $31/£20

WOOD, NICHOLAS. A Practical Treatise on Railroads, and Interior Communication in General. London, 1831. 2nd ed. 16pp ads, 23,(4),530pp; 8 fldg copper plts, 3 full-pg wood engrs, 2 tables (1 fldg). Untrimmed. New leather spine, black lettering piece, marbled bds. (New eps, tp corner clipped, repaired, blindstamps, plts foxed), o/w VG. *Scribe's Perch*.* $150/£96

WOOD, P. Diseases of the Heart and Circulation. 1956. 2nd ed. (Few pp crinkled, ink sig fep; sm nick spine.) *Whitehart.* $39/£25

WOOD, RICHARD G. Stephen Harriman Long, 1784-1864, Army Engineer, Explorer, Inventor. Glendale: A.H. Clark, 1966. Frontis port. Blue cl. Fine in plain dj. *Bohling.* $25/£16

WOOD, RICHARD G. Stephen Harriman Long, 1784-1864. Glendale, 1966. 1st ed. Fine. *Pratt.* $25/£16

WOOD, RICHARD G. Stephen Harriman Long, 1784-1864. Glendale: A.H. Clark, 1966. 1st ed. Frontis, fldg map. Blue cl, gilt. NF. *Parmer.* $50/£32

WOOD, STANLEY. Over the Range to the Golden Gate. Chicago: R.R. Donnelley, 1896. 283pp. Good. *Hayman.* $25/£16

WOOD, STANLEY. Over the Range to the Golden Gate. Chicago: Donnelley, 1900. Pict lt olive cl, gilt. *Yudkin*.* $30/£19

WOOD, THOMAS. An Institute of the Laws of England.... London, 1772. 10th ed. 657pp + table (ink name eradicated tp, lt foxed, browned, old professional tape repair tp). Later calf (fr bd + prelims detached, joints repaired w/mod non-archival tape, heavily worn). *King.* $250/£160

WOOD, WILLIAM. Remarks on the Plea of Insanity and on the Management of Criminal Lunatics. London, 1852. 2nd ed. Fine. *Argosy.* $75/£48

WOODBERRY, GEORGE. Nathaniel Hawthorne. Boston: Houghton, Mifflin, 1902. 1st ed. Ltd to 600. Uncut. Blue cl, label. Fine. BAL IV:34:col.2. *Macdonnell.* $75/£48

WOODBURY, DAVID O. The Colorado Conquest. NY, 1941. 1st ed. Tan cl. (Hinges tender, sl flaws), else VG. *Five Quail.* $35/£22

WOODCOCK, E. N. Fifty Years a Hunter and Trapper. A. R. Harding (ed). Columbus: Harding, 1941. VG + in white illus wraps (lt soiled). *Bowman.* $30/£19

WOODFORD, JACK. Sin and Such. NY: Privately pt by Panurge, (1930). One of 1500 numbered. Good. *Hayman.* $20/£13

WOODFORDE, JAMES. The Diary of a Country Parson. John Beresford (ed). OUP, 1926-1931. Vol 1 3rd issue; others 1st eds. 5 vols. Frontis each vol. Ptd paper spine labels (rubbed). Good set (ink names). *Bickersteth.* $203/£130

WOODHOUSE, CHARLES PLATTEN. Old English Toby Jugs. London: Mountrose Press, 1949. 1st ed. 12 plts. (Fr flyleaf removed; spine rather worn.) *Hollett.* $39/£25

WOODHOUSE, ROBERT. The Principles of Analytical Calculation. CUP, 1803. 1st ed. (8),xxxiv,219pp. Contemp tree calf (rebacked), raised bands, red morocco spine label. VG (tp edges browned, text lt browned). *Glaser.* $475/£304

WOODLAND, W. LLOYD. The Story of Winchester. London, 1932. 1st ed thus. Gilt-dec cl (sl soiled). *Edwards.* $19/£12

WOODLEY, THOMAS FREDERICK. Thaddeus Stevens. Harrisburg, PA, 1934. 1st ed. VG. *Mcclintock.* $42/£27

WOODRELL, DANIEL. Muscle for the Wing. NY: Henry Holt, 1988. 1st ed. VF in dj. *Mordida.* $35/£22

WOODRELL, DANIEL. Woe to Live On. NY: Henry Holt, 1987. 1st ed. VF in dj. *Mordida.* $35/£22

WOODRUFF, H. The Trotting Horse of America. C. J. Foster (ed). NY: Ford, 1869. 1st ed. Frontis port, 412pp + ads. Blind-stamped gilt-dec cl. VG. *Mikesh.* $45/£29

WOODRUFF, JANETTE. Indian Oasis. Caxton, 1939. 1st ed. Frontis. VG. *Oregon.* $30/£19

WOODS, CAROLINE H. Woman in Prison. NY: Hurd & Houghton, 1869. 1st ed. 193pp. VG (cl faded). *Second Life.* $225/£144

WOODS, JAMES. Recollections of Pioneer Work in California. SF: Joseph Winterburn, 1878. 1st ed. 260pp (ink name). Gilt-lettered grn cl (lt worn). VG. *Argonaut.* $60/£38

WOODS, JOHN. Two Years' Residence in the Settlement of the English Prairie, in the Illinois Country, United States.... London, 1822. 1st ed. (4),310pp; 3 maps (2 fldg). Contemp 1/2 morocco. Howes W654. *Ginsberg.* $1,250/£801

WOODS, JOHN. Two Years' Residence on the English Prairie of Illinois. Chicago: R.R. Donnelley/Lakeside, 1968. VG. *Lien.* $20/£13

WOODS, JOHN. Two Years' Residence on the English Prairie of Illinois. Paul M. Angle (ed). Chicago: Lakeside, Christmas, 1968. Dk blue cl (sm spots upper cvr). *Sadlon.* $15/£10

WOODS, S. Lights and Shadows of Life on the Pacific Coast. NY: Funk & Wagnalls, 1910. 1st ed. Frontis port. Yellow cl (lt soil, sl worn). *Shasky.* $30/£19

WOODS, STUART. Chiefs. NY: W.W. Norton, 1981. 1st ed. Fine in dj (crease inner fr flap). *Mordida.* $100/£64

WOODS, STUART. Grass Roots. NY, 1989. 1st ed. Fine in Fine dj. *Smith.* $20/£13

WOODS, STUART. Under the Lake. NY, 1987. 1st ed. Fine in Fine dj. *Smith.* $20/£13

WOODS, STUART. Under the Lake. NY: S&S, 1987. 1st ed. Inscribed. VF in dj. *Mordida.* $45/£29

WOODSON, CARTER G. The Negro in Our History. Washington: Associated Publishers, (1922). 1st ed. Frontis; 2 maps. Maroon cl (spine ends rubbed). *Petrilla.* $125/£80

WOODSON, ROBERT E. et al. Rauwolfia. Boston, 1957. Frontis. VG + in dj (sl chipped). *Brooks.* $36/£23

Woodstock. (By Walter Scott.) Edinburgh/London: Archibald Constable/Longman et al, 1826. 1st ed. 3 vols. 2nd state vol 3 pp167-8 cancel leaf. Orig drab bds, red cl spines, ptd labels. Good+ set (spine labels heavily rubbed, extrems sl worn). *Sumner & Stillman.* $125/£80

Woodstock. (By Walter Scott.) Edinburgh: Constable, 1826. 1st ed. 3 vols. xvi,315; (4),332; (2),370pp, 1/2 titles vols 1-2. Good set (bkpls) in contemp 1/2 calf (hinges broken, inner hinge reinforced, rubbed, sl worn). *Cox.* $59/£38

WOODTHORPE, R. C. Death in a Little Town. DCC, 1935. 1st ed. (Lt cvr wear), else NF. *Murder By The Book.* $35/£22

WOODWARD, ARTHUR. Camels and Surveyors in Death Valley. Palm Desert: Desert Ptrs, (1961). 1st ed. Fine in wraps. *Book Market.* $20/£13

WOODWARD, ARTHUR. Denominators of the Fur Trade. Pasadena: Westernlore, (1979). 2nd ptg, rev. VF in pict dj. *Argonaut.* $60/£38

WOODWARD, ARTHUR. Feud on the Colorado. L.A.: Westernlore, (1955). 10 full-pg illus. Dj. *Dawson.* $40/£26

WOODWARD, ARTHUR. Feud on the Colorado. Westernlore, 1955. 1st ed. Red cl. Fine in VG + dj. *Five Quail.* $45/£29

WOODWARD, C. VANN. Reunion and Reaction, the Compromise of 1877 and the End of Reconstruction. Boston, 1951. 1st ed. Fine in dj (lt worn, tear). *Pratt.* $25/£16

WOODWARD, GEORGE E. and F.W. Graperies and Horticultural Buildings. NY, (1865). 139pp. (Spine ends frayed; cvrs stained.) *King.* $65/£42

WOODWARD, H. B. The Geology of England and Wales. London: Longmans, Green, 1876. 1st ed. xx,476pp. VG (sm notation). *Blake.* $100/£64

WOODWARD, H. B. The Geology of England and Wales.... London, 1887. 2nd ed. Fldg color map mtd on linen in pocket. *Maggs.* $62/£40

WOODWARD, JOSEPH et al. The Medical and Surgical History of the War of Rebellion, 1861-65. Washington, 1870-88. 1st ed, 1st & 2nd ptgs. 6 vols. Grn cl. VG (inner hinges cracked). *Fye.* $2,500/£1,603

WOODWORTH, JOHN M. Cholera Epidemic of 1873 in the United States. Washington: HD95, 1875. 1st ed. (2),1025pp. New cl, leather label. *Ginsberg.* $125/£80

WOODWORTH, R. S. Psychological Issues. NY: Columbia Univ, 1939. 1st ed. Signed. Frontis port. Grn cl. NF. *Gach.* $65/£42

WOOFTER, THOMAS JACKSON, JR. Black Yeomanry: Life on St. Helena Island. NY: Henry Holt, (1930). 1st ed. VG (cl sl rubbed, spine sunned). *Mcgowan.* $45/£29

WOOFTER, THOMAS JACKSON, JR. Landlord and Tenant on the Cotton Plantation. Washington: 1936. 1st ed. VG in orig stiff ptd wrappers. *Mcgowan.* $75/£48

WOOLEY, CHARLES. A Two Years Journal in New York, and Part of Its Territories in America. NY: Wm. Gowans, 1860. New ed. 97pp + 20pp pub's cat. Gilt-stamped cl. Nice (spine faded, lt rubbed). *Bohling.* $35/£22

WOOLEY, ROGER. The Fly-Fisher's Flies. Fishing Gazette, 1948. 2nd ed. *Petersfield.* $33/£21

WOOLEY, ROGER. Modern Trout Fly Dressing. London, 1932. 1st ed. *Petersfield.* $55/£35

WOOLEY, ROGER. Modern Trout Fly Dressings. London, 1932. 1st ed. (Backstrip sl rubbed.) *Petersfield.* $55/£35

WOOLF, CECIL and BROCARD SEWELL (eds). New Quests for Corvo. London: Icon Books, 1965. 1st trade ed. Card wrappers. *Clearwater.* $39/£25

WOOLF, DOUGLAS. Wall to Wall. NY: Grove Press, 1962. 1st ed. Fine (tape mks eps) in NF dj. *Beasley.* $35/£22

WOOLF, H. (ed). Some Strangeness in Proportion. 1980. (Spine sl defective), o/w VG. *Whitehart.* $39/£25

WOOLF, LEONARD. Barbarians at the Gate. London: Left Bk Club/Gollancz, 1939. 1st ed. Red paper-cvrd bds. NF. *Beasley.* $25/£16

WOOLF, VIRGINIA. Beau Brummell. NY: Rimington & Hooper, 1930. 1st ed. #336/550. Signed. Paper-cvrd bds (soil, edges rubbed). *Metropolitan*.* $287/£184

WOOLF, VIRGINIA. Between the Acts. London, 1941. 1st Eng ed. Nice (inscrip; spine sl faded). *Clearwater.* $39/£25

WOOLF, VIRGINIA. Between the Acts. NY: Harcourt, Brace, n.d. (1941). 1st Amer ed. (Eps browned; cvrs sl faded at top edge, spine), o/w VG in dj (sl browned, chipped). *Virgo.* $125/£80

WOOLF, VIRGINIA. Books and Portraits. NY: Harcourt Brace, 1978. 1st Amer ed. (Long inscrip fep), o/w Nice in dj. *Virgo.* $28/£18

WOOLF, VIRGINIA. The Captain's Death Bed and Other Essays. NY: Harcourt, (1950). 1st Amer ed. Nice in dj (2 creased tears spine crown). *Reese.* $60/£38

WOOLF, VIRGINIA. The Captain's Death Bed and Other Essays. NY: Harcourt, Brace, (1950). 1st Amer ed. One of 5000 ptd. NF in dj (spine, edges browned). *Antic Hay.* $125/£80

WOOLF, VIRGINIA. The Captain's Death Bed and Other Essays. NY, 1950. 1st Amer ed. Fine (sl rubbed) in dj (price-clipped). *Polyanthos.* $100/£64

WOOLF, VIRGINIA. The Captain's Death Bed. London: Hogarth, 1950. 1st U.K. ed. (Eps offsetting, pg edges sl spotted, inscrip; top cvr edges sl faded), o/w VG in dj (browned,   soiled, chipped, price-clipped). *Virgo.* $78/£50

WOOLF, VIRGINIA. The Captain's Death Bed. NY, 1950. 1st Amer ed. Fine (lower edges sl rubbed) in dj (price-clipped). *Polyanthos.* $75/£48

WOOLF, VIRGINIA. The Captain's Death Bed. NY: Harcourt, Brace, 1950. 1st Amer ed. (Sig), else NF in dj (price-clipped, spine dknd). *Cahan.* $75/£48

WOOLF, VIRGINIA. The Death of the Moth: And Other Essays. London: Hogarth, 1942. 1st ed. (Eps sl spotted), else VG in illus dj (spine ends chipped). *Cahan.* $125/£80

WOOLF, VIRGINIA. Flush, a Biography. London: Hogarth, 1933. 1st ed (one of 12,680). Frontis. (Cl edges sl tanned), o/w Very Nice in dj (tanned, nicks, sm edge tear mended on verso). *Reese.* $125/£80

WOOLF, VIRGINIA. Granite and Rainbow. NY: Harcourt, Brace, (1958). 1st Amer ed. (Faded strip top edge cl), else NF in dj (spine browned). *Antic Hay.* $50/£32

WOOLF, VIRGINIA. Granite and Rainbow. Hogarth, 1958. 1st ed. (Margins lt browned.) Dj (chipped, sl loss spine head, edges lt browned). *Edwards.* $55/£35

WOOLF, VIRGINIA. Granite and Rainbow. London: Hogarth, 1958. 1st ed. Very Nice in dj (sl soiled, browned, chipped, 2-inch closed tear top edge). *Virgo.* $78/£50

WOOLF, VIRGINIA. Granite and Rainbow. London: Hogarth, 1958. 1st ed. One of 6000. NF (sl wear) in dj (lt wear, dknd, chip fr panel). *Antic Hay.* $85/£54

WOOLF, VIRGINIA. Granite and Rainbow. London: Hogarth, 1958. 1st ed. VG in dj (lt worn, dknd, short closed tear). *Hermitage.* $100/£64

WOOLF, VIRGINIA. A Haunted House and Other Short Stories. London: Hogarth, 1943. 1st ed. (Paper tanned, spine extrems sunned), else Good in dj (tanned, chips to spine, tear mended on verso). *Reese.* $55/£35

WOOLF, VIRGINIA. A Letter to a Young Poet. London: Hogarth, 1932. 1st ed. Dec wrappers. (Sl browned.) *Metropolitan*.* $115/£74

WOOLF, VIRGINIA. The Letters of Virginia Woolf. Nigel Nicolson & Joanne Troutmann (eds). London: Hogarth, 1976/1980. 1st eds. 6 vols complete. (Names), o/w VG set in djs (sl faded, vol 1 corners nicked). *Virgo.* $312/£200

WOOLF, VIRGINIA. The Moment and Other Essays. Hogarth, 1947. 1st ed. VG in dj (sl faded, frayed, sm splits). *Cox.* $62/£40

WOOLF, VIRGINIA. Monday or Tuesday. Richmond: Hogarth, 1921. 1st ed. One of 1000. Vanessa Bell (illus). 8vo. White paper bds (sl rubbed), brn cl spine. *Sotheby's*.* $646/£414

WOOLF, VIRGINIA. Mr. Bennett and Mrs. Brown. London: Hogarth, 1924. 1st ed. One of 1000 ptd. Good (few leaves lt foxed) in pict stiff wrappers (edges tanned, chip spine crown). *Reese.* $125/£80

WOOLF, VIRGINIA. Mrs. Dalloway. NY: Modern Library, 1928. Good in dj (chipped). *Clearwater.* $39/£25

WOOLF, VIRGINIA. Orlando: a Biography. London: Hogarth, 1928. 1st trade ed. Port. (Bkpl, top edge foxed), o/w Nice in dj (patchy, long tears internally mended). *Reese.* $85/£54

WOOLF, VIRGINIA. Orlando: A Biography. NY: Crosby Gaige, 1928. 1st ed. One of 861 signed. (Corner sl bumped), o/w Fine w/o dj, as issued. *Captain's Bookshelf.* $850/£545

WOOLF, VIRGINIA. Orlando: A Biography. NY: Crosby Gaige, 1928. One of 800 (of 861) numbered, signed. (Spine faded), o/w Excellent. *Gekoski.* $1,170/£750

WOOLF, VIRGINIA. Roger Fry. Hogarth, 1940. 1st UK ed. VG (spine faded from dj chips) in dj (chipped, lacks spine top removing most of title). *Williams.* $62/£40

WOOLF, VIRGINIA. Roger Fry. London: Hogarth, 1940. 1st Eng ed. Clippings, sections of dj loosely inserted. Good (faded). *Clearwater.* $78/£50

WOOLF, VIRGINIA. The Sickle Side of the Moon. Nigel Nicolson (ed). London: Hogarth, 1979. 1st ed. Vol 5. (Sl bumped), o/w NF in dj. *Virgo.* $39/£25

WOOLF, VIRGINIA. Street Haunting. SF: Westgate, 1930. #120/500. Signed. 1/2 leather, dec paper. (Spine dknd, head rubbed.) Pub's slipcase. *Metropolitan*.* $460/£295

WOOLF, VIRGINIA. Three Guineas. NY: Harcourt, (1938). 1st Amer ed (7500 ptd). VG in dj (spine tanned, sm spots). *Reese.* $75/£48

WOOLF, VIRGINIA. Three Guineas. Hogarth, 1938. 1st ed. (Feps sl browned; sm spine patch sl discolored.) Dj (lt spotted, edges sl chipped w/spine loss). *Edwards.* $101/£65

WOOLF, VIRGINIA. To the Lighthouse. Hogarth, 1927. 1st ed. (Sl dull, discolored, spine dknd, foxing, esp edges.) *Ash.* $78/£50

WOOLF, VIRGINIA. Virginia Woolf and Lytton Strachey: Letters. Leonard Woolf & James Strachey (eds). London: Hogarth/C&W, 1956. 1st ed. (Sl shelfwear), o/w VG in VG dj (corners, spine ends sl worn). *Virgo.* $125/£80

WOOLF, VIRGINIA. The Waves. London: Hogarth, 1931. 1st Eng ed. (Foxed, esp fore-edges; mkd, stained.) *Clearwater.* $55/£35

WOOLF, VIRGINIA. The Waves. London: Hogarth, 1931. 1st ed. Very Nice in Good dj (spine tanned, internal repair). *Reese.* $275/£176

WOOLF, VIRGINIA. A Writer's Diary. Leonard Woolf (ed). Hogarth, 1953. 1st ed. VG (few pencil notes, sidelines) in dj (sl faded, turn-ins tipped to eps). *Cox.* $55/£35

WOOLF, VIRGINIA. A Writer's Diary. Leonard Woolf (ed). London: Hogarth, 1953. 1st ed. Nice in dj (spine tanned, sm chip). *Reese.* $35/£22

WOOLF, VIRGINIA. A Writer's Diary. Leonard Woolf (ed). London: Hogarth, 1963. 1st ed. (Eps, fore-edges sl spotted), o/w VG in dj (soiled, browned, sl nicked). *Virgo.* $78/£50

WOOLF, VIRGINIA. The Years. NY: Editions for the Armed Services, (1945). 1st ASE ptg. NF in illus wrappers. *Turtle Island.* $45/£29

WOOLF, VIRGINIA. The Years. Hogarth, 1937. 1st ed. (Cl lt soiled, edge-rubbed; lacks dj.) *Edwards.* $39/£25

WOOLF, VIRGINIA. The Years. London: Hogarth, 1937. 1st ed. (Pg edges sl browned, sl offsetting, spotting to eps; cvrs sl soiled, rubbed), o/w VG in dj (browned, spotted, chipped, top edge frayed). *Virgo.* $312/£200

WOOLF, VIRGINIA. The Years. London: Hogarth, 1937. 1st ed. Pale grn cl. VF (mod bkpl) in dj (lt foxing). *Bromer.* $475/£304

WOOLFOLK, GEORGE RUBLE. Cotton Regency. NY: Bookman Associates, (1958). VG. *Bohling.* $15/£10

WOOLLCOTT, ALEXANDER. Woollcott's Second Reader. NY, 1937. One of 1500 signed. White bds, leather labels. Fine in pub's bd slipcase. *Argosy.* $175/£112

WOOLLEY, C. LEONARD and MAX MALLOWAN. The Old Babylonian Period. London/NY: British Museum/Univ of PA, 1976. 129 plts. Good. *Archaeologia.* $250/£160

WOOLLEY, C. LEONARD. The Royal Cemetery: A Report on the Predynastic and Sargonid Graves Excavated Between 1926 and 1931. NY: British Museum/Univ of PA, 1934. 2 vols complete. Sm folio. 273 plts. Good in orig ptd wrappers. *Archaeologia.* $650/£417

WOOLLEY, C. LEONARD. The Ziggurat and Its Surroundings. Oxford: British Museum/Univ of PA, 1939. Sm folio. 88 plts. (Sig.) Orig cl-backed ptd bds (corners rubbed). *Archaeologia.* $650/£417

WOOLLEY, LEE H. California 1849-1913...Sixty-Four Years' Residence in that State. Oakland: DeWitt & Snelling, 1913. Frontis port. Ptd lt-blue wrappers (sunned overall). *Dawson.* $50/£32

WOOLLEY, LEE H. California, 1849-1913; or, The Rambling Sketches and Experiences of Sixty-Four Years' Residence in That State. Oakland: De Witt and Snelling, 1913. 1st ed. Frontis port. (Spine faded), else Fine in gray ptd wrappers. *Argonaut.* $45/£29

WOOLMAN, JOHN. A Journal of the Life, Gospel Labours, and Christian Experiences of That Faithful Minister of Jesus Christ.... London: Ptd by William Phillips, 1824. New ed. 416pp. (Pp 1-16 affixed to inner margin, tp lettering sl obscured, text split pp16-17, sl browned, fep lacks corner; upper hinge cracked, lacks backstrip.) *Edwards.* $148/£95

WOOLMAN, JOHN. A Journal of the Life, Gospel Labours, and Christian Experiences, of That Faithful Minister of Jesus Christ, John Woolman.... Phila: T.E. Chapman, 1837. 396pp. Calf, spine rules. VG. Howes W669. *Petrilla.* $60/£38

WOOLNER, THOMAS. Pygmalion. London: Macmillan, 1881. 1st ed. (viii),208pp. Blue cl (spine ends frayed), gilt. *Burmester.* $55/£35

WOOLRICH, CORNELL. Beyond the Night. Avon, (1959). Pb orig. Fine. *Certo.* $40/£26

WOOLRICH, CORNELL. Children of the Ritz. NY: Boni & Liveright, 1927. 1st ed. (Extrems lt worn.) Striking dj (closed tears, nicks, creases to edges, speckles of fading). *Metropolitan*.* $1,035/£663

WOOLRICH, CORNELL. The Doom Stone. Avon, (1960). Pb orig. Fine. *Certo.* $35/£22

WOOLRICH, CORNELL. Hotel Room. NY, 1958. 1st ed. NF in VG dj. *Warren.* $75/£48

WOOLRICH, CORNELL. Hotel Room. NY: Random House, 1958. 1st ed. VG in illus dj. *Cahan.* $65/£42

WOOLRICH, CORNELL. I Wouldn't Be in Your Shoes. Lippincott, 1943. 1st ed. Blue spine (faded). VG in supplied color copy dj, orig fr dj flap laid in. *Certo.* $75/£48

WOOLRICH, CORNELL. Nightwebs. NY: Harper & Row, 1971. 1st ed. Fine in dj (spine ends, corners sl worn). *Mordida.* $85/£54

WOOLRICH, CORNELL. Nightwebs. Francis M. Nevins, Jr. (ed). NY: Harper & Row, 1971. 1st ed. NF in dj (edgewear, spine extrems lt chipping). *Janus.* $45/£29

WOOLSON, ABBA GOOLD. George Eliot and Her Heroines. NY: Harper, 1886. 1st ed. 177pp + ads. Nice. *Second Life.* $85/£54

WOOLWORTH, SOLOMON. Experiences in the Civil War. Newark, NJ, 1904. 2nd ed. Frontis port. Orig ptd illus wraps. VG. *Wantagh.* $85/£54

WOOSTER, DAVID. Alpine Plants, Figures and Descriptions of the Most Striking and Beautiful of the Alpine Flowers. London: Bell & Daldy, 1872. 1st ed. ix,152pp (lt foxed, aged); 54 chromolitho plts (few lt foxed, few w/edges lt worn), guards. Marbled eps; aeg. Early full brn morocco (sl shelfworn, sl scuffed), raised bands, gilt. *Baltimore*.* $250/£160

WOOSTER, DAVID. Alpine Plants. London, 1874. 2 vols. Vol 1 2nd ed. 108 color plts. Blue cl (spines faded, sl worn; sl shaken), gilt. *Maggs.* $312/£200

WOOSTER, DAVID. Alpine Plants. London: George Bell, 1874. 2nd ed. 2 vols. 10pp pub's ads at end. 108 plts. (Lt soil, spotting, 1 plt lt spotted.) Teg. Contemp grn 1/2 morocco (spines rubbed, faded). *Christie's*.* $262/£168

WOOSTER, DAVID. The Gold Rush. Mount Pleasant, MI, (1972). One of 487. Fine. *Hayman.* $20/£13

WORCESTER, DEAN C. The Phillipine Islands and Their People. NY, 1901. Fldg map. (Ex-lib, bkpl, ink stamps feps.) Dec cl (sm dent fore-edge upper bd, bkpl remains lower bd). *Edwards.* $47/£30

WORCESTER, G. R. G. The Junks and Sampans of the Yangtze. London, 1947. Frontis, fldg map, 83 plts. Grn cl. *Edwards.* $117/£75

WORDSWORTH, WILLIAM. A Guide Through the District of the Lakes. Kendal: John Hudson, 1835. 5th ed. xxiv,140,(ii,ad leaf)pp, engr fldg map (panel torn). Pub's pebble-grained cl, gilt, paper spine label. Nice. *Hollett.* $250/£160

WORDSWORTH, WILLIAM. The Poetical Works of William Wordsworth. Edward Moxon, 1836-1837. New ed. 6 vols. Frontis port vol 1. Aeg. Contemp full leather (hinges rubbed; upper hinges vols 1, 4, 5 starting; vol 6 skillfully rebacked, orig backstrip), gilt. Internally VG (bkpls). *Tiger.* $624/£400

WORDSWORTH, WILLIAM. The Poetical Works.... London: Edward Moxon, 1857. New ed. 6 vols. Engr port. Brn cl (sl rubbed, spines dull, mkd). *Burmester.* $390/£250

WORDSWORTH, WILLIAM. The Recluse. London: Macmillan, 1888. 1st ed. Grn cl, gilt. (Lt spotted, rubbed), else VG. *Macdonnell.* $100/£64

WORK, JOHN W., JR. (ed). American Negro Songs and Spirituals. NY: Crown, (1940). 1st ed. Buckram (stained). *Petrilla.* $50/£32

WORK, JOHN. The Snake Country Expedition of 1830-1831. Francis D. Haines, Jr. (ed). Norman: Univ of OK, (1971). 1st ed. VG in dj. *Lien.* $40/£26

WORKMAN, FANNY BULLOCK and WILLIAM HUNTER WORKMAN. The Call of the Snowy Hispar. London, 1910. 1st ed. 2 maps (1 w/hinge sl torn). Pict cl. (Inner fr hinge cracked, top edge spotted, cvrs worn.) *King.* $650/£417

WORKMAN, FANNY BULLOCK and WILLIAM HUNTER WORKMAN. Icebound Heights of the Mustagh. London, 1908. 1st ed. 9.5x6. 2 maps (1 w/tear at hinge). Teg. Pict cl (heavily soiled, spotted, edge soiled, sl dented). *King.* $600/£385

WORLEY, E. D. Iron Horses of the Santa Fe Trail. (Dallas): Southwest Railroad Hist Soc, (1965). 1st ed. Pict eps. Blue cl, gilt. Fine in NF dj. *Harrington.* $80/£51

WORMALD, FRANCIS. English Drawings of the Tenth and Eleventh Centuries. London, 1952. Color frontis, 41 plts. Good. *Washton.* $75/£48

WORRELL, JOHN. A Diamond in the Rough Embracing Anecdote, Biography, Romance, and History. Indianapolis, 1906. 1st ed. Howes W679. *Ginsberg.* $200/£128

WORRINGER, WILHELM. Egyptian Art. London: Putnam, (1928). 1st Eng ed. 29 plts. Good. *Archaeologia.* $45/£29

WORSLEY, ETTA BLANCHARD. Columbus on the Chattahoochee. Columbus, GA: Columbus Office Supply Co, 1951. (Lt rubbed; lt foxing), else VG. *Cahan.* $75/£48

WORSLEY, F. Endurance. London: Geoffrey Bles, 1939. 2nd ed. Good (lacks fep). *High Latitude.* $30/£19

WORSLEY, F. Under Sail in the Frozen North. Phila: David McKay, 1927. Lg fldg map. VG. *High Latitude.* $50/£32

WORSWICK, CLARK and JONATHAN SPENCE. Imperial China: Photographs 1850-1912. NY: Pennwick/Crown, 1978. 1st ed. (Owner stamp), else NF in illus dj. *Cahan.* $45/£29

WORTHINGTON, HOOKER. Homeopathy. NY: Scribner, 1851. 1st ed. 146 pp. (Top spine cut), o/w VG. *Middle Earth.* $75/£48

WORTLEY, EMMELINE STUART. Travels in the United States, etc., During 1849 and 1850. London, 1851. 3 vols. Half-title vol 2. Later 3/4 morocco, bds. VG. Howes W687. *Reese.* $250/£160

WORTLEY, EMMELINE STUART. Travels in the United States, etc., During 1849 and 1850. NY, 1851. 1st Amer ed. 463pp + ads. Pub's dec cl, gilt. (Foxed, fr hinge cracked, fep excised), else Good. Howes W687. *Reese.* $200/£128

WORTLEY, EMMELINE STUART. Travels in the United States...1849 and 1850. NY: Harper, 1851. 1st US ed. 463pp + ads. Good (cl worn, sl foxed, water stain). Howes W687. *Second Life.* $125/£80

WOUK, HERMAN. The Caine Mutiny. GC: Doubleday, 1951. 1st ed. Blue cl. Fine in VG pict dj (sl worn, rubbed; few tiny chips spine top). *Cummins.* $250/£160

WOUK, HERMAN. Marjorie Morningstar. GC: Doubleday, 1955. 1st ed. Fine in dj (sl rubbing). *Between The Covers.* $150/£96

WOUK, HERMAN. War and Remembrance. Boston: Little Brown, (1978). One of unknown # for friends of author and pub w/extra leaf tipped in so stating. Signed. Fine in Fine dj, slipcase. *Lenz.* $85/£54

WOUK, HERMAN. Youngblood Hawke. London: Collins, 1962. 1st UK ed. Fine in dj (lt worn). *Hermitage.* $40/£26

WREN, P. C. Beau Geste. London/NY, 1927. #221/1000 signed. 20 tipped-in illus by Helen McKie, incl 4 color. Good (leaf starting). *Scribe's Perch*.* $20/£13

WREN, P. C. Beau Ideal. London: John Murray, 1928. 1st UK ed. NF (bkpl) in VG pict dj. *Williams.* $148/£95

WREN, P. C. The Mammon of Righteousness. London: Murray, 1930. Colonial ed. VG in dj (sl worn, rubbed). *Williams.* $133/£85

WRIGHT, A. H. and A. A. Handbook of Snakes of the U.S. and Canada, Volume II. Ithaca: Comstock, (1970). Gilt-dec cl. VG+ in Good+ dj. *Mikesh.* $37/£24

WRIGHT, ANDREW. Court Hand Restored. London, 1778. 2nd ed. (A)tp,(A2)ded,(A3-A4)subs,7pp, 20 plts; C sub-title,(11-99pp)). (Feps sl foxed; pp1-7 sl browned; bkpl). Gilt-edged calf (spine rubbed, joints starting to crack), morocco spine label. *Edwards.* $140/£90

WRIGHT, ANDREW. Court-Hand Restored. London: Stevens, 1912. 10th ed. 30 plts, 30 leaves decriptions. VG (backstrip faded). *Cox.* $47/£30

WRIGHT, BRUCE S. High Tide and an East Wind. Harrisburg: Stackpole/Wildlife Mgmt Co, 1954. 1st ed. Pict eps. Blue cl. Fine in Fine pict dj. *Biscotti.* $45/£29

WRIGHT, CAROLYN and CLARENCE. Tiny Hinsdale of the Silvery San Juans. Denver: Big Mountain, 1964. Map. *Dumont.* $30/£19

WRIGHT, CHARLES. The Wig. NY: FSG, (1966). 1st ed. Fine in dj. *Hermitage.* $30/£19

WRIGHT, CHARLES. The Wig: A Mirror Image. NY: FSG, 1966. 1st ed. Cl-backed paper over bds, blind emb. NF in dj (lt rubbed). *Cahan.* $50/£32

WRIGHT, E. W. (ed). Lewis and Dryden's Marine History of the Pacific Northwest. Portland, OR, 1895. Aeg. Pub's gilt-stamped leather (rubbed, spine tips chipped, joints worn). Internally Sound. *Oinonen*.* $175/£112

WRIGHT, E. W. (ed). Lewis and Dryden's Marine History of the Pacific Northwest. 1961. Ltd to 750. VG. *King.* $100/£64

WRIGHT, E. W. (ed). Lewis and Dryden's Marine History of the Pacific Northwest. NY, 1961. Ltd to 750. Howes W693. *Ginsberg*. $175/£112

WRIGHT, EDWARD. The Ferriby Boats: Seacraft of the Bronze Age. London/NY: Routledge, (1990). 1st ed. VF. *Lefkowicz*. $125/£80

WRIGHT, FRANCES. A Few Days in Athens.... NY: Wright & Owen, 1831. Frontis, 141pp (foxed, lib label eps). Cl-backed bds, paper label (soiled). *M & S*. $150/£96

WRIGHT, FRANK LLOYD. An American Architecture. Edgar Kaufmann (ed). NY: Horizon Press, 1955. 1st ed. VG in dj (sl worn, faded). *Hermitage*. $150/£96

WRIGHT, FRANK LLOYD. The Disappearing City. NY: William Farquhar Payson, 1932. 1st ed, 2nd binding. Blue cl, ptd label. (Name, eps sl dknd; faded, label sl worn), else Good. *Cahan*. $125/£80

WRIGHT, FRANK LLOYD. Frank Lloyd Wright, An Autobiography. NY: Duell, Sloan, 1943. 1st ed. Sound. *Ars Artis*. $55/£35

WRIGHT, FRANK LLOYD. The Future of Architecture. NY, 1953. 1st ed. Dj (top edge sl worn). *Swann**. $258/£165

WRIGHT, FRANK LLOYD. The Future of Architecture. NY: Horizon, 1953. 1st ed. Full-pg frontis port. Red w/white cl. (Cl, eps lt foxed), else VG in dj (lt soiled, worn). *Cahan*. $100/£64

WRIGHT, FRANK LLOYD. The Future of Architecture. NY: Horizon, 1953. 1st ed. Frontis. NF in Good dj (creased chips lower edge, soiled, price-clipped). *Reese*. $125/£80

WRIGHT, FRANK LLOYD. The Japanese Print. An Interpretation. NY: Horizon Press, (1967). 1st ed. 32 full-pg color plts. Beige cl (spine soiled). Pub's ptd slipcase (edges soiled). *Karmiole*. $200/£128

WRIGHT, FRANK LLOYD. Modern Architecture, Being the Kahn Lectures for 1930. Princeton Univ, 1931. 1st ed. Color pict bds (worn). *Argosy*. $200/£128

WRIGHT, FRANK LLOYD. The Natural House. NY, 1954. Dj (chips, edge tears). *Swann**. $92/£59

WRIGHT, FRANK LLOYD. The Natural House. NY: Horizon, 1954. 1st ed. (Name; cl spine sl dknd), else VG in dj (closed tear, tips chipped). *Cahan*. $125/£80

WRIGHT, FRANK LLOYD. The Story of the Tower: The Tree That Escaped the Crowded Forest. NY: Horizon, 1956. 1st ed. Frontis port. Red/black cl. (Lt rubbed), else VG. *Cahan*. $125/£80

WRIGHT, FRANK LLOYD. A Testament. NY: Horizon, (1957). 1st ed. Folio. 4-pg fold-out. Linen, dec cvr. NF in pict dj. *Cahan*. $125/£80

WRIGHT, FRANK LLOYD. The Work of Frank Lloyd Wright. Horizon, 1965. Fine in illus pub's slipcase (sunned, bumped). *Metropolitan**. $150/£96

WRIGHT, FRANK LLOYD. The Work of Frank Lloyd Wright. Horizon, 1965. (Ex-lib, ink stamps, label, cellotape mks pastdowns; cl sl soiled, spine #s; lacks dj.) *Edwards*. $156/£100

WRIGHT, G. FREDERICK. The Ice Age in North America and Its Bearings upon the Antiquity of Man. NY: D. Appleton, 1889. 1st ed. Frontis, xviii,622pp,(1) ads; 3 fldg maps. Teg. Gilt/grn pict lt blue cl (lt soiled); teg. Fine. *House*. $150/£96

WRIGHT, G. FREDERICK. The Ice Age in North America. NY: D. Appleton, 1891. xviii,18-648pp. Pict cl. VG. *Adelson*. $50/£32

WRIGHT, HAROLD BELL. The Re-Creation of Brian Kent. Chicago: Book Supply, (1919). 1st ed. NF. *Antic Hay*. $25/£16

WRIGHT, HELEN S. The Great White North. NY: Macmillan, 1910. 1st ed. Pict grn cl (spine rubbed, sl dusty; lt aged, ink stamps), gilt. *Baltimore**. $20/£13

WRIGHT, J. Where Copper Was King. Boston: Small, Maynard, c 1905. Pict cl. VG. *Blake*. $125/£80

WRIGHT, JAY. Dimensions of History. (Santa Cruz: Kayak, 1976.) One of 1000. Fine in illus wrappers. *Dermont*. $75/£48

WRIGHT, JOHN COUCHOIS. Crooked Tree, Indian Legends and a Short History of the Little Traverse Bay Region. Harbor Springs, MI: C. Fayette Erwin, (1917). 39 plts. Black-stamped grn cl. VG in dj (sl soiled, frayed). *Bohling*. $45/£29

WRIGHT, JOHN. The Flower Grower's Guide. London, n.d. (1897). 3 vols in 6 bindings. 1104pp (sl foxing); 46 color plts (tissue guard torn). Aeg. Dec blue cl (2 spines rubbed), beveled edges. Well Preserved set. *Brooks*. $195/£125

WRIGHT, JOHN. The Fruit Grower's Guide. London: J.S. Virtue, (1891-94). 3 vols in 6 orig divisions. 4to. 3 chromolitho titles, 43 chromolitho plts (lt spotted). Gilt edges. Pict cl. *Christie's**. $1,264/£810

WRIGHT, JOSEPH. The English Dialect Dictionary. London: Henry Frowde, 1898-1905. 1st ed. 6 vols. Pub's cl (shelfworn). *Oinonen**. $500/£321

WRIGHT, MURIEL H. A Guide to the Indian Tribes of Oklahoma. Norman: Univ of OK, 1951. Stated 1st ed. Good in Good dj. *Scribe's Perch**. $25/£16

WRIGHT, O. L. Our House. NY: Horizon, 1959. 1st ed. Gilt-emb cl. VG. *Cahan*. $30/£19

WRIGHT, O. L. and F. L. Frank Lloyd Wright Architecture. London: Macdonald, 1963. Sound in dj. *Ars Artis*. $55/£35

WRIGHT, O. L. and F. L. An Organic Architecture. London, 1939. 20 plts. Sound. *Ars Artis*. $55/£35

WRIGHT, RICHARD B. The Weekend Man. NY: FSG, (1971). 1st ed, 1st bk. Fine in dj (crease fr flap, sm tear). *Antic Hay*. $25/£16

WRIGHT, RICHARD. The Color Curtain. Cleveland, 1956. 1st Amer ed. Fine in Fine dj. *Polyanthos*. $75/£48

WRIGHT, RICHARD. The Long Dream. GC: Doubleday, 1958. 1st ed. NF in VG+ dj (chip, short edgetear). *Lame Duck*. $50/£32

WRIGHT, RICHARD. Native Son. NY, 1940. 1st ed. VG+ 2nd-state binding (gray cl) in Good 1st-state yellow/green dj (piece missing at lower-fr panel and spine, sm tears). *Warren*. $95/£61

WRIGHT, RICHARD. Pagan Spain. London, 1960. 1st British ed. Fine in NF dj. *Warren*. $75/£48

WRIGHT, RICHARD. Twelve Million Black Voices: A Folk History.... London: Lindsay Drummond, 1947. 1st UK ed. Brn cl, gilt spine lettering. VG. *Petrilla*. $65/£42

WRIGHT, RICHARD. White Man, Listen! GC: Doubleday, 1957. 1st ed. Black cl, white/orange lettering. VG. *Petrilla*. $35/£22

WRIGHT, RICHARDSON. Hawkers and Walkers in Early America. Phila: Lippincott, 1927. Stated 1st ed. Dec cvr. Good. *Scribe's Perch**. $36/£23

WRIGHT, ROBERT. A Memoir of General James Oglethorpe.... London: Chapman, 1867. 1st ed. (16),424pp; map. (Fr cvr, spine sl worn.) Howes W705. *Ginsberg*. $150/£96

WRIGHT, ROY V. and PORTER WRIGHT. Locomotive Dictionary. NY/Chicago: Simmons/Boardman, 1912. (3rd ed.) Full morocco, gilt logo. *Cullen*. $225/£144

WRIGHT, S. FOWLER. The Island of Cape Sparrow. Gollancz, 1928. 1st UK ed. Fine (lacks dj). *Williams*. $39/£25

WRIGHT, S. FOWLER. Spiders' War. NY: Abelard, (1954). 1st ed. NF (top, fore-edge spotted) in dj (wear, soil, price-clipped). *Antic Hay*. $25/£16

WRIGHT, S. FOWLER. The Throne of Saturn. Sauk City: Arkham House, 1949. 1st ed. VG (eps browned) in dj (sl wear, chip). *Antic Hay.* $50/£32

WRIGHT, SOLOMON ALEXANDER. My Rambles as East Texas Cowboy, Hunter, Fisherman, Tie-Cutter. Austin: TX Folklore Soc, 1942. VG + (sl bumped). *Bohling.* $40/£26

WRIGHT, STEPHEN. Meditations in Green. NY: Scribners, (1983). 1st ed, 1st bk. Fine in dj. *Between The Covers.* $85/£54

WRIGHT, STEPHEN. Meditations in Green. NY: Scribner, 1983. 1st ed, 1st bk. (Sm damp mk), else Fine in Fine dj. *Else Fine.* $45/£29

WRIGHT, THOMAS. The Life of Edward Fitzgerald. Grant Richards, 1904. 1st ed. 2 vols. 56 plts. Uncut. (Spine faded, labels worn), o/w VG. *Poetry Bookshop.* $62/£40

WRIGHT, THOMAS. The Life of Walter Pater. NY/London, 1907. 1st ed. 2 vols. 78 plts. Teg; uncut. VG. *Argosy.* $125/£80

WRIGHT, THOMAS. Narratives of Sorcery and Magic. NY: Redfield, 1852. 1st ed. 420pp. VG + (rebound). *Middle Earth.* $195/£125

WRIGHT, W. B. The Quaternary Ice Age. London: Macmillan, (1937). 2nd ed. 23 plts. (Rear cvr stained), else VG + . *Mikesh.* $25/£16

WRIGHT, W. H. The Grizzly Bear. NY: Scribner, Sept 1909. 1st ed. Dec cvr (spine bumped). Good. *Scribe's Perch*.* $35/£22

WRIGHT, W. P. Garden Trees and Shrubs. London, 1928. 2nd ed. 24 color, 49 plain plts, fldg plan. (Ends, edges sl foxed), o/w Fine. *Henly.* $33/£21

WRIGHT, W. SWIFT. Pastime Sketches: Scenes and Events at 'The Mouth of the Eel' on the Historic Wabash.... (Logansport, IN), 1907. 1st ed. *Ginsberg.* $125/£80

WRIGHTSON, BERNI. Berni Wrightson: A Look Back. Christopher Zavisa (ed). Novato/Lancaster: Underwood Miller, 1991. One of 700 numbered. Dj, cl fldg case. *Swann*.* $57/£37

WRIGHTSON, JOHN. The Principles of Agricultural Practice.... London: Chapman & Hall, 1893. 3rd ed. Color frontis, 228pp; map. Excellent. *Second Life.* $65/£42

Writers Take Sides. Letters About the War in Spain from 418 American Authors. NY: League of Amer Writers, (1938). 1st ed. NF in ptd wrappers (spine sl tanned). *Reese.* $100/£64

WROTH, LAWRENCE C. The Colonial Printer. Portland, ME: Southworth, 1938. 2nd ed. One of 1500 ptd. Box. *Ginsberg.* $150/£96

WROTH, LAWRENCE C. The Colonial Printer. Portland: Southworth-Anthoensen, 1938. (Spine sl cracked.) *Rostenberg & Stern.* $75/£48

WROTH, LAWRENCE C. First Century of the John Carter Brown Library. Providence, 1946. Cl-backed marbled bds. VG. *Truepenny.* $45/£29

WROTTESLEY, GEORGE. Life and Correspondence of Field Marshal Sir John Burgoyne, Bart. London, 1873. 2 vols. Port, facs letter frontispieces, 506; 508pp. Red cl (mkd), gilt. *Maggs.* $226/£145

WROTTESLEY, JOHN. The Great Northern Railway. Batsford, 1979-81. 1st eds. 3 vols. Djs. *Edwards.* $55/£35

WU, G. D. Prehistoric Pottery in China. London: Kegan Paul et al, (1938). 1st ed. 2 maps. Black cl, gilt spine. Good in dj. *Karmiole.* $75/£48

WUERTH, LOUIS A. Catalogue of the Etchings of Joseph Pennell. Boston: Little, Brown, 1928. #408/465. Frontis etching. Calf-backed cl bds. NF in dj (sm tear, top edge sl chipped). *New Hampshire*.* $310/£199

WUERTH, LOUIS A. Catalogue of the Etchings of Joseph Pennell. SF, 1988. Folio. Dj. *Swann*.* $115/£74

WULMARTH, M. GRACE. Lexicon of Geologic Names of the United States. GPO, 1938. 2 vols. Orig ptd wraps. *Cullen.* $50/£32

WUNDERLICH, CAROL. On the Temperature in Diseases. W. B. Woodman (trans). London: New Sydenham Soc, 1871. xii,468pp; 40 woodcuts, 7 lithos. Brn cl. (Tp, index sl spotted), o/w VG. *White.* $47/£30

WUNDERLICH, CAROL. On the Temperature in Diseases. London: New Sydenham Soc, 1871. 1st Eng ed. New cl. VG. *Goodrich.* $125/£80

WUORIO, EVA-LIS. The Land of Right Up and Down. Dobson, 1968. 1st Eng ed. Edward Ardizzone (illus). 4to. 61pp; 3 dbl-pg color pictures, 21 b/w illus. Color pict bds. VG + . *Bookmark.* $27/£17

WURLITZER, RUDOLPH. Nog. NY, 1968. 1st ed, 1st bk. VG + in VG dj (edgeworn). *Warren.* $35/£22

WURTENBERGER, FRANSZEPP. Mannerism. The European Style of the Sixteenth Century. NY, 1963. (Backstrip bottom worn), o/w VG. *Washton.* $75/£48

Wuthering Heights. (By Emily Bronte.) NY: Harper, 1848. 1st Amer ed, wrappered issue. 2 vols. 12mo. Ptd buff wrappers (vol 2 spine chipped, affecting part of title; lt foxed, early sig fr cvr each vol). Blue morocco fldg box. *Swann*.* $2,760/£1,769

WYCHERLEY, WILLIAM. The Complete Works. Montague Summers (ed). Nonesuch, 1924. 1st ed. #496/900. 4 vols. Uncut, partly unopened. Good in buckram-backed bds, paper labels (1 chipped); 1 backstrip sl darker brn, as issued. *Cox.* $172/£110

WYETH, BETSY JAMES. Wyeth at Kuerners. Boston: Houghton Mifflin, 1976. 1st ed. Fine in Fine dj. *New Hampshire*.* $65/£42

WYETH, JOHN A. A Textbook on Surgery, General, Operative, and Mechanical. NY: Appleton, 1887. 1st ed. x,777pp. New 1/4 calf. Good. *Goodrich.* $250/£160

WYETH, JOHN A. A Textbook on Surgery, General, Operative, and Mechanical. NY: Appleton, 1888. 1st ed, 2nd ptg. x,777pp. Orig cl (recased, lt rubbed). Internally Fine. *Goodrich.* $195/£125

WYETH, NATHANIEL J. The Correspondence and Journals of Captain Nathaniel J. Wyeth 1831-6. F. G. Young (ed). Eugene: University Press, 1899. 1st ed. xx,262pp; 3 maps. Orig ptd wraps. (Chip spine head, sl rubbed), else Good. Howes W718. *Brown.* $100/£64

WYKE, JOHN. A Catalogue of Tools for Watch and Clock Makers. Charlottesville, VA, (1978). 62 plts. VG in dj. *Weber.* $45/£29

WYKES, ALAN. Snake Man. 1960. 1st ed. Frontis port. Dj (sl rubbed). *Edwards.* $25/£16

WYLIE, ELINOR. Mr. Hodge and Mr. Hazard. NY: Knopf, 1928. 1st ed. NF in dj (spine tanned, sl chipped). *Turtle Island.* $45/£29

WYLIE, ELINOR. Mr. Hodge and Mr. Hazard. NY: Knopf, 1928. One of 145 numbered, signed. Unopened. Blue cl, silver stamping. Fine in pub's slipcase. *Dermont.* $250/£160

WYLIE, ELINOR. Trivial Breath. London/NY, 1928. 1st issue. #90/100 signed. Uncut, partly unopened. (Spine sl sunned, extrems sl rubbed.) *Polyanthos.* $35/£22

WYLLIE, JOHN. Tumours of the Cerebellum. London: H.K. Lewis, 1908. (Text sl browned), else VG. *Goodrich.* $195/£125

WYLLYS, RUFUS K. Arizona, History of a Frontier State. Phoenix, 1950. 1st ed. One of 400. Fine in Fine dj (internally reinforced w/archival tape). *Turpen.* $50/£32

WYLLYS, RUFUS K. Arizona: The History of a Frontier State. Phoenix: Hobson and Herr, (1950). 1st ed w/spelling error in 1/2-title. Signed. 8 maps. (Bkpl, sig), else Fine in dj (lt worn). Argonaut. $65/£42

WYNDHAM, JOHN. The Chrysalids. London: Michael Joseph, 1955. 1st ed. (Sm bkstore stamp fep), else Fine in dj. Associates. $250/£160

WYNDHAM, JOHN. The Midwich Cuckoos. Ballantine, 1957. 1st ed. VG- in dj (sl frayed). Madle. $50/£32

WYNDHAM, JOHN. The Seeds of Time. London: Michael Joseph, 1956. 1st UK ed. VG (bkshop label) in Good+ dj (sl dusty, rubbed, sl loss spine top). Williams. $39/£25

WYNDHAM, JOHN. Web. Joseph, 1979. 1st UK ed. Mint in Mint dj. Martin. $25/£16

WYNDHAM, RICHARD. A Book of Towers and Other Buildings of Southern Europe. London: Frederick Etchells & Hugh MacDonald, 1928. 24 etchings. (Lt dampstained; bds dknd, hinge starting, chipped.) Metropolitan*. $20/£13

WYNDHAM, ROBERT. Chinese Mother Goose Rhymes. Cleveland: World, 1968. 1st ed. Ed Young (illus). 10 3/4 x 8 1/4. 48pp. Fine in dj. Cattermole. $45/£29

WYNN, MARCIA RITTENHOUSE. Desert Bonanza: The Story of Early Randsburg.... Glendale: Clark, 1963. 2nd ed. One of 2112. Brn cl. Fine. Argonaut. $50/£32

WYNNE, JAMES. Private Libraries of New York. NY: French, 1860. Engr frontis, 417pp (foxing). Uncut, unopened. (Binding rubbed.) Internally VG. Goodrich. $95/£61

WYNNE, JOHN HUDDLESTONE. Fables of Flowers for the Female Sex. London: George Riley, 1773. 1st ed. ix,173pp,(3); 30 engr plts. Full contemp calf. Well Preserved. Quest. $250/£160

WYNNE, JOHN HUDDLESTONE. Tales for Youth; in Thirty Poems: to Which Are Annexed, Historical Remarks.... London: Newberry, 1794. 8vo. John Bewick (illus). Frontis, x,158pp + (2)pp ads. Contemp speckled calf (spine worm damage, fr joint cracked but firm), gilt. Bromer. $750/£481

WYSONG, THOMAS TURNER. The Rocks of Deer Creek, Hartford County, Maryland. Balt: Sherwood, 1879. 1st ed. 78pp. (Extrems worn), else NF. Mcgowan. $85/£54

X

X, MALCOLM. (Pseud of Malcolm Little.) with ALEX HALEY. The Autobiography of Malcolm X. NY: Grove, (1964). 1st ptg. Fine in NF dj (lt soiled, sm scratch fr panel). Between The Covers. $750/£481

XANTHUS, JANOS. Letters from North America. Detroit, 1976. 1st ed in English. Map. Fine in Fine dj. Turpen. $38/£24

Y

YADIN, YIGAEL. The Art of Warfare in Biblical Lands.... NY: McGraw-Hill, (1963). 2 vols. 1/2 cl. Good in slipcase. Archaeologia. $175/£112

YARDLEY, HERBERT. The American Black Chamber. Indianapolis: B-M, (1931). 1st ed. Good (ink note, pencil notes). Agvent. $40/£26

YARNALL, M. Catalogue of Stars Observed at the United States Naval Observatory During the Years 1845 to 1877. Washington: GPO, 1878. 2nd ed. xxi,281pp. Old 1/4 calf, marbled bds, black title label. (Scuffed, extrems worn), else VG. Weber. $125/£80

YARRELL, WILLIAM. A History of British Birds. London, 1843. 1st ed. 3 vols. 520 woodcut engrs. Vol 3 w/pub's cat at end, w/further 16 woodcuts. (Bkpl.) Henly. $175/£112

YARRELL, WILLIAM. A History of British Fishes. London, 1841. 2nd ed. 2 vols. xlvii,464; (ii),628pp, 500 wood engrs. (Marginal browning; hinges tender, vol 2 gathering sl loose; worn, chipped.) Edwards. $70/£45

YARRELL, WILLIAM. A History of British Fishes. London, 1841. 2 vols. Petersfield. $86/£55

YARRELL, WILLIAM. A History of British Fishes. John Richardson (ed). London: John van Voorst, 1859. 3rd ed. 3 vols (2 vols + supp vol). Frontis ports. xxxviii, 675; 670pp. (Lt spotting, margins lt browned; cl sl rubbed, lower bd vol 2 dampstained; supp vol faded, lt soiled, spine chipped.) Edwards. $133/£85

YATES, DORNFORD. And Berry Came Too. Ward Lock, 1936. 1st UK ed. NF in VG dj (sl edgewear, dusty, nicked, price-clipped). Williams. $55/£35

YATES, DORNFORD. The Berry Scene. Ward, Lock, (1947). 1st ed. (Heavily inscribed), else Nice in dj (worn, chipped). Ash. $31/£20

YATES, ELIZABETH. The Christmas Story. NY: Aladdin Books, 1949. 1st ed. Nora Unwin (illus). 8vo. 54pp. VG in dj (sl loss bottom spine edge). Dower. $45/£29

YATES, FRANCES A. The Valois Tapestries. London, 1975. 2nd ed. 48 plts. Edwards. $39/£25

YATES, RICHARD. Eleven Kinds of Loneliness. Boston: Little, Brown, (1962). 1st ed. VG in dj (lt edgewear). Reese. $50/£32

YATES, WILLIAM and CHARLES MACLEAN. A View of the Science of Life. Phila, 1797. 232pp. Old bds (newly rebacked; foxing). Goodrich. $50/£32

YATO, TAMOTSU. Young Samurai: Bodybuilders of Japan. Keizo Aizawa (ed). NY: Grove, 1967. 1st US ed. Fine in pict dj (lt worn). Cahan. $150/£96

YAVNO, MAX. The Los Angeles Book. Lee Shippey (text). Boston: Houghton Mifflin, 1950. 1st ed. VG in dj (chipped, worn). Cahan. $40/£26

YAVNO, MAX. The Story of Wine in California. Berkeley: Univ of CA, 1962. 1st ed. NF in VG+ dj. Smith. $60/£38

Year 1200. II. A Background Survey. NY: MMA, 1970. Good in wrappers. Washton. $85/£54

Year's Pictorial History of the American Negro. Year's Pictorial History of the American Negro. Charles H. Wesley (forward). (Maplewood, NJ/NY: C.S. Hammond/Year, 1965.) 1st ed. Fine in pict wrappers. Between The Covers. $50/£32

YEATS, G. D. Some Observations on the Duodenum, or Second Stomach.... 1820. 54pp (scattered foxing); 2 fldg plts. (Rebound in 1/2 cl.) Marbled bds. Whitehart. $101/£65

YEATS, W. B. The Death of Synge. Dublin: Cuala, 1928. One of 400. 1/4 linen, gray paper bds (lt soiled, spine sl dknd). VG (paper sl age-toned). Waverly*. $110/£71

YEATS, W. B. Dramatis Personae 1896-1902. Macmillan, 1936. 1st ed thus. Uncut. 1/4 cl. (Edges dknd), o/w VG in dj (dknd). Poetry Bookshop. $86/£55

YEATS, W. B. Dramatis Personae 1896-1902.... Macmillan, 1936. 1st British trade ed. Frontis port. Cl-backed patterned bds. VG in dj (sl nicked, dusty). *Ash.* $55/£35

YEATS, W. B. Early Poems and Stories. Macmillan, 1925. #87/250. Signed. Uncut. Acetate wrapper (worn). *Yudkin*.* $375/£240

YEATS, W. B. Explorations. Mrs W.B. Yeats (selected by). London: Macmillan, 1962. 1st ed as such. Frontis port. (Bkpl), else NF in dj (lt worn). *Cahan.* $50/£32

YEATS, W. B. The Herne's Egg, a Stage Play. London: Macmillan, 1938. 1st ed (1600 ptd). (Edges sl rubbed), o/w NF in NF dj (sl nicks). *Reese.* $125/£80

YEATS, W. B. (ed). Irish Folk Tales. Avon, CT: LEC, 1973. One of 2000 signed by Ted Gensamer (decs). 12 color mtd plts. VG in bd slipcase. *Argosy.* $150/£96

YEATS, W. B. The King of the Great Clock Tower, Commentaries and Poems. NY: Macmillan, 1935. 1st Amer ed. VG in Good dj (spine chip, nicks, mended tear verso). *Reese.* $85/£54

YEATS, W. B. Last Poems and Plays. NY: Macmillan, 1940. 1st Amer ed. (Eps sl foxed), o/w NF in dj (spine sl tanned, sm nick). *Reese.* $125/£80

YEATS, W. B. Later Poems. Macmillan, March 1924. #104/250. Signed. Uncut. Acetate wrapper. *Yudkin*.* $400/£256

YEATS, W. B. The Player Queen. London: Macmillan, 1922. 1st ed (1000 ptd). (Inscrip), else Good in parchment-like wrappers (spine chipped, mended). *Reese.* $50/£32

YEATS, W. B. Plays in Prose and Verse. Macmillan, March 1924. #2/250. Signed. Uncut. Acetate wrapper. *Yudkin*.* $400/£256

YEATS, W. B. Poems. London: T. Fisher Unwin, (1922). Signed, dated. Frontis port. Blue cl, gilt. Fine. *Appelfeld.* $350/£224

YEATS, W. B. Responsibilities. Dundrum: Cuala Press, 1914. 1st ed. One of 400 ptd. Gray bds, linen spine. Fine. *Appelfeld.* $300/£192

YEATS, W. B. The Secret Rose. London: Lawrence & Bullen, 1897. 1st ed. Blue cl, gilt. Nice. *Appelfeld.* $325/£208

YEATS, W. B. Stories of Michael Robartes and His Friends. Dublin: Cuala, 1931. One of 450. Unopened. 1/4 linen, blue paper bds. VG (cvrs sl bowed, edges lt soiled, lower corner sl worn). *Waverly*.* $132/£85

YEATS, W. B. Three Things. London: Faber, 1929. One of 500 numbered, signed. Paper-cvrd bds (toned, rubbed, back fold cracked, sl chipped). Contents VG. *Waverly*.* $253/£162

YEATS, W. B. The Tower. Macmillan, 1928. 1st ed. 2000 ptd. Dec cl, gilt. VG (edges sl spotted) in dj. *Ash.* $226/£145

YEATS, W. B. The Tower. London: Macmillan, 1928. 1st ed. Dec cl. Fine in dj (spine head chipped, fr fold split). *Jaffe.* $450/£288

YEATS, W. B. The Tower. NY: Macmillan, 1928. 1st Amer ed. Heavily gilt pict cl. VG (ink name, date; lt rubbing). *Reese.* $150/£96

YEATS, W. B. The Unicorn from the Stars. NY: Macmillan, 1908. 1st Amer ed. Blue cl, gilt. NF. *Macdonnell.* $85/£54

YEATS, W. B. Wheels and Butterflies. Macmillan, 1934. 1st ed. VG (top edge sl dusty) in dj (sl browned, rubbed). *Ash.* $94/£60

YEATS, W. B. The Wild Swans at Coole. NY: Macmillan, 1919. 1st Amer ed. Dec gray paper bds stamped in black. (Sl loss spine crown), o/w Very Nice in dj (2 sm chips, short closed tear). *Reese.* $225/£144

YEATS, W. B. The Winding Stair and Other Poems. Macmillan, 1933. 1st trade ed. 2000 ptd. (Cvr fore-edges sl discolored), o/w Nice in dj (split, repaired). *Ash.* $78/£50

YEATS, W. B. The Winding Stair and Other Poems. London, 1933. 1st ed. Grn emb cl, gilt. (Sl rubbed), o/w VG. *Words Etc.* $47/£30

YEATS, W. B. The Winding Stair. NY: Fountain, 1929. 1st ed. One of 642 signed. NF in dec cl, morocco spine labels. *Captain's Bookshelf.* $650/£417

YEE, CHIANG. The Silent Traveller in Japan. NY: Norton, 1972. 1st ed. 16 color plts. NF in dj. *Worldwide.* $20/£13

YEE, CHIANG. The Silent Traveller in Oxford. 1944. 1st ed. VG in dj (creased, spine browned, ends sl torn). *Words Etc.* $16/£10

YEE, CHIANG. The Silent Traveller in War Time. London: Country Life, 1939. 1st Eng ed. Very Nice (inscrip) in dj (sl nicked). *Clearwater.* $39/£25

YEE, CHIANG. Yebbin. Methuen, 1947. 1st ed. Tall 8vo. 143pp; 4 color plts. VG in pict dj (worn). *Bookmark.* $23/£15

YELD, GEORGE. Scrambles on the Eastern Graians 1878-1897. London, 1900. 1st ed. 20 plts, fldg map. Teg. (Feps lt browned; cl sl worn.) *Edwards.* $148/£95

YELLEN, SAMUEL. In the House and Out. Bloomington, 1952. 1st ed. Signed. VG + in VG + dj. *Smith.* $25/£16

Yellow Book. London/NY, 1894-97. 13 vols (all issued). 8vo. Orig pict yellow cl (soiled). *Swann*.* $805/£516

Yellow Book: An Illustrated Quarterly. London: James Lane, 1894-1897. 13 vols. Black-stamped yellow cl. NF (ex-lib, lib stamps eps). *Argosy.* $850/£545

YEOMANS, FRANK C. Proctology. NY: Appleton, 1936. (Inner hinges taped.) *Goodrich.* $25/£16

YERBY, FRANK. The Saracen Blade. NY: Dial, 1952. 1st ed. (Sm name), else Fine in Fine dj (faint stain inside). *Between The Covers.* $85/£54

YERKES, ROBERT M. The Mind of a Gorilla: Part II: Mental Development. Worcester, MA: Clark Univ, 1927. 1st ed. Presentation copy. Crimson cl. VG. *Gach.* $65/£42

YEVTUSHENKO, YEVGENY. Selected Poems. Milner-Gulland & Levi (trans). NY: Dutton, 1962. 1st ed. NF in dj (lt used, price-clipped). *Antic Hay.* $25/£16

YEVTUSHENKO, YEVGENY. Selected Poems. NY: Dutton, 1962. 1st US ed. Fine in dj (sm scratches). *Lame Duck.* $35/£22

YEVTUSHENKO, YEVGENY. Stolen Apples. GC: Doubleday, 1971. Ltd to 250 numbered, signed. Fine in orig cardbd slipcase. *Antic Hay.* $100/£64

YOAKUM, H. History of Texas from Its First Settlement in 1685 to Its Annexation to the United States in 1846. NY: Redfield, 1856. 1st ed, 2nd issue. 2 vols. 482; 576pp (scattered foxing). 5 plts, 4 maps (1 fldg), fldg facs (long tear repaired). Brn cl (extrems lt worn), gilt-lettered spine. VG. *Argonaut.* $500/£321

YOINHE, C. M. A Year on the Great Barrier Reef. London, 1930. 1st ed. Presentation copy. 70 plts, 6 maps (5 fldg). (Cl sl soiled.) *Edwards.* $55/£35

YOLEN, JANE. The Emperor and the Kite. Cleveland: World, 1967. 1st ed. Ed Young (illus), 9 1/2 x 8 1/4. 32pp. Fine in dj. *Cattermole.* $35/£22

YONGE, CHARLOTTE M. The Lances of Lynwood. Macmillan, 1929. 1st ed. Marguerite de Angeli (illus). 6x7.5. 217pp. (Owner stamp ep, dj corner), o/w VG in dj (ragged). *My Bookhouse.* $35/£22

YONGE, CHARLOTTE M. Magnum Bonum or Mother Carey's Brood. Macmillan, 1879. 1st ed. 3 vols. Ad leaf vol 3, (ink inscrip top margin tp vols 2&3, lt red ink stain upper margin pg [iii] vol 1). No 1/2 titles called for. Grn cl, blocked in black/gilt/blind, spines gilt. *Bickersteth*. $86/£55

YONGE, CHARLOTTE M. The Sea Shore. London, 1949. 1st ed. 72 plts (40 color). Good. *Henly*. $23/£15

YONGE, CHARLOTTE M. Unknown to History. Macmillan, 1882. 1st ed. 2 vols. ix,(i),312; vii,(i),277,(3)pp, ad leaf (bk labels pasted to eps). *Cox*. $39/£25

YONGE, JAMES. The Journal of James Yonge (1647-1721) Plymouth Surgeon. F. N. L. Poynter (ed). London: Longmans, Green, 1963. Blue cl. VG in dj (worn). *Parmer*. $45/£29

YORICK, MR. (Pseud of Laurence Sterne.) A Sentimental Journey Through France and Italy. London: T. Becket and P.A. de Hondt, 1768. 1st ed. 2 vols. 12mo. xx,203; (4),208pp, 1/2-titles present. 18th cent calf (hinges rubbed, vol 2 spine chipped), gilt, red calf labels, marbled eps. Nice set. *Karmiole*. $1,250/£801

YORICK, MR. (Pseud of Laurence Sterne.) A Sentimental Journey Through France and Italy. London: T. Becket, etc., 1768. 1st ed w/1/2-titles and rare ad leaf promising 2 more vols that never appeared. 2 vols. Old brn calf (extrems worn, crack at top hinge vol 1; eps browned), gilt-paneled spines, raised bands, red/grn leather labels. Good. *Appelfeld*. $650/£417

YORICK, MR. (Pseud of Laurence Sterne.) A Sentimental Journey Through France and Italy. London: A. Millar/J. Hodges, 1782. 2 vols. 159;159pp + engr port. Old speckled calf (edges restored, rebacked to match), raised bands. *Hollett*. $101/£65

YORICK, MR. (Pseud of Laurence Sterne.) A Sentimental Journey Through France and Italy. London, 1809. New ed. 2 color plts. Uncut. Contemp bds. VG. *Argosy*. $150/£96

YORICK, MR. (Pseud of Laurence Sterne.) A Sentimental Journey Through France and Italy. NY, 1885. Facs of 1st ed. One of 100 numbered. 2 vols. 203; 208pp. (Spine labels defective, cvrs worn, chipped; hinges splitting.) *King*. $100/£64

YORICK, MR. (Pseud of Laurence Sterne.) A Sentimental Journey Through Italy and France. London: Tegg, 1809. 'New ed.' 1st ed thus. 2 hand-colored engrs by Thomas Rowlandson. Later full polished tan calf (neatly rebacked, orig spine laid down), gilt extra. *Swann**. $126/£81

YORINKS, ARTHUR. Hey, Al. NY: FSG, 1986. 1st ed. Richard Egielski (illus). 9 1/4 x 10 1/4. 32pp. Fine in dj. *Cattermole*. $60/£38

YOSHINOBU, TOKUGAWA. The Tokugawa Collection: No Robes and Masks. (NY): Japan Soc, (1977). Wrappers. *Freeman**. $30/£19

YOST, KARL and FREDERIC G. RENNER (comps). A Bibliography of the Published Works of Charles M. Russell. Lincoln: Univ of NE, (1971). Fine in Fine dj. *Book Market*. $100/£64

YOST, NELLIE SNYDER. The Call of the Range. Denver: Sage Books, (1966). 1st ed. Fine in pict dj. *Argonaut*. $60/£38

YOUATT, WILLIAM. Sheep. NY: Moore, (1848). 159pp. Pub's cl (sl water-stained). *Second Life*. $75/£48

YOUMANS, EDWARD L. Alcohol and the Constitution of Man.... NY, 1854. VG. *Argosy*. $75/£48

YOUMANS, ELIZA A. The First Book of Botany. NY: Appleton, 1873. New, enlgd ed. 202pp + ads (foxed). Leather-backed bds (rubbed). VG. *Second Life*. $25/£16

Young Lady's Book. Boston: Lilly et al, 1833. 3rd ed. Engr frontis, 505pp. Blind-stamped full calf (1-inch tear spine top). VG. *Second Life*. $125/£80

Young Lady's Equestrian Manual. Phila/New Orleans: Haswell, Barrington & Haswell/Towar, 1839. (4)102pp; plt. (Cl faded.) *M & S*. $275/£176

Young Samurai Bodybuilders of Japan. NY: Grove, 1967. 1st Amer ed. Fine in NF dj (chips). *Warren*. $75/£48

YOUNG, ANDREW. The White Blackbird. London, 1935. 1st Eng ed. Fine in dj (closed tear). *Clearwater*. $47/£30

YOUNG, ANDREW. Winter Harvest. London: Nonesuch, 1933. 1st Eng ed. Buckram-backed bds. Fine (name) in dj (sl torn, mkd). *Clearwater*. $55/£35

YOUNG, ARTHUR. Travels During the Years 1787, 1788, and 1789. London: W. Richardson & Bury St. Edmunds, 1794. 2 vols. Fldg frontis map (torn w/o loss), viii,629; (ii),336,(iv)pp; 2 fldg maps. (Some leaves vol 1 shaved, ex-lib, bkpls, ink stamps.) Marbled eps. Early 1/2 calf, marbled bds (sl worn, rebacked in mod calf), orig labels laid down. *Edwards*. $312/£200

YOUNG, ARTHUR. Travels in France During the Years 1787, 1788, 1789. George Bell, 1890. 3rd ed. Frontis, lx,366pp + cat. (Tp lt spotting), o/w VG in blind-stamped cl. *Cox*. $23/£15

YOUNG, BENNETT H. Confederate Wizards of the Saddle. Boston: Chapple, 1914. 1st ed. Red cl (professionally recased, sl soiled). VG. Howes Y21. *Captain's Bookshelf*. $300/£192

YOUNG, BETTY LOU and THOMAS R. YOUNG. Rustic Canyon and the Story of the Uplifters. Santa Monica: Casa Vieja, 1975. Gray cl (bowed). Dj (short tear). *Dawson*. $125/£80

YOUNG, ED. Lon Po Po. NY: Philomel, 1989. 1st ed. 8 1/4 x 10 1/4. 32pp. Fine in dj. *Cattermole*. $45/£29

YOUNG, EDWARD. Night Thoughts, on Life, Death, and Immortality. London, 1802. 8 engr plts. (Sl foxed, lt pencil marginalia.) Vellum (stained), black gilt label. *Yudkin**. $100/£64

YOUNG, EGERTON R. By Canoe and Dog Train Among the Cree and Salteaux Indians. NY/Cincinnati: Eaton & Mains, (1891). Signed w/author's Indian name and pen name. Grn pict cl (Lt soil, wear), o/w VG. *Glenn*. $65/£42

YOUNG, EGERTON R. By Canoe and Dog-Train Among the Cree and Salteaux Indians. NY/Cincinnati: Hunt & Eaton/Cranston & Curts, 1890. 267pp. Blue-grn cl (worn, soiled), gilt. *Parmer*. $125/£80

YOUNG, ELLA. The Tangle-Coated Horse. NY: MacKay, 1967. Vera Bock (illus). 186pp. Fine in dj. *Cattermole*. $50/£32

YOUNG, ELLA. The Wondersmith and His Son. NY: MacKay, 1964. Boris Artzybasheff (illus). 5 1/2 x 8 1/4. Fair (ex-lib, mks). *Cattermole*. $30/£19

YOUNG, ERNEST. North American Excursion. London: Edward Arnold, (1947). 1st ed. Red cl, gilt. VG in dj (lt soiled). *Bohling*. $27/£17

YOUNG, EVELYN. The Tale of Tai. NY: OUP, 1940. 1st ed. 6 1/4 x 6 3/4. 40pp. Good in dj. *Cattermole*. $45/£29

YOUNG, FRANCIS BRETT. Portrait of a Village. 1937. 1st ed. 30 wood engrs by Joan Hassall. VG (sl foxing, cvrs sl mkd) in dj (worn). *Whittle*. $28/£18

YOUNG, FRANCIS BRETT. Portrait of a Village. London: Heinemann, 1937. 1st ed. 30 wood engrs. (Sl mkd.) *Hollett*. $39/£25

YOUNG, G. O. Alaska Yukon Trophies Won and Lost. Huntington, WV: Standards, 1947. Dec cl. (Blind stamp tp), else VG. *High Latitude*. $115/£74

YOUNG, G. O. Alaskan Trophies Won and Lost. Boston, (1928). 1st ed. (Shelfworn, spine sl frayed.) Oinonen*. $190/£122

YOUNG, GAVIN. Iraq. London, 1980. 1st Eng ed. Fine in dj. Clearwater. $78/£50

YOUNG, GAVIN. Return to the Marshes. London, 1977. 1st Eng ed, 1st bk. Very Nice (sm stain fep from adhesive label) in dj. Clearwater. $62/£40

YOUNG, GEORGE. A Treatise on Opium, Founded on Practical Observations. A. Millar, 1753. 1st ed. 8vo. xv,(i),182pp + ad leaf. Orig calf (rebacked, orig spine label, eps preserved). Bickersteth. $515/£330

YOUNG, HARRY. Hard Knocks: A Life Story of the Vanishing West. Chicago: Laird & Lee, (1915). 1st ed. Good in dj (sl worn). Howes H27. Lien. $75/£48

YOUNG, HUGH. Hugh Young: A Surgeon's Autobiography. NY, 1940. 1st ed. Color frontis, 2 plts. VG. Doctor's Library. $50/£32

YOUNG, HUGH. A Surgeon's Autobiography. NY: Harcourt, Brace, 1940. (3rd ptg.) 3 color plts. Good. Goodrich. $30/£19

YOUNG, J. H. Caesarean Section. 1944. (Sm tears 2pp, sm ink sig, 1 section cracked; cl sl mkd, worn.) Whitehart. $62/£40

YOUNG, JAMES HARVEY. The Toadstool Millionaires. Princeton, 1961. VG. Fye. $50/£32

YOUNG, JAMES HARVEY. The Toadstool Millionaires. Princeton: Princeton Univ, 1961. 1st ed. Fine in dj. Cahan. $25/£16

YOUNG, JEAN and MICHAEL LANG. Woodstock Festival Remembered. NY: Ballantine, 1979. 1st ed. NF in wraps. Sclanders. $23/£15

YOUNG, JESSE BOWMAN. What a Boy Saw in the Army. NY: Hunt & Eaton, (1894). 1st ed. Patterned eps. Gilt-stamped blue pict cl (sl rubbed). VG. Houle. $150/£96

YOUNG, JOHN P. Journalism in California: Pacific Coast and Exposition Biographies. SF: Chronicle, (1915). 1st bk ed. Marbled eps. Grey cl (sl edgewear, spine dknd), gilt. NF. Harrington. $60/£38

YOUNG, JOHN RUSSELL. Around the World with General Grant. American News, (1879). 2 vols. Marbled edges. (Fr hinge both vols cracked.) 1/4 leather (scuffed), marbled bds. Yudkin*. $40/£26

YOUNG, LOT D. Reminiscences of a Soldier of the Orphan Brigade. (Louisville, KY: Courier-Journal, 1922.) 1st ed. VG in ptd wrappers. Mcgowan. $95/£61

YOUNG, MARGUERITE. Miss MacIntosh, My Darling. NY: Scribner, (1965). 1st ed. Fine in dj (nicked). Hermitage. $35/£22

YOUNG, NORWOOD. The Story of Rome. London, 1905. 4th ed. 4 fldg plans. Teg. Gilt-dec cl (spine sl discolored). Edwards. $19/£12

YOUNG, OTIS E. The First Military Escort on the Santa Fe Trail 1829.... Glendale, 1952. 1st ed. One of 1005. Frontis. Fine. Turpen. $125/£80

YOUNG, OTIS E. The First Military Escort on the Santa Fe Trail, 1829. Glendale: A.H. Clark, 1952. 1st ed. Map. Teg, mostly unopened. Red cl (spine faded, foot bumped). VG+. Harrington. $100/£64

YOUNG, OTIS E. The First Military Escort on the Santa Fe Trail, 1829. Glendale: Clark, 1952. 1st ed. One of 1005. 4 plts, fldg map. Teg. Red cl (spine ends lt rubbed), gilt-lettered spine. Fine. Argonaut. $125/£80

YOUNG, OTIS E. The West of Philip St. George Cooke 1809-1895. Glendale, 1955. 1st ed. One of 1249. Fldg map. Top edge red, others untrimmed. VF. No dj as issued. Turpen. $95/£61

YOUNG, OTIS E. The West of Philip St. George Cooke, 1809-1895. Glendale: Clark, 1955. 1st ed. Map. Ginsberg. $125/£80

YOUNG, OTIS E. The West of Philip St. George Cooke, 1809-1895. Glendale: Clark, 1955. 1st ed. One of 1249. Frontis port, 9 plts, fldg map. Maroon cl, gilt-lettered spine. Fine. Argonaut. $125/£80

YOUNG, PAUL H. Making and Using the Fly and Leader. N.p. (Michigan): PP, 1935. 2nd ed. Price list laid in. VG+. Bowman. $100/£64

YOUNG, PERRY. The Mistick Krewe. New Orleans: Carnival Press, 1931. 30 color plts. VG (inscrip; sl worn). Waverly*. $33/£21

YOUNG, S. HALL. Hall Young of Alaska, 'The Mushing Parson.' NY: Fleming H. Revell, (1927). 1st ed. Gilt-lettered grn cl. (Extrems sl rubbed), else Fine. Argonaut. $35/£22

YOUNG, STANLEY P. The Bobcat of North America. Harrisburg: Stackpole/Wildlife Mgmt Co, 1958. 1st ed. Color frontis. Yellow cl. Fine in Fine pict dj. Biscotti. $40/£26

YOUNG, STANLEY P. and E. A. GOLDMAN. The Puma. Washington, DC: Amer Wildlife Inst, 1946. 1st ed. Color frontis, 92 photo plts. Grn cl, gilt. VG in dj (taped). Price. $34/£22

YOUNG, STANLEY P. and E. A. GOLDMAN. The Puma: Mysterious American Cat. Washington, 1946. 1st ed. Gilt-dec cl. NF in VG dj. Mikesh. $60/£38

YOUNG, STANLEY P. and HARTLEY H. T. JACKSON. The Clever Coyote. Harrisburg: Stackpole/Wildlife Mgmt Co, 1951. 1st ed. Color frontis. Red cl, gilt. Fine in Fine pict dj. Biscotti. $45/£29

YOUNG, WILLIAM B. The Practical Interest Calculator; or Book of Interest.... AR: G. W. Beasley, 1860. 94pp. Stamped leather. (Text lt toned, stained; worn, lacks most of spine, bds sl buckled), else Good. Brown. $75/£48

YOUNG, WILLIAM E. Shark! Shark! Horace S. Mazet (ed). NY: Gotham House, 1933. Gilt-titled 1/2 shark leather, tan rough-weave cl emb w/shark. VF. Bowman. $125/£80

YOUNGBLOOD, CHARLES L. A Mighty Hunter. Chicago: Rand, 1890. Rpt of 1882 ed. Frontis, 362,(4)pp; 47 plts. Pict cl. Howes Y34. Ginsberg. $200/£128

YOUNGBLOOD, CHARLES L. A Mighty Hunter: The Adventures of Charles L. Youngblood.... Chicago: Rand, McNally, 1890. 362pp (few pp loose). Pict cl (worn). Howes Y34. Lien. $35/£22

YOUNGHUSBAND, F. The Heart of a Continent. NY: Scribner, 1896. 1st Amer ed. Frontis, xviv,409pp; 4 fldg maps (incl pocket map at end). Grn gilt-dec cl. VG. Terramedia. $400/£256

YOUNGHUSBAND, F. Kashmir. London: A&C Black, 1917. 3rd ptg. Fldg map. Dec lt brn cl, gilt. (Sl wear), else VG. Terramedia. $50/£32

YOUNGSON, A. J. The Making of Classical Edinburgh. Univ of Edinburgh, 1966. 1st ed. VG in dj. Hadley. $62/£40

YOUNT, GEORGE C. George C. Yount and His Chronicles of the West. Denver: Old West, 1966. One of 1250. Color frontis, fldg map. Pict cl. Fine. Harrington. $85/£54

YOUNT, JOHN. Wolf at the Door. NY: Random House, (1967). 1st ed, 1st bk. Fine in Fine dj. Bernard. $50/£32

YOURCENAR, MARGUERITE. The Dark Brain of Piranesi and Other Essays. Richard Howard (trans). NY: FSG, (1984). 1st ed. Fine in NF dj. Antic Hay. $25/£16

YOURCENAR, MARGUERITE. The Dark Brain of Piranesi and Other Essays. NY, 1984. 1st ed. Fine in Fine dj. Smith. $20/£13

YOURCENAR, MARGUERITE. Fires. NY: FSG, (1981). 1st ed. Fine in Fine dj. Dermont. $25/£16

Youth's History of the Great Civil War in the United States from 1861 to 1865. NY, 1866. 1st ed. 384pp. VG (sl internal soiling). *Pratt.* $45/£29

YULE, HENRY (ed). The Book of Ser Marco Polo, the Venetian, Concerning the Kingdoms and Marvels of the East. London: Murray, 1875. 2nd ed. 2 vols. xlii,444; xxii,606pp. (Cl sl rubbed, fr cvr vol 2 damp soiled), o/w VG. *Worldwide.* $250/£160

YULE, HENRY (ed). The Book of Ser Marco Polo, the Venetian. London: Murray, 1903. 3rd ed. 2 vols. Grn dec cl. (Sl rubbed), else VG. *Terramedia.* $200/£128

YURDIN, BETTY. The Tiger in the Teapot. NY: Holt, 1968. 1st ed. William Pene Du Bois (illus). 5 1/4 x 7 1/4. 32pp. Pict bds. VG in dj. *Cattermole.* $30/£19

YUTANG, LIN. Chinatown Family. NY, 1948. 1st ed. VG (dent) in VG dj. *Smith.* $20/£13

Z

ZADKIEL. The Grammar of Astrology. London, 1840. 2nd ed. x,178pp + 64pp. VG + (rebound). *Middle Earth.* $145/£93

ZADKIEL. The Handbook of Astrology. Volume II. London, (1863). xii,75 + 33pp. Dec cvr. VG-. *Middle Earth.* $99/£63

ZAFRIS, NANCY. The People I Know. Athens, GA, 1990. 1st ed, 1st bk. VF in VF dj. *Else Fine.* $35/£22

ZANGWILL, ISRAEL. Dreamers of the Ghetto. Heinemann, 1898. 1st ed. Orange cl (sl worn, sl mks, sm abrasions rear cvr). Good (eps cracking; sl shaken). *Ash.* $39/£25

ZANGWILL, ISRAEL. Dreamers of the Ghetto. NY: Harper, 1899. 1st Amer ed. Dec purple cl. VG. *Antic Hay.* $45/£29

ZANGWILL, ISRAEL. The King of Schnorrers. London: Rodale, 1954. 1st UK ed. Dec cl. VG. *Hollett.* $47/£30

ZANGWILL, ISRAEL. The Master. NY: Harper, 1895. 1st Amer ed. Dec cl. VG (sl soil, sm stain fr cvr). *Antic Hay.* $40/£26

ZANGWILL, ISRAEL. The Old Maid's Club. William Heinemann, 1892. 4th thousand. Ad leaf. Good (ink inscrip, lt spotted; spine bumped, chipped, corners rubbed). *Tiger.* $16/£10

ZANGWILL, ISRAEL. Without Prejudice. NY, 1897. 1st Amer ed. Uncut. Dec cvrs, gilt. Fine (spine sl sunned) in dj (spine sunned, chipped). *Polyanthos.* $60/£38

ZAPF, HERMANN. Manuale Typographicum. Frankfurt/NY, 1968. 1/4 imitation vellum. VG (ex-lib). *Swann*.* $172/£110

ZATURENSKA, MARYA. Christina Rossetti. NY, 1949. 1st ed. Fine in VG dj. *Mcclintock.* $20/£13

ZEIGLER, WILBUR G. and BEN S. GROSSCUP. The Heart of the Alleghanies or Western North Carolina.... Raleigh, NC: Alfred Williams, (1883). 1st ed. Fldg map. Pict cl (extrems lt rubbed), gilt. *Sadlon.* $275/£176

ZEISLER, SIGMUND. Reminiscences of the Anarchist Case. Chicago: Chicago Literary Club, 1927. 1st ed. Pb. NF (sm corner chip, edge tears). *Beasley.* $125/£80

ZELAZNY, ROGER. Blood of Amber. NY, (1986). 1st ed. Signed. VG in dj. *King.* $35/£22

ZELAZNY, ROGER. The Doors of His Face, the Lamps of His Mouth. London: Faber & Faber, (1971). 1st Eng ed. Fine in Fine dj. *Certo.* $40/£26

ZELAZNY, ROGER. Isle of the Dead. Andre Deutsch, 1970. 1st UK ed. Signed. Dj. *Edwards.* $31/£20

ZELAZNY, ROGER. Lord of Light. GC: Doubleday, 1967. 1st ed. Signed presentation. Bulked edges (sl soiled). Navy cl (sl edgeworn; sl spread), silver spine lettering. VG pict dj (sl edgeworn). *Baltimore*.* $300/£192

ZELAZNY, ROGER. Lord of Light. GC: Doubleday, 1967. 1st ed. NF (extrems sl rubbed) in dj (extrems worn, sm chips). *Metropolitan*.* $373/£239

ZELAZNY, ROGER. Sign of the Unicorn. GC: Doubleday, 1975. 1st ed. Rev copy. NF in VG dj (sl faded, lt soil rear panel). *Metropolitan*.* $40/£26

ZELINSKY, PAUL O. The Maid and the Mouse and the Odd-Shaped House. NY: Dodd, Mead, 1981. 2nd ed. 9 1/4 x 11 1/4. 32pp. Fine in dj. *Cattermole.* $25/£16

ZEMACH, HARVE. Duffy and the Devil. NY: FSG, 1973. 1st ed. Margot Zemach (illus). 8 3/4 x 10 3/4. 32pp. VG in dj (home-laminated). *Cattermole.* $75/£48

ZEMACH, MARGOT. Self-Portrait. Reading, MA: Addison-Wesley, 1978. 8vo. 32pp. Good+ in Good+ dj (price-clipped). *Scribe's Perch*.* $14/£9

ZENKERT, CHARLES A. Flora of the Niagara Frontier Region. Buffalo, 1934. Fldg color map. Cl back (new), paper over bds (worn). Servicable. *Brooks.* $24/£15

ZENZINOV, VLADIMIR and ISAAC DON LEVINE. The Road to Oblivion. NY: McBride, 1931. 1st ed. (Cl edges rubbed), o/w VG. *Worldwide.* $18/£12

ZERVOS, CHRISTIAN. Pablo Picasso. Vol 1. Works from 1895 to 1906. Paris/NY, (1932). Uncut. Stiff wrappers (sl worn, loose in casing). *Oinonen*.* $40/£26

ZIEGLER, PHILIP. The Black Death. London, 1969. 1st ed. Frontis. (Newspaper clippings.) Dj (sl chipped). *Edwards.* $23/£15

ZIEGLER, RICHARD. Judith the Widow of Bethulia. London: Dennis Dobson, (1946). One of 700 numbered. 4to. (41)pp (sm stains tp, rear pastedown). Deckle-edged. Pict cream bds (bumped, soiled, warped, edges dknd). VG. Internally NF. *Blue Mountain.* $20/£13

ZIGROSSER, CARL. The Expressionists. A Survey of Their Graphic Art. Braziller, 1957. Dj (sl tear). *Metropolitan*.* $57/£37

ZIGROSSER, CARL. Rockwellkentiana. NY, 1933. 1st ed. Pict cl (wear, spotting). *Freeman*.* $20/£13

ZILBOORG, GREGORY. A History of Medical Psychology. NY: Norton, (1941). 1st ed. 17 half-tones. Black cl. VG in dj (edgeworn). *Gach.* $65/£42

ZIMMERMAN, R. D. Mindscream. NY: Donald I. Fine, 1989. 1st ed. VF in dj. *Mordida.* $30/£19

ZIMMERMAN, R. D. Nightfall in Berlin. NY: Donald I. Fine, 1990. 1st ed. Signed. VF in dj. *Mordida.* $35/£22

ZINDEL, PAUL. A Begonia for Miss Applebaum. NY: Harper, 1989. 1st ed. 5 3/4 x 8 1/2. 180pp. Fine in dj. *Cattermole.* $35/£22

ZINSSER, HANS. Rats, Lice and History. London: Routledge, 1935. 1st ed. Red cl. VG. *White.* $23/£15

ZOBELL, ALBERT, JR. Sentinel in the East. Salt Lake City: N. Morgan, 1965. 1st ed. Fine in VG- dj (rubbed). *Archer.* $30/£19

ZOCCHI, GIUSEPPE. Views of Florence. NY: Walker, 1976. 1st ed. Ltd to 950 numbered. 27 plts. (Lt soiled.) Contents Fine in cl case. *Waverly*.* $22/£14

Zodiac. (Gehenna Press), 1963. One of 320 numbered (of 350). 12 engrs of Sante Graziani. 1/4 cl, paper over bds. Fine in slipcase. *Heller.* $275/£176

ZOGBAUM, RUFUS F. Horse, Foot, and Dragoons. NY: Harper, 1888. 1st ed. 176pp (pencil sigs, ink handstamps, sl aged). Brn coated eps. Dk blue-grn pict cl (frayed, sl worn). *Baltimore**. $60/£38

ZOLA, EMILE. Assomoir: The Prelude to Nana. London: Vizatelli, 1884. 1st ed in English. (Half-title margins chipped), else VG. *Lame Duck.* $200/£128

ZOLA, EMILE. The Monomaniac. Edward Vizetelly (ed). Hutchinson, 1902. 2nd ed. Frontis. Good (rebacked, orig backstrip relaid). *Tiger.* $16/£10

ZOLA, EMILE. Piping Hot. Vizetelly, 1885. 8 full-pg b/w plts. Pub's cat dated Sept 1884. Pict cl (spine bumped, dulled). Good (fore-edge lt spotted). *Tiger.* $140/£90

ZOLA, EMILE. Therese Raquin. London: Vizetelly, 1886. 1st British ed, 1st ed in English. VG+ in illus bds (worn). *Lame Duck.* $275/£176

ZOLLERS, GEORGE O. Thrilling Incidents on Sea and Land. Mount Morris, IL, 1892. 1st ed. 400pp. Dec cl. *Ginsberg.* $175/£112

ZOLLINGER, JAMES PETER. Sutter, the Man and His Empire. NY/London/Toronto: OUP, 1939. 1st ed. Frontis port. Yellow cl. (Soiled), o/w VG. *Pacific**. $23/£15

ZOLLINGER, JAMES PETER. Sutter: The Man and His Empire. NY: OUP, 1939. 1st ed. VG in dj (worn; tape repaired). *Lien.* $30/£19

ZOOLOGICAL SOCIETY OF LONDON. Catalogue of the Library. London, 1902. 5th ed. (Owner stamp tp, pencil marginalia, browned.) Mod cl. *Oinonen**. $120/£77

ZORACH, WILLIAM. Art Is My Life. Cleveland/NY: World, 1967. 1st ed. (Name ep), else VG in dj (crown chipped, rubbed). *Cahan.* $45/£29

ZOUCH, THOMAS. Memoirs of the Life and Writings of Sir Philip Sidney. York: Ptd by Thomas Wilson, 1809. 2nd ed. Copper-engr frontis port, 400pp (foxed; bkpl). 1/2 calf (ca 1900), purple cl (spine rubbed, fr outer hinge partly cracked), black morocco spine label. *Karmiole.* $175/£112

ZUCKERMAN, S. The Social Life of Monkeys and Apes. London, 1932. 24 plts. *Edwards.* $39/£25

ZUKOFSKY, LOUIS. Catullus Fragmenta. Turret Books, 1969. Ltd to 100. This copy unnumbered, unsigned. Fine in wrappers. *Words Etc.* $19/£12

ZUKOFSKY, LOUIS. Little: A Fragment for Careenagers. (L.A.): Black Sparrow, 1967. One of 250 numbered, signed. Fine in Fine wrappers. *Lenz.* $125/£80

ZUKOFSKY, LOUIS. Prepositions. London, 1967. 1st ed. #137/150 signed. Fine in dj (sm nick, price-clipped). *Polyanthos.* $75/£48

ZWEIG, ARNOLD. Education Before Verdun. Eric Sutton (trans). NY: Viking, 1936. 1st Amer ed. Fine in dj (lt used). *Antic Hay.* $30/£19